KU-480-884

Racehorse Record

JUMPS 2003-2004

Sponsored by:

Established 1973

Production Editor	Ashley Rumney
Comments by	David Bellingham, Mark Brown, Steffan Edwards
	Walter Glynn, Keith Hewitt, Steve Jones,
	Richard Lowther, David Orton, Ashley Rumney,
	Ronald Wood, Richard Young
Development	Phillip Lamphee, Dan Di Pol

Typeset and Published by Raceform Ltd,
Compton, Newbury, Berkshire, RG20 6NL
Tel: 01635 578080
Fax: 01635 578101
Web http://www.raceform.co.uk
EMail: raceform@raceform.co.uk
Printed by William Clowes Ltd, Beccles

ISBN 1 904317 55 3

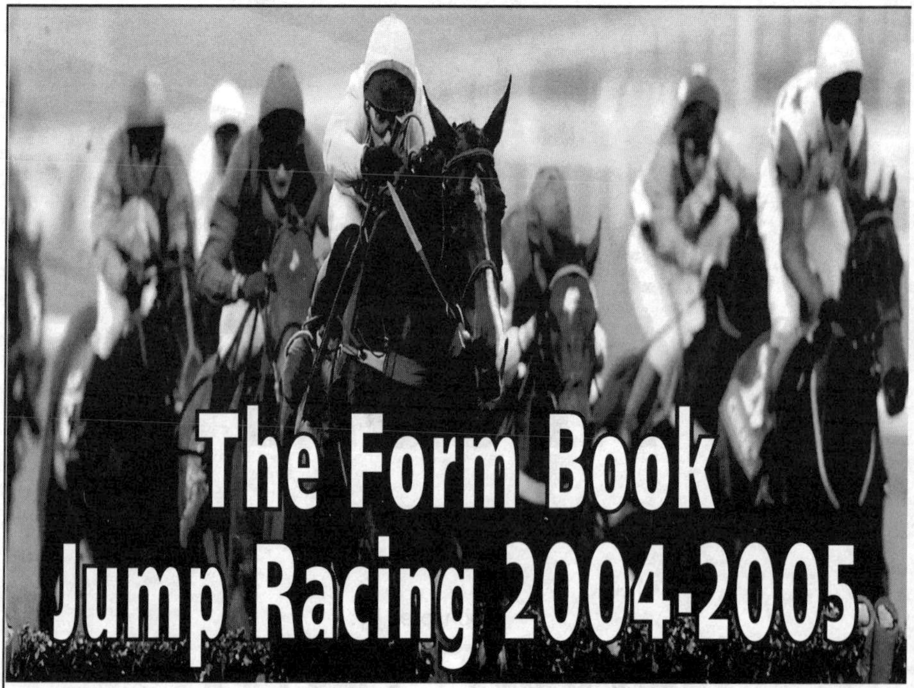

CONTENTS

Full details of all Raceform services and publications are available from
Raceform, Compton, Newbury, Berkshire RG20 6NL.
Tel: 01635 578080 Fax: 01635 578101.
Web http://www.raceform.co.uk
Email: raceform@raceform.co.uk

Cover Photo: Puntal (Danny Howard, left),
leads Kings Mistral over the Pond Fence on his way to victory
in the BetFred Gold Cup at Sandown, 24th April 2004

INTRODUCTION

Raceform's *Racehorse Record* has been designed not only as an historical reference, but also as a guide to the future, with the aim being to provide factual information about individual horses that ran under Jump racing Rules in Britain during the 2003-2004 season, and also to pinpoint conditions that are likely to prove conducive to future success.

For full season's results and ratings, refer to the *Chaseform Jumps Annual 2003-2004*.

The horses are listed in alphabetical order.

KEY TO HORSE RECORDS

Best Mate (IRE) ——— Name of horse, plus country of origin suffix in brackets

117   (155h) **178** —— Master Split Second speed rating on left, Raceform rating on right (hurdles ratings in brackets)

9-y-o b g Un Desperado (FR)-Katday (FR) (Miller's Mate)
Miss H C Knight Jim Lewis

Age, colour, sex and pedigree. The sire's name is followed by the dam's name, then the dam's sire's name in brackets

Placings: 71221/1112/1221/111-211   (4424)

Trainer's name in bold (plus date of transfer and previous trainer's name if the horse changed stables during the season), followed by the owner's name

2003/04: 20²GS, 24¹YS, 26¹G,

	Starts	**1st**	**2nd**	**3rd**	**Win & Pl**
Chases	3	2	1	0	277312
Career Total	19	13	6	0	964665

Complete list of the horse's placings, starting with its first recorded race. Bumper outings are in italic, hurdles outings in roman type and chase or hunter chase outings in bold type. A slash '/' or dash '-' indicates a change of season. This is followed in brackets by the Raceform number of the last race in the Form Book in which the horse competed

174	3/04	Chel	3m2f110yA Ch	GD	£203000
172	12/03	Leop	3m	Ch	Y-S	£63311
178	3/03	Chel	3m2f110yA Ch	GD	£203000
173	12/02	Kemp	3m	A Ch	SFT	£87000
171	11/02	Hntg	2m4f110yA Ch	G-S	£32725
176	3/02	Chel	3m2f110yA Ch	GD	£174000
172	11/01	Extr	2m1f110yA HCh	G-F	£21000
167	2/01	Sand	2m4f110yA Ch	HVY	£24000
156	11/00	Chel	2m	A Ch	G-S	£15000
151	10/00	Extr	2m1f110yD Ch	GD	£3926
146	4/00	Aint	2m4f	A Hdl	GD	£21000
137	12/99	Sand	2m110y D Hdl	G-S	£3688
133	11/99		2m110y B NHF	GD	£7197

2003-2004 season's record, broken down into race types followed by career record

Total win prize-money £858841

Career wins, showing (left to right) winning Raceform rating, date of win (month/year), course, distance, race conditions and type, going, win prize money

Going: Sf: 0-0 GS: 0-1 Gd: 0-1 GF: - Fm: 0-0
Distance: 2m/2m3: 0-0 2m4-2m7: 0-1 **3m: 2-2**
Track: LH: **2-2** RH: 0-1 Tight: 0-0 **Gall: 1-2**
Aids: Bl: 0-0 Vi: 0-0 Tstrap: 0-0 Ckp: 0-0
Best Rating: 178 3/03 Chel 3m2f110y good Ch

Going record for the season (wins-runs)

Distance record for the season

Track type record for the season

Aids record for the season (blinkers, visor, tongue strap, cheekpieces)

Best Raceform rating achieved during the season, followed by the relevant date, course, distance, going and race type

Brilliant chaser; the best staying chaser in training; has never been out of the first two over hurdles or fences and is the first horse since Arkle to win three Cheltenham Gold Cups; below his best when beaten in the 2003 Peterborough Chase by Jair Du Cochet, but bounced back by taking the Grade One Ericsson Chase at Leopardstown in December with ease, having run there rather than the King George at Kempton; completed an historic Gold Cup hat-trick, but his half-length defeat of Sir Rembrandt does not mark the form he showed in the previous two renewals; has an excellent cruising pace, jumps well, has a fine turn of foot and acts on any ground; proved at Cheltenham that he can battle; effective from 2m 4f to 3m 2f and on any type of track.

Raceform master comment on selected horses only. (These comments may refer in some instances to races which have already taken place during the 2004-2005 season).

Scale of Weight for Age for Steeple Chases and Hurdle Races

HURDLE RACES

The allowances, assessed in lbs, which three-year-olds and four-year-olds will receive from five-year-olds and upwards

Distance Miles	Age	JAN 1/15	JAN 16/31	FEB 1/14	FEB 15/29	MAR 1/15	MAR 16/31	APR 1/15	APR 16/30	MAY 1/15	MAY 16/31	JUNE 1/15	JUNE 16/30	JULY 1/15	JULY 16/31	AUG 1/15	AUG 16/31	SEPT 1/15	SEPT 16/30	OCT 1/15	OCT 16/31	NOV 1/15	NOV 16/30	DEC 1/15	DEC 16/31
2	3	-	-	-	-	-	-	-	-	-	-	-	-	21	21	20	20	19	19	18	18	17	16	15	14
	4	12	11	10	9	8	7	6	5	4	4	3	3	3	3	2	2	1	1	-	-	-	-	-	-
2.5	3	-	-	-	-	-	-	-	-	-	-	-	-	22	22	21	21	20	20	19	19	18	17	16	15
	4	13	12	11	10	9	8	7	6	5	5	4	4	5	4	4	3	3	2	2	1	-	-	-	-
3	3	-	-	-	-	-	-	-	-	-	-	-	-	22	22	21	21	20	20	19	18	17	16	15	14
	4	14	13	12	11	10	10	9	8	7	6	6	5	5	5	4	4	3	3	2	2	1	1	-	-

Scale of Weight for Age for Steeple Chases and Hurdle Races

STEEPLE CHASES

The allowances, assessed in lbs, which four-year-olds and five-year-olds will receive from six-year-olds and upwards

Distance Miles	Age	JAN 1/15	JAN 16/31	FEB 1/14	FEB 15/29	MAR 1/15	MAR 16/31	APR 1/15	APR 16/30	MAY 1/15	MAY 16/31	JUNE 1/15	JUNE 16/30	JULY 1/15	JULY 16/31	AUG 1/15	AUG 16/31	SEPT 1/15	SEPT 16/30	OCT 1/15	OCT 16/31	NOV 1/15	NOV 16/30	DEC 1/15	DEC 16/31
2	4	-	-	-	-	-	-	-	-	-	-	-	-	16	16	15	15	14	14	13	13	12	12	11	10
	5	9	8	7	6	5	4	3	3	2	2	1	1	-	-	-	-	-	-	-	-	-	-	-	-
2.5	4	-	-	-	-	-	-	-	-	-	-	-	-	17	17	16	16	15	15	14	14	13	12	12	11
	5	10	9	8	7	6	5	4	4	3	3	2	2	1	1	-	-	-	-	-	-	-	-	-	-
3	4	-	-	-	-	-	-	-	-	-	-	-	-	17	17	16	16	15	15	14	14	13	13	13	13
	5	12	12	11	11	10	10	9	8	7	7	6	6	5	5	4	4	3	3	2	2	1	1	-	-

RACEFORM RATINGS

Raceform Ratings for each horse are listed after the Starting Price and indicate the actual level of performance attained in that race. The figure in the back index represents the BEST public form that Raceform's Handicappers still believe the horse capable of reproducing.

To use the ratings constructively in determining those horses best-in in future events, the following procedures should be followed:

(i) In races where all runners are set to carry the same weight, no calculations are necessary. The horse with the highest rating is best in.

(ii) In races where all runners are set to carry different weights, add one point to the Raceform Rating for every pound less than 12 st to be carried; deduct one point for every pound more than 12 st.

For example,

Horse	Age & Weight	Adjustment from 12st	RR base rating	Adjusted rating
Flagship Uberalles	8-12-00	0	172	172
Edredon Bleu	10-11-12	+2	168	170
Fadalko	9-11-10	+4	168	172
Cenkos	8-11-06	+8	166	174

Therefore Cenkos is top-rated (best-in)

NB No adjustments are made for weight for age in Chaseform ratings. The official weight for age scale is displayed for information purposes while any live weight for age conditions are displayed underneath each individual result.

The following symbols are used in conjunction with the ratings:
++ almost certain to prove better
+ likely to prove better
d disappointing (has run well below best recently)
? form hard to evaluate, may prove unreliable
t tentative rating based on race-time

Weight adjusted ratings for every race are published daily in Raceform Private Handicap, and on our new service, Raceform Private Handicap ONLINE (www.raceform.co.uk). For subscription terms please contact the Subscription Department on (01635) 578080.

REVIEW OF THE SEASON

by Richard Lowther

The 2003-2004 jumps season saw Best Mate enter the record books as the first horse since Arkle to win three Cheltenham Gold Cups, becoming a household name in the process. Ginger McCain was back in the winner's enclosure at Aintree, and it was business as usual for Martin Pipe and Tony McCoy, although not without some scares along the way.

Graham Lee rode a remarkable four-timer at Wetherby on November 1, spearheaded by the success of Ballybough Rasher in the featured Bet365 Charlie Hall Chase. Lee was to enjoy plenty more highlights in a fantastic season in the saddle.

REBRANDED

Cheltenham's Open meeting in mid-November was rebranded, with Paddy Power taking over sponsorship. The big race, formerly known as the Mackeson, the Murphy's and the Thomas Pink, became the Paddy Power Gold Cup, and it was won in good style by Fondmort, from the Nicky Henderson yard and ridden by Mick Fitzgerald. The following day's Greatwood Hurdle, a valuable two-mile handicap, went to 33/1-shot Rigmarole, who had been in action since the start of the season and was having his tenth run of the campaign.

The following weekend attentions turned to Huntingdon where Best Mate was in action for the first time since winning Gold Cup number two. Starting odds-on for the Tote Peterborough Chase, he produced a somewhat laboured display and was beaten fair and square into second by the French raider Jair Du Cochet, who now looked a serious pretender to Best Mate's Gold Cup crown.

Also on November 22, Nicky Henderson snaffled another nice prize when Iris Royal won the First National Gold Cup Chase at Ascot, ridden by Marcus Foley. On the same card, Andrew Thornton produced perhaps the ride of the season on Kingscliff in the coral.co.uk Handicap Chase. After just three fences the reins broke on the former champion hunter chaser, leaving Thornton with virtually no steering for the remainder of the three-mile journey. Having survived a lurch into the rails when the reins initially snapped, the partnership made most of the running to beat Horus by 17 lengths.

CRACKING FINISH

Aintree's Tote Becher Chase on November 23 produced a cracking finish. The course was shorn of one of its most fearsome obstacles when the decision was made to omit the Chair fence due to the low sun, and the race was off 13 minutes late. Amberleigh House, the Becher winner of 2001, looked set to win again, but was pipped right on the line by Clan Royal, from the Jonjo O'Neill yard. The winner, ridden by Liam Cooper in the J P McManus colours, had won the Topham Trophy over the big fences the previous season.

The Hennessy Cognac Gold Cup took place at Newbury on November 29 with controversy over the previous year's running still going on. The 2002 victor, Be My Royal, was eventually disqualified after testing positive to morphine, but his connections have lodged an appeal so runner-up Gingembre has yet to be officially awarded the race.

Strong Flow, from the Paul Nicholls yard, became the first novice other than Be My Royal to win the Hennessy. The six-year-old was running for only the fifth time over fences and he betrayed his inexperience with a terrible blunder at the ninth fence, but he jumped well otherwise and went on to beat Joss Naylor in hugely impressive style. Connections now had to consider whether to aim their new star at the Gold Cup or keep him to the novice division.

NO MORE BUSINESS

A jumping great bowed out at Chepstow on December 6. After finishing a well beaten fourth on his seasonal debut in the John Hughes Rehearsal Chase, See More Business was retired by owners Paul Barber and Sir Robert Ogden. Now a 13-year-old, See More Business had won the 1999 Cheltenham Gold Cup as well as the King George VI Chase twice.

Sir Rembrandt, an early casualty in the previous week's Hennessy, confirmed himself a smart young chaser when beating Bindaree in the Rehearsal. The pair would renew rivalry back at Chepstow in the Welsh National.

The William Hill - Tingle Creek Trophy Chase at Sandown on December 6 saw reigning two-mile champ Moscow Flyer maintain his record of having won all his completed starts over fences. He beat young pretender Azertyuiop, the previous season's Arkle winner, by an impressive four lengths.

Iris Royal landed his second big pre-Christmas chase when taking the Tripleprint Gold Cup at Cheltenham on December 13. Sir Robert Ogden's battler, ridden by Mick Fitzgerald, just held off Risk Accessor by a head.

Rigmarole notched another long-priced Cheltenham victory when winning the Tote Bula Hurdle at 25/1. Champion Hurdler Rooster Booster finished fifth after being totally unsuited by the lack of pace.

FARCE

The run-up to Christmas saw two minor races reduced to farce. On December 15 at Towcester, all bar three of the field in an amateurs' chase bypassed a marker on the wrong side with a circuit to go. The first five home all had to be disqualified and the race was awarded to Stormhill Stag, who had finished a distant sixth. Just three days later, most of the field in a selling hurdle at Ludlow took the wrong route into the home straight, leading to bans for seven jockeys. In both cases the confusion had resulted from obstacles being omitted, and highlighted the difficult job facing both riders and Stewards.

Best Mate had been expected to tackle the Pertemps King George VI Chase at Kempton on Boxing Day but his connections eventually decided to run him instead in the Ericsson Chase at Leopardstown two days later, where the ground was more suitable. Remarkably, owner Jim Lewis, trainer Henrietta Knight and rider Jim Culloty were to land the King George anyway when veteran Edredon Bleu rallied in game fashion to

beat Tiutchev and First Gold. A 25/1-shot at Kempton, Edredon Bleu won all five of his races before his season ended in February as there were no suitable targets left for him. In Best Mate's absence, Jair Du Cochet had been expected to cash in at Kempton, but the 2/1 favourite had a 'bad day at the office' and was pulled up. Best Mate was back to his best at Leopardstown, coming home in splendid isolation for an impressive win, and was now as low as 4/5 for the Gold Cup.

Strong Flow's season also ended prematurely, as he sustained a serious leg injury when winning the Network Design Feltham Novices' Chase at Kempton on Boxing Day. All being well this tremendous prospect will be back in the new season. Feltham runner-up Ballycassidy was the season's winning-most horse with seven victories to his name.

Intersky Falcon won his second successive Jobs@Pertemps City Christmas Hurdle at Kempton, a change to hold-up tactics enabling him to beat Rooster Booster by two and a half lengths. Rooster Booster had a pacemaker in the field to ensure that there was no repeat of the dawdle that had ruined his chance in the Bula, but the pacemaker failed to do his job and this race turned into another sprint.

The Coral Welsh National at Chepstow on December 27 was run in very testing conditions as the rain lashed down. Bindaree handled the ground better than most and wore down old rival Sir Rembrandt on the run-in, the pair finishing well clear.

EPIC DUEL

The Victor Chandler Chase at Ascot on January 10 was surely one of the races of the season. After an epic duel, Isio beat Azertyuiop, who was conceding 19lb, by a neck. The runner-up now looked the only serious challenger to Moscow Flyer at Cheltenham.

On the same afternoon at Warwick, the Henrietta Knight-trained Southern Star, ridden by Graham Lee, landed the £63,000 Tote Classic Chase. Sadly, the victory was overshadowed by the deaths of two fine chasers, Behrajan and Take Control.

Tony McCoy made history once again when becoming the first jump jockey to ride 2,000 winners in Britain. The incomparable A P reached the landmark aboard Magical Bailiwick, trained appropriately by Martin Pipe, at Wincanton on January 17.

Jair Du Cochet, and his under-fire rider Jacques Ricou, restored their reputations with a brilliant win in Cheltenham's Pillar Property Chase on January 24. Only two of the six starters completed the course, among the non-finishers being Sir Rembrandt, pulled up after never travelling, and Martin Pipe's exciting novice Therealbandit, a faller on only his third run over fences.

Mick Fitzgerald broke his left arm in a fall at Sandown on February 7, an injury that was to cost him some big winners. Fitzgerald had happier memories of a trip to Sandown in November, when a victory on Orswell Crest was his 1,000th in Britain.

FOUR FOR FLORIDA

Florida Pearl won Leopardstown's Hennessy Cognac Gold Cup for the fourth time on February 8. Willie Mullins' popular chaser, left clear by the departure of Harbour Pilot at the second last, was later forced to miss the Cheltenham Gold Cup after incurring a leg problem.

A field of 25 lined up for the Tote Gold Trophy at Newbury on February 14, Rooster Booster giving the best part of a stone away. Sent off the 9/2 favourite, the grey almost pulled it off, but was caught right on the line by 16/1 chance Geos, who had won the Newbury showpiece back in 2000. Geos, partnered by Marcus Foley, was yet another big Saturday winner for Nicky Henderson.

Rigmarole strengthened his Champion Hurdle claims when beating Intersky Falcon fair and square in the Axminster Kingwell Hurdle at Wincanton on February 21. Paul Nicholls's gelding now appeared the major danger to Rooster Booster in the big one.

Trained by Richard Guest, Tyneandthyneagain won his second big handicap of the season when surviving mistakes to win the Tote Eider Chase at Newcastle on February 21. The nine-year-old had earlier won the Skybet Chase at Doncaster, a race better known to traditionalists as the Great Yorkshire.

Nicky Henderson produced another Saturday special when old stager Marlborough won the Racing Post Chase at Kempton on February 28. The 8/1 shot, who beat previous winner Gunther McBride by four lengths, was a chance ride for Ruby Walsh. In the continued absence of Mick Fitzgerald, Walsh had been booked to ride the stable's main hope Irish Hussar, but he was withdrawn an hour before the race due to the ground. Barry Fenton had been due to partner Marlborough, but was injured in a fall earlier in the day leaving Walsh to step in.

The Henderson yard repeated the trick the following weekend, when Isio landed the inaugural and highly valuable Vodafone Gold Cup Chase at Newbury. Barry Geraghty was in the saddle this time.

A fit-again Barry Fenton partnered Scorned to victory in the big pre-Cheltenham hurdle at Sandown, the Sunderlands Imperial Cup, for the Andew Balding stable. The following week, riding at Huntingdon, Fenton's season was ended by a broken leg.

EMOTIONAL VICTORY

The previous season's winners of the big four races at the Cheltenham Festival, Rooster Booster, Moscow Flyer, Baracouda and Best Mate, all returned to defend their crowns. First up was Rooster Booster who started 11/8 favourite for the Smurfit Champion Hurdle. All looked to be going to plan for the grey's followers as he ranged up alongside leader Hardy Eustace at the last flight, but to the surprise of nearly everyone the 33/1 outsider pulled away on the run-in to win by five lengths. Intersky Falcon was third, with Rigmarole slightly lame back in eighth. Irish raider Hardy Eustace, trained by Dessie Hughes and ridden by Conor O'Dwyer, was a late addition to the Champion Hurdle field having originally been going to run in the Coral Cup. It was a highly emotional victory as jockey Kieran Kelly, who had won the Royal & SunAlliance Hurdle on Hardy Eustace at the 2003 Festival, had died after a fall at Kilbeggan in August, aged 25.

Earlier on day one of the Festival, Martin Pipe and Tony McCoy teamed up to take the Irish Independent Arkle Challenge Trophy Chase with Well Chief. Hot favourite for the two-mile novices' championship, Thisthatandtother, was a faller at the second.

On the Wednesday, Moscow Flyer became the second champion to be beaten, as Jessica Harrington's star blundered away rider Barry Geraghty at the last ditch in the Queen Mother Champion Chase. This left the way clear for Azertyuiop, who beat former champion Flagship Uberalles by nine lengths in the hands of Ruby Walsh. The win gave

the Paul Nicholls team ample compensation for their disappointment with Thisthatandtother the previous day.

Having won the Arkle with Well Chief, Pipe, McCoy and owner David Johnson had high hopes of adding the Royal & SunAlliance Chase for staying novices. Their Our Vic was sent off a warm favourite, but he faded to finish third behind surprise Irish winner Rule Supreme from the Willie Mullins yard.

Philip Hobbs and Richard Johnson, out of luck with Rooster Booster, were on target in the Coral Cup with Monkerhostin on the Wednesday, as well as Thursday's opener, the JCB Triumph Hurdle, with 20/1 chance Made In Japan.

IRIS'S REVENGE

Going into the Bonusprint.com Stayers' Hurdle Baracouda had a sensational record of 14 wins from his last 15 runs, including a defeat of young pretender Iris's Gift in the previous year's version, but the grey took his revenge after a fine duel. Iris's Gift, who came to Cheltenham with just a single run under his belt, drew the sting out of Baracouda before beating the French star by a length and a half.

Best Mate's Gold Cup chances were boosted in an unwelcome manner just days before the race when his main rival Jair Du Cochet was killed on the gallops at trainer Guillaume Macaire's yard. The tragedy saw Best Mate sent off at 8/11, with Therealbandit next best at 15/2 in a field of ten. Best Mate travelled well behind the leaders as First Gold made the running. There was an anxious moment for the favourite's supporters as he was hemmed in by Harbour Pilot on the home turn, but Jim Culloty stayed cool and switched him into the clear. He was soon in front, but had to show real grit to hold off Harbour Pilot up the final hill, with Sir Rembrandt finishing strongly to divide the pair. Therealbandit was a well beaten seventh. There were emotional scenes as trainer Henrietta Knight and her husband Terry Biddlecombe greeted their star.

The Aintree Grand National meeting, the last under the sponsorship of Martell, opened on April 1 with a new race, the Liverpool Hurdle, which had previously been known as the Long Distance Hurdle and run at Ascot. Iris's Gift made virtually all the running to beat the novice Royal Rosa by two and a half lengths. The runner-up was owned by Graham Wylie, a very wealthy businessman who, having sold his computer software company, moved into jump racing in a big way and assembled a squad of expensive purchases under the care of Durham trainer Howard Johnson.

The versatile Tiutchev, who had been placed in both the King George and the Queen Mother Champion Chase, gained a deserved victory in the Martell Cognac Cup, at the main expense of the previous year's winner First Gold. It was the fifth Grade One success of Tiutchev's career.

Made In Japan made a brave attempt to become the first horse to complete the Triumph Hurdle/Anniversary Hurdle double since Pollardstown in 1979, but the 4lb penalty told in the end and he went down by three parts of a length to Irish raider Al Eile, who had finished only 15th at Cheltenham.

Moscow Flyer was back to winning ways in the Martell Cognac Melling Chase on day two at Aintree, beating Isio by six lengths. From 17 starts over fences he now had twelve wins to his name, but had failed to get round on the other five occasions.

Arkle winner Well Chief followed up in the opening race of the Saturday card, the Maghull Novices' Chase, under a confident ride from Tony McCoy. Runner-up Thisthatandtother never stopped fighting but was beaten on merit.

COWBOY GUNS DOWN ROOSTER

Rooster Booster suffered another setback in a frustrating season as he was beaten into second by Rhinestone Cowboy in the Martell Cognac Aintree Hurdle. The Jonjo O'Neill-trained winner was partnered, as he had been all season, by the owner's son J P Magnier, an amateur rider who was unable to claim in such a valuable event.

The Martell Cognac Grand National invariably produces a great story and the 2004 running didn't disappoint. When the weights were unveiled in February, trainer Ginger McCain had been characteristically bullish about the chances of Amberleigh House, whose fine record at Aintree included a third in the big race twelve months earlier. Carrying 10st 10lb, the twelve-year-old was given a lovely patient ride by Graham Lee, and the pair swept into the lead at the elbow to beat favourite Clan Royal, whose rider Liam Cooper had lost his whip, and outsider Lord Atterbury. The 2003 winner Monty's Pass was a long way back in fourth in a race which produced plenty of grief, including no fewer than nine casualties at Becher's Brook on the first circuit. Amberleigh House was McCain's fourth winner of the big race, following the legendary Red Rum in 1973, 1974 and 1977, and meant that McCain had now equalled Fred Rimell's National record.

There was an English success in the Powers Gold Label Irish Grand National on Easter Monday, April 12, when 33/1 shot Granit D'Estruval, trained in Yorkshire by Ferdie Murphy, got home by half a length in the hands of Brian Harding.

'ABBEY' NATIONAL

Granit D'Estruval made a bold bid to follow up just five days later in the Gala Casinos Daily Record Scottish Grand National but came down at the final fence when disputing the lead. This left the highly popular Ayr specialist Grey Abbey, trained by Howard Johnson, to come home alone, giving Graham Lee another big winner in a memorable season.

The campaign ended on April 24 with the first running of the BetFred Gold Cup at Sandown, a race run of late as the Attheraces Gold Cup but still the Whitbread to many people. In a cracking finish, the novice Puntal, trained by Martin Pipe, just held on from the Paul Nicholls runner Royal Auclair. Puntal's Irish jockey Danny Howard was winning his first race in Britain.

Going into the Grand National meeting Paul Nicholls had held a narrow lead over Martin Pipe in the trainers' championship, but Pipe moved ahead over the course of the three days and never relinquished his grip on the title afterwards. It was Pipe's ninth consecutive title and 14th overall, but Nicholls will be wondering if he is ever going to be champion trainer.

Tony McCoy was champion jockey again with 209 winners, 21 ahead of his nearest rival Richard Johnson. McCoy retained his title despite having missed three and a half months of the season due to injury and suspension, the longest lay-off coming in June when he broke his left arm in a fall at Worcester. Johnson was able to build an early lead over McCoy, but could never get clear.

Martin Pipe's leading owner David Johnson was champion once more, his horses picking up £924,000 in win and place prize money. Champion conditional was Jamie Moore, also attached to the Pipe yard. Sam Thomas, who turned professional in November, was one winner behind Moore.

Jumping mourned the death of the great Fred Winter in April at the age of 77. Champion jockey four times and champion trainer on eight occasions, he won the Grand National twice as a rider, on Sundew and Kilmore, and twice as a trainer with Jay Trump and Anglo. He rode Gold Cup winners Saffron Tartan and Mandarin, and sent out Midnight Court to win in 1978.

Anne, Duchess of Westminster, owner of the legendary Arkle, died in September at the age of 88. Her yellow and black colours were also carried to victory in another Gold Cup by Ten Up and in a Grand National by Last Suspect.

Ken Cundell, trainer of that fine grey chaser Stalbridge Colonist, one of the few horses to beat Arkle over fences, died in October aged 88.

Norman Williamson retired from the saddle in October. A great stylist, he won both the Champion Hurdle and Gold Cup in 1995, on Alderbrook and Master Oats respectively.

Nick Gaselee, best known as the trainer of 1992 Grand National winner Party Politics, retired at the end of the season.

Notes

A Few Bob Back (IRE)

99(106h)   (123 h)**92**

8-y-o b g Bob Back (USA)-Kottna (USA) (Lyphard (USA))
D Eddy Brian Chicken

Placings:0005/5P41F0012P/1133060-F303F4   **(4274)**
2003/04: 20FG, 223S, 240GS, 213GS, 23FS, 204G,

	Starts	1st	2nd	3rd	Win & Pl
Hurdles	3	0	0	1	883
Chases	3	0	0	1	1265
Career Total	27	4	1	4	25476

120	11/02	Ayr	2m4f	C(0-130)HHdl	SFT	£6851
114	11/02	Kels	2m6f110yD(0-125)HHdl	SFT	£4199
108	1/02	Newc	3m	D(0-125)HHdl	SFT	£3542
99	8/01	Slig	2m4f	(0-95)HHdl	SH	£4312

Total win prize-money £18905

Going: Sf: 0-2 GS: 0-2 Gd: 0-2 GF: - Fm: 0-0
Distance: 2m/2m3: 0-0 2m4-2m7: 0-4 3m+: 0-2
Track: LH: 0-4 RH: 0-1 Tight: 0-2 Gall: 0-0
Aids: Bl: 0-0 Vi: 0-0 Tstrap: 0-0 Ckp: 0-4
Best Rating: 120 12/02 Muss 3m   gd-fm Hdl

Fair handicap hurdler; good third on chasing debut at Sedgefield in January; acts on a soft surface and stays three miles; has worn cheekpieces and blinkers.

A Fine Story

8-y-o b/br g Le Moss-Kelly's Story (Netherkelly)
H Hill Broderick Munro-Wilson

Placings:P   **(4308)**
2003/04: 24PG,

	Starts	1st	2nd	3rd	Win & Pl
Chases	1	0	0	0	
Career Total	1	0	0	0	

Going: Sf: 0-0 GS: 0-0 Gd: 0-1 GF: - Fm: 0-0
Distance: 2m/2m3: 0-0 2m4-2m7: 0-0 3m+: 0-1
Track: LH: 0-0 RH: 0-1 Tight: 0-0 Gall: 0-0
Aids: Bl: 0-0 Vi: 0-0 Tstrap: 0-0 Ckp: 0-0
Best Rating: 0 3/04 Sand 3m110y good Ch

A Glass In Thyne (IRE)

85   **103**

6-y-o br g Glacial Storm (USA)-River Thyne (IRE) (Good Thyne (USA))
B N Pollock J B Dale

Placings:32   **(3271)**
2003/04: 193G, 202S,

	Starts	1st	2nd	3rd	Win & Pl
Hurdles	2	0	1	1	2342
Career Total	2	0	1	1	2342

Going: Sf: 0-1 GS: 0-0 Gd: 0-1 GF: - Fm: 0-0
Distance: 2m/2m3: 0-0 2m4-2m7: 0-2 3m+: 0-0
Track: LH: 0-1 RH: 0-1 Tight: 0-1 Gall: 0-0
Aids: Bl: 0-0 Vi: 0-0 Tstrap: 0-0 Ckp: 0-0
Best Rating: 108 1/04 Asct 2m4f soft Hdl

Placed in novice hurdles; stays 2m 4f; effective in soft ground.

A Piece Of Cake (IRE)

94   **147**

11-y-o gr g Roselier (FR)-Boreen Bro (Boreen (FR))
Mrs M Reveley Lightbody Celebration Cakes Ltd

Placings:0/15F2123131/6F1450/U21U11-54   **(3004)**
2003/04: 255S, 254GS,

	Starts	1st	2nd	3rd	Win & Pl
Chases	2	0	0	0	2014
Career Total	25	8	3	2	101227

147	3/03	Kels	4m	C(0-135)HCh	GD	£30856
136	2/03	Ayr	2m4f	B(0-145)HCh	SFT	£13312
136	1/03	Ayr	2m4f	B(0-140)HCh	HVY	£12096
134	2/02	Newc	2m4f	B(0-140)HCh	SFT	£8853
134	4/01	Asct	2m3f110yC(0-130)HCh	SFT	£14040
122	1/01	Newc	2m4f	E Ch	HVY	£3120
110	11/00	Kels	2m6f110yE Ch	SFT	£3315
89	5/00	Weth	2m4f110yD Hdl	G-F	£3432

Total win prize-money £89026

Going: Sf: 0-1 GS: 0-1 Gd: 0-0 GF: - Fm: 0-0
Distance: 2m/2m3: 0-0 2m4-2m7: 0-0 3m+: 0-2
Track: LH: 0-2 RH: 0-0 Tight: 0-1 Gall: 0-0
Aids: Bl: 0-0 Vi: 0-0 Tstrap: 0-0 Ckp: 0-0
Best Rating: 147 3/03 Kels 4m   good Ch

Very useful chaser; most of best form over two miles four, but managed to win a valuable chase over four miles at Kelso in March 2003; best on soft ground; has tended to make mistakes in the past.

A Pound Down (IRE)

7-y-o b g Treasure Hunter-Ann's Queen (IRE) (Rhoman Rule (USA))
N G Ayliffe Derek Walker

Placings:P   **(4695)**
2003/04: 23PG,

	Starts	1st	2nd	3rd	Win & Pl
Chases	1	0	0	0	
Career Total	1	0	0	0	

Going: Sf: 0-0 GS: 0-0 Gd: 0-1 GF: - Fm: 0-0
Distance: 2m/2m3: 0-0 2m4-2m7: 0-0 3m+: 0-1
Track: LH: 0-0 RH: 0-1 Tight: 0-0 Gall: 0-0
Aids: Bl: 0-0 Vi: 0-0 Tstrap: 0-0 Ckp: 0-0
Best Rating: 0 4/04 Extr 2m7f110y good Ch

A Romp Too Far (IRE)

8-y-o b g Eurobus-Saxa Princess (IRE) (Lancastrian)
M Ranger G M Julian

Placings:06/P0PP-P   **(3792)**
2003/04: 25PG,

	Starts	1st	2nd	3rd	Win & Pl
Chases	1	0	0	0	
Career Total	7	0	0	0	0

Going: Sf: 0-0 GS: 0-0 Gd: 0-1 GF: - Fm: 0-0
Distance: 2m/2m3: 0-0 2m4-2m7: 0-0 3m+: 0-1
Track: LH: 0-0 RH: 0-1 Tight: 0-0 Gall: 0-0
Aids: Bl: 0-0 Vi: 0-0 Tstrap: 0-0 Ckp: 0-0
Best Rating: 98 10/01 Chel 2m110y good NHF

A Toi A Moi (FR)

87   **103**

4-y-o ch g Cyborg (FR)-Peperonelle (FR) (Dom Pasquini (FR))
Miss Venetia Williams (T Civel 8/10) T England

Placings:2240   **(3485)**
2003/04: 152G, 182HO, 164S, 170GS,

	Starts	1st	2nd	3rd	Win & Pl
Hurdles	4	0	2	0	11157
Career Total	4	0	2	0	11157

Going: Sf: 0-1 GS: 0-1 Gd: 0-1 GF: - Fm: 0-0
Distance: 2m/2m3: 0-3 2m4-2m7: 0-0 3m+: 0-0
Track: LH: 0-2 RH: 0-0 Tight: 0-0 Gall: 0-1
Aids: Bl: 0-0 Vi: 0-0 Tstrap: 0-0 Ckp: 0-0
Best Rating: 103 1/04 Chel 2m1f   gd-sft Hdl

Juvenile hurdler; ex-French; distant fourth in a Grade One event at Chepstow on his British debut; again well held next time; acts with cut in the ground; stays 2m2f.

Ababou (FR)

8-y-o ch g Synefos (USA)-Racine Carree (FR) (Dom Racine (FR))
Mrs Lucy Latchford Mrs Lucy Latchford

Placings:00P6/0405046P/6-1P   **(4607)**
2003/04: 251GS, 25PGS,

	Starts	1st	2nd	3rd	Win & Pl
Chases	2	1	0	0	1341
Career Total	15	1	0	0	2349

| 90 | 3/04 | MRas | 3m1f | H Ch | G-S | £1340 |

Total win prize-money £1341

Going: Sf: 0-0 GS: 1-2 Gd: 0-0 GF: - Fm: 0-0
Distance: 2m/2m3: 0-0 2m4-2m7: 0-0 3m+: 1-2
Track: LH: 0-0 RH: 1-2 Tight: 1-2 Gall: 0-0
Aids: Bl: 0-0 Vi: 0-0 Tstrap: 0-0 Ckp: 0-0
Best Rating: 90 3/04 MRas 3m1f   gd-sft Ch

Winner of six points; struggled to last home in poor hunters' chase at Market Rasen in March; stays three miles; not a good jumper under Rules.

Abajany

97   **93**

10-y-o b g Akarad (FR)-Miss Ivory Coast (USA) (Sir Ivor)
R J Baker Graham Brown

Placings:P45/260/3/4/03000/060-3   **(1222)**
2003/04: 173GF,

	Starts	1st	2nd	3rd	Win & Pl
Hurdles	1	0	0	1	535
Career Total	17	0	1	3	4002

Going: Sf: 0-0 GS: 0-0 Gd: 0-0 GF: - Fm: 0-1
Distance: 2m/2m3: 0-1 2m4-2m7: 0-0 3m+: 0-0
Track: LH: 0-1 RH: 0-0 Tight: 0-1 Gall: 0-0
Aids: Bl: 0-0 Vi: 0-0 Tstrap: 0-0 Ckp: 0-0
Best Rating: 106 10/98 Plum 2m1f   good Hdl

A Flat winner, he has shown bits and pieces of form over timber and looks to need a sound surface; probably only just stays 2m.

Abalvino (FR)

107   **136**

10-y-o ch g Sillery (USA)-Abalvina (FR) (Abdos)

P R Webber I M S Racing & Noel Cronin

Placings:*3130*/45/F3124321/15132U0/F332210-0F434020

(4575)

2003/04: 17⁰GS, 16ᶠG, 16⁴G, 16³HY, 16⁴S, 16⁰G, 17²G, 18⁰G,

	Starts	1st	2nd	3rd	Win & Pl
Chases	8	0	1	1	6712
Career Total	36	6	6	8	58244

136	2/03	Newb	2m1f	C(0-135)HCh	SFT	£8190
130	12/01	Strf	2m1f110yD(0-120)HCh		SFT	£8580
130	5/01	Hntg	2m110y E Ch		GD	£3752
130	4/01	MRas	2m1f110yD Ch		G-S	£4849
117	12/00	Leic	2m	E(0-135)HCh	G-S	£3133
114	1/99	Towc	2m	H NHF	HVY	£1420

Total win prize-money £29924

Going:	Sf: 0-2 GS: 0-1 Gd: 0-5 GF: - Fm: 0-0
Distance:	2m/2m3: 0-8 2m4-2m7: 0-0 3m+: 0-0
Track:	LH: 0-5 RH: 0-3 Tight: 0-0 Gall: 0-4
Aids:	Bl: 0-0 Vi: 0-0 Tstrap: 0-6 Ckp: 0-2
Best Rating:	136 2/03 Newb 2m1f soft Ch

Useful handicap chaser; front-runner; effective at around two miles and acts on good and soft ground; wears a tongue strap.

Abbey's Girl (IRE)
(0c)**34**

8-y-o b m Elbio-Abbey Trinity (IRE) (Tender King)
J D Frost (K J Burke 15/5) Dead Loss Racing

Placings:000/00/F-00P

(1120)

2003/04: 24⁰S, 19⁰G, 19ᶠGF,

	Starts	1st	2nd	3rd	Win & Pl
Hurdles	3	0	0	0	
Career Total	9	0	0	0	

Going:	Sf: 0-1 GS: 0-0 Gd: 0-1 GF: - Fm: 0-1
Distance:	2m/2m3: 0-2 2m4-2m7: 0-0 3m+: 0-1
Track:	LH: 0-0 RH: 0-0 Tight: 0-0 Gall: 0-0
Aids:	Bl: 0-0 Vi: 0-0 Tstrap: 0-0 Ckp: 0-1
Best Rating:	46 4/00 Cork 2m soft Hdl

Abbeyknock Boy (IRE)
(94h) (75h)**80**

7-y-o b/br g Alphabatim (USA)-Haha Dash (IRE) (Lord Ha Ha)
M F Harris Pat Owens

Placings:4/04U/0034P00303-6

(0138)

2003/04: 24ᶠG,

	Starts	1st	2nd	3rd	Win & Pl
Chases	1	0	0	0	0
Career Total	15	0	0	3	1867

Going:	Sf: 0-0 GS: 0-0 Gd: 0-1 GF: - Fm: 0-0
Distance:	2m/2m3: 0-0 2m4-2m7: 0-0 3m+: 0-1
Track:	LH: 0-0 RH: 0-1 Tight: 0-1 Gall: 0-0
Aids:	Bl: 0-0 Vi: 0-0 Tstrap: 0-1 Ckp: 0-0
Best Rating:	80 3/03 Wwck 3m110y gd-fm Ch

Moderate chaser; poor maiden over hurdles; stays three miles; effective at fast ground.

Abbeytown (IRE)
101 **124+**

7-y-o ch g Over The River (FR)-Call Queen (Callernish)
K Riordan Miss M L Estby

Placings:0025

(4398)

2003/04: 24⁰SH, 20⁰S, 24²GY, 32⁸G,

	Starts	1st	2nd	3rd	Win & Pl
Chases	4	0	1	0	2611
Career Total	4	0	1	0	2611

Going:	Sf: 0-1 GS: 0-0 Gd: 0-1 GF: - Fm: 0-0
Distance:	2m/2m3: 0-0 2m4-2m7: 0-1 3m+: 0-0
Track:	LH: 0-1 RH: 0-2 Tight: 0-0 Gall: 0-1
Aids:	Bl: 0-0 Vi: 0-0 Tstrap: 0-0 Ckp: 0-0
Best Rating:	124 3/04 Chel 4m good Ch

Irish novice chaser; stays three miles; acts with cut in the ground.

Abbots Court (IRE)

9-y-o b g Hallowed Turf (USA)-Coronea Sea Queen (IRE) (Bassompierre)
R H Alner H Wellstead

Placings:0/0PP/4-F

(1511)

2003/04: 26ᶠGF,

	Starts	1st	2nd	3rd	Win & Pl
Chases	1	0	0	0	
Career Total	5	0	0	0	260

Going:	Sf: 0-0 GS: 0-0 Gd: 0-0 GF: - Fm: 0-1
Distance:	2m/2m3: 0-0 2m4-2m7: 0-0 3m+: 0-1
Track:	LH: 0-1 RH: 0-0 Tight: 0-0 Gall: 0-0
Aids:	Bl: 0-0 Vi: 0-0 Tstrap: 0-0 Ckp: 0-0
Best Rating:	95 3/01 Hntg 2m110y soft NHF

A winner of point-to-points in 2000; most disapointing over fences; should stay well.

Aberdare
96f **86f**

5-y-o b m Overbury (IRE)-Temple Heights (Shirley Heights)
J R Bewley R Bewley

Placings:0400

(3982)

2003/04: 16⁸G, 16⁴HY, 17⁰GS, 17⁰G,

	Starts	1st	2nd	3rd	Win & Pl
NH Flat	4	0	0	0	0
Career Total	4	0	0	0	0

Going:	Sf: 0-1 GS: 0-1 Gd: 0-2 GF: - Fm: 0-0
Distance:	2m/2m3: 0-4 2m4-2m7: 0-0 3m+: 0-0
Track:	LH: 0-3 RH: 0-1 Tight: 0-1 Gall: 0-0
Aids:	Bl: 0-0 Vi: 0-0 Tstrap: 0-0 Ckp: 0-0
Best Rating:	86 1/04 Newc 2m heavy NHF

Abernant Lady
70 **40**

7-y-o gr m Absalom-Hosting (Thatching)
A G Newcombe Derek Walker

Placings:4-0

(0869)

2003/04: 22⁰GF,

	Starts	1st	2nd	3rd	Win & Pl
Hurdles	1	0	0	0	
Career Total	2	0	0	0	310

Going:	Sf: 0-0 GS: 0-0 Gd: 0-0 GF: - Fm: 0-1
Distance:	2m/2m3: 0-0 2m4-2m7: 0-1 3m+: 0-0
Track:	LH: 0-1 RH: 0-0 Tight: 0-1 Gall: 0-0

Aids:	Bl: 0-0 Vi: 0-0 Tstrap: 0-0 Ckp: 0-0
Best Rating:	40 10/02 Extr 2m3f firm Hdl

Aberthatch (FR)
102

5-y-o b m Thatching-Academy Angel (FR) (Royal Academy (USA))
M J Ryan Avondale Construction Ltd

Placings:32-PP

(3928)

2003/04: 17ᴾGS, 16ᴾG,

	Starts	1st	2nd	3rd	Win & Pl
Hurdles	2	0	0	0	
Career Total	4	0	1	1	2786

Going:	Sf: 0-0 GS: 0-1 Gd: 0-1 GF: - Fm: 0-0
Distance:	2m/2m3: 0-2 2m4-2m7: 0-0 3m+: 0-0
Track:	LH: 0-0 RH: 0-2 Tight: 0-1 Gall: 0-0
Aids:	Bl: 0-0 Vi: 0-0 Tstrap: 0-0 Ckp: 0-0
Best Rating:	98 11/02 Hntg 2m110y gd-sft Hdl

Moderate performer on the Flat, she has shown ability in novice hurdles.

Abigail
92f **69f**

4-y-o gr f Simply Great (FR)-Stormy Gal (IRE) (Strong Gale)
T D Easterby Mrs Anne Henson

Placings:0

(4962)

2003/04: 17⁰G,

	Starts	1st	2nd	3rd	Win & Pl
NH Flat	1	0	0	0	
Career Total	1	0	0	0	

Going:	Sf: 0-0 GS: 0-0 Gd: 0-1 GF: - Fm: 0-0
Distance:	2m/2m3: 0-1 2m4-2m7: 0-0 3m+: 0-0
Track:	LH: 0-0 RH: 0-1 Tight: 0-0 Gall: 0-0
Aids:	Bl: 0-0 Vi: 0-0 Tstrap: 0-0 Ckp: 0-0
Best Rating:	69 4/04 MRas 2m1f110y good NHF

Ability
55 **31**

5-y-o b g Alflora (IRE)-Beatle Song (Song)
S C Burrough Mrs Christine Priest

Placings:0

(4812)

2003/04: 16⁰G,

	Starts	1st	2nd	3rd	Win & Pl
Hurdles	1	0	0	0	
Career Total	1	0	0	0	

Going:	Sf: 0-0 GS: 0-0 Gd: 0-1 GF: - Fm: 0-0
Distance:	2m/2m3: 0-1 2m4-2m7: 0-0 3m+: 0-0
Track:	LH: 0-1 RH: 0-0 Tight: 0-0 Gall: 0-0
Aids:	Bl: 0-0 Vi: 0-0 Tstrap: 0-0 Ckp: 0-0
Best Rating:	31 4/04 Chep 2m110y good Hdl

Able Native (IRE)
104(101c) (95c)**111**

7-y-o b m Thatching-Native Joy (IRE) (Be My Native (USA))
R C Guest N B Mason

Placings:204/0051342122055133/24560616223-U54120

(0715)

2003/04: 20^{U}HY, 16^{S}G, 20^{4}G, 16^{1}G, 20^{2}HY, 16^{0}G,

	Starts	1st	2nd	3rd	Win & Pl
Hurdles	4	1	1	0	7320
Chases	2	0	0	0	0
Career Total	36	5	8	4	32075

112	5/03	Hexm	2m110y	E(0-110)HHdl	GD £3426
95	10/02	Fknm	3m110y	F(0-90)HCh	GD £4007
113	3/02	Newc	2m4f	E(0-110)HHdl	HVY £3493
104	1/02	Fknm	2m	E(0-110)HHdl	SFT £2408
100	10/01	Fknm	2m	F(0-105)HHdl	SFT £3342

Total win prize-money £16679

Going: Sf: 0-2 GS: 0-0 Gd: 1-4 GF: - Fm: 0-0
Distance: 2m/2m3: 1-3 2m4-2m7: 0-3 3m+: 0-0
Track: LH: 1-4 RH: 0-2 Tight: 0-0 Gall: 0-0
Aids: Bl: 1-3 Vi: 0-0 Tstrap: 1-2 Ckp: 0-3
Best Rating: 113 3/02 Newc 2m4f heavy Hdl

Moderate hurdler; goes well with cut and likes a sharp track; best over two miles, stays two and a half; goes well at Fakenham, where she won over fences in October 2002; acts on ground good and softer.

Abou Zulu
43
4-y-o ch g Abou Zouz (USA)-Mary From Dunlow (Nicholas Bill)
H A McWilliams J J Wright

Placings:40 (1603)
2003/04: 16^{4}F, 17^{9}GF,

	Starts	1st	2nd	3rd	Win & Pl
Hurdles	2	0	0	0	0
Career Total	2	0	0	0	0

Going: Sf: 0-0 GS: 0-0 Gd: 0-0 GF: 0-2
Distance: 2m/2m3: 0-2 2m4-2m7: 0-0 3m+: 0-0
Track: LH: 0-0 RH: 0-1 Tight: 0-0 Gall: 0-0
Aids: Bl: 0-1 Vi: 0-0 Tstrap: 0-0 Ckp: 0-1
Best Rating: 43 10/03 Kels 2m firm Hdl

Above The Cut (USA)
105   99
12-y-o ch g Topsider (USA)-Placer Queen (Habitat)
C P Morlock J P M & J W Cook

Placings:25662152/216/64/253606645/22244/0005201421 05/061230363-01145 (0754)
2003/04: 22^{9}G, 24^{1}GF, 27^{1}GF, 22^{4}G, 27^{5}GF,

	Starts	1st	2nd	3rd	Win & Pl
Hurdles	5	2	0	0	8845
Career Total	53	7	11	4	36646

99	6/03	NAbb	3m3f	G(0-110)HHdl	G-F £4772
96	5/03	Extr	3m110y	F(0-100)HHdl	G-F £3549
99	7/02	MRas	3m	G(0-95)HHdl	GD £2289
99	12/01	Tntn	3m110y	D(0-120)HHdl	G-S £3510
99	10/01	Ludl	3m	F(0-95)HHdl	G-F £3209
110	5/97	Towc	2m	D(0-125)HHdl	GD £2840
106	3/97	Ludl	2m	E(0-115)HHdl	G-F £2584

Total win prize-money £22754

Going: Sf: 0-0 GS: 0-0 Gd: 0-2 GF: - Fm: 2-3
Distance: 2m/2m3: 0-0 2m4-2m7: 0-2 3m+: 2-3
Track: LH: 1-3 RH: 0-2 Tight: 1-3 Gall: 0-0
Aids: Bl: 0-0 Vi: 0-0 Tstrap: 0-0 Ckp: 0-0
Best Rating: 110 5/97 Towc 2m good Hdl

Plating class hurdler; in good form in 2003 registering back-to-back wins at Exeter and Newton Abbot in May and June; fair handicap chaser; does not want the ground too soft; acts on a sound surface; stays 3m 3f.

Abraham Smith
70f
4-y-o b g Lord Americo-Alice Smith (Alias Smith (USA))
B J Eckley Brian Eckley

Placings:4 (4509)
2003/04: 14^{4}GS,

	Starts	1st	2nd	3rd	Win & Pl
NH Flat	1	0	0	0	0
Career Total	1	0	0	0	0

Going: Sf: 0-0 GS: 0-1 Gd: 0-0 GF: - Fm: 0-0
Distance: 2m/2m3: 0-0 2m4-2m7: 0-0 3m+: 0-0
Track: LH: 0-0 RH: 0-0 Tight: 0-0 Gall: 0-0
Aids: Bl: 0-0 Vi: 0-0 Tstrap: 0-0 Ckp: 0-0
Best Rating: 70 3/04 Hrfd 1m6f gd-sft NHF

Absolutely Hopeful
11-y-o ch g Nearly A Hand-Owena Deep (Deep Run)
Simon Jones Simon Jones

Placings:304/0/022PP/2FP5556PP/4536410P/FP-5 (3845)
2003/04: 25^{5}GS,

	Starts	1st	2nd	3rd	Win & Pl
Chases	1	0	0	0	0
Career Total	29	1	3	2	6063

89	2/02	Folk	2m6f110yE(0-110)HHdl		SFT £2555

Total win prize-money £2555

Going: Sf: 0-0 GS: 0-1 Gd: 0-0 GF: - Fm: 0-0
Distance: 2m/2m3: 0-0 2m4-2m7: 0-0 3m+: 0-1
Track: LH: 0-0 RH: 0-1 Tight: 0-0 Gall: 0-0
Aids: Bl: 0-1 Vi: 0-0 Tstrap: 0-0 Ckp: 0-0
Best Rating: 89 2/02 Folk 2m6f110y soft Hdl

Inconsistent staying hurdler; hunter chasing now; goes well in soft ground.

Abuelos
5-y-o b g Sabrehill (USA)-Miss Oasis (Green Desert (USA))
T P McGovern (S Dow 16/2) J Noonan

Placings:P (2336)
2003/04: 16^{P}S,

	Starts	1st	2nd	3rd	Win & Pl
Hurdles	1	0	0	0	
Career Total	1	0	0	0	

Going: Sf: 0-1 GS: 0-0 Gd: 0-0 GF: - Fm: 0-0
Distance: 2m/2m3: 0-1 2m4-2m7: 0-0 3m+: 0-0
Track: LH: 0-1 RH: 0-0 Tight: 0-1 Gall: 0-0
Aids: Bl: 0-0 Vi: 0-0 Tstrap: 0-0 Ckp: 0-0
Best Rating: 0 11/03 Plum 2m soft Hdl

Abzuson
111   100
7-y-o b g Abzu-Mellouise (Handsome Sailor)
J R Norton Abzuson Syndicate

Placings:241/6FU2-0F6232 (4515)
2003/04: 20^{4}G, 19^{F}G, 21^{6}GS, 20^{2}GS, 20^{3}S, 25^{2}GS,

	Starts	1st	2nd	3rd	Win & Pl
Hurdles	6	0	2	1	2631
Career Total	13	1	4	1	5893

102	4/02	Hexm	2m110y H NHF		GD £1624

Total win prize-money £1624

Going: Sf: 0-1 GS: 0-3 Gd: 0-2 GF: - Fm: 0-0
Distance: 2m/2m3: 0-0 2m4-2m7: 0-5 3m+: 0-1
Track: LH: 0-6 RH: 0-0 Tight: 0-1 Gall: 0-2
Aids: Bl: 0-0 Vi: 0-0 Tstrap: 0-0 Ckp: 0-0
Best Rating: 102 4/02 Hexm 2m110y good NHF

Bumper winner at Hexham, looked a threat when last flight casualty at Newcastle in January; placed at Newcastle twice since.

Academic Gold (IRE)
6-y-o ch g Royal Academy (USA)-Penultimate (USA) (Roberto (USA))
R D Tudor R D Tudor

Placings:P (3314)
2003/04: 16^{P}S,

	Starts	1st	2nd	3rd	Win & Pl
Hurdles	1	0	0	0	
Career Total	1	0	0	0	

Going: Sf: 0-1 GS: 0-0 Gd: 0-0 GF: - Fm: 0-0
Distance: 2m/2m3: 0-1 2m4-2m7: 0-0 3m+: 0-0
Track: LH: 0-0 RH: 0-0 Tight: 0-0 Gall: 0-0
Aids: Bl: 0-0 Vi: 0-0 Tstrap: 0-0 Ckp: 0-0
Best Rating: 0 1/04 Leic 2m soft Hdl

Academy Brief (IRE)
93   70
4-y-o b g Brief Truce (USA)-Stylish Academy (IRE) (Royal Academy (USA))
J W Mullins Mrs Sally Mullins

Placings:P342 (1472)
2003/04: 16^{P}G, 17^{3}G, 17^{4}GF, 17^{2}F,

	Starts	1st	2nd	3rd	Win & Pl
Hurdles	4	0	1	1	1556
Career Total	4	0	1	1	1556

Going: Sf: 0-0 GS: 0-0 Gd: 0-2 GF: - Fm: 0-2
Distance: 2m/2m3: 0-4 2m4-2m7: 0-0 3m+: 0-0
Track: LH: 0-3 RH: 0-1 Tight: 0-3 Gall: 0-0
Aids: Bl: 0-0 Vi: 0-0 Tstrap: 0-0 Ckp: 0-0
Best Rating: 70 9/03 Extr 2m1f firm Hdl

Plating-class hurdler; looks a doubtful stayer.

Acamani (GER)
7-y-o b g Winged Love (IRE)-Adjani (Surumu (GER))
C Von Der Recke Gestut Park Wiedingen

Placings:2/23-P (1830)
2003/04: 21^{P}G,

	Starts	1st	2nd	3rd	Win & Pl
Hurdles	1	0	0	0	
Career Total	4	0	2	1	4662

Going: Sf: 0-0 GS: 0-0 Gd: 0-0 GF: - Fm: 0-1
Distance: 2m/2m3: 0-0 2m4-2m7: 0-1 3m+: 0-0
Track: LH: 0-1 RH: 0-0 Tight: 0-0 Gall: 0-1
Aids: Bl: 0-0 Vi: 0-0 Tstrap: 0-0 Ckp: 0-0
Best Rating: 0 10/03 Chel 2m5f gd-fm Hdl

German trained gelding; stays two miles four.

Accademic (IRE)

(95h)   (95h)

7-y-o ch g Accordion-Giolla's Bone (Pitpan)
S E H Sherwood Lady Thompson

Placings:05P-PF   (4442)
2003/04: 21^{P}G, 20^{F}GS,

	Starts	1st	2nd	3rd	Win & Pl
Hurdles	1	0	0	0	0
Chases	1	0	0	0	0
Career Total	5	0	0	0	0

Going: Sf: 0-0 GS: 0-1 Gd: 0-1 GF: - Fm: 0-0
Distance: 2m/2m3: 0-0 2m4-2m7: 0-2 3m+: 0-0
Track: LH: 0-2 RH: 0-0 Tight: 0-0 Gall: 0-0
Aids: Bl: 0-0 Vi: 0-0 Tstrap: 0-0 Ckp: 0-0
Best Rating: 98 12/02 Extr 2m3f   gd-sft Hdl

Acceleration (IRE)
93   81

4-y-o b g Groom Dancer (USA)-Overdrive (Shirley Heights)
R Allan (Sir Mark Prescott 20/10) Kim Marshall, Sue Rigby, Susan Warren

Placings:605456   (4310)
2003/04: 16^{R}G, 16^{Q}GS, 16^{S}S, 18^{4}HY, 16^{S}G, 16^{R}GF,

	Starts	1st	2nd	3rd	Win & Pl
Hurdles	6	0	0	0	270
Career Total	6	0	0	0	270

Going: Sf: 0-2 GS: 0-1 Gd: 0-2 GF: - Fm: 0-1
Distance: 2m/2m3: 0-6 2m4-2m7: 0-0 3m+: 0-0
Track: LH: 0-4 RH: 0-2 Tight: 0-3 Gall: 0-0
Aids: Bl: 0-0 Vi: 0-1 Tstrap: 0-0 Ckp: 0-3
Best Rating: 81 2/04 Muss 2m   good Hdl

Maiden hurdler; has worn cheekpieces and a visor.

Accepting
105   104

7-y-o b g Mtoto-D'Azy (Persian Bold)
J Mackie M T Bloore & Mrs J E Lockwood

Placings:0350-415P4540   (4405)
2003/04: 21^{4}GF, 26^{1}GF, 24^{5}G, 24^{P}GF, 24^{4}GS, 23^{5}GS, 26^{4}G, 26^{9}G,

	Starts	1st	2nd	3rd	Win & Pl
Hurdles	8	1	0	1	3997
Career Total	12	1	0	1	4503
104 5/03 Hntg 3m2f		E(0-105)HHdl		G-F	£3458

Total win prize-money £3458

Going: Sf: 0-0 GS: 0-2 Gd: 0-3 GF: - Fm: 1-3
Distance: 2m/2m3: 0-0 2m4-2m7: 0-0 3m+: 1-7
Track: LH: 0-3 RH: 1-5 Tight: 0-0 Gall: 1-3
Aids: Bl: 0-0 Vi: 0-0 Tstrap: 0-0 Ckp: 0-4
Best Rating: 104 5/03 Hntg 3m2f   gd-fm Hdl

Moderate hurdler; stayer on the level, and there seems no end to his stamina over jumps; acts well on fast ground.

Access Overseas
91   84d

7-y-o b m Access Ski-Access Advantage (Infantry)
J D Frost Miss Elaine D Williams

Placings:45/1U4040/3340-546300   (4714)
2003/04: 19^{5}G, 19^{4}GF, 22^{8}GF, 16^{3}G, 16^{9}GS, 16^{9}G,

	Starts	1st	2nd	3rd	Win & Pl
Hurdles	6	0	0	1	376

Career Total   18   1   0   3   3579
91   6/01 NAbb 2m1f   G Hdl   GD   £2275
                     Total win prize-money £2275

Going: Sf: 0-0 GS: 0-1 Gd: 0-3 GF: - Fm: 0-2
Distance: 2m/2m3: 0-5 2m4-2m7: 0-1 3m+: 0-0
Track: LH: 0-2 RH: 0-2 Tight: 0-1 Gall: 0-0
Aids: Bl: 0-0 Vi: 0-0 Tstrap: 0-0 Ckp: 0-0
Best Rating: 91 6/01 NAbb 2m1f   good Hdl

Plating-class hurdler at around two miles; acts on good ground.

Accipiter
109   149+

5-y-o b g Polar Falcon (USA)-Accuracy (Gunner B)
G B Balding Miss B Swire

Placings:533-1211511   (4641)
2003/04: 17^{3}S, 17^{1}G, 16^{2}GS, 22^{1}GS, 19^{1}GS, 20^{5}S, 20^{1}GS, 24^{1}G,

	Starts	1st	2nd	3rd	Win & Pl
NH Flat	2	1	0	1	3429
Hurdles	6	4	1	0	82566
Career Total	10	5	1	2	86288
149 4/04 Aint	3m110y	A Hdl		GD	£46400
143 3/04 Asct	2m4f	B(0-140)HHdl		G-S	£23200
125 1/04 Tntn	2m3f110yD Hdl			G-S	£6483
127 1/04 Winc	2m6f	E Hdl		G-S	£3794
109 11/03 NAbb	2m1f	H NHF		GD	£2989

Total win prize-money £82867

Going: Sf: 0-2 GS: 3-4 Gd: 2-2 GF: - Fm: 0-0
Distance: 2m/2m3: 1-3 **2m4-2m7: 3-4** 3m+: 1-1
Track: LH: 2-4 **RH: 3-4** Tight: 3-4 Gall: 0-0
Aids: Bl: 0-0 Vi: 0-0 Tstrap: 0-0 Ckp: 0-0
Best Rating: 149 4/04 Aint 3m110y   good Hdl

Smart novice hurdler; landed a Grade One novices' contest at Aintree; was a fair bumper performer; from a very successful family, especially on soft ground; stays three miles; tough and progressive.

Accordion Girl (IRE)

6-y-o b m Accordion-Triple D'Or (Golden Love)
J W Mullins Denis J Barry

Placings:3-4P   (0707)
2003/04: 16^{4}G, 22^{P}GF,

	Starts	1st	2nd	3rd	Win & Pl
NH Flat	1	0	0	0	0
Hurdles	1	0	0	0	0
Career Total	3	0	0	1	279

Going: Sf: 0-0 GS: 0-0 Gd: 0-1 GF: - Fm: 0-1
Distance: 2m/2m3: 0-1 2m4-2m7: 0-1 3m+: 0-0
Track: LH: 0-2 RH: 0-0 Tight: 0-0 Gall: 0-0
Aids: Bl: 0-0 Vi: 0-0 Tstrap: 0-0 Ckp: 0-0
Best Rating: 88 5/03 Worc 2m   good NHF

Fair debut in a modest bumper at Fontwell in April 2003.

Acertack (IRE)
96(89h)   (65h)84

7-y-o b g Supreme Leader-Ask The Madam (Strong Gale)
R Rowe Keith Hunter

Placings:000-P0F3562   (4576)
2003/04: 21^{P}GF, 16^{9}G, 16^{F}G, 20^{3}S, 17^{5}GS, 24^{6}G, 18^{2}G,

	Starts	1st	2nd	3rd	Win & Pl
Chases	7	0	1	1	2034
Career Total	10	0	1	1	2034

Going: Sf: 0-1 GS: 0-1 Gd: 0-4 GF: - Fm: 0-1
Distance: 2m/2m3: 0-4 2m4-2m7: 0-2 3m+: 0-1
Track: LH: 0-3 RH: 0-4 Tight: 0-4 Gall: 0-1
Aids: Bl: 0-0 Vi: 0-0 Tstrap: 0-0 Ckp: 0-0
Best Rating: 84 3/04 Newb 2m2f110y good Ch

Plating-class chaser; showed little in good novice hurdles; should do better now he is handicapped.

Aces Four (IRE)
98f   97f

5-y-o ch g Fourstars Allstar (USA)-Special Trix (IRE) (Peacock (FR))
W McKeown J Molloy

Placings:225   (4866)
2003/04: 16^{2}S, 16^{2}GF, 16^{5}S,

	Starts	1st	2nd	3rd	Win & Pl
NH Flat	3	0	2	0	1184
Career Total	3	0	2	0	1184

Going: Sf: 0-2 GS: 0-0 Gd: 0-0 GF: - Fm: 0-1
Distance: 2m/2m3: 0-3 2m4-2m7: 0-0 3m+: 0-0
Track: LH: 0-3 RH: 0-0 Tight: 0-0 Gall: 0-0
Aids: Bl: 0-0 Vi: 0-0 Tstrap: 0-0 Ckp: 0-0
Best Rating: 97 1/04 Weth 2m   soft NHF

Fair efforts in bumpers at Wetherby and Ayr but hung markedly left on both occasions and below that level in better event at Ayr in April; handles soft and fast ground and, although he has the ability to win a race, looks one to tread carefully with.

Achilles Wings (USA)
98   112

8-y-o b g Irish River (FR)-Shirley Valentine (Shirley Heights)
Miss K M George Exterior Profiles Ltd

Placings:20/43P41U1153/30P-54135   (2955)
2003/04: 20^{5}G, 20^{4}G, 22^{1}G, 22^{3}G, 22^{5}G,

	Starts	1st	2nd	3rd	Win & Pl
Hurdles	5	1	0	1	5870
Career Total	20	4	1	4	22839
104 11/03 NAbb	2m6f	C(0-135)HHdl	GD	£4676
127 2/02 Winc	2m	D(0-125)HHdl	SFT	£3514
118 1/02 Winc	2m	D(0-125)HHdl	G-S	£6890
114 11/01 Hrfd	2m3f110yF(0-100)HHdl	GD	£2639

Total win prize-money £17720

Going: Sf: 0-0 GS: 0-0 Gd: 1-5 GF: - Fm: 0-0
Distance: 2m/2m3: 0-0 **2m4-2m7: 1-5** 3m+: 0-0
Track: LH: 1-4 RH: 0-1 **Tight: 1-4** Gall: 0-0
Aids: Bl: 0-0 Vi: 0-0 Tstrap: 0-0 **Ckp: 1-3**
Best Rating: 127 4/02 Chep 2m110y   gd-sft Hdl

Modest handicap hurdler; stays two miles six, but effective at shorter; acts on soft ground.

Acoustic (IRE)
102   (88h)97

10-y-o br g Orchestra-Rambling Ivy (Mandalus)
O Brennan Lady Anne Bentinck

Placings:3/0054/4P446-23   (4436)
2003/04: 24^{2}GF, 24^{3}GS,

	Starts	1st	2nd	3rd	Win & Pl
Chases	2	0	1	1	2411
Career Total	12	0	1	2	4352

Going: Sf: 0-0 GS: 0-1 Gd: 0-0 GF: - Fm: 0-1
Distance: 2m/2m3: 0-0 2m4-2m7: 0-0 3m+: 0-2
Track: LH: 0-2 RH: 0-0 Tight: 0-2 Gall: 0-0
Aids: Bl: 0-0 Vi: 0-0 Tstrap: 0-0 Ckp: 0-0
Best Rating: 97　5/03　Fknm　3m110y　gd-fm　Ch

A winning point-to-pointer, he has made little impact under Rules so far.

Acquired (IRE)
89f　　　　　79f
6-y-o b/br m Presenting-The Scarlet Dragon (Oats)
Mrs H Dalton　Michael Scott & Martin Timlin

Placings: 055　　　　　　　　　　(4144)
2003/04: 16⁶GF, 16⁵GF, 16⁶G,

	Starts	1st	2nd	3rd	Win & Pl
NH Flat	3	0	0	0	0
Career Total	3	0	0	0	0

Going: Sf: 0-0 GS: 0-0 Gd: 0-1 GF: - Fm: 0-2
Distance: 2m/2m3: 0-3 2m4-2m7: 0-0 3m+: 0-0
Track: LH: 0-1 RH: 0-2 Tight: 0-0 Gall: 0-0
Aids: Bl: 0-0 Vi: 0-0 Tstrap: 0-0 Ckp: 0-0
Best Rating: 79　3/04　Ludl　2m　good　NHF

Across The Water
81　　　　　59
10-y-o b m Slip Anchor-Stara (Star Appeal)
G H Jones　Mike Mifflin

Placings: PP/060　　　　　　　　(4375)
2003/04: 16⁰G, 19⁶GS, 19⁹G,

	Starts	1st	2nd	3rd	Win & Pl
Hurdles	3	0	0	0	0
Career Total	5	0	0	0	0

Going: Sf: 0-0 GS: 0-1 Gd: 0-2 GF: - Fm: 0-0
Distance: 2m/2m3: 0-1 2m4-2m7: 0-2 3m+: 0-0
Track: LH: 0-0 RH: 0-3 Tight: 0-1 Gall: 0-0
Aids: Bl: 0-0 Vi: 0-0 Tstrap: 0-0 Ckp: 0-0
Best Rating: 59　2/04　Hrfd　2m3f110y　gd-sft　Hdl

Act In Time (IRE)
110(94h)　　　(95h)113
12-y-o b g Actinium (FR)-Anvil Chorus (Levanter)
T R George　T R George

Placings: 0P/424/1P2251/515200/4U4415/1P501532/P4- (4941)
22P36220
2003/04: 22²G, 22²G, 30PG, 26³G, 24⁶GS, 24²G, 24²G, 31⁹GS,

	Starts	1st	2nd	3rd	Win & Pl
Hurdles	1	0	1	0	900
Chases	7	0	3	1	5848
Career Total	41	6	9	2	58941
118	12/01	Ludl	3m3f110yD(0-120)HCh	GD	£7956
118	5/01	Sedg	3m4f	D(0-125)HCh	GD £11163
118	2/01	Fknm	3m110y	F(0-100)HCh	SFT £4046
121	12/99	Winc	3m1f110yC(0-130)HCh	SFT £8976
125	4/99	Chel	2m5f	D(0-115)HCh	GD £5836
106	12/98	Chel	2m5f	E(0-125)HCh	GD £3452
			Total win prize-money £41431

Going: Sf: 0-0 GS: 0-2 Gd: 0-6 GF: - Fm: 0-0
Distance: 2m/2m3: 0-0 2m4-2m7: 0-0 3m+: 0-6
Track: LH: 0-3 RH: 0-3 Tight: 0-4 Gall: 0-0
Aids: Bl: 0-0 Vi: 0-0 Tstrap: 0-0 Ckp: 0-1
Best Rating: 125　4/99　Chel　2m5f　good　Ch

Hunter chaser; suited by three miles plus and best on good ground.

Active Account (USA)
69　　　　　39
7-y-o b/br g Unaccounted For (USA)-Ameritop (USA) (Topsider (USA))
Mrs H Dalton　Mrs Heather Dalton

Placings: 6P/0-0　　　　　　　　(0308)
2003/04: 17⁰G,

	Starts	1st	2nd	3rd	Win & Pl
Hurdles	1	0	0	0	
Career Total	4	0	0	0	0

Going: Sf: 0-0 GS: 0-0 Gd: 0-1 GF: - Fm: 0-0
Distance: 2m/2m3: 0-1 2m4-2m7: 0-0 3m+: 0-0
Track: LH: 0-1 RH: 0-0 Tight: 0-1 Gall: 0-0
Aids: Bl: 0-0 Vi: 0-0 Tstrap: 0-0 Ckp: 0-0
Best Rating: 73　12/01　Muss　2m　good　NHF

Acushnet
78f　　　　　50f
5-y-o b g Ezzoud (IRE)-Flitcham (Elegant Air)
N B King　Dean Bostock And Raymond Bostock

Placings: 0　　　　　　　　　　(4934)
2003/04: 18⁰G,

	Starts	1st	2nd	3rd	Win & Pl
NH Flat	1	0	0	0	
Career Total	1	0	0	0	

Going: Sf: 0-0 GS: 0-0 Gd: 0-1 GF: - Fm: 0-0
Distance: 2m/2m3: 0-1 2m4-2m7: 0-0 3m+: 0-0
Track: LH: 0-1 RH: 0-0 Tight: 0-1 Gall: 0-0
Aids: Bl: 0-0 Vi: 0-0 Tstrap: 0-0 Ckp: 0-0
Best Rating: 50　4/04　Font　2m2f110y　good　NHF

Acuteangle (IRE)

8-y-o b/br m Cataldi-Sharp Mama Vii (Damsire Unregistered)
Mrs S Wall　J P C Wall

Placings: 0/U　　　　　　　　　(4122)
2003/04: 21UG,

	Starts	1st	2nd	3rd	Win & Pl
Chases	1	0	0	0	
Career Total	2	0	0	0	

Going: Sf: 0-0 GS: 0-0 Gd: 0-1 GF: - Fm: 0-0
Distance: 2m/2m3: 0-0 2m4-2m7: 0-1 3m+: 0-0
Track: LH: 0-0 RH: 0-1 Tight: 0-1 Gall: 0-0
Aids: Bl: 0-0 Vi: 0-0 Tstrap: 0-0 Ckp: 0-0
Best Rating: 12　5/01　Hntg　2m110y　gd-fm　Hdl

Ad Astra
101f　　　　　104f
5-y-o b g Alhijaz-So It Goes (Free State)
M Bradstock　Mrs Mary E Fitzpatrick

Placings: 3　　　　　　　　　　(2797)
2003/04: 17³GS,

	Starts	1st	2nd	3rd	Win & Pl
NH Flat	1	0	0	1	298

Career Total 　1　0　0　1　298

Going: Sf: 0-0 GS: 0-1 Gd: 0-0 GF: - Fm: 0-0
Distance: 2m/2m3: 0-1 2m4-2m7: 0-0 3m+: 0-0
Track: LH: 0-1 RH: 0-0 Tight: 0-1 Gall: 0-0
Aids: Bl: 0-0 Vi: 0-0 Tstrap: 0-0 Ckp: 0-0
Best Rating: 104　12/03　Bang　2m1f　gd-sft　NHF

Ad Hoc (IRE)
106(105h)　　(146h)162
10-y-o b g Strong Gale-Knockarctic (Quayside)
P F Nicholls　Sir Robert Ogden

Placings: 3111/FFP521/053B4/51233U1-66F　(3291)
2003/04: 27⁶G, 24⁶S, 29⁷GS,

	Starts	1st	2nd	3rd	Win & Pl
Chases	3	0	0	0	1500
Career Total	25	6	2	4	251861
158	4/03	Sand	3m5f110yA HCh	GD	£87000
146	11/02	Asct	3m	D Hdl	HVY	£5109
158	4/01	Sand	3m5f110yA HCh	SFT	£72500
149	4/00	Ayr	3m1f	C HCh	GD	£21970
113	1/00	Ayr	2m5f110yD Ch	SFT	£3945
106	12/99	Leic	2m7f110yE Ch	G-F	£3613
			Total win prize-money £194138

Going: Sf: 0-1 GS: 0-1 Gd: 0-1 GF: - Fm: 0-0
Distance: 2m/2m3: 0-0 2m4-2m7: 0-0 3m+: 0-3
Track: LH: 0-2 RH: 0-1 Tight: 0-0 Gall: 0-1
Aids: Bl: 0-0 Vi: 0-0 Tstrap: 0-0 Ckp: 0-0
Best Rating: 158　4/03　Sand　3m5f110y　good　Ch

Smart chaser; full of running when knocked out of the Grand National four out in 2002 and unseated in 2003; confined to hurdles in 2002/3 prior to finishing third in the National Hunt Handicap Chase at Cheltenham; ended season with a second win in the Attheraces Gold Cup; shaped well on his return this season but disappointing subsequently; stays extended three miles five; acts on most types of ground.

Adalie
101(98h)　　　(91 h)98+
10-y-o b m Absalom-Allied Newcastle (Crooner)
P J Hobbs (J Joseph 23/11)　Jack Joseph

Placings: 001/0F32/0503213-O020163P　(4919)
2003/04: 20⁰HY, 16⁰S, 19²G, 19⁰GS, 19¹HY, 19⁶GS, 19³GS,
20PGS,

	Starts	1st	2nd	3rd	Win & Pl
Hurdles	2	0	0	0	0
Chases	6	1	1	1	5874
Career Total	22	2	3	4	14625
98	2/04	Hrfd	2m3f	E(0-100)HCh	HVY	£4527
91	3/03	Font	2m2f110yF(0-100)HHdl	SFT	£3367
105	4/00	NAbb	2m1f	H NHF	HVY	£1771
			Total win prize-money £9665

Going: Sf: 1-3 GS: 0-4 Gd: 0-1 GF: - Fm: 0-0
Distance: 2m/2m3: 1-4 2m4-2m7: 0-4 3m+: 0-0
Track: LH: 0-3 RH: 1-4 Tight: 0-2 Gall: 0-0
Aids: Bl: 0-0 Vi: 0-0 Tstrap: 0-0 Ckp: 0-0
Best Rating: 106　2/00　Kemp　2m　soft　NHF

Moderate bumper and hurdle winner; winning chaser; acts in soft ground; best at around two and a half miles; has a tendency to race lazily.

Adalpour (IRE)
101　　　　　88+
6-y-o b g Kahyasi-Adalya (IRE) (Darshaan)
C W Moore (D M Lloyd 22/3)　C W Moore

Placings:02-23P4   (4688)
2003/04: 19⁵GS, 17³GF, 19⁴GS, 16⁴G,

	Starts	1st	2nd	3rd	Win & Pl
Hurdles	4	0	1	1	1542
Career Total	6	0	2	1	2216

Going: Sf: 0-0 GS: 0-2 Gd: 0-1 GF: - Fm: 0-1
Distance: 2m/2m3: 0-2 2m4-2m7: 0-2 3m+: 0-0
Track: LH: 0-1 RH: 0-3 Tight: 0-1 Gall: 0-0
Aids: Bl: 0-0 Vi: 0-0 Tstrap: 0-0 Ckp: 0-0
Best Rating: 88 2/04 Hrfd 2m3f110y gd-sft Hdl

Plating-class hurdler; AW winner; stays 2m 4f.

Adamant Approach (IRE)

95(111h)   (142h)150
10-y-o b g Mandalus-Crash Approach (Crash Course)
W P Mullins Greenstar Syndicate

Placings:1/P2422/152413F35/41F1F-50620   (4428)
2003/04: 16⁵GY, 20⁴GS, 16⁸YS, 18²Y, 17⁹G,

	Starts	1st	2nd	3rd	Win & Pl
Hurdles	2	0	0	0	0
Chases	3	0	1	0	3094
Career Total	25	5	5	2	102153
129 3/03 Cork	2m		Ch	G-Y	£9285
150 12/02 Punc	2m		Ch	HVY	£6773
139 1/02 Leop	2m		(0-140)HHdl	Y-S	£48251
107 10/01 Fair	2m		Hdl	GD	£5564
136 2/00 Leop	2m		NHF	YLD	£4140

Total win prize-money £74016

Going: Sf: 0-0 GS: 0-1 Gd: 0-1 GF: - Fm: 0-0
Distance: 2m/2m3: 0-4 2m4-2m7: 0-1 3m+: 0-0
Track: LH: 0-3 RH: 0-1 Tight: 0-0 Gall: 0-2
Aids: Bl: 0-0 Vi: 0-0 Tstrap: 0-0 Ckp: 0-0
Best Rating: 152 3/02 Chel 2m110y gd-sft Hdl

Smart performer; looked likely winner of Supreme Novices' Hurdle at Cheltenham Festival in 2002 when falling at last; twice a winner over fences in 2002/2003 and fell in the Arkle in between; fifth on seasonal return; stays 2m 4f and suited by cut in the ground; races prominently.

Adamant James (IRE)

5-y-o b g Sri Pekan (USA)-Classic Romance (Cadeaux Genereux)
S Dow (T D McCarthy 5/6) James Etheridge

Placings:P   (2336)
2003/04: 16⁷S,

	Starts	1st	2nd	3rd	Win & Pl
Hurdles	1	0	0	0	
Career Total	1	0	0	0	

Going: Sf: 0-1 GS: 0-0 Gd: 0-0 GF: - Fm: 0-0
Distance: 2m/2m3: 0-1 2m4-2m7: 0-0 3m+: 0-0
Track: LH: 0-1 RH: 0-0 Tight: 0-1 Gall: 0-0
Aids: Bl: 0-0 Vi: 0-0 Tstrap: 0-0 Ckp: 0-0
Best Rating: 0 11/03 Plum 2m soft Hdl

Added Dimension (IRE)

88   87
13-y-o b g Top Ville-Lassalia (Sallust)

N A Dunger N A Dunger

Placings:P/P42636/031112/0/00/303/425014/F00-1 (1852)
2003/04: 16¹G,

	Starts	1st	2nd	3rd	Win & Pl
Hurdles	1	1	0	0	2629
Career Total	29	5	3	4	14662
87 10/03 Towc	2m	F(0-100)HHdl	GD	£2628
96 12/01 Towc	2m	G(0-95)HHdl	HVY	£1659
111 2/97 Tntn	2m1f	F(0-105)HHdl	GD	£1962
104 2/97 Hrfd	2m1f	F(0-105)HHdl	G-S	£2318
98 1/97 Folk	2m1f110yF(0-105)HHdl	SFT	£2180

Total win prize-money £10749

Going: Sf: 0-0 GS: 0-0 Gd: 1-1 GF: - Fm: 0-0
Distance: 2m/2m3: 1-1 2m4-2m7: 0-0 3m+: 0-0
Track: LH: 0-0 RH: 1-1 Tight: 0-0 Gall: 0-0
Aids: Bl: 0-0 Vi: 0-0 Tstrap: 0-0 Ckp: 0-0
Best Rating: 111 3/97 Hrfd 2m1f good Hdl

Modest veteran; lightly raced in recent seasons; suited by two miles and easy ground.

Adecco (IRE)

78   104d
5-y-o b g Eagle Eyed (USA)-Kharaliya (FR) (Doyoun)
R C Guest N J Jones

Placings:16P3-0   (0099)
2003/04: 20⁹G,

	Starts	1st	2nd	3rd	Win & Pl
Hurdles	1	0	0	0	
Career Total	5	1	0	1	4375
101 10/02 Ludl	2m	E Hdl	FRM	£3523

Total win prize-money £3523

Going: Sf: 0-0 GS: 0-0 Gd: 0-1 GF: - Fm: 0-0
Distance: 2m/2m3: 0-0 2m4-2m7: 0-1 3m+: 0-0
Track: LH: 0-1 RH: 0-0 Tight: 0-0 Gall: 0-0
Aids: Bl: 0-0 Vi: 0-0 Tstrap: 0-0 Ckp: 0-0
Best Rating: 101 10/02 Ludl 2m firm Hdl

A winner on the Flat in Germany. Bought by Venetia Williams after making a successful hurdling debut for Christian Von Der Recke at Ludlow October 2002. Found things a lot tougher in valuable event at Wetherby a week later.

Adele

79f   60f
4-y-o b f Cloudings (IRE)-Sharp Practice (Broadsword (USA)
J G O'Neill J G O'Neill

Placings:00   (4345)
2003/04: 16⁰HY, 16⁹GS,

	Starts	1st	2nd	3rd	Win & Pl
NH Flat	2	0	0	0	
Career Total	2	0	0	0	

Going: Sf: 0-1 GS: 0-1 Gd: 0-0 GF: - Fm: 0-0
Distance: 2m/2m3: 0-1 2m4-2m7: 0-0 3m+: 0-0
Track: LH: 0-1 RH: 0-1 Tight: 0-0 Gall: 0-0
Aids: Bl: 0-0 Vi: 0-0 Tstrap: 0-0 Ckp: 0-0
Best Rating: 54 3/04 Wwck 2m gd-sft NHF

Adelphi Boy (IRE)

103   107
8-y-o ch g Ballad Rock-Toda (Absalom)
M Todhunter Barry Brown

Placings:2-12   (1203)
2003/04: 16¹GF, 22²G,

	Starts	1st	2nd	3rd	Win & Pl
Hurdles	2	1	1	0	5322
Career Total	3	1	2	0	6094
107 6/03 Prth	2m110y E Hdl	G-F	£4149

Total win prize-money £4150

Going: Sf: 0-0 GS: 0-0 Gd: 0-1 GF: - Fm: 1-1
Distance: 2m/2m3: 1-1 2m4-2m7: 0-1 3m+: 0-0
Track: LH: 0-1 RH: 1-1 Tight: 0-1 Gall: 0-0
Aids: Bl: 0-0 Vi: 0-0 Tstrap: 0-0 Ckp: 0-0
Best Rating: 107 8/03 Ctml 2m6f good Hdl

Novice hurdler; successful on second start at Perth in June; broke down when narrowly beaten at Cartmel two months later; stays two mile six; acts on fast ground.

Adelphie Lass

57f
4-y-o b f Theatrical Charmer-Miss Adventure (Adonijah)
M R Hoad Mrs Julie Hoad

Placings:0   (2101)
2003/04: 12⁰GF,

	Starts	1st	2nd	3rd	Win & Pl
NH Flat	1	0	0	0	
Career Total	1	0	0	0	

Going: Sf: 0-0 GS: 0-0 Gd: 0-0 GF: - Fm: 0-1
Distance: 2m/2m3: 0-0 2m4-2m7: 0-0 3m+: 0-0
Track: LH: 0-1 RH: 0-0 Tight: 0-0 Gall: 0-0
Aids: Bl: 0-0 Vi: 0-0 Tstrap: 0-0 Ckp: 0-0
Best Rating: 57 11/03 Newb 1m4f110y gd-fm NHF

Adiemus

60   54
6-y-o b g Green Desert (USA)-Anodyne (Dominion)
J Noseda (R T Phillips 29/11) G Lansbury

Placings:0   (2449)
2003/04: 16⁰GS,

	Starts	1st	2nd	3rd	Win & Pl
Hurdles	1	0	0	0	
Career Total	1	0	0	0	

Going: Sf: 0-0 GS: 0-1 Gd: 0-0 GF: - Fm: 0-0
Distance: 2m/2m3: 0-1 2m4-2m7: 0-0 3m+: 0-0
Track: LH: 0-1 RH: 0-0 Tight: 0-0 Gall: 0-1
Aids: Bl: 0-0 Vi: 0-0 Tstrap: 0-0 Ckp: 0-0
Best Rating: 54 11/03 Newb 2m110y gd-sft Hdl

Very useful Flat performer; well held in warm race on hurdles debut. (DEAD)

Adiysha (IRE)

106   81
7-y-o b m Namaqualand (USA)-Adira (IRE) (Ballad Rock)
D A Rees (Paul Nolan 11/7) D A Rees & P Harris

Placings:0000/250P00/200-60622555233   (2411)
2003/04: 16⁶YS, 16⁹F, 16⁸GF, 16²F, 17²GF, 19⁵GF, 17⁵GF, 16⁵GF, 16²G, 16³GF, 19³GF,

	Starts	1st	2nd	3rd	Win & Pl
Hurdles	11	0	3	2	4323
Career Total	24	0	5	2	6512

Going: Sf: 0-0 GS: 0-0 Gd: 0-1 GF: - Fm: 0-9
Distance: 2m/2m3: 0-9 2m4-2m7: 0-2 3m+: 0-0

Track: LH: 0-2 RH: 0-5 Tight: 0-5 Gall: 0-0
Aids: Bl: 0-0 Vi: 0-0 Tstrap: 0-0 Ckp: 0-0
Best Rating: 86 5/01 Rosc 2m   gd-fm Hdl

Plating-class hurdler; acts on fast ground; effective over two miles.

Adjiram (IRE)
96   79
8-y-o b g Be My Guest (USA)-Adjriyna (Top Ville)
A W Carroll K Marshall

Placings:2P/0/0406/640-06   (4266)
2003/04: 16⁶G, 16⁸GF,

	Starts	1st	2nd	3rd	Win & Pl
Hurdles	2	0	0	0	0
Career Total	12	0	1	0	744

Going: Sf: 0-0 GS: 0-0 Gd: 0-1 GF: - Fm: 0-1
Distance: 2m/2m3: 0-2 2m4-2m7: 0-0 3m+: 0-0
Track: LH: 0-1 RH: 0-1 Tight: 0-0 Gall: 0-0
Aids: Bl: 0-0 Vi: 0-0 Tstrap: 0-0 Ckp: 0-0
Best Rating: 79 6/02 Font 2m2f110y gd-fm Hdl

Admiral Peary (IRE)
100   106
8-y-o b/br g Lord Americo-Arctic Brief (Buckskin (FR))
C R Egerton M Haynes

Placings:33/13PU324611502F-2P   (0290)
2003/04: 26²GF, 27⁷G,

	Starts	1st	2nd	3rd	Win & Pl
Hurdles	2	0	1	0	2100
Career Total	18	3	3	4	13330
108 12/02 Plum	3m1f110yE(0-105)HHdl		HVY	£2957
94 11/02 NAbb	2m6f	E(0-100)HHdl	SFT	£2912
86 7/02 Strf	2m110y	H NHF	G-F	£2212

Total win prize-money £8082

Going: Sf: 0-0 GS: 0-0 Gd: 0-1 GF: - Fm: 0-1
Distance: 2m/2m3: 0-0 2m4-2m7: 0-0 3m+: 0-2
Track: LH: 0-1 RH: 0-1 Tight: 0-1 Gall: 0-1
Aids: Bl: 0-0 Vi: 0-0 Tstrap: 0-0 Ckp: 0-0
Best Rating: 115 2/02 Font 2m2f110y soft NHF

Modest hurdler; effective in soft ground; stays three miles two but effective at shorter.

Adopted Hero (IRE)
108   127+
4-y-o b g Sadler's Wells (USA)-Lady Liberty (NZ) (Noble Bijou (USA))
G L Moore (J H M Gosden 4/10) N J Jones, Phil Collins

Placings:3160   (4625)
2003/04: 16³S, 16¹GF, 17⁶G, 16⁹G,

	Starts	1st	2nd	3rd	Win & Pl
Hurdles	4	1	0	1	15348
Career Total	4	1	0	1	15348
119 2/04 Hntg	2m110y	B Hdl		G-S	£10218

Total win prize-money £10218

Going: Sf: 0-1 GS: 1-1 Gd: 0-2 GF: - Fm: 0-0
Distance: 2m/2m3: 1-4 2m4-2m7: 0-0 3m+: 0-0
Track: LH: 0-3 RH: 1-1 Tight: 0-1 Gall: 1-2
Aids: Bl: 0-0 Vi: 0-0 Tstrap: 0-0 Ckp: 0-0
Best Rating: 127 3/04 Chel 2m1f   good Hdl

Juvenile hurdler; smart on the Flat; appreciates cut in the ground; sixth in the Triumph.

Adradee (IRE)
87(101h)   (87h)87
10-y-o b m Ajraas (USA)-Miss Tan A Dee (Tanfirion)
M J Weeden Mrs E A Haycock

Placings:06/00063003*20/261643431116U0/6506036/0604-
65635035P   (4674)
2003/04: 16⁶GF, 18⁵GF, 17⁶GF, 19³G, 17⁵GF, 22⁹GF, 21³GF,
19⁵GF, 16⁹G,

	Starts	1st	2nd	3rd	Win & Pl
Hurdles	6	0	0	1	529
Chases	3	0	0	1	622
Career Total	46	4	2	7	16192
114 10/99 DRoy	2m	(0-116)HHdl	Y-S	£2464
99 9/99 Clon	2m	(0-102)HHdl	G-F	£2217
95 8/99 Tral	2m	(0-109)HHdl	YLD	£3388
89 6/99 Tral	2m	(0-116)HHdl	GD	£3683

Total win prize-money £11753

Going: Sf: 0-0 GS: 0-0 Gd: 0-2 GF: - Fm: 0-7
Distance: 2m/2m3: 0-7 2m4-2m7: 0-2 3m+: 0-0
Track: LH: 0-3 RH: 0-5 Tight: 0-4 Gall: 0-0
Aids: Bl: 0-0 Vi: 0-0 Tstrap: 0-0 Ckp: 0-0
Best Rating: 114 10/99 DRoy 2m   yld-sft Hdl

Won four handicap hurdles in Ireland in 1999; disappointing since coming to this country; lightly-raced of late.

Adronikus (IRE)
60   93
7-y-o ch g Monsun (GER)-Arionette (Lombard (GER))
D J Wintle Mrs B Grainger

Placings:0P/061130-0   (0187)
2003/04: 22⁹GF,

	Starts	1st	2nd	3rd	Win & Pl
Hurdles	1	0	0	0	
Career Total	9	2	0	1	7339
91 10/02 Fknm	2m	F(0-100)HHdl	GD	£3357
83 7/02 MRas	2m1f110yE(0-105)HHdl		G-F	£3556

Total win prize-money £6913

Going: Sf: 0-0 GS: 0-0 Gd: 0-0 GF: - Fm: 0-0
Distance: 2m/2m3: 0-0 2m4-2m7: 0-1 3m+: 0-0
Track: LH: 0-0 RH: 0-1 Tight: 0-0 Gall: 0-0
Aids: Bl: 0-1 Vi: 0-0 Tstrap: 0-1 Ckp: 0-0
Best Rating: 93 10/02 Plum 2m   good Hdl

Moderate hurdler, effective on good or fast ground at around two miles.

Advocatus (GER)
80   73
6-y-o b g Law Society (USA)-Aguilas (Konigsstuhl (GER))
A G Hobbs Three Counties Racing 2

Placings:54-0PPP00   (3226)
2003/04: 26⁹GS, 24⁷GF, 26⁶G, 21⁸G, 26⁹GS, 26⁹GS,

	Starts	1st	2nd	3rd	Win & Pl
Hurdles	6	0	0	0	
Career Total	8	0	0	0	349

Going: Sf: 0-0 GS: 0-3 Gd: 0-2 GF: - Fm: 0-1
Distance: 2m/2m3: 0-0 2m4-2m7: 0-1 3m+: 0-5
Track: LH: 0-3 RH: 0-3 Tight: 0-0 Gall: 0-0
Aids: Bl: 0-2 Vi: 0-0 Tstrap: 0-0 Ckp: 0-1
Best Rating: 73 3/03 Hntg 2m4f110y good Hdl

Adyton (GER)
4-y-o c Second Set (IRE)-Alliance (GER) (Milford)
Mario Hofer Stall Cohiba-Bar

Placings:P   (2764)
2003/04: 16⁷GS,

	Starts	1st	2nd	3rd	Win & Pl
Hurdles	1	0	0	0	
Career Total	1	0	0	0	

Going: Sf: 0-0 GS: 0-1 Gd: 0-0 GF: - Fm: 0-0
Distance: 2m/2m3: 0-1 2m4-2m7: 0-0 3m+: 0-0
Track: LH: 0-1 RH: 0-0 Tight: 0-1 Gall: 0-0
Aids: Bl: 0-0 Vi: 0-0 Tstrap: 0-1 Ckp: 0-0
Best Rating: 0 12/03 Plum 2m   gd-sft Hdl

Listed winner on the All-Weather in Germany; pulled up on hurdles debut.

Aegean
104   112
10-y-o b g Rock Hopper-Sayulita (Habitat)
Mrs S J Smith Mrs Alicia Skene & W S Skene

Placings:43030/3251112/0332444/P21-36   (0383)
2003/04: 25³GS, 25⁸G,

	Starts	1st	2nd	3rd	Win & Pl
Chases	2	0	0	1	1402
Career Total	24	4	4	6	43179
112 8/02 Prth	3m	C(0-135)HCh	G-S	£16968
116 8/00 Worc	2m7f110yE(0-105)HCh		G-F	£3454
110 7/00 Worc	2m7f110yE H Ch		G-F	£3376
96 6/00 Hexm	3m1f	E(0-105)HCh	G-F	£3120

Total win prize-money £26920

Going: Sf: 0-0 GS: 0-1 Gd: 0-1 GF: - Fm: 0-0
Distance: 2m/2m3: 0-0 2m4-2m7: 0-0 3m+: 0-2
Track: LH: 0-2 RH: 0-0 Tight: 0-2 Gall: 0-0
Aids: Bl: 0-0 Vi: 0-0 Tstrap: 0-0 Ckp: 0-0
Best Rating: 116 10/00 Aint 3m1f   good Ch

Modest handicap chaser, effective over three miles and on a sound surface.

Aegean Pirate (IRE)
82f   55f
7-y-o b g Polykratis-Rusheen Na Corra (IRE) (Burslem)
C J Hemsley Keith McKay

Placings:P-003   (1594)
2003/04: 16⁸GF, 17⁹GF, 16³GF,

	Starts	1st	2nd	3rd	Win & Pl
NH Flat	3	0	0	1	260
Career Total	4	0	0	1	260

Going: Sf: 0-0 GS: 0-0 Gd: 0-0 GF: - Fm: 0-3
Distance: 2m/2m3: 0-3 2m4-2m7: 0-0 3m+: 0-0
Track: LH: 0-1 RH: 0-2 Tight: 0-0 Gall: 0-0
Aids: Bl: 0-0 Vi: 0-0 Tstrap: 0-0 Ckp: 0-0
Best Rating: 55 7/03 Worc 2m   gd-fm NHF

Aegean Sunrise
99   96
6-y-o ch g Deploy-Dizzydaisy (Sharpo)
Jamie Poulton Dr David Chapman-Jones

Placings:2/002P   (4486)
2003/04: 21⁰GS, 20⁹GS, 16²GS, 18⁸G,

	Starts	1st	2nd	3rd	Win & Pl
Hurdles	4	0	1	0	1102
Career Total	5	0	2	0	1790

Going:	Sf: 0-0 GS: 0-3 Gd: 0-1 GF: - Fm: 0-0
Distance:	2m/2m3: 0-2 2m4-2m7: 0-2 3m+: 0-0
Track:	LH: 0-1 RH: 0-3 Tight: 0-2 Gall: 0-0
Aids:	Bl: 0-0 Vi: 0-0 Tstrap: 0-0 Ckp: 0-0
Best Rating:	96 3/04 Towc 2m gd-sft Hdl

Moderate hurdler; acts on good ground.

Aelred

109(99h)   (83h)125+

11-y-o b g Ovac (ITY)-Sponsorship (Sparkler)
R Johnson J L Gledson

Placings:000/556043463642/1212320125/3P23216050/426
323104260-4031515515F   (4640)
2003/04: 17⁴G, 20⁰G, 20³G, 16¹GF, 16⁵S, 20¹GS, 20⁵S, 20⁵HY,
20¹G, 22⁵GS, 21⁶G,

	Starts	1st	2nd	3rd	Win & Pl
Chases	11	3	0	1	21700
Career Total	58	8	10	8	59517
125 2/04	Newc	2m4f	C(0-130)HCh	GD	£10237
122 1/04	Newc	2m4f	D(0-125)HCh	G-S	£6773
111 12/03	Sthl	2m	E(0-110)HCh	G-F	£2936
119 12/02	Newc	2m110y	D(0-120)HCh	SFT	£5642
116 1/02	Newc	2m110y	E(0-110)HCh	SFT	£3370
105 1/01	Newc	2m110y	F(0-110)HCh	SFT	£2912
98 5/00	Ctml	2m1f110y		F(0-100)HCh	
GD £2990					
99 5/00	Kels	2m1f	E Ch	G-S	£3445
			Total win prize-money £38308		

Going:	Sf: 0-3 GS: 1-2 Gd: 1-5 GF: - 3m+: 0-0
Distance:	2m/2m3: 1-3 **2m4-2m7: 2-8** 3m+: 0-0
Track:	**LH: 3-10** RH: 0-1 Tight: 1-5 **Gall: 2-2**
Aids:	Bl: 0-0 Vi: 0-0 Tstrap: 0-0 Ckp: 0-2
Best Rating:	125 2/04 Newc 2m4f good Ch

Modest chaser; best over two miles but has won over two
and a half miles; suited by cut in the ground; best with forcing tactics; suited by going left-handed and goes well at
Newcastle; has been tried in cheekpieces and a tongue tie.

Aerleon Pete (IRE)

100   (95c)95

10-y-o b g Caerleon (USA)-Bristle (Thatch (USA))
Jonjo O'Neill John P McManus

Placings:04640/0206/3636020004/01101133PP06/3300U3
5/5F0-FP00505   (1249)
2003/04: 16ᶠGF, 20ᴾGF, 16⁰G, 16⁹GF, 16⁵G, 22⁹GF, 19⁵GF,

	Starts	1st	2nd	3rd	Win & Pl
Hurdles	5	0	0	0	0
Chases	2	0	0	0	0
Career Total	48	4	2	7	45271
145 7/00	MRas	2m1f110yB(0-140)HHdl	G-F	£17225
118 6/00	Kbgn	2m3f	(0-123)HHdl	G-F	£7728
123 6/00	Naas	2m	(0-109)HHdl	YLD	£3312
120 5/00	Kbgn	2m3f	(0-116)HHdl	GD	£6624
			Total win prize-money £34889		

Going:	Sf: 0-0 GS: 0-0 Gd: 0-2 GF: - Fm: 0-5
Distance:	2m/2m3: 0-4 2m4-2m7: 0-3 3m+: 0-0
Track:	LH: 0-3 RH: 0-4 Tight: 0-3 Gall: 0-1
Aids:	Bl: 0-0 Vi: 0-0 Tstrap: 0-1 Ckp: 0-2
Best Rating:	145 7/00 MRas 2m1f110y gd-fm Hdl

One time very useful hurdler in Ireland; disappointing over
both hurdles and fences since joining Jonjo O'Neill; best on
good ground or faster; stays two and a half miles.

Afadan (IRE)

96   97

6-y-o br g Royal Academy (USA)-Afasara (IRE) (Shardari)
J R Jenkins St Albans Chasers

Placings:P1PP/0200-4P   (2156)
2003/04: 16⁴GF, 16ᴾGS,

	Starts	1st	2nd	3rd	Win & Pl
Hurdles	2	0	0	0	0
Career Total	10	1	1	0	4780
110 12/01	Sand	2m110y	D Hdl	SFT	£3526
			Total win prize-money £3526		

Going:	Sf: 0-0 GS: 0-1 Gd: 0-0 GF: - Fm: 0-1
Distance:	2m/2m3: 0-2 2m4-2m7: 0-0 3m+: 0-0
Track:	LH: 0-2 RH: 0-0 Tight: 0-0 Gall: 0-0
Aids:	Bl: 0-0 Vi: 0-0 Tstrap: 0-0 Ckp: 0-0
Best Rating:	110 11/02 Hntg 2m110y gd-sft Hdl

Afarad (IRE)

9-y-o b g Slip Anchor-Afasara (IRE) (Shardari)
Jonjo O'Neill John P McManus

Placings:31323/1610/466056/31P/00-P   (4917)
2003/04: 20ᴾGS,

	Starts	1st	2nd	3rd	Win & Pl
Hurdles	1	0	0	0	
Career Total	21	4	1	4	45004
97 6/01	Kbgn	2m4f	Ch	GD	£5564
108 2/00	Clon	2m	Hdl	SH	£3864
140 11/99	Naas	2m	Hdl	Y-S	£4928
132 12/98	Leop	2m	Hdl	HVY	£4184
			Total win prize-money £18543		

Going:	Sf: 0-0 GS: 0-1 Gd: 0-0 GF: - Fm: 0-0
Distance:	2m/2m3: 0-0 2m4-2m7: 0-1 3m+: 0-0
Track:	LH: 0-1 RH: 0-0 Tight: 0-0 Gall: 0-0
Aids:	Bl: 0-0 Vi: 0-0 Tstrap: 0-0 Ckp: 0-0
Best Rating:	146 4/99 Aint 2m110y gd-sft Hdl

Afeef (USA)

87   73

5-y-o b/br g Dayjur (USA)-Jah (USA) (Relaunch (USA))
R T Phillips Ellangowan Racing Partners II

Placings:050P   (4634)
2003/04: 17⁵GS, 17⁵GS, 16⁹G, 19ᴾG,

	Starts	1st	2nd	3rd	Win & Pl
Hurdles	4	0	0	0	0
Career Total	4	0	0	0	0

Going:	Sf: 0-0 GS: 0-2 Gd: 0-2 GF: - Fm: 0-0
Distance:	2m/2m3: 0-3 2m4-2m7: 0-1 3m+: 0-0
Track:	LH: 0-0 RH: 0-0 Tight: 0-3 Gall: 0-0
Aids:	Bl: 0-0 Vi: 0-0 Tstrap: 0-0 Ckp: 0-0
Best Rating:	73 1/04 Tntn 2m1f gd-sft Hdl

Aficionado (IRE)

91   72

10-y-o b g Marju (IRE)-Haneena (Habitat)
R Williams R Williams

Placings:3B5560/00060/06064/000/6/6-6636   (0632)
2003/04: 19⁶GS, 19⁶GF, 23⁵GF, 21⁶GF,

	Starts	1st	2nd	3rd	Win & Pl
Chases	4	0	0	1	833
Career Total	25	0	0	2	1093

Going:	Sf: 0-0 GS: 0-1 Gd: 0-0 GF: - Fm: 0-3
Distance:	2m/2m3: 0-2 2m4-2m7: 0-1 3m+: 0-1
Track:	LH: 0-2 RH: 0-2 Tight: 0-1 Gall: 0-0
Aids:	Bl: 0-0 Vi: 0-0 Tstrap: 0-0 Ckp: 0-0
Best Rating:	73 11/98 Hrfd 2m1f good Hdl

African Sunset (IRE)

94   81

4-y-o b g Danehill Dancer (IRE)-Nizamiya (Darshaan)
J W F Aynsley (Anthony Mullins 13/12) J W F Aynsley

Placings:F0P   (4187)
2003/04: 16ᶠY, 16⁰S, 16ᴾGS,

	Starts	1st	2nd	3rd	Win & Pl
Hurdles	3	0	0	0	
Career Total	3	0	0	0	

Going:	Sf: 0-1 GS: 0-1 Gd: 0-0 GF: - Fm: 0-0
Distance:	2m/2m3: 0-3 2m4-2m7: 0-0 3m+: 0-0
Track:	LH: 0-1 RH: 0-1 Tight: 0-1 Gall: 0-0
Aids:	Bl: 0-0 Vi: 0-0 Tstrap: 0-0 Ckp: 0-0
Best Rating:	81 12/03 Fair 2m soft Hdl

Afro Man

103   108+

6-y-o b g Commanche Run-Lady Elle (IRE) (Persian Mews)
C J Mann J E Brown, E Good & R Lucas

Placings:0064-1   (1946)
2003/04: 21¹G,

	Starts	1st	2nd	3rd	Win & Pl
Hurdles	1	1	0	0	3531
Career Total	5	1	0	0	3797
108 11/03	Kemp	2m5f	D Hdl	GD	£3530
			Total win prize-money £3531		

Going:	Sf: 0-0 GS: 0-0 Gd: 1-1 GF: - Fm: 0-0
Distance:	2m/2m3: 0-0 2m4-2m7: 1-1 3m+: 0-0
Track:	LH: 0-0 **RH: 1-1** Tight: 0-0 Gall: 0-0
Aids:	Bl: 0-0 Vi: 0-0 Tstrap: 0-0 Ckp: 0-0
Best Rating:	108 11/03 Kemp 2m5f good Hdl

Moderate hurdler; off the mark at Kempton in November
2003; stays two miles five; acts on good ground.

After Eight (GER)

106   116

4-y-o br c Sir Felix (FR)-Amrei (Ardross)
M F Harris (C Von Der Recke 28/10) Let's Live Racing

Placings:2142   (2987)
2003/04: 16²GF, 16¹GS, 16⁴GS, 16²G,

	Starts	1st	2nd	3rd	Win & Pl
Hurdles	4	1	2	0	19327
Career Total	4	1	2	0	19327
111 11/03	Hntg	2m110y	B Hdl	G-S	£13487
			Total win prize-money £13488		

Going:	Sf: 0-0 GS: 1-2 Gd: 0-1 GF: - Fm: 0-1
Distance:	**2m/2m3: 1-4** 2m4-2m7: 0-0 3m+: 0-0
Track:	LH: 0-2 **RH: 1-2** Tight: 0-0 **Gall: 1-1**
Aids:	Bl: 0-0 Vi: 0-0 Tstrap: 0-0 Ckp: 0-0
Best Rating:	113 10/03 Chel 2m110y gd-fm Hdl

Fair juvenile hurdler; won Grade B hurdle at Huntingdon in
November 2003; effective over two miles; acts on good
ground.

After Galway (IRE)
84   83+
8-y-o b g Camden Town-Money For Honey (New Brig)
Miss V Scott A Butler

Placings:3/0/U0P4   (4937)
2003/04: 17^{U}GS, 18^{0}GS, 20^{P}S, 16^{4}GS,

	Starts	1st	2nd	3rd	Win & Pl
Hurdles	4	0	0	0	443
Career Total	6	0	0	1	684

Going:	Sf: 0-1 GS: 0-3 Gd: 0-0 GF: - Fm: 0-0
Distance:	2m/2m3: 0-3 2m4-2m7: 0-1 3m+: 0-0
Track:	LH: 0-3 RH: 0-1 Tight: 0-2 Gall: 0-1
Aids:	Bl: 0-0 Vi: 0-0 Tstrap: 0-0 Ckp: 0-0
Best Rating:	107 4/01 Muss 2m1f gd-fm NHF

After Me Boys
100   127+
10-y-o b g Arzanni-Realm Wood (Precipice Wood)
Mrs S J Smith   Keith Nicholson

Placings:21421/212P/21-301   (4176)
2003/04: 20^{3}S, 20^{6}S, 24^{1}G,

	Starts	1st	2nd	3rd	Win & Pl
Hurdles	3	1	0	1	15994
Career Total	14	5	5	1	41289
127	3/04	Donc	3m110y	B(0-140)HHdl	GD	£13889
124	3/03	Newc	3m	C(0-130)HHdl	G-S	£10120
112	8/01	Sthl	2m4f110yE(0-115)HHdl		G-F	£2380
110	4/01	MRas	2m3f110yD Hdl		HVY	£4403
109	6/00	Hexm	2m	H NHF		G-F	£1641
				Total win prize-money £32436

Going:	Sf: 0-2 GS: 0-0 Gd: 1-1 GF: - Fm: 0-0
Distance:	2m/2m3: 0-0 2m4-2m7: 0-2 3m+: 1-1
Track:	LH: 1-3 RH: 0-0 Tight: 0-0 Gall: 1-1
Aids:	Bl: 0-0 Vi: 0-0 Tstrap: 0-0 Ckp: 0-0
Best Rating:	127 3/04 Donc 3m110y good Hdl

Fair hurdler; stays three miles and acts on any ground.

After Puck (IRE)
101   99
6-y-o ch m Un Desperado (FR)-Domitor's Lass (Domitor (USA))
Michael Hourigan   Three K's Syndicate

Placings:000330-03024   (0859a)
2003/04: 18^{0}Y, 16^{3}G, 20^{0}F, 16^{2}GF, 20^{4}F,

	Starts	1st	2nd	3rd	Win & Pl
NH Flat	1	0	0	0	0
Hurdles	4	0	1	1	3124
Career Total	11	0	1	3	4078

Going:	Sf: 0-0 GS: 0-0 Gd: 0-0 GF: - Fm: 0-3
Distance:	2m/2m3: 0-3 2m4-2m7: 0-2 3m+: 0-0
Track:	LH: 0-1 RH: 0-0 Tight: 0-1 Gall: 0-0
Aids:	Bl: 0-0 Vi: 0-0 Tstrap: 0-0 Ckp: 0-0
Best Rating:	99 7/03 Limk 2m gd-fm Hdl

Plating-class performer; effective at two miles; acts on good ground.

After The Blue (IRE)
74   100
7-y-o b g Last Tycoon-Sudden Interest (FR) (Highest Honor (FR))
K G Wingrove   L T Woodhouse

Placings:544442P/F1-0PPPP   (4781)
2003/04: 20^{0}GF, 17^{P}GS, 17^{P}GS, 24^{P}GS, 16^{P}G,

	Starts	1st	2nd	3rd	Win & Pl
Hurdles	5	0	0	0	
Career Total	14	1	1	0	3841
100	6/02	Hntg	2m4f110yE Hdl		G-F	£2499
			Total win prize-money £2499

Going:	Sf: 0-0 GS: 0-3 Gd: 0-1 GF: - Fm: 0-1
Distance:	2m/2m3: 0-3 2m4-2m7: 0-1 3m+: 0-1
Track:	LH: 0-1 RH: 0-4 Tight: 0-0 Gall: 0-1
Aids:	Bl: 0-0 Vi: 0-1 Tstrap: 0-4 Ckp: 0-0
Best Rating:	100 6/02 Hntg 2m4f110y gd-fm Hdl

Moderate hurdler; effective at 2m 4f; acts on fast ground; wears a tongue tie.

Afzal Rose
76f   53f
4-y-o b f Afzal-Fortria Rosie Dawn (Derring Rose)
M Scudamore   M J and W J Fenn

Placings:0   (4608)
2003/04: 17^{0}G,

	Starts	1st	2nd	3rd	Win & Pl
NH Flat	1	0	0	0	
Career Total	1	0	0	0	

Going:	Sf: 0-0 GS: 0-0 Gd: 0-0 GF: - Fm: 0-0
Distance:	2m/2m3: 0-0 2m4-2m7: 0-0 3m+: 0-0
Track:	LH: 0-0 RH: 0-0 Tight: 0-1 Gall: 0-0
Aids:	Bl: 0-0 Vi: 0-0 Tstrap: 0-0 Ckp: 0-0
Best Rating:	55 3/04 MRas 2m1f110y good NHF

Again Jane
73f   52f
4-y-o ch f Then Again-Janie-O (Hittite Glory)
J M Jefferson   P Nelson

Placings:050   (3438)
2003/04: 13^{0}GF, 13^{5}S, 16^{0}HY,

	Starts	1st	2nd	3rd	Win & Pl
NH Flat	3	0	0	0	0
Career Total	3	0	0	0	0

Going:	Sf: 0-2 GS: 0-0 Gd: 0-0 GF: - Fm: 0-1
Distance:	2m/2m3: 0-1 2m4-2m7: 0-0 3m+: 0-0
Track:	LH: 0-1 RH: 0-0 Tight: 0-0 Gall: 0-0
Aids:	Bl: 0-0 Vi: 0-0 Tstrap: 0-0 Ckp: 0-0
Best Rating:	52 12/03 Towc 1m5f110y soft NHF

Agile King
13-y-o b g Rakaposhi King-My Aisling (John De Coombe)
A J Tizzard   A J Tizzard

Placings:6/5/P-   (0020)
2003/04: 26^{P}S,

	Starts	1st	2nd	3rd	Win & Pl
Chases	1	0	0	0	
Career Total	3	0	0	0	0

Going:	Sf: 0-1 GS: 0-0 Gd: 0-0 GF: - Fm: 0-0
Distance:	2m/2m3: 0-0 2m4-2m7: 0-0 3m+: 0-1
Track:	LH: 0-1 RH: 0-0 Tight: 0-1 Gall: 0-0
Aids:	Bl: 0-0 Vi: 0-0 Tstrap: 0-0 Ckp: 0-0
Best Rating:	70 5/01 Hntg 2m4f110y gd-fm Ch

Agincourt (IRE)
102(99h)   (79h)95+
8-y-o b g Alphabatim (USA)-Miss Brantridge (Riboboy (USA))
John R Upson   Middleham Park Racing Xxi

Placings:000/065100P/432144-1UPP   (3710)
2003/04: 25^{1}GS, 29^{U}G, 28^{P}G, 24^{P}HY,

	Starts	1st	2nd	3rd	Win & Pl
Chases	4	1	0	0	2401
Career Total	20	3	1	1	12676
96	11/03	Towc	3m1f	F(0-100)HCh	G-S	£2401
91	1/03	Ludl	3m	E(0-105)HCh	SFT	£4901
79	12/01	Weth	3m1f	F(0-95)HHdl	G-S	£2688
				Total win prize-money £9990

Going:	Sf: 0-1 GS: 1-1 Gd: 0-2 GF: - Fm: 0-0
Distance:	2m/2m3: 0-0 2m4-2m7: 0-0 3m+: 1-4
Track:	LH: 0-1 RH: 1-1 Tight: 0-0 Gall: 0-0
Aids:	Bl: 0-0 Vi: 0-0 Tstrap: 0-0 Ckp: 0-0
Best Rating:	96 11/03 Towc 3m1f gd-sft Ch

Moderate chaser; stays three miles; acts on soft ground.

Agitando (IRE)
111   113
8-y-o b g Tenby-Crown Rose (Dara Monarch)
B De Haan   The Inspirations Partnership

Placings:511/3030633F-6F53   (4813)
2003/04: 16^{6}GS, 16^{F}GF, 16^{5}G, 16^{3}G,

	Starts	1st	2nd	3rd	Win & Pl
Hurdles	4	0	0	1	1116
Career Total	15	2	0	5	11106
122	4/02	MRas	2m1f110yD Hdl		GD	£3836
111	4/02	Uttx	2m	E Hdl		GD	£2702
			Total win prize-money £6538

Going:	Sf: 0-0 GS: 0-1 Gd: 0-2 GF: - Fm: 0-1
Distance:	2m/2m3: 0-4 2m4-2m7: 0-0 3m+: 0-0
Track:	LH: 0-2 RH: 0-2 Tight: 0-1 Gall: 0-1
Aids:	Bl: 0-0 Vi: 0-0 Tstrap: 0-0 Ckp: 0-1
Best Rating:	122 12/02 Kemp 2m soft Hdl

Fair hurdler; best over two miles; acts on soft ground, but much better on a decent surface; has worn cheekpieces.

Agnese
92f   73f
4-y-o ch f Abou Zouz (USA)-Efizia (Efisio)
G M Moore   Mrs H I S Calzini

Placings:00   (4323)
2003/04: 16^{6}G, 16^{0}S,

	Starts	1st	2nd	3rd	Win & Pl
NH Flat	2	0	0	0	
Career Total	2	0	0	0	

Going:	Sf: 0-1 GS: 0-0 Gd: 0-1 GF: - Fm: 0-0
Distance:	2m/2m3: 0-2 2m4-2m7: 0-0 3m+: 0-0
Track:	LH: 0-1 RH: 0-1 Tight: 0-0 Gall: 0-0
Aids:	Bl: 0-0 Vi: 0-0 Tstrap: 0-0 Ckp: 0-0
Best Rating:	76 3/04 Newc 2m soft NHF

Ah Yeah (IRE)
106(89h)   (70h)96
7-y-o b g Roselier (FR)-Serena Bay (Furry Glen)
K C Bailey   Dream Makers Partnership

Placings:5006525S   (4855)

2003/04: 16^5GS, 21^9GS, 16^9G, 17^6HY, 25^5G, 25^2G, 19^5GS, 24^5GF,

	Starts	1st	2nd	3rd	Win & Pl
NH Flat	1	0	0	0	0
Hurdles	3	0	0	0	0
Chases	4	0	1	0	1090
Career Total	8	0	1	0	1090

Going: Sf: 0-1 GS: 0-3 Gd: 0-3 GF: - Fm: 0-1
Distance: 2m/2m3: 0-3 2m4-2m7: 0-2 3m+: 0-3
Track: LH: 0-1 RH: 0-6 Tight: 0-2 Gall: 0-2
Aids: Bl: 0-0 Vi: 0-0 Tstrap: 0-0 Ckp: 0-4
Best Rating: 96   3/04   Towc   3m1f   good   Ch

Winning Irish pointer; improved by switch to fences and fitting of cheekpieces; acts on fast ground.

Aide De Camp (FR)
94f   **91+f**
5-y-o b g Saint Preuil (FR)-Baraka De Thaix Ii (FR) (Olmeto)
P F Nicholls   Sir Robert Ogden

Placings:1   (4738)
2003/04: 17^1G,

	Starts	1st	2nd	3rd	Win & Pl
NH Flat	1	1	0	0	2975
Career Total	1	1	0	0	2975

91   4/04   NAbb   2m1f   H NHF   GD   £2975
Total win prize-money £2975

Going: Sf: 0-0 GS: 0-0 Gd: 1-1 GF: - Fm: 0-0
Distance: 2m/2m3: 1-1 2m4-2m7: 0-0 3m+: 0-0
Track: LH: 1-1 RH: 0-0 Tight: 1-1 Gall: 0-0
Aids: Bl: 0-0 Vi: 0-0 Tstrap: 0-0 Ckp: 0-0
Best Rating: 91   4/04   NAbb   2m1f   good   NHF

Aiden (IRE)
74   **98**
10-y-o b g Supreme Leader-Chevaux-Vapeur (Le Moss)
Mrs L Richards   The Aiden Partnership

Placings:0463/233044P/0PPPP   (4367)
2003/04: 21^0S, 25^9S, 22^9GS, 24^6G, 25^9GS,

	Starts	1st	2nd	3rd	Win & Pl
Hurdles	5	0	0	0	
Career Total	16	0	1	3	2786

Going: Sf: 0-2 GS: 0-2 Gd: 0-1 GF: - Fm: 0-0
Distance: 2m/2m3: 0-0 2m4-2m7: 0-2 3m+: 0-3
Track: LH: 0-2 RH: 0-2 Tight: 0-2 Gall: 0-0
Aids: Bl: 0-1 Vi: 0-3 Tstrap: 0-0 Ckp: 0-0
Best Rating: 98   2/02   Kemp   3m110y   soft   Hdl

Aifung (IRE)
95   **72+**
6-y-o ch m Bigstone (IRE)-Palmyra (GER) (Arratos (FR))
R H Buckler   Mrs P J Buckler

Placings:2611-54130   (4574)
2003/04: 20^5S, 19^4GF, 22^1GF, 21^3GS, 21^9G,

	Starts	1st	2nd	3rd	Win & Pl
Hurdles	5	1	0	1	5291
Career Total	9	3	1	1	10517

78   7/03   NAbb   2m6f   D Hdl   G-F   £4760
100   4/03   NAbb   2m1f   H NHF   GD   £2996
90   10/02   Hntg   2m110y   H NHF   G-F   £1764
Total win prize-money £9521

Going: Sf: 0-1 GS: 0-1 Gd: 0-1 GF: - Fm: 1-2
Distance: 2m/2m3: 0-0 2m4-2m7: 1-5 3m+: 0-0

Track: LH: 1-3 RH: 0-2 Tight: 1-2 Gall: 0-1
Aids: Bl: 0-0 Vi: 0-0 Tstrap: 0-0 Ckp: 0-0
Best Rating: 100   4/03   NAbb   2m1f   good   NHF

Won bumpers at Huntingdon October 2002 and Newton Abbot April 2003; appreciated step up in distance when landing 2m 6f mares' only novice hurdle at Newton Abbot in July; stays well; acts on ground good and faster.

Ain Tecbalet (FR)
102(95h)   (88h)**108**
6-y-o b g Riverquest (FR)-La Chance Au Roy (FR) (Rex Magna (FR))
N J Henderson   The French Connection

Placings:40/2224/43130500-22P2P4P   (4941)
2003/04: 19^2GF, 20^2S, 21^8GS, 26^2G, 24^8GS, 25^4GF, 31^8GS,

	Starts	1st	2nd	3rd	Win & Pl
Chases	7	0	3	0	4343
Career Total	21	1	6	2	17303

7/02   Mesl   2m1f110y   Ch   GD   £3239
Total win prize-money £3239

Going: Sf: 0-1 GS: 0-3 Gd: 0-1 GF: - Fm: 0-2
Distance: 2m/2m3: 0-1 2m4-2m7: 0-2 3m+: 0-4
Track: LH: 0-3 RH: 0-3 Tight: 0-3 Gall: 0-0
Aids: Bl: 0-0 Vi: 0-0 Tstrap: 0-0 Ckp: 0-0
Best Rating: 108   4/04   Extr   3m1f110y   gd-fm   Ch

Moderate ex-French chaser; yet to win in this country; stays 2m 4f; may be better suited by decent ground.

Aine Dubh (IRE)
117   **146+**
7-y-o b m Bob Back (USA)-Deep Thyne (IRE) (Good Thyne (USA))
Kevin F O'Donnell   Kevin O'Donnell

Placings:4221/301360-110404063   (4623)
2003/04: 16^9GY, 20^1YS, 21^1Y, 20^9GY, 20^4GF, 20^5S, 16^4YS, 20^9Y, 21^6G, 24^3G,

	Starts	1st	2nd	3rd	Win & Pl
Hurdles	10	2	0	1	37854
Career Total	19	4	2	3	56275

128   8/03   Gway   2m5f190y   HHdl   YLD   £21103
118   5/03   Punc   2m4f   Hdl   Y-S   £7840
98   3/03   Tram   2m4f   Hdl   SFT   £5824
99   11/01   Punc   2m   NHF   SFT   £4451
Total win prize-money £39222

Going: Sf: 0-1 GS: 0-0 Gd: 0-2 GF: - Fm: 0-1
Distance: 2m/2m3: 0-2 2m4-2m7: 2-7 3m+: 0-1
Track: LH: 0-3 RH: 1-4 Tight: 1-0 Gall: 0-1
Aids: Bl: 0-0 Vi: 0-0 Tstrap: 0-0 Ckp: 0-1
Best Rating: 146   4/04   Aint   3m110y   good   Hdl

Useful Irish-trained handicap hurdler; probably flattered when running way above her previous form when third to Iris's Gift at Aintree; stays two miles five; acts on yielding ground.

Air Attache (USA)
9-y-o b g Sky Classic (CAN)-Diplomatic Cover (USA) (Roberto (USA))
K R Pearce   Keith R Pearce

Placings:1341121/1231-1   (0262)
2003/04: 20^1GF,

	Starts	1st	2nd	3rd	Win & Pl
Chases	1	1	0	0	3094

Track: LH: 1-3 RH: 1-2 Tight: 1-2 Gall: 0-1
Aids: Bl: 0-0 Vi: 0-0 Tstrap: 0-0 Ckp: 0-0
Best Rating: 100   4/03   NAbb   2m1f   good   NHF

Career Total	12	7	2	2	23177
109	5/03	Ludl	2m4f	H Ch	G-F £3094
111	4/03	Hrfd	2m3f	H Ch	G-F £1666
116	6/02	Hrfd	2m	E Ch	G-F £3110
126	8/00	Uttx	2m	D(0-125)HHdl	G-F £3022
118	7/00	Worc	2m	D Hdl	G-F £2899
112	7/00	NAbb	2m1f	D(0-120)HHdl	G-F £3018
104	5/00	MRas	2m1f110yE Hdl		G-F £2702

Total win prize-money £19513

Going: Sf: 0-0 GS: 0-0 Gd: 0-0 GF: - Fm: 1-1
Distance: 2m/2m3: 0-0 2m4-2m7: 1-1 3m+: 0-0
Track: LH: 0-0 RH: 1-1 Tight: 1-1 Gall: 0-0
Aids: Bl: 0-0 Vi: 0-0 Tstrap: 1-1 Ckp: 0-0
Best Rating: 126   8/00   Uttx   2m   gd-fm   Hdl

Useful novice hurdler in 2000; overcame two-year absence to score on chasing debut in June 2002 when trained by Charlie Mann; won hunter chase at Hereford in April 2003 on first run for new yard after long lay-off; followed up less impressively at Ludlow; effective at up to 2m 4f; suited by fast ground.

Air Of Confusion
100   **94+**
6-y-o b g Mr Confusion (IRE)-First Born (Be My Native (USA))
Mrs K Walton   John Harper

Placings:0-3P413   (1599)
2003/04: 16^5G, 20^PG, 17^4GF, 17^1G, 17^3GF,

	Starts	1st	2nd	3rd	Win & Pl
Hurdles	5	1	0	2	4389
Career Total	6	1	0	2	4389

94   9/03   Bang   2m1f   E Hdl   GD   £3510
Total win prize-money £3510

Going: Sf: 0-0 GS: 0-0 Gd: 1-3 GF: - Fm: 0-2
Distance: 2m/2m3: 1-4 2m4-2m7: 0-1 3m+: 0-0
Track: LH: 1-3 RH: 0-2 Tight: 1-2 Gall: 0-0
Aids: Bl: 0-1 Vi: 0-0 Tstrap: 0-0 Ckp: 0-0
Best Rating: 94   10/03   Carl   2m1f   gd-fm   Hdl

Moderate novice hurdler; strong chasing type; acts on a sound surface; effective at around two miles.

Aircon (IRE)
100   (44h)**89**
9-y-o ch g Moscow Society (USA)-Corrielek (Menelek)
R Dickin   G Hutsby

Placings:5/56613/FUF5P300P22/S25PP-42242430   (1854)
2003/04: 20^4G, 21^2GF, 21^4GF, 24^4GF, 21^2GF, 20^4GF, 19^3GF, 25^9G,

	Starts	1st	2nd	3rd	Win & Pl
Chases	8	0	3	1	5085
Career Total	30	1	6	3	15037

109   2/01   Wwck   2m4f110yD Ch   SFT   £5008
Total win prize-money £5008

Going: Sf: 0-0 GS: 0-0 Gd: 0-3 GF: - Fm: 0-5
Distance: 2m/2m3: 0-0 2m4-2m7: 0-6 3m+: 0-2
Track: LH: 0-6 RH: 0-2 Tight: 0-0 Gall: 0-1
Aids: Bl: 0-0 Vi: 0-8 Tstrap: 0-0 Ckp: 0-0
Best Rating: 109   5/01   NAbb   3m2f110y   gd-fm   Ch

Moderate handicap chaser; stays three miles; regularly visored.

Aisle
7-y-o b g Arazi (USA)-Chancel (USA) (Al Nasr (FR))
L R James   Mrs Carol Lloyd-James

Placings:P   (0467)
2003/04: 16^{P}G,

	Starts	1st	2nd	3rd	Win & Pl
Hurdles	1	0	0	0	
Career Total	1	0	0	0	

Going: Sf: 0-0 GS: 0-0 Gd: 0-1 GF: - Fm: 0-0
Distance: 2m/2m3: 0-1 2m4-2m7: 0-0 3m+: 0-0
Track: LH: 0-1 RH: 0-0 Tight: 0-0 Gall: 0-0
Aids: Bl: 0-0 Vi: 0-0 Tstrap: 0-0 Ckp: 0-0
Best Rating: 0   5/03 Hexm 2m110y   good   Hdl

Akarus (FR)
145
9-y-o b g Labus (FR)-Meris (FR) (Amarko (FR))
M C Pipe A J White

Placings:6040000/030040010F02P0/23320054B655206/00 200316P02-FPF   (4647)
2003/04: 29^{F}S, 29^{P}GS, 36^{F}G,

	Starts	1st	2nd	3rd	Win & Pl
Chases	3	0	0	0	
Career Total	50	2	6	4	132305
10/02 Autl 2m7f110y HCh				VS	£48312
12/00 Pari 2m4f110y Ch				HLD	£4323

Total win prize-money £52635

Going: Sf: 0-1 GS: 0-1 Gd: 0-1 GF: - Fm: 0-0
Distance: 2m/2m3: 0-0 2m4-2m7: 0-0 3m+: 0-3
Track: LH: 0-3 RH: 0-0 Tight: 0-1 Gall: 0-0
Aids: Bl: 0-0 Vi: 0-0 Tstrap: 0-0 Ckp: 0-0
Best Rating: 145   3/03 Uttx 4m2f   soft   Ch

Very useful chaser, ex-French; ran a blinder on only his third start in this country when runner-up in the Midlands National; going well when fell in the Welsh National in 2003; suited by soft ground.

Akina (NZ)
13-y-o b g Ivory Hunter (USA)-Wairoa Belle (NZ) (Bold Venture (NZ))
B J Llewellyn N Brookes

Placings:1F4F0/F0UP/0FP/FU0F2U2PP/FP-PF   (1194)
2003/04: 25^{P}GF, 20^{F}GF,

	Starts	1st	2nd	3rd	Win & Pl
Chases	2	0	0	0	
Career Total	25	1	2	0	3927
8/98 Awap 1m5f Hdl				HVY	£2060

Total win prize-money £2060

Going: Sf: 0-0 GS: 0-0 Gd: 0-0 GF: - Fm: 0-2
Distance: 2m/2m3: 0-0 2m4-2m7: 0-1 3m+: 0-1
Track: LH: 0-1 RH: 0-1 Tight: 0-0 Gall: 0-0
Aids: Bl: 0-0 Vi: 0-0 Tstrap: 0-0 Ckp: 0-2
Best Rating: 91   3/99 Chep 2m110y   gd-sft   Hdl

Al Eile (IRE)
114   136
4-y-o b g Alzao (USA)-Kilcsem Eile (IRE) (Commanche Run)
John Queally (Miss S Collins 31/7) M A Ryan

Placings:11201   (4625)
2003/04: 16^{1}GF, 16^{1}G, 16^{2}S, 17^{0}G, 16^{1}G,

	Starts	1st	2nd	3rd	Win & Pl
Hurdles	5	3	1	0	90886
Career Total	5	3	1	0	90886
136 4/04 Aint 2m110y A Hdl				GD	£63800

116 11/03 Chel 2m110y B Hdl GD £12852
102 9/03 List 2m Hdl G-F £8064
Total win prize-money £84717

Going: Sf: 0-1 GS: 0-0 Gd: 2-3 GF: - Fm: 1-1
Distance: 2m/2m3: 3-5 2m4-2m7: 0-0 3m+: 0-0
Track: LH: 3-5 RH: 0-0 Tight: 1-1 Gall: 0-1
Aids: Bl: 0-0 Vi: 0-0 Tstrap: 0-0 Ckp: 0-1
Best Rating: 136   4/04 Aint 2m110y   good   Hdl

Smart Irish juvenile hurdler; good winner at Cheltenham in November; narrow conqueror of Triumph winner Made In Japan in Grade 2 event at Aintree; acts on a sound surface, although handled easier ground on the Flat.

Al Mabrook (IRE)
107   95+
9-y-o b g Rainbows For Life (CAN)-Sky Lover (Ela-Mana-Mou)
N G Richards Hale Racing Limited

Placings:2P26332/60P-2305F6111   (3763)
2003/04: 17^{2}G, 21^{3}G, 18^{0}G, 18^{5}S, 16^{6}GS, 21^{6}G, 17^{1}GS, 19^{1}G, 17^{1}GS,

	Starts	1st	2nd	3rd	Win & Pl
Hurdles	9	3	1	1	11493
Career Total	19	3	4	3	16413
91 2/04 Sedg 2m1f E(0-110)HHdl				G-S	£4930
95 2/04 Catt 2m3f G(0-90)HHdl				G-S	£2394
92 1/04 Sedg 2m1f G(0-85)HHdl				G-S	£2394

Total win prize-money £9718

Going: Sf: 0-1 GS: 2-3 Gd: 1-5 GF: - Fm: 0-0
Distance: 2m/2m3: 3-7 2m4-2m7: 0-0 3m+: 0-0
Track: LH: 3-9 RH: 0-0 Tight: 3-8 Gall: 0-0
Aids: Bl: 0-0 Vi: 0-1 Tstrap: 0-0 Ckp: 0-0
Best Rating: 95   2/04 Catt 2m3f   good   Hdl

Plating-class hurdler; stays trips of around two and a half miles and suited by good ground or softer; has been quirky in the past, but does go well for an inexperienced rider.

Alaared (USA)
94   70
4-y-o b g King Of Kings (IRE)-Celtic Loot (USA) (Irish River (FR))
D R Gandolfo (J L Dunlop 15/9) Matty Williams

Placings:P60   (4788)
2003/04: 16^{P}G, 18^{6}G, 16^{0}G,

	Starts	1st	2nd	3rd	Win & Pl
Hurdles	3	0	0	0	
Career Total	3	0	0	0	

Going: Sf: 0-0 GS: 0-0 Gd: 0-3 GF: - Fm: 0-0
Distance: 2m/2m3: 0-3 2m4-2m7: 0-0 3m+: 0-0
Track: LH: 0-3 RH: 0-0 Tight: 0-2 Gall: 0-1
Aids: Bl: 0-0 Vi: 0-0 Tstrap: 0-0 Ckp: 0-0
Best Rating: 70   4/04 Font 2m2f110y   good   Hdl

Alabaster
9-y-o gr m Gran Alba (USA)-Last Ditch (Ben Novus)
N J Hawke Mrs D R Whigham

Placings:PP/4   (4247)
2003/04: 25^{4}GF,

	Starts	1st	2nd	3rd	Win & Pl
Chases	1	0	0	0	309
Career Total	3	0	0	0	309

Going: Sf: 0-0 GS: 0-0 Gd: 0-0 GF: - Fm: 0-1
Distance: 2m/2m3: 0-0 2m4-2m7: 0-0 3m+: 0-1
Track: LH: 0-0 RH: 0-1 Tight: 0-0 Gall: 0-0
Aids: Bl: 0-0 Vi: 0-0 Tstrap: 0-0 Ckp: 0-1
Best Rating: 0   3/04 Hrfd 3m1f110y   gd-fm   Ch

Alagazam
89   67
6-y-o ch g Alhijaz-Maziere (Mazilier (USA))
B I Case Mrs M Howlett

Placings:0/0-500P   (0854)
2003/04: 23^{5}GF, 21^{0}GF, 22^{0}G, 22^{P}GF,

	Starts	1st	2nd	3rd	Win & Pl
Hurdles	4	0	0	0	0
Career Total	6	0	0	0	0

Going: Sf: 0-0 GS: 0-0 Gd: 0-1 GF: - Fm: 0-3
Distance: 2m/2m3: 0-0 2m4-2m7: 0-0 3m+: 0-1
Track: LH: 0-3 RH: 0-1 Tight: 0-3 Gall: 0-1
Aids: Bl: 0-0 Vi: 0-0 Tstrap: 0-0 Ckp: 0-0
Best Rating: 67   5/03 Fknm 2m7f110y   gd-fm   Hdl

Alakdar (CAN)
105(101h)   (77h)**98**
10-y-o ch g Green Dancer (USA)-Population (General Assembly (USA))
C J Down Ms L Stark

Placings:00/30/0464235/25300/010602F443P/062-011533P   (2420)
2003/04: 24^{0}GF, 23^{1}G, 21^{1}G, 26^{5}GF, 22^{3}G, 22^{3}GS, 24^{P}GS,

	Starts	1st	2nd	3rd	Win & Pl
Hurdles	1	0	0	0	0
Chases	6	2	0	2	8272
Career Total	37	3	4	6	17682
96 7/03 NAbb 2m5f110yF(0-90)Ch				GD	£4075
98 7/03 Worc 2m7f110yF(0-100)HCh				GD	£3445
88 6/01 NAbb 2m7f110yD Ch				G-S	£4202

Total win prize-money £11723

Going: Sf: 0-0 GS: 0-2 Gd: 2-3 GF: - Fm: 0-2
Distance: 2m/2m3: 0-0 2m4-2m7: 1-3 3m+: 1-4
Track: LH: 2-6 RH: 0-1 Tight: 1-2 Gall: 0-0
Aids: Bl: 0-0 Vi: 0-1 Tstrap: 0-0 Ckp: 0-0
Best Rating: 98   11/03 Hayd 2m6f   gd-sft   Ch

Moderate chaser; stays three miles two well and is suited by stamina test; likes fast ground.

Alam (USA)
108   114+
5-y-o b g Silver Hawk (USA)-Ghashtah (USA) (Nijinsky (CAN))
P Monteith G M Cowan

Placings:2211-663630   (3978)
2003/04: 17^{6}GS, 17^{6}HY, 16^{3}S, 16^{6}S, 20^{3}HY, 20^{0}G,

	Starts	1st	2nd	3rd	Win & Pl
Hurdles	6	0	0	2	2358
Career Total	10	2	2	2	11633
104 3/03 Kels 2m110y E Hdl				G-S	£3627
114 1/03 Ayr 2m E Hdl				SFT	£3510

Total win prize-money £7137

Going: Sf: 0-4 GS: 0-1 Gd: 0-1 GF: - Fm: 0-0
Distance: 2m/2m3: 0-4 2m4-2m7: 0-2 3m+: 0-0
Track: LH: 0-3 RH: 0-3 Tight: 0-1 Gall: 0-0
Aids: Bl: 0-0 Vi: 0-0 Tstrap: 0-0 Ckp: 0-0
Best Rating: 114   1/03 Ayr 2m   soft   Hdl

Alasil (USA)

Fair hurdler; best over two miles and acts on soft ground.

86   **66**

4-y-o b/br g Swain (IRE)-Asl (USA) (Caro)
Mrs N Smith (J L Dunlop 13/10) Tony Hayward And Barry Fulton

Placings:050   (4097)
2003/04: 16⁰G, 18⁵G, 16⁶G,

	Starts	1st	2nd	3rd	Win & Pl
Hurdles	3	0	0	0	0
Career Total	3	0	0	0	0

Going:	Sf: 0-0 GS: 0-0 Gd: 0-3 GF: - Fm: 0-0
Distance:	2m/2m3: 0-3 2m4-2m7: 0-0 3m+: 0-0
Track:	LH: 0-2 RH: 0-1 Tight: 0-2 Gall: 0-0
Aids:	BI: 0-0 Vi: 0-0 Tstrap: 0-0 Ckp: 0-0
Best Rating:	71 1/04 Font 2m2f110y good Hdl

Alayzeass (IRE)

88f   **31f**

5-y-o b m Aahsaylad-In Reverse (IRE) (Cardinal Flower)
J S Moore   Mrs Amanda Killick

Placings:0   (2489)
2003/04: 16⁰GS,

	Starts	1st	2nd	3rd	Win & Pl
NH Flat	1	0	0	0	
Career Total	1	0	0	0	

Going:	Sf: 0-0 GS: 0-1 Gd: 0-0 GF: - Fm: 0-0
Distance:	2m/2m3: 0-1 2m4-2m7: 0-0 3m+: 0-0
Track:	LH: 0-1 RH: 0-0 Tight: 0-0 Gall: 0-1
Aids:	BI: 0-0 Vi: 0-0 Tstrap: 0-0 Ckp: 0-0
Best Rating:	31 11/03 Newb 2m110y gd-sft NHF

Alba Rose

78f   **62f**

5-y-o gr m Overbury (IRE)-Belle Rose (IRE) (Roselier (FR))
J N R Billinge   Mrs V Gilmour

Placings:0   (3887)
2003/04: 16⁰G,

	Starts	1st	2nd	3rd	Win & Pl
NH Flat	1	0	0	0	
Career Total	1	0	0	0	

Going:	Sf: 0-0 GS: 0-0 Gd: 0-1 GF: - Fm: 0-0
Distance:	2m/2m3: 0-1 2m4-2m7: 0-0 3m+: 0-0
Track:	LH: 0-0 RH: 0-1 Tight: 0-1 Gall: 0-0
Aids:	BI: 0-0 Vi: 0-0 Tstrap: 0-0 Ckp: 0-0
Best Rating:	66 2/04 Muss 2m good NHF

Albamart Wood

        80

8-y-o gr g Gran Alba (USA)-Marty's Round (Martinmas)
R J Hodges   Lt Col E L Stocker

Placings:F366-B   (0274)
2003/04: 16⁸GF,

	Starts	1st	2nd	3rd	Win & Pl
Chases	1	0	0	0	
Career Total	5	0	0	1	1704

Albany (IRE)

100   **114**

4-y-o ch g Alhaarth (IRE)-Tochar Ban (USA) (Assert)
J Howard Johnson (Mrs J R Ramsden 8/8) Andrea & Graham Wylie

Placings:131P   (4853)
2003/04: 16¹G, 16³S, 24¹G, 22⁸GS,

	Starts	1st	2nd	3rd	Win & Pl		
Hurdles	4	2	0	1	8559		
Career Total	4	2	0	1	8559		
114 3/04	Hexm	3m		E Hdl		GD	£3493
93 2/04	Catt	2m		E Hdl		GD	£3489
					Total win prize-money £6983		

Going:	Sf: 0-1 GS: 0-1 Gd: 2-2 GF: - Fm: 0-0
Distance:	2m/2m3: 1-2 2m4-2m7: 0-1 3m+: 1-1
Track:	LH: 2-4 RH: 0-0 Tight: 1-1 Gall: 0-0
Aids:	BI: 0-0 Vi: 0-0 Tstrap: 0-0 Ckp: 0-0
Best Rating:	114 3/04 Hexm 3m good Hdl

Useful fast-ground stayer on the Flat; narrow winner on his hurdling debut at Catterick in February; creditable third in much stronger company at Haydock a week later; handles heavy ground but may be better suited by good ground; should stay further than two miles.

Albert House (IRE)

97   **94**

6-y-o ch g Carroll House-Action Plan (Creative Plan (USA))
R H Alner   David O Moon

Placings:00-5FF05   (4361)
2003/04: 20⁵S, 21⁶G, 20⁶GS, 21⁰G, 21⁵GS,

	Starts	1st	2nd	3rd	Win & Pl
Hurdles	5	0	0	0	0
Career Total	7	0	0	0	0

Going:	Sf: 0-1 GS: 0-2 Gd: 0-2 GF: - Fm: 0-0
Distance:	2m/2m3: 0-0 2m4-2m7: 0-5 3m+: 0-0
Track:	LH: 0-3 RH: 0-2 Tight: 0-1 Gall: 0-0
Aids:	BI: 0-0 Vi: 0-0 Tstrap: 0-0 Ckp: 0-0
Best Rating:	94 12/03 Leic 2m4f110y gd-sft Hdl

Albert Square (IRE)

85   **79**

7-y-o b g Alflora (IRE)-Place Stephanie (IRE) (Hatim (USA))
R Rowe   J C H Berry

Placings:60-404P   (4716)
2003/04: 17⁴G, 19⁰S, 20⁴G, 21⁸G,

	Starts	1st	2nd	3rd	Win & Pl
Hurdles	4	0	0	0	0
Career Total	6	0	0	0	0

Going:	Sf: 0-1 GS: 0-0 Gd: 0-3 GF: - Fm: 0-0
Distance:	2m/2m3: 0-1 2m4-2m7: 0-3 3m+: 0-0
Track:	LH: 0-1 RH: 0-2 Tight: 0-3 Gall: 0-0
Aids:	BI: 0-0 Vi: 0-0 Tstrap: 0-0 Ckp: 0-0
Best Rating:	93 12/03 Font 2m4f good Hdl

Albertino Lad

98   **84**

7-y-o ch g Mystiko (USA)-Siokra (Kris)
L Lungo   R J Gilbert

Placings:5/4-436   (4946)
2003/04: 16⁴G, 16³S, 16⁶GS,

	Starts	1st	2nd	3rd	Win & Pl
NH Flat	1	0	0	0	0
Hurdles	2	0	0	1	268
Career Total	5	0	0	1	268

Going:	Sf: 0-1 GS: 0-1 Gd: 0-1 GF: - Fm: 0-0
Distance:	2m/2m3: 0-3 2m4-2m7: 0-0 3m+: 0-0
Track:	LH: 0-2 RH: 0-1 Tight: 0-0 Gall: 0-0
Aids:	BI: 0-0 Vi: 0-0 Tstrap: 0-0 Ckp: 0-0
Best Rating:	102 2/03 Ayr 2m gd-sft NHF

Moderate form in bumpers on good and easy ground; bit better than bare form of hurdles debut suggests but will need to brush up jumping to progress over hurdles.

Albuhera (IRE)

110   **139**

6-y-o b g Desert Style (IRE)-Morning Welcome (IRE) (Be My Guest (USA))
P F Nicholls (M Johnston 9/8) D J & F A Jackson

Placings:6111621151002   (4847)
2003/04: 16⁶GF, 17¹GF, 16¹GF, 16¹GF, 16⁶GF, 16²GF, 16¹GS, 17¹G, 16⁵G, 16¹G, 16⁹G, 16⁰G, 16²GS,

	Starts	1st	2nd	3rd	Win & Pl		
Hurdles	13	6	2	0	46813		
Career Total	13	6	2	0	46813		
139 2/04	Newb	2m110y		C Hdl		GD	£7540
119 12/03	Tntn	2m1f		C Hdl		GD	£5622
129 11/03	Newb	2m110y		C Hdl		G-S	£6612
131 10/03	Chel	2m110y		B HHdl		G-F	£11031
106 10/03	Chep	2m110y		E Hdl		G-F	£2590
106 10/03	Extr	2m1f		E Hdl		G-F	£3332
					Total win prize-money £36729		

Going:	Sf: 0-0 GS: 1-2 Gd: 2-5 GF: - Fm: 3-6
Distance:	2m/2m3: 6-13 2m4-2m7: 0-0 3m+: 0-0
Track:	LH: 4-9 RH: 2-4 Tight: 1-2 Gall: 2-2
Aids:	BI: 0-0 Vi: 0-0 Tstrap: 6-13 Ckp: 0-0
Best Rating:	139 2/04 Newb 2m110y good Hdl

Very useful novice hurdler; former smart Flat performer at best; won six times in 2003/2004 and been placed in Graded company; suited by a fast-run two miles; prefers fast ground, but can act with cut; wears a tongue tie; progressive and tough.

Albundy (IRE)

98   **86**

5-y-o b g Alzao (USA)-Grove Daffodil (IRE) (Salt Dome (USA))
B Mactaggart   P H Betts (holdings) Ltd

Placings:F640-F63   (0690)
2003/04: 20⁶G, 18⁶G, 20³GF,

	Starts	1st	2nd	3rd	Win & Pl
Hurdles	3	0	0	1	727
Career Total	7	0	0	1	727

Going:	Sf: 0-0 GS: 0-0 Gd: 0-2 GF: - Fm: 0-1
Distance:	2m/2m3: 0-1 2m4-2m7: 0-2 3m+: 0-0
Track:	LH: 0-3 RH: 0-0 Tight: 0-1 Gall: 0-0
Aids:	BI: 0-0 Vi: 0-0 Tstrap: 0-0 Ckp: 0-3
Best Rating:	86 5/03 Kels 2m2f good Hdl

Plating-class novice hurdler.

Alcapone (IRE)

112   (113h)**154**
10-y-o b g Roselier (FR)-Ann's Cap (IRE) (Cardinal Flower)
M F Morris Mrs A M Daly

Placings:0F263121436/**F55U21F031/34523FPP/031U5PF5 624-2555P1P**   (4647)
2003/04: 20²GF, 25⁵G, 20⁵YS, 24⁵YS, 24⁵S, 18¹Y, 36⁸G,

	Starts	1st	2nd	3rd	Win & Pl
Chases	7	1	1	0	17596
Career Total	49	6	6	6	109013
154 3/04 Thur	2m2f		Ch	YLD	£10544
152 11/02 Navn	2m		Ch	Y-S	£15950
143 4/01 Fair	2m		Ch	Y-S	£32500
130 12/00 Fair	2m100y		Ch	SFT	£3864
112 2/00 Clon	2m		(0-95)Hdl	SFT	£2760
103 1/00 Tram	2m		Ch	Y-S	£3588
			Total win prize-money £69207

Going:	Sf: 0-1 GS: 0-0 Gd: 0-2 GF: - Fm: 0-1
Distance:	2m/2m3: 1-1 2m4-2m7: 0-2 3m+: 0-4
Track:	LH: 0-4 RH: 1-3 Tight: 0-1 Gall: 0-0
Aids:	Bl: 0-0 Vi: 0-0 Tstrap: 0-0 Ckp: 0-0
Best Rating:	154 3/04 Thur 2m2f yield Ch

Smart Irish chaser; stays three miles but is probably better over slightly shorter trips; suited by cut in the ground.

Alcatras (IRE)

103(82h)   (68h)**107+**
7-y-o b/br g Corrouge (USA)-Kisco (IRE) (Henbit (USA))
B J M Ryall I & Mrs K G Fawcett

Placings:0R0-4FF2250   (4933)
2003/04: 21⁴G, 23⁵G, 24⁶G, 24²GS, 24²G, 25⁵GS, 26⁰G,

	Starts	1st	2nd	3rd	Win & Pl
Chases	7	0	2	0	3384
Career Total	10	0	2	0	3384

Going:	Sf: 0-0 GS: 0-2 Gd: 0-5 GF: - Fm: 0-0
Distance:	2m/2m3: 0-0 2m4-2m7: 0-1 3m+: 0-6
Track:	LH: 0-1 RH: 0-5 Tight: 0-5 Gall: 0-0
Aids:	Bl: 0-0 Vi: 0-0 Tstrap: 0-0 Ckp: 0-0
Best Rating:	107 3/04 Tntn 3m good Ch

Modest novice chaser; hint of ability over fences; stays three miles; acts on good ground or softer.

Alchemystic (IRE)

102   **106**
4-y-o b g In The Wings-Kama Tashoof (Mtoto)
G L Moore (Mrs A J Perrett 9/9) N J Jones

Placings:5145   (4573)
2003/04: 16⁵GS, 18¹G, 18⁴G, 19⁵G,

	Starts	1st	2nd	3rd	Win & Pl
Hurdles	4	1	0	0	2883
Career Total	4	1	0	0	2883
104 12/03 Font	2m2f110yE Hdl		GD	£2625
			Total win prize-money £2625

Going:	Sf: 0-0 GS: 0-1 Gd: 1-3 GF: - Fm: 0-0
Distance:	2m/2m3: 1-4 2m4-2m7: 0-0 3m+: 0-0
Track:	LH: 1-4 RH: 0-0 Tight: 1-2 Gall: 0-2
Aids:	Bl: 0-0 Vi: 0-0 Tstrap: 0-0 Ckp: 0-0
Best Rating:	104 12/03 Font 2m2f110y good Hdl

Alcopop

104f   **98f**
5-y-o b g Alderbrook-Albaciyna (Hotfoot)

Miss Venetia Williams P S & Mrs B M Willcocks

Placings:234   (4264)
2003/04: 17²G, 17³GF, 16⁴GF,

	Starts	1st	2nd	3rd	Win & Pl
NH Flat	3	0	1	1	684
Career Total	3	0	1	1	684

Going:	Sf: 0-0 GS: 0-0 Gd: 0-1 GF: - Fm: 0-2
Distance:	2m/2m3: 0-3 2m4-2m7: 0-0 3m+: 0-0
Track:	LH: 0-2 RH: 0-1 Tight: 0-2 Gall: 0-0
Aids:	Bl: 0-0 Vi: 0-0 Tstrap: 0-0 Ckp: 0-0
Best Rating:	98 11/03 Hrfd 2m1f gd-fm NHF

Has shown ability in bumpers but is proving expensive to follow.

Alcris

80f   **89f**
5-y-o b/br g Alderbrook-One Of Those Days (Soviet Lad (USA))
Jonjo O'Neill Home Run Syndicate Ltd

Placings:0   (4179)
2003/04: 16⁰G,

	Starts	1st	2nd	3rd	Win & Pl
NH Flat	1	0	0	0	
Career Total	1	0	0	0	

Going:	Sf: 0-0 GS: 0-0 Gd: 0-1 GF: - Fm: 0-0
Distance:	2m/2m3: 0-1 2m4-2m7: 0-0 3m+: 0-0
Track:	LH: 0-1 RH: 0-0 Tight: 0-0 Gall: 0-1
Aids:	Bl: 0-0 Vi: 0-0 Tstrap: 0-0 Ckp: 0-0
Best Rating:	89 3/04 Donc 2m110y good NHF

Alderburn

95f   **101f**
5-y-o b g Alderbrook-Threewaygirl (Orange Bay)
H D Daly Mrs D P G Flory

Placings:203   (4787)
2003/04: 17²GF, 16⁰G, 16³G,

	Starts	1st	2nd	3rd	Win & Pl
NH Flat	3	0	1	1	748
Career Total	3	0	1	1	748

Going:	Sf: 0-0 GS: 0-0 Gd: 0-2 GF: - Fm: 0-1
Distance:	2m/2m3: 0-3 2m4-2m7: 0-0 3m+: 0-0
Track:	LH: 0-0 RH: 0-3 Tight: 0-0 Gall: 0-1
Aids:	Bl: 0-0 Vi: 0-0 Tstrap: 0-0 Ckp: 0-0
Best Rating:	101 4/04 Hntg 2m110y good NHF

Promising bumper debut; pulled hard and lay out of his ground next time; well beaten third at Huntingdon in April.

Aldiruos (IRE)

90   **69**
4-y-o g c Bigstone (IRE)-Ball Cat (FR) (Cricket Ball (USA))
P J Hobbs (Y-M Porzier 2/5) Aramis Racing Syndicate

Placings:550P0   (4697)
2003/04: 16⁵G, 17⁵G, 16⁰GF, 16⁹S, 17⁰G,

	Starts	1st	2nd	3rd	Win & Pl
Hurdles	5	0	0	0	0
Career Total	5	0	0	0	0

Going:	Sf: 0-2 GS: 0-0 Gd: 0-2 GF: - Fm: 0-0
Distance:	2m/2m3: 0-0 2m4-2m7: 0-0 3m+: 0-7

Track:	LH: 0-4 RH: 0-1 Tight: 0-3 Gall: 0-0
Aids:	Bl: 0-2 Vi: 0-0 Tstrap: 0-1 Ckp: 0-0
Best Rating:	69 7/03 Strf 2m110y good Hdl

Ex-French hurdler; won a mile and a half claimer on soft ground at Longchamp in April; no great promise to date.

Aleemdar (IRE)

85   **89**
7-y-o b g Doyoun-Aleema (Red God)
A E Jones (Miss K Marks 18/6) John Spence

Placings:030500/22110400455-00PPPP   (4262)
2003/04: 20⁰HY, 16⁰GF, 20⁰GF, 16⁰FG, 16⁰GS, 19⁰GF,

	Starts	1st	2nd	3rd	Win & Pl
Hurdles	6	0	0	0	
Career Total	23	2	2	1	15484
113 7/02 Klny	2m1f		Hdl	GD	£5503
104 7/02 Naas	2m		Hdl	G-Y	£7196
			Total win prize-money £12699

Going:	Sf: 0-1 GS: 0-1 Gd: 0-1 GF: - Fm: 0-3
Distance:	2m/2m3: 0-4 2m4-2m7: 0-2 3m+: 0-0
Track:	LH: 0-4 RH: 0-0 Tight: 0-2 Gall: 0-0
Aids:	Bl: 0-1 Vi: 0-1 Tstrap: 0-2 Ckp: 0-0
Best Rating:	113 7/02 Klny 2m1f good Hdl

Alessandro Severo

93   **81**
5-y-o gr g Brief Truce (USA)-Altaia (FR) (Sicyos (USA))
Mrs D A Hamer (N P Littmoden 10/10) Mike Thomas

Placings:40P   (4242)
2003/04: 20⁴GF, 17⁰GS, 24⁵G,

	Starts	1st	2nd	3rd	Win & Pl
Hurdles	3	0	0	0	293
Career Total	3	0	0	0	293

Going:	Sf: 0-0 GS: 0-1 Gd: 0-1 GF: - Fm: 0-1
Distance:	2m/2m3: 0-1 2m4-2m7: 0-1 3m+: 0-1
Track:	LH: 0-0 RH: 0-3 Tight: 0-1 Gall: 0-1
Aids:	Bl: 0-0 Vi: 0-0 Tstrap: 0-0 Ckp: 0-0
Best Rating:	82 2/04 Tntn 2m1f gd-sft Hdl

Alexander Banquet (IRE)

113   **156**
11-y-o b g Glacial Storm (USA)-Black Nancy (Monksfield)
W P Mullins Mrs N O'Callaghan

Placings:11/11110/1144512/32/316U3/660420F   (4647)
2003/04: 24⁶YS, 24⁶S, 24⁰S, 24⁴YS, 25²Y, 26⁰G, 36⁶G,

	Starts	1st	2nd	3rd	Win & Pl
Chases	7	0	1	0	8158
Career Total	28	10	3	3	249354
168 2/02 Leop	3m		Ch	HVY	£61411
150 2/00 Naas	2m4f		Ch	SFT	£10400
147 11/99 Fair	2m4f		Ch	SFT	£26116
140 11/99 Naas	2m3f		Ch	Y-S	£4620
146 2/99 Leop	2m2f		Hdl	SH	£17343
148 11/98 Fair	2m		Hdl	Y-S	£16956
116 11/98 Punc	2m		Hdl	HVY	£4483
120 11/98 Fair	2m4f		Hdl	Y-S	£2690
142 3/98 Chel	2m110y	A NHF		GD	£18448
115 2/98 Gowr	2m1f		NHF	YLD	£2978
			Total win prize-money £165449

Going:	Sf: 0-2 GS: 0-0 Gd: 0-2 GF: - Fm: 0-0
Distance:	2m/2m3: 0-0 2m4-2m7: 0-0 3m+: 0-7

Track: LH: 0-5 RH: 0-2 Tight: 0-1 Gall: 0-1
Aids: Bl: 0-0 Vi: 0-0 Tstrap: 0-0 Ckp: 0-0
Best Rating: 168 2/02 Leop 3m   heavy   Ch

Smart chaser; won the Festival bumper in 1998; runner-up in the Royal & SunAlliance Chase in 2000; suffered a strained tendon in 2001, but came back to win the Hennessy at Leopardstown in 2002; off for 20 months before trailing last of the finishers in the 2003 Ericsson Chase; has run some good races without success since, but tailed off in the Gold Cup and fell at Aintree; acts well in testing ground; stays three miles.

Alexander Milenium (IRE)

(0c)**108**

8-y-o b g Be My Native (USA)-Kissowen (Pitpan)
Jonjo O'Neill (W P Mullins 15/5) Mrs N O'Callaghan

Placings: 1P2/F65-03P   (2283)
2003/04: 16⁶G, 16³YS, 17⁶G

	Starts	1st	2nd	3rd	Win & Pl
NH Flat	1	0	0	0	0
Hurdles	2	0	0	1	500
Career Total	9	1	1	1	9561
136 12/01 Leop 2m		NHF		YLD	£5564

Total win prize-money £5565

Going: Sf: 0-0 GS: 0-0 Gd: 0-2 GF: - Fm: 0-0
Distance: 2m/2m3: 0-3 2m4-2m7: 0-0 3m+: 0-0
Track: LH: 0-0 RH: 0-2 Tight: 0-0 Gall: 0-0
Aids: Bl: 0-0 Vi: 0-0 Tstrap: 0-0 Ckp: 0-0
Best Rating: 136 12/01 Leop 2m   yield   NHF

A useful bumper performer, hurdler and promising novice chaser; best around two miles; acts on an easy surface.

Alexander Musical (IRE)

76   81

6-y-o b/br g Accordion-Love For Lydia (IRE) (Law Society (USA))
S T Lewis (J G Burns 24/6) Simon T Lewis

Placings: 0-00P4   (4630)
2003/04: 16⁹F, 16⁹G, 25⁶G, 17⁴G,

	Starts	1st	2nd	3rd	Win & Pl
NH Flat	2	0	0	0	0
Hurdles	2	0	0	0	286
Career Total	5	0	0	0	286

Going: Sf: 0-0 GS: 0-0 Gd: 0-3 GF: - Fm: 0-1
Distance: 2m/2m3: 0-2 2m4-2m7: 0-3 3m+: 0-1
Track: LH: 0-2 RH: 0-1 Tight: 0-1 Gall: 0-1
Aids: Bl: 0-1 Vi: 0-0 Tstrap: 0-0 Ckp: 0-0
Best Rating: 95 4/03 List 2m   gd-fm   NHF

Alexander Park (IRE)

7-y-o b g Yashgan-Lady Laramie (IRE) (Le Bavard (FR))
John R Upson Middleham Park Racing Iv

Placings: P000-PPP   (3963)
2003/04: 21⁶GS, 24⁶S, 24⁶GS,

	Starts	1st	2nd	3rd	Win & Pl
Hurdles	2	0	0	0	0
Chases	1	0	0	0	0
Career Total	7	0	0	0	0

Going: Sf: 0-1 GS: 0-2 Gd: 0-0 GF: - Fm: 0-0
Distance: 2m/2m3: 0-2 2m4-2m7: 0-1 3m+: 0-2
Track: LH: 0-2 RH: 0-1 Tight: 0-1 Gall: 0-0
Aids: Bl: 0-0 Vi: 0-0 Tstrap: 0-0 Ckp: 0-0
Best Rating: 0 2/04 Towc 3m   gd-sft   Hdl

Alexanderthegreat (IRE)

113   142

6-y-o b g Supreme Leader-Sandy Jayne (IRE) (Royal Fountain)
P F Nicholls The Irish Connection

Placings: 121303   (4386)
2003/04: 21¹GS, 19²S, 24¹GS, 22³S, 23⁰S, 25³G,

	Starts	1st	2nd	3rd	Win & Pl
Hurdles	6	2	1	2	20822
Career Total	6	2	1	2	20822
109 1/04 Extr	3m110y	E Hdl		G-S	£3605
107 12/03 Plum	2m5f	E Hdl		G-S	£2849

Total win prize-money £6454

Going: Sf: 0-3 GS: 2-2 Gd: 0-1 GF: - Fm: 0-0
Distance: 2m/2m3: 0-1 2m4-2m7: 1-2 3m+: 1-3
Track: LH: 1-3 RH: 1-3 Tight: 1-1 Gall: 0-1
Aids: Bl: 0-0 Vi: 0-0 Tstrap: 0-0 Ckp: 0-0
Best Rating: 143 3/04 Chel 3m1f110y good   Hdl

Useful novice hurdler; winning pointer; placed in the Pertemps Final at Cheltenham; acts in soft ground; stays three miles two.

Alexandra Parade (IRE)

103   105

7-y-o b m Mister Lord (USA)-Ballyanihan (Le Moss)
Mrs J C McGregor   Campbell Ross

Placings: 515/524P   (3812)
2003/04: 20⁵G, 20²S, 224HY, 20⁶GS,

	Starts	1st	2nd	3rd	Win & Pl
Hurdles	4	0	1	0	1449
Career Total	7	1	1	0	2997
96 2/02 Fknm 2m		H NHF		G-S	£1548

Total win prize-money £1548

Going: Sf: 0-2 GS: 0-1 Gd: 0-1 GF: - Fm: 0-0
Distance: 2m/2m3: 0-0 2m4-2m7: 0-4 3m+: 0-0
Track: LH: 0-3 RH: 0-1 Tight: 0-0 Gall: 0-0
Aids: Bl: 0-0 Vi: 0-0 Tstrap: 0-0 Ckp: 0-0
Best Rating: 109 4/02 Chel 2m1f   good   NHF

Half-sister to winning stayer Cottstown Boy, won her second bumper at Fakenham and ran best race over hurdles at Ayr in December 2003; may be capable of a bit better.

Alf Lauren

74f   96f

6-y-o b g Alflora (IRE)-Gokatiego (Huntercombe)
A King Helen Loggin & Richard Preston

Placings: 1-0   (2223)
2003/04: 17⁰G,

	Starts	1st	2nd	3rd	Win & Pl
NH Flat	1	0	0	0	
Career Total	2	1	0	0	2030
96 3/03 Bang 2m1f		H NHF		GD	£2030

Total win prize-money £2030

Going: Sf: 0-0 GS: 0-0 Gd: 0-1 GF: - Fm: 0-0

Distance: 2m/2m3: 0-1 2m4-2m7: 0-0 3m+: 0-0
Track: LH: 0-1 RH: 0-0 Tight: 0-1 Gall: 0-0
Aids: Bl: 0-0 Vi: 0-0 Tstrap: 0-0 Ckp: 0-0
Best Rating: 96 3/03 Bang 2m1f   good   NHF

Alfa Sunrise

105   103

7-y-o b g Alflora (IRE)-Gipsy Dawn (Lighter)
R H Buckler   Tony Fiorillo

Placings: 5/210-56420F   (4268)
2003/04: 21⁵S, 19⁶GF, 20⁴G, 19²S, 24⁰G, 24⁶GF,

	Starts	1st	2nd	3rd	Win & Pl
Hurdles	6	0	1	0	1120
Career Total	10	1	2	0	3916
120 12/02 Font	2m2f110yH NHF			SFT	£2226

Total win prize-money £2226

Going: Sf: 0-2 GS: 0-0 Gd: 0-2 GF: - Fm: 0-0
Distance: 2m/2m3: 0-2 2m4-2m7: 0-2 3m+: 0-0
Track: LH: 0-4 RH: 0-1 Tight: 0-2 Gall: 0-2
Aids: Bl: 0-0 Vi: 0-0 Tstrap: 0-0 Ckp: 0-0
Best Rating: 120 12/02 Font 2m2f110y soft   NHF

Moderate novice hurdler; acts on soft ground; effective over two and a half miles, but looks to need further.

Alfie (IRE)

67   34

6-y-o b g Alphabatim (USA)-Brave Bavard (Le Bavard (FR))
Miss Lucinda V Russell   A R Trotter

Placings: 0   (1840)
2003/04: 17⁰G,

	Starts	1st	2nd	3rd	Win & Pl
Hurdles	1	0	0	0	
Career Total	1	0	0	0	

Going: Sf: 0-0 GS: 0-0 Gd: 0-1 GF: - Fm: 0-0
Distance: 2m/2m3: 0-1 2m4-2m7: 0-0 3m+: 0-0
Track: LH: 0-1 RH: 0-0 Tight: 0-1 Gall: 0-0
Aids: Bl: 0-0 Vi: 0-0 Tstrap: 0-0 Ckp: 0-0
Best Rating: 34 10/03 Sedg 2m1f   good   Hdl

Alfie Bright

53   15

6-y-o ch g Alflora (IRE)-Candlebright (Lighter)
Mrs L B Normile   J M Crichton and Mrs D A Whitaker

Placings: 0PP   (4908)
2003/04: 17⁰HY, 20⁶HY, 20⁶S,

	Starts	1st	2nd	3rd	Win & Pl
Hurdles	3	0	0	0	
Career Total	3	0	0	0	

Going: Sf: 0-3 GS: 0-0 Gd: 0-0 GF: - Fm: 0-0
Distance: 2m/2m3: 0-1 2m4-2m7: 0-2 3m+: 0-0
Track: LH: 0-1 RH: 0-2 Tight: 0-0 Gall: 0-0
Aids: Bl: 0-0 Vi: 0-0 Tstrap: 0-0 Ckp: 0-0
Best Rating: 15 11/03 Carl 2m1f   heavy   Hdl

Alfie Plunkett

5-y-o b g Mind Games-River Of Fortune (IRE) (Lahib (USA))
Mrs Jane Galpin   The Artemis Partnership

Placings:0PP (4856)
2003/04: 16^{0}GS, 17^{P}G, 19^{P}GF,

	Starts	1st	2nd	3rd	Win & Pl
NH Flat	1	0	0	0	0
Hurdles	2	0	0	0	0
Career Total	3	0	0	0	

Going: Sf: 0-0 GS: 0-1 Gd: 0-1 GF: - Fm: 0-1
Distance: 2m/2m3: 0-2 2m4-2m7: 0-1 3m+: 0-0
Track: LH: 0-1 RH: 0-2 Tight: 0-1 Gall: 0-0
Aids: Bl: 0-0 Vi: 0-0 Tstrap: 0-0 Ckp: 0-0
Best Rating: 0 4/04 Tntn 2m3f110y gd-fm Hdl

Alfie Twofourtwo (IRE)

(76h) (74h)
8-y-o b g Jolly Jake (NZ)-Spin N' Win (Cardinal Flower)
Ferdy Murphy Mrs G P Seymour

Placings:005003/5PPPLP (4390)
2003/04: 20^{5}GS, 24^{P}GS, 21^{P}GS, 25^{P}G, 20^{L}G, 27^{P}G,

	Starts	1st	2nd	3rd	Win & Pl
Hurdles	3	0	0	0	0
Chases	3	0	0	0	0
Career Total	12	0	0	1	344

Going: Sf: 0-0 GS: 0-2 Gd: 0-4 GF: - Fm: 0-0
Distance: 2m/2m3: 0-0 2m4-2m7: 0-3 3m+: 0-3
Track: LH: 0-4 RH: 0-2 Tight: 0-4 Gall: 0-0
Aids: Bl: 0-0 Vi: 0-1 Tstrap: 0-0 Ckp: 0-1
Best Rating: 91 3/02 Clon 2m2f heavy NHF

Alfie Valentine
74   57
8-y-o b g Alflora (IRE)-My Aisling (John De Coombe)
Mrs P Ford K R Ford

Placings:00P (4756)
2003/04: 24^{0}GF, 16^{0}GS, 19^{P}S,

	Starts	1st	2nd	3rd	Win & Pl
Hurdles	3	0	0	0	0
Career Total	3	0	0	0	

Going: Sf: 0-1 GS: 0-1 Gd: 0-0 GF: - Fm: 0-1
Distance: 2m/2m3: 0-1 2m4-2m7: 0-1 3m+: 0-1
Track: LH: 0-2 RH: 0-0 Tight: 0-0 Gall: 0-0
Aids: Bl: 0-0 Vi: 0-0 Tstrap: 0-0 Ckp: 0-0
Best Rating: 57 3/04 Chep 2m110y gd-sft Hdl

Alfie's Sun
95f   99f
5-y-o b g Alflora (IRE)-Sun Dante (IRE) (Phardante (FR))
D E Cantillon I A Low

Placings:052 (3649)
2003/04: 16^{0}GS, 16^{5}S, 16^{2}GS,

	Starts	1st	2nd	3rd	Win & Pl
NH Flat	3	0	1	0	708
Career Total	3	0	1	0	708

Going: Sf: 0-1 GS: 0-2 Gd: 0-0 GF: - Fm: 0-0
Distance: 2m/2m3: 0-3 2m4-2m7: 0-0 3m+: 0-0
Track: LH: 0-1 RH: 0-2 Tight: 0-0 Gall: 0-2
Aids: Bl: 0-0 Vi: 0-0 Tstrap: 0-0 Ckp: 0-0
Best Rating: 99 2/04 Kemp 2m gd-sft NHF

Has shown ability in bumpers.

Alfloriano
64f   42f
5-y-o b g Alflora (IRE)-Swallowfield (Wattlefield)
O Sherwood The Chamberlain Addiscott Partnership

Placings:0 (4284)
2003/04: 16^{0}GS,

	Starts	1st	2nd	3rd	Win & Pl
NH Flat	1	0	0	0	
Career Total	1	0	0	0	

Going: Sf: 0-0 GS: 0-1 Gd: 0-0 GF: - Fm: 0-0
Distance: 2m/2m3: 0-1 2m4-2m7: 0-0 3m+: 0-0
Track: LH: 0-0 RH: 0-1 Tight: 0-0 Gall: 0-0
Aids: Bl: 0-0 Vi: 0-0 Tstrap: 0-0 Ckp: 0-0
Best Rating: 42 3/04 Towc 2m gd-sft NHF

Alfy Rich
104   87
8-y-o b g Alflora (IRE)-Weareagrandmother (Prince Tenderfoot (USA))
P M Rich P M Rich

Placings:006/P210-P05B43406 (4873)
2003/04: 22^{0}S, 24^{P}GS, 26^{0}GS, 21^{5}S, 19^{B}S, 17^{4}G, 19^{3}G, 17^{4}GS, 17^{0}G, 20^{6}GS,

	Starts	1st	2nd	3rd	Win & Pl
Hurdles	10	0	0	1	1291
Career Total	16	1	1	1	4758

78 3/03 Hntg 2m5f110yG(0-90)HHdl GD £2555
Total win prize-money £2555

Going: Sf: 0-3 GS: 0-4 Gd: 0-3 GF: - Fm: 0-0
Distance: 2m/2m3: 0-4 2m4-2m7: 0-4 3m+: 0-2
Track: LH: 0-3 RH: 0-7 Tight: 0-4 Gall: 0-1
Aids: Bl: 0-0 Vi: 0-0 Tstrap: 0-0 Ckp: 0-0
Best Rating: 87 3/03 Extr 2m1f soft Hdl

Plating-class hurdler; effective on good and softer.

Algarve
107   100
7-y-o b g Alflora (IRE)-Garvenish (Balinger)
H D Daly Trevor Hemmings

Placings:600-21P4 (3272)
2003/04: 20^{5}GS, 20^{1}GS, 20^{P}G, 22^{4}G,

	Starts	1st	2nd	3rd	Win & Pl
Hurdles	4	1	1	0	6185
Career Total	7	1	1	0	6185

100 11/03 Aint 2m4f E(0-100)HHdl G-S £4264
Total win prize-money £4264

Going: Sf: 0-0 GS: 1-2 Gd: 0-2 GF: - Fm: 0-0
Distance: 2m/2m3: 0-0 2m4-2m7: 1-4 3m+: 0-0
Track: LH: 1-4 RH: 0-0 Tight: 1-2 Gall: 0-0
Aids: Bl: 0-0 Vi: 0-0 Tstrap: 0-0 Ckp: 0-0
Best Rating: 100 1/04 Hayd 2m6f good Hdl

Moderate novice hurdler; winner at Aintree in November; ran badly next time but back to form at Haydock, even if a non-stayer; stays 2m 4f.

Algenon (DEN)
95f   93f
4-y-o br g Asaasy (USA)-La Natte (FR) (Native Guile (USA))
Ferdy Murphy R Sunter

Placings:35 (4594)
2003/04: 16^{3}G, 16^{5}G,

	Starts	1st	2nd	3rd	Win & Pl
NH Flat	2	0	0	1	312
Career Total	2	0	0	1	312

Going: Sf: 0-0 GS: 0-0 Gd: 0-2 GF: - Fm: 0-0
Distance: 2m/2m3: 0-2 2m4-2m7: 0-0 3m+: 0-0
Track: LH: 0-1 RH: 0-1 Tight: 0-0 Gall: 0-1
Aids: Bl: 0-0 Vi: 0-0 Tstrap: 0-0 Ckp: 0-0
Best Rating: 92 2/04 Hayd 2m good NHF

Danish-bred; well backed at long odds when promising third on debut in bumper at Haydock in February.

Algymo

4-y-o b f Tamure (IRE)-Red Point (Reference Point)
S C Burrough Mrs Maureen Emery

Placings:000 (4918)
2003/04: 16^{0}GS, 17^{0}G, 20^{4}GS,

	Starts	1st	2nd	3rd	Win & Pl
NH Flat	2	0	0	0	0
Hurdles	1	0	0	0	0
Career Total	3	0	0	0	

Going: Sf: 0-0 GS: 0-2 Gd: 0-1 GF: - Fm: 0-0
Distance: 2m/2m3: 0-2 2m4-2m7: 0-1 3m+: 0-0
Track: LH: 0-1 RH: 0-1 Tight: 0-0 Gall: 0-0
Aids: Bl: 0-0 Vi: 0-0 Tstrap: 0-0 Ckp: 0-0
Best Rating: 61 3/04 Asct 2m110y gd-sft NHF

Ali Bruce
77f   47f
4-y-o b g Cadeaux Genereux-Actualite (Polish Precedent (USA))
D E Cantillon Mrs Edward Cantillon

Placings:0 (3446)
2003/04: 16^{0}G,

	Starts	1st	2nd	3rd	Win & Pl
NH Flat	1	0	0	0	
Career Total	1	0	0	0	

Going: Sf: 0-0 GS: 0-0 Gd: 0-1 GF: - Fm: 0-0
Distance: 2m/2m3: 0-1 2m4-2m7: 0-0 3m+: 0-0
Track: LH: 0-0 RH: 0-1 Tight: 0-0 Gall: 0-0
Aids: Bl: 0-0 Vi: 0-0 Tstrap: 0-0 Ckp: 0-0
Best Rating: 51 1/04 Ludl 2m good NHF

Aliabad (IRE)
106   77
9-y-o b/br g Doyoun-Alannya (FR) (Relko)
J G M O'Shea N G H Ayliffe

Placings:600534/2032300503P/0/0/3433302P044 (4246)
2003/04: 20^{3}GF, 22^{4}GF, 21^{3}GF, 24^{3}F, 22^{3}GF, 21^{0}G, 21^{2}GF, 26^{P}GS, 16^{0}G, 19^{4}G, 17^{4}GF,

	Starts	1st	2nd	3rd	Win & Pl
Hurdles	11	0	1	4	2639
Career Total	30	0	3	8	5661

Going: Sf: 0-0 GS: 0-1 Gd: 0-3 GF: 0-7
Distance: 2m/2m3: 0-2 2m4-2m7: 0-7 3m+: 0-2
Track: LH: 0-3 RH: 0-8 Tight: 0-4 Gall: 0-1
Aids: Bl: 0-0 Vi: 0-2 Tstrap: 0-0 Ckp: 0-0
Best Rating: 87 4/00 Ludl 2m5f good Hdl

Poor maiden hurdler at up to 3m 2f; acts on a sound surface.

Alias (IRE)

89(66h)   (30h)**75+**

6-y-o br g Allegoric (USA)-Snowdrifter (Strong Gale)
P T Dalton C Corbin

Placings:40PP326F55P6   **(4590)**
2003/04: 17⁴GF, 20⁰G, 26⁰G, 16ᴾGS, 23³F, 24²G, 23⁶GF, 24ᶠG, 27⁵GS, 24⁵G, 24ᴾG, 24⁶G,

	Starts	1st	2nd	3rd	Win & Pl
NH Flat	1	0	0	0	0
Hurdles	2	0	0	0	0
Chases	9	0	1	1	1675
Career Total	12	0	1	1	1675

Going: Sf: 0-0 GS: 0-2 Gd: 0-7 GF: - Fm: 0-3
Distance: 2m/2m3: 0-2 2m4-2m7: 0-1 3m+: 0-9
Track: LH: 0-8 RH: 0-4 Tight: 0-4 Gall: 0-4
Aids: Bl: 0-3 Vi: 0-1 Tstrap: 0-0 Ckp: 0-4
Best Rating: 75   2/04   Fknm   3m110y   good   Ch

Alisa (IRE)

50f

4-y-o b f Slip Anchor-Ariadne (GER) (King's Lake (USA))
B I Case Fools And Horses

Placings:000   **(2675)**
2003/04: 12⁰GF, 14⁰G, 12⁰GF,

	Starts	1st	2nd	3rd	Win & Pl
NH Flat	3	0	0	0	
Career Total	3	0	0	0	

Going: Sf: 0-0 GS: 0-0 Gd: 0-1 GF: - Fm: 0-2
Distance: 2m/2m3: 0-0 2m4-2m7: 0-0 3m+: 0-0
Track: LH: 0-3 RH: 0-0 Tight: 0-0 Gall: 0-0
Aids: Bl: 0-0 Vi: 0-0 Tstrap: 0-0 Ckp: 0-1
Best Rating: 50   12/03   Newb   1m4f110y   gd-fm   NHF

Alittlemoreaction

52   **10**

6-y-o b g Alflora (IRE)-Ilderton Road (Noalto)
M J Roberts Mike Roberts

Placings:000-000   **(4755)**
2003/04: 20⁰GS, 21⁰GS, 21⁰G,

	Starts	1st	2nd	3rd	Win & Pl
Hurdles	3	0	0	0	
Career Total	6	0	0	0	

Going: Sf: 0-0 GS: 0-2 Gd: 0-1 GF: - Fm: 0-0
Distance: 2m/2m3: 0-0 2m4-2m7: 0-3 3m+: 0-0
Track: LH: 0-2 RH: 0-1 Tight: 0-3 Gall: 0-0
Aids: Bl: 0-0 Vi: 0-0 Tstrap: 0-0 Ckp: 0-0
Best Rating: 10   3/04   Plum   2m5f   gd-sft   Hdl

Alizarin (IRE)

5-y-o b m Tagula (IRE)-Persian Empress (IRE) (Persian Bold)
A C Wilson (R E Barr 12/5) Cooper Wilson

Placings:P   **(1370)**
2003/04: 20ᴾF,

	Starts	1st	2nd	3rd	Win & Pl
Hurdles	1	0	0	0	
Career Total	1	0	0	0	

Going: Sf: 0-0 GS: 0-0 Gd: 0-0 GF: - Fm: 0-1
Distance: 2m/2m3: 0-0 2m4-2m7: 0-1 3m+: 0-0
Track: LH: 0-1 RH: 0-0 Tight: 0-0 Gall: 0-0
Aids: Bl: 0-0 Vi: 0-0 Tstrap: 0-0 Ckp: 0-0
Best Rating: 0   9/03   Hexm   2m4f110y   firm   Hdl

Alka International

96(95c)   (110c)**121**

12-y-o b g Northern State (USA)-Cachucha (Gay Fandango (USA))
Mrs P Townsley Paul Townsley

Placings:3240/242P/3212532/262360/11240/0/5246615/53 50-406F   **(3747)**
2003/04: 16⁴S, 16⁰S, 23⁶HY, 18ᶠGS,

	Starts	1st	2nd	3rd	Win & Pl
Hurdles	42	4	10	5	31669
Career Total	42	4	10	5	31669
121	2/02	Plum	2m	D(0-115)HHdl	HVY	£3430
133	12/99	Ling	2m110y	D(0-125)HHdl	SFT	£2851
133	12/99	Font	2m2f110yC(0-130)HHdl	GD	£7002
103	12/97	Hayd	2m	E(0-120)HHdl	SFT	£2221
				Total win prize-money £15506		

Going: Sf: 0-3 GS: 0-1 Gd: 0-0 GF: - Fm: 0-0
Distance: 2m/2m3: 0-3 2m4-2m7: 0-0 3m+: 0-1
Track: LH: 0-3 RH: 0-1 Tight: 0-2 Gall: 0-0
Aids: Bl: 0-4 Vi: 0-0 Tstrap: 0-0 Ckp: 0-0
Best Rating: 133   12/99   Kemp   2m   soft   Hdl

Fair, but fragile handicap hurdler; looks best over two miles, but does get further; suited by cut in the ground; often fitted with blinkers.

All Bleevable

102   **100**

7-y-o b g Presidium-Eve's Treasure (Bustino)
Mrs S Lamyman Mike & Tony Blee And Roy Allerston

Placings:6P005/PP20/234-34224113   **(4438)**
2003/04: 16³GF, 17⁴GF, 17²GF, 17²G, 16⁴GS, 16¹G, 16¹G, 16³GS,

	Starts	1st	2nd	3rd	Win & Pl
Hurdles	8	2	2	2	9533
Career Total	20	2	4	3	10874
100	3/04	Donc	2m110y	E(0-105)HHdl	GD	£3686
92	2/04	Fknm	2m	G(0-90)HHdl	GD	£2696
				Total win prize-money £6383		

Going: Sf: 0-0 GS: 0-2 Gd: 2-3 GF: - Fm: 0-3
Distance: 2m/2m3: 2-8 2m4-2m7: 0-0 3m+: 0-0
Track: LH: 2-8 RH: 0-0 Tight: 1-4 Gall: 1-1
Aids: Bl: 0-0 Vi: 0-0 Tstrap: 0-0 Ckp: 0-0
Best Rating: 100   3/04   Donc   2m110y   good   Hdl

Plating-class hurdler; suited by a sharp track and a sound surface; effective at around two miles; suited by forcing tactics.

All But (IRE)

96(93h)   (70h)**72**

12-y-o b g Roselier (FR)-Cloncunny (Teofane)
J Clements (J Parkes 6/2) James Clements

Placings:0/4/F0064523B24P/46S0064/PFU040500F0/0640 F-355PPP36   **(4661)**
2003/04: 20³G, 20⁵S, 27⁵G, 21ᴾGS, 19ᴾG, 28ᴾGY, 24³Y, 25⁶S,

	Starts	1st	2nd	3rd	Win & Pl
Hurdles	1	0	0	0	
Career Total	1	0	0	0	

	Starts	1st	2nd	3rd	Win & Pl
Hurdles	1	0	0	0	0
Chases	7	0	0	2	977
Career Total	45	0	2	3	6634

Plating-class maiden ex-Irish chaser, stays three miles.

All Eyez On Me (IRE)

(86c)   (66c)**52**

7-y-o b g Torus-Ella Rosa (Le Bavard (FR))
Dr P Pritchard A J Whiting

Placings:000/FPUUP0P6-0   **(0681)**
2003/04: 24⁰GF,

	Starts	1st	2nd	3rd	Win & Pl
Hurdles	1	0	0	0	
Career Total	12	0	0	0	0

Going: Sf: 0-0 GS: 0-0 Gd: 0-0 GF: - Fm: 0-1
Distance: 2m/2m3: 0-0 2m4-2m7: 0-0 3m+: 0-1
Track: LH: 0-1 RH: 0-0 Tight: 0-0 Gall: 0-0
Aids: Bl: 0-0 Vi: 0-0 Tstrap: 0-0 Ckp: 0-1
Best Rating: 66   1/03   Ludl   2m4f   soft   Ch

All Honey (IRE)

97   (0c)**76**

7-y-o ch m Fourstars Allstar (USA)-A Bit Of Honey (The Parson)
Miss K Marks Nick Shutts

Placings:61/433540/234540UP0-31F0055   **(2418)**
2003/04: 20³S, 16¹G, 16ᶠG, 16⁰GF, 22⁰GF, 16⁵G, 16⁵GS,

	Starts	1st	2nd	3rd	Win & Pl
Hurdles	7	1	0	1	2911
Career Total	24	2	1	4	9910
76	5/03	Uttx	2m	G Hdl	GD	£2548
105	4/01	List	2m	NHF	HVY	£3895
				Total win prize-money £6443		

Going: Sf: 0-1 GS: 0-1 Gd: 1-3 GF: - Fm: 0-2
Distance: 2m/2m3: 1-5 2m4-2m7: 0-2 3m+: 0-0
Track: LH: 1-7 RH: 0-0 Tight: 0-2 Gall: 0-0
Aids: Bl: 0-0 Vi: 0-0 Tstrap: 0-0 Ckp: 0-0
Best Rating: 105   4/01   List   2m   heavy   NHF

A bumper winner in Ireland; plating-class hurdler.

All In The Stars (IRE)

100   **111**

6-y-o ch g Fourstars Allstar (USA)-Luton Flyer (Condorcet (FR))
D P Keane Avon Thoroughbreds Ltd

Placings:O-P4U2P55   **(4405)**
2003/04: 21ᴾS, 20⁴GS, 24ᵁGS, 22²S, 24ᴾS, 26⁵GS, 26⁵G,

	Starts	1st	2nd	3rd	Win & Pl
Hurdles	7	0	1	0	1068
Career Total	8	0	1	0	1068

Going: Sf: 0-3 GS: 0-3 Gd: 0-1 GF: - Fm: 0-0

Distance: 2m/2m3: 0-0 2m4-2m7: 0-3 3m+: 0-4
Track: LH: 0-3 RH: 0-4 Tight: 0-0 Gall: 0-3
Aids: Bl: 0-0 Vi: 0-2 Tstrap: 0-0 Ckp: 0-0
Best Rating: 108 1/04 Extr 2m6f110y soft Hdl

Moderate hurdler; point winner February 2003; stays well; effective in soft ground; has worn visor.

All On My Own (USA)

83   67

9-y-o ch g Unbridled (USA)-Someforall (USA) (One For All (USA))
I W McInnes Ian McInnes

Placings: 450/000P00/0006/2P   (2842)
2003/04: 16²GS, 16°GS,

	Starts	1st	2nd	3rd	Win & Pl
Hurdles	2	0	1	0	544
Career Total	15	0	1	0	544

Going: Sf: 0-0 GS: 0-2 Gd: 0-0 GF: - Fm: 0-0
Distance: 2m/2m3: 0-2 2m4-2m7: 0-0 3m+: 0-0
Track: LH: 0-2 RH: 0-0 Tight: 0-1 Gall: 0-0
Aids: Bl: 0-0 Vi: 0-0 Tstrap: 0-0 Ckp: 0-0
Best Rating: 90 10/99 Hexm 2m   good NHF

Plating-class hurdler; yet to win a race of any sort.

All Right For Time

6-y-o b m Sula Bula-Penny Falls (Push On)
C C Bealby G H Dook

Placings: 0P   (2867)
2003/04: 16°GS, 25°S,

	Starts	1st	2nd	3rd	Win & Pl
NH Flat	1	0	0	0	0
Hurdles	1	0	0	0	0
Career Total	2	0	0	0	0

Going: Sf: 0-1 GS: 0-1 Gd: 0-0 GF: - Fm: 0-0
Distance: 2m/2m3: 0-1 2m4-2m7: 0-0 3m+: 0-1
Track: LH: 0-2 RH: 0-0 Tight: 0-0 Gall: 0-0
Aids: Bl: 0-0 Vi: 0-0 Tstrap: 0-0 Ckp: 0-0
Best Rating: 32 11/03 Uttx 2m   gd-sft NHF

All Rock Hard (NZ)

104   103

6-y-o ch g Bigstone (IRE)-My Lady Gray (NZ) (Otehi Bay (AUS))
R C Guest Paul Beck

Placings: 5230030   (4178)
2003/04: 16⁵S, 19²G, 16³GF, 16⁰G, 16⁰GS, 16³F, 16⁰G,

	Starts	1st	2nd	3rd	Win & Pl
Hurdles	7	0	1	2	1623
Career Total	7	0	1	2	1623

Going: Sf: 0-1 GS: 0-1 Gd: 0-3 GF: - Fm: 0-2
Distance: 2m/2m3: 0-6 2m4-2m7: 0-1 3m+: 0-0
Track: LH: 0-3 RH: 0-4 Tight: 0-4 Gall: 0-2
Aids: Bl: 0-1 Vi: 0-0 Tstrap: 0-0 Ckp: 0-0
Best Rating: 103 2/04 Muss 2m   firm   Hdl

Plating-class novice hurdler; dual winner on the level in Australasia; placed in novice events; stays two and a half miles.

All Sewn Up

12-y-o ch g Jazetas-Rose Of Bradford (Levanter)
R J Baker Neil & Susie Dalgren

Placings: 6/0630P/6/P   (0751)
2003/04: 16ᴾGF,

	Starts	1st	2nd	3rd	Win & Pl
Chases	1	0	0	0	
Career Total	8	0	0	1	381

Going: Sf: 0-0 GS: 0-0 Gd: 0-0 GF: - Fm: 0-1
Distance: 2m/2m3: 0-1 2m4-2m7: 0-0 3m+: 0-0
Track: LH: 0-1 RH: 0-0 Tight: 0-1 Gall: 0-0
Aids: Bl: 0-0 Vi: 0-0 Tstrap: 0-0 Ckp: 0-0
Best Rating: 66 10/96 Chel 2m110y firm Hdl

All Sonsilver (FR)

103   (102h) 119+

7-y-o b g Son Of Silver-All Licette (FR) (Native Guile (USA))
M Todhunter Sir Robert Ogden

Placings: 011/P2351-321136   (4320)
2003/04: 24³S, 25²S, 20¹HY, 24¹HY, 20³G, 24⁶S,

	Starts	1st	2nd	3rd	Win & Pl
Chases	6	2	1	2	12808
Career Total	14	5	2	3	25922
119 2/04 Newc	3m		E(0-110)HCh	HVY	£5099
112 1/04 Newc	2m4f		E(0-105)HCh	HVY	£4371
106 2/03 Ayr		2m5f110yE(0-105)HCh		G-S	£4114
102 4/02 Hexm	2m110y		E(0-110)HHdl	GD	£3360
95 3/02 Kels		2m110y E Hdl		SFT	£3062
			Total win prize-money £20008		

Going: Sf: 2-5 GS: 0-0 Gd: 0-1 GF: - Fm: 0-0
Distance: 2m/2m3: 0-0 2m4-2m7: 1-2 3m+: 1-4
Track: LH: 2-6 RH: 0-0 Tight: 0-0 Gall: 2-4
Aids: Bl: 0-0 Vi: 0-0 Tstrap: 0-0 Ckp: 0-0
Best Rating: 119 2/04 Newc 3m   heavy   Ch

Modest chaser; tends to idle in front; stays three miles and one furlong; suited by soft and heavy ground.

All Things Equal (IRE)

70f   95f

5-y-o b g Supreme Leader-Angel's Dream (King's Ride)
S E H Sherwood J Hales

Placings: 20   (4649)
2003/04: 16²G, 17⁰G,

	Starts	1st	2nd	3rd	Win & Pl
NH Flat	2	0	1	0	1126
Career Total	2	0	1	0	1126

Going: Sf: 0-0 GS: 0-0 Gd: 0-2 GF: - Fm: 0-0
Distance: 2m/2m3: 0-2 2m4-2m7: 0-0 3m+: 0-0
Track: LH: 0-0 RH: 0-1 Tight: 0-0 Gall: 0-0
Aids: Bl: 0-0 Vi: 0-0 Tstrap: 0-0 Ckp: 0-0
Best Rating: 95 2/04 Kemp 2m   good   NHF

Alleged Affair (IRE)

93f   89f

7-y-o gr g Safety Catch (USA)-Wren's Princess (Wrens Hill)
B D Leavy E G Ashford

Placings: 0-5   (1665)

2003/04: 16⁵GF,

	Starts	1st	2nd	3rd	Win & Pl
NH Flat	1	0	0	0	0
Career Total	2	0	0	0	0

Going: Sf: 0-0 GS: 0-0 Gd: 0-0 GF: - Fm: 0-1
Distance: 2m/2m3: 0-1 2m4-2m7: 0-0 3m+: 0-0
Track: LH: 0-1 RH: 0-0 Tight: 0-0 Gall: 0-0
Aids: Bl: 0-0 Vi: 0-0 Tstrap: 0-0 Ckp: 0-0
Best Rating: 92 12/02 Donc 2m110y   gd-sft NHF

Some promise in bumpers; hung on fast ground second start.

Alleged Slave (IRE)

101 (103h)   (110 h) 116

9-y-o ch g Husyan (USA)-Lek Dawn (Menelek)
A King Mrs Peter Prowting

Placings: 2/265-PP3221   (4786)
2003/04: 24ᴾGS, 22ᴾS, 20³G, 19⁴HY, 20²G, 16¹G,

	Starts	1st	2nd	3rd	Win & Pl
Chases	6	1	2	1	7532
Career Total	10	1	4	1	8812
116 4/04 Hntg		2m110y E(0-105)HCh		GD	£3946
			Total win prize-money £3947		

Going: Sf: 0-2 GS: 0-1 Gd: 1-3 GF: - Fm: 0-0
Distance: 2m/2m3: 1-2 2m4-2m7: 0-3 3m+: 0-1
Track: LH: 0-2 RH: 1-4 Tight: 0-1 Gall: 1-3
Aids: Bl: 0-0 Vi: 0-0 Tstrap: 0-0 Ckp: 0-0
Best Rating: 117 4/00 Hntg 2m110y good NHF

Moderate chaser; finally off the mark with decisive success at Huntingdon in April; best at two miles but stays three miles; acts on soft ground.

Allegedly Red

99   81

5-y-o ch m Sabrehill (USA)-Tendency (Ballad Rock)
Mrs A Duffield Mrs L J Tounsend & S & G Scaffolding

Placings: 66F4-1054P4   (4258)
2003/04: 19¹GF, 20⁰G, 17⁵G, 16⁴G, 19ᴾG, 16⁴GF,

	Starts	1st	2nd	3rd	Win & Pl
Hurdles	6	1	0	0	0
Career Total	10	1	0	0	0

Going: Sf: 0-0 GS: 0-0 Gd: 0-4 GF: - Fm: 1-2
Distance: 2m/2m3: 1-5 2m4-2m7: 0-1 3m+: 0-0
Track: LH: 1-5 RH: 0-1 Tight: 1-5 Gall: 0-0
Aids: Bl: 0-0 Vi: 0-0 Tstrap: 0-1 Ckp: 0-0
Best Rating: 85 12/03 MRas 2m1f110y good Hdl

Dead-heated in poor mares' only novices' hurdle at Catterick in November; suited by two and a half miles.

Allegiance

84   61

9-y-o b g Rock Hopper-So Precise (FR) (Balidar)
P Wegmann P Wegmann

Placings: P15000532040/000/11626430P0/0-00450 (3880)
2003/04: 16⁰GS, 16⁰GS, 16⁴GS, 17⁵HY, 16⁰S,

	Starts	1st	2nd	3rd	Win & Pl
Hurdles	5	0	0	0	298
Career Total	31	3	2	5	10897
100 11/00 Wwck	2m		F(0-100)HHdl	HVY	£1940
100 11/00 NAbb	2m1f		F(0-110)HHdl	HVY	£2678
79 9/98 MRas		2m1f110yG Hdl		GD	£1562
			Total win prize-money £6180		

Going: Sf: 0-2 GS: 0-3 Gd: 0-0 GF: - Fm: 0-0
Distance: 2m/2m3: 0-5 2m4-2m7: 0-0 3m+: 0-0
Track: LH: 0-3 RH: 0-2 Tight: 0-1 Gall: 0-0
Aids: Bl: 0-0 Vi: 0-0 Tstrap: 0-0 Ckp: 0-0
Best Rating: 100   12/00   Chep   2m110y   soft   Hdl

Aller Moor (IRE)
100

13-y-o b g Dry Dock-Boggy Peak (Shirley Heights)
C J Gray   G Keirle

Placings:060/1122113/5422P/42220P/11P-PPP   (3052)
2003/04: 25PGF, 25PGS, 24PG,

	Starts	1st	2nd	3rd	Win & Pl
Chases	3	0	0	0	
Career Total	27	6	7	1	36512
100	3/03	Extr	3m1f110yH Ch		GD	£3549
100	3/03	Hrfd	3m1f110yH Ch		SFT	£1526
131	3/98	Winc	3m1f110yD(0-120)HCh		GD	£4384
131	1/98	Winc	3m1f110yC(0-135)HCh		GD	£5225
113	11/97	Winc	3m1f110yD(0-105)HCh		GD	£3550
109	5/97	Strf	3m	H Ch		GD	£2976

Total win prize-money £21210

Going: Sf: 0-0 GS: 0-1 Gd: 0-1 GF: - Fm: 0-1
Distance: 2m/2m3: 0-0 2m4-2m7: 0-0 3m+: 0-3
Track: LH: 0-0 RH: 0-3 Tight: 0-1 Gall: 0-0
Aids: Bl: 0-0 Vi: 0-0 Tstrap: 0-0 Ckp: 0-0
Best Rating: 131   3/98   Winc   3m1f110y   good   Ch

Allez Mousson
92   **82**

6-y-o b g Hernando (FR)-Rynechra (Blakeney)
A Bailey   Dr K Kaye

Placings:00   (3976)
2003/04: 24DS, 20DG,

	Starts	1st	2nd	3rd	Win & Pl
Hurdles	2	0	0	0	
Career Total	2	0	0	0	

Going: Sf: 0-1 GS: 0-0 Gd: 0-1 GF: - Fm: 0-0
Distance: 2m/2m3: 0-0 2m4-2m7: 0-1 3m+: 0-1
Track: LH: 0-1 RH: 0-1 Tight: 0-0 Gall: 0-0
Aids: Bl: 0-0 Vi: 0-0 Tstrap: 0-0 Ckp: 0-0
Best Rating: 82   2/04   Carl   2m4f   good   Hdl

Allez Scotia
96   **66**

5-y-o ch m Minster Son-Allez (Move Off)
R Nixon   G R S Nixon

Placings:000303   (4909)
2003/04: 16HY, 16DG, 16DG, 17DHY, 16DG, 24DS,

	Starts	1st	2nd	3rd	Win & Pl
NH Flat	4	0	0	1	274
Hurdles	2	0	0	1	856
Career Total	6	0	0	2	1130

Going: Sf: 0-3 GS: 0-0 Gd: 0-3 GF: - Fm: 0-0
Distance: 2m/2m3: 0-5 2m4-2m7: 0-0 3m+: 0-1
Track: LH: 0-2 RH: 0-4 Tight: 0-0 Gall: 0-0
Aids: Bl: 0-0 Vi: 0-0 Tstrap: 0-0 Ckp: 0-0
Best Rating: 84   3/04   Carl   2m1f   heavy   NHF

Allez Toujours (IRE)
       (58c)

9-y-o b g Castle Keep-Adapan (Pitpan)
M Sheppard   Simon Gegg

Placings:035/5/430PBP3-PP   (0487)
2003/04: 20PG, 22PGF,

	Starts	1st	2nd	3rd	Win & Pl
Hurdles	2	0	0	0	
Career Total	13	0	0	3	1626

Going: Sf: 0-0 GS: 0-0 Gd: 0-0 GF: - Fm: 0-1
Distance: 2m/2m3: 0-0 2m4-2m7: 0-2 3m+: 0-0
Track: LH: 0-2 RH: 0-0 Tight: 0-1 Gall: 0-0
Aids: Bl: 0-1 Vi: 0-0 Tstrap: 0-0 Ckp: 0-0
Best Rating: 104   12/00   Cork   2m   soft   Hdl

Allfriends
74f   **47f**

5-y-o b/br g Alflora (IRE)-Three Friends (IRE) (The Parson)
H P Hogarth   Hogarth Racing

Placings:00   (3724)
2003/04: 16DGS, 16DS,

	Starts	1st	2nd	3rd	Win & Pl
NH Flat	2	0	0	0	
Career Total	2	0	0	0	

Going: Sf: 0-1 GS: 0-1 Gd: 0-0 GF: - Fm: 0-0
Distance: 2m/2m3: 0-2 2m4-2m7: 0-0 3m+: 0-0
Track: LH: 0-2 RH: 0-0 Tight: 0-0 Gall: 0-0
Aids: Bl: 0-0 Vi: 0-0 Tstrap: 0-0 Ckp: 0-0
Best Rating: 47   1/04   Catt   2m   gd-sft   NHF

Allimac (IRE)
103   (104h)**123**

7-y-o b g Alphabatim (USA)-Firewood (IRE) (Brush Aside (USA))
Miss H C Knight   Mrs T P Radford

Placings:20/2204/1213P1-33P   (2996)
2003/04: 20³GF, 16³GF, 20PGF,

	Starts	1st	2nd	3rd	Win & Pl
Chases	3	0	0	2	1424
Career Total	15	3	4	3	20704
105	4/03	MRas	2m4f	Ch		GD	£5810
123	10/02	Ludl	2m4f	E Ch		FRM	£4108
111	5/02	Hrfd	2m3f	D Ch		G-F	£4875

Total win prize-money £14793

Going: Sf: 0-0 GS: 0-0 Gd: 0-0 GF: - Fm: 0-3
Distance: 2m/2m3: 0-1 2m4-2m7: 0-2 3m+: 0-0
Track: LH: 0-0 RH: 0-3 Tight: 0-0 Gall: 0-1
Aids: Bl: 0-0 Vi: 0-0 Tstrap: 0-0 Ckp: 0-0
Best Rating: 123   11/02   Kemp   2m   good   Ch

Fair chaser; bled twice before taking a weak event at Market Rasen in April 2003; effective on fast ground.

Allotrope (IRE)

9-y-o b g Nashwan (USA)-Graphite (USA) (Mr Prospector (USA))
Lady Susan Brooke   Lady Susan Brooke

Placings:525/3P05430/10/05P-P   (0073)
2003/04: 24PS,

	Starts	1st	2nd	3rd	Win & Pl
Chases	1	0	0	0	
Career Total	16	1	1	2	4099
86	10/01	Kels	2m6f110yF(0-105)HHdl		GD	£2856

Total win prize-money £2856

Going: Sf: 0-1 GS: 0-0 Gd: 0-0 GF: - Fm: 0-0
Distance: 2m/2m3: 0-0 2m4-2m7: 0-0 3m+: 0-1
Track: LH: 0-1 RH: 0-0 Tight: 0-1 Gall: 0-0
Aids: Bl: 0-1 Vi: 0-0 Tstrap: 0-0 Ckp: 0-0
Best Rating: 98   10/99   Kels   2m6f110y   good   Hdl

Allstar Leader (IRE)
97   **83**

7-y-o b g Fourstars Allstar (USA)-Rugged Leader (Supreme Leader)
J J Lambe (Seamus O'Farrell 4/5)   Seamus O'Farrell

Placings:505/0F0000006-52212   (0938)
2003/04: 17⁵Y, 16²F, 24²G, 20¹F, 21²GF,

	Starts	1st	2nd	3rd	Win & Pl
Hurdles	5	1	3	0	8791
Career Total	17	1	3	0	8791
75	7/03	Slig	(67-95)HHdl		FRM	£5376

Total win prize-money £5377

Going: Sf: 0-0 GS: 0-0 Gd: 0-1 GF: - Fm: 1-3
Distance: 2m/2m3: 0-0 2m4-2m7: 1-2 3m+: 0-1
Track: LH: 0-1 RH: 0-2 Tight: 0-1 Gall: 0-0
Aids: Bl: 0-0 Vi: 0-0 Tstrap: 0-0 Ckp: 0-0
Best Rating: 100   4/03   Fair   2m   good   NHF

Moderate hurdler; acts on fast ground; stays three miles.

Alltime Dancer (IRE)
52

12-y-o b g Waajib-Dance On Lady (Grundy)
Mrs C F Lambert   Major Charles Lambert

Placings:1213141144/5450003651/6/4540/05-0   (4306)
2003/04: 24DG,

	Starts	1st	2nd	3rd	Win & Pl
Chases	1	0	0	0	
Career Total	28	6	1	2	21185
118	4/97	Plum	2m4f	E(0-115)HHdl		G-F	£2241
114	3/96	Newb	2m110y	D Hdl		G-S	£2941
126	12/95	Sand	2m110y	C Hdl		GD	£3525
126	11/95	Sand	2m110y	C Hdl		G-F	£3355
114	10/95	Extr	2m1f110yE Hdl		GD	£2122
87	7/95	MRas	2m1f110yD Hdl		G-F	£2630

Total win prize-money £16816

Going: Sf: 0-0 GS: 0-0 Gd: 0-1 GF: - Fm: 0-0
Distance: 2m/2m3: 0-0 2m4-2m7: 0-0 3m+: 0-1
Track: LH: 0-0 RH: 0-1 Tight: 0-0 Gall: 0-1
Aids: Bl: 0-0 Vi: 0-0 Tstrap: 0-0 Ckp: 0-0
Best Rating: 127   10/96   Chep   2m110y   good   Hdl

Allude (IRE)
107   **112**

5-y-o b g Darshaan-Ahliyat (USA) (Irish River (FR))
C J Mann   Abbott Racing Limited

Placings:36520-1112   (0856)
2003/04: 16¹G, 17¹G, 16¹G, 16²GF,

	Starts	1st	2nd	3rd	Win & Pl
Hurdles	4	3	1	0	14610
Career Total	9	3	2	1	16624
106	6/03	Prth	2m110y	D Hdl		GD	£5538

96	5/03	Ctml	2m1f110yE Hdl		GD	£3484
97	5/03	Worc	2m	E Hdl	GD	£3486
				Total win prize-money £12508		

Going: Sf: 0-0 GS: 0-0 Gd: 3-3 GF: - Fm: 0-1
Distance: 2m/2m3: 3-4 2m4-2m7: 0-0 3m+: 0-0
Track: LH: 2-3 RH: 1-1 Tight: 1-2 Gall: 0-0
Aids: Bl: 0-0 Vi: 0-0 Tstrap: 0-0 Ckp: 3-4
Best Rating: 112 4/03 Aint 2m110y good Hdl

Modest hurdler; Flat winner in Ireland; landed three-timer in spring 2003; acts on good and good to firm ground.

Allumee
97f   103f

5-y-o ch g Alflora (IRE)-Coire Vannich (Celtic Cone)
P J Hobbs High Spirits

Placings: 5500   (4824)
2003/04: 16⁵GS, 17⁵S, 16⁹G, 17⁰GF,

	Starts	1st	2nd	3rd	Win & Pl
NH Flat	4	0	0	0	0
Career Total	4	0	0	0	0

Going: Sf: 0-1 GS: 0-1 Gd: 0-1 GF: - Fm: 0-1
Distance: 2m/2m3: 0-4 2m4-2m7: 0-0 3m+: 0-0
Track: LH: 0-1 RH: 0-2 Tight: 0-0 Gall: 0-1
Aids: Bl: 0-0 Vi: 0-0 Tstrap: 0-0 Ckp: 0-0
Best Rating: 103 2/04 Asct 2m110y good NHF

Has shown a fair level of ability in bumpers.

Almanoso
92   62

8-y-o b m Teenoso (USA)-Almanot (Remainder Man)
R Curtis Guildings Racing Club

Placings: 6/40550/6230U/P5-P3PP2P0   (4632)
2003/04: 21ᴾG, 22³G, 20ᴾG, 26ᴾGS, 22²G, 22ᴾGS, 24⁰G,

	Starts	1st	2nd	3rd	Win & Pl
Hurdles	6	0	1	1	1043
Chases	1	0	0	0	0
Career Total	20	0	2	2	1897

Going: Sf: 0-0 GS: 0-2 Gd: 0-5 GF: - Fm: 0-0
Distance: 2m/2m3: 0-0 2m4-2m7: 0-0 3m+: 0-2
Track: LH: 0-2 RH: 0-3 Tight: 0-5 Gall: 0-0
Aids: Bl: 0-3 Vi: 0-0 Tstrap: 0-0 Ckp: 0-0
Best Rating: 99 4/00 Asct 2m110y soft NHF

Plating-class hurdler; stays really well.

Almaravide (GER)
107   130+

8-y-o ch g Orfano (GER)-Allerleirauh (GER) (Espresso)
M Bradstock P J Constable

Placings: 11/44/0-2130   (4397)
2003/04: 16²GS, 20¹S, 20³HY, 21⁰G,

	Starts	1st	2nd	3rd	Win & Pl
Hurdles	4	1	1	1	18753
Career Total	9	3	1	1	29897
126	1/04	Asct	2m4f	C(0-135)HHdl	SFT	£10354
100	4/00	MRas	2m3f110yD Hdl		SFT	£3253
137	4/00	Chel	2m1f	C Hdl	SFT	£6971
				Total win prize-money £20580		

Going: Sf: 1-2 GS: 0-1 Gd: 0-1 GF: - Fm: 0-0
Distance: 2m/2m3: 0-1 2m4-2m7: 1-3 3m+: 0-0
Track: LH: 0-1 RH: 1-3 Tight: 0-0 Gall: 0-1
Aids: Bl: 0-0 Vi: 0-0

Best Rating: 137 4/00 Chel 2m1f   soft   Hdl

Useful handicap hurdler; races prominently; acts best on soft ground; stays 2m 4f; open to further progression.

Almaydan
107   127

6-y-o b g Marju (IRE)-Cunning (Bustino)
R Lee George Brookes & Family

Placings: 42121   (4691)
2003/04: 17⁴G, 19²G, 17¹GS, 16²G, 17¹G,

	Starts	1st	2nd	3rd	Win & Pl
Hurdles	5	2	2	0	12436
Career Total	5	2	2	0	12436
129	4/04	Extr	2m1f	E Hdl		£4355
113	2/04	Tntn	2m1f	D Hdl	G-S	£5057
				Total win prize-money £9412		

Going: Sf: 0-0 GS: 1-1 Gd: 1-4 GF: - Fm: 0-0
Distance: 2m/2m3: 2-4 2m4-2m7: 0-1 3m+: 0-0
Track: LH: 0-2 RH: 2-3 Tight: 1-1 Gall: 0-1
Aids: Bl: 0-0 Vi: 0-0 Tstrap: 0-0 Ckp: 0-0
Best Rating: 129 4/04 Extr 2m1f good Hdl

Useful novice hurdler; suited by two miles but stays further; progressive.

Almier (IRE)
69   68

6-y-o gr g Phardante (FR)-Stepfaster (Step Together (USA))
Michael Hourigan C Maune

Placings: 000-5f50   (2153)
2003/04: 16⁵GY, 16¹S, 20⁵G, 16⁰G,

	Starts	1st	2nd	3rd	Win & Pl
NH Flat	2	1	0	0	5825
Hurdles	2	0	0	0	0
Career Total	7	1	0	0	5825
97	9/03	List	2m	NHF	SFT	£5824
				Total win prize-money £5825		

Going: Sf: 1-1 GS: 0-0 Gd: 0-2 GF: - Fm: 0-0
Distance: 2m/2m3: 1-3 2m4-2m7: 0-1 3m+: 0-0
Track: LH: 0-1 RH: 0-0 Tight: 0-0 Gall: 0-0
Aids: Bl: 0-0 Vi: 0-0 Tstrap: 0-0 Ckp: 0-0
Best Rating: 102 9/03 Gway 2m   gd-yld NHF

Plating-class Irish-trained hurdler; winner of a bumper; still a maiden over hurdles; acts in soft ground.

Almire Du Lia (FR)
101 (96h)   (92h) 118

6-y-o ch g Beyssac (FR)-Lita (FR) (Big John (FR))
Mrs S C Bradburne Hardie, Cochrane, Paterson & Steel

Placings: 26512-0313P   (4947)
2003/04: 20⁰S, 20³GS, 20¹HY, 25³G, 20ᴾGS,

	Starts	1st	2nd	3rd	Win & Pl
Hurdles	1	0	0	0	0
Chases	4	1	0	2	6540
Career Total	10	2	2	2	13184
100	3/04	Newc	2m4f	E Ch	HVY	£4361
96	3/03	Newc	2m4f	E(0-105)HHdl	G-S	£4212
				Total win prize-money £8574		

Going: Sf: 1-2 GS: 0-2 Gd: 0-1 GF: - Fm: 0-0
Distance: 2m/2m3: 0-2 2m4-2m7: 1-4 3m+: 0-1
Track: LH: 1-4 RH: 0-1 Tight: 0-1 Gall: 1-1
Aids: Bl: 0-0 Vi: 1-4 Tstrap: 0-0 Ckp: 0-0
Best Rating: 118 3/04 Kels 3m1f good Ch

Moderate staying hurdler/novice chaser who got off the

mark over fences at Newcastle in March; much improved effort when good third in better company at Kelso a week later; stays three miles well; acts on heavy and fast ground; usually wears sheepskin cheekpieces and has been visored over fences.

Almnadia (IRE)
104   107

5-y-o b m Alhaarth (IRE)-Mnaafa (IRE) (Darshaan)
S Gollings J Hennessy

Placings: 2643126416P035-300046540   (4842)
2003/04: 22³GF, 21⁰G, 20⁰G, 16⁰S, 19⁴G, 22⁶G, 21⁵G, 24⁴G, 21⁰G,

	Starts	1st	2nd	3rd	Win & Pl
Hurdles	9	0	0	1	4573
Career Total	23	2	2	3	21835
101	12/02	Fknm	2m	E Hdl	G-S	£3465
107	10/02	Chel	2m110y	C Hdl	G-F	£6826
				Total win prize-money £10292		

Going: Sf: 0-1 GS: 0-0 Gd: 0-7 GF: - Fm: 0-1
Distance: 2m/2m3: 0-1 2m4-2m7: 0-7 3m+: 0-1
Track: LH: 0-4 RH: 0-4 Tight: 0-0 Gall: 0-2
Aids: Bl: 0-0 Vi: 0-0 Tstrap: 0-0 Ckp: 0-0
Best Rating: 107 4/04 Chel 2m5f110y good Hdl

Modest hurdler; handles fast ground, not as effective on a soft surface; stays two mi

Almontasir (IRE)
35f   6f

6-y-o b g Distinctly North (USA)-My Blue (Scenic)
T P McGovern Ahmed Abdel-Khaleq

Placings: PP-0   (0087)
2003/04: 16⁰GS,

	Starts	1st	2nd	3rd	Win & Pl
NH Flat	1	0	0	0	
Career Total	3	0	0	0	

Going: Sf: 0-0 GS: 0-1 Gd: 0-0 GF: - Fm: 0-0
Distance: 2m/2m3: 0-1 2m4-2m7: 0-0 3m+: 0-0
Track: LH: 0-1 RH: 0-0 Tight: 0-0 Gall: 0-0
Aids: Bl: 0-0 Vi: 0-0 Tstrap: 0-0 Ckp: 0-1
Best Rating: 16 5/03 Worc 2m   gd-sft NHF

Almost An Angel (IRE)

14-y-o ch g Lancastrian-Ballykytton (Signa Infesta)
S T Lewis Simon T Lewis

Placings: 0P00/PPPP0/P   (0032)
2003/04: 25ᴾG,

	Starts	1st	2nd	3rd	Win & Pl
Chases	1	0	0	0	
Career Total	10	0	0	0	

Going: Sf: 0-0 GS: 0-0 Gd: 0-0 GF: - Fm: 0-0
Distance: 2m/2m3: 0-0 2m4-2m7: 0-0 3m+: 0-1
Track: LH: 0-1 RH: 0-0 Tight: 0-0 Gall: 0-1
Aids: Bl: 0-0 Vi: 0-0 Tstrap: 0-0 Ckp: 0-0
Best Rating: 70 7/98 Limk 2m2f yield Hdl

Alph
86   86

7-y-o b g Alflora (IRE)-Royal Birthday (St Paddy)

R Ingram Friends of the Turf Racing Limited

Placings:0   (3897)
2003/04: 16⁰GS,

	Starts	1st	2nd	3rd	Win & Pl
Hurdles	1	0	0	0	
Career Total	1	0	0	0	

Going: Sf: 0-0 GS: 0-1 Gd: 0-0 GF: - Fm: 0-0
Distance: 2m/2m3: 0-1 2m4-2m7: 0-0 3m+: 0-0
Track: LH: 0-0 RH: 0-1 Tight: 0-0 Gall: 0-0
Aids: Bl: 0-0 Vi: 0-0 Tstrap: 0-0 Ckp: 0-0
Best Rating: **86** 2/04 Sand 2m110y gd-sft Hdl

Alpha Centauri (IRE)

10-y-o ch g Alphabatim (USA)-Barna Glen (Furry Glen)
P Butler Mrs J Butler

Placings:0/1P/P5PP-PF   (4453)
2003/04: 24PG, 19FGS,

	Starts	1st	2nd	3rd	Win & Pl
Chases	2	0	0	0	
Career Total	9	1	0	0	3312
104 11/00 Naas 2m				NHF	Y-S £3312

Total win prize-money £3312

Going: Sf: 0-0 GS: 0-1 Gd: 0-1 GF: - Fm: 0-0
Distance: 2m/2m3: 0-0 2m4-2m7: 0-1 3m+: 0-1
Track: LH: 0-1 RH: 0-1 Tight: 0-0 Gall: 0-1
Aids: Bl: 0-0 Vi: 0-0 Tstrap: 0-0 Ckp: 0-0
Best Rating: **104** 11/00 Naas 2m yld-sft NHF

Alpha Gioconda (IRE)

7-y-o b g Alphabatim (USA)-Rio Dulce (Rio Carmelo (FR))
N J Henderson Parr Thoroughbred Racing I

Placings:0   (4167)
2003/04: 21⁰G,

	Starts	1st	2nd	3rd	Win & Pl
Hurdles	1	0	0	0	
Career Total	1	0	0	0	

Going: Sf: 0-0 GS: 0-0 Gd: 0-1 GF: - Fm: 0-0
Distance: 2m/2m3: 0-0 2m4-2m7: 0-1 3m+: 0-0
Track: LH: 0-1 RH: 0-0 Tight: 0-0 Gall: 0-1
Aids: Bl: 0-0 Vi: 0-0 Tstrap: 0-0 Ckp: 0-0
Best Rating: **0** 3/04 Newb 2m5f good Hdl

Alpha Gold (IRE)
(71h)**97**

9-y-o ch g Alphabatim (USA)-Show M How (Ashmore (FR))
H D Daly Alpha Gold Partnership

Placings:60P21U2FU/P   (4652)
2003/04: 25PG,

	Starts	1st	2nd	3rd	Win & Pl
Chases	1	0	0	0	
Career Total	10	1	2	0	4905
87 3/02 Hntg 3m			F(0-90)HCh	SFT	£2646

Total win prize-money £2646

Going: Sf: 0-0 GS: 0-0 Gd: 0-1 GF: - Fm: 0-0
Distance: 2m/2m3: 0-0 2m4-2m7: 0-0 3m+: 0-1

Track: LH: 0-0 RH: 0-1 Tight: 0-0 Gall: 0-0
Aids: Bl: 0-0 Vi: 0-0 Tstrap: 0-0 Ckp: 0-0
Best Rating: 87 4/02 Wwck 3m110y gd-fm Ch

Ex-pointer, confirmed promise he showed on chasing debut with a win over three miles in a weak event in March 2002. Acts on soft ground, but has handled faster.

Alpha Image (IRE)

5-y-o b g Alphabatim (USA)-Happy Image (Le Moss)
Mrs L Williamson John Riley

Placings:PP   (3280)
2003/04: 20PGS, 24PHY,

	Starts	1st	2nd	3rd	Win & Pl
Hurdles	2	0	0	0	
Career Total	2	0	0	0	

Going: Sf: 0-1 GS: 0-1 Gd: 0-0 GF: - Fm: 0-0
Distance: 2m/2m3: 0-0 2m4-2m7: 0-1 3m+: 0-1
Track: LH: 0-2 RH: 0-0 Tight: 0-0 Gall: 0-0
Aids: Bl: 0-0 Vi: 0-0 Tstrap: 0-0 Ckp: 0-0
Best Rating: **0** 1/04 Uttx 3m110y heavy Hdl

Alpha Leather

13-y-o gr g Zambrano-Harvey's Choice (Whistlefield)
Mark J Grassick Mrs C J Lloyd

Placings:6400000/B605555/2632P400/306S5064545U0/P6
000/P454-U0P   (0361)
2003/04: 25UG, 24⁰GF, 34PHY,

	Starts	1st	2nd	3rd	Win & Pl
Chases	3	0	0	0	
Career Total	47	0	2	2	3299

Going: Sf: 0-1 GS: 0-0 Gd: 0-0 GF: - Fm: 0-1
Distance: 2m/2m3: 0-0 2m4-2m7: 0-0 3m+: 0-3
Track: LH: 0-3 RH: 0-0 Tight: 0-0 Gall: 0-1
Aids: Bl: 0-0 Vi: 0-0 Tstrap: 0-0 Ckp: 0-0
Best Rating: **89** 11/95 Uttx 2m gd-fm NHF

Alpha Noble (GER)
95

7-y-o b g Lando (GER)-Alpha (GER) (Frontal)
Miss Venetia Williams Richard Abbott & Mario Stavrou

Placings:4-F   (1361)
2003/04: 16FGF,

	Starts	1st	2nd	3rd	Win & Pl
Hurdles	1	0	0	0	
Career Total	2	0	0	0	0

Going: Sf: 0-0 GS: 0-0 Gd: 0-0 GF: - Fm: 0-1
Distance: 2m/2m3: 0-1 2m4-2m7: 0-0 3m+: 0-0
Track: LH: 0-1 RH: 0-0 Tight: 0-0 Gall: 0-0
Aids: Bl: 0-0 Vi: 0-0 Tstrap: 0-0 Ckp: 0-0
Best Rating: **95** 12/02 Uttx 2m soft Hdl

Winner three times on the Flat in Germany, showed some promise though well beaten on debut over hurdles at Uttoxeter in December.

Alpha Romana (IRE)
93   **106**

10-y-o b g Alphabatim (USA)-Stella Romana (Roman Warrior)

Mrs S E Busby Mrs Susan E Busby

Placings:06056/0030/P21/1PP0F2-151PP   (4701)
2003/04: 16¹G, 16⁵G, 20¹G, 20PG, 22PG,

	Starts	1st	2nd	3rd	Win & Pl
Chases	5	2	0	0	5066
Career Total	23	4	2	1	12278
99 5/03 Hexm	2m4f110yH Ch			GD	£1540
106 4/03 Chel	2m110y H Ch			GD	£3526
106 5/02 Chel	2m110y H Ch			G-F	£3675
89 4/02 Fknm	2m5f110yH Ch			GD	£2212

Total win prize-money £10953

Going: Sf: 0-0 GS: 0-0 Gd: 2-5 GF: - Fm: 0-0
Distance: 2m/2m3: 1-2 2m4-2m7: 1-3 3m+: 0-0
Track: LH: 2-3 RH: 0-1 Tight: 0-2 Gall: 1-1
Aids: Bl: 0-0 Vi: 0-0 Tstrap: 0-0 Ckp: 0-0
Best Rating: **106** 4/03 Chel 2m110y good Ch

Hunter chaser; effective at below three miles; suited by good/fast ground.

Alpha Rose
107   **97**

7-y-o ch m Inchinor-Philgwyn (Milford)
C R Egerton S Myatt

Placings:2051   (1587)
2003/04: 16²GF, 20⁰S, 17⁵GF, 16¹GF,

	Starts	1st	2nd	3rd	Win & Pl
Hurdles	4	1	1	0	3906
Career Total	4	1	1	0	3906
100 10/03 Hntg	2m110y F(0-95)HHdl			G-F	£2870

Total win prize-money £2870

Going: Sf: 0-1 GS: 0-0 Gd: 0-0 GF: - Fm: 1-3
Distance: 2m/2m3: 1-3 2m4-2m7: 0-1 3m+: 0-0
Track: LH: 0-3 RH: 1-1 Tight: 0-2 Gall: 1-1
Aids: Bl: 0-0 Vi: 0-0 Tstrap: 0-0 Ckp: 0-0
Best Rating: **100** 10/03 Hntg 2m110y gd-fm Hdl

Prolific winner in moderate company on the Flat; runner-up on hurdling bow at Wetherby May 2003; disappointing on soft ground next time and won back on fast on fourth start; best around two miles.

Alphabetic
107   **98**

7-y-o ch g Alflora (IRE)-Incamelia (St Columbus)
N J Henderson Mrs D A Henderson

Placings:303-33   (2673)
2003/04: 20³GF, 19³GF,

	Starts	1st	2nd	3rd	Win & Pl
Hurdles	2	0	0	2	1672
Career Total	5	0	0	4	2305

Going: Sf: 0-0 GS: 0-0 Gd: 0-0 GF: - Fm: 0-2
Distance: 2m/2m3: 0-1 2m4-2m7: 0-1 3m+: 0-0
Track: LH: 0-2 RH: 0-0 Tight: 0-0 Gall: 0-1
Aids: Bl: 0-0 Vi: 0-0 Tstrap: 0-0 Ckp: 0-0
Best Rating: **98** 4/03 Asct 2m110y good NHF

Fair novice hurdler; some form in bumpers; acts on fast ground and may need trips beyond two and a half miles over hurdles.

Alphasupreme (IRE)
80f

7-y-o ch m Alphabatim (USA)-Railway Rabbit (IRE) (Supreme Leader)
C J Down Mrs P M Underhill

Placings:45-P   (0251)
2003/04: 17PGF,

	Starts	1st	2nd	3rd	Win & Pl
NH Flat	1	0	0	0	
Career Total	3	0	0	0	0

Going: Sf: 0-0 GS: 0-0 Gd: 0-0 GF: - Fm: 0-1
Distance: 2m/2m3: 0-1 2m4-2m7: 0-0 3m+: 0-0
Track: LH: 0-0 RH: 0-1 Tight: 0-0 Gall: 0-0
Aids: Bl: 0-0 Vi: 0-0 Tstrap: 0-0 Ckp: 0-0
Best Rating: 80 7/02 NAbb 2m1f   gd-fm NHF

Alpine Fox
101   111+
7-y-o b g Risk Me (FR)-Hill Vixen (Goldhill)
T R George Mrs A D Williams

Placings:21122   (2488)
2003/04: 162GS, 161G, 161GF, 162G, 162GS,

	Starts	1st	2nd	3rd	Win & Pl
NH Flat	4	2	2	0	8213
Hurdles	1	0	1	0	2510
Career Total	5	2	3	0	10723
125 6/03 Worc 2m		H NHF		G-F	£1979
113 5/03 Worc 2m		H NHF		GD	£1884

Total win prize-money £3864

Going: Sf: 0-0 GS: 0-2 Gd: 1-2 GF: - Fm: 1-1
Distance: 2m/2m3: 2-5 2m4-2m7: 0-0 3m+: 0-0
Track: LH: 2-5 RH: 0-0 Tight: 0-0 Gall: 0-1
Aids: Bl: 0-0 Vi: 0-0 Tstrap: 0-0 Ckp: 0-0
Best Rating: 125 6/03 Worc 2m   gd-fm NHF

Useful bumper performer; likes fast ground; runner-up on hurdles debut.

Alpine Hideaway (IRE)
105   85
11-y-o b g Tirol-Arbour (USA) (Graustark)
J S Wainwright Peter Easterby

Placings:534341/1135PP6050/34/0/554000/546-04214
        (1248)
2003/04: 16OGF, 174GF, 172GF, 171GF, 174GF,

	Starts	1st	2nd	3rd	Win & Pl
Hurdles	5	1	1	0	3089
Career Total	33	4	1	4	11921
85 8/03 Sedg 2m1f		G(0-95)HHdl		G-F	£2359
113 6/98 MRas		2m1f110yE(0-110)HHdl		GD	£2903
112 5/98 Weth 2m		D Hdl		G-F	£2897
102 3/98 Newc 2m		F Hdl		G-F	£1896

Total win prize-money £10056

Going: Sf: 0-0 GS: 0-0 Gd: 0-0 GF: - Fm: 1-5
Distance: 2m/2m3: 1-5 2m4-2m7: 0-0 3m+: 0-0
Track: LH: 1-2 RH: 0-3 Tight: 1-4 Gall: 0-0
Aids: Bl: 0-0 Vi: 0-0 Tstrap: 0-0 Ckp: 1-5
Best Rating: 113 9/98 Sedg 2m1f   good Hdl

Plating-class hurdler; recorded first win for over five years at Sedgefield in August 2003; best at two miles; suited by fast ground.

Alpine Panther (IRE)

11-y-o b g Tirol-Kentucky Wildcat (Be My Guest (USA))
C R Cox C R Cox

Placings:12501/11120F/24F34/PPF50-P   (0030)
2003/04: 33PG,

	Starts	1st	2nd	3rd	Win & Pl
Chases	1	0	0	0	
Career Total	22	5	3	1	24562
136 12/98 Bang 3m		B(0-140)HHdl		G-S	£6983
130 12/98 Newc 3m		D(0-125)HHdl		SFT	£2773
119 11/98 Plum		2m4f		F Hdl	SFT	£3550
98 4/98 Carl		2m4f110yE Hdl		GD	£2010
111 12/97 Newc 2m		E Hdl		GD	£2274

Total win prize-money £17590

Going: Sf: 0-0 GS: 0-0 Gd: 0-1 GF: - Fm: 0-0
Distance: 2m/2m3: 0-0 2m4-2m7: 0-0 3m+: 0-1
Track: LH: 0-1 RH: 0-0 Tight: 0-0 Gall: 0-1
Aids: Bl: 0-1 Vi: 0-0 Tstrap: 0-0 Ckp: 0-0
Best Rating: 136 1/99 Chel 2m5f110y gd-sft Hdl

Alpine Slave
105(107h)   (112h)112+
7-y-o ch g Afflora (IRE)-Celtic Slave (Celtic Cone)
N J Gifford Mrs J T Gifford

Placings:6F13-P44231   (4888)
2003/04: 20PGS, 254GS, 224G, 262GS, 243GS, 241GF,

	Starts	1st	2nd	3rd	Win & Pl
Chases	6	1	1		8715
Career Total	10	2	1	2	13112
102 4/04 Strf	3m		D Ch		G-F	£5538
91 3/03 Font		2m2f110yE Hdl		SFT	£3601

Total win prize-money £9139

Going: Sf: 0-0 GS: 0-4 Gd: 0-1 GF: - Fm: 1-1
Distance: 2m/2m3: 0-0 2m4-2m7: 0-2 3m+: 1-4
Track: LH: 1-2 RH: 0-2 Tight: 1-4 Gall: 0-1
Aids: Bl: 0-0 Vi: 0-0 Tstrap: 0-0 Ckp: 0-0
Best Rating: 112 2/04 Font 3m2f110y gd-sft Ch

Modest half-brother to the smart chaser Young Spartacus; won once over hurdles, but has looked better over fences without winning; stays three miles, but also effective over shorter; acts on soft ground.

Alrida (IRE)
96   94
5-y-o b g Ali-Royal (IRE)-Ride Bold (USA) (J O Tobin (USA))
R A Fahey (W Jarvis 16/9) Mark S Russell Partnership

Placings:2   (4220)
2003/04: 172G,

	Starts	1st	2nd	3rd	Win & Pl
Hurdles	1	0	1	0	1031
Career Total	1	0	1	0	1031

Going: Sf: 0-0 GS: 0-0 Gd: 0-1 GF: - Fm: 0-0
Distance: 2m/2m3: 0-1 2m4-2m7: 0-0 3m+: 0-0
Track: LH: 0-0 RH: 0-1 Tight: 0-1 Gall: 0-0
Aids: Bl: 0-0 Vi: 0-0 Tstrap: 0-0 Ckp: 0-0
Best Rating: 97 3/04 MRas 2m1f110y good Hdl

Fair but disappointing handicapper on the Flat; well backed when runner-up on hurdling debut at Market Rasen in March.

Alscot Foxy Lady (IRE)
82(84h)   (43h)80
7-y-o b m Foxhound (USA)-Arena (Sallust)
R Dickin Warwick Members Two

Placings:0F00/00P-035   (0834)
2003/04: 16OGS, 163GF, 165GF,

	Starts	1st	2nd	3rd	Win & Pl
Hurdles	1	0	0	0	0
Chases	2	0	0	1	621
Career Total	10	0	0	1	621

Going: Sf: 0-0 GS: 0-1 Gd: 0-0 GF: - Fm: 0-2
Distance: 2m/2m3: 0-3 2m4-2m7: 0-0 3m+: 0-0
Track: LH: 0-2 RH: 0-1 Tight: 0-0 Gall: 0-0
Aids: Bl: 0-1 Vi: 0-0 Tstrap: 0-0 Ckp: 0-0
Best Rating: 80 5/03 Hrfd 2m   gd-fm Ch

Plating-class hurdler; not disgraced on chase debut.

Alsina

13-y-o b g Alias Smith (USA)-Tersina (Lighter)
Peter Innes Peter Innes

Placings:P/2PP0-0   (0101)
2003/04: 25OG,

	Starts	1st	2nd	3rd	Win & Pl
Chases	1	0	0	0	
Career Total	6	0	1	0	856

Going: Sf: 0-0 GS: 0-0 Gd: 0-1 GF: - Fm: 0-0
Distance: 2m/2m3: 0-0 2m4-2m7: 0-0 3m+: 0-1
Track: LH: 0-1 RH: 0-0 Tight: 0-0 Gall: 0-0
Aids: Bl: 0-0 Vi: 0-0 Tstrap: 0-0 Ckp: 0-0
Best Rating: 89 5/02 Hexm 3m1f   gd-sft Ch

Alska (FR)

11-y-o b/br m Leading Counsel (USA)-Kolkwitzia (FR) (The Wonder (FR))
P L Southcombe P L Southcombe

Placings:P00UUP00/332/U05P6P/3U02U/44406-545251
       (4858)
2003/04: 216S, 255GF, 314GF, 245G, 252GF, 255G, 241GF,

	Starts	1st	2nd	3rd	Win & Pl
Chases	7	1	1	0	3394
Career Total	33	1	3	3	6740
75 4/04 Tntn	3m		H Ch		G-F	£2383

Total win prize-money £2384

Going: Sf: 0-1 GS: 0-0 Gd: 0-2 GF: - Fm: 1-4
Distance: 2m/2m3: 0-0 2m4-2m7: 0-1 3m+: 1-6
Track: LH: 0-1 RH: 1-6 Tight: 1-3 Gall: 0-0
Aids: Bl: 0-0 Vi: 0-0 Tstrap: 0-0 Ckp: 0-0
Best Rating: 76 5/99 Winc 2m5f   firm Ch

Modest hunter chaser; finally broke her duck when coming from a seemingly hopeless position in 3m hunter chase at Taunton April 2004; acts on a sound surface.

Alston Wonder Man (IRE)
93   (0c)86+
9-y-o ch g Husyan (USA)-Welsh Thorn (Welsh Saint)
Mrs J R Buckley (S Kirk 30/8) Mrs J R Buckley

Placings:0-1P   (1760)
2003/04: 171GF, 20PG,

	Starts	1st	2nd	3rd	Win & Pl
Hurdles	2	1	0	0	2436
Career Total	3	1	0	0	2436

86 8/03 MRas 2m1f110yG Hdl G-F £2436
Total win prize-money £2436

Going:	Sf: 0-0 GS: 0-0 Gd: 0-1 GF: - Fm: 1-1
Distance:	2m/2m3: 1-1 2m4-2m7: 0-1 3m+: 0-0
Track:	LH: 0-1 RH: 1-1 Tight: 1-2 Gall: 0-0
Aids:	Bl: 0-0 Vi: 0-0 Tstrap: 0-0 Ckp: 0-0
Best Rating:	86 8/03 MRas 2m1f110y gd-fm Hdl

Showed some ability in Irish points; landed a gamble in selling hurdle at Market Rasen in August on first outing here; pulled up lame next time; best at two miles; acts on fast ground.

Alsyati

103   94

6-y-o ch g Salse (USA)-Rubbiyati (Cadeaux Genereux)
D Burchell (C E Brittain 3/10) Mrs Linda Cognet

Placings:00P1   (4266)
2003/04: 17⁰GS, 16⁰S, 16ᴾHY, 16¹GF,

	Starts	1st	2nd	3rd	Win & Pl
Hurdles	4	1	0	0	2492
Career Total	4	1	0	0	2492
88 3/04 Chep 2m110y G(0-90)HHdl G-F £2492					

Total win prize-money £2492

Going:	Sf: 0-2 GS: 0-1 Gd: 0-0 GF: - Fm: 1-1
Distance:	2m/2m3: 1-4 2m4-2m7: 0-0 3m+: 0-0
Track:	LH: 1-1 RH: 0-3 Tight: 0-1 Gall: 0-0
Aids:	Bl: 0-0 Vi: 0-0 Tstrap: 0-0 Ckp: 0-0
Best Rating:	88 3/04 Chep 2m110y gd-fm Hdl

Plating-class hurdler; acts on fast ground.

Altareek (USA)

105   97

7-y-o b g Alleged (USA)-Black Tulip (FR) (Fabulous Dancer (USA))
J M Jefferson Dean Bostock And Raymond Bostock

Placings:100/3P0-42240P   (4948)
2003/04: 16⁴G, 20²GS, 21²GS, 26⁴GS, 26⁹G, 27ᴾGS,

	Starts	1st	2nd	3rd	Win & Pl
Hurdles	6	0	2	0	1782
Career Total	12	4	2	1	4047
110 3/02 MRas 2m1f110yH NHF				G-S	£1743

Total win prize-money £1743

Going:	Sf: 0-0 GS: 0-4 Gd: 0-2 GF: - Fm: 0-0
Distance:	2m/2m3: 0-1 2m4-2m7: 0-2 3m+: 0-3
Track:	LH: 0-1 RH: 0-4 Tight: 0-1 Gall: 0-3
Aids:	Bl: 0-6 Vi: 0-0 Tstrap: 0-0 Ckp: 0-0
Best Rating:	110 3/02 MRas 2m1f110y gd-sft NHF

Moderate hurdler; bumper winner; stays three miles.

Altay

112   129

7-y-o b g Erin's Isle-Aliuska (IRE) (Fijar Tango (FR))
R A Fahey R M Jeffs & J Potter

Placings:0/1212-1602   (4077)
2003/04: 16¹GS, 16⁶G, 16⁰G, 16²F,

	Starts	1st	2nd	3rd	Win & Pl
Hurdles	4	1	1	0	44434
Career Total	9	3	3	0	65425
129 5/03 Hayd 2m A HHdl G-S £40600					
123 3/03 Weth 2m D(0-125)HHdl G-F £6831					
109 12/02 Muss 2m E HHdl G-F £4221					

Total win prize-money £51654

| Going: | Sf: 0-0 GS: 1-1 Gd: 0-2 GF: - Fm: 0-1 |

Distance:	2m/2m3: 1-4 2m4-2m7: 0-0 3m+: 0-0
Track:	LH: 1-2 RH: 0-2 Tight: 0-1 Gall: 0-0
Aids:	Bl: 0-0 Vi: 0-0 Tstrap: 0-0 Ckp: 0-0
Best Rating:	129 2/04 Muss 2m firm Hdl

Useful hurdler; better known as a fair middle-distance handicapper on the Flat, he has done well in his few outings over hurdles, taking the Grade Three Swinton Hurdle in May 2003; suited to two miles and a sound surface.

Althrey Ruler (IRE)

98(108h)   (84h)84

11-y-o b g Phardante (FR)-Keego's Aunt (Tyrant (USA))
W M Brisbourne (W Clay 4/10) F Lloyd

Placings:0062F/020P1/660/F5P55P440026P/0035P25-
PP23F   (2117)
2003/04: 24ᴾG, 16ᴾGF, 16²GF, 17³G, 20ᶠF,

	Starts	1st	2nd	3rd	Win & Pl
Hurdles	1	0	0	0	0
Chases	4	0	1	1	1789
Career Total	38	1	5	2	8889
97 3/00 Uttx 2m F(0-100)HHdl GD £2789					

Total win prize-money £2790

Going:	Sf: 0-0 GS: 0-0 Gd: 0-2 GF: - Fm: 0-3
Distance:	2m/2m3: 0-3 2m4-2m7: 0-1 3m+: 0-1
Track:	LH: 0-4 RH: 0-1 Tight: 0-3 Gall: 0-0
Aids:	Bl: 0-0 Vi: 0-0 Tstrap: 0-0 Ckp: 0-0
Best Rating:	97 3/00 Uttx 2m good Hdl

Plating-class hurdler; pulled up on chase debut; tubed when well beaten runner-up at Uttoxeter in October; acts on most types of ground; best over two miles.

Altitude Dancer (IRE)

104   89+

4-y-o b g Sadler's Wells (USA)-Height Of Passion (Shirley Heights)
P A Blockley (B Ellison 10/1) J D Cotterill

Placings:2630   (3272)
2003/04: 17²GF, 16⁶G, 16³G, 22⁰G,

	Starts	1st	2nd	3rd	Win & Pl
Hurdles	4	0	1	1	1289
Career Total	4	0	1	1	1289

Going:	Sf: 0-0 GS: 0-0 Gd: 0-3 GF: - Fm: 0-1
Distance:	2m/2m3: 0-3 2m4-2m7: 0-1 3m+: 0-0
Track:	LH: 0-2 RH: 0-2 Tight: 0-0 Gall: 0-0
Aids:	Bl: 0-0 Vi: 0-0 Tstrap: 0-0 Ckp: 0-0
Best Rating:	89 12/03 Leic 2m good Hdl

Novice hurdler; effective over two miles, but needs further; acts on fast ground.

Alva Glen (USA)

99   94+

7-y-o b g Gulch (USA)-Domludge (USA) (Lyphard (USA))
Miss Venetia Williams Exors of the late M J Morris

Placings:U3F00U00   (4697)
2003/04: 17ᵁGF, 20³GF, 16ᶠGF, 16⁰G, 16⁰GF, 16ᵁGF, 17⁰GS, 17⁰G,

	Starts	1st	2nd	3rd	Win & Pl
Hurdles	8	0	0	1	499
Career Total	8	0	0	1	499

| Going: | Sf: 0-0 GS: 0-1 Gd: 0-2 GF: - Fm: 0-5 |

Distance:	2m/2m3: 0-7 2m4-2m7: 0-1 3m+: 0-0
Track:	LH: 0-7 RH: 0-1 Tight: 0-3 Gall: 0-0
Aids:	Bl: 0-0 Vi: 0-0 Tstrap: 0-0 Ckp: 0-0
Best Rating:	94 12/03 Bang 2m1f gd-sft Hdl

One-time useful performer on the Flat; disappointing maiden over hurdles; poor jumper.

Alvaro (IRE)

93(104h)   (88h)88

7-y-o ch g Priolo (USA)-Gezalle (Shareef Dancer (USA))
D J Wintle Caerphilly Building Supplies Ltd

Placings:60R0/60/03P3313600200003P04-2354   (1191)
2003/04: 27²GF, 24³GF, 22⁵GF, 23⁴GF,

	Starts	1st	2nd	3rd	Win & Pl
Hurdles	3	0	1	1	1987
Chases	1	0	0	0	312
Career Total	29	1	2	6	9694
88 8/02 Ctml 2m6f E Hdl GD £3752					

Total win prize-money £3752

Going:	Sf: 0-0 GS: 0-0 Gd: 0-0 GF: - Fm: 0-4
Distance:	2m/2m3: 0-0 2m4-2m7: 0-1 3m+: 0-3
Track:	LH: 0-4 RH: 0-0 Tight: 0-2 Gall: 0-0
Aids:	Bl: 0-0 Vi: 0-0 Tstrap: 0-0 Ckp: 0-0
Best Rating:	88 4/03 Hrfd 3m2f gd-fm Hdl

Plating-class hurdler; has been let down by his jumping over fences; stays 3m 3f; acts on a sound surface.

Alvino

109(100h)   (109+h)130+

7-y-o b g Alflora (IRE)-Rose Ravine (Deep Run)
Miss H C Knight Martin Broughton

Placings:110/31-21P14   (4955)
2003/04: 20²GF, 17¹GS, 20⁵G, 21¹GF, 20⁴G,

	Starts	1st	2nd	3rd	Win & Pl
Chases	5	2	1	0	12283
Career Total	10	5	1	1	29694
130 3/04 Winc 2m5f D Ch G-F £5827					
117 12/03 MRas 2m1f110yD Ch G-S £3770					
109 4/03 Ludl 2m D Hdl GD £4875					
130 12/01 Asct 2m110y B NHF GD £10426					
114 11/01 Ludl 2m H NHF G-F £1519					

Total win prize-money £26418

Going:	Sf: 0-0 GS: 1-1 Gd: 0-2 GF: - Fm: 1-2
Distance:	2m/2m3: 1-1 2m4-2m7: 1-4 3m+: 0-0
Track:	LH: 0-0 RH: 2-5 Tight: 1-1 Gall: 0-1
Aids:	Bl: 0-0 Vi: 0-0 Tstrap: 0-0 Ckp: 0-0
Best Rating:	130 3/04 Winc 2m5f gd-fm Ch

Fair novice chaser; bumper and novice hurdle winner; has suffered from wind problems; off the mark over fences at Market Rasen in December 2003; needs a level right-handed track; best over two miles; acts on fast and easy ground.

Always Believe (USA)

8-y-o b g Carr De Naskra (USA)-Wonder Mar (USA) (Fire Dancer (USA))
Mrs P Ford (M R Bosley 14/6) R S Herbert

Placings:P   (4915)
2003/04: 16ᴾGS,

	Starts	1st	2nd	3rd	Win & Pl
Hurdles	1	0	0	0	
Career Total	1	0	0	0	

Going:	Sf: 0-0 GS: 0-1 Gd: 0-0 GF: - Fm: 0-0
Distance:	2m/2m3: 0-1 2m4-2m7: 0-0 3m+: 0-0
Track:	LH: 0-1 RH: 0-0 Tight: 0-0 Gall: 0-0
Aids:	Bl: 0-0 Vi: 0-0 Tstrap: 0-1 Ckp: 0-0
Best Rating:	0 4/04 Worc 2m gd-sft Hdl

Always In Debt (IRE)
89f   92f
5-y-o b g Norwich-Forever In Debt (Pragmatic)
P J Hobbs Mrs Karola Vann

Placings:6   (4454)
2003/04: 16⁶GS,

	Starts	1st	2nd	3rd	Win & Pl
NH Flat	1	0	0	0	0
Career Total	1	0	0	0	0

Going:	Sf: 0-0 GS: 0-1 Gd: 0-0 GF: - Fm: 0-0
Distance:	2m/2m3: 0-1 2m4-2m7: 0-0 3m+: 0-0
Track:	LH: 0-0 RH: 0-1 Tight: 0-0 Gall: 0-0
Aids:	Bl: 0-0 Vi: 0-0 Tstrap: 0-0 Ckp: 0-0
Best Rating:	92 3/04 Asct 2m110y gd-sft NHF

Showed promise on debut.

Always On The Line (IRE)
10-y-o gr g Arapahos (FR)-Fiona's Waltz (General Ironside)
R Barber Mrs M Merriam

Placings:0/5/FU3   (4823)
2003/04: 26⁶G, 24⁴UG, 23⁸GF,

	Starts	1st	2nd	3rd	Win & Pl
Chases	3	0	0	1	428
Career Total	5	0	0	1	428

Going:	Sf: 0-0 GS: 0-0 Gd: 0-2 GF: - Fm: 0-1
Distance:	2m/2m3: 0-0 2m4-2m7: 0-0 3m+: 0-3
Track:	LH: 0-1 RH: 0-2 Tight: 0-1 Gall: 0-1
Aids:	Bl: 0-0 Vi: 0-0 Tstrap: 0-0 Ckp: 0-0
Best Rating:	102 4/04 Extr 2m7f110y gd-fm Ch

Always Rainbows (IRE)
101   (62c)95
6-y-o b g Rainbows For Life (CAN)-Maura's Guest (IRE) (Be My Guest (USA))
B S Rothwell J Eddings

Placings:1F1200-0P00005320   (4513)
2003/04: 16⁹G, 22⁸PS, 16⁹G, 16⁵OS, 20⁴S, 16⁵S, 17⁵GS, 17³G,
19²GF, 16⁶GS,

	Starts	1st	2nd	3rd	Win & Pl
Hurdles	9	0	1	1	1553
Chases	1	0	0	0	0
Career Total	16	2	2	1	16749
118 12/02 Weth 2m		D Hdl		SFT	£4615
110 11/02 Weth 2m		D Hdl		G-S	£3981

Total win prize-money £8596

Going:	Sf: 0-4 GS: 0-2 Gd: 0-3 GF: - Fm: 0-1
Distance:	2m/2m3: 0-8 2m4-2m7: 0-2 3m+: 0-0
Track:	LH: 0-9 RH: 0-1 Tight: 0-2 Gall: 0-1
Aids:	Bl: 0-3 Vi: 0-3 Tstrap: 0-0 Ckp: 0-1
Best Rating:	118 2/03 Weth 2m gd-sft Hdl

Modest hurdler; both wins have come at Wetherby; stays two miles three; effective on good or soft ground; often visored.

Always Something (IRE)
86   64
7-y-o b/br m Insan (USA)-Lizzie Simms (IRE) (Phardante (FR))
Mrs M Reveley (Michael Condon 1/6) The Mary Reveley Racing Club

Placings:0-605P   (4432)
2003/04: 20⁶G, 21⁰GS, 25⁵GF, 32⁸G,

	Starts	1st	2nd	3rd	Win & Pl
Chases	4	0	0	0	0
Career Total	5	0	0	0	0

Going:	Sf: 0-0 GS: 0-1 Gd: 0-2 GF: - Fm: 0-1
Distance:	2m/2m3: 0-0 2m4-2m7: 0-2 3m+: 0-2
Track:	LH: 0-3 RH: 0-1 Tight: 0-3 Gall: 0-0
Aids:	Bl: 0-1 Vi: 0-0 Tstrap: 0-0 Ckp: 0-0
Best Rating:	64 4/03 Gowr 2m4f gd-fm Ch

Always Wayward
90   49
9-y-o br g Terimon-Forever Together (Hawaiian Return (USA))
Mrs S Wall Penny Gyte,Tom Wood,Fiona Wood,Wilson

Placings:13/0P0F460524/0   (2781)
2003/04: 16⁹G,

	Starts	1st	2nd	3rd	Win & Pl
Chases	1	0	0	0	0
Career Total	13	1	1	1	4008
90 1/99 MRas 1m5f110yH NHF			SFT		£1430

Total win prize-money £1431

Going:	Sf: 0-0 GS: 0-0 Gd: 0-1 GF: - Fm: 0-0
Distance:	2m/2m3: 0-0 2m4-2m7: 0-0 3m+: 0-0
Track:	LH: 0-0 RH: 0-1 Tight: 0-1 Gall: 0-0
Aids:	Bl: 0-0 Vi: 0-0 Tstrap: 0-0 Ckp: 0-0
Best Rating:	122 4/99 Aint 2m110y good NHF

Amacita
41
6-y-o b m Shareef Dancer (USA)-Kina (USA) (Bering)
K G Wingrove M M Foulger

Placings:4P0P0-P   (0442)
2003/04: 19⁸GF,

	Starts	1st	2nd	3rd	Win & Pl
Hurdles	1	0	0	0	0
Career Total	6	0	0	0	0

Going:	Sf: 0-0 GS: 0-0 Gd: 0-0 GF: - Fm: 0-1
Distance:	2m/2m3: 0-0 2m4-2m7: 0-1 3m+: 0-0
Track:	LH: 0-0 RH: 0-1 Tight: 0-0 Gall: 0-0
Aids:	Bl: 0-0 Vi: 0-1 Tstrap: 0-1 Ckp: 0-0
Best Rating:	88 9/02 Hrfd 2m1f gd-fm Hdl

Amanda Kasakova
51
8-y-o ch m Kasakov-Manna Green (Bustino)
J R Norton Mrs Hazel Tattersall

Placings:0/00-P   (0098)
2003/04: 16⁸G,

	Starts	1st	2nd	3rd	Win & Pl
Hurdles	1	0	0	0	
Career Total	4	0	0	0	

Going:	Sf: 0-0 GS: 0-0 Gd: 0-1 GF: - Fm: 0-0
Distance:	2m/2m3: 0-1 2m4-2m7: 0-0 3m+: 0-0
Track:	LH: 0-1 RH: 0-0 Tight: 0-0 Gall: 0-0
Aids:	Bl: 0-0 Vi: 0-0 Tstrap: 0-0 Ckp: 0-0
Best Rating:	74 6/00 Hexm 2m gd-fm NHF

Amandari (FR)
91   70
8-y-o ch g Petit Loup (USA)-Baby Sitting (FR) (Son Of Silver)
J K Hunter K Hunter

Placings:P/203PF/066P-05P6   (4796)
2003/04: 19⁰GS, 25⁵G, 24⁷PHY, 21⁶G,

	Starts	1st	2nd	3rd	Win & Pl
Hurdles	4	0	0	0	0
Career Total	14	0	1	1	1633

Going:	Sf: 0-1 GS: 0-1 Gd: 0-2 GF: - Fm: 0-0
Distance:	2m/2m3: 0-1 2m4-2m7: 0-1 3m+: 0-2
Track:	LH: 0-3 RH: 0-1 Tight: 0-3 Gall: 0-0
Aids:	Bl: 0-0 Vi: 0-0 Tstrap: 0-0 Ckp: 0-0
Best Rating:	74 2/03 Newc 3m soft Hdl

Amanpuri (GER)
104
6-y-o b g Fairy King (USA)-Aratika (FR) (Zino)
P A Blockley (Miss Gay Kelleway 1/3) J T Billson

Placings:2F   (3901)
2003/04: 16²SH, 17⁸GS,

	Starts	1st	2nd	3rd	Win & Pl
Hurdles	2	0	1	0	1091
Career Total	2	0	1	0	1091

Going:	Sf: 0-0 GS: 0-1 Gd: 0-0 GF: - Fm: 0-0
Distance:	2m/2m3: 0-2 2m4-2m7: 0-0 3m+: 0-0
Track:	LH: 0-0 RH: 0-1 Tight: 0-1 Gall: 0-0
Aids:	Bl: 0-0 Vi: 0-0 Tstrap: 0-0 Ckp: 0-0
Best Rating:	104 6/03 Baln 2m sft-hvy Hdl

Amaraku
5-y-o b g Kylian (USA)-Shernborne (Kalaglow)
A L Forbes Tony Forbes

Placings:56P   (1663)
2003/04: 17⁵GF, 24⁶GF, 20⁸GF,

	Starts	1st	2nd	3rd	Win & Pl
Hurdles	3	0	0	0	0
Career Total	3	0	0	0	0

Going:	Sf: 0-0 GS: 0-0 Gd: 0-0 GF: - Fm: 0-3
Distance:	2m/2m3: 0-1 2m4-2m7: 0-1 3m+: 0-1
Track:	LH: 0-2 RH: 0-1 Tight: 0-1 Gall: 0-0
Aids:	Bl: 0-0 Vi: 0-0 Tstrap: 0-0 Ckp: 0-0
Best Rating:	0 10/03 Uttx 2m4f110y gd-fm Hdl

Amari (IRE)

(75c)   (27c)**29**

9-y-o ch g Grand Plaisir (IRE)-Teazle (Quayside)
A G Hobbs Jason Parfitt

Placings:5543/P6/**5660**/00P0-P0P   (3226)
2003/04: 24PGS, 24QGF, 26FGS,

	Starts	1st	2nd	3rd	Win & Pl
Hurdles	2	0	0	0	0
Chases	1	0	0	0	0
Career Total	17	0	0	1	523

Going: Sf: 0-0 GS: 0-2 Gd: 0-0 GF: - Fm: 0-1
Distance: 2m/2m3: 0-2 2m4-2m7: 0-0 3m+: 0-3
Track: LH: 0-1 RH: 0-2 Tight: 0-0 Gall: 0-0
Aids: Bl: 0-0 Vi: 0-2 Tstrap: 0-0 Ckp: 0-0
Best Rating: 101 3/00 Uttx 2m4f110y good Hdl

Amber Dawn

85f   80f

5-y-o ch m Weld-Scrambird (Dubassoff (USA))
B J Llewellyn Maenllwyd Racing Club

Placings:0   (4846)
2003/04: 17QG,

	Starts	1st	2nd	3rd	Win & Pl
NH Flat	1	0	0	0	
Career Total	1	0	0	0	

Going: Sf: 0-0 GS: 0-0 Gd: 0-1 GF: - Fm: 0-0
Distance: 2m/2m3: 0-1 2m4-2m7: 0-0 3m+: 0-0
Track: LH: 0-1 RH: 0-0 Tight: 0-0 Gall: 0-1
Aids: Bl: 0-0 Vi: 0-0 Tstrap: 0-0 Ckp: 0-0
Best Rating: 80 4/04 Chel 2m1f good NHF

Amber Go Go

101(86c)   (49c)**55**

7-y-o ch m Rudimentary (USA)-Plaything (High Top)
James Moffatt (K W Hogg 14/10) Ian Macleod

Placings:O/00PP/0010P4-P5F043   (4390)
2003/04: 16PG, 215G, 21FG, 16QG, 19QG, 273G,

	Starts	1st	2nd	3rd	Win & Pl
Hurdles	5	0	0	1	337
Chases	1	0	0	0	0
Career Total	17	1	0	1	4510
71	6/02	Ctml	2m1f110yD Hdl	G-S	£3913
			Total win prize-money £3913		

Going: Sf: 0-0 GS: 0-0 Gd: 0-6 GF: - Fm: 0-0
Distance: 2m/2m3: 0-3 2m4-2m7: 0-2 3m+: 0-1
Track: LH: 0-6 RH: 0-0 Tight: 0-5 Gall: 0-0
Aids: Bl: 0-0 Vi: 0-0 Tstrap: 0-0 Ckp: 0-0
Best Rating: 71 6/02 Ctml 2m1f110y gd-sft Hdl

Plating-class hurdler; winner on soft ground in 2002; stays well.

Amber Gold

6-y-o b m Tragic Role (USA)-Dark Amber (Formidable (USA))
Mrs S M Johnson Evans, Compton, Matthews & Matthews

Placings:0-056P   (2851)
2003/04: 17QG, 16FGF, 19GGS, 19FGS,

	Starts	1st	2nd	3rd	Win & Pl
NH Flat	2	0	0	0	0

Hurdles   2   0   0   0   0
Career Total   5   0   0   0   0

Going: Sf: 0-0 GS: 0-2 Gd: 0-1 GF: - Fm: 0-1
Distance: 2m/2m3: 0-2 2m4-2m7: 0-2 3m+: 0-0
Track: LH: 0-2 RH: 0-2 Tight: 0-1 Gall: 0-0
Aids: Bl: 0-0 Vi: 0-0 Tstrap: 0-0 Ckp: 0-0
Best Rating: 74 11/03 Worc 2m gd-fm NHF

Amber Lily

83   58

12-y-o ch m Librate-Just Bluffing (Green Shoon)
S T Lewis T G Williams

Placings:00/0P1P030P000/F263050/P/PPP3F6-56 (1852)
2003/04: 17QGF, 16QG,

	Starts	1st	2nd	3rd	Win & Pl
Hurdles	2	0	0	0	0
Career Total	29	1	1	3	3259
96	9/99	Hrfd	2m1f	E Hdl	GD £1954
			Total win prize-money £1954		

Going: Sf: 0-0 GS: 0-0 Gd: 0-1 GF: - Fm: 0-0
Distance: 2m/2m3: 0-2 2m4-2m7: 0-0 3m+: 0-0
Track: LH: 0-0 RH: 0-2 Tight: 0-0 Gall: 0-0
Aids: Bl: 0-0 Vi: 0-0 Tstrap: 0-0 Ckp: 0-0
Best Rating: 96 9/99 Hrfd 2m1f good Hdl

Amber Moss

91(99c)   (93c)**81**

9-y-o ch g Phardante (FR)-Queen's Darling (Le Moss)
Mrs C J Kerr Mrs C J Kerr

Placings:00*52311*/F33U0PF/242P26332P/U646440336-06FP020U2   (4913)
2003/04: 25QG, 20GGS, 22FG, 20PG, 20QGS, 273F, 24QG, 25UG, 242S,

	Starts	1st	2nd	3rd	Win & Pl
Hurdles	4	0	2	0	2584
Chases	5	0	0	0	0
Career Total	43	2	7	7	25324
116	4/00	Ayr	2m6f	C HHdl	GD £7488
113	3/00	Uttx	2m4f110yD Hdl	GD	£3802
			Total win prize-money £11291		

Going: Sf: 0-1 GS: 0-2 Gd: 0-5 GF: - Fm: 0-1
Distance: 2m/2m3: 0-0 2m4-2m7: 0-4 3m+: 0-5
Track: LH: 0-6 RH: 0-3 Tight: 0-2 Gall: 0-0
Aids: Bl: 0-0 Vi: 0-0 Tstrap: 0-0 Ckp: 0-9
Best Rating: 116 4/00 Ayr 2m6f good Hdl

Amber Starlight

98   85

6-y-o b m Binary Star (USA)-Stupid Cupid (Idiots Delight)
R Rowe The Exclusive Partnership

Placings:6   (2576)
2003/04: 16GGS,

	Starts	1st	2nd	3rd	Win & Pl
Hurdles	1	0	0	0	0
Career Total	1	0	0	0	0

Going: Sf: 0-0 GS: 0-1 Gd: 0-0 GF: - Fm: 0-0
Distance: 2m/2m3: 0-1 2m4-2m7: 0-0 3m+: 0-0
Track: LH: 0-0 RH: 0-1 Tight: 0-0 Gall: 0-0
Aids: Bl: 0-0 Vi: 0-0 Tstrap: 0-0 Ckp: 0-0
Best Rating: 85 12/03 Sand 2m110y gd-sft Hdl

Amberleigh House (IRE)

113(103h)   (111h)**154**

12-y-o br g Buckskin (FR)-Chancy Gal (Al Sirat)
D McCain Halewood International Ltd

Placings:00/36 13213144024/**2145345B**/622F43210/1550P B/5216501/36324033-342P51   (4647)
2003/04: 233GF, 244GF, 272G, 20PS, 245G, 361G,

	Starts	1st	2nd	3rd	Win & Pl
Hurdles	2	0	0	1	544
Chases	4	1	1	0	365391
Career Total	59	9	9	10	551662
154	4/04	Aint	4m4f	A HCh	GD £348000
140	4/02	Bang	3m110y	C(0-135)HCh	GD £7572
132	11/01	Aint	3m3f	B HCh	SFT £29000
145	5/00	Punc	2m4f	HCh	GD £11440
143	2/00	Thur	2m4f	Ch	HVY £13000
118	10/98	Gowr	2m1f	Ch	Y-S £2989
129	2/98	Leop	2m	HHdl	Y-S £5956
120	1/98	Navn	2m	Hdl	HVY £2680
111	11/97	Naas	2m	NHF	SH £3051
			Total win prize-money £423691		

Going: Sf: 0-1 GS: 0-0 Gd: 1-3 GF: - Fm: 0-2
Distance: 2m/2m3: 0-0 2m4-2m7: 0-1 3m+: 1-5
Track: LH: 1-5 RH: 0-1 Tight: 1-2 Gall: 0-1
Aids: Bl: 0-0 Vi: 0-0 Tstrap: 0-0 Ckp: 0-0
Best Rating: 154 4/04 Aint 4m4f good Ch

Smart staying chaser; best in decent races receiving weight rather than giving weight away; loves the big Aintree fences; winner of the Becher Chase in November 2001 and runner-up in both 2002 and 2003; excellent third in the 2003 Grand National; took the 2004 renewal; not very big but jumps well; stays extreme distances.

Ambience

89f

7-y-o ch g Wolfhound (USA)-Amber Fizz (USA) (Effervescing (USA))
M J Gingell Going Grey Partnership

Placings:0/50-0   (0675)
2003/04: 17QGF,

	Starts	1st	2nd	3rd	Win & Pl
NH Flat	1	0	0	0	
Career Total	4	0	0	0	0

Going: Sf: 0-0 GS: 0-0 Gd: 0-0 GF: - Fm: 0-0
Distance: 2m/2m3: 0-1 2m4-2m7: 0-0 3m+: 0-0
Track: LH: 0-1 RH: 0-0 Tight: 0-0 Gall: 0-0
Aids: Bl: 0-0 Vi: 0-0 Tstrap: 0-0 Ckp: 0-0
Best Rating: 89 3/03 Hrfd 1m6f gd-fm NHF

Ambience Lady

101(92h)   (92 h)**104+**

8-y-o b m Batshoof-Upper Caen (High Top)
J W Mullins First Impressions Racing Group 2

Placings:140/4U03P-231222P5   (3443)
2003/04: 172GF, 173GF, 201GF, 212GF, 212G, 192G, 21PG, 205G,

	Starts	1st	2nd	3rd	Win & Pl
Chases	8	1	4	1	7799
Career Total	16	2	4	2	10092
104	11/03	Worc	2m4f110yF(0-90)HCh	G-F	£2905
86	1/00	Folk	2m1f110yH NHF	SFT	£1505
			Total win prize-money £4410		

Going: Sf: 0-0 GS: 0-0 Gd: 0-4 GF: - Fm: 1-4

Distance:	2m/2m3: 0-2 **2m4-2m7**: **1-6** 3m+: 0-0
Track:	LH: **1-3** RH: 0-5 Tight: 0-3 Gall: 0-0
Aids:	Bl: 0-0 Vi: 0-0 Tstrap: 0-0 Ckp: 0-0
Best Rating:	**104** 12/03 Winc 2m5f　good　Ch

Plating-class hurdler/novice chaser; soft ground bumper winner, but acts on fast ground.

Ambition Royal (FR)
91f　　96+f
4-y-o ch g Cyborg (FR)-Before Royale (FR) (Dauphin Du Bourg (FR))
Mrs L B Normile (N J Henderson 1/1) J Petterson

Placings:14　　　　　　　　　　(4867)
2003/04: 14¹G, 16⁴S,

	Starts	1st	2nd	3rd	Win & Pl
NH Flat	2	1	0	0	3007
Career Total	2	1	0	0	3007
96	11/03 Wwck 1m6f	H NHF	GD		£2733

Total win prize-money £2734

Going:	Sf: 0-1 GS: 0-0 Gd: 1-1 GF: - Fm: 0-0
Distance:	2m/2m3: 0-2 2m4-2m7: 0-0 3m+: 0-0
Track:	LH: **1-2** RH: 0-0 Tight: 0-0 Gall: 0-0
Aids:	Bl: 0-0 Vi: 0-0 Tstrap: 0-0 Ckp: 0-0
Best Rating:	**96** 11/03 Wwck 1m6f　good　NHF

Made a winning debut in a bumper at Warwick in November 2003 and not disgraced over 2m on next start at Ayr in April following year; effective over a mile six; acts on good and soft ground; shapes as though a good test of stamina will suit.

Ambry
110　　124
7-y-o br g Machiavellian (USA)-Alkaffeyeh (IRE) (Sadler's Wells (USA))
Mrs S J Smith Raymond Gross, Ms Adrienne Gross

Placings:2124/0230210/116U00-4112425　　(2949)
2003/04: 17⁴GF, 20¹G, 20¹GF, 20²GF, 21⁴GF, 25²G, 25⁵G,

	Starts	1st	2nd	3rd	Win & Pl
Hurdles	7	2	2	0	21227
Career Total	24	6	6	1	39912
123	9/03 Worc	2m4f	D(0-125)HHdl	G-F	£3464
114	8/03 Bang	2m4f	D(0-115)HHdl	GD	£5476
124	5/02 Towc	2m	D(0-125)HHdl	G-F	£3150
124	5/02 Font	2m2f110yD(0-120)HHdl		G-F	£3430
122	3/02 Font	2m2f110yE(0-110)HHdl		SFT	£2646
94	3/01 Plum	2m	E Hdl	HVY	£3304

Total win prize-money £21471

Going:	Sf: 0-0 GS: 0-0 Gd: 1-3 GF: - Fm: 1-4
Distance:	2m/2m3: 0-1 **2m4-2m7**: **2-4** 3m+: 0-2
Track:	LH: **2-7** RH: 0-0 Tight: **1-1** Gall: 0-2
Aids:	Bl: 0-0 Vi: 0-0 Tstrap: 0-0 Ckp: 0-0
Best Rating:	**124** 11/03 Chel 3m1f110y good　Hdl

Fair handicap hurdler, suited by trips up to two and a half miles; acts on fast and soft ground; running well for new yard in the summer of 2003, winning twice; has worn blinkers.

Ambushed (IRE)
101(105h)　　　(103h)100
8-y-o b g Indian Ridge-Surprise Move (IRE) (Simply Great (FR))
P Monteith Melville/Stewart

Placings:343/230/F32140-36100064　　(4430)
2003/04: 16³G, 16⁶G, 16¹G, 16⁰G, 17⁰G, 16⁰G, 16⁶G, 16⁴G,

	Starts	1st	2nd	3rd	Win & Pl
Hurdles	6	1	0	1	6835
Chases	2	0	0	0	299
Career Total	20	2	2	5	20851
103	6/03 Prth	2m110y	D(0-115)HHdl	GD	£6090
95	11/02 Ayr	2m	D Hdl	SFT	£9200

Total win prize-money £15291

Going:	Sf: 0-0 GS: 0-0 Gd: 1-8 GF: - Fm: 0-0
Distance:	2m/2m3: 1-8 2m4-2m7: 0-0 3m+: 0-0
Track:	LH: 0-2 **RH: 1-6** Tight: 0-3 Gall: 0-0
Aids:	Bl: 0-0 Vi: 0-0 Tstrap: 0-0 Ckp: 0-0
Best Rating:	**103** 6/03 Prth　2m110y　good　Hdl

Moderate hurdler/chaser; best at two miles; acts on good ground or softer.

Ameras (IRE)
104　　　78
6-y-o b m Hamas (IRE)-Amerindian (Commanche Run)
Miss S E Forster A G & Mrs E J Bell

Placings:P03620455520　　　　(4690)
2003/04: 16²GF, 16⁶G, 16³GF, 17⁶G, 20²GF, 18⁰S, 24⁴S, 21⁵GS, 16⁵HY, 20⁵GS, 16²G, 22⁰G,

	Starts	1st	2nd	3rd	Win & Pl
Hurdles	12	0	2	1	1916
Career Total	12	0	2	1	1916

Going:	Sf: 0-3 GS: 0-2 Gd: 0-4 GF: - Fm: 0-3
Distance:	2m/2m3: 0-7 2m4-2m7: 0-4 3m+: 0-1
Track:	LH: 0-10 RH: 0-2 Tight: 0-5 Gall: 0-0
Aids:	Bl: 0-0 Vi: 0-0 Tstrap: 0-1 Ckp: 0-0
Best Rating:	**78** 2/04 Ayr　2m4f　gd-sft　Hdl

Selling hurdler; headstrong; stays three miles and acts on soft.

Americanconnection (IRE)
107　　　(81c)102
8-y-o b g Lord Americo-Ballyea Jacki (Straight Lad)
M C Pipe Henderson, George, Pitman

Placings:0/000-135　　　　　(1933)
2003/04: 22¹GF, 25³GF, 24⁵G,

	Starts	1st	2nd	3rd	Win & Pl
Hurdles	3	1	0	1	4165
Career Total	7	1	0	1	4165
102	10/03 Extr	2m6f110yE Hdl		G-F	£3010

Total win prize-money £3010

Going:	Sf: 0-0 GS: 0-0 Gd: 0-1 GF: - Fm: 1-2
Distance:	2m/2m3: 0-0 **2m4-2m7**: **1-1** 3m+: 0-2
Track:	LH: 0-1 **RH: 1-2** Tight: 0-0 Gall: 0-1
Aids:	Bl: 0-0 Vi: 0-0 Tstrap: 0-0 Ckp: 0-0
Best Rating:	**102** 10/03 Extr　2m6f110y　gd-fm　Hdl

Ex-Irish gelding; narrow winner of novice hurdle at Exeter in October; stays three miles; acts on good ground.

Amicelli (GER)
106　　　107
5-y-o b g Goofalik (USA)-Arratonia (GER) (Arratos (FR))
C J Mann Jack Joseph

Placings:635　　　　　　　(4560)
2003/04: 16⁶G, 20³GF, 21⁵GS,

	Starts	1st	2nd	3rd	Win & Pl
Hurdles	3	0	0	1	838
Career Total	3	0	0	1	838

A winner on the Flat in Germany; satisfactory effort in decent novice event at Newbury in February on good ground; fair third next time over two and a half miles; strong sort, should win races.

Amjad
99(100h)
7-y-o ch g Cadeaux Genereux-Babita (Habitat)
Miss Kate Milligan Miss Kate Milligan

Placings:F3410/44461660-P05363　　(1768)
2003/04: 16⁵G, 17⁰G, 16⁵GF, 16³F, 16⁶GF, 16³G,

	Starts	1st	2nd	3rd	Win & Pl
Hurdles	2	0	0	0	0
Chases	4	0	0	2	954
Career Total	19	2	0	3	7115
92	10/02 Carl	2m1f	E(0-115)HHdl	G-F	£3143
102	12/01 Donc	2m110y	G Hdl	GD	£2331

Total win prize-money £5474

Going:	Sf: 0-0 GS: 0-0 Gd: 0-3 GF: - Fm: 0-3
Distance:	2m/2m3: 0-6 2m4-2m7: 0-0 3m+: 0-0
Track:	LH: 0-5 RH: 0-1 Tight: 0-1 Gall: 0-0
Aids:	Bl: 0-0 Vi: 0-0 Tstrap: 0-0 Ckp: 0-0
Best Rating:	**102** 12/01 Donc　2m110y　good　Hdl

Moderate hurdler, not a good jumper of fences; best over two miles; suited by a sound surface.

Ammonias (GER)
101　　　119
5-y-o b h Monsun (GER)-Augreta (GER) (Simply Great (FR))
C J Mann (P Schiergen 27/9) J E Brown & P Randall

Placings:4320　　　　　　(4394)
2003/04: 16⁴GS, 21³G, 21²GS, 21⁰G,

	Starts	1st	2nd	3rd	Win & Pl
Hurdles	4	0	1	1	3393
Career Total	4	0	1	1	3393

Going:	Sf: 0-0 GS: 0-2 Gd: 0-2 GF: - Fm: 0-0
Distance:	2m/2m3: 0-1 2m4-2m7: 0-3 3m+: 0-0
Track:	LH: 0-2 RH: 0-0 Tight: 0-0 Gall: 0-0
Aids:	Bl: 0-0 Vi: 0-0 Tstrap: 0-0 Ckp: 0-0
Best Rating:	**119** 3/04 Chel　2m5f　good　Hdl

Promising novice hurdler; stays 2m 5f; formerly smart middle-distance performer on the Flat in Germany.

Among Equals
110　　　114
7-y-o b g Sadler's Wells (USA)-Epicure's Garden (USA) (Affirmed (USA))
M Meade (R T Phillips 30/11) Ladyswood Stud

Placings:011/023　　　　　(4559)
2003/04: 16⁹GS, 18²G, 16³GS,

	Starts	1st	2nd	3rd	Win & Pl
Hurdles	3	0	1	1	3956
Career Total	6	2	1	1	12070
126	2/01 Hayd	2m	C(0-125)HHdl	SFT	£5486
126	1/01 Wwck	2m	E Hdl	HVY	£2628

Total win prize-money £8115

Going: Sf: 0-0 GS: 0-2 Gd: 0-1 GF: - Fm: 0-0
Distance: 2m/2m3: 0-3 2m4-2m7: 0-0 3m+: 0-0
Track: LH: 0-3 RH: 0-0 Tight: 0-1 Gall: 0-2
Aids: Bl: 0-0 Vi: 0-0 Tstrap: 0-0 Ckp: 0-0
Best Rating: 126 2/01   Hayd 2m   soft   Hdl

Modest hurdler; lightly raced; has scope to stay two and a half miles; effective in heavy ground; has been tried in blinkers on the Flat.

Amplifi (IRE)

101(105h)   (106h)97

7-y-o b g Phardante (FR)-Season's Delight (Idiots Delight)
P J Hobbs C K Watkins

Placings:20-F40U3F0P0   (4917)
2003/04: 16FG, 19⁴G, 17⁰G, 16ᵁHY, 16³G, 18FG, 20⁰G, 20ᴾG, 20ᴾGS,

	Starts	1st	2nd	3rd	Win & Pl
Hurdles	4	0	0	0	301
Chases	5	0	1	1	638
Career Total	11	0	1	1	2259

Going: Sf: 0-1 GS: 0-1 Gd: 0-7 GF: - Fm: 0-0
Distance: 2m/2m3: 0-6 2m4-2m7: 0-3 3m+: 0-0
Track: LH: 0-5 RH: 0-4 Tight: 0-2 Gall: 0-2
Aids: Bl: 0-0 Vi: 0-0 Tstrap: 0-0 Ckp: 0-0
Best Rating: 106 11/02   Newb 2m110y   soft   Hdl

Modest novice hurdler/chaser; still a maiden; seems best on good ground; raced mainly at around two miles.

Amptina (IRE)

109   (72h)81

9-y-o b g Shardari-Cotton Gale (Strong Gale)
Mrs S J Smith Worcester Racing Club

Placings:0/0S5305060P/30-144413   (2263)
2003/04: 17¹G, 17⁴GS, 16⁴GF, 16⁴G, 17¹G, 17³G,

	Starts	1st	2nd	3rd	Win & Pl
Chases	6	2	0	1	9153
Career Total	19	2	0	3	10810
78 11/03 Sthl	2m1f	E(0-100)HCh		GD	£2957
81 8/03 Bang	2m1f110yE(0-105)HCh		GD	£5073
			Total win prize-money £8031

Going: Sf: 0-0 GS: 0-1 Gd: 2-4 GF: - Fm: 0-1
Distance: 2m/2m3: 2-6 2m4-2m7: 0-0 3m+: 0-0
Track: LH: 2-4 RH: 0-2 Tight: 1-2 Gall: 0-0
Aids: Bl: 0-0 Vi: 0-0 Tstrap: 0-0 Ckp: 0-0
Best Rating: 97 11/01 DRoy 2m   yield   Ch

Ex-Irish; won on British debut from 6lb out of handicap at Bangor in August; regained winning thread with narrow success at Southwell in Noevmber; best over two miles; fast ground suits.

Amritsar

95   76

7-y-o ch g Indian Ridge-Trying For Gold (USA) (Northern Baby (CAN))
K G Wingrove L T Woodhouse

Placings:P6002   (0996)
2003/04: 17ᴾGF, 16⁶GF, 16⁹G, 16⁰GF, 16²G,

	Starts	1st	2nd	3rd	Win & Pl
Hurdles	5	0	1	0	852
Career Total	5	0	1	0	852

Going: Sf: 0-0 GS: 0-0 Gd: 0-2 GF: - Fm: 0-3
Distance: 2m/2m3: 0-5 2m4-2m7: 0-0 3m+: 0-0

Track: LH: 0-4 RH: 0-1 Tight: 0-1 Gall: 0-0
Aids: Bl: 0-0 Vi: 0-0 Tstrap: 0-1 Ckp: 0-0
Best Rating: 76 7/03   Strf   2m110y   good   Hdl

Plating-class hurdler; longstanding maiden; appears to act on any ground.

Amusement

75d

8-y-o ch g Mystiko (USA)-Jolies Eaux (Shirley Heights)
D G Bridgwater Daltagh Construction Ltd

Placings:00/200/604P-P   (0060)
2003/04: 17ᴾGS,

	Starts	1st	2nd	3rd	Win & Pl
Hurdles	1	0	0	0	
Career Total	10	0	1	0	827

Going: Sf: 0-0 GS: 0-1 Gd: 0-0 GF: - Fm: 0-0
Distance: 2m/2m3: 0-1 2m4-2m7: 0-0 3m+: 0-0
Track: LH: 0-0 RH: 0-1 Tight: 0-0 Gall: 0-0
Aids: Bl: 0-0 Vi: 0-0 Tstrap: 0-0 Ckp: 0-1
Best Rating: 89 8/01   Hntg   2m110y   gd-fm   NHF

Amy Lewis

79f   87f

6-y-o b m Sir Harry Lewis (USA)-Trecento (Precious Metal)
J Mackie F A Dickinson

Placings:0   (4050)
2003/04: 16⁰G,

	Starts	1st	2nd	3rd	Win & Pl
NH Flat	1	0	0	0	
Career Total	1	0	0	0	

Going: Sf: 0-0 GS: 0-0 Gd: 0-1 GF: - Fm: 0-0
Distance: 2m/2m3: 0-1 2m4-2m7: 0-0 3m+: 0-0
Track: LH: 0-1 RH: 0-0 Tight: 0-0 Gall: 0-0
Aids: Bl: 0-0 Vi: 0-0 Tstrap: 0-0 Ckp: 0-0
Best Rating: 86 2/04   Hayd   2m   good   NHF

An Girseach (IRE)

96   54

7-y-o b m Roselier (FR)-Elfi (IRE) (Le Moss)
M C Pipe P J Finn

Placings:40   (2389)
2003/04: 20⁴GF, 20⁰G,

	Starts	1st	2nd	3rd	Win & Pl
Hurdles	2	0	0	0	0
Career Total	2	0	0	0	0

Going: Sf: 0-0 GS: 0-0 Gd: 0-1 GF: - Fm: 0-1
Distance: 2m/2m3: 0-0 2m4-2m7: 0-2 3m+: 0-0
Track: LH: 0-2 RH: 0-0 Tight: 0-0 Gall: 0-0
Aids: Bl: 0-0 Vi: 0-0 Tstrap: 0-0 Ckp: 0-0
Best Rating: 59 7/03   Worc   2m4f   gd-fm   Hdl

Irish point winner; fourth on hurdling debut over 2m 4f at Worcester July 2003; may do better over a longer trip.

Analogy (IRE)

108   119

4-y-o ch g Bahhare (USA)-Anna Comnena (IRE) (Shareef Dancer (USA))
C J Mann (Sir Mark Prescott 28/7) Hugh Villiers

Placings:126012   (4931)
2003/04: 18¹GF, 17²G, 16⁶G, 17⁹G, 24¹G, 22²G,

	Starts	1st	2nd	3rd	Win & Pl
Hurdles	6	2	2	0	11603
Career Total	6	2	2	0	11603
119 4/04 Ludl	3m	D Hdl		GD	£5595
101 8/03 Font	2m2f110yE Hdl		G-F	£3360
			Total win prize-money £8956

Going: Sf: 0-0 GS: 0-0 Gd: 1-5 GF: - Fm: 1-1
Distance: 2m/2m3: 1-4 2m4-2m7: 0-1 3m+: 1-1
Track: LH: 1-4 RH: 1-2 Tight: 1-3 Gall: 0-1
Aids: Bl: 0-1 Vi: 0-0 Tstrap: 2-4 Ckp: 0-0
Best Rating: 119 4/04   Font   2m6f110y   good   Hdl

Fair novice hurdler; moderate winning stayer on the level; stays three miles two; acts on decent ground; sometimes fitted with a tongue tie.

Analyze (FR)

101   103+

6-y-o b g Anabaa (USA)-Bramosia (Forzando)
B G Powell (M R Channon 11/9) The Arkle Bar Partnership

Placings:3230P   (2590)
2003/04: 16³F, 17²GF, 16³GF, 16⁰G, 16ᴾGS,

	Starts	1st	2nd	3rd	Win & Pl
Hurdles	5	0	1	2	4313
Career Total	5	0	1	2	4313

Going: Sf: 0-0 GS: 0-1 Gd: 0-1 GF: - Fm: 0-3
Distance: 2m/2m3: 0-5 2m4-2m7: 0-0 3m+: 0-0
Track: LH: 0-3 RH: 0-2 Tight: 0-0 Gall: 0-0
Aids: Bl: 0-0 Vi: 0-0 Tstrap: 0-0 Ckp: 0-0
Best Rating: 103 10/03   Chel   2m110y   gd-fm   Hdl

Moderate hurdler; fair handicapper on the Flat; failed to stay after pulling hard first two starts; given his head a ran better next time; best on fast ground.

Anatar (IRE)

102   132

6-y-o b g Caerleon (USA)-Anaza (Darshaan)
M C Pipe Eminence Grise Partnership

Placings:050/011211001-0040005   (4704)
2003/04: 22⁹G, 20⁰GS, 20⁴S, 17⁰GS, 20⁰S, 21⁰G, 18⁵G,

	Starts	1st	2nd	3rd	Win & Pl
Hurdles	7	0	0	0	797
Career Total	19	5	1	0	29931
128 3/03 Asct	2m4f	C(0-130)HHdl	GD	£6971
132 12/02 Uttx	2m	C(0-130)HHdl	SFT	£8076
129 12/02 Sand	2m110y	D(0-110)HHdl	SFT	£7052
105 10/02 Plum	2m	E(0-100)HHdl	GD	£2978
97 9/02 NAbb	2m1f	F(0-100)HHdl	GD	£2996
			Total win prize-money £28075

Going: Sf: 0-2 GS: 0-2 Gd: 0-3 GF: - Fm: 0-0
Distance: 2m/2m3: 0-2 2m4-2m7: 0-5 3m+: 0-0
Track: LH: 0-6 RH: 0-1 Tight: 0-2 Gall: 0-2
Aids: Bl: 0-0 Vi: 0-0 Tstrap: 0-0 Ckp: 0-0
Best Rating: 132 12/02 Uttx   2m   soft   Hdl

Fair hurdler; stays two and a half miles; suited by ground good or softer.

Andaleer (IRE)

(87h)   (83h)82

9-y-o b m Phardante (FR)-Dunleer Duchess (Our Mirage)
Mrs H Dalton M Richards And G Stone

Placings:4/23333/2P-4P   (3516)
2003/04: 19⁴GF, 18ᴾG,

	Starts	1st	2nd	3rd	Win & Pl
Hurdles	1	0	0	0	0
Chases	1	0	0	0	0
Career Total	10	0	2	4	2763

Going:	Sf: 0-0 GS: 0-0 Gd: 0-1 GF: - Fm: 0-1
Distance:	2m/2m3: 0-0 2m4-2m7: 0-0 3m+: 0-0
Track:	LH: 0-1 RH: 0-0 Tight: 0-2 Gall: 0-0
Aids:	Bl: 0-0 Vi: 0-0 Tstrap: 0-2 Ckp: 0-0
Best Rating:	93 5/01 Bang 2m1f gd-sft NHF

Andreas (FR)
91   102
4-y-o b g Marchand De Sable (USA)-Muscova Dancer (FR)
(Muscovite (USA))
P F Nicholls Mark Tincknell

Placings:313130   (4863)
2003/04: 16³G, 16¹G, 17³VS, 18¹G, 18³G, 16⁰S,

	Starts	1st	2nd	3rd	Win & Pl
Hurdles	6	2	0	3	16364
Career Total	6	2	0	3	16364
12/03	Cagn	2m2f	Hdl		GD	£8104
7/03	Divo	2m	Hdl		GD	£2805
			Total win prize-money £10909

Going:	Sf: 0-1 GS: 0-0 Gd: 2-4 GF: - Fm: 0-0
Distance:	2m/2m3: 2-6 2m4-2m7: 0-0 3m+: 0-0
Track:	LH: 0-1 RH: 0-0 Tight: 0-0 Gall: 0-0
Aids:	Bl: 0-0 Vi: 0-0 Tstrap: 0-0 Ckp: 0-0
Best Rating:	102 4/04 Ayr 2m soft Hdl

Andrew Doble
95(102h)   (89h)71
5-y-o ch g Sabrehill (USA)-Verchinina (Star Appeal)
Miss Venetia Williams Knightsbridge Bc

Placings:600U31303-P4P4P   (1453)
2003/04: 17³S, 17ᴾGF, 19⁴G, 21ᴾS, 20⁴G, 17ᴾGF,

	Starts	1st	2nd	3rd	Win & Pl
Hurdles	4	0	0	1	888
Chases	2	0	0	0	313
Career Total	14	1	0	3	5774
86	1/03	Fknm	2m	E(0-105)HHdl	SFT	£3458
			Total win prize-money £3458

Going:	Sf: 0-1 GS: 0-1 Gd: 0-2 GF: - Fm: 0-0
Distance:	2m/2m3: 0-4 2m4-2m7: 0-2 3m+: 0-0
Track:	LH: 0-5 RH: 0-0 Tight: 0-4 Gall: 0-0
Aids:	Bl: 0-0 Vi: 0-0 Tstrap: 0-0 Ckp: 0-0
Best Rating:	89 4/03 NAbb 2m1f soft Hdl

Showed tremendous improvement when third from 7lb 'wrong' in 2m novices handicap at Ludlow January 2003; disappointing since, including over fences.

Andromache
101   79+
5-y-o ch m Hector Protector (USA)-South Sea Bubble (IRE)
(Bustino)
G B Balding J T Brown

Placings:3-30P020   (3352)
2003/04: 19³GF, 17⁰G, 16ᴾG, 16⁰G, 17²HY, 16⁰S,

	Starts	1st	2nd	3rd	Win & Pl
Hurdles	6	0	1	1	1506
Career Total	7	0	1	2	2024

Going:	Sf: 0-2 GS: 0-0 Gd: 0-3 GF: - Fm: 0-1
Distance:	2m/2m3: 0-6 2m4-2m7: 0-0 3m+: 0-0
Track:	LH: 0-1 RH: 0-5 Tight: 0-1 Gall: 0-1
Aids:	Bl: 0-0 Vi: 0-2 Tstrap: 0-1 Ckp: 0-0
Best Rating:	79 1/04 Folk 2m1f110y heavy Hdl

Plating-class hurdler; stays two miles-three; acts on any ground.

Andy Gin (FR)
91   104
5-y-o b g Ski Chief (USA)-Love Love Kate (FR) (Saint Andrews (FR))
P J Hobbs Terry Warner

Placings:10-050P   (3921)
2003/04: 16⁵G, 19⁵G, 16⁰G, 16ᴾGS,

	Starts	1st	2nd	3rd	Win & Pl
Hurdles	4	0	0	0	0
Career Total	6	1	0	0	4784
104	1/03	Extr	2m1f	D Hdl	G-S	£4784
			Total win prize-money £4784

Going:	Sf: 0-0 GS: 0-1 Gd: 0-3 GF: - Fm: 0-0
Distance:	2m/2m3: 0-4 2m4-2m7: 0-0 3m+: 0-0
Track:	LH: 0-1 RH: 0-3 Tight: 0-0 Gall: 0-0
Aids:	Bl: 0-0 Vi: 0-0 Tstrap: 0-0 Ckp: 0-0
Best Rating:	104 1/03 Extr 2m1f gd-sft Hdl

Fair hurdler; ex-French; winner on his British debut at Exeter but down the field in the 2003 Triumph Hurdle; held since; effective on soft ground.

Andy's Birthday (IRE)
92(84h)   (47h)102
13-y-o ch g King Luthier-Clonroche Abendego (Pauper)
Miss S J Wilton John Pointon And Sons

Placings:0P0/1F254P1/P23P6/PP42131/4PP-06146 (4525)
2003/04: 20⁰GS, 24⁶GS, 25¹GS, 25⁴HY, 24⁶GS,

	Starts	1st	2nd	3rd	Win & Pl
Hurdles	1	0	0	0	0
Chases	4	1	0	0	4303
Career Total	30	5	3	2	27620
102	1/04	Hrfd	3m1f110yF(0-95)HCh	G-S	£3926
103	3/02	Uttx	2m7f	D(0-115)HCh	HVY	£5068
102	2/02	Kemp	3m	D(0-115)HCh	SFT	£3640
109	4/00	Uttx	3m	D(0-125)HCh	SFT	£4567
107	12/99	Uttx	3m	E(0-105)HCh	SFT	£3288
			Total win prize-money £20491

Going:	Sf: 0-1 GS: 1-4 Gd: 0-0 GF: - Fm: 0-0
Distance:	2m/2m3: 0-0 2m4-2m7: 0-1 3m+: 1-4
Track:	LH: 0-3 RH: 1-2 Tight: 0-0 Gall: 0-0
Aids:	Bl: 0-0 Vi: 0-0 Tstrap: 0-0 Ckp: 1-5
Best Rating:	109 4/00 Uttx 3m soft Ch

Fair staying chaser when on song. Goes well in soft ground and has benefited from the fitting of a tongue-strap this year.

Anflora
97f   70f
7-y-o b m Alflora (IRE)-Ancella (Tycoon Ii)
B J Llewellyn Maenllwyd Racing Club

Placings:4   (1156)
2003/04: 18⁴GF,

	Starts	1st	2nd	3rd	Win & Pl
NH Flat	1	0	0	0	0
Career Total	1	0	0	0	0

Going:	Sf: 0-0 GS: 0-0 Gd: 0-0 GF: - Fm: 0-1
Distance:	2m/2m3: 0-0 2m4-2m7: 0-0 3m+: 0-0
Track:	LH: 0-1 RH: 0-0 Tight: 0-0 Gall: 0-0
Aids:	Bl: 0-0 Vi: 0-0 Tstrap: 0-0 Ckp: 0-0
Best Rating:	70 8/03 Font 2m2f110y gd-fm NHF

Angel Delight
97(105h)   (97 h)105+
8-y-o gr m Seymour Hicks (FR)-Bird's Custard (Birdbrook)
Miss Venetia Williams Croome Cavaliers

Placings:6/560/5510533-2   (2767)
2003/04: 20²GS,

	Starts	1st	2nd	3rd	Win & Pl
Chases	1	0	1	0	936
Career Total	12	1	1	2	10466
100	2/03	Kemp	2m5f	D(0-115)HHdl	G-S	£6467
			Total win prize-money £6467

Going:	Sf: 0-0 GS: 0-1 Gd: 0-0 GF: - Fm: 0-0
Distance:	2m/2m3: 0-0 2m4-2m7: 0-1 3m+: 0-0
Track:	LH: 0-1 RH: 0-0 Tight: 0-1 Gall: 0-0
Aids:	Bl: 0-0 Vi: 0-0 Tstrap: 0-0 Ckp: 0-0
Best Rating:	105 12/03 Plum 2m4f gd-sft Ch

Modest hurdler; second on chase debut; stays two miles five; acts on good and yielding ground; tends not to find a great deal.

Angelena Ballerina
(88h)   (63h)
6-y-o gr m Roselier (FR)-True Clown (True Song)
Mrs H Dalton Mr & Mrs Peter Orton

Placings:0F6P-P6F   (3967)
2003/04: 21ᴾS, 19⁶HY, 25ᶠGS,

	Starts	1st	2nd	3rd	Win & Pl
Hurdles	2	0	0	0	0
Chases	1	0	0	0	0
Career Total	7	0	0	0	0

Going:	Sf: 0-2 GS: 0-1 Gd: 0-0 GF: - Fm: 0-0
Distance:	2m/2m3: 0-0 2m4-2m7: 0-2 3m+: 0-1
Track:	LH: 0-0 RH: 0-3 Tight: 0-0 Gall: 0-0
Aids:	Bl: 0-0 Vi: 0-0 Tstrap: 0-1 Ckp: 0-0
Best Rating:	77 5/02 Extr 2m1f good NHF

Angello
67   58+
7-y-o ch g Selkirk (USA)-Pomorie (IRE) (Be My Guest (USA))
J A B Old Mrs Anne Yearley

Placings:0   (0149)
2003/04: 20⁰GF,

	Starts	1st	2nd	3rd	Win & Pl
Hurdles	1	0	0	0	
Career Total	1	0	0	0	

Going:	Sf: 0-0 GS: 0-0 Gd: 0-0 GF: 0-0 Fm: 0-1
Distance:	2m/2m3: 0-0 2m4-2m7: 0-1 3m+: 0-0
Track:	LH: 0-1 RH: 0-0 Tight: 0-0 Gall: 0-0
Aids:	Bl: 0-0 Vi: 0-0 Tstrap: 0-0 Ckp: 0-0
Best Rating:	58 5/03 Chep 2m4f gd-fm Hdl

Angels Venture
111   115+
8-y-o ch g Unfuwain (USA)-City Of Angels (Woodman (USA))
J R Jenkins   Mrs Wendy Jenkins

Placings:1033/5P5/634/33255122   (2269)
2003/04: 17³GF, 17³GF, 16²GF, 16⁵GF, 16⁵GF, 16¹F, 16²GF, 16²GF,

	Starts	1st	2nd	3rd	Win & Pl
Hurdles	8	1	3	2	7945
Career Total	18	2	3	5	12824
115 10/03 Winc	2m	E(0-110)HHdl		FRM	£3423
100 11/99 Uttx	2m	E Hdl		G-S	£2347
		Total win prize-money £5771			

Going: Sf: 0-0 GS: 0-0 Gd: 0-0 GF: - Fm: 1-8
Distance: 2m/2m3: 1-8 2m4-2m7: 0-0 3m+: 0-0
Track: LH: 0-5 RH: 1-3 Tight: 0-0 Gall: 0-1
Aids: Bl: 0-0 Vi: 0-0 Tstrap: 0-0 Ckp: 0-1
Best Rating: 117 4/02 Asct   2m110y   gd-fm   Hdl

Modest hurdler; acts on most types of ground; best at around two miles.

Angie Gold
84   53
7-y-o b m Mesleh-Gold Duchess (Sonnen Gold)
Mrs S J Smith   Town Moor Golf Racing Syndicate

Placings:0/006044-4   (0472)
2003/04: 20⁴G, 17⁴GS,

	Starts	1st	2nd	3rd	Win & Pl
Hurdles	2	0	0	0	0
Career Total	8	0	0	0	0

Going: Sf: 0-0 GS: 0-1 Gd: 0-1 GF: - Fm: 0-0
Distance: 2m/2m3: 0-1 2m4-2m7: 0-1 3m+: 0-0
Track: LH: 0-2 RH: 0-0 Tight: 0-1 Gall: 0-0
Aids: Bl: 0-0 Vi: 0-0 Tstrap: 0-0 Ckp: 0-0
Best Rating: 69 3/03 Sthl   2m   gd-fm   NHF

Maiden hurdler; has not shown much so far.

Angiolini (USA)
85
7-y-o ch g Woodman (USA)-Danse Royale (IRE) (Caerleon (USA))
A E Jones (N F Glynn 13/11) N F Glynn

Placings:0/000000/4005-00P   (4148)
2003/04: 16⁰G, 16⁰GF, 19⁰PG,

	Starts	1st	2nd	3rd	Win & Pl
Hurdles	3	0	0	0	0
Career Total	14	0	0	0	0

Going: Sf: 0-0 GS: 0-0 Gd: 0-2 GF: - Fm: 0-1
Distance: 2m/2m3: 0-2 2m4-2m7: 0-1 3m+: 0-0
Track: LH: 0-1 RH: 0-2 Tight: 0-2 Gall: 0-0
Aids: Bl: 0-0 Vi: 0-0 Tstrap: 0-0 Ckp: 0-0
Best Rating: 85 5/02 Uttx   2m4f110y   good   Hdl

Anguilla
93   78
9-y-o b g Rudimentary (USA)-More Wise (Ballymore)
P T Dalton   Mrs Lucia Farmer

Placings:4/0/0P02-U0P   (4914)
2003/04: 21ᵁS, 21⁰G, 24ᴾGS,

	Starts	1st	2nd	3rd	Win & Pl
Hurdles	3	0	0	0	
Career Total	9	0	1	0	878

Going: Sf: 0-1 GS: 0-1 Gd: 0-1 GF: - Fm: 0-0
Distance: 2m/2m3: 0-0 2m4-2m7: 0-2 3m+: 0-1
Track: LH: 0-1 RH: 0-2 Tight: 0-0 Gall: 0-2
Aids: Bl: 0-0 Vi: 0-0 Tstrap: 0-0 Ckp: 0-0
Best Rating: 78 3/04 Hntg   2m5f110y   good   Hdl

Plating-class hurdler; stays two and a half miles.

Animal Magic
82   53
4-y-o b f Shareef Dancer (USA)-Blessed Lass (HOL) (Good Times (ITY))
C J Down   Mrs A E Baker

Placings:P0   (3773)
2003/04: 16²G, 16⁰G,

	Starts	1st	2nd	3rd	Win & Pl
Hurdles	2	0	0	0	
Career Total	2	0	0	0	

Going: Sf: 0-0 GS: 0-0 Gd: 0-2 GF: - Fm: 0-0
Distance: 2m/2m3: 0-2 2m4-2m7: 0-0 3m+: 0-0
Track: LH: 0-0 RH: 0-2 Tight: 0-0 Gall: 0-0
Aids: Bl: 0-0 Vi: 0-0 Tstrap: 0-0 Ckp: 0-0
Best Rating: 57 2/04 Ludl   2m   good   Hdl

Ankles Back (IRE)
100   107+
7-y-o b g Seclude (USA)-Pedalo (Legal Tender)
Mrs H Dalton   Ray Bailey

Placings:5-P11PP   (4841)
2003/04: 20ᴾS, 23¹GF, 23¹G, 24ᴾG, 21ᴾG,

	Starts	1st	2nd	3rd	Win & Pl
Hurdles	1	0	0	0	0
Chases	4	2	0	0	9770
Career Total	6	2	0	0	9770
116 1/04 Leic	2m7f110yD(0-110)HCh			GD	£5824
100 12/03 Leic	2m7f110yE Ch			G-F	£3945
	Total win prize-money £9770				

Going: Sf: 0-1 GS: 0-0 Gd: 1-3 GF: - Fm: 1-1
Distance: 2m/2m3: 0-0 2m4-2m7: 0-0 3m+: 2-3
Track: LH: 0-2 RH: 2-3 Tight: 0-0 Gall: 0-1
Aids: Bl: 0-0 Vi: 0-0 Tstrap: 0-0 Ckp: 0-0
Best Rating: 116 1/04   Leic   2m7f110y   good   Ch

Moderate chaser; stays three miles; acts on fast ground.

Anna Almost
70
6-y-o b m Tragic Role (USA)-Princess Hotpot (IRE) (King's Ride)
T Wall   D B Roberts

Placings:006/4P3U-P   (0082)
2003/04: 16ᴾGS,

	Starts	1st	2nd	3rd	Win & Pl
Hurdles	1	0	0	0	
Career Total	8	0	0	1	374

Going: Sf: 0-0 GS: 0-0 Gd: 0-0 GF: - Fm: 0-0
Distance: 2m/2m3: 0-1 2m4-2m7: 0-0 3m+: 0-0
Track: LH: 0-1 RH: 0-0 Tight: 0-0 Gall: 0-0
Aids: Bl: 0-0 Vi: 0-0 Tstrap: 0-0 Ckp: 0-0

Best Rating: 74 4/02   Fknm   2m   good   NHF

Anna Walhaan (IRE)
101   87
5-y-o b g Green Desert (USA)-Queens Music (USA) (Dixieland Band (USA))
Ian Williams (M R Channon 3/7) A J Cresser

Placings:306   (2069)
2003/04: 16³GF, 16⁰G, 16⁶GF,

	Starts	1st	2nd	3rd	Win & Pl
Hurdles	3	0	0	1	483
Career Total	3	0	0	1	483

Going: Sf: 0-0 GS: 0-0 Gd: 0-1 GF: - Fm: 0-2
Distance: 2m/2m3: 0-3 2m4-2m7: 0-0 3m+: 0-0
Track: LH: 0-2 RH: 0-1 Tight: 0-1 Gall: 0-1
Aids: Bl: 0-0 Vi: 0-0 Tstrap: 0-0 Ckp: 0-0
Best Rating: 87 10/03 Uttx   2m   gd-fm   Hdl

Winner in modest company at up to a mile on the Flat; last of three finishers on hurdling debut at Uttoxeter in October.

Annabee
7-y-o gr m Norton Challenger-Annaway (New Brig)
B I Case (Mrs L Wadham 2/5) P P Hall

Placings:0P/PPFP   (3779)
2003/04: 23ᴾGS, 25ᴾGS, 24ᶠS, 21ᴾG,

	Starts	1st	2nd	3rd	Win & Pl
Hurdles	1	0	0	0	
Chases	3	0	0	0	
Career Total	6	0	0	0	

Going: Sf: 0-1 GS: 0-2 Gd: 0-1 GF: - Fm: 0-0
Distance: 2m/2m3: 0-0 2m4-2m7: 0-1 3m+: 0-3
Track: LH: 0-1 RH: 0-3 Tight: 0-0 Gall: 0-1
Aids: Bl: 0-0 Vi: 0-0 Tstrap: 0-0 Ckp: 0-0
Best Rating: 0 2/04 Ludl   2m5f   good   Hdl

Annaghmore Gale (IRE)
10-y-o br g Strong Gale-Kept In The Dark (Kemal (FR))
Miss Sarah George   The A J's Partnership

Placings:4/6004O/60F5L6/21C133PSPP/6F232F1P2RU-0   (0031)
2003/04: 21⁰G,

	Starts	1st	2nd	3rd	Win & Pl
Chases	1	0	0	0	
Career Total	34	3	4	3	29361
110 8/02 Baln	2m4f	(0-109)HCh		G-F	£7975
112 7/01 Baln	2m1f	Ch		Y-S	£6120
97 5/01 Navn	2m1f	Ch		FRM	£5286
	Total win prize-money £19382				

Going: Sf: 0-0 GS: 0-0 Gd: 0-1 GF: - Fm: 0-0
Distance: 2m/2m3: 0-0 2m4-2m7: 0-1 3m+: 0-0
Track: LH: 0-1 RH: 0-0 Tight: 0-0 Gall: 0-1
Aids: Bl: 0-0 Vi: 0-0 Tstrap: 0-0 Ckp: 0-0
Best Rating: 113 8/01 Rosc   2m5f   yield   Ch

Anneka Louise

10-y-o ch m Jendali (USA)-Scotgavotte (FR) (Dunbeath (USA))
R J Jackson F S Jackson

Placings:00560/P   (0416)
2003/04: 22PG,

	Starts	1st	2nd	3rd	Win & Pl
Chases	1	0	0	0	
Career Total	6	0	0	0	0

Going: Sf: 0-0 GS: 0-0 Gd: 0-1 GF: - Fm: 0-0
Distance: 2m/2m3: 0-0 2m4-2m7: 0-1 3m+: 0-0
Track: LH: 0-0 RH: 0-1 Tight: 0-1 Gall: 0-0
Aids: Bl: 0-0 Vi: 0-0 Tstrap: 0-0 Ckp: 0-0
Best Rating: 42 7/98 Sedg 2m5f110y good   Hdl

Annie Byers
105(99h)   (107+h)108+

8-y-o ch m Sula Bula-Tuneful Flutter (Orchestra)
J G Portman M J Vandenberghe

Placings:2004535-311521   (4676)
2003/04: 20³GF, 20¹GF, 20¹G, 22⁵GS, 20²G, 22¹G,

	Starts	1st	2nd	3rd	Win & Pl
Hurdles	3	2	0	1	7841
Chases	3	1	1	0	7368
Career Total	13	3	2	2	16992
107	4/04	Winc	2m6f	E(0-100)HHdl	GD	£3678
104	12/03	Sand	2m4f110yD(0-110)HCh	GD	£5408
85	11/03	Leic	2m4f110yE(0-100)HHdl	G-F	£3474

Total win prize-money £12561

Going: Sf: 0-0 GS: 0-0 Gd: 2-3 GF: - Fm: 1-2
Distance: 2m/2m3: 0-0 2m4-2m7: 3-6 3m+: 0-0
Track: LH: 0-0 RH: 3-5 Tight: 0-1 Gall: 0-1
Aids: Bl: 0-0 Vi: 0-0 Tstrap: 0-0 Ckp: 0-0
Best Rating: 108 2/04 MRas 2m4f   good   Ch

Moderate hurdler/chaser; suited by two and a half miles; acts on decent ground.

Annie Dipper
92   69

9-y-o ch m Weld-Honey Dipper (Golden Dipper)
C J Gray P Popham, F D Popham, T Bartlett

Placings:P5252   (4737)
2003/04: 25PS, 26⁵S, 24²GF, 22⁵G, 21²G,

	Starts	1st	2nd	3rd	Win & Pl
Chases	5	0	2	0	2232
Career Total	5	0	2	0	2232

Going: Sf: 0-2 GS: 0-0 Gd: 0-2 GF: - Fm: 0-1
Distance: 2m/2m3: 0-0 2m4-2m7: 0-2 3m+: 0-3
Track: LH: 0-3 RH: 0-1 Tight: 0-2 Gall: 0-0
Aids: Bl: 0-0 Vi: 0-0 Tstrap: 0-0 Ckp: 0-0
Best Rating: 69 4/04 NAbb 2m5f110y good   Ch

Annie Fleetwood
91   87

6-y-o ch m Anshan-Gold Luck (USA) (Slew O'Gold (USA))
C P Morlock J P M & J W Cook

Placings:064-30   (0250)
2003/04: 22³G, 24⁰GF,

	Starts	1st	2nd	3rd	Win & Pl
Hurdles	2	0	0	1	450

Career Total   5   0   0   1   450   C F Swan N O'Flaherty

Going: Sf: 0-0 GS: 0-0 Gd: 0-1 GF: - Fm: 0-1
Distance: 2m/2m3: 0-0 2m4-2m7: 0-1 3m+: 0-1
Track: LH: 0-0 RH: 0-2 Tight: 0-0 Gall: 0-0
Aids: Bl: 0-0 Vi: 0-0 Tstrap: 0-0 Ckp: 0-0
Best Rating: 87 4/03 Extr 2m6f110y good   Hdl

Modest form in novice hurdles at up to 2m 6f.

Annie Greenlaw
(87h)   (64h)67

8-y-o b m Petoski-Cascabel (Matahawk)
P R Hedger B J Champion

Placings:003F   (4751)
2003/04: 16⁰S, 16⁰G, 16³GS, 17FG,

	Starts	1st	2nd	3rd	Win & Pl
Hurdles	2	0	0	0	0
Chases	2	0	0	1	825
Career Total	4	0	0	1	825

Going: Sf: 0-1 GS: 0-1 Gd: 0-2 GF: - Fm: 0-0
Distance: 2m/2m3: 0-0 2m4-2m7: 0-0 3m+: 0-0
Track: LH: 0-3 RH: 0-1 Tight: 0-3 Gall: 0-0
Aids: Bl: 0-0 Vi: 0-0 Tstrap: 0-0 Ckp: 0-0
Best Rating: 67 3/04 Winc 2m   gd-sft   Ch

Annies Gold (IRE)

8-y-o b m Spanish Place (USA)-Leventos (Le Moss)
Mrs S M Johnson Colin Thomson

Placings:P-PP   (2939)
2003/04: 21PGF, 20PGS,

	Starts	1st	2nd	3rd	Win & Pl
Hurdles	2	0	0	0	
Career Total	3	0	0	0	

Going: Sf: 0-0 GS: 0-1 Gd: 0-0 GF: - Fm: 0-1
Distance: 2m/2m3: 0-0 2m4-2m7: 0-2 3m+: 0-0
Track: LH: 0-1 RH: 0-1 Tight: 0-0 Gall: 0-0
Aids: Bl: 0-1 Vi: 0-0 Tstrap: 0-0 Ckp: 0-0
Best Rating: 0 12/03 Uttx 2m4f110y gd-sft   Hdl

Annies Theme
60f   51f

6-y-o b m Weld-Metannee (The Brianstan)
Dr J R J Naylor Mrs B Bishop

Placings:0   (0087)
2003/04: 16⁰GS,

	Starts	1st	2nd	3rd	Win & Pl
NH Flat	1	0	0	0	
Career Total	1	0	0	0	

Going: Sf: 0-0 GS: 0-1 Gd: 0-0 GF: - Fm: 0-0
Distance: 2m/2m3: 0-0 2m4-2m7: 0-0 3m+: 0-0
Track: LH: 0-1 RH: 0-0 Tight: 0-0 Gall: 0-0
Aids: Bl: 0-0 Vi: 0-0 Tstrap: 0-0 Ckp: 0-0
Best Rating: 61 5/03 Worc 2m   gd-sft   NHF

Anno Jubilo (GER)
89   117

7-y-o b/br g Lando (GER)-Anna Maria (GER) (Night Shift (USA))

Placings:21412-600   (4804a)
2003/04: 16⁶S, 16⁰G, 16⁰Y,

	Starts	1st	2nd	3rd	Win & Pl
Hurdles	3	0	0	0	
Career Total	8	2	2	0	12156
114	8/02	Rosc	2m	Hdl	YLD	£5079
99	7/02	Baln	2m	Hdl	GD	£4021

Total win prize-money £9101

Going: Sf: 0-1 GS: 0-0 Gd: 0-1 GF: - Fm: 0-0
Distance: 2m/2m3: 0-3 2m4-2m7: 0-0 3m+: 0-0
Track: LH: 0-1 RH: 0-1 Tight: 0-1 Gall: 0-0
Aids: Bl: 0-0 Vi: 0-0 Tstrap: 0-0 Ckp: 0-0
Best Rating: 117 4/04 Fair 2m   yield   Hdl

Fair Irish-trained hurdler; best at two miles; acts well on good or softer ground.

Annodyce
79   73

6-y-o b m Faustus (USA)-Coleford (USA) (Secreto (USA))
Miss Z C Davison Mrs J Irvine

Placings:4/PP5054-00   (4120)
2003/04: 16⁶GS, 17⁰G,

	Starts	1st	2nd	3rd	Win & Pl
Hurdles	2	0	0	0	
Career Total	9	0	0	0	260

Going: Sf: 0-0 GS: 0-1 Gd: 0-1 GF: - Fm: 0-0
Distance: 2m/2m3: 0-2 2m4-2m7: 0-0 3m+: 0-0
Track: LH: 0-1 RH: 0-1 Tight: 0-1 Gall: 0-0
Aids: Bl: 0-0 Vi: 0-0 Tstrap: 0-0 Ckp: 0-0
Best Rating: 73 4/03 Plum 2m   gd-fm   Hdl

Plating-class hurdler; made a promising enough debut at Huntingdon over two miles on good to firm; poor form since.

Anns Girl
99   87

11-y-o br m Newski (USA)-Nearly Married (Nearly A Hand)
J C Fox Mrs J A Cleary

Placings:061022413/6563F3P000/2454432111F460/P000/
P55000055050-130   (0491)
2003/04: 16¹GS, 16³G, 17⁰GF,

	Starts	1st	2nd	3rd	Win & Pl
Hurdles	3	1	0	1	3163
Career Total	52	6	4	5	21834
85	5/03	Worc	2m	G(0-95)HHdl	G-S	£2646
111	10/00	Extr	2m1f	D(0-125)HHdl	GD	£3419
105	9/00	Extr	2m1f	D(0-120)HHdl	GD	£3159
98	9/00	Worc	2m	G(0-115)HHdl	G-F	£2765
104	4/99	NAbb	2m1f	E Hdl	GD	£2421
83	6/98	Worc	2m	H NHF	GD	£1213

Total win prize-money £15625

Going: Sf: 0-0 GS: 1-1 Gd: 0-1 GF: - Fm: 0-1
Distance: 2m/2m3: 1-3 2m4-2m7: 0-0 3m+: 0-0
Track: LH: 1-3 RH: 0-0 Tight: 0-1 Gall: 0-0
Aids: Bl: 1-3 Vi: 0-0 Tstrap: 0-0 Ckp: 0-0
Best Rating: 111 11/00 Newb 2m3f   soft   Hdl

Moderate hurdler; won seller at Worcester May 2003; acts on good ground

Anonymity
(80h)   (95+h)4

6-y-o ch h Exit To Nowhere (USA)-Wind Of Roses (USA) (Lomond (USA))

G T Lynch B Keane

Placings:000014/001-03210000   (4928a)
2003/04: 19⁰F, 18³Y, 20²GF, 24¹G, 24⁰GF, 21⁰G, 16⁰GY, 18⁰HY,

	Starts	1st	2nd	3rd	Win & Pl
Hurdles	6	1	1	1	12130
Chases	2	0	0	0	0
Career Total	17	3	1	1	20641
95	9/03	List	3m	(81-123)HHdl	GD	£8441
86	4/03	Thur	2m2f	(67-95)HHdl	G-F	£4480
84	4/02	Clon	2m	(60-88)HHdl	G-Y	£3809

Total win prize-money £16733

Going: Sf: 0-1 GS: 0-0 Gd: 1-2 GF: - Fm: 0-3
Distance: 2m/2m3: 0-4 2m4-2m7: 0-2 3m+: 1-2
Track: LH: 0-2 RH: 0-2 Tight: 0-0 Gall: 0-1
Aids: Bl: 0-0 Vi: 0-0 Tstrap: 1-7 Ckp: 0-0
Best Rating: 95 9/03 List 3m   good   Hdl

Another Bally

(51h)
8-y-o gr g Neltino-Michele My Belle (Lochnager)
Mrs H Dalton Felix Sheridan

Placings:0F/P-F3P   (4918)
2003/04: 19³G, 17³GS, 20⁰GS,

	Starts	1st	2nd	3rd	Win & Pl
Hurdles	1	0	0	0	0
Chases	2	0	0	1	833
Career Total	6	0	0	1	833

Going: Sf: 0-0 GS: 0-2 Gd: 0-1 GF: - Fm: 0-0
Distance: 2m/2m3: 0-2 2m4-2m7: 0-1 3m+: 0-0
Track: LH: 0-3 RH: 0-0 Tight: 0-1 Gall: 0-0
Aids: Bl: 0-0 Vi: 0-0 Tstrap: 0-0 Ckp: 0-0
Best Rating: 51 10/01 Gowr 2m1f   good   Hdl

Another Chance

102(107h)   (118h)113+
9-y-o b g Golden Heights-Lapopie (Deep Run)
J M Jefferson North South Partnership

Placings:33/326F/22F2122140/P326356   (4947)
2003/04: 22³PS, 20³HY, 24²G, 25⁶GS, 20³HY, 20⁵S, 20⁶GS,

	Starts	1st	2nd	3rd	Win & Pl
Hurdles	2	0	0	0	0
Chases	5	0	1	2	2948
Career Total	23	2	7	5	24992
132	2/02	Hntg	2m4f110yB Hdl	SFT	£10504
125	10/01	Bang	2m4f	F(0-110)HHdl	SFT	£3510

Total win prize-money £14014

Going: Sf: 0-4 GS: 0-2 Gd: 0-1 GF: - Fm: 0-0
Distance: 2m/2m3: 0-0 2m4-2m7: 0-5 3m+: 0-2
Track: LH: 0-3 RH: 0-4 Tight: 0-2 Gall: 0-0
Aids: Bl: 0-0 Vi: 0-0 Tstrap: 0-0 Ckp: 0-0
Best Rating: 132 2/02 Hntg 2m4f110y soft   Hdl

Useful front-running hurdler at his best; lightly-raced of late;
easily best effort over fences when runner-up at
Musselburgh in February; stays three miles; best suited by
cut in the ground.

Another Club Royal

91   74+
5-y-o b g Overbury (IRE)-Miss Club Royal (Avocat)
D McCain Halewood International Ltd

Placings:140   (4171)
2003/04: 16¹GF, 16⁴GF, 19⁰G,

	Starts	1st	2nd	3rd	Win & Pl
Hurdles	3	1	0	0	2695
Career Total	3	1	0	0	2695
74	11/03	Uttx	2m	E Hdl	G-F	£2695

Total win prize-money £2695

Going: Sf: 0-0 GS: 0-0 Gd: 0-1 GF: - Fm: 1-2
Distance: 2m/2m3: 1-3 2m4-2m7: 0-0 3m+: 0-0
Track: LH: 1-3 RH: 0-0 Tight: 0-1 Gall: 0-1
Aids: Bl: 0-0 Vi: 0-0 Tstrap: 0-0 Ckp: 0-0
Best Rating: 74 11/03 Uttx 2m   gd-fm   Hdl

Won on racecourse debut at Uttoxeter in a poor contest over
two miles on good to firm in November 2003; should stay
further; looks a chasing type.

Another Conquest

89   71
5-y-o b m El Conquistador-Kellys Special (Netherkelly)
J W Mullins F G Matthews

Placings:5P6   (4736)
2003/04: 16⁵GS, 21⁵GS, 17⁶G,

	Starts	1st	2nd	3rd	Win & Pl
NH Flat	1	0	0	0	0
Hurdles	2	0	0	0	0
Career Total	3	0	0	0	0

Going: Sf: 0-0 GS: 0-2 Gd: 0-1 GF: - Fm: 0-0
Distance: 2m/2m3: 0-2 2m4-2m7: 0-1 3m+: 0-0
Track: LH: 0-1 RH: 0-2 Tight: 0-1 Gall: 0-0
Aids: Bl: 0-0 Vi: 0-0 Tstrap: 0-0 Ckp: 0-0
Best Rating: 76 4/04 NAbb 2m1f   good   Hdl

Another Copper

93(102h)   (90dh)87
8-y-o ch g Bandmaster (USA)-Letitica (Deep Run)
C J Down Mrs E J Taplin

Placings:301/5FP2F56-F32P464P2   (4792)
2003/04: 27⁶S, 21⁵GF, 26³GF, 22²GF, 24⁴HY, 24⁴GS, 24⁶G,
20⁴S, 26⁴G,

	Starts	1st	2nd	3rd	Win & Pl
Hurdles	7	0	1	1	2305
Chases	3	0	1	0	972
Career Total	19	1	3	2	8592
77	4/02	Extr	2m7f110yE Ch	FRM	£3640

Total win prize-money £3640

Going: Sf: 0-3 GS: 0-1 Gd: 0-3 GF: - Fm: 0-3
Distance: 2m/2m3: 0-0 2m4-2m7: 0-3 3m+: 0-7
Track: LH: 0-6 RH: 0-4 Tight: 0-5 Gall: 0-0
Aids: Bl: 0-5 Vi: 0-0 Tstrap: 0-0 Ckp: 0-0
Best Rating: 90 1/04 Extr 3m110y   gd-sft   Hdl

Moderate hurdler/plating-class chaser; got off the mark in a
poor novice chase on his chasing debut at Exeter April
2002; subsequently disappointing over fences; appreciates
fast ground; has worn blinkers.

Another Dude (IRE)

108   121+
7-y-o br g Shardari-Gemma's Fridge (Frigid Aire)
J Howard Johnson Maurice Hutchinson

Placings:0442P/21221P-0P31P3   (4883)
2003/04: 20⁴GS, 16⁵GS, 16³G, 16¹G, 16⁶G, 17³GS,

	Starts	1st	2nd	3rd	Win & Pl
Hurdles	6	1	0	2	8668
Career Total	17	3	4	2	20020
121	2/04	Muss	2m	D(0-120)HHdl	GD	£6838

| 109 | 2/03 | Catt | 2m3f | E Hdl | GD | £3698 |
| 115 | 11/02 | Catt | 2m | E(0-100)HHdl | GD | £2908 |

Total win prize-money £13446

Going: Sf: 0-0 GS: 0-3 Gd: 1-3 GF: - Fm: 0-0
Distance: 2m/2m3: 1-5 2m4-2m7: 0-1 3m+: 0-0
Track: LH: 0-2 RH: 1-4 Tight: 1-4 Gall: 0-0
Aids: Bl: 0-1 Vi: 0-0 Tstrap: 0-0 Ckp: 0-0
Best Rating: 121 2/04 Muss 2m   good   Hdl

Modest hurdler; stays 2m 4f, but effective at shorter; suited
by good ground; will make a chaser in time.

Another General (IRE)

(134h)119
9-y-o b g Glacial Storm (USA)-What's In A Name (IRE) (Le
Moss)
R T Phillips Paul Duffy, Alan Beard, Brian Beard

Placings:14/1111P/211-PPPF   (4101)
2003/04: 26⁵HY, 24²G, 24²S, 26²G,

	Starts	1st	2nd	3rd	Win & Pl
Chases	4	0	0	0	
Career Total	14	7	1	0	33430
119	3/03	Ayr	3m1f	D Ch	SFT	£5810
119	1/03	Donc	3m	E Ch	GD	£4290
133	3/02	Newb	3m110y	D Hdl	G-S	£4641
134	2/02	Winc	2m6f	B Hdl	SFT	£9282
113	1/02	Folk	2m6f110yE Hdl	HVY	£2667
105	12/01	Leic	2m4f110yD Hdl	HVY	£3588
116	12/00	Towc	2m	H NHF	HVY	£1652

Total win prize-money £31930

Going: Sf: 0-2 GS: 0-0 Gd: 0-2 GF: - Fm: 0-0
Distance: 2m/2m3: 0-0 2m4-2m7: 0-0 3m+: 0-4
Track: LH: 0-3 RH: 0-1 Tight: 0-1 Gall: 0-0
Aids: Bl: 0-0 Vi: 0-0 Tstrap: 0-0 Ckp: 0-0
Best Rating: 134 2/02 Winc 2m6f   soft   Hdl

Fair chaser; also quite useful over hurdles; acts on testing
ground but has won on good; stays very well; has been well
out of form this term.

Another Graduate (IRE)

70   36
6-y-o ch g Naheez (USA)-Another Daisy (Major Point)
John R Upson The Nap Hand Partnership

Placings:0-00   (2838)
2003/04: 17⁰GS, 20⁰GS,

	Starts	1st	2nd	3rd	Win & Pl
Hurdles	2	0	0	0	
Career Total	3	0	0	0	

Going: Sf: 0-0 GS: 0-1 Gd: 0-1 GF: - Fm: 0-0
Distance: 2m/2m3: 0-1 2m4-2m7: 0-1 3m+: 0-0
Track: LH: 0-1 RH: 0-1 Tight: 0-1 Gall: 0-0
Aids: Bl: 0-0 Vi: 0-0 Tstrap: 0-0 Ckp: 0-0
Best Rating: 45 2/03 Kemp 2m   good   NHF

Another Islay

13-y-o b g Tobin Lad (USA)-Coincidence Girl (Manacle)
K Robson Mrs M Armstrong

Placings:0/00/P5/0/P/P0P343PPP4/P   (0079)
2003/04: 21⁵PS,

	Starts	1st	2nd	3rd	Win & Pl
Chases	1	0	0	0	

Career Total	18	0	0	2	1552

Going:	Sf: 0-1 GS: 0-0 Gd: 0-0 GF: - Fm: 0-0
Distance:	2m/2m3: 0-0 2m4-2m7: 0-1 3m+: 0-0
Track:	LH: 0-1 RH: 0-0 Tight: 0-1 Gall: 0-0
Aids:	Bl: 0-1 Vi: 0-0 Tstrap: 0-0 Ckp: 0-0
Best Rating:	74 5/01 Hexm 2m110y firm Ch

Another Joker
104(82h)   (97h)110
9-y-o b g Commanche Run-Just For A Laugh (Idiots Delight)
J L Needham Miss Joanna Needham

Placings:0/20U02/0054-126162P					(3999)
2003/04: 19¹GF, 16²G, 21⁶GF, 16¹GF, 18⁶GS, 16²G, 16⁹G,					
	Starts	1st	2nd	3rd	Win & Pl
Hurdles	1	0	0	0	
Chases	6	2	2	0	10724
Career Total	17	2	4	0	12467
110 10/03 Hayd	2m	E Ch		G-F	£3406
109 5/03 Hrfd	2m3f	F Ch		G-F	£3406
			Total win prize-money £6812		

Going:	Sf: 0-0 GS: 0-1 Gd: 0-3 GF: - Fm: 2-3
Distance:	2m/2m3: 2-6 2m4-2m7: 0-1 3m+: 0-0
Track:	LH: 1-4 RH: 1-3 Tight: 0-1 Gall: 0-2
Aids:	Bl: 0-0 Vi: 0-0 Tstrap: 0-0 Ckp: 0-0
Best Rating:	110 10/03 Hayd 2m gd-fm Ch

Modest chaser, acts on fast ground; stays two and a half miles.

Another Justice (IRE)

8-y-o ch g Dolphin Street (FR)-Unheard Melody (Lomond (USA))
R V Westwood R V Westwood

Placings:000/PP					(4078)
2003/04: 20⁵G, 24⁵F,					
	Starts	1st	2nd	3rd	Win & Pl
Chases	2	0	0	0	
Career Total	5	0	0	0	

Going:	Sf: 0-0 GS: 0-0 Gd: 0-1 GF: - Fm: 0-1
Distance:	2m/2m3: 0-0 2m4-2m7: 0-1 3m+: 0-1
Track:	LH: 0-0 RH: 0-2 Tight: 0-1 Gall: 0-0
Aids:	Bl: 0-0 Vi: 0-0 Tstrap: 0-0 Ckp: 0-0
Best Rating:	66 8/99 Rosc 2m gd-yld Hdl

Another Moose (IRE)
105(102c)   (114c)119+
9-y-o b g Mister Lord (USA)-Moose (IRE) (Royal Fountain)
Miss E C Lavelle Remenham Racing

Placings:5212/02-FP40F					(4052)
2003/04: 22⁶GS, 25⁶G, 21⁴G, 23⁰S, 24⁶G,					
	Starts	1st	2nd	3rd	Win & Pl
Hurdles	3	0	0	0	534
Chases	2	0	0	0	
Career Total	11	1	3	0	7081
130 3/01 Hntg	2m4f110yE Hdl			SFT	£2327
		Total win prize-money £2328			

Going:	Sf: 0-1 GS: 0-1 Gd: 0-3 GF: - Fm: 0-0
Distance:	2m/2m3: 0-0 2m4-2m7: 0-2 3m+: 0-3

Track: LH: 0-2 RH: 0-3 Tight: 0-0 Gall: 0-1
Aids: Bl: 0-0 Vi: 0-0 Tstrap: 0-0 Ckp: 0-0
Best Rating: 130 3/01 Hntg 2m4f110y soft Hdl

Fair hurdler/novice chaser; stays three miles two; best on soft ground.

Another Promise (IRE)
91   81
5-y-o b g Presenting-Snape (IRE) (Strong Gale)
J A Supple Geoff Hubbard Racing

Placings:055					(4216)
2003/04: 21⁰GF, 19⁵G, 22⁵G,					
	Starts	1st	2nd	3rd	Win & Pl
Hurdles	3	0	0	0	0
Career Total	3	0	0	0	0

Going:	Sf: 0-0 GS: 0-0 Gd: 0-2 GF: - Fm: 0-1
Distance:	2m/2m3: 0-0 2m4-2m7: 0-3 3m+: 0-0
Track:	LH: 0-0 RH: 0-2 Tight: 0-1 Gall: 0-0
Aids:	Bl: 0-0 Vi: 0-0 Tstrap: 0-0 Ckp: 0-0
Best Rating:	81 3/04 MRas 2m6f good Hdl

Another Rum (IRE)
104   118
6-y-o b g Zaffaran (USA)-Sharp Fashion Vii (Damsire Unregistered)
I A Duncan Ronald Lilley

Placings:533-31031262					(4853)
2003/04: 18³Y, 22¹G, 24⁰Y, 20³S, 24¹GS, 24²Y, 22⁶Y, 22²GS,					
	Starts	1st	2nd	3rd	Win & Pl
NH Flat	1	0	0	1	455
Hurdles	7	2	2	1	19588
Career Total	11	2	2	4	20770
112 2/04 Ayr	3m110y E Hdl		G-S	£3640
106 11/03 Ayr	2m6f	E Hdl		GD	£3532
		Total win prize-money £7173		

Going:	Sf: 0-1 GS: 1-2 Gd: 1-1 GF: - Fm: 0-0
Distance:	2m/2m3: 0-1 2m4-2m7: 1-4 3m+: 1-3
Track:	LH: 2-4 RH: 0-2 Tight: 0-0 Gall: 0-0
Aids:	Bl: 0-0 Vi: 0-0 Tstrap: 0-0 Ckp: 0-0
Best Rating:	118 4/04 Ayr 2m6f gd-sft Hdl

Fair hurdles winner at Ayr (over two miles and six and over three miles) and showed right attitude to win there in February 2004; only relatively lightly raced, goes on easy ground and may be capable of better in handicaps.

Anshabil (IRE)
101f   109+f
5-y-o br g Anshan-Billeragh Thyne (IRE) (Good Thyne (USA))
A King Jerry Wright

Placings:35					(4447)
2003/04: 16³G, 16⁵S,					
	Starts	1st	2nd	3rd	Win & Pl
NH Flat	2	0	0	1	348
Career Total	2	0	0	1	348

Going:	Sf: 0-1 GS: 0-0 Gd: 0-1 GF: - Fm: 0-0
Distance:	2m/2m3: 0-2 2m4-2m7: 0-0 3m+: 0-0
Track:	LH: 0-1 RH: 0-1 Tight: 0-0 Gall: 0-0
Aids:	Bl: 0-0 Vi: 0-0 Tstrap: 0-0 Ckp: 0-0
Best Rating:	109 2/04 Asct 2m110y good NHF

Good third in Ascot bumper on debut in February; left the impression he needs a stiffer track when not disgraced on softer ground at Warwick next time.

Answered Promise (FR)

5-y-o ro g Highest Honor (FR)-Answered Prayer (Green Desert (USA))
A W Carroll (I Semple 6/9) Andy Taylor

Placings:P					(2444)
2003/04: 16⁶S,					
	Starts	1st	2nd	3rd	Win & Pl
Hurdles	1	0	0	0	
Career Total	1	0	0	0	

Going:	Sf: 0-1 GS: 0-0 Gd: 0-0 GF: - Fm: 0-0
Distance:	2m/2m3: 0-1 2m4-2m7: 0-0 3m+: 0-0
Track:	LH: 0-1 RH: 0-0 Tight: 0-0 Gall: 0-0
Aids:	Bl: 0-0 Vi: 0-0 Tstrap: 0-0 Ckp: 0-0
Best Rating:	0 11/03 Hayd 2m soft Hdl

Antartic Prince (IRE)
100   102+
8-y-o ch g Glacial Storm (USA)-Clonea Fog (Laurence O)
P J Hobbs M J Tuckey

Placings:6/000/2					(3353)
2003/04: 24²S,					
	Starts	1st	2nd	3rd	Win & Pl
Chases	1	0	1	0	1305
Career Total	5	0	1	0	1305

Going:	Sf: 0-1 GS: 0-0 Gd: 0-0 GF: - Fm: 0-0
Distance:	2m/2m3: 0-0 2m4-2m7: 0-0 3m+: 0-1
Track:	LH: 0-0 RH: 0-1 Tight: 0-0 Gall: 0-1
Aids:	Bl: 0-0 Vi: 0-0 Tstrap: 0-0 Ckp: 0-0
Best Rating:	107 5/01 Fair 2m good NHF

Antique Gold
59
10-y-o b g Gildoran-Chanelle (The Parson)
R Allan R Allan

Placings:52/22/6/P					(4292)
2003/04: 16⁶GF,					
	Starts	1st	2nd	3rd	Win & Pl
Hurdles	1	0	0	0	
Career Total	6	0	3	0	3158

Going:	Sf: 0-0 GS: 0-0 Gd: 0-0 GF: - Fm: 0-1
Distance:	2m/2m3: 0-1 2m4-2m7: 0-0 3m+: 0-0
Track:	LH: 0-1 RH: 0-0 Tight: 0-0 Gall: 0-0
Aids:	Bl: 0-0 Vi: 0-0 Tstrap: 0-0 Ckp: 0-0
Best Rating:	125 11/99 Asct 3m good Hdl

Antonine
96f   93f
4-y-o ch g Selkirk (USA)-Eversince (USA) (Foolish Pleasure (USA))
C J Mann John Hersey-Walker

Placings: *4*   (4816)
2003/04: 16⁴G,

	Starts	1st	2nd	3rd	Win & Pl
NH Flat	1	0	0	0	0
Career Total	1	0	0	0	0

Going:	Sf: 0-0 GS: 0-0 Gd: 0-1 GF: - Fm: 0-0
Distance:	2m/2m3: 0-1 2m4-2m7: 0-0 3m+: 0-0
Track:	LH: 0-1 RH: 0-0 Tight: 0-0 Gall: 0-0
Aids:	Bl: 0-0 Vi: 0-0 Tstrap: 0-0 Ckp: 0-0
Best Rating:	93 4/04 Chep 2m110y good NHF

Half-brother to high-class German middle-distance performer; weakened in closing stages in Chepstow bumper on his debut.

Antony Ebeneezer
103   94
5-y-o ch h Hurricane Sky (AUS)-Captivating (IRE) (Wolfhound (USA))
C R Dore Castles UK

Placings: F50-41455535   (4892)
2003/04: 16⁴GF, 16¹G, 16⁴GF, 16⁵GF, 16⁵F, 16⁵GF, 16³G, 16⁵GF,

	Starts	1st	2nd	3rd	Win & Pl
Hurdles	8	1	0	1	6496
Career Total	11	1	0	1	6496
89 7/03 Strf	2m110y	E(0-105)HHdl		GD	£4095

Total win prize-money £4095

Going:	Sf: 0-0 GS: 0-0 Gd: 1-2 GF: - Fm: 0-6
Distance:	2m/2m3: 1-8 2m4-2m7: 0-0 3m+: 0-0
Track:	LH: 1-7 RH: 0-1 Tight: 1-5 Gall: 0-1
Aids:	Bl: 0-0 Vi: 0-0 Tstrap: 1-6 Ckp: 0-0
Best Rating:	94 3/04 Newb 2m110y good Hdl

Plating-class hurdler; showed significant improvement for being fitted with a tongue tie when readily winning a handicap hurdle at Stratford July 2003; best at two miles; effective on good ground.

Any News
88
7-y-o ch g Karinga Bay-D'Egliere (FR) (Port Etienne (FR))
P A Blockley H C C Racing Partnership

Placings: *44/0/000-PP*   (0908)
2003/04: 20ᴾG, 17ᴾGF,

	Starts	1st	2nd	3rd	Win & Pl
Hurdles	2	0	0	0	
Career Total	8	0	0	0	548

Going:	Sf: 0-0 GS: 0-0 Gd: 0-1 GF: - Fm: 0-1
Distance:	2m/2m3: 0-1 2m4-2m7: 0-1 3m+: 0-0
Track:	LH: 0-2 RH: 0-0 Tight: 0-0 Gall: 0-0
Aids:	Bl: 0-0 Vi: 0-0 Tstrap: 0-0 Ckp: 0-0
Best Rating:	103 1/01 Leop 2m soft NHF

Anzal (IRE)
101   95+
6-y-o b g Kahyasi-Anazara (USA) (Trempolino (USA))
D R Gandolfo Peter Melotti & Andy Chalmers

Placings: *0/PPPF4016-151PPP*   (4917)
2003/04: 19¹GF, 22⁵GF, 20¹G, 22ᴿGF, 19ᴾGF, 20ᴾGS,

	Starts	1st	2nd	3rd	Win & Pl
Hurdles	6	2	0	0	6370
Career Total	15	3	0	0	9958
95 6/03 Worc	2m4f	F(0-105)HHdl		GD	£2660
88 5/03 Extr	2m3f	E(0-100)HHdl		G-F	£3710

---

90   4/03   Extr   2m3f   F(0-90)HHdl   G-F   £3588

Total win prize-money £9958

Going:	Sf: 0-0 GS: 0-1 Gd: 1-1 GF: - Fm: 1-4
Distance:	2m/2m3: 1-2 2m4-2m7: 1-4 3m+: 0-0
Track:	LH: 1-3 RH: 1-2 Tight: 0-1 Gall: 0-0
Aids:	Bl: 0-1 Vi: 0-0 Tstrap: 0-0 Ckp: 0-0
Best Rating:	95 6/03 Worc 2m4f good Hdl

Moderate hurdler; benefited from a wind operation with three wins in 2003; a rather in and out performer who apparently needs time between races; suited by a sound surface; effective up to 2m 4f.

Aoiferob (IRE)

6-y-o b g Commanche Run-Lancana (IRE) (Lancastrian)
B G Powell W T Racing Syndicate

Placings: PPF   (4672)
2003/04: 25ᴾS, 26ᴾS, 25ᶠG,

	Starts	1st	2nd	3rd	Win & Pl
Chases	3	0	0	0	
Career Total	3	0	0	0	

Going:	Sf: 0-2 GS: 0-0 Gd: 0-1 GF: - Fm: 0-0
Distance:	2m/2m3: 0-0 2m4-2m7: 0-0 3m+: 0-3
Track:	LH: 0-1 RH: 0-2 Tight: 0-0 Gall: 0-0
Aids:	Bl: 0-0 Vi: 0-1 Tstrap: 0-0 Ckp: 0-0
Best Rating:	0 4/04 Winc 3m1f110y good Ch

Apadi (USA)
(105h)   (97h) 78
8-y-o ch g Diesis-Ixtapa (USA) (Chief's Crown (USA))
R C Guest (M C Chapman 5/10) Mrs Anna Kenny

Placings: 6403/521511620F6000F0/23245U243F36F54255
-R1365054   (3667)
2003/04: 16ᴿGF, 17¹GF, 17³G, 16ᴿGF, 16⁵G, 16⁹GS, 16⁵HY,
16⁴HY,

	Starts	1st	2nd	3rd	Win & Pl
Hurdles	7	1	0	1	3455
Chases	1	0	0	0	314
Career Total	46	4	6	5	23609
97 6/03 MRas	2m1f110yG(0-90)HHdl		G-F		£2555
102 9/01 Worc	2m	E(0-115)HHdl		G-F	£3083
95 8/01 Ctml	2m1f110yG(0-90)HHdl		GD	£3657
86 7/01 Sthl	2m	G Hdl		G-F	£1596

Total win prize-money £10893

Going:	Sf: 0-2 GS: 0-1 Gd: 0-2 GF: - Fm: 1-3
Distance:	2m/2m3: 1-8 2m4-2m7: 0-0 3m+: 0-0
Track:	LH: 0-7 RH: 1-1 Tight: 1-4 Gall: 0-2
Aids:	Bl: 0-0 Vi: 0-0 Tstrap: 0-0 Ckp: 0-1
Best Rating:	106 10/01 MRas 2m1f110y gd-sft Hdl

Modest and frustrating handicap hurdler; best at two miles on a sound surface; suited by a strong pace but becoming hard to win with.

Apollo Theatre
101   107+
6-y-o b g Sadler's Wells (USA)-Threatening (Warning)
R Rowe The Encore Partnership II

Placings: *533-343*   (4560)
2003/04: 17³GS, 20⁴G, 21³GS,

	Starts	1st	2nd	3rd	Win & Pl
Hurdles	3	0	0	2	2165
Career Total	6	0	0	4	2744

Going:	Sf: 0-0 GS: 0-2 Gd: 0-1 GF: - Fm: 0-0
Distance:	2m/2m3: 0-1 2m4-2m7: 0-0 3m+: 0-0
Track:	LH: 0-2 RH: 0-1 Tight: 0-2 Gall: 0-1
Aids:	Bl: 0-0 Vi: 0-0 Tstrap: 0-0 Ckp: 0-1
Best Rating:	108 3/04 Newb 2m5f gd-sft Hdl

Has performed creditably on all starts to date in bumpers and over hurdles; stays to and a half miles; acts on most ground types.

Apollo Victoria (FR)
93   93
7-y-o b g Sadler's Wells (USA)-Dame Solitaire (CAN) (Halo (USA))
B G Powell R J T 290 Limited

Placings: P0   (3042)
2003/04: 16ᴾS, 16⁹GS,

	Starts	1st	2nd	3rd	Win & Pl
Hurdles	2	0	0	0	
Career Total	2	0	0	0	

Going:	Sf: 0-1 GS: 0-1 Gd: 0-0 GF: - Fm: 0-0
Distance:	2m/2m3: 0-2 2m4-2m7: 0-0 3m+: 0-0
Track:	LH: 0-1 RH: 0-1 Tight: 0-0 Gall: 0-1
Aids:	Bl: 0-0 Vi: 0-0 Tstrap: 0-0 Ckp: 0-0
Best Rating:	102 12/03 Newb 2m110y gd-sft Hdl

Apple Joe
102   (41h) 90
8-y-o b g Sula Bula-Hazelwain (Hard Fact)
A J Whiting A J Whiting

Placings: FP304/536344-536124U3   (4667)
2003/04: 24⁵G, 25³GS, 24⁶GS, 26¹S, 24²HY, 26⁴G, 24ᵁGS, 24³S,

	Starts	1st	2nd	3rd	Win & Pl
Chases	8	1	1	2	5248
Career Total	19	1	1	5	7761
90 12/03 Plum	3m2f	F(0-100)HCh		SFT	£2576

Total win prize-money £2576

Going:	Sf: 1-3 GS: 0-3 Gd: 0-2 GF: - Fm: 0-0
Distance:	2m/2m3: 0-0 2m4-2m7: 0-0 3m+: 1-8
Track:	LH: 1-6 RH: 0-1 Tight: 1-4 Gall: 0-0
Aids:	Bl: 0-0 Vi: 0-0 Tstrap: 0-0 Ckp: 1-5
Best Rating:	90 4/04 Ling 3m soft Ch

Modest staying chaser; got off the mark when romping home in 3m 2f amateur riders' handicap at Plumpton December 2003; sound effort when runner-up off 7lb higher mark next time; stays 3m 2f; acts in soft ground.

April Ace
79   46
8-y-o ch g First Trump-Champ D'Avril (Northfields (USA))
R J Baker Graham Brown

Placings: 0/000-0   (4246)
2003/04: 17⁹GF,

	Starts	1st	2nd	3rd	Win & Pl
Hurdles	1	0	0	0	
Career Total	5	0	0	0	

Going:	Sf: 0-0 GS: 0-0 Gd: 0-0 GF: - Fm: 0-1
Distance:	2m/2m3: 0-1 2m4-2m7: 0-0 3m+: 0-0
Track:	LH: 0-0 RH: 0-1 Tight: 0-0 Gall: 0-0
Aids:	Bl: 0-0 Vi: 0-0 Tstrap: 0-0 Ckp: 0-0
Best Rating:	48 7/02 Strf 2m110y gd-fm Hdl

April Allegro (FR)

(114h)   (129h)**102**
8-y-o br g Doyoun-April Lee (USA) (Lyphard (USA))
Michael Hourigan T J Doran

Placings:P2310/6030/002P61100110**000R/5P**01-04003040
(1288a)
2003/04: 24[0]YS, 22[4]G, 24[0]GF, 20[0]GF, 20[3]GY, 22[0]S, 25[4]GF, 25[0]GF,

	Starts	1st	2nd	3rd	Win & Pl
Hurdles	4	0	0	0	1298
Chases	4	0	0	1	997
Career Total	37	6	2	3	72429
129 4/03	Fair	2m6f	HHdl	GD	£14772
137 10/01	Gowr	3m	HHdl	GD	£13104
133 9/01	List	2m4f	HHdl	G-F	£13104
125 7/01	Cork	2m4f	HHdl	G-F	£13104
125 6/01	Kbgn	2m3f	(0-123)HHdl	GD	£9435
104 2/00	MRas	2m1f110yD	Hdl	G-S	£3308

Total win prize-money £66832

Going: Sf: 0-1 GS: 0-0 Gd: 0-1 GF: - Fm: 0-4
Distance: 2m/2m3: 0-0 2m4-2m7: 0-4 3m+: 0-4
Track: LH: 0-2 RH: 0-4 Tight: 0-1 Gall: 0-0
Aids: Bl: 0-0 Vi: 0-0 Tstrap: 0-0 Ckp: 0-0
Best Rating: 137 10/01 Gowr 3m   good   Hdl

Useful Irish trained hurdler; stays three miles; acts on decent ground.

April Louise

81   **65**
8-y-o b m Meqdaam (USA)-California Dreamin (Slip Anchor)
T Wall D Bunn

Placings:0000630/3420505 1023/4330P-60   (0207)
2003/04: 17[6]S, 16[0]GF,

	Starts	1st	2nd	3rd	Win & Pl
Hurdles	2	0	0	0	0
Career Total	25	1	2	5	15260
109 2/02	Ludl	2m	D(0-115)HHdl	SFT	£4056

Total win prize-money £4056

Going: Sf: 0-1 GS: 0-0 Gd: 0-0 GF: - Fm: 0-1
Distance: 2m/2m3: 0-2 2m4-2m7: 0-0 3m+: 0-0
Track: LH: 0-2 RH: 0-0 Tight: 0-1 Gall: 0-0
Aids: Bl: 0-0 Vi: 0-0 Tstrap: 0-0 Ckp: 0-0
Best Rating: 117 4/02 Aint 2m10y good   Hdl

Modest handicapper; acts on soft ground; effective over two miles.

April Miss (FR)

93   **75+**
4-y-o bl f Averti (IRE)-Lady Of Jakarta (USA) (Procida (USA))
Mrs L Wadham (John Allen 9/6) Dingley Dell Racing Ltd

Placings:53256   (2071)
2003/04: 18[5]GF, 16[3]GF, 18[2]GF, 16[5]GF, 16[6]GF,

	Starts	1st	2nd	3rd	Win & Pl
Hurdles	5	0	1	1	1199
Career Total	5	0	1	1	1199

Going: Sf: 0-0 GS: 0-0 Gd: 0-0 GF: - Fm: 0-5
Distance: 2m/2m3: 0-5 2m4-2m7: 0-0 3m+: 0-0
Track: LH: 0-3 RH: 0-2 Tight: 0-2 Gall: 0-2
Aids: Bl: 0-0 Vi: 0-1 Tstrap: 0-0 Ckp: 0-0
Best Rating: 75 9/03 Font 2m2f110y gd-fm   Hdl

Modest juvenile hurdler; showed little on the Flat; looks a little better over hurdles; stays two miles two; acts on fast ground.

April Spirit

(80h)**97**
9-y-o b m Nomination-Seraphim (FR) (Lashkari)
Mrs S J Smith Mrs B Ramsden

Placings:06/24533230/03/4051F546/010322035-2141
(1343)
2003/04: 23[2]G, 21[1]G, 21[4]GF, 26[1]GF,

	Starts	1st	2nd	3rd	Win & Pl
Chases	4	2	1	0	7795
Career Total	33	4	5	6	20422
97 9/03	Sthl	3m2f	E(0-110)HCh	G-F	£3241
97 8/03	Sthl	2m5f110yF(0-90)HCh	GD	£3248
91 7/02	Worc	2m7f110yF(0-100)HCh	GD	£3230
97 8/01	Worc	2m4f110yE(0-105)HCh	G-F	£3484

Total win prize-money £13204

Going: Sf: 0-0 GS: 0-0 Gd: 1-2 GF: - Fm: 1-2
Distance: 2m/2m3: 0-2 2m4-2m7: 1-2 3m+: 1-2
Track: LH: 2-4 RH: 0-0 Tight: 0-0 Gall: 0-0
Aids: Bl: 0-0 Vi: 0-0 Tstrap: 0-0 Ckp: 0-0
Best Rating: 97 9/03 Sthl 3m2f   gd-fm   Ch

Moderate staying chaser, stays three miles-plus, acts on a sound surface; suited by a flat track.

April Treasure

(70c)**73**
9-y-o b m Stani (USA)-Eleri (Rolfe (USA))
Mrs P Ford K R Ford

Placings:PP0/P0F25P050P/65005/42P4600P4F-0P5P
(1362)
2003/04: 20[0]GF, 20[P]GF, 26[5]GF, 16[P]GF,

	Starts	1st	2nd	3rd	Win & Pl
Hurdles	4	0	0	0	0
Career Total	32	0	2	0	1642

Going: Sf: 0-0 GS: 0-0 Gd: 0-0 GF: - Fm: 0-4
Distance: 2m/2m3: 0-1 2m4-2m7: 0-2 3m+: 0-1
Track: LH: 0-4 RH: 0-0 Tight: 0-0 Gall: 0-0
Aids: Bl: 0-0 Vi: 0-0 Tstrap: 0-0 Ckp: 0-0
Best Rating: 77 10/00 Strf 2m110y soft   Hdl

Plating-class hurdler.

Aqribaa (IRE)

94   **68**
6-y-o b g Pennekamp (USA)-Karayb (IRE) (Last Tycoon)
A J Lockwood A J Lockwood

Placings:3P/560-0   (2163)
2003/04: 16[0]G,

	Starts	1st	2nd	3rd	Win & Pl
Hurdles	1	0	0	0	
Career Total	6	0	0	1	486

Going: Sf: 0-0 GS: 0-0 Gd: 0-1 GF: - Fm: 0-0
Distance: 2m/2m3: 0-1 2m4-2m7: 0-0 3m+: 0-0
Track: LH: 0-1 RH: 0-0 Tight: 0-0 Gall: 0-0
Aids: Bl: 0-0 Vi: 0-0 Tstrap: 0-0 Ckp: 0-0
Best Rating: 68 9/02 Hexm 2m110y   gd-fm   Hdl

Aqua Pura (GER)

89   **62**
5-y-o b g Acatenango (GER)-Actraphane (Shareef Dancer (USA))
B J Curley Mrs B J Curley

Placings:0-03P4   (4280)
2003/04: 21[0]G, 16[3]HY, 24[P]GS, 16[4]GS,

	Starts	1st	2nd	3rd	Win & Pl
Hurdles	4	0	0	1	915
Career Total	5	0	0	1	915

Going: Sf: 0-1 GS: 0-2 Gd: 0-1 GF: - Fm: 0-0
Distance: 2m/2m3: 0-2 2m4-2m7: 0-1 3m+: 0-1
Track: LH: 0-1 RH: 0-3 Tight: 0-0 Gall: 0-0
Aids: Bl: 0-0 Vi: 0-0 Tstrap: 0-0 Ckp: 0-0
Best Rating: 66 12/03 Wwck 2m5f   good   Hdl

Of little account over hurdles.

Ar Muin Na Muice (IRE)

110(109c)   (122c)**142+**
8-y-o ch m Executive Perk-Raashideah (Dancer's Image (USA))
Jonjo O'Neill Mrs G Smith

Placings:0/111/1F211-2F55   (4386)
2003/04: 24[2]S, 24[F]GS, 23[6]S, 25[6]S,

	Starts	1st	2nd	3rd	Win & Pl
Hurdles	2	0	0	0	1500
Chases	2	0	1	0	1426
Career Total	13	6	2	0	59200
145 3/03	Newb	2m5f	HHdl	GD	£29000
127 2/03	Weth	2m4f110yD	Hdl	GD	£5570
104 10/02	Bang	2m4f	D Hdl	SFT	£4264
127 12/01	Leop	2m	NHF	YLD	£6677
118 12/01	Navn	2m	NHF	Y-S	£5564
105 5/01	Gowr	2m	NHF	YLD	£3616

Total win prize-money £54694

Going: Sf: 0-2 GS: 0-1 Gd: 0-1 GF: - Fm: 0-0
Distance: 2m/2m3: 0-0 2m4-2m7: 0-0 3m+: 0-4
Track: LH: 0-4 RH: 0-0 Tight: 0-0 Gall: 0-1
Aids: Bl: 0-0 Vi: 0-0 Tstrap: 0-0 Ckp: 0-0
Best Rating: 145 3/03 Newb 2m5f   good   Hdl

Useful hurdler; won the 2003 Mares Final at Newbury; not disgraced when narrowly beaten by Rum Pointer on chasing debut at Uttoxeter on Boxing Day 2003; fell nexty time; just about stays 3m, though better at shorter; best on good and soft ground, not extremes.

Arabian Moon (IRE)

92(95c)   (114c)**119**
8-y-o ch g Barathea (IRE)-Excellent Alibi (USA) (Exceller (USA))
M C Pipe (S Dow 28/10) No Dramas Partnership

Placings:46/111023/110P-11205P560   (3489)
2003/04: 20[1]GF, 18[1]GF, 21[2]GF, 24[0]GF, 21[5]GF, 20[P]S, 24[5]GF, 22[6]G, 17[0]GS,

	Starts	1st	2nd	3rd	Win & Pl
Hurdles	4	0	0	0	611
Chases	5	2	1	0	10445
Career Total	21	7	2	1	38507
112 8/03	Font	2m2f	E Ch	G-F	£4944
114 8/03	Font	2m4f	E Ch	G-F	£4017
137 10/02	Chel	2m5f	B(0-145)HHdl	G-F	£9323
127 10/02	Font	2m2f110yC(0-130)HHdl	GD	£6217
110 8/01	Uttx	2m4f110yD Hdl	G-F	£3360
110 8/01	Strf	2m6f110yD Hdl	GD	£3523
115 5/01	Fknm	2m7f110yE Hdl	G-F	£2374

Total win prize-money £33759

Going: Sf: 0-1 GS: 0-1 Gd: 0-1 GF: - Fm: 2-6
Distance: 2m/2m3: 1-2 2m4-2m7: 1-5 3m+: 0-2
Track: LH: 0-4 RH: 0-3 Tight: 2-6 Gall: 0-2
Aids: Bl: 0-0 Vi: 0-3 Tstrap: 0-0 Ckp: 0-1

Best Rating: 137 10/02 Chel 2m5f   gd-fm Hdl

Useful hurdler/novice chaser; stays three miles, but better over a shorter trip; won first two starts over fences in minor events at Fontwell; acts on ground good or faster.

Araf
101   91
5-y-o b g Millkom-Euphyllia (Superpower)
N Wilson W R S

Placings:0F55-P00   (0895)
2003/04: 17^{P}GF, 16^{0}GF, 17^{0}GF,

	Starts	1st	2nd	3rd	Win & Pl
Hurdles	3	0	0	0	
Career Total	7	0	0	0	0

Going:	Sf: 0-0 GS: 0-0 Gd: 0-0 GF: - Fm: 0-3
Distance:	2m/2m3: 0-3 2m4-2m7: 0-0 3m+: 0-0
Track:	LH: 0-2 RH: 0-1 Tight: 0-2 Gall: 0-0
Aids:	Bl: 0-0 Vi: 0-0 Tstrap: 0-0 Ckp: 0-0
Best Rating:	83 11/02 Newc 2m gd-sft Hdl

Selling winner on the Flat but very limited ability to far over hurdles.

Araglin
105   98+
5-y-o b g Sadler's Wells (USA)-River Caro (USA) (Irish River (FR))
Miss S J Wilton John Pointon And Sons

Placings:0F600-13025060   (4785)
2003/04: 19^{1}GF, 16^{X}GF, 20^{X}GS, 21^{2}GF, 19^{9}G, 19^{9}G, 21^{6}GS, 21^{0}G,

	Starts	1st	2nd	3rd	Win & Pl
Hurdles	8	1	1	1	4638
Career Total	13	1	1	1	4638
98 10/03 MRas 2m3f110yE Hdl			G-F		£3125

Total win prize-money £3126

Going:	Sf: 0-0 GS: 0-2 Gd: 0-3 GF: - Fm: 1-3
Distance:	2m/2m3: 0-1 2m4-2m7: 1-7 3m+: 0-0
Track:	LH: 0-3 RH: 1-5 Tight: 1-2 Gall: 0-1
Aids:	Bl: 0-0 Vi: 0-0 Tstrap: 0-0 Ckp: 0-0
Best Rating:	98 11/03 Ludl 2m5f gd-fm Hdl

Stepped up on previous efforts when winning weakly contested 2m 3f maiden hurdle at Market Rasen October 2003; acts on good to firm.

Arawak Prince (IRE)
                         (89h)
8-y-o ch g College Chapel-Alpine Symphony (Northern Dancer)
G Prodromou George Prodromou

Placings:P1045/140P60/124P-F   (1629)
2003/04: 17^{F}GF,

	Starts	1st	2nd	3rd	Win & Pl
Chases	1	0	0	0	
Career Total	16	3	1	0	8636
89 8/02 Sthl 2m1f G Hdl			G-F		£2223
106 5/01 Hrfd 2m1f G(0-95)HHdl			GD		£2100
107 3/00 Plum 2m E Hdl			GD		£2338

Total win prize-money £6661

Going:	Sf: 0-0 GS: 0-0 Gd: 0-0 GF: - Fm: 0-1
Distance:	2m/2m3: 0-1 2m4-2m7: 0-0 3m+: 0-0
Track:	LH: 0-1 RH: 0-0 Tight: 0-0 Gall: 0-0
Aids:	Bl: 0-0 Vi: 0-1 Tstrap: 0-0 Ckp: 0-0
Best Rating:	107 3/00 Plum 2m good Hdl

Arbie (CAN)

5-y-o b g Mountain Cat (USA)-Empress Of Love (USA) (Czaravich (USA))
Mrs L C Jewell Peter Oppenheimer

Placings:P   (1417)
2003/04: 18^{P}GF,

	Starts	1st	2nd	3rd	Win & Pl
Hurdles	1	0	0	0	
Career Total	1	0	0	0	

Going:	Sf: 0-0 GS: 0-0 Gd: 0-0 GF: - Fm: 0-1
Distance:	2m/2m3: 0-1 2m4-2m7: 0-0 3m+: 0-0
Track:	LH: 0-1 RH: 0-0 Tight: 0-1 Gall: 0-0
Aids:	Bl: 0-0 Vi: 0-0 Tstrap: 0-0 Ckp: 0-1
Best Rating:	0 9/03 Font 2m2f110y gd-fm Hdl

Arc En Ciel
70   55
6-y-o b g Rainbow Quest (USA)-Nadia Nerina (CAN) (Northern Dancer)
G L Moore Mrs M J George

Placings:0-0   (3831)
2003/04: 16^{0}G,

	Starts	1st	2nd	3rd	Win & Pl
Hurdles	1	0	0	0	
Career Total	2	0	0	0	

Going:	Sf: 0-0 GS: 0-0 Gd: 0-1 GF: - Fm: 0-0
Distance:	2m/2m3: 0-1 2m4-2m7: 0-0 3m+: 0-0
Track:	LH: 0-1 RH: 0-0 Tight: 0-0 Gall: 0-1
Aids:	Bl: 0-0 Vi: 0-0 Tstrap: 0-0 Ckp: 0-0
Best Rating:	60 2/04 Newb 2m110y good Hdl

Arceye

7-y-o b g Weld-Flower Of Tintem (Free State)
M G Rimell Mark Rimell

Placings:00P   (4511)
2003/04: 17^{0}GF, 16^{0}GS, 20^{P}GS,

	Starts	1st	2nd	3rd	Win & Pl
NH Flat	2	0	0	0	0
Hurdles	1	0	0	0	0
Career Total	3	0	0	0	0

Going:	Sf: 0-0 GS: 0-2 Gd: 0-0 GF: - Fm: 0-1
Distance:	2m/2m3: 0-2 2m4-2m7: 0-1 3m+: 0-0
Track:	LH: 0-1 RH: 0-2 Tight: 0-0 Gall: 0-1
Aids:	Bl: 0-0 Vi: 0-0 Tstrap: 0-0 Ckp: 0-0
Best Rating:	69 12/03 Hntg 2m110y gd-sft NHF

Arch Caper (IRE)
                         41f
7-y-o b m Archway (IRE)-African Caper (IRE) (Brush Aside (USA))
C N Kellett J W Ellis

Placings:0   (0334)
2003/04: 17^{0}GF,

	Starts	1st	2nd	3rd	Win & Pl
NH Flat	1	0	0	0	
Career Total	1	0	0	0	

Going:	Sf: 0-0 GS: 0-0 Gd: 0-0 GF: - Fm: 0-1
Distance:	2m/2m3: 0-1 2m4-2m7: 0-0 3m+: 0-0
Track:	LH: 0-1 RH: 0-0 Tight: 0-1 Gall: 0-0
Aids:	Bl: 0-0 Vi: 0-0 Tstrap: 0-0 Ckp: 0-1
Best Rating:	41 5/03 Sthl 2m1f gd-fm NHF

Arch Stanton (IRE)
118   140+
6-y-o b g Lahib (USA)-Sweet Repose (High Top)
W P Mullins John J Brennan

Placings:5322S-215462   (4804a)
2003/04: 16^{2}Y, 16^{1}YS, 16^{2}S, 18^{4}S, 16^{6}G, 16^{2}Y,

	Starts	1st	2nd	3rd	Win & Pl
Hurdles	6	1	2	0	16681
Career Total	11	1	4	1	20674
123 12/03 Leop 2m Hdl			Y-S		£6720

Total win prize-money £6721

Going:	Sf: 0-2 GS: 0-0 Gd: 0-1 GF: - Fm: 0-0
Distance:	2m/2m3: 1-6 2m4-2m7: 0-0 3m+: 0-0
Track:	LH: 1-4 RH: 0-1 Tight: 0-0 Gall: 0-0
Aids:	Bl: 0-0 Vi: 0-0 Tstrap: 0-0 Ckp: 0-0
Best Rating:	140 4/04 Fair 2m yield Hdl

Useful Irish-trained novice hurdler; suited by two miles and cut in the ground.

Archenko
46f   74f
4-y-o b g Weldnaas (USA)-Silverdale Rose (Nomination)
A Berry Anthony White

Placings:0   (4316)
2003/04: 16^{0}GF,

	Starts	1st	2nd	3rd	Win & Pl
NH Flat	1	0	0	0	
Career Total	1	0	0	0	

Going:	Sf: 0-0 GS: 0-0 Gd: 0-0 GF: - Fm: 0-1
Distance:	2m/2m3: 0-1 2m4-2m7: 0-0 3m+: 0-0
Track:	LH: 0-1 RH: 0-0 Tight: 0-0 Gall: 0-0
Aids:	Bl: 0-0 Vi: 0-0 Tstrap: 0-0 Ckp: 0-0
Best Rating:	74 3/04 Ayr 2m gd-fm NHF

Archias (GER)
99   86
5-y-o b g Darshaan-Arionette (Lombard (GER))
R C Guest G & J Racing

Placings:00600   (3935)
2003/04: 16^{0}GF, 16^{0}GS, 16^{6}GF, 16^{6}G, 16^{0}GS,

	Starts	1st	2nd	3rd	Win & Pl
Hurdles	5	0	0	0	0
Career Total	5	0	0	0	0

Going:	Sf: 0-0 GS: 0-2 Gd: 0-1 GF: - Fm: 0-2
Distance:	2m/2m3: 0-5 2m4-2m7: 0-0 3m+: 0-0
Track:	LH: 0-2 RH: 0-3 Tight: 0-4 Gall: 0-1
Aids:	Bl: 0-0 Vi: 0-0 Tstrap: 0-1 Ckp: 0-0
Best Rating:	92 1/04 Muss 2m gd-fm Hdl

Archie Babe (IRE)
107   122
8-y-o ch g Archway (IRE)-Frensham Manor (Le Johnstan)
J J Quinn Bowett Lamb & Kelly

Placings:F44-1423   (3607)
2003/04: 16¹GS, 16⁴S, 16²G, 16³S,

	Starts	1st	2nd	3rd	Win & Pl
Hurdles	4	1	1	1	6583
Career Total	7	1	1	1	6856
122 11/03 Weth	2m		D Hdl	G-S	£4069
			Total win prize-money		£4069

Going:	Sf: 0-2 GS: 1-1 Gd: 0-1 GF: - Fm: 0-0
Distance:	2m/2m3: 1-4 2m4-2m7: 0-0 3m+: 0-0
Track:	LH: 1-4 RH: 0-0 Tight: 0-0 Gall: 0-1
Aids:	Bl: 0-0 Vi: 0-0 Tstrap: 0-0 Ckp: 0-0
Best Rating:	122 11/03 Weth 2m gd-sft Hdl

Fair novice hurdler; ran away with a competitive novices' handicap at Wetherby in November; big disappointment in ordinary event at Hexham following month; back to his best when runner-up to useful sort at Wetherby on Boxing Day; best with cut in the ground.

Archirondel

6-y-o b g Bin Ajwaad (IRE)-Penang Rose (NZ) (Kingdom Bay (NZ))
M D Hammond (John Berry 12/10) The Archi Partnership

Placings:0   (3403)
2003/04: 19⁰G,

	Starts	1st	2nd	3rd	Win & Pl
Hurdles	1	0	0	0	
Career Total	1	0	0	0	

Going:	Sf: 0-0 GS: 0-0 Gd: 0-1 GF: - Fm: 0-0
Distance:	2m/2m3: 0-0 2m4-2m7: 0-1 3m+: 0-0
Track:	LH: 0-1 RH: 0-0 Tight: 0-0 Gall: 0-0
Aids:	Bl: 0-0 Vi: 0-0 Tstrap: 0-0 Ckp: 0-0
Best Rating:	0 1/04 Donc 2m3f110y good Hdl

Arctic Blue
73   33
4-y-o b g Polar Prince (IRE)-Miss Sarajane (Skyliner)
J S Moore Tom Yates,Mrs Evelyn Yates,J S Moore

Placings:0   (0958)
2003/04: 16⁰G,

	Starts	1st	2nd	3rd	Win & Pl
Hurdles	1	0	0	0	
Career Total	1	0	0	0	

Going:	Sf: 0-0 GS: 0-0 Gd: 0-1 GF: - Fm: 0-0
Distance:	2m/2m3: 0-1 2m4-2m7: 0-0 3m+: 0-0
Track:	LH: 0-1 RH: 0-0 Tight: 0-1 Gall: 0-0
Aids:	Bl: 0-0 Vi: 0-0 Tstrap: 0-0 Ckp: 0-0
Best Rating:	33 7/03 Strf 2m110y good Hdl

Arctic Burner (IRE)
55   84
10-y-o b g Glacial Storm (USA)-Lucky Appeal (Star Appeal)
J C Tuck Mrs J Chapman

Placings:00/06006/4240241U/PR515500/0   (0676)
2003/04: 16⁰GF,

	Starts	1st	2nd	3rd	Win & Pl
Hurdles	1	0	0	0	
Career Total	24	2	2	0	7367
81 7/01 Strf	2m3f		E(0-105)HHdl	GD	£3010
90 9/00 NAbb	2m110y		F(0-100)HCh	G-F	£2527
			Total win prize-money		£5537

Going:	Sf: 0-0 GS: 0-0 Gd: 0-0 GF: - Fm: 0-1
Distance:	2m/2m3: 0-1 2m4-2m7: 0-0 3m+: 0-0
Track:	LH: 0-1 RH: 0-0 Tight: 0-0 Gall: 0-0
Aids:	Bl: 0-0 Vi: 0-1 Tstrap: 0-0 Ckp: 0-0
Best Rating:	96 6/00 Strf 2m110y gd-sft Hdl

Arctic Challenge (IRE)
111   131
10-y-o b g Glacial Storm (USA)-Ruckinge Girl (Eborneezer)
K R Burke I & Mrs A Russell

Placings:4/33/3336/2013P01P2/14242P-1U3   (2870)
2003/04: 21¹G, 20⁰GF, 20³G,

	Starts	1st	2nd	3rd	Win & Pl
Chases	3	1	0	1	12777
Career Total	25	4	4	7	40466
131 5/03 Strf	2m5f110yB(0-140)HCh			GD	£11728
126 5/02 Worc	2m4f110yD(0-125)HCh			GD	£4065
111 4/02 Hntg	2m4f110yE Ch			G-F	£3078
129 11/01 Kemp	2m4f110yD Ch			GD	£4936
			Total win prize-money		£23810

Going:	Sf: 0-0 GS: 0-0 Gd: 1-2 GF: - Fm: 0-1
Distance:	2m/2m3: 0-0 2m4-2m7: 1-3 3m+: 0-0
Track:	LH: 1-3 RH: 0-0 Tight: 1-1 Gall: 0-0
Aids:	Bl: 0-0 Vi: 0-0 Tstrap: 0-0 Ckp: 1-2
Best Rating:	131 5/03 Strf 2m5f110y good Ch

Useful handicap chaser; bounced back to form in cheekpieces when winning 2m 5f handicap at Stratford May 2003; unseated next time; best at two and a half miles; acts on ground good or faster; suited by a flat track; has not always been convincing in a tight finish; has been tried in cheekpieces.

Arctic Fancy (USA)
108   130
11-y-o ch g Arctic Tern (USA)-Fit And Fancy (USA) (Vaguely Noble)
Miss H C Knight Another Chance Partnership

Placings:21135/12151/63550/4402224/10-2P305U   (4784)
2003/04: 20²S, 19⁰S, 20³GS, 20⁰G, 20⁵GS, 24⁰G,

	Starts	1st	2nd	3rd	Win & Pl
Chases	6	0	1	1	3861
Career Total	30	6	6	3	48760
130 1/03 Donc	2m3f		C(0-130)HCh	GD	£8300
135 4/00 Chep	2m110y		E Ch	SFT	£3575
137 1/00 Donc	2m110y		D Ch	G-F	£3789
127 11/99 Chep	2m110y		E Ch	GD	£2989
125 2/99 Folk	2m4f110yE Hdl			SFT	£2853
119 1/99 Plum	2m1f		E Hdl	HVY	£2407
			Total win prize-money		£23918

Going:	Sf: 0-2 GS: 0-2 Gd: 0-2 GF: - Fm: 0-0
Distance:	2m/2m3: 0-0 2m4-2m7: 0-5 3m+: 0-1
Track:	LH: 0-4 RH: 0-2 Tight: 0-3 Gall: 0-1
Aids:	Bl: 0-0 Vi: 0-0 Tstrap: 0-0 Ckp: 0-0
Best Rating:	139 5/00 Punc 2m good Ch

Fair handicap chaser; successful on return in 2m 3f handicap chase at Doncaster January 2003; acts on good and soft ground; needs a sound surface to be effective beyond 2m.

Arctic Gamble
102
12-y-o b g Arctic Lord-Honey Gamble (Gambling Debt)
L G Cottrell Miss Sally Lock

Placings:42F/26411-0   (4820)
2003/04: 25⁰GF,

	Starts	1st	2nd	3rd	Win & Pl
Chases	1	0	0	0	
Career Total	9	2	2	0	11884
108 4/03 Winc	3m1f110yE Ch			FRM	£4137
108 3/03 Tntn	3m		F(0-90)HCh	FRM	£3705
			Total win prize-money		£7842

Moderate chaser; broke his duck in modest novices handicap at Taunton March 2003; followed up next time; stays three miles; appreciates a sound surface.

Arctic Glow
85   56
5-y-o ch m Weld-Arctic Mission (The Parson)
Mrs H Pudd Mrs H Pudd

Placings:P00   (4856)
2003/04: 19⁰S, 19⁰G, 19⁰GF,

	Starts	1st	2nd	3rd	Win & Pl
Hurdles	3	0	0	0	
Career Total	3	0	0	0	

Going:	Sf: 0-1 GS: 0-0 Gd: 0-1 GF: - Fm: 0-0
Distance:	2m/2m3: 0-2 2m4-2m7: 0-1 3m+: 0-0
Track:	LH: 0-0 RH: 0-3 Tight: 0-1 Gall: 0-0
Aids:	Bl: 0-0 Vi: 0-0 Tstrap: 0-0 Ckp: 0-0
Best Rating:	56 4/04 Tntn 2m3f110y gd-fm Hdl

Arctic King

11-y-o b g Arctic Lord-Dunsilly Bell (London Bells (CAN))
A M Lloyd A M Lloyd

Placings:06/4636U/02P3F5P/P5P/F-3   (3845)
2003/04: 25³GS,

	Starts	1st	2nd	3rd	Win & Pl
Chases	1	0	0	1	260
Career Total	19	0	1	3	2920

Going:	Sf: 0-0 GS: 0-1 Gd: 0-0 GF: - Fm: 0-0
Distance:	2m/2m3: 0-0 2m4-2m7: 0-0 3m+: 0-1
Track:	LH: 0-0 RH: 0-1 Tight: 0-0 Gall: 0-0
Aids:	Bl: 0-0 Vi: 0-0 Tstrap: 0-0 Ckp: 0-0
Best Rating:	88 2/04 Hrfd 3m1f110y gd-sft Ch

Arctic Lagoon (IRE)
107(100h)   (81h)110
5-y-o ch g Bering-Lake Pleasant (IRE) (Elegant Air)
Mrs S C Bradburne Strath Pack Partnership

Placings:040P-3536322P042   (4293)
2003/04: 16³G, 16⁵G, 20³G, 20⁶G, 21³S, 16²S, 20²GS, 21PGS, 16⁹G, 19⁴G, 20²GF,

	Starts	1st	2nd	3rd	Win & Pl
Hurdles	4	0	0	2	1192
Chases	7	0	3	1	4660
Career Total	15	0	3	3	6277

Going:	Sf: 0-1 GS: 0-2 Gd: 0-7 GF: - Fm: 0-1
Distance:	2m/2m3: 0-5 2m4-2m7: 0-6 3m+: 0-0

Track: LH: 0-7 RH: 0-4 Tight: 0-4 Gall: 0-0
Aids: Bl: 0-0 Vi: 0-1 Tstrap: 0-6 Ckp: 0-0
Best Rating: 110 12/03 Hexm 2m110y soft Ch

Moderate hurdler/chaser; still a maiden; effective between two and two and a half miles; suited by a sound surface.

Arctic Moss (IRE)
92f   90f

5-y-o ch m Moscow Society (USA)-Arctic Match (Royal Match)
G A Swinbank Yarm Skip Alliance

Placings: 10   (4328)
2003/04: 16¹G, 16⁰S,

	Starts	1st	2nd	3rd	Win & Pl
NH Flat	2	1	0	0	2982
Career Total	2	1	0	0	2982
94 2/04 Muss 2m			H NHF		GD	£2982

Total win prize-money £2982

Going: Sf: 0-1 GS: 0-0 Gd: 1-1 GF: - Fm: 0-0
Distance: 2m/2m3: 1-2 2m4-2m7: 0-0 3m+: 0-0
Track: LH: 0-0 RH: 1-2 Tight: 1-1 Gall: 0-0
Aids: Bl: 0-0 Vi: 0-0 Tstrap: 0-0 Ckp: 0-0
Best Rating: 94 2/04 Muss 2m   good NHF

Winner of a mares only bumper at Musselburgh on her debut, doing it in good style, and can only improve; effective at two miles; acts on a sound surface.

Arctic Playboy
77   42

8-y-o b g Petoski-Arctic Oats (Oats)
Ian Williams R P Dineen

Placings: 0/O3/340-00   (2865)
2003/04: 20⁰GS, 19⁰GS,

	Starts	1st	2nd	3rd	Win & Pl
Hurdles	2	0	0	0	
Career Total	8	0	0	2	791

Going: Sf: 0-0 GS: 0-2 Gd: 0-0 GF: - Fm: 0-0
Distance: 2m/2m3: 0-1 2m4-2m7: 0-1 3m+: 0-0
Track: LH: 0-2 RH: 0-0 Tight: 0-0 Gall: 0-0
Aids: Bl: 0-0 Vi: 0-0 Tstrap: 0-0 Ckp: 0-0
Best Rating: 98 12/02 Newc 2m   soft NHF

Arctic Rainbow (IRE)
101   104

6-y-o b g King's Ride-Arctic Chatter (Le Bavard (FR))
D B Feek The Hon Mrs C Cameron

Placings: 44044   (4309)
2003/04: 17⁴GS, 21⁴GS, 22⁰HY, 20⁴GS, 16⁴G,

	Starts	1st	2nd	3rd	Win & Pl
NH Flat	1	0	0	0	
Hurdles	4	0	0	0	386
Career Total	5	0	0	0	386

Going: Sf: 0-1 GS: 0-3 Gd: 0-1 GF: - Fm: 0-0
Distance: 2m/2m3: 0-2 2m4-2m7: 0-3 3m+: 0-0
Track: LH: 0-1 RH: 0-4 Tight: 0-4 Gall: 0-0
Aids: Bl: 0-0 Vi: 0-0 Tstrap: 0-0 Ckp: 0-0
Best Rating: 104 12/03 Plum 2m5f   gd-sft Hdl

Stayed on well on bumper debut; showed promise on first start over hurdles.

Arctic Sky (IRE)
92(108h)   (110+h)122+

7-y-o b g Arctic Lord-Lake Garden Park (Comedy Star (USA))
N J Henderson Mrs Christopher Pugh

Placings: 0/6122001-1   (1948)
2003/04: 20¹GF,

	Starts	1st	2nd	3rd	Win & Pl
Chases	1	1	0	0	4920
Career Total	9	3	2	0	11992
122 11/03 Kemp 2m4f110yD Ch				G-F	£4920
110 4/03 Hntg 2m5f110yE(0-110)HHdl				G-F	£3542
100 6/02 Hrfd 2m1f		H NHF		G-F	£1631

Total win prize-money £10093

Going: Sf: 0-0 GS: 0-0 Gd: 0-0 GF: - Fm: 1-1
Distance: 2m/2m3: 0-0 2m4-2m7: 1-1 3m+: 0-0
Track: LH: 0-0 RH: 1-1 Tight: 0-0 Gall: 0-0
Aids: Bl: 0-0 Vi: 0-0 Tstrap: 0-0 Ckp: 0-0
Best Rating: 122 11/03 Kemp 2m4f110y gd-fm Ch

Modest hurdler/novice chaser; made a winning start to his chase career in a two-runner event at Kempton in November 2003; handles cut, but best on fast ground; stays two and a half miles and should get further; suited by forcing tactics.

Arctic Spirit
(102h)   (78h)103

9-y-o b g Arctic Lord-Dickies Girl (Saxon Farm)
R Dickin The Lordy Racing Partnership

Placings: 0P005/60246532/0001U1F561/2P031636-3   (4760)
2003/04: 16⁵S,

	Starts	1st	2nd	3rd	Win & Pl
Hurdles	1	0	0	1	778
Career Total	32	4	3	4	18799
103 1/03 Sthl 2m	F(0-105)HCh		G-S	£3374
103 4/02 Towc 2m110y	E(0-105)HCh		GD	£4202
96 12/01 Leic 2m	E(0-105)HCh		G-F	£3146
82 11/01 Wwck 2m110y	F(0-100)HCh		GD	£2562

Total win prize-money £13284

Going: Sf: 0-1 GS: 0-0 Gd: 0-0 GF: - Fm: 0-0
Distance: 2m/2m3: 0-1 2m4-2m7: 0-0 3m+: 0-0
Track: LH: 0-0 RH: 0-1 Tight: 0-0 Gall: 0-0
Aids: Bl: 0-0 Vi: 0-0 Tstrap: 0-0 Ckp: 0-0
Best Rating: 103 1/03 Sthl 2m   gd-sft Ch

An effective sort in modest handicap chases at around two miles; likes to dominate.

Arctic Times (IRE)

8-y-o ch g Montelimar (USA)-Miss Penguin (General Assembly (USA))
Eugene M O'Sullivan Trevor Hemmings

Placings: 40/0F40/212-51F   (4425)
2003/04: 24⁵GF, 24¹GF, 26⁴G,

	Starts	1st	2nd	3rd	Win & Pl
Chases	3	1	0	0	4032
Career Total	12	2	2	0	13716
103 5/03 Wxfd 3m	Ch		G-F	£4032
100 3/03 Limk 3m	Ch		YLD	£5152

Total win prize-money £9185

Going: Sf: 0-0 GS: 0-0 Gd: 0-1 GF: - Fm: 1-2
Distance: 2m/2m3: 0-0 2m4-2m7: 0-0 3m+: 1-3
Track: LH: 0-1 RH: 1-2 Tight: 0-0 Gall: 0-1
Aids: Bl: 0-0 Vi: 0-0 Tstrap: 0-0 Ckp: 0-0
Best Rating: 103 5/03 Wxfd 3m   gd-fm Ch

Point winner in Ireland; has shown fair form in hunter chases; runner-up to a smart Lord Atterbury at Aintree in April 2003; acts on most going, but has shown best form on quick ground; stays three miles.

Ardashir (FR)
110   128+

5-y-o b g Simon Du Desert (FR)-Antea (FR) (Esprit Du Nord (USA))
N A Twiston-Davies Miss Caroline Wilson

Placings: 0P-0202010   (4963)
2003/04: 20⁵G, 16²GS, 17⁰GS, 20⁴S, 24⁰G, 24¹GS, 20⁰G,

	Starts	1st	2nd	3rd	Win & Pl
Hurdles	7	1	2	0	8189
Career Total	9	1	2	0	8189
128 4/04 Bang 3m	D(0-120)HHdl		G-S	£5369

Total win prize-money £5369

Going: Sf: 0-1 GS: 1-3 Gd: 0-3 GF: - Fm: 0-0
Distance: 2m/2m3: 0-2 2m4-2m7: 0-3 3m+: 1-2
Track: LH: 1-3 RH: 0-4 Tight: 1-2 Gall: 0-1
Aids: Bl: 0-0 Vi: 0-0 Tstrap: 0-0 Ckp: 0-0
Best Rating: 128 4/04 Bang 3m   gd-sft Hdl

Modest handicap hurdler; improving; stays three miles; acts on soft ground.

Arden Hills (IRE)
89(104h)   (85h)65+

10-y-o b g Supreme Leader-Pisa (IRE) (Carlingford Castle)
J D Frost Christine And Aubrey Loze

Placings: RBP/0R614-62653004   (4737)
2003/04: 20⁶GF, 22²GF, 17⁶GF, 22⁵GF, 22³GS, 22⁰GF, 21⁰GS, 21⁴G,

	Starts	1st	2nd	3rd	Win & Pl
Hurdles	6	0	1	1	1225
Chases	2	0	0	0	
Career Total	16	1	1	1	3954
85 2/03 Chep 2m110y	G(0-90)HHdl		HVY	£2450

Total win prize-money £2450

Going: Sf: 0-0 GS: 0-2 Gd: 0-1 GF: - Fm: 0-5
Distance: 2m/2m3: 0-1 2m4-2m7: 0-7 3m+: 0-0
Track: LH: 0-8 RH: 0-0 Tight: 0-7 Gall: 0-0
Aids: Bl: 0-0 Vi: 0-0 Tstrap: 0-0 Ckp: 0-0
Best Rating: 85 6/03 NAbb 2m6f   gd-fm Hdl

Failed to complete on each of his four starts over fences, but won a selling hurdle at Chepstow in February 2003; suited by soft ground; seems to handle a faster surface but probably needs further than 2m on it.

Ardent Scout
112   145

12-y-o b g Ardross-Vidette (Billion (USA))
Mrs S J Smith Mrs Alicia Skene & W S Skene

Placings: 53³F013104B/1U31P32PP/32134/123PP/3403P50/1332120-4344000   (4871)
2003/04: 20⁴G, 27³G, 29⁴GS, 24⁴S, 33⁰G, 36⁰G, 24⁰S,

	Starts	1st	2nd	3rd	Win & Pl
Chases	7	0	0	1	15442
Career Total	50	8	5	12	143437
145 11/02 Aint	3m3f	B HCh	G-S	£37700
115 5/02 Uttx	3m	B HCh	GD	£11485
129 11/00 Ayr	3m1f	C(0-135)HCh	G-S	£6942
114 11/99 Bang	3m110y	C(0-130)HCh	HVY	£6087
133 12/98 Weth	3m1f	D Ch	SFT	£3756
115 11/98 Carl	2m4f110yD Ch		SFT	£3501
114 12/97 Weth	2m4f110yD(0-110)HHdl		SFT	£3304

96 11/97 Carl 2m4f110yE Hdl   GD £2500
Total win prize-money £75277

Going:	Sf: 0-2 GS: 0-1 Gd: 0-4 GF: - Fm: 0-0
Distance:	2m/2m3: 0-0 2m4-2m7: 0-1 3m+: 0-6
Track:	LH: 0-7 RH: 0-0 Tight: 0-3 Gall: 0-1
Aids:	Bl: 0-0 Vi: 0-0 Tstrap: 0-0 Ckp: 0-0
Best Rating:	145 11/02 Aint 3m3f gd-sft Ch

Useful staying chaser; a sound jumper and goes well under testing conditions; won the Becher Chase at Aintree in November 2002; suffered a leg injury in March 2003; stays extreme distances; acts on most ground, although better with cut.

Ardstown 115

13-y-o b m Ardross-Booterstown (Master Owen)
R F Knipe Mrs R F Knipe

Placings:232/113122/21/04P/6 (3463)
2003/04: 24⁶S,

	Starts	1st	2nd	3rd	Win & Pl
Chases	1	0	0	0	
Career Total	15	4	5	2	28723
131 3/01 Newb 3m	B(0-140)HCh			HVY	£10152
106 3/00 Leic	2m7f110yH Ch			G-S	£5018
111 2/00 Chep 3m	H Ch			SFT	£1785
94 5/99 Strf 3m	H Ch			GD	£2784

Total win prize-money £19741

Going:	Sf: 0-1 GS: 0-0 Gd: 0-0 GF: - Fm: 0-0
Distance:	2m/2m3: 0-0 2m4-2m7: 0-0 3m+: 0-1
Track:	LH: 0-1 RH: 0-0 Tight: 0-0 Gall: 0-0
Aids:	Bl: 0-0 Vi: 0-0 Tstrap: 0-0 Ckp: 0-0
Best Rating:	131 3/01 Newb 3m heavy Ch

Ardwelshin (FR) 96 76+

6-y-o b g Ajdayt (USA)-Reem Dubai (IRE) (Nashwan (USA))
C J Down (Mrs P Townsley 26/7) Ken Field

Placings:0P-0P3PP (4518)
2003/04: 17⁰G, 16ᴾG, 16³GS, 17ᴾG, 17ᴾGS,

	Starts	1st	2nd	3rd	Win & Pl
Hurdles	5	0	0	1	430
Career Total	7	0	0	1	430

Going:	Sf: 0-0 GS: 0-2 Gd: 0-3 GF: - Fm: 0-0
Distance:	2m/2m3: 0-5 2m4-2m7: 0-0 3m+: 0-0
Track:	LH: 0-1 RH: 0-4 Tight: 0-2 Gall: 0-0
Aids:	Bl: 0-1 Vi: 0-0 Tstrap: 0-0 Ckp: 0-0
Best Rating:	78 12/03 Strf 2m110y gd-sft Hdl

Argento 107(104h) (117h)120

7-y-o b g Weldnaas (USA)-Four M'S (Majestic Maharaj)
G M Moore J B Wallwin

Placings:654/32311222662-F313FU04 (4604)
2003/04: 16⁶G, 16³G, 16¹GF, 17³GS, 16⁵GS, 19ᵁG, 17⁰GS, 17⁴GS,

	Starts	1st	2nd	3rd	Win & Pl
Chases	8	1	0	2	5945
Career Total	22	3	5	4	19543
117 11/03 Catt 2m	E Ch			G-F	£4144
108 10/02 Sedg 2m1f	E Hdl			GD	£3307
97 10/02 Hexm 2m110y	E Hdl			G-F	£2877

Total win prize-money £10329

Going:	Sf: 0-0 GS: 0-4 Gd: 0-3 GF: - Fm: 1-1
Distance:	2m/2m3: 1-8 2m4-2m7: 0-0 3m+: 0-0
Track:	LH: 1-4 RH: 0-4 Tight: 1-5 Gall: 0-1
Aids:	Bl: 0-0 Vi: 0-0 Tstrap: 0-0 Ckp: 0-0
Best Rating:	120 12/03 Newc 2m110y gd-sft Ch

Fair novice chaser; left virtually alone when opening account over fences at Catterick in November; best over trips of around two miles; handles cut in the ground, but best on good or faster; goes well on undulating tracks.

Arijaz 102 86+

7-y-o b g Teenoso (USA)-Zajira (IRE) (Ela-Mana-Mou)
Mrs L B Normile (P R Webber 2/5) L B N Racing Club

Placings:6/4-00P13 (4312)
2003/04: 16⁰GS, 16⁹GF, 16ᴾGF, 20¹F, 24³GF,

	Starts	1st	2nd	3rd	Win & Pl
NH Flat	1	0	0	0	0
Hurdles	4	1	0	1	6321
Career Total	7	1	0	1	6595
86 2/04 Muss 2m4f	D Hdl			FRM	£5551

Total win prize-money £5551

Going:	Sf: 0-0 GS: 0-1 Gd: 0-0 GF: - Fm: 1-4
Distance:	2m/2m3: 0-3 2m4-2m7: 1-1 3m+: 0-1
Track:	LH: 0-2 RH: 1-3 Tight: 1-3 Gall: 0-0
Aids:	Bl: 0-0 Vi: 0-0 Tstrap: 0-0 Ckp: 0-0
Best Rating:	93 3/03 Plum 2m2f gd-fm NHF

Modest hurdler who won over two and a half miles at Musselburgh on fast ground in February and not totally disgraced on handicap debut at Ayr following month upped to three miles; may be capable of better and judging by his physique, he should do well over fences in due course.

Arimero (GER) 101 110

4-y-o b g Monsun (GER)-Averna (Heraldiste (USA))
C F Swan Robert Sinclair

Placings:4060 (4625)
2003/04: 16⁴S, 16⁰S, 16⁶G, 16⁰G,

	Starts	1st	2nd	3rd	Win & Pl
Hurdles	4	0	0	0	451
Career Total	4	0	0	0	451

Going:	Sf: 0-2 GS: 0-0 Gd: 0-2 GF: - Fm: 0-0
Distance:	2m/2m3: 0-4 2m4-2m7: 0-0 3m+: 0-0
Track:	LH: 0-3 RH: 0-0 Tight: 0-1 Gall: 0-0
Aids:	Bl: 0-0 Vi: 0-0 Tstrap: 0-0 Ckp: 0-0
Best Rating:	110 4/04 Aint 2m110y good Hdl

Modest Irish-trained novice hurdler; formerly trained in Germany; yet to win over hurdles.

Aristoxene (FR) 99 98+

4-y-o b g Start Fast (FR)-Petite Folie (Salmon Leap (USA))
G Macaire R P C Hoad

Placings:123 (3603)
2003/04: 16¹GS, 16²GS, 16³S,

	Starts	1st	2nd	3rd	Win & Pl
Hurdles	3	1	1	1	10652
Career Total	3	1	1	1	10652
11/03 Fntb 2m	Hdl			G-S	£5195

Total win prize-money £5195

Going:	Sf: 0-1 GS: 1-2 Gd: 0-0 GF: - Fm: 0-0
Distance:	2m/2m3: 1-3 2m4-2m7: 0-0 3m+: 0-0
Track:	LH: 0-2 RH: 0-0 Tight: 0-0 Gall: 0-1
Aids:	Bl: 0-0 Vi: 0-0 Tstrap: 0-0 Ckp: 0-0
Best Rating:	98 1/04 Donc 2m110y soft Hdl

French-trained hurdler; suited by two miles; effective with cut in the ground.

Arjay

6-y-o b g Shaamit (IRE)-Jenny's Call (Petong)
Andrew Turnell Dr John Holliowood

Placings:P (2154)
2003/04: 16ᴾGS,

	Starts	1st	2nd	3rd	Win & Pl
Hurdles	1	0	0	0	
Career Total	1	0	0	0	

Going:	Sf: 0-0 GS: 0-1 Gd: 0-0 GF: - Fm: 0-0
Distance:	2m/2m3: 0-1 2m4-2m7: 0-0 3m+: 0-0
Track:	LH: 0-1 RH: 0-0 Tight: 0-0 Gall: 0-0
Aids:	Bl: 0-0 Vi: 0-0 Tstrap: 0-0 Ckp: 0-0
Best Rating:	0 11/03 Uttx 2m gd-sft Hdl

Arjaypear (IRE) 93 85

5-y-o b g Petardia-Lila Pedigo (IRE) (Classic Secret (USA))
A King T R Pearson

Placings:P50-U2220 (1333)
2003/04: 16ᵁGF, 16²G, 16²GF, 20²GF, 19⁹GF,

	Starts	1st	2nd	3rd	Win & Pl
Hurdles	5	0	3	0	2838
Career Total	8	0	3	0	2838

Showed improved form when staying on 50/1 second in modest 2m novice hurdle at Worcester July 2003; runner-up in similar event at the same course next time; may appreciated a longer trip.

Ark Admiral 101 94+

5-y-o b g Inchinor-Kelimutu (Top Ville)
P F Nicholls (B J Meehan 28/7) Miss A L Mayo

Placings:33 (4893)
2003/04: 17³G, 16³G,

	Starts	1st	2nd	3rd	Win & Pl
Hurdles	2	0	0	2	1081
Career Total	2	0	0	2	1081

Going:	Sf: 0-0 GS: 0-0 Gd: 0-2 GF: - Fm: 0-0
Distance:	2m/2m3: 0-2 2m4-2m7: 0-0 3m+: 0-0
Track:	LH: 0-0 RH: 0-2 Tight: 0-0 Gall: 0-0
Aids:	Bl: 0-0 Vi: 0-0 Tstrap: 0-2 Ckp: 0-0
Best Rating:	94 4/04 Tntn 2m1f good Hdl

Arlas (FR) 100 105

9-y-o b g Northern Fashion (USA)-Ribbon In Her Hair (USA) (Sauce Boat (USA))

M C Pipe Matt Archer & Miss Jean Broadhurst

Placings:2P316462/51F12424/P1U0P/1211124/P66P
                    (4694)
2003/04: 26^{P}GS, 25^{R}G, 24^{R}G, 23^{P}G,

		Starts	1st	2nd	3rd	Win & Pl
Chases		4	0	0	0	0
Career Total		32	8	6	1	121922
147	9/01	Worc	2m7f110yC(0-135)HCh		G-F	£6864
143	8/01	Worc	2m7f110yC(0-130)HCh		G-F	£6745
142	7/01	NAbb	3m2f110yC(0-135)HCh		G-F	£5846
123	5/01	Hrfd	2m3f110yG Hdl		GD	£2044
127	11/00	NAbb	2m6f	C(0-130)HHdl	HVY	£6743
119	1/00	Font	2m6f	D Ch	GD	£3906
	5/99	Autl	2m5f110y Ch		HLD	£53821
	12/98	Cagn	2m1f110y Hdl		GD	£6061

Total win prize-money £92034

Going:	Sf: 0-0 GS: 0-1 Gd: 0-3 GF: - Fm: 0-0
Distance:	2m/2m3: 0-0 2m4-2m7: 0-0 3m+: 0-4
Track:	LH: 0-2 RH: 0-2 Tight: 0-1 Gall: 0-2
Aids:	Bl: 0-0 Vi: 0-1 Tstrap: 0-1 Ckp: 0-2
Best Rating:	147 10/01 Chep 3m good Ch

Very useful chaser/hurdler back in 2001, but off the track for two years prior to pulling up in the 2003 Hennessy; has not recaptured his best since; suited by trips of around three miles, he has won on heavy ground over hurdles, but is especially well suited by faster conditions; has worn blinkers.

Arlequin De Sou (FR)

10-y-o b g Sir Brink (FR)-Colombine (USA) (Empery (USA))
Miss Polly Curling Mrs Karola Vann

Placings:1141356/2112P5/1321433F/002/1F206-6 (4002)
2003/04: 20^{R}G,

		Starts	1st	2nd	3rd	Win & Pl
Chases		1	0	0	0	0
Career Total		30	8	5	4	63043
131	10/02	Hayd	2m6f	D(0-125)HCh	GD	£5206
137	12/00	Chel	2m5f	E(0-125)HCh	SFT	£7247
121	11/00	Winc	2m6f	E(0-115)HHdl	G-S	£4426
116	2/00	Font	2m6f110yD(0-125)HHdl		G-S	£5499
105	2/00	Chep	2m4f	D(0-115)HHdl	SFT	£3087
	12/98	Autl	2m1f110y Ch		HVY	£6566
	11/98	Engh	2m2f	Ch	VS	£6566
	10/98	Autl	2m4f110y Ch		HLD	£6566

Total win prize-money £45167

Going:	Sf: 0-0 GS: 0-0 Gd: 0-1 GF: - Fm: 0-0
Distance:	2m/2m3: 0-0 2m4-2m7: 0-1 3m+: 0-0
Track:	LH: 0-0 RH: 0-1 Tight: 0-1 Gall: 0-0
Aids:	Bl: 0-1 Vi: 0-0 Tstrap: 0-0 Ckp: 0-0
Best Rating:	137 12/00 Chel 2m5f soft Ch

Useful chaser; best when bullying the opposition from the front; wears blinkers; suited by trips of around two and a half miles on easy and good ground.

Armagh South (IRE)
86   83

5-y-o ch g Topanoora-Mogen (Adonijah)
J Howard Johnson M McKernan

Placings:0600   (4595)
2003/04: 16°G, 20^{R}G, 20°S, 22^{R}G,

	Starts	1st	2nd	3rd	Win & Pl
NH Flat	1	0	0	0	0
Hurdles	3	0	0	0	0
Career Total	4	0	0	0	0

Going: Sf: 0-1 GS: 0-0 Gd: 0-3 GF: - Fm: 0-0
Distance: 2m/2m3: 0-1 2m4-2m7: 0-3 3m+: 0-0
Track: LH: 0-2 RH: 0-2 Tight: 0-2 Gall: 0-1
Aids: Bl: 0-0 Vi: 0-0 Tstrap: 0-0 Ckp: 0-0
Best Rating: 83   2/04   Carl   2m4f   good   Hdl

Armaguedon (FR)
95   124+

6-y-o b g Garde Royale-Miss Dundee (FR) (Esprit Du Nord (USA))
L Lungo Ashleybank Investments Limited

Placings:3/1130-21   (4292)
2003/04: 19^{Q}GS, 16^{T}GF,

		Starts	1st	2nd	3rd	Win & Pl
Hurdles		2	1	1	0	4261
Career Total		7	3	1	2	11843
124	3/04	Ayr	2m	F Hdl	G-F	£3262
127	12/02	Ayr	1m6f	H NHF	G-S	£2618
125	11/02	Newc	1m6f	H NHF	G-S	£2646

Total win prize-money £8526

Going:	Sf: 0-0 GS: 0-1 Gd: 0-0 GF: - Fm: 1-1
Distance:	2m/2m3: 1-2 2m4-2m7: 0-0 3m+: 0-0
Track:	LH: 1-2 RH: 0-0 Tight: 0-1 Gall: 0-0
Aids:	Bl: 0-0 Vi: 0-0 Tstrap: 0-0 Ckp: 0-0
Best Rating:	127 12/02 Ayr 1m6f gd-sft NHF

Fair novice hurdler; decent in bumpers; may not stay much beyond two miles over hurdles; still has scope.

Armaturk (FR)
116   (151h)157

7-y-o g g Baby Turk-Armalita (FR) (Goodland (FR))
P F Nicholls B C Marshall

Placings:332111/3121131/342100-56412624 (4864)
2003/04: 24^{S}GF, 20^{Q}GS, 21^{4}G, 16^{1}S, 17^{Q}G, 16^{Q}G, 16^{2}G, 16^{4}S,

		Starts	1st	2nd	3rd	Win & Pl
Hurdles		1	0	0	0	383
Chases		7	1	2	0	44582
Career Total		27	9	5	5	187848
156	1/04	Donc	2m110y	B(0-140)HCh	SFT	£13639
144	2/03	Winc	2m5f	B Ch	G-S	£11979
157	4/02	Aint	2m	A Ch	GD	£46500
142	2/02	Wwck	2m110y	A Ch	SFT	£18000
139	12/01	Newb	2m2f110yD Ch		GD	£5905
151	10/01	Kemp	2m	B Hdl	G-S	£6890
130	4/01	Kemp	2m	D Hdl	GD	£3939
128	4/01	Plum	2m	E Hdl	HVY	£2513
	1/01	Pau	2m110y	Hdl	SFT	£6305

Total win prize-money £115672

Going:	Sf: 1-2 GS: 0-1 Gd: 0-4 GF: - Fm: 0-1
Distance:	2m/2m3: 1-5 2m4-2m7: 0-2 3m+: 0-0
Track:	LH: 1-8 RH: 0-0 Tight: 0-1 Gall: 1-4
Aids:	Bl: 0-0 Vi: 0-0 Tstrap: 1-7 Ckp: 0-0
Best Rating:	157 4/04 Aint 2m good Ch

Very useful chaser; likes to front run; has worn a tongue tie; effective at two miles but stays two miles five; versatile regarding ground.

Armen (FR)
90(104h)   (135h)105+

7-y-o b g Kaldoun (FR)-Anna Edes (FR) (Fabulous Dancer (USA))
M C Pipe T M Hely-Hutchinson

Placings:132/032PF   (4631)
2003/04: 17^{Q}G, 24^{3}G, 19^{2}G, 19^{P}GS, 19^{F}G,

	Starts	1st	2nd	3rd	Win & Pl
Hurdles	1	0	0	0	0
Chases	4	0	1	1	2530
Career Total	8	1	2	2	16820
135 2/01 Plum	2m	E Hdl		SFT	£2075

Total win prize-money £2076

Going: Sf: 0-0 GS: 0-1 Gd: 0-4 GF: - Fm: 0-0
Distance: 2m/2m3: 0-3 2m4-2m7: 0-1 3m+: 0-1
Track: LH: 0-3 RH: 0-2 Tight: 0-1 Gall: 0-2
Aids: Bl: 0-0 Vi: 0-1 Tstrap: 0-0 Ckp: 0-0
Best Rating: 135 4/01 Aint 2m110y   soft   Hdl

Showed useful form as a juvenile hurdler in 2000/1; missed the next two seasons; probably stays 3m; acts well in soft ground.

Arms Acrossthesea
70   86

5-y-o b g Namaqualand (USA)-Zolica (Beveled (USA))
F P Murtagh J Clayton

Placings:F54P45-0   (0428)
2003/04: 17^{Q}G,

	Starts	1st	2nd	3rd	Win & Pl
Hurdles	1	0	0	0	0
Career Total	7	0	0	0	271

Going: Sf: 0-0 GS: 0-0 Gd: 0-1 GF: - Fm: 0-0
Distance: 2m/2m3: 0-1 2m4-2m7: 0-0 3m+: 0-0
Track: LH: 0-1 RH: 0-0 Tight: 0-1 Gall: 0-0
Aids: Bl: 0-0 Vi: 0-0 Tstrap: 0-0 Ckp: 0-0
Best Rating: 86 11/02 Catt 2m   good   Hdl

Yet to prove he stays two miles over hurdles.

Aroseforclare
87   31

8-y-o b m Royal Vulcan-Lovelyroseofclare (Torus)
Miss K M George Kevin David Kerslake

Placings:06/000/0PU-0P5   (0805)
2003/04: 21^{Q}G, 22^{P}GF, 26^{S}G,

	Starts	1st	2nd	3rd	Win & Pl
Hurdles	3	0	0	0	0
Career Total	11	0	0	0	0

Going: Sf: 0-0 GS: 0-0 Gd: 0-2 GF: - Fm: 0-1
Distance: 2m/2m3: 0-0 2m4-2m7: 0-2 3m+: 0-1
Track: LH: 0-2 RH: 0-1 Tight: 0-1 Gall: 0-0
Aids: Bl: 0-0 Vi: 0-0 Tstrap: 0-0 Ckp: 0-0
Best Rating: 62 5/01 Extr 2m1f   firm   NHF

Poor hurdler; shown little so far.

Around Before (IRE)
107(101h)   (103+h)118

7-y-o ch g Be My Native (USA)-Glynn Cross (IRE) (Mister Lord (USA))
Jonjo O'Neill (E Bolger 29/6) John P McManus

Placings:54U-6F40211211   (1677)
2003/04: 25^{R}YS, 24^{F}Y, 20^{4}GF, 24^{Q}GF, 26^{2}GF, 24^{1}GF, 26^{1}GF, 24^{2}GF, 26^{1}GF, 24^{1}F,

		Starts	1st	2nd	3rd	Win & Pl
Hurdles		5	2	1	0	7442
Chases		5	2	1	0	10870
Career Total		13	4	2	0	18623
108	10/03	Towc	3m	E(0-110)HHdl	FRM	£3346
99	10/03	Hntg	3m2f	E(0-110)HHdl	G-F	£2695
114	8/03	Font	3m2f110yE(0-105)HCh		G-F	£4953

105 8/03 Uttx 3m   E(0-110)HCh G-F £5031
Total win prize-money £16025

Going:	Sf: 0-0 GS: 0-0 Gd: 0-0 GF: - Fm: 4-8
Distance:	2m/2m3: 0-0 2m4-2m7: 0-1 3m+: 4-9
Track:	LH: 1-5 RH: 2-4 Tight: 1-1 Gall: 1-2
Aids:	Bl: 0-0 Vi: 0-0 Tstrap: 4-6 Ckp: 0-0
Best Rating:	118 9/03 Hntg 3m gd-fm Ch

Moderate chaser; progressing nicely with present connections after disappointing as a pointer for Enda Bolger in Ireland; won back-to-back staying handicaps when reverting to hurdles in October 2003; stays three miles two; acts on a sound surface.

Arribilo (GER)

92   (90c)**91**

10-y-o b g Top Ville-Arborea (GER) (Priamos (GER))
B P J Baugh I J Hooper

Placings:0/P62P045/265PF031-0   (0057)
2003/04: 17⁹GS,

	Starts	1st	2nd	3rd	Win & Pl
Hurdles	1	0	0	0	
Career Total	17	1	2	1	4557
91 4/03 Hntg 2m110y G(0-90)HHdl G-F £2413					
			Total win prize-money £2414		

Going:	Sf: 0-0 GS: 0-1 Gd: 0-0 GF: - Fm: 0-0
Distance:	2m/2m3: 0-1 2m4-2m7: 0-0 3m+: 0-0
Track:	LH: 0-0 RH: 0-1 Tight: 0-0 Gall: 0-0
Aids:	Bl: 0-0 Vi: 0-0 Tstrap: 0-0 Ckp: 0-0
Best Rating:	91 4/03 Hntg 2m110y gd-fm Hdl

Modest form over hurdles, including claimers; took a selling handicap hurdle on fast ground at Huntingdon in April 2003; best over two miles.

Art Expert (FR)

6-y-o b g Pursuit Of Love-Celtic Wing (Midyan (USA))
Mrs N Macauley Classic Glass & Dishwashing Systems Ltd

Placings:P0-PP   (0806)
2003/04: 23⁹G, 26ᴾG,

	Starts	1st	2nd	3rd	Win & Pl
Hurdles	2	0	0	0	
Career Total	4	0	0	0	

Going:	Sf: 0-0 GS: 0-0 Gd: 0-2 GF: - Fm: 0-0
Distance:	2m/2m3: 0-0 2m4-2m7: 0-1 3m+: 0-1
Track:	LH: 0-2 RH: 0-0 Tight: 0-0 Gall: 0-0
Aids:	Bl: 0-0 Vi: 0-0 Tstrap: 0-0 Ckp: 0-1
Best Rating:	73 3/03 Hntg 2m110y gd-fm Hdl

Arte Et Labore (IRE)

76   **28**

4-y-o b f Raphane (USA)-Bouffant (High Top)
K A Ryan John W Howarth

Placings:00   (2302)
2003/04: 16⁹G, 16⁹GF,

	Starts	1st	2nd	3rd	Win & Pl
Hurdles	2	0	0	0	
Career Total	2	0	0	0	

Going:	Sf: 0-0 GS: 0-0 Gd: 0-1 GF: - Fm: 0-1
Distance:	2m/2m3: 0-2 2m4-2m7: 0-0 3m+: 0-0
Track:	LH: 0-2 RH: 0-0 Tight: 0-1 Gall: 0-1

Aids: Bl: 0-0 Vi: 0-0 Tstrap: 0-0 Ckp: 0-0
Best Rating: 28 11/03 Catt 2m   gd-fm Hdl

Artemesia

101(103c)   (97c)**101**

9-y-o b m Teenoso (USA)-Annicombe Run (Deep Run)
Ferdy Murphy Beautifully Bred Partnership

Placings:3/024/03U6R4/2120001-142440   (2929)
2003/04: 20¹GF, 22⁴GS, 20²GF, 21⁴GF, 21⁴GF, 21⁰G,

	Starts	1st	2nd	3rd	Win & Pl
Hurdles	4	1	0	0	3520
Chases	2	0	1	0	1505
Career Total	23	3	4	2	13916
101 5/03 Fknm 2m4f F(0-95)HHdl G-F £2757					
95 4/03 Fknm 2m4f E(0-105)HHdl G-F £3423					
91 5/02 Fknm 2m7f110yE(0-100)HHdl G-S £2996					
			Total win prize-money £9176		

Going:	Sf: 0-0 GS: 0-1 Gd: 0-1 GF: - Fm: 1-4
Distance:	2m/2m3: 0-0 2m4-2m7: 1-6 3m+: 0-0
Track:	LH: 1-6 RH: 0-0 Tight: 1-5 Gall: 0-0
Aids:	Bl: 0-0 Vi: 0-0 Tstrap: 0-0 Ckp: 0-0
Best Rating:	102 1/01 Fknm 2m soft NHF

Plating-class handicap hurdler; good second on her first try over fences at Hexham in June; stays three miles and acts on a good or slightly softer surface; goes well at Fakenham; game.

Artemise (FR)

106   **103+**

6-y-o b m Cyborg (FR)-Articule (FR) (Art Francais (USA))
A King J A H West

Placings:00P2P-20105   (4339)
2003/04: 17²G, 19⁰GS, 16¹G, 16⁹S, 16⁵G,

	Starts	1st	2nd	3rd	Win & Pl
Hurdles	5	1	1	0	3560
Career Total	10	1	2	0	4423
103 12/03 Winc 2m F(0-95)HHdl GD £2492					
			Total win prize-money £2492		

Going:	Sf: 0-1 GS: 0-1 Gd: 1-3 GF: - Fm: 0-0
Distance:	2m/2m3: 1-5 2m4-2m7: 0-0 3m+: 0-0
Track:	LH: 0-2 RH: 1-3 Tight: 0-0 Gall: 0-0
Aids:	Bl: 0-0 Vi: 0-0 Tstrap: 0-0 Ckp: 0-0
Best Rating:	103 12/03 Winc 2m good Hdl

Modest novice hurdler; runner-up in mares' only race at Southwell in November and scored at Wincanton the following month; suited by good ground.

Arthur Daly (IRE)

95   (89h)**110+**

7-y-o b g Lord Americo-Time Talker (IRE) (Stalker)
Denis P Murphy Colm Hearne

Placings:000/023-0332BF34035   (4837)
2003/04: 20⁰G, 20³YS, 19³GF, 24²S, 24⁸F, 22ᶠGF, 20³G, 28⁴G, 24⁰GY, 20³S, 25⁶GF,

	Starts	1st	2nd	3rd	Win & Pl
Hurdles	3	0	1	1	1919
Chases	8	0	0	3	3510
Career Total	17	0	2	5	6785

Going:	Sf: 0-2 GS: 0-1 Gd: 0-3 GF: - Fm: 0-4
Distance:	2m/2m3: 0-1 2m4-2m7: 0-5 3m+: 0-5
Track:	LH: 0-1 RH: 0-3 Tight: 0-0 Gall: 0-1
Aids:	Bl: 0-0 Vi: 0-0 Tstrap: 0-0 Ckp: 0-0
Best Rating:	110 4/04 Chel 3m1f110y gd-fm Ch

Arthur Pendragon

4-y-o b g Botanic (USA)-Blue Room (Gorytus (USA))
Jonjo O'Neill G J Hicks

Placings:P   (3511)
2003/04: 18ᴾG,

	Starts	1st	2nd	3rd	Win & Pl
Hurdles	1	0	0	0	
Career Total	1	0	0	0	

Going:	Sf: 0-0 GS: 0-0 Gd: 0-1 GF: - Fm: 0-0
Distance:	2m/2m3: 0-1 2m4-2m7: 0-0 3m+: 0-0
Track:	LH: 0-1 RH: 0-0 Tight: 0-1 Gall: 0-0
Aids:	Bl: 0-0 Vi: 0-0 Tstrap: 0-0 Ckp: 0-0
Best Rating:	0 1/04 Font 2m2f110y good Hdl

Arthurs Kingdom (IRE)

90(99h)   (79 h)**88+**

8-y-o b g Roi Danzig (USA)-Merrie Moment (IRE) (Taufan (USA))
Miss Kate Milligan Dr Roy Palmer

Placings:603450/05325105P/P2053310-U2U4P50 (4794)
2003/04: 27ᵁG, 27²GF, 25ᵁS, 27⁴GS, 27ᴾG, 25⁵S, 21⁰G,

	Starts	1st	2nd	3rd	Win & Pl
Hurdles	2	0	0	0	0
Chases	5	0	1	0	1086
Career Total	30	2	3	4	9123
79 3/03 Sedg 3m3f110yG(0-90)HHdl SFT £2443					
79 8/01 Ctml 2m6f G(0-90)HHdl G-S £2772					
			Total win prize-money £5215		

Going:	Sf: 0-2 GS: 0-1 Gd: 0-3 GF: - Fm: 0-1
Distance:	2m/2m3: 0-0 2m4-2m7: 0-1 3m+: 0-6
Track:	LH: 0-7 RH: 0-0 Tight: 0-5 Gall: 0-0
Aids:	Bl: 0-0 Vi: 0-0 Tstrap: 0-0 Ckp: 0-4
Best Rating:	90 9/00 Sedg 2m1f soft Hdl

Plating-class staying hurdler/chaser, stays marathon trips; seems to handle any ground; has worn cheekpieces.

Artic Jack (FR)

112   **158**

8-y-o b g Cadoudal (FR)-Si Jamais (FR) (Arctic Tern (USA))
Mrs S J Smith Trevor Hemmings

Placings:2/616/2F114PU3/1313FP   (4805a)
2003/04: 28¹S, 25³GS, 24¹G, 28³G, 28ᶠG, 29ᴾY,

	Starts	1st	2nd	3rd	Win & Pl
Chases	6	2	0	2	60785
Career Total	18	5	2	3	91820
155 1/04 Hayd 3m A HCh GD £37200					
155 11/03 Hayd 3m4f110yC(0-135)HCh SFT £7085					
140 1/02 Asct 3m110y B Ch GD £9035					
111 12/01 Folk 2m5f D Ch GD £4459					
126 1/01 Hayd 2m D Hdl SFT £3612					
			Total win prize-money £61391		

Going:	Sf: 1-1 GS: 0-1 Gd: 1-3 GF: - Fm: 0-0
Distance:	2m/2m3: 0-0 2m4-2m7: 0-0 3m+: 2-5
Track:	LH: 2-5 RH: 0-1 Tight: 0-1 Gall: 0-0
Aids:	Bl: 0-0 Vi: 0-0 Tstrap: 0-0 Ckp: 0-0
Best Rating:	155 1/04 Hayd 3m good Ch

Smart handicap chaser; jumped well when decisive winner on return to action for new stable at Haydock in November 2003; held next time in desperate conditions, but bounced back to beat Kingscliff in the Peter Marsh Chase in January

back at Haydock; has won on soft and good ground; stays three and a half miles; front runner.

Artic Reason (IRE)
105   **84**
5-y-o b g Perugino (USA)-Vendetta Valentino (USA) (Bering)
E McNamara Mrs K L Jarvey

Placings:050-3O0400   (4943a)
2003/04: 16²S, 18ᵁGF, 16⁰G, 16⁴S, 19⁰S, 16⁰SH,

	Starts	1st	2nd	3rd	Win & Pl
Hurdles	6	0	0	1	782
Career Total	9	0	0	1	782

Going:	Sf: 0-3 GS: 0-0 Gd: 0-1 GF: - Fm: 0-1
Distance:	2m/2m3: 0-6 2m4-2m7: 0-0 3m+: 0-0
Track:	LH: 0-3 RH: 0-0 Tight: 0-0 Gall: 0-0
Aids:	Bl: 0-1 Vi: 0-0 Tstrap: 0-0 Ckp: 0-0
Best Rating:	97 12/02 Fair 2m soft Hdl

Plating-class Irish-trained hurdler; still a maiden; ran out fifth start.

Aruba Dam (IRE)
77   **72**
6-y-o br m Be My Native (USA)-Arumah (Arapaho)
P F Nicholls Mrs Kathy Stuart

Placings:0-33   (2013)
2003/04: 16³GF, 16³GF,

	Starts	1st	2nd	3rd	Win & Pl
NH Flat	1	0	0	1	279
Hurdles	1	0	0	1	420
Career Total	3	0	0	2	699

Going:	Sf: 0-0 GS: 0-0 Gd: 0-0 GF: - Fm: 0-2
Distance:	2m/2m3: 0-2 2m4-2m7: 0-0 3m+: 0-0
Track:	LH: 0-1 RH: 0-1 Tight: 0-0 Gall: 0-0
Aids:	Bl: 0-0 Vi: 0-0 Tstrap: 0-0 Ckp: 0-0
Best Rating:	75 11/03 Winc 2m gd-fm Hdl

Third in poor Chepstow bumper second start.

Arzillo
93   **87**
8-y-o b g Forzando-Titania's Dance (IRE) (Fairy King (USA))
J M Bradley Miss D Guilding

Placings:FUP543   (1309)
2003/04: 16ᶠGF, 16ᵁGF, 17ᴾG, 16⁵G, 16⁴GF, 16³GF,

	Starts	1st	2nd	3rd	Win & Pl
Hurdles	6	0	0	1	339
Career Total	6	0	0	1	339

Going:	Sf: 0-0 GS: 0-0 Gd: 0-2 GF: - Fm: 0-4
Distance:	2m/2m3: 0-6 2m4-2m7: 0-0 3m+: 0-0
Track:	LH: 0-6 RH: 0-0 Tight: 0-0 Gall: 0-0
Aids:	Bl: 0-0 Vi: 0-0 Tstrap: 0-0 Ckp: 0-3
Best Rating:	87 8/03 Worc 2m gd-fm Hdl

Better effort when fourth at Worcester August 2003; probably going to struggle to stay 2m over hurdles.

Asador (FR)
(104c)   (141c) **90+**
8-y-o ch g Kadounor (FR)-Apos (FR) (Baillamont (USA))
A G Juckes (P F Nicholls 2/12) Dennis Skinner

Placings:1110/**1F1P/1FF**0-FP   (4120)
2003/04: 17ᶠGS, 17ᴾG,

	Starts	1st	2nd	3rd	Win & Pl
Hurdles	2	0	0	0	
Career Total	14	6	0	0	39006

137	11/02	Chep	2m3f110yC(0-130)HCh	HVY	£7345
130	2/02	Plum	2m1f E Ch	HVY	£3360
130	12/01	NAbb	2m110y D Ch	HVY	£3740
	2/00	Ange	2m1f110y Hdl	VS	£10567
	1/00	Pau	2m2f Hdl	VS	£7535
	12/99	Pau	2m110y Hdl	HVY	£6459
			Total win prize-money £39006		

Going:	Sf: 0-0 GS: 0-1 Gd: 0-1 GF: - Fm: 0-0
Distance:	2m/2m3: 0-2 2m4-2m7: 0-0 3m+: 0-0
Track:	LH: 0-0 RH: 0-2 Tight: 0-1 Gall: 0-0
Aids:	Bl: 0-0 Vi: 0-0 Tstrap: 0-0 Ckp: 0-0
Best Rating:	141 1/03 Chep 2m110y heavy Ch

One time useful chaser/hurdler; still in the lead but tiring when falling at the last in 2m 1f selling hurdle at Hereford December 2003; subsequently claimed for £5,000; effective at 2m to 2m 4f; suited by a left-handed track; well suited by soft ground; not a good jumper of fences.

Ascari
79   **83**
8-y-o br g Presidium-Ping Pong (Petong)
A L Forbes Ernie Jackson

Placings:0P4/6/F/20PP6   (2415)
2003/04: 17²GF, 16⁹G, 17ᴾGF, 26ᴾG, 16⁶GS,

	Starts	1st	2nd	3rd	Win & Pl
Hurdles	5	0	1	0	1010
Career Total	10	0	1	0	1010

Going:	Sf: 0-0 GS: 0-1 Gd: 0-2 GF: - Fm: 0-2
Distance:	2m/2m3: 0-4 2m4-2m7: 0-0 3m+: 0-1
Track:	LH: 0-4 RH: 0-1 Tight: 0-2 Gall: 0-0
Aids:	Bl: 0-0 Vi: 0-0 Tstrap: 0-0 Ckp: 0-0
Best Rating:	83 5/03 Sthl 2m1f gd-fm Hdl

Ascoolasice
6-y-o b g Thethingaboutitis (USA)-Frozen Pipe (Majestic Maharaj)
Miss L J Brewer Alan Brewer

Placings:P   (3785)
2003/04: 24ᴾS,

	Starts	1st	2nd	3rd	Win & Pl
Chases	1	0	0	0	
Career Total	1	0	0	0	

Going:	Sf: 0-1 GS: 0-0 Gd: 0-0 GF: - Fm: 0-0
Distance:	2m/2m3: 0-0 2m4-2m7: 0-0 3m+: 0-0
Track:	LH: 0-0 RH: 0-1 Tight: 0-0 Gall: 0-1
Aids:	Bl: 0-0 Vi: 0-0 Tstrap: 0-0 Ckp: 0-0
Best Rating:	0 2/04 Hntg 3m soft Ch

Ashfield Jake (IRE)
12-y-o br g Jolly Jake (NZ)-Ashfield Rose (Mon Capitaine)
S T Lewis Simon T Lewis

Placings:0U00P/PP-PP   (0613)
2003/04: 16ᴾG, 25ᴾGF,

	Starts	1st	2nd	3rd	Win & Pl
Chases	2	0	0	0	

Career Total	9	0	0	0

Going:	Sf: 0-0 GS: 0-0 Gd: 0-1 GF: - Fm: 0-1
Distance:	2m/2m3: 0-1 2m4-2m7: 0-0 3m+: 0-1
Track:	LH: 0-1 RH: 0-1 Tight: 0-0 Gall: 0-1
Aids:	Bl: 0-0 Vi: 0-0 Tstrap: 0-0 Ckp: 0-0

Ashgar (USA)
111 (103c)   (98c)**95**
8-y-o ch g Bien Bien (USA)-Ardisia (USA) (Affirmed (USA))
M D Hammond Jay Dee Bloodstock Limited

Placings:2/1124023/**314F2P**2261P5P-22305   (4796)
2003/04: 26²GS, 21²F, 16³G, 27⁰GS, 21⁵G,

	Starts	1st	2nd	3rd	Win & Pl
Hurdles	5	0	2	1	1565
Career Total	26	4	8	3	24448

107	11/02	Weth	2m7f G Hdl	HVY	£2215
93	5/02	Uttx	3m2f E Ch	GD	£3391
109	11/01	Ludl	2m5f E Hdl	G-F	£2803
109	11/01	Ludl	2m5f E Hdl	G-F	£2712
			Total win prize-money £11125		

Going:	Sf: 0-0 GS: 0-2 Gd: 0-2 GF: - Fm: 0-1
Distance:	2m/2m3: 0-1 2m4-2m7: 0-2 3m+: 0-2
Track:	LH: 0-3 RH: 0-2 Tight: 0-2 Gall: 0-0
Aids:	Bl: 0-4 Vi: 0-0 Tstrap: 0-0 Ckp: 0-0
Best Rating:	122 4/02 Chel 3m gd-fm Hdl

Plating-class hurdler; stays well; acts on fast ground; recently suffered breathing problems.

Ashgreen
7-y-o b g Afzal-Space Kate (Space King)
S Turner S Turner

Placings:FP50P/0   (0028)
2003/04: 21⁰G,

	Starts	1st	2nd	3rd	Win & Pl
Chases	1	0	0	0	
Career Total	6	0	0	0	0

Going:	Sf: 0-0 GS: 0-0 Gd: 0-1 GF: - Fm: 0-0
Distance:	2m/2m3: 0-0 2m4-2m7: 0-1 3m+: 0-0
Track:	LH: 0-1 RH: 0-0 Tight: 0-0 Gall: 0-1
Aids:	Bl: 0-0 Vi: 0-0 Tstrap: 0-0 Ckp: 0-0
Best Rating:	85 4/03 Chel 2m5f good Ch

Ashley Brook (IRE)
106   **123+**
6-y-o ch g Magical Wonder (USA)-Seamill (IRE) (Lafontaine (USA))
K Bishop Mrs E K Ellis

Placings:23410-12135   (4833)
2003/04: 17¹G, 17²G, 19¹G, 19³GS, 21⁵GF,

	Starts	1st	2nd	3rd	Win & Pl
Hurdles	5	2	1	1	10278
Career Total	10	3	2	2	11321

123	12/03	Tntn	2m3f110yE Hdl	GD	£2744
112	11/03	Extr	2m1f D Hdl	GD	£4056
			Total win prize-money £6800		

Going:	Sf: 0-0 GS: 0-1 Gd: 2-3 GF: - Fm: 0-1
Distance:	2m/2m3: 1-2 2m4-2m7: 1-3 3m+: 0-0
Track:	LH: 0-1 RH: 2-4 Tight: 1-3 Gall: 0-1
Aids:	Bl: 0-0 Vi: 0-0 Tstrap: 0-0 Ckp: 0-0

Best Rating: 123 12/03 Tntn 2m3f110y good Hdl

Fair novice hurdler; free running sort; stays two miles-three; acts on good and soft ground; progressive.

Ashley Marsh
77   45
6-y-o b g Alflora (IRE)-Annapurna (Rakaposhi King)
T R George M J Hoskins

Placings:P000P					(4697)
2003/04: 19⁰GS, 19⁰S, 19⁰GS, 22⁰GS, 17ᴾG,					

	Starts	1st	2nd	3rd	Win & Pl
Hurdles	5	0	0	0	
Career Total	5	0	0	0	

Going:	Sf: 0-1 GS: 0-3 Gd: 0-1 GF: - Fm: 0-0
Distance:	2m/2m3: 0-2 2m4-2m7: 0-3 3m+: 0-0
Track:	LH: 0-4 RH: 0-5 Tight: 0-1 Gall: 0-0
Aids:	Bl: 0-0 Vi: 0-0 Tstrap: 0-0 Ckp: 0-0
Best Rating: 45	1/04 Extr 2m3f soft Hdl

Ashley Muck
103   (126h)122
11-y-o b g Gunner B-Miss Muck (Balinger)
M C Pipe Matt Archer & Miss Jean Broadhurst

Placings:U/5/32F12/3/50P13/21111123/F443-423					(0679)
2003/04: 20⁴G, 20²GF, 20³GF,					

	Starts	1st	2nd	3rd	Win & Pl
Chases	3	0	1	1	3594
Career Total	28	7	5	6	48975
136	9/01	Uttx	2m5f		D(0-125)HCh	GD	£4920
136	8/01	Uttx	2m5f		C(0-135)HCh	G-F	£5872
136	8/01	NAbb	2m5f110yD Ch		GD	£3721
131	7/01	NAbb	2m5f110yE Ch		G-F	£3376
112	6/01	NAbb	2m5f110yD Ch		G-F	£3840
123	3/01	Strf	2m110y	D(0-125)HHdl	SFT	£7436
126	11/98	Extr	2m1f	E Hdl	SFT	£2805
				Total win prize-money £31973	

Going:	Sf: 0-0 GS: 0-0 Gd: 0-1 GF: - Fm: 0-2
Distance:	2m/2m3: 0-2 2m4-2m7: 0-3 3m+: 0-0
Track:	LH: 0-3 RH: 0-0 Tight: 0-0 Gall: 0-0
Aids:	Bl: 0-0 Vi: 0-0 Tstrap: 0-0 Ckp: 0-0
Best Rating: 136	9/01 Uttx 2m5f good Ch

Fair handicap chaser; has plenty of ability, but has temperament problems and sometimes loses ground at the start; acts on fast ground; suited by trips of around two and a half miles.

Ashleybank House (IRE)
105   111+
7-y-o b g Lord Americo-Deep Perk (IRE) (Deep Run)
L Lungo Ashleybank Investments Limited

Placings:045-P011PU					(4731)
2003/04: 20ᴾG, 20ᴾHY, 16¹S, 24¹HY, 22ᴾGS, 20ᵁG,					

	Starts	1st	2nd	3rd	Win & Pl
Hurdles	6	2	0	0	8398
Career Total	9	2	0	0	8398
112	1/04	Ayr	3m110y	D(0-110)HHdl	HVY	£4862
103	12/03	Ayr	2m	E(0-105)HHdl	SFT	£3536
				Total win prize-money £8398	

Going:	Sf: 2-3 GS: 0-1 Gd: 0-2 GF: - Fm: 0-0
Distance:	2m/2m3: 1-1 2m4-2m7: 0-4 3m+: 1-1
Track:	LH: 2-3 RH: 0-3 Tight: 0-1 Gall: 0-0

Aids: Bl: 0-0 Vi: 0-0 Tstrap: 0-0 Ckp: 0-0
Best Rating: 112 1/04 Ayr 3m110y heavy Hdl

Big, chasing-type; showed some ability in bumpers and turned in improved effort on soft ground when winning at Ayr in December; duly improved for step up to three miles when successful at same course following month; most disappointing at Kelso in March, never going; stays well; suited by soft ground.

Ashnaya (FR)
108   98+
6-y-o b m Ashkalani (IRE)-Upend (Main Reef)
W Storey B P Bradshaw

Placings:065/F21PP0-4104					(2138)
2003/04: 16⁴G, 20¹G, 21⁰G, 20⁴G,					

	Starts	1st	2nd	3rd	Win & Pl
Hurdles	4	1	0	0	4139
Career Total	13	2	1	0	8701
98	5/03	Hexm	2m4f110yE(0-110)HHdl	GD	£3458
91	8/02	Ctml	2m1f110yE(0-100)HHdl	GD	£3738
			Total win prize-money £7196	

Going:	Sf: 0-0 GS: 0-0 Gd: 1-4 GF: - Fm: 0-0
Distance:	2m/2m3: 0-1 2m4-2m7: 1-3 3m+: 0-0
Track:	LH: 1-3 RH: 0-1 Tight: 0-1 Gall: 0-1
Aids:	Bl: 0-0 Vi: 0-0 Tstrap: 0-0 Ckp: 1-4
Best Rating: 98	5/03 Hexm 2m4f110y good Hdl

Plating-class hurdler; stays two and a half miles; acts on most types of ground.

Ashtaroute (USA)
101   80+
4-y-o b f Holy Bull (USA)-Beating The Buzz (IRE) (Bluebird (USA))
M C Chapman Twinacre Nurseries Ltd

Placings:06					(4260)
2003/04: 19⁰G, 16⁶GF,					

	Starts	1st	2nd	3rd	Win & Pl
Hurdles	2	0	0	0	0
Career Total	2	0	0	0	0

Going:	Sf: 0-0 GS: 0-0 Gd: 0-1 GF: - Fm: 0-1
Distance:	2m/2m3: 0-1 2m4-2m7: 0-1 3m+: 0-0
Track:	LH: 0-2 RH: 0-0 Tight: 0-1 Gall: 0-0
Aids:	Bl: 0-0 Vi: 0-0 Tstrap: 0-0 Ckp: 0-0
Best Rating: 80	3/04 Catt 2m gd-fm Hdl

Ashton Vale
98
5-y-o ch g Ashkalani (IRE)-My Valentina (Royal Academy (USA))
M A Barnes J T Davidson

Placings:1231533-P0					(2931)
2003/04: 17ᴾGF, 17⁰G,					

	Starts	1st	2nd	3rd	Win & Pl
Hurdles	2	0	0	0	0
Career Total	9	2	1	3	9121
97	10/02	Winc	2m	E Hdl	FRM	£3108
100	9/02	NAbb	2m1f	E Hdl	GD	£3136
			Total win prize-money £6245	

Going:	Sf: 0-0 GS: 0-0 Gd: 0-1 GF: - Fm: 0-1
Distance:	2m/2m3: 0-2 2m4-2m7: 0-1 3m+: 0-0
Track:	LH: 0-2 RH: 0-0 Tight: 0-2 Gall: 0-0
Aids:	Bl: 0-0 Vi: 0-0 Tstrap: 0-2 Ckp: 0-0
Best Rating: 101	10/02 Chep 2m110y gd-fm Hdl

Aids: Bl: 0-0 Vi: 0-0 Tstrap: 0-0 Ckp: 0-0
Best Rating: 112 1/04 Ayr 3m110y heavy Hdl

Modest juvenile hurdler; made a winning debut over hurdles at Newton Abbot in August 2002 and won a non-event at Wincanton in October; best on a sound surface; usually wears a tongue tie.

Ashtoreth (IRE)
93   70
5-y-o ch m Ashkalani (IRE)-Sally Chase (Sallust)
D McCain D McCain

Placings:3P02PP5-625P6					(0976)
2003/04: 16⁶G, 17²GS, 16⁵GF, 17ᴾGF, 17⁶GF,					

	Starts	1st	2nd	3rd	Win & Pl
Hurdles	5	0	1	0	757
Career Total	12	0	2	1	2017

Going:	Sf: 0-0 GS: 0-1 Gd: 0-1 GF: - Fm: 0-3
Distance:	2m/2m3: 0-5 2m4-2m7: 0-0 3m+: 0-0
Track:	LH: 0-4 RH: 0-1 Tight: 0-3 Gall: 0-0
Aids:	Bl: 0-0 Vi: 0-0 Tstrap: 0-0 Ckp: 0-1
Best Rating: 70	6/03 Uttx 2m gd-fm Hdl

Plating-class maiden hurdler.

Ashwell (IRE)
101   98
5-y-o gr g Anshan-Willshego (Welsh Captain)
C C Bealby C Ireland Mrs R Bingley W Skelton

Placings:045F					(4511)
2003/04: 16⁶GS, 19⁴G, 19⁵G, 20ᶠGS,					

	Starts	1st	2nd	3rd	Win & Pl
NH Flat	1	0	0	0	0
Hurdles	3	0	0	0	434
Career Total	4	0	0	0	434

Going:	Sf: 0-0 GS: 0-2 Gd: 0-2 GF: - Fm: 0-0
Distance:	2m/2m3: 0-1 2m4-2m7: 0-3 3m+: 0-0
Track:	LH: 0-3 RH: 0-1 Tight: 0-1 Gall: 0-0
Aids:	Bl: 0-0 Vi: 0-0 Tstrap: 0-0 Ckp: 0-0
Best Rating: 97	2/04 MRas 2m3f110y good Hdl

Remote fourth on hurdling debut at Market Rasen in February; will stay well.

Ashwicke Gambler

8-y-o b g Tout Ensemble-Miss Dollymouse (Nader)
J W Mullins Mrs Sally Mullins

Placings:P0P					(0635)
2003/04: 22ᴾGS, 22⁰GF, 22ᴾGF,					

	Starts	1st	2nd	3rd	Win & Pl
Hurdles	3	0	0	0	
Career Total	3	0	0	0	

Going:	Sf: 0-0 GS: 0-0 Gd: 0-1 GF: - Fm: 0-2
Distance:	2m/2m3: 0-0 2m4-2m7: 0-3 3m+: 0-0
Track:	LH: 0-3 RH: 0-0 Tight: 0-3 Gall: 0-0
Aids:	Bl: 0-0 Vi: 0-0 Tstrap: 0-0 Ckp: 0-0
Best Rating: 0	6/03 NAbb 2m6f gd-fm Hdl

Ask For Luck (IRE)
94   86
7-y-o b g Camden Town-French Thistle (Kemal (FR))
J G Portman Anthony Boswood

Placings:00B3-0 (4897)
2003/04: 22^{Q}G,

	Starts	1st	2nd	3rd	Win & Pl
Hurdles	1	0	0	0	
Career Total	5	0	0	1	811

Going: Sf: 0-0 GS: 0-0 Gd: 0-1 GF: - Fm: 0-0
Distance: 2m/2m3: 0-0 2m4-2m7: 0-1 3m+: 0-0
Track: LH: 0-0 RH: 0-1 Tight: 0-0 Gall: 0-0
Aids: Bl: 0-0 Vi: 0-0 Tstrap: 0-0 Ckp: 0-0
Best Rating: 94 12/02 Wwck 2m soft NHF

Modest novice hurdler; stays three miles.

Ask Me What (IRE)
(101h) (103+h)
7-y-o b m Shernazar-Laffan's Bridge (IRE) (Mandalus)
Miss Venetia Williams The Turf Club

Placings:4/143120-235UU (4759)
2003/04: 16^{2}GF, 20^{3}GS, 16^{5}G, 20^{U}US, 16^{U}S,

	Starts	1st	2nd	3rd	Win & Pl
Hurdles	3	0	1	1	1700
Chases	2	0	0	0	0
Career Total	12	2	2	2	9347
104 3/03 Bang	2m1f	E Hdl		SFT	£3432
102 12/02 Folk	2m1f110yH	NHF		HVY	£1918

Total win prize-money £5350

Going: Sf: 0-1 GS: 0-2 Gd: 0-1 GF: - Fm: 0-1
Distance: 2m/2m3: 0-3 2m4-2m7: 0-2 3m+: 0-0
Track: LH: 0-1 RH: 0-4 Tight: 0-1 Gall: 0-1
Aids: Bl: 0-1 Vi: 0-0 Tstrap: 0-0 Ckp: 0-0
Best Rating: 104 11/03 Hntg 2m110y gd-fm Hdl

Moderate hurdler; effective at two miles but stays further; acts on soft ground.

Ask The Gatherer (IRE)
97　　102+
6-y-o b g Be My Native (USA)-Shean Bracken (IRE) (Le Moss)
P F Nicholls (W J Burke 9/5) Mrs Toni S Tipper

Placings:13 (2652)
2003/04: 16^{1}G, 20^{3}G,

	Starts	1st	2nd	3rd	Win & Pl
NH Flat	1	1	0	0	3584
Hurdles	1	0	0	1	394
Career Total	2	1	0	1	3978
96 5/03 Wxfd	2m	NHF		GD	£3584

Total win prize-money £3584

Going: Sf: 0-0 GS: 0-0 Gd: 1-2 GF: - Fm: 0-0
Distance: 2m/2m3: 1-1 2m4-2m7: 0-1 3m+: 0-0
Track: LH: 0-0 RH: 0-0 Tight: 0-1 Gall: 0-0
Aids: Bl: 0-0 Vi: 0-0 Tstrap: 0-0 Ckp: 0-0
Best Rating: 102 12/03 Font 2m4f good Hdl

Irish bumper winner; shaped with plenty of promise on hurdling debut.

Aslapoftheeuro (IRE)
80　　30
6-y-o b g Eurobus-Slapoftheballot (Ragapan)
M C Pipe P J Finn

Placings:0P000 (0833)
2003/04: 20^{0}GF, 26^{0}GF, 22^{0}GF, 22^{0}G, 24^{0}GF,

	Starts	1st	2nd	3rd	Win & Pl
Hurdles	5	0	0	0	
Career Total	5	0	0	0	

Going: Sf: 0-0 GS: 0-0 Gd: 0-1 GF: - Fm: 0-4
Distance: 2m/2m3: 0-0 2m4-2m7: 0-3 3m+: 0-1
Track: LH: 0-4 RH: 0-1 Tight: 0-2 Gall: 0-0
Aids: Bl: 0-0 Vi: 0-1 Tstrap: 0-0 Ckp: 0-0
Best Rating: 30 6/03 NAbb 2m6f gd-fm Hdl

Asparagus (IRE)
108 (115h) 127
10-y-o b g Roselier (FR)-Arctic Bead (IRE) (Le Moss)
M Sheppard Simon Gegg

Placings:23FF/F1434211/232331-4P2314 (4871)
2003/04: 20^{4}GS, 16^{2}S, 16^{2}HY, 20^{3}S, 20^{1}GS, 24^{4}S,

	Starts	1st	2nd	3rd	Win & Pl
Chases	6	1	1	1	20112
Career Total	24	5	5	6	52050
125 3/04 Bang	2m4f110y	C(0-135)HCh		G-S	£10562
127 3/03 Uttx	2m5f	C(0-135)HCh		SFT	£9399
115 3/02 Uttx	2m5f	F(0-100)HCh		HVY	£3445
110 3/02 Chep	2m110y	F(0-95)HCh		SFT	£2989
115 11/01 Uttx	2m	E Hdl		HVY	£2730

Total win prize-money £29126

Going: Sf: 0-4 GS: 1-2 Gd: 0-0 GF: - Fm: 0-0
Distance: 2m/2m3: 0-2 **2m4-2m7: 1-3** 3m+: 0-1
Track: **LH: 1-6** RH: 0-0 **Tight: 1-2** Gall: 0-1
Aids: Bl: 0-0 Vi: 0-0 **Tstrap: 1-6** Ckp: 0-0
Best Rating: 127 3/03 Uttx 2m5f soft Ch

Fair chaser; won at Uttoxeter in March 2003, but suffered in the weights as a result; effective at up to two miles five and should stay farther; loves the mud; wears a tongue tie.

Assignation
67　　50
4-y-o b g Compton Place-Hug Me (Shareef Dancer (USA))
Miss M Bragg (B R Millman 13/10) Friends Of Rock Park

Placings:00 (3947)
2003/04: 17^{0}GS, 16^{0}G,

	Starts	1st	2nd	3rd	Win & Pl
Hurdles	2	0	0	0	
Career Total	2	0	0	0	

Going: Sf: 0-0 GS: 0-1 Gd: 0-1 GF: - Fm: 0-0
Distance: 2m/2m3: 0-2 2m4-2m7: 0-0 3m+: 0-0
Track: LH: 0-0 RH: 0-2 Tight: 0-1 Gall: 0-0
Aids: Bl: 0-0 Vi: 0-0 Tstrap: 0-0 Ckp: 0-0
Best Rating: 56 2/04 Winc 2m good Hdl

Assoon
103　　102
5-y-o b g Ezzoud (IRE)-Handy Dancer (Green God)
G L Moore Bryan Pennick

Placings:2122 (1520)
2003/04: 17^{2}GF, 16^{1}GF, 19^{2}GF, 18^{2}G,

	Starts	1st	2nd	3rd	Win & Pl
NH Flat	2	1	1	0	2455
Hurdles	2	0	2	0	1836
Career Total	4	1	3	0	4291
86 7/03 Worc	2m	H NHF		G-F	£1906

Total win prize-money £1907

Going: Sf: 0-0 GS: 0-0 Gd: 0-1 GF: - Fm: 1-3
Distance: 2m/2m3: 1-3 2m4-2m7: 0-1 3m+: 0-0
Track: LH: 1-2 RH: 0-2 Tight: 0-3 Gall: 0-0
Aids: Bl: 0-0 Vi: 0-0 Tstrap: 0-0 Ckp: 0-0
Best Rating: 102 10/03 Font 2m2f110y good Hdl

Took a modest bumper at Worcester in July on second start; runner-up twice over hurdles; suited by two and a half miles and will stays further; acts on fast ground.

Assumetheposition (FR)
83
4-y-o gr g Cyborg (FR)-Jeanne Grey (FR) (Fast Topaze (USA))
R C Guest D V Racing

Placings:400 (4179)
2003/04: 16^{4}HY, 17^{0}G, 16^{0}G,

	Starts	1st	2nd	3rd	Win & Pl
NH Flat	3	0	0	0	0
Career Total	3	0	0	0	0

Going: Sf: 0-1 GS: 0-0 Gd: 0-2 GF: - Fm: 0-0
Distance: 2m/2m3: 0-3 2m4-2m7: 0-0 3m+: 0-0
Track: LH: 0-2 RH: 0-1 Tight: 0-0 Gall: 0-1
Aids: Bl: 0-0 Vi: 0-0 Tstrap: 0-0 Ckp: 0-0
Best Rating: 79 2/04 Carl 2m1f good NHF

Assured Movements (USA)
91　　84
8-y-o b g Northern Flagship (USA)-Love At Dawn (USA) (Grey Dawn Ii)
Mrs D A Hamer Twelly Davies

Placings:623F02/4035/0312/4-60 (0761)
2003/04: 19^{6}GF, 16^{0}G,

	Starts	1st	2nd	3rd	Win & Pl
Hurdles	2	0	0	0	
Career Total	17	1	3	3	6677
91 4/02 Chep	2m110y	E Hdl		G-F	£2856

Total win prize-money £2856

Going: Sf: 0-0 GS: 0-0 Gd: 0-1 GF: - Fm: 0-1
Distance: 2m/2m3: 0-1 2m4-2m7: 0-1 3m+: 0-0
Track: LH: 0-1 RH: 0-1 Tight: 0-0 Gall: 0-0
Aids: Bl: 0-0 Vi: 0-1 Tstrap: 0-1 Ckp: 0-1
Best Rating: 95 5/02 Extr 2m6f110y good Hdl

Astafort (FR)
100　　86
5-y-o ch g Kendor (FR)-Tres Chic (USA) (Northern Fashion (USA))
A C Whillans Mrs Murray Scott

Placings:043025U-443003 (4911)
2003/04: 16^{4}G, 16^{4}G, 18^{3}G, 20^{4}G, 20^{0}S, 16^{3}S,

	Starts	1st	2nd	3rd	Win & Pl
Hurdles	6	0	0	2	2318
Career Total	13	0	1	3	3758

Going: Sf: 0-2 GS: 0-0 Gd: 0-4 GF: - Fm: 0-0
Distance: 2m/2m3: 0-4 2m4-2m7: 0-2 3m+: 0-0
Track: LH: 0-5 RH: 0-1 Tight: 0-3 Gall: 0-0
Aids: Bl: 0-0 Vi: 0-0 Tstrap: 0-0 Ckp: 0-0
Best Rating: 86 4/04 Prth 2m110y soft Hdl

Plating-class; fair efforts over hurdles in ordinary company, looking likely to appreciate a longer trip; effective at two miles though; acts on good ground.

Astle (IRE)

6-y-o ch g Spectrum (IRE)-Very Sophisticated (USA) (Affirmed (USA))
Mrs N Macauley W Murdoch

Placings:P				(0623)

2003/04: 17^PG,

	Starts	1st	2nd	3rd	Win & Pl
Hurdles	1	0	0	0	
Career Total	1	0	0	0	

Going:	Sf: 0-0 GS: 0-0 Gd: 0-1 GF: - Fm: 0-0
Distance:	2m/2m3: 0-1 2m4-2m7: 0-0 3m+: 0-0
Track:	LH: 0-0 RH: 0-1 Tight: 0-1 Gall: 0-0
Aids:	Bl: 0-0 Vi: 0-0 Tstrap: 0-0 Ckp: 0-0
Best Rating:	0 6/03 MRas 2m1f110y good Hdl

Aston (USA)
101   90

4-y-o b g Bahri (USA)-Halholah (USA) (Secreto (USA))
C F Swan (Noel Meade 5/8) Mrs Paul Duffin

Placings:4560				(4742a)

2003/04: 16^4G, 16^5GF, 16^8Y, 16^9Y,

	Starts	1st	2nd	3rd	Win & Pl
Hurdles	4	0	0	0	286
Career Total	4	0	0	0	286

Going:	Sf: 0-0 GS: 0-0 Gd: 0-1 GF: - Fm: 0-1
Distance:	2m/2m3: 0-4 2m4-2m7: 0-0 3m+: 0-0
Track:	LH: 0-0 RH: 0-1 Tight: 0-1 Gall: 0-0
Aids:	Bl: 0-1 Vi: 0-0 Tstrap: 0-0 Ckp: 0-0
Best Rating:	90 8/03 Rosc 2m good Hdl

Aston Mara
102   103

7-y-o b g Bering-Coigach (Niniski (USA))
M A Buckley Mrs D J Buckley

Placings:42003/0144230624/504036-3114464F0	(3759)

2003/04: 20^3G, 21^11GF, 19^1G, 20^4GF, 21^4GF, 19^6GF, 19^4GF, 22^FGF, 22^0G,

	Starts	1st	2nd	3rd	Win & Pl
Hurdles	9	2	0	1	9286
Career Total	30	3	3	4	16870
103	6/03	MRas	2m3f110yD(0-120)HHdl	GD	£5590
103	5/03	Hntg	2m5f110yG(0-95)HHdl	G-F	£2497
101	6/01	Prth	2m4f110yE Hdl	FRM	£2961

Total win prize-money £11049

Going:	Sf: 0-0 GS: 0-0 Gd: 1-3 GF: - Fm: 1-6
Distance:	2m/2m3: 0-0 2m4-2m7: 2-9 3m+: 0-0
Track:	LH: 0-4 RH: 2-4 Tight: 1-5 Gall: 1-1
Aids:	Bl: 0-0 Vi: 0-0 Tstrap: 0-0 Ckp: 0-0
Best Rating:	103 6/03 MRas 2m3f110y good Hdl

Moderate hurdler; best at around two and a half miles, but stays three; suited by fast ground.

Astormydayiscoming
94   81

6-y-o b g Alhaatmi-Valentine Song (Pas De Seul)

G F Bridgwater Out Of The Frying Pan Partnership

Placings:2442-0006FP6P	(1300)

2003/04: 16^0GS, 16^0G, 20^0G, 19^6G, 22^FGF, 22^PG, 26^6GS, 16^PGF,

	Starts	1st	2nd	3rd	Win & Pl
Hurdles	8	0	0	0	0
Career Total	12	0	2	0	1613

Going:	Sf: 0-0 GS: 0-2 Gd: 0-4 GF: - Fm: 0-2
Distance:	2m/2m3: 0-4 2m4-2m7: 0-3 3m+: 0-1
Track:	LH: 0-7 RH: 0-1 Tight: 0-3 Gall: 0-0
Aids:	Bl: 0-1 Vi: 0-0 Tstrap: 0-0 Ckp: 0-5
Best Rating:	87 11/02 Ludl 2m gd-sft Hdl

Astral Affair (IRE)

5-y-o br m Norwich-Jupiters Jill (Jupiter Pluvius)
P A Pritchard Woodland Generators

Placings:0-240PP	(4340)

2003/04: 16^2GF, 16^4GF, 17^0GS, 22^PGS, 25^PG,

	Starts	1st	2nd	3rd	Win & Pl
NH Flat	3	0	1	0	558
Hurdles	2	0	0	0	0
Career Total	6	0	1	0	558

Going:	Sf: 0-0 GS: 0-2 Gd: 0-1 GF: - Fm: 0-2
Distance:	2m/2m3: 0-3 2m4-2m7: 0-1 3m+: 0-1
Track:	LH: 0-4 RH: 0-1 Tight: 0-1 Gall: 0-0
Aids:	Bl: 0-0 Vi: 0-0 Tstrap: 0-0 Ckp: 0-0
Best Rating:	84 11/03 Wwck 2m gd-fm NHF

Runner-up despite tack problems in poor Chepstow bumper October 2003.

Astral Dancer (IRE)
73f   64f

4-y-o ch g Fourstars Allstar (USA)-Walk N'Dance (IRE) (Pennine Walk)
J Mackie The Festival Dream Partnership

Placings:6	(4885)

2003/04: 17^6GS,

	Starts	1st	2nd	3rd	Win & Pl
NH Flat	1	0	0	0	0
Career Total	1	0	0	0	0

Going:	Sf: 0-0 GS: 0-1 Gd: 0-0 GF: - Fm: 0-0
Distance:	2m/2m3: 0-1 2m4-2m7: 0-0 3m+: 0-0
Track:	LH: 0-0 RH: 0-1 Tight: 0-0 Gall: 0-0
Aids:	Bl: 0-0 Vi: 0-0 Tstrap: 0-0 Ckp: 0-0
Best Rating:	64 4/04 Carl 2m1f gd-sft NHF

Poor selling hudler.

Astral Prince
101(93h)   (62h)83

6-y-o ch g Efisio-Val D'Erica (Ashmore (FR))
Mrs K Walton (A Crook 18/6) D E Reeves & P W Colley

Placings:006/0460-56U42256	(4786)

2003/04: 16^5G, 17^6G, 20^UG, 17^4GF, 17^2GS, 17^2GF, 17^5GF, 16^9G,

	Starts	1st	2nd	3rd	Win & Pl
Hurdles	2	0	0	0	0
Chases	6	0	2	0	2531
Career Total	15	0	2	0	2531

Going:	Sf: 0-0 GS: 0-1 Gd: 0-4 GF: - Fm: 0-3
Distance:	2m/2m3: 0-7 2m4-2m7: 0-1 3m+: 0-0

Track:	LH: 0-6 RH: 0-2 Tight: 0-2 Gall: 0-1
Aids:	Bl: 0-0 Vi: 0-0 Tstrap: 0-0 Ckp: 0-6
Best Rating:	83 10/03 Sthl 2m1f gd-fm Ch

Plating-class chaser/hurdler; best at around two miles; acts on fast and easy ground; wears cheekpieces.

Astro Glide (IRE)

8-y-o ch m Star Quest-Polly-Glide (Pollerton)
Mrs L B Normile L B N Racing Club

Placings:PP	(3321)

2003/04: 20^PG, 21^PGS,

	Starts	1st	2nd	3rd	Win & Pl
Hurdles	2	0	0	0	
Career Total	2	0	0	0	

Going:	Sf: 0-0 GS: 0-1 Gd: 0-1 GF: - Fm: 0-0
Distance:	2m/2m3: 0-0 2m4-2m7: 0-2 3m+: 0-0
Track:	LH: 0-1 RH: 0-1 Tight: 0-1 Gall: 0-0
Aids:	Bl: 0-0 Vi: 0-0 Tstrap: 0-0 Ckp: 0-0
Best Rating:	0 1/04 Sedg 2m5f110y gd-sft Hdl

Astronaut
103   94+

7-y-o b g Sri Pekan (USA)-Wild Abandon (USA) (Graustark)
A E Jones Amos Eaton

Placings:4R6/40/041	(1059)

2003/04: 16^9GF, 16^4GF, 20^1GF,

	Starts	1st	2nd	3rd	Win & Pl
Hurdles	3	1	0	0	2345
Career Total	8	1	0	0	2345
94	8/03	Uttx	2m4f110yG(0-95)HHdl	G-F	£2345

Total win prize-money £2345

Going:	Sf: 0-0 GS: 0-0 Gd: 0-0 GF: - Fm: 1-3
Distance:	2m/2m3: 0-2 2m4-2m7: 1-1 3m+: 0-0
Track:	LH: 1-3 RH: 0-0 Tight: 0-0 Gall: 0-0
Aids:	Bl: 0-0 Vi: 0-0 Tstrap: 0-0 Ckp: 0-0
Best Rating:	103 5/01 Font 2m2f110y gd-fm Hdl

Atahuelpa
93   105

4-y-o b g Hernando (FR)-Certain Story (Known Fact (USA))
M F Harris (P F I Cole 23/8) Let's Live Racing

Placings:F2P4	(1901)

2003/04: 16^FGF, 16^2GF, 16^PGF, 16^4GF,

	Starts	1st	2nd	3rd	Win & Pl
Hurdles	4	0	1	0	1060
Career Total	4	0	1	0	1060

Going:	Sf: 0-0 GS: 0-0 Gd: 0-0 GF: - Fm: 0-4
Distance:	2m/2m3: 0-4 2m4-2m7: 0-0 3m+: 0-0
Track:	LH: 0-2 RH: 0-2 Tight: 0-2 Gall: 0-1
Aids:	Bl: 0-0 Vi: 0-0 Tstrap: 0-1 Ckp: 0-0
Best Rating:	105 9/03 Strf 2m110y gd-fm Hdl

Juvenile hurdler; useful performer on the Flat; desperately unlucky not to make winning debut over hurdles when falling at the last at Stratford in September; touched off next time; keen sort.

Atalanta Surprise (IRE)

90(98h)   (79 h)**86+**
7-y-o ch g Phardante (FR)-Curragh Breeze (Furry Glen)
R H Buckler Martyn Forrester

Placings:003640PP-30P0F   (4265)
2003/04: 21³G, 20⁰G, 24PHY, 21⁰G, 26FGF,

	Starts	1st	2nd	3rd	Win & Pl
Hurdles	1	0	0	0	0
Chases	4	0	0	1	462
Career Total	13	0	0	2	1170

Going:	Sf: 0-1 GS: 0-0 Gd: 0-3 GF: - Fm: 0-1
Distance:	2m/2m3: 0-0 2m4-2m7: 0-3 3m+: 0-2
Track:	LH: 0-4 RH: 0-1 Tight: 0-2 Gall: 0-0
Aids:	Bl: 0-0 Vi: 0-0 Tstrap: 0-0 Ckp: 0-0
Best Rating:	86 11/03 NAbb 2m5f110y good Ch

Atalya

72(100c)   (85c)**102**
7-y-o ch g Afzal-Sandy Looks (Music Boy)
S T Lewis Simon T Lewis

Placings:0024313/23P/40P33-PP05000   (4526)
2003/04: 16PGS, 17PG, 16⁰GF, 19⁵G, 17⁰GS, 16⁰GS, 16⁰GS,

	Starts	1st	2nd	3rd	Win & Pl
Hurdles	4	0	0	0	0
Chases	3	0	0	0	0
Career Total	22	1	2	5	7072
88	1/01 Winc 2m			F Hdl	SFT £2513
					Total win prize-money £2513

Going:	Sf: 0-0 GS: 0-4 Gd: 0-2 GF: - Fm: 0-1
Distance:	2m/2m3: 0-2 2m4-2m7: 0-1 3m+: 0-0
Track:	LH: 0-4 RH: 0-2 Tight: 0-3 Gall: 0-0
Aids:	Bl: 0-0 Vi: 0-0 Tstrap: 0-0 Ckp: 0-0
Best Rating:	102 5/01 Hntg 2m110y gd-fm Hdl

Athenian Law

104   **105+**
7-y-o br g Darshaan-Titania's Way (Fairy King (USA))
P J Hobbs Richard Green (fine Paintings)

Placings:11/3-P2   (0835)
2003/04: 17PGF, 16²GF,

	Starts	1st	2nd	3rd	Win & Pl
Hurdles	2	0	1	0	1045
Career Total	5	2	1	1	6730
95	11/01 MRas 2m1f110yE Hdl			G-S	£2996
99	10/01 Hrfd 2m1f			H NHF	GD £1596
					Total win prize-money £4592

Going:	Sf: 0-0 GS: 0-0 Gd: 0-0 GF: - Fm: 0-2
Distance:	2m/2m3: 0-2 2m4-2m7: 0-0 3m+: 0-0
Track:	LH: 0-2 RH: 0-0 Tight: 0-1 Gall: 0-0
Aids:	Bl: 0-0 Vi: 0-0 Tstrap: 0-0 Ckp: 0-0
Best Rating:	107 7/03 Worc 2m gd-fm Hdl

Made winning debut in Hereford bumper October 2001; odds-on when making successful transition to hurdles in weak event at Market Rasen the following month; not seen until third in Perth handicap April 2003; pulled up after losing action at Newton Abbot in May; bounced back when narrowly beaten at Worcester in July; effective at 2m; acts on a sound surface.

Athenry Gent (IRE)

82   **55**
5-y-o ch g Fourstars Allstar (USA)-Covette (Master Owen)
J Howard Johnson J R McAleese

Placings:005   (4074)
2003/04: 25⁰GS, 16⁰GF, 20⁵F,

	Starts	1st	2nd	3rd	Win & Pl
Hurdles	3	0	0	0	0
Career Total	3	0	0	0	0

Going:	Sf: 0-0 GS: 0-1 Gd: 0-0 GF: - Fm: 0-2
Distance:	2m/2m3: 0-1 2m4-2m7: 0-1 3m+: 0-1
Track:	LH: 0-1 RH: 0-2 Tight: 0-2 Gall: 0-0
Aids:	Bl: 0-0 Vi: 0-0 Tstrap: 0-0 Ckp: 0-0
Best Rating:	54 2/04 Muss 2m4f firm Hdl

Athnowen (IRE)

110   **97**
12-y-o b g Lord Americo-Lady Bluebird (Arapaho)
J R Payne R J Payne

Placings:PF6510U2344/05365FU/P0P1/2F6322R2-0421F2U22   (4694)
2003/04: 16⁰GF, 21⁴GF, 16²GF, 20¹GS, 21FGS, 21²S, 21UG, 19²GS, 23²G,

	Starts	1st	2nd	3rd	Win & Pl
Chases	9	1	4	0	12745
Career Total	39	3	9	3	26754
92	12/03 Uttx 2m4f	F(0-100)HCh	G-S	£4940
84	3/02 NAbb 2m5f110yG(0-95)HCh		GD	£2282
95	1/00 Hrfd 2m	E(0-105)HCh	G-S	£3103
					Total win prize-money £10326

Going:	Sf: 0-1 GS: 1-3 Gd: 0-2 GF: - Fm: 0-3
Distance:	2m/2m3: 0-2 **2m4-2m7:** 1-6 3m+: 0-1
Track:	**LH:** 1-5 RH: 0-3 Tight: 0-4 Gall: 0-0
Aids:	Bl: 0-0 Vi: 0-0 Tstrap: 0-0 Ckp: 0-0
Best Rating:	101 3/00 Tntn 2m3f good Ch

Plating-class chaser; returned to winning ways at Uttoxeter in December 2003; unlucky not to follow up off 7lb higher mark when falling two out at Uttoxeter next time; stays 2m 6f, effective at shorter; acts on most types of ground.

Atlantic Crossing (IRE)

98(98c)   (95+c)**113+**
7-y-o b g Roselier (FR)-Ocean Mist (IRE) (Crash Course)
P Beaumont N W A Bannister

Placings:000/U110-P2UF6F000   (4870)
2003/04: 20PYS, 20²S, 20UGS, 20FGS, 21GGS, 20FGS, 24⁰G, 20⁰S, 24⁰GS,

	Starts	1st	2nd	3rd	Win & Pl
Hurdles	4	0	0	0	0
Chases	5	0	1	0	1072
Career Total	16	2	1	0	8703
112	12/02 Hayd 2m4f	D Hdl	GD	£4056
113	11/02 Carl 2m4f	E Hdl	HVY	£3575
					Total win prize-money £7631

Going:	Sf: 0-2 GS: 0-5 Gd: 0-1 GF: - Fm: 0-0
Distance:	2m/2m3: 0-0 2m4-2m7: 0-7 3m+: 0-2
Track:	LH: 0-8 RH: 0-1 Tight: 0-4 Gall: 0-0
Aids:	Bl: 0-1 Vi: 0-0 Tstrap: 0-0 Ckp: 0-0
Best Rating:	113 11/02 Carl 2m4f heavy Hdl

Fair novice chaser; stays 2m 4f; effective in testing ground; has worn blinkers.

Atlantic Hawk

6-y-o b g Daar Alzamaan (IRE)-Pyewacket (Belfort (FR))
Ferdy Murphy R Sunter

Placings:045-UU   (4660)
2003/04: 20UGS, 24US,

	Starts	1st	2nd	3rd	Win & Pl
Hurdles	2	0	0	0	0
Career Total	5	0	0	0	0

Going:	Sf: 0-1 GS: 0-1 Gd: 0-0 GF: - Fm: 0-0
Distance:	2m/2m3: 0-1 2m4-2m7: 0-0 3m+: 0-1
Track:	LH: 0-2 RH: 0-0 Tight: 0-0 Gall: 0-0
Aids:	Bl: 0-0 Vi: 0-0 Tstrap: 0-0 Ckp: 0-0
Best Rating:	88 4/03 Ayr 2m good NHF

Bumper performer; has shown promise in three starts; will have to learn to settle better.

Atlantic Lady (GER)

90   **89**
6-y-o br m Dashing Blade-Atlantic City (GER) (Medicus (GER))
Mrs N S Sharpe J Pritchard

Placings:3F2F6P0-00   (2516)
2003/04: 16⁰G, 17⁰GS,

	Starts	1st	2nd	3rd	Win & Pl
Hurdles	2	0	0	0	
Career Total	9	0	1	1	1350

Going:	Sf: 0-0 GS: 0-1 Gd: 0-1 GF: - Fm: 0-0
Distance:	2m/2m3: 0-2 2m4-2m7: 0-0 3m+: 0-0
Track:	LH: 0-1 RH: 0-1 Tight: 0-1 Gall: 0-0
Aids:	Bl: 0-0 Vi: 0-0 Tstrap: 0-0 Ckp: 0-0
Best Rating:	89 12/02 Uttx 2m soft Hdl

Atlanticus (IRE)

(92h)   (102h)**84**
8-y-o b g King's Lake (USA)-Amazonia (GER) (Alpenkonig (GER))
Mrs E Slack (C Grant 17/1) A Slack

Placings:06004350/14-0PF00   (4275)
2003/04: 17⁰GS, 21PG, 20FGF, 16⁰S, 20⁰G,

	Starts	1st	2nd	3rd	Win & Pl
Hurdles	2	0	0	0	0
Chases	3	0	0	0	0
Career Total	15	1	0	1	3831
87	10/02 Fknm 2m4f	G Hdl	GD	£2215
					Total win prize-money £2216

Going:	Sf: 0-1 GS: 0-1 Gd: 0-2 GF: - Fm: 0-1
Distance:	2m/2m3: 0-2 2m4-2m7: 0-3 3m+: 0-0
Track:	LH: 0-2 RH: 0-3 Tight: 0-3 Gall: 0-0
Aids:	Bl: 0-0 Vi: 0-0 Tstrap: 0-3 Ckp: 0-0
Best Rating:	102 12/01 Leop 2m yield Hdl

Atlastaboy (IRE)

107(103h)   (108h)**123+**
8-y-o b g Phardante (FR)-Corcaigh (Town And Country)
T R George Timothy N Chick

Placings:33561-31PU   (4398)
2003/04: 25³GS, 27¹GS, 23PG, 32UG,

	Starts	1st	2nd	3rd	Win & Pl
Chases	4	1	0	1	8829

Career Total	9	2	0	3	14761
123 1/04 Tntn	3m3f	C(0-130)HCh		G-S	£8170
108 2/03 Hntg	3m2f	D(0-115)HHdl		GD	£4979
				Total win prize-money £13150

Going:	Sf: 0-0 GS: 1-2 Gd: 0-2 GF: - Fm: 0-0
Distance:	2m/2m3: 0-0 2m4-2m7: 0-0 3m+: 1-4
Track:	LH: 0-1 RH: 1-3 Tight: 1-2 Gall: 0-1
Aids:	Bl: 0-0 Vi: 0-0 Tstrap: 0-0 Ckp: 0-0
Best Rating:	123 1/04 Tntn 3m3f gd-sft Ch

Modest hurdler, but looked much better over fences; acted on good ground; stayed very well. (DEAD)

Atomic Breeze (IRE)

10-y-o b/br g Strong Gale-Atomic Lady (Over The River (FR))
D M Forster D M Forster

Placings:0P/0P/0P3P/F45PP423P51-PPPP5422F	(4626)
2003/04: 25PG, 24FG, 25PGF, 26PGF, 25SGF, 27⁴GF, 28²GF, 27²G, 21FG,	

	Starts	1st	2nd	3rd	Win & Pl
Chases	9	0	2	0	1923
Career Total	28	1	3	2	10774
78 4/03 Carl	3m2f	F(0-95)HCh		G-F	£5954
				Total win prize-money £5954

Going:	Sf: 0-0 GS: 0-0 Gd: 0-4 GF: - Fm: 0-5
Distance:	2m/2m3: 0-0 2m4-2m7: 0-1 3m+: 0-8
Track:	LH: 0-6 RH: 0-3 Tight: 0-6 Gall: 0-1
Aids:	Bl: 0-0 Vi: 0-0 Tstrap: 0-0 Ckp: 0-0
Best Rating:	88 4/02 Sedg 2m5f gd-fm Ch

Plating-class staying chaser, ran quite well in the autumn of 2002; got off the mark at Carlisle in April 2003; yet to win since; stays three miles-three; acts on a sound surface.

Atoski

10-y-o b g Petoski-Culm Valley (Port Corsair)
Mrs H Dalton (A N Dalton 30/4) Paternosters Racing

Placings:0U5/P	(0704)
2003/04: 22PGF,	

	Starts	1st	2nd	3rd	Win & Pl
Chases	1	0	0		
Career Total	4	0	0	0	0

Going:	Sf: 0-0 GS: 0-0 Gd: 0-0 GF: - Fm: 0-1
Distance:	2m/2m3: 0-0 2m4-2m7: 0-1 3m+: 0-0
Track:	LH: 0-0 RH: 0-1 Tight: 0-1 Gall: 0-0
Aids:	Bl: 0-0 Vi: 0-0 Tstrap: 0-0 Ckp: 0-0
Best Rating:	21 4/01 Plum 2m4f soft Ch

Attack

8-y-o gr g Sabrehill (USA)-Butsova (Formidable (USA))
Mrs Julie Read (P J Hobbs 6/9) Mrs P King

Placings:0010-33P	(3919)
2003/04: 16³GF, 21³GF, 21PG,	

	Starts	1st	2nd	3rd	Win & Pl
Chases	3	0	2		1480
Career Total	7	1	0	2	7829
88 10/02 Limk	2m	Hdl	G-F	£6349
			Total win prize-money £6350

Going:	Sf: 0-0 GS: 0-0 Gd: 0-1 GF: - Fm: 0-2
Distance:	2m/2m3: 0-1 2m4-2m7: 0-2 3m+: 0-0

Track:	LH: 0-3 RH: 0-0 Tight: 0-3 Gall: 0-0
Aids:	Bl: 0-1 Vi: 0-0 Tstrap: 0-3 Ckp: 0-0
Best Rating:	88 10/02 Limk 2m gd-fm Hdl

Atticus Finch (IRE)

97(100h)   (91h)109+

7-y-o b g Witness Box (USA)-Dramatic Loop (IRE) (Balinger)
Mrs M Stirk Mrs M Stirk

Placings:3544P31UF-1425331F1U	(4726)
2003/04: 17¹GF, 21⁴GF, 16²GF, 20⁵GF, 19³GF, 20³GF, 25¹GS, 24FS, 20¹GS, 24UG,	

	Starts	1st	2nd	3rd	Win & Pl
Hurdles	3	1	1	0	5075
Chases	7	2	0	2	8912
Career Total	19	4	1	4	20216
109 3/04 MRas	2m4f	E(0-110)HCh	G-S	£3876
105 1/04 Catt	3m1f110yE(0-105)HCh	G-S	£3981
90 5/03 Sthl	2m1f	E Hdl	G-F	£3535
91 3/03 Weth	2m	E(0-105)HCh	G-F	£4017
			Total win prize-money £15410

Going:	Sf: 0-1 GS: 2-2 Gd: 0-1 GF: - Fm: 1-6
Distance:	2m/2m3: 1-3 2m4-2m7: 1-4 3m+: 1-3
Track:	LH: 2-6 RH: 1-4 Tight: 2-4 Gall: 0-1
Aids:	Bl: 0-0 Vi: 0-0 Tstrap: 0-0 Ckp: 0-0
Best Rating:	109 3/04 MRas 2m4f gd-soft Ch

Moderate chaser; winning pointer; stays three miles one; keen sort; chancy jumper.

Attorney General (IRE)

113   119

5-y-o b g Sadler's Wells (USA)-Her Ladyship (Polish Precedent (USA))
J A B Old W E Sturt

Placings:1F34	(4559)
2003/04: 17¹G, 16FS, 17³GS, 16⁴GS,	

	Starts	1st	2nd	3rd	Win & Pl
Hurdles	4	1	0	1	6445
Career Total	4	1	0	1	6445
95 11/03 NAbb	2m1f	E Hdl	GD	£3409
			Total win prize-money £3409

Going:	Sf: 0-1 GS: 0-2 Gd: 1-1 GF: - Fm: 0-0
Distance:	2m/2m3: 1-4 2m4-2m7: 0-0 3m+: 0-0
Track:	LH: 1-3 RH: 0-1 Tight: 1-1 Gall: 0-2
Aids:	Bl: 0-0 Vi: 0-0 Tstrap: 0-0 Ckp: 0-0
Best Rating:	119 1/04 Chel 2m1f gd-sft Hdl

Modest novice hurdler; effective at around two miles; acts on most ground.

Atum Re (IRE)

113(107h)   (117+h)140

7-y-o br g Be My Native (USA)-Collopy's Cross (Pragmatic)
P R Webber Paul Green

Placings:10/P165-2B132321	(4869)
2003/04: 19²GS, 16⁶G, 17¹GF, 16³G, 16²G, 16³G, 20²G, 17¹S,	

	Starts	1st	2nd	3rd	Win & Pl
Chases	8	2	3	2	34104
Career Total	14	4	3	2	41844
135 4/04 Bang	2m1f110yD Ch	SFT	£5999
127 10/03 MRas	2m1f110yC Ch	G-F	£7328
117 2/03 Winc	2m	D Hdl	G-S	£5687
108 12/01 Ludl	2m	H NHF	G-F	£1603
			Total win prize-money £20619

Track:	LH: 0-3 RH: 0-0 Tight: 0-3 Gall: 0-0
Aids:	Bl: 0-1 Vi: 0-0 Tstrap: 0-3 Ckp: 0-0
Best Rating:	88 10/02 Limk 2m gd-fm Hdl

Going:	Sf: 1-1 GS: 0-1 Gd: 0-5 GF: - Fm: 1-1
Distance:	2m/2m3: 2-7 2m4-2m7: 0-1 3m+: 0-0
Track:	LH: 1-2 RH: 1-6 Tight: 2-2 Gall: 0-1
Aids:	Bl: 0-0 Vi: 0-0 Tstrap: 0-0 Ckp: 0-0
Best Rating:	140 2/04 Kemp 2m4f110y good Ch

Very useful novice chaser; effective at up to two and a half miles; acts on good and good to soft ground; should be capable of better still.

Auburn Duke

71f   71f

4-y-o ch g Inchinor-Dakota Girl (Northern State (USA))
W Jenks B Perkins

Placings:6	(4543)
2003/04: 16⁶GS,	

	Starts	1st	2nd	3rd	Win & Pl
NH Flat	1	0	0		0
Career Total	1	0	0	0	0

Going:	Sf: 0-0 GS: 0-1 Gd: 0-0 GF: - Fm: 0-0
Distance:	2m/2m3: 0-1 2m4-2m7: 0-0 3m+: 0-0
Track:	LH: 0-0 RH: 0-1 Tight: 0-0 Gall: 0-0
Aids:	Bl: 0-0 Vi: 0-0 Tstrap: 0-0 Ckp: 0-0
Best Rating:	71 3/04 Ludl 2m gd-sft NHF

Auburn Spirit

109(95h)   (82h)112+

9-y-o ch g Teamster-Spirit Of Youth (Kind Of Hush)
M D I Usher G A Summers

Placings:04/5000/514306/6031463/FP2621-4222016221432	(4749)
2003/04: 24⁴G, 25²GS, 25²S, 25²S, 25⁶GS, 16⁴HY, 24⁶S, 24²G, 26²GF, 29¹GS, 29⁴GS, 23³GS, 25²G,	

	Starts	1st	2nd	3rd	Win & Pl
Hurdles	3	0	1	1	1361
Chases	10	2	5	0	15578
Career Total	38	5	8	4	29345
112 3/04 Wwck	3m5f	D(0-125)HCh	G-S	£5905
112 1/04 Font	3m2f110yE(0-110)HCh	HVY	£4381
91 4/03 Plum	3m2f	F(0-90)HCh	G-F	£3360
91 2/02 Hrfd	2m3f	E(0-105)HCh	HVY	£3237
68 11/00 Winc	2m6f	F(0-100)HHdl	SFT	£2639
			Total win prize-money £19522

Going:	Sf: 1-4 GS: 1-5 Gd: 0-3 GF: - Fm: 0-1
Distance:	2m/2m3: 0-0 2m4-2m7: 0-1 3m+: 2-12
Track:	LH: 1-4 RH: 0-6 Tight: 1-4 Gall: 0-0
Aids:	Bl: 0-0 Vi: 0-0 Tstrap: 0-0 Ckp: 0-0
Best Rating:	112 3/04 Wwck 3m5f gd-sft Ch

Moderate staying chaser; progressive in early 2004 with wins at Fontwell and Warwick; stays 3m 5f; acts on soft ground.

Audiostreetdotcom

93(110h)   (98h)85

7-y-o ch g Risk Me (FR)-Ballagarrow Girl (North Stoke)
G B Balding Audiostreetdotcom Partnership

Placings:426/0U34236441/4603015306326F-023P45306P	(4737)
2003/04: 22FS, 22⁶G, 20²G, 20³HY, 18PG, 20⁴HY, 21⁵S, 21³G, 21⁵GS, 21⁶GS, 21PG,	

	Starts	1st	2nd	3rd	Win & Pl
Hurdles	8	0	1	2	3789
Chases	3	0	0	0	

Career Total	37	2	4	7	17361
98	12/02 Newb	2m3f	E(0-110)HHdl	HVY	£3150
98	3/02 NAbb	2m6f	E(0-105)HHdl	£3136

Total win prize-money £6286

Going:	Sf: 0-4 GS: 0-2 Gd: 0-5 GF: - Fm: 0-0
Distance:	2m2m3: 0-1 2m4-2m7: 0-10 3m+: 0-0
Track:	LH: 0-8 RH: 0-0 Tight: 0-8 Gall: 0-1
Aids:	Bl: 0-0 Vi: 0-0 Tstrap: 0-0 Ckp: 0-11
Best Rating:	105 1/01 Wwck 2m soft Hdl

Modest hurdler; quirky sort; suited by soft ground; stays two miles six, wears sheepskin cheekpieces and a hood.

Auditor

66(84h)   (59+h)46

5-y-o b g Polish Precedent (USA)-Annaba (IRE) (In The Wings)
S T Lewis Simon T Lewis

Placings:6P65P4   (3441)
2003/04: 17⁶GF, 16⁹GF, 19⁶G, 16⁵GF, 16⁹HY, 20⁴G,

	Starts	1st	2nd	3rd	Win & Pl
Hurdles	5	0	0	0	0
Chases	1	0	0	0	340
Career Total	6	0	0	0	340

Going:	Sf: 0-1 GS: 0-0 Gd: 0-2 GF: - Fm: 0-3
Distance:	2m2m3: 0-5 2m4-2m7: 0-1 3m+: 0-0
Track:	LH: 0-2 RH: 0-4 Tight: 0-1 Gall: 0-0
Aids:	Bl: 0-1 Vi: 0-0 Tstrap: 0-0 Ckp: 0-0
Best Rating:	60 11/03 Leic 2m gd-fm Hdl

Auditty (IRE)

103   108

11-y-o b g Montelimar (USA)-Tax Code (Workboy)
W Jenks Michael Stoddart

Placings:060/0605F/F410150/P1521565/2310121U0P/243 34504-F31230P   (2190)
2003/04: 16⁶GF, 20³GF, 16¹GF, 16²G, 17³G, 20⁰G, 22⁰GS,

	Starts	1st	2nd	3rd	Win & Pl
Chases	7	1	1	2	8194
Career Total	48	8	5	5	55140
100	9/03 Worc	2m	D(0-125)HCh	G-F	£5011
121	9/01 List	2m	(0-130)HCh	G-F	£7790
121	8/01 Tram	2m	(0-109)HCh	GD	£7233
108	6/01 Tram	2m	(0-123)HCh	FRM	£6399
109	8/00 Tram	2m4f	(0-109)HCh	G-F	£5520
85	6/00 Dund	2m1f	(0-102)HCh	G-Y	£4140
92	10/99 Navn	2m1f	(0-102)HCh	GD	£3388
82	9/99 Dund	2m3f	(0-102)HCh	FRM	£2464

Total win prize-money £41947

Going:	Sf: 0-0 GS: 0-1 Gd: 0-3 GF: - Fm: 1-3
Distance:	2m2m3: 1-4 2m4-2m7: 0-3 3m+: 0-0
Track:	LH: 1-5 RH: 0-2 Tight: 0-2 Gall: 0-1
Aids:	Bl: 0-0 Vi: 0-0 Tstrap: 0-0 Ckp: 0-1
Best Rating:	121 6/02 Tram 2m good Ch

Moderate ex-Irish chaser; all out to win strongly-run two-mile handicap chase at Worcester in September 2003; in the frame off higher marks since; loves fast ground; effective at up to two miles four.

Auetaler (GER)

93   119

10-y-o gr g Niniski (USA)-Astica (GER) (Surumu (GER))
E McNamara James McNamara

Placings:1023/1110341242/06/1F1434P0/45005600 (2135)

2003/04: 16⁴G, 20⁵GF, 16⁶S, 16⁰Y, 22⁵F, 20⁶S, 20⁹GF, 21⁰G,

	Starts	1st	2nd	3rd	Win & Pl
Hurdles	8	0	0	0	468
Career Total	32	7	3	3	59104
101	8/01 NAbb	2m110y	E Ch	G-F	£3342
114	5/01 NAbb	2m5f110yD Ch		G-F	£4270
151	2/00 Sand	2m110y	B Hdl	G-S	£8112
114	5/99 Uttx	2m	E Hdl	GD	£2472
122	5/99 Strf	2m6f110yD Hdl		GD	£3428
115	5/99 Aint	2m4f	D Hdl	G-S	£2983
128	2/99 Tntn	2m1f	E Hdl	G-S	£2472

Total win prize-money £27082

Going:	Sf: 0-2 GS: 0-0 Gd: 0-2 GF: - Fm: 0-3
Distance:	2m2m3: 0-3 2m4-2m7: 0-5 3m+: 0-0
Track:	LH: 0-2 RH: 0-2 Tight: 0-0 Gall: 0-1
Aids:	Bl: 0-1 Vi: 0-0 Tstrap: 0-0 Ckp: 0-0
Best Rating:	158 4/00 Aint 2m4f good Hdl

Modest hurdler; fell just below top class over hurdles when with Martin Pipe; not convincing over fences despite winning two of his first four starts in the summer of 2001; on the downgrade now and has shown little since switching to Ireland.

Aughmor River (IRE)

9-y-o b g Over The River (FR)-Morego (Way Up North)
R W Gardiner B Belchem

Placings:5P/P   (4607)
2003/04: 25⁰GS,

	Starts	1st	2nd	3rd	Win & Pl
Chases	1	0	0	0	
Career Total	3	0	0	0	

Going:	Sf: 0-0 GS: 0-1 Gd: 0-0 GF: - Fm: 0-0
Distance:	2m2m3: 0-0 2m4-2m7: 0-0 3m+: 0-1
Track:	LH: 0-0 RH: 0-1 Tight: 0-1 Gall: 0-0
Aids:	Bl: 0-0 Vi: 0-0 Tstrap: 0-0 Ckp: 0-0
Best Rating:	50 2/00 Clon 3m sft-hvy Ch

Auld Nick (IRE)

88   78

6-y-o b g Old Vic-Grey Tor (Ahonoora)
M C Pipe Sean Lucey

Placings:0-4450P   (4142)
2003/04: 16⁴G, 21⁴S, 19⁵GS, 26⁹GS, 24⁷G,

	Starts	1st	2nd	3rd	Win & Pl
Hurdles	5	0	0	0	1132
Career Total	6	0	0	0	1132

Going:	Sf: 0-1 GS: 0-2 Gd: 0-2 GF: - Fm: 0-0
Distance:	2m2m3: 0-1 2m4-2m7: 0-2 3m+: 0-2
Track:	LH: 0-2 RH: 0-1 Tight: 0-0 Gall: 0-1
Aids:	Bl: 0-0 Vi: 0-1 Tstrap: 0-0 Ckp: 0-0
Best Rating:	85 12/02 Wwck 2m soft NHF

Auld Thynes Sake (IRE)

92   87

7-y-o b g Good Thyne (USA)-La Fairy (IRE) (Lafontaine (USA))
Mrs Merrita Jones Speed 2911 Ltd

Placings:430-000   (4167)

2003/04: 20⁰G, 16⁹GF, 21⁰G,

	Starts	1st	2nd	3rd	Win & Pl
Hurdles	3	0	0	0	
Career Total	6	0	0	1	635

Going:	Sf: 0-0 GS: 0-0 Gd: 0-2 GF: - Fm: 0-1
Distance:	2m2m3: 0-1 2m4-2m7: 0-2 3m+: 0-0
Track:	LH: 0-3 RH: 0-0 Tight: 0-0 Gall: 0-2
Aids:	Bl: 0-0 Vi: 0-0 Tstrap: 0-0 Ckp: 0-0
Best Rating:	102 10/02 Chel 2m110y good NHF

Promising efforts in bumpers.

Aunt Hilda

96   67

5-y-o b m Distant Relative-Aloha Jane (USA) (Hawaii)
M F Harris Mrs Susan Keable

Placings:503330PP-0500440   (1469)
2003/04: 16⁶GF, 16⁵G, 16⁹GF, 16⁹GF, 16⁴GF, 17⁴GF, 17⁰F,

	Starts	1st	2nd	3rd	Win & Pl
Hurdles	7	0	0	0	267
Career Total	15	0	0	3	1587

Going:	Sf: 0-0 GS: 0-0 Gd: 0-1 GF: - Fm: 0-6
Distance:	2m2m3: 0-7 2m4-2m7: 0-0 3m+: 0-0
Track:	LH: 0-4 RH: 0-3 Tight: 0-3 Gall: 0-1
Aids:	Bl: 0-5 Vi: 0-0 Tstrap: 0-0 Ckp: 0-1
Best Rating:	80 11/02 Hntg 2m110y gd-sft Hdl

Plating-class novice hurdler.

Auntie Alba

6-y-o b m Gran Alba (USA)-Auntie Lorna (Uncle Pokey)
N J Pomfret R P Brett

Placings:PP   (0484)
2003/04: 20⁵PS, 16⁹GF,

	Starts	1st	2nd	3rd	Win & Pl
Hurdles	2	0	0	0	
Career Total	2	0	0	0	

Going:	Sf: 0-1 GS: 0-0 Gd: 0-0 GF: - Fm: 0-1
Distance:	2m2m3: 0-1 2m4-2m7: 0-1 3m+: 0-0
Track:	LH: 0-1 RH: 0-1 Tight: 0-0 Gall: 0-0
Aids:	Bl: 0-0 Vi: 0-0 Tstrap: 0-0 Ckp: 0-0
Best Rating:	0 5/03 Hntg 2m110y gd-fm Hdl

Auntie Jachinta

71f   69f

6-y-o b m Governor General-Hopeful Alda (Kambalda)
J A Supple Geoff Hubbard Racing

Placings:00   (3920)
2003/04: 17⁹HY, 16⁰G,

	Starts	1st	2nd	3rd	Win & Pl
NH Flat	2	0	0	0	
Career Total	2	0	0	0	

Going:	Sf: 0-1 GS: 0-0 Gd: 0-1 GF: - Fm: 0-0
Distance:	2m2m3: 0-2 2m4-2m7: 0-0 3m+: 0-0
Track:	LH: 0-1 RH: 0-1 Tight: 0-2 Gall: 0-0
Aids:	Bl: 0-0 Vi: 0-0 Tstrap: 0-0 Ckp: 0-0
Best Rating:	69 1/04 Folk 2m1f110y heavy NHF

Aurazure (IRE)
91f   103f
6-y-o gr g Roselier (FR)-Siul Currach (Deep Run)
C R Egerton   Mrs Sandra A Roe

Placings:44   (3874)
2003/04: 16⁴GS, 17⁴GS,

	Starts	1st	2nd	3rd	Win & Pl
NH Flat	2	0	0	0	0
Career Total	2	0	0	0	0

Going:	Sf: 0-0 GS: 0-2 Gd: 0-0 GF: - Fm: 0-0
Distance:	2m/2m3: 0-2 2m4-2m7: 0-0 3m+: 0-0
Track:	LH: 0-0 RH: 0-2 Tight: 0-1 Gall: 0-0
Aids:	Bl: 0-0 Vi: 0-0 Tstrap: 0-0 Ckp: 0-0
Best Rating:	103 2/04 Folk 2m1f110y gd-sft NHF

Autcaesar Autnihil (IRE)
(82h)70
9-y-o b g Supreme Leader-Monagey (Pimpernel's Tune)
A G Juckes   Whistlejacket Partnership

Placings:000/6P4F-PF   (0453)
2003/04: 26⁵HY, 23⁵FHY,

	Starts	1st	2nd	3rd	Win & Pl
Chases	2	0	0	0	
Career Total	9	0	0	0	323

Going:	Sf: 0-2 GS: 0-0 Gd: 0-0 GF: - Fm: 0-0
Distance:	2m/2m3: 0-0 2m4-2m7: 0-0 3m+: 0-1
Track:	LH: 0-2 RH: 0-0 Tight: 0-0 Gall: 0-0
Aids:	Bl: 0-0 Vi: 0-1 Tstrap: 0-0 Ckp: 0-0
Best Rating:	82 3/02 Newb 2m5f soft Hdl

Autumn Rain (USA)
97+
7-y-o br g Dynaformer (USA)-Edda (USA) (Ogygian (USA))
D L Williams   Ridgeway Farm Racing

Placings:P063-P   (1940)
2003/04: 22⁵G,

	Starts	1st	2nd	3rd	Win & Pl
Hurdles	1	0	0	0	
Career Total	5	0	0	1	456

Going:	Sf: 0-0 GS: 0-0 Gd: 0-1 GF: - Fm: 0-0
Distance:	2m/2m3: 0-0 2m4-2m7: 0-1 3m+: 0-0
Track:	LH: 0-0 RH: 0-1 Tight: 0-1 Gall: 0-0
Aids:	Bl: 0-0 Vi: 0-0 Tstrap: 0-0 Ckp: 0-0
Best Rating:	97 12/02 Wwck 3m1f soft Hdl

A fair handicapper on the Flat, he has shown ability over hurdles.

Avadi (IRE)
83   80+
6-y-o b g Un Desperado (FR)-Flamewood (Touching Wood (USA))
Mrs H Dalton   Mrs Julie Martin

Placings:0-40656   (4650)
2003/04: 16⁴GF, 17⁰GS, 20⁶GS, 24⁵GF, 19⁶G,

	Starts	1st	2nd	3rd	Win & Pl
NH Flat	2	0	0	0	0
Hurdles	3	0	0	0	0

Career Total   6   0   0   0   0

Going:	Sf: 0-0 GS: 0-2 Gd: 0-1 GF: - Fm: 0-2
Distance:	2m/2m3: 0-2 2m4-2m7: 0-2 3m+: 0-1
Track:	LH: 0-3 RH: 0-2 Tight: 0-0 Gall: 0-0
Aids:	Bl: 0-0 Vi: 0-0 Tstrap: 0-0 Ckp: 0-0
Best Rating:	87 3/04 Chep 3m gd-fm Hdl

Novice hurdler; poor form so far; looked doubtful stayer when tried at 3m; acts on most ground.

Avalanche (FR)
115(105h)   (111+h)136
7-y-o gr g Highest Honor (FR)-Fairy Gold (Golden Fleece (USA))
J R Best   The Downhill Partnership

Placings:200/U3P/1F110U4-634231331   (4864)
2003/04: 20⁶GS, 19³G, 24⁴G, 20²G, 20³G, 20¹G, 21³GS, 20³GS, 16¹S,

	Starts	1st	2nd	3rd	Win & Pl
Hurdles	1	0	0	1	596
Chases	8	2	1	3	38764
Career Total	22	5	2	5	70880

136	4/04	Ayr	2m	B HCh	SFT	£13546
136	2/04	Kemp	2m4f110yC(0-130)HCh	GD	£12064
135	2/03	Kemp	2m4f110yC(0-130)HCh	GD	£12760
124	2/03	Kemp	2m4f110yC(0-135)HCh	G-S	£9657
111	1/03	Leic	2m4f110yE Ch	SFT	£4927

Total win prize-money £52954

Going:	Sf: 1-1 GS: 0-3 Gd: 1-5 GF: - Fm: 0-0
Distance:	2m/2m3: 1-1 2m4-2m7: 1-7 3m+: 0-1
Track:	LH: 1-4 RH: 1-5 Tight: 0-0 Gall: 0-1
Aids:	Bl: 0-0 Vi: 0-0 Tstrap: 0-0 Ckp: 0-0
Best Rating:	136 4/04 Ayr 2m soft Ch

Fair chaser; stays two and a half miles and acts on soft ground; has a fine record at Kempton but efforts on consecutive days at Ayr in April 2004 show he is fully effective on left-handed tracks; consistent.

Avalon Buck (IRE)
106   107
11-y-o b g Buckskin (FR)-Lilly's Way (Golden Love)
Miss Venetia Williams   Dean Shakespeare

Placings:1/2211134/1PP/F0-662PP5   (1091)
2003/04: 23⁶G, 24⁶GS, 26²G, 26²GF, 22⁶G, 24⁵G,

	Starts	1st	2nd	3rd	Win & Pl
Hurdles	1	0	0	0	0
Chases	5	0	1	0	1648
Career Total	19	5	3	1	17947

123	12/01	Sthl	3m110y E Ch	SFT	£3475
116	2/01	Uttx	2m4f110yD Hdl	SFT	£3475
111	1/01	Chep	2m4f E Hdl	G-S	£2439
124	1/01	Extr	2m1f E Hdl	HVY	£2136
110	12/99	Wwck	2m	H NHF	SFT	£1912

Total win prize-money £13440

Going:	Sf: 0-0 GS: 0-1 Gd: 0-4 GF: - Fm: 0-1
Distance:	2m/2m3: 0-0 2m4-2m7: 0-1 3m+: 0-5
Track:	LH: 0-5 RH: 0-1 Tight: 0-4 Gall: 0-0
Aids:	Bl: 0-3 Vi: 0-0 Tstrap: 0-0 Ckp: 0-1
Best Rating:	124 1/01 Extr 2m1f heavy Hdl

Moderate performer; stays three miles plus; suited by soft ground.

Avanti Tiger (IRE)
79   39
5-y-o b/br g Supreme Leader-Reign Of Terror (IRE) (Orchestra)

C C Bealby   C Martin

Placings:00   (4588)
2003/04: 16⁰S, 21⁰G,

	Starts	1st	2nd	3rd	Win & Pl
NH Flat	1	0	0	0	0
Hurdles	1	0	0	0	0
Career Total	2	0	0	0	0

Going:	Sf: 0-1 GS: 0-0 Gd: 0-1 GF: - Fm: 0-0
Distance:	2m/2m3: 0-1 2m4-2m7: 0-1 3m+: 0-0
Track:	LH: 0-0 RH: 0-2 Tight: 0-0 Gall: 0-2
Aids:	Bl: 0-0 Vi: 0-0 Tstrap: 0-0 Ckp: 0-0
Best Rating:	84 1/04 Hntg 2m110y soft NHF

Avas Delight (IRE)
101   93
6-y-o b g Ajraas (USA)-Whothatis (Creative Plan (USA))
R H Alner (S J Treacy 7/7)   P M De Wilde

Placings:055000412   (4818)
2003/04: 18⁰Y, 16⁵G, 20⁵YS, 17⁹G, 20⁰S, 16⁰S, 17⁴G, 16¹GS, 17²GF,

	Starts	1st	2nd	3rd	Win & Pl
NH Flat	3	0	0	0	0
Hurdles	6	1	1	0	4867
Career Total	9	1	1	0	4867

90	3/04	Winc	2m	E(0-105)HHdl	G-S	£3437

Total win prize-money £3437

Going:	Sf: 0-2 GS: 1-1 Gd: 0-3 GF: - Fm: 0-1
Distance:	2m/2m3: 1-7 2m4-2m7: 0-2 3m+: 0-0
Track:	LH: 0-2 RH: 1-4 Tight: 0-2 Gall: 0-0
Aids:	Bl: 0-0 Vi: 0-0 Tstrap: 0-0 Ckp: 0-0
Best Rating:	97 6/03 Rosc 2m4f yld-sft NHF

Avebury
97(105h)   (98h)90
8-y-o b g Fairy King (USA)-Circle Of Chalk (FR) (Kris)
G M Moore   The Tupgill Partnership

Placings:20/331102-   (0010)
2003/04: 16²GF,

	Starts	1st	2nd	3rd	Win & Pl
Chases	1	0	1	0	1224
Career Total	8	2	2	2	8437

98	8/02	Sedg	2m1f	E Hdl	GD	£2905
95	7/02	Sedg	2m1f	E Hdl	G-F	£2954

Total win prize-money £5859

Going:	Sf: 0-0 GS: 0-0 Gd: 0-0 GF: - Fm: 0-1
Distance:	2m/2m3: 0-1 2m4-2m7: 0-3 3m+: 0-0
Track:	LH: 0-1 RH: 0-0 Tight: 0-0 Gall: 0-1
Aids:	Bl: 0-0 Vi: 0-0 Tstrap: 0-1 Ckp: 0-0
Best Rating:	105 12/00 Muss 2m good NHF

Avec Plaisir (IRE)

9-y-o ch g Grand Plaisir (IRE)-Ballinellard Lady (Fine Blade (USA))
T R George   Mrs Christine Davies

Placings:0/52/PPP-P   (0493)
2003/04: 25⁵PG,

	Starts	1st	2nd	3rd	Win & Pl
Chases	1	0	0	0	0
Career Total	7	0	1	0	1072

Going:	Sf: 0-0 GS: 0-0 Gd: 0-1 GF: - Fm: 0-0
Distance:	2m/2m3: 0-0 2m4-2m7: 0-0 3m+: 0-1
Track:	LH: 0-1 RH: 0-0 Tight: 0-0 Gall: 0-0
Aids:	Bl: 0-1 Vi: 0-0 Tstrap: 0-0 Ckp: 0-0
Best Rating:	110 1/01 Donc 3m110y good Hdl

Aveiro (IRE)

8-y-o b g Darshaan-Avila (Ajdal (USA))
Miss Gay Kelleway (B G Powell 19/2) This Time Next Year Racing

Placings:PP/P (1481)
2003/04: 19^{P}GF,

	Starts	1st	2nd	3rd	Win & Pl
Hurdles	1	0	0	0	
Career Total	3	0	0	0	

Going:	Sf: 0-0 GS: 0-0 Gd: 0-0 GF: - Fm: 0-1
Distance:	2m/2m3: 0-0 2m4-2m7: 0-1 3m+: 0-0
Track:	LH: 0-0 RH: 0-1 Tight: 0-0 Gall: 0-0
Aids:	Bl: 0-1 Vi: 0-0 Tstrap: 0-0 Ckp: 0-0
Best Rating:	0 10/03 Hrfd 2m3f110y gd-fm Hdl

Avenel

12-y-o b m Decent Fellow-Mermaid (Furry Glen)
R Allan Mrs M Wilson

Placings:0/P (3987)
2003/04: 21^{P}GS,

	Starts	1st	2nd	3rd	Win & Pl
Chases	1	0	0	0	
Career Total	2	0	0	0	

Going:	Sf: 0-0 GS: 0-1 Gd: 0-0 GF: - Fm: 0-0
Distance:	2m/2m3: 0-0 2m4-2m7: 0-1 3m+: 0-0
Track:	LH: 0-1 RH: 0-0 Tight: 0-0 Gall: 0-0
Aids:	Bl: 0-0 Vi: 0-0 Tstrap: 0-0 Ckp: 0-0
Best Rating:	63 5/98 DRoy 2m good Hdl

Averse (USA)
105f   88+f

5-y-o b m Lord Avie (USA)-Averti (USA) (Known Fact (USA))
N G Richards Kevin Johnston

Placings:20 (4328)
2003/04: 16^{2}GS, 16^{5}S,

	Starts	1st	2nd	3rd	Win & Pl
NH Flat	2	0	1	0	676
Career Total	2	0	1	0	676

Going:	Sf: 0-1 GS: 0-1 Gd: 0-0 GF: - Fm: 0-0
Distance:	2m/2m3: 0-2 2m4-2m7: 0-0 3m+: 0-0
Track:	LH: 0-1 RH: 0-1 Tight: 0-0 Gall: 0-0
Aids:	Bl: 0-0 Vi: 0-0 Tstrap: 0-0 Ckp: 0-0
Best Rating:	88 11/03 Weth 2m gd-sft NHF

Promising second in a Wetherby bumper; should do better over obstacles when upped in trip; acts on easy going.

Avitta (IRE)
101   117+

5-y-o b m Pennekamp (USA)-Alinova (USA) (Alleged (USA))

Miss Venetia Williams P A Deal, A Hirschfeld & M Graham

Placings:12-3F5F2362 (4849)
2003/04: 18^{3}G, 16^{F}G, 16^{5}GS, 17^{F}GS, 16^{2}S, 16^{3}G, 16^{6}G, 16^{2}GS,

	Starts	1st	2nd	3rd	Win & Pl
Hurdles	8	0	2	2	11915
Career Total	10	1	3	2	17884
104 1/03 Fknm 2m		D Hdl		SFT	£4881
				Total win prize-money	£4882

Going:	Sf: 0-1 GS: 0-3 Gd: 0-4 GF: - Fm: 0-0
Distance:	2m/2m3: 0-8 2m4-2m7: 0-0 3m+: 0-0
Track:	LH: 0-5 RH: 0-3 Tight: 0-1 Gall: 0-2
Aids:	Bl: 0-1 Vi: 0-0 Tstrap: 0-0 Ckp: 0-0
Best Rating:	117 2/04 Weth 2m soft Hdl

Modest hurdler; keen sort; worn down when runner-up at Wetherby in February; acts on good and soft ground; unlikely to stay beyond two miles.

Awesome Wells (IRE)
99   82+

10-y-o b g Sadler's Wells (USA)-Shadywood (Habitat)
D J Wintle M Tuerks

Placings:P/P/044P1-P0030 (4632)
2003/04: 20^{P}S, 16^{6}S, 16^{0}G, 16^{3}G, 24^{0}G,

	Starts	1st	2nd	3rd	Win & Pl
Hurdles	5	0	0	1	369
Career Total	12	1	0	1	3581
85 3/03 Wwck 2m		F(0-100)HHdl		SFT	£2838
				Total win prize-money	£2839

Going:	Sf: 0-2 GS: 0-0 Gd: 0-3 GF: - Fm: 0-0
Distance:	2m/2m3: 0-3 2m4-2m7: 0-1 3m+: 0-1
Track:	LH: 0-1 RH: 0-4 Tight: 0-1 Gall: 0-1
Aids:	Bl: 0-0 Vi: 0-0 Tstrap: 0-2 Ckp: 0-0
Best Rating:	85 3/03 Wwck 2m soft Hdl

Winning hurdler; acts on soft ground;

Ay Carumba

7-y-o b g Seymour Hicks (FR)-Aldington Peach (Creetown)
J F Panvert J F Panvert

Placings:U/000-PP (2237)
2003/04: 19^{P}G, 16^{P}G,

	Starts	1st	2nd	3rd	Win & Pl
Hurdles	2	0	0	0	
Career Total	6	0	0	0	

Going:	Sf: 0-0 GS: 0-0 Gd: 0-2 GF: - Fm: 0-0
Distance:	2m/2m3: 0-1 2m4-2m7: 0-1 3m+: 0-0
Track:	LH: 0-1 RH: 0-1 Tight: 0-1 Gall: 0-0
Aids:	Bl: 0-0 Vi: 0-0 Tstrap: 0-0 Ckp: 0-0
Best Rating:	0 11/03 Kemp 2m good Hdl

Aye Aye Popeye (IRE)
107   119

6-y-o ch g Imperial Frontier (USA)-Boskovice (IRE) (Flash Of Steel)
Mrs John Harrington Vincent Clynch

Placings:245/14060F06-1000020 (4828a)
2003/04: 16^{1}G, 17^{0}G, 16^{0}Y, 16^{0}GY, 16^{0}GS, 16^{2}YS, 16^{0}Y,

	Starts	1st	2nd	3rd	Win & Pl
Hurdles	7	1	1	0	12581

Career Total	18	2	2	0	19102
119 4/03 Punc 2m		Hdl		GD	£9496
110 5/02 Clon 2m		Hdl		Y-S	£4233
				Total win prize-money	£13730

Going:	Sf: 0-0 GS: 0-1 Gd: 1-2 GF: - Fm: 0-0
Distance:	2m/2m3: 1-7 2m4-2m7: 0-0 3m+: 0-0
Track:	LH: 0-1 RH: 1-5 Tight: 0-0 Gall: 0-0
Aids:	Bl: 0-2 Vi: 0-0 Tstrap: 0-0 Ckp: 0-0
Best Rating:	119 12/03 Leop 2m yld-sft Hdl

Fair Irish-trained hurdler; effective at two miles; acts on good and soft ground.

Aye Surely (IRE)
97(84c)   (99c)98

10-y-o b g Legal Circles (USA)-Uno Navarro (Raga Navarro (ITY))
Mrs A M Thorpe Don Jones

Placings:12506/034/0U0F40P/01F0BFF405442-6P (1606)
2003/04: 24^{6}GF, 26^{6}PG,

	Starts	1st	2nd	3rd	Win & Pl
Hurdles	2	0	0	0	0
Career Total	30	2	2	1	14384
110 7/02 Limk 2m4f		(0-109)HCh		SFT	£7619
93 6/99 Slig 2m		Hdl		HVY	£2209
				Total win prize-money	£9830

Going:	Sf: 0-0 GS: 0-0 Gd: 0-0 GF: - Fm: 0-2
Distance:	2m/2m3: 0-0 2m4-2m7: 0-0 3m+: 0-2
Track:	LH: 0-0 RH: 0-2 Tight: 0-1 Gall: 0-1
Aids:	Bl: 0-0 Vi: 0-0 Tstrap: 0-0 Ckp: 0-0
Best Rating:	110 7/02 Limk 2m4f soft Ch

Modest ex-Irish hurdler/chaser; stays three miles three; usually wore blinkers in Ireland but left off so far by current connections.

Azertyuiop (FR)
121   (162h)176+

7-y-o b g Baby Turk-Temara (FR) (Rex Magna (FR))
P F Nicholls J Hales

Placings:112/1545/1111-U2211 (4396)
2003/04: 17^{U}G, 16^{2}G, 16^{2}GS, 17^{1}G, 16^{1}G,

	Starts	1st	2nd	3rd	Win & Pl
Chases	5	2	2	0	225300
Career Total	16	9	3	0	418660
176 3/04 Chel	2m	A Ch		GD	£145000
166 2/04 Newb	2m1f	A Ch		GD	£31900
166 3/03 Chel	2m	A Ch		GD	£81200
165 2/03 Winc	2m	C Ch		G-S	£8946
160 11/02 Chel	2m	A Ch		G-S	£17400
125 10/02 MRas	2m1f110y	C Ch		G-S	£8190
162 11/01 Winc	2m	A HHdl		GD	£15000
155 2/01 Winc	2m	A HHdl		GD	£21000
10/00 Autl	1m7f	Hdl		VS	£13449
				Total win prize-money	£342085

Going:	Sf: 0-0 GS: 0-1 Gd: 2-4 GF: - Fm: 0-0
Distance:	2m/2m3: 2-5 2m4-2m7: 0-0 3m+: 0-0
Track:	LH: 2-2 RH: 0-3 Tight: 0-0 Gall: 2-2
Aids:	Bl: 0-0 Vi: 0-0 Tstrap: 0-0 Ckp: 0-0
Best Rating:	176 3/04 Chel 2m good Ch

Top-class chaser; formerly high-class hurdler; wide-margin winner of all four outings over fences as a novice, including Arkle Challenge Trophy at Cheltenham by 11 lengths; unseated at the first in the Haldon Gold Cup on his reappearance, before running second to Moscow Flyer in the Tingle Creek; just beaten by Isio (who was getting 19lb) in Victor Chandler in January, and hacked up at Newbury subsequently and took the Queen Mother Chase at Cheltenham

in emphatic fashion (main rival unseated); suited by two miles; acts on good and soft ground; jumps well; races enthusiastically.

Azzemour (FR)
93f   84f

5-y-o ch g Morespeed-Tarde (FR) (Kashtan (FR))
P F Nicholls Tony Hayward And Barry Fulton

Placings:4   (4936)
2003/04: 18⁴G,

	Starts	1st	2nd	3rd	Win & Pl
NH Flat	1	0	0	0	0
Career Total	1	0	0	0	0

Going:	Sf: 0-0 GS: 0-0 Gd: 0-1 GF: - Fm: 0-0
Distance:	2m/2m3: 0-1 2m4-2m7: 0-0 3m+: 0-0
Track:	LH: 0-1 RH: 0-0 Tight: 0-1 Gall: 0-0
Aids:	Bl: 0-0 Vi: 0-0 Tstrap: 0-0 Ckp: 0-0
Best Rating:	84 4/04 Font 2m2f110y good NHF

Baby Gee
105   98

10-y-o ch m King Among Kings-Market Blues (Porto Bello)
D W Whillans Chas N Whillans

Placings:004/011123/4123-41651600   (4599)
2003/04: 16³G, 16⁴G, 20¹GF, 16⁶G, 21⁵GS, 16¹G, 16⁶S, 16⁹G, 18⁰G,

	Starts	1st	2nd	3rd	Win & Pl
Hurdles	9	2	0	1	13207
Career Total	21	6	2	2	31243
98	1/04	Catt	2m	C(0-130)HHdl	GD	£6870
92	6/03	Prth	2m4f110y	D(0-115)HHdl	G-F	£5499
92	2/03	Sedg	2m1f	E(0-110)HHdl	HVY	£4745
81	2/02	Muss	2m	G(0-105)HHdl	G-S	£2996
80	1/02	Newc	2m	E(0-100)HHdl	SFT	£2534
73	1/02	Catt	2m	G(0-90)HHdl	G-S	£1764
				Total win prize-money		£24409

Going:	Sf: 0-1 GS: 0-1 Gd: 1-6 GF: - Fm: 1-1
Distance:	2m/2m3: 1-7 2m4-2m7: 1-2 3m+: 0-0
Track:	LH: 1-7 RH: 1-2 Tight: 1-3 Gall: 0-2
Aids:	Bl: 0-0 Vi: 0-0 Tstrap: 0-0 Ckp: 0-0
Best Rating:	98 1/04 Catt 2m good Hdl

Moderate hurdler; effective from two to two and a half miles and seems to go on any ground.

Baby Jane
91   69+

10-y-o b m Old Vic-Sutosky (Great Nephew)
R Johnson Geoff Pickering

Placings:3/6P06P   (3317)
2003/04: 20⁶GF, 17⁸GF, 19⁰GF, 16⁶GF, 16⁸S,

	Starts	1st	2nd	3rd	Win & Pl
Hurdles	5	0	0	0	0
Career Total	6	0	0	1	308

Going:	Sf: 0-1 GS: 0-0 Gd: 0-0 GF: - Fm: 0-4
Distance:	2m/2m3: 0-4 2m4-2m7: 0-1 3m+: 0-0
Track:	LH: 0-3 RH: 0-2 Tight: 0-3 Gall: 0-0
Aids:	Bl: 0-0 Vi: 0-0 Tstrap: 0-0 Ckp: 0-1
Best Rating:	84 8/97 Prth 2m110y good Hdl

Baby Run (FR)
108f   109+f

4-y-o b g Baby Turk-Run For Laborie (FR) (Lesotho (USA))
N A Twiston-Davies Mr & Mrs Peter Orton

Placings:3125   (3632)
2003/04: 12³GF, 13¹GS, 12²G, 16⁵G,

	Starts	1st	2nd	3rd	Win & Pl
NH Flat	4	1	1	1	4936
Career Total	4	1	1	1	4936
103	12/03	Extr	1m5f	H NHF	G-S	£2268
				Total win prize-money		£2268

Going:	Sf: 0-0 GS: 1-1 Gd: 0-2 GF: - Fm: 0-1
Distance:	2m/2m3: 0-1 2m4-2m7: 0-0 3m+: 0-0
Track:	LH: 0-2 RH: 1-1 Tight: 0-0 Gall: 0-1
Aids:	Bl: 0-0 Vi: 0-0 Tstrap: 0-0 Ckp: 0-0
Best Rating:	112 2/04 Newb 2m110y good NHF

Scopey sort; bumper winner; suited by trips of around 12 furlongs in bumpers, but should stay two miles over hurdles.

Baby Sister
95f   84f

5-y-o ch m King Among Kings-Market Blues (Porto Bello)
D W Whillans Chas N Whillans

Placings:62   (3738)
2003/04: 16⁶G, 16²G,

	Starts	1st	2nd	3rd	Win & Pl
NH Flat	2	0	1	0	842
Career Total	2	0	1	0	842

Going:	Sf: 0-0 GS: 0-0 Gd: 0-2 GF: - Fm: 0-0
Distance:	2m/2m3: 0-2 2m4-2m7: 0-0 3m+: 0-0
Track:	LH: 0-0 RH: 0-2 Tight: 0-1 Gall: 0-0
Aids:	Bl: 0-0 Vi: 0-0 Tstrap: 0-0 Ckp: 0-0
Best Rating:	84 2/04 Muss 2m good NHF

Bacardi Boy (IRE)
103(98h)   (112h)107

8-y-o b g Lord Americo-Little Welly (Little Buskins)
T R George Allan Stennett & Terry Warner

Placings:13332/130-33U353   (4590)
2003/04: 26³HY, 26³G, 24ᵁS, 24³G, 24⁴S, 24³G,

	Starts	1st	2nd	3rd	Win & Pl
Chases	6	0	0	4	2958
Career Total	14	2	1	8	13325
112	1/03	Chep	3m	F Hdl	HVY	£2772
118	11/01	Carl	2m1f	H NHF	SFT	£1610
				Total win prize-money		£4382

Going:	Sf: 0-3 GS: 0-0 Gd: 0-3 GF: - Fm: 0-0
Distance:	2m/2m3: 0-2 2m4-2m7: 0-0 3m+: 0-6
Track:	LH: 0-3 RH: 0-3 Tight: 0-2 Gall: 0-2
Aids:	Bl: 0-0 Vi: 0-0 Tstrap: 0-0 Ckp: 0-0
Best Rating:	126 12/01 Chep 2m110y gd-sft NHF

Fair novice chaser; stays three miles plus; best on soft ground.

Baccarat (IRE)

10-y-o b g Bob Back (USA)-Sarahlee (Sayyaf)
Lady Susan Brooke (T J Fitzgerald 7/5) Lady Susan Brooke

Placings:1230/4/F33/3/PP3P-P   (3845)
2003/04: 25⁵GS,

	Starts	1st	2nd	3rd	Win & Pl
Chases	1	0	0	0	
Career Total	14	1	1	5	4926
115	12/98	Donc	2m110y	H NHF	GD	£1413
				Total win prize-money		£1413

Going:	Sf: 0-0 GS: 0-1 Gd: 0-0 GF: - Fm: 0-0
Distance:	2m/2m3: 0-0 2m4-2m7: 0-0 3m+: 0-1
Track:	LH: 0-0 RH: 0-1 Tight: 0-0 Gall: 0-0
Aids:	Bl: 0-0 Vi: 0-0 Tstrap: 0-1 Ckp: 0-0
Best Rating:	123 3/99 Chel 2m110y gd-sft NHF

Bachelor's Tonic (IRE)
86f   81f

6-y-o b g Fayruz-Dance Alone (USA) (Monteverdi)
K A Morgan (C J Mann 23/7) S & M Giles & M Hawkins

Placings:0/063   (2115)
2003/04: 16⁰G, 16⁶G, 16³G,

	Starts	1st	2nd	3rd	Win & Pl
NH Flat	3	0	0	1	210
Career Total	4	0	0	1	210

Going:	Sf: 0-0 GS: 0-0 Gd: 0-3 GF: - Fm: 0-0
Distance:	2m/2m3: 0-3 2m4-2m7: 0-0 3m+: 0-0
Track:	LH: 0-3 RH: 0-0 Tight: 0-2 Gall: 0-0
Aids:	Bl: 0-0 Vi: 0-0 Tstrap: 0-0 Ckp: 0-0
Best Rating:	81 2/02 Kemp 2m good NHF

Bachelors Pad
99   80

10-y-o b g Pursuit Of Love-Note Book (Mummy's Pet)
Miss S J Wilton John Pointon And Sons

Placings:05/00155361030/026040-04364533U000 (4401)
2003/04: 16⁸G, 19⁴GF, 17³GF, 17⁶GF, 16⁴GF, 17⁵GF, 16³GS, 16³GS, 16¹S, 16⁶G, 16⁶S, 21⁰G,

	Starts	1st	2nd	3rd	Win & Pl
Hurdles	12	0	0	3	883
Career Total	31	2	1	5	5972
86	12/01	Strf	2m110y	G(0-95)HHdl	SFT	£2002
86	10/01	Fknm	2m	G(0-90)HHdl	SFT	£1862
				Total win prize-money		£3865

Going:	Sf: 0-2 GS: 0-2 Gd: 0-3 GF: - Fm: 0-5
Distance:	2m/2m3: 0-11 2m4-2m7: 0-1 3m+: 0-0
Track:	LH: 0-5 RH: 0-7 Tight: 0-2 Gall: 0-1
Aids:	Bl: 0-0 Vi: 0-0 Tstrap: 0-0 Ckp: 0-11
Best Rating:	86 12/01 Strf 2m110y soft Hdl

Plating-class hurdler; acts on soft ground; effective over two miles; has worn cheekpieces.

Back In The Game
51   18

8-y-o ch g Phountzi (USA)-Chasmarella (Yukon Eric (CAN))
Miss Z C Davison Mrs J Irvine

Placings:0P0   (4268)
2003/04: 16⁶G, 20⁸GS, 24⁸G,

	Starts	1st	2nd	3rd	Win & Pl
Hurdles	3	0	0	0	
Career Total	3	0	0	0	

Going:	Sf: 0-0 GS: 0-1 Gd: 0-1 GF: - Fm: 0-1
Distance:	2m/2m3: 0-1 2m4-2m7: 0-1 3m+: 0-1
Track:	LH: 0-1 RH: 0-2 Tight: 0-1 Gall: 0-1

Aids: Bl: 0-0 Vi: 0-0 Tstrap: 0-0 Ckp: 0-0
Best Rating: 18   11/03   Towc   2m   good   Hdl

Back On Song (IRE)
56   26

5-y-o b m Bob Back (USA)-No Blues (IRE) (Orchestra)
J Howard Johnson Dr B Mayoh

Placings: 0F00   (3468)
2003/04: 16⁰GF, 19ᶠGS, 16⁰GS, 20⁰GF,

	Starts	1st	2nd	3rd	Win & Pl
NH Flat	1	0	0	0	0
Hurdles	3	0	0	0	0
Career Total	**4**	**0**	**0**	**0**	

Going: Sf: 0-0 GS: 0-2 Gd: 0-0 GF: - Fm: 0-2
Distance: 2m/2m3: 0-3 2m4-2m7: 0-1 3m+: 0-0
Track: LH: 0-3 RH: 0-1 Tight: 0-2 Gall: 0-0
Aids: Bl: 0-0 Vi: 0-0 Tstrap: 0-0 Ckp: 0-0
Best Rating: 53   11/03   Hexm   2m110y   gd-fm   NHF

Back On Top (IRE)
116(108h)   (128h) 140

10-y-o b g Bob Back (USA)-Top Girl (IRE) (High Top)
J L Hassett Mrs John Magnier

Placings: P000011/10/P0/10/4012-1400PP   (4805a)
2003/04: 25¹GY, 22⁴Y, 24⁰S, 25⁰G, 20⁰PG, 29ᴾY,

	Starts	1st	2nd	3rd	Win & Pl
Hurdles	2	0	0	0	0
Chases	4	1	0	0	24269
Career Total	**24**	**6**	**1**	**0**	**69951**
133	5/03	Punc	3m1f	HCh	G-Y £21103
119	2/03	Gowr	2m4f	(0-123)HHdl	YLD £8441
112	3/02	Limk	2m2f	Ch	SFT £8042
125	5/99	Klny	2m1f	HHdl	SFT £14453
110	4/99	Punc	2m2f	(0-116)HHdl	YLD £7366
91	4/99	Cork	2m	(0-102)HHdl	SFT £3989

Total win prize-money £63398

Going: Sf: 0-1 GS: 0-0 Gd: 0-2 GF: - Fm: 0-0
Distance: 2m/2m3: 0-0 2m4-2m7: 0-2 3m+: 1-4
Track: LH: 0-3 RH: 1-3 Tight: 0-0 Gall: 0-2
Aids: Bl: 0-0 Vi: 0-0 Tstrap: 0-0 Ckp: 0-0
Best Rating: 140   7/03   Gway   2m6f   yield   Ch

Fair hurdler/chaser; stays three miles; acts on soft ground.

Back To Ben Alder (IRE)
98   111+

7-y-o b g Bob Back (USA)-Winter Fox (Martinmas)
N J Henderson Mrs Christopher Hanbury

Placings: 10-1   (4309)
2003/04: 16¹G,

	Starts	1st	2nd	3rd	Win & Pl
Hurdles	1	1	0	0	5018
Career Total	**3**	**2**	**0**	**0**	**7412**
111	3/04	Sand	2m110y	D Hdl	GD £5018
118	1/03	Kemp	2m	H NHF	G-S £2394

Total win prize-money £7412

Going: Sf: 0-0 GS: 0-0 Gd: 1-1 GF: - Fm: 0-0
Distance: 2m/2m3: 1-1 2m4-2m7: 0-0 3m+: 0-0
Track: LH: 0-0 RH: 1-1 Tight: 0-0 Gall: 0-0
Aids: Bl: 0-0 Vi: 0-0 Tstrap: 0-0 Ckp: 0-0
Best Rating: 118   1/03   Kemp   2m   gd-sft   NHF

Fair novice hurdler; useful bumper performer; struck into when disappointing in the 2003 Festival Bumper; made a winning debut over hurdles at Sandown in March 2004; acts well with cut in the ground.

Backbeat (IRE)
(101h)   (111 h)

7-y-o ch g Bob Back (USA)-Pinata (Deep Run)
D R C Elsworth W V & Mrs E S Robins

Placings: 240/41P-P   (2484)
2003/04: 18ᶠGS,

	Starts	1st	2nd	3rd	Win & Pl
Chases	1	0	0	0	
Career Total	**7**	**1**	**1**	**0**	**5985**
111	2/03	Newb	2m3f	D Hdl	SFT £5583

Total win prize-money £5584

Going: Sf: 0-0 GS: 0-1 Gd: 0-0 GF: - Fm: 0-0
Distance: 2m/2m3: 0-1 2m4-2m7: 0-0 3m+: 0-0
Track: LH: 0-1 RH: 0-0 Tight: 0-0 Gall: 0-1
Aids: Bl: 0-1 Vi: 0-0 Tstrap: 0-0 Ckp: 0-0
Best Rating: 121   12/01   Asct   2m110y   good   NHF

Modest hurdler; likes to front run; pulled up on chase debut after jumping to the right; blinkered for the first time on that occasion; effective on good/soft ground.

Backcraft (IRE)
104   113+

6-y-o b g Bob Back (USA)-Bawnanell (Viking (USA))
L Lungo M Magowan

Placings: 313/14P6P0P-5210   (0794)
2003/04: 17⁵G, 20²GF, 16¹GF, 16⁰G,

	Starts	1st	2nd	3rd	Win & Pl
Hurdles	4	1	1	0	5150
Career Total	**14**	**3**	**1**	**2**	**13395**
116	6/03	Hexm	2m110y	E(0-105)HHdl	G-F £3458
120	5/02	Weth	2m	D(0-115)HHdl	G-F £3447
102	3/02	Kels	2m2f	E Hdl	HVY £2786

Total win prize-money £9692

Going: Sf: 0-0 GS: 0-0 Gd: 0-2 GF: - Fm: 1-2
Distance: 2m/2m3: 1-3 2m4-2m7: 0-1 3m+: 0-0
Track: LH: 1-2 RH: 0-2 Tight: 0-1 Gall: 0-0
Aids: Bl: 0-0 Vi: 0-0 Tstrap: 0-0 Ckp: 0-0
Best Rating: 120   5/02   Weth   2m   gd-fm   Hdl

Modest hurdler; stays two and a half miles; seems to go on any ground.

Backscratcher
95(97h)   (83+h) 81

10-y-o b g Backchat (USA)-Tiernee Quintana (Artaius (USA))
John R Upson The Fourways Partnership

Placings: 000/0406003-4036P1006FP   (4494)
2003/04: 24⁴GF, 24⁰GF, 24³GF, 24⁶GF, 20ᶠF, 24¹GS, 26⁰G, 23⁰G, 25⁶GS, 25ᶠG, 24ᴾGS,

	Starts	1st	2nd	3rd	Win & Pl
Hurdles	3	0	0	1	371
Chases	8	1	0	0	2847
Career Total	**21**	**1**	**0**	**2**	**3667**
83	12/03	Uttx	3m	F(0-90)HCh	G-S £2847

Total win prize-money £2847

Going: Sf: 0-0 GS: 1-3 Gd: 0-3 GF: - Fm: 0-5
Distance: 2m/2m3: 0-0 2m4-2m7: 0-1 3m+: 1-10
Track: LH: 1-3 RH: 0-7 Tight: 0-3 Gall: 0-1
Aids: Bl: 0-2 Vi: 0-0 Tstrap: 0-0 Ckp: 0-0
Best Rating: 83   12/03   Uttx   3m   gd-sft   Ch

Very moderate over both hurdles and fences; narrow winner of a modest novices' handicap chase at Uttoxeter in December; stays three miles.

Bacyan (IRE)
103   102

7-y-o ch g Denel (FR)-Naycab (Le Moss)
Mrs A Hamilton Ian Hamilton

Placings: 15321P   (3814)
2003/04: 17¹G, 24⁵GS, 16³S, 25²GS, 25¹G, 24ᴾGS,

	Starts	1st	2nd	3rd	Win & Pl
NH Flat	1	0	0	0	1968
Hurdles	5	1	1	1	4613
Career Total	**6**	**2**	**1**	**1**	**6581**
100	1/04	Catt	3m1f110y	E Hdl	GD £3562
100	10/03	Carl	2m1f	H NHF	GD £1968

Total win prize-money £5530

Going: Sf: 0-1 GS: 0-3 Gd: 2-2 GF: - Fm: 0-0
Distance: 2m/2m3: 1-2 2m4-2m7: 0-0 3m+: 1-4
Track: LH: 1-4 RH: 1-2 Tight: 1-1 Gall: 0-0
Aids: Bl: 0-0 Vi: 0-0 Tstrap: 0-0 Ckp: 0-0
Best Rating: 100   1/04   Catt   3m1f110y   good   Hdl

Point winner in March 2003 who won ordinary bumper on debut under rules at Carlisle in October; clear second best in novices' hurdle over three miles at Wetherby in January; eventual wide-margin winner at Catterick two weeks later; stays really well; will be suited by fences in due course.

Baden Vugie (IRE)
71   (47h) 48

7-y-o bl g Hamas (IRE)-Bag Lady (Be My Guest) (USA)
S T Lewis Simon T Lewis

Placings: 00/000/0045-UP   (4570)
2003/04: 16ᵁGS, 24ᴾGS,

	Starts	1st	2nd	3rd	Win & Pl
Chases	2	0	0	0	
Career Total	**11**	**0**	**0**	**0**	**374**

Going: Sf: 0-0 GS: 0-2 Gd: 0-0 GF: - Fm: 0-0
Distance: 2m/2m3: 0-1 2m4-2m7: 0-0 3m+: 0-1
Track: LH: 0-2 RH: 0-0 Tight: 0-1 Gall: 0-0
Aids: Bl: 0-0 Vi: 0-0 Tstrap: 0-0 Ckp: 0-0
Best Rating: 58   2/01   Wwck   2m   soft   NHF

Badger Beer
12-y-o b g Town And Country-Panda Pops (Cornuto)
J W Dufosee Mrs R H Woodhouse

Placings: 4/43P/20P/014P0B4/3P-2F   (4289)
2003/04: 25²GF, 25ᶠGS,

	Starts	1st	2nd	3rd	Win & Pl
Chases	2	0	1	0	1033
Career Total	**18**	**1**	**2**	**2**	**5098**
95	5/01	Winc	2m5f	H Ch	G-F £2222

Total win prize-money £2223

Going: Sf: 0-0 GS: 0-0 Gd: 0-0 GF: - Fm: 0-2
Distance: 2m/2m3: 0-0 2m4-2m7: 0-0 3m+: 0-2
Track: LH: 0-0 RH: 0-2 Tight: 0-0 Gall: 0-0
Aids: Bl: 0-0 Vi: 0-0 Tstrap: 0-0 Ckp: 0-0
Best Rating: 98   5/03   Winc   3m1f110y   gd-fm   Ch

Hunter chaser; likes fast ground; stays well.

Badgers Glory

77   **62**

8-y-o gr/ro g Neltino-Shedid (St Columbus)
G P Enright Frederick Gray

Placings:00PP4P/4P-6   (4791)
2003/04: 20⁶G,

	Starts	1st	2nd	3rd	Win & Pl
Chases	1	0	0	0	0
Career Total	9	0	0	0	480

Going:	Sf: 0-0 GS: 0-0 Gd: 0-1 GF: - Fm: 0-0
Distance:	2m/2m3: 0-0 2m4-2m7: 0-1 3m+: 0-0
Track:	LH: 0-1 RH: 0-0 Tight: 0-1 Gall: 0-0
Aids:	Bl: 0-0 Vi: 0-0 Tstrap: 0-0 Ckp: 0-0
Best Rating:	71 5/01 Folk 2m1f110y gd-sft NHF

Badrinath (IRE)

10-y-o b g Imperial Frontier (USA)-Badedra (King's Lake (USA))
H J Collingridge D T Thom

Placings:0/P   (2542)
2003/04: 16⁶G,

	Starts	1st	2nd	3rd	Win & Pl
Hurdles	1	0	0	0	
Career Total	2	0	0	0	

Going:	Sf: 0-0 GS: 0-0 Gd: 0-1 GF: - Fm: 0-0
Distance:	2m/2m3: 0-1 2m4-2m7: 0-0 3m+: 0-0
Track:	LH: 0-0 RH: 0-1 Tight: 0-0 Gall: 0-0
Aids:	Bl: 0-0 Vi: 0-0 Tstrap: 0-0 Ckp: 0-0
Best Rating:	34 12/00 Fknm 2m gd-sft Hdl

Badworth Gale (IRE)

10-y-o br g Strong Gale-Badsworth Madam (Over The River (FR))
J E Dillon J E Dillon

Placings:P64/0P-PP   (4775)
2003/04: 25PGS, 21PG,

	Starts	1st	2nd	3rd	Win & Pl
Chases	2	0	0	0	
Career Total	7	0	0	0	269

Going:	Sf: 0-0 GS: 0-1 Gd: 0-1 GF: - Fm: 0-0
Distance:	2m/2m3: 0-0 2m4-2m7: 0-0 3m+: 0-1
Track:	LH: 0-1 RH: 0-1 Tight: 0-2 Gall: 0-0
Aids:	Bl: 0-0 Vi: 0-0 Tstrap: 0-0 Ckp: 0-0
Best Rating:	61 6/02 MRas 2m6f110y gd-fm Ch

Baganite (AUS)

5-y-o ch g Grand Lodge (USA)-Lady Triscanny (AUS) (Sir Tristram)
Jonjo O'Neill A Purvis

Placings:00P   (4197)
2003/04: 16⁰HY, 16⁰GS, 24PG,

	Starts	1st	2nd	3rd	Win & Pl
NH Flat	2	0	0	0	0
Hurdles	1	0	0	0	0

Bahlino (IRE)

102   **87**

4-y-o gr g Bahhare (USA)-Azulino (IRE) (Bluebird (USA))
J Howard Johnson (W Jarvis 13/10) Andrea & Graham Wylie

Placings:34   (4260)
2003/04: 16³G, 16⁴GF,

	Starts	1st	2nd	3rd	Win & Pl
Hurdles	2	0	0	1	499
Career Total	2	0	0	1	499

Going:	Sf: 0-0 GS: 0-0 Gd: 0-1 GF: - Fm: 0-1
Distance:	2m/2m3: 0-2 2m4-2m7: 0-0 3m+: 0-0
Track:	LH: 0-2 RH: 0-0 Tight: 0-2 Gall: 0-0
Aids:	Bl: 0-0 Vi: 0-0 Tstrap: 0-1 Ckp: 0-0
Best Rating:	87 3/04 Catt 2m gd-fm Hdl

Baie D'Along (FR)

5-y-o b m Tel Quel (FR)-County Kerry (FR) (Comrade In Arms)
N J Hawke Mrs D R Whigham

Placings:5-P   (0871)
2003/04: 17PGF,

	Starts	1st	2nd	3rd	Win & Pl
NH Flat	1	0	0	0	
Career Total	2	0	0	0	0

Going:	Sf: 0-0 GS: 0-0 Gd: 0-0 GF: - Fm: 0-1
Distance:	2m/2m3: 0-1 2m4-2m7: 0-0 3m+: 0-0
Track:	LH: 0-1 RH: 0-0 Tight: 0-1 Gall: 0-0
Aids:	Bl: 0-0 Vi: 0-0 Tstrap: 0-0 Ckp: 0-0
Best Rating:	0 7/03 NAbb 2m1f gd-fm NHF

Baie Des Singes

79   **71**

10-y-o b g Royal Vulcan-Mikey's Monkey (Monksfield)
M J M Evans M J M Evans

Placings:2/0343F5/24P4FP/5/44F04   (4566)
2003/04: 17⁴GS, 20⁴S, 19⁵HY, 16⁶G, 17⁴GS,

	Starts	1st	2nd	3rd	Win & Pl
Chases	5	0	0	0	1033
Career Total	19	0	2	2	5588

Going:	Sf: 0-2 GS: 0-2 Gd: 0-1 GF: - Fm: 0-0
Distance:	2m/2m3: 0-4 2m4-2m7: 0-1 3m+: 0-0
Track:	LH: 0-3 RH: 0-2 Tight: 0-2 Gall: 0-0
Aids:	Bl: 0-0 Vi: 0-0 Tstrap: 0-0 Ckp: 0-0
Best Rating:	109 2/99 Wwck 2m gd-sft NHF

Maiden staying hurdler/chaser.

Baikaline (FR)

72   **55**

5-y-o b m Cadoudal (FR)-Advantage (FR) (Antheus (USA))
Ian Williams Ian Williams

Placings:3220FP-6   (3279)
2003/04: 16⁶HY,

	Starts	1st	2nd	3rd	Win & Pl
Hurdles	1	0	0	0	0
Career Total	7	0	2	1	15951

Going:	Sf: 0-1 GS: 0-0 Gd: 0-0 GF: - Fm: 0-0
Distance:	2m/2m3: 0-1 2m4-2m7: 0-0 3m+: 0-0
Track:	LH: 0-1 RH: 0-0 Tight: 0-0 Gall: 0-0
Aids:	Bl: 0-0 Vi: 0-0 Tstrap: 0-0 Ckp: 0-0
Best Rating:	55 1/04 Uttx 2m heavy Hdl

Ex-French hurdler; acts on testing ground.

Bailey Contract

6-y-o b m Contract Law (USA)-Megabucks (Buckskin (FR))
A C Whillans Mrs L M Whillans

Placings:0U   (4881)
2003/04: 17⁰HY, 17ᵁGS,

	Starts	1st	2nd	3rd	Win & Pl
NH Flat	1	0	0	0	0
Hurdles	1	0	0	0	0
Career Total	2	0	0	0	

Going:	Sf: 0-1 GS: 0-1 Gd: 0-0 GF: - Fm: 0-0
Distance:	2m/2m3: 0-2 2m4-2m7: 0-0 3m+: 0-0
Track:	LH: 0-0 RH: 0-2 Tight: 0-0 Gall: 0-0
Aids:	Bl: 0-0 Vi: 0-0 Tstrap: 0-0 Ckp: 0-0
Best Rating:	0 4/04 Carl 2m1f gd-sft Hdl

Bailey's Bro (IRE)

7-y-o br g Castle Keep-Boreen Bro (Boreen (FR))
M Bradstock The Frankly Intolerable

Placings:0P-P   (3084)
2003/04: 22PGS,

	Starts	1st	2nd	3rd	Win & Pl
Hurdles	1	0	0	0	
Career Total	3	0	0	0	

Going:	Sf: 0-0 GS: 0-1 Gd: 0-0 GF: - Fm: 0-0
Distance:	2m/2m3: 0-0 2m4-2m7: 0-1 3m+: 0-0
Track:	LH: 0-1 RH: 0-0 Tight: 0-1 Gall: 0-0
Aids:	Bl: 0-0 Vi: 0-0 Tstrap: 0-0 Ckp: 0-0
Best Rating:	64 12/02 Newb 2m110y heavy NHF

Baileys Prize (USA)

97   **95**

7-y-o ch g Mister Baileys-Mar Mar (USA) (Forever Casting (USA))
B J Llewellyn (C J Gray 23/3) Mrs Elizabeth Heal

Placings:6434020-0000   (4818)
2003/04: 19⁰S, 19⁰G, 17⁰GS, 17⁰GF,

	Starts	1st	2nd	3rd	Win & Pl
Hurdles	3	0	0	0	0
Chases	1	0	0	0	0
Career Total	11	0	1	1	1753

Going:	Sf: 0-1 GS: 0-1 Gd: 0-1 GF: - Fm: 0-0
Distance:	2m/2m3: 0-3 2m4-2m7: 0-1 3m+: 0-0
Track:	LH: 0-1 RH: 0-3 Tight: 0-0 Gall: 0-1
Aids:	Bl: 0-1 Vi: 0-1 Tstrap: 0-1 Ckp: 0-0
Best Rating:	95 1/03 Extr 2m3f gd-sft Hdl

Bajan Girl (FR)

80f

4-y-o b f Emperor Jones (USA)-Lovely Noor (USA)
(Fappiano (USA))
M C Pipe D A Johnson

Placings:030   (2675)
2003/04: 12⁰GF, 14³G, 12⁰GF,

	Starts	1st	2nd	3rd	Win & Pl
NH Flat	3	0	0	1	391
Career Total	3	0	0	1	391

Going:	Sf: 0-0 GS: 0-0 Gd: 0-1 GF: - Fm: 0-2
Distance:	2m/2m3: 0-0 2m4-2m7: 0-0 3m+: 0-0
Track:	LH: 0-3 RH: 0-0 Tight: 0-0 Gall: 0-0
Aids:	Bl: 0-0 Vi: 0-1 Tstrap: 0-0 Ckp: 0-0
Best Rating:	80 11/03 Wwck 1m6f good NHF

Half-sister to Wahiba Sands and Medaille Militaire; disappointed on bumper debut; only modest form next time.

Bak On Board

8-y-o b g Sula Bula-Kirstins Pride (Silly Prices)
Miss L Gardner D V Gardner

Placings:000/05P35/P5-   (0020)
2003/04: 26⁵S,

	Starts	1st	2nd	3rd	Win & Pl
Chases	1	0	0	0	0
Career Total	10	0	0	1	400

Going:	Sf: 0-1 GS: 0-0 Gd: 0-0 GF: - Fm: 0-0
Distance:	2m/2m3: 0-0 2m4-2m7: 0-0 3m+: 0-1
Track:	LH: 0-1 RH: 0-0 Tight: 0-1 Gall: 0-0
Aids:	Bl: 0-0 Vi: 0-0 Tstrap: 0-0 Ckp: 0-0
Best Rating:	74 1/01 Kemp 2m soft NHF

Lacks stamina over hurdles, despite being tried at various trips.

Bak To Bill

105(116h)   (122 h)119+

9-y-o b g Nicholas Bill-Kirstins Pride (Silly Prices)
Mrs S Gardner D V Gardner

Placings:4/63ROP2PP/2062P3065425412/23212344-
U5U220243U2   (4888)
2003/04: 22⁴S, 23ᵁGF, 22⁵G, 24ᵁGF, 23²G, 24²G, 23⁰G, 23²GS,
19⁴S, 24³G, 23ᵁGS, 24²GF,

	Starts	1st	2nd	3rd	Win & Pl
Hurdles	2	0	0	0	491
Chases	10	0	4	1	6441
Career Total	43	2	12	5	33208
115	1/03	Leic	2m4f110yD(0-120)HHdl	HVY	£6909
105	3/02	Winc	2m6f	F(0-100)HHdl GD	£3402
			Total win prize-money		£10312

Going:	Sf: 0-2 GS: 0-2 Gd: 0-5 GF: - Fm: 0-3
Distance:	2m/2m3: 0-1 2m4-2m7: 0-2 3m+: 0-9
Track:	LH: 0-2 RH: 0-9 Tight: 0-5 Gall: 0-0
Aids:	Bl: 0-0 Vi: 0-0 Tstrap: 0-0 Ckp: 0-2
Best Rating:	120 3/03 Uttx 2m6f110y soft Hdl

Fair hurdler/chaser; acts on good and heavy ground; effective at two miles four to two miles six; not the most fluent jumper of fences; goes well for his lady rider.

Bakers Dozen

48   3

4-y-o ch g Whittingham (IRE)-Blue Empress (Blue
Cashmere)

T R George L H Ballinger

Placings:0   (2253)
2003/04: 17⁰GF,

	Starts	1st	2nd	3rd	Win & Pl
Hurdles	1	0	0	0	
Career Total	1	0	0	0	

Going:	Sf: 0-0 GS: 0-0 Gd: 0-0 GF: - Fm: 0-1
Distance:	2m/2m3: 0-1 2m4-2m7: 0-0 3m+: 0-0
Track:	LH: 0-0 RH: 0-1 Tight: 0-0 Gall: 0-0
Aids:	Bl: 0-0 Vi: 0-0 Tstrap: 0-0 Ckp: 0-0
Best Rating:	3 11/03 Hrld 2m1f gd-fm Hdl

Bakiri (IRE)

101   91+

6-y-o b g Doyoun-Bakiya (USA) (Trempolino (USA))
Andrew Reid (R T Phillips 15/3) A S Reid

Placings:000-500012   (4370)
2003/04: 22⁵GF, 20⁰GS, 16⁰GS, 20⁰GS, 19¹G, 19²GF,

	Starts	1st	2nd	3rd	Win & Pl
Hurdles	6	1	1	0	3359
Career Total	9	1	1	0	3359
91	3/04	Tntn	2m3f110yG(0-95)HHdl	GD	£2527
			Total win prize-money		£2527

Going:	Sf: 0-0 GS: 0-3 Gd: 1-1 GF: - Fm: 0-2
Distance:	2m/2m3: 0-2 2m4-2m7: 1-4 3m+: 0-0
Track:	LH: 0-4 RH: 1-2 Tight: 1-4 Gall: 0-1
Aids:	Bl: 0-0 Vi: 0-0 Tstrap: 0-1 Ckp: 0-0
Best Rating:	91 3/04 Strf 2m3f gd-fm Hdl

Modest hurdler; suited by two and a half miles and good ground.

Bal De Nuit (FR)

112(107h)   (119h)137

5-y-o gr g Balleroy (USA)-Eoline (FR) (In Fijar (USA))
P F Nicholls Mrs Monica Hackett

Placings:F0321F1-2113   (3491)
2003/04: 20²GS, 18¹GS, 16¹GS, 16³HY,

	Starts	1st	2nd	3rd	Win & Pl
Chases	4	2	1	1	32058
Career Total	11	4	2	2	58824
137	1/04	Asct	2m	A Ch	G-S	£23450
137	12/03	Newb	2m2f110yD Ch	G-S	£5694
129	4/03	Chel	2m1f	D Hdl	GD	£9744
119	1/03	Kemp	2m	D Hdl	GD	£5255
			Total win prize-money		£44143

Going:	Sf: 0-1 GS: 2-3 Gd: 0-0 GF: - Fm: 0-0
Distance:	2m/2m3: 2-3 2m4-2m7: 0-1 3m+: 0-0
Track:	LH: 1-2 RH: 1-2 Tight: 0-0 Gall: 1-2
Aids:	Bl: 0-0 Vi: 0-0 Tstrap: 0-0 Ckp: 0-0
Best Rating:	137 1/04 Asct 2m gd-sft Ch

Very useful novice chaser; ex-French; suited by two miles, but does stay further; handles good ground, but best with some cut; likes to race prominently.

Balakar (IRE)

102   96

8-y-o b g Doyoun-Balaniya (USA) (Diesis)
M F Harris D M Robb

Placings:0/05043/P30101-3   (0420)
2003/04: 17³GF,

	Starts	1st	2nd	3rd	Win & Pl
Hurdles	1	0	0	1	453

Career Total		13	2	0	3	9251
94	4/03	Plum	2m	F(0-90)Hdl G-F	£2618
94	3/03	Wwck	2m	D(0-120)HHdl G-F	£4823
			Total win prize-money		£7441

Going:	Sf: 0-0 GS: 0-0 Gd: 0-0 GF: - Fm: 0-1
Distance:	2m/2m3: 0-1 2m4-2m7: 0-0 3m+: 0-0
Track:	LH: 0-0 RH: 0-1 Tight: 0-1 Gall: 0-0
Aids:	Bl: 0-0 Vi: 0-0 Tstrap: 0-1 Ckp: 0-0
Best Rating:	103 10/00 Punc 2m gd-yld Hdl

Moderate hurdler; effective in soft and fast ground ; suited by trips of around two miles.

Balapour (IRE)

117   137

6-y-o b g Kahyasi-Balanina (USA) (Diesis)
Patrick O Brady Miss Rita Shah

Placings:51031000423/0U534BF20F-06U0444   (4804a)
2003/04: 16⁰GY, 19⁶S, 16ᵁS, 16⁰YS, 16⁴G, 17⁴G, 16⁴Y,

	Starts	1st	2nd	3rd	Win & Pl
Hurdles	7	0	0	0	4221
Career Total	28	2	2	3	57749
119	12/01	Fair	2m	Hdl	YLD	£13104
111	9/01	Fair	2m	Hdl	FRM	£5564
			Total win prize-money		£18670

Going:	Sf: 0-2 GS: 0-0 Gd: 0-2 GF: - Fm: 0-0
Distance:	2m/2m3: 0-7 2m4-2m7: 0-0 3m+: 0-0
Track:	LH: 0-4 RH: 0-2 Tight: 0-0 Gall: 0-1
Aids:	Bl: 0-0 Vi: 0-0 Tstrap: 0-7 Ckp: 0-0
Best Rating:	137 3/04 Chel 2m1f good Hdl

Useful Irish-trained hurdler; stayed on into creditable fourth in 2002 Triumph Hurdle, and showed his liking for the track when returning to finish runner-up in the County Hurdle in 2003; does not have a great winning record, but does not get his conditions very often; best form over 2m; seems best on a sound surface and in a strongly-run race.

Balinahinch Castle (IRE)

120

7-y-o b g Good Thyne (USA)-Emerald Flair (Flair Path)
Mrs L B Normile K J Fehilly

Placings:11P5-P   (1426)
2003/04: 24⁴G,

	Starts	1st	2nd	3rd	Win & Pl
Hurdles	1	0	0	0	
Career Total	5	2	0	0	7535
120	11/02	Wwck	3m1f	D Hdl	GD	£3835
120	10/02	Extr	2m6f110yE Hdl	GD	£3377
			Total win prize-money		£7213

Going:	Sf: 0-0 GS: 0-0 Gd: 0-1 GF: - Fm: 0-0
Distance:	2m/2m3: 0-0 2m4-2m7: 0-0 3m+: 0-1
Track:	LH: 0-0 RH: 0-1 Tight: 0-0 Gall: 0-0
Aids:	Bl: 0-0 Vi: 0-0 Tstrap: 0-0 Ckp: 0-0
Best Rating:	120 11/02 Wwck 3m1f good Hdl

Ex-Irish pointer, stayed on well to win a novice hurdle at Exeter on his British debut and put up another staying performance to win at Warwick; stays beyond three miles and is a chaser in the making; clearly prefers good ground.

Balisteros (FR)

99(103c)   (104c)63

15-y-o b g Bad Conduct (USA)-Oldbury (FR) (Fin Bon)
Mrs B K Thomson Mrs B K Thomson

Placings:00/005FU50/2/35/112/124F4P/2353/3-216 (0579)
2003/04: 25^{2}G, 24^{1}G, 24^{6}G,

	Starts	1st	2nd	3rd	Win & Pl
Hurdles	1	0	0	0	0
Chases	2	1	1	0	4732
Career Total	29	4	5	4	19415
104 5/03 Strf	3m		H Ch	GD	£3659
117 5/00 Uttx	3m2f		H Ch	G-F	£3393
103 3/00 Kels	3m1f		H Ch	G-S	£1960
105 2/00 Sedg	2m5f		H Ch	G-S	£1582

Total win prize-money £10596

Going: Sf: 0-0 GS: 0-0 Gd: 1-3 GF: - Fm: 0-0
Distance: 2m/2m3: 0-0 2m4-2m7: 0-0 3m+: 1-3
Track: LH: 1-2 RH: 0-1 Tight: 1-1 Gall: 0-0
Aids: Bl: 0-0 Vi: 0-0 Tstrap: 0-0 Ckp: 0-0
Best Rating: 118 6/00 Strf 3m4f good Ch

Fair pointer/hunter chaser; prolific points winner in his prime, but in the veteran stage now; showed he is still capable of winning when landing fast-run 3m ladies event at Stratford May 2003; can make mistakes; stays well; seems to go on any ground.

Balkirk
77   89d
7-y-o ch g Selkirk (USA)-Balenare (Pharly (FR))
Mrs H M Bridges   Mrs H M Bridges

Placings:006/443PP-PP300 (2818)
2003/04: 16^{6}GF, 22^{P}G, 19^{3}GF, 17^{0}GS, 19^{9}G,

	Starts	1st	2nd	3rd	Win & Pl
Hurdles	5	0	0	1	446
Career Total	13	0	0	2	2209

Going: Sf: 0-0 GS: 0-1 Gd: 0-2 GF: - Fm: 0-2
Distance: 2m/2m3: 0-3 2m4-2m7: 0-2 3m+: 0-0
Track: LH: 0-3 RH: 0-3 Tight: 0-3 Gall: 0-0
Aids: Bl: 0-1 Vi: 0-0 Tstrap: 0-2 Ckp: 0-1
Best Rating: 89 12/02 Sand 2m110y soft Hdl

Plating-class hurdler; stays 2m 4f, has worn a tongue-strap.

Ball Games
101   83
6-y-o b g Mind Games-Deb's Ball (Glenstal (USA))
James Moffatt   Jennie Moffatt, Evan Munro

Placings:00/553-0042P (2526)
2003/04: 16^{0}G, 17^{0}GS, 17^{4}G, 16^{2}GF, 16^{P}GS,

	Starts	1st	2nd	3rd	Win & Pl
Hurdles	5	0	1	0	524
Career Total	10	0	1	1	1084

Going: Sf: 0-0 GS: 0-2 Gd: 0-2 GF: - Fm: 0-1
Distance: 2m/2m3: 0-5 2m4-2m7: 0-0 3m+: 0-0
Track: LH: 0-5 RH: 0-0 Tight: 0-3 Gall: 0-0
Aids: Bl: 0-0 Vi: 0-3 Tstrap: 0-0 Ckp: 0-1
Best Rating: 84 8/02 Ctml 2m1f110y good Hdl

Plating-class maiden hurdler; suited by a sound surface; often wears a visor or cheekpieces.

Balla D'Aire (IRE)
95(73h)   (83h)83
9-y-o b/br g Balla Cove-Silius (Junius (USA))
K F Clutterbuck   K F Clutterbuck

Placings:324/P0044/00545P/5/P-6214 (3917)
2003/04: 16^{6}G, 21^{2}G, 23^{1}F, 24^{4}G,

	Starts	1st	2nd	3rd	Win & Pl
Hurdles	1	0	0	0	0
Chases	3	1	1	0	6400
Career Total	20	1	2	1	7784
83 12/03 Leic	2m7f110yE Ch			FRM	£4410

Total win prize-money £4410

Going: Sf: 0-0 GS: 0-0 Gd: 0-3 GF: - Fm: 1-1
Distance: 2m/2m3: 0-1 2m4-2m7: 0-1 3m+: 1-2
Track: LH: 0-3 RH: 1-1 Tight: 0-3 Gall: 0-0
Aids: Bl: 0-0 Vi: 0-0 Tstrap: 0-0 Ckp: 0-0
Best Rating: 91 2/99 Plum 2m1f gd-sft Hdl

Ballad Minstrel (IRE)
12-y-o gr g Ballad Rock-Sashi Woo (Rusticaro (FR))
Miss J E Foster (T J Fitzgerald 17/5) Miss J E Foster

Placings:14/20/301B4/22122213/30F0/P0014/0-PP (4542)
2003/04: 21^{P}S, 20^{P}GS,

	Starts	1st	2nd	3rd	Win & Pl
Chases	2	0	0	0	
Career Total	29	5	6	3	30080
122 2/01 Weth	2m	E(0-115)HCh	SFT		£3484
126 3/99 Bang	2m4f110yC(0-130)HCh		SFT		£5680
124 12/98 Catt	2m	E Ch	GD		£3148
107 2/98 Newc	2m	E Hdl	GD		£2442
110 2/96 Hayd	2m	H NHF	HVY		£1745

Total win prize-money £16501

Going: Sf: 0-1 GS: 0-1 Gd: 0-0 GF: - Fm: 0-0
Distance: 2m/2m3: 0-0 2m4-2m7: 0-2 3m+: 0-0
Track: LH: 0-1 RH: 0-0 Tight: 0-2 Gall: 0-0
Aids: Bl: 0-0 Vi: 0-0 Tstrap: 0-0 Ckp: 0-0
Best Rating: 126 3/99 Bang 2m4f110y soft Ch

Balladeer (IRE)
103   115+
6-y-o b g King's Theatre (IRE)-Carousel Music (On Your Mark)
Miss H C Knight   Scott Hardy Partnership

Placings:F3226-21410P0 (4870)
2003/04: 20^{2}GF, 22^{1}F, 21^{4}G, 21^{1}GF, 21^{0}G, 24^{P}GS, 24^{0}GS,

	Starts	1st	2nd	3rd	Win & Pl
Hurdles	7	2	1	0	9286
Career Total	12	2	3	1	14831
112 11/03 Ludl	2m5f	D Hdl	G-F		£3711
112 10/03 Winc	2m6f	E Hdl	FRM		£3297

Total win prize-money £7009

Going: Sf: 0-0 GS: 0-2 Gd: 0-2 GF: - Fm: 2-3
Distance: 2m/2m3: 0-0 2m4-2m7: 2-5 3m+: 0-2
Track: LH: 0-2 RH: 2-5 Tight: 0-1 Gall: 0-2
Aids: Bl: 0-0 Vi: 0-0 Tstrap: 0-0 Ckp: 0-0
Best Rating: 115 11/03 Chel 2m5f good Hdl

Fair staying hurdler; should stay three miles; acts on any ground; normally a front runner.

Ballards Boy (FR)
70   60
5-y-o b g Sleeping Car (FR)-Anita (FR) (Olmeto)
N J Pomfret   Mrs Liz Deacon

Placings:0-0 (0210)
2003/04: 16^{0}G,

	Starts	1st	2nd	3rd	Win & Pl
Hurdles	1	0	0	0	
Career Total	2	0	0	0	

Going: Sf: 0-0 GS: 0-0 Gd: 0-1 GF: - Fm: 0-0
Distance: 2m/2m3: 0-1 2m4-2m7: 0-0 3m+: 0-0
Track: LH: 0-1 RH: 0-0 Tight: 0-0 Gall: 0-0
Aids: Bl: 0-0 Vi: 0-0 Tstrap: 0-0 Ckp: 0-0
Best Rating: 60 5/03 Worc 2m good Hdl

Ballet-K
83   (147h)116+
10-y-o ch m Gunner B-Nicolene (Nice Music)
C Roberts   Gallagher Enterprises Ltd

Placings:1115/F120212/6320/46200P/P61 (3143)
2003/04: 21^{P}GF, 22^{6}S, 25^{1}S,

	Starts	1st	2nd	3rd	Win & Pl
Chases	3	1	0		4371
Career Total	24	6	5	1	47161
116 1/04 Extr	3m1f110yE Ch		SFT		£4371
130 4/00 Chep	2m4f	E Hdl	SFT		£2170
129 2/00 Uttx	2m	D Hdl	SFT		£3672
114 2/99 Donc	2m110y	H NHF	G-F		£1514
95 2/99 Ayr	2m	H NHF	SFT		£1464
96 6/98 MRas	1m5f110yH NHF		G-F		£1308

Total win prize-money £14501

Going: Sf: 1-2 GS: 0-0 Gd: 0-0 GF: - Fm: 0-1
Distance: 2m/2m3: 0-0 2m4-2m7: 0-0 3m+: 1-1
Track: LH: 0-1 RH: 1-2 Tight: 0-0 Gall: 0-0
Aids: Bl: 0-0 Vi: 0-0 Tstrap: 0-0 Ckp: 0-0
Best Rating: 150 2/01 Sand 2m6f heavy Hdl

Fair novice chaser; very useful staying handicap hurdler in her pomp; surprise winner of a weak novice chase at Exeter in January 2004; stays three miles plus and suited by soft ground.

Ballinclay King (IRE)
102   145
10-y-o b g Asir-Clonroche Artic (Pauper)
Ferdy Murphy   I Guise, B Leatherday & N L Spence

Placings:14/115102/1314214/04PP/P3314P-P3060PP (4598)
2003/04: 24^{P}G, 25^{3}GS, 20^{0}GS, 21^{6}G, 21^{0}GS, 24^{P}S, 32^{6}G,

	Starts	1st	2nd	3rd	Win & Pl
Hurdles	1	0	0	0	
Chases	6	0	0	1	2861
Career Total	32	8	2	4	111946
145 1/03 Chel	2m5f	B HCh	HVY		£23200
152 4/01 Aint	2m	A Ch	HVY		£46500
144 12/00 Ayr	2m	D Ch	SFT		£3705
145 10/00 Weth	2m	E Ch	G-S		£3206
131 2/00 Ayr	2m4f	E Hdl	HVY		£2747
116 12/99 Hayd	2m	D Hdl	HVY		£3322
122 11/99 Ayr	2m	E Hdl	GD		£2670
130 4/99 Ayr	2m	H NHF	SFT		£3548

Total win prize-money £88900

Going: Sf: 0-2 GS: 0-2 Gd: 0-3 GF: - Fm: 0-0
Distance: 2m/2m3: 0-2 2m4-2m7: 0-4 3m+: 0-0
Track: LH: 0-7 RH: 0-0 Tight: 0-3 Gall: 0-3
Aids: Bl: 0-0 Vi: 0-0 Tstrap: 0-0 Ckp: 0-0
Best Rating: 152 4/01 Aint 2m heavy Ch

Very useful chaser; best at two and a half miles; acts well on soft ground.

Ballinure Boy (IRE)

11-y-o b g Meneval (USA)-Sweet Cahore (General Ironside)
Mrs S J Hickman Mrs E Smith

Placings:1-4   (4301)
2003/04: 23⁴G,

	Starts	1st	2nd	3rd	Win & Pl
Chases	1	0	0	0	528
Career Total	2	1	0	0	1958
90 5/02 Folk	2m5f	H Ch		GD	£1430
				Total win prize-money	£1430

Going:	Sf: 0-0 GS: 0-0 Gd: 0-1 GF: - Fm: 0-0
Distance:	2m/2m3: 0-0 2m4-2m7: 0-0 3m+: 0-1
Track:	LH: 0-0 RH: 0-1 Tight: 0-0 Gall: 0-0
Aids:	Bl: 0-0 Vi: 0-0 Tstrap: 0-0 Ckp: 0-0
Best Rating:	90 5/02 Folk 2m5f good Ch

Comfortable winner of a maiden hunter chase at Folkestone in May 2002.

Ballistic Boy
75   35

7-y-o ch g First Trump-Be Discreet (Junius (USA))
R W Thomson R W Thomson

Placings:2/525211/0P   (4690)
2003/04: 22⁰GS, 22⁰G,

	Starts	1st	2nd	3rd	Win & Pl
Hurdles	2	0	0	0	
Career Total	9	2	3	0	8167
100 8/01 Worc	3m	F(0-95)HHdl	G-F	£1946
92 8/01 Bang	2m4f	F(0-105)HHdl	GD	£3688
			Total win prize-money	£5635

Going:	Sf: 0-0 GS: 0-1 Gd: 0-1 GF: - Fm: 0-0
Distance:	2m/2m3: 0-0 2m4-2m7: 0-2 3m+: 0-0
Track:	LH: 0-2 RH: 0-0 Tight: 0-2 Gall: 0-0
Aids:	Bl: 0-0 Vi: 0-0 Tstrap: 0-0 Ckp: 0-0
Best Rating:	100 8/01 Worc 3m gd-fm Hdl

Ballofasop (IRE)

7-y-o b g Shalford (IRE)-Sosalolomome (IRE) (Salse (USA))
A J Whiting A J Whiting

Placings:00PP0   (3789)
2003/04: 16⁶GF, 18⁹G, 21⁸S, 21⁹S, 22⁰G,

	Starts	1st	2nd	3rd	Win & Pl
NH Flat	2	0	0	0	0
Hurdles	3	0	0	0	0
Career Total	5	0	0	0	0

Going:	Sf: 0-2 GS: 0-0 Gd: 0-2 GF: - Fm: 0-1
Distance:	2m/2m3: 0-2 2m4-2m7: 0-3 3m+: 0-0
Track:	LH: 0-4 RH: 0-0 Tight: 0-2 Gall: 0-0
Aids:	Bl: 0-1 Vi: 0-0 Tstrap: 0-1 Ckp: 0-1
Best Rating:	66 9/03 Worc 2m gd-fm NHF

Bally Good

6-y-o b g Alderbrook-Another Debt (Pitpan)
B G Powell Jubert Family

Placings:0   (2537)
2003/04: 18⁰S,

	Starts	1st	2nd	3rd	Win & Pl
NH Flat	1	0	0	0	

Career Total   1   0   0   0

Going:	Sf: 0-1 GS: 0-0 Gd: 0-0 GF: - Fm: 0-0
Distance:	2m/2m3: 0-1 2m4-2m7: 0-0 3m+: 0-0
Track:	LH: 0-1 RH: 0-0 Tight: 0-0 Gall: 0-0
Aids:	Bl: 0-0 Vi: 0-0 Tstrap: 0-0 Ckp: 0-0
Best Rating:	0 12/03 Plum 2m2f soft NHF

Bally Lir Lady
98   74

10-y-o b m Lir-Ballyorney Girl (New Member)
S C Burrough P R Rodford

Placings:0540/P/F363056/0450   (1015)
2003/04: 17⁰GF, 22⁴GF, 22⁵GF, 20⁰GF,

	Starts	1st	2nd	3rd	Win & Pl
Hurdles	4	0	0	0	270
Career Total	16	0	0	2	912

Going:	Sf: 0-0 GS: 0-0 Gd: 0-0 GF: - Fm: 0-4
Distance:	2m/2m3: 0-1 2m4-2m7: 0-3 3m+: 0-0
Track:	LH: 0-4 RH: 0-0 Tight: 0-3 Gall: 0-0
Aids:	Bl: 0-4 Vi: 0-0 Tstrap: 0-0 Ckp: 0-0
Best Rating:	76 8/01 Worc 2m4f gd-fm Hdl

Modest form at up to 2m 6f in novice hurdles.

Bally Lira
121

12-y-o b m Lir-Ballyorney Girl (New Member)
P R Rodford Victor Thorne

Placings:633045521/24P36541U33/6343P242/322635101/
65U0356/505135-0P003   (4265)
2003/04: 32⁰G, 25⁸S, 24⁹S, 26⁰HY, 26⁹GF,

	Starts	1st	2nd	3rd	Win & Pl
Chases	5	0	0	1	535
Career Total	55	5	6	12	43591
115 2/03 Chep	3m2f110yC(0-135)HCh	HVY	£8303
109 4/01 Extr	3m1f110yE(0-115)HCh	SFT	£4355
113 3/01 Wwck	3m2f	F(0-100)HCh	HVY	£2786
97 3/99 Chep	3m	D Ch	HVY	£3870
89 3/98 Extr	3m2f	D(0-125)HHdl	G-S	£3353
			Total win prize-money	£22668

Going:	Sf: 0-3 GS: 0-0 Gd: 0-1 GF: - Fm: 0-1
Distance:	2m/2m3: 0-0 2m4-2m7: 0-0 3m+: 0-5
Track:	LH: 0-3 RH: 0-2 Tight: 0-0 Gall: 0-0
Aids:	Bl: 0-0 Vi: 0-0 Tstrap: 0-0 Ckp: 0-2
Best Rating:	115 2/03 Chep 3m2f110y heavy Ch

Fair chaser; stays forever, but is painfully slow and would ideally like five miles in treacle; won easily when leading all the way at Chepstow in February 2003, causing a shock under a fine ride from 13lb out of the handicap.

Bally's Bak
98   93

6-y-o ch m Bob Back (USA)-Whatagale (Strong Gale)
Mrs S J Smith Formulated Polymer Products Ltd

Placings:03500-U330FP00   (4879)
2003/04: 17⁰G, 20⁵G, 24⁵S, 25⁰GS, 22⁰HY, 24⁵GF, 24⁰HY, 20⁰GS,

	Starts	1st	2nd	3rd	Win & Pl
Hurdles	8	0	0	2	843
Career Total	13	0	0	3	1114

Going:	Sf: 0-3 GS: 0-2 Gd: 0-2 GF: - Fm: 0-1
Distance:	2m/2m3: 0-1 2m4-2m7: 0-3 3m+: 0-4

Ballyaahbutt (IRE)
85f   64f

5-y-o b g Good Thyne (USA)-Lady Henbit (IRE) (Henbit (USA))
B G Powell Mrs A Ellis

Placings:00   (3215)
2003/04: 16⁰G, 16⁰GS,

	Starts	1st	2nd	3rd	Win & Pl
NH Flat	2	0	0	0	
Career Total	2	0	0	0	

Going:	Sf: 0-0 GS: 0-1 Gd: 0-1 GF: - Fm: 0-0
Distance:	2m/2m3: 0-2 2m4-2m7: 0-0 3m+: 0-0
Track:	LH: 0-2 RH: 0-0 Tight: 0-0 Gall: 0-0
Aids:	Bl: 0-0 Vi: 0-0 Tstrap: 0-0 Ckp: 0-0
Best Rating:	64 12/03 Wwck 2m good NHF

Ballyadam (IRE)
60f   14f

6-y-o b g Eve's Error-Rugged View (Rugged Man)
G B Balding Baldings (training) Ltd

Placings:0   (4199)
2003/04: 16⁶G,

	Starts	1st	2nd	3rd	Win & Pl
NH Flat	1	0	0	0	
Career Total	1	0	0	0	

Going:	Sf: 0-0 GS: 0-0 Gd: 0-1 GF: - Fm: 0-0
Distance:	2m/2m3: 0-1 2m4-2m7: 0-0 3m+: 0-0
Track:	LH: 0-1 RH: 0-0 Tight: 0-0 Gall: 0-1
Aids:	Bl: 0-0 Vi: 0-0 Tstrap: 0-0 Ckp: 0-0
Best Rating:	14 3/04 Newb 2m110y good NHF

Ballyalbany (IRE)
89   25

6-y-o b g Lord Americo-Raisin Turf (IRE) (Phardante (FR))
Mrs Susan Nock Gerard Nock

Placings:3000   (4324)
2003/04: 17⁹GS, 16⁰G, 16⁰G, 20⁰S,

	Starts	1st	2nd	3rd	Win & Pl
NH Flat	3	0	0	1	242
Hurdles	1	0	0	0	0
Career Total	4	0	0	1	242

Going:	Sf: 0-1 GS: 0-1 Gd: 0-2 GF: - Fm: 0-0
Distance:	2m/2m3: 0-3 2m4-2m7: 0-1 3m+: 0-0
Track:	LH: 0-2 RH: 0-2 Tight: 0-0 Gall: 0-2
Aids:	Bl: 0-0 Vi: 0-0 Tstrap: 0-0 Ckp: 0-0
Best Rating:	99 12/03 Hrfd 2m1f gd-sft NHF

Ballyards (IRE)
80   69

6-y-o gr g Roselier (FR)-Another Partner (Le Bavard (FR))
Mrs S J Smith Widdop Wanderers

Career Total (Ballinure Boy)

Career Total	1	0	0	0

Track:	LH: 0-6 RH: 0-2 Tight: 0-0 Gall: 0-0
Aids:	Bl: 0-0 Vi: 0-0 Tstrap: 0-0 Ckp: 0-0
Best Rating:	93 1/04 Hayd 2m6f heavy Hdl

Very modest novice hurdler; best effort when third in weak event at Wetherby in November; should stay well.

Placings:F00P (4515)
2003/04: 19^F G, 20^0 G, 22^0 G, 25^P GS,

	Starts	1st	2nd	3rd	Win & Pl
Hurdles	4	0	0	0	
Career Total	4	0	0	0	

Going: Sf: 0-0 GS: 0-1 Gd: 0-3 GF: - Fm: 0-0
Distance: 2m/2m3: 0-1 2m4-2m7: 0-2 3m+: 0-1
Track: LH: 0-2 RH: 0-1 Tight: 0-1 Gall: 0-0
Aids: Bl: 0-0 Vi: 0-0 Tstrap: 0-0 Ckp: 0-0
Best Rating: 69 2/04 Carl 2m4f good Hdl

Ballybough Rasher (IRE)
125(112h) (113h)**150**
9-y-o b g Broken Hearted-Chat Her Up (Proverb)
J Howard Johnson Comtake-Welding Engineering Specialists

Placings:0001/1F121PP/3U1UP4P-21 (1882)
2003/04: 24^2 G, 25^1 G,

	Starts	1st	2nd	3rd	Win & Pl
Hurdles	1	0	1	0	2072
Chases	1	1	0	0	35700
Career Total	20	6	2	1	68352
150	11/03	Weth	3m1f	A Ch	GD £35700
143	11/02	Aint	2m4f	D(0-125)HCh	GD £7215
130	1/02	Donc	3m	D Ch	GD £4273
122	10/01	Aint	3m1f	C Ch	GD £7252
108	5/01	Hexm	3m	F(0-100)HHdl	G-F £2231
100	2/01	Catt	3m1f110y	F(0-100)HHdl	SFT £2002

Total win prize-money £58675

Going: Sf: 0-0 GS: 0-0 Gd: 1-2 GF: - Fm: 0-0
Distance: 2m/2m3: 0-0 2m4-2m7: 0-0 3m+: 1-2
Track: LH: 1-2 RH: 0-0 Tight: 0-1 Gall: 0-0
Aids: Bl: 0-0 Vi: 0-0 Tstrap: 0-0 Ckp: 0-0
Best Rating: 150 11/03 Weth 3m1f good Ch

Smart chaser/modest hurdler; made a promising seasonal debut when second over hurdles at Aintree in October; 40/1 shot when taking Grade 2 Charlie Hall Chase at Wetherby a week later; effective from two and a half to three miles; acts on any ground.

Ballybrophy (IRE)
105 **135+**
9-y-o gr g Roselier (FR)-Bavardmore (Le Bavard (FR))
S E H Sherwood Keith Berry

Placings:P10/211-1PP10F0 (4861)
2003/04: 25^1 GS, 28^P S, 24^F GS, 24^1 S, 24^0 S, 32^F G, 33^0 GS,

	Starts	1st	2nd	3rd	Win & Pl
Chases	7	2	0	0	11440
Career Total	13	5	1	0	27594
135	1/04	Chep	3m	D(0-125)HCh	SFT £5850
118	5/03	Aint	3m1f	D(0-120)HCh	G-S £5590
119	3/03	Wwck	3m5f	D(0-125)HCh	G-S £6886
123	2/03	Asct	3m110y	E(0-110)HCh	G-S £5616
103	12/00	Hntg	3m2f	E Hdl	HVY £2634

Total win prize-money £26578

Going: Sf: 1-3 GS: 1-3 Gd: 0-1 GF: - Fm: 0-0
Distance: 2m/2m3: 0-0 2m4-2m7: 0-0 3m+: 2-7
Track: LH: 2-6 RH: 0-1 Tight: 1-2 Gall: 0-1
Aids: Bl: 0-2 Vi: 1-2 Tstrap: 0-0 Ckp: 0-1
Best Rating: 135 1/04 Chep 3m soft Ch

Useful chaser; progressive in the spring of 2003; back to form in a first-time visor when winning at Chepstow in January; stays three miles five; suited to soft ground; has worn a visor/blinkers.

Ballycassidy (IRE)
117 (131dh)**152**
8-y-o br g Insan (USA)-Bitofabreeze (IRE) (Callernish)
P Bowen R Owen & P Fullagar

Placings:2233/111F2310/2220-1110131112P (3721)
2003/04: 21^1 GF, 24^1 GF, 20^1 GF, 22^0 Y, 22^1 GF, 19^3 GF, 25^1 G, 24^1 GS, 24^1 GF, 24^2 G, 25^P S,

	Starts	1st	2nd	3rd	Win & Pl
Chases	11	7	1	1	120161
Career Total	27	11	7	4	154144
145	12/03	Newb	3m	C Ch	G-F £10280
148	11/03	Newb	3m	A Ch	G-S £23450
143	10/03	Aint	3m1f	C Ch	GD £11675
143	9/03	MRas	2m6f110y	C Ch	G-F £8700
141	7/03	MRas	2m4f	B(0-145)HCh	G-F £40600
138	7/03	Strf	3m	D Ch	G-F £5852
106	6/03	NAbb	2m5f110y	D Ch	G-F £6223
131	1/02	Hntg	3m2f	A Hdl	G-S £12127
129	6/01	Strf	3m3f	D(0-125)HHdl	G-F £3666
122	5/01	Strf	2m6f110y	D Hdl	GD £3900
108	5/01	Hrfd	3m2f	E Hdl	GD £2800

Total win prize-money £129275

Going: Sf: 0-1 GS: 1-1 Gd: 1-2 GF: - Fm: 5-6
Distance: 2m/2m3: 0-0 2m4-2m7: 3-5 3m+: 4-6
Track: LH: 5-7 RH: 2-4 Tight: 5-5 Gall: 2-2
Aids: Bl: 0-0 Vi: 0-0 Tstrap: 0-0 Ckp: 0-0
Best Rating: 152 12/03 Kemp 3m good Ch

Smart chaser; won six of first eight starts over fences including a valuable Market Rasen handicap and a Grade Two at Newbury; chased home Strong Flow in the Feltham; effective between two and a half miles and three miles; unsuited by testing conditions; has been tried in blinkers.

Ballyconnell (IRE)
107 (90h)**124+**
8-y-o b g Insan (USA)-Stormy Skies (Strong Gale)
Miss Venetia Williams (D K Weld 17/9) Gallant Denco Wallace Whittle

Placings:2U5U5-2221P410 (4385)
2003/04: 20^2 F, 22^2 S, 23^2 G, 20^1 F, 24^P G, 25^4 G, 21^1 GS, 24^0 G,

	Starts	1st	2nd	3rd	Win & Pl
Hurdles	1	0	1	0	1039
Chases	7	2	2	0	23412
Career Total	8	2	4	0	26120
133	1/04	Chel	2m5f	B HCh	G-S £12852
115	8/03	Tral	2m4f	C Ch	FRM £5600

Total win prize-money £18453

Going: Sf: 0-1 GS: 1-1 Gd: 0-4 GF: - Fm: 1-2
Distance: 2m/2m3: 0-0 2m4-2m7: 2-5 3m+: 0-3
Track: LH: 1-4 RH: 0-1 Tight: 0-0 Gall: 1-3
Aids: Bl: 0-0 Vi: 0-0 Tstrap: 0-0 Ckp: 0-0
Best Rating: 133 1/04 Chel 2m5f gd-sft Ch

Ex-Irish; fair chaser; made a pleasing British debut when fourth in a good race at Cheltenham; bloodless winner at the same track next time; stays up to three miles; best on a sound surface.

Ballycreen Euphony (IRE)

7-y-o b g Nearly A Nose (USA)-My Faery Fey VII (Damsire Unregistered)
J C Tuck Miss Rosalind Emmet

Placings:0 (4692)
2003/04: 17^0 G,

	Starts	1st	2nd	3rd	Win & Pl
Hurdles	1	0	0	0	
Career Total	1	0	0	0	

Going: Sf: 0-0 GS: 0-0 Gd: 0-1 GF: - Fm: 0-0
Distance: 2m/2m3: 0-1 2m4-2m7: 0-0 3m+: 0-0
Track: LH: 0-0 RH: 0-1 Tight: 0-0 Gall: 0-0
Aids: Bl: 0-0 Vi: 0-0 Tstrap: 0-0 Ckp: 0-0
Best Rating: 0 4/04 Extr 2m1f good Hdl

Ballydavid (IRE)
65
12-y-o br g Lord Americo-Arctic Bavard (Le Bavard (FR))
G B Balding Mrs Alurie O'Sullivan

Placings:300/405PP/5/4-F (0152)
2003/04: 20^F GF,

	Starts	1st	2nd	3rd	Win & Pl
Hurdles	1	0	0	0	
Career Total	11	0	0	1	350

Going: Sf: 0-0 GS: 0-0 Gd: 0-0 GF: - Fm: 0-1
Distance: 2m/2m3: 0-0 2m4-2m7: 0-1 3m+: 0-0
Track: LH: 0-1 RH: 0-0 Tight: 0-0 Gall: 0-0
Aids: Bl: 0-0 Vi: 0-0 Tstrap: 0-0 Ckp: 0-0
Best Rating: 88 2/98 Sedg 2m5f110y good Hdl

Plating-class-hurdler at around two and a half miles.

Ballyhand
91f **78f**
7-y-o b g Nearly A Hand-Ballynora (Ballacashtal (CAN))
W J Reed W J Reed

Placings:0/06 (0871)
2003/04: 17^0 G, 17^6 G,

	Starts	1st	2nd	3rd	Win & Pl
NH Flat	2	0	0	0	0
Career Total	3	0	0	0	0

Going: Sf: 0-0 GS: 0-0 Gd: 0-1 GF: - Fm: 0-1
Distance: 2m/2m3: 0-2 2m4-2m7: 0-0 3m+: 0-0
Track: LH: 0-2 RH: 0-0 Tight: 0-2 Gall: 0-0
Aids: Bl: 0-0 Vi: 0-0 Tstrap: 0-0 Ckp: 0-0
Best Rating: 78 7/03 NAbb 2m1f gd-fm NHF

Ballyhannon (IRE)

15-y-o b g Strong Gale-Chestnut Fire (Deep Run)
Miss J Froggatt E W Froggatt

Placings:52005/U/P5/UUPPP/P (0361)
2003/04: 34^P HY,

	Starts	1st	2nd	3rd	Win & Pl
Chases	1	0	0	0	
Career Total	14	0	1	0	482

Going: Sf: 0-1 GS: 0-0 Gd: 0-0 GF: - Fm: 0-0
Distance: 2m/2m3: 0-0 2m4-2m7: 0-0 3m+: 0-1
Track: LH: 0-1 RH: 0-0 Tight: 0-0 Gall: 0-0
Aids: Bl: 0-0 Vi: 0-0 Tstrap: 0-0 Ckp: 0-0
Best Rating: 82 10/94 Tipp 2m soft NHF

Ballykettrail (IRE)

90   120

8-y-o b g Catrail (USA)-Ballykett Lady (USA) (Sir Ivor (USA))
Jonjo O'Neill   John P McManus

Placings:*33¹11124/350006002-F6P*   (4942)
2003/04: 20^FS, 20^RGF, 20^PGS,

	Starts	1st	2nd	3rd	Win & Pl
Hurdles	3	0	0	0	0
Career Total	19	3	2	3	20603
119 8/01	Baln	2m4f	Hdl	GD	£4451
112 7/01	Klny	2m1f	NHF	GD	£4451
115 6/01	Naas	2m	NHF	G-Y	£3895

Total win prize-money £12799

Going:	Sf: 0-1 GS: 0-1 Gd: 0-0 GF: - Fm: 0-1
Distance:	2m/2m3: 0-0 2m4-2m7: 0-3 3m+: 0-0
Track:	LH: 0-2 RH: 0-1 Tight: 0-0 Gall: 0-0
Aids:	Bl: 0-1 Vi: 0-0 Tstrap: 0-0 Ckp: 0-1
Best Rating:	127 12/01 Leop 2m yield Hdl

Fair hurdler; won two bumpers and a two and a half mile maiden hurdle in Ireland in 2001; promising first run for Jonjo O'Neill when second to Ragdale Hall at Stratford April 2003; unsuited by soft ground.

Ballylusky (IRE)

111(114h)   (135h)122

7-y-o b g Lord Americo-Blackbushe Place (IRE) (Buckskin (FR))
Jonjo O'Neill   Black Sheep Racing

Placings:*5/001232F3UF62/523112340-1F410*   (3714)
2003/04: 25¹G, 24^FS, 24⁴G, 23¹HY, 22⁶S,

	Starts	1st	2nd	3rd	Win & Pl
Hurdles	2	1	0	0	12058
Chases	3	1	0	0	13190
Career Total	27	5	5	4	66428
135 1/04	Hayd	2m7f110yB	HHdl	HVY	£12058
122 11/03	Aint	3m1f	B HCh	GD	£11887
124 11/02	MRas	2m5f110y	HHdl	G-S	£10075
120 11/03	Weth	2m4f110yC(0-130)HHdl		G-S	£7046
100 9/01	List	2m	Hdl	G-F	£5842

Total win prize-money £46909

Going:	Sf: 1-3 GS: 0-0 Gd: 1-2 GF: - Fm: 0-0
Distance:	2m/2m3: 0-0 2m4-2m7: 0-1 3m+: 2-4
Track:	LH: 2-3 RH: 0-2 Tight: 1-1 Gall: 0-0
Aids:	Bl: 0-0 Vi: 0-0 Tstrap: 0-0 Ckp: 0-0
Best Rating:	135 1/04 Hayd 2m7f110y heavy Hdl

Fair hurdler/moderate chaser; ex-Irish; not a good jumper of fences; stays three miles one and suited by cut in the ground; appreciates being ridden aggressively; tough.

Ballymenagh (IRE)

12-y-o br g Buckskin (FR)-Breeze Dancer (Torus)
K Robson   Mrs M Armstrong

Placings:*02001PF00/60*54P0/003/U   (4600)
2003/04: 25^UG,

	Starts	1st	2nd	3rd	Win & Pl
Chases	1	0	0	0	
Career Total	19	1	1	1	2078
92 8/98	Dpat	2m1f172y	NHF	G-F	£1494

Total win prize-money £1495

Going:	Sf: 0-0 GS: 0-0 Gd: 0-1 GF: - Fm: 0-0
Distance:	2m/2m3: 0-0 2m4-2m7: 0-0 3m+: 0-1
Track:	LH: 0-1 RH: 0-0 Tight: 0-1 Gall: 0-0
Aids:	Bl: 0-0 Vi: 0-0 Tstrap: 0-0 Ckp: 0-0
Best Rating:	92 8/98 Dpat 2m1f172y gd-fm NHF

Ballynattin Blue (IRE)

82   116

11-y-o ch g Good Thyne (USA)-Ballynattin Moss (Le Moss)
J N R Billinge   J N R Billinge

Placings:*505*412/410P4/14P6/360-5P   (3326)
2003/04: 20⁵G, 21^PGS,

	Starts	1st	2nd	3rd	Win & Pl
Hurdles	2	0	0	0	0
Career Total	20	3	1	1	15802
116 10/01	Aint	3m110y	C(0-135)HHdl	GD	£6870
111 1/01	Ayr	3m110y	F(0-100)HHdl	SFT	£3094
102 3/00	Kels	2m6f110yE	Hdl	G-S	£2044

Total win prize-money £12009

Going:	Sf: 0-0 GS: 0-1 Gd: 0-1 GF: - Fm: 0-0
Distance:	2m/2m3: 0-0 2m4-2m7: 0-2 3m+: 0-0
Track:	LH: 0-2 RH: 0-0 Tight: 0-1 Gall: 0-0
Aids:	Bl: 0-0 Vi: 0-0 Tstrap: 0-0 Ckp: 0-0
Best Rating:	116 10/01 Aint 3m110y good Hdl

Ballyrobert (IRE)

101(95h)   (89 h)113+

7-y-o b/br g Bob's Return (IRE)-Line Abreast (High Line)
N A Gaselee   The Saxon Partnership

Placings:40460-111F5U   (4576)
2003/04: 16¹G, 18¹GS, 16¹G, 21^FGS, 18⁵G, 18^UG,

	Starts	1st	2nd	3rd	Win & Pl
Chases	6	3	0	0	18458
Career Total	11	3	0	0	19172
112 11/03	Asct	2m	D(0-110)HCh	GD	£7210
112 11/03	Newb	2m2f110yD(0-110)HCh		G-S	£8700
112 11/03	Towc	2m110y	E Ch	GD	£2548

Total win prize-money £18458

Going:	Sf: 0-0 GS: 1-2 Gd: 2-4 GF: - Fm: 0-0
Distance:	2m/2m3: 3-5 2m4-2m7: 0-1 3m+: 0-0
Track:	LH: 1-4 RH: 2-2 Tight: 0-0 Gall: 1-4
Aids:	Bl: 0-0 Vi: 0-0 Tstrap: 0-0 Ckp: 0-0
Best Rating:	112 12/03 Asct 2m good Ch

Fair chaser; Irish point-to-point winner, struggled to progress on useful British debut run until winning at Towcester in November 2003; followed up at Newbury and completed the hat-trick when scoring at Ascot; fell at Cheltenham in January 2004; suited by stiff two miles; acts on good to soft; had injury problems in 2002/03; progressing well.

Ballystone (IRE)

103(108h)   (112 h)126

11-y-o ch g Roselier (FR)-Gusserane Princess (Paddy's Stream)
L Lungo   Andrew W B Duncan & S E Constable

Placings:266F2/1121P/2U10/P2U21U12-5U5034   (4726)
2003/04: 30⁵G, 25^UG, 24⁵G, 25⁰G, 20³G, 24⁴G,

	Starts	1st	2nd	3rd	Win & Pl
Hurdles	2	0	0	0	0
Chases	4	0	1	0	1967
Career Total	28	6	7	1	40963
112 3/03	Carl	3m110y	E Hdl	SFT	£3542
126 12/02	Muss	3m	D(0-120)HCh	G-F	£6678
126 12/01	Catt	3m1f110yD(0-120)HCh		GD	£4982
122 2/01	Carl	3m2f	D(0-125)HCh	SFT	£4270
122 11/00	Newc	3m	D Ch	SFT	£4580
117 11/00	Ayr	2m5f110yD(0-110)HCh		SFT	£3861

Total win prize-money £27915

Going:	Sf: 0-0 GS: 0-0 Gd: 0-6 GF: - Fm: 0-0
Distance:	2m/2m3: 0-0 2m4-2m7: 0-1 3m+: 0-5
Track:	LH: 0-3 RH: 0-2 Tight: 0-2 Gall: 0-0
Aids:	Bl: 0-0 Vi: 0-0 Tstrap: 0-0 Ckp: 0-1
Best Rating:	126 4/03 Carl 3m gd-fm Ch

Fair staying chaser/hurdler; tends to make the odd mistake over fences; stays three and a quarter miles; has won on soft ground and good to firm; has worn cheekpieces.

Ballyvaddy (IRE)

110(110h)   (126h)109+

8-y-o gr g Roselier (FR)-Bodalmore Kit (Bargello)
G B Balding   Lady G Wates

Placings:0/4UP312/120431-1121   (4916)
2003/04: 24¹G, 21¹GF, 24²GF, 23¹GS,

	Starts	1st	2nd	3rd	Win & Pl
Hurdles	2	1	1	0	7436
Chases	2	2	0	0	11453
Career Total	17	6	3	2	39298
109 4/04	Worc	2m7f110yE(0-105)HCh		G-S	£4563
120 10/03	Kemp	2m5f	D(0-125)HHdl	G-F	£4065
92 5/03	Ludl	3m	E(0-105)HCh	GD	£6690
118 4/03	Ludl	2m5f	D(0-105)HHdl	GD	£5499
101 10/02	Kemp	2m5f	D(0-125)HHdl	GD	£5073
96 4/02	Winc	2m6f	D(0-105)HHdl	GD	£3458

Total win prize-money £29549

Going:	Sf: 0-0 GS: 1-1 Gd: 1-1 GF: - Fm: 1-2
Distance:	2m/2m3: 0-0 2m4-2m7: 1-2 3m+: 2-3
Track:	LH: 1-2 RH: 2-2 Tight: 1-1 Gall: 0-0
Aids:	Bl: 0-0 Vi: 0-0 Tstrap: 0-0 Ckp: 0-0
Best Rating:	126 11/03 Chep 3m gd-fm Hdl

Lightly-raced, progressive hurdler/chaser, better over hurdles and won Kempton handicap for second year running in October; returned from five months off to win over fences at Worcester in April; consistent; stays two miles-six over hurdles, but three miles over fences, acts on good and good to soft ground, has worn a visor and sheepskin cheekpieces.

Ballywalter (IRE)

85(99h)   (81 h)60

8-y-o ch g Commanche Run-Call Me Honey (Le Bavard (FR))
N A Gaselee   Barry Marsden

Placings:F*55055-0P*   (1674)
2003/04: 22⁰G, 19^PF,

	Starts	1st	2nd	3rd	Win & Pl
Chases	2	0	0	0	0
Career Total	8	0	0	0	0

Going:	Sf: 0-0 GS: 0-0 Gd: 0-1 GF: - Fm: 0-1
Distance:	2m/2m3: 0-0 2m4-2m7: 0-2 3m+: 0-0
Track:	LH: 0-0 RH: 0-0 Tight: 0-1 Gall: 0-0
Aids:	Bl: 0-0 Vi: 0-0 Tstrap: 0-0 Ckp: 0-0
Best Rating:	81 3/03 Plum 3m1f110y gd-fm Hdl

Balmoral Queen

77   57

4-y-o br f Wizard King-Balmoral Princess (Thethingaboutitis (USA))
D McCain   Mrs D McCain

Placings:*000*FP   (4758)
2003/04: 14⁰G, 17⁰GS, 17⁰G, 17^FGS, 16^PS,

	Starts	1st	2nd	3rd	Win & Pl
NH Flat	1	0	0	0	0

Hurdles	4	0	0	0	0
Career Total	5	0	0	0	

Going:	Sf: 0-1 GS: 0-2 Gd: 0-2 GF: - Fm: 0-0
Distance:	2m/2m3: 0-4 2m4-2m7: 0-0 3m+: 0-0
Track:	LH: 0-3 RH: 0-2 Tight: 0-2 Gall: 0-0
Aids:	Bl: 0-0 Vi: 0-0 Tstrap: 0-0 Ckp: 0-0
Best Rating:	68 11/03 Wwck 1m6f good NHF

Baloo

97(105h)   (110 h)**96**

8-y-o b g Morpeth-Moorland Nell (Neltino)
J D Frost Cloud Nine-Premier Cru

Placings:3540550/3364104/1340-2152**233**   (2654)
2003/04: 22²GF, 27¹GF, 24⁵GF, 24²GF, 24⁴GF, 24³GS, 22³G,

	Starts	1st	2nd	3rd	Win & Pl
Hurdles	3	1	1	0	8013
Chases	4	0	2	2	3830
Career Total	25	3	3	6	19500
110	6/03	NAbb 3m3f	D(C-125)HHdl	G-F	£6075
102	7/02	NAbb 3m3f	E(0-105)HHdl	G-F	£2933
87	11/01	Extr	2m6f110yE(0-105)HHdl	G-F	£2520
		Total win prize-money £11528			

Going:	Sf: 0-0 GS: 0-1 Gd: 0-1 GF: - Fm: 1-5
Distance:	2m/2m3: 0-0 2m4-2m7: 0-2 3m+: 1-5
Track:	LH: 1-5 RH: 0-1 Tight: 1-6 Gall: 0-0
Aids:	Bl: 0-0 Vi: 0-0 Tstrap: 0-0 Ckp: 0-0
Best Rating:	110 6/03 NAbb 3m3f gd-fm Hdl

Modest staying hurdler; third career win at Newton Abbot June 2003; not disgraced on chasing debut when runner-up over 3m at Stratford in October but exposed since; stays 3m 3f; likes top of the ground.

Bambi De L'Orme (FR)

99   **115+**

5-y-o gr g True Brave (USA)-Princesse Ira (FR) (Less Ice)
Ian Williams (G Chaignon 23/11) B Boutoul

Placings:0/P1F152-16342132   (4653)
2003/04: 17¹VS, 17⁶VS, 17³HO, 17⁴VS, 17²VS, 16¹G, 16³G, 19²G,

	Starts	1st	2nd	3rd	Win & Pl
Hurdles	2	1	0	0	15840
Chases	6	1	2	2	18128
Career Total	15	4	3	2	43082
115	2/04	Newc	2m110y E Ch	GD	£4739
	5/03	Nant	2m1f110y Hdl	VS	£11221
	11/02	Sbri	1m7f	Hdl	HVY	£3239
	9/02	Vire	2m	Hdl	GD	£2945
		Total win prize-money £22144			

Going:	Sf: 0-0 GS: 0-0 Gd: 1-3 GF: - Fm: 0-0
Distance:	2m/2m3: 2-8 2m4-2m7: 0-3 3m+: 0-0
Track:	LH: 1-1 RH: 0-2 Tight: 0-0 Gall: 1-2
Aids:	Bl: 0-0 Vi: 0-0 Tstrap: 0-0 Ckp: 0-0
Best Rating:	115 3/04 Hntg 2m110y good Ch

Fair novice chaser; ex-French; won three times over hurdles in France and fluent chasing debut on first run for new year in uncompetitive event at Newcastle in February 2004; ran well next time; effective at two miles; acts on good ground; type to improve again.

Ban Dubh

82f   **83f**

5-y-o b m Syrtos-Hatherley (Deep Run)
J Rudge J De Lisle Wells

Placings:00   (4571)
2003/04: 16⁶G, 17⁰GS,

	Starts	1st	2nd	3rd	Win & Pl
NH Flat	2	0	0	0	
Career Total	2	0	0	0	

Going:	Sf: 0-0 GS: 0-1 Gd: 0-1 GF: - Fm: 0-0
Distance:	2m/2m3: 0-2 2m4-2m7: 0-0 3m+: 0-0
Track:	LH: 0-1 RH: 0-1 Tight: 0-1 Gall: 0-1
Aids:	Bl: 0-0 Vi: 0-0 Tstrap: 0-0 Ckp: 0-0
Best Rating:	83 3/04 Hntg 2m110y good NHF

Banana Ridge

95f   **83f**

6-y-o ch m Primitive Rising (USA)-Madison Girl (Last Fandango)
T D Walford Peter Maddison

Placings:4   (0705)
2003/04: 17⁴GF,

	Starts	1st	2nd	3rd	Win & Pl
NH Flat	1	0	0	0	0
Career Total	1	0	0	0	0

Going:	Sf: 0-0 GS: 0-0 Gd: 0-0 GF: - Fm: 0-1
Distance:	2m/2m3: 0-1 2m4-2m7: 0-0 3m+: 0-0
Track:	LH: 0-0 RH: 0-0 Tight: 0-1 Gall: 0-0
Aids:	Bl: 0-0 Vi: 0-0 Tstrap: 0-0 Ckp: 0-0
Best Rating:	83 6/03 MRas 2m1f110y gd-fm NHF

Bandit Brown (IRE)

103   (91h)**96+**

8-y-o b g Supreme Leader-Parkroe Lady (IRE) (Deep Run)
P Winkworth R D Barber & R J B Blake

Placings:4043/2   (4534)
2003/04: 22²GS,

	Starts	1st	2nd	3rd	Win & Pl
Chases	1	0	1	0	1215
Career Total	5	0	1	1	1566

Going:	Sf: 0-0 GS: 0-1 Gd: 0-0 GF: - Fm: 0-0
Distance:	2m/2m3: 0-0 2m4-2m7: 0-1 3m+: 0-0
Track:	LH: 0-0 RH: 0-0 Tight: 0-0 Gall: 0-0
Aids:	Bl: 0-0 Vi: 0-0 Tstrap: 0-0 Ckp: 0-0
Best Rating:	96 3/04 Towc 2m6f gd-sft Ch

Bangor Erris (IRE)

(50h)**91**

11-y-o ch g Executive Perk-Dawn Infidel (IRE) (Fidel)
A J Chamberlain A C Ledbury

Placings:4FPP/43/236/004F36P51F5P4/P   (1000)
2003/04: 22³G,

	Starts	1st	2nd	3rd	Win & Pl
Hurdles	1	0	0	0	
Career Total	23	1	1	3	5270
81	1/02	Font	2m6f	F(0-90)HCh	GD	£3220
		Total win prize-money £3220			

Going:	Sf: 0-0 GS: 0-0 Gd: 0-1 GF: - Fm: 0-0
Distance:	2m/2m3: 0-0 2m4-2m7: 0-1 3m+: 0-0
Track:	LH: 0-1 RH: 0-0 Tight: 0-0 Gall: 0-0
Aids:	Bl: 0-0 Vi: 0-0 Tstrap: 0-0 Ckp: 0-0
Best Rating:	82 10/99 Plum 2m5f gd-fm Hdl

Banjo Hill

111(104h)   (100h)**116**

10-y-o b g Arctic Lord-Just Hannah (Macmillion)
Miss E C Lavelle John B Hobbs

Placings:454000016/12200/1/P/2353325511-16654P
                                              (4694)
2003/04: 23¹G, 20⁶GF, 24⁶GF, 20⁵GF, 26⁴GF, 23⁶G,

	Starts	1st	2nd	3rd	Win & Pl
Chases	6	1	0	0	10320
Career Total	32	6	4	3	41870
116	4/03	Extr	2m7f110yC(0-135)HCh	GD	£8775
116	4/03	Chel	2m6f110yD(0-115)HCh	GD	£13050
115	3/03	Hntg	2m4f110yF(0-95)HCh	G-F	£3601
105	5/00	Extr	2m6f	D(0-120)HHdl	FRM	£3692
99	9/99	Font	2m6f110yE(0-115)HHdl	GD	£2267
89	4/99	Winc	2m6f	F(0-105)HHdl	GD	£2570
		Total win prize-money £33956			

Going:	Sf: 0-0 GS: 0-0 Gd: 1-2 GF: - Fm: 0-4
Distance:	2m/2m3: 0-0 2m4-2m7: 0-2 3m+: 1-4
Track:	LH: 0-1 RH: 1-4 Tight: 0-3 Gall: 0-1
Aids:	Bl: 0-0 Vi: 0-0 Tstrap: 0-0 Ckp: 0-0
Best Rating:	116 4/03 Extr 2m7f110y good Ch

Moderate hurdler/chaser; won novices' handicap chase in March 2003 on first run for Emma Lavelle; overcame a 14lb rise in the weights when following up at Cheltenham next time and completed the hat-trick at Exeter; stays nearly three miles; effective at 2m4f; acts on a sound surface.

Banker Count

108   **130+**

12-y-o b g Lord Bud-Gilzie Bank (New Brig)
Miss Venetia Williams Mrs H Brown

Placings:6632/1/P221F/13/FB2121/12132U0/P0PP2
                                              (4889)
2003/04: 20²GS, 24⁰S, 24²G, 24²PG, 20²GF,

	Starts	1st	2nd	3rd	Win & Pl
Chases	5	0	1	0	3599
Career Total	30	7	8	3	89307
157	12/01	Weth	2m4f110yB(0-145)HCh	SFT	£10436
142	11/01	Weth	2m4f110yB(0-150)HCh	GD	£10656
134	4/01	Weth	3m1f	B(0-150)HCh	G-S	£7215
125	2/01	Kels	2m6f110yC(0-130)HCh	SFT	£7020
119	12/99	Donc	2m110y	C(0-130)HCh	GF	£5743
100	3/99	Catt	2m3f	C Ch	SFT	£2979
113	11/97	Weth	2m	C Hdl	G-F	£3652
		Total win prize-money £47703			

Going:	Sf: 0-1 GS: 0-1 Gd: 0-2 GF: - Fm: 0-1
Distance:	2m/2m3: 0-2 2m4-2m7: 0-2 3m+: 0-3
Track:	LH: 0-3 RH: 0-2 Tight: 0-1 Gall: 0-2
Aids:	Bl: 0-0 Vi: 0-0 Tstrap: 0-0 Ckp: 0-0
Best Rating:	157 12/01 Weth 2m4f110y soft Ch

Useful chaser; finished ninth in the Nakayama Grand Jump in April 2002; had previously been capable of showing very useful form, but regressed since; stays around three miles, but better at shorter; acts well on soft ground.

Bankersdraft

93   **62**

9-y-o ch g Mazaad-Overdraft (Bustino)
R C Guest N B Mason

Placings:0PP6/PP0/6F3-6   (0133)
2003/04: 24⁶GF,

	Starts	1st	2nd	3rd	Win & Pl
Chases	1	0	0	0	0
Career Total	11	0	0	1	554

Going: Sf: 0-0 GS: 0-0 Gd: 0-0 GF: - Fm: 0-1
Distance: 2m/2m3: 0-0 2m4-2m7: 0-0 3m+: 0-1
Track: LH: 0-0 RH: 0-1 Tight: 0-0 Gall: 0-1
Aids: Bl: 0-0 Vi: 0-0 Tstrap: 0-0 Ckp: 0-1
Best Rating: 62   3/03   Hntg   2m4f110y   gd-fm   Ch

Plating-class novice chaser.

Banneret (USA)

(0c)

11-y-o b g Imperial Falcon (CAN)-Dashing Partner
(Formidable (USA))
K G Wingrove (F L Matthews 15/5) A Bourne

Placings:334/0/FRF/06R-RR   (2516)
2003/04: 20PGF, 17RGS,

	Starts	1st	2nd	3rd	Win & Pl
Hurdles	1	0	0	0	0
Chases	1	0	0	0	0
Career Total	12	0	0	2	450

Going: Sf: 0-0 GS: 0-1 Gd: 0-0 GF: - Fm: 0-1
Distance: 2m/2m3: 0-1 2m4-2m7: 0-1 3m+: 0-0
Track: LH: 0-0 RH: 0-2 Tight: 0-1 Gall: 0-0
Aids: Bl: 0-0 Vi: 0-0 Tstrap: 0-1 Ckp: 0-0
Best Rating: 83   1/00   Ludl   2m   gd-sft   Hdl

Banningham Blaze
101   79+

4-y-o b f Averti (IRE)-Ma Pavlova (USA) (Irish River (FR))
C R Dore Crown Select

Placings:4223PP652P   (4776)
2003/04: 16AGF, 16PGF, 16ZF, 16RF, 16PG, 16PS, 19SGS, 16ZG, 20PG,

	Starts	1st	2nd	3rd	Win & Pl
Hurdles	10	0	3	1	3346
Career Total	10	0	3	1	3346

Going: Sf: 0-1 GS: 0-0 Gd: 0-4 GF: - Fm: 0-5
Distance: 2m/2m3: 0-9 2m4-2m7: 0-1 3m+: 0-0
Track: LH: 0-6 RH: 0-3 Tight: 0-4 Gall: 0-3
Aids: Bl: 0-1 Vi: 0-0 Tstrap: 0-0 Ckp: 0-0
Best Rating: 79   3/04   Hntg   2m110y   good   Hdl

Modest form over hurdles on a sound surface.

Bansha Bru (IRE)
60   22

4-y-o b g Fumo Di Londra (IRE)-Pride Of Duneane (IRE)
(Anita's Prince)
Miss E C Lavelle The Bawz Partnership

Placings:00   (4309)
2003/04: 17PS, 16PG,

	Starts	1st	2nd	3rd	Win & Pl
NH Flat	1	0	0	0	0
Hurdles	1	0	0	0	0
Career Total	2	0	0	0	

Going: Sf: 0-1 GS: 0-0 Gd: 0-1 GF: - Fm: 0-1
Distance: 2m/2m3: 0-2 2m4-2m7: 0-0 3m+: 0-0
Track: LH: 0-0 RH: 0-1 Tight: 0-0 Gall: 0-0
Aids: Bl: 0-0 Vi: 0-0 Tstrap: 0-0 Ckp: 0-0
Best Rating: 22   3/04   Sand   2m110y   good   Hdl

Barabbas (USA)
94f   92f

5-y-o b g Royal Academy (USA)-Kamsi (USA) (Afleet
(CAN))
R F Johnson Houghton Philip Newton

Placings:20   (3948)
2003/04: 16ZGF, 16RG,

	Starts	1st	2nd	3rd	Win & Pl
NH Flat	2	0	1	0	545
Career Total	2	0	1	0	545

Going: Sf: 0-0 GS: 0-0 Gd: 0-1 GF: - Fm: 0-1
Distance: 2m/2m3: 0-2 2m4-2m7: 0-0 3m+: 0-0
Track: LH: 0-0 RH: 0-2 Tight: 0-0 Gall: 0-0
Aids: Bl: 0-0 Vi: 0-0 Tstrap: 0-0 Ckp: 0-0
Best Rating: 92   11/03   Winc   2m   gd-fm   NHF

Baracouda (FR)
120   176

9-y-o b g Alesso (USA)-Peche Aubar (FR) (Zino)
F Doumen John P McManus

Placings:52/112211111/1111/121-1112   (4423)
2003/04: 24TGS, 25TG, 22TS, 24ZG,

	Starts	1st	2nd	3rd	Win & Pl
Hurdles	4	3	1	0	129400
Career Total	22	16	5	0	641988

174	2/04	Sand	2m6f	A HHdl	SFT	£34800
176	12/03	Asct	3m1f110yA Hdl	GD	£40600
159	11/03	Newb	3m110y	A Hdl	G-S	£23200
176	3/03	Chel	3m	A Hdl	GD	£85260
158	11/02	Asct	2m4f	A Hdl	HVY	£18600
171	3/02	Chel	3m	A Hdl	GD	£72500
156	2/02	Kemp	3m110y	A Hdl	GD	£15000
176	12/01	Asct	3m1f110yA Hdl	GD	£33000
171	11/01	Asct	2m4f	A Hdl	GD	£15600
155	4/01	Sand	3m	A Hdl	G-S	£37700
	3/01	Autl	2m3f110y Hdl	HVY	£31038
161	2/01	Font	2m4f	B Hdl	G-S	£14365
175	12/00	Asct	3m1f110yA Hdl	HVY	£33000
	11/00	Autl	2m4f110y Hdl	HVY	£48031
	7/00	Autl	2m2f	Hdl	HLD	£14409
	5/00	Autl	2m3f110y HHdl	VS	£25937

Total win prize-money £543040

Going: Sf: 1-1 GS: 1-1 Gd: 1-2 GF: - Fm: 0-0
Distance: 2m/2m3: 0-0 2m4-2m7: 0-0 3m+: **3m+: 2-3**
Track: LH: 1-2 **RH: 2-2** Tight: 0-0 **Gall: 1-2**
Aids: Bl: 0-0 Vi: 0-0 Tstrap: 0-0 Ckp: 0-0
Best Rating: 176   12/03   Asct   3m1f110y   good   Hdl

Top-class staying hurdler; he won ten consecutive races
over hurdles including two Long Walk Hurdles at Ascot and
the 2002 Stayers' Hurdle at the Festival; given a lot to do at
Ascot in his first two starts of the 2002/03 season, just getting up to win the first, but being beaten by Deano's Beeno
on his attempt to win a third Long Walk; bounced back to
win Stayers' again at Cheltenham; won his first two starts in
the 2003/4 season before putting up a fantastic weight-car-
rying-performance in a Sandown handicap; runner-up in the
2004 Stayers' Hurdle; acts on any ground; prefers a true
test; usually only ever does just enough.

Barbed Broach
(IRE)

11-y-o b g Waajib-Miss Galwegian (Sandford Lad)
N W Padfield N W Padfield

Placings:0U54OP60/U66/P   (0353)
2003/04: 21PGF,

	Starts	1st	2nd	3rd	Win & Pl
Chases	1	0	0	0	
Career Total	12	0	0	0	234

Going: Sf: 0-0 GS: 0-0 Gd: 0-0 GF: - Fm: 0-1
Distance: 2m/2m3: 0-0 2m4-2m7: 0-1 3m+: 0-0
Track: LH: 0-0 RH: 0-1 Tight: 0-1 Gall: 0-0
Aids: Bl: 0-0 Vi: 0-0 Tstrap: 0-0 Ckp: 0-0
Best Rating: 84   9/00   Baln   2m1f   gd-yld   Ch

Barbizon (NZ)
95   (87h)96

10-y-o b g Oregon (USA)-Fleece Tum (NZ) (Umteen (NZ))
B De Haan Plough Racing

Placings:0660/3F01/1PF/60P/1-U2   (0446)
2003/04: 24UGF, 24ZG,

	Starts	1st	2nd	3rd	Win & Pl
Chases	2	0	1	0	954
Career Total	17	3	1	1	10124

96	11/02	Ludl	2m4f	E(0-105)HCh	GD	£4173
96	5/00	Ludl	2m5f	E(0-105)HHdl	GD	£2600
96	4/00	Towc	2m5f	F Hdl	GD	£1909

Total win prize-money £8683

Going: Sf: 0-0 GS: 0-0 Gd: 0-1 GF: - Fm: 0-0
Distance: 2m/2m3: 0-0 2m4-2m7: 0-0 3m+: 0-2
Track: LH: 0-0 RH: 0-2 Tight: 0-0 Gall: 0-2
Aids: Bl: 0-0 Vi: 0-0 Tstrap: 0-2 Ckp: 0-0
Best Rating: 96   11/02   Ludl   2m4f   good   Ch

Moderate chaser; returning from a long lay-off to win a
novices' handicap chase in November 2002. Effective at two
and a half miles.

Barcelona
109   116

7-y-o b g Barathea (IRE)-Pipitina (Bustino)
G L Moore RFG Investments Ltd

Placings:1406541/52464030-1245   (2653)
2003/04: 22TG, 22ZGF, 20AGF, 18SG,

	Starts	1st	2nd	3rd	Win & Pl
Hurdles	4	1	1	0	5888
Career Total	19	3	2	1	29866

115	5/03	Font	2m6f110yE(0-110)HHdl	GD	£3516
110	4/02	Asct	2m4f	B Hdl	G-F	£17400
115	10/01	Font	2m2f110yE HHdl	G-S	£2460

Total win prize-money £23378

Going: Sf: 0-0 GS: 0-0 Gd: 0-1 GF: - Fm: 0-2
Distance: 2m/2m3: 0-1 **2m4-2m7: 1-3** 3m+: 0-0
Track: LH: **1-4** RH: 0-0 Tight: 1-3 Gall: 0-0
Aids: Bl: 0-0 Vi: 0-0 Tstrap: 0-0 **Ckp: 1-3**
Best Rating: 116   6/03   Worc   2m4f   gd-fm   Hdl

A fair stayer on the level, he made a winning debut over hurdles at Fontwell and scored on fast ground at Ascot in April
2002; stays two and a half miles, but does not want the
ground too soft.

Barcham Again
(IRE)
98(107h)   (97h)91

7-y-o b g Aristocracy-Dante's Thatch (IRE) (Phardante (FR))
K C Bailey D Allen

Placings:02P-56U05633FP1P   (4666)

2003/04: 22⁵S, 20⁶G, 25ᵁGS, 24⁰GS, 21⁵G, 26⁶GS, 20³S, 19³HY, 25ᶠGS, 24ᴾG, 25¹G, 20ᴾS,

	Starts	1st	2nd	3rd	Win & Pl
Hurdles	4	0	0	0	0
Chases	8	1	0	2	5195
Career Total	15	1	1	2	6291

91 3/04 Hrfd 3m1f110yF(0-90)HCh GD £3965
Total win prize-money £3965

Going:	Sf: 0-4 GS: 0-4 Gd: 1-4 GF: - Fm: 0-0
Distance:	2m/2m3: 0-1 2m4-2m7: 0-5 3m+: 1-6
Track:	LH: 0-4 RH: 1-8 Tight: 0-2 Gall: 0-2
Aids:	Bl: 0-0 Vi: 0-0 Tstrap: 0-0 Ckp: 1-8
Best Rating:	97 11/02 Ludl 2m5f good Hdl

Plating-class chaser; stays 2m 5f.

Bard Of Drumcoo (IRE)

9-y-o ch g Orange Reef-Sporting Houdini (Monseigneur (USA))
M A Kemp Mr & Mrs J R M Ridge

Placings:0P6/F6-5 (0202)
2003/04: 30⁵GF,

	Starts	1st	2nd	3rd	Win & Pl
Chases	1	0	0	0	0
Career Total	6	0	0	0	0

Going:	Sf: 0-0 GS: 0-0 Gd: 0-0 GF: - Fm: 0-1
Distance:	2m/2m3: 0-0 2m4-2m7: 0-0 3m+: 0-1
Track:	LH: 0-0 RH: 0-1 Tight: 0-0 Gall: 0-1
Aids:	Bl: 0-0 Vi: 0-0 Tstrap: 0-0 Ckp: 0-0
Best Rating:	69 4/03 Fknm 3m110y good Ch

Bardon Boy

10-y-o ch g Rakaposhi King-Paper Dice (Le Dauphin)
Mrs Monica Tory Mrs Monica Tory,Norman Tory,A Tory

Placings:U03P0/45FF54/P3-46 (0509)
2003/04: 26³S, 24⁴GS, 28⁶GS,

	Starts	1st	2nd	3rd	Win & Pl
Chases	3	0	0	1	526
Career Total	15	0	0	2	1188

Going:	Sf: 0-1 GS: 0-1 Gd: 0-0 GF: - Fm: 0-1
Distance:	2m/2m3: 0-0 2m4-2m7: 0-0 3m+: 0-3
Track:	LH: 0-3 RH: 0-0 Tight: 0-2 Gall: 0-0
Aids:	Bl: 0-0 Vi: 0-0 Tstrap: 0-0 Ckp: 0-0
Best Rating:	79 5/03 Chep 3m gd-fm Ch

Barfleur (IRE)
92f   87f

4-y-o b f Anshan-Lulu Buck (Buckskin (FR))
Miss E C Lavelle Switch International Trailers UK Ltd

Placings:0 (4846)
2003/04: 17⁰G,

	Starts	1st	2nd	3rd	Win & Pl
NH Flat	1	0	0	0	
Career Total	1	0	0	0	

Going:	Sf: 0-0 GS: 0-0 Gd: 0-1 GF: - Fm: 0-0
Distance:	2m/2m3: 0-1 2m4-2m7: 0-0 3m+: 0-0
Track:	LH: 0-1 RH: 0-0 Tight: 0-0 Gall: 0-1

Aids: Bl: 0-0 Vi: 0-0 Tstrap: 0-0 Ckp: 0-0
Best Rating: 87 4/04 Chel 2m1f good NHF

Barito (GER)
103   (126h)136

7-y-o b g Winged Love (IRE)-Blumme (CHI) (Jadar (CHI))
C Von Der Recke Gestut Karlshof

Placings:31121301560/4216-621513PF (4640)
2003/04: 21⁶VS, 22²G, 19¹G, 25⁵S, 20¹GF, 24³G, 20ᴾG, 21ᶠG,

	Starts	1st	2nd	3rd	Win & Pl
Chases	8	2	1	1	26480
Career Total	23	7	3	3	61448

136	10/03	Chel	2m4f110yC(0-135)HCh	G-F	£12702
	8/03	Maia	2m3f110y Ch	GD	£9150
130	1/03	Plum	2m4f D Ch	SFT	£8260
126	12/01	Kemp	2m B Hdl	GD	£7085
	9/01	Maia	2m110y Hdl	GD	£6212
	7/01	Aabe	2m1f HHdl	SFT	£1607
	7/01	Aabe	2m1f Hdl	SFT	£1607

Total win prize-money £46623

Going:	Sf: 0-1 GS: 0-0 Gd: 1-5 GF: - Fm: 1-1
Distance:	2m/2m3: 0-0 2m4-2m7: 2-6 3m+: 0-2
Track:	LH: 1-2 RH: 0-3 Tight: 0-1 Gall: 1-1
Aids:	Bl: 0-0 Vi: 0-0 Tstrap: 0-0 Ckp: 0-0
Best Rating:	136 12/03 Sand 3m110y good Ch

Useful chaser; stays two miles four; acts on most ground.

Barnards Green (IRE)
102(90h)   (79h)98

6-y-o ch g Florida Son-Pearly Castle (IRE) (Carlingford Castle)
R H Alner T H Chadney

Placings:0-360P03FP (4527)
2003/04: 16³GF, 17⁶GF, 17⁰G, 22ᴾG, 19⁴G, 16³G, 24ᶠG, 19ᴾGS,

	Starts	1st	2nd	3rd	Win & Pl
Hurdles	4	0	0	1	500
Chases	4	0	0	1	530
Career Total	9	0	0	2	1030

Going:	Sf: 0-0 GS: 0-1 Gd: 0-5 GF: - Fm: 0-2
Distance:	2m/2m3: 0-5 2m4-2m7: 0-2 3m+: 0-1
Track:	LH: 0-2 RH: 0-6 Tight: 0-4 Gall: 0-0
Aids:	Bl: 0-0 Vi: 0-0 Tstrap: 0-0 Ckp: 0-0
Best Rating:	98 3/04 Folk 2m good Ch

Barnes Green
70f   38f

6-y-o br g Teenoso (USA)-Almanot (Remainder Man)
L Wells P A Sells

Placings:0 (0216)
2003/04: 16⁰G,

	Starts	1st	2nd	3rd	Win & Pl
NH Flat	1	0	0	0	
Career Total	1	0	0	0	

Going:	Sf: 0-0 GS: 0-0 Gd: 0-1 GF: - Fm: 0-0
Distance:	2m/2m3: 0-1 2m4-2m7: 0-0 3m+: 0-0
Track:	LH: 0-1 RH: 0-0 Tight: 0-0 Gall: 0-0
Aids:	Bl: 0-0 Vi: 0-0 Tstrap: 0-0 Ckp: 0-0
Best Rating:	41 5/03 Worc 2m good NHF

Barney Radetzky (IRE)
(57h)

8-y-o b g Jurado (USA)-Clarrie (Ballyciptic)
I A Duncan Alan Steele

Placings:0/0/0000/BF-P (0469)
2003/04: 16ᴾG,

	Starts	1st	2nd	3rd	Win & Pl
Chases	1	0	0	0	
Career Total	9	0	0	0	

Going:	Sf: 0-0 GS: 0-0 Gd: 0-1 GF: - Fm: 0-0
Distance:	2m/2m3: 0-1 2m4-2m7: 0-0 3m+: 0-0
Track:	LH: 0-1 RH: 0-0 Tight: 0-0 Gall: 0-0
Aids:	Bl: 0-0 Vi: 0-0 Tstrap: 0-0 Ckp: 0-0
Best Rating:	65 12/01 Navn 2m yield NHF

Barneys Lyric
101   107

4-y-o ch g Hector Protector (USA)-Anchorage (IRE) (Slip Anchor)
N A Twiston-Davies (R Charlton 3/7) Mr & Mrs Peter Orton

Placings:U1133634 (4948)
2003/04: 17ᵁGF, 17¹G, 16¹G, 16³GF, 16³G, 16⁶GS, 24³GS, 24⁶GS,

	Starts	1st	2nd	3rd	Win & Pl
Hurdles	8	2	0	3	11739
Career Total	8	2	0	3	11739

107	9/03	Prth	2m110y E Hdl	GD	£2954
107	9/03	Bang	2m1f E Hdl	GD	£3591

Total win prize-money £6545

Going:	Sf: 0-0 GS: 0-3 Gd: 2-3 GF: - Fm: 0-2
Distance:	2m/2m3: 2-6 2m4-2m7: 0-0 3m+: 0-2
Track:	LH: 1-5 RH: 1-2 Tight: 1-2 Gall: 0-0
Aids:	Bl: 0-0 Vi: 0-0 Tstrap: 0-0 Ckp: 0-0
Best Rating:	107 3/04 Asct 3m gd-sft Hdl

Fair juvenile hurdler; unseated on debut, but won next two; likes to blaze a trail but held up when tried over three miles; acts on a sound surface.

Barneys Reflection
95   75

4-y-o b g Petoski-Annaberg (IRE) (Tirol)
Mrs L Wadham Mrs C Bailey

Placings:006 (4588)
2003/04: 13⁰S, 21⁰G, 21⁵G,

	Starts	1st	2nd	3rd	Win & Pl
NH Flat	1	0	0	0	0
Hurdles	2	0	0	0	0
Career Total	3	0	0	0	0

Going:	Sf: 0-1 GS: 0-0 Gd: 0-2 GF: - Fm: 0-0
Distance:	2m/2m3: 0-0 2m4-2m7: 0-2 3m+: 0-0
Track:	LH: 0-1 RH: 0-1 Tight: 0-1 Gall: 0-1
Aids:	Bl: 0-0 Vi: 0-0 Tstrap: 0-0 Ckp: 0-0
Best Rating:	75 3/04 Hntg 2m5f110y good Hdl

Barneysian
(74h)

8-y-o b g Petoski-Rosemoss (Le Moss)
R Dickin Mrs Margaret James

Placings:0/05/000-P (0212)

2003/04: 23PG,

	Starts	1st	2nd	3rd	Win & Pl
Chases	1	0	0	0	
Career Total	7	0	0	0	0

Going:	Sf: 0-0 GS: 0-0 Gd: 0-1 GF: - Fm: 0-0
Distance:	2m/2m3: 0-0 2m4-2m7: 0-0 3m+: 0-1
Track:	LH: 0-1 RH: 0-0 Tight: 0-0 Gall: 0-0
Aids:	Bl: 0-0 Vi: 0-0 Tstrap: 0-0 Ckp: 0-0
Best Rating:	74 2/02 MRas 2m3f110y gd-sft Hdl

Baron Allfours
106   78

12-y-o gr g Baron Blakeney-Georgian Quickstep (Dubassoff (USA))
Miss Z C Davison The Secret Circle

Placings: O/0P/2U25F3PP/PPPPPP34454P2F/P-0P3212
(1213)
2003/04: 24⁰GF, 26PGF, 24³G, 26²GF, 22¹GF, 20²GF,

	Starts	1st	2nd	3rd	Win & Pl
Chases	6	1	2	1	6562
Career Total	32	1	5	3	10975

78 8/03 Font 2m6f   E Ch   G-F £4007
Total win prize-money £4007

Going:	Sf: 0-0 GS: 0-0 Gd: 0-1 GF: - Fm: 1-5
Distance:	2m/2m3: 0-0 2m4-2m7: 1-2 3m+: 0-4
Track:	LH: 0-2 RH: 0-2 Tight: 1-3 Gall: 0-2
Aids:	Bl: 0-0 Vi: 0-0 Tstrap: 0-0 Ckp: 0-0
Best Rating:	86 7/00 MRas 2m6f110y good Ch

Plating-class chaser, stays three miles plus.

Baron Aron (IRE)
91   (98h)104

9-y-o br g Lord Americo-Eleika (Camden Town)
B N Pollock (Donal Hassett 20/7) Baroness Pitkeathley and Charles Wilson

Placings: 615P00-1F1P3P05FF
(4531)
2003/04: 16¹GY, 20FGY, 17¹Y, 16PGF, 17³GS, 20PGS, 16⁹GF, 16⁵G, 17FG, 16FGS,

	Starts	1st	2nd	3rd	Win & Pl
Hurdles	1	1	0	0	4929
Chases	9	1	0	1	6485
Career Total	16	3	0	1	15223

104 7/03 Baln 2m1f   Ch   YLD £6048
98 6/03 Clon 2m   (74-95)HHdl   G-Y £4928
90 12/02 Tram 2m   Hdl   HVY £3809
Total win prize-money £14788

Going:	Sf: 0-0 GS: 0-3 Gd: 0-2 GF: - Fm: 0-2
Distance:	**2m/2m3: 2-8** 2m4-2m7: 0-2 3m+: 0-0
Track:	LH: 0-5 RH: 0-2 Tight: 0-2 Gall: 0-1
Aids:	Bl: 0-4 Vi: 0-0 Tstrap: 0-0 Ckp: 0-0
Best Rating:	104 7/03 Baln 2m1f yield Ch

Baron Blitzkrieg
88   67

6-y-o b g Sir Harry Lewis (USA)-Steel Typhoon (General Ironside)
Jonjo O'Neill Mrs Ann Bish

Placings: 56P
(2770)
2003/04: 16FGS, 20PGS, 16PS,

	Starts	1st	2nd	3rd	Win & Pl
NH Flat	1	0	0	0	0
Hurdles	2	0	0	0	0
Career Total	3	0	0	0	0

Going:	Sf: 0-1 GS: 0-2 Gd: 0-0 GF: - Fm: 0-0
Distance:	2m/2m3: 0-2 2m4-2m7: 0-1 3m+: 0-0
Track:	LH: 0-2 RH: 0-1 Tight: 0-0 Gall: 0-0
Aids:	Bl: 0-0 Vi: 0-0 Tstrap: 0-0 Ckp: 0-0
Best Rating:	80 11/03 Uttx 2m gd-sft NHF

Baron Steane (IRE)
86f   91f

5-y-o b g Lord Americo-Lottosprite (IRE) (Sandalay)
Lady Connell Mrs Lisa Gregory

Placings: 45
(4787)
2003/04: 16⁴GS, 16⁵G,

	Starts	1st	2nd	3rd	Win & Pl
NH Flat	2	0	0	0	0
Career Total	2	0	0	0	0

Going:	Sf: 0-0 GS: 0-1 Gd: 0-1 GF: - Fm: 0-0
Distance:	2m/2m3: 0-2 2m4-2m7: 0-0 3m+: 0-0
Track:	LH: 0-1 RH: 0-1 Tight: 0-0 Gall: 0-1
Aids:	Bl: 0-0 Vi: 0-0 Tstrap: 0-0 Ckp: 0-0
Best Rating:	91 3/04 Chep 2m110y gd-sft NHF

Baron Windrush
93   125+

6-y-o b g Alderbrook-Dame Scarlet (Blakeney)
N A Twiston-Davies The Double Octagon Partnership

Placings: 0-6113
(4931)
2003/04: 20⁶S, 22¹G, 25¹GS, 22³G,

	Starts	1st	2nd	3rd	Win & Pl
Hurdles	4	2	0	1	7707
Career Total	5	2	0	1	7707

125 3/04 Weth 3m1f   E Hdl   G-S £3472
110 3/04 MRas 2m6f   E Hdl   GD £3689
Total win prize-money £7161

Going:	Sf: 0-1 GS: 1-1 Gd: 1-2 GF: - Fm: 0-0
Distance:	2m/2m3: 0-0 2m4-2m7: 1-3 3m+: 1-1
Track:	**LH: 1-2** RH: 0-1 Tight: 0-1 Gall: 0-0
Aids:	Bl: 0-0 Vi: 0-0 Tstrap: 0-0 Ckp: 0-0
Best Rating:	125 3/04 Weth 3m1f gd-sft Hdl

Fair hurdler; much improved effort when decisive winner of novices' hurdle at Market Rasen in March despite hanging violently left; very easy winner at Wetherby two weeks later; suited by give; stays well.

Baron's Pharaoh (IRE)
85   106

9-y-o b g Phardante (FR)-Katomi (Monksfield)
A W Carroll R H Harris & Barry Veasey

Placings: 000/11/P0F05
(4605)
2003/04: 20PGS, 16⁰GS, 19FG, 21⁰GS, 22⁵G,

	Starts	1st	2nd	3rd	Win & Pl
Hurdles	5	0	0	0	0
Career Total	10	2	0	0	6019

106 7/01 MRas 2m3f110yD Hdl   GD £3558
96 5/01 Wwck 2m   F Hdl   GD £2460
Total win prize-money £6020

Going:	Sf: 0-0 GS: 0-3 Gd: 0-2 GF: - Fm: 0-0
Distance:	2m/2m3: 0-1 2m4-2m7: 0-4 3m+: 0-0
Track:	LH: 0-3 RH: 0-1 Tight: 0-0 Gall: 0-0
Aids:	Bl: 0-0 Vi: 0-0 Tstrap: 0-0 Ckp: 0-0
Best Rating:	106 7/01 MRas 2m3f110y good Hdl

Barons Pharjan (IRE)

7-y-o b g Phardante (FR)-Widden Fields (Shy Groom (USA))
A W Carroll Barry Veasey

Placings: PP0P
(4369)
2003/04: 22PG, 19PG, 19⁰G, 20PG,

	Starts	1st	2nd	3rd	Win & Pl
Hurdles	3	0	0	0	0
Chases	1	0	0	0	0
Career Total	4	0	0	0	0

Going:	Sf: 0-0 GS: 0-0 Gd: 0-4 GF: - Fm: 0-0
Distance:	2m/2m3: 0-0 2m4-2m7: 0-4 3m+: 0-0
Track:	LH: 0-4 RH: 0-0 Tight: 0-2 Gall: 0-0
Aids:	Bl: 0-0 Vi: 0-0 Tstrap: 0-0 Ckp: 0-0
Best Rating:	0 3/04 Strf 2m4f good Ch

Barracat (IRE)

7-y-o b g Good Thyne (USA)-Helens Fashion (IRE) (Over The River (FR))
B W Hills D C G Gyle-Thompson

Placings: 1-P
(3871)
2003/04: 17PGS,

	Starts	1st	2nd	3rd	Win & Pl
Hurdles	1	0	0	0	
Career Total	2	1	0	0	1803

110 5/02 Hrfd 2m1f   H NHF   GD £1802
Total win prize-money £1803

Going:	Sf: 0-0 GS: 0-1 Gd: 0-0 GF: - Fm: 0-0
Distance:	2m/2m3: 0-1 2m4-2m7: 0-0 3m+: 0-0
Track:	LH: 0-0 RH: 0-1 Tight: 0-1 Gall: 0-0
Aids:	Bl: 0-0 Vi: 0-0 Tstrap: 0-0 Ckp: 0-0
Best Rating:	110 5/02 Hrfd 2m1f good NHF

Barren Lands
(95h)   (120h)121

9-y-o b g Green Desert (USA)-Current Raiser (Filiberto (USA))
K Bishop Mrs E K Ellis

Placings: 62314102/031P106/2004342F22/15615-0P
(4449)
2003/04: 21⁰G, 20PGS,

	Starts	1st	2nd	3rd	Win & Pl
Hurdles	2	0	0	0	
Career Total	32	6	6	3	37724

121 11/02 Hrfd 2m3f   D(0-115)HCh   SFT £6773
121 5/02 Aint 2m3f   D(0-145)HHdl   GD £6148
116 1/01 Tntn 2m1f   D(0-120)HHdl   SFT £3575
116 10/00 Winc 2m   E(0-110)HHdl   G-S £3250
104 1/00 Tntn 2m1f   D(0-120)HHdl   GD £3526
109 12/99 Winc 2m   F(0-100)HHdl   SFT £2402
Total win prize-money £25674

Going:	Sf: 0-0 GS: 0-1 Gd: 0-1 GF: - Fm: 0-0
Distance:	2m/2m3: 0-0 2m4-2m7: 0-2 3m+: 0-0
Track:	LH: 0-1 RH: 0-1 Tight: 0-0 Gall: 0-1
Aids:	Bl: 0-0 Vi: 0-0 Tstrap: 0-0 Ckp: 0-0
Best Rating:	121 11/02 Hrfd 2m3f soft Ch

Fair hurdler/chaser, he is best on a right-handed track with give in the ground; stays two miles three.

Barresbo
104   122
10-y-o b g Barrys Gamble-Bo' Babbity (Strong Gale)
A C Whillans E Waugh

Placings:0/2023044/1/22302142/12-P3000   (2608)
2003/04: 24PG, 22³GS, 22²G, 20⁴GS, 16⁴G,

	Starts	1st	2nd	3rd	Win & Pl
Hurdles	5	0	0	1	903
Career Total	24	3	7	3	20366
111 5/02 Kels	2m6f110yD(0-125)HHdl			G-S	£3458
115 2/02 Ayr	2m4f F(0-95)HHdl			HVY	£3150
104 4/01 Prth	2m110y G Hdl			HVY	£3614
			Total win prize-money		£10222

Going: Sf: 0-0 GS: 0-2 Gd: 0-3 GF: - Fm: 0-0
Distance: 2m/2m3: 0-1 2m4-2m7: 0-3 3m+: 0-1
Track: LH: 0-4 RH: 0-1 Tight: 0-3 Gall: 0-0
Aids: Bl: 0-0 Vi: 0-0 Tstrap: 0-0 Ckp: 0-0
Best Rating: 122 5/03 Ctml 2m6f   gd-sft Hdl

Fair hurdler; likes to race prominently; effective at up to three miles; likes soft ground but handles faster; suffered severe leg injury at Wetherby in December.

Barrons Pike
72f   59f
5-y-o ch g Jumbo Hirt (USA)-Bromley Rose (Rubor)
F S Storey F S Storey

Placings:00   (2858)
2003/04: 16⁶S, 16⁰GS,

	Starts	1st	2nd	3rd	Win & Pl
NH Flat	2	0	0	0	
Career Total	2	0	0	0	

Going: Sf: 0-1 GS: 0-1 Gd: 0-0 GF: - Fm: 0-0
Distance: 2m/2m3: 0-2 2m4-2m7: 0-0 3m+: 0-0
Track: LH: 0-2 RH: 0-0 Tight: 0-0 Gall: 0-0
Aids: Bl: 0-0 Vi: 0-0 Tstrap: 0-0 Ckp: 0-0
Best Rating: 59 11/03 Ayr 2m   soft NHF

Barrosa
83   70+
5-y-o b m Sabrehill (USA)-Shehana (USA) (The Minstrel (CAN))
Miss K M George A B Parr

Placings:6-6345   (2411)
2003/04: 16⁶GF, 17³G, 16⁴GF, 19⁵GF,

	Starts	1st	2nd	3rd	Win & Pl
Hurdles	4	0	0	1	674
Career Total	5	0	0	1	674

Going: Sf: 0-0 GS: 0-0 Gd: 0-1 GF: - Fm: 0-3
Distance: 2m/2m3: 0-3 2m4-2m7: 0-1 3m+: 0-0
Track: LH: 0-1 RH: 0-3 Tight: 0-2 Gall: 0-0
Aids: Bl: 0-0 Vi: 0-0 Tstrap: 0-0 Ckp: 0-0
Best Rating: 70 11/03 Winc 2m   gd-fm Hdl

Barrow (SWI)
97
7-y-o br g Caerleon (USA)-Bestow (Shirley Heights)
Ferdy Murphy Janet And Myrtle

Placings:4324/2/01-P   (0158)
2003/04: 23PGF,

	Starts	1st	2nd	3rd	Win & Pl
Hurdles	1	0	0	0	

Career Total	8	1	2	1	7124
97 4/03 Hntg	2m5f110yE Hdl			G-F	£3626
			Total win prize-money		£3626

Going: Sf: 0-0 GS: 0-0 Gd: 0-0 GF: - Fm: 0-1
Distance: 2m/2m3: 0-0 2m4-2m7: 0-0 3m+: 0-1
Track: LH: 0-1 RH: 0-0 Tight: 0-1 Gall: 0-0
Aids: Bl: 0-0 Vi: 0-0 Tstrap: 0-0 Ckp: 0-0
Best Rating: 113 5/01 Ayr 2m6f   gd-fm Hdl

Modest hurdler; finally broke his duck in poor company on fast ground at Huntingdon in April 2003; suited by two mile six.

Barrow Drive
117   (140h)152
8-y-o b g Gunner B-Fille De Soleil (Sunyboy)
Anthony Mullins Exors of the late Mrs B Lenihan

Placings:3111166/F2111112213F-33611404   (4580a)
2003/04: 20⁶GY, 25³G, 24³F, 26⁶GS, 22¹SH, 20¹YS, 18⁴Y, 20⁰G, 20⁴Y,

	Starts	1st	2nd	3rd	Win & Pl
Chases	9	2	0	2	46955
Career Total	27	12	3	4	210664
150 2/04 Gowr	2m4f	Ch		Y-S	£17191
145 1/04 Tram	2m6f	Ch		SH	£12130
145 2/03 Leop	2m5f	Ch		Y-S	£44318
139 11/02 Punc	2m4f	Ch		SFT	£15398
137 10/02 Gowr	2m4f	Ch		GD	£15950
109 9/02 Gway	2m1f	Ch		SFT	£7975
120 7/02 Gway	2m4f	Ch		YLD	£10368
104 7/02 Kbgn	2m4f	Ch		Y-S	£6561
140 12/01 Cork	3m	Hdl		Y-S	£15725
125 11/01 Cork	2m	Hdl		Y-S	£6677
120 9/01 Gway	2m3f	NHF		GD	£5842
114 8/01 Kbgn	2m3f	NHF		GD	£3895
			Total win prize-money		£162035

Going: Sf: 0-0 GS: 0-0 Gd: 0-2 GF: - Fm: 0-1
Distance: 2m/2m3: 0-1 2m4-2m7: 2-5 3m+: 0-1
Track: LH: 0-4 RH: 2-4 Tight: 0-0 Gall: 0-2
Aids: Bl: 0-0 Vi: 0-0 Tstrap: 2-9 Ckp: 0-0
Best Rating: 150 2/04 Gowr 2m4f   yld-sft Ch

Smart Irish-trained chaser; won Grade One P. J. Moriarty Chase at Leopardstown in 2003; effective at up to two miles six; acts on soft ground; wears a tongue tie.

Barry Island
5-y-o b g Turtle Island (IRE)-Pine Ridge (High Top)
D R C Elsworth Matthew Green

Placings:P   (2449)
2003/04: 16PGS,

	Starts	1st	2nd	3rd	Win & Pl
Hurdles	1	0	0	0	
Career Total	1	0	0	0	

Going: Sf: 0-0 GS: 0-1 Gd: 0-0 GF: - Fm: 0-0
Distance: 2m/2m3: 0-1 2m4-2m7: 0-0 3m+: 0-0
Track: LH: 0-1 RH: 0-0 Tight: 0-0 Gall: 0-1
Aids: Bl: 0-0 Vi: 0-0 Tstrap: 0-0 Ckp: 0-0
Best Rating: 0 11/03 Newb 2m110y   gd-sft Hdl

Bartlet
5-y-o b g Infantry-Deviji (Mansingh (USA))
M A Allen Andy Holder

Placings:0   (0372)
2003/04: 16⁰G,

	Starts	1st	2nd	3rd	Win & Pl
NH Flat	1	0	0	0	
Career Total	1	0	0	0	

Going: Sf: 0-0 GS: 0-0 Gd: 0-1 GF: - Fm: 0-0
Distance: 2m/2m3: 0-1 2m4-2m7: 0-0 3m+: 0-0
Track: LH: 0-1 RH: 0-0 Tight: 0-0 Gall: 0-0
Aids: Bl: 0-0 Vi: 0-0 Tstrap: 0-0 Ckp: 0-0
Best Rating: 0 5/03 Worc 2m   good NHF

Barton
109   (170h)145
11-y-o ch g Port Etienne (FR)-Peanuts (FR) (Mistigri)
T D Easterby Sir Stanley Clarke

Placings:02/1111111/12514/2111101/0366-2   (1885)
2003/04: 20²G,

	Starts	1st	2nd	3rd	Win & Pl
Chases	1	0	1	0	3166
Career Total	26	14	4	1	295047
160 4/02 Aint	3m1f	A Ch		GD	£46500
139 1/02 Newc	2m4f	A Ch		SFT	£14875
139 12/01 Weth	2m	C Ch		G-S	£6376
147 12/01 Newc	3m	C Ch		G-S	£6711
129 11/01 Newc	2m4f	E Ch		GD	£3110
170 4/01 Aint	2m4f	A Hdl		HVY	£71400
163 11/00 Newc	2m	A Hdl		SFT	£22200
163 4/99 Aint	2m4f	A Hdl		GD	£17850
160 3/99 Chel	2m5f	A Hdl		G-S	£45960
158 1/99 Donc	2m4f	A Hdl		GD	£10087
149 12/98 Sand	2m6f	A Hdl		GD	£9689
148 11/98 Uttx	2m4f110yA Hdl			GD	£9419
119 10/98 Weth	2m7f	C Hdl		SFT	£4185
113 10/98 Weth	2m4f110yD Hdl			GD	£3037
			Total win prize-money		£271404

Going: Sf: 0-0 GS: 0-0 Gd: 0-1 GF: - Fm: 0-0
Distance: 2m/2m3: 0-0 2m4-2m7: 0-1 3m+: 0-0
Track: LH: 0-1 RH: 0-0 Tight: 0-0 Gall: 0-0
Aids: Bl: 0-0 Vi: 0-0 Tstrap: 0-0 Ckp: 0-0
Best Rating: 170 4/01 Aint 2m4f   heavy Hdl

Former top-class hurdler/novice chaser; won the Royal and SunAlliance Hurdle at the Cheltenham Festival in 2001 and the Grade 2 Mildmay Novices' Chase at Aintree in April 2002; not at his best in 2002/3; made a very pleasing return when narrowly held over two and a half miles at Wetherby in November, but not seen since; acts on good and soft ground; stays three miles plus.

Barton Bandit
76   (78h)4
8-y-o ch g Sula Bula-Yamrah (Milford)
J M Bradley Leeway Group Limited

Placings:4/0P4PF4/522PP4P-P0   (1018)
2003/04: 23PG, 20⁰G,

	Starts	1st	2nd	3rd	Win & Pl
Chases	2	0	0	0	
Career Total	16	0	2	0	2900

Going: Sf: 0-0 GS: 0-0 Gd: 0-2 GF: - Fm: 0-0
Distance: 2m/2m3: 0-0 2m4-2m7: 0-1 3m+: 0-1
Track: LH: 0-2 RH: 0-0 Tight: 0-0 Gall: 0-0
Aids: Bl: 0-0 Vi: 0-0 Tstrap: 0-0 Ckp: 0-0
Best Rating: 90 5/02 Aint 2m4f   good Ch

Barton Baron (IRE)

90   **84**

6-y-o b g Phardante (FR)-Boolavogue (IRE) (Torus)
D P Keane   Sir Stanley Clarke

Placings:*00*-P000   (3846)
2003/04: 20^PGS, 16^0GS, 16^0S, 17^0GS,

	Starts	1st	2nd	3rd	Win & Pl
Hurdles	4	0	0	0	
Career Total	6	0	0	0	

Going: Sf: 0-1 GS: 0-3 Gd: 0-0 GF: - Fm: 0-0
Distance: 2m/2m3: 0-3 2m4-2m7: 0-1 3m+: 0-0
Track: LH: 0-3 RH: 0-1 Tight: 0-1 Gall: 0-0
Aids: Bl: 0-0 Vi: 0-0 Tstrap: 0-0 Ckp: 0-0
Best Rating: 84   12/03   Hayd   2m   gd-sft   Hdl

Barton Bog (IRE)

                   (89h)**72**

10-y-o gr g Roselier (FR)-Al's Niece (Al Sirat)
M J M Evans (J R Cornwall 5/3)   Mrs J Z Munday

Placings:630232/23523P0/5-P533PP   (4570)
2003/04: 24^PGS, 25^5HY, 24^3HY, 23^3GF, 24^PG, 24^PGS,

	Starts	1st	2nd	3rd	Win & Pl
Chases	6	0	4	6	1726
Career Total	20	0	4	6	7124

Going: Sf: 0-2 GS: 0-2 Gd: 0-1 GF: - Fm: 0-1
Distance: 2m/2m3: 0-0 2m4-2m7: 0-0 3m+: 0-6
Track: LH: 0-3 RH: 0-3 Tight: 0-1 Gall: 0-0
Aids: Bl: 0-3 Vi: 0-0 Tstrap: 0-0 Ckp: 0-0
Best Rating: 89   4/01   Prth   3m110y   heavy   Hdl

Barton Dante

97   **111**

7-y-o b m Phardante (FR)-Cindie Girl (Orchestra)
M W Easterby   Sir Stanley Clarke

Placings:*22/2*131210/3U-42   (0412)
2003/04: 20^4G, 20^2G,

	Starts	1st	2nd	3rd	Win & Pl
Hurdles	2	0	1	0	1364
Career Total	13	3	5	2	11536
107	1/02	Sedg	2m5f110y E Hdl	HVY	£2450
105	11/01	Catt	2m3f	F Hdl	G-F	£1907
97	10/01	Bang	2m1f	H NHF	GD	£1767

            Total win prize-money £6126

Going: Sf: 0-0 GS: 0-0 Gd: 0-2 GF: - Fm: 0-0
Distance: 2m/2m3: 0-0 2m4-2m7: 0-2 3m+: 0-0
Track: LH: 0-2 RH: 0-0 Tight: 0-0 Gall: 0-0
Aids: Bl: 0-0 Vi: 0-0 Tstrap: 0-0 Ckp: 0-0
Best Rating: 111   5/03   Hexm   2m4f110y   good   Hdl

Modest hurdler; stays two and a half miles; acts on any ground.

Barton Gate

103   **110**

6-y-o b g Rock Hopper-Ruth's River (Young Man (FR))
D P Keane   Sir Stanley Clarke

Placings:*5036*-P41136   (4565)
2003/04: 16^PGS, 19^4GS, 16^1GS, 16^1GS, 16^3GS, 17^6GS,

	Starts	1st	2nd	3rd	Win & Pl
Hurdles	6	2	0	1	7368
Career Total	10	2	0	2	7656

---

105   12/03   Uttx   2m   E(0-105)HHdl   G-S   £3867
94   12/03   Uttx   2m   F(0-85)HHdl   G-S   £2051
           Total win prize-money £5919

Going: Sf: 0-0 GS: 2-6 Gd: 0-0 GF: - Fm: 0-0
Distance: 2m/2m3: 2-5 2m4-2m7: 0-1 3m+: 0-0
Track: LH: 2-5 RH: 0-1 Tight: 0-1 Gall: 0-0
Aids: Bl: 0-0 Vi: 2-5 Tstrap: 0-0 Ckp: 0-0
Best Rating: 110   1/04   Wwck   2m   gd-sft   Hdl

Modest performer; improved form for new stable with back-to-back wins in 2m handicap hurdles at Uttoxeter in December 2003; third off 22lb higher mark next time; wears a visor; best suited by 2m; looks well treated at the moment.

Barton Hill

100   **106**

7-y-o b g Nicholas Bill-Home From The Hill (IRE) (Jareer (USA))
T D Easterby   Sir Stanley Clarke

Placings:5P04-1506   (4459)
2003/04: 19^1G, 24^5HY, 20^6HY, 20^6HY,

	Starts	1st	2nd	3rd	Win & Pl
Hurdles	4	1	0	0	2285
Career Total	8	1	0	0	2679
92	12/03	MRas	2m3f110y F Hdl		GD	£2284

           Total win prize-money £2285

Going: Sf: 0-3 GS: 0-0 Gd: 1-1 GF: - Fm: 0-0
Distance: 2m/2m3: 0-0 2m4-2m7: 1-3 3m+: 0-1
Track: LH: 0-3 RH: 1-1 Tight: 1-1 Gall: 0-2
Aids: Bl: 0-0 Vi: 0-0 Tstrap: 0-0 Ckp: 0-0
Best Rating: 106   3/03   Uttx   2m   soft   Hdl

Modest novice hurdler; promise in bumpers and hurdles in 2002/2003; showed a good attitude when making a winning reappearance at Market Rasen in December; stays at least two miles three.

Barton May

96   **86**

5-y-o ch m Midnight Legend-Yamrah (Milford)
D P Keane   Westfield Racing

Placings:05430   (4668)
2003/04: 19^0S, 20^5G, 20^4HY, 22^3G, 23^0GS,

	Starts	1st	2nd	3rd	Win & Pl
Hurdles	5	0	0	1	693
Career Total	5	0	0	1	693

Going: Sf: 0-2 GS: 0-1 Gd: 0-2 GF: - Fm: 0-0
Distance: 2m/2m3: 0-1 2m4-2m7: 0-4 3m+: 0-0
Track: LH: 0-4 RH: 0-0 Tight: 0-3 Gall: 0-1
Aids: Bl: 0-0 Vi: 0-0 Tstrap: 0-0 Ckp: 0-0
Best Rating: 86   3/04   Font   2m6f110y   good   Hdl

Modest form in novice hurdles at around 2m 4f.

Barton Nic

101(111h)   (118+h)**90+**

11-y-o b g Nicholas Bill-Dutch Majesty (Homing)
D P Keane   Proverbial Optimists

Placings:*4625*/0/0P/*2F*/51315-1P14F0014   (4666)
2003/04: 20^1S, 22^PGS, 16^1GS, 18^4G, 20^PHY, 20^0S, 17^0G, 16^1GS, 20^4S,

	Starts	1st	2nd	3rd	Win & Pl
Hurdles	7	2	0	0	6314
Chases	2	1	0	0	3642
Career Total	23	5	2	1	16313
90	3/04	Chep	2m110y	F(0-90)HCh	G-S	£3360

---

116   12/03   Plum   2m   E(0-110)HHdl   G-S   £3031
100   5/03   Bang   2m4f   G(0-95)HHdl   SFT   £2891
104   2/03   Plum   2m   F(0-90)HHdl   HVY   £2576
84   12/02   Uttx   3m110y   F(0-100)HHdl   SFT   £2653
          Total win prize-money £14512

Going: Sf: 1-4 GS: 2-3 Gd: 0-2 GF: - Fm: 0-0
Distance: 2m/2m3: 2-4 2m4-2m7: 1-5 3m+: 0-0
Track: LH: 3-8 RH: 0-1 Tight: 2-5 Gall: 0-1
Aids: Bl: 3-8 Vi: 0-0 Tstrap: 0-0 Ckp: 0-1
Best Rating: 118   2/04   Chep   2m4f   heavy   Hdl

Fair hurdler; took advantage of being thrown in on his hurdles form when making a successful return to fences in Class F 2m handicap at Chepstow March 2004; has won over 2m and 3m; goes well on a soft surface; often fitted with either sheepskin cheekpieces or blinkers.

Barton Sands (IRE)

80   **62**

7-y-o b g Tenby-Hetty Green (Bay Express)
M C Pipe   Stuart M Mercer

Placings:P0P0   (4246)
2003/04: 17^PGF, 16^0GF, 16^PGS, 17^0GF,

	Starts	1st	2nd	3rd	Win & Pl
Hurdles	4	0	0	0	
Career Total	4	0	0	0	

Going: Sf: 0-0 GS: 0-1 Gd: 0-0 GF: - Fm: 0-3
Distance: 2m/2m3: 0-4 2m4-2m7: 0-0 3m+: 0-0
Track: LH: 0-2 RH: 0-2 Tight: 0-1 Gall: 0-1
Aids: Bl: 0-0 Vi: 0-3 Tstrap: 0-3 Ckp: 0-0
Best Rating: 62   12/03   Newb   2m110y   gd-fm   Hdl

Barton Sun (IRE)

87f   **74f**

5-y-o b g Indian Ridge-Sun Screen (Caerleon (USA))
R N Bevis   Steve Corbett

Placings:*00*   (4920)
2003/04: 16^0HY, 16^0GS,

	Starts	1st	2nd	3rd	Win & Pl
NH Flat	2	0	0	0	
Career Total	2	0	0	0	

Going: Sf: 0-1 GS: 0-1 Gd: 0-0 GF: - Fm: 0-0
Distance: 2m/2m3: 0-2 2m4-2m7: 0-0 3m+: 0-0
Track: LH: 0-2 RH: 0-0 Tight: 0-0 Gall: 0-0
Aids: Bl: 0-0 Vi: 0-0 Tstrap: 0-0 Ckp: 0-0
Best Rating: 74   4/04   Worc   2m   gd-sft   NHF

Basil

  (59h)   (7h)**88+**

11-y-o br g Lighter-Thrupence (Royal Highway)
R H Buckler   Mrs C J Dunn

Placings:PU00/RU3P5/0531F-UPRF1P   (3413)
2003/04: 24^UG, 25^PG, 24^PGS, 26^FGS, 29^1S, 26^PS,

	Starts	1st	2nd	3rd	Win & Pl
Chases	6	1	0	0	5187
Career Total	20	2	0	2	9867
87	1/04	Plum	3m5f	E(0-105)HCh	SFT	£5187
87	1/03	Wwck	3m2f	F(0-95)HCh	SFT	£3556

          Total win prize-money £8743

Going: Sf: 1-2 GS: 0-1 Gd: 0-3 GF: - Fm: 0-0
Distance: 2m/2m3: 0-0 2m4-2m7: 0-0 3m+: 1-6
Track: LH: 1-4 RH: 0-2 Tight: 1-4 Gall: 0-0

Aids: Bl: 0-0 Vi: 0-0 Tstrap: 0-0 Ckp: 0-0
Best Rating: 87 1/04 Plum 3m5f soft Ch

Modest handicap chaser; ended long losing run when successful at Warwick in January 2003; acts in testing conditions; stays three and a quarter miles.

Basinet

101   95

6-y-o b g Alzao (USA)-Valiancy (Grundy)
J J Quinn Tara Leisure

Placings:2F3   (1480)
2003/04: 17²GF, 17FG, 17³G,

	Starts	1st	2nd	3rd	Win & Pl
Hurdles	3	0	1	1	1349
Career Total	3	0	1	1	1349

Going: Sf: 0-0 GS: 0-0 Gd: 0-2 GF: - Fm: 0-1
Distance: 2m/2m3: 0-2 2m4-2m7: 0-0 3m+: 0-0
Track: LH: 0-3 RH: 0-0 Tight: 0-3 Gall: 0-0
Aids: Bl: 0-0 Vi: 0-0 Tstrap: 0-0 Ckp: 0-0
Best Rating: 95 8/03 Sedg 2m1f gd-fm Hdl

Moderate handicapper at up to nine furlongs on the Flat; runner-up on hurdling debut at Sedgefield in August; poised to challenge when falling two out at Cartmel two weeks later.

Bassano (USA)

95   83

10-y-o b g Alwasmi (USA)-Marittima (USA) (L'Emigrant (USA))
S C Burrough Mrs Christine Priest

Placings:5644/40/63322P5/6304-2P5B36   (1304)
2003/04: 23²GF, 26PGF, 21⁵G, 20⁶GF, 23³GF, 20⁶GF,

	Starts	1st	2nd	3rd	Win & Pl
Chases	6	0	1	1	1821
Career Total	23	0	3	4	5362

Going: Sf: 0-0 GS: 0-0 Gd: 0-1 GF: - Fm: 0-5
Distance: 2m/2m3: 0-0 2m4-2m7: 0-3 3m+: 0-3
Track: LH: 0-6 RH: 0-0 Tight: 0-0 Gall: 0-0
Aids: Bl: 0-0 Vi: 0-0 Tstrap: 0-2 Ckp: 0-0
Best Rating: 107 1/01 Font 2m6f110y soft Hdl

Plating-class novice chaser; not the most fluent of jumpers; stays three miles.

Bassey (IRE)

11-y-o b g Be My Native (USA)-Evergreen Lady (Smartset)
Miss Fiona-Jane Hatfield M Hemphill

Placings:4124/4430/21/F   (3785)
2003/04: 24FS,

	Starts	1st	2nd	3rd	Win & Pl
Chases	1	0	0	0	
Career Total	11	2	2	1	7368
102 1/01 Fknm	2m7f110yE Hdl			SFT	£2380
106 12/97 Bang	2m1f	H NHF		GD	£1318
			Total win prize-money £3699		

Going: Sf: 0-1 GS: 0-0 Gd: 0-0 GF: - Fm: 0-0
Distance: 2m/2m3: 0-0 2m4-2m7: 0-0 3m+: 0-1
Track: LH: 0-0 RH: 0-1 Tight: 0-0 Gall: 0-1
Aids: Bl: 0-0 Vi: 0-0 Tstrap: 0-0 Ckp: 0-0
Best Rating: 113 1/00 Kemp 2m5f good Hdl

Bath House Boy (IRE)

99   (0c)89

11-y-o b g Don't Forget Me-Domiciliate (King's Lake (USA))
Mrs Pippa Bickerton David Bickerton

Placings:3010P4/4F2P4540/0/030020/P3P3   (1627)
2003/04: 24PG, 26⁰GF, 25PGF, 24³GF,

	Starts	1st	2nd	3rd	Win & Pl
Hurdles	3	0	0	2	832
Chases	1	0	0	0	0
Career Total	25	1	2	4	6363
109 12/98 Uttx	2m4f110yE Hdl			G-S	£1955
			Total win prize-money £1956		

Going: Sf: 0-0 GS: 0-0 Gd: 0-1 GF: - Fm: 0-3
Distance: 2m/2m3: 0-0 2m4-2m7: 0-0 3m+: 0-4
Track: LH: 0-3 RH: 0-1 Tight: 0-1 Gall: 0-0
Aids: Bl: 0-0 Vi: 0-0 Tstrap: 0-0 Ckp: 0-0
Best Rating: 110 12/99 Towc 2m6f good Ch

Moderate hurdler; over fences has shown little as well; tends to run in snatches and is a frustrating sort; suited by fast going.

Bathsheba

76   41

5-y-o b m Overbury (IRE)-Winnow (Oats)
K Bishop Miss Marie Steele

Placings:0-000   (4375)
2003/04: 16⁹S, 17⁹GS, 19⁰G,

	Starts	1st	2nd	3rd	Win & Pl
Hurdles	3	0	0	0	
Career Total	4	0	0	0	

Going: Sf: 0-1 GS: 0-1 Gd: 0-1 GF: - Fm: 0-0
Distance: 2m/2m3: 0-2 2m4-2m7: 0-1 3m+: 0-0
Track: LH: 0-0 RH: 0-3 Tight: 0-2 Gall: 0-0
Aids: Bl: 0-0 Vi: 0-0 Tstrap: 0-0 Ckp: 0-0
Best Rating: 42 2/04 Tntn 2m1f gd-sft Hdl

Bathwick Annie

103(108h)   (97 h)128+

8-y-o ch m Sula Bula-Lily Mab (FR) (Prince Mab (FR))
D P Keane W Clifford

Placings:24035-6111P   (4610a)
2003/04: 20⁶GS, 24¹GS, 22¹GS, 20¹G, 22PYS,

	Starts	1st	2nd	3rd	Win & Pl
Hurdles	1	0	0	0	
Chases	4	3	0	0	17693
Career Total	10	3	1	1	19349
117 2/04 MRas	2m4f	D Ch		GD	£6370
130 12/03 Newb	2m6f110yD(0-110)HCh			G-S	£6552
130 12/03 Hntg	3m	D(0-110)HCh		G-S	£4770
			Total win prize-money £17693		

Going: Sf: 0-0 GS: 2-3 Gd: 1-1 GF: - Fm: 0-0
Distance: 2m/2m3: 0-0 2m4-2m7: 2-4 3m+: 1-1
Track: LH: 1-2 RH: 2-2 Tight: 1-2 Gall: 2-2
Aids: Bl: 0-0 Vi: 0-0 Tstrap: 0-0 Ckp: 0-0
Best Rating: 130 12/03 Newb 2m6f110y gd-sft Ch

Progressive novice chaser; former maiden pointer/hurdler; winner of all three novice chases to date; suited by two and a half miles and will stay a lot further; best going right-handed; tough mare.

Baton Charge (IRE)

94   99+

6-y-o b g Gildoran-Frizzball (IRE) (Orchestra)
T R George (Lady A Maxwell 8/5) John Dyson

Placings:6042P   (4631)
2003/04: 18⁶Y, 16⁰S, 24⁴G, 20²G, 19PG,

	Starts	1st	2nd	3rd	Win & Pl
NH Flat	2	0	0	0	0
Chases	3	0	1	0	2730
Career Total	5	0	1	0	2730

Going: Sf: 0-1 GS: 0-0 Gd: 0-3 GF: - Fm: 0-0
Distance: 2m/2m3: 0-3 2m4-2m7: 0-1 3m+: 0-1
Track: LH: 0-1 RH: 0-3 Tight: 0-1 Gall: 0-1
Aids: Bl: 0-0 Vi: 0-0 Tstrap: 0-0 Ckp: 0-0
Best Rating: 99 3/04 Kemp 2m4f110y good Ch

Batoutoftheblue

11-y-o br g Batshoof-Action Belle (Auction Ring (USA))
K Robson Mrs M Armstrong

Placings:333220/2B3/1/P-U   (0475)
2003/04: 26⁴GS,

	Starts	1st	2nd	3rd	Win & Pl
Chases	1	0	0	0	
Career Total	12	1	3	4	7265
120 5/01 Ayr	2m6f	E Hdl		G-F	£2968
			Total win prize-money £2968		

Going: Sf: 0-0 GS: 0-1 Gd: 0-0 GF: - Fm: 0-0
Distance: 2m/2m3: 0-0 2m4-2m7: 0-0 3m+: 0-1
Track: LH: 0-1 RH: 0-0 Tight: 0-1 Gall: 0-0
Aids: Bl: 0-0 Vi: 0-0 Tstrap: 0-0 Ckp: 0-0
Best Rating: 120 5/01 Ayr 2m6f gd-fm Hdl

Batswing

97(107c)   (130c)130d

9-y-o b g Batshoof-Magic Milly (Simply Great (FR))
B Ellison Ashley Carr

Placings:13/4/21B3/300112041/6PO405-3224P6P50000   (3885)
2003/04: 16³YG, 17²G, 21²G, 16⁴GF, 20PGF, 16⁶GF, 16PG, 19⁵GF, 16⁶G, 16⁵GS, 16⁰G,

	Starts	1st	2nd	3rd	Win & Pl
Hurdles	5	0	0	0	
Chases	7	0	2	1	10409
Career Total	34	5	4	4	54637
134 4/02 Punc	2m	(0-127)HCh		G-Y	£9969
114 1/02 Muss	2m	E Ch		SFT	£3107
107 1/02 Muss	2m	D Ch		GD	£4192
122 2/01 Donc	2m110y	C(0-130)HHdl		GD	£5534
113 3/99 Tntn	2m3f110y			E Hdl	SFT
£2452					
			Total win prize-money £25257		

Going: Sf: 0-0 GS: 0-1 Gd: 0-6 GF: - Fm: 0-4
Distance: 2m/2m3: 0-9 2m4-2m7: 0-3 3m+: 0-0
Track: LH: 0-9 RH: 0-3 Tight: 0-5 Gall: 0-1
Aids: Bl: 0-1 Vi: 0-0 Tstrap: 0-4 Ckp: 0-0
Best Rating: 134 4/02 Punc 2m gd-yld Ch

Fair chaser/hurdler; acts well with cut in the ground; two miles is his trip; has worn cheekpieces and a tongue tie.

Battle Line

96   **87**

5-y-o b g Brief Truce (USA)-Forest Heights (Slip Anchor)
E McNamara Aidan Ryan

Placings:00B00-62030   (2135)
2003/04: 16⁶GF, 20²S, 20⁹GF, 18³GF, 21⁰G,

	Starts	1st	2nd	3rd	Win & Pl
Hurdles	5	0	1	1	2013
Career Total	10	0	1	1	2013

Going: Sf: 0-1 GS: 0-0 Gd: 0-1 GF: - Fm: 0-3
Distance: 2m/2m3: 0-2 2m4-2m7: 0-3 3m+: 0-0
Track: LH: 0-2 RH: 0-1 Tight: 0-0 Gall: 0-1
Aids: Bl: 0-0 Vi: 0-0 Tstrap: 0-0 Ckp: 0-0
Best Rating: 87 11/03 Thur 2m2f   gd-fm   Hdl

Battle Warning

117   **149+**

9-y-o b g Warning-Royal Ballet (IRE) (Sadler's Wells (USA))
P Bowen P Bowen

Placings:2P1224P-111   (2708)
2003/04: 24¹G, 24¹S, 25¹G,

	Starts	1st	2nd	3rd	Win & Pl
Hurdles	3	3	0	0	35652
Career Total	10	4	3	0	54085
149 12/03 Chel	3m1f110yB HHdl		GD	£11546	
136 11/03 Asct	3m	C(0-130)HHdl	SFT	£17371	
140 10/03 Aint	3m110y	C(0-130)HHdl	GD	£6734	
121 1/03 Donc	2m3f110yE Hdl		G-S	£3532	

Total win prize-money £39185

Going: Sf: 1-1 GS: 0-0 Gd: 2-2 GF: - Fm: 0-0
Distance: 2m/2m3: 0-0 2m4-2m7: 0-0 **3m+: 3-3**
Track: **LH: 2-2** RH: 1-1 Tight: 1-1 Gall: 1-1
Aids: Bl: 0-0 Vi: 0-0 Tstrap: 0-0 Ckp: 0-0
Best Rating: 149 12/03 Chel 3m1f110y good   Hdl

Smart hurdler, improving staying hurdler; winning stayer on the Flat; stays three miles plus; acts on any ground; has worn blinkers.

Batto

86   **77+**

4-y-o b g Slip Anchor-Frog (Akarad (FR))
G M Moore (W J Haggas 26/8) Mrs I I Plumb

Placings:045   (3976)
2003/04: 16⁹GS, 21⁴GS, 20⁹G,

	Starts	1st	2nd	3rd	Win & Pl
Hurdles	3	0	0	0	279
Career Total	3	0	0	0	279

Going: Sf: 0-0 GS: 0-2 Gd: 0-1 GF: - Fm: 0-0
Distance: 2m/2m3: 0-1 2m4-2m7: 0-2 3m+: 0-0
Track: LH: 0-2 RH: 0-1 Tight: 0-1 Gall: 0-0
Aids: Bl: 0-0 Vi: 0-0 Tstrap: 0-0 Ckp: 0-0
Best Rating: 77 2/04 Sedg 2m5f110y gd-sft   Hdl

Bay Caster

11-y-o b g Gunner B-Marina Bird (Julio Mariner)
P R Webber D P Barrie & M J Rees

Placings:1/PP   (4560)
2003/04: 21³G, 21⁰GS,

	Starts	1st	2nd	3rd	Win & Pl
Hurdles	2	0	0	0	

| Career Total | 3 | 1 | 0 | 0 | 1201 |
| 103 5/98 | Hntg | 2m110y | H NHF | G-F | £1201 |

Total win prize-money £1201

Going: Sf: 0-0 GS: 0-1 Gd: 0-1 GF: - Fm: 0-0
Distance: 2m/2m3: 0-0 2m4-2m7: 0-2 3m+: 0-0
Track: LH: 0-2 RH: 0-0 Tight: 0-0 Gall: 0-2
Aids: Bl: 0-0 Vi: 0-0 Tstrap: 0-0 Ckp: 0-0
Best Rating: 103 5/98 Hntg 2m110y   gd-fm   NHF

Bay Kenny

106   **115**

6-y-o b g Karinga Bay-Erica Superba (Langton Heath)
K C Bailey I F W Buchan

Placings:46146142   (4712)
2003/04: 16⁴G, 17⁶G, 17¹GF, 20⁴G, 22⁶HY, 21¹G, 24⁴GS, 24²G,

	Starts	1st	2nd	3rd	Win & Pl
NH Flat	3	1	0	0	1624
Hurdles	5	1	1	0	8632
Career Total	8	2	1	0	10256
112 3/04 Plum	2m5f	D Hdl	GD	£5980	
99 11/03 Hrfd	2m1f	H NHF	G-F	£1624	

Total win prize-money £7604

Going: Sf: 0-1 GS: 0-1 Gd: 1-5 GF: - Fm: 1-1
Distance: 2m/2m3: 1-3 2m4-2m7: 1-3 3m+: 0-2
Track: LH: 1-4 RH: 1-4 **Tight: 1-3** Gall: 0-1
Aids: Bl: 0-0 Vi: 0-0 Tstrap: 0-0 Ckp: 0-0
Best Rating: 119 4/04 Ludl 3m   good   Hdl

Modest hurdler; half-brother to staying chaser Lord Seamus; won Hereford bumper on third start; fair efforts over hurdles; acts on a sound surface.

Bay Magic (IRE)

95(101h)   **(91h)106**

11-y-o b g Ela-Mana-Mou-Come In (Be My Guest (USA))
Miss Lucinda V Russell A R Trotter

Placings:61/4502245000/32/2P4344/2545/31F5424625-U2P3030   (3359)
2003/04: 24ᵁG, 24²G, 24ᴾGS, 22³G, 23⁰G, 20³S, 25⁰S,

	Starts	1st	2nd	3rd	Win & Pl
Hurdles	6	0	1	2	2355
Chases	1	0	0	0	0
Career Total	41	2	8	5	20434
106 11/02 Hexm	2m4f110yE(0-105)HCh	HVY	£3523	
112 9/97 List	2m	NHF	SFT	£3730	

Total win prize-money £7253

Going: Sf: 0-2 GS: 0-1 Gd: 0-4 GF: - Fm: 0-0
Distance: 2m/2m3: 0-0 2m4-2m7: 0-3 3m+: 0-4
Track: LH: 0-5 RH: 0-2 Tight: 0-1 Gall: 0-0
Aids: Bl: 0-0 Vi: 0-1 Tstrap: 0-0 Ckp: 0-4
Best Rating: 112 5/98 Leop 2m   gd-fm   NHF

Bay Maid

98f   **71f**

6-y-o b m Karinga Bay-Maid To Match (Matching Pair)
Lady Connell Sir Michael Connell

Placings:00/3   (1156)
2003/04: 18³GF,

	Starts	1st	2nd	3rd	Win & Pl
NH Flat	1	0	0	1	264
Career Total	3	0	0	1	264

Going: Sf: 0-0 GS: 0-0 Gd: 0-0 GF: - Fm: 0-1
Distance: 2m/2m3: 0-1 2m4-2m7: 0-0 3m+: 0-1

Battle Line / continued (right column top)

Track: LH: 0-1 RH: 0-0 Tight: 0-1 Gall: 0-0
Aids: Bl: 0-0 Vi: 0-0 Tstrap: 0-0 Ckp: 0-0
Best Rating: 71 8/03 Font 2m2f110y gd-fm NHF

Bdellium

93(83h)   **(55h)93**

6-y-o b m Royal Vulcan-Kelly's Logic (Netherkelly)
B I Case Neil Hutley

Placings:00-60P663P   (4485)
2003/04: 16⁶G, 21⁰G, 16⁶S, 21⁶GS, 21⁶S, 20³G, 22ᴾG,

	Starts	1st	2nd	3rd	Win & Pl
Hurdles	5	0	0	0	0
Chases	2	0	0	1	980
Career Total	9	0	0	1	980

Going: Sf: 0-2 GS: 0-1 Gd: 0-4 GF: - Fm: 0-0
Distance: 2m/2m3: 0-2 2m4-2m7: 0-5 3m+: 0-0
Track: LH: 0-1 RH: 0-5 Tight: 0-2 Gall: 0-2
Aids: Bl: 0-0 Vi: 0-0 Tstrap: 0-0 Ckp: 0-0
Best Rating: 93 2/04 MRas 2m4f   good   Ch

Poor hurdler; modest third on chasing debut at Market Rasen in February; suited by two and a half miles.

Be Bop Bentley

9-y-o br g Arms And The Man-Playful Touch (Lepanto (GER))
P Maskill P Maskill

Placings:0R   (4891)
2003/04: 16⁰G, 24ᴿGF,

	Starts	1st	2nd	3rd	Win & Pl
Chases	2	0	0	0	
Career Total	2	0	0	0	

Going: Sf: 0-0 GS: 0-0 Gd: 0-1 GF: - Fm: 0-1
Distance: 2m/2m3: 0-1 2m4-2m7: 0-0 3m+: 0-1
Track: LH: 0-1 RH: 0-1 Tight: 0-1 Gall: 0-0
Aids: Bl: 0-0 Vi: 0-0 Tstrap: 0-0 Ckp: 0-0

Be Fair

107   **128+**

6-y-o br g Blushing Flame (USA)-Tokyo (Mtoto)
D E Cantillon Mrs Edward Cantillon

Placings:1/11402-111   (1902)
2003/04: 16¹GF, 16¹GF, 21¹GF,

	Starts	1st	2nd	3rd	Win & Pl
Hurdles	3	3	0	0	9877
Career Total	9	6	1	0	23443
128 11/03 Hntg	2m5f110yE Hdl		G-F	£2891	
116 5/03 Hntg	2m110y E Hdl		G-F	£3542	
103 5/03 Hntg	2m110y E Hdl		G-F	£3444	
117 9/02 Worc	2m	H NHF	GD	£1990	
117 9/02 NAbb	2m1f	H NHF	GD	£2184	
104 4/02 Hntg	2m110y H NHF		G-F	£1792	

Total win prize-money £15843

Going: Sf: 0-0 GS: 0-0 Gd: 0-0 GF: - Fm: 3-3
Distance: **2m/2m3: 2-2** 2m4-2m7: 1-1 3m+: 0-0
Track: LH: 0-0 **RH: 3-3** Tight: 0-0 **Gall: 3-3**
Aids: Bl: 0-0 Vi: 0-0 Tstrap: 0-0 Ckp: 0-0
Best Rating: 128 11/03 Hntg 2m5f110y gd-fm   Hdl

Useful novice hurdler; won his first three bumpers and finished well clear of the others when runner-up in Grade Two bumper at Aintree; won first three novice hurdles, all at

Huntingdon; acts on fast ground; stays 2m 5f; has plenty of pace.

Be Merry (IRE)
50f   84f
5-y-o ch m Broken Hearted-Charlies Rising (IRE) (Rising)
I A Gault   I A Gault

Placings:6   (4316)
2003/04: 16⁶GF,

	Starts	1st	2nd	3rd	Win & Pl
NH Flat	1	0	0	0	0
Career Total	1	0	0	0	0

Going:	Sf: 0-0 GS: 0-0 Gd: 0-0 GF: - Fm: 0-1
Distance:	2m/2m3: 0-1 2m4-2m7: 0-0 3m+: 0-0
Track:	LH: 0-1 RH: 0-0 Tight: 0-0 Gall: 0-0
Aids:	Bl: 0-0 Vi: 0-0 Tstrap: 0-0 Ckp: 0-0
Best Rating:	84 3/04 Ayr 2m gd-fm NHF

Showed ability in slowly run bumper (pulled far too hard) on debut at Ayr in March 2004; may do better in due course.

Be My Adelina (IRE)
95f   105+f
6-y-o b m Be My Native (USA)-Adelinas Leader (IRE) (Supreme Leader)
P F Nicholls   Jeffrey Hordle

Placings:3-1   (0309)
2003/04: 17¹G,

	Starts	1st	2nd	3rd	Win & Pl
NH Flat	1	1	0	0	2030
Career Total	2	1	0	1	2462
105 5/03 Bang 2m1f	H NHF			GD	£2030
Total win prize-money £2030					

Going:	Sf: 0-0 GS: 0-0 Gd: 1-1 GF: - Fm: 0-0
Distance:	2m/2m3: 1-1 2m4-2m7: 0-0 3m+: 0-0
Track:	LH: 1-1 RH: 0-0 Tight: 1-1 Gall: 0-0
Aids:	Bl: 0-0 Vi: 0-0 Tstrap: 0-0 Ckp: 0-0
Best Rating:	105 5/03 Bang 2m1f good NHF

Just tapped for speed in slowly-run bumper at Exeter on her debut; won at Bangor next time.

Be My Belle (IRE)
108(115h)   (140h)141
8-y-o b m Be My Native (USA)-Boreen Belle (Boreen (FR))
S J Treacy   Mrs M Aherne

Placings:01/0504211140140/21413132-4P2256   (3744a)
2003/04: 24⁴F, 26⁶PGS, 24²YS, 24⁵S, 24⁶YS,

	Starts	1st	2nd	3rd	Win & Pl
Hurdles	1	0	1	0	6169
Chases	5	0	1	0	16741
Career Total	29	8	5	2	125180
144 1/03 Gowr 3m	HCh			SH	£31655
132 12/02 Leop 3m	Ch			HVY	£17944
133 12/02 Fair 3m1f	Ch			SFT	£6773
140 3/02 Punc 3m	Hdl			SFT	£7975
111 1/02 Thur 2m6f	Hdl			HVY	£6138
138 1/02 Gowr 3m	Hdl			HVY	£7196
119 1/02 DRoy 2m4f	Hdl			SFT	£4868
112 2/01 Gowr 2m1f	NHF			HVY	£4173
Total win prize-money £86724					

Going:	Sf: 0-2 GS: 0-1 Gd: 0-0 GF: - Fm: 0-1
Distance:	2m/2m3: 0-0 2m4-2m7: 0-0 3m+: 0-6
Track:	LH: 0-4 RH: 0-1 Tight: 0-0 Gall: 0-1
Aids:	Bl: 0-0 Vi: 0-0 Tstrap: 0-0 Ckp: 0-0
Best Rating:	144 1/03 Gowr 3m sft-hvy Ch

Very useful Irish-trained mare; stays three miles plus; well suited by testing ground.

Be My Destiny (IRE)
109(107h)   (115 h)133+
7-y-o b g Be My Native (USA)-Miss Cali (Young Man (FR))
M Pitman   Mrs Elizabeth Pearce

Placings:206/02125-F2361F   (4195)
2003/04: 17⁵FS, 18²GS, 16³G, 20⁶G, 24¹G, 24⁴FG,

	Starts	1st	2nd	3rd	Win & Pl
Chases	6	1	1	1	10816
Career Total	14	2	4	1	18001
133 2/04 Newb 3m	C Ch			GD	£8320
115 1/03 Folk	2m1f110yE Hdl			HVY	£3577
Total win prize-money £11897					

Going:	Sf: 0-1 GS: 0-1 Gd: 1-4 GF: - Fm: 0-0
Distance:	2m/2m3: 0-3 2m4-2m7: 0-1 3m+: 1-2
Track:	LH: 1-4 RH: 0-2 Tight: 0-1 Gall: 1-3
Aids:	Bl: 0-0 Vi: 0-0 Tstrap: 0-0 Ckp: 0-0
Best Rating:	133 2/04 Newb 3m good Ch

Fair hurdler/novice chaser; effective at two to three miles; acts on most types of ground; going the right way over fences.

Be My Dream (IRE)

9-y-o b g Be My Native (USA)-Dream Toi (Carlburg)
R J Webb   C W Booth

Placings:06/31132/2122254-30   (0483)
2003/04: 25³GS, 24⁰GF,

	Starts	1st	2nd	3rd	Win & Pl
Chases	2	0	0	1	231
Career Total	16	3	5	3	19232
117 6/02 Uttx	3m	D Ch		HVY	£4147
111 10/01 Weth	3m1f	F(0-90)HHdl		GD	£2492
111 10/01 MRas	3m	F(0-100)HHdl		G-S	£2712
Total win prize-money £9352					

Going:	Sf: 0-0 GS: 0-1 Gd: 0-0 GF: - Fm: 0-1
Distance:	2m/2m3: 0-0 2m4-2m7: 0-0 3m+: 0-2
Track:	LH: 0-0 RH: 0-2 Tight: 0-0 Gall: 0-1
Aids:	Bl: 0-0 Vi: 0-1 Tstrap: 0-0 Ckp: 0-1
Best Rating:	117 8/02 Bang 3m110y soft Ch

Modest hunter chaser; stays well; acts on good ground.

Be My Friend (IRE)
115
8-y-o ch g Be My Native (USA)-Miss Lamb (Relkino)
Mrs H Dalton   J Hales

Placings:351-FP   (2313)
2003/04: 20⁶GF, 16⁸PGS,

	Starts	1st	2nd	3rd	Win & Pl
Hurdles	1	0	0	0	0
Chases	1	0	0	0	0
Career Total	5	1	0	1	4504
115 3/03 Bang 2m1f	E Hdl			GD	£3916
Total win prize-money £3916					

Going:	Sf: 0-0 GS: 0-1 Gd: 0-0 GF: - Fm: 0-1
Distance:	2m/2m3: 0-1 2m4-2m7: 0-1 3m+: 0-0
Track:	LH: 0-0 RH: 0-2 Tight: 0-0 Gall: 0-0
Aids:	Bl: 0-0 Vi: 0-0 Tstrap: 0-0 Ckp: 0-0
Best Rating:	115 3/03 Bang 2m1f good Hdl

Moderate performer; effective over two miles one, should stay further; acts on good ground.

Be My Manager (IRE)
109   134
9-y-o b g Be My Native (USA)-Fahy Quay (Quayside)
M Todhunter   Brian Murfin

Placings:2143/11/P4F/5303000-11PP   (4294)
2003/04: 24¹G, 20¹G, 20²G, 22²GF,

	Starts	1st	2nd	3rd	Win & Pl
Hurdles	1	0	0	0	0
Chases	3	2	0	0	13852
Career Total	20	5	1	3	43568
139 12/03 Weth	2m4f110yC(0-135)HCh			GD	£7020
129 9/03 Perth	3m	D(0-115)HCh		GD	£6831
146 1/01 Chel	2m5f	C HCh		SFT	£11212
120 10/00 Tntn	2m3f	D Ch		GD	£5642
117 1/00 Leic	2m4f110yD Hdl			SFT	£3705
Total win prize-money £34412					

Going:	Sf: 0-0 GS: 0-0 Gd: 2-3 GF: - Fm: 0-1
Distance:	2m/2m3: 0-0 2m4-2m7: 1-3 3m+: 1-1
Track:	LH: 1-2 RH: 1-2 Tight: 0-0 Gall: 0-0
Aids:	Bl: 0-0 Vi: 0-0 Tstrap: 0-0 Ckp: 0-0
Best Rating:	146 1/01 Chel 2m5f soft Ch

Useful chaser; well regarded, but became disappointing for Henrietta Knight; made a winning debut for Martin Todhunter at Perth in September 2003; followed up at Wetherby in December but returned lame next time; acts on good ground; stays three miles but equally effective over shorter.

Be My Own (IRE)
92   71
8-y-o b g Lord Americo-No Slow (King's Ride)
R H Buckler   R H Buckler

Placings:40P00B0/0PF2U   (4895)
2003/04: 22⁰GS, 22²PGF, 16⁶GF, 20²G, 22⁴G,

	Starts	1st	2nd	3rd	Win & Pl
Hurdles	5	0	1	0	672
Career Total	12	0	1	0	672

Going:	Sf: 0-0 GS: 0-1 Gd: 0-2 GF: - Fm: 0-2
Distance:	2m/2m3: 0-1 2m4-2m7: 0-4 3m+: 0-0
Track:	LH: 0-3 RH: 0-1 Tight: 0-3 Gall: 0-0
Aids:	Bl: 0-0 Vi: 0-0 Tstrap: 0-0 Ckp: 0-0
Best Rating:	82 10/01 Hrfd 2m1f good NHF

Be My Valentine (IRE)
79   45
6-y-o b m Be My Native (USA)-Valantonia (IRE) (Over The River (FR))
C R Egerton   M Haynes

Placings:400   (3321)
2003/04: 16⁴G, 16⁶GS, 21⁰GS,

	Starts	1st	2nd	3rd	Win & Pl
NH Flat	2	0	0	0	0
Hurdles	1	0	0	0	0
Career Total	3	0	0	0	0

Going:	Sf: 0-0 GS: 0-2 Gd: 0-1 GF: - Fm: 0-0
Distance:	2m/2m3: 0-2 2m4-2m7: 0-1 3m+: 0-0
Track:	LH: 0-2 RH: 0-1 Tight: 0-1 Gall: 0-1
Aids:	Bl: 0-0 Vi: 0-0 Tstrap: 0-0 Ckp: 0-0
Best Rating:	86 12/03 Newb 2m110y gd-sft NHF

Be Off With You
66f 28f
5-y-o b m Nalchik (USA)-Tilstock Maid (Rolfe (USA))
B R Foster Michael Brownrigg

Placings:*00*					(1195)
2003/04: 16⁰GF, 16⁰GF,					

	Starts	1st	2nd	3rd	Win & Pl
NH Flat	2	0	0	0	
Career Total	2	0	0	0	

Going:	Sf: 0-0 GS: 0-0 Gd: 0-0 GF: - Fm: 0-2
Distance:	2m/2m3: 0-2 2m4-2m7: 0-0 3m+: 0-0
Track:	LH: 0-2 RH: 0-0 Tight: 0-0 Gall: 0-0
Aids:	Bl: 0-0 Vi: 0-0 Tstrap: 0-0 Ckp: 0-0
Best Rating:	28 7/03 Worc 2m gd-fm NHF

Be Swift

5-y-o ch g Millkom-Conwy (Rock City)
A J Chamberlain N F B P L Racing

Placings:*6*					(1481)
2003/04: 19⁶GF,					

	Starts	1st	2nd	3rd	Win & Pl
Hurdles	1	0	0	0	0
Career Total	1	0	0	0	0

Going:	Sf: 0-0 GS: 0-0 Gd: 0-0 GF: - Fm: 0-1
Distance:	2m/2m3: 0-0 2m4-2m7: 0-1 3m+: 0-0
Track:	LH: 0-0 RH: 0-1 Tight: 0-0 Gall: 0-0
Aids:	Bl: 0-0 Vi: 0-0 Tstrap: 0-0 Ckp: 0-0
Best Rating:	0 10/03 Hrfd 2m3f110y gd-fm Hdl

Be The Tops (IRE)
(105h) (92h)
6-y-o br g Topanoora-Be The One (IRE) (Supreme Leader)
Jonjo O'Neill John P McManus

Placings:*5311P0P*					(4941)
2003/04: 20⁵S, 20³GF, 20¹G, 22¹GF, 24ᴾG, 22⁰G, 31ᴾGS,					

	Starts	1st	2nd	3rd	Win & Pl
Hurdles	5	2	0	1	9530
Chases	2	0	0	0	0
Career Total	7	2	0	1	9530
92 7/03 Ctml	2m6f		E Hdl	G-F	£3386
89 6/03 Prth	2m4f110yD Hdl			G-S	£5512
		Total win prize-money £8899			

Going:	Sf: 0-1 GS: 0-1 Gd: 1-3 GF: - Fm: 1-2
Distance:	2m/2m3: 0-0 **2m4-2m7: 2-5** 3m+: 0-2
Track:	LH: 1-5 RH: 1-1 **Tight: 1-3** Gall: 0-0
Aids:	Bl: 0-1 Vi: 0-0 Tstrap: 0-0 **Ckp: 1-3**
Best Rating:	92 7/03 Ctml 2m6f gd-fm Hdl

Ex-Irish point winner; off the mark over hurdles here at Perth in June 2003; followed up narrowly at Cartmel the following month; suited by two miles six; has worn cheekpieces.

Be Upstanding
103(96h) (106h)120
9-y-o ch g Hubbly Bubbly (USA)-Two Travellers (Deep Run)
Ferdy Murphy M Holmes

Placings:UF/01345/6331021S-U523UF3					(4221)
2003/04: 25ᵁG, 24⁴GS, 25²GS, 24³G, 25ᵁGS, 27ᶠGS, 22³GS,					

	Starts	1st	2nd	3rd	Win & Pl
Chases	7	0	1	2	4057

Career Total	22	3	2	5	19486
117 4/03 Uttx	3m	E(0-110)HCh	GD	£4416	
111 1/03 Fknm	2m5f110yE(0-100)HCh		SFT	£3806	
86 2/02 Fknm	2m4f	D Hdl	G-S	£3343	
		Total win prize-money £11566			

Going:	Sf: 0-0 GS: 0-5 Gd: 0-2 GF: - Fm: 0-0
Distance:	2m/2m3: 0-0 2m4-2m7: 0-1 3m+: 0-6
Track:	LH: 0-6 RH: 0-1 Tight: 0-3 Gall: 0-1
Aids:	Bl: 0-0 Vi: 0-0 Tstrap: 0-0 Ckp: 0-3
Best Rating:	117 4/03 Uttx 3m good Ch

Modest chaser; stays three miles; acts on soft ground; wears cheekpieces.

Beachcomber

9-y-o b g Kuwait Beach (USA)-Miss Rupert (Solar Topic)
J Groucott Frank Peate

Placings:FO					(4717)
2003/04: 24ᶠS, 24⁰G,					

	Starts	1st	2nd	3rd	Win & Pl
Chases	2	0	0	0	0
Career Total	2	0	0	0	0

Going:	Sf: 0-1 GS: 0-0 Gd: 0-1 GF: - Fm: 0-0
Distance:	2m/2m3: 0-0 2m4-2m7: 0-0 3m+: 0-2
Track:	LH: 0-0 RH: 0-2 Tight: 0-1 Gall: 0-1
Aids:	Bl: 0-0 Vi: 0-0 Tstrap: 0-0 Ckp: 0-0
Best Rating:	0 4/04 Ludl 3m good Ch

Beacon Of Light (IRE)
96 81
6-y-o b m Lake Coniston (IRE)-Deydarika (IRE) (Kahyasi)
Ferdy Murphy Paul T Murphy

Placings:66166002					(4388)
2003/04: 17⁶G, 20⁶GS, 21¹GF, 19⁶GF, 21⁶GS, 23⁰S, 24⁰GS, 21²G,					

	Starts	1st	2nd	3rd	Win & Pl
Hurdles	8	1	1	0	2846
Career Total	8	1	1	0	2846
77 11/03 Sedg	2m5f110yG Hdl		G-F	£1820	
		Total win prize-money £1820			

Going:	Sf: 0-1 GS: 0-3 Gd: 0-2 GF: - Fm: 1-2
Distance:	2m/2m3: 0-1 **2m4-2m7: 1-6** 3m+: 0-1
Track:	**LH: 1-7** RH: 0-1 **Tight: 1-4** Gall: 0-1
Aids:	Bl: 0-0 Vi: 0-0 Tstrap: 0-0 **Ckp: 1-7**
Best Rating:	81 3/04 Sedg 2m5f110y good Hdl

Selling-class novice hurdler; won at Sedgefield in November; handles most types of ground; stays two mile five.

Beamish Prince
105 89
5-y-o ch g Bijou D'Inde-Unconditional Love (IRE) (Polish Patriot (USA))
G M Moore (M Johnston 24/7) Geoff & Sandra Turnbull

Placings:4665F					(4258)
2003/04: 16⁴GS, 16⁶GF, 16⁶GS, 17⁵GS, 16ᶠGF,					

	Starts	1st	2nd	3rd	Win & Pl
Hurdles	5	0	0	0	0
Career Total	5	0	0	0	0

Going:	Sf: 0-0 GS: 0-3 Gd: 0-0 GF: - Fm: 0-2

Distance:	2m/2m3: 0-5 2m4-2m7: 0-0 3m+: 0-0
Track:	LH: 0-4 RH: 0-1 Tight: 0-4 Gall: 0-1
Aids:	Bl: 0-0 Vi: 0-0 Tstrap: 0-0 Ckp: 0-0
Best Rating:	89 3/04 Catt 2m gd-fm Hdl

Modest handicapper on the Flat; has shown very limited ability over hurdles; booked for second spot when falling two out in seller at Catterick in March.

Bear On Board (IRE)
109 136+
9-y-o b g Black Monday-Under The River (Over The River (FR))
A King J E Brown

Placings:122/P3312-P11120					(4647)
2003/04: 26ᴾHY, 24¹S, 30¹GS, 33¹G, 28²G, 36⁰G,					

	Starts	1st	2nd	3rd	Win & Pl
Chases	6	3	1	0	48280
Career Total	14	5	4	2	66722
136 1/04 Chel	4m1f	B(0-145)HCh	GD	£12562	
134 12/03 Bang	3m6f	D(0-120)HCh	G-S	£5551	
126 11/03 Hayd	3m	D(0-115)HCh	SFT	£3766	
114 3/03 Bang	3m110y	D(0-120)HCh	SFT	£5838	
115 11/00 Uttx	2m6f110y		E Hdl	HVY	£2485
		Total win prize-money £30203			

Going:	Sf: 1-2 GS: 1-1 Gd: 1-3 GF: - Fm: 0-0
Distance:	2m/2m3: 0-0 2m4-2m7: 0-0 **3m+: 3-6**
Track:	**LH: 3-6** RH: 0-0 Tight: 0-0 Gall: 1-1
Aids:	Bl: 0-0 Vi: 0-0 Tstrap: 0-0 Ckp: 0-0
Best Rating:	136 1/04 Chel 4m1f good Ch

Useful chaser; progressive; stays extreme distances really well and acts on most types of ground.

Bearaway (IRE)
102 102+
7-y-o b g Fourstars Allstar (USA)-Cruiseaway (Torus)
Mrs H Dalton Paternosters Racing

Placings:51213415					(1833)
2003/04: 16⁵G, 17¹GF, 16²G, 16¹G, 16³GF, 17⁴GF, 16¹F, 16⁵GF,					

	Starts	1st	2nd	3rd	Win & Pl
NH Flat	3	1	0	0	2547
Hurdles	5	2	0	1	8536
Career Total	8	3	1	1	11083
104 10/03 Towc	2m	D Hdl	FRM	£4143	
81 7/03 Worc	2m	E Hdl	GD	£3406	
111 6/03 Sthl	2m1f	H NHF	G-F	£1925	
		Total win prize-money £9475			

Going:	Sf: 0-0 GS: 0-0 Gd: 1-3 GF: - Fm: 2-5
Distance:	**2m/2m3: 3-8** 2m4-2m7: 0-0 3m+: 0-0
Track:	**LH: 2-6** RH: 1-2 Tight: 0-0 Gall: 0-0
Aids:	Bl: 0-0 Vi: 0-0 Tstrap: 0-0 Ckp: 0-1
Best Rating:	111 6/03 Sthl 2m1f gd-fm NHF

Modest novice hurdler; placed once from three starts in Irish points; comfortable winner of modest Southwell bumper June 2003; made successful switch to hurdles when winning weak 2m event at Worcester the following month; acts on fast ground; improving.

Beare Necessities (IRE)
91 82
5-y-o ch g Presenting-Lady Laburnum (Carlingford Castle)
A Ennis A T A Wates

Placings:0	(2283)

2003/04: 17⁹G,

	Starts	1st	2nd	3rd	Win & Pl
Hurdles	1	0	0	0	
Career Total	1	0	0	0	

Going:	Sf: 0-0 GS: 0-0 Gd: 0-1 GF: - Fm: 0-0
Distance:	2m2m3: 0-1 2m4-2m7: 0-0 3m+: 0-0
Track:	LH: 0-0 RH: 0-1 Tight: 0-0 Gall: 0-0
Aids:	Bl: 0-0 Vi: 0-0 Tstrap: 0-0 Ckp: 0-0
Best Rating:	82 11/03 Extr 2m1f good Hdl

Beasley
92 / 75
5-y-o b g First Trump-Le Shuttle (Presidium)
D McCain Centaur Racing Ltd

Placings: F43004-5465 (1136)
2003/04: 17⁵GF, 17⁴GF, 20⁶GF, 20⁵G,

	Starts	1st	2nd	3rd	Win & Pl
Hurdles	4	0	0	0	0
Career Total	10	0	0	1	444

Going:	Sf: 0-0 GS: 0-0 Gd: 0-1 GF: - Fm: 0-3
Distance:	2m2m3: 0-2 2m4-2m7: 0-2 3m+: 0-0
Track:	LH: 0-4 RH: 0-0 Tight: 0-3 Gall: 0-0
Aids:	Bl: 0-1 Vi: 0-0 Tstrap: 0-0 Ckp: 0-0
Best Rating:	75 7/03 Sedg 2m1f gd-fm Hdl

Poor selling hurdler.

Beat The Bank (IRE)
9-y-o br g Good Thyne (USA)-Must Clear (Al Sirat)
O Sherwood Chris Munro

Placings: U3PP (4916)
2003/04: 24⁹US, 23³GS, 24⁴PG, 23⁹GS,

	Starts	1st	2nd	3rd	Win & Pl
Chases	4	0	0	1	611
Career Total	4	0	0	1	611

Going:	Sf: 0-1 GS: 0-2 Gd: 0-1 GF: - Fm: 0-0
Distance:	2m2m3: 0-0 2m4-2m7: 0-0 3m+: 0-4
Track:	LH: 0-1 RH: 0-3 Tight: 0-1 Gall: 0-1
Aids:	Bl: 0-0 Vi: 0-0 Tstrap: 0-0 Ckp: 0-1
Best Rating:	0 4/04 Worc 2m7f110y gd-sft Ch

Three-mile point winner; moderate chaser.

Beat The Heat (IRE)
104 / 121
6-y-o b g Salse (USA)-Summer Trysting (USA) (Alleged (USA))
Jedd O'Keeffe Richard Berry

Placings: 3235-11233P (4326)
2003/04: 16¹G, 16¹G, 16²G, 16³S, 16³GS, 16⁹S,

	Starts	1st	2nd	3rd	Win & Pl
Hurdles	6	2	1	2	19194
Career Total	10	2	2	4	22219
114 11/03 Kels	2m110y D(0-125)HHdl		GD		£10432
104 10/03 Aint	2m110y D Hdl		GD		£3757
				Total win prize-money	£14190

Going:	Sf: 0-2 GS: 0-1 Gd: 2-3 GF: - Fm: 0-0
Distance:	2m/2m3: 2-6 2m4-2m7: 0-0 3m+: 0-0
Track:	LH: 2-5 RH: 0-1 Tight: 2-2 Gall: 0-1
Aids:	Bl: 0-0 Vi: 0-0 Tstrap: 0-0 Ckp: 0-0
Best Rating:	121 2/04 Newc 2m gd-sft Hdl

Fair hurdler; winner at Aintree and Kelso in the autumn and placed in handicaps since; stays two and a half miles; suited by decent ground.

Beat The Retreat
(95h) / (90h)91
9-y-o b g Terimon-Carpet Slippers (Daring March)
A King Mrs Peter Mason

Placings: 43/33/3PP3P02-U3 (0450)
2003/04: 19¹⁴GF, 20³GF,

	Starts	1st	2nd	3rd	Win & Pl
Chases	2	0	0	1	589
Career Total	13	0	1	6	4527

Going:	Sf: 0-0 GS: 0-0 Gd: 0-0 GF: - Fm: 0-2
Distance:	2m/2m3: 0-1 2m4-2m7: 0-1 3m+: 0-0
Track:	LH: 0-0 RH: 0-2 Tight: 0-0 Gall: 0-1
Aids:	Bl: 0-0 Vi: 0-0 Tstrap: 0-0 Ckp: 0-0
Best Rating:	107 1/02 Hntg 2m110y gd-sft Hdl

Modest maiden hurdler; runner-up on debut over fences at Huntingdon in April; effective at up to two miles six; acts on good and soft ground.

Beau Artiste
101 / 88
4-y-o ch g Peintre Celebre (USA)-Belle Esprit (Warning)
J Howard Johnson (Jedd O'Keeffe 27/10) G F Bear

Placings: 22 (4795)
2003/04: 16²GF, 17²G,

	Starts	1st	2nd	3rd	Win & Pl
Hurdles	2	0	2	0	2090
Career Total	2	0	2	0	2090

Going:	Sf: 0-0 GS: 0-0 Gd: 0-1 GF: - Fm: 0-1
Distance:	2m/2m3: 0-2 2m4-2m7: 0-0 3m+: 0-0
Track:	LH: 0-1 RH: 0-1 Tight: 0-2 Gall: 0-0
Aids:	Bl: 0-0 Vi: 0-0 Tstrap: 0-0 Ckp: 0-0
Best Rating:	88 4/04 Sedg 2m1f good Hdl

Frustrating maiden on the level; satisfactory hurdling efforts on a sound surface.

Beau Brun (FR)
8-y-o b/br g Cadoudal (FR)-Atakaia (FR) (Ataxerxes (GER))
G B Balding Roe Racing Ltd

Placings: P53/P/PP-P (0086)
2003/04: 23⁹GS,

	Starts	1st	2nd	3rd	Win & Pl
Chases	1	0	0	0	
Career Total	7	0	0	1	675

Going:	Sf: 0-0 GS: 0-1 Gd: 0-0 GF: - Fm: 0-0
Distance:	2m/2m3: 0-0 2m4-2m7: 0-0 3m+: 0-1
Track:	LH: 0-1 RH: 0-0 Tight: 0-0 Gall: 0-0
Aids:	Bl: 0-0 Vi: 0-0 Tstrap: 0-0 Ckp: 0-0
Best Rating:	55 11/99 Hntg 2m110y good Hdl

Beau Chasseur (FR)
92 / 80+
6-y-o ch g Cyborg (FR)-Safari Girl (FR) (Far Away Son (USA))

P Winkworth (N G Richards 24/5) P Winkworth

Placings: 5/121PF06-0P0PP (3440)
2003/04: 16⁹GF, 17⁵G, 16⁹G, 17⁶GF, 16⁶G,

	Starts	1st	2nd	3rd	Win & Pl
Hurdles	5	0	0	0	
Career Total	13	2	1	0	8781
6/02 Diep	2m1f110y Ch		GD		£4123
5/02 Lrsy	2m1f Ch		SFT		£2945
				Total win prize-money	£7068

Going:	Sf: 0-0 GS: 0-1 Gd: 0-3 GF: - Fm: 0-1
Distance:	2m/2m3: 0-5 2m4-2m7: 0-0 3m+: 0-0
Track:	LH: 0-3 RH: 0-2 Tight: 0-2 Gall: 0-0
Aids:	Bl: 0-0 Vi: 0-0 Tstrap: 0-0 Ckp: 0-0
Best Rating:	80 11/03 Wwck 2m good Hdl

Beau Coup
94 / 100
7-y-o b g Toulon-Energance (IRE) (Salmon Leap (USA))
John R Upson Mrs Ann Key

Placings: 635/45U55P5P (4676)
2003/04: 21⁴GF, 21⁵GS, 20ᵁGS, 20⁵G, 17⁵HY, 24⁵PGS, 22⁶GS, 22⁹G,

	Starts	1st	2nd	3rd	Win & Pl
Hurdles	8	0	0	0	0
Career Total	11	0	0	1	504

Going:	Sf: 0-1 GS: 0-4 Gd: 0-2 GF: - Fm: 0-1
Distance:	2m/2m3: 0-1 2m4-2m7: 0-6 3m+: 0-1
Track:	LH: 0-1 RH: 0-6 Tight: 0-2 Gall: 0-1
Aids:	Bl: 0-0 Vi: 0-0 Tstrap: 0-0 Ckp: 0-0
Best Rating:	100 3/02 Font 2m2f110y soft Hdl

Beau Jake (IRE)
(90h) / (79h)99
9-y-o b g Jolly Jake (NZ)-Cool Mary (Beau Charmeur (FR))
N M Babbage John Cantrill

Placings: 44003000/55F63-6 (0153)
2003/04: 24⁶GF,

	Starts	1st	2nd	3rd	Win & Pl
Hurdles	1	0	0	0	0
Career Total	14	0	0	2	1301

Going:	Sf: 0-0 GS: 0-0 Gd: 0-0 GF: - Fm: 0-1
Distance:	2m/2m3: 0-0 2m4-2m7: 0-0 3m+: 0-1
Track:	LH: 0-1 RH: 0-0 Tight: 0-0 Gall: 0-0
Aids:	Bl: 0-0 Vi: 0-0 Tstrap: 0-0 Ckp: 0-0
Best Rating:	99 2/03 Tntn 3m soft Ch

Beau Supreme (IRE)
105 / 106
7-y-o b g Supreme Leader-Miss Sabreur (Avocat)
C J Down Mrs R E Vicary

Placings: 2340 (4895)
2003/04: 21²G, 21³G, 21⁴GS, 22⁰G,

	Starts	1st	2nd	3rd	Win & Pl
Hurdles	4	0	1	1	2692
Career Total	4	0	1	1	2692

Going:	Sf: 0-0 GS: 0-1 Gd: 0-3 GF: - Fm: 0-0
Distance:	2m/2m3: 0-0 2m4-2m7: 0-4 3m+: 0-0
Track:	LH: 0-2 RH: 0-2 Tight: 0-0 Gall: 0-2
Aids:	Bl: 0-0 Vi: 0-0 Tstrap: 0-0 Ckp: 0-0

Best Rating: 106 3/04 Newb 2m5f gd-sft Hdl

Fair novice hurdler; placed in points; plenty of promise in novice hurdles; effective at up to two mile five; acts on good ground.

Beau Torero (FR)

101(92c) (82c)**96+**
6-y-o gr g True Brave (USA)-Brave Lola (FR) (Dom Pasquini (FR))
B N Pollock Mrs K Lloyd Mrs L Pollock L Stilwell

Placings:3000005-312 (2952)
2003/04: 16³GF, 19¹GF, 16²G,

	Starts	1st	2nd	3rd	Win & Pl
Hurdles	3	1	1	1	5355
Career Total	10	1	1	2	5607
93 11/03 Tntn	2m3f110yF(0-90)HHdl			G-F	£4026

Total win prize-money £4027

Going:	Sf: 0-0 GS: 0-0 Gd: 0-1 GF: - Fm: 1-2
Distance:	2m/2m3: 0-2 2m4-2m7: 1-1 3m+: 0-0
Track:	LH: 0-0 RH: 1-3 Tight: 1-1 Gall: 0-0
Aids:	Bl: 0-0 Vi: 0-0 Tstrap: 0-0 Ckp: 0-0
Best Rating:	96 12/03 Winc 2m good Hdl

Poor novice chaser/hurdler; did not jump well on his chase debut; off the mark over jumps in November 2003 at Taunton over 2m3f on fast ground.

Beauchamp Gigi (IRE)

90f **97+f**
6-y-o b m Bob Back (USA)-Beauchamp Grace (Ardross)
J Howard Johnson (John E Kiely 19/10) Andrea & Graham Wylie

Placings:14 (3887)
2003/04: 16¹F, 16⁴G,

	Starts	1st	2nd	3rd	Win & Pl
NH Flat	2	1	0	0	4481
Career Total	2	1	0	0	4481
97 10/03 Cork	2m	NHF		FRM	£4480

Total win prize-money £4481

Going:	Sf: 0-0 GS: 0-0 Gd: 0-1 GF: - Fm: 1-1
Distance:	2m/2m3: 1-2 2m4-2m7: 0-0 3m+: 0-0
Track:	LH: 0-0 RH: 0-1 Tight: 0-1 Gall: 0-0
Aids:	Bl: 0-0 Vi: 0-0 Tstrap: 0-0 Ckp: 0-0
Best Rating:	97 2/04 Muss 2m good NHF

Cork bumper winner; has since joined Howard Johnson; finished fourth in a mares only bumper at Musselburgh; will stay further over hurdles; acts on decent ground.

Beauchamp Magic

(88h) (57h)
9-y-o b g Northern Park (USA)-Beauchamp Buzz (High Top)
K G Wingrove A Bourne

Placings:0P/0/600-P (3252)
2003/04: 16⁵PG,

	Starts	1st	2nd	3rd	Win & Pl
Chases	1	0	0	0	0
Career Total	7	0	0	0	0

Going:	Sf: 0-0 GS: 0-0 Gd: 0-1 GF: - Fm: 0-0
Distance:	2m/2m3: 0-1 2m4-2m7: 0-0 3m+: 0-0
Track:	LH: 0-0 RH: 0-0 Tight: 0-1 Gall: 0-0
Aids:	Bl: 0-0 Vi: 0-0 Tstrap: 0-1 Ckp: 0-0
Best Rating:	75 10/00 Font 2m4f good Hdl

Beauchamp Q

96f **91f**
5-y-o b g Inchinor-Beauchamp Buzz (High Top)
A P Jones Mrs K T Pilkington

Placings:4000 (4199)
2003/04: 16⁴G, 16⁰HY, 16⁹G, 16⁹G,

	Starts	1st	2nd	3rd	Win & Pl
NH Flat	4	0	0	0	0
Career Total	4	0	0	0	0

Going:	Sf: 0-1 GS: 0-0 Gd: 0-3 GF: - Fm: 0-0
Distance:	2m/2m3: 0-4 2m4-2m7: 0-0 3m+: 0-0
Track:	LH: 0-3 RH: 0-1 Tight: 0-0 Gall: 0-1
Aids:	Bl: 0-0 Vi: 0-0 Tstrap: 0-0 Ckp: 0-1
Best Rating:	91 12/03 Wwck 2m good NHF

Beauchamp Quest

5-y-o b g Pharly (FR)-Beauchamp Kate (Petoski)
A P Jones Mrs K T Pilkington

Placings:0 (4739)
2003/04: 17⁰G,

	Starts	1st	2nd	3rd	Win & Pl
NH Flat	1	0	0	0	
Career Total	1	0	0	0	

Going:	Sf: 0-0 GS: 0-0 Gd: 0-1 GF: - Fm: 0-0
Distance:	2m/2m3: 0-1 2m4-2m7: 0-0 3m+: 0-0
Track:	LH: 0-1 RH: 0-0 Tight: 0-1 Gall: 0-0
Aids:	Bl: 0-0 Vi: 0-0 Tstrap: 0-0 Ckp: 0-0
Best Rating:	0 4/04 NAbb 2m1f good NHF

Beauly (IRE)

100 **82+**
9-y-o b g Beau Sher-Woodland Theory (Sheer Grit)
J G M O'Shea K A Wells

Placings:00013-5415 (2791)
2003/04: 21⁵GF, 19⁴G, 16¹G, 17⁵GS,

	Starts	1st	2nd	3rd	Win & Pl
Hurdles	4	1	0	0	3126
Career Total	9	2	0	1	3126
82 12/03 Wwck	2m	E(0-105)HHdl		GD	£3125
72 3/03 Extr	2m1f	E(0-100)HHdl		FRM	£4013

Total win prize-money £7140

Going:	Sf: 0-0 GS: 0-1 Gd: 1-2 GF: - Fm: 0-1
Distance:	2m/2m3: 1-3 2m4-2m7: 0-1 3m+: 0-0
Track:	LH: 1-4 RH: 0-0 Tight: 0-1 Gall: 0-0
Aids:	Bl: 0-0 Vi: 0-0 Tstrap: 0-0 Ckp: 0-0
Best Rating:	82 12/03 Bang 2m1f gd-sft Hdl

Moderate hurdler; acts on fast ground.

Beausejour (USA)

103 **89**
6-y-o ch m Diesis-Libeccio (NZ) (Danzatore (CAN))
J Gallagher (B G Powell 31/12) Miss K Mundy

Placings:F500-36401454526 (4890)
2003/04: 16³GS, 16⁶G, 18⁴GF, 16⁰GF, 16¹GF, 16⁴GF, 16⁵G, 18⁴G, 16⁵G, 19²G, 19⁶GF,

	Starts	1st	2nd	3rd	Win & Pl
Hurdles	11	1	1	1	5485
Career Total	15	1	1	1	5485
87 6/03 Worc	2m	F Hdl		G-F	£2716

Total win prize-money £2716

Plating-class hurdler; off the mark in 2m novices' claiming hurdle at Worcester June 2003; acts on fast ground; best at 2m; has worn cheekpieces; inclined to run too freely.

Beaver Lodge (IRE)

100(105h) (120 h)**111**
7-y-o gr g Grand Lodge (USA)-Thistlewood (Kalamoun)
B P J Baugh (C J Mann 23/7) J H Chrimes And Mr & Mrs G W Hannam

Placings:0234/445011/61400-3223P (1359)
2003/04: 19³G, 20²G, 23²G, 23³GF, 20⁸G,

	Starts	1st	2nd	3rd	Win & Pl
Hurdles	1	0	0	1	860
Chases	4	0	2	1	3160
Career Total	20	3	3	3	20505
119 12/02 MRas	2m3f110yD(0-125)HHdl			G-S	£5037
113 4/02 Bang	2m4f	E Hdl		GD	£3962
112 4/02 MRas	2m3f110yD(0-120)HHdl			G-F	£3500

Total win prize-money £12500

Going:	Sf: 0-0 GS: 0-0 Gd: 0-4 GF: - Fm: 0-1
Distance:	2m/2m3: 0-0 2m4-2m7: 0-4 3m+: 0-0
Track:	LH: 0-3 RH: 0-2 Tight: 0-3 Gall: 0-0
Aids:	Bl: 0-0 Vi: 0-0 Tstrap: 0-0 Ckp: 0-0
Best Rating:	120 6/03 MRas 2m3f110y good Hdl

Fair, ex-Irish handicap hurdler; did well in this country in 2002, improving gradually and winning three times; just held on chasing debut at Market Rasen in July 2003; eventually well beaten by Stromness over 3m next time; suited by trips of around 2m 4f; goes on any ground.

Bebe Bleu (IRE)

8-y-o b m Terimon-Fu's Lady (Netherkelly)
M C Pipe Mrs Angie Malde

Placings:20F/PU (0485)
2003/04: 20⁸S, 22⁰GF,

	Starts	1st	2nd	3rd	Win & Pl
Hurdles	2	0	0	0	
Career Total	5	0	1	0	446

Going:	Sf: 0-1 GS: 0-0 Gd: 0-0 GF: - Fm: 0-0
Distance:	2m/2m3: 0-0 2m4-2m7: 0-2 3m+: 0-0
Track:	LH: 0-2 RH: 0-0 Tight: 0-2 Gall: 0-0
Aids:	Bl: 0-0 Vi: 0-0 Tstrap: 0-0 Ckp: 0-0
Best Rating:	100 11/01 Wwck 2m good NHF

Bed Bug (FR)

102 **104**
6-y-o b g Double Bed (FR)-Cotation (FR) (Recitation (USA))
N J Henderson The Barrow Boys Iv

Placings:045031-243P6 (4210)
2003/04: 20²GF, 16⁴G, 21³G, 19⁶G, 16⁶G,

	Starts	1st	2nd	3rd	Win & Pl
Hurdles	5	0	1	1	2524
Career Total	11	1	1	2	8538
100 4/03 Fknm	2m	D(0-110)HHdl		GD	£5445

Total win prize-money £5446

Going:	Sf: 0-0 GS: 0-0 Gd: 0-4 GF: - Fm: 0-1	
Distance:	2m/2m3: 0-2 2m4-2m7: 0-3 3m+: 0-0	
Track:	LH: 0-2 RH: 0-3 Tight: 0-1 Gall: 0-0	
Aids:	Bl: 0-0 Vi: 0-0 Tstrap: 0-0 Ckp: 0-0	
Best Rating:	104 12/03 Kemp 2m5f good Hdl	

Modest hurdler; stays 2m 5f; best on good ground.

Bedford Leader
101   74
6-y-o b m Bedford (USA)-Neladar (Ardar)
A P Jones B W Bedford

Placings:*00-052630*   (3904)
2003/04: 22⁰GF, 26⁵GF, 16²S, 21⁶S, 24³S, 24⁰GS,

	Starts	1st	2nd	3rd	Win & Pl
Hurdles	6	0	1	1	1053
Career Total	8	0	1	1	1053

Going:	Sf: 0-3 GS: 0-1 Gd: 0-0 GF: - Fm: 0-2	
Distance:	2m/2m3: 0-1 2m4-2m7: 0-2 3m+: 0-3	
Track:	LH: 0-2 RH: 0-4 Tight: 0-2 Gall: 0-0	
Aids:	Bl: 0-0 Vi: 0-0 Tstrap: 0-0 Ckp: 0-0	
Best Rating:	74 1/04 Chep 3m soft Hdl	

Moderate novice hurdler; struggling to find optimum trip; just fails to get home over three miles; acts on soft ground.

Bee An Bee (IRE)
111(105h)   (115h)131+
7-y-o b g Phardante (FR)-Portia's Delight (IRE) (The Parson)
T R George Stan Moore

Placings:*2200/6421024F-12F141U*   (4871)
2003/04: 24¹GS, 24²G, 25⁵G, 25¹S, 25⁴S, 24¹G, 24ᵁS,

	Starts	1st	2nd	3rd	Win & Pl
Chases	7	3	1	0	31767
Career Total	19	4	5	0	39674
131	3/04	Newb	3m	C(0-135)HCh	GD £16425
125	1/04	Folk	3m1f	E(0-110)HCh	SFT £8092
114	11/03	Uttx	3m	E Ch	G-S £3367
106	12/02	Extr	2m1f	E(0-100)HHdl	G-S £3486
			Total win prize-money £31372		

Going:	Sf: 1-3 GS: 1-1 Gd: 1-3 GF: - Fm: 0-0	
Distance:	2m/2m3: 0-0 2m4-2m7: 0-0 3m+: 3-7	
Track:	LH: 2-6 RH: 1-1 Tight: 1-2 Gall: 1-2	
Aids:	Bl: 0-0 Vi: 0-0 Tstrap: 0-0 Ckp: 0-0	
Best Rating:	131 3/04 Newb 3m good Ch	

Fair chaser; progressing with experience; stays three miles; acts on soft ground; has worn a visor.

Beechbrook Gale (IRE)
20
8-y-o b g Toulon-Swan Upping (Lord Gayle (USA))
John R Upson Jim Bath & Martin Tucker

Placings:*5FP3/F6-5P*   (1788)
2003/04: 21⁵G, 24ᴾGF,

	Starts	1st	2nd	3rd	Win & Pl
Hurdles	1	0	0	0	0
Chases	1	0	0	0	0
Career Total	8	0	0	1	943

Going:	Sf: 0-0 GS: 0-0 Gd: 0-1 GF: - Fm: 0-1	
Distance:	2m/2m3: 0-0 2m4-2m7: 0-0 3m+: 0-1	
Track:	LH: 0-1 RH: 0-1 Tight: 0-1 Gall: 0-0	

Aids:	Bl: 0-0 Vi: 0-0 Tstrap: 0-0 Ckp: 0-0	
Best Rating:	83 3/02 Towc 2m110y gd-sft Ch	

Beechwood
94   87+
6-y-o b g Fraam-Standard Rose (Ile De Bourbon (USA))
Miss H C Knight Peter Taplin

Placings:*4434-P500*   (4546)
2003/04: 16ᶠG, 17⁵GS, 17⁰GS, 16⁹GS,

	Starts	1st	2nd	3rd	Win & Pl
Hurdles	4	0	0	0	0
Career Total	8	0	0	1	353

Going:	Sf: 0-0 GS: 0-3 Gd: 0-1 GF: - Fm: 0-0	
Distance:	2m/2m3: 0-4 2m4-2m7: 0-0 3m+: 0-0	
Track:	LH: 0-0 RH: 0-4 Tight: 0-2 Gall: 0-0	
Aids:	Bl: 0-0 Vi: 0-0 Tstrap: 0-0 Ckp: 0-0	
Best Rating:	107 2/03 Winc 2m gd-sft NHF	

Has shown ability in bumpers; has proved too headstrong so far over hurdles.

Beedulup
96(103h)   (80h)80
9-y-o br g Perpendicular-Biloela (Nicholas Bill)
P Wegmann P Wegmann

Placings:*040/P/5P06122254-050025U*   (1589)
2003/04: 22⁰GF, 21⁵G, 22⁰GF, 27⁰G, 20²GF, 20⁵GF, 20ᵁGF,

	Starts	1st	2nd	3rd	Win & Pl
Hurdles	4	0	0	0	0
Chases	3	0	1	0	1173
Career Total	21	1	4	0	6521
69	8/02	Ctml	2m6f	G(0-90)HHdl	GD £2772
			Total win prize-money £2772		

Going:	Sf: 0-0 GS: 0-0 Gd: 0-2 GF: - Fm: 0-5	
Distance:	2m/2m3: 0-0 2m4-2m7: 0-6 3m+: 0-1	
Track:	LH: 0-6 RH: 0-1 Tight: 0-4 Gall: 0-0	
Aids:	Bl: 0-0 Vi: 0-0 Tstrap: 0-0 Ckp: 0-2	
Best Rating:	98 1/00 Newc 2m soft NHF	

Beef Or Salmon (IRE)
115   (118h)169
8-y-o ch g Cajetano (USA)-Farinella (IRE) (Salmon Leap (USA))
Michael Hourigan B J Craig

Placings:*312F11050/1111F-31134*   (4424)
2003/04: 20⁹YS, 20¹Y, 16¹YS, 24³YS, 26⁴G,

	Starts	1st	2nd	3rd	Win & Pl
Chases	5	2	0	2	88864
Career Total	19	9	1	3	275968
158	12/03	Cork	2m	Ch	Y-S £21103
169	12/03	Punc	2m4f	Ch	YLD £37987
164	2/03	Leop	3m	Ch	Y-S £67597
163	12/02	Leop	2m	Ch	HVY £59815
146	12/02	Cork	2m	Ch	SFT £15950
152	11/02	Clon	2m4f	Ch	HVY £23912
118	1/02	Gowr	2m2f	Hdl	HVY £7975
120	1/02	Cork	2m	NHF	SFT £4868
123	11/01	Clon	2m	NHF	SFT £4173
			Total win prize-money £241404		

Going:	Sf: 0-0 GS: 0-0 Gd: 0-1 GF: - Fm: 0-0	
Distance:	2m/2m3: 1-1 2m4-2m7: 1-2 3m+: 0-2	
Track:	LH: 0-2 RH: 1-2 Tight: 0-0 Gall: 0-1	

Aids:	Bl: 0-0 Vi: 0-0 Tstrap: 0-0 Ckp: 0-0	
Best Rating:	169 3/04 Chel 3m2f110y good Ch	

Top-class Irish-trained chaser; progressed quickly in his first season over fences in 2002/03 to become the rising star of Irish chasing; won his first four chases, culminating in the Ericsson Chase and Hennessy Gold Cup at Leopardstown; well fancied for Cheltenham Gold Cup, but fell at the third; had an up and down 2003/04 season but stayed on well when fourth in the Gold Cup; stays 3m 2f, effective at shorter; goes well in soft and heavy ground; usually held up and has a turn of foot.

Beefy Nova
104   84
12-y-o ch g Ra Nova-Cherry Sip (Nearly A Hand)
G H Yardley Philip Jones

Placings:*3322032/50642P/UU4415150/2FP2/3604405-2665523114*   (4403)
2003/04: 21²GF, 21⁶GF, 23⁶G, 22⁵G, 24⁵GS, 22²G, 21³GS, 22¹GS, 24¹G, 24⁴G,

	Starts	1st	2nd	3rd	Win & Pl
Chases	10	2	2	1	9374
Career Total	43	4	8	5	27845
84	3/04	Hntg	3m	F(0-90)HCh	GD £3444
74	2/04	Font	2m6f	F(0-90)HCh	G-S £3416
117	2/00	Ludl	2m4f	D(0-125)HCh	G-F £4095
114	12/99	Hrfd	2m3f	D(0-110)HCh	HVY £4344
			Total win prize-money £15300		

Going:	Sf: 0-0 GS: 1-3 Gd: 1-5 GF: - Fm: 0-2	
Distance:	2m/2m3: 0-0 2m4-2m7: 1-6 3m+: 1-4	
Track:	LH: 0-4 RH: 1-4 Tight: 1-5 Gall: 1-2	
Aids:	Bl: 0-0 Vi: 0-0 Tstrap: 0-0 Ckp: 0-0	
Best Rating:	120 11/00 Aint 2m4f gd-sft Ch	

Plating-class chaser; stays three miles; acts on both extremes of going.

Beehive Lad
92(90h)   (51h)82
10-y-o b g Then Again-Steel Typhoon (General Ironside)
R Ford Dave Teasdale

Placings:*00/034/24F/003*   (0408)
2003/04: 20⁰S, 16⁶G, 17³G,

	Starts	1st	2nd	3rd	Win & Pl
Hurdles	2	0	0	0	0
Chases	1	0	0	1	740
Career Total	11	0	1	2	2062

Going:	Sf: 0-1 GS: 0-0 Gd: 0-2 GF: - Fm: 0-0	
Distance:	2m/2m3: 0-0 2m4-2m7: 0-1 3m+: 0-0	
Track:	LH: 0-2 RH: 0-1 Tight: 0-2 Gall: 0-0	
Aids:	Bl: 0-0 Vi: 0-0 Tstrap: 0-0 Ckp: 0-0	
Best Rating:	98 3/01 MRas 2m1f110y gd-sft Hdl	

Been Here Before
4-y-o ch g Fearless Action (USA)-Mistral Magic (Crofter (USA))
D W Barker S Johnson/J Johnson/G Willis/J Griffiths

Placings:*00*   (4663)
2003/04: 16⁰G, 16⁰S,

	Starts	1st	2nd	3rd	Win & Pl
NH Flat	2	0	0	0	
Career Total	2	0	0	0	

Going: Sf: 0-1 GS: 0-0 Gd: 0-1 GF: - Fm: 0-0
Distance: 2m/2m3: 0-2 2m4-2m7: 0-0 3m+: 0-0
Track: LH: 0-2 RH: 0-0 Tight: 0-0 Gall: 0-1
Aids: Bl: 0-0 Vi: 0-0 Tstrap: 0-0 Ckp: 0-0

Beetle Bug
95   57+
4-y-o br f Robellino (USA)-Special Beat (Bustino)
A M Hales (J G Portman 25/8) The Cornish 'Crac'
Partnership

Placings:65UP5   (4774)
2003/04: 16⁶GS, 19⁵GS, 17ᵁG, 19ᴾGF, 16⁵G,

	Starts	1st	2nd	3rd	Win & Pl
Hurdles	5	0	0	0	0
Career Total	5	0	0	0	0

Going: Sf: 0-0 GS: 0-2 Gd: 0-2 GF: - Fm: 0-1
Distance: 2m/2m3: 0-4 2m4-2m7: 0-1 3m+: 0-0
Track: LH: 0-4 RH: 0-1 Tight: 0-4 Gall: 0-0
Aids: Bl: 0-0 Vi: 0-0 Tstrap: 0-4 Ckp: 0-0
Best Rating: 57 4/04 Fknm 2m   good Hdl

Before Dark (IRE)
110f   102f
6-y-o b g Phardante (FR)-Menebeans (IRE) (Duky)
Mrs M Dalton C B Compton

Placings:230   (4050)
2003/04: 16²GS, 17³GS, 16⁶G,

	Starts	1st	2nd	3rd	Win & Pl
NH Flat	3	0	1	1	744
Career Total	3	0	1	1	744

Going: Sf: 0-0 GS: 0-2 Gd: 0-1 GF: - Fm: 0-0
Distance: 2m/2m3: 0-3 2m4-2m7: 0-0 3m+: 0-0
Track: LH: 0-1 RH: 0-2 Tight: 0-0 Gall: 0-1
Aids: Bl: 0-0 Vi: 0-0 Tstrap: 0-0 Ckp: 0-0
Best Rating: 107 1/04 Extr 2m1f   gd-sft NHF

Half-brother to Dalcassian Buck; runner-up in bumper on
debut to above-average rival and another good performance
on his next start at Exeter.

Before The Mast (IRE)
80+
7-y-o br g Broken Hearted-Kings Reserve (King's Ride)
Noel T Chance A D Weller

Placings:2/3-1P3   (2589)
2003/04: 16¹GF, 17ᴾG, 16³GS,

	Starts	1st	2nd	3rd	Win & Pl
NH Flat	1	1	0	0	1481
Hurdles	2	0	0	1	523
Career Total	5	1	1	2	2939
116	10/03	Hntg	2m110y	H NHF	G-F £1480

Total win prize-money £1481

Going: Sf: 0-0 GS: 0-1 Gd: 0-1 GF: - Fm: 1-1
Distance: 2m/2m3: 1-3 2m4-2m7: 0-0 3m+: 0-0
Track: LH: 0-1 RH: 1-2 Tight: 0-1 Gall: 1-1
Aids: Bl: 0-0 Vi: 0-0 Tstrap: 0-0 Ckp: 0-0
Best Rating: 116 10/03 Hntg 2m110y   gd-fm NHF

Promising efforts in bumpers; pulled up after racing too
keenly on hurdling debut; also pulled too hard when a distant third at Chepstow next time.

Begsy's Bullet
(103h)   (96+h)69
9-y-o b m Primitive Rising (USA)-Seeker's Sister (Ashmore
(FR))
D McCain Mrs D McCain

Placings:020251/0F1502-FP3P1   (3348)
2003/04: 20ᶠHY, 21ᴾHY, 20³S, 20ᶠGS, 21¹S,

	Starts	1st	2nd	3rd	Win & Pl
Hurdles	2	1	0	1	3130
Chases	3	0	0	0	0
Career Total	17	3	3	1	14174
96	1/04	Hntg	2m5f110yF(0-95)HHdl	SFT	£2800
85	1/03	Sedg	2m5f110yE Hdl	HVY	£3465
81	2/01	Sedg	2m5f	D Ch	SFT	£4740

Total win prize-money £11005

Going: Sf: 1-4 GS: 0-1 Gd: 0-0 GF: - Fm: 0-0
Distance: 2m/2m3: 0-0 2m4-2m7: 1-5 3m+: 0-0
Track: LH: 0-4 RH: 1-1 Tight: 0-0 Gall: 1-1
Aids: Bl: 0-0 Vi: 0-0 Tstrap: 0-0 Ckp: 0-0
Best Rating: 96 1/04 Hntg 2m5f110y soft Hdl

Moderate hurdler/chaser; landed a modest mares' only
novices' hurdle at Sedgefield in January; acts on soft
ground.

Behan
79   66
5-y-o ch g Rainbows For Life (CAN)-With Finesse (Be My
Guest (USA))
A Crook (G M Moore 14/5) Keith Nicholson

Placings:00   (2361)
2003/04: 16⁰G, 16⁰GF,

	Starts	1st	2nd	3rd	Win & Pl
Hurdles	2	0	0	0	0
Career Total	2	0	0	0	0

Going: Sf: 0-0 GS: 0-0 Gd: 0-1 GF: - Fm: 0-1
Distance: 2m/2m3: 0-2 2m4-2m7: 0-0 3m+: 0-0
Track: LH: 0-1 RH: 0-1 Tight: 0-0 Gall: 0-0
Aids: Bl: 0-2 Vi: 0-0 Tstrap: 0-0 Ckp: 0-0
Best Rating: 67 11/03 Ayr 2m   good Hdl

Behavingbadly (IRE)
83(94h)   (125h)125
9-y-o b g Lord Americo-Audrey's Turn (Strong Gale)
A Parker H Henderson

Placings:521122/03F43210-UF001   (4941)
2003/04: 25ᵁS, 30ᶠG, 20⁰G, 26⁰G, 31¹GS,

	Starts	1st	2nd	3rd	Win & Pl
Hurdles	1	0	0	0	0
Chases	4	1	0	0	12760
Career Total	19	4	4	2	33445
114	4/04	Prth	3m7f	E(0-110)HCh	G-S £12760
120	3/03	Ayr	3m1f	D(0-125)HCh	SFT £6531
112	1/02	Catt	3m1f110yE Hdl	G-S £2807
95	12/01	Hexm	3m	E Hdl	SFT £2439

Total win prize-money £24538

Going: Sf: 1-4 GS: 1-1 Gd: 0-3 GF: - Fm: 0-0
Distance: 2m/2m3: 0-2 2m4-2m7: 0-1 3m+: 1-4
Track: LH: 0-2 RH: 0-2 Tight: 0-1 Gall: 0-0
Aids: Bl: 0-0 Vi: 0-0 Tstrap: 0-0 Ckp: 0-0
Best Rating: 125 4/02 Prth 3m110y   good Hdl

Fair hurdler/maiden chaser; stays three miles plus; suited by
soft ground.

Behrajan (IRE)
113
9-y-o b/br g Arazi (USA)-Behera (Mill Reef (USA))
H D Daly The Behrajan Partnership

Placings:11215/52113/112213/33212P/61150-2F (3291)
2003/04: 24²S, 29ᶠGS,

	Starts	1st	2nd	3rd	Win & Pl
Chases	2	0	1	0	11000
Career Total	29	11	7	4	261774
168	1/03	Chel	3m1f110yA Ch	G-S £49600
166	12/02	Asct	3m110y A HCh	SFT £31000
148	12/01	Weth	3m1f	A HCh	G-S £19053
144	3/01	Hntg	3m	E Ch	SFT £3562
122	11/00	Extr	2m7f110yD Ch	G-S £5330
140	10/00	Weth	3m1f	D Ch	G-S £4186
164	1/00	Hayd	2m7f110yA Hdl	SFT £15000
167	12/99	Chel	3m	B Hdl	SFT £8286
138	2/99	Wwck	2m4f110yB Hdl	G-S £7385
138	1/99	Sand	2m110y A Hdl	SFT £15699
125	12/98	Wwck	2m	E Hdl	G-S £2792

Total win prize-money £161896

Going: Sf: 0-1 GS: 0-1 Gd: 0-0 GF: - Fm: 0-0
Distance: 2m/2m3: 0-0 2m4-2m7: 0-0 3m+: 0-2
Track: LH: 0-1 RH: 0-1 Tight: 0-0 Gall: 0-0
Aids: Bl: 0-0 Vi: 0-0 Tstrap: 0-0 Ckp: 0-0
Best Rating: 168 12/03 Asct 3m110y soft Ch

High-class chaser; runner-up in the Hennessy Gold Cups at
both Newbury and Leopardstown in 2001/2; disappointed in
the 2002 Gold Cup and fifth in the 2003 running; suited by
3m plus and easy ground; an out and out galloper; did not
find a great deal when in front. (DEAD)

Behzad (IRE)
104   83
5-y-o b g Kahyasi-Behriya (IRE) (Kenmare (FR))
D McCain Daren Brown

Placings:30-3322P   (0878)
2003/04: 16³GF, 17³G, 20²GF, 20²G, 20ᴾGF,

	Starts	1st	2nd	3rd	Win & Pl
Hurdles	5	0	2	2	4116
Career Total	7	0	2	3	4406

Going: Sf: 0-0 GS: 0-0 Gd: 0-2 GF: - Fm: 0-3
Distance: 2m/2m3: 0-2 2m4-2m7: 0-3 3m+: 0-0
Track: LH: 0-3 RH: 0-2 Tight: 0-1 Gall: 0-0
Aids: Bl: 0-0 Vi: 0-0 Tstrap: 0-0 Ckp: 0-0
Best Rating: 87 3/03 Bang 2m1f   good NHF

Showed a little ability in bumpers and hurdles.

Bekstar
94   77
9-y-o br m Nicholas Bill-Murex (Royalty)
J C Tuck Mrs J Chapman

Placings:400/0064/0031F46/41255000-560 (3103)
2003/04: 17⁵G, 19⁶G, 18⁰G,

	Starts	1st	2nd	3rd	Win & Pl
Hurdles	3	0	0	0	0
Career Total	25	2	1	1	5953
100	6/02	NAbb	2m6f	E(0-105)HHdl	GD	£2639
91	10/01	Extr	2m1f	G(0-95)HHdl	G-F	£1792

Total win prize-money £4431

Going: Sf: 0-0 GS: 0-0 Gd: 0-3 GF: - Fm: 0-0
Distance: 2m/2m3: 0-2 2m4-2m7: 0-1 3m+: 0-0
Track: LH: 0-2 RH: 0-1 Tight: 0-3 Gall: 0-0
Aids: Bl: 0-0 Vi: 0-0 Tstrap: 0-0 Ckp: 0-0

Best Rating: 101 6/02 NAbb 2m6f   good   Hdl

Bel Ombre (FR)

4-y-o b g Nikos-Danse Du Soleil (FR) (Morespeed)
O Sherwood   P Deal, J Tyndall, M St Quinton

Placings:*P*   (4934)
2003/04: 18PG,

	Starts	1st	2nd	3rd	Win & Pl
NH Flat	1	0	0	0	
Career Total	1	0	0	0	

Going:	Sf: 0-0 GS: 0-0 Gd: 0-1 GF: - Fm: 0-0
Distance:	2m/2m3: 0-1 2m4-2m7: 0-0 3m+: 0-0
Track:	LH: 0-1 RH: 0-0 Tight: 0-1 Gall: 0-0
Aids:	Bl: 0-0 Vi: 0-0 Tstrap: 0-0 Ckp: 0-0
Best Rating:	0 4/04 Font 2m2f110y good NHF

Belalcazar

78f   62f

5-y-o b g El Conquistador-Ruby Celebration (New Member)
Miss I E Craig   Mr and Mrs P R Ensor

Placings:*0*   (4739)
2003/04: 17PG,

	Starts	1st	2nd	3rd	Win & Pl
NH Flat	1	0	0	0	
Career Total	1	0	0	0	

Going:	Sf: 0-0 GS: 0-0 Gd: 0-1 GF: - Fm: 0-0
Distance:	2m/2m3: 0-1 2m4-2m7: 0-0 3m+: 0-0
Track:	LH: 0-1 RH: 0-0 Tight: 0-1 Gall: 0-0
Aids:	Bl: 0-0 Vi: 0-0 Tstrap: 0-0 Ckp: 0-0
Best Rating:	62 4/04 NAbb 2m1f good NHF

Belcaro (GER)

94   103+

5-y-o b g Dashing Blade-Bella Carolina (GER) (Surumu (GER))
C J Mann   Lee Bolingbroke & Partners IV

Placings:613   (4793)
2003/04: 16RG, 17TG, 16RG,

	Starts	1st	2nd	3rd	Win & Pl
Hurdles	3	1	0	1	4232
Career Total	3	1	0	1	4232
103	4/04	Tntn	2m1f	E Hdl	GD £3718

Total win prize-money £3718

Going:	Sf: 0-0 GS: 0-0 Gd: 1-3 GF: - Fm: 0-0
Distance:	2m/2m3: 1-3 2m4-2m7: 0-0 3m+: 0-0
Track:	LH: 0-1 RH: 1-2 Tight: 1-2 Gall: 0-0
Aids:	Bl: 0-0 Vi: 0-0 Tstrap: 0-0 Ckp: 0-0
Best Rating:	103 4/04 Tntn 2m1f good Hdl

Fair hurdler; ex-German; won moderate race at Taunton in April 2004; suited by two miles and good ground.

Belfast Boy (IRE)

72

6-y-o b g Forest Wind (USA)-Abadila (IRE) (Shernazar)
Patrick J Flynn (J Clements 14/5) J Clements

Placings:000-P4   (1196a)
2003/04: 20PG, 20⁴F,

	Starts	1st	2nd	3rd	Win & Pl
Hurdles	2	0	0	0	312
Career Total	5	0	0	0	312

Going:	Sf: 0-0 GS: 0-0 Gd: 0-1 GF: - Fm: 0-1
Distance:	2m/2m3: 0-0 2m4-2m7: 0-2 3m+: 0-0
Track:	LH: 0-0 RH: 0-1 Tight: 0-0 Gall: 0-0
Aids:	Bl: 0-0 Vi: 0-0 Tstrap: 0-0 Ckp: 0-0
Best Rating:	72 8/03 Cork 2m4f firm Hdl

Belisario (IRE)

105   127+

10-y-o b/br g Distinctly North (USA)-Bold Kate (Bold Lad (IRE))
M W Easterby   Paul G Jacobs

Placings:413/562/1F/3131/20-1   (4320)
2003/04: 24TS,

	Starts	1st	2nd	3rd	Win & Pl
Chases	1	1	0	0	6773
Career Total	15	5	2	3	21108
127	3/04	Newc	3m	D(0-120)HCh	SFT £6773
115	3/02	Donc	3m	E Ch	SFT £3302
119	1/02	Weth	2m7f110yE Ch		G-S £3363
112	10/00	Weth	2m7f	F(0-100)HHdl	G-S £1970
106	3/98	MRas	1m5f110yH NHF		G-S £1287

Total win prize-money £16697

Going:	Sf: 1-1 GS: 0-0 Gd: 0-0 GF: - Fm: 0-0
Distance:	2m/2m3: 0-0 2m4-2m7: 0-0 3m+: 1-1
Track:	LH: 1-1 RH: 0-0 Tight: 0-0 Gall: 1-1
Aids:	Bl: 0-0 Vi: 0-0 Tstrap: 0-0 Ckp: 0-0
Best Rating:	127 3/04 Newc 3m soft Ch

Fair chaser; lightly raced, has taken well to fences but does not stand much racing; won easily on first outing for a year at Newcastle in March 2004; stays three miles; acts on good to soft.

Bell Lane Lad (IRE)

109   109+

7-y-o b g Wakashan-Busti Lass (IRE) (Bustineto)
A King   Jack McGrath

Placings:*0*/000P1-142   (2833)
2003/04: 22TGS, 22⁴GS, 20²G,

	Starts	1st	2nd	3rd	Win & Pl
Hurdles	3	1	1	0	5681
Career Total	9	2	1	0	11199
107	11/03	Uttx	2m6f110yE(0-110)HHdl		G-S £3490
86	4/03	Bang	2m4f	F(0-100)HHdl	G-F £5518

Total win prize-money £9010

Going:	Sf: 0-0 GS: 1-2 Gd: 0-1 GF: - Fm: 0-0
Distance:	2m/2m3: 0-0 2m4-2m7: 1-3 3m+: 0-0
Track:	LH: 1-1 RH: 0-2 Tight: 0-1 Gall: 0-0
Aids:	Bl: 0-0 Vi: 0-0 Tstrap: 0-0 Ckp: 0-0
Best Rating:	109 12/03 Asct 2m4f good Hdl

Modest hurdler; acts on fast and easy ground; stays two miles six.

Bell Tex (IRE)

95   63

12-y-o br g Orchestra-Lyngard (Balliol)
J C Fox   Shirley M & Peter G Palmer

Placings:P/P040/2/0-005   (0676)
2003/04: 16PGF, 17PG, 16RGF,

	Starts	1st	2nd	3rd	Win & Pl
Hurdles	3	0	0	0	0

Career Total	10	0	1	0	582

Going:	Sf: 0-0 GS: 0-0 Gd: 0-1 GF: - Fm: 0-2
Distance:	2m/2m3: 0-3 2m4-2m7: 0-0 3m+: 0-0
Track:	LH: 0-3 RH: 0-0 Tight: 0-1 Gall: 0-0
Aids:	Bl: 0-0 Vi: 0-0 Tstrap: 0-0 Ckp: 0-0
Best Rating:	85 5/01 Folk 2m4f110y gd-fm Hdl

Bell Tor (IRE)

90   85

7-y-o b m King's Ride-Shannon Juliette (Julio Mariner)
D R Gandolfo   Starlight Racing

Placings:6/PP26-520   (2656)
2003/04: 21⁵G, 21²G, 22⁰G,

	Starts	1st	2nd	3rd	Win & Pl
Hurdles	3	0	1	0	969
Career Total	8	0	2	0	2011

Going:	Sf: 0-0 GS: 0-0 Gd: 0-3 GF: - Fm: 0-0
Distance:	2m/2m3: 0-0 2m4-2m7: 0-3 3m+: 0-0
Track:	LH: 0-3 RH: 0-0 Tight: 0-2 Gall: 0-0
Aids:	Bl: 0-0 Vi: 0-0 Tstrap: 0-0 Ckp: 0-0
Best Rating:	88 11/03 Wwck 2m5f good Hdl

Moderate novice hurdler; stays two and a half miles; acts on good ground.

Bella Bambina

100   85

4-y-o b f Turtle Island (IRE)-Lady Eurolink (Kala Shikari)
M C Pipe (J L Dunlop 3/9) Eurolink Group Plc

Placings:362   (3196)
2003/04: 16³GF, 16RG, 16²S,

	Starts	1st	2nd	3rd	Win & Pl
Hurdles	3	0	1	1	1537
Career Total	3	0	1	1	1537

Going:	Sf: 0-1 GS: 0-0 Gd: 0-1 GF: - Fm: 0-1
Distance:	2m/2m3: 0-3 2m4-2m7: 0-0 3m+: 0-0
Track:	LH: 0-1 RH: 0-2 Tight: 0-1 Gall: 0-0
Aids:	Bl: 0-0 Vi: 0-2 Tstrap: 0-0 Ckp: 0-0
Best Rating:	85 1/04 Plum 2m soft Hdl

Visored for hurdling debut when badly interefered with prior to finishing third.

Bella Castana

4-y-o ch f Efisio-Simple Logic (Aragon)
A Charlton   Miss Juliet E Reed

Placings:U   (2483)
2003/04: 16UGS,

	Starts	1st	2nd	3rd	Win & Pl
Hurdles	1	0	0	0	
Career Total	1	0	0	0	

Going:	Sf: 0-0 GS: 0-1 Gd: 0-0 GF: - Fm: 0-0
Distance:	2m/2m3: 0-1 2m4-2m7: 0-0 3m+: 0-0
Track:	LH: 0-1 RH: 0-0 Tight: 0-0 Gall: 0-1
Aids:	Bl: 0-0 Vi: 0-0 Tstrap: 0-0 Ckp: 0-0
Best Rating:	0 11/03 Newb 2m110y gd-sft Hdl

Bella Liana (IRE)
32f
4-y-o b f Sesaro (USA)-Bella Galiana (ITY) (Don Roberto (USA))
J Parkes Derrick Mossop

Placings:0   (2482)
2003/04: 13⁰GF,

	Starts	1st	2nd	3rd	Win & Pl
NH Flat	1	0	0	0	
Career Total	1	0	0	0	

Going:	Sf: 0-0 GS: 0-0 Gd: 0-0 GF: - Fm: 0-1
Distance:	2m/2m3: 0-0 2m4-2m7: 0-0 3m+: 0-0
Track:	LH: 0-0 RH: 0-0 Tight: 0-0 Gall: 0-0
Aids:	Bl: 0-0 Vi: 0-0 Tstrap: 0-0 Ckp: 0-0
Best Rating:	35 11/03 Donc 1m5f gd-fm NHF

Bella Mary
92(91c)   (72c)78
9-y-o b m Derrylin-Pro-Token (Proverb)
C T Pogson C T Pogson

Placings:0P0/4P320P0P-533PPP5000   (4592)
2003/04: 20⁵HY, 21³GF, 22³GF, 24PGF, 20PGS, 25PGS, 16⁵S, 22⁰G, 21⁰G, 26⁸G,

	Starts	1st	2nd	3rd	Win & Pl
Hurdles	4	0	0	0	0
Chases	6	0	0	2	1082
Career Total	21	0	1	3	2847

Going:	Sf: 0-2 GS: 0-2 Gd: 0-3 GF: - Fm: 0-3
Distance:	2m/2m3: 0-1 2m4-2m7: 0-6 3m+: 0-3
Track:	LH: 0-3 RH: 0-6 Tight: 0-0 Gall: 0-4
Aids:	Bl: 0-0 Vi: 0-0 Tstrap: 0-0 Ckp: 0-0
Best Rating:	82 12/02 Sthl 2m gd-sft Hdl

Bella Pavlina

6-y-o ch m Sure Blade (USA)-Pab's Choice (Telsmoss)
W M Brisbourne (M Todhunter 7/5) The Cartmel Syndicate

Placings:FP   (0168)
2003/04: 16FG, 16PGF,

	Starts	1st	2nd	3rd	Win & Pl
Hurdles	2	0	0	0	
Career Total	2	0	0	0	

Going:	Sf: 0-0 GS: 0-0 Gd: 0-1 GF: - Fm: 0-1
Distance:	2m/2m3: 0-0 2m4-2m7: 0-0 3m+: 0-0
Track:	LH: 0-2 RH: 0-0 Tight: 0-1 Gall: 0-0
Aids:	Bl: 0-0 Vi: 0-0 Tstrap: 0-0 Ckp: 0-0

Bellacaccia (IRE)
98   90+
8-y-o ch m Beau Sher-Game Gambler (IRE) (Long Pond)
C W Thornton D B Dennison

Placings:4/324/64BF031-   (0013)
2003/04: 24¹GF,

	Starts	1st	2nd	3rd	Win & Pl
Hurdles	1	1	0	0	2723
Career Total	11	1	1	2	4116
90   4/03   Newc   3m   F(0-90)Hdl   G-F   £2723

Total win prize-money £2723

Bellaport Girl
85f   55f
6-y-o b m Supreme Leader-Derry Nell (Derrylin)
Dr J R J Naylor Gallery Racing

Placings:000   (1156)
2003/04: 17⁰GF, 16⁰GF, 18⁰GF,

	Starts	1st	2nd	3rd	Win & Pl
NH Flat	3	0	0	0	
Career Total	3	0	0	0	

Going:	Sf: 0-0 GS: 0-0 Gd: 0-0 GF: - Fm: 0-3
Distance:	2m/2m3: 0-3 2m4-2m7: 0-0 3m+: 0-0
Track:	LH: 0-2 RH: 0-1 Tight: 0-1 Gall: 0-0
Aids:	Bl: 0-0 Vi: 0-0 Tstrap: 0-0 Ckp: 0-0
Best Rating:	55 7/03 Worc 2m gd-fm NHF

Bellefleur
90   76+
7-y-o b m Alflora (IRE)-Isabeau (Law Society (USA))
J M Jefferson Pryke Hygiene Group,P Wilkinson,B Wade

Placings:055/045P3-6F0PP   (3317)
2003/04: 17⁶G, 21FGF, 23⁹GS, 24PGS, 16PS,

	Starts	1st	2nd	3rd	Win & Pl
Hurdles	4	0	0	0	0
Chases	1	0	0	0	0
Career Total	13	0	0	1	822

Going:	Sf: 0-1 GS: 0-2 Gd: 0-1 GF: - Fm: 0-1
Distance:	2m/2m3: 0-2 2m4-2m7: 0-2 3m+: 0-1
Track:	LH: 0-4 RH: 0-1 Tight: 0-2 Gall: 0-0
Aids:	Bl: 0-0 Vi: 0-1 Tstrap: 0-0 Ckp: 0-0
Best Rating:	81 2/02 Donc 2m110y soft NHF

Bellino Empresario (IRE)
88   67
6-y-o b g Robellino (USA)-The Last Empress (IRE) (Last Tycoon)
B Llewellyn Mrs M Llewellyn

Placings:P-000P   (2250)
2003/04: 16⁹GS, 17⁰GF, 16⁰GF, 19PGF,

	Starts	1st	2nd	3rd	Win & Pl
Hurdles	4	0	0	0	
Career Total	5	0	0	0	

Going:	Sf: 0-0 GS: 0-0 Gd: 0-0 GF: - Fm: 0-3
Distance:	2m/2m3: 0-3 2m4-2m7: 0-1 3m+: 0-0
Track:	LH: 0-2 RH: 0-2 Tight: 0-0 Gall: 0-0
Aids:	Bl: 0-0 Vi: 0-0 Tstrap: 0-0 Ckp: 0-0
Best Rating:	67 5/03 Hrfd 2m1f gd-fm Hdl

Selling hurdler, keen sort and not getting home at present.

Belski
105   110+
11-y-o b g Arctic Lord-Belkino (Relkino)
C L Tizzard The Butterwick Syndicate

Placings:2P222-3131P1P   (4820)
2003/04: 22³G, 23¹G, 23³G, 25¹S, 24PGS, 23¹GS, 25PGF,

	Starts	1st	2nd	3rd	Win & Pl
Chases	7	3	0	2	17102
Career Total	12	3	4	2	21740
110	3/04	Extr	2m7f110yD(0-110)HCh	G-S	£5804
110	2/04	Extr	3m1f110yE(0-105)HCh	SFT	£5135
110	12/03	Extr	2m7f110yD Ch	GD	£4847

Total win prize-money £15788

Going:	Sf: 1-1 GS: 1-2 Gd: 1-3 GF: - Fm: 0-1
Distance:	2m/2m3: 0-0 2m4-2m7: 0-1 3m+: 3-6
Track:	LH: 0-0 RH: 3-6 Tight: 0-2 Gall: 0-0
Aids:	Bl: 0-0 Vi: 0-0 Tstrap: 0-0 Ckp: 0-0
Best Rating:	110 3/04 Extr 2m7f110y gd-sft Ch

Fair chaser; winning pointer; stays three miles; acts on soft ground.

Beluga (IRE)
71f   46f
5-y-o gr g John French-Mesena (Pals Passage)
M Pitman Malcolm C Denmark

Placings:0   (3927)
2003/04: 16⁰GS,

	Starts	1st	2nd	3rd	Win & Pl
NH Flat	1	0	0	0	
Career Total	1	0	0	0	

Going:	Sf: 0-0 GS: 0-0 Gd: 0-0 GF: - Fm: 0-0
Distance:	2m/2m3: 0-1 2m4-2m7: 0-0 3m+: 0-0
Track:	LH: 0-0 RH: 0-1 Tight: 0-0 Gall: 0-0
Aids:	Bl: 0-0 Vi: 0-0 Tstrap: 0-0 Ckp: 0-0
Best Rating:	46 2/04 Sand 2m110y gd-sft NHF

Placed in a Polytrack bumper on his debut and disappointed on next outing in Sandown bumper when running very keen.

Belvento (IRE)
100   97
12-y-o b g Strong Gale-Salufair (Salluceva)
N J Gifford Mrs Jean Plackett

Placings:00/5050/PF4/P/1P2P4-524   (0704)
2003/04: 26⁵G, 25²GF, 22⁴GF,

	Starts	1st	2nd	3rd	Win & Pl
Chases	3	0	1	0	874
Career Total	18	1	2	0	3291
101	5/02	Folk	3m2f	H Ch	GD	£1436

Total win prize-money £1437

Going:	Sf: 0-0 GS: 0-0 Gd: 0-1 GF: - Fm: 0-2
Distance:	2m/2m3: 0-0 2m4-2m7: 0-1 3m+: 0-2
Track:	LH: 0-0 RH: 0-2 Tight: 0-3 Gall: 0-0
Aids:	Bl: 0-0 Vi: 0-0 Tstrap: 0-0 Ckp: 0-0
Best Rating:	101 5/02 Folk 3m2f good Ch

Modest chaser; prolific winner between the flags; stays three miles two; suited by a sound surface.

Ben Britten
82   82
5-y-o ch g Sabrehill (USA)-Golden Panda (Music Boy)
N G Richards Brian Robb

Fair hurdler; stays three miles; has won on fast ground, but is probably better with cut.

Placings:0					(4732)
2003/04: 17ᴰG,					

	Starts	1st	2nd	3rd	Win & Pl
Hurdles	1	0	0	0	
Career Total	1	0	0	0	

Going:	Sf: 0-0 GS: 0-0 Gd: 0-1 GF: - Fm: 0-0
Distance:	2m/2m3: 0-1 2m4-2m7: 0-0 3m+: 0-0
Track:	LH: 0-0 RH: 0-1 Tight: 0-0 Gall: 0-0
Aids:	Bl: 0-0 Vi: 0-0 Tstrap: 0-0 Ckp: 0-0
Best Rating:	80 4/04 Carl 2m1f good Hdl

Ben Ewar
102   112

10-y-o b g Old Vic-Sunset Reef (Mill Reef (USA))
K O Cunningham-Brown   A J Richards

Placings:16501/035/4P5P0423-4U6P20					(4704)
2003/04: 16⁴G, 20ᵁG, 16⁶G, 16ᴾHY, 16²GS, 18⁹G,					

	Starts	1st	2nd	3rd	Win & Pl
Hurdles	6	0	1	0	3151
Career Total	22	2	2	2	48047
4/01	Engh	2m1f110y Hdl		HVY	£19399
128 12/00	Asct	2m110y A Hdl		HVY	£9600
			Total win prize-money £28999		

Going:	Sf: 0-1 GS: 0-1 Gd: 0-4 GF: - Fm: 0-0
Distance:	2m/2m3: 0-5 2m4-2m7: 0-1 3m+: 0-0
Track:	LH: 0-4 RH: 0-2 Tight: 0-2 Gall: 0-0
Aids:	Bl: 0-0 Vi: 0-0 Tstrap: 0-0 Ckp: 0-0
Best Rating:	139 3/02 Chel 2m1f good Hdl

Modest hurdler; formerly high-class performer on the Flat and over hurdles; stays two and a half miles and handles most types of ground; not the most trustworthy and is one to steer clear of; handles most ground; has worn a tongue-tie.

Ben From Ketton

9-y-o b g Cruise Missile-Saucy Girl (Saucy Kit)
S J Robinson   S J Robinson

Placings:P/0					(0101)
2003/04: 25ᴾG,					

	Starts	1st	2nd	3rd	Win & Pl
Chases	1	0	0	0	
Career Total	2	0	0	0	

Going:	Sf: 0-0 GS: 0-0 Gd: 0-1 GF: - Fm: 0-0
Distance:	2m/2m3: 0-0 2m4-2m7: 0-0 3m+: 0-1
Track:	LH: 0-1 RH: 0-0 Tight: 0-0 Gall: 0-0
Aids:	Bl: 0-0 Vi: 0-0 Tstrap: 0-0 Ckp: 0-0
Best Rating:	0 5/03 Hexm 3m1f good Ch

Ben More
98   81

6-y-o b g Seymour Hicks (FR)-Stac-Pollaidh (Tina's Pet)
Miss K Marks (J S King 25/2) Nick Shutts

Placings:35042-P330523P					(4700)
2003/04: 22ᴾGF, 20³GF, 19³G, 16⁵G, 21²G, 22³GF, 20ᴾG,					

	Starts	1st	2nd	3rd	Win & Pl
Hurdles	8	0	1	3	1828
Career Total	13	0	2	4	3503

Going:	Sf: 0-0 GS: 0-0 Gd: 0-5 GF: - Fm: 0-3
Distance:	2m/2m3: 0-3 2m4-2m7: 0-5 3m+: 0-0
Track:	LH: 0-3 RH: 0-3 Tight: 0-3 Gall: 0-0

Aids:	Bl: 0-0 Vi: 0-0 Tstrap: 0-0 Ckp: 0-0
Best Rating:	90 12/02 Hrfd 2m1f good NHF

Plating-class novice hurdler; stays two miles-six; best on a sound surface.

Benbecula (IRE)
103(109h)   (116+h)104+

7-y-o b g Glacial Storm (USA)-Lough View (Radical)
P R Webber   J Dougall

Placings:20/53223-P32F					(4274)
2003/04: 22ᴾS, 21³GS, 24²G, 20ᶠG,					

	Starts	1st	2nd	3rd	Win & Pl
Chases	4	0	1	1	2325
Career Total	11	0	4	3	13176

Going:	Sf: 0-1 GS: 0-1 Gd: 0-2 GF: - Fm: 0-0
Distance:	2m/2m3: 0-0 2m4-2m7: 0-3 3m+: 0-1
Track:	LH: 0-0 RH: 0-4 Tight: 0-1 Gall: 0-0
Aids:	Bl: 0-0 Vi: 0-4 Tstrap: 0-0 Ckp: 0-0
Best Rating:	116 3/03 Sand 2m4f110y heavy Hdl

Maiden over hurdles and fences; placed in bumpers and novices' hurdles; stays two miles five; acts on decent ground.

Benbow
80

7-y-o ch g Gunner B-Juno Away (Strong Gale)
F Jordan   D Pugh

Placings:0534-P					(0054)
2003/04: 26ᴾGS,					

	Starts	1st	2nd	3rd	Win & Pl
Hurdles	1	0	0	0	
Career Total	5	0	0	1	918

Going:	Sf: 0-0 GS: 0-1 Gd: 0-0 GF: - Fm: 0-0
Distance:	2m/2m3: 0-0 2m4-2m7: 0-0 3m+: 0-1
Track:	LH: 0-0 RH: 0-1 Tight: 0-0 Gall: 0-0
Aids:	Bl: 0-0 Vi: 0-0 Tstrap: 0-0 Ckp: 0-0
Best Rating:	80 4/03 Ludl 3m good Hdl

Benbyas
114   151

7-y-o b g Rambo Dancer (CAN)-Light The Way (Nicholas Bill)
D Carroll   C H Stephenson & Partners

Placings:223/21113340/4013250-501062					(4862)
2003/04: 16⁵G, 16⁶S, 16¹HY, 16⁰G, 17⁶G, 16²GS,					

	Starts	1st	2nd	3rd	Win & Pl
Hurdles	6	1	1	0	18820
Career Total	24	5	5	4	95582
146	1/04	Uttx	2m	B(0-140)HHdl	HVY	£9044
146	12/02	Donc	2m110y	B(0-140)HHdl	SFT	£8151
133	12/01	Chel	2m1f	C(0-135)HHdl	GD	£17875
113	11/01	Weth	2m	D Hdl	GD	£3948
117	11/01	Weth	2m	C Hdl	GD	£5635
			Total win prize-money £44655		

Going:	Sf: 1-2 GS: 0-1 Gd: 0-3 GF: - Fm: 0-0
Distance:	2m/2m3: 1-6 2m4-2m7: 0-0 3m+: 0-0
Track:	LH: 1-5 RH: 0-1 Tight: 0-0 Gall: 0-2
Aids:	Bl: 0-0 Vi: 0-0 Tstrap: 0-0 Ckp: 0-0
Best Rating:	146 4/04 Ayr 2m gd-sft Hdl

Smart hurdler; back to form with a bang when facile winner at Uttoxeter in January 2004; suited by the minimum trip and

best on soft ground; likes to make the running; in good form on the Flat in the spring of 2004.

Benefit
98(104h)   (87h)86

10-y-o b g Primitive Rising (USA)-Sobriquet (Roan Rocket)
Miss L C Siddall   Mrs D Ibbotson

Placings:34/213040206/13534P5/P043P2F100-0P0453					(4514)
2003/04: 21⁰G, 21ᴾGS, 21⁰GS, 23⁴G, 24⁵G, 25³GS,					

	Starts	1st	2nd	3rd	Win & Pl
Hurdles	3	0	0	0	494
Chases	3	0	0	1	628
Career Total	34	3	3	6	17508
86	3/03	MRas	2m6f	D(0-115)HHdl	GD	£4797
89	5/01	Wwck	2m5f	F(0-90)HHdl	GD	£2597
103	6/00	Uttx	2m4f110yD Hdl		GD	£2947
			Total win prize-money £10342		

Going:	Sf: 0-0 GS: 0-3 Gd: 0-3 GF: - Fm: 0-0
Distance:	2m/2m3: 0-0 2m4-2m7: 0-3 3m+: 0-3
Track:	LH: 0-5 RH: 0-1 Tight: 0-5 Gall: 0-0
Aids:	Bl: 0-0 Vi: 0-0 Tstrap: 0-0 Ckp: 0-0
Best Rating:	103 6/00 Uttx 2m4f110y good Hdl

Inconsistent very moderate hurdler/chaser; stays three miles.

Bengal Boy
100(100h)   (86h)93

8-y-o b g Gildoran-Bengal Lady (Celtic Cone)
P Beaumont   Brandsby Racing

Placings:0004P/PP46P2U5315/03U246645664-UP403P					(1074)
2003/04: 20ᵁGS, 20ᴾGF, 16⁴G, 22⁰GF, 21³GF, 21ᴾGF,					

	Starts	1st	2nd	3rd	Win & Pl
Hurdles	1	0	0	0	0
Chases	5	0	0	1	1185
Career Total	34	1	2	3	9721
97	3/02	Bang	2m1f110yD Ch		SFT	£4340
			Total win prize-money £4340		

Going:	Sf: 0-0 GS: 0-1 Gd: 0-1 GF: - Fm: 0-4
Distance:	2m/2m3: 0-1 2m4-2m7: 0-5 3m+: 0-0
Track:	LH: 0-3 RH: 0-3 Tight: 0-3 Gall: 0-0
Aids:	Bl: 0-2 Vi: 0-0 Tstrap: 0-0 Ckp: 0-0
Best Rating:	98 6/02 Ctml 2m1f110y good Hdl

Moderate hurdler/chaser; prone to jumping errors and made mistakes before winning a terrible Bangor novice chase by a wide margin in March 2002; handles soft and fast ground and should stay two and a half miles.

Benjamin (IRE)
94   63

6-y-o b g Night Shift (USA)-Best Academy (USA) (Roberto (USA))
Jane Southcombe   Mark Savill

Placings:00PP0-00					(1543)
2003/04: 17⁰F, 16⁰GF,					

	Starts	1st	2nd	3rd	Win & Pl
Hurdles	2	0	0	0	
Career Total	7	0	0	0	

Going:	Sf: 0-0 GS: 0-0 Gd: 0-1 GF: - Fm: 0-2
Distance:	2m/2m3: 0-2 2m4-2m7: 0-0 3m+: 0-0
Track:	LH: 0-1 RH: 0-1 Tight: 0-1 Gall: 0-0
Aids:	Bl: 0-0 Vi: 0-0 Tstrap: 0-2 Ckp: 0-0
Best Rating:	63 9/03 Extr 2m1f firm Hdl

Benjamin Buckram (IRE)

60f   **97f**

5-y-o b g Topanoora-Red Bit (IRE) (Henbit (USA))
C R Egerton M Haynes

Placings:*0*   (3934)
2003/04: 16⁰G,

	Starts	1st	2nd	3rd	Win & Pl
NH Flat	1	0	0	0	
Career Total	1	0	0	0	

Going: Sf: 0-0 GS: 0-0 Gd: 0-1 GF: - Fm: 0-0
Distance: 2m/2m3: 0-1 2m4-2m7: 0-0 3m+: 0-0
Track: LH: 0-0 RH: 0-1 Tight: 0-0 Gall: 0-0
Aids: Bl: 0-0 Vi: 0-0 Tstrap: 0-0 Ckp: 0-0
Best Rating: 97 2/04 Asct 2m110y good NHF

Benji

99   **87**

13-y-o b g High Kicker (USA)-Snap Tin (Jimmy Reppin)
R Ingram A A W Jackson

Placings:00PUF05P/633U40/P642/135/P3P31P   (1418)
2003/04: 16PGF, 20³G, 17PG, 18³GF, 19¹GF, 20PGF,

	Starts	1st	2nd	3rd	Win & Pl
Chases	6	1	0	2	4445
Career Total	27	2	1	5	9262
87	9/03	Hrfd	2m3f	E(0-110)HCh	G-F	£3297
103	5/00	Folk	2m	F(0-90)Ch	GD	£2380

Total win prize-money £5677

Going: Sf: 0-0 GS: 0-0 Gd: 0-2 GF: - Fm: 1-4
Distance: 2m/2m3: 1-4 2m4-2m7: 0-2 3m+: 0-0
Track: LH: 0-2 **RH: 1-2** Tight: 0-4 Gall: 0-1
Aids: Bl: 0-0 Vi: 0-0 Tstrap: 0-0 Ckp: 0-0
Best Rating: 103 6/00 Folk 2m good Ch

Bennanabaa

5-y-o b g Anabaa (USA)-Arc Empress Jane (IRE) (Rainbow Quest (USA))
S C Burrough Mr & Mrs Charles Hill

Placings:*6*   (1734)
2003/04: 16⁶GF,

	Starts	1st	2nd	3rd	Win & Pl
NH Flat	1	0	0	0	0
Career Total	1	0	0	0	0

Going: Sf: 0-0 GS: 0-0 Gd: 0-0 GF: - Fm: 0-1
Distance: 2m/2m3: 0-1 2m4-2m7: 0-0 3m+: 0-0
Track: LH: 0-1 RH: 0-0 Tight: 0-0 Gall: 0-0
Aids: Bl: 0-0 Vi: 0-0 Tstrap: 0-0 Ckp: 0-0
Best Rating: 0 10/03 Chep 2m110y gd-fm NHF

Beno (IRE)

5-y-o b g Ridgewood Ben-Future Romance (Distant Relative)
Mrs H O Graham Mrs H O Graham

Placings:*0000P*   (4685)
2003/04: 16⁶G, 16⁰GS, 16⁰G, 17⁰HY, 16PG,

	Starts	1st	2nd	3rd	Win & Pl
NH Flat	4	0	0	0	0

Hurdles	1	0	0	0	0
Career Total	5	0	0	0	

Going: Sf: 0-1 GS: 0-1 Gd: 0-3 GF: - Fm: 0-0
Distance: 2m/2m3: 0-2 2m4-2m7: 0-0 3m+: 0-0
Track: LH: 0-3 RH: 0-2 Tight: 0-2 Gall: 0-0
Aids: Bl: 0-0 Vi: 0-0 Tstrap: 0-0 Ckp: 0-0
Best Rating: 70 11/03 Ayr 2m good NHF

Benova Boy

98   **71**

12-y-o ch g Ra Nova-Alithorne (Kinglet)
S J Gilmore Mrs J M Gurney

Placings:6/F0630/0533F436   (1191)
2003/04: 24⁰GF, 23⁵GF, 23³GF, 24³G, 21FGF, 24⁴G, 26³G, 23⁶GF,

	Starts	1st	2nd	3rd	Win & Pl
Chases	8	0	0	3	2202
Career Total	14	0	0	4	2534

Going: Sf: 0-0 GS: 0-0 Gd: 0-3 GF: - Fm: 0-5
Distance: 2m/2m3: 0-0 2m4-2m7: 0-1 3m+: 0-7
Track: LH: 0-7 RH: 0-1 Tight: 0-3 Gall: 0-1
Aids: Bl: 0-4 Vi: 0-3 Tstrap: 0-0 Ckp: 0-1
Best Rating: 71 6/03 Strf 3m good Ch

Plating-class novice chaser; still a maiden; best on a sound surface.

Benrajah (IRE)

108(110h)   (100h)**115+**

7-y-o b g Lord Americo-Andy's Fancy (IRE) (Andretti)
M Todhunter Brian Murfin

Placings:2/335013-F1214236   (4648)
2003/04: 21FGF, 25¹F, 26²GF, 25¹GS, 20⁴GS, 24²G, 22³GS, 20⁶G,

	Starts	1st	2nd	3rd	Win & Pl
Chases	8	2	2	1	11543
Career Total	15	3	3	4	17344
115	12/03	Catt	3m1f110yE(0-110)HCh	G-S	£3415
106	10/03	Kels	3m1f	E Ch	FRM	£3598
100	3/03	Wwck	3m1f	E Hdl	G-F	£3571

Total win prize-money £10586

Going: Sf: 0-0 GS: 1-3 Gd: 0-2 GF: - Fm: 1-3
Distance: 2m/2m3: 0-0 2m4-2m7: 0-4 **3m+: 2-4**
Track: **LH: 2-7** RH: 0-1 **Tight: 2-5** Gall: 0-0
Aids: Bl: 0-0 Vi: 0-0 Tstrap: 0-0 Ckp: 0-0
Best Rating: 115 3/04 Kels 2m6f110y gd-sft Ch

Modest hurdler/chaser; acts on fast ground; stays beyond three miles and best when able to dominate; mainly creditable efforts this year and is the type to win more races.

Benson (IRE)

9-y-o b/br g Hawkstone (IRE)-Erin St Helen (IRE) (Seclude (USA))
J W Mullins Miss Dinah Wilkins

Placings:4P5/6/1530F1P-0FP   (4717)
2003/04: 25⁰GS, 20FG, 24PG,

	Starts	1st	2nd	3rd	Win & Pl
Chases	3	0	0	0	
Career Total	14	2	0	1	10990
105	3/03	Wwck	2m4f110yD(0-120)HCh	G-F	£5754
112	10/02	Hrfd	2m3f	E(0-105)HCh	GD	£4160

Total win prize-money £9914

Going: Sf: 0-0 GS: 0-1 Gd: 0-2 GF: - Fm: 0-0

Distance: 2m/2m3: 0-0 2m4-2m7: 0-1 3m+: 0-2
Track: LH: 0-0 RH: 0-2 Tight: 0-2 Gall: 0-0
Aids: Bl: 0-0 Vi: 0-0 Tstrap: 0-0 Ckp: 0-0
Best Rating: 112 10/02 Hrfd 2m3f good Ch

Modest chaser; effective at two and a half miles; acts on good and fast ground.

Bentyheath Lane

87(104h)   (78h)**71**

7-y-o b g Puissance-Eye Sight (Roscoe Blake)
M Mullineaux The Hon Mrs S Pakenham

Placings:500P/P32200-40320506   (1747)
2003/04: 16⁴GS, 16⁰GF, 16³GF, 17²G, 17⁰G, 16⁵GF, 17⁰GF, 16⁸GF,

	Starts	1st	2nd	3rd	Win & Pl
Hurdles	7	0	1	1	2399
Chases	1	0	0	0	
Career Total	18	0	3	2	5079

Going: Sf: 0-0 GS: 1-0 Gd: 0-2 GF: - Fm: 0-5
Distance: 2m/2m3: 0-8 2m4-2m7: 0-4 3m+: 0-0
Track: LH: 0-7 RH: 0-1 Tight: 0-3 Gall: 0-0
Aids: Bl: 0-0 Vi: 0-0 Tstrap: 0-0 Ckp: 0-0
Best Rating: 78 8/03 Bang 2m1f good Hdl

Poor maiden hurdler; placed several times; best effort last time out; seems best on fast ground.

Benvolio

(48h)**65**

7-y-o br g Cidrax (FR)-Miss Capulet (Commanche Run)
P L Clinton (C N Kellett 3/5) 7 A.D. Racing

Placings:0P000000/00000PP/0R3P5P4P5PP3-PP0 (1253)
2003/04: 26PHY, 26PGF, 22⁰GF,

	Starts	1st	2nd	3rd	Win & Pl
Hurdles	2	0	0	0	0
Chases	1	0	0	0	0
Career Total	30	0	0	2	1554

Going: Sf: 0-1 GS: 0-0 Gd: 0-0 GF: - Fm: 0-2
Distance: 2m/2m3: 0-0 2m4-2m7: 0-1 3m+: 0-2
Track: LH: 0-2 RH: 0-0 Tight: 0-0 Gall: 0-0
Aids: Bl: 0-0 Vi: 0-0 Tstrap: 0-0 Ckp: 0-1
Best Rating: 69 5/01 Hrfd 2m3f110y good Hdl

Berengario (IRE)

93   **67**

4-y-o b g Mark Of Esteem (IRE)-Ivrea (Sadler's Wells (USA))
S C Burrough Mrs Deborah Potter

Placings:0000306   (4546)
2003/04: 12⁰GF, 16⁰S, 17⁰GS, 16⁰S, 17³GS, 16⁰G, 16⁶GS,

	Starts	1st	2nd	3rd	Win & Pl
NH Flat	1	0	0	0	0
Hurdles	6	0	0	1	478
Career Total	7	0	0	1	478

Going: Sf: 0-2 GS: 0-3 Gd: 0-1 GF: - Fm: 0-0
Distance: 2m/2m3: 0-6 2m4-2m7: 0-0 3m+: 0-0
Track: LH: 0-3 RH: 0-4 Tight: 0-0 Gall: 0-1
Aids: Bl: 0-2 Vi: 0-0 Tstrap: 0-0 Ckp: 0-0
Best Rating: 67 2/04 Hrfd 2m1f gd-sft Hdl

Bergamo
107   **104**
8-y-o b g Robellino (USA)-Pretty Thing (Star Appeal)
B Ellison Rasen Goes Racing

Placings:0324P/21423124/526054-402322523   (4796)
2003/04: 20⁴HY, 24⁰G, 21²G, 21³GF, 16²G, 17²GS, 19⁵G, 16²GF, 21³G,

	Starts	1st	2nd	3rd	Win & Pl
Hurdles	9	0	4	2	5210
Career Total	28	2	9	4	21874
109	3/02	Fknm	2m		D(0-120)HHdl	GD	£5408
103	12/01	Muss	2m4f		E Hdl	GD	£3052

Total win prize-money £8460

Going: Sf: 0-1 GS: 0-1 Gd: 0-5 GF: - Fm: 0-2
Distance: 2m/2m3: 0-3 2m4-2m7: 0-5 3m+: 0-1
Track: LH: 0-6 RH: 0-3 Tight: 0-6 Gall: 0-1
Aids: Bl: 0-7 Vi: 0-0 Tstrap: 0-0 Ckp: 0-2
Best Rating: 109 9/02 Prth 2m110y gd-fm Hdl

Moderate hurdler; fair performer at his best; suited by a sound surface and a sharp track; goes well at Musselburgh; wears blinkers or cheekpieces; usually held up.

Bering Gifts (IRE)

9-y-o b g Bering-Bobbysoxer (Valiyar)
Mrs T J Hill Alan Hill

Placings:6/3601F0/10512140/0414034235-0   (4775)
2003/04: 21⁰G,

	Starts	1st	2nd	3rd	Win & Pl
Chases	1	0	0	0	
Career Total	26	5	2	3	17923
118	6/02	Strf	2m110y	D(0-120)HHdl	G-F	£3562
118	8/01	Hntg	2m110y	F(0-110)HHdl	G-F	£1946
107	7/01	NAbb	2m11	D(0-120)HHdl	G-F	£3114
113	5/01	Hntg	2m110y	E Hdl	G-F	£3136
100	8/00	Worc	2m	F Hdl	G-F	£1897

Total win prize-money £13655

Going: Sf: 0-0 GS: 0-0 Gd: 0-1 GF: - Fm: 0-0
Distance: 2m/2m3: 0-0 2m4-2m7: 0-1 3m+: 0-0
Track: LH: 0-1 RH: 0-0 Tight: 0-1 Gall: 0-0
Aids: Bl: 0-0 Vi: 0-0 Tstrap: 0-0 Ckp: 0-0
Best Rating: 118 7/02 Strf 2m110y gd-fm Hdl

Formerly fair handicap hurdler for Charlie Mann; likes fast ground; needs to be produced late; best at distances around two and a half miles.

Berkeley Hall
104   **85**
7-y-o b m Saddlers' Hall (IRE)-Serious Affair (Valiyar)
R Lee Richard Edwards

Placings:60-25P   (1136)
2003/04: 16²G, 16⁵G, 20⁰G,

	Starts	1st	2nd	3rd	Win & Pl
Hurdles	3	0	1	0	852
Career Total	5	0	1	0	852

Going: Sf: 0-0 GS: 0-0 Gd: 0-3 GF: - Fm: 0-0
Distance: 2m/2m3: 0-2 2m4-2m7: 0-1 3m+: 0-0
Track: LH: 0-3 RH: 0-0 Tight: 0-3 Gall: 0-0
Aids: Bl: 0-0 Vi: 0-0 Tstrap: 0-0 Ckp: 0-1
Best Rating: 85 5/03 Strf 2m110y good Hdl

Plating class at up to 7f on the Flat; runner-up in 2m mares only novices' seller at Stratford May 2003.

Berlin Blue
104   **126**
11-y-o b g Belmez (USA)-Blue Brocade (Reform)
R M Stronge Peter J Douglas Engineering

Placings:444F0/52116/642322/4111/54/03PF-66   (0767)
2003/04: 24⁶GF, 32⁶GF,

	Starts	1st	2nd	3rd	Win & Pl
Chases	2	0	0	0	900
Career Total	28	5	4	2	51509
129	7/00	Uttx	4m110y	B(0-140)HCh	G-F	£26000
115	6/00	Uttx	3m	D Ch	G-F	£3718
110	5/00	Uttx	3m2f	E Ch	G-F	£3159
119	3/99	Newb	3m110y	D Hdl	G-F	£2997
113	2/99	Hntg	2m4f110yE(0-105)HHdl	G-S	£2808

Total win prize-money £38683

Going: Sf: 0-0 GS: 0-0 Gd: 0-0 GF: - Fm: 0-2
Distance: 2m/2m3: 0-0 2m4-2m7: 0-0 3m+: 0-2
Track: LH: 0-1 RH: 0-0 Tight: 0-0 Gall: 0-0
Aids: Bl: 0-0 Vi: 0-0 Tstrap: 0-0 Ckp: 0-0
Best Rating: 129 7/00 Uttx 4m110y gd-fm Ch

Fair hurdler/decent chaser; scored a hat-trick over fences at Uttoxeter in the summer of 2000; lightly raced since; stays four miles; best on good ground or faster; sound jumper.

Bermuda (IRE)
95   **66**
5-y-o b g Sadler's Wells (USA)-Sequel (IRE) (Law Society (USA))
G F Edwards (W Jenks 5/5) G F Edwards

Placings:055PP00   (3789)
2003/04: 16⁶G, 17⁵GF, 20⁵GF, 16⁵S, 20⁵GS, 24⁰G, 22⁰G,

	Starts	1st	2nd	3rd	Win & Pl
NH Flat	2	0	0	0	0
Hurdles	5	0	0	0	750
Career Total	7	0	0	0	750

Going: Sf: 0-1 GS: 0-1 Gd: 0-3 GF: - Fm: 0-2
Distance: 2m/2m3: 0-3 2m4-2m7: 0-3 3m+: 0-1
Track: LH: 0-3 RH: 0-4 Tight: 0-2 Gall: 0-0
Aids: Bl: 0-2 Vi: 0-0 Tstrap: 0-0 Ckp: 0-1
Best Rating: 84 5/03 Ludl 2m good NHF

Bernardon (GER)
109   **131**
8-y-o b g Suave Dancer (USA)-Bejaria (GER) (Konigsstuhl (GER))
R C Guest The Macca & Growler Partnership

Placings:1F0/124000P0-P4P436   (4813)
2003/04: 16⁶G, 16⁴S, 16⁶S, 16⁴GS, 18³G, 16⁶G,

	Starts	1st	2nd	3rd	Win & Pl
Hurdles	6	0	0	1	2178
Career Total	17	2	1	1	22215
136	6/02	Worc	2m	B(0-140)HHdl	SFT	£13897
111	2/02	Tntn	2m1f	D Hdl	SFT	£3815

Total win prize-money £17712

Going: Sf: 0-2 GS: 0-1 Gd: 0-3 GF: - Fm: 0-0
Distance: 2m/2m3: 0-4 2m4-2m7: 0-0 3m+: 0-0
Track: LH: 0-5 RH: 0-1 Tight: 0-2 Gall: 0-0
Aids: Bl: 0-0 Vi: 0-0 Tstrap: 0-0 Ckp: 0-1
Best Rating: 136 8/02 Sthl 2m1f gd-fm Hdl

Fair ex-German hurdler; effective at around two miles; at his best with a little cut in the ground; has worn a visor.

Bernini (IRE)
96   **102**
4-y-o b g Grand Lodge (USA)-Alsahah (IRE) (Unfuwain (USA))
N J Henderson (M L W Bell 23/6) Mrs Maureen Buckley

Placings:3530   (4573)
2003/04: 16⁵S, 16⁵GS, 17³G, 19⁰G,

	Starts	1st	2nd	3rd	Win & Pl
Hurdles	4	0	0	2	1055
Career Total	4	0	0	2	1055

Going: Sf: 0-1 GS: 0-1 Gd: 0-2 GF: - Fm: 0-0
Distance: 2m/2m3: 0-4 2m4-2m7: 0-0 3m+: 0-0
Track: LH: 0-3 RH: 0-1 Tight: 0-1 Gall: 0-3
Aids: Bl: 0-0 Vi: 0-0 Tstrap: 0-0 Ckp: 0-0
Best Rating: 101 1/04 Newb 2m110y soft Hdl

Novice hurdler; Flat winner at 1m 4f; effective over two miles.

Berrington (NZ)

7-y-o b g Fort Prospect (USA)-Calamity (NZ) (Bally Royal)
A J Deakin A J Deakin

Placings:00/P-P   (0367)
2003/04: 16⁶G,

	Starts	1st	2nd	3rd	Win & Pl
Hurdles	1	0	0		
Career Total	4	0	0		

Going: Sf: 0-0 GS: 0-0 Gd: 0-1 GF: - Fm: 0-0
Distance: 2m/2m3: 0-1 2m4-2m7: 0-0 3m+: 0-0
Track: LH: 0-1 RH: 0-0 Tight: 0-0 Gall: 0-0
Aids: Bl: 0-0 Vi: 0-0 Tstrap: 0-0 Ckp: 0-0
Best Rating: 50 12/01 Ludl 2m good NHF

Berrywhite (IRE)

6-y-o ch g Barathea (IRE)-Berryville (USA) (Hatchet Man (USA))
C Grant Mrs A Meller

Placings:P0   (3767)
2003/04: 19⁰G, 17⁰HY,

	Starts	1st	2nd	3rd	Win & Pl
Hurdles	2	0	0		
Career Total	2	0	0		

Going: Sf: 0-1 GS: 0-0 Gd: 0-1 GF: - Fm: 0-0
Distance: 2m/2m3: 0-1 2m4-2m7: 0-1 3m+: 0-0
Track: LH: 0-0 RH: 0-2 Tight: 0-1 Gall: 0-0
Aids: Bl: 0-0 Vi: 0-0 Tstrap: 0-0 Ckp: 0-0
Best Rating: 0 2/04 Carl 2m1f heavy Hdl

Bertie Arms

4-y-o b f Cloudings (IRE)-Pugilistic (Hard Fought)
J M Jefferson P F Birch

Placings:0   (4780)
2003/04: 16⁶S,

	Starts	1st	2nd	3rd	Win & Pl
NH Flat	1	0	0		
Career Total	1	0	0		

Going: Sf: 0-1 GS: 0-0 Gd: 0-0 GF: - Fm: 0-0
Distance: 2m/2m3: 0-1 2m4-2m7: 0-0 3m+: 0-0
Track: LH: 0-1 RH: 0-0 Tight: 0-1 Gall: 0-0
Aids: Bl: 0-0 Vi: 0-0 Tstrap: 0-0 Ckp: 0-0

Bertie O'Toole

(59h)   (7h)
10-y-o b g Jendali (USA)-Young Mary (Young Generation)
Mrs R L Elliot Alan Guthrie

Placings: 0/0000/00PU   (4616)
2003/04: 20⁵HY, 24⁸GS, 24⁸G, 21UG,

	Starts	1st	2nd	3rd	Win & Pl
Hurdles	3	0	0	0	0
Chases	1	0	0	0	0
Career Total	9	0	0	0	0

Going: Sf: 0-1 GS: 0-1 Gd: 0-2 GF: - Fm: 0-0
Distance: 2m/2m3: 0-0 2m4-2m7: 0-2 3m+: 0-2
Track: LH: 0-4 RH: 0-0 Tight: 0-1 Gall: 0-1
Aids: Bl: 0-0 Vi: 0-0 Tstrap: 0-3 Ckp: 0-0
Best Rating: 70 11/99 Ayr 2m good NHF

Bertiebanoo (IRE)
103   **115**
6-y-o ch g Be My Native (USA)-Gemeleks Gem (IRE)
(Carlingford Castle)
P J Hobbs P A Newey

Placings: 0-1520   (4870)
2003/04: 17⁰S, 21¹S, 24⁵S, 25²S, 24⁰GS,

	Starts	1st	2nd	3rd	Win & Pl
NH Flat	1	0	0	0	
Hurdles	4	1	1	0	4806
Career Total	5	1	1	0	4806
111 11/03 Plum	2m5f	E Hdl		SFT	£3718

Total win prize-money £3718

Going: Sf: 1-4 GS: 0-1 Gd: 0-0 GF: - Fm: 0-0
Distance: 2m/2m3: 0-0 **2m4-2m7: 1-1** 3m+: 0-3
Track: **LH: 1-4** RH: 0-1 Tight: 1-4 Gall: 0-0
Aids: Bl: 0-0 Vi: 0-0 Tstrap: 0-0 Ckp: 0-0
Best Rating: 115 3/04 Wwck 3m1f soft Hdl

Fair novice hurdler; brave winner of 2m 5f novice hurdle in bad ground at Plumpton in November 2003; good effort when runner-up at Warwick under a penalty; stays three miles; future chaser.

Beseiged (USA)
105   **114+**
7-y-o ch g Cadeaux Genereux-Munnaya (USA) (Nijinsky (CAN))
R A Fahey Mike Caulfield

Placings: 525/111-11P00   (3885)
2003/04: 16¹G, 16¹G, 16PGS, 16⁰S, 16⁰G,

	Starts	1st	2nd	3rd	Win & Pl
Hurdles	5	2	0	0	8182
Career Total	11	5	1	0	19211
114 5/03 Prth	2m110y	E(0-105)HHdl		GD	£4841
113 5/03 Kels	2m110y	E(0-120)HHdl		GD	£3341
114 4/03 MRas	2m3f110yD Hdl			G-F	£5320
102 6/02 Prth	2m110y	E Hdl		G-S	£2898
98 5/02 Prth	2m110y	H NHF		G-F	£2345

Total win prize-money £18745

Going: Sf: 0-1 GS: 0-1 Gd: 2-3 GF: - Fm: 0-0
Distance: 2m/2m3: 2-5 2m4-2m7: 0-0 3m+: 0-0
Track: LH: 1-3 RH: 1-2 Tight: 1-2 Gall: 0-2
Aids: Bl: 0-0 Vi: 0-0 Tstrap: 0-0 Ckp: 0-0

Best Rating: 114 5/03 Prth 2m110y good Hdl

Fair hurdler; fair form in bumpers, winning at Perth in May 2002; off the mark over hurdles at the same course the following month and returned from nearly a year off to win at Market Rasen; won another two and looked progressive, but out of the frame in better races since; suited by a sound surface.

Bessie Bunter

63
8-y-o b m Rakaposhi King-Black H'Penny (Town And Country)
J A B Old Bessie Bunter Partnership

Placings: 500/55006-0   (0366)
2003/04: 24⁰S,

	Starts	1st	2nd	3rd	Win & Pl
Hurdles	1	0	0	0	
Career Total	9	0	0	0	0

Going: Sf: 0-1 GS: 0-0 Gd: 0-0 GF: - Fm: 0-0
Distance: 2m/2m3: 0-0 2m4-2m7: 0-0 3m+: 0-1
Track: LH: 0-1 RH: 0-0 Tight: 0-0 Gall: 0-0
Aids: Bl: 0-0 Vi: 0-0 Tstrap: 0-0 Ckp: 0-0
Best Rating: 82 12/02 Chep 2m110y soft Hdl

Fair debut effort in a Taunton bumper.

Best Mate (IRE)
117   (155h)**178**
9-y-o b g Un Desperado (FR)-Katday (FR) (Miller's Mate)
Miss H C Knight Jim Lewis

Placings: f1221/1112/1221/111-211   (4424)
2003/04: 20²GS, 24¹YS, 26¹G,

	Starts	1st	2nd	3rd	Win & Pl
Chases	3	2	1	0	277312
Career Total	19	13	6	0	964665
174 3/04 Chel	3m2f110yA Ch		GD	£203000
172 12/03 Leop	3m	Ch	Y-S	£63311
178 3/03 Chel	3m2f110yA Ch		GD	£203000
173 12/02 Kemp	3m	A Ch	SFT	£87000
171 11/02 Hntg	2m4f110yA Ch		G-S	£32725
176 3/02 Chel	3m2f110yA Ch		GD	£174000
172 11/01 Extr	2m1f110yA HCh		G-F	£21000
167 2/01 Sand	2m4f110yA Ch		HVY	£24000
156 11/00 Chel	2m	A Ch	G-S	£15000
151 10/00 Extr	2m1f110yD Ch		GD	£3926
146 4/00 Aint	2m4f	A Hdl	GD	£21000
137 12/99 Sand	2m110y	D Hdl	G-S	£3680
133 11/99 Chel	2m110y	B NHF	GD	£7197

Total win prize-money £858841

Going: Sf: 0-0 GS: 0-1 Gd: 1-1 GF: - Fm: 0-0
Distance: 2m/2m3: 0-0 2m4-2m7: 0-1 **3m+: 2-2**
Track: LH: 2-2 RH: 0-1 Tight: 0-0 Gall: 1-2
Aids: Bl: 0-0 Vi: 0-0 Tstrap: 0-0 Ckp: 0-0
Best Rating: 178 3/03 Chel 3m2f110y good Ch

Brilliant chaser; the best staying chaser in training; has never been out of the first two over hurdles or fences and is the first horse since Arkle to win three Cheltenham Gold Cups; below his best when beaten in the 2003 Peterborough Chase by Jair Du Cochet, but bounced back by taking the Grade One Ericsson Chase at Leopardstown in December with ease, having run there rather than the King George at Kempton; completed an historic Gold Cup hat-trick, but his half-length defeat of Sir Rembrandt did not match the form he showed in the previous two renewals; has an excellent cruising pace, jumps well, has a fine turn of foot and acts on any ground; proved at Cheltenham that he can battle; effective from 2m 4f to 3m 2f and on any type of track.

Best Wait (IRE)
109(109h)   (114 h)**105**
7-y-o b m Insan (USA)-Greek Melody (IRE) (Trojan Fort)
T Hogan (P F Nicholls 23/5) J M Ryan

Placings: 6f241530305F0/614263-324F056525622F
    (4413a)
2003/04: 17³G, 16²G, 16⁴GS, 17FSH, 16⁰S, 16⁵GY, 16⁶S, 16⁵Y, 16²GY, 20⁵S, 16⁶S, 16²GY, 18²GY, 20FY,

	Starts	1st	2nd	3rd	Win & Pl
Hurdles	9	0	2	0	4458
Chases	5	0	2	1	3681
Career Total	33	3	6	4	38723
108 9/02 Rosc	2m	(74-116)HHdl	G-Y	£4239
105 10/01 Limk	2m	Hdl	YLD	£8387
101 7/01 Cork	2m	NHF	FRM	£5564

Total win prize-money £18191

Going: Sf: 0-4 GS: 0-1 Gd: 0-2 GF: - Fm: 0-0
Distance: 2m/2m3: 0-2 2m4-2m7: 0-2 3m+: 0-0
Track: LH: 0-2 RH: 0-8 Tight: 0-0 Gall: 0-0
Aids: Bl: 0-0 Vi: 0-0 Tstrap: 0-8 Ckp: 0-6
Best Rating: 125 12/01 Fair 2m yield Hdl

Fair hurdler; ex-Irish; effective at two miles and seems to handle any ground; wears a tongue tie.

Best World (FR)
75   **63**
4-y-o b g Lost World (IRE)-Katevana (FR) (Cadoudal (FR))
Paul John Gilligan B Walsh

Placings: 500   (4200a)
2003/04: 16⁵G, 16⁰YS, 16⁰YS,

	Starts	1st	2nd	3rd	Win & Pl
Hurdles	3	0	0	0	540
Career Total	3	0	0	0	540

Going: Sf: 0-0 GS: 0-0 Gd: 0-1 GF: - Fm: 0-0
Distance: 2m/2m3: 0-3 2m4-2m7: 0-0 3m+: 0-0
Track: LH: 0-2 RH: 0-0 Tight: 0-0 Gall: 0-0
Aids: Bl: 0-0 Vi: 0-0 Tstrap: 0-0 Ckp: 0-0
Best Rating: 63 2/04 Gowr 2m yld-sft Hdl

Besuto (IRE)

7-y-o br g Fourstars Allstar (USA)-Mabbots Own (Royal Trip)
D D Scott Mrs D D Scott

Placings: 456-PP   (4895)
2003/04: 16PG, 22PG,

	Starts	1st	2nd	3rd	Win & Pl
Hurdles	2	0	0	0	
Career Total	5	0	0	0	0

Going: Sf: 0-0 GS: 0-0 Gd: 0-2 GF: - Fm: 0-0
Distance: 2m/2m3: 0-1 2m4-2m7: 0-1 3m+: 0-0
Track: LH: 0-0 RH: 0-2 Tight: 0-0 Gall: 0-0
Aids: Bl: 0-0 Vi: 0-0 Tstrap: 0-0 Ckp: 0-0
Best Rating: 89 11/02 Tntn 2m1f gd-sft NHF

Betabatim (IRE)
(100h)   (94h)**94**
9-y-o b g Alphabatim (USA)-Lucy Platter (FR) (Record Token)
J E Brockbank J E Brockbank

Placings:5/P/P0FP54/155UP-P (2232)
2003/04: 16PG,

	Starts	1st	2nd	3rd	Win & Pl
Chases	1	0	0	0	
Career Total	14	1	0	0	2940

94 5/02 Kels 2m110y E Hdl G-S £2940
Total win prize-money £2940

Going: Sf: 0-0 GS: 0-0 Gd: 0-1 GF: - Fm: 0-0
Distance: 2m/2m3: 0-1 2m4-2m7: 0-0 3m+: 0-0
Track: LH: 0-1 RH: 0-0 Tight: 0-0 Gall: 0-0
Aids: Bl: 0-0 Vi: 0-0 Tstrap: 0-0 Ckp: 0-0
Best Rating: 95 4/00 Carl 2m1f gd-sft NHF

Bethilda
78   **47**
8-y-o br m Joligeneration-Woodland Firefly (Min's Baby)
C J Down Mrs J Gillespie

Placings:5 (1122)
2003/04: 22⁵GF,

	Starts	1st	2nd	3rd	Win & Pl
Hurdles	1	0	0	0	0
Career Total	1	0	0	0	0

Going: Sf: 0-0 GS: 0-0 Gd: 0-0 GF: - Fm: 0-1
Distance: 2m/2m3: 0-0 2m4-2m7: 0-1 3m+: 0-0
Track: LH: 0-1 RH: 0-0 Tight: 0-0 Gall: 0-0
Aids: Bl: 0-0 Vi: 0-0 Tstrap: 0-0 Ckp: 0-0
Best Rating: 51 8/03 NAbb 2m6f gd-fm Hdl

Better Days (IRE)
104   (122h)**141**
8-y-o b g Supreme Leader-Kilkilrun (Deep Run)
Mrs S J Smith Trevor Hemmings

Placings:2/160/P-1F315P053 (4860)
2003/04: 21¹G, 20⁵S, 16³GS, 20¹GS, 20⁵G, 24⁴G, 21⁰G, 20⁵GS, 20³GS,

	Starts	1st	2nd	3rd	Win & Pl
Chases	9	2	0	2	16668
Career Total	14	3	1	2	21825

141 12/03 Hayd 2m4f C Ch G-S £8778
121 11/03 Sthl 2m5f110yE Ch GD £2756
115 11/01 Aint 2m110y D Hdl G-S £4212
Total win prize-money £15746

Going: Sf: 0-2 GS: 1-3 Gd: 1-4 GF: - Fm: 0-0
Distance: 2m/2m3: 0-0 2m4-2m7: 2-7 3m+: 0-1
Track: LH: 2-4 RH: 0-1 Tight: 0-0 Gall: 0-0
Aids: Bl: 0-0 Vi: 0-0 Tstrap: 0-0 Ckp: 0-0
Best Rating: 141 12/03 Hayd 2m4f gd-sft Ch

Fair chaser; stays two miles five and will get further; acts on good and good to soft ground.

Better Moment (IRE)
96   (92+c)**100**
7-y-o b g Turtle Island (IRE)-Snoozeandyoulose (IRE) (Scenic)
M C Pipe M C Pipe

Placings:0105434/3U2/2441615364-041231 (1231)
2003/04: 17⁰GF, 16⁴G, 17¹G, 20²GF, 19³GF, 17¹GF,

	Starts	1st	2nd	3rd	Win & Pl
Hurdles	6	2	1	1	6325
Career Total	26	5	3	4	15492

100 8/03 Sthl 2m1f G Hdl G-F £2597
100 7/03 Sthl 2m1f G Hdl GD £2639
96 7/02 NAbb 2m1f F(0-90)Hdl G-F £2653
96 6/02 Worc 2m G Hdl G-F £2054
86 1/01 Catt 2m G Hdl G-S £1596
Total win prize-money £11540

Going: Sf: 0-0 GS: 0-0 Gd: 1-2 GF: - Fm: 1-4
Distance: 2m/2m3: 2-5 2m4-2m7: 0-1 3m+: 0-0
Track: LH: 2-5 RH: 0-0 Tight: 0-1 Gall: 0-0
Aids: Bl: 0-0 Vi: 2-6 Tstrap: 0-0 Ckp: 0-0
Best Rating: 100 8/03 Sthl 2m1f gd-fm Hdl

Selling hurdler; best at around two miles; acts on fast ground but has scored on good to soft; needs plenty of driving; usually wears a visor.

Better Think Again (IRE)
116   **110**
10-y-o b g Brush Aside (USA)-Ride The Rapids (Bulldozer)
Mrs Edwina Finn (D P Kelly 11/10) J Doherty

Placings:1/13P/63P0/2F300/64-30532 (2760a)
2003/04: 24³YS, 24⁰Y, 24⁵GF, 21³G, 24²S,

	Starts	1st	2nd	3rd	Win & Pl
Hurdles	5	0	1	2	5975
Career Total	20	2	2	5	22739

127 11/99 Chep 2m4f C Hdl G-S £5356
121 4/99 Punc 2m NHF YLD £6138
Total win prize-money £11495

Going: Sf: 0-1 GS: 0-0 Gd: 0-1 GF: - Fm: 0-1
Distance: 2m/2m3: 0-0 2m4-2m7: 0-1 3m+: 0-4
Track: LH: 0-3 RH: 0-1 Tight: 0-0 Gall: 0-0
Aids: Bl: 0-0 Vi: 0-0 Tstrap: 0-0 Ckp: 0-0
Best Rating: 127 4/01 Kemp 3m110y good Hdl

Fair Irish hurdler; formerly trained in Britain; has shown mixed form at up to three miles two including over fences; handles cut but is effective on a sound surface.

Better Thyne (IRE)
97(108h)   (108h)**121**
8-y-o ch g Good Thyne (USA)-Cailin Cainnteach (Le Bavard (FR))
V R A Dartnall R F Woodward

Placings:P3310/1UF6P-0 (2775)
2003/04: 25⁵S,

	Starts	1st	2nd	3rd	Win & Pl
Chases	1	0	0	0	
Career Total	11	2	0	2	7367

108 12/02 Tntn 3m110y D(0-120)HHdl G-S £4277
102 1/02 Uttx 3m110y F Hdl HVY £1974
Total win prize-money £6251

Going: Sf: 0-1 GS: 0-0 Gd: 0-0 GF: - Fm: 0-0
Distance: 2m/2m3: 0-2 2m4-2m7: 0-0 3m+: 0-1
Track: LH: 0-0 RH: 0-1 Tight: 0-0 Gall: 0-0
Aids: Bl: 0-0 Vi: 0-0 Tstrap: 0-0 Ckp: 0-0
Best Rating: 121 1/03 Extr 2m7f110y gd-sft Ch

Betterthedeviluno
5-y-o b g Hector Protector (USA)-Aquaglow (Caerleon (USA))
D McCain D McCain

Placings:P (4378)
2003/04: 17PG,

	Starts	1st	2nd	3rd	Win & Pl
Hurdles	1	0	0	0	
Career Total	1	0	0	0	

Going: Sf: 0-0 GS: 0-0 Gd: 0-1 GF: - Fm: 0-0
Distance: 2m/2m3: 0-1 2m4-2m7: 0-0 3m+: 0-0
Track: LH: 0-0 RH: 0-1 Tight: 0-1 Gall: 0-1
Aids: Bl: 0-0 Vi: 0-0 Tstrap: 0-0 Ckp: 0-0
Best Rating: 0 3/04 Tntn 2m1f good Hdl

Betterware Boy
83   **73**
4-y-o ch g Barathea (IRE)-Crystal Drop (Cadeaux Genereux)
P M Phelan (Mrs A J Perrett 8/7) Andrew L Cohen

Placings:000 (3422)
2003/04: 16⁰S, 17⁰G, 17⁰HY,

	Starts	1st	2nd	3rd	Win & Pl
Hurdles	3	0	0	0	
Career Total	3	0	0	0	

Going: Sf: 0-2 GS: 0-0 Gd: 0-1 GF: - Fm: 0-0
Distance: 2m/2m3: 0-3 2m4-2m7: 0-0 3m+: 0-0
Track: LH: 0-2 RH: 0-1 Tight: 0-1 Gall: 0-1
Aids: Bl: 0-0 Vi: 0-0 Tstrap: 0-0 Ckp: 0-0
Best Rating: 73 1/04 Chel 2m1f good Hdl

Modest form shown on both start over hurdles to date; gets two miles.

Bexley (IRE)
88   **74+**
6-y-o b g Torus-Regency Charm (IRE) (Prince Regent (FR))
C Grant Trevor Hemmings

Placings:0406P (4731)
2003/04: 16⁰HY, 16⁴S, 20⁰G, 20⁶GS, 20PG,

	Starts	1st	2nd	3rd	Win & Pl
NH Flat	2	0	0	0	0
Hurdles	3	0	0	0	0
Career Total	5	0	0	0	0

Going: Sf: 0-2 GS: 0-1 Gd: 0-2 GF: - Fm: 0-0
Distance: 2m/2m3: 0-2 2m4-2m7: 0-3 3m+: 0-0
Track: LH: 0-3 RH: 0-2 Tight: 0-0 Gall: 0-0
Aids: Bl: 0-0 Vi: 0-0 Tstrap: 0-0 Ckp: 0-0
Best Rating: 88 2/04 Weth 2m soft NHF

Big, chasing-type; has shown some ability in bumpers; will stays well.

Beyond Borders (USA)
103   **100**
6-y-o b/br g Pleasant Colony (USA)-Welcome Proposal (Be My Guest (USA))
S Gollings Quickfall Racing

Placings:236/0032064626-030304350 (4956)
2003/04: 16⁰G, 19³G, 16⁰S, 16²S, 17⁰GS, 16⁴G, 18³G, 19⁵GF, 22⁰G,

	Starts	1st	2nd	3rd	Win & Pl
Hurdles	9	0	0	3	1617
Career Total	22	0	3	5	6446

Going: Sf: 0-2 GS: 0-1 Gd: 0-5 GF: - Fm: 0-1
Distance: 2m/2m3: 0-7 2m4-2m7: 0-2 3m+: 0-0
Track: LH: 0-5 RH: 0-5 Tight: 0-3 Gall: 0-1

Aids: Bl: 0-1 Vi: 0-0 Tstrap: 0-0 Ckp: 0-0
Best Rating: 113 2/02 Naas 2m　　heavy　Hdl

Moderate maiden hurdler; ex-Irish; effective at two miles; usually wears blinkers.

Beyond Control (IRE)
104　　　　　　　　(0c)126
9-y-o b g Supreme Leader-Bucktina (Buckskin (FR))
C L Tizzard Anthony Knott

Placings: F31P/PU1101P-40　　　　(3942)
2003/04: 25⁴G, 22⁰G,

	Starts	1st	2nd	3rd	Win & Pl
Hurdles	2	0	0	0	3500
Career Total	13	4	0	1	24055
126	3/03	Sand	2m6f	D(0-120)HHdl	HVY	£9419
126	1/03	Kemp	3m110y	D(0-120)HHdl	G-S	£5073
112	1/03	Folk	2m6f110yG Hdl		HVY	£2366
112	2/02	Tntn	3m110y E Hdl		SFT	£3087
				Total win prize-money £19945

Going: Sf: 0-0 GS: 0-0 Gd: 0-2 GF: - Fm: 0-0
Distance: 2m/2m3: 0-0 2m4-2m7: 0-1 3m+: 0-1
Track: LH: 0-0 RH: 0-2 Tight: 0-0 Gall: 0-0
Aids: Bl: 0-0 Vi: 0-0 Tstrap: 0-0 Ckp: 0-0
Best Rating: 126 12/03 Asct 3m1f110y good　Hdl

Useful hurdler; not always the most fluent jumper of fences; has been a revelation since going back hurdling; outclassed in graded company recently; stays three miles plus; well suited by soft ground.

Beyond The Pole (USA)
95　　　　　　　　81+
6-y-o b g Ghazi (USA)-North Of Sunset (USA) (Northern Baby (CAN))
B R Johnson Tann Racing

Placings: 0P0　　　　　　(3414)
2003/04: 16⁰S, 22ᴾGS, 16⁰S,

	Starts	1st	2nd	3rd	Win & Pl
Hurdles	3	0	0	0	
Career Total	3	0	0	0	

Going: Sf: 0-2 GS: 0-1 Gd: 0-0 GF: - Fm: 0-0
Distance: 2m/2m3: 0-2 2m4-2m7: 0-1 3m+: 0-0
Track: LH: 0-2 RH: 0-1 Tight: 0-3 Gall: 0-0
Aids: Bl: 0-0 Vi: 0-0 Tstrap: 0-0 Ckp: 0-0
Best Rating: 81 1/04 Plum 2m　　soft　Hdl

Beyondtherealm
89　　　　　　　　90
6-y-o b g Morpeth-Workamiracle (Teamwork)
J D Frost Singing In The Rain

Placings: 005　　　　　　(4524)
2003/04: 16⁰S, 18⁰HY, 16⁵GS,

	Starts	1st	2nd	3rd	Win & Pl
NH Flat	2	0	0	0	0
Hurdles	1	0	0	0	0
Career Total	3	0	0	0	0

Going: Sf: 0-2 GS: 0-1 Gd: 0-0 GF: - Fm: 0-0
Distance: 2m/2m3: 0-3 2m4-2m7: 0-1 3m+: 0-0
Track: LH: 0-3 RH: 0-0 Tight: 0-1 Gall: 0-0
Aids: Bl: 0-0 Vi: 0-0 Tstrap: 0-0 Ckp: 0-0

Best Rating: 97 12/03 Chep 2m110y　soft　NHF

Winning pointer over 2m4f on good ground; signs of ability in soft ground bumpers and on hurdling debut; should improve on a sounder surface.

Bhanoyi (IRE)
86　　　　　　　　48
5-y-o ch g Perugino (USA)-Bourgeonette (Mummy's Pet)
Mrs C A Dunnett (P S McEntee 29/5) College Farm Thoroughbreds

Placings: 0　　　　　　(0484)
2003/04: 16⁰GF,

	Starts	1st	2nd	3rd	Win & Pl
Hurdles	1	0	0	0	
Career Total	1	0	0	0	

Going: Sf: 0-0 GS: 0-0 Gd: 0-0 GF: - Fm: 0-1
Distance: 2m/2m3: 0-1 2m4-2m7: 0-0 3m+: 0-0
Track: LH: 0-0 RH: 0-1 Tight: 0-0 Gall: 0-0
Aids: Bl: 0-0 Vi: 0-0 Tstrap: 0-0 Ckp: 0-0
Best Rating: 54 5/03 Hntg 2m110y　gd-fm　Hdl

Bicycle Thief (IRE)
(93h)　　　　(116h)123
11-y-o ch g Archway (IRE)-Push Bike (Ballad Rock)
Miss Venetia Williams B Moore & E C Stephens

Placings: 52/13110/0014/0046/F32231-FF0　(4870)
2003/04: 24ᶠG, 24ᶠG, 24⁰GS,

	Starts	1st	2nd	3rd	Win & Pl
Hurdles	1	0	0	0	0
Chases	2	0	0	0	0
Career Total	24	5	3	3	36630
110	3/03	Bang	3m110y	D Ch	GD	£5950
138	3/01	Ling	2m3f110yB(0-140)HHdl	HVY	£14040
127	1/00	Kemp	2m5f	D Hdl	GD	£3835
125	12/99	Hrfd	2m3f110yE Hdl	HVY	£2850
129	12/99	Hrfd	2m3f110yE Hdl	GD	£2682
				Total win prize-money £29357

Going: Sf: 0-0 GS: 0-1 Gd: 0-2 GF: - Fm: 0-0
Distance: 2m/2m3: 0-0 2m4-2m7: 0-0 3m+: 0-3
Track: LH: 0-3 RH: 0-0 Tight: 0-2 Gall: 0-1
Aids: Bl: 0-0 Vi: 0-0 Tstrap: 0-0 Ckp: 0-0
Best Rating: 138 3/01 Ling　2m3f110y　heavy　Hdl

Decent handicap hurdler/fair novice chaser, but not a natural over fences; suited by trips of around two and a half miles; acts in soft ground; off for a year after March 2003.

Bid For Fame (USA)
99　　　　　　　　110
7-y-o b/br g Quest For Fame-Shroud (USA) (Vaguely Noble)
N Tinkler (N J Henderson 3/12) Elite Racing Club

Placings: 43-31343　　　　(2279)
2003/04: 16³GS, 16¹GF, 20³G, 25⁴G, 20³G,

	Starts	1st	2nd	3rd	Win & Pl
Hurdles	5	1	0	3	5471
Career Total	7	1	0	4	7038
105	10/03	Uttx	2m	E Hdl	G-F	£3381
				Total win prize-money £3381

Going: Sf: 0-0 GS: 0-1 Gd: 0-3 GF: - Fm: 1-1
Distance: 2m/2m3: 1-2 2m4-2m7: 0-2 3m+: 0-0
Track: LH: 1-3 RH: 0-2 Tight: 0-1 Gall: 0-0
Aids: Bl: 0-0 Vi: 0-0 Tstrap: 0-0 Ckp: 0-0
Best Rating: 110 11/03 Asct　2m4f　good　Hdl

Modest hurdler; yet to really shine beyond two miles; best on fast ground.

Bid Spotter (IRE)
104　　　　　　　　75
5-y-o b g Eagle Eyed (USA)-Bebe Auction (IRE) (Auction Ring (USA))
Mrs Lucinda Featherstone Heart Of England Racing

Placings: 0P42PP0　　　　(4785)
2003/04: 16⁰GF, 20ᴾGS, 20⁴GS, 16²S, 16ᴾS, 17ᴾG, 21⁰G,

	Starts	1st	2nd	3rd	Win & Pl
Hurdles	7	0	1	0	1289
Career Total	7	0	1	0	1289

Going: Sf: 0-2 GS: 0-2 Gd: 0-2 GF: - Fm: 0-1
Distance: 2m/2m3: 0-4 2m4-2m7: 0-3 3m+: 0-0
Track: LH: 0-1 RH: 0-6 Tight: 0-1 Gall: 0-3
Aids: Bl: 0-0 Vi: 0-0 Tstrap: 0-0 Ckp: 0-0
Best Rating: 75 1/04 Hntg　2m110y　soft　Hdl

Big Atoll (NZ)
86　　　　　　　　28
12-y-o b g Coral Reef (FR)-Medamac (NZ) (Yipp)
Miss C Dyson Miss C Dyson

Placings: 00321/062/PP/0　　(0630)
2003/04: 17⁰GF,

	Starts	1st	2nd	3rd	Win & Pl
Hurdles	1	0	0	0	
Career Total	11	1	2	1	4804
108	4/99	Uttx	2m	E(0-105)HHdl	G-S	£2715
				Total win prize-money £2715

Going: Sf: 0-0 GS: 0-0 Gd: 0-0 GF: - Fm: 0-1
Distance: 2m/2m3: 0-1 2m4-2m7: 0-0 3m+: 0-0
Track: LH: 0-1 RH: 0-0 Tight: 0-1 Gall: 0-0
Aids: Bl: 0-0 Vi: 0-0 Tstrap: 0-0 Ckp: 0-0
Best Rating: 108 4/99 Uttx　2m　　gd-sft　Hdl

Big Bone (FR)
97f　　　　　　　88f
4-y-o b g Zayyani-Bone Crasher (FR) (Cadoudal (FR))
T P Tate T P Tate

Placings: 351　　　　　(4323)
2003/04: 16³G, 17⁵G, 16¹S,

	Starts	1st	2nd	3rd	Win & Pl
NH Flat	3	1	0	1	2433
Career Total	3	1	0	1	2433
91	3/04	Newc	2m	H NHF	SFT	£2142
				Total win prize-money £2142

Going: Sf: 1-1 GS: 0-0 Gd: 0-2 GF: - Fm: 0-0
Distance: 2m/2m3: 1-3 2m4-2m7: 0-0 3m+: 0-0
Track: LH: 1-2 RH: 0-1 Tight: 0-1 Gall: 0-0
Aids: Bl: 0-0 Vi: 0-0 Tstrap: 0-0 Ckp: 0-0
Best Rating: 91 3/04 Newc 2m　　soft　NHF

Third in bumper on debut at Catterick in January; game winner at Newcastle in March; suited by give.

Big Max
105(106c)　　　　(97+c)100
9-y-o b g Rakaposhi King-Edwina's Dawn (Space King)
Miss K M George Exterior Profiles Ltd

Placings: 0P414/1231/364P013/2P4U53P-4524125P (4897)

2003/04: 21⁴G, 26⁵G, 19²GS, 20⁴G, 19¹S, 21²S, 19⁵G, 22²G,

	Starts	1st	2nd	3rd	Win & Pl
Hurdles	4	1	1	0	4376
Chases	4	0	1	0	1423
Career Total	**31**	**5**	**4**	**4**	**25507**
100	2/04	Extr	2m3f	F(0-100)HHdl	SFT £3556
100	3/02	MRas	2m5f110y	D(0-120)HHdl	G-S £4069
113	4/01	Muss	3m	F(0-100)HHdl	G-F £3251
104	10/00	MRas	3m	F(0-100)HHdl	GD £2646
85	1/00	Muss	2m4f	F(0-100)HHdl	GD £3493

Total win prize-money £17017

Going:	Sf: 1-2 GS: 0-1 Gd: 0-5 GF: - Fm: 0-0
Distance:	2m/2m3: 1-2 2m4-2m7: 0-5 3m+: 0-1
Track:	LH: 0-3 RH: 1-5 Tight: 0-4 Gall: 0-0
Aids:	Bl: 0-0 Vi: 0-0 Tstrap: 0-0 Ckp: 0-0
Best Rating:	113 4/01 Muss 3m gd-fm Hdl

Modest handicap hurdler at between 2m4f and 3m; best effort over fences when second to easy winner over 2m3f at Hereford December 2003 on ground softer than ideal; a free-runner, he seems to appreciate a sharp right-handed track and good or fast ground.

Big Moment

121   **147**

6-y-o ch g Be My Guest (USA)-Petralona (USA) (Alleged (USA))
Mrs A J Perrett R Doel,A Black,Dr J Howells & D Broad

Placings:11235 (4394)
2003/04: 16¹S, 20¹G, 21²GS, 20³G, 21⁵G,

	Starts	1st	2nd	3rd	Win & Pl
Hurdles	5	2	1	1	23089
Career Total	**5**	**2**	**1**	**1**	**23089**
127	12/03	Font	2m4f	E Hdl	GD £2758
133	11/03	Plum	2m	D Hdl	SFT £4631

Total win prize-money £7389

Going:	Sf: 1-1 GS: 0-1 Gd: 1-3 GF: - Fm: 0-0
Distance:	2m/2m3: 1-1 2m4-2m7: 1-4 3m+: 0-0
Track:	LH: 1-3 RH: 0-0 Tight: 2-3 Gall: 0-2
Aids:	Bl: 0-0 Vi: 0-0 Tstrap: 0-0 Ckp: 0-0
Best Rating:	147 3/04 Chel 2m5f good Hdl

Smart novice hurdler; useful stayer on the Flat; successful in his first two starts over hurdles and only just beaten by Cornish Rebel in Grade One Challow Hurdle; good effort against experienced opposition at Fontwell and in the Royal & SunAlliance Hurdle; acts on any ground; gets 2m5f; likeable sort.

Big Perks (IRE)

12-y-o ch g Executive Perk-Secret Ocean (Most Secret)
P T Dalton R A H Perkins

Placings:21/0333/4/22262/02/0 (1621)
2003/04: 17⁰G,

	Starts	1st	2nd	3rd	Win & Pl
Chases	1	0	0	0	
Career Total	**15**	**1**	**6**	**3**	**9244**
102	1/97	Wwck	2m	H NHF	G-F £1476

Total win prize-money £1476

Going:	Sf: 0-0 GS: 0-0 Gd: 0-1 GF: - Fm: 0-0
Distance:	2m/2m3: 0-1 2m4-2m7: 0-0 3m+: 0-0
Track:	LH: 0-1 RH: 0-0 Tight: 0-1 Gall: 0-0
Aids:	Bl: 0-0 Vi: 0-0 Tstrap: 0-0 Ckp: 0-0
Best Rating:	116 1/01 Donc 2m110y good Ch

Runner-up on his first three starts over fences, he disappointed next time on unsuitably soft ground.

Big Quick (IRE)

101

9-y-o ch g Glacial Storm (USA)-Furryvale (Furry Glen)
L Wells R A Gadd

Placings:32/22002314-P (0436)
2003/04: 22⁷GF,

	Starts	1st	2nd	3rd	Win & Pl
Hurdles	1	0	0	0	
Career Total	**11**	**1**	**4**	**2**	**9718**
101	4/03	Extr	3m110y	E(0-110)HHdl	G-F £4810

Total win prize-money £4810

Going:	Sf: 0-0 GS: 0-0 Gd: 0-0 GF: - Fm: 0-1
Distance:	2m/2m3: 0-0 2m4-2m7: 0-1 3m+: 0-0
Track:	LH: 0-1 RH: 0-0 Tight: 0-1 Gall: 0-0
Aids:	Bl: 0-0 Vi: 0-0 Tstrap: 0-0 Ckp: 0-0
Best Rating:	102 5/01 NAbb 2m1f gd-fm NHF

Despite his saddle having slipped badly lost his maiden tag over hurdles in 3m fast ground handicap at Exeter April 2003.

Big Rob (IRE)

86   **88+**

5-y-o b g Bob Back (USA)-Native Shore (IRE) (Be My Native (USA))
B G Powell P H Betts

Placings:56P (4167)
2003/04: 16⁵GS, 16⁶GS, 21⁷PG,

	Starts	1st	2nd	3rd	Win & Pl
NH Flat	1	0	0	0	
Hurdles	2	0	0	0	
Career Total	**3**	**0**	**0**	**0**	

Going:	Sf: 0-0 GS: 0-2 Gd: 0-1 GF: - Fm: 0-0
Distance:	2m/2m3: 0-2 2m4-2m7: 0-1 3m+: 0-0
Track:	LH: 0-1 RH: 0-2 Tight: 0-0 Gall: 0-2
Aids:	Bl: 0-0 Vi: 0-0 Tstrap: 0-0 Ckp: 0-0
Best Rating:	89 12/03 Hntg 2m110y gd-sft NHF

Big Smoke (IRE)

65   **31**

4-y-o gr g Perugino (USA)-Lightning Bug (Prince Bee)
J Howard Johnson (B J Meehan 6/10) M McKernan

Placings:000 (4461)
2003/04: 16⁰G, 16⁰G, 16⁰HY,

	Starts	1st	2nd	3rd	Win & Pl
Hurdles	3	0	0	0	
Career Total	**3**	**0**	**0**	**0**	

Going:	Sf: 0-1 GS: 0-0 Gd: 0-2 GF: - Fm: 0-0
Distance:	2m/2m3: 0-3 2m4-2m7: 0-0 3m+: 0-0
Track:	LH: 0-1 RH: 0-2 Tight: 0-2 Gall: 0-1
Aids:	Bl: 0-0 Vi: 0-0 Tstrap: 0-0 Ckp: 0-0
Best Rating:	31 2/04 Muss 2m good Hdl

Big Star (IRE)

94   **67**

7-y-o ro g Fourstars Allstar (USA)-Dame Blakeney (IRE) (Blakeney)
M A Barnes (J S Haldane 15/5) Gordon Davidson & Russell Hall

Placings:0/00-005 (4881)
2003/04: 16⁰G, 16⁰G, 17⁵GS,

	Starts	1st	2nd	3rd	Win & Pl
NH Flat	1	0	0	0	0
Hurdles	2	0	0	0	0
Career Total	**6**	**0**	**0**	**0**	**0**

Going:	Sf: 0-0 GS: 0-1 Gd: 0-2 GF: - Fm: 0-0
Distance:	2m/2m3: 0-3 2m4-2m7: 0-0 3m+: 0-0
Track:	LH: 0-1 RH: 0-2 Tight: 0-1 Gall: 0-0
Aids:	Bl: 0-0 Vi: 0-0 Tstrap: 0-0 Ckp: 0-0
Best Rating:	69 4/04 Kels 2m110y good Hdl

Big Tree (FR)

87   **62**

6-y-o ch g Apple Tree (FR)-Maria Cara (FR) (Trepan (FR))
J M Jefferson Mr & Mrs Raymond Anderson Green

Placings:52P00 (3356)
2003/04: 17⁵GF, 17²G, 22⁶PG, 16⁶GF, 18⁶S,

	Starts	1st	2nd	3rd	Win & Pl
NH Flat	2	0	1	0	562
Hurdles	3	0	0	0	0
Career Total	**5**	**0**	**1**	**0**	**562**

Going:	Sf: 0-1 GS: 0-0 Gd: 0-2 GF: - Fm: 0-2
Distance:	2m/2m3: 0-4 2m4-2m7: 0-1 3m+: 0-0
Track:	LH: 0-2 RH: 0-3 Tight: 0-2 Gall: 0-0
Aids:	Bl: 0-0 Vi: 0-0 Tstrap: 0-0 Ckp: 0-0
Best Rating:	98 10/03 Carl 2m1f good NHF

Related to a French Flat winner and has shown enough in two starts in bumpers at Carlisle in autumn of 2003 to suggest he can win races, especially when sent chasing in due course.

Big Wheel

98(92c)   (94c)**115**

9-y-o ch g Mujtahid (USA)-Numuthej (USA) (Nureyev (USA))
N G Richards Hale Racing Limited

Placings:45/1041113/F001P3P/F512-43211 (1686)
2003/04: 16⁴G, 20³G, 17²GF, 16¹F, 16¹GF,

	Starts	1st	2nd	3rd	Win & Pl
Hurdles	5	2	1	1	10741
Career Total	**25**	**8**	**2**	**3**	**26968**
115	10/03	Kels	2m	D(0-115)HHdl	G-F £3419
107	10/03	Kels	2m	D(0-120)HHdl	FRM £5434
105	3/03	Sedg	2m1f	G(0-90)HHdl	GD £2408
105	1/01	Tntn	2m3f110y	F(0-105)HHdl	SFT £2604
103	3/00	Ludl	2m	F Hdl	GD £2730
109	3/00	Hrfd	2m1f	G Hdl	GD £2128
100	1/00	Winc	2m	F Hdl	G-S £1939
102	11/99	Ludl	2m	G Hdl	GD £1968

Total win prize-money £22630

Going:	Sf: 0-0 GS: 0-0 Gd: 0-2 GF: - Fm: 2-3
Distance:	2m/2m3: 2-4 2m4-2m7: 0-1 3m+: 0-0
Track:	LH: 0-1 RH: 0-2 Tight: 0-1 Gall: 0-0
Aids:	Bl: 0-0 Vi: 0-0 Tstrap: 0-0 Ckp: 0-0
Best Rating:	115 10/03 Kels 2m gd-fm Hdl

Moderate hurdler; effective on a sound surface or softer; stays two miles-three but outstayed when tried over an extended two miles-five; well suited by a sharp track; goes well fresh.

Bigwig (IRE)

95   **81**

11-y-o ch g Thatching-Sabaah (USA) (Nureyev (USA))
G L Moore Mrs Elizabeth Kiernan

Placings:6504/405P0034/511562026/62O250411/06F3301
2/044060116/005300004-130   **(0602)**
2003/04: 22¹GF, 21³GF, 22⁰G,

	Starts	1st	2nd	3rd	Win & Pl
Hurdles	3	1	0	1	3563
Career Total	**59**	**8**	**5**	**5**	**26931**
86	5/03	Winc	2m6f	F(0-100)HHdl	G-F	£3206
99	4/02	Plum	2m5f	E(0-105)HHdl	G-F	£2975
95	3/02	Plum	2m5f	F(0-90)Hdl	G-S	£1928
104	4/01	Plum	2m5f	F(0-105)HHdl	HVY	£2901
110	4/00	Plum	2m5f	E(0-105)HHdl	G-S	£2800
110	4/00	Plum	2m5f	F Hdl	G-S	£2758
97	8/98	Worc	2m2f	E(0-115)HHdl	GD	£2442
78	5/98	Hntg	2m110y	G(0-95)HHdl	G-F	£1716

Total win prize-money £20729

Going:	Sf: 0-0 GS: 0-0 Gd: 0-1 GF: - Fm: 1-2
Distance:	2m/2m3: 0-0 **2m4-2m7: 1-3** 3m+: 0-0
Track:	LH: 0-0 **RH: 1-2** Tight: 0-1 Gall: 0-1
Aids:	**Bl: 1-3** Vi: 0-0 Tstrap: 0-0 Ckp: 0-0
Best Rating:	110 4/00 Plum 2m5f gd-sft Hdl

Plating-class hurdler; fair sort at best, but on the decline now; course specialist a Plumpton; suited by testing ground, but acts on faster; usually wears blinkers; best in the spring.

Biliverdin (IRE)
105   **136**
10-y-o b g Bob Back (USA)-Straw Beret (USA) (Chief's Crown (USA))
G B Balding   Theo Waddington And Bernard Keay

Placings:21/100/00/1P25/FF3234/6111   **(4955)**
2003/04: 17⁶G, 19¹GS, 23¹G, 20¹G,

	Starts	1st	2nd	3rd	Win & Pl
Chases	4	3	0	0	29041
Career Total	**21**	**6**	**3**	**2**	**79298**
135	4/04	Sand	2m4f110yB HCh		GD	£16616
136	4/04	Extr	2m7f110yD Ch		GD	£7504
122	3/04	Extr	2m3f110yE Ch		G-S	£4920
105	5/00	Hntg	2m110y E Hdl		GD	£2564
124	2/99	Punc	2m	NHF		HVY	£3683
116	4/98	Punc	2m	NHF		G-Y	£25652

Total win prize-money £60941

Going:	Sf: 0-0 GS: 1-1 Gd: 2-3 GF: - Fm: 0-0
Distance:	2m/2m3: 0-1 **2m4-2m7: 2-2** 3m+: 1-1
Track:	LH: 0-0 **RH: 3-4** Tight: 0-0 Gall: 0-0
Aids:	Bl: 0-0 Vi: 0-0 Tstrap: 0-0 Ckp: 0-0
Best Rating:	136 4/04 Extr 2m7f110y good Ch

Useful novice chaser; lightly raced due to injury problems; returned after missing a season to win three in the spring of 2004; stays 3m, effective at 2m 4f; acts on a good or softer.

Bill Brown
91   **76**
6-y-o b g North Briton-Dickies Girl (Saxon Farm)
R Dickin   The Lordy Racing Partnership

Placings:0006   **(4844)**
2003/04: 16⁶G, 16⁰G, 16⁰G, 17⁶G,

	Starts	1st	2nd	3rd	Win & Pl
NH Flat	1	0	0	0	0
Hurdles	3	0	0	0	254
Career Total	**4**	**0**	**0**	**0**	**254**

Going:	Sf: 0-1 GS: 0-0 Gd: 0-3 GF: - Fm: 0-0
Distance:	2m/2m3: 0-4 2m4-2m7: 0-0 3m+: 0-0
Track:	LH: 0-2 RH: 0-2 Tight: 0-0 Gall: 0-3
Aids:	Bl: 0-0 Vi: 0-0 Tstrap: 0-0 Ckp: 0-0
Best Rating:	76 3/04 Hntg 2m110y good Hdl

Bill Haze
8-y-o ch g Romany Rye-Brilliant Haze Vii (Damsire Unregistered)
P Dando   P Dando

Placings:P   **(4815)**
2003/04: 24⁰G,

	Starts	1st	2nd	3rd	Win & Pl
Chases	1	0	0	0	
Career Total	**1**	**0**	**0**	**0**	

Going:	Sf: 0-0 GS: 0-0 Gd: 0-1 GF: - Fm: 0-0
Distance:	2m/2m3: 0-0 2m4-2m7: 0-0 3m+: 0-1
Track:	LH: 0-1 RH: 0-0 Tight: 0-0 Gall: 0-0
Aids:	Bl: 0-1 Vi: 0-0 Tstrap: 0-0 Ckp: 0-0

Bill Me Up (IRE)
8-y-o b g Shardari-Little Credit (Little Buskins)
J Heard   J Heard

Placings:0000/U-2   **(4696)**
2003/04: 19²G,

	Starts	1st	2nd	3rd	Win & Pl
Chases	1	0	1	0	1132
Career Total	**6**	**0**	**1**	**0**	**1132**

Going:	Sf: 0-0 GS: 0-0 Gd: 0-1 GF: - Fm: 0-0
Distance:	2m/2m3: 0-0 2m4-2m7: 0-1 3m+: 0-0
Track:	LH: 0-0 RH: 0-1 Tight: 0-0 Gall: 0-0
Aids:	Bl: 0-0 Vi: 0-0 Tstrap: 0-0 Ckp: 0-0
Best Rating:	103 4/04 Extr 2m3f110y good Ch

Bill Owen
103   **85**
8-y-o ch g Nicholas Bill-Pollys Owen (Master Owen)
D P Keane   Tim/Mary Barton & Wadswickcountrystore

Placings:P54-P1   **(1169)**
2003/04: 25⁰GS, 18¹GF,

	Starts	1st	2nd	3rd	Win & Pl
Chases	2	1	0	0	3348
Career Total	**5**	**1**	**0**	**0**	**3783**
85	8/03	Font	2m2f	F(0-90)HCh	G-F	£3347

Total win prize-money £3348

Going:	Sf: 0-0 GS: 0-1 Gd: 0-0 GF: - Fm: 1-1
Distance:	**2m/2m3: 1-1** 2m4-2m7: 0-0 3m+: 0-1
Track:	LH: 0-0 RH: 0-1 **Tight: 1-1** Gall: 0-0
Aids:	Bl: 0-0 Vi: 0-0 Tstrap: 0-0 Ckp: 0-0
Best Rating:	85 8/03 Font 2m2f gd-fm Ch

Bill's Echo
(99h)   **(90+h)**
5-y-o br g Double Eclipse (IRE)-Bit On Edge (Henbit (USA))
R C Guest   Burns Partnership

Placings:5504-36F643F   **(4593)**
2003/04: 19³G, 16⁶G, 16⁵F, 20⁶G, 19⁴G, 17³G, 16⁶G,

	Starts	1st	2nd	3rd	Win & Pl
Hurdles	6	0	0	2	843
Chases	1	0	0	0	0
Career Total	**11**	**0**	**0**	**2**	**843**

Going:	Sf: 0-1 GS: 0-0 Gd: 0-6 GF: - Fm: 0-0

Distance:	2m/2m3: 0-4 2m4-2m7: 0-3 3m+: 0-0
Track:	LH: 0-4 RH: 0-0 Tight: 0-3 Gall: 0-2
Aids:	Bl: 0-0 Vi: 0-0 Tstrap: 0-0 Ckp: 0-0
Best Rating:	100 3/04 Hntg 2m110y good Ch

Moderate novice hurdler; finds little under pressure.

Billesey (IRE)
                         89f
6-y-o b g King's Ride-Rose Runner (IRE) (Roselier (FR))
S E H Sherwood   Aiden Murphy

Placings:1   **(4495)**
2003/04: 16¹G,

	Starts	1st	2nd	3rd	Win & Pl
NH Flat	1	1	0	0	1876
Career Total	**1**	**1**	**0**	**0**	**1876**
89	3/04	Strf	2m110y H NHF		GD	£1876

Total win prize-money £1876

Going:	Sf: 0-0 GS: 0-0 Gd: 1-1 GF: - Fm: 0-0
Distance:	**2m/2m3: 1-1** 2m4-2m7: 0-0 3m+: 0-0
Track:	LH: 0-0 RH: 0-0 Tight: 0-0 Gall: 0-0
Aids:	Bl: 0-0 Vi: 0-0 Tstrap: 0-0 Ckp: 0-0
Best Rating:	89 3/04 Strf 2m110y good NHF

Billie John (IRE)
107(96h)   (103+h)**115**
9-y-o ch g Boyne Valley-Lovestream (Sandy Creek)
Mrs K Walton   Mrs Patricia M Wilson

Placings:0/60620/14241-13F1443   **(1767)**
2003/04: 17¹G, 16³G, 16⁶GF, 16¹GF, 17⁴G, 17⁴GF, 17³G,

	Starts	1st	2nd	3rd	Win & Pl
Hurdles	1	0	0	1	2155
Chases	6	2	0	1	11590
Career Total	**18**	**4**	**2**	**2**	**22247**
114	7/03	Sedg	2m110y	E(0-110)HCh	G-F	£4667
98	4/03	Kels	2m1f	D Ch	GD	£5317
103	9/02	Bang	2m1f	D Hdl	GD	£3818
96	5/02	Hexm	2m110y	E Hdl	GD	£2548

Total win prize-money £16351

Going:	Sf: 0-0 GS: 0-0 Gd: 1-4 GF: - Fm: 1-3
Distance:	**2m/2m3: 2-7** 2m4-2m7: 0-0 3m+: 0-0
Track:	**LH: 2-4** RH: 0-3 **Tight: 2-4** Gall: 0-0
Aids:	Bl: 0-0 Vi: 0-0 Tstrap: 0-0 Ckp: 0-0
Best Rating:	115 9/03 MRas 2m1f110y gd-fm Ch

Modest chaser; acts on fast ground; best at around two miles.

Billy Ballbreaker (IRE)
98(92c)   (73+c)**93**
8-y-o br g Good Thyne (USA)-Droichead Dhamhile (IRE) (The Parson)
C L Tizzard   E Vickery & R Dibble

Placings:50/6-035360200   **(4242)**
2003/04: 22⁰G, 22³G, 22⁵GF, 24³G, 26⁶G, 24⁰G, 24²GS, 24⁰S, 24⁰G,

	Starts	1st	2nd	3rd	Win & Pl
Hurdles	6	0	1	1	1766
Chases	3	0	0	1	528
Career Total	**12**	**0**	**1**	**2**	**2294**

Going:	Sf: 0-1 GS: 0-1 Gd: 0-5 GF: - Fm: 0-2
Distance:	2m/2m3: 0-0 2m4-2m7: 0-3 3m+: 0-6
Track:	LH: 0-5 RH: 0-4 Tight: 0-7 Gall: 0-0

Aids: Bl: 0-0 Vi: 0-3 Tstrap: 0-0 Ckp: 0-0
Best Rating: 106 12/01 Newb 2m110y good NHF

Showed promise in bumpers late in 2001; moderate form at up to three miles over hurdles; did not take to fences; can pull hard.

Billy Brick

6-y-o b g Nalchik (USA)-Tilstock Maid (Rolfe (USA))
B R Foster Michael Brownrigg

Placings:0P (1136)
2003/04: 16⁰GF, 20⁰PG,

	Starts	1st	2nd	3rd	Win & Pl
NH Flat	1	0	0	0	0
Hurdles	1	0	0	0	0
Career Total	2	0	0	0	

Going: Sf: 0-0 GS: 0-0 Gd: 0-1 GF: - Fm: 0-1
Distance: 2m/2m3: 0-1 2m4-2m7: 0-1 3m+: 0-0
Track: LH: 0-2 RH: 0-0 Tight: 0-1 Gall: 0-0
Aids: Bl: 0-0 Vi: 0-0 Tstrap: 0-0 Ckp: 0-0
Best Rating: 42 7/03 Worc 2m gd-fm NHF

Billy Two Rivers (IRE)
100   78

5-y-o ch g Woodborough (USA)-Good Visibility (IRE) (Electric)
D R MacLeod Maurice W Chapman

Placings:0006P (4950)
2003/04: 16⁰GF, 16⁰S, 20⁰GS, 16⁰G, 20⁰GS,

	Starts	1st	2nd	3rd	Win & Pl
Hurdles	5	0	0	0	0
Career Total	5	0	0	0	

Going: Sf: 0-1 GS: 0-2 Gd: 0-1 GF: - Fm: 0-1
Distance: 2m/2m3: 0-3 2m4-2m7: 0-2 3m+: 0-0
Track: LH: 0-3 RH: 0-2 Tight: 0-3 Gall: 0-0
Aids: Bl: 0-0 Vi: 0-0 Tstrap: 0-0 Ckp: 0-0
Best Rating: 78 4/04 Kels 2m110y good Hdl

Billyvoddan (IRE)
98   92+

5-y-o b g Accordion-Derryclare (Pollerton)
H D Daly Trevor Hemmings

Placings:03363 (4181)
2003/04: 17⁰G, 16³GS, 16³S, 20⁶S, 16³G,

	Starts	1st	2nd	3rd	Win & Pl
NH Flat	2	0	0	1	272
Hurdles	3	0	0	2	1023
Career Total	5	0	0	3	1295

Going: Sf: 0-2 GS: 0-1 Gd: 0-2 GF: - Fm: 0-0
Distance: 2m/2m3: 0-4 2m4-2m7: 0-1 3m+: 0-0
Track: LH: 0-2 RH: 0-0 Tight: 0-0 Gall: 0-1
Aids: Bl: 0-0 Vi: 0-0 Tstrap: 0-0 Ckp: 0-0
Best Rating: 92 3/04 Hntg 2m110y good Hdl

Very modest form in bumpers and novice hurdles.

Billywill (IRE)
100(83h)   (72h)108+

10-y-o b/br g Topanoora-Sandy Maid (Sandy Creek)

J W Mullins (V Bowens 24/6) P F Kehoe

Placings:211265/5/353/000PFF0046-PP2123P (4398)
2003/04: 18⁸GY, 21⁸PG, 21²GF, 19¹GS, 20⁵S, 16³S, 32²PG,

	Starts	1st	2nd	3rd	Win & Pl
Chases	7	1	2	1	5427
Career Total	27	3	4	3	15054
108 12/03 Hrfd	2m3f	E(0-105)HCh	G-S	£2877	
115 11/98 Naas	2m	NHF	YLD	£2391	
101 10/98 Naas	2m	NHF	YLD	£3885	
				Total win prize-money	£9154

Going: Sf: 0-2 GS: 1-1 Gd: 0-2 GF: - Fm: 0-1
Distance: 2m/2m3: 1-3 2m4-2m7: 0-3 3m+: 0-1
Track: LH: 0-2 RH: 1-5 Tight: 0-3 Gall: 0-2
Aids: Bl: 0-0 Vi: 0-0 Tstrap: 1-4 Ckp: 0-1
Best Rating: 134 3/99 Chel 2m110y gd-sft NHF

Moderate chaser; improved form over fences since being fitted with a tongue-tie to correct a breathing problem; easy winner of weakly contested handicap at Hereford December 2003; stays two and half miles; acts on soft ground; has worn cheekpieces.

Bindaree (IRE)
116(91h)   (112+h)153+

10-y-o ch g Roselier (FR)-Flowing Tide (Main Reef)
N A Twiston-Davies H R Mould

Placings:31111240/1213U124U/0533601/0FU2406-F216U (4647)
2003/04: 27⁶FG, 26²GS, 29¹S, 29⁶GS, 36⁰UG,

	Starts	1st	2nd	3rd	Win & Pl
Chases	5	1	1	0	58050
Career Total	36	9	5	4	477366
153 12/03 Chep	3m5f110yA HCh	SFT	£47600		
148 4/02 Aint	4m4f A HCh	GD	£290000		
144 1/01 Asct	3m110y B Ch	G-S	£8807		
133 11/00 Chep	2m3f110yA Ch	SFT	£18000		
136 9/00 Prth	2m4f110yD Ch	HVY	£4771		
153 12/99 Chel	2m5f110yA Hdl	SFT	£16375		
153 12/99 Chel	3m A Hdl	G-S	£9525		
141 11/99 Chep	3m B Hdl	SFT	£7132		
135 10/99 Carl	3m110y E Hdl	GD	£2346		
			Total win prize-money	£404558	

Going: Sf: 1-1 GS: 0-2 Gd: 0-2 GF: - Fm: 0-0
Distance: 2m/2m3: 0-2 2m4-2m7: 0-0 3m+: 1-5
Track: LH: 1-5 RH: 0-0 Tight: 0-0 Gall: 0-0
Aids: Bl: 0-0 Vi: 0-0 Tstrap: 0-0 Ckp: 0-0
Best Rating: 153 12/03 Chep 3m5f110y soft Ch

Smart chaser; winner of the Grand National in 2002 and Welsh National in 2003, emphasising that he jumps well and stays forever; suited by going left-handed; effective on good and soft ground.

Bindy Bondy
95   65+

7-y-o b m Beveled (USA)-Rockmount Rose (Proverb)
J R Best Mrs V Palmer

Placings:000P-0506 (1081)
2003/04: 20⁰GF, 16⁵GF, 17⁰GF, 16⁶GF,

	Starts	1st	2nd	3rd	Win & Pl
Hurdles	4	0	0	0	0
Career Total	8	0	0	0	

Going: Sf: 0-0 GS: 0-0 Gd: 0-0 GF: - Fm: 0-4
Distance: 2m/2m3: 0-3 2m4-2m7: 0-1 3m+: 0-0
Track: LH: 0-3 RH: 0-1 Tight: 0-2 Gall: 0-0
Aids: Bl: 0-0 Vi: 0-0 Tstrap: 0-0 Ckp: 0-0
Best Rating: 82 2/03 Ludl 2m good NHF

Poor form in novice hurdles at up to 2m 4f; twice beaten in selling handicaps August 2003.

Binny Bay
99(99h)   (85 h)90

8-y-o b m Karinga Bay-Binny Grove (Sunyboy)
D McCain D McCain

Placings:000030034612/15623443-414PP05 (4139)
2003/04: 19⁴GF, 20¹G, 20⁴G, 20⁰PG, 25⁸PGS, 21⁰GS, 20⁰S,

	Starts	1st	2nd	3rd	Win & Pl
Chases	7	1	0	0	7894
Career Total	27	3	2	4	17933
90 7/03 Prth	2m4f110yE(0-105)HCh	GD	£7140		
90 5/02 Bang	2m4f D(0-110)HHdl	SFT	£3724		
85 4/02 Uttx	2m G Hdl	G-F	£1946		
			Total win prize-money	£12810	

Going: Sf: 0-0 GS: 0-2 Gd: 1-4 GF: - Fm: 0-1
Distance: 2m/2m3: 0-2 2m4-2m7: 1-5 3m+: 0-1
Track: LH: 0-3 RH: 1-4 Tight: 0-4 Gall: 0-0
Aids: Bl: 0-2 Vi: 0-0 Tstrap: 0-2 Ckp: 0-0
Best Rating: 90 7/03 Prth 2m4f110y good Ch

Modest novice chaser; stays two and a half miles; acts on any ground; has worn a tongue tie.

Bint St James
72   58+

9-y-o b m Shareef Dancer (USA)-St James's Antigua (IRE) (Law Society (USA))
W Clay Mrs Janet Dutton

Placings:550/P4U3F0P01P/402FPP0/005-P0 (4603)
2003/04: 20²HY, 17⁰G,

	Starts	1st	2nd	3rd	Win & Pl
Hurdles	2	0	0	0	
Career Total	25	1	1	1	2443
85 11/99 MRas	2m3f110yG(0-90)HHdl	G-S	£1490		
			Total win prize-money	£1490	

Going: Sf: 0-1 GS: 0-0 Gd: 0-1 GF: - Fm: 0-0
Distance: 2m/2m3: 0-1 2m4-2m7: 0-1 3m+: 0-0
Track: LH: 0-1 RH: 0-1 Tight: 0-1 Gall: 0-0
Aids: Bl: 0-0 Vi: 0-0 Tstrap: 0-0 Ckp: 0-0
Best Rating: 85 11/99 MRas 2m3f110y gd-sft Hdl

Birchall Belle (IRE)
92f   74+f

6-y-o b m Presenting-Queenford Belle (Celtic Cone)
P D Evans Mrs Claire Massey

Placings:0-6P (2945)
2003/04: 16⁶G, 16⁰PS,

	Starts	1st	2nd	3rd	Win & Pl
NH Flat	2	0	0	0	0
Career Total	3	0	0	0	

Going: Sf: 0-0 GS: 0-1 Gd: 0-1 GF: - Fm: 0-0
Distance: 2m/2m3: 0-2 2m4-2m7: 0-0 3m+: 0-0
Track: LH: 0-1 RH: 0-1 Tight: 0-0 Gall: 0-0
Aids: Bl: 0-0 Vi: 0-0 Tstrap: 0-0 Ckp: 0-0
Best Rating: 74 12/03 Ludl 2m good NHF

Birdwatch
98   93

6-y-o b g Minshaanshu Amad (USA)-Eider (Niniski (USA))
Mrs M Reveley Jeremy Mitchell And Janet Powney

Placings:63235 (4852)
2003/04: 16⁶G, 16³GS, 16²HY, 16³S, 20⁵GS,

	Starts	1st	2nd	3rd	Win & Pl
NH Flat	4	0	1	2	1147
Hurdles	1	0	0	0	0
Career Total	5	0	1	2	1147

Going: Sf: 0-2 GS: 0-2 Gd: 0-1 GF: - Fm: 0-0
Distance: 2m/2m3: 0-4 2m4-2m7: 0-1 3m+: 0-0
Track: LH: 0-5 RH: 0-0 Tight: 0-0 Gall: 0-0
Aids: Bl: 0-0 Vi: 0-0 Tstrap: 0-0 Ckp: 0-0
Best Rating: 107 1/04 Ayr 2m heavy NHF

Has shown ability in bumpers, placed three times.

Birkdale (IRE)

(99h) (103h)
13-y-o gr g Roselier (FR)-Clonroche Lady (Charlottesvilles Flyer)
Ferdy Murphy Miss J V Morgan

Placings:02/221111P/215211134/4511101P/50/232P0/36P
P (4272)
2003/04: 24³GS, 25⁶G, 25ᴾGS, 26ᴾG,

	Starts	1st	2nd	3rd	Win & Pl
Hurdles	1	0	0	1	415
Chases	3	0	0	0	0
Career Total	37	12	7	3	66137
134	3/00	Ayr	3m1f	D(0-125)HCh	HVY	£5215
134	1/00	Kels	3m1f	D(0-125)HCh	GD	£3867
129	12/99	Ayr	3m1f	D(0-125)HCh	HVY	£4198
155	12/99	Hayd	2m4f	B HHdl	HVY	£6781
148	2/99	Weth	2m7f	C(0-135)HHdl	GD	£4435
152	1/99	Weth	3m1f	D(0-125)HHdl	SFT	£2786
145	1/99	Newc	3m	D(0-125)HHdl	SFT	£2775
125	11/98	Kels	2m6f110yE Ch		HVY	£3290
127	3/98	Ayr	3m110y	D(0-125)HHdl	SFT	£2747
120	1/98	Catt	3m1f110yE Hdl		SFT	£2598
118	12/97	Sedg	3m3f110yE Hdl		SFT	£2355
103	12/97	Hexm	3m	E Hdl	SFT	£2511

Total win prize-money £43560

Going: Sf: 0-0 GS: 0-2 Gd: 0-2 GF: - Fm: 0-0
Distance: 2m/2m3: 0-0 2m4-2m7: 0-0 3m+: 0-4
Track: LH: 0-3 RH: 0-1 Tight: 0-0 Gall: 0-0
Aids: Bl: 0-0 Vi: 0-0 Tstrap: 0-0 Ckp: 0-0
Best Rating: 155 12/99 Hayd 2m4f heavy Hdl

Formerly useful chaser/smart hurdler; fair sort these days; genuine front-running stayer; best suited by a soft surface; stays three miles plus.

Birth Of The Blues
87 51
8-y-o ch g Efisio-Great Steps (Vaigly Great)
A Charlton J M Sancaster

Placings:P000/0-0 (2238)
2003/04: 16⁰G,

	Starts	1st	2nd	3rd	Win & Pl
Hurdles	1	0	0	0	
Career Total	6	0	0	0	

Going: Sf: 0-0 GS: 0-0 Gd: 0-1 GF: - Fm: 0-0
Distance: 2m/2m3: 0-1 2m4-2m7: 0-0 3m+: 0-0
Track: LH: 0-0 RH: 0-1 Tight: 0-0 Gall: 0-0
Aids: Bl: 0-0 Vi: 0-0 Tstrap: 0-0 Ckp: 0-0
Best Rating: 57 12/00 Fknm 2m gd-sft Hdl

Bishop's Blade
60
7-y-o b g Sure Blade (USA)-Myrtilla (Beldale Flutter (USA))
E Retter Edward Retter

Placings:0-4 (1519)
2003/04: 20⁴G,

	Starts	1st	2nd	3rd	Win & Pl
Hurdles	1	0	0	0	0
Career Total	2	0	0	0	0

Going: Sf: 0-0 GS: 0-0 Gd: 0-1 GF: - Fm: 0-0
Distance: 2m/2m3: 0-0 2m4-2m7: 0-1 3m+: 0-0
Track: LH: 0-0 RH: 0-0 Tight: 0-1 Gall: 0-0
Aids: Bl: 0-1 Vi: 0-0 Tstrap: 0-0 Ckp: 0-0
Best Rating: 60 1/03 Extr 2m3f gd-sft Hdl

Poor staying maiden on the Flat for Jeff King; only moderate form to date over hurdles; wears blinkers.

Bishop's Bridge (IRE)
106f 100f
6-y-o b g Norwich-River Swell (IRE) (Over The River (FR))
Andrew Turnell Mrs M R Taylor

Placings:0-230 (4920)
2003/04: 16²G, 16³GS, 16⁰GS,

	Starts	1st	2nd	3rd	Win & Pl
NH Flat	3	0	1	1	1005
Career Total	4	0	1	1	1005

Going: Sf: 0-0 GS: 0-2 Gd: 0-1 GF: - Fm: 0-0
Distance: 2m/2m3: 0-3 2m4-2m7: 0-0 3m+: 0-0
Track: LH: 0-2 RH: 0-1 Tight: 0-0 Gall: 0-0
Aids: Bl: 0-0 Vi: 0-0 Tstrap: 0-0 Ckp: 0-0
Best Rating: 100 3/04 Kemp 2m good NHF

Placed in bumpers at Kempton in March and Wetherby two weeks later.

Bison King (IRE)
101 109
7-y-o b g King's Ride-Valantonia (IRE) (Over The River (FR))
C R Egerton Mrs Evelyn Hankinson

Placings:20-331530 (4451)
2003/04: 20³GS, 20³G, 26¹GS, 24³G, 24³G, 24⁰GS,

	Starts	1st	2nd	3rd	Win & Pl
Hurdles	6	1	0	3	5445
Career Total	8	1	1	3	6159
108	12/03	Hntg	3m2f	E Hdl		G-S	£3101

Total win prize-money £3101

Going: Sf: 0-0 GS: 1-3 Gd: 0-3 GF: - Fm: 0-0
Distance: 2m/2m3: 0-0 2m4-2m7: 0-2 3m+: 1-4
Track: LH: 0-2 RH: 1-4 Tight: 0-1 Gall: 1-1
Aids: Bl: 0-0 Vi: 0-0 Tstrap: 0-0 Ckp: 0-0
Best Rating: 109 3/04 Bang 3m good Hdl

Modest hurdler; stays well; acts on good ground.

Bisquet-De-Bouche
101 (0c)72
10-y-o ch m Most Welcome-Larive (Blakeney)
A W Carroll Martin Brook

Placings:0/0202B12P/63641/35/05P5P-463 (0487)

Bishop's Blade

2003/04: 24⁴G, 27⁵G, 22³GF,

	Starts	1st	2nd	3rd	Win & Pl
Hurdles	3	0	0	1	438
Career Total	24	2	3	3	9628
97	4/01	Winc	2m6f	F(0-105)HHdl	SFT	£3724
87	2/00	Catt	3m1f110y			F(0-100)HHdl
GD	£2012					

Total win prize-money £5737

Going: Sf: 0-0 GS: 0-0 Gd: 0-2 GF: - Fm: 0-1
Distance: 2m/2m3: 0-0 2m4-2m7: 0-1 3m+: 0-2
Track: LH: 0-3 RH: 0-0 Tight: 0-2 Gall: 0-0
Aids: Bl: 0-0 Vi: 0-0 Tstrap: 0-0 Ckp: 0-0
Best Rating: 97 4/01 Winc 2m6f soft Hdl

Plating-class hurdler; possibly a shade unlucky when close third despite finishing lame in 2m 6f selling handicap Newton Abbot May 2003; never a factor when tried over fences; best on a sound surface; stays three miles.

Bit O Magic (IRE)
110 107
12-y-o ch g Henbit (USA)-Arpal Magic (Master Owen)
Ferdy Murphy Geoff Adam

Placings:1/20/4F15344/650/31/U2P41/323030F122F-3FF (0648)
2003/04: 22³G, 17ᶠG, 20ᶠGF,

	Starts	1st	2nd	3rd	Win & Pl
Chases	3	0	0	1	1257
Career Total	34	5	5	6	26555
107	1/03	Muss	2m4f	E(0-110)HCh	GD	£5343
101	4/02	Hntg	2m110y	D(0-115)HCh	G-F	£4059
101	10/00	Kels	2m2f	F(0-110)HHdl	SFT	£1879
88	12/98	Muss	2m4f	E Hdl	GD	£2262
99	5/96	Prth	2m110y	H NHF	FRM	£1966

Total win prize-money £15510

Going: Sf: 0-0 GS: 0-0 Gd: 0-2 GF: - Fm: 0-1
Distance: 2m/2m3: 0-1 2m4-2m7: 0-2 3m+: 0-0
Track: LH: 0-3 RH: 0-0 Tight: 0-2 Gall: 0-0
Aids: Bl: 0-0 Vi: 0-0 Tstrap: 0-0 Ckp: 0-0
Best Rating: 107 4/03 Kels 2m1f good Ch

Modest handicap chaser; winner at Musselburgh in January; stays two miles four; seems to act on most ground; has worn blinkers.

Bit O' Gold
52 1
6-y-o b g Henbit (USA)-Run Of Gold (Deep Run)
Mrs K B Mactaggart Mrs J Roncoroni

Placings:0000-0 (0040)
2003/04: 16⁰G,

	Starts	1st	2nd	3rd	Win & Pl
Hurdles	1	0	0	0	
Career Total	5	0	0	0	

Going: Sf: 0-0 GS: 0-0 Gd: 0-1 GF: - Fm: 0-0
Distance: 2m/2m3: 0-1 2m4-2m7: 0-0 3m+: 0-0
Track: LH: 0-1 RH: 0-0 Tight: 0-1 Gall: 0-0
Aids: Bl: 0-0 Vi: 0-0 Tstrap: 0-0 Ckp: 0-0
Best Rating: 55 6/02 Hexm 2m110y good NHF

Bit O'Speed (IRE)
13-y-o b g Henbit (USA)-Speedy Debbie (Pollerton)
Mrs S Richardson James Richardson

Placings:0/00/143331/525545PP/42/13-P (0204)

2003/04: 20PGF;

	Starts	1st	2nd	3rd	Win & Pl
Chases	1	0	0	0	
Career Total	22	3	2	4	10839
106 4/03 Strf	3m		H Ch	GD	£2898
108 9/97 Gway	2m1f		Ch	Y-S	£3391
90 5/97 Dpat	2m1f172y		Hdl	GF	£1695
				Total win prize-money	£7985

Going:	Sf: 0-0 GS: 0-0 Gd: 0-0 GF: - Fm: 0-1
Distance:	2m/2m3: 0-0 2m4-2m7: 0-1 3m+: 0-0
Track:	LH: 0-1 RH: 0-0 Tight: 0-0 Gall: 0-0
Aids:	Bl: 0-0 Vi: 0-0 Tstrap: 0-0 Ckp: 0-0
Best Rating:	115 5/98 Wxfd 2m4f good Ch

Hunter chaser; winning hurdler and chaser in his native Ireland; made all to land a Stratford hunter chase in April 2003; found 2m 5f inadequate when third at the same venue a week later; suited by a sound surface and three miles.

Bit Of A Broad

7-y-o b m Tudor Diver-Broad Appeal (Star Appeal)
R Shiels R Shiels

Placings:0PP (0690)
2003/04: 16DG, 24PGF, 20PGF,

	Starts	1st	2nd	3rd	Win & Pl
NH Flat	1	0	0	0	0
Hurdles	2	0	0	0	0
Career Total	3	0	0	0	

Going:	Sf: 0-0 GS: 0-0 Gd: 0-1 GF: - Fm: 0-2
Distance:	2m/2m3: 0-1 2m4-2m7: 0-0 3m+: 0-1
Track:	LH: 0-1 RH: 0-1 Tight: 0-0 Gall: 0-0
Aids:	Bl: 0-0 Vi: 0-0 Tstrap: 0-0 Ckp: 0-0
Best Rating:	51 5/03 Kels 2m110y good NHF

Bit Of A Snob
106(59h)   73
13-y-o b g St Columbus-Classey (Dubassoff (USA))
J S King Miss S Douglas-Pennant

Placings:PP02043/1P1313P/P01/PPP0-P032FP0 (3876)
2003/04: 21PG, 19DG, 19DGF, 18PGF, 16FGF, 16PG, 20PG,

	Starts	1st	2nd	3rd	Win & Pl
Hurdles	1	0	0	0	0
Chases	6	0	1	1	1010
Career Total	24	4	2	4	15672
98 8/01 Hntg	2m110y	F(0-100)HCh		G-F	£2660
104 8/00 NAbb	2m110y	F(0-110)HCh		G-F	£4065
98 6/00 Hrfd	2m	E Ch		G-F	£3110
100 5/00 Winc	2m	E Hdl		FRM	£2751
				Total win prize-money	£12587

Going:	Sf: 0-0 GS: 0-0 Gd: 0-3 GF: - Fm: 0-4
Distance:	2m/2m3: 0-4 2m4-2m7: 0-0 3-3m+: 0-0
Track:	LH: 0-3 RH: 0-3 Tight: 0-2 Gall: 0-0
Aids:	Bl: 0-5 Vi: 0-0 Tstrap: 0-0 Ckp: 0-0
Best Rating:	104 8/00 NAbb 2m110y good Ch

Has been on the decline since winning 2m handicap chase at Huntingdon in August 2001; acts on a sound surface.

Bitofamixup (IRE)

13-y-o br g Strong Gale-Geeaway (Gala Performance (ZIM))
M J Roberts Mike Roberts

Placings:011/12122/164U/P2PP/63P3/06UU-11PFP (4626)
2003/04: 25TGF, 28TG, 26PG, 24FG, 21PG,

	Starts	1st	2nd	3rd	Win & Pl
Chases	5	2	0	0	22354
Career Total	29	7	4	2	56965
116 5/03 Strf	3m4f	B Ch		GD	£20436
112 5/03 Folk	3m1f	H Ch		G-F	£1918
140 5/98 Worc	2m7f110yE Ch			GD	£3566
131 2/98 Font	3m2f110yD Ch			GD	£3975
126 5/97 Bang	3m110y	H Ch		GD	£1548
137 4/97 Aint	3m1f	B Ch		GD	£7107
108 2/97 Hntg	3m	H Ch		G-S	£1262
				Total win prize-money	£39813

Going:	Sf: 0-0 GS: 0-0 Gd: 1-4 GF: - Fm: 1-1
Distance:	2m/2m3: 0-0 2m4-2m7: 0-1 3m+: 2-4
Track:	LH: 1-3 RH: 1-1 Tight: 2-5 Gall: 0-0
Aids:	Bl: 0-0 Vi: 0-0 Tstrap: 2-4 Ckp: 0-0
Best Rating:	146 4/98 Ayr 3m1f good Ch

Formerly smart hunter chaser; seems to have benefitted from having his tongue tied again and won hunter chase at Folkestone May 2003; showed he is still a force to be reckoned with when springing 25/1 surprise in 'Horse and Hound Cup' at Stratford next time; disappointing since; stays three and a half miles; acts well on a sound surface.

Bitter Sweet
102   104
8-y-o g m Deploy-Julia Flyte (Drone (USA))
J L Spearing Masonaires

Placings:000/132403/2224135-325 (1609)
2003/04: 16DGF, 17PGF, 16PGF,

	Starts	1st	2nd	3rd	Win & Pl
Hurdles	3	0	1	1	1545
Career Total	19	2	5	4	15615
103 11/02 Wwck	2m	D(0-125)HHdl		GD	£3770
83 9/01 Worc	2m	E Hdl		G-F	£2443
				Total win prize-money	£6213

Going:	Sf: 0-0 GS: 0-0 Gd: 0-0 GF: - Fm: 0-3
Distance:	2m/2m3: 0-3 2m4-2m7: 0-0 3m+: 0-0
Track:	LH: 0-1 RH: 0-2 Tight: 0-1 Gall: 0-1
Aids:	Bl: 0-0 Vi: 0-0 Tstrap: 0-0 Ckp: 0-0
Best Rating:	104 5/03 Wwck 2m gd-fm Hdl

Modest handicap hurdler; suited by good or faster ground and likes to be produced late.

Black Bob (IRE)
67   52
7-y-o b g Good Thyne (USA)-Midsummer Blends (IRE) (Duky)
J S Haldane John & Mary Stenhouse

Placings:P0P (3825)
2003/04: 20PS, 20PGS, 20PS,

	Starts	1st	2nd	3rd	Win & Pl
Hurdles	3	0	0	0	
Career Total	3	0	0	0	

Going:	Sf: 0-2 GS: 0-1 Gd: 0-0 GF: - Fm: 0-0
Distance:	2m/2m3: 0-0 2m4-2m7: 0-3 3m+: 0-0
Track:	LH: 0-3 RH: 0-0 Tight: 0-0 Gall: 0-0
Aids:	Bl: 0-0 Vi: 0-0 Tstrap: 0-0 Ckp: 0-0
Best Rating:	52 12/03 Hayd 2m4f gd-sft Hdl

Black Church Lad (IRE)
111   106
8-y-o gr g Ashmolean (USA)-Petit Guest (Northern Guest (USA))

Michael Hourigan Mrs F Hewitt-Murphy

Placings:300006.5200/21460S24303-212304P000 (4372)
2003/04: 18PG, 20TG, 16PYS, 16PG, 20PS, 20PY, 24PS, 20PHY, 20PY, 16PGF,

	Starts	1st	2nd	3rd	Win & Pl
Hurdles	10	1	2	1	11468
Career Total	31	2	5	4	22687
107 5/03 Klny	2m4f	(74-109)HHdl		GD	£6272
89 5/02 Clon	2m	(74-109)HHdl		Y-S	£4868
				Total win prize-money	£11141

Going:	Sf: 0-3 GS: 0-0 Gd: 1-3 GF: - Fm: 0-1
Distance:	2m/2m3: 0-4 2m4-2m7: 1-5 3m+: 0-1
Track:	LH: 0-2 RH: 0-5 Tight: 0-1 Gall: 0-0
Aids:	Bl: 0-0 Vi: 0-0 Tstrap: 0-0 Ckp: 0-1
Best Rating:	108 5/03 Punc 2m yld-sft Hdl

Black Collar
97f   87f
5-y-o br m Bob's Return (IRE)-Rosemoss (Le Moss)
T D Walford Neil Watson

Placings:6 (4962)
2003/04: 17PG,

	Starts	1st	2nd	3rd	Win & Pl
NH Flat	1	0	0	0	0
Career Total	1	0	0	0	0

Going:	Sf: 0-0 GS: 0-0 Gd: 0-0 GF: - Fm: 0-0
Distance:	2m/2m3: 0-1 2m4-2m7: 0-0 3m+: 0-0
Track:	LH: 0-0 RH: 0-1 Tight: 0-1 Gall: 0-0
Aids:	Bl: 0-0 Vi: 0-0 Tstrap: 0-0 Ckp: 0-0
Best Rating:	87 4/04 MRas 2m1f110y good NHF

Black De Bessy (FR)
99   120+
6-y-o b g Perrault-Emerald City (Top Ville)
D R C Elsworth (J Bertran De Balanda 6/1) Mrs Derek Fletcher

Placings:14/305P0042-3511242304313 (4930)
2003/04: 17PG, 19PG, 18TGF, 19TG, 19PGS, 20PG, 20PG, 20PHO, 19PG, 18PGS, 19PG, 18TG, 22PG,

	Starts	1st	2nd	3rd	Win & Pl
Hurdles	4	1	0	1	9263
Chases	9	2	2	3	19293
Career Total	23	4	3	5	40871
120 4/04 Font	2m2f	E Ch		GD	£4351
8/03 Vich	2m3f110y	HHdl		GD	£7169
7/03 Aixl	2m2f	Ch		G-F	£3117
3/02 Pari	2m1f	Hdl		G-S	£5258
				Total win prize-money	£19896

Going:	Sf: 0-0 GS: 0-2 Gd: 2-9 GF: - Fm: 1-1
Distance:	2m/2m3: 2-7 2m4-2m7: 1-6 3m+: 0-0
Track:	LH: 0-0 RH: 0-1 Tight: 1-2 Gall: 0-0
Aids:	Bl: 0-0 Vi: 0-0 Tstrap: 0-0 Ckp: 0-0
Best Rating:	120 4/04 Font 2m2f good Ch

Fair novice chaser; ex-French; suited by trips of around two miles and good ground.

Black Frost (IRE)
99(105h)   (115h)121+
8-y-o ch g Glacial Storm (USA)-Black Tulip (Pals Passage)
Mrs S J Smith Trevor Hemmings

Placings:23/50/351P1-1441FU   (4648)
2003/04: 22¹GS, 20⁴G, 19⁴S, 22¹G, 25ᶠGF, 20ᵁG,

	Starts	1st	2nd	3rd	Win & Pl
Chases	6	2	0		16366
Career Total	15	4	1	2	26327
127 2/04 Hayd 2m6f	D(0-120)HCh	GD	£6864
114 11/03 Hayd 2m6f	C Ch	G-S	£8186
103 4/03 Carl 2m4f	E Hdl	G-F	£3500
115 1/03 Hayd 2m4f	D Hdl	G-S	£5083

Total win prize-money £23634

Going: Sf: 0-1 GS: 1-1 Gd: 1-3 GF: - Fm: 0-1
Distance: 2m/2m3: 0-1 **2m4-2m7: 2-4** 3m+: 0-1
Track: LH: **2-6** RH: 0-0 Tight: 0-1 Gall: 0-1
Aids: Bl: 0-0 Vi: 0-0 Tstrap: 0-0 Ckp: 0-0
Best Rating: **127** 2/04 Hayd 2m6f   good   Ch

Fair novice chaser/modest hurdler; stays two miles six, but sure to get further and looks a real stayer; handles any ground.

Black Legend (IRE)
87   91
5-y-o b g Marju (IRE)-Lamping (Warning)
R Lee Jon Waldman and Partners

Placings:006   (4138)
2003/04: 17ᵁGS, 21ᵁG, 16ᶠG,

	Starts	1st	2nd	3rd	Win & Pl
Hurdles	3	0	0	0	0
Career Total	3	0	0	0	0

Going: Sf: 0-0 GS: 0-1 Gd: 0-2 GF: - Fm: 0-0
Distance: 2m/2m3: 0-2 2m4-2m7: 0-1 3m+: 0-0
Track: LH: 0-1 RH: 0-2 Tight: 0-1 Gall: 0-0
Aids: Bl: 0-0 Vi: 0-0 Tstrap: 0-0 Ckp: 0-0
Best Rating: **91** 3/04 Ludl 2m   good   Hdl

Black Leopard (IRE)
62   27
5-y-o b/br g Presenting-Glen Laura (Kambalda)
P D Niven P J Finn

Placings:0   (4881)
2003/04: 17ᵁGS,

	Starts	1st	2nd	3rd	Win & Pl
Hurdles	1	0	0	0	
Career Total	1	0	0	0	

Going: Sf: 0-0 GS: 0-1 Gd: 0-0 GF: - Fm: 0-0
Distance: 2m/2m3: 0-1 2m4-2m7: 0-0 3m+: 0-0
Track: LH: 0-0 RH: 0-1 Tight: 0-0 Gall: 0-0
Aids: Bl: 0-0 Vi: 0-0 Tstrap: 0-0 Ckp: 0-0
Best Rating: **22** 4/04 Carl 2m1f   gd-sft   Hdl

Black Marquess (IRE)
7-y-o b g Great Marquess-Kitty Wren (Warpath)
I A Duncan I A Duncan

Placings:06004   (4847)
2003/04: 19ᵁYS, 16ᶠGF, 16ᵁS, 16ᵁS, 16⁴GS,

	Starts	1st	2nd	3rd	Win & Pl
NH Flat	4	0	0	0	0
Hurdles	1	0	0	0	565
Career Total	5	0	0	0	565

Going: Sf: 0-2 GS: 0-1 Gd: 0-0 GF: - Fm: 0-1
Distance: 2m/2m3: 0-5 2m4-2m7: 0-0 3m+: 0-0
Track: LH: 0-1 RH: 0-0 Tight: 0-0 Gall: 0-0
Aids: Bl: 0-0 Vi: 0-0 Tstrap: 0-0 Ckp: 0-0
Best Rating: **86** 11/03 DRoy 2m   gd-fm   NHF

Black Saint
73
7-y-o b g Perpendicular-Fool's Errand (Milford)
P Wegmann P Wegmann

Placings:300P/PF   (4756)
2003/04: 16ᶠGS, 19ᶠS,

	Starts	1st	2nd	3rd	Win & Pl
Hurdles	2	0	0		
Career Total	6	0	0	1	339

Going: Sf: 0-1 GS: 0-1 Gd: 0-0 GF: - Fm: 0-0
Distance: 2m/2m3: 0-1 2m4-2m7: 0-1 3m+: 0-0
Track: LH: 0-0 RH: 0-1 Tight: 0-0 Gall: 0-0
Aids: Bl: 0-0 Vi: 0-0 Tstrap: 0-0 Ckp: 0-0
Best Rating: **73** 7/01 Wolv 2m   gd-sft   Hdl

Black Smoke (IRE)
7-y-o gr g Ala Hounak-Korean Citizen (IRE) (Mister Lord (USA))
R C Guest R Burridge

Placings:00221   (4884)
2003/04: 20ᵁHY, 20ᵁGS, 24²G, 23²G, 24¹GS,

	Starts	1st	2nd	3rd	Win & Pl
Hurdles	2	0	0		0
Chases	3	1	2	0	4094
Career Total	5	1	2	0	4094
95 4/04 Carl 3m	H Ch	G-S	£1624

Total win prize-money £1624

Going: Sf: 0-1 GS: 1-2 Gd: 0-2 GF: - Fm: 0-0
Distance: 2m/2m3: 0-0 2m4-2m7: 0-2 **3m+: 1-3**
Track: LH: 0-2 **RH: 1-3** Tight: 0-0 Gall: 0-1
Aids: Bl: 0-0 Vi: 0-0 Tstrap: 0-0 Ckp: 0-0
Best Rating: **95** 4/04 Carl 3m   gd-sft   Ch

Modest form over regulation fences and opened account over three miles in modest hunters chase at Carlisle in April 2004; acts on good and good to soft ground.

Black Stripe Lady
6-y-o b m Karinga Bay-Garvenish (Balinger)
R Ford (M Todhunter 28/4) Black Stripe Racing

Placings:440-0   (3322)
2003/04: 16ᵁG, 21ᵁGS,

	Starts	1st	2nd	3rd	Win & Pl
NH Flat	1	0	0	0	0
Hurdles	1	0	0	0	0
Career Total	4	0	0	0	0

Going: Sf: 0-0 GS: 0-1 Gd: 0-1 GF: - Fm: 0-0
Distance: 2m/2m3: 0-1 2m4-2m7: 0-1 3m+: 0-0
Track: LH: 0-2 RH: 0-0 Tight: 0-1 Gall: 0-0
Aids: Bl: 0-0 Vi: 0-0 Tstrap: 0-0 Ckp: 0-0
Best Rating: **85** 3/03 Hayd 2m   good   NHF

Black Swan (IRE)
66   33
4-y-o b g Nashwan (USA)-Sea Spray (IRE) (Royal Academy (USA))
G A Ham Colin B Taylor

Placings:6000   (4444)
2003/04: 16ᶠGF, 17ᵁGF, 16ᵁG, 16ᵁS,

	Starts	1st	2nd	3rd	Win & Pl
Hurdles	4	0	0	0	0
Career Total	4	0	0	0	0

Going: Sf: 0-1 GS: 0-0 Gd: 0-1 GF: - Fm: 0-2
Distance: 2m/2m3: 0-4 2m4-2m7: 0-0 3m+: 0-0
Track: LH: 0-3 RH: 0-1 Tight: 0-0 Gall: 0-2
Aids: Bl: 0-0 Vi: 0-0 Tstrap: 0-0 Ckp: 0-0
Best Rating: **33** 11/03 Hrfd 2m1f   gd-fm   Hdl

Little from over hurdles or on the Flat.

Blackberry Way
10-y-o ch m Almoojid-Prickly Path (Royal Match)
Ms Louise Cullen Chris And Stella Watson

Placings:P/5/13435P-033P   (4872)
2003/04: 21ᴾS, 20ᵁG, 25³GF, 22³G, 24ᴾS,

	Starts	1st	2nd	3rd	Win & Pl
Chases	5	0	0	2	486
Career Total	12	1	0	4	2338
78 5/02 Hntg 2m4f110yH Ch		G-F	£1352

Total win prize-money £1352

Going: Sf: 0-2 GS: 0-0 Gd: 0-2 GF: - Fm: 0-1
Distance: 2m/2m3: 0-0 2m4-2m7: 0-3 3m+: 0-2
Track: LH: 0-3 RH: 0-2 Tight: 0-0 Gall: 0-1
Aids: Bl: 0-0 Vi: 0-0 Tstrap: 0-2 Ckp: 0-0
Best Rating: **91** 3/04 Newb 2m6f110y   good   Ch

Blackchurch Lass (IRE)
(89h)   (56h)
6-y-o b m Taum Go Leor (IRE)-Melons Lady (IRE) (The Noble Player (USA))
Evan Williams Kevin Glastonbury

Placings:03P/45F4   (1589)
2003/04: 21⁴GF, 18⁵GF, 19ᶠGF, 20⁴GF,

	Starts	1st	2nd	3rd	Win & Pl
Hurdles	2	0	0	0	0
Chases	2	0	0	0	258
Career Total	7	0	0	1	704

Going: Sf: 0-0 GS: 0-0 Gd: 0-0 GF: - Fm: 0-4
Distance: 2m/2m3: 0-2 2m4-2m7: 0-2 3m+: 0-0
Track: LH: 0-2 RH: 0-2 Tight: 0-2 Gall: 0-0
Aids: Bl: 0-0 Vi: 0-0 Tstrap: 0-0 Ckp: 0-0
Best Rating: **56** 9/03 Font 2m2f110y   gd-fm   Hdl

Blackchurch Mist (IRE)
109(105c)   (113c)113
7-y-o b m Erin's Isle-Diandra (Shardari)
B W Duke Brendan W Duke Racing

Placings:0/30332P11P5-15243112P05P   (4307)

2003/04: 21^1GF, 21^5GF, 22^2GF, 22^4G, 21^3GS, 20^1GF, 21^1GF, 22^2GF, 21^8F, 24^0G, 20^5G, 22^8G,

	Starts	1st	2nd	3rd	Win & Pl
Hurdles	8	2	1	1	12632
Chases	4	1	1	0	7369
Career Total	23	5	3	4	29933

113	9/03	Strf	2m5f110yD Ch		G-F	£5194
110	8/03	Worc	2m4f D(0-120)HHdl		G-F	£5122
113	5/03	Wwck	2m5f E(0-110)HHdl		G-F	£3990
103	3/03	Folk	2m4f110yE Hdl		GD	£3542
98	12/02	Winc	2m6f E(0-100)HHdl		G-S	£3388
				Total win prize-money		£21237

Going: Sf: 0-0 GS: 0-1 Gd: 0-4 GF: - Fm: 3-7
Distance: 2m/2m3: 0-0 2m4-2m7: 3-11 3m+: 0-1
Track: LH: 3-5 RH: 0-5 Tight: 1-3 Gall: 0-1
Aids: Bl: 0-0 Vi: 0-0 Tstrap: 3-11 Ckp: 0-1
Best Rating: 113 9/03 MRas 2m6f110y gd-fm Ch

Modest hurdler/novice chaser; races enthusiastically; made a successful transition to fences when left clear at the last at Stratford in September 2003; held subsequently; stays two miles six; has suffered from breathing trouble; is usually tongue tied; probably does not act on really soft ground.

Blackcountry Lad

9-y-o b g Henbit (USA)-Cupids Bower (Owen Dudley)
A P James T N Siviter

Placings:OOO/PP-0 (0764)
2003/04: 20^0GF,

	Starts	1st	2nd	3rd	Win & Pl
Hurdles	1	0	0	0	
Career Total	6	0	0	0	

Going: Sf: 0-0 GS: 0-0 Gd: 0-0 GF: - Fm: 0-1
Distance: 2m/2m3: 0-0 2m4-2m7: 0-1 3m+: 0-0
Track: LH: 0-1 RH: 0-0 Tight: 0-0 Gall: 0-0
Aids: Bl: 0-0 Vi: 0-0 Tstrap: 0-0 Ckp: 0-0
Best Rating: 17 12/00 Hrfd 2m1f heavy NHF

Blackergreen
89f   89+f
5-y-o b g Zaffaran (USA)-Ballinderry Moss (Le Moss)
Mrs M Reveley P England

Placings:2 (4952)
2003/04: 16^2GS,

	Starts	1st	2nd	3rd	Win & Pl
NH Flat	1	0	1	0	984
Career Total	1	0	1	0	984

Going: Sf: 0-0 GS: 0-1 Gd: 0-0 GF: - Fm: 0-0
Distance: 2m/2m3: 0-1 2m4-2m7: 0-0 3m+: 0-0
Track: LH: 0-0 RH: 0-0 Tight: 0-0 Gall: 0-0
Aids: Bl: 0-0 Vi: 0-0 Tstrap: 0-0 Ckp: 0-0
Best Rating: 89 4/04 Prth 2m10y gd-sft NHF

Has winners in pedigree and shaped well on racecourse debut in Perth bumper in April 2004; sure to improve.

Blackies All (USA)
99   105+
6-y-o b g Hazaam (USA)-Allijess (USA) (Tom Rolfe)
W M Brisbourne (Andrew Lee 18/1) D Shenton Syndicate

Placings:33/040-03001 (4605)
2003/04: 20^0G, 24^3Y, 24^0S, 24^0S, 22^1G,

	Starts	1st	2nd	3rd	Win & Pl
Hurdles	5	1	0	1	5502

Career Total	10	1	0	3		6950
105	3/04	MRas	2m6f D(0-115)HHdl		GD	£5047
			Total win prize-money			£5047

Going: Sf: 0-2 GS: 0-0 Gd: 1-2 GF: - Fm: 0-0
Distance: 2m/2m3: 0-0 2m4-2m7: 1-2 3m+: 0-3
Track: LH: 0-0 RH: 0-1 Tight: 0-0 Gall: 0-0
Aids: Bl: 0-0 Vi: 0-0 Tstrap: 0-0 Ckp: 0-0
Best Rating: 105 3/04 MRas 2m6f good Hdl

Blackout (IRE)
95   75+
9-y-o b g Black Monday-Fine Bess (Fine Blade (USA))
J Barclay Jim Barclay

Placings:6/0605PP/45435-3PPF4PP (4684)
2003/04: 25^3GS, 24^2GF, 20^2S, 25^5HY, 25^4GF, 25^5G, 25^5G,

	Starts	1st	2nd	3rd	Win & Pl
Chases	7	0	0	1	906
Career Total	19	0	0	2	3082

Going: Sf: 0-2 GS: 0-1 Gd: 0-2 GF: - Fm: 0-2
Distance: 2m/2m3: 0-0 2m4-2m7: 0-1 3m+: 0-6
Track: LH: 0-6 RH: 0-1 Tight: 0-4 Gall: 0-0
Aids: Bl: 0-0 Vi: 0-0 Tstrap: 0-0 Ckp: 0-0
Best Rating: 83 1/01 Ayr 3m10y gd-sft Hdl

Modest hurdler/novice chaser. Yet to win a race of any sort.

Blairgowrie (IRE)
95f   109f
5-y-o b g Supreme Leader-Parsons Term (IRE) (The Parson)
J Howard Johnson M McKernan

Placings:2 (4886)
2003/04: 17^2GS,

	Starts	1st	2nd	3rd	Win & Pl
NH Flat	1	0	1	0	594
Career Total	1	0	1	0	594

Going: Sf: 0-0 GS: 0-1 Gd: 0-0 GF: - Fm: 0-0
Distance: 2m/2m3: 0-1 2m4-2m7: 0-0 3m+: 0-0
Track: LH: 0-1 RH: 0-1 Tight: 0-0 Gall: 0-0
Aids: Bl: 0-0 Vi: 0-0 Tstrap: 0-0 Ckp: 0-0
Best Rating: 108 4/04 Carl 2m1f gd-sft NHF

Out of a dam who won in bumper and over hurdles; satisfactory debut when second to impressive winner at Carlisle in bumper in April 2004; likely to improve.

Blakeney Coast (IRE)
108(89h)   (75+h)108
7-y-o b g Satco (FR)-Up To More Trix (IRE) (Torus)
C L Tizzard (Mrs M Reveley 28/6) The Jam Boys

Placings:660/056PP32-13U511 (1547)
2003/04: 20^1GF, 20^3G, 17^4GF, 24^5G, 17^1GF, 17^1GF,

	Starts	1st	2nd	3rd	Win & Pl
Hurdles	1	0	0	0	
Chases	5	3	0	1	14089
Career Total	16	3	1	2	15694

100	10/03	Plum	2m1f E(0-100)HCh		G-F	£3012
108	9/03	Plum	2m1f E(0-105)HCh		G-F	£3648
96	5/03	Weth	2m4f110yD(0-110)HCh		G-F	£6808
			Total win prize-money			£13253

Going: Sf: 0-0 GS: 0-0 Gd: 0-2 GF: - Fm: 3-4
Distance: 2m/2m3: 2-3 2m4-2m7: 1-2 3m+: 0-1
Track: LH: 3-6 RH: 0-0 Tight: 2-2 Gall: 0-0
Aids: Bl: 0-0 Vi: 0-0 Tstrap: 0-0 Ckp: 0-0
Best Rating: 108 9/03 Plum 2m1f gd-fm Ch

Moderate novice chaser; jumps soundly; acts on firm ground; stays two miles four.

Blakes Road (IRE)
93f   67f
7-y-o b/br g Be My Native (USA)-Joyau (IRE) (Roselier (FR))
Miss Venetia Williams Lady Harris

Placings:06 (1195)
2003/04: 16^0G, 16^6GF,

	Starts	1st	2nd	3rd	Win & Pl
NH Flat	2	0	0	0	0
Career Total	2	0	0	0	0

Going: Sf: 0-0 GS: 0-0 Gd: 0-1 GF: - Fm: 0-1
Distance: 2m/2m3: 0-2 2m4-2m7: 0-0 3m+: 0-0
Track: LH: 0-1 RH: 0-1 Tight: 0-0 Gall: 0-0
Aids: Bl: 0-0 Vi: 0-0 Tstrap: 0-0 Ckp: 0-0
Best Rating: 67 8/03 Worc 2m gd-fm NHF

Blank Canvas (IRE)
102f   93+f
6-y-o b g Presenting-Strong Cloth (IRE) (Strong Gale)
K C Bailey D Allen

Placings:60 (4578)
2003/04: 17^6GS, 16^0G,

	Starts	1st	2nd	3rd	Win & Pl
NH Flat	2	0	0	0	0
Career Total	2	0	0	0	0

Going: Sf: 0-0 GS: 0-1 Gd: 0-1 GF: - Fm: 0-0
Distance: 2m/2m3: 0-2 2m4-2m7: 0-0 3m+: 0-0
Track: LH: 0-1 RH: 0-1 Tight: 0-0 Gall: 0-1
Aids: Bl: 0-0 Vi: 0-0 Tstrap: 0-0 Ckp: 0-0
Best Rating: 93 3/04 Newb 2m110y good NHF

Blasket Sound (IRE)
101   100
12-y-o b g Lancastrian-June's Friend (Laurence O)
D J Wintle R H L Barnes

Placings:541235331/464UP64320145FU/45PU3F1143/264
221P0/20P0P216/00253-45143 (4508)
2003/04: 27^4G, 24^5S, 24^1GS, 22^4HY, 26^3GS,

	Starts	1st	2nd	3rd	Win & Pl
Hurdles	5	1	0	1	4006
Career Total	60	8	8	8	36478

96	12/03	Uttx	3m110y F(0-100)HHdl		G-S	£3094
100	2/02	Hntg	3m2f E(0-110)HHdl		SFT	£2576
113	3/01	Hntg	3m2f D(0-110)HHdl		SFT	£2051
105	3/00	Towc	3m1f D(0-120)HCh		SFT	£3848
100	3/00	Chep	3m2f110yE(0-115)HCh		HVY	£2879
104	1/99	Naas	3m (0-116)HCh		HVY	£3989
101	4/98	Clon	3m Ch		HVY	£1935
104	11/97	Limk	2m4f Hdl		HVY	£2712
			Total win prize-money			£23088

Going: Sf: 0-2 GS: 1-2 Gd: 0-1 GF: - Fm: 0-0
Distance: 2m/2m3: 0-2 2m4-2m7: 0-1 3m+: 1-4
Track: LH: 1-2 RH: 0-3 Tight: 0-2 Gall: 0-0
Aids: Bl: 0-0 Vi: 0-0 Tstrap: 0-0 Ckp: 0-0
Best Rating: 113 3/01 Hntg 3m2f soft Hdl

Modest staying hurdler; showed he is no backnumber when winning Class F handicap at Uttoxeter Boxing Day 2003; acts on an easy surface; best around 3m 2f.

Blau Grau (GER)

84   62

7-y-o gr g Neshad (USA)-Belle Orfana (GER) (Orfano (GER))
K A Morgan (P A Blockley 8/5) D S Cooper

Placings:45   (2691)
2003/04: 16⁴GF, 16⁵G,

	Starts	1st	2nd	3rd	Win & Pl
Hurdles	2	0	0	0	0
Career Total	2	0	0	0	0

Going:	Sf: 0-0 GS: 0-0 Gd: 0-1 GF: - Fm: 0-1
Distance:	2m/2m3: 0-2 2m4-2m7: 0-0 3m+: 0-0
Track:	LH: 0-1 RH: 0-1 Tight: 0-1 Gall: 0-0
Aids:	Bl: 0-0 Vi: 0-0 Tstrap: 0-0 Ckp: 0-0
Best Rating:	68 7/03 Strf 2m110y gd-fm Hdl

Plating-class hurdler; fourth in a seller on his jumps debut; multiple winner on the Flat in his native Germany; has worn blinkers on the Flat.

Blazeaway (USA)

95   77

4-y-o b/br g Hansel (USA)-Alessia's Song (USA) (Air Forbes Won (USA))
R S Brookhouse (M Johnston 17/7) Mrs S J Brookhouse

Placings:25P0P   (4915)
2003/04: 17²G, 16⁵GF, 17⁸G, 17⁹GF, 16⁹GS,

	Starts	1st	2nd	3rd	Win & Pl
Hurdles	5	0	1	0	1056
Career Total	5	0	1	0	1056

Going:	Sf: 0-0 GS: 0-1 Gd: 0-2 GF: - Fm: 0-2
Distance:	2m/2m3: 0-5 2m4-2m7: 0-0 3m+: 0-2
Track:	LH: 0-3 RH: 0-2 Tight: 0-3 Gall: 0-0
Aids:	Bl: 0-2 Vi: 0-0 Tstrap: 0-0 Ckp: 0-0
Best Rating:	77 9/03 Strf 2m110y gd-fm Hdl

Plating-class over hurdles.

Blazing Batman

105(105h)   (74h) 111

11-y-o ch g Shaab-Cottage Blaze (Sunyboy)
Dr P Pritchard Jumping Jokers

Placings:50/42/F/FP04/PU415P41542PP0/444632360-203FP5P3531322533520   (4640)
2003/04: 23²GF, 24⁰GF, 26³GF, 26⁶GS, 26⁶GF, 27⁵GF, 22⁶GF, 26³GF, 23⁵GF, 28³GF, 23¹F, 26³GF, 25²GF, 24²GF, 26⁵GS, 25³HY, 16³S, 17⁵G, 24²GS, 21⁰G,

	Starts	1st	2nd	3rd	Win & Pl
Hurdles	3	0	1	0	1044
Chases	17	1	3	6	14971
Career Total	52	3	7	8	31337
77	10/03 Extr	2m7f110yE(0-105)HCh	FRM	£4960
93	11/01 Fknm	3m5f110yF(0-100)HCh	SFT	£4123
93	7/01 Sthl	3m110y E Ch	G-F	£3406
		Total win prize-money £12490		

Going:	Sf: 0-2 GS: 0-3 Gd: 0-2 GF: - Fm: 1-13
Distance:	2m/2m3: 0-2 2m4-2m7: 0-2 3m+: 1-16
Track:	LH: 0-13 RH: 1-5 Tight: 0-10 Gall: 0-6
Aids:	Bl: 0-0 Vi: 0-0 Tstrap: 0-0 Ckp: 0-0
Best Rating:	111 3/04 Strf 3m gd-sft Ch

Blazing Fiddle (IRE)

35f

5-y-o b g Anshan-Second Violin (IRE) (Cataldi)
J M Jefferson P Gaffney & J N Stevenson

Placings:0   (4952)
2003/04: 16⁰GS,

	Starts	1st	2nd	3rd	Win & Pl
NH Flat	1	0	0	0	
Career Total	1	0	0	0	

Going:	Sf: 0-0 GS: 0-1 Gd: 0-0 GF: - Fm: 0-0
Distance:	2m/2m3: 0-1 2m4-2m7: 0-0 3m+: 0-0
Track:	LH: 0-0 RH: 0-1 Tight: 0-0 Gall: 0-0
Aids:	Bl: 0-0 Vi: 0-0 Tstrap: 0-0 Ckp: 0-0

Blazing Guns (IRE)

93f   97f

5-y-o ch g Un Desperado (FR)-Quefort (Quayside)
Miss H C Knight Jim Lewis

Placings:60   (3649)
2003/04: 16⁶GS, 16⁰GS,

	Starts	1st	2nd	3rd	Win & Pl
NH Flat	2	0	0	0	
Career Total	2	0	0	0	

Going:	Sf: 0-0 GS: 0-2 Gd: 0-0 GF: - Fm: 0-0
Distance:	2m/2m3: 0-2 2m4-2m7: 0-0 3m+: 0-0
Track:	LH: 0-1 RH: 0-1 Tight: 0-0 Gall: 0-1
Aids:	Bl: 0-0 Vi: 0-0 Tstrap: 0-0 Ckp: 0-0
Best Rating:	97 12/03 Newb 2m110y gd-sft NHF

A huge individual; highly-regarded brother to smart hurdler Unarmed; ran promisingly in hot bumper on debut at Newbury in December; does not want the ground too soft.

Blazing Hills

95   93+

8-y-o ch g Shaab-Cottage Blaze (Sunyboy)
P T Dalton Mrs Julie Martin

Placings:0/5623B115/065U   (4443)
2003/04: 25⁰S, 25⁶GS, 24⁵G, 29ᵁGS,

	Starts	1st	2nd	3rd	Win & Pl
Chases	4	0	0	0	
Career Total	13	2	1	1	7913
100	10/01 Towc	3m1f	F(0-90)HCh	GD	£3562
91	9/01 Uttx	3m2f	E Ch	G-F	£3012
			Total win prize-money £6575		

Going:	Sf: 0-1 GS: 0-2 Gd: 0-1 GF: - Fm: 0-0
Distance:	2m/2m3: 0-2 2m4-2m7: 0-0 3m+: 0-4
Track:	LH: 0-2 RH: 0-2 Tight: 0-1 Gall: 0-0
Aids:	Bl: 0-4 Vi: 0-0 Tstrap: 0-0 Ckp: 0-0
Best Rating:	100 10/01 Towc 3m1f good Ch

Moderate staying chaser, he won at Uttoxeter before defying 12 stone in first-time blinkers at Towcester; has had his problems since then; acts on good ground.

Blazing Liss (IRE)

91f   119+f

5-y-o b m Supreme Leader-Liss De Paor (IRE) (Phardante (FR))

Modest staying chaser/hurdler; stays extreme distances; acts on most types of ground.

John E Kiely Mrs N Flynn

Placings:111F   (4400)
2003/04: 16¹GY, 16¹GF, 16¹S, 16²G,

	Starts	1st	2nd	3rd	Win & Pl
NH Flat	4	3	0	0	21659
Career Total	4	3	0	0	21659
119	12/03 Navn	2m	NHF	SFT	£8441
107	10/03 Gway	2m	NHF	G-F	£6048
116	5/03 Punc	2m	NHF	G-Y	£7168
			Total win prize-money £21660		

Going:	Sf: 1-1 GS: 0-0 Gd: 0-1 GF: - Fm: 1-1
Distance:	2m/2m3: 3-4 2m4-2m7: 0-0 3m+: 0-0
Track:	LH: 0-0 RH: 1-1 Tight: 0-0 Gall: 0-0
Aids:	Bl: 0-0 Vi: 0-0 Tstrap: 0-0 Ckp: 0-0
Best Rating:	119 12/03 Navn 2m soft NHF

Exciting half-sister to very smart hurdler Liss A Paoraigh; impressive winner of all her three bumpers to date; has won on both fast and soft ground.

Blazing Saddles (IRE)

93   71

5-y-o b g Sadler's Wells (USA)-Dalawara (IRE) (Top Ville)
Mrs J Candlish (P R Hedger 3/6) Racing For You Limited

Placings:002-0000P   (4245)
2003/04: 16⁹G, 16⁶GS, 19⁰G, 26ᴾGF,

	Starts	1st	2nd	3rd	Win & Pl
Hurdles	5	0	0	0	
Career Total	8	0	1	0	1075

Going:	Sf: 0-1 GS: 0-1 Gd: 0-2 GF: - Fm: 0-1
Distance:	2m/2m3: 0-4 2m4-2m7: 0-0 3m+: 0-1
Track:	LH: 0-3 RH: 0-2 Tight: 0-1 Gall: 0-1
Aids:	Bl: 0-0 Vi: 0-0 Tstrap: 0-0 Ckp: 0-5
Best Rating:	71 12/03 Wwck 2m good Hdl

Poor hurdler; yet to show any worthwhile form; has worn cheekpieces.

Blencathra

74f   56f

5-y-o b m Midnight Legend-April City (Lidhame)
C Smith T I Gourley

Placings:0   (4608)
2003/04: 17⁰G,

	Starts	1st	2nd	3rd	Win & Pl
NH Flat	1	0	0	0	
Career Total	1	0	0	0	

Going:	Sf: 0-0 GS: 0-0 Gd: 0-1 GF: - Fm: 0-0
Distance:	2m/2m3: 0-1 2m4-2m7: 0-0 3m+: 0-0
Track:	LH: 0-0 RH: 0-1 Tight: 0-1 Gall: 0-0
Aids:	Bl: 0-0 Vi: 0-0 Tstrap: 0-0 Ckp: 0-0
Best Rating:	58 3/04 MRas 2m1f110y good NHF

Bleu Superbe (FR)

115   149+

9-y-o b g Epervier Bleu-Brett's Dream (FR) (Pharly (FR))
Miss Venetia Williams P A Deal, A Hirschfeld & J Tyndall

Placings:111113/F603P122/5PPP13P/F3P/11PP11PPP-P13633PF   (4864)
2003/04: 17⁶G, 16¹G, 16³S, 16⁶GS, 16³S, 16³G, 16⁶G, 16⁴S,

	Starts	1st	2nd	3rd	Win & Pl
Chases	8	1	0	3	24352

Career Total	41	12	2	7	166465
149	11/03	Asct	2m	B(0-145)HCh	GD	£11674
149	11/03	Donc	2m11y	B(0-150)HCh	GD	£13585
142	11/02	Newb	2m1f	C(0-135)HCh	G-S	£9326
144	5/02	Towc	2m11y	C(0-135)HCh	GD	£5850
131	5/02	Aint	2m	D(0-125)HCh	GD	£5167
140	3/01	Hayd	2m	D(0-120)HCh	HVY	£7117
	1/00	Cagn	2m7f	Ch	SFT	£21133
	3/99	Pau	2m2f110y	Ch	VS	£7535
	1/99	Pau	2m2f	Hdl	VS	£15070
	1/99	Pau	2m2f	Hdl	HVY	£7535
	12/98	Bord	2m2f	Hdl	VS	£5051
	11/98	Bord	2m2f	Hdl	VS	£3030

Total win prize-money £112075

Going: Sf: 0-3 GS: 0-1 Gd: 1-4 GF: - Fm: 0-0
Distance: 2m/2m3: 1-8 2m4-2m7: 0-0 3m+: 0-0
Track: LH: 0-4 RH: 1-4 Tight: 0-2 Gall: 0-0
Aids: Bl: 0-0 Vi: 0-0 Tstrap: 0-1 Ckp: 0-0
Best Rating: 149 11/03 Asct 2m good Ch

Smart handicap chaser; best at around two miles; acts on good and soft going; has found his consistency this year, having previously developed a habit of pulling up; has been tried in a tongue tie.

Blind Smart (IRE)
87f   81f
6-y-o br g Phardante (FR)-Smart Chick (True Song)
M F Harris C J Courage

Placings:00   (0617)
2003/04: 17⁰GF, 17⁰GF,

	Starts	1st	2nd	3rd	Win & Pl
NH Flat	2	0	0	0	
Career Total	2	0	0	0	

Going: Sf: 0-0 GS: 0-0 Gd: 0-0 GF: - Fm: 0-2
Distance: 2m/2m3: 0-2 2m4-2m7: 0-0 3m+: 0-0
Track: LH: 0-0 RH: 0-2 Tight: 0-1 Gall: 0-0
Aids: Bl: 0-0 Vi: 0-0 Tstrap: 0-0 Ckp: 0-0
Best Rating: 81 5/03 MRas 2m1f110y gd-fm NHF

Blood Sub (IRE)
(103h)   (111+h)
7-y-o b g Roselier (FR)-Clearwater Glen (Furry Glen)
Jonjo O'Neill John P McManus

Placings:251-FP   (2719)
2003/04: 20⁵S, 20⁰GS,

	Starts	1st	2nd	3rd	Win & Pl
Chases	2	0	0	0	
Career Total	5	1	1	0	5091
111	3/03	Uttx	2m4f110yE Hdl	SFT	£4537

Total win prize-money £4537

Going: Sf: 0-1 GS: 0-1 Gd: 0-0 GF: - Fm: 0-0
Distance: 2m/2m3: 0-0 2m4-2m7: 0-0 3m+: 0-0
Track: LH: 0-2 RH: 0-0 Tight: 0-0 Gall: 0-1
Aids: Bl: 0-0 Vi: 0-0 Tstrap: 0-0 Ckp: 0-0
Best Rating: 111 3/03 Uttx 2m4f110y soft Hdl

Fair novice hurdler; casualty on chasing debut; suited by two and a half miles and soft ground; still has plenty of scope.

Blossom Whispers
89   80
7-y-o b m Ezzoud (IRE)-Springs Welcome (Blakeney)
N G Ayliffe (Mrs M Reveley 2/5) D T Hooper

Placings:053006F-4600   (3748)

2003/04: 27⁴S, 24⁶G, 22⁰G, 22⁰GS,

	Starts	1st	2nd	3rd	Win & Pl
Hurdles	4	0	0	0	0
Career Total	11	0	0	1	697

Going: Sf: 0-1 GS: 0-1 Gd: 0-2 GF: - Fm: 0-0
Distance: 2m/2m3: 0-0 2m4-2m7: 0-2 3m+: 0-2
Track: LH: 0-2 RH: 0-1 Tight: 0-2 Gall: 0-0
Aids: Bl: 0-0 Vi: 0-0 Tstrap: 0-0 Ckp: 0-1
Best Rating: 80 4/03 Weth 2m7f gd-fm Hdl

Plating-class hurdler; looked sure to be involved in the finish before falling two out in a seller at Wetherby in April 2003; suited by a test of stamina.

Blow Me Down
74   35
5-y-o b m Overbury (IRE)-Chinook's Daughter (IRE) (Strong Gale)
F Jordan Mrs K Roberts-Hindle

Placings:5006P00P   (3997)
2003/04: 18⁵GF, 17⁰GF, 17⁰GF, 16⁶Gd, 16⁶PS, 16⁰GS, 16⁰S, 21⁰PG,

	Starts	1st	2nd	3rd	Win & Pl
NH Flat	4	0	0	0	0
Hurdles	4	0	0	0	0
Career Total	8	0	0	0	0

Going: Sf: 0-2 GS: 0-1 Gd: 0-1 GF: - Fm: 0-4
Distance: 2m/2m3: 0-7 2m4-2m7: 0-1 3m+: 0-0
Track: LH: 0-3 RH: 0-5 Tight: 0-2 Gall: 0-0
Aids: Bl: 0-0 Vi: 0-0 Tstrap: 0-0 Ckp: 0-0
Best Rating: 79 11/03 Wwck 2m gd-fm NHF

Blowing Away (IRE)
(96h)   (56h)
10-y-o b/br m Last Tycoon-Taken By Force (Persian Bold)
Julian Poulton Mrs Elizabeth Reed

Placings:301/6365F/664300-0F   (0481)
2003/04: 16⁰GS, 16⁶GF,

	Starts	1st	2nd	3rd	Win & Pl
Hurdles	1	0	0	0	0
Chases	1	0	0	0	0
Career Total	16	1	0	3	2945
71	3/98	Uttx	2m	G Hdl	GD	£1595

Total win prize-money £1595

Going: Sf: 0-0 GS: 0-1 Gd: 0-0 GF: - Fm: 0-1
Distance: 2m/2m3: 0-2 2m4-2m7: 0-0 3m+: 0-0
Track: LH: 0-1 RH: 0-1 Tight: 0-0 Gall: 0-1
Aids: Bl: 0-0 Vi: 0-1 Tstrap: 0-0 Ckp: 0-0
Best Rating: 80 2/98 Catt 2m good Hdl

Blowing Wind (FR)
102   126
11-y-o b/br g Fabulous Dancer (USA)-Bassita (Bustino)
M C Pipe P A Deal

Placings:02403111/4F2B0/4112106/303113/P513/36000-40RR0   (4953)
2003/04: 20⁴G, 19⁰GS, 24⁶S, 36⁶G, 20⁰G,

	Starts	1st	2nd	3rd	Win & Pl
Chases	5	0	0	0	794
Career Total	40	9	3	6	286833
147	3/02	Chel	2m4f110yA HCh	G-S	£45500
134	2/01	Sand	2m	B HCh	HVY	£10071
147	1/01	Donc	2m3f110yC(0-130)HCh	GD	£6545
140	2/00	Asct	2m3f110yB Ch	G-S	£10114

138	1/00	Leic	2m	E Ch	GD	£3315
118	12/99	Ludl	2m	E Ch	G-S	£3048
155	4/98	Ayr	2m	A HHdl	GD	£15669
156	3/98	Chel	2m1f	A HHdl	GD	£26974
147	3/98	Sand	2m110y	B(0-150)HHdl	SFT	£21495

Total win prize-money £142735

Going: Sf: 0-1 GS: 0-1 Gd: 0-3 GF: - Fm: 0-0
Distance: 2m/2m3: 0-0 2m4-2m7: 0-3 3m+: 0-2
Track: LH: 0-1 RH: 0-4 Tight: 0-1 Gall: 0-0
Aids: Bl: 0-0 Vi: 0-0 Tstrap: 0-0 Ckp: 0-0
Best Rating: 158 2/99 Hayd 2m soft Hdl

Fair chaser; third in the 2001 and 2002 Grand Nationals and a surprise winner of the Mildmay of Flete at the 2002 Festival; best around two and a half miles; acts on good ground or softer; refused at Sandown in February and again in the Grand National; probably on the downgrade.

Blue Americo (IRE)
103   116+
6-y-o br g Lord Americo-Princess Menelek (Menelek)
P F Nicholls Mrs Angela Tincknell

Placings:0-351623   (4671)
2003/04: 17³G, 16⁵S, 17¹S, 19⁶GS, 16²G, 16³G,

	Starts	1st	2nd	3rd	Win & Pl
Hurdles	6	1	1	2	8874
Career Total	7	1	1	2	8874
116	2/04	Tntn	2m1f	E Hdl	SFT	£4303

Total win prize-money £4303

Going: Sf: 1-2 GS: 0-1 Gd: 0-3 GF: - Fm: 0-0
Distance: 2m/2m3: 1-5 2m4-2m7: 0-1 3m+: 0-0
Track: LH: 0-1 RH: 1-5 Tight: 1-3 Gall: 0-0
Aids: Bl: 0-0 Vi: 0-0 Tstrap: 0-0 Ckp: 0-0
Best Rating: 116 3/04 Winc 2m good Hdl

Modest hurdler; was highly regarded last season; best at around two miles; acts on soft; can race keenly.

Blue Away (IRE)
111   112+
6-y-o b g Blues Traveller (IRE)-Lomond Heights (IRE) (Lomond (USA))
P Hughes Astolfi Syndicate

Placings:0050040341-10   (4806a)
2003/04: 20¹GY, 21¹G, 22⁰Y,

	Starts	1st	2nd	3rd	Win & Pl
Hurdles	3	2	0	0	31230
Career Total	12	2	0	1	32325
112	11/03	Chel	2m5f	C(0-135)HHdl	GD	£16457
100	4/03	Punc	2m4f	(0-140)HHdl	G-Y	£14772

Total win prize-money £31230

Going: Sf: 0-0 GS: 0-0 Gd: 1-1 GF: - Fm: 0-0
Distance: 2m/2m3: 0-0 2m4-2m7: 2-3 3m+: 0-0
Track: LH: 1-1 RH: 1-2 Tight: 0-0 Gall: 1-1
Aids: Bl: 0-0 Vi: 1-1 Tstrap: 0-0 Ckp: 0-0
Best Rating: 112 11/03 Chel 2m5f good Hdl

Modest Irish-trained hurdler; won at Cheltenham in November; stays two miles five, but effective at shorter; acts on soft ground; has been tried in blinkers/visor.

Blue Bar
69   44
6-y-o gr m Norton Challenger-Royal Scarlet (Royal Fountain)
Mrs R L Elliot J P H Wight and J J Cockburn

Placings:0PFPP   (4913)

2003/04: 17⁰HY, 16⁵S, 24ᶠGS, 22ᴾGS, 24ᴾS,

	Starts	1st	2nd	3rd	Win & Pl
Hurdles	5	0	0	0	
Career Total	5	0	0	0	

Going:	Sf: 0-3 GS: 0-2 Gd: 0-0 GF: - Fm: 0-0
Distance:	2m/2m3: 0-2 2m4-2m7: 0-1 3m+: 0-2
Track:	LH: 0-3 RH: 0-2 Tight: 0-1 Gall: 0-0
Aids:	Bl: 0-0 Vi: 0-0 Tstrap: 0-0 Ckp: 0-0
Best Rating:	44 11/03 Carl 2m1f heavy Hdl

Ex-pointer; well beaten on hurdling debut.

Blue Brook

84f   77f

5-y-o ch g Alderbrook-Connaught's Pride (Hubbly Bubbly (USA))
Mrs S D Williams Mrs Angela Tincknell

Placings:00   (4291)
2003/04: 16⁰HY, 16⁰G,

	Starts	1st	2nd	3rd	Win & Pl
NH Flat	2	0	0	0	
Career Total	2	0	0	0	

Going:	Sf: 0-1 GS: 0-0 Gd: 0-1 GF: - Fm: 0-0
Distance:	2m/2m3: 0-2 2m4-2m7: 0-0 3m+: 0-0
Track:	LH: 0-0 RH: 0-2 Tight: 0-0 Gall: 0-0
Aids:	Bl: 0-0 Vi: 0-0 Tstrap: 0-0 Ckp: 0-0
Best Rating:	76 3/04 Winc 2m good NHF

Blue Business

107   103

6-y-o br g Roselier (FR)-Miss Redlands (Dubassoff (USA))
P F Nicholls Mrs Angela Tincknell

Placings:20323   (4895)
2003/04: 16²GF, 20⁰GS, 22³G, 24²G, 22³G,

	Starts	1st	2nd	3rd	Win & Pl
NH Flat	1	0	1	0	574
Hurdles	4	0	1	2	3286
Career Total	5	0	2	2	3860

Going:	Sf: 0-0 GS: 0-1 Gd: 0-3 GF: - Fm: 0-1
Distance:	2m/2m3: 0-1 2m4-2m7: 0-3 3m+: 0-1
Track:	LH: 0-2 RH: 0-3 Tight: 0-1 Gall: 0-0
Aids:	Bl: 0-0 Vi: 0-0 Tstrap: 0-0 Ckp: 0-0
Best Rating:	103 4/04 Winc 2m6f good Hdl

Half-brother to See More Business; looks a real stayer.

Blue Buster

85f   82f

4-y-o b g Young Buster (IRE)-Lazybird Blue (IRE) (Bluebird (USA))
M W Easterby John Connor

Placings:6   (4277)
2003/04: 17⁶G,

	Starts	1st	2nd	3rd	Win & Pl
NH Flat	1	0	0	0	0
Career Total	1	0	0	0	0

Going:	Sf: 0-0 GS: 0-0 Gd: 0-1 GF: - Fm: 0-0
Distance:	2m/2m3: 0-1 2m4-2m7: 0-0 3m+: 0-0
Track:	LH: 0-0 RH: 0-1 Tight: 0-0 Gall: 0-0
Aids:	Bl: 0-0 Vi: 0-0 Tstrap: 0-0 Ckp: 0-0
Best Rating:	82 3/04 Carl 2m1f good NHF

Blue Canyon (IRE)

89   82

6-y-o b g Phardante (FR)-Miss Gosling (Prince Bee)
B De Haan Willsford Racing Incorporated

Placings:00-0P4   (4539)
2003/04: 20⁰GS, 20⁰GS, 21⁴GS,

	Starts	1st	2nd	3rd	Win & Pl
Hurdles	3	0	0	0	326
Career Total	5	0	0	0	326

Going:	Sf: 0-0 GS: 0-3 Gd: 0-0 GF: - Fm: 0-0
Distance:	2m/2m3: 0-0 2m4-2m7: 0-3 3m+: 0-0
Track:	LH: 0-1 RH: 0-2 Tight: 0-0 Gall: 0-0
Aids:	Bl: 0-0 Vi: 0-0 Tstrap: 0-1 Ckp: 0-0
Best Rating:	90 3/03 Wwck 2m good NHF

Blue Cascade (IRE)

5-y-o b g Royal Academy (USA)-Blaine (USA) (Lyphard's Wish (FR))
G E Jones G Elwyn Jones

Placings:PP   (1588)
2003/04: 17⁰GF, 16⁰GF,

	Starts	1st	2nd	3rd	Win & Pl
Hurdles	2	0	0	0	
Career Total	2	0	0	0	

Going:	Sf: 0-0 GS: 0-0 Gd: 0-0 GF: - Fm: 0-2
Distance:	2m/2m3: 0-2 2m4-2m7: 0-0 3m+: 0-0
Track:	LH: 0-0 RH: 0-2 Tight: 0-0 Gall: 0-0
Aids:	Bl: 0-0 Vi: 0-0 Tstrap: 0-2 Ckp: 0-0
Best Rating:	0 10/03 Ludl 2m gd-fm Hdl

Blue Circle

4-y-o b c Whittingham (IRE)-Reshift (Night Shift (USA))
M Mullineaux T Clarke

Placings:P   (2871)
2003/04: 16ᴾS,

	Starts	1st	2nd	3rd	Win & Pl
Hurdles	1	0	0	0	
Career Total	1	0	0	0	

Going:	Sf: 0-1 GS: 0-0 Gd: 0-0 GF: - Fm: 0-0
Distance:	2m/2m3: 0-1 2m4-2m7: 0-0 3m+: 0-0
Track:	LH: 0-1 RH: 0-0 Tight: 0-0 Gall: 0-0
Aids:	Bl: 0-0 Vi: 0-0 Tstrap: 0-0 Ckp: 0-0
Best Rating:	0 12/03 Wwck 2m soft Hdl

Blue Dance

78   42

5-y-o b h Danzig Connection (USA)-Blues Player (Jaazeiro (USA))
N A Twiston-Davies M K F Seymour

Placings:6   (4918)
2003/04: 20⁶GS,

	Starts	1st	2nd	3rd	Win & Pl
Hurdles	1	0	0	0	0
Career Total	1	0	0	0	0

Going:	Sf: 0-0 GS: 0-1 Gd: 0-0 GF: - Fm: 0-0

Distance:	2m/2m3: 0-0 2m4-2m7: 0-1 3m+: 0-0
Track:	LH: 0-1 RH: 0-0 Tight: 0-0 Gall: 0-0
Aids:	Bl: 0-0 Vi: 0-0 Tstrap: 0-0 Ckp: 0-0
Best Rating:	42 4/04 Worc 2m4f gd-sft Hdl

Jumped poorly but hinted at ability on hurdling debut.

Blue Derby (IRE)

103   106

6-y-o b g Supreme Leader-Minigirls Niece (IRE) (Strong Gale)
Ms Bridget Nicholls (P J Hobbs 22/1) Mrs Angela Tincknell

Placings:01-601565   (4895)
2003/04: 22⁶G, 17⁰G, 17¹GS, 19⁵S, 19⁶GS, 22⁵G,

	Starts	1st	2nd	3rd	Win & Pl
Hurdles	6	1	0	0	3836
Career Total	8	2	0	0	5705
112	12/03 Extr	2m1f	E Hdl		G-S £3836
84	3/03 Tntn	2m1f	H NHF		FRM £1869
				Total win prize-money £5705	

Going:	Sf: 0-1 GS: 1-2 Gd: 0-3 GF: - Fm: 0-0
Distance:	2m/2m3: 1-3 2m4-2m7: 0-3 3m+: 0-0
Track:	LH: 0-0 RH: 1-6 Tight: 0-1 Gall: 0-0
Aids:	Bl: 0-0 Vi: 0-0 Tstrap: 0-1 Ckp: 0-0
Best Rating:	112 12/03 Extr 2m1f gd-sft Hdl

Fair novice hurdler; bumper winner; suited by two miles and should get further; acts on most types of ground.

Blue Endeavour (IRE)

102   112

6-y-o b g Endeavour (USA)-Jingle Bells (FR) (In The Mood (FR))
P F Nicholls Mrs Angela Tincknell

Placings:4-4543   (4819)
2003/04: 17⁴GF, 19⁵S, 17⁴G, 22³GF,

	Starts	1st	2nd	3rd	Win & Pl
NH Flat	1	0	0	0	0
Hurdles	3	0	0	1	975
Career Total	5	0	0	1	975

Going:	Sf: 0-0 GS: 0-0 Gd: 0-2 GF: - Fm: 0-2
Distance:	2m/2m3: 0-3 2m4-2m7: 0-1 3m+: 0-0
Track:	LH: 0-0 RH: 0-4 Tight: 0-0 Gall: 0-0
Aids:	Bl: 0-0 Vi: 0-0 Tstrap: 0-0 Ckp: 0-0
Best Rating:	111 4/04 Extr 2m1f good Hdl

From good jumping family; tapped for speed when fourth in first two bumpers; likely to need further over obstacles.

Blue Ette (IRE)

91f   60f

4-y-o b g Blues Traveller (IRE)-Princess Roxanne (Prince Tenderfoot (USA))
G A Swinbank Elsa Crankshaw & G Allan li

Placings:00   (4571)
2003/04: 16⁰GF, 17⁰GS,

	Starts	1st	2nd	3rd	Win & Pl
NH Flat	2	0	0	0	
Career Total	2	0	0	0	

Going:	Sf: 0-0 GS: 0-1 Gd: 0-0 GF: - Fm: 0-1
Distance:	2m/2m3: 0-2 2m4-2m7: 0-0 3m+: 0-0
Track:	LH: 0-2 RH: 0-0 Tight: 0-0 Gall: 0-2

Aids: Bl: 0-0 Vi: 0-0 Tstrap: 0-0 Ckp: 0-0
Best Rating: 60 3/04 Catt 2m   gd-fm NHF

Blue Hawk (IRE)
105   94+
7-y-o ch g Prince Of Birds (USA)-Classic Queen (IRE) (Classic Secret (USA))
Miss L V Davis Miss Louise Davis

Placings:222/13   (1811)
2003/04: 16¹GF, 17³G,

	Starts	1st	2nd	3rd	Win & Pl
Hurdles	2	1	0	1	2278
Career Total	5	1	3	1	4260
94	9/03	Uttx	2m		G Hdl	G-F £1925

Total win prize-money £1925

Going: Sf: 0-0 GS: 0-0 Gd: 0-0 GF: - Fm: 1-1
Distance: 2m/2m3: 1-2 2m4-2m7: 0-0 3m+: 0-0
Track: LH: 1-2 RH: 0-0 Tight: 0-1 Gall: 0-0
Aids: Bl: 0-0 Vi: 0-0 Tstrap: 0-0 Ckp: 0-0
Best Rating: 102 10/00 Ludl 2m   gd-fm Hdl

Poor on the level; has been much better over hurdles; won on first start for nearly a year in selling race at Uttoxeter in September 2003; acts on sound surface.

Blue Irish (IRE)
(105h)   (95h)95
13-y-o gr g Roselier (FR)-Grannie No (Brave Invader (USA))
Ferdy Murphy Miss J V Morgan

Placings:2066353/141/41/4FPP3UP/U/F/4260262P-2P
                                                (0898)
2003/04: 25³G, 30²G, 26⁶GF,

	Starts	1st	2nd	3rd	Win & Pl
Chases	3	0	1	0	2540
Career Total	31	3	5	3	25356
120	11/98	Carl	3m2f	C(0-130)HCh	HVY £4856
125	2/98	Naas	3m	Ch	Y-S £5956
118	11/97	Navn	2m4f	Ch	HVY £4069

Total win prize-money £14882

Going: Sf: 0-0 GS: 0-0 Gd: 0-2 GF: - Fm: 0-1
Distance: 2m/2m3: 0-0 2m4-2m7: 0-0 3m+: 0-3
Track: LH: 0-2 RH: 0-0 Tight: 0-1 Gall: 0-0
Aids: Bl: 0-0 Vi: 0-0 Tstrap: 0-0 Ckp: 0-3
Best Rating: 128 11/99 DRoy 3m1f   soft Ch

Moderate hurdler; one-time useful chaser in Ireland; runner-up in old boys chase at Cartmel in May; stays well; goes best at Sedgefield.

Blue Jar
66   36
6-y-o b g Royal Abjar (USA)-Artist's Glory (Rarity)
M Mullineaux T Clarke

Placings:00PBPP-P0   (0135)
2003/04: 17⁸S, 16⁰G,

	Starts	1st	2nd	3rd	Win & Pl
Hurdles	2	0	0	0	
Career Total	8	0	0	0	

Going: Sf: 0-1 GS: 0-0 Gd: 0-1 GF: - Fm: 0-0
Distance: 2m/2m3: 0-2 2m4-2m7: 0-0 3m+: 0-0
Track: LH: 0-1 RH: 0-1 Tight: 0-1 Gall: 0-0
Aids: Bl: 0-0 Vi: 0-0 Tstrap: 0-0 Ckp: 0-0
Best Rating: 65 3/02 Hntg 2m110y gd-fm NHF

Blue Leader (IRE)
103   88+
5-y-o b g Cadeaux Genereux-Blue Duster (USA) (Danzig (USA))
G Brown Mrs Amanda Killick

Placings:000P-151   (4404)
2003/04: 16¹G, 18⁵GF, 16¹G,

	Starts	1st	2nd	3rd	Win & Pl
Hurdles	3	2	0	0	4423
Career Total	7	2	0	0	4423
88	3/04	Hntg	2m110y	F(0-100)HHdl	GD £2583
77	10/03	Fknm	2m	G(0-90)HHdl	GD £1839

Total win prize-money £4423

Going: Sf: 0-0 GS: 0-0 Gd: 2-2 GF: - Fm: 0-1
Distance: 2m/2m3: 2-3 2m4-2m7: 0-0 3m+: 0-0
Track: LH: 1-2 RH: 1-0 Tight: 1-2 Gall: 1-1
Aids: Bl: 0-0 Vi: 0-0 Tstrap: 0-0 Ckp: 0-1
Best Rating: 88 3/04 Hntg 2m110y good Hdl

Plating-class hurdler; best around two miles; acts on good ground.

Blue Lizard (IRE)
(87h)   (53h)
7-y-o b g Roselier (FR)-Rathsallagh Tartan (Strong Gale)
Ferdy Murphy A Bloom

Placings:40-P   (3325)
2003/04: 21⁵GS,

	Starts	1st	2nd	3rd	Win & Pl
Chases	1	0	0	0	
Career Total	3	0	0	0	306

Going: Sf: 0-0 GS: 0-1 Gd: 0-0 GF: - Fm: 0-0
Distance: 2m/2m3: 0-0 2m4-2m7: 0-0 3m+: 0-0
Track: LH: 0-1 RH: 0-0 Tight: 0-1 Gall: 0-0
Aids: Bl: 0-0 Vi: 0-0 Tstrap: 0-0 Ckp: 0-0
Best Rating: 53 12/02 Weth 2m7f   gd-sft Hdl

Blue Maine (IRE)
7-y-o b m Doubletour (USA)-Bluejama (Windjammer (USA))
R A Curran R McGaw

Placings:00P   (4868)
2003/04: 16⁰Y, 16⁰Y, 20⁰GS,

	Starts	1st	2nd	3rd	Win & Pl
NH Flat	2	0	0	0	0
Hurdles	1	0	0	0	0
Career Total	3	0	0	0	0

Going: Sf: 0-0 GS: 0-1 Gd: 0-0 GF: - Fm: 0-0
Distance: 2m/2m3: 0-2 2m4-2m7: 0-1 3m+: 0-0
Track: LH: 0-1 RH: 0-0 Tight: 0-1 Gall: 0-0
Aids: Bl: 0-0 Vi: 0-0 Tstrap: 0-0 Ckp: 0-0
Best Rating: 70 3/04 Navn 2m   yield NHF

Blue Morning
72   68
6-y-o b m Balnibarbi-Bad Start (USA) (Bold Bidder)
Mrs J C McGregor Mrs Daphne Pease

Placings:00-060P   (3676)
2003/04: 16⁶G, 16⁶G, 16⁰GF, 16⁰HY,

	Starts	1st	2nd	3rd	Win & Pl
NH Flat	1	0	0	0	0

Hurdles 3 0 0 0   0
Career Total 6 0 0 0   0

Going: Sf: 0-1 GS: 0-0 Gd: 0-2 GF: - Fm: 0-1
Distance: 2m/2m3: 0-4 2m4-2m7: 0-0 3m+: 0-0
Track: LH: 0-2 RH: 0-2 Tight: 0-2 Gall: 0-0
Aids: Bl: 0-0 Vi: 0-0 Tstrap: 0-0 Ckp: 0-0
Best Rating: 69 11/03 Ayr 2m   good Hdl

Blue Orleans
72
6-y-o b g Dancing Spree (USA)-Blues Player (Jaazeiro (USA))
R Brotherton Advanced Marketing Services Ltd

Placings:1P/P   (0746)
2003/04: 16⁰G,

	Starts	1st	2nd	3rd	Win & Pl
Hurdles	1	0	0	0	
Career Total	3	1	0	0	2979
72	7/01	Strf	2m110y	E Hdl	GD £2978

Total win prize-money £2979

Going: Sf: 0-0 GS: 0-0 Gd: 0-1 GF: - Fm: 0-0
Distance: 2m/2m3: 0-1 2m4-2m7: 0-0 3m+: 0-0
Track: LH: 0-1 RH: 0-0 Tight: 0-1 Gall: 0-0
Aids: Bl: 0-0 Vi: 0-0 Tstrap: 0-0 Ckp: 0-0
Best Rating: 72 7/01 Strf 2m110y good Hdl

Blue Planet (IRE)
96
6-y-o b g Bluebird (USA)-Millie Musique (Miller's Mate)
P G Murphy Miss J Collison

Placings:30/442-P0   (3099)
2003/04: 22⁰GS, 20⁰G,

	Starts	1st	2nd	3rd	Win & Pl
Hurdles	2	0	0	0	
Career Total	7	0	1	1	1313

Going: Sf: 0-0 GS: 0-1 Gd: 0-1 GF: - Fm: 0-0
Distance: 2m/2m3: 0-0 2m4-2m7: 0-2 3m+: 0-0
Track: LH: 0-0 RH: 0-1 Tight: 0-2 Gall: 0-0
Aids: Bl: 0-0 Vi: 0-0 Tstrap: 0-0 Ckp: 0-0
Best Rating: 96 3/03 Font 2m4f   soft Hdl

Novice hurdler; stays 2m 4f; acts in soft ground.

Blue Ride (IRE)
105   127
7-y-o b m King's Ride-Charmere's Beauty (IRE) (Phardante (FR))
P F Nicholls Mrs Angela Tincknell

Placings:1/21131-25   (2150)
2003/04: 22²GF, 25⁵G,

	Starts	1st	2nd	3rd	Win & Pl
Hurdles	2	0	1	0	7848
Career Total	8	4	2	1	42069
133	4/03	Chel	2m5f110yA HHdl	GD £16240
121	2/03	Winc	2m6f	D Hdl	G-S £5389
98	12/02	Winc	2m	E Hdl	G-S £3010
96	4/02	Ludl	2m	H NHF	G-F £2222

Total win prize-money £26842

Going: Sf: 0-0 GS: 0-0 Gd: 0-1 GF: - Fm: 0-1
Distance: 2m/2m3: 0-0 2m4-2m7: 0-1 3m+: 0-1
Track: LH: 0-1 RH: 0-1 Tight: 0-0 Gall: 0-1
Aids: Bl: 0-0 Vi: 0-0 Tstrap: 0-0 Ckp: 0-0

Best Rating: 133 4/03 Chel 2m5f110y good Hdl

Useful hurdler; winner twice at Wincanton; landed Listed mares only handicap at Cheltenham April 2003; stays two miles six; acts on fast and yielding ground; looks most progressive.

Blue Romance (IRE)
97   80

6-y-o b m Bob Back (USA)-Double Symphony (IRE) (Orchestra)
P F Nicholls Mrs Angela Tincknell

Placings:1F5   (3256)
2003/04: 16¹GF, 16⁶G, 21⁵GS,

	Starts	1st	2nd	3rd	Win & Pl
NH Flat	1	1	0	0	1907
Hurdles	2	0	0	0	0
Career Total	3	1	0	0	1907
88	11/03 Winc	2m	H NHF		G-F £1906
			Total win prize-money £1907		

Going:	Sf: 0-0 GS: 0-1 Gd: 0-1 GF: - Fm: 1-1
Distance:	2m/2m3: 1-2 2m4-2m7: 0-1 3m+: 0-0
Track:	LH: 0-0 RH: 1-3 Tight: 0-0 Gall: 0-0
Aids:	Bl: 0-0 Vi: 0-0 Tstrap: 0-1 Ckp: 0-0
Best Rating:	88 11/03 Winc 2m gd-fm NHF

Blue Rondo (IRE)

4-y-o b g Hernando (FR)-Blueberry Walk (Green Desert (USA))
Ian Williams (R Charlton 5/5) Sky Blues Racing

Placings:R   (3875)
2003/04: 16ᴿS,

	Starts	1st	2nd	3rd	Win & Pl
Hurdles	1	0	0	0	
Career Total	1	0	0	0	

Going:	Sf: 0-1 GS: 0-0 Gd: 0-0 GF: 0-0 Fm: 0-0
Distance:	2m/2m3: 0-1 2m4-2m7: 0-0 3m+: 0-0
Track:	LH: 0-0 RH: 0-1 Tight: 0-0 Gall: 0-0
Aids:	Bl: 0-1 Vi: 0-0 Tstrap: 0-0 Ckp: 0-0
Best Rating:	0 2/04 Leic 2m soft Hdl

Blue Savanna
93   69+

4-y-o ch g Bluegrass Prince (IRE)-Dusk In Daytona (Beveled (USA))
J G Portman A S B Portman

Placings:5205   (4378)
2003/04: 16⁵GF, 17²GF, 16⁰G, 17⁵G,

	Starts	1st	2nd	3rd	Win & Pl
Hurdles	4	0	1	0	532
Career Total	4	0	1	0	532

Going:	Sf: 0-0 GS: 0-0 Gd: 0-1 GF: - Fm: 0-3
Distance:	2m/2m3: 0-4 2m4-2m7: 0-0 3m+: 0-0
Track:	LH: 0-1 RH: 0-3 Tight: 0-2 Gall: 0-1
Aids:	Bl: 0-2 Vi: 0-0 Tstrap: 0-0 Ckp: 0-1
Best Rating:	69 11/03 Tntn 2m1f gd-fm Hdl

Blue Shannon (IRE)
71   20

6-y-o b m Be My Native (USA)-Shannon Foam (Le Bavard (FR))

Ms Bridget Nicholls Mrs Angela Tincknell

Placings:204-0P   (2013)
2003/04: 20⁰G, 16ᴾGF,

	Starts	1st	2nd	3rd	Win & Pl
Hurdles	2	0	0	0	
Career Total	5	0	1	0	734

Going:	Sf: 0-0 GS: 0-0 Gd: 0-1 GF: - Fm: 0-1
Distance:	2m/2m3: 0-1 2m4-2m7: 0-1 3m+: 0-0
Track:	LH: 0-1 RH: 0-1 Tight: 0-1 Gall: 0-0
Aids:	Bl: 0-0 Vi: 0-0 Tstrap: 0-0 Ckp: 0-0
Best Rating:	92 3/03 Ludl 2m gd-fm NHF

Blue Streak (IRE)
104   103+

7-y-o ch g Bluebird (USA)-Fleet Amour (USA) (Afleet (CAN))
G L Moore D R Hunnisett

Placings:4162160-0123500   (4790)
2003/04: 18⁹GF, 16¹GF, 16²GF, 16³S, 18⁵G, 21⁰S, 21⁰G,

	Starts	1st	2nd	3rd	Win & Pl
Hurdles	7	1	1	1	2935
Career Total	14	3	2	1	9803
103	10/03 Plum	2m	F Hdl		G-F £1848
100	11/02 Plum	2m	E(0-110)HHdl		SFT £3094
100	10/02 Plum	2m	F Hdl		G-F £2926
			Total win prize-money £7868		

Going:	Sf: 0-2 GS: 0-0 Gd: 0-2 GF: - Fm: 1-3
Distance:	2m/2m3: 1-5 2m4-2m7: 0-2 3m+: 0-0
Track:	LH: 1-7 RH: 0-0 Tight: 1-7 Gall: 0-0
Aids:	Bl: 0-4 Vi: 0-0 Tstrap: 0-0 Ckp: 0-0
Best Rating:	103 10/03 Plum 2m gd-fm Hdl

Moderate hurdler, won in first-time eyeshield; suited by two miles; effective on fast ground.

Blue Venture (IRE)
81   87+

4-y-o ch g Alhaarth (IRE)-September Tide (IRE) (Thatching)
P C Haslam Blue Lion Racing

Placings:1P   (1355)
2003/04: 17¹GF, 17ᴾG,

	Starts	1st	2nd	3rd	Win & Pl
Hurdles	2	1	0	0	5525
Career Total	2	1	0	0	5525
87	7/03 MRas	2m1f110yD Hdl		G-F £5525	
		Total win prize-money £5525			

Going:	Sf: 0-0 GS: 0-0 Gd: 0-1 GF: - Fm: 1-1
Distance:	2m/2m3: 1-2 2m4-2m7: 0-0 3m+: 0-0
Track:	LH: 0-1 RH: 1-1 Tight: 1-2 Gall: 0-0
Aids:	Bl: 0-0 Vi: 0-0 Tstrap: 0-0 Ckp: 0-0
Best Rating:	87 7/03 MRas 2m1f110y gd-fm Hdl

Made a winning hurdles debut at Market Rasen in July; jumped right and pulled up next time.

Blue Yonder
47f

4-y-o b f Terimon-Areal (IRE) (Roselier (FR))
Mrs N S Sharpe The Blue Yonder Partnership

Placings:0   (3649)
2003/04: 16⁰GS,

	Starts	1st	2nd	3rd	Win & Pl
NH Flat	1	0	0	0	
Career Total	1	0	0	0	

Going:	Sf: 0-0 GS: 0-1 Gd: 0-0 GF: - Fm: 0-0
Distance:	2m/2m3: 0-1 2m4-2m7: 0-0 3m+: 0-0
Track:	LH: 0-0 RH: 0-1 Tight: 0-0 Gall: 0-0
Aids:	Bl: 0-0 Vi: 0-0 Tstrap: 0-0 Ckp: 0-0

Bluegrass Beau
75   66+

4-y-o ch g Bluegrass Prince (IRE)-Blushing Belle (Local Suitor (USA))
B G Powell (I A Wood 14/5) Christopher Shankland

Placings:4   (1414)
2003/04: 18⁴GF,

	Starts	1st	2nd	3rd	Win & Pl
Hurdles	1	0	0	0	0
Career Total	1	0	0	0	0

Going:	Sf: 0-0 GS: 0-0 Gd: 0-0 GF: - Fm: 0-1
Distance:	2m/2m3: 0-1 2m4-2m7: 0-0 3m+: 0-0
Track:	LH: 0-1 RH: 0-0 Tight: 0-1 Gall: 0-0
Aids:	Bl: 0-0 Vi: 0-0 Tstrap: 0-0 Ckp: 0-0
Best Rating:	66 9/03 Font 2m2f110y gd-fm Hdl

Juvenile hurdler; fair handicapper, but had become disappointing on the Flat; well beaten on hurdling debut.

Blues Story (FR)
81(92h)   (92 h)58

6-y-o b g Pistolet Bleu (IRE)-Herbe Sucree (FR) (Tiffauges)
R Ford (P R Webber 2/5) D F Price

Placings:00/44-50400P   (4256)
2003/04: 16⁵GS, 20⁰G, 20⁴GS, 17⁰GS, 16⁰G, 20ᴾG,

	Starts	1st	2nd	3rd	Win & Pl
Hurdles	4	0	0	0	328
Chases	2	0	0	0	0
Career Total	10	0	0	0	983

Going:	Sf: 0-0 GS: 0-3 Gd: 0-3 GF: - Fm: 0-0
Distance:	2m/2m3: 0-3 2m4-2m7: 0-3 3m+: 0-0
Track:	LH: 0-6 RH: 0-0 Tight: 0-5 Gall: 0-0
Aids:	Bl: 0-0 Vi: 0-0 Tstrap: 0-0 Ckp: 0-0
Best Rating:	92 5/03 Worc 2m gd-sft Hdl

Blunham
83   47

4-y-o b g Danzig Connection (USA)-Relatively Sharp (Sharpen Up)
M C Chapman (C W Fairhurst 9/7) Twinacre Nurseries Ltd

Placings:0   (4258)
2003/04: 16⁰GF,

	Starts	1st	2nd	3rd	Win & Pl
Hurdles	1	0	0	0	
Career Total	1	0	0	0	

Going:	Sf: 0-0 GS: 0-0 Gd: 0-0 GF: - Fm: 0-1
Distance:	2m/2m3: 0-1 2m4-2m7: 0-0 3m+: 0-0
Track:	LH: 0-1 RH: 0-0 Tight: 0-1 Gall: 0-0
Aids:	Bl: 0-0 Vi: 0-0 Tstrap: 0-0 Ckp: 0-0
Best Rating:	47 3/04 Catt 2m gd-fm Hdl

Blunham Hill (IRE)
105(104h)   (101h)102+

6-y-o ch g Over The River (FR)-Bronach (Beau Charmeur (FR))

John R Upson The Reserved Judgment Partnership

Placings:53P5-02P2431   (4534)
2003/04: 20⁰GS, 21²S, 21³PS, 23²GS, 20⁴S, 25³GS, 22¹GS,

	Starts	1st	2nd	3rd	Win & Pl
Hurdles	5	0	2	0	2006
Chases	2	1	0	1	4558
Career Total	11	1	2	2	7188
102 3/04 Towc 2m6f		E Ch		G-S	£3948

Total win prize-money £3949

Going:	Sf: 0-3 GS: 1-4 Gd: 0-0 GF: - Fm: 0-0
Distance:	2m/2m3: 0-0 2m4-2m7: 1-5 3m+: 0-2
Track:	LH: 0-3 RH: 1-4 Tight: 0-1 Gall: 0-0
Aids:	Bl: 0-0 Vi: 0-0 Tstrap: 0-0 Ckp: 0-0
Best Rating:	102 3/04 Towc 2m6f gd-sft Ch

Moderate chaser/hurdler, stays two and a half miles and will be suited by further.

Blushing Bull
111f   111f
5-y-o b g Makbul-Blush (Gildoran)
P F Nicholls Richard Barber

Placings:202   (4529)
2003/04: 16²HY, 16⁰G, 16²GS,

	Starts	1st	2nd	3rd	Win & Pl
NH Flat	3	0	2	0	1202
Career Total	3	0	2	0	1202

Going:	Sf: 0-1 GS: 1-0 Gd: 0-1 GF: - Fm: 0-0
Distance:	2m/2m3: 0-3 2m4-2m7: 0-0 3m+: 0-0
Track:	LH: 0-3 RH: 0-0 Tight: 0-0 Gall: 0-1
Aids:	Bl: 0-0 Vi: 0-0 Tstrap: 0-0 Ckp: 0-0
Best Rating:	111 3/04 Chep 2m110y gd-sft NHF

Fair form in bumpers; narrowly denied on debut in bumper at Uttoxeter in January 2004 (first two well clear); disappointing in hot contest on faster ground next time; returned to form when runner-up in soft ground at Chepstow; acts on soft ground.

Blushing Prince (IRE)
98   91
6-y-o b g Priolo (USA)-Eliade (IRE) (Flash Of Steel)
Mrs L Stubbs Des Thurlby

Placings:2163   (2366)
2003/04: 17²GF, 16¹F, 16⁶G, 21³GF,

	Starts	1st	2nd	3rd	Win & Pl
Hurdles	4	1	1	1	5550
Career Total	4	1	1	1	5550
91 10/03 Weth 2m		D Hdl		FRM	£4026

Total win prize-money £4027

Going:	Sf: 0-0 GS: 0-0 Gd: 0-1 GF: - Fm: 1-3
Distance:	2m/2m3: 1-3 2m4-2m7: 0-1 3m+: 0-0
Track:	LH: 1-2 RH: 0-2 Tight: 0-0 Gall: 0-0
Aids:	Bl: 0-0 Vi: 0-0 Tstrap: 1-4 Ckp: 0-0
Best Rating:	91 11/03 Weth 2m good Hdl

Novice hurdler, plating-class on the Flat; flattered when runner-up on debut; went one better next time; wears tongue tie; acts on firm ground.

Blyth Brook

12-y-o b g Meadowbrook-The Bean-Goose (King Sitric)
W T Reed Mrs S A Sutton

Placings:000/25P2/65/03P1-1P1PF   (4626)
2003/04: 20¹GF, 20¹G, 20⁰G, 24¹G, 21³PGF, 21⁴FS,

	Starts	1st	2nd	3rd	Win & Pl
Chases	6	3	0	0	6987
Career Total	18	3	2	1	9230
105 2/04 Muss 3m				GD	£2170
101 5/03 Prth 2m4f110yH Ch				GD	£3347
86 4/03 Newc 2m4f H Ch				G-F	£1469

Total win prize-money £6987

Going:	Sf: 0-0 GS: 0-0 Gd: 2-4 GF: - Fm: 1-2
Distance:	2m/2m3: 0-0 2m4-2m7: 2-5 3m+: 1-1
Track:	LH: 1-4 RH: 2-2 Tight: 1-2 Gall: 1-1
Aids:	Bl: 0-0 Vi: 0-0 Tstrap: 0-0 Ckp: 0-0
Best Rating:	105 2/04 Muss 3m good Ch

Fair hunter chaser, effective from two and a half miles upwards and suited by fast ground; can be headstrong.

Boardroom Dancer (IRE)
75   97
7-y-o b g Executive Perk-Dancing Course (IRE) (Crash Course)
D J Caro D J Caro

Placings:466-P31   (2577)
2003/04: 24⁴S, 25³G, 24¹GF,

	Starts	1st	2nd	3rd	Win & Pl
Hurdles	1	0	0	0	0
Chases	2	1	0	1	3844
Career Total	6	1	0	1	3844
97 12/03 Sthl		3m110y E Ch		G-F	£3146

Total win prize-money £3147

Going:	Sf: 0-1 GS: 0-0 Gd: 0-1 GF: - Fm: 1-1
Distance:	2m/2m3: 0-0 2m4-2m7: 0-0 3m+: 1-3
Track:	LH: 1-3 RH: 0-0 Tight: 1-2 Gall: 0-0
Aids:	Bl: 0-0 Vi: 0-0 Tstrap: 0-0 Ckp: 0-0
Best Rating:	97 12/03 Sthl 3m110y gd-fm Ch

Novice chaser; headstrong; won a poor race easily second time over fences.

Boardwalk Knight (IRE)
83   (98?h)57
7-y-o b g Shardari-Takhiyra (Vayrann)
M Todhunter Abbadis Racing Club

Placings:002F/0100P-0   (1072)
2003/04: 16⁰GF,

	Starts	1st	2nd	3rd	Win & Pl
Chases	1	0	0	0	0
Career Total	10	1	1	0	5100
92 8/02 Wxfd 2m			Hdl	G-Y	£3809

Total win prize-money £3810

Going:	Sf: 0-0 GS: 0-0 Gd: 0-0 GF: - Fm: 0-1
Distance:	2m/2m3: 0-1 2m4-2m7: 0-0 3m+: 0-0
Track:	LH: 0-1 RH: 0-0 Tight: 0-1 Gall: 0-0
Aids:	Bl: 0-0 Vi: 0-0 Tstrap: 0-0 Ckp: 0-0
Best Rating:	98 10/02 Rosc 2m good Hdl

Boater
91   76
10-y-o b g Batshoof-Velvet Beret (IRE) (Dominion)
R J Baker Christine And Aubrey Loze

Placings:23/42P61/02211402/3F5/032252426/16F4-000   (0633)

2003/04: 16⁰G, 17⁰GF, 22⁰GF,

	Starts	1st	2nd	3rd	Win & Pl
Hurdles	3	0	0	0	
Career Total	34	4	9	3	22865
111 5/02 NAbb 2m1f		E(0-105)HHdl		G-S	£2562
118 8/99 NAbb 2m1f		C(0-130)HHdl		GD	£4662
112 7/99 NAbb 2m1f		F(0-100)HHdl		G-F	£2640
99 4/99 Tntn 2m1f		F(0-100)HHdl		G-S	£1966

Total win prize-money £11830

Going:	Sf: 0-0 GS: 0-0 Gd: 0-1 GF: - Fm: 0-2
Distance:	2m/2m3: 0-2 2m4-2m7: 0-1 3m+: 0-0
Track:	LH: 0-0 RH: 0-0 Tight: 0-2 Gall: 0-0
Aids:	Bl: 0-2 Vi: 0-0 Tstrap: 0-0 Ckp: 0-0
Best Rating:	122 7/00 NAbb 2m1f gd-fm Hdl

Fair handicap hurdler; suited by fast ground but acts on easier; returned after a five month absence to narrowly win a Class E handicap at Newton Abbot May 2002; lightly raced since; usually wears blinkers.

Bob Ar Aghaidh (IRE)
102   115+
8-y-o b g Bob Back (USA)-Shuil Ar Aghaidh (The Parson)
C Tinkler George Ward

Placings:260/5232-1FP0F   (4819)
2003/04: 20¹GS, 19⁴S, 21⁶S, 20⁰S, 22⁶GF,

	Starts	1st	2nd	3rd	Win & Pl
Hurdles	5	1	0	0	2765
Career Total	12	1	3	1	5877
115 11/03 Uttx 2m4f110y				E Hdl	G-S

£2765

Total win prize-money £2765

Going:	Sf: 0-3 GS: 1-1 Gd: 0-0 GF: - Fm: 0-1
Distance:	2m/2m3: 0-0 2m4-2m7: 1-5 3m+: 0-0
Track:	LH: 1-3 RH: 0-0 Tight: 0-1 Gall: 0-0
Aids:	Bl: 0-0 Vi: 0-0 Tstrap: 0-0 Ckp: 0-0
Best Rating:	115 11/03 Uttx 2m4f110y gd-sft Hdl

Fair hurdler; off the mark when winning at Uttoxeter in November; fell next time; stays two and a half miles; acts on soft ground; open to some improvement.

Bob Bob Bobbin
113f   117f
5-y-o gr g Bob Back (USA)-Absalom's Lady (Absalom)
C L Tizzard Mrs Sarah Tizzard

Placings:24   (3832)
2003/04: 16²S, 16⁴G,

	Starts	1st	2nd	3rd	Win & Pl
NH Flat	2	0	1	0	4435
Career Total	2	0	1	0	4435

Going:	Sf: 0-1 GS: 0-0 Gd: 0-1 GF: - Fm: 0-0
Distance:	2m/2m3: 0-2 2m4-2m7: 0-0 3m+: 0-0
Track:	LH: 0-2 RH: 0-0 Tight: 0-0 Gall: 0-1
Aids:	Bl: 0-0 Vi: 0-0 Tstrap: 0-0 Ckp: 0-0
Best Rating:	120 2/04 Newb 2m110y good NHF

Son of Bob Back who ran a blinder on his debut at Chepstow in Grade Two bumper in December 2003 on soft ground.

Bob Le Gaoth (IRE)
74   84
8-y-o br g Bob Back (USA)-Shuil Le Gaoth (IRE) (Strong Gale)

C Tinkler Bonusprint

Placings:*31/U/F-30P*   (4519)
2003/04: 22³HY, 20⁰GS, 22ᴾGS,

	Starts	1st	2nd	3rd	Win & Pl
Hurdles	3	0	0	1	528
Career Total	7	1	0	2	3358
110 4/01	NAbb	2m1f		H NHF	SFT £2450

Total win prize-money £2450

Going:	Sf: 0-1 GS: 0-2 Gd: 0-0 GF: - Fm: 0-0
Distance:	2m/2m3: 0-0 2m4-2m7: 0-3 3m+: 0-0
Track:	LH: 0-0 RH: 0-2 Tight: 0-1 Gall: 0-0
Aids:	Bl: 0-0 Vi: 0-0 Tstrap: 0-0 Ckp: 0-0
Best Rating:	110 4/01 NAbb 2m1f soft NHF

Soft ground bumper winner in 2001; lightly-raced since; has been placed over hurdles; stays 2m4f.

Bob The Piler
107   124+

8-y-o b g Jendali (USA)-Laxay (Laxton)
N G Richards Taranto De Pol

Placings:*415/4-311020*   (4662)
2003/04: 20³G, 17¹HY, 16¹HY, 20⁰HY, 16²HY, 20⁰S,

	Starts	1st	2nd	3rd	Win & Pl
Hurdles	6	2	1	1	7991
Career Total	10	3	1	1	9580
124 1/04	Newc 2m	E(0-105)HHdl	HVY	£3490
107 11/03	Carl 2m1f	E Hdl	HVY	£2759
108 2/01	Sedg 2m1f	H NHF	SFT	£1589

Total win prize-money £7839

Going:	Sf: 2-5 GS: 0-0 Gd: 0-1 GF: - Fm: 0-0
Distance:	2m/2m3: 2-3 2m4-2m7: 0-3 3m+: 0-0
Track:	LH: 1-3 RH: 1-3 Tight: 0-0 Gall: 1-2
Aids:	Bl: 0-0 Vi: 0-0 Tstrap: 0-0 Ckp: 0-0
Best Rating:	124 1/04 Newc 2m heavy Hdl

Modest hurdler; acts on soft ground; should be suited by further than two miles; progressive.

Bob's Buster
109(93h)   (61h)115+

8-y-o b g Bob's Return (IRE)-Saltina (Bustino)
R Johnson Mrs Geraldine Jones

Placings:*FP0/02053444/252F43313/045-014113123336*
         (4938)
2003/04: 17⁰S, 16¹GF, 16⁴GF, 16¹G, 16¹G, 16³GS, 17¹S, 16²HY, 16³GS, 17³GS, 16³GS, 16ᴾGS,

	Starts	1st	2nd	3rd	Win & Pl
Hurdles	1	0	0	0	0
Chases	11	4	1	4	18197
Career Total	35	5	4	8	27401
115 1/04	Kels 2m1f	E(0-110)HCh	SFT	£4160
115 12/03	Sedg 2m110y	E(0-105)HCh	GD	£3269
101 12/03	Donc 2m110y	D(0-115)HCh	GD	£3347
110 11/03	Hexm 2m110y	F(0-95)HCh	G-F	£2372
90 4/02	Hexm 2m110y	E(0-110)HHdl	GD	£3052

Total win prize-money £16202

Going:	Sf: 1-3 GS: 0-5 Gd: 2-2 GF: - Fm: 1-2
Distance:	2m/2m3: 4-12 2m4-2m7: 0-0 3m+: 0-0
Track:	LH: 4-10 RH: 0-2 Tight: 2-6 Gall: 1-1
Aids:	Bl: 0-0 Vi: 0-0 Tstrap: 0-0 Ckp: 2-8
Best Rating:	115 1/04 Kels 2m1f soft Ch

Moderate chaser; has won on soft but suited by a sound surface and best suited by two miles; has a good strike rate over fences and may be capable of better; has worn sheepskin cheekpieces.

Bob's Gone (IRE)
105   105

6-y-o ch g Eurobus-Bob's Girl (IRE) (Bob Back (USA))
R J Smith Team Cobra Racing Syndicate

Placings:*F35241P/U044-1P*   (2469)
2003/04: 22¹G, 24ᴾS,

	Starts	1st	2nd	3rd	Win & Pl
Hurdles	2	1	0	0	6165
Career Total	13	2	1	1	15244
107 7/03	Strf	2m6f110yD(0-115)HHdl	GD	£6165
105 12/01	Limk 2m	Hdl	GD	£6120

Total win prize-money £12286

Going:	Sf: 0-1 GS: 0-0 Gd: 1-1 GF: - Fm: 0-0
Distance:	2m/2m3: 0-0 2m4-2m7: 1-1 3m+: 0-1
Track:	LH: 1-1 RH: 0-1 Tight: 1-1 Gall: 0-0
Aids:	Bl: 0-0 Vi: 0-0 Tstrap: 0-0 Ckp: 0-0
Best Rating:	107 7/03 Strf 2m6f110y good Hdl

Moderate hurdler; won over two miles on the Flat in Ireland; lightly-raced since; landed gamble when making most in two miles six Stratford handicap in July 2003; stays well; likes cut in the ground.

Bob's Sherie
86   48

5-y-o b m Bob's Return (IRE)-Sheraton Girl (Mon Tresor)
W M Brisbourne Happy Times Ahead Partnership

Placings:*F05P00*   (4569)
2003/04: 20ᶠGS, 21⁰GS, 16⁵S, 16ᴾGS, 17⁰GF, 17⁰GS,

	Starts	1st	2nd	3rd	Win & Pl
Hurdles	6	0	0	0	0
Career Total	6	0	0	0	0

Going:	Sf: 0-1 GS: 0-4 Gd: 0-0 GF: - Fm: 0-1
Distance:	2m/2m3: 0-4 2m4-2m7: 0-2 3m+: 0-0
Track:	LH: 0-2 RH: 0-4 Tight: 0-1 Gall: 0-0
Aids:	Bl: 0-0 Vi: 0-0 Tstrap: 0-0 Ckp: 0-0
Best Rating:	49 1/04 Leic 2m soft Hdl

Bob's Temptation

5-y-o br g Bob's Return (IRE)-Temptation (IRE) (Clearly Bust)
A J Wilson The Cotswold Partnership

Placings:*0*   (4571)
2003/04: 17⁰GS,

	Starts	1st	2nd	3rd	Win & Pl
NH Flat	1	0	0	0	0
Career Total	1	0	0	0	0

Going:	Sf: 0-0 GS: 0-1 Gd: 0-0 GF: - Fm: 0-0
Distance:	2m/2m3: 0-1 2m4-2m7: 0-0 3m+: 0-0
Track:	LH: 0-1 RH: 0-0 Tight: 0-1 Gall: 0-0
Aids:	Bl: 0-0 Vi: 0-0 Tstrap: 0-0 Ckp: 0-0

Bob's The Business (IRE)
103   106+

10-y-o b g Bob Back (USA)-Kiora (Camden Town)
Ian Williams Christopher Harris

Placings:*1P*   (4342)
2003/04: 25¹GS, 29ᴾGS,

	Starts	1st	2nd	3rd	Win & Pl
Chases	2	1	0	0	3959
Career Total	2	1	0	0	3959
106 2/04	Towc	3m1f	E Ch	G-S £3958

Total win prize-money £3959

Going:	Sf: 0-0 GS: 1-2 Gd: 0-0 GF: - Fm: 0-0
Distance:	2m/2m3: 0-0 2m4-2m7: 0-0 3m+: 1-2
Track:	LH: 0-1 RH: 1-1 Tight: 0-0 Gall: 0-0
Aids:	Bl: 0-0 Vi: 0-0 Tstrap: 0-0 Ckp: 0-0
Best Rating:	106 2/04 Towc 3m1f gd-sft Ch

Triple point-to-point winner; made a winning chase debut at Towcester in February 2004; disappointed next time; stays 3m; acts on soft ground.

Bobalong (IRE)
108   99

7-y-o b g Bob's Return (IRE)-Northern Wind (Northfields (USA))
C P Morlock Pell-Mell Partners

Placings:*0-06P1PP*   (4561)
2003/04: 20⁰GS, 22⁶GS, 22ᴾHY, 24¹S, 25ᴾG, 24ᴾGS,

	Starts	1st	2nd	3rd	Win & Pl
Hurdles	6	1	0	0	2667
Career Total	7	1	0	0	2667
99 1/04	Chep 3m	F Hdl	SFT	£2667

Total win prize-money £2667

Going:	Sf: 1-2 GS: 0-3 Gd: 0-1 GF: - Fm: 0-0
Distance:	2m/2m3: 0-0 2m4-2m7: 0-3 3m+: 1-3
Track:	LH: 1-4 RH: 0-2 Tight: 0-2 Gall: 0-1
Aids:	Bl: 0-0 Vi: 0-0 Tstrap: 0-1 Ckp: 0-0
Best Rating:	99 1/04 Chep 3m soft Hdl

Modest novice hurdler; improved massively on fourth outing over hurdles when upped to three miles on soft ground at Chepstow in January; likes to force the pace.

Bobanvi
103   74+

6-y-o b m Timeless Times (USA)-Bobanlyn (IRE) (Dance Of Life (USA))
J S Wainwright S Pedersen

Placings:*0002044P/P2500063-3015445P*   (3000)
2003/04: 27³S, 20⁰G, 22¹G, 21⁵GF, 20⁴GF, 22⁴G, 24⁵GF, 25ᴾGS,

	Starts	1st	2nd	3rd	Win & Pl
Hurdles	8	1	0	1	3535
Career Total	24	1	2	2	5411
74 8/03	Ctml	2m6f	G(0-90)HHdl	GD £3041

Total win prize-money £3042

Going:	Sf: 0-1 GS: 0-1 Gd: 1-3 GF: - Fm: 0-3
Distance:	2m/2m3: 0-0 2m4-2m7: 1-5 3m+: 0-3
Track:	LH: 1-6 RH: 0-1 Tight: 1-3 Gall: 0-1
Aids:	Bl: 0-0 Vi: 1-5 Tstrap: 0-0 Ckp: 0-2
Best Rating:	77 11/03 MRas 2m6f good Hdl

Poor hurdler; visored for the first time when breaking her duck in selling handicap hurdle at Cartmel in August; stays two mile six.

Bobayaro (IRE)
103(92h)   (108h)132

8-y-o b g Bob Back (USA)-Instanter (Morston (FR))
N G Richards It's A Bargain Syndicate

Placings:*2/6413321/232F421-11F*   (0784)
2003/04: 23¹G, 24¹GF, 24ᶠG,

	Starts	1st	2nd	3rd	Win & Pl
Chases	3	2	0	0	10738

Career Total		18	5	5	3	36670
132	6/03 Prth 3m	D Ch			G-F	£6812
132	5/03 Weth	2m7f110yE Ch			GD	£3926
97	4/03 Prth 3m	C Ch			GD	£9065
108	4/02 Prth	2m4f110yD Hdl			GD	£3718
99	9/01 Gway 2m	NHF			G-F	£5008
		Total win prize-money £28529				

Going:	Sf: 0-0 GS: 0-0 Gd: 1-2 GF: - Fm: 1-1
Distance:	2m/2m3: 0-0 2m4-2m7: 0-0 **3m+: 2-3**
Track:	LH: 0-0 **RH: 1-2** Tight: 0-0 Gall: 0-0
Aids:	Bl: 0-0 Vi: 0-0 Tstrap: 0-0 Ckp: 0-0
Best Rating:	132 6/03 Prth 3m gd-fm Ch

Fair chaser; successful over hurdles; rattled up a hat-trick between April and June 2003; stays 3 miles; best on decent ground.

Bobbi Rose Red
91(102h)   (76h)**72**
7-y-o ch m Bob Back (USA)-Lady Rosanna (Kind Of Hush)
P T Dalton Mrs Julie Martin

Placings:536/05F4-4345P065   (3693)
2003/04: 24⁴S, 20³G, 16⁴G, 22⁵GS, 21ᴾS, 22⁰G, 20⁶HY, 19⁵G,

	Starts	1st	2nd	3rd	Win & Pl
Hurdles	7	0	0	1	1113
Chases	1	0	0	0	0
Career Total	15	0	0	2	1336

Going:	Sf: 0-3 GS: 0-1 Gd: 0-4 GF: - Fm: 0-0
Distance:	2m/2m3: 0-2 2m4-2m7: 0-5 3m+: 0-1
Track:	LH: 0-6 RH: 0-2 Tight: 0-3 Gall: 0-0
Aids:	Bl: 0-0 Vi: 0-0 Tstrap: 0-0 Ckp: 0-0
Best Rating:	83 3/02 Towc 2m soft NHF

Plating-class novice hurdler; stays three miles.

Bobbie James (IRE)

8-y-o ch g Roselier (FR)-Brown Forest (Brave Invader (USA))
J Mackie Mrs D E H Turner

Placings:00-P   (0205)
2003/04: 21ᴾGF,

	Starts	1st	2nd	3rd	Win & Pl
Hurdles	1	0	0	0	
Career Total	3	0	0	0	

Going:	Sf: 0-0 GS: 0-0 Gd: 0-0 GF: - Fm: 0-1
Distance:	2m/2m3: 0-0 2m4-2m7: 0-1 3m+: 0-0
Track:	LH: 0-1 RH: 0-0 Tight: 0-0 Gall: 0-0
Aids:	Bl: 0-0 Vi: 0-0 Tstrap: 0-0 Ckp: 0-0
Best Rating:	59 10/02 Chel 2m110y good NHF

Bobby Blakeney
86   **45**
9-y-o gr g Baron Blakeney-Coming Out (Fair Season)
Miss L V Davis Miss Louise Davis

Placings:P-0P   (0531)
2003/04: 22⁰S, 20ᴾGF,

	Starts	1st	2nd	3rd	Win & Pl
Hurdles	2	0	0	0	
Career Total	3	0	0	0	

Going:	Sf: 0-1 GS: 0-0 Gd: 0-0 GF: - Fm: 0-1
Distance:	2m/2m3: 0-0 2m4-2m7: 0-2 3m+: 0-0

Track:	LH: 0-2 RH: 0-0 Tight: 0-0 Gall: 0-0
Aids:	Bl: 0-0 Vi: 0-0 Tstrap: 0-0 Ckp: 0-0
Best Rating:	45 5/03 Uttx 2m6f110y soft Hdl

Bobby Dazzler
107   **110+**
5-y-o b g Bob's Return (IRE)-Preachers Popsy (The Parson)
N A Twiston-Davies Our Friends In The North

Placings:05021   (4908)
2003/04: 17⁰G, 20⁵S, 21⁰GS, 21²G, 20¹S,

	Starts	1st	2nd	3rd	Win & Pl
NH Flat	1	0	0	0	0
Hurdles	4	1	1	0	8197
Career Total	5	1	1	0	8197
107	4/04 Prth	2m4f110yD Hdl	SFT	£5837	
	Total win prize-money £5837				

Going:	Sf: 1-2 GS: 0-1 Gd: 0-2 GF: - Fm: 0-0
Distance:	2m/2m3: 0-1 **2m4-2m7: 1-4** 3m+: 0-0
Track:	LH: 0-0 **RH: 1-4** Tight: 0-0 Gall: 0-0
Aids:	Bl: 0-0 Vi: 0-0 Tstrap: 0-0 Ckp: 0-0
Best Rating:	110 2/04 Kemp 2m5f good Hdl

Modest hurdler; has been progressing with racing; effective at up to two mile five; acts on good and soft ground.

Bobby Grant
144
13-y-o ch g Gunner B-Goldaw (Gala Performance (ZIM))
P Beaumont John J Thompson

Placings:3f115/2/2F2310/121124/251/6/3240-P   (2445)
2003/04: 28ᴾS,

	Starts	1st	2nd	3rd	Win & Pl
Chases	1	0	0	0	
Career Total	27	8	7	3	132102
163	12/00 Hayd 3m	A Ch	HVY	£25200	
153	1/00 Hayd 3m	B(0-140)HCh	SFT	£8827	
160	12/99 Hayd 3m	A Ch	HVY	£25000	
137	11/99 Newc 2m4f	D(0-125)HCh	GD	£3810	
142	1/99 Newc 2m4f	A Ch	SFT	£12834	
112	2/97 Newc 2m4f	E Hdl	GD	£2473	
101	1/97 Weth	2m4f110yE Hdl	GD	£2587	
100	12/96 Hexm 2m	H NHF	G-S	£1406	
	Total win prize-money £82139				

Going:	Sf: 0-1 GS: 0-0 Gd: 0-0 GF: - Fm: 0-0
Distance:	2m/2m3: 0-0 2m4-2m7: 0-0 3m+: 0-1
Track:	LH: 0-0 RH: 0-0 Tight: 0-0 Gall: 0-0
Aids:	Bl: 0-0 Vi: 0-0 Tstrap: 0-0 Ckp: 0-0
Best Rating:	163 12/00 Hayd 3m heavy Ch

Smart staying chaser; lightly raced these days; stays beyond three miles; effective in soft ground; goes well at Haydock. Sadly broke a leg at that track in November 2003. (DEAD)

Bobosh
90   **103**
8-y-o b g Devil's Jump-Jane Craig (Rapid Pass)
R Dickin Haydn Gott

Placings:00/0/0250255234040210/504440-6   (4760)
2003/04: 16⁶S,

	Starts	1st	2nd	3rd	Win & Pl
Hurdles	1	0	0	0	
Career Total	26	1	4	1	11971
102	4/02 Ludl	2m5f	D(0-120)HHdl	G-F	£4336
	Total win prize-money £4337				

Going:	Sf: 0-1 GS: 0-0 Gd: 0-0 GF: - Fm: 0-0

Track:	LH: 0-2 RH: 0-0 Tight: 0-0 Gall: 0-0
Aids:	Bl: 0-0 Vi: 0-0 Tstrap: 0-0 Ckp: 0-0
Best Rating:	45 5/03 Uttx 2m6f110y soft Hdl

Distance:	2m/2m3: 0-1 2m4-2m7: 0-0 3m+: 0-0
Track:	LH: 0-0 RH: 0-1 Tight: 0-0 Gall: 0-0
Aids:	Bl: 0-0 Vi: 0-0 Tstrap: 0-0 Ckp: 0-0
Best Rating:	102 4/02 Ludl 2m5f gd-fm Hdl

Modest hurdler; seems to act on any surface but lacks a change of gear.

Bobsbest (IRE)
108(83c)   (59c)**84**
8-y-o b g Lashkari-Bobs (Warpath)
R J Price (R Dickin 16/10) R A Jefferies

Placings:0400/06634040/5200P0F1P2-226345B554 (4142)
2003/04: 21²GF, 20²GF, 22⁸GF, 20³G, 24⁴F, 24⁵GF, 22⁸GS,
19⁵GS, 20⁵S, 24⁴G,

	Starts	1st	2nd	3rd	Win & Pl
Hurdles	9	0	2	1	3300
Chases	1	0	0	0	0
Career Total	32	1	4	2	8825
75	3/03 MRas 2m6f	F(0-95)HHdl	GD	£3241	
	Total win prize-money £3241				

Going:	Sf: 0-1 GS: 0-2 Gd: 0-2 GF: - Fm: 0-5
Distance:	2m/2m3: 0-0 2m4-2m7: 0-7 3m+: 0-3
Track:	LH: 0-2 RH: 0-8 Tight: 0-1 Gall: 0-0
Aids:	Bl: 0-0 Vi: 0-0 Tstrap: 0-0 Ckp: 0-0
Best Rating:	88 10/00 Chel 2m110y good NHF

Plating-class hurdler/chaser; stays well and suited by decent ground; has worn visor.

Bobsleigh
105   **111**
5-y-o b g Robellino (USA)-Do Run Run (Commanche Run)
Mrs A J Perrett A Ogilvy And Mrs F Ogilvy

Placings:22164   (3956)
2003/04: 17²GS, 20²G, 16¹S, 20⁶S, 22⁴G,

	Starts	1st	2nd	3rd	Win & Pl
Hurdles	5	1	2	0	6945
Career Total	5	1	2	0	6945
99	1/04 Plum 2m	D Hdl	SFT	£4992	
	Total win prize-money £4992				

Going:	Sf: 1-2 GS: 0-1 Gd: 0-2 GF: - Fm: 0-0
Distance:	**2m/2m3: 1-2** 2m4-2m7: 0-3 3m+: 0-0
Track:	**LH: 1-2** RH: 0-2 **Tight: 1-4** Gall: 0-0
Aids:	Bl: 0-0 Vi: 0-0 Tstrap: 0-0 Ckp: 0-0
Best Rating:	111 2/04 Font 2m6f110y good Hdl

Modest novice hurdler; fair stayer on the Flat; stays two miles; acts on good to soft ground.

Bodfari Creek
108   **114**
7-y-o ch g In The Wings-Cormorant Creek (Gorytus (USA))
J G Portman (P R Webber 16/7) Pump Technology Limited

Placings:1/2F-2211143   (1364)
2003/04: 16²G, 20²GF, 24¹GF, 24¹G, 22¹GF, 24⁴GF, 20³GF,

	Starts	1st	2nd	3rd	Win & Pl
Hurdles	7	3	2	1	13646
Career Total	10	4	3	1	16886
111	8/03 Font	2m6f110yE Hdl	G-F	£3334
98	7/03 Worc 3m	E Hdl	GD	£3437
96	6/03 Worc 3m	E Hdl	G-F	£3542
98	3/02 Hayd 2m	H NHF	GD	£1932
	Total win prize-money £12246				

Going:	Sf: 0-0 GS: 0-0 Gd: 1-2 GF: - Fm: 2-5
Distance:	2m/2m3: 1-0 2m4-2m7: 1-3 **3m+: 2-3**
Track:	LH: 3-6 RH: 0-1 Tight: 1-2 Gall: 0-0

Aids: Bl: 0-0 Vi: 0-0 Tstrap: 0-0 Ckp: 0-0
Best Rating: 114 9/03   Worc   2m4f   gd-fm   Hdl

Successful on debut in Haydock bumper March 2002; failed to achieve much with back-to-back wins at Worcester over 3m in the summer; easy winner at Fontwell in August for new stable; well beaten on handicap bow two weeks later; stays 3m; acts on fast ground.

Bodfari Rose
102   92
5-y-o ch m Indian Ridge-Royale Rose (FR) (Bering)
A Bailey   Mrs J Bailey

Placings:332P-22326P   (1357)
2003/04: 17²G, 17²S, 16³GF, 16²GF, 20⁶G, 20⁶G,

	Starts	1st	2nd	3rd	Win & Pl
Hurdles	6	0	3	1	4039
Career Total	10	0	4	3	5991

Going: Sf: 0-1 GS: 0-0 Gd: 0-3 GF: - Fm: 0-2
Distance: 2m/2m3: 0-4 2m4-2m7: 0-2 3m+: 0-0
Track: LH: 0-5 RH: 0-1 Tight: 0-3 Gall: 0-0
Aids: Bl: 0-0 Vi: 0-0 Tstrap: 0-0 Ckp: 0-6
Best Rating: 89   6/03   Uttx   2m   gd-fm   Hdl

Moderate maiden hurdler; regularly in the frame without getting her head in front.

Bodfari Signet
109   112
8-y-o ch g King's Signet (USA)-Darakah (Doulab (USA))
Mrs S C Bradburne   Strath Pack Partnership

Placings:4130P/00F316/4F541422246/212455065233-
P5434142422300   (4729)
2003/04: 20⁶G, 20⁵GF, 20⁴G, 20³G, 22⁴F, 22¹GF, 22⁴G, 20²GF, 24⁴GF, 16²G, 16²G, 16³F, 18⁰G, 20⁰G,

	Starts	1st	2nd	3rd	Win & Pl
Hurdles	14	1	3	2	12408
Career Total	48	5	9	6	38524
99	10/03 Kels	2m6f110yF(0-100)HHdl	G-F	£3445
104	5/02 Prth	2m4f110yE(0-110)HHdl	G-F	£4182
103	12/01 Muss	2m1f	G(0-95)HHdl	G-F	£2341
92	4/01 Muss	2m1f	F(0-100)HHdl	G-F	£3230
91	9/99 Strf	2m10y E Hdl	G-F	£3096
		Total win prize-money £16298

Going: Sf: 0-0 GS: 0-0 Gd: 0-8 GF: - Fm: 1-6
Distance: 2m/2m3: 0-4 2m4-2m7: 1-9 3m+: 0-0
Track: LH: 1-4 RH: 0-9 Tight: 1-8 Gall: 0-0
Aids: Bl: 0-0 Vi: 0-1 Tstrap: 0-0 Ckp: 0-0
Best Rating: 112 2/04   Muss   2m   good   Hdl

Moderate hurdler; best at up to two miles and six furlongs, acts on any ground, likes Musselburgh.

Bogie Bogey
42f
4-y-o b f Royal Applause-Classic Colleen (IRE) (Sadler's Wells (USA))
G B Balding   Mrs Helen Bogie & Mrs Julia Harvey

Placings:0P   (2675)
2003/04: 12⁰GF, 12⁰GF,

	Starts	1st	2nd	3rd	Win & Pl
NH Flat	2	0	0	0	
Career Total	2	0	0	0	

Going: Sf: 0-0 GS: 0-0 Gd: 0-0 GF: - Fm: 0-2
Distance: 2m/2m3: 0-0 2m4-2m7: 0-0 3m+: 0-0

Track: LH: 0-2 RH: 0-0 Tight: 0-0 Gall: 0-0
Aids: Bl: 0-0 Vi: 0-0 Tstrap: 0-0 Ckp: 0-0
Best Rating: 42   11/03   Newb   1m4f110y   gd-fm   NHF

Bohemian Boy (IRE)
104   114+
6-y-o gr g Roselier (FR)-Right Hand (Oats)
M Pitman   S D Hemstock

Placings:122   (3411)
2003/04: 22¹GS, 22²HY, 21²S,

	Starts	1st	2nd	3rd	Win & Pl
Hurdles	3	1	2	0	5534
Career Total	3	1	2	0	5534
111	12/03 Folk	2m6f110yF Hdl	G-S	£2828
		Total win prize-money £2828

Going: Sf: 0-2 GS: 1-1 Gd: 0-0 GF: - Fm: 0-0
Distance: 2m/2m3: 0-4 2m4-2m7: 1-3 3m+: 0-0
Track: LH: 0-1 RH: 1-2 Tight: 1-3 Gall: 0-0
Aids: Bl: 0-0 Vi: 0-0 Tstrap: 0-0 Ckp: 0-0
Best Rating: 120 1/04   Plum   2m5f   soft   Hdl

Modest novice hurdler; made a winning debut at Folkestone in December 2003; stays two miles six; acts on easy ground.

Bohemian Spirit (IRE)

6-y-o b g Eagle Eyed (USA)-Tuesday Morning (Sadler's Wells (USA))
M J Brown   Peter Armitage

Placings:U1P1   (4775)
2003/04: 24ᵁS, 21¹GF, 20⁰GS, 21¹G,

	Starts	1st	2nd	3rd	Win & Pl
Chases	4	2	0	0	5361
Career Total	4	2	0	0	5361
103	4/04 Fknm	2m5f110yH Ch	GD	£3421
103	3/04 Ayr	2m5f110yH Ch	G-F	£1939
		Total win prize-money £5361

Going: Sf: 0-1 GS: 0-1 Gd: 1-1 GF: - Fm: 1-1
Distance: 2m/2m3: 0-0 2m4-2m7: 2-3 3m+: 0-1
Track: LH: 2-2 RH: 0-2 Tight: 1-2 Gall: 0-1
Aids: Bl: 0-0 Vi: 0-0 Tstrap: 0-0 Ckp: 0-0
Best Rating: 103 4/04   Fknm   2m5f110y   good   Ch

Fair hunter; seems best at around two and a half miles under Rules and best on a sound surface.

Bohill Lad (IRE)
100(105c)   (0c)117
10-y-o b g Contract Law (USA)-La Sass (Sassafras (FR))
J D Frost   Mrs J McCormack

Placings:000/444 00000/U343P3015/1534422UP/12122631
2/513PP60501-0456   (1473)
2003/04: 16⁰G, 17⁴GF, 20⁵GF, 17⁶F,

	Starts	1st	2nd	3rd	Win & Pl
Hurdles	4	0	0	0	1035
Career Total	52	7	6	8	38521
117	4/03 Extr	2m3f	D(0-125)HHdl	G-F	£4810
120	7/02 NAbb	2m110y	D(0-125)HCh	G-F	£4530
118	3/02 Extr	2m3f	D(0-115)HHdl	GD	£3542
120	7/01 NAbb	2m110y	D Ch	GD	£4057
105	6/01 NAbb	2m1f	F(0-105)HHdl	G-F	£3073
103	5/00 Extr	2m1f	E(0-115)HHdl	G-F	£3201
97	3/00 Tntn	2m1f	G Hdl	G-F	£1526
		Total win prize-money £24740

Going: Sf: 0-0 GS: 0-0 Gd: 0-1 GF: - Fm: 0-3
Distance: 2m/2m3: 0-3 2m4-2m7: 0-1 3m+: 0-0
Track: LH: 0-3 RH: 0-1 Tight: 0-1 Gall: 0-0
Aids: Bl: 0-0 Vi: 0-0 Tstrap: 0-0 Ckp: 0-0
Best Rating: 120 7/02   NAbb   2m110y   gd-fm   Ch

He mixes hurdling and chasing these days and is a fair tool under both codes around the minor tracks; suited by two to two and a half miles and though he has run well on soft ground, is better on faster; benefitted from a change of tactics when making all in 2m 3f handicap hurdle at Exeter April 2003; ran much better than finishing position suggests next time.

Boing Boing (IRE)
101   96
4-y-o b g King's Theatre (IRE)-Limerick Princess (IRE) (Polish Patriot (USA))
Miss S J Wilton (J W Hills 22/9)   John Pointon And Sons

Placings:1P3500   (4892)
2003/04: 16¹GF, 16²GF, 17³G, 16⁵S, 16⁰S, 16⁰GF,

	Starts	1st	2nd	3rd	Win & Pl
Hurdles	6	1	0	1	4641
Career Total	6	1	0	1	4641
96	10/03 Strf	2m110y D Hdl	G-F	£4173
		Total win prize-money £4173

Going: Sf: 0-2 GS: 0-0 Gd: 0-1 GF: - Fm: 1-3
Distance: 2m/2m3: 1-6 2m4-2m7: 0-0 3m+: 0-0
Track: LH: 1-5 RH: 0-1 Tight: 1-3 Gall: 0-0
Aids: Bl: 0-0 Vi: 0-0 Tstrap: 0-0 Ckp: 0-0
Best Rating: 96   11/03   Bang   2m1f   good   Hdl

Started off well over hurdles when winning at Stratford in October 2003; held since; effective at two miles; acts on fast ground; has been tried in visor on the Flat.

Bold Action (IRE)

13-y-o b g Denel (FR)-Loughan-Na-Curry (No Argument)
Jon Trice-Rolph   D P Smith

Placings:223/306/1/4214UP224P/64P23/011460/2PPR3P1
P/P   (0227)
2003/04: 24⁰G,

	Starts	1st	2nd	3rd	Win & Pl
Chases	1	0	0	0	
Career Total	37	5	7	4	27744
93	4/02 Carl	3m2f	F(0-95)HCh	G-S	£3997
101	1/01 Weth	3m1f	E(0-115)HCh	HVY	£3360
94	12/00 Towc	3m1f	F(0-110)HCh	HVY	£5018
105	11/98 Hexm	3m1f	E(0-105)HCh	HVY	£3425
92	11/97 Hexm	2m4f110yE Hdl	G-F	£2532
		Total win prize-money £18333

Bold Affair
72f   53f
5-y-o ch g Bold Arrangement-So Curious (Gildoran)
Mrs L Williamson   Dennis Hutchinson

Placings:00   (4213)
2003/04: 16⁰G, 16⁰G,

	Starts	1st	2nd	3rd	Win & Pl
NH Flat	2	0	0	0	

	Starts	1st	2nd	3rd
Career Total	2	0	0	0

Going: Sf: 0-0 GS: 0-0 Gd: 0-2 GF: - Fm: 0-0
Distance: 2m/2m3: 0-2 2m4-2m7: 0-0 3m+: 0-0
Track: LH: 0-0 RH: 0-2 Tight: 0-0 Gall: 0-0
Aids: Bl: 0-0 Vi: 0-0 Tstrap: 0-0 Ckp: 0-0
Best Rating: 53 2/04 Winc 2m good NHF

Bold Bishop (IRE)

115 149+

7-y-o b g Religiously (USA)-Ladybojangles (IRE) (Buckskin (FR))
Jonjo O'Neill Mrs G Smith

Placings: *1/404*-2121126 (4638)
2003/04: 16^{2}GS, 17^{1}GS, 20^{2}GS, 16^{1}GS, 16^{1}GS, 16^{2}S, 16^{6}G,

	Starts	1st	2nd	3rd	Win & Pl
Hurdles	7	3	3	0	27951
Career Total	**11**	**4**	**3**	**0**	**32801**

122	2/04	Sand	2m110y	D Hdl	G-S	£5044
126	12/03	Strf	2m110y	D Hdl	G-S	£5187
112	12/03	MRas	2m1f110y	D Hdl	G-S	£3478
111	4/02	Weth	2m	H NHF	G-F	£1939

Total win prize-money £15648

Going: Sf: 0-1 GS: 3-5 Gd: 0-1 GF: - Fm: 0-0
Distance: **2m/2m3: 3-6** 2m4-2m7: 0-1 3m+: 0-0
Track: LH: 1-4 **RH: 2-3 Tight: 2-4** Gall: 0-0
Aids: Bl: 0-0 Vi: 0-0 Tstrap: 0-0 Ckp: 0-0
Best Rating: 149 3/04 Sand 2m110y soft Hdl

Smart novice hurdler; fourth in the 2003 Festival bumper; effective from two to two and a half miles; won a bumper on fast ground, but best hurdles form has been on soft; runner-up in the 2004 Imperial Cup but disappointing at Aintree subsequently; progressing well but may be a bit 'soft'.

Bold Cardowan (IRE)

96 86

8-y-o b g Persian Bold-Moving Trend (IRE) (Be My Guest (USA))
John Berry J McCarthy

Placings: 340/036201/13P003053-06 (0896)
2003/04: 24^{3}GF, 24^{0}G, 22^{6}GF,

	Starts	1st	2nd	3rd	Win & Pl
Hurdles	3	0	0	1	389
Career Total	**20**	**2**	**1**	**5**	**7499**

93	5/02	Hexm	3m	E Hdl	G-S	£2702
91	4/02	Newc	2m4f	F(0-90)Hdl	GD	£2226

Total win prize-money £4928

Going: Sf: 0-0 GS: 0-0 Gd: 0-1 GF: - Fm: 0-2
Distance: 2m/2m3: 0-0 2m4-2m7: 0-1 3m+: 0-2
Track: LH: 0-3 RH: 0-0 Tight: 0-1 Gall: 0-1
Aids: Bl: 0-0 Vi: 0-0 Tstrap: 0-0 Ckp: 0-0
Best Rating: 93 6/02 Hexm 2m4f110y good Hdl

Fair hurdler at his best, stays three miles and effective on good ground; finds nothing off the bridle and needs plenty of kidding.

Bold Century

77

7-y-o b g Casteddu-Bold Green (FR) (Green Dancer (USA))
S C Burrough Hill, Kemp and Hill

Placings: F (1951)
2003/04: 17^{F}G,

	Starts	1st	2nd	3rd	Win & Pl
Hurdles	1	0	0	0	
Career Total	**1**	**0**	**0**	**0**	

Going: Sf: 0-0 GS: 0-0 Gd: 0-1 GF: - Fm: 0-0
Distance: 2m/2m3: 0-1 2m4-2m7: 0-0 3m+: 0-0
Track: LH: 0-1 RH: 0-0 Tight: 0-1 Gall: 0-0
Aids: Bl: 0-0 Vi: 0-0 Tstrap: 0-0 Ckp: 0-0
Best Rating: 77 11/03 NAbb 2m1f good Hdl

Bold Classic (IRE)

11-y-o b g Persian Bold-Bay Street (Grundy)
C Grant Chris Grant

Placings: 5023/11164/2PP5/300/P001420/5523 (4851)
2003/04: 25^{5}S, 25^{5}G, 25^{2}S, 27^{3}GS,

	Starts	1st	2nd	3rd	Win & Pl
Chases	4	0	1	1	1276
Career Total	**27**	**4**	**4**	**3**	**19630**

100	8/01	Ctml	3m2f	E Ch	GD	£3428
127	3/98	Uttx	3m110y	B(0-140)HHdl	GD	£5103
112	1/98	Sand	2m6f	D(0-110)HHdl	SFT	£3095
107	11/97	Carl	2m4f110y	F(0-105)HHdl	GD	£2052

Total win prize-money £13680

Going: Sf: 0-2 GS: 0-1 Gd: 0-1 GF: - Fm: 0-0
Distance: 2m/2m3: 0-0 2m4-2m7: 0-0 3m+: 0-4
Track: LH: 0-4 RH: 0-0 Tight: 0-1 Gall: 0-0
Aids: Bl: 0-0 Vi: 0-0 Tstrap: 0-0 Ckp: 0-0
Best Rating: 127 3/98 Uttx 3m110y good Hdl

Lightly-raced over recent years; does not look the same horse over fences as he was over hurdles; goes on most ground.

Bold Hunter

83(100c) (86c)66

10-y-o b g Polish Precedent (USA)-Pumpona (USA) (Sharpen Up)
M J M Evans M J M Evans

Placings: 0U/2126453/06404P53/00P035/1353F5P5-P02000 (4278)
2003/04: 16^{P}GS, 17^{0}G, 16^{2}S, 16^{0}GS, 16^{0}GS, 19^{0}GS,

	Starts	1st	2nd	3rd	Win & Pl
Hurdles	6	0	1	0	544
Career Total	**37**	**2**	**3**	**5**	**11483**

84	5/02	Bang	2m1f110y	E(0-100)HCh	GD	£4329
96	8/99	Strf	2m110y	E Hdl	GD	£2537

Total win prize-money £6867

Going: Sf: 0-1 GS: 0-4 Gd: 0-1 GF: - Fm: 0-0
Distance: 2m/2m3: 0-5 2m4-2m7: 0-1 3m+: 0-0
Track: LH: 0-3 RH: 0-2 Tight: 0-2 Gall: 0-0
Aids: Bl: 0-0 Vi: 0-0 Tstrap: 0-0 Ckp: 0-0
Best Rating: 97 8/99 NAbb 2m1f good Hdl

Modest winning chaser. Got off the mark at Bangor in May 2002.

Bold Jogger (IRE)

83 75d

7-y-o b g Persian Bold-Mouette (FR) (Fabulous Dancer (USA))
M J Gingell B Dowling

Placings: 000-0P (0588)
2003/04: 20^{0}G, 24^{P}GF,

	Starts	1st	2nd	3rd	Win & Pl
Hurdles	2	0	0	0	
Career Total	**5**	**0**	**0**	**0**	

Going: Sf: 0-0 GS: 0-0 Gd: 0-1 GF: - Fm: 0-1
Distance: 2m/2m3: 0-0 2m4-2m7: 0-1 3m+: 0-1
Track: LH: 0-2 RH: 0-0 Tight: 0-0 Gall: 0-0
Aids: Bl: 0-0 Vi: 0-0 Tstrap: 0-0 Ckp: 0-0
Best Rating: 75 12/02 Newb 2m110y good Hdl

Bold King (FR)

9-y-o gr g Turgeon (USA)-Vanila Fudge (USA) (Bold Bidder)
Paul Morris (Ian Williams 29/6) Mrs N J Roberts

Placings: 1050000/46112/11235/5413212035/3P230001341-2406P (4143)
2003/04: 24^{2}S, 28^{4}GS, 32^{0}GF, 25^{6}GS, 25^{P}G,

	Starts	1st	2nd	3rd	Win & Pl
Chases	5	0	1	0	2230
Career Total	**43**	**9**	**6**	**6**	**56463**

111	4/03	Uttx	3m2f	E(0-110)HCh	GD	£5381
96	3/03	Wwck	2m5f	F Hdl	GD	£2702
114	1/02	Ludl	3m	D(0-115)HHdl	GD	£3415
109	11/01	Extr	2m3f	D(0-125)HHdl	G-F	£3510
127	11/00	Leic	2m	E Ch	G-S	£3022
107	10/00	Towc	2m110y	D Ch	GD	£3835
101	3/00	Ludl	2m	F(0-105)HHdl	GD	£4111
101	3/00	Hntg	2m110y	F(0-110)HHdl	G-F	£1806
	6/98	Autl	1m7f	Hdl	VS	£10101

Total win prize-money £37885

Going: Sf: 0-1 GS: 0-2 Gd: 0-1 GF: - Fm: 0-1
Distance: 2m/2m3: 0-0 2m4-2m7: 0-0 3m+: 0-5
Track: LH: 0-2 RH: 0-1 Tight: 0-2 Gall: 0-0
Aids: Bl: 0-0 Vi: 0-0 Tstrap: 0-0 Ckp: 0-1
Best Rating: 127 11/00 Newb 2m1f heavy Ch

Moderate hurdler/chaser; stays three miles plus and appreciates decent ground.

Bold Momento

84f 69f

5-y-o b g Never So Bold-Native Of Huppel (IRE) (Be My Native (USA))
B De Haan William A Tyrer

Placings: *0-0* (0705)
2003/04: 17^{0}GF,

	Starts	1st	2nd	3rd	Win & Pl
NH Flat	1	0	0	0	
Career Total	**2**	**0**	**0**	**0**	

Going: Sf: 0-0 GS: 0-0 Gd: 0-0 GF: - Fm: 0-1
Distance: 2m/2m3: 0-1 2m4-2m7: 0-0 3m+: 0-0
Track: LH: 0-0 RH: 0-1 Tight: 0-1 Gall: 0-0
Aids: Bl: 0-0 Vi: 0-0 Tstrap: 0-0 Ckp: 0-0
Best Rating: 69 3/03 Newb 2m110y good NHF

Bold Navigator

102 99

14-y-o b g Lighter-Drummond Lass (Peacock (FR))
A M Crow A M Crow

Placings: P/0/5P/141U-U15P (4272)
2003/04: 30^{U}G, 27^{1}G, 27^{5}GS, 26^{P}G,

	Starts	1st	2nd	3rd	Win & Pl
Chases	4	1	0	0	2611
Career Total	**12**	**3**	**0**	**0**	**10172**

99	12/03	Sedg	3m3f	F(0-95)HCh	GD	£2611
99	3/03	Carl	3m	F(0-95)HCh	SFT	£3513

85 10/02 Hexm 3m1f E Ch GD £3780
Total win prize-money £9904

Going: Sf: 0-0 GS: 0-1 Gd: 1-3 GF: - Fm: 0-0
Distance: 2m/2m3: 0-0 2m4-2m7: 0-0 3m+: 1-4
Track: LH: 1-3 RH: 0-1 Tight: 1-2 Gall: 0-0
Aids: Bl: 0-0 Vi: 0-0 Tstrap: 0-0 Ckp: 0-0
Best Rating: 99 12/03 Sedg 3m3f good Ch

Moderate chaser; ex-eventer and point-to-pointer; stays three miles-three; acts on good and soft ground.

Bold Statement

12-y-o ch g Kris-Bold Fantasy (Bold Lad (IRE))
S Flook S Flook

Placings: 52/01U4512/11253U31/23145UF/U0-243 (0506)
2003/04: 25²GS, 24⁴G, 24³GS,

	Starts	1st	2nd	3rd	Win & Pl
Chases	3	0	1	1	1227
Career Total	29	6	5	4	24765
110	12/98	Tntn	3m	E(0-110)HCh	GD	£3317
109	4/98	Prth	3m	D(0-110)HCh	HVY	£5196
115	5/97	Ctml	2m1f110yE Hdl		GD	£3072
119	5/97	Hexm	2m	E Hdl	G-F	£2607
105	3/97	Hexm	2m	E Hdl	SFT	£2917
104	11/96	Hexm	2m	H NHF	GD	£1343
				Total win prize-money £18454		

Going: Sf: 0-0 GS: 0-2 Gd: 0-1 GF: - Fm: 0-0
Distance: 2m/2m3: 0-0 2m4-2m7: 0-0 3m+: 0-3
Track: LH: 0-2 RH: 0-1 Tight: 0-0 Gall: 0-0
Aids: Bl: 0-0 Vi: 0-0 Tstrap: 0-0 Ckp: 0-3
Best Rating: 119 5/97 Hexm 2m gd-fm Hdl

Bold Tactics (IRE)

8-y-o br g Jurado (USA)-Bold Lyndsey (Be My Native (USA))
Mrs P Grainger (F A Hutsby 12/5) Nick Shutts

Placings: 235-2224 (4655)
2003/04: 21²G, 21²G, 19²GS, 16⁴G,

	Starts	1st	2nd	3rd	Win & Pl
Chases	4	0	3	0	2432
Career Total	7	0	4	1	3209

Going: Sf: 0-0 GS: 0-1 Gd: 0-3 GF: - Fm: 0-0
Distance: 2m/2m3: 0-1 2m4-2m7: 0-3 3m+: 0-0
Track: LH: 0-2 RH: 0-2 Tight: 0-0 Gall: 0-1
Aids: Bl: 0-0 Vi: 0-0 Tstrap: 0-0 Ckp: 0-0
Best Rating: 96 3/04 Asct 2m3f110y gd-sft Ch

Promising pointer/hunter chaser; stayed three miles; acts on good ground or softer.

Bolshie Baron
85   67

15-y-o b g Baron Blakeney-Contrary Lady (Conwyn)
B N Doran (H W Wheeler 10/5) H W Wheeler

Placings: 6620422/P0P50P/4/P2PP/43P3/B6P-46 (0613)
2003/04: 30⁴GF, 25⁶GF,

	Starts	1st	2nd	3rd	Win & Pl
Chases	2	0	0	0	0
Career Total	27	0	4	2	5405

Going: Sf: 0-0 GS: 0-0 Gd: 0-0 GF: - Fm: 0-2
Distance: 2m/2m3: 0-0 2m4-2m7: 0-0 3m+: 0-2

Track: LH: 0-0 RH: 0-2 Tight: 0-0 Gall: 0-1
Aids: Bl: 0-0 Vi: 0-0 Tstrap: 0-0 Ckp: 0-0
Best Rating: 82 5/00 Folk 3m7f good Ch

A modest pointer and poor hunter.

Bolshoi Ballet
107   105

6-y-o b g Dancing Spree (USA)-Broom Isle (Damister (USA))
J Mackie The M A S Partnership

Placings: 050P1-412005 (3005)
2003/04: 20⁴S, 16¹GF, 16²G, 16⁹GS, 19⁰G, 16⁵GS,

	Starts	1st	2nd	3rd	Win & Pl
Hurdles	6	1	1	0	7469
Career Total	11	2	1	0	12740
100	11/03	Hayd	2m	D(0-120)HHdl	G-F	£3789
105	3/03	Newb	2m110y	D(0-110)HHdl	SFT	£5271
				Total win prize-money £9062		

Going: Sf: 0-1 GS: 0-2 Gd: 0-2 GF: - Fm: 1-1
Distance: 2m/2m3: 1-4 2m4-2m7: 0-2 3m+: 0-0
Track: LH: 1-6 RH: 0-0 Tight: 0-0 Gall: 0-1
Aids: Bl: 0-0 Vi: 0-0 Tstrap: 0-0 Ckp: 1-5
Best Rating: 105 11/03 Weth 2m good Hdl

Moderate hurdler; mixes hurdling with Flat racing; won in first-time cheekpieces at Haydock in November 2003; acts on soft and fast ground.

Bolton Barrie (IRE)
111   (0c)97

6-y-o b g Broken Hearted-Ballyduggan Queen (IRE) (King Luthier)
R C Guest Glenn Roberts

Placings: 0630-053011BP362 (3235)
2003/04: 16⁶G, 17⁵GF, 20³G, 16⁰G, 20¹GF, 25¹F, 16⁸GF, 16⁸G, 19³G, 20⁸G, 24²GF,

	Starts	1st	2nd	3rd	Win & Pl
Hurdles	10	2	1	2	7164
Chases	1	0	0	0	0
Career Total	15	2	1	2	7436
92	10/03	Weth	3m1f	E(0-90)HHdl	FRM	£2212
92	10/03	Carl	2m4f	E(0-100)HHdl	G-F	£2670
				Total win prize-money £4883		

Going: Sf: 0-0 GS: 0-0 Gd: 0-6 GF: - Fm: 2-5
Distance: 2m/2m3: 0-5 2m4-2m7: 1-4 3m+: 1-2
Track: LH: 1-7 RH: 1-2 Tight: 0-1 Gall: 0-0
Aids: Bl: 0-0 Vi: 0-0 Tstrap: 0-0 Ckp: 0-1
Best Rating: 97 1/04 Muss 3m110y gd-fm Hdl

Plating-class hurdler; stays 3m 1f; acts on fast ground.

Bolton Castle
82f   66f

7-y-o b g Royal Fountain-Elegant Mary (Grey Ghost)
G A Harker P I Harker

Placings: 0 (2858)
2003/04: 16⁰GS,

	Starts	1st	2nd	3rd	Win & Pl
NH Flat	1	0	0	0	
Career Total	1	0	0	0	

Going: Sf: 0-0 GS: 0-1 Gd: 0-0 GF: - Fm: 0-0
Distance: 2m/2m3: 0-1 2m4-2m7: 0-0 3m+: 0-0
Track: LH: 0-1 RH: 0-0 Tight: 0-0 Gall: 0-0
Aids: Bl: 0-0 Vi: 0-0 Tstrap: 0-0 Ckp: 0-0
Best Rating: 66 12/03 Newc 2m gd-sft NHF

Bolton Forest (IRE)
                                                75

11-y-o b g Be My Native (USA)-Tickenor Wood (Le Bavard (FR))
Miss S E Forster Mrs C Strang Steel

Placings: 0/ f2200/04413055P/51/16204/6/50-P (4480)
2003/04: 20⁰HY,

	Starts	1st	2nd	3rd	Win & Pl
Chases	1	0	0	0	
Career Total	26	4	3	1	17093
115	5/00	MRas	2m6f110yE Ch		G-F	£3526
107	4/00	Font	2m4f	F(0-100)HHdl	GD	£2744
93	7/98	Limk	2m2f	Hdl	YLD	£2989
100	9/97	List	2m	NHF	G-Y	£4069
				Total win prize-money £13328		

Going: Sf: 0-1 GS: 0-0 Gd: 0-0 GF: - Fm: 0-0
Distance: 2m/2m3: 0-0 2m4-2m7: 0-1 3m+: 0-0
Track: LH: 0-0 RH: 0-1 Tight: 0-0 Gall: 0-0
Aids: Bl: 0-0 Vi: 0-0 Tstrap: 0-1 Ckp: 0-0
Best Rating: 115 5/00 MRas 2m6f110y gd-fm Ch

Bomba Charger

12-y-o b g Prince Of Peace-Lady Guinevere (Tormento)
Mrs R Welch Mrs R Welch

Placings: 06/P03PF6/4/0/24-P (0030)
2003/04: 33⁰FG,

	Starts	1st	2nd	3rd	Win & Pl
Chases	1	0	0	0	
Career Total	13	0	1	1	1447

Going: Sf: 0-0 GS: 0-0 Gd: 0-1 GF: - Fm: 0-0
Distance: 2m/2m3: 0-0 2m4-2m7: 0-1 3m+: 0-1
Track: LH: 0-1 RH: 0-0 Tight: 0-0 Gall: 0-1
Aids: Bl: 0-1 Vi: 0-0 Tstrap: 0-0 Ckp: 0-0
Best Rating: 89 5/00 Chep 3m firm Ch

Bond Diamond
70   28

7-y-o gr g Prince Sabo-Alsiba (Northfields (USA))
P R Webber Cresta Run

Placings: 0 (0882)
2003/04: 16⁰GS,

	Starts	1st	2nd	3rd	Win & Pl
Hurdles	1	0	0	0	
Career Total	1	0	0	0	

Going: Sf: 0-0 GS: 0-0 Gd: 0-0 GF: - Fm: 0-1
Distance: 2m/2m3: 0-1 2m4-2m7: 0-0 3m+: 0-0
Track: LH: 0-1 RH: 0-0 Tight: 0-0 Gall: 0-0
Aids: Bl: 0-0 Vi: 0-0 Tstrap: 0-0 Ckp: 0-0
Best Rating: 33 7/03 Uttx 2m gd-fm Hdl

Multiple handicap winner on the flat; didn't impress with his jumping when well beaten on hurdling bow at Uttoxeter in July.

Bonfire Night (IRE)
80(95h)   (61h)55+

8-y-o b m Air Display (USA)-Smokey Path (IRE) (Scallywag)
R Dickin Mrs A L Merry

Placings: 0-00403003 (4531)
2003/04: 16⁰GS, 22⁰G, 16⁴G, 21⁰G, 16³F, 25⁰GS, 20⁰S, 16³GS,

	Starts	1st	2nd	3rd	Win & Pl
Hurdles	4	0	0	0	278
Chases	4	0	0	2	1097
Career Total	9	0	0	2	1375

Going: Sf: 0-1 GS: 0-3 Gd: 0-3 GF: - Fm: 0-1
Distance: 2m/2m3: 0-4 2m4-2m7: 0-3 3m+: 0-1
Track: LH: 0-3 RH: 0-5 Tight: 0-1 Gall: 0-1
Aids: Bl: 0-0 Vi: 0-0 Tstrap: 0-0 Ckp: 0-0
Best Rating: 65 11/03 Wwck 2m5f   good   Hdl

Bonito

90   **67**
6-y-o ch g Pivotal-Bonita (Primo Dominie)
P C Haslam P C Haslam

Placings:6 (1878)
2003/04: 16RG,

	Starts	1st	2nd	3rd	Win & Pl
Hurdles	1	0	0	0	0
Career Total	1	0	0	0	0

Going: Sf: 0-0 GS: 0-0 Gd: 0-1 GF: - Fm: 0-0
Distance: 2m/2m3: 0-1 2m4-2m7: 0-0 3m+: 0-0
Track: LH: 0-1 RH: 0-0 Tight: 0-0 Gall: 0-0
Aids: Bl: 0-0 Vi: 0-0 Tstrap: 0-0 Ckp: 0-0
Best Rating: 69 11/03 Kels 2m110y   good   Hdl

Bonnet's Pieces

5-y-o b m Alderbrook-Chichell's Hurst (Oats)
Mrs P Sly The Stablemates II

Placings:00PP (3897)
2003/04: 17QGS, 20QGS, 19PG, 16FGS,

	Starts	1st	2nd	3rd	Win & Pl
NH Flat	1	0	0	0	0
Hurdles	3	0	0	0	0
Career Total	4	0	0	0	0

Going: Sf: 0-0 GS: 0-3 Gd: 0-1 GF: - Fm: 0-0
Distance: 2m/2m3: 0-2 2m4-2m7: 0-2 3m+: 0-0
Track: LH: 0-0 RH: 0-4 Tight: 0-2 Gall: 0-1
Aids: Bl: 0-0 Vi: 0-0 Tstrap: 0-0 Ckp: 0-0
Best Rating: 43 11/03 Folk 2m1f110y gd-sft NHF

Bonnie Flora

84   **59**
8-y-o b m Then Again-My Minnie (Kind Of Hush)
J W Mullins New Forest Racing Partnership

Placings:0P00F (4818)
2003/04: 17QG, 19PS, 16QS, 22QGS, 17FGF,

	Starts	1st	2nd	3rd	Win & Pl
Hurdles	5	0	0	0	0
Career Total	5	0	0	0	0

Going: Sf: 0-2 GS: 0-1 Gd: 0-1 GF: - Fm: 0-1
Distance: 2m/2m3: 0-4 2m4-2m7: 0-1 3m+: 0-0
Track: LH: 0-2 RH: 0-3 Tight: 0-2 Gall: 0-1
Aids: Bl: 0-0 Vi: 0-0 Tstrap: 0-0 Ckp: 0-0
Best Rating: 65 12/03 Tntn 2m1f   good   Hdl

Bonnie Parker (IRE)

100   **93+**
5-y-o b m Un Desperado (FR)-Strong Gara (IRE) (Strong Gale)
Ferdy Murphy Racegoers Club Owners Group

Placings:050P165UPP (4909)
2003/04: 17QG, 16FGF, 21QGS, 27PG, 211GS, 20FGF, 22FG, 21UG, 24PS, 24PS,

	Starts	1st	2nd	3rd	Win & Pl
NH Flat	2	0	0	0	0
Hurdles	8	1	0	0	3361
Career Total	10	1	0	0	3361
93 1/04 Sedg 2m5f110yE Hdl			G-S		£3360

Total win prize-money £3361

Going: Sf: 0-2 GS: 1-2 Gd: 0-4 GF: - Fm: 0-2
Distance: 2m/2m3: 0-2 2m4-2m7: 1-5 3m+: 0-3
Track: LH: 1-6 RH: 0-4 Tight: 1-6 Gall: 0-0
Aids: Bl: 0-0 Vi: 0-0 Tstrap: 0-0 Ckp: 0-0
Best Rating: 93 1/04 Sedg 2m5f110y gd-sft Hdl

First worthwhile form when shock winner of very modest mares' only novices' hurdle at Sedgefield in January; swerved badly in front; stays two mile six; handles heavy ground.

Bonny Boy (IRE)

88   **75**
9-y-o b g Bustino-Dingle Bay (Petingo)
D A Rees D Rees

Placings:2/03P-PP40U6 (4484)
2003/04: 26PG, 26PGF, 244HY, 25QG, 26UGF, 286G,

	Starts	1st	2nd	3rd	Win & Pl
Hurdles	1	0	0	0	0
Chases	5	0	0	0	265
Career Total	10	0	1	1	1695

Going: Sf: 0-1 GS: 0-0 Gd: 0-3 GF: - Fm: 0-2
Distance: 2m/2m3: 0-0 2m4-2m7: 0-0 3m+: 0-6
Track: LH: 0-4 RH: 0-1 Tight: 0-2 Gall: 0-0
Aids: Bl: 0-0 Vi: 0-0 Tstrap: 0-1 Ckp: 0-2
Best Rating: 75 3/03 Font 3m2f110y soft   Ch

Completed four-timer in points in 2001; disappointing so far under Rules.

Bonny Busona

           55f
4-y-o b f Abou Zouz (USA)-La Busona (IRE) (Broken Hearted)
K F Clutterbuck The T Class Partnership

Placings:0 (2482)
2003/04: 13QGF,

	Starts	1st	2nd	3rd	Win & Pl
NH Flat	1	0	0	0	0
Career Total	1	0	0	0	0

Going: Sf: 0-0 GS: 0-0 Gd: 0-0 GF: - Fm: 0-1
Distance: 2m/2m3: 0-0 2m4-2m7: 0-0 3m+: 0-0
Track: LH: 0-0 RH: 0-0 Tight: 0-0 Gall: 0-0
Aids: Bl: 0-0 Vi: 0-0 Tstrap: 0-0 Ckp: 0-0
Best Rating: 58 11/03 Donc 1m5f   gd-fm   NHF

Bonny Grey

101f   **96f**
6-y-o gr m Seymour Hicks (FR)-Sky Wave (Idiots Delight)

P D Evans P D Evans

Placings:U1 (4920)
2003/04: 16UG, 161GS,

	Starts	1st	2nd	3rd	Win & Pl
NH Flat	2	1	0	0	2153
Career Total	2	1	0	0	2153
96 4/04 Worc 2m H NHF			G-S		£2153

Total win prize-money £2153

Going: Sf: 0-0 GS: 1-1 Gd: 0-1 GF: - Fm: 0-0
Distance: 2m/2m3: 1-2 2m4-2m7: 0-0 3m+: 0-0
Track: LH: 1-1 RH: 0-1 Tight: 0-0 Gall: 0-0
Aids: Bl: 0-0 Vi: 0-0 Tstrap: 0-0 Ckp: 0-0
Best Rating: 96 4/04 Worc 2m   gd-sft NHF

Came from last to first to win bumper on second start; acts in yielding ground.

Bonny Grove

4-y-o b g Bonny Scot (IRE)-Binny Grove (Sunyboy)
G A Harker D Holmes

Placings:0 (2776)
2003/04: 13QS,

	Starts	1st	2nd	3rd	Win & Pl
NH Flat	1	0	0	0	0
Career Total	1	0	0	0	0

Going: Sf: 0-1 GS: 0-0 Gd: 0-0 GF: - Fm: 0-0
Distance: 2m/2m3: 0-0 2m4-2m7: 0-0 3m+: 0-0
Track: LH: 0-0 RH: 0-0 Tight: 0-0 Gall: 0-0
Aids: Bl: 0-0 Vi: 0-0 Tstrap: 0-0 Ckp: 0-0
Best Rating: 0 12/03 Towc 1m5f110y soft   NHF

Bonnybridge (IRE)

70   **(17h)75**
7-y-o ch m Zaffaran (USA)-Oralee (Prominer)
Liam Lennon Liam Lennon

Placings:0040055-4006600 (4413a)
2003/04: 224G, 20QG, 20QGF, 23FGF, 216GS, 18QGY, 20QY,

	Starts	1st	2nd	3rd	Win & Pl
Chases	7	0	0	0	338
Career Total	14	0	0	0	534

Going: Sf: 0-0 GS: 0-1 Gd: 0-2 GF: - Fm: 0-2
Distance: 2m/2m3: 0-1 2m4-2m7: 0-6 3m+: 0-0
Track: LH: 0-2 RH: 0-1 Tight: 0-1 Gall: 0-0
Aids: Bl: 0-6 Vi: 0-0 Tstrap: 0-0 Ckp: 0-0
Best Rating: 77 2/03 Muss 2m   good   NHF

Bonnyjo (FR)

90f   **90f**
5-y-o br g Cyborg (FR)-Argument Facile (FR) (Argument (FR))
P R Webber The Branners & Guido Partnership

Placings:40 (4787)
2003/04: 184S, 16QG,

	Starts	1st	2nd	3rd	Win & Pl
NH Flat	2	0	0	0	0
Career Total	2	0	0	0	0

Going: Sf: 0-1 GS: 0-0 Gd: 0-1 GF: - Fm: 0-0
Distance: 2m/2m3: 0-2 2m4-2m7: 0-0 3m+: 0-0
Track: LH: 0-1 RH: 0-1 Tight: 0-0 Gall: 0-1

Aids: Bl: 0-0 Vi: 0-0 Tstrap: 0-0 Ckp: 0-0
Best Rating: 90 2/04 Plum 2m2f   soft   NHF

French bred gelding; outpaced on debut at Plumpton in February over 2m 2f in a fair bumper; will improve for better ground.

Bonus Bridge (IRE)
111   (108h)141+
9-y-o b g Executive Perk-Corivia (Over The River (FR))
H D Daly   Lady Knutsford

Placings:34/123P4/25222-3221134P   (4869)
2003/04: 23³GS, 20²GF, 20²G, 16¹GS, 16¹G, 16³S, 16⁴G, 17⁴S,

	Starts	1st	2nd	3rd	Win & Pl
Chases	8	2	2	2	17483
Career Total	20	3	7	4	30266
141 1/04 Ludl	2m	E Ch		GD	£5131
127 11/03 Chep	2m10y	E Ch		G-S	£2996
103 10/01 Hrfd	2m1f	E Hdl		SFT	£3328

Total win prize-money £11457

Going: Sf: 0-2 GS: 1-2 Gd: 1-3 GF: - Fm: 0-1
Distance: 2m/2m3: 2-5 2m4-2m7: 0-2 3m+: 0-1
Track: LH: 1-5 RH: 1-3 Tight: 1-4 Gall: 0-1
Aids: Bl: 0-0 Vi: 0-0 Tstrap: 0-0 Ckp: 0-0
Best Rating: 141 4/04 Aint 2m   good   Ch

Useful novice chaser; stays two miles three; acts on soft ground, but handles a sounder surface.

Bonus Trix (IRE)
91   93
8-y-o b g Executive Perk-Black Trix (Peacock (FR))
C Tinkler (A J Lidderdale 15/11)   Team George I

Placings:P/10/06P-64   (2564)
2003/04: 20⁶GS, 19⁴GS,

	Starts	1st	2nd	3rd	Win & Pl
Hurdles	2	0	0	0	0
Career Total	8	1	0	0	1666
95 5/01 Bang	2m1f	H NHF		GD	£1666

Total win prize-money £1666

Going: Sf: 0-0 GS: 0-2 Gd: 0-0 GF: - Fm: 0-0
Distance: 2m/2m3: 0-1 2m4-2m7: 0-1 3m+: 0-0
Track: LH: 0-1 RH: 0-1 Tight: 0-0 Gall: 0-0
Aids: Bl: 0-0 Vi: 0-0 Tstrap: 0-1 Ckp: 0-0
Best Rating: 95 3/02 Newb 2m110y   gd-sft   NHF

Some ability over hurdles; has suffered breathing problems.

Boobee (IRE)
84   72
8-y-o b g Mister Lord (USA)-Who's She (Tall Noble (USA))
P M Phelan   Andrew L Cohen

Placings:0P   (3810)
2003/04: 20⁰G, 24ᴾG,

	Starts	1st	2nd	3rd	Win & Pl
Hurdles	2	0	0	0	
Career Total	2	0	0	0	

Going: Sf: 0-0 GS: 0-0 Gd: 0-2 GF: - Fm: 0-0
Distance: 2m/2m3: 0-0 2m4-2m7: 0-1 3m+: 0-1
Track: LH: 0-0 RH: 0-2 Tight: 0-0 Gall: 0-0
Aids: Bl: 0-0 Vi: 0-0 Tstrap: 0-0 Ckp: 0-0
Best Rating: 72 11/03 Asct 2m4f   good   Hdl

Boogy Woogy
8-y-o ch g Rock Hopper-Primulette (Mummy's Pet)
Robert Bowling   A Bowling

Placings:312/13P00643/450/33243-P   (3723)
2003/04: 25ᴾS,

	Starts	1st	2nd	3rd	Win & Pl
Chases	1	0	0	0	
Career Total	20	2	2	6	16490
125 10/00 Weth	2m	D(0-125)HHdl		G-S	£2957
90 11/99 MRas	2m1f110yD Hdl			G-S	£3504

Total win prize-money £6462

Going: Sf: 0-1 GS: 0-0 Gd: 0-0 GF: - Fm: 0-0
Distance: 2m/2m3: 0-0 2m4-2m7: 0-0 3m+: 0-1
Track: LH: 0-1 RH: 0-0 Tight: 0-0 Gall: 0-0
Aids: Bl: 0-1 Vi: 0-0 Tstrap: 0-0 Ckp: 0-0
Best Rating: 125 10/00 Weth 2m   gd-sft   Hdl

Hunter chaser; winning hurdler at around two miles; effective on any ground; often looks out of love with the game.

Book's Way
78(108h)   (70h)69
8-y-o br g Afzal-In A Whirl (USA) (Island Whirl (USA))
D W Thompson (Mrs D A Hamer 27/6)   J A Moore

Placings:006/PP-0003214U405PP00   (4914)
2003/04: 16⁶GF, 22⁰G, 22⁹G, 21³GF, 26²GF, 24¹GF, 22⁴GF, 23ᵁGF, 24⁴GS, 24⁰GF, 20⁵GF, 27ᴾG, 24ᴾG, 21⁰G, 24⁰GS,

	Starts	1st	2nd	3rd	Win & Pl
Hurdles	12	1	1	1	3411
Chases	3	0	0	0	
Career Total	20	1	1	1	3411
70 10/03 Hexm	3m	E Hdl		G-F	£2236

Total win prize-money £2237

Going: Sf: 0-0 GS: 0-2 Gd: 0-5 GF: - Fm: 1-8
Distance: 2m/2m3: 0-1 2m4-2m7: 0-7 3m+: 1-7
Track: LH: 1-11 RH: 0-4 Tight: 0-8 Gall: 0-2
Aids: Bl: 0-1 Vi: 0-0 Tstrap: 0-0 Ckp: 0-1
Best Rating: 70 10/03 Kels 2m6f110y   gd-fm   Hdl

Plating-class hurdler/chaser; made the most of a good opportunity in a poor novices' hurdle at Hexham in October; stays three miles; handles fast ground.

Books Law
6-y-o b g Contract Law (USA)-In A Whirl (USA) (Island Whirl (USA))
Mrs D A Hamer   Power Units (1953) Ltd

Placings:PP-P   (1013)
2003/04: 20ᴾGF,

	Starts	1st	2nd	3rd	Win & Pl
Hurdles	1	0	0	0	
Career Total	3	0	0	0	

Going: Sf: 0-0 GS: 0-0 Gd: 0-0 GF: - Fm: 0-1
Distance: 2m/2m3: 0-0 2m4-2m7: 0-1 3m+: 0-0
Track: LH: 0-1 RH: 0-0 Tight: 0-0 Gall: 0-0
Aids: Bl: 0-0 Vi: 0-0 Tstrap: 0-0 Ckp: 0-1
Best Rating: 0 8/03 Worc 2m4f   gd-fm   Hdl

Books Whirl
7-y-o b m Henbit (USA)-In A Whirl (USA) (Island Whirl (USA))

Mrs D A Hamer   Gwynne Phillips

Placings:00/P   (0941)
2003/04: 20ᴾG,

	Starts	1st	2nd	3rd	Win & Pl
Hurdles	1	0	0	0	
Career Total	3	0	0	0	

Going: Sf: 0-0 GS: 0-0 Gd: 0-1 GF: - Fm: 0-0
Distance: 2m/2m3: 0-0 2m4-2m7: 0-1 3m+: 0-0
Track: LH: 0-1 RH: 0-0 Tight: 0-0 Gall: 0-0
Aids: Bl: 0-0 Vi: 0-0 Tstrap: 0-0 Ckp: 0-0
Best Rating: 44 9/01 Hrfd 2m1f   gd-fm   NHF

Boom Or Bust (IRE)
100   88
5-y-o ch g Entrepreneur-Classic Affair (USA) (Trempolino (USA))
Miss K M George   The Westwoods

Placings:5P3FP-F43054   (4898)
2003/04: 16⁶GF, 17⁴GF, 16³GS, 16⁶G, 17⁵G, 16⁴G,

	Starts	1st	2nd	3rd	Win & Pl
Hurdles	6	0	0	1	554
Career Total	11	0	0	2	1484

Going: Sf: 0-0 GS: 0-1 Gd: 0-3 GF: - Fm: 0-2
Distance: 2m/2m3: 0-6 2m4-2m7: 0-0 3m+: 0-0
Track: LH: 0-2 RH: 0-4 Tight: 0-2 Gall: 0-0
Aids: Bl: 0-1 Vi: 0-0 Tstrap: 0-0 Ckp: 0-1
Best Rating: 88 3/04 Tntn 2m1f   good   Hdl

Poor handicap hurdler; unlikely to stay beyond two miles.

Boon Companion
70   68
5-y-o b g Sure Blade (USA)-Pea Green (Try My Best (USA))
John Berry   Miss Amanda Rawding

Placings:05P   (2421)
2003/04: 20⁰G, 20⁵G, 20ᴾGS,

	Starts	1st	2nd	3rd	Win & Pl
Hurdles	3	0	0	0	0
Career Total	3	0	0	0	0

Going: Sf: 0-0 GS: 0-1 Gd: 0-2 GF: - Fm: 0-0
Distance: 2m/2m3: 0-0 2m4-2m7: 0-3 3m+: 0-0
Track: LH: 0-3 RH: 0-0 Tight: 0-0 Gall: 0-0
Aids: Bl: 0-0 Vi: 0-0 Tstrap: 0-0 Ckp: 0-0
Best Rating: 68 10/03 Fknm 2m4f   good   Hdl

Boozy Douz
75   35
4-y-o ch f Abou Zouz (USA)-Ackcontent (USA) (Key To Content (USA))
H S Howe   R J Sage

Placings:P040   (2669)
2003/04: 16ᴾGF, 16⁰GF, 17⁴GF, 16⁰GF,

	Starts	1st	2nd	3rd	Win & Pl
Hurdles	4	0	0	0	0
Career Total	4	0	0	0	0

Going: Sf: 0-0 GS: 0-0 Gd: 0-0 GF: - Fm: 0-4
Distance: 2m/2m3: 0-4 2m4-2m7: 0-0 3m+: 0-0
Track: LH: 0-2 RH: 0-2 Tight: 0-2 Gall: 0-2
Aids: Bl: 0-0 Vi: 0-0 Tstrap: 0-0 Ckp: 0-0

Best Rating: 35   11/03   Tntn   2m1f   gd-fm   Hdl

Border Bandit (IRE)
91f   79f
5-y-o b g Shahanndeh-Mwanamio (Sole Mio (USA))
A Crook W Graham & J Gordon

Placings: 430P   (4952)
2003/04: 16⁴GF, 16³GF, 17⁹G, 16⁸GS,

	Starts	1st	2nd	3rd	Win & Pl
NH Flat	4	0	0	1	323
Career Total	4	0	0	1	323

Going: Sf: 0-0 GS: 0-1 Gd: 0-1 GF: - Fm: 0-2
Distance: 2m2m3: 0-2 2m4-2m7: 0-0 3m+: 0-0
Track: LH: 0-0 RH: 0-4 Tight: 0-0 Gall: 0-0
Aids: Bl: 0-0 Vi: 0-0 Tstrap: 0-0 Ckp: 0-0
Best Rating: 79   2/04   Carl   2m1f   good   NHF

Showed ability in bumpers.

Border Burn
65
10-y-o ch g Safawan-Burning Ryme (Rymer)
M J Gingell J M Valdes-Scott

Placings: 6P/450/40-4   (0329)
2003/04: 26⁴GF,

	Starts	1st	2nd	3rd	Win & Pl
Chases	1	0	0	0	271
Career Total	8	0	0	0	485

Going: Sf: 0-0 GS: 0-0 Gd: 0-0 GF: - Fm: 0-1
Distance: 2m2m3: 0-0 2m4-2m7: 0-0 3m+: 0-1
Track: LH: 0-1 RH: 0-0 Tight: 0-0 Gall: 0-0
Aids: Bl: 0-0 Vi: 0-0 Tstrap: 0-0 Ckp: 0-0
Best Rating: 81   5/02   Hexm   3m1f   gd-sft   Ch

Border Farmer (IRE)
81   55
11-y-o b g Riverhead (USA)-Double Figures (FR) (Double Form)
Mrs S Richardson (James Richardson 21/5) James Richardson

Placings: 006/04P/06/U26/U-6UP5   (0677)
2003/04: 25⁶G, 25⁵UG, 31⁵PGF, 23⁵GF,

	Starts	1st	2nd	3rd	Win & Pl
Chases	4	0	0	0	0
Career Total	16	0	1	0	530

Going: Sf: 0-0 GS: 0-0 Gd: 0-2 GF: - Fm: 0-2
Distance: 2m2m3: 0-0 2m4-2m7: 0-0 3m+: 0-4
Track: LH: 0-2 RH: 0-2 Tight: 0-1 Gall: 0-1
Aids: Bl: 0-0 Vi: 0-0 Tstrap: 0-0 Ckp: 0-0
Best Rating: 79   5/01   Strf   3m   gd-fm   Ch

Border Glen
41
8-y-o b g Selkirk (USA)-Sulitelma (USA) (The Minstrel (CAN))
P Wegmann P Wegmann

Placings: PP060-P   (0442)
2003/04: 19⁵GF,

	Starts	1st	2nd	3rd	Win & Pl
Hurdles	1	0	0	0	
Career Total	6	0	0	0	0

Going: Sf: 0-0 GS: 0-0 Gd: 0-0 GF: - Fm: 0-1
Distance: 2m2m3: 0-0 2m4-2m7: 0-1 3m+: 0-0
Track: LH: 0-0 RH: 0-1 Tight: 0-0 Gall: 0-0
Aids: Bl: 0-0 Vi: 0-0 Tstrap: 0-0 Ckp: 0-0
Best Rating: 41   4/03   Ludl   2m   good   Hdl

Border Light
11-y-o ch g Lighter-Border Cherry (Deep Run)
H J Manners H J Manners

Placings: 0/0/45P/03PP/3P-6   (0275)
2003/04: 25⁶GF,

	Starts	1st	2nd	3rd	Win & Pl
Chases	1	0	0	0	0
Career Total	12	0	0	2	1069

Going: Sf: 0-0 GS: 0-0 Gd: 0-0 GF: - Fm: 0-1
Distance: 2m2m3: 0-0 2m4-2m7: 0-0 3m+: 0-1
Track: LH: 0-0 RH: 0-1 Tight: 0-0 Gall: 0-0
Aids: Bl: 0-0 Vi: 0-0 Tstrap: 0-0 Ckp: 0-0
Best Rating: 83   3/03   Plum   3m2f   soft   Ch

Border Star (IRE)
98   (0c)94+
7-y-o b g Parthian Springs-Tengello (Bargello)
J M Jefferson Mrs Kathleen Campey

Placings: O655005/461436-P660P040   (4956)
2003/04: 17⁵PG, 17⁶G, 17⁶GS, 19⁰GS, 23⁵PS, 27⁰GS, 22⁴G, 22⁰G,

	Starts	1st	2nd	3rd	Win & Pl
Hurdles	7	0	0	0	334
Chases	1	0	0	0	
Career Total	21	1	0	0	4401
87   8/02   Strf   2m110y   E(0-105)HHdl   G-S   £3601
Total win prize-money £3601

Going: Sf: 0-1 GS: 0-3 Gd: 0-4 GF: - Fm: 0-0
Distance: 2m2m3: 0-4 2m4-2m7: 0-3 3m+: 0-1
Track: LH: 0-7 RH: 0-0 Tight: 0-6 Gall: 0-0
Aids: Bl: 0-5 Vi: 0-0 Tstrap: 0-0 Ckp: 0-2
Best Rating: 94   11/02   Newc   2m   gd-sft   Hdl

Border Tale
102   114
4-y-o b g Selkirk (USA)-Likely Story (IRE) (Night Shift (USA))
C Weedon (M L W Bell 1/8) Chadwick, Dyer & Flynn

Placings: 31PP300   (4422)
2003/04: 17³G, 16¹GF, 16⁸G, 16⁸PS, 16³G, 16⁸S, 17⁰G,

	Starts	1st	2nd	3rd	Win & Pl
Hurdles	7	1	0	2	4767
Career Total	7	1	0	2	4767
94   11/03   Hayd   2m   D Hdl   G-F   £3454
Total win prize-money £3455

Going: Sf: 0-2 GS: 0-0 Gd: 0-4 GF: - Fm: 1-1
Distance: 2m2m3: 1-7 2m4-2m7: 0-0 3m+: 0-0
Track: LH: 1-6 RH: 0-1 Tight: 0-1 Gall: 0-2
Aids: Bl: 0-0 Vi: 0-0 Tstrap: 0-0 Ckp: 0-0
Best Rating: 114   3/04   Chel   2m1f   good   Hdl

Fair juvenile hurdler; useful handicapper on the Flat; effective over two miles; acts on a sound surface.

Borehill Joker
104(108h)   (86h)82
8-y-o ch g Pure Melody (USA)-Queen Matilda (Castle Keep)
E Haddock Miss H M Newell

Placings: 3/0021P3062115/4154524522366/140P030-30455P0P5   (4760)
2003/04: 19³GS, 16⁸GS, 16⁴S, 16⁵GF, 16⁵G, 19⁵PS, 19⁰GS, 19⁰PG, 16⁵S,

	Starts	1st	2nd	3rd	Win & Pl
Hurdles	1	0	0	0	0
Chases	8	0	0	1	948
Career Total	42	5	5	5	18625
104   5/02   Towc   2m   D(0-120)HHdl   SFT   £3740
104   10/01   Sthl   2m   F(0-105)HHdl   GD   £2240
102   1/01   Leic   2m   F Hdl   HVY   £2646
101   1/01   Leic   2m   G(0-90)HHdl   HVY   £1967
89   10/00   Towc   2m   G Hdl   G-S   £1575
Total win prize-money £12169

Going: Sf: 0-3 GS: 0-3 Gd: 0-2 GF: - Fm: 0-1
Distance: 2m2m3: 0-8 2m4-2m7: 0-1 3m+: 0-0
Track: LH: 0-0 RH: 0-9 Tight: 0-0 Gall: 0-0
Aids: Bl: 0-1 Vi: 0-0 Tstrap: 0-9 Ckp: 0-0
Best Rating: 104   5/02   Towc   2m   good   Hdl

Plating-class hurdler/novice chaser, suited by a right-handed track and soft ground.

Boring Goring (IRE)
73(104c)   (90c)90
10-y-o b g Aristocracy-Coolrusk (IRE) (Millfontaine)
Miss A M Newton-Smith Goring Hotel

Placings: 40/0P2P54/44FF/PUF2161/0B4320-2FP0   (3959)
2003/04: 25²GQ, 25⁵GF, 24⁴PS, 22⁰G,

	Starts	1st	2nd	3rd	Win & Pl
Hurdles	2	0	0	0	0
Chases	2	0	1	0	857
Career Total	29	2	4	1	10707
90   3/02   Plum   2m5f   E Hdl   GD   £2719
90   11/01   Extr   2m6f110yF(0-100)HHdl   G-F   £2727
Total win prize-money £5447

Going: Sf: 0-1 GS: 0-0 Gd: 0-1 GF: - Fm: 0-0
Distance: 2m2m3: 0-0 2m4-2m7: 0-1 3m+: 0-3
Track: LH: 0-1 RH: 0-3 Tight: 0-4 Gall: 0-0
Aids: Bl: 0-0 Vi: 0-0 Tstrap: 0-0 Ckp: 0-2
Best Rating: 95   2/99   Folk   2m1f110y   soft   NHF

Moderate hurdler; has shown ability over fences without winning; stays two miles five furlongs and likes fast ground.

Born Leader (IRE)
94   90+
6-y-o b g Supreme Leader-Real Lace (Kampala)
A King Nigel Bunter & Jules Sigler

Placings: 62030   (4560)
2003/04: 17⁶GS, 16²GS, 16⁰S, 21³G, 21⁰GS,

	Starts	1st	2nd	3rd	Win & Pl
NH Flat	2	0	1	0	586
Hurdles	3	0	0	1	1180
Career Total	5	0	1	1	1766

Going: Sf: 0-1 GS: 0-3 Gd: 0-1 GF: - Fm: 0-0
Distance: 2m2m3: 0-3 2m4-2m7: 0-2 3m+: 0-0
Track: LH: 0-4 RH: 0-1 Tight: 0-1 Gall: 0-1
Aids: Bl: 0-0 Vi: 0-0 Tstrap: 0-0 Ckp: 0-0
Best Rating: 100   1/04   Weth   2m   gd-sft   NHF

Has shown ability in bumpers and novice hurdles; will stay three miles over fences; acts on good and soft ground.

Border Farmer top-right fragment

	Starts	1st	2nd	3rd	Win & Pl
Hurdles	1	0	0	0	
Career Total	6	0	0	0	0

Boro Sovereign (IRE)

89   **101**

11-y-o b g King's Ride-Boro Penny (Normandy)
M Scudamore Mrs P De W Johnson

Placings: 1/ 122/13/402/21PPU230F0/P4P6UP   (4715)
2003/04: 21PG, 24⁴S, 25³HY, 20⁶G, 19UGS, 20PG,

	Starts	1st	2nd	3rd	Win & Pl
Chases	6	0	0	0	450
Career Total	25	4	5	2	18895
115	9/01	Bang	2m4f110yD Ch	GD	£4309
106	12/99	Towc	2m	E Hdl	SFT	£2740
109	12/98	Hntg	2m110y	H NHF	SFT	£1392
105	4/97	Tipp	2m	NHF	GD	£2712

Total win prize-money £11155

Going:	Sf: 0-2 GS: 0-1 Gd: 0-3 GF: - Fm: 0-0
Distance:	2m/2m3: 0-2 2m4-2m7: 0-4 3m+: 0-2
Track:	LH: 0-1 RH: 0-4 Tight: 0-1 Gall: 0-0
Aids:	Bl: 0-0 Vi: 0-0 Tstrap: 0-0 Ckp: 0-0
Best Rating:	129 11/01 Chep 3m soft Hdl

Modest hurdler/moderate chaser; formerly useful bumper horse; not seen since March 2002; stays 2m4f; seems to act on any ground.

Borora

106   **103+**

5-y-o gr g Shareef Dancer (USA)-Bustling Nelly (Bustino)
R Lee Mrs E M Clarke

Placings: 0-F513F26   (4493)
2003/04: 17FGF, 16⁵GF, 17¹GF, 16³G, 17FGS, 17²GS, 16⁶G,

	Starts	1st	2nd	3rd	Win & Pl
Hurdles	7	1	1	1	4422
Career Total	8	1	1	1	4422
82	10/03	Hrfd	2m1f	E(0-100)HHdl	G-F	£2478

Total win prize-money £2478

Going:	Sf: 0-0 GS: 0-0 Gd: 0-2 GF: - Fm: 1-3
Distance:	2m/2m3: 1-7 2m4-2m7: 0-0 3m+: 0-0
Track:	LH: 0-2 RH: 1-5 Tight: 0-3 Gall: 0-1
Aids:	Bl: 0-0 Vi: 0-0 Tstrap: 0-0 Ckp: 0-0
Best Rating:	103 12/03 Hrfd 2m1f gd-sft Hdl

Plating-class hurdler; keen sort; effective at 2m; acts on fast ground.

Borzov (IRE)

103   (76h) **101**

11-y-o ch g Kefaah (USA)-Esquire Lady (Be My Guest (USA))
T J Taaffe Christopher Power Smith

Placings: 00/0000/010F3UUP/0B1U5FF/0/00F51-PP10   (1199a)
2003/04: 24PG, 25PF, 25¹GF, 24UF,

	Starts	1st	2nd	3rd	Win & Pl
Chases	4	1	0	0	4082
Career Total	31	4	0	1	19928
101	8/03	MRas	3m1f	E(0-110)HCh	G-F	£4082
98	4/03	Fair	3m1f	(0-116)HCh	G-F	£8441
98	6/00	Rosc	3m100y	(0-116)HCh	GD	£3864
98	6/99	Tral	2m6f	Ch	GD	£2915

Total win prize-money £19304

Going:	Sf: 0-0 GS: 0-0 Gd: 0-1 GF: - Fm: 1-3
Distance:	2m/2m3: 0-0 2m4-2m7: 0-0 3m+: 1-4
Track:	LH: 0-0 RH: 1-1 Tight: 1-1 Gall: 0-0
Aids:	Bl: 0-0 Vi: 0-0 Tstrap: 0-0 Ckp: 0-0
Best Rating:	101 8/03 MRas 3m1f gd-fm Ch

Moderate irish chaser; stays three miles one furlong; acts on good ground or faster; suiting by hold-up tactics.

Bosham Mill

108   **132+**

6-y-o ch g Nashwan (USA)-Mill On The Floss (Mill Reef (USA))
Jonjo O'Neill (Ian Williams 1/6) GPS Racing

Placings: 14211P   (2722)
2003/04: 20¹GF, 22⁴G, 20²G, 24¹GF, 25¹G, 25PGS,

	Starts	1st	2nd	3rd	Win & Pl
Hurdles	6	3	1	0	12885
Career Total	6	3	1	0	12885
132	11/03	Kemp	3m1f	D(0-120)HHdl	GD	£3398
114	10/03	Carl	3m110y	E Hdl	G-F	£3094
102	5/03	Chep	2m4f	D Hdl	G-F	£5268

Total win prize-money £11760

Going:	Sf: 0-0 GS: 0-1 Gd: 1-3 GF: - Fm: 2-2
Distance:	2m/2m3: 0-0 2m4-2m7: 1-3 3m+: 2-3
Track:	LH: 1-4 RH: 2-2 Tight: 0-2 Gall: 0-1
Aids:	Bl: 0-0 Vi: 0-0 Tstrap: 0-0 Ckp: 0-0
Best Rating:	132 11/03 Kemp 3m1f good Hdl

Modest hurdler; smart but ultimately disappointing on the Flat and not entirely straightforward; made winning debut over hurdles over 2m 4f at Chepstow in May 2003 for Ian Williams; won ordinary Carlisle novice event on second start for Jonjo O'Neill; suited by fast ground; stays 3m.

Bosphorus

5-y-o b g Polish Precedent (USA)-Ancara (Dancing Brave (USA))
D G Bridgwater Led Astray Again Partnership

Placings: 0-34   (1729)
2003/04: 16³F, 20⁴GF,

	Starts	1st	2nd	3rd	Win & Pl
Hurdles	2	0	0	1	638
Career Total	3	0	0	1	638

Going:	Sf: 0-0 GS: 0-0 Gd: 0-0 GF: - Fm: 0-2
Distance:	2m/2m3: 0-1 2m4-2m7: 0-1 3m+: 0-0
Track:	LH: 0-1 RH: 0-1 Tight: 0-0 Gall: 0-0
Aids:	Bl: 0-0 Vi: 0-0 Tstrap: 0-0 Ckp: 0-0
Best Rating:	58 12/02 Newb 1m4f110y good NHF

Plater on the Flat, has shown little ability so far over jumps; acts on fast ground; should stay at least 2m4f.

Boss Man (IRE)

74   **37**

4-y-o b g Entrepreneur-Triste Oeil (USA) (Raise A Cup (USA))
T D Easterby D F Sills

Placings: 0   (1007)
2003/04: 17⁰G,

	Starts	1st	2nd	3rd	Win & Pl
Hurdles	1	0	0	0	
Career Total	1	0	0	0	

Going:	Sf: 0-0 GS: 0-0 Gd: 0-0 GF: - Fm: 0-0
Distance:	2m/2m3: 0-1 2m4-2m7: 0-0 3m+: 0-0
Track:	LH: 0-1 RH: 0-0 Tight: 0-1 Gall: 0-0
Aids:	Bl: 0-0 Vi: 0-0 Tstrap: 0-0 Ckp: 0-0
Best Rating:	37 8/03 Bang 2m1f good Hdl

Boss Royal

103   (90h) **87+**

7-y-o ch g Afzal-Born Bossy (Ebomeezer)
G A Ham The Holmes Office

Placings: P/0003P341/PFU-003P06   (4896)
2003/04: 19⁰G, 16⁰G, 19³GS, 18PG, 16PGS, 16⁶G,

	Starts	1st	2nd	3rd	Win & Pl
Chases	6	0	0	1	865
Career Total	18	1	0	3	6887
90	4/02	Bang	2m4f	F(0-100)HHdl	GD	£5245

Total win prize-money £5246

Going:	Sf: 0-0 GS: 0-2 Gd: 0-4 GF: - Fm: 0-0
Distance:	2m/2m3: 0-6 2m4-2m7: 0-0 3m+: 0-0
Track:	LH: 0-1 RH: 0-4 Tight: 0-3 Gall: 0-0
Aids:	Bl: 0-0 Vi: 0-0 Tstrap: 0-5 Ckp: 0-0
Best Rating:	90 4/02 Bang 2m4f good Hdl

Boss Tweed (IRE)

95   **91**

7-y-o b g Persian Bold-Betty Kenwood (Dominion)
B Mactaggart Graeme Renton

Placings: 02/46-033P   (1140)
2003/04: 16⁸G, 16³GF, 16³G, 16PGF,

	Starts	1st	2nd	3rd	Win & Pl
Hurdles	4	0	0	2	1490
Career Total	8	0	1	2	3322

Going:	Sf: 0-0 GS: 0-0 Gd: 0-2 GF: - Fm: 0-2
Distance:	2m/2m3: 0-4 2m4-2m7: 0-3 3m+: 0-0
Track:	LH: 0-1 RH: 0-3 Tight: 0-1 Gall: 0-0
Aids:	Bl: 0-0 Vi: 0-0 Tstrap: 0-4 Ckp: 0-0
Best Rating:	104 5/02 Kels 2m110y good Hdl

Plating-class hurdler; suited by good ground; only raced at two miles; usually wears tongue tie.

Boston Lass

107 (98h)   (72h) **85**

7-y-o br m Terimon-Larksmore (Royal Fountain)
R D E Woodhouse M K Oldham

Placings: 4004P063/0452302P-2P2PF565   (4533)
2003/04: 21²S, 22PG, 26²G, 22PS, 27FGS, 20⁵G, 24⁶HY, 22⁵GS,

	Starts	1st	2nd	3rd	Win & Pl
Chases	8	0	2	0	2619
Career Total	24	0	4	2	6103

Going:	Sf: 0-3 GS: 0-2 Gd: 0-3 GF: - Fm: 0-0
Distance:	2m/2m3: 0-0 2m4-2m7: 0-5 3m+: 0-3
Track:	LH: 0-7 RH: 0-1 Tight: 0-6 Gall: 0-1
Aids:	Bl: 0-0 Vi: 0-0 Tstrap: 0-0 Ckp: 0-3
Best Rating:	85 5/03 Ctml 3m2f good Ch

Moderate hurdler/chaser; stays three miles, but may prefer shorter; suited by soft; has worn cheekpieces.

Bosuns Mate

11-y-o ch g Yachtsman (USA)-Langton Lass (Nearly A Hand)
M Keighley M Keighley

Placings: 41/1211200/0U361231/FPPF032/P1656/123-PU3U5   (4635)
2003/04: 28PG, 22US, 20³G, 26¹UG, 24⁵G,

	Starts	1st	2nd	3rd	Win & Pl
Chases	5	0	0	1	333
Career Total	37	8	5	5	72637
90 2/03 Sand	2m4f110yH Ch			SFT	£2373
126 10/01 Extr	3m1f110yD(0-120)HCh			G-F	£5440
145 4/00 Sand	3m110y B Ch			SFT	£16883
145 3/00 Bang	3m110y D Ch			GD	£4719
137 1/99 Newb	3m110y C Hdl			HVY	£4781
137 12/98 Chel	3m	A Hdl		GD	£9375
113 5/98 Worc	2m	H NHF		G-F	£1560
101 3/98 Ludl	2m	H NHF		GD	£1203
		Total win prize-money £46336			

Going: Sf: 0-1 GS: 0-0 Gd: 0-4 GF: - Fm: 0-0
Distance: 2m/2m3: 0-0 2m4-2m7: 0-2 3m+: 0-3
Track: LH: 0-3 RH: 0-2 Tight: 0-2 Gall: 0-1
Aids: Bl: 0-2 Vi: 0-0 Tstrap: 0-0 Ckp: 0-1
Best Rating: 145 4/00   Sand   3m110y   soft   Ch

Bosworth Boy

6-y-o b g Deploy-Krill (Kris)
J Gallagher   John L Marriott

Placings:630/0-4   (1136)
2003/04: 20⁴G,

	Starts	1st	2nd	3rd	Win & Pl
Hurdles	1	0	0	0	274
Career Total	5	0	0	1	661

Going: Sf: 0-0 GS: 0-0 Gd: 0-1 GF: - Fm: 0-0
Distance: 2m/2m3: 0-0 2m4-2m7: 0-1 3m+: 0-0
Track: LH: 0-1 RH: 0-0 Tight: 0-1 Gall: 0-0
Aids: Bl: 0-0 Vi: 0-0 Tstrap: 0-0 Ckp: 0-0
Best Rating: 87 4/02   Asct   2m110y   gd-fm   NHF

Flat off-cast who made his debut in a bumper; little shown since; acts on most ground.

Bosworth Dixie (IRE)

4-y-o b f Turtle Island (IRE)-Alice En Ballade (Tap On Wood)
Miss J S Davis (J Gallagher 13/8)   Miss J Davis

Placings:P   (1502)
2003/04: 16ᴾGF,

	Starts	1st	2nd	3rd	Win & Pl
Hurdles	1	0	0	0	
Career Total	1	0	0	0	

Going: Sf: 0-0 GS: 0-0 Gd: 0-0 GF: - Fm: 0-1
Distance: 2m/2m3: 0-1 2m4-2m7: 0-0 3m+: 0-0
Track: LH: 0-1 RH: 0-0 Tight: 0-0 Gall: 0-0
Aids: Bl: 0-0 Vi: 0-0 Tstrap: 0-0 Ckp: 0-0

Bosworth Gypsy (IRE)
85f   85f

6-y-o b m Aahsaylad-Googly (Sunley Builds)
J Gallagher   J L Marriott and A L Marriott

Placings:50   (3285)
2003/04: 16⁵GS, 16⁰HY,

	Starts	1st	2nd	3rd	Win & Pl
NH Flat	2	0	0	0	0
Career Total	2	0	0	0	0

Going: Sf: 0-1 GS: 0-1 Gd: 0-0 GF: - Fm: 0-0
Track: LH: 0-2 RH: 0-0 Tight: 0-0 Gall: 0-1
Aids: Bl: 0-0 Vi: 0-0 Tstrap: 0-0 Ckp: 0-1
Best Rating: 85 12/03 Uttx   2m   gd-sft NHF

Boulta (IRE)

10-y-o ch g Commanche Run-Boulta View (Beau Chapeau)
Mrs Clare Moore   Mrs Clare Moore

Placings:0/250P026-244   (4687)
2003/04: 20⁶GF, 25²GS, 24⁴HY, 25⁴G,

	Starts	1st	2nd	3rd	Win & Pl
Chases	4	0	1	0	595
Career Total	11	0	3	0	2315

Going: Sf: 0-1 GS: 0-1 Gd: 0-1 GF: - Fm: 0-1
Distance: 2m/2m3: 0-0 2m4-2m7: 0-1 3m+: 0-3
Track: LH: 0-4 RH: 0-0 Tight: 0-2 Gall: 0-2
Aids: Bl: 0-0 Vi: 0-0 Tstrap: 0-0 Ckp: 0-4
Best Rating: 91 5/02   Prth   2m4f110y   gd-fm   Ch

Modest hunter chaser; handles any ground; has worn a tongue tie and cheekpieces.

Bounce Again (FR)
92f   86f

4-y-o b g Jeune Homme (USA)-Lattaquie (FR) (Fast Topaze (USA))
M C Pipe   Mrs Belinda Harvey

Placings:30   (4571)
2003/04: 18³S, 17⁰GS,

	Starts	1st	2nd	3rd	Win & Pl
NH Flat	2	0	0	1	327
Career Total	2	0	0	1	327

Going: Sf: 0-1 GS: 0-1 Gd: 0-0 GF: - Fm: 0-0
Distance: 2m/2m3: 0-2 2m4-2m7: 0-0 3m+: 0-0
Track: LH: 0-2 RH: 0-0 Tight: 0-1 Gall: 0-0
Aids: Bl: 0-0 Vi: 0-0 Tstrap: 0-0 Ckp: 0-0
Best Rating: 86 2/04   Plum   2m2f   soft   NHF

Half-brother to stable's Whitbread winner Bounce Back; showed promise on debut in soft ground bumper at Plumpton in February over 2m 2f.

Bounce Back (USA)
95   (153h)146

8-y-o ch g Trempolino (USA)-Lattaquie (FR) (Fast Topaze (USA))
M C Pipe   Mrs Belinda Harvey

Placings:21F/1332224/2321433561/0P6-3PF0   (4965)
2003/04: 29³G, 29ᴾS, 36⁵G, 29⁹GF,

	Starts	1st	2nd	3rd	Win & Pl
Chases	4	0	1	0	4950
Career Total	27	4	6	6	262707
156 4/02 Sand	3m5f110yA HCh			GD	£72500
139 12/01 Chep	2m3f110yD Ch			SFT	£4124
5/00 Autl	3m1f110y Hdl			VS	£28818
3/00 Engh	2m3f110y Hdl			HLD	£11527
		Total win prize-money £116969			

Going: Sf: 0-1 GS: 0-0 Gd: 0-2 GF: - Fm: 0-1
Distance: 2m/2m3: 0-0 2m4-2m7: 0-0 3m+: 0-4
Track: LH: 0-2 RH: 0-2 Tight: 0-1 Gall: 0-0
Aids: Bl: 0-1 Vi: 0-0 Tstrap: 0-0 Ckp: 0-0
Best Rating: 156 4/02   Sand   3m5f110y   good   Ch

Formerly a high-class hurdler in France; very useful chaser; proved a revelation when stepped up to three miles five in the Attheraces Gold Cup at Sandown in April 2002; below form since; ideally suited by at least three miles; best on a decent surface; blinkered when falling in the Grand National; has worn a visor in the past.

Bound
114   130+

6-y-o b g Kris-Tender Moment (IRE) (Caerleon (USA))
Mrs L Wadham   Hebomapa

Placings:3P203112/3023000-F13200   (4628)
2003/04: 17ᶠGS, 16¹GS, 17³G, 17²GS, 17⁰G, 20⁰G,

	Starts	1st	2nd	3rd	Win & Pl
Hurdles	6	1	1	1	21657
Career Total	21	3	4	5	36909
125 12/03 Hntg	2m110y D(0-125)HHdl		G-S	£13747
110 4/02 Plum	2m	E Hdl	G-F	£2698
106 3/02 MRas	2m1f110yD Hdl		G-S	£3672
		Total win prize-money £20120			

Going: Sf: 0-0 GS: 1-3 Gd: 0-3 GF: - Fm: 0-0
Distance: 2m/2m3: 1-5 2m4-2m7: 0-1 3m+: 0-0
Track: LH: 0-4 RH: 1-2 Tight: 0-2 Gall: 1-4
Aids: Bl: 0-0 Vi: 0-0 Tstrap: 0-1 Ckp: 0-0
Best Rating: 130 1/04   Chel   2m1f   gd-sft   Hdl

Useful handicap hurdler; out on his own when falling at the last at Market Rasen in December 2003; good efforts since; suited by forcing tactics; effective over two miles; acts on fast and easy ground; has worn a tongue tie.

Boundary House

6-y-o ch g Afflora (IRE)-Preacher's Gem (The Parson)
J A B Old   Nick Viney

Placings:00P   (4650)
2003/04: 16⁰S, 16⁶GS, 19⁰G,

	Starts	1st	2nd	3rd	Win & Pl
NH Flat	2	0	0	0	0
Hurdles	1	0	0	0	0
Career Total	3	0	0	0	

Going: Sf: 0-1 GS: 0-1 Gd: 0-1 GF: - Fm: 0-0
Distance: 2m/2m3: 0-2 2m4-2m7: 0-1 3m+: 0-0
Track: LH: 0-1 RH: 0-2 Tight: 0-0 Gall: 0-0
Aids: Bl: 0-0 Vi: 0-0 Tstrap: 0-0 Ckp: 0-0
Best Rating: 92 2/04   Kemp   2m   gd-sft   NHF

Bourbon Manhattan
112   138+

6-y-o b g Afflora (IRE)-Vanina Ii (FR) (Italic (FR))
A King   A Longman, T Warner, R devereux & Ptnrs

Placings:116-123201   (4852)
2003/04: 16¹GS, 16²S, 16³GS, 16²G, 16⁰G, 20¹GS,

	Starts	1st	2nd	3rd	Win & Pl
Hurdles	6	2	2	1	19885
Career Total	9	4	2	1	26169
135 4/04 Ayr	2m4f	C Hdl	G-S	£7715
129 11/03 Aint	2m110y D Hdl		G-S	£5005
129 3/03 Newb	2m110y H NHF		SFT	£3248
110 11/02 Tntn	2m1f	H NHF	G-S	£2436
		Total win prize-money £18405			

Going: Sf: 0-1 GS: 2-3 Gd: 0-2 GF: - Fm: 0-0
Distance: 2m/2m3: 1-5 2m4-2m7: 1-1 3m+: 0-0

Track: LH: 2-3 RH: 0-3 Tight: 1-1 Gall: 0-0
Aids: Bl: 0-0 Vi: 0-0 Tstrap: 0-0 Ckp: 0-0
Best Rating: 138 3/04 Chel 2m110y good Hdl

Useful novice hurdler; formerly useful bumper horse, made a winning hurdling debut, but disappointing afterwards; suited by some cut and may prefer a flat track.

Bourgeois

109   115

7-y-o ch g Sanglamore (USA)-Bourbon Girl (Ile De Bourbon (USA))
T D Easterby C H Stevens

Placings:01P2   (4260)
2003/04: 20⁵GS, 16¹GS, 16⁶S, 16²GF,

	Starts	1st	2nd	3rd	Win & Pl
Hurdles	4	1	1	0	4787
Career Total	4	1	1	0	4787
104	1/04	Catt	2m	E Hdl	G-S £3741

Total win prize-money £3742

Going: Sf: 0-1 GS: 1-2 Gd: 0-0 GF: - Fm: 0-1
Distance: 2m/2m3: 1-3 2m4-2m7: 0-1 3m+: 0-0
Track: LH: 1-4 RH: 0-0 Tight: 1-2 Gall: 0-0
Aids: Bl: 0-0 Vi: 0-0 Tstrap: 0-0 Ckp: 0-0
Best Rating: 115 3/04 Catt 2m gd-fm Hdl

Useful handicapper on the Flat; improved a good deal on initial effort when decisive winner at Catterick in January; ran as if something amiss and eventually pulled up a week later; runner-up on return at Catterick in March; seems best suited by two miles.

Bow Strada

110(112c)   (136c)135

7-y-o ch g Rainbow Quest (USA)-La Strada (Niniski (USA))
P J Hobbs M J Tuckey

Placings:23/11F01/2231014-0BP   (4840)
2003/04: 21⁰G, 24⁸G, 24⁴G,

	Starts	1st	2nd	3rd	Win & Pl
Hurdles	3	0	0	0	
Career Total	17	5	3	2	31351
136	3/03	Asct	2m3f110yD Ch		GD £5356
130	11/02	Leic	2m	E Ch	G-F £4046
135	4/02	Extr	2m3f	D(0-125)HHdl	FRM £3575
121	12/01	Tntn	2m1f	D Hdl	G-S £5528
123	12/01	Donc	2m110y	E Hdl	GD £3290

Total win prize-money £21795

Going: Sf: 0-0 GS: 0-0 Gd: 0-3 GF: - Fm: 0-0
Distance: 2m/2m3: 0-0 2m4-2m7: 0-1 3m+: 0-2
Track: LH: 0-3 RH: 0-0 Tight: 0-1 Gall: 0-2
Aids: Bl: 0-0 Vi: 0-0 Tstrap: 0-0 Ckp: 0-0
Best Rating: 136 3/03 Asct 2m3f110y good Ch

Useful handicap hurdler/novice chaser; stays two and a half miles; suited by a sound surface.

Bowcliffe Court (IRE)

65   64

12-y-o b g Slip Anchor-Res Nova (USA) (Blushing Groom (FR))
G H Jones John Priday Construction Ltd

Placings:P130/6443/511/P600/0-0   (0761)
2003/04: 16⁰G,

	Starts	1st	2nd	3rd	Win & Pl
Hurdles	1	0	0	0	
Career Total	17	3	0	2	10295

113	12/98	Leic	2m	E(0-110)HHdl	SFT £3028
104	12/98	Leic	2m	E(0-110)HHdl	G-S £2206
98	12/96	Chep	2m110y	D Hdl	SFT £2693

Total win prize-money £7928

Going: Sf: 0-0 GS: 0-0 Gd: 0-0 GF: - Fm: 0-0
Distance: 2m/2m3: 0-1 2m4-2m7: 0-0 3m+: 0-0
Track: LH: 0-1 RH: 0-0 Tight: 0-0 Gall: 0-0
Aids: Bl: 0-0 Vi: 0-0 Tstrap: 0-0 Ckp: 0-0
Best Rating: 113 12/98 Leic 2m soft Hdl

Bowd Lane Joe

81   67

5-y-o gr g Mazaad-Race To The Rhythm (Deep Run)
A W Carroll R H Fox

Placings:030   (3408)
2003/04: 16⁰GS, 20³GS, 16⁰G,

	Starts	1st	2nd	3rd	Win & Pl
Hurdles	3	0	0	1	547
Career Total	3	0	0	1	547

Going: Sf: 0-0 GS: 0-2 Gd: 0-1 GF: - Fm: 0-0
Distance: 2m/2m3: 0-2 2m4-2m7: 0-1 3m+: 0-0
Track: LH: 0-2 RH: 0-1 Tight: 0-0 Gall: 0-2
Aids: Bl: 0-0 Vi: 0-0 Tstrap: 0-0 Ckp: 0-0
Best Rating: 76 12/03 Leic 2m4f110y gd-sft Hdl

Very moderate novice hurdler; handles cut in the ground.

Bowfell

78   41

6-y-o b m Alflora (IRE)-April City (Lidhame)
M E Sowersby J Payne

Placings:0FUU/00   (4958)
2003/04: 21⁰G, 17⁰G,

	Starts	1st	2nd	3rd	Win & Pl
Hurdles	2	0	0	0	
Career Total	6	0	0	0	0

Going: Sf: 0-0 GS: 0-0 Gd: 0-2 GF: - Fm: 0-0
Distance: 2m/2m3: 0-1 2m4-2m7: 0-0 3m+: 0-0
Track: LH: 0-1 RH: 0-0 Tight: 0-2 Gall: 0-0
Aids: Bl: 0-1 Vi: 0-1 Tstrap: 0-0 Ckp: 0-0
Best Rating: 54 2/02 MRas 2m1f110y gd-sft Hdl

Bowleaze (IRE)

95   93+

5-y-o br g Right Win (IRE)-Mrs Cullen (Over The River (FR))
R H Alner Martin Short

Placings:1-4   (2218)
2003/04: 17⁴G,

	Starts	1st	2nd	3rd	Win & Pl
Hurdles	1	0	0	0	329
Career Total	2	1	0	0	3591
91	4/03	Extr	2m1f	H NHF	G-F £3262

Total win prize-money £3262

Going: Sf: 0-0 GS: 0-0 Gd: 0-1 GF: - Fm: 0-0
Distance: 2m/2m3: 0-1 2m4-2m7: 0-0 3m+: 0-0
Track: LH: 0-1 RH: 0-0 Tight: 0-1 Gall: 0-0
Aids: Bl: 0-0 Vi: 0-0 Tstrap: 0-0 Ckp: 0-0
Best Rating: 98 11/03 NAbb 2m1f good Hdl

Easy winner of six-runner fast ground bumper on his debut at Exeter April 2003; promise over hurdles.

Bowles Patrol (IRE)

89   (75h)94

12-y-o gr g Roselier (FR)-Another Dud (Le Bavard (FR))
John R Upson Bill Ellis

Placings:00F3/00022/3/UP12134414/12235FP31/1U36523
5/0P61103/545F-6   (0056)
2003/04: 25⁶GS,

	Starts	1st	2nd	3rd	Win & Pl
Chases	1	0	0	0	
Career Total	49	8	6	8	38159
103	12/01	Tntn	3m	F(0-105)HCh	G-S £3802
98	11/01	Sedg	3m3f	F(0-105)HCh	SFT £2863
111	5/00	Hntg	2m5f110yF(0-110)HHdl		GD £2710
112	4/00	MRas	2m5f110yF(0-100)HHdl		SFT £1542
101	11/99	NAbb	2m5f110yF(0-100)HCh		SFT £3120
107	3/99	Newb	2m5f	E(0-115)HHdl	SFT £3057
91	12/98	Plum	3m110y	E(0-105)HHdl	G-S £2775
86	11/98	Carl	2m4f110yE(0-100)HHdl		SFT £2402

Total win prize-money £22274

Going: Sf: 0-0 GS: 0-1 Gd: 0-0 GF: - Fm: 0-0
Distance: 2m/2m3: 0-0 2m4-2m7: 0-0 3m+: 0-1
Track: LH: 0-0 RH: 0-1 Tight: 0-0 Gall: 0-0
Aids: Bl: 0-0 Vi: 0-0 Tstrap: 0-0 Ckp: 0-0
Best Rating: 112 1/01 Leic 2m4f110y heavy Hdl

Staying chaser, genuine if a little one-paced.

Bowling Beauty

77   36

6-y-o br m Alderbrook-Bowling Fort (Bowling Pin)
Miss S E Forster A G & Mrs E J Bell

Placings:6-0   (0472)
2003/04: 17⁰GS,

	Starts	1st	2nd	3rd	Win & Pl
Hurdles	1	0	0	0	
Career Total	2	0	0	0	0

Going: Sf: 0-0 GS: 0-1 Gd: 0-0 GF: - Fm: 0-0
Distance: 2m/2m3: 0-1 2m4-2m7: 0-0 3m+: 0-0
Track: LH: 0-1 RH: 0-0 Tight: 0-1 Gall: 0-0
Aids: Bl: 0-0 Vi: 0-0 Tstrap: 0-0 Ckp: 0-0
Best Rating: 76 3/03 Hexm 2m110y good NHF

Bowsprit

4-y-o ch g Fleetwood (IRE)-Longwood Lady (Rudimentary (USA))
B G Powell (M R Channon 9/5) The Three Bears Racing

Placings:P   (2436)
2003/04: 17⁰G,

	Starts	1st	2nd	3rd	Win & Pl
Hurdles	1	0	0	0	
Career Total	1	0	0	0	

Going: Sf: 0-0 GS: 0-0 Gd: 0-1 GF: - Fm: 0-0
Distance: 2m/2m3: 0-0 2m4-2m7: 0-0 3m+: 0-0
Track: LH: 0-1 RH: 0-0 Tight: 0-0 Gall: 0-0
Aids: Bl: 0-0 Vi: 0-0 Tstrap: 0-0 Ckp: 0-0
Best Rating: 0 11/03 Bang 2m1f good Hdl

Pulled up on hurdling debut at Bangor; may be capable of better.

Box Builder

98   (0c)110

7-y-o ch g Fraam-Ena Olley (Le Moss)

H Morrison M Hutchinson

Placings:4025/122410P-5   (4176)
2003/04: 24⁵G,

	Starts	1st	2nd	3rd	Win & Pl
Hurdles	1	0	0	0	0
Career Total	12	2	3	0	9284
102 8/02	NAbb	2m6f		E Hdl	G-F	£2898
110 5/02	Aint	2m4f		D Hdl	GD	£3588

Total win prize-money £6486

Going:	Sf: 0-0 GS: 0-0 Gd: 0-1 GF: - Fm: 0-0
Distance:	2m/2m3: 0-0 2m4-2m7: 0-0 3m+: 0-1
Track:	LH: 0-1 RH: 0-0 Tight: 0-0 Gall: 0-1
Aids:	Bl: 0-0 Vi: 0-0 Tstrap: 0-0 Ckp: 0-0
Best Rating:	110 3/04 Donc 3m110y good Hdl

Effective over hurdles at around two miles six furlongs. Acts on a sound surface, and did not take to chasing when tried in August 2002. Regularly tongue tied.

Boxer's Double

61(83h)   (56h)55
7-y-o b g Petoski-Grayrose Double (Celtic Cone)
G A Ham K C White

Placings:6000PP/P05340060R-043P   (2284)
2003/04: 22⁰G, 17⁴G, 20³F, 19⁶G,

	Starts	1st	2nd	3rd	Win & Pl
Hurdles	2	0	0	0	0
Chases	2	0	0	1	562
Career Total	20	0	0	2	840

Going:	Sf: 0-0 GS: 0-0 Gd: 0-2 GF: - Fm: 0-2
Distance:	2m/2m3: 0-1 2m4-2m7: 0-0 3m+: 0-2
Track:	LH: 0-1 RH: 0-0 Tight: 0-2 Gall: 0-0
Aids:	Bl: 0-0 Vi: 0-2 Tstrap: 0-0 Ckp: 0-0
Best Rating:	76 10/01 Hrfd 2m1f good NHF

Boy's Hurrah (IRE)

97   110+
8-y-o b g Phardante (FR)-Gorryelm (Arctic Slave)
J Howard Johnson (J A Berry 26/10) Woolpack Farm Partnership

Placings:0041-12P   (4398)
2003/04: 24¹GF, 20²F, 32⁶G,

	Starts	1st	2nd	3rd	Win & Pl
Chases	3	1	1	0	6132
Career Total	7	2	1	0	11644
110 1/04	Muss	3m		E Ch	G-F	£4075
98 9/02	List	2m4f		NHF	FRM	£5291

Total win prize-money £9367

Going:	Sf: 0-0 GS: 0-0 Gd: 0-1 GF: - Fm: 1-2
Distance:	2m/2m3: 0-0 2m4-2m7: 0-0 3m+: 1-2
Track:	LH: 0-1 RH: 1-2 Tight: 1-2 Gall: 0-1
Aids:	Bl: 0-0 Vi: 0-0 Tstrap: 0-0 Ckp: 0-0
Best Rating:	110 2/04 Muss 2m4f firm Ch

Bumper and multiple point winner in Ireland; jumped well when ready winner of novices' chase at Musselburgh in January.

Boyne Banks (IRE)

92
9-y-o ch g Boyne Valley-Pallatess (Pall Mall)
N A Twiston-Davies James Cheetham

Placings:P/640P-P   (0056)
2003/04: 25⁰GS,

	Starts	1st	2nd	3rd	Win & Pl
Chases	1	0	0	0	
Career Total	6	0	0	0	392

Going:	Sf: 0-0 GS: 0-1 Gd: 0-0 GF: - Fm: 0-0
Distance:	2m/2m3: 0-0 2m4-2m7: 0-0 3m+: 0-1
Track:	LH: 0-0 RH: 0-1 Tight: 0-0 Gall: 0-0
Aids:	Bl: 0-1 Vi: 0-0 Tstrap: 0-0 Ckp: 0-0
Best Rating:	92 12/02 Wwck 3m110y gd-sft Ch

Bracey Run (IRE)

100   106
14-y-o b g The Parson-Outdoor Ivy (Deep Run)
A J Lidderdale Bonusprint

Placings:2/31334P/FF/33203/311U/40004/41426-30 (0527)
2003/04: 21³GF, 20⁰GF,

	Starts	1st	2nd	3rd	Win & Pl
Hurdles	2	0	0	1	513
Career Total	30	4	3	8	25288
112 5/02	Sthl	2m4f110yE(0-105)HHdl	G-S	£2639
126 5/00	Uttx	2m4f110yB(0-140)HHdl	G-F	£6227
119 5/00	Hrfd	2m3f110yD(0-120)HHdl	GD	£3269
110 12/97	Towc	2m	E Hdl	SFT	£2705

Total win prize-money £14842

Going:	Sf: 0-0 GS: 0-0 Gd: 0-0 GF: - Fm: 0-2
Distance:	2m/2m3: 0-0 2m4-2m7: 0-2 3m+: 0-0
Track:	LH: 0-2 RH: 0-0 Tight: 0-0 Gall: 0-0
Aids:	Bl: 0-0 Vi: 0-0 Tstrap: 0-0 Ckp: 0-0
Best Rating:	130 2/98 Chep 2m4f110y gd-sft Hdl

Veteran hurdler, on the downgrade. Had slipped to a useful mark when winning moderate handicap at Southwell in May 2002; third in same race this time; acts on all types of ground.

Brachvogel (GER)

97   (109h)101
10-y-o gr g Val Des Pres (FR)-Bastei (GER) (Authi)
J D Frost Miss A Sirett

Placings:600/2433200500/2   (4631)
2003/04: 19²G,

	Starts	1st	2nd	3rd	Win & Pl
Chases	1	0	1	0	1692
Career Total	14	0	3	2	5361

Going:	Sf: 0-0 GS: 0-0 Gd: 0-1 GF: - Fm: 0-0
Distance:	2m/2m3: 0-1 2m4-2m7: 0-0 3m+: 0-0
Track:	LH: 0-0 RH: 0-1 Tight: 0-1 Gall: 0-0
Aids:	Bl: 0-0 Vi: 0-0 Tstrap: 0-0 Ckp: 0-0
Best Rating:	109 7/01 Klny 2m1f good Hdl

Bracken Run (IRE)

10-y-o b g Commanche Run-Stable Lass (Golden Love)
David Pearson David Pearson

Placings:P/0/PP   (0531)
2003/04: 24⁰PS, 20⁰GF,

	Starts	1st	2nd	3rd	Win & Pl
Hurdles	2	0	0	0	
Career Total	4	0	0	0	

Going:	Sf: 0-1 GS: 0-0 Gd: 0-0 GF: - Fm: 0-1
Distance:	2m/2m3: 0-0 2m4-2m7: 0-0 3m+: 0-1
Track:	LH: 0-2 RH: 0-0 Tight: 0-1 Gall: 0-0
Aids:	Bl: 0-0 Vi: 0-0 Tstrap: 0-0 Ckp: 0-0
Best Rating:	0 6/03 Worc 2m4f gd-fm Hdl

Brackenheath (IRE)

13-y-o b g Le Moss-Stable Lass (Golden Love)
Mrs D M Grissell John Grist

Placings:0220/F142120/P022F240/3F5/PP/1R/3P-4 (0351)
2003/04: 25⁴GF,

	Starts	1st	2nd	3rd	Win & Pl
Chases	1	0	0	0	
Career Total	29	3	7	2	24850
100 5/01	Folk	3m2f		H Ch	GD	£1462
118 2/98	Folk	2m6f110yE Hdl	G-F	£2731
109 11/97	Asct	3m		C Hdl	SFT	£3582

Total win prize-money £7778

Going:	Sf: 0-0 GS: 0-0 Gd: 0-0 GF: - Fm: 0-1
Distance:	2m/2m3: 0-0 2m4-2m7: 0-0 3m+: 0-1
Track:	LH: 0-0 RH: 0-1 Tight: 0-1 Gall: 0-0
Aids:	Bl: 0-1 Vi: 0-0 Tstrap: 0-0 Ckp: 0-0
Best Rating:	139 4/98 Aint 3m110y soft Hdl

Formerly useful hurdler.chaser, now hunter chasing. Best on a sound surface although handles softer, likes Folkestone.

Brackney Boy (IRE)

103   (92c)89
10-y-o b g Zaffaran (USA)-Donard Lily (Master Buck)
I A Duncan Dr Stephen Sinclair

Placings:5220/001246/F60F30-022   (0471)
2003/04: 24⁰Y, 24²Y, 24²G,

	Starts	1st	2nd	3rd	Win & Pl
Hurdles	3	0	2	0	3234
Career Total	19	1	5	1	17057
102 11/01	DRoy	2m6f		Hdl	YLD	£6677

Total win prize-money £6677

Going:	Sf: 0-0 GS: 0-0 Gd: 0-1 GF: - Fm: 0-0
Distance:	2m/2m3: 0-0 2m4-2m7: 0-0 3m+: 0-3
Track:	LH: 0-2 RH: 0-1 Tight: 0-0 Gall: 0-0
Aids:	Bl: 0-3 Vi: 0-0 Tstrap: 0-0 Ckp: 0-0
Best Rating:	112 11/01 Navn 3m yld-sft Hdl

Got off the mark over hurdles in a maiden on Yielding ground over two miles six and put up a good effort after that on his step up to three miles.

Brad

(80h)   (70h)
6-y-o b g Deploy-Celia Brady (Last Tycoon)
P R Webber Mrs David Blackburn

Placings:20/5-56PU   (4369)
2003/04: 17⁵GF, 20⁶GS, 18⁸GS, 20⁴G,

	Starts	1st	2nd	3rd	Win & Pl
NH Flat	1	0	0	0	0
Hurdles	2	0	0	0	0
Chases	1	0	0	0	0
Career Total	7	0	1	0	662

Going:	Sf: 0-0 GS: 0-2 Gd: 0-1 GF: - Fm: 0-1
Distance:	2m/2m3: 0-2 2m4-2m7: 0-2 3m+: 0-0
Track:	LH: 0-2 RH: 0-2 Tight: 0-2 Gall: 0-0
Aids:	Bl: 0-0 Vi: 0-0 Tstrap: 0-0 Ckp: 0-0
Best Rating:	97 11/02 Chep 2m110y heavy NHF

Showed promise in bumper company; acts in testing ground.

Bradford Bridge

11-y-o ch m Cruise Missile-Opt Out (Spartan General)
W S Kittow Dhobiwallah Racing

Placings:P-　　　　　　　　　　　　　　(0015)
2003/04: 21PS,

	Starts	1st	2nd	3rd	Win & Pl
Chases	1	0	0	0	
Career Total	1	0	0	0	

Going:	Sf: 0-1 GS: 0-0 Gd: 0-0 GF: - Fm: 0-0	
Distance:	2m/2m3: 0-0 2m4-2m7: 0-1 3m+: 0-0	
Track:	LH: 0-1 RH: 0-0 Tight: 0-1 Gall: 0-0	
Aids:	Bl: 0-0 Vi: 0-0 Tstrap: 0-0 Ckp: 0-0	
Best Rating:	0　4/03　NAbb　2m5f110y　soft	Ch

Bradley My Boy (IRE)

81　　　　　　　　　　　　　　　　81

8-y-o ch g Treasure Hunter-Clonaslee Baby (Konigssee)
Mrs A M Naughton A P Brady

Placings:45/10050/000FP5-00　　　　　(1368)
2003/04: 16PG, 16PG,

	Starts	1st	2nd	3rd	Win & Pl
Hurdles	2	0	0	0	
Career Total	15	1	0	0	1886
103　5/01　NAbb　2m1f　H NHF　G-F　£1694					
Total win prize-money £1694					

Going:	Sf: 0-0 GS: 0-0 Gd: 0-1 GF: - Fm: 0-1	
Distance:	2m/2m3: 0-2 2m4-2m7: 0-0 3m+: 0-0	
Track:	LH: 0-2 RH: 0-0 Tight: 0-1 Gall: 0-0	
Aids:	Bl: 0-0 Vi: 0-0 Tstrap: 0-0 Ckp: 0-0	
Best Rating:	103　5/01　NAbb　2m1f　gd-fm NHF

Moderate ex-Irish hurdler; poor form since arriving in Britain.

Brady Boys (USA)

105(98h)　　　　　　　　　(87h)90

7-y-o b g Cozzene (USA)-Elvia (USA) (Roberto (USA))
J G M O'Shea D Cound and R Davies

Placings:5P/4042010-0254024　　　　(4653)
2003/04: 20PG, 202GF, 165GF, 204F, 199GS, 162G, 194G,

	Starts	1st	2nd	3rd	Win & Pl
Hurdles	3	0	1	0	754
Chases	4	0	1	0	1941
Career Total	16	1	3	0	5955
87　3/03　Tntn　2m1f　G Hdl　HVY　£2373					
Total win prize-money £2373					

Going:	Sf: 0-0 GS: 0-1 Gd: 0-3 GF: - Fm: 0-3	
Distance:	2m/2m3: 0-4 2m4-2m7: 0-3 3m+: 0-0	
Track:	LH: 0-2 RH: 0-4 Tight: 0-5 Gall: 0-0	
Aids:	Bl: 0-0 Vi: 0-2 Tstrap: 0-0 Ckp: 0-0	
Best Rating:	90　4/04　Hrfd　2m3f　good	Ch

Plating-class hurdler; inconsistent and runs best when fresh;
acts on soft ground; has worn visor.

Braeburn

99　　　　　　　　　　　　　　　　88

9-y-o b g Petoski-Great Granny Smith (Fine Blue)
R T Phillips Mrs T Stopford-Sackville

Placings:2P/FP-P64　　　　　　　　　(3526)
2003/04: 19PGS, 206G, 234G,

	Starts	1st	2nd	3rd	Win & Pl
Chases	3	0	0	0	328
Career Total	7	0	1	0	1570

Going:	Sf: 0-0 GS: 0-1 Gd: 0-2 GF: - Fm: 0-0	
Distance:	2m/2m3: 0-1 2m4-2m7: 0-1 3m+: 0-1	
Track:	LH: 0-0 RH: 0-3 Tight: 0-1 Gall: 0-0	
Aids:	Bl: 0-0 Vi: 0-0 Tstrap: 0-0 Ckp: 0-0	
Best Rating:	95　3/02　Ludl　3m　gd-sft	Ch

Braes Of Mar

14-y-o b g Bustino-Barbella (Barolo)
C R McEwen The Queen

Placings:163/11133FP/64F0/122/42341/4/4P/0　　(4308)
2003/04: 240G,

	Starts	1st	2nd	3rd	Win & Pl
Chases	1	0	0	0	
Career Total	26	6	3	4	19557
94　4/99　Folk　3m2f　H Ch　G-F　£1123					
90　3/98　Sand　3m110y　H Ch　G-S　£2081					
115　11/95　Hrfd　2m3f　E Ch　G-S　£2775					
120　11/95　Leic　2m4f110yD(0-120)HHdl　GD　£2709					
91　5/95　MRas　2m1f110yD Hdl　G-F　£2756					
114　12/94　Sand　2m110y　Hdl　GD　£2948					
Total win prize-money £14393					

Going:	Sf: 0-0 GS: 0-0 Gd: 0-1 GF: - Fm: 0-0	
Distance:	2m/2m3: 0-0 2m4-2m7: 0-0 3m+: 0-1	
Track:	LH: 0-0 RH: 0-1 Tight: 0-0 Gall: 0-0	
Aids:	Bl: 0-0 Vi: 0-0 Tstrap: 0-0 Ckp: 0-0	
Best Rating:	120　11/95　Leic　2m4f110y　good	Hdl

Bramblehill Duke (IRE)

105　　　　　　　　　　　　　136

12-y-o b g Kambalda-Scat-Cat (Furry Glen)
Miss Venetia Williams Mel Davies

Placings:f43P/11331/F2R21/5P1165/03P20/312000F-
P6P3250R　　　　　　　　　　　　(4647)
2003/04: 25PGY, 246S, 26PG, 243S, 272GS, 265HY, 289G, 36RG,

	Starts	1st	2nd	3rd	Win & Pl
Chases	8	0	1	1	3602
Career Total	40	8	5	6	67747
135　11/02　Bang　3m110y　C(0-130)HCh　HVY　£7377					
135　1/01　Wwck　2m4f110yC(0-135)HCh　SFT　£8424					
140　1/01　Uttx　2m4f　B(0-140)HCh　HVY　£10426					
125　2/00　Hayd　2m6f　C Ch　HVY　£7315					
119　11/98　Newb　2m5f　E(0-110)HHdl　GD　£3566					
109　5/98　Towc　2m110y　E Hdl　G-F　£2460					
109　5/98　Chep　2m110y　E(0-100)HHdl　GD　£2416					
107　11/97　Hayd　3m　H NHF　GD　£1278					
Total win prize-money £43263					

Going:	Sf: 0-3 GS: 0-1 Gd: 0-3 GF: - Fm: 0-0	
Distance:	2m/2m3: 0-0 2m4-2m7: 0-0 3m+: 0-8	
Track:	LH: 0-4 RH: 0-4 Tight: 0-2 Gall: 0-2	
Aids:	Bl: 0-0 Vi: 0-0 Tstrap: 0-0 Ckp: 0-0	
Best Rating:	140　1/01　Uttx　2m4f　heavy	Ch

Fair handicap chaser; stays three miles, although effective
at shorter; acts on most types of ground, but probably best
on soft; falling in the weights.

Bramlynn Brook (FR)

108　　　　　　　　　　　112

6-y-o ch g Apple Tree (FR)-Sainte Lys (FR) (Don Roberto
(USA))
Miss Venetia Williams Christopher Drury

Placings:522-f1226　　　　　　　　(4325)
2003/04: 181G, 211S, 202G, 212GS, 206S,

	Starts	1st	2nd	3rd	Win & Pl
NH Flat	1	1	0	0	2352
Hurdles	4	1	2	0	5752
Career Total	8	2	4	0	9769
107　11/03　Towc　2m5f　E Hdl　SFT　£2989					
107　11/03　Plum　2m2f　H NHF　GD　£2352					
Total win prize-money £5341					

Going:	Sf: 1-2 GS: 0-1 Gd: 1-2 GF: - Fm: 0-0	
Distance:	2m/2m3: 1-1 2m4-2m7: 1-4 3m+: 0-0	
Track:	LH: 1-2 RH: 1-2 Tight: 0-2 Gall: 0-0	
Aids:	Bl: 0-0 Vi: 0-0 Tstrap: 0-0 Ckp: 0-0	
Best Rating:	113　12/03　Font　2m4f　good	Hdl

Modest novice hurdler; won at Towcester and Plumpton;
stays two miles five; acts on good, but best with cut; resolute
galloper.

Brandeston Ron (IRE)

5-y-o b g Presenting-Boolavogue (IRE) (Torus)
Jonjo O'Neill Ron George

Placings:00P　　　　　　　　　　（4887)
2003/04: 16PG, 16PG, 22PGF,

	Starts	1st	2nd	3rd	Win & Pl
NH Flat	2	0	0	0	0
Hurdles	1	0	0	0	0
Career Total	3	0	0	0	0

Going:	Sf: 0-0 GS: 0-0 Gd: 0-2 GF: - Fm: 0-1	
Distance:	2m/2m3: 0-2 2m4-2m7: 0-1 3m+: 0-0	
Track:	LH: 0-2 RH: 0-1 Tight: 0-1 Gall: 0-1	
Aids:	Bl: 0-0 Vi: 0-0 Tstrap: 0-0 Ckp: 0-0	
Best Rating:	58　3/04　Hntg　2m110y　good	NHF

Brandsby Stripe

100(94h)　　　　　　　　(72h)75

9-y-o ch g Nomadic Way (USA)-I'm Fine (Fitzwilliam (USA))
P Beaumont The Foulrice Twenty

Placings:0/60P4-1PPU6P4P0　　　　(4796)
2003/04: 171S, 20PS, 25PS, 16UGS, 16RG, 24PG, 204G, 20PG,
219G,

	Starts	1st	2nd	3rd	Win & Pl
Hurdles	1	0	0	0	
Chases	8	1	0	0	4603
Career Total	14	1	0	0	4603
69　5/03　Bang　2m1f110yE(0-100)HCh　SFT　£4270					
Total win prize-money £4271					

Going:	Sf: 1-3 GS: 0-1 Gd: 0-5 GF: - Fm: 0-0	
Distance:	2m/2m3: 1-3 2m4-2m7: 0-4 3m+: 0-2	
Track:	LH: 1-8 RH: 0-1 Tight: 1-7 Gall: 0-0	
Aids:	Bl: 0-3 Vi: 0-0 Tstrap: 0-0 Ckp: 0-1	
Best Rating:	75　3/04　Bang　2m4f110y　good	Ch

Plating-class maiden hurdler/chaser.

Brandy Wine (IRE)

81   **68**

6-y-o b g Roselier (FR)-Sakonnet (IRE) (Mandalus)
L Lungo Ashleybank Investments Limited

Placings:60   (3494)
2003/04: 16⁶S, 20⁹HY,

	Starts	1st	2nd	3rd	Win & Pl
NH Flat	1	0	0	0	0
Hurdles	1	0	0	0	0
Career Total	2	0	0	0	0

Going:	Sf: 0-2 GS: 0-0 Gd: 0-0 GF: - Fm: 0-0
Distance:	2m/2m3: 0-1 2m4-2m7: 0-1 3m+: 0-0
Track:	LH: 0-2 RH: 0-0 Tight: 0-0 Gall: 0-0
Aids:	Bl: 0-0 Vi: 0-0 Tstrap: 0-0 Ckp: 0-0
Best Rating:	83 1/04 Weth 2m soft NHF

Started favourite when never dangerous on debut in bumper at Wetherby in January.

Branston Nell

5-y-o b m Classic Cliche (IRE)-Indefinite Article (IRE) (Indian Ridge)
C R Dore (I A Wood 8/9) Castles UK

Placings:P   (4180)
2003/04: 20⁸G,

	Starts	1st	2nd	3rd	Win & Pl
Hurdles	1	0	0	0	
Career Total	1	0	0	0	

Going:	Sf: 0-0 GS: 0-0 Gd: 0-0 GF: - Fm: 0-0
Distance:	2m/2m3: 0-0 2m4-2m7: 0-1 3m+: 0-0
Track:	LH: 0-0 RH: 0-0 Tight: 0-0 Gall: 0-1
Aids:	Bl: 0-0 Vi: 0-0 Tstrap: 0-0 Ckp: 0-0

Branston Tiger

5-y-o b h Mark Of Esteem (IRE)-Tuxford Hideaway (Cawston's Clown)
J G Given (G A Swinbank 1/12) J David Abell

Placings:5   (2505)
2003/04: 16⁵S,

	Starts	1st	2nd	3rd	Win & Pl
Hurdles	1	0	0	0	0
Career Total	1	0	0	0	0

Going:	Sf: 0-1 GS: 0-0 Gd: 0-0 GF: - Fm: 0-0
Distance:	2m/2m3: 0-1 2m4-2m7: 0-0 3m+: 0-0
Track:	LH: 0-1 RH: 0-0 Tight: 0-1 Gall: 0-0
Aids:	Bl: 0-0 Vi: 0-0 Tstrap: 0-0 Ckp: 0-0

Brassie

103f   **113+f**

5-y-o b g Celtic Swing-Gong (Bustino)
R M Beckett A D G Oldrey

Placings:120   (4400)
2003/04: 16¹GS, 16²G, 16⁹G,

	Starts	1st	2nd	3rd	Win & Pl
NH Flat	3	1	1	0	2932
Career Total	3	1	1	0	2932
113 12/03 Uttx	2m		H NHF	G-S	£2142

Total win prize-money £2142

Brassis Hill (IRE)

13-y-o b g Marktingo-Mystery Woman (Tula Rocket)
Mrs D M Grissell T Hunter Blair

Placings:0/40400/1655/6020P/2/3234/5300P3/6-5   (0354)
2003/04: 21⁵GF,

	Starts	1st	2nd	3rd	Win & Pl
Chases	1	0	0	0	0
Career Total	28	1	3	4	6868
95 5/97 Clon	2m		NHF	GD	£2204

Total win prize-money £2204

Going:	Sf: 0-0 GS: 0-0 Gd: 0-0 GF: - Fm: 0-1
Distance:	2m/2m3: 0-0 2m4-2m7: 0-1 3m+: 0-0
Track:	LH: 0-0 RH: 0-1 Tight: 0-0 Gall: 0-0
Aids:	Bl: 0-1 Vi: 0-0 Tstrap: 0-0 Ckp: 0-0
Best Rating:	95 5/97 Clon 2m good NHF

Moderate chaser, seems to handle any ground, usually tongue tied.

Brathay Majic

10-y-o ch m Totem (USA)-Roches Roost (Pauper)
W S Coltherd Mrs L J McLeod

Placings:00/0P   (4271)
2003/04: 20⁸G,

	Starts	1st	2nd	3rd	Win & Pl
Hurdles	1	0	0	0	
Career Total	4	0	0	0	

Going:	Sf: 0-0 GS: 0-0 Gd: 0-0 GF: - Fm: 0-0
Distance:	2m/2m3: 0-0 2m4-2m7: 0-1 3m+: 0-0
Track:	LH: 0-0 RH: 0-1 Tight: 0-0 Gall: 0-0
Aids:	Bl: 0-0 Vi: 0-0 Tstrap: 0-0 Ckp: 0-0
Best Rating:	63 2/99 Donc 2m110y gd-fm NHF

Brave Caradoc (IRE)

96   **92+**

6-y-o b g Un Desperado (FR)-Drivers Bureau (Proverb)
G L Moore M K George

Placings:3-066P25   (4914)
2003/04: 20⁶G, 20⁶GS, 21⁶G, 25⁵GS, 23²GS, 24⁵GS,

	Starts	1st	2nd	3rd	Win & Pl
Hurdles	6	0	1	0	1129
Career Total	7	0	1	1	1470

Going:	Sf: 0-0 GS: 0-4 Gd: 0-2 GF: - Fm: 0-0
Distance:	2m/2m3: 0-0 2m4-2m7: 0-4 3m+: 0-2
Track:	LH: 0-3 RH: 0-1 Tight: 0-4 Gall: 0-0
Aids:	Bl: 0-0 Vi: 0-0 Tstrap: 0-0 Ckp: 0-0
Best Rating:	92 4/04 Ling 2m7f gd-sft Hdl

Brave Dane (IRE)

98   **90**

6-y-o b g Danehill (USA)-Nuriva (USA) (Woodman (USA))
A W Carroll (J L Spearing 21/7) Gordon W Day

Placings:0PF05/U0   (3286)
2003/04: 17ᵁGS, 16⁹GS,

	Starts	1st	2nd	3rd	Win & Pl
Hurdles	2	0	0	0	
Career Total	7	0	0	0	0

Going:	Sf: 0-0 GS: 0-2 Gd: 0-0 GF: - Fm: 0-0
Distance:	2m/2m3: 0-2 2m4-2m7: 0-0 3m+: 0-0
Track:	LH: 0-1 RH: 0-1 Tight: 0-0 Gall: 0-0
Aids:	Bl: 0-0 Vi: 0-0 Tstrap: 0-0 Ckp: 0-0
Best Rating:	90 12/03 Hrfd 2m1f gd-sft Hdl

Failed to complete two of his first four starts, otherwise well held. Has yet to show he stays further than the minimum trip.

Brave Effect (IRE)

(101c)   (95c) **102**

8-y-o br g Bravefoot-Crupney Lass (Ardoon)
M Todhunter P E Sowerby, K A Sowerby, R E Bell

Placings:2/0P4401-BP2P4   (1604)
2003/04: 20⁸G, 22⁷GS, 16²F, 20⁶G, 17⁴GF,

	Starts	1st	2nd	3rd	Win & Pl
Hurdles	3	0	0	0	0
Chases	2	0	1	0	838
Career Total	12	1	2	0	5894
102 4/03 Carl	2m4f		E(0-105)HHdl	G-F	£3934

Total win prize-money £3934

Going:	Sf: 0-0 GS: 0-1 Gd: 0-2 GF: - Fm: 0-2
Distance:	2m/2m3: 0-2 2m4-2m7: 0-3 3m+: 0-0
Track:	LH: 0-3 RH: 0-2 Tight: 0-1 Gall: 0-0
Aids:	Bl: 0-0 Vi: 0-0 Tstrap: 0-0 Ckp: 0-0
Best Rating:	102 4/03 Carl 2m4f gd-fm Hdl

Moderate hurdler; stays two and a half miles; suited by a sound surface; has worn a tongue strap.

Brave Inca (IRE)

118   **152**

6-y-o b g Good Thyne (USA)-Wigwam Mam (IRE) (Commanche Run)
C A Murphy Novices Syndicate

Placings:00/0011-1111   (4381)
2003/04: 20¹S, 16¹S, 18¹S, 16¹G,

	Starts	1st	2nd	3rd	Win & Pl
Hurdles	4	4	0	0	110613
Career Total	10	6	0	0	121366
152 3/04 Chel	2m110y	A Hdl	GD	£58000
145 2/04 Leop	2m2f	Hdl	SFT	£36619
118 12/03 Navn	2m	(0-130)HHdl	SFT	£9496
107 11/03 Fair	2m4f	(74-109)HHdl	SFT	£6496
127 3/03 Navn	2m	NHF	G-Y	£4928
127 3/03 Fair	2m	NHF	HVY	£5824

Total win prize-money £121368

Going:	Sf: 3-3 GS: 0-0 Gd: 1-1 GF: - Fm: 0-0
Distance:	2m/2m3: 3-3 2m4-2m7: 1-1 3m+: 0-0
Track:	LH: 3-3 RH: 1-1 Tight: 0-0 Gall: 0-0
Aids:	Bl: 0-0 Vi: 0-0 Tstrap: 0-0 Ckp: 0-0
Best Rating:	152 3/04 Chel 2m110y good Hdl

Smart Irish-trained novice hurdler; dual bumper winner; won four times over hurdles in 2003/4, culminating in a Grade One success at Leopardstown and the Supreme Novices' at

Big type; wide margin winner of bumper on racecourse debut at Uttoxeter in December; runner up under a penalty on next start; best on good ground; looks useful prospect.

Cheltenham; stays two and a half miles and best on soft ground; has a sweet turn of foot; progressive and tough.

Brave Knight

91(92h)   (60h)**75**

7-y-o b g Presidium-Agnes Jane (Sweet Monday)
N Bycroft Piers Casimir-Mrowczynski

Placings:5/2PP-62   **(1906)**
2003/04: 17⁵GF, 24²GF,

	Starts	1st	2nd	3rd	Win & Pl
Hurdles	1	0	0	0	0
Chases	1	0	1	0	888
Career Total	6	0	2	0	3408

Going:	Sf: 0-0 GS: 0-0 Gd: 0-0 GF: - Fm: 0-2	
Distance:	2m/2m3: 0-1 2m4-2m7: 0-0 3m+: 0-1	
Track:	LH: 0-0 RH: 0-2 Tight: 0-1 Gall: 0-1	
Aids:	Bl: 0-0 Vi: 0-0 Tstrap: 0-0 Ckp: 0-0	
Best Rating:	75 10/02 MRas 2m1f110y gd-sft	Ch

A poor maiden on the Flat, who has been beaten over hurdles, over fences and in a point-to-point

Brave Lord (IRE)

93   **94+**

7-y-o ch g Mister Lord (USA)-Artic Squaw (IRE) (Buckskin (FR))
L Lungo Solway Stayers

Placings:6-10P02   **(4595)**
2003/04: 24¹G, 17⁹HY, 20²S, 20⁹G, 22²G,

	Starts	1st	2nd	3rd	Win & Pl
Hurdles	5	1	1	0	5216
Career Total	6	1	1	0	5216
94 5/03 Prth	3m110y E Hdl			GD	£4124
			Total win prize-money £4124		

Going:	Sf: 0-2 GS: 0-0 Gd: 1-3 GF: - Fm: 0-0	
Distance:	2m/2m3: 0-1 2m4-2m7: 0-0 3m+: 1-1	
Track:	LH: 0-3 RH: 1-2 Tight: 0-1 Gall: 0-1	
Aids:	Bl: 0-0 Vi: 0-0 Tstrap: 0-0 Ckp: 0-0	
Best Rating:	94 3/04 Kels 2m6f110y good	Hdl

Won modest three mile hurdle on good ground at Perth in May but well beaten since in much softer conditions; runner-up to wide margin winner at Kelso in April.

Brave Spirit (FR)

101(97h)   (82h)**83+**

6-y-o b g Legend Of France (USA)-Guerre Ou Paix (FR) (Comrade In Arms)
Ian Williams Sir Robert Ogden

Placings:00-500FP2   **(4403)**
2003/04: 17⁵G, 17⁰G, 16⁰S, 20⁵S, 25⁵G, 24²G,

	Starts	1st	2nd	3rd	Win & Pl
Hurdles	3	0	0	0	0
Chases	3	0	1	0	974
Career Total	8	0	1	0	974

Going:	Sf: 0-2 GS: 0-0 Gd: 0-4 GF: - Fm: 0-0	
Distance:	2m/2m3: 0-3 2m4-2m7: 0-1 3m+: 0-0	
Track:	LH: 0-1 RH: 0-5 Tight: 0-1 Gall: 0-2	
Aids:	Bl: 0-0 Vi: 0-0 Tstrap: 0-0 Ckp: 0-1	
Best Rating:	83 3/04 Hntg 3m good	Ch

Promise in first completed start at the third attempt over fences; stays three miles; acts on good ground.

Brave Thought (IRE)

105(107h)   (130h)**112+**

9-y-o b g Commanche Run-Bristol Fairy (Smartset)
P Monteith Hamilton House Limited

Placings:16433/F06313435-F2414522   **(4947)**
2003/04: 16⁶S, 16²GS, 16⁴HY, 16¹HY, 20⁴GS, 17⁵GS, 20²HY, 20⁶GS,

	Starts	1st	2nd	3rd	Win & Pl
Chases	8	1	3	0	12153
Career Total	22	3	3	5	27718
108 1/04 Ayr	2m	E Ch		HVY	£5152
117 12/02 Thur	2m	Hdl		YLD	£8042
117 5/01 Tipp	2m	NHF		HVY	£3895
			Total win prize-money £17090		

Going:	Sf: 1-4 GS: 0-4 Gd: 0-0 GF: - Fm: 0-0	
Distance:	2m/2m3: 1-5 2m4-2m7: 0-3 3m+: 0-0	
Track:	LH: 1-6 RH: 0-2 Tight: 0-1 Gall: 0-1	
Aids:	Bl: 0-0 Vi: 0-0 Tstrap: 0-0 Ckp: 0-0	
Best Rating:	128 1/03 Navn 2m soft	Hdl

Moderate hurdler/novice chaser; won at Ayr on heavy ground in January 2004; effective up to two and a half miles; acts with give in the ground.

Bravura

96   **81+**

6-y-o ch g Never So Bold-Sylvan Song (Song)
G L Moore R Kiernan

Placings:4   **(0484)**
2003/04: 16⁴GF,

	Starts	1st	2nd	3rd	Win & Pl
Hurdles	1	0	0	0	0
Career Total	1	0	0	0	0

Going:	Sf: 0-0 GS: 0-0 Gd: 0-0 GF: - Fm: 0-1	
Distance:	2m/2m3: 0-1 2m4-2m7: 0-0 3m+: 0-1	
Track:	LH: 0-0 RH: 0-1 Tight: 0-0 Gall: 0-1	
Aids:	Bl: 0-0 Vi: 0-0 Tstrap: 0-0 Ckp: 0-1	
Best Rating:	87 5/03 Hntg 2m110y gd-fm	Hdl

Brazil (IRE)

81(60h)   (86h)**62**

6-y-o b g Germany (USA)-Alberta Rose (IRE) (Phardante (FR))
T R George Mrs Sharon C Nelson

Placings:000-FP00UF   **(4119)**
2003/04: 16⁶GF, 16²GF, 19⁴G, 16⁹G, 16⁰GS, 16⁶G,

	Starts	1st	2nd	3rd	Win & Pl
Hurdles	3	0	0	0	0
Chases	3	0	0	0	0
Career Total	9	0	0	0	0

Going:	Sf: 0-0 GS: 0-1 Gd: 0-3 GF: - Fm: 0-2	
Distance:	2m/2m3: 0-5 2m4-2m7: 0-1 3m+: 0-0	
Track:	LH: 0-2 RH: 0-4 Tight: 0-2 Gall: 0-1	
Aids:	Bl: 0-0 Vi: 0-0 Tstrap: 0-0 Ckp: 0-0	
Best Rating:	86 5/03 Winc 2m gd-fm	Hdl

Breaking Breeze (IRE)

(91h)   (105h)**114+**

9-y-o b g Mandalus-Knockacool Breeze (Buckskin (FR))
J S King H Porter, N Rich, V Askew

Placings:1040/321400/014311-P   **(4935)**
2003/04: 18²G,

	Starts	1st	2nd	3rd	Win & Pl
Chases	1	0	0	0	
Career Total	17	5	1	2	21161
114 9/02 Hrfd	2m3f	E(0-110)HCh		G-F	£4338
105 8/02 Hntg	2m4f110yE Ch			G-F	£3487
105 6/02 Hntg	2m4f110yE Ch			G-F	£2977
103 12/01 Ludl	2m	E(0-115)HHdl		GD	£4046
111 8/00 Cork	2m	NHF		Y-S	£3588
			Total win prize-money £18437		

Going:	Sf: 0-0 GS: 0-0 Gd: 0-1 GF: - Fm: 0-0	
Distance:	2m/2m3: 0-1 2m4-2m7: 0-0 3m+: 0-0	
Track:	LH: 0-0 RH: 0-0 Tight: 0-1 Gall: 0-0	
Aids:	Bl: 0-0 Vi: 0-0 Tstrap: 0-0 Ckp: 0-0	
Best Rating:	114 9/02 Hrfd 2m3f gd-fm	Ch

Breathoffreshair (IRE)

7-y-o ch g Fresh Breeze (USA)-Carl Louise (Invited (USA))
J Gallagher (C J Price 10/5) G Ivall

Placings:0P   **(2838)**
2003/04: 16⁰G, 20ᴾGS,

	Starts	1st	2nd	3rd	Win & Pl
NH Flat	1	0	0	0	0
Hurdles	1	0	0	0	0
Career Total	2	0	0	0	

Going:	Sf: 0-0 GS: 0-1 Gd: 0-1 GF: - Fm: 0-0	
Distance:	2m/2m3: 0-1 2m4-2m7: 0-1 3m+: 0-0	
Track:	LH: 0-2 RH: 0-0 Tight: 0-0 Gall: 0-0	
Aids:	Bl: 0-0 Vi: 0-0 Tstrap: 0-0 Ckp: 0-0	
Best Rating:	0 12/03 Uttx 2m4f110y gd-sft	Hdl

Breathtaking View (USA)

107   **93**

8-y-o b g Country Pine (USA)-Lituya Bay (USA) (Empery (USA))
G Prodromou Mrs B Macalister

Placings:5003-01156523   **(1758)**
2003/04: 16⁸GF, 19¹G, 17¹G, 17⁵GF, 19⁶G, 16⁵GF, 19²GF, 16³G,

	Starts	1st	2nd	3rd	Win & Pl
Hurdles	8	2	1	1	7630
Career Total	12	2	1	2	8468
92 7/03 MRas	2m1f110yE(0-105)HHdl			GD	£3532
83 6/03 MRas	2m3f110yG(0-90)HHdl			GD	£2565
			Total win prize-money £6099		

Going:	Sf: 0-0 GS: 0-0 Gd: 2-4 GF: - Fm: 0-4	
Distance:	2m/2m3: 1-6 2m4-2m7: 1-2 3m+: 0-0	
Track:	LH: 0-5 RH: 2-3 Tight: 2-7 Gall: 0-0	
Aids:	Bl: 0-0 Vi: 0-0 Tstrap: 0-1 Ckp: 0-0	
Best Rating:	93 10/03 Fknm 2m good	Hdl

Moderate hurdler; took a selling hurdle at Market Rasen in June 2003; has run well in strong company there since; stays two and a half miles; acts on a sound surface; has worn cheekpieces.

Breema Donna

85f   **55**f

6-y-o b m Sir Harry Lewis (USA)-Donna Del Lago (King's Lake (USA))

R Dickin M Maccarthy

| Placings:6 | | | | | (1334) |
| 2003/04: 17⁶GF, | | | | | |

	Starts	1st	2nd	3rd	Win & Pl
NH Flat	1	0	0	0	0
Career Total	1	0	0	0	0

Going:	Sf: 0-0 GS: 0-0 Gd: 0-0 GF: - Fm: 0-1
Distance:	2m/2m3: 0-1 2m4-2m7: 0-0 3m+: 0-0
Track:	LH: 0-0 RH: 0-1 Tight: 0-0 Gall: 0-0
Aids:	Bl: 0-0 Vi: 0-0 Tstrap: 0-0 Ckp: 0-0
Best Rating:	55 9/03 Hrfd 2m1f gd-fm NHF

Breeze Home
100   95

8-y-o b g Homo Sapien-Poppy's Pride (Uncle Pokey)
Ian Williams Mrs M Mann

| Placings:P0/6011 | | | | | (2691) |
| 2003/04: 16⁶GF, 19⁰GF, 17¹GF, 16¹G, | | | | | |

	Starts	1st	2nd	3rd	Win & Pl
Hurdles	4	2	0	0	5551
Career Total	6	2	0	0	5551
95 12/03 Ludl	2m		F Hdl	GD	£2765
86 10/03 MRas	2m1f110yF(0-100)HHdl			G-F	£2786

Total win prize-money £5551

Going:	Sf: 0-0 GS: 0-0 Gd: 1-1 GF: - Fm: 1-3
Distance:	2m/2m3: 2-3 2m4-2m7: 0-1 3m+: 0-0
Track:	LH: 0-0 RH: 2-4 Tight: 1-1 Gall: 0-1
Aids:	Bl: 0-0 Vi: 0-0 Tstrap: 0-0 Ckp: 0-0
Best Rating:	95 12/03 Ludl 2m good Hdl

Lightly-raced hurdler; missed the whole of 2002; won at
Market Rasen and Ludlow late in 2003; needs fast ground.

Breezer
88   85

4-y-o b g Forzando-Lady Lacey (Kampala)
G B Balding Mrs P Gulliver Mrs K Perrin G Balding

| Placings:4000 | | | | | (4591) |
| 2003/04: 16⁴G, 18⁰G, 16⁰G, 16⁰G, | | | | | |

	Starts	1st	2nd	3rd	Win & Pl
Hurdles	4	0	0	0	0
Career Total	4	0	0	0	0

Going:	Sf: 0-0 GS: 0-0 Gd: 0-4 GF: - Fm: 0-0
Distance:	2m/2m3: 0-4 2m4-2m7: 0-0 3m+: 0-0
Track:	LH: 0-2 RH: 0-2 Tight: 0-1 Gall: 0-2
Aids:	Bl: 0-0 Vi: 0-1 Tstrap: 0-0 Ckp: 0-0
Best Rating:	85 12/03 Winc 2m good Hdl

Modest novice hurdler; yet to win a race of any sort.

Breezy Warrior (IRE)

5-y-o b g Commanche Run-Another Crash (Crash Course)
E W Tuer E Tuer

| Placings:464PPP | | | | | (3212) |
| 2003/04: 16⁴GF, 17⁶G, 17⁴G, 19⁰GS, 19⁰GS, 20⁰GS, | | | | | |

	Starts	1st	2nd	3rd	Win & Pl
NH Flat	3	0	0	0	0
Hurdles	3	0	0	0	0
Career Total	6	0	0	0	0

Going:	Sf: 0-0 GS: 0-3 Gd: 0-2 GF: - Fm: 0-1
Distance:	2m/2m3: 0-4 2m4-2m7: 0-2 3m+: 0-0
Track:	LH: 0-6 RH: 0-0 Tight: 0-3 Gall: 0-0
Aids:	Bl: 0-0 Vi: 0-0 Tstrap: 0-0 Ckp: 0-1
Best Rating:	80 10/03 Sedg 2m1f good NHF

Breknen Le Noir (FR)
111   128+

6-y-o b g Pelder (IRE)-Roziyna (Reform)
P J Hobbs P Deal & M St Quinton

| Placings:23410P21 | | | | | (4874) |
| 2003/04: 16²G, 16³GS, 16⁴S, 16¹HY, 16⁰S, 20⁰GS, 17²G, 20¹GS, | | | | | |

	Starts	1st	2nd	3rd	Win & Pl
Hurdles	8	2	2	1	11370
Career Total	8	2	2	1	11370
117 4/04 Bang	2m4f		E Hdl	G-S	£3737
128 1/04 Asct	2m110y	D(0-120)HHdl		HVY	£4823

Total win prize-money £8561

Going:	Sf: 1-3 GS: 1-3 Gd: 0-2 GF: - Fm: 0-0
Distance:	2m/2m3: 1-6 2m4-2m7: 1-2 3m+: 0-0
Track:	LH: 1-2 RH: 1-6 Tight: 1-1 Gall: 0-0
Aids:	Bl: 2-5 Vi: 0-0 Tstrap: 0-0 Ckp: 0-0
Best Rating:	128 1/04 Asct 2m110y heavy Hdl

Ex-French Flat racer; disappointed on first three starts over
hurdles before bolting up on handicap debut at Ascot when
having blinkers applied for the first time over hurdles; went
off too fast next time, and failed to stay the trip latest; capable of better; best at two miles; acts well in soft ground; usually wears blinkers.

Brereton (IRE)
102(97h)   (83h)106

8-y-o b g Be My Native (USA)-Society News (Law Society
(USA))
M C Pipe (N J Henderson 18/5) D A Johnson

| Placings:20⁵/400-614F | | | | | (0627) |
| 2003/04: 21⁶G, 21¹GF, 21⁴GS, 24²GF, | | | | | |

	Starts	1st	2nd	3rd	Win & Pl
Hurdles	1	0	0	0	0
Chases	3	1	0	0	4866
Career Total	10	1	1	0	5354
106 5/03 Fknm	2m5f110yF(0-100)HCh			G-F	£4444

Total win prize-money £4445

Going:	Sf: 0-0 GS: 0-1 Gd: 0-1 GF: - Fm: 1-2
Distance:	2m/2m3: 0-0 2m4-2m7: 1-3 3m+: 0-1
Track:	LH: 1-3 RH: 0-1 Tight: 1-2 Gall: 0-0
Aids:	Bl: 0-0 Vi: 0-1 Tstrap: 0-0 Ckp: 0-0
Best Rating:	120 12/01 Wwck 2m soft NHF

Moderate hurdler; encouraging debut in a Warwick bumper;
looked to need further when fifth on his hurdles bow over
two miles five; acts on soft ground; has suffered from
breathing problems.

Bressbee (USA)
102   97

6-y-o ch g Twining (USA)-Bressray (USA) (Nureyev (USA))
N P Littmoden (J W Unett 17/3) Nigel Shields

| Placings:3 | | | | | (1702) |
| 2003/04: 16³GF, | | | | | |

	Starts	1st	2nd	3rd	Win & Pl
Hurdles	1	0	0	1	806
Career Total	1	0	0	1	806

Brevity
60   22

9-y-o b g Tenby-Rive (USA) (Riverman (USA))
J M Bradley E A Hayward

| Placings:0 | | | | | (1457) |
| 2003/04: 16⁰GF, | | | | | |

	Starts	1st	2nd	3rd	Win & Pl
Hurdles	1	0	0	0	0
Career Total	1	0	0	0	0

Going:	Sf: 0-0 GS: 0-0 Gd: 0-0 GF: - Fm: 0-1
Distance:	2m/2m3: 0-1 2m4-2m7: 0-0 3m+: 0-0
Track:	LH: 0-1 RH: 0-0 Tight: 0-1 Gall: 0-0
Aids:	Bl: 0-0 Vi: 0-1 Tstrap: 0-0 Ckp: 0-0
Best Rating:	22 9/03 Plum 2m gd-fm Hdl

Brewster (IRE)
114   137

7-y-o b g Roselier (FR)-Aelia Paetina (Buckskin (FR))
Ian Williams Mr & Mrs John Poynton

| Placings:1/322-403 | | | | | (4833) |
| 2003/04: 23⁴S, 25⁰G, 21³GF, | | | | | |

	Starts	1st	2nd	3rd	Win & Pl
Hurdles	3	0	0	1	4290
Career Total	7	1	2	2	10822
117 4/02 Slig	2m		NHF	HVY	£3386

Total win prize-money £3387

Going:	Sf: 0-1 GS: 0-0 Gd: 0-1 GF: - Fm: 0-1
Distance:	2m/2m3: 0-0 2m4-2m7: 0-1 3m+: 0-2
Track:	LH: 0-3 RH: 0-0 Tight: 0-0 Gall: 0-2
Aids:	Bl: 0-0 Vi: 0-0 Tstrap: 0-0 Ckp: 0-0
Best Rating:	137 2/04 Hayd 2m7f110y soft Hdl

Irish bumper winner; decent novice hurdler; 35lb out of the
handicap when excellent fourth at Haydock in February;
stays three miles; effective in testing ground.

Brian James
(77c)   (36c)86

10-y-o ch g River God (USA)-Rose Orchard (Rouser)
F P Murtagh F P Murtagh

| Placings:04PPP/45216FP3/23332/040PP3P-PP | | | | | (0431) |
| 2003/04: 25⁰G, 26⁰G, | | | | | |

	Starts	1st	2nd	3rd	Win & Pl
Hurdles	1	0	0	0	0
Chases	1	0	0	0	0
Career Total	27	1	3	5	7226
102 12/00 Sedg	3m3f110yE Hdl			SFT	£2380

Total win prize-money £2380

Going:	Sf: 0-0 GS: 0-0 Gd: 0-2 GF: - Fm: 0-0
Distance:	2m/2m3: 0-0 2m4-2m7: 0-0 3m+: 0-2
Track:	LH: 0-2 RH: 0-0 Tight: 0-1 Gall: 0-0
Aids:	Bl: 0-0 Vi: 0-0 Tstrap: 0-0 Ckp: 0-0
Best Rating:	102 11/01 Sedg 3m3f110y good Hdl

Moderate staying hurdler; stays extreme distances; has
worn cheekpieces.

(Brevity top note continued) Multiple winner at up to 10f on the Flat; well held when third
in strongly run Stratford 2m maiden hurdle on hurdling debut
October 2003.

Briar (CZE)

98 **94**

5-y-o b h House Rules (USA)-Bright Angel (AUT) (Antuco (GER))
M Pitman J F Garrett

Placings:04143420-60 **(3334)**
2003/04: 26⁶GF, 24⁰S,

	Starts	1st	2nd	3rd	Win & Pl
Hurdles	2	0	0	0	
Career Total	10	1	1	1	6264
94	11/02 Folk	2m1f110yE Hdl		SFT	£3094
			Total win prize-money £3094		

Going: Sf: 0-1 GS: 0-0 Gd: 0-0 GF: - Fm: 0-1
Distance: 2m/2m3: 0-0 2m4-2m7: 0-0 3m+: 0-2
Track: LH: 0-1 RH: 0-1 Tight: 0-2 Gall: 0-2
Aids: Bl: 0-0 Vi: 0-0 Tstrap: 0-0 Ckp: 0-1
Best Rating: 94 3/03 Sand 2m4f110y heavy Hdl

Briar Rose (IRE)

108 **93+**

9-y-o gr m Roselier (FR)-Born Lucky (Deep Run)
N M L Ewart N M L Ewart

Placings:PP00/P6P023P-541010P **(4272)**
2003/04: 24⁷GF, 25⁵G, 25⁴G, 30¹G, 25⁵S, 25¹HY, 33⁰G, 26⁷G,

	Starts	1st	2nd	3rd	Win & Pl
Chases	8	2	0	0	6815
Career Total	18	2	1	1	8369
93	2/04 Kels	3m1f	F(0-90)HCh	HVY	£3549
81	11/03 Newc	3m6f	E(0-105)HCh	GD	£3265
			Total win prize-money £6815		

Going: Sf: 1-2 GS: 0-0 Gd: 1-5 GF: - Fm: 0-1
Distance: 2m/2m3: 0-0 2m4-2m7: 0-0 3m+: 2-8
Track: LH: 2-7 RH: 0-1 Tight: 1-1 Gall: 1-3
Aids: Bl: 0-0 Vi: 0-0 Tstrap: 0-0 Ckp: 0-0
Best Rating: 93 2/04 Kels 3m1f heavy Ch

Plating-class chaser; got off the mark over three miles six at Newcastle in November 2003; acts on most types of ground; needs a thorough test.

Briary Boy (IRE)

12-y-o ch g Mister Lord (USA)-Aprolon Princess (IRE) (Duky)
Miss M Taylor Miss M Taylor

Placings:000/FP/U- **(0020)**
2003/04: 26ᵁS,

	Starts	1st	2nd	3rd	Win & Pl
Chases	1	0	0	0	
Career Total	6	0	0	0	

Going: Sf: 0-1 GS: 0-0 Gd: 0-0 GF: - Fm: 0-0
Distance: 2m/2m3: 0-0 2m4-2m7: 0-0 3m+: 0-1
Track: LH: 0-1 RH: 0-0 Tight: 0-1 Gall: 0-0
Aids: Bl: 0-0 Vi: 0-0 Tstrap: 0-0 Ckp: 0-0
Best Rating: 51 12/97 Cork 2m yld-sft Hdl

Bric A Brac

74 **30**

7-y-o ch m Minster Son-Greenhill's Girl (Radetzky)
W G Young W G Young

Placings:000/06-00P0 **(0897)**
2003/04: 20⁶G, 16⁰G, 17⁰GS, 16ᴾG, 17⁰GF,

	Starts	1st	2nd	3rd	Win & Pl
Hurdles	5	0	0	0	0
Career Total	9	0	0	0	0

Going: Sf: 0-0 GS: 0-1 Gd: 0-3 GF: - Fm: 0-1
Distance: 2m/2m3: 0-4 2m4-2m7: 0-1 3m+: 0-0
Track: LH: 0-4 RH: 0-1 Tight: 0-2 Gall: 0-0
Aids: Bl: 0-0 Vi: 0-0 Tstrap: 0-0 Ckp: 0-0
Best Rating: 31 5/03 Ctml 2m1f110y gd-sft Hdl

Bridgend Blue (IRE)

66

8-y-o b g Up And At 'Em-Sperrin Mist (Camden Town)
J S Hubbuck J S Hubbuck

Placings:53P/P60P00P06P050/0505-65 **(1491)**
2003/04: 20⁶GF, 16⁵GF,

	Starts	1st	2nd	3rd	Win & Pl
Hurdles	2	0	0	0	
Career Total	22	0	0	1	341

Going: Sf: 0-0 GS: 0-0 Gd: 0-0 GF: - Fm: 0-2
Distance: 2m/2m3: 0-1 2m4-2m7: 0-1 3m+: 0-0
Track: LH: 0-2 RH: 0-0 Tight: 0-0 Gall: 0-0
Aids: Bl: 0-0 Vi: 0-0 Tstrap: 0-0 Ckp: 0-0
Best Rating: 71 9/99 Hntg 2m110y good Hdl

Modest hurdler.

Brief Contact (IRE)

76

6-y-o b g Brief Truce (USA)-Incommunicado (IRE) (Sadler's Wells (USA))
Jamie Poulton George H Gibson

Placings:025/P **(2773)**
2003/04: 16ᴾS,

	Starts	1st	2nd	3rd	Win & Pl
Hurdles	1	0	0	0	
Career Total	4	0	1	0	975

Going: Sf: 0-1 GS: 0-0 Gd: 0-0 GF: - Fm: 0-0
Distance: 2m/2m3: 0-1 2m4-2m7: 0-0 3m+: 0-0
Track: LH: 0-0 RH: 0-1 Tight: 0-0 Gall: 0-0
Aids: Bl: 0-1 Vi: 0-0 Tstrap: 0-0 Ckp: 0-0
Best Rating: 76 10/01 Chep 2m110y good Hdl

Improved on his debut when runner-up in a moderate Plumpton juvenile event in September.

Briery Mec

77 **37**

9-y-o b g Ron's Victory (USA)-Briery Fille (Sayyaf)
H J Collingridge N H Gardner

Placings:0 **(4402)**
2003/04: 16⁰G,

	Starts	1st	2nd	3rd	Win & Pl
Hurdles	1	0	0	0	
Career Total	1	0	0	0	

Going: Sf: 0-0 GS: 0-0 Gd: 0-0 GF: - Fm: 0-0
Distance: 2m/2m3: 0-1 2m4-2m7: 0-0 3m+: 0-0
Track: LH: 0-0 RH: 0-1 Tight: 0-0 Gall: 0-1
Aids: Bl: 0-0 Vi: 0-0 Tstrap: 0-0 Ckp: 0-0
Best Rating: 39 3/04 Hntg 2m110y good Hdl

Brigade Charge (USA)

95(78h) (63h)**120**

9-y-o b g Affirmed (USA)-Fairy Footsteps (Mill Reef (USA))
Jonjo O'Neill John P McManus

Placings:40/30022132/4/2B11/63-6PP0 **(4170)**
2003/04: 17⁶GS, 20ᴾG, 20ᴾGS, 21⁰G,

	Starts	1st	2nd	3rd	Win & Pl
Hurdles	1	0	0	0	
Chases	3	0	0	0	239
Career Total	21	3	4	3	43357
125	3/02 Navn	2m1f	Ch	SH	£6773
115	2/02 Fair	2m2f	Ch	SFT	£7831
115	12/99 Leop	2m	Ch	SH	£4620
			Total win prize-money £19225		

Going: Sf: 0-0 GS: 0-2 Gd: 0-2 GF: - Fm: 0-0
Distance: 2m/2m3: 0-1 2m4-2m7: 0-3 3m+: 0-0
Track: LH: 0-4 RH: 0-0 Tight: 0-0 Gall: 0-2
Aids: Bl: 0-1 Vi: 0-0 Tstrap: 0-0 Ckp: 0-1
Best Rating: 129 5/00 Hayd 2m good Hdl

Fair chaser; ex-Irish; stays beyond two miles and acts in soft ground; yet to hit top form in Britain.

Brigadier Du Bois (FR)

92 **85+**

5-y-o gr g Apeldoorn (FR)-Artic Night (FR) (Kaldoun (FR))
Mrs L Wadham Hebomapa

Placings:2030-0P3 **(3880)**
2003/04: 16⁶GS, 16ᴾHY, 16⁵GS,

	Starts	1st	2nd	3rd	Win & Pl
Hurdles	3	0	0	1	657
Career Total	7	0	1	2	8736

Going: Sf: 0-2 GS: 0-1 Gd: 0-0 GF: - Fm: 0-0
Distance: 2m/2m3: 0-3 2m4-2m7: 0-0 3m+: 0-0
Track: LH: 0-1 RH: 0-2 Tight: 0-0 Gall: 0-0
Aids: Bl: 0-1 Vi: 0-0 Tstrap: 0-1 Ckp: 0-0
Best Rating: 85 2/04 Leic 2m soft Hdl

Has been placed on the Flat and over hurdles in France; acts on soft ground.

Brigante Girl (IRE)

102f **100f**

6-y-o b m Old Vic-Strong Winds (IRE) (Strong Gale)
N G Richards Kevin Johnston

Placings:23-6 **(1622)**
2003/04: 17⁶G,

	Starts	1st	2nd	3rd	Win & Pl
NH Flat	1	0	0	0	0
Career Total	3	0	1	1	909

Going: Sf: 0-0 GS: 0-0 Gd: 0-0 GF: - Fm: 0-0
Distance: 2m/2m3: 0-1 2m4-2m7: 0-0 3m+: 0-0
Track: LH: 0-1 RH: 0-0 Tight: 0-1 Gall: 0-0
Aids: Bl: 0-0 Vi: 0-0 Tstrap: 0-0 Ckp: 0-0
Best Rating: 100 10/02 Bang 2m1f gd-sft NHF

Beat the others out of sight when well beaten by the promising Priests Bridge in a Bangor bumper October 2002. Fair run next time.

Bright Approach (IRE)

11-y-o gr g Roselier (FR)-Dysart Lady (King's Ride)
J G Cann (Mrs O Bush 18/3) J H Burbidge

Placings:5/141P66/12122-U12P01   (4845)
2003/04: 33ᵁG, 31¹GF, 28²G, 25ᴾG, 26⁶G, 26¹G,

	Starts	1st	2nd	3rd	Win & Pl
Chases	6	2	1	0	14709
Career Total	18	6	4	0	41708
133	4/04	Chel	3m2f110yH Ch		GD	£4936
116	5/03	Folk	3m7f	H Ch	G-F	£3484
112	2/03	Ludl	3m3f110yH Ch		GD	£3010
121	5/02	Chel	4m1f	H Ch	G-F	£5603
103	5/01	Chel	4m1f	H Ch	GD	£5528
98	5/01	Extr	2m7f110yH Ch		GD	£1715
			Total win prize-money £24277			

Going:	Sf: 0-0 GS: 0-0 Gd: 1-5 GF: - Fm: 1-1
Distance:	2m/2m3: 0-0 2m4-2m7: 0-0 3m+: 2-6
Track:	LH: 1-4 RH: 1-2 Tight: 1-2 Gall: 1-3
Aids:	Bl: 0-0 Vi: 0-0 Tstrap: 0-0 Ckp: 0-0
Best Rating:	133 4/04 Chel 3m2f110y good Ch

Useful hunter chaser, in good form in 2003 when runner-up in the Cheltenham Foxhunters' and 'Horse and Hound Cup'; stays 4m; needs a test of stamina; likes fast ground.

Bright Eagle (IRE)
91   67

4-y-o ch g Eagle Eyed (USA)-Lumiere (USA) (Northjet)
R Lee (C F Wall 20/9) Rex Norton

Placings:0   (4602)
2003/04: 17⁰G,

	Starts	1st	2nd	3rd	Win & Pl
Hurdles	1	0	0	0	
Career Total	1	0	0	0	

Going:	Sf: 0-0 GS: 0-0 Gd: 0-1 GF: - Fm: 0-0
Distance:	2m/2m3: 0-1 2m4-2m7: 0-0 3m+: 0-0
Track:	LH: 0-0 RH: 0-1 Tight: 0-0 Gall: 0-0
Aids:	Bl: 0-0 Vi: 0-0 Tstrap: 0-0 Ckp: 0-0
Best Rating:	67 3/04 MRas 2m1f110y good Hdl

Bright Green
100   99+

5-y-o b g Green Desert (USA)-Shining High (Shirley Heights)
J A B Old W E Sturt

Placings:5104   (4735)
2003/04: 16⁵GS, 16¹HY, 16⁰GS, 17⁴G,

	Starts	1st	2nd	3rd	Win & Pl
Hurdles	4	1	0	0	5070
Career Total	4	1	0	0	5070
99	2/04	Chep	2m110y	E Hdl	HVY	£4693
			Total win prize-money £4693			

Going:	Sf: 1-1 GS: 0-2 Gd: 0-1 GF: - Fm: 0-0
Distance:	2m/2m3: 1-4 2m4-2m7: 0-0 3m+: 0-0
Track:	LH: 1-3 RH: 0-1 Tight: 0-1 Gall: 0-0
Aids:	Bl: 0-0 Vi: 0-0 Tstrap: 0-0 Ckp: 0-0
Best Rating:	99 2/04 Chep 2m110y heavy Hdl

Jumped better than on his hurdling debut when winning 2m novice hurdle on heavy ground at Chepstow second start.

Bright November

13-y-o b g Niniski (USA)-Brigata (Brigadier Gerard)
D Fortt Mrs C Skipworth

Placings:05522216/110/3F/2P/11115/24P/F-4   (0031)
2003/04: 21⁴G,

	Starts	1st	2nd	3rd	Win & Pl
Chases	1	0	0	0	296
Career Total	25	7	5	1	41836
134	2/01	Asct	2m3f110yB Ch		SFT	£10166
130	11/00	Kemp	2m	D Ch	SFT	£4251
134	11/00	Kemp	2m4f110yD Ch		SFT	£5096
124	10/00	Hrfd	2m	F(0-110)HCh	GD	£3711
118	4/98	Uttx	2m	B(0-140)HHdl	G-S	£5003
107	4/98	Hrfd	2m1f	F(0-105)HHdl	SFT	£3048
91	4/96	Hrfd	2m3f110yF(0-95)HHdl		G-F	£2906
			Total win prize-money £34183			

Going:	Sf: 0-0 GS: 0-0 Gd: 0-1 GF: - Fm: 0-0
Distance:	2m/2m3: 0-0 2m4-2m7: 0-1 3m+: 0-0
Track:	LH: 0-1 RH: 0-0 Tight: 0-0 Gall: 0-0
Aids:	Bl: 0-0 Vi: 0-0 Tstrap: 0-0 Ckp: 0-0
Best Rating:	134 2/01 Asct 2m3f110y soft Ch

Bright Steel (IRE)
84   64

7-y-o gr g Roselier (FR)-Ikeathy (Be Friendly)
A Parker Mr & Mrs Raymond Anderson Green

Placings:0/00-54P   (3000)
2003/04: 17⁵GF, 22⁴G, 25ᴾGS,

	Starts	1st	2nd	3rd	Win & Pl
Hurdles	3	0	0	0	269
Career Total	6	0	0	0	269

Going:	Sf: 0-0 GS: 0-1 Gd: 0-1 GF: - Fm: 0-1
Distance:	2m/2m3: 0-1 2m4-2m7: 0-1 3m+: 0-1
Track:	LH: 0-2 RH: 0-1 Tight: 0-1 Gall: 0-0
Aids:	Bl: 0-0 Vi: 0-0 Tstrap: 0-0 Ckp: 0-0
Best Rating:	64 10/03 Carl 2m1f gd-fm Hdl

Bright Times Ahead (IRE)
67f   54f

6-y-o ch m Rainbows For Life (CAN)-Just A Second (Jimsun)
C J Drewe W P Long

Placings:00   (4529)
2003/04: 16⁰G, 16⁰GS,

	Starts	1st	2nd	3rd	Win & Pl
NH Flat	2	0	0	0	
Career Total	2	0	0	0	

Going:	Sf: 0-0 GS: 0-1 Gd: 0-1 GF: - Fm: 0-0
Distance:	2m/2m3: 0-2 2m4-2m7: 0-0 3m+: 0-0
Track:	LH: 0-1 RH: 0-1 Tight: 0-0 Gall: 0-1
Aids:	Bl: 0-0 Vi: 0-0 Tstrap: 0-0 Ckp: 0-0
Best Rating:	54 3/04 Hntg 2m110y good NHF

Brilliantrio
94   61+

6-y-o ch m Selkirk (USA)-Loucoum (FR) (Iron Duke (FR))
M C Chapman (J G M O'Shea 26/6) Jack Wilson

Placings:P00   (2069)
2003/04: 16ᴾGF, 17⁰GF, 16⁹GF,

	Starts	1st	2nd	3rd	Win & Pl
Hurdles	3	0	0	0	
Career Total	3	0	0	0	

Going:	Sf: 0-0 GS: 0-0 Gd: 0-0 GF: - Fm: 0-3
Distance:	2m/2m3: 0-3 2m4-2m7: 0-0 3m+: 0-0
Track:	LH: 0-1 RH: 0-2 Tight: 0-1 Gall: 0-1
Aids:	Bl: 0-0 Vi: 0-0 Tstrap: 0-1 Ckp: 0-0
Best Rating:	64 11/03 Hntg 2m10y gd-fm Hdl

Brillyant Dancer
85   59+

6-y-o b m Environment Friend-Brillyant Glen (IRE) (Glenstal (USA))
Mrs A Duffield Clarks New Town

Placings:50   (3433)
2003/04: 17⁵HY, 16⁰HY,

	Starts	1st	2nd	3rd	Win & Pl
Hurdles	2	0	0	0	0
Career Total	2	0	0	0	0

Going:	Sf: 0-2 GS: 0-0 Gd: 0-0 GF: - Fm: 0-0
Distance:	2m/2m3: 0-2 2m4-2m7: 0-0 3m+: 0-0
Track:	LH: 0-1 RH: 0-1 Tight: 0-0 Gall: 0-1
Aids:	Bl: 0-0 Vi: 0-0 Tstrap: 0-0 Ckp: 0-0
Best Rating:	59 11/03 Carl 2m1f heavy Hdl

Bringontheclowns (IRE)
98   109

5-y-o b g Entrepreneur-Circus Maid (IRE) (High Top)
M F Harris (Anthony Mullins 30/8) Joking Around Partnership

Placings:024-10305F   (2553)
2003/04: 16¹GF, 16⁰S, 16³F, 16⁰F, 16⁵G, 16⁷G,

	Starts	1st	2nd	3rd	Win & Pl
Hurdles	6	1	0	1	5766
Career Total	9	1	1	1	7478
106	6/03	Wxfd	2m	Hdl	G-F	£4480
			Total win prize-money £4481			

Going:	Sf: 0-1 GS: 0-0 Gd: 0-2 GF: - Fm: 1-3
Distance:	2m/2m3: 1-6 2m4-2m7: 0-0 3m+: 0-0
Track:	LH: 0-1 RH: 0-2 Tight: 0-0 Gall: 0-0
Aids:	Bl: 0-0 Vi: 0-0 Tstrap: 0-2 Ckp: 0-0
Best Rating:	110 1/03 Gowr 2m sft-hvy Hdl

Moderate ex-Irish hurdler; best around two miles; acts on a sound surface; has worn a tongue tie.

Brios Boy
86   60

4-y-o ch g My Best Valentine-Rose Elegance (Bairn (USA))
G A Harker (R Bastiman 21/8) P Savignano

Placings:U50P   (2712)
2003/04: 16ᵁG, 16⁵GF, 16⁹GS, 16ᴾGS,

	Starts	1st	2nd	3rd	Win & Pl
Hurdles	4	0	0	0	0
Career Total	4	0	0	0	0

Going:	Sf: 0-0 GS: 0-2 Gd: 0-1 GF: - Fm: 0-1
Distance:	2m/2m3: 0-4 2m4-2m7: 0-0 3m+: 0-0

Track: LH: 0-4 RH: 0-0 Tight: 0-2 Gall: 0-2
Aids: Bl: 0-1 Vi: 0-0 Tstrap: 0-0 Ckp: 0-1
Best Rating: 60 11/03 Catt 2m   gd-fm Hdl

Broadbrook Lass
96   95+

10-y-o ch m Broadsword (USA)-Netherbrook Lass (Netherkelly)
Mrs H Dalton Michael H Ings

Placings:21F1P-P4   (4961)
2003/04: 24PGS, 20⁴GS,

	Starts	1st	2nd	3rd	Win & Pl
Chases	2	0	0	0	299
Career Total	7	2	1	0	10542

| 105 | 8/02 | Bang | 2m4f110yD Ch | | SFT | £4845 |
| 111 | 6/02 | Uttx | 2m5f | D Ch | G-S | £4121 |

Total win prize-money £8967

Going: Sf: 0-0 GS: 0-1 Gd: 0-1 GF: - Fm: 0-0
Distance: 2m/2m3: 0-0 2m4-2m7: 0-1 3m+: 0-1
Track: LH: 0-0 RH: 0-2 Tight: 0-1 Gall: 0-1
Aids: Bl: 0-0 Vi: 0-0 Tstrap: 0-2 Ckp: 0-0
Best Rating: 111 6/02 Uttx 2m5f   gd-sft Ch

Dual winning pointer; won a couple of novice chases on soft ground at around two and a half miles in the summer of 2002; acts on any ground; a bit of a tail swisher; possibly unsuited to right-handed courses.

Broadgate Flyer (IRE)
110(98h)   (84h)101

10-y-o b g Silver Kite (USA)-Fabulous Pet (Somethingfabulous (USA))
Miss Lucinda V Russell D G Pryde

Placings:343165/R05P00UF/4005P450616/P6026/P54626
0P/5330U4411-53144P314   (1687)
2003/04: 24¹GF, 22⁵G, 24³GS, 24¹G, 24⁴G, 16⁴GF, 24PGF, 24³G, 25¹F, 25⁴GF,

	Starts	1st	2nd	3rd	Win & Pl
Chases	10	3	0	2	19452
Career Total	56	6	2	6	35143

95	10/03	Kels	3m1f	D(0-115)HCh	FRM	£4017
101	6/03	Prth	3m	D(0-115)HCh	GD	£8092
101	4/03	Newc	3m	E(0-105)HCh	G-F	£4143
84	4/03	Carl	2m4f	E(0-110)HCh	G-F	£4348
80	3/00	Sedg	2m110y	D Ch	G-F	£4119
72	10/97	Kels	2m110y	E Hdl	FRM	£2192

Total win prize-money £26915

Going: Sf: 0-0 GS: 0-1 Gd: 1-4 GF: - Fm: 2-5
Distance: 2m/2m3: 0-1 2m4-2m7: 0-1 3m+: 3-8
Track: LH: 2-7 RH: 1-3 Tight: 1-5 Gall: 1-1
Aids: Bl: 0-0 Vi: 0-0 Tstrap: 3-10 Ckp: 0-0
Best Rating: 101 6/03 Prth 3m   good Ch

Plating-class chaser; stays three miles; very much suited by fast ground; usually tongue tied.

Broadstone Road (IRE)
98   (114h)124

7-y-o ch g Magical Wonder (USA)-Administer (Damister (USA))
Paul John Gilligan Thomas Gibbons

Placings:00/002100/053155010-534103240111P   (2148)
2003/04: 16⁵Y, 20³YS, 17⁴Y, 20¹F, 22⁰S, 21³F, 19²F, 22⁴F, 20⁰S, 19¹S, 20¹F, 22¹GF, 20PG,

Starts	1st	2nd	3rd	Win & Pl

	Starts	1st	2nd	3rd	Win & Pl
Hurdles	3	0	1	0	1779
Chases	10	4	0	2	58299
Career Total	30	7	2	3	84359

124	10/03	Gway	2m6f	HCh	G-F	£18993
124	10/03	Cork	2m4f	Ch	FRM	£11818
116	9/03	List	2m3f	(0-140)HCh	SFT	£16883
124	6/03	Navn	2m4f	Ch	FRM	£8441
108	9/02	List	2m4f	HHdl	FRM	£13957
110	8/02	Kbgn	2m3f	(0-116)HHdl	Y-S	£4239
114	7/01	Kbgn	2m	Hdl	GD	£4451

Total win prize-money £78785

Going: Sf: 1-3 GS: 0-0 Gd: 0-1 GF: - Fm: 3-6
Distance: 2m/2m3: 1-4 2m4-2m7: 3-9 3m+: 0-0
Track: LH: 1-3 RH: 1-2 Tight: 0-0 Gall: 0-1
Aids: Bl: 0-0 Vi: 0-0 Tstrap: 0-0 Ckp: 0-0
Best Rating: 124 10/03 Gway 2m6f   gd-fm Ch

Irish novice chaser; effective from 2m 3f - 2m 6f; acts on soft and fast ground.

Broadway Bay
97   70

6-y-o b g Karinga Bay-Brownscroft (Dubassoff (USA))
G A Ham Mrs W D Smith

Placings:00000   (4147)
2003/04: 16⁰G, 16⁰GS, 16⁰G, 17⁰GS, 24⁰G,

	Starts	1st	2nd	3rd	Win & Pl
NH Flat	3	0	0	0	0
Hurdles	2	0	0	0	0
Career Total	5	0	0	0	0

Going: Sf: 0-0 GS: 0-2 Gd: 0-3 GF: - Fm: 0-0
Distance: 2m/2m3: 0-4 2m4-2m7: 0-0 3m+: 0-1
Track: LH: 0-1 RH: 0-4 Tight: 0-2 Gall: 0-0
Aids: Bl: 0-0 Vi: 0-0 Tstrap: 0-5 Ckp: 0-0
Best Rating: 70 3/04 Tntn 3m110y   Hdl

Brochrua (IRE)
96   70

4-y-o b f Hernando (FR)-Severine (USA) (Trempolino (USA))
J D Frost (R Donohoe 20/8) Ms H Vernon-Jones

Placings:066   (4854)
2003/04: 16⁰S, 19⁶G, 17⁶GF,

	Starts	1st	2nd	3rd	Win & Pl
Hurdles	3	0	0	0	0
Career Total	3	0	0	0	0

Going: Sf: 0-1 GS: 0-0 Gd: 0-1 GF: - Fm: 0-1
Distance: 2m/2m3: 0-2 2m4-2m7: 0-1 3m+: 0-0
Track: LH: 0-1 RH: 0-2 Tight: 0-3 Gall: 0-0
Aids: Bl: 0-0 Vi: 0-0 Tstrap: 0-0 Ckp: 0-0
Best Rating: 70 3/04 Tntn 2m3f110y   good Hdl

Brockton Mist (IRE)
85(105h)   (114h)123

9-y-o ch g Mister Lord (USA)-Glens Princess (Prince Hansel)
P J Hobbs Mrs D A La Trobe

Placings:2/050/21122F3U3-2   (0369)
2003/04: 23²G,

	Starts	1st	2nd	3rd	Win & Pl
Chases	1	0	1	0	1218
Career Total	14	2	5	2	14676

| 100 | 9/02 | Prth | 3m110y | E Hdl | G-F | £4134 |
| 114 | 5/02 | Weth | 2m7f | D Hdl | GD | £3535 |

Total win prize-money £7669

Going: Sf: 0-0 GS: 0-0 Gd: 0-1 GF: - Fm: 0-0
Distance: 2m/2m3: 0-0 2m4-2m7: 0-0 3m+: 0-1
Track: LH: 0-1 RH: 0-0 Tight: 0-0 Gall: 0-0
Aids: Bl: 0-0 Vi: 0-0 Tstrap: 0-0 Ckp: 0-0
Best Rating: 123 11/02 Hayd 3m   good Ch

A half-brother to Grand National winner Papillon; won 3m novice hurdles at Wetherby and Perth 2002; subsequently become disappointing over fences; acts on ground good and faster.

Broctune Melody
98f   85f

5-y-o b/br g Merdon Melody-Eider (Niniski (USA))
Mrs M Reveley D Playforth + D Young

Placings:006   (3482)
2003/04: 17⁰GF, 16⁰GS, 16⁶G,

	Starts	1st	2nd	3rd	Win & Pl
NH Flat	3	0	0	0	0
Career Total	3	0	0	0	0

Going: Sf: 0-0 GS: 0-1 Gd: 0-1 GF: - Fm: 0-1
Distance: 2m/2m3: 0-3 2m4-2m7: 0-0 3m+: 0-0
Track: LH: 0-2 RH: 0-1 Tight: 0-1 Gall: 0-0
Aids: Bl: 0-0 Vi: 0-0 Tstrap: 0-0 Ckp: 0-0
Best Rating: 85 1/04 Weth 2m   gd-sft NHF

Big-type; well beaten in bumpers.

Broguestown Breeze (IRE)
96   (92h)100

11-y-o b g Montelimar (USA)-Spin A Coin (Torus)
R Dean Richard Dean

Placings:0321/P00P25/34PP/3/2-5F006650   (4792)
2003/04: 20⁵GS, 21FGS, 22⁰GS, 25⁰GS, 25⁶G, 24⁶G, 28⁵G, 26⁰G,

	Starts	1st	2nd	3rd	Win & Pl
Chases	8	0	0	0	0
Career Total	24	1	3	3	8099

| 105 | 1/99 | DRoy | 2m4f | Ch | HVY | £3376 |

Total win prize-money £3376

Going: Sf: 0-0 GS: 0-4 Gd: 0-4 GF: - Fm: 0-0
Distance: 2m/2m3: 0-0 2m4-2m7: 0-3 3m+: 0-5
Track: LH: 0-2 RH: 0-4 Tight: 0-6 Gall: 0-1
Aids: Bl: 0-0 Vi: 0-0 Tstrap: 0-0 Ckp: 0-1
Best Rating: 105 1/99 DRoy 2m4f   heavy Ch

Plating-class chaser; lightly raced; stays 3m 2f; acts on most types of ground.

Broken Dream (IRE)
104   (97h)112

7-y-o b g Broken Hearted-A Little Further (Mandalus)
P R Rodford (Miss H C Knight 5/11) Les Trott

Placings:204/23UP-054U35   (4916)
2003/04: 21⁰G, 22⁵S, 20⁴G, 24UGS, 26³G, 23⁵GS,

	Starts	1st	2nd	3rd	Win & Pl
Chases	6	0	0	1	1389
Career Total	13	0	2	2	4374

Going: Sf: 0-1 GS: 0-2 Gd: 0-3 GF: - Fm: 0-0
Distance: 2m/2m3: 0-0 2m4-2m7: 0-3 3m+: 0-3

Track:	LH: 0-5 RH: 0-1 Tight: 0-3 Gall: 0-1
Aids:	Bl: 0-0 Vi: 0-0 Tstrap: 0-0 Ckp: 0-0
Best Rating:	112 12/02 Plum 2m4f heavy Ch

Fair novice hurdler/disappointing chaser; suited by decent ground; stays 2m 4f.

Bromley Abbey
67f   53f
6-y-o ch m Minster Son-Little Bromley (Riberetto)
R Ford Mrs A Eubank

Placings:*0-6*   (1964)
2003/04: 16⁰G, 16⁶GF,

	Starts	1st	2nd	3rd	Win & Pl
NH Flat	2	0	0	0	0
Career Total	2	0	0	0	0

Going:	Sf: 0-0 GS: 0-0 Gd: 0-1 GF: - Fm: 0-1
Distance:	2m/2m3: 0-2 2m4-2m7: 0-0 3m+: 0-0
Track:	LH: 0-2 RH: 0-0 Tight: 0-0 Gall: 0-0
Aids:	Bl: 0-0 Vi: 0-0 Tstrap: 0-0 Ckp: 0-0
Best Rating:	53 11/03 Hayd 2m gd-fm NHF

Bronco Style (IRE)
74f   44f
6-y-o ch g Executive Perk-Name A Reason (IRE) (Buckskin (FR))
C J Gray A G Fear

Placings:*00*   (1378)
2003/04: 17⁰GF, 16⁰GF,

	Starts	1st	2nd	3rd	Win & Pl
NH Flat	2	0	0	0	
Career Total	2	0	0	0	

Going:	Sf: 0-0 GS: 0-0 Gd: 0-0 GF: - Fm: 0-2
Distance:	2m/2m3: 0-2 2m4-2m7: 0-0 3m+: 0-0
Track:	LH: 0-2 RH: 0-0 Tight: 0-1 Gall: 0-0
Aids:	Bl: 0-0 Vi: 0-0 Tstrap: 0-0 Ckp: 0-0
Best Rating:	44 9/03 Worc 2m gd-fm NHF

Bronhallow
108(97h)   (60h)88
11-y-o b g Belmez (USA)-Grey Twig (Godswalk (USA))
Mrs Barbara Waring R Parker,E Davies,L Nicholls,Mrs R Field

Placings:50P0025P/023P43355P4125/4356556/46433/00P
000634-P021P   (0857)
2003/04: 23⁹GF, 25⁰GF, 21²GS, 24¹G, 21⁵PGF,

	Starts	1st	2nd	3rd	Win & Pl
Chases	5	1	1	0	5730
Career Total	48	2	4	7	14164
79	6/03	Strf	3m	E Ch		GD	£4046
101	4/99	Uttx	3m110y	F(0-100)HHdl		G-S	£3061
				Total win prize-money £7107

Going:	Sf: 0-0 GS: 0-2 Gd: 1-1 GF: - Fm: 0-2
Distance:	2m/2m3: 0-0 2m4-2m7: 0-2 3m+: 1-3
Track:	LH: 1-4 RH: 0-1 Tight: 1-5 Gall: 0-0
Aids:	Bl: 1-3 Vi: 0-1 Tstrap: 0-0 Ckp: 0-0
Best Rating:	102 11/99 Uttx 3m110y soft Hdl

Plating-class hurdler/novice chaser; acts on most ground; has worn blinkers; stays 3m.

Bronzesmith
100   110
8-y-o b g Greensmith-Bronze Age (Celtic Cone)
B J M Ryall Mrs M E Ash

Placings:*062/*13/3F24U-452PB4P   (3452)
2003/04: 21ᵁS, 23⁴GS, 20⁵G, 16²GF, 17⁶G, 19⁸S, 19⁴GS, 19⁶GS,

	Starts	1st	2nd	3rd	Win & Pl
Chases	8	0	1	0	2360
Career Total	17	1	3	2	9585
89	10/01	Extr	2m1f	E Hdl		G-F	£2765
				Total win prize-money £2765

Going:	Sf: 0-2 GS: 0-3 Gd: 0-2 GF: - Fm: 0-1
Distance:	2m/2m3: 0-4 2m4-2m7: 0-3 3m+: 0-1
Track:	LH: 0-4 RH: 0-4 Tight: 0-3 Gall: 0-0
Aids:	Bl: 0-0 Vi: 0-0 Tstrap: 0-1 Ckp: 0-0
Best Rating:	110 1/04 Hrfd 2m3f gd-sft Ch

Won 2m 1f novice hurdle on fast ground at Exeter October 2001; disappointing over fences but is not badly handicapped now on some of his form; best at up to 2m 4f.

Brook Street
92   75
7-y-o b g Cruise Missile-Sweet Spice (Native Bazaar)
C L Tizzard C L Tizzard

Placings:*45/06-34*   (3195)
2003/04: 21³S, 21⁴S,

	Starts	1st	2nd	3rd	Win & Pl
Hurdles	2	0	0	1	697
Career Total	6	0	0	1	697

Going:	Sf: 0-2 GS: 0-0 Gd: 0-0 GF: - Fm: 0-0
Distance:	2m/2m3: 0-4 2m4-2m7: 0-2 3m+: 0-0
Track:	LH: 0-1 RH: 0-1 Tight: 0-1 Gall: 0-0
Aids:	Bl: 0-0 Vi: 0-0 Tstrap: 0-0 Ckp: 0-0
Best Rating:	89 3/02 Winc 2m soft NHF

Brooklands Lad
82(103h)   (96h)81
7-y-o b g North Col-Sancal (Whistlefield)
J W Mullins B R Edgeley

Placings:*4002-3P065*   (2820)
2003/04: 22³GF, 20⁵PGF, 22⁰G, 17⁶G, 20⁵GF,

	Starts	1st	2nd	3rd	Win & Pl
Hurdles	3	0	0	1	518
Chases	2	0	0	0	0
Career Total	6	0	1	1	1378

Going:	Sf: 0-0 GS: 0-0 Gd: 0-2 GF: - Fm: 0-3
Distance:	2m/2m3: 0-1 2m4-2m7: 0-4 3m+: 0-0
Track:	LH: 0-2 RH: 0-3 Tight: 0-2 Gall: 0-0
Aids:	Bl: 0-0 Vi: 0-0 Tstrap: 0-2 Ckp: 0-0
Best Rating:	96 4/03 Strf 2m3f gd-fm Hdl

Novice hurdler/chaser stays 2m 4f; unsuited by soft ground.

Brooklyn Breeze (IRE)
105(108h)   (133+h)140+
7-y-o b/br g Be My Native (USA)-Moss Gale (Strong Gale)
L Lungo Ashleybank Investments Limited

Placings:*4/1111-1*   (2404)
2003/04: 20¹S,

	Starts	1st	2nd	3rd	Win & Pl
Chases	1	1	0	0	5772
Career Total	6	5	0	0	28324
140	11/03	Carl	2m4f	D Ch		SFT	£5772
133	4/03	Prth	3m110y	C Hdl		GD	£7482
124	4/03	Ayr	2m4f	C Hdl		GD	£7657
95	11/03	Muss	2m	E Hdl		GD	£4056
107	11/02	Aint	2m1f	H NHF		GD	£3356
				Total win prize-money £28325

Going:	Sf: 1-1 GS: 0-0 Gd: 0-0 GF: - Fm: 0-0
Distance:	2m/2m3: 0-0 2m4-2m7: 1-1 3m+: 1-0
Track:	LH: 0-0 RH: 1-1 Tight: 0-0 Gall: 0-0
Aids:	Bl: 0-0 Vi: 0-0 Tstrap: 0-0 Ckp: 0-0
Best Rating:	140 11/03 Carl 2m4f soft Ch

Useful novice chaser/hurdler; bumper winner; unbeaten in three starts over hurdles; jumped well when winning chase debut; stays three miles; suited by good and soft ground; likes to be held up; highly progressive.

Brooklyn Brownie (IRE)
79f   99+f
5-y-o b g Presenting-In The Brownies (IRE) (Lafontaine (USA))
J M Jefferson P Gaffney & J N Stevenson

Placings:*0100*   (4481)
2003/04: 16⁰G, 16¹GF, 16⁹G, 17⁰HY,

	Starts	1st	2nd	3rd	Win & Pl
NH Flat	4	1	0	0	1862
Career Total	4	1	0	0	1862
99	6/03	Hexm	2m110y	H NHF		G-F	£1862
				Total win prize-money £1862

Going:	Sf: 0-1 GS: 0-0 Gd: 0-2 GF: - Fm: 1-1
Distance:	2m/2m3: 1-4 2m4-2m7: 0-0 3m+: 0-0
Track:	LH: 1-2 RH: 0-1 Tight: 0-0 Gall: 0-0
Aids:	Bl: 0-0 Vi: 0-0 Tstrap: 0-0 Ckp: 0-0
Best Rating:	99 6/03 Hexm 2m110y gd-fm NHF

Brooklyn's Gold (USA)
106(101c)   (114c)130
9-y-o b g Seeking The Gold (USA)-Brooklyn's Dance (FR) (Shirley Heights)
Ian Williams Terry Warner

Placings:*0/60F1254222/12144133-0025660*   (4372)
2003/04: 16⁹GS, 16⁰GF, 16²GGS, 16⁵G, 16⁹G, 16⁶G, 16⁸G,

	Starts	1st	2nd	3rd	Win & Pl
Hurdles	5	0	0	0	2239
Chases	2	0	1	0	796
Career Total	26	4	6	2	47806
126	2/03	Kemp	2m	C(0-135)HHdl		GD	£10092
118	11/02	Hntg	2m110y	D(0-120)HHdl		G-S	£8326
117	10/02	Hrfd	2m1f	D(0-120)HHdl		GD	£3955
107	11/02	Wwck	2m	D(0-110)HHdl		SFT	£5174
				Total win prize-money £27548

Going:	Sf: 0-0 GS: 0-2 Gd: 0-3 GF: - Fm: 0-2
Distance:	2m/2m3: 0-7 2m4-2m7: 0-0 3m+: 0-0
Track:	LH: 0-3 RH: 0-4 Tight: 0-1 Gall: 0-1
Aids:	Bl: 0-0 Vi: 0-0 Tstrap: 0-0 Ckp: 0-0
Best Rating:	130 4/03 Aint 2m110y good Hdl

Useful handicap hurdler; very consistent in 2002/3; no match for the progressive Kalca Mome on chasing debut at Hereford in December 2003; unplaced in a Flat race, hurdle and chase since; suited by two miles and good ground.

Brooks

94   105

8-y-o b g Minster Son-Melody Moon (Philip Of Spain)
John R Upson T L Brooks

Placings:FP45   (4653)
2003/04: 19FG, 21PGS, 20⁴G, 19⁵G,

	Starts	1st	2nd	3rd	Win & Pl
Chases	4	0	0	0	428
Career Total	4	0	0	0	428

Going:	Sf: 0-0 GS: 0-1 Gd: 0-3 GF: - Fm: 0-0
Distance:	2m/2m3: 0-2 2m4-2m7: 0-2 3m+: 0-0
Track:	LH: 0-2 RH: 0-2 Tight: 0-3 Gall: 0-0
Aids:	Bl: 0-0 Vi: 0-0 Tstrap: 0-0 Ckp: 0-0
Best Rating:	**105** 1/04 Catt 2m3f good Ch

Winning pointer; jumped well in front for a long way on return to action in novices' chase at Catterick in January but beaten when falling at the last.

Brooksie

97   102

9-y-o b g Efisio-Elkie Brooks (Relkino)
Miss K M George Stableline

Placings:00030330/64366P0/313663262/00023463P31/25
11-04P005056P   (4735)
2003/04: 20⁰G, 16⁴GF, 16PG, 19⁰GS, 19⁰HY, 16⁵GS, 17⁰G, 19⁵G,
19⁵G, 17PG,

	Starts	1st	2nd	3rd	Win & Pl
Hurdles	10	0	0	0	0
Career Total	49	4	4	10	20453
102	7/02	NAbb	2m1f	D(0-120)HHdl	G-F	£3546
102	7/02	Worc	2m	D(0-115)HHdl	GD	£3591
102	4/02	Tntn	2m1f	E(0-110)HHdl	GD	£2674
91	1/01	Tntn	2m3f110yG Hdl	HVY	£1596

Total win prize-money £11407

Going:	Sf: 0-1 GS: 0-2 Gd: 0-6 GF: - Fm: 0-1
Distance:	2m/2m3: 0-5 2m4-2m7: 0-5 3m+: 0-0
Track:	LH: 0-2 RH: 0-8 Tight: 0-5 Gall: 0-1
Aids:	Bl: 0-1 Vi: 0-9 Tstrap: 0-0 Ckp: 0-0
Best Rating:	**102** 7/02 NAbb 2m1f gd-fm Hdl

Modest hurdler between two and two and a half miles; appears to like Taunton; seems to handle most types of ground.

Brooksy Dove

6-y-o ch g Alderbrook-Coney Dove (Celtic Cone)
A E Price M G Racing

Placings:PP   (4340)
2003/04: 17PHY, 25PG,

	Starts	1st	2nd	3rd	Win & Pl
Hurdles	2	0	0	0	0
Career Total	2	0	0	0	0

Going:	Sf: 0-1 GS: 0-0 Gd: 0-1 GF: - Fm: 0-0
Distance:	2m/2m3: 0-1 2m4-2m7: 0-0 3m+: 0-1
Track:	LH: 0-1 RH: 0-1 Tight: 0-0 Gall: 0-0
Aids:	Bl: 0-0 Vi: 0-0 Tstrap: 0-0 Ckp: 0-0
Best Rating:	**0** 3/04 Wwck 3m1f good Hdl

Broom Close (IRE)

(104h)   (89 h)90

10-y-o b g Yashgan-Pick Nine (Tumble Wind (USA))

R Johnson / Jack Thornton

Placings:4P/0/12654140-PP   (0429)
2003/04: 24⁰GF, 21PGF, 21PG,

	Starts	1st	2nd	3rd	Win & Pl
Hurdles	1	0	0	0	0
Chases	2	0	0	0	0
Career Total	13	2	1	0	7104
89	2/03	Newc	2m4f	F(0-90)HHdl	SFT	£2765
82	10/02	Carl	2m4f	E(0-105)HHdl	SFT	£3206

Total win prize-money £5971

Going:	Sf: 0-0 GS: 0-0 Gd: 0-1 GF: - Fm: 0-2
Distance:	2m/2m3: 0-0 2m4-2m7: 0-2 3m+: 0-1
Track:	LH: 0-3 RH: 0-0 Tight: 0-1 Gall: 0-1
Aids:	Bl: 0-0 Vi: 0-0 Tstrap: 0-0 Ckp: 0-1
Best Rating:	**90** 1/03 Newc 2m110y heavy Ch

Moderate handicap hurdler; winner at Carlisle and Newcastle this time; best at up to two and a half miles.

Broomers Hill (IRE)

95f   84f

4-y-o b g Sadler's Wells (USA)-Bella Vitessa (IRE) (Thatching)
L A Dace The Tuesday Syndicate

Placings:240   (4578)
2003/04: 12²S, 13⁴S, 16⁰G,

	Starts	1st	2nd	3rd	Win & Pl
NH Flat	3	0	1	0	724
Career Total	3	0	1	0	724

Going:	Sf: 0-2 GS: 0-0 Gd: 0-1 GF: - Fm: 0-0
Distance:	2m/2m3: 0-1 2m4-2m7: 0-0 3m+: 0-0
Track:	LH: 0-1 RH: 0-0 Tight: 0-0 Gall: 0-1
Aids:	Bl: 0-0 Vi: 0-0 Tstrap: 0-0 Ckp: 0-0
Best Rating:	**84** 11/03 Asct 1m4f soft NHF

Very promising debut in an Ascot bumper.

Brophys Sonnet (IRE)

9-y-o b/br m Homo Sapien-Shanna Golden (IRE) (Le Bavard (FR))
I A Duncan I A Duncan

Placings:0   (0467)
2003/04: 16⁰G,

	Starts	1st	2nd	3rd	Win & Pl
Hurdles	1	0	0	0	0
Career Total	1	0	0	0	0

Going:	Sf: 0-0 GS: 0-0 Gd: 0-1 GF: - Fm: 0-0
Distance:	2m/2m3: 0-1 2m4-2m7: 0-0 3m+: 0-0
Track:	LH: 0-1 RH: 0-0 Tight: 0-0 Gall: 0-0
Aids:	Bl: 0-0 Vi: 0-0 Tstrap: 0-0 Ckp: 0-0

Brother Joe (NZ)

109(108h)   (144 h)153+

10-y-o ch g Hula Town (NZ)-Olivia Rose (NZ) (Travolta (FR))
P J Hobbs Sir Robert Ogden

Placings:2111/F55F1/123U023/16P05P-211F11111F   (2148)
2003/04: 23⁰G, 16¹GF, 21¹GF, 20FGF, 21¹GF, 20¹GF, 19¹GF, 21¹G, 19¹GF, 20FG,

---

	Starts	1st	2nd	3rd	Win & Pl
Chases	10	7	1	0	64973
Career Total	32	13	4	2	140951
153	11/03	Chep	2m3f110y Ch	G-F	£27300
122	10/03	Fknm	2m5f110yC Ch	GD	£8359
144	10/03	Chep	2m3f110yC Ch	G-F	£8320
120	8/03	Hntg	2m4f110yC Ch	G-F	£4728
126	8/03	NAbb	2m5f110yD Ch	G-F	£5395
128	6/03	Uttx	2m5f	E Ch	G-F	£5167
109	6/03	Worc	2m	E Ch	G-F	£3948
160	11/02	Weth	3m1f	A Hdl	G-S	£17400
155	10/01	Chel	2m5f	B(0-145)HHdl	GD	£9282
142	4/01	Ayr	2m6f	B(0-150)HHdl	GD	£7124
140	4/00	Ayr	2m6f	B HHdl	GD	£6988
140	3/00	Chep	2m4f	B(0-140)HHdl	G-S	£6825
110	11/99	Folk	2m4f110yF Hdl	G-S	£1499

Total win prize-money £112338

Going:	Sf: 0-0 GS: 0-0 Gd: 1-3 GF: - Fm: 6-7
Distance:	2m/2m3: 1-1 **2m4-2m7: 6-8** 3m+: 0-1
Track:	**LH: 6-8** RH: 1-2 **Tight: 2-3** Gall: 1-2
Aids:	Bl: 0-0 Vi: 0-0 Tstrap: 0-0 Ckp: 0-0
Best Rating:	**160** 11/02 Weth 3m1f gd-sft Hdl

Smart novice chaser; smart staying hurdler when in the mood; won seven times over fences; showed a tendency to jump right; stayed 3m but considered best at around 2m 4f over fences; best on fast; was suited by racing prominently (DEAD).

Brother Ted

69   49

7-y-o b g Henbit (USA)-Will Be Wanton (Palm Track)
J K Cresswell J K S Cresswell

Placings:0500-6   (0624)
2003/04: 20⁶GF,

	Starts	1st	2nd	3rd	Win & Pl
Hurdles	1	0	0	0	0
Career Total	5	0	0	0	0

Going:	Sf: 0-0 GS: 0-0 Gd: 0-0 GF: - Fm: 0-0
Distance:	2m/2m3: 0-0 2m4-2m7: 0-1 3m+: 0-0
Track:	LH: 0-1 RH: 0-0 Tight: 0-0 Gall: 0-0
Aids:	Bl: 0-0 Vi: 0-0 Tstrap: 0-0 Ckp: 0-0
Best Rating:	**86** 7/02 Strf 2m110y gd-fm NHF

Broughton Knows

98   80

7-y-o b g Most Welcome-Broughtons Pet (IRE) (Cyrano De Bergerac)
W J Musson Broughton Thermal Insulation

Placings:45   (0507)
2003/04: 16⁴GF, 16⁵G,

	Starts	1st	2nd	3rd	Win & Pl
Hurdles	2	0	0	0	0
Career Total	2	0	0	0	0

Going:	Sf: 0-0 GS: 0-0 Gd: 0-1 GF: - Fm: 0-1
Distance:	2m/2m3: 0-2 2m4-2m7: 0-0 3m+: 0-0
Track:	LH: 0-1 RH: 0-1 Tight: 0-1 Gall: 0-0
Aids:	Bl: 0-0 Vi: 0-0 Tstrap: 0-0 Ckp: 0-0
Best Rating:	**80** 5/03 Hntg 2m110y gd-fm Hdl

Broughtons Mill

97   63

9-y-o gr g Ron's Victory (USA)-Sandra's Desire (Grey Desire)

J A Supple (Mrs A M Naughton 14/5) Geoff Hubbard Racing

Placings:U/000264					(4774)
2003/04: 16⁰G, 16⁰G, 16⁰S, 16²GS, 17⁶G, 16⁴G,					

2003/04: 16⁰G, 16⁰G, 16⁰S, 16²GS, 17⁶G, 16⁴G,

	Starts	1st	2nd	3rd	Win & Pl
Hurdles	6	0	1	0	776
Career Total	7	0	1	0	776

Going:	Sf: 0-1 GS: 0-1 Gd: 0-4 GF: - Fm: 0-0
Distance:	2m/2m3: 0-6 2m4-2m7: 0-0 3m+: 0-0
Track:	LH: 0-5 RH: 0-1 Tight: 0-6 Gall: 0-0
Aids:	Bl: 0-0 Vi: 0-0 Tstrap: 0-0 Ckp: 0-2
Best Rating:	62 4/04 Fknm 2m good Hdl

Brown Ben

92   **77**

10-y-o b g General Gambul-City Sunset (Sunyboy)
D P Keane Mrs H R Cross

Placings:F3440					(2513)
2003/04: 20⁶GF, 21³GF, 26⁴GF, 16⁴GS, 16⁰GS,					

	Starts	1st	2nd	3rd	Win & Pl
Chases	5	0	0	1	1367
Career Total	5	0	0	1	1367

Going:	Sf: 0-0 GS: 0-2 Gd: 0-0 GF: - Fm: 0-3
Distance:	2m/2m3: 0-2 2m4-2m7: 0-2 3m+: 0-1
Track:	LH: 0-3 RH: 0-2 Tight: 0-2 Gall: 0-0
Aids:	Bl: 0-0 Vi: 0-0 Tstrap: 0-0 Ckp: 0-0
Best Rating:	77 8/03 NAbb 2m5f110y gd-fm Ch

Brown Chieftain (IRE)

11-y-o b g Meneval (USA)-Brown Trout (IRE) (Beau Charmeur (FR))
A W G Geering A W G Geering

Placings:00000/P-P					(0490)
2003/04: 26⁶GF,					

	Starts	1st	2nd	3rd	Win & Pl
Chases	1	0	0	0	
Career Total	7	0	0	0	

Going:	Sf: 0-0 GS: 0-0 Gd: 0-0 GF: - Fm: 0-1
Distance:	2m/2m3: 0-0 2m4-2m7: 0-0 3m+: 0-1
Track:	LH: 0-1 RH: 0-0 Tight: 0-1 Gall: 0-0
Aids:	Bl: 0-0 Vi: 0-0 Tstrap: 0-0 Ckp: 0-0
Best Rating:	56 8/00 Kbgn 2m4f gd-fm Ch

Brown Esquire

13-y-o b g Broadleaf-Ana Brown (Souvran)
Miss G Dewhurst Miss G Dewhurst

Placings:0PP/PP/2/6P-P					(4143)
2003/04: 25⁶G,					

	Starts	1st	2nd	3rd	Win & Pl
Chases	1	0	0	0	
Career Total	9	0	1	0	751

Going:	Sf: 0-0 GS: 0-0 Gd: 0-1 GF: - Fm: 0-0
Distance:	2m/2m3: 0-0 2m4-2m7: 0-0 3m+: 0-1
Track:	LH: 0-0 RH: 0-0 Tight: 0-0 Gall: 0-0

Aids:	Bl: 0-0 Vi: 0-0 Tstrap: 0-0 Ckp: 0-0
Best Rating:	89 4/02 Ludl 3m gd-fm Ch

Brown Flyer

84   **48**

7-y-o gr g Baron Blakeney-Brown Veil (Don't Look)
H D Daly Mrs A G Lawe

Placings:600					(4511)
2003/04: 20⁶G, 17⁰HY, 20⁰GS,					

	Starts	1st	2nd	3rd	Win & Pl
Hurdles	3	0	0	0	0
Career Total	3	0	0	0	0

Going:	Sf: 0-1 GS: 0-1 Gd: 0-1 GF: - Fm: 0-0
Distance:	2m/2m3: 0-1 2m4-2m7: 0-2 3m+: 0-0
Track:	LH: 0-2 RH: 0-1 Tight: 0-0 Gall: 0-0
Aids:	Bl: 0-0 Vi: 0-0 Tstrap: 0-0 Ckp: 0-0
Best Rating:	48 11/03 Chep 2m4f good Hdl

Brown Teddy

99   **111+**

7-y-o b g Afzal-Quadrapol (Pollerton)
R Ford G B Barlow

Placings:4/044115-1					(2525)
2003/04: 19¹GS,					

	Starts	1st	2nd	3rd	Win & Pl
Hurdles	1	1	0	0	3392
Career Total	8	3	0	0	10453
111	12/03	Catt	2m3f	E(0-110)HHdl	G-S	£3391
102	3/03	Hntg	2m110y	F(0-100)HHdl	GD	£2681
101	1/03	Muss	2m	E Hdl	GD	£4056
				Total win prize-money £10129		

Going:	Sf: 0-0 GS: 1-1 Gd: 0-0 GF: - Fm: 0-0
Distance:	**2m/2m3:** 1-1 2m4-2m7: 0-0 3m+: 0-0
Track:	**LH:** 1-1 RH: 0-0 **Tight:** 1-1 Gall: 0-0
Aids:	Bl: 0-0 Vi: 0-0 Tstrap: 0-0 Ckp: 0-0
Best Rating:	111 12/03 Catt 2m3f gd-sft Hdl

Modest performer; chasing bred, he won twice as a novice over two miles; scored after two miles three on seasonal debut in December 2003; best on good ground or slightly softer; open to further improvement.

Browneyes Blue (IRE)

92f   **71f**

6-y-o b g Satco (FR)-Bawnard Lady (Ragapan)
D R MacLeod Maurice W Chapman

Placings:005					(4952)
2003/04: 16⁰HY, 16⁰GS, 16⁵GS,					

	Starts	1st	2nd	3rd	Win & Pl
NH Flat	3	0	0	0	0
Career Total	3	0	0	0	0

Going:	Sf: 0-1 GS: 0-2 Gd: 0-0 GF: - Fm: 0-0
Distance:	2m/2m3: 0-3 2m4-2m7: 0-0 3m+: 0-0
Track:	LH: 0-2 RH: 0-1 Tight: 0-0 Gall: 0-0
Aids:	Bl: 0-0 Vi: 0-0 Tstrap: 0-0 Ckp: 0-0
Best Rating:	71 2/04 Ayr 2m gd-sft NHF

Brownings Express

5-y-o b g Elmaamul (USA)-Chushan Venture (Pursuit Of Love)
M W Easterby L P S Racing

Placings:00P					(4660)
2003/04: 16⁰GS, 16⁰GF, 24⁰PS,					

	Starts	1st	2nd	3rd	Win & Pl
NH Flat	2	0	0	0	0
Hurdles	1	0	0	0	0
Career Total	3	0	0	0	

Going:	Sf: 0-1 GS: 0-1 Gd: 0-0 GF: - Fm: 0-1
Distance:	2m/2m3: 0-2 2m4-2m7: 0-0 3m+: 0-0
Track:	LH: 0-3 RH: 0-0 Tight: 0-2 Gall: 0-0
Aids:	Bl: 0-0 Vi: 0-0 Tstrap: 0-0 Ckp: 0-0
Best Rating:	60 3/04 Catt 2m gd-fm NHF

Bruern (IRE)

77   **58**

7-y-o b g Aahsaylad-Bob's Girl (IRE) (Bob Back (USA))
Mrs Mary Hambro Richard Hambro

Placings:0-00					(3350)
2003/04: 16⁰GS, 16⁰S,					

	Starts	1st	2nd	3rd	Win & Pl
NH Flat	1	0	0	0	0
Hurdles	1	0	0	0	0
Career Total	3	0	0	0	

Going:	Sf: 0-1 GS: 0-1 Gd: 0-0 GF: - Fm: 0-0
Distance:	2m/2m3: 0-2 2m4-2m7: 0-0 3m+: 0-0
Track:	LH: 0-1 RH: 0-1 Tight: 0-0 Gall: 0-2
Aids:	Bl: 0-0 Vi: 0-0 Tstrap: 0-0 Ckp: 0-0
Best Rating:	69 12/03 Newb 2m110y gd-sft NHF

Brunston Castle

4-y-o b g Hector Protector (USA)-Villella (Sadler's Wells (USA))
B R Millman Seasons Holidays

Placings:P					(3637)
2003/04: 19⁰PS,					

	Starts	1st	2nd	3rd	Win & Pl
Hurdles	1	0	0	0	
Career Total	1	0	0	0	

Going:	Sf: 0-1 GS: 0-0 Gd: 0-0 GF: - Fm: 0-0
Distance:	2m/2m3: 0-1 2m4-2m7: 0-0 3m+: 0-0
Track:	LH: 0-0 RH: 0-1 Tight: 0-0 Gall: 0-0
Aids:	Bl: 0-0 Vi: 0-0 Tstrap: 0-1 Ckp: 0-0

Brush A King

109(82c)   (67c)**93**

9-y-o b g Derrylin-Colonial Princess (Roscoe Blake)
C T Pogson C T Pogson

Placings:560/03/00P/3PP046151-2210634005					(3918)
2003/04: 21²GF, 25²G, 26¹GF, 25⁰G, 26⁵GS, 26³GF, 20⁴F, 16⁰GS, 25⁰G, 23⁵G,					

	Starts	1st	2nd	3rd	Win & Pl
Hurdles	8	1	2	0	6053
Chases	2	0	0	1	1543
Career Total	27	3	2	3	16413

93	6/03	Sthl	3m2f	F(0-95)HHdl	G-F £3549
93	4/03	Sedg	2m5f110yG(0-100)HHdl	G-F £5584
78	2/03	Catt	2m3f	G(0-90)HHdl	GD £2450
				Total win prize-money	£11584

Going:	Sf: 0-0 GS: 0-2 Gd: 0-4 GF: - Fm: 1-4
Distance:	2m/2m3: 0-1 2m4-2m7: 0-2 **3m+: 1-7**
Track:	**LH: 1-8** RH: 0-1 Tight: 0-2 Gall: 0-2
Aids:	Bl: 0-1 Vi: 0-0 Tstrap: 0-0 Ckp: 0-0
Best Rating:	**96** 11/00 Weth 2m heavy NHF

Moderate hurdler; stays two miles-five; suited by a sound surface.

Brush The Ark
97   97+

10-y-o b m Brush Aside (USA)-Expensive Lark (Sir Lark)
J S Smith Donald Smith

Placings:125/362PP04/3222-030   (4574)
2003/04: 19⁰G, 17³G, 21⁰G,

	Starts	1st	2nd	3rd	Win & Pl
Hurdles	3	0	0	1	522
Career Total	17	1	5	3	7748
100	10/00	Bang	2m1f	H NHF	SFT £1704
				Total win prize-money	£1705

Going:	Sf: 0-0 GS: 0-1 Gd: 0-2 GF: - Fm: 0-0
Distance:	2m/2m3: 0-1 2m4-2m7: 0-2 3m+: 0-0
Track:	LH: 0-2 RH: 0-1 Tight: 0-1 Gall: 0-1
Aids:	Bl: 0-0 Vi: 0-0 Tstrap: 0-0 Ckp: 0-0
Best Rating:	**100** 10/00 Bang 2m1f soft NHF

Novice hurdler; bumper winner; placed in novice hurdles; acts on soft ground; stays 3m 2f.

Bruthuinne (IRE)
111

9-y-o ch g Vaquillo (USA)-Portane Miss (Salluceva)
B G Powell Martin Broughton

Placings:63/34/4PU3223P/114F-PP   (0532)
2003/04: 20⁰G, 23⁰GF,

	Starts	1st	2nd	3rd	Win & Pl
Chases	2	0	0	0	
Career Total	18	2	2	4	16162
109	10/02	Plum	3m2f	D(0-120)HCh	GD £5950
95	10/02	Hrfd	3m1f110yE Ch	G-F £3874
				Total win prize-money	£9825

Going:	Sf: 0-0 GS: 0-0 Gd: 0-1 GF: - Fm: 0-0
Distance:	2m/2m3: 0-0 2m4-2m7: 0-1 3m+: 0-1
Track:	LH: 0-2 RH: 0-0 Tight: 0-0 Gall: 0-0
Aids:	Bl: 0-0 Vi: 0-0 Tstrap: 0-0 Ckp: 0-0
Best Rating:	**111** 11/00 Kemp 2m soft Ch

Buadhach (IRE)

8-y-o b g Petoski-Viking Rocket (Viking (USA))
M A Hill M A Hill

Placings:P20/0P0210P0/0-F   (0033)
2003/04: 16⁶G,

	Starts	1st	2nd	3rd	Win & Pl
Chases	1	0	0	0	
Career Total	13	1	2	0	4643
84	11/01	Ayr	2m4f	D(0-110)HHdl	G-S £3402
				Total win prize-money	£3402

Going:	Sf: 0-0 GS: 0-0 Gd: 0-1 GF: - Fm: 0-0
Distance:	2m/2m3: 0-1 2m4-2m7: 0-0 3m+: 0-0
Track:	LH: 0-1 RH: 0-0 Tight: 0-0 Gall: 0-1

Aids:	Bl: 0-0 Vi: 0-0 Tstrap: 0-0 Ckp: 0-0
Best Rating:	**103** 6/00 Hexm 2m gd-fm NHF

Bualadhbos (IRE)
54

5-y-o b g Royal Applause-Goodnight Girl (IRE) (Alzao (USA))
F Jordan F K Jennings

Placings:6-0P   (0854)
2003/04: 16⁶G, 22⁶GF,

	Starts	1st	2nd	3rd	Win & Pl
Hurdles	2	0	0	0	
Career Total	3	0	0	0	

Going:	Sf: 0-0 GS: 0-0 Gd: 0-1 GF: - Fm: 0-1
Distance:	2m/2m3: 0-1 2m4-2m7: 0-1 3m+: 0-0
Track:	LH: 0-2 RH: 0-0 Tight: 0-2 Gall: 0-0
Aids:	Bl: 0-0 Vi: 0-0 Tstrap: 0-0 Ckp: 0-0
Best Rating:	**48** 11/02 Hntg 2m110y gd-sft Hdl

Bubba Boy (IRE)
74f   101+f

4-y-o b/br g Anshan-Royal Patrol (IRE) (Phardante (FR))
M C Pipe D A Johnson

Placings:2   (4824)
2003/04: 17²GF,

	Starts	1st	2nd	3rd	Win & Pl
NH Flat	1	0	1	0	792
Career Total	1	0	1	0	792

Going:	Sf: 0-0 GS: 0-0 Gd: 0-0 GF: - Fm: 0-1
Distance:	2m/2m3: 0-1 2m4-2m7: 0-0 3m+: 0-0
Track:	LH: 0-0 RH: 0-1 Tight: 0-0 Gall: 0-0
Aids:	Bl: 0-0 Vi: 0-0 Tstrap: 0-0 Ckp: 0-0
Best Rating:	**101** 4/04 Extr 2m1f gd-fm NHF

Bubble Boy (IRE)
70f   97f

5-y-o ch g Hubbly Bubbly (USA)-Cool Charm (Beau Charmeur (FR))
B G Powell John Plackett

Placings:5   (4824)
2003/04: 17⁵GF,

	Starts	1st	2nd	3rd	Win & Pl
NH Flat	1	0	0	0	0
Career Total	1	0	0	0	0

Going:	Sf: 0-0 GS: 0-0 Gd: 0-0 GF: - Fm: 0-1
Distance:	2m/2m3: 0-1 2m4-2m7: 0-0 3m+: 0-0
Track:	LH: 0-0 RH: 0-1 Tight: 0-0 Gall: 0-0
Aids:	Bl: 0-0 Vi: 0-0 Tstrap: 0-0 Ckp: 0-0
Best Rating:	**97** 4/04 Extr 2m1f gd-fm NHF

Bubble Brook

6-y-o b g Alderbrook-Leinster Girl (Don)
H J Manners A J & Mrs A Moffatt

Placings:0   (0373)
2003/04: 16⁹G,

	Starts	1st	2nd	3rd	Win & Pl
NH Flat	1	0	0	0	

Career Total	**1** **0** **0** **0**

Going:	Sf: 0-0 GS: 0-0 Gd: 0-1 GF: - Fm: 0-0
Distance:	2m/2m3: 0-1 2m4-2m7: 0-0 3m+: 0-0
Track:	LH: 0-1 RH: 0-0 Tight: 0-0 Gall: 0-0
Aids:	Bl: 0-0 Vi: 0-0 Tstrap: 0-0 Ckp: 0-0

Bubble Up (IRE)
100   76

5-y-o b m Nicolotte-Mousseux (IRE) (Jareer (USA))
J G Portman Mrs S J Portman

Placings:3F   (1309)
2003/04: 16³G, 16⁶GF,

	Starts	1st	2nd	3rd	Win & Pl
Hurdles	2	0	0	1	426
Career Total	2	0	0	1	426

Going:	Sf: 0-0 GS: 0-0 Gd: 0-1 GF: - Fm: 0-1
Distance:	2m/2m3: 0-2 2m4-2m7: 0-0 3m+: 0-0
Track:	LH: 0-2 RH: 0-0 Tight: 0-1 Gall: 0-0
Aids:	Bl: 0-0 Vi: 0-0 Tstrap: 0-1 Ckp: 0-0
Best Rating:	**86** 9/03 Worc 2m gd-fm Hdl

Showed ability at up to a mile on the Flat; twice refused to enter the stalls prior to finishing third in mares only novices seller on hurdling debut; would have been placed but for falling next time.

Buckby Lane
109(106h)   (120+h)139+

8-y-o b g Nomadic Way (USA)-Buckby Folly (Netherkelly)
P R Webber Mrs P Starkey

Placings:4P/2U311-21   (2719)
2003/04: 20²GS, 20¹GS,

	Starts	1st	2nd	3rd	Win & Pl
Chases	2	1	1	0	33594
Career Total	9	3	2	1	56673
139	12/03	Chel	2m4f110yB Ch	G-S £29000
126	4/03	Chel	2m5f110yB Hdl	GD £17400
120	3/03	Plum	2m5f	E Hdl	HVY £3474
				Total win prize-money	£49874

Going:	Sf: 0-0 GS: 1-2 Gd: 0-0 GF: - Fm: 0-0
Distance:	2m/2m3: 0-0 **2m4-2m7: 1-2** 3m+: 0-0
Track:	**LH: 1-2** RH: 0-0 Tight: 0-0 **Gall: 1-2**
Aids:	Bl: 0-0 Vi: 0-0 Tstrap: 0-0 Ckp: 0-0
Best Rating:	**139** 12/03 Chel 2m4f110y gd-sft Ch

Useful novice chaser; fair sort over hurdles; needed to run when second of two to Puntal on chasing debut; stepped up to win at Cheltenham next time; has scope to do well over fences; stays 2m 5f and acts on good and soft ground; suited by forcing tactics.

Buckland Knight (IRE)

8-y-o b/br g Commanche Run-Myra Gaye (Buckskin (FR))
Mrs Laura J Young Mrs Laura J Young & Mrs Sally White

Placings:400/U1P/0PU5P-UFFF   (4872)
2003/04: 25ᵁGS, 26⁶GS, 25⁶FS, 24⁶FS,

	Starts	1st	2nd	3rd	Win & Pl
Chases	4	0	0	0	
Career Total	15	1	0	0	2744
115	1/02	Folk	2m1f110yE Hdl	HVY £2744

Total win prize-money £2744

Going:	Sf: 0-2 GS: 0-1 Gd: 0-0 GF: - Fm: 0-1
Distance:	2m/2m3: 0-0 2m4-2m7: 0-0 3m+: 0-4
Track:	LH: 0-2 RH: 0-2 Tight: 0-1 Gall: 0-0
Aids:	Bl: 0-0 Vi: 0-0 Tstrap: 0-0 Ckp: 0-0
Best Rating:	115 1/02 Folk 2m1f110y heavy Hdl

Buckland Lad (IRE)

13-y-o ch g Phardante (FR)-Belcraig (Foggy Bell)
Mrs D M Grissell Mrs D M Grissell

Placings:0/054312/3121/21/1214112/3F12/25RP/P/10
(0521)
2003/04: 21¹GF, 24⁰G,

	Starts	1st	2nd	3rd	Win & Pl
Chases	2	1	0	0	
Career Total	31	10	7	3	56689
88	05/03	Folk	Hun Ch		G-F	£1238
120	12/99	Kemp	2m4f110yD(0-120)HCh	SFT	£11040
117	3/99	Folk	2m	D(0-125)HCh	GD	£3622
127	3/99	Newb	2m1f	C(0-135)HCh	SFT	£5970
117	1/99	Kemp	2m	C(0-130)HCh	SFT	£5420
107	12/98	Wind	2m	D(0-125)HCh	G-S	£3418
114	12/97	Font	2m3f	D(0-120)HCh	SFT	£3557
95	3/97	Ling	2m	F(0-95)HCh	G-F	£2467
91	2/97	Folk	2m	F(0-100)HCh	SFT	£2612
93	4/96	Folk	2m1f110yE(0-100)HHdl	G-F	£2678
			Total win prize-money £42026

Going:	Sf: 0-0 GS: 0-0 Gd: 0-1 GF: - Fm: 1-1
Distance:	2m/2m3: 0-0 2m4-2m7: 1-1 3m+: 0-1
Track:	LH: 1-1 RH: 1-1 Tight: 1-2 Gall: 0-0
Aids:	Bl: 0-0 Vi: 0-0 Tstrap: 0-0 Ckp: 0-0
Best Rating:	127 3/99 Newb 2m1f soft Ch

Formerly genuine and reliable chaser; won a hunter at Folkestone in May 2003; goes well at Kempton; stays two miles five; acts on any ground.

Buckskin Lad (IRE)
87

9-y-o b/br g Buckskin (FR)-Loverush (Golden Love)
Mrs N S Sharpe (C Roberts 7/5) The Blue Yonder Partnership

Placings:2/6PP126-PP
(3227)
2003/04: 24⁴GS, 26⁰GS,

	Starts	1st	2nd	3rd	Win & Pl
Hurdles	2	0	0	0	
Career Total	9	1	2	0	4866
87	2/03	Catt	3m1f110yE(0-100)HHdl	GD	£3562
			Total win prize-money £3562

Going:	Sf: 0-0 GS: 0-2 Gd: 0-0 GF: - Fm: 0-0
Distance:	2m/2m3: 0-0 2m4-2m7: 0-0 3m+: 0-2
Track:	LH: 0-1 RH: 0-1 Tight: 0-0 Gall: 0-0
Aids:	Bl: 0-0 Vi: 0-0 Tstrap: 0-0 Ckp: 0-0
Best Rating:	97 5/00 Worc 2m gd-fm NHF

Runner-up in a bumper; shock winner at Catterick in February 2003 appreciating the better ground; good effort when second under a penalty on softer ground at Hereford next time; stays three miles plus.

Buddy Girie

11-y-o b g Lord Bud-Hatsu-Girie (Ascertain (USA))
P Cornforth J Cornforth

Placings:F/4-225
(0509)

2003/04: 21²S, 26²G, 28⁵GS,

	Starts	1st	2nd	3rd	Win & Pl
Chases	3	0	2	0	1102
Career Total	5	0	2	0	1102

Going:	Sf: 0-1 GS: 0-1 Gd: 0-1 GF: - Fm: 0-0
Distance:	2m/2m3: 0-0 2m4-2m7: 0-1 3m+: 0-2
Track:	LH: 0-3 RH: 0-0 Tight: 0-3 Gall: 0-0
Aids:	Bl: 0-0 Vi: 0-0 Tstrap: 0-0 Ckp: 0-0
Best Rating:	91 5/03 Sedg 2m5f soft Ch

Multiple point winner but one paced under Rules.

Bude
76(103h)   (94h)91

5-y-o gr g Environment Friend-Gay Da Cheen (IRE) (Tenby)
S A Brookshaw Laurie Briggs Jnr

Placings:52466001P23-034105U3P3
(4142)
2003/04: 21⁰GF, 16³GF, 16⁴G, 16¹GF, 19⁰GF, 17⁵G, 17⁰G, 16³GF, 20⁶GF, 24³G,

	Starts	1st	2nd	3rd	Win & Pl
Hurdles	7	1	0	2	6336
Chases	3	0	1	0	1020
Career Total	21	2	2	4	14269
91	8/03	Uttx	2m	E(0-110)HHdl	G-F	£3799
85	3/03	Ludl	2m	E(0-105)HHdl	G-F	£4017
			Total win prize-money £7816

Going:	Sf: 0-0 GS: 0-0 Gd: 0-0 GF: - Fm: 1-6
Distance:	2m/2m3: 1-6 2m4-2m7: 0-3 3m+: 0-1
Track:	LH: 1-6 RH: 0-4 Tight: 0-4 Gall: 0-0
Aids:	Bl: 0-2 Vi: 0-0 Tstrap: 0-0 Ckp: 0-1
Best Rating:	91 3/04 Ludl 3m good Hdl

Moderate hurdler/novice chaser; acts on ground good and faster; has worn blinkers, but left off recently.

Bula's Quest
97f   93f

5-y-o b g Sula Bula-Dinkies Quest (Sergeant Drummer (USA))
L G Cottrell David Cocks

Placings:13
(1378)
2003/04: 17¹GF, 16³GF,

	Starts	1st	2nd	3rd	Win & Pl
NH Flat	2	1	0	1	3646
Career Total	2	1	0	1	3646
93	8/03	NAbb	2m1f	H NHF	G-F	£3427
			Total win prize-money £3427

Going:	Sf: 0-0 GS: 0-0 Gd: 0-0 GF: - Fm: 1-2
Distance:	2m/2m3: 1-2 2m4-2m7: 0-0 3m+: 0-1
Track:	LH: 1-2 RH: 0-0 Tight: 1-1 Gall: 0-0
Aids:	Bl: 0-0 Vi: 0-0 Tstrap: 0-0 Ckp: 0-0
Best Rating:	96 9/03 Worc 2m gd-fm NHF

Probably failed to achieve much when 20/1 winner on debut in Newton Abbot bumper August 2003; set slow pace when third at Worcester next time.

Bulgaria Moon

4-y-o ch g Groom Dancer (USA)-Gai Bulga (Kris)
C Grant Chris Grant

Placings:0
(1183)
2003/04: 17⁰G,

	Starts	1st	2nd	3rd	Win & Pl
Hurdles	1	0	0	0	
Career Total	1	0	0	0	

Going:	Sf: 0-0 GS: 0-0 Gd: 0-1 GF: - Fm: 0-0
Distance:	2m/2m3: 0-0 2m4-2m7: 0-0 3m+: 0-0
Track:	LH: 0-1 RH: 0-0 Tight: 0-1 Gall: 0-0
Aids:	Bl: 0-0 Vi: 0-0 Tstrap: 0-0 Ckp: 0-0
Best Rating:	0 8/03 Ctml 2m1f110y good Hdl

Bungee Jumper
111   104

14-y-o b g Idiots Delight-Catherine Bridge (Pitpan)
B D Leavy Trevor Farrow

Placings:20/002/2113/00/P40/42P26P0/2F431/3/P/P-B1531
(1093)
2003/04: 16⁸GF, 16¹GF, 16⁵GF, 17⁹GF, 17¹G,

	Starts	1st	2nd	3rd	Win & Pl
Chases	5	2	0	1	15491
Career Total	34	5	6	4	30482
104	8/03	Strf	2m1f110yD(0-125)HCh	GD	£8141
104	6/03	Uttx	2m	D(0-120)HCh	GF	£6090
105	7/99	Strf	2m1f110yD Ch	GD	£4318
104	10/95	Ludl	2m	E Hdl	FRM	£2332
97	9/95	Hntg	2m110y	E Hdl	G-F	£2442
			Total win prize-money £23325

Going:	Sf: 0-0 GS: 0-0 Gd: 1-1 GF: - Fm: 1-4
Distance:	2m/2m3: 2-5 2m4-2m7: 0-0 3m+: 0-0
Track:	LH: 2-3 RH: 0-2 Tight: 1-3 Gall: 0-1
Aids:	Bl: 0-0 Vi: 0-0 Tstrap: 0-0 Ckp: 0-1
Best Rating:	109 5/00 Worc 2m gd-fm Ch

Moderate chaser; lightly raced veteran; one-time fairly useful novice for Tim Forster; back to form after a long spell in the doldrums when winning modest handicap chases at Uttoxeter in June and Stratford in August 2003; best at around two miles; likes fast ground.

Bunkum
105(105h)   (125 h)111

6-y-o b g Robellino (USA)-Spinning Mouse (Bustino)
R Lee John Jackson And Maggie Pope

Placings:441/1-5645F2P
(4653)
2003/04: 20⁵S, 20⁵S, 19⁴S, 16⁵S, 24⁵S, 21²G, 19⁵G,

	Starts	1st	2nd	3rd	Win & Pl
Hurdles	2	0	0	0	403
Chases	5	0	1	0	1689
Career Total	11	2	1	0	9783
122	2/03	Chep	2m4f	D(0-125)HHdl	HVY	£5024
118	3/02	Chep	2m110y	E Hdl	SFT	£2667
			Total win prize-money £7692

Going:	Sf: 0-5 GS: 0-0 Gd: 0-2 GF: - Fm: 0-0
Distance:	2m/2m3: 0-2 2m4-2m7: 0-4 3m+: 0-1
Track:	LH: 0-4 RH: 0-3 Tight: 0-1 Gall: 0-1
Aids:	Bl: 0-0 Vi: 0-0 Tstrap: 0-0 Ckp: 0-0
Best Rating:	122 2/03 Chep 2m4f heavy Hdl

Modest chaser/fair hurdler; effective at two and a half miles; acts on soft/heavy ground.

Bunratty's Sole (IRE)

6-y-o br g Phardante (FR)-Bucks Gift (IRE) (Buckley)
N M Bloom R P Fryer

Placings:6
(4779)
2003/04: 24⁶S,

	Starts	1st	2nd	3rd	Win & Pl
Chases	1	0	0	0	0

Career Total   1   0   0   0   0

Going:	Sf: 0-1 GS: 0-0 Gd: 0-0 GF: - Fm: 0-0
Distance:	2m/2m3: 0-0 2m4-2m7: 0-0 3m+: 0-1
Track:	LH: 0-1 RH: 0-0 Tight: 0-1 Gall: 0-0
Aids:	Bl: 0-0 Vi: 0-0 Tstrap: 0-0 Ckp: 0-1
Best Rating:	73 4/04 Fknm 3m110y soft Ch

Burdens Boy
107
8-y-o b g Alflora (IRE)-Dalbeattie (Phardante (FR))
H D Daly Furrows Ltd

Placings:36/1F/F   (3906)
2003/04: 19FGS,

	Starts	1st	2nd	3rd	Win & Pl
Hurdles	1	0	0	0	
Career Total	5	1	0	1	4543
107 10/01 Towc	2m		D Hdl		SFT £4290

Total win prize-money £4290

Going:	Sf: 0-0 GS: 0-1 Gd: 0-0 GF: - Fm: 0-0
Distance:	2m/2m3: 0-0 2m4-2m7: 0-1 3m+: 0-0
Track:	LH: 0-0 RH: 0-1 Tight: 0-1 Gall: 0-0
Aids:	Bl: 0-0 Vi: 0-0 Tstrap: 0-0 Ckp: 0-0
Best Rating:	107 2/04 Tntn 2m3f110y gd-sft Hdl

Burdens Girl
109   100+
7-y-o ch m Alflora (IRE)-Dalbeattie (Phardante (FR))
H D Daly Furrows Ltd

Placings:44/00-P2611   (4651)
2003/04: 19PGS, 212GF, 216G, 171G, 171G,

	Starts	1st	2nd	3rd	Win & Pl
Hurdles	5	2	1	0	16142
Career Total	9	2	1	0	16142
106 4/04 Hrfd	2m1f		D(0-115)HHdl	GD	£10491
95 3/04 Tntn	2m1f		F(0-95)HHdl	GD	£4387

Total win prize-money £14879

Going:	Sf: 0-0 GS: 0-1 Gd: 2-3 GF: - Fm: 0-1
Distance:	2m/2m3: 2-2 2m4-2m7: 0-3 3m+: 0-0
Track:	LH: 0-0 RH: 2-5 Tight: 1-1 Gall: 0-0
Aids:	Bl: 0-0 Vi: 0-0 Tstrap: 0-0 Ckp: 0-0
Best Rating:	106 4/04 Hrfd 2m1f good Hdl

Plating -class novice hurdler; stays 2m 5f but effective at shorter; acts best on a sound surface.

Burley Don Carlos

8-y-o b g Neltino-Burley Bianca (Kinglet)
D Pipe Mrs Henry Llewellyn

Placings:U   (4675)
2003/04: 25UG,

	Starts	1st	2nd	3rd	Win & Pl
Chases	1	0	0	0	
Career Total	1	0	0	0	

Going:	Sf: 0-0 GS: 0-0 Gd: 0-1 GF: - Fm: 0-0
Distance:	2m/2m3: 0-0 2m4-2m7: 0-0 3m+: 0-1
Track:	LH: 0-0 RH: 0-1 Tight: 0-0 Gall: 0-0
Aids:	Bl: 0-0 Vi: 0-0 Tstrap: 0-0 Ckp: 0-0

Burning Gold

6-y-o b g Gildoran-Regan (USA) (Lear Fan (USA))
Mrs S D Williams William Peto

Placings:PP   (3146)
2003/04: 21PS, 19PS,

	Starts	1st	2nd	3rd	Win & Pl
Hurdles	2	0	0	0	
Career Total	2	0	0	0	

Going:	Sf: 0-2 GS: 0-0 Gd: 0-0 GF: - Fm: 0-0
Distance:	2m/2m3: 0-1 2m4-2m7: 0-1 3m+: 0-0
Track:	LH: 0-0 RH: 0-2 Tight: 0-0 Gall: 0-0
Aids:	Bl: 0-0 Vi: 0-0 Tstrap: 0-0 Ckp: 0-0

Burning Shore (IRE)
105   81
4-y-o b f Desert King (IRE)-Gerante (USA) (Private Account (USA))
Mrs L Wadham The Not Over Big Partnership

Placings:332253   (4777)
2003/04: 163GF, 163GF, 162G, 172G, 205G, 233G,

	Starts	1st	2nd	3rd	Win & Pl
Hurdles	6	0	2	3	4715
Career Total	6	0	2	3	4715

Going:	Sf: 0-0 GS: 0-0 Gd: 0-0 GF: - Fm: 0-2
Distance:	2m/2m3: 0-4 2m4-2m7: 0-1 3m+: 0-1
Track:	LH: 0-3 RH: 0-3 Tight: 0-4 Gall: 0-2
Aids:	Bl: 0-0 Vi: 0-0 Tstrap: 0-0 Ckp: 0-0
Best Rating:	81 4/04 Fknm 2m7f110y good Hdl

Plating-class hurdler; acts on good.

Burning Truth (USA)
108 (105h)   (115h)115
10-y-o ch g Known Fact (USA)-Galega (Sure Blade (USA))
M Sheppard G Jones

Placings:0/0/4512114-442223F221   (1589)
2003/04: 164G, 194G, 162GF, 162GF, 162GF, 173G, 16FGF, 162GF, 192GF, 201GF,

	Starts	1st	2nd	3rd	Win & Pl
Hurdles	2	0	0	0	706
Chases	8	1	5	1	11076
Career Total	19	4	6	1	28537
112 10/03 Ludl	2m4f		E Ch	G-F	£3347
115 4/03 Strf	2m110y		D(0-120)HHdl	G-F	£5512
104 10/02 Ludl	2m		D(0-120)HHdl	FRM	£6776
99 10/02 Hrfd	2m1f		E(0-100)HHdl	G-F	£3034

Total win prize-money £18671

Going:	Sf: 0-0 GS: 0-0 Gd: 0-3 GF: - Fm: 1-7
Distance:	2m/2m3: 0-8 2m4-2m7: 1-2 3m+: 0-0
Track:	LH: 0-4 RH: 1-6 Tight: 1-3 Gall: 0-0
Aids:	Bl: 0-0 Vi: 0-0 Tstrap: 0-0 Ckp: 0-0
Best Rating:	115 10/03 Hrfd 2m3f gd-fm Ch

Modest chaser; fair front-running hurdler; ended a frustrating run of seconds when winning a weakly contested 2m 4f beginners' chase at Ludlow October 2003; suited by fast ground; stays 2m 4f.

Burnt Copper (IRE)
84   78
4-y-o b g College Chapel-Try My Rosie (Try My Best (USA))
J R Best R Blake, B Blake, N webberley, R Sackett

Burning Gold (continued — right column)

Placings:35P5   (2764)
2003/04: 163GF, 16FGF, 17PG, 16FGS,

	Starts	1st	2nd	3rd	Win & Pl
Hurdles	4	0	0	1	921
Career Total	4	0	0	1	921

Going:	Sf: 0-0 GS: 0-1 Gd: 0-1 GF: - Fm: 0-2
Distance:	2m/2m3: 0-4 2m4-2m7: 0-0 3m+: 0-0
Track:	LH: 0-2 RH: 0-2 Tight: 0-3 Gall: 0-0
Aids:	Bl: 0-0 Vi: 0-0 Tstrap: 0-0 Ckp: 0-0
Best Rating:	78 12/03 Plum 2m gd-sft Hdl

Moderate juvenile hurdler; modest handicapper on the Flat, best on Polytrack.

Burundi (IRE)
104 (107h)   (120 h)115+
10-y-o b g Danehill (USA)-Sofala (Home Guard (USA))
A W Carroll R G Owens

Placings:1162/P40/223P436/1305F01205-23123224   (4562)
2003/04: 202GF, 203G, 171GS, 202G, 203G, 222G, 202G, 224G,

	Starts	1st	2nd	3rd	Win & Pl
Chases	8		1	4	2	16033
Career Total	32	5	8	5	40407
103 7/03 Strf	2m1f110yE Ch		G-S	£4732
120 2/03 Weth	2m4f110yD(0-125)HHdl		GD	£4940
120 5/02 Folk	2m1f110yE(0-110)HHdl		GD	£2968
120 12/98 Leic	2m		E Hdl	G-S	£2882
109 11/98 Leic	2m		E Hdl	SFT	£2903

Total win prize-money £18425

Going:	Sf: 0-0 GS: 1-1 Gd: 0-6 GF: - Fm: 0-1
Distance:	2m/2m3: 1-1 2m4-2m7: 0-7 3m+: 0-0
Track:	LH: 1-5 RH: 0-3 Tight: 1-2 Gall: 0-1
Aids:	Bl: 0-0 Vi: 0-0 Tstrap: 0-0 Ckp: 0-0
Best Rating:	120 3/03 Chep 2m4f good Hdl

Modest chaser; stays two and a half miles and suited by good ground; best when held up; has not always jumped fluently over fences and has twice been reported to have suffered from breathing problems; stays two mile six, but effective at shorter; acts on fast ground good and softer.

Burwood Breeze (IRE)
104   (100h)111
8-y-o b g Fresh Breeze (USA)-Shuil Le Cheile (Quayside)
T R George David & Lesley Byrne

Placings:544420/F5522-2F22O312   (4817)
2003/04: 242GF, 242G, 24FGS, 232S, 242G, 240S, 243G, 241GS, 242G,

	Starts	1st	2nd	3rd	Win & Pl
Chases	9	1	5	1	14797
Career Total	19	1	7	1	17922
105 3/04 Bang	3m110y D Ch		G-S	£5541

Total win prize-money £5541

Going:	Sf: 0-2 GS: 1-2 Gd: 0-4 GF: - Fm: 0-1
Distance:	2m/2m3: 0-0 2m4-2m7: 0-0 3m+: 1-9
Track:	LH: 1-3 RH: 0-6 Tight: 1-2 Gall: 0-3
Aids:	Bl: 0-0 Vi: 0-0 Tstrap: 0-0 Ckp: 0-0
Best Rating:	111 4/04 Chep 3m good Ch

Moderate chaser; finally broke his duck in 3m novice chase at Bangor March 2004; good effort when runner-up in Chepstow handicap next time; stays three miles; acts on good and good to soft ground.

Bus

(69h)   (54h)
9-y-o ch g Weld-Roaring Breeze (Roaring Riva)
Mrs L Williamson M Williamson

Placings:000P0/106F040/34F2-45   (1042)
2003/04: 17⁴GS, 16⁵GF,

	Starts	1st	2nd	3rd	Win & Pl
Chases	2	0	0	0	364
Career Total	18	1	1	1	3941
70 5/00 Hexm 2m		F(0-95)HHdl		GD	£1919

Total win prize-money £1919

Going:	Sf: 0-0 GS: 0-1 Gd: 0-0 GF: - Fm: 0-1
Distance:	2m/2m3: 0-2 2m4-2m7: 0-0 3m+: 0-0
Track:	LH: 0-2 RH: 0-0 Tight: 0-2 Gall: 0-0
Aids:	Bl: 0-0 Vi: 0-0 Tstrap: 0-0 Ckp: 0-0
Best Rating:	96 7/02 Strf 2m1f110y good Ch

Moderate hurdler, suited by fast ground.

Bush Hill Bandit (IRE)

9-y-o b/br g Executive Perk-Baby Isle (Menelek)
Mrs Anne-Marie Hays C J Hays

Placings:06/006/P/1-3055   (4779)
2003/04: 24³GF, 28⁰GS, 26⁵G, 24⁴S,

	Starts	1st	2nd	3rd	Win & Pl
Chases	4	0	0	1	312
Career Total	11	1	0	1	3190
94 4/03 Fknm 3m110y		H Ch		GD	£2878

Total win prize-money £2878

Going:	Sf: 0-1 GS: 0-1 Gd: 0-1 GF: - Fm: 0-1
Distance:	2m/2m3: 0-0 2m4-2m7: 0-0 3m+: 0-4
Track:	LH: 0-3 RH: 0-0 Tight: 0-4 Gall: 0-0
Aids:	Bl: 0-0 Vi: 0-0 Tstrap: 0-0 Ckp: 0-0
Best Rating:	94 4/04 Fknm 3m110y soft Ch

Modest pointer/hunter chaser; completed a hat-trick on hunter-chase debut at Fakenham in April 2003; stays three miles; best on a sound surface.

Bush Park (IRE)

109(103h)   (105h)123
9-y-o b g Be My Native (USA)-By All Means (Pitpan)
R H Alner H Wellstead

Placings:325/3503/0012312310/014B310F-5552221234PP
                                           (4195)
2003/04: 23⁵G, 24⁵S, 21⁵GF, 24²GF, 25²GF, 20²G, 19¹GS, 22²GF,
24³GS, 21⁴S, 21⁷G, 24⁶G,

	Starts	1st	2nd	3rd	Win & Pl
Hurdles	2	0	2	0	2280
Chases	10	1	2	1	10570
Career Total	37	6	7	7	44534
115 11/03 Chep 2m3f110yD(0-115)HCh		G-S	£4085
123 12/02 Plum 2m4f		D(0-125)HCh	HVY	£5362
117 10/02 Uttx 2m5f		D(0-125)HCh	G-F	£7800
105 3/02 Winc 2m		E(0-105)HHdl	SFT	£2730
112 11/01 Hrfd 2m3f		E(0-115)HCh	GD	£3435
101 10/01 Sthl 2m		F(0-100)HCh	GD	£2756

Total win prize-money £26169

Going:	Sf: 0-2 GS: 1-2 Gd: 0-4 GF: - Fm: 0-4
Distance:	2m/2m3: 0-0 2m4-2m7: 1-6 3m+: 0-6
Track:	LH: 1-7 RH: 0-4 Tight: 0-2 Gall: 0-3
Aids:	Bl: 0-1 Vi: 0-1 Tstrap: 1-2 Ckp: 0-0
Best Rating:	123 12/02 Plum 2m4f heavy Ch

Modest hurdler/chaser; stays three miles, but effective at shorter; handles good ground or softer; rarely runs a bad race.

Bushido (IRE)

107   119+
5-y-o br g Brief Truce (USA)-Pheopotstown (Henbit (USA))
Mrs S J Smith Mrs B Ramsden

Placings:0221213-602513P0   (4662)
2003/04: 17⁶G, 17⁰HY, 19²G, 16⁵S, 19¹GS, 19³S, 20⁴GS, 20⁰S,

	Starts	1st	2nd	3rd	Win & Pl
Hurdles	8	1	1	1	5695
Career Total	15	3	4	2	17280
122 1/04 Catt	2m3f	E(0-110)HHdl	G-S	£3563
104 3/03 Hexm	2m110y	F Hdl	GD	£3887
95 3/03 Carl	2m1f	F Hdl	G-S	£2660

Total win prize-money £10110

Going:	Sf: 0-4 GS: 1-2 Gd: 0-2 GF: - Fm: 0-0
Distance:	2m/2m3: 1-4 2m4-2m7: 0-0 3m+: 0-0
Track:	LH: 1-6 RH: 0-0 Tight: 1-2 Gall: 0-0
Aids:	Bl: 0-0 Vi: 0-0 Tstrap: 0-0 Ckp: 0-0
Best Rating:	122 1/04 Catt 2m3f gd-sft Hdl

Fair hurdler; acts on good and good to soft; stays two and a half miles.

Business Class (NZ)

101(90h)   (76h)107
12-y-o b g Accountant (NZ)-Fury's Princess (NZ) (Our Kungfu (NZ))
Mrs M Reveley Exors of the late E Fenwick

Placings:5531104/212F063P3-0024413325U52   (4961)
2003/04: 21⁰GF, 21⁹G, 16²G, 22⁴GF, 20⁴GF, 20¹F, 20³F, 20⁹GF,
24²GF, 22⁵G, 20⁵GS, 21⁵G, 20²GS,

	Starts	1st	2nd	3rd	Win & Pl
Hurdles	1	0	0	0	0
Chases	12	1	3	2	9571
Career Total	29	4	5	5	26106
106 11/03 Leic	2m4f110yF(0-100)HCh	FRM	£4240
106 6/02 MRas	2m6f110yF(0-100)HCh	G-F	£3526
105 4/02 Sedg	2m5f	D Ch	G-F	£3883
94 3/02 Catt	2m	D Ch	G-S	£4192

Total win prize-money £15843

Going:	Sf: 0-0 GS: 0-2 Gd: 0-4 GF: - Fm: 1-7
Distance:	2m/2m3: 0-2 2m4-2m7: 1-11 3m+: 0-1
Track:	LH: 0-6 RH: 1-7 Tight: 0-8 Gall: 0-0
Aids:	Bl: 0-0 Vi: 0-0 Tstrap: 0-0 Ckp: 0-1
Best Rating:	109 7/02 MRas 2m6f110y good Ch

Moderate chaser; effective over two and a half miles, but gets further; acts on a sound surface.

Business Traveller (IRE)

107   98+
4-y-o ch g Titus Livius (FR)-Dancing Venus (Pursuit Of Love)
R J Price (G A Swinbank 1/8) Karl and Patricia Reece

Placings:U05410   (4887)
2003/04: 16⁰S, 16⁹S, 16⁵G, 16⁴S, 19¹G, 22⁰GF,

	Starts	1st	2nd	3rd	Win & Pl
Hurdles	6	1	0	0	5358
Career Total	6	1	0	0	5358
98 3/04 Newb	2m3f	D(0-115)HHdl	GD	£5073

Total win prize-money £5073

Going:	Sf: 0-3 GS: 0-0 Gd: 1-2 GF: - Fm: 0-1

Distance:	2m/2m3: 1-5 2m4-2m7: 0-1 3m+: 0-0
Track:	LH: 1-5 RH: 0-1 Tight: 0-1 Gall: 1-1
Aids:	Bl: 0-0 Vi: 0-0 Tstrap: 0-0 Ckp: 0-0
Best Rating:	98 3/04 Newb 2m3f good Hdl

Moderate novice hurdler; yet to win a race of any sort.

Busman (IRE)

15-y-o ch g Be My Guest (USA)-Cistus (Sun Prince)
K R Pearce Mrs E K Jones

Placings:26/F312062120/35/2/1313/1515/446/P (0055)
2003/04: 25ᴾGS,

	Starts	1st	2nd	3rd	Win & Pl
Chases	1	0	0	0	
Career Total	27	6	5	4	13536
105 4/98 Asct	2m3f110yH Ch		GD	£2801
90 2/98 Ludl	2m4f	H Ch	GD	£1203
106 3/97 Font	2m3f	H Ch	G-F	£1562
103 5/96 Bang	3m110y	H Ch	SFT	£1658
88 12/93 Chep	2m4f110y	Hdl	SFT	£1702

Total win prize-money £8927

Going:	Sf: 0-0 GS: 0-1 Gd: 0-0 GF: - Fm: 0-0
Distance:	2m/2m3: 0-0 2m4-2m7: 0-0 3m+: 0-1
Track:	LH: 0-0 RH: 0-1 Tight: 0-0 Gall: 0-0
Aids:	Bl: 0-0 Vi: 0-0 Tstrap: 0-0 Ckp: 0-0
Best Rating:	106 3/97 Font 2m3f gd-fm Ch

Buster (IRE)

89   62
5-y-o ch g Presenting-Chez Georges (Welsh Saint)
M J Ryan Extraman Ltd, Duncan Sykes, Gary Waller

Placings:00P   (4588)
2003/04: 16⁵S, 16⁹G, 21ᴾG,

	Starts	1st	2nd	3rd	Win & Pl
NH Flat	1	0	0	0	0
Hurdles	2	0	0	0	0
Career Total	3	0	0	0	

Going:	Sf: 0-1 GS: 0-0 Gd: 0-2 GF: - Fm: 0-0
Distance:	2m/2m3: 0-2 2m4-2m7: 0-0 3m+: 0-0
Track:	LH: 0-0 RH: 0-3 Tight: 0-0 Gall: 0-3
Aids:	Bl: 0-0 Vi: 0-0 Tstrap: 0-0 Ckp: 0-0
Best Rating:	64 3/04 Hntg 2m110y good Hdl

Buster Buttons

12-y-o b g Lord Bud-Lady Buttons (New Brig)
R E Barr S G Jones

Placings:P   (0477)
2003/04: 26ᴾGS,

	Starts	1st	2nd	3rd	Win & Pl
Hurdles	1	0	0	0	
Career Total	1	0	0	0	

Going:	Sf: 0-0 GS: 0-1 Gd: 0-0 GF: - Fm: 0-0
Distance:	2m/2m3: 0-0 2m4-2m7: 0-0 3m+: 0-1
Track:	LH: 0-1 RH: 0-0 Tight: 0-1 Gall: 0-0
Aids:	Bl: 0-1 Vi: 0-1 Tstrap: 0-0 Ckp: 0-0

Buster Clyde (IRE)

7-y-o b g Bustomi-The Red Mare (Sagaro)

J R Bewley R Bewley

Placings:*0-0*   (1899)
2003/04: 20⁰GS,

	Starts	1st	2nd	3rd	Win & Pl
Hurdles	1	0	0	0	
Career Total	2	0	0	0	

Going:	Sf: 0-0 GS: 0-1 Gd: 0-0 GF: - Fm: 0-0
Distance:	2m/2m3: 0-0 2m4-2m7: 0-1 3m+: 0-0
Track:	LH: 0-0 RH: 0-1 Tight: 0-0 Gall: 0-0
Aids:	Bl: 0-0 Vi: 0-0 Tstrap: 0-0 Ckp: 0-0
Best Rating:	56 12/02 Newc 2m soft NHF

Bustisu

97   **79**

7-y-o b m Rakaposhi King-Tasmin Gayle (IRE) (Strong Gale)
D J Wintle John W Egan

Placings:*63-P003*   (4100)
2003/04: 16⁵S, 16⁰G, 16⁶GS, 21³G,

	Starts	1st	2nd	3rd	Win & Pl
Hurdles	4	0	0	1	541
Career Total	6	0	0	2	815

Going:	Sf: 0-1 GS: 0-1 Gd: 0-2 GF: - Fm: 0-0
Distance:	2m/2m3: 0-3 2m4-2m7: 0-1 3m+: 0-0
Track:	LH: 0-2 RH: 0-2 Tight: 0-1 Gall: 0-0
Aids:	Bl: 0-0 Vi: 0-0 Tstrap: 0-0 Ckp: 0-0
Best Rating:	82 12/02 Folk 2m1f110y heavy NHF

Bustling Rio (IRE)

98   (109c)**123**

8-y-o b g Up And At 'Em-Une Venitienne (FR) (Green Dancer (USA))
P C Haslam Rio Stainless Engineering Limited

Placings:*111/14120/0-006*   (4275)
2003/04: 20⁰GS, 19⁰G, 20⁶G,

	Starts	1st	2nd	3rd	Win & Pl
Hurdles	3			0	
Career Total	12	5	1	0	17751
99	3/02	Hntg	2m4f110yE Ch		G-F	£3035
99	11/01	Newc	2m4f	E Ch	G-S	£3168
124	1/01	Weth	2m7f	E Hdl	HVY	£2660
120	10/00	Aint	2m4f	E Hdl	GD	£3120
113	10/00	MRas	2m3f110yE Hdl		GD	£2912
			Total win prize-money £14897

Going:	Sf: 0-0 GS: 0-1 Gd: 0-2 GF: - Fm: 0-0
Distance:	2m/2m3: 0-0 2m4-2m7: 0-3 3m+: 0-0
Track:	LH: 0-2 RH: 0-1 Tight: 0-0 Gall: 0-0
Aids:	Bl: 0-0 Vi: 0-0 Tstrap: 0-0 Ckp: 0-0
Best Rating:	124 1/01 Weth 2m7f heavy Hdl

Fair hurdler/chaser; winner on the Flat on both turf and sand; very versatile; probably best over trips of around two and a half miles though does stay further; acts on any ground.

Bustyerbubble

4-y-o b f Sri Pekan (USA)-South Sea Bubble (IRE) (Bustino)
C N Kellett Miss E J Redford

Placings:*P*   (2226)
2003/04: 16⁶GS,

	Starts	1st	2nd	3rd	Win & Pl
Hurdles	1	0	0	0	

Career Total   1   0   0   0

Going:	Sf: 0-0 GS: 0-1 Gd: 0-0 GF: - Fm: 0-0
Distance:	2m/2m3: 0-1 2m4-2m7: 0-0 3m+: 0-0
Track:	LH: 0-0 RH: 0-1 Tight: 0-0 Gall: 0-0
Aids:	Bl: 0-0 Vi: 0-0 Tstrap: 0-0 Ckp: 0-0

Butleigh Rose

9-y-o ch m Nicholas Bill-Mistress McKenzie (Deep Run)
Miss N Stephens N Searle and R Napper

Placings:*0FP/P/F*   (0249)
2003/04: 19⁶GF,

	Starts	1st	2nd	3rd	Win & Pl
Chases	1	0	0	0	
Career Total	5	0	0	0	

Going:	Sf: 0-0 GS: 0-0 Gd: 0-0 GF: - Fm: 0-1
Distance:	2m/2m3: 0-0 2m4-2m7: 0-1 3m+: 0-0
Track:	LH: 0-0 RH: 0-1 Tight: 0-0 Gall: 0-0
Aids:	Bl: 0-0 Vi: 0-0 Tstrap: 0-0 Ckp: 0-0

Buttress

104f   **95+f**

5-y-o b h Zamindar (USA)-Furnish (Green Desert (USA))
M W Easterby G H Sparkes

Placings:*320*   (4517)
2003/04: 16³G, 16²GF, 16⁶GS,

	Starts	1st	2nd	3rd	Win & Pl
NH Flat	3	0	1	1	860
Career Total	3	0	1	1	860

Going:	Sf: 0-0 GS: 0-1 Gd: 0-1 GF: - Fm: 0-1
Distance:	2m/2m3: 0-3 2m4-2m7: 0-0 3m+: 0-0
Track:	LH: 0-3 RH: 0-0 Tight: 0-1 Gall: 0-0
Aids:	Bl: 0-0 Vi: 0-0 Tstrap: 0-0 Ckp: 0-0
Best Rating:	95 3/04 Catt 2m gd-fm NHF

Travelled strongly but just held in bumper at Catterick in March on second outing.

Buz Kiri (USA)

97   **83**

6-y-o b g Gulch (USA)-Whitecorners (USA) (Caro)
A W Carroll Serafino Agodino

Placings:*0-44002220*   (2710)
2003/04: 20⁴G, 20⁴GF, 24⁰GF, 16⁰G, 16²GS, 16²GS, 16²GS, 16⁶GS,

	Starts	1st	2nd	3rd	Win & Pl
Hurdles	8	0	3	0	1806
Career Total	9	0	3	0	1806

Going:	Sf: 0-0 GS: 0-1 Gd: 0-5 GF: - Fm: 0-2
Distance:	2m/2m3: 0-5 2m4-2m7: 0-2 3m+: 0-1
Track:	LH: 0-6 RH: 0-2 Tight: 0-3 Gall: 0-2
Aids:	Bl: 0-0 Vi: 0-0 Tstrap: 0-0 Ckp: 0-0
Best Rating:	83 11/03 Fknm 2m good Hdl

Plating-class hurdler; stays two miles four; effective on good ground; has worn tongue tie.

Buzybakson (IRE)

108(97h)   (102+h)**107**

7-y-o b/br g Bob Back (USA)-Middle Verde (USA) (Sham (USA))

J R Cornwall J R Cornwall

Placings:*06F13-P54P0254P*   (4642)
2003/04: 17⁶GF, 20⁵GS, 20⁴GS, 24⁶GS, 20⁶G, 24²S, 24⁵G, 25⁴GS, 25⁶G,

	Starts	1st	2nd	3rd	Win & Pl
Hurdles	1	0	0	0	
Chases	8	0	1	0	4279
Career Total	14	1	1	1	7757
102	12/02	MRas	2m3f110yF Hdl		G-S	£2964
			Total win prize-money £2965

Going:	Sf: 0-1 GS: 0-4 Gd: 0-3 GF: - Fm: 0-1
Distance:	2m/2m3: 0-1 2m4-2m7: 0-3 3m+: 0-5
Track:	LH: 0-4 RH: 0-5 Tight: 0-4 Gall: 0-2
Aids:	Bl: 0-0 Vi: 0-0 Tstrap: 0-0 Ckp: 0-0
Best Rating:	107 2/04 Hntg 3m soft Ch

Moderate hurdler/novice chaser; acts on soft ground.

By Definition (IRE)

85   **44**

6-y-o gr m Definite Article-Miss Goodbody (Castle Keep)
J C Tuck (J M Bradley 13/9) Paul & Ann de Weck

Placings:*P0P-P000*   (2952)
2003/04: 16⁶GF, 16⁰GF, 16⁰GF, 16⁰G,

	Starts	1st	2nd	3rd	Win & Pl
Hurdles	4	0	0	0	
Career Total	7	0	0	0	

Going:	Sf: 0-0 GS: 0-0 Gd: 0-1 GF: - Fm: 0-3
Distance:	2m/2m3: 0-4 2m4-2m7: 0-0 3m+: 0-0
Track:	LH: 0-2 RH: 0-2 Tight: 0-0 Gall: 0-0
Aids:	Bl: 0-0 Vi: 0-0 Tstrap: 0-0 Ckp: 0-0
Best Rating:	44 12/03 Winc 2m good Hdl

Bygone

96f   **89f**

6-y-o b g Past Glories-Meltonby (Sayf El Arab (USA))
J Hetherton N Hetherton

Placings:*2-60*   (4962)
2003/04: 17⁶GS, 17⁰G,

	Starts	1st	2nd	3rd	Win & Pl
NH Flat	2	0	0	0	0
Career Total	3	0	1	0	526

Going:	Sf: 0-0 GS: 0-1 Gd: 0-1 GF: - Fm: 0-0
Distance:	2m/2m3: 0-2 2m4-2m7: 0-0 3m+: 0-0
Track:	LH: 0-1 RH: 0-1 Tight: 0-2 Gall: 0-0
Aids:	Bl: 0-0 Vi: 0-0 Tstrap: 0-0 Ckp: 0-0
Best Rating:	89 4/04 MRas 2m1f110y good NHF

Byron Lamb

106   (122h)**136+**

7-y-o b g Rambo Dancer (CAN)-Caroline Lamb (Hotfoot)
N G Richards Edward Melville

Placings:*f3111/12121-24UP*   (4399)
2003/04: 16²G, 19⁴GS, 20⁴HY, 20⁰G,

	Starts	1st	2nd	3rd	Win & Pl
Chases	4	0	0	0	3363
Career Total	14	7	3	1	32527
134	3/03	Hexm	2m110y	E Ch	GD	£3880
121	1/03	Ayr	2m	D Ch	HVY	£5453
122	12/02	Ayr	2m	D Ch	G-S	£4914
113	3/02	Carl	2m1f	E Hdl	G-S	£3094
122	3/02	Ayr	2m	D Hdl	SFT	£3465

112	3/02	Ayr	2m	F Hdl		HVY	£2478
112	11/01	Ayr	2m	H NHF		G-S	£1788
				Total win prize-money £25075			

Going:	Sf: 0-1 GS: 0-1 Gd: 0-2 GF: - Fm: 0-0
Distance:	2m/2m3: 0-1 2m4-2m7: 0-3 3m+: 0-0
Track:	LH: 0-3 RH: 0-1 Tight: 0-0 Gall: 0-1
Aids:	Bl: 0-0 Vi: 0-0 Tstrap: 0-0 Ckp: 0-0
Best Rating:	136 1/04 Asct 2m3f110y gd-sft Ch

Useful chaser; formerly decent novice hurdler; has a fine record at Ayr; adequate rather than neat jumper; best over two miles, but stays further; suited by cut in the ground.

Bywell Beau (IRE)
88f   84f

5-y-o b g Lord Americo-Early Dalus (IRE) (Mandalus)
J I A Charlton W F Trueman

Placings:43	(4952)
2003/04: 16⁴G, 16³GS,	

	Starts	1st	2nd	3rd	Win & Pl
NH Flat	2	0	0	1	492
Career Total	2	0	0	1	492

Going:	Sf: 0-0 GS: 0-1 Gd: 0-1 GF: - Fm: 0-0
Distance:	2m/2m3: 0-2 2m4-2m7: 0-0 3m+: 0-0
Track:	LH: 0-0 RH: 0-2 Tight: 0-0 Gall: 0-1
Aids:	Bl: 0-0 Vi: 0-0 Tstrap: 0-0 Ckp: 0-0
Best Rating:	84 4/04 Prth 2m110y gd-sft NHF

Half-brother to useful staying chaser Rugged River; has shaped quite well on both starts in bumpers; acts on good and easy ground; should win a small race.

Ca Na Trona (IRE)
102   98+

5-y-o b g Accordion-Sterna Star (Corvaro (USA))
N J Henderson Lady Lloyd-Webber

Placings:0540	(4561)
2003/04: 16⁰GS, 16⁵G, 21⁴G, 24⁰GS,	

	Starts	1st	2nd	3rd	Win & Pl
NH Flat	1	0	0	0	0
Hurdles	3	0	0	0	466
Career Total	4	0	0	0	466

Going:	Sf: 0-0 GS: 0-2 Gd: 0-2 GF: - Fm: 0-0
Distance:	2m/2m3: 0-2 2m4-2m7: 0-1 3m+: 0-1
Track:	LH: 0-3 RH: 0-1 Tight: 0-0 Gall: 0-3
Aids:	Bl: 0-0 Vi: 0-0 Tstrap: 0-0 Ckp: 0-0
Best Rating:	99 3/04 Newb 2m5f good Hdl

Moderate hurdler; half-brother to high-class hurdler Hardy Eustace; ran green on debut in hot bumper at Newbury in December; held over hurdles.

Ca Ne Fait Rien (IRE)

8-y-o gr g Denel (FR)-Fairytale-Ending (Sweet Story)
N M Babbage B & M Babbage & Co Ltd

Placings:04/4-0	(1618)
2003/04: 20⁰G,	

	Starts	1st	2nd	3rd	Win & Pl
Hurdles	1	0	0	0	
Career Total	4	0	0	0	0

Going:	Sf: 0-0 GS: 0-0 Gd: 0-1 GF: - Fm: 0-0
Distance:	2m/2m3: 0-0 2m4-2m7: 0-1 3m+: 0-0
Track:	LH: 0-1 RH: 0-0 Tight: 0-1 Gall: 0-0
Aids:	Bl: 0-0 Vi: 0-0 Tstrap: 0-0 Ckp: 0-0
Best Rating:	85 5/02 Worc 2m gd-fm NHF

Caballe (USA)
71

7-y-o ch m Opening Verse (USA)-Attirance (FR) (Crowned Prince (USA))
Dr P Pritchard B S Hicks

Placings:133350/14050005-0	(0333)
2003/04: 21⁰GF,	

	Starts	1st	2nd	3rd	Win & Pl
Hurdles	1	0	0	0	
Career Total	15	2	0	3	7781
106	11/02	Hntg	2m110y	D(0-115)HHdl		G-S	£4075
114	12/01	Plum	2m	E Hdl		SFT	£2492
			Total win prize-money £6568				

Going:	Sf: 0-0 GS: 0-0 Gd: 0-0 GF: - Fm: 0-1
Distance:	2m/2m3: 0-2 2m4-2m7: 0-1 3m+: 0-0
Track:	LH: 0-1 RH: 0-0 Tight: 0-0 Gall: 0-0
Aids:	Bl: 0-0 Vi: 0-0 Tstrap: 0-0 Ckp: 0-0
Best Rating:	114 12/01 Bang 2m1f gd-sft Hdl

Modest handicap hurdler at her best;. effective over two miles and acts on a soft surface.

Cabaret Quest
(96h)   (62h)

8-y-o ch g Pursuit Of Love-Cabaret Artiste (Shareef Dancer (USA))
R C Guest Miss S Howell

Placings:0P40F0/FP-06F	(0762)
2003/04: 16⁰GF, 16⁶G, 16⁶G,	

	Starts	1st	2nd	3rd	Win & Pl
Hurdles	1	0	0	0	0
Chases	2	0	0	0	0
Career Total	11	0	0	0	0

Going:	Sf: 0-0 GS: 0-0 Gd: 0-2 GF: - Fm: 0-1
Distance:	2m/2m3: 0-3 2m4-2m7: 0-0 3m+: 0-0
Track:	LH: 0-2 RH: 0-1 Tight: 0-1 Gall: 0-0
Aids:	Bl: 0-0 Vi: 0-0 Tstrap: 0-1 Ckp: 0-1
Best Rating:	68 9/01 Worc 2m gd-fm Hdl

Caber (IRE)
90   65

4-y-o b g Celtic Swing-Arusha (IRE) (Dance Of Life (USA))
O Sherwood Raymond Tooth

Placings:02	(4918)
2003/04: 16⁰G, 20²GS,	

	Starts	1st	2nd	3rd	Win & Pl
NH Flat	1	0	0	0	0
Hurdles	1	0	1	0	938
Career Total	2	0	1	0	938

Going:	Sf: 0-0 GS: 0-1 Gd: 0-1 GF: - Fm: 0-0
Distance:	2m/2m3: 0-1 2m4-2m7: 0-1 3m+: 0-0
Track:	LH: 0-1 RH: 0-1 Tight: 0-0 Gall: 0-0
Aids:	Bl: 0-0 Vi: 0-0 Tstrap: 0-0 Ckp: 0-0
Best Rating:	65 4/04 Worc 2m4f gd-sft Hdl

Runner-up in weak novice hurdle in April; probably stays 2m 4f.

Cabille (FR)

12-y-o ch g Lesotho (USA)-Ironique (FR) (Riverman (USA))
H H G Owen H H G Owen

Placings:/023P/0P40/PU-PPPP	(0836)
2003/04: 23⁰GS, 22⁰G, 20⁰GF, 23⁰GF,	

	Starts	1st	2nd	3rd	Win & Pl
Hurdles	2	0	0	0	0
Chases	2	0	0	0	0
Career Total	14	0	1	1	1788

Going:	Sf: 0-0 GS: 0-1 Gd: 0-1 GF: - Fm: 0-2
Distance:	2m/2m3: 0-0 2m4-2m7: 0-2 3m+: 0-2
Track:	LH: 0-4 RH: 0-0 Tight: 0-1 Gall: 0-0
Aids:	Bl: 0-2 Vi: 0-0 Tstrap: 0-0 Ckp: 0-2
Best Rating:	94 3/98 Donc 2m10y soft Ch

Cadrillon (FR)

14-y-o br g Le Pontet (FR)-Jenvraie (FR) (Night And Day)
Miss J E Foster Yorkshire Point-to-Point Club

Placings:4000F4/0/13P45326P0/54P4545443P/6464P2550 P0P/PP/52P-3	(0389)
2003/04: 25³G,	

	Starts	1st	2nd	3rd	Win & Pl
Chases	1	0	0	1	536
Career Total	46	1	3	4	9681
93	5/98	Hexm	3m1f			G-S	£2583
			Total win prize-money £2583				

Going:	Sf: 0-0 GS: 0-0 Gd: 0-1 GF: - Fm: 0-0
Distance:	2m/2m3: 0-0 2m4-2m7: 0-0 3m+: 0-1
Track:	LH: 0-1 RH: 0-0 Tight: 0-0 Gall: 0-0
Aids:	Bl: 0-0 Vi: 0-0 Tstrap: 0-0 Ckp: 0-1
Best Rating:	93 5/98 Hexm 3m1f gd-sft Ch

Plating-class chaser but better pointer; stays really well.

Caesar's Palace (GER)
107   106

7-y-o ch g Lomitas-Caraveine (FR) (Nikos)
Miss Lucinda V Russell Peter J S Russell

Placings:111156/25000P4410/1231626024-450423333262	(4948)
2003/04: 24⁴G, 22⁵GS, 20⁰GF, 24⁴G, 24²GF, 24³G, 24³HY, 24³GS, 22²GF, 24⁶HY, 27²GS,	

	Starts	1st	2nd	3rd	Win & Pl
Hurdles	12	0	3	4	8043
Career Total	38	7	5	8	41401
96	8/02	Strf	2m6f110yF Hdl		G-S	£3073
127	5/02	Chep	3m	E(0-115)HHdl	G-F	£2681
125	4/02	Extr	3m110y	D(0-120)HHdl	FRM	£5401
124	12/00	Chel	2m1f	B Hdl	SFT	£7150
119	11/00	Newb	2m110y	D Hdl	SFT	£3887
119	9/00	Plum	2m	E Hdl	G-F	£2352
105	8/00	Font	2m2f110yE Hdl		G-F	£2254
			Total win prize-money £26799				

Going:	Sf: 0-2 GS: 0-3 Gd: 0-4 GF: - Fm: 0-3
Distance:	2m/2m3: 0-0 2m4-2m7: 0-3 3m+: 0-9
Track:	LH: 0-7 RH: 0-4 Tight: 0-2 Gall: 0-3
Aids:	Bl: 0-0 Vi: 0-0 Tstrap: 0-0 Ckp: 0-3
Best Rating:	127 5/02 Chep 3m gd-fm Hdl

Moderate hurdler; prolific novice hurdle winner for Martin Pipe in 2000; has not won since leaving the champion in 2002; stays three miles; acts on any ground; at his best

when making the running; has worn a visor, blinkers or cheekpieces.

Caesarean Hunter (USA)

81   **63**

5-y-o ch g Jade Hunter (USA)-Grey Fay (USA) (Grey Dawn Ii)
R T Phillips (S Kirk 1/10) A A Wickham

Placings:000   (4793)
2003/04: 17⁰GS, 16⁰G, 16⁰G,

	Starts	1st	2nd	3rd	Win & Pl
Hurdles	3	0	0	0	
Career Total	3	0	0	0	

Going: Sf: 0-0 GS: 0-1 Gd: 0-2 GF: - Fm: 0-0
Distance: 2m/2m3: 0-3 2m4-2m7: 0-0 3m+: 0-0
Track: LH: 0-2 RH: 0-1 Tight: 0-3 Gall: 0-0
Aids: Bl: 0-0 Vi: 0-0 Tstrap: 0-0 Ckp: 0-0
Best Rating: 63 2/04 Folk 2m1f110y gd-sft Hdl

Caged Tiger

85f   **91f**

5-y-o b g Classic Cliche (IRE)-Run Tiger (IRE) (Commanche Run)
T P Tate T P Tate

Placings:4   (4277)
2003/04: 17⁴G,

	Starts	1st	2nd	3rd	Win & Pl
NH Flat	1	0	0	0	0
Career Total	1	0	0	0	0

Going: Sf: 0-0 GS: 0-0 Gd: 0-1 GF: - Fm: 0-0
Distance: 2m/2m3: 0-1 2m4-2m7: 0-0 3m+: 0-0
Track: LH: 0-0 RH: 0-0 Tight: 0-0 Gall: 0-0
Aids: Bl: 0-0 Vi: 0-0 Tstrap: 0-0 Ckp: 0-0
Best Rating: 91 3/04 Carl 2m1f good NHF

Caher Society (IRE)

12-y-o ch g Moscow Society (USA)-Dame's Delight (Ballymoss)
Paul Morris Roy Swinburne

Placings:0/05/P33P0P/35F/261P/40-5U33   (4655)
2003/04: 24⁵GS, 24⁴G, 20⁵GS, 16⁴G,

	Starts	1st	2nd	3rd	Win & Pl
Chases	4	0	0	2	762
Career Total	22	1	1	5	6084
106 3/02 Ludl	2m4f		H Ch	SFT	£2786

Total win prize-money £2786

Going: Sf: 0-0 GS: 0-1 Gd: 0-3 GF: - Fm: 0-0
Distance: 2m/2m3: 0-1 2m4-2m7: 0-0 3m+: 0-2
Track: LH: 0-1 RH: 0-3 Tight: 0-3 Gall: 0-0
Aids: Bl: 0-0 Vi: 0-0 Tstrap: 0-0 Ckp: 0-0
Best Rating: 106 3/02 Ludl 2m4f soft Ch

Modest pointer/hunter chaser.

Caitland

80   **40**

5-y-o b m Puissance-Lorlanne (Bustino)
R Allan David Doughty

Placings:0   (1431)
2003/04: 16⁰G,

	Starts	1st	2nd	3rd	Win & Pl
Hurdles	1	0	0	0	
Career Total	1	0	0	0	

Going: Sf: 0-0 GS: 0-0 Gd: 0-1 GF: - Fm: 0-0
Distance: 2m/2m3: 0-1 2m4-2m7: 0-0 3m-: 0-0
Track: LH: 0-0 RH: 0-1 Tight: 0-0 Gall: 0-0
Aids: Bl: 0-0 Vi: 0-0 Tstrap: 0-0 Ckp: 0-0
Best Rating: 42 9/03 Prth 2m110y good Hdl

Caitriona's Choice (IRE)

107   **116**

13-y-o b g Carmelite House (USA)-Muligatawny (Malacate (USA))
P Monteith The Dregs Of Humanity

Placings:165322/0223162316/06/0604022/512/B0/6453B6 04/16062P0-512254P23P060P   (4458)
2003/04: 16⁵G, 16¹GS, 17²GS, 16²GF, 16⁵G, 17⁴G, 16⁹G, 18²G, 16³S, 16⁸S, 17⁰S, 16⁸HY, 16⁹G, 16⁸HY,

	Starts	1st	2nd	3rd	Win & Pl
Chases	14	1	3	1	14536
Career Total	59	6	12	5	49447
116 5/03 Prth	2m	C(0-135)HCh	G-S	£8011
109 6/02 Navn	2m1f	(0-116)HCh	SH	£6773
96 7/99 Gway	2m1f	Ch	G-F	£4910
123 1/97 Punc	2m	(0-116)HHdl	YLD	£3051
110 10/96 Rosc	2m	Hdl	YLD	£4237
116 5/95 Baln	2m	NHF	GD	£2204

Total win prize-money £29188

Going: Sf: 0-5 GS: 1-2 Gd: 0-6 GF: - Fm: 0-1
Distance: 2m/2m3: 1-14 2m4-2m7: 0-0 3m+: 0-0
Track: LH: 0-10 RH: 1-4 Tight: 0-4 Gall: 0-1
Aids: Bl: 0-0 Vi: 0-0 Tstrap: 0-0 Ckp: 0-0
Best Rating: 123 1/97 Punc 2m yield Hdl

Modest chaser, formerly trained in Ireland; has won on fast ground and with cut; suited by two miles.

Cake It Easy (IRE)

92   **91**

4-y-o ch f Kendor (FR)-Diese Memory (USA) (Diesis)
Mrs M Reveley (M Johnston 3/7) Lightbody Celebration Cakes Ltd

Placings:0   (4863)
2003/04: 16⁰S,

	Starts	1st	2nd	3rd	Win & Pl
Hurdles	1	0	0	0	
Career Total	1	0	0	0	

Going: Sf: 0-1 GS: 0-0 Gd: 0-0 GF: - Fm: 0-0
Distance: 2m/2m3: 0-1 2m4-2m7: 0-0 3m+: 0-0
Track: LH: 0-1 RH: 0-0 Tight: 0-1 Gall: 0-0
Aids: Bl: 0-0 Vi: 0-0 Tstrap: 0-0 Ckp: 0-0
Best Rating: 91 4/04 Ayr 2m soft Hdl

Cal Mac

83   **89+**

5-y-o b g Botanic (USA)-Shifting Mist (Night Shift (USA))
John G Carr (H Morrison 25/10) W Hennessy

Placings:00B03   (4958)
2003/04: 16⁶S, 16⁰S, 16⁸Y, 20⁰S, 17³G,

	Starts	1st	2nd	3rd	Win & Pl
Hurdles	5	0	0	1	339
Career Total	5	0	0	1	339

Going: Sf: 0-3 GS: 0-0 Gd: 0-1 GF: - Fm: 0-0
Distance: 2m/2m3: 0-4 2m4-2m7: 0-1 3m+: 0-0
Track: LH: 0-2 RH: 0-3 Tight: 0-1 Gall: 0-0
Aids: Bl: 0-0 Vi: 0-0 Tstrap: 0-0 Ckp: 0-0
Best Rating: 89 4/04 MRas 2m1f110y good Hdl

Calamint

    19

5-y-o gr g Kaldoun (FR)-Coigach (Niniski (USA))
K C Bailey Sootys Racing Club

Placings:00P-P   (0057)
2003/04: 17⁰GS,

	Starts	1st	2nd	3rd	Win & Pl
Hurdles	1	0	0	0	
Career Total	4	0	0	0	

Going: Sf: 0-0 GS: 0-1 Gd: 0-0 GF: - Fm: 0-0
Distance: 2m/2m3: 0-1 2m4-2m7: 0-0 3m+: 0-0
Track: LH: 0-0 RH: 0-1 Tight: 0-0 Gall: 0-0
Aids: Bl: 0-0 Vi: 0-0 Tstrap: 0-0 Ckp: 0-0
Best Rating: 19 12/02 Wwck 2m soft Hdl

Calamintha

108   **111+**

4-y-o b f Mtoto-Calendula (Be My Guest (USA))
M C Pipe (R M Beckett 29/10) David Jenks

Placings:1210F   (4368)
2003/04: 17¹G, 18²G, 16¹S, 22⁰G, 16⁶GF,

	Starts	1st	2nd	3rd	Win & Pl
Hurdles	5	2	1	0	7601
Career Total	5	2	1	0	7601
112 1/04 Leic	2m	E Hdl	SFT	£3575
108 11/03 Bang	2m1f	E Hdl	GD	£3276

Total win prize-money £6851

Going: Sf: 1-1 GS: 0-0 Gd: 1-3 GF: - Fm: 0-1
Distance: 2m/2m3: 2-4 2m4-2m7: 0-1 3m+: 0-0
Track: LH: 1-3 RH: 1-2 Tight: 1-4 Gall: 0-0
Aids: Bl: 0-0 Vi: 1-3 Tstrap: 0-0 Ckp: 0-0
Best Rating: 112 1/04 Leic 2m soft Hdl

Fair hurdler; successful on her hurdling debut; beaten next time when saddle slipped, but bounced back to win easily at Leicester; best at around two miles; prefers testing ground.

Calatagan (IRE)

106   **119+**

5-y-o ch g Danzig Connection (USA)-Calachuchi (Martinmas)
J M Jefferson Mr & Mrs J M Davenport

Placings:1F-130661   (4372)
2003/04: 17¹GF, 17³GS, 16⁰S, 16⁶G, 16⁶G, 16¹GF,

	Starts	1st	2nd	3rd	Win & Pl
Hurdles	6	2	0	1	12328
Career Total	8	3	0	1	16163
122 3/04 Strf	2m110y	D(0-125)HHdl	G-F	£8482
116 11/03 Sedg	2m1f	E(0-110)HHdl	G-F	£3318
114 12/02 Catt	2m	D Hdl	G-S	£3835

Total win prize-money £15636

Going: Sf: 0-1 GS: 0-1 Gd: 0-2 GF: - Fm: 2-2
Distance: 2m/2m3: 2-6 2m4-2m7: 0-0 3m+: 0-0

Track: LH: 2-4 RH: 0-2 **Tight:** 2-5 Gall: 0-0
Aids: Bl: 0-0 Vi: 0-0 Tstrap: 0-0 Ckp: 0-0
Best Rating: 122 3/04 Strf 2m110y gd-fm Hdl

Fair hurdler; suited by two miles and fast ground.

Calcot Flyer
102   89
6-y-o br g Anshan-Lady Catcher (Free Boy)
A King Miss J M Bodycote

Placings: 00-450   (3810)
2003/04: 22⁴S, 26⁵G, 24⁰G,

	Starts	1st	2nd	3rd	Win & Pl
Hurdles	3	0	0	0	281
Career Total	5	0	0	0	281

Going: Sf: 0-1 GS: 0-0 Gd: 0-2 GF: - Fm: 0-0
Distance: 2m/2m3: 0-0 2m4-2m7: 0-1 3m+: 0-2
Track: LH: 0-2 RH: 0-1 Tight: 0-0 Gall: 0-0
Aids: Bl: 0-0 Vi: 0-0 Tstrap: 0-0 Ckp: 0-0
Best Rating: 92 1/03 Hayd 2m gd-sft NHF

Caldamus

12-y-o gr g Scallywag-Portodamus (Porto Bello)
Miss S Waugh Miss R D Elliott

Placings: 465/3514/B46/P2/1-P   (4289)
2003/04: 25ᴾGF,

	Starts	1st	2nd	3rd	Win & Pl
Chases	1	0	0	0	
Career Total	14	2	1	1	5609
99 3/03 Winc 3m1f110yH Ch				SFT	£1456
110 2/99 Sedg 2m5f110yE Hdl				GD	£2582
Total win prize-money £4039					

Going: Sf: 0-0 GS: 0-0 Gd: 0-0 GF: - Fm: 0-1
Distance: 2m/2m3: 0-0 2m4-2m7: 0-0 3m+: 0-1
Track: LH: 0-0 RH: 0-1 Tight: 0-0 Gall: 0-0
Aids: Bl: 0-0 Vi: 0-0 Tstrap: 0-0 Ckp: 0-0
Best Rating: 110 2/99 Sedg 2m5f110y good Hdl

Fair form in point-to-points and hunter chases; effective from 2m 4f to 3m; handles soft ground, but best on good.

Calder River
87   102
6-y-o b m Alderbrook-Calametta (Oats)
Mrs Sandra McCarthy Mrs Sandra McCarthy

Placings: B-3056660F   (3974a)
2003/04: 16⁸GY, 17³G, 20⁹GF, 17⁵G, 16⁶GY, 16⁸Y, 24⁸Y, 20⁰Y, 24ᶠY,

	Starts	1st	2nd	3rd	Win & Pl
NH Flat	4	0	0	1	290
Hurdles	5	0	0	0	0
Career Total	9	0	0	1	290

Going: Sf: 0-0 GS: 0-0 Gd: 0-2 GF: - Fm: 0-1
Distance: 2m/2m3: 0-5 2m4-2m7: 0-2 3m+: 0-2
Track: LH: 0-4 RH: 0-1 Tight: 0-2 Gall: 0-0
Aids: Bl: 0-0 Vi: 0-0 Tstrap: 0-6 Ckp: 0-0
Best Rating: 102 12/03 Cork 3m yield Hdl

California Son (IRE)
88   78
8-y-o ch g Lycius (USA)-Madame Nureyev (USA) (Nureyev (USA))

Ms K Stenefeldt (C L Popham 18/10) Ch S Racing

Placings: 3033234   (4111)
2003/04: 16³G, 17⁰G, 19³G, 16³G, 17²G, 16³S, 16⁴GF,

	Starts	1st	2nd	3rd	Win & Pl
Hurdles	4	0	0	3	1660
Chases	3	0	1	1	1825
Career Total	7	0	1	4	3484

Going: Sf: 0-1 GS: 0-0 Gd: 0-5 GF: - Fm: 0-1
Distance: 2m/2m3: 0-7 2m4-2m7: 0-0 3m+: 0-0
Track: LH: 0-1 RH: 0-1 Tight: 0-0 Gall: 0-0
Aids: Bl: 0-0 Vi: 0-0 Tstrap: 0-0 Ckp: 0-0
Best Rating: 78 3/04 Leic 2m gd-fm Ch

Plating-class hurdler/chaser; well beaten third in novice chase at Wetherby in January; best suited by two miles.

Caliwag (IRE)
86   (74h) 98
8-y-o b g Lahib (USA)-Mitsubishi Style (Try My Best (USA))
Jamie Poulton Lottie Collins Partnership

Placings: 006/3-5344   (1697)
2003/04: 16⁵GF, 20³GF, 17⁴GF, 24⁴GF,

	Starts	1st	2nd	3rd	Win & Pl
Chases	4	0	0	1	1483
Career Total	8	0	0	2	2505

Going: Sf: 0-0 GS: 0-0 Gd: 0-0 GF: - Fm: 0-4
Distance: 2m/2m3: 0-2 2m4-2m7: 0-1 3m+: 0-0
Track: LH: 0-3 RH: 0-1 Tight: 0-3 Gall: 0-0
Aids: Bl: 0-1 Vi: 0-0 Tstrap: 0-2 Ckp: 0-0
Best Rating: 98 3/03 Sand 2m soft Ch

Moderate novice chaser; showed little in novice hurdles in 2000/1; outclassed in three starts over fences.

Call Me Jack (IRE)
89 (97h)   (94h) 103
8-y-o b g Lord Americo-Tawney Rose (Tarqogan)
J Hetherton R G Fell

Placings: 6/026521/431F/P3F24-4PFF3U2U5   (4957)
2003/04: 16⁴G, 16⁴GS, 16⁸S, 19ᶠG, 16ᶠG, 16³G, 16ᵁGF, 17²GS, 16ᵁS, 17⁵GS,

	Starts	1st	2nd	3rd	Win & Pl
Hurdles	1	0	0	0	264
Chases	9	0	1	1	2977
Career Total	25	2	4	3	13350
102 11/01 Sedg 2m1f E(0-115)HHdl			SFT	£2338	
97 4/01 Prth 2m110y D Hdl			HVY	£3332	
Total win prize-money £5670					

Going: Sf: 0-2 GS: 0-3 Gd: 0-4 GF: - Fm: 0-1
Distance: 2m/2m3: 0-0 2m4-2m7: 0-0 3m+: 0-0
Track: LH: 0-7 RH: 0-3 Tight: 0-4 Gall: 0-1
Aids: Bl: 0-0 Vi: 0-0 Tstrap: 0-7 Ckp: 0-0
Best Rating: 108 3/01 MRas 2m1f110y gd-sft Hdl

Modest hurdler/novice chaser; suited by two miles over hurdles in soft ground.

Call Me Sonic
(84h)   (92h) 74
8-y-o b g Henbit (USA)-Call-Me-Dinky (Mart Lane)
R H Alner C A Fuller

Placings: 0P45/3P5-P   (0183)
2003/04: 21ᴾGF,

	Starts	1st	2nd	3rd	Win & Pl
Chases	1	0	0	0	
Career Total	8	0	0	1	0

Call Of The Wild
71   73
4-y-o ch g Wolfhound (USA)-Biba (IRE) (Superlative)
R A Fahey Lets Go Racing 1

Placings: 6F   (3690)
2003/04: 16⁶S, 16⁷G,

	Starts	1st	2nd	3rd	Win & Pl
Hurdles	2	0	0	0	0
Career Total	2	0	0	0	0

Going: Sf: 0-1 GS: 0-0 Gd: 0-1 GF: - Fm: 0-0
Distance: 2m/2m3: 0-2 2m4-2m7: 0-0 3m+: 0-0
Track: LH: 0-2 RH: 0-0 Tight: 0-1 Gall: 0-1
Aids: Bl: 0-0 Vi: 0-0 Tstrap: 0-0 Ckp: 0-0
Best Rating: 73 2/04 Catt 2m good Hdl

Call The Mark (IRE)
89   56
5-y-o b g Goldmark (USA)-Shalerina (USA) (Shalford (IRE))
C N Kellett Sean A Taylor

Placings: 00P   (0761)
2003/04: 16⁰GF, 16⁰GF, 16ᴾGF,

	Starts	1st	2nd	3rd	Win & Pl
Hurdles	3	0	0	0	
Career Total	3	0	0	0	

Going: Sf: 0-0 GS: 0-0 Gd: 0-1 GF: - Fm: 0-2
Distance: 2m/2m3: 0-3 2m4-2m7: 0-0 3m+: 0-0
Track: LH: 0-2 RH: 0-1 Tight: 0-0 Gall: 0-1
Aids: Bl: 0-0 Vi: 0-0 Tstrap: 0-1 Ckp: 0-0
Best Rating: 62 5/03 Hntg 2m110y gd-fm Hdl

Calling Brave (IRE)
116 (111h)   (143+h) 153+
8-y-o ch g Bob Back (USA)-Queenie Kelly (The Parson)
N J Henderson Sir Robert Ogden

Placings: 1420/1U12200-1111U   (4395)
2003/04: 24¹G, 25¹G, 20¹G, 20¹G, 24ᵁG,

	Starts	1st	2nd	3rd	Win & Pl
Hurdles	1	1	0	0	13443
Chases	4	3	0	0	35192
Career Total	16	7	3	0	71783
153 2/04 Kemp 2m4f110yA Ch				GD	£21700
149 1/04 Sand 2m4f110yC Ch				GD	£10371
131 12/03 Folk 3m1f E Ch				GD	£3120
143 11/03 Aint 3m110y B HHdl				GD	£13443
121 12/02 Newb 2m3f D Hdl				GD	£4927
114 11/02 Kemp 2m D Hdl				GD	£4251
132 11/01 Aint 2m1f H NHF				G-S	£2149
Total win prize-money £59962					

Going: Sf: 0-0 GS: 0-0 Gd: 4-5 GF: - Fm: 0-0
Distance: 2m/2m3: 0-0 2m4-2m7: 2-2 3m+: 2-3
Track: LH: 1-2 RH: 3-3 Tight: 2-2 Gall: 0-1

Aids: Bl: 0-0 Vi: 0-0 Tstrap: 0-0 Ckp: 0-0
Best Rating: 153 2/04 Kemp 2m4f110y good Ch

Smart hurdler/novicechaser; made a successful debut over fences at Folkestone in December 2003 and followed up at Sandown; won the Pendil in style before unseating in the Royal & SunAlliance Chase; stays three miles, effective at shorter; best on good ground, but has been placed on heavy; still open to improvement.

Callmecozmo (IRE)
97f   113f
6-y-o ch g Zaffaran (USA)-Call Me Connie (IRE) (Combine Harvester)
P R Webber Mollington House racing

Placings: 1   (4529)
2003/04: 16¹GS,

	Starts	1st	2nd	3rd	Win & Pl
NH Flat	1	1	0	0	2009
Career Total	1	1	0	0	2009
113 3/04 Chep 2m110y H NHF				G-S	£2009
Total win prize-money £2009					

Going: Sf: 0-0 GS: 1-1 Gd: 0-0 GF: - Fm: 0-0
Distance: 2m/2m3: 1-1 2m4-2m7: 0-0 3m+: 0-0
Track: LH: 1-1 RH: 0-0 Tight: 0-0 Gall: 0-0
Aids: Bl: 0-0 Vi: 0-0 Tstrap: 0-0 Ckp: 0-0
Best Rating: 113 3/04 Chep 2m110y gd-sft NHF

Out of a sister to a bumper winner; showed the right sort of attitude when making all on debut in soft ground Chepstow bumper March 2004.

Calon Lan (IRE)
90   68
13-y-o b g Bustineto-Cherish (Bargello)
R Williams R Williams

Placings: 3/F/4P13/233P12/41545/1/0P004P/PP24-0P365P
                                             (3255)
2003/04: 16⁰GF, 16²GF, 19³GF, 20⁶GF, 19⁵GS, 24²PG,

	Starts	1st	2nd	3rd	Win & Pl
Chases	6	0	0	1	299
Career Total	34	4	3	5	29679
105 3/01 Hntg 2m110y D(0-125)HCh			SFT	£4108
116 10/99 Strf 2m1f110yD(0-120)HCh			G-F	£3821
109 4/99 Ayr 2m C Ch			HVY	£5865
112 3/98 Newb 2m110y C Hdl			SFT	£4237
Total win prize-money £18031					

Going: Sf: 0-0 GS: 0-1 Gd: 0-1 GF: - Fm: 0-4
Distance: 2m/2m3: 0-4 2m4-2m7: 0-1 3m+: 0-1
Track: LH: 0-3 RH: 0-3 Tight: 0-0 Gall: 0-0
Aids: Bl: 0-0 Vi: 0-0 Tstrap: 0-0 Ckp: 0-0
Best Rating: 125 11/98 Chep 2m3f110y gd-sft Ch

Plating-class chaser; without a win since March 2001; stays two miles five and acts on any ground; suited by forcing tactics; has worn blinkers.

Calvados (USA)
63(100c)   (99+c)94
5-y-o b h Seattle Slew (USA)-A Votre Sante (USA) (Irish River (FR))
John A Quinn Ormonde Racing Syndicate

Placings: 0F05252   (4111)
2003/04: 18⁰G, 22²GY, 16⁶S, 16⁵S, 16²HY, 20⁵V, 16²GF,

	Starts	1st	2nd	3rd	Win & Pl
Hurdles	4	0	1	0	1577
Chases	3	0	1	0	1272
Career Total	7	0	2	0	2849

Going: Sf: 0-3 GS: 0-0 Gd: 0-1 GF: - Fm: 0-1
Distance: 2m/2m3: 0-5 2m4-2m7: 0-2 3m+: 0-0
Track: LH: 0-0 RH: 0-3 Tight: 0-0 Gall: 0-0
Aids: Bl: 0-0 Vi: 0-0 Tstrap: 0-0 Ckp: 0-0
Best Rating: 99 3/04 Leic 2m gd-fm Ch

Calvic (IRE)
103   104
6-y-o ch g Old Vic-Calishee (IRE) (Callernish)
T R George The Alchabas Partnership

Placings: 66130   (3717)
2003/04: 16⁶GF, 20⁶GS, 21¹S, 21³S, 20⁰S,

	Starts	1st	2nd	3rd	Win & Pl
NH Flat	1	0	0	0	0
Hurdles	4	1	0	1	3421
Career Total	5	1	0	1	3421
104 11/03 Towc 2m5f	E Hdl		SFT	£2989
Total win prize-money £2989					

Going: Sf: 1-3 GS: 0-1 Gd: 0-0 GF: - Fm: 0-1
Distance: 2m/2m3: 0-1 2m4-2m7: 1-4 3m+: 0-0
Track: LH: 0-2 RH: 1-3 Tight: 0-0 Gall: 0-0
Aids: Bl: 0-0 Vi: 0-0 Tstrap: 0-0 Ckp: 0-0
Best Rating: 104 12/03 Towc 2m5f soft Hdl

Fair novice hurdler; stays beyond two and a half miles and acts on soft ground; still has scope.

Camaderry (IRE)
90   85+
6-y-o ch g Dr Devious (IRE)-Rathvindon (Realm)
Mrs A M Naughton Famous Five Racing

Placings: 63-00P   (4603)
2003/04: 17⁹GS, 16⁹GF, 17⁵G,

	Starts	1st	2nd	3rd	Win & Pl
Hurdles	3	0	0	0	0
Career Total	5	0	0	1	354

Going: Sf: 0-0 GS: 0-1 Gd: 0-1 GF: - Fm: 0-1
Distance: 2m/2m3: 0-3 2m4-2m7: 0-0 3m+: 0-0
Track: LH: 0-2 RH: 0-1 Tight: 0-3 Gall: 0-0
Aids: Bl: 0-0 Vi: 0-0 Tstrap: 0-0 Ckp: 0-0
Best Rating: 85 5/02 Font 2m2f110y gd-fm Hdl

Camaraderie
(100h)   (92 h)
8-y-o b g Most Welcome-Secret Valentine (Wollow)
A G Juckes Mrs K C Price

Placings: 010/6/2214-60U   (4604)
2003/04: 20⁶G, 16⁰G, 17ᵁGS,

	Starts	1st	2nd	3rd	Win & Pl
Hurdles	2	0	0	0	0
Chases	1	0	0	0	0
Career Total	11	2	2	2	6145
92 3/03 Chep 2m110y G Hdl			GD	£2366
104 10/00 Kels 2m110y G Hdl			SFT	£2373
Total win prize-money £4739					

Going: Sf: 0-0 GS: 0-1 Gd: 0-2 GF: - Fm: 0-0
Distance: 2m/2m3: 0-2 2m4-2m7: 0-1 3m+: 0-0
Track: LH: 0-0 RH: 0-2 Tight: 0-2 Gall: 0-0
Aids: Bl: 0-1 Vi: 0-0 Tstrap: 0-0 Ckp: 0-0
Best Rating: 104 10/00 Kels 2m110y soft Hdl

Moderate hurdler; acts on good or softer.

Camdenation (IRE)
93   94
8-y-o b g Camden Town-Out The Nav (IRE) (Over The River (FR))
N J Gifford Unstable Companions

Placings: 50/012350-4   (4790)
2003/04: 21⁴G,

	Starts	1st	2nd	3rd	Win & Pl
Hurdles	1	0	0	0	280
Career Total	9	1	1	1	5077
102 11/02 Folk 2m6f110yE Hdl			G-S	£2989
Total win prize-money £2989					

Going: Sf: 0-0 GS: 0-0 Gd: 0-1 GF: - Fm: 0-0
Distance: 2m/2m3: 0-0 2m4-2m7: 0-1 3m+: 0-0
Track: LH: 0-1 RH: 0-0 Tight: 0-1 Gall: 0-0
Aids: Bl: 0-0 Vi: 0-0 Tstrap: 0-0 Ckp: 0-0
Best Rating: 102 12/02 Font 2m4f soft Hdl

Moderate hurdler; stays two miles-six; acts on soft ground.

Cameron Bridge (IRE)
105(109h)   (108h)142
8-y-o b g Camden Town-Arctic Raheen (Over The River (FR))
P J Hobbs The Country Side

Placings: F5/55532112/F363541414-11566F5   (4953)
2003/04: 19¹GF, 20¹GF, 16⁵GS, 20⁵G, 20⁶GS, 20⁴GF, 20⁵G,

	Starts	1st	2nd	3rd	Win & Pl
Hurdles	1	0	0	0	600
Chases	6	2	0	0	14329
Career Total	27	6	2	3	37399
140 11/03 Kemp 2m4f110yB(0-140)HCh			G-F	£8073
138 10/03 Chep 2m3f110yD(0-125)HCh			G-F	£4686
107 4/03 Hrfd 2m3f E Ch			SFT	£5187
115 3/03 Extr 3m3f110yE Ch			SFT	£4901
101 1/02 Winc E Hdl			G-S	£3136
105 1/02 Winc 2m E(0-110)HHdl			GD	£2989
Total win prize-money £28973					

Going: Sf: 0-0 GS: 0-2 Gd: 0-2 GF: - Fm: 2-3
Distance: 2m/2m3: 0-1 2m4-2m7: 2-6 3m+: 0-0
Track: LH: 1-3 RH: 1-4 Tight: 0-1 Gall: 0-1
Aids: Bl: 0-0 Vi: 0-0 Tstrap: 0-0 Ckp: 0-0
Best Rating: 140 11/03 Kemp 2m4f110y gd-fm Ch

Useful chaser; stays two and a half miles on sharp tracks; acts on any ground; goes well fresh.

Cameron Jack
100(101c)   (80c)96+
9-y-o b g Elmaamul (USA)-Ile De Reine (Ile De Bourbon (USA))
Miss Kate Milligan The Aunts

Placings: 2/0/5U36P2-03113P   (4690)
2003/04: 20⁰G, 20³GF, 26¹G, 26¹GF, 27³GF, 22⁶G,

	Starts	1st	2nd	3rd	Win & Pl
Hurdles	5	2	0	2	7862
Chases	1	0	0	0	0
Career Total	14	2	2	3	10043
98 7/03 Sthl 3m2f F(0-90)HHdl			G-F	£3479
93 7/03 Sthl 3m2f E Hdl			GD	£3395
Total win prize-money £6874					

Going: Sf: 0-0 GS: 0-0 Gd: 1-3 GF: - Fm: 1-3
Distance: 2m/2m3: 0-0 2m4-2m7: 0-3 3m+: 2-3
Track: LH: 2-6 RH: 0-0 Tight: 0-2 Gall: 0-0
Aids: Bl: 0-0 Vi: 0-0 Tstrap: 0-0 Ckp: 0-0

Best Rating: 98 7/03 Sthl 3m2f gd-fm Hdl

Plating-class chaser; low grade hurdler; poor jumper; rejuvenated since switching back to hurdles with back-to-back wins over 3m2f at Southwell July 2003; acts on good ground; stays well.

Camitrov (FR)

14-y-o b g Sharken (FR)-Emitrovna (FR) (Buisson D'Or)
D Line G R Kerr

Placings:022211341/42/55/3/243F/1/2UP/6-5P (4542)
2003/04: 20^{5}G, 20^{2}GS,

	Starts	1st	2nd	3rd	Win & Pl
Chases	2	0	0	0	
Career Total	25	4	6	3	48501
118 3/00 Sand 3m110y E Ch				GD	£6380
125 4/95 Punc 2m4f Ch				YLD	£12871
97 12/94 MRas 2m1f110y Ch				SFT	£4056
112 11/94 Wwck 2m Ch				G-S	£3600
			Total win prize-money		£26908

Going: Sf: 0-0 GS: 0-1 Gd: 0-1 GF: - Fm: 0-0
Distance: 2m/2m3: 0-0 2m4-2m7: 0-2 3m+: 0-0
Track: LH: 0-0 RH: 0-2 Tight: 0-1 Gall: 0-0
Aids: Bl: 0-0 Vi: 0-0 Tstrap: 0-0 Ckp: 0-0
Best Rating: 144 3/95 Chel 2m soft Ch

Formerly a useful chaser, but is now just an ordinary pointer/hunter.

Camp Hill

112(75h) (94h)94
10-y-o gr g Ra Nova-Baytino (Neltino)
J S Haldane Mrs Hugh Fraser

Placings:00/6P00/P5542/50436U42F/P60412U23-6P0PP51610P (4882)
2003/04: 16^{6}G, 22^{6}G, 17^{0}HY, 20^{5}S, 24^{5}HY, 25^{5}HY, 20^{1}HY, 26^{6}G, 20^{1}HY, 20^{0}G, 26^{6}GS,

	Starts	1st	2nd	3rd	Win & Pl
Hurdles	1	0	0	0	0
Chases	10	2	0	0	7982
Career Total	40	3	4	2	19493
94 3/04 Carl 2m4f E(0-110)HCh				HVY	£4309
84 2/04 Carl 2m4f F(0-100)HCh				HVY	£3672
94 12/02 Ayr 2m4f F(0-90)Ch				SFT	£3038
			Total win prize-money		£11021

Going: Sf: 2-6 GS: 0-1 Gd: 0-4 GF: - Fm: 0-0
Distance: 2m/2m3: 0-2 2m4-2m7: 2-5 3m+: 0-4
Track: LH: 0-5 RH: 2-6 Tight: 0-2 Gall: 0-1
Aids: Bl: 0-0 Vi: 0-0 Tstrap: 0-0 Ckp: 0-0
Best Rating: 94 3/04 Carl 2m4f heavy Ch

Moderate chaser, suited by two and a half miles and soft ground.

Campaign Trail (IRE)

109 134
6-y-o b g Sadler's Wells (USA)-Campestral (USA) (Alleged (USA))
Jonjo O'Neill M Tabor

Placings:5660/11-112 (3292)
2003/04: 24^{1}GS, 25^{1}G, 25^{2}GS,

	Starts	1st	2nd	3rd	Win & Pl
Hurdles	3	2	1	0	27907
Career Total	9	4	1	0	36877
134 12/03 Weth 3m1f B(0-140)HHdl				GD	£14046
137 12/03 Bang 3m C(0-135)HHdl				G-S	£8580
117 1/03 Sthl 2m4f110yD Hdl				G-S	£5070
126 10/02 Carl 2m1f D(0-115)HHdl				SFT	£3900
			Total win prize-money		£31597

Going: Sf: 0-0 GS: 1-2 Gd: 1-1 GF: - Fm: 0-0
Distance: 2m/2m3: 0-0 2m4-2m7: 0-0 3m+: 2-3
Track: LH: 2-3 RH: 0-0 Tight: 1-1 Gall: 0-0
Aids: Bl: 0-0 Vi: 0-0 Tstrap: 0-0 Ckp: 0-0
Best Rating: 137 12/03 Bang 3m gd-sft Hdl

Fair hurdler; made a successful debut in handicap company at Carlisle in October 2002 and followed up very easily in novice company at Southwell; completed a four-timer in handicaps in December 2003; not disgraced having gone up a total of 11lb when second at Warwick the following month; suited by soft ground; stays 3m.

Camross

99 89
8-y-o b g Teenoso (USA)-Arizona Belle (Arab Chieftain)
J C Fox Shannon Racing Partnership

Placings:0003R0/16 (3963)
2003/04: 21^{1}S, 24^{6}GS,

	Starts	1st	2nd	3rd	Win & Pl
Hurdles	2	1	0	0	3024
Career Total	8	1	0	1	3306
89 12/03 Towc 2m5f E(0-105)HHdl				SFT	£3024
			Total win prize-money		£3024

Going: Sf: 1-1 GS: 0-1 Gd: 0-0 GF: - Fm: 0-0
Distance: 2m/2m3: 0-0 2m4-2m7: 1-1 3m+: 0-1
Track: LH: 0-0 RH: 1-2 Tight: 0-0 Gall: 0-0
Aids: Bl: 0-0 Vi: 0-0 Tstrap: 0-0 Ckp: 0-0
Best Rating: 89 12/03 Towc 2m5f soft Hdl

Plating-class hurdler; stays two miles -five; acts on soft.

Can't Be Scrabble

93 (0c)89+
11-y-o b g Gargoor-Scribble Along (Supergrey)
C J Down J Selby

Placings:F-221P444 (1307)
2003/04: 24^{2}GF, 20^{2}GF, 22^{1}GF, 22^{6}GF, 22^{4}GF, 19^{4}GF, 24^{5}GF,

	Starts	1st	2nd	3rd	Win & Pl
Hurdles	7	1	2	0	8381
Career Total	8	1	2	0	8381
94 7/03 Strf 2m6f110yD Hdl				G-F	£5486
			Total win prize-money		£5486

Going: Sf: 0-0 GS: 0-0 Gd: 0-0 GF: - Fm: 1-7
Distance: 2m/2m3: 0-0 2m4-2m7: 1-3 3m+: 0-0
Track: LH: 1-6 RH: 0-0 Tight: 1-3 Gall: 0-0
Aids: Bl: 0-0 Vi: 0-0 Tstrap: 0-0 Ckp: 0-0
Best Rating: 94 7/03 Strf 2m6f110y gd-fm Hdl

Novice hurdler; winning pointer; had things his own way when landing modest 2m 6f novices' hurdle at Stratford July 2003; stays 3m; best on fast ground; looks a tricky ride.

Canada

140+
6-y-o b g Ezzoud (IRE)-Chancel (USA) (Al Nasr (FR))
M C Pipe W J Gredley

Placings:1P/243-1 (0924)
2003/04: 22^{1}GF,

	Starts	1st	2nd	3rd	Win & Pl
Hurdles	1	1	0	0	8138
Career Total	6	2	1	1	20495
140 7/03 MRas 2m6f D(0-125)HHdl				G-F	£8138
109 2/02 Hayd 2m D Hdl				HVY	£3902
			Total win prize-money		£12041

Going: Sf: 0-0 GS: 0-0 Gd: 0-0 GF: - Fm: 1-1
Distance: 2m/2m3: 0-0 2m4-2m7: 1-1 3m+: 0-0
Track: LH: 0-0 RH: 0-0 Tight: 0-0 Gall: 0-0
Aids: Bl: 0-0 Vi: 0-0 Tstrap: 0-0 Ckp: 0-0
Best Rating: 140 7/03 MRas 2m6f gd-fm Hdl

Useful hurdler; stays 2m 6f; seems to handle any ground; mixes hurdling with Flat racing.

Canada Road (IRE)

6-y-o b g Great Marquess-New Technique (FR) (Formidable (USA))
R J Smith Oliver Ryan, Kieran Ryan, Janet Baker

Placings:5-00P0 (3698)
2003/04: 17^{0}G, 16^{0}G, 21^{0}S, 17^{0}HY,

	Starts	1st	2nd	3rd	Win & Pl
NH Flat	2	0	0	0	0
Hurdles	2	0	0	0	0
Career Total	5	0	0	0	0

Going: Sf: 0-2 GS: 0-0 Gd: 0-2 GF: - Fm: 0-0
Distance: 2m/2m3: 0-3 2m4-2m7: 0-1 3m+: 0-0
Track: LH: 0-2 RH: 0-2 Tight: 0-1 Gall: 0-0
Aids: Bl: 0-0 Vi: 0-0 Tstrap: 0-0 Ckp: 0-0
Best Rating: 87 4/03 Hntg 2m110y gd-fm NHF

Canadiane (FR)

107(101h) (123h)120
9-y-o ch m Nikos-Carmonera (FR) (Carmont (FR))
M C Pipe D A Johnson

Placings:664F/454562125/06503242P4/3121213231333244121U5-6244404103 (3656)
2003/04: 20^{6}G, 21^{2}GF, 20^{4}GF, 17^{4}GF, 21^{4}GF, 20^{9}GF, 20^{4}G, 16^{1}GF, 20^{0}G, 19^{3}S,

	Starts	1st	2nd	3rd	Win & Pl
Chases	10	1	1	1	9326
Career Total	53	8	10	7	78820
119 11/03 Chep 2m110y D(0-120)HCh				G-F	£4336
117 3/03 Hayd 2m D(0-120)HCh				G-F	£8368
121 1/03 Tntn 2m1f D(0-120)HHdl				SFT	£5167
120 8/02 Font 2m4f E Ch				G-F	£4431
118 7/02 Strf 2m1f110yE Ch				GD	£3640
112 6/02 Hrfd 2m3f E Ch				GD	£3045
102 5/02 Ludl 2m4f D Ch				G-F	£4026
120 12/99 Chep 2m110y D Hdl				G-S	£3347
			Total win prize-money		£36364

Going: Sf: 0-1 GS: 0-0 Gd: 0-3 GF: - Fm: 1-6
Distance: 2m/2m3: 1-3 2m4-2m7: 0-7 3m+: 0-0
Track: LH: 1-6 RH: 0-4 Tight: 0-7 Gall: 0-2
Aids: Bl: 0-0 Vi: 1-3 Tstrap: 0-0 Ckp: 0-1
Best Rating: 121 4/03 Extr 2m3f gd-fm Hdl

Moderate chaser; effective over two to two and a half miles and acts on most ground; jumps well; can be moody.

Canal End (IRE)

94 90
7-y-o b g Montelimar (USA)-Miss Cripps (IRE) (Lafontaine (USA))
Jonjo O'Neill Mrs Jonjo O'Neill

Placings:000026-450 (0706)
2003/04: 22^{4}GF, 24^{5}GF, 22^{0}GF,

	Starts	1st	2nd	3rd	Win & Pl
Hurdles	3	0	0	0	0
Career Total	9	0	1	0	1068

Going:	Sf: 0-0 GS: 0-0 Gd: 0-0 GF: - Fm: 0-3
Distance:	2m2m3: 0-0 2m4-2m7: 0-2 3m+: 0-1
Track:	LH: 0-2 RH: 0-1 Tight: 0-1 Gall: 0-0
Aids:	Bl: 0-0 Vi: 0-0 Tstrap: 0-0 Ckp: 0-0
Best Rating:	90 6/03 Worc 3m gd-fm Hdl

Canatrice (IRE)
91   90

4-y-o gr f Brief Truce (USA)-Cantata (IRE) (Saddlers' Hall (IRE))
T D McCarthy (B R Johnson 28/8) The One For The Ditch Partnership

Placings:43P004   (4839)
2003/04: 16⁴G, 16³GS, 16⁶S, 21⁰G, 20⁹GF, 17⁴GF,

	Starts	1st	2nd	3rd	Win & Pl
Hurdles	6	0	0	1	2693
Career Total	6	0	0	1	2693

Going:	Sf: 0-1 GS: 0-1 Gd: 0-2 GF: - Fm: 0-2
Distance:	2m2m3: 0-4 2m4-2m7: 0-2 3m+: 0-0
Track:	LH: 0-3 RH: 0-2 Tight: 0-2 Gall: 0-2
Aids:	Bl: 0-0 Vi: 0-0 Tstrap: 0-0 Ckp: 0-6
Best Rating:	90 4/04 Chel 2m1f gd-fm Hdl

Has shown some ability in juvenile hurdles; winner over middle distances on the Flat; usually wears cheekpieces; has worn a visor.

Cancun Caribe (IRE)
97   102+

7-y-o ch g Port Lucaya-Miss Tuko (Good Times (ITY))
Evan Williams Dapper Racing Syndicate

Placings:001-1   (4752)
2003/04: 16¹G,

	Starts	1st	2nd	3rd	Win & Pl
Hurdles	1	1	0	0	2786
Career Total	4	2	0	0	5145
102	4/04	Plum	2m	F(0-90)Hdl	GD £2786
97	3/03	Hrfd	2m3f110yG Hdl	G-F	£2359
				Total win prize-money £5145

Going:	Sf: 0-0 GS: 0-0 Gd: 1-1 GF: - Fm: 0-0
Distance:	2m2/3: 1-1 2m4-2m7: 0-0 3m+: 0-0
Track:	LH: 1-1 RH: 0-0 Tight: 1-1 Gall: 0-0
Aids:	Bl: 0-0 Vi: 0-0 Tstrap: 0-0 Ckp: 0-0
Best Rating:	102 4/04 Plum 2m good Hdl

Plating-class hurdler; got off the mark in a Hereford seller in March 2003; scored after 13 month absence in 2004; stays two and a half miles; acts on a sound surface.

Candarli (IRE)
100   118+

8-y-o ch g Polish Precedent (USA)-Calounia (IRE) (Pharly (FR))
D R Gandolfo A E Frost

Placings:5/301/302P-564306   (4718)
2003/04: 16⁵GS, 16⁶G, 16⁴G, 16³GS, 16⁰GS, 16⁶G,

	Starts	1st	2nd	3rd	Win & Pl
Hurdles	6	0	0	1	3143
Career Total	14	1	1	3	12294
106	3/02	Winc	2m	D(0-125)HHdl	GD £5261
				Total win prize-money £5262

Going:	Sf: 0-0 GS: 0-3 Gd: 0-3 GF: - Fm: 0-0
Distance:	2m/2m3: 0-6 2m4-2m7: 0-0 3m+: 0-0
Track:	LH: 0-1 RH: 0-5 Tight: 0-0 Gall: 0-1
Aids:	Bl: 0-0 Vi: 0-0 Tstrap: 0-0 Ckp: 0-0
Best Rating:	116 12/03 Chel 2m110y good Hdl

Modest hurdler; effective over two miles; acts well on good ground.

Candello
101f   104+f

6-y-o b m Supreme Leader-Oubava (FR) (Groom Dancer (USA))
N J Henderson Erik Thorbek

Placings:1   (4144)
2003/04: 16¹G,

	Starts	1st	2nd	3rd	Win & Pl
NH Flat	1	1	0	0	2681
Career Total	1	1	0	0	2681
104	3/04	Ludl	2m	H NHF	GD £2681
				Total win prize-money £2681

Going:	Sf: 0-0 GS: 0-0 Gd: 1-1 GF: - Fm: 0-0
Distance:	2m/2m3: 1-1 2m4-2m7: 0-0 3m+: 0-0
Track:	LH: 0-0 RH: 1-1 Tight: 0-0 Gall: 0-0
Aids:	Bl: 0-0 Vi: 0-0 Tstrap: 0-0 Ckp: 0-0
Best Rating:	104 3/04 Ludl 2m good NHF

Won on debut at Ludlow in mares-only bumper on good ground in March.

Canny Chiftane
79   30

8-y-o b g Be My Chief (USA)-Prudence (Grundy)
Miss C J E Caroe Miss C J E Caroe

Placings:04461/30PP5/0P0PP16400P/P-0PP0PPP0 (4401)
2003/04: 20⁶S, 20⁶HY, 20⁶G, 20⁶HY, 22⁶HY, 21⁰G,

	Starts	1st	2nd	3rd	Win & Pl
Hurdles	7	0	0	0	
Career Total	29	2	0	1	4135
86	11/01	Fknm	2m4f	G(0-95)HHdl	SFT £1867
77	4/00	Newc	2m	F Hdl	G-S £1897
				Total win prize-money £3765

Going:	Sf: 0-4 GS: 0-0 Gd: 0-3 GF: - Fm: 0-0
Distance:	2m/2m3: 0-0 2m4-2m7: 0-7 3m+: 0-0
Track:	LH: 0-4 RH: 0-3 Tight: 0-2 Gall: 0-1
Aids:	Bl: 0-1 Vi: 0-3 Tstrap: 0-0 Ckp: 0-0
Best Rating:	86 11/01 Fknm 2m4f soft Hdl

Canny Scot
97   90+

7-y-o b g Slip Anchor-Pomade (Luthier)
R Curtis Studley Racing Partnership

Placings:S/4000-2011   (2288)
2003/04: 18²GF, 16⁶GF, 22¹G, 22¹G,

	Starts	1st	2nd	3rd	Win & Pl
Hurdles	4	2	1	0	7132
Career Total	9	2	1	0	7451
90	11/03	Extr	2m6f110yE(0-100)HHdl	GD £3094
85	11/03	NAbb	2m6f	E(0-100)HHdl	GD £3290
				Total win prize-money £6384

Going:	Sf: 0-0 GS: 0-0 Gd: 2-2 GF: - Fm: 0-0
Distance:	2m/2m3: 0-2 2m4-2m7: 2-2 3m+: 0-0
Track:	LH: 1-3 RH: 1-1 Tight: 1-3 Gall: 0-0
Aids:	Bl: 0-0 Vi: 0-0 Tstrap: 0-0 Ckp: 0-0
Best Rating:	101 10/02 Gway 2m heavy NHF

Moderate hurdler; stays two miles-six; acts on good ground.

Canon Barney (IRE)
92(107c)   (118c)111

9-y-o b g Salluceva-Debbie's Candy (Candy Cane)
Jonjo O'Neill John P McManus

Placings:3F/64153F41/3U41-0P0F5   (4451)
2003/04: 20⁰GS, 24⁶PS, 24⁰S, 24⁶G, 24⁵GS,

	Starts	1st	2nd	3rd	Win & Pl
Hurdles	3	0	0	0	0
Chases	2	0	0	0	0
Career Total	19	3	0	3	26687
123	3/03	Uttx	3m2f	B HCh	SFT £12342
111	2/02	Navn	2m2f	Hdl	SFT £5503
102	11/01	Navn	2m	NHF	YLD £5008
				Total win prize-money £22853

Going:	Sf: 0-2 GS: 0-2 Gd: 0-1 GF: - Fm: 0-0
Distance:	2m/2m3: 0-0 2m4-2m7: 0-1 3m+: 0-4
Track:	LH: 0-2 RH: 0-3 Tight: 0-1 Gall: 0-0
Aids:	Bl: 0-0 Vi: 0-0 Tstrap: 0-0 Ckp: 0-2
Best Rating:	123 3/03 Uttx 3m2f soft Ch

Modest hurdler/chaser; ex-Irish; stays well; acts on soft ground; has worn cheekpieces.

Canon McCarthy (IRE)
69   89

8-y-o ch g Be My Native (USA)-Archetype (Over The River (FR))
S T Lewis Simon T Lewis

Placings:34563/0332/246-33P   (3419)
2003/04: 24³GF, 25³S, 23⁶GS,

	Starts	1st	2nd	3rd	Win & Pl
Chases	3	0	0	2	913
Career Total	15	0	2	6	6427

Going:	Sf: 0-1 GS: 0-1 Gd: 0-0 GF: - Fm: 0-1
Distance:	2m/2m3: 0-0 2m4-2m7: 0-0 3m+: 0-3
Track:	LH: 0-1 RH: 0-2 Tight: 0-1 Gall: 0-0
Aids:	Bl: 0-1 Vi: 0-0 Tstrap: 0-0 Ckp: 0-0
Best Rating:	96 10/00 Font 2m4f good Hdl

Moderate form in novice and handicap chases; stays three miles; acts on good.

Cansalrun (IRE)
89   77+

5-y-o b m Anshan-Monamandy (IRE) (Mandalus)
J W Mullins Mrs Josephine S Blackwell

Placings:6240P5   (2652)
2003/04: 17⁶G, 17²GF, 16⁴GF, 17⁰G, 21⁰GS, 20⁵G,

	Starts	1st	2nd	3rd	Win & Pl
NH Flat	3	0	1	0	450
Hurdles	3	0	0	0	0
Career Total	6	0	1	0	450

Going:	Sf: 0-0 GS: 0-1 Gd: 0-3 GF: - Fm: 0-2
Distance:	2m/2m3: 0-4 2m4-2m7: 0-2 3m+: 0-0
Track:	LH: 0-2 RH: 0-3 Tight: 0-3 Gall: 0-0
Aids:	Bl: 0-0 Vi: 0-0 Tstrap: 0-0 Ckp: 0-0
Best Rating:	77 12/03 Font 2m4f good Hdl

Runner-up in Hereford bumper September 2003; failed to confirm the form with the fourth at Chepstow the following month.

Cantarinho

6-y-o b g Alderbrook-Hot Hostess (Silly Season)
D J Kemp Mrs M M Harrison

Placings:2-1   (4779)
2003/04: 24¹S,

	Starts	1st	2nd	3rd	Win & Pl
Chases	1	1	0	0	3328
Career Total	2	1	1	0	3958
122 4/04 Fknm	3m110y H Ch			SFT	£3328
				Total win prize-money £3328

Going:	Sf: 1-1 GS: 0-0 Gd: 0-0 GF: - Fm: 0-0
Distance:	2m/2m3: 0-0 2m4-2m7: 0-0 3m+: 1-1
Track:	LH: 1-1 RH: 0-0 Tight: 1-1 Gall: 0-0
Aids:	Bl: 0-0 Vi: 0-0 Tstrap: 0-0 Ckp: 0-0
Best Rating:	122 4/04 Fknm 3m110y soft Ch

Fair pointer/hunter; stays three miles and handles most types of ground; still has scope.

Canterbury Jack (IRE)

7-y-o b g Supreme Leader-Crest Of The Hill (Prince Regent (FR))
D Pipe P J Finn

Placings:0/223-P   (4298)
2003/04: 23PG,

	Starts	1st	2nd	3rd	Win & Pl
Chases	1	0	0	0	
Career Total	5	0	2	1	2024

Going:	Sf: 0-0 GS: 0-0 Gd: 0-1 GF: - Fm: 0-0
Distance:	2m/2m3: 0-0 2m4-2m7: 0-0 3m+: 0-1
Track:	LH: 0-0 RH: 0-1 Tight: 0-0 Gall: 0-0
Aids:	Bl: 0-0 Vi: 0-1 Tstrap: 0-0 Ckp: 0-0
Best Rating:	103 9/02 Worc 3m good Hdl

Cantoris
89   58

4-y-o b g Unfuwain (USA)-Choir Mistress (Chief Singer)
C L Popham (M Johnston 18/10) H J W Davies, Rodney Peacock

Placings:P00056   (4856)
2003/04: 16PS, 16QG, 16QG, 21QG, 17SG, 19QGF,

	Starts	1st	2nd	3rd	Win & Pl
Hurdles	6	0	0	0	0
Career Total	6	0	0	0	0

Going:	Sf: 0-1 GS: 0-1 Gd: 0-3 GF: - Fm: 0-1
Distance:	2m/2m3: 0-4 2m4-2m7: 0-2 3m+: 0-0
Track:	LH: 0-0 RH: 0-6 Tight: 0-1 Gall: 0-0
Aids:	Bl: 0-2 Vi: 0-0 Tstrap: 0-1 Ckp: 0-0
Best Rating:	58 4/04 Tntn 2m3f110y gd-fm Hdl

Cantys Brig (IRE)
80   49

7-y-o gr g Roselier (FR)-Call Catherine (IRE) (Strong Gale)
Miss L C Siddall Mrs D Ibbotson

Placings:0/60030-060P   (4756)
2003/04: 20QHY, 24⁶G, 24QHY, 19PS,

	Starts	1st	2nd	3rd	Win & Pl
Hurdles	4	0	0	0	0

Career Total   10   0   0   1   514

Going:	Sf: 0-3 GS: 0-0 Gd: 0-1 GF: - Fm: 0-0
Distance:	2m/2m3: 0-0 2m4-2m7: 0-2 3m+: 0-2
Track:	LH: 0-1 RH: 0-2 Tight: 0-0 Gall: 0-1
Aids:	Bl: 0-0 Vi: 0-0 Tstrap: 0-0 Ckp: 0-0
Best Rating:	59 1/03 Newc 2m heavy NHF

Cap Classique
102f   84+f

5-y-o b g Classic Cliche (IRE)-Champenoise (Forzando)
Simon Earle Lovely Bubbly Racing

Placings:041   (1334)
2003/04: 16⁹G, 16⁴GF, 17¹GF,

	Starts	1st	2nd	3rd	Win & Pl
NH Flat	3	1	0	0	1575
Career Total	3	1	0	0	1575
84 9/03 Hrfd	2m1f	H NHF		G-F	£1575
				Total win prize-money £1575

Going:	Sf: 0-0 GS: 0-0 Gd: 0-1 GF: - Fm: 1-2
Distance:	2m/2m3: 1-3 2m4-2m7: 0-0 3m+: 0-0
Track:	LH: 0-2 RH: 1-1 Tight: 0-0 Gall: 0-0
Aids:	Bl: 0-0 Vi: 0-0 Tstrap: 0-0 Ckp: 0-0
Best Rating:	84 9/03 Hrfd 2m1f gd-fm NHF

Came from a long way back and rider banned seven days for riding an ill-judged race when fourth in weak Worcester bumper second start; won at Hereford next time; acts on fast.

Cap In Hand
85   55

12-y-o ch g Nearly A Hand-Beringa Bee (Sunley Builds)
Mrs S J Smith A P Russell

Placings:00/F0/50/153/400-05   (0387)
2003/04: 16⁶G, 20⁵G,

	Starts	1st	2nd	3rd	Win & Pl
Hurdles	2	0	0	0	0
Career Total	14	1	0	1	2046
82 9/00 Sedg	2m5f110yG(0-95)HHdl		GD	£1673
				Total win prize-money £1673

Going:	Sf: 0-0 GS: 0-0 Gd: 0-2 GF: - Fm: 0-0
Distance:	2m/2m3: 0-1 2m4-2m7: 0-1 3m+: 0-0
Track:	LH: 0-2 RH: 0-0 Tight: 0-0 Gall: 0-0
Aids:	Bl: 0-0 Vi: 0-0 Tstrap: 0-0 Ckp: 0-0
Best Rating:	82 9/00 Sedg 2m5f110y good Hdl

Capacoostic
                                                                            51

7-y-o ch m Savahra Sound-Cocked Hat Girl (Ballacashtal (CAN))
A G Juckes C A Cavanagh

Placings:00-P   (0680)
2003/04: 16PGF,

	Starts	1st	2nd	3rd	Win & Pl
Hurdles	1	0	0	0	0
Career Total	3	0	0	0	

Going:	Sf: 0-0 GS: 0-0 Gd: 0-0 GF: - Fm: 0-1
Distance:	2m/2m3: 0-1 2m4-2m7: 0-0 3m+: 0-0
Track:	LH: 0-1 RH: 0-0 Tight: 0-0 Gall: 0-0
Aids:	Bl: 0-0 Vi: 0-0 Tstrap: 0-0 Ckp: 0-0
Best Rating:	51 12/02 Ludl 2m good Hdl

Cape Canaveral (IRE)
98   114d

5-y-o b g Sadler's Wells (USA)-Emmaline (USA) (Affirmed (USA))
G L Moore Gillespie Brothers

Placings:20555-1300   (3717)
2003/04: 20¹GF, 19³S, 20⁹G, 20⁹S,

	Starts	1st	2nd	3rd	Win & Pl
Hurdles	4	1	0	1	3141
Career Total	9	1	1	1	4264
110 11/03 Font	2m4f	E Hdl		G-F	£2639
				Total win prize-money £2639

Going:	Sf: 0-2 GS: 0-0 Gd: 0-1 GF: - Fm: 1-1
Distance:	2m/2m3: 0-0 2m4-2m7: 1-4 3m+: 0-0
Track:	LH: 0-1 RH: 0-1 Tight: 1-3 Gall: 0-0
Aids:	Bl: 0-0 Vi: 0-0 Tstrap: 0-0 Ckp: 0-0
Best Rating:	114 12/02 Font 2m2f110y good Hdl

Fair hurdler; stays two miles four; acts on a sound surface and soft ground.

Cape Coast (IRE)
88   63

7-y-o b g Common Grounds-Strike It Rich (FR) (Rheingold)
P D Evans M W Lawrence

Placings:F00   (1698)
2003/04: 19¹⁰GF, 16⁹GF, 16⁶GF,

	Starts	1st	2nd	3rd	Win & Pl
Hurdles	3	0	0	0	
Career Total	3	0	0	0	

Going:	Sf: 0-0 GS: 0-0 Gd: 0-0 GF: - Fm: 0-3
Distance:	2m/2m3: 0-3 2m4-2m7: 0-0 3m+: 0-0
Track:	LH: 0-2 RH: 0-1 Tight: 0-2 Gall: 0-0
Aids:	Bl: 0-0 Vi: 0-0 Tstrap: 0-2 Ckp: 0-0
Best Rating:	63 10/03 Ludl 2m gd-fm Hdl

Cape Stormer (IRE)

9-y-o b g Be My Native (USA)-My Sunny South (Strong Gale)
Mrs C M Gorman M Gorman

Placings:0P225/121316102-410   (4626)
2003/04: 20⁴G, 20¹G, 21⁹G,

	Starts	1st	2nd	3rd	Win & Pl
Chases	3	1	0	0	2681
Career Total	17	5	4	1	36013
117 3/04 Leic	2m4f110yH Ch			GD	£2681
124 3/03 Newb	2m6f110yD(0-120)HCh		GD	£7085
121 12/02 Ludl	2m4f D(0-120)HCh		GD	£6695
121 10/02 Chel	2m4f110yD(0-110)HCh		GD	£9700
109 5/02 Font	2m4f E Hdl			G-F	£2593
				Total win prize-money £28755

Going:	Sf: 0-0 GS: 0-0 Gd: 1-3 GF: - Fm: 0-0
Distance:	2m/2m3: 0-0 2m4-2m7: 1-3 3m+: 0-0
Track:	LH: 0-1 RH: 1-2 Tight: 0-1 Gall: 0-0
Aids:	Bl: 0-0 Vi: 0-0 Tstrap: 0-0 Ckp: 0-0
Best Rating:	124 3/03 Newb 2m6f110y good Ch

Formerly decent novice chaser, now hunter chasing and won at Leicester; effective from 2m 4f to 2m 6f and well suited by a sound surface; consistent.

Cappadrummin (IRE)

97   **110**

7-y-o ch g Bob Back (USA)-Out And About (Orchestra)
N J Henderson   Lady Lloyd-Webber

Placings:1/5F-04   (3250)
2003/04: 20⁰G, 16⁴S,

	Starts	1st	2nd	3rd	Win & Pl
Hurdles	2	0	0	0	305
Career Total	5	1	0	0	3161

112 2/02 Kemp 2m   H NHF   GD   £2562
Total win prize-money £2562

Going: Sf: 0-1 GS: 0-0 Gd: 0-1 GF: - Fm: 0-0
Distance: 2m/2m3: 0-1 2m4-2m7: 0-1 3m+: 0-0
Track: LH: 0-0 RH: 0-2 Tight: 0-0 Gall: 0-0
Aids: Bl: 0-0 Vi: 0-0 Tstrap: 0-0 Ckp: 0-0
Best Rating: **112** 2/02 Kemp 2m   good   NHF

A brother to the smart chaser Whattabob, he is a good-ground bumper winner and ran a promising race on his hurdling debut, but has gone backwards since; not the best of jumpers.

Capriccio (IRE)

100   **100**

7-y-o gr g Robellino (USA)-Yamamah (Siberian Express (USA))
Mrs S C Bradburne   Lord Cochrane And Partners

Placings:11/0660/6   (1426)
2003/04: 24⁶G,

	Starts	1st	2nd	3rd	Win & Pl
Hurdles	1	0	0	0	0
Career Total	7	2	0	0	5457

117 2/01 Wwck 2m   E Hdl   SFT   £2870
115 1/01 Folk   2m1f110yE Hdl   HVY   £2586
Total win prize-money £5457

Going: Sf: 0-0 GS: 0-0 Gd: 0-1 GF: - Fm: 0-0
Distance: 2m/2m3: 0-0 2m4-2m7: 0-0 3m+: 0-1
Track: LH: 0-0 RH: 0-1 Tight: 0-0 Gall: 0-0
Aids: Bl: 0-0 Vi: 0-0 Tstrap: 0-0 Ckp: 0-0
Best Rating: **117** 2/01 Wwck 2m   soft   Hdl

Moderate hurdler; twice a winner over hurdles in the mud at the beginning of 2001, little form since, including in blinkers; effective at two miles.

Capricorn Princess

105(113h)   (124h)**87**

10-y-o b m Nicholas Bill-Yamrah (Milford)
B D Leavy   Capricorn Hospitality

Placings:00P635/424112/0230P5/1-0324   (1629)
2003/04: 16⁶GS, 20³GF, 21²GF, 17⁴GF,

	Starts	1st	2nd	3rd	Win & Pl
Hurdles	2	0	0	1	780
Chases	2	0	1	0	1800
Career Total	23	3	4	3	20821

119 4/03 Uttx 2m   D(0-125)HHdl   GD   £5878
95 8/00 Bang 2m1f   D Hdl   GD   £3477
93 7/00 Uttx 2m   E(0-105)HHdl   G-F   £3552
Total win prize-money £12909

Going: Sf: 0-0 GS: 0-1 Gd: 0-0 GF: - Fm: 0-3
Distance: 2m/2m3: 0-2 2m4-2m7: 0-2 3m+: 0-0
Track: LH: 0-4 RH: 0-0 Tight: 0-1 Gall: 0-0
Aids: Bl: 0-0 Vi: 0-0 Tstrap: 0-1 Ckp: 0-0
Best Rating: **119** 4/03 Uttx 2m   good   Hdl

Fair hurdler; landed a touch on return from injury at Uttoxeter in April 2003; finished lame when well-beaten second on chase debut; suited by a sound surface; best at around two miles.

Capriolo (IRE)

102   **105**

8-y-o ch g Priolo (USA)-Carroll's Canyon (IRE) (Hatim (USA))
P G Murphy   S J Kingshott

Placings:040P/4213235050-22452034600   (4790)
2003/04: 20²G, 18²GF, 22⁴GF, 20⁵G, 20²G, 20⁰G, 18³G, 20⁴HY, 18⁶G, 19⁰G, 21⁰G,

	Starts	1st	2nd	3rd	Win & Pl
Hurdles	11	0	3	1	4518
Career Total	25	1	5	3	11390

104 11/02 Plum 2m   F Hdl   SFT   £2968
Total win prize-money £2968

Going: Sf: 0-1 GS: 0-0 Gd: 0-8 GF: - Fm: 0-2
Distance: 2m/2m3: 0-3 2m4-2m7: 0-8 3m+: 0-0
Track: LH: 0-5 RH: 0-4 Tight: 0-8 Gall: 0-0
Aids: Bl: 0-0 Vi: 0-0 Tstrap: 0-0 Ckp: 0-11
Best Rating: **105** 11/02 Font   2m2f110y   gd-sft   Hdl

Moderate performer; acts on any ground; effective at around two miles and two and a half miles.

Capt Pugwash

98f   **103f**

6-y-o ch g Karinga Bay-Spire Belle (Final Straw)
B W Hills   Miss T Sturgis

Placings:2   (2012)
2003/04: 16²G,

	Starts	1st	2nd	3rd	Win & Pl
NH Flat	1	0	1	0	458
Career Total	1	0	1	0	458

Going: Sf: 0-0 GS: 0-0 Gd: 0-1 GF: - Fm: 0-0
Distance: 2m/2m3: 0-1 2m4-2m7: 0-0 3m+: 0-0
Track: LH: 0-0 RH: 0-1 Tight: 0-0 Gall: 0-0
Aids: Bl: 0-0 Vi: 0-0 Tstrap: 0-0 Ckp: 0-0
Best Rating: **103** 11/03 Sand   2m110y   good   NHF

Fair effort on bumper debut.

Captain Clooney (IRE)

96   **94**

11-y-o b g Supreme Leader-Capincur Lady (Over The River (FR))
N R Mitchell   Michael Green

Placings:42⁵51000/40/5P/0PU/1FP-260P4P5   (4737)
2003/04: 26²S, 29⁶S, 26⁰S, 25⁶GS, 26⁴GF, 24⁶GS, 21⁵G,

	Starts	1st	2nd	3rd	Win & Pl
Chases	7	0	1	0	1004
Career Total	25	2	2	0	10279

94 12/02 Plum 3m2f   F(0-100)HCh   HVY   £4069
116 1/99 Punc 3m   Hdl   HVY   £3989
Total win prize-money £8059

Going: Sf: 0-3 GS: 0-2 Gd: 0-1 GF: - Fm: 0-1
Distance: 2m/2m3: 0-0 2m4-2m7: 0-1 3m+: 0-6
Track: LH: 0-6 RH: 0-1 Tight: 0-5 Gall: 0-0
Aids: Bl: 0-0 Vi: 0-0 Tstrap: 0-0 Ckp: 0-0
Best Rating: **116** 1/99 Punc 3m   heavy   Hdl

Plating-class chaser; makes mistakes; acts in heavy ground; stays three and a quarter miles.

Captain Corelli

99   **94**

7-y-o b g Weld-Deaconess (The Parson)
M Pitman   Patrick Bancroft

Placings:30/462   (4181)
2003/04: 16⁴S, 20⁶S, 16²G,

	Starts	1st	2nd	3rd	Win & Pl
NH Flat	1	0	0	0	798
Hurdles	2	0	1	0	1036
Career Total	5	0	1	1	2078

Going: Sf: 0-2 GS: 0-0 Gd: 0-1 GF: - Fm: 0-0
Distance: 2m/2m3: 0-2 2m4-2m7: 0-1 3m+: 0-0
Track: LH: 0-1 RH: 0-2 Tight: 0-0 Gall: 0-1
Aids: Bl: 0-0 Vi: 0-0 Tstrap: 0-0 Ckp: 0-0
Best Rating: **104** 12/03 Chep   2m110y   soft   NHF

Decent bumper performer; well beaten on hurdles debut.

Captain Darling (IRE)

4-y-o b g Pennekamp (USA)-Gale Warning (IRE) (Last Tycoon)
R M H Cowell   A Dunmore

Placings:5   (1901)
2003/04: 16⁵GF,

	Starts	1st	2nd	3rd	Win & Pl
Hurdles	1	0	0	0	0
Career Total	1	0	0	0	0

Going: Sf: 0-0 GS: 0-0 Gd: 0-0 GF: - Fm: 0-1
Distance: 2m/2m3: 0-1 2m4-2m7: 0-0 3m+: 0-0
Track: LH: 0-0 RH: 0-1 Tight: 0-0 Gall: 0-1
Aids: Bl: 0-0 Vi: 0-0 Tstrap: 0-0 Ckp: 0-0
Best Rating: **0** 11/03 Hntg   2m110y   gd-fm   Hdl

Captain Flinders (IRE)

100   **101**

7-y-o b g Satco (FR)-Auburn Queen (Kinglet)
Miss H C Knight   P M Warren

Placings:02-53   (3646)
2003/04: 17⁵G, 21³GS,

	Starts	1st	2nd	3rd	Win & Pl
Hurdles	2	0	0	1	770
Career Total	4	0	1	1	1336

Going: Sf: 0-0 GS: 0-1 Gd: 0-1 GF: - Fm: 0-0
Distance: 2m/2m3: 0-1 2m4-2m7: 0-1 3m+: 0-0
Track: LH: 0-0 RH: 0-2 Tight: 0-0 Gall: 0-0
Aids: Bl: 0-0 Vi: 0-0 Tstrap: 0-0 Ckp: 0-0
Best Rating: **106** 2/04 Kemp   2m5f   gd-sft   Hdl

Has shown good form in bumpers; promise in novice hurdles; stays 2m 5f.

Captain Ginger

4-y-o ch g Muhtarram (USA)-Brand (Shareef Dancer (USA))
H Morrison (A M Balding 24/8)   The Queen

Placings:P   (3329)

2003/04: 16⁰S,

	Starts	1st	2nd	3rd	Win & Pl
Hurdles	1	0	0	0	
Career Total	**1**	**0**	**0**	**0**	

Going:	Sf: 0-1 GS: 0-0 Gd: 0-0 GF: - Fm: 0-0
Distance:	2m/2m3: 0-1 2m4-2m7: 0-0 3m+: 0-0
Track:	LH: 0-1 RH: 0-0 Tight: 0-0 Gall: 0-1
Aids:	Bl: 0-0 Vi: 0-0 Tstrap: 0-0 Ckp: 0-0

Far too keen and eventually pulled up on hurdles debut.

Captain Hardy (IRE)
103   90+
4-y-o b g Victory Note (USA)-Airey Fairy (IRE) (Alzao (USA))
G Brown (S Kirk 14/10) A B Dix

Placings: 06021   (4898)
2003/04: 16⁰S, 18⁶G, 16⁰S, 17²G, 16¹G,

	Starts	1st	2nd	3rd	Win & Pl
Hurdles	5	1	1	0	4470
Career Total	**5**	**1**	**1**	**0**	**4470**
89	4/04	Winc	2m		E(0-110)HHdl	GD	£3584
				Total win prize-money £3584		

Going:	Sf: 0-2 GS: 0-0 Gd: 1-3 GF: - Fm: 0-0
Distance:	**2m/2m3: 1-5** 2m4-2m7: 0-0 3m+: 0-0
Track:	LH: 0-2 **RH: 1-3** Tight: 0-2 Gall: 0-1
Aids:	Bl: 0-0 Vi: 0-0 Tstrap: 0-0 Ckp: 0-0
Best Rating:	**89** 4/04 Winc 2m good Hdl

Moderate novice hurdler; winner on the Flat; suited to a sound surface.

Captain Jake
95   84
9-y-o b g Phardante (FR)-Cherry Crest (Pollerton)
M Appleby Clovers

Placings: 66/PP-U2PP   (2937)
2003/04: 24ᵁGF, 25²GF, 25ᴾG, 25ᴾS,

	Starts	1st	2nd	3rd	Win & Pl
Chases	4	0	1	0	830
Career Total	**8**	**0**	**1**	**0**	**830**

Going:	Sf: 0-1 GS: 0-0 Gd: 0-1 GF: - Fm: 0-2
Distance:	2m/2m3: 0-0 2m4-2m7: 0-0 3m+: 0-4
Track:	LH: 0-0 RH: 0-4 Tight: 0-2 Gall: 0-1
Aids:	Bl: 0-0 Vi: 0-0 Tstrap: 0-0 Ckp: 0-3
Best Rating:	**86** 1/01 Hayd 2m6f soft Hdl

Plating-class novice chaser.

Captain Maduck (IRE)
76f   60f
6-y-o b g Distinctly North (USA)-Avril's Choice (Montelimar (USA))
M Pitman S D Hemstock

Placings: 00   (3046)
2003/04: 16⁰GS, 16⁰GS,

	Starts	1st	2nd	3rd	Win & Pl
NH Flat	2	0	0	0	
Career Total	**2**	**0**	**0**	**0**	

Going:	Sf: 0-0 GS: 0-2 Gd: 0-0 GF: - Fm: 0-0
Distance:	2m/2m3: 0-2 2m4-2m7: 0-0 3m+: 0-0

Track:	LH: 0-1 RH: 0-1 Tight: 0-0 Gall: 0-2
Aids:	Bl: 0-0 Vi: 0-0 Tstrap: 0-0 Ckp: 0-0
Best Rating:	**60** 12/03 Newb 2m110y gd-sft NHF

Captain Murphy (IRE)
105f   101f
6-y-o b g Executive Perk-Laura Daisy (Buckskin (FR))
J I A Charlton M H Walton

Placings: 0422   (4867)
2003/04: 16⁰S, 16⁴GS, 16²GS, 16²S,

	Starts	1st	2nd	3rd	Win & Pl
NH Flat	4	0	2	0	1652
Career Total	**4**	**0**	**2**	**0**	**1652**

Going:	Sf: 0-2 GS: 0-2 Gd: 0-0 GF: - Fm: 0-0
Distance:	2m/2m3: 0-4 2m4-2m7: 0-0 3m+: 0-0
Track:	LH: 0-3 RH: 0-1 Tight: 0-0 Gall: 0-0
Aids:	Bl: 0-0 Vi: 0-0 Tstrap: 0-0 Ckp: 0-0
Best Rating:	**101** 4/04 Ayr 2m soft NHF

Has shown ability in bumpers on easy ground and looks the type to jump obstacles in due course; sure to win a race.

Captain O'Neill
87(101h)   (90h)50
10-y-o b g Welsh Captain-The Last Tune (Gunner B)
A W Carroll D Joyce

Placings: 600P303P/36/001PP0P/51034F323P0F002-P2P02PPPP   (2442)
2003/04: 20⁵S, 20²GF, 24⁶GF, 20⁰G, 20²GF, 25ᴾGF, 25ᴾGF, 19¹GF, 20⁵S,

	Starts	1st	2nd	3rd	Win & Pl
Hurdles	4	0	1	0	732
Chases	5	0	1	0	1182
Career Total	**41**	**2**	**4**	**6**	**10877**
87	5/02	Chep	2m4f		G(0-90)HHdl	G-F	£2079
90	12/01	Chep	2m4f		G Hdl	SFT	£1946
				Total win prize-money £4025		

Going:	Sf: 0-2 GS: 0-0 Gd: 0-1 GF: - Fm: 0-6
Distance:	2m/2m3: 0-0 2m4-2m7: 0-6 3m+: 0-3
Track:	LH: 0-6 RH: 0-3 Tight: 0-1 Gall: 0-1
Aids:	Bl: 0-0 Vi: 0-1 Tstrap: 0-0 Ckp: 0-0
Best Rating:	**91** 8/02 Worc 2m4f110y good Ch

Plating-class hurdler; won twice over 2m 4f at Chepstow; struggles to stay 3m over fences.

Captain Rawlings
86   51
5-y-o ch g Lancastrian-Coombesbury Lane (Torus)
H D Daly N F Williams

Placings: 0F00   (4887)
2003/04: 16⁰GS, 19⁰F, 16⁰G, 22⁰GF,

	Starts	1st	2nd	3rd	Win & Pl
NH Flat	1	0	0	0	0
Hurdles	3	0	0	0	0
Career Total	**4**	**0**	**0**	**0**	

Going:	Sf: 0-0 GS: 0-1 Gd: 0-2 GF: - Fm: 0-1
Distance:	2m/2m3: 0-2 2m4-2m7: 0-2 3m+: 0-0
Track:	LH: 0-2 RH: 0-2 Tight: 0-1 Gall: 0-1
Aids:	Bl: 0-0 Vi: 0-0 Tstrap: 0-0 Ckp: 0-0
Best Rating:	**72** 1/04 Ludl 2m gd-sft NHF

Captain Robin (IRE)
88
10-y-o b g Supreme Leader-Gentle Madam (Camden Town)
N A Twiston-Davies H R Mould

Placings: 102/04P-0   (0359)
2003/04: 22⁰G,

	Starts	1st	2nd	3rd	Win & Pl
Hurdles	1	0	0	0	
Career Total	**7**	**1**	**0**	**0**	**2653**
106	11/99	NAbb	2m1f		H NHF	G-S	£1945
				Total win prize-money £1945		

Going:	Sf: 0-0 GS: 0-0 Gd: 0-1 GF: - Fm: 0-0
Distance:	2m/2m3: 0-0 2m4-2m7: 0-0 3m+: 0-0
Track:	LH: 0-1 RH: 0-0 Tight: 0-1 Gall: 0-0
Aids:	Bl: 0-0 Vi: 0-0 Tstrap: 0-0 Ckp: 0-0
Best Rating:	**106** 3/00 Newb 2m110y soft NHF

Fair bumper performer but has struggled over hurdles; effective at around two miles; acts well with cut in the ground.

Captain Ron (IRE)
73(69c)   (36c)18
8-y-o b g Marju (IRE)-Callas Star (Chief Singer)
Mrs S M Johnson (S Lloyd 12/5) N E Powell

Placings: 0/0-P0P0   (4290)
2003/04: 21ᴾG, 19⁰S, 21ᴾG, 22⁰G,

	Starts	1st	2nd	3rd	Win & Pl
Hurdles	3	0	0	0	0
Chases	1	0	0	0	0
Career Total	**6**	**0**	**0**	**0**	

Going:	Sf: 0-1 GS: 0-0 Gd: 0-3 GF: - Fm: 0-0
Distance:	2m/2m3: 0-1 2m4-2m7: 0-3 3m+: 0-0
Track:	LH: 0-1 RH: 0-3 Tight: 0-0 Gall: 0-0
Aids:	Bl: 0-0 Vi: 0-0 Tstrap: 0-0 Ckp: 0-0
Best Rating:	**47** 7/01 Strf 2m6f110y gd-fm Hdl

Captain Smoothy
72f
4-y-o b g Charmer-The Lady Captain (Neltino)
M J Gingell P Cranney

Placings: 660   (3139)
2003/04: 12⁶GF, 13⁶GF, 12⁰G,

	Starts	1st	2nd	3rd	Win & Pl
NH Flat	3	0	0	0	0
Career Total	**3**	**0**	**0**	**0**	**0**

Going:	Sf: 0-0 GS: 0-0 Gd: 0-1 GF: - Fm: 0-2
Distance:	2m/2m3: 0-0 2m4-2m7: 0-0 3m+: 0-0
Track:	LH: 0-1 RH: 0-0 Tight: 0-0 Gall: 0-0
Aids:	Bl: 0-0 Vi: 0-0 Tstrap: 0-0 Ckp: 0-0
Best Rating:	**75** 11/03 Donc 1m5f gd-fm NHF

Captain Valiant (IRE)
81f   99f
6-y-o b g Supreme Leader-Anna Valley (Gleason (USA))
G B Balding Miss B Swire

Placings: 032-0   (0141)
2003/04: 16⁰G,

	Starts	1st	2nd	3rd	Win & Pl
NH Flat	1	0	0	0	

| Career Total | 4 | 0 | 1 | 1 | 1115 |

Going:	Sf: 0-0 GS: 0-0 Gd: 0-1 GF: - Fm: 0-0
Distance:	2m/2m3: 0-1 2m4-2m7: 0-0 3m+: 0-0
Track:	LH: 0-0 RH: 0-1 Tight: 0-0 Gall: 0-0
Aids:	Bl: 0-0 Vi: 0-0 Tstrap: 0-0 Ckp: 0-0
Best Rating:	99 4/03 Ludl 2m good NHF

Good jumping pedigree; twice placed in modest bumpers at Ludlow spring 2003.

Captain Zinzan (NZ)
113(99c)   (101c)**128+**
9-y-o b g Zabeel (NZ)-Lady Springfield (NZ) (Sharivari (USA))
L A Dace The Tuesday Syndicate

Placings:44/121/2/33F543-2111   (0760)
2003/04: 22²GF, 21¹GF, 20¹GF, 20¹G,

	Starts	1st	2nd	3rd	Win & Pl
Hurdles	4	3	1	0	17969
Career Total	16	5	3	3	27420
128 6/03 Worc	2m4f	C(0-130)HHdl	GD	£6828
118 6/03 Worc	2m4f	D(0-125)HHdl	G-F	£5460
104 5/03 Hntg	2m5f110yD(0-125)HHdl	G-F	£4764
119 1/01 Donc	2m110y E Hdl	GD	£3080
108 8/00 Hntg	2m110y H NHF	G-F	£1477
			Total win prize-money £21610

Going:	Sf: 0-0 GS: 0-0 Gd: 1-1 GF: - Fm: 2-3
Distance:	2m/2m3: 0-0 2m4-2m7: 3-4 3m+: 0-0
Track:	LH: 2-2 RH: 1-2 Tight: 0-0 Gall: 1-1
Aids:	Bl: 0-0 Vi: 0-0 Tstrap: 0-0 Ckp: 0-0
Best Rating:	128 6/03 Worc 2m4f good Hdl

Remarkable improvement over hurdles in June 2003 and hacked up when completing a hat-trick; has managed to keep ahead of the Handicapper despite having gone up a stone; seems sure to be in for another hefty rise in the ratings; best on a sound surface; stays 2m 4f.

Captain's Leap (IRE)
92   **90**
8-y-o ch g Grand Plaisir (IRE)-Ballingowan Star (Le Moss)
L Lungo J Regan

Placings:216/5-P604P   (4658)
2003/04: 16⁶S, 16⁶S, 17⁰GS, 24⁴G, 20⁴S,

	Starts	1st	2nd	3rd	Win & Pl
Hurdles	5	0	0	0	0
Career Total	9	1	1	0	2002
99 12/01 Muss	2m	H NHF	GD	£1554
			Total win prize-money £1554

Going:	Sf: 0-3 GS: 0-1 Gd: 0-1 GF: - Fm: 0-0
Distance:	2m/2m3: 0-3 2m4-2m7: 0-1 3m+: 0-0
Track:	LH: 0-5 RH: 0-0 Tight: 0-2 Gall: 0-0
Aids:	Bl: 0-0 Vi: 0-0 Tstrap: 0-0 Ckp: 0-0
Best Rating:	102 3/02 Ayr 2m soft NHF

Captain's Walk
32
8-y-o b g Seymour Hicks (FR)-Mayina (Idiots Delight)
P Bowen John O'Sullivan

Placings:60/40P/P6-P   (0250)
2003/04: 24⁰GF,

	Starts	1st	2nd	3rd	Win & Pl
Hurdles	1	0	0	0	

| Career Total | 8 | 0 | 0 | 0 | 0 |

Going:	Sf: 0-0 GS: 0-0 Gd: 0-0 GF: - Fm: 0-1
Distance:	2m/2m3: 0-0 2m4-2m7: 0-0 3m+: 0-1
Track:	LH: 0-0 RH: 0-1 Tight: 0-0 Gall: 0-0
Aids:	Bl: 0-0 Vi: 0-0 Tstrap: 0-0 Ckp: 0-0
Best Rating:	91 5/01 Extr 2m1f firm NHF

Captains Table
88   **118**
11-y-o b g Welsh Captain-Wensum Girl (Ballymoss)
R Dickin Les Pike

Placings:6/21P223F-0   (2242)
2003/04: 20⁰GF,

	Starts	1st	2nd	3rd	Win & Pl
Chases	1	0	0	0	
Career Total	9	1	3	1	9551
111 12/02 Donc	2m110y D Ch	GD	£4741
			Total win prize-money £4741

Going:	Sf: 0-0 GS: 0-0 Gd: 0-0 GF: - Fm: 0-1
Distance:	2m/2m3: 0-0 2m4-2m7: 0-0 3m+: 0-1
Track:	LH: 0-0 RH: 0-1 Tight: 0-0 Gall: 0-0
Aids:	Bl: 0-0 Vi: 0-0 Tstrap: 0-0 Ckp: 0-0
Best Rating:	118 2/03 Leic 2m gd-sft Ch

Fair chaser; ex-eventer; jumped soundly when making all in novices' chase at Doncaster in December 2002; acts on a sound surface; likes to make the running; effective at two miles.

Captaintwothousand
91(79h)   (92h)**98**
9-y-o b g Milieu-Royal Scarlet (Royal Fountain)
C W Fairhurst Mrs A M Leggett

Placings:0/2P6U50/0P22123/52566-645U5PUP   (4605)
2003/04: 19⁶GS, 24⁴GS, 21⁵GS, 16¹UG, 16⁵HY, 22⁵GS, 21⁵UG, 22⁵PG,

	Starts	1st	2nd	3rd	Win & Pl
Hurdles	2	0	0	0	
Chases	6	0	0	0	334
Career Total	27	1	5	1	7697
92 3/02 Catt	2m3f	F(0-100)HHdl	G-S	£2096
			Total win prize-money £2097

Going:	Sf: 0-1 GS: 0-4 Gd: 0-3 GF: - Fm: 0-0
Distance:	2m/2m3: 0-3 2m4-2m7: 0-4 3m+: 0-1
Track:	LH: 0-6 RH: 0-1 Tight: 0-4 Gall: 0-2
Aids:	Bl: 0-1 Vi: 0-0 Tstrap: 0-0 Ckp: 0-0
Best Rating:	106 10/00 Sedg 2m1f gd-sft NHF

Moderate novice chaser; stays 2m 4f.

Caracciola (GER)
103(113h)   (136h)**150**
7-y-o b g Lando (GER)-Capitolina (FR) (Empery (USA))
N J Henderson P J D Pottinger

Placings:21313P-121120   (4382)
2003/04: 16¹G, 16²G, 16¹S, 16¹G, 16²G, 16⁰G,

	Starts	1st	2nd	3rd	Win & Pl
Hurdles	2	1	1	0	16499
Chases	4	2	1	0	21968
Career Total	12	5	3	2	56179
150 12/03 Kemp	2m	B Ch	GD	£10495
150 12/03 Hayd	2m	C Ch	SFT	£8988
135 11/03 Sand	2m110y D(0-125)HHdl	GD	£5499
125 2/03 Newb	2m110y C Hdl	GD	£7384
113 12/02 Newb	2m110y D Hdl	GD	£4738
			Total win prize-money £37106

| Career Total | 8 | 0 | 0 | 0 | 0 |

Going:	Sf: 0-0 GS: 0-0 Gd: 0-0 GF: - Fm: 0-1
Distance:	2m/2m3: 0-0 2m4-2m7: 0-0 3m+: 0-1
Track:	LH: 0-0 RH: 0-1 Tight: 0-0 Gall: 0-1
Aids:	Bl: 0-0 Vi: 0-0 Tstrap: 0-0 Ckp: 0-0
Best Rating:	91 5/01 Extr 2m1f firm NHF

Going:	Sf: 1-1 GS: 0-0 Gd: 2-5 GF: - Fm: 0-0
Distance:	2m/2m3: 3-6 2m4-2m7: 0-3 3m+: 0-0
Track:	LH: 1-3 RH: 2-3 Tight: 0-0 Gall: 0-1
Aids:	Bl: 0-0 Vi: 0-0 Tstrap: 0-0 Ckp: 0-0
Best Rating:	150 12/03 Kemp 2m good Ch

Smart novice chaser; very useful hurdler; ex-German; made a winning chasing debut at Haydock in December 2003 and lowered Thisthatandtother's colours at Kempton over Christmas; beaten by Palua at that track next time; last in the Arkle at Cheltenham; best over two miles; best on good but acts on soft ground; suited by waiting tactics.

Carapuce (FR)
100   **117+**
5-y-o ch g Bigstone (IRE)-Treasure City (FR) (Moulin)
L Lungo Mr & Mrs Raymond Anderson Green

Placings:50B0-01131P   (4641)
2003/04: 16⁶G, 20¹G, 20¹G, 24³GS, 17¹HY, 24⁰PG,

	Starts	1st	2nd	3rd	Win & Pl
Hurdles	6	3	0	1	16026
Career Total	10	3	0	1	16026
117 2/04 Carl	2m1f	D Hdl	HVY	£5255
112 11/03 Hexm	2m4f110yB HHdl	GD	£4615
97 11/03 Ayr	2m4f	D(0-110)HHdl	GD	£4836
			Total win prize-money £14706

Going:	Sf: 1-1 GS: 0-1 Gd: 2-4 GF: - Fm: 0-0
Distance:	2m/2m3: 1-2 2m4-2m7: 2-1 3m+: 0-2
Track:	LH: 2-4 RH: 1-2 Tight: 0-2 Gall: 0-0
Aids:	Bl: 0-0 Vi: 0-0 Tstrap: 0-0 Ckp: 0-0
Best Rating:	117 2/04 Carl 2m1f heavy Hdl

Useful hurdler; in good form in novice company in 2003/4; stays two and a half miles; acts on good and heavy ground.

Carbonado
10-y-o b g Anshan-Virevoite (Shareef Dancer (USA))
H R Tuck Mrs M J Tuck

Placings:546F0/42/42PP5-2644P   (4373)
2003/04: 25²G, 20⁶GF, 24⁴G, 25⁴G, 24⁵PG,

	Starts	1st	2nd	3rd	Win & Pl
Chases	5	0	1	0	1308
Career Total	17	0	3	0	3070

Going:	Sf: 0-0 GS: 0-0 Gd: 0-4 GF: - Fm: 0-1
Distance:	2m/2m3: 0-0 2m4-2m7: 0-1 3m+: 0-4
Track:	LH: 0-2 RH: 0-2 Tight: 0-3 Gall: 0-1
Aids:	Bl: 0-0 Vi: 0-0 Tstrap: 0-5 Ckp: 0-0
Best Rating:	96 3/04 Ludl 3m1f110y good Ch

Hunter chaser, effective over three miles on a sound surface.

Carbury Cross (IRE)
102   (105h)**151**
10-y-o b g Mandalus-Brickey Gazette (Fine Blade (USA))
Jonjo O'Neill Mrs Jonjo O'Neill

Placings:41306/211/111/62021U6/P5P00P0-2PU4FP   (3291)
2003/04: 21²GF, 27⁵PG, 27⁰UG, 29⁴G, 33⁵G, 29⁵GS,

	Starts	1st	2nd	3rd	Win & Pl
Chases	6	0	1	0	4722
Career Total	31	7	4	1	95130
153 4/02 Aint	3m1f	B HCh	GD	£26000
134 4/01 Ayr	3m1f	B HCh	G-F	£21385
130 2/01 Donc	3m	E Ch	GD	£3225

124	1/01	Muss	3m	E Ch	G-S	£3575
122	11/99	Hayd	2m7f110yD(0-120)HHdl		GD	£3078
126	10/99	Carl	3m110y E(0-115)HHdl		GD	£2402
108	1/99	Weth	2m4f110yD Hdl		SFT	£3116

Total win prize-money £62782

Going:	Sf: 0-0 GS: 0-1 Gd: 0-4 GF: - Fm: 0-1
Distance:	2m/2m3: 0-0 2m4-2m7: 0-1 3m+: 0-5
Track:	LH: 0-5 RH: 0-1 Tight: 0-2 Gall: 0-2
Aids:	Bl: 0-4 Vi: 0-0 Tstrap: 0-0 Ckp: 0-0
Best Rating:	153 4/02 Aint 3m1f good Ch

Useful chaser; winner of a valuable event at Aintree in April 2002; well below par in 2002/3 but creditable seventh in the Grand National; started the season off well with a second at Stratford, but disappointing since; stays at least 3m 4f; acts on fast and soft ground; has been blinkered.

Cardenas (GER)
110   143
5-y-o b g Acatenango (GER)-Cocorna (Night Shift (USA))
C R Egerton (Mario Hofer 15/2) Dr G Madan Mohan

Placings:21140   (4629)
2003/04: 17²S, 16¹GS, 20¹G, 16⁴G, 20⁶G,

	Starts	1st	2nd	3rd	Win & Pl
Hurdles	5	2	1	0	64105
Career Total	5	2	1	0	64105

| | 2/04 | Capa | 2m4f110y Hdl | | GD | £40141 |
| 131 | 12/03 | Newb | 2m110y B Hdl | | G-S | £12470 |

Total win prize-money £52611

Going:	Sf: 0-1 GS: 1-1 Gd: 1-3 GF: - Fm: 0-0
Distance:	2m/2m3: 1-3 2m4-2m7: 1-2 3m+: 0-0
Track:	LH: 1-3 RH: 0-0 Tight: 0-1 Gall: 1-1
Aids:	Bl: 0-0 Vi: 0-0 Tstrap: 0-0 Ckp: 0-0
Best Rating:	143 3/04 Chel 2m110y good Hdl

Useful novice hurdler; a winner three times on the Flat in Germany; second on his hurdling debut in Italy in December 2003 and successful on his next two outings at Newbury and again in Italy; ran well in the Supreme Novices' on debut for new connections, but disappointing at Aintree next time; stays 2m 4f and effective on good ground, but prefers cut; tough sort who should improve further.

Cardinal Mark (IRE)
104(102h)   (103h)92
10-y-o b g Ardross-Sister Of Gold (The Parson)
Mrs S J Smith G T Pierse

Placings:1P013/60/41300635FF002P/45430-436231
(4616)
2003/04: 25⁴GF, 21³GS, 20⁶HY, 24²GS, 20³G, 21¹G,

	Starts	1st	2nd	3rd	Win & Pl
Hurdles	3	0	1	1	1500
Chases	3	1	0	1	4019
Career Total	32	4	2	6	24448

88	3/04	Sedg	2m5f	F(0-95)HCh	GD	£3490
114	5/01	Baln	2m4f	Ch	G-Y	£5286
89	3/00	Clon	2m	Hdl	G-Y	£2980
101	10/99	Cork	2m1f	NHF	Y-S	£3388

Total win prize-money £15146

Going:	Sf: 0-1 GS: 0-2 Gd: 1-2 GF: - Fm: 0-1
Distance:	2m/2m3: 0-0 2m4-2m7: 1-4 3m+: 0-1
Track:	LH: 1-4 RH: 0-2 Tight: 1-3 Gall: 0-1
Aids:	Bl: 0-0 Vi: 0-0 Tstrap: 0-0 Ckp: 0-0
Best Rating:	114 5/01 Baln 2m4f gd-yld Ch

Moderate ex-Irish chaser/hurdler, suited by two and a half to three miles; handles any ground.

Cardington
94   96
5-y-o b g Saddlers' Hall (IRE)-Passionelle (Nashwan (USA))
Mrs S J Smith W J Dobson

Placings:54342   (4881)
2003/04: 17⁵GF, 17⁴GF, 17³G, 16⁴GS, 17²GS,

	Starts	1st	2nd	3rd	Win & Pl
NH Flat	3	0	0	1	281
Hurdles	2	0	1	0	1545
Career Total	5	0	1	1	1826

Going:	Sf: 0-0 GS: 0-2 Gd: 0-1 GF: - Fm: 0-2
Distance:	2m/2m3: 0-5 2m4-2m7: 0-0 3m+: 0-0
Track:	LH: 0-1 RH: 0-4 Tight: 0-2 Gall: 0-0
Aids:	Bl: 0-0 Vi: 0-0 Tstrap: 0-0 Ckp: 0-0
Best Rating:	97 10/03 Carl 2m1f good NHF

Fair form in bumpers in 2003; modest form in novice hurdles.

Carew
96(87h)   (59h)70
8-y-o b g Minster Son-The White Lion (Flying Tyke)
C Grant D Vic Roper

Placings:52B/40/004-2523   (1477)
2003/04: 17²GF, 21⁵GF, 26²G, 21³G,

	Starts	1st	2nd	3rd	Win & Pl
Chases	4	0	2	1	3171
Career Total	12	0	3	1	3621

Going:	Sf: 0-0 GS: 0-0 Gd: 0-2 GF: - Fm: 0-2
Distance:	2m/2m3: 0-1 2m4-2m7: 0-2 3m+: 0-1
Track:	LH: 0-4 RH: 0-0 Tight: 0-4 Gall: 0-0
Aids:	Bl: 0-0 Vi: 0-0 Tstrap: 0-0 Ckp: 0-0
Best Rating:	102 12/00 Muss 2m good NHF

Plating-class novice chaser; acts on a sound surface.

Carew Lad
83   60+
8-y-o b g Arzanni-Miss Skindles (Taufan (USA))
Mrs D A Hamer Mrs Mandy Hinchliffe

Placings:6-6   (0758)
2003/04: 24⁶G,

	Starts	1st	2nd	3rd	Win & Pl
Hurdles	1	0	0	0	0
Career Total	2	0	0	0	0

Going:	Sf: 0-0 GS: 0-0 Gd: 0-1 GF: - Fm: 0-0
Distance:	2m/2m3: 0-0 2m4-2m7: 0-0 3m+: 0-1
Track:	LH: 0-1 RH: 0-0 Tight: 0-0 Gall: 0-0
Aids:	Bl: 0-0 Vi: 0-0 Tstrap: 0-0 Ckp: 0-0
Best Rating:	81 7/02 Worc 2m good NHF

Careysville (IRE)
112
13-y-o b g Carmelite House (USA)-Kavali (Blakeney)
Miss Venetia Williams Miss V M Williams

Placings:6500P/06/5F11PF5/2101/F424/3/02/52P-4 (0454)
2003/04: 26⁴HY,

	Starts	1st	2nd	3rd	Win & Pl
Chases	1	0	0	0	456
Career Total	29	4	4	1	30569

| 129 | 3/99 | Newb | 3m | C(0-135)HCh | SFT | £5524 |
| 129 | 1/99 | Folk | 3m2f | D(0-125)HCh | SFT | £7335 |

| 118 | 1/98 | Ludl | 3m | E(0-115)HCh | G-S | £3048 |
| 122 | 12/97 | Font | 3m2f110yE(0-100)HCh | | SFT | £3603 |

Total win prize-money £19511

Going:	Sf: 0-1 GS: 0-0 Gd: 0-0 GF: - Fm: 0-0
Distance:	2m/2m3: 0-0 2m4-2m7: 0-0 3m+: 0-1
Track:	LH: 0-1 RH: 0-0 Tight: 0-0 Gall: 0-0
Aids:	Bl: 0-0 Vi: 0-0 Tstrap: 0-0 Ckp: 0-0
Best Rating:	129 3/99 Newb 3m soft Ch

Moderate chaser; runner-up in the Grand Military Gold Cup in both 2002 and 2003; stays 3m 4f and is effective on soft ground.

Caribbean Cove (IRE)
100   (90c)109+
6-y-o gr g Norwich-Peaceful Rose (Roselier (FR))
Miss H C Knight Trevor Hemmings

Placings:00031-1FP530P   (4870)
2003/04: 21¹GF, 21²G, 20²G, 19⁵S, 20³S, 21⁰G, 24²PGS,

	Starts	1st	2nd	3rd	Win & Pl
Hurdles	5	1	0	1	4997
Chases	2	0	0	0	0
Career Total	12	2	0	2	9577

| 92 | 5/03 | Wwck | 2m5f | E Hdl | G-F | £3867 |
| 106 | 4/03 | Bang | 2m4f | E Hdl | G-F | £3721 |

Total win prize-money £7589

Going:	Sf: 0-2 GS: 0-1 Gd: 0-3 GF: - Fm: 1-1
Distance:	2m/2m3: 0-0 2m4-2m7: 1-6 3m+: 0-1
Track:	LH: 1-6 RH: 0-1 Tight: 0-3 Gall: 0-1
Aids:	Bl: 0-0 Vi: 0-0 Tstrap: 0-0 Ckp: 0-0
Best Rating:	109 2/04 Hayd 2m4f soft Hdl

Modest novice hurdler; won back-to-back novice hurdles in the spring of 2003; stays 2m5f; seems best on good to firm, but has been placed on soft.

Caribbean Lad (IRE)
77
8-y-o ch g Denel (FR)-Daisy Star (Star Appeal)
J R Turner J W Daniel

Placings:00/0F/PPP   (2477)
2003/04: 22⁵G, 17⁵GF, 24⁶GF,

	Starts	1st	2nd	3rd	Win & Pl
Hurdles	3	0	0	0	
Career Total	7	0	0	0	

Going:	Sf: 0-0 GS: 0-0 Gd: 0-1 GF: - Fm: 0-2
Distance:	2m/2m3: 0-1 2m4-2m7: 0-1 3m+: 0-1
Track:	LH: 0-3 RH: 0-0 Tight: 0-2 Gall: 0-1
Aids:	Bl: 0-0 Vi: 0-0 Tstrap: 0-0 Ckp: 0-0
Best Rating:	77 10/01 Carl 2m1f gd-sft Hdl

Caribbean Man
85   78+
4-y-o b g Hector Protector (USA)-Caribbean Star (Soviet Star (USA))
B J Llewellyn (Sir Michael Stoute 11/6) Maenllwyd Racing Club

Placings:3642   (3317)
2003/04: 16³G, 17⁶GF, 16⁴GS, 16²S,

	Starts	1st	2nd	3rd	Win & Pl
Hurdles	4	0	1	1	1301
Career Total	4	0	1	1	1301

Going:	Sf: 0-1 GS: 0-1 Gd: 0-0 GF: - Fm: 0-2
Distance:	2m/2m3: 0-4 2m4-2m7: 0-0 3m+: 0-0
Track:	LH: 0-2 RH: 0-2 Tight: 0-0 Gall: 0-0
Aids:	Bl: 0-0 Vi: 0-0 Tstrap: 0-0 Ckp: 0-1
Best Rating:	78 1/04 Leic 2m soft Hdl

Plating-class hurdler; acts on any ground.

Caribbean Sun (IRE)

4-y-o b c Grand Lodge (USA)-Carranita (IRE) (Anita's Prince)
B Palling Albert Yemm

Placings:P					(2871)
2003/04: 16PS,					

	Starts	1st	2nd	3rd	Win & Pl
Hurdles	1	0	0	0	
Career Total	1	0	0	0	

Going:	Sf: 0-1 GS: 0-0 Gd: 0-0 GF: - Fm: 0-0
Distance:	2m/2m3: 0-0 2m4-2m7: 0-0 3m+: 0-0
Track:	LH: 0-1 RH: 0-0 Tight: 0-0 Gall: 0-0
Aids:	Bl: 0-0 Vi: 0-0 Tstrap: 0-0 Ckp: 0-0
Best Rating:	0 12/03 Wwck 2m soft Hdl

Did show promise on the Flat; may be capable of better over hurdles.

Caribean Dream

9-y-o ch m Afzal-Lovelek (Golden Love)
G E Jones G Elwyn Jones

Placings:P-P					(0376)
2003/04: 20PS,					

	Starts	1st	2nd	3rd	Win & Pl
Hurdles	1	0	0	0	
Career Total	2	0	0	0	

Going:	Sf: 0-1 GS: 0-0 Gd: 0-0 GF: - Fm: 0-0
Distance:	2m/2m3: 0-0 2m4-2m7: 0-0 3m+: 0-0
Track:	LH: 0-1 RH: 0-0 Tight: 0-1 Gall: 0-0
Aids:	Bl: 0-0 Vi: 0-0 Tstrap: 0-0 Ckp: 0-0

Carlotta
69   24

7-y-o b m Carlingford Castle-Baryta (Nishapour (FR))
N J Gifford Lime Street Racing Syndicate

Placings:60PP					(4361)
2003/04: 16PS, 18PGS, 16PG, 21PGS,					

	Starts	1st	2nd	3rd	Win & Pl
NH Flat	1	0	0	0	0
Hurdles	3	0	0	0	0
Career Total	4	0	0	0	0

Going:	Sf: 0-1 GS: 0-2 Gd: 0-1 GF: - Fm: 0-0
Distance:	2m/2m3: 0-3 2m4-2m7: 0-1 3m+: 0-0
Track:	LH: 0-3 RH: 0-1 Tight: 0-3 Gall: 0-0
Aids:	Bl: 0-0 Vi: 0-0 Tstrap: 0-0 Ckp: 0-0
Best Rating:	69 12/03 Towc 2m soft NHF

Carlovent (FR)
104   120

9-y-o b g Cadoudal (FR)-Carlaya (FR) (Carmarthen (FR))

M C Pipe C M , B J & R F Batterham

Placings:11F113/1111FF11160/514PU612/543535034/503	
4P50133-00356P00	(4963)
2003/04: 239GS, 25G, 223G, 205S, 226S, 25PG, 24G, 20PG,	

	Starts	1st	2nd	3rd	Win & Pl
Hurdles	8	0	0	1	2427
Career Total	52	14	1	8	181738
142 4/03	Aint	3m110y	A HHdl		GD	£23200
149 4/01	Aint	3m110y	B HHdl		SFT	£26000
144 11/00	Asct	2m	B HCh		G-S	£13312
136 11/99	Chep	2m110y	B Hdl		G-S	£6710
147 11/99	Chep	2m4f	B HHdl		SFT	£22073
142 10/99	Chep	2m110y	B HHdl		SFT	£6710
134 7/99	Wolv	2m4f110yC(0-130)HHdl		G-F	£6563
6/99	Autl	2m1f110y	Ch		SFT	£6997
6/99	Toul	2m1f110y	Hdl		GD	£3767
5/99	Dax	2m3f	Ch		SFT	£3767
10/98	Mesl	2m1f110y	Ch		HVY	£3535
9/98	Jarn	2m	Hdl		GD	£1515
7/98	Pomp	1m5f110y	Hdl		GD	£2828
6/98	Pomp	1m5f110y	Hdl		GD	£2525

Total win prize-money £129503

Going:	Sf: 0-2 GS: 0-1 Gd: 0-5 GF: - Fm: 0-0
Distance:	2m/2m3: 0-0 2m4-2m7: 0-4 3m+: 0-4
Track:	LH: 0-4 RH: 0-4 Tight: 0-1 Gall: 0-2
Aids:	Bl: 0-0 Vi: 0-8 Tstrap: 0-0 Ckp: 0-0
Best Rating:	150 2/02 Sand 2m6f soft Hdl

Fair hurdler; multiple winner in both France and here; took a three-mile handicap hurdle at Aintree for the second time in three years in April 2003; acts on any ground; best at around three miles; reportedly blind in one eye; usually wears a visor; has been let down by his hurdling.

Carlton Cracker

12-y-o b g Primitive Rising (USA)-Miss Cracker Jack (Ancient Monro)
C N Kellett J E Titley

Placings:3F/PUP5321/P					(2464)
2003/04: 22PS,					

	Starts	1st	2nd	3rd	Win & Pl
Chases	1	0	0	0	
Career Total	10	1	1	2	5878
100 4/02	MRas	3m1f	F(0-95)Ch	GD	£3556

Total win prize-money £3556

Going:	Sf: 0-1 GS: 0-0 Gd: 0-0 GF: - Fm: 0-0
Distance:	2m/2m3: 0-0 2m4-2m7: 0-1 3m+: 0-0
Track:	LH: 0-0 RH: 0-1 Tight: 0-0 Gall: 0-0
Aids:	Bl: 0-0 Vi: 0-0 Tstrap: 0-0 Ckp: 0-0
Best Rating:	100 4/02 MRas 3m1f good Ch

Carluccios Quest
82f   50f

6-y-o gr g Terimon-Jindabyne (Good Times (ITY))
Mrs H Dalton Mrs C S Wilson

Placings:0					(1817)
2003/04: 17G,					

	Starts	1st	2nd	3rd	Win & Pl
NH Flat	1	0	0	0	
Career Total	1	0	0	0	

Going:	Sf: 0-0 GS: 0-0 Gd: 0-1 GF: - Fm: 0-0
Distance:	2m/2m3: 0-1 2m4-2m7: 0-0 3m+: 0-0
Track:	LH: 0-1 RH: 0-0 Tight: 0-1 Gall: 0-0
Aids:	Bl: 0-0 Vi: 0-0 Tstrap: 0-0 Ckp: 0-0
Best Rating:	51 10/03 Bang 2m1f good NHF

Carly Bay
103   109+

6-y-o b m Carlton (GER)-Polly Minor (Sunley Builds)
G P Enright A O Ashford

Placings:0/44415-F4P23P					(4102)
2003/04: 16FS, 184G, 24PG, 16?S, 21?S, 16PG,					

	Starts	1st	2nd	3rd	Win & Pl
Hurdles	6	0	1	1	2919
Career Total	12	1	1	1	6720
109 2/03	Plum	2m	E Hdl	HVY	£3532

Total win prize-money £3533

Going:	Sf: 0-3 GS: 0-0 Gd: 0-3 GF: - Fm: 0-0
Distance:	2m/2m3: 0-4 2m4-2m7: 0-1 3m+: 0-1
Track:	LH: 0-5 RH: 0-1 Tight: 0-5 Gall: 0-0
Aids:	Bl: 0-0 Vi: 0-0 Tstrap: 0-0 Ckp: 0-0
Best Rating:	109 1/04 Plum 2m soft Hdl

Modest novice hurdler; got off the mark in an ordinary novice hurdle at Plumpton; acts on heavy ground; effective over two miles.

Carlys Quest
104   97

10-y-o ch g Primo Dominie-Tuppy (USA) (Sharpen Up)
Ferdy Murphy Yorkeys Knob Racing Club

Placings:050/220/304					(4879)
2003/04: 233GS, 21G, 204GS,					

	Starts	1st	2nd	3rd	Win & Pl
Hurdles	3	0	0	1	673
Career Total	9	0	2	1	2226

Going:	Sf: 0-0 GS: 0-2 Gd: 0-1 GF: - Fm: 0-0
Distance:	2m/2m3: 0-0 2m4-2m7: 0-2 3m+: 0-1
Track:	LH: 0-2 RH: 0-1 Tight: 0-2 Gall: 0-0
Aids:	Bl: 0-1 Vi: 0-2 Tstrap: 0-3 Ckp: 0-0
Best Rating:	111 3/99 Chel 2m110y gd-sft Hdl

Modest hurdler; he has shown ability over hurdles, but does not find a great deal off the bridle; usually wears visor or blinkers.

Carmelite (IRE)
(63c)105

9-y-o ch g Good Thyne (USA)-Monks Lass (IRE) (Monksfield)
Mrs S Wall J P C Wall

Placings:10/0FS013113P5/P63FP61U/0PPP00-P					(2486)
2003/04: 16PGS,					

	Starts	1st	2nd	3rd	Win & Pl
Hurdles	1	0	0	0	
Career Total	28	5	0	3	30731
112 1/02	Cork	2m	Ch	SFT	£7407
127 11/00	Punc	2m4f	Hdl	SFT	£5520
121 10/00	Gway	2m4f	Hdl	HVY	£6624
112 9/00	List	2m4f	Hdl	HVY	£4416
98 9/99	List	2m	NHF	HVY	£4466

Total win prize-money £28435

Going:	Sf: 0-0 GS: 0-1 Gd: 0-0 GF: - Fm: 0-0
Distance:	2m/2m3: 0-0 2m4-2m7: 0-0 3m+: 0-0
Track:	LH: 0-1 RH: 0-0 Tight: 0-0 Gall: 0-1
Aids:	Bl: 0-0 Vi: 0-0 Tstrap: 0-0 Ckp: 0-0
Best Rating:	127 11/00 Navn 2m4f soft Hdl

Carn Rivers (IRE)

58   **77**

9-y-o ch g Over The River (FR)-Carnowen (Deep Run)
Mrs S J Smith Mrs S Smith

Placings:63   (1620)
2003/04: 20⁶GF, 17³G,

	Starts	1st	2nd	3rd	Win & Pl
Hurdles	2	0	0	1	472
Career Total	**2**	**0**	**0**	**1**	**472**

Going:	Sf: 0-0 GS: 0-0 Gd: 0-1 GF: - Fm: 0-1
Distance:	2m/2m3: 0-1 2m4-2m7: 0-1 3m+: 0-0
Track:	LH: 0-2 RH: 0-0 Tight: 0-1 Gall: 0-0
Aids:	Bl: 0-0 Vi: 0-0 Tstrap: 0-0 Ckp: 0-0
Best Rating:	77 10/03 Bang 2m1f good Hdl

Beaten for speed when third in slowly-run novice hurdle at Bangor October 2003.

Carnacrack

108   **95**

10-y-o b g Le Coq D'Or-Carney (New Brig)
Miss S E Forster C Storey

Placings:21021F4033-64132336   (3340)
2003/04: 22⁶G, 24⁴G, 26¹GF, 25³F, 25²GF, 28³G, 27³GF, 25⁶GS,

	Starts	1st	2nd	3rd	Win & Pl
Chases	8	1	1	3	8450
Career Total	**18**	**3**	**3**	**5**	**20370**
93	7/03	Ctrnl	3m2f	E(0-105)HCh	G-F	£4459
95	11/02	Kels	3m1f	F(0-100)HCh	HVY	£4026
86	6/02	Ctrnl	3m2f	E Ch	GD	£3146
				Total win prize-money £11632		

Going:	Sf: 0-0 GS: 0-1 Gd: 0-3 GF: - Fm: 1-4
Distance:	2m/2m3: 0-0 2m4-2m7: 0-1 3m+: 1-7
Track:	LH: 1-7 RH: 0-0 Tight: 1-7 Gall: 0-0
Aids:	Bl: 0-0 Vi: 0-0 Tstrap: 0-0 Ckp: 1-7
Best Rating:	95 11/03 Kels 3m4f good Ch

Moderate chaser; stays three miles plus; suited by some cut.

Carnaney Girl

(74h)   (32h)

6-y-o ch m Primitive Rising (USA)-Mossberry Fair (Mossberry)
A E Jones Miss Sophie Parmentier

Placings:PP0R0PF   (3653)
2003/04: 16⁸G, 17⁶GF, 16⁹GF, 17⁸GF, 16⁹GF, 21⁹GF, 16⁴S,

	Starts	1st	2nd	3rd	Win & Pl
Hurdles	6	0	0	0	0
Chases	1	0	0	0	0
Career Total	**7**	**0**	**0**	**0**	

Going:	Sf: 0-1 GS: 0-0 Gd: 0-1 GF: - Fm: 0-5
Distance:	2m/2m3: 0-6 2m4-2m7: 0-1 3m+: 0-0
Track:	LH: 0-6 RH: 0-1 Tight: 0-4 Gall: 0-1
Aids:	Bl: 0-0 Vi: 0-0 Tstrap: 0-0 Ckp: 0-0
Best Rating:	32 9/03 Worc 2m gd-fm Hdl

Plating-class hurdler/chaser; has failed to complete on most starts.

Carnoustie (USA)

95   **92**

6-y-o gr m Ezzoud (IRE)-Sarba (USA) (Persepolis (FR))
R T Phillips Dozen Dreamers Partnership

Placings:3/3412403521-250P   (4370)
2003/04: 26²GF, 22⁵GF, 20⁹GS, 19⁹GF,

	Starts	1st	2nd	3rd	Win & Pl
Hurdles	4	0	1	0	744
Career Total	**15**	**2**	**3**	**3**	**10066**
89	3/03	Strf	2m3f	G Hdl	G-S	£2947
98	6/02	NAbb	2m1f	D Hdl	G-F	£3419
				Total win prize-money £6366		

Going:	Sf: 0-0 GS: 0-1 Gd: 0-0 GF: - Fm: 0-3
Distance:	2m/2m3: 0-1 2m4-2m7: 0-2 3m+: 0-1
Track:	LH: 0-2 RH: 0-0 Tight: 0-2 Gall: 0-2
Aids:	Bl: 0-0 Vi: 0-0 Tstrap: 0-0 Ckp: 0-2
Best Rating:	98 6/02 NAbb 2m1f gd-fm Hdl

Moderate novice hurdler; stays two and a half miles; has worn cheekpieces.

Caroline's Rose

91   **69+**

6-y-o br m Fraam-Just Rosie (Sula Bula)
A P Jones The Lambourn Racing Club

Placings:0-0P563566   (2691)
2003/04: 17⁰GF, 19⁰GF, 17⁵GF, 16⁶G, 16³GF, 16⁵G, 16⁶GF, 16⁶G,

	Starts	1st	2nd	3rd	Win & Pl
Hurdles	8	0	0	1	320
Career Total	**9**	**0**	**0**	**1**	**320**

Going:	Sf: 0-0 GS: 0-0 Gd: 0-4 GF: - Fm: 0-4
Distance:	2m/2m3: 0-7 2m4-2m7: 0-1 3m+: 0-0
Track:	LH: 0-4 RH: 0-4 Tight: 0-1 Gall: 0-0
Aids:	Bl: 0-0 Vi: 0-0 Tstrap: 0-1 Ckp: 0-0
Best Rating:	69 10/03 Ludl 2m gd-fm Hdl

Free-running novice hurdler; best effort when third in Ludlow seller October 2003.

Caroubier (IRE)

93   **93+**

4-y-o ch g Woodborough (USA)-Patsy Grimes (Beveled (USA))
J Gallagher (T D Barron 9/2) C R Marks (banbury)

Placings:4515   (2436)
2003/04: 17⁴G, 16⁵GF, 16¹GF, 17⁵G,

	Starts	1st	2nd	3rd	Win & Pl
Hurdles	4	1	0	0	3441
Career Total	**4**	**1**	**0**	**0**	**3441**
93	11/03	Wwck	2m	E Hdl	G-F	£3146
				Total win prize-money £3147		

Going:	Sf: 0-0 GS: 0-0 Gd: 0-2 GF: - Fm: 1-2
Distance:	2m/2m3: 1-4 2m4-2m7: 0-0 3m+: 0-0
Track:	LH: 1-4 RH: 0-0 Tight: 0-3 Gall: 0-0
Aids:	Bl: 1-2 Vi: 0-0 Tstrap: 0-0 Ckp: 0-0
Best Rating:	93 11/03 Wwck 2m gd-fm Hdl

Juvenile hurdler; winner five times on the Flat; made all in blinkers third hurdles start; acts on fast.

Carpenters Boy

92f   **76f**

4-y-o b g Nomination-Jolly Girl (Jolly Me)
Mrs A M Thorpe Mrs A M Thorpe

Placings:00   (4571)
2003/04: 16⁹G, 17⁹GS,

	Starts	1st	2nd	3rd	Win & Pl
NH Flat	2	0	0	0	
Career Total	**2**	**0**	**0**	**0**	

Going:	Sf: 0-0 GS: 0-1 Gd: 0-1 GF: - Fm: 0-0
Distance:	2m/2m3: 0-2 2m4-2m7: 0-0 3m+: 0-0
Track:	LH: 0-2 RH: 0-0 Tight: 0-1 Gall: 0-1
Aids:	Bl: 0-0 Vi: 0-0 Tstrap: 0-0 Ckp: 0-0
Best Rating:	76 3/04 Bang 2m1f gd-sft NHF

Carraig Brol (IRE)

10-y-o b g Cataldi-Davy's Hall (Weavers Hall)
W S Coltherd Mrs L J McLeod

Placings:4/PPP   (4659)
2003/04: 25⁵GF, 20⁸HY, 16⁸S,

	Starts	1st	2nd	3rd	Win & Pl
Chases	3	0	0	0	
Career Total	**4**	**0**	**0**	**0**	**163**

Going:	Sf: 0-2 GS: 0-0 Gd: 0-0 GF: - Fm: 0-1
Distance:	2m/2m3: 0-1 2m4-2m7: 0-1 3m+: 0-1
Track:	LH: 0-2 RH: 0-0 Tight: 0-0 Gall: 0-0
Aids:	Bl: 0-0 Vi: 0-0 Tstrap: 0-0 Ckp: 0-1
Best Rating:	80 5/00 Folk 2m5f good Ch

Carriage Ride (IRE)

98   **87**

6-y-o b g Tidaro (USA)-Casakurali (Gleason (USA))
N G Richards James Callow & David Wesley Yates

Placings:0-00P20   (4879)
2003/04: 20⁰G, 18⁰S, 17⁰GS, 20²S, 20⁰GS,

	Starts	1st	2nd	3rd	Win & Pl
Hurdles	5	0	1	0	1081
Career Total	**6**	**0**	**1**	**0**	**1081**

Going:	Sf: 0-2 GS: 0-2 Gd: 0-1 GF: - Fm: 0-0
Distance:	2m/2m3: 0-2 2m4-2m7: 0-3 3m+: 0-0
Track:	LH: 0-4 RH: 0-1 Tight: 0-3 Gall: 0-0
Aids:	Bl: 0-0 Vi: 0-0 Tstrap: 0-0 Ckp: 0-0
Best Rating:	90 4/04 Hexm 2m4f110y soft Hdl

Carrick Troop (IRE)

115   **132+**

11-y-o gr g Roselier (FR)-Over The Pond (IRE) (Over The River (FR))
Mrs M Reveley Major J C K Young

Placings:P4/6B112/322PPU3P/P13B114/1430504-621   (2451)

2003/04: 17⁶G, 20²G, 17¹GS,

	Starts	1st	2nd	3rd	Win & Pl
Chases	3	1	1	0	11215
Career Total	**32**	**7**	**4**	**4**	**62749**
132	11/03	Newb	2m1f	C(0-135)HCh	G-S	£9228
128	11/02	Weth	2m	C(0-135)HCh	GD	£8200
128	3/02	Newb	2m2f110yD(0-125)HCh	G-S	£7182
118	3/02	Newb	2m1f	C(0-135)HCh	SFT	£8268
114	12/01	Hayd	2m	D(0-125)HCh	SFT	£9051
116	1/00	Sedg	3m3f	F(0-105)HCh	SFT	£2873
110	12/99	MRas	3m1f	C(0-105)HCh	G-S	£3481
				Total win prize-money £48286		

Going:	Sf: 0-0 GS: 1-1 Gd: 0-2 GF: - Fm: 0-0
Distance:	2m/2m3: 1-2 2m4-2m7: 0-1 3m+: 0-0
Track:	LH: 1-3 RH: 0-0 Tight: 0-1 Gall: 1-1
Aids:	Bl: 0-0 Vi: 0-0 Tstrap: 0-0 Ckp: 0-0
Best Rating:	132 11/03 Newb 2m1f gd-sft Ch

Decent handicap chaser who used to race over three miles plus but now seems perfectly capable at trips around two miles; suited by soft ground; needs a strong pace in order to show his best.

Carrig Boy (IRE)

14-y-o ch g Long Pond-Shining Brightly (Giolla Mear)
I Anderson Ian Anderson

Placings:00/PB/1   (0294)
2003/04: 20¹GS,

	Starts	1st	2nd	3rd	Win & Pl
Chases	1	1	0	0	2789
Career Total	5	1	0	0	2789
86 5/03 Strf	2m4f	H Ch		G-S	£2788

Total win prize-money £2789

Going:	Sf: 0-0 GS: 1-1 Gd: 0-0 GF: - Fm: 0-0
Distance:	2m/2m3: 0-0 2m4-2m7: 1-1 3m+: 0-0
Track:	LH: 1-1 RH: 0-0 Tight: 1-1 Gall: 0-0
Aids:	Bl: 0-0 Vi: 0-0 Tstrap: 0-0 Ckp: 0-0
Best Rating:	86 5/03 Strf 2m4f gd-sft Ch

Winner of three points; took advantage of Executive Park's fall when coming from a long way back to win 2m 4f hunter chase at Stratford May 2003.

Carrigafoyle

80   **80**

9-y-o b g Young Senor (USA)-Miss Skindles (Taufan (USA))
O Brennan O Brennan

Placings:40/06/02050PP-30   (0479)
2003/04: 20³GF, 21⁰GF,

	Starts	1st	2nd	3rd	Win & Pl
Hurdles	2	0	0	1	508
Career Total	13	0	1	1	1394

Going:	Sf: 0-0 GS: 0-0 Gd: 0-0 GF: - Fm: 0-2
Distance:	2m/2m3: 0-0 2m4-2m7: 0-2 3m+: 0-0
Track:	LH: 0-0 RH: 0-2 Tight: 0-0 Gall: 0-2
Aids:	Bl: 0-0 Vi: 0-0 Tstrap: 0-0 Ckp: 0-0
Best Rating:	93 1/03 Donc 2m110y gd-sft Hdl

Moderate hurdler; acts on a soft surface; has never raced beyond two miles three; still a maiden.

Carroll's Gold (IRE)

94   **74**

6-y-o br g Carroll House-Missfethard-On-Sea (Deep Run)
E L James Mrs M M Stobart

Placings:500-2F   (1082)
2003/04: 16²GF, 16ᶠGF,

	Starts	1st	2nd	3rd	Win & Pl
Hurdles	2	0	1	0	1036
Career Total	5	0	1	0	1036

Going:	Sf: 0-0 GS: 0-0 Gd: 0-0 GF: - Fm: 0-2
Distance:	2m/2m3: 0-2 2m4-2m7: 0-0 3m+: 0-0
Track:	LH: 0-2 RH: 0-0 Tight: 0-0 Gall: 0-0
Aids:	Bl: 0-0 Vi: 0-0 Tstrap: 0-0 Ckp: 0-0
Best Rating:	93 5/02 Extr 2m1f good NHF

Poor form in bumpers; well beaten runner-up on hurdling debut at Uttoxeter in July.

Carryonharry (IRE)

98   (132h)**133**

10-y-o gr g Roselier (FR)-Bluebell Avenue (Boreen Beag)
M C Pipe Drs' D Silk J Castro M Gillard P Walker

Placings:663113/1133/1110F/P10P46P-640000   (4965)
2003/04: 24⁶G, 24⁴S, 33⁰G, 30⁰G, 33⁰GS, 29⁰GF,

		Starts	1st	2nd	3rd	Win & Pl
Chases		6	0	0	0	3100
Career Total		28	8	0	4	73569
133	12/02 Kemp 3m	C(0-135)HCh		SFT	£29000
124	12/01 Extr	2m7f110yD Ch		GD	£5538
122	11/01 Extr	2m7f110yD Ch		G-F	£5681
133	11/01 Font	2m6f	E Ch		G-S	£3185
133	11/00 Chep	3m	C(0-130)HHdl	HVY	£5057
130	11/00 Kemp	3m110y D(0-120)HHdl		SFT	£4212
114	2/00	Wwck 2m4f110yD Hdl		GD	£3685
106	1/00	Plum 2m5f	E Hdl		SFT	£2415

Total win prize-money £58774

Going:	Sf: 0-1 GS: 0-1 Gd: 0-3 GF: - Fm: 0-1
Distance:	2m/2m3: 0-0 2m4-2m7: 0-0 3m+: 0-6
Track:	LH: 0-3 RH: 0-3 Tight: 0-0 Gall: 0-2
Aids:	Bl: 0-0 Vi: 0-4 Tstrap: 0-0 Ckp: 0-0
Best Rating:	133 12/02 Kemp 3m soft Ch

Fair chaser; effective at three miles; has won on good and soft ground; sometimes visored.

Casayana

4-y-o b f Sir Harry Lewis (USA)-Five And Four (IRE) (Green Desert (USA))
D McCain The Rum Partnership

Placings:0P   (3754)
2003/04: 16⁰G, 17ᴾG,

	Starts	1st	2nd	3rd	Win & Pl
NH Flat	1	0	0	0	0
Hurdles	1	0	0	0	0
Career Total	2	0	0	0	

Going:	Sf: 0-0 GS: 0-0 Gd: 0-2 GF: - Fm: 0-0
Distance:	2m/2m3: 0-2 2m4-2m7: 0-0 3m+: 0-0
Track:	LH: 0-1 RH: 0-1 Tight: 0-1 Gall: 0-0
Aids:	Bl: 0-0 Vi: 0-0 Tstrap: 0-0 Ckp: 0-0

Case Of Poteen (IRE)

97(103h)   (95+h)**90**

8-y-o b/br m Witness Box (USA)-On The Hooch (Over The River (FR))
Mrs S C Bradburne Mrs P Grant

Placings:60/3232503/043246/FC4230-2416   (3733)
2003/04: 24²S, 25⁴GS, 20¹GF, 24⁶G,

	Starts	1st	2nd	3rd	Win & Pl
Hurdles	3	1	1	0	4124
Chases	1	0	0	0	0
Career Total	25	1	5	5	10393
95 1/04 Muss	2m4f	E Hdl		G-F	£3454

Total win prize-money £3455

Going:	Sf: 0-1 GS: 0-1 Gd: 0-1 GF: - Fm: 1-1
Distance:	2m/2m3: 0-0 2m4-2m7: 1-1 3m+: 0-3
Track:	LH: 0-2 RH: 1-2 Tight: 1-2 Gall: 0-0
Aids:	Bl: 0-0 Vi: 0-0 Tstrap: 0-0 Ckp: 0-0
Best Rating:	103 1/01 Newc 2m4f heavy Hdl

Moderate staying hurdler who continues to fall short; fully exposed.

Cash 'N' Credit

97(100h)   (70h)**79**

6-y-o b m Homo Sapien-Not Enough (Balinger)
R Dickin The Cash 'N' Creditors

Placings:00/534-145000254   (4919)
2003/04: 16¹G, 16⁴G, 17⁵GS, 16⁰GS, 20⁰G, 19⁰GS, 25²GF, 25⁵G, 20⁴GS,

	Starts	1st	2nd	3rd	Win & Pl
Chases	9	1	1	0	5324
Career Total	14	1	1	1	5822
79 6/03 Worc 2m	F(0-95)HCh		GD	£3542

Total win prize-money £3543

Going:	Sf: 0-0 GS: 0-4 Gd: 1-4 GF: - Fm: 0-1
Distance:	2m/2m3: 1-5 2m4-2m7: 0-2 3m+: 0-2
Track:	LH: 1-4 RH: 0-5 Tight: 0-1 Gall: 0-0
Aids:	Bl: 0-0 Vi: 0-0 Tstrap: 0-0 Ckp: 0-3
Best Rating:	79 3/04 Hrfd 3m1f110y gd-fm Ch

Stepped up on previous efforts when making winning debut over fences off low weight in 2m novices' handicap at Worcester June 2003; held since; acts on a sound surface; sometimes wears cheekpieces.

Cash Return

90   **62**

5-y-o b m Bob's Return (IRE)-We're In The Money (Billion (USA))
B G Powell Berkeley Square Racing

Placings:00000-U50   (4232)
2003/04: 20ᵁG, 24⁵G, 20⁰GF,

	Starts	1st	2nd	3rd	Win & Pl
Hurdles	3	0	0	0	0
Career Total	8	0	0	0	0

Going:	Sf: 0-0 GS: 0-0 Gd: 0-1 GF: - Fm: 0-2
Distance:	2m/2m3: 0-0 2m4-2m7: 0-2 3m+: 0-1
Track:	LH: 0-2 RH: 0-0 Tight: 0-1 Gall: 0-0
Aids:	Bl: 0-0 Vi: 0-0 Tstrap: 0-0 Ckp: 0-0
Best Rating:	64 3/04 Font 2m4f gd-fm Hdl

Cashel Dancer

105   **94**

5-y-o b m Bishop Of Cashel-Dancing Debut (Polar Falcon (USA))
S A Brookshaw Ken Edwards

Placings:440-13143320630   (4716)
2003/04: 19¹GS, 17³GF, 20¹GF, 19⁴G, 19³GS, 17³GF, 20²GF, 16⁰GS, 21⁶G, 16³GS, 21⁰G,

	Starts	1st	2nd	3rd	Win & Pl
Hurdles	11	2	1	4	11166
Career Total	14	2	1	4	11750
68 6/03 Uttx	2m4f110yE Hdl		G-F	£4165
78 5/03 Hrfd	2m3f110yE Hdl		G-S	£3906

Total win prize-money £8072

Going:	Sf: 0-0 GS: 1-3 Gd: 0-3 GF: - Fm: 1-5
Distance:	2m/2m3: 0-5 2m4-2m7: 2-6 3m+: 0-0
Track:	LH: 1-4 RH: 1-7 Tight: 0-1 Gall: 0-0
Aids:	Bl: 0-0 Vi: 0-0 Tstrap: 0-0 Ckp: 0-0
Best Rating:	94 10/03 Hrfd 2m1f gd-fm Hdl

Plating-class hurdler; in the frame in weak novice hurdles before accounting for a depleted field at Uttoxeter in June 2003; stays two and a half miles.

Cassia Heights
106   (79h)122+
9-y-o b g Montelimar (USA)-Cloncoose (IRE) (Remainder Man)
S A Brookshaw B Ridge & D Hewitt

Placings:000/0200P/0542U4P311331/22422426304-21423P21   (4640)
2003/04: 24²G, 22¹GF, 21⁴GS, 31²G, 24³GS, 24³G, 24²G, 21¹G,

	Starts	1st	2nd	3rd	Win & Pl
Chases	8	2	3	1	59528
Career Total	40	5	10	5	96459
122	4/04	Aint	2m5f110yB(0-150)HCh	GD	£40600
112	10/03	Hayd	2m6f	D(0-120)HCh	G-F	£3542
111	3/02	Hayd	3m	D(0-125)HCh	GD	£7085
91	1/02	Donc	3m	D(0-115)HCh	SFT	£4290
95	1/02	Ludl	3m	E(0-105)HCh	GD	£3581
				Total win prize-money	£59100

Going: Sf: 0-0 GS: 0-2 Gd: 1-5 GF: - Fm: 1-1
Distance: 2m/2m3: 0-0 2m4-2m7: 2-3 3m+: 0-5
Track: LH: 2-6 RH: 0-1 Tight: 1-4 Gall: 0-1
Aids: Bl: 0-0 Vi: 0-0 Tstrap: 2-8 Ckp: 0-0
Best Rating: 122 4/04 Aint   2m5f110y good   Ch

Modest chaser; fifth career win in Topham Chase at Aintree; probably stays 3m 7f; acts on most types of ground; seems suited by a flat track; regularly tongue tied.

Castanet
105   88
5-y-o b m Pennekamp (USA)-Addaya (IRE) (Persian Bold)
A E Price Mrs Carol Davis

Placings:246-6055340   (4716)
2003/04: 16⁶GF, 16⁰GS, 17⁵HY, 21⁵G, 21³G, 16⁴G, 21⁰G,

	Starts	1st	2nd	3rd	Win & Pl
Hurdles	7	0	0	1	1943
Career Total	10	0	1	1	3649

Going: Sf: 0-1 GS: 0-1 Gd: 0-4 GF: - Fm: 0-1
Distance: 2m/2m3: 0-4 2m4-2m7: 0-3 3m+: 0-0
Track: LH: 0-1 RH: 0-6 Tight: 0-1 Gall: 0-2
Aids: Bl: 0-1 Vi: 0-0 Tstrap: 0-0 Ckp: 0-0
Best Rating: 88 3/04 Donc 2m110y good   Hdl

Plating-class hurdler; seems best on a soft surface.

Castle Folly (IRE)
71   91
12-y-o b g Carlingford Castle-Air Plane (Arratos (FR))
J White Nick Quesnel

Placings:P/0P4/F3211-000   (4530)
2003/04: 22⁰HY, 18⁰GS, 16⁰GS,

	Starts	1st	2nd	3rd	Win & Pl
Chases	3	0	0	0	
Career Total	12	2	1	1	9008
91	10/02	Font	2m6f	F(0-95)HCh	GD	£3745
91	9/02	Sthl	2m5f110yE Ch	GD	£3506
				Total win prize-money	£7252

Going: Sf: 0-1 GS: 0-2 Gd: 0-0 GF: - Fm: 0-0
Distance: 2m/2m3: 0-2 2m4-2m7: 0-1 3m+: 0-0
Track: LH: 0-1 RH: 0-0 Tight: 0-2 Gall: 0-0
Aids: Bl: 0-1 Vi: 0-0 Tstrap: 0-0 Ckp: 0-0
Best Rating: 91 10/02 Font 2m6f good   Ch

Multiple winning pointer who likes to force the pace and stays three and a quarter miles. Off the mark under rules in weak contest at Southwell and followed up at Fontwell in October.

Castle Hatim
6-y-o b m Hatim (USA)-Castle Fountain (Royal Fountain)
W Amos Mrs C A Warden

Placings:00PP   (4601)
2003/04: 16⁰GF, 16⁰GF, 24⁰GS, 22⁰GS,

	Starts	1st	2nd	3rd	Win & Pl
NH Flat	2	0	0	0	0
Hurdles	2	0	0	0	0
Career Total	4	0	0	0	

Going: Sf: 0-0 GS: 0-2 Gd: 0-0 GF: - Fm: 0-2
Distance: 2m/2m3: 0-2 2m4-2m7: 0-1 3m+: 0-1
Track: LH: 0-2 RH: 0-0 Tight: 0-3 Gall: 0-0
Aids: Bl: 0-0 Vi: 0-0 Tstrap: 0-0 Ckp: 0-0
Best Rating: 45 12/03 Muss 2m   gd-fm NHF

Castle Prince (IRE)
113   121
10-y-o b g Homo Sapien-Lisaleen Lady (Miners Lamp)
R J Hodges The Gardens Entertainments Ltd

Placings:66000/2432F2/33144515/23455U34002-435564   (4896)
2003/04: 16⁴GF, 16³GF, 17⁵G, 16⁵GF, 16⁶G, 16⁴G,

	Starts	1st	2nd	3rd	Win & Pl
Chases	6	0	0	1	6699
Career Total	36	2	5	6	37297
115	4/02	Winc	2m	D(0-115)HCh	GD	£4368
102	1/02	Folk	2m	E(0-105)HCh	SFT	£3367
				Total win prize-money	£7735

Going: Sf: 0-0 GS: 0-0 Gd: 0-3 GF: - Fm: 0-3
Distance: 2m/2m3: 0-4 2m4-2m7: 0-0 3m+: 0-0
Track: LH: 0-1 RH: 0-5 Tight: 0-0 Gall: 0-0
Aids: Bl: 0-0 Vi: 0-0 Tstrap: 0-0 Ckp: 0-0
Best Rating: 140 4/02 Sand 2m   good   Ch

Fair handicap chaser; usually out of his depth in small-field conditions events; suited by two to two and a half miles; acts on any ground.

Castle Richard (IRE)
102(90c)   (111c)112
7-y-o gr g Sexton Blake-Miss McCormick (IRE) (Roselier (FR))
G M Moore Mrs Mary And Miss Susan Hatfield

Placings:6512P-22FU003   (4729)
2003/04: 20²G, 25²G, 20⁰G, 21⁰U, 25⁰G, 20⁰G, 20³G,

	Starts	1st	2nd	3rd	Win & Pl
Hurdles	3	0	0	1	1180
Chases	4	0	2	0	3105
Career Total	12	1	3	1	8793
112	12/02	Sedg	2m5f110yE Hdl		SFT	£3388
				Total win prize-money	£3388

Going: Sf: 0-0 GS: 0-0 Gd: 0-7 GF: - Fm: 0-0
Distance: 2m/2m3: 0-0 2m4-2m7: 0-2 3m+: 0-2
Track: LH: 0-5 RH: 0-2 Tight: 0-2 Gall: 0-0
Aids: Bl: 0-1 Vi: 0-0 Tstrap: 0-0 Ckp: 0-0
Best Rating: 112 11/03 Ayr 2m4f   good   Ch

Modest novice chaser/hurdler; stays two miles five, acts on a soft surface; has worn blinkers.

Castle Ring
93   93
5-y-o b g Sri Pekan (USA)-Understudy (In The Wings)
R Hollinshead R Hollinshead

Placings:3   (2257)
2003/04: 17³G,

	Starts	1st	2nd	3rd	Win & Pl
Hurdles	1	0	0	1	431
Career Total	1	0	0	1	431

Going: Sf: 0-0 GS: 0-0 Gd: 0-1 GF: - Fm: 0-0
Distance: 2m/2m3: 0-1 2m4-2m7: 0-0 3m+: 0-0
Track: LH: 0-0 RH: 0-1 Tight: 0-1 Gall: 0-0
Aids: Bl: 0-0 Vi: 0-0 Tstrap: 0-0 Ckp: 0-0
Best Rating: 93 11/03 MRas 2m1f110y good   Hdl

Plater on the Flat; well beaten third on hurdling debut at Market Rasen in November.

Castle River (USA)
102   96
5-y-o b g Irish River (FR)-Castellina (USA) (Danzig Connection (USA))
B G Powell H C T Racing

Placings:0-21404P   (2238)
2003/04: 16²GF, 16¹F, 16⁴GF, 16⁰GF, 16⁴GF, 16⁶PG,

	Starts	1st	2nd	3rd	Win & Pl
Hurdles	6	1	1	0	4704
Career Total	7	1	1	0	4704
84	10/03	Towc	2m	E Hdl		FRM	£3402
				Total win prize-money	£3402

Going: Sf: 0-0 GS: 0-0 Gd: 0-1 GF: - Fm: 1-5
Distance: 2m/2m3: 1-6 2m4-2m7: 0-0 3m+: 0-0
Track: LH: 0-3 RH: 1-3 Tight: 0-0 Gall: 0-1
Aids: Bl: 0-0 Vi: 0-0 Tstrap: 0-0 Ckp: 0-0
Best Rating: 96 11/03 Hntg 2m110y gd-fm Hdl

Disappointing type on the level; runner-up at an easy winner at Uttoxeter in October 2003; went one better when over-coming mistake at the last at Towcester next time; acts on fast ground.

Castle Weir (IRE)
7-y-o b g Lord Americo-Alchymya (Cosmo)
W P Mullins Castle Racing Club

Placings:14-234P2   (4708a)
2003/04: 24²S, 24³YS, 25⁴Y, 26⁰G, 24²YS,

	Starts	1st	2nd	3rd	Win & Pl
Chases	5	0	2	1	5628
Career Total	7	1	2	1	10121
78	5/02	Navn	3m	Ch		SFT	£4233
				Total win prize-money	£4233

Going: Sf: 0-1 GS: 0-0 Gd: 0-1 GF: - Fm: 0-0
Distance: 2m/2m3: 0-0 2m4-2m7: 0-0 3m+: 0-5
Track: LH: 0-2 RH: 0-3 Tight: 0-0 Gall: 0-1
Aids: Bl: 0-0 Vi: 0-0 Tstrap: 0-0 Ckp: 0-0
Best Rating: 112 2/04 Leop 3m   yld-sft Ch

Fair hunter chaser; has not won since his debut at Navan in 2002; stays three miles; acts on most ground.

Castleboy (IRE)
81f   69f
6-y-o b g King's Ride-Bissie's Jayla (Zambrano)
P J Hobbs Mrs D L Whateley

Placings:0   (3927)
2003/04: 16³GS,

	Starts	1st	2nd	3rd	Win & Pl
NH Flat	1	0	0	0	
Career Total	1	0	0	0	

Going:	Sf: 0-0 GS: 0-1 Gd: 0-0 GF: - Fm: 0-0
Distance:	2m/2m3: 0-1 2m4-2m7: 0-0 3m+: 0-0
Track:	LH: 0-0 RH: 0-1 Tight: 0-0 Gall: 0-0
Aids:	Bl: 0-0 Vi: 0-0 Tstrap: 0-0 Ckp: 0-0
Best Rating:	69 2/04 Sand 2m10y gd-sft NHF

Castlebridge
54

7-y-o b g Batshoof-Super Sisters (AUS) (Call Report (USA))
K R Burke P Sweeting

Placings:3/0/0300-P   (2114)
2003/04: 16²G,

	Starts	1st	2nd	3rd	Win & Pl
Hurdles	1	0	0	0	
Career Total	7	0	0	2	650

Going:	Sf: 0-0 GS: 0-0 Gd: 0-1 GF: - Fm: 0-0
Distance:	2m/2m3: 0-1 2m4-2m7: 0-0 3m+: 0-0
Track:	LH: 0-1 RH: 0-0 Tight: 0-0 Gall: 0-0
Aids:	Bl: 0-0 Vi: 0-1 Tstrap: 0-0 Ckp: 0-0
Best Rating:	68 8/00 Bang 2m1f good Hdl

Castlediva

7-y-o ch m Carlingford Castle-Bivadell (Bivouac)
B N Pollock Stuart A Blyth

Placings:0   (4668)
2003/04: 23⁰GS,

	Starts	1st	2nd	3rd	Win & Pl
Hurdles	1	0	0	0	
Career Total	1	0	0	0	

Going:	Sf: 0-0 GS: 0-1 Gd: 0-0 GF: - Fm: 0-0
Distance:	2m/2m3: 0-0 2m4-2m7: 0-1 3m+: 0-0
Track:	LH: 0-1 RH: 0-0 Tight: 0-0 Gall: 0-0
Aids:	Bl: 0-0 Vi: 0-0 Tstrap: 0-0 Ckp: 0-0
Best Rating:	0 4/04 Ling 2m7f gd-sft Hdl

Castleford (IRE)
97(103c)   (92c)95+

6-y-o b g Be My Native (USA)-Commanche Bay (IRE)
(Commanche Run)
P J Hobbs Mrs D Whateley, Mrs L Field, A Murphy

Placings:05-3000333   (4656)
2003/04: 24³G, 21⁰G, 19⁰G, 22⁰S, 24³G, 22³GS, 26³G,

	Starts	1st	2nd	3rd	Win & Pl
Hurdles	6	0	0	3	2006
Chases	1	0	0	1	1075
Career Total	9	0	0	4	3081

Going:	Sf: 0-1 GS: 0-1 Gd: 0-5 GF: - Fm: 0-0
Distance:	2m/2m3: 0-1 2m4-2m7: 0-3 3m+: 0-3
Track:	LH: 0-1 RH: 0-6 Tight: 0-0 Gall: 0-0
Aids:	Bl: 0-0 Vi: 0-0 Tstrap: 0-0 Ckp: 0-0
Best Rating:	101 3/03 Chep 2m110y good NHF

Modest gelding; out of an unraced half-sister to Topsham Bay, has shown ability in bumpers and novice hurdles; stays three miles.

Castlemore (IRE)
102   102

6-y-o b g Be My Native (USA)-Parsonetta (The Parson)
P J Hobbs Castlemore Securities Limited

Placings:44-22503   (4539)
2003/04: 16²G, 21²G, 20⁵G, 20⁰G, 21³GS,

	Starts	1st	2nd	3rd	Win & Pl
NH Flat	1	0	1	0	793
Hurdles	4	0	1	1	1739
Career Total	7	0	2	1	2532

Going:	Sf: 0-0 GS: 0-1 Gd: 0-4 GF: - Fm: 0-0
Distance:	2m/2m3: 0-1 2m4-2m7: 0-4 3m+: 0-0
Track:	LH: 0-1 RH: 0-4 Tight: 0-0 Gall: 0-0
Aids:	Bl: 0-0 Vi: 0-0 Tstrap: 0-0 Ckp: 0-0
Best Rating:	102 3/04 Ludl 2m5f gd-sft Hdl

Modest novice hurdler; stays 2m5f; acts on good ground.

Castleshane (IRE)
107   134

7-y-o b g Kris-Ahbab (IRE) (Ajdal (USA))
S Gollings W Hobson,J King,G King,P Winfrow

Placings:2340P/F51242053/2501-3   (2014)
2003/04: 16³GF,

	Starts	1st	2nd	3rd	Win & Pl
Hurdles	1	0	0	1	3300
Career Total	19	2	4	3	38743
134 4/03 Chep 2m110y C(0-135)HHdl G-F £7231
106 10/01 Chel 2m110y D Hdl GD £7345
Total win prize-money £14576

Going:	Sf: 0-0 GS: 0-0 Gd: 0-0 GF: - Fm: 0-1
Distance:	2m/2m3: 0-1 2m4-2m7: 0-0 3m+: 0-0
Track:	LH: 0-0 RH: 0-1 Tight: 0-0 Gall: 0-0
Aids:	Bl: 0-0 Vi: 0-0 Tstrap: 0-0 Ckp: 0-0
Best Rating:	134 11/03 Winc 2m gd-fm Hdl

Useful hurdler; useful on the Flat as well; likes his own way out in front, otherwise he can tend to sulk; suited by two miles; best on a sound surface.

Catch The Perk (IRE)
97(90h)   (74h)90

7-y-o b g Executive Perk-Kilbally Quilty (IRE) (Montelimar (USA))
Miss Lucinda V Russell A A Bissett

Placings:6425046-50P0P1   (4434)
2003/04: 16⁵GS, 20⁰GF, 22⁵S, 20⁰GF, 16⁰GF, 20¹G,

	Starts	1st	2nd	3rd	Win & Pl
Hurdles	2	0	0	0	0
Chases	4	1	0	0	3325
Career Total	13	1	1	0	4762
90 3/04 Hexm 2m4f110yF(0-100)HCh GD £3325
Total win prize-money £3325

Going:	Sf: 0-1 GS: 0-1 Gd: 1-1 GF: - Fm: 0-3
Distance:	2m/2m3: 0-2 2m4-2m7: 1-4 3m+: 0-0
Track:	LH: 1-2 RH: 0-4 Tight: 0-3 Gall: 0-0
Aids:	Bl: 0-0 Vi: 0-0 Tstrap: 0-0 Ckp: 1-1
Best Rating:	98 12/02 Muss 2m gd-fm NHF

Catchatan (IRE)
89   99

9-y-o b g Cataldi-Snowtan (IRE) (Tanfirion)
P R Webber Dennis Yardy

Placings:P4/P21045-4PP   (0946)
2003/04: 24⁴GF, 23⁰PG,

	Starts	1st	2nd	3rd	Win & Pl
Chases	3	0	0	0	390
Career Total	11	1	1	0	6828
98 12/02 Leic 2m D(0-110)HCh G-S £4849
Total win prize-money £4849

Going:	Sf: 0-0 GS: 0-0 Gd: 0-2 GF: - Fm: 0-1
Distance:	2m/2m3: 0-0 2m4-2m7: 0-0 3m+: 0-3
Track:	LH: 0-3 RH: 0-0 Tight: 0-0 Gall: 0-0
Aids:	Bl: 0-0 Vi: 0-0 Tstrap: 0-2 Ckp: 0-0
Best Rating:	99 2/03 Leic 2m gd-sft Ch

Cateel Bay
72   61

6-y-o ch m Most Welcome-Calachuchi (Martinmas)
H Alexander Mrs C D Bruce

Placings:06U06P000-0   (0472)
2003/04: 16⁶GF, 17⁰GS,

	Starts	1st	2nd	3rd	Win & Pl
Hurdles	2	0	0	0	
Career Total	10	0	0	0	0

Going:	Sf: 0-0 GS: 0-1 Gd: 0-0 GF: - Fm: 0-1
Distance:	2m/2m3: 0-2 2m4-2m7: 0-0 3m+: 0-0
Track:	LH: 0-2 RH: 0-0 Tight: 0-1 Gall: 0-1
Aids:	Bl: 0-0 Vi: 0-0 Tstrap: 0-0 Ckp: 0-0
Best Rating:	62 1/03 Catt 2m good Hdl

Winner of a claimer on the Flat at three, poor form in selling hurdles so far.

Catfish Hunter

4-y-o b g Safawan-Secret Account (Blakeney)
Mrs L P Baker Mrs L P Baker

Placings:0   (4407)
2003/04: 16⁰G,

	Starts	1st	2nd	3rd	Win & Pl
NH Flat	1	0	0	0	
Career Total	1	0	0	0	

Going:	Sf: 0-0 GS: 0-0 Gd: 0-1 GF: - Fm: 0-0
Distance:	2m/2m3: 0-1 2m4-2m7: 0-0 3m+: 0-0
Track:	LH: 0-0 RH: 0-1 Tight: 0-0 Gall: 0-1
Aids:	Bl: 0-0 Vi: 0-0 Tstrap: 0-0 Ckp: 0-0

Catherine's Way (IRE)

12-y-o b g Mandalus-Sharp Approach (Crash Course)
Martin Ward Martin Ward

Placings:0/405F/42141/1P/U4/2P5/PP-U   (3919)
2003/04: 21⁰G,

	Starts	1st	2nd	3rd	Win & Pl
Chases	1	0	0	0	
Career Total	20	3	2	0	12875
120 2/00 MRas 2m6f110yD(0-125)HCh G-S £4536

115 3/99 Leic 2m4f110yE(0-105)HCh SFT £3496
111 12/98 Hntg 2m110y E(0-105)HCh SFT £2901
Total win prize-money £10934

Going:	Sf: 0-0 GS: 0-0 Gd: 0-1 GF: - Fm: 0-0
Distance:	2m/2m3: 0-0 2m4-2m7: 0-1 3m+: 0-0
Track:	LH: 0-1 RH: 0-0 Tight: 0-1 Gall: 0-0
Aids:	Bl: 0-0 Vi: 0-0 Tstrap: 0-0 Ckp: 0-0
Best Rating:	120 2/00 MRas 2m6f110y gd-sft Ch

Caucasian (IRE)

89   75

6-y-o g g Leading Counsel (USA)-Kemal's Princess (Kemal (FR))
Ian Williams   Ian Williams

Placings:*0-0000*   (2730)
2003/04: 16⁰G, 16⁰G, 16⁰GS, 16⁰S,

	Starts	1st	2nd	3rd	Win & Pl
NH Flat	1	0	0	0	0
Hurdles	3	0	0	0	0
Career Total	5	0	0	0	0

Going:	Sf: 0-1 GS: 0-1 Gd: 0-2 GF: - Fm: 0-0
Distance:	2m/2m3: 0-4 2m4-2m7: 0-0 3m+: 0-0
Track:	LH: 0-3 RH: 0-1 Tight: 0-2 Gall: 0-0
Aids:	Bl: 0-0 Vi: 0-0 Tstrap: 0-0 Ckp: 0-0
Best Rating:	75 10/03 Aint 2m110y good Hdl

Cavvies Niece

6-y-o b m Ballet Royal (USA)-Cavisoir (Afzal)
H J Manners   H J Manners

Placings:*0P-P*   (0058)
2003/04: 19PGS,

	Starts	1st	2nd	3rd	Win & Pl
Hurdles	1	0	0	0	
Career Total	3	0	0	0	

Going:	Sf: 0-0 GS: 0-1 Gd: 0-0 GF: - Fm: 0-0
Distance:	2m/2m3: 0-0 2m4-2m7: 0-0 3m+: 0-0
Track:	LH: 0-0 RH: 0-1 Tight: 0-0 Gall: 0-0
Aids:	Bl: 0-0 Vi: 0-0 Tstrap: 0-0 Ckp: 0-0
Best Rating:	0 5/03 Hrld 2m3f110y gd-sft Hdl

Caymans Gift

4-y-o ch g Cayman Kai (IRE)-Gymcrak Cyrano (IRE) (Cyrano De Bergerac)
A C Whillans   I Campbell

Placings:*0F6*   (4908)
2003/04: 16⁰G, 16FG, 20⁶S,

	Starts	1st	2nd	3rd	Win & Pl
NH Flat	1	0	0	0	0
Hurdles	2	0	0	0	0
Career Total	3	0	0	0	0

Going:	Sf: 0-1 GS: 0-0 Gd: 0-2 GF: - Fm: 0-0
Distance:	2m/2m3: 0-2 2m4-2m7: 0-1 3m+: 0-0
Track:	LH: 0-1 RH: 0-2 Tight: 0-2 Gall: 0-0
Aids:	Bl: 0-0 Vi: 0-0 Tstrap: 0-0 Ckp: 0-0
Best Rating:	56 2/04 Muss 2m good NHF

Ceanannas Mor (IRE)

103   132+

10-y-o b/br g Strong Gale-Game Sunset (Menelek)
N J Henderson   Major Christopher Hanbury

Placings:*033/14FF/164032/54PP-P11*   (2132)
2003/04: 33PG, 231G, 321GF,

	Starts	1st	2nd	3rd	Win & Pl
Chases	3	2	0	0	14964
Career Total	20	4	1	3	48568
132	11/03 Chel	4m	C(0-130)HCh	G-F	£9549
122	11/03 Extr	2m7f110yD(0-125)HCh	GD	£5414
132	10/01 Kemp	3m	B(0-145)HCh	G-S	£17400
120	11/00 Leic	2m7f110yE CH	G-S	£3302
			Total win prize-money £35667

Going:	Sf: 0-0 GS: 0-0 Gd: 1-2 GF: - Fm: 1-1
Distance:	2m/2m3: 0-0 2m4-2m7: 0-0 3m+: 2-3
Track:	LH: 1-1 RH: 1-2 Tight: 0-0 Gall: 1-1
Aids:	Bl: 0-0 Vi: 0-0 Tstrap: 0-0 Ckp: 0-0
Best Rating:	132 11/03 Chel 4m gd-fm Ch

Fair handicap chaser; had a successful breathing operation during 2003; stays four miles and suited by good ground or softer.

Ceasers Reign (IRE)

12-y-o ch g Rhoman Rule (USA)-Dora Gayle (Lord Gayle (USA))
T D B Underwood   T D B Underwood

Placings:*0/0000600/00P/U/6*   (0186)
2003/04: 25⁶GF,

	Starts	1st	2nd	3rd	Win & Pl
Chases	1	0	0	0	0
Career Total	13	0	0	0	0

Going:	Sf: 0-0 GS: 0-0 Gd: 0-0 GF: - Fm: 0-1
Distance:	2m/2m3: 0-0 2m4-2m7: 0-0 3m+: 0-1
Track:	LH: 0-0 RH: 0-1 Tight: 0-0 Gall: 0-0
Aids:	Bl: 0-0 Vi: 0-0 Tstrap: 0-0 Ckp: 0-0
Best Rating:	86 11/97 Thur 2m yld-sft Hdl

Cedar

71(86h)   (80h)36

7-y-o gr g Absalom-Setai's Palace (Royal Palace)
R Dickin   D J Jackson

Placings:*F4-P3F0*   (4369)
2003/04: 22PS, 163HY, 19FG, 20⁴G,

	Starts	1st	2nd	3rd	Win & Pl
Hurdles	2	0	0	1	639
Chases	2	0	0	0	0
Career Total	6	0	0	1	967

Going:	Sf: 0-3 GS: 0-0 Gd: 0-1 GF: - Fm: 0-0
Distance:	2m/2m3: 0-2 2m4-2m7: 0-2 3m+: 0-0
Track:	LH: 0-2 RH: 0-2 Tight: 0-1 Gall: 0-0
Aids:	Bl: 0-2 Vi: 0-0 Tstrap: 0-0 Ckp: 0-0
Best Rating:	80 1/04 Towc 2m heavy Hdl

Placed in modest novice hurdles.

Cedar Chief

7-y-o b g Saddlers' Hall (IRE)-Dame Ashfield (Grundy)

K Tork   K Tork

Placings:243044/F45410PF026/6U0-5606   (4453)
2003/04: 25⁵GF, 24⁶G, 24⁹G, 19⁶GS,

	Starts	1st	2nd	3rd	Win & Pl
Chases	4	0	0	0	0
Career Total	24	1	2	1	3099
85	10/01 Folk	2m6f110yG(0-95)HHdl	HVY	£1561
			Total win prize-money £1561

Going:	Sf: 0-0 GS: 0-1 Gd: 0-2 GF: - Fm: 0-1
Distance:	2m/2m3: 0-0 2m4-2m7: 0-1 3m+: 0-3
Track:	LH: 0-0 RH: 0-4 Tight: 0-1 Gall: 0-0
Aids:	Bl: 0-4 Vi: 0-0 Tstrap: 0-0 Ckp: 0-0
Best Rating:	85 10/01 Folk 2m6f110y heavy Hdl

Cedar Green

105   125

10-y-o br g Bustino-Explosiva (USA) (Explodent (USA))
K C Bailey   J Perriss

Placings:*0*P41R23PP/F12126/3512-PPP1PP   (4598)
2003/04: 24PHY, 30PGS, 30PGS, 251S, 24PS, 32PG,

	Starts	1st	2nd	3rd	Win & Pl
Chases	6	1	0	0	5551
Career Total	25	5	4	2	37364
124	1/04 Weth	3m1f	D(0-115)HCh	SFT	£5551
125	2/03 Font	3m2f110yD(0-125)HCh	G-S	£5668
119	1/02 Carl	3m4f	C(0-130)Ch	SFT	£7020
109	12/01 Wwck	3m2f	D(0-130)HCh	SFT	£3932
113	12/00 Towc	2m6f	D Ch	HVY	£4130
			Total win prize-money £26302

Going:	Sf: 1-3 GS: 0-2 Gd: 0-1 GF: - Fm: 0-0
Distance:	2m/2m3: 0-0 2m4-2m7: 0-0 3m+: 1-6
Track:	LH: 1-5 RH: 0-1 Tight: 0-2 Gall: 0-2
Aids:	Bl: 1-5 Vi: 0-0 Tstrap: 0-0 Ckp: 0-1
Best Rating:	125 3/03 Extr 3m6f110y soft Ch

Decent chaser; has scored several times in the mud, but does not always look the most reliable ride; stays extreme distances; scored at Fontwell in February 2003; good second off 7lb higher mark in Devon National at Exeter next time; bounced back after being pulled up three times when recording fifth career win at Wetherby in January; wears blinkers.

Cedar Master (IRE)

97   102+

7-y-o b g Soviet Lad (USA)-Samriah (IRE) (Wassl)
J R Boyle (R J O'Sullivan 24/5)   Robert Allen

Placings:03246-312   (1420)
2003/04: 16⁹GF, 19¹GF, 22²GF,

	Starts	1st	2nd	3rd	Win & Pl
Hurdles	3	1	1	1	4741
Career Total	8	1	2	2	6239
98	8/03 MRas	2m3f110yE Hdl	G-F	£3464
			Total win prize-money £3465

Going:	Sf: 0-0 GS: 0-0 Gd: 0-0 GF: - Fm: 1-3
Distance:	2m/2m3: 0-1 2m4-2m7: 1-2 3m+: 0-0
Track:	LH: 0-1 RH: 1-2 Tight: 1-2 Gall: 0-0
Aids:	Bl: 1-3 Vi: 0-0 Tstrap: 1-2 Ckp: 0-0
Best Rating:	105 9/03 Font 2m6f110y gd-fm Hdl

Moderate hurdler; best over two and a half miles and suited by a sound surface.

Cedar Rangers (USA)

95   **83+**

6-y-o b g Anabaa (USA)-Chelsea (USA) (Miswaki (USA))
G F Edwards   G F Edwards

Placings:043304305   (4714)
2003/04: 16⁰GF, 16⁴GF, 16³GF, 17³GF, 16⁰GF, 19⁴GF, 19³G,
18⁰G, 16⁵G,

	Starts	1st	2nd	3rd	Win & Pl
Hurdles	9	0	0	3	1567
Career Total	9	0	0	3	1567

Going:	Sf: 0-0 GS: 0-0 Gd: 0-3 GF: - Fm: 0-6
Distance:	2m/2m3: 0-7 2m4-2m7: 0-2 3m+: 0-0
Track:	LH: 0-5 RH: 0-4 Tight: 0-5 Gall: 0-0
Aids:	Bl: 0-0 Vi: 0-0 Tstrap: 0-0 Ckp: 0-0
Best Rating:	**83** 4/04 Ludl 2m good Hdl

Novice hurdler; pulls very hard.

Celebration Town (IRE)

105   **110+**

7-y-o b/br g Case Law-Battle Queen (Kind Of Hush)
N G Richards   Greystoke Stables Ltd

Placings:00-26101330   (4688)
2003/04: 16²G, 16⁶GF, 16⁹G, 16¹GF, 16³GF, 16³GF, 16⁹G,

	Starts	1st	2nd	3rd	Win & Pl
Hurdles	8	2	1	2	7964
Career Total	10	2	1	2	7964
106	10/03	Hayd	2m	E(0-105)HHdl	G-F	2467
102	6/03	Hexm	2m110y	E(0-110)HHdl	G-F	3430
				Total win prize-money £5898		

Going:	Sf: 0-0 GS: 0-0 Gd: 0-3 GF: - Fm: 2-5
Distance:	**2m/2m3: 2-8** 2m4-2m7: 0-0 3m+: 0-0
Track:	**LH: 2-6** RH: 0-2 Tight: 0-1 Gall: 0-0
Aids:	Bl: 0-0 Vi: 0-0 Tstrap: 0-0 Ckp: 0-0
Best Rating:	**106** 10/03 Hayd 2m gd-fm Hdl

Modest hurdler; formerly useful on the Flat; best at around two miles and very much suited by fast ground.

Celestial Gold (IRE)

105   **144**

6-y-o br g Persian Mews-What A Queen (King's Ride)
M C Pipe   D A Johnson

Placings:13321   (4837)
2003/04: 22¹GS, 24³GS, 24³GS, 32²G, 25¹GF,

	Starts	1st	2nd	3rd	Win & Pl
Chases	5	2	1	2	29686
Career Total	5	2	1	2	29686
134	4/04	Chel	3m11f110yB Ch		G-F	11137
125	11/03	Towc	2m6f	E Ch	G-S	2947
				Total win prize-money £14084		

Going:	Sf: 0-0 GS: 1-3 Gd: 0-1 GF: - Fm: 1-1
Distance:	2m/2m3: 0-0 2m4-2m7: 1-1 3m+: 1-4
Track:	LH: 1-4 RH: 1-1 Tight: 0-1 **Gall: 1-3**
Aids:	Bl: 0-0 Vi: 0-0 Tstrap: 0-0 Ckp: 0-0
Best Rating:	**144** 3/04 Chel 4m good Ch

Useful chaser; a smart pointer in 2003; runner-up in National Hunt Chase at Cheltenham in 2004 and went one better at the track next time over shorter; stays 4m; effective on fast and soft ground; has worn a visor.

Celibate (IRE)

95   **130**

13-y-o ch g Shy Groom (USA)-Dance Alone (USA)
(Monteverdi)
C J Mann   Stamford Bridge Partnership

Placings:25213664/0521210446F0/2111123F2/1545124/02
31531/33433226B/03P1355265/10403236P/34-0   (3647)
2003/04: 24⁰GS,

	Starts	1st	2nd	3rd	Win & Pl
Chases	1	0	0	0	
Career Total	74	13	13	13	269696
143	10/01	Winc	2m5f	A HCh	GD	£21000
147	12/00	Asct	2m	B HCh	SFT	£9339
157	4/99	Punc	2m	Ch	YLD	£32098
157	2/99	Newb	2m1f	A Ch	G-S	£18503
160	12/97	Asct	2m	B HCh	G-S	£9403
153	10/97	Kemp	2m	B(0-150)HCh	GD	£4429
134	11/96	Chel	2m	A Ch	GD	£11780
120	10/96	Chel	2m	D Ch	FRM	£3701
134	10/96	Kemp	2m	D Ch	GD	£3436
110	9/96	Worc	2m	D Ch	G-F	£3562
122	12/95	Hayd	2m	C(0-135)HHdl	GD	£3728
117	11/95	Towc	2m	D(0-120)HHdl	G-F	£2756
108	11/94	Clon	2m	Hdl	SFT	£2120
				Total win prize-money £125857		

Going:	Sf: 0-0 GS: 0-1 Gd: 0-0 GF: - Fm: 0-0
Distance:	2m/2m3: 0-0 2m4-2m7: 0-0 3m+: 0-1
Track:	LH: 0-0 RH: 0-1 Tight: 0-1 Gall: 0-0
Aids:	Bl: 0-0 Vi: 0-0 Tstrap: 0-0 Ckp: 0-0
Best Rating:	**160** 1/98 Asct 2m soft Ch

Useful chaser; admirably consistent in his day; reportedly retired.

Celioso (IRE)

113(103h)   (84 h) **125**

7-y-o b g Celio Rufo-Bettons Rose (Roselier (FR))
Mrs S J Smith   Leigh Musketeer Racing Club

Placings:00P/P4414-F05122112   (3479)
2003/04: 25⁰G, 22⁰GS, 22⁵GF, 21¹G, 24²G, 20²G, 21¹GF, 28¹G,
30²G,

	Starts	1st	2nd	3rd	Win & Pl
Hurdles	1	0	0	0	0
Chases	8	3	3	0	20343
Career Total	17	4	3	0	24311
125	12/03	MRas	3m4f110yC(0-130)HCh	GD	£7003
125	11/03	Sedg	2m5f	E Ch	G-F	£4128
113	9/03	Sedg	2m5f	E Ch	GD	£3220
84	3/03	Carl	3m110y	E(0-105)HHdl	GD	£2482
				Total win prize-money £18020		

Going:	Sf: 0-0 GS: 0-1 Gd: 2-6 GF: - Fm: 1-2
Distance:	2m/2m3: 0-0 **2m4-2m7: 2-5** 3m+: 1-4
Track:	**LH: 2-7** RH: 1-2 **Tight: 3-7** Gall: 0-0
Aids:	Bl: 0-0 Vi: 0-0 Tstrap: 0-0 Ckp: 0-0
Best Rating:	**125** 1/04 Catt 3m6f good Ch

Fair chaser; progressing well in 2003/4; suited by decent ground; stays three miles four; unexposed over staying trips.

Celta Vigo (IRE)

6-y-o b m Executive Perk-Alice Freyne (IRE) (Lancastrian)
Mrs L B Normile   Mrs Janice M Fraser

Placings:00P   (2927)
2003/04: 16⁰G, 16⁰GS, 27⁰G,

	Starts	1st	2nd	3rd	Win & Pl
NH Flat	1	0	0	0	0
Hurdles	2	0	0	0	0

Career Total	3 0 0 0

Going:	Sf: 0-0 GS: 0-1 Gd: 0-2 GF: - Fm: 0-0
Distance:	2m/2m3: 0-2 2m4-2m7: 0-0 3m+: 0-1
Track:	LH: 0-1 RH: 0-2 Tight: 0-1 Gall: 0-0
Aids:	Bl: 0-0 Vi: 0-0 Tstrap: 0-0 Ckp: 0-0
Best Rating:	**36** 5/03 Prth 2m110y good NHF

Celtic Action

11-y-o b g Fearless Action (USA)-Llanon (Owen Dudley)
D R Wellicome   D R Wellicome

Placings:P   (2388)
2003/04: 20⁰G,

	Starts	1st	2nd	3rd	Win & Pl
Hurdles	1	0	0	0	0
Career Total	1	0	0	0	0

Going:	Sf: 0-0 GS: 0-0 Gd: 0-1 GF: - Fm: 0-0
Distance:	2m/2m3: 0-0 2m4-2m7: 0-1 3m+: 0-0
Track:	LH: 0-1 RH: 0-0 Tight: 0-0 Gall: 0-0
Aids:	Bl: 0-0 Vi: 0-0 Tstrap: 0-0 Ckp: 0-0

Celtic Blaze (IRE)

101   **97**

5-y-o b m Charente River (IRE)-Firdaunt (Tanfirion)
B S Rothwell   Cleaning And Paper Disposables Ltd

Placings:22-0244066   (4429)
2003/04: 17⁰GF, 16⁴GS, 21⁴GS, 16⁰G, 16⁶GS, 16⁶G,

	Starts	1st	2nd	3rd	Win & Pl
Hurdles	7	0	1	0	2591
Career Total	9	0	3	0	5475

Going:	Sf: 0-1 GS: 0-3 Gd: 0-2 GF: - Fm: 0-1
Distance:	2m/2m3: 0-6 2m4-2m7: 0-1 3m+: 0-0
Track:	LH: 0-5 RH: 0-2 Tight: 0-3 Gall: 0-0
Aids:	Bl: 0-0 Vi: 0-0 Tstrap: 0-0 Ckp: 0-2
Best Rating:	**100** 1/04 Sand 2m110y gd-sft Hdl

Moderate novice hurdler; suited by easy ground.

Celtic Boy (IRE)

96   **85**

6-y-o b g Arctic Lord-Laugh Away (Furry Glen)
P Bowen   Walters Plant Hire Ltd

Placings:661   (4918)
2003/04: 16⁶G, 24⁶G, 20¹G,

	Starts	1st	2nd	3rd	Win & Pl
NH Flat	1	0	0	0	0
Hurdles	2	1	0	0	3283
Career Total	3	1	0	0	3283
85	4/04	Worc	2m4f	F Hdl	G-S	£3283
				Total win prize-money £3283		

Going:	Sf: 0-0 GS: 1-1 Gd: 0-2 GF: - Fm: 0-0
Distance:	2m/2m3: 0-1 **2m4-2m7: 1-1** 3m+: 0-1
Track:	**LH: 1-1** RH: 0-2 Tight: 0-0 Gall: 0-0
Aids:	Bl: 0-0 Vi: 0-0 Tstrap: 0-0 Ckp: 0-0
Best Rating:	**85** 4/04 Worc 2m4f gd-sft Hdl

Maiden pointer; winning novice hurdler; stays 2m 4f; quirky sort.

Celtic Duke

12-y-o b g Strong Gale-Celtic Cygnet (Celtic Cone)
J M Turner J M Turner

Placings:030/2363/13521/212/2PP/2-144   (4779)
2003/04: 24¹GF, 25⁴G, 24⁴S,

	Starts	1st	2nd	3rd	Win & Pl
Chases	3	1	0	0	2708
Career Total	22	4	6	4	25543

95	5/03	Fknm	3m110y	H Ch	G-F	£2184
114	11/99	Kels	3m4f	D(0-120)HCh	GD	£3779
105	4/99	Kels	3m1f	D(0-120)HCh	G-F	£4071
90	6/98	Prth	3m	D Ch	G-F	£3501

Total win prize-money £13536

Going:	Sf: 0-1 GS: 0-0 Gd: 0-1 GF: - Fm: 1-1
Distance:	2m/2m3: 0-0 2m4-2m7: 0-0 3m+: 1-3
Track:	LH: 1-3 RH: 0-0 Tight: 1-2 Gall: 0-0
Aids:	Bl: 0-0 Vi: 0-0 Tstrap: 0-0 Ckp: 0-0
Best Rating:	114 5/00 Sedg 3m4f gd-fm Ch

Moderate hunter chaser/point-to-pointer; former staying handicapper; stays three miles; goes well on top of the ground.

Celtic Flow

94(92h)   (68h)59
6-y-o b m Primitive Rising (USA)-Celtic Lane (Welsh Captain)
C R Wilson W R Wilson

Placings:5006-5056625F   (4882)
2003/04: 21⁵S, 16⁰G, 21⁵GF, 17⁶GS, 19⁶G, 25²GF, 24⁵G, 26^FGS,

	Starts	1st	2nd	3rd	Win & Pl
Hurdles	6	0	0	0	0
Chases	2	0	1	0	1230
Career Total	12	0	1	0	1230

Going:	Sf: 0-1 GS: 0-2 Gd: 0-3 GF: - Fm: 0-2
Distance:	2m/2m3: 0-3 2m4-2m7: 0-2 3m+: 0-3
Track:	LH: 0-7 RH: 0-1 Tight: 0-5 Gall: 0-0
Aids:	Bl: 0-0 Vi: 0-0 Tstrap: 0-0 Ckp: 0-0
Best Rating:	75 1/03 Sedg 2m1f heavy NHF

Selling hurdler; well beaten runner-up in weak event on chasing bow at Catterick in March; suited by three miles.

Celtic Legend (FR)

82(90h)   (82 h)76
5-y-o br g Celtic Swing-Another Legend (USA) (Lyphard's Wish (FR))
Mrs M Reveley Jemm Partnership Limited

Placings:064-00620   (4164)
2003/04: 16⁰G, 20⁰G, 25⁶GS, 16²GF, 19⁰G,

	Starts	1st	2nd	3rd	Win & Pl
Hurdles	3	0	0	0	0
Chases	2	0	1	0	1248
Career Total	8	0	1	0	1570

Going:	Sf: 0-0 GS: 0-1 Gd: 0-3 GF: - Fm: 0-1
Distance:	2m/2m3: 0-3 2m4-2m7: 0-0 3m+: 0-1
Track:	LH: 0-4 RH: 0-1 Tight: 0-2 Gall: 0-0
Aids:	Bl: 0-0 Vi: 0-0 Tstrap: 0-0 Ckp: 0-0
Best Rating:	80 3/03 Kels 2m2f good Hdl

Juvenile hurdler, well beaten so far but might do better in handicap company in due course.

Celtic Major (IRE)

90   93
6-y-o gr g Roselier (FR)-Dun Oengus (IRE) (Strong Gale)
Jonjo O'Neill Walters Plant Hire Ltd

Placings:2505   (3923)
2003/04: 18²G, 16⁵HY, 16⁹HY, 16⁶GS,

	Starts	1st	2nd	3rd	Win & Pl
NH Flat	2	0	1	0	672
Hurdles	2	0	0	0	0
Career Total	4	0	1	0	672

Going:	Sf: 0-2 GS: 0-1 Gd: 0-1 GF: - Fm: 0-0
Distance:	2m/2m3: 0-4 2m4-2m7: 0-0 3m+: 0-0
Track:	LH: 0-3 RH: 0-1 Tight: 0-0 Gall: 0-0
Aids:	Bl: 0-0 Vi: 0-0 Tstrap: 0-0 Ckp: 0-0
Best Rating:	104 11/03 Plum 2m2f good NHF

Runner-up in ordinary bumper on debut at Plumpton in November; well beaten since.

Celtic Pride (IRE)

97   (137h)117
9-y-o gr g Roselier (FR)-Grannie No (Brave Invader (USA))
P Bowen Walters Plant Hire Ltd

Placings:0110/P10/3-U34   (0362)
2003/04: 23^UGS, 23³G, 26⁴HY,

	Starts	1st	2nd	3rd	Win & Pl
Chases	3	0	0	1	1193
Career Total	11	3	0	2	22441

137	2/02	Hayd	2m7f110yB HHdl	HVY	£8782
125	1/01	Navn	2m6f	Hdl	SFT	£6677
110	1/01	Fair	2m6f	Hdl	HVY	£5008

Total win prize-money £20468

Going:	Sf: 0-1 GS: 0-1 Gd: 0-1 GF: - Fm: 0-0
Distance:	2m/2m3: 0-0 2m4-2m7: 0-0 3m+: 0-3
Track:	LH: 0-3 RH: 0-0 Tight: 0-0 Gall: 0-0
Aids:	Bl: 0-0 Vi: 0-0 Tstrap: 0-0 Ckp: 0-0
Best Rating:	137 2/02 Hayd 2m7f110y heavy Hdl

A decent Irish novice hurdler in 2000/2001; won 3m handicap hurdle at Haydock Febraury 2002; lightly-raced since; modest form in 3m novice chases.

Celtic Ruffian (IRE)

49   12
6-y-o b g Celio Rufo-Candid Lady (Arctic Lord)
R Rowe Mrs P V Crocker

Placings:20UP0P0   (4932)
2003/04: 18²GF, 17⁰GS, 20^UG, 22^PHY, 22⁰G, 22^PG, 27⁰G,

	Starts	1st	2nd	3rd	Win & Pl
NH Flat	2	0	1	0	642
Hurdles	5	0	0	0	0
Career Total	7	0	1	0	642

Going:	Sf: 0-1 GS: 0-1 Gd: 0-4 GF: - Fm: 0-1
Distance:	2m/2m3: 0-2 2m4-2m7: 0-4 3m+: 0-1
Track:	LH: 0-3 RH: 0-2 Tight: 0-5 Gall: 0-0
Aids:	Bl: 0-0 Vi: 0-0 Tstrap: 0-0 Ckp: 0-0
Best Rating:	68 10/03 Plum 2m2f gd-fm NHF

Celtic Son (FR)

106f   117+f
5-y-o b g Celtic Arms (FR)-For Kicks (FR) (Top Ville)
M C Pipe D A Johnson

Celtic Star (IRE)

73(105h)   (109+h)59
6-y-o b g Celtic Swing-Recherche (Rainbow Quest (USA))
Miss K M George (Nick Williams 18/11) Exterior Profiles Ltd

Placings:3243226/0313P66-P03331UPP5   (4811)
2003/04: 17^PG, 20⁴GF, 20³GF, 21³GF, 22³GF, 17¹G, 16^UGS, 16^PHY, 17^PG, 24⁵G,

	Starts	1st	2nd	3rd	Win & Pl
Hurdles	7	1	0	3	5643
Chases	3	0	0	0	0
Career Total	24	2	3	7	15902

109	11/03	NAbb	2m1f	E(0-110)HHdl	GD	£2961
100	9/02	Font	2m2f110yE Hdl		G-F	£3136

Total win prize-money £6097

Going:	Sf: 0-1 GS: 0-1 Gd: 1-4 GF: - Fm: 0-4
Distance:	2m/2m3: 1-5 2m4-2m7: 0-4 3m+: 0-1
Track:	LH: 1-10 RH: 0-0 Tight: 1-4 Gall: 0-1
Aids:	Bl: 0-0 Vi: 0-3 Tstrap: 0-0 Ckp: 0-1
Best Rating:	109 11/03 NAbb 2m1f good Hdl

Moderate hurdler; stays two and a half miles; acts on most types of ground; has worn a visor; a quirky sort.

Celtic Tanner (IRE)

75   53
5-y-o b g Royal Abjar (USA)-Mills Pride (IRE) (Posen (USA))
D J Wintle G M McGuinness

Placings:0-0P   (2771)
2003/04: 16⁰GS, 16^PS,

	Starts	1st	2nd	3rd	Win & Pl
Hurdles	2	0	0	0	
Career Total	3	0	0	0	

Going:	Sf: 0-1 GS: 0-1 Gd: 0-0 GF: - Fm: 0-0
Distance:	2m/2m3: 0-2 2m4-2m7: 0-0 3m+: 0-0
Track:	LH: 0-1 RH: 0-1 Tight: 0-0 Gall: 0-1
Aids:	Bl: 0-0 Vi: 0-0 Tstrap: 0-0 Ckp: 0-0
Best Rating:	74 2/03 Kemp 2m good NHF

Celtic Ted

72   42
6-y-o b g Celtic Swing-Careful Dancer (Gorytus (USA))
P Butler Christopher W Wilson

Placings:0/0   (0417)
2003/04: 17⁰G,

Placings:1-640   (4400)
2003/04: 16⁶G, 16⁴G, 16⁹G,

	Starts	1st	2nd	3rd	Win & Pl
NH Flat	3	0	0	0	0
Career Total	4	1	0	0	3584

117	2/03	Thur	2m	NHF	SH	£3584

Total win prize-money £3584

Going:	Sf: 0-0 GS: 0-0 Gd: 0-3 GF: - Fm: 0-0
Distance:	2m/2m3: 0-3 2m4-2m7: 0-0 3m+: 0-0
Track:	LH: 0-3 RH: 0-0 Tight: 0-0 Gall: 0-2
Aids:	Bl: 0-0 Vi: 0-0 Tstrap: 0-0 Ckp: 0-0
Best Rating:	117 2/03 Thur 2m sft-hvy NHF

Winner of a bumper in his only start in Ireland; sixth in a Grade Two bumper run on fast ground at Newbury on British debut, but well beaten in 2004 Championship Bumper at Cheltenham; suited by soft ground; shapes like a stayer; should improve when faced with hurdles.

	Starts	1st	2nd	3rd	Win & Pl
Hurdles	1	0	0	0	
Career Total	2	0	0	0	

Going: Sf: 0-0 GS: 0-0 Gd: 0-1 GF: - Fm: 0-0
Distance: 2m/2m3: 0-1 2m4-2m7: 0-0 3m+: 0-0
Track: LH: 0-0 RH: 0-1 Tight: 0-1 Gall: 0-0
Aids: Bl: 0-0 Vi: 0-0 Tstrap: 0-0 Ckp: 0-1
Best Rating: 40 5/03 MRas 2m1f110y good Hdl

Celtic Vision (IRE)
91(92c) (106c)120+
8-y-o b g Be My Native (USA)-Dream Run (Deep Run)
M Appleby (Jonjo O'Neill 11/12) P & P J Hughes

Placings:3/1020/212P1-53332FP0PF000 (4248)
2003/04: 24^6G, 16^3GF, 16^3GF, 21^3G, 21^2G, 24^FGS, 20^PF, 16^6GS, 25^PGS, 21^FG, 22^6G, 21^6G, 19^6GF,

	Starts	1st	2nd	3rd	Win & Pl
Hurdles	7	0	0	0	
Chases	6	0	1	3	2435
Career Total	23	3	4	4	22047
120	3/03	Kels	2m2f	C(0-135)HHdl	GD £10257
117	11/02	Sthl	2m4f110yD Hdl		G-S £4212
112	12/01	NAbb	2m1f	H NHF	HVY £2317
				Total win prize-money	£16786

Going: Sf: 0-0 GS: 0-3 Gd: 0-6 GF: - Fm: 0-4
Distance: 2m/2m3: 0-3 2m4-2m7: 0-7 3m+: 0-3
Track: LH: 0-8 RH: 0-5 Tight: 0-3 Gall: 0-2
Aids: Bl: 0-3 Vi: 0-0 Tstrap: 0-3 Ckp: 0-1
Best Rating: 120 3/03 Kels 2m2f good Hdl

Fair hurdler; showed ability, but had jumping problems over fences; stays two and a half miles; suited by cut in the ground; has worn blinkers, cheekpieces and a tongue tie.

Cenkos (FR)
118(99h) (129h)168
10-y-o ch g Nikos-Vincenza (Grundy)
P F Nicholls Mrs J Stewart

Placings:111/4/PF1F121121/244423P/14444351/12342-16154441 (4964)
2003/04: 16^1GF, 16^6G, 16^1GF, 16^5G, 16^4S, 16^4G, 20^4G, 16^1GF,

	Starts	1st	2nd	3rd	Win & Pl
Hurdles	1	0	0	0	0
Chases	7	3	0	0	113212
Career Total	42	14	6	3	532600
165	4/04	Sand	2m	B Ch	G-F £58000
167	11/03	Chel	2m	B HCh	G-F £16236
164	5/03	Wwck	2m110y	B Ch	G-F £13975
167	12/02	Sand	2m	A Ch	SFT £59500
166	4/02	Sand	2m	B Ch	GD £44625
154	5/01	Wwck	2m110y	B Ch	G-F £10952
155	4/00	Aint	2m	A Ch	GD £36000
158	3/00	Wwck	2m	A Ch	SFT £14410
152	1/00	Kemp	2m	D Ch	GD £5908
140	12/99	Sthl	2m	B(0-140)HCh	SFT £8651
123	12/99	Plum	2m	E Ch	GD £2900
	4/98	Engh	2m1f	Hdl	HVY £15152
	3/98	Engh	2m2f	Hdl	VS £10101
	3/98	Engh	2m110y	Hdl	HLD £10101
				Total win prize-money	£306514

Going: Sf: 0-1 GS: 0-0 Gd: 0-4 GF: - Fm: 3-3
Distance: 2m/2m3: 3-7 2m4-2m7: 0-1 3m+: 0-0
Track: LH: 2-5 RH: 1-3 Tight: 0-1 Gall: 1-2
Aids: Bl: 0-0 Vi: 0-0 Tstrap: 0-0 Ckp: 0-0
Best Rating: 167 3/04 Chel 2m good Ch

High-class chaser; third in both the 2002 and 2003 runnings

of the Queen Mother Champion Chase; won the Queen Mother Celebration Chase at Sandown in 2002 and 2004; fourth in the Queen Mother and the Melling Chase in 2004; best at two miles, stays 2m 4f; best on fast ground; likes the sun on his back; often goes well at Sandown.

Centaur Komet
6-y-o b g Komaite (USA)-Rather Gorgeous (Billion (USA))
D McCain Centaur Racing Ltd

Placings:0 (2159)
2003/04: 16^0GS,

	Starts	1st	2nd	3rd	Win & Pl
NH Flat	1	0	0	0	
Career Total	1	0	0	0	

Going: Sf: 0-0 GS: 0-1 Gd: 0-0 GF: - Fm: 0-0
Distance: 2m/2m3: 0-1 2m4-2m7: 0-0 3m+: 0-0
Track: LH: 0-1 RH: 0-0 Tight: 0-0 Gall: 0-0
Aids: Bl: 0-0 Vi: 0-0 Tstrap: 0-1 Ckp: 0-0

Central Committee (IRE)
71 111
9-y-o ch g Royal Academy (USA)-Idle Chat (USA) (Assert)
R T Phillips The Escape Committee

Placings:464B5P/21/56113314-000 (4785)
2003/04: 22^9G, 22^9G, 21^0G,

	Starts	1st	2nd	3rd	Win & Pl
Hurdles	3	0	0	0	
Career Total	19	4	1	2	17577
111	2/03	Font	2m6f110yE(0-110)HHdl		G-S £4173
98	10/02	Sedg	2m5f110yE(0-105)HHdl		GD £3391
98	9/02	Bang	2m4f	E(0-110)HHdl	GD £5187
103	6/00	Worc	2m4f	E Hdl	G-F £2506
				Total win prize-money	£15258

Going: Sf: 0-0 GS: 0-0 Gd: 0-3 GF: - Fm: 0-0
Distance: 2m/2m3: 0-0 2m4-2m7: 0-3 3m+: 0-0
Track: LH: 0-1 RH: 0-1 Tight: 0-1 Gall: 0-1
Aids: Bl: 0-0 Vi: 0-0 Tstrap: 0-0 Ckp: 0-0
Best Rating: 111 3/03 MRas 3m gd-sft Hdl

Modest hurdler; has had injury and wind problems; suited by two and a half miles and fast ground; game sort.

Central House
118(120h) (139h)147
7-y-o b g Alflora (IRE)-Fantasy World (Kemal (FR))
D T Hughes John F Kenny

Placings:323/f11122326-2112U4 (4827a)
2003/04: 16^6GY, 20^2GY, 17^1S, 17^1S, 17^2YS, 16^1G, 20^4Y,

	Starts	1st	2nd	3rd	Win & Pl
Hurdles	1	0	0	0	
Chases	6	2	2	6	64917
Career Total	17	5	6	3	106885
147	12/03	Leop	2m1f	Ch	SFT £42207
128	11/03	Fair	2m1f	Ch	SFT £8441
126	12/02	Cork	2m	Hdl	SFT £7407
130	11/02	Clon	2m	Hdl	SFT £3809
108	11/02	Punc	2m	NHF	SFT £4444
				Total win prize-money	£66313

Going: Sf: 2-2 GS: 0-1 Gd: 0-1 GF: - Fm: 0-0
Distance: 2m/2m3: 2-5 2m4-2m7: 0-2 3m+: 0-0
Track: LH: 1-3 RH: 1-4 Tight: 0-0 Gall: 0-1
Aids: Bl: 0-0 Vi: 0-0 Tstrap: 0-0 Ckp: 0-0

Best Rating: 147 1/04 Leop 2m1f yld-sft Ch

Useful Irish-trained novice chaser; suited by 2m and soft ground; likes to race prominently.

Ceol Na Sraide (IRE)
99 87
5-y-o b m King's Theatre (IRE)-My Lady's Key (USA) (Key To The Mint (USA))
B S Rothwell (J S Bolger 25/5) J Eddings

Placings:632660U (4163)
2003/04: 16^6GS, 16^3S, 16^2G, 16^6S, 16^6S, 16^9G, 16^4G,

	Starts	1st	2nd	3rd	Win & Pl
Hurdles	7	0	1	1	1711
Career Total	7	0	1	1	1711

Going: Sf: 0-3 GS: 0-1 Gd: 0-3 GF: - Fm: 0-0
Distance: 2m/2m3: 0-7 2m4-2m7: 0-0 3m+: 0-0
Track: LH: 0-5 RH: 0-2 Tight: 0-2 Gall: 0-1
Aids: Bl: 0-0 Vi: 0-0 Tstrap: 0-0 Ckp: 0-0
Best Rating: 87 1/04 Kels 2m110y soft Hdl

Moderate novice hurdler; effective over two miles; acts on easy ground.

Ceresfield (NZ)
105(102h) (99h)112+
8-y-o br m Westminster (NZ)-Audrey Rose (NZ) (Blue Razor (USA))
R C Guest Keith Middleton

Placings:63341/2450521-32522132150625154 (4516)
2003/04: 16^1G, 16^3G, 17^2GF, 20^5G, 20^2G, 17^2G, 17^1GF, 17^3G, 16^2GF, 16^1GF, 16^5GF, 17^0GF, 17^6GF, 17^2GF, 16^6G, 16^1G, 16^5G, 16^4GS,

	Starts	1st	2nd	3rd	Win & Pl
Chases	18	4	5	2	27453
Career Total	29	5	7	4	30810
112	2/04	Muss	2m	D(0-110)HCh	GD £6773
112	9/03	Uttx	2m	F(0-100)HCh	G-F £3066
102	7/03	Ctml	2m1f110yE Ch		G-F £4472
107	4/03	Hexm	2m110y	E(0-105)HCh	GD £4026
	4/02	Araw	1m6f	Hdl	FRM £1250
				Total win prize-money	£19588

Going: Sf: 0-0 GS: 0-1 Gd: 2-9 GF: - Fm: 0-0
Distance: 2m/2m3: 4-16 2m4-2m7: 0-2 3m+: 0-0
Track: LH: 3-12 RH: 1-6 Tight: 2-8 Gall: 0-2
Aids: Bl: 0-0 Vi: 0-0 Tstrap: 0-0 Ckp: 3-14
Best Rating: 112 2/04 Muss 2m good Ch

Moderate chaser; winner on the Flat and over jumps in New Zealand; consistent sort; likes to front run, but sometimes goes off too fast; best at around two miles; acts on a sound surface; usually wears cheekpieces and a tongue tie.

Cesare Borgia (IRE)
86 53
4-y-o ch c Dr Devious (IRE)-Prospering (Prince Sabo)
R Johnson (A Berry 7/8) Robert Johnson

Placings:P6F0 (3337)
2003/04: 16^PG, 16^6GF, 16^FGS, 16^9GS,

	Starts	1st	2nd	3rd	Win & Pl
Hurdles	4	0	0	0	0
Career Total	4	0	0	0	0

Going: Sf: 0-0 GS: 0-2 Gd: 0-1 GF: - Fm: 0-1

Distance:	2m/2m3: 0-4 2m4-2m7: 0-0 3m+: 0-0
Track:	LH: 0-4 RH: 0-0 Tight: 0-3 Gall: 0-1
Aids:	Bl: 0-0 Vi: 0-0 Tstrap: 0-0 Ckp: 0-0
Best Rating:	53 11/03 Catt 2m gd-fm Hdl

Cetti's Warbler
108   **98+**

6-y-o gr m Sir Harry Lewis (USA)-Sedge Warbler (Scallywag)
Mrs P Robeson Mrs P Robeson

Placings:*0*-031356P   (4574)
2003/04: 20⁰G, 21³GS, 16¹S, 21³GS, 22⁵HY, 20⁶GS, 21⁷G,

	Starts	1st	2nd	3rd	Win & Pl
Hurdles	7	1	0	2	3266
Career Total	8	1	0	2	3266
98 12/03 Towc 2m		E Hdl		SFT	£2317
				Total win prize-money	£2317

Going:	Sf: 1-2 GS: 0-3 Gd: 0-2 GF: - Fm: 0-0
Distance:	2m/2m3: 1-1 2m4-2m7: 0-0 3m+: 0-0
Track:	LH: 0-4 RH: 1-3 Tight: 0-1 Gall: 0-2
Aids:	Bl: 0-0 Vi: 0-0 Tstrap: 0-0 Ckp: 0-0
Best Rating:	98 12/03 Newb 2m5f gd-sft Hdl

Moderate novice hurdler; has come on with experience, but looks only moderate; stays 2m5f; acts on good ground.

Cha Cha Cha Dancer
90   **96**

4-y-o ch g Groom Dancer (USA)-Amber Fizz (USA) (Effervescing (USA))
G A Swinbank Scotnorth Racing Ltd

Placings:603   (4597)
2003/04: 17⁶GS, 16⁰GF, 16³G,

	Starts	1st	2nd	3rd	Win & Pl
Hurdles	3	0	0	1	644
Career Total	3	0	0	1	644

Going:	Sf: 0-0 GS: 0-1 Gd: 0-1 GF: - Fm: 0-1
Distance:	2m/2m3: 0-3 2m4-2m7: 0-0 3m+: 0-0
Track:	LH: 0-3 RH: 0-0 Tight: 0-3 Gall: 0-0
Aids:	Bl: 0-0 Vi: 0-0 Tstrap: 0-0 Ckp: 0-0
Best Rating:	96 3/04 Kels 2m110y good Hdl

Juvenile hurdler; modest third at Kelso in March.

Chabrimal Minster
108   **104+**

7-y-o b g Minster Son-Bromley Rose (Rubor)
R Ford B Mills, C Roberts, M & M Burrows

Placings:2-1   (4273)
2003/04: 24¹G,

	Starts	1st	2nd	3rd	Win & Pl
Hurdles	1	1	0	0	3949
Career Total	2	1	1	0	4977
109 3/04 Carl 3m110y E Hdl				GD	£3948
				Total win prize-money	£3949

Going:	Sf: 0-0 GS: 0-0 Gd: 1-1 GF: - Fm: 0-0
Distance:	2m/2m3: 0-0 2m4-2m7: 0-0 3m+: 1-1
Track:	LH: 0-0 RH: 1-1 Tight: 0-0 Gall: 0-0
Aids:	Bl: 0-0 Vi: 0-0 Tstrap: 0-0 Ckp: 0-0
Best Rating:	109 3/04 Carl 3m110y good Hdl

Novice hurdler; stays three miles; acts on good ground.

Chadswell (IRE)
96(104c)   (108c)**108**

11-y-o b g Lord Americo-Marita Ann (Crozier)
R Ford Mike Proudfoot Partnership

Placings:543461/10P/24F531142/1P1P03-00   (0431)
2003/04: 24⁰G, 26⁰G,

	Starts	1st	2nd	3rd	Win & Pl
Hurdles	2	0	0	0	
Career Total	26	6	2	3	26487
108 11/02 Sedg 3m3f	E(0-105)HCh	SFT	£3997
108 6/02 Ctml 3m3f	D(0-125)HHdl	HVY	£4745
108 3/02 Sedg 3m4f	D(0-115)HCh	SFT	£4007
101 2/02 Sedg 3m3f	E(0-110)HCh	SFT	£3297
102 5/00 Ctml 2m6f	F(0-95)HHdl	G-S	£3068
99 4/00 Carl 2m4f110yE Hdl		G-S	£2562
		Total win prize-money £21677	

Going:	Sf: 0-0 GS: 0-0 Gd: 0-2 GF: - Fm: 0-0
Distance:	2m/2m3: 0-0 2m4-2m7: 0-0 3m+: 0-2
Track:	LH: 0-1 RH: 0-1 Tight: 0-1 Gall: 0-0
Aids:	Bl: 0-0 Vi: 0-0 Tstrap: 0-1 Ckp: 0-0
Best Rating:	108 11/02 Sedg 3m3f soft Ch

Modest chaser/hurdler; needs three miles plus and soft ground; likes a sharp track.

Chain Line

14-y-o br g Relkino-Housemistress (New Member)
J W F Aynsley J W F Aynsley

Placings:*0*/060/0P0/PP5/400P000/1FP0PFP/00P5P/F5PP/0FPPPP-4   (0694)
2003/04: 16⁴GF,

	Starts	1st	2nd	3rd	Win & Pl
Hurdles	1	0	0	0	0
Career Total	40	1	0	0	2668
88 6/99 Hexm 2m		E Hdl	G-F	£2668
			Total win prize-money	£2668

Going:	Sf: 0-0 GS: 0-0 Gd: 0-0 GF: - Fm: 0-1
Distance:	2m/2m3: 0-0 2m4-2m7: 0-0 3m+: 0-0
Track:	LH: 0-1 RH: 0-0 Tight: 0-0 Gall: 0-0
Aids:	Bl: 0-0 Vi: 0-0 Tstrap: 0-0 Ckp: 0-0
Best Rating:	88 6/99 Hexm 2m gd-fm Hdl

Chakra
88   **64**

10-y-o gr g Mystiko (USA)-Maracuja (USA) (Riverman (USA))
C J Gray R L Squire

Placings:0P0   (3448)
2003/04: 17⁰G, 16⁷GS, 17⁰GS,

	Starts	1st	2nd	3rd	Win & Pl
Hurdles	3	0	0	0	
Career Total	3	0	0	0	

Going:	Sf: 0-0 GS: 0-2 Gd: 0-1 GF: - Fm: 0-0
Distance:	2m/2m3: 0-3 2m4-2m7: 0-0 3m+: 0-0
Track:	LH: 0-0 RH: 0-3 Tight: 0-2 Gall: 0-0
Aids:	Bl: 0-0 Vi: 0-0 Tstrap: 0-0 Ckp: 0-0
Best Rating:	64 12/03 Tntn 2m1f good Hdl

Chalford Mill
    40f

4-y-o b g Blushing Flame (USA)-Crambella (IRE) (Red Sunset)

C W Thornton Mrs Sheila Oakes

Placings:*0*   (2776)
2003/04: 13⁰S,

	Starts	1st	2nd	3rd	Win & Pl
NH Flat	1	0	0	0	
Career Total	1	0	0	0	

Going:	Sf: 0-1 GS: 0-0 Gd: 0-0 GF: - Fm: 0-0
Distance:	2m/2m3: 0-0 2m4-2m7: 0-0 3m+: 0-0
Track:	LH: 0-0 RH: 0-0 Tight: 0-0 Gall: 0-0
Aids:	Bl: 0-0 Vi: 0-0 Tstrap: 0-0 Ckp: 0-0
Best Rating:	40 12/03 Towc 1m5f110y soft NHF

Chalom (IRE)
94   **76**

6-y-o b g Mujadil (USA)-The Poachers Lady (IRE) (Salmon Leap (USA))
O Sherwood (B J Meehan 30/4) Maagar Uk Ltd

Placings:0006   (4781)
2003/04: 17⁰G, 21⁰GS, 19⁰G, 16⁶G,

	Starts	1st	2nd	3rd	Win & Pl
Hurdles	4	0	0	0	0
Career Total	4	0	0	0	0

Going:	Sf: 0-0 GS: 0-1 Gd: 0-3 GF: - Fm: 0-0
Distance:	2m/2m3: 0-2 2m4-2m7: 0-2 3m+: 0-0
Track:	LH: 0-2 RH: 0-2 Tight: 0-1 Gall: 0-1
Aids:	Bl: 0-0 Vi: 0-0 Tstrap: 0-0 Ckp: 0-0
Best Rating:	76 4/04 Hntg 2m110y good Hdl

Chamoss Royale (FR)
106   **115+**

4-y-o ch f Garde Royale-Chamoss (FR) (Tip Moss (FR))
P F Nicholls Mrs Kathy Stuart

Placings:11   (4544)
2003/04: 17¹HY, 22¹GS,

	Starts	1st	2nd	3rd	Win & Pl
Hurdles	2	2	0	0	13684
Career Total	2	2	0	0	13684
115 3/04 Winc 2m6f		E Hdl	G-S	£3542
1/04 Pau 2m1f110y Hdl			HVY	£10141
			Total win prize-money	£13684

Going:	Sf: 1-1 GS: 1-1 Gd: 0-0 GF: - Fm: 0-0
Distance:	2m/2m3: 1-1 2m4-2m7: 1-1 3m+: 0-0
Track:	LH: 0-0 RH: 1-1 Tight: 0-0 Gall: 0-0
Aids:	Bl: 0-0 Vi: 0-0 Tstrap: 0-0 Ckp: 0-0
Best Rating:	115 3/04 Winc 2m6f gd-sft Hdl

Fair hurdler; ex-French; stays 2m 6f; acts on soft ground.

Champagne Harry
111   **134**

6-y-o b g Sir Harry Lewis (USA)-Sparkling Cinders (Netherkelly)
N A Twiston-Davies Gavin Macechern

Placings:30U-4121121313356035   (4840)
2003/04: 16⁴GS, 17¹GF, 20⁵S, 20¹GF, 20¹GF, 24²G, 24¹G, 21³GF, 20¹GF, 21³G, 25³GS, 24⁵G, 24⁶S, 21⁰G, 24³G, 24⁵G,

	Starts	1st	2nd	3rd	Win & Pl
Hurdles	16	5	2	4	51196
Career Total	19	5	2	5	51465
134 11/03 Chep 2m4f		A Hdl	G-F	£17850

122	9/03	Prth	3m110y	D Hdl	GD	£2982
110	6/03	Uttx	2m4f110yE Hdl		G-F	£4104
106	6/03	Worc	2m4f	E Hdl	G-F	£3493
105	5/03	Hrfd	2m1f	E Hdl	G-F	£3477
				Total win prize-money £31908		

Going:	Sf: 0-2 GS: 0-2 Gd: 1-7 GF: - Fm: 4-5
Distance:	2m/2m3: 1-2 **2m4-2m7: 3-7** 3m+: 1-7
Track:	**LH: 3-14** RH: 2-2 Tight: 0-1 Gall: 0-7
Aids:	Bl: 0-0 Vi: 0-0 Tstrap: 0-0 Ckp: 0-0
Best Rating:	**134** 4/04 Aint 3m110y good Hdl

Useful novice hurdler; won Grade Two contest at Chepstow in November 2003; held in good company since; handles cut, but best on fast ground; stays three miles; will make a chaser.

Champagne Lil

94(112h)   (109h)**86+**

7-y-o gr m Terimon-Sparkling Cinders (Netherkelly)

N A Twiston-Davies Mrs Janey Mordaunt

Placings:4f1U53/6042P3-112243400   (4693)
2003/04: 21¹G, 19¹GF, 20²GF, 24²G, 20⁴GF, 25³G, 20⁴GS, 19⁰GS, 22⁰G,

	Starts	1st	2nd	3rd	Win & Pl
Hurdles	6	2	2	0	10867
Chases	3	0	0	1	1096
Career Total	20	3	3	3	17944

109	5/03	Hrfd	2m3f110yE(0-110)HHdl	G-F	£3367
99	5/03	Ludl	2m5f	E(0-105)HHdl	GD	£4225
96	10/01	Chep	2m110y	H NHF	GD	£1617
				Total win prize-money £9209	

Going:	Sf: 0-0 GS: 0-2 Gd: 1-4 GF: - Fm: 1-3
Distance:	2m/2m3: 0-1 **2m4-2m7: 2-6** 3m+: 0-2
Track:	LH: 0-2 **RH: 2-7** Tight: 0-1 Gall: 0-1
Aids:	Bl: 0-0 Vi: 0-0 Tstrap: 0-0 Ckp: 0-0
Best Rating:	**109** 10/03 Chep 2m4f gd-fm Hdl

Modest hurdler; stays three miles; acts on a sound surface, but is effective with cut in the ground.

Champagne Lou Lou

81f   **85f**

6-y-o b m Supreme Leader-Highfrith (Deep Run)

A Parker Derrick Mossop

Placings:60   (3669)
2003/04: 16⁶GS, 16⁰HY,

	Starts	1st	2nd	3rd	Win & Pl
NH Flat	2	0	0	0	0
Career Total	2	0	0	0	0

Going:	Sf: 0-1 GS: 0-0 Gd: 0-1 GF: - Fm: 0-0
Distance:	2m/2m3: 0-2 2m4-2m7: 0-0 3m+: 0-0
Track:	LH: 0-2 RH: 0-0 Tight: 0-0 Gall: 0-0
Aids:	Bl: 0-0 Vi: 0-0 Tstrap: 0-0 Ckp: 0-0
Best Rating:	**70** 1/04 Hayd 2m good NHF

Champagne Sundae (IRE)

84f   **86f**

6-y-o b g Supreme Leader-Partners In Crime (Crofthall)

P Winkworth Sundae Best

Placings:6P   (4636)
2003/04: 17⁵GS, 17⁰G,

	Starts	1st	2nd	3rd	Win & Pl
NH Flat	2	0	0	0	0

Career Total	2	0	0	0	0

Going:	Sf: 0-0 GS: 0-1 Gd: 0-1 GF: - Fm: 0-0
Distance:	2m/2m3: 0-2 2m4-2m7: 0-0 3m+: 0-0
Track:	LH: 0-0 RH: 0-1 Tight: 0-0 Gall: 0-0
Aids:	Bl: 0-0 Vi: 0-0 Tstrap: 0-0 Ckp: 0-0
Best Rating:	**86** 2/04 Folk 2m1f110y gd-sft NHF

Champetre (FR)

94   **78**

6-y-o ch g Pursuit Of Love-Fermiere (FR) (General Holme (USA))

Miss Victoria Roberts The Champetre Partnership

Placings:304   (4812)
2003/04: 17³G, 17⁰G, 16⁴G,

	Starts	1st	2nd	3rd	Win & Pl
Hurdles	3	0	0	1	611
Career Total	3	0	0	1	611

Going:	Sf: 0-0 GS: 0-0 Gd: 0-3 GF: - Fm: 0-0
Distance:	2m/2m3: 0-3 2m4-2m7: 0-0 3m+: 0-0
Track:	LH: 0-1 RH: 0-2 Tight: 0-2 Gall: 0-0
Aids:	Bl: 0-0 Vi: 0-0 Tstrap: 0-0 Ckp: 0-0
Best Rating:	**78** 4/04 Chep 2m110y good Hdl

Heavy ground Flat winner in France in 2000; has been beaten in a seller; will need to settle better to get two miles over hurdles.

Chan Move

101   **73**

12-y-o b g Move Off-Kanisa (Chantro)

W J Smith W J Smith

Placings:000/0P000F0PP0/PP/P025520/P00/00R/5-PP06P0P   (0935)
2003/04: 21⁵PS, 20⁰PG, 17⁰GS, 19⁰G, 22⁶PGF, 17⁰GF, 21⁵PGF,

	Starts	1st	2nd	3rd	Win & Pl
Hurdles	7	0	0	0	0
Career Total	36	0	2	0	986

Going:	Sf: 0-1 GS: 0-1 Gd: 0-2 GF: - Fm: 0-3
Distance:	2m/2m3: 0-2 2m4-2m7: 0-5 3m+: 0-0
Track:	LH: 0-6 RH: 0-1 Tight: 0-5 Gall: 0-0
Aids:	Bl: 0-6 Vi: 0-0 Tstrap: 0-0 Ckp: 0-0
Best Rating:	**84** 4/00 Newc 2m gd-sft Hdl

Chance Flight

79f   **53f**

4-y-o b f Busy Flight-Castle Maid (Castle Keep)

R J Hodges R T Sercombe

Placings:0   (4291)
2003/04: 16⁰G,

	Starts	1st	2nd	3rd	Win & Pl
NH Flat	1	0	0	0	0
Career Total	1	0	0	0	0

Going:	Sf: 0-0 GS: 0-0 Gd: 0-1 GF: - Fm: 0-0
Distance:	2m/2m3: 0-1 2m4-2m7: 0-0 3m+: 0-0
Track:	LH: 0-0 RH: 0-1 Tight: 0-0 Gall: 0-0
Aids:	Bl: 0-0 Vi: 0-0 Tstrap: 0-0 Ckp: 0-0
Best Rating:	**53** 3/04 Winc 2m good NHF

Chance Meeting

53   **20**

6-y-o b m Overbury (IRE)-Pepper Star (IRE) (Salt Dome (USA))

A King The Golden Anorak Partnership

Placings:60   (3213)
2003/04: 17⁶GS, 16⁰GS,

	Starts	1st	2nd	3rd	Win & Pl
NH Flat	1	0	0	0	0
Hurdles	1	0	0	0	0
Career Total	2	0	0	0	0

Going:	Sf: 0-0 GS: 0-2 Gd: 0-0 GF: - Fm: 0-0
Distance:	2m/2m3: 0-2 2m4-2m7: 0-0 3m+: 0-0
Track:	LH: 0-1 RH: 0-1 Tight: 0-1 Gall: 0-0
Aids:	Bl: 0-0 Vi: 0-0 Tstrap: 0-0 Ckp: 0-0
Best Rating:	**66** 12/03 Folk 2m1f110y gd-sft NHF

Chancers Dante (IRE)

(108h)   (92+h)

8-y-o b g Phardante (FR)-Own Acre (Linacre)

Ferdy Murphy Mrs P B Symes

Placings:1/0003/06P0-213FP   (2908)
2003/04: 24²G, 24¹G, 21³G, 16⁵F, 24⁵GS,

	Starts	1st	2nd	3rd	Win & Pl
Hurdles	2	1	1	0	3461
Chases	3	0	0	1	1286
Career Total	14	2	1	2	9827

92	5/03	Hexm	3m	F(0-100)HHdl	GD	£2681
101	6/01	Cork	2m4f	NHF	GD	£4729
				Total win prize-money £7411	

Going:	Sf: 0-1 GS: 0-1 Gd: 1-3 GF: - Fm: 0-0
Distance:	2m/2m3: 0-1 2m4-2m7: 0-1 **3m+: 1-3**
Track:	**LH: 1-3** RH: 0-2 Tight: 0-1 Gall: 0-1
Aids:	Bl: 0-1 Vi: 0-0 Tstrap: 0-0 Ckp: 0-0
Best Rating:	**101** 6/01 Cork 2m4f good NHF

Plating-class hurdler; stays three miles; effective on ground from good to heavy.

Chandelier

4-y-o ch g Sabrehill (USA)-La Noisette (Rock Hopper)

M S Saunders Chris Scott & Peter Hall

Placings:P0   (2764)
2003/04: 16⁶GF, 16⁰GS,

	Starts	1st	2nd	3rd	Win & Pl
Hurdles	2	0	0	0	0
Career Total	2	0	0	0	0

Going:	Sf: 0-0 GS: 0-1 Gd: 0-0 GF: - Fm: 0-0
Distance:	2m/2m3: 0-2 2m4-2m7: 0-0 3m+: 0-0
Track:	LH: 0-2 RH: 0-0 Tight: 0-1 Gall: 0-0
Aids:	Bl: 0-0 Vi: 0-0 Tstrap: 0-0 Ckp: 0-1

Changed Times (IRE)

                92

6-y-o br g Semillon-Miss Ivy (IRE) (Le Bavard (FR))

Liam Lennon Michael Dominic Sands

Placings:2F4P5   **(4410a)**
2003/04: 24²G, 25⁴S, 27⁴GS, 24ᴾGY, 16⁵Y,

	Starts	1st	2nd	3rd	Win & Pl
Chases	5	0	1	0	1585
Career Total	5	0	1	0	1585

Going:	Sf: 0-1 GS: 0-1 Gd: 0-1 GF: - Fm: 0-0
Distance:	2m/2m3: 0-1 2m4-2m7: 0-0 3m+: 0-4
Track:	LH: 0-1 RH: 0-1 Tight: 0-1 Gall: 0-0
Aids:	Bl: 0-0 Vi: 0-0 Tstrap: 0-0 Ckp: 0-0
Best Rating:	92 3/04 DRoy 2m100y yield Ch

Channahrlie (IRE)
110   (93h) **107**
10-y-o gr g Celio Rufo-Derravarragh Lady (IRE) (Radical)
R Dickin J C Clemmow

Placings:034/20610/551224PF16/02222221PP-3111123P   **(4141)**
2003/04: 25³F, 26¹GF, 20¹G, 24¹GF, 23¹F, 24²GS, 23³G, 24ᴾG,

	Starts	1st	2nd	3rd	Win & Pl
Chases	8	4	1	2	25670
Career Total	36	8	10	3	53136
107	12/03 Leic	2m7H110yD(0-125)HCh	FRM	£6720
102	11/03 Ludl	3m	D(0-120)HCh	G-F	£7144
95	11/03 Ling	2m4f110yF(0-90)Ch	GD	£3605
107	11/03 Wwck	3m2f	F(0-100)HCh	G-F	£2926
91	3/03 Sthl	3m110y	D(0-110)HCh	G-F	£4347
93	4/02 Hrfd	3m2f	E(0-105)HHdl	G-F	£2912
90	8/01 Bang	3m110y	D(0-125)HCh	GD	£5382
90	12/00 Leic	2m	D(0-110)HCh	G-S	£4241
			Total win prize-money £37273	

Going:	Sf: 0-0 GS: 0-1 Gd: 1-3 GF: - Fm: 3-4
Distance:	2m/2m3: 0-0 2m4-2m7: 1-1 3m+: 3-7
Track:	LH: 2-3 RH: 2-5 Tight: 2-3 Gall: 0-1
Aids:	Bl: 0-0 Vi: 0-0 Tstrap: 0-0 Ckp: 4-5
Best Rating:	107 12/03 Newb 3m gd-sft Ch

Modest chaser; completed a four-timer in late 2003; stays beyond three miles; acts on a sound surface; often wears cheekpieces; has worn a visor.

Channel Highlander
(85c)   (53+c)
9-y-o b g Jendali (USA)-Young Mary (Young Generation)
L Lungo R Flynn

Placings:600/0540350U/6604/P-3P   **(2140)**
2003/04: 16ᴾG, 16³GF, 20ᴾG,

	Starts	1st	2nd	3rd	Win & Pl
Hurdles	1	0	0	0	0
Chases	2	0	0	1	365
Career Total	18	0	0	2	683

Going:	Sf: 0-0 GS: 0-0 Gd: 0-2 GF: - Fm: 0-1
Distance:	2m/2m3: 0-2 2m4-2m7: 0-1 3m+: 0-0
Track:	LH: 0-3 RH: 0-0 Tight: 0-0 Gall: 0-1
Aids:	Bl: 0-0 Vi: 0-0 Tstrap: 0-0 Ckp: 0-0
Best Rating:	86 10/01 Carl 2m4f gd-sft Hdl

Poor chaser/hurdler; has broken blood vessels.

Chanticlier
107   **113+**
7-y-o b g Roselier (FR)-Cherry Crest (Pollerton)
K C Bailey Mrs Jane Lane

Placings:2/65-32   **(1968)**
2003/04: 26³GS, 21²G,

	Starts	1st	2nd	3rd	Win & Pl
Hurdles	2	0	1	1	1379
Career Total	5	0	2	1	2985

Going:	Sf: 0-0 GS: 0-1 Gd: 0-1 GF: - Fm: 0-0
Distance:	2m/2m3: 0-0 2m4-2m7: 0-1 3m+: 0-1
Track:	LH: 0-0 RH: 0-2 Tight: 0-0 Gall: 0-0
Aids:	Bl: 0-0 Vi: 0-0 Tstrap: 0-0 Ckp: 0-0
Best Rating:	116 3/02 Sand 2m110y gd-sft NHF

Modest hurdler; gve a hotpot a real fright on his debut in a Sandown bumper and was not disgraced on his hurdling debut; highly tried first two starts over hurdles; third when dropped in class over 3m 2f at Hereford May 2003.

Chaparro Amargoso (IRE)
11-y-o b g Ela-Mana-Mou-Champanera (Top Ville)
F L Matthews J E Wood

Placings:1/3/3P6/12F43446052/12334-0U   **(4510)**
2003/04: 20⁰G, 19ᵁGS,

	Starts	1st	2nd	3rd	Win & Pl
Chases	2	0	0	0	
Career Total	23	3	3	5	16667
104	5/02 Weth	2m	D(0-115)HCh	G-F	£4069
108	7/01 Sedg	2m110y	E Ch	G-F	£3152
110	10/97 Hexm	2m	H NHF	G-F	£1187
			Total win prize-money £8409	

Going:	Sf: 0-0 GS: 0-1 Gd: 0-1 GF: - Fm: 0-0
Distance:	2m/2m3: 0-1 2m4-2m7: 0-1 3m+: 0-0
Track:	LH: 0-0 RH: 0-2 Tight: 0-1 Gall: 0-0
Aids:	Bl: 0-0 Vi: 0-0 Tstrap: 0-0 Ckp: 0-0
Best Rating:	110 7/02 Wolv 2m gd-sft Ch

A consistent performer in modest handicap chases, he is best suited by two miles and fast ground.

Chapel Royale (IRE)
94   **88**
7-y-o gr g College Chapel-Merci Royale (Fairy King (USA))
Mrs N S Sharpe (Evan Williams 20/10) The Blue Yonder Partnership

Placings:000-05   **(1717)**
2003/04: 17⁰GF, 16⁵GF,

	Starts	1st	2nd	3rd	Win & Pl
Hurdles	2	0	0	0	0
Career Total	5	0	0	0	0

Going:	Sf: 0-0 GS: 0-0 Gd: 0-0 GF: - Fm: 0-2
Distance:	2m/2m3: 0-2 2m4-2m7: 0-0 3m+: 0-0
Track:	LH: 0-1 RH: 0-1 Tight: 0-1 Gall: 0-0
Aids:	Bl: 0-0 Vi: 0-0 Tstrap: 0-2 Ckp: 0-0
Best Rating:	88 2/03 Weth 2m good Hdl

Plating-class hurdler; modest handicapper on the Flat; no worthwhile form over hurdles.

Chapel Times (IRE)
85f   **96+f**
5-y-o b g Supreme Leader-Dippers Daughter (Strong Gale)
H D Daly Trevor Hemmings

Placings:3   **(4481)**
2003/04: 17³HY,

	Starts	1st	2nd	3rd	Win & Pl
NH Flat	1	0	0	1	275

Career Total	1	0	0	1	275

Going:	Sf: 0-1 GS: 0-0 Gd: 0-0 GF: - Fm: 0-0
Distance:	2m/2m3: 0-1 2m4-2m7: 0-0 3m+: 0-0
Track:	LH: 0-0 RH: 0-1 Tight: 0-0 Gall: 0-0
Aids:	Bl: 0-0 Vi: 0-0 Tstrap: 0-0 Ckp: 0-0
Best Rating:	101 3/04 Carl 2m1f heavy NHF

Chapeltown (IRE)
107(92h)   (114h)**115+**
12-y-o b g Denel (FR)-Lady Dunsford (Torus)
N J Henderson Newbury Racehorse Owners Group Ii

Placings:066630/213/1513/41/U-012   **(4821)**
2003/04: 16⁶G, 19¹G, 19²GF,

	Starts	1st	2nd	3rd	Win & Pl
Hurdles	1	0	0	0	0
Chases	2	1	1	0	6849
Career Total	19	5	2	3	30855
113	4/04 Tntn	2m3f	D Ch	GD	£5499
135	11/01 Newb	2m3f	C(0-135)HHdl	GD	£7150
130	3/01 Newb	2m110y	D Hdl	HVY	£4738
135	11/00 Newb	2m110y	C Hdl	HVY	£5720
99	5/98 DRoy	2m	NHF	GD	£1489
			Total win prize-money £24597	

Going:	Sf: 0-0 GS: 0-0 Gd: 1-2 GF: - Fm: 0-1
Distance:	2m/2m3: 1-2 2m4-2m7: 0-1 3m+: 0-0
Track:	LH: 0-1 RH: 1-2 Tight: 1-1 Gall: 0-1
Aids:	Bl: 0-0 Vi: 0-0 Tstrap: 0-0 Ckp: 0-0
Best Rating:	135 11/01 Newb 2m3f good Hdl

Useful hurdler; very lightly raced in recent years; won a very moderate event on his belated chasing debut; goes well at Newbury; effective at up to just short of two and a half miles; acts on good and heavy ground.

Chapter House (USA)
87   **85+**
5-y-o b g Pulpit (USA)-Lilian Bayliss (IRE) (Sadler's Wells (USA))
M W Easterby (D Nicholls 25/9) Lord Daresbury

Placings:5U000   **(4688)**
2003/04: 16⁵S, 16ᵁGS, 20⁰GS, 20⁰GS, 16⁰G,

	Starts	1st	2nd	3rd	Win & Pl
Hurdles	5	0	0	0	0
Career Total	5	0	0	0	0

Going:	Sf: 0-1 GS: 0-3 Gd: 0-1 GF: - Fm: 0-0
Distance:	2m/2m3: 0-3 2m4-2m7: 0-2 3m+: 0-0
Track:	LH: 0-5 RH: 0-0 Tight: 0-1 Gall: 0-0
Aids:	Bl: 0-1 Vi: 0-0 Tstrap: 0-0 Ckp: 0-0
Best Rating:	85 12/03 Hayd 2m soft Hdl

Charlatan (IRE)
87   **77**
6-y-o b g Charnwood Forest (IRE)-Taajreh (IRE) (Mtoto)
Mrs C A Dunnett Andy Middleton

Placings:000-60   **(4774)**
2003/04: 16⁶GS, 16⁰G,

	Starts	1st	2nd	3rd	Win & Pl
Hurdles	2	0	0	0	0
Career Total	5	0	0	0	0

Going:	Sf: 0-0 GS: 0-1 Gd: 0-1 GF: - Fm: 0-0

Distance:	2m/2m3: 0-2 2m4-2m7: 0-0 3m+: 0-0
Track:	LH: 0-2 RH: 0-0 Tight: 0-2 Gall: 0-0
Aids:	Bl: 0-0 Vi: 0-0 Tstrap: 0-0 Ckp: 0-0
Best Rating:	77 1/03 Hntg 2m110y soft Hdl

Charlie

74   53

6-y-o b g Pharly (FR)-Leave It To Lib (Tender King)
N A Twiston-Davies   N A Twiston-Davies

Placings:456   (1360)
2003/04: 16⁴G, 16⁵GF, 17⁶G,

	Starts	1st	2nd	3rd	Win & Pl
NH Flat	2	0	0	0	265
Hurdles	1	0	0	0	0
Career Total	3	0	0	0	265

Going:	Sf: 0-0 GS: 0-0 Gd: 0-2 GF: - Fm: 0-1
Distance:	2m/2m3: 0-3 2m4-2m7: 0-0 3m+: 0-0
Track:	LH: 0-2 RH: 0-0 Tight: 0-1 Gall: 0-0
Aids:	Bl: 0-0 Vi: 0-0 Tstrap: 0-0 Ckp: 0-0
Best Rating:	94 5/03 Kels 2m110y good NHF

Made a promising debut when fourth in a decent Kelso bumper in May 2003; rather disappointing after; acts on good ground.

Charlie Bubbles (IRE)

86   57

7-y-o b g Un Desperado (FR)-Bounty (IRE) (Cataldi)
B De Haan   Flora Charlie Limited

Placings:0-00   (4812)
2003/04: 16⁶G, 16⁹G,

	Starts	1st	2nd	3rd	Win & Pl
Hurdles	2	0	0	0	
Career Total	3	0	0	0	

Going:	Sf: 0-0 GS: 0-0 Gd: 0-2 GF: - Fm: 0-0
Distance:	2m/2m3: 0-2 2m4-2m7: 0-0 3m+: 0-0
Track:	LH: 0-1 RH: 0-1 Tight: 0-0 Gall: 0-1
Aids:	Bl: 0-0 Vi: 0-0 Tstrap: 0-0 Ckp: 0-0
Best Rating:	59 3/04 Hntg 2m110y good Hdl

Charlie Castallan

80f   61f

4-y-o gr g Wace (USA)-Castle Cary (Castle Keep)
N J Hawke   Mrs D A Wetherall

Placings:00   (4550)
2003/04: 16⁰G, 16⁰GS,

	Starts	1st	2nd	3rd	Win & Pl
NH Flat	2	0	0	0	
Career Total	2	0	0	0	

Going:	Sf: 0-0 GS: 0-1 Gd: 0-1 GF: - Fm: 0-0
Distance:	2m/2m3: 0-2 2m4-2m7: 0-0 3m+: 0-0
Track:	LH: 0-0 RH: 0-2 Tight: 0-0 Gall: 0-0
Aids:	Bl: 0-0 Vi: 0-0 Tstrap: 0-0 Ckp: 0-0
Best Rating:	61 3/04 Winc 2m good NHF

Charlie Chapel

95f   90f

5-y-o b g College Chapel-Lightino (Bustino)

W M Brisbourne   D Shenton Syndicate

Placings:P50   (4571)
2003/04: 16⁵GS, 16⁵G, 17⁰GS,

	Starts	1st	2nd	3rd	Win & Pl
NH Flat	3	0	0	0	0
Career Total	3	0	0	0	0

Charlie Moon (IRE)

56f   21f

5-y-o gr g Moonax (IRE)-Charlottes Lot (Fine Blade (USA))
Jonjo O'Neill   Trevor Hemmings

Placings:0   (3649)
2003/04: 16⁰G,

	Starts	1st	2nd	3rd	Win & Pl
NH Flat	1	0	0	0	
Career Total	1	0	0	0	

Going:	Sf: 0-0 GS: 0-0 Gd: 0-0 GF: - Fm: 0-0
Distance:	2m/2m3: 0-1 2m4-2m7: 0-0 3m+: 0-0
Track:	LH: 0-0 RH: 0-1 Tight: 0-0 Gall: 0-0
Aids:	Bl: 0-0 Vi: 0-0 Tstrap: 0-0 Ckp: 0-0
Best Rating:	21 2/04 Kemp 2m gd-sft NHF

Charlie Strong (IRE)

11-y-o b g Strong Gale-The Village Vixen (Buckskin (FR))
R Kelvin-Hughes   R Kelvin-Hughes

Placings:6/1/63/1P-P   (4425)
2003/04: 26⁶PG,

	Starts	1st	2nd	3rd	Win & Pl
Chases	1	0	0	0	
Career Total	7	2	0	1	8908
108 5/02	Winc	2m5f	H Ch		G-F £6795
109 4/01	Extr	2m7f110yH Ch			G-S £1790
				Total win prize-money £8587	

Going:	Sf: 0-0 GS: 0-0 Gd: 0-1 GF: - Fm: 0-0
Distance:	2m/2m3: 0-0 2m4-2m7: 0-0 3m+: 0-1
Track:	LH: 0-1 RH: 0-0 Tight: 0-0 Gall: 0-1
Aids:	Bl: 0-0 Vi: 0-0 Tstrap: 0-0 Ckp: 0-0
Best Rating:	109 4/01 Extr 2m7f110y gd-sft Ch

Charlie Whitestone

72f

5-y-o b g Sovereign Water (FR)-Khatti Hawk (Hittite Glory)
R D E Woodhouse   P Hampshire

Placings:00   (0649)
2003/04: 16⁰G, 16⁰GF,

	Starts	1st	2nd	3rd	Win & Pl
NH Flat	2	0	0	0	
Career Total	2	0	0	0	

Going:	Sf: 0-0 GS: 0-0 Gd: 0-1 GF: - Fm: 0-1
Distance:	2m/2m3: 0-0 2m4-2m7: 0-0 3m+: 0-0
Track:	LH: 0-1 RH: 0-0 Tight: 0-0 Gall: 0-0
Aids:	Bl: 0-0 Vi: 0-0 Tstrap: 0-0 Ckp: 0-0
Best Rating:	72 5/03 Kels 2m110y good NHF

Charlie's Angel

6-y-o gr m Rakaposhi King-Dunnoholm (Kalaglow)
P York (R H York 11/8)   C Cheesman

Placings:50⁄55   (4302)
2003/04: 16⁵GF, 16⁰GF, 17⁵GS, 20⁵G,

	Starts	1st	2nd	3rd	Win & Pl
NH Flat	2	0	0	0	0
Hurdles	1	0	0	0	0
Chases	1	0	0	0	0
Career Total	4	0	0	0	0

Going:	Sf: 0-0 GS: 0-1 Gd: 0-1 GF: - Fm: 0-2
Distance:	2m/2m3: 0-3 2m4-2m7: 0-1 3m+: 0-0
Track:	LH: 0-3 RH: 0-1 Tight: 0-0 Gall: 0-0
Aids:	Bl: 0-0 Vi: 0-0 Tstrap: 0-0 Ckp: 0-0
Best Rating:	75 7/03 Worc 2m gd-fm NHF

Charlie's Double

67f   43f

5-y-o b g Double Eclipse (IRE)-Pendil's Niece (Roscoe Blake)
J R Best   The Highly Hopeful Club

Placings:0   (3482)
2003/04: 16⁰G,

	Starts	1st	2nd	3rd	Win & Pl
NH Flat	1	0	0	0	
Career Total	1	0	0	0	

Going:	Sf: 0-0 GS: 0-0 Gd: 0-1 GF: - Fm: 0-0
Distance:	2m/2m3: 0-1 2m4-2m7: 0-0 3m+: 0-0
Track:	LH: 0-1 RH: 0-0 Tight: 0-1 Gall: 0-0
Aids:	Bl: 0-0 Vi: 0-0 Tstrap: 0-0 Ckp: 0-0
Best Rating:	43 1/04 Catt 2m good NHF

Charlieadams (IRE)

14-y-o b g Carlingford Castle-Lucy Platter (FR) (Record Token)
J F W Muir   J F W Muir

Placings:0⁄000P0/2/4U3/50F3/O116UUP/2FU1112226-P60   (4689)

2003/04: 24⁸F, 21⁶GF, 25⁹G,

	Starts	1st	2nd	3rd	Win & Pl
Chases	3	0	0	0	
Career Total	34	5	5	2	26011
110 8/02	Prth	2m4f110yD(0-115)HCh		GD	£6760
114 8/02	Sedg	2m5f	D(0-120)HCh	GD	£4784
101 7/02	Sedg	2m5f	E(0-110)HCh	G-F	£4124
88 5/01	Hexm	2m4f110yH Ch		G-F	£1337
88 5/01	Prth	2m4f110yH Ch		SFT	£2317
			Total win prize-money £19322		

Going:	Sf: 0-0 GS: 0-0 Gd: 0-1 GF: - Fm: 0-2
Distance:	2m/2m3: 0-0 2m4-2m7: 0-1 3m+: 0-2
Track:	LH: 0-2 RH: 0-1 Tight: 0-2 Gall: 0-0
Aids:	Bl: 0-0 Vi: 0-0 Tstrap: 0-0 Ckp: 0-0
Best Rating:	114 10/02 Kels 3m1f good Ch

Charlies Bride (IRE)

79   46

9-y-o b/br m Rich Charlie-Nordic Bride (IRE) (Nordico (USA))
M A Barnes   Pointerfarm Racing Partnership

Placings:25/P0 (3476)
2003/04: 17^6HY, 16^6G,

	Starts	1st	2nd	3rd	Win & Pl
Hurdles	2	0	0	0	
Career Total	4	0	1	0	902

Going:	Sf: 0-1 GS: 0-0 Gd: 0-1 GF: - Fm: 0-0
Distance:	2m/2m3: 0-2 2m4-2m7: 0-0 3m+: 0-0
Track:	LH: 0-4 RH: 0-1 Tight: 0-1 Gall: 0-0
Aids:	Bl: 0-0 Vi: 0-0 Tstrap: 0-2 Ckp: 0-0
Best Rating:	90 7/99 Strf 2m110y good Hdl

Charlies Future
110(108h)   (107 h)**113**
6-y-o b g Democratic (USA)-Fausterelie (Faustus (USA))
S C Burrough M L Lewis-Jones

Placings:55003/06402153-54332 (3638)
2003/04: 22^3S, 22^5G, 19^4GS, 19^3S, 19^3GS, 19^2S,

	Starts	1st	2nd	3rd	Win & Pl
Hurdles	2	0	0	1	983
Chases	4	0	1	2	3018
Career Total	18	1	2	4	9581
107 3/03 Tntn	2m3f110yE(0-105)HHdl			HVY	£3887
				Total win prize-money	£3887

Going:	Sf: 0-3 GS: 0-2 Gd: 0-1 GF: - Fm: 0-0
Distance:	2m/2m3: 0-1 2m4-2m7: 0-0 3m+: 0-0
Track:	LH: 0-4 RH: 0-2 Tight: 0-2 Gall: 0-0
Aids:	Bl: 0-0 Vi: 0-0 Tstrap: 0-0 Ckp: 0-0
Best Rating:	113 2/04 Extr 2m3f110y soft Ch

Modest hurdler; easy winner of ordinary handicap at Taunton March 2003; not disgraced over fences; acts on soft ground; stays two miles six.

Charlies Memory
106   **103+**
5-y-o b g Blushing Flame (USA)-Hat Hill (Roan Rocket)
M W Easterby J W P Curtis

Placings:055033 (4618)
2003/04: 16^0GS, 16^5S, 16^5G, 20^4GS, 16^3GF, 21^3G,

	Starts	1st	2nd	3rd	Win & Pl
NH Flat	3	0	0	0	0
Hurdles	3	0	0	2	1042
Career Total	6	0	0	2	1042

Going:	Sf: 0-1 GS: 0-2 Gd: 0-2 GF: - Fm: 0-1
Distance:	2m/2m3: 0-4 2m4-2m7: 0-2 3m+: 0-0
Track:	LH: 0-6 RH: 0-0 Tight: 0-3 Gall: 0-1
Aids:	Bl: 0-0 Vi: 0-0 Tstrap: 0-1 Ckp: 0-0
Best Rating:	103 3/04 Catt 2m gd-fm Hdl

Modest form in bumpers and hurdles; seems to be suited by a sound surface and two miles.

Charliesmedarlin
103   **90**
13-y-o b g Macmillion-Top Cover (High Top)
Mrs Barbara Waring E S Chivers

Placings:00/P/4UPL06P3P/30/11/U-PP313 (0708)
2003/04: 25^5GS, 26^6GF, 21^3GF, 24^1GF, 21^3GF,

	Starts	1st	2nd	3rd	Win & Pl
Chases	5	1	0	2	6455
Career Total	22	3	0	4	15350
90 6/03 Uttx 3m	E(0-110)HCh			G-F	£5070
104 7/00 Strf	2m5f110yE(0-105)HCh			G-F	£3428

91 7/00 Worc 2m7f110yF(0-110)HCh GD £4306
Total win prize-money £12805

Going:	Sf: 0-0 GS: 0-1 Gd: 0-0 GF: - Fm: 1-4
Distance:	2m/2m3: 0-0 2m4-2m7: 0-2 3m+: 1-3
Track:	LH: 1-4 RH: 0-1 Tight: 0-2 Gall: 0-0
Aids:	Bl: 0-0 Vi: 0-0 Tstrap: 0-0 Ckp: 0-0
Best Rating:	104 7/00 Strf 2m5f110y gd-fm Ch

Moderate handicap chaser; off course for nearly three years after winning back-to-back handicaps July 2000; failed to complete first three starts after comeback; much better effort having been dropped 15lb when third at Newton Abbot June 2003; scored from 6lb out of the handicap at Uttoxeter next time; stays 3m; acts on a sound surface.

Charlotte Lamb
39f
4-y-o gr f Pharly (FR)-Caroline Lamb (Hotfoot)
Miss S E Hall Miss S E Hall

Placings:0 (2482)
2003/04: 13^0GF,

	Starts	1st	2nd	3rd	Win & Pl
NH Flat	1	0	0	0	
Career Total	1	0	0	0	

Going:	Sf: 0-0 GS: 0-0 Gd: 0-0 GF: - Fm: 0-1
Distance:	2m/2m3: 0-0 2m4-2m7: 0-0 3m+: 0-0
Track:	LH: 0-0 RH: 0-0 Tight: 0-0 Gall: 0-0
Aids:	Bl: 0-0 Vi: 0-0 Tstrap: 0-0 Ckp: 0-0
Best Rating:	42 11/03 Donc 1m5f gd-fm NHF

Charly Bomber
6-y-o ch g Lancastrian-Charlycia (Good Times (ITY))
Miss M Bragg Friends Of Rock Park

Placings:0 (4739)
2003/04: 17^0G,

	Starts	1st	2nd	3rd	Win & Pl
NH Flat	1	0	0	0	
Career Total	1	0	0	0	

Going:	Sf: 0-0 GS: 0-0 Gd: 0-0 GF: - Fm: 0-0
Distance:	2m/2m3: 0-1 2m4-2m7: 0-0 3m+: 0-0
Track:	LH: 0-1 RH: 0-0 Tight: 0-1 Gall: 0-0
Aids:	Bl: 0-0 Vi: 0-0 Tstrap: 0-0 Ckp: 0-0

Charly Jack
5-y-o b g Alderbrook-Reperage (USA) (Key To Content (USA))
Ferdy Murphy Lee M Symes

Placings:0 (2912)
2003/04: 16^0GS,

	Starts	1st	2nd	3rd	Win & Pl
NH Flat	1	0	0	0	
Career Total	1	0	0	0	

Going:	Sf: 0-0 GS: 0-1 Gd: 0-0 GF: - Fm: 0-0
Distance:	2m/2m3: 0-1 2m4-2m7: 0-0 3m+: 0-0
Track:	LH: 0-0 RH: 0-1 Tight: 0-0 Gall: 0-1
Aids:	Bl: 0-0 Vi: 0-0 Tstrap: 0-0 Ckp: 0-0

Charm Offensive
94   **85**
6-y-o b m Zieten (USA)-Shoag (USA) (Affirmed (USA))
C J Gray What Racing

Placings:500-431P0060 (4488)
2003/04: 22^4GF, 22^3F, 24^1G, 24^4GS, 24^0G, 26^9GS, 24^6GF, 22^0G,

	Starts	1st	2nd	3rd	Win & Pl
Hurdles	8	1	0	1	2683
Career Total	11	1	0	1	2683
85 11/03 Towc 3m	F(0-90)Hdl			GD	£2212
				Total win prize-money	£2212

Going:	Sf: 0-0 GS: 0-2 Gd: 1-3 GF: - Fm: 0-3
Distance:	2m/2m3: 0-0 2m4-2m7: 0-3 3m+: 1-5
Track:	LH: 0-2 RH: 1-6 Tight: 0-2 Gall: 0-0
Aids:	Bl: 0-0 Vi: 0-0 Tstrap: 0-0 Ckp: 0-0
Best Rating:	85 11/03 Towc 3m good Hdl

Very modest novice hurdler; acts on good ground; stays three miles.

Charming Admiral (IRE)
103(87h)   (86h)**99**
11-y-o b g Shareef Dancer (USA)-Lilac Charm (Bustino)
Mrs A Duffield The Old Spice Girls

Placings:4312013/3014F2/116P/50/51P61-0530P (4457)
2003/04: 20^0HY, 25^5GS, 25^3S, 20^4HY, 24^5HY,

	Starts	1st	2nd	3rd	Win & Pl
Hurdles	1	0	0	0	0
Chases	4	0	0	1	854
Career Total	29	7	2	4	28338
99 3/03 Hexm	2m4f110yF(0-100)HCh			SFT	£3276
92 12/02 Catt	3m1f110yE(0-110)HCh			G-S	£4192
109 9/00 Sedg	2m5f E(0-115)HCh			SFT	£4153
109 8/00 Ctml	2m5f110yF(0-110)HCh			G-S	£3461
100 2/99 Carl	2m4f110yD Ch			HVY	£3964
126 4/98 Kels	2m110y D(0-125)HHdl			HVY	£2762
124 1/98 Catt	2m3f E Hdl			G-S	£2092
				Total win prize-money	£23903

Going:	Sf: 0-4 GS: 0-1 Gd: 0-0 GF: - Fm: 0-0
Distance:	2m/2m3: 0-0 2m4-2m7: 0-2 3m+: 0-3
Track:	LH: 0-3 RH: 0-2 Tight: 0-1 Gall: 0-1
Aids:	Bl: 0-5 Vi: 0-0 Tstrap: 0-0 Ckp: 0-0
Best Rating:	126 4/98 Kels 2m110y heavy Hdl

Moderate chaser; stays really well, but is unreliable; suited by soft ground; wears blinkers.

Charmouth Forest
79
8-y-o ch g Lir-Crimson Lady (Crimson Beau)
C J Gray D J Staddon

Placings:00/650/55564P- (0017)
2003/04: 27^0PS,

	Starts	1st	2nd	3rd	Win & Pl
Hurdles	1	0	0	0	
Career Total	11	0	0	0	456

Going:	Sf: 0-1 GS: 0-0 Gd: 0-0 GF: - Fm: 0-0
Distance:	2m/2m3: 0-0 2m4-2m7: 0-0 3m+: 0-1
Track:	LH: 0-1 RH: 0-0 Tight: 0-1 Gall: 0-0
Aids:	Bl: 0-0 Vi: 0-0 Tstrap: 0-1 Ckp: 0-0
Best Rating:	82 1/03 Extr 2m3f gd-sft Hdl

Moderate hurdler; yet to make the frame.

Charnwood Street (IRE)

95   **73**

5-y-o b g Charnwood Forest (IRE)-La Vigie (King Of Clubs)
D Shaw Swann Racing Ltd

Placings:005-005P0550   (2477)
2003/04: 20⁰G, 17⁰GF, 16⁵HY, 21⁵G, 24⁹G, 20⁵G, 26⁵GS, 24⁹GF,

	Starts	1st	2nd	3rd	Win & Pl
Hurdles	8	0	0	0	0
Career Total	11	0	0	0	0

Going:	Sf: 0-1 GS: 0-1 Gd: 0-4 GF: - Fm: 0-2
Distance:	2m/2m3: 0-2 2m4-2m7: 0-3 3m+: 0-3
Track:	LH: 0-5 RH: 0-3 Tight: 0-4 Gall: 0-2
Aids:	Bl: 0-0 Vi: 0-7 Tstrap: 0-0 Ckp: 0-0
Best Rating:	74 11/03 Hntg 3m2f gd-sft Hdl

Moderate hurdler.

Charter Royal (FR)

93(91h)   (71h) **71**

9-y-o gr g Royal Charter (FR)-Tadjmine (FR) (Tadj (FR))
A R Dicken Got To Be In It To Win It Partnership

Placings:650/050300/2241F0F/60145053400U/P63P00P-
0604P   (3736)
2003/04: 16⁰G, 21⁶GF, 19⁰GS, 24⁴GF, 24⁴P'G,

	Starts	1st	2nd	3rd	Win & Pl
Hurdles	2	0	0	0	0
Chases	3	0	0	0	254
Career Total	40	2	2	3	8358
80	11/01 Sedg	2m110y F(0-110)HCh		SFT	£2520
80	1/01 Catt	2m F(0-100)HCh		G-S	£2401
		Total win prize-money £4922			

Going:	Sf: 0-0 GS: 0-1 Gd: 0-2 GF: - Fm: 0-2
Distance:	2m/2m3: 0-2 2m4-2m7: 0-1 3m+: 0-2
Track:	LH: 0-3 RH: 0-2 Tight: 0-4 Gall: 0-0
Aids:	Bl: 0-0 Vi: 0-0 Tstrap: 0-0 Ckp: 0-0
Best Rating:	84 10/00 Carl 2m gd-sft Ch

Very moderate handicap chaser, he acts on soft ground and
is effective over two to three miles.

Chase The Sunset (IRE)

108   **98**

6-y-o ch g Un Desperado (FR)-Cherry Chase (IRE) (Red
Sunset)
Miss H C Knight Jim Lewis

Placings:04-25203   (3899)
2003/04: 16²GF, 16⁵GS, 17²G, 17⁰GS, 20³GS,

	Starts	1st	2nd	3rd	Win & Pl
Hurdles	5	0	2	1	5353
Career Total	7	0	2	1	5685

Going:	Sf: 0-0 GS: 0-3 Gd: 0-1 GF: - Fm: 0-1
Distance:	2m/2m3: 0-4 2m4-2m7: 0-1 3m+: 0-0
Track:	LH: 0-2 RH: 0-3 Tight: 0-0 Gall: 0-2
Aids:	Bl: 0-0 Vi: 0-0 Tstrap: 0-0 Ckp: 0-0
Best Rating:	98 2/04 Sand 2m4f110y gd-sft Hdl

Moderate hurdler; some promise so far; will jump fences in
time; stays two miles one, but should be suited by farther.

Chasing The Bride

11-y-o b g Gildoran-Bride (Remainder Man)
Miss A Goschen Miss A Goschen

Placings:U/22116/22/PU04P/511   (4891)
2003/04: 24⁵G, 25¹GF, 24¹GF,

	Starts	1st	2nd	3rd	Win & Pl
Chases	3	2	0	0	4396
Career Total	15	4	4	0	11246
112	4/04	Strf	3m	H Ch	G-F	£2926
112	3/04	Winc	3m1f110y	H Ch	G-F	£1470
104	4/00	Asct	3m110y	H Ch	GD	£2697
102	3/00	Winc	3m1f110y	H Ch	G-S	£1557
				Total win prize-money £8652		

Going:	Sf: 0-0 GS: 0-0 Gd: 0-1 GF: - Fm: 2-2
Distance:	2m/2m3: 0-0 2m4-2m7: 0-0 3m+: 2-3
Track:	LH: 1-2 RH: 1-1 Tight: 1-1 Gall: 0-1
Aids:	Bl: 0-0 Vi: 0-0 Tstrap: 0-0 Ckp: 0-0
Best Rating:	117 2/01 Kemp 3m good Ch

A smart hunter chaser in his day; not so good these days,
but still winning races; stays three miles plus; acts well on a
sound surface.

Chateau Rose (IRE)

105(105c)   (116c) **107**

8-y-o b g Roselier (FR)-Claycastle (IRE) (Carlingford Castle)
N A Gaselee The Southern Set

Placings:30/32220/43133U-5F4P044   (4519)
2003/04: 30⁵GS, 22⁵GF, 24⁴GS, 24⁵P'S, 20⁰GS, 24⁴G, 22⁴GS,

	Starts	1st	2nd	3rd	Win & Pl
Hurdles	3	0	0	0	699
Chases	4	0	0	0	880
Career Total	20	1	3	5	11971
116	1/03	Leic	2m7f110yE Ch		SFT	£4192
				Total win prize-money £4193		

Going:	Sf: 0-2 GS: 0-3 Gd: 0-1 GF: - Fm: 0-1
Distance:	2m/2m3: 0-0 2m4-2m7: 0-3 3m+: 0-4
Track:	LH: 0-3 RH: 0-4 Tight: 0-1 Gall: 0-3
Aids:	Bl: 0-1 Vi: 0-0 Tstrap: 0-0 Ckp: 0-0
Best Rating:	116 12/03 Newb 2m6f110y gd-fm Ch

Modest hurdler/chaser; got off the mark when winning at
Leicester in January 2003; needs soft ground; stays well.

Chater Flair

91   **102**

7-y-o b g Efisio-Native Flair (Be My Native (USA))
D Burchell M T Hughes

Placings:2/U20-FU0P   (4508)
2003/04: 16⁶S, 19ᵁGS, 20⁰G, 26ᴾGS,

	Starts	1st	2nd	3rd	Win & Pl
Hurdles	4	0	0	0	
Career Total	8	0	2	0	2590

Going:	Sf: 0-1 GS: 0-2 Gd: 0-1 GF: - Fm: 0-0
Distance:	2m/2m3: 0-1 2m4-2m7: 0-2 3m+: 0-1
Track:	LH: 0-0 RH: 0-4 Tight: 0-0 Gall: 0-1
Aids:	Bl: 0-0 Vi: 0-2 Tstrap: 0-0 Ckp: 0-0
Best Rating:	102 6/02 Strf 2m6f110y gd-fm Hdl

Plating-class hurdler; stays 2m 6f; acts on fast ground.

Chauvinist (IRE)

110(111h)   (145 h) **132+**

9-y-o b g Roselier (FR)-Sacajawea (Tanfirion)

N J Henderson Mrs E Roberts & Nick Roberts

Placings:1/224/11303-3   (2592)
2003/04: 16³G,

	Starts	1st	2nd	3rd	Win & Pl
Chases	1	0	0	1	3300
Career Total	10	3	2	3	87024
145	12/02	Asct	2m110y	A(0-150)HHdl	HVY	£58000
121	11/02	Newb	2m110y	D Hdl	SFT	£4290
118	2/01	Kemp	2m	H NHF	G-S	£2541
				Total win prize-money £64831		

Going:	Sf: 0-0 GS: 0-0 Gd: 0-1 GF: - Fm: 0-0
Distance:	2m/2m3: 0-1 2m4-2m7: 0-0 3m+: 0-0
Track:	LH: 0-0 RH: 0-1 Tight: 0-0 Gall: 0-0
Aids:	Bl: 0-0 Vi: 0-0 Tstrap: 0-0 Ckp: 0-0
Best Rating:	145 12/02 Asct 2m110y heavy Hdl

Very useful hurdler; third in Grade Two on chasing debut;
winner of the 2002 Ladbroke Hurdle at Ascot and third in the
Supreme Novices' at Cheltenham; stays 2m 4f although
probably best over shorter; suited by cut in the ground.

Cheeky Boy Danny

52f   **29f**

6-y-o ch g Formidable (USA)-Moments Joy (Adonijah)
R D E Woodhouse Mrs Jayne E Benn

Placings:00   (4886)
2003/04: 16⁰GS, 17⁰GS,

	Starts	1st	2nd	3rd	Win & Pl
NH Flat	2	0	0	0	
Career Total	2	0	0	0	

Going:	Sf: 0-0 GS: 0-2 Gd: 0-0 GF: - Fm: 0-0
Distance:	2m/2m3: 0-2 2m4-2m7: 0-0 3m+: 0-0
Track:	LH: 0-1 RH: 0-1 Tight: 0-0 Gall: 0-0
Aids:	Bl: 0-0 Vi: 0-0 Tstrap: 0-0 Ckp: 0-0
Best Rating:	23 3/04 Weth 2m gd-sft NHF

Cheery Martyr

82   **68**

6-y-o b m Perpendicular-Kate O'Kirkham (Le Bavard (FR))
P Needham P Needham

Placings:054   (4881)
2003/04: 17⁰HY, 16⁵S, 17⁴GS,

	Starts	1st	2nd	3rd	Win & Pl
NH Flat	2	0	0	0	0
Hurdles	1	0	0	0	290
Career Total	3	0	0	0	290

Going:	Sf: 0-2 GS: 0-1 Gd: 0-0 GF: - Fm: 0-0
Distance:	2m/2m3: 0-3 2m4-2m7: 0-0 3m+: 0-0
Track:	LH: 0-1 RH: 0-2 Tight: 0-0 Gall: 0-0
Aids:	Bl: 0-0 Vi: 0-0 Tstrap: 0-0 Ckp: 0-0
Best Rating:	79 4/04 Hexm 2m110y soft NHF

Chelsea's Diamond

4-y-o b f Man Among Men (IRE)-Sharp Thistle (Sharpo)
J Akehurst Chelsea Artisans Ltd

Placings:0   (4934)
2003/04: 18⁰G,

	Starts	1st	2nd	3rd	Win & Pl
NH Flat	1	0	0	0	
Career Total	1	0	0	0	

Going:	Sf: 0-0 GS: 0-0 Gd: 0-1 GF: - Fm: 0-0
Distance:	2m/2m3: 0-1 2m4-2m7: 0-0 3m+: 0-0
Track:	LH: 0-1 RH: 0-0 Tight: 0-1 Gall: 0-0
Aids:	Bl: 0-0 Vi: 0-0 Tstrap: 0-0 Ckp: 0-0

Chem's Truce (IRE)

106   **118**

7-y-o b g Brief Truce (USA)-In The Rigging (USA) (Topsider (USA))
Miss Venetia Williams O P Dakin

Placings:P60/1226-P3224650   (4194)
2003/04: 17PG, 163GF, 172G, 162G, 164GS, 176G, 165S, 160G,

	Starts	1st	2nd	3rd	Win & Pl
Hurdles	8	0	2	1	10904
Career Total	15	1	4	1	16190
107	10/02	Hayd	2m		E(0-105)HHdl	GD	£3080
				Total win prize-money	£3080

Going:	Sf: 0-1 GS: 0-1 Gd: 0-5 GF: - Fm: 0-1
Distance:	2m/2m3: 0-8 2m4-2m7: 0-0 3m+: 0-0
Track:	LH: 0-5 RH: 0-1 Tight: 0-3 Gall: 0-3
Aids:	Bl: 0-0 Vi: 0-0 Tstrap: 0-0 Ckp: 0-0
Best Rating:	118	11/03	Kels	2m110y	good	Hdl

Fair hurdler; useful handicapper on the Flat; effective at around two miles over hurdles; effective on soft and fast ground.

Chemicalreaction

90   **80+**

4-y-o b g Definite Article-Ewar Snowflake (Snow Chief (USA))
R A Fahey G & K Murray

Placings:B40300   (3337)
2003/04: 17PG, 164F, 160GF, 163GF, 160GS, 160GS,

	Starts	1st	2nd	3rd	Win & Pl
Hurdles	6	0	0	1	598
Career Total	6	0	0	1	598

Going:	Sf: 0-0 GS: 0-2 Gd: 0-0 GF: - Fm: 0-4
Distance:	2m/2m3: 0-6 2m4-2m7: 0-0 3m+: 0-0
Track:	LH: 0-5 RH: 0-1 Tight: 0-4 Gall: 0-0
Aids:	Bl: 0-2 Vi: 0-1 Tstrap: 0-0 Ckp: 0-0
Best Rating:	80	10/03	Weth	2m	firm	Hdl

Plating-class juvenile hurdler.

Chergan (IRE)

111   **127**

11-y-o b g Yashgan-Cherry Bright (IRE) (Miners Lamp)
Mrs S C Bradburne Copland, Hardie And Steel

Placings:PF3/P35042U222/23P42114P/32P62222214/511 52350202-3F15242105   (4938)
2003/04: 20³GF, 21FGF, 251GF, 20⁵G, 162GF, 164G, 242GF, 191G, 21⁹G, 165GS,

	Starts	1st	2nd	3rd	Win & Pl
Chases	10	2	2	1	19368
Career Total	54	7	17	6	83991
127	3/04	Donc	2m3f	D(0-125)HCh	GD	£6864
124	10/03	Kels	2m3f	D(0-125)HCh	G-F	£5434
122	10/02	Weth	2m4f110yB(0-145)HCh	G-F	£10888
114	9/02	Prth	2m	D(0-115)HCh	GD	£8151
117	3/02	Hayd	2m	D(0-120)HCh	GD	£7052
116	1/01	Muss	2m4f	F(0-110)HCh	G-S	£4858
106	1/01	Muss	2m4f	F(0-110)HCh	GD	£3601
				Total win prize-money	£46851

| Going: | Sf: 0-0 GS: 0-1 Gd: 1-4 GF: - Fm: 1-5 |

Distance:	2m/2m3: 1-4 2m4-2m7: 0-4 3m+: 1-2
Track:	LH: 2-7 RH: 0-3 Tight: 1-5 Gall: 0-0
Aids:	Bl: 0-0 Vi: 0-0 Tstrap: 0-0 Ckp: 0-0
Best Rating:	127	3/04	Donc	2m3f	good	Ch

Fair handicap chaser; effective at two to three miles, but is possibly best over two and a half; acts on any ground but best on a sound surface.

Cherokee Bay

102   **94+**

4-y-o b f Primo Dominie-Me Cherokee (Persian Bold)
G L Moore (J A Osborne 29/9) P Iron Ltd

Placings:53242   (4929)
2003/04: 16⁵GS, 16³G, 19²G, 164G, 18²G,

	Starts	1st	2nd	3rd	Win & Pl
Hurdles	5	0	2	1	2833
Career Total	5	0	2	1	2833

Going:	Sf: 0-0 GS: 0-1 Gd: 0-4 GF: - Fm: 0-0
Distance:	2m/2m3: 0-4 2m4-2m7: 0-1 3m+: 0-0
Track:	LH: 0-4 RH: 0-1 Tight: 0-5 Gall: 0-0
Aids:	Bl: 0-0 Vi: 0-0 Tstrap: 0-0 Ckp: 0-0
Best Rating:	94	4/04	Font	2m2f110y	good	Hdl

Plating-class hurdler; stays two miles three; acts on good ground.

Cherokee Run (IRE)

10-y-o b g Commanche Run-Hampton Grange (Boreen (FR))
A J Tizzard A J Tizzard

Placings:41PP   (3792)
2003/04: 254GF, 251GF, 28PGS, 25PG,

	Starts	1st	2nd	3rd	Win & Pl
Chases	4	1	0	0	3619
Career Total	4	1	0	0	3619
95	5/03	Winc	3m1f110yH Ch	G-F	£3357
				Total win prize-money	£3357

Going:	Sf: 0-0 GS: 0-1 Gd: 0-1 GF: - Fm: 1-2
Distance:	2m/2m3: 0-0 2m4-2m7: 0-0 3m+: 1-4
Track:	LH: 0-0 RH: 1-3 Tight: 0-1 Gall: 0-0
Aids:	Bl: 0-0 Vi: 0-0 Tstrap: 0-0 Ckp: 0-0
Best Rating:	95	5/03	Winc	3m1f110y	gd-fm	Ch

Hunter chaser; stays well; acts on decent ground.

Cherry Gold

10-y-o b g Rakaposhi King-Merry Cherry (Deep Run)
Evan Williams R Mason

Placings:1-131434U1   (4815)
2003/04: 241GF, 22³G, 241GF, 264GF, 243GF, 254GF, 24UGS, 241G,

	Starts	1st	2nd	3rd	Win & Pl
Hurdles	3	1	0	2	5916
Chases	5	2	0	0	5203
Career Total	9	4	0	2	14525
118	4/04	Chep	3m	H Ch	GD	£3367
90	8/03	MRas	3m	D Hdl	G-F	£4719
104	5/03	Chep	3m	H Ch	G-F	£1456
105	4/03	Chep	3m	H Ch	G-F	£3406
				Total win prize-money	£12948

Going:	Sf: 0-0 GS: 0-1 Gd: 1-2 GF: - Fm: 2-5
Distance:	2m/2m3: 0-0 2m4-2m7: 0-1 3m+: 3-7
Track:	LH: 2-5 RH: 1-2 Tight: 1-3 Gall: 0-0

| Aids: | Bl: 0-0 Vi: 0-0 Tstrap: 0-0 Ckp: 1-2 |
| Best Rating: | 118 | 4/04 | Chep | 3m | good | Ch |

Modest hunter chaser/hurdler; prolific winner between the flags; won the Dunraven Windows point-to-point championship at Chepstow in both 2003 and 2004; stays three miles and handles fast ground, though he may prefer it easier; suited by forcing tactics.

Cherry Queen

6-y-o ch m Royal Vulcan-Cherry Sip (Nearly A Hand)
C N Kellett Mrs Helen Herrick

Placings:00P   (2688)
2003/04: 160GF, 160GS, 20PGS,

	Starts	1st	2nd	3rd	Win & Pl
NH Flat	2	0	0	0	0
Hurdles	1	0	0	0	0
Career Total	3	0	0	0	

Going:	Sf: 0-0 GS: 0-2 Gd: 0-0 GF: - Fm: 0-1
Distance:	2m/2m3: 0-2 2m4-2m7: 0-1 3m+: 0-0
Track:	LH: 0-2 RH: 0-1 Tight: 0-0 Gall: 0-1
Aids:	Bl: 0-0 Vi: 0-0 Tstrap: 0-0 Ckp: 0-0

Cherub (GER)

113   **136**

4-y-o b c Winged Love (IRE)-Chalkidiki (GER) (Nebos (GER))
Jonjo O'Neill (A Schutz 27/9) Atlantic Joinery Limited

Placings:4240   (4625)
2003/04: 164G, 162S, 174G, 160G,

	Starts	1st	2nd	3rd	Win & Pl
Hurdles	4	0	1	0	7734
Career Total	4	0	1	0	7734

Going:	Sf: 0-1 GS: 0-0 Gd: 0-3 GF: - Fm: 0-0
Distance:	2m/2m3: 0-4 2m4-2m7: 0-0 3m+: 0-0
Track:	LH: 0-2 RH: 0-0 Tight: 0-2 Gall: 0-1
Aids:	Bl: 0-0 Vi: 0-0 Tstrap: 0-3 Ckp: 0-0
Best Rating:	136	3/04	Chel	2m1f	good	Hdl

Juvenile hurdler; mile winner on the Flat in Germany on soft ground; effective over two miles; acts on soft ground; has worn a tongue tie.

Chester Park

80f   **53f**

6-y-o ch g King's Signet (USA)-Good Skills (Bustino)
K Bishop K Bishop

Placings:0-0   (0871)
2003/04: 170GF,

	Starts	1st	2nd	3rd	Win & Pl
NH Flat	1	0	0	0	
Career Total	2	0	0	0	

Going:	Sf: 0-0 GS: 0-0 Gd: 0-0 GF: - Fm: 0-1
Distance:	2m/2m3: 0-1 2m4-2m7: 0-0 3m+: 0-0
Track:	LH: 0-1 RH: 0-0 Tight: 0-1 Gall: 0-0
Aids:	Bl: 0-0 Vi: 0-0 Tstrap: 0-0 Ckp: 0-0
Best Rating:	53	7/03	NAbb	2m1f	gd-fm	NHF

Chevalier Errant (IRE)

109   **119**

11-y-o b/br g Strong Gale-Luminous Run (Deep Run)
M Todhunter   James R Adam

Placings:0531/235333532/24114326/11B/1U05F605-F34F
                                   (4295)

2003/04: 20FG, 22³G, 19⁴G, 20FGF,

	Starts	1st	2nd	3rd	Win & Pl
Chases	4	0	0	1	1634
Career Total	36	6	4	8	56596
128 6/02 Strf	2m5f110yB(0-140)HCh			G-F	£10108
128 6/01 MRas	2m C(0-135)HCh			G-F	£10476
128 6/01 Strf	2m1f110yC(0-135)HCh			G-F	£6864
120 12/00 Donc	2m110y C(0-130)HCh			HVY	£6022
119 11/00 Ayr	2m C(0-130)HCh			SFT	£6118
102 4/99 Kels	2m110y E Hdl			G-F	£3025

                         Total win prize-money £42615

Going:	Sf: 0-0 GS: 0-0 Gd: 0-3 GF: - Fm: 0-1
Distance:	2m/2m3: 0-0 2m4-2m7: 0-4 3m+: 0-0
Track:	LH: 0-3 RH: 0-1 Tight: 0-2 Gall: 0-0
Aids:	Bl: 0-0 Vi: 0-0 Tstrap: 0-0 Ckp: 0-0
Best Rating:	128 6/02 Strf 2m5f110y gd-fm Ch

Modest chaser; formerly useful at his best; stays two miles six and acts on good or faster ground.

Chevet Girl (IRE)

106   **(102c)116**

9-y-o ch m Roselier (FR)-Vulcash (IRE) (Callernish)
J Howard Johnson   D M Gibbons

Placings:0663/5115510/1PF003-0F54   (2725)
2003/04: 17⁰G, 16FG, 16⁵S, 16⁴G,

	Starts	1st	2nd	3rd	Win & Pl
Hurdles	3	0	0	0	1154
Chases	1	0	0	0	0
Career Total	21	4	0	2	14307
116 11/02 Weth	2m E(0-110)HHdl			GD	£3066
99 4/02 Kels	2m110y D(0-125)HHdl			G-F	£3591
103 11/01 Weth	2m C(0-105)HHdl			SFT	£3052
85 10/01 Carl	2m1f E(0-115)HHdl			G-S	£2441

                         Total win prize-money £12151

Going:	Sf: 0-1 GS: 0-0 Gd: 0-3 GF: 0-0
Distance:	2m/2m3: 0-4 2m4-2m7: 0-0 3m+: 0-0
Track:	LH: 0-3 RH: 0-0 Tight: 0-0 Gall: 0-1
Aids:	Bl: 0-0 Vi: 0-0 Tstrap: 0-0 Ckp: 0-0
Best Rating:	116 11/02 Weth 2m good Hdl

Moderate handicap hurdler; best over two miles on a sound surface; has fallen on both outings over fences; goes well fresh.

Cheyenne Chief

                                  95d

5-y-o b g Be My Chief (USA)-Cartuccia (IRE) (Doyoun)
G M Moore   John Lishman

Placings:524F1440P-0   (0098)
2003/04: 16⁰G,

	Starts	1st	2nd	3rd	Win & Pl
Hurdles	1	0	0	0	
Career Total	10	1	1	0	4874
96 11/02 Newc	2m E Hdl			SFT	£3423

                         Total win prize-money £3423

Going:	Sf: 0-0 GS: 0-0 Gd: 0-1 GF: - Fm: 0-0
Distance:	2m/2m3: 0-1 2m4-2m7: 0-0 3m+: 0-0
Track:	LH: 0-1 RH: 0-0 Tight: 0-0 Gall: 0-0

Chica Bonita

80f   **47f**

5-y-o ch m Blushing Flame (USA)-Lutine Royal (Formidable (USA))
J E Long   Amaroni Racing

Placings:00   (4447)
2003/04: 17⁰HY, 16⁰S,

	Starts	1st	2nd	3rd	Win & Pl
NH Flat	2	0	0	0	
Career Total	2	0	0	0	

Going:	Sf: 0-2 GS: 0-0 Gd: 0-0 GF: - Fm: 0-0
Distance:	2m/2m3: 0-2 2m4-2m7: 0-0 3m+: 0-0
Track:	LH: 0-1 RH: 0-1 Tight: 0-1 Gall: 0-0
Aids:	Bl: 0-0 Vi: 0-0 Tstrap: 0-0 Ckp: 0-0
Best Rating:	47 3/04 Wwck 2m soft NHF

Chicago Breeze (IRE)

(96h)   **(78h)**

7-y-o b m Lord Americo-Anguillita (IRE) (King Of Clubs)
Ferdy Murphy   W Winlow, Mrs C Seymour, E Whalley

Placings:0/40520303/4UP   (4616)
2003/04: 27⁴GF, 16⁰G, 21FG,

	Starts	1st	2nd	3rd	Win & Pl
Hurdles	1	0	0	0	
Chases	2	0	0	0	
Career Total	12	0	1	2	2623

Going:	Sf: 0-0 GS: 0-0 Gd: 0-2 GF: - Fm: 0-0
Distance:	2m/2m3: 0-1 2m4-2m7: 0-1 3m+: 0-1
Track:	LH: 0-3 RH: 0-0 Tight: 0-2 Gall: 0-0
Aids:	Bl: 0-0 Vi: 0-0 Tstrap: 0-0 Ckp: 0-0
Best Rating:	96 1/02 Fair 2m2f yld-sft Hdl

Chicago Bulls (IRE)

111(108h)   (128+h)**130+**

6-y-o b g Darshaan-Celestial Melody (USA) (The Minstrel (CAN))
A King   A M Armitage

Placings:54455110/2324005-133U540   (4840)
2003/04: 22⁵S, 21¹G, 24³S, 24⁵S, 24Us, 24⁴GS, 24⁰G,

	Starts	1st	2nd	3rd	Win & Pl
Hurdles	4	1	0	1	5599
Chases	4	0	0	1	3010
Career Total	22	3	2	3	30801
129 11/03 Towc	2m5f D(0-125)HHdl			GD	£2926
120 3/02 Ludl	2m5f E Hdl			SFT	£3125
113 2/02 Donc	2m4f E Hdl			SFT	£3164

                       Total win prize-money £9216

Going:	Sf: 0-3 GS: 0-2 Gd: 1-3 GF: - Fm: 0-0
Distance:	2m/2m3: 0-0 2m4-2m7: 1-2 3m+: 0-6
Track:	LH: 0-3 RH: 1-5 Tight: 0-1 Gall: 0-3
Aids:	Bl: 0-1 Vi: 0-0 Tstrap: 0-0 Ckp: 0-0
Best Rating:	130 12/03 Chel 3m1f110y good Ch

Useful hurdler, stays three miles and acts on soft ground; ran a promising race on chase debut when finishing third to Therealbandit at Cheltenham; has not built on that since.

Chicago City (IRE)

11-y-o br g Strong Gale-Orchardstown (Pollerton)
N J Gifford   S N J Embiricos

Placings:023/432P/4144134/F6P/5114P/205F   (4891)
2003/04: 21²G, 24⁰G, 19⁵GS, 24⁷GF,

	Starts	1st	2nd	3rd	Win & Pl
Chases	4	0	1	0	740
Career Total	26	4	3	3	25153
118 11/01 Newb	2m4f D(0-125)HCh			GD	£7215
115 10/01 Font	2m4f F(0-105)HCh			G-S	£3010
118 2/00 Sand	2m4f110yD Ch			G-S	£5096
98 11/99 Folk	2m E Ch			G-F	£3466

                       Total win prize-money £18787

Going:	Sf: 0-0 GS: 0-1 Gd: 0-2 GF: - Fm: 0-1
Distance:	2m/2m3: 0-0 2m4-2m7: 0-2 3m+: 0-2
Track:	LH: 0-3 RH: 0-1 Tight: 0-1 Gall: 0-1
Aids:	Bl: 0-0 Vi: 0-0 Tstrap: 0-0 Ckp: 0-0
Best Rating:	123 10/00 Chel 2m4f110y good Ch

Hunter Chaser; probably best around two and a half miles, he does not want the ground too soft; suited to galloping tracks.

Chicuelo (FR)

114(108h)   (132h)**149**

8-y-o b g Mansonnien (FR)-Dovapas (FR) (Paseo (FR))
M C Pipe   Mrs Belinda Harvey

Placings:03/512F023/222433210/225025/1P11P01-0113204055P   (4861)
2003/04: 20⁰GF, 24¹GF, 24¹GF, 25³GF, 24²G, 24⁰GS, 21⁴GS, 22⁰S, 24⁵G, 24⁵G, 33PGS,

	Starts	1st	2nd	3rd	Win & Pl
Hurdles	3	1	0	0	6744
Chases	8	1	1	1	26085
Career Total	42	8	10	5	240529
149 11/03 Asct	3m110y B(0-140)HCh			G-F	£11583
132 8/03 Worc	3m C(0-135)HHdl			G-F	£6743
146 3/03 Extr	3m1f110yD Ch			FRM	£7046
149 1/03 Hntg	3m E Ch			SFT	£5208
141 12/02 Asct	2m3f110yB(0-140)HCh			G-S	£13494
149 7/02 MRas	3m B(0-140)HCh			G-S	£37700
4/01 Autl	2m2f Hdl			HVY	£14549
7/99 Autl	1m1f110y Hdl				HLD

£10764

                       Total win prize-money £107088

Going:	Sf: 0-1 GS: 0-3 Gd: 0-3 GF: - Fm: 2-4
Distance:	2m/2m3: 0-0 2m4-2m7: 0-3 3m+: 2-8
Track:	LH: 1-5 RH: 1-6 Tight: 0-2 Gall: 0-2
Aids:	Bl: 0-0 Vi: 2-11 Tstrap: 0-0 Ckp: 0-0
Best Rating:	149 11/03 Winc 3m1f110y gd-fm Ch

Smart chaser/decent over hurdles; ex-French; effective from two and a half to three miles; appears to handle all types of going; sometimes makes mistakes; suited by small fields and going right-handed; usually wears a visor.

Chief Mouse

11-y-o b g Be My Chief (USA)-Top Mouse (High Top)
J E Price   J E Price

Placings:12106P111/5634030/P05424310000/PU155/331321/P/035063-PP   (4510)
2003/04: 26⁰GS, 19⁷GS,

	Starts	1st	2nd	3rd	Win & Pl
Chases	2	0	0	0	
Career Total	48	9	3	8	42465
104 7/00 Strf	3m D(0-120)HCh			G-F	£4810

101	6/00	Uttx	2m	D(0-120)HCh	G-F	£3692
89	10/99	Ludl	2m4f	D(0-110)HCh	G-F	£4162
90	9/98	Bang	2m4f	E(0-110)HHdl	GD	£3631
108	4/97	Asct	2m110y	D(0-110)HHdl	G-F	£3420
108	4/97	Chel	2m4f110yC	HHdl	G-F	£4788
90	3/97	Ludl	2m	F Hdl	G-F	£2094
106	11/96	MRas	2m1f110yD	Hdl	GD	£3148
88	8/96	Hrfd	2m1f	E Hdl	G-F	£2444

Total win prize-money £32190

Going: Sf: 0-0 GS: 0-2 Gd: 0-0 GF: - Fm: 0-0
Distance: 2m/2m3: 0-1 2m4-2m7: 0-0 3m+: 0-1
Track: LH: 0-1 RH: 0-1 Tight: 0-0 Gall: 0-0
Aids: Bl: 0-0 Vi: 0-0 Tstrap: 0-0 Ckp: 0-1
Best Rating: 109 1/97 Tntn 2m1f   good   Hdl

Chief Of Justice

7-y-o b g Be My Chief (USA)-Clare Court (Glint Of Gold)
Mrs Laura J Young Mrs Laura J Young

Placings:40   (3898)
2003/04: 20⁴G, 20⁹G,

	Starts	1st	2nd	3rd	Win & Pl
Chases	2	0	0	0	0
Career Total	2	0	0	0	0

Going: Sf: 0-0 GS: 0-0 Gd: 0-2 GF: 0-0 Fm: 0-0
Distance: 2m/2m3: 0-0 2m4-2m7: 0-2 3m+: 0-0
Track: LH: 0-1 RH: 0-1 Tight: 0-0 Gall: 0-0
Aids: Bl: 0-0 Vi: 0-0 Tstrap: 0-0 Ckp: 0-0
Best Rating: 74 5/03 Hexm 2m4f110y good   Ch

Chief Suspect (IRE)

12-y-o b g Yashgan-Clerihan Miss (Tarqogan)
Michael Blake Staverton Owners Group

Placings:0F/0   (0354)
2003/04: 21⁰GF,

	Starts	1st	2nd	3rd	Win & Pl
Chases	1	0	0	0	
Career Total	3	0	0		

Going: Sf: 0-0 GS: 0-0 Gd: 0-0 GF: - Fm: 0-1
Distance: 2m/2m3: 0-0 2m4-2m7: 0-0 3m+: 0-0
Track: LH: 0-0 RH: 0-1 Tight: 0-1 Gall: 0-0
Aids: Bl: 0-0 Vi: 0-0 Tstrap: 0-0 Ckp: 0-0
Best Rating: 37 5/03 Folk 2m5f   gd-fm   Ch

Chief Wardance
77   (104h)75+

10-y-o ch g Profilic-Dolly Wardance (Warpath)
C N Kellett Mrs Jennifer Woodward

Placings:50/12F4214/4265/14F23/005/U4   (3001)
2003/04: 16⁰GS, 16⁴GS,

	Starts	1st	2nd	3rd	Win & Pl
Chases	2	0	0	0	421
Career Total	23	3	4	1	12667
120	5/00	Weth	2m	E(0-115)HHdl	G-F	£2842
106	2/99	Newc	2m	E Hdl	G-S	£2431
95	5/98	Uttx	2m	H NHF	G-F	£1413

Total win prize-money £6687

Going: Sf: 0-0 GS: 0-2 Gd: 0-0 GF: - Fm: 0-0
Distance: 2m/2m3: 0-2 2m4-2m7: 0-0 3m+: 0-0
Track: LH: 0-2 RH: 0-0 Tight: 0-0 Gall: 0-0

Aids: Bl: 0-0 Vi: 0-0 Tstrap: 0-0 Ckp: 0-0
Best Rating: 120 7/00 Sthl 2m   gd-fm   Hdl

Chief Yeoman
114   138

4-y-o br g Machiavellian (USA)-Step Aloft (Shirley Heights)
Miss Venetia Williams (Sir Michael Stoute 4/8) B Moore &
E C Stephens

Placings:1241223   (4839)
2003/04: 16¹GF, 16²G, 16⁴GS, 16¹S, 16²GS, 17²G, 17³GF,

	Starts	1st	2nd	3rd	Win & Pl
Hurdles	7	2	3	1	43879
Career Total	7	2	3	1	43879
120	1/04	Newb	2m110y	E Hdl	SFT	£3916
100	10/03	Kemp	2m	D Hdl	G-F	£9065

Total win prize-money £12981

Going: Sf: 1-1 GS: 0-2 Gd: 0-2 GF: - Fm: 1-2
Distance: 2m/2m3: 2-7 2m4-2m7: 0-0 3m+: 0-0
Track: LH: 1-4 RH: 1-3 Tight: 0-0 Gall: 1-5
Aids: Bl: 0-0 Vi: 0-0 Tstrap: 0-0 Ckp: 0-0
Best Rating: 138 3/04 Chel 2m1f   good   Hdl

Useful juvenile hurdler; formerly useful handicapper on the
Flat; second in the 2004 Triumph Hurdle; suited by two
miles; seems best on good ground, but has won on soft.

China Chase (IRE)
84f   77f

5-y-o b g Anshan-Hannies Girl (IRE) (Invited (USA))
J L Spearing T N Siviter

Placings:06   (4291)
2003/04: 16⁰G, 16⁶G,

	Starts	1st	2nd	3rd	Win & Pl
NH Flat	2	0	0	0	0
Career Total	2	0	0	0	0

Going: Sf: 0-0 GS: 0-0 Gd: 0-2 GF: - Fm: 0-0
Distance: 2m/2m3: 0-2 2m4-2m7: 0-0 3m+: 0-0
Track: LH: 0-0 RH: 0-2 Tight: 0-0 Gall: 0-0
Aids: Bl: 0-0 Vi: 0-0 Tstrap: 0-0 Ckp: 0-0
Best Rating: 77 3/04 Winc 2m   good   NHF

Chism (IRE)

13-y-o br g Euphemism-Melody Gayle Vii (Damsire
Unregistered)
R J King Mrs S King

Placings:324/43132P/PP5/63/P/P   (0030)
2003/04: 33ᴾG,

	Starts	1st	2nd	3rd	Win & Pl
Chases	1	0	0	0	
Career Total	16	1	2	4	3757
96	3/99	Winc	2m5f	H Ch	GD	£1203

Total win prize-money £1204

Going: Sf: 0-0 GS: 0-0 Gd: 0-1 GF: - Fm: 0-0
Distance: 2m/2m3: 0-0 2m4-2m7: 0-0 3m+: 0-1
Track: LH: 0-1 RH: 0-0 Tight: 0-0 Gall: 0-1
Aids: Bl: 0-0 Vi: 0-0 Tstrap: 0-0 Ckp: 0-0
Best Rating: 99 3/98 Winc 3m1f110y good   Ch

Chita's Flight
51f

4-y-o gr f Busy Flight-Chita's Cone (Celtic Cone)

Aids: Bl: 0-0 Vi: 0-0 Tstrap: 0-0 Ckp: 0-0
Best Rating: 120 7/00 Sthl 2m   gd-fm   Hdl

S C Burrough I M Ham

Placings:60   (4738)
2003/04: 14⁶GS, 17⁰G,

	Starts	1st	2nd	3rd	Win & Pl
NH Flat	2	0	0	0	0
Career Total	2	0	0	0	0

Going: Sf: 0-0 GS: 0-1 Gd: 0-1 GF: - Fm: 0-0
Distance: 2m/2m3: 0-1 2m4-2m7: 0-0 3m+: 0-0
Track: LH: 0-1 RH: 0-0 Tight: 0-1 Gall: 0-0
Aids: Bl: 0-0 Vi: 0-0 Tstrap: 0-0 Ckp: 0-0
Best Rating: 51 3/04 Hrfd 1m6f   gd-sft   NHF

Chivalry
105   135+

5-y-o b g Mark Of Esteem (IRE)-Gai Bulga (Kris)
J Howard Johnson (Sir Mark Prescott 4/10) Andrea &
Graham Wylie

Placings:1141   (4847)
2003/04: 16¹GS, 16¹S, 18⁴GS, 16¹GS,

	Starts	1st	2nd	3rd	Win & Pl
Hurdles	4	3	0	0	31023
Career Total	4	3	0	0	31023
135	4/04	Ayr	2m	C Hdl	G-S	£7345
132	1/04	Kels	2m110y	C(0-135)HHdl	SFT	£8554
94	11/03	Ayr	2m	B Hdl	GD	£13624

Total win prize-money £29523

Going: Sf: 1-1 GS: 1-2 Gd: 1-1 GF: - Fm: 0-0
Distance: 2m/2m3: 3-4 2m4-2m7: 0-0 3m+: 0-0
Track: LH: 3-4 RH: 0-0 Tight: 1-2 Gall: 0-0
Aids: Bl: 1-1 Vi: 0-0 Tstrap: 0-0 Ckp: 0-0
Best Rating: 135 4/04 Ayr 2m   gd-sft   Hdl

Useful hurdler; very smart on the Flat; winner of the 2003
Cambridgeshire; won a slowly-run contest on his hurdles
debut at Ayr in November 2003; followed up in a Kelso
handicap, but disappointed back at same course in valuable
Grade Two; won uncompetitive Ayr event in April; plenty of
room for improvement with his jumping technique but
shapes as though the step up to two and a half miles will
suit.

Chives (IRE)
90   164

9-y-o b g Good Thyne (USA)-Chatty Actress (Le Bavard
(FR))
Miss H C Knight Trevor Hemmings

Placings:15/11/31F133/2220P-4P   (2983)
2003/04: 24⁴S, 29ᴾS,

	Starts	1st	2nd	3rd	Win & Pl
Chases	2	0	0	0	3000
Career Total	17	5	3	3	79565
143	2/02	Winc	3m1f110y	D Ch	SFT	£4368
126	12/01	Strf	3m	D Ch	SFT	£5154
130	11/00	Kemp	2m5f	D Hdl	SFT	£3753
105	10/00	Hrfd	2m1f	E Hdl	GD	£2684
116	2/00	Sand	2m110y	N NHF	SFT	£1746

Total win prize-money £17709

Going: Sf: 0-2 GS: 0-0 Gd: 0-0 GF: - Fm: 0-0
Distance: 2m/2m3: 0-0 2m4-2m7: 0-0 3m+: 0-2
Track: LH: 0-2 RH: 0-0 Tight: 0-0 Gall: 0-0
Aids: Bl: 0-0 Vi: 0-0 Tstrap: 0-0 Ckp: 0-0
Best Rating: 164 12/02 Chep 3m5f110y heavy   Ch

High-class staying chaser; scored twice over fences in the
2001/2002 in season and ran a blinder to finish third in the

Royal & SunAlliance Chase at the Festival; runner-up under a big weight in the Welsh National in 2002; faded into seventh in the Cheltenham Gold Cup having run prominently for a long way; broke a blood vessel when soon pulled up in the Grand National; suited by soft and heavy ground; stays at least 3m 5f; honest and genuine, but has not won since February 2002.

Chivite (IRE)
110   121+
5-y-o b g Alhaarth (IRE)-Laura Margaret (Persian Bold)
P J Hobbs I Russell

Placings:023-2131200141   (4822)
2003/04: 18²G, 20¹GF, 24³G, 20¹GF, 18²GF, 21⁰G, 22⁰GS, 19¹G, 17⁴G, 19¹GF,

	Starts	1st	2nd	3rd	Win & Pl
Hurdles	10	4	2	1	19605
Career Total	**13**	**4**	**3**	**2**	**21225**
121 4/04 Extr	2m3f	D(0-125)HHdl		G-F	£4972
112 12/03 Tntn	2m3f110yD(0-120)HHdl			GD	£3809
111 7/03 Uttx	2m4f110yE Hdl			G-F	£3598
115 5/03 Hntg	2m4f110yE Hdl			G-F	£3556
			Total win prize-money £15936		

Going:	Sf: 0-0 GS: 0-1 Gd: 1-5 GF: - Fm: 3-4
Distance:	2m/2m3: 1-4 2m4-2m7: 3-5 3m+: 0-1
Track:	LH: 1-6 RH: 3-4 Tight: 1-3 Gall: 1-2
Aids:	Bl: 0-0 Vi: 0-0 Tstrap: 0-0 Ckp: 0-0
Best Rating:	121 4/04 Extr 2m3f gd-fm Hdl

Fair hurdler; generally consistent; stays two and a half miles; acts on fast ground.

Chockdee (FR)
105   118+
4-y-o b g King's Theatre (IRE)-Chagrin D'Amour (IRE) (Last Tycoon)
P F Nicholls (F Rohaut 15/6) Mr And Mrs J D Cotton

Placings:540   (4863)
2003/04: 16⁵G, 16⁴G, 16⁰S,

	Starts	1st	2nd	3rd	Win & Pl
Hurdles	3	0	0	0	1500
Career Total	**3**	**0**	**0**	**0**	**1500**

Going:	Sf: 0-1 GS: 0-0 Gd: 0-2 GF: - Fm: 0-0
Distance:	2m/2m3: 0-3 2m4-2m7: 0-0 3m+: 0-0
Track:	LH: 0-1 RH: 0-2 Tight: 0-0 Gall: 0-0
Aids:	Bl: 0-0 Vi: 0-0 Tstrap: 0-0 Ckp: 0-0
Best Rating:	118 2/04 Kemp 2m good Hdl

Fair hurdler; fifth on British hurdle debut at Kempton in February; acts on most ground; should improve.

Choco Roco
74   43
7-y-o b g Faustus (USA)-Leilaway (Scallywag)
D Burchell The Cross Crusaders

Placings:00PP0   (4490)
2003/04: 16⁰GS, 17⁰GS, 22³GS, 24²PG, 16⁰G,

	Starts	1st	2nd	3rd	Win & Pl
NH Flat	2	0	0	0	0
Hurdles	3	0	0	0	0
Career Total	**5**	**0**	**0**	**0**	

Going:	Sf: 0-0 GS: 0-3 Gd: 0-2 GF: - Fm: 0-0
Distance:	2m/2m3: 0-3 2m4-2m7: 0-1 3m+: 0-1
Track:	LH: 0-2 RH: 0-3 Tight: 0-1 Gall: 0-0
Aids:	Bl: 0-0 Vi: 0-0 Tstrap: 0-0 Ckp: 0-0

Best Rating: 43 3/04 Strf 2m110y good Hdl

Chocolate Soldier (IRE)
92   72+
6-y-o ch g Mister Lord (USA)-Traditional Lady (Carlingford Castle)
Evan Williams A J Reid

Placings:0/5-114   (1373)
2003/04: 17¹GF, 16¹GF, 24⁴GF,

	Starts	1st	2nd	3rd	Win & Pl
NH Flat	2	2	0	0	3688
Hurdles	1	0	0	0	0
Career Total	**5**	**2**	**0**	**0**	**3688**
105 8/03 Worc	2m	H NHF		G-F	£1867
105 7/03 Sedg	2m1f	H NHF		G-F	£1820
		Total win prize-money £3688			

Going:	Sf: 0-0 GS: 0-0 Gd: 0-0 GF: - Fm: 2-3
Distance:	2m/2m3: 2-2 2m4-2m7: 0-0 3m+: 0-1
Track:	LH: 2-3 RH: 0-0 Tight: 1-1 Gall: 0-0
Aids:	Bl: 2-3 Vi: 0-0 Tstrap: 0-0 Ckp: 0-0
Best Rating:	105 8/03 Worc 2m gd-fm NHF

Showed signs of temperament in point-to-points; made all in a poor bumper at Sedgefield in July 2003; defied a penalty in weak event at Worcester the following month; reported to have finished distressed when fourth in 3m maiden hurdle at the same venue next time; handles fast ground.

Choisty (IRE)
99   91
14-y-o ch g Callernish-Rosemount Rose (Ashmore (FR))
H E Haynes H Edward Haynes

Placings:5C32/2UF11U/F1FP/4PR041U1/22142F/0/PPP21P3/P4-P5P3   (4652)
2003/04: 24²GF, 28⁵GS, 26⁰G, 25³G,

	Starts	1st	2nd	3rd	Win & Pl
Chases	4	0	0	1	1080
Career Total	**42**	**7**	**6**	**3**	**60446**
120 3/02 Wwck	3m5f	C(0-135)HCh	GD	£6857
135 1/00 Wwck	3m5f	B(0-145)HCh	SFT	£14014
126 5/99 Hrfd	3m1f110yE(0-115)HCh	GD	£3525
131 3/99 Chep	3m	D(0-120)HCh	G-S	£7002
123 3/98 Wwck	3m5f	C(0-135)HCh	SFT	£8550
117 1/97 Weth	3m1f	E Ch	GD	£3077
108 1/97 Carl	3m	D Ch	GD	£3842
		Total win prize-money £46871		

Going:	Sf: 0-0 GS: 0-1 Gd: 0-2 GF: - Fm: 0-1
Distance:	2m/2m3: 0-0 2m4-2m7: 0-0 3m+: 0-4
Track:	LH: 0-3 RH: 0-1 Tight: 0-2 Gall: 0-0
Aids:	Bl: 0-0 Vi: 0-0 Tstrap: 0-0 Ckp: 0-0
Best Rating:	135 3/00 Wwck 3m5f soft Ch

Veteran staying chaser; acts on soft ground.

Chris And Ryan (IRE)
6-y-o b g Goldmark (USA)-Beautyofthepeace (IRE) (Exactly Sharp (USA))
Mrs L B Normile Allan A Grant

Placings:0-0P   (4565)
2003/04: 16⁰S, 17⁰GS,

	Starts	1st	2nd	3rd	Win & Pl
NH Flat	1	0	0	0	0
Hurdles	1	0	0	0	0

Going:	Sf: 0-1 GS: 0-1 Gd: 0-0 GF: - Fm: 0-0
Distance:	2m/2m3: 0-2 2m4-2m7: 0-0 3m+: 0-0
Track:	LH: 0-2 RH: 0-0 Tight: 0-1 Gall: 0-0
Aids:	Bl: 0-0 Vi: 0-0 Tstrap: 0-0 Ckp: 0-0
Best Rating:	57 3/04 Newc 2m soft NHF

Christinas Cottage (IRE)
73   48
10-y-o ch m Abednego-Inverdonan (Our Mirage)
Graham John McKeever Patrick Joseph McCartan

Placings:0/0   (0194)
2003/04: 20⁰G,

	Starts	1st	2nd	3rd	Win & Pl
Hurdles	1	0	0	0	
Career Total	**2**	**0**	**0**	**0**	

Going:	Sf: 0-0 GS: 0-0 Gd: 0-1 GF: - Fm: 0-0
Distance:	2m/2m3: 0-0 2m4-2m7: 0-1 3m+: 0-0
Track:	LH: 0-1 RH: 0-0 Tight: 0-0 Gall: 0-0
Aids:	Bl: 0-0 Vi: 0-0 Tstrap: 0-0 Ckp: 0-0
Best Rating:	65 5/99 Dpat 2m4f110y gd-fm NHF

Christmas Truce (IRE)
96   95
5-y-o b g Brief Truce (USA)-Superflash (Superlative)
Ian Williams (M H Tompkins 27/6) M Murphy

Placings:4-53456   (4785)
2003/04: 22⁵G, 16³S, 19⁴GS, 21⁵G, 21⁶G,

	Starts	1st	2nd	3rd	Win & Pl
Hurdles	5	0	0	1	713
Career Total	**6**	**0**	**0**	**1**	**1085**

Going:	Sf: 0-1 GS: 0-1 Gd: 0-3 GF: - Fm: -
Distance:	2m/2m3: 0-1 2m4-2m7: 0-4 3m+: 0-0
Track:	LH: 0-2 RH: 0-3 Tight: 0-2 Gall: 0-2
Aids:	Bl: 0-0 Vi: 0-0 Tstrap: 0-0 Ckp: 0-3
Best Rating:	95 2/04 Hrfd 2m3f110y gd-sft Hdl

Fair middle-distance handicapper on the Flat; in the frame in novice hurdles.

Christopher
106(105h)   (116h)121+
7-y-o gr g Arzanni-Forest Nymph (NZ) (Oak Ridge (FR))
P J Hobbs Allan Stennett

Placings:10263/114F0-5315   (3528)
2003/04: 21⁵G, 20³G, 19¹S, 20⁵G,

	Starts	1st	2nd	3rd	Win & Pl
Hurdles	2	0	0	1	1348
Chases	2	1	0	0	4469
Career Total	**14**	**4**	**1**	**2**	**15073**
121 1/04 Extr	2m3f110yE Ch			SFT	£4468
116 5/02 Uttx	2m4f110yE Hdl			GD	£2667
112 5/02 Extr	2m1f	E Hdl		GD	£2856
101 5/01 Hrfd	2m1f	H NHF		GD	£1956
		Total win prize-money £11949			

Going:	Sf: 1-1 GS: 0-0 Gd: 0-3 GF: - Fm: 0-0
Distance:	2m/2m3: 0-0 2m4-2m7: 1-4 3m+: 0-0
Track:	LH: 0-1 RH: 1-3 Tight: 0-0 Gall: 0-1

Career Total   3   0   0   0

Aids: Bl: 0-0 Vi: 0-0 Tstrap: 0-0 Ckp: 0-0
Best Rating: 121 1/04　Leic　2m4f110y　good　Ch

Fair novice chaser/moderate hurdler; bumper winner; showed a good attitude to win on his chasing debut; stays two and a half miles; acts on good and soft ground.

Christy Jnr (IRE)

93(88c)　　　　　　　　　　(68c)67

10-y-o b g Andretti-Rare Currency (Rarity)
C J Teague Mrs J H Burn

Placings: 0/00/0045-04653UB006　　(4390)
2003/04: 24⁰G, 27⁴S, 26⁶GF, 27⁵GF, 22³S, 24ᵁGS, 24⁸S, 24⁰GF, 24⁰GS, 27⁶G,

	Starts	1st	2nd	3rd	Win & Pl
Hurdles	5	0	0	0	0
Chases	5	0	0	1	544
Career Total	17	0	0	1	544

Going:	Sf: 0-3 GS: 0-2 Gd: 0-2 GF: - Fm: 0-3
Distance:	2m2m3: 0-0 2m4-2m7: 0-1 3m+: 0-9
Track:	LH: 0-9 RH: 0-1 Tight: 0-5 Gall: 0-2
Aids:	Bl: 0-0 Vi: 0-0 Tstrap: 0-0 Ckp: 0-0
Best Rating:	79 4/99 Clon 2m4f heavy Hdl

Christy Senior (IRE)

97　　　　　　　　　　　　　(0c)85

9-y-o b g Erin's Isle-Persian Sparkler (Persian Bold)
J J Lambe J P Kearney

Placings: 02442/4U40P0/50/0P-P603650P　　(1402a)
2003/04: 20⁰G, 16⁶GF, 17⁰GF, 17³GF, 16⁶GF, 17⁵G, 17⁰GF, 18³GF,

	Starts	1st	2nd	3rd	Win & Pl
Hurdles	8	0	0	1	337
Career Total	23	0	2	1	3116

Going:	Sf: 0-0 GS: 0-0 Gd: 0-2 GF: - Fm: 0-6
Distance:	2m2m3: 0-7 2m4-2m7: 0-1 3m+: 0-0
Track:	LH: 0-4 RH: 0-4 Tight: 0-3 Gall: 0-0
Aids:	Bl: 0-1 Vi: 0-0 Tstrap: 0-8 Ckp: 0-0
Best Rating:	104 5/00 Punc 2m good Hdl

Plating-class hurdler.

Christy's Pride (IRE)

(96h)　　　　　　　　　　　(77h)

12-y-o ch m Kambalda-Caddy Shack (Precipice Wood)
C Weedon Bill Hinge

Placings: 05/512321/P4/40-PP00　　(3334)
2003/04: 30⁰G, 24⁴S, 24⁰G, 24⁰S,

	Starts	1st	2nd	3rd	Win & Pl
Hurdles	2	0	0	0	0
Chases	2	0	0	0	0
Career Total	16	2	2	1	12896
109 4/01	Asct	3m	C(0-135)HHdl	HVY	£6288
104 1/01	Font	2m6f110yF(0-90)HHdl	SFT	£2562
			Total win prize-money £8851		

Going:	Sf: 0-2 GS: 0-0 Gd: 0-2 GF: - Fm: 0-0
Distance:	2m2m3: 0-0 2m4-2m7: 0-0 3m+: 0-4
Track:	LH: 0-2 RH: 0-1 Tight: 0-1 Gall: 0-1
Aids:	Bl: 0-0 Vi: 0-0 Tstrap: 0-0 Ckp: 0-0
Best Rating:	109 4/01 Asct 3m heavy Hdl

Moderate hurdler/chaser; loves the mud; stays three miles.

Chromazone

69　　　　　　　　　　　　　　30

7-y-o gr m Roselier (FR)-Gold Bash (Golden Love)
D J Caro Mrs Jan Smith

Placings: 0U0　　　　　　　　　　(0449)
2003/04: 17⁰G, 20ᵁS, 20⁰GF,

	Starts	1st	2nd	3rd	Win & Pl
Hurdles	3	0	0	0	
Career Total	3	0	0	0	

Going:	Sf: 0-1 GS: 0-0 Gd: 0-1 GF: - Fm: 0-1
Distance:	2m2m3: 0-1 2m4-2m7: 0-2 3m+: 0-0
Track:	LH: 0-1 RH: 0-0 Tight: 0-1 Gall: 0-1
Aids:	Bl: 0-0 Vi: 0-0 Tstrap: 0-0 Ckp: 0-0
Best Rating:	30 4/03 Extr 2m1f good Hdl

Churchtown Glen (IRE)

(89h)　　　　　　　　　　　(78h)84

11-y-o b/br g Be My Native (USA)-Hill Side Glen (Goldhill)
Ian Williams C J Tipton

Placings: 0163533/130115002/533133334P/P233F050P/31PP26/54654-6　　(0629)
2003/04: 24⁶GF,

	Starts	1st	2nd	3rd	Win & Pl
Hurdles	1	0	0	0	0
Career Total	47	6	3	13	40864
101 11/01	Uttx	3m2f	F(0-95)HCh	SFT	£3031
98 11/99	Newb	2m4f	D Ch	G-F	£5336
117 12/98	Hayd	2m4f	B HHdl	SFT	£6827
117 11/98	Hayd	2m6f	B HHdl	HVY	£5022
118 10/98	Strf	2m3f	C(0-135)HHdl	GD	£3743
97 11/97	Ludl	2m5f110yE Hdl		GD	£2346
			Total win prize-money £26305		

Going:	Sf: 0-0 GS: 0-0 Gd: 0-0 GF: - Fm: 0-1
Distance:	2m2m3: 0-0 2m4-2m7: 0-0 3m+: 0-1
Track:	LH: 0-1 RH: 0-0 Tight: 0-0 Gall: 0-0
Aids:	Bl: 0-0 Vi: 0-0 Tstrap: 0-0 Ckp: 0-0
Best Rating:	119 5/99 Uttx 3m110y good Hdl

Modest chaser; stays three miles plus; has had breathing problems; acts on soft/heavy ground; has won on faster.

Churlish Lad (IRE)

7-y-o b g Commanche Run-Pennyala (Skyliner)
M Bradstock The Frankly Intolerable

Placings: 1/U-0OP　　　　　　　　(4098)
2003/04: 16⁰G, 16⁰S, 21⁰G,

	Starts	1st	2nd	3rd	Win & Pl
NH Flat	2	0	0	0	0
Hurdles	1	0	0	0	0
Career Total	5	1	0	0	1708
94 4/02	Plum	2m2f	H NHF	GD	£1708
			Total win prize-money £1708		

Going:	Sf: 0-1 GS: 0-0 Gd: 0-2 GF: - Fm: 0-0
Distance:	2m2m3: 0-2 2m4-2m7: 0-1 3m+: 0-0
Track:	LH: 0-2 RH: 0-1 Tight: 0-1 Gall: 0-0
Aids:	Bl: 0-0 Vi: 0-0 Tstrap: 0-0 Ckp: 0-1
Best Rating:	94 4/02 Plum 2m2f good NHF

Cigarillo (IRE)

101　　　　　　　　　　　　106

6-y-o br g Vestris Abu-Rose-Anore (Roselier (FR))
Noel T Chance C C Shand Kydd

Placings: 6/3302P3311　　　　　　(4612)
2003/04: 16³G, 16³GF, 20⁰GF, 16²GF, 19⁶S, 19³S, 20³G, 19¹G, 21¹G,

	Starts	1st	2nd	3rd	Win & Pl
NH Flat	2	0	0	2	561
Hurdles	7	2	1	2	10421
Career Total	10	2	1	4	10981
104 3/04	Sedg	2m5f110yE Hdl		GD	£3380
106 3/04	Newb	2m3f	E(0-105)HHdl	GD	£3934
			Total win prize-money £7314		

Going:	Sf: 0-2 GS: 0-0 Gd: 2-4 GF: - Fm: 0-3
Distance:	2m2m3: 1-6 2m4-2m7: 1-3 3m+: 0-0
Track:	LH: 2-7 RH: 0-2 Tight: 1-2 Gall: 1-4
Aids:	Bl: 0-0 Vi: 0-0 Tstrap: 0-0 Ckp: 0-0
Best Rating:	106 3/04 Newb 2m3f good Hdl

Modest hurdler; winner at Newbury and Sedgefield in March; stays two and a half miles; suited by good ground and a galloping track; excellent mount for an inexperienced rider..

Cill Churnain (IRE)

107(107c)　　　　　　(123+c)127

11-y-o b g Arctic Cider (USA)-The Dozer (IRE) (Bulldozer)
Mrs S J Smith Keith Middleton

Placings: PO/PUR2U3U2O24531/421131124-612311316　　(2949)
2003/04: 20⁶G, 21¹GF, 24²GF, 21³GF, 24¹GF, 20¹G, 24³G, 25¹S, 25⁶G,

	Starts	1st	2nd	3rd	Win & Pl
Hurdles	5	1	1	1	10848
Chases	4	3	0	1	34984
Career Total	34	9	6	5	75655
118 12/03	Kels	3m1f	B(0-145)HCh	GD	£11919
126 10/03	Aint	2m4f	C(0-130)HCh	GD	£15520
127 9/03	MRas	3m	C(0-135)HHdl	G-F	£6704
120 7/03	Uttx	2m5f	E(0-110)HCh	G-F	£6669
109 9/02	Worc	2m4f	C(0-135)HHdl	GD	£5968
118 9/02	Sthl	2m5f110yD(0-125)HHdl		GD	£5109
108 7/02	Sedg	2m5f110yD(0-125)HHdl		G-F	£3672
110 6/02	Worc	3m	E Hdl		G-F	£2632
108 3/02	Sedg	2m5f	E Ch		SFT	£3051
			Total win prize-money £61248		

Going:	Sf: 1-1 GS: 0-0 Gd: 1-4 GF: - Fm: 2-4
Distance:	2m2m3: 0-0 2m4-2m7: 2-4 3m+: 2-5
Track:	LH: 3-8 RH: 1-1 Tight: 3-4 Gall: 0-0
Aids:	Bl: 0-0 Vi: 0-0 Tstrap: 0-0 Ckp: 0-0
Best Rating:	127 11/03 Aint 3m110y good Hdl

Useful handicap hurdler/moderate, but well handicapped chaser; back over fences after a successful spell over hurdles when easy winner at Uttoxeter in July 2003; added another hurdle race success at Market Rasen in September; scored over fences at Aintree the following month; stays three miles well but effective over shorter; handles the soft but is considered best on a sounder surface.

Cillamon

91f　　　　　　　　　　　　85f

7-y-o b m Terimon-Dubacilla (Dubassoff (USA))
L G Cottrell Henry T Cole

Placings: 6-3　　　　　　　　　　(0154)
2003/04: 16³GF,

	Starts	1st	2nd	3rd	Win & Pl
NH Flat	1	0	0	1	287
Career Total	2	0	0	1	287

Going: Sf: 0-0 GS: 0-0 Gd: 0-0 GF: - Fm: 0-1
Distance: 2m/2m3: 0-1 2m4-2m7: 0-0 3m+: 0-0
Track: LH: 0-1 RH: 0-0 Tight: 0-0 Gall: 0-0
Aids: Bl: 0-0 Vi: 0-0 Tstrap: 0-0 Ckp: 0-0
Best Rating: 92 5/03 Chep 2m10y gd-fm NHF

Daughter of high-class chaser Dubacilla; won 2m 4f point February 2003.

Cimarrone Cove (IRE)

9-y-o gr g Roselier (FR)-Sugarstown (Sassafras (FR))
M W Easterby (David M Easterby 11/3) The Grand National Racing Club Limited

Placings:2/4124/P4611F3/3606P/532FP-6FP (4542)
2003/04: 24^6G, 25^6G, 20^5GS,

	Starts	1st	2nd	3rd	Win & Pl
Chases	3	0	0	0	
Career Total	25	3	3	3	19958
130 12/00 Newb 3m	D Ch		SFT	£4348
119 12/00 Donc 3m	D Ch		HVY	£5118
114 12/99 Hntg 3m2f	E Hdl		G-S	£2757

Total win prize-money £12226

Going: Sf: 0-0 GS: 0-1 Gd: 0-2 GF: - Fm: 0-0
Distance: 2m/2m3: 0-0 2m4-2m7: 0-1 3m+: 0-2
Track: LH: 0-1 RH: 0-2 Tight: 0-1 Gall: 0-1
Aids: Bl: 0-2 Vi: 0-0 Tstrap: 0-0 Ckp: 0-0
Best Rating: 130 2/01 Newb 3m soft Ch

Fair staying handicap chaser, suited by soft ground. has worn headgear.

Cinnamon Club

12-y-o b m Derrylin-Cinnamon Run (Deep Run)
Mrs Ruth Hayter Mrs A Villar

Placings:05/25533/5001U/P-5 (0201)
2003/04: 24^5GF,

	Starts	1st	2nd	3rd	Win & Pl
Chases	1	0	0	0	
Career Total	14	1	1	2	3170
87 6/98 Worc 2m	F Hdl		GD	£2136

Total win prize-money £2136

Going: Sf: 0-0 GS: 0-0 Gd: 0-0 GF: - Fm: 0-1
Distance: 2m/2m3: 0-0 2m4-2m7: 0-0 3m+: 0-1
Track: LH: 0-0 RH: 0-1 Tight: 0-0 Gall: 0-1
Aids: Bl: 0-0 Vi: 0-0 Tstrap: 0-1 Ckp: 0-0
Best Rating: 94 5/97 Hrfd 2m1f good NHF

Cinnamon Line
96   99

8-y-o ch g Derrylin-Cinnamon Run (Deep Run)
R H Alner Club Ten

Placings:24/3350/6F35-F4 (4733)
2003/04: 24^6G, 22^4G,

	Starts	1st	2nd	3rd	Win & Pl
Hurdles	2	0	0	0	276
Career Total	12	0	1	3	2540

Going: Sf: 0-0 GS: 0-0 Gd: 0-2 GF: - Fm: 0-0
Distance: 2m/2m3: 0-0 2m4-2m7: 0-1 3m+: 0-1
Track: LH: 0-2 RH: 0-0 Tight: 0-1 Gall: 0-1
Aids: Bl: 0-0 Vi: 0-0 Tstrap: 0-0 Ckp: 0-0
Best Rating: 110 3/01 Newb 2m10y heavy NHF

A chaser in the making; has not translated his bumper form to hurdles; better effort when third in a three mile handicap at Taunton January 2003; acts on soft/heavy ground.

Cintra Ruby (IRE)
95   84

6-y-o b m Phardante (FR)-Ardfallon (IRE) (Supreme Leader)
W K Goldsworthy Bruce McKay

Placings:03PP06 (3777)
2003/04: 17^9G, 16^3G, 16^6GS, 17^9GS, 16^9G, 16^6G,

	Starts	1st	2nd	3rd	Win & Pl
Hurdles	6	0	0	1	529
Career Total	6	0	0	1	529

Going: Sf: 0-0 GS: 0-2 Gd: 0-4 GF: - Fm: 0-0
Distance: 2m/2m3: 0-6 2m4-2m7: 0-0 3m+: 0-0
Track: LH: 0-2 RH: 0-4 Tight: 0-1 Gall: 0-0
Aids: Bl: 0-0 Vi: 0-0 Tstrap: 0-0 Ckp: 0-0
Best Rating: 85 1/04 Ludl 2m good Hdl

Novice hurdler; pulled up in two points; first sign of ability second start when third at Kempton.

Cionn Mhalanna (IRE)
89   76

6-y-o b g Corrouge (USA)-Pennyland (Le Bavard (FR))
P Beaumont D R Brown & Miss E E Toland

Placings:05-06004P (4660)
2003/04: 16^9G, 19^6GS, 20^9GS, 20^9GS, 24^4G, 24^6PS,

	Starts	1st	2nd	3rd	Win & Pl
NH Flat	1	0	0	0	0
Hurdles	5	0	0	0	0
Career Total	8	0	0	0	0

Going: Sf: 0-1 GS: 0-3 Gd: 0-2 GF: - Fm: 0-0
Distance: 2m/2m3: 0-2 2m4-2m7: 0-2 3m+: 0-2
Track: LH: 0-6 RH: 0-0 Tight: 0-1 Gall: 0-0
Aids: Bl: 0-0 Vi: 0-0 Tstrap: 0-0 Ckp: 0-0
Best Rating: 97 3/03 Carl 2m1f gd-sft NHF

Modest form over hurdles; stays three miles; acts on a sound surface.

Circle Of Wolves
105   96+

6-y-o ch g Wolfhound (USA)-Misty Halo (High Top)
M J Gingell Mrs J M Penney

Placings:5543/545205003-334P031300 (4790)
2003/04: 23^3GF, 20^3GF, 20^4GF, 22^6G, 22^6GF, 21^3GF, 21^1G, 20^3G, 22^6G, 21^9G,

	Starts	1st	2nd	3rd	Win & Pl
Hurdles	10	1	0	4	3737
Career Total	23	1	1	6	7932
96 11/03 Plum 2m5f	F(0-90)HHdl		GD	£1869

Total win prize-money £1869

Going: Sf: 0-0 GS: 0-0 Gd: 1-5 GF: - Fm: 0-5
Distance: 2m/2m3: 0-0 2m4-2m7: 1-9 3m+: 0-1
Track: LH: 1-9 RH: 0-0 Tight: 1-8 Gall: 0-0
Aids: Bl: 0-0 Vi: 0-0 Tstrap: 0-0 Ckp: 0-0

Best Rating: 96 11/03 Plum 2m5f good Hdl

Moderate hurdler; off the mark at the 20th attempt at Plumpton in October 2003 over 2m5f; suited by cut in the ground.

Circumstance

6-y-o ch m Beveled (USA)-Instant Pleasure (Bairn (USA))
R Dickin Rush Green Partnership

Placings:UP-P (0440)
2003/04: 17^9GF,

	Starts	1st	2nd	3rd	Win & Pl
Hurdles	1	0	0	0	
Career Total	3	0	0	0	

Going: Sf: 0-0 GS: 0-0 Gd: 0-0 GF: - Fm: 0-1
Distance: 2m/2m3: 0-1 2m4-2m7: 0-0 3m+: 0-0
Track: LH: 0-0 RH: 0-1 Tight: 0-0 Gall: 0-0
Aids: Bl: 0-0 Vi: 0-0 Tstrap: 0-0 Ckp: 0-0

Circus Maximus (USA)
101 (96h)   (118h) 104

7-y-o b g Pleasant Colony (USA)-Crockadore (USA) (Nijinsky (CAN))
Ian Williams Christopher McHale

Placings:42164/3P/0066P-11P2 (4759)
2003/04: 24^1GF, 20^1S, 24^8S, 16^2S,

	Starts	1st	2nd	3rd	Win & Pl
Hurdles	1	1	0	0	2961
Chases	3	1	1	0	7040
Career Total	16	3	2	1	19887
118 1/04 Leic 2m4f110yF Hdl			SFT	£2961
104 10/03 Hntg 3m	D Ch		G-F	£5344
120 2/01 Naas 2m	Hdl		SH	£4729

Total win prize-money £13035

Going: Sf: 1-3 GS: 0-0 Gd: 0-0 GF: - Fm: 1-1
Distance: 2m/2m3: 0-1 2m4-2m7: 1-13 3m+: 1-2
Track: LH: 0-0 RH: 2-4 Tight: 0-0 Gall: 1-2
Aids: Bl: 1-3 Vi: 0-0 Tstrap: 0-0 Ckp: 0-0
Best Rating: 123 1/01 Gowr 2m soft Hdl

Fair hurdler; made a winning chase debut October 2003; ex-Irish; stays 3m; acts on most types of ground; has worn blinkers.

Cisco
89   74

6-y-o b g Shambo-School Run (Deep Run)
B Mactaggart Harlequin Racing

Placings:050/66U50-6 (4595)
2003/04: 22^6G,

	Starts	1st	2nd	3rd	Win & Pl
Hurdles	1	0	0	0	0
Career Total	9	0	0	0	0

Going: Sf: 0-0 GS: 0-0 Gd: 0-1 GF: - Fm: 0-0
Distance: 2m/2m3: 0-0 2m4-2m7: 0-1 3m+: 0-0
Track: LH: 0-1 RH: 0-0 Tight: 0-1 Gall: 0-0
Aids: Bl: 0-0 Vi: 0-0 Tstrap: 0-0 Ckp: 0-0
Best Rating: 74 3/04 Kels 2m6f110y good Hdl

Very limited ability so far.

Cita Verda (FR)

110   125

6-y-o b m Take Risks (FR)-Mossita (FR) (Tip Moss (FR))
P Monteith   Mr & Mrs Raymond Anderson Green

Placings:1102/3155411-63336   (2848)
2003/04: 16⁶GS, 16³GS, 16³G, 16³S, 16⁶S,

	Starts	1st	2nd	3rd	Win & Pl
Hurdles	5	0	0	3	7692
Career Total	16	5	1	4	43957
122 4/03	Ayr	2m	B HHdl		GD £17664
119 1/03	Ayr	2m	D(0-120)HHdl		HVY £5278
119 5/02	Prth	2m110y	E Hdl		G-F £2978
115 3/02	Ayr	2m	E Hdl		HVY £3024
85 2/02	Muss	2m	E Hdl		SFT £2660
				Total win prize-money £31605

Going:	Sf: 0-2 GS: 0-2 Gd: 0-1 GF: - Fm: 0-0
Distance:	2m/2m3: 0-5 2m4-2m7: 0-0 3m+: 0-0
Track:	LH: 0-3 RH: 0-2 Tight: 0-1 Gall: 0-0
Aids:	Bl: 0-0 Vi: 0-0 Tstrap: 0-0 Ckp: 0-0
Best Rating:	125 11/03 Kels 2m110y good Hdl

Fair handicap hurdler; goes well at Ayr; stays two miles; acts on any ground.

Citiman (AUS)

7-y-o b g Citidancer-Taimian (NZ) (Taipan (USA))
A J Whitehead   A J Whitehead

Placings:0   (3779)
2003/04: 21⁹G,

	Starts	1st	2nd	3rd	Win & Pl
Hurdles	1	0	0	0	
Career Total	1	0	0	0	

Going:	Sf: 0-0 GS: 0-0 Gd: 0-0 GF: - Fm: 0-0
Distance:	2m/2m3: 0-0 2m4-2m7: 0-1 3m+: 0-0
Track:	LH: 0-0 RH: 0-1 Tight: 0-0 Gall: 0-0
Aids:	Bl: 0-0 Vi: 0-0 Tstrap: 0-0 Ckp: 0-0

City Flyer

88   54

7-y-o br g Night Shift (USA)-Al Guswa (Shernazar)
Miss J Feilden   Mrs P Gooden

Placings:65/U0   (0445)
2003/04: 16ᵁG, 16⁶G,

	Starts	1st	2nd	3rd	Win & Pl
Hurdles	2	0	0	0	
Career Total	4	0	0	0	0

Going:	Sf: 0-0 GS: 0-0 Gd: 0-1 GF: - Fm: 0-1
Distance:	2m/2m3: 0-2 2m4-2m7: 0-0 3m+: 0-0
Track:	LH: 0-0 RH: 0-2 Tight: 0-0 Gall: 0-2
Aids:	Bl: 0-0 Vi: 0-0 Tstrap: 0-0 Ckp: 0-0
Best Rating:	74 11/01 Hntg 2m110y good Hdl

City Gent

98   87

10-y-o b g Primitive Rising (USA)-Classy Lassy (Class Distinction)
N Wilson   J McGuinness

Placings:050SF/PUF535/2364P211/665PP400/5534U42-2P   (0421)
2003/04: 16²G, 17ᴾGF,

	Starts	1st	2nd	3rd	Win & Pl
Chases	2	0	1	0	1038
Career Total	36	2	4	3	15997
98 4/01	MRas	2m1f110yE(0-105)HCh		HVY £3932
98 2/01	Muss	2m	D(0-110)HCh		GD £4823
			Total win prize-money £8756

Going:	Sf: 0-0 GS: 0-0 Gd: 0-1 GF: - Fm: 0-1
Distance:	2m/2m3: 0-2 2m4-2m7: 0-0 3m+: 0-0
Track:	LH: 0-1 RH: 0-1 Tight: 0-1 Gall: 0-0
Aids:	Bl: 0-0 Vi: 0-0 Tstrap: 0-0 Ckp: 0-0
Best Rating:	98 4/01 MRas 2m1f110y heavy Ch

Plating-class chaser; best at two miles but stays further.

City Reach

81   66

8-y-o b g Petong-Azola (IRE) (Alzao (USA))
Miss M Bragg   W H Whitley

Placings:PP-040P   (0975)
2003/04: 16⁹G, 17⁴GF, 16⁶G, 17⁷GS,

	Starts	1st	2nd	3rd	Win & Pl
Hurdles	4	0	0	0	270
Career Total	6	0	0	0	270

Going:	Sf: 0-0 GS: 0-1 Gd: 0-2 GF: - Fm: 0-1
Distance:	2m/2m3: 0-4 2m4-2m7: 0-0 3m+: 0-0
Track:	LH: 0-4 RH: 0-0 Tight: 0-2 Gall: 0-0
Aids:	Bl: 0-0 Vi: 0-0 Tstrap: 0-3 Ckp: 0-0
Best Rating:	66 6/03 NAbb 2m1f gd-fm Hdl

Clan Law (IRE)

52f   7f

6-y-o b g Danehill (USA)-My-O-My (IRE) (Waajib)
Mrs L B Normile   Mrs L Normile

Placings:0   (4952)
2003/04: 16⁹GS,

	Starts	1st	2nd	3rd	Win & Pl
NH Flat	1	0	0	0	
Career Total	1	0	0	0	

Going:	Sf: 0-0 GS: 0-1 Gd: 0-0 GF: - Fm: 0-0
Distance:	2m/2m3: 0-1 2m4-2m7: 0-0 3m+: 0-0
Track:	LH: 0-0 RH: 0-1 Tight: 0-0 Gall: 0-0
Aids:	Bl: 0-0 Vi: 0-0 Tstrap: 0-0 Ckp: 0-0
Best Rating:	7 4/04 Prth 2m110y gd-sft NHF

Clan Royal (FR)

112   (104h)151+

9-y-o b g Chef De Clan Ii (FR)-Allee Du Roy (FR) (Rex Magna (FR))
Jonjo O'Neill   John P McManus

Placings:00/311332/1343/351411-12   (4647)
2003/04: 27¹G, 36²G,

	Starts	1st	2nd	3rd	Win & Pl
Chases	2	1	1	0	178500
Career Total	20	7	2	6	252980
147 11/03	Aint	3m3f	B HCh		GD £46500
133 4/03	Aint	2m5f110yB(0-150)HCh		GD £40600
129 3/03	Newb	2m4f	D(0-125)HCh		SFT £10037
117 2/03	Font	2m2f	E(0-105)HCh		SFT £4046
112 6/01	Navn	2m	(0-116)HCh		FRM £6955
101 7/00	Baln	2m1f	Ch		G-F £3588
103 7/00	Bell	2m1f	Hdl		G-F £3174
			Total win prize-money £114902

Going:	Sf: 0-0 GS: 0-0 Gd: 1-2 GF: - Fm: 0-0
Distance:	2m/2m3: 0-0 2m4-2m7: 0-0 3m+: 1-2
Track:	LH: 1-2 RH: 0-0 Tight: 1-2 Gall: 0-0
Aids:	Bl: 0-0 Vi: 0-0 Tstrap: 0-0 Ckp: 0-0
Best Rating:	151 4/04 Aint 4m4f good Ch

Smart ex-Irish chaser; handles the Grand National fences well having won the Topham and Becher Chases at Aintree in 2003; somewhat unfortunate runner-up in the Grand National; stays really well; acts on any ground.

Clandestino (FR)

84f   74f

5-y-o b g General Holme (USA)-Corolina (USA) (Nashua)
Mrs K Walton   Stan Clough and Dudley Bendall

Placings:0P00   (4866)
2003/04: 16⁶S, 17ᴾGF, 17⁹G, 16⁶S,

	Starts	1st	2nd	3rd	Win & Pl
NH Flat	4	0	0	0	
Career Total	4	0	0	0	

Going:	Sf: 0-2 GS: 0-0 Gd: 0-1 GF: - Fm: 0-1
Distance:	2m/2m3: 0-4 2m4-2m7: 0-0 3m+: 0-0
Track:	LH: 0-3 RH: 0-1 Tight: 0-2 Gall: 0-0
Aids:	Bl: 0-0 Vi: 0-0 Tstrap: 0-0 Ckp: 0-0
Best Rating:	74 10/03 Sedg 2m1f good NHF

Clarendon (IRE)

(107h)   (112 h)95

8-y-o ch g Forest Wind (USA)-Sparkish (IRE) (Persian Bold)
P J Hobbs   The Plus Fours

Placings:43/11/1000-2F   (0710)
2003/04: 17²GF, 16ᶠGF,

	Starts	1st	2nd	3rd	Win & Pl
Hurdles	1	0	1	0	1049
Chases	1	0	0	0	0
Career Total	10	3	1	1	14711
125 7/02	Strf	2m110y	D(0-125)HHdl		G-F £6831
108 6/01	NAbb	2m1f	D Hdl		G-F £3554
106 6/01	Worc	2m	E Hdl		G-F £2562
			Total win prize-money £12948

Going:	Sf: 0-0 GS: 0-0 Gd: 0-0 GF: - Fm: 0-2
Distance:	2m/2m3: 0-2 2m4-2m7: 0-0 3m+: 0-0
Track:	LH: 0-2 RH: 0-0 Tight: 0-2 Gall: 0-0
Aids:	Bl: 0-0 Vi: 0-0 Tstrap: 0-0 Ckp: 0-0
Best Rating:	125 7/02 Strf 2m110y gd-fm Hdl

Fair hurdler; runner-up in claimer at Newton Abbot June 2003; well-backed when falling at the last with a length lead on chasing debut at the same course next time; appreciates fast ground; effective at around 2m.

Class Of Ninetytwo (IRE)

15-y-o b g Lancastrian-Lothian Lassie (Precipice Wood)
S Wynne   J E Stockton

Placings:050/65000/P11113/212/PF5P/P/P21/23P-4 (0307)
2003/04: 24⁴G,

	Starts	1st	2nd	3rd	Win & Pl
Chases	1	0	0	0	324
Career Total	29	6	4	2	31105
92 3/02	Bang	3m110y	H Ch		SFT £1498
127 11/96	Wwck	3m2f	B(0-145)HCh		GD £6736
124 2/96	Chep	3m2f110yD(0-125)HCh		GD £4099
119 1/96	Leic	3m	F(0-105)HCh		GD £3236

110	12/95	Ludl	3m	F(0-100)HCh	G-F	£2775
113	11/95	Wwck	3m2f	D Ch	GD	£3756
				Total win prize-money £22100		

Going:	Sf: 0-0 GS: 0-0 Gd: 0-1 GF: - Fm: 0-0
Distance:	2m/2m3: 0-0 2m4-2m7: 0-0 3m+: 0-1
Track:	LH: 0-1 RH: 0-0 Tight: 0-1 Gall: 0-0
Aids:	Bl: 0-0 Vi: 0-0 Tstrap: 0-0 Ckp: 0-0
Best Rating:	127 11/96 Wwck 3m2f good Ch

One-time fair staying handicapper; modest hunter chaser these days; likes to dominate; stays very well.

Classi Maureen

87   **43**

4-y-o ch f Among Men (USA)-Hi-Hannah (Red Sunset)
Mrs S M Johnson S A Hughes

Placings:00   (4854)
2003/04: 17⁰G, 17⁰GF,

	Starts	1st	2nd	3rd	Win & Pl
Hurdles	2	0	0	0	
Career Total	2	0	0	0	

Going:	Sf: 0-0 GS: 0-0 Gd: 0-1 GF: - Fm: 0-1
Distance:	2m/2m3: 0-2 2m4-2m7: 0-0 3m+: 0-0
Track:	LH: 0-0 RH: 0-2 Tight: 0-2 Gall: 0-0
Aids:	Bl: 0-0 Vi: 0-0 Tstrap: 0-0 Ckp: 0-0
Best Rating:	43 4/04 Tntn 2m1f gd-fm Hdl

Classic Calvados (FR)

87   **94**

5-y-o br/br g Thatching-Mountain Stage (IRE) (Pennine Walk)
P D Niven David H Cox

Placings:P04   (4732)
2003/04: 16⁶GS, 16⁰GF, 17⁴G,

	Starts	1st	2nd	3rd	Win & Pl
Hurdles	3	0	0	0	284
Career Total	3	0	0	0	284

Going:	Sf: 0-0 GS: 0-1 Gd: 0-1 GF: - Fm: 0-1
Distance:	2m/2m3: 0-3 2m4-2m7: 0-0 3m+: 0-0
Track:	LH: 0-1 RH: 0-2 Tight: 0-1 Gall: 0-1
Aids:	Bl: 0-0 Vi: 0-0 Tstrap: 0-1 Ckp: 0-0
Best Rating:	93 4/04 Carl 2m1f good Hdl

Classic Capers

98f   **101+f**

5-y-o ch g Classic Cliche (IRE)-Jobiska (Dunbeath (USA))
J M Jefferson Richard Collins

Placings:154   (4886)
2003/04: 16¹GS, 16⁵S, 17⁴GS,

	Starts	1st	2nd	3rd	Win & Pl
NH Flat	3	1	0	0	1960
Career Total	3	1	0	0	1960
101	2/04	Ayr	2m	H NHF	G-S	£1960
				Total win prize-money £1960		

Going:	Sf: 0-1 GS: 1-2 Gd: 0-0 GF: - Fm: 0-0
Distance:	2m/2m3: 1-3 2m4-2m7: 0-0 3m+: 0-0
Track:	LH: 1-2 RH: 0-1 Tight: 0-0 Gall: 0-0
Aids:	Bl: 0-0 Vi: 0-0 Tstrap: 0-0 Ckp: 0-0
Best Rating:	101 3/04 Newc 2m soft NHF

Dam a half sister to a smart miler and herself has bred a couple of Flat winners; pleasing introduction when winning Ayr bumper on debut; respectable fifth under a penalty at Newcastle in March.

Classic China

89   **92+**

7-y-o ch m Karinga Bay-Chanelle (The Parson)
J W Mullins P C And Mrs S I Fry

Placings:22-1F565   (4668)
2003/04: 23¹G, 22⁴HY, 22⁵G, 24⁵G, 23⁵GS,

	Starts	1st	2nd	3rd	Win & Pl
Hurdles	5	1	0	0	2937
Career Total	7	1	2	0	4111
92	11/03	Ling	2m7f	E Hdl	GD	£2936
				Total win prize-money £2937		

Going:	Sf: 0-1 GS: 0-1 Gd: 1-3 GF: - Fm: 0-0
Distance:	2m/2m3: 0-0 2m4-2m7: 0-0 3m+: 0-1
Track:	LH: 1-3 RH: 0-2 Tight: 1-2 Gall: 0-0
Aids:	Bl: 0-0 Vi: 0-0 Tstrap: 0-0 Ckp: 0-0
Best Rating:	100 1/03 Folk 2m1f110y heavy NHF

Second in two average bumpers before winning hurdle debut at Lingfield in November 2003; stays 2m7f; acts on most ground; has worn cheekpieces.

Classic Conkers (IRE)

99   **92**

10-y-o b g Conquering Hero (USA)-Erck (Sun Prince)
Miss J Feilden Steven Rees

Placings:0/234-0F   (0681)
2003/04: 20⁹GF, 24⁴GF,

	Starts	1st	2nd	3rd	Win & Pl
Hurdles	2	0	0	0	
Career Total	6	0	1	1	1599

Going:	Sf: 0-0 GS: 0-0 Gd: 0-0 GF: - Fm: 0-2
Distance:	2m/2m3: 0-0 2m4-2m7: 0-1 3m+: 0-1
Track:	LH: 0-2 RH: 0-0 Tight: 0-0 Gall: 0-0
Aids:	Bl: 0-0 Vi: 0-0 Tstrap: 0-0 Ckp: 0-0
Best Rating:	92 11/02 Weth 2m4f110y heavy Hdl

Modest on the Flat, he has shown some ability in his few attempts over hurdles. Needs at least two and a half miles.

Classic Lash (IRE)

110   (92h)**103**

8-y-o b g Classic Cheer (IRE)-Khaiylasha (IRE) (Kahyasi)
P Needham P Needham

Placings:000030216F0300/P05502114P**35312-342F3**
                             (0785)
2003/04: 21³S, 20⁴G, 20²GF, 20⁵G, 20³G,

	Starts	1st	2nd	3rd	Win & Pl
Chases	5	0	1	2	4495
Career Total	34	4	4	6	28985
102	4/03	Sedg	2m5f	E Ch	GD	£4056
92	10/02	Limk	3m	(60-95)HHdl	GD	£6561
85	10/02	Dpat	2m6f	(60-95)HHdl	G-F	£3809
93	9/01	DRoy	3m	(0-102)HHdl	FRM	£3895
				Total win prize-money £18322		

Going:	Sf: 0-1 GS: 0-0 Gd: 0-3 GF: - Fm: 0-1
Distance:	2m/2m3: 0-0 2m4-2m7: 0-5 3m+: 0-0
Track:	LH: 0-2 RH: 0-3 Tight: 0-1 Gall: 0-0
Aids:	Bl: 0-0 Vi: 0-0 Tstrap: 0-0 Ckp: 0-0
Best Rating:	103 6/03 Prth 2m4f110y good Ch

Moderate chaser; winning hurdler in his native Ireland; off the mark over fences when successful at Sedgefield in April 2003; stays three miles, best on a sound surface.

Classic Lin (FR)

4-y-o gr f Linamix (FR)-Classic Storm (Belfort (FR))
A Berry D J Ayres

Placings:0   (3278)
2003/04: 16⁰G,

	Starts	1st	2nd	3rd	Win & Pl
NH Flat	1	0	0	0	
Career Total	1	0	0	0	

Going:	Sf: 0-0 GS: 0-0 Gd: 0-1 GF: - Fm: 0-0
Distance:	2m/2m3: 0-1 2m4-2m7: 0-0 3m+: 0-0
Track:	LH: 0-1 RH: 0-0 Tight: 0-0 Gall: 0-0
Aids:	Bl: 0-0 Vi: 0-0 Tstrap: 0-0 Ckp: 0-0

Classic Native (IRE)

107   **116+**

6-y-o b/br g Be My Native (USA)-Thats Irish (Furry Glen)
Jonjo O'Neill Ray & Sue Dodd Partnership

Placings:101-2465   (4255)
2003/04: 20²G, 20⁴GS, 19⁶G, 24⁵G,

	Starts	1st	2nd	3rd	Win & Pl
Hurdles	4	0	1	0	2162
Career Total	7	2	1	0	21564
131	4/03	Aint	2m1f	A NHF	GD	£17400
113	12/02	Wwck	2m	H NHF	SFT	£2002
				Total win prize-money £19402		

Going:	Sf: 0-0 GS: 0-1 Gd: 0-3 GF: - Fm: 0-0
Distance:	2m/2m3: 0-2 2m4-2m7: 0-3 3m+: 0-1
Track:	LH: 0-3 RH: 0-1 Tight: 0-3 Gall: 0-0
Aids:	Bl: 0-0 Vi: 0-0 Tstrap: 0-0 Ckp: 0-0
Best Rating:	131 4/03 Aint 2m1f good NHF

Very useful bumper horse in 2002/3; not as good over hurdles; seems to get three miles; suited by soft ground.

Classic Quartet

91   **67+**

4-y-o b f Classic Cliche (IRE)-Carolside (Music Maestro)
Mrs L Williamson K Carbery

Placings:2   (1298)
2003/04: 16²GF,

	Starts	1st	2nd	3rd	Win & Pl
Hurdles	1	0	1	0	946
Career Total	1	0	1	0	946

Going:	Sf: 0-0 GS: 0-0 Gd: 0-0 GF: - Fm: 0-1
Distance:	2m/2m3: 0-1 2m4-2m7: 0-0 3m+: 0-0
Track:	LH: 0-1 RH: 0-0 Tight: 0-0 Gall: 0-0
Aids:	Bl: 0-0 Vi: 0-0 Tstrap: 0-0 Ckp: 0-1
Best Rating:	76 9/03 Uttx 2m gd-fm Hdl

Fair debut effort at Uttoxeter in September over two miles; should stay further; wears cheekpieces.

Classic Revival

6-y-o ch g Elmaamul (USA)-Sweet Revival (Claude Monet (USA))
Mrs A Price Mrs A Price

Placings:0PP (2032)
2003/04: 16⁰GF, 19ᴾGF, 20ᴾGF,

	Starts	1st	2nd	3rd	Win & Pl
NH Flat	1	0	0	0	0
Hurdles	2	0	0	0	0
Career Total	3	0	0	0	

Going:	Sf: 0-0 GS: 0-0 Gd: 0-0 GF: - Fm: 0-3
Distance:	2m/2m3: 0-1 2m4-2m7: 0-2 3m+: 0-0
Track:	LH: 0-0 RH: 0-1 Tight: 0-0 Gall: 0-0
Aids:	Bl: 0-0 Vi: 0-0 Tstrap: 0-0 Ckp: 0-0
Best Rating:	28 6/03 Worc 2m gd-fm NHF

Classic Rock
68 **83+**

5-y-o b g Classic Cliche (IRE)-Ruby Vision (IRE) (Vision (USA))
J W Unett G J G Roberts

Placings:00-1P (4676)
2003/04: 19¹GF, 22ᴾG,

	Starts	1st	2nd	3rd	Win & Pl
Hurdles	2	1	0	0	3634
Career Total	4	1	0	0	3634
83 3/04 Hrfd	2m3f110yE Hdl			G-F	£3633

Total win prize-money £3633

Going:	Sf: 0-0 GS: 0-0 Gd: 0-0 GF: 0- Fm: 1-1
Distance:	2m/2m3: 0-0 2m4-2m7: 1-2 3m+: 0-0
Track:	LH: 0-0 RH: 1-2 Tight: 0-0 Gall: 0-0
Aids:	Bl: 0-0 Vi: 0-0 Tstrap: 0-0 Ckp: 0-0
Best Rating:	83 3/04 Hrfd 2m3f110y gd-fm Hdl

Classic Ruby
95f **70f**

4-y-o b f Classic Cliche (IRE)-Burmese Ruby (Good Times (ITY))
M R Bosley Mrs Jean M O'Connor

Placings:0 (4447)
2003/04: 16⁰S,

	Starts	1st	2nd	3rd	Win & Pl
NH Flat	1	0	0	0	
Career Total	1	0	0	0	

Going:	Sf: 0-1 GS: 0-0 Gd: 0-0 GF: - Fm: 0-0
Distance:	2m/2m3: 0-1 2m4-2m7: 0-0 3m+: 0-0
Track:	LH: 0-1 RH: 0-0 Tight: 0-0 Gall: 0-0
Aids:	Bl: 0-0 Vi: 0-0 Tstrap: 0-0 Ckp: 0-0
Best Rating:	70 3/04 Wwck 2m soft NHF

Classical Ben
104 **97+**

6-y-o ch g Most Welcome-Stoproveritate (Scorpio (FR))
R A Fahey J D Clark And Partners

Placings:31-314 (3692)
2003/04: 16³G, 16¹GS, 19⁴G,

	Starts	1st	2nd	3rd	Win & Pl
NH Flat	2	1	0	1	2453
Hurdles	1	0	0	0	307
Career Total	5	2	0	2	4958
103 1/04 Catt	2m	H NHF		G-S	£2023
97 4/03 Hexm	2m110y	H NHF		GD	£1904

Total win prize-money £3927

Going:	Sf: 0-0 GS: 1-1 Gd: 0-2 GF: - Fm: 0-0
Distance:	2m/2m3: 1-3 2m4-2m7: 0-0 3m+: 0-0
Track:	LH: 1-2 RH: 0-1 Tight: 1-2 Gall: 0-0
	Bl: 0-0 Vi: 0-0 Tstrap: 0-0 Ckp: 0-0
Best Rating:	103 1/04 Catt 2m gd-sft NHF

Dual bumper winner; genuine and should stay well over hurdles.

Classify
105 **101+**

5-y-o b g Classic Cliche (IRE)-Slmaat (Sharpo)
P F Nicholls Mrs P Pullin, J Pullin & A Bank

Placings:32-F35 (4931)
2003/04: 17ᶠHY, 18³G, 22⁵G,

	Starts	1st	2nd	3rd	Win & Pl
Hurdles	3	0	0	1	537
Career Total	5	0	1	2	1802

Going:	Sf: 0-1 GS: 0-0 Gd: 0-2 GF: - Fm: 0-0
Distance:	2m/2m3: 0-2 2m4-2m7: 0-1 3m+: 0-0
Track:	LH: 0-2 RH: 0-1 Tight: 0-2 Gall: 0-0
Aids:	Bl: 0-0 Vi: 0-0 Tstrap: 0-0 Ckp: 0-0
Best Rating:	101 3/04 Font 2m2f110y good Hdl

Placed in two fast ground bumpers and over hurdles.

Classy Clare

6-y-o b m Nicholas Bill-Clare's Choice (Pragmatic)
J M Bradley John Brookman

Placings:PP-P (0528)
2003/04: 16ᴾGF,

	Starts	1st	2nd	3rd	Win & Pl
Hurdles	1	0	0	0	
Career Total	3	0	0	0	

Going:	Sf: 0-0 GS: 0-0 Gd: 0-0 GF: - Fm: 0-0
Distance:	2m/2m3: 0-1 2m4-2m7: 0-0 3m+: 0-0
Track:	LH: 0-1 RH: 0-0 Tight: 0-0 Gall: 0-0
Aids:	Bl: 0-0 Vi: 0-0 Tstrap: 0-0 Ckp: 0-0

Classy Clarence (IRE)
90 **63**

7-y-o ch g Un Desperado (FR)-Winscarlet North (Garland Knight)
C Tinkler J Fishpool

Placings:0-500P0 (4592)
2003/04: 22⁵GS, 22⁰HY, 24⁰G, 22ᴾG, 26⁹G,

	Starts	1st	2nd	3rd	Win & Pl
Hurdles	5	0	0	0	0
Career Total	6	0	0	0	0

Going:	Sf: 0-1 GS: 0-1 Gd: 0-3 GF: - Fm: 0-0
Distance:	2m/2m3: 0-2 2m4-2m7: 0-3 3m+: 0-2
Track:	LH: 0-1 RH: 0-4 Tight: 0-3 Gall: 0-1
Aids:	Bl: 0-1 Vi: 0-0 Tstrap: 0-0 Ckp: 0-0
Best Rating:	76 3/03 Wwck 2m good NHF

Claude Greengrass
100(92c) **(95c)112+**

8-y-o ch g Shalford (IRE)-Rainbow Brite (BEL) (Captain's Treasure)
Jonjo O'Neill John P McManus

Placings:0000000/0215F2-10B0BP (4813)
2003/04: 17¹GS, 18⁰GS, 16⁸G, 17⁰GS, 16⁸GF, 16ᴾG,

	Starts	1st	2nd	3rd	Win & Pl
Hurdles	5	1	0	0	3705
Chases	1	0	0	0	0
Career Total	19	2	2	0	10971
112 11/03 Carl	2m1f	D(0-115)HHdl		G-S	£3705
97 1/03 Donc	2m110y	H(0-100)HHdl		G-S	£3630

Total win prize-money £7335

Going:	Sf: 0-0 GS: 1-3 Gd: 0-2 GF: - Fm: 0-1
Distance:	2m/2m3: 1-6 2m4-2m7: 0-0 3m+: 0-0
Track:	LH: 0-5 RH: 1-1 Tight: 0-1 Gall: 0-2
Aids:	Bl: 1-3 Vi: 0-0 Tstrap: 0-0 Ckp: 0-0
Best Rating:	112 11/03 Carl 2m1f gd-sft Hdl

Moderate hurdler; well held when tried over fences; has run well in blinkers; best over two miles; suited by cut in the ground

Claydon Cavalier
69f **33f**

5-y-o b g Regal Embers (IRE)-Marsdale (Royal Palace)
J R Jenkins Ms L M Bartlett

Placings:0 (4594)
2003/04: 16⁰G,

	Starts	1st	2nd	3rd	Win & Pl
NH Flat	1	0	0	0	
Career Total	1	0	0	0	

Going:	Sf: 0-0 GS: 0-0 Gd: 0-1 GF: - Fm: 0-0
Distance:	2m/2m3: 0-1 2m4-2m7: 0-0 3m+: 0-0
Track:	LH: 0-0 RH: 0-1 Tight: 0-0 Gall: 0-1
Aids:	Bl: 0-0 Vi: 0-0 Tstrap: 0-0 Ckp: 0-0
Best Rating:	33 3/04 Hntg 2m110y good NHF

Claylord (IRE)

10-y-o b g Lord Americo-Princess Seal (Prince Tenderfoot (USA))
Mrs L B Normile Stephen Ramsay

Placings:00/0/P (4258)
2003/04: 16ᴾGF,

	Starts	1st	2nd	3rd	Win & Pl
Hurdles	1	0	0	0	
Career Total	4	0	0	0	

Going:	Sf: 0-0 GS: 0-0 Gd: 0-0 GF: - Fm: 0-1
Distance:	2m/2m3: 0-1 2m4-2m7: 0-0 3m+: 0-0
Track:	LH: 0-1 RH: 0-0 Tight: 0-1 Gall: 0-0
Aids:	Bl: 0-0 Vi: 0-0 Tstrap: 0-0 Ckp: 0-0
Best Rating:	86 1/99 Donc 2m110y good NHF

Claymore (IRE)
112(110c) **(145+c)140**

8-y-o b g Broadsword (USA)-Mazza (Mazilier (USA))
O Sherwood B T Stewart-Brown

Placings:010F12P3/314131UP-12F120B5 (4853)
2003/04: 19¹G, 20²GS, 19ᶠS, 20¹S, 20²G, 21⁰G, 24ᴮG, 22⁵GS,

	Starts	1st	2nd	3rd	Win & Pl
Hurdles	6	2	1	0	21266
Chases	2	0	1	0	8800
Career Total	24	7	3	3	63873
138 1/04 Weth	2m4f110yB HHdl			SFT	£11095
138 11/03 Extr	2m3f	D(0-125)HHdl		GD	£4241

145	2/03	Hayd	2m6f	D Ch	G-S	£5551
145	12/02	Chep	2m3f110yC(0-135)HCh	HVY	£9984
144	11/02	Uttx	2m	D Ch	HVY	£5252
115	1/02	Font	2m2f110yE Hdl	GD	£2730
111	11/01	Plum	2m2f	H NHF	G-S	£1652
				Total win prize-money		£40505

Going:	Sf: 1-2 GS: 0-2 Gd: 1-4 GF: - Fm: 0-0
Distance:	2m/2m3: 1-1 2m4-2m7: 1-6 3m+: 0-1
Track:	LH: 1-7 RH: 1-1 Tight: 0-1 Gall: 0-2
Aids:	Bl: 0-0 Vi: 0-0 Tstrap: 0-0 Ckp: 0-0
Best Rating:	145 12/03 Chep 2m3f110y soft Ch

Useful chaser/very useful hurdler; made a winning return in 2003/04 over hurdles at Wetherby in January; stays two miles six; acts on good ground or softer; tends to make mistakes over fences.

Clayphento

66   **24**

6-y-o b m Lyphento (USA)-Canny Member (New Member)
R H Alner H John Irish

Placings:0FP   (0550)
2003/04: 17²G, 17FGF, 17PGF,

	Starts	1st	2nd	3rd	Win & Pl
Hurdles	3	0	0	0	
Career Total	3	0	0	0	

Going:	Sf: 0-0 GS: 0-0 Gd: 0-1 GF: - Fm: 0-2
Distance:	2m/2m3: 0-3 2m4-2m7: 0-0 3m+: 0-0
Track:	LH: 0-1 RH: 0-2 Tight: 0-1 Gall: 0-0
Aids:	Bl: 0-1 Vi: 0-0 Tstrap: 0-0 Ckp: 0-0
Best Rating:	24 4/03 Extr 2m1f good Hdl

Clear Dawn (IRE)

106   (95h)**115+**

9-y-o b g Clearly Bust-Cobra Queen (Dawn Review)
J M Jefferson Mr & Mrs J M Davenport

Placings:P66/530331035/331/62300-0431PU3   (4778)
2003/04: 24⁹G, 24⁴G, 22³GS, 24¹GF, 25PGS, 22UHY, 21³G,

	Starts	1st	2nd	3rd	Win & Pl
Chases	7	1	0	2	7209
Career Total	27	3	1	3	21087
115	12/03	Muss	3m	D(0-120)HCh	G-F	£5369
100	10/01	Weth	2m7f110yE(0-105)HCh	GD	£3542
100	1/01	Muss	3m	F(0-105)HHdl	GD	£3721
				Total win prize-money		£12633

Going:	Sf: 0-1 GS: 0-2 Gd: 0-3 GF: - Fm: 1-1
Distance:	2m/2m3: 0-0 2m4-2m7: 0-3 3m+: 1-4
Track:	LH: 0-5 RH: 1-2 Tight: 1-6 Gall: 0-0
Aids:	Bl: 0-0 Vi: 0-0 Tstrap: 0-0 Ckp: 0-0
Best Rating:	115 12/03 Muss 3m gd-fm Ch

Modest chaser; stays three miles; best on good ground.

Cleopatras Therapy (IRE)

92   **95**

7-y-o b g Gone Fishin-Nec Precario (Krayyan)
T H Caldwell T H Caldwell

Placings:152-5PP4400   (4870)
2003/04: 16⁵GF, 20²G, 20PHY, 19⁴G, 20⁴GS, 20⁰G, 24⁰GS,

	Starts	1st	2nd	3rd	Win & Pl
NH Flat	1	0	0	0	0
Hurdles	6	0	0	0	
Career Total	10	1	1	0	3402

| 90 | 1/03 | Ludl | 2m | H NHF | SFT | £2828 |
| | | | | Total win prize-money | | £2828 |

Going:	Sf: 0-1 GS: 0-2 Gd: 0-3 GF: - Fm: 0-1
Distance:	2m/2m3: 0-1 2m4-2m7: 0-5 3m+: 0-1
Track:	LH: 0-6 RH: 0-1 Tight: 0-1 Gall: 0-0
Aids:	Bl: 0-0 Vi: 0-0 Tstrap: 0-0 Ckp: 0-0
Best Rating:	95 3/04 Donc 2m3f110y good Hdl

Made a winning debut in a Ludlow bumper in 2003; struggling to make much impact over hurdles.

Clettwr Girl (IRE)

76f   **38f**

6-y-o gr m Roselier (FR)-Spring Bavard (Le Bavard (FR))
K R Pearce Mrs E K Jones

Placings:0   (0947)
2003/04: 16⁰G,

	Starts	1st	2nd	3rd	Win & Pl
NH Flat	1	0	0	0	
Career Total	1	0	0	0	

Going:	Sf: 0-0 GS: 0-0 Gd: 0-1 GF: - Fm: 0-0
Distance:	2m/2m3: 0-1 2m4-2m7: 0-0 3m+: 0-0
Track:	LH: 0-1 RH: 0-0 Tight: 0-0 Gall: 0-0
Aids:	Bl: 0-0 Vi: 0-0 Tstrap: 0-0 Ckp: 0-0
Best Rating:	41 7/03 Worc 2m good NHF

Clever Thyne (IRE)

91   (0c)**105**

7-y-o b g Good Thyne (USA)-Clever Milly (Precipice Wood)
H D Daly Mrs Geoffrey Churton

Placings:4555/2F23F4-1   (0054)
2003/04: 26¹GS,

	Starts	1st	2nd	3rd	Win & Pl
Hurdles	1	1	0	0	3530
Career Total	11	1	2	1	6494
105	5/03	Hrfd	3m2f	E Hdl	G-S	£3529
				Total win prize-money		£3530

Going:	Sf: 0-0 GS: 1-1 Gd: 0-0 GF: - Fm: 0-0
Distance:	2m/2m3: 0-0 2m4-2m7: 0-0 3m+: 1-1
Track:	LH: 0-0 RH: 1-1 Tight: 0-0 Gall: 0-0
Aids:	Bl: 0-0 Vi: 0-0 Tstrap: 0-0 Ckp: 0-0
Best Rating:	105 5/03 Hrfd 3m2f gd-sft Hdl

Appreciated a longer trip when winning 3m 2f maiden hurdle at Hereford May 2003; has been let down by his hurdling in the past and fell in his only novice chase to date.

Cleymor House (IRE)

94(87h)   (54h)**71**

6-y-o ch g Duky-Deise Lady (Le Bavard (FR))
John R Upson The Nap Hand Partnership

Placings:000-04500   (4185)
2003/04: 20⁰GS, 21⁴GS, 21⁵GS, 20⁰S, 24⁰G,

	Starts	1st	2nd	3rd	Win & Pl
Hurdles	1	0	0	0	0
Chases	4	0	0	0	263
Career Total	8	0	0	0	263

Going:	Sf: 0-1 GS: 0-3 Gd: 0-1 GF: - Fm: 0-0
Distance:	2m/2m3: 0-0 2m4-2m7: 0-4 3m+: 0-1
Track:	LH: 0-1 RH: 0-4 Tight: 0-2 Gall: 0-2
Aids:	Bl: 0-0 Vi: 0-0 Tstrap: 0-0 Ckp: 0-0

Best Rating:	65 1/04 Folk 2m5f gd-sft Ch

Clichy

99f   **81f**

4-y-o b f Classic Cliche (IRE)-Kentucky Tears (USA) (Cougar (CHI))
M Dods N A Riddell

Placings:306   (4482)
2003/04: 16³HY, 16⁶G, 17⁶HY,

	Starts	1st	2nd	3rd	Win & Pl
NH Flat	3	0	0	1	282
Career Total	3	0	0	1	282

Going:	Sf: 0-2 GS: 0-0 Gd: 0-1 GF: - Fm: 0-0
Distance:	2m/2m3: 0-3 2m4-2m7: 0-0 3m+: 0-0
Track:	LH: 0-1 RH: 0-2 Tight: 0-0 Gall: 0-0
Aids:	Bl: 0-0 Vi: 0-0 Tstrap: 0-0 Ckp: 0-0
Best Rating:	81 1/04 Newc 2m heavy NHF

Promise on bumper debut.

Clifton Mist

105   **91**

8-y-o gr m Lyphento (USA)-Brave Maiden (Three Legs)
H S Howe Richard Garrard

Placings:U5P5/R44/600445600/1P100-423444   (3644)
2003/04: 16⁶GF, 19²GF, 16³G, 19⁴S, 17⁴GS, 24⁴GS,

	Starts	1st	2nd	3rd	Win & Pl
Hurdles	6	0	1	1	3359
Career Total	27	2	1	1	10015
91	12/02	Tntn	2m3f110yF(0-95)HHdl	SFT	£3757
85	10/02	Tntn	2m3f110yG(0-90)HHdl	FRM	£1946
				Total win prize-money		£5703

Going:	Sf: 0-1 GS: 0-2 Gd: 0-1 GF: - Fm: 0-2
Distance:	2m/2m3: 0-4 2m4-2m7: 0-1 3m+: 0-1
Track:	LH: 0-0 RH: 0-6 Tight: 0-0 Gall: 0-1
Aids:	Bl: 0-0 Vi: 0-0 Tstrap: 0-0 Ckp: 0-0
Best Rating:	91 2/04 Kemp 3m110y gd-sft Hdl

Moderate hurdler, stays two and a half miles, acts on fast ground.

Clingstone

98(97h)   (98dh)**98**

8-y-o b m Henbit (USA)-Linen Leaf (Bold Owl)
T R George Timothy N Chick

Placings:06²25P-46   (2252)
2003/04: 16⁶GF, 16⁶GF,

	Starts	1st	2nd	3rd	Win & Pl
Chases	2	0	0	0	276
Career Total	7	0	1	0	1136

Going:	Sf: 0-0 GS: 0-0 Gd: 0-0 GF: - Fm: 0-2
Distance:	2m/2m3: 0-2 2m4-2m7: 0-0 3m+: 0-0
Track:	LH: 0-0 RH: 0-2 Tight: 0-0 Gall: 0-0
Aids:	Bl: 0-0 Vi: 0-0 Tstrap: 0-0 Ckp: 0-0
Best Rating:	98 11/03 Carl 2m gd-fm Ch

Moderate chaser; best at 2m.

Cliquey

103   **94+**

5-y-o b g Muhtarram (USA)-Meet Again (Lomond (USA))
R H Buckler (B J Llewellyn 15/3) M J Hallett

Placings:3U2441P10   (4898)
2003/04: 16⁹GF, 20ᵁG, 20²GF, 19⁴GF, 16⁴G, 16¹GF, 17⁹GS, 19¹GF, 16⁹G,

	Starts	1st	2nd	3rd	Win & Pl
Hurdles	9	2	1	1	6069
Career Total	9	2	1	1	6069
94	3/04	Strf	2m3f		G Hdl	G-F £2912
94	11/03	Leic	2m		G Hdl	G-F £2254

Total win prize-money £5166

Going: Sf: 0-0 GS: 0-1 Gd: 0-3 GF: - Fm: 2-5
Distance: 2m/2m3: 2-6 2m4-2m7: 0-3 3m+: 0-0
Track: LH: 1-4 RH: 1-4 Tight: 1-5 Gall: 0-0
Aids: Bl: 1-2 Vi: 0-0 Tstrap: 1-1 Ckp: 0-0
Best Rating: 94 3/04 Strf 2m3f gd-fm Hdl

Moderate novice hurdler; won over seven furlongs on the Flat; dual selling hurdle winner on fastish ground.

Clodoald (FR)

86(109h)   (110+h)65
7-y-o b g Beaudelaire (USA)-Mint Stick (FR) (Tropular)
A Crook (M C Pipe 2/10) Stef Stefanou

Placings:6/02F032255640132000/302300000P44/2P41113
B-PPP050   (4605)
2003/04: 20⁶G, 17⁸GF, 22⁸GF, 21⁰GF, 19⁵GF, 22⁰G,

	Starts	1st	2nd	3rd	Win & Pl
Hurdles	1	0	0	0	0
Chases	5	0	0	0	0
Career Total	45	4	6	5	38900
108	9/02	Hntg	2m4f110yD(0-120)HHdl	G-F	£4114
106	8/02	Worc	2m4f	G Hdl	GD	£2934
106	7/02	Uttx	2m	G(0-95)HHdl	G-F	£2086
	12/00	Engh	2m1f	Ch	HVY	£6244

Total win prize-money £15379

Going: Sf: 0-0 GS: 0-0 Gd: 0-2 GF: - Fm: 0-4
Distance: 2m/2m3: 0-2 2m4-2m7: 0-4 3m+: 0-0
Track: LH: 0-2 RH: 0-1 Tight: 0-3 Gall: 0-0
Aids: Bl: 0-0 Vi: 0-1 Tstrap: 0-5 Ckp: 0-0
Best Rating: 108 9/02 Hntg 2m4f110y gd-fm Hdl

Moderate chaser; acts on a sound surface; stays two miles five furlongs.

Clonmel's Minella (IRE)

111   126
13-y-o b g Strong Gale-Martones Chance (Golden Love)
Michael Hourigan John J Nallen

Placings:1/130/U40F/211F320U-4223643S   (1648a)
2003/04: 25⁴G, 25²G, 20²YS, 22³Y, 20⁶F, 22⁴G, 19³S, 24⁵GF,

	Starts	1st	2nd	3rd	Win & Pl
Chases	8	0	2	2	14930
Career Total	24	4	4	4	53573
99	10/02	Cork	2m6f	(0-116)HCh	GD	£7975
91	9/02	List	2m3f	(0-95)HCh	FRM	£6984
126	11/00	Naas	2m	Hdl	SH	£4416
116	4/98	List	2m4f	NHF	Y-S	£2978

Total win prize-money £22354

Going: Sf: 0-1 GS: 0-0 Gd: 0-3 GF: - Fm: 0-2
Distance: 2m/2m3: 0-1 2m4-2m7: 0-4 3m+: 0-3
Track: LH: 0-1 RH: 0-4 Tight: 0-1 Gall: 0-0
Aids: Bl: 0-2 Vi: 0-0 Tstrap: 0-0 Ckp: 0-0
Best Rating: 126 9/03 List 2m3f soft Ch

Modest Irish chaser at up to two and three-quarter miles; effective on most ground.

Clonroche Vinyls (IRE)

98   89
9-y-o ch m Rashar (USA)-Clonroche Beggar (Pauper)
Ferdy Murphy Nicholas Butterly

Placings:13024/630605-523F   (2799)
2003/04: 20⁵G, 24²GS, 24³S, 24⁶S,

	Starts	1st	2nd	3rd	Win & Pl
Hurdles	4	0	1	1	1059
Career Total	15	1	2	3	4423
100	12/01	Folk	2m1f110yH NHF	HVY	£1589

Total win prize-money £1589

Going: Sf: 0-2 GS: 0-1 Gd: 0-1 GF: - Fm: 0-0
Distance: 2m/2m3: 0-0 2m4-2m7: 0-1 3m+: 0-3
Track: LH: 0-2 RH: 0-2 Tight: 0-0 Gall: 0-1
Aids: Bl: 0-0 Vi: 0-0 Tstrap: 0-0 Ckp: 0-0
Best Rating: 100 12/01 Folk 2m1f110y heavy NHF

Plating-class hurdler; stays 3m; acts on soft ground.

Cloone Express

5-y-o ch g Polar Falcon (USA)-Simple Logic (Aragon)
Mrs L C Jewell Gallagher Equine Ltd

Placings:P   (4097)
2003/04: 16⁸G,

	Starts	1st	2nd	3rd	Win & Pl
Hurdles	1	0	0	0	
Career Total	1	0	0	0	

Going: Sf: 0-0 GS: 0-0 Gd: 0-1 GF: - Fm: 0-0
Distance: 2m/2m3: 0-1 2m4-2m7: 0-0 3m+: 0-0
Track: LH: 0-1 RH: 0-0 Tight: 0-1 Gall: 0-0
Aids: Bl: 0-0 Vi: 0-0 Tstrap: 0-1 Ckp: 0-0

Cloonloo Annie

5-y-o ch m Be My Chief (USA)-Don't Be Late (Pollerton)
M Todhunter Mrs Loretta Kilroe

Placings:00P   (3433)
2003/04: 16⁹G, 16⁹G, 16⁷HY,

	Starts	1st	2nd	3rd	Win & Pl
NH Flat	2	0	0	0	0
Hurdles	1	0	0	0	0
Career Total	3	0	0	0	

Going: Sf: 0-1 GS: 0-1 Gd: 0-1 GF: - Fm: 0-0
Distance: 2m/2m3: 0-3 2m4-2m7: 0-0 3m+: 0-0
Track: LH: 0-3 RH: 0-0 Tight: 0-0 Gall: 0-1
Aids: Bl: 0-0 Vi: 0-0 Tstrap: 0-0 Ckp: 0-0
Best Rating: 52 1/04 Hayd 2m good NHF

Cloth Of Gold

74   122
7-y-o b g Barathea (IRE)-Bustinetta (Bustino)
Lady Herries Mrs H A Cameron-Rose

Placings:461/1-0   (4693)
2003/04: 22⁰G,

	Starts	1st	2nd	3rd	Win & Pl
Hurdles	1	0	0	0	
Career Total	5	2	0	0	6145
122	6/02	NAbb	2m6f	D(0-120)HHdl	GD	£3309

| 96 | 4/02 | Hntg | 2m5f110yE Hdl | G-F | £2835 |

Total win prize-money £6145

Going: Sf: 0-0 GS: 0-0 Gd: 0-1 GF: - Fm: 0-0
Distance: 2m/2m3: 0-0 2m4-2m7: 0-1 3m+: 0-0
Track: LH: 0-0 RH: 0-1 Tight: 0-0 Gall: 0-0
Aids: Bl: 0-0 Vi: 0-0 Tstrap: 0-0 Ckp: 0-0
Best Rating: 122 6/02 NAbb 2m6f good Hdl

Clouding Over

86f   69f
4-y-o gr f Cloudings (IRE)-Wellwotdouthink (Rymer)
Mrs M Reveley W D Hockenhull

Placings:60   (4780)
2003/04: 16⁶GS, 16⁹S,

	Starts	1st	2nd	3rd	Win & Pl
NH Flat	2	0	0	0	0
Career Total	2	0	0	0	0

Going: Sf: 0-1 GS: 0-1 Gd: 0-0 GF: - Fm: 0-0
Distance: 2m/2m3: 0-2 2m4-2m7: 0-0 3m+: 0-0
Track: LH: 0-2 RH: 0-0 Tight: 0-1 Gall: 0-0
Aids: Bl: 0-0 Vi: 0-0 Tstrap: 0-0 Ckp: 0-0
Best Rating: 69 3/04 Wwck 2m gd-sft NHF

Cloudy Bay Boy

6-y-o gr g Petoski-Smoke (Rusticaro (FR))
Mrs Caroline Bailey William Roe

Placings:F   (4655)
2003/04: 16⁶G,

	Starts	1st	2nd	3rd	Win & Pl
Chases	1	0	0	0	
Career Total	1	0	0	0	

Going: Sf: 0-0 GS: 0-0 Gd: 0-1 GF: - Fm: 0-0
Distance: 2m/2m3: 0-1 2m4-2m7: 0-0 3m+: 0-0
Track: LH: 0-0 RH: 0-1 Tight: 0-0 Gall: 0-0
Aids: Bl: 0-0 Vi: 0-0 Tstrap: 0-0 Ckp: 0-0
Best Rating: 69 4/04 Hrfd 2m good Ch

Cloudy Blues (IRE)

79f   68f
6-y-o ro g Glacial Storm (USA)-Chataka Blues (IRE) (Sexton Blake)
R H Buckler Mrs R L Haskins

Placings:0   (3046)
2003/04: 16⁹GS,

	Starts	1st	2nd	3rd	Win & Pl
NH Flat	1	0	0	0	
Career Total	1	0	0	0	

Going: Sf: 0-0 GS: 0-1 Gd: 0-0 GF: - Fm: 0-0
Distance: 2m/2m3: 0-1 2m4-2m7: 0-0 3m+: 0-0
Track: LH: 0-1 RH: 0-0 Tight: 0-0 Gall: 0-1
Aids: Bl: 0-0 Vi: 0-0 Tstrap: 0-0 Ckp: 0-0
Best Rating: 68 12/03 Newb 2m110y gd-sft NHF

Cloudy Creek (IRE)

10-y-o gr g Roselier (FR)-Jacob's Creek (IRE) (Buckskin (FR))

Miss E Leppard Prof D B A Silk

Placings:10/4F6P-3P   (4373)
2003/04: 25³GS, 24PG,

	Starts	1st	2nd	3rd	Win & Pl
Chases	2	0	0	1	223
Career Total	8	1	0	1	3087
99 3/02 Plum 2m5f E Hdl			G-S		£2488

Total win prize-money £2489

Going:	Sf: 0-0 GS: 0-1 Gd: 0-1 GF: - Fm: 0-0
Distance:	2m/2m3: 0-0 2m4-2m7: 0-0 3m+: 0-2
Track:	LH: 0-1 RH: 0-1 Tight: 0-2 Gall: 0-0
Aids:	Bl: 0-0 Vi: 0-0 Tstrap: 0-0 Ckp: 0-0
Best Rating:	107 12/02 Tntn 3m gd-sft Ch

Cloudy Grey (IRE)
114   134+

7-y-o gr g Roselier (FR)-Dear Limousin (Pollerton)
Miss E C Lavelle Mrs J R Lavelle & Mrs A Hepworth

Placings:4112-1   (3265)
2003/04: 16¹S,

	Starts	1st	2nd	3rd	Win & Pl
Hurdles	1	1	0	0	5356
Career Total	5	3	1	0	13837
134 1/04 Asct 2m110y D Hdl			SFT		£5356
128 1/03 Hayd 2m H NHF			G-S		£2121
109 12/02 Hrfd 2m1f H NHF			GD		£1960

Total win prize-money £9437

Going:	Sf: 1-1 GS: 0-0 Gd: 0-0 GF: - Fm: 0-0
Distance:	2m/2m3: 1-1 2m4-2m7: 0-0 3m+: 0-0
Track:	LH: 0-0 RH: 1-1 Tight: 0-1 Gall: 0-0
Aids:	Bl: 0-0 Vi: 0-0 Tstrap: 0-0 Ckp: 0-0
Best Rating:	134 1/04 Asct 2m110y soft Hdl

Useful novice hurdler; formerly leading bumper performer; impressive winner on hurdling debut at Ascot; should stay at least two and a half miles; acts in soft ground; a bright prospect.

Clownfish

10-y-o b g Silly Prices-Sea Sand (Sousa)
A R Dicken Got To Be In It To Win It Partnership

Placings:0PF5/43F/30P/UP   (1875)
2003/04: 24ᵁG, 22PG,

	Starts	1st	2nd	3rd	Win & Pl
Chases	2	0	0	0	
Career Total	12	0	0	2	1359

Going:	Sf: 0-0 GS: 0-0 Gd: 0-2 GF: - Fm: 0-0
Distance:	2m/2m3: 0-0 2m4-2m7: 0-1 3m+: 0-1
Track:	LH: 0-1 RH: 0-1 Tight: 0-1 Gall: 0-0
Aids:	Bl: 0-0 Vi: 0-0 Tstrap: 0-0 Ckp: 0-0
Best Rating:	90 1/00 Newc 2m soft NHF

Very moderate placed form over fences.

Club Royal
100(96h)   (80 h)80

7-y-o b g Alflora (IRE)-Miss Club Royal (Avocat)
D McCain Halewood International Ltd

Placings:P6402-1P34PP4PU   (4075)
2003/04: 21¹S, 21PS, 20³G, 20⁴G, 27PGF, 24PGF, 16⁴G, 21PGS, 24ᵁF,

	Starts	1st	2nd	3rd	Win & Pl
Hurdles	3	1	0	0	3465

			Chases	6	0	0	1	1742
			Career Total	14	1	1	1	6489
80 5/03 Sedg 2m5f110yE Hdl						SFT		£3465

Total win prize-money £3465

Going:	Sf: 1-2 GS: 0-1 Gd: 0-3 GF: - Fm: 0-3
Distance:	2m/2m3: 0-1 2m4-2m7: 1-5 3m+: 0-3
Track:	LH: 1-5 RH: 0-4 Tight: 1-6 Gall: 0-1
Aids:	Bl: 0-1 Vi: 0-0 Tstrap: 0-0 Ckp: 0-0
Best Rating:	80 6/03 Prth 2m4f110y good Ch

Plating-class novice hurdler; won a weak novices' hurdle at Sedgefield in May; third on debut over fences at Market Rasen the following month; stays two and a half miles.

Coachman (IRE)
73   48

6-y-o b g King's Ride-Royal Shares (IRE) (Royal Fountain)
A J Lockwood A J Lockwood

Placings:0-500PPU   (4958)
2003/04: 17⁵GS, 20⁰G, 19⁰GS, 25PGS, 17PGS, 17ᵁG,

	Starts	1st	2nd	3rd	Win & Pl
Hurdles	6	0	0	0	0
Career Total	7	0	0	0	0

Going:	Sf: 0-0 GS: 0-3 Gd: 0-3 GF: - Fm: 0-0
Distance:	2m/2m3: 0-4 2m4-2m7: 0-1 3m+: 0-1
Track:	LH: 0-5 RH: 0-1 Tight: 0-4 Gall: 0-0
Aids:	Bl: 0-0 Vi: 0-0 Tstrap: 0-0 Ckp: 0-0
Best Rating:	50 10/03 Sedg 2m1f good Hdl

Coastguard (IRE)
92(95h)   (90h)89

10-y-o b g Satco (FR)-Godlike (Godswalk (USA))
David Pearson (C J Mann 9/6) David Pearson

Placings:526311P/53UP214651/3U3003P-43065PP   (4478)
2003/04: 21⁴GF, 22³GF, 22⁰G, 25PG, 20⁵GF, 22PG, 20PHY,

	Starts	1st	2nd	3rd	Win & Pl
Hurdles	3	0	0	1	780
Chases	4	0	0	0	288
Career Total	31	4	2	6	22087
105 3/02 Newb 2m6f110yD(0-120)HCh			G-S		£7247
101 12/01 Strf 2m5f110yF(0-110)HCh			SFT		£3549
97 3/01 Plum 2m5f F(0-90)Hdl			HVY		£2320
96 2/01 Folk 2m6f110yF(0-110)HHdl			HVY		£1985

Total win prize-money £15103

Going:	Sf: 0-1 GS: 0-0 Gd: 0-3 GF: - Fm: 0-3
Distance:	2m/2m3: 0-0 2m4-2m7: 0-6 3m+: 0-1
Track:	LH: 0-5 RH: 0-2 Tight: 0-5 Gall: 0-0
Aids:	Bl: 0-3 Vi: 0-0 Tstrap: 0-0 Ckp: 0-0
Best Rating:	105 3/02 Newb 2m6f110y gd-sft Ch

Modest handicap chaser; suited by two and half to three miles and soft ground.

Cobbet (CZE)
112(87h)   (127h)126

8-y-o b g Favoured Nations (IRE)-Creace (CZE) (Sirano (CZE))
T R George Timothy N Chick

Placings:101122344/62331-115434   (4843)
2003/04: 17¹G, 16¹G, 20⁵GF, 17⁴G, 18³G, 16⁴G,

	Starts	1st	2nd	3rd	Win & Pl
Chases	6	2	0	1	15368
Career Total	20	6	3	4	46480
119 6/03 Prth 2m D Ch			GD		£6734
118 5/03 Kels 2m1f E Ch			GD		£4420

---

126 4/03 Chel 2m110y C(0-135)HCh			GD		£12760
115 10/01 Winc 2m F(0-110)HHdl			GD		£3250
104 10/01 Winc 2m F(0-110)HHdl			G-F		£2485
100 5/01 Fknm 2m G Hdl			G-F		£1596

Total win prize-money £31245

Going:	Sf: 0-0 GS: 0-0 Gd: 2-5 GF: - Fm: 0-1
Distance:	2m/2m3: 2-5 2m4-2m7: 0-1 3m+: 0-0
Track:	LH: 1-4 RH: 1-2 Tight: 1-3 Gall: 0-2
Aids:	Bl: 0-0 Vi: 0-0 Tstrap: 0-0 Ckp: 0-0
Best Rating:	126 4/03 Chel 2m110y good Ch

Fair novice chaser; ex-Polish-trained; landed a hat-trick of chases between April and June 2003; two miles is his trip; best on decent ground; goes well fresh.

Cobreces
106   123

6-y-o b g Environment Friend-Oleada (IRE) (Tirol)
P F Nicholls Gerry Mizel & Terry Warner

Placings:1143/13005211-560625   (4633)
2003/04: 19⁵S, 20⁶GS, 24⁰S, 24⁶G, 20²GS, 24⁵G,

	Starts	1st	2nd	3rd	Win & Pl
Chases	6	0	1	0	2048
Career Total	18	5	2	2	68257
118 3/03 Font 2m4f D Ch			G-F		£6104
123 3/03 Wwck 2m4f110yE Ch			GD		£4252
5/02 Autl 2m2f Ch			VS		£12368
11/01 Autl 1m7f Hdl			VS		£12124
10/01 Autl 1m7f Hdl			VS		£14549

Total win prize-money £49398

Going:	Sf: 0-2 GS: 0-2 Gd: 0-2 GF: - Fm: 0-3
Distance:	2m/2m3: 0-0 2m4-2m7: 0-3 3m+: 0-3
Track:	LH: 0-3 RH: 0-3 Tight: 0-3 Gall: 0-0
Aids:	Bl: 0-3 Vi: 0-0 Tstrap: 0-2 Ckp: 0-0
Best Rating:	123 3/03 Wwck 2m4f110y good Ch

Modest chaser; acts on both fast and soft ground; effective at around two and a half miles; starting to frustrate; has been tried in blinkers and a tongue tie.

Cock Of The Roost (IRE)
75(82h)   (24h)61

7-y-o b g Executive Perk-Sly Maid (Rapid River)
S T Lewis Simon T Lewis

Placings:00050P0P6-P04PPPP   (1935)
2003/04: 20PGF, 17⁰GF, 16⁴GF, 21PGF, 20PGF, 19PGF, 19PG,

	Starts	1st	2nd	3rd	Win & Pl
Hurdles	2	0	0	0	0
Chases	5	0	0	0	0
Career Total	16	0	0	0	0

Going:	Sf: 0-0 GS: 0-0 Gd: 0-1 GF: - Fm: 0-6
Distance:	2m/2m3: 0-2 2m4-2m7: 0-5 3m+: 0-0
Track:	LH: 0-5 RH: 0-2 Tight: 0-2 Gall: 0-0
Aids:	Bl: 0-1 Vi: 0-0 Tstrap: 0-2 Ckp: 0-0
Best Rating:	76 10/02 Hrfd 2m1f gd-fm NHF

Plating-class novice chaser; has shown over hurdles or fences.

Cockatoo Ridge
97   100

7-y-o ch g Riverwise (USA)-Came Cottage (Nearly A Hand)
N R Mitchell Mrs E Mitchell

Placings:051-00446P   (4895)

2003/04: 16⁰GS, 19⁰G, 22⁴G, 24⁴G, 21⁶GS, 22ᴾG,

	Starts	1st	2nd	3rd	Win & Pl
Hurdles	6	0	0	0	1129
Career Total	9	1	0	0	3082
91 4/03 Font	2m2f110yH NHF			G-F	£1953

Total win prize-money £1953

Going:	Sf: 0-0 GS: 0-2 Gd: 0-4 GF: - Fm: 0-0
Distance:	2m/2m3: 0-2 2m4-2m7: 0-3 3m+: 0-1
Track:	LH: 0-2 RH: 0-4 Tight: 0-0 Gall: 0-2
Aids:	Bl: 0-0 Vi: 0-0 Tstrap: 0-0 Ckp: 0-0
Best Rating:	100 2/04 Winc 2m6f good Hdl

Modest hurdler; half-brother to Champion hurdler Rooster Booster; scored in bumper at Fontwell in April 2003: has run well over hurdles without winning; probably best at two and a half miles; acts on fast ground.

Coctail Lady (IRE)
101   76
4-y-o ch f Piccolo-Last Ambition (IRE) (Cadeaux Genereux)
B W Duke Oak Green Racing Partnership

Placings: 16P464P   (2716)
2003/04: 16¹G, 16⁶GF, 18ᴾGF, 16⁴GF, 16⁶GF, 16⁴GF, 16ᴾGS,

	Starts	1st	2nd	3rd	Win & Pl
Hurdles	7	1	0	0	5934
Career Total	7	1	0	0	5934
87 7/03 Strf	2m110y D Hdl			GD	£5447

Total win prize-money £5447

Going:	Sf: 0-0 GS: 0-1 Gd: 1-1 GF: - Fm: 0-5
Distance:	2m/2m3: 1-7 2m4-2m7: 0-0 3m+: 0-0
Track:	LH: 1-7 RH: 0-0 Tight: 1-4 Gall: 0-0
Aids:	Bl: 0-1 Vi: 0-0 Tstrap: 0-0 Ckp: 0-0
Best Rating:	87 7/03 Strf 2m110y good Hdl

Had schooled well prior to causing 100/1 shock on hurdling debut at Stratford July 2003; has struggled since.

Code Sign (USA)
102   98+
5-y-o b g Gulch (USA)-Karasavina (IRE) (Sadler's Wells (USA))
P J Hobbs Denise Winton and Elizabeth Hodgson

Placings: 600-1523P   (1333)
2003/04: 16¹G, 17⁵GF, 16²GF, 18³GF, 19ᴾGF,

	Starts	1st	2nd	3rd	Win & Pl
Hurdles	5	1	1	1	5273
Career Total	8	1	1	1	5273
92 5/03 Worc	2m	E(0-105)HHdl		GD	£3619

Total win prize-money £3619

Going:	Sf: 0-0 GS: 0-0 Gd: 1-1 GF: - Fm: 0-4
Distance:	2m/2m3: 1-4 2m4-2m7: 0-1 3m+: 0-0
Track:	LH: 1-4 RH: 0-1 Tight: 0-2 Gall: 0-0
Aids:	Bl: 0-1 Vi: 0-0 Tstrap: 0-0 Ckp: 0-0
Best Rating:	98 8/03 Font 2m2f110y gd-fm Hdl

Useful but frustrating maiden on the Flat; took advantage of being handicapped on unsuitably soft ground when winning over 2m at Worcester May 2003; beaten off an 11lb higher mark next time; much better effort when second back at Worcester in August.

Cody
101   86+
5-y-o ch g Zilzal (USA)-Ibtihaj (USA) (Raja Baba (USA))
G A Ham P A Dales

Placings: 000000-004204F6F0420P   (4914)
2003/04: 16⁰G, 16⁰GS, 17⁴GS, 19²G, 24⁰G, 16⁴GS, 22ᴾG, 17⁶GS,

21ᶠG, 16⁰GF, 19⁴GS, 24²G, 22⁰G, 24ᴾGS,

	Starts	1st	2nd	3rd	Win & Pl
Hurdles	14	0	2	0	1368
Career Total	20	0	2	0	1368

Going:	Sf: 0-0 GS: 0-6 Gd: 0-7 GF: - Fm: 0-1
Distance:	2m/2m3: 0-6 2m4-2m7: 0-5 3m+: 0-3
Track:	LH: 0-5 RH: 0-9 Tight: 0-6 Gall: 0-0
Aids:	Bl: 0-0 Vi: 0-4 Tstrap: 0-0 Ckp: 0-0
Best Rating:	86 4/04 Tntn 3m110y good Hdl

Plating class hurdler; limited promise so far.

Codys Castle
12-y-o b g Ascendant-Hurricane Lizzie (Kalimnos)
Mrs E M Collinson Mrs E M Collinson

Placings: 00/0   (4303)
2003/04: 16⁰G,

	Starts	1st	2nd	3rd	Win & Pl
Chases	1	0	0	0	
Career Total	3	0	0	0	

Going:	Sf: 0-0 GS: 0-0 Gd: 0-1 GF: - Fm: 0-0
Distance:	2m/2m3: 0-1 2m4-2m7: 0-0 3m+: 0-0
Track:	LH: 0-0 RH: 0-1 Tight: 0-0 Gall: 0-0
Aids:	Bl: 0-1 Vi: 0-0 Tstrap: 0-0 Ckp: 0-0
Best Rating:	19 4/00 Clon 2m4f good Hdl

Coercion (IRE)
68   41
6-y-o b g Ilium-Nicholas Ferry (Floriferous)
R F Fisher Great Head House Estates Limited

Placings: 0000   (4881)
2003/04: 16⁰GS, 17⁰G, 16⁰S, 17⁰GS,

	Starts	1st	2nd	3rd	Win & Pl
NH Flat	3	0	0	0	
Hurdles	1	0	0	0	0
Career Total	4	0	0	0	

Going:	Sf: 0-1 GS: 0-2 Gd: 0-1 GF: - Fm: 0-0
Distance:	2m/2m3: 0-4 2m4-2m7: 0-0 3m+: 0-0
Track:	LH: 0-2 RH: 0-2 Tight: 0-1 Gall: 0-0
Aids:	Bl: 0-0 Vi: 0-0 Tstrap: 0-0 Ckp: 0-0
Best Rating:	50 1/04 Catt 2m gd-sft NHF

Colca Canyon (IRE)
117(93h)   (112h)144
7-y-o b g Un Desperado (FR)-Golden Flats (Sonnen Gold)
Mrs John Harrington Philip F Myerscough

Placings: 000/04-11121U2352   (4769a)
2003/04: 16¹GY, 16¹G, 16¹G, 16²F, 19¹GF, 16ᵁS, 21²F, 17³YS, 16⁵G, 17²Y,

	Starts	1st	2nd	3rd	Win & Pl
NH Flat	1	1	0	0	3808
Hurdles	2	2	0	0	13218
Chases	7	1	3	1	33791
Career Total	15	4	3	1	51247
124 9/03 List	2m3f	Ch		G-F	£7168
112 7/03 Limk	2m	Hdl		GD	£7392
101 7/03 Navn	2m	Hdl		G-F	£5824
99 7/03 Baln	2m	NHF		G-Y	£3808

Total win prize-money £24195

Going:	Sf: 0-1 GS: 0-0 Gd: 1-2 GF: - Fm: 2-4

Distance: 2m/2m3: 4-9 2m4-2m7: 0-1 3m+: 0-0

Track:	LH: 1-4 RH: 0-1 Tight: 0-0 Gall: 0-1
Aids:	Bl: 0-0 Vi: 0-0 Tstrap: 0-0 Ckp: 0-0
Best Rating:	144 4/04 Fair 2m1f yield Ch

Useful Irish novice chaser; best at around 2m, but gets farther; effective on most types of ground.

Colca's Date
5-y-o br m Sovereign Water (FR)-Rabdanna (Rabdan)
J Gallagher Smith Wadley Homes Ltd

Placings: 00   (4402)
2003/04: 16⁰S, 16⁰G,

	Starts	1st	2nd	3rd	Win & Pl
NH Flat	1	0	0	0	0
Hurdles	1	0	0	0	0
Career Total	2	0	0	0	0

Going:	Sf: 0-1 GS: 0-0 Gd: 0-1 GF: - Fm: 0-0
Distance:	2m/2m3: 0-2 2m4-2m7: 0-0 3m+: 0-0
Track:	LH: 0-0 RH: 0-2 Tight: 0-0 Gall: 0-2
Aids:	Bl: 0-0 Vi: 0-0 Tstrap: 0-0 Ckp: 0-0

Cold Class (IRE)
11-y-o b g Glacial Storm (USA)-Cameo Class (Roi Guillaume (FR))
Miss A M Newton-Smith Tomorrows Easy Partnership

Placings: 506/4F3/0P   (0803)
2003/04: 24⁰GF, 21²G,

	Starts	1st	2nd	3rd	Win & Pl
Hurdles	2	0	0	0	
Career Total	8	0	0	1	380

Going:	Sf: 0-0 GS: 0-0 Gd: 0-1 GF: - Fm: 0-1
Distance:	2m/2m3: 0-0 2m4-2m7: 0-1 3m+: 0-1
Track:	LH: 0-2 RH: 0-0 Tight: 0-0 Gall: 0-0
Aids:	Bl: 0-0 Vi: 0-0 Tstrap: 0-0 Ckp: 0-0
Best Rating:	101 12/99 Folk 2m6f110y soft Hdl

Cold Comfort
74
12-y-o b g Arctic Lord-Main Brand (Main Reef)
I R Brown I R Brown

Placings: U6/F-P   (0761)
2003/04: 16ᴾG,

	Starts	1st	2nd	3rd	Win & Pl
Hurdles	1	0	0	0	
Career Total	4	0	0	0	0

Going:	Sf: 0-0 GS: 0-0 Gd: 0-1 GF: - Fm: 0-0
Distance:	2m/2m3: 0-1 2m4-2m7: 0-0 3m+: 0-0
Track:	LH: 0-1 RH: 0-0 Tight: 0-0 Gall: 0-0
Aids:	Bl: 0-0 Vi: 0-0 Tstrap: 0-0 Ckp: 0-0
Best Rating:	74 4/02 Chep 2m110y gd-fm Hdl

Cold Encounter (IRE)
106(94h)   (61h)101+
9-y-o ch g Polar Falcon (USA)-Scene Galante (FR) (Sicyos (USA))

R M Stronge Anthony Hibbard And Joe Baker

Placings:3222005P/454/122142/50P1112P4P0   (4933)
2003/04: 21^5GF, 24^0GF, 28^8GF, 24^1G, 24^1GF, 26^1GF, 25^2GF, 24^8S, 25^4G, 24^8S, 26^9G,

	Starts	1st	2nd	3rd	Win & Pl
Hurdles	1	0	0	0	0
Chases	10	3	1	0	14812
Career Total	28	5	7	1	27276
101 11/03 Font	3m2f110yD(0-125)HCh			G-F	£3987
101 11/03 Kemp	3m D(0-120)HCh			G-F	£5768
101 10/03 Bang	3m110y E(0-105)HCh			GD	£3575
110 7/01 MRas	2m4f E Ch			G-S	£3428
88 5/01 Hntg	3m F(0-100)HCh			G-F	£2824
				Total win prize-money	£19585

Going: Sf: 0-2 GS: 0-0 Gd: 1-3 GF: - Fm: 2-6
Distance: 2m/2m3: 0-0 2m4-2m7: 0-1 **3m+: 3-10**
Track: LH: 1-5 RH: 1-4 **Tight: 2-6** Gall: 0-1
Aids: Bl: 0-0 Vi: 0-0 Tstrap: 0-0 Ckp: 0-0
Best Rating: 110 7/01 MRas 2m4f gd-sft Ch

Moderate chaser; completed a quick hat-trick in October and November 2003; acts on good/good to firm; stays three miles; likes to front run.

Coleham
70f   60f
6-y-o b m Saddlers' Hall (IRE)-Katie Scarlett (Lochnager)
W M Brisbourne Barry Baggott

Placings:14/2-0   (0309)
2003/04: 17^0G,

	Starts	1st	2nd	3rd	Win & Pl
NH Flat	1	0	0	0	
Career Total	4	1	1	0	2478
94 2/02 Ludl	2m H NHF			GD	£2033
				Total win prize-money	£2034

Going: Sf: 0-0 GS: 0-0 Gd: 0-1 GF: - Fm: 0-0
Distance: 2m/2m3: 0-4 2m4-2m7: 0-0 3m+: 0-0
Track: LH: 0-1 RH: 0-0 Tight: 0-1 Gall: 0-0
Aids: Bl: 0-0 Vi: 0-0 Tstrap: 0-0 Ckp: 0-0
Best Rating: 94 3/02 Ludl 2m soft NHF

Coleshill Lad
60   62+
4-y-o br g Wizard King-Hallowed Ground (IRE) (Godswalk (USA))
J Joseph (M Scudamore 7/1) Jack Joseph

Placings:0050P   (4363)
2003/04: 12^0S, 16^0GS, 16^5GS, 17^0GS, 16^0GS,

	Starts	1st	2nd	3rd	Win & Pl
NH Flat	1	0	0	0	0
Hurdles	4	0	0	0	0
Career Total	5	0	0	0	0

Going: Sf: 0-1 GS: 0-3 Gd: 0-1 GF: - Fm: 0-0
Distance: 2m/2m3: 0-4 2m4-2m7: 0-0 3m+: 0-0
Track: LH: 0-3 RH: 0-1 Tight: 0-1 Gall: 0-0
Aids: Bl: 0-0 Vi: 0-0 Tstrap: 0-0 Ckp: 0-0
Best Rating: 62 12/03 Uttx 2m gd-sft Hdl

Collective Dream
9-y-o b g North Col-Tournanova (High Line)
R Curtis Collective Dreamers

Placings:PP-0PFF   (4278)

2003/04: 27^8S, 21^0G, 20^0G, 16^8GS, 19^8GS,

	Starts	1st	2nd	3rd	Win & Pl
Hurdles	5	0	0	0	
Career Total	6	0	0	0	

Going: Sf: 0-1 GS: 0-2 Gd: 0-2 GF: - Fm: 0-0
Distance: 2m/2m3: 0-1 2m4-2m7: 0-3 3m+: 0-1
Track: LH: 0-3 RH: 0-1 Tight: 0-2 Gall: 0-0
Aids: Bl: 0-0 Vi: 0-0 Tstrap: 0-0 Ckp: 0-0

College City (IRE)
91   88
5-y-o b g College Chapel-Polish Crack (IRE) (Polish Patriot (USA))
R C Guest Mrs Anna Kenny

Placings:000126-00   (1376)
2003/04: 16^6G, 16^0G, 16^0GF,

	Starts	1st	2nd	3rd	Win & Pl
Hurdles	3	0	0	0	0
Career Total	8	1	1	0	3153
87 2/03 Newc	2m G(0-95)HHdl			SFT	£2387
				Total win prize-money	£2387

Going: Sf: 0-0 GS: 0-0 Gd: 0-2 GF: - Fm: 0-1
Distance: 2m/2m3: 0-3 2m4-2m7: 0-0 3m+: 0-0
Track: LH: 0-3 RH: 0-0 Tight: 0-0 Gall: 0-0
Aids: Bl: 0-0 Vi: 0-0 Tstrap: 0-0 Ckp: 0-1
Best Rating: 87 2/03 Newc 2m soft Hdl

Plating-class hurdler; acts on soft.

College Cracker
6-y-o b m Environment Friend-Primo Panache (Primo Dominie)
J F Coupland J F Coupland

Placings:00   (2945)
2003/04: 16^0GS, 16^0GS,

	Starts	1st	2nd	3rd	Win & Pl
NH Flat	2	0	0	0	
Career Total	2	0	0	0	

Going: Sf: 0-0 GS: 0-2 Gd: 0-0 GF: - Fm: 0-0
Distance: 2m/2m3: 0-2 2m4-2m7: 0-0 3m+: 0-0
Track: LH: 0-2 RH: 0-0 Tight: 0-0 Gall: 0-0
Aids: Bl: 0-0 Vi: 0-0 Tstrap: 0-0 Ckp: 0-0

Collier Hill
111   117+
6-y-o ch g Dr Devious (IRE)-Polar Queen (Polish Precedent (USA))
G A Swinbank Ashley Young

Placings:1/1236   (4190)
2003/04: 16^1S, 16^2G, 16^3GF, 18^8GS,

	Starts	1st	2nd	3rd	Win & Pl
Hurdles	4	1	1	1	8854
Career Total	5	2	1	1	10576
117 12/03 Kels	2m110y E Hdl			SFT	£3178
93 3/02 Catt	2m H NHF			G-S	£1722
				Total win prize-money	£4900

Going: Sf: 1-1 GS: 0-1 Gd: 0-1 GF: - Fm: 0-1
Distance: 2m/2m3: 0-4 2m4-2m7: 0-0 3m+: 0-0
Track: LH: 1-3 RH: 0-1 Tight: 1-3 Gall: 0-1
Aids: Bl: 0-0 Vi: 0-0 Tstrap: 0-0 Ckp: 0-0
Best Rating: 120 12/03 Donc 2m110y good Hdl

Bumper winner who won on hurdles debut at Kelso; not the most fluent when beaten by 97-rated Flat horse under penalty at Doncaster in December; still room for improvement in jumping.

Colliers Court
7-y-o b g Puget (USA)-Rag Time Belle (Raga Navarro (ITY))
Mrs L Williamson The Castle Bend Syndicate

Placings:600-P   (4874)
2003/04: 20^0GS,

	Starts	1st	2nd	3rd	Win & Pl
Hurdles	1	0	0	0	
Career Total	4	0	0	0	

Going: Sf: 0-0 GS: 0-1 Gd: 0-0 GF: - Fm: 0-0
Distance: 2m/2m3: 0-0 2m4-2m7: 0-1 3m+: 0-0
Track: LH: 0-1 RH: 0-0 Tight: 0-1 Gall: 0-0
Aids: Bl: 0-0 Vi: 0-0 Tstrap: 0-0 Ckp: 0-0
Best Rating: 86 12/02 Uttx 2m soft NHF

Colliers Quay (IRE)
113
8-y-o b g Warcraft (USA)-Francois's Crumpet (IRE) (Strong Gale)
Miss Venetia Williams The Quay Quintet

Placings:60/001412050-P   (4693)
2003/04: 22^8G,

	Starts	1st	2nd	3rd	Win & Pl
Hurdles	1	0	0	0	
Career Total	12	2	1	0	11885
113 9/02 Sthl	3m2f E Hdl			GD	£2891
106 7/02 Cork	3m Hdl			G-F	£7619
				Total win prize-money	£10511

Going: Sf: 0-0 GS: 0-0 Gd: 0-1 GF: - Fm: 0-0
Distance: 2m/2m3: 0-3 2m4-2m7: 0-0 3m+: 0-1
Track: LH: 0-0 RH: 0-1 Tight: 0-0 Gall: 0-0
Aids: Bl: 0-0 Vi: 0-0 Tstrap: 0-0 Ckp: 0-0
Best Rating: 113 10/02 Plum 2m5f good Hdl

Fair staying hurdler; suited to a sound surface.

Colne Valley Amy
69   41
7-y-o b m Mizoram (USA)-Panchellita (USA) (Pancho Villa (USA))
G L Moore Raymond Gross, Ms Adrienne Gross

Placings:P06   (4365)
2003/04: 17^0GS, 16^0GS, 16^6GS,

	Starts	1st	2nd	3rd	Win & Pl
Hurdles	3	0	0	0	0
Career Total	3	0	0	0	0

Going: Sf: 0-0 GS: 0-3 Gd: 0-0 GF: - Fm: 0-0
Distance: 2m/2m3: 0-3 2m4-2m7: 0-0 3m+: 0-0
Track: LH: 0-1 RH: 0-2 Tight: 0-2 Gall: 0-0
Aids: Bl: 0-0 Vi: 0-0 Tstrap: 0-0 Ckp: 0-0
Best Rating: 52 1/04 Winc 2m gd-sft Hdl

Colnside Brook
99   95
5-y-o br m Sovereign Water (FR)-Armagnac Messenger (Pony Express)

B G Powell A Cutler

Placings:204   (4895)
2003/04: 16²GF, 20⁰GS, 224G,

	Starts	1st	2nd	3rd	Win & Pl
NH Flat	1	0	1	0	666
Hurdles	2	0	0	0	0
Career Total	3	0	1	0	666

Going:	Sf: 0-0 GS: 0-1 Gd: 0-1 GF: - Fm: 0-1
Distance:	2m/2m3: 0-1 2m4-2m7: 0-2 3m+: 0-0
Track:	LH: 0-1 RH: 0-2 Tight: 0-0 Gall: 0-1
Aids:	Bl: 0-0 Vi: 0-0 Tstrap: 0-0 Ckp: 0-0
Best Rating:	95 4/04 Winc 2m6f good Hdl

Some ability over hurdles.

Colombian Green (IRE)

10-y-o b g Sadler's Wells (USA)-Sharaya (USA) (Youth (USA))
P Greenwood (D R Gandolfo 30/10) T J Whitley

Placings:0/2F242/1346/3634P4-044   (4675)
2003/04: 16⁸G, 19⁴G, 254G,

	Starts	1st	2nd	3rd	Win & Pl
Chases	3	0	0	0	502
Career Total	19	1	3	3	12920
123 10/01 Hrfd 2m1f	D(0-120)HHdl SFT £3311
				Total win prize-money £3311

Going:	Sf: 0-0 GS: 0-0 Gd: 0-2 GF: - Fm: 0-1
Distance:	2m/2m3: 0-1 2m4-2m7: 0-1 3m+: 0-1
Track:	LH: 0-0 RH: 0-2 Tight: 0-0 Gall: 0-1
Aids:	Bl: 0-0 Vi: 0-0 Tstrap: 0-0 Ckp: 0-0
Best Rating:	123 11/01 Asct 2m110y good Hdl

Fair novice chaser/decent winning hurdler; acts on soft ground and is suited by around two miles; regularly held up; fell on his chasing debut; better effort on his next try over fences two years later, but well beaten in two starts since.

Colonel Blazer

12-y-o b g Jupiter Island-Glen Dancer (Furry Glen)
Miss Elaine Bywater Miss Elaine Bywater

Placings:103/01P1/44141F/2436062/113450/46/4/P (3845)
2003/04: 25ᴾGS,

	Starts	1st	2nd	3rd	Win & Pl
Chases	1	0	0	0	
Career Total	30	7	2	3	27808
108 5/99 Towc 2m110y D(0-125)HCh	G-F	£4027
110 5/99 Extr 2m1f E(0-115)HCh	G-F	£4342
112 2/98 Leic 2m4f110yE(0-115)HCh	GD	£3379
112 1/98 Wind 2m E(0-100)HCh	G-S	£2823
85 4/97 Extr 2m2f E Hdl	G-S	£2367
104 2/97 Tntn 2m3f110yD Hdl	G-S	£2567
108 1/96 Kemp 2m H NHF	GD	£1581
				Total win prize-money £21089

Going:	Sf: 0-0 GS: 0-1 Gd: 0-0 GF: - Fm: 0-0
Distance:	2m/2m3: 0-0 2m4-2m7: 0-0 3m+: 0-1
Track:	LH: 0-0 RH: 0-1 Tight: 0-0 Gall: 0-0
Aids:	Bl: 0-0 Vi: 0-0 Tstrap: 0-0 Ckp: 0-1
Best Rating:	113 4/96 Worc 2m gd-fm NHF

Colonel Brown (IRE)

69   (0c)19

8-y-o b g Scenic-Musical Smoke (IRE) (Orchestra)

A G Hobbs R S And R J Lanchbury

Placings:0/0006000/5201P4/P6P-F00   (0676)
2003/04: 16⁶GS, 20⁰G, 16⁶GF,

	Starts	1st	2nd	3rd	Win & Pl
Hurdles	2	0	0	0	0
Chases	1	0	0	0	0
Career Total	20	1	1	0	6170
99 7/01 Dund 2m1f	Ch	FRM £5008
				Total win prize-money £5008

Going:	Sf: 0-0 GS: 0-1 Gd: 0-1 GF: - Fm: 0-1
Distance:	2m/2m3: 0-2 2m4-2m7: 0-1 3m+: 0-0
Track:	LH: 0-3 RH: 0-0 Tight: 0-0 Gall: 0-0
Aids:	Bl: 0-0 Vi: 0-0 Tstrap: 0-2 Ckp: 0-0
Best Rating:	99 7/01 Dund 2m1f firm Ch

Colonel Frank

116(103h)   (113 h)139+

7-y-o b g Toulon-Fit For Firing (FR) (In Fijar (USA))
B G Powell The Hambledon Hunters

Placings:0/34612-521   (3308)
2003/04: 19⁵GF, 24²GF, 20¹HY,

	Starts	1st	2nd	3rd	Win & Pl
Hurdles	1	0	0	0	0
Chases	2	1	1	0	7278
Career Total	9	2	2	1	12439
139 1/04 Font 2m4f E Ch	HVY	£4707
111 3/03 Font 2m2f110yE Hdl	GD	£3464
				Total win prize-money £8173

Going:	Sf: 1-1 GS: 0-0 Gd: 0-0 GF: - Fm: 0-2
Distance:	2m/2m3: 0-1 **2m4-2m7: 1-1** 3m+: 0-1
Track:	LH: 0-2 RH: 0-0 **Tight: 1-1** Gall: 0-2
Aids:	Bl: 0-0 Vi: 0-0 Tstrap: 0-0 Ckp: 0-0
Best Rating:	139 1/04 Font 2m4f heavy Ch

Fair novice hurdler; front runner; stays 2m 4f; suited by a sound surface.

Colonel Kurtz (USA)

6-y-o b g Slip Anchor-Rustaka (USA) (Riverman (USA))
J S King R B Denny

Placings:P-P   (0054)
2003/04: 26ᴾGS,

	Starts	1st	2nd	3rd	Win & Pl
Hurdles	1	0	0	0	
Career Total	2	0	0	0	

Going:	Sf: 0-0 GS: 0-1 Gd: 0-0 GF: - Fm: 0-0
Distance:	2m/2m3: 0-0 2m4-2m7: 0-0 3m+: 0-1
Track:	LH: 0-0 RH: 0-1 Tight: 0-0 Gall: 0-0
Aids:	Bl: 0-0 Vi: 0-0 Tstrap: 0-0 Ckp: 0-0

Colonial Rule (USA)

94   94

7-y-o b g Pleasant Colony (USA)-Musicale (USA) (The Minstrel (CAN))
Mrs L B Normile A K Collins and D J Hindmarsh

Placings:022F1P/P/02P433P2P0-6464   (3283)
2003/04: 22⁶G, 24⁴GS, 20⁶GF, 20⁴HY,

	Starts	1st	2nd	3rd	Win & Pl
Hurdles	3	0	0	0	0
Chases	1	0	0	0	0
Career Total	21	1	4	2	5329
93 2/01 Catt 2m3f	G(0-90)HHdl SFT £1708
				Total win prize-money £1708

Going:	Sf: 0-1 GS: 0-1 Gd: 0-1 GF: - Fm: 0-1
Distance:	2m/2m3: 0-0 2m4-2m7: 0-3 3m+: 0-1
Track:	LH: 0-2 RH: 0-1 Tight: 0-1 Gall: 0-0
Aids:	Bl: 0-1 Vi: 0-0 Tstrap: 0-2 Ckp: 0-0
Best Rating:	94 3/03 Hntg 2m5f110y good Hdl

Plating-class hurdler; has been tried in blinkers and a visor; looks best at around two miles six, but stays further; acts on testing ground.

Colonial Sunset (IRE)

(99h)   (93h)105

10-y-o b g Lancastrian-Thai Nang (Tap On Wood)
A J Whiting (Dr P Pritchard 22/5) A J Whiting

Placings:200/0212P60/000/00/2/P500552320236-P23 (2340)
2003/04: 23ᴾGF, 26²G, 17³S,

	Starts	1st	2nd	3rd	Win & Pl
Chases	3	0	1	1	2001
Career Total	32	1	8	3	16751
106 12/98 Leop 2m	Hdl	SFT £4184
				Total win prize-money £4185

Going:	Sf: 0-1 GS: 0-0 Gd: 0-1 GF: - Fm: 0-1
Distance:	2m/2m3: 0-1 2m4-2m7: 0-0 3m+: 0-2
Track:	LH: 0-3 RH: 0-0 Tight: 0-2 Gall: 0-0
Aids:	Bl: 0-0 Vi: 0-0 Tstrap: 0-0 Ckp: 0-1
Best Rating:	118 1/99 Leop 2m heavy Hdl

Plating-class hurdler/novice chaser; acts on soft ground; stays two and a half miles.

Colonnade

89   70

5-y-o b m Blushing Flame (USA)-White Palace (Shirley Heights)
C Grant Ian W Glenton

Placings:40   (2508)
2003/04: 20⁴G, 16⁶S,

	Starts	1st	2nd	3rd	Win & Pl
Hurdles	2	0	0	0	0
Career Total	2	0	0	0	0

Going:	Sf: 0-1 GS: 0-0 Gd: 0-1 GF: - Fm: 0-0
Distance:	2m/2m3: 0-1 2m4-2m7: 0-1 3m+: 0-0
Track:	LH: 0-2 RH: 0-0 Tight: 0-1 Gall: 0-0
Aids:	Bl: 0-0 Vi: 0-0 Tstrap: 0-0 Ckp: 0-0
Best Rating:	76 11/03 Weth 2m4f110y good Hdl

Poor maiden on the flat; fourth in weak novices' hurdle on debut at Wetherby in November; stays two and a half miles.

Colorado Falls (IRE)

103   114

6-y-o b g Nashwan (USA)-Ballet Shoes (IRE) (Ela-Mana-Mou)
P Monteith J W D Campbell

Placings:1-352   (3980)
2003/04: 16⁵S, 18⁵HY, 17²G,

	Starts	1st	2nd	3rd	Win & Pl
Hurdles	3	0	1	1	2870
Career Total	4	1	1	1	6328
104 6/02 Ctml 2m1f110yD Hdl	HVY	£3458
				Total win prize-money £3458

Going:	Sf: 0-2 GS: 0-0 Gd: 0-1 GF: - Fm: 0-0

Distance: 2m/2m3: 0-3 2m4-2m7: 0-0 3m+: 0-0
Track: LH: 0-2 RH: 0-1 Tight: 0-2 Gall: 0-0
Aids: Bl: 0-0 Vi: 0-0 Tstrap: 0-0 Ckp: 0-0
Best Rating: 114 2/04 Carl 2m1f good Hdl

Won on his hurdling debut on heavy ground in June 2002; lightly raced since.

Colourful Life (IRE)
113 (132c)**125**
8-y-o ch g Rainbows For Life (CAN)-Rasmara (Kalaglow)
Mrs M Reveley Andy Peake & David Jackson

Placings:4225/1U1F14F114/5022606-0005342 (4840)
2003/04: 16⁰GS, 20⁰GS, 20⁹S, 20⁵GS, 20³G, 20⁴G, 24²G,

	Starts	1st	2nd	Win & Pl
Hurdles	7	0	1	9787
Career Total	28	5	5	66580
116	2/02	Kemp	2m	C(0-135)HHdl	G-S	£10920
111	2/02	Newc	2m	B HHdl	SFT	£8489
120	11/01	Uttx	2m	D Ch	HVY	£4944
122	11/01	Weth	2m4f110yD(0-115)HCh	GD	£5372
96	5/01	Weth	2m4f110yD Hdl	GD	£4011
			Total win prize-money £33736

Going: Sf: 0-1 GS: 0-3 Gd: 0-3 GF: - Fm: 0-0
Distance: 2m/2m3: 0-1 2m4-2m7: 0-5 3m+: 0-1
Track: LH: 0-7 RH: 0-0 Tight: 0-2 Gall: 0-2
Aids: Bl: 0-0 Vi: 0-0 Tstrap: 0-0 Ckp: 0-1
Best Rating: 125 4/04 Chel 3m good Hdl

Fair hurdler/chaser; runner-up in 2003 Pierse Hurdle; effective at up to two and a half miles; acts on most types of ground; not won since early 2002.

Colquhoun
105 **110**
10-y-o b g Rakaposhi King-Red Rambler (Rymer)
T R George B A Kilpatrick

Placings:2P5P1P/P2/F2U-33223 (1008)
2003/04: 21³G, 21³GF, 21²GF, 20²GF, 20³G,

	Starts	1st	2nd	Win & Pl
Chases	5	0	2	3	7481
Career Total	16	1	5	3	13724
117	3/00	Chep	2m4f	D Ch	G-S	£3191
			Total win prize-money £3192

Going: Sf: 0-0 GS: 0-0 Gd: 0-2 GF: - Fm: 0-3
Distance: 2m/2m3: 0-0 2m4-2m7: 0-5 3m+: 0-0
Track: LH: 0-4 RH: 0-0 Tight: 0-5 Gall: 0-0
Aids: Bl: 0-0 Vi: 0-0 Tstrap: 0-0 Ckp: 0-1
Best Rating: 117 3/00 Chep 2m4f gd-sft Ch

Modest novice chaser; regularly placed without winning; iffy jumper; stays 2m 6f; suited by good ground; may need headgear.

Coltminator
93 **75+**
4-y-o b c Robellino (USA)-Darshay (FR) (Darshaan)
Frau E Mader Stall Capricorn

Placings:363 (3856)
2003/04: 16³S, 16⁶G, 16³S,

	Starts	1st	2nd	3rd	Win & Pl
Hurdles	3	0	0	2	2589
Career Total	3	0	0	2	2589

Going: Sf: 0-2 GS: 0-0 Gd: 0-1 GF: - Fm: 0-0
Distance: 2m/2m3: 0-3 2m4-2m7: 0-0 3m+: 0-0
Track: LH: 0-1 RH: 0-0 Tight: 0-1 Gall: 0-0

Aids: Bl: 0-0 Vi: 0-0 Tstrap: 0-0 Ckp: 0-0
Best Rating: 80 2/04 Plum 2m soft Hdl

Columbus (IRE)
117 **119**
7-y-o b g Sadler's Wells (USA)-Northern Script (USA) (Arts And Letters (USA))
Mrs J Candlish Racing For You Limited

Placings:32126P/4262222-2P55203 (4948)
2003/04: 24²YS, 25⁵G, 24⁵GS, 25⁵GS, 25²G, 25⁹G, 27³GS,

	Starts	1st	2nd	Win & Pl
Hurdles	7	0	2	1	6334
Career Total	20	1	9	2	20969
93	1/01	Ayr	2m	E Hdl	SFT	£2814
			Total win prize-money £2814

Going: Sf: 0-0 GS: 0-3 Gd: 0-3 GF: - Fm: 0-0
Distance: 2m/2m3: 0-1 2m4-2m7: 0-5 3m+: 0-1
Track: LH: 0-4 RH: 0-2 Tight: 0-2 Gall: 0-1
Aids: Bl: 0-2 Vi: 0-5 Tstrap: 0-0 Ckp: 0-0
Best Rating: 119 2/04 Catt 3m1f110y good Hdl

Fair hurdler; has frequently changed stables; suited by cut in the ground, but also handles a sound surface; stays 3m; by no means reliable; usually wears a visor or blinkers.

Colvada
72 (0c)**2**
8-y-o b m North Col-Prevada (Soldier Rose)
Ian Williams Mr & Mrs M R Paul

Placings:FPP/PP-0P0 (4401)
2003/04: 21⁰S, 22³GS, 21⁰G,

	Starts	1st	2nd	3rd	Win & Pl
Hurdles	3	0	0	0	
Career Total	8	0	0	0	

Going: Sf: 0-1 GS: 0-1 Gd: 0-1 GF: - Fm: 0-0
Distance: 2m/2m3: 0-0 2m4-2m7: 0-3 3m+: 0-0
Track: LH: 0-0 RH: 0-3 Tight: 0-1 Gall: 0-2
Aids: Bl: 0-0 Vi: 0-0 Tstrap: 0-0 Ckp: 0-0
Best Rating: 88 1/02 Hrfd 2m3f110y soft Hdl

Colway Ritz
99 **82**
10-y-o b g Rudimentary (USA)-Million Heiress (Auction Ring (USA))
W Storey Mrs M Tindale & Tom Park

Placings:060/2 (2140)
2003/04: 20²G,

	Starts	1st	2nd	3rd	Win & Pl
Hurdles	1	0	1	0	614
Career Total	4	0	1	0	614

Going: Sf: 0-0 GS: 0-0 Gd: 0-1 GF: - Fm: 0-0
Distance: 2m/2m3: 0-0 2m4-2m7: 0-1 3m+: 0-0
Track: LH: 0-1 RH: 0-0 Tight: 0-0 Gall: 0-1
Aids: Bl: 0-0 Vi: 0-0 Tstrap: 0-0 Ckp: 0-0
Best Rating: 82 11/03 Newc 2m4f good Hdl

Lightly raced over hurdles; stays 2m 4f.

Comanche War Paint (IRE)
111(88h) (94 h)**129+**
7-y-o b g Commanche Run-Galeshula (Strong Gale)

P F Nicholls
Tony Fear & Tim Hawkins

Placings:62F-51121242 (4240)
2003/04: 26⁵GS, 25¹GF, 23¹GF, 25²GF, 25¹GF, 25²G, 27⁴GS, 30²G,

	Starts	1st	2nd	Win & Pl
Hurdles	1	0	0	0	
Chases	7	3	3	0	31499
Career Total	11	3	4	0	32249
125	11/03	Winc	3m1f110yC(0-135)HCh	G-F	£8715
94	6/03	Worc	2m7f110yE Ch	G-F	£3861
116	5/03	Winc	3m1f110yD Ch	G-F	£6640
			Total win prize-money £19216

Going: Sf: 0-0 GS: 0-2 Gd: 0-2 GF: - Fm: 3-4
Distance: 2m/2m3: 0-0 2m4-2m7: 0-0 3m+: 3-8
Track: LH: 1-1 RH: 2-7 Tight: 0-1 Gall: 0-0
Aids: Bl: 0-0 Vi: 0-0 Tstrap: 0-0 Ckp: 0-0
Best Rating: 129 12/03 Winc 3m1f110y good Ch

Fair hurdler/chaser; acts on fast ground; stays beyond three miles.

Combe Castle
99(99c) (49c)**87**
9-y-o gr g Carlingford Castle-Silver Cirrus (General Ironside)
N B King (K C Bailey 5/5) Major R G Wilson

Placings:0/0UPP/U0R6P-PU2PP0 (4405)
2003/04: 24PGF, 21UGF, 24²PHY, 24PHY, 24PGS, 26⁰G,

	Starts	1st	2nd	3rd	Win & Pl
Hurdles	4	0	1	0	1293
Chases	2	0	0	0	
Career Total	16	0	1	0	1293

Going: Sf: 0-2 GS: 0-1 Gd: 0-1 GF: - Fm: 0-2
Distance: 2m/2m3: 0-0 2m4-2m7: 0-1 3m+: 0-5
Track: LH: 0-1 RH: 0-5 Tight: 0-1 Gall: 0-3
Aids: Bl: 0-1 Vi: 0-0 Tstrap: 0-0 Ckp: 0-3
Best Rating: 87 1/04 Towc 3m heavy Hdl

Plating-class hurdler/chaser; probably flattered when second at 100/1 at Towcester in January 2004.

Combined Venture (IRE)
96(93h) (65h)**81**
8-y-o b h Dolphin Street (FR)-Centinela (Caerleon (USA))
P T Dalton Mrs Joanne Woods

Placings:F002U/P/PP05PP0-06256 (1105)
2003/04: 17⁰GF, 16⁶G, 16²G, 20⁵G, 17⁶GS,

	Starts	1st	2nd	3rd	Win & Pl
Hurdles	1	0	0	0	
Chases	4	0	1	0	1054
Career Total	18	0	2	0	1500

Going: Sf: 0-0 GS: 0-1 Gd: 0-3 GF: - Fm: 0-1
Distance: 2m/2m3: 0-4 2m4-2m7: 0-1 3m+: 0-0
Track: LH: 0-4 RH: 0-1 Tight: 0-1 Gall: 0-0
Aids: Bl: 0-0 Vi: 0-0 Tstrap: 0-0 Ckp: 0-0
Best Rating: 81 7/03 Worc 2m good Ch

Improved on chasing debut when caught close home from 5lb out of the handicap in 2m Worcester novices handicap July 2003; can continue to progress.

Come Bye (IRE)
99 **82**
8-y-o b g Star Quest-Boreen Dubh (Boreen (FR))

Miss A M Newton-Smith (W J Burke 16/6) Pps Racing

Placings:0-334B0P2000   (4588)
2003/04: 18³Y, 20³HY, 16⁴G, 21⁸S, 21⁰GS, 22⁷HY, 18²GS, 17⁰G,
17⁹G, 21⁹G,

	Starts	1st	2nd	3rd	Win & Pl
NH Flat	3	0	0	2	1133
Hurdles	7	0	1	0	1284
Career Total	11	0	1	2	2417

Going: Sf: 0-3 GS: 0-2 Gd: 0-4 GF: - Fm: 0-0
Distance: 2m/2m3: 0-5 2m4-2m7: 0-5 3m+: 0-0
Track: LH: 0-3 RH: 0-4 Tight: 0-0 Gall: 0-1
Aids: Bl: 0-0 Vi: 0-2 Tstrap: 0-0 Ckp: 0-1
Best Rating: 91 6/03 Rosc 2m   good NHF

Plating-class ex-Irish maiden; best effort in Britain was at Fontwell in February when second from 20lb out of the handicap; stays 2m 4f; acts on soft ground.

Come On Boy

10-y-o ch g Henbit (USA)-Miss Rewarde (Andy Rew)
Mark Doyle T G Williams

Placings:P-PP   (4655)
2003/04: 20⁸G, 16⁸G,

	Starts	1st	2nd	3rd	Win & Pl
Chases	2	0	0	0	
Career Total	3	0	0	0	

Going: Sf: 0-0 GS: 0-0 Gd: 0-2 GF: - Fm: 0-0
Distance: 2m/2m3: 0-1 2m4-2m7: 0-1 3m+: 0-0
Track: LH: 0-0 RH: 0-2 Tight: 0-0 Gall: 0-0
Aids: Bl: 0-1 Vi: 0-0 Tstrap: 0-0 Ckp: 0-0

Come On George (IRE)

8-y-o b g Barathea (IRE)-Lacovia (USA) (Majestic Light (USA))
S E H Sherwood S Gray & Mrs P Treadgold

Placings:00P/0/P-P   (4505)
2003/04: 25⁸G,

	Starts	1st	2nd	3rd	Win & Pl
Chases	1	0	0	0	
Career Total	6	0	0	0	

Going: Sf: 0-0 GS: 0-0 Gd: 0-1 GF: - Fm: 0-0
Distance: 2m/2m3: 0-0 2m4-2m7: 0-0 3m+: 0-0
Track: LH: 0-0 RH: 0-1 Tight: 0-0 Gall: 0-0
Aids: Bl: 0-0 Vi: 0-0 Tstrap: 0-0 Ckp: 0-0
Best Rating: 57 2/00 Wwck 2m   good Hdl

Come The Dawn

8-y-o b m Gunner B-Herald The Dawn (Dubassoff (USA))
M Sheppard The Dawn Raiders

Placings:46/P   (4650)
2003/04: 19⁸G,

	Starts	1st	2nd	3rd	Win & Pl
Hurdles	1	0	0	0	
Career Total	3	0	0	0	0

Placings: | (2080)
2003/04: 23⁸G,

	Starts	1st	2nd	3rd	Win & Pl
Hurdles	1	0	0	0	
Career Total	11	1	0	1	4182
97	3/03	MRas	2m5f110yE Hdl		G-S	£3380

Total win prize-money £3380

Comete Du Lac (FR)
95(88c)   (87c)**81+**

7-y-o ch m Comte Du Bourg (FR)-Line Du Nord (FR) (Esprit Du Nord (USA))
Mrs N Macauley (M D Hammond 27/9) Andy Peake

Placings:FF/P46234FF4F/2112121P/313F24R0-
00P5P0100P   (4911)
2003/04: 17⁰G, 17⁰GF, 19⁸GF, 16⁵GF, 21⁸GS, 19⁰GS, 16¹S, 16⁰G,
16⁹G, 16⁸S,

	Starts	1st	2nd	3rd	Win & Pl
Hurdles	10	1	0	0	2842
Career Total	38	4	5	3	55265
82	1/04	Chep	2m110y	F(0-95)HHdl	SFT	£2842
	6/02	Autl	2m2f110y	Ch	VS	£12368
	12/01	Cagn	2m2f	Hdl	SFT	£6719
	10/01	Toul	2m1f110y	Ch	GD	£4850
	8/01	Toul	2m1f110y	Ch	GD	£1649
	7/01	Auri	2m1f110y	Ch	GD	£1649

Total win prize-money £30077

Going: Sf: 1-2 GS: 0-2 Gd: 0-3 GF: - Fm: 0-3
Distance: 2m/2m3: 1-7 2m4-2m7: 0-3 3m+: 0-0
Track: LH: 1-4 RH: 0-6 Tight: 0-0 Gall: 0-2
Aids: Bl: 1-7 Vi: 0-2 Tstrap: 0-0 Ckp: 0-0
Best Rating: 87 11/02 Ayr 2m   soft Ch

Moderate ex-French hurdler/chaser; successful over hurdles and four times over fences in France; best at around two miles; acts on good and soft ground; has worn blinkers and a visor.

Comfortable Call
104   **86+**

6-y-o ch g Nashwan (USA)-High Standard (Kris)
H Alexander Paul J Dixon

Placings:6P00431-42210   (4796)
2003/04: 16⁴G, 19²G, 20²GF, 20¹S, 21⁰G,

	Starts	1st	2nd	3rd	Win & Pl
Hurdles	5	1	2	0	4059
Career Total	12	2	2	1	6811
86	3/04	Newc	2m4f	G(0-95)HHdl	SFT	£2394
74	4/03	MRas	2m1f110yG(0-95)HHdl	GD	£2399

Total win prize-money £4794

Going: Sf: 1-1 GS: 0-0 Gd: 0-3 GF: - Fm: 0-1
Distance: 2m/2m3: 0-1 2m4-2m7: 1-4 3m+: 0-0
Track: LH: 1-3 RH: 0-2 Tight: 0-2 Gall: 1-1
Aids: Bl: 0-0 Vi: 0-0 Tstrap: 1-5 Ckp: 0-0
Best Rating: 86 3/04 Newc 2m4f   soft Hdl

Plating-class hurdler; handed when clear leader fell at the last at Market Rasen in April; successfull in similar event at Newcastle in March and again at Wetherby the following month; suited by a galloping track; stays two and a half miles.

Commanche General (IRE)
97

7-y-o b g Commanche Run-Shannon Amber (IRE) (Phardante (FR))
J F Panvert J F Panvert

Placings:00/443P0614-P   (2080)
2003/04: 23⁸G,

Going: Sf: 0-0 GS: 0-0 Gd: 0-1 GF: - Fm: 0-0
Distance: 2m/2m3: 0-0 2m4-2m7: 0-1 3m+: 0-0
Track: LH: 0-1 RH: 0-0 Tight: 0-1 Gall: 0-0
Aids: Bl: 0-0 Vi: 0-0 Tstrap: 0-0 Ckp: 0-0
Best Rating: 97 3/03 MRas 2m5f110y   gd-sft Hdl

Moderate novice hurdler; all the way winner at Market Rasen in March 2003; suited by cut; stays two miles five.

Commanche Hero (IRE)
108(105h)   (92h)**105**

11-y-o ch g Cardinal Flower-Fair Bavard (Le Bavard (FR))
R J Price Pete Holder

Placings:104/64F0043/00/00F3F46334/3P050123-
2221153203   (4701)
2003/04: 25²GS, 25²GF, 24²GF, 24¹GF, 24¹G, 25⁵G, 24³GF,
30²GS, 32⁰G, 22³G,

	Starts	1st	2nd	3rd	Win & Pl
Hurdles	2	0	1	0	1076
Chases	8	2	3	1	19423
Career Total	40	4	5	8	29679
105	10/03	Bang	3m110y	D(0-120)HCh	SFT	£10968
103	9/03	Hntg	3m	E(0-110)HCh	G-F	£3101
85	3/03	Hntg	3m	F(0-95)HCh	GD	£3477
103	1/98	Font	2m2f	H NHF	SFT	£1434

Total win prize-money £18982

Going: Sf: 0-0 GS: 0-2 Gd: 1-4 GF: - Fm: 1-4
Distance: 2m/2m3: 0-0 2m4-2m7: 0-1 3m+: 2-9
Track: LH: 1-4 RH: 1-5 Tight: 1-3 Gall: 1-2
Aids: Bl: 0-0 Vi: 0-0 Tstrap: 0-0 Ckp: 0-0
Best Rating: 105 11/03 Hntg 3m6f110y gd-sft Ch

Plating-class hurdler; has really come into his own since being sent chasing in 2003 winning twice at Huntingdon; best effort when landing Class D handicap at Bangor in October; stays three miles; acts on good ground and softer.

Commanche Jim (IRE)
107(85h)   (103h)**120**

8-y-o b g Commanche Run-On A Dream (Balinger)
R H Alner David O Moon

Placings:5/0/0644145P0/4F215116-32P5364   (4734)
2003/04: 26⁹G, 29²G, 25⁸G, 27⁵GS, 26⁹HY, 29⁶GS, 26⁴G,

	Starts	1st	2nd	3rd	Win & Pl
Chases	7	0	2	2	3350
Career Total	26	4	2	2	21976
120	3/03	Font	3m2f110yE(0-110)HCh	SFT	£4381
107	2/03	Tntn	3m	D(0-115)HCh	SFT	£5765
103	12/02	Folk	2m5f	F(0-95)HCh	SFT	£3493
101	12/01	Plum	3m1f110yE(0-105)HHdl	SFT	£2418

Total win prize-money £16060

Going: Sf: 0-1 GS: 0-2 Gd: 0-4 GF: - Fm: 0-0
Distance: 2m/2m3: 0-0 2m4-2m7: 0-0 3m+: 0-7
Track: LH: 0-5 RH: 0-2 Tight: 0-3 Gall: 0-0
Aids: Bl: 0-0 Vi: 0-0 Tstrap: 0-0 Ckp: 0-0
Best Rating: 120 2/04 Chep 3m2f110y heavy Ch

Modest staying chaser; won back-to-back handicaps February 2003; sound effort when close third in heavy

ground over extended 3m 2f at Chepstow February 2004; acts on soft ground.

Commanche Quest (IRE)

107(102h)   (104h)**111**

8-y-o b g Commanche Run-Conna Dodger (IRE) (Kemal (FR))
Mrs M Reveley The Eleven O'Clock Club

Placings:642534/35F6P34-12342   (3359)
2003/04: 25¹G, 24²GS, 25³G, 25⁴S, 25²S,

	Starts	1st	2nd	3rd	Win & Pl
Hurdles	1	0	1	0	792
Chases	4	1	1	1	7649
Career Total	18	1	3	4	13404
106 5/03 Hexm 3m1f		E Ch		GD	£3870
			Total win prize-money £3871

Going:	Sf: 0-2 GS: 0-1 Gd: 1-2 GF: - Fm: 0-0
Distance:	2m/2m3: 0-0 2m4-2m7: 0-0 3m+: 1-5
Track:	LH: 1-4 RH: 0-1 Tight: 0-2 Gall: 0-0
Aids:	Bl: 0-0 Vi: 0-0 Tstrap: 0-0 Ckp: 0-0
Best Rating:	111 1/04 Kels 3m1f soft Ch

Modest form over hurdles; has shown some ability over fences; stays three miles and acts with give in the ground.

Commanche Spirit (IRE)

10-y-o b g Commanche Run-Emmett's Lass (Deep Run)
Mrs Sue Bell Mrs Sue Bell

Placings:PPP/4P/P   (4392)
2003/04: 27PG,

	Starts	1st	2nd	3rd	Win & Pl
Chases	1	0	0	0	
Career Total	6	0	0	0	0

Going:	Sf: 0-0 GS: 0-0 Gd: 0-1 GF: - Fm: 0-0
Distance:	2m/2m3: 0-0 2m4-2m7: 0-0 3m+: 0-1
Track:	LH: 0-1 RH: 0-0 Tight: 0-1 Gall: 0-0
Aids:	Bl: 0-0 Vi: 0-0 Tstrap: 0-0 Ckp: 0-0
Best Rating:	54 4/02 Sedg 3m3f gd-fm Ch

Commanche Summer

98(94c)   (76c)**83**

10-y-o b m Commanche Run-Royal Typhoon (Royal Fountain)
J D Frost E M Treneer

Placings:0U23/6/460P4/40P40436/046330-424   (0549)
2003/04: 22⁴G, 24²GF, 27⁴GF,

	Starts	1st	2nd	3rd	Win & Pl
Hurdles	3	0	1	0	1393
Career Total	27	0	2	4	5516

Going:	Sf: 0-0 GS: 0-0 Gd: 0-1 GF: - Fm: 0-2
Distance:	2m/2m3: 0-0 2m4-2m7: 0-0 3m+: 0-2
Track:	LH: 0-2 RH: 0-1 Tight: 0-1 Gall: 0-0
Aids:	Bl: 0-0 Vi: 0-0 Tstrap: 0-0 Ckp: 0-0
Best Rating:	83 5/03 Chep 3m gd-fm Hdl

Maiden selling hurdler/chaser; paid the penalty in the ratings for a good effort from a stone out of the handicap in 3m amateur riders hurdle at Chepstow May 2003; seems to handle all types of ground.

Commanche Wind (IRE)

93   **94**

9-y-o b g Commanche Run-Delko (Decent Fellow)
E W Tuer E Tuer

Placings:0/0060300/5F/101324P-5F6   (1143)
2003/04: 22⁵G, 19⁶G, 20⁶GF,

	Starts	1st	2nd	3rd	Win & Pl
Hurdles	3	0	0	0	
Career Total	20	2	1	2	8338
107 5/02 Weth	2m4f110yD(0-120)HHdl	G-S	£3360
96 5/02 Sedg	2m5f110yE Hdl	G-F	£2569
		Total win prize-money £5929

Going:	Sf: 0-0 GS: 0-0 Gd: 0-2 GF: - Fm: 0-1
Distance:	2m/2m3: 0-0 2m4-2m7: 0-3 3m+: 0-1
Track:	LH: 0-1 RH: 0-2 Tight: 0-2 Gall: 0-0
Aids:	Bl: 0-0 Vi: 0-0 Tstrap: 0-0 Ckp: 0-0
Best Rating:	107 7/02 Sedg 2m5f110y gd-fm Hdl

Modest hurdler, stays two and a half miles.

Commercial Flyer (IRE)

102   **96**

5-y-o ch g Carroll House-Shabra Princess (Buckskin (FR))
M C Pipe D A Johnson

Placings:420   (3775)
2003/04: 20⁴S, 19²S, 16⁹G,

	Starts	1st	2nd	3rd	Win & Pl
Hurdles	3	0	1	0	1136
Career Total	3	0	1	0	1136

Going:	Sf: 0-2 GS: 0-0 Gd: 0-1 GF: - Fm: 0-0
Distance:	2m/2m3: 0-2 2m4-2m7: 0-1 3m+: 0-0
Track:	LH: 0-1 RH: 0-2 Tight: 0-0 Gall: 0-0
Aids:	Bl: 0-0 Vi: 0-0 Tstrap: 0-0 Ckp: 0-0
Best Rating:	96 2/04 Extr 2m3f soft Hdl

Novice hurdler; half-brother to stable's very smart Our Vic; well regarded; showed promise on his debut at Chepstow over two miles four.

Common Girl (IRE)

83

6-y-o gr m Roselier (FR)-Rumups Debut (IRE) (Good Thyne (USA))
O Brennan J W Hardy

Placings:53-04   (4407)
2003/04: 16⁶GS, 16⁴G,

	Starts	1st	2nd	3rd	Win & Pl
NH Flat	2	0	0	0	0
Career Total	4	0	0	1	272

Going:	Sf: 0-0 GS: 0-1 Gd: 0-1 GF: - Fm: 0-0
Distance:	2m/2m3: 0-2 2m4-2m7: 0-0 3m+: 0-0
Track:	LH: 0-0 RH: 0-0 Tight: 0-0 Gall: 0-2
Aids:	Bl: 0-0 Vi: 0-0 Tstrap: 0-0 Ckp: 0-0
Best Rating:	87 3/04 Hntg 2m110y good NHF

Moderate bumper performer; has shown some ability on a sound surface.

Commonwealth (IRE)

105   **94**

8-y-o b g Common Grounds-Silver Slipper (Indian Ridge)

Mrs J Candlish J T Summerfield

Placings:20/12225/0/45   (3844)
2003/04: 17⁴G, 17⁵GS,

	Starts	1st	2nd	3rd	Win & Pl
Hurdles	2	0	0	0	308
Career Total	10	1	4	0	6227
103 5/00 Kels	2m110y E Hdl	GD	£2380
		Total win prize-money £2380

Going:	Sf: 0-0 GS: 0-1 Gd: 0-1 GF: - Fm: 0-0
Distance:	2m/2m3: 0-2 2m4-2m7: 0-0 3m+: 0-0
Track:	LH: 0-1 RH: 0-1 Tight: 0-1 Gall: 0-0
Aids:	Bl: 0-0 Vi: 0-0 Tstrap: 0-0 Ckp: 0-0
Best Rating:	103 2/01 Muss 2m good Hdl

Useful juvenile hurdler but lightly-raced since; effective at 2m.

Compadre

97(92h)   (84h)**93**

6-y-o gr g Environment Friend-Cardinal Press (Sharrood (USA))
P Beaumont J Stephenson

Placings:P5-443335   (3884)
2003/04: 16⁵G, 16⁴GF, 16⁴GF, 16³GF, 16³G, 16⁵G,

	Starts	1st	2nd	3rd	Win & Pl
Hurdles	3	0	0	0	759
Chases	4	0	0	3	1748
Career Total	8	0	0	3	2507

Going:	Sf: 0-0 GS: 0-0 Gd: 0-5 GF: - Fm: 0-2
Distance:	2m/2m3: 0-7 2m4-2m7: 0-0 3m+: 0-0
Track:	LH: 0-4 RH: 0-3 Tight: 0-3 Gall: 0-2
Aids:	Bl: 0-0 Vi: 0-0 Tstrap: 0-0 Ckp: 0-0
Best Rating:	93 1/04 Donc 2m110y good Ch

Maiden hurdler/novice chaser; best effort when well beaten third in novices' handicap at Doncaster in January.

Companion

6-y-o b m Most Welcome-Benazir (High Top)
T D McCarthy (Miss Gay Kelleway 9/9) Custom Racing

Placings:P   (2777)
2003/04: 17PGS,

	Starts	1st	2nd	3rd	Win & Pl
Hurdles	1	0	0	0	
Career Total	1	0	0	0	

Going:	Sf: 0-0 GS: 0-1 Gd: 0-0 GF: - Fm: 0-0
Distance:	2m/2m3: 0-1 2m4-2m7: 0-0 3m+: 0-0
Track:	LH: 0-0 RH: 0-1 Tight: 0-1 Gall: 0-0
Aids:	Bl: 0-0 Vi: 0-0 Tstrap: 0-0 Ckp: 0-1

Complete Outsider

66   **27**

6-y-o b g Opera Ghost-Alice Passthorn (Rapid Pass)
Nick Williams Mike Ford

Placings:13U0   (4490)
2003/04: 17¹GF, 16³GS, 24⁴G, 16⁹G,

	Starts	1st	2nd	3rd	Win & Pl
NH Flat	2	1	0	1	2689
Hurdles	2	0	0	0	0
Career Total	4	1	0	1	2689
88 10/03 Extr	2m1f	H NHF	G-F	£2373
		Total win prize-money £2373

Going: Sf: 0-0 GS: 0-0 Gd: 0-2 GF: - Fm: 1-2
Distance: 2m/2m3: 1-2 2m4-2m7: 0-0 3m+: 0-1
Track: LH: 0-2 RH: 1-2 Tight: 0-1 Gall: 0-0
Aids: Bl: 0-0 Vi: 0-0 Tstrap: 0-0 Ckp: 0-0
Best Rating: 95 11/03 Worc 2m   gd-fm NHF

Made a winning debut in an Exeter bumper; held since.

Comply Or Die (IRE)
115   150
5-y-o b g Old Vic-Madam Madcap (Furry Glen)
M C Pipe D A Johnson

Placings:11214					(4394)
2003/04: 16¹GF, 21¹GF, 20²GF, 25¹GS, 21⁴G,					

	Starts	1st	2nd	3rd	Win & Pl
Hurdles	5	3	1	0	36086
Career Total	5	3	1	0	36086
134	12/03	Chel	3m1f110yA Hdl		G-S	£17400
123	10/03	Plum	2m5f	E Hdl	G-F	£3423
123	10/03	Chep	2m110y	D Hdl	G-F	£3662

Total win prize-money £24486

Going: Sf: 0-0 GS: 1-1 Gd: 0-1 GF: - Fm: 2-3
Distance: 2m/2m3: 1-1 2m4-2m7: 0-0 3m+: 0-0
Track: LH: 3-5 RH: 0-0 Tight: 0-1 Gall: 1-2
Aids: Bl: 0-0 Vi: 0-0 Tstrap: 0-0 Ckp: 0-0
Best Rating: 150 3/04 Chel 2m5f   good Hdl

Smart novice hurdler; created favourable impression when making winning debut at Chepstow in October 2003; unable to recover from a bad mistake when runner-up in Grade Two at the same course the following month, but won a three mile-one Grade Two at Cheltenham subsequently before a good effort in the Royal & SunAlliance Hurdle; stamina is his strong suit.

Compton Aviator
99   77+
8-y-o ch g First Trump-Rifada (Ela-Mana-Mou)
A W Carroll Gary S Nichol

Placings:5					(1731)
2003/04: 16⁵GF,					

	Starts	1st	2nd	3rd	Win & Pl
Hurdles	1	0	0	0	0
Career Total	1	0	0	0	0

Going: Sf: 0-0 GS: 0-0 Gd: 0-0 GF: - Fm: 0-1
Distance: 2m/2m3: 0-1 2m4-2m7: 0-0 3m+: 0-0
Track: LH: 0-1 RH: 0-0 Tight: 0-0 Gall: 0-0
Aids: Bl: 0-0 Vi: 0-0 Tstrap: 0-1 Ckp: 0-0
Best Rating: 79 10/03 Chep 2m110y   gd-fm Hdl

Compton Chick (IRE)
103(95h)   (96dh)94
6-y-o b m Dolphin Street (FR)-Cecina (Welsh Saint)
J W Mullins New Forest Racing Partnership

Placings:355/42542044-142U3153243P					(2015)
2003/04: 20¹G, 25⁴GF, 20²GF, 26⁰GF, 22³GF, 20¹G, 23⁵GF, 26²GF, 22²GF, 22⁴G, 25³GF, 25⁵GF,					

	Starts	1st	2nd	3rd	Win & Pl
Hurdles	1	0	0	1	732
Chases	11	2	2	3	13779
Career Total	23	2	4	4	17036
94	8/03	Worc	2m4f110yE(0-105)HCh	GD	£4114
75	5/03	Ludl	2m4f	D Ch	GD	£5796

Total win prize-money £9911

Going: Sf: 0-0 GS: 0-0 Gd: 2-3 GF: - Fm: 0-9
Distance: 2m/2m3: 0-2 2m4-2m7: 2-5 3m+: 0-7
Track: LH: 1-5 RH: 1-5 Tight: 1-6 Gall: 0-0
Aids: Bl: 0-0 Vi: 0-5 Tstrap: 0-5 **Ckp: 2-7**
Best Rating: 96 11/02 Leic 2m4f110y heavy Hdl

Moderate chaser; best at two and a half miles, stays three; acts on a sound surface.

Compton Commander
101   90
6-y-o ch g Barathea (IRE)-Triode (USA) (Sharpen Up)
Ian Williams (G A Butler 6/5) Mark Gichero

Placings:000664					(4716)
2003/04: 16⁹GF, 16⁰G, 16⁹GS, 16⁶G, 16⁶G, 21⁴G,					

	Starts	1st	2nd	3rd	Win & Pl
Hurdles	6	0	0	0	438
Career Total	6	0	0	0	438

Going: Sf: 0-0 GS: 0-1 Gd: 0-4 GF: - Fm: 0-1
Distance: 2m/2m3: 0-5 2m4-2m7: 0-1 3m+: 0-0
Track: LH: 0-3 RH: 0-3 Tight: 0-2 Gall: 0-1
Aids: Bl: 0-0 Vi: 0-1 Tstrap: 0-0 Ckp: 0-0
Best Rating: 90 10/03 Aint 2m110y   good Hdl

Moderate hurdler; best at two miles; acts on most ground; sometimes wears a visor.

Comte De Chambord
82(68h)   (28h)59
8-y-o gr g Baron Blakeney-Show Rose (Coliseum)
Mark Campion A M Campion

Placings:305-3060UU6					(4477)
2003/04: 20³G, 21⁰GF, 19⁹G, 16⁰G, 20⁰HY, 21⁰G, 20⁶HY,					

	Starts	1st	2nd	3rd	Win & Pl
Hurdles	4	0	0	1	739
Chases	3	0	0	0	0
Career Total	10	0	0	2	957

Going: Sf: 0-2 GS: 0-0 Gd: 0-4 GF: - Fm: 0-1
Distance: 2m/2m3: 0-1 2m4-2m7: 0-6 3m+: 0-1
Track: LH: 0-5 RH: 0-2 Tight: 0-2 Gall: 0-2
Aids: Bl: 0-0 Vi: 0-0 Tstrap: 0-0 Ckp: 0-0
Best Rating: 92 6/02 Worc 2m   soft NHF

Con Tricks
101   (103h)107
11-y-o b g El Conquistador-Dame Nellie (Dominion)
J W Mullins Shildon Racing

Placings:0/0/6P45F1/42426243/2/1F1					(3100)
2003/04: 20¹GS, 22²S, 26¹G,					

	Starts	1st	2nd	3rd	Win & Pl
Chases	3	2	0	0	6104
Career Total	20	3	4	1	16707
107	12/03	Font	3m2f110yE(0-100)HCh	GD	£2827
103	12/03	Plum	2m4f	F(0-100)HCh	G-S	£3276
103	4/00	Towc	2m5f	F Hdl	GD	£1922

Total win prize-money £8026

Going: Sf: 0-1 GS: 1-1 Gd: 1-1 GF: - Fm: 0-6
Distance: 2m/2m3: 0-0 2m4-2m7: 1-2 3m+: 1-1
Track: LH: 1-1 RH: 0-1 Tight: 2-2 Gall: 0-0
Aids: Bl: 0-0 Vi: 0-0 Tstrap: 0-0 Ckp: 0-0

Best Rating: 107 12/03 Font 3m2f110y good   Ch

Moderate chaser; won at Plumpton in December 2003 after lengthy absence; stays 3m; suited by soft ground.

Conchita
107+f
7-y-o b m St Ninian-Carnetto (Le Coq D'Or)
G A Harker Mrs G E Brewis

Placings:331-1					(0007)
2003/04: 16¹G,					

	Starts	1st	2nd	3rd	Win & Pl
NH Flat	1	1	0	0	1876
Career Total	4	2	0	2	4467
107	4/03	Hexm	2m110y	H NHF	GD	£1876
102	3/03	Hexm	2m110y	H NHF	GD	£2037

Total win prize-money £3913

Going: Sf: 0-0 GS: 0-0 Gd: 1-1 GF: - Fm: 0-0
Distance: 2m/2m3: 1-1 2m4-2m7: 0-0 3m+: 0-0
Track: LH: 1-1 RH: 0-0 Tight: 0-0 Gall: 0-0
Aids: Bl: 0-0 Vi: 0-0 Tstrap: 0-0 Ckp: 0-0
Best Rating: 107 4/03 Hexm 2m110y   good NHF

Jump-bred, third first time in a bumper at Newcastle in January and occupied same position at Carlisle two months later; has since won twice at Hexham; should make her mark over hurdles in time.

Condoyle (IRE)
70   (86h)64
11-y-o b g Rare One-Worthy Gale (Strong Gale)
R J Baker Percy Buckingham

Placings:F5B4335056/64P2-0					(0762)
2003/04: 16⁰G,					

	Starts	1st	2nd	3rd	Win & Pl
Chases	1	0	0	0	0
Career Total	15	0	1	2	2132

Going: Sf: 0-0 GS: 0-0 Gd: 0-1 GF: - Fm: 0-0
Distance: 2m/2m3: 0-1 2m4-2m7: 0-0 3m+: 0-0
Track: LH: 0-1 RH: 0-0 Tight: 0-0 Gall: 0-0
Aids: Bl: 0-0 Vi: 0-0 Tstrap: 0-0 Ckp: 0-0
Best Rating: 86 7/01 Worc 2m4f   good Hdl

Very modest chaser, wears headgear.

Conor's Pride (IRE)
98   (0c)101
7-y-o ch g Phardante (FR)-Surely Madam (Torenaga)
B Mactaggart (Michael Hourigan 12/10) Harlequin Racing

Placings:0P/P006F-003135056600					(4688)
2003/04: 16⁶G, 22⁰Y, 17³GF, 16¹F, 19³F, 17⁵F, 17⁰GF, 16⁵F, 20⁶GF, 16⁶GF, 18⁰G, 16⁰G,					

	Starts	1st	2nd	3rd	Win & Pl
NH Flat	1	0	0	0	0
Hurdles	10	1	0	2	5997
Chases	1	0	0	0	0
Career Total	19	1	0	2	5997
89	8/03	Tram	2m	Hdl	FRM	£4928

Total win prize-money £4929

Going: Sf: 0-0 GS: 0-0 Gd: 0-3 GF: - Fm: 1-8
Distance: 2m/2m3: 1-10 2m4-2m7: 0-2 3m+: 0-0
Track: LH: 0-3 RH: 0-3 Tight: 0-3 Gall: 0-0
Aids: Bl: 0-0 Vi: 0-0 Tstrap: 0-0 Ckp: 0-0
Best Rating: 101 1/04 Muss 2m   gd-fm Hdl

Ex-Irish very moderate winning novice hurdler and novice chaser.

Conquer (IRE)

102   **110**

9-y-o b g Phardante (FR)-Tullow Performance (Gala Performance (ZIM))
H D Daly M Ward-Thomas

Placings:334/3/UP-2F202   (4782)
2003/04: 24²GS, 24ᶠGS, 22²G, 24⁰G, 24²G,

	Starts	1st	2nd	3rd	Win & Pl
Chases	5	0	3	0	3387
Career Total	11	0	3	3	4816

Going:	Sf: 0-0 GS: 0-2 Gd: 0-3 GF: – Fm: 0-0
Distance:	2m/2m3: 0-0 2m4-2m7: 0-1 3m+: 0-4
Track:	LH: 0-0 RH: 0-4 Tight: 0-1 Gall: 0-2
Aids:	Bl: 0-0 Vi: 0-0 Tstrap: 0-0 Ckp: 0-0
Best Rating:	110 4/04 Hntg 3m good Ch

Point winner in the past; hard to keep sound; runner-up in handicap chase at Market Rasen in February and novice event at Huntingdon in April; suited by three miles.

Conroy

102   **93+**

5-y-o b g Greensmith-Highland Spirit (Scottish Reel)
F Jordan D Ancil

Placings:453-02232   (1060)
2003/04: 16⁶G, 16²GF, 16²G, 17³GS, 16²GF,

	Starts	1st	2nd	3rd	Win & Pl
NH Flat	1	0	0	0	0
Hurdles	4	0	3	1	3985
Career Total	8	0	3	2	4403

Going:	Sf: 0-0 GS: 0-1 Gd: 0-2 GF: – Fm: 0-2
Distance:	2m/2m3: 0-5 2m4-2m7: 0-0 3m+: 0-0
Track:	LH: 0-3 RH: 0-2 Tight: 0-2 Gall: 0-1
Aids:	Bl: 0-0 Vi: 0-0 Tstrap: 0-0 Ckp: 0-0
Best Rating:	93 6/03 Strf 2m110y good Hdl

Fair jumping pedigree; has not performed at all badly in bumper and hurdle races.

Constant Husband

11-y-o gr g Le Solaret (FR)-Miss Mirror (Magic Mirror)
R N Bevis Steve Corbett

Placings:00/00062/1F12/4/6   (0289)
2003/04: 20⁶GS,

	Starts	1st	2nd	3rd	Win & Pl
Hurdles	1	0	0	0	0
Career Total	13	2	2	0	8092
91	7/99	MRas	2m4f	F(0-100)HCh	G-F	£3166
94	5/99	Towc	2m110y	E(0-105)HCh	SFT	£3020
				Total win prize-money £6187

Going:	Sf: 0-0 GS: 0-1 Gd: 0-0 GF: – Fm: 0-0
Distance:	2m/2m3: 0-0 2m4-2m7: 0-0 3m+: 0-0
Track:	LH: 0-1 RH: 0-0 Tight: 0-1 Gall: 0-0
Aids:	Bl: 0-0 Vi: 0-0 Tstrap: 0-0 Ckp: 0-0
Best Rating:	94 5/99 Towc 2m110y soft Ch

Constantine

103   **105**

4-y-o gr g Linamix (FR)-Speremm (IRE) (Sadler's Wells (USA))
G L Moore (J S Goldie 30/9) Mrs B Quinn

Placings:60143   (4591)
2003/04: 16⁶GF, 16⁶GS, 17¹HY, 16⁴GS, 16³G,

	Starts	1st	2nd	3rd	Win & Pl
Hurdles	5	1	0	1	4934
Career Total	5	1	0	1	4934
101	1/04	Folk	2m1f110yE Hdl		HVY	£3528
				Total win prize-money £3528

Going:	Sf: 1-1 GS: 0-2 Gd: 0-1 GF: – Fm: 0-1
Distance:	2m/2m3: 1-5 2m4-2m7: 0-0 3m+: 0-0
Track:	LH: 0-1 RH: 1-4 Tight: 1-1 Gall: 0-2
Aids:	Bl: 0-0 Vi: 0-0 Tstrap: 0-0 Ckp: 0-0
Best Rating:	105 3/04 Hntg 2m110y good Hdl

Moderate hurdler; best around 2m; acts on good ground or softer.

Contemporary Art

70   **(0c)66**

6-y-o b g Blushing Flame (USA)-Marie La Rose (FR) (Night Shift (USA))
M C Pipe (J E Hammond 29/6) Cave Equum

Placings:6P101-06PP6   (1506)
2003/04: 20⁰GS, 18⁶G, 20⁶G, 20ᶠGF, 16⁶GF,

	Starts	1st	2nd	3rd	Win & Pl
Hurdles	3	0	0	0	0
Chases	2	0	0	0	0
Career Total	10	2	0	0	8416
4/03	Comp	2m1f110y Ch		GD	£4052
3/03	Lyrh	2m2f55y Hdl		GD	£4364
			Total win prize-money £8416

Going:	Sf: 0-0 GS: 0-1 Gd: 0-2 GF: – Fm: 0-2
Distance:	2m/2m3: 0-2 2m4-2m7: 0-3 3m+: 0-0
Track:	LH: 0-3 RH: 0-0 Tight: 0-1 Gall: 0-0
Aids:	Bl: 0-0 Vi: 0-0 Tstrap: 0-0 Ckp: 0-0
Best Rating:	66 10/03 Uttx 2m gd-fm Hdl

Ex-French hurdler/chaser; looks to have lost his way here.

Continental (IRE)

102f   **96f**

6-y-o ch g Rashar (USA)-Twilight Katie (Stubbs Gazette)
P J Hobbs Aiden Murphy

Placings:6-2   (4447)
2003/04: 16²S,

	Starts	1st	2nd	3rd	Win & Pl
NH Flat	1	0	1	0	658
Career Total	2	0	1	0	658

Going:	Sf: 0-1 GS: 0-0 Gd: 0-0 GF: – Fm: 0-0
Distance:	2m/2m3: 0-1 2m4-2m7: 0-0 3m+: 0-0
Track:	LH: 0-1 RH: 0-0 Tight: 0-0 Gall: 0-0
Aids:	Bl: 0-0 Vi: 0-0 Tstrap: 0-0 Ckp: 0-0
Best Rating:	96 3/04 Wwck 2m soft NHF

Out of a mare who won two bumpers; showed signs of ability at Gowran Park October 2002; promising effort when narrowly beaten at Warwick March 2004; seems sure to go on to better things.

Contraband

113   **145+**

6-y-o b g Red Ransom (USA)-Shortfall (Last Tycoon)
M C Pipe (W J Haggas 16/10) D A Johnson

Placings:311120021   (4844)
2003/04: 16³GF, 17¹GF, 16¹GF, 16¹G, 16²HY, 16⁹G, 21⁰G, 16²G, 17¹G,

	Starts	1st	2nd	3rd	Win & Pl
Hurdles	9	4	2	1	39365

Career Total	9	4	2	1	39365
145	4/04	Chel	2m1f	B Hdl	GD	£9831
134	12/03	Kemp	2m	C Hdl	GD	£6162
114	12/03	Muss	2m	E Hdl	G-F	£3073
128	11/03	Tntn	2m1f	D Hdl	G-F	£4459
					Total win prize-money £23525

Going:	Sf: 0-1 GS: 0-0 Gd: 2-5 GF: – Fm: 2-3
Distance:	2m/2m3: 4-8 2m4-2m7: 0-1 3m+: 0-0
Track:	LH: 1-5 RH: 3-4 Tight: 2-3 Gall: 1-3
Aids:	Bl: 0-0 Vi: 0-0 Tstrap: 0-0 Ckp: 0-0
Best Rating:	145 4/04 Chel 2m1f good Hdl

Very useful novice hurdler; formerly useful middle-distance handicapper on the Flat; completed a hat-trick at the end of 2003; just worn down in Grade 2 at Aintree, but gained compensation at Cheltenham next time; suited by two miles and a quick surface; likes to make the running; keen sort; genuine.

Control Man (IRE)

115   **137+**

6-y-o ch g Glacial Storm (USA)-Got To Fly (IRE) (Kemal (FR))
M C Pipe D A Johnson

Placings:115-13411P   (4641)
2003/04: 17¹G, 20³GS, 21⁴GS, 18¹GS, 20¹S, 24ᴾG,

	Starts	1st	2nd	3rd	Win & Pl
Hurdles	6	3	0	1	47045
Career Total	9	5	0	1	59518
137	3/04	Sand	2m4f110yA HHdl		SFT	£34800
119	2/04	Font	2m2f110yE Hdl		G-S	£3464
114	11/03	NAbb	2m1f	E Hdl	GD	£4280
131	12/02	Chep	2m110y	A NHF	HVY	£9600
116	12/02	Plum	2m2f	H NHF	HVY	£2373
					Total win prize-money £54518

Going:	Sf: 1-1 GS: 1-3 Gd: 1-2 GF: – Fm: 0-0
Distance:	2m/2m3: 2-2 2m4-2m7: 1-3 3m+: 0-1
Track:	LH: 2-4 RH: 1-2 Tight: 2-3 Gall: 0-1
Aids:	Bl: 0-0 Vi: 1-2 Tstrap: 0-0 Ckp: 0-0
Best Rating:	137 3/04 Sand 2m4f110y soft Hdl

Useful novice hurdler; former decent bumper horse; outstayed his rivals when winning the EBF Final at Sandown on testing ground; stays two and a half miles; best on soft ground; tough; has worn a visor.

Conundrum (IRE)

6-y-o ch g Dr Devious (IRE)-Wasabi (IRE) (Polar Falcon (USA))
A C Wilson Cooper Wilson

Placings:O   (1248)
2003/04: 17⁰GF,

	Starts	1st	2nd	3rd	Win & Pl
Hurdles	1	0	0	0	
Career Total	1	0	0	0	

Going:	Sf: 0-0 GS: 0-0 Gd: 0-0 GF: – Fm: 0-1
Distance:	2m/2m3: 0-1 2m4-2m7: 0-0 3m+: 0-0
Track:	LH: 0-0 RH: 0-1 Tight: 0-1 Gall: 0-0
Aids:	Bl: 0-0 Vi: 0-0 Tstrap: 0-0 Ckp: 0-0

Cook O'Hawick (IRE)

94   **82**

7-y-o b g King's Ride-Miner's Yank (Miners Lamp)

L Lungo Ashleybank Investments Limited

Placings:050-26 (3369)
2003/04: 16²GS, 16⁶S,

	Starts	1st	2nd	3rd	Win & Pl
Hurdles	2	0	1	0	1448
Career Total	5	0	1	0	1448

Going:	Sf: 0-1 GS: 0-1 Gd: 0-0 GF: - Fm: 0-0
Distance:	2m2/m3: 0-2 2m4-2m7: 0-0 3m+: 0-0
Track:	LH: 0-1 RH: 0-1 Tight: 0-0 Gall: 0-0
Aids:	Bl: 0-0 Vi: 0-0 Tstrap: 0-0 Ckp: 0-0
Best Rating:	82 5/03 Prth 2m110y gd-sft Hdl

Cookies Bank
91   90

6-y-o b g Broadsword (USA)-Kitty Come Home (Monsanto (FR))
Mrs S D Williams Berry Racing

Placings:5-3U0P (4519)
2003/04: 19³G, 24ᵁGS, 17⁹GS, 22ᴾGS,

	Starts	1st	2nd	3rd	Win & Pl
Hurdles	4	0	0	1	392
Career Total	5	0	0	1	392

Going:	Sf: 0-0 GS: 0-3 Gd: 0-1 GF: - Fm: 0-0
Distance:	2m2/m3: 0-1 2m4-2m7: 0-3 3m+: 0-1
Track:	LH: 0-0 RH: 0-4 Tight: 0-2 Gall: 0-4
Aids:	Bl: 0-0 Vi: 0-0 Tstrap: 0-0 Ckp: 0-0
Best Rating:	90 12/03 Tntn 2m3f110y good Hdl

Showed promise on hurdling debut.

Cool Degree (IRE)

6-y-o br g Arctic Lord-Ballyfin Maid (IRE) (Boreen (FR))
Ferdy Murphy Trevor Hemmings

Placings:44-6 (2177)
2003/04: 22⁶G,

	Starts	1st	2nd	3rd	Win & Pl
Hurdles	1	0	0	0	0
Career Total	3	0	0	0	0

Going:	Sf: 0-0 GS: 0-0 Gd: 0-1 GF: - Fm: 0-0
Distance:	2m2/m3: 0-0 2m4-2m7: 0-1 3m+: 0-0
Track:	LH: 0-1 RH: 0-0 Tight: 0-0 Gall: 0-0
Aids:	Bl: 0-0 Vi: 0-0 Tstrap: 0-0 Ckp: 0-0
Best Rating:	94 3/03 Carl 2m1f soft NHF

Well beaten fourth in weak bumper on debut.

Cool Investment (IRE)
91(108h)   (109h)130

7-y-o b g Prince Of Birds (USA)-Superb Investment (IRE) (Hatim (USA))
R M Stronge A P Holland

Placings:4003333/40211-5FU0P0PP (4508)
2003/04: 20⁵GS, 29⁵S, 29ᵁG, 24⁹GS, 24ᴾS, 26⁹GS, 29ᴾGS, 26ᴾGS,

	Starts	1st	2nd	3rd	Win & Pl
Hurdles	3	0	0	0	0
Chases	5	0	0	0	0
Career Total	20	2	1	4	17619
125 12/02 Newb	2m6f110yD(0-110)HCh		SFT	£5421	

119 12/02 Wwck 3m110y C Ch G-S £7735
Total win prize-money £13156

Going:	Sf: 0-2 GS: 0-5 Gd: 0-1 GF: - Fm: 0-0
Distance:	2m2/m3: 0-0 2m4-2m7: 0-1 3m+: 0-7
Track:	LH: 0-5 RH: 0-3 Tight: 0-1 Gall: 0-3
Aids:	Bl: 0-0 Vi: 0-0 Tstrap: 0-0 Ckp: 0-1
Best Rating:	130 11/03 Plum 3m5f soft Ch

Fair chaser/modest hurdler; stays three miles; acts on most types of ground but suited by soft; has been tried in tongue-tie and blinkers.

Cool Mate (IRE)
95   87

6-y-o br g Montelimar (USA)-Another Advantage (IRE) (Roselier (FR))
Mrs Dianne Sayer (Mrs E Slack 6/1) A Slack

Placings:064P004 (3767)
2003/04: 17⁰G, 17⁵G, 20⁴GS, 20ᴾS, 20⁰GS, 16⁰HY, 17⁴HY,

	Starts	1st	2nd	3rd	Win & Pl
NH Flat	2	0	0	0	0
Hurdles	5	0	0	0	404
Career Total	7	0	0	0	404

Going:	Sf: 0-3 GS: 0-2 Gd: 0-2 GF: - Fm: 0-0
Distance:	2m2/m3: 0-0 2m4-2m7: 0-3 3m+: 0-0
Track:	LH: 0-4 RH: 0-3 Tight: 0-2 Gall: 0-0
Aids:	Bl: 0-0 Vi: 0-0 Tstrap: 0-0 Ckp: 0-0
Best Rating:	87 11/03 Carl 2m4f gd-sft Hdl

Moderate bumper form on good ground or softer.

Cool Monty (IRE)
105   (122h)128+

10-y-o ch g Montelimar (USA)-Rose Ground (Over The River (FR))
A M Balding Guy Luck

Placings:0/44/202/P1P-P1614 (4057)
2003/04: 17⁹GS, 16¹GS, 16⁶GS, 17¹G, 20⁴G,

	Starts	1st	2nd	3rd	Win & Pl
Chases	5	2	0	0	9375
Career Total	14	3	2	0	17584
128 2/04 MRas	2m1f110yD(0-115)HCh		GD	£5324	
115 12/03 Hntg	2m110y E(0-105)HCh		GD	£3010	
103 12/02 MRas	2m1f110yD Ch		SFT	£4784	

Total win prize-money £13119

Going:	Sf: 0-0 GS: 1-3 Gd: 1-2 GF: - Fm: 0-0
Distance:	2m2/m3: 2-4 2m4-2m7: 0-1 3m+: 0-0
Track:	LH: 0-2 RH: 2-3 Tight: 1-2 Gall: 1-2
Aids:	Bl: 0-0 Vi: 0-0 Tstrap: 0-0 Ckp: 0-0
Best Rating:	128 2/04 MRas 2m1f110y good Ch

Modest chaser; recorded third career success with easy wide margin victory at Market Rasen in February; head-strong and best suited by two miles; suited by easy ground.

Cool Roxy
108   121+

7-y-o b g Environment Friend-Roxy River (Ardross)
A G Blackmore A G Blackmore

Placings:00F/P444412216-661553115 (4836)
2003/04: 16⁶GS, 16⁶GF, 16¹G, 21⁵G, 22⁵GS, 20³G, 23¹G, 16¹GS, 21⁵GF,

	Starts	1st	2nd	3rd	Win & Pl
Hurdles	9	3	0	1	18343
Career Total	22	5	2	1	31258
121 3/04 Fknm	2m D(0-120)HHdl		G-S	£6656	

116 2/04 Fknm 2m7f110yD(0-115)HHdl GD £6422
101 10/03 Fknm 2m E(0-105)HHdl GD £3402
105 3/03 Fknm 2m D(0-120)HHdl GD £6207
96 11/02 Fknm 2m E(0-105)HHdl G-S £3415
Total win prize-money £26104

Going:	Sf: 0-0 GS: 1-3 Gd: 2-4 GF: - Fm: 0-2
Distance:	2m2/m3: 2-4 2m4-2m7: 0-4 3m+: 1-1
Track:	LH: 3-6 RH: 0-2 Tight: 3-4 Gall: 0-3
Aids:	Bl: 0-0 Vi: 0-0 Tstrap: 0-0 Ckp: 0-0
Best Rating:	121 4/04 Chel 2m5f110y gd-fm Hdl

Modest hurdler; goes well at Fakenham; stays two miles seven; acts on most ground; likes to race prominently.

Cool Song
103(88h)   (80h)74

8-y-o ch g Michelozzo (USA)-Vi's Delight (New Member)
D J Caro M J Weaver

Placings:5/55-F01P (2548)
2003/04: 22ᶠG, 22⁰S, 25¹G, 28ᴾGS,

	Starts	1st	2nd	3rd	Win & Pl
Hurdles	2	0	0	0	0
Chases	2	1	0	0	3241
Career Total	7	1	0	0	3241
83 11/03 MRas	3m1f E Ch		GD	£3241	

Total win prize-money £3241

Going:	Sf: 0-1 GS: 0-1 Gd: 1-2 GF: - Fm: 0-0
Distance:	2m2/m3: 0-2 2m4-2m7: 1-3 3m+: 1-2
Track:	LH: 0-1 RH: 1-3 Tight: 1-2 Gall: 0-0
Aids:	Bl: 0-0 Vi: 0-0 Tstrap: 0-0 Ckp: 0-0
Best Rating:	91 10/02 MRas 2m1f110y good NHF

Successful on chasing bow in weak event at Market Rasen in November; stays three miles.

Cool Spice
111   119+

7-y-o b m Karinga Bay-Cool Run (Deep Run)
P J Hobbs Celtic Racing

Placings:21305516 (4842)
2003/04: 16²GF, 16¹GF, 16⁹G, 16⁹GS, 17⁵GS, 19⁵GF, 19¹G, 21⁶G,

	Starts	1st	2nd	3rd	Win & Pl
Hurdles	8	2	1	2	22619
Career Total	8	2	1	2	22619
129 4/04 Tntn	2m3f110yE(0-110)HHdl		GD	£3705	
107 10/03 Chel	2m110y D Hdl		G-F	£12971	

Total win prize-money £16676

Going:	Sf: 0-0 GS: 0-2 Gd: 1-3 GF: - Fm: 1-3
Distance:	2m2/m3: 1-5 2m4-2m7: 1-3 3m+: 0-0
Track:	LH: 1-4 RH: 1-4 Tight: 1-1 Gall: 0-2
Aids:	Bl: 0-0 Vi: 0-0 Tstrap: 0-0 Ckp: 0-0
Best Rating:	129 4/04 Tntn 2m3f110y good Hdl

Modest novice hurdler; stays two and a half miles and acts on a sound surface.

Coolbythepool
91   72

4-y-o b g Bijou D'Inde-Alchi (USA) (Alleged (USA))
Ian Williams (M Johnston 28/9) Webtack Racing

Placings:6 (4490)
2003/04: 16⁶G,

	Starts	1st	2nd	3rd	Win & Pl
Hurdles	1	0	0	0	0
Career Total	1	0	0	0	0

Going:	Sf: 0-0 GS: 0-0 Gd: 0-1 GF: - Fm: 0-0
Distance:	2m/2m3: 0-1 2m4-2m7: 0-0 3m+: 0-0
Track:	LH: 0-1 RH: 0-0 Tight: 0-0 Gall: 0-0
Aids:	Bl: 0-0 Vi: 0-0 Tstrap: 0-0 Ckp: 0-0
Best Rating:	**72** 3/04 Strf 2m110y good Hdl

Cooldine King (IRE)
98   90+

5-y-o b g Germany (USA)-Tara's Serenade (IRE)
(Orchestra)
P R Webber Mrs Mary O'Connor

Placings:	f23FP				(4651)

2003/04: 16¹G, 19²S, 21³GS, 16⁶G, 17⁹G,

	Starts	1st	2nd	3rd	Win & Pl
NH Flat	1	1	0	0	1603
Hurdles	4	0	1	1	1569
Career Total	**5**	**1**	**1**	**1**	**3172**
105	11/03	Sand	2m110y	H NHF	GD £1603
			Total win prize-money £1603

Going:	Sf: 0-1 GS: 0-1 Gd: 1-3 GF: - Fm: 0-0
Distance:	2m/2m3: 1-3 2m4-2m7: 0-2 3m+: 0-0
Track:	LH: 0-2 RH: 1-3 Tight: 0-1 Gall: 0-1
Aids:	Bl: 0-0 Vi: 0-0 Tstrap: 0-0 Ckp: 0-0
Best Rating:	**105** 11/03 Sand 2m110y good NHF

Moderate novice hurdler; bumper winner; stays trips of around two and a half miles; suited by ground good or softer.

Coole Presence (IRE)

5-y-o b m Presenting-Eleanors Joy (Sheer Grit)
R Johnson Mrs Fiona Thompson

Placings:	P				(3468)

2003/04: 20⁰GF,

	Starts	1st	2nd	3rd	Win & Pl
Hurdles	1	0	0	0	
Career Total	**1**	**0**	**0**	**0**	

Going:	Sf: 0-0 GS: 0-0 Gd: 0-0 GF: - Fm: 0-1
Distance:	2m/2m3: 0-0 2m4-2m7: 0-1 3m+: 0-0
Track:	LH: 0-0 RH: 0-0 Tight: 0-1 Gall: 0-0
Aids:	Bl: 0-0 Vi: 0-0 Tstrap: 0-0 Ckp: 0-0

Coole Spirit (IRE)
134

11-y-o b g All Haste (USA)-Chocolatebiscuit (Biskrah)
Miss E C Lavelle Coole And The Gang

Placings:	2105/4323F/11/1P-3P				(2989)

2003/04: 29³S, 24⁸G,

	Starts	1st	2nd	3rd	Win & Pl
Chases	2	0	0	1	3524
Career Total	**15**	**4**	**2**	**3**	**29634**
134	1/03	Kemp	3m	D(0-125)HCh	G-S £10871
123	11/01	Uttx	3m	E Ch	SFT £3523
112	10/01	Font	3m2f110yE Ch		G-S £3120
108	12/99	Leic	2m4f110yD Hdl		GD £3665
			Total win prize-money £21179

Going:	Sf: 0-1 GS: 0-0 Gd: 0-1 GF: - Fm: 0-0
Distance:	2m/2m3: 0-0 2m4-2m7: 0-0 3m+: 0-2
Track:	LH: 0-1 RH: 0-1 Tight: 0-1 Gall: 0-0
Aids:	Bl: 0-0 Vi: 0-0 Tstrap: 0-0 Ckp: 0-0
Best Rating:	**134** 1/03 Kemp 3m gd-sft Ch

Useful handicap chaser; returned from a lengthy absence to win at Kempton in January 2003; stays beyond three miles; effective on soft ground.

Coole Venture (IRE)

10-y-o b g Satco (FR)-Mandavard (IRE) (Mandalus)
Mrs Edward Crow J Aled Griffiths

Placings:	66/32				(0509)

2003/04: 24³G, 28²GS,

	Starts	1st	2nd	3rd	Win & Pl
Chases	2	0	1	1	4388
Career Total	**4**	**0**	**1**	**1**	**4388**

Going:	Sf: 0-0 GS: 0-1 Gd: 0-1 GF: - Fm: 0-0
Distance:	2m/2m3: 0-0 2m4-2m7: 0-0 3m+: 0-2
Track:	LH: 0-2 RH: 0-0 Tight: 0-2 Gall: 0-0
Aids:	Bl: 0-0 Vi: 0-0 Tstrap: 0-0 Ckp: 0-0
Best Rating:	**105** 5/03 Strf 3m4f gd-sft Ch

Useful pointer; beaten favourite in hunter chase May 2003.

Coolers Quest
81 (86h)   (69h) 48+

5-y-o b m Saddlers' Hall (IRE)-Lucidity (Vision (USA))
P C Ritchens Mrs K A Davis

Placings:	000045				(4791)

2003/04: 16⁰G, 19⁰GS, 19⁰G, 16⁰S, 16⁴GS, 20⁵G,

	Starts	1st	2nd	3rd	Win & Pl
Hurdles	4	0	0	0	0
Chases	2	0	0	0	240
Career Total	**6**	**0**	**0**	**0**	**240**

Going:	Sf: 0-1 GS: 0-2 Gd: 0-3 GF: - Fm: 0-0
Distance:	2m/2m3: 0-5 2m4-2m7: 0-1 3m+: 0-0
Track:	LH: 0-4 RH: 0-2 Tight: 0-0 Gall: 0-0
Aids:	Bl: 0-0 Vi: 0-0 Tstrap: 0-0 Ckp: 0-0
Best Rating:	**69** 12/03 Extr 2m3f good Hdl

Cooling Castle (FR)
99   88+

8-y-o ch g Sanglamore (USA)-Syphaly (USA) (Lyphard
(USA))
Ronald Thompson B Bruce

Placings:	2P/30/51005				(4603)

2003/04: 16⁵G, 17¹GF, 16⁹GS, 16⁰G, 17⁵G,

	Starts	1st	2nd	3rd	Win & Pl
Hurdles	5	1	0	0	1911
Career Total	**9**	**1**	**1**	**3**	**3146**
88	11/03	Sedg	2m1f	G(0-95)HHdl	G-F £1911
			Total win prize-money £1911

Going:	Sf: 0-0 GS: 0-1 Gd: 0-3 GF: - Fm: 1-1
Distance:	2m/2m3: 1-5 2m4-2m7: 0-0 3m+: 0-0
Track:	LH: 1-4 RH: 0-1 Tight: 1-2 Gall: 0-2
Aids:	Bl: 0-0 Vi: 0-0 Tstrap: 0-0 Ckp: 0-0
Best Rating:	**93** 11/99 Weth 2m good Hdl

Plating-class hurdler; got off the mark in a selling handicap hurdle at Sedgefield; effective on good to firm.

Cooling Off (IRE)
100   91

7-y-o b m Brief Truce (USA)-Lovers' Parlour (Beldale Flutter (USA))

J R Jenkins Ms Sandra Yuill

Placings:	214405P/6PP1550-3P104				(2684)

2003/04: 20³GF, 26⁸GF, 19¹G, 16⁹G, 21⁴GS,

	Starts	1st	2nd	3rd	Win & Pl
Hurdles	5	1	0	1	2718
Career Total	**19**	**3**	**1**	**1**	**8966**
91	11/03	Wwck	2m3f	F(0-100)HHdl	GD £2324
95	12/02	Font	2m2f110yG Hdl		GD £2219
102	10/01	Fknm	2m4f	D Hdl	SFT £3326
			Total win prize-money £7869

Going:	Sf: 0-0 GS: 0-1 Gd: 1-2 GF: - Fm: 0-2
Distance:	2m/2m3: 1-2 2m4-2m7: 0-2 3m+: 0-0
Track:	LH: 1-4 RH: 0-1 Tight: 0-1 Gall: 0-1
Aids:	Bl: 0-0 Vi: 0-0 Tstrap: 0-0 Ckp: 0-0
Best Rating:	**102** 10/01 Fknm 2m4f soft Hdl

Moderate hurdler; suited by two and a half miles; acts on most types of ground.

Coolteen Hero (IRE)
84

14-y-o b g King Luthier-Running Stream (Paddy's Stream)
R H Alner J Browne,Mrs C Robertson,Mrs E Woodhouse

Placings:	612U5U12212/F11222F3233/315B534FP/F52120				
3235/431432253/05425113063/00F32431FF-P				(0056)

2003/04: 25⁸GS,

	Starts	1st	2nd	3rd	Win & Pl
Chases	1	0	0	0	
Career Total	**72**	**11**	**15**	**14**	**61690**
84	11/02	Leic	2m7f110yF(0-100)HCh	GD £3425
91	11/01	Leic	2m7f110yF(0-105)HCh	G-F £3020
92	11/01	Chep	3m	F(0-110)HCh	G-S £2555
106	11/00	Leic	2m4f110yF(0-110)HCh	G-S £2889
110	11/99	Hrld	2m3f	F(0-110)HCh	GD £3525
113	11/98	Plum	2m	E(0-110)HCh	SFT £3442
116	10/97	Bang	2m1f110yE(0-115)HCh	GD £4135
112	9/97	Extr	2m1f110yE(0-115)HCh	G-F £3436
106	4/97	Extr	2m3f110yD(0-125)HCh	FRM £3629
100	2/97	Plum	2m	E Ch	G-S £3303
80	10/96	Tntn	2m110y	E Ch	G-F £2828
			Total win prize-money £36082

Going:	Sf: 0-0 GS: 0-1 Gd: 0-0 GF: - Fm: 0-0
Distance:	2m/2m3: 0-0 2m4-2m7: 0-0 3m+: 0-1
Track:	LH: 0-0 RH: 0-1 Tight: 0-0 Gall: 0-0
Aids:	Bl: 0-0 Vi: 0-0 Tstrap: 0-0 Ckp: 0-0
Best Rating:	**119** 3/98 Folk 2m good Ch

Veteran front-running handicapper; stays three miles; acts on a sound surface, but handles soft.

Coombe Gold (IRE)
87   75

7-y-o b/br g Insan (USA)-Augustaeliza (IRE) (Callernish)
N J Gifford D S Norden & R S Norden

Placings:	064/0				(1919)

2003/04: 21⁰G,

	Starts	1st	2nd	3rd	Win & Pl
Hurdles	1	0	0	0	0
Career Total	**4**	**0**	**0**	**0**	**0**

Going:	Sf: 0-0 GS: 0-0 Gd: 0-1 GF: - Fm: 0-0
Distance:	2m/2m3: 0-0 2m4-2m7: 0-1 3m+: 0-0
Track:	LH: 0-1 RH: 0-0 Tight: 0-1 Gall: 0-0
Aids:	Bl: 0-0 Vi: 0-0 Tstrap: 0-0 Ckp: 0-0
Best Rating:	**75** 4/02 Chep 2m4f gd-fm Hdl

Copeland

118(80c) (113c)**152+**

9-y-o b g Generous (IRE)-Whitehaven (Top Ville)
M C Pipe Professor D B A Silk & Mrs Heather Silk

Placings:211202/3635053/211202U1/0F62-340301 **(4862)**
2003/04: 17^{3}GS, 16^{4}G, 16^{0}G, 17^{3}G, 20^{0}G, 16^{1}GS,

	Starts	1st	2nd	3rd	Win & Pl
Hurdles	5	1	0	1	32350
Chases	1	0	0	1	646
Career Total	**31**	**6**	**7**	**5**	**260146**

152	4/04	Ayr	2m	A HHdl	G-S	£23200
159	4/02	Sand	2m110y	B Hdl	GD	£35700
163	2/02	Newb	2m110y	A HHdl	SFT	£63800
163	1/02	Chel	2m1f	B(0-145)HHdl	HVY	£10257
143	12/99	Sand	2m110y	B HHdl	G-S	£34900
128	11/99	Wwck	2m2f110yD Hdl		GD	£4146

Total win prize-money £172003

Going: Sf: 0-0 GS: 1-2 Gd: 0-4 GF: - Fm: 0-0
Distance: **2m/2m3: 1-5** 2m4-2m7: 0-1 3m+: 0-0
Track: **LH: 1-6** RH: 0-0 Tight: 0-2 Gall: 0-2
Aids: Bl: 0-0 **Vi: 1-6** Tstrap: 0-0 Ckp: 0-0
Best Rating: **163** 2/02 Winc 2m gd-sft Hdl

High-class hurdler; winner of the Tote Gold Trophy and short-head winner from Intersky Falcon in Masai Hurdle at Sandown in 2002; slightly disappointing on chase debut in December 2003; excellent third in the 2004 County Hurdle at Cheltenham and returned to winning ways at Ayr the following month; best over 2m and suited by the ground good or softer; usually wears a visor.

Coppeen Cross (IRE)

103 (84h)**84**

10-y-o b g Phardante (FR)-Greek Opal (Furry Glen)
O Brennan O Brennan

Placings:60/62P6 **(0821)**
2003/04: 21^{6}GF, 20^{2}G, 22^{P}GF, 20^{6}G,

	Starts	1st	2nd	3rd	Win & Pl
Chases	4	0	1	0	1326
Career Total	**6**	**0**	**1**	**0**	**1326**

Going: Sf: 0-0 GS: 0-0 Gd: 0-2 GF: - Fm: 0-2
Distance: 2m/2m3: 0-0 2m4-2m7: 0-4 3m+: 0-0
Track: LH: 0-1 RH: 0-3 Tight: 0-3 Gall: 0-0
Aids: Bl: 0-0 Vi: 0-0 Tstrap: 0-0 Ckp: 0-0
Best Rating: **84** 7/03 MRas 2m4f good Ch

Irish point winner; poor form here including when runner-up in a novices chase at Market Rasen in June 2003.

Copper Shell

101(67h) (46h)**93**

10-y-o ch g Beveled (USA)-Luly My Love (Hello Gorgeous (USA))
Miss A M Newton-Smith Brighton Racing Club

Placings:5P230/400604/504/51210P/553P26/340320-54U6610 **(4525)**
2003/04: 19^{5}G, 20^{4}GS, 24^{U}GS, 21^{6}GS, 26^{6}S, 25^{1}GS, 24^{0}GS,

	Starts	1st	2nd	3rd	Win & Pl
Chases	7	1	0	0	3552
Career Total	**39**	**3**	**4**	**4**	**16360**

79	2/04	Folk	3m1f	F(0-90)HCh	G-S	£3552
107	4/01	Plum	2m1f	E Ch	SFT	£3883
100	1/01	Folk	2m	E(0-105)HCh	HVY	£2912

Total win prize-money £10348

Going: Sf: 0-1 GS: 1-5 Gd: 0-1 GF: - Fm: 0-0
Distance: 2m/2m3: 0-0 2m4-2m7: 0-3 **3m+: 1-4**
Track: LH: 0-3 **RH: 1-4 Tight: 1-4** Gall: 0-1
Aids: Bl: 1-2 Vi: 0-1 Tstrap: 1-3 Ckp: 0-4
Best Rating: **107** 4/01 Plum 2m1f soft Ch

Plating-class chaser; acts on a soft surface; effective at around two miles; often wears cheekpieces and/or a tongue tie.

Copplestone (IRE)

103 **103**

8-y-o b g Second Set (IRE)-Queen Of The Brush (Averof)
W Storey J D Wright

Placings:44/4612U54P1-12445000040PP **(4883)**
2003/04: 16^{1}GF, 16^{1}G, 17^{2}G, 16^{4}G, 17^{4}G, 17^{5}GS, 20^{0}G, 16^{0}S, 19^{0}GS, 16^{0}HY, 18^{4}HY, 19^{0}GF, 20^{P}HY, 17^{P}GS,

	Starts	1st	2nd	3rd	Win & Pl
Hurdles	14	2	1	0	8543
Career Total	**24**	**3**	**2**	**0**	**13075**

103	5/03	Hexm	2m110y	G(0-95)HHdl	GD	£2471
93	4/03	Newc	2m	G(0-95)HHdl	G-F	£2436
87	12/02	Catt	2m	G(0-95)HHdl	G-S	£3623

Total win prize-money £8531

Going: Sf: 0-4 GS: 0-3 Gd: 1-5 GF: - Fm: 1-2
Distance: **2m/2m3: 2-12** 2m4-2m7: 0-2 3m+: 0-0
Track: **LH: 2-9** RH: 0-5 Tight: 0-4 **Gall: 1-3**
Aids: Bl: 0-0 Vi: 0-0 Tstrap: 0-0 **Ckp: 2-14**
Best Rating: **103** 5/03 Hexm 2m110y good Hdl

Plating-class hurdler, likes a left-handed track and goes well at Catterick; suited by two miles; acts on any ground; wears cheekpieces.

Copsale Lad

106 **123**

7-y-o ch g Karinga Bay-Squeaky Cottage (True Song)
N J Henderson Swallow Partnership

Placings:5P-1301 **(4833)**
2003/04: 19^{1}S, 18^{3}GS, 20^{0}S, 21^{1}GF,

	Starts	1st	2nd	3rd	Win & Pl
Hurdles	4	2	0	1	21729
Career Total	**6**	**2**	**0**	**1**	**21729**

123	4/04	Chel	2m5f110yB Hdl		G-F	£17400
122	1/04	Extr	2m3f	E Hdl	SFT	£3796

Total win prize-money £21196

Going: Sf: 1-2 GS: 0-1 Gd: 0-0 GF: - Fm: 1-1
Distance: 2m/2m3: 1-2 2m4-2m7: 1-2 3m+: 0-0
Track: LH: 1-2 RH: 1-2 Tight: 0-1 **Gall: 1-1**
Aids: Bl: 0-0 Vi: 0-0 Tstrap: 0-0 Ckp: 0-0
Best Rating: **123** 4/04 Chel 2m5f110y gd-fm Hdl

Fair novice hurdler; won his first start for Nicky Henderson, but held in third on next start; previously suffered from heart problems; stays two miles five; effective on any ground.

Coq De Mirande (FR)

(113h)**106**

10-y-o gr g Gairloch-Carmonera (FR) (Carmont (FR))
Miss K Marks (A L T Moore 4/10) Nick Shutts

Placings:FF1/P344F/11221/P-L0266RP **(2824)**
2003/04: 17^{L}F, 17^{0}GF, 16^{2}GF, 16^{6}G, 16^{6}GF, 16^{R}GF, 16^{P}GF,

	Starts	1st	2nd	3rd	Win & Pl
Hurdles	2	0	1	0	1818
Chases	5	0	0	0	0
Career Total	**21**	**4**	**3**	**1**	**31402**

123	9/01	List	2m	Ch	G-F	£7862
120	6/01	Navn	2m1f	Ch	GD	£7862
115	5/01	Klny	2m1f	Ch	G-F	£6399
100	4/00	DRoy	2m	Hdl	G-F	£2760

Total win prize-money £24885

Going: Sf: 0-0 GS: 0-0 Gd: 0-1 GF: - Fm: 0-6
Distance: 2m/2m3: 0-7 2m4-2m7: 0-0 3m+: 0-0
Track: LH: 0-1 RH: 0-3 Tight: 0-1 Gall: 0-0
Aids: Bl: 0-0 Vi: 0-0 Tstrap: 0-1 Ckp: 0-0
Best Rating: **123** 9/01 List 2m gd-fm Ch

Ex-Irish; former winning novice chaser; showed temperament when refusing to race on British debut in selling hurdle; best around two miles; acts on fast ground; likes to race handily.

Coral Island

92(91h) (93h)**113**

10-y-o b g Charmer-Misowni (Niniski (USA))
R M Stronge Mrs Bernice Stronge

Placings:1130/00600/F016100/001412164P/5U663P1-00 **(3858)**
2003/04: 20^{0}GF, 21^{0}S,

	Starts	1st	2nd	3rd	Win & Pl
Hurdles	1	0	0	0	0
Chases	1	0	0	0	0
Career Total	**35**	**8**	**1**	**2**	**35779**

110	3/03	Newb	2m2f110yD(0-125)HCh		GD	£7085
128	1/02	Donc	2m3f110yD Ch		SFT	£4431
117	12/01	Plum	2m1f	D Ch	GD	£4030
114	12/01	Wwck	2m110y	D Ch	SFT	£4004
117	12/99	Font	2m6f110yC(0-130)HHdl		G-S	£4742
106	10/99	Font	2m6f110yE(0-115)HHdl		GD	£2285
103	9/97	Sedg	2m1f	E Hdl	G-F	£2320
103	8/97	Prth	2m110y	E Hdl	GD	£2276

Total win prize-money £31174

Going: Sf: 0-1 GS: 0-0 Gd: 0-0 GF: - Fm: 0-1
Distance: 2m/2m3: 0-0 2m4-2m7: 0-2 3m+: 0-0
Track: LH: 0-2 RH: 0-0 Tight: 0-1 Gall: 0-1
Aids: Bl: 0-0 Vi: 0-0 Tstrap: 0-0 Ckp: 0-0
Best Rating: **128** 1/02 Donc 2m3f110y soft Ch

Fair chaser; effective at up to two miles six; acts on any ground.

Coralbrook

79f **75f**

4-y-o b g Alderbrook-Coral Delight (Idiots Delight)
Mrs P Robeson Mrs P Robeson

Placings:0 **(4407)**
2003/04: 16^{0}G,

	Starts	1st	2nd	3rd	Win & Pl
NH Flat	1	0	0	0	
Career Total	**1**	**0**	**0**	**0**	

Going: Sf: 0-0 GS: 0-0 Gd: 0-1 GF: - Fm: 0-0
Distance: 2m/2m3: 0-1 2m4-2m7: 0-0 3m+: 0-0
Track: LH: 0-0 RH: 0-1 Tight: 0-0 Gall: 0-1
Aids: Bl: 0-0 Vi: 0-0 Tstrap: 0-0 Ckp: 0-0
Best Rating: **75** 3/04 Hntg 2m110y good NHF

Corazonado (FR)

4-y-o b g Pistolet Bleu (IRE)-Heleda (FR) (Zino)
R H York G W Plummer

Placings:0 **(4936)**

2003/04: 18⁰G,

	Starts	1st	2nd	3rd	Win & Pl
NH Flat	1	0	0	0	
Career Total	1	0	0	0	

Going:	Sf: 0-0 GS: 0-0 Gd: 0-1 GF: - Fm: 0-0
Distance:	2m/2m3: 0-1 2m4-2m7: 0-0 3m+: 0-0
Track:	LH: 0-1 RH: 0-0 Tight: 0-1 Gall: 0-0
Aids:	Bl: 0-0 Vi: 0-0 Tstrap: 0-0 Ckp: 0-0

Corbie Lynn

103   95+

7-y-o ch m Jumbo Hirt (USA)-Kilkenny Gorge (Deep Run)
W S Coltherd   J R Cheyne

Placings: 0232011   (4601)
2003/04: 17⁰G, 16²GF, 16³G, 22²G, 20⁶G, 22¹GS, 22¹GS,

	Starts	1st	2nd	3rd	Win & Pl
NH Flat	1	0	0	0	0
Hurdles	6	2	2	1	9958
Career Total	7	2	2	1	9958
104 3/04	Kels	2m6f110yE Hdl		G-S	£3549
97 3/04	Kels	2m6f110yE (0-110)HHdl		G-S	£3990
		Total win prize-money £7539			

Going:	Sf: 0-0 GS: 2-2 Gd: 0-3 GF: - Fm: 0-2
Distance:	2m/2m3: 0-3 **2m4-2m7:** 2-4 3m+: 0-0
Track:	**LH:** 2-4 RH: 0-2 **Tight:** 2-4 Gall: 0-0
Aids:	Bl: 0-0 Vi: 0-0 Tstrap: 0-0 Ckp: 0-0
Best Rating:	104 3/04 Kels 2m6f110y gd-sft Hdl

Modest novice hurdler; had the run of the race when winning at Kelso in March; narrow but game winner there three weeks later; stays 2m6f; acts on easy ground.

Cordilla (IRE)

101   110+

6-y-o b g Accordion-Tumble Heather (Tumble Wind (USA))
N G Richards   Trevor Hemmings

Placings: 2-0511P1   (4950)
2003/04: 20⁰S, 20⁵S, 20¹S, 17¹HY, 20²G, 20¹GS,

	Starts	1st	2nd	3rd	Win & Pl
Hurdles	6	3	0	0	14095
Career Total	7	3	1	0	14728
110 4/04	Prth	2m4f110yD(0-110)HHdl		G-S	£7046
106 2/04	Carl	2m1f	E(0-105)HHdl	HVY	£3526
96 12/03	Ayr	2m4f	E Hdl	SFT	£3523
		Total win prize-money £14095			

Going:	Sf: 2-4 GS: 1-1 Gd: 0-1 GF: - Fm: 0-0
Distance:	2m/2m3: 1-1 **2m4-2m7:** 2-5 3m+: 0-0
Track:	LH: 1-4 **RH: 2-2** Tight: 0-0 Gall: 0-0
Aids:	Bl: 0-0 Vi: 0-0 Tstrap: 0-0 Ckp: 0-0
Best Rating:	110 4/04 Prth 2m4f110y gd-sft Hdl

Fair form in bumper and over hurdles at up to two and a half miles on soft ground; improved effort when winning at Ayr in December 2003; likely to improve again, especially over three miles.

Core Of Silver (IRE)

86   58

5-y-o b g Nucleon (USA)-My Silversmith (IRE) (Cyrano De Bergerac)
P Monteith   Mrs G Smyth

Placings: 0-0U0   (1878)
2003/04: 17⁰GF, 16ᵁGF, 16⁰G,

	Starts	1st	2nd	3rd	Win & Pl
NH Flat	1	0	0	0	0

	Starts	1st	2nd	3rd	Win & Pl
Hurdles	2	0	0	0	0
Career Total	4	0	0	0	

Going:	Sf: 0-0 GS: 0-0 Gd: 0-1 GF: - Fm: 0-2
Distance:	2m/2m3: 0-3 2m4-2m7: 0-0 3m+: 0-0
Track:	LH: 0-1 RH: 0-1 Tight: 0-1 Gall: 0-0
Aids:	Bl: 0-0 Vi: 0-0 Tstrap: 0-0 Ckp: 0-0
Best Rating:	60 11/03 Kels 2m110y good Hdl

Cork Harbour (FR)

92   97+

8-y-o ch g Grand Lodge (USA)-Irish Sea (Irish River (FR))
P Bowen   Marshall James

Placings: 6/00-U1   (1690)
2003/04: 17ᵁGF, 17¹GF,

	Starts	1st	2nd	3rd	Win & Pl
Hurdles	2	1	0	0	1842
Career Total	5	1	0	0	1842
96 10/03	MRas	2m1f110yG(0-95)HHdl		G-F	£1842
		Total win prize-money £1842			

Going:	Sf: 0-0 GS: 0-0 Gd: 0-0 GF: - Fm: 1-2
Distance:	**2m/2m3:** 1-2 2m4-2m7: 0-0 3m+: 0-0
Track:	LH: 0-1 **RH: 1-1 Tight:** 1-2 Gall: 0-0
Aids:	**Bl:** 1-2 Vi: 0-0 Tstrap: 0-0 Ckp: 0-0
Best Rating:	96 10/03 MRas 2m1f110y gd-fm Hdl

Selling-class hurdler; best around 2m; acts on fast.

Corkan (IRE)

89   71

10-y-o b g Torus-Broad Tab (Cantab)
J Cullinan   D G Marshall

Placings: 066P/533P4/2P441/125P-00PUP   (1816)
2003/04: 20⁰G, 25⁰GF, 23⁶GF, 26ᵁGF, 24²G,

	Starts	1st	2nd	3rd	Win & Pl
Chases	5	0	0	0	
Career Total	23	2	2	2	9891
91 5/02	Font	3m2f110yE(0-105)HCh		G-F	£3514
83 3/02	Plum	3m2f	F(0-95)HCh	GD	£2509
		Total win prize-money £6023			

Going:	Sf: 0-0 GS: 0-0 Gd: 0-2 GF: - Fm: 0-3
Distance:	2m/2m3: 0-0 2m4-2m7: 0-1 3m+: 0-4
Track:	LH: 0-3 RH: 0-1 Tight: 0-3 Gall: 0-0
Aids:	Bl: 0-0 Vi: 0-0 Tstrap: 0-0 Ckp: 0-2
Best Rating:	91 6/02 Hntg 3m gd-fm Ch

Ex-Irish gelding; modest chaser; won 3m 2f handicaps at Plumpton March 2002 and Fontwell in May; returned to form in first-time cheekpieces and was going well when falling four out in 3m 2f handicap at Newton Abbot August 2003; stays well; acts on ground good and faster.

Corletto (POL)

92   (91h) 95

7-y-o b g Professional (IRE)-Cortesia (POL) (Who Knows)
T R George   B A Kilpatrick

Placings: P65115/3203P-5PP   (0975)
2003/04: 16⁵G, 16⁰GF, 17ᴾGS,

	Starts	1st	2nd	3rd	Win & Pl
Hurdles	1	0	0	0	0
Chases	2	0	0	0	0
Career Total	14	2	1	2	9568
91 4/02	Hrfd	2m1f	D(0-115)HHdl	G-F	£3896
85 3/02	Tntn	2m1f	F(0-95)HHdl	SFT	£2933
		Total win prize-money £6830			

Going:	Sf: 0-0 GS: 0-1 Gd: 0-1 GF: - Fm: 0-1
Distance:	2m/2m3: 0-3 2m4-2m7: 0-0 3m+: 0-0
Track:	LH: 0-3 RH: 0-0 Tight: 0-3 Gall: 0-0
Aids:	Bl: 0-1 Vi: 0-0 Tstrap: 0-0 Ckp: 0-0
Best Rating:	95 11/02 MRas 2m1f110y gd-sft Ch

Moderate chaser; best at around two miles.

Corn Bunting

76   64

7-y-o b/br m Teenoso (USA)-Annie Kelly (Oats)
B N Pollock   Mrs R Hoare

Placings: 5/6   (2029)
2003/04: 17⁶G,

	Starts	1st	2nd	3rd	Win & Pl
Hurdles	1	0	0	0	0
Career Total	2	0	0	0	0

Going:	Sf: 0-0 GS: 0-0 Gd: 0-1 GF: - Fm: 0-0
Distance:	2m/2m3: 0-1 2m4-2m7: 0-0 3m+: 0-0
Track:	LH: 0-1 RH: 0-0 Tight: 0-0 Gall: 0-0
Aids:	Bl: 0-0 Vi: 0-0 Tstrap: 0-0 Ckp: 0-0
Best Rating:	77 6/01 Worc 2m gd-fm NHF

Cornish Gale (IRE)

95 (92h)   (110+h) 133

10-y-o br g Strong Gale-Seanaphobal Lady (Kambalda)
P F Nicholls   C G Roach

Placings: 0/22P/53111/PF0-1120UP   (4195)
2003/04: 22¹GF, 16¹GF, 20²G, 20⁰G, 22ᵁG, 24ᴾG,

	Starts	1st	2nd	3rd	Win & Pl
Hurdles	4	2	1	0	8604
Chases	2	0	0	0	0
Career Total	18	5	3	1	38562
109 5/03	Winc	2m	E Hdl	G-F	£3500
110 5/03	Winc	2m6f	E Hdl	G-F	£3626
126 12/01	Asct	2m	C(0-125)HCh	GD	£10166
139 11/01	Chel	2m4f110yB Ch		GD	£12754
123 11/01	Extr	2m3f110yD Ch		G-F	£5395
		Total win prize-money £35441			

Going:	Sf: 0-0 GS: 0-0 Gd: 0-4 GF: - Fm: 2-2
Distance:	2m/2m3: 1-1 2m4-2m7: 1-4 3m+: 0-1
Track:	LH: 0-2 **RH: 2-4** Tight: 0-0 Gall: 0-1
Aids:	Bl: 0-0 Vi: 0-0 Tstrap: 0-0 Ckp: 0-0
Best Rating:	139 11/01 Chel 2m4f110y good Ch

Fair chaser/hurdler; stays two miles six, but effective at shorter; needs decent ground.

Cornish Jester

95f   90f

5-y-o b g Slip Anchor-Fortune's Girl (Ardross)
P J Hobbs   P J Hobbs

Placings: 60   (4920)
2003/04: 16⁶GS, 16⁰GS,

	Starts	1st	2nd	3rd	Win & Pl
NH Flat	2	0	0	0	0
Career Total	2	0	0	0	0

Going:	Sf: 0-1 GS: 0-1 Gd: 0-0 GF: - Fm: 0-0
Distance:	2m/2m3: 0-2 2m4-2m7: 0-0 3m+: 0-0
Track:	LH: 0-1 RH: 0-1 Tight: 0-0 Gall: 0-1
Aids:	Bl: 0-0 Vi: 0-0 Tstrap: 0-0 Ckp: 0-0
Best Rating:	90 1/04 Hntg 2m110y soft NHF

Cornish Rebel (IRE)

122   **152+**

7-y-o br g Un Desperado (FR)-Katday (FR) (Miller's Mate)
P F Nicholls C G Roach

Placings:*10*-110   (4641)
2003/04: 20¹G, 21¹GS, 24⁰G,

	Starts	1st	2nd	3rd	Win & Pl
Hurdles	3	2	0	0	22974
Career Total	5	3	0	0	34574
152 12/03 Newb 2m5f		A Hdl		G-S	£20300
123 11/03 Chep 2m4f		E Hdl		GD	£2674
138 2/03 Newb 2m110y		A NHF		GD	£11600
				Total win prize-money £34574

Going:	Sf: 0-0 GS: 1-1 Gd: 1-2 GF: - Fm: 0-0
Distance:	2m/2m3: 0-0 2m4-2m7: 2-2 3m+: 0-1
Track:	LH: 2-3 RH: 0-0 Tight: 0-1 Gall: 1-1
Aids:	Bl: 0-0 Vi: 0-0 Tstrap: 0-0 Ckp: 0-0
Best Rating:	152 12/03 Newb 2m5f gd-sft Hdl

Smart novice hurdler; full-brother to Best Mate and Inca Trail; impressive winner of a Grade Two Newbury bumper on his debut, but below form in the Cheltenham bumper of 2003; successful on hurdling debut and won hot Grade One Challow Hurdle at Newbury on his next outing; disappointing at Aintree on quicker ground; stays 2m5f; acts on good, but prefers soft ground; has masses of potential, but is still immature.

Corporate Player (IRE)

94   **101+**

6-y-o b g Zaffaran (USA)-Khazna (Stanford)
Noel T Chance A D Weller

Placings:*6*-155   (4483)
2003/04: 16¹S, 16⁵GS, 18⁵G,

	Starts	1st	2nd	3rd	Win & Pl
Hurdles	3	1	0	0	3532
Career Total	4	1	0	0	3532
101 1/04 Winc 2m		E Hdl		SFT	£3531
				Total win prize-money £3531

Going:	Sf: 1-1 GS: 0-1 Gd: 0-1 GF: - Fm: 0-0
Distance:	2m/2m3: 1-3 2m4-2m7: 0-0 3m+: 0-0
Track:	LH: 0-0 RH: 1-2 Tight: 0-1 Gall: 0-0
Aids:	Bl: 0-0 Vi: 0-0 Tstrap: 0-1 Ckp: 0-0
Best Rating:	101 2/04 Sand 2m110y gd-sft Hdl

Novice hurdler; effective in soft ground.

Corrage (IRE)

106   **90+**

7-y-o b g Corrouge (USA)-Cora Gold (Goldhill)
R T Phillips Michael Gates

Placings:*0/2*   (0990)
2003/04: 22²G,

	Starts	1st	2nd	3rd	Win & Pl
Hurdles	1	0	1	0	1472
Career Total	2	0	1	0	1472

Going:	Sf: 0-0 GS: 0-0 Gd: 0-1 GF: - Fm: 0-0
Distance:	2m/2m3: 0-0 2m4-2m7: 0-1 3m+: 0-0
Track:	LH: 0-1 RH: 0-0 Tight: 0-1 Gall: 0-0
Aids:	Bl: 0-0 Vi: 0-0 Tstrap: 0-0 Ckp: 0-0
Best Rating:	90 7/03 NAbb 2m6f good Hdl

Had one run over hurdles for Nigel Twiston-Davies in February 2002; looked all over the winner until apparently

---

blowing up after refusing to settle early on in 2m 6f maiden hurdle at Newton Abbot July 2003; can take a similar event.

Corrare (IRE)

68   **68**

7-y-o b m Corrouge (USA)-Granig Rarity (Rarity)
J R Boyle John Hopkins (t/a South Hatch Racing)

Placings:*0P03*-P0   (2531)
2003/04: 26²PGF, 21⁰S,

	Starts	1st	2nd	3rd	Win & Pl
Hurdles	2	0	0	0	
Career Total	6	0	0	1	350

Going:	Sf: 0-1 GS: 0-0 Gd: 0-0 GF: - Fm: 0-1
Distance:	2m/2m3: 0-0 2m4-2m7: 0-1 3m+: 0-1
Track:	LH: 0-1 RH: 0-1 Tight: 0-1 Gall: 0-1
Aids:	Bl: 0-2 Vi: 0-0 Tstrap: 0-0 Ckp: 0-0
Best Rating:	68 4/03 Plum 2m5f gd-fm Hdl

Poor hurdler; first sign of ability when third in a moderate Plumpton seller in first-time blinkers in April 2003.

Corrib Eclipse

107f   **121f**

5-y-o b g Double Eclipse (IRE)-Last Night's Fun (IRE) (Law Society (USA))
Jamie Poulton M Ioannou

Placings:*1200*   (4400)
2003/04: 16¹GF, 16²S, 16⁰G, 16⁰G,

	Starts	1st	2nd	3rd	Win & Pl
NH Flat	4	1	1	0	3755
Career Total	4	1	1	0	3755
93 9/03 Worc 2m		H NHF		G-F	£1529
				Total win prize-money £1530

Going:	Sf: 0-1 GS: 0-0 Gd: 0-2 GF: - Fm: 1-1
Distance:	2m/2m3: 1-4 2m4-2m7: 0-0 3m+: 0-0
Track:	LH: 1-3 RH: 0-1 Tight: 0-0 Gall: 0-1
Aids:	Bl: 0-0 Vi: 0-0 Tstrap: 0-0 Ckp: 0-0
Best Rating:	121 3/04 Chel 2m110y good NHF

Staying pedigree; 20/1 shock winner when narrowly beating the odds-on Renvyle in slowly-run Worcester bumper on debut September 2003; acts on fast.

Corrib Lad (IRE)

90   **79**

6-y-o b/br g Supreme Leader-Nun So Game (The Parson)
P J Hobbs Ms C Hehir

Placings:*03*-000   (3079)
2003/04: 17⁰G, 17⁰GS, 16⁰GS,

	Starts	1st	2nd	3rd	Win & Pl
Hurdles	3	0	0	0	
Career Total	5	0	0	1	303

Going:	Sf: 0-0 GS: 0-2 Gd: 0-1 GF: - Fm: 0-0
Distance:	2m/2m3: 0-3 2m4-2m7: 0-0 3m+: 0-0
Track:	LH: 0-2 RH: 0-1 Tight: 0-2 Gall: 0-0
Aids:	Bl: 0-0 Vi: 0-0 Tstrap: 0-0 Ckp: 0-0
Best Rating:	106 3/03 Wwck 2m good NHF

Corrie Mor (IRE)

9-y-o ch g Moscow Society (USA)-Corrie Lough (IRE) (The Parson)

Mrs S E Busby Mrs Susan E Busby

Placings:*0/006P/2P*   (4823)
2003/04: 25²GF, 23⁰GF,

	Starts	1st	2nd	3rd	Win & Pl
Chases	2	0	1	0	337
Career Total	7	0	1	0	337

Going:	Sf: 0-0 GS: 0-0 Gd: 0-0 GF: - Fm: 0-2
Distance:	2m/2m3: 0-0 2m4-2m7: 0-0 3m+: 0-2
Track:	LH: 0-1 RH: 0-1 Tight: 0-1 Gall: 0-0
Aids:	Bl: 0-0 Vi: 0-0 Tstrap: 0-0 Ckp: 0-0
Best Rating:	92 3/04 Catt 3m1f110y gd-fm Ch

Point winner; well beaten runner-up in hunter chase at Catterick in March.

Corries Wood (IRE)

96   **85**

5-y-o b g Corrouge (USA)-Ewood Park (Wishing Star)
J J Lambe (Daniel J Murphy 4/6) Edward O'Connor

Placings:*0*-04235   (1348a)
2003/04: 16⁰G, 16⁴F, 21²GF, 17³G, 17⁵GF,

	Starts	1st	2nd	3rd	Win & Pl
Hurdles	5	0	1	1	1829
Career Total	6	0	1	1	1829

Going:	Sf: 0-0 GS: 0-0 Gd: 0-2 GF: - Fm: 0-3
Distance:	2m/2m3: 0-4 2m4-2m7: 0-1 3m+: 0-0
Track:	LH: 0-2 RH: 0-2 Tight: 0-2 Gall: 0-0
Aids:	Bl: 0-0 Vi: 0-0 Tstrap: 0-0 Ckp: 0-0
Best Rating:	85 8/03 Ctml 2m1f110y good Hdl

Moderate novice hurdler; stays 2m 5f.

Corroboree (IRE)

92(104h)   **(106+h)91+**

7-y-o b g Corrouge (USA)-Laura's Toi (Quayside)
N A Twiston-Davies The Corroborators

Placings:*32000/10*-16   (2571)
2003/04: 16¹G, 20⁶G,

	Starts	1st	2nd	3rd	Win & Pl
Hurdles	1	1	0	0	3437
Chases	0	0	0	0	0
Career Total	9	2	1	1	7806
110 11/03 Kemp 2m		E(0-110)HHdl		GD	£3437
106 11/02 Kemp 2m		E(0-110)HHdl		SFT	£3445
				Total win prize-money £6882

Going:	Sf: 0-0 GS: 0-0 Gd: 1-2 GF: - Fm: 0-0
Distance:	2m/2m3: 1-1 2m4-2m7: 0-1 3m+: 0-0
Track:	LH: 0-0 RH: 1-2 Tight: 0-0 Gall: 0-0
Aids:	Bl: 0-0 Vi: 0-0 Tstrap: 0-0 Ckp: 0-0
Best Rating:	110 11/03 Kemp 2m good Hdl

Moderate hurdler; got off the mark in a small Kempton handicap in November 2002; off for nearly a year when winning the same race in 2003; effective at two miles, but should stay further; acts on most ground; should make a nice chaser.

Coscoroba (IRE)

79   **32**

10-y-o ch m Shalford (IRE)-Tameeza (USA) (Shahrastani (USA))
D W Whillans D W Whillans

Placings:*606/22U00/00*   (4614)
2003/04: 20⁰S, 17⁰G,

	Starts	1st	2nd	3rd	Win & Pl
Hurdles	2	0	0	0	
Career Total	10	0	2	0	1460

Going:	Sf: 0-1 GS: 0-0 Gd: 0-1 GF: - Fm: 0-0
Distance:	2m/2m3: 0-1 2m4-2m7: 0-1 3m+: 0-0
Track:	LH: 0-2 RH: 0-0 Tight: 0-1 Gall: 0-1
Aids:	Bl: 0-0 Vi: 0-0 Tstrap: 0-0 Ckp: 0-1
Best Rating:	81 10/99 Kels 2m110y good Hdl

Cosi Celeste (FR)

85   **87**

7-y-o b g Apeldoorn (FR)-Lemixikoa (FR) (Mendez (FR))
John Allen John Allen

Placings:00P6   (4959)
2003/04: 16⁰G, 16⁰G, 25⁹S, 19⁶G,

	Starts	1st	2nd	3rd	Win & Pl
Hurdles	4	0	0	0	0
Career Total	4	0	0	0	0

Going:	Sf: 0-1 GS: 0-1 Gd: 0-2 GF: - Fm: 0-0
Distance:	2m/2m3: 0-2 2m4-2m7: 0-1 3m+: 0-1
Track:	LH: 0-1 RH: 0-3 Tight: 0-1 Gall: 0-0
Aids:	Bl: 0-0 Vi: 0-0 Tstrap: 0-0 Ckp: 0-0
Best Rating:	87 4/04 MRas 2m3f110y good Hdl

Cosmic Case

112   **112**

9-y-o b m Casteddu-La Fontainova (IRE) (Lafontaine (USA))
J S Goldie The Cosmic Cases

Placings:4000560416/53225101P/12B110665-F12023200000   (4849)
2003/04: 20⁶G, 16¹GS, 16²G, 16⁹G, 16²G, 17³GF, 20²GF, 16⁹S, 16⁸S, 16⁹S, 16⁰G, 16⁹GS,

	Starts	1st	2nd	3rd	Win & Pl
Hurdles	12	1	3	1	16756
Career Total	40	7	6	2	50849

107	5/03	Prth	2m110y	D(0-125)HHdl	G-S	£4696
105	10/02	Kels	2m110y	D(0-120)HHdl	G-F	£8053
103	9/02	Prth	2m110y	D(0-115)HHdl	G-F	£5564
94	8/02	Prth	2m110y	D(0-115)HHdl	G-S	£5434
94	2/01	Kels	2m2f	E(0-115)HHdl	SFT	£6500
94	12/00	Muss	2m	G(0-95)HHdl	GD	£2331
92	2/00	Catt	2m	F(0-95)Hdl	GD	£1928

Total win prize-money £34508

Going:	Sf: 0-3 GS: 1-2 Gd: 0-5 GF: - Fm: 0-2
Distance:	2m/2m3: 1-10 2m4-2m7: 0-2 3m+: 0-0
Track:	LH: 0-4 RH: 1-8 Tight: 0-3 Gall: 0-0
Aids:	Bl: 0-0 Vi: 0-0 Tstrap: 0-0 Ckp: 0-0
Best Rating:	111 8/03 Prth 2m4f110y gd-fm Hdl

Modest hurdler; tends to mix hurdling with Flat; stays two and a half miles, handles most ground; best going right-handed.

Cosmic Flight (IRE)

76   **41**

8-y-o b g Torus-Palatine Lady (Pauper)
N M Babbage Richard Coates

Placings:0/50/30P-0   (0442)
2003/04: 19⁰GF,

	Starts	1st	2nd	3rd	Win & Pl
Hurdles	1	0	0	0	
Career Total	7	0	0	1	260

Going:	Sf: 0-0 GS: 0-0 Gd: 0-0 GF: - Fm: 0-1
Distance:	2m/2m3: 0-2 2m4-2m7: 0-1 3m+: 0-0
Track:	LH: 0-1 RH: 0-1 Tight: 0-0 Gall: 0-0
Aids:	Bl: 0-0 Vi: 0-0 Tstrap: 0-0 Ckp: 0-1
Best Rating:	84 7/02 Worc 2m gd-fm NHF

Cosmic Ranger

90(100h)   (64h)**73**

6-y-o b g Magic Ring (IRE)-Lismore (Relkino)
H Alexander Mrs Hamish Alexander

Placings:6P04004-020PP4F0   (4613)
2003/04: 16⁴GF, 16⁹G, 17²G, 17⁰GF, 21⁶G, 21⁶GS, 16⁴S, 16⁶HY, 16⁹G,

	Starts	1st	2nd	3rd	Win & Pl
Hurdles	4	0	1	0	808
Chases	5	0	0	0	306
Career Total	15	0	1	0	1114

Going:	Sf: 0-2 GS: 0-1 Gd: 0-4 GF: - Fm: 0-2
Distance:	2m/2m3: 0-7 2m4-2m7: 0-2 3m+: 0-0
Track:	LH: 0-7 RH: 0-2 Tight: 0-5 Gall: 0-2
Aids:	Bl: 0-0 Vi: 0-0 Tstrap: 0-0 Ckp: 0-0
Best Rating:	73 1/04 Weth 2m soft Ch

First worthwhile form when runner-up in selling handicap hurdle at Cartmel in May 2003; held over fences.

Cosmic Song

99   **80**

7-y-o b m Cosmonaut-Hotaria (Sizzling Melody)
R M Whitaker Country Lane Partnership

Placings:P4-460   (0618)
2003/04: 16⁴GF, 16⁶G, 19⁰G,

	Starts	1st	2nd	3rd	Win & Pl
Hurdles	3	0	0	0	0
Career Total	5	0	0	0	0

Going:	Sf: 0-0 GS: 0-0 Gd: 0-2 GF: - Fm: 0-1
Distance:	2m/2m3: 0-2 2m4-2m7: 0-1 3m+: 0-0
Track:	LH: 0-2 RH: 0-1 Tight: 0-2 Gall: 0-0
Aids:	Bl: 0-0 Vi: 0-0 Tstrap: 0-0 Ckp: 0-0
Best Rating:	80 5/03 Kels 2m110y good Hdl

Winner of three selling races on the Flat; best race over hurdles on third start when well beaten fourth at Wetherby in May 2003.

Cosmocrat

106   **105**

6-y-o b g Cosmonaut-Bella Coola (Northern State (USA))
R M Stronge Peter J Douglas Engineering

Placings:6F/200F-130P   (4813)
2003/04: 16¹GS, 16⁹HY, 20⁶GS, 16²G,

	Starts	1st	2nd	3rd	Win & Pl
Hurdles	4	1	0	1	4669
Career Total	10	1	1	1	5762

105	11/03	Uttx	2m	E(0-110)HHdl	G-S	£2954

Total win prize-money £2954

Going:	Sf: 0-1 GS: 1-2 Gd: 0-1 GF: - Fm: 0-0
Distance:	2m/2m3: 1-3 2m4-2m7: 0-1 3m+: 0-0
Track:	LH: 1-3 RH: 0-1 Tight: 0-0 Gall: 0-0
Aids:	Bl: 0-0 Vi: 0-0 Tstrap: 0-0 Ckp: 0-0
Best Rating:	105 11/03 Uttx 2m gd-sft Hdl

Modest hurdler; fair performer on the Flat; acts in soft ground.

Cossack Dancer (IRE)

109f   **101f**

6-y-o b g Moscow Society (USA)-Merry Lesa (Dalesa)
M Bradstock The United Front Partnership

Placings:630   (3832)
2003/04: 16⁶S, 16³GS, 16⁰G,

	Starts	1st	2nd	3rd	Win & Pl
NH Flat	3	0	0	1	235
Career Total	3	0	0	1	235

Going:	Sf: 0-1 GS: 0-1 Gd: 0-1 GF: - Fm: 0-0
Distance:	2m/2m3: 0-3 2m4-2m7: 0-0 3m+: 0-0
Track:	LH: 0-2 RH: 0-1 Tight: 0-0 Gall: 0-2
Aids:	Bl: 0-0 Vi: 0-0 Tstrap: 0-0 Ckp: 0-0
Best Rating:	101 12/03 Hntg 2m110y gd-sft NHF

Showed promise in fair bumper on second outing.

Cotopaxi (IRE)

103   **133**

8-y-o b g Turtle Island (IRE)-Ullapool (Dominion)
Miss Venetia Williams Mrs Kathy Stuart

Placings:061440/4015500/004400/0513114-01 (3366)
2003/04: 16⁶GS, 21¹G,

	Starts	1st	2nd	3rd	Win & Pl
Hurdles	2	1	0	0	6191
Career Total	28	6	0	1	39487

133	1/04	Kemp	2m5f	C(0-130)HHdl	GD	£6191
130	8/02	Sthl	2m1f	C(0-130)HHdl	G-F	£5882
129	8/02	MRas	2m3f110y	C(0-130)HHdl	G-S	£6130
116	7/02	Worc	2m4f110y	D(0-125)HHdl	GD	£4046
121	8/00	Gway	2m	Hdl	G-Y	£4692
103	11/99	Navn	2m	Hdl	Y-S	£4004

Total win prize-money £30947

Going:	Sf: 0-0 GS: 0-1 Gd: 1-1 GF: - Fm: 0-0
Distance:	2m/2m3: 0-1 2m4-2m7: 1-1 3m+: 0-0
Track:	LH: 0-0 RH: 1-2 Tight: 0-0 Gall: 0-0
Aids:	Bl: 0-0 Vi: 0-0 Tstrap: 0-0 Ckp: 0-0
Best Rating:	133 1/04 Kemp 2m5f good Hdl

Useful ex-Irish hurdler; effective at up to two and a half miles; acts on fast and soft going.

Cottage Hill

5-y-o b m Primitive Rising (USA)-Celtic Lane (Welsh Captain)
C R Wilson W R Wilson

Placings:00   (4959)
2003/04: 16⁰G, 19⁰G,

	Starts	1st	2nd	3rd	Win & Pl
NH Flat	1	0	0	0	0
Hurdles	1	0	0	0	0
Career Total	2	0	0	0	

Going:	Sf: 0-0 GS: 0-0 Gd: 0-1 GF: - Fm: 0-1
Distance:	2m/2m3: 0-1 2m4-2m7: 0-1 3m+: 0-0
Track:	LH: 0-1 RH: 0-1 Tight: 0-2 Gall: 0-0
Aids:	Bl: 0-0 Vi: 0-0 Tstrap: 0-0 Ckp: 0-0
Best Rating:	29 3/04 Catt 2m gd-fm NHF

Cottam Grange

98   **85**

4-y-o b c River Falls-Karminski (Pitskelly)

M W Easterby Peter Easterby

Placings:6640340   (4879)
2003/04: 16⁶GF, 16⁶S, 16⁴G, 16⁹G, 24³G, 21⁴G, 20⁰GS,

	Starts	1st	2nd	3rd	Win & Pl
Hurdles	7	0	0	1	650
Career Total	7	0	0	1	650

Going: Sf: 0-1 GS: 0-1 Gd: 0-4 GF: - Fm: 0-1
Distance: 2m/2m3: 0-4 2m4-2m7: 0-2 3m+: 0-1
Track: LH: 0-6 RH: 0-1 Tight: 0-2 Gall: 0-1
Aids: Bl: 0-0 Vi: 0-0 Tstrap: 0-0 Ckp: 0-0
Best Rating: 85 3/04 Sedg 2m5f110y good Hdl

Modest form over hurdles at best but ran right up to best over three miles at Hexham in March 2004; may well be capable of better.

Cotty's Rock (IRE)
57f   34f
5-y-o ch g Beneficial-Its Good Ere (Import)
J Howard Johnson Andrea & Graham Wylie

Placings:0   (4885)
2003/04: 17⁰GS,

	Starts	1st	2nd	3rd	Win & Pl
NH Flat	1	0	0	0	
Career Total	1	0	0	0	

Going: Sf: 0-0 GS: 0-1 Gd: 0-0 GF: - Fm: 0-0
Distance: 2m/2m3: 0-1 2m4-2m7: 0-0 3m+: 0-0
Track: LH: 0-0 RH: 0-1 Tight: 0-0 Gall: 0-0
Aids: Bl: 0-0 Vi: 0-0 Tstrap: 0-0 Ckp: 0-0
Best Rating: 34 4/04 Carl 2m1f gd-sft NHF

Cougar (IRE)
92   84
4-y-o b g Sadler's Wells (USA)-Pieds De Plume (FR)
(Seattle Slew (USA))
R Rowe Capt A Pratt

Placings:6062P   (4573)
2003/04: 16⁶S, 16⁰GS, 18⁶G, 19²G, 19ᴾG,

	Starts	1st	2nd	3rd	Win & Pl
Hurdles	5	0	1	0	1499
Career Total	5	0	1	0	1499

Going: Sf: 0-1 GS: 0-1 Gd: 0-3 GF: - Fm: 0-0
Distance: 2m/2m3: 0-5 2m4-2m7: 0-0 3m+: 0-0
Track: LH: 0-4 RH: 0-1 Tight: 0-2 Gall: 0-2
Aids: Bl: 0-0 Vi: 0-0 Tstrap: 0-0 Ckp: 0-0
Best Rating: 84 1/04 Sand 2m110y gd-sft Hdl

Could Be Class
19f
5-y-o b m Gildoran-Olympic Rose (IRE) (Roselier (FR))
A Ennis Peter Crate

Placings:0   (4495)
2003/04: 16⁰G,

	Starts	1st	2nd	3rd	Win & Pl
NH Flat	1	0	0	0	
Career Total	1	0	0	0	

Going: Sf: 0-0 GS: 0-0 Gd: 0-1 GF: - Fm: 0-0
Distance: 2m/2m3: 0-1 2m4-2m7: 0-0 3m+: 0-0
Track: LH: 0-0 RH: 0-0 Tight: 0-0 Gall: 0-0

Aids: Bl: 0-0 Vi: 0-0 Tstrap: 0-0 Ckp: 0-0
Best Rating: 19 3/04 Strf 2m110y good NHF

Could It Be Legal
80   44
7-y-o b g Roviris-Miss Gaylord (Cavo Doro)
P M Rich B Meadmore

Placings:0-U00   (4145)
2003/04: 19ᵁGS, 17ᵁHY, 19⁰G,

	Starts	1st	2nd	3rd	Win & Pl
Hurdles	3	0	0	0	
Career Total	4	0	0	0	

Going: Sf: 0-1 GS: 0-1 Gd: 0-1 GF: - Fm: 0-0
Distance: 2m/2m3: 0-1 2m4-2m7: 0-2 3m+: 0-0
Track: LH: 0-0 RH: 0-3 Tight: 0-1 Gall: 0-0
Aids: Bl: 0-0 Vi: 0-0 Tstrap: 0-0 Ckp: 0-0
Best Rating: 76 12/02 Wwck 2m soft NHF

Couldn't Be Phar (IRE)
97   70
7-y-o ch g Phardante (FR)-Queenford Belle (Celtic Cone)
D R Gandolfo Starlight Racing

Placings:00-3PP   (2851)
2003/04: 16⁵G, 21ᴾS, 19ᴾGS,

	Starts	1st	2nd	3rd	Win & Pl
Hurdles	3	0	0	1	556
Career Total	5	0	0	1	556

Going: Sf: 0-1 GS: 0-1 Gd: 0-1 GF: - Fm: 0-0
Distance: 2m/2m3: 0-1 2m4-2m7: 0-2 3m+: 0-0
Track: LH: 0-0 RH: 0-3 Tight: 0-1 Gall: 0-0
Aids: Bl: 0-0 Vi: 0-0 Tstrap: 0-0 Ckp: 0-0
Best Rating: 71 10/03 Towc 2m good Hdl

Almost refused to race before finishing a remote third on his hurdling debut.

Coulters Candy
92   92
6-y-o ch g Clantime-Heldigvis (Hot Grove)
A C Whillans 7 Up Partnership

Placings:200506-530P   (0783)
2003/04: 16⁵G, 16³GS, 16⁰GF, 20ᴾG,

	Starts	1st	2nd	3rd	Win & Pl
Hurdles	4	0	0	1	724
Career Total	10	0	1	1	1239

Going: Sf: 0-0 GS: 0-1 Gd: 0-2 GF: - Fm: 0-1
Distance: 2m/2m3: 0-3 2m4-2m7: 0-1 3m+: 0-0
Track: LH: 0-1 RH: 0-3 Tight: 0-0 Gall: 0-0
Aids: Bl: 0-0 Vi: 0-0 Tstrap: 0-0 Ckp: 0-0
Best Rating: 93 7/02 Worc 2m good NHF

Modest form in bumpers, suited by fast ground.

Coulthard (IRE)
86(102h)   (112h)102
11-y-o ch g Glenstal (USA)-Royal Aunt (Martinmas)
Mrs P Sly R Brazier

Placings:033/52332FF4151/612162/0320/000F/234353F0/
330423-304052P   (4786)
2003/04: 16³G, 16⁰GS, 16⁴S, 16⁰HY, 16⁵GS, 16²G, 16ᴾG,

	Starts	1st	2nd	3rd	Win & Pl
Hurdles	5	0	0	1	1362
Chases	2	0	1	0	1248
Career Total	49	4	8	12	40253

130 1/99 Wwck 2m   D(0-125)HHdl SFT £2838
121 11/98 Towc 2m   D(0-125)HHdl SFT £2745
112 4/98 Asct 2m110y D(0-110)HHdl SFT £3647
109 3/98 Limk 2m   (0-123)HHdl   SFT £3573
                    Total win prize-money £12806

Going: Sf: 0-2 GS: 0-2 Gd: 0-3 GF: - Fm: 0-0
Distance: 2m/2m3: 0-7 2m4-2m7: 0-0 3m+: 0-0
Track: LH: 0-2 RH: 0-5 Tight: 0-1 Gall: 0-2
Aids: Bl: 0-0 Vi: 0-0 Tstrap: 0-0 Ckp: 0-0
Best Rating: 130 1/00 Chel 2m1f gd-sft Hdl

Modest hurdler/chaser; acts well with cut in the ground; best over two miles; without a win since 1999.

Counsel
79   77
9-y-o ch g Most Welcome-My Polished Corner (IRE) (Tate Gallery (USA))
J C Tuck J C T Racing Club

Placings:000P/10020/P06   (4142)
2003/04: 20ᴾG, 16⁰GF, 24⁶G,

	Starts	1st	2nd	3rd	Win & Pl
Hurdles	3	0	0	0	
Career Total	12	1	1	0	2982

73 8/01 Font 2m4f   F(0-90)HHdl   G-F £2299
                    Total win prize-money £2300

Going: Sf: 0-0 GS: 0-0 Gd: 0-2 GF: - Fm: 0-1
Distance: 2m/2m3: 0-1 2m4-2m7: 0-1 3m+: 0-1
Track: LH: 0-1 RH: 0-2 Tight: 0-1 Gall: 0-0
Aids: Bl: 0-0 Vi: 0-0 Tstrap: 0-0 Ckp: 0-0
Best Rating: 77 12/01 Extr 2m6f110y good Hdl

Has won a couple of point to points and has modest form over hurdles. Should have a change of fortune when switched to fences.

Count Campioni (IRE)
105(108h)   (135h)117+
10-y-o br g Brush Aside (USA)-Emerald Flair (Flair Path)
M Pitman J F Garrett

Placings:11132/123330/13345/0/431   (3705)
2003/04: 24⁴GS, 24³G, 26¹HY,

	Starts	1st	2nd	3rd	Win & Pl
Hurdles	2	0	0	1	4354
Chases	1	1	0	0	6942
Career Total	20	6	2	7	55346

117 2/04 Chep 3m2f110yD(0-125)HCh HVY £6942
126 9/00 Uttx 3m   D Ch   G-S £4381
147 11/99 Newb 2m110y B Hdl   G-F £6453
110 2/99 Fknm 2m4f   D Hdl   G-S £2666
105 1/99 Ludl 2m   H NHF   SFT £1598
105 11/98 Ludl 2m   H NHF   GD   £1276
                     Total win prize-money £23319

Going: Sf: 1-1 GS: 0-1 Gd: 0-1 GF: - Fm: 0-0
Distance: 2m/2m3: 0-0 2m4-2m7: 0-0 3m+: 1-3
Track: LH: 1-3 RH: 0-0 Tight: 0-0 Gall: 0-2
Aids: Bl: 0-0 Vi: 0-0 Tstrap: 0-0 Ckp: 0-0
Best Rating: 152 1/00 Chel 2m5f110y gd-sft Hdl

Former smart staying hurdler/useful novice chaser; off the track for two and a half years with leg trouble prior to running a couple of blinders over hurdles; fine effort on return to fences when winning extended 3m 2f handicap chase in heavy ground at Chepstow February 2004.

Count Fosco

102   **85+**

6-y-o b g Alflora (IRE)-Carrikins (Buckskin (FR))
T J Fitzgerald Lady Lloyd-Webber

Placings:505   (4685)
2003/04: 16⁵G, 20⁰S, 16⁵G,

	Starts	1st	2nd	3rd	Win & Pl
NH Flat	1	0	0	0	0
Hurdles	2	0	0	0	0
Career Total	3	0	0	0	0

Going:	Sf: 0-1 GS: 0-0 Gd: 0-2 GF: - Fm: 0-0
Distance:	2m/2m3: 0-2 2m4-2m7: 0-1 3m+: 0-0
Track:	LH: 0-2 RH: 0-2 Tight: 0-1 Gall: 0-1
Aids:	Bl: 0-0 Vi: 0-0 Tstrap: 0-0 Ckp: 0-0
Best Rating:	87 4/04 Kels 2m110y good Hdl

Count Oski

103(86h)   (92h)**100**

8-y-o b g Petoski-Sea Countess (Ercolano (USA))
M J Ryan The Laodiceans

Placings:0/05500/0FF541P-5U33   (4784)
2003/04: 24⁵GF, 24ᵁG, 24³GF, 24³G,

	Starts	1st	2nd	3rd	Win & Pl
Chases	4	0	0	2	1656
Career Total	17	1	0	2	7540
100 3/03 Asct	3m110y	D(0-110)HCh	GD	£5460

Total win prize-money £5460

Going:	Sf: 0-0 GS: 0-0 Gd: 0-2 GF: - Fm: 0-2
Distance:	2m/2m3: 0-0 2m4-2m7: 0-0 3m+: 0-4
Track:	LH: 0-2 RH: 0-2 Tight: 0-1 Gall: 0-2
Aids:	Bl: 0-1 Vi: 0-0 Tstrap: 0-0 Ckp: 0-0
Best Rating:	100 5/03 Hntg 3m good Ch

Moderate chaser; stays three miles; suited by decent ground; at his best in the spring.

Count The Cost (IRE)

98   **89**

5-y-o ch g Old Vic-Roseaustin (IRE) (Roselier (FR))
J Wade John Wade

Placings:P524   (2403)
2003/04: 17ᴾGF, 21⁵G, 20²G, 17⁴HY,

	Starts	1st	2nd	3rd	Win & Pl
Hurdles	4	0	1	0	1017
Career Total	4	0	1	0	1017

Going:	Sf: 0-1 GS: 0-0 Gd: 0-2 GF: - Fm: 0-1
Distance:	2m/2m3: 0-2 2m4-2m7: 0-2 3m+: 0-0
Track:	LH: 0-3 RH: 0-1 Tight: 0-0 Gall: 0-0
Aids:	Bl: 0-0 Vi: 0-0 Tstrap: 0-0 Ckp: 0-0
Best Rating:	89 11/03 Carl 2m1f heavy Hdl

Modest novice hurdler; probably best effort when runner-up in weak novices' hurdle at Wetherby in November; should stay well.

Count Tirol (IRE)

     (24h)

7-y-o b g Tirol-Bid High (IRE) (High Estate)
J R Payne J R Payne

Placings:00P/0PP   (3638)

2003/04: 19⁰G, 22ᴾS, 19ᴾS,

	Starts	1st	2nd	3rd	Win & Pl
Hurdles	2	0	0	0	0
Chases	1	0	0	0	0
Career Total	6	0	0	0	

Going:	Sf: 0-2 GS: 0-0 Gd: 0-1 GF: - Fm: 0-0
Distance:	2m/2m3: 0-1 2m4-2m7: 0-2 3m+: 0-0
Track:	LH: 0-0 RH: 0-3 Tight: 0-0 Gall: 0-0
Aids:	Bl: 0-0 Vi: 0-0 Tstrap: 0-0 Ckp: 0-0
Best Rating:	24 12/01 Tntn 2m1f gd-sft Hdl

Count Tony

105   (0c)**121+**

10-y-o ch g Keen-Turtle Dove (Gyr (USA))
P Bowen (J Gallagher 11/8) T W Raymond

Placings:412165/1200/02210P/2P0/5F0F30/P-
PP4055111616   (3942)
2003/04: 23ᴾG, 20ᴾGF, 20⁴G, 22⁰G, 21⁵GS, 20⁵G, 22¹G, 22¹G,
21¹G, 20⁶S, 19¹S, 22⁶G,

	Starts	1st	2nd	3rd	Win & Pl
Hurdles	11	4	0	0	18317
Chases	1	0	0	0	0
Career Total	38	8	5	1	40330
121 1/04 Donc	2m3f110yC(0-135)HHdl	SFT	£6968
114 12/03 Kemp	2m5f	C(0-135)HHdl	GD	£6162
107 12/03 Font	2m6f110yE(0-105)HHdl	GD	£2618
96 11/03 MRas	2m4f	G(0-90)HHdl	GD	£1809
117 6/99 Worc	2m4f	C(0-135)HHdl	G-F	£4705
112 5/98 Prth	2m110y	E Hdl	G-F	£2598
110 2/98 Catt	2m	E Hdl	GD	£2332
108 11/97 Ayr	2m	E Hdl	G-S	£2262

Total win prize-money £29455

Going:	Sf: 1-2 GS: 0-1 Gd: 3-8 GF: - Fm: 0-1
Distance:	2m/2m3: 0-0 2m4-2m7: 4-11 3m+: 0-1
Track:	LH: 2-8 RH: 1-3 Tight: 1-3 Gall: 0-0
Aids:	Bl: 0-0 Vi: 0-0 Tstrap: 0-0 Ckp: 4-6
Best Rating:	121 1/04 Donc 2m3f110y soft Hdl

Fair handicap hurdler; having a good season in 2003/4; best on fast ground, but acts in soft; stays two miles six well; effective in sheepskin cheekpieces.

Countash

5-y-o b g Botanic (USA)-Jenny Mere (Brigadier Gerard)
D Burchell (A P James 9/7) Jim Tew

Placings:SPP   (3698)
2003/04: 16⁵G, 16ᴾGF, 17ᴾHY,

	Starts	1st	2nd	3rd	Win & Pl
NH Flat	2	0	0	0	0
Hurdles	1	0	0	0	0
Career Total	3	0	0	0	

Going:	Sf: 0-1 GS: 0-0 Gd: 0-1 GF: - Fm: 0-1
Distance:	2m/2m3: 0-3 2m4-2m7: 0-0 3m+: 0-0
Track:	LH: 0-2 RH: 0-1 Tight: 0-0 Gall: 0-0
Aids:	Bl: 0-0 Vi: 0-0 Tstrap: 0-0 Ckp: 0-0

Countback (FR)

97   **75**

5-y-o b g Anabaa (USA)-Count Me Out (FR) (Kaldoun (FR))
C C Bealby Blake Kennedy Partnership

Placings:6-0P0025   (4958)
2003/04: 17⁰G, 16ᴾS, 16⁶S, 17⁰GS, 16²G, 17⁵G,

		Starts	1st	2nd	3rd	Win & Pl
NH Flat		1	0	0	0	0
Hurdles		5	0	1	0	778
Career Total		7	0	1	0	778

Going:	Sf: 0-2 GS: 0-1 Gd: 0-3 GF: - Fm: 0-0
Distance:	2m/2m3: 0-6 2m4-2m7: 0-0 3m+: 0-0
Track:	LH: 0-2 RH: 0-4 Tight: 0-4 Gall: 0-1
Aids:	Bl: 0-1 Vi: 0-0 Tstrap: 0-0 Ckp: 0-2
Best Rating:	78 4/03 MRas 2m1f110y good NHF

Countess Camilla

109   **114+**

7-y-o br m Bob's Return (IRE)-Forest Pride (IRE) (Be My Native (USA))
K C Bailey The Fingers Crossed partnership

Placings:411-31211P   (4574)
2003/04: 21³GS, 16¹S, 16²GS, 22¹HY, 20¹HY, 21ᴾG,

	Starts	1st	2nd	3rd	Win & Pl
Hurdles	6	3	1	1	13071
Career Total	9	5	1	1	16942
105 2/04 Carl	2m4f	D Hdl	HVY	£4845
114 1/04 Hayd	2m6f	D Hdl	HVY	£4745
105 12/03 Towc	2m	E Hdl	SFT	£2317
110 2/03 Hntg	2m110y	H NHF	GD	£1988
110 1/03 Folk	2m1f110y	H NHF	HVY	£1883

Total win prize-money £15779

Going:	Sf: 3-4 GS: 0-1 Gd: 0-1 GF: - Fm: 0-0
Distance:	2m/2m3: 1-2 2m4-2m7: 2-4 3m+: 0-0
Track:	LH: 1-2 RH: 2-4 Tight: 0-0 Gall: 0-1
Aids:	Bl: 0-0 Vi: 0-0 Tstrap: 0-0 Ckp: 0-0
Best Rating:	114 1/04 Hayd 2m6f heavy Hdl

Useful novice hurdler; future chasing type; stays two and a half miles and acts on both good and heavy ground.

Countess Elton (IRE)

78   **55**

4-y-o ch f Mukaddamah (USA)-Be Prepared (IRE) (Be My Guest (USA))
R E Barr (K A Ryan 6/8) P Cartmell

Placings:000   (2528)
2003/04: 16⁵G, 16⁰GS, 16⁰GS,

	Starts	1st	2nd	3rd	Win & Pl
Hurdles	3	0	0	0	0
Career Total	3	0	0	0	0

Going:	Sf: 0-0 GS: 0-2 Gd: 0-1 GF: - Fm: 0-0
Distance:	2m/2m3: 0-3 2m4-2m7: 0-0 3m+: 0-0
Track:	LH: 0-3 RH: 0-0 Tight: 0-1 Gall: 0-1
Aids:	Bl: 0-0 Vi: 0-0 Tstrap: 0-0 Ckp: 0-0
Best Rating:	52 11/03 Weth 2m gd-sft Hdl

Countess Kiri

96f   **94f**

6-y-o b m Opera Ghost-Ballagh Countess (King's Ride)
P Bowen David J Evans

Placings:634   (0533)
2003/04: 16⁶G, 17³G, 16⁴GF,

	Starts	1st	2nd	3rd	Win & Pl
NH Flat	3	0	0	1	287
Career Total	3	0	0	1	287

Going:	Sf: 0-0 GS: 0-0 Gd: 0-2 GF: - Fm: 0-1
Distance:	2m/2m3: 0-3 2m4-2m7: 0-0 3m+: 0-0
Track:	LH: 0-1 RH: 0-2 Tight: 0-0 Gall: 0-0
Aids:	Bl: 0-0 Vi: 0-0 Tstrap: 0-0 Ckp: 0-0
Best Rating:	94 5/03 Ludl 2m good NHF

Modest form in bumpers.

Countess Point

107f   **110f**

6-y-o ch m Karinga Bay-Rempstone (Coronash)
C L Tizzard Mrs J E Purdie

Placings:2143   (4846)
2003/04: 16²HY, 18¹G, 16⁴S, 17³G,

	Starts	1st	2nd	3rd	Win & Pl
NH Flat	4	1	1	1	5389
Career Total	4	1	1	1	5389
99	2/04	Font	2m2f110yH NHF	GD	£2968

Total win prize-money £2968

Going:	Sf: 0-2 GS: 0-0 Gd: 1-2 GF: - Fm: 0-0
Distance:	2m/2m3: 1-4 2m4-2m7: 0-0 3m+: 0-0
Track:	LH: 1-3 RH: 0-1 Tight: 1-1 Gall: 0-1
Aids:	Bl: 0-0 Vi: 0-0 Tstrap: 0-0 Ckp: 0-0
Best Rating:	110 3/04 Sand 2m110y soft NHF

Full-sister to heavy ground bumper winner Earl's Kitchen; had a hard race when narrowly beaten on debut in heavy ground bumper at Chepstow February 2004; improved on that when winning next time at Fontwell; will stay further over hurdles; acts on both good and soft ground.

Counting

9-y-o ch m Minster Son-Elitist (Keren)
L P Grassick Graham Brookhouse

Placings:P   (0758)
2003/04: 24⁰G,

	Starts	1st	2nd	3rd	Win & Pl
Hurdles	1	0	0	0	
Career Total	1	0	0	0	

Going:	Sf: 0-0 GS: 0-0 Gd: 0-1 GF: - Fm: 0-0
Distance:	2m/2m3: 0-0 2m4-2m7: 0-0 3m+: 0-1
Track:	LH: 0-1 RH: 0-0 Tight: 0-0 Gall: 0-0
Aids:	Bl: 0-0 Vi: 0-0 Tstrap: 0-0 Ckp: 0-0

Country Kris

86   **77**

12-y-o b g Town And Country-Mariban (Mummy's Pet)
B J M Ryall B J M Ryall

Placings:042/4240/3622/0202PP66/560/0201000/00-0P
                                             (4697)
2003/04: 22⁰G, 17³G,

	Starts	1st	2nd	3rd	Win & Pl
Hurdles	2	0	0	0	
Career Total	33	1	7	1	7484
104	10/01	Strf	2m110y	F(0-100)HHdl	G-S	£2303

Total win prize-money £2303

Going:	Sf: 0-0 GS: 0-0 Gd: 0-2 GF: - Fm: 0-0
Distance:	2m/2m3: 0-1 2m4-2m7: 0-1 3m+: 0-0
Track:	LH: 0-1 RH: 0-1 Tight: 0-1 Gall: 0-0
Aids:	Bl: 0-0 Vi: 0-0 Tstrap: 0-0 Ckp: 0-0
Best Rating:	106 11/99 Extr 2m6f gd-sft Hdl

Country Lad

4-y-o br g Rock City-Northern Line (Camden Town)
Ferdy Murphy Mrs R Morley

Placings:P   (4284)
2003/04: 16⁰GS,

	Starts	1st	2nd	3rd	Win & Pl
NH Flat	1	0	0	0	
Career Total	1	0	0	0	

Going:	Sf: 0-0 GS: 0-1 Gd: 0-0 GF: - Fm: 0-0
Distance:	2m/2m3: 0-1 2m4-2m7: 0-0 3m+: 0-0
Track:	LH: 0-0 RH: 0-1 Tight: 0-0 Gall: 0-0
Aids:	Bl: 0-0 Vi: 0-0 Tstrap: 0-0 Ckp: 0-0

Countryside Friend

7-y-o ch g Sabrehill (USA)-Well Proud (IRE) (Sadler's Wells (USA))
D L Williams Miss L Horner

Placings:PP0   (1519)
2003/04: 16⁶GF, 19⁶F, 20⁰G,

	Starts	1st	2nd	3rd	Win & Pl
Hurdles	3	0	0	0	
Career Total	3	0	0	0	

Going:	Sf: 0-0 GS: 0-0 Gd: 0-1 GF: - Fm: 0-2
Distance:	2m/2m3: 0-2 2m4-2m7: 0-1 3m+: 0-0
Track:	LH: 0-1 RH: 0-1 Tight: 0-1 Gall: 0-0
Aids:	Bl: 0-0 Vi: 0-0 Tstrap: 0-0 Ckp: 0-0

Countrywide Star (IRE)

94   **68**

6-y-o ch g Common Grounds-Silver Slipper (Indian Ridge)
C N Kellett J E Titley

Placings:0P/030P-U030   (4774)
2003/04: 17⁰UG, 16⁰GF, 16³GS, 16⁰G,

	Starts	1st	2nd	3rd	Win & Pl
Hurdles	4	0	0	1	388
Career Total	10	0	0	2	818

Going:	Sf: 0-0 GS: 0-1 Gd: 0-2 GF: - Fm: 0-1
Distance:	2m/2m3: 0-4 2m4-2m7: 0-0 3m+: 0-0
Track:	LH: 0-3 RH: 0-1 Tight: 0-3 Gall: 0-0
Aids:	Bl: 0-0 Vi: 0-4 Tstrap: 0-0 Ckp: 0-0
Best Rating:	68 10/02 Strf 2m110y good Hdl

Lightly raced hurdler, third in a ladies' race in October 2002.

County Classic

98   **85**

5-y-o b m Noble Patriarch-Cumbrian Rhapsody (Sharrood (USA))
T D Easterby T J Benson

Placings:2-313642   (3322)
2003/04: 17³GF, 17¹G, 16³G, 19⁶GF, 16⁴GS, 21²GS,

	Starts	1st	2nd	3rd	Win & Pl
NH Flat	3	1	0	2	2049
Hurdles	3	0	1	0	1374
Career Total	7	1	2	2	4179
90	10/03	Sedg	2m1f	H NHF	GD	£1568

Total win prize-money £1568

Going:	Sf: 0-0 GS: 0-2 Gd: 1-2 GF: - Fm: 0-2
Distance:	2m/2m3: 1-5 2m4-2m7: 0-1 3m+: 0-0
Track:	LH: 1-5 RH: 0-1 Tight: 1-4 Gall: 0-0
Aids:	Bl: 0-0 Vi: 0-0 Tstrap: 0-0 Ckp: 0-0
Best Rating:	105 11/03 Newc 2m good NHF

Modest bumper winner; best effort over hurdles when fourth in mares' only novices' event at Wetherby in January.

County Derry

11-y-o b g Derrylin-Colonial Princess (Roscoe Blake)
J R Scott G T Lever

Placings:PP/14523/1425-211P134   (4845)
2003/04: 26²G, 24¹G, 26¹HY, 28⁶G, 26¹G, 26³G, 26⁴G,

	Starts	1st	2nd	3rd	Win & Pl
Chases	7	3	1	1	20800
Career Total	18	5	3	2	34988
132	2/04	Font	3m2f110yH Ch		GD	£4065
120	5/03	Uttx	3m2f	H Ch	HVY	£6682
120	5/03	Uttx	3m	H Ch	GD	£3328
132	5/02	Towc	3m1f	H Ch	SFT	£6857
100	5/01	Strf	3m4f	H Ch	G-F	£2614

Total win prize-money £23549

Going:	Sf: 1-1 GS: 0-0 Gd: 2-6 GF: - Fm: 0-0
Distance:	2m/2m3: 0-0 2m4-2m7: 0-0 3m+: 3-7
Track:	LH: 2-6 RH: 0-0 Tight: 1-2 Gall: 0-3
Aids:	Bl: 0-0 Vi: 0-0 Tstrap: 0-0 Ckp: 1-3
Best Rating:	132 2/04 Font 3m2f110y good Ch

Useful pointer/hunter chaser; third in the 2004 Cheltenham Foxhunters'; has been let down on occasions by his jumping, goes well in cheekpieces; stays well; acts on any ground.

County Flyer

106(95h)   (77+h)**95**

11-y-o b g Cruise Missile-Random Select (Random Shot)
J S Smith R J Heathman (county Contractors) Ltd

Placings:00/P0/43003/44461/P56-1P3P33P   (3526)
2003/04: 25¹GS, 22²PG, 22³G, 24⁴PG, 22³G, 24³G, 23⁰G,

	Starts	1st	2nd	3rd	Win & Pl
Hurdles	2	0	0	2	805
Chases	5	1	0	1	5454
Career Total	24	2	0	5	11712
95	5/03	Hrfd	3m1f110yE(0-105)HCh	G-S	£4940
91	12/01	Extr	2m7f110yE(0-105)HCh	G-S	£3796

Total win prize-money £8736

Going:	Sf: 0-0 GS: 1-2 Gd: 0-5 GF: - Fm: 0-0
Distance:	2m/2m3: 0-0 2m4-2m7: 0-2 3m+: 1-5
Track:	LH: 0-2 RH: 1-5 Tight: 0-2 Gall: 0-0
Aids:	Bl: 0-0 Vi: 0-0 Tstrap: 0-0 Ckp: 0-0
Best Rating:	99 3/99 Asct 2m110y gd-fm NHF

Plating-class chaser; stays beyond three miles and suited by ground good or softer.

Countykat (IRE)

78   **55**

4-y-o b g Woodborough (USA)-Kitty Kildare (USA) (Seattle Dancer (USA))
K R Burke I Russell

Placings:0   (2871)
2003/04: 16⁰S,

	Starts	1st	2nd	3rd	Win & Pl
Hurdles	1	0	0	0	

| Career Total | 1 | 0 | 0 | 0 |

Going:	Sf: 0-1 GS: 0-0 Gd: 0-0 GF: - Fm: 0-0	
Distance:	2m/2m3: 0-1 2m4-2m7: 0-0 3m+: 0-0	
Track:	LH: 0-1 RH: 0-0 Tight: 0-0 Gall: 0-0	
Aids:	Bl: 0-0 Vi: 0-0 Tstrap: 0-0 Ckp: 0-0	
Best Rating:	55 12/03 Wwck 2m	soft Hdl

Fair performer on the Flat; may be the type to do well over hurdles if lasting out.

Courage Under Fire

9-y-o b g Risk Me (FR)-Dreamtime Quest (Blakeney)
C C Bealby T P Radford

Placings:0/65P05/01/53P3336122P/1213P-F252   (4779)
2003/04: 25²S, 23²G, 24⁵G, 24²S,

	Starts	1st	2nd	3rd	Win & Pl
Chases	4	0	2	0	3863
Career Total	28	4	5	5	33142
124 11/02 Font	3m2f110yD(0-125)HCh		G-S	£5726	
124 10/02 MRas	3m1f	C(0-130)HCh	G-S	£10335	
118 2/02 MRas	2m6f110yE(0-105)HCh		SFT	£3444	
102 4/01 Fknm	3m110y H Ch		G-S	£2200	
			Total win prize-money £21706		

Going:	Sf: 0-2 GS: 0-0 Gd: 0-2 GF: - Fm: 0-0	
Distance:	2m/2m3: 0-0 2m4-2m7: 0-0 3m+: 0-4	
Track:	LH: 0-3 RH: 0-1 Tight: 0-1 Gall: 0-1	
Aids:	Bl: 0-4 Vi: 0-0 Tstrap: 0-0 Ckp: 0-0	
Best Rating:	124 11/02 Font 3m2f110y gd-sft Ch	

Modest handicap chaser, stays well and best with cut in the ground; usually wears blinkers.

Coursing Run (IRE)
105   (117h)**130+**

8-y-o ch g Glacial Storm (USA)-Let The Hare Run (IRE) (Tale Quale)
H D Daly The Hon Mrs A E Heber-Percy

Placings:21P5/1-1P16P   (4342)
2003/04: 24¹GS, 30°PGS, 24¹S, 24⁶S, 29°GS,

	Starts	1st	2nd	3rd	Win & Pl
Chases	5	2	0	0	14515
Career Total	10	4	1	0	23552
127 1/04 Newb	3m	D(0-125)HCh	SFT	£7072	
124 11/03 Bang	3m110y	C(0-130)HCh	G-S	£7442	
117 11/02 Sthl	3m110y	E Ch	G-S	£4424	
117 11/01 Chep	2m4f	D Hdl	SFT	£3493	
			Total win prize-money £22433		

Going:	Sf: 1-2 GS: 1-3 Gd: 0-0 GF: - Fm: 0-0	
Distance:	2m/2m3: 0-0 2m4-2m7: 0-0 3m+: 2-5	
Track:	LH: 2-5 RH: 0-0 Tight: 1-2 Gall: 1-1	
Aids:	Bl: 0-0 Vi: 0-1 Tstrap: 0-0 Ckp: 0-0	
Best Rating:	127 1/04 Newb 3m soft Ch	

Fair chaser; third career win at Newbury in January; stays three miles; acts on soft ground; looked progressive until poor effort at Haydock in February latest.

Court Champagne
105   **98**

8-y-o b m Batshoof-Fairfield's Breeze (Buckskin (FR))
R J Price Derek & Cheryl Holder

Placings:611P6/0143/B60F2-01P   (0444)
2003/04: 16°G, 20¹S, 19°GF,

	Starts	1st	2nd	3rd	Win & Pl
Hurdles	3	1	0	0	6877

Career Total	17	4	1	1	18254
98 5/03 Uttx	2m4f110y		D(0-120)HHdl	SFT	£6877
91 5/01 Wwck	2m	E(0-115)HHdl	G-F	£2625
96 2/01 Ludl	2m	E(0-115)HHdl	G-S	£4124
76 6/00 Strf	2m110y	D Hdl	GD	£3250
			Total win prize-money £16876		

Going:	Sf: 1-1 GS: 1-0 Gd: 0-1 GF: - Fm: 0-1	
Distance:	2m/2m3: 0-1 2m4-2m7: 1-2 3m+: 0-0	
Track:	LH: 1-2 RH: 0-1 Tight: 0-0 Gall: 0-0	
Aids:	Bl: 0-0 Vi: 0-0 Tstrap: 0-0 Ckp: 1-3	
Best Rating:	98 5/03 Uttx 2m4f110y soft Hdl	

Moderate hurdler; won in the mud in game style at Uttoxeter in May; equally effective on fast ground; best over two miles but stays further.

Court Emperor
92f   **62f**

4-y-o b g Mtoto-Fairfields Cone (Celtic Cone)
R J Price Derek & Cheryl Holder

Placings:0000   (4213)
2003/04: 14°G, 13°GS, 16°G, 16°G,

	Starts	1st	2nd	3rd	Win & Pl
NH Flat	4	0	0	0	
Career Total	4	0	0	0	

Going:	Sf: 0-0 GS: 0-1 Gd: 0-3 GF: - Fm: 0-0	
Distance:	2m/2m3: 0-2 2m4-2m7: 0-0 3m+: 0-0	
Track:	LH: 0-1 RH: 0-3 Tight: 0-0 Gall: 0-0	
Aids:	Bl: 0-0 Vi: 0-0 Tstrap: 0-0 Ckp: 0-0	
Best Rating:	62 3/04 Kemp 2m good NHF	

Court Empress
88   **80**

7-y-o ch m Emperor Fountain-Tudor Sunset (Sunyboy)
P D Purdy P D Purdy

Placings:0-05   (4929)
2003/04: 17°G, 18⁵G,

	Starts	1st	2nd	3rd	Win & Pl
Hurdles	2	0	0	0	
Career Total	3	0	0	0	

Going:	Sf: 0-0 GS: 0-0 Gd: 0-2 GF: - Fm: 0-0	
Distance:	2m/2m3: 0-2 2m4-2m7: 0-0 3m+: 0-0	
Track:	LH: 0-2 RH: 0-0 Tight: 0-2 Gall: 0-0	
Aids:	Bl: 0-0 Vi: 0-0 Tstrap: 0-0 Ckp: 0-0	
Best Rating:	80 4/04 Font 2m2f110y good Hdl	

Court Leney (IRE)
91(92h)   (83h)**58**

9-y-o b g Commanche Run-Dont Call Me Lady (Le Bavard (FR))
G Prodromou What R U Like Partnership

Placings:0/3001P6UP05   (4750)
2003/04: 26⁵GF, 20⁴G, 24⁸G, 29¹G, 29⁶S, 21⁶GS, 25⁴GS, 24²G, 17°G, 21⁵G,

	Starts	1st	2nd	3rd	Win & Pl
Hurdles	5	0	0	1	366
Chases	5	1	0	1	4160
Career Total	11	1	0	1	4526
11/03 Fknm	3m5f110yF(0-100)HCh		GD	£4160	
			Total win prize-money £4160		

Going:	Sf: 0-1 GS: 0-2 Gd: 1-6 GF: - Fm: 0-1	

Distance:	2m/2m3: 0-1 2m4-2m7: 0-3 3m+: 1-6	
Track:	LH: 0-6 RH: 0-3 Tight: 0-7 Gall: 0-0	
Aids:	Bl: 0-0 Vi: 0-0 Tstrap: 0-0 Ckp: 0-1	
Best Rating:	81 10/03 Sthl 3m2f gd-fm Hdl	

Plating-class performer; stays three miles; acts on good ground.

Court Music (IRE)

5-y-o b/br m Revoque (IRE)-Lute And Lyre (IRE) (The Noble Player (USA))
R E Barr G Thornton

Placings:P   (2087)
2003/04: 17°GF,

	Starts	1st	2nd	3rd	Win & Pl
Hurdles	1	0	0	0	
Career Total	1	0	0	0	

Going:	Sf: 0-0 GS: 0-0 Gd: 0-0 GF: - Fm: 0-1	
Distance:	2m/2m3: 0-1 2m4-2m7: 0-0 3m+: 0-0	
Track:	LH: 0-1 RH: 0-0 Tight: 0-1 Gall: 0-0	
Aids:	Bl: 0-0 Vi: 0-0 Tstrap: 0-0 Ckp: 0-0	

Court Of Justice (USA)
93(110h)   (117h)**83**

8-y-o b g Alleged (USA)-Captive Island (Northfields (USA))
K A Morgan Roemex Ltd

Placings:142/246/143-5401026   (4960)
2003/04: 20⁵GS, 16⁴G, 16⁶S, 16¹S, 16⁹HY, 16²S, 20⁶GS,

	Starts	1st	2nd	3rd	Win & Pl
Hurdles	6	1	1	0	4615
Chases	1	0	0	0	0
Career Total	16	3	3	1	14652
117 1/04 Leic	2m	E(0-110)HHdl	SFT	£3513	
103 12/02 Leic	2m	G Hdl	HVY	£2359	
113 11/00 Weth	2m	D Hdl	SFT	£3308	
			Total win prize-money £9181		

Going:	Sf: 1-4 GS: 1-0 Gd: 0-2 GF: - Fm: 0-0	
Distance:	2m/2m3: 1-5 2m4-2m7: 0-2 3m+: 0-0	
Track:	LH: 0-4 RH: 1-3 Tight: 0-1 Gall: 0-0	
Aids:	Bl: 0-0 Vi: 0-0 Tstrap: 0-0 Ckp: 1-4	
Best Rating:	117 1/04 Leic 2m soft Hdl	

Fair hurdler; stays two to two and a half miles; suited by soft ground; has worn cheekpieces.

Court Ordeal (IRE)

9-y-o ch g Kris-In Review (Ela-Mana-Mou)
R N Bevis Miss N C Taylor

Placings:65304F15/4050P/232P4F/530P0/0   (2791)
2003/04: 17°GS,

	Starts	1st	2nd	3rd	Win & Pl
Hurdles	1	0	0	0	
Career Total	25	1	2	3	5191
93 2/99 Carl	2m1f	E Hdl	HVY	£2346	
			Total win prize-money £2346		

Going:	Sf: 0-0 GS: 0-1 Gd: 0-0 GF: - Fm: 0-0	
Distance:	2m/2m3: 0-1 2m4-2m7: 0-0 3m+: 0-0	
Track:	LH: 0-1 RH: 0-0 Tight: 0-1 Gall: 0-0	
Aids:	Bl: 0-0 Vi: 0-0 Tstrap: 0-0 Ckp: 0-0	
Best Rating:	101 12/99 Hrfd 2m3f110y heavy Hdl	

Court Shareef

119   **143**

9-y-o b g Shareef Dancer (USA)-Fairfields Cone (Celtic Cone)
R J Price Derek & Cheryl Holder

Placings:20FP/2221234236   (4862)
2003/04: 16²GS, 17²GF, 16²G, 20¹GF, 21²GF, 20⁹GF, 20⁴G, 21²G, 20³G, 16⁶GS,

	Starts	1st	2nd	3rd	Win & Pl
Hurdles	10	1	5	2	38934
Career Total	14	1	6	2	39754
129 9/03 Worc 2m4f			C(0-135)HHdl		G-F £5050

Total win prize-money £5051

Going: Sf: 0-0 GS: 0-2 Gd: 0-4 GF: 0-4 Fm: 1-4
Distance: 2m2/2m3: 0-4 **2m4-2m7: 1-6** 3m+: 0-0
Track: LH: 1-8 RH: 0-2 Tight: 0-2 Gall: 0-2
Aids: Bl: 0-0 Vi: 0-0 Tstrap: 0-0 Ckp: 0-0
Best Rating: **143** 4/04 Aint 2m4f   good   Hdl

Smart hurdler; ran a massive race from a stone out of the handicap to finish second in the 2004 Coral Cup; good third in Grade Two novice contest at Aintree next time; well suited by two and a half miles on fast ground.

Courtcard

69   **25**

5-y-o b m Persian Bold-Hafhafah (Shirley Heights)
Mrs Lucinda Featherstone Heart Of England Racing

Placings:P-F0PPP   (3348)
2003/04: 16FGF, 17PGF, 19PGF, 16PS, 21PS,

	Starts	1st	2nd	3rd	Win & Pl
Hurdles	5	0	0	0	
Career Total	6	0	0	0	

Going: Sf: 0-2 GS: 0-0 Gd: 0-0 GF: - Fm: 0-3
Distance: 2m2/2m3: 0-3 2m4-2m7: 0-2 3m+: 0-0
Track: LH: 0-1 RH: 0-4 Tight: 0-3 Gall: 0-1
Aids: Bl: 0-0 Vi: 0-0 Tstrap: 0-0 Ckp: 0-0
Best Rating: **25** 8/03 MRas 2m1f110y   gd-fm   Hdl

Courtelimorr

75   **26**

4-y-o b f Defacto (USA)-Auntie Fay (IRE) (Fayruz)
B S Rothwell Ms Denise S Doyle

Placings:U0P   (1448)
2003/04: 17UGF, 17OGF, 17PGF,

	Starts	1st	2nd	3rd	Win & Pl
Hurdles	3	0	0	0	
Career Total	3	0	0	0	

Going: Sf: 0-0 GS: 0-0 Gd: 0-0 GF: 0-0 Fm: 0-3
Distance: 2m2/2m3: 0-3 2m4-2m7: 0-0 3m+: 0-0
Track: LH: 0-1 RH: 0-2 Tight: 0-3 Gall: 0-0
Aids: Bl: 0-0 Vi 0-0 Tstrap: 0-0 Ckp: 0-2
Best Rating: **30** 8/03 Sedg 2m1f   gd-fm   Hdl

Courtledge

(89h)   **(78h)**

9-y-o b g Unfuwain (USA)-Tremellick (Mummy's Pet)
M J Gingell Going Grey Partnership

Placings:P605040601163/314PPPP-PPP0   (4774)
2003/04: 24PG, 21PGS, 20PS, 16PG,

	Starts	1st	2nd	3rd	Win & Pl
Hurdles	1	0	0	0	0

Chases	3	0	0	0	0
Career Total	24	3	0	2	12904
102 7/02 Wolv	2m4f110yE(0-105)HCh			G-S	£3604
102 4/02 Fknm	2m5f110yE(0-110)HCh			GD	£4114
91 3/02 Fknm	3m110y D Ch			GD	£4165

Total win prize-money £11884

Going: Sf: 0-1 GS: 0-1 Gd: 0-2 GF: - Fm: 0-0
Distance: 2m2/2m3: 0-1 2m4-2m7: 0-2 3m+: 0-1
Track: LH: 0-4 RH: 0-0 Tight: 0-4 Gall: 0-0
Aids: Bl: 0-0 Vi: 0-1 Tstrap: 0-0 Ckp: 0-1
Best Rating: **102** 7/02 Wolv 2m4f110y gd-sft Ch

Coustou (IRE)

4-y-o b g In Command (IRE)-Carranza (IRE) (Lead On Time (USA))
A R Dicken (M A Jarvis 10/8) Mr & Mrs Raymond Anderson Green

Placings:U   (3732)
2003/04: 16UG,

	Starts	1st	2nd	3rd	Win & Pl
Hurdles	1	0	0	0	
Career Total	1	0	0	0	

Going: Sf: 0-0 GS: 0-0 Gd: 0-1 GF: - Fm: 0-0
Distance: 2m2/2m3: 0-1 2m4-2m7: 0-0 3m+: 0-0
Track: LH: 0-0 RH: 0-1 Tight: 0-1 Gall: 0-0
Aids: Bl: 0-0 Vi: 0-0 Tstrap: 0-0 Ckp: 0-0

Covent Garden

102   **132+**

6-y-o b g Sadler's Wells (USA)-Temple Row (Ardross)
J Howard Johnson Ada Partnership

Placings:U60/11111-3   (2591)
2003/04: 22³GS,

	Starts	1st	2nd	3rd	Win & Pl
Hurdles	1	0	0	1	848
Career Total	9	5	0	1	45215
132 3/03 Kels	2m2f	A Hdl		G-S	£17400
129 12/02 Muss	3m	D(0-125)HHdl		G-F	£6760
121 11/02 Aint	2m4f	C(0-130)HHdl		GD	£14300
104 10/02 Carl	2m4f	E(0-100)HHdl		G-F	£2931
78 9/02 Hexm	2m110y	E(0-100)HHdl		G-F	£2975

Total win prize-money £44367

Going: Sf: 0-0 GS: 0-1 Gd: 0-0 GF: - Fm: 0-0
Distance: 2m2/2m3: 0-0 2m4-2m7: 0-1 3m+: 0-0
Track: LH: 0-0 RH: 0-1 Tight: 0-0 Gall: 0-0
Aids: Bl: 0-0 Vi: 0-0 Tstrap: 0-0 Ckp: 0-0
Best Rating: **132** 3/03 Kels 2m2f   gd-sft Hdl

Useful hurdler; winner on the Flat; completed a five-timer in 2002/3 despite a huge rise in the handicap, won a Grade Two event on last occasion; good third on reappearance; effective at between two and three miles; especially effective on fast ground.

Cowboyboots (IRE)

96(103h)   (115h)**104**

6-y-o b g Lord Americo-Little Welly (Little Buskins)
L Wells David Gower

Placings:523/3213P-P0FB50   (4840)
2003/04: 25PGS, 20OG, 20FG, 22BGS, 22⁵G, 24OG,

	Starts	1st	2nd	3rd	Win & Pl
Hurdles	3	0	0	0	0
Chases	3	0	0	0	0

Career Total	14	1	2	3	9027
115 1/03 Font	2m6f110yE Hdl		HVY	£3591

Total win prize-money £3591

Going: Sf: 0-0 GS: 0-2 Gd: 0-4 GF: - Fm: 0-0
Distance: 2m2/2m3: 0-0 2m4-2m7: 0-4 3m+: 0-2
Track: LH: 0-3 RH: 0-3 Tight: 0-1 Gall: 0-1
Aids: Bl: 0-0 Vi: 0-0 Tstrap: 0-0 Ckp: 0-0
Best Rating: **115** 1/03 Font 2m6f110y heavy Hdl

Fair hurdler; won a novice event at Fontwell in January 2003; stays three miles; acts in testing ground.

Coxwell Cossack

86   **89**

11-y-o ch g Gildoran-Stepout (Sagaro)
Mark Campion F S W Partnership

Placings:3/3P2/0445FF5/412221124045/30052/P   (4404)
2003/04: 16PG,

	Starts	1st	2nd	3rd	Win & Pl
Hurdles	1	0	0	0	
Career Total	29	3	6	3	19392
116 8/00 MRas	2m3f110yC(0-130)HHdl		G-F	£5920
116 7/00 MRas	2m1f110yD Hdl		G-F	£3421
104 6/00 MRas	2m1f110yE Hdl		GD	£2590

Total win prize-money £11932

Going: Sf: 0-0 GS: 0-0 Gd: 0-1 GF: - Fm: 0-0
Distance: 2m2/2m3: 0-1 2m4-2m7: 0-0 3m+: 0-0
Track: LH: 0-0 RH: 0-1 Tight: 0-0 Gall: 0-1
Aids: Bl: 0-0 Vi: 0-0 Tstrap: 0-0 Ckp: 0-0
Best Rating: **116** 8/00 MRas 2m3f110y   gd-fm   Hdl

Coy Lad (IRE)

90   **73**

7-y-o ch g Be My Native (USA)-Don't Tutch Me (The Parson)
T J Fitzgerald Mr & Mrs Raymond Anderson Green

Placings:44/64-U003   (3881)
2003/04: 16UG, 17OGS, 16OG, 24³G,

	Starts	1st	2nd	3rd	Win & Pl
Hurdles	4	0	0	1	724
Career Total	8	0	0	1	1867

Going: Sf: 0-0 GS: 0-1 Gd: 0-3 GF: - Fm: 0-0
Distance: 2m2/2m3: 0-3 2m4-2m7: 0-0 3m+: 0-1
Track: LH: 0-3 RH: 0-0 Tight: 0-2 Gall: 0-0
Aids: Bl: 0-0 Vi: 0-0 Tstrap: 0-0 Ckp: 0-0
Best Rating: **106** 2/02 Newb 2m110y   soft   NHF

Plating-class hurdler; yet to prove he stays beyond two miles.

Coyote Lakes

61f   **25f**

5-y-o ch g Be My Chief (USA)-Oakbrook Tern (USA) (Arctic Tern (USA))
Mrs L C Jewell Gallagher Equine Ltd

Placings:0   (3927)
2003/04: 16OGS,

	Starts	1st	2nd	3rd	Win & Pl
NH Flat	1	0	0	0	
Career Total	1	0	0	0	

Going: Sf: 0-0 GS: 0-1 Gd: 0-0 GF: - Fm: 0-0
Distance: 2m2/2m3: 0-1 2m4-2m7: 0-0 3m+: 0-0
Track: LH: 0-0 RH: 0-1 Tight: 0-0 Gall: 0-0

Aids: Bl: 0-0 Vi: 0-0 Tstrap: 0-0 Ckp: 0-0
Best Rating: 25   2/04   Sand   2m110y   gd-sft   NHF

Crack On Cheryl

10-y-o b m Rakaposhi King-Furstin (Furry Glen)
V Y Gethin   V Y Gethin

Placings:000UPPPP/0/PFPPF   (4888)
2003/04: 19PGS, 26FG, 24PG, 25PGS, 24FGF,

	Starts	1st	2nd	3rd	Win & Pl
Hurdles	3	0	0	0	0
Chases	2	0	0	0	
Career Total	**14**	**0**	**0**	**0**	

Going: Sf: 0-0 GS: 0-2 Gd: 0-2 GF: - Fm: 0-1
Distance: 2m/2m3: 0-1 2m4-2m7: 0-0 3m+: 0-4
Track: LH: 0-1 RH: 0-0 Tight: 0-1 Gall: 0-0
Aids: Bl: 0-0 Vi: 0-0 Tstrap: 0-0 Ckp: 0-0
Best Rating: 14   9/99   Worc   2m   gd-fm   NHF

Cracking Dawn (IRE)

                    (132h)**135**
9-y-o b g Be My Native (USA)-Rare Coin (Kemal (FR))
R H Alner   Peter Bonner

Placings:0/012/1-PP   (3037)
2003/04: 20PGS, 24FGS,

	Starts	1st	2nd	3rd	Win & Pl
Chases	2	0	0	0	
Career Total	**7**	**2**	**1**	**0**	**10118**
135	11/02	Hayd	3m	D Ch	GD	£5460
125	2/02	Font	2m6f110yE Hdl	SFT	£3332
			Total win prize-money £8792		

Going: Sf: 0-0 GS: 0-2 Gd: 0-0 GF: - Fm: 0-0
Distance: 2m/2m3: 0-0 2m4-2m7: 0-1 3m+: 0-1
Track: LH: 0-2 RH: 0-0 Tight: 0-0 Gall: 0-1
Aids: Bl: 0-0 Vi: 0-0 Tstrap: 0-0 Ckp: 0-0
Best Rating: 135   11/02   Hayd   3m   good   Ch

Fair chaser; winner of Irish point-to-points, won a Fontwell novice hurdle on his British debut in February 2002 and was very impressive on his chase debut at Haydock in November 2002; off the track for over a year and pulled up on return when jumping poorly (bruised foot); stays three miles and acts on good ground or softer.

Cracking Walker (IRE)

69   86
8-y-o ch g Rashar (USA)-Futile Walk (Crash Course)
G B Balding   J Harvey, H Bogie, R Spencer & T Geake

Placings:4/0FU   (4290)
2003/04: 21DGS, 24FG, 22UG,

	Starts	1st	2nd	3rd	Win & Pl
Hurdles	3	0	0	0	
Career Total	**4**	**0**	**0**	**0**	**0**

Going: Sf: 0-0 GS: 0-1 Gd: 0-2 GF: - Fm: 0-0
Distance: 2m/2m3: 0-0 2m4-2m7: 0-2 3m+: 0-1
Track: LH: 0-0 RH: 0-3 Tight: 0-0 Gall: 0-0
Aids: Bl: 0-0 Vi: 0-0 Tstrap: 0-0 Ckp: 0-0
Best Rating: 86   4/01   Winc   2m6f   soft   Hdl

Crackrattle (IRE)

10-y-o ch g Montelimar (USA)-Gaye Le Moss (Le Moss)
B N Pollock   Mrs P Polito, L Stilwell, S P Russel

Placings:6/P/60-P   (0416)
2003/04: 22FG,

	Starts	1st	2nd	3rd	Win & Pl
Chases	1	0	0	0	
Career Total	**5**	**0**	**0**	**0**	**0**

Going: Sf: 0-0 GS: 0-0 Gd: 0-1 GF: - Fm: 0-0
Distance: 2m/2m3: 0-0 2m4-2m7: 0-1 3m+: 0-0
Track: LH: 0-0 RH: 0-1 Tight: 0-1 Gall: 0-0
Aids: Bl: 0-0 Vi: 0-0 Tstrap: 0-0 Ckp: 0-1
Best Rating: 66   4/99   Towc   2m   good   NHF

Crafty Miss (IRE)

5-y-o b/br m Warcraft (USA)-Mrs Rumpole (IRE) (Strong Gale)
C J Down   M D Rusden

Placings:0   (4550)
2003/04: 16DGS,

	Starts	1st	2nd	3rd	Win & Pl
NH Flat	1	0	0	0	
Career Total	**1**	**0**	**0**	**0**	

Going: Sf: 0-0 GS: 0-1 Gd: 0-0 GF: - Fm: 0-0
Distance: 2m/2m3: 0-1 2m4-2m7: 0-0 3m+: 0-0
Track: LH: 0-0 RH: 0-1 Tight: 0-0 Gall: 0-0
Aids: Bl: 0-0 Vi: 0-0 Tstrap: 0-0 Ckp: 0-0

Crafty Monkey (IRE)

81   70
7-y-o b g Warcraft (USA)-Mikey's Monkey (Monksfield)
M Pitman   G Pascoe & S Brewer

Placings:6-000P   (4895)
2003/04: 16DG, 16DG, 16DG, 22PG,

	Starts	1st	2nd	3rd	Win & Pl
Hurdles	4	0	0	0	
Career Total	**5**	**0**	**0**	**0**	**0**

Going: Sf: 0-0 GS: 0-0 Gd: 0-4 GF: - Fm: 0-0
Distance: 2m/2m3: 0-3 2m4-2m7: 0-1 3m+: 0-0
Track: LH: 0-1 RH: 0-3 Tight: 0-0 Gall: 0-3
Aids: Bl: 0-0 Vi: 0-0 Tstrap: 0-0 Ckp: 0-0
Best Rating: 87   10/02   Fknm   2m   gd-sft   NHF

Cragg Prince (IRE)

99f   97f
5-y-o b g Roselier (FR)-Ivory Queen (Teenoso (USA))
Mrs S J Smith   Widdop Wanderers

Placings:02   (4571)
2003/04: 16DG, 172GS,

	Starts	1st	2nd	3rd	Win & Pl
NH Flat	2	0	1	0	598
Career Total	**2**	**0**	**1**	**0**	**598**

Going: Sf: 0-0 GS: 0-1 Gd: 0-1 GF: - Fm: 0-0
Distance: 2m/2m3: 0-2 2m4-2m7: 0-0 3m+: 0-0
Track: LH: 0-2 RH: 0-0 Tight: 0-1 Gall: 0-1

Aids: Bl: 0-0 Vi: 0-0 Tstrap: 0-0 Ckp: 0-0
Best Rating: 97   3/04   Bang   2m1f   gd-sft   NHF

Craigmor

80   71
4-y-o br g Polar Falcon (USA)-Western Horizon (USA) (Gone West (USA))
M F Harris   M Harris

Placings:00500   (2819)
2003/04: 16DGF, 16DG, 16DG, 16DGS, 16DGF,

	Starts	1st	2nd	3rd	Win & Pl
Hurdles	5	0	0	0	0
Career Total	**5**	**0**	**0**	**0**	

Going: Sf: 0-0 GS: 0-1 Gd: 0-2 GF: - Fm: 0-2
Distance: 2m/2m3: 0-5 2m4-2m7: 0-0 3m+: 0-0
Track: LH: 0-2 RH: 0-3 Tight: 0-1 Gall: 0-2
Aids: Bl: 0-0 Vi: 0-0 Tstrap: 0-0 Ckp: 0-0
Best Rating: 71   12/03   Winc   2m   good   Hdl

Cramond (IRE)

103f   87f
6-y-o b g Lord America-Rullahola (Blue Rullah)
A Parker   R A Bartlett

Placings:6-4   (3474)
2003/04: 16FGF,

	Starts	1st	2nd	3rd	Win & Pl
NH Flat	1	0	0	0	0
Career Total	**2**	**0**	**0**	**0**	**0**

Going: Sf: 0-0 GS: 0-0 Gd: 0-0 GF: - Fm: 0-1
Distance: 2m/2m3: 0-1 2m4-2m7: 0-0 3m+: 0-0
Track: LH: 0-0 RH: 0-1 Tight: 0-1 Gall: 0-0
Aids: Bl: 0-0 Vi: 0-0 Tstrap: 0-0 Ckp: 0-0
Best Rating: 87   1/04   Muss   2m   gd-fm   NHF

Cranborne (IRE)

7-y-o b m King's Ride-Random Wind (Random Shot)
A H Mactaggart   A H Mactaggart

Placings:00-00   (3356)
2003/04: 16DGF, 18DS,

	Starts	1st	2nd	3rd	Win & Pl
NH Flat	1	0	0	0	0
Hurdles	1	0	0	0	0
Career Total	**4**	**0**	**0**	**0**	

Going: Sf: 0-1 GS: 0-0 Gd: 0-0 GF: - Fm: 0-1
Distance: 2m/2m3: 0-2 2m4-2m7: 0-0 3m+: 0-0
Track: LH: 0-2 RH: 0-0 Tight: 0-1 Gall: 0-0
Aids: Bl: 0-0 Vi: 0-0 Tstrap: 0-0 Ckp: 0-0
Best Rating: 31   1/03   Tntn   2m1f   soft   NHF

Craobh Rua (IRE)

108   97
7-y-o b g Lord America-Addies Lass (Little Buskins)
R H Alner (Michael Cunningham 17/1)   R W Humphreys

Placings:00/0-5004062   (4899)
2003/04: 16FGF, 16DGY, 20DS, 16FS, 20DHY, 16FG, 16DG,

	Starts	1st	2nd	3rd	Win & Pl
NH Flat	1	0	0	0	0

Hurdles	6	0	1	0	1508
Career Total	10	0	1	0	1508

Going: Sf: 0-3 GS: 0-0 Gd: 0-2 GF: - Fm: 0-1
Distance: 2m/2m3: 0-5 2m4-2m7: 0-2 3m+: 0-0
Track: LH: 0-0 RH: 0-0 Tight: 0-0 Gall: 0-0
Aids: Bl: 0-0 Vi: 0-0 Tstrap: 0-0 Ckp: 0-0
Best Rating: 97 11/03 Punc 2m   gd-yld Hdl

Moderate ex-Irish hurdler; seems to handle most ground.

Crarae Jack

6-y-o b g Gran Alba (USA)-Double Dose (Al Sirat)
H P Hogarth Hogarth Racing

Placings:0-FP   (4273)
2003/04: 19FG, 24PG,

	Starts	1st	2nd	3rd	Win & Pl
Hurdles	2	0	0	0	
Career Total	3	0	0	0	

Going: Sf: 0-0 GS: 0-0 Gd: 0-2 GF: - Fm: 0-0
Distance: 2m/2m3: 0-1 2m4-2m7: 0-0 3m+: 0-1
Track: LH: 0-1 RH: 0-1 Tight: 0-1 Gall: 0-0
Aids: Bl: 0-0 Vi: 0-0 Tstrap: 0-0 Ckp: 0-0
Best Rating: 83 4/03 Ayr 2m   good NHF

Crazy Horse (IRE)
107   140
11-y-o b g Little Bighorn-Our Dorcet (Condorcet (FR))
L Lungo Ashleybank Investments Limited

Placings:P101/2211213/5U2220/3U31/1/P6P-4PP0 (4628)
2003/04: 234GS, 23PG, 23PHY, 20PG,

	Starts	1st	2nd	3rd	Win & Pl
Hurdles	4	0	0	0	1294
Career Total	29	7	6	3	77889
152 5/01 Hayd	2m7f110yB Hdl			GD	£10237
159 4/01 Aint	2m4f B HHdl			SFT	£26000
150 3/99 Kels	2m2f B Hdl			SFT	£13680
125 1/99 Kels	2m110y D Hdl			HVY	£2932
133 12/98 Ayr	2m E Hdl			HVY	£2682
120 4/98 Ayr	2m H NHF			GD	£3598
128 2/98 Weth	2m H NHF			GD	£1434
			Total win prize-money		£60566

Going: Sf: 0-1 GS: 0-1 Gd: 0-2 GF: - Fm: 0-0
Distance: 2m/2m3: 0-2 2m4-2m7: 0-1 3m+: 0-3
Track: LH: 0-4 RH: 0-0 Tight: 0-1 Gall: 0-0
Aids: Bl: 0-0 Vi: 0-0 Tstrap: 0-0 Ckp: 0-0
Best Rating: 159 4/01 Aint 2m4f   soft Hdl

Very useful hurdler at his best; stays three miles; acts on good and soft ground; has to be produced late.

Crazy Mazie
88   77
7-y-o b m Risk Me (FR)-Post Impressionist (IRE) (Ahonoora)
K A Morgan Le Tricolore

Placings:6663/004F-3P2P40   (4669)
2003/04: 263FG, 24PG, 212S, 16PS, 194GS, 239GS,

	Starts	1st	2nd	3rd	Win & Pl
Hurdles	6	0	1	1	1172
Career Total	14	0	1	2	1702

Going: Sf: 0-2 GS: 0-2 Gd: 0-1 GF: - Fm: 0-1
Distance: 2m/2m3: 0-1 2m4-2m7: 0-3 3m+: 0-2

Track: LH: 0-1 RH: 0-4 Tight: 0-2 Gall: 0-2
Aids: Bl: 0-0 Vi: 0-0 Tstrap: 0-0 Ckp: 0-0
Best Rating: 83 4/02 MRas 2m1f110y   good NHF

Cream Cracker
88f   80f
6-y-o b m Sir Harry Lewis (USA)-Cream By Post (Torus)
Ms Bridget Nicholls Ridge Racing

Placings:50   (4509)
2003/04: 16FG, 14DGS,

	Starts	1st	2nd	3rd	Win & Pl
NH Flat	2	0	0	0	0
Career Total	2	0	0	0	0

Going: Sf: 0-0 GS: 0-1 Gd: 0-1 GF: - Fm: 0-0
Distance: 2m/2m3: 0-1 2m4-2m7: 0-0 3m+: 0-0
Track: LH: 0-0 RH: 0-1 Tight: 0-0 Gall: 0-0
Aids: Bl: 0-2 Vi: 0-0 Tstrap: 0-0 Ckp: 0-0
Best Rating: 80 3/04 Winc 2m   good NHF

Creative Time (IRE)
105   (66h)115
8-y-o b g Houmayoun (FR)-Creative Princess (IRE) (Creative Plan (USA))
Miss H C Knight Mrs G M Sturges & H Stephen Smith

Placings:3334/20P-4P1P   (4916)
2003/04: 244G, 24PGS, 241G, 23PGS,

	Starts	1st	2nd	3rd	Win & Pl
Chases	4	1	0	0	11034
Career Total	11	1	1	3	15247
104 3/04 Strf	3m D(0-120)HCh			GD	£10504
			Total win prize-money		£10504

Going: Sf: 0-0 GS: 0-2 Gd: 1-2 GF: - Fm: 0-0
Distance: 2m/2m3: 0-0 2m4-2m7: 0-0 3m+: 1-4
Track: LH: 1-2 RH: 0-2 Tight: 1-2 Gall: 0-0
Aids: Bl: 0-0 Vi: 0-0 Tstrap: 0-0 Ckp: 0-0
Best Rating: 115 1/03 Ludl 3m   gd-sft Ch

Modest chaser; has shown form at up to three miles on both fast and soft ground.

Creed (IRE)
71   65
4-y-o ch g Entrepreneur-Ardent Range (IRE) (Archway (IRE))
F P Murtagh (R A Fahey 19/7) Hurst Farm Racing

Placings:4P   (1525)
2003/04: 174GF, 16PF,

	Starts	1st	2nd	3rd	Win & Pl
Hurdles	2	0	0	0	425
Career Total	2	0	0	0	425

Going: Sf: 0-0 GS: 0-0 Gd: 0-0 GF: - Fm: 0-2
Distance: 2m/2m3: 0-2 2m4-2m7: 0-0 3m+: 0-0
Track: LH: 0-0 RH: 0-0 Tight: 0-1 Gall: 0-0
Aids: Bl: 0-0 Vi: 0-0 Tstrap: 0-0 Ckp: 0-0
Best Rating: 65 7/03 MRas 2m1f110y   gd-fm Hdl

Stayer on the Flat; showed promise on debut and backed when pulled up lame next time.

Cregg House (IRE)
100(101h)   (115 h)131?
9-y-o ch g King Persian-Loyal River (Over The River (FR))

S Donohoe (P Mullins 18/5) Mrs Kathleen Kennedy

Placings:0223446/3F421136/PP4024222R/310324532P06 04R5-000034   (3631a)
2003/04: 16DY, 23DGF, 22DY, 24DYG, 20DG, 20DS,

	Starts	1st	2nd	3rd	Win & Pl
Hurdles	1	0	0	0	
Chases	5	0	0	1	2921
Career Total	47	3	9	7	78601
113 6/02 Navn	2m Hdl			SFT	£5714
116 2/01 Fair	3m1f HCh			YLD	£10483
104 1/01 Fair	2m5f120y Ch			HVY	£5564
			Total win prize-money		£21764

Going: Sf: 0-1 GS: 0-0 Gd: 0-1 GF: - Fm: 0-0
Distance: 2m/2m3: 0-1 2m4-2m7: 0-3 3m+: 0-1
Track: LH: 0-3 RH: 0-2 Tight: 0-0 Gall: 0-1
Aids: Bl: 0-2 Vi: 0-0 Tstrap: 0-0 Ckp: 0-2
Best Rating: 156 3/02 Chel 2m5f   good Ch

Useful Irish chaser; runner-up in the Cathcart in 2002 and ran well at the Festival in 2003 when fourth in the Mildmay Of Flete, but little form since; travels well but tends to find little off the bridle; suited by cut in the ground; best at two to two and a half miles.

Creon
111(102c)   (119c)130
9-y-o b g Saddlers' Hall (IRE)-Creake (Derring Do)
Jonjo O'Neill John P McManus

Placings:004/04P120/0003F05001164/3002430061/016-300P61   (4386)
2003/04: 223S, 25DG, 24DS, 23PHY, 20PHY, 251G,

	Starts	1st	2nd	3rd	Win & Pl
Hurdles	4	1	0	0	34800
Chases	2	0	0	1	470
Career Total	41	6	2	4	65806
124 3/04 Chel	3m1f110yA HHdl			GD	£34800
130 11/02 Chep	3m C(0-130)HHdl			HVY	£6158
109 4/02 Prth	3m2f110yF(0-90)HCh			GD	£5330
134 1/01 Kemp	3m110y D(0-120)HHdl			SFT	£5187
134 12/00 Weth	2m7f C(0-130)HHdl			SFT	£4992
90 9/99 Baln	2m Hdl			G-F	£2957
			Total win prize-money		£59425

Going: Sf: 0-4 GS: 0-0 Gd: 1-2 GF: - Fm: 0-0
Distance: 2m/2m3: 0-0 2m4-2m7: 0-2 3m+: 1-4
Track: LH: 1-5 RH: 0-1 Tight: 0-0 Gall: 1-2
Aids: Bl: 0-0 Vi: 0-0 Tstrap: 0-0 Ckp: 1-1
Best Rating: 134 1/01 Kemp 3m110y   soft Hdl

Fair hurdler/moderate chaser; can look very good on his day, but does not always produce it; shock winner of Pertemps Hurdle Final at Cheltenham in 2004; acts on soft ground and handles faster; stays three miles two; has worn cheekpieces.

Cresswell Gold
99   77
7-y-o b m Homo Sapien-Running For Gold (Rymer)
D A Rees D A Rees & P Harris

Placings:0/05P6PPP-04U4P055   (1329)
2003/04: 19DG, 194GF, 17DG, 224GF, 20PGF, 22DGF, 195GF, 195GF,

	Starts	1st	2nd	3rd	Win & Pl
Hurdles	8	0	0	0	0
Career Total	16	0	0	0	0

Going: Sf: 0-0 GS: 0-0 Gd: 0-2 GF: - Fm: 0-6
Distance: 2m/2m3: 0-2 2m4-2m7: 0-6 3m+: 0-0
Track: LH: 0-4 RH: 0-3 Tight: 0-3 Gall: 0-0

Aids: Bl: 0-0 Vi: 0-0 Tstrap: 0-2 Ckp: 0-6
Best Rating: 84　12/02 Chep 2m4f　soft　Hdl

Cresswell Katie (IRE)
40

6-y-o b m King's Ride-Romantic Rose (IRE) (Strong Gale)
W K Goldsworthy (P Bowen 7/6) Bruce McKay

Placings:00-0P　　　　　　　　　　(1373)
2003/04: 16⁰YS, 24ᴾGF,

	Starts	1st	2nd	3rd	Win & Pl
Hurdles	2	0	0	0	
Career Total	4	0	0	0	

Going: Sf: 0-0 GS: 0-0 Gd: 0-0 GF: - Fm: 0-1
Distance: 2m/2m3: 0-1 2m4-2m7: 0-0 3m+: 0-1
Track: LH: 0-1 RH: 0-0 Tight: 0-0 Gall: 0-0
Aids: Bl: 0-0 Vi: 0-0 Tstrap: 0-0 Ckp: 0-0
Best Rating: 40　5/03 Gowr 2m　yld-sft　Hdl

Cresswell Quay
105　　　　129+

11-y-o ch g Bold Fox-Karatina (FR) (Dilettante Ii)
W K Goldsworthy (P Bowen 10/3) Bruce McKay

Placings:60/50650/5/4313/F46P/11121-1065P　(4871)
2003/04: 26¹GS, 26⁰G, 24⁶S, 24⁴S, 24ᴾS,

	Starts	1st	2nd	3rd	Win & Pl
Chases	5	1	0	0	4081
Career Total	26	6	1	2	29122
124	12/03 Plum	3m2f	E(0-110)HCh	G-S	£4081
118	1/03 Folk	3m1f	E(0-110)HCh	SFT	£8173
102	12/02 Font	2m6f	F(0-90)HCh	GD	£4104
84	11/02 Wwck	3m2f	F(0-95)HCh	GD	£3083
105	11/02 NAbb	3m2f110y (0-105)HCh	HVY	£4261
94	7/00 Wolv	3m1f	E Hdl	G-S	£2293

Total win prize-money £25999

Going: Sf: 0-2 GS: 1-1 Gd: 0-2 GF: - Fm: 0-0
Distance: 2m/2m3: 0-0 2m4-2m7: 0-0 3m+: 1-5
Track: LH: 1-5 RH: 0-0 Tight: 1-3 Gall: 0-2
Aids: Bl: 0-0 Vi: 0-0 Tstrap: 0-0 Ckp: 0-0
Best Rating: 124　12/03 Plum 3m2f　gd-sft　Ch

Fair staying chaser; formed a formidable partnership with Timmy Murphy in 2002/3; needs to be produced with precise timing; suited by soft ground; stays 3m 2f.

Crimson Dancer
107　　　　100+

4-y-o b f Groom Dancer (USA)-Crimson Rosella (Polar Falcon) (USA)
Miss S J Wilton (W J Haggas 14/10) John Pointon And Sons

Placings:2P22U　　　　　　　　　　(4504)
2003/04: 17²GF, 16ᴾG, 16²GS, 16²G, 17ᵁG,

	Starts	1st	2nd	3rd	Win & Pl
Hurdles	5	0	3	0	3684
Career Total	5	0	3	0	3684

Going: Sf: 0-0 GS: 0-1 Gd: 0-3 GF: - Fm: 0-1
Distance: 2m/2m3: 0-5 2m4-2m7: 0-0 3m+: 0-0
Track: LH: 0-1 RH: 0-4 Tight: 0-1 Gall: 0-0
Aids: Bl: 0-0 Vi: 0-0 Tstrap: 0-3 Ckp: 0-0
Best Rating: 100　3/04 Hrfd 2m1f　good　Hdl

Crinan (IRE)
96　　　　79

6-y-o ch g Carroll House-Esther (Persian Bold)
Mrs P Sly Mrs V M Edmonson

Placings:00-0450　　　　　　　　　(4564)
2003/04: 17⁰GS, 16⁴S, 16⁶S, 19⁰GS,

	Starts	1st	2nd	3rd	Win & Pl
Hurdles	4	0	0	0	0
Career Total	6	0	0	0	0

Going: Sf: 0-2 GS: 0-2 Gd: 0-0 GF: - Fm: 0-0
Distance: 2m/2m3: 0-4 2m4-2m7: 0-0 3m+: 0-0
Track: LH: 0-1 RH: 0-3 Tight: 0-1 Gall: 0-2
Aids: Bl: 0-0 Vi: 0-0 Tstrap: 0-0 Ckp: 0-0
Best Rating: 79　1/04 Hntg 2m110y　soft　Hdl

Crisis (IRE)
88　　　　61

8-y-o b g Second Set (IRE)-Special Offer (IRE) (Shy Groom (USA))
P T Dalton Mrs R S Perkins

Placings:2433134/331/6/00　　　　　(4343)
2003/04: 23⁰GS, 21⁰GS,

	Starts	1st	2nd	3rd	Win & Pl
Hurdles	2	0	0	0	
Career Total	13	2	1	5	10879
108	11/00 Uttx	2m4f110yE(0-115)HHdl	HVY	£2338
95	1/00 Leic	2m4f110yE HHdl	SFT	£3588

Total win prize-money £5926

Going: Sf: 0-0 GS: 0-2 Gd: 0-0 GF: - Fm: 0-0
Distance: 2m/2m3: 0-0 2m4-2m7: 0-1 3m+: 0-1
Track: LH: 0-2 RH: 0-0 Tight: 0-0 Gall: 0-0
Aids: Bl: 0-0 Vi: 0-0 Tstrap: 0-0 Ckp: 0-0
Best Rating: 108　11/00 Uttx 2m4f110y　heavy　Hdl

Cristoforo (IRE)
105　　　　103+

7-y-o b g Perugino (USA)-Red Barons Lady (IRE) (Electric)
B J Curley P Byrne

Placings:000/0-5122　　　　　　　(2238)
2003/04: 17⁵GF, 16¹GF, 16²G, 16²G,

	Starts	1st	2nd	3rd	Win & Pl
Hurdles	4	1	2	0	8592
Career Total	8	1	2	0	8592
90	10/03 Plum	2m	F(0-90)HHdl	G-F	£2649

Total win prize-money £2650

Going: Sf: 0-0 GS: 0-0 Gd: 0-2 GF: - Fm: 1-2
Distance: 2m/2m3: 1-4 2m4-2m7: 0-0 3m+: 0-0
Track: LH: 1-2 RH: 0-2 Tight: 1-2 Gall: 0-0
Aids: Bl: 0-0 Vi: 0-0 Tstrap: 0-0 Ckp: 0-0
Best Rating: 103　11/03 Kemp 2m　good　Hdl

Plating-class hurdler; likes to blaze a trail; landed a hat-trick on the Flat in 2002; took advantage of lowly mark to land a gamble at Plumpton in October 2003; faded approaching the last when runner-up at Cheltenham and Kempton next two starts.

Cristophe
101　　　　(0c)84+

6-y-o b g Kris-Our Shirley (Shirley Heights)

Mrs A M Thorpe (Mrs B K Thomson 28/7) Mrs A M Thorpe

Placings:000P0/360224-40P0004000411　(4914)
2003/04: 24⁴GS, 20⁰GF, 20ᴾGF, 22⁰GF, 17⁹GF, 22⁵HV, 19⁴S, 16⁸S, 21⁰G, 17⁰G, 17⁴GS, 21¹G, 24¹GS,

	Starts	1st	2nd	3rd	Win & Pl
Hurdles	12	2	0	0	6318
Chases	1	0	0	0	
Career Total	24	2	2	1	8041
84	4/04 Worc	3m	F(0-95)HHdl	G-S	£3150
76	4/04 Plum	2m5f	G(0-90)HHdl	GD	£2523

Total win prize-money £5674

Going: Sf: 0-3 GS: 1-3 Gd: 1-3 GF: - Fm: 0-4
Distance: 2m/2m3: 0-5 2m4-2m7: 1-6 3m+: 1-2
Track: LH: 2-8 RH: 0-5 Tight: 1-5 Gall: 0-0
Aids: Bl: 0-1 Vi: 0-0 Tstrap: 0-0 Ckp: 0-2
Best Rating: 84　4/04 Worc 3m　gd-sft　Hdl

Plating-class hurdler; long-standing maiden under both codes until winning a Plumpton seller on his 34th start; followed up at Worcester; stays three miles; acts on good and easy ground.

Croaghnacree (IRE)

7-y-o b m Mister Lord (USA)-Castle Flame (IRE) (Carlingford Castle)
S J Marshall S J Marshall

Placings:00P-PPF　　　　　　　　　(3435)
2003/04: 20ᴾGS, 20ᴾG, 20ᶠHY,

	Starts	1st	2nd	3rd	Win & Pl
Hurdles	3	0	0	0	
Career Total	6	0	0	0	

Going: Sf: 0-1 GS: 0-1 Gd: 0-1 GF: - Fm: 0-0
Distance: 2m/2m3: 0-0 2m4-2m7: 0-3 3m+: 0-0
Track: LH: 0-2 RH: 0-1 Tight: 0-0 Gall: 0-2
Aids: Bl: 0-0 Vi: 0-0 Tstrap: 0-0 Ckp: 0-0
Best Rating: 51　1/03 Newc 2m　heavy　NHF

Croc An Oir (IRE)
112(72h)　　　(69h)98

7-y-o ch g Treasure Hunter-Cool Mary (Beau Charmeur (FR))
Miss Venetia Williams Miss V M Williams

Placings:03-431　　　　　　　　　(1040)
2003/04: 23⁴GF, 26³G, 26¹GF,

	Starts	1st	2nd	3rd	Win & Pl
Hurdles	2	0	0	1	786
Chases	1	1	0	0	3394
Career Total	5	1	0	2	4802
98	8/03 NAbb	3m2f110yF(0-90)HCh	G-F	£3393

Total win prize-money £3394

Going: Sf: 0-0 GS: 0-0 Gd: 0-1 GF: - Fm: 1-2
Distance: 2m/2m3: 0-0 2m4-2m7: 0-0 3m+: 1-3
Track: LH: 1-3 RH: 0-0 Tight: 1-2 Gall: 0-0
Aids: Bl: 0-0 Vi: 0-0 Tstrap: 0-0 Ckp: 0-0
Best Rating: 98　8/03 NAbb 3m2f110y　gd-fm　Ch

Irish point winner; poor novice hurdler; probably unsuited by soft ground when beaten odds-on favourite on chasing debut; left clear four out when winning extended 3m 2f conditional jockeys' handicap at Newton Abbot August 2003; stays really well.

Croc En Bouche (USA)

80f　　　　　　　　　　81f

5-y-o b g Broad Brush (USA)-Supercook (USA) (Best Turn (USA))
Mrs H Dalton G A Roberts

| Placings:00-0 | | | | | (0251) |
| 2003/04: 17ºGF, | | | | | |

	Starts	1st	2nd	3rd	Win & Pl
NH Flat	1	0	0	0	
Career Total	3	0	0	0	

Going:	Sf: 0-0 GS: 0-0 Gd: 0-0 GF: - Fm: 0-1
Distance:	2m/2m3: 0-1 2m4-2m7: 0-0 3m+: 0-0
Track:	LH: 0-0 RH: 0-1 Tight: 0-0 Gall: 0-0
Aids:	Bl: 0-0 Vi: 0-0 Tstrap: 0-0 Ckp: 0-0
Best Rating:	75 5/03 Extr 2m1f gd-fm NHF

Crocadee

(101h)　　　　　　　　　　(126+h)

11-y-o b g Rakaposhi King-Raise The Dawn (Rymer)
Miss Venetia Williams Favourites Racing

| Placings:20/12/1121016/311FU212/F-35 | | | | | (4528) |
| 2003/04: 21³G, 20⁵GS, | | | | | |

	Starts	1st	2nd	3rd	Win & Pl
Hurdles	2	0	0	1	3300
Career Total	22	8	5	2	82911
146	2/01	Kemp	2m4f110yA Ch		GD	£13200
140	12/00	Hayd	2m	A Ch	HVY	£12000
145	11/00	Hayd	2m4f	B Ch	HVY	£11180
143	2/00	Hntg	2m4f110yB Hdl		SFT	£6968
142	2/00	Leic	2m4f110yD Hdl		G-S	£4446
152	11/99	Hayd	2m4f	C Hdl	G-S	£5472
113	11/99	Hayd	2m4f	D Hdl	GD	£3095
129	3/99	Bang	2m1f	H NHF	G-S	£1630
			Total win prize-money £57991			

Going:	Sf: 0-0 GS: 0-1 Gd: 0-1 GF: - Fm: 0-0
Distance:	2m/2m3: 0-0 2m4-2m7: 0-2 3m+: 0-0
Track:	LH: 0-1 RH: 0-1 Tight: 0-0 Gall: 0-0
Aids:	Bl: 0-0 Vi: 0-0 Tstrap: 0-0 Ckp: 0-0
Best Rating:	152 2/01 Sand 2m4f110y heavy Ch

Useful hurdler; one time very useful chaser; returned from a tendon injury to show some ability in 2004; effective at around 2m 4f; effective with cut in the ground.

Crocodiles Den (IRE)

8-y-o b g Alphabatim (USA)-Misty Gold (Arizona Duke)
P A Blockley Richard R H Whiting

| Placings:00/3UP-P | | | | | (0328) |
| 2003/04: 21ºGF, | | | | | |

	Starts	1st	2nd	3rd	Win & Pl
Chases	1	0	0	0	
Career Total	6	0	0	1	632

Going:	Sf: 0-0 GS: 0-0 Gd: 0-0 GF: - Fm: 0-1
Distance:	2m/2m3: 0-0 2m4-2m7: 0-1 3m+: 0-0
Track:	LH: 0-1 RH: 0-0 Tight: 0-0 Gall: 0-0
Aids:	Bl: 0-0 Vi: 0-0 Tstrap: 0-1 Ckp: 0-0
Best Rating:	71 5/01 Klny 2m1f good NHF

Croft Court

13-y-o b g Crofthall-Queen Of Dara (Dara Monarch)
Nick Seal D J Renney

| Placings:F/41/P0/6 | | | | | (0055) |
| 2003/04: 25⁶GS, | | | | | |

	Starts	1st	2nd	3rd	Win & Pl
Chases	1	0	0	0	
Career Total	6	1	0	0	3705
96	4/01	Plum	3m2f	E Ch	G-S	£3315
			Total win prize-money £3315			

Going:	Sf: 0-0 GS: 0-1 Gd: 0-0 GF: - Fm: 0-0
Distance:	2m/2m3: 0-0 2m4-2m7: 0-0 3m+: 0-1
Track:	LH: 0-0 RH: 0-1 Tight: 0-0 Gall: 0-0
Aids:	Bl: 0-1 Vi: 0-0 Tstrap: 0-0 Ckp: 0-0
Best Rating:	96 4/01 Plum 3m2f gd-sft Ch

Croix De Guerre (IRE)

107　　　　　　　　　　106+

4-y-o gr g Highest Honor (FR)-Esclava (USA) (Nureyev (USA))
P J Hobbs (Sir Mark Prescott 2/10) Jack Joseph

| Placings:224222 | | | | | (4698) |
| 2003/04: 16²G, 18²G, 16⁴G, 20²GF, 16²GS, 18²G, | | | | | |

	Starts	1st	2nd	3rd	Win & Pl
Hurdles	6	0	5	0	5576
Career Total	6	0	5	0	5576

Going:	Sf: 0-0 GS: 0-1 Gd: 0-0 GF: - Fm: 0-1
Distance:	2m/2m3: 0-5 2m4-2m7: 0-1 3m+: 0-0
Track:	LH: 0-2 RH: 0-3 Tight: 0-3 Gall: 0-0
Aids:	Bl: 0-3 Vi: 0-0 Tstrap: 0-0 Ckp: 0-0
Best Rating:	106 3/04 Asct 2m110y gd-sft Hdl

Modest novice hurdler; has finished runner-up rather too often; effective at around two miles and suited by a sound surface; usually wears blinkers.

Croker (IRE)

(105h)　　　　　　　　　　(100 h)

9-y-o ch g Rainbows For Life (CAN)-Almagest (Dike (USA))
S T Lewis Simon T Lewis

| Placings:4313/3344/P66033P/0001400/311200-0P | | | | | (4376) |
| 2003/04: 19ºS, 16ºG, | | | | | |

	Starts	1st	2nd	3rd	Win & Pl
Hurdles	1	0	0	0	0
Chases	1	0	0	0	0
Career Total	30	4	1	2	14446
100	12/02	Bang	2m	F(0-100)HHdl	G-S	£2404
89	12/02	Leic	2m	F(0-105)HHdl	HVY	£3031
81	8/01	Bang	2m1f	G(0-95)HHdl	GD	£2383
110	11/98	Uttx	2m	E Hdl	SFT	£2295
			Total win prize-money £10115			

Going:	Sf: 0-1 GS: 0-0 Gd: 0-1 GF: - Fm: 0-0
Distance:	2m/2m3: 0-2 2m4-2m7: 0-0 3m+: 0-0
Track:	LH: 0-0 RH: 0-2 Tight: 0-1 Gall: 0-0
Aids:	Bl: 0-0 Vi: 0-0 Tstrap: 0-0 Ckp: 0-0
Best Rating:	113 12/98 Wwck 2m gd-sft Hdl

Cromer Pier

100　　　　　　　　　　83d

9-y-o b g Reprimand-Fleur Du Val (Valiyar)

G Fierro G Fierro

| Placings:605001/PP0P1002P00/0/00-030PF00 | | | | | (3440) |
| 2003/04: 16⁰G, 19³GF, 19⁰G, 26⁸GF, 16⁶S, 17⁰G, 16⁸G, | | | | | |

	Starts	1st	2nd	3rd	Win & Pl
Hurdles	7	0	0	1	347
Career Total	27	2	1	1	3891
83	10/00	MRas	2m1f110yG(0-95)HHdl	GD	£1456
93	4/00	MRas	2m1f110yG Hdl	SFT	£1519
			Total win prize-money £2975		

Going:	Sf: 0-1 GS: 0-1 Gd: 0-0 GF: - Fm: 0-2
Distance:	2m/2m3: 0-4 2m4-2m7: 0-2 3m+: 0-1
Track:	LH: 0-2 RH: 0-5 Tight: 0-2 Gall: 0-0
Aids:	Bl: 0-1 Vi: 0-0 Tstrap: 0-0 Ckp: 0-0
Best Rating:	93 4/00 MRas 2m1f110y soft Hdl

Plating-class hurdler; stays 2m 4f.

Cromwell (IRE)

103　　　　　(69h)93

9-y-o b g Last Tycoon-Catherine Parr (USA) (Riverman (USA))
M C Chapman Sir Stanley Clarke

| Placings:06054/344111453640644551/323612441P61410/0236P/UPP-06264154356 | | | | | (3437) |
| 2003/04: 21⁰G, 17⁶GF, 25²GF, 27⁶GF, 21⁴G, 28¹GF, 24⁵GF, 28⁴G, 28³GS, 28⁵G, 24⁸HY, | | | | | |

	Starts	1st	2nd	3rd	Win & Pl
Hurdles	1	0	0	0	0
Chases	10	1	1	1	5231
Career Total	57	9	4	6	44161
93	10/03	MRas	3m4f110yE(0-110)HCh	G-F	£3227
113	3/01	MRas	3m1f	D Ch	HVY	£5303
107	2/01	Catt	3m1f110yE Ch	SFT	£3745
107	11/00	MRas	3m1f	E(0-115)HCh	G-S	£4329
102	10/00	MRas	3m1f	D Ch	GD	£5096
107	4/00	MRas	2m3f110yD Hdl	SFT	£3000
103	8/99	MRas	3m	D Hdl	G-F	£3109
103	7/99	MRas	2m1f110yD Hdl	G-F	£3070
106	7/99	MRas	2m5f110yE Hdl	G-F	£2316
			Total win prize-money £33197		

Going:	Sf: 0-1 GS: 0-1 Gd: 0-4 GF: - Fm: 1-5
Distance:	2m/2m3: 0-1 2m4-2m7: 0-2 3m+: 1-8
Track:	LH: 0-4 RH: 1-7 Tight: 1-8 Gall: 0-2
Aids:	Bl: 1-10 Vi: 0-0 Tstrap: 0-0 Ckp: 0-0
Best Rating:	113 5/01 Weth 3m1f firm Ch

Moderate chaser; multiple course winner at Market Rasen; seems able to cope with most surfaces; stays well.

Crookstown Castle (IRE)

82　　　　　　　　　　83+

6-y-o gr g Castle Keep-Moorstown Rose (IRE) (Roselier (FR))
Noel T Chance Mrs M C Sweeney

| Placings:2450 | | | | | (3646) |
| 2003/04: 16²GS, 19⁴GF, 22⁵HY, 21⁰GS, | | | | | |

	Starts	1st	2nd	3rd	Win & Pl
NH Flat	1	0	1	0	538
Hurdles	3	0	0	0	386
Career Total	4	0	1	0	925

Going:	Sf: 0-1 GS: 0-1 Gd: 0-1 GF: - Fm: 0-1
Distance:	2m/2m3: 0-2 2m4-2m7: 0-2 3m+: 0-0
Track:	LH: 0-3 RH: 0-1 Tight: 0-1 Gall: 0-1
Aids:	Bl: 0-0 Vi: 0-0 Tstrap: 0-0 Ckp: 0-0
Best Rating:	102 5/03 Worc 2m good NHF

Satisfactory debut when eventually well held by Alpine Fox in Worcester bumper May 2003, made jumping mistakes on hurdles debut.

Crosby Dancer

5-y-o b g Glory Of Dancer-Mary Macblain (Damister (USA))
W S Coltherd B Confrey

| Placings:PU | | | | | (4727) |
| 2003/04: 16PHY, 17UG, | | | | | |

	Starts	1st	2nd	3rd	Win & Pl
Hurdles	2	0	0	0	
Career Total	2	0	0	0	

Going:	Sf: 0-1 GS: 0-0 Gd: 0-1 GF: - Fm: 0-0
Distance:	2m/2m3: 0-2 2m4-2m7: 0-0 3m+: 0-0
Track:	LH: 0-1 RH: 0-1 Tight: 0-0 Gall: 0-1
Aids:	Bl: 0-0 Vi: 0-0 Tstrap: 0-0 Ckp: 0-0

Crosby Don

88(81h)   (33h)75
9-y-o b g Alhijaz-Evening Star (Red Sunset)
J R Weymes Don Raper

| Placings:6034P0/06FF6/434/5B00023-0 | | | | | (4960) |
| 2003/04: 16GGF, 20QGS, | | | | | |

	Starts	1st	2nd	3rd	Win & Pl
Chases	2	0	0	1	612
Career Total	22	0	1	3	3304

Going:	Sf: 0-0 GS: 0-1 Gd: 0-0 GF: - Fm: 0-1
Distance:	2m/2m3: 0-1 2m4-2m7: 0-1 3m+: 0-0
Track:	LH: 0-1 RH: 0-1 Tight: 0-0 Gall: 0-1
Aids:	Bl: 0-0 Vi: 0-0 Tstrap: 0-0 Ckp: 0-0
Best Rating:	92 11/98 Newc 2m good Hdl

Poor novice hurdler, novice chaser.

Crosby Donjohn

79   67
7-y-o ch g Magic Ring (IRE)-Ovideo (Domynsky)
J R Weymes Don Raper

| Placings:0PP-2F | | | | | (1531) |
| 2003/04: 17QGF, 17FGF, | | | | | |

	Starts	1st	2nd	3rd	Win & Pl
Hurdles	2	0	1	0	776
Career Total	5	0	1	0	776

Going:	Sf: 0-0 GS: 0-0 Gd: 0-0 GF: - Fm: 0-2
Distance:	2m/2m3: 0-2 2m4-2m7: 0-0 3m+: 0-0
Track:	LH: 0-1 RH: 0-1 Tight: 0-2 Gall: 0-0
Aids:	Bl: 0-0 Vi: 0-0 Tstrap: 0-0 Ckp: 0-0
Best Rating:	73 10/03 MRas 2m1f110y gd-fm Hdl

Plating-class hurdler; yet to prove he gets two miles.

Crosby Rocker

6-y-o b m Rock Hopper-Mary Macblain (Damister (USA))
John A Harris D Jackson

| Placings:P | | | | | (2305) |
| 2003/04: 19PGF, | | | | | |

	Starts	1st	2nd	3rd	Win & Pl
Hurdles	1	0	0	0	

| Career Total | 1 | 0 | 0 | 0 | |

Going:	Sf: 0-0 GS: 0-0 Gd: 0-0 GF: - Fm: 0-1
Distance:	2m/2m3: 0-1 2m4-2m7: 0-0 3m+: 0-0
Track:	LH: 0-1 RH: 0-0 Tight: 0-0 Gall: 0-0
Aids:	Bl: 0-0 Vi: 0-0 Tstrap: 0-0 Ckp: 0-0
Best Rating:	0 11/03 Catt 2m3f gd-fm Hdl

Cross River

9-y-o b g Reprimand-River Maiden (USA) (Riverman (USA))
Joss Saville Mrs S Smith

| Placings:000/00/0P/P | | | | | (4302) |
| 2003/04: 20PG, | | | | | |

	Starts	1st	2nd	3rd	Win & Pl
Chases	1	0	0	0	
Career Total	8	0	0	0	

Going:	Sf: 0-0 GS: 0-0 Gd: 0-0 GF: - Fm: 0-0
Distance:	2m/2m3: 0-0 2m4-2m7: 0-1 3m+: 0-0
Track:	LH: 0-0 RH: 0-1 Tight: 0-0 Gall: 0-0
Aids:	Bl: 0-0 Vi: 0-0 Tstrap: 0-0 Ckp: 0-0
Best Rating:	63 10/99 Chel 2m10y good NHF

Crossbow Creek

99   108+
6-y-o b g Lugana Beach-Roxy River (Ardross)
M G Rimell Mrs M R T Rimell

| Placings:10-662144 | | | | | (4893) |
| 2003/04: 16RGS, 16RGS, 16²S, 16¹G, 16⁴G, 16⁴G, | | | | | |

	Starts	1st	2nd	3rd	Win & Pl
NH Flat	2	0	0	0	
Hurdles	4	1	1	0	5417
Career Total	8	2	1	0	7853
107	2/04	Ludl	2m	E Hdl	GD	£4033
111	2/03	Weth	2m	H NHF	G-S	£2436
					Total win prize-money £6469

Going:	Sf: 0-1 GS: 0-2 Gd: 1-3 GF: - Fm: 0-0
Distance:	2m/2m3: 1-6 2m4-2m7: 0-0 3m+: 0-0
Track:	LH: 0-1 RH: 1-5 Tight: 0-0 Gall: 0-2
Aids:	Bl: 0-0 Vi: 0-0 Tstrap: 0-0 Ckp: 0-0
Best Rating:	116 3/03 Chel 2m110y good NHF

Novice hurdler; big sort; won a fair contest at Ludlow on his second start over hurdles; acts on good and soft ground.

Crow Creek (IRE)

6-y-o br g Presenting-Rossacrowe Gale (IRE) (Strong Gale)
T P Walshe (B N Doran 13/5) Mrs Penny Walshe

| Placings:3-50P00P | | | | | (4245) |
| 2003/04: 17⁵G, 16⁰GS, 24PGF, 19⁰GS, 21⁰G, 26PGF, | | | | | |

	Starts	1st	2nd	3rd	Win & Pl
NH Flat	2	0	0	0	0
Hurdles	4	0	0	0	0
Career Total	7	0	0	1	288

Going:	Sf: 0-0 GS: 0-2 Gd: 0-2 GF: - Fm: 0-0
Distance:	2m/2m3: 0-2 2m4-2m7: 0-2 3m+: 0-0
Track:	LH: 0-1 RH: 0-0 Tight: 0-1 Gall: 0-0
Aids:	Bl: 0-1 Vi: 0-0 Tstrap: 0-0 Ckp: 0-0
Best Rating:	85 5/03 Hrfd 2m1f good NHF

Crown And Cushion

11-y-o b g High Adventure-Soulieana (Manado)
Mrs Kim Sly Mrs N R Matthews

| Placings:10PP/345131/52F1U/P/PU456/P | | | | | (4344) |
| 2003/04: 26RGS, | | | | | |

	Starts	1st	2nd	3rd	Win & Pl
Chases	1	0	0	0	
Career Total	22	4	1	2	17450
100	3/00	Strf	3m	D(0-120)HCh	GD	£7319
87	4/98	Fknm	2m4f	F(0-100)HHdl	G-S	£3670
89	12/97	Sthl	2m4f110yF(0-100)HHdl	GD	£2197
91	11/96	Hrfd	2m1f	E Hdl	G-S	£2486
					Total win prize-money £15674

Going:	Sf: 0-0 GS: 0-1 Gd: 0-0 GF: - Fm: 0-0
Distance:	2m/2m3: 0-0 2m4-2m7: 0-0 3m+: 0-1
Track:	LH: 0-1 RH: 0-0 Tight: 0-0 Gall: 0-0
Aids:	Bl: 0-0 Vi: 0-0 Tstrap: 0-0 Ckp: 0-0
Best Rating:	100 3/00 Strf 3m good Ch

Crownfield

97   99
5-y-o b g Blushing Flame (USA)-Chief Island (Be My Chief (USA))
Mrs M Reveley Bill Brown

| Placings:04P02-1 | | | | | (0168) |
| 2003/04: 16¹GF, | | | | | |

	Starts	1st	2nd	3rd	Win & Pl
Hurdles	1	1	0	0	3626
Career Total	6	1	1	0	8780
99	5/03	Weth	2m	E Hdl	G-F	£3626
					Total win prize-money £3626

Going:	Sf: 0-0 GS: 0-0 Gd: 0-0 GF: - Fm: 1-1
Distance:	2m/2m3: 1-1 2m4-2m7: 0-0 3m+: 0-0
Track:	LH: 1-1 RH: 0-0 Tight: 0-0 Gall: 0-0
Aids:	Bl: 0-0 Vi: 0-0 Tstrap: 0-0 Ckp: 0-0
Best Rating:	99 5/03 Weth 2m gd-fm Hdl

Improving and opened account over hurdles on firm ground at Wetherby in May 2003.

Cruise Leader (IRE)

101   125
9-y-o b g Supreme Leader-Ormskirk Mover (Deep Run)
C Grant Trevor Hemmings

| Placings:10/13241/U11 | | | | | (3372) |
| 2003/04: 22US, 20¹GS, 20¹S, | | | | | |

	Starts	1st	2nd	3rd	Win & Pl
Chases	3	2	0	0	11365
Career Total	10	5	1	1	20143
123	1/04	Weth	2m4f110yD(0-120)HCh	SFT	£5629
124	12/03	Weth	2m4f110yD(0-110)HCh	G-S	£5736
114	2/01	Ludl	2m	E Hdl	G-S	£2233
110	10/00	Bang	2m1f	E Hdl	SFT	£2768
108	12/99	Hntg	2m110y	H NHF	G-S	£2066
					Total win prize-money £18432

Going:	Sf: 1-2 GS: 1-1 Gd: 0-0 GF: - Fm: 0-0
Distance:	2m/2m3: 0-0 2m4-2m7: 2-3 3m+: 0-0
Track:	LH: 2-3 RH: 0-0 Tight: 0-1 Gall: 0-0
Aids:	Bl: 0-0 Vi: 0-0 Tstrap: 0-0 Ckp: 0-0
Best Rating:	124 12/03 Weth 2m4f110y gd-sft Ch

Fair chaser; has changed stable and was back on the winning trail at Wetherby in December; followed up in handicap chase there the following month; suited by two and a half miles; best in soft ground.

Cruise The Fairway (IRE)

8-y-o b g Insan (USA)-Tickhill (General Assembly (USA))
B G Powell R J T 290 Limited

Placings:*10*/1413346/3412/P (2453)
2003/04: 26PGS,

	Starts	1st	2nd	3rd	Win & Pl
Chases	1	0	0	0	
Career Total	14	4	1	3	24384
125 12/01 Newb	3m		C Ch		GD £8287
111 1/01 Extr	2m1f		E Hdl		HVY £2119
113 11/00 Aint	2m110y		D Hdl		G-S £4309
103 3/00 Newb	2m110y		H NHF		SFT £2478
				Total win prize-money £17196	

Going:	Sf: 0-1 GS: 0-1 Gd: 0-0 GF: - Fm: 0-0
Distance:	2m/2m3: 0-0 2m4-2m7: 0-0 3m+: 0-1
Track:	LH: 0-0 RH: 0-0 Tight: 0-0 Gall: 0-1
Aids:	Bl: 0-0 Vi: 0-0 Tstrap: 0-0 Ckp: 0-0
Best Rating:	130 1/02 Newb 2m6f110y good Ch

Cruising Along

61f   17f

6-y-o gr m Thethingaboutitis (USA)-Cruising On (Cruise Missile)
P T Dalton Mrs J E Goodall

Placings:*00* (4920)
2003/04: 16PGS, 16PGS,

	Starts	1st	2nd	3rd	Win & Pl
NH Flat	2	0	0	0	
Career Total	2	0	0	0	

Going:	Sf: 0-1 GS: 0-1 Gd: 0-0 GF: - Fm: 0-0
Distance:	2m/2m3: 0-2 2m4-2m7: 0-0 3m+: 0-0
Track:	LH: 0-2 RH: 0-0 Tight: 0-0 Gall: 0-0
Aids:	Bl: 0-0 Vi: 0-0 Tstrap: 0-0 Ckp: 0-0
Best Rating:	17 4/04 Worc 2m gd-sft NHF

Cruising Clyde

97f   102f

5-y-o ch g Karinga Bay-Bournel (Sunley Builds)
E Retter Edward Retter

Placings:*01* (3948)
2003/04: 16PS, 16¹G,

	Starts	1st	2nd	3rd	Win & Pl
NH Flat	2	1	0	0	2443
Career Total	2	1	0	0	2443
102 2/04 Winc	2m		H NHF		GD £2443
				Total win prize-money £2443	

Going:	Sf: 0-1 GS: 0-0 Gd: 1-1 GF: - Fm: 0-0
Distance:	2m/2m3: 1-2 2m4-2m7: 0-0 3m+: 0-0
Track:	LH: 0-0 RH: 1-2 Tight: 0-0 Gall: 0-0
Aids:	Bl: 0-0 Vi: 0-0 Tstrap: 0-0 Ckp: 0-0
Best Rating:	102 2/04 Winc 2m good NHF

Well beaten on Bumper debut at Ascot in December on testing ground.

Crumbs

76f   46f

4-y-o b f Puissance-Norska (Northfields (USA))
B Mactaggart In The Pink Syndicate

Placings:*0* (4867)
2003/04: 16⁰S,

	Starts	1st	2nd	3rd	Win & Pl
NH Flat	1	0	0	0	
Career Total	1	0	0	0	

Going:	Sf: 0-1 GS: 0-0 Gd: 0-0 GF: - Fm: 0-0
Distance:	2m/2m3: 0-1 2m4-2m7: 0-0 3m+: 0-0
Track:	LH: 0-1 RH: 0-0 Tight: 0-0 Gall: 0-0
Aids:	Bl: 0-0 Vi: 0-0 Tstrap: 0-0 Ckp: 0-0
Best Rating:	46 4/04 Ayr 2m soft NHF

Crunchy (IRE)

92   100

6-y-o ch g Common Grounds-Credit Crunch (IRE) (Caerleon (USA))
B Ellison The Half Moon Club

Placings:024-33PP03 (4959)
2003/04: 16³GF, 16³G, 16PS, 17PGS, 17⁰GS, 19³G,

	Starts	1st	2nd	3rd	Win & Pl
Hurdles	6	0	0	3	2173
Career Total	9	0	1	3	3591

Going:	Sf: 0-1 GS: 0-2 Gd: 0-2 GF: - Fm: 0-1
Distance:	2m/2m3: 0-5 2m4-2m7: 0-1 3m+: 0-0
Track:	LH: 0-4 RH: 0-2 Tight: 0-4 Gall: 0-0
Aids:	Bl: 0-0 Vi: 0-0 Tstrap: 0-3 Ckp: 0-2
Best Rating:	100 3/03 Catt 2m soft Hdl

Moderate hurdler; appreciated the better ground and just held at bay in novices' hurdle at Catterick in March; had been in good form on the All-Weather previously; best at around two miles; acts on fast ground.

Crusoe (IRE)

45

7-y-o b g Turtle Island (IRE)-Self Reliance (Never So Bold)
A Sadik A Sadik

Placings:P0004P/0-P (2866)
2003/04: 16PS,

	Starts	1st	2nd	3rd	Win & Pl
Hurdles	1	0	0	0	
Career Total	8	0	0	0	0

Going:	Sf: 0-0 GS: 0-1 Gd: 0-0 GF: - Fm: 0-0
Distance:	2m/2m3: 0-1 2m4-2m7: 0-0 3m+: 0-0
Track:	LH: 0-1 RH: 0-0 Tight: 0-0 Gall: 0-0
Aids:	Bl: 0-1 Vi: 0-0 Tstrap: 0-0 Ckp: 0-0
Best Rating:	49 11/02 Hrfd 2m1f soft Hdl

Cryptogam

76   51

4-y-o b f Zamindar (USA)-Moss (Alzao (USA))
M E Sowersby (Mrs A J Perrett 19/5) R D Seldon

Placings:*00* (2528)
2003/04: 16⁰GS, 16⁰GS,

	Starts	1st	2nd	3rd	Win & Pl
Hurdles	2	0	0	0	
Career Total	2	0	0	0	

Going:	Sf: 0-0 GS: 0-2 Gd: 0-0 GF: - Fm: 0-0
Distance:	2m/2m3: 0-2 2m4-2m7: 0-0 3m+: 0-0
Track:	LH: 0-2 RH: 0-0 Tight: 0-1 Gall: 0-0
Aids:	Bl: 0-0 Vi: 0-0 Tstrap: 0-0 Ckp: 0-0

Crystal Brook

6-y-o b m Alderbrook-Earles-Field (Wolverlife)
Colin Staley (Evan Williams 13/9) Colin Staley

Placings:0PP (4655)
2003/04: 17⁰GF, 16PGF, 16PG,

	Starts	1st	2nd	3rd	Win & Pl
NH Flat	1	0	0	0	0
Hurdles	1	0	0	0	0
Chases	1	0	0	0	0
Career Total	3	0	0	0	

Going:	Sf: 0-0 GS: 0-0 Gd: 0-1 GF: - Fm: 0-2
Distance:	2m/2m3: 0-3 2m4-2m7: 0-0 3m+: 0-0
Track:	LH: 0-2 RH: 0-1 Tight: 0-1 Gall: 0-0
Aids:	Bl: 0-0 Vi: 0-0 Tstrap: 0-0 Ckp: 0-0
Best Rating:	40 9/03 NAbb 2m1f gd-fm NHF

Crystal D'Ainay (FR)

128   (0c)162

5-y-o b g Saint Preuil (FR)-Guendale (FR) (Cadoudal (FR))
A King Tony Fisher & Mrs Jeni Fisher

Placings:4112212-212134 (4623)
2003/04: 20²GS, 21¹GS, 24²G, 20¹GS, 24³G, 24⁴G,

	Starts	1st	2nd	3rd	Win & Pl
Hurdles	6	2	2	1	67690
Career Total	13	5	5	1	99904
156 1/04 Chel	2m4f110yA Hdl				G-S £29000
157 12/03 Chel	2m5f		B Hdl		G-S £12122
125 3/03 Uttx	2m		D Hdl		SFT £5128
12/02 Ange	2m2f110y Ch				HLD £4712
11/02 Bord	2m1f		Hdl		HLD £4417
				Total win prize-money £55380	

Going:	Sf: 0-0 GS: 2-3 Gd: 0-3 GF: - Fm: 0-0
Distance:	2m/2m3: 0-0 **2m4-2m7: 2-3** 3m+: 0-3
Track:	**LH: 2-6** RH: 0-0 Tight: 0-2 **Gall: 2-4**
Aids:	Bl: 0-0 Vi: 0-0 Tstrap: 0-0 Ckp: 0-0
Best Rating:	162 3/04 Chel 3m good Hdl

High-class hurdler; winner over hurdles and fences in France; won Cleeve Hurdle at Cheltenham in January; third in the Stayers' Hurdle behind the top-class Iris's Gift, and fourth behind the same rival at Aintree; stays three miles; effective in soft ground; tough and progressing well; has a big future.

Crystal Dance (FR)

89   (0c)72

4-y-o gr g Loup Solitaire (USA)-Somptueuse (FR) (Crystal Palace (FR))
C Grant (J-Y Artu 5/11) Lord Daresbury

Placings:55-033000430606 (4795)
2003/04: 17⁰VS, 17³VS, 17³S, 17⁰S, 15⁰S, 15⁰VS, 17⁴VS, 17³VS, 16⁶S, 16⁶GS, 20⁴GS, 17⁶G,

	Starts	1st	2nd	3rd	Win & Pl
Hurdles	8	0	0	1	1909
Chases	4	0	0	2	2659
Career Total	14	0	0	3	6964

Going:	Sf: 0-4 GS: 0-2 Gd: 0-1 GF: - Fm: 0-0
Distance:	2m/2m3: 0-9 2m4-2m7: 0-1 3m+: 0-0
Track:	LH: 0-4 RH: 0-0 Tight: 0-3 Gall: 0-0
Aids:	Bl: 0-0 Vi: 0-0 Tstrap: 0-0 Ckp: 0-0

Best Rating: 72 3/04 Kels 2m110y gd-sft Hdl

Crystal Gift

111   **121**

12-y-o b g Dominion-Grain Lady (USA) (Greinton)
A C Whillans Mrs L M Whillans

Placings:43221/226/12441/26052F11/004066014/330214/6
242   **(4662)**
2003/04: 20⁶S, 20²HY, 20⁴S, 20²S,

	Starts	1st	2nd	3rd	Win & Pl
Hurdles	4	0	2	0	5347
Career Total	40	7	10	3	63001
121	3/02	Ayr	2m4f	C(0-135)HHdl	SFT	£6831
121	4/01	Hayd	2m	B(0-140)HHdl	SFT	£10046
125	3/00	Kels	2m2f	C(0-135)HHdl	G-S	£8658
118	3/00	Ayr	2m4f	D(0-125)HHdl	HVY	£3016
111	3/99	Hexm	2m4f110yD(0-125)HHdl	G-S	£2768
103	1/99	Ayr	2m	C(0-135)HHdl	HVY	£4445
105	5/96	Kels	2m110y D Hdl	SFT	£3053

Total win prize-money £38818

Going:	Sf: 0-4 GS: 0-0 Gd: 0-0 GF: - Fm: 0-0
Distance:	2m/2m3: 0-0 2m4-2m7: 0-4 3m+: 0-0
Track:	LH: 0-4 RH: 0-0 Tight: 0-0 Gall: 0-0
Aids:	Bl: 0-0 Vi: 0-0 Tstrap: 0-0 Ckp: 0-0
Best Rating: 125	3/00 Kels 2m2f gd-sft Hdl

Fair handicap hurdler; tends to show his best form in the spring; effective from two to three miles and showed he retains most of his ability on his second run after long break at Ayr in January 2004; must have soft ground.

Culbann (IRE)

93f   **97f**

5-y-o b m Religiously (USA)-Persian Gem (IRE) (Persian Heights)
G A Harker R Rae

Placings:4   **(4846)**
2003/04: 17⁴G,

	Starts	1st	2nd	3rd	Win & Pl
NH Flat	1	0	0	0	298
Career Total	1	0	0	0	298

Going:	Sf: 0-0 GS: 0-0 Gd: 0-1 GF: - Fm: 0-0
Distance:	2m/2m3: 0-1 2m4-2m7: 0-0 3m+: 0-0
Track:	LH: 0-1 RH: 0-0 Tight: 0-0 Gall: 0-1
Aids:	Bl: 0-0 Vi: 0-0 Tstrap: 0-0 Ckp: 0-0
Best Rating: 97	4/04 Chel 2m1f good NHF

Culcabock (IRE)

107   **89**

4-y-o b g Unfuwain (USA)-Evidently (IRE) (Slip Anchor)
P Monteith (Joseph Crowley 15/7) Mrs Elizabeth Ferguson

Placings:13034342   **(4657)**
2003/04: 16¹G, 16³G, 16⁹GF, 18³HY, 17⁴GS, 16³GS, 16⁴GF, 16²S,

	Starts	1st	2nd	3rd	Win & Pl
Hurdles	8	1	1	3	6750
Career Total	8	1	1	3	6750
104	11/03 Ayr	2m	E Hdl	GD	£3435

Total win prize-money £3435

Going:	Sf: 0-2 GS: 0-2 Gd: 1-2 GF: - Fm: 0-2
Distance:	2m/2m3: 1-8 2m4-2m7: 0-0 3m+: 0-0
Track:	LH: 1-7 RH: 0-1 Tight: 0-4 Gall: 0-1
Aids:	Bl: 0-0 Vi: 0-0 Tstrap: 0-0 Ckp: 0-0
Best Rating: 104	11/03 Ayr 2m good Hdl

Had the run of the race when winning poor race at Ayr in November and probably ran to similar level at Newcastle in defeat later that month; stays two miles; can make the running.

Cullen Road (IRE)

89   **76**

6-y-o b g Wakashan-My Wings (Erin's Hope)
J R Jenkins Jack McGrath

Placings:6005F5-30   **(0701)**
2003/04: 16³GF, 17⁰GF,

	Starts	1st	2nd	3rd	Win & Pl
Hurdles	2	0	0	1	521
Career Total	8	0	0	1	521

Going:	Sf: 0-0 GS: 0-0 Gd: 0-0 GF: - Fm: 0-2
Distance:	2m/2m3: 0-2 2m4-2m7: 0-0 3m+: 0-0
Track:	LH: 0-1 RH: 0-1 Tight: 0-1 Gall: 0-0
Aids:	Bl: 0-0 Vi: 0-0 Tstrap: 0-0 Ckp: 0-1
Best Rating: 86	10/02 Hntg 2m110y gd-fm NHF

Modest form in bumpers and novice hurdles; best on a sound surface.

Cullian

102(91c)   (90c)**97**

7-y-o b m Missed Flight-Diamond Gig (Pitskelly)
J G M O'Shea (Mrs N Smith 12/1) Bill Tyler

Placings:0504/1P010-3P0P2   **(4673)**
2003/04: 22⁰S, 16³G, 25⁵GF, 20⁰G, 20⁰HY, 16²G,

	Starts	1st	2nd	3rd	Win & Pl
Hurdles	4	0	1	0	1081
Chases	2	0	0	0	460
Career Total	14	2	1	1	8106
94	2/03 Plum	2m5f	E(0-105)HHdl	SFT	£3523
95	11/02 Folk	2m1f110yE Hdl	G-S	£3041

Total win prize-money £6565

Going:	Sf: 0-2 GS: 0-0 Gd: 0-3 GF: - Fm: 0-1
Distance:	2m/2m3: 0-2 2m4-2m7: 0-3 3m+: 0-1
Track:	LH: 0-2 RH: 0-3 Tight: 0-4 Gall: 0-0
Aids:	Bl: 0-1 Vi: 0-0 Tstrap: 0-0 Ckp: 0-2
Best Rating: 97	4/04 Winc 2m good Hdl

Modest novice hurdler; stays two miles five; effective in soft ground; has worn cheekpieces.

Cumbrian Knight (IRE)

110   **111+**

6-y-o b g Presenting-Crashrun (Crash Course)
J M Jefferson Cumbrian Industrials Ltd

Placings:4231440-412420P02   **(4883)**
2003/04: 16⁴G, 17¹G, 17²G, 20⁴HY, 20⁶S, 16⁶GS, 16⁹G, 17²GS,

	Starts	1st	2nd	3rd	Win & Pl
Hurdles	9	1	3	0	7396
Career Total	16	2	4	1	11077
91	10/03 Bang	2m1f	E Hdl	GD	£3304
97	11/02 Hayd	2m	H NHF	GD	£2138

Total win prize-money £5443

Going:	Sf: 0-0 GS: 0-3 Gd: 1-4 GF: - Fm: 0-0
Distance:	2m/2m3: 1-8 2m4-2m7: 0-1 3m+: 0-0
Track:	LH: 1-5 RH: 0-4 Tight: 1-3 Gall: 0-0
Aids:	Bl: 0-0 Vi: 0-0 Tstrap: 0-0 Ckp: 0-0
Best Rating: 111	4/04 Carl 2m1f gd-sft Hdl

Promise in bumpers on fast ground, before getting off the mark at Haydock in November 2002; odds-on winner of slowly-run 2m 1f weakly contested novice hurdle at Bangor in October 2003; acts on good ground.

Cupla Cairde

107   **119**

4-y-o b c Double Eclipse (IRE)-Four-Legged Friend (Aragon)
D T Hughes Ceathrar Le Ceile Syndicate

Placings:623212613   **(4802a)**
2003/04: 16⁶GF, 16²GY, 16³S, 16²S, 16¹HY, 16²S, 16⁶S, 16¹GF, 16³Y,

	Starts	1st	2nd	3rd	Win & Pl
Hurdles	9	2	3	2	27582
Career Total	9	2	3	2	27582
118	3/04 Strf	2m110y D Hdl	G-F	£5681
112	1/04 Punc	2m	Hdl	HVY	£14647

Total win prize-money £20329

Going:	Sf: 1-5 GS: 0-0 Gd: 0-0 GF: - Fm: 1-2
Distance:	2m/2m3: 2-9 2m4-2m7: 0-0 3m+: 0-0
Track:	LH: 1-5 RH: 1-4 Tight: 1-1 Gall: 0-0
Aids:	Bl: 2-4 Vi: 0-0 Tstrap: 0-0 Ckp: 0-0
Best Rating: 118	4/04 Fair 2m yield Hdl

Decent Irish juvenile hurdler; handles most types of ground; has worn blinkers.

Curiositski

70   **65**

8-y-o b m Petoski-Nosey's Daughter (Song)
D A Rees D Rees

Placings:0/40405/0   **(0869)**
2003/04: 22⁰GF,

	Starts	1st	2nd	3rd	Win & Pl
Hurdles	1	0	0	0	
Career Total	7	0	0	0	

Going:	Sf: 0-0 GS: 0-0 Gd: 0-0 GF: - Fm: 0-1
Distance:	2m/2m3: 0-0 2m4-2m7: 0-1 3m+: 0-0
Track:	LH: 0-1 RH: 0-0 Tight: 0-1 Gall: 0-0
Aids:	Bl: 0-0 Vi: 0-0 Tstrap: 0-0 Ckp: 0-0
Best Rating: 70	5/01 Bang 2m1f good NHF

Curly Spencer (IRE)

111(100h)   (116 h)**121**

10-y-o br g Yashgan-Tim's Brief (Avocat)
A Parker Mr & Mrs Raymond Anderson Green

Placings:00/543051100/1U/PF2422/51114-P344P2P3   **(4912)**
2003/04: 24³PG, 20³GF, 20⁴S, 22⁴HY, 22⁵GS, 20²HY, 24³G, 20⁶S,

	Starts	1st	2nd	3rd	Win & Pl
Chases	8	0	1	2	5878
Career Total	32	6	4	3	43215
121	1/03 Ayr	2m4f	C(0-130)HCh	SFT	£8034
113	11/02 Newc	2m4f	D(0-125)HCh	G-S	£10582
116	11/02 Carl	2m4f	E(0-100)HHdl	G-S	£2898
116	2/01 Carl	2m4f110yF(0-100)HCh	HVY	£3271
109	3/00 Hexm	2m4f110yF(0-100)HCh	SFT	£3107
103	3/00 Carl	2m	E(0-115)HCh	HVY	£3380

Total win prize-money £31722

Going:	Sf: 0-4 GS: 0-1 Gd: 0-2 GF: - Fm: 0-1
Distance:	2m/2m3: 0-0 2m4-2m7: 0-6 3m+: 0-2
Track:	LH: 0-3 RH: 0-5 Tight: 0-2 Gall: 0-0
Aids:	Bl: 0-0 Vi: 0-0 Tstrap: 0-0 Ckp: 0-0
Best Rating: 121	1/03 Ayr 2m4f soft Ch

Fair chaser; suited by forcing tactics; best over two and a half miles; appreciates cut in the ground.

Curragh Gold (IRE)
98   75

4-y-o b f Flying Spur (AUS)-Go Indigo (IRE) (Cyrano De Bergerac)
Mrs P N Dutfield The Goldrush Partners

Placings:0002P   (4733)
2003/04: 16⁰S, 17⁰HY, 16⁰S, 19²G, 22PG,

	Starts	1st	2nd	3rd	Win & Pl
Hurdles	5	0	1	0	722
Career Total	5	0	1	0	722

Going:	Sf: 0-3 GS: 0-0 Gd: 0-2 GF: - Fm: 0-0
Distance:	2m/2m3: 0-3 2m4-2m7: 0-2 3m+: 0-0
Track:	LH: 0-3 RH: 0-2 Tight: 0-5 Gall: 0-0
Aids:	Bl: 0-2 Vi: 0-0 Tstrap: 0-0 Ckp: 0-0
Best Rating:	75 3/04 Tntn 2m3f110y good Hdl

Curtins Hill (IRE)
109(103h)   (107 h)117

10-y-o b g Roi Guillaume (FR)-Kinallen Lady (IRE) (Abednego)
T R George Mrs Elizabeth Pitman

Placings:0050/611402-34302213   (4169)
2003/04: 24³G, 20⁴GF, 20³G, 18³GS, 23²G, 21²GS, 24¹G, 23³G,

	Starts	1st	2nd	3rd	Win & Pl
Chases	8	1	2	3	19346
Career Total	18	3	3	3	33532
116	2/04	Sand	3m110y	D(0-115)HCh	GD	£6987
107	12/02	Chel	2m1f	D(0-120)HHdl	SFT	£9265
98	12/02	Ludl	2m5f	E(0-105)HHdl	GD	£3484
			Total win prize-money £19737			

Going:	Sf: 0-0 GS: 0-2 Gd: 1-5 GF: - Fm: 0-1
Distance:	2m/2m3: 0-1 2m4-2m7: 0-4 3m+: 1-3
Track:	LH: 0-5 RH: 1-3 Tight: 0-1 Gall: 0-5
Aids:	Bl: 0-0 Vi: 0-0 Tstrap: 0-0 Ckp: 0-0
Best Rating:	116 2/04 Sand 3m110y good Ch

Modest ex-Irish hurdler/novice chaser; effective at two miles to two miles five; acts on good and soft ground; not a straightforward ride.

Cush Jewel (IRE)
105   (0c)91

8-y-o b m Executive Perk-Shannon Jewel (IRE) (Le Bavard (FR))
J G M O'Shea (David Fenton 8/6) The Cross Racing Club

Placings:0000-0343132F2550   (3808)
2003/04: 20⁴G, 24³GF, 21⁴GF, 26³GF, 21¹F, 24³GF, 19²G, 26FG, 20²GF, 21⁵GF, 19⁵HY, 21⁰G,

	Starts	1st	2nd	3rd	Win & Pl
Hurdles	11	1	2	3	6795
Chases	1	0	0	0	0
Career Total	16	1	2	3	6795
91	10/03	Towc	2m5f	E(0-105)HHdl	FRM	£3721
			Total win prize-money £3721			

Going:	Sf: 0-1 GS: 0-0 Gd: 0-4 GF: - Fm: 1-7
Distance:	2m/2m3: 0-0 2m4-2m7: 1-8 3m+: 0-4
Track:	LH: 0-3 RH: 1-8 Tight: 0-2 Gall: 0-1
Aids:	Bl: 0-0 Vi: 0-0 Tstrap: 0-0 Ckp: 0-1
Best Rating:	91 11/03 Leic 2m4f110y gd-fm Hdl

Modest hurdler; stays three miles and acts on fast ground.

Cusp
94   73

4-y-o b f Pivotal-Bambolona (Bustino)
C W Thornton Mrs C Wilson

Placings:06U0   (4732)
2003/04: 16⁰GS, 16⁶HY, 16UG, 17⁰G,

	Starts	1st	2nd	3rd	Win & Pl
Hurdles	4	0	0	0	0
Career Total	4	0	0	0	0

Going:	Sf: 0-1 GS: 0-1 Gd: 0-2 GF: - Fm: 0-0
Distance:	2m/2m3: 0-4 2m4-2m7: 0-0 3m+: 0-0
Track:	LH: 0-3 RH: 0-1 Tight: 0-1 Gall: 0-1
Aids:	Bl: 0-0 Vi: 0-0 Tstrap: 0-0 Ckp: 0-0
Best Rating:	73 2/04 Catt 2m good Hdl

Cut Throat Jake
72   47

7-y-o ch g Karinga Bay-French Lip (Scorpio (FR))
S J Gilmore Pieces Of Eight

Placings:0/PP00U   (1190)
2003/04: 24PGF, 26PG, 16⁹G, 20⁹GF, 20UGF,

	Starts	1st	2nd	3rd	Win & Pl
Hurdles	5	0	0		
Career Total	6	0	0		

Going:	Sf: 0-0 GS: 0-0 Gd: 0-2 GF: - Fm: 0-3
Distance:	2m/2m3: 0-1 2m4-2m7: 0-2 3m+: 0-2
Track:	LH: 0-5 RH: 0-0 Tight: 0-0 Gall: 0-0
Aids:	Bl: 0-0 Vi: 0-0 Tstrap: 0-0 Ckp: 0-0
Best Rating:	53 8/03 Worc 2m4f gd-fm Hdl

Cuthill Hope (IRE)
96   119

13-y-o gr g Peacock (FR)-Sicilian Princess (Sicilian Prince)
A C Whillans Stephen Gilchrist

Placings:441/331F6F1/143O/12U/50P1P5/531-P45U   (3675)
2003/04: 20PG, 25⁴S, 25⁵S, 22UHY,

	Starts	1st	2nd	3rd	Win & Pl
Chases	4	0	0		306
Career Total	30	7	1	4	36386
119	11/02	Kels	2m6f110yD(0-120)HCh	SFT	£6773
119	3/02	Kels	3m1f	D(0-120)HCh	SFT	£5427
118	11/00	Ayr	3m1f	D(0-125)HCh	G-S	£3750
114	5/98	Aint	2m	D(0-125)HCh	G-F	£4622
126	4/98	Kels	3m1f	D Ch	SFT	£3403
126	1/98	Donc	2m3f110yD Ch	GD	£4237
105	3/97	Plum	2m1f	E Hdl	GS	£2553
			Total win prize-money £30768			

Going:	Sf: 0-3 GS: 0-0 Gd: 0-1 GF: - Fm: 0-0
Distance:	2m/2m3: 0-0 2m4-2m7: 0-2 3m+: 0-2
Track:	LH: 0-4 RH: 0-0 Tight: 0-3 Gall: 0-0
Aids:	Bl: 0-0 Vi: 0-0 Tstrap: 0-0 Ckp: 0-0
Best Rating:	126 4/98 Kels 2m1f soft Ch

Useful handicap chaser; stays three miles plus and acts on most types of ground; has worn a visor; likes to make the running.

Cutthroat
78f   84+f

4-y-o ch g Kris-Could Have Been (Nomination)
T P Tate T P Tate

Placings:3   (4543)
2003/04: 16³GS,

	Starts	1st	2nd	3rd	Win & Pl
NH Flat	1	0	0	1	366
Career Total	1	0	0	1	366

Going:	Sf: 0-0 GS: 0-1 Gd: 0-0 GF: - Fm: 0-0
Distance:	2m/2m3: 0-1 2m4-2m7: 0-0 3m+: 0-0
Track:	LH: 0-0 RH: 0-1 Tight: 0-0 Gall: 0-0
Aids:	Bl: 0-0 Vi: 0-0 Tstrap: 0-0 Ckp: 0-0
Best Rating:	84 3/04 Ludl 2m gd-sft NHF

Cutthroat Kid (IRE)
80

14-y-o b g Last Tycoon-Get Ahead (Silly Season)
T R Greathead Mrs S Greathead

Placings:12/12631415/3140/00042/1025/03003/045440/0   (4750)
2003/04: 21⁰G,

	Starts	1st	2nd	3rd	Win & Pl
Hurdles	1	0	0		
Career Total	35	6	4	4	19089
93	12/99	Hntg	2m5f110yF(0-100)HHdl	G-S	£2108
101	3/97	MRas	2m3f110yF Hdl	GD	£1994
115	1/96	Ayr	2m6f	E(0-115)HHdl	GD	£2631
115	1/96	Sedg	2m5f110yD(0-120)HHdl	G-F	£2860
92	5/95	Sedg	2m5f110yE Hdl	FRM	£2318
107	12/94	Donc	2m4f	Hdl	GD	£2485
			Total win prize-money £14399			

Going:	Sf: 0-0 GS: 0-0 Gd: 0-1 GF: - Fm: 0-0
Distance:	2m/2m3: 0-0 2m4-2m7: 0-1 3m+: 0-0
Track:	LH: 0-1 RH: 0-0 Tight: 0-1 Gall: 0-0
Aids:	Bl: 0-0 Vi: 0-0 Tstrap: 0-0 Ckp: 0-0
Best Rating:	118 1/96 Newc 2m4f good Hdl

Veteran, plating-class staying hurdler; suited by a sharp track.

Cyanara
107(103h)   (61h)83

8-y-o b m Jupiter Island-Shamana (Broadsword (USA))
Dr P Pritchard Steven R Hanney

Placings:0/P/P061P00P0/00O0-535FP5263433B250230   (4648)
2003/04: 16⁵GF, 21³GF, 24⁵G, 20FGF, 26PGF, 26⁵GF, 26²GF, 22⁶G, 26³GF, 24⁴GF, 20³GF, 19³G, 19⁶G, 22²HY, 19⁵HY, 24⁰GS, 22²GF, 22³G, 20⁰G,

	Starts	1st	2nd	3rd	Win & Pl
Hurdles	1	0	0	0	0
Chases	18	0	3	5	7220
Career Total	34	1	3	5	10454
76	11/01	Fknm	2m	E(0-105)HHdl	SFT	£3234
			Total win prize-money £3234			

Going:	Sf: 0-2 GS: 0-1 Gd: 0-6 GF: - Fm: 0-10
Distance:	2m/2m3: 0-3 2m4-2m7: 0-9 3m+: 0-7
Track:	LH: 0-10 RH: 0-5 Tight: 0-9 Gall: 0-1
Aids:	Bl: 0-0 Vi: 0-0 Tstrap: 0-0 Ckp: 0-0
Best Rating:	76 3/04 Font 2m6f gd-fm Ch

Plating-class novice chaser.

Cybele Eria (FR)
(96h)   (117h)105

7-y-o b m Johann Quatz (FR)-Money Can't Buy (Thatching)
John Allen (N J Henderson 10/5) Avon Estates Ltd

Placings:23/2241/F25003212-46   (3418)
2003/04: 16⁴GF, 17⁶GS,

	Starts	1st	2nd	3rd	Win & Pl
Hurdles	2	0	0	0	0
Career Total	17	2	6	2	15810
84 3/03 Wwck 2m110y E Ch				G-F	£4036
117 3/02 Hrfd 2m1f E Hdl				SFT	£2849
				Total win prize-money	£6886

Going: Sf: 0-0 GS: 0-1 Gd: 0-0 GF: - Fm: 0-1
Distance: 2m/2m3: 0-2 2m4-2m7: 0-0 3m+: 0-0
Track: LH: 0-1 RH: 0-1 Tight: 0-0 Gall: 0-0
Aids: Bl: 0-0 Vi: 0-0 Tstrap: 0-0 Ckp: 0-0
Best Rating: 117 11/02 Hayd 2m good Hdl

Modest hurdler/novice chaser; acts on soft ground; does not find much off the bridle.

Cyborg De Sou (FR)
108   105+
6-y-o b g Cyborg (FR)-Moomaw (Akarad (FR))
G A Harker (J F C Maxwell 15/1) John J Maguire

Placings:4/0-0004261   (4946)
2003/04: 16⁹G, 16⁶G, 16⁵S, 16⁴S, 17²GS, 16⁶HY, 16¹GS,

	Starts	1st	2nd	3rd	Win & Pl
NH Flat	2	0	0	0	
Hurdles	5	1	1	0	7010
Career Total	9	1	1	0	7169
105 4/04 Prth 2m110y D Hdl				G-S	£5668
				Total win prize-money	£5668

Going: Sf: 0-3 GS: 1-2 Gd: 0-2 GF: - Fm: 0-0
Distance: 2m/2m3: 1-7 2m4-2m7: 0-0 3m+: 0-0
Track: LH: 0-2 RH: 1-1 Tight: 0-1 Gall: 0-1
Aids: Bl: 0-0 Vi: 0-0 Tstrap: 0-0 Ckp: 0-0
Best Rating: 105 4/04 Prth 2m110y gd-sft Hdl

Modest hurdler who got off the mark at Perth in April 2004; acts on soft ground but well beaten on heavy; only raced around two miles over hurdles but worth a try over a bit further.

Cyfor Malta (FR)
102   145
11-y-o b g Cyborg (FR)-Force Nine (FR) (Luthier)
M C Pipe D A Johnson

Placings:32111211/11/3/1402P/14U-56PP0   (4835)
2003/04: 20⁵GS, 25⁶G, 20⁵G, 25⁶G, 21⁰GF,

	Starts	1st	2nd	3rd	Win & Pl
Chases	5	0	0	0	3350
Career Total	24	9	3	2	308711
169 11/02 Chel 2m4f110yA HCh				G-S	£58000
162 12/01 Newb 2m4f B(0-145)HCh				SFT	£20300
169 1/99 Chel 3m1f110yA Ch				SFT	£18390
163 11/98 Chel 2m4f110yA HCh				GD	£47260
158 4/98 Aint 2m6f B(0-145)HCh				SFT	£25072
147 3/98 Chel 2m5f B Ch				GD	£33500
146 1/98 Sand 2m4f110yD Ch				G-S	£4485
11/97 Autl 2m4f110y Ch				HLD	£22447
10/97 Autl 2m1f110y Ch				VS	£13468
				Total win prize-money	£242923

Going: Sf: 0-0 GS: 0-0 Gd: 0-4 GF: - Fm: 0-1
Distance: 2m/2m3: 0-0 2m4-2m7: 0-3 3m+: 0-2
Track: LH: 0-5 RH: 0-0 Tight: 0-1 Gall: 0-4
Aids: Bl: 0-0 Vi: 0-0 Tstrap: 0-0 Ckp: 0-0
Best Rating: 169 11/02 Chel 2m4f110y gd-sft Ch

Smart chaser, formerly high-class several years ago; landed the Murphy's Gold Cup and the Pillar Chase in 1998/9; a leg injury then kept him off the track for two years, but back to his best when landing the Thomas Pink on his seasonal debut in November 2002, four years on from his first success in the same race; not at his best in 2003/04 season; stays 3m 1f, although he is fully effective at shorter; best when allowed to get his toe in a little; has worn a visor.

Cyindien (FR)
100(91c)   (80c)107
7-y-o b/br g Cyborg (FR)-Indiana Rose (FR) (Cadoudal (FR))
Ms Bridget Nicholls Ms Bridget Nicholls

Placings:5/222-3046003   (4897)
2003/04: 20³GS, 22⁹GS, 20⁴S, 24⁶GS, 20⁰G, 17⁰G, 22³G,

	Starts	1st	2nd	3rd	Win & Pl
Hurdles	5	0	0	2	1098
Chases	2	0	0	0	313
Career Total	11	0	3	2	4085

Going: Sf: 0-1 GS: 0-3 Gd: 0-3 GF: - Fm: 0-0
Distance: 2m/2m3: 0-1 2m4-2m7: 0-5 3m+: 0-1
Track: LH: 0-5 RH: 0-2 Tight: 0-1 Gall: 0-1
Aids: Bl: 0-1 Vi: 0-0 Tstrap: 0-0 Ckp: 0-1
Best Rating: 107 12/02 Wwck 3m1f soft Hdl

Moderate hurdler; well beaten in chases; stays three miles, acts with cut in the ground.

Cyrium (IRE)
93f   80f
5-y-o b g Woodborough (USA)-Jarmar Moon (Unfuwain (USA))
C J Mann (R F Fisher 15/5) Colin And Pauline Sturgeon

Placings:0-40   (4213)
2003/04: 16⁴GF, 16⁰G,

	Starts	1st	2nd	3rd	Win & Pl
NH Flat	2	0	0	0	0
Career Total	3	0	0	0	0

Going: Sf: 0-0 GS: 0-0 Gd: 0-1 GF: - Fm: 0-1
Distance: 2m/2m3: 0-2 2m4-2m7: 0-0 3m+: 0-0
Track: LH: 0-0 RH: 0-2 Tight: 0-0 Gall: 0-0
Aids: Bl: 0-0 Vi: 0-0 Tstrap: 0-0 Ckp: 0-0
Best Rating: 80 5/03 Ludl 2m gd-fm NHF

D'Argent (IRE)
103(96h)   (119h)155
7-y-o gr g Roselier (FR)-Money Galore (IRE) (Monksfield)
A King Nigel Bunter

Placings:0211/00-351115P   (4642)
2003/04: 22³G, 22⁵G, 26¹G, 24¹G, 24¹GS, 25⁵G, 25⁵G,

	Starts	1st	2nd	3rd	Win & Pl
Hurdles	2	0	0	1	720
Chases	5	3	0	0	25703
Career Total	13	5	1	1	33134
155 1/04 Wwck 3m110y B Ch				G-S	£14040
136 12/03 Wwck 3m110y C Ch				GD	£6929
126 12/03 Wwck 3m2f E Ch				GD	£3484
119 3/02 Extr 2m3f E Hdl				GD	£2842
119 3/02 Donc 2m4f E Hdl				SFT	£3122
				Total win prize-money	£30417

Going: Sf: 0-0 GS: 1-1 Gd: 2-6 GF: - Fm: 0-0
Distance: 2m/2m3: 0-0 2m4-2m7: 0-2 3m+: 3-5
Track: LH: 3-6 RH: 0-1 Tight: 0-3 Gall: 0-0
Aids: Bl: 0-0 Vi: 0-0 Tstrap: 0-0 Ckp: 0-0
Best Rating: 155 1/04 Wwck 3m110y gd-sft Ch

Smart and unbeaten staying novice chaser; completed a hat-trick of wins at Warwick when landing a Class B event in January 2004; rather disappointing against experienced rivals at Wincanton and jumped poorly at Aintree; may be best going left-handed; stays 3m 2f; acts on good and soft ground.

D'Issan (IRE)
74f   50f
6-y-o br g Commanche Run-Loch Phar (IRE) (Phardante (FR))
B J M Ryall J J Boulter

Placings:0   (0606)
2003/04: 17⁰G,

	Starts	1st	2nd	3rd	Win & Pl
NH Flat	1	0	0	0	
Career Total	1	0	0	0	

Going: Sf: 0-0 GS: 0-0 Gd: 0-1 GF: - Fm: 0-0
Distance: 2m/2m3: 0-1 2m4-2m7: 0-0 3m+: 0-0
Track: LH: 0-1 RH: 0-0 Tight: 0-1 Gall: 0-0
Aids: Bl: 0-0 Vi: 0-0 Tstrap: 0-0 Ckp: 0-0
Best Rating: 51 6/03 NAbb 2m1f good NHF

Dabarpour (IRE)
96(84c)   (69c)96
8-y-o b/br g Alzao (USA)-Dabara (IRE) (Shardari)
M A Barnes (J G M O'Shea 13/7) J G Graham

Placings:4050/32500/120003124/14624-0544240600   (3735)
2003/04: 16⁹GS, 20⁵G, 19⁴G, 17⁴S, 17²GF, 17⁴G, 16⁶GF, 16⁶GF, 16⁰GS, 16⁰G,

	Starts	1st	2nd	3rd	Win & Pl
Hurdles	9	0	1	0	1044
Chases	1	0	0	0	418
Career Total	33	3	5	2	15964
112 5/02 Wwck 2m D(0-115)HHdl				FRM	£3349
103 11/01 Hntg 2m110y E(0-115)HHdl				GD	£2429
100 6/01 Strf 2m110y E(0-105)HHdl				G-F	£3209
				Total win prize-money	£8989

Going: Sf: 0-1 GS: 0-2 Gd: 0-4 GF: - Fm: 0-3
Distance: 2m/2m3: 0-8 2m4-2m7: 0-2 3m+: 0-0
Track: LH: 0-7 RH: 0-2 Tight: 0-5 Gall: 0-0
Aids: Bl: 0-0 Vi: 0-1 Tstrap: 0-2 Ckp: 0-3
Best Rating: 112 5/02 Wwck 2m firm Hdl

Modest handicap hurdler; disappointing on only start over fences; acts on fast ground; seems best at around 2m.

Dabus
108   (0c)98
9-y-o b g Kris-Licorne (Sadler's Wells (USA))
M C Chapman J C Greenway

Placings:PP03606/125211425/3202303F-0RU015   (1476)
2003/04: 16⁰G, 19⁶R, 16⁴GF, 17⁰G, 17¹GF, 17⁵G,

	Starts	1st	2nd	3rd	Win & Pl
Hurdles	6	1	0	0	1848
Career Total	30	4	5	4	19574
94 9/03 Sedg 2m1f G(0-95)HHdl				G-F	£1848
111 7/00 Sthl 2m D(0-120)HHdl				G-F	£5499
111 7/00 MRas 2m1f110yE(0-105)HHdl				GD	£2886
91 5/00 Strf 2m110y F(0-100)HHdl				GD	£2982
				Total win prize-money	£13215

Going: Sf: 0-0 GS: 0-0 Gd: 0-4 GF: - Fm: 1-2
Distance: 2m/2m3: 1-5 2m4-2m7: 0-1 3m+: 0-0
Track: LH: 1-5 RH: 0-1 Tight: 1-4 Gall: 0-0
Aids: Bl: 0-0 Vi: 0-0 Tstrap: 0-0 Ckp: 0-0

Best Rating: 111 7/00 Strf 2m3f   gd-fm Hdl

Plating-class hurdler; effective at around two miles; acts on decent ground.

Dad's Elect (GER)

99   **110+**

5-y-o b g Lomitas-Diamond Lake (USA) (Cox's Ridge (USA))
C J Mann A L R Morton

Placings:0243012150   (4638)
2003/04: 17⁰G, 18²G, 17⁴G, 16³G, 16⁰G, 18¹HY, 20²G, 17¹G, 20⁵G, 16⁰G,

	Starts	1st	2nd	3rd	Win & Pl
Hurdles	10	2	2	1	36260
Career Total	10	2	2	1	36260
12/03 Capa	2m1f110y Hdl			GD	£12987
11/03 Siro	2m2f	HHdl		HVY	£12987
	Total win prize-money £25974				

Going:	Sf: 1-2 GS: 0-0 Gd: 1-8 GF: - Fm: 0-0
Distance:	2m/2m3: 2-8 2m4-2m7: 0-2 3m+: 0-0
Track:	LH: 0-1 RH: 0-1 Tight: 0-1 Gall: 0-0
Aids:	Bl: 1-2 Vi: 0-0 Tstrap: 0-0 Ckp: 0-0
Best Rating: 110 4/04 Aint 2m110y good Hdl

Fair novice hurdler; dual winner over hurdles in Italy, now with Charlie Mann; stays two and a half miles and acts on ground good or softer; has worn blinkers.

Dads Gift

85f   **82f**

6-y-o ch g Ajjaj-Lyricist (Averof)
R L Brown S R Brown

Placings:200   (4816)
2003/04: 14²GS, 17⁰G, 16⁰G,

	Starts	1st	2nd	3rd	Win & Pl
NH Flat	3	0	1	0	568
Career Total	3	0	1	0	568

Going:	Sf: 0-0 GS: 0-1 Gd: 0-2 GF: - Fm: 0-0
Distance:	2m/2m3: 0-2 2m4-2m7: 0-0 3m+: 0-0
Track:	LH: 0-2 RH: 0-0 Tight: 0-1 Gall: 0-0
Aids:	Bl: 0-0 Vi: 0-0 Tstrap: 0-0 Ckp: 0-0
Best Rating: 82 3/04 Hrfd 1m6f gd-sft NHF

Dads Lad (IRE)

103   **106+**

10-y-o b g Supreme Leader-Furryvale (Furry Glen)
Miss Suzy Smith Miss Suzy Smith

Placings:4334/304514/03F4B3-21P13   (3425)
2003/04: 26²HY, 28¹GS, 28⁰PG, 24¹GS, 25³G,

	Starts	1st	2nd	3rd	Win & Pl
Chases	5	2	1		13201
Career Total	21	3	1	6	22498
106 1/04 Asct	3m110y D(0-115)HCh	G-S	£6864
99 12/03 MRas	3m4f110yD(0-110)HCh	G-S	£3267
100 3/02 Bang	3m110y D(0-110)HCh	SFT	£4231
	Total win prize-money £14364				

Going:	Sf: 0-2 GS: 2-2 Gd: 0-1 GF: - Fm: 0-0
Distance:	2m/2m3: 0-0 2m4-2m7: 0-0 3m+: 2-5
Track:	LH: 0-1 RH: 2-4 Tight: 1-3 Gall: 0-0
Aids:	Bl: 2-5 Vi: 0-0 Tstrap: 0-0 Ckp: 0-0
Best Rating: 106 1/04 Asct 3m110y gd-sft Ch

Moderate handicap chaser, suited by soft ground, stays 3m plus; wears blinkers.

Daily Run (IRE)

76   **43**

6-y-o b g Supreme Leader-Rugged Run (Deep Run)
G M Moore A J Coupland

Placings:000P   (4727)
2003/04: 16⁸S, 20⁹HY, 20⁰GS, 17⁷G,

	Starts	1st	2nd	3rd	Win & Pl
NH Flat	1	0	0	0	0
Hurdles	3	0	0	0	0
Career Total	4	0	0	0	0

Going:	Sf: 0-2 GS: 0-1 Gd: 0-1 GF: - Fm: 0-0
Distance:	2m/2m3: 0-2 2m4-2m7: 0-2 3m+: 0-0
Track:	LH: 0-1 RH: 0-1 Tight: 0-0 Gall: 0-2
Aids:	Bl: 0-0 Vi: 0-0 Tstrap: 0-0 Ckp: 0-0
Best Rating: 69 11/03 Ayr 2m soft NHF

Daisy Dale

91   **73**

6-y-o gr m Terimon-Quetta's Girl (Orchestra)
K Bishop N K Allin

Placings:00O/64240   (2693)
2003/04: 17⁰GS, 16⁴GF, 16²F, 19⁴GF, 16⁰G,

	Starts	1st	2nd	3rd	Win & Pl
NH Flat	1	0	0	0	0
Hurdles	4	0	1	0	1366
Career Total	8	0	1	0	1366

Going:	Sf: 0-0 GS: 0-0 Gd: 0-0 GF: - Fm: 0-4
Distance:	2m/2m3: 0-4 2m4-2m7: 0-1 3m+: 0-0
Track:	LH: 0-1 RH: 0-4 Tight: 0-1 Gall: 0-0
Aids:	Bl: 0-0 Vi: 0-0 Tstrap: 0-0 Ckp: 0-0
Best Rating: 73 11/03 Tntn 2m3f110y gd-fm Hdl

Has not shown much worthwhile form in bumpers or hurdle races to date.

Dajazar (IRE)

                                         (95dc)**32**

8-y-o b g Seattle Dancer (USA)-Dajarra (IRE) (Blushing Groom (FR))
Miss V Scott Mr & Mrs Aynsley & M Abercrombie

Placings:0530P/2310023/030412P00-F   (0042)
2003/04: 18²FG,

	Starts	1st	2nd	3rd	Win & Pl
Hurdles	1	0	0	0	
Career Total	22	2	3	4	16409
106 8/02 Tral	2m6f	(81-123)HHdl	GD	£7407
107 7/01 Dund	2m135y Hdl		FRM	£3895
	Total win prize-money £11303				

Going:	Sf: 0-0 GS: 0-0 Gd: 0-1 GF: - Fm: 0-0
Distance:	2m/2m3: 0-1 2m4-2m7: 0-0 3m+: 0-0
Track:	LH: 0-1 RH: 0-0 Tight: 0-1 Gall: 0-0
Aids:	Bl: 0-0 Vi: 0-0 Tstrap: 0-0 Ckp: 0-0
Best Rating: 116 2/01 Naas 2m sft-hvy Hdl

Dalaram (IRE)

104   **124+**

4-y-o b c Sadler's Wells (USA)-Dalara (IRE) (Doyoun)
J Howard Johnson (Sir Michael Stoute 2/10) Andrea & Graham Wylie

Placings:0101   (4863)
2003/04: 17⁰GS, 16¹G, 16⁰G, 16¹S,

	Starts	1st	2nd	3rd	Win & Pl
Hurdles	4	2	0	0	10940
Career Total	4	2	0	0	10940
124 4/04 Ayr	2m	C Hdl	SFT	£7481
101 2/04 Muss	2m	E Hdl	GD	£3458
	Total win prize-money £10940				

Going:	Sf: 1-1 GS: 0-1 Gd: 1-2 GF: - Fm: 0-0
Distance:	2m/2m3: 2-4 2m4-2m7: 0-0 3m+: 0-0
Track:	LH: 1-3 RH: 1-1 Tight: 1-2 Gall: 0-1
Aids:	Bl: 0-0 Vi: 0-0 Tstrap: 1-3 Ckp: 0-0
Best Rating: 124 4/04 Ayr 2m soft Hdl

Smart performer on the Flat; eventual wide-margin winner on second start over hurdles at Musselburgh in February and had the run of the race when showing improved form at Ayr in April; should stay further than two miles; effective with or without a tongue strap.

Dalawan

95f   **90f**

5-y-o b g Nashwan (USA)-Magdala (IRE) (Sadler's Wells (USA))
A J Chamberlain F J Brennan

Placings:2   (1226)
2003/04: 17²GF,

	Starts	1st	2nd	3rd	Win & Pl
NH Flat	1	0	1	0	1055
Career Total	1	0	1	0	1055

Going:	Sf: 0-0 GS: 0-0 Gd: 0-0 GF: - Fm: 0-1
Distance:	2m/2m3: 0-1 2m4-2m7: 0-0 3m+: 0-0
Track:	LH: 0-1 RH: 0-0 Tight: 0-1 Gall: 0-0
Aids:	Bl: 0-0 Vi: 0-0 Tstrap: 0-0 Ckp: 0-0
Best Rating: 90 8/03 NAbb 2m1f gd-fm NHF

Son of Nashwan out of a Sadler's Wells mare; runner-up in modest Newton Abbot bumper on debut August 2003.

Dalblair (IRE)

100   **92+**

5-y-o b g Lake Coniston (IRE)-Cartagena Lady (IRE) (Prince Rupert (FR))
M Todhunter (J A Glover 6/10) Abbadis Racing Club

Placings:34   (3230)
2003/04: 16³G, 16⁴GF,

	Starts	1st	2nd	3rd	Win & Pl
Hurdles	2	0	0	1	2357
Career Total	2	0	0	1	2357

Going:	Sf: 0-0 GS: 0-0 Gd: 0-1 GF: - Fm: 0-0
Distance:	2m/2m3: 0-2 2m4-2m7: 0-0 3m+: 0-0
Track:	LH: 0-1 RH: 0-1 Tight: 0-1 Gall: 0-0
Aids:	Bl: 0-0 Vi: 0-0 Tstrap: 0-0 Ckp: 0-0
Best Rating: 98 1/04 Muss 2m gd-fm Hdl

Showed ability in both starts over hurdles so far; should stay two and a half miles and may well be capable of better; wore headgear on the Flat.

Dalcassian Buck (IRE)

99(99h)   (93 h)**93**

10-y-o ch g Buckskin (FR)-Menebeans (IRE) (Duky)
C L Popham The Four Bucks

Placings:F4P6P1/446PP4F3-P6203U4P   (4855)
2003/04: 21³S, 17⁸G, 21⁸G, 24²GS, 25⁰HY, 21³G, 24⁰G, 21⁴GS, 24⁰PGF,

	Starts	1st	2nd	3rd	Win & Pl
Chases	9	0	1	2	3932
Career Total	22	1	1	2	8002

93 4/02 Towc 2m   E Hdl   G-S £3146
Total win prize-money £3147

Going:	Sf: 0-2 GS: 0-2 Gd: 0-4 GF: - Fm: 0-1
Distance:	2m/2m3: 0-1 2m4-2m7: 0-4 3m+: 0-4
Track:	LH: 0-2 RH: 0-7 Tight: 0-3 Gall: 0-0
Aids:	Bl: 0-0 Vi: 0-0 Tstrap: 0-0 Ckp: 0-1
Best Rating:	93 2/04 Winc 2m5f good Ch

Modest hurdler/chaser; stays three miles; acts on good and easy ground.

Dalcassian King (IRE)
104   91

11-y-o b g King's Ride-Niagara Lass (Prince Hansel)
P Wegmann   P Wegmann

Placings:4P56/0/PP2540000P605   (4888)
2003/04: 17FG, 16PGF, 16²F, 16⁵GS, 16⁴G, 16⁰GF, 16⁰GS, 19⁰HY, 16⁸G, 19⁴G, 25⁶G, 19⁰G, 24⁵GF,

	Starts	1st	2nd	3rd	Win & Pl
Hurdles	3	0	0	0	0
Chases	10	0	1	0	1492
Career Total	18	0	1	0	1775

Going:	Sf: 0-1 GS: 0-2 Gd: 0-6 GF: - Fm: 0-4
Distance:	2m/2m3: 0-9 2m4-2m7: 0-2 3m+: 0-2
Track:	LH: 0-6 RH: 0-7 Tight: 0-5 Gall: 0-1
Aids:	Bl: 0-1 Vi: 0-0 Tstrap: 0-0 Ckp: 0-1
Best Rating:	97 11/98 Newb 3m110y good Hdl

Irish point. winner; on the downgrade over fences here.

Dale Creek (IRE)
100   95

9-y-o b g Mandalus-Typhoon Signal (Aristocracy)
R H Alner   David O Moon

Placings:0/0PF0/0U60/54256415/FPPU042-64UP   (1335)
2003/04: 23⁶G, 26⁴GF, 26ᵁGF, 19⁹GF,

	Starts	1st	2nd	3rd	Win & Pl
Chases	4	0	0	0	361
Career Total	28	1	2	0	10535

95 8/01 Kbgn 3m1f   Ch   GD £6677
Total win prize-money £6677

Going:	Sf: 0-0 GS: 0-0 Gd: 0-1 GF: - Fm: 0-3
Distance:	2m/2m3: 0-1 2m4-2m7: 0-0 3m+: 0-3
Track:	LH: 0-2 RH: 0-1 Tight: 0-2 Gall: 0-0
Aids:	Bl: 0-0 Vi: 0-0 Tstrap: 0-0 Ckp: 0-0
Best Rating:	99 6/01 Kbgn 2m3f good NHF

Plating-class chaser; possibly best in good ground.

Dalkeys Lad
100f   84f

4-y-o b g Supreme Leader-Dalkey Sound (Crash Course)
Mrs L B Normile   G S Brown

Placings:330   (4277)
2003/04: 16³HY, 16³GS, 17⁰G,

	Starts	1st	2nd	3rd	Win & Pl
NH Flat	3	0	0	2	554
Career Total	3	0	0	2	554

Going:	Sf: 0-1 GS: 0-1 Gd: 0-1 GF: - Fm: 0-0

Distance: 2m/2m3: 0-3 2m4-2m7: 0-0 3m+: 0-0
Track: LH: 0-2 RH: 0-1 Tight: 0-0 Gall: 0-0
Aids: Bl: 0-0 Vi: 0-0 Tstrap: 0-0 Ckp: 0-0
Best Rating: 84   2/04   Ayr   2m   gd-sft   NHF

Half-brother to winning hurdler This Thyne and shaped creditably on racecourse debut in heavy ground Ayr bumper in January 2004; confirmed that promise over same course and distance following month and type to do better over further when sent hurdling.

Dallington Brook

5-y-o b g Bluegrass Prince (IRE)-Valetta (Faustus (USA))
Dr J R J Naylor   Dr J R J Naylor

Placings:00   (4495)
2003/04: 17⁰G, 16⁰G,

	Starts	1st	2nd	3rd	Win & Pl
NH Flat	2	0	0	0	
Career Total	2	0	0	0	

Going:	Sf: 0-1 GS: 0-0 Gd: 0-1 GF: - Fm: 0-0
Distance:	2m/2m3: 0-2 2m4-2m7: 0-0 3m+: 0-0
Track:	LH: 0-0 RH: 0-0 Tight: 0-0 Gall: 0-0
Aids:	Bl: 0-1 Vi: 0-0 Tstrap: 0-0 Ckp: 0-0

Dalriath
76   72+

5-y-o b m Fraam-Alsiba (Northfields (USA))
M C Chapman (Patrick J Flynn 17/9) M B Giełty

Placings:0F   (4214)
2003/04: 16⁰HY, 17FG,

	Starts	1st	2nd	3rd	Win & Pl
Hurdles	2	0	0	0	
Career Total	2	0	0	0	

Going:	Sf: 0-1 GS: 0-0 Gd: 0-1 GF: - Fm: 0-0
Distance:	2m/2m3: 0-2 2m4-2m7: 0-0 3m+: 0-0
Track:	LH: 0-1 RH: 0-1 Tight: 0-0 Gall: 0-1
Aids:	Bl: 0-0 Vi: 0-0 Tstrap: 0-0 Ckp: 0-0
Best Rating:	72 3/04 MRas 2m1f110y good Hdl

Dalus Park (IRE)
106   113+

9-y-o b g Mandalus-Pollerton Park (Pollerton)
C C Bealby   The Huntingdon Hopefuls

Placings:2/20-31P436   (4941)
2003/04: 24³GS, 25¹HY, 25PS, 24⁴S, 24³HY, 31⁶GS,

	Starts	1st	2nd	3rd	Win & Pl
Chases	6	1	0	2	5967
Career Total	9	1	2	2	7501

113 1/04 Towc 3m1f   F(0-95)HCh   HVY   £3445
Total win prize-money £3445

Going:	Sf: 1-4 GS: 0-2 Gd: 0-0 GF: - Fm: 0-0
Distance:	2m/2m3: 0-0 2m4-2m7: 0-0 3m+: 1-6
Track:	LH: 0-2 RH: 1-3 Tight: 0-0 Gall: 0-1
Aids:	Bl: 0-0 Vi: 0-0 Tstrap: 0-0 Ckp: 0-0
Best Rating:	113 1/04 Towc 3m1f heavy Ch

Moderate chaser; winning pointer; stays three miles; suited by testing ground.

Dalymacandoyleline (IRE)

8-y-o b g Boyne Valley-Gerties Pride (The Parson)
N F Glynn   N F Glynn

Placings:O00/PF0   (0738a)
2003/04: 19⁰GS, 22FGY, 23⁰F,

	Starts	1st	2nd	3rd	Win & Pl
Chases	3	0	0	0	
Career Total	6	0	0	0	

Going:	Sf: 0-0 GS: 0-1 Gd: 0-0 GF: - Fm: 0-1
Distance:	2m/2m3: 0-1 2m4-2m7: 0-2 3m+: 0-0
Track:	LH: 0-0 RH: 0-1 Tight: 0-0 Gall: 0-0
Aids:	Bl: 0-1 Vi: 0-0 Tstrap: 0-0 Ckp: 0-0
Best Rating:	59 4/02 List 2m4f gd-fm NHF

Dam The Breeze

11-y-o b g Ikdam-Cool Breeze (Windjammer (USA))
Evan Williams   Kevin Glastonbury

Placings:FPP/45F21601/112/0F-161P3026   (4626)
2003/04: 25¹GF, 24⁶G, 24¹GF, 25PGF, 26³GF, 24⁰GF, 25²G, 21⁶G,

	Starts	1st	2nd	3rd	Win & Pl
Hurdles	2	1	0	1	3749
Chases	6	1	1	0	5887
Career Total	24	4	3	1	26653

108	7/03	Uttx	3m110y	E(0-105)HHdl	G-F	£3373
117	5/03	Hrfd	3m1f110y	E(0-105)HCh	G-F	£4527
111	5/01	Hntg	3m2f	F(0-95)HHdl	G-F	£2520
111	5/01	Hntg	3m	E(0-115)HCh	GD	£4329
105	4/01	MRas	3m1f	F(0-95)Ch	G-S	£3906
113	8/00	Worc	2m7f110yE Ch		G-S	£3347

Total win prize-money £22004

Going:	Sf: 0-0 GS: 0-0 Gd: 0-3 GF: - Fm: 2-5
Distance:	2m/2m3: 0-0 2m4-2m7: 0-1 3m+: 2-7
Track:	LH: 1-3 RH: 1-1 Tight: 0-2 Gall: 0-0
Aids:	Bl: 0-0 Vi: 0-0 Tstrap: 0-0 Ckp: 0-0
Best Rating:	117 5/03 Hrfd 3m1f110y gd-fm Ch

Modest staying hurdler/chaser; stays 3m 2f; appreciates a decent surface; front runner; usually amateur ridden.

Damarisco (FR)
70   55

4-y-o b g Scribe (IRE)-Blanche Dame (FR) (Saint Cyrien (FR))
P J Hobbs   The Kingpins

Placings:0   (2483)
2003/04: 16⁰GS,

	Starts	1st	2nd	3rd	Win & Pl
Hurdles	1	0	0	0	
Career Total	1	0	0	0	

Going:	Sf: 0-0 GS: 0-1 Gd: 0-0 GF: - Fm: 0-0
Distance:	2m/2m3: 0-1 2m4-2m7: 0-0 3m+: 0-0
Track:	LH: 0-1 RH: 0-0 Tight: 0-0 Gall: 0-1
Aids:	Bl: 0-0 Vi: 0-0 Tstrap: 0-0 Ckp: 0-0
Best Rating:	55 11/03 Newb 2m110y gd-sft Hdl

Down the field on hurdles debut at Ascot; likely to be capable of better; is in the right hands to win races; wore blinkers on the Flat in France.

Dame Edna (FR)

71   **46**

4-y-o b f Octagonal (NZ)-Mohave Desert (USA) (Diesis)
Miss Sheena West D Naylor

Placings:0P   (3196)
2003/04: 16⁰GS, 16ᴾS,

	Starts	1st	2nd	3rd	Win & Pl
Hurdles	2	0	0	0	
Career Total	2	0	0	0	

Going:	Sf: 0-1 GS: 0-1 Gd: 0-0 GF: - Fm: 0-0
Distance:	2m/2m3: 0-2 2m4-2m7: 0-0 3m+: 0-0
Track:	LH: 0-2 RH: 0-0 Tight: 0-2 Gall: 0-0
Aids:	Bl: 0-0 Vi: 0-0 Tstrap: 0-0 Ckp: 0-0
Best Rating:	46 12/03 Plum 2m gd-sft Hdl

Dame Margaret

57   **23**

4-y-o ch f Elmaamul (USA)-Pomorie (IRE) (Be My Guest (USA))
J A B Old (M L W Bell 12/11) Mrs Anne Yearley

Placings:0   (3364)
2003/04: 16⁰G,

	Starts	1st	2nd	3rd	Win & Pl
Hurdles	1	0	0	0	
Career Total	1	0	0	0	

Going:	Sf: 0-0 GS: 0-0 Gd: 0-1 GF: - Fm: 0-0
Distance:	2m/2m3: 0-1 2m4-2m7: 0-0 3m+: 0-0
Track:	LH: 0-0 RH: 0-1 Tight: 0-0 Gall: 0-0
Aids:	Bl: 0-0 Vi: 0-0 Tstrap: 0-0 Ckp: 0-0
Best Rating:	23 1/04 Kemp 2m good Hdl

Plating-class on the Flat, best form shown at middle distances.

Damien's Choice (IRE)

93(111c)   (113c)**108**

12-y-o b g Erin's Hope-Reenoga (Tug Of War)
Dr P Pritchard (G A Swinbank 14/6) Norwester Racing Club

Placings:264/43/525P0P240/04126/40650/21P112266/52U
F55211-000P00R4500   (4673)
2003/04: 17⁰G, 16⁰GF, 16⁰GF, 16ᴾG, 17⁰G, 16ᴿGS, 16⁴GS, 19⁵G, 16⁰G, 16⁰G,

	Starts	1st	2nd	3rd	Win & Pl
Hurdles	5	0	0	0	0
Chases	6	0	0	0	0
Career Total	55	9	6	2	37770
113	4/03	Prth	2m	D(0-125)HCh	GD	£8255
108	4/03	Kels	2m1f	E(0-110)HCh	GD	£6948
102	12/01	Catt	2m	F(0-105)HCh	SFT	£3965
94	11/01	Sedg	2m110y	F(0-100)HCh	SFT	£2884
108	6/01	Hexm	2m	E(0-115)HHdl	GD	£2366
81	11/99	Kels	2m110y	F(0-95)HHdl	GD	£3039
				Total win prize-money £27458

Going:	Sf: 0-1 GS: 0-2 Gd: 0-6 GF: - Fm: 0-2
Distance:	2m/2m3: 0-10 2m4-2m7: 0-1 3m+: 0-0
Track:	LH: 0-6 RH: 0-5 Tight: 0-6 Gall: 0-0
Aids:	Bl: 0-0 Vi: 0-0 Tstrap: 0-0 Ckp: 0-2
Best Rating:	113 4/03 Prth 2m good Ch

Modest chaser, best over two miles; acts on any ground; sometimes wears cheekpieces.

Damiens Pride (IRE)

14-y-o b g Bulldozer-Riopoless (Royal And Regal (USA))
Mrs S J Batchelor Mrs S J Batchelor

Placings:302P/213F-04R   (0490)
2003/04: 21⁰G, 25⁴GF, 26ᴿGF,

	Starts	1st	2nd	3rd	Win & Pl
Chases	3	0	0	0	258
Career Total	11	1	2	2	5139
92	5/02	Extr	2m3f110yH Ch	GD	£1586
			Total win prize-money £1586

Going:	Sf: 0-0 GS: 0-0 Gd: 0-1 GF: - Fm: 0-2
Distance:	2m/2m3: 0-0 2m4-2m7: 0-1 3m+: 0-2
Track:	LH: 0-2 RH: 0-1 Tight: 0-1 Gall: 0-1
Aids:	Bl: 0-0 Vi: 0-0 Tstrap: 0-0 Ckp: 0-0
Best Rating:	100 5/02 Chel 2m5f gd-fm Ch

Damus (GER)

91(98h)   (118h)**127**

10-y-o br g Surumu (GER)-Dawn Side (CAN) (Bold Forbes (USA))
Mrs J C McGregor (M C Pipe 18/12) The Good To Soft Firm

Placings:203/1322U/1311300/1221P5/F624443-04P25P
       (4911)
2003/04: 20⁰G, 19⁴GF, 17ᴾG, 16²GF, 16⁵GF, 16ᴾS,

	Starts	1st	2nd	3rd	Win & Pl
Hurdles	1	0	0	0	0
Chases	5	0	1	0	1291
Career Total	34	6	7	5	53246
130	12/01	Sthl	2m	B(0-140)HCh	GD	£13848
118	10/01	MRas	2m1f110yD(0-120)HHdl	G-S	£5551
130	12/00	Fknm	2m110y	E Ch	G-S	£3003
128	7/00	Wolv	2m	C(0-135)HCh	G-S	£7928
115	5/00	Hrfd	2m	E Ch	G-S	£3051
123	10/99	Plum	2m	E(0-105)HHdl	G-F	£3176
				Total win prize-money £36559

Going:	Sf: 0-0 GS: 0-0 Gd: 0-2 GF: - Fm: 0-3
Distance:	2m/2m3: 0-4 2m4-2m7: 0-2 3m+: 0-0
Track:	LH: 0-4 RH: 0-2 Tight: 0-2 Gall: 0-0
Aids:	Bl: 0-0 Vi: 0-3 Tstrap: 0-0 Ckp: 0-0
Best Rating:	130 6/02 Strf 2m1f110y gd-fm Ch

Modest chaser; effective over hurdles too; effective at around two miles; acts on good to soft ground.

Dan De Man (IRE)

101(101h)   (79h)**73**

13-y-o b g Phardante (FR)-Slave De (Arctic Slave)
Miss L C Siddall Miss L C Siddall

Placings:05/060F5/3P0151225/41123360/4560404P51/040
P400/03P100024000/P0P065P2-F640030   (4814)
2003/04: 20²G, 20⁵S, 16⁴GS, 21⁰GS, 17ᴾHY, 21³G, 19⁰G,

	Starts	1st	2nd	3rd	Win & Pl
Hurdles	3	0	0	0	279
Chases	4	0	0	1	537
Career Total	68	6	5	5	24089
92	11/01	Hayd	2m4f	F(0-110)HHdl	SFT	£2758
97	4/00	Newc	2m110y	E Ch	G-S	£3458
115	12/98	Newc	2m	E(0-110)HHdl	SFT	£2211
112	11/98	Weth	2m4f110yE(0-110)HHdl	GD	£2407
97	1/98	Donc	2m110y	F(0-110)HHdl	GD	£2356
84	12/97	Newc	2m	F(0-100)HHdl	GD	£1934
				Total win prize-money £15127

Going:	Sf: 0-2 GS: 0-2 Gd: 0-3 GF: - Fm: 0-0
Distance:	2m/2m3: 0-2 2m4-2m7: 0-5 3m+: 0-0

Damiens Pride — (right column top)

Track:	LH: 0-6 RH: 0-1 Tight: 0-2 Gall: 0-0
Aids:	Bl: 0-0 Vi: 0-0 Tstrap: 0-0 Ckp: 0-0
Best Rating:	117 1/00 Weth 2m soft Hdl

Plating-class hurdler/chaser; generally inconsistent; effective on a soft surface; stays 2m 4f.

Dana Anne (IRE)

7-y-o ch m Abednego-Joyful Rosanna (Kernal (FR))
J K Magee J K Magee

Placings:0   (1372)
2003/04: 16⁰F,

	Starts	1st	2nd	3rd	Win & Pl
NH Flat	1	0	0	0	
Career Total	1	0	0	0	

Going:	Sf: 0-0 GS: 0-0 Gd: 0-0 GF: - Fm: 0-1
Distance:	2m/2m3: 0-1 2m4-2m7: 0-0 3m+: 0-0
Track:	LH: 0-1 RH: 0-0 Tight: 0-0 Gall: 0-0
Aids:	Bl: 0-0 Vi: 0-0 Tstrap: 0-0 Ckp: 0-0

Danabu (IRE)

6-y-o b g Un Desperado (FR)-Ishtar Abu (St Chad)
C Grant Trevor Hemmings

Placings:P   (3766)
2003/04: 17ᴾGS,

	Starts	1st	2nd	3rd	Win & Pl
NH Flat	1	0	0	0	
Career Total	1	0	0	0	

Going:	Sf: 0-0 GS: 0-1 Gd: 0-0 GF: - Fm: 0-0
Distance:	2m/2m3: 0-1 2m4-2m7: 0-0 3m+: 0-0
Track:	LH: 0-1 RH: 0-0 Tight: 0-1 Gall: 0-0
Aids:	Bl: 0-0 Vi: 0-0 Tstrap: 0-0 Ckp: 0-0

Danakil

106   **95+**

9-y-o b g Warning-Danilova (USA) (Lyphard (USA))
S Dow The Danakilists

Placings:44   (2381)
2003/04: 16⁴GS, 16⁴G,

	Starts	1st	2nd	3rd	Win & Pl
Hurdles	2	0	0	0	0
Career Total	2	0	0	0	0

Going:	Sf: 0-0 GS: 0-0 Gd: 0-1 GF: - Fm: 0-1
Distance:	2m/2m3: 0-2 2m4-2m7: 0-0 3m+: 0-0
Track:	LH: 0-1 RH: 0-1 Tight: 0-0 Gall: 0-1
Aids:	Bl: 0-0 Vi: 0-0 Tstrap: 0-0 Ckp: 0-0
Best Rating:	95 11/03 Wwck 2m good Hdl

Novice hurdler; modest middle-distance horse on the Flat; effective over two miles; may be better over further; acts on good ground.

Dance All Night

5-y-o b g Suave Dancer (USA)-Lyndseylee (Swing Easy (USA))
C W Moore C W Moore

Placings:U0 (4732)
2003/04: 17UG, 17PG,

	Starts	1st	2nd	3rd	Win & Pl
Hurdles	2	0	0	0	
Career Total	2	0	0		

Going: Sf: 0-0 GS: 0-0 Gd: 0-2 GF: - Fm: 0-0
Distance: 2m/2m3: 0-2 2m4-2m7: 0-0 3m+: 0-0
Track: LH: 0-0 RH: 0-2 Tight: 0-1 Gall: 0-0
Aids: Bl: 0-0 Vi: 0-0 Tstrap: 0-0 Ckp: 0-0

Dance In Tune
87(107h)   (105 h)**99**
7-y-o b g Mujtahid (USA)-Dancing Prize (IRE) (Sadler's Wells (USA))
P J Hobbs Major And Mrs P I C Payne

Placings:11643-53 (0486)
2003/04: 16SG, 16JG,

	Starts	1st	2nd	3rd	Win & Pl
Hurdles	1	0	0	0	0
Chases	1	0	0	1	832
Career Total	7	2	0	2	8511
111 8/02 Worc 2m		E Hdl		G-F	£3157
102 8/02 NAbb 2m1f		D Hdl		G-F	£3766
				Total win prize-money	£6923

Going: Sf: 0-0 GS: 0-0 Gd: 0-1 GF: - Fm: 0-1
Distance: 2m/2m3: 0-2 2m4-2m7: 0-0 3m+: 0-0
Track: LH: 0-1 RH: 0-1 Tight: 0-1 Gall: 0-0
Aids: Bl: 0-0 Vi: 0-0 Tstrap: 0-0 Ckp: 0-0
Best Rating: 111 8/02 Worc 2m gd-fm Hdl

Fair hurdler; promising debut over fences when third in 2m handicap chase at Newton Abbot May 2003; seems sure to improve; suited by fast ground; may require a stiffer 2m now.

Dance Of Life
96 **78**
5-y-o b m Shareef Dancer (USA)-Regan (USA) (Lear Fan (USA))
S Gollings Mrs Shirley Brasher

Placings:P600F-05PP00 (4569)
2003/04: 17QG, 17SGF, 17PGF, 16PG, 16QGS, 17QGS,

	Starts	1st	2nd	3rd	Win & Pl
Hurdles	6	0	0	0	0
Career Total	11	0	0	0	0

Going: Sf: 0-0 GS: 0-0 Gd: 0-2 GF: - Fm: 0-2
Distance: 2m/2m3: 0-0 2m4-2m7: 0-0 3m+: 0-2
Track: LH: 0-4 RH: 0-2 Tight: 0-5 Gall: 0-1
Aids: Bl: 0-5 Vi: 0-0 Tstrap: 0-0 Ckp: 0-0
Best Rating: 78 7/03 MRas 2m1f110y good Hdl

Plating-class hurdler; in a seller for the first time was clear when falling at the last at Market Rasen in April.

Dancer Life (POL)
113 **108**
5-y-o b h Professional (IRE)-Dyktatorka (POL) (Kastet (POL))
Jonjo O'Neill John P McManus

Placings:F0140F0 (4210)
2003/04: 16FG, 17QG, 161GF, 164GS, 17QG, 17PGS, 16QG,

	Starts	1st	2nd	3rd	Win & Pl
Hurdles	7	1	0	0	3246
Career Total	7	1	0	0	3246

107 11/03 Hntg 2m110y E Hdl G-F £2870
Total win prize-money £2870

Going: Sf: 0-0 GS: 0-2 Gd: 0-4 GF: - Fm: 1-1
Distance: 2m/2m3: 1-7 2m4-2m7: 0-0 3m+: 0-0
Track: LH: 0-3 RH: 1-4 Tight: 0-2 Gall: 1-2
Aids: Bl: 0-2 Vi: 0-0 Tstrap: 0-0 Ckp: 0-0
Best Rating: 108 12/03 Sand 2m110y gd-sft Hdl

Modest performer; best around two miles; acts on fast ground.

Dancer Polish (POL)
85 **66**
6-y-o b g Professional (IRE)-Doloreska (POL) (Who Knows)
A Sadik A Sadik

Placings:4213P5-P66PP (2665)
2003/04: 16PGF, 16SGF, 19QGF, 22PGS, 16PG,

	Starts	1st	2nd	3rd	Win & Pl
Hurdles	5	0	0	0	0
Career Total	11	1	1	1	4546
94 10/02 Uttx 2m		E Hdl		G-F	£3250
				Total win prize-money	£3250

Going: Sf: 0-0 GS: 0-1 Gd: 0-1 GF: - Fm: 0-3
Distance: 2m/2m3: 0-3 2m4-2m7: 0-2 3m+: 0-0
Track: LH: 0-3 RH: 0-2 Tight: 0-2 Gall: 0-0
Aids: Bl: 0-2 Vi: 0-0 Tstrap: 0-0 Ckp: 0-0
Best Rating: 94 11/02 Hntg 2m110y gd-sft Hdl

Moderate hurdler; dual winner on the Flat in Poland; suited by a sound surface; yet to prove he stays further than two miles.

Dancing Bay
111 **133+**
7-y-o b g Suave Dancer (USA)-Kabayil (Dancing Brave (USA))
N J Henderson Elite Racing Club

Placings:2F/1410-16010 (4628)
2003/04: 161S, 16PHY, 16QS, 161GS, 20QG,

	Starts	1st	2nd	3rd	Win & Pl
Hurdles	5	2	0	0	18500
Career Total	11	4	1	0	33543
133 3/04 Newb 2m110y	B(0-140)HHdl		G-S		£12442
133 12/03 Hexm 2m110y	D(0-125)HHdl		SFT		£5824
122 2/03 Plum 2m5f	C Hdl		SFT		£6857
127 1/03 Plum 2m	D Hdl		SFT		£5590
			Total win prize-money		£30714

Going: Sf: 1-3 GS: 1-1 Gd: 0-1 GF: - Fm: 0-0
Distance: 2m/2m3: 2-4 2m4-2m7: 0-1 3m+: 0-0
Track: LH: 2-4 RH: 0-1 Tight: 0-1 Gall: 1-1
Aids: Bl: 0-0 Vi: 0-0 Tstrap: 0-0 Ckp: 0-0
Best Rating: 133 3/04 Newb 2m110y gd-sft Hdl

Useful handicap hurdler; stayer on the Flat; effective at up to two miles five, but better over shorter; suited by testing ground.

Dancing Danoli
48f
4-y-o f Bin Ajwaad (IRE)-Wave Dancer (Dance In Time (CAN))
M Wellings G K Gordon

Placings:00 (3709)
2003/04: 12QGF, 16PHY,

	Starts	1st	2nd	3rd	Win & Pl
NH Flat	2	0	0	0	
Career Total	2	0	0	0	

Going: Sf: 0-1 GS: 0-0 Gd: 0-0 GF: - Fm: 0-1
Distance: 2m/2m3: 0-2 2m4-2m7: 0-0 3m+: 0-0
Track: LH: 0-2 RH: 0-0 Tight: 0-0 Gall: 0-0
Aids: Bl: 0-0 Vi: 0-0 Tstrap: 0-0 Ckp: 0-0
Best Rating: 48 12/03 Newb 1m4f110y gd-fm NHF

Dancing Dill
90
9-y-o b m Dancing High-Some Shiela (Remainder Man)
J P Dodds J R Jeffreys

Placings:3/3624/P/P (0781)
2003/04: 20PG,

	Starts	1st	2nd	3rd	Win & Pl
Hurdles	1	0	0	0	
Career Total	7	0	1	2	1754

Going: Sf: 0-0 GS: 0-0 Gd: 0-1 GF: - Fm: 0-0
Distance: 2m/2m3: 0-0 2m4-2m7: 0-1 3m+: 0-0
Track: LH: 0-0 RH: 0-1 Tight: 0-0 Gall: 0-0
Aids: Bl: 0-0 Vi: 0-0 Tstrap: 0-0 Ckp: 0-0
Best Rating: 90 5/01 Prth 2m4f110y gd-fm Hdl

Dancing Fosenby
8-y-o b g Terimon-Wave Dancer (Dance In Time (CAN))
Miss P C Lownds Mrs Heather Flaherty

Placings:4PP0043/604-4 (0350)
2003/04: 214GF,

	Starts	1st	2nd	3rd	Win & Pl
Chases	1	0	0	0	163
Career Total	11	0	0	1	932

Going: Sf: 0-0 GS: 0-0 Gd: 0-0 GF: - Fm: 0-1
Distance: 2m/2m3: 0-0 2m4-2m7: 0-1 3m+: 0-0
Track: LH: 0-0 RH: 0-1 Tight: 0-1 Gall: 0-0
Aids: Bl: 0-0 Vi: 0-0 Tstrap: 0-0 Ckp: 0-0
Best Rating: 79 5/03 Folk 2m5f gd-fm Ch

Dancing Hill
98 **67**
5-y-o b m Piccolo-Ryewater Dream (Touching Wood (USA))
Mrs E B Scott Mrs E B Scott

Placings:00 (4375)
2003/04: 24QG, 19QG,

	Starts	1st	2nd	3rd	Win & Pl
Hurdles	2	0	0	0	
Career Total	2	0	0	0	

Going: Sf: 0-0 GS: 0-0 Gd: 0-2 GF: - Fm: 0-0
Distance: 2m/2m3: 0-0 2m4-2m7: 0-1 3m+: 0-1
Track: LH: 0-0 RH: 0-2 Tight: 0-2 Gall: 0-0
Aids: Bl: 0-0 Vi: 0-0 Tstrap: 0-1 Ckp: 0-0
Best Rating: 67 3/04 Tntn 3m110y good Hdl

Dancing Pearl
107 **123**
6-y-o ch m Dancing Spree (USA)-Elegant Rose (Noalto)
C J Price J E Heymans

Placings:344/44116-22214 (4849)

2003/04: 17²G, 16²G, 16²GS, 16¹G, 16⁴GS,

	Starts	1st	2nd	3rd	Win & Pl
Hurdles	5	1	3	0	21556
Career Total	13	3	3	1	30998
123 3/04 Donc	2m110y D(0-120)HHdl			GD	£10237
92 3/03 Sthl	2m	E Hdl		G-F	£3486
100 1/03 Sthl	2m	E Hdl		G-S	£3542
			Total win prize-money £17266		

Going:	Sf: 0-0 GS: 0-2 Gd: 1-3 GF: - Fm: 0-0
Distance:	2m/2m3: 1-5 2m4-2m7: 0-0 3m+: 0-0
Track:	LH: 1-3 RH: 0-2 Tight: 0-0 Gall: 1-1
Aids:	Bl: 0-0 Vi: 0-0 Tstrap: 0-0 Ckp: 0-0
Best Rating:	123 3/04 Donc 2m110y good Hdl

Modest hurdler; recorded third career win with wide-margin success at Doncaster in March; acts on good and easy ground; consistent sort; best suited by a flat track.

Dancing Phantom
101   95
9-y-o b g Darshaan-Dancing Prize (IRE) (Sadler's Wells (USA))
James Moffatt Bernard Bargh, Jeff Hamer, Steve Henshaw

Placings:1/0/P/00   (2801)
2003/04: 17⁰HY, 16⁹S,

	Starts	1st	2nd	3rd	Win & Pl
Hurdles	2	0	0	0	
Career Total	5	1	0	0	3168
127 11/99 Weth	2m	D Hdl		GD	£3168
			Total win prize-money £3168		

Going:	Sf: 0-2 GS: 0-0 Gd: 0-0 GF: - Fm: 0-0
Distance:	2m/2m3: 0-2 2m4-2m7: 0-0 3m+: 0-0
Track:	LH: 0-1 RH: 0-1 Tight: 0-0 Gall: 0-0
Aids:	Bl: 0-0 Vi: 0-0 Tstrap: 0-0 Ckp: 0-0
Best Rating:	127 11/99 Weth 2m good Hdl

He won on his debut over hurdles in 1999 but has been lightly raced since, both on the Flat and over the sticks.

Dancing Tilly
85   65
6-y-o b m Dancing Spree (USA)-L'Ancressaan (Dalsaan)
R A Fahey The 'We Believe In Miracles' Partnership

Placings:05B   (2691)
2003/04: 19⁰GF, 16⁵GF, 16⁸G,

	Starts	1st	2nd	3rd	Win & Pl
Hurdles	3	0	0	0	
Career Total	3	0	0	0	

Going:	Sf: 0-0 GS: 0-0 Gd: 0-1 GF: - Fm: 0-2
Distance:	2m/2m3: 0-3 2m4-2m7: 0-0 3m+: 0-0
Track:	LH: 0-2 RH: 0-1 Tight: 0-2 Gall: 0-0
Aids:	Bl: 0-0 Vi: 0-0 Tstrap: 0-0 Ckp: 0-1
Best Rating:	65 12/03 Sthl 2m gd-fm Hdl

Looks no better over timber than she was on the Flat.

Danebank (IRE)
57   13
4-y-o b g Danehill (USA)-Snow Bank (IRE) (Law Society (USA))
J Mackie (J W Hills 27/10) Ms L A Machin

Placings:0   (4368)
2003/04: 16⁹GF,

	Starts	1st	2nd	3rd	Win & Pl
Hurdles	1	0	0	0	
Career Total	1	0	0	0	

Going:	Sf: 0-0 GS: 0-0 Gd: 0-0 GF: - Fm: 0-1
Distance:	2m/2m3: 0-1 2m4-2m7: 0-0 3m+: 0-0
Track:	LH: 0-1 RH: 0-0 Tight: 0-1 Gall: 0-0
Aids:	Bl: 0-0 Vi: 0-0 Tstrap: 0-0 Ckp: 0-0
Best Rating:	12 3/04 Strf 2m110y gd-fm Hdl

Dangerous Dan McGo (IRE)
99f   106f
6-y-o b g Un Desperado (FR)-Sharnad (IRE) (Shardari)
M C Pipe J J Whelan

Placings:40   (4454)
2003/04: 16⁴GS, 16⁹GS,

	Starts	1st	2nd	3rd	Win & Pl
NH Flat	2	0	0	0	0
Career Total	2	0	0	0	0

Going:	Sf: 0-0 GS: 0-2 Gd: 0-0 GF: - Fm: 0-0
Distance:	2m/2m3: 0-2 2m4-2m7: 0-0 3m+: 0-0
Track:	LH: 0-0 RH: 0-2 Tight: 0-0 Gall: 0-0
Aids:	Bl: 0-0 Vi: 0-0 Tstrap: 0-0 Ckp: 0-0
Best Rating:	106 2/04 Sand 2m110y gd-sft NHF

Promising bumper debut in a fair contest but disappointing favourite next time.

Dangerously Good
109   125+
6-y-o b g Shareef Dancer (USA)-Ecologically Kind (Alleged (USA))
G L Moore (R C Guest 4/5) N J Jones

Placings:50-31102   (4836)
2003/04: 16³S, 21¹GS, 22²G, 20⁹GS, 21²GF,

	Starts	1st	2nd	3rd	Win & Pl
Hurdles	5	2	1	1	14646
Career Total	7	2	1	1	14646
121 2/04 Font	2m6f110yE Hdl			GD	£4348
115 2/04 Kemp	2m5f	D Hdl		G-S	£5005
			Total win prize-money £9354		

Going:	Sf: 0-1 GS: 1-2 Gd: 1-1 GF: - Fm: 0-1
Distance:	2m/2m3: 0-2 2m4-2m7: 2-4 3m+: 0-0
Track:	LH: 1-2 RH: 1-3 Tight: 1-1 Gall: 0-1
Aids:	Bl: 2-5 Vi: 0-0 Tstrap: 0-0 Ckp: 0-0
Best Rating:	129 4/04 Chel 2m5f110y gd-fm Hdl

Decent novice hurdler; lightly-raced performer on the Flat; has won on sand in Spain; stays 2m 6f; has worn blinkers/visor and cheekpieces.

Danish Decorum (IRE)
100   91
5-y-o ch g Danehill Dancer (IRE)-Dignified Air (FR) (Wolver Hollow)
Evan Williams (C G Cox 25/6) W Ralph Thomas

Placings:646   (1951)
2003/04: 19⁶GF, 16⁴GF, 17⁶G,

	Starts	1st	2nd	3rd	Win & Pl
Hurdles	3	0	0	0	403
Career Total	3	0	0	0	403

Going:	Sf: 0-0 GS: 0-0 Gd: 0-1 GF: - Fm: 0-2
Distance:	2m/2m3: 0-2 2m4-2m7: 0-1 3m+: 0-0
Track:	LH: 0-2 RH: 0-1 Tight: 0-2 Gall: 0-0

Aids:	Bl: 0-0 Vi: 0-0 Tstrap: 0-0 Ckp: 0-0
Best Rating:	91 10/03 Strf 2m110y gd-fm Hdl

Last of six on debut over hurdles at Hereford in September 2003; weakened into fourth after setting good gallop at Stratford next time.

Danny Leahy (FR)
88   78
4-y-o b g Danehill (USA)-Paloma Bay (IRE) (Alzao (USA))
M D Hammond (J G Given 16/10) D Green

Placings:040   (4271)
2003/04: 16⁹G, 20⁴G, 20⁹G,

	Starts	1st	2nd	3rd	Win & Pl
Hurdles	3	0	0	0	303
Career Total	3	0	0	0	303

Going:	Sf: 0-0 GS: 0-0 Gd: 0-3 GF: - Fm: 0-0
Distance:	2m/2m3: 0-1 2m4-2m7: 0-2 3m+: 0-0
Track:	LH: 0-1 RH: 0-2 Tight: 0-1 Gall: 0-0
Aids:	Bl: 0-0 Vi: 0-0 Tstrap: 0-0 Ckp: 0-0
Best Rating:	78 2/04 Carl 2m4f good Hdl

Has shown a little ability so far over hurdles.

Dans Pride (IRE)
95f   104f
6-y-o b g Presenting-Mindyourown (IRE) (Town And Country)
Noel T Chance Brian Jacobs

Placings:44   (3948)
2003/04: 16⁴HY, 16⁴G,

	Starts	1st	2nd	3rd	Win & Pl
NH Flat	2	0	0	0	0
Career Total	2	0	0	0	0

Going:	Sf: 0-1 GS: 0-0 Gd: 0-1 GF: - Fm: 0-0
Distance:	2m/2m3: 0-2 2m4-2m7: 0-0 3m+: 0-0
Track:	LH: 0-0 RH: 0-2 Tight: 0-0 Gall: 0-0
Aids:	Bl: 0-0 Vi: 0-0 Tstrap: 0-0 Ckp: 0-0
Best Rating:	99 2/04 Winc 2m good NHF

Danse Slave (FR)
88   90
5-y-o b m Broadway Flyer (USA)-Snow Girl (FR) (River Mist (USA))
R H Alner S W D Partnership

Placings:024021-PP6   (4859)
2003/04: 22⁸GS, 22²G, 19⁶GF,

	Starts	1st	2nd	3rd	Win & Pl
Hurdles	3	0	0	0	0
Career Total	9	1	2	0	7472
82 4/03 Extr	2m3f	D Hdl		G-F	£5122
			Total win prize-money £5122		

Going:	Sf: 0-0 GS: 0-1 Gd: 0-1 GF: - Fm: 0-0
Distance:	2m/2m3: 0-0 2m4-2m7: 0-3 3m+: 0-0
Track:	LH: 0-0 RH: 0-3 Tight: 0-2 Gall: 0-0
Aids:	Bl: 0-0 Vi: 0-0 Tstrap: 0-0 Ckp: 0-0
Best Rating:	90 12/02 Wwck 2m soft Hdl

Built on some fair performances when winning 19 furlong mares only novices hurdle at Exeter on fast ground April 2003.

Dante Citizen (IRE)

103(96h)   (97h)**111+**

6-y-o ch g Phardante (FR)-Boreen Citizen (Boreen (FR))
T R George Ryder Racing Ltd

Placings:0-055250315   (4713)
2003/04: 17³G, 16⁵GS, 16⁶GS, 24²GS, 22⁵S, 26⁶GS, 20³G, 24¹GS, 24⁶G,

	Starts	1st	2nd	3rd	Win & Pl
Hurdles	6	0	1	0	884
Chases	3	1	0	0	5523
Career Total	10	1	1	0	6407
111 3/04 Ludl	3m		E Ch	G-S	£4667
			Total win prize-money £4667		

Going:	Sf: 0-1 GS: 1-5 Gd: 0-3 GF: - Fm: 0-0
Distance:	2m/2m3: 0-3 2m4-2m7: 0-2 3m+: 1-4
Track:	LH: 0-5 RH: 1-4 Tight: 1-5 Gall: 0-1
Aids:	Bl: 0-0 Vi: 0-0 Tstrap: 0-0 Ckp: 0-0
Best Rating:	111 3/04 Ludl 3m gd-sft Ch

Moderate novice chaser; former Irish pointer; stays three miles and should get further; acts with cut in the ground.

Dante's Banker (IRE)

(106h)   (86h)

8-y-o ch g Phardante (FR)-Nancy Myles (The Parson)
C C Bealby Mrs J A C Lundgren

Placings:0/42F   (1861)
2003/04: 22⁴GF, 26²GF, 25ᶠGF,

	Starts	1st	2nd	3rd	Win & Pl
Hurdles	2	0	1	0	820
Chases	1	0	0	0	0
Career Total	4	0	1	0	820

Going:	Sf: 0-0 GS: 0-0 Gd: 0-0 GF: - Fm: 0-3
Distance:	2m/2m3: 0-0 2m4-2m7: 0-1 3m+: 0-2
Track:	LH: 0-2 RH: 0-1 Tight: 0-0 Gall: 0-1
Aids:	Bl: 0-0 Vi: 0-0 Tstrap: 0-0 Ckp: 0-0
Best Rating:	86 10/03 Hntg 3m2f gd-fm Hdl

Irish point winner; well beaten on first outing here at Uttoxeter in October after a lengthy absence; fell next time.

Dante's Battle (IRE)

(101h)   (100h)

12-y-o b/br g Phardante (FR)-No Battle (Khalkis)
Miss K Marks Nick Shutts

Placings:060/20220/011403200/11244/110/02F32F/455P-
P001153144P   (4737)
2003/04: 17ᴾGF, 16⁰G, 16⁰GF, 19¹GF, 20¹GF, 17⁵GF, 19³GF,
19¹GF, 17⁴G, 24⁴GF, 21ᴾG,

	Starts	1st	2nd	3rd	Win & Pl
Hurdles	8	3	0	1	7905
Chases	3	0	0	0	823
Career Total	46	9	7	3	47657
100 10/03 Strf	2m3f	G Hdl		G-F	£2247
94 8/03 Hntg	2m4f110y	G Hdl		G-F	£2394
90 8/03 NAbb	2m3f	G(0-95)HHdl		G-F	£2933
133 5/00 Rosc	2m5f	Ch		FRM	£5536
117 5/00 Tipp	2m4f	Ch		FRM	£4140
131 6/99 Gowr	2m	(0-140)HHdl		GD	£6138
110 5/99 Bain	2m1f	Ch		GD	£3683
121 7/98 Naas	2m	(0-123)HHdl		GD	£2989
108 6/98 Thur	2m	Hdl		GD	£1935
			Total win prize-money £31996		

Going:	Sf: 0-0 GS: 0-0 Gd: 0-3 GF: - Fm: 3-8

Distance

Distance:	2m/2m3: 2-7 2m4-2m7: 1-3 3m+: 0-1
Track:	LH: 1-7 RH: 1-3 Tight: 1-6 Gall: 1-1
Aids:	Bl: 0-0 Vi: 0-0 Tstrap: 0-0 Ckp: 0-0
Best Rating:	133 8/01 Gway 2m1f gd-yld Ch

Plating-class hurdler; formerly useful over hurdles and fences in Ireland; goes well on firm ground; stays two miles four; goes well on a decent surface; has broken blood vessels in the past.

Dante's Brook (IRE)

106   **82**

10-y-o ch g Phardante (FR)-Arborfield Brook (Over The River (FR))
B Mactaggart Jim Jeffrey

Placings:0/5600/343P0/334P-5PU325   (1367)
2003/04: 16⁵G, 16ᴾG, 17ᵁGF, 17³G, 16²GF, 16⁵F,

	Starts	1st	2nd	3rd	Win & Pl
Chases	6	0	1	1	2809
Career Total	20	0	1	5	5687

Going:	Sf: 0-0 GS: 0-0 Gd: 0-3 GF: - Fm: 0-3
Distance:	2m/2m3: 0-6 2m4-2m7: 0-0 3m+: 0-0
Track:	LH: 0-3 RH: 0-3 Tight: 0-2 Gall: 0-0
Aids:	Bl: 0-0 Vi: 0-0 Tstrap: 0-3 Ckp: 0-0
Best Rating:	86 5/00 Kels 2m110y gd-fm Hdl

Moderate hurdler/chaser at around two miles.

Dante's Porridge (IRE)

85   **78+**

8-y-o b g Phardante (FR)-Canal Street (Oats)
Mrs S J Smith Mrs S Smith

Placings:2   (1963)
2003/04: 16²GF,

	Starts	1st	2nd	3rd	Win & Pl
Hurdles	1	0	1	0	1111
Career Total	1	0	1	0	1111

Going:	Sf: 0-0 GS: 0-0 Gd: 0-0 GF: - Fm: 0-1
Distance:	2m/2m3: 0-1 2m4-2m7: 0-0 3m+: 0-0
Track:	LH: 0-1 RH: 0-0 Tight: 0-0 Gall: 0-0
Aids:	Bl: 0-0 Vi: 0-0 Tstrap: 0-0 Ckp: 0-0
Best Rating:	78 11/03 Hayd 2m gd-fm Hdl

Danteco

106(104h)   (95 h)**100**

9-y-o gr g Phardante (FR)-Up Cooke (Deep Run)
Miss Kate Milligan Mrs J M L Milligan

Placings:3/6056/P00O/1FF14212P4-0P6333   (2789)
2003/04: 20⁶G, 20ᴾGF, 21⁶G, 27³G, 27³G, 24ᴾGF,

	Starts	1st	2nd	3rd	Win & Pl
Hurdles	2	0	0	0	0
Chases	4	0	3	2	1558
Career Total	25	3	2	4	12970
94 9/02 Hexm	2m4f110yE(0-110)HCh		G-F	£3503
95 8/02 Sedg	2m5f110yE(0-100)HHdl		GD	£2905
94 6/02 Hexm	2m4f110yF Ch		G-F	£2184
		Total win prize-money £8593		

Going:	Sf: 0-0 GS: 0-0 Gd: 0-4 GF: - Fm: 0-2
Distance:	2m/2m3: 0-2 2m4-2m7: 0-3 3m+: 0-3
Track:	LH: 0-4 RH: 0-2 Tight: 0-4 Gall: 0-0
Aids:	Bl: 0-0 Vi: 0-0 Tstrap: 0-0 Ckp: 0-1
Best Rating:	100 10/02 Sedg 2m5f gd-fm Hdl

Modest chaser/hurdler; headstrong type; equally effective over hurdles and fences; stays two miles five furlongs; acts on a sound surface.

Dantes Reef (IRE)

97(114h)   (123h)**114**

8-y-o b g Phardante (FR)-Thousand Flowers (Take A Reef)
A J Martin T McGoldrick

Placings:0U023/203.2410-23F0113   (4449)
2003/04: 17²G, 20³GY, 20ᶠGY, 16⁶S, 17¹S, 20¹GY, 20³GS,

	Starts	1st	2nd	3rd	Win & Pl
Hurdles	4	1	1	2	20923
Chases	3	1	0	0	6813
Career Total	19	3	4	4	37023
123 2/04 Fair	2m4f	(81-123)HHdl	G-Y	£9169
114 2/04 Navn	2m1f	Ch	SFT	£6812
109 3/03 DRoy	2m	Hdl	YLD	£4480
		Total win prize-money £20463		

Going:	Sf: 1-2 GS: 0-1 Gd: 0-1 GF: - Fm: 0-0
Distance:	2m/2m3: 1-3 2m4-2m7: 1-4 3m+: 0-0
Track:	LH: 1-3 RH: 1-2 Tight: 0-0 Gall: 0-0
Aids:	Bl: 0-0 Vi: 0-0 Tstrap: 0-0 Ckp: 0-0
Best Rating:	128 3/04 Asct 2m4f gd-sft Hdl

Fair Irish hurdler; winning chaser; likes soft ground and is seemingly best at the around two miles, although stays further.

Dantes Venture (IRE)

99(94c)   (104+c)**104**

7-y-o b g Phardante (FR)-Fast Adventure (Deep Run)
D J Caro Mrs J F Billington

Placings:005/223020-23P4P4   (4897)
2003/04: 26²GS, 21³G, 24ᴾS, 22⁴G, 24ᴾGS, 22⁴G,

	Starts	1st	2nd	3rd	Win & Pl
Hurdles	5	0	1	0	1354
Chases	1	0	0	1	424
Career Total	15	0	4	2	5897

Going:	Sf: 0-1 GS: 0-2 Gd: 0-3 GF: - Fm: 0-0
Distance:	2m/2m3: 0-0 2m4-2m7: 0-3 3m+: 0-3
Track:	LH: 0-2 RH: 0-3 Tight: 0-0 Gall: 0-1
Aids:	Bl: 0-0 Vi: 0-2 Tstrap: 0-0 Ckp: 0-0
Best Rating:	106 2/04 MRas 2m6f good Hdl

Moderate novice hurdler; well beaten third behind two useful types on his chasing debut at Southwell in November; will be suited by three miles.

Dantie Boy (IRE)

8-y-o br g Phardante (FR)-Ballybride Gale (IRE) (Strong Gale)
A W Congdon (P J Hobbs 7/9) A W Congdon

Placings:521/51213266-252F222   (4858)
2003/04: 19²G, 20⁵GF, 20²G, 20ᶠGF, 21²GF, 20²GF, 24²GF,

	Starts	1st	2nd	3rd	Win & Pl
Hurdles	3	0	2	0	2588
Chases	4	0	3	0	3599
Career Total	18	3	8	1	22881
122 10/02 Tntn	2m3f	D Ch	G-F	£5427
86 9/02 Worc	2m4f	E Hdl	GD	£3073
109 4/02 Extr	2m6f110yE Hdl		FRM	£3071
		Total win prize-money £11573		

Going:	Sf: 0-0 GS: 0-0 Gd: 0-2 GF: - Fm: 0-5

Distance:	2m/2m3: 0-0 2m4-2m7: 0-6 3m+: 0-1
Track:	LH: 0-5 RH: 0-2 Tight: 0-4 Gall: 0-0
Aids:	Bl: 0-0 Vi: 0-0 Tstrap: 0-0 Ckp: 0-0
Best Rating:	122 6/03 Strf 2m4f good Ch

One time fair hurdler/chaser; often let down by his jumping over fences; caught on the line in 3m hunter chase at Taunton April 2004; acts on fast ground.

Danzig Flyer (IRE)
85   43

9-y-o b g Roi Danzig (USA)-Fenland Express (IRE) (Reasonable (FR))
B D Leavy Mrs Renee Farrington-Kirkham

Placings:000/6P0/600/0F-00   (0768)
2003/04: 16⁰GF, 22⁰GF,

	Starts	1st	2nd	3rd	Win & Pl
Hurdles	2	0	0	0	
Career Total	13	0	0	0	0

Going:	Sf: 0-0 GS: 0-0 Gd: 0-0 GF: - Fm: 0-2
Distance:	2m/2m3: 0-0 2m4-2m7: 0-1 3m+: 0-0
Track:	LH: 0-2 RH: 0-0 Tight: 0-0 Gall: 0-0
Aids:	Bl: 0-0 Vi: 0-0 Tstrap: 0-0 Ckp: 0-0
Best Rating:	65 11/01 Strf 2m110y soft Hdl

Danzig Prince
88   78

5-y-o b g Danzig Connection (USA)-Lovely Greek Lady (Ela-Mana-Mou)
K A Morgan Wentdale Limited

Placings:P324050P   (3915)
2003/04: 20⁰GF, 21³GF, 20²GF, 19⁴GF, 20⁰GS, 16⁵GS, 16⁰G, 16⁰G,

	Starts	1st	2nd	3rd	Win & Pl
Hurdles	8	0	1	1	1514
Career Total	8	0	1	1	1514

Going:	Sf: 0-0 GS: 0-2 Gd: 0-2 GF: - Fm: 0-4
Distance:	2m/2m3: 0-3 2m4-2m7: 0-5 3m+: 0-0
Track:	LH: 0-6 RH: 0-2 Tight: 0-1 Gall: 0-1
Aids:	Bl: 0-4 Vi: 0-2 Tstrap: 0-0 Ckp: 0-1
Best Rating:	78 8/03 Uttx 2m4f110y gd-fm Hdl

Plating-class hurdler; has shown little so far; has been tried in blinkers and a visor.

Daphne's Doll (IRE)
84   55

9-y-o b m Polish Patriot (USA)-Helietta (Tyrnavos)
Dr J R J Naylor Mrs S P Elphick

Placings:000P0   (4100)
2003/04: 17⁰G, 16⁰G, 20⁰G, 24⁰GS, 21⁰G,

	Starts	1st	2nd	3rd	Win & Pl
Hurdles	5	0	0	0	
Career Total	5	0	0	0	

Going:	Sf: 0-0 GS: 0-1 Gd: 0-4 GF: - Fm: 0-0
Distance:	2m/2m3: 0-2 2m4-2m7: 0-2 3m+: 0-1
Track:	LH: 0-1 RH: 0-3 Tight: 0-3 Gall: 0-0
Aids:	Bl: 0-0 Vi: 0-0 Tstrap: 0-0 Ckp: 0-0
Best Rating:	55 12/03 Leic 2m good Hdl

Dara Capall (IRE)
103f   85f

4-y-o b g Simply Great (FR)-She's Pretty (Furry Glen)
Mrs M Reveley Revival Racing Ltd

Placings:03   (4264)
2003/04: 16⁶G, 16³GF,

	Starts	1st	2nd	3rd	Win & Pl
NH Flat	2	0	0	1	294
Career Total	2	0	0	1	294

Going:	Sf: 0-0 GS: 0-0 Gd: 0-1 GF: - Fm: 0-0
Distance:	2m/2m3: 0-2 2m4-2m7: 0-0 3m+: 0-0
Track:	LH: 0-1 RH: 0-1 Tight: 0-2 Gall: 0-0
Aids:	Bl: 0-0 Vi: 0-0 Tstrap: 0-0 Ckp: 0-0
Best Rating:	85 3/04 Catt 2m gd-fm NHF

Strong finishing third on second start in bumper at Catterick in March; should improve again.

Darab (POL)
96   95

4-y-o ch g Alywar (USA)-Damara (POL) (Pyjama Hunt)
T R George Ryder Racing Ltd

Placings:0   (4368)
2003/04: 16⁰GF,

	Starts	1st	2nd	3rd	Win & Pl
Hurdles	1	0	0	0	
Career Total	1	0	0	0	

Going:	Sf: 0-0 GS: 0-0 Gd: 0-0 GF: - Fm: 0-1
Distance:	2m/2m3: 0-1 2m4-2m7: 0-0 3m+: 0-0
Track:	LH: 0-1 RH: 0-0 Tight: 0-1 Gall: 0-0
Aids:	Bl: 0-0 Vi: 0-0 Tstrap: 0-0 Ckp: 0-0
Best Rating:	15 3/04 Strf 2m110y gd-fm Hdl

Dardanus
(100h)   (103+h)100

6-y-o ch g Komaite (USA)-Dance On A Cloud (USA) (Capote (USA))
C J Mann M J & C G Cruddace

Placings:14220-F   (0371)
2003/04: 20⁵G,

	Starts	1st	2nd	3rd	Win & Pl
Chases	1	0	0	0	
Career Total	6	1	2	0	4752
100 8/02 Font 2m2f110yE Hdl				G-F	£2968
			Total win prize-money		£2968

Going:	Sf: 0-0 GS: 0-0 Gd: 0-1 GF: - Fm: 0-0
Distance:	2m/2m3: 0-0 2m4-2m7: 0-1 3m+: 0-0
Track:	LH: 0-1 RH: 0-0 Tight: 0-0 Gall: 0-0
Aids:	Bl: 0-0 Vi: 0-0 Tstrap: 0-0 Ckp: 0-0
Best Rating:	103 10/02 Font 2m2f110y good Hdl

Fair middle-distance handicapper on the Flat; made a winning debut over hurdles in August 2002; in third place when falling at the last on chasing debut in 2m 4f handicap at Worcester May 2003.

Dareneur (IRE)
64f

4-y-o ch f Entrepreneur-Darayna (IRE) (Shernazar)
W M Brisbourne Preece Haden Partnership

Placings:0   (2675)
2003/04: 12⁰G,

	Starts	1st	2nd	3rd	Win & Pl
NH Flat	1	0	0	0	
Career Total	1	0	0	0	

Going:	Sf: 0-0 GS: 0-0 Gd: 0-0 GF: - Fm: 0-1
Distance:	2m/2m3: 0-0 2m4-2m7: 0-0 3m+: 0-1
Track:	LH: 0-1 RH: 0-0 Tight: 0-0 Gall: 0-0
Aids:	Bl: 0-0 Vi: 0-0 Tstrap: 0-0 Ckp: 0-0
Best Rating:	64 12/03 Newb 1m4f110y gd-fm NHF

Darjeeling (IRE)
97f   80+f

5-y-o b m Presenting-Afternoon Tea (IRE) (Decent Fellow)
Mrs S Gardner D V Gardner

Placings:000   (4213)
2003/04: 16⁰S, 17⁰S, 16⁰G,

	Starts	1st	2nd	3rd	Win & Pl
NH Flat	3	0	0	0	
Career Total	3	0	0	0	

Going:	Sf: 0-2 GS: 0-0 Gd: 0-1 GF: - Fm: 0-0
Distance:	2m/2m3: 0-3 2m4-2m7: 0-0 3m+: 0-0
Track:	LH: 0-0 RH: 0-2 Tight: 0-0 Gall: 0-0
Aids:	Bl: 0-0 Vi: 0-0 Tstrap: 0-0 Ckp: 0-0
Best Rating:	80 3/04 Kemp 2m good NHF

Dark Ben (FR)
30f   75f

4-y-o b g Solar One (FR)-Reine D'Auteuil (FR) (Cap Martin (FR))
Miss Kate Milligan J D Gordon

Placings:0   (4482)
2003/04: 17⁰HY,

	Starts	1st	2nd	3rd	Win & Pl
NH Flat	1	0	0	0	
Career Total	1	0	0	0	

Going:	Sf: 0-1 GS: 0-0 Gd: 0-0 GF: - Fm: 0-0
Distance:	2m/2m3: 0-1 2m4-2m7: 0-0 3m+: 0-0
Track:	LH: 0-0 RH: 0-1 Tight: 0-0 Gall: 0-0
Aids:	Bl: 0-0 Vi: 0-0 Tstrap: 0-0 Ckp: 0-0
Best Rating:	75 3/04 Carl 2m1f heavy NHF

Dark Character
87   89+

5-y-o b g Reprimand-Poyle Jezebelle (Sharpo)
G A Swinbank Leading Star Racing Group

Placings:216-1R3   (2530)
2003/04: 17¹G, 16⁶G, 19³GS,

	Starts	1st	2nd	3rd	Win & Pl
NH Flat	1	1	0	0	1582
Hurdles	2	0	0	1	500
Career Total	6	2	1	1	5075
112 10/03 Bang 2m1f H NHF				GD	£1582
99 3/03 Sthl 2m H NHF				G-F	£1967
			Total win prize-money		£3549

Going:	Sf: 0-0 GS: 0-1 Gd: 1-2 GF: - Fm: 0-0
Distance:	2m/2m3: 1-3 2m4-2m7: 0-0 3m+: 0-0
Track:	LH: 1-3 RH: 0-0 Tight: 1-2 Gall: 0-0
Aids:	Bl: 0-0 Vi: 0-0 Tstrap: 0-0 Ckp: 0-0
Best Rating:	112 10/03 Bang 2m1f good NHF

Fair novice hurdler; good form in bumpers; has shown mulish tendencies over timber; may not stay beyond two miles.

Dark Crusader (IRE)

(69h)

9-y-o br g Cajetano (USA)-Glissade (Furry Glen)
Miss Lucinda V Russell Brahms & Liszt

Placings:42204P/4311PP/44PPP/P-0U5P   (2902)
2003/04: 20⁰G, 21ᵁG, 22⁵S, 21ᴾS,

	Starts	1st	2nd	3rd	Win & Pl
Hurdles	1	0	0	0	0
Chases	3	0	0	0	0
Career Total	**22**	**2**	**2**	**1**	**7782**
118 12/00 Folk	2m4f110yE Hdl			HVY	£2621
118 11/00 Towc	2m5f	E Hdl		SFT	£2275
		Total win prize-money £4897

Going:	Sf: 0-2 GS: 0-0 Gd: 0-2 GF: - Fm: 0-0
Distance:	2m/2m3: 0-0 2m4-2m7: 0-4 3m+: 0-0
Track:	LH: 0-3 RH: 0-1 Tight: 0-1 Gall: 0-0
Aids:	Bl: 0-0 Vi: 0-2 Tstrap: 0-0 Ckp: 0-0
Best Rating:	118 12/00 Folk 2m4f110y heavy Hdl

Dark Dolores

6-y-o b/br m Inchinor-Pingin (Corvaro (USA))
J R Boyle (N P Littmoden 3/7) Friends of the Turf Racing Limited

Placings:UP   (2777)
2003/04: 16ᵁGF, 17ᴾGS,

	Starts	1st	2nd	3rd	Win & Pl
Hurdles	2	0	0	0	0
Career Total	**2**	**0**	**0**	**0**	

Going:	Sf: 0-0 GS: 0-1 Gd: 0-0 GF: - Fm: 0-1
Distance:	2m/2m3: 0-2 2m4-2m7: 0-0 3m+: 0-0
Track:	LH: 0-1 RH: 0-1 Tight: 0-2 Gall: 0-0
Aids:	Bl: 0-1 Vi: 0-0 Tstrap: 0-0 Ckp: 0-0

Dark Island

65(75h)   (12h)17

9-y-o b g Silver Season-Isle Maree (Star Appeal)
Mary Meek Mrs Mary Meek

Placings:P-3600   (4791)
2003/04: 26³GF, 22ᴿGF, 16⁹GF, 20⁰G,

	Starts	1st	2nd	3rd	Win & Pl
Hurdles	3	0	0	1	410
Chases	1	0	0	0	0
Career Total	**5**	**0**	**0**	**1**	**410**

Going:	Sf: 0-0 GS: 0-0 Gd: 0-1 GF: - Fm: 0-3
Distance:	2m/2m3: 0-1 2m4-2m7: 0-2 3m+: 0-1
Track:	LH: 0-2 RH: 0-2 Tight: 0-1 Gall: 0-1
Aids:	Bl: 0-0 Vi: 0-0 Tstrap: 0-0 Ckp: 0-0
Best Rating:	17 4/04 Plum 2m4f good Ch

Dark Mandate (IRE)

(67h)   (47h)

6-y-o b/br m Mandalus-Ceoltoir Dubh (Black Minstrel)
J S Haldane Mrs Hugh Fraser

Placings:P-PP0PP   (4613)
2003/04: 20ᴾG, 20ᴾS, 20⁰GS, 16ᴾG, 16ᴾG,

	Starts	1st	2nd	3rd	Win & Pl
Hurdles	3	0	0	0	0
Chases	2	0	0	0	0
Career Total	**6**	**0**	**0**	**0**	

Going:	Sf: 0-1 GS: 0-1 Gd: 0-3 GF: - Fm: 0-0
Distance:	2m/2m3: 0-2 2m4-2m7: 0-3 3m+: 0-0
Track:	LH: 0-4 RH: 0-1 Tight: 0-1 Gall: 0-0
Aids:	Bl: 0-0 Vi: 0-0 Tstrap: 0-0 Ckp: 0-0
Best Rating:	47 12/03 Hayd 2m4f gd-sft Hdl

Dark Room (IRE)

105   122+

7-y-o b g Toulon-Maudlin Bridge (IRE) (Strong Gale)
Jonjo O'Neill John P McManus

Placings:U/6U51223P0-410PF   (4640)
2003/04: 20⁴GF, 21¹GS, 24⁰S, 33ᴾG, 21ᶠG,

	Starts	1st	2nd	3rd	Win & Pl
Chases	5	1	0	0	25051
Career Total	**15**	**2**	**2**	**1**	**33447**
123 11/03 Aint	2m5f110yC(0-130)HCh			G-S	£24522
116 12/02 MRas	3m1f	E(0-105)HCh		SFT	£4212
		Total win prize-money £28734

Going:	Sf: 0-1 GS: 1-1 Gd: 0-2 GF: - Fm: 0-1
Distance:	2m/2m3: 0-0 **2m4-2m7:** 1-3 3m+: 0-2
Track:	**LH:** 1-4 RH: 0-1 **Tight:** 1-2 Gall: 0-2
Aids:	Bl: 0-0 Vi: 0-0 Tstrap: 0-0 Ckp: 0-0
Best Rating:	123 11/03 Aint 2m5f110y gd-sft Ch

Fair chaser; effective at around two miles six but stays marathon trips; won valuable handicap over the Grand National fences in November 2003; acts on soft ground.

Dark Shadows

97   101

9-y-o b g Machiavellian (USA)-Instant Desire (USA) (Northern Dancer)
W Storey D O Cremin

Placings:4020/066/2PP2-26342   (2137)
2003/04: 20²G, 22⁶G, 20³G, 20⁴G, 24²G,

	Starts	1st	2nd	3rd	Win & Pl
Hurdles	5	0	2	1	2787
Career Total	**16**	**0**	**5**	**1**	**5016**

Going:	Sf: 0-0 GS: 0-0 Gd: 0-5 GF: - Fm: 0-0
Distance:	2m/2m3: 0-0 2m4-2m7: 0-4 3m+: 0-1
Track:	LH: 0-3 RH: 0-2 Tight: 0-2 Gall: 0-1
Aids:	Bl: 0-0 Vi: 0-0 Tstrap: 0-0 Ckp: 0-0
Best Rating:	106 3/00 MRas 1m5f110y gd-fm NHF

Modest hurdler; pretty exposed; acts on good ground; stays 3m.

Dark Slaney (IRE)

68   39

9-y-o b g Meneval (USA)-Black Valley (IRE) (Good Thyne (USA))
P D Niven David Bamber

Placings:P0P   (3481)
2003/04: 20ᴾS, 25⁰GS, 25ᴾG,

	Starts	1st	2nd	3rd	Win & Pl
Hurdles	3	0	0	0	0
Career Total	**3**	**0**	**0**	**0**	

Going:	Sf: 0-1 GS: 0-1 Gd: 0-1 GF: - Fm: 0-0
Distance:	2m/2m3: 0-0 2m4-2m7: 0-1 3m+: 0-2
Track:	LH: 0-3 RH: 0-0 Tight: 0-1 Gall: 0-0
Aids:	Bl: 0-0 Vi: 0-0 Tstrap: 0-0 Ckp: 0-0
Best Rating:	39 1/04 Weth 3m1f gd-sft Hdl

Dark Stranger (FR)

13-y-o b g Iveday (FR)-Abeille Royale (USA) (Turn To Mars (USA))
M C Pipe Terry Neill

Placings:412F2/34P/11201P1/24P11U/03P3R4/25600032/0   (4384)
2003/04: 24⁰G,

	Starts	1st	2nd	3rd	Win & Pl
Chases	1	0	0	0	
Career Total	**36**	**7**	**6**	**4**	**138323**
149 3/00 Chel	2m4f110yB HCh			GD	£35750
135 2/00 Leic	2m4f110yD(0-125)HCh			GD	£5135
144 4/99 Sand	2m4f110yC HCh			GD	£13851
139 4/99 Asct	2m3f110yC Ch			G-F	£6840
131 1/99 Ling	2m4f110yD(0-110)HCh			HVY	£3794
127 1/99 Ludl	2m4f	F(0-100)HCh		G-S	£2450
118 2/96 Hayd	2m	D Hdl		SFT	£3235
		Total win prize-money £71056

Going:	Sf: 0-0 GS: 0-0 Gd: 0-1 GF: - Fm: 0-0
Distance:	2m/2m3: 0-0 2m4-2m7: 0-0 3m+: 0-1
Track:	LH: 0-1 RH: 0-0 Tight: 0-0 Gall: 0-1
Aids:	Bl: 0-1 Vi: 0-0 Tstrap: 0-0 Ckp: 0-0
Best Rating:	149 3/00 Chel 2m4f110y good Ch

Useful handicap chaser; took the Mildmay of Flete at the 2000 Festival; did not enjoy the best of luck in either the 2000 and 2001 Grand Nationals, but ran really well to be second in the attheraces Gold Cup in April 2002; not seen since; stays well; appears to need top-of-the-ground these days; usually blinkered.

Dark Thunder (IRE)

71   61

7-y-o b/br g Religiously (USA)-Culkeern (Master Buck)
T P McGovern Anthony O'Gorman

Placings:P036   (4361)
2003/04: 26ᴾGS, 21⁰G, 22³GF, 21⁶GS,

	Starts	1st	2nd	3rd	Win & Pl
Hurdles	3	0	0	1	518
Chases	1	0	0	0	0
Career Total	**4**	**0**	**0**	**1**	**518**

Going:	Sf: 0-0 GS: 0-0 Gd: 0-1 GF: - Fm: 0-1
Distance:	2m/2m3: 0-2 2m4-2m7: 0-3 3m+: 0-1
Track:	LH: 0-3 RH: 0-0 Tight: 0-4 Gall: 0-0
Aids:	Bl: 0-0 Vi: 0-0 Tstrap: 0-0 Ckp: 0-0
Best Rating:	61 3/04 Plum 2m5f gd-sft Hdl

Dark Vocation (IRE)

101   97

4-y-o b g College Chapel-Shadia (USA) (Naskra (USA))
F J Bowles Mrs C Connolly

Placings:043000   (4802a)
2003/04: 16⁹GY, 16⁴G, 16³S, 16⁰Y, 16⁰YS, 16⁰Y,

	Starts	1st	2nd	3rd	Win & Pl
Hurdles	6	0	0	1	1964
Career Total	**6**	**0**	**0**	**1**	**1964**

Going:	Sf: 0-1 GS: 0-0 Gd: 0-1 GF: - Fm: 0-0
Distance:	2m/2m3: 0-6 2m4-2m7: 0-0 3m+: 0-0
Track:	LH: 0-4 RH: 0-1 Tight: 0-0 Gall: 0-0
Aids:	Bl: 0-0 Vi: 0-0 Tstrap: 0-6 Ckp: 0-0
Best Rating:	97 11/03 Navn 2m gd-yld Hdl

Dark Whisper (IRE)
97f   89f
5-y-o b g Ali-Royal (IRE)-Bolino Star (IRE) (Stalker)
Ian Williams Ten Away Partnership

Placings:*4352*   (1019)
2003/04: 17⁴G, 17³GF, 16⁵G, 16²GF,

	Starts	1st	2nd	3rd	Win & Pl
NH Flat	4	0	1	1	274
Career Total	4	0	1	1	274

Going:	Sf: 0-0 GS: 0-0 Gd: 0-2 GF: - Fm: 0-2
Distance:	2m/2m3: 0-4 2m4-2m7: 0-0 3m+: 0-0
Track:	LH: 0-2 RH: 0-2 Tight: 0-1 Gall: 0-0
Aids:	Bl: 0-0 Vi: 0-0 Tstrap: 0-0 Ckp: 0-0
Best Rating:	89 8/03 Worc 2m gd-fm NHF

Consistent form in modest bumpers; very unlucky third start.

Darkness
105f   109f
5-y-o ch g Accordion-Winnowing (IRE) (Strong Gale)
C R Egerton Lady Lloyd-Webber

Placings:*3*   (4199)
2003/04: 16³G,

	Starts	1st	2nd	3rd	Win & Pl
NH Flat	1	0	0	1	381
Career Total	1	0	0	1	381

Going:	Sf: 0-0 GS: 0-0 Gd: 0-1 GF: - Fm: 0-0
Distance:	2m/2m3: 0-1 2m4-2m7: 0-0 3m+: 0-0
Track:	LH: 0-1 RH: 0-0 Tight: 0-0 Gall: 0-1
Aids:	Bl: 0-0 Vi: 0-0 Tstrap: 0-0 Ckp: 0-0
Best Rating:	109 3/04 Newb 2m110y good NHF

Darnley
110(103h)   (104 h)109+
7-y-o b/br g Henbit (USA)-Reeling (Relkino)
J N R Billinge Sceptre House Golf Society

Placings:*0/0PF34-11404*   (4940)
2003/04: 16¹GS, 16¹GS, 16⁴G, 17⁰GS, 16⁴GS,

	Starts	1st	2nd	3rd	Win & Pl
Hurdles	1	1	0	0	4706
Chases	4	1	0	0	4157
Career Total	11	2	0	1	10434
104	12/03 Newc	2m110y E Ch		G-S	£3080
101	5/03 Prth	2m110y D Hdl		G-S	£4706
		Total win prize-money £7786			

Going:	Sf: 0-0 GS: 2-4 Gd: 0-1 GF: - Fm: 0-0
Distance:	2m/2m3: 2-5 2m4-2m7: 0-0 3m+: 0-0
Track:	LH: 1-2 RH: 1-3 Tight: 0-2 **Gall: 1-1**
Aids:	Bl: 0-0 Vi: 0-0 Tstrap: 0-0 Ckp: 0-0
Best Rating:	109 2/04 Muss 2m good Ch

Moderate novice hurdler; best efforts on good ground; fortunate winner on chasing debut at Newcastle in December; may be capable of better.

Dashing Charm
66   36
5-y-o b g Charmer-New Cruiser (Le Solaret (FR))
C C Bealby City Racing Club

Placings:*000*   (4783)
2003/04: 16⁹GF, 16⁰G, 21⁹GS,

	Starts	1st	2nd	3rd	Win & Pl
NH Flat	2	0	0	0	0
Hurdles	1	0	0	0	0
Career Total	3	0	0	0	

Going:	Sf: 0-0 GS: 0-0 Gd: 0-2 GF: - Fm: 0-1
Distance:	2m/2m3: 0-2 2m4-2m7: 0-1 3m+: 0-0
Track:	LH: 0-1 RH: 0-2 Tight: 0-0 Gall: 0-2
Aids:	Bl: 0-0 Vi: 0-0 Tstrap: 0-0 Ckp: 0-0
Best Rating:	63 3/04 Hntg 2m110y good NHF

Dashing Dollar (IRE)
96   77
13-y-o b g Lord Americo-Cora Swan (Tarqogan)
J R Payne R J Payne

Placings:*0/06 f120/440/1/F00113/0U0065/10P405020/5PF*
0P5-F03620PP   (4632)
2003/04: 20⁰GF, 22⁰GF, 16³S, 24⁶G, 19²HY, 22⁰G, 24⁵PGS, 24⁵PG,

	Starts	1st	2nd	3rd	Win & Pl
Hurdles	8	0	1	1	1132
Career Total	46	6	3	2	24844
119	5/01 Extr	2m6f110yE(0-115)HHdl	G-S	£3346
121	4/00 Extr	2m3f110yD(0-125)HHdl	HVY	£3753
114	3/00 Extr	2m7f	E(0-115)HHdl	G-S	£3315
116	11/98 Wind	2m6f110yD(0-125)HHdl	GD	£5303
114	11/96 Clon	2m	Hdl	Y-S	£2295
118	11/96 Clon	2m	NHF	YLD	£2648
		Total win prize-money £20661			

Going:	Sf: 0-2 GS: 0-1 Gd: 0-3 GF: - Fm: 0-2
Distance:	2m/2m3: 0-1 2m4-2m7: 0-1 3m+: 0-3
Track:	LH: 0-3 RH: 0-4 Tight: 0-4 Gall: 0-0
Aids:	Bl: 0-0 Vi: 0-0 Tstrap: 0-0 Ckp: 0-0
Best Rating:	121 4/00 Extr 2m3f110y heavy Hdl

Modest hurdler; stays two miles-six; goes well at Exeter.

Dashing Spur (IRE)
4-y-o b g Flying Spur (AUS)-Glamour Stock (USA) (Marfa (USA))
Miss Victoria Roberts D C Roberts

Placings:*P*   (2205)
2003/04: 17⁰G,

	Starts	1st	2nd	3rd	Win & Pl
Hurdles	1	0	0	0	
Career Total	1	0	0	0	

Going:	Sf: 0-0 GS: 0-0 Gd: 0-0 GF: - Fm: 0-0
Distance:	2m/2m3: 0-1 2m4-2m7: 0-0 3m+: 0-0
Track:	LH: 0-0 RH: 0-1 Tight: 0-0 Gall: 0-0
Aids:	Bl: 0-0 Vi: 0-0 Tstrap: 0-0 Ckp: 0-0

Dashing Steve
45
5-y-o b g Danzig Connection (USA)-Blazing Sunset (Blazing Saddles (AUS))
Mrs A M Thorpe D A Jones

Placings:*00P-P*   (0130)
2003/04: 16⁹GF,

	Starts	1st	2nd	3rd	Win & Pl
Hurdles	1	0	0	0	
Career Total	4	0	0	0	

Going:	Sf: 0-0 GS: 0-0 Gd: 0-0 GF: - Fm: 0-1

Dat My Horse (IRE)
98(101c)   (99c)122
10-y-o b g All Haste (USA)-Toposki (FR) (Top Ville)
Evan Williams A Lowrie & Mrs J Lowrie

Placings:*F5/P/FF/111023034P-0P5*   (4822)
2003/04: 27⁰GF, 22⁰GF, 19⁵GF,

	Starts	1st	2nd	3rd	Win & Pl
Hurdles	3	0	0	0	0
Career Total	18	3	1	2	13969
122	6/02 MRas	3m	E Hdl	G-F	£2565
113	5/02 Towc	3m	D Hdl	GD	£3250
116	5/02 Hrfd	3m2f	D Hdl	G-F	£3150
		Total win prize-money £8966			

Going:	Sf: 0-0 GS: 0-0 Gd: 0-0 GF: - Fm: 0-3
Distance:	2m/2m3: 0-1 2m4-2m7: 0-1 3m+: 0-1
Track:	LH: 0-1 RH: 0-1 Tight: 0-1 Gall: 0-0
Aids:	Bl: 0-0 Vi: 0-0 Tstrap: 0-0 Ckp: 0-0
Best Rating:	122 11/02 Hrfd 2m3f110y good Hdl

Winning pointer; modest hurdler; stays 3m 2f; acts on fast ground, handles softer.

Datbandito (IRE)
103f   101f
5-y-o gr g Un Desperado (FR)-Most Of All (Absalom)
L Lungo P E Truscott

Placings:*534*   (4316)
2003/04: 17⁵GS, 16³GF, 16⁴GF,

	Starts	1st	2nd	3rd	Win & Pl
NH Flat	3	0	0	1	422
Career Total	3	0	0	1	422

Going:	Sf: 0-0 GS: 0-1 Gd: 0-0 GF: - Fm: 0-2
Distance:	2m/2m3: 0-3 2m4-2m7: 0-0 3m+: 0-0
Track:	LH: 0-2 RH: 0-1 Tight: 0-0 Gall: 0-0
Aids:	Bl: 0-0 Vi: 0-0 Tstrap: 0-0 Ckp: 0-0
Best Rating:	101 12/03 Bang 2m1f gd-sft NHF

Full brother to Irish bumper/hurdles winner and has shown promise in bumpers on fast ground; type to win races, especially granted a stiffer test over obstacles.

Datito (IRE)
92   99
9-y-o b g Over The River (FR)-Crash Call (Crash Course)
R T Phillips G Lansbury

Placings:*1/42/3*   (3314)
2003/04: 16³S,

	Starts	1st	2nd	3rd	Win & Pl
Hurdles	1	0	0	1	786
Career Total	4	1	1	1	3638
126	3/01 Hayd	2m	H NHF	HVY	£1708
		Total win prize-money £1708			

Going:	Sf: 0-1 GS: 0-0 Gd: 0-0 GF: - Fm: 0-0
Distance:	2m/2m3: 0-1 2m4-2m7: 0-0 3m+: 0-0
Track:	LH: 0-0 RH: 0-1 Tight: 0-0 Gall: 0-0
Aids:	Bl: 0-0 Vi: 0-0 Tstrap: 0-0 Ckp: 0-0
Best Rating:	126 3/01 Hayd 2m heavy NHF

Lightly-raced performer; former Irish point-to-point winner, made a winning debut under Rules in a bumper at Haydock

in March 2001 on heavy ground; beaten twice over hurdles on faster ground after a year's absence; fair return form similar absence in February at Leicester when third on soft ground; stays 2m 4f.

Davenport Milenium (IRE)

109   154

8-y-o b g Insan (USA)-Society Belle (Callernish)
W P Mullins   Mrs N O'Callaghan

Placings:12/1F5111/3-4250   (4383)
2003/04: 20⁴S, 16²GS, 16⁵Y, 16⁹G,

	Starts	1st	2nd	3rd	Win & Pl
Hurdles	4	0	1	0	17961
Career Total	13	5	2	1	134952
158	4/02	Punc	2m	Hdl		G-Y £49693
154	4/02	Punc	2m4f	Hdl		GD £34233
140	3/02	Fair	2m2f	Hdl		G-Y £7975
120	12/01	Fair	2m2f	Hdl		YLD £6677
132	2/01	Leop	2m	NHF		HVY £5564

Total win prize-money £104143

Going:	Sf: 0-1 GS: 0-1 Gd: 0-1 GF: - Fm: 0-0
Distance:	2m/2m3: 0-3 2m4-2m7: 0-1 3m+: 0-0
Track:	LH: 0-3 RH: 0-1 Tight: 0-0 Gall: 0-0
Aids:	Bl: 0-0 Vi: 0-0 Tstrap: 0-0 Ckp: 0-0
Best Rating:	158 4/02 Punc 2m gd-yld Hdl

Smart Irish hurdler; scored three times in the spring of 2002, including two Grade Ones within the space of three days at the Punchestown Festival; off the track for ten months before returning in November 2003; ran well in the Bula subsequently and not disgraced in the Irish Champion Hurdle; effective from 2m to 2m 4f; best on a sound surface.

Davids Lad (IRE)

108   (91h)153

10-y-o b g Yashgan-Cool Nora (IRE) (Lafontaine (USA))
A J Martin   Eddie Joe's Racing Syndicate

Placings:0000S.501/14F504P5114P6/00110F61/111543F/4
04-356260   (4647)
2003/04: 20³GY, 22⁵SH, 17⁶S, 20²S, 18⁶Y, 36⁹G,

	Starts	1st	2nd	3rd	Win & Pl
Chases	6	0	1	1	8064
Career Total	45	10	1	2	163032
147	10/01	Rosc	2m	Ch		YLD £7862
154	5/01	Navn	3m	HCh		GD £16693
148	5/01	Fair	3m5f	HCh		GD £65725
150	4/01	Fair	2m4f	HCh		SFT £19395
124	11/00	Chel	2m4f110y	D(0-125)HCh		G-S £11505
111	10/00	Navn	2m4f	(0-116)HCh		YLD £5520
109	1/00	Navn	2m4f	(0-102)HHdl		SFT £4416
111	1/00	Muss	3m	F(0-105)HHdl		GD £3591
97	5/99	Prth	2m4f110yF(0-110)HHdl			HVY £3793
91	4/99	DRoy	2m4f	(0-102)HHdl		YLD £2823

Total win prize-money £141328

Going:	Sf: 0-2 GS: 0-0 Gd: 0-1 GF: - Fm: 0-0
Distance:	2m/2m3: 0-2 2m4-2m7: 0-3 3m+: 0-1
Track:	LH: 0-2 RH: 0-4 Tight: 0-1 Gall: 0-0
Aids:	Bl: 0-0 Vi: 0-0 Tstrap: 0-1 Ckp: 0-0
Best Rating:	154 5/01 Navn 3m good Ch

Smart Irish chaser; won Powers Gold Label Irish Grand National at Fairyhouse in 2001; fell when going well in the following year's Aintree National; has form on all sorts of ground; has won at distances from two miles to three miles five; sometimes wears a tongue strap.

Davoski

103(101h)   (122h)155

10-y-o b g Niniski (USA)-Pamela Peach (Habitat)
Ms Bridget Nicholls   Sir Robert Ogden

Placings:113132142210/1/16120/34/13430-P533   (4843)
2003/04: 20⁰GS, 19⁵G, 17³G, 16⁵G,

	Starts	1st	2nd	3rd	Win & Pl
Chases	4	0	0	2	3818
Career Total	29	9	4	7	103863
155	11/02	Asct	2m	A(0-150)HCh	G-S	£17835
152	12/00	Chel	2m110y	B HCh	SFT	£13663
140	10/00	Strf	2m5f110yC(0-135)HCh	SFT	£6890
134	10/99	Fknm	2m5f110yC Ch	GD	£8135
136	4/99	Uttx	2m	C(0-135)HHdl	G-S	£5083
134	1/99	Kemp	2m	D Hdl	SFT	£2944
121	11/98	NAbb	2m1f	E(0-110)HHdl	SFT	£2684
114	10/98	Uttx	2m	E Hdl	GD	£2431
98	9/98	Hrfd	2m1f	E Hdl	G-F	£2430

Total win prize-money £62097

Going:	Sf: 0-1 GS: 0-1 Gd: 0-3 GF: - Fm: 0-0
Distance:	2m/2m3: 0-2 2m4-2m7: 0-2 3m+: 0-0
Track:	LH: 0-3 RH: 0-1 Tight: 0-0 Gall: 0-2
Aids:	Bl: 0-0 Vi: 0-0 Tstrap: 0-0 Ckp: 0-0
Best Rating:	155 11/02 Asct 2m gd-sft Ch

Very useful chaser; developed into a really good handicapper in 2000/2001 before being sidelined for a year with leg trouble; stays two miles five, but seems most effective at the minimum trip; effective on all ground; best when fresh.

Dawn's Cognac (IRE)

11-y-o b g Glacial Storm (USA)-Misty Venture (Foggy Bell)
D Brace   David Brace

Placings:U/PP-0F   (4815)
2003/04: 21⁰G, 24²FG,

	Starts	1st	2nd	3rd	Win & Pl
Chases	2	0	0	0	0
Career Total	5	0	0	0	0

Going:	Sf: 0-0 GS: 0-0 Gd: 0-2 GF: - Fm: 0-0
Distance:	2m/2m3: 0-0 2m4-2m7: 0-1 3m+: 0-1
Track:	LH: 0-2 RH: 0-0 Tight: 0-0 Gall: 0-1
Aids:	Bl: 0-0 Vi: 0-0 Tstrap: 0-0 Ckp: 0-0
Best Rating:	56 4/03 Chel 2m5f good Ch

Dawton (POL)

83   67

6-y-o br h Greinton-Da Wega (POL) (Who Knows)
T R George   B A Kilpatrick

Placings:0   (2671)
2003/04: 16⁰GF,

	Starts	1st	2nd	3rd	Win & Pl
Hurdles	1	0	0	0	
Career Total	1	0	0	0	

Going:	Sf: 0-0 GS: 0-0 Gd: 0-0 GF: - Fm: 0-1
Distance:	2m/2m3: 0-1 2m4-2m7: 0-0 3m+: 0-0
Track:	LH: 0-1 RH: 0-0 Tight: 0-0 Gall: 0-0
Aids:	Bl: 0-0 Vi: 0-0 Tstrap: 0-0 Ckp: 0-0
Best Rating:	67 12/03 Newb 2m110y gd-fm Hdl

Day Du Roy (FR)

107(107h)   (108h)120+

6-y-o b g Ajdayt (USA)-Rose Pomme (FR) (Rose Laurel)
Jonjo O'Neill   Mrs Mo Done

Placings:001PP-252153363421   (4889)
2003/04: 17²G, 17⁵G, 17²G, 20¹GF, 19⁵G, 17³G, 20³G, 19⁶S, 20³GS, 20⁴G, 17²G, 20¹GF,

	Starts	1st	2nd	3rd	Win & Pl
Hurdles	9	1	3	2	11632
Chases	3	1	0	1	10527
Career Total	17	3	3	3	26871
120	4/04	Strf	2m4f	C(0-130)HCh	G-F	£9488
106	11/03	Hayd	2m4f	E(0-110)HHdl	G-F	£2999
	11/02	Fntb	2m3f	Ch	HLD	£4712

Total win prize-money £17201

Going:	Sf: 0-1 GS: 0-1 Gd: 0-8 GF: - Fm: 2-2
Distance:	2m/2m3: 0-6 2m4-2m7: 2-6 3m+: 0-0
Track:	LH: 2-8 RH: 0-4 Tight: 1-6 Gall: 0-1
Aids:	Bl: 0-1 Vi: 0-0 Tstrap: 0-1 Ckp: 0-0
Best Rating:	120 4/04 Strf 2m4f gd-fm Ch

Modest hurdler/chaser; winner of a four-year-olds' chase in France in November 2002; stays 2m 4f; acts on fast and soft ground; does not find much off the bridle; has worn blinkers and a tongue strap.

Dayenoo (FR)

35f   85f

4-y-o b g Subotica (FR)-La Cenomane (FR) (Master Thatch)
M W Easterby   G H Sparkes

Placings:2   (4482)
2003/04: 17²HY,

	Starts	1st	2nd	3rd	Win & Pl
NH Flat	1	0	1	0	548
Career Total	1	0	1	0	548

Going:	Sf: 0-1 GS: 0-0 Gd: 0-0 GF: - Fm: 0-0
Distance:	2m/2m3: 0-1 2m4-2m7: 0-0 3m+: 0-0
Track:	LH: 0-0 RH: 0-1 Tight: 0-0 Gall: 0-0
Aids:	Bl: 0-0 Vi: 0-0 Tstrap: 0-0 Ckp: 0-0
Best Rating:	85 3/04 Carl 2m1f heavy NHF

Daytime Arrival (IRE)

59

6-y-o ch g Lucky Guest-Daymer Bay (Lomond (USA))
Keith Thomas   Mrs M A Holt

Placings:00000-PP   (2929)
2003/04: 16⁹GS, 21⁹G,

	Starts	1st	2nd	3rd	Win & Pl
Hurdles	2	0	0	0	
Career Total	7	0	0	0	

Going:	Sf: 0-0 GS: 0-1 Gd: 0-1 GF: - Fm: 0-0
Distance:	2m/2m3: 0-1 2m4-2m7: 0-1 3m+: 0-0
Track:	LH: 0-2 RH: 0-0 Tight: 0-1 Gall: 0-1
Aids:	Bl: 0-0 Vi: 0-0 Tstrap: 0-0 Ckp: 0-0
Best Rating:	59 8/02 Tipp 2m gd-fm Hdl

Daytime Dawn (IRE)

13-y-o b g Rashar (USA)-Ard Clos (Ardoon)
R N C Wale   R N C Wale

Placings: F0/564/00/U1/1/0/4/PP-P0   (0354)
2003/04: 16PG, 21OGF,

	Starts	1st	2nd	3rd	Win & Pl
Chases	2	0	0	0	
Career Total	16	2	0	0	4455
108 4/00 Hrfd	2m	H Ch		GD	£2012
88 4/99 Hrfd	2m3f	H Ch		G-F	£2442
			Total win prize-money £4455		

Going: Sf: 0-0 GS: 0-0 Gd: 0-1 GF: - Fm: 0-1
Distance: 2m/2m3: 0-1 2m4-2m7: 0-1 3m+: 0-0
Track: LH: 0-1 RH: 0-1 Tight: 0-1 Gall: 0-1
Aids: Bl: 0-0 Vi: 0-0 Tstrap: 0-1 Ckp: 0-0
Best Rating: 108 4/00 Hrfd 2m good Ch

Dazzling Rio (IRE)
99   94
5-y-o b g Ashkalani (IRE)-Dazzling Fire (IRE) (Bluebird (USA))
Miss Kate Milligan Mrs A Roddis

Placings: P2634-242440P   (2710)
2003/04: 17²GF, 17⁴G, 21²GF, 21⁴G, 20⁴GF, 16⁰G, 16FGS,

	Starts	1st	2nd	3rd	Win & Pl
Hurdles	7	0	2	0	2104
Career Total	12	0	3	1	3679

Going: Sf: 0-0 GS: 0-1 Gd: 0-3 GF: - Fm: 0-3
Distance: 2m/2m3: 0-4 2m4-2m7: 0-3 3m+: 0-0
Track: LH: 0-7 RH: 0-0 Tight: 0-5 Gall: 0-1
Aids: Bl: 0-0 Vi: 0-0 Tstrap: 0-0 Ckp: 0-1
Best Rating: 94 9/03 Sedg 2m5f110y gd-fm Hdl

Moderate hurdler; running consistently without success; stays two miles five; acts on a sound surface.

Dd's Glenalla (IRE)
105   97
7-y-o b m Be My Native (USA)-Willowho Pride (Arapaho)
N A Twiston-Davies Mrs Caroline Beresford-Wylie

Placings: 0620P-26450203   (4914)
2003/04: 20²G, 23⁶G, 21⁴GF, 20⁵HY, 21⁰G, 26²GF, 21⁰G, 24³GS,

	Starts	1st	2nd	3rd	Win & Pl
Hurdles	8	0	2	1	2736
Career Total	13	0	3	1	3288

Going: Sf: 0-1 GS: 0-2 Gd: 0-4 GF: - Fm: 0-1
Distance: 2m/2m3: 0-0 2m4-2m7: 0-6 3m+: 0-2
Track: LH: 0-7 RH: 0-0 Tight: 0-3 Gall: 0-2
Aids: Bl: 0-0 Vi: 0-0 Tstrap: 0-0 Ckp: 0-0
Best Rating: 97 4/04 Worc 3m gd-sft Hdl

Modest bumper form; placed in novice hurdles; stays 3m 2f; effective on fast ground.

De Blanc (IRE)
103   98+
4-y-o b f Revoque (IRE)-Queen's Share (Main Reef)
Miss Venetia Williams (A Renzoni 29/11) Mrs Kathy Stuart

Placings: 51   (4489)
2003/04: 16⁵G, 16¹G,

	Starts	1st	2nd	3rd	Win & Pl
Hurdles	2	1	0	0	3445
Career Total	2	1	0	0	3445
98 3/04 Strf	2m110y	E Hdl		GD	£3445
			Total win prize-money £3445		

Going: Sf: 0-0 GS: 0-0 Gd: 1-2 GF: - Fm: 0-0
Distance: 2m/2m3: 1-2 2m4-2m7: 0-0 3m+: 0-0

Dead-Eyed Dick (IRE)
101(80h)   109
8-y-o b g Un Desperado (FR)-Glendale Charmer (Down The Hatch)
Nick Williams Mrs Jane Williams

Placings: 00/05P/01FP6P-31FP   (3710)
2003/04: 24³GF, 19¹G, 19FGS, 24PHY,

	Starts	1st	2nd	3rd	Win & Pl
Chases	4	1	0	1	4006
Career Total	15	2	0	1	8472
102 11/03 Extr	2m3f110yF(0-95)HCh		GD	£3570
102 12/02 Extr	2m7f110yD(0-105)HCh		G-S	£4465
			Total win prize-money £8036		

Going: Sf: 0-1 GS: 0-1 Gd: 1-1 GF: - Fm: 0-0
Distance: 2m/2m3: 0-0 2m4-2m7: 1-2 3m+: 0-2
Track: LH: 0-3 RH: 1-1 Tight: 0-0 Gall: 0-0
Aids: Bl: 0-0 Vi: 0-0 Tstrap: 0-0 Ckp: 0-0
Best Rating: 109 12/02 Chel 2m5f good Ch

Modest chaser; stays three miles; acts on good or softer; likes Exeter.

Deadly Doris
70   63
10-y-o b m Ron's Victory (USA)-Camp Chair (Ela-Mana-Mou)
N A Smith Stan Hey And Partners

Placings: 540/55600/5042U25355/15655/40P-0   (3703)
2003/04: 19⁰HY,

	Starts	1st	2nd	3rd	Win & Pl
Hurdles	1	0	0	0	
Career Total	27	1	2	1	4195
92 11/01 Towc	2m	E Hdl		SFT	£2618
			Total win prize-money £2618		

Going: Sf: 0-1 GS: 0-0 Gd: 0-0 GF: - Fm: 0-0
Distance: 2m/2m3: 0-0 2m4-2m7: 0-1 3m+: 0-0
Track: LH: 0-0 RH: 0-1 Tight: 0-0 Gall: 0-0
Aids: Bl: 0-0 Vi: 0-0 Tstrap: 0-0 Ckp: 0-0
Best Rating: 94 1/99 Hntg 2m110y soft NHF

Dealer Del
111   103
10-y-o b g Deltic (USA)-No Deal (Sharp Deal)
C J Down Mrs Hazel Leeves

Placings: 053/51P2UP-1P1F   (4532)
2003/04: 25¹GF, 25PGF, 26¹GF, 25FGS,

	Starts	1st	2nd	3rd	Win & Pl
Chases	4	2	0	0	6911
Career Total	13	3	1	1	11604
103 6/03 NAbb	3m2f110yF(0-95)HCh		G-F	£3368
100 5/03 Hrfd	3m1f110yF(0-95)HCh		G-F	£3542
103 5/02 Towc	2m6f	H Ch		GD	£2847
			Total win prize-money £9758		

Going: Sf: 0-0 GS: 0-1 Gd: 0-0 GF: - Fm: 2-3
Distance: 2m/2m3: 0-0 2m4-2m7: 0-0 3m+: 2-4
Track: LH: 1-1 RH: 0-1 Tight: 1-1 Gall: 0-0
Aids: Bl: 0-0 Vi: 0-0 Tstrap: 0-0 Ckp: 0-0
Best Rating: 103 6/03 NAbb 3m2f110y gd-fm Ch

Dealer's Choice (IRE)
105(103h)   (109+h)121
10-y-o gr g Roselier (FR)-Cam Flower Vii (Damsire Unregistered)
Miss Victoria Roberts (M Pitman 29/4) P Duffy, G King, D Roberts, B Savage

Placings: 1/2F65F5/U/261P1P/21PFU1-6P1060   (4715)
2003/04: 27¹S, 24⁶GS, 20PG, 20¹G, 24⁰G, 20⁶GS, 20⁰G,

	Starts	1st	2nd	3rd	Win & Pl
Hurdles	2	1	0	0	3537
Chases	5	1	0	0	6825
Career Total	26	6	3	0	29100
116 2/04 Ludl	2m4f	D(0-125)HCh	GD	£6825
109 4/03 Ludl	3m3f	E Hdl	SFT	£3537
121 12/02 Folk	2m5f	D(0-120)HCh	SFT	£5200
121 3/02 Ludl	2m4f	D(0-115)HCh	SFT	£5148
108 12/01 Ludl	2m4f	F(0-95)HCh	GD	£3887
97 4/99 Font	2m2f110yH NHF		SFT	£1567
			Total win prize-money £26164		

Going: Sf: 1-1 GS: 2-2 Gd: 1-4 GF: - Fm: 0-0
Distance: 2m/2m3: 0-0 2m4-2m7: 1-4 3m+: 1-3
Track: LH: 1-3 RH: 1-4 Tight: 2-5 Gall: 0-1
Aids: Bl: 0-0 Vi: 0-0 Tstrap: 0-0 Ckp: 0-0
Best Rating: 121 12/02 Folk 2m5f soft Ch

Modest chaser; stays three miles three furlongs, but effective at two miles four; suited by an easy surface and a sharp track; has a good record at Ludlow.

Deano's Beeno
112   160
12-y-o b g Far North (CAN)-Sans Dot (Busted)
M C Pipe Axom

Placings: 105/111/2105/12215/1210/00/23121612-623430
                                                           (4623)
2003/04: 23⁶GS, 24²GS, 25³G, 24⁴G, 24³G, 24⁰G,

	Starts	1st	2nd	3rd	Win & Pl
Hurdles	6	0	1	2	22358
Career Total	35	12	8	3	255200
157 4/03 Asct	3m	A Hdl		GD	£23200
160 2/03 Kemp	3m110y	A Hdl		GD	£23800
164 12/02 Asct	3m1f110yA Hdl		SFT	£40200
176 1/01 Donc	3m110y	A Hdl		GD	£15780
176 11/00 Newb	3m110y	A Hdl		SFT	£13800
153 2/00 Newb	3m	C Ch		G-S	£6474
176 11/99 Newb	3m110y	A Hdl		G-S	£13100
174 1/99 Hayd	2m7f110yA Hdl		SFT	£12440
153 12/97 Bang	3m	B(0-140)HHdl		GD	£4783
154 11/97 Hayd	2m6f	B HHdl		SFT	£4883
148 11/97 NAbb	2m6f	D(0-125)HHdl	SFT	£2762
134 12/96 NAbb	2m1f	D Hdl		SFT	£2911
			Total win prize-money £164135		

Going: Sf: 0-0 GS: 0-2 Gd: 0-4 GF: - Fm: 0-0
Distance: 2m/2m3: 0-0 2m4-2m7: 0-0 3m+: 0-6
Track: LH: 0-4 RH: 0-2 Tight: 0-1 Gall: 0-2
Aids: Bl: 0-2 Vi: 0-1 Tstrap: 0-0 Ckp: 0-0
Best Rating: 176 1/01 Donc 3m110y good Hdl

Smart staying hurdler; took the scalp of Baracouda in the Long Walk Hurdle at Ascot in December 2002 under an inspired McCoy ride and landed Grade Two Rendlesham Hurdle at Kempton in February 2003; returned to Ascot to land the Long Distance Hurdle in April; fair reappearance at Newbury in November 2003, but disappointing sort; often

Track: LH: 1-2 RH: 0-0 Tight: 1-1 Gall: 0-1
Aids: Bl: 0-0 Vi: 0-0 Tstrap: 0-0 Ckp: 0-0
Best Rating: 98 3/04 Strf 2m110y good Hdl

Moderate hunter/handicap chaser; pulled up between winning at Hereford and Newton Abbot in May/June 2003; stays 3m 2f; acts on any ground; inconsistent and suffers from back problems.

shows signs of temperament; goes well fresh; prefers to dominate. Reportedly retired.

Dear Boy

50   **26**

5-y-o ch g Anshan-Kev's Lass (IRE) (Kemal (FR))
J A Supple   Geoff Hubbard Racing

Placings:POP   (2712)
2003/04: 21PGF, 16QGS, 16PGS,

	Starts	1st	2nd	3rd	Win & Pl
Hurdles	3	0	0	0	
Career Total	3	0	0	0	

Going:	Sf: 0-0 GS: 0-2 Gd: 0-0 GF: - Fm: 0-1
Distance:	2m/2m3: 0-2 2m4-2m7: 0-0 3m+: 0-0
Track:	LH: 0-2 RH: 0-2 Tight: 0-0 Gall: 0-2
Aids:	Bl: 0-0 Vi: 0-0 Tstrap: 0-0 Ckp: 0-0
Best Rating:	31 11/03 Towc 2m gd-sft Hdl

Dear Deal

107   **133**

11-y-o b g Sharp Deal-The Deer Hound (Cash And Carry)
C L Tizzard   J A G Meaden

Placings:665/2443/11/32P4/2220S22P-125361263 (4837)
2003/04: 241GF, 242GF, 255G, 243S, 33RG, 241GS, 242G, 326G, 253GF,

	Starts	1st	2nd	3rd	Win & Pl
Chases	9	2	2	2	35493
Career Total	30	4	9	4	53304
133 2/04 Kemp	3m	D(0-125)HCh	G-S	£9303
126 10/03 Chel	3m110y	C Ch	G-F	£9811
121 10/00 Winc	2m6f	E Hdl	G-S	£2506
118 9/00 Extr	2m6f110yE Hdl		GD	£2632

Total win prize-money £24253

Going:	Sf: 0-1 GS: 1-1 Gd: 0-4 GF: - Fm: 1-3
Distance:	2m/2m3: 0-0 2m4-2m7: 0-0 3m+: 2-9
Track:	LH: 1-7 RH: 1-2 Tight: 0-0 Gall: 1-7
Aids:	Bl: 0-0 Vi: 0-0 Tstrap: 0-3 Ckp: 1-0
Best Rating:	133 4/04 Chel 3m1f110y gd-fm Ch

Useful chaser; stays three miles plus; acts on most types of ground, but probably best on soft ground; consistent.

Dear Sir (IRE)

92   **89**

4-y-o ch g Among Men (USA)-Deerussa (IRE) (Jareer (USA))
Mrs P N Dutfield   Unity Farm Holiday Centre Ltd

Placings:031P   (2483)
2003/04: 17QG, 173F, 161GF, 16PGS,

	Starts	1st	2nd	3rd	Win & Pl
Hurdles	4	1	0	1	4304
Career Total	4	1	0	1	4304
89 11/03 Hntg	2m110y D Hdl		G-F	£3789

Total win prize-money £3790

Going:	Sf: 0-0 GS: 0-1 Gd: 0-1 GF: - Fm: 1-2
Distance:	2m/2m3: 1-4 2m4-2m7: 0-0 3m+: 0-0
Track:	LH: 0-2 RH: 1-2 Tight: 0-0 Gall: 1-2
Aids:	Bl: 0-0 Vi: 0-0 Tstrap: 0-0 Ckp: 0-0
Best Rating:	89 11/03 Hntg 2m110y gd-fm Hdl

Deb's Son

96   **86**

7-y-o b g Minster Son-Deb's Ball (Glenstal (USA))

James Moffatt   F A Wilson

Placings:32403/613040/6P014-06020   (2799)
2003/04: 244GF, 26QG, 24RG, 22QG, 212GF, 240S,

	Starts	1st	2nd	3rd	Win & Pl
Hurdles	6	0	1	0	520
Career Total	21	2	2	3	8088
89 4/03 Sedg	2m5f110yG(0-100)HHdl	GD	£2352
100 8/01 Ctml	2m6f	E Hdl	G-S	£3115

Total win prize-money £5467

Going:	Sf: 0-1 GS: 0-0 Gd: 0-3 GF: - Fm: 0-2
Distance:	2m/2m3: 0-2 2m4-2m7: 0-2 3m+: 0-4
Track:	LH: 0-5 RH: 0-1 Tight: 0-4 Gall: 0-1
Aids:	Bl: 0-0 Vi: 0-4 Tstrap: 0-0 Ckp: 0-2
Best Rating:	100 8/01 Ctml 2m6f gd-sft Hdl

Modest hurdler, won a seller in first-time visor at Sedgefield in April 2003; stays two miles-six plus, suited by cut in the ground; has worn cheekpieces.

Debandy Boy

4-y-o b g Timeless Times (USA)-Judys Girl (IRE) (Simply Great (FR))
J S Wainwright   T W Heseltine

Placings:PP   (1071)
2003/04: 17PGF, 17PGF,

	Starts	1st	2nd	3rd	Win & Pl
Hurdles	2	0	0	0	
Career Total	2	0	0	0	

Going:	Sf: 0-0 GS: 0-0 Gd: 0-0 GF: - Fm: 0-2
Distance:	2m/2m3: 0-2 2m4-2m7: 0-0 3m+: 0-0
Track:	LH: 0-1 RH: 0-1 Tight: 0-2 Gall: 0-0
Aids:	Bl: 0-0 Vi: 0-0 Tstrap: 0-0 Ckp: 0-1

Debatable

111f   **110+f**

5-y-o ch g Deploy-Questionable (Rainbow Quest (USA))
P R Webber   K Abdulla

Placings:1   (0763)
2003/04: 161G,

	Starts	1st	2nd	3rd	Win & Pl
NH Flat	1	1	0	0	1912
Career Total	1	1	0	0	1912
110 6/03 Worc	2m	H NHF	GD	£1912

Total win prize-money £1912

Going:	Sf: 0-0 GS: 0-0 Gd: 1-1 GF: - Fm: 0-0
Distance:	2m/2m3: 1-1 2m4-2m7: 0-0 3m+: 0-0
Track:	LH: 1-1 RH: 0-0 Tight: 0-0 Gall: 0-0
Aids:	Bl: 0-0 Vi: 0-0 Tstrap: 0-0 Ckp: 0-0
Best Rating:	110 6/03 Worc 2m good NHF

Brother to In Question who has won on the Flat and both over hurdles and fences; made winning debut in Worcester bumper June 2003; should be able to go on to better things.

Debbie

99   **81**

5-y-o b m Deploy-Elita (Sharpo)
B D Leavy (I A Wood 1/10)   Bevan Holmes Underwood and Partners

Placings:6F   (4630)
2003/04: 16RG, 17FG,

	Starts	1st	2nd	3rd	Win & Pl
Hurdles	2	0	0	0	0

Career Total   2   0   0   0   0

Going:	Sf: 0-0 GS: 0-0 Gd: 0-2 GF: - Fm: 0-0
Distance:	2m/2m3: 0-2 2m4-2m7: 0-0 3m+: 0-0
Track:	LH: 0-0 RH: 0-2 Tight: 0-1 Gall: 0-1
Aids:	Bl: 0-0 Vi: 0-0 Tstrap: 0-0 Ckp: 0-0
Best Rating:	81 4/04 Tntn 2m1f good Hdl

Decent Bond (IRE)

7-y-o b g Witness Box (USA)-Decent Skin (IRE) (Buckskin (FR))
V Thompson   V Thompson

Placings:U   (4687)
2003/04: 25UG,

	Starts	1st	2nd	3rd	Win & Pl
Chases	1	0	0	0	
Career Total	1	0	0	0	

Going:	Sf: 0-0 GS: 0-0 Gd: 0-1 GF: - Fm: 0-0
Distance:	2m/2m3: 0-0 2m4-2m7: 0-0 3m+: 0-1
Track:	LH: 0-1 RH: 0-0 Tight: 0-1 Gall: 0-0
Aids:	Bl: 0-0 Vi: 0-0 Tstrap: 0-0 Ckp: 0-0

Decent Rose (IRE)

6-y-o ch m Roselier (FR)-Decent Banker (Decent Fellow)
J I A Charlton   Sydney Ramsey & Partners

Placings:50PP   (4731)
2003/04: 165GF, 16QGS, 18PS, 20PG,

	Starts	1st	2nd	3rd	Win & Pl
NH Flat	2	0	0	0	
Hurdles	2	0	0	0	
Career Total	4	0	0	0	

Going:	Sf: 0-1 GS: 0-1 Gd: 0-1 GF: - Fm: 0-1
Distance:	2m/2m3: 0-3 2m4-2m7: 0-1 3m+: 0-0
Track:	LH: 0-3 RH: 0-1 Tight: 0-1 Gall: 0-0
Aids:	Bl: 0-0 Vi: 0-0 Tstrap: 0-0 Ckp: 0-0
Best Rating:	85 6/03 Hexm 2m110y gd-fm NHF

Deco Star (IRE)

83   **53**

5-y-o b g Dolphin Street (FR)-Ecco Mi (IRE) (Priolo (USA))
C J Gray   A C Heal

Placings:0P4   (4378)
2003/04: 17QG, 19PGS, 174G,

	Starts	1st	2nd	3rd	Win & Pl
Hurdles	3	0	0	0	0
Career Total	3	0	0	0	0

Going:	Sf: 0-0 GS: 0-1 Gd: 0-2 GF: - Fm: 0-0
Distance:	2m/2m3: 0-2 2m4-2m7: 0-1 3m+: 0-0
Track:	LH: 0-0 RH: 0-3 Tight: 0-2 Gall: 0-0
Aids:	Bl: 0-0 Vi: 0-0 Tstrap: 0-2 Ckp: 0-0
Best Rating:	53 3/04 Tntn 2m1f good Hdl

Decoded

8-y-o ch g Deploy-Golden Panda (Music Boy)

Mrs Sarah L Dent Mrs H E Aitkin

Placings:431260/56/**663F65/14P-FU5**   (4949)
2003/04: 25FG, 27UG, 26SGS,

	Starts	1st	2nd	3rd	Win & Pl
Chases	3	0	0	0	0
Career Total	20	2	1	2	9221
85	10/02 Kels	3m1f	E Ch	G-F	£4056
94	1/00 Ayr	2m4f	E Hdl	SFT	£2723
				Total win prize-money £6779

Going:	Sf: 0-0 GS: 0-1 Gd: 0-2 GF: - Fm: 0-0
Distance:	2m/2m3: 0-0 2m4-2m7: 0-0 3m+: 0-3
Track:	LH: 0-2 RH: 0-0 Tight: 0-2 Gall: 0-0
Aids:	Bl: 0-0 Vi: 0-0 Tstrap: 0-0 Ckp: 0-2
Best Rating:	94 1/00 Ayr 2m4f soft Hdl

Plating-class chaser; stays three miles one furlong; acts on any ground; has worn cheekpieces.

Dee Dee Bea

6-y-o b m Bustino-Dante's Delight (Idiots Delight)
L Wells W A Scott

Placings:0   (1622)
2003/04: 17QG,

	Starts	1st	2nd	3rd	Win & Pl
NH Flat	1	0	0	0	
Career Total	1	0	0	0	

Going:	Sf: 0-0 GS: 0-0 Gd: 0-1 GF: - Fm: 0-0
Distance:	2m/2m3: 0-1 2m4-2m7: 0-0 3m+: 0-0
Track:	LH: 0-1 RH: 0-0 Tight: 0-1 Gall: 0-0
Aids:	Bl: 0-0 Vi: 0-0 Tstrap: 0-0 Ckp: 0-0

Deep King (IRE)
94   94

9-y-o b/br g King's Ride-Splendid Run (Deep Run)
J W Mullins Miss Dinah Wilkins

Placings:143OUP3-P4P3   (4935)
2003/04: 21PG, 16AGS, 20PGF, 18SG,

	Starts	1st	2nd	3rd	Win & Pl
Chases	4	0	0	1	1013
Career Total	11	1	0	3	8406
80	7/02 Wxfd	2m4f	Ch	G-F	£5291
				Total win prize-money £5291

Going:	Sf: 0-0 GS: 0-1 Gd: 0-2 GF: - Fm: 0-1
Distance:	2m/2m3: 0-2 2m4-2m7: 0-2 3m+: 0-1
Track:	LH: 0-1 RH: 0-2 Tight: 0-1 Gall: 0-1
Aids:	Bl: 0-0 Vi: 0-0 Tstrap: 0-0 Ckp: 0-0
Best Rating:	100 8/02 Tipp 2m7f firm Ch

Modest chaser; winner over fences in Ireland; no promise in this country; stays two and a half miles.

Deep Quest
88   63

5-y-o g El Conquistador-Ten Deep (Deep Run)
S C Burrough Five Deep Partnership

Placings:0   (2698)
2003/04: 17QG,

	Starts	1st	2nd	3rd	Win & Pl
Hurdles	1	0	0	0	
Career Total	1	0	0	0	

Going:	Sf: 0-0 GS: 0-0 Gd: 0-1 GF: - Fm: 0-0

Deep Sigh
89   72

7-y-o b g Weld-At Long Last (John French)
D R Gandolfo Mrs John Lee

Placings:50P-P020FRU   (4774)
2003/04: 21PS, 16QGS, 16QGS, 16QS, 20FG, 18RG, 16UG,

	Starts	1st	2nd	3rd	Win & Pl
Hurdles	5	0	1	0	586
Chases	2	0	0	0	0
Career Total	10	0	1	0	586

Going:	Sf: 0-2 GS: 0-2 Gd: 0-3 GF: - Fm: 0-0
Distance:	2m/2m3: 0-5 2m4-2m7: 0-2 3m+: 0-0
Track:	LH: 0-6 RH: 0-1 Tight: 0-3 Gall: 0-2
Aids:	Bl: 0-0 Vi: 0-0 Tstrap: 0-0 Ckp: 0-0
Best Rating:	84 11/02 NAbb 2m1f heavy NHF

Best effort over hurdles when runner-up in novices' handicap at Uttoxeter in December.

Deep Water (USA)
105(110h)   (122h) 128

10-y-o b g Diesis-Water Course (USA) (Irish River (FR))
M D Hammond The County Set

Placings:1121/5/410/0211F0P/03336/4032411-462104   (4951)
2003/04: 16AGS, 22SGS, 20QS, 19IG, 22QGS, 24AGS,

	Starts	1st	2nd	3rd	Win & Pl
Chases	6	1	1	0	9364
Career Total	33	9	4	4	95414
126	2/04 Catt	2m3f	D(0-120)HCh	GD	£5460
126	3/03 Weth	2m	D(0-120)HCh	G-F	£5378
126	3/03 MRas	2m1f110yD(0-120)HCh	SFT	£5343
123	12/00 MRas	2m1f110yD Ch	SFT	£5421
115	11/00 Catt	2m	D Ch	GD	£4173
140	2/00 Hayd	2m	B Hdl	SFT	£14490
146	4/98 Aint	2m110y	A Hdl	GD	£28334
126	2/98 Kels	2m110y	C Hdl	G-S	£4065
100	1/98 Kels	2m110y	D Hdl	HVY	£3025
				Total win prize-money £75690

Going:	Sf: 0-1 GS: 0-4 Gd: 1-1 GF: - Fm: 0-0
Distance:	**2m/2m3: 1-2** 2m4-2m7: 0-3 3m+: 0-1
Track:	LH: 1-3 RH: 0-3 Tight: 1-3 Gall: 0-0
Aids:	Bl: 0-0 Vi: 0-0 Tstrap: 0-0 Ckp: 0-0
Best Rating:	146 4/98 Aint 2m110y good Hdl

Useful chaser; formerly smart hurdler; stays two and a half miles plus; acts on good and soft ground; Tony Dobbin has built up a good relationship with him.

Deepastheocean
85   57

5-y-o b h Kris-Dance On A Cloud (USA) (Capote (USA))
M D Hammond G Shiel and SCB Ltd

Placings:04060   (4946)
2003/04: 16PS, 16AGF, 16QGF, 20FF, 16QGS,

	Starts	1st	2nd	3rd	Win & Pl
NH Flat	3	0	0	0	0
Hurdles	2	0	0	0	0
Career Total	5	0	0	0	0

Deer Dancer
97   94

4-y-o b g Tamure (IRE)-Anatomic (Deerhound (USA))
J D Frost Mrs J F Bury

Placings:33213   (4692)
2003/04: 13QGS, 13SS, 17QGS, 17IS, 17QG,

	Starts	1st	2nd	3rd	Win & Pl
NH Flat	2	0	0	2	608
Hurdles	3	1	1	1	5056
Career Total	5	1	1	3	5664
91	2/04 Extr	2m1f	E Hdl	SFT	£3406
				Total win prize-money £3406

Going:	Sf: 1-2 GS: 0-2 Gd: 0-1 GF: - Fm: 0-0
Distance:	**2m/2m3: 1-3** 2m4-2m7: 0-0 3m+: 0-0
Track:	LH: 0-0 **RH: 1-4** Tight: 0-0 Gall: 0-0
Aids:	Bl: 0-0 Vi: 0-0 Tstrap: 0-0 Ckp: 0-0
Best Rating:	94 4/04 Extr 2m1f good Hdl

Modest bumper and novice hurdling form to date.

Deer Dolly (IRE)

7-y-o b m Welsh Term-Wild Deer (Royal Buck)
P Butler Mrs E Lucey-Butler

Placings:P-PP   (2500)
2003/04: 21PS, 25PGF,

	Starts	1st	2nd	3rd	Win & Pl
Hurdles	1	0	0	0	0
Chases	1	0	0	0	0
Career Total	3	0	0	0	

Going:	Sf: 0-1 GS: 0-0 Gd: 0-0 GF: - Fm: 0-1
Distance:	2m/2m3: 0-0 2m4-2m7: 0-1 3m+: 0-1
Track:	LH: 0-1 RH: 0-1 Tight: 0-2 Gall: 0-0
Aids:	Bl: 0-0 Vi: 0-0 Tstrap: 0-0 Ckp: 0-1

Deewaar (IRE)
87   67

4-y-o b g Ashkalani (IRE)-Chandni (IRE) (Ahonoora)
J C Fox (J S Moore 27/8) Metropolitan Masonry Limited

Placings:0   (4577)
2003/04: 16QG,

	Starts	1st	2nd	3rd	Win & Pl
Hurdles	1	0	0	0	
Career Total	1	0	0	0	

Going:	Sf: 0-0 GS: 0-0 Gd: 0-1 GF: - Fm: 0-0
Distance:	2m/2m3: 0-1 2m4-2m7: 0-0 3m+: 0-0
Track:	LH: 0-1 RH: 0-0 Tight: 0-0 Gall: 0-1
Aids:	Bl: 0-0 Vi: 0-0 Tstrap: 0-0 Ckp: 0-0
Best Rating:	72 3/04 Newb 2m110y good Hdl

Defendtherealm
(83h) 119

13-y-o br g Derring Rose-Armagnac Princess (Armagnac Monarch)

Distance: 2m/2m3: 0-1 2m4-2m7: 0-0 3m+: 0-0
Track: LH: 0-0 RH: 0-1 Tight: 0-1 Gall: 0-0
Aids: Bl: 0-0 Vi: 0-0 Tstrap: 0-0 Ckp: 0-0
Best Rating: 63 12/03 Tntn 2m1f good Hdl

Going: Sf: 0-1 GS: 0-1 Gd: 0-0 GF: - Fm: 0-3
Distance: 2m/2m3: 0-4 2m4-2m7: 0-1 3m+: 0-0
Track: LH: 0-1 RH: 0-1 Tight: 0-3 Gall: 0-0
Aids: Bl: 0-0 Vi: 0-0 Tstrap: 0-0 Ckp: 0-0
Best Rating: 73 12/03 Muss 2m gd-fm NHF

J D Frost J D Frost

Placings:503231/3430U122/54F5F1U1/34245/213PP53/4P U5/P   **(0988)**
2003/04: 27PG,

	Starts	1st	2nd	3rd	Win & Pl
Hurdles	1	0	0	0	
Career Total	39	5	5	7	27197
110	8/00	NAbb	3m2f110yD(0-120)HCh		G-F	£4284
114	4/99	Extr	2m7f110yE(0-105)HCh		SFT	£3965
114	3/99	Extr	2m3f	D Ch	SFT	£3710
93	3/98	NAbb	2m6f	D(0-120)HHdl	SFT	£2805
96	3/97	NAbb	2m6f	E Hdl	HVY	£2284
				Total win prize-money £17052		

Going: Sf: 0-0 GS: 0-0 Gd: 0-1 GF: - Fm: 0-0
Distance: 2m/2m3: 0-0 2m4-2m7: 0-0 3m+: 0-1
Track: LH: 0-1 RH: 0-0 Tight: 0-0 Gall: 0-0
Aids: Bl: 0-0 Vi: 0-0 Tstrap: 0-0 Ckp: 0-0
Best Rating: 114 4/99   Extr   2m7f110y   soft   Ch

He is an effective sort in modest handicap chases in the West country.

Deferlant (FR)

98(108c)   (113c)108
7-y-o ch g Bering-Sail Storm (USA) (Topsider (USA))
K Bell (Mrs H Dalton 17/5) Mrs G McNeela

Placings:123120/622224300/342111F40040F-0050 **(4651)**
2003/04: 17PG, 21PG, 18PG, 17PG,

	Starts	1st	2nd	3rd	Win & Pl
Hurdles	4	0	0	0	0
Career Total	32	5	7	3	34945
125	8/02	Worc	2m4f110yE Ch		G-S	£3575
101	8/02	Prth	2m	Ch	G-S	£6695
114	7/02	Strf	2m1f110yD Ch		GD	£4728
115	12/00	Newb	2m110y D Hdl		SFT	£3786
110	7/00	MRas	2m1f110yD Hdl		G-F	£3477
				Total win prize-money £22263		

Going: Sf: 0-0 GS: 0-0 Gd: 0-4 GF: - Fm: 0-0
Distance: 2m/2m3: 0-3 2m4-2m7: 0-1 3m+: 0-0
Track: LH: 0-2 RH: 0-2 Tight: 0-2 Gall: 0-0
Aids: Bl: 0-0 Vi: 0-4 Tstrap: 0-0 Ckp: 0-0
Best Rating: 130 8/01   Strf   2m110y   gd-fm   Hdl

Modest hurdler, fair chaser; often finishes weakly over fences; stays in excess of two and a half miles; usually visored, generally jumps well.

Deja Vu (IRE)

103   87+
5-y-o b g Lord Americo-Khalkeys Shoon (Green Shoon)
J Howard Johnson The Sgs Partnership

Placings:5401P   **(3734)**
2003/04: 17PGF, 24PG, 24PS, 20PGF, 20PG,

	Starts	1st	2nd	3rd	Win & Pl
Hurdles	5	1	0	0	3754
Career Total	5	1	0	0	3754
89	1/04	Muss	2m4f	E(0-100)HHdl	G-F	£3445
				Total win prize-money £3445		

Going: Sf: 0-1 GS: 0-0 Gd: 0-2 GF: - Fm: 1-2
Distance: 2m/2m3: 0-1 2m4-2m7: 1-2 3m+: 0-2
Track: LH: 0-3 RH: 1-2 Tight: 1-3 Gall: 0-1
Aids: Bl: 0-0 Vi: 0-0 Tstrap: 0-0 Ckp: 0-0
Best Rating: 89 1/04   Muss   2m4f   gd-fm   Hdl

Moderate handicap hurdler; effective over two and a half miles; acts on fast ground.

Del Trotter (IRE)

107(98c)   (113c)99
9-y-o b g King Luthier-Arctic Alice (Brave Invader (USA))
J Howard Johnson Group Captain J A Prideaux

Placings:006f40/50000S01/F163435-24450 **(4459)**
2003/04: 16²GF, 16⁴G, 19⁴GS, 24⁵HY, 20⁰HY,

	Starts	1st	2nd	3rd	Win & Pl
Hurdles	4	0	1	0	640
Chases	1	0	0	0	
Career Total	26	3	1	2	16585
113	11/02	Sedg	2m110y	E(0-110)HCh	SFT	£4056
113	3/02	Wxfd	2m	Ch	SFT	£7407
108	12/00	Clon	2m	NHF	SH	£3312
				Total win prize-money £14776		

Going: Sf: 0-2 GS: 0-1 Gd: 0-1 GF: - Fm: 0-1
Distance: 2m/2m3: 0-3 2m4-2m7: 0-1 3m+: 0-1
Track: LH: 0-5 RH: 0-0 Tight: 0-2 Gall: 0-2
Aids: Bl: 0-1 Vi: 0-0 Tstrap: 0-0 Ckp: 0-0
Best Rating: 113 11/02   Sedg   2m110y   soft   Ch

Plating-class; seemingly better on a soft surface; effective at around two and a half miles.

Delaware Bay

100(99h)   (87h)76
5-y-o ch g Karinga Bay-Galacia (IRE) (Gallic League)
R H Alner A P Hedditch

Placings:0545-503P   **(4241)**
2003/04: 19⁵G, 22⁵S, 19³S, 19PG,

	Starts	1st	2nd	3rd	Win & Pl
Hurdles	2	0	0	0	0
Chases	2	0	0	0	660
Career Total	8	0	0	0	660

Going: Sf: 0-2 GS: 0-0 Gd: 0-2 GF: - Fm: 0-0
Distance: 2m/2m3: 0-1 2m4-2m7: 0-3 3m+: 0-0
Track: LH: 0-0 RH: 0-4 Tight: 0-0 Gall: 0-0
Aids: Bl: 0-0 Vi: 0-0 Tstrap: 0-0 Ckp: 0-0
Best Rating: 87 12/02   Winc   2m   gd-sft   Hdl

Delgany Royal (IRE)

12-y-o b g Denel (FR)-Glen Of Erin (Furry Glen)
Mrs Nicola Pollock (D T Hughes 5/5) C M Wilson

Placings:0/0P1PP0/440F06/P23U11212350P/6310P04/643 64U45600-P1P   **(4845)**
2003/04: 24PG, 23¹G, 26PG,

	Starts	1st	2nd	3rd	Win & Pl
Chases	3	1	0	0	6864
Career Total	47	6	3	4	61120
103	3/04	Leic	2m7f110yH Ch		GD	£6864
131	12/01	Fair	3m1f	HCh	YLD	£15725
118	12/00	Leop	2m5f	(0-116)HCh	SH	£6072
114	11/00	Punc	2m2f	(0-116)HCh	HVY	£4968
109	10/00	Fair	2m4f	(0-109)HCh	GD	£3312
99	2/99	Gowr	2m2f	Ch	SH	£5217
				Total win prize-money £42160		

Going: Sf: 0-0 GS: 0-0 Gd: 0-0 GF: 1-3 GF: - Fm: 0-0
Distance: 2m/2m3: 0-0 2m4-2m7: 0-0 3m+: 1-3
Track: LH: 0-1 RH: 1-1 Tight: 0-0 Gall: 0-1
Aids: Bl: 0-0 Vi: 0-0 Tstrap: 0-0 Ckp: 0-1
Best Rating: 131 12/01   Fair   3m1f   yield   Ch

Best at around three miles, he has a good weight-carrying record and is suited by testing conditions. Jumps soundly.

Deliceo (IRE)

108   105
11-y-o br g Roselier (FR)-Grey's Delight (Decent Fellow)
M Sheppard The Blues Partnership

Placings:1//0035204/36332412P4P/21462443FP/U14010-2U13134   **(4540)**
2003/04: 22²G, 24UGS, 19¹GS, 19³GS, 20¹G, 20³G, 20⁴GS,

	Starts	1st	2nd	3rd	Win & Pl
Chases	7	2	1	2	12659
Career Total	42	7	6	7	39953
102	1/04	Ludl	2m4f	D(0-115)HCh	GD	£6747
99	12/03	Hrfd	2m3f	E(0-110)HCh	G-S	£3297
96	2/03	Leic	2m4f110yE(0-105)HCh		G-S	£4953
82	11/02	Hrfd	2m4f	(0-105)HCh	GD	£4147
84	11/01	Towc	2m6f	F(0-105)HCh	SFT	£3753
89	12/00	Ludl	2m4f	(0-105)HCh	SFT	£5012
92	10/98	Carl	2m1f	H NHF	GF	£1255
				Total win prize-money £29166		

Going: Sf: 0-0 GS: 1-4 Gd: 1-3 GF: - Fm: 0-0
Distance: 2m/2m3: 1-2 2m4-2m7: 1-4 3m+: 0-1
Track: LH: 0-1 RH: 2-6 Tight: 1-3 Gall: 0-1
Aids: Bl: 0-0 Vi: 0-0 Tstrap: 0-0 Ckp: 0-0
Best Rating: 105 2/04   Ludl   2m4f   good   Ch

Moderate chaser; in-and-out performer; effective at between 2m 3f and 3m; suited by soft ground; usually comes to form in November/December.

Dellone

89   (0c)65
12-y-o b g Gunner B-Coire Vannich (Celtic Cone)
T R George M C Houghton

Placings:R/F4/62U32P32P/6441041F6/00U44U-6 **(3855)**
2003/04: 16⁶S,

	Starts	1st	2nd	3rd	Win & Pl
Hurdles	1	0	0	0	0
Career Total	28	2	3	2	9352
92	2/02	Hrfd	2m1f	E(0-100)HHdl	HVY	£2702
88	12/01	Hrfd	2m1f	E(0-105)HHdl	SFT	£2418
				Total win prize-money £5121		

Going: Sf: 0-1 GS: 0-0 Gd: 0-0 GF: - Fm: 0-0
Distance: 2m/2m3: 0-1 2m4-2m7: 0-0 3m+: 0-0
Track: LH: 0-1 RH: 0-0 Tight: 0-1 Gall: 0-0
Aids: Bl: 0-0 Vi: 0-0 Tstrap: 0-0 Ckp: 0-0
Best Rating: 92 2/02   Folk   2m1f110y   soft   Hdl

Plating-class hurdler and a moderate maiden over fences; effective at around two miles one; acts well on a soft surface; likes to make the running.

Delphi

72   90
8-y-o ch g Grand Lodge (USA)-Euridice (IRE) (Woodman (USA))
B G Powell Philip Banfield

Placings:2/F60/34500/450000003-0   **(0480)**
2003/04: 26⁰GF,

	Starts	1st	2nd	3rd	Win & Pl
Hurdles	1	0	0	0	
Career Total	19	0	1	2	2333

Going: Sf: 0-0 GS: 0-0 Gd: 0-0 GF: - Fm: 0-1
Distance: 2m/2m3: 0-0 2m4-2m7: 0-0 3m+: 0-1
Track: LH: 0-0 RH: 0-1 Tight: 0-0 Gall: 0-1
Aids: Bl: 0-0 Vi: 0-0 Tstrap: 0-0 Ckp: 0-0
Best Rating: 106 9/01   List   2m   gd-fm   Hdl

Delphine

92f   **94f**

5-y-o ch m Old Vic-Oh So Bright (Celtic Cone)
T R George   Mrs A E Goodwin

Placings:6   (4846)
2003/04: 17⁶G,

	Starts	1st	2nd	3rd	Win & Pl
NH Flat	1	0	0	0	0
Career Total	1	0	0	0	0

Going:	Sf: 0-0 GS: 0-0 Gd: 0-1 GF: - Fm: 0-0
Distance:	2m2m3: 0-1 2m4-2m7: 0-0 3m+: 0-0
Track:	LH: 0-1 RH: 0-0 Tight: 0-0 Gall: 0-1
Aids:	Bl: 0-0 Vi: 0-0 Tstrap: 0-0 Ckp: 0-0
Best Rating:	94 4/04 Chel 2m1f good NHF

Demarco (IRE)

114f   **124f**

6-y-o ch g Old Vic-Peas (IRE) (Little Wolf)
N J Henderson   R A Bartlett

Placings:130   (4400)
2003/04: 16¹G, 16³G, 16⁰G,

	Starts	1st	2nd	3rd	Win & Pl
NH Flat	3	1	0	1	5065
Career Total	3	1	0	1	5065
122	1/04	Ludl	2m	NHF	GD	£2765

Total win prize-money £2765

Going:	Sf: 0-0 GS: 0-0 Gd: 1-3 GF: - Fm: 0-0
Distance:	2m2m3: 1-3 2m4-2m7: 0-0 3m+: 0-0
Track:	LH: 0-0 RH: 1-1 Tight: 0-0 Gall: 0-1
Aids:	Bl: 0-0 Vi: 0-0 Tstrap: 0-0 Ckp: 0-0
Best Rating:	125 2/04 Newb 2m110y good NHF

Demasta (NZ)

105   **131**

13-y-o ch g Northerly Native (USA)-Hit It Gold (AUS) (Hit It Benny (AUS))
Ms A E Embiricos (N J Henderson 10/5) P S Johnson

Placings:1113/1/114/11611/1PP445-P3F   (4182)
2003/04: 20⁰G, 16³GS, 16⁶G,

	Starts	1st	2nd	3rd	Win & Pl
Chases	3	0	0	1	1126
Career Total	22	11	0	2	86113
140	5/02	Wwck	2m110y	B Ch		FRM £11816
140	4/02	Sand	2m	B(0-145)HCh	GD	£17400
132	4/02	Chel	2m110y	C(0-135)HCh	GD	£12662
123	7/01	MRas	2m4f	D Ch	GD	£5466
114	6/01	NAbb	2m1f	D Ch	G-F	£3876
	8/99	Maia	2m1f110y Hdl		GD	£8201
	8/99	Maia	2m1f110y Hdl		GD	£7290
	5/99	Elle	1m6f175y Hdl		SFT	£2381
	9/97	Awap	1m6f	Hdl	SFT	£2048
	9/97	Araw	1m6f	Hdl	SFT	£1775
	8/97	Hast	1m4f110y Hdl		G-S	£2101

Total win prize-money £75018

Going:	Sf: 0-0 GS: 0-1 Gd: 0-2 GF: - Fm: 0-0
Distance:	2m/2m3: 0-2 2m4-2m7: 0-1 3m+: 0-0
Track:	LH: 0-2 RH: 0-1 Tight: 0-1 Gall: 0-1
Aids:	Bl: 0-0 Vi: 0-0 Tstrap: 0-0 Ckp: 0-1
Best Rating:	140 5/02 Wwck 2m110y firm Ch

Very useful handicap chaser; likes to force the pace; can go well fresh; effective at up to two and a half miles on ground good or faster.

Demi Beau

116   **135**

6-y-o b g Dr Devious (IRE)-Charming Life (NZ) (Sir Tristram)
C J Mann   Hugh Villiers

Placings:144-510F   (4644)
2003/04: 17⁵G, 17¹G, 17⁹G, 16⁶G,

	Starts	1st	2nd	3rd	Win & Pl
Hurdles	4	1	0	0	16066
Career Total	7	2	0	0	21698
134	12/03	Chel	2m1f	C(0-135)HHdl	GD	£16066
126	1/03	Donc	2m110y	E Hdl	G-S	£3562

Total win prize-money £19628

Going:	Sf: 0-0 GS: 0-0 Gd: 1-4 GF: - Fm: 0-0
Distance:	2m/2m3: 1-4 2m4-2m7: 0-0 3m+: 0-0
Track:	LH: 1-3 RH: 0-1 Tight: 0-0 Gall: 1-2
Aids:	Bl: 0-0 Vi: 0-0 Tstrap: 0-0 Ckp: 0-0
Best Rating:	135 4/04 Aint 2m110y good Hdl

Very useful hurdler; suited by two miles and acts on any ground; likes to race prominently.

Dempsey (IRE)

107   **136+**

6-y-o b g Lord Americo-Kyle Cailin (Over The River (FR))
M Pitman   Mrs T Brown

Placings:3P0-111F1   (4671)
2003/04: 17¹GF, 17¹G, 17¹GS, 16²F, 16¹G,

	Starts	1st	2nd	3rd	Win & Pl
NH Flat	1	1	0	0	1519
Hurdles	4	3	0	0	9209
Career Total	8	4	0	1	11330
121	4/04	Winc	2m	E Hdl	GD	£3594
131	12/03	Folk	2m1f110y	E Hdl	G-S	£2604
136	11/03	Folk	2m1f110y	E Hdl	GD	£3010
107	10/03	Hrld	2m1f	N HHF	G-F	£1519

Total win prize-money £10728

Going:	Sf: 0-0 GS: 1-1 Gd: 2-3 GF: - Fm: 1-1
Distance:	2m/2m3: 4-5 2m4-2m7: 0-0 3m+: 0-0
Track:	LH: 0-0 RH: 4-5 Tight: 2-2 Gall: 0-0
Aids:	Bl: 0-0 Vi: 0-0 Tstrap: 0-0 Ckp: 0-0
Best Rating:	136 11/03 Folk 2m1f110y good Hdl

Full-brother to former useful Irish-trained chaser Puget Blue; useful bumper performer, easy winner of first two runs over hurdles; held by winner when falling in a better race next time; ; back to form at Wincanton; best going right-handed.

Denby (IRE)

4-y-o b g Sri Pekan (USA)-Latch Key Lady (USA) (Tejano (USA))
M W Easterby   David Scott

Placings:05   (4317)
2003/04: 16⁰S, 16⁵S,

	Starts	1st	2nd	3rd	Win & Pl
NH Flat	1	0	0	0	0
Hurdles	1	0	0	0	0
Career Total	2	0	0	0	0

Going:	Sf: 0-2 GS: 0-0 Gd: 0-0 GF: - Fm: 0-0
Distance:	2m/2m3: 0-2 2m4-2m7: 0-0 3m+: 0-0
Track:	LH: 0-2 RH: 0-0 Tight: 0-0 Gall: 0-0
Aids:	Bl: 0-0 Vi: 0-0 Tstrap: 0-0 Ckp: 0-0
Best Rating:	50 1/04 Weth 2m soft NHF

Dene View (IRE)

96(105h)   (98h)**101+**

9-y-o br g Good Thyne (USA)-The Furnituremaker (Mandalus)
R A Fahey   C H Stevens

Placings:00/00/4433305P/1312P3-0405   (3473)
2003/04: 17⁰S, 16⁴GS, 16⁹GS, 20⁵GF,

	Starts	1st	2nd	3rd	Win & Pl
Hurdles	2	0	0	0	0
Chases	2	0	0	1	258
Career Total	22	2	1	5	10530
95	1/03	Donc	2m110y	E(0-105)HCh	GD	£4110
98	12/02	Catt	2m3f	E(0-110)HHdl	G-S	£2929

Total win prize-money £7041

Going:	Sf: 0-1 GS: 0-2 Gd: 0-0 GF: - Fm: 0-1
Distance:	2m/2m3: 0-3 2m4-2m7: 0-1 3m+: 0-0
Track:	LH: 0-3 RH: 0-1 Tight: 0-3 Gall: 0-0
Aids:	Bl: 0-0 Vi: 0-0 Tstrap: 0-0 Ckp: 0-0
Best Rating:	101 12/03 Catt 2m gd-sft Ch

Modest hurdler/chaser; stays two and a half miles and best on a sound surface.

Deneises Blossom (IRE)

99(100c)   (75c)**75**

11-y-o b m Beau Sher-Lindabell (Over The River (FR))
G A Harker (W Storey 20/12) John J Maguire

Placings:45B/P/6024003503/0623463204B0-30540 (3476)
2003/04: 27³GS, 22⁰S, 24⁵GS, 17⁴GS, 16⁰G,

	Starts	1st	2nd	3rd	Win & Pl
Hurdles	3	0	0	0	0
Chases	2	0	0	1	360
Career Total	31	0	3	5	5081

Going:	Sf: 0-1 GS: 0-2 Gd: 0-1 GF: - Fm: 0-1
Distance:	2m/2m3: 0-2 2m4-2m7: 0-1 3m+: 0-2
Track:	LH: 0-5 RH: 0-0 Tight: 0-4 Gall: 0-1
Aids:	Bl: 0-0 Vi: 0-0 Tstrap: 0-0 Ckp: 0-1
Best Rating:	81 1/02 Newc 2m soft Hdl

Moderate maiden hurdler/chaser; stays two miles-six, appreciates cut in the ground.

Denney's Well (IRE)

                   59

9-y-o ch g Good Thyne (USA)-Julias Well (Golden Love)
R Ford   Black Stripe Racing

Placings:35-550   (4525)
2003/04: 20⁵HY, 26⁵GF, 24⁰GS,

	Starts	1st	2nd	3rd	Win & Pl
Chases	3	0	0	0	0
Career Total	5	0	0	1	354

Going:	Sf: 0-1 GS: 0-1 Gd: 0-0 GF: - Fm: 0-1
Distance:	2m/2m3: 0-0 2m4-2m7: 0-1 3m+: 0-2
Track:	LH: 0-3 RH: 0-0 Tight: 0-0 Gall: 0-0
Aids:	Bl: 0-0 Vi: 0-0 Tstrap: 0-0 Ckp: 0-1
Best Rating:	69 6/02 Ctml 3m2f good Ch

Dennis The Mennis (IRE)

                   7f

5-y-o b g Fourstars Allstar (USA)-Farm Approach (Tug Of War)

Mrs A M Thorpe Mrs A M Thorpe

Placings:000   (4936)
2003/04: 14⁰GS, 17⁰G, 18⁰G,

	Starts	1st	2nd	3rd	Win & Pl
NH Flat	3	0	0	0	
Career Total	3	0	0	0	

Going:	Sf: 0-0 GS: 0-1 Gd: 0-2 GF: - Fm: 0-0
Distance:	2m/2m3: 0-2 2m4-2m7: 0-0 3m+: 0-0
Track:	LH: 0-2 RH: 0-0 Tight: 0-2 Gall: 0-0
Aids:	Bl: 0-0 Vi: 0-0 Tstrap: 0-0 Ckp: 0-0
Best Rating:	7 3/04 Hrfd 1m6f gd-sft NHF

Denny Island

8-y-o b g Rock Hopper-Bara Peg (Random Shot)
J W Mullins D H Smith

Placings:PPPP   (3051)
2003/04: 16ᴾGF, 21ᴾS, 22ᴾG, 19ᴾG,

	Starts	1st	2nd	3rd	Win & Pl
Hurdles	3	0	0	0	
Chases	1	0	0	0	
Career Total	4	0	0	0	

Going:	Sf: 0-1 GS: 0-0 Gd: 0-2 GF: - Fm: 0-1
Distance:	2m/2m3: 0-1 2m4-2m7: 0-0 3-3m+: 0-0
Track:	LH: 0-1 RH: 0-2 Tight: 0-3 Gall: 0-0
Aids:	Bl: 0-0 Vi: 0-0 Tstrap: 0-0 Ckp: 0-0

Deoch An Dorais (IRE)

88   (115h)**111**
9-y-o b g Supreme Leader-General Rain (General Ironside)
N J Henderson Park Lane Racing AG Switzerland

Placings:6/0053122/33/3F00/2U22UP-3P   (2239)
2003/04: 17³G, 25ᴾG,

	Starts	1st	2nd	3rd	Win & Pl
Hurdles	1	0	0	0	0
Chases	1	0	0	1	464
Career Total	22	1	5	5	13764
101 1/00 Naas 2m		NHF		SFT	£3312

Total win prize-money £3312

Going:	Sf: 0-0 GS: 0-0 Gd: 0-2 GF: - Fm: 0-0
Distance:	2m/2m3: 0-1 2m4-2m7: 0-0 3m+: 0-1
Track:	LH: 0-1 RH: 0-1 Tight: 0-1 Gall: 0-0
Aids:	Bl: 0-0 Vi: 0-0 Tstrap: 0-0 Ckp: 0-0
Best Rating:	115 12/01 Newb 2m110y soft Hdl

Modest hurdler/chaser; strong sort; has suffered from back problems; best at around two miles on an easy surface.

Deptford (IRE)

99f   **100f**
5-y-o ch g Un Desperado (FR)-Katty London (Camden Town)
P R Chamings Mrs V K Shaw

Placings:60   (4578)
2003/04: 16⁶GS, 16⁰G,

	Starts	1st	2nd	3rd	Win & Pl
NH Flat	2	0	0	0	
Career Total	2	0	0	0	

Deputy Leader (IRE)

12-y-o b g Florida Son-Larne (Giolla Mear)
K Hunter K Hunter

Placings:5365/F/4U660F-666   (0475)
2003/04: 21⁶S, 20⁶G, 26⁶GS,

	Starts	1st	2nd	3rd	Win & Pl
Chases	3	0	0	0	0
Career Total	14	0	0	1	182

Going:	Sf: 0-0 GS: 0-1 Gd: 0-1 GF: - Fm: 0-0
Distance:	2m/2m3: 0-2 2m4-2m7: 0-2 3m+: 0-1
Track:	LH: 0-3 RH: 0-0 Tight: 0-0 Gall: 0-0
Aids:	Bl: 0-0 Vi: 0-0 Tstrap: 0-0 Ckp: 0-0
Best Rating:	107 12/97 Towc 2m soft NHF

Dere Street

10-y-o b g Derring Rose-Jed Again (Cagirama)
Mrs R L Elliot D Davidson

Placings:4   (0101)
2003/04: 25⁴G,

	Starts	1st	2nd	3rd	Win & Pl
Chases	1	0	0	0	192
Career Total	1	0	0	0	192

Going:	Sf: 0-0 GS: 0-0 Gd: 0-1 GF: - Fm: 0-0
Distance:	2m/2m3: 0-0 2m4-2m7: 0-0 3m+: 0-1
Track:	LH: 0-1 RH: 0-0 Tight: 0-0 Gall: 0-0
Aids:	Bl: 0-0 Vi: 0-0 Tstrap: 0-0 Ckp: 0-0
Best Rating:	62 5/03 Hexm 3m1f good Ch

Derek Trotter

5-y-o b g Cosmonaut-Cinderella Derek (Hittite Glory)
A D Smith Miss Kerensa Pluess

Placings:0-0   (0154)
2003/04: 16⁰GF,

	Starts	1st	2nd	3rd	Win & Pl
NH Flat	1	0	0	0	
Career Total	2	0	0	0	

Going:	Sf: 0-0 GS: 0-0 Gd: 0-0 GF: - Fm: 0-1
Distance:	2m/2m3: 0-1 2m4-2m7: 0-0 3m+: 0-0
Track:	LH: 0-1 RH: 0-0 Tight: 0-0 Gall: 0-0
Aids:	Bl: 0-0 Vi: 0-0 Tstrap: 0-0 Ckp: 0-0

Derivative (IRE)

113   **130+**
6-y-o b/br g Erin's Isle-Our Hope (Dancing Brave (USA))
Miss Venetia Williams P Ryan

Placings:20/32615-15451302000   (4840)
2003/04: 20¹G, 19⁵G, 21⁴G, 20⁵GS, 22¹G, 21³G, 20⁰S, 24²G, 25⁰G, 24⁰G, 24⁰G,

	Starts	1st	2nd	3rd	Win & Pl
Hurdles	11	2	1	1	20872
Career Total	18	3	3	2	28107
130 12/03 Winc 2m6f		B Hdl		GD	£8051
112 5/03 Prth 2m4f110yE(0-110)HHdl				GD	£5564
106 2/03 Ayr 2m4f		E Hdl		HVY	£3640

Total win prize-money £17256

Going:	Sf: 0-1 GS: 0-1 Gd: 2-9 GF: - Fm: 0-0
Distance:	2m/2m3: 0-0 2m4-2m7: 2-7 3m+: 0-4
Track:	LH: 0-8 RH: 2-3 Tight: 0-2 Gall: 0-5
Aids:	Bl: 0-1 Vi: 0-0 Tstrap: 0-0 Ckp: 0-0
Best Rating:	130 2/04 Newb 3m110y good Hdl

Useful hurdler; stays three miles, but effective at two and a half miles; handles good but appreciates much softer ground; has worn blinkers.

Derring Bridge

104   (107c)**103**
14-y-o b g Derring Rose-Bridge Ash (Normandy)
Mrs S M Johnson I K Johnson

Placings:0P51U0F/040055P4/031U654300642/223111321 1436/4222221143/4002113342120F/1244435F/63514R0/31 RP-0325354450   (2793)
2003/04: 22⁰GF, 27³GF, 24²G, 24⁵GF, 24³GF, 26⁵GF, 23⁴GF, 24⁴GF, 24⁵GS, 24⁰GS,

	Starts	1st	2nd	3rd	Win & Pl
Hurdles	10	0	1	2	3752
Career Total	94	15	14	13	90024
103 8/02 Worc 3m		C(0-135)HHdl		GD	£5921
102 7/01 Worc 3m		D(0-125)HHdl		GD	£4017
116 6/00 Worc 2m7f110yC(0-135)HCh				G-F	£7046
114 9/99 Hntg 3m		E(0-115)HCh		GD	£3601
116 7/99 NAbb 3m2f110yD(0-125)HCh				G-F	£3543
106 7/99 Worc 2m7f110yF(0-110)HCh				G-F	£2497
109 9/98 NAbb 3m2f110yD(0-120)HCh				G-F	£3355
98 8/98 Worc 2m7f110yE Ch				G-F	£2951
107 9/97 MRas 3m		D(0-130)HHdl		GD	£3717
111 9/97 NAbb 3m3f		D(0-120)HHdl		G-S	£2655
104 7/97 Worc 3m		D(0-125)HHdl		G-F	£2756
107 6/97 Uttx 3m110y		D(0-135)HHdl		G-S	£3436
111 6/97 Sthl 3m110y		E(0-110)HHdl		G-S	£2390
91 6/96 Sthl 3m110y		E(0-110)HHdl		G-S	£3054
87 3/95 Ludl 2m5f110yE Hdl				G-S	£2626

Total win prize-money £53569

Going:	Sf: 0-0 GS: 0-2 Gd: 0-1 GF: - Fm: 0-7
Distance:	2m/2m3: 0-0 2m4-2m7: 0-1 3m+: 0-9
Track:	LH: 0-9 RH: 0-1 Tight: 0-3 Gall: 0-1
Aids:	Bl: 0-0 Vi: 0-0 Tstrap: 0-0 Ckp: 0-0
Best Rating:	116 6/00 Worc 2m7f110y gd-fm Ch

Moderate hurdler now in the veteran stage; out and out stayer; goes well on fast ground; good record at Worcester.

Derring Dove

12-y-o b g Derring Rose-Shadey Dove (Deadly Nightshade)
H W Lavis H W Lavis

Placings:0/P05/P/4432P/400/P233-P3P   (0521)
2003/04: 21ᴾG, 24³G, 24ᴾG,

	Starts	1st	2nd	3rd	Win & Pl
Chases	3	0	0	1	1038
Career Total	20	0	2	4	3718

Going:	Sf: 0-0 GS: 0-0 Gd: 0-3 GF: - Fm: 0-0
Distance:	2m/2m3: 0-0 2m4-2m7: 0-1 3m+: 0-5
Track:	LH: 0-3 RH: 0-0 Tight: 0-1 Gall: 0-1
Aids:	Bl: 0-0 Vi: 0-0 Tstrap: 0-0 Ckp: 0-0
Best Rating:	99 2/01 Ludl 3m gd-sft Ch

Derrintogher Yank (IRE)

(97h)   (103h) **133+**
10-y-o b g Lord Americo-Glenmalur (Black Minstrel)
S E H Sherwood Con O'Connor

Placings:23/411221/05/P1-3FF   (2956)
2003/04: 21³G, 24FGS, 25FG,

	Starts	1st	2nd	3rd	Win & Pl
Hurdles	1	0	0	1	418
Chases	2	0	0	0	0
Career Total	15	4	3	2	18534
123 11/02 Ludl	3m		D Ch		GD £5473
126 3/00 Strf	2m6f110yD Hdl			GD £3971
127 11/99 Kemp	2m5f		D Hdl		GD £3217
112 10/99 Chep	2m4f		E Hdl		GD £2052

Total win prize-money £14714

Going:	Sf: 0-0 GS: 0-1 Gd: 0-2 GF: - Fm: 0-0
Distance:	2m/2m3: 0-0 2m4-2m7: 0-1 3m+: 0-2
Track:	LH: 0-1 RH: 0-2 Tight: 0-1 Gall: 0-0
Aids:	Bl: 0-0 Vi: 0-0 Tstrap: 0-0 Ckp: 0-0
Best Rating:	133 11/03 Bang 3m110y gd-sft Ch

Useful chaser; stays three miles; acts on good ground.

Derry Ann
78

8-y-o b m Derrylin-Ancat Girl (Politico (USA))
G P Kelly C I Ratcliffe

Placings:040/330-PP   (0449)
2003/04: 19PGS, 20PGF,

	Starts	1st	2nd	3rd	Win & Pl
Hurdles	2	0	0	0	
Career Total	8	0	0	2	899

Going:	Sf: 0-0 GS: 0-1 Gd: 0-0 GF: - Fm: 0-1
Distance:	2m/2m3: 0-0 2m4-2m7: 0-2 3m+: 0-0
Track:	LH: 0-0 RH: 0-2 Tight: 0-0 Gall: 0-1
Aids:	Bl: 0-0 Vi: 0-0 Tstrap: 0-0 Ckp: 0-0
Best Rating:	91 5/02 Chep 2m110y gd-fm NHF

Glimmer of ability in bumpers.

Derry Dice
89   **82**

8-y-o b g Derrylin-Paper Dice (Le Dauphin)
C T Pogson C T Pogson

Placings:00460U-026   (2854)
2003/04: 20FGS, 24²GS, 26PGS,

	Starts	1st	2nd	3rd	Win & Pl
Hurdles	3	0	1	0	780
Career Total	9	0	1	0	780

Going:	Sf: 0-0 GS: 0-2 Gd: 0-0 GF: - Fm: 0-1
Distance:	2m/2m3: 0-0 2m4-2m7: 0-1 3m+: 0-2
Track:	LH: 0-2 RH: 0-1 Tight: 0-1 Gall: 0-0
Aids:	Bl: 0-3 Vi: 0-0 Tstrap: 0-0 Ckp: 0-0
Best Rating:	85 1/03 Stfl 2m good NHF

Blinkered, has shown strictly limited ability in bumpers.

Derryquin
99+

9-y-o b g Lion Cavern (USA)-Top Berry (High Top)
Miss E C Lavelle Lady Bland

Placings:142-P   (1219)
2003/04: 16PGF,

	Starts	1st	2nd	3rd	Win & Pl
Hurdles	1	0	0	0	
Career Total	4	1	1	0	4603
99 7/02 NAbb	2m1f	D Hdl		G-F £3757

Total win prize-money £3757

Going:	Sf: 0-0 GS: 0-0 Gd: 0-0 GF: - Fm: 0-1
Distance:	2m/2m3: 0-1 2m4-2m7: 0-0 3m+: 0-0
Track:	LH: 0-0 RH: 0-1 Tight: 0-0 Gall: 0-1
Aids:	Bl: 0-0 Vi: 0-0 Tstrap: 0-0 Ckp: 0-0
Best Rating:	99 9/02 Stfl 2m1f good Hdl

A fair mile handicapper on the Flat; overcame some novicey jumping early on to make quite an impressive winning debut over hurdles at Newton Abbot July 2002, but well beaten next time under a penalty.

Dervalloc (IRE)

(85h)   (75h)
7-y-o b g Zaffaran (USA)-Keeping Company (Kings Company)
P Winkworth P Winkworth

Placings:04-0600P   (4281)
2003/04: 21³G, 20⁶G, 21⁰S, 22⁰GS, 22PG,

	Starts	1st	2nd	3rd	Win & Pl
Hurdles	4	0	0	0	0
Chases	1	0	0	0	0
Career Total	7	0	0	0	331

Going:	Sf: 0-1 GS: 0-1 Gd: 0-3 GF: - Fm: 0-0
Distance:	2m/2m3: 0-0 2m4-2m7: 0-5 3m+: 0-0
Track:	LH: 0-2 RH: 0-3 Tight: 0-2 Gall: 0-1
Aids:	Bl: 0-1 Vi: 0-0 Tstrap: 0-0 Ckp: 0-0
Best Rating:	86 2/03 Sand 2m110y heavy NHF

Desailly
113   **140+**

10-y-o ch g Teamster-G W Superstar (Rymer)
G B Balding The Team

Placings:452/3U3U1/22564-1232P   (4861)
2003/04: 24¹GS, 24²S, 24³G, 24²G, 33PGS,

	Starts	1st	2nd	3rd	Win & Pl
Chases	5	1	2	1	31782
Career Total	18	2	5	3	46710
129 12/03 Newb	3m	D(0-125)HCh		G-S £11440
127 3/02 Extr	2m7f110yD(0-125)HCh		G-F £4914

Total win prize-money £16354

Going:	Sf: 0-1 GS: 1-2 Gd: 0-2 GF: - Fm: 0-0
Distance:	2m/2m3: 0-0 2m4-2m7: 0-0 3m+: 1-5
Track:	LH: 1-4 RH: 0-1 Tight: 0-0 Gall: 1-3
Aids:	Bl: 0-0 Vi: 0-0 Tstrap: 0-0 Ckp: 0-0
Best Rating:	140 3/04 Newb 3m good Ch

Useful chaser; fairly lightly raced; regularly held up; stays three miles; acts well on good ground.

Desert Air (JPN)
105   **121**

5-y-o ch g Desert King (IRE)-Greek Air (IRE) (Ela-Mana-Mou)
M C Pipe Mrs Belinda Harvey

Placings:213-00   (4644)
2003/04: 16⁰S, 16⁰G,

	Starts	1st	2nd	3rd	Win & Pl
Hurdles	2	0	0	0	

Career Total	5	1	1	1	6352
121 1/03 Tntn	2m1f	E Hdl		SFT £4530

Total win prize-money £4531

Going:	Sf: 0-1 GS: 0-0 Gd: 0-1 GF: - Fm: 0-0
Distance:	2m/2m3: 0-2 2m4-2m7: 0-0 3m+: 0-0
Track:	LH: 0-1 RH: 0-1 Tight: 0-1 Gall: 0-0
Aids:	Bl: 0-0 Vi: 0-2 Tstrap: 0-2 Ckp: 0-0
Best Rating:	121 2/03 Kemp 2m gd-sft Hdl

Useful juvenile hurdler in 2002/3; best at two miles; effective in soft ground; tends to jump to the right; wears a visor.

Desert Spa (USA)
74   **46**

9-y-o b g Sheikh Albadou-Healing Waters (USA) (Temperence Hill (USA))
G E Jones (Andrew Reid 15/8) G Elwyn Jones

Placings:5P   (2512)
2003/04: 24⁵GF, 19PGS,

	Starts	1st	2nd	3rd	Win & Pl
Hurdles	2	0	0	0	0
Career Total	2	0	0	0	0

Going:	Sf: 0-0 GS: 0-1 Gd: 0-0 GF: - Fm: 0-1
Distance:	2m/2m3: 0-0 2m4-2m7: 0-1 3m+: 0-0
Track:	LH: 0-1 RH: 0-0 Tight: 0-0 Gall: 0-0
Aids:	Bl: 0-0 Vi: 0-0 Tstrap: 0-0 Ckp: 0-0
Best Rating:	57 11/03 Chep 3m gd-fm Hdl

Desert Traveller (IRE)
62

6-y-o b g Desert Style (IRE)-Cellatica (USA) (Sir Ivor)
R J Baker R J Baker

Placings:00P000/04-PP   (3049)
2003/04: 22PG, 24PG,

	Starts	1st	2nd	3rd	Win & Pl
Hurdles	2	0	0	0	
Career Total	10	0	0	0	0

Going:	Sf: 0-0 GS: 0-0 Gd: 0-2 GF: - Fm: 0-0
Distance:	2m/2m3: 0-0 2m4-2m7: 0-1 3m+: 0-1
Track:	LH: 0-0 RH: 0-2 Tight: 0-1 Gall: 0-0
Aids:	Bl: 0-2 Vi: 0-0 Tstrap: 0-0 Ckp: 0-0
Best Rating:	62 10/02 Extr 2m6f110y firm Hdl

Designer Label (IRE)
89(108h)   (79h) **105**

8-y-o ch g Insan (USA)-Belle Babillard (IRE) (Le Bavard (FR))
M Pitman Mrs Sue Venton

Placings:636/63P/421   (1330)
2003/04: 20⁴GF, 22²GF, 25¹GF,

	Starts	1st	2nd	3rd	Win & Pl
Hurdles	2	0	1	0	1988
Chases	1	0	0	0	2808
Career Total	9	1	1	2	5811
105 9/03 Hrfd	3m1f110yE(0-105)HCh		G-F £2808

Total win prize-money £2808

Going:	Sf: 0-0 GS: 0-0 Gd: 0-0 GF: - Fm: 1-3
Distance:	2m/2m3: 0-0 2m4-2m7: 0-0 3m+: 1-1
Track:	LH: 0-2 RH: 1-1 Tight: 0-1 Gall: 0-0

Aids: Bl: 0-0 Vi: 0-0 Tstrap: 0-0 Ckp: 0-0
Best Rating: 108 11/00 Kemp 2m soft Hdl

Had shown modest ability at up to 2m 6f in novice hurdles, prior to winning on chasing bow at Hereford in September 2003; stays three miles; effective on fast ground.

Desmond Tutu (IRE)
110

7-y-o b g Be My Native (USA)-Amy Fairy (The Parson)
P F Nicholls D J Nichols

Placings:1/12232121-P (1504)
2003/04: 20PGF,

	Starts	1st	2nd	3rd	Win & Pl
Hurdles	1	0	0	0	
Career Total	10	4	4	1	17956

113	4/03	Winc	2m6f	E Hdl		FRM	£3647
87	3/03	Extr	2m3f	E Hdl		FRM	£5011
119	10/02	Chep	2m110y	H NHF		GD	£1995
113	4/02	Font	2m2f110yH NHF		G-F	£2065

Total win prize-money £12719

Going: Sf: 0-0 GS: 0-0 Gd: 0-0 GF: - Fm: 0-1
Distance: 2m/2m3: 0-0 2m4-2m7: 0-1 3m+: 0-0
Track: LH: 0-1 RH: 0-0 Tight: 0-0 Gall: 0-0
Aids: Bl: 0-0 Vi: 0-0 Tstrap: 0-0 Ckp: 0-0
Best Rating: 119 10/02 Chep 2m110y good NHF

Fair hurdler; stays 2m 6f; best on ground good or faster.

Desperate Measures
89(104h) (73h)56
8-y-o ch m Kasakov-Precious Ballerina (Ballacashtal (CAN))
Miss Lucinda V Russell A D Stewart

Placings:04050/U363P-5 (0041)
2003/04: 17SG,

	Starts	1st	2nd	3rd	Win & Pl
Chases	1	0	0	0	0
Career Total	11	0	0	2	1164

Going: Sf: 0-0 GS: 0-0 Gd: 0-1 GF: - Fm: 0-0
Distance: 2m/2m3: 0-1 2m4-2m7: 0-0 3m+: 0-0
Track: LH: 0-1 RH: 0-0 Tight: 0-1 Gall: 0-0
Aids: Bl: 0-0 Vi: 0-0 Tstrap: 0-0 Ckp: 0-0
Best Rating: 92 12/01 Muss 2m1f gd-fm NHF

Destino
88 65
5-y-o ch g Keen-Hanajir (IRE) (Cadeaux Genereux)
Mrs S J Smith Mrs Enid Brindle

Placings:60330 (2920)
2003/04: 16PGF, 16QGF, 16QGF, 16QG, 19QG,

	Starts	1st	2nd	3rd	Win & Pl
NH Flat	3	0	0	1	210
Hurdles	2	0	0	1	368
Career Total	5	0	0	2	578

Going: Sf: 0-0 GS: 0-0 Gd: 0-2 GF: - Fm: 0-3
Distance: 2m/2m3: 0-4 2m4-2m7: 0-1 3m+: 0-0
Track: LH: 0-4 RH: 0-1 Tight: 0-1 Gall: 0-0
Aids: Bl: 0-0 Vi: 0-0 Tstrap: 0-0 Ckp: 0-0
Best Rating: 81 10/03 Hexm 2m110y gd-fm NHF

Modest form in bumpers.

Detonateur (FR)
101 110

6-y-o b g Pistolet Bleu (IRE)-Soviet Princess (IRE) (Soviet Lad (USA))
Ian Williams Mr & Mrs John Poynton

Placings:020/054302-60 (1454)
2003/04: 17SGF, 16QGF,

	Starts	1st	2nd	3rd	Win & Pl
Hurdles	2	0	0	0	0
Career Total	11	0	2	1	6061

Going: Sf: 0-1 GS: 0-0 Gd: 0-0 GF: - Fm: 0-2
Distance: 2m/2m3: 0-2 2m4-2m7: 0-0 3m+: 0-0
Track: LH: 0-2 RH: 0-0 Tight: 0-0 Gall: 0-0
Aids: Bl: 0-1 Vi: 0-0 Tstrap: 0-0 Ckp: 0-0
Best Rating: 116 3/02 Chel 2m110y gd-sft Hdl

Modest hurdler; French import; suited by soft ground; yet to win a race, but has faced some stiff tasks; tends to race freely and looked most reluctant when only sixth at long-odds on in first-time blinkers at Southwell in May 2003.

Deux Bons Amis

6-y-o b g Roselier (FR)-Rippling Melody (Ardross)
P J Hobbs Celtic Racing

Placings:P0 (2845)
2003/04: 20PGS, 24QS,

	Starts	1st	2nd	3rd	Win & Pl
Hurdles	2	0	0	0	
Career Total	2	0	0	0	

Going: Sf: 0-1 GS: 0-1 Gd: 0-0 GF: - Fm: 0-0
Distance: 2m/2m3: 0-0 2m4-2m7: 0-1 3m+: 0-1
Track: LH: 0-1 RH: 0-0 Tight: 0-1 Gall: 0-0
Aids: Bl: 0-0 Vi: 0-0 Tstrap: 0-0 Ckp: 0-0

Devil's Perk (IRE)
70 16

6-y-o b g Executive Perk-She Devil (Le Moss)
J Wade John Wade

Placings:0 (1424)
2003/04: 20QG,

	Starts	1st	2nd	3rd	Win & Pl
Hurdles	1	0	0	0	
Career Total	1	0	0	0	

Going: Sf: 0-0 GS: 0-0 Gd: 0-1 GF: - Fm: 0-0
Distance: 2m/2m3: 0-0 2m4-2m7: 0-1 3m+: 0-0
Track: LH: 0-0 RH: 0-1 Tight: 0-0 Gall: 0-0
Aids: Bl: 0-0 Vi: 0-0 Tstrap: 0-0 Ckp: 0-0
Best Rating: 24 9/03 Prth 2m4f110y good Hdl

Devil's Run (IRE)
99(93h) (112h)114
8-y-o b g Commanche Run-She Devil (Le Moss)
J Wade John Wade

Placings:004/0331134/6F423212-246 (3522)
2003/04: 25QG, 23QG, 25QS,

	Starts	1st	2nd	3rd	Win & Pl
Chases	3	0	1	0	2020
Career Total	21	3	4	4	24731

112 3/03 Sedg 2m5f E(0-110)HCh SFT £4657

112 2/02 Newc 2m4f B(0-140)HHdl SFT £6753
108 1/02 Weth 2m4f110y D(0-
115)HHdl G-S £3500

Total win prize-money £14911

Going: Sf: 0-1 GS: 0-0 Gd: 0-2 GF: - Fm: 0-0
Distance: 2m/2m3: 0-4 2m4-2m7: 0-0 3m+: 0-3
Track: LH: 0-2 RH: 0-0 Tight: 0-0 Gall: 0-0
Aids: Bl: 0-0 Vi: 0-0 Tstrap: 0-0 Ckp: 0-0
Best Rating: 114 11/03 Weth 2m7f110y good Ch

Modest chaser; winner twice over hurdles; broke his duck over fences when successful at Sedgefield in March 2003; acts on soft and looked unsuited by fast when disappointing runner-up at Carlisle two weeks later; stays two miles five.

Devil's Teardrop
70 41

4-y-o ch g Hernando (FR)-River Divine (USA) (Irish River (FR))
C J Mann (D J S Cosgrove 16/5) The Happy Go Lucky Partnership

Placings:4 (4899)
2003/04: 16QG,

	Starts	1st	2nd	3rd	Win & Pl
Hurdles	1	0	0	0	0
Career Total	1	0	0	0	0

Going: Sf: 0-0 GS: 0-0 Gd: 0-1 GF: - Fm: 0-0
Distance: 2m/2m3: 0-1 2m4-2m7: 0-0 3m+: 0-0
Track: LH: 0-0 RH: 0-1 Tight: 0-0 Gall: 0-0
Aids: Bl: 0-0 Vi: 0-0 Tstrap: 0-0 Ckp: 0-0
Best Rating: 41 4/04 Winc 2m good Hdl

Well beaten on hurdling debut.

Devon Maid
64f 15f

5-y-o ch m Fraam-Sharp Dance (Dance Of Life (USA))
R J Hodges Mrs Angela Tincknell

Placings:0 (2697)
2003/04: 16QG,

	Starts	1st	2nd	3rd	Win & Pl
NH Flat	1	0	0	0	
Career Total	1	0	0	0	

Going: Sf: 0-0 GS: 0-0 Gd: 0-1 GF: - Fm: 0-0
Distance: 2m/2m3: 0-1 2m4-2m7: 0-0 3m+: 0-0
Track: LH: 0-0 RH: 0-1 Tight: 0-0 Gall: 0-0
Aids: Bl: 0-0 Vi: 0-0 Tstrap: 0-0 Ckp: 0-0
Best Rating: 15 12/03 Ludl 2m good NHF

Devon View (IRE)
108 139

10-y-o b g Jolly Jake (NZ)-Skipaside (Quayside)
P F Nicholls Jeffrey Hordle

Placings:P/212122/3113U32-23 (2454)
2003/04: 16QGS, 20QGS,

	Starts	1st	2nd	3rd	Win & Pl
Chases	2	0	1	1	6865
Career Total	16	4	6	4	43112

137	12/02	Wwck	2m110y	C(0-130)HCh	G-S	£7345
136	11/02	Chep	2m110y	D(0-120)HCh	SFT	£4758
113	3/02	Chep	2m3f110yE Ch	SFT	£3081
129	2/02	Leic	2m	E Ch	SFT	£3406

Total win prize-money £18590

Going: Sf: 0-0 GS: 0-2 Gd: 0-0 GF: - Fm: 0-0
Distance: 2m/2m3: 0-1 2m4-2m7: 0-1 3m+: 0-0
Track: LH: 0-1 RH: 0-1 Tight: 0-0 Gall: 0-1
Aids: Bl: 0-0 Vi: 0-0 Tstrap: 0-0 Ckp: 0-0
Best Rating: 139 4/03 Sand 2m4f110y good Ch

Useful handicap chaser; stays two and a half miles, but effective at shorter; acts on soft ground; likes to race prominently.

Devote
99   95

6-y-o b g Pennekamp (USA)-Radiant Bride (USA) (Blushing Groom (FR))
J D Frost The Welsh Valleys Syndicate

Placings:35420213/003422-556415   (4526)
2003/04: 16⁵G, 16⁵GS, 19⁶S, 17⁴GS, 17¹G, 16⁵GS,

	Starts	1st	2nd	3rd	Win & Pl
Hurdles	6	1	0	0	2338
Career Total	20	2	4	3	10123
95	3/04	Tntn	2m1f		G Hdl	GD £2338
95	2/02	Tntn	2m3f110yE(0-110)HHdl		SFT	£3388

Total win prize-money £5726

Going: Sf: 0-1 GS: 0-3 Gd: 1-2 GF: - Fm: 0-0
Distance: 2m/2m3: 1-2 2m4-2m7: 0-0 3m+: 0-0
Track: LH: 0-1 RH: 1-5 Tight: 1-2 Gall: 0-0
Aids: Bl: 1-4 Vi: 0-0 Tstrap: 0-0 Ckp: 0-1
Best Rating: 95 3/04 Tntn 2m1f good Hdl

Dewasentah (IRE)
74f   94+f

5-y-o b m Supreme Leader-Our Sioux (IRE) (Jolly Jake (NZ))
J M Jefferson Mrs J U Hales & Mrs L M Joicey

Placings:01   (4663)
2003/04: 16⁵G, 16¹S,

	Starts	1st	2nd	3rd	Win & Pl
NH Flat	2	1	0	0	2051
Career Total	2	1	0	0	2051
94	4/04	Hexm	2m110y	H NHF	SFT	£2051

Total win prize-money £2051

Going: Sf: 1-1 GS: 0-0 Gd: 0-1 GF: - Fm: 0-0
Distance: 2m/2m3: 1-2 2m4-2m7: 0-0 3m+: 0-0
Track: LH: 1-2 RH: 0-0 Tight: 0-0 Gall: 0-0
Aids: Bl: 0-0 Vi: 0-0 Tstrap: 0-0 Ckp: 0-0
Best Rating: 94 4/04 Hexm 2m110y soft NHF

Bettered debut form when winning soft ground Hexham bumper in April 2004; travelled strongly for long way that day and may be capable of better.

Dextra Lighting
86   99

5-y-o b g Then Again-Celtic Dove (Celtic Cone)
C L Tizzard Dextra Lighting Systems

Placings:60F   (3462)
2003/04: 16⁶GS, 22⁰GS, 24⁵S,

	Starts	1st	2nd	3rd	Win & Pl
NH Flat	1	0	0	0	0
Hurdles	2	0	0	0	0
Career Total	3	0	0	0	0

Going: Sf: 0-1 GS: 0-2 Gd: 0-0 GF: - Fm: 0-0
Distance: 2m/2m3: 0-1 2m4-2m7: 0-1 3m+: 0-1
Track: LH: 0-2 RH: 0-1 Tight: 0-0 Gall: 0-1
Aids: Bl: 0-0 Vi: 0-0 Tstrap: 0-0 Ckp: 0-0

Best Rating: 110 1/04 Chep 3m   soft   Hdl

Di's Dilemma
102   92

6-y-o b m Teenoso (USA)-Reve En Rose (Revlow)
C C Bealby T W R Bayley

Placings:30-2FF464   (4776)
2003/04: 16²G, 16⁵S, 19⁶G, 16⁴S, 21⁶G, 20⁴G,

	Starts	1st	2nd	3rd	Win & Pl
Hurdles	6	0	1	0	1106
Career Total	8	0	1	1	1368

Going: Sf: 0-2 GS: 0-0 Gd: 0-4 GF: - Fm: 0-0
Distance: 2m/2m3: 0-3 2m4-2m7: 0-3 3m+: 0-0
Track: LH: 0-1 RH: 0-5 Tight: 0-2 Gall: 0-1
Aids: Bl: 0-0 Vi: 0-0 Tstrap: 0-0 Ckp: 0-0
Best Rating: 92 1/04 Hntg 2m110y soft Hdl

Stoutly-bred, close third in ordinary mares' only bumper on debut at Market Rasen in March; well beaten on a sound surface subsequently.

Diamant Noir
109   142

6-y-o b m Sir Harry Lewis (USA)-Free Travel (Royalty)
Jonjo O'Neill D J Burke

Placings:211-11211F   (4045)
2003/04: 16¹G, 21¹¹GS, 20²GS, 24¹G, 24¹S, 23⁶G,

	Starts	1st	2nd	3rd	Win & Pl
Hurdles	6	4	1	0	35318
Career Total	9	6	2	0	40758
142	1/04	Donc	3m110y	A Hdl	SFT	£17400
137	12/03	Kemp	3m110y	B HHdl	GD	£12122
123	11/03	Towc	2m5f	E Hdl	G-S	£2079
108	11/03	Towc	2m	E Hdl	GD	£2212
103	3/03	Hayd	2m	H NHF	G-F	£2870
108	3/03	Wwck	2m	H NHF	SFT	£2002

Total win prize-money £38685

Going: Sf: 1-1 GS: 1-2 Gd: 2-3 GF: - Fm: 0-0
Distance: 2m/2m3: 1-1 2m4-2m7: 1-2 3m+: 2-3
Track: LH: 1-2 RH: 3-4 Tight: 0-0 Gall: 1-2
Aids: Bl: 0-0 Vi: 0-0 Tstrap: 0-0 Ckp: 0-0
Best Rating: 142 1/04 Donc 3m110y soft Hdl

Very useful novice hurdler; bumper winner; stays three miles; acts on fast and easy ground; has a fair turn of foot.

Diamond Darren (IRE)
91   88

5-y-o ch g Dolphin Street (FR)-Deerussa (IRE) (Jareer (USA))
Miss Victoria Roberts (R D E Woodhouse 7/5) A Smith

Placings:434230-P040   (2701)
2003/04: 22⁶G, 20⁰GS, 19⁴GF, 24⁰G,

	Starts	1st	2nd	3rd	Win & Pl
Hurdles	4	0	0	0	0
Career Total	10	0	1	2	2149

Going: Sf: 0-0 GS: 0-1 Gd: 0-2 GF: - Fm: 0-1
Distance: 2m/2m3: 0-0 2m4-2m7: 0-4 3m+: 0-1
Track: LH: 0-2 RH: 0-2 Tight: 0-2 Gall: 0-0
Aids: Bl: 0-0 Vi: 0-0 Tstrap: 0-2 Ckp: 0-0
Best Rating: 88 10/02 Ludl 2m   firm   Hdl

Plating-class hurdler; best at two miles.

Diamond Dazzler
89   53

6-y-o br g Sula Bula-Dancing Diamond (IRE) (Alzao (USA))
D P Keane Dajam & Damian Burbidge

Placings:00-050P6   (3081)
2003/04: 16⁰GF, 16⁵GF, 20⁰GF, 20⁶GS, 16⁶GS,

	Starts	1st	2nd	3rd	Win & Pl
NH Flat	1	0	0	0	0
Hurdles	4	0	0	0	545
Career Total	7	0	0	0	545

Going: Sf: 0-0 GS: 0-2 Gd: 0-0 GF: - Fm: 0-3
Distance: 2m/2m3: 0-3 2m4-2m7: 0-2 3m+: 0-0
Track: LH: 0-3 RH: 0-2 Tight: 0-2 Gall: 0-1
Aids: Bl: 0-1 Vi: 0-0 Tstrap: 0-0 Ckp: 0-0
Best Rating: 70 2/03 Folk 2m1f110y heavy NHF

Poor hurdler; blinkered for first time when dropped into seller at Stratford December 2003.

Diamond Dynasty
71   62

7-y-o b g Son Pardo-Reperage (USA) (Key To Content (USA))
J N R Billinge J N R Billinge

Placings:000PP/P000-0P0F0   (4074)
2003/04: 18⁰G, 20⁰G, 18⁰S, 20²GF, 20⁰F,

	Starts	1st	2nd	3rd	Win & Pl
Hurdles	5	0	0	0	
Career Total	14	0	0	0	

Going: Sf: 0-1 GS: 0-0 Gd: 0-2 GF: - Fm: 0-2
Distance: 2m/2m3: 0-2 2m4-2m7: 0-3 3m+: 0-0
Track: LH: 0-2 RH: 0-3 Tight: 0-4 Gall: 0-0
Aids: Bl: 0-1 Vi: 0-0 Tstrap: 0-0 Ckp: 0-1
Best Rating: 62 4/03 Prth 2m10y good Hdl

Diamond Hall
90(98h)   (102h)86

11-y-o b g Lapierre-Willitwin (Majestic Maharaj)
R D Tudor R D Tudor

Placings:51/1200/3/1/40P633F/UP5235050303-PU02P   (4527)
2003/04: 20⁰GF, 23⁴ᴿG, 20⁰GF, 22²G, 19⁶PGS,

	Starts	1st	2nd	3rd	Win & Pl
Chases	5	0	1	0	1884
Career Total	32	3	3	6	14813
102	5/99	Strf	2m110y	F(0-100)HHdl	G-S	£2682
91	10/97	Ludl	2m	H NHF	G-F	£1213
86	4/97	Chep	2m110y	H NHF	FRM	£1686

Total win prize-money £5582

Going: Sf: 0-0 GS: 0-1 Gd: 0-2 GF: - Fm: 0-2
Distance: 2m/2m3: 0-0 2m4-2m7: 0-4 3m+: 0-1
Track: LH: 0-1 RH: 0-4 Tight: 0-1 Gall: 0-0
Aids: Bl: 0-0 Vi: 0-0 Tstrap: 0-0 Ckp: 0-0
Best Rating: 102 5/01 Sedg 2m1f   good   Hdl

Fair hurdler; best effort over fences when third in 2m 5f novices handicap at Cheltenham in April when 8lb 'wrong'.

Diamond Joshua (IRE)
90   94

6-y-o b g Mujadil (USA)-Elminya (IRE) (Sure Blade (USA))

M Scudamore (M E Sowersby 8/2) Hereford Journal Racing Club

Placings:1333P/6040P3-400000　　　　(4917)
2003/04: 20⁴G, 16⁰G, 19⁰G, 16⁰S, 20⁰G, 20⁰GS,

	Starts	1st	2nd	3rd	Win & Pl
Hurdles	6	0	0	0	528
Career Total	17	1	0	4	17829
101	10/01	Weth	2m	D Hdl	GD	£3843

Total win prize-money £3843

Going:	Sf: 0-1 GS: 0-1 Gd: 0-4 GF: - Fm: 0-0
Distance:	2m/2m3: 0-2 2m4-2m7: 0-4 3m+: 0-0
Track:	LH: 0-5 RH: 0-1 Tight: 0-1 Gall: 0-0
Aids:	Bl: 0-1 Vi: 0-0 Tstrap: 0-5 Ckp: 0-0
Best Rating:	131 3/02 Chel 2m1f good Hdl

Moderate hurdler at his best; staying-on third in the Triumph Hurdle in 2002; has changed stables and found things tough since; best avoided; stays 2m 4f; usually wears a tongue tie.

Diamond Maxine (IRE)
110　　　　89+
4-y-o b f Turtle Island (IRE)-Kawther (Tap On Wood)
John Berry Diamond Racing Ltd

Placings:1　　　　　　(2331)
2003/04: 16¹G,

	Starts	1st	2nd	3rd	Win & Pl
Hurdles	1	1	0	0	4472
Career Total	1	1	0	0	4472
89	11/03	Fknm	2m	D Hdl	GD	£4472

Total win prize-money £4472

Going:	Sf: 0-0 GS: 0-0 Gd: 1-1 GF: - Fm: 0-0
Distance:	2m/2m3: 1-1 2m4-2m7: 0-0 3m+: 0-0
Track:	LH: 1-1 RH: 0-0 Tight: 1-1 Gall: 0-0
Aids:	Bl: 0-0 Vi: 0-0 Tstrap: 0-0 Ckp: 0-0
Best Rating:	89 11/03 Fknm 2m good Hdl

Won a weak race on her hurdling debut at Fakenham.

Diamond Merchant
107f　　　　109f
5-y-o ch g Vettori (IRE)-Tosca (Be My Guest (USA))
A King T J & Mrs H Parrott

Placings:240　　　　　　(3948)
2003/04: 16²GS, 18⁴HY, 16⁰G,

	Starts	1st	2nd	3rd	Win & Pl
NH Flat	3	0	1	0	451
Career Total	3	0	1	0	451

Going:	Sf: 0-1 GS: 0-1 Gd: 0-1 GF: - Fm: 0-0
Distance:	2m/2m3: 0-3 2m4-2m7: 0-0 3m+: 0-0
Track:	LH: 0-1 RH: 0-2 Tight: 0-1 Gall: 0-1
Aids:	Bl: 0-0 Vi: 0-0 Tstrap: 0-0 Ckp: 0-0
Best Rating:	109 12/03 Hntg 2m110y gd-sft NHF

Has shown ability in bumper outings to date; unsuited by heavy ground.

Diamond Mick
91　　　　88
4-y-o ch g Pivotal-Miss Poll Flinders (Swing Easy (USA))
R Johnson (G G Margarson 28/10) Norcroft Park Stud

Placings:0002　　　　　　(4758)
2003/04: 16⁰GS, 16⁰GS, 16⁰GS, 16²S,

	Starts	1st	2nd	3rd	Win & Pl
Hurdles	4	0	1	0	1466

Career Total　　　　4　　0　　1　　0　　1466

Aids:	Bl: 0-0 Vi: 0-0 Tstrap: 0-0 Ckp: 0-0
Best Rating:	106 4/04 Aint 2m1f good NHF

Going:　Sf: 0-1 GS: 0-3 Gd: 0-0 GF: - Fm: 0-0
Distance:　2m/2m3: 0-4 2m4-2m7: 0-0 3m+: 0-0
Track:　LH: 0-2 RH: 0-2 Tight: 0-1 Gall: 0-1
Aids:　Bl: 0-0 Vi: 0-0 Tstrap: 0-0 Ckp: 0-3
Best Rating:　88 2/04 Hntg 2m110y gd-sft Hdl

Diamond Monroe (IRE)
94(102h)　　(100+h)100+
8-y-o ch g Treasure Hunter-Star Of Monroe (Derring Rose)
N J Henderson Newbury Racehorse Owners Group

Placings:50552-2421335　　　　(4113)
2003/04: 23²GF, 24⁴GF, 22²G, 24¹GF, 24³G, 24³GS, 23⁵GF,

	Starts	1st	2nd	3rd	Win & Pl
Hurdles	5	1	2	1	6779
Chases	2	0	0	1	834
Career Total	12	1	3	2	8667
99	11/03	Ludl	3m	F(0-100)HHdl	G-F	£4036

Total win prize-money £4037

Going:	Sf: 0-0 GS: 0-1 Gd: 0-2 GF: - Fm: 1-4
Distance:	2m/2m3: 0-0 2m4-2m7: 0-1 3m+: 1-6
Track:	LH: 0-4 RH: 1-3 Tight: 0-4 Gall: 0-0
Aids:	Bl: 0-0 Vi: 0-0 Tstrap: 0-0 Ckp: 0-0
Best Rating:	101 11/03 NAbb 2m6f good Hdl

Moderate hurdler; limited promise so far; stays three miles; acts on good ground.

Diamond Orchid (IRE)
104　　　　109+
4-y-o gr f Victory Note (USA)-Olivia's Pride (IRE) (Digamist (USA))
P D Evans (D Carroll 27/6) Diamond Racing Ltd

Placings:020　　　　　　(4489)
2003/04: 16⁰GF, 16²GF, 16⁰G,

	Starts	1st	2nd	3rd	Win & Pl
Hurdles	3	0	1	0	1748
Career Total	3	0	1	0	1748

Going:	Sf: 0-0 GS: 0-0 Gd: 0-1 GF: - Fm: 0-2
Distance:	2m/2m3: 0-3 2m4-2m7: 0-0 3m+: 0-0
Track:	LH: 0-2 RH: 0-1 Tight: 0-2 Gall: 0-0
Aids:	Bl: 0-0 Vi: 0-2 Tstrap: 0-0 Ckp: 0-0
Best Rating:	109 3/04 Strf 2m110y gd-fm Hdl

Modest hurdler; acts on a sound surface.

Diamond Sal
99f　　　　106f
6-y-o b m Bob Back (USA)-Fortune's Girl (Ardross)
Mrs M Reveley R Haggas

Placings:2-2251　　　　(4649)
2003/04: 16²G, 16²HY, 16⁵S, 17¹G,

	Starts	1st	2nd	3rd	Win & Pl
NH Flat	4	1	2	0	19011
Career Total	5	1	3	0	19707
106	4/04	Aint	2m1f	A NHF	GD	£17400

Total win prize-money £17400

Going:	Sf: 0-2 GS: 0-0 Gd: 1-2 GF: - Fm: 0-0
Distance:	2m/2m3: 1-4 2m4-2m7: 0-0 3m+: 0-0
Track:	LH: 0-2 RH: 0-1 Tight: 0-0 Gall: 0-0

Career Total　　4　　0　　1　　0　　1466

Aids:	Bl: 0-0 Vi: 0-0 Tstrap: 0-0 Ckp: 0-0
Best Rating:	106 4/04 Aint 2m1f good NHF

Shock winner of the Aintree Champion Bumper; had previously been placed in ordinary events; should stay further over hurdles; acts on most ground.

Diamond Vein
84　　　　52
5-y-o b g Green Dancer (USA)-Blushing Sunrise (USA) (Cox's Ridge (USA))
S P Griffiths J Lavelle

Placings:0010-P0P　　　　(4660)
2003/04: 21⁰GS, 20⁰GS, 24⁰S,

	Starts	1st	2nd	3rd	Win & Pl
Hurdles	3	0	0	0	
Career Total	7	1	0	0	2016
86	2/03	Sedg	2m1f	H NHF	HVY	£2016

Total win prize-money £2016

Going:	Sf: 0-1 GS: 0-2 Gd: 0-0 GF: - Fm: 0-0
Distance:	2m/2m3: 0-0 2m4-2m7: 0-2 3m+: 0-1
Track:	LH: 0-3 RH: 0-0 Tight: 0-1 Gall: 0-0
Aids:	Bl: 0-0 Vi: 0-0 Tstrap: 0-0 Ckp: 0-0
Best Rating:	86 2/03 Sedg 2m1f heavy NHF

Diamondalternative (IRE)
94　　　　76+
9-y-o gr g Be My Native (USA)-Dame Blakeney (IRE) (Blakeney)
C R Egerton Mrs A Ross

Placings:1/3510　　　　(1374)
2003/04: 24³S, 22⁵GF, 26¹G, 24⁰GF,

	Starts	1st	2nd	3rd	Win & Pl
Hurdles	4	1	0	1	3962
Career Total	5	2	0	1	5600
64	7/03	Sthl	3m2f	E Hdl	GD	£3388
108	1/01	Font	2m2f110yH NHF		SFT	£1638

Total win prize-money £5026

Going:	Sf: 0-1 GS: 0-0 Gd: 1-1 GF: - Fm: 0-2
Distance:	2m/2m3: 0-0 2m4-2m7: 0-1 3m+: 1-3
Track:	LH: 1-4 RH: 0-0 Tight: 0-2 Gall: 0-0
Aids:	Bl: 0-0 Vi: 0-0 Tstrap: 0-0 Ckp: 0-0
Best Rating:	108 1/01 Font 2m2f110y soft NHF

Bumper winner; struggled home in poor novices' hurdle at Southwell in June; stays really well.

Diamonds Will Do (IRE)
106　　　　108
7-y-o b m Bigstone (IRE)-Clear Ability (IRE) (Be My Guest (USA))
Miss Venetia Williams Geraldine Mapp & Lawrence Degville

Placings:65510/05423300-153360　　　　(3200)
2003/04: 20¹G, 20⁵GF, 20³G, 21³G, 24⁶GS, 16⁰S,

	Starts	1st	2nd	3rd	Win & Pl
Hurdles	6	1	0	2	4648
Career Total	19	2	1	4	11627
100	8/03	Bang	2m4f	E(0-105)HHdl	GD	£3549
104	3/02	DRoy	2m	Hdl	G-Y	£3809

Total win prize-money £7359

Going:	Sf: 0-1 GS: 0-1 Gd: 1-3 GF: - Fm: 0-1
Distance:	2m/2m3: 0-1 2m4-2m7: 1-4 3m+: 0-1

Track: LH: 1-6 RH: 0-0 Tight: 1-3 Gall: 0-0
Aids: Bl: 0-0 Vi: 0-0 Tstrap: 0-0 Ckp: 0-0
Best Rating: 108 12/02 Fknm 2m   gd-sft Hdl

Ex-Irish hurdler; won 2m maiden hurdle at Down Royal March 2003; disappointing until winning 2m 4f Amateur riders' handicap at Bangor August 2003; acts on good and easy ground.

Diceman (IRE)
105   (109h)**129+**
9-y-o b g Supreme Leader-Henry's Gamble (IRE) (Carlingford Castle)
Mrs S J Smith John Veitch,Graham Allen,Patrick Veitch

Placings:332/3/0/12311-F41P1FU   (2950)
2003/04: 25FG, 254G, 20¹GF, 20PG, 20¹G, 19FG, 20UG,

	Starts	1st	2nd	3rd	Win & Pl
Chases	7	2	0	0	15657
Career Total	17	5	2	4	31745
132	11/03	Newc	2m4f	D(0-120)HCh	GD	£6643
123	11/03	Carl	2m4f	D(0-125)HCh	GF	£7475
115	3/03	Newc	2m4f	E Ch	G-S	£4017
115	3/03	Carl	2m4f	E Ch	SFT	£4212
109	12/02	Donc	2m3f110yE Hdl		G-S	£3178
			Total win prize-money £25525			

Going: Sf: 0-0 GS: 0-0 Gd: 1-6 GF: - Fm: 1-1
Distance: 2m/2m3: 0-1 2m4-2m7: 2-4 3m+: 0-2
Track: LH: 1-5 RH: 1-2 Tight: 0-1 Gall: 1-2
Aids: Bl: 0-0 Vi: 0-0 Tstrap: 0-0 Ckp: 0-0
Best Rating: 132 11/03 Newc 2m4f   good Ch

Fair chaser; best at 2m4f; acts on all ground bar extremes; progressive and tough.

Dick McCarthy (IRE)
102
12-y-o b g Lancastrian-Waltzing Shoon (Green Shoon)
R Rowe Anthony D Kerman

Placings:50050/0222/003/132162310/2360/424226322/335 P522-4   (0325)
2003/04: 24⁴GF,

	Starts	1st	2nd	3rd	Win & Pl
Chases	1	0	0	0	572
Career Total	42	3	13	7	35585
115	3/00	Newb	2m6f110yD(0-120)HCh	G-F	£7247
115	12/99	Plum	2m1f	E Ch	SFT	£3895
106	10/99	Plum	2m4f	D(0-115)HCh	G-F	£5365
			Total win prize-money £16509			

Going: Sf: 0-0 GS: 0-0 Gd: 0-0 GF: - Fm: 0-1
Distance: 2m/2m3: 0-0 2m4-2m7: 0-0 3m+: 0-1
Track: LH: 0-1 RH: 0-0 Tight: 0-1 Gall: 0-0
Aids: Bl: 0-0 Vi: 0-0 Tstrap: 0-0 Ckp: 0-0
Best Rating: 118 1/00 Plum 2m4f   soft Ch

Fair chaser; stays three miles plus; acts on any ground; consistently placed but difficult to win with.

Dick The Taxi
102(91h)   (130h)**111+**
10-y-o b g Karlinsky (USA)-Another Galaxy (IRE) (Anita's Prince)
R J Smith Dicks Backers

Placings:101/0321P1/0P6/61P-3P221   (4957)
2003/04: 16³S, 16PHY, 16²G, 16²G, 17¹GS,

	Starts	1st	2nd	3rd	Win & Pl
Chases	5	1	2	1	7394
Career Total	20	6	3	2	24733
111	4/04	MRas	2m1f110yE(0-105)HCh	G-S	£3829

120	6/02	Strf	2m110y	C(0-135)HHdl	G-F	£6838
130	4/01	Fknm	2m	D(0-110)HHdl	G-S	£3291
117	2/01	Tntn	2m1f	E Hdl	HVY	£2702
122	4/00	MRas	1m5f110yH NHF	SFT	£1533
119	5/99	Worc	2m	H NHF	G-S	£1735
			Total win prize-money £19929			

Going: Sf: 0-2 GS: 1-1 Gd: 0-2 GF: - Fm: 0-0
Distance: 2m/2m3: 1-5 2m4-2m7: 0-0 3m+: 0-0
Track: LH: 0-1 RH: 1-4 Tight: 1-3 Gall: 0-1
Aids: Bl: 0-0 Vi: 0-0 Tstrap: 0-0 Ckp: 0-0
Best Rating: 130 4/01 Fknm 2m   gd-sft Hdl

Fair hurdler, winner on the Flat; has shown ability over fences this season; best over 2m; acts on any ground.

Dick Turpin (USA)
109   109
10-y-o br g Red Ransom (USA)-Turn To Money (USA) (Turn To Mars (USA))
Mrs L Wadham The Dyball Partnership

Placings:P/31602412-1P   (0418)
2003/04: 16¹G, 19PG,

	Starts	1st	2nd	3rd	Win & Pl
Hurdles	2	1	0	0	3692
Career Total	11	3	2	1	19812
109	5/03	Uttx	2m	D(0-120)HHdl	GD	£3692
100	3/03	MRas	2m1f110yD(0-120)HHdl	GD	£8437
96	12/02	Fknm	2m4f	E Hdl	G-S	£3475
			Total win prize-money £15605			

Going: Sf: 0-0 GS: 0-0 Gd: 1-2 GF: - Fm: 0-0
Distance: 2m/2m3: 1-1 2m4-2m7: 0-1 3m+: 0-0
Track: LH: 1-1 RH: 0-1 Tight: 0-0 Gall: 0-0
Aids: Bl: 0-0 Vi: 0-0 Tstrap: 0-0 Ckp: 0-0
Best Rating: 109 5/03 Uttx 2m   good Hdl

Moderate hurdler, stays two and a half miles; acts on good and good to soft ground.

Dickens (USA)
103   112+
4-y-o ch g King Of Kings (IRE)-Dellagrazia (USA) (Trempolino (USA))
Miss Venetia Williams George Houghton

Placings:301   (3187)
2003/04: 16³G, 16⁰S, 16¹GS,

	Starts	1st	2nd	3rd	Win & Pl
Hurdles	3	1	0	1	7232
Career Total	3	1	0	1	7232
112	1/04	Sand	2m110y	D Hdl	G-S	£5642
			Total win prize-money £5642			

Going: Sf: 0-1 GS: 1-1 Gd: 0-1 GF: - Fm: 0-0
Distance: 2m/2m3: 1-3 2m4-2m7: 0-0 3m+: 0-0
Track: LH: 0-2 RH: 1-1 Tight: 0-0 Gall: 0-0
Aids: Bl: 0-0 Vi: 0-0 Tstrap: 0-0 Ckp: 0-0
Best Rating: 112 1/04 Sand 2m110y   gd-sft Hdl

Modest juvenile hurdler; ex-Irish; well beaten on first two outings before winning at Sandown; suited by good or easy ground.

Dickensbury Lad (FR)
103   108+
4-y-o b g Luchiroverte (IRE)-Voltige De Cotte (FR) (Saumon (FR))
N A Twiston-Davies Thomas D Goodman

Placings:1233   (4874)
2003/04: 17¹G, 17²G, 16³G, 20³GS,

	Starts	1st	2nd	3rd	Win & Pl
Hurdles	4	1	1	2	6800
Career Total	4	1	1	2	6800
84	2/04	MRas	2m1f110yD Hdl	GD	£4657
			Total win prize-money £4657			

Going: Sf: 0-0 GS: 0-1 Gd: 1-3 GF: - Fm: 0-0
Distance: 2m/2m3: 1-3 2m4-2m7: 0-0 3m+: 0-0
Track: LH: 0-2 RH: 1-2 Tight: 1-4 Gall: 0-0
Aids: Bl: 0-0 Vi: 0-0 Tstrap: 0-0 Ckp: 0-0
Best Rating: 108 4/04 Bang 2m4f   gd-sft Hdl

Modest hurdler, successful on debut over hurdles at Market Rasen in February despite looking very inexperienced; stayed on well when runner-up there next time; will be suited by two and a half miles.

Dickie Lewis
(71h)   (49h)
6-y-o b g Well Beloved-Moneyacre (Veloski)
D McCain D McCain

Placings:004P56   (3820)
2003/04: 16⁰G, 20⁰G, 214GF, 22PS, 26⁵GS, 22⁶S,

	Starts	1st	2nd	3rd	Win & Pl
NH Flat	1	0	0	0	0
Hurdles	3	0	0	0	0
Chases	2	0	0	0	0
Career Total	6	0	0	0	0

Going: Sf: 0-2 GS: 0-1 Gd: 0-1 GF: - Fm: 0-2
Distance: 2m/2m3: 0-3 2m4-2m7: 0-4 3m+: 0-1
Track: LH: 0-4 RH: 0-2 Tight: 0-2 Gall: 0-0
Aids: Bl: 0-0 Vi: 0-0 Tstrap: 0-0 Ckp: 0-0
Best Rating: 62 6/03 Worc 2m   gd-fm NHF

Dickinsons Bay
6-y-o b m Arrasas (USA)-Lb's Girl (My Treasure Chest)
G P Enright Joseph Taylor

Placings:00PP   (4929)
2003/04: 17⁰HY, 18⁰S, 19PGS, 18PG,

	Starts	1st	2nd	3rd	Win & Pl
NH Flat	2	0	0	0	0
Hurdles	2	0	0	0	0
Career Total	4	0	0	0	0

Going: Sf: 0-2 GS: 0-1 Gd: 0-1 GF: - Fm: 0-0
Distance: 2m/2m3: 0-3 2m4-2m7: 0-1 3m+: 0-0
Track: LH: 0-3 RH: 0-1 Tight: 0-1 Gall: 0-0
Aids: Bl: 0-0 Vi: 0-2 Tstrap: 0-0 Ckp: 0-0
Best Rating: 45 1/04 Folk 2m1f110y heavy NHF

Dictum (GER)
107   136
6-y-o ch g Secret 'n Classy (CAN)-Doretta (GER) (Aspros (GER))
Mrs Susan Nock Gerard Nock

Placings:214P   (4381)
2003/04: 16²GS, 16¹HY, 16⁴G, 16PG,

	Starts	1st	2nd	3rd	Win & Pl
Hurdles	4	1	1	0	6624
Career Total	4	1	1	0	6624
136	1/04	Asct	2m110y	D Hdl	HVY	£5005
			Total win prize-money £5005			

Going: Sf: 1-1 GS: 0-1 Gd: 0-2 GF: - Fm: 0-0
Distance: 2m/2m3: 1-4 2m4-2m7: 0-0 3m+: 0-0
Track: LH: 0-2 RH: 1-2 Tight: 0-0 Gall: 0-1
Aids: Bl: 0-0 Vi: 0-0 Tstrap: 0-0 Ckp: 0-0
Best Rating: 136 1/04 Asct 2m110y heavy Hdl

Useful novice hurdler; formerly Group class middle-distance performer in Germany; suited by two miles; best on soft ground.

Did'ntsleepawink (IRE)

(93h)　　　　　　　　　　(80h)
8-y-o b g Dromod Hill-Kamalee (Kambalda)
Jonjo O'Neill John P McManus

Placings:000562/5050-P　　　　　　(0236)
2003/04: 25PGF,

	Starts	1st	2nd	3rd	Win & Pl
Chases	1	0	0	0	
Career Total	11	0	1	0	1472

Going: Sf: 0-0 GS: 0-0 Gd: 0-0 GF: - Fm: 0-1
Distance: 2m/2m3: 0-0 2m4-2m7: 0-0 3m+: 0-1
Track: LH: 0-0 RH: 0-1 Tight: 0-0 Gall: 0-0
Aids: Bl: 0-0 Vi: 0-0 Tstrap: 0-0 Ckp: 0-0
Best Rating: 105 4/02 Fair 2m yield NHF

Didcot

96f　　　　　　　　　　　　90f
5-y-o ch g Roselier (FR)-Astromis (IRE) (Torus)
J Rudge Tom Hayes

Placings:00　　　　　　　　　　(4920)
2003/04: 17PGS, 16PGS,

	Starts	1st	2nd	3rd	Win & Pl
NH Flat	2	0	0	0	
Career Total	2	0	0	0	

Going: Sf: 0-0 GS: 0-2 Gd: 0-0 GF: - Fm: 0-0
Distance: 2m/2m3: 0-2 2m4-2m7: 0-0 3m+: 0-0
Track: LH: 0-2 RH: 0-0 Tight: 0-1 Gall: 0-0
Aids: Bl: 0-0 Vi: 0-0 Tstrap: 0-0 Ckp: 0-0
Best Rating: 90 3/04 Bang 2m1f gd-sft NHF

Didifon

107(103h)　　　　　　(116h)110
9-y-o b g Zafonic (USA)-Didicoy (USA) (Danzig (USA))
N P McCormack (C W Fairhurst 17/8) Mrs D McCormack

Placings:0/61506/360000/603312-4601　(2379)
2003/04: 17⁴GS, 16⁶GF, 21⁹GS, 16¹GF,

	Starts	1st	2nd	3rd	Win & Pl
Chases	4	1	0	0	3275
Career Total	22	3	1	3	19441
107	11/03	Sedg	2m110y	F(0-100)HCh	G-F	£2751
110	3/03	Sedg	2m110y	E Ch	GD	£4665
119	11/00	DRoy	2m	Hdl	Y-S	£5520

Total win prize-money £12937

Going: Sf: 0-0 GS: 0-1 Gd: 0-0 GF: - Fm: 1-3
Distance: 2m/2m3: 1-3 2m4-2m7: 0-1 3m+: 0-0
Track: LH: 1-4 RH: 0-0 Tight: 0-0 Gall: 0-0
Aids: Bl: 0-0 Vi: 0-0 Tstrap: 0-0 Ckp: 1-3
Best Rating: 122 10/01 Gway 2m sft-hvy Hdl

Moderate chaser; best at around two miles; likes fast ground; usually wears cheekpieces.

Die Fledermaus (IRE)

108(85h)　　　　　　　　　　104
10-y-o b g Batshoof-Top Mouse (High Top)
D J Wintle L & P Partnership

Placings:60F0/23440/3113124/141231200/363024105/214
P04P-R05331124　　　　　　　　(1678)
2003/04: 23PGF, 21PGD, 20⁵G, 21³GF, 24³G, 20¹GF, 23¹GF, 25²GF, 25⁴F,

	Starts	1st	2nd	3rd	Win & Pl
Chases	9	2	1	2	9256
Career Total	50	10	7	8	51603
95	9/03	Worc	2m7f110yF(0-90)HCh	G-F	£2975
98	8/03	Worc	2m4f110yF(0-100)HCh	G-F	£3425
110	7/02	Wolv	3m1f	D(0-115)HCh	GD	£4928
109	11/01	Tntn	3m	F(0-105)HCh	GD	£3080
108	8/00	Sthl	3m110y	E(0-115)HCh	GD	£4357
115	7/00	Worc	2m4f110yD(0-125)HHdl	GD	£6711
105	6/00	NAbb	2m5f110yD Ch	G-F	£3760
111	10/99	Chep	2m4f	D(0-125)HHdl	SFT	£2842
106	8/99	Ctml	2m6f	E Hdl	GD	£2915
104	8/99	Bang	2m4f	E Hdl	GD	£1882

Total win prize-money £37098

Going: Sf: 0-0 GS: 0-0 Gd: 0-2 GF: - Fm: 2-7
Distance: 2m/2m3: 0-0 2m4-2m7: 1-4 3m+: 1-5
Track: LH: 2-8 RH: 0-1 Tight: 0-3 Gall: 0-0
Aids: Bl: 0-1 Vi: 0-0 Tstrap: 0-0 Ckp: 0-0
Best Rating: 115 7/00 Wolv 2m4f110y good Hdl

Low-grade handicap chaser; winner twice at Worcester this summer; finds 2m 4f on the short side these days and suited by three miles; acts on easy ground and good to firm ground.

Digger (IRE)

80　　　　　　　　　　　　78+
5-y-o ch g Danzig Connection (USA)-Baliana (Midyan (USA))
Miss Gay Kelleway The Inside Rail

Placings:0　　　　　　　　　　(3900)
2003/04: 17PGS,

	Starts	1st	2nd	3rd	Win & Pl
Hurdles	1	0	0	0	
Career Total	1	0	0	0	

Going: Sf: 0-0 GS: 0-1 Gd: 0-0 GF: - Fm: 0-0
Distance: 2m/2m3: 0-1 2m4-2m7: 0-0 3m+: 0-0
Track: LH: 0-0 RH: 0-1 Tight: 0-1 Gall: 0-0
Aids: Bl: 0-0 Vi: 0-0 Tstrap: 0-0 Ckp: 0-0
Best Rating: 80 2/04 Tntn 2m1f gd-sft Hdl

Digging Deep

8-y-o ch m Scorpio (FR)-Two Travellers (Deep Run)
Ferdy Murphy Mrs Elaine Holmes

Placings:0　　　　　　　　　　(3321)
2003/04: 21PGS,

	Starts	1st	2nd	3rd	Win & Pl
Hurdles	1	0	0	0	
Career Total	1	0	0	0	

Going: Sf: 0-0 GS: 0-1 Gd: 0-0 GF: - Fm: 0-0
Distance: 2m/2m3: 0-0 2m4-2m7: 0-1 3m+: 0-0
Track: LH: 0-1 RH: 0-0 Tight: 0-1 Gall: 0-0
Aids: Bl: 0-0 Vi: 0-0 Tstrap: 0-0 Ckp: 0-0

Diklers Rose (IRE)

81f　　　　　　　　　　　　82f
5-y-o gr m Roselier (FR)-Diklers Run (Deep Run)
Mrs M Reveley The Mary Reveley Racing Club

Placings:4　　　　　　　　　　(4481)
2003/04: 17⁴HY,

	Starts	1st	2nd	3rd	Win & Pl
NH Flat	1	0	0	0	0
Career Total	1	0	0	0	0

Going: Sf: 0-1 GS: 0-0 Gd: 0-0 GF: - Fm: 0-0
Distance: 2m/2m3: 0-1 2m4-2m7: 0-0 3m+: 0-0
Track: LH: 0-0 RH: 0-0 Tight: 0-0 Gall: 0-0
Aids: Bl: 0-0 Vi: 0-0 Tstrap: 0-0 Ckp: 0-0
Best Rating: 87 3/04 Carl 2m1f heavy NHF

Dileer (IRE)

99　　　　　　　　　　　　105
5-y-o b g Barathea (IRE)-Stay Sharpe (USA) (Sharpen Up)
D J Wintle (L M Cumani 25/10) Court Roof Tiling Ltd

Placings:52F　　　　　　　　　　(3767)
2003/04: 17⁵G, 17²GS, 17FHY,

	Starts	1st	2nd	3rd	Win & Pl
Hurdles	3	0	1	0	1304
Career Total	3	0	1	0	1304

Going: Sf: 0-1 GS: 0-1 Gd: 0-1 GF: - Fm: 0-0
Distance: 2m/2m3: 0-3 2m4-2m7: 0-0 3m+: 0-0
Track: LH: 0-0 RH: 0-3 Tight: 0-2 Gall: 0-0
Aids: Bl: 0-0 Vi: 0-0 Tstrap: 0-0 Ckp: 0-0
Best Rating: 105 2/04 Carl 2m1f heavy Hdl

Ability in novice hurdles; suited by a stiff track.

Dilsaa

99　　　　　　　　　　　　98
7-y-o ch g Night Shift (USA)-Llia (Shirley Heights)
K A Ryan Yorkshire Racing Club V

Placings:331241　　　　　　　　(1623)
2003/04: 17³GF, 17³GF, 17¹G, 17²GF, 17⁴G, 20¹GF,

	Starts	1st	2nd	3rd	Win & Pl
Hurdles	6	2	1	2	8257
Career Total	6	2	1	2	8257
98	10/03	Hexm	2m4f110yE Hdl	G-F	£2226
92	8/03	Ctml	2m1f110yE Hdl	GD	£3737

Total win prize-money £5964

Going: Sf: 0-0 GS: 0-0 Gd: 1-2 GF: - Fm: 1-4
Distance: 2m/2m3: 1-5 2m4-2m7: 1-1 3m+: 0-0
Track: LH: 2-5 RH: 0-1 Tight: 1-4 Gall: 0-0
Aids: Bl: 0-0 Vi: 0-0 Tstrap: 0-0 Ckp: 0-0
Best Rating: 98 10/03 Hexm 2m4f110y gd-fm Hdl

Moderate novice hurdler; plater on the Flat; fair efforts in the summer of 2003 and took modest events at Cartmel in August and Hexham in October; stays two and a half miles; acts on fast ground.

Dilys

5-y-o b m Efisio-Ramajana (USA) (Shadeed (USA))
W S Kittow Mrs Jenny Hopkins

Placings:P　　　　　　　　　　(3047)
2003/04: 17PG,

	Starts	1st	2nd	3rd	Win & Pl
Hurdles	1	0	0	0	
Career Total	1	0	0	0	

Going:	Sf: 0-0 GS: 0-0 Gd: 0-1 GF: - Fm: 0-0
Distance:	2m/2m3: 0-1 2m4-2m7: 0-0 3m+: 0-0
Track:	LH: 0-0 RH: 0-1 Tight: 0-1 Gall: 0-0
Aids:	Bl: 0-0 Vi: 0-0 Tstrap: 0-0 Ckp: 0-0

Dimitri (IRE)

(99h)   (97+h)

7-y-o gr g Roselier (FR)-Treidlia (Mandalus)
S Gollings J B Webb

Placings:0230P   (4436)
2003/04: 16PS, 24PHY, 24GS, 24QG, 24PGS,

	Starts	1st	2nd	3rd	Win & Pl
NH Flat	1	0	0	0	0
Hurdles	3	0	1	1	1831
Chases	1	0	0	0	0
Career Total	5	0	1	1	1831

Going:	Sf: 0-3 GS: 0-1 Gd: 0-1 GF: - Fm: 0-0
Distance:	2m/2m3: 0-1 2m4-2m7: 0-0 3m+: 0-4
Track:	LH: 0-4 RH: 0-1 Tight: 0-1 Gall: 0-0
Aids:	Bl: 0-0 Vi: 0-0 Tstrap: 0-0 Ckp: 0-0
Best Rating:	97 1/04 Uttx 3m110y heavy Hdl

Irish point winner; game runner-up in novices' hurdle in testing conditions at Uttoxeter in January; stays exceptionally well.

Dinarelli (FR)

92   91

5-y-o gr g Linamix (FR)-Dixiella (FR) (Fabulous Dancer (USA))
M C Pipe (F Head 26/8) Lord Donoughmore & Countess Donoughmore

Placings:00405   (4541)
2003/04: 17QGS, 17QGS, 16KG, 17QG, 16PGS,

	Starts	1st	2nd	3rd	Win & Pl
Hurdles	5	0	0	0	0
Career Total	5	0	0	0	0

Going:	Sf: 0-0 GS: 0-3 Gd: 0-2 GF: - Fm: 0-0
Distance:	2m/2m3: 0-5 2m4-2m7: 0-0 3m+: 0-0
Track:	LH: 0-4 RH: 0-1 Tight: 0-4 Gall: 0-0
Aids:	Bl: 0-0 Vi: 0-2 Tstrap: 0-0 Ckp: 0-0
Best Rating:	94 3/04 Plum 2m good Hdl

Dinofelis

105   81

6-y-o b g Rainbow Quest (USA)-Revonda (IRE) (Sadler's Wells (USA))
W M Brisbourne Mark Brisbourne

Placings:6PPP02-34601050   (2361)
2003/04: 16QG, 16KGF, 16PGS, 16QGF, 16¹GF, 16QGF, 16SGF, 16QGF,

	Starts	1st	2nd	3rd	Win & Pl
Hurdles	8	1	0	1	2661
Career Total	14	1	1	1	3337
79	10/03	Ludl	2m	G Hdl	G-F £2242

Total win prize-money £2243

Going:	Sf: 0-0 GS: 0-0 Gd: 0-2 GF: - Fm: 1-6
Distance:	2m/2m3: 1-8 2m4-2m7: 0-0 3m+: 0-0

Track:	LH: 0-4 RH: 1-4 Tight: 0-2 Gall: 0-1
Aids:	Bl: 0-0 Vi: 0-0 Tstrap: 0-0 Ckp: 1-8
Best Rating:	81 5/03 Fknm 2m gd-fm Hdl

Poor plater; won weakly contested 2m seller at Ludlow September 2003; best efforts on fast ground and sharp tracks.

Dinsey Finnegan (IRE)

9-y-o b g Fresh Breeze (USA)-Rose Of Solway (Derring Rose)
Simon Bloss J G Phillips

Placings:00/P4-66   (4298)
2003/04: 21SG, 23QG,

	Starts	1st	2nd	3rd	Win & Pl
Chases	2	0	0	0	0
Career Total	6	0	0	0	167

Going:	Sf: 0-0 GS: 0-0 Gd: 0-2 GF: - Fm: 0-0
Distance:	2m/2m3: 0-0 2m4-2m7: 0-1 3m+: 0-0
Track:	LH: 0-1 RH: 0-1 Tight: 0-0 Gall: 0-1
Aids:	Bl: 0-0 Vi: 0-0 Tstrap: 0-0 Ckp: 0-2
Best Rating:	86 4/03 Chel 2m5f good Ch

Dionn Righ (IRE)

98   111

9-y-o b g Asir-Happy Eliza (Laurence O)
J Howard Johnson Gordon Brown/bert Watson

Placings:4U/P11P2-P4PPF   (4615)
2003/04: 29PG, 25⁴S, 24PHY, 33PG, 28FG,

	Starts	1st	2nd	3rd	Win & Pl
Chases	5	0	0	0	327
Career Total	12	2	1	0	10221
111	2/03	Sedg	3m3f	E Ch	HVY £4046
105	12/02	Sedg	3m3f	E Ch	SFT £4351

Total win prize-money £8398

Going:	Sf: 0-2 GS: 0-0 Gd: 0-3 GF: - Fm: 0-0
Distance:	2m/2m3: 0-0 2m4-2m7: 0-0 3m+: 0-5
Track:	LH: 0-4 RH: 0-1 Tight: 0-2 Gall: 0-2
Aids:	Bl: 0-0 Vi: 0-0 Tstrap: 0-0 Ckp: 0-1
Best Rating:	111 2/03 Sedg 3m3f heavy Ch

Modest chaser; outslogged rivals when winning at Sedgefield in February; stays three miles-three; acts on soft ground but handles faster; has worn blinkers.

Dionysian (IRE)

85   70

5-y-o ch g Be My Guest (USA)-Justitia (Dunbeath (USA))
R H Alner Paul Murphy & Frank Watson

Placings:000   (4180)
2003/04: 16QGS, 16QG, 20QG,

	Starts	1st	2nd	3rd	Win & Pl
NH Flat	1	0	0	0	0
Hurdles	2	0	0	0	0
Career Total	3	0	0	0	0

Going:	Sf: 0-0 GS: 0-1 Gd: 0-2 GF: - Fm: 0-0
Distance:	2m/2m3: 0-2 2m4-2m7: 0-1 3m+: 0-0
Track:	LH: 0-2 RH: 0-1 Tight: 0-1 Gall: 0-2
Aids:	Bl: 0-0 Vi: 0-0 Tstrap: 0-0 Ckp: 0-0
Best Rating:	70 3/04 Plum 2m good Hdl

Diorama (GER)

79(98h)   (81h)73

9-y-o b m Bakharoff (USA)-Dosha (FR) (Sharpman)
L A Dace Mrs K Tobin And Miss R Kennedy

Placings:0/000605/0000/160P04F-P336   (2501)
2003/04: 24PF, 21³G, 22³GF, 21⁶GF,

	Starts	1st	2nd	3rd	Win & Pl
Hurdles	2	0	0	1	267
Chases	2	0	1	0	413
Career Total	22	1	0	2	3746
86	11/02	Plum	2m5f	F(0-90)HHdl	SFT £3066

Total win prize-money £3066

Going:	Sf: 0-0 GS: 0-0 Gd: 0-1 GF: - Fm: 0-3
Distance:	2m/2m3: 0-0 2m4-2m7: 0-3 3m+: 0-1
Track:	LH: 0-1 RH: 0-2 Tight: 0-3 Gall: 0-0
Aids:	Bl: 0-2 Vi: 0-0 Tstrap: 0-0 Ckp: 0-0
Best Rating:	86 11/02 Plum 2m5f soft Hdl

Plating-class hurdler; landed a gamble in ordinary handicap hurdle at Plumpton in November.

Diplomatic Daisy (IRE)

73f   57f

5-y-o b m Alflora (IRE)-Landa's Counsel (Pragmatic)
D R Gandolfo James Blackshaw

Placings:0   (4529)
2003/04: 16QGS,

	Starts	1st	2nd	3rd	Win & Pl
NH Flat	1	0	0	0	
Career Total	1	0	0	0	

Going:	Sf: 0-0 GS: 0-1 Gd: 0-0 GF: - Fm: 0-0
Distance:	2m/2m3: 0-1 2m4-2m7: 0-0 3m+: 0-0
Track:	LH: 0-1 RH: 0-0 Tight: 0-0 Gall: 0-0
Aids:	Bl: 0-0 Vi: 0-0 Tstrap: 0-0 Ckp: 0-0
Best Rating:	57 3/04 Chep 2m110y gd-sft NHF

Direct Access (IRE)

99   147

9-y-o ch g Roselier (FR)-Spanish Flame (IRE) (Spanish Place (USA))
L Lungo Ashleybank Investments Limited

Placings:1111/11F24/1P-P6P4   (3936)
2003/04: 26PG, 25⁶S, 20PG, 20⁴G,

	Starts	1st	2nd	3rd	Win & Pl
Chases	4	0	0	0	1096
Career Total	15	7	1	0	50773
147	11/02	Kels	3m1f	C(0-130)HCh	SFT £8014
136	11/01	Carl	2m4f	D Ch	HVY £5187
113	11/01	Carl	2m	D Ch	SFT £4823
143	3/01	Sand	2m4f110yA HHdl	HVY £18560
143	2/01	Kels	2m6f110yE Hdl	SFT £2730
142	1/01	Ayr	2m4f	D Hdl	G-S £3423
122	12/00	Ayr	2m4f	E Hdl	SFT £2380

Total win prize-money £45118

Going:	Sf: 0-1 GS: 0-0 Gd: 0-3 GF: - Fm: 0-0
Distance:	2m/2m3: 0-0 2m4-2m7: 0-2 3m+: 0-2
Track:	LH: 0-3 RH: 0-1 Tight: 0-1 Gall: 0-1
Aids:	Bl: 0-1 Vi: 0-0 Tstrap: 0-1 Ckp: 0-0
Best Rating:	147 11/02 Kels 3m1f soft Ch

Fair chaser; very useful novice chaser in 2001/2, but not as good nowadays; stays three miles plus, acts on soft ground; becoming disappointing and pulled up in first time blinkers at Wetherby in December.

Direct Descendant (IRE)

104   **93+**

5-y-o ch g Be My Guest (USA)-Prague Spring (Salse (USA))
J J Quinn Miss D A Johnson

Placings:1003-0531245   (2376)
2003/04: 17⁰GF, 21⁵GF, 17³G, 16¹GF, 16²GF, 16⁴GF, 17⁵GF,

	Starts	1st	2nd	3rd	Win & Pl
Hurdles	7	1	1	1	3132
Career Total	11	2	1	2	5608
95	10/03 Hexm	2m110y G Hdl		G-F	£1834
74	9/02 MRas	2m1f110yG Hdl		G-F	£2044
		Total win prize-money £3878			

Going:	Sf: 0-0 GS: 0-0 Gd: 0-1 GF: - Fm: 1-6
Distance:	2m/2m3: 1-6 2m4-2m7: 0-1 3m+: 0-0
Track:	LH: 1-7 RH: 0-0 Tight: 0-5 Gall: 0-0
Aids:	Bl: 0-0 Vi: 0-1 Tstrap: 0-0 Ckp: 0-0
Best Rating:	95 10/03 Hexm 2m110y gd-fm Hdl

Selling hurdler; best over 2m; suited by fast ground.

Direct Flight (IRE)

97   **97+**

6-y-o ch g Dry Dock-Midnight Mistress (Midsummer Night li)
Noel T Chance Top Flight Racing

Placings: f2P6   (4167)
2003/04: 16¹G, 17²G, 20⁰GS, 21⁶G,

	Starts	1st	2nd	3rd	Win & Pl
NH Flat	1	1	0	0	1467
Hurdles	3	0	1	0	862
Career Total	4	1	1	0	2329
105	10/03 Fknm	2m	H NHF	GD	£1467
		Total win prize-money £1467			

Going:	Sf: 0-0 GS: 0-1 Gd: 1-3 GF: - Fm: 0-0
Distance:	2m/2m3: 1-2 2m4-2m7: 0-2 3m+: 0-0
Track:	LH: 1-3 RH: 0-1 Tight: 1-2 Gall: 0-1
Aids:	Bl: 0-0 Vi: 0-0 Tstrap: 0-0 Ckp: 0-0
Best Rating:	105 10/03 Fknm 2m good NHF

Made a successful debut in a Fakenham bumper in October; runner-up on hurdling bow at Market Rasen the following month.

Direction

74   **65**

6-y-o b m Lahib (USA)-Theme (IRE) (Sadler's Wells (USA))
K A Morgan J Sheridan,G S Alcock,Miss S M Cosgrove

Placings:1/0240-0040   (4592)
2003/04: 17⁰GS, 20⁰GS, 23⁴GS, 26⁰G,

	Starts	1st	2nd	3rd	Win & Pl
Hurdles	4	0	0	0	0
Career Total	9	1	1	0	2483
93	3/02 MRas	2m1f110yH NHF		G-S	£1617
		Total win prize-money £1617			

Going:	Sf: 0-0 GS: 0-3 Gd: 0-1 GF: - Fm: 0-0
Distance:	2m/2m3: 0-1 2m4-2m7: 0-1 3m+: 0-2
Track:	LH: 0-2 RH: 0-2 Tight: 0-2 Gall: 0-1
Aids:	Bl: 0-0 Vi: 0-0 Tstrap: 0-0 Ckp: 0-0
Best Rating:	97 3/03 MRas 2m1f110y good NHF

Bumper winner; no show over hurdles yet.

Dirk Cove (IRE)

106(90h)   (89h)**108**

10-y-o ch g Montelimar (USA)-Another Miller (Gala

Performance (USA))
R Rowe Dr B Alexander

Placings:543/11205/36/334P405341-424330P0   (4525)
2003/04: 24⁴GF, 26²GF, 22⁴G, 30³GS, 32³G, 28⁰G, 26⁵GF, 24⁰GS,

	Starts	1st	2nd	3rd	Win & Pl
Chases	8	0	1	2	4557
Career Total	28	3	2	7	21212
105	4/03 Font	2m6f	E Ch	G-F	£4371
107	12/00 Tntn	3m110y	D(0-120)HHdl	SFT	£3575
104	11/00 Towc	2m5f	E(0-115)HHdl	SFT	£2240
		Total win prize-money £10186			

Going:	Sf: 0-0 GS: 0-2 Gd: 0-3 GF: - Fm: 0-3
Distance:	2m/2m3: 0-0 2m4-2m7: 0-1 3m+: 0-7
Track:	LH: 0-3 RH: 0-3 Tight: 0-2 Gall: 0-1
Aids:	Bl: 0-5 Vi: 0-0 Tstrap: 0-0 Ckp: 0-0
Best Rating:	113 1/01 Kemp 3m110y soft Hdl

Modest staying hurdler/chaser, suited by soft ground, but acts on a sound surface; stays three miles; has worn blinkers.

Disco King

10-y-o b g Rakaposhi King-Divine Affair (IRE) (The Parson)
O O'Neill Derek Baxter

Placings:0/P/P   (0516)
2003/04: 22⁰G,

	Starts	1st	2nd	3rd	Win & Pl
Hurdles	1	0	0	0	0
Career Total	3	0	0	0	0

Going:	Sf: 0-0 GS: 0-0 Gd: 0-1 GF: - Fm: 0-0
Distance:	2m/2m3: 0-0 2m4-2m7: 0-1 3m+: 0-0
Track:	LH: 0-1 RH: 0-0 Tight: 0-1 Gall: 0-0
Aids:	Bl: 0-0 Vi: 0-0 Tstrap: 0-0 Ckp: 0-0
Best Rating:	80 2/99 Ludl 2m good Hdl

Discreet Girl

5-y-o b m Mistertopogigo (IRE)-Pillow Talk (IRE) (Taufan (USA))
Mrs S Lamyman P Lamyman

Placings:00P-P   (0802)
2003/04: 17⁰G,

	Starts	1st	2nd	3rd	Win & Pl
Hurdles	1	0	0	0	0
Career Total	4	0	0	0	0

Going:	Sf: 0-0 GS: 0-0 Gd: 0-1 GF: - Fm: 0-0
Distance:	2m/2m3: 0-1 2m4-2m7: 0-0 3m+: 0-0
Track:	LH: 0-1 RH: 0-0 Tight: 0-0 Gall: 0-0
Aids:	Bl: 0-0 Vi: 0-0 Tstrap: 0-0 Ckp: 0-0

Disgrace

89   **73**

4-y-o b g Distinctly North (USA)-Ace Girl (Stanford)
Mrs S J Smith (A Berry 25/6) Paul J Dixon

Placings:40003   (2712)
2003/04: 17⁴G, 16⁰GF, 16⁰G, 17⁰G, 16³GS,

	Starts	1st	2nd	3rd	Win & Pl
Hurdles	5	0	0	1	602
Career Total	5	0	0	1	602

Going:	Sf: 0-0 GS: 0-1 Gd: 0-3 GF: - Fm: 0-1
Distance:	2m/2m3: 0-5 2m4-2m7: 0-0 3m+: 0-0
Track:	LH: 0-5 RH: 0-0 Tight: 0-2 Gall: 0-2
Aids:	Bl: 0-0 Vi: 0-0 Tstrap: 0-0 Ckp: 0-0
Best Rating:	73 12/03 Donc 2m110y gd-sft Hdl

Plating-class juvenile hurdler.

Dispol Rock (IRE)

72   **97**

8-y-o b g Ballad Rock-Havana Moon (Ela-Mana-Mou)
Dr P Pritchard Dr P Pritchard

Placings:5U00F543310-0   (2183)
2003/04: 21⁰G,

	Starts	1st	2nd	3rd	Win & Pl
Hurdles	1	0	0	0	0
Career Total	12	1	0	2	7076
97	3/03 Tntn	2m1f	F(0-95)HHdl	HVY	£4371
		Total win prize-money £4371			

Going:	Sf: 0-0 GS: 0-0 Gd: 0-1 GF: - Fm: 0-0
Distance:	2m/2m3: 0-0 2m4-2m7: 0-1 3m+: 0-0
Track:	LH: 0-1 RH: 0-0 Tight: 0-0 Gall: 0-1
Aids:	Bl: 0-0 Vi: 0-0 Tstrap: 0-0 Ckp: 0-0
Best Rating:	97 3/03 Tntn 2m1f heavy Hdl

Moderate hurdler; easy winner of weak extended two mile handicap at Taunton March 2003; acts on soft ground.

Distant Prospect (IRE)

103   **123**

7-y-o b g Namaqualand (USA)-Ukraine's Affair (USA) (The Minstrel (CAN))
A M Balding The Rae Smiths And Pauline Gale

Placings:2165   (3489)
2003/04: 16²GS, 16¹GF, 21⁶GS, 17⁵GS,

	Starts	1st	2nd	3rd	Win & Pl
Hurdles	4	1	1	0	8896
Career Total	4	1	1	0	8896
116	12/03 Newb	2m110y	D Hdl	G-F	£5310
		Total win prize-money £5311			

Going:	Sf: 0-0 GS: 0-3 Gd: 0-0 GF: - Fm: 1-1
Distance:	2m/2m3: 1-3 2m4-2m7: 0-1 3m+: 0-0
Track:	LH: 1-4 RH: 0-0 Tight: 0-0 Gall: 1-4
Aids:	Bl: 0-0 Vi: 0-0 Tstrap: 0-0 Ckp: 0-0
Best Rating:	123 1/04 Chel 2m1f gd-sft Hdl

Useful novice hurdler; very useful staying handicapper on the level; made a pleasing start over timber; has won over two miles, but likely to prove suited by further; acts on most types of ground.

Distant Romance

(91h)   (72h)

7-y-o br m Phardante (FR)-Rhine Aria (Workboy)
Miss Z C Davison A A Goldson

Placings:0P-P50P   (3171)
2003/04: 16⁰G, 17⁵GS, 16⁰G, 16⁵GS,

	Starts	1st	2nd	3rd	Win & Pl
Hurdles	3	0	0	0	0
Chases	1	0	0	0	0
Career Total	6	0	0	0	0

Going:	Sf: 0-0 GS: 0-2 Gd: 0-2 GF: - Fm: 0-0
Distance:	2m/2m3: 0-4 2m4-2m7: 0-0 3m+: 0-0
Track:	LH: 0-0 RH: 0-4 Tight: 0-2 Gall: 0-0

Aids: Bl: 0-0 Vi: 0-0 Tstrap: 0-0 Ckp: 0-0
Best Rating: 72 12/03 Leic 2m   good   Hdl

Distant Sky (USA)
80

7-y-o ch g Distant View (USA)-Nijinsky Star (USA) (Nijinsky (CAN))
Miss J S Davis Miss J Davis

Placings:B00-P   (0140)
2003/04: 21PG,

	Starts	1st	2nd	3rd	Win & Pl
Hurdles	1	0	0	0	
Career Total	4	0	0	0	

Going: Sf: 0-0 GS: 0-0 Gd: 0-0 GF: - Fm: 0-0
Distance: 2m/2m3: 0-0 2m4-2m7: 0-1 3m+: 0-0
Track: LH: 0-0 RH: 0-1 Tight: 0-0 Gall: 0-0
Aids: Bl: 0-0 Vi: 0-0 Tstrap: 0-0 Ckp: 0-0
Best Rating: 80 12/02 Kemp 2m   soft   Hdl

Distant Thunder (IRE)
102   114+

6-y-o b g Phardante (FR)-Park Breeze (IRE) (Strong Gale)
R H Alner Old Moss Farm

Placings:24-41FP10   (4629)
2003/04: 17AGS, 20LS, 21FGS, 23PS, 20AG,

	Starts	1st	2nd	3rd	Win & Pl
Hurdles	6	2	0	0	8607
Career Total	8	2	1	0	9589
114	3/04	Sand	2m4f110yD Hdl		SFT	£5044
125	12/03	Chep	2m4f	D Hdl	SFT	£3563
			Total win prize-money £8607			

Going: Sf: 2-3 GS: 0-2 Gd: 0-1 GF: - Fm: 0-0
Distance: 2m/2m3: 0-1 2m4-2m7: 2-4 3m+: 0-1
Track: LH: 1-4 RH: 1-2 Tight: 0-1 Gall: 0-0
Aids: Bl: 0-0 Vi: 0-0 Tstrap: 0-0 Ckp: 0-0
Best Rating: 125 12/03 Chep 2m4f   soft   Hdl

Useful hurdler; half-brother to Moving Earth and Fork Lightning; fair form in two Kempton bumpers early in 2003; relished the testing ground when winning at Chepstow and Sandown; stays two miles four.

Distinctly Well (IRE)
84   72

7-y-o b g Distinctly North (USA)-Brandywell (Skyliner)
M Sheppard Miss A Bevan

Placings:000-PO00   (3773)
2003/04: 17PGS, 19PGS, 16QGS, 16PG,

	Starts	1st	2nd	3rd	Win & Pl
Hurdles	4	0	0	0	
Career Total	7	0	0	0	

Going: Sf: 0-0 GS: 0-3 Gd: 0-1 GF: - Fm: 0-0
Distance: 2m/2m3: 0-0 2m4-2m7: 0-0 3m+: 0-0
Track: LH: 0-2 RH: 0-2 Tight: 0-1 Gall: 0-0
Aids: Bl: 0-0 Vi: 0-0 Tstrap: 0-0 Ckp: 0-0
Best Rating: 76 2/04 Ludl 2m   good   Hdl

Diva Dancer
88   65

4-y-o ch f Dr Devious (IRE)-Catina (Nureyev (USA))

J Hetherton 21st Century Racing 2

Placings:00C   (4657)
2003/04: 16QGS, 16QG, 16CS,

	Starts	1st	2nd	3rd	Win & Pl
Hurdles	3	0	0	0	
Career Total	3	0	0	0	

Going: Sf: 0-1 GS: 0-1 Gd: 0-1 GF: - Fm: 0-0
Distance: 2m/2m3: 0-3 2m4-2m7: 0-0 3m+: 0-0
Track: LH: 0-3 RH: 0-0 Tight: 0-2 Gall: 0-0
Aids: Bl: 0-0 Vi: 0-0 Tstrap: 0-0 Ckp: 0-0
Best Rating: 65 3/04 Kels 2m10y gd-sft Hdl

Diversity (IRE)
101   93

6-y-o ch g Over The River (FR)-Ballymas (Martinmas)
Jonjo O'Neill Home Run Syndicate Ltd

Placings:FP00U4P   (4592)
2003/04: 20PGS, 16PGF, 17QG, 17QGS, 19UGS, 26AG, 26PG,

	Starts	1st	2nd	3rd	Win & Pl
Hurdles	6	0	0	0	0
Chases	1	0	0	0	
Career Total	7	0	0	0	

Going: Sf: 0-0 GS: 0-3 Gd: 0-3 GF: - Fm: 0-1
Distance: 2m/2m3: 0-4 2m4-2m7: 0-1 3m+: 0-2
Track: LH: 0-1 RH: 0-6 Tight: 0-0 Gall: 0-3
Aids: Bl: 0-0 Vi: 0-0 Tstrap: 0-0 Ckp: 0-0
Best Rating: 93 3/04 Hntg 3m2f   good   Hdl

Divet Hill
108(106h)   (106+h)126

10-y-o b g Milieu-Bargello's Lady (Bargello)
Mrs A Hamilton Ian Hamilton

Placings:5P/4O12221133/1122311141514-2P4P   (2863)
2003/04: 25QGF, 21PGS, 20AGF, 20PGS,

	Starts	1st	2nd	3rd	Win & Pl
Hurdles	1	0	0	0	520
Chases	3	0	1	0	2265
Career Total	29	10	6	3	69571
120	4/03	Aint	2m5f110yB Ch		GD	£24375
126	10/02	Kels	3m1f	D(0-125)HCh	G-F	£5434
104	8/02	Prth	2m4f110yD Hdl		GD	£4043
104	7/02	Sedg	2m5f110yE Hdl		G-F	£2940
92	7/02	Sedg	2m5f110yE Hdl		G-F	£2940
124	5/02	Prth	2m4f110yD(0-115)HCh		G-F	£5512
104	5/02	Hexm	3m1f	H Ch	G-S	£2310
121	9/01	Sedg	2m5f	E Ch	G-F	£3282
98	8/01	Prth	2m	D Ch	GD	£4056
115	5/01	Newc	3m	E Ch	G-F	£3668
			Total win prize-money £58561			

Going: Sf: 0-0 GS: 0-2 Gd: 0-0 GF: - Fm: 0-2
Distance: 2m/2m3: 0-0 2m4-2m7: 0-3 3m+: 0-1
Track: LH: 0-2 RH: 0-2 Tight: 0-3 Gall: 0-1
Aids: Bl: 0-0 Vi: 0-0 Tstrap: 0-0 Ckp: 0-0
Best Rating: 126 10/02 Kels 3m1f   gd-fm   Ch

Fair chaser/hurdler; effective at two and a half to three miles plus; good jumper and excelled himself when taking the Foxhunters' at Aintree in 2003; suited by fast ground; genuine sort.

Divine Mist (IRE)
94+

7-y-o br g Roselier (FR)-Tate Divinity (IRE) (Tate Gallery (USA))

Jonjo O'Neill Trevor Hemmings

Placings:00/20F-P   (1307)
2003/04: 24PGF,

	Starts	1st	2nd	3rd	Win & Pl
Hurdles	1	0	0	0	
Career Total	6	0	1	0	574

Going: Sf: 0-0 GS: 0-0 Gd: 0-0 GF: - Fm: 0-1
Distance: 2m/2m3: 0-0 2m4-2m7: 0-0 3m+: 0-1
Track: LH: 0-1 RH: 0-0 Tight: 0-0 Gall: 0-0
Aids: Bl: 0-0 Vi: 0-0 Tstrap: 0-0 Ckp: 0-0
Best Rating: 94 2/03 Extr 2m6f110y gd-sft Hdl

Runner-up in a bumper; no real form over hurdles so far; should stay three miles.

Divorce Action (IRE)
(75c)117

8-y-o b g Common Grounds-Overdue Reaction (Be My Guest (USA))
S R Bowring M T Hughes

Placings:26510/406/413456/53304-F   (1531)
2003/04: 17FGF,

	Starts	1st	2nd	3rd	Win & Pl
Hurdles	1	0	0	0	
Career Total	20	2	1	3	14204
117	7/01	Sthl	2m	D(0-120)HHdl	G-F	£5395
99	3/00	Newb	2m110y	D(0-120)HHdl	G-F	£5362
			Total win prize-money £10758			

Going: Sf: 0-0 GS: 0-0 Gd: 0-0 GF: - Fm: 0-0
Distance: 2m/2m3: 0-1 2m4-2m7: 0-0 3m+: 0-0
Track: LH: 0-0 RH: 0-1 Tight: 0-1 Gall: 0-0
Aids: Bl: 0-0 Vi: 0-0 Tstrap: 0-0 Ckp: 0-0
Best Rating: 117 7/01 Sthl 2m   gd-fm   Hdl

Fair handicap hurdler at the minimum trip on fast ground.

Divulge (USA)
103(81c)   (74c)90

7-y-o b g Diesis-Avira (Dancing Brave (USA))
A Crook Jay Dee Bloodstock Limited

Placings:000/03F6/FU425530-42520005   (1756)
2003/04: 16AG, 16QG, 19SG, 17FGF, 16QGF, 17QGF, 17QGF, 16AG,

	Starts	1st	2nd	3rd	Win & Pl
Hurdles	8	0	2	0	1382
Career Total	23	0	3	2	3366

Going: Sf: 0-0 GS: 0-0 Gd: 0-0 GF: - Fm: 0-4
Distance: 2m/2m3: 0-7 2m4-2m7: 0-1 3m+: 0-0
Track: LH: 0-4 RH: 0-4 Tight: 0-4 Gall: 0-1
Aids: Bl: 0-0 Vi: 0-3 Tstrap: 0-0 Ckp: 0-4
Best Rating: 91 11/01 Strf 2m110y   soft   Hdl

Frustrating plating-class hurdler/chaser who has let been down his jumping on early chasing starts; has worn visor.

Dix Bay
103(81c)   (76c)112

9-y-o b g Teenoso (USA)-Cooks Lawn (The Parson)
M W Easterby Lord Daresbury

Placings:042/1213/2061/U5P-P240   (4729)
2003/04: 20PS, 16QGS, 16AGS, 20QG,

	Starts	1st	2nd	3rd	Win & Pl
Hurdles	4	0	1	0	792

Career Total	18	3	4	1	13441
112 4/02 Weth	2m4f110yD(0-115)HHdl			G-F	£4277
106 1/01 Weth	2m4f110yD Hdl			G-S	£3759
108 10/00 MRas	2m1f110yH NHF			GD	£1554

Total win prize-money £9590

Going:	Sf: 0-1 GS: 0-2 Gd: 0-1 GF: - Fm: 0-0
Distance:	2m/2m3: 0-2 2m4-2m7: 0-2 3m+: 0-0
Track:	LH: 0-1 RH: 0-3 Tight: 0-0 Gall: 0-1
Aids:	Bl: 0-0 Vi: 0-0 Tstrap: 0-0 Ckp: 0-0
Best Rating:	112 2/04 Hntg 2m110y gd-sft Hdl

Modest hurdler; effective at up to two and a half miles; acts on most going; can go well fresh.

Dixcart Valley
94(101h)   (75h)65

8-y-o b g Carlingford Castle-Renshaw Wood (Ascertain (USA))

P Beaumont Mrs J M Plummer

Placings:PP5500P-6PP3P   (0977)

2003/04: 25RG, 26PG, 24PG, 17³GF, 21PGF,

	Starts	1st	2nd	3rd	Win & Pl
Chases	5	0	0	1	688
Career Total	12	0	0	1	688

Going:	Sf: 0-0 GS: 0-0 Gd: 0-3 GF: - Fm: 0-2
Distance:	2m/2m3: 0-1 2m4-2m7: 0-1 3m+: 0-3
Track:	LH: 0-4 RH: 0-1 Tight: 0-3 Gall: 0-0
Aids:	Bl: 0-1 Vi: 0-0 Tstrap: 0-0 Ckp: 0-0
Best Rating:	75 2/03 Catt 3m1f110y good Hdl

Poor novice hurdler/chaser.

Dixon Varner (IRE)

14-y-o b g Sheer Grit-Raise The Bells (Belfalas)

Mrs D M Grissell F Marshall

Placings:F/F1F1/1/P13/2-PP   (0352)

2003/04: 33PG, 31PGF,

	Starts	1st	2nd	3rd	Win & Pl
Chases	2	0	0	0	
Career Total	12	4	1	1	22321
128 2/99 Thur	3m	Ch		HVY	£3222
114 5/97 Kbgn	3m1f	Ch		GD	£2204
127 4/97 Punc	3m1f	Ch		GD	£12871
110 2/97 Thur	3m	Ch		SFT	£3391

Total win prize-money £21689

Going:	Sf: 0-0 GS: 0-0 Gd: 0-1 GF: - Fm: 0-1
Distance:	2m/2m3: 0-0 2m4-2m7: 0-0 3m+: 0-2
Track:	LH: 0-1 RH: 0-1 Tight: 0-1 Gall: 0-1
Aids:	Bl: 0-0 Vi: 0-0 Tstrap: 0-0 Ckp: 0-1
Best Rating:	128 2/99 Thur 3m heavy Ch

Dizzy Lad (IRE)
90   81

8-y-o b g Alphabatim (USA)-Court Session (Seymour Hicks (FR))

J S King Kingsbridge Racing Club

Placings:06/4-66P   (0833)

2003/04: 20RG, 22RG, 24PGF,

	Starts	1st	2nd	3rd	Win & Pl
Hurdles	3	0	0	0	
Career Total	6	0	0	0	268

Going:	Sf: 0-0 GS: 0-0 Gd: 0-0 GF: - Fm: 0-3
Distance:	2m/2m3: 0-0 2m4-2m7: 0-2 3m+: 0-1
Track:	LH: 0-3 RH: 0-0 Tight: 0-1 Gall: 0-0
Aids:	Bl: 0-0 Vi: 0-0 Tstrap: 0-0 Ckp: 0-0
Best Rating:	92 4/01 Font 2m2f110y good Hdl

Dizzy Tart (IRE)
104   102

5-y-o b m Definite Article-Tizzy (Formidable (USA))

Mrs P N Dutfield Darren C Mercer

Placings:23102035-32F   (2017)

2003/04: 16³GF, 17²GF, 22²GF,

	Starts	1st	2nd	3rd	Win & Pl
Hurdles	3	0	1	1	1610
Career Total	11	1	3	3	7813
85 9/02 Hntg	2m110y E Hdl			G-F	£3031

Total win prize-money £3031

Going:	Sf: 0-0 GS: 0-0 Gd: 0-0 GF: - Fm: 0-3
Distance:	2m/2m3: 0-0 2m4-2m7: 0-1 3m+: 0-0
Track:	LH: 0-1 RH: 0-2 Tight: 0-1 Gall: 0-0
Aids:	Bl: 0-0 Vi: 0-0 Tstrap: 0-0 Ckp: 0-0
Best Rating:	102 11/03 Winc 2m6f gd-fm Hdl

Plating-class hurdler, acts on a sound surface; effective at around two miles; usually held up.

Do It On Dani
110   (0c)116

9-y-o br m Weld-Dark City (Sweet Monday)

Mrs A M Thorpe Mrs A M Thorpe

Placings:34050/6042342/2312214110P64-4PP443103   (2001)

2003/04: 26⁴GF, 20²GF, 26PG, 27⁴GF, 24⁴G, 24³GF, 24¹GF, 21¹⁰GF, 24³GF,

	Starts	1st	2nd	3rd	Win & Pl
Hurdles	7	1	0	2	8548
Chases	2	0	0	0	0
Career Total	34	5	5	5	36422
116 10/03 Ludl	3m	D(0-125)HHdl	G-F	£4396
119 10/02 Plum	3m1f110yD(0-120)HHdl		GD	£4108
112 9/02 MRas	3m	C(0-135)HHdl	G-F	£8235
104 8/02 Uttx	3m110y E Hdl		G-F	£3328
95 6/02 NAbb	3m3f	C(0-130)HHdl	G-F	£5044

Total win prize-money £25113

Going:	Sf: 0-0 GS: 0-0 Gd: 0-0 GF: - Fm: 1-7
Distance:	2m/2m3: 0-0 2m4-2m7: 0-2 3m+: 1-7
Track:	LH: 0-6 RH: 1-4 Tight: 0-3 Gall: 0-3
Aids:	Bl: 0-0 Vi: 0-0 Tstrap: 0-0 Ckp: 0-0
Best Rating:	119 4/03 Aint 3m110y good Hdl

Fair hurdler; in good form in 2002 and shot up the ratings after four victories; returned to form when winning 3-runner Ludlow handicap October 2003; stays beyond 3m; acts on fast ground; consistent; pulled up both starts over fences.

Do L'Enfant D'Eau (FR)
105   134

5-y-o ch g Minds Music (USA)-L'Eau Sauvage (Saumarez)

P J Hobbs Terry Warner

Placings:3/3131431110-044   (2717)

2003/04: 16⁵G, 16⁴GS, 14GS, 4⁴GS,

	Starts	1st	2nd	3rd	Win & Pl
Hurdles	3	0	0	0	2295
Career Total	14	5	0	4	53374
134 3/03 Wwck	2m	B HHdl	GD	£17991
127 3/03 Newb	2m110y C(0-130)HHdl		SFT	£12272
119 2/03 Hrfd	2m1f	D(0-110)HHdl	GD	£4745
100 12/02 Folk	2m1f110yE Hdl		HVY	£3643
96 11/02 Hrfd	2m1f	E Hdl	SFT	£3475

Total win prize-money £42130

Going:	Sf: 0-0 GS: 0-2 Gd: 0-1 GF: - Fm: 1-0
Distance:	2m/2m3: 0-2 2m4-2m7: 0-1 3m+: 0-0
Track:	LH: 0-3 RH: 0-0 Tight: 0-0 Gall: 0-2
Aids:	Bl: 0-0 Vi: 0-0 Tstrap: 0-0 Ckp: 0-0
Best Rating:	134 12/03 Chel 2m5f gd-sft Hdl

Useful hurdler; French import; best at around two miles; effective in soft ground but handles good; genuine sort.

Doberman (IRE)
102(103h)   (100h)92

9-y-o br g Dilum (USA)-Switch Blade (IRE) (Robellino (USA))

P D Evans (W M Brisbourne 30/5) P D Evans

Placings:520/43-402331233334   (1799)

2003/04: 17⁴GS, 16⁹GF, 16²G, 16³GF, 16³GF, 18¹GF, 19²GF, 20³GF, 19³GF, 17³GF, 20³GF, 16⁴F,

	Starts	1st	2nd	3rd	Win & Pl
Hurdles	9	1	2	3	5694
Chases	3	0	0	3	2019
Career Total	17	1	3	7	9155
100 8/03 Font	2m2f110yG Hdl		G-F	£2359

Total win prize-money £2359

Going:	Sf: 0-0 GS: 0-1 Gd: 0-1 GF: - Fm: 1-10
Distance:	2m/2m3: 1-9 2m4-2m7: 0-3 3m+: 0-0
Track:	LH: 1-6 RH: 0-6 Tight: 1-5 Gall: 0-1
Aids:	Bl: 0-2 Vi: 1-8 Tstrap: 0-0 Ckp: 0-0
Best Rating:	100 9/03 Hrfd 2m3f110y gd-fm Hdl

Plating-class hurdler; respectable efforts on first two outings over fences without his usual visor but no sign of improvement when headgear refitted next time; a bit of a character; acts on most types of ground; best at around 2m.

Doce Vida (IRE)
100   102

6-y-o b m Montelimar (USA)-Miss The Post (Bustino)

A King Mrs R J Skan

Placings:521026   (4692)

2003/04: 16⁵G, 16²G, 16¹GS, 17⁰GS, 17²G, 17⁶G,

	Starts	1st	2nd	3rd	Win & Pl
NH Flat	2	0	1	0	996
Hurdles	4	1	1	0	5464
Career Total	6	1	2	0	6460
101 1/04 Weth	2m	E Hdl	G-S	£4420

Total win prize-money £4420

Going:	Sf: 0-0 GS: 1-2 Gd: 0-4 GF: - Fm: 0-0
Distance:	2m/2m3: 1-6 2m4-2m7: 0-0 3m+: 0-0
Track:	LH: 1-4 RH: 0-2 Tight: 0-1 Gall: 0-1
Aids:	Bl: 0-0 Vi: 0-0 Tstrap: 0-0 Ckp: 0-0
Best Rating:	102 3/04 Bang 2m1f good Hdl

Moderate novice hurdler; should stay beyond two miles; suited by give.

Doctor John
82   96

7-y-o ch g Handsome Sailor-Bollin Sophie (Efisio)

Andrew Turnell Dr John Hollowood

Placings:6/050-0PP0   (3527)

2003/04: 20⁰GS, 22PGS, 20PGS, 20⁰S,

	Starts	1st	2nd	3rd	Win & Pl
Hurdles	2	0	0	0	0

Chases	2	0	0	0	0
Career Total	8	0	0	0	0

Fair form in bumpers/hurdles; fair form in novice chases; off the mark at Catterick in March; jumps soundly; stays well.

Going:	Sf: 0-1 GS: 0-3 Gd: 0-0 GF: - Fm: 0-0
Distance:	2m/2m3: 0-2 2m4-2m7: 0-4 3m+: 0-0
Track:	LH: 0-2 RH: 0-2 Tight: 0-0 Gall: 0-0
Aids:	Bl: 0-0 Vi: 0-0 Tstrap: 0-0 Ckp: 0-0
Best Rating:	96 1/03 Donc 2m110y gd-sft Hdl

Plater on the Flat; moderate over hurdles; broke blood vessel on chase debut.

Dodger (IRE)

4-y-o b g Among Men (USA)-Hazy Image (Ahonoora)
Jamie Poulton Ormonde Racing

Placings:P					(1211)
2003/04: 18PGF,					
	Starts	1st	2nd	3rd	Win & Pl
Hurdles	1	0	0	0	0
Career Total	1	0	0	0	0

Going:	Sf: 0-0 GS: 0-0 Gd: 0-0 GF: - Fm: 0-1
Distance:	2m/2m3: 0-1 2m4-2m7: 0-0 3m+: 0-0
Track:	LH: 0-1 RH: 0-0 Tight: 0-1 Gall: 0-0
Aids:	Bl: 0-0 Vi: 0-0 Tstrap: 0-0 Ckp: 0-0

Dodger McCartney
71f   86f

6-y-o ch g Karinga Bay-Redgrave Girl (Deep Run)
K Bishop W O J Davies

Placings:2					(1728)
2003/04: 172GF,					
	Starts	1st	2nd	3rd	Win & Pl
NH Flat	1	0	1	0	678
Career Total	1	0	1	0	678

Going:	Sf: 0-0 GS: 0-0 Gd: 0-0 GF: - Fm: 0-1
Distance:	2m/2m3: 0-1 2m4-2m7: 0-0 3m+: 0-0
Track:	LH: 0-0 RH: 0-1 Tight: 0-0 Gall: 0-0
Aids:	Bl: 0-0 Vi: 0-0 Tstrap: 0-1 Ckp: 0-0
Best Rating:	86 10/03 Extr 2m1f gd-fm NHF

Out of a useful jumps mare; runner-up on debut in a bumper.

Doe Nal Rua (IRE)
100(105h)   (89h)110+

7-y-o b g Mister Lord (USA)-Phardante Girl (IRE) (Phardante (FR))
T D Easterby The G-Guck Group

Placings:30003-O0432331					(4259)
2003/04: 20OG, 20PHY, 234G, 242GS, 252S, 253HY, 223G, 251GF,					
	Starts	1st	2nd	3rd	Win & Pl
Hurdles	3	0	0	0	336
Chases	5	1	1	3	7687
Career Total	13	1	1	5	8894
110 3/04 Catt 3m1f110yE(0-100)HCh G-F £3997					
				Total win prize-money £3998	

Going:	Sf: 0-3 GS: 0-1 Gd: 0-3 GF: - Fm: 1-1
Distance:	2m/2m3: 0-0 2m4-2m7: 0-4 **3m+:** 1-3
Track:	**LH:** 1-7 RH: 0-1 **Tight:** 1-2 Gall: 0-1
Aids:	Bl: 0-0 Vi: 0-0 Tstrap: 0-0 Ckp: 0-0
Best Rating:	110 3/04 Catt 3m1f110y gd-fm Ch

Does It Matter
(59h)   (24h)

7-y-o b g Carlingford Castle-Flopsy Mopsy (Full Of Hope)
P C Ritchens John Pearl

Placings:000P-0560					(0614)
2003/04: 16OGS, 19SGF, 166GF, 16OGF,					
	Starts	1st	2nd	3rd	Win & Pl
Hurdles	1	0	0	0	0
Chases	3	0	0	0	0
Career Total	8	0	0	0	0

Going:	Sf: 0-0 GS: 0-1 Gd: 0-0 GF: - Fm: 0-3
Distance:	2m/2m3: 0-4 2m4-2m7: 0-0 3m+: 0-0
Track:	LH: 0-2 RH: 0-2 Tight: 0-0 Gall: 0-0
Aids:	Bl: 0-0 Vi: 0-0 Tstrap: 0-0 Ckp: 0-0
Best Rating:	62 7/02 Strf 2m110y gd-fm NHF

Doigts D'Or (FR)
98   90

9-y-o b g Sanglamore (USA)-Doigts De Fee (USA) (L'Emigrant (USA))
P R Webber Mrs Fiona Gregory

Placings:502/15040/5/44-53PP					(1105)
2003/04: 17OG, 163GF, 17PG, 17PGS,					
	Starts	1st	2nd	3rd	Win & Pl
Chases	4	0	0	1	776
Career Total	15	1	1	1	5191
110 11/99 Hntg 2m110y E Hdl GD £2635					
				Total win prize-money £2635	

Going:	Sf: 0-0 GS: 0-1 Gd: 0-2 GF: - Fm: 0-1
Distance:	2m/2m3: 0-4 2m4-2m7: 0-0 3m+: 0-0
Track:	LH: 0-3 RH: 0-1 Tight: 0-2 Gall: 0-0
Aids:	Bl: 0-0 Vi: 0-0 Tstrap: 0-0 Ckp: 0-0
Best Rating:	110 1/00 Kemp 2m good Hdl

Winning novice hurdler but poor novice chaser; best over two miles; acts on fast ground.

Doli Cygnus
84   72

6-y-o gr m Bedford (USA)-Damsong (Petong)
E L James Exors of the late Mrs D Hardy

Placings:53-000000					(4733)
2003/04: 16OS, 21OG, 16OG, 16OG, 19OG, 22OG,					
	Starts	1st	2nd	3rd	Win & Pl
NH Flat	1	0	0	0	0
Hurdles	5	0	0	0	0
Career Total	8	0	0	1	268

Going:	Sf: 0-1 GS: 0-0 Gd: 0-5 GF: - Fm: 0-0
Distance:	2m/2m3: 0-4 2m4-2m7: 0-2 3m+: 0-0
Track:	LH: 0-2 RH: 0-4 Tight: 0-1 Gall: 0-1
Aids:	Bl: 0-0 Vi: 0-0 Tstrap: 0-0 Ckp: 0-1
Best Rating:	95 11/02 Hrfd 2m1f soft NHF

Staying on well in bumpers on her first two runs.

Dolly Bell (IRE)

6-y-o b m Commanche Run-Rosey Park (Boreen (FR))

J G M O'Shea K W Bell & Son Ltd

Placings:000P					(4736)
2003/04: 16OS, 16OHY, 16OGS, 17PG,					
	Starts	1st	2nd	3rd	Win & Pl
NH Flat	3	0	0	0	0
Hurdles	1	0	0	0	0
Career Total	4	0	0	0	0

Going:	Sf: 0-2 GS: 0-1 Gd: 0-1 GF: - Fm: 0-0
Distance:	2m/2m3: 0-4 2m4-2m7: 0-0 3m+: 0-0
Track:	LH: 0-4 RH: 0-0 Tight: 0-0 Gall: 0-0
Aids:	Bl: 0-0 Vi: 0-0 Tstrap: 0-0 Ckp: 0-0
Best Rating:	62 3/04 Wwck 2m gd-sft NHF

Dolly Dove
61   41

9-y-o b m Gran Alba (USA)-Celtic Dove (Celtic Cone)
C J Price Ryan Price

Placings:00/00/00					(3467)
2003/04: 16OGS, 16OS,					
	Starts	1st	2nd	3rd	Win & Pl
Hurdles	2	0	0	0	0
Career Total	6	0	0	0	0

Going:	Sf: 0-1 GS: 0-1 Gd: 0-0 GF: - Fm: 0-0
Distance:	2m/2m3: 0-2 2m4-2m7: 0-3 3m+: 0-0
Track:	LH: 0-2 RH: 0-0 Tight: 0-0 Gall: 0-0
Aids:	Bl: 0-0 Vi: 0-0 Tstrap: 0-0 Ckp: 0-0
Best Rating:	41 7/01 Worc 2m4f good Hdl

Dolzago
62   9

4-y-o b g Pursuit Of Love-Doctor's Glory (USA) (Elmaamul (USA))
G L Moore (P W Harris 3/9) R Kiernan, Paul Chapman

Placings:0					(3422)
2003/04: 17OHY,					
	Starts	1st	2nd	3rd	Win & Pl
Hurdles	1	0	0	0	0
Career Total	1	0	0	0	0

Going:	Sf: 0-1 GS: 0-0 Gd: 0-0 GF: - Fm: 0-0
Distance:	2m/2m3: 0-1 2m4-2m7: 0-0 3m+: 0-0
Track:	LH: 0-0 RH: 0-1 Tight: 0-0 Gall: 0-0
Aids:	Bl: 0-0 Vi: 0-0 Tstrap: 0-0 Ckp: 0-0
Best Rating:	9 1/04 Folk 2m1f110y heavy Hdl

Dom D'Orgeval (FR)
78   68

4-y-o b g Belmez (USA)-Marie D'Orgeval (FR) (Bourbon (FR))
Nick Williams Mrs Jane Williams

Placings:00060					(3224)
2003/04: 12OGF, 12OS, 16OG, 16OS, 17OGS,					
	Starts	1st	2nd	3rd	Win & Pl
NH Flat	2	0	0	0	0
Hurdles	3	0	0	0	495
Career Total	5	0	0	0	495

Going:	Sf: 0-2 GS: 0-1 Gd: 0-1 GF: - Fm: 0-1
Distance:	2m/2m3: 0-3 2m4-2m7: 0-0 3m+: 0-0
Track:	LH: 0-2 RH: 0-2 Tight: 0-0 Gall: 0-0

Aids: Bl: 0-0 Vi: 0-0 Tstrap: 0-0 Ckp: 0-0
Best Rating: 68 12/03 Chep 2m110y soft Hdl

Little ability shown in two bumpers and one outing over hurdles to date.

Dom Shadeed

57

9-y-o b g Shadeed (USA)-Fair Dominion (Dominion)
R J Baker Graham Brown

Placings:60/0R-0   (0245)
2003/04: 17³GF,

	Starts	1st	2nd	3rd	Win & Pl
Hurdles	1	0	0	0	
Career Total	5	0	0	0	0

Going: Sf: 0-0 GS: 0-0 Gd: 0-0 GF: - Fm: 0-1
Distance: 2m/2m3: 0-1 2m4-2m7: 0-0 3m+: 0-0
Track: LH: 0-0 RH: 0-1 Tight: 0-0 Gall: 0-0
Aids: Bl: 0-0 Vi: 0-0 Tstrap: 0-0 Ckp: 0-0
Best Rating: 61 9/99 Tntn 2m3f110y gd-fm Hdl

Domenico (IRE)

105   123

6-y-o b g Sadler's Wells (USA)-Russian Ballet (USA) (Nijinsky (CAN))
J R Jenkins American Horse Racing Club Ltd

Placings:02/1535-1012635F0   (2686)
2003/04: 17¹GS, 20⁰GF, 17¹GF, 16²GF, 16⁶F, 16³GF, 16⁵G, 19³GF, 16⁹GS,

	Starts	1st	2nd	3rd	Win & Pl
Hurdles	9	2	1	1	14749
Career Total	15	3	2	2	20326
118 9/03 Sthl	2m1f	D(0-115)HHdl		G-F	£3393
110 8/03 Sthl	2m1f	D(0-125)HHdl		G-S	£5018
114 11/02 Uttx	2m	E Hdl		SFT	£3643
		Total win prize-money £12055			

Going: Sf: 0-0 GS: 1-2 Gd: 0-1 GF: - Fm: 1-6
Distance: **2m/2m3: 2-8** 2m4-2m7: 0-1 3m+: 0-0
Track: **LH: 2-6** RH: 0-3 Tight: 0-1 Gall: 0-2
Aids: Bl: 0-0 Vi: 0-0 Tstrap: 0-0 Ckp: 0-0
Best Rating: 123 9/03 Plum 2m gd-fm Hdl

Fair hurdler; best at around two miles; effective on easy ground, but handles faster; has won only two starts at Southwell.

Dominican Monk (IRE)

107f   105f

5-y-o b g Lord Americo-Ballyveg Katie (IRE) (Roselier (FR))
C Tinkler (A J Lidderdale 21/5) George Ward

Placings:3164   (4594)
2003/04: 16³G, 16¹GF, 16⁶G, 16⁴G,

	Starts	1st	2nd	3rd	Win & Pl
NH Flat	4	1	0	1	2991
Career Total	4	1	0	1	2991
105 12/03 Ludl	2m	H NHF		G-F	£2723
		Total win prize-money £2723			

Going: Sf: 0-0 GS: 0-0 Gd: 0-3 GF: - Fm: 1-1
Distance: **2m/2m3: 1-4** 2m4-2m7: 0-0 3m+: 0-0
Track: LH: 0-1 **RH: 1-3** Tight: 0-0 Gall: 0-1
Aids: Bl: 0-0 Vi: 0-0 Tstrap: 0-0 Ckp: 0-0
Best Rating: 105 2/04 Winc 2m good NHF

Out of a sister to The Grey Monk; swerved badly left when third on debut in Worcester bumper; won next time at Ludlow.

Dominikus

109   (105h)125

7-y-o b g Second Set (IRE)-Dolce Vita (GER) (Windwurf (GER))
Ferdy Murphy The Aarons Archer Partnership

Placings:405/116066420/5212-532145   (4834)
2003/04: 16⁵G, 24³G, 20²G, 24¹G, 24⁴G, 26⁵GF,

	Starts	1st	2nd	3rd	Win & Pl
Chases	6	1	1	1	23992
Career Total	22	4	4	1	37263
125 6/03 Prth	3m	B(0-140)HCh	GD	£18739
106 7/02 MRas	2m4f	E Ch	GD	£3997
89 6/01 Hexm	2m	D Hdl	GD	£3353
89 5/01 Hexm	2m	F(0-95)HHdl	FRM	£2017
		Total win prize-money £28108		

Going: Sf: 0-0 GS: 0-0 Gd: 1-5 GF: - Fm: 0-1
Distance: 2m/2m3: 0-1 2m4-2m7: 0-1 **3m+: 1-4**
Track: LH: 0-4 RH: 0-0 Tight: 0-0 Gall: 0-0
Aids: Bl: 0-0 Vi: 0-0 Tstrap: 0-0 Ckp: 0-0
Best Rating: 125 6/03 Prth 3m good Ch

Fair chaser; good fourth in Kim Muir at Festival on first start since June; stays three miles; acts on fast ground.

Domquista D'Or

98   66

7-y-o b g Superpower-Gild The Lily (Ile De Bourbon (USA))
G A Ham Colin B Taylor

Placings:P0653035/P032PP50-6F   (0069)
2003/04: 20⁶S, 16⁶G,

	Starts	1st	2nd	3rd	Win & Pl
Hurdles	2	0	0	0	0
Career Total	18	0	1	3	1788

Going: Sf: 0-1 GS: 0-0 Gd: 0-1 GF: - Fm: 0-0
Distance: 2m/2m3: 0-1 2m4-2m7: 0-1 3m+: 0-0
Track: LH: 0-2 RH: 0-0 Tight: 0-0 Gall: 0-0
Aids: Bl: 0-0 Vi: 0-0 Tstrap: 0-0 Ckp: 0-0
Best Rating: 82 4/02 Wwck 2m gd-fm Hdl

Don Fayruz (IRE)

12-y-o b g Fayruz-Gobolino (Don)
B N Doran (Mrs A J Bowlby 11/7) J A Danahar

Placings:1265/P0/P   (3081)
2003/04: 16⁶GS,

	Starts	1st	2nd	3rd	Win & Pl
Hurdles	1	0	0	0	
Career Total	7	1	1	0	3080
108 10/98 Winc	2m	E Hdl	G-S	£1730
		Total win prize-money £1730		

Going: Sf: 0-0 GS: 0-1 Gd: 0-0 GF: - Fm: 0-0
Distance: 2m/2m3: 0-1 2m4-2m7: 0-0 3m+: 0-0
Track: LH: 0-1 RH: 0-0 Tight: 0-1 Gall: 0-0
Aids: Bl: 0-0 Vi: 0-0 Tstrap: 0-0 Ckp: 0-0
Best Rating: 110 11/98 Wwck 2m soft Hdl

Don Fernando

104(103h)   (133 h)121+

5-y-o b h Zilzal (USA)-Teulada (USA) (Riverman (USA))

M C Pipe Lucayan Stud

Placings:112B0-33215   (4427)
2003/04: 17³GF, 16³GF, 19²S, 20¹G, 21⁵G,

	Starts	1st	2nd	3rd	Win & Pl
Hurdles	2	0	0	2	4319
Chases	3	1	1	0	10994
Career Total	10	3	2	2	43039
116 3/04 Plum	2m4f	D Ch	GD	£6873
136 12/02 Chel	2m1f	A Hdl	GD	£11600
127 11/02 Chel	2m110y	B Hdl	G-S	£9526
		Total win prize-money £28000		

Going: Sf: 0-1 GS: 0-0 Gd: 1-2 GF: - Fm: 0-2
Distance: 2m/2m3: 0-3 **2m4-2m7: 1-2** 3m+: 0-0
Track: LH: 1-5 RH: 0-0 Tight: 1-2 Gall: 0-1
Aids: Bl: 0-0 Vi: 0-0 Tstrap: 0-0 Ckp: 0-0
Best Rating: 136 8/03 NAbb 2m1f gd-fm Hdl

Fair novice chaser/useful hurdler; stays 2m 4f; acts well with cut in the ground; has worn a visor.

Don Ido (ARG)

89

8-y-o b g Lazy Boy (ARG)-She's Goy You (ARG) (Indalecio (ARG))
J A B Old Mrs Janet Dacey

Placings:U/435-PPP   (2710)
2003/04: 16⁶G, 16⁶G, 16⁶GS,

	Starts	1st	2nd	3rd	Win & Pl
Hurdles	3	0	0	0	
Career Total	7	0	0	1	1009

Going: Sf: 0-0 GS: 0-1 Gd: 0-2 GF: - Fm: 0-0
Distance: 2m/2m3: 0-3 2m4-2m7: 0-0 3m+: 0-0
Track: LH: 0-3 RH: 0-0 Tight: 0-1 Gall: 0-1
Aids: Bl: 0-0 Vi: 0-0 Tstrap: 0-0 Ckp: 0-0
Best Rating: 89 10/02 Chel 2m110y gd-fm Hdl

Don Royal

10-y-o b g Rakaposhi King-Donna Farina (Little Buskins)
J R Scott G T Lever

Placings:3PP4-335   (4563)
2003/04: 26⁴G, 21³G, 24³G, 22⁵G,

	Starts	1st	2nd	3rd	Win & Pl
Chases	4	0	0	2	971
Career Total	7	0	0	3	1399

Going: Sf: 0-1 GS: 0-0 Gd: 0-3 GF: - Fm: 0-0
Distance: 2m/2m3: 0-0 2m4-2m7: 0-2 3m+: 0-2
Track: LH: 0-4 RH: 0-0 Tight: 0-2 Gall: 0-1
Aids: Bl: 0-0 Vi: 0-0 Tstrap: 0-0 Ckp: 0-0
Best Rating: 95 3/04 Strf 3m good Ch

Winning pointer; seems to act on most types of ground;

Don Rubini

6-y-o b g Emarati (USA)-Emerald Ring (Auction Ring (USA))
W K Goldsworthy Mrs L A Goldsworthy

Placings:F   (0033)
2003/04: 16⁶G,

	Starts	1st	2nd	3rd	Win & Pl
Chases	1	0	0	0	
Career Total	1	0	0	0	

Going:	Sf: 0-0 GS: 0-0 Gd: 0-1 GF: - Fm: 0-0
Distance:	2m/2m3: 0-1 2m4-2m7: 0-0 3m+: 0-0
Track:	LH: 0-1 RH: 0-0 Tight: 0-0 Gall: 0-1
Aids:	Bl: 0-0 Vi: 0-0 Tstrap: 0-1 Ckp: 0-0

Don Valentino (POL)
98   110
5-y-o ch g Duke Valentino-Dona (POL) (Dakota)
T R George Sir Stanley Clarke

Placings:0-14120   (3483)
2003/04: 16¹GF, 16⁴GS, 16¹GS, 18²G, 17⁰GS,

	Starts	1st	2nd	3rd	Win & Pl
Hurdles	5	2	1	0	7282
Career Total	6	2	1	0	7282
105	12/03	Donc	2m110y E(0-100)HHdl	G-S	£2275
82	11/03	Hayd	2m	D Hdl	G-F	£3888

Total win prize-money £6164

Going:	Sf: 0-0 GS: 1-3 Gd: 0-1 GF: - Fm: 1-1
Distance:	2m/2m3: 2-5 2m4-2m7: 0-0 3m+: 0-0
Track:	LH: 2-5 RH: 0-1 Tight: 0-1 Gall: 1-2
Aids:	Bl: 0-0 Vi: 0-0 Tstrap: 0-0 Ckp: 0-0
Best Rating:	110 12/03 Font 2m2f110y good Hdl

Modest hurdler; best at around two miles; effective in softish ground.

Don't Sioux Me (IRE)
111   120
6-y-o b g Sadler's Wells (USA)-Commanche Belle (Shirley Heights)
C R Dore L Cohen

Placings:623-2321411530056F20   (4628)
2003/04: 17²GS, 19³G, 17²GF, 16¹GF, 17⁴GF, 17¹GF, 17¹GS, 16⁵GF, 16³GF, 16⁰GS, 16⁰GS, 17⁵G, 17⁵GS, 16⁵GF, 16²GS, 16⁰GS,

	Starts	1st	2nd	3rd	Win & Pl
Hurdles	16	3	3	2	21649
Career Total	19	3	4	3	23312
109	8/03	Sthl	2m1f	E Hdl	G-S	£3416
120	8/03	MRas	2m1f110yD Hdl	G-F	£4823
115	6/03	Hexm	2m110y E Hdl	G-F	£3402

Total win prize-money £11641

Going:	Sf: 0-0 GS: 1-6 Gd: 0-3 GF: - Fm: 2-7
Distance:	2m/2m3: 3-14 2m4-2m7: 0-2 3m+: 0-0
Track:	LH: 2-8 RH: 1-8 Tight: 1-6 Gall: 0-4
Aids:	Bl: 0-0 Vi: 0-0 Tstrap: 3-13 Ckp: 0-0
Best Rating:	120 1/04 Chel 2m1f gd-sft Hdl

Modest hurdler, likes to front run; effective over two miles and handles most types of ground; often tongue tied; consistent.

Donadino (IRE)
97(97h)   (98h)93
11-y-o br br g Be My Native (USA)-Atteses (Smooth Stepper)
Jonjo O'Neill John P McManus

Placings:25/20F14/31313/B143/1FU06B/3P103-6 (0215)
2003/04: 20⁶G,

	Starts	1st	2nd	3rd	Win & Pl
Chases	1	0	0	0	
Career Total	28	6	2	6	49595
122	8/02	Gway	2m1f	HCh	YLD	£14355
120	5/01	Rosc	2m5f	Ch	G-F	£7862
110	6/00	Rosc	2m	Hdl	GD	£3864
97	3/00	Naas	2m	Ch	Y-S	£4736
123	9/99	Baln	2m1f	Ch	G-F	£6160

117 3/99 Leop 2m   Hdl   YLD £3069
Total win prize-money £40049

Going:	Sf: 0-0 GS: 0-0 Gd: 0-1 GF: - Fm: 0-0
Distance:	2m/2m3: 0-0 2m4-2m7: 0-1 3m+: 0-0
Track:	LH: 0-1 RH: 0-0 Tight: 0-0 Gall: 0-0
Aids:	Bl: 0-0 Vi: 0-0 Tstrap: 0-0 Ckp: 0-0
Best Rating:	130 5/00 Punc 2m gd-fm Ch

Fair chaser at around two and a half miles, suited by fast ground but acts on softer.

Donatus (IRE)
92   103
8-y-o b g Royal Academy (USA)-La Dame Du Lac (USA) (Round Table)
Miss K M George Stableline

Placings:22240/41P/0SPP3F/2463P-P0P0F050   (4898)
2003/04: 19⁵GS, 17⁰G, 16⁴PS, 16⁵G, 17⁴GS, 17⁵G, 16⁰G,

	Starts	1st	2nd	3rd	Win & Pl
Hurdles	8	0	0	0	0
Career Total	27	1	4	2	10377
111	10/00	Fknm	2m4f	D Hdl	GD	£2990

Total win prize-money £2990

Going:	Sf: 0-1 GS: 0-2 Gd: 0-5 GF: - Fm: 0-0
Distance:	2m/2m3: 0-6 2m4-2m7: 0-2 3m+: 0-0
Track:	LH: 0-0 RH: 0-8 Tight: 0-2 Gall: 0-1
Aids:	Bl: 0-0 Vi: 0-0 Tstrap: 0-0 Ckp: 0-5
Best Rating:	130 3/00 Chel 2m1f gd-fm Hdl

Frustrating sort over hurdles, often there or thereabouts but on a long losing run. Still better than he was on the Flat.

Donegal Shore (IRE)
89   72
5-y-o b h Mujadil (USA)-Distant Shore (IRE) (Jareer (USA))
Mrs J Candlish Racing For You Limited

Placings:000P-4040   (1217)
2003/04: 16⁴G, 16⁰G, 20⁴GF, 16⁰GF,

	Starts	1st	2nd	3rd	Win & Pl
Hurdles	4	0	0	0	286
Career Total	8	0	0	0	286

Going:	Sf: 0-0 GS: 0-0 Gd: 0-2 GF: - Fm: 0-2
Distance:	2m/2m3: 0-3 2m4-2m7: 0-1 3m+: 0-0
Track:	LH: 0-2 RH: 0-2 Tight: 0-0 Gall: 0-1
Aids:	Bl: 0-0 Vi: 0-0 Tstrap: 0-2 Ckp: 0-0
Best Rating:	73 8/03 Hntg 2m110y gd-fm Hdl

Donie Dooley (IRE)
95   91+
6-y-o ch g Be My Native (USA)-Bridgeofallen (IRE) (Torus)
P T Dalton Mrs Julie Martin

Placings:43/0-0F510   (2838)
2003/04: 16⁶S, 20⁴S, 16⁵GF, 20¹GF, 20⁰GS,

	Starts	1st	2nd	3rd	Win & Pl
NH Flat	1	0	0	0	0
Hurdles	4	1	0	0	5285
Career Total	8	1	0	1	7137
93	6/03	Uttx	2m4f110yD Hdl	G-F	£5284

Total win prize-money £5285

Going:	Sf: 0-2 GS: 0-1 Gd: 0-0 GF: - Fm: 1-2
Distance:	2m/2m3: 0-2 2m4-2m7: 1-3 3m+: 0-0
Track:	LH: 1-5 RH: 0-0 Tight: 0-0 Gall: 0-0
Aids:	Bl: 0-0 Vi: 0-0 Tstrap: 0-0 Ckp: 0-0
Best Rating:	93 6/03 Uttx 2m4f110y gd-fm Hdl

Moderate novice hurdler; ex-Irish'; won at Uttoxeter in June; stays 2m 4f; acts on fast ground.

Donnegale (IRE)
12-y-o b g Strong Gale-Marys Gift (Monksfield)
Miss J E Foster Miss J E Foster

Placings:60406/4/P31140/1P/F0123/PP142430P/3 (0475)
2003/04: 26³GS,

	Starts	1st	2nd	3rd	Win & Pl
Chases	1	0	0	1	338
Career Total	29	5	2	4	20127
95	10/01	Sedg	3m3f	F(0-100)HCh	G-S	£3626
107	2/01	Catt	3m1f110yE(0-115)HHdl	SFT	£5307
93	3/00	Catt	3m1f110yH Ch	G-F	£1553
101	2/99	Catt	3m1f110y(0-105)HHdl	GD	£2444
89	12/98	Sedg	3m3f110yE Hdl	GD	£2460

Total win prize-money £15391

Going:	Sf: 0-0 GS: 0-1 Gd: 0-0 GF: - Fm: 0-0
Distance:	2m/2m3: 0-0 2m4-2m7: 0-0 3m+: 0-1
Track:	LH: 0-1 RH: 0-0 Tight: 0-1 Gall: 0-0
Aids:	Bl: 0-0 Vi: 0-0 Tstrap: 0-0 Ckp: 0-1
Best Rating:	107 4/01 Muss 3m gd-fm Hdl

Hunter chaser; formerly a moderate chaser; his jumping is not always up to scratch; acts on a soft surface.

Donny Bowling
94   82
4-y-o b f Sesaro (USA)-Breakfast Creek (Hallgate)
M E Sowersby M E Sowersby

Placings:4P404P0P540   (4958)
2003/04: 17⁴GF, 16⁰GF, 16⁴G, 16⁰GS, 16⁴GS, 16⁰G, 16⁰G, 17⁰G, 17⁰S, 17⁰G,

	Starts	1st	2nd	3rd	Win & Pl
Hurdles	11	0	0	0	645
Career Total	11	0	0	0	645

Going:	Sf: 0-1 GS: 0-2 Gd: 0-6 GF: - Fm: 0-2
Distance:	2m/2m3: 0-0 2m4-2m7: 0-0 3m+: 0-0
Track:	LH: 0-5 RH: 0-6 Tight: 0-8 Gall: 0-0
Aids:	Bl: 0-0 Vi: 0-0 Tstrap: 0-0 Ckp: 0-0
Best Rating:	69 3/04 MRas 2m1f110y good Hdl

Donnybrook (IRE)
91   116
11-y-o ch g Riot Helmet-Evening Bun (Baragoi)
R D E Woodhouse R D E Woodhouse

Placings:00/433P042/151144300/3221315/P40240/503403
410/04514404-PP50P40   (4941)
2003/04: 22⁵G, 20⁵G, 20⁵G, 20⁰G, 24⁵GS, 24⁴G, 31⁹GS,

	Starts	1st	2nd	3rd	Win & Pl
Chases	7	0	0	0	518
Career Total	55	7	4	7	56832
116	11/02	Hayd	2m4f	D(0-125)HCh	GD	£4803
116	3/02	Newc	2m110y	D(0-125)HCh	HVY	£4728
121	1/00	Newc	2m	A Ch	SFT	£19500
115	12/99	Uttx	2m	D Ch	SFT	£4182
102	10/98	Weth	2m	E(0-105)HHdl	SFT	£3745
93	10/98	MRas	2m3f110yE Hdl	SFT	£2845
95	5/98	Hexm	2m	E Hdl	GD	£2033

Total win prize-money £41269

Going:	Sf: 0-0 GS: 0-2 Gd: 0-5 GF: - Fm: 0-0
Distance:	2m/2m3: 0-0 2m4-2m7: 0-4 3m+: 0-3
Track:	LH: 0-5 RH: 0-1 Tight: 0-3 Gall: 0-0
Aids:	Bl: 0-0 Vi: 0-0 Tstrap: 0-0 Ckp: 0-1

Best Rating: 121 1/00 Newc 2m4f soft Ch

Fair handicap chaser; jumps well; best on soft ground; stays three miles; by no means consistent.

Donovan (NZ)
97 79

5-y-o b g Stark South (USA)-Agent Jane (NZ) (Sound Reason (CAN))
R C Guest Concertina Racing Too

Placings: 5060P0PP00 (4690)
2003/04: 16⁵GF, 17⁰GF, 17⁶GF, 20⁰G, 20⁶G, 16⁰S, 16⁶GS, 22⁸GS, 19⁰GF, 22⁰G,

	Starts	1st	2nd	3rd	Win & Pl
NH Flat	3	0	0	0	0
Hurdles	6	0	0	0	0
Chases	1	0	0	0	0
Career Total	10	0	0	0	0

Going: Sf: 0-1 GS: 0-2 Gd: 0-3 GF: - Fm: 0-4
Distance: 2m/2m3: 0-6 2m4-2m7: 0-4 3m+: 0-0
Track: LH: 0-7 RH: 0-3 Tight: 0-6 Gall: 0-0
Aids: Bl: 0-0 Vi: 0-0 Tstrap: 0-0 Ckp: 0-2
Best Rating: 86 10/03 Carl 2m1f gd-fm NHF

Dooberry Firkin
68 49

6-y-o b m Presenting-Shipley Bridge (Town And Country)
Mrs S Gardner S Osborne

Placings: 360650 (3320)
2003/04: 16³GF, 16⁶G, 20⁹GS, 24⁶S, 19⁵S, 16⁰S,

	Starts	1st	2nd	3rd	Win & Pl
NH Flat	2	0	0	1	818
Hurdles	4	0	0	0	0
Career Total	6	0	0	1	818

Going: Sf: 0-3 GS: 0-1 Gd: 0-1 GF: - Fm: 0-1
Distance: 2m/2m3: 0-4 2m4-2m7: 0-1 3m+: 0-1
Track: LH: 0-2 RH: 0-4 Tight: 0-0 Gall: 0-0
Aids: Bl: 0-0 Vi: 0-0 Tstrap: 0-0 Ckp: 0-0
Best Rating: 92 11/03 Chel 2m110y good NHF

Dooley Gate

7-y-o b g Petoski-High 'B' (Gunner B)
F P Murtagh F P Murtagh

Placings: 0-P (2903)
2003/04: 20⁰S,

	Starts	1st	2nd	3rd	Win & Pl
Hurdles	1	0	0	0	0
Career Total	2	0	0	0	0

Going: Sf: 0-1 GS: 0-0 Gd: 0-0 GF: - Fm: 0-0
Distance: 2m/2m3: 0-0 2m4-2m7: 0-1 3m+: 0-0
Track: LH: 0-1 RH: 0-0 Tight: 0-0 Gall: 0-0
Aids: Bl: 0-0 Vi: 0-0 Tstrap: 0-0 Ckp: 0-0
Best Rating: 58 12/02 Newc 2m soft NHF

Door Of Knowledge (USA)
94 90+

4-y-o b/br g Theatrical-Mynador (USA) (Forty Niner (USA))

M F Harris (D K Weld 7/9) M Harris

Placings: 3545P500 (4444)
2003/04: 16³GF, 16⁵GF, 16⁴G, 16⁵S, 16⁸G, 16⁵G, 16⁰G, 16⁰S,

	Starts	1st	2nd	3rd	Win & Pl
Hurdles	8	0	0	1	1530
Career Total	8	0	0	1	1530

Going: Sf: 0-2 GS: 0-0 Gd: 0-4 GF: - Fm: 0-2
Distance: 2m/2m3: 0-8 2m4-2m7: 0-0 3m+: 0-0
Track: LH: 0-6 RH: 0-2 Tight: 0-1 Gall: 0-0
Aids: Bl: 0-7 Vi: 0-0 Tstrap: 0-7 Ckp: 0-0
Best Rating: 85 11/03 Asct 2m10y soft Hdl

Modest juvenile hurdler; Flat winner in Ireland; often wears blinkers and has been tongue tied; best form is on fast ground.

Dorans Gold
(94h) (81h)133

10-y-o b g Gildoran-Cindie Girl (Orchestra)
Miss Venetia Williams (P F Nicholls 13/6) D E Harrison

Placings: 2/1P50/11F2F42/12P/1P120-4F6UPP (4726)
2003/04: 20⁴S, 20⁰G, 22⁶GF, 24⁰GS, 20⁰GS, 24⁰G,

	Starts	1st	2nd	3rd	Win & Pl
Hurdles	1	0	0	0	0
Chases	5	0	0	0	639
Career Total	26	6	5	0	82435
133	12/02	Wwck	2m4f110y	C(0-130)	HCh	G-S	£11235
130	10/02	Bang	2m4f110y	D(0-125)	HCh	SFT	£6727
124	7/01	MRas	2m4f	B(0-140)	HCh	G-S	£37297
118	10/00	Hntg	2m4f110y	E	Ch	G-F	£2951
103	5/00	Extr	2m3f	E(0-105)	HCh	GD	£3136
112	11/99	Aint	2m110y	D	Hdl	GD	£3993
			Total win prize-money £65341				

Going: Sf: 0-1 GS: 0-2 Gd: 0-2 GF: - Fm: 0-1
Distance: 2m/2m3: 0-0 2m4-2m7: 0-4 3m+: 0-2
Track: LH: 0-4 RH: 0-2 Tight: 0-3 Gall: 0-0
Aids: Bl: 0-1 Vi: 0-0 Tstrap: 0-0 Ckp: 0-0
Best Rating: 133 12/02 Wwck 2m4f110y gd-sft Ch

Fair chaser; previously with Paul Nicholls; best over two and a half miles; suited by soft ground.

Dorans Magic

9-y-o b g Gildoran-Mearlin (Giolla Mear)
Miss A Armitage N W A Bannister

Placings: 64/02241/054102P/2F (4949)
2003/04: 25²G, 26⁴GS,

	Starts	1st	2nd	3rd	Win & Pl
Chases	2	0	1	0	892
Career Total	16	2	4	0	12607
109	2/02	Wwck	2m4f110y	D	Ch	HVY	£4069
114	4/01	Hayd	2m6f	D	Hdl	SFT	£3877
			Total win prize-money £7946				

Going: Sf: 0-0 GS: 0-1 Gd: 0-1 GF: - Fm: 0-0
Distance: 2m/2m3: 0-0 2m4-2m7: 0-0 3m+: 0-2
Track: LH: 0-1 RH: 0-0 Tight: 0-1 Gall: 0-0
Aids: Bl: 0-0 Vi: 0-0 Tstrap: 0-0 Ckp: 0-0
Best Rating: 114 4/01 Hayd 2m6f soft Hdl

Modest hunter chaser; formerly useful hurdler; stays three miles; acts well on decent ground.

Dormy Two (IRE)
98 79

4-y-o b f Eagle Eyed (USA)-Tartan Lady (IRE) (Taufan (USA))

J S Wainwright (Mrs P N Dutfield 6/10) Anthony D Copley

Placings: 563035 (4795)
2003/04: 16⁵GS, 16⁶GS, 16³GS, 17⁰G, 17³G, 17⁵G,

	Starts	1st	2nd	3rd	Win & Pl
Hurdles	6	0	0	2	1511
Career Total	6	0	0	2	1511

Going: Sf: 0-0 GS: 0-3 Gd: 0-3 GF: - Fm: 0-0
Distance: 2m/2m3: 0-6 2m4-2m7: 0-0 3m+: 0-0
Track: LH: 0-4 RH: 0-2 Tight: 0-4 Gall: 0-0
Aids: Bl: 0-0 Vi: 0-0 Tstrap: 0-0 Ckp: 0-2
Best Rating: 79 3/04 MRas 2m1f110y good Hdl

Maiden on the Flat; modest form in juvenile hurdles.

Dorooss (IRE)
98f 81f

4-y-o b g Charnwood Forest (IRE)-Catherinofaragon (USA) (Chief's Crown (USA))
Ian Williams C N Barnes

Placings: 0 (4447)
2003/04: 16⁰S,

	Starts	1st	2nd	3rd	Win & Pl
NH Flat	1	0	0	0	
Career Total	1	0	0	0	

Going: Sf: 0-1 GS: 0-0 Gd: 0-0 GF: - Fm: 0-0
Distance: 2m/2m3: 0-1 2m4-2m7: 0-0 3m+: 0-0
Track: LH: 0-1 RH: 0-0 Tight: 0-0 Gall: 0-0
Aids: Bl: 0-0 Vi: 0-0 Tstrap: 0-0 Ckp: 0-0
Best Rating: 81 3/04 Wwck 2m soft NHF

Dorset Fern (IRE)
(92c) (47c)76

8-y-o b m Tirol-La Duse (Junius (USA))
J K Price J K Price

Placings: 060/00/00000003UP0/P203004-P0 (1231)
2003/04: 22⁸GF, 17⁰GF,

	Starts	1st	2nd	3rd	Win & Pl
Hurdles	1	0	0	0	0
Chases	1	0	0	0	0
Career Total	25	0	1	2	1428

Going: Sf: 0-0 GS: 0-0 Gd: 0-0 GF: - Fm: 0-2
Distance: 2m/2m3: 0-1 2m4-2m7: 0-1 3m+: 0-0
Track: LH: 0-1 RH: 0-0 Tight: 0-1 Gall: 0-0
Aids: Bl: 0-1 Vi: 0-0 Tstrap: 0-0 Ckp: 0-0
Best Rating: 76 12/02 Tntn 2m3f110y gd-sft Hdl

Dottie Digger (IRE)
93 68

5-y-o b m Catrail (USA)-Hint-Of-Romance (IRE) (Treasure Kay)
Miss Lucinda V Russell Dig In Racing

Placings: 00B6P-50014P (2511)
2003/04: 16⁵S, 16⁰GF, 16⁰G, 16¹G, 16⁴G, 18⁰S,

	Starts	1st	2nd	3rd	Win & Pl
Hurdles	6	1	0	0	2940
Career Total	11	1	0	0	2940
70	11/03	Kels	2m110y	G	Hdl	GD	£2660
			Total win prize-money £2660				

Going: Sf: 0-1 GS: 0-0 Gd: 1-4 GF: - Fm: 0-1
Distance: 2m/2m3: 1-6 2m4-2m7: 0-0 3m+: 0-0

Track: LH: 1-3 RH: 0-3 **Tight:** 1-3 Gall: 0-0
Aids: Bl: 0-0 Vi: 1-6 Tstrap: 0-0 Ckp: 0-0
Best Rating: 70 11/03 Kels 2m110y good Hdl

Poor hurdler who won very weak seller over two miles at Kelso in November when making all the running; should stay further.

Double Account (FR)

109   (112b)**122**

9-y-o b g Sillery (USA)-Fabulous Account (USA) (Private Account (USA))
C J Mann M J & C G Cruddace

Placings:3/120500165/3024040/103321/105-15   (2708)
2003/04: 26¹GF, 25⁵G,

	Starts	1st	2nd	3rd	Win & Pl
Hurdles	2	1	0	0	7323
Career Total	28	6	3	4	47501
122 5/03 Hntg	3m2f	C(0-130)HHdl		G-F	£6825
119 2/03 Kemp	2m2f	C(0-130)HHdl		GD	£13340
96 5/01 Clon	2m2f	Ch		GD	£5286
108 1/00 Punc	2m	(0-137)HHdl		Y-S	£4968
104 5/99 Navn	2m	Hdl		GD	£5524
			Total win prize-money £35944		

Going: Sf: 0-0 GS: 0-0 Gd: 0-1 GF: - Fm: 1-1
Distance: 2m/2m3: 0-0 2m4-2m7: 0-0 3m+: 1-2
Track: LH: 0-0 RH: 1-1 **Tight:** 0-0 Gall: 1-2
Aids: Bl: 1-1 Vi: 0-0 Tstrap: 0-0 Ckp: 0-0
Best Rating: 122 5/03 Hntg 3m2f gd-fm Hdl

Fair Ex-Irish hurdler/chaser; effective over two and a half miles, but stays a lot further; acts on good or easy ground.

Double Agent

94   100

11-y-o ch g Niniski (USA)-Rexana (Relko)
Miss A M Newton-Smith E J Farrant

Placings:611F03/50315360/3002562/3/0P5013/P-1P4
                  (4749)

2003/04: 22¹HY, 23PGS, 25⁴G,

	Starts	1st	2nd	3rd	Win & Pl
Hurdles	3	1	0	0	2569
Career Total	32	5	2	6	17239
93 1/04 Folk	2m6f110yG Hdl			HVY	£2569
100 1/02 Folk	2m6f110yG Hdl			SFT	£2275
103 12/97 Newc	2m4f	C(0-135)HHdl		GD	£3273
105 2/97 Muss	2m	C(0-105)HHdl		GD	£2560
103 2/97 Muss	2m	E Hdl		G-F	£2399
			Total win prize-money £13077		

Going: Sf: 1-1 GS: 0-1 Gd: 0-1 GF: - Fm: 0-0
Distance: 2m/2m3: 0-0 **2m4-2m7:** 1-2 3m+: 0-1
Track: LH: 0-0 RH: 1-1 **Tight:** 1-2 Gall: 0-0
Aids: Bl: 0-0 Vi: 0-0 Tstrap: 0-0 Ckp: 0-0
Best Rating: 105 4/97 Prth 2m110y good Hdl

Plating-class hurdler; fair hurdler on good ground a few years ago; suffered with injury and had little racing recently; made most to win at Folkestone in January 2002 and repeated that victory in the corresponding race in 2004 after a long absence; stays two miles-six; acts on a sound surface but has won in heavy ground.

Double Blade

82(106h)   (121h)99

9-y-o b g Kris-Sesame (Derrylin)
N Wilson (Mrs M Reveley 30/9) Razor Sharp Partnership

Placings:11110/4300/313/5113-322211523   (2859)
2003/04: 16³G, 20²G, 16²GF, 16²G, 17¹G, 16¹GF, 16⁵GF, 16²GF, 16³GS,

	Starts	1st	2nd	3rd	Win & Pl
Hurdles	7	2	3	1	7140
Chases	2	0	1	1	1476
Career Total	25	9	4	6	40609
112 10/03 Plum	2m	F Hdl		G-F	£1932
109 9/03 Sedg	2m1f	F Hdl		GD	£1981
120 10/02 Sedg	2m1f	F Hdl		G-F	£2646
114 9/02 Prth	2m110y	F Hdl		G-F	£4199
123 11/01 Weth	2m	C(0-135)HHdl		GD	£5395
130 11/99 Sedg	2m1f	C Hdl		GD	£4696
130 10/99 Weth	2m	C Hdl		GD	£4955
119 10/99 Sedg	2m1f	E Hdl		G-F	£2635
106 9/99 Sedg	2m1f	E Hdl		G-F	£2407
			Total win prize-money £30848		

Going: Sf: 0-0 GS: 0-1 Gd: 1-4 GF: - Fm: 1-4
Distance: **2m/2m3:** 2-8 2m4-2m7: 0-1 3m+: 0-0
Track: **LH:** 2-7 RH: 0-2 **Tight:** 2-3 Gall: 0-1
Aids: Bl: 0-0 Vi: 0-0 Tstrap: 0-0 Ckp: 0-0
Best Rating: 130 10/00 Weth 2m gd-sft Hdl

Modest hurdler; suited by a sound surface; effective at around two miles; usually held up and doesn't always find as much as expected off the bridle; doesn't look a natural jumper of fences.

Double Bogey Blues (IRE)

97   (108?h)**108**

8-y-o b g Celio Rufo-Belmount Star (IRE) (Good Thyne (USA))
M Mullineaux The Hon Mrs S Pakenham

Placings:05/41F6054P03/565121P-P40   (4652)
2003/04: 20PS, 24⁴G, 25⁰G,

	Starts	1st	2nd	3rd	Win & Pl
Chases	3	0	0	0	425
Career Total	22	3	1	1	19379
108 3/03 Ludl	3m	D Ch		G-F	£5740
108 2/03 Hrfd	3m1f110yE(0-135)HCh		GD	£4212
105 11/01 Thur	2m6f	Hdl		Y-S	£5564
			Total win prize-money £15517		

Going: Sf: 0-1 GS: 0-0 Gd: 0-2 GF: - Fm: 0-0
Distance: 2m/2m3: 0-0 2m4-2m7: 0-1 3m+: 0-2
Track: LH: 0-2 RH: 0-1 **Tight:** 0-1 Gall: 0-0
Aids: Bl: 0-0 Vi: 0-0 Tstrap: 0-0 Ckp: 0-0
Best Rating: 108 3/03 Ludl 3m gd-fm Ch

Moderate ex-Irish chaser; stays well and acts on most types of ground.

Double Bubble (IRE)

6-y-o b/br g Mandalus-Double Talk (Dublin Taxi)
C N Kellett Rob Woodward

Placings:0-0   (1450)
2003/04: 17⁰GF,

	Starts	1st	2nd	3rd	Win & Pl
NH Flat	1	0	0	0	
Career Total	2	0	0	0	

Going: Sf: 0-0 GS: 0-0 Gd: 0-0 GF: - Fm: 0-1
Distance: 2m/2m3: 0-1 2m4-2m7: 0-0 3m+: 0-0
Track: LH: 0-0 RH: 1: 0-1 **Tight:** 0-1 Gall: 0-0
Aids: Bl: 0-0 Vi: 0-0 Tstrap: 0-0 Ckp: 0-0

Double Deal

99   86+

5-y-o ch m Keen-Close The Deal (Nicholas Bill)
M W Easterby R S Cockerill (Farms) Ltd

Placings:06302P5   (4732)
2003/04: 17⁰GF, 17⁶G, 16³GS, 16⁰GS, 16²HY, 17⁰G, 17⁵G,

	Starts	1st	2nd	3rd	Win & Pl
NH Flat	3	0	0	1	237
Hurdles	4	0	0	1	1072
Career Total	7	0	1	1	1309

Going: Sf: 0-1 GS: 0-2 Gd: 0-3 GF: - Fm: 0-1
Distance: 2m/2m3: 0-7 2m4-2m7: 0-0 3m+: 0-0
Track: LH: 0-5 RH: 0-2 **Tight:** 0-3 Gall: 0-1
Aids: Bl: 0-0 Vi: 0-0 Tstrap: 0-0 Ckp: 0-0
Best Rating: 86 1/04 Newc 2m heavy Hdl

Modest form to date in bumpers and novice hurdles; acts in easy ground.

Double Destiny

96   94

8-y-o b g Anshan-Double Gift (Cragador)
Miss E C Lavelle Mrs P Scott-Dunn

Placings:025-4P   (0593)
2003/04: 19⁴GF, 20PGF,

	Starts	1st	2nd	3rd	Win & Pl
Hurdles	2	0	0	0	0
Career Total	5	0	1	0	1255

Going: Sf: 0-0 GS: 0-0 Gd: 0-0 GF: - Fm: 0-2
Distance: 2m/2m3: 0-1 2m4-2m7: 0-1 3m+: 0-0
Track: LH: 0-1 RH: 0-1 **Tight:** 0-0 Gall: 0-0
Aids: Bl: 0-0 Vi: 0-0 Tstrap: 0-0 Ckp: 0-2
Best Rating: 94 5/03 Extr 2m3f gd-fm Hdl

Stepped up on hurdling debut when second to easy winner Double Honour at Exeter; adopted front-running tactics in first-time cheekpieces when stepped up to 2m 3f at Exeter May 2003.

Double Diplomacy

8-y-o b g State Diplomacy (USA)-Malmo (Free State)
P Beaumont Mrs E Dixon

Placings:PPP-P   (2377)
2003/04: 21PGF,

	Starts	1st	2nd	3rd	Win & Pl
Chases	1	0	0	0	
Career Total	4	0	0	0	

Going: Sf: 0-0 GS: 0-0 Gd: 0-0 GF: - Fm: 0-1
Distance: 2m/2m3: 0-0 2m4-2m7: 0-1 3m+: 0-0
Track: LH: 0-1 RH: 0-0 **Tight:** 0-1 Gall: 0-0
Aids: Bl: 0-0 Vi: 0-0 Tstrap: 0-0 Ckp: 0-0

Double Em

61   58

5-y-o b g Balnibarbi-Something Speedy (IRE) (Sayf El Arab (USA))
D W Thompson David Bartlett

Placings:P00-P0F0   (4614)
2003/04: 20PHY, 16⁵G, 24⁴G, 17⁰G,

	Starts	1st	2nd	3rd	Win & Pl
Hurdles	3	0	0	0	0

	Starts	1st	2nd	3rd	Win & Pl
Chases	1	0	0	0	0
Career Total	7	0	0	0	

Going: Sf: 0-1 GS: 0-0 Gd: 0-3 GF: - Fm: 0-0
Distance: 2m/2m3: 0-2 2m4-2m7: 0-1 3m+: 0-1
Track: LH: 0-3 RH: 0-1 Tight: 0-3 Gall: 0-0
Aids: Bl: 0-0 Vi: 0-0 Tstrap: 0-0 Ckp: 0-1
Best Rating: 58 8/02 Sedg 2m1f good Hdl

Double Emblem (IRE)

52f

7-y-o ch m Weld-Sultry (Sula Bula)
B R Foster Michael Brownrigg

Placings:0-0 (1665)
2003/04: 16⁰GF,

	Starts	1st	2nd	3rd	Win & Pl
NH Flat	1	0	0	0	
Career Total	2	0	0	0	

Going: Sf: 0-0 GS: 0-0 Gd: 0-0 GF: - Fm: 0-1
Distance: 2m/2m3: 0-1 2m4-2m7: 0-0 3m+: 0-0
Track: LH: 0-1 RH: 0-0 Tight: 0-0 Gall: 0-0
Aids: Bl: 0-0 Vi: 0-0 Tstrap: 0-0 Ckp: 0-0
Best Rating: 61 8/02 Worc 2m gd-fm NHF

Double Header (IRE)

95f   97f

5-y-o b g Old Vic-Ballybeggan Lady (IRE) (Le Bavard (FR))
Mrs S D Williams Dick Williamson

Placings:30 (4816)
2003/04: 16³GS, 16⁰G,

	Starts	1st	2nd	3rd	Win & Pl
NH Flat	2	0	0	1	341
Career Total	2	0	0	1	341

Going: Sf: 0-0 GS: 0-1 Gd: 0-1 GF: - Fm: 0-0
Distance: 2m/2m3: 0-2 2m4-2m7: 0-0 3m+: 0-0
Track: LH: 0-1 RH: 0-1 Tight: 0-0 Gall: 0-0
Aids: Bl: 0-0 Vi: 0-0 Tstrap: 0-0 Ckp: 0-0
Best Rating: 97 3/04 Winc 2m gd-sft NHF

Double Helix

97   85

5-y-o b g Marju (IRE)-Totham (Shernazar)
M E Sowersby A Milner

Placings:500640050P2 (4958)
2003/04: 16⁵G, 16⁰GS, 16⁰GS, 20⁶G, 19⁴G, 19⁰GS, 20⁰G, 17⁵G, 17⁰G, 16⁸S, 17²G,

	Starts	1st	2nd	3rd	Win & Pl
Hurdles	11	0	1	0	678
Career Total	11	0	1	0	678

Going: Sf: 0-1 GS: 0-3 Gd: 0-7 GF: - Fm: 0-0
Distance: 2m/2m3: 0-8 2m4-2m7: 0-3 3m+: 0-0
Track: LH: 0-5 RH: 0-6 Tight: 0-6 Gall: 0-0
Aids: Bl: 0-4 Vi: 0-3 Tstrap: 0-0 Ckp: 0-0
Best Rating: 85 3/04 MRas 2m1f110y good Hdl

Double Honour (FR)

109(110h)   (136h)136

6-y-o gr g Highest Honor (FR)-Silver Cobra (USA) (Silver Hawk (USA))
P J Hobbs The 4th Middleham Partnership

Placings:11301-022313131 (4910)
2003/04: 20⁰YS, 20²GS, 20²S, 19³GS, 22¹S, 24³G, 24¹G, 25³G, 24¹S,

	Starts	1st	2nd	3rd	Win & Pl
Hurdles	3	0	2	0	10858
Chases	6	3	0	3	33319
Career Total	14	6	2	4	57030
136 4/04	Prth	3m	C Ch		SFT £10492
131 3/04	Tntn	3m	E Ch		GD £4225
136 1/04	Newb	2m6f110yD Ch			SFT £5772
118 4/03	Extr	2m1f	E Hdl		G-F £4078
135 1/03	Extr	2m3f	E Hdl		G-S £3808
132 1/03	Hntg	2m110y E Hdl			SFT £3668
					Total win prize-money £32044

Going: Sf: 2-3 GS: 0-2 Gd: 1-3 GF: - Fm: 0-0
Distance: 2m/2m3: 0-1 2m4-2m7: 1-4 **3m+:** 2-4
Track: LH: 1-4 **RH:** 2-5 Tight: 1-2 Gall: 1-1
Aids: Bl: 0-0 Vi: 0-0 Tstrap: 0-0 Ckp: 0-0
Best Rating: 136 4/04 Prth 3m soft Ch

Useful novice chaser; out-and-out stayer on the Flat; stays three miles and acts on any ground, but probably at his best on a soft surface; suited by forcing tactics.

Double Scoop

70   33

5-y-o b g Double Eclipse (IRE)-Grayrose Double (Celtic Cone)
B G Powell P H Betts

Placings:20 (2652)
2003/04: 16²G, 20⁰G,

	Starts	1st	2nd	3rd	Win & Pl
NH Flat	1	0	1	0	420
Hurdles	1	0	0	0	0
Career Total	2	0	1	0	420

Going: Sf: 0-0 GS: 0-0 Gd: 0-2 GF: - Fm: 0-0
Distance: 2m/2m3: 0-1 2m4-2m7: 0-1 3m+: 0-0
Track: LH: 0-1 RH: 0-0 Tight: 0-2 Gall: 0-0
Aids: Bl: 0-0 Vi: 0-0 Tstrap: 0-0 Ckp: 0-0
Best Rating: 94 11/03 Fknm 2m good NHF

Double Spey

95

5-y-o b g Atraf-Yankee Special (Bold Lad (IRE))
P C Haslam Mrs B M Hawkins & A Dixon

Placings:40-5 (0806)
2003/04: 26⁵G,

	Starts	1st	2nd	3rd	Win & Pl
Hurdles	1	0	0	0	0
Career Total	3	0	0	0	303

Going: Sf: 0-0 GS: 0-0 Gd: 0-1 GF: - Fm: 0-0
Distance: 2m/2m3: 0-0 2m4-2m7: 0-0 3m+: 0-1
Track: LH: 0-1 RH: 0-0 Tight: 0-0 Gall: 0-0
Aids: Bl: 0-0 Vi: 0-0 Tstrap: 0-0 Ckp: 0-0
Best Rating: 95 10/02 Weth 2m gd-fm Hdl

Double Tee (IRE)

83   (77h)46

8-y-o br g Jurado (USA)-Monkeylane (Monksfield)
N J Hawke N J Hawke

Placings:60/000660UP/0P-U4P6 (4146)
2003/04: 24ᵁG, 21⁴S, 24⁹GS, 24⁶G,

	Starts	1st	2nd	3rd	Win & Pl
Chases	4	0	0	0	269
Career Total	16	0	0	0	269

Going: Sf: 0-1 GS: 0-1 Gd: 0-2 GF: - Fm: 0-0
Distance: 2m/2m3: 0-0 2m4-2m7: 0-1 3m+: 0-3
Track: LH: 0-0 RH: 0-4 Tight: 0-4 Gall: 0-0
Aids: Bl: 0-0 Vi: 0-0 Tstrap: 0-0 Ckp: 0-1
Best Rating: 77 12/01 Winc 2m6f good Hdl

Double Timer (IRE)

72   (110h)53

9-y-o ch g Doubletour (USA)-Midnightattheoasis (IRE) (King Persian)
Jonjo O'Neill John P McManus

Placings:1/164211/6 (2404)
2003/04: 20⁶S,

	Starts	1st	2nd	3rd	Win & Pl
Chases	1	0	0	0	0
Career Total	8	4	1	0	12189
115 1/02	Kemp	3m110y D(0-120)HHdl		SFT	£5050
105 12/01	Sthl	3m110y E Hdl		SFT	£2436
102 9/01	Prth	2m110y H NHF		GD	£2282
111 10/00	Sedg	2m1f	H NHF		G-S	£1662
					Total win prize-money £11432

Going: Sf: 0-1 GS: 0-0 Gd: 0-0 GF: - Fm: 0-0
Distance: 2m/2m3: 0-0 2m4-2m7: 0-1 3m+: 0-0
Track: LH: 0-0 RH: 0-1 Tight: 0-0 Gall: 0-0
Aids: Bl: 0-0 Vi: 0-0 Tstrap: 0-0 Ckp: 0-0
Best Rating: 115 1/02 Kemp 3m110y soft Hdl

Double Whirl

8-y-o ch g Destroyer-Priceless Peril (Silly Prices)
R Ford Mrs David Marshall

Placings:P/SPP (4273)
2003/04: 22⁵G, 20⁰G, 24ᴾG,

	Starts	1st	2nd	3rd	Win & Pl
Hurdles	3	0	0	0	
Career Total	4	0	0	0	

Going: Sf: 0-0 GS: 0-0 Gd: 0-3 GF: - Fm: 0-0
Distance: 2m/2m3: 0-0 2m4-2m7: 0-2 3m+: 0-1
Track: LH: 0-2 RH: 0-1 Tight: 0-1 Gall: 0-0
Aids: Bl: 0-0 Vi: 0-0 Tstrap: 0-0 Ckp: 0-0

Double Wish (IRE)

79   61

6-y-o b h Barathea (IRE)-Love Bateta (IRE) (Caerleon (USA))
Miss M E Rowland Miss M E Rowland

Placings:P0-00PF (0945)
2003/04: 19⁰G, 19⁰GF, 16ᴾGF, 16ᶠG,

	Starts	1st	2nd	3rd	Win & Pl
Hurdles	4	0	0	0	
Career Total	6	0	0	0	

Going: Sf: 0-0 GS: 0-0 Gd: 0-2 GF: - Fm: 0-2
Distance: 2m/2m3: 0-2 2m4-2m7: 0-2 3m+: 0-0
Track: LH: 0-2 RH: 0-2 Tight: 0-0 Gall: 0-0
Aids: Bl: 0-0 Vi: 0-0 Tstrap: 0-3 Ckp: 0-1
Best Rating: 62　5/03　Hrfd　2m3f110y　good　Hdl

Double You Cubed
108(101h)　　(77h)100+
10-y-o b g Destroyer-Bright Suggestion (Magnate)
J S Goldie Mrs D I Goldie

Placings:P5PP/5U-U4P63PB2162P　　(4947)
2003/04: 25UG, 25⁴G, 25⁶G, 20⁶GS, 25³S, 21PGS, 25BHY, 20PGS,
20¹GF, 16⁶GF, 20²G, 20PGS,

	Starts	1st	2nd	3rd	Win & Pl
Hurdles	1	0	1	0	1012
Chases	11	1	1	1	6221
Career Total	18	1	2	1	7233

100　3/04　Ayr　2m4f　E(0-110)HCh　G-F　£4357
　　　　　　　　　　Total win prize-money £4358

Going: Sf: 0-2 GS: 0-4 Gd: 0-4 GF: - Fm: 1-2
Distance: 2m/2m3: 0-1 2m4-2m7: 1-6 3m+: 0-5
Track: LH: 1-11 RH: 0-1 Tight: 0-2 Gall: 0-0
Aids: Bl: 0-0 Vi: 0-0 Tstrap: 0-0 Ckp: 0-0
Best Rating: 100　3/04　Hexm　2m4f110y　good　Ch

Plating-class chaser/hurdler; poor form to date but did shape better returned to hurdles in February 2004 and confirmed that promise when winning back over fences at Ayr following month; inconsistent.

Doublewood (IRE)
66f　　40f
6-y-o b m Charnwood Forest (IRE)-Double On (IRE) (Doubletour (USA))
J A B Old W E Sturt

Placings:04　　(3968)
2003/04: 17⁹GS, 16⁴GS,

	Starts	1st	2nd	3rd	Win & Pl
NH Flat	2	0	0	0	0
Career Total	2	0	0	0	0

Going: Sf: 0-0 GS: 0-2 Gd: 0-0 GF: - Fm: 0-0
Distance: 2m/2m3: 0-2 2m4-2m7: 0-0 3m+: 0-0
Track: LH: 0-0 RH: 0-2 Tight: 0-1 Gall: 0-0
Aids: Bl: 0-0 Vi: 0-0 Tstrap: 0-0 Ckp: 0-0
Best Rating: 40　2/04　Towc　2m　gd-sft　NHF

Douceur Des Songes (FR)
109(89c)　　(86+c)93
7-y-o b m Art Francais (USA)-Ma Poetesse (FR) (Sorrento (FR))
A L Forbes (M C Pipe 10/11) Tony Forbes

Placings:4004/P002331/123245P23P06-55631426614P　　(4890)
2003/04: 17⁵GF, 16⁵G, 17⁶G, 20³GF, 20¹GF, 22⁴GF, 18²GF, 22⁶F,
16⁶GF, 20¹GF, 18⁴GF, 19PGF,

	Starts	1st	2nd	3rd	Win & Pl
Hurdles	11	2	1	1	5721
Chases	1	0	0	0	0
Career Total	35	4	5	5	24654

93　10/03　Uttx　2m4f110yG Hdl　G-F　£1848
93　8/03　Worc　2m4f　F Hdl　G-F　£2975
105　6/02　Uttx　2m　D Hdl　HVY　£3454

105　4/02　Font　2m2f110yE Hdl　G-F　£2709
　　　　　　　　　　Total win prize-money £10987

Going: Sf: 0-0 GS: 0-0 Gd: 0-2 GF: - Fm: 2-10
Distance: 2m/2m3: 0-7 2m4-2m7: 2-5 3m+: 0-0
Track: LH: 2-10 RH: 0-1 Tight: 0-6 Gall: 0-0
Aids: Bl: 0-0 Vi: 1-2 Tstrap: 0-0 Ckp: 0-0
Best Rating: 112　7/02　Worc　2m　good　Hdl

Plating-class hurdler; suited by trips of around two and a half miles and fast ground; unreliable; has worn a visor and cheekpieces.

Dovedale
89f　　82f
4-y-o b f Groom Dancer (USA)-Peetsie (IRE) (Fairy King (USA))
Mrs Mary Hambro Richard Hambro

Placings:0　　(4846)
2003/04: 17⁰G,

	Starts	1st	2nd	3rd	Win & Pl
NH Flat	1	0	0	0	
Career Total	1	0	0	0	

Going: Sf: 0-0 GS: 0-0 Gd: 0-1 GF: - Fm: 0-0
Distance: 2m/2m3: 0-1 2m4-2m7: 0-0 3m+: 0-0
Track: LH: 0-1 RH: 0-0 Tight: 0-0 Gall: 0-1
Aids: Bl: 0-0 Vi: 0-0 Tstrap: 0-0 Ckp: 0-0
Best Rating: 82　4/04　Chel　2m1f　good　NHF

Dovetto
15-y-o ch g Riberetto-Shadey Dove (Deadly Nightshade)
A E Price Mrs M Price

Placings:0/555/0/0/30/0464102422/3544442312/06353P12
55/50200031/3420P36P5/P-0　　(0521)
2003/04: 24⁰G,

	Starts	1st	2nd	3rd	Win & Pl
Chases	1	0	0	0	
Career Total	57	4	8	8	26088

87　4/01　Plum　2m4f　F(0-100)HCh　SFT　£3542
85　3/00　Hrfd　2m　E(0-115)HCh　GD　£4381
86　3/99　Chep　2m3f110yD(0-110)HCh　G-S　£3772
86　1/98　Extr　2m2f　E(0-100)HHdl　HVY　£2565
　　　　　　　　　　Total win prize-money £14261

Going: Sf: 0-0 GS: 0-0 Gd: 0-1 GF: - Fm: 0-0
Distance: 2m/2m3: 0-0 2m4-2m7: 0-0 3m+: 0-1
Track: LH: 0-1 RH: 0-0 Tight: 0-1 Gall: 0-0
Aids: Bl: 0-0 Vi: 0-0 Tstrap: 0-0 Ckp: 0-0
Best Rating: 91　2/99　Carl　2m　heavy　Ch

Down To The Woods (USA)
70　　45
6-y-o ch g Woodman (USA)-Riviera Wonder (USA) (Batonnier (USA))
R D E Woodhouse (M J Polglase 28/9) M A Sawyer

Placings:0　　(1309)
2003/04: 16⁰GF,

	Starts	1st	2nd	3rd	Win & Pl
Hurdles	1	0	0	0	
Career Total	1	0	0	0	

Going: Sf: 0-0 GS: 0-0 Gd: 0-0 GF: - Fm: 0-0
Distance: 2m/2m3: 0-1 2m4-2m7: 0-0 3m+: 0-0

Track: LH: 0-1 RH: 0-0 Tight: 0-0 Gall: 0-0
Aids: Bl: 0-0 Vi: 0-0 Tstrap: 0-0 Ckp: 0-0
Best Rating: 55　9/03　Worc　2m　gd-fm　Hdl

Downpour (USA)
111　　135+
6-y-o b g Torrential (USA)-Juliac (USA) (Accipiter (USA))
Ian Williams Favourites Racing

Placings:0/103-10　　(4428)
2003/04: 16¹G, 17⁰G,

	Starts	1st	2nd	3rd	Win & Pl
Hurdles	2	1	0	0	6871
Career Total	6	2	0	1	11060

135　11/03　Asct　2m110y　C(0-130)HHdl　GD　£6870
100　5/02　Hrfd　2m3f110yD Hdl　G-F　£3150
　　　　　　　　　　Total win prize-money £10021

Going: Sf: 0-0 GS: 0-0 Gd: 1-2 GF: - Fm: 0-0
Distance: 2m/2m3: 1-2 2m4-2m7: 0-0 3m+: 0-0
Track: LH: 0-1 RH: 1-1 Tight: 0-0 Gall: 0-1
Aids: Bl: 0-0 Vi: 0-0 Tstrap: 0-0 Ckp: 0-0
Best Rating: 135　11/03　Asct　2m110y　good　Hdl

Fair hurdler; stays 2m 4f; suited by fast ground, although does act on soft.

Downtherefordancin (IRE)
102　　106+
4-y-o b g Groom Dancer (USA)-Merlin's Fancy (Caerleon (USA))
M C Pipe (S Dow 29/5) The Reims Partnership

Placings:2U132525320405　　(4859)
2003/04: 17²G, 17⁴G, 17¹GF, 18³GF, 16²F, 20⁵GF, 16²GS, 17⁵G,
16³S, 17²S, 20⁰GS, 16⁴GF, 19⁰G, 19⁵GF,

	Starts	1st	2nd	3rd	Win & Pl
Hurdles	14	1	4	2	9094
Career Total	14	1	4	2	9094

91　9/03　NAbb　2m1f　E Hdl　G-F　£2877
　　　　　　　　　　Total win prize-money £2877

Going: Sf: 0-2 GS: 0-2 Gd: 0-4 GF: - Fm: 1-6
Distance: 2m/2m3: 1-11 2m4-2m7: 0-3 3m+: 0-0
Track: LH: 1-8 RH: 0-6 Tight: 1-6 Gall: 0-2
Aids: Bl: 0-0 Vi: 1-12 Tstrap: 0-0 Ckp: 0-0
Best Rating: 106　2/04　Tntn　2m1f　soft　Hdl

Moderate hurdler; stays beyond two miles, but is not a fluent jumper; acts on fast and soft ground; wears a visor.

Dr Charlie
103　　107
6-y-o ch g Dr Devious (IRE)-Miss Toot (Ardross)
Miss C Dyson (C J Mann 21/5) Miss C Dyson

Placings:61/55404-0P014565P2　　(4897)
2003/04: 20⁰S, 20PG, 22⁰G, 19¹GF, 20⁴G, 19⁵G, 19⁶GS, 21⁵GS,
21PGS, 22²G,

	Starts	1st	2nd	3rd	Win & Pl
Hurdles	10	1	1	0	3389
Career Total	17	2	1	0	7067

93　10/03　Hrfd　2m3f110yE(0-110)HHdl　G-F　£2317
101　4/02　Wwck　2m3f　E Hdl　G-F　£2922
　　　　　　　　　　Total win prize-money £5240

Going: Sf: 0-1 GS: 0-3 Gd: 0-5 GF: - Fm: 1-1
Distance: 2m/2m3: 0-1 2m4-2m7: 1-9 3m+: 0-0
Track: LH: 0-6 RH: 1-4 Tight: 0-2 Gall: 0-1
Aids: Bl: 0-1 Vi: 0-0 Tstrap: 0-0 Ckp: 0-0

Best Rating: 104 2/03 Chep 2m4f   heavy   Hdl

Modest hurdler; stays two and a half miles; effective on most types of ground but best on fast.

Dr Deductible

12-y-o b g Derrylin-Tantrum (Leading Man)
J E Brockbank Mrs J E Brockbank

Placings:PP3UFP5/5-142   (0475)
2003/04: 25¹G, 25⁴G, 26⁶GS,

	Starts	1st	2nd	3rd	Win & Pl
Chases	3	1	1	0	3657
Career Total	11	1	1	1	4069
86	4/03	Kels	3m1f	H Ch	GD	£2982

Total win prize-money £2982

Going:	Sf: 0-0 GS: 0-0 Gd: 1-2 GF: - Fm: 0-0
Distance:	2m/2m3: 0-0 2m4-2m7: 0-0 **3m+:** 1-3
Track:	**LH:** 1-3 RH: 0-0 **Tight:** 1-3 Gall: 0-0
Aids:	**Bl:** 1-3 Vi: 0-0 Tstrap: 0-0 Ckp: 0-0
Best Rating:	86 5/03 Ctml 3m2f gd-sft Ch

Modest hunter chaser; stays three miles; acts well on fast ground.

Dr Raj

5-y-o ch g In The Wings-Tawaaded (IRE) (Nashwan (USA))
B A McMahon C G Conway

Placings:0-0P   (3315)
2003/04: 17⁰G, 16⁶S,

	Starts	1st	2nd	3rd	Win & Pl
NH Flat	1	0	0	0	0
Hurdles	1	0	0	0	0
Career Total	3	0	0	0	

Going:	Sf: 0-1 GS: 0-0 Gd: 0-0 GF: - Fm: 0-1
Distance:	2m/2m3: 0-2 2m4-2m7: 0-0 3m+: 0-0
Track:	LH: 0-1 RH: 0-1 Tight: 0-0 Gall: 0-0
Aids:	Bl: 0-0 Vi: 0-0 Tstrap: 0-1 Ckp: 0-0
Best Rating:	64 5/03 Sthl 2m1f gd-fm NHF

Dr Sharp (IRE)
101   106+

4-y-o ch g Dr Devious (IRE)-Stoned Imaculate (IRE) (Durgam (USA))
T P Tate The Ivy Syndicate

Placings:1UU2   (4732)
2003/04: 18¹HY, 18⁴US, 16⁴S, 17²G,

	Starts	1st	2nd	3rd	Win & Pl
Hurdles	4	1	1	0	4645
Career Total	4	1	1	0	4645
106	2/04	Kels	2m2f	E Hdl	HVY	£3510

Total win prize-money £3510

Going:	Sf: 1-2 GS: 0-1 Gd: 0-1 GF: - Fm: 0-0
Distance:	**2m/2m3:** 1-4 2m4-2m7: 0-0 3m+: 0-0
Track:	**LH:** 1-3 RH: 0-0 **Tight:** 1-2 Gall: 0-0
Aids:	Bl: 0-0 Vi: 0-0 Tstrap: 0-0 Ckp: 0-0
Best Rating:	106 4/04 Carl 2m1f good Hdl

Fair middle distance performer on the Flat; won in good style on his hurdle debut in February at Kelso on Heavy ground but let down by jumping on next two starts; will have to brush up hurdles technique to progress.

Dracaena
90   72

7-y-o b m State Diplomacy (USA)-Jay-Dee-Jay (Mijet)
P Beaumont S W Knowles

Placings:60P400   (4732)
2003/04: 17⁶HY, 19⁰G, 21⁶GS, 16⁴HY, 17⁰G, 17⁰G,

	Starts	1st	2nd	3rd	Win & Pl
Hurdles	6	0	0	0	259
Career Total	6	0	0	0	259

Going:	Sf: 0-2 GS: 0-1 Gd: 0-3 GF: - Fm: 0-0
Distance:	2m/2m3: 0-4 2m4-2m7: 0-2 3m+: 0-0
Track:	LH: 0-3 RH: 0-3 Tight: 0-3 Gall: 0-1
Aids:	Bl: 0-0 Vi: 0-0 Tstrap: 0-0 Ckp: 0-0
Best Rating:	70 4/04 Carl 2m1f good Hdl

Dragon Hunter (IRE)
95   (110h)103+

9-y-o b g Welsh Term-Sahob (Roselier (FR))
C R Egerton Douglas, Davis, Urquhart

Placings:421P/F-P402   (4448)
2003/04: 25⁶PG, 24⁴GS, 24⁰G, 24²GS,

	Starts	1st	2nd	3rd	Win & Pl
Chases	4	0	1	0	3019
Career Total	9	1	2	0	6802
110	3/02	Font	3m3f	E Hdl	SFT	£2509

Total win prize-money £2510

Going:	Sf: 0-0 GS: 0-2 Gd: 0-2 GF: - Fm: 0-0
Distance:	2m/2m3: 0-0 2m4-2m7: 0-0 **3m+:** 0-4
Track:	LH: 0-1 RH: 0-3 Tight: 0-0 Gall: 0-0
Aids:	Bl: 0-0 Vi: 0-0 Tstrap: 0-0 Ckp: 0-0
Best Rating:	110 3/02 Font 3m3f soft Hdl

Modest novice chaser; effective in soft ground; stays extreme distances.

Dragon King
111   111+

12-y-o b g Rakaposhi King-Dunsilly Bell (London Bells (CAN))
P Bowen R Greenway

Placings:2/050046110/032031353302/5P33231311303304
53U440220/22253250400/04131103/4042142414F1-
S22353511P0354   (4484)
2003/04: 27⁴SS, 24²GF, 22⁶GF, 22³G, 22⁵G, 26³GF, 25⁵G, 25¹GF, 25¹GF, 31⁸G, 28⁰G, 27³GS, 24⁵GS, 28⁴G,

	Starts	1st	2nd	3rd	Win & Pl
Chases	14	2	2	3	11881
Career Total	92	14	14	19	70138
111	12/03	Folk	3m1f	E(0-110)HCh	G-F	£3307
111	11/03	Hrfd	3m1f110yF(0-90)HCh	G-F	£2191
100	4/03	Font	3m2f110yF(0-100)HCh	G-F	£3334
99	2/03	Font	2m6f	F(0-90)HCh	SFT	£3381
80	7/02	NAbb	2m5f110yF(0-90)Ch	G-F	£2947
92	9/01	MRas	3m1f	F(0-110)HCh	G-F	£4114
92	8/01	NAbb	3m2f110yF(0-100)HCh	G-F	£2947
86	7/01	Worc	2m4f110yF(0-100)HCh	SFT	£2975
111	9/99	Sedg	2m5f	D(0-120)HCh	G-F	£3699
111	9/99	NAbb	2m5f110yF(0-125)HCh	G-F	£3765
90	8/99	NAbb	2m110y	D Ch	GD	£3838
98	11/98	Wind	2m	E(0-110)HHdl	G-S	£2880
94	3/98	Tntn	2m1f	F(0-95)HHdl	G-S	£2050
84	3/98	Tntn	2m1f	F(0-105)HHdl	G-S	£1903

Total win prize-money £43373

Going:	Sf: 0-1 GS: 0-2 Gd: 0-6 GF: - Fm: 2-5
Distance:	2m/2m3: 0-0 2m4-2m7: 0-3 **3m+:** 2-11

Track:
Aids:
Best Rating: 111 1/04 Tntn 3m3f   gd-sft   Ch

LH: 0-3 RH: 2-7 Tight: 1-9 Gall: 0-0
Bl: 2-14 Vi: 0-0 Tstrap: 0-0 Ckp: 0-0

Moderate chaser; very sound jumper; often jumps right, but effective left-handed; stays three miles two; acts on fast ground and with give.

Dragon Prince
51   46

4-y-o b g Zamindar (USA)-Nawafell (Kris)
R C Guest Blaydon Racers Partnership

Placings:6   (4597)
2003/04: 16⁶G,

	Starts	1st	2nd	3rd	Win & Pl
Hurdles	1	0	0	0	0
Career Total	1	0	0	0	0

Going:	Sf: 0-0 GS: 0-0 Gd: 0-1 GF: - Fm: 0-0
Distance:	2m/2m3: 0-1 2m4-2m7: 0-0 3m+: 0-0
Track:	LH: 0-1 RH: 0-0 Tight: 0-1 Gall: 0-0
Aids:	Bl: 0-0 Vi: 0-0 Tstrap: 0-0 Ckp: 0-0
Best Rating:	46 3/04 Kels 2m110y good Hdl

Dragon's Dream
101   91+

6-y-o b g Afzal-Another Relation (Relkino)
P F Nicholls Richard Barber

Placings:2U0   (4147)
2003/04: 17²G, 19⁴UG, 24⁰G,

	Starts	1st	2nd	3rd	Win & Pl
NH Flat	1	0	1	0	842
Hurdles	2	0	0	0	0
Career Total	3	0	1	0	842

Going:	Sf: 0-0 GS: 0-0 Gd: 0-2 GF: - Fm: 0-1
Distance:	2m/2m3: 0-1 2m4-2m7: 0-1 3m+: 0-1
Track:	LH: 0-1 RH: 0-2 Tight: 0-3 Gall: 0-0
Aids:	Bl: 0-0 Vi: 0-0 Tstrap: 0-0 Ckp: 0-0
Best Rating:	91 3/04 Tntn 3m110y good Hdl

Easy winner of only completed point; caught close home in Newton Abbot bumper July 2003; unseated next time; acts on a sound surface.

Dragut Torghoud (IRE)
89

8-y-o b g Persian Mews-Artist's Jewel (Le Moss)
N M Babbage Ford Associated Racing Team li

Placings:4P462-P   (0140)
2003/04: 21⁶PG,

	Starts	1st	2nd	3rd	Win & Pl
Hurdles	1	0	0	0	
Career Total	6	0	1	0	2049

Going:	Sf: 0-0 GS: 0-0 Gd: 0-1 GF: - Fm: 0-0
Distance:	2m/2m3: 0-0 2m4-2m7: 0-1 3m+: 0-0
Track:	LH: 0-0 RH: 0-1 Tight: 0-0 Gall: 0-0
Aids:	Bl: 0-0 Vi: 0-0 Tstrap: 0-0 Ckp: 0-0
Best Rating:	89 4/03 Ludl 2m5f good Hdl

Moderate novice hurdler; first form when chasing home fair sort at Ludlow in April 2003; stays two miles five.

Drakestone

108   **98**

13-y-o b g Motivate-Lyricist (Averof)
R L Brown R L Brown

Placings:06034/030033/52/306/**F3U54P0**113/2/4013440P2
/0-211P   **(0760)**
2003/04: 20²S, 19¹GF, 17¹GF, 20³G,

	Starts	1st	2nd	3rd	Win & Pl
Hurdles	4	2	1	0	6603
Career Total	41	5	4	8	20498
98	6/03	Hrfd	2m1f	E(0-110)HHdl	G-F	3347
91	5/03	Hrfd	2m3f110yG Hdl		G-F	2429
103	8/01	Worc	2m4f	F Hdl	G-F	1897
97	2/00	Bang	2m1f	F(0-110)HHdl	G-S	3623
75	1/00	Hrfd	2m1f	F Hdl	G-S	2324

Total win prize-money £13622

Going:	Sf: 0-1 GS: 0-0 Gd: 0-1 GF: - Fm: 2-2
Distance:	2m/2m3: 1-1 2m4-2m7: 1-3 3m+: 0-0
Track:	LH: 0-2 **RH: 2-2** Tight: 0-1 Gall: 0-0
Aids:	Bl: 0-0 Vi: 0-0 Tstrap: 0-0 Ckp: 0-0
Best Rating:	105 10/01 Chep 2m4f good Hdl

Moderate handicap hurdler; returned as good as ever after a year off with leg trouble with wins at Hereford in May and June 2003; stays 2m 4f, suited by a sound surface although has won with cut in the ground.

Drama King

82   **86**

12-y-o b g Tragic Role (USA)-Consistent Queen (Queens Hussar)
B J Llewellyn Alan J Williams

Placings:F5142/0612/501/00P/36416500P/05P15040-6
     (0106)
2003/04: 20⁶S,

	Starts	1st	2nd	3rd	Win & Pl
Hurdles	1	0	0	0	0
Career Total	33	5	2	1	12902
86	11/02	Uttx	2m	G(0-90)HHdl	SFT	1960
96	12/01	Folk	2m4f110yF(0-100)HHdl	SFT	1820
96	1/00	Uttx	2m4f110yG(0-95)HHdl	SFT	2191
100	7/98	Worc	2m4f	E(0-115)HHdl	SFT	2337
95	3/98	Strf	2m3f	G Hdl	GD	2901

Total win prize-money £11211

Going:	Sf: 0-1 GS: 0-0 Gd: 0-0 GF: - Fm: 0-0
Distance:	2m/2m3: 0-0 2m4-2m7: 0-1 3m+: 0-0
Track:	LH: 0-1 RH: 0-0 Tight: 0-0 Gall: 0-0
Aids:	Bl: 0-1 Vi: 0-0 Tstrap: 0-0 Ckp: 0-0
Best Rating:	100 7/98 Strf 2m6f110y gd-fm Hdl

Dramatic Approach (IRE)

10-y-o b g Dry Dock-Gayles Approach (Strong Gale)
B G Powell John Plackett

Placings:0/F   **(3419)**
2003/04: 23FGS,

	Starts	1st	2nd	3rd	Win & Pl
Chases	1	0	0	0	0
Career Total	2	0	0	0	

Going:	Sf: 0-0 GS: 0-1 Gd: 0-0 GF: - Fm: 0-0
Distance:	2m/2m3: 0-0 2m4-2m7: 0-0 3m+: 0-1
Track:	LH: 0-0 RH: 0-1 Tight: 0-0 Gall: 0-0
Aids:	Bl: 0-0 Vi: 0-0 Tstrap: 0-0 Ckp: 0-0

Best Rating: 83   11/00   Asct   3m   soft   Hdl

Drat

90f   **95f**

5-y-o b g Faustus (USA)-Heresy (IRE) (Black Minstrel)
R Mathew Robin Mathew

Placings:4   **(4454)**
2003/04: 16⁴GS,

	Starts	1st	2nd	3rd	Win & Pl
NH Flat	1	0	0	0	0
Career Total	1	0	0	0	0

Going:	Sf: 0-0 GS: 0-1 Gd: 0-0 GF: - Fm: 0-0
Distance:	2m/2m3: 0-1 2m4-2m7: 0-0 3m+: 0-0
Track:	LH: 0-0 RH: 0-1 Tight: 0-0 Gall: 0-0
Aids:	Bl: 0-0 Vi: 0-0 Tstrap: 0-0 Ckp: 0-0
Best Rating:	95 3/04 Asct 2m110y gd-sft NHF

Showed promise on debut in an Ascot bumper.

Dream Castle (IRE)

90   **82**

10-y-o b g Poet's Dream (IRE)-Kerry's Castle (Deep Run)
Lindsay Woods William M Brown

Placings:505030/6/0103-0503   **(4133a)**
2003/04: 16⁰Y, 20⁵G, 22⁰G, 18³GY,

	Starts	1st	2nd	3rd	Win & Pl
Hurdles	4	0	0	1	450
Career Total	15	1	0	3	5175
91	3/03	Dpat	2m1f172y (67-88)HHdl	SFT	4032

Total win prize-money £4032

Going:	Sf: 0-0 GS: 0-0 Gd: 0-2 GF: - Fm: 0-0
Distance:	2m/2m3: 0-2 2m4-2m7: 0-2 3m+: 0-0
Track:	LH: 0-0 RH: 0-2 Tight: 0-0 Gall: 0-0
Aids:	Bl: 0-0 Vi: 0-0 Tstrap: 0-0 Ckp: 0-0
Best Rating:	91 3/03 Dpat 2m1f172y soft Hdl

Dream Falcon

106   **97+**

4-y-o b g Polar Falcon (USA)-Pip's Dream (Glint Of Gold)
R J Hodges P E Axon

Placings:1130   **(3966)**
2003/04: 16¹GF, 16¹GS, 17³GS, 16⁰GS,

	Starts	1st	2nd	3rd	Win & Pl
Hurdles	4	2	0	1	7324
Career Total	4	2	0	1	7324
97	1/04	Ludl	2m	E(0-105)HHdl	G-S	3828
89	12/03	Ludl	2m	G Hdl	G-F	2740

Total win prize-money £6570

Going:	Sf: 0-0 GS: 1-3 Gd: 0-0 GF: - Fm: 1-1
Distance:	**2m/2m3: 2-4** 2m4-2m7: 0-0 3m+: 0-0
Track:	LH: 0-0 **RH: 2-4** Tight: 0-1 Gall: 0-0
Aids:	Bl: 0-0 Vi: 0-0 Tstrap: 0-0 Ckp: 0-0
Best Rating:	97 1/04 Ludl 2m gd-sft Hdl

Moderate hurdler; acts on fast ground.

Dream King (IRE)

61   **9**

4-y-o b g Petardia-Barinia (Corvaro (USA))
Miss S E Forster (M J Polglase 13/10) Should Be Fun Racing

—

Placings:00   **(4187)**
2003/04: 18⁰HY, 16⁰GS,

	Starts	1st	2nd	3rd	Win & Pl
Hurdles	2	0	0	0	
Career Total	2	0	0	0	

Going:	Sf: 0-1 GS: 0-1 Gd: 0-0 GF: - Fm: 0-0
Distance:	2m/2m3: 0-2 2m4-2m7: 0-0 3m+: 0-0
Track:	LH: 0-2 RH: 0-0 Tight: 0-2 Gall: 0-0
Aids:	Bl: 0-0 Vi: 0-0 Tstrap: 0-0 Ckp: 0-0
Best Rating:	9 2/04 Kels 2m2f heavy Hdl

Dream On Willie (IRE)

114(104h)   (83dh)**108**

7-y-o b g Synefos (USA)-Mrs Mahon's Toy (IRE) (Roselier (FR))
E A Elliott Eric A Elliott

Placings:62035-65U21222P24   **(4947)**
2003/04: 24⁶G, 20⁵G, 20⁰G, 21²G, 20¹G, 21²G, 20²G, 20²G, 24P⁰GS, 21²G, 20⁴GS,

	Starts	1st	2nd	3rd	Win & Pl
Hurdles	2	0	0	0	0
Chases	9	1	5	0	14710
Career Total	16	1	6	0	16564
102	11/03	Weth	2m4f110yD(0-115)HCh	GD	5531

Total win prize-money £5532

Going:	Sf: 0-0 GS: 0-2 Gd: 1-9 GF: - Fm: 0-0
Distance:	2m/2m3: 0-0 **2m4-2m7: 1-9** 3m+: 0-2
Track:	**LH: 1-10** RH: 0-1 Tight: 0-2 Gall: 0-1
Aids:	Bl: 0-0 Vi: 0-0 Tstrap: 0-0 Ckp: 0-0
Best Rating:	108 4/04 Sedg 2m5f good Ch

Moderate chaser; suited by two and a half miles; acts on fast ground.

Dream With Me (FR)

101(112h)   (124 h)**118**

7-y-o b g Johann Quatz (FR)-Midnight Ride (FR) (Fast Topaze (USA))
M C Pipe Dr G Madan Mohan

Placings:256/111116P0-145532   **(1726)**
2003/04: 20¹GF, 21⁴GF, 20⁵GF, 16⁵GF, 17³GF, 17²F,

	Starts	1st	2nd	3rd	Win & Pl
Chases	6	1	1	1	9498
Career Total	17	6	2	1	35177
118	5/03	MRas	2m4f	D Ch	G-F	5967
138	11/02	Asct	2m110y	C(0-135)HHdl	G-S	6743
129	10/02	Bang	2m1f	D(0-135)HHdl	G-F	7312
118	10/02	Hrfd	2m3f110yE Hdl	G-F	3024
105	8/02	Uttx	2m	E Hdl	G-F	3454
121	6/02	Strf	2m110y	E(0-105)HHdl	G-F	3614

Total win prize-money £30118

Going:	Sf: 0-0 GS: 0-0 Gd: 0-0 GF: - Fm: 1-6
Distance:	2m/2m3: 0-3 **2m4-2m7: 1-3** 3m+: 0-0
Track:	LH: 0-3 **RH: 1-3** Tight: 1-5 Gall: 0-0
Aids:	Bl: 0-0 Vi: 0-0 **Tstrap: 1-6** Ckp: 0-0
Best Rating:	138 11/02 Asct 2m110y gd-sft Hdl

Useful ex-French novice hurdler; won his first five starts of the 2002/2003 season; won three-runner novice chase at Market Rasen May 2003; has become disappointing over fences and was once tried in a visor; effective on fast and yielding ground; stays 2m 4f; wears a tongue tie.

Dreaming Diva

5-y-o ch m Whittingham (IRE)-Any Dream (IRE) (Shernazar)
J C Fox Mrs Alicia Aldis And Simon Caunce

Placings:P				(2671)
2003/04: 16PGF,				

	Starts	1st	2nd	Win & Pl
Hurdles	1	0	0	
Career Total	1	0	0	

Going:	Sf: 0-0 GS: 0-0 Gd: 0-0 GF: - Fm: 0-1
Distance:	2m/2m3: 0-1 2m4-2m7: 0-0 3m+: 0-0
Track:	LH: 0-1 RH: 0-0 Tight: 0-0 Gall: 0-1
Aids:	Bl: 0-0 Vi: 0-0 Tstrap: 0-0 Ckp: 0-0

Drift Away (USA)
99   99

4-y-o b f Dehere (USA)-Flying Blind (IRE) (Silver Kite (USA))
J J Lambe (P J Prendergast 12/7) J J Lambe

Placings:250510				(2470a)
2003/04: 172GF, 175G, 169GF, 165G, 161GF, 169S,				

	Starts	1st	2nd	Win & Pl
Hurdles	6	1	1	7721
Career Total	6	1	1	7721
99	11/03	DRoy	2m	Hdl		G-F	£6720

Total win prize-money £6721

Going:	Sf: 0-1 GS: 0-0 Gd: 0-2 GF: - Fm: 1-3
Distance:	2m/2m3: 1-6 2m4-2m7: 0-0 3m+: 0-0
Track:	LH: 0-2 RH: 0-3 Tight: 0-2 Gall: 0-0
Aids:	Bl: 0-2 Vi: 0-0 Tstrap: 0-0 Ckp: 0-0
Best Rating:	99	11/03	DRoy	2m	gd-fm	Hdl

Irish juvenile hurdler; just denied when runner-up on debut over hurdles at Sedgefield in August; won at Down Royal in November; effective on fast ground; has worn blinkers.

Drom Wood (IRE)
105   100+

8-y-o ch g Be My Native (USA)-Try Your Case (Proverb)
T R George Mrs M Devine

Placings:0104/0F6-1414P5				(3052)
2003/04: 246GS, 201GF, 254G, 241GF, 304GS, 24PGS, 245G,				

	Starts	1st	2nd	Win & Pl
Hurdles	1	0	0	0
Chases	6	2	0	7934
Career Total	13	3	0	12047
105	11/03	Chep	3m	F(0-100)HCh	G-F	£3052
84	5/03	Hntg	2m4f110y	E(0-100)HCh	G-F	£4087
100	7/01	Bell	2m1f	NHF	G-F	£3756

Total win prize-money £10895

Going:	Sf: 0-0 GS: 0-2 Gd: 0-2 GF: - Fm: 2-3
Distance:	2m/2m3: 0-0 2m4-2m7: 1-1 3m+: 1-6
Track:	LH: 1-3 RH: 1-4 Tight: 0-2 Gall: 1-4
Aids:	Bl: 0-0 Vi: 0-0 Tstrap: 0-0 Ckp: 0-0
Best Rating:	105	11/03	Chep	3m	gd-fm	Ch

Moderate hurdler and chaser; won a bumper in his native Ireland; won novice chase at Huntingdon May 2003; jumped right-handed when going clear for easy win at Chepstow in November; stays 3m; acts well and seems best served by fast ground.

Drombeag (IRE)
104   134

6-y-o b g Presenting-Bula Beag (IRE) (Brush Aside (USA))

Jonjo O'Neill John P McManus

Placings:31-223				(4398)
2003/04: 242GS, 252G, 323G,				

	Starts	1st	2nd	3rd	Win & Pl
Chases	3	0	2	1	7846
Career Total	5	1	2	2	10072
108	3/03	Carl	2m1f	H NHF		SFT	£1932

Total win prize-money £1932

Going:	Sf: 0-0 GS: 0-1 Gd: 0-2 GF: - Fm: 0-0
Distance:	2m/2m3: 0-0 2m4-2m7: 0-0 3m+: 0-3
Track:	LH: 0-2 RH: 0-1 Tight: 0-0 Gall: 0-1
Aids:	Bl: 0-0 Vi: 0-0 Tstrap: 0-0 Ckp: 0-0
Best Rating:	134	3/04	Chel	4m	good	Ch

Fair novice chaser; acts on soft ground; stays extreme distances; still has scope.

Dromlease Express (IRE)
(126h)   (132+h)112

6-y-o ch g Fourstars Allstar (USA)-Niat Supreme (IRE) (Supreme Leader)
C Byrnes RDS Syndicate

Placings:04F5103-01102				(4741a)
2003/04: 200S, 161GY, 161S, 210G, 242YS,				

	Starts	1st	2nd	3rd	Win & Pl
Hurdles	4	2	0		63829
Chases	1	0	1	0	5380
Career Total	12	3	1		76843
134	1/04	Leop	2m	(0-140)HHdl	SFT	£55387
116	11/03	Naas	2m	(88-130)HHdl	G-Y	£8441
120	2/03	Gowr	2m	Hdl	YLD	£6720

Total win prize-money £70550

Going:	Sf: 1-2 GS: 0-0 Gd: 0-1 GF: - Fm: 0-0
Distance:	2m/2m3: 2-2 2m4-2m7: 0-2 3m+: 0-1
Track:	LH: 2-4 RH: 0-0 Tight: 0-0 Gall: 0-1
Aids:	Bl: 0-0 Vi: 0-0 Tstrap: 0-0 Ckp: 0-0
Best Rating:	134	1/04	Leop	2m	soft	Hdl

Useful Irish-trained handicap hurdler, winner of the 2004 Pierse Hurdle; effective over two miles but stays farther; suited by some cut in the ground; progressive.

Druid's Glen (IRE)
(114h)135

8-y-o br g Un Desperado (FR)-Fais Vite (USA) (Sharpen Up)
Jonjo O'Neill John P McManus

Placings:253411/11P202-P				(2297)
2003/04: 24PS,				

	Starts	1st	2nd	3rd	Win & Pl
Chases	1	0	0	0	
Career Total	13	4	3	1	29162
139	12/02	Sthl	3m110y	E Ch	G-S	£4389
121	11/02	MRas	3m1f	D Ch	SFT	£4793
114	4/02	Strf	2m6f110y	E Hdl	GD	£3220
113	3/02	Strf	2m6f110y	D Hdl	G-S	£4173

Total win prize-money £16576

Going:	Sf: 0-1 GS: 0-0 Gd: 0-0 GF: - Fm: 0-0
Distance:	2m/2m3: 0-0 2m4-2m7: 0-0 3m+: 0-1
Track:	LH: 0-0 RH: 0-1 Tight: 0-0 Gall: 0-0
Aids:	Bl: 0-0 Vi: 0-0 Tstrap: 0-0 Ckp: 0-0
Best Rating:	139	11/03	Asct	3m110y	soft	Ch

Useful chaser; looks best over three miles but effective at shorter; suited by a sharp track; acts on good and soft ground.

Druids Confederacy (IRE)
97   116+

6-y-o ch m Great Marquess-Winsome Blends (IRE) (Zaffaran (USA))
C R Egerton Bush Syndicate

Placings:210P				(3490)
2003/04: 172GS, 161S, 169GS, 22PHY,				

	Starts	1st	2nd	3rd	Win & Pl
NH Flat	1	0	1	0	448
Hurdles	3	1	0		3031
Career Total	4	1	1	0	3479
116	12/03	Towc	2m	E Hdl	SFT	£3031

Total win prize-money £3031

Going:	Sf: 1-2 GS: 0-2 Gd: 0-0 GF: - Fm: 0-0
Distance:	2m/2m3: 1-3 2m4-2m7: 0-1 3m+: 0-0
Track:	LH: 0-2 RH: 1-2 Tight: 0-1 Gall: 0-0
Aids:	Bl: 0-0 Vi: 0-0 Tstrap: 0-0 Ckp: 0-0
Best Rating:	116	12/03	Towc	2m	soft	Hdl

Made a very pleasing debut when second in a mares' only bumper at Folkestone on debut in November; odds-on most disappointing at Wetherby two months later.

Drumdowney Lad (IRE)

5-y-o b g Darnay-Alpencrocus (IRE) (Waajib)
R H York M Power

Placings:00-5P				(4655)
2003/04: 165G, 16PG,				

	Starts	1st	2nd	3rd	Win & Pl
Chases	2	0	0	0	0
Career Total	4	0	0	0	0

Going:	Sf: 0-0 GS: 0-0 Gd: 0-2 GF: - Fm: 0-0
Distance:	2m/2m3: 0-2 2m4-2m7: 0-0 3m+: 0-0
Track:	LH: 0-0 RH: 0-2 Tight: 0-1 Gall: 0-0
Aids:	Bl: 0-0 Vi: 0-0 Tstrap: 0-0 Ckp: 0-0
Best Rating:	80	2/03	Punc	2m	sft-hvy	NHF

Dry Old Party (IRE)
85f   70f

5-y-o ch g Un Desperado (FR)-The Vine Browne (IRE) (Torus)
P Winkworth P Winkworth

Placings:00				(3354)
2003/04: 169G, 169S,				

	Starts	1st	2nd	3rd	Win & Pl
NH Flat	2	0	0	0	
Career Total	2	0	0	0	

Going:	Sf: 0-1 GS: 0-0 Gd: 0-1 GF: - Fm: 0-0
Distance:	2m/2m3: 0-2 2m4-2m7: 0-0 3m+: 0-0
Track:	LH: 0-1 RH: 0-1 Tight: 0-0 Gall: 0-1
Aids:	Bl: 0-0 Vi: 0-0 Tstrap: 0-0 Ckp: 0-0
Best Rating:	70	1/04	Hntg	2m110y	soft	NHF

Dual Star (IRE)
105(84h)   (99h)95

9-y-o ch g Warning-Sizes Vary (Be My Guest (USA))
L Waring (P J Hobbs 10/9) Mrs J Waring

Placings:0040/410P/040266051500/0306006200F46F/011
P53046-5541355603P5   (4857)
2003/04: 17⁹GF, 16⁵GF, 18⁴GF, 16¹GF, 19³GF, 17⁵GF, 19⁵GF,
17⁶G, 16⁰G, 16³GF, 18⁶G, 19⁵GF,

	Starts	1st	2nd	3rd	Win & Pl
Chases	12	1	0	2	5379
Career Total	55	5	2	4	21346
94	8/03	Hntg	2m110y F(0-100)HCh	G-F	£3234
94	8/02	NAbb	2m110y E(0-110)HCh	G-F	£3675
89	7/02	NAbb	2m110y F(0-100)HCh	G-F	£3283
105	10/00	Dpat	2m1f172y C(0-102)HHdl	YLD	£2345
86	8/99	Dpat	2m1f87y Hdl	G-F	£2002
			Total win prize-money £14540		

Going:	Sf: 0-0 GS: 0-0 Gd: 0-3 GF: - Fm: 1-9
Distance:	2m/2m3: 1-11 2m4-2m7: 0-1 3m+: 0-0
Track:	LH: 0-4 RH: 1-7 Tight: 0-5 Gall: 1-2
Aids:	Bl: 0-0 Vi: 0-0 Tstrap: 1-10 Ckp: 0-0
Best Rating:	105 10/00 Dpat 2m1f172y yield Hdl

Plating-class chaser; completed back-back wins in extended 2m handicaps at Newton Abbot summer of 2002; first win in 2003 came in August at Huntingdon over two miles; effective at two miles; acts on fast ground.

Dubai Seven Stars

95   121

6-y-o m Suave Dancer (USA)-Her Honour (Teenoso (USA))
M C Pipe   M C Pipe

Placings:1P10/2400-01P500   (4634)
2003/04: 24⁰GS, 19¹G, 22²FG, 20⁵S, 24⁰S, 19⁰G,

	Starts	1st	2nd	3rd	Win & Pl
Hurdles	6	1	0	0	2373
Career Total	14	3	1	0	11229
104	12/03	Tntn	2m3f110yG Hdl	GD	£2373
103	1/02	Tntn	2m1f	E Hdl	SFT	£2631
115	12/01	Plum	2m	E Hdl	GD	£2439
			Total win prize-money £7444		

Going:	Sf: 0-2 GS: 0-1 Gd: 1-3 GF: - Fm: 0-0
Distance:	2m/2m3: 0-0 2m4-2m7: 1-4 3m+: 0-2
Track:	LH: 0-1 RH: 1-5 Tight: 1-3 Gall: 0-0
Aids:	Bl: 0-0 Vi: 1-6 Tstrap: 0-0 Ckp: 0-0
Best Rating:	130 11/02 Chep 3m soft Hdl

Moderate hurdler; effective over two but stays three miles; third in the 2002 Cesarewitch on the Flat; has won on good ground and heavy.

Duchamp (USA)

103   (110h)131

7-y-o b g Pine Bluff (USA)-Higher Learning (USA) (Fappiano (USA))
A M Balding   R & E H Investments Ltd

Placings:35/21213132F/5425U03F2-21P   (1784)
2003/04: 20²GF, 21¹GF, 20⁰G,

	Starts	1st	2nd	3rd	Win & Pl
Chases	3	1	1	0	9494
Career Total	23	4	6	4	34818
129	10/03	Strf	2m5f110yC(0-135)HCh	G-F	£8034
131	12/01	Donc	2m3f110yD Ch	GD	£4407
110	11/01	Towc	2m110y E Ch	SFT	£3822
110	5/01	Font	2m2f110yE Hdl	G-F	£2418
			Total win prize-money £18682		

Going:	Sf: 0-0 GS: 0-0 Gd: 0-1 GF: - Fm: 1-2
Distance:	2m/2m3: 0-0 2m4-2m7: 1-3 3m+: 0-0
Track:	LH: 1-3 RH: 0-0 Tight: 1-3 Gall: 0-0
Aids:	Bl: 0-0 Vi: 1-1 Tstrap: 0-0 Ckp: 0-0
Best Rating:	131 11/02 Kemp 2m4f110y good Ch

Modest chaser; winner on the Flat, over hurdles and fences; best at around 2m 4f; likes fast ground; has worn a visor.

Duke Of Brittany (FR)

93   78

5-y-o b g Rifapour (IRE)-Fox Trot V (FR) (Abdonski (FR))
Mrs M Reveley   Sir Robert Ogden

Placings:02606   (3881)
2003/04: 17⁰G, 16²G, 27⁶G, 16⁰GF, 24⁶G,

	Starts	1st	2nd	3rd	Win & Pl
NH Flat	1	0	0	0	0
Hurdles	4	0	1	0	736
Career Total	5	0	1	0	736

Going:	Sf: 0-0 GS: 0-0 Gd: 0-4 GF: - Fm: 0-1
Distance:	2m/2m3: 0-3 2m4-2m7: 0-0 3m+: 0-2
Track:	LH: 0-2 RH: 0-2 Tight: 0-2 Gall: 0-0
Aids:	Bl: 0-0 Vi: 0-0 Tstrap: 0-0 Ckp: 0-0
Best Rating:	73 11/03 Hexm 2m110y good Hdl

Duke Of Buckingham (IRE)

113   147+

8-y-o b g Phardante (FR)-Deselby's Choice (Crash Course)
P R Webber   C W Booth

Placings:3/3/32344-11012211164   (4964)
2003/04: 16¹GF, 16¹GF, 20⁴GF, 16¹GF, 17²GF, 16²GF, 16¹GF,
16¹GF, 16¹G, 16⁶G, 16⁴GF,

	Starts	1st	2nd	3rd	Win & Pl
Chases	11	6	2	0	41928
Career Total	17	6	3	3	48341
144	12/03	Wwck	2m110y D(0-125)HCh	GD	£4410
136	11/03	Kemp	2m	D Ch	G-F	£4326
	11/03	Folk	2m	D(0-125)HCh	G-F	£6140
124	8/03	Prth	2m	D Ch	G-F	£7098
120	5/03	Hntg	2m110y E Ch	G-F	£4309
117	5/03	Wwck	2m110y E Ch	G-F	£4078
			Total win prize-money £30362		

Going:	Sf: 0-0 GS: 0-0 Gd: 1-2 GF: - Fm: 5-9
Distance:	2m/2m3: 6-10 2m4-2m7: 0-1 3m+: 0-0
Track:	LH: 2-4 RH: 4-7 Tight: 1-4 Gall: 1-2
Aids:	Bl: 0-0 Vi: 0-0 Tstrap: 0-0 Ckp: 0-0
Best Rating:	147 4/04 Sand 2m gd-fm Ch

Useful chaser; sound jumper; free-running type; best at around two miles; best on a sound surface and thought not to like soft ground.

Duke Of Earl (IRE)

92   127+

5-y-o ch g Ali-Royal (IRE)-Faye (Monsanto (FR))
S Kirk   Speedith Group

Placings:15330-1   (1500)
2003/04: 16¹GF,

	Starts	1st	2nd	3rd	Win & Pl
Hurdles	1	1	0	0	10765
Career Total	6	2	0	2	25761
127	10/03	Chep	2m110y B HHdl	G-F	£10764
115	11/02	Hntg	2m110y B Hdl	G-S	£10374
			Total win prize-money £21139		

Going:	Sf: 0-0 GS: 0-0 Gd: 0-0 GF: - Fm: 1-1
Distance:	2m/2m3: 1-1 2m4-2m7: 0-0 3m+: 0-0

Track:	LH: 1-1 RH: 0-0 Tight: 0-0 Gall: 0-0
Aids:	Bl: 0-0 Vi: 0-0 Tstrap: 0-0 Ckp: 0-0
Best Rating:	127 10/03 Chep 2m110y gd-fm Hdl

Fair hurdler; belied his trainer's concerns about the fast ground when landing Free Handicap Hurdle at Chepstow October 2003; seems best suited by decent ground, although has run well on heavy; should stay further than 2m.

Dun An Doras (IRE)

99(105h)   (101 h)110

8-y-o br g Glacial Storm (USA)-Doorslammer (Avocat)
J D Frost   Cloud Nine-Premier Cru

Placings:0/0/5023544-12212315P   (4521)
2003/04: 27⁴S, 22¹GF, 22²GS, 19²GF, 19¹GF, 19²G, 21³G, 20¹F,
19⁵G, 19⁵GS,

	Starts	1st	2nd	3rd	Win & Pl
Hurdles	5	2	2	0	10460
Chases	5	1	1	1	6162
Career Total	18	3	4	2	18510
113	12/03	Leic	2m4f110yE Ch	FRM	£4046
100	9/03	NAbb	2m3f	E Hdl	G-F	£2905
96	6/03	NAbb	2m6f	E Hdl	G-F	£3503
			Total win prize-money £10455		

Going:	Sf: 0-1 GS: 0-2 Gd: 0-3 GF: - Fm: 3-4
Distance:	2m/2m3: 1-2 2m4-2m7: 2-7 3m+: 0-1
Track:	LH: 1-4 RH: 1-3 Tight: 1-4 Gall: 0-0
Aids:	Bl: 0-0 Vi: 0-0 Tstrap: 0-0 Ckp: 0-0
Best Rating:	113 12/03 Leic 2m4f110y firm Ch

Modest hurdler/novice chaser; won maiden point in Ireland; effective over trips of around two and a half to two and three-quarter miles.

Dun Victory

9-y-o b g Destroyer-Dun Gay Lass (Rolfe (USA))
Mrs P Claxton   Mrs P Claxton

Placings:P   (4687)
2003/04: 25°G,

	Starts	1st	2nd	3rd	Win & Pl
Chases	1	0	0	0	
Career Total	1	0	0	0	

Going:	Sf: 0-0 GS: 0-0 Gd: 0-1 GF: - Fm: 0-0
Distance:	2m/2m3: 0-0 2m4-2m7: 0-0 3m+: 0-1
Track:	LH: 0-1 RH: 0-0 Tight: 0-0 Gall: 0-0
Aids:	Bl: 0-0 Vi: 0-0 Tstrap: 0-0 Ckp: 0-0

Dunbay

10-y-o b g Dunbeath (USA)-Lekuti (Le Coq D'Or)
Mrs Peter Shaw   Mrs Jilly Kelly

Placings:0/0/FP   (0151)
2003/04: 16²G, 24ᴾGF,

	Starts	1st	2nd	3rd	Win & Pl
Chases	2	0	0	0	
Career Total	4	0	0	0	

Going:	Sf: 0-0 GS: 0-0 Gd: 0-1 GF: - Fm: 0-1
Distance:	2m/2m3: 0-1 2m4-2m7: 0-0 3m+: 0-1
Track:	LH: 0-2 RH: 0-0 Tight: 0-0 Gall: 0-1
Aids:	Bl: 0-0 Vi: 0-0 Tstrap: 0-0 Ckp: 0-0
Best Rating:	22 4/00 Carl 2m1f gd-sft NHF

Duncliffe

99   **96+**

7-y-o b g Executive Perk-Ida Melba (Idiots Delight)
R H Alner   Lady Cobham

Placings:42   (4665)
2003/04: 19⁴GS, 24²S,

	Starts	1st	2nd	3rd	Win & Pl
Chases	2	0	1	0	1648
Career Total	2	0	1	0	1648

Going:	Sf: 0-1 GS: 0-1 Gd: 0-0 GF: - Fm: 0-0
Distance:	2m/2m3: 0-0 2m4-2m7: 0-1 3m+: 0-1
Track:	LH: 0-1 RH: 0-1 Tight: 0-1 Gall: 0-0
Aids:	Bl: 0-0 Vi: 0-0 Tstrap: 0-0 Ckp: 0-0
Best Rating:	96 4/04 Ling 3m soft Ch

Duncrievie Gale

                               60

7-y-o gr g Gildoran-The Whirlie Weevil (Scallywag)
Miss Lucinda V Russell   Masons Arms Racing Club & D Fu Tong

Placings:0/P-2U   (4910)
2003/04: 20²PHY, 24ᵁS,

	Starts	1st	2nd	3rd	Win & Pl
Chases	2	0	1	0	1342
Career Total	4	0	1	0	1342

Going:	Sf: 0-2 GS: 0-0 Gd: 0-0 GF: - Fm: 0-0
Distance:	2m/2m3: 0-0 2m4-2m7: 0-1 3m+: 0-1
Track:	LH: 0-1 RH: 0-1 Tight: 0-0 Gall: 0-1
Aids:	Bl: 0-0 Vi: 0-0 Tstrap: 0-0 Ckp: 0-0
Best Rating:	80 4/02 Ayr 2m good NHF

Dundonald

65   **50**

5-y-o ch g Magic Ring (IRE)-Cal Norma's Lady (IRE) (Lyphard's Special (USA))
M Appleby (A W Carroll 11/8)   Michael Appleby

Placings:00-0PP   (2691)
2003/04: 16⁰GS, 17ᴾGF, 16ᴾG,

	Starts	1st	2nd	3rd	Win & Pl
Hurdles	3	0	0	0	
Career Total	5	0	0	0	

Going:	Sf: 0-0 GS: 0-1 Gd: 0-1 GF: - Fm: 0-1
Distance:	2m/2m3: 0-3 2m4-2m7: 0-0 3m+: 0-0
Track:	LH: 0-1 RH: 0-2 Tight: 0-1 Gall: 0-0
Aids:	Bl: 0-0 Vi: 0-0 Tstrap: 0-2 Ckp: 0-1
Best Rating:	50 4/03 Sedg 2m1f good Hdl

Dundridge Native

97f   **77f**

6-y-o b m Be My Native (USA)-Fra Mau (Wolver Hollow)
M Madgwick   C L Hood

Placings:50   (4291)
2003/04: 16⁵HY, 16⁰G,

	Starts	1st	2nd	3rd	Win & Pl
NH Flat	2	0	0	0	0
Career Total	2	0	0	0	0

Going:	Sf: 0-1 GS: 0-0 Gd: 0-1 GF: - Fm: 0-0

Dundrod

7-y-o ch g Riverwise (USA)-Pallanda (Pablond)
F P Murtagh   Sam Hamilton

Placings:06PP   (3358)
2003/04: 17⁰G, 20⁶G, 17ᴾHY, 16ᴾS,

	Starts	1st	2nd	3rd	Win & Pl
NH Flat	1	0	0	0	0
Hurdles	3	0	0	0	0
Career Total	4	0	0	0	0

Going:	Sf: 0-2 GS: 0-0 Gd: 0-2 GF: - Fm: 0-0
Distance:	2m/2m3: 0-3 2m4-2m7: 0-1 3m+: 0-0
Track:	LH: 0-3 RH: 0-1 Tight: 0-2 Gall: 0-1
Aids:	Bl: 0-0 Vi: 0-0 Tstrap: 0-0 Ckp: 0-0
Best Rating:	64 10/03 Sedg 2m1f good NHF

Dungarvans Choice (IRE)

92(101c)   (126c)**139**

9-y-o ch g Orchestra-Marys Gift (Monksfield)
N J Henderson   Elite Racing Club

Placings:2014/2110/2P12-0   (0104)
2003/04: 20⁰S,

	Starts	1st	2nd	3rd	Win & Pl
Hurdles	1	0	0	0	
Career Total	13	4	4	0	21759
137	2/03	Newb	2m5f	D(0-125)HHdl	SFT	£5882
124	2/02	Sand	2m110y	D Hdl	HVY	£4660
126	1/02	Hntg	2m110y	E Hdl	G-S	£2569
109	1/01	Chep	2m110y	H NHF	G-S	£1491

Total win prize-money £14604

Going:	Sf: 0-1 GS: 0-0 Gd: 0-0 GF: - Fm: 0-0
Distance:	2m/2m3: 0-0 2m4-2m7: 0-1 3m+: 0-0
Track:	LH: 0-1 RH: 0-0 Tight: 0-0 Gall: 0-0
Aids:	Bl: 0-0 Vi: 0-0 Tstrap: 0-0 Ckp: 0-0
Best Rating:	137 3/03 Uttx 2m6f110y soft Hdl

Decent form in bumpers and over hurdles; did not take to jumping fences; effective at up to two and a half miles; appreciates cut in the ground.

Dunkerron

94(99h)   (80h)**90**

7-y-o b g Pursuit Of Love-Top Berry (High Top)
P J Hobbs (J Joseph 8/10)   Jack Joseph

Placings:3P053/5002530P-1U5064142   (2286)
2003/04: 16¹G, 16ᵁGF, 16⁵G, 16⁹GF, 16⁶GF, 16⁴F, 17¹GF, 16⁴GF, 17²G,

	Starts	1st	2nd	3rd	Win & Pl
Hurdles	6	1	0	0	2747
Chases	3	1	0	0	5328
Career Total	22	2	2	3	10273
90	10/03	Plum	2m1f	D(0-110)HCh	G-F	£4340
80	5/03	Hntg	2m110y	G(0-95)HHdl	GD	£2436

Total win prize-money £6776

Going:	Sf: 0-0 GS: 0-0 Gd: 0-3 GF: - Fm: 1-6
Distance:	2m/2m3: 2-9 2m4-2m7: 0-0 3m+: 0-0
Track:	LH: 1-6 RH: 1-3 Tight: 1-1 Gall: 1-1

Dunlea (IRE)

106(109h)   (98+h)**112**

8-y-o b h Common Grounds-No Distractions (Tap On Wood)
John G Carr   A-One Syndicate

Placings:0053310/00003/0000/6400-10000405P (4681a)
2003/04: 24¹GF, 21⁹G, 20⁰Y, 19⁰YS, 17⁰S, 17⁴S, 22⁰S, 20⁵G, 16ᴾYS,

	Starts	1st	2nd	3rd	Win & Pl
Hurdles	2	1	0	0	2184
Chases	7	0	0	3	451
Career Total	29	2	0	3	9203
108	10/03	Hexm	3m	F(0-100)HHdl	G-F	£2184
87	3/00	Navn	2m	Hdl	YLD	£4416

Total win prize-money £6600

Going:	Sf: 0-3 GS: 0-0 Gd: 0-2 GF: - Fm: 1-1
Distance:	2m/2m3: 0-4 2m4-2m7: 0-4 3m+: 1-1
Track:	LH: 1-5 RH: 0-2 Tight: 0-1 Gall: 0-1
Aids:	Bl: 0-0 Vi: 0-0 Tstrap: 0-0 Ckp: 0-0
Best Rating:	112 1/04 Fair 2m1f soft Ch

Modest Irish-trained chaser/hurdler; stays three miles, effective at shorter; acts on fast ground.

Dunmanus Bay (IRE)

7-y-o gr g Mandalus-Baby Fane (IRE) (Buckskin (FR))
Mrs Julie Read (M C Pipe 23/9)   Mrs P King

Placings:0330F6-10F0P5621PPP   (4779)
2003/04: 19¹G, 25⁰GF, 21²GF, 21⁰GF, 21ᴾGF, 21⁵GF, 27⁶G, 26²GF, 26¹GF, 26ᴾGF, 25ᴾGS, 24ᴾS,

	Starts	1st	2nd	3rd	Win & Pl
Hurdles	1	0	0	0	
Chases	11	2	1	0	8223
Career Total	18	2	1	2	9300
103	9/03	NAbb	3m2f110yE(0-110)HCh	G-F	£3347
93	4/03	Extr	2m3f110yF(0-95)HCh	GD	£3432

Total win prize-money £6780

Going:	Sf: 0-1 GS: 0-1 Gd: 1-2 GF: - Fm: 1-8
Distance:	2m/2m3: 0-0 2m4-2m7: 1-5 3m+: 1-7
Track:	LH: 1-8 RH: 1-3 Tight: 1-9 Gall: 0-0
Aids:	Bl: 0-2 Vi: 2-9 Tstrap: 0-0 Ckp: 0-0
Best Rating:	103 9/03 NAbb 3m2f110y gd-fm Ch

Moderate chaser; often let down by his jumping; won in first-time visor at Exeter April 2003; has since joined Martin Pipe; benefited from the McCoy treatment when winning at Newton Abbot in September; acts on good ground; stays three miles two.

Dunnet Head (IRE)

105f   **116+f**

5-y-o ch g Shernazar-Kabarda (Relkino)
L Lungo   Mr & Mrs Raymond Anderson Green

Placings:1   (4867)
2003/04: 16¹S,

	Starts	1st	2nd	3rd	Win & Pl
NH Flat	1	1	0	0	3549
Career Total	1	1	0	0	3549

Aids: Bl: 0-0 Vi: 0-0 Tstrap: 0-0 Ckp: 0-0
Best Rating: 90   11/03   Wwck   2m110y   gd-fm   Ch

Modest hurdler, took advantage of a lenient mark when beating a large field in 2m Huntingdon conditional seller May 2003; disappointing since; suited by a sound surface and a positive ride.

116 4/04 Ayr   2m   H NHF   SFT   £3549
                        Total win prize-money £3549

Going: Sf: 1-1 GS: 0-0 Gd: 0-0 GF: - Fm: 0-0
Distance: 2m/2m3: 1-1 2m4-2m7: 0-0 3m+: 0-0
Track: LH: 1-1 RH: 0-0 Tight: 0-0 Gall: 0-0
Aids: Bl: 0-0 Vi: 0-0 Tstrap: 0-0 Ckp: 0-0
Best Rating: 116 4/04 Ayr 2m   soft   NHF

Half-brother to ordinary winning hurdler Delgany Royal; created very favourable impression when sluicing up in ordinary bumper at Ayr on debut in April 2004; travelled strongly that day and powered clear under hands and heels riding; exciting prospect.

Dunnicks Chance
71

9-y-o b m Greensmith-Field Chance (Whistlefield)
F G Tucker F G Tucker

Placings:0F50/60/P3P6002-P6   (2957)
2003/04: 19^PGS, 16^RG,

	Starts	1st	2nd	3rd	Win & Pl
Hurdles	2	0	0	0	0
Career Total	15	0	1	1	1537

Going: Sf: 0-0 GS: 0-1 Gd: 0-1 GF: - Fm: 0-0
Distance: 2m/2m3: 0-1 2m4-2m7: 0-1 3m+: 0-0
Track: LH: 0-0 RH: 0-2 Tight: 0-0 Gall: 0-0
Aids: Bl: 0-0 Vi: 0-0 Tstrap: 0-0 Ckp: 0-0
Best Rating: 71 4/03 NAbb 2m1f   gd-fm   Hdl

Poor hurdler; handed second place in a maiden hurdle at Newton Abbot in April 2003.

Dunnicks Head

8-y-o b m Greensmith-Country Magic (National Trust)
F G Tucker F G Tucker

Placings:0/P   (3787)
2003/04: 22^PG,

	Starts	1st	2nd	3rd	Win & Pl
Hurdles	1	0	0	0	
Career Total	2	0	0	0	

Going: Sf: 0-0 GS: 0-0 Gd: 0-1 GF: - Fm: 0-0
Distance: 2m/2m3: 0-0 2m4-2m7: 0-1 3m+: 0-0
Track: LH: 0-0 RH: 0-1 Tight: 0-0 Gall: 0-0
Aids: Bl: 0-0 Vi: 0-0 Tstrap: 0-0 Ckp: 0-0

Dunnicks Trust

6-y-o b g Greensmith-Country Magic (National Trust)
F G Tucker F G Tucker

Placings:00-0PP   (3247)
2003/04: 16^RGS, 19^PS, 22^PGS,

	Starts	1st	2nd	3rd	Win & Pl
NH Flat	1	0	0	0	0
Hurdles	2	0	0	0	0
Career Total	5	0	0	0	

Going: Sf: 0-1 GS: 0-2 Gd: 0-0 GF: - Fm: 0-0
Distance: 2m/2m3: 0-2 2m4-2m7: 0-1 3m+: 0-0
Track: LH: 0-1 RH: 0-2 Tight: 0-0 Gall: 0-0
Aids: Bl: 0-0 Vi: 0-0 Tstrap: 0-0 Ckp: 0-0
Best Rating: 54 2/03 Winc 2m   gd-sft   NHF

Dunnicks View
93   80

15-y-o b g Sula Bula-Country Magic (National Trust)
F G Tucker F G Tucker

Placings:55/6050/P0P02/P43/3U3403P/F4F34622435/456
2165P33/6521026/000222536/6355-56P   (3710)
2003/04: 21^SG, 24^6G, 24^PHY,

	Starts	1st	2nd	3rd	Win & Pl
Chases	3	0	0	0	0
Career Total	65	2	9	10	23622
87	12/00 Tntn	3m	F(0-105)HCh	SFT	£3461
91	1/00 Tntn	3m	F(0-95)HCh	SFT	£3077
			Total win prize-money £6539		

Going: Sf: 0-1 GS: 0-0 Gd: 0-2 GF: - Fm: 0-0
Distance: 2m/2m3: 0-0 2m4-2m7: 0-1 3m+: 0-2
Track: LH: 0-1 RH: 0-2 Tight: 0-1 Gall: 0-0
Aids: Bl: 0-0 Vi: 0-0 Tstrap: 0-0 Ckp: 0-0
Best Rating: 100 1/94 Chel 2m1f   soft   Hdl

Modest staying chaser, tends to reserve his best for Taunton; stays three and a quarter miles; acts on soft ground.

Dunowen (IRE)
101(99h)   (92h)99

9-y-o b g Be My Native (USA)-Lulu Buck (Buckskin (FR))
J M P Eustace Mrs T S Matthews

Placings:0U4/00040463/3221F4-2350P   (4117)
2003/04: 20^2GS, 21^3G, 16^5GS, 20^PS, 22^PG,

	Starts	1st	2nd	3rd	Win & Pl
Hurdles	2	0	1	0	1312
Chases	3	0	0	1	538
Career Total	22	1	3	3	14065
99	2/03 Limk	2m4f	(0-109)HCh	SFT	£6720
			Total win prize-money £6721		

Going: Sf: 0-1 GS: 0-2 Gd: 0-2 GF: - Fm: 0-0
Distance: 2m/2m3: 0-1 2m4-2m7: 0-0 3m+: 0-0
Track: LH: 0-2 RH: 0-3 Tight: 0-4 Gall: 0-1
Aids: Bl: 0-2 Vi: 0-1 Tstrap: 0-0 Ckp: 0-0
Best Rating: 99 12/03 Folk 2m5f   good   Ch

Brother to high-class chaser Lord Sam; best effort on third outing over two miles at Towcester on good ground in April 2004; should act on soft ground; likely to be best suited by 2m 4f plus.

Dunraven
108(103c)   (82c)92+

9-y-o b g Perpendicular-Politique (Politico (USA))
M J Gingell Fare Dealing Partnership

Placings:6F6/0503P500/401104033U3-
0244353003140OU5   (4781)
2003/04: 16^6G, 16^2GF, 19^4G, 17^4GF, 16^3G, 21^5G, 16^3F, 19^6G,
16^6G, 16^6S, 16^1S, 16^4S, 16^6GS, 16^6GS, 16^6G,

	Starts	1st	2nd	3rd	Win & Pl
Hurdles	13	1	1	2	4882
Chases	3	0	1	0	617
Career Total	38	3	1	7	14237
92	1/04 Leic	2m	G(0-90)HHdl	SFT	£2639
85	10/02 Fknm	2m	E(0-105)HHdl	G-S	£3740
86	10/02 Sthl	2m1f	G(0-95)HHdl	GD	£2317
			Total win prize-money £8697		

Going: Sf: 1-3 GS: 0-2 Gd: 0-8 GF: - Fm: 0-3
Distance: 2m/2m3: 1-15 2m4-2m7: 0-1 3m+: 0-0
Track: LH: 0-9 RH: 1-7 Tight: 0-6 Gall: 0-2
Aids: Bl: 0-0 Vi: 1-5 Tstrap: 0-0 Ckp: 0-1
Best Rating: 92 1/04 Leic 2m   soft   Hdl

Plating-class hurdler; little impact over fences; best at 2m; suited by give underfoot.

Dunsemore
88f   60f

4-y-o b f Prince Daniel (USA)-Admire-A-More (Le Coq D'Or)
P Monteith Mrs A F Tullie

Placings:00   (4952)
2003/04: 16^0HY, 16^0GS,

	Starts	1st	2nd	3rd	Win & Pl
NH Flat	2	0	0	0	
Career Total	2	0	0	0	

Going: Sf: 0-1 GS: 0-1 Gd: 0-0 GF: - Fm: 0-0
Distance: 2m/2m3: 0-2 2m4-2m7: 0-0 3m+: 0-0
Track: LH: 0-1 RH: 0-1 Tight: 0-0 Gall: 0-0
Aids: Bl: 0-0 Vi: 0-0 Tstrap: 0-0 Ckp: 0-0
Best Rating: 60 1/04 Newc 2m   heavy   NHF

Dunshaughlin (IRE)
102   90

7-y-o b g Supreme Leader-Russian Gale (IRE) (Strong Gale)
J A B Old W E Sturt

Placings:6-0   (4691)
2003/04: 17^6S, 17^0G,

	Starts	1st	2nd	3rd	Win & Pl
NH Flat	1	0	0	0	0
Hurdles	1	0	0	0	0
Career Total	2	0	0	0	0

Going: Sf: 0-1 GS: 0-0 Gd: 0-1 GF: - Fm: 0-0
Distance: 2m/2m3: 0-2 2m4-2m7: 0-0 3m+: 0-0
Track: LH: 0-1 RH: 0-1 Tight: 0-1 Gall: 0-0
Aids: Bl: 0-0 Vi: 0-0 Tstrap: 0-0 Ckp: 0-0
Best Rating: 98 4/03 NAbb 2m1f   soft   NHF

Brother to high-class chaser Lord Sam; best effort on third outing over two miles at Towcester on good ground in April 2004; should act on soft ground; likely to be best suited by 2m 4f plus.

Dunster Castle
110   (106h)119

9-y-o ch g Carlingford Castle-Gay Edition (New Member)
P J Hobbs Mrs D L Whateley

Placings:1/25F/32631/3P21-1P2F   (1828)
2003/04: 26^1G, 23^PGF, 25^2F, 24^FGF,

	Starts	1st	2nd	3rd	Win & Pl
Chases	4	1	1	0	5480
Career Total	17	4	4	3	21722
119	5/03 Font	3m2f110yE Ch		GD	£4095
119	4/03 Ludl	3m	D Ch	GD	£6300
105	4/02 Winc	2m6f	E Hdl	GD	£3052
105	3/00 Chep	2m110y	H NHF	GD	£1757
			Total win prize-money £15204		

Going: Sf: 0-0 GS: 0-0 Gd: 0-0 GF: 1-1 Fm: 0-3
Distance: 2m/2m3: 0-0 2m4-2m7: 0-0 3m+: 1-4
Track: LH: 0-2 RH: 0-1 Tight: 1-1 Gall: 0-1
Aids: Bl: 0-0 Vi: 0-0 Tstrap: 0-0 Ckp: 0-0
Best Rating: 119 10/03 Towc 3m1f   firm   Ch

Modest hurdler/chaser; in good form when winning novice chases and Ludlow and Fontwell in the spring of 2003; acts well on good ground; stays well.

Dunston Bill

107   (73h)**122**

10-y-o b g Sizzling Melody-Fardella (ITY) (Molvedo)
C J Mann All For One And One For All Partnership

Placings:624/20P31/325P041/642144124F/21U23P-46P33
(4871)
2003/04: 20⁴G, 24⁶G, 24⁴PGS, 24³GS, 24³S,

	Starts	1st	2nd	3rd	Win & Pl
Chases	5	0	0	2	3203
Career Total	36	5	7	5	38337
122	11/02	MRas	2m6f110yD(0-120)HCh	SFT	£5512
119	1/02	Kemp	2m4f110yD(0-115)HCh	SFT	£5096
112	11/02	NAbb	2m5f110yE(0-105)HCh	HVY	£3427
106	4/00	Hrfd	2m1f	E(0-115)HHdl	GD	£4082
98	4/99	Towc	2m	F(0-105)HHdl	SFT	£1933
			Total win prize-money £20050		

Going:	Sf: 0-1 GS: 0-2 Gd: 0-2 GF: - Fm: 0-0
Distance:	2m/2m3: 0-0 2m4-2m7: 0-1 3m+: 0-4
Track:	LH: 0-3 RH: 0-2 Tight: 0-2 Gall: 0-1
Aids:	Bl: 0-5 Vi: 0-0 Tstrap: 0-0 Ckp: 0-0
Best Rating:	122 11/02 MRas 2m6f110y soft Ch

Fair chaser; best over trips around two and a half miles or a bit further; suited by cut in the ground; suited by sharp tracks; best going right-handed; usually wears blinkers.

Duraid (IRE)

12-y-o ch g Irish River (FR)-Fateful Princess (USA) (Vaguely Noble)
C Grant A Suddes

Placings:1/11124/4/54/P   (0897)
2003/04: 17PGF,

	Starts	1st	2nd	3rd	Win & Pl
Hurdles	1	0	0	0	
Career Total	10	4	1	0	6521
113	10/96	Weth	2m	H NHF	GD	£1406
107	10/96	Sedg	2m1f	H NHF	G-F	£1259
99	9/96	Carl	2m1f	H NHF	FRM	£1224
104	4/96	Sedg	2m	H NHF	G-F	£1385
			Total win prize-money £5274		

Going:	Sf: 0-0 GS: 0-0 Gd: 0-0 GF: - Fm: 0-1
Distance:	2m/2m3: 0-1 2m4-2m7: 0-0 3m+: 0-0
Track:	LH: 0-1 RH: 0-0 Tight: 0-1 Gall: 0-0
Aids:	Bl: 0-0 Vi: 0-0 Tstrap: 0-0 Ckp: 0-0
Best Rating:	113 10/96 Weth 2m good NHF

Durante (IRE)

97f   **81f**

6-y-o ch g Shernazar-Sweet Tune (Welsh Chanter)
J A B Old W E Sturt

Placings:0   (4578)
2003/04: 16⁰G,

	Starts	1st	2nd	3rd	Win & Pl
NH Flat	1	0	0	0	
Career Total	1	0	0	0	

Going:	Sf: 0-0 GS: 0-0 Gd: 0-0 GF: 0-1 Fm: 0-0
Distance:	2m/2m3: 0-1 2m4-2m7: 0-0 3m+: 0-0
Track:	LH: 0-1 RH: 0-0 Tight: 0-0 Gall: 0-1
Aids:	Bl: 0-0 Vi: 0-0 Tstrap: 0-0 Ckp: 0-0
Best Rating:	81 3/04 Newb 2m110y good NHF

Durham Dandy

100(96h)   (73h)**84**

8-y-o b g Inchinor-Disco Girl (FR) (Green Dancer (USA))
M W Easterby (Miss J E Foster 24/5) John Dwyer

Placings:43022/54/4P/20P6226   (1837)
2003/04: 20²GS, 20⁰G, 22PGF, 20⁶G, 22²PGF, 20²GF, 27⁶G,

	Starts	1st	2nd	3rd	Win & Pl
Hurdles	2	0	0	0	0
Chases	5	0	3	0	3966
Career Total	16	0	5	1	6005

Going:	Sf: 0-0 GS: 0-1 Gd: 0-3 GF: - Fm: 0-3
Distance:	2m/2m3: 0-0 2m4-2m7: 0-6 3m+: 0-1
Track:	LH: 0-3 RH: 0-4 Tight: 0-4 Gall: 0-0
Aids:	Bl: 0-0 Vi: 0-0 Tstrap: 0-0 Ckp: 0-7
Best Rating:	85 12/99 Catt 2m gd-fm Hdl

Plating-class chaser; winner of two points; could not take full advantage of Executive Park's fall when caught on the run-in in two miles four hunter chase at Stratford May 2003; usually wears cheekpieces; has been tried in blinkers.

Duringthenight (IRE)

5-y-o b g Namaqualand (USA)-Legend Of Spain (USA) (Alleged (USA))
G A Swinbank Amie Flower

Placings:6222-F   (1535)
2003/04: 19PGF,

	Starts	1st	2nd	3rd	Win & Pl
Hurdles	1	0	0	0	
Career Total	5	0	3	0	2138

Going:	Sf: 0-0 GS: 0-0 Gd: 0-0 GF: - Fm: 0-1
Distance:	2m/2m3: 0-0 2m4-2m7: 0-1 3m+: 0-0
Track:	LH: 0-0 RH: 0-1 Tight: 0-1 Gall: 0-0
Aids:	Bl: 0-0 Vi: 0-0 Tstrap: 0-0 Ckp: 0-0
Best Rating:	96 4/03 Prth 2m110y good NHF

Modest bumper performer; runner-up three times in spring of 2003; acts on good ground.

Durkar Star (IRE)

6-y-o b g Bin Ajwaad (IRE)-Faith Alone (Safawan)
M C Chapman Eric Knowles

Placings:0   (0628)
2003/04: 16⁰GF,

	Starts	1st	2nd	3rd	Win & Pl
Hurdles	1	0	0	0	
Career Total	1	0	0	0	

Going:	Sf: 0-0 GS: 0-0 Gd: 0-0 GF: - Fm: 0-1
Distance:	2m/2m3: 0-1 2m4-2m7: 0-0 3m+: 0-0
Track:	LH: 0-1 RH: 0-0 Tight: 0-0 Gall: 0-0
Aids:	Bl: 0-0 Vi: 0-0 Tstrap: 0-0 Ckp: 0-0

Dushaan

(76h)   (23h)

9-y-o ch g Anshan-Soon To Be (Hot Spark)
Mrs L B Normile Out The Box Racing

Placings:5/3400405P1/10P/0-0500PP   (3324)

2003/04: 16⁰G, 16⁵G, 17⁰G, 16⁶S, 21PS, 17PGS,

	Starts	1st	2nd	3rd	Win & Pl
Hurdles	3	0	0	0	0
Chases	3	0	0	0	0
Career Total	20	2	0	1	6333
96	5/01	Prth	2m110y	E(0-105)HHdl	SFT	£3445
96	4/01	Weth	2m	F(0-100)HHdl	G-S	£2614
			Total win prize-money £6060		

Going:	Sf: 0-2 GS: 0-1 Gd: 0-3 GF: - Fm: 0-0
Distance:	2m/2m3: 0-5 2m4-2m7: 0-1 3m+: 0-0
Track:	LH: 0-4 RH: 0-2 Tight: 0-2 Gall: 0-0
Aids:	Bl: 0-1 Vi: 0-0 Tstrap: 0-0 Ckp: 0-0
Best Rating:	101 5/00 Prth 2m110y gd-sft NHF

Moderate hurdler, showed progressive form in the spring of 2001, winning at Wetherby and Perth. Suited by soft ground.

Dusky Light

84   **83**

6-y-o b m Gildoran-Starawak (Star Appeal)
P F Nicholls Richard Barber

Placings:34-605   (4700)
2003/04: 16⁶G, 17⁰GS, 20⁵G,

	Starts	1st	2nd	3rd	Win & Pl
Hurdles	3	0	0	0	0
Career Total	5	0	0	1	818

Going:	Sf: 0-0 GS: 0-1 Gd: 0-2 GF: - Fm: 0-0
Distance:	2m/2m3: 0-2 2m4-2m7: 0-1 3m+: 0-0
Track:	LH: 0-2 RH: 0-0 Tight: 0-3 Gall: 0-0
Aids:	Bl: 0-0 Vi: 0-0 Tstrap: 0-0 Ckp: 0-0
Best Rating:	90 11/02 Tntn 2m1f gd-sft NHF

Dusky Lord

94f   **89f**

5-y-o b g Lord Americo-Red Dusk (Deep Run)
N J Gifford The American Dream

Placings:3   (4934)
2003/04: 18³G,

	Starts	1st	2nd	3rd	Win & Pl
NH Flat	1	0	0	1	274
Career Total	1	0	0	1	274

Going:	Sf: 0-0 GS: 0-0 Gd: 0-1 GF: - Fm: 0-0
Distance:	2m/2m3: 0-1 2m4-2m7: 0-0 3m+: 0-0
Track:	LH: 0-1 RH: 0-0 Tight: 0-1 Gall: 0-0
Aids:	Bl: 0-0 Vi: 0-0 Tstrap: 0-0 Ckp: 0-0
Best Rating:	89 4/04 Font 2m2f110y good NHF

Dusty Bandit (IRE)

101   **95+**

6-y-o ch g Un Desperado (FR)-Marble Miller (IRE) (Mister Lord (USA))
P F Nicholls Mrs J Stewart

Placings:53P   (4931)
2003/04: 18⁵GS, 19³G, 22PG,

	Starts	1st	2nd	3rd	Win & Pl
Hurdles	3	0	0	1	1024
Career Total	3	0	0	1	1024

Going:	Sf: 0-0 GS: 0-1 Gd: 0-2 GF: - Fm: 0-0
Distance:	2m/2m3: 0-1 2m4-2m7: 0-2 3m+: 0-0
Track:	LH: 0-2 RH: 0-1 Tight: 0-3 Gall: 0-0
Aids:	Bl: 0-0 Vi: 0-0 Tstrap: 0-0 Ckp: 0-0

Best Rating: 95   3/04   Tntn   2m3f110y   good   Hdl

A brother to decent Irish bumper winner Kymadjen; green on debut at Fontwell in fair novice hurdle; respectable effort next time; will stay two and a half miles; acts on good ground.

Dusty Too

108   **104+**

6-y-o gr m Terimon-Princess Florine (USA) (Our Native (USA))
Mrs A J Perrett S P Tindall

Placings: 1140-113   (3513)
2003/04: 18¹GF, 21¹GF, 20³G,

	Starts	1st	2nd	3rd	Win & Pl
Hurdles	3	2	0	1	5728
Career Total	7	4	0	1	9881

90	10/03	Plum	2m5f	E Hdl	G-F	£2586
104	9/03	Font	2m2f110yE Hdl		G-F	£2618
97	8/02	Worc	2m	H NHF		£1887
101	8/02	Worc	2m	H NHF	GD	£2266
				Total win prize-money £9359

Going: Sf: 0-0 GS: 0-0 Gd: 0-1 GF: - Fm: 2-2
Distance: 2m/2m3: 1-1 2m4-2m7: 1-2 3m+: 0-0
Track: LH: 2-2 RH: 0-0 Tight: 2-3 Gall: 0-0
Aids: Bl: 0-0 Vi: 0-0 Tstrap: 0-0 Ckp: 0-0
Best Rating: 117 1/04 Font 2m4f good Hdl

Moderate novice hurdler; half-sister to a couple of bumper winners in Ireland; dual bumper winner; landed two weak hurdles in the autumn of 2003; acts on fast ground; stays two miles five.

Dutch Star

67f   **40f**

5-y-o b m Alflora (IRE)-Double Dutch (Nicholas Bill)
G P Enright McManus/Fuller

Placings: 0   (4454)
2003/04: 16⁰GS,

	Starts	1st	2nd	3rd	Win & Pl
NH Flat	1	0	0	0	
Career Total	1	0	0	0	

Going: Sf: 0-0 GS: 0-1 Gd: 0-0 GF: - Fm: 0-0
Distance: 2m/2m3: 0-1 2m4-2m7: 0-0 3m+: 0-0
Track: LH: 0-0 RH: 0-1 Tight: 0-0 Gall: 0-0
Aids: Bl: 0-0 Vi: 0-0 Tstrap: 0-0 Ckp: 0-0
Best Rating: 40 3/04 Asct 2m110y gd-sft NHF

Dylan The Villain

63f   **29f**

5-y-o b g Overbury (IRE)-Radmore Brandy (Derrylin)
G A Ham J R Salter

Placings: 000   (4738)
2003/04: 18⁰S, 16⁰G, 17⁰G,

	Starts	1st	2nd	3rd	Win & Pl
NH Flat	3	0	0	0	
Career Total	3	0	0	0	

Going: Sf: 0-1 GS: 0-0 Gd: 0-2 GF: - Fm: 0-0
Distance: 2m/2m3: 0-3 2m4-2m7: 0-0 3m+: 0-0
Track: LH: 0-2 RH: 0-1 Tight: 0-1 Gall: 0-0
Aids: Bl: 0-0 Vi: 0-0 Tstrap: 0-0 Ckp: 0-0
Best Rating: 29 2/04 Plum 2m2f soft NHF

Dynamic Lifter (IRE)

104   **95**

6-y-o ch g Be My Native (USA)-Best Trump (Le Bavard (FR))
Jonjo O'Neill John P McManus

Placings: 006032-322P   (0858)
2003/04: 24³S, 24²GF, 27²GF, 22⁰GF,

	Starts	1st	2nd	3rd	Win & Pl
Hurdles	4	0	2	1	3773
Career Total	10	0	3	2	5231

Going: Sf: 0-1 GS: 0-0 Gd: 0-0 GF: - Fm: 0-3
Distance: 2m/2m3: 0-0 2m4-2m7: 0-1 3m+: 0-3
Track: LH: 0-4 RH: 0-0 Tight: 0-2 Gall: 0-0
Aids: Bl: 0-1 Vi: 0-0 Tstrap: 0-0 Ckp: 0-0
Best Rating: 95 6/03 NAbb 3m3f gd-fm Hdl

Moderate hurdler; stays 3m 3f; acts on fast ground; running well in the summer of 2003.

Eagle Eye Boy

10-y-o b/br g Roscoe Blake-Hayburnwyke (Pretty Form)
G F Bridgwater Mrs Gail Bridgwater

Placings: 0   (2032)
2003/04: 20⁰GF,

	Starts	1st	2nd	3rd	Win & Pl
Hurdles	1	0	0	0	
Career Total	1	0	0	0	

Going: Sf: 0-0 GS: 0-0 Gd: 0-0 GF: - Fm: 0-1
Distance: 2m/2m3: 0-0 2m4-2m7: 0-0 3m+: 0-0
Track: LH: 0-1 RH: 0-0 Tight: 0-0 Gall: 0-0
Aids: Bl: 0-0 Vi: 0-0 Tstrap: 0-0 Ckp: 0-0

Eagles High (IRE)

106   **111**

5-y-o ch g Eagle Eyed (USA)-Bint Al Balad (IRE) (Ahonoora)
Patrick O Brady Miss Rita Shah

Placings: 1-503L044233F3303   (4372)
2003/04: 16²G, 17⁰G, 16³YS, 19⁰GF, 20⁰GF, 16⁴GY, 16⁴S, 16²YS, 20⁰S, 17³S, 16⁴S, 16³S, 20³Y, 19⁰Y, 16³GF,

	Starts	1st	2nd	3rd	Win & Pl
Hurdles	15	0	1	6	11719
Career Total	16	1	1	6	16647
99	3/03	Navn	2m	Hdl	HVY £4928
				Total win prize-money £4929

Going: Sf: 0-5 GS: 0-0 Gd: 0-2 GF: - Fm: 0-3
Distance: 2m/2m3: 0-12 2m4-2m7: 0-3 3m+: 0-0
Track: LH: 0-9 RH: 0-1 Tight: 0-1 Gall: 0-0
Aids: Bl: 0-0 Vi: 0-0 Tstrap: 0-0 Ckp: 0-0
Best Rating: 111 3/04 Strf 2m110y gd-fm Hdl

Irish hurdles winner on heavy ground.

Eaglet (IRE)

95   **77**

6-y-o b g Eagle Eyed (USA)-Justice System (USA) (Criminal Type (USA))
Miss V Scott A Scott (Northumberland)

Placings: 06U   (1653)
2003/04: 16⁰G, 16⁰YS, 17⁰UG,

	Starts	1st	2nd	3rd	Win & Pl
Hurdles	3	0	0	0	0

Career Total   3   0   0   0   0

Going: Sf: 0-0 GS: 0-0 Gd: 0-2 GF: - Fm: 0-1
Distance: 2m/2m3: 0-3 2m4-2m7: 0-0 3m+: 0-0
Track: LH: 0-2 RH: 0-0 Tight: 0-1 Gall: 0-0
Aids: Bl: 0-0 Vi: 0-0 Tstrap: 0-0 Ckp: 0-0
Best Rating: 77 10/03 Hexm 2m110y gd-fm Hdl

Poor maiden on the Flat and over hurdles; headstrong.

Ear To The Ground (IRE)

95(82c)   (0c)**93**

11-y-o gr m Roselier (FR)-Shanagale Vii (Damsire Unregistered)
P J Rothwell Reins Of Fire Syndicate

Placings: F/12104404000/3360000-P30B20   (3014a)
2003/04: 20⁰GF, 20³G, 21⁰G, 20⁰S, 24²S, 22⁰S,

	Starts	1st	2nd	3rd	Win & Pl
Hurdles	5	0	1	1	1539
Chases	1	0	0	0	0
Career Total	25	2	2	3	17449
115	7/01	Kbgn	2m4f	Ch	GD £6677
105	6/01	Tram	2m6f	Hdl	FRM £4451
				Total win prize-money £11129

Going: Sf: 0-3 GS: 0-0 Gd: 0-2 GF: - Fm: 0-1
Distance: 2m/2m3: 0-0 2m4-2m7: 0-5 3m+: 0-1
Track: LH: 0-1 RH: 0-0 Tight: 0-0 Gall: 0-1
Aids: Bl: 0-0 Vi: 0-0 Tstrap: 0-0 Ckp: 0-5
Best Rating: 122 7/01 Naas 2m3f good Hdl

Earl Sigurd (IRE)

109   **106**

6-y-o ch g High Kicker (USA)-My Kind (Mon Tresor)
L Lungo Queens House

Placings: 3131/00P-24   (0412)
2003/04: 17²G, 20⁴G,

	Starts	1st	2nd	3rd	Win & Pl
Hurdles	2	0	1	0	1556
Career Total	9	2	1	2	8965
103	12/01	Catt	2m	D Hdl	SFT £3997
88	10/01	Kels	2m110y	E Hdl	GD £2618
				Total win prize-money £6616

Going: Sf: 0-0 GS: 0-0 Gd: 0-2 GF: - Fm: 0-0
Distance: 2m/2m3: 0-1 2m4-2m7: 0-1 3m+: 0-0
Track: LH: 0-2 RH: 0-0 Tight: 0-1 Gall: 0-0
Aids: Bl: 0-0 Vi: 0-0 Tstrap: 0-0 Ckp: 0-0
Best Rating: 103 5/03 Bang 2m1f good Hdl

Moderate hurdler; best at two miles; has won on a sound surface and soft ground.

Earl Token

8-y-o b g Primitive Rising (USA)-Lady Token (Roscoe Blake)
R J Armson R J Armson

Placings: PP-P   (0619)
2003/04: 24²G,

	Starts	1st	2nd	3rd	Win & Pl
Hurdles	1	0	0	0	
Career Total	3	0	0	0	

Going: Sf: 0-0 GS: 0-0 Gd: 0-1 GF: - Fm: 0-0
Distance: 2m/2m3: 0-0 2m4-2m7: 0-0 3m+: 0-1

Career Total   3   0   0   0   0

Track: LH: 0-0 RH: 0-1 Tight: 0-1 Gall: 0-0
Aids: Bl: 0-0 Vi: 0-0 Tstrap: 0-0 Ckp: 0-0

Earls Rock

93   74+

6-y-o b g Gunner B-Will Be Wanton (Palm Track)
J K Cresswell J K S Cresswell

Placings:040000   (4887)
2003/04: 16⁰G, 16⁴GF, 17⁰G, 20⁰GS, 19⁰G, 22⁰GF,

	Starts	1st	2nd	3rd	Win & Pl
NH Flat	3	0	0	0	0
Hurdles	3	0	0	0	0
Career Total	6	0	0	0	0

Going: Sf: 0-0 GS: 0-1 Gd: 0-3 GF: - Fm: 0-2
Distance: 2m/2m3: 0-3 2m4-2m7: 0-3 3m+: 0-0
Track: LH: 0-5 RH: 0-1 Tight: 0-2 Gall: 0-0
Aids: Bl: 0-0 Vi: 0-0 Tstrap: 0-0 Ckp: 0-0
Best Rating: 79 10/03 Bang 2m1f good NHF

Earlsfield Raider

99   103

4-y-o ch g Double Trigger (IRE)-Harlequin Walk (IRE)
(Pennine Walk)
G L Moore (R J O'Sullivan 27/5) Mrs R J Doorgachurn

Placings:123451   (4755)
2003/04: 16¹G, 16²S, 16³GS, 16⁴S, 16⁵GS, 21¹G,

	Starts	1st	2nd	3rd	Win & Pl
Hurdles	6	2	1	1	15408
Career Total	6	2	1	1	15408
95	4/04	Plum	2m5f	E Hdl	GD £3920
94	11/03	Sand	2m110y	B Hdl	GD £8955
			Total win prize-money £12875		

Going: Sf: 0-2 GS: 0-2 Gd: 2-2 GF: - Fm: 0-0
Distance: 2m/2m3: 1-5 2m4-2m7: 1-1 3m+: 0-0
Track: LH: 1-1 RH: 1-5 Tight: 1-1 Gall: 0-0
Aids: Bl: 0-0 Vi: 0-0 Tstrap: 0-0 Ckp: 0-0
Best Rating: 103 3/04 Asct 2m110y gd-sft Hdl

Moderate novice hurdler; effective over two miles; acts on good and soft ground.

Early Edition

104(96h)   (93+h)104+

8-y-o b g Primitive Rising (USA)-Ottery News (Pony Express)
O J Carter (P F Nicholls 2/4) O J Carter

Placings:PF-416PPU03P00F1F   (4642)
2003/04: 17⁴GF, 17¹GS, 20⁶G, 17⁵G, 20⁰GS, 20ᵁGS, 20⁰S, 21³S, 24¹PHY, 17⁰GS, 19⁰S, 22⁴G, 25¹GS, 25²FG,

	Starts	1st	2nd	3rd	Win & Pl
Hurdles	10	1	0	1	5086
Chases	4	1	0	0	6910
Career Total	16	2	0	1	11995
104	3/04	Winc	3m1f110yE(0-110)HCh	G-S	£6909
93	7/03	NAbb	2m1f	E Hdl	G-S £4114
			Total win prize-money £11025		

Going: Sf: 0-4 GS: 2-5 Gd: 0-4 GF: - Fm: 0-1
Distance: 2m/2m3: 1-5 2m4-2m7: 0-6 3m+: 1-3
Track: LH: 1-8 RH: 1-6 Tight: 1-7 Gall: 0-1
Aids: Bl: 0-0 Vi: 0-0 Tstrap: 0-1 Ckp: 0-0
Best Rating: 104 3/04 Winc 3m1f110y gd-sft Ch

Former pointer; won weak novices' hurdle at Newton Abbot

---

in July 2003; survived mistakes to win handicap chase at Wincanton in March; stays 3m 1f; effective on easy ground.

Early Morning

9-y-o ch g Cruise Missile-Sparkling Tarqua (Never Die Dancing)
C J Down Dhobiwallah Racing

Placings:PF   (0546)
2003/04: 23⁰G, 21ᶠGF,

	Starts	1st	2nd	3rd	Win & Pl
Chases	2	0	0	0	
Career Total	2	0	0	0	

Going: Sf: 0-0 GS: 0-0 Gd: 0-1 GF: - Fm: 0-1
Distance: 2m/2m3: 0-0 2m4-2m7: 0-1 3m+: 0-1
Track: LH: 0-2 RH: 0-0 Tight: 0-1 Gall: 0-0
Aids: Bl: 0-0 Vi: 0-0 Tstrap: 0-0 Ckp: 0-0

Early Rivers

80f   63f

5-y-o b m Teenoso (USA)-Cherry Morello (Bargello)
C J Down Dr S G F Cave

Placings:00   (4738)
2003/04: 16⁰GS, 17⁰G,

	Starts	1st	2nd	3rd	Win & Pl
NH Flat	2	0	0	0	
Career Total	2	0	0	0	

Going: Sf: 0-0 GS: 0-1 Gd: 0-1 GF: - Fm: 0-0
Distance: 2m/2m3: 0-2 2m4-2m7: 0-0 3m+: 0-0
Track: LH: 0-1 RH: 0-1 Tight: 0-1 Gall: 0-0
Aids: Bl: 0-0 Vi: 0-0 Tstrap: 0-0 Ckp: 0-0
Best Rating: 63 3/04 Ludl 2m gd-sft NHF

Early Start

107   101

6-y-o ch m Husyan (USA)-Gipsy Dawn (Lighter)
J W Mullins Adam Day

Placings:13-2   (1970)
2003/04: 16²G,

	Starts	1st	2nd	3rd	Win & Pl
Hurdles	1	0	1	0	632
Career Total	3	1	1	1	5314
102	2/03	Font	2m2f110yH NHF	SFT	£1932
			Total win prize-money £1932		

Going: Sf: 0-0 GS: 0-0 Gd: 0-1 GF: - Fm: 0-0
Distance: 2m/2m3: 0-1 2m4-2m7: 0-0 3m+: 0-0
Track: LH: 0-0 RH: 0-1 Tight: 0-0 Gall: 0-0
Aids: Bl: 0-0 Vi: 0-0 Tstrap: 0-0 Ckp: 0-0
Best Rating: 102 11/03 Towc 2m good Hdl

Won a soft ground Fontwell bumper on her debut in February 2003; creditable third in mares only Listed event at Cheltenham in April on a sounder surface; absent since runner-up on hurdles debut in November 2003.

Earth Man (IRE)

100f   103f

5-y-o b g Hamas (IRE)-Rajaura (IRE) (Storm Bird (CAN))
P F Nicholls R M Penny

Placings:62   (4934)

2003/04: 16⁶GS, 18²G,

	Starts	1st	2nd	3rd	Win & Pl
NH Flat	2	0	1	0	548
Career Total	2	0	1	0	548

Going: Sf: 0-0 GS: 0-1 Gd: 0-1 GF: - Fm: 0-0
Distance: 2m/2m3: 0-2 2m4-2m7: 0-0 3m+: 0-0
Track: LH: 0-1 RH: 0-1 Tight: 0-1 Gall: 0-0
Aids: Bl: 0-0 Vi: 0-0 Tstrap: 0-0 Ckp: 0-0
Best Rating: 103 4/04 Font 2m2f110y good NHF

Runnerup in bumper on second outing.

Earthmover (IRE)

13-y-o ch g Mister Lord (USA)-Clare's Crystal (Tekoah)
P F Nicholls R M Penny

Placings:11111/FU0P/511536F/112233U0/1342P3/P11411
-11P213   (4845)
2003/04: 26¹G, 24¹G, 28ᴾG, 26²G, 26¹G, 26³G,

	Starts	1st	2nd	3rd	Win & Pl
Chases	6	3	1	1	39281
Career Total	42	17	4	6	180851
140	3/04	Chel	3m2f110yB Ch	GD	£23200
113	5/03	Uttx	3m	H Ch	GD	£7266
140	4/03	Chel	3m2f110yH Ch	GD	£6804
140	4/03	Chel	3m2f110yH Ch	GD	£6698
140	4/03	Ayr	3m3f110yH Ch	GD	£3575
134	2/03	Chep	3m2f110yH Ch	HVY	£1561
140	2/03	Weth	3m1f	H Ch	G-S	£1526
150	10/01	Chep	3m	B(0-145)HCh	GD	£9937
152	5/00	Weth	3m1f	B(0-145)HCh	G-S	£9486
148	5/00	Chep	3m	B(0-145)HCh	FRM	£8703
151	11/99	Chep	3m	B(0-150)HHdl	SFT	£6824
141	10/99	Chel	3m1f110yD Hdl	GD	£4531
159	3/98	Chel	3m2f110yB Ch	GD	£18957
133	3/98	Newb	3m	H Ch	SFT	£1576
127	2/98	Wwck	3m2f	H Ch	GD	£1086
119	5/97	Strf	3m4f	H Ch	GD	£4272
112	5/97	Chep	3m	H Ch	G-S	£3434
			Total win prize-money £119441		

Going: Sf: 0-0 GS: 0-0 Gd: 3-6 GF: - Fm: 0-0
Distance: 2m/2m3: 0-0 2m4-2m7: 0-0 3m+: 3-6
Track: LH: 3-5 RH: 0-0 Tight: 0-2 Gall: 2-3
Aids: Bl: 0-0 Vi: 0-0 Tstrap: 0-0 Ckp: 0-0
Best Rating: 159 3/98 Chel 3m2f110y good Ch

Leading hunter chaser; winner of the 1998 Foxhunters' at Cheltenham and successful in the same race in 2004; needs a left-handed track; stays well; acts on most ground; very genuine; a credit to connections.

Easibrook Jane

103   110

6-y-o b m Alderbrook-Relatively Easy (Relkino)
C L Tizzard R G Tizzard

Placings:05320-11606   (4833)
2003/04: 21¹S, 19¹S, 21⁶GS, 21⁰G, 21⁶GF,

	Starts	1st	2nd	3rd	Win & Pl
Hurdles	5	2	0	0	7695
Career Total	10	2	1	1	9853
107	12/03	Ling	2m3f110yE Hdl	SFT	£3514
110	11/03	Plum	2m5f	E Hdl	SFT	£3731
			Total win prize-money £7245		

Going: Sf: 2-2 GS: 0-1 Gd: 0-1 GF: - Fm: 0-0
Distance: 2m/2m3: 0-0 2m4-2m7: 2-5 3m+: 0-0
Track: LH: 2-5 RH: 0-0 Tight: 2-2 Gall: 0-3
Aids: Bl: 0-0 Vi: 0-0 Tstrap: 0-0 Ckp: 0-0
Best Rating: 110 4/04 Chel 2m5f110y gd-fm Hdl

Fair novice hurdler; stays two miles five; has shown form on a soft surface.

East Hill (IRE)

105   **107+**

8-y-o b g Satco (FR)-Sharmalyne (FR) (Melyno)
G B Balding Leon Best

Placings:341/2240/40452-3140220050   (3514)
2003/04: 18³G, 20¹G, 21⁴G, 21⁰G, 22²GF, 19²G, 20⁰G, 20⁰G, 21⁵G, 18⁰G,

	Starts	1st	2nd	3rd	Win & Pl
Hurdles	10	1	2	1	6921
Career Total	22	2	5	2	13157
107 10/03	Bang	2m4f	E(0-110)HHdl	GD	£3562
106 4/01	Font	2m2f110yH NHF		GD	£1914
			Total win prize-money £5477

Going: Sf: 0-0 GS: 0-0 Gd: 1-9 GF: - Fm: 0-1
Distance: 2m/2m3: 0-2 2m4-2m7: 1-8 3m+: 0-0
Track: LH: 1-5 RH: 0-4 Tight: 1-6 Gall: 0-1
Aids: Bl: 0-0 Vi: 0-0 Tstrap: 0-0 Ckp: 0-0
Best Rating: 107 12/03 Tntn 2m3f110y good Hdl

Modest novice hurdler; bumper winner; stays 2m 5f and best on good ground; likes to front run.

East Lawyer (FR)

90   **82**

5-y-o b g Homme De Loi (IRE)-East Riding (FR) (Fabulous Dancer (USA))
P F Nicholls (M Rolland 10/6) Champneys Partnership

Placings:5320-1PP6   (3708)
2003/04: 18¹VS, 20²GF, 20⁰G, 16⁸HY,

	Starts	1st	2nd	3rd	Win & Pl
Hurdles	4	1	0	0	23377
Career Total	8	1	1	1	39261
5/03	Autl	2m2f	HHdl		VS	£23377
			Total win prize-money £23377

Going: Sf: 0-1 GS: 0-0 Gd: 0-1 GF: - Fm: 0-1
Distance: 2m/2m3: 1-2 2m4-2m7: 0-2 3m+: 0-0
Track: LH: 0-2 RH: 0-0 Tight: 0-1 Gall: 0-0
Aids: Bl: 1-2 Vi: 0-0 Tstrap: 0-1 Ckp: 0-0
Best Rating: 82 2/04 Chep 2m110y heavy Hdl

A winner over hurdles in France; pulled up on British debut; stays two miles two; wore blinkers in France.

East Tycoon (IRE)

106   **122+**

5-y-o ch g Bigstone (IRE)-Princesse Sharpo (USA) (Trempolino (USA))
Jonjo O'Neill Mrs G Smith

Placings:141-60   (2594)
2003/04: 20⁶GS, 16⁰GS,

	Starts	1st	2nd	3rd	Win & Pl
Hurdles	2	0	0	0	0
Career Total	5	2	0	0	14299
128 3/03	Strf	2m110y D Hdl		G-S	£5577
120 1/03	Donc	2m110y C Hdl		G-S	£7221
			Total win prize-money £12799

Going: Sf: 0-0 GS: 0-2 Gd: 0-0 GF: - Fm: 0-0
Distance: 2m/2m3: 0-1 2m4-2m7: 0-1 3m+: 0-0
Track: LH: 0-1 RH: 0-1 Tight: 0-1 Gall: 0-0
Aids: Bl: 0-0 Vi: 0-0 Tstrap: 0-0 Ckp: 0-0
Best Rating: 128 3/03 Strf 2m110y gd-sft Hdl

Fair ex-Irish hurdler; effective at two miles; acts on most ground; has worn blinkers.

Easter Present (IRE)

100   **106**

5-y-o br g Presenting-Spring Fiddler (IRE) (Fidel)
Miss H C Knight Mrs R A Humphries

Placings:3-4122   (3775)
2003/04: 16⁴GS, 17¹GS, 16²S, 16²G,

	Starts	1st	2nd	3rd	Win & Pl
NH Flat	2	1	0	0	2370
Hurdles	2	0	2	0	2746
Career Total	5	1	2	1	5401
101 12/03	Hrfd	2m1f	H NHF		G-S	£1785
			Total win prize-money £1785

Going: Sf: 0-1 GS: 1-2 Gd: 0-1 GF: - Fm: 0-0
Distance: 2m/2m3: 1-4 2m4-2m7: 0-0 3m+: 0-0
Track: LH: 0-1 RH: 1-3 Tight: 0-0 Gall: 0-2
Aids: Bl: 0-0 Vi: 0-0 Tstrap: 0-0 Ckp: 0-0
Best Rating: 108 11/03 Newb 2m110y gd-sft NHF

Modest novice hurdler; bumper winner; has shown a fair bit of promise over hurdles; acts on good and soft ground.

Eastern Point

10-y-o b m Buckskin (FR)-Deep Creek (Deep Run)
P York (R H York 2/8) Mrs K H York

Placings:30043P21   (4298)
2003/04: 21³GF, 28⁰GS, 20⁰G, 21⁴GF, 23³G, 20²G, 21²G, 23¹G,

	Starts	1st	2nd	3rd	Win & Pl
Chases	8	1	1	2	3982
Career Total	8	1	1	2	3982
100 3/04	Leic	2m7f110yH CH		GD	£2203
			Total win prize-money £2204

Going: Sf: 0-0 GS: 0-1 Gd: 1-5 GF: - Fm: 0-2
Distance: 2m/2m3: 0-0 2m4-2m7: 0-5 3m+: 1-3
Track: LH: 0-4 RH: 1-4 Tight: 0-5 Gall: 0-0
Aids: Bl: 0-0 Vi: 0-0 Tstrap: 0-0 Ckp: 0-0
Best Rating: 100 3/04 Leic 2m7f110y good Ch

Moderate hunter chaser; stays three miles; acts on good.

Eastern Tribute (USA)

110(114h)   (125 h)**115+**

8-y-o b g Affirmed (USA)-Mia Duchessa (USA) (Nijinsky (CAN))
A C Whillans John J Elliot

Placings:33F44/51410202/033225P42/1U42601FP-UP21PPP   (4912)
2003/04: 16⁰S, 21⁸S, 21²GS, 16¹HY, 20²G, 16⁸S, 20⁸S,

	Starts	1st	2nd	3rd	Win & Pl
Chases	7	1	1	0	5382
Career Total	38	5	7	4	40806
115 1/04	Newc	2m110y E Ch		HVY	£3997
122 1/03	Ayr	2m4f	B(0-150)HHdl	HVY	£10159
113 5/02	Kels	2m2f	D(0-125)HHdl	G-S	£6201
110 1/01	Ayr	2m	D(0-125)HHdl	SFT	£3388
98 11/00	Ayr	2m	E Hdl	SFT	£1974
			Total win prize-money £25721

Going: Sf: 1-5 GS: 0-1 Gd: 0-1 GF: - Fm: 0-0
Distance: 2m/2m3: 1-3 2m4-2m7: 0-4 3m+: 0-0
Track: LH: 1-6 RH: 0-1 Tight: 0-1 Gall: 1-3
Aids: Bl: 0-0 Vi: 0-0 Tstrap: 0-0 Ckp: 0-0
Best Rating: 122 1/03 Ayr 2m4f heavy Hdl

Fair chaser; formerly fair handicap hurdler; suited by soft and heavy ground; effective at up to two and a half miles.

Easternking

95   **71+**

5-y-o ch m Sabrehill (USA)-Kshessinskaya (Hadeer)
J S Wainwright Peter Easterby

Placings:0056520-400   (4603)
2003/04: 24⁴GF, 24⁰GF, 17⁰G,

	Starts	1st	2nd	3rd	Win & Pl
Hurdles	3	0	0	1	266
Career Total	10	0	1	0	966

Going: Sf: 0-0 GS: 0-0 Gd: 0-1 GF: - Fm: 0-2
Distance: 2m/2m3: 0-1 2m4-2m7: 0-0 3m+: 0-2
Track: LH: 0-1 RH: 0-2 Tight: 0-2 Gall: 0-1
Aids: Bl: 0-0 Vi: 0-3 Tstrap: 0-0 Ckp: 0-0
Best Rating: 71 10/03 MRas 3m gd-fm Hdl

Plating-class hurdler.

Eastwell Manor

97   **72**

6-y-o b g Dancing Spree (USA)-Kinchenjunga (Darshaan)
Miss M Bragg Friends Of Rock Park

Placings:PP/3F-0   (0491)
2003/04: 17⁰GF,

	Starts	1st	2nd	3rd	Win & Pl
Hurdles	1	0	0	0	
Career Total	5	0	0	1	579

Going: Sf: 0-0 GS: 0-0 Gd: 0-0 GF: - Fm: 0-1
Distance: 2m/2m3: 0-1 2m4-2m7: 0-0 3m+: 0-0
Track: LH: 0-1 RH: 0-0 Tight: 0-1 Gall: 0-0
Aids: Bl: 0-0 Vi: 0-0 Tstrap: 0-0 Ckp: 0-0
Best Rating: 72 8/02 NAbb 2m1f gd-fm Hdl

Eastwell Violet

4-y-o b f Danzig Connection (USA)-Kinchenjunga (Darshaan)
R T Phillips (S Dow 10/7) Eastwell Manor Racing Ltd

Placings:0   (2205)
2003/04: 17⁰G,

	Starts	1st	2nd	3rd	Win & Pl
Hurdles	1	0	0	0	
Career Total	1	0	0	0	

Going: Sf: 0-0 GS: 0-0 Gd: 0-0 GF: - Fm: 0-0
Distance: 2m/2m3: 0-1 2m4-2m7: 0-0 3m+: 0-0
Track: LH: 0-1 RH: 0-1 Tight: 0-1 Gall: 0-0
Aids: Bl: 0-0 Vi: 0-0 Tstrap: 0-0 Ckp: 0-0

Easy Rider (IRE)

87   **60**

4-y-o b g Blues Traveller (IRE)-Curie Express (IRE) (Fayruz)
E L James Tantivy Racing Partnership 2

Placings:3   (1267)
2003/04: 17³GF,

	Starts	1st	2nd	3rd	Win & Pl
Hurdles	1	0	0	1	411
Career Total	1	0	0	1	411

Going:	Sf: 0-0 GS: 0-0 Gd: 0-0 GF: - Fm: 0-1
Distance:	2m/2m3: 0-1 2m4-2m7: 0-0 3m+: 0-0
Track:	LH: 0-1 RH: 0-0 Tight: 0-1 Gall: 0-0
Aids:	Bl: 0-0 Vi: 0-0 Tstrap: 0-1 Ckp: 0-0
Best Rating:	65 9/03 NAbb 2m1f gd-fm Hdl

Runner-up five times on the Flat at up to a mile; shaped like a non-stayer when well beaten third on hurdling debut.

Easy Squeezy

(92h)   (72h)
7-y-o b g Alflora (IRE)-Easy Horse (FR) (Carmarthen (FR))
N A Twiston-Davies The Yes - No - Wait Sorries

Placings:500-3666PFPF   (1189)
2003/04: 22³G, 26⁶GF, 26⁶GF, 20⁶G, 23⁹GF, 23⁷G, 24²G, 24⁶GF,

	Starts	1st	2nd	3rd	Win & Pl
Hurdles	5	0	0	1	900
Chases	3	0	0	0	
Career Total	11	0	0	1	900

Going:	Sf: 0-0 GS: 0-0 Gd: 0-4 GF: - Fm: 0-4
Distance:	2m/2m3: 0-0 2m4-2m7: 0-1 3m+: 0-6
Track:	LH: 0-7 RH: 0-1 Tight: 0-2 Gall: 0-4
Aids:	Bl: 0-4 Vi: 0-0 Tstrap: 0-0 Ckp: 0-0
Best Rating:	87 1/03 Sthl 2m good NHF

Plating-class hurdler; benefitted from waiting tactics when a strong finishing third in 2m 6f novice hurdle at Stratford May 2003; tried to run out next time; should stay 3m; acts on fast ground.

Easy Tiger (FR)

6-y-o ch g Sillery (USA)-Extreme Dream (FR) (Zino)
Jonjo O'Neill Team Tiger

Placings:0/5-P   (2941)
2003/04: 16⁹GS,

	Starts	1st	2nd	3rd	Win & Pl
Hurdles	1	0	0	0	
Career Total	3	0	0	0	0

Going:	Sf: 0-0 GS: 0-1 Gd: 0-0 GF: - Fm: 0-0
Distance:	2m/2m3: 0-1 2m4-2m7: 0-0 3m+: 0-0
Track:	LH: 0-1 RH: 0-0 Tight: 0-0 Gall: 0-0
Aids:	Bl: 0-0 Vi: 0-0 Tstrap: 0-0 Ckp: 0-0
Best Rating:	76 5/02 Folk 2m1f110y good NHF

Eau De Cologne

105   139
12-y-o b g Persian Bold-No More Rosies (Warpath)
B G Powell Dr M Evans

Placings:3212/1F2342611/42/2116/42113/20P32UP/66340
502112-43U0   (4572)
2003/04: 25⁴G, 24³GF, 27⁴G, 24⁹G,

	Starts	1st	2nd	3rd	Win & Pl
Chases	4	0	0	1	4126
Career Total	46	10	11	6	145237
139	3/03	Hayd	3m	D(0-125)HCh	G-F	£8628
126	3/03	Newb	3m	C(0-135)HCh	GD	£16158
149	3/01	Asct	2m3f110yB HCh		SFT	£10088
143	12/00	Kemp	3m	C(0-130)HCh	G-S	£11310
144	3/00	Newb	3m	C(0-140)HCh	G-F	£10520
137	3/00	Winc	2m5f	D Ch	G-S	£4387
138	4/98	Asct	3m	B HHdl	SFT	£5193
141	2/98	Newb	3m110y	C(0-130)HHdl	GD	£4130
115	5/97	Hrfd	2m3f110yE Hdl		GD	£2070
109	3/97	Plum	2m4f	E Hdl	G-F	£2826
			Total win prize-money £75314			

Going:	Sf: 0-0 GS: 0-0 Gd: 0-3 GF: - Fm: 0-1
Distance:	2m/2m3: 0-0 2m4-2m7: 0-0 3m+: 0-4
Track:	LH: 0-3 RH: 0-1 Tight: 0-2 Gall: 0-1
Aids:	Bl: 0-3 Vi: 0-1 Tstrap: 0-0 Ckp: 0-0
Best Rating:	149 10/01 Winc 2m5f good Ch

Useful chaser; stays beyond three miles and acts on most types of ground; goes well in a visor/ blinkers; established a good partnership with James Davies.Reportedly retired.

Eau Pure (FR)

102   98+
7-y-o b m Epervier Bleu-Eau De Nuit (King's Lake (USA))
G L Moore (B A Pearce 2/1) Trevor Painting

Placings:005/0FP4613000/P404P001132U4   (4917)
2003/04: 17⁵GF, 16⁴HY, 20⁶GF, 23⁴G, 16⁶S, 19⁰S, 17⁰HY, 18¹GF,
19¹GS, 17³G, 23²GS, 21⁴UG, 20⁴GS,

	Starts	1st	2nd	3rd	Win & Pl
Hurdles	13	2	1	1	8608
Career Total	26	3	1	2	16948
96	3/04	Towc	2m3f110yF(0-100)HHdl		G-S	£2975
90	3/04	Font	2m2f110yF(0-100)HHdl		G-F	£3451
8/01	Diep	2m1f110y Ch		SFT	£3686
		Total win prize-money £10112			

Going:	Sf: 0-4 GS: 1-3 Gd: 0-3 GF: - Fm: 1-3
Distance:	2m/2m3: 1-6 2m4-2m7: 1-7 3m+: 0-0
Track:	LH: 1-8 RH: 0-4 Tight: 1-7 Gall: 0-0
Aids:	Bl: 0-0 Vi: 0-0 Tstrap: 0-0 Ckp: 0-1
Best Rating:	98 4/04 Ling 2m7f gd-sft Hdl

Moderate hurdler; dual winner in March 2004; stays 2 1/2 miles; acts on fast and easy ground.

Eau So Sloe

13-y-o b g Baron Blakeney-Final Attraction (Jalmood (USA))
F L Matthews Mrs L Danton

Placings:5/0PF4F4P/2/PP0P/PPPP/PPPUP/0PP00-P
                                                                      (0483)
2003/04: 24PGF,

	Starts	1st	2nd	3rd	Win & Pl
Chases	1	0	0	0	
Career Total	28	0	1	0	1075

Going:	Sf: 0-0 GS: 0-0 Gd: 0-0 GF: - Fm: 0-1
Distance:	2m/2m3: 0-0 2m4-2m7: 0-0 3m+: 0-1
Track:	LH: 0-0 RH: 0-1 Tight: 0-0 Gall: 0-1
Aids:	Bl: 0-1 Vi: 0-1 Tstrap: 0-0 Ckp: 0-0
Best Rating:	90 12/95 Folk 2m1f110y good NHF

Ebinzayd (IRE)

111   126+
8-y-o b g Tenby-Sharakawa (IRE) (Darshaan)
L Lungo R J Gilbert

Placings:0/12113/2U0/20500-100P1   (4883)
2003/04: 18¹G, 16⁶S, 20⁶G, 20³GF, 17¹GS,

	Starts	1st	2nd	3rd	Win & Pl
Hurdles	5	2	0	0	11762
Career Total	19	5	3	1	25595
126	4/04	Carl	2m1f	D(0-120)HHdl	G-S	£5027
122	4/03	Kels	2m2f	D(0-125)HHdl	GD	£6734
119	4/01	Muss	2m1f	D Hdl	G-F	£3822
109	1/01	Muss	2m	E Hdl	G-S	£2254
116	11/00	Kels	2m110y	E Hdl	SFT	£2964
		Total win prize-money £20802			

Going:	Sf: 0-1 GS: 1-1 Gd: 1-2 GF: - Fm: 0-1
Distance:	2m/2m3: 2-3 2m4-2m7: 0-2 3m+: 0-0
Track:	LH: 1-3 RH: 1-2 Tight: 1-2 Gall: 0-0
Aids:	Bl: 0-0 Vi: 0-0 Tstrap: 0-0 Ckp: 0-0
Best Rating:	126 4/04 Carl 2m1f gd-sft Hdl

Fair but temperamental hurdler; recorded fifth career win at Carlisle in April; stays two and a half miles; acts on any ground; jumped badly when tried over fences.

Ebitda (IRE)

73f   71f
6-y-o ch g Executive Perk-Ursula's Choice (Cracksman)
Miss K Marks Nick Shutts

Placings:00   (0263)
2003/04: 16⁹G, 16⁸GF,

	Starts	1st	2nd	3rd	Win & Pl
NH Flat	2	0	0	0	
Career Total	2	0	0	0	

Going:	Sf: 0-0 GS: 0-0 Gd: 0-1 GF: - Fm: 0-1
Distance:	2m/2m3: 0-2 2m4-2m7: 0-0 3m+: 0-0
Track:	LH: 0-0 RH: 0-2 Tight: 0-0 Gall: 0-0
Aids:	Bl: 0-0 Vi: 0-0 Tstrap: 0-0 Ckp: 0-0
Best Rating:	71 5/03 Ludl 2m good NHF

Ebony Light (IRE)

108(100h)   (101h)146
8-y-o br g Buckskin (FR)-Amelioras Daughter (General Ironside)
D McCain Roger Bellamy

Placings:40213/3334F1F114-31P4P4P6   (4726)
2003/04: 20³G, 26¹G, 29⁶G, 24⁴G, 24⁶HY, 28⁴G, 32⁶G, 24⁶G,

	Starts	1st	2nd	3rd	Win & Pl
Chases	8	1	0	1	18242
Career Total	23	5	1	5	42373
137	11/03	Carl	3m2f	C(0-135)HCh	GD	£8385
139	3/03	Carl	2m4f	C Ch	SFT	£9065
125	2/03	Newc	2m4f	E Ch	SFT	£4134
110	1/03	Newc	2m4f	E Ch	HVY	£4026
100	3/02	Uttx	3m110y	E Hdl	HVY	£2702
			Total win prize-money £28313			

Going:	Sf: 0-1 GS: 0-0 Gd: 1-7 GF: - Fm: 0-0
Distance:	2m/2m3: 0-0 2m4-2m7: 0-1 3m+: 1-7
Track:	LH: 0-5 RH: 1-3 Tight: 0-2 Gall: 0-0
Aids:	Bl: 0-0 Vi: 0-0 Tstrap: 0-0 Ckp: 0-0
Best Rating:	139 3/03 Carl 2m4f soft Ch

Fair front-running chaser; stays three and a half miles; handles testing conditions; best on right-handed tracks.

Eccentricity

95   80
6-y-o b m Emarati (USA)-Lady Electric (Electric)
A King A J Coombes & J L Frampton

Placings:35   (3859)
2003/04: 17³GS, 16⁵S,

	Starts	1st	2nd	3rd	Win & Pl
Hurdles	2	0	0	1	652
Career Total	2	0	0	1	652

Going:	Sf: 0-1 GS: 0-1 Gd: 0-0 GF: - Fm: 0-0
Distance:	2m/2m3: 0-0 2m4-2m7: 0-0 3m+: 0-0
Track:	LH: 0-1 RH: 0-1 Tight: 0-2 Gall: 0-0
Aids:	Bl: 0-0 Vi: 0-0 Tstrap: 0-0 Ckp: 0-0
Best Rating:	80 2/04 Plum 2m soft Hdl

Echo Du Lac (FR)

104 (113h)**116**

8-y-o b g Matahawk-Love Dream (FR) (Platonic Love)
A King Jerry Wright

Placings:46/3P10/P3/F1P234-02PP (4734)
2003/04: 24⁰G, 24²G, 25ᴾGS, 26ᴾG,

	Starts	1st	2nd	3rd	Win & Pl
Chases	4	0	1	0	1700
Career Total	18	2	2	3	14586
116 12/02 Sthl	3m110y	D(0-115)HCh	G-S	£5148
110 3/01 Ling	2m110y	E(0-105)HHdl	HVY	£2933
		Total win prize-money £8081

Going:	Sf: 0-0 GS: 0-1 Gd: 0-3 GF: - Fm: 0-0
Distance:	2m/2m3: 0-0 2m4-2m7: 0-0 3m+: 0-0
Track:	LH: 0-2 RH: 0-0 Tight: 0-2 Gall: 0-0
Aids:	Bl: 0-0 Vi: 0-0 Tstrap: 0-3 Ckp: 0-0
Best Rating:	116 3/04 Bang 3m110y good Ch

Modest chaser; stays three miles; cannot have the ground too soft; usually wears tongue tie.

Echo's Of Dawn (IRE)

73 **123**

12-y-o ch g Duky-Nicenames (IRE) (Decent Fellow)
John R Upson Middleham Park Racing Xvii

Placings:UP532/4112U153/1626P/31P0P-P0P (4494)
2003/04: 24ᴾGS, 24⁰G, 24ᴾGS,

	Starts	1st	2nd	3rd	Win & Pl
Chases	3	0	0	0	
Career Total	26	5	3	3	39723
123 12/02 Uttx	3m	D(0-125)HCh	SFT	£5733
124 11/01 Bang	3m110y	C(0-130)HCh	SFT	£6955
124 1/00 Ludl	3m	E(0-105)HCh	GD	£3818
117 11/99 Uttx	2m5f	E(0-115)HCh	G-S	£4182
109 11/99 Uttx	2m4f	E(0-105)HCh	SFT	£2957
		Total win prize-money £23646

Going:	Sf: 0-0 GS: 0-3 Gd: 0-0 GF: - Fm: 0-0
Distance:	2m/2m3: 0-0 2m4-2m7: 0-0 3m+: 0-3
Track:	LH: 0-2 RH: 0-1 Tight: 0-2 Gall: 0-0
Aids:	Bl: 0-0 Vi: 0-0 Tstrap: 0-0 Ckp: 0-0
Best Rating:	124 2/02 Sand 3m110y gd-sft Ch

Modest chaser these days; stays 3m; acts in soft ground.

Ede'Iff

105(104h) (98h)**109**

7-y-o b m Tragic Role (USA)-Flying Amy (Norwick (USA))
W G M Turner Hawks And Doves Racing Syndicate

Placings:P400/5/656U2141130-35642512 (4674)
2003/04: 16³G, 16⁵GF, 18⁶G, 16⁴G, 16⁵HY, 20¹G, 16²G,

	Starts	1st	2nd	3rd	Win & Pl
Hurdles	3	0	0	1	788
Chases	5	1	2	0	10383
Career Total	24	4	3	2	21828
104 3/04 Ludl	2m4f	D Ch	GD	£6669
95 2/03 Leic	2m	F Hdl	HVY	£3503
85 1/03 Ludl	2m	G(75-95)Hdl	SFT	£3104
83 12/02 Ludl	2m	F Hdl	GD	£3115
		Total win prize-money £16393

Going:	Sf: 0-1 GS: 0-0 Gd: 1-6 GF: - Fm: 0-0
Distance:	2m/2m3: 0-7 2m4-2m7: 1-1 3m+: 0-0
Track:	LH: 0-2 RH: 1-6 Tight: 1-3 Gall: 0-0
Aids:	Bl: 0-0 Vi: 0-0 Tstrap: 1-8 Ckp: 0-0
Best Rating:	110 4/04 Winc 2m good Ch

Moderate hurdler/novice chaser; successful three times in selling and plating company; stays two and a half miles; effective at two; acts on good and soft ground.

Ede's

96 **79**

4-y-o ch g Bijou D'Inde-Ballagarrow Girl (North Stoke)
W G M Turner Tony Smith

Placings:210 (4788)
2003/04: 16²GF, 16¹GS, 16⁰G,

	Starts	1st	2nd	3rd	Win & Pl
Hurdles	3	1	1	0	4252
Career Total	3	1	1	0	4252
65 3/04 Plum	2m	F Hdl	G-S	£2548
		Total win prize-money £2548

Going:	Sf: 0-0 GS: 1-1 Gd: 0-1 GF: - Fm: 0-1
Distance:	2m/2m3: 1-3 2m4-2m7: 0-0 3m+: 0-0
Track:	LH: 1-3 RH: 0-0 Tight: 1-3 Gall: 0-0
Aids:	Bl: 0-0 Vi: 0-0 Tstrap: 0-0 Ckp: 0-0
Best Rating:	79 8/03 Strf 2m110y gd-fm Hdl

Lightly-raced on the Flat; ran well when runner-up on his hurdling debut at Stratford in August 2003; acts on fast ground.

Edgar Gink (IRE)

10-y-o ch g Step Together (USA)-Turbo Run (Deep Run)
L Corcoran The A T P Racing Partnership

Placings:5P/4P53/23-0 (0028)
2003/04: 21⁰G,

	Starts	1st	2nd	3rd	Win & Pl
Chases	1	0	0	0	
Career Total	9	0	1	2	3357

Going:	Sf: 0-0 GS: 0-0 Gd: 0-1 GF: - Fm: 0-0
Distance:	2m/2m3: 0-0 2m4-2m7: 0-1 3m+: 0-0
Track:	LH: 0-1 RH: 0-0 Tight: 0-0 Gall: 0-1
Aids:	Bl: 0-0 Vi: 0-0 Tstrap: 0-0 Ckp: 0-0
Best Rating:	100 4/03 Aint 3m1f good Ch

Won weak point March 2003; unlucky not to win Taunton Hunter Chase eight days later when over confidently ridden; acts on ground good and faster.

Edgemoor Princess

83f **61f**

6-y-o b m Broadsword (USA)-Stubbin Moor (Kinglet)
R J Armson R J Armson

Placings:00 (4920)
2003/04: 16⁵GF, 16⁰GS,

	Starts	1st	2nd	3rd	Win & Pl
NH Flat	2	0	0	0	
Career Total	2	0	0	0	

Going:	Sf: 0-0 GS: 0-1 Gd: 0-0 GF: - Fm: 0-1
Distance:	2m/2m3: 0-2 2m4-2m7: 0-0 3m+: 0-0
Track:	LH: 0-1 RH: 0-0 Tight: 0-0 Gall: 0-0
Aids:	Bl: 0-0 Vi: 0-0 Tstrap: 0-0 Ckp: 0-0
Best Rating:	61 4/04 Worc 2m gd-sft NHF

Edginswell Lass

75 **57**

6-y-o b m Morpeth-Oribi Gorge (IRE) (Heraldiste (USA))

Ian Williams Terry Sanders

Placings:00-00 (4118)
2003/04: 17⁰GS, 22⁰G,

	Starts	1st	2nd	3rd	Win & Pl
Hurdles	2	0	0	0	
Career Total	4	0	0	0	

Going:	Sf: 0-0 GS: 0-1 Gd: 0-1 GF: - Fm: 0-0
Distance:	2m/2m3: 0-1 2m4-2m7: 0-1 3m+: 0-0
Track:	LH: 0-0 RH: 0-2 Tight: 0-2 Gall: 0-0
Aids:	Bl: 0-0 Vi: 0-0 Tstrap: 0-0 Ckp: 0-0
Best Rating:	76 10/02 Hntg 2m110y gd-fm NHF

Edipo Re

92(77c) (43c)**74**

12-y-o b g Slip Anchor-Lady Barrister (Law Society (USA))
Ian Williams (B R Summers 12/5) Tony Eaves

Placings:0/6001/2/1165/60 (0942)
2003/04: 16⁶G, 16⁰G,

	Starts	1st	2nd	3rd	Win & Pl
Hurdles	1	0	0	0	0
Chases	1	0	0	0	0
Career Total	12	3	1	0	6704
93 5/01 Weth	2m	F(0-100)HHdl	FRM	£2100
90 5/01 Hntg	2m110y	F(0-100)HHdl	G-F	£2467
79 4/00 Hntg	2m110y	G(0-95)HHdl	GD	£1666
		Total win prize-money £6234

Going:	Sf: 0-0 GS: 0-0 Gd: 0-2 GF: - Fm: 0-0
Distance:	2m/2m3: 0-2 2m4-2m7: 0-0 3m+: 0-0
Track:	LH: 0-2 RH: 0-0 Tight: 0-0 Gall: 0-0
Aids:	Bl: 0-0 Vi: 0-0 Tstrap: 0-0 Ckp: 0-0
Best Rating:	95 1/97 Hayd 2m gd-fm Hdl

Very moderate handicap hurdler, suited by two miles and fast ground.

Edition Francaise (FR)

6-y-o ch g Garde Royale-Bull Finch Aulmes (FR) (Rose Laurel)
P F Nicholls Sir Robert Ogden

Placings:P (1830)
2003/04: 21ᴾGF,

	Starts	1st	2nd	3rd	Win & Pl
Hurdles	1	0	0	0	
Career Total	1	0	0	0	

Going:	Sf: 0-0 GS: 0-0 Gd: 0-0 GF: - Fm: 0-1
Distance:	2m/2m3: 0-0 2m4-2m7: 0-1 3m+: 0-0
Track:	LH: 0-1 RH: 0-0 Tight: 0-0 Gall: 0-1
Aids:	Bl: 0-0 Vi: 0-0 Tstrap: 0-0 Ckp: 0-0

Edmo Heights

109(118h) (124h)**114**

8-y-o ch g Keen-Bodham (Bustino)
T D Easterby Edmolift Uk Ltd

Placings:13/4P211154O-010331361 (4318)
2003/04: 16⁶GS, 16¹GS, 16⁹G, 17³GF, 17³G, 16¹S, 19³G, 17⁶GS, 16¹S,

	Starts	1st	2nd	3rd	Win & Pl
Hurdles	4	1	0	1	12171
Chases	5	2	0	2	9502

			Starts	1st	2nd	3rd	Win & Pl
Career Total		20	7	1	4		45101
114 3/04 Newc	2m110y	E Ch				SFT	£4342
100 1/04 Weth	2m	E Ch				SFT	£3981
124 5/03 Aint	2m110y	C(0-135)HHdl				G-S	£9593
122 2/03 Catt	2m	C(0-130)HHdl				GD	£6948
111 1/03 Catt	2m	E(0-110)HHdl				GD	£7085
103 12/02 Hayd	2m	E(0-110)HHdl				GD	£3192
98 8/00 Sedg	2m1f	E Hdl				GD	£2338

Total win prize-money £37480

Going:	Sf: 2-2 GS: 1-3 Gd: 0-3 GF: - Fm: 0-1
Distance:	2m/2m3: 3-9 2m4-2m7: 0-0 3m+: 0-0
Track:	LH: 3-7 RH: 0-2 Tight: 1-6 Gall: 1-1
Aids:	Bl: 0-0 Vi: 0-0 Tstrap: 0-0 Ckp: 0-0
Best Rating:	126 6/03 MRas 2m1f110y gd-fm Hdl

Fair novice chaser/fair hurdler; off the mark on second attempt over fences at Wetherby in January; had luck on his side when narrow winner at Newcastle in March; best over two miles; suited by give.

Edmo Yewkay (IRE)
103 112

4-y-o b/br g Sri Pekan (USA)-Mannequin (IRE) (In The Wings)

T D Easterby Edmolift Uk Ltd

Placings:612414P (4422)

2003/04: 16⁶G, 16¹G, 16²S, 16⁴GS, 16¹S, 16⁴GS, 17⁶G,

			Starts	1st	2nd	3rd	Win & Pl
Hurdles			7	2	1	0	13005
Career Total			7	2	1	0	13005
107 1/04 Donc	2m110y	C Hdl				SFT	£7104
99 11/03 Newc	2m	D Hdl				GD	£3614

Total win prize-money £10719

Going:	Sf: 1-2 GS: 0-2 Gd: 1-3 GF: - Fm: 0-0
Distance:	2m/2m3: 2-7 2m4-2m7: 0-0 3m+: 0-0
Track:	LH: 2-6 RH: 0-1 Tight: 0-0 Gall: 2-5
Aids:	Bl: 0-0 Vi: 0-0 Tstrap: 0-0 Ckp: 0-0
Best Rating:	107 2/04 Hntg 2m110y gd-sft Hdl

Fair juvenile hurdler; effective over two miles, but should stay further; acts well on fast and soft ground; wore blinkers on the Flat.

Edredon Bleu (FR)
117 172

12-y-o b g Grand Tresor (FR)-Nuit Bleue Iii (FR) (Le Pontet (FR))

Miss H C Knight Jim Lewis

Placings:1/21111520P/41111F/41212/51331/3161/1243/12
1166-11111 (3790)

2003/04: 21¹F, 17¹G, 20¹YS, 24¹G, 21¹G,

			Starts	1st	2nd	3rd	Win & Pl
Chases			5	5	0	0	179207
Career Total			45	24	6	4	723011
137 2/04 Winc	2m5f	B Ch				GD	£10382
172 12/03 Kemp	3m	A Ch				GD	£92800
157 11/03 Clon	2m4f	Ch				Y-S	£25324
171 11/03 Extr	2m1f110yA	HCh				GD	£29000
172 10/03 Winc	2m5f	A HCh				FRM	£21700
165 1/03 Winc	2m5f	B Ch				G-S	£16042
168 12/02 Winc	2m5f	B Ch				G-S	£11928
172 11/02 Extr	2m1f110yA	HCh				GD	£24360
168 11/01 Hntg	2m4f110yA	Ch				G-S	£30000
164 4/01 Sand	2m	A Ch				G-S	£49300
168 11/00 Hntg	2m4f110yA	Ch				G-S	£27000
166 3/00 Chel	2m	A Ch				GD	£107300
163 11/99 Hntg	2m4f110yA	Ch				G-F	£23750
167 2/99 Sand	2m	B HCh				GD	£8036
164 11/98 Hntg	2m4f110yA	HCh				GD	£18211
154 3/98 Chel	2m110y	B HCh				GD	£29611
152 2/98 Sand	2m	B(0-145)HCh				G-F	£7578
142 12/97 Kemp	2m4f110yB	HCh				SFT	£12741
138 12/97 Leic	2m4f110yC(0-130)HCh					GD	£4945
9/96 Autl	2m2f	Ch				GD	£15810
8/96 LE L	2m4f	Ch				GD	£7905
7/96 LE L	2m1f	Ch				G-S	£3952
7/96 LE L	2m1f	Ch				SFT	£3952
3/96 Seic	2m1f	Ch				SFT	£3952

Total win prize-money £585587

Going:	Sf: 0-0 GS: 0-0 Gd: 3-3 GF: - Fm: 1-1
Distance:	2m/2m3: 1-1 2m4-2m7: 3-3 3m+: 1-1
Track:	LH: 0-0 RH: 5-5 Tight: 0-0 Gall: 0-0
Aids:	Bl: 0-0 Vi: 0-0 Tstrap: 5-5 Ckp: 0-0
Best Rating:	172 12/03 Kemp 3m good Ch

Top-class chaser, winner of the Queen Mother Champion Chase in 2000 and King George in 2003, and four-time winner of the Peterborough Chase at Huntingdon; probably best over two and a half miles these days, but was still good enough to land the Haldon Gold Cup over two miles in November 2003 and cause a surprise by winning the King George over three miles; one of the best jumpers around; his attacking style of racing is best suited to fast conditions; wears a tongue tie.

Effectual
90(103c) (115c)134

11-y-o b g Efisio-Moharabuiee (Pas De Seul)

Miss Venetia Williams B C Dice

Placings:311211145/3311564/201255343/20/6600/35501-4P (4948)

2003/04: 22⁴G, 27⁶GS,

			Starts	1st	2nd	3rd	Win & Pl
Hurdles			2	0	0	0	391
Career Total			38	9	4	6	94040
115 3/03 Font	3m2f110yE	Ch				SFT	£5082
156 12/99 Chel	3m	B HHdl				GD	£6911
140 1/99 Font	2m2f110yC(0-130)HHdl					SFT	£4735
138 12/98 Donc	2m110y	B Hdl				GD	£5020
136 3/98 Donc	2m110y	B Hdl				SFT	£13745
132 3/98 Donc	2m110y	C(0-135)Hdl				SFT	£4090
130 2/98 Weth	2m	B(0-145)HHdl				GD	£5455
127 12/97 Tntn	2m1f	B Hdl				GD	£3018
125 12/97 NAbb	2m1f	E Hdl				HVY	£2148

Total win prize-money £50207

Going:	Sf: 0-0 GS: 0-1 Gd: 0-1 GF: - Fm: 0-0
Distance:	2m/2m3: 0-0 2m4-2m7: 0-1 3m+: 0-1
Track:	LH: 0-0 RH: 0-1 Tight: 0-0 Gall: 0-0
Aids:	Bl: 0-0 Vi: 0-0 Tstrap: 0-0 Ckp: 0-0
Best Rating:	159 5/00 Punc 3m good Hdl

Useful hurdler/chaser; has not always looked a straightforward ride; fourth to Bacchanal in the 2000 Stayers' Hurdle at the Cheltenham Festival, but has not looked the same horse since returning from a year off with a tendon injury; stays three miles plus; has won on good and soft ground.

Effie Gray
90 77

5-y-o b m Sri Pekan (USA)-Rose Bouquet (General Assembly (USA))

P R Johnson (J W Unett 5/3) P Johnson

Placings:0046-360P0 (4493)

2003/04: 17³GF, 17⁶GF, 16⁶GF, 20⁶G, 16⁹G,

			Starts	1st	2nd	3rd	Win & Pl
Hurdles			9	0	0	1	494
Career Total			9	0	0	1	494

Going:	Sf: 0-0 GS: 0-0 Gd: 0-2 GF: - Fm: 0-3
Distance:	2m/2m3: 0-4 2m4-2m7: 0-1 3m+: 0-0
Track:	LH: 0-3 RH: 0-2 Tight: 0-3 Gall: 0-0
Aids:	Bl: 0-0 Vi: 0-0 Tstrap: 0-0 Ckp: 0-1
Best Rating:	77 7/03 Sedg 2m1f gd-fm Hdl

Very moderate novice hurdler; easily best effort when close third at Sedgefield in July.

Effusive
90(94h) (126dh)94

11-y-o b g Phardante (FR)-Bubbling (Tremblant)

Jonjo O'Neill John P McManus

Placings:24/16/5561213/BF6020/6P-464U (0857)

2003/04: 16⁴GF, 17⁶S, 16⁴G, 21⁴GF,

			Starts	1st	2nd	3rd	Win & Pl
Chases			4	0	0	0	933
Career Total			23	3	3	1	14298
126 8/00 Rosc	2m	(0-116)HHdl				FRM	£4140
121 7/00 Klny	2m1f	(0-102)HHdl				GD	£3312
92 8/99 Wxfd	2m	Hdl				GD	£2679

Total win prize-money £10132

Going:	Sf: 0-1 GS: 0-0 Gd: 0-1 GF: - Fm: 0-2
Distance:	2m/2m3: 0-3 2m4-2m7: 0-1 3m+: 0-0
Track:	LH: 0-3 RH: 0-1 Tight: 0-2 Gall: 0-0
Aids:	Bl: 0-0 Vi: 0-0 Tstrap: 0-0 Ckp: 0-0
Best Rating:	126 8/01 Naas 2m gd-yld Hdl

Ex-Irish handicap hurdler, effective at around two miles on good ground or faster. Now with Jonjo O'Neill.

Eggmount (IRE)
97f 109+f

6-y-o b g Riberetto-Brigade Leader (IRE) (Supreme Leader)

T R George R P Foden

Placings:1 (4952)

2003/04: 16¹GS,

			Starts	1st	2nd	3rd	Win & Pl
NH Flat			1	1	0	0	3444
Career Total			1	1	0	0	3444
109 4/04 Prth	2m110y	H NHF				G-S	£3444

Total win prize-money £3444

Going:	Sf: 0-0 GS: 1-1 Gd: 0-0 GF: - Fm: 0-0
Distance:	2m/2m3: 1-1 2m4-2m7: 0-0 3m+: 0-0
Track:	LH: 0-0 RH: 1-1 Tight: 0-0 Gall: 0-0
Aids:	Bl: 0-0 Vi: 0-0 Tstrap: 0-0 Ckp: 0-0
Best Rating:	109 4/04 Prth 2m110y gd-sft NHF

Irish point winner who ran out the wide margin winner of Perth bumper in April 2004; plenty of scope for improvement and sure to win races over obstacles.

Egypt Point (IRE)
94 73

7-y-o b g Jurado (USA)-Cherry Jubilee (Le Bavard (FR))

D G Bridgwater Long Hill Partnership

Placings:0/6-0 (4712)

2003/04: 24⁰G,

			Starts	1st	2nd	3rd	Win & Pl
Hurdles			1	0	0	0	
Career Total			3	0	0	0	0

Going:	Sf: 0-0 GS: 0-0 Gd: 0-1 GF: - Fm: 0-0
Distance:	2m/2m3: 0-2 2m4-2m7: 0-0 3m+: 0-1
Track:	LH: 0-0 RH: 0-1 Tight: 0-0 Gall: 0-0
Aids:	Bl: 0-0 Vi: 0-0 Tstrap: 0-0 Ckp: 0-0
Best Rating:	77 4/04 Ludl 3m good Hdl

Ehab (IRE)

100   91+

5-y-o b g Cadeaux Genereux-Dernier Cri (Slip Anchor)
G L Moore (P J Makin 26/9) The Go For Brokers Partnership

Placings:0400   (4210)
2003/04: 16⁰GS, 17⁴GS, 16⁶S, 16⁹G,

	Starts	1st	2nd	3rd	Win & Pl
Hurdles	4	0	0	0	0
Career Total	4	0	0	0	0

Going:	Sf: 0-1 GS: 0-2 Gd: 0-1 GF: - Fm: 0-0
Distance:	2m/2m3: 0-4 2m4-2m7: 0-0 3m+: 0-0
Track:	LH: 0-1 RH: 0-3 Tight: 0-0 Gall: 0-1
Aids:	Bl: 0-0 Vi: 0-0 Tstrap: 0-0 Ckp: 0-0
Best Rating:	91 12/03 Folk 2m1f110y gd-sft Hdl

Ei Ei

116(107h)   (121 h)148

9-y-o b g North Briton-Branitska (Mummy's Pet)
M C Chapman Mrs S M Richards

Placings:0641121111540246032/3512463514215113061-31142022413443002465 3   (4953)
2003/04: 16³GF, 20¹G, 17¹G, 19⁴G, 17²GF, 16⁹G, 20²GF, 16²G, 19⁴GF, 17¹G, 19³GF, 16⁴F, 16⁴GF, 20³G, 20⁰GF, 20⁰GS, 19²GS, 16⁴S, 16⁶G, 16⁵G, 20³G,

	Starts	1st	2nd	3rd	Win & Pl
Hurdles	10	1	2	1	15903
Chases	11	2	2	3	63916
Career Total	59	15	9	8	170410
121	8/03	Ctml	2m1f110yD(0-120)HHdl	GD	£5850
143	5/03	Strf	2m4f110yD(0-135)HCh	GD	£8141
138	5/03	Weth	2m4f110yB(0-145)HCh	GD	£11576
135	4/03	Sand	2m B(0-145)HCh	G-F	£18600
121	1/03	Sthl	2m E(0-110)HCh	G-S	£3605
103	12/02	Hntg	2m110y D(0-125)HHdl	G-S	£8287
140	11/02	Sthl	2m C(0-135)HCh	G-S	£10010
129	9/02	Worc	2m C(0-135)HCh	GF	£7174
130	6/02	Ctml	2m1f110yD(0-125)HCh	G-S	£4355
128	10/01	Sthl	2m E(0-115)HCh	GD	£3386
112	10/01	Sedg	2m110y E(0-115)HCh	GD	£3265
127	9/01	MRas	2m4f F(0-110)HCh	SFT	£3916
129	9/01	Strf	2m1f110yD(0-120)HCh	G-F	£4127
92	8/01	Sthl	2m E(0-110)HCh	G-F	£2775
91	7/01	Strf	2m110y G Hdl	G-F	£1967
			Total win prize-money		£97041

Going:	Sf: 0-1 GS: 0-2 Gd: 3-10 GF: - Fm: 0-8
Distance:	2m/2m3: 2-11 2m4-2m7: 1-10 3m+: 0-0
Track:	LH: 3-13 RH: 0-8 Tight: 2-11 Gall: 0-3
Aids:	Bl: 0-0 Vi: 0-0 Tstrap: 0-0 Ckp: 0-0
Best Rating:	146 4/04 Sand 2m4f110y good Ch

Smart chaser; tough and consistent front-runner; best at around two miles, but stayed two and a half; did not want the ground too soft; sadly took a fatal fall at Market rasen early in the new season. (DEAD)

Eight (IRE)

96   83

8-y-o ch g Thatching-Up To You (Sallust)
C G Cox Charles Curtis

Placings:P/00-30   (2564)
2003/04: 16⁰G, 19⁰GS,

	Starts	1st	2nd	3rd	Win & Pl
Hurdles	2	0	0	1	419
Career Total	5	0	0	1	419

Going:	Sf: 0-0 GS: 0-1 Gd: 0-1 GF: - Fm: 0-0
Distance:	2m/2m3: 0-2 2m4-2m7: 0-0 3m+: 0-0
Track:	LH: 0-0 RH: 0-2 Tight: 0-0 Gall: 0-0
Aids:	Bl: 0-0 Vi: 0-0 Tstrap: 0-0 Ckp: 0-0
Best Rating:	83 11/03 Kemp 2m good Hdl

Plating-class hurdler; first sign of ability when well-beaten third at Kempton.

Eisenhower (IRE)

(78h)   (62h)

5-y-o b g Erin's Isle-Lyphard Abu (IRE) (Lyphard's Special (USA))
J Wade John Wade

Placings:00P   (4684)
2003/04: 17⁰GS, 20⁰S, 25⁰G,

	Starts	1st	2nd	3rd	Win & Pl
Hurdles	2	0	0	0	
Chases	1	0	0	0	
Career Total	3	0	0	0	

Going:	Sf: 0-1 GS: 0-1 Gd: 0-1 GF: - Fm: 0-0
Distance:	2m/2m3: 0-1 2m4-2m7: 0-1 3m+: 0-1
Track:	LH: 0-3 RH: 0-0 Tight: 0-0 Gall: 0-1
Aids:	Bl: 0-1 Vi: 0-0 Tstrap: 0-0 Ckp: 0-0
Best Rating:	62 2/04 Sedg 2m1f gd-sft Hdl

El Bandito (IRE)

102   (87h)114+

10-y-o ch g Un Desperado (FR)-Red Marble (Le Bavard (FR))
R Lee The Another Comedy Partnership

Placings:52/1330/4P55F00/PP11-2P41210   (4953)
2003/04: 22³GS, 19²GS, 16⁴S, 20¹G, 19⁴GF, 18¹G, 20⁰G,

	Starts	1st	2nd	3rd	Win & Pl
Chases	7	2	2	0	12900
Career Total	24	5	3	2	25786
114	3/04	Newb	2m1f10yD(0-125)HCh	GD	£5694
110	2/04	Leic	2m4f110yE(0-105)HCh	GD	£4202
108	3/03	Chep	2m3f110yD(0-110)HCh	GD	£5622
93	2/03	Leic	2m4f110yF(0-95)HCh	G-S	£4299
105	5/00	Extr	2m1f H NHF	G-F	£1767
			Total win prize-money		£21587

Going:	Sf: 0-1 GS: 0-2 Gd: 2-3 GF: - Fm: 0-1
Distance:	2m/2m3: 1-3 2m4-2m7: 1-4 3m+: 0-0
Track:	LH: 1-4 RH: 1-3 Tight: 0-0 **Gall: 1-1**
Aids:	Bl: 0-0 Vi: 0-0 Tstrap: 0-0 Ckp: 0-0
Best Rating:	114 3/04 Newb 2m2f110y good Ch

Modest chaser; stays two and a half miles; best on good ground, but handles a bit of cut; considered best suited to left-handed courses; regularly held up.

El Blade

98   (120h)110

7-y-o b g Dashing Blade-Elisha (GER) (Konigsstuhl (GER))
B G Powell Favourites Racing

Placings:F2151/45F   (3452)
2003/04: 19⁴GS, 19⁵GS, 19⁵GS,

	Starts	1st	2nd	3rd	Win & Pl
Chases	3	0	0	0	0
Career Total	8	2	1	0	6731
120	3/02	Hrfd	2m3f110yD(0-120)HHdl	GD	£3454
107	12/01	Hrfd	2m3f110yE Hdl	GD	£2513
			Total win prize-money		£5968

Going:	Sf: 0-0 GS: 0-3 Gd: 0-0 GF: - Fm: 0-0

Distance / Track (El Blade continued — right column)

Distance:	2m/2m3: 0-3 2m4-2m7: 0-0 3m+: 0-0
Track:	LH: 0-0 RH: 0-3 Tight: 0-1 Gall: 0-0
Aids:	Bl: 0-0 Vi: 0-0 Tstrap: 0-0 Ckp: 0-0
Best Rating:	120 3/02 Hrfd 2m3f110y good Hdl

Front-running hurdler/chaser; stays 2m 4f; goes well at Hereford; acts on good and soft ground.

El Cordobes (IRE)

106(83h)   (82h)98

13-y-o b g Torus-Queens Tricks (Le Bavard (FR))
Mrs J R Buckley Mrs J R Buckley

Placings:3/005000/0/2P55445/13154213/32010/6654P400/14P421F3433-33445211PP6F   (3917)
2003/04: 21⁵GF, 17⁹GF, 21⁴GF, 21⁴G, 24⁵GF, 20²F, 24¹G, 24¹G, 19⁵GS, 25⁹GS, 22⁶G, 24⁴G,

	Starts	1st	2nd	3rd	Win & Pl
Hurdles	2	0	1	0	1310
Chases	10	2	2	2	8749
Career Total	59	8	5	9	46105
98	11/03	Fknm	3m110y E(0-105)HCh	GD	£2915
94	10/03	Fknm	3m110y E(0-110)HCh	GD	£4286
98	12/02	MRas	2m6f110yD(0-120)HCh	SFT	£5894
90	5/02	Fknm	2m5f110yF(0-100)HCh	GD	£3444
99	10/00	Fknm	2m5f110yF(0-100)HCh	GD	£3563
94	3/00	Donc	2m110y D(0-110)HCh	G-S	£4134
92	9/99	Hntg	2m110y E(0-115)HCh	G-F	£3109
94	5/99	Hntg	2m4f110yF(0-100)HCh	G-F	£3406
			Total win prize-money		£30755

Going:	Sf: 0-0 GS: 0-2 Gd: 2-5 GF: - Fm: 0-5
Distance:	2m/2m3: 0-1 2m4-2m7: 0-6 **3m+: 2-5**
Track:	**LH: 2-9** RH: 0-3 Tight: **2-8** Gall: 0-1
Aids:	Bl: 0-0 Vi: 0-0 Tstrap: 0-0 Ckp: 0-0
Best Rating:	98 11/03 Fknm 3m110y good Ch

Moderate handicap chaser; headstrong front-runner; effective from two to three miles; acts on a sound surface, but also handles cut in the ground.

El Don

91(84h)   (62h)61

12-y-o b g High Kicker (USA)-Madam Gerard (Brigadier Gerard)
B Scriven B Scriven

Placings:0/12214P13/55142/P0F/FP600/F5F0/00/P0P5-   (0015)
2003/04: 21⁵S,

	Starts	1st	2nd	3rd	Win & Pl
Chases	1	0	0	0	
Career Total	32	4	3	1	18037
111	10/97	Font	2m2f110yD(0-125)HHdl	GD	£3416
113	4/97	Chep	2m4f110yC(0-135)HHdl	FRM	£3533
104	11/96	Weth	2m B(0-145)HHdl	GD	£4825
104	5/96	Font	2m2f E Hdl	G-F	£2427
			Total win prize-money		£14202

Going:	Sf: 0-1 GS: 0-0 Gd: 0-0 GF: - Fm: 0-0
Distance:	2m/2m3: 0-0 2m4-2m7: 0-1 3m+: 0-0
Track:	LH: 0-1 RH: 0-0 Tight: 0-1 Gall: 0-0
Aids:	Bl: 0-0 Vi: 0-0 Tstrap: 0-0 Ckp: 0-0
Best Rating:	114 4/99 Fknm 2m4f good Hdl

El Giza (USA)

64   50

6-y-o ch g Cozzene (USA)-Gazayil (USA) (Irish River (FR))
J M Bradley Raymond Tooth

Placings:0   (4812)
2003/04: 16⁰G,

	Starts	1st	2nd	3rd	Win & Pl
Hurdles	1	0	0	0	
Career Total	1	0	0	0	

Going: Sf: 0-0 GS: 0-0 Gd: 0-1 GF: - Fm: 0-0
Distance: 2m/2m3: 0-1 2m4-2m7: 0-0 3m+: 0-0
Track: LH: 0-1 RH: 0-0 Tight: 0-0 Gall: 0-0
Aids: Bl: 0-0 Vi: 0-0 Tstrap: 0-0 Ckp: 0-0
Best Rating: 50   4/04   Chep   2m110y   good   Hdl

El Gran Hombre (USA)

8-y-o ch g El Gran Senor (USA)-Conquistress (USA) (Conquistador Cielo (USA))
Miss Kariana Key   Miss Kariana Key

Placings:0P/P   (1208)
2003/04: 17PG,

	Starts	1st	2nd	3rd	Win & Pl
Hurdles	1	0	0	0	
Career Total	3	0	0	0	

Going: Sf: 0-0 GS: 0-0 Gd: 0-1 GF: - Fm: 0-0
Distance: 2m/2m3: 0-1 2m4-2m7: 0-0 3m+: 0-0
Track: LH: 0-1 RH: 0-0 Tight: 0-1 Gall: 0-0
Aids: Bl: 0-0 Vi: 0-0 Tstrap: 0-0 Ckp: 0-0
Best Rating: 18   12/00   Fknm   2m   gd-sft   Hdl

El Hombre

96(83h)   (68h)80
6-y-o b g Afzal-Dunsilly Bell (London Bells (CAN))
C C Bealby   Michael Hill

Placings:03-03P643F   (4403)
2003/04: 17OG, 173G, 20PGS, 16RGS, 204S, 203GF, 24FG,

	Starts	1st	2nd	3rd	Win & Pl
Hurdles	4	0	0	1	435
Chases	3	0	0	1	575
Career Total	9	0	0	3	1297

Going: Sf: 0-1 GS: 0-2 Gd: 0-3 GF: - Fm: 0-1
Distance: 2m/2m3: 0-3 2m4-2m7: 0-3 3m+: 0-1
Track: LH: 0-4 RH: 0-3 Tight: 0-2 Gall: 0-2
Aids: Bl: 0-0 Vi: 0-0 Tstrap: 0-0 Ckp: 0-0
Best Rating: 89   12/02   Fknm   2m   gd-sft   NHF

El Hombre Del Rio (IRE)

107(107h)   (100 h)120+
7-y-o ch g Over The River (FR)-Hug In A Fog (IRE) (Strong Gale)
R H Alner   Perpetual Pub's Lazy Punters Black Book

Placings:0P/242232-23FP3612   (4667)
2003/04: 262S, 263G, 24FGS, 23PG, 243S, 24RG, 281G, 24RS,

	Starts	1st	2nd	3rd	Win & Pl
Chases	8	1	2	2	9469
Career Total	16	1	6	3	15826
117	3/04	Font	3m4f	E(0-105)HCh	GD	4459
				Total win prize-money £4459	

Going: Sf: 0-3 GS: 0-1 Gd: 1-4 GF: - Fm: 0-0
Distance: 2m/2m3: 0-0 2m4-2m7: 0-0 3m+: 1-8
Track: LH: 0-4 RH: 0-3 Tight: 0-2 Gall: 0-1
Aids: Bl: 0-0 Vi: 0-0 Tstrap: 0-0 Ckp: 0-0

Best Rating: 120 4/04   Ling   3m   soft   Ch

Moderate chaser; stays three miles two, will get further if required; acts on soft ground.

El Nombre

5-y-o b g El Conquistador-Worth Matravers (National Trust)
R J Hodges   M H Dare

Placings:0   (4550)
2003/04: 16OGS,

	Starts	1st	2nd	3rd	Win & Pl
NH Flat	1	0	0	0	
Career Total	1	0	0	0	

Going: Sf: 0-0 GS: 0-1 Gd: 0-0 GF: - Fm: 0-0
Distance: 2m/2m3: 0-1 2m4-2m7: 0-0 3m+: 0-0
Track: LH: 0-0 RH: 0-1 Tight: 0-0 Gall: 0-0
Aids: Bl: 0-0 Vi: 0-0 Tstrap: 0-0 Ckp: 0-0

El Pedro

89   87
5-y-o b g Piccolo-Standard Rose (Ile De Bourbon (USA))
N E Berry (M R Channon 9/10)   Box 40 Racing

Placings:000-0   (1587)
2003/04: 16OGF,

	Starts	1st	2nd	3rd	Win & Pl
Hurdles	1	0	0	0	
Career Total	4	0	0	0	

Going: Sf: 0-0 GS: 0-0 Gd: 0-0 GF: - Fm: 0-1
Distance: 2m/2m3: 0-1 2m4-2m7: 0-0 3m+: 0-0
Track: LH: 0-0 RH: 0-1 Tight: 0-0 Gall: 0-1
Aids: Bl: 0-0 Vi: 0-0 Tstrap: 0-0 Ckp: 0-0
Best Rating: 78   11/02   Newb   2m110y   soft   Hdl

El Penyon

7-y-o b g Rock Hopper-Capel Lass (The Brianstan)
J W Mullins   Patrick Everard

Placings:000-5P   (2203)
2003/04: 17SGF, 17PG,

	Starts	1st	2nd	3rd	Win & Pl
Hurdles	2	0	0	0	0
Career Total	5	0	0	0	0

Going: Sf: 0-0 GS: 0-0 Gd: 0-1 GF: - Fm: 0-1
Distance: 2m/2m3: 0-2 2m4-2m7: 0-0 3m+: 0-0
Track: LH: 0-0 RH: 0-2 Tight: 0-1 Gall: 0-0
Aids: Bl: 0-0 Vi: 0-0 Tstrap: 0-1 Ckp: 0-0
Best Rating: 55   11/02   Winc   2m   good   NHF

El Vaquero (IRE)

105   117+
6-y-o ch g Un Desperado (FR)-Marble Fontaine (Lafontaine (USA))
Miss H C Knight   T M Curtis

Placings:10-332F1   (4895)
2003/04: 173GS, 163GS, 162GS, 20FS, 221G,

	Starts	1st	2nd	3rd	Win & Pl
Hurdles	5	1	1	2	6933

Career Total	7	2	1	2	8914
116	4/04	Winc	2m6f	E Hdl	GD	£4014
102	12/02	Hntg	2m110y	H NHF	G-S	£1981
				Total win prize-money £5996	

Going: Sf: 0-1 GS: 0-3 Gd: 1-1 GF: - Fm: 0-0
Distance: 2m/2m3: 0-3 2m4-2m7: 1-2 3m+: 0-0
Track: LH: 0-1 RH: 1-4 Tight: 0-1 Gall: 0-0
Aids: Bl: 0-0 Vi: 0-0 Tstrap: 0-0 Ckp: 0-0
Best Rating: 117   2/04   Sand   2m110y   gd-sft   Hdl

Fair novice hurdler; stays two mile six and acts on good ground.

Ela Agori Mou (IRE)

103   82
7-y-o ch g Ela-Mana-Mou-La Courant (USA) (Little Current (USA))
D Eddy   Brian Chicken

Placings:0/2010/P65463   (3734)
2003/04: 20PGS, 16RS, 16SGS, 204GF, 24RGF, 203G,

	Starts	1st	2nd	3rd	Win & Pl
Hurdles	6	0	0	1	704
Career Total	11	1	1	1	2710
82	9/01	Hrfd	2m1f	H NHF	G-F	£1568
				Total win prize-money £1568	

Going: Sf: 0-1 GS: 0-2 Gd: 0-1 GF: - Fm: 0-2
Distance: 2m/2m3: 0-2 2m4-2m7: 0-3 3m+: 0-1
Track: LH: 0-2 RH: 0-3 Tight: 0-3 Gall: 0-1
Aids: Bl: 0-0 Vi: 0-0 Tstrap: 0-0 Ckp: 0-4
Best Rating: 103   5/01   Newc   2m   gd-fm   NHF

Moderate bumper winner on fast ground; best effort over hurdles when third in handicap company at Musselburgh in February; suited by two and a half miles; has worn cheek-pieces.

Ela D'Argent (IRE)

102   102
5-y-o b m Ela-Mana-Mou-Petite-D-Argent (Noalto)
Miss K Marks (M C Pipe 3/6)   Nick Shutts

Placings:U11051-4P   (2997)
2003/04: 174GF, 16PGS,

	Starts	1st	2nd	3rd	Win & Pl
Hurdles	2	0	0	0	262
Career Total	8	3	0	0	11289
102	3/03	Plum	2m	F Hdl	G-F	£2765
102	10/02	Chep	2m110y	D Hdl	G-F	£4075
101	9/02	Prth	2m110y	D Hdl	G-F	£4186
				Total win prize-money £11027	

Going: Sf: 0-0 GS: 0-1 Gd: 0-0 GF: - Fm: 0-1
Distance: 2m/2m3: 0-2 2m4-2m7: 0-0 3m+: 0-0
Track: LH: 0-1 RH: 0-1 Tight: 0-1 Gall: 0-0
Aids: Bl: 0-0 Vi: 0-0 Tstrap: 0-0 Ckp: 0-0
Best Rating: 102   3/03   Plum   2m   gd-fm   Hdl

Modest hurdler; front-runner; did not achieve much when winning Plumpton claimer in March 2003; acts on fast ground; effective at two miles.

Ela Jay

101   105
5-y-o b m Double Eclipse (IRE)-Papirusa (IRE) (Pennine Walk)
H Morrison   J & L Wetherald - M & M Glover

Placings:U-1640P   (3366)
2003/04: 171G, 216GS, 164G, 169GS, 21PG,

	Starts	1st	2nd	3rd	Win & Pl
Hurdles	5	1	0	0	3453
Career Total	6	1	0	0	3453
91 11/03 Folk 2m1f110yE Hdl				GD	£2933
				Total win prize-money	£2933

Going: Sf: 0-0 GS: 0-2 Gd: 1-3 GF: - Fm: 0-0
Distance: 2m/2m3: 1-3 2m4-2m7: 0-2 3m+: 0-0
Track: LH: 0-0 RH: 1-5 Tight: 1-1 Gall: 0-0
Aids: Bl: 0-0 Vi: 0-0 Tstrap: 0-0 Ckp: 0-0
Best Rating: 105 12/03 Ludl 2m   good Hdl

Modest novice hurdler; looks best at around two miles; suited by fast ground.

Ela La Senza (IRE)
112(73c)   (45c)98
7-y-o br g Lord Americo-Diamond Glow (Kalaglow)
N A Twiston-Davies Xunely Limited

Placings:45560U-531201230P   (4656)
2003/04: 16[5]GF, 20[3]G, 20[1]GF, 22[2]G, 24[9]GF, 20[1]G, 22[2]GF, 21[3]GF, 19[9]GS, 26[0]G,

	Starts	1st	2nd	3rd	Win & Pl
Hurdles	9	2	2	2	10454
Chases	1	0	0	0	0
Career Total	16	2	2	2	10694
97 9/03 Prth 2m4f110yF(0-100)HHdl				GD	£3562
90 6/03 Worc 2m4f E(0-110)HHdl				G-F	£3581
				Total win prize-money	£7144

Going: Sf: 0-0 GS: 0-1 Gd: 1-4 GF: - Fm: 1-5
Distance: 2m/2m3: 0-0 **2m4-2m7: 2-6** 3m+: 0-2
Track: LH: 1-6 RH: 1-4 Tight: 0-0 Gall: 0-0
Aids: Bl: 0-0 Vi: 0-0 Tstrap: 0-0 Ckp: 0-0
Best Rating: 98 10/03 Kemp 2m5f   gd-fm Hdl

Modest hurdler; in good form in summer 2003; stays two and a half miles; acts on most types of ground; can take a keen hold.

Ela Re
114   117
5-y-o ch g Sabrehill (USA)-Lucia Tarditi (FR) (Crystal Glitters (USA))
C R Dore L Cohen

Placings:02O30-11634310   (4054)
2003/04: 17[1]G, 17[1]G, 17[6]GF, 17[3]GF, 16[4]GF, 17[3]GF, 17[1]GS, 21[0]G,

	Starts	1st	2nd	3rd	Win & Pl
Hurdles	8	3	0	2	19704
Career Total	13	3	1	3	22274
117 1/04 Chel 2m1f D(0-120)HHdl				G-S	£10353
107 6/03 MRas 2m1f110yE Hdl				GD	£3737
103 5/03 MRas 2m1f110yE Hdl				GD	£3883
				Total win prize-money	£17975

Going: Sf: 0-0 GS: 1-1 Gd: 2-3 GF: - Fm: 0-4
Distance: **2m/2m3: 3-7** 2m4-2m7: 0-1 3m+: 0-0
Track: LH: 1-2 **RH: 2-6** Tight: 2-6 Gall: 1-1
Aids: Bl: 0-0 Vi: 0-0 Tstrap: 0-0 Ckp: 0-0
Best Rating: 117 1/04 Chel 2m1f   gd-sft Hdl

Fair hurdler; won competitive novices' handicap at Cheltenham in January 2004; suited by trips of around 2m; effective on good ground.

Electric Nellie
7-y-o gr m Neltino-Alternation (FR) (Electric)
J F Panvert J F Panvert

Placings:U5030-6P5   (3928)

2003/04: 20[6]G, 19[2P]GS, 16[5]G,

	Starts	1st	2nd	3rd	Win & Pl
Hurdles	3	0	0	0	0
Career Total	8	0	0	1	447

Going: Sf: 0-0 GS: 0-1 Gd: 0-2 GF: - Fm: 0-0
Distance: 2m/2m3: 0-1 2m4-2m7: 0-2 3m+: 0-0
Track: LH: 0-0 RH: 0-2 Tight: 0-1 Gall: 0-0
Aids: Bl: 0-0 Vi: 0-0 Tstrap: 0-0 Ckp: 0-0
Best Rating: 85 2/03 Ludl 2m   good NHF

Poor form in bumpers and novices' hurdles.

Electrique (IRE)
                                  92+
4-y-o b g Elmaamul (USA)-Majmu (USA) (Al Nasr (FR))
J A Osborne Paul J Dixon

Placings:F   (3732)
2003/04: 16[6]G,

	Starts	1st	2nd	3rd	Win & Pl
Hurdles	1	0	0	0	
Career Total	1	0	0	0	

Going: Sf: 0-0 GS: 0-0 Gd: 0-1 GF: - Fm: 0-0
Distance: 2m/2m3: 0-1 2m4-2m7: 0-0 3m+: 0-0
Track: LH: 0-0 RH: 0-1 Tight: 0-1 Gall: 0-0
Aids: Bl: 0-0 Vi: 0-0 Tstrap: 0-0 Ckp: 0-0
Best Rating: 97 2/04 Muss 2m   good Hdl

Fair sort on the Flat; a winner over ten furlongs; keen, booked for clear second spot when crashing out at the last on hurdling bow at Musselburgh in February.

Elegant Accord (IRE)
70f   35f
6-y-o b m Accordion-Swan Bridge (IRE) (Supreme Leader)
Mrs P Ford J T Jones

Placings:00   (4920)
2003/04: 17[0]GS, 16[0]GS,

	Starts	1st	2nd	3rd	Win & Pl
NH Flat	2	0	0	0	
Career Total	2	0	0	0	

Going: Sf: 0-0 GS: 0-2 Gd: 0-0 GF: - Fm: 0-0
Distance: 2m/2m3: 0-2 2m4-2m7: 0-0 3m+: 0-0
Track: LH: 0-2 RH: 0-0 Tight: 0-1 Gall: 0-0
Aids: Bl: 0-0 Vi: 0-0 Tstrap: 0-0 Ckp: 0-0
Best Rating: 35 4/04 Worc 2m   gd-sft NHF

Elegant Clutter (IRE)
106   87+
6-y-o b g Petorius-Mountain Hop (IRE) (Tirol)
R N Bevis Kelvin Briggs

Placings:0655/0P-01   (1811)
2003/04: 22[8]G, 17[1]G,

	Starts	1st	2nd	3rd	Win & Pl
Hurdles	2	1	0	0	2471
Career Total	8	1	0	0	2471
91 10/03 Bang 2m1f E(0-105)HHdl				GD	£2471
				Total win prize-money	£2471

Going: Sf: 0-0 GS: 0-0 Gd: 1-2 GF: - Fm: 0-0
Distance: 2m/2m3: 1-1 2m4-2m7: 0-1 3m+: 0-0

Track: LH: 1-2 RH: 0-0 Tight: 1-2 Gall: 0-0
Aids: Bl: 0-0 Vi: 0-0 Tstrap: 0-0 Ckp: 0-0
Best Rating: 96 11/01 Thur 2m   yld-sft Hdl

Elenas River (IRE)
111   (112h)130+
8-y-o br g Over The River (FR)-Elena's Beauty (Targogan)
P J Hobbs (Miss H C Knight 5/5) Ian David Limited

Placings:556/02213/FU402[3]-2211   (4894)
2003/04: 26[2]G, 24[4]G, 24[1]GS, 25[1]G,

	Starts	1st	2nd	3rd	Win & Pl
Chases	4	2	2	0	15637
Career Total	18	3	5	2	30640
130 4/04 Winc 3m1f110yE Ch				GD	£4800
130 3/04 Asct 3m110y C Ch				G-S	£8092
99 2/02 Ludl 2m5f D(0-120)HHdl				GD	£5187
				Total win prize-money	£18080

Going: Sf: 0-0 GS: 1-1 Gd: 1-3 GF: - Fm: 0-0
Distance: 2m/2m3: 0-0 2m4-2m7: 0-0 **3m+: 2-4**
Track: LH: 0-0 **RH: 2-3** Tight: 0-2 Gall: 0-0
Aids: Bl: 0-0 Vi: 0-0 Tstrap: 0-0 Ckp: 0-0
Best Rating: 130 4/04 Winc 3m1f110y good Ch

Fair chaser; gradually improving over fences; stays 3m and suited by good ground.

Elfeet Bay (IRE)
98(92h)   (71h)83
9-y-o b g Yashgan-Marjoram (Warpath)
Mrs L Williamson J M Davies

Placings:00006/00/60-452455C   (0899)
2003/04: 17[4]S, 17[5]S, 17[2]G, 16[4]G, 16[5]GF, 16[5]G, 17[0]GF,

	Starts	1st	2nd	3rd	Win & Pl
Chases	7	0	1	0	2327
Career Total	16	0	1	0	2327

Going: Sf: 0-2 GS: 0-0 Gd: 0-3 GF: - Fm: 0-2
Distance: 2m/2m3: 0-7 2m4-2m7: 0-0 3m+: 0-0
Track: LH: 0-0 RH: 0-0 Tight: 0-4 Gall: 0-0
Aids: Bl: 0-0 Vi: 0-0 Tstrap: 0-0 Ckp: 0-3
Best Rating: 86 3/00 Thur 2m   good NHF

Poor hurdler; runner-up in modest chase at Cartmel in May.

Elfkirk (IRE)
88f   95f
5-y-o b m Zaffaran (USA)-Winter Sunset (Celio Rufo)
J I A Charlton M H Walton

Placings:1   (4885)
2003/04: 17[1]GS,

	Starts	1st	2nd	3rd	Win & Pl
NH Flat	1	1	0	0	2078
Career Total	1	1	0	0	2078
95 4/04 Carl 2m1f H NHF				G-S	£2077
				Total win prize-money	£2078

Going: Sf: 0-0 GS: 1-1 Gd: 0-0 GF: - Fm: 0-0
Distance: 2m/2m3: 1-1 2m4-2m7: 0-0 3m+: 0-0
Track: LH: 0-0 **RH: 1-1** Tight: 0-0 Gall: 0-0
Aids: Bl: 0-0 Vi: 0-0 Tstrap: 0-0 Ckp: 0-0
Best Rating: 95 4/04 Carl 2m1f   gd-sft NHF

National Hunt bred; took a modest bumper on debut at Carlisle in April; handles testing conditions.

Elgar

92(103h)   (94h)**109+**
7-y-o ch g Alflora (IRE)-School Run (Deep Run)
M Scudamore (G H Yardley 3/5) Mrs S Tainton

Placings:02/0-33P1P5F   (4782)
2003/04: 22³S, 17³G, 18²GS, 19¹S, 20²S, 20⁵G, 24FG,

	Starts	1st	2nd	3rd	Win & Pl
Hurdles	2	0	0	1	562
Chases	5	1	0	1	3455
Career Total	10	1	1	2	5585
113 12/03 Towc	2m3f110yF(0-100)HCh		SFT		£2961

Total win prize-money £2961

Going:	Sf: 1-3 GS: 0-1 Gd: 0-3 GF: - Fm: 0-0
Distance:	2m/2m3: 0-2 2m4-2m7: 1-4 3m+: 0-1
Track:	LH: 0-2 RH: 0-4 Tight: 0-0 Gall: 0-2
Aids:	Bl: 0-0 Vi: 0-0 Tstrap: 1-1 Ckp: 0-0
Best Rating:	113 12/03 Towc 2m3f110y soft Ch

Moderate performer; off the mark over fences on weak handicap at Towcester in December 2003 in first time tongue tie; pulled up back over hurdles latest; stays 2m 6f; seems best on soft ground.

Elheba (IRE)

106   **98+**
5-y-o b/br g Elbio-Fireheba (ITY) (Fire Of Life (USA))
C J Down (M Wigham 13/11) Three To One

Placings:5550L1   (4654)
2003/04: 19⁵S, 17⁵GS, 16⁵G, 17⁹G, 21ᴸGS, 17¹G,

	Starts	1st	2nd	3rd	Win & Pl
Hurdles	6	1	0	0	2499
Career Total	6	1	0	0	2499
98 4/04 Hrfd	2m1f	G Hdl		GD	£2499

Total win prize-money £2499

Going:	Sf: 0-1 GS: 0-2 Gd: 1-3 GF: - Fm: 0-0
Distance:	2m/2m3: 1-5 2m4-2m7: 0-1 3m+: 0-0
Track:	LH: 0-1 RH: 1-5 Tight: 0-3 Gall: 0-0
Aids:	Bl: 0-2 Vi: 0-0 Tstrap: 0-0 Ckp: 0-0
Best Rating:	98 4/04 Hrfd 2m1f good Hdl

Eliipop

     49
6-y-o b g First Trump-Hasty Key (USA) (Key To The Mint (USA))
R J Price Fox And Cub Partnership

Placings:00/P   (0996)
2003/04: 16²G,

	Starts	1st	2nd	3rd	Win & Pl
Hurdles	1	0	0	0	
Career Total	3	0	0	0	

Going:	Sf: 0-0 GS: 0-0 Gd: 0-1 GF: - Fm: 0-0
Distance:	2m/2m3: 0-1 2m4-2m7: 0-0 3m+: 0-0
Track:	LH: 0-1 RH: 0-0 Tight: 0-1 Gall: 0-0
Aids:	Bl: 0-0 Vi: 0-0 Tstrap: 0-0 Ckp: 0-0
Best Rating:	49 10/01 Kemp 2m gd-sft Hdl

Eljay's Boy

98   **84**
6-y-o b g Sir Harry Lewis (USA)-Woodland Flower (Furry Glen)
P F Nicholls Stephen Purdew And Des Nichols

Placings:02-40F430   (4654)

2003/04: 21⁴S, 19⁰G, 18FHY, 22⁴G, 16⁹GS, 17⁰G,

	Starts	1st	2nd	3rd	Win & Pl
Hurdles	6	0	0	1	777
Career Total	8	0	1	1	1693

Going:	Sf: 0-2 GS: 0-1 Gd: 0-3 GF: - Fm: 0-0
Distance:	2m/2m3: 0-3 2m4-2m7: 0-3 3m+: 0-0
Track:	LH: 0-2 RH: 0-4 Tight: 0-3 Gall: 0-0
Aids:	Bl: 0-2 Vi: 0-0 Tstrap: 0-0 Ckp: 0-0
Best Rating:	97 4/03 NAbb 2m1f gd-fm NHF

Half-brother to Stamparland Hill; moderate efforts in bumpers and hurdles.

Ella Falls (IRE)

101(94c)   (81+c)**81**
9-y-o b m Dancing Dissident (USA)-Over Swing (FR) (Saint Cyrien (FR))
Mrs H Dalton Ray Bailey

Placings:F0P/0/1350/0U/3335   (3229)
2003/04: 24³G, 20⁰G, 24³GF, 19⁵GS,

	Starts	1st	2nd	3rd	Win & Pl
Hurdles	3	0	0	2	948
Chases	1	0	0	1	311
Career Total	14	1	0	4	3482
88 7/00 Worc	3m	F(0-100)HHdl		G-F	£1897

Total win prize-money £1897

Going:	Sf: 0-0 GS: 0-1 Gd: 0-1 GF: - Fm: 0-0
Distance:	2m/2m3: 0-0 2m4-2m7: 0-2 3m+: 0-2
Track:	LH: 0-2 RH: 0-2 Tight: 0-0 Gall: 0-0
Aids:	Bl: 0-0 Vi: 0-0 Tstrap: 0-0 Ckp: 0-0
Best Rating:	88 7/00 Sthl 3m110y gd-fm Hdl

Dual point-to-point winner; lightly-raced over hurdles since winning 3m novices' handicap in July 2000.

Ellabury

88f   **66f**
5-y-o b m Overbury (IRE)-Kayella (Fine Blade (USA))
R Dickin Mrs J Cumiskey, M Doocey, T Joyce

Placings:00   (1931)
2003/04: 16⁹GF, 16⁹GF,

	Starts	1st	2nd	3rd	Win & Pl
NH Flat	2	0	0	0	
Career Total	2	0	0	0	

Going:	Sf: 0-0 GS: 0-0 Gd: 0-0 GF: - Fm: 0-2
Distance:	2m/2m3: 0-2 2m4-2m7: 0-0 3m+: 0-0
Track:	LH: 0-2 RH: 0-0 Tight: 0-0 Gall: 0-0
Aids:	Bl: 0-0 Vi: 0-0 Tstrap: 0-0 Ckp: 0-0
Best Rating:	66 11/03 Wwck 2m gd-fm NHF

Ellamine

97   (98c)**85**
10-y-o b m Warrshan (USA)-Anhaar (Ela-Mana-Mou)
M C Pipe Orchard Partnership

Placings:621322/3/0400440122143F00/130222P05-2   (0444)

2003/04: 19²GF,

	Starts	1st	2nd	3rd	Win & Pl
Hurdles	1	0	1	0	1036
Career Total	33	4	9	4	19007
105 6/02 NAbb	2m6f	G(0-95)HHdl		G-F	£2317
98 10/01 Strf	2m110y	G Hdl		G-S	£2023
99 9/01 Font	2m2f110yG(0-95)HHdl		G-F		£2436
94 7/98 Wolv	2m	E Hdl		GD	£2207

Total win prize-money £8983

Going:	Sf: 0-0 GS: 0-0 Gd: 0-0 GF: - Fm: 0-1
Distance:	2m/2m3: 0-0 2m4-2m7: 0-1 3m+: 0-0
Track:	LH: 0-0 RH: 0-1 Tight: 0-0 Gall: 0-0
Aids:	Bl: 0-0 Vi: 0-0 Tstrap: 0-1 Ckp: 0-0
Best Rating:	105 6/02 NAbb 2m6f gd-fm Hdl

Selling-class hurdler, stays two miles six; acts on most surfaces, often tongue tied.

Elle Roseador

81f   **80f**
5-y-o b m El Conquistador-The Hon Rose (Baron Blakeney)
M Madgwick Mrs Monica Yates

Placings:42-4   (1944)
2003/04: 17⁴G,

	Starts	1st	2nd	3rd	Win & Pl
NH Flat	1	0	0	0	0
Career Total	3	0	1	0	558

Going:	Sf: 0-0 GS: 0-0 Gd: 0-1 GF: - Fm: 0-0
Distance:	2m/2m3: 0-1 2m4-2m7: 0-0 3m+: 0-0
Track:	LH: 0-0 RH: 0-1 Tight: 0-1 Gall: 0-0
Aids:	Bl: 0-0 Vi: 0-0 Tstrap: 0-0 Ckp: 0-0
Best Rating:	80 4/03 Font 2m2f110y gd-fm NHF

Modest bumper performer; acts on fast ground.

Elle Royal (IRE)

92   **69**
5-y-o b m Ali-Royal (IRE)-Silvretta (IRE) (Tirol)
T P McGovern Steve Major

Placings:05U0-50   (0676)
2003/04: 16⁵G, 16⁹GF,

	Starts	1st	2nd	3rd	Win & Pl
Hurdles	2	0	0	0	0
Career Total	6	0	0	0	0

Going:	Sf: 0-0 GS: 0-0 Gd: 0-1 GF: - Fm: 0-1
Distance:	2m/2m3: 0-2 2m4-2m7: 0-0 3m+: 0-0
Track:	LH: 0-1 RH: 0-1 Tight: 0-0 Gall: 0-1
Aids:	Bl: 0-0 Vi: 0-0 Tstrap: 0-0 Ckp: 0-0
Best Rating:	69 5/03 Hntg 2m110y good Hdl

Ello Ollie (IRE)

88   (101c)**94**
9-y-o b g Roselier (FR)-Kayanna (Torenaga)
Andrew Turnell Dr John Hollowood

Placings:3022U50/06P1F222/5-050P   (4914)
2003/04: 20⁴GS, 24⁵GS, 24⁰G, 24FGS,

	Starts	1st	2nd	3rd	Win & Pl
Hurdles	4	0	0	0	0
Career Total	20	1	5	1	8441
91 1/02 Leic	2m7f110yF(0-95)HCh		GD		£3913

Total win prize-money £3913

Going:	Sf: 0-0 GS: 0-3 Gd: 0-1 GF: - Fm: 0-0
Distance:	2m/2m3: 0-0 2m4-2m7: 0-1 3m+: 0-3
Track:	LH: 0-3 RH: 0-1 Tight: 0-0 Gall: 0-2
Aids:	Bl: 0-0 Vi: 0-0 Tstrap: 0-0 Ckp: 0-0
Best Rating:	99 2/00 Newc 2m4f soft Hdl

Ellway Prospect

98   **72**
4-y-o ch f Pivotal-Littlemisstrouble (USA) (My Gallant (USA))

Miss I E Craig C H Bothway

Placings:563466   (4897)
2003/04: 16⁶GS, 21⁶GS, 16⁹S, 21⁴G, 26⁶GS, 22⁶G,

	Starts	1st	2nd	3rd	Win & Pl
Hurdles	6	0	0	1	820
Career Total	6	0	0	1	820

Going: Sf: 0-1 GS: 0-3 Gd: 0-2 GF: - Fm: 0-0
Distance: 2m/2m3: 0-2 2m4-2m7: 0-3 3m+: 0-1
Track: LH: 0-1 RH: 0-5 Tight: 0-1 Gall: 0-0
Aids: Bl: 0-0 Vi: 0-0 Tstrap: 0-0 Ckp: 0-0
Best Rating: 72 3/04 Hrfd 3m2f   gd-sft Hdl

Well beaten on hurdling debut.

Eltringham

4-y-o b f Milieu-Whosgotsillyssense (Pragmatic)
C R Wilson Mrs S Martin

Placings:0   (4886)
2003/04: 17⁹GS,

	Starts	1st	2nd	3rd	Win & Pl
NH Flat	1	0	0	0	
Career Total	1	0	0	0	

Going: Sf: 0-0 GS: 0-1 Gd: 0-0 GF: - Fm: 0-0
Distance: 2m/2m3: 0-1 2m4-2m7: 0-0 3m+: 0-0
Track: LH: 0-0 RH: 0-1 Tight: 0-0 Gall: 0-0
Aids: Bl: 0-0 Vi: 0-0 Tstrap: 0-0 Ckp: 0-0

Eluna

(103c)   (94c) **112**
6-y-o ch m Unfuwain (USA)-Elisha (GER) (Konigsstuhl (GER))
Ian Williams Mr & Mrs John Poynton

Placings:21100/45P6-PP   (3819)
2003/04: 20ᴾHY, 23ᴾS,

	Starts	1st	2nd	3rd	Win & Pl
Hurdles	1	0	0	0	0
Chases	1	0	0	0	0
Career Total	11	2	1	0	6666
124	2/02	Wwck	2m		E Hdl	HVY	£2954
124	1/02	Wwck	2m		E Hdl	HVY	£2740

Total win prize-money £5695

Going: Sf: 0-2 GS: 0-0 Gd: 0-0 GF: - Fm: 0-0
Distance: 2m/2m3: 0-0 2m4-2m7: 0-1 3m+: 0-1
Track: LH: 0-2 RH: 0-0 Tight: 0-0 Gall: 0-0
Aids: Bl: 0-0 Vi: 0-0 Tstrap: 0-1 Ckp: 0-0
Best Rating: 124 2/02 Wwck 2m   heavy Hdl

Fair ex-German-trained filly; won twice at Warwick at the start of 2002; joined Ian Williams and has struggled both over hurdles and fences; acts on heavy ground; has worn a tongue tie.

Elvera

71f   **87f**
6-y-o b m Elmaamul (USA)-Bewitch (Idiots Delight)
J M Bradley J H Lee

Placings:00-0   (1334)
2003/04: 17⁹GF,

	Starts	1st	2nd	3rd	Win & Pl
NH Flat	1	0	0	0	
Career Total	3	0	0	0	

Going: Sf: 0-0 GS: 0-0 Gd: 0-0 GF: - Fm: 0-1
Distance: 2m/2m3: 0-1 2m4-2m7: 0-0 3m+: 0-0
Track: LH: 0-0 RH: 0-1 Tight: 0-0 Gall: 0-0
Aids: Bl: 0-0 Vi: 0-0 Tstrap: 0-0 Ckp: 0-0
Best Rating: 87 3/03 Ludl 2m   good NHF

Elvis

99   (97c)**95**
11-y-o b g Southern Music-Tyqueen (Tycoon Ii)
L Wells The Chap Quartet

Placings:60/P0P/660511/003/233F/F406B02-0463B (4266)
2003/04: 16⁹G, 17⁴GS, 17⁸HY, 18³GS, 16⁸GF,

	Starts	1st	2nd	3rd	Win & Pl
Hurdles	5	0	0	1	642
Career Total	30	2	2	4	9919
98	12/99	Font	2m2f110yD(0-120)HHdl	G-S	£3070
101	12/99	Font	2m2f110yG Hdl	GD	£2867

Total win prize-money £5939

Going: Sf: 0-1 GS: 0-2 Gd: 0-1 GF: - Fm: 0-1
Distance: 2m/2m3: 0-5 2m4-2m7: 0-0 3m+: 0-0
Track: LH: 0-2 RH: 0-3 Tight: 0-3 Gall: 0-0
Aids: Bl: 0-0 Vi: 0-0 Tstrap: 0-0 Ckp: 0-0
Best Rating: 101 5/01 NAbb 2m1f   gd-fm Hdl

Moderate hurdler; stays two miles-two; suited by good or slightly softer; has been tried unsuccessfully over fences; does not find much for pressure.

Elvis Reigns

99(85h)   (92h)**102**
8-y-o b g Rock City-Free Rein (Sagaro)
M D Hammond A G Chappell

Placings:231UPP00/P/004/0135624403533-03   (0474)
2003/04: 16⁶GF, 17³GS,

	Starts	1st	2nd	3rd	Win & Pl
Chases	2	0	0	1	1048
Career Total	27	2	2	6	31694
106	6/02	Ctml	2m1f110yE(0-100)HCh	HVY	£3419
	7/99	Autl	2m1f110y Hdl	SFT	£11840

Total win prize-money £15259

Going: Sf: 0-0 GS: 0-1 Gd: 0-0 GF: - Fm: 0-1
Distance: 2m/2m3: 0-2 2m4-2m7: 0-0 3m+: 0-1
Track: LH: 0-2 RH: 0-0 Tight: 0-1 Gall: 0-0
Aids: Bl: 0-1 Vi: 0-1 Tstrap: 0-0 Ckp: 0-0
Best Rating: 106 7/02 Limk 2m4f   soft Ch

Moderate chaser; effective at 2m to 2m 4f; has worn blinkers and cheekpieces.

Elvis Returns

100
6-y-o b g Alhaatmi-Buckmist Blue (IRE) (Buckskin (FR))
J M Jefferson J Cleeve

Placings:602   (4216)
2003/04: 16⁶S, 16⁹GS, 22²G,

	Starts	1st	2nd	3rd	Win & Pl
NH Flat	2	0	0	0	0
Hurdles	1	0	1	0	1054
Career Total	3	0	1	0	1054

Going: Sf: 0-1 GS: 0-1 Gd: 0-1 GF: - Fm: 0-0
Distance: 2m/2m3: 0-2 2m4-2m7: 0-1 3m+: 0-0
Track: LH: 0-1 RH: 0-1 Tight: 0-0 Gall: 0-1
Aids: Bl: 0-0 Vi: 0-0 Tstrap: 0-0 Ckp: 0-0
Best Rating: 100 3/04 MRas 2m6f   good Hdl

Runner-up in weak novices' hurdle at Market Rasen in March on jumping debut; will stay three miles.

Em's Guy

6-y-o b g Royal Fountain-Gaelic Empress (Regular Guy)
A Parker J John Paterson

Placings:0PP   (4601)
2003/04: 16⁹GS, 20ᴾG, 22ᴾGS,

	Starts	1st	2nd	3rd	Win & Pl
NH Flat	1	0	0	0	0
Hurdles	2	0	0	0	0
Career Total	3	0	0	0	

Going: Sf: 0-0 GS: 0-2 Gd: 0-1 GF: - Fm: 0-0
Distance: 2m/2m3: 0-1 2m4-2m7: 0-2 3m+: 0-0
Track: LH: 0-2 RH: 0-1 Tight: 0-2 Gall: 0-0
Aids: Bl: 0-0 Vi: 0-0 Tstrap: 0-0 Ckp: 0-0
Best Rating: 68 1/04 Catt 2m   gd-sft NHF

Em's Royalty

99   **101**
7-y-o b g Royal Fountain-Gaelic Empress (Regular Guy)
A Parker J John Paterson

Placings:3-3   (2429)
2003/04: 24³GS,

	Starts	1st	2nd	3rd	Win & Pl
Hurdles	1	0	0	1	432
Career Total	2	0	0	2	992

Going: Sf: 0-0 GS: 0-1 Gd: 0-0 GF: - Fm: 0-0
Distance: 2m/2m3: 0-0 2m4-2m7: 0-0 3m+: 0-1
Track: LH: 0-1 RH: 0-0 Tight: 0-0 Gall: 0-0
Aids: Bl: 0-0 Vi: 0-0 Tstrap: 0-0 Ckp: 0-0
Best Rating: 101 11/03 Ayr 3m110y   gd-sft Hdl

Modest novice hurdler; stays three miles; acts on soft ground.

Emanate

90f   **87f**
6-y-o ch g Nicholas Bill-Sleepline Princess (Royal Palace)
P F Nicholls G Z Mizel

Placings:602   (4291)
2003/04: 17⁶GF, 16⁰G, 16²G,

	Starts	1st	2nd	3rd	Win & Pl
NH Flat	3	0	1	0	574
Career Total	3	0	1	0	574

Going: Sf: 0-0 GS: 0-0 Gd: 0-2 GF: - Fm: 0-1
Distance: 2m/2m3: 0-3 2m4-2m7: 0-0 3m+: 0-0
Track: LH: 0-0 RH: 0-3 Tight: 0-0 Gall: 0-0
Aids: Bl: 0-0 Vi: 0-0 Tstrap: 0-0 Ckp: 0-0
Best Rating: 87 3/04 Winc 2m   good NHF

Emanic (FR)

102   **113**
4-y-o b g Video Rock (FR)-Una Volta (FR) (Toujours Pret (USA))
A King (G Macaire 8/9) Million In Mind Partnership

Placings:13433   (4863)
2003/04: 16¹S, 16³GS, 16⁴S, 16³GF, 16²S,

	Starts	1st	2nd	3rd	Win & Pl
Hurdles	5	1	0	3	6957
Career Total	5	1	0	3	6957
113 12/03 Wwck 2m	E Hdl			SFT	£3230

Total win prize-money £3231

Going:	Sf: 1-3 GS: 0-1 Gd: 0-0 GF: - Fm: 0-1
Distance:	2m/2m3: 1-5 2m4-2m7: 0-0 3m+: 0-0
Track:	LH: 1-5 RH: 0-0 Tight: 0-1 Gall: 0-1
Aids:	Bl: 0-0 Vi: 0-0 Tstrap: 0-0 Ckp: 0-0
Best Rating:	113 4/04 Ayr 2m soft Hdl

Dual winner over 1m 4f on good ground in France; impressive winner on hurdling debut in the mud at Warwick December 2003; disappointing subsequently; suited by two miles.

Emarati's Image

6-y-o b g Emarati (USA)-Choir's Image (Lochnager)
R M Stronge (J O'Reilly 19/6) Mrs Bernice Stronge

Placings:P					(2336)
2003/04: 16PS,					
	Starts	1st	2nd	3rd	Win & Pl
Hurdles	1	0	0	0	
Career Total	1	0	0	0	

Going:	Sf: 0-1 GS: 0-0 Gd: 0-0 GF: - Fm: 0-0
Distance:	2m/2m3: 0-1 2m4-2m7: 0-0 3m+: 0-0
Track:	LH: 0-1 RH: 0-0 Tight: 0-1 Gall: 0-0
Aids:	Bl: 0-0 Vi: 0-0 Tstrap: 0-0 Ckp: 0-0

Ember Days
66   21

5-y-o gr m Reprimand-Evening Falls (Beveled (USA))
J L Spearing Mrs Carol J Welch

Placings:P0					(4220)
2003/04: 16PG, 17PG,					
	Starts	1st	2nd	3rd	Win & Pl
Hurdles	2	0	0	0	
Career Total	2	0	0	0	

Going:	Sf: 0-0 GS: 0-0 Gd: 0-2 GF: - Fm: 0-0
Distance:	2m/2m3: 0-2 2m4-2m7: 0-0 3m+: 0-0
Track:	LH: 0-0 RH: 0-2 Tight: 0-1 Gall: 0-0
Aids:	Bl: 0-0 Vi: 0-0 Tstrap: 0-0 Ckp: 0-0
Best Rating:	24 3/04 MRas 2m1f110y good Hdl

Ember King

6-y-o b g Regal Embers (IRE)-Innocent Princess (NZ) (Full On Aces (AUS))
A P James Dr Anne E Ramkaran

Placings:0					(1019)
2003/04: 16QGF,					
	Starts	1st	2nd	3rd	Win & Pl
NH Flat	1	0	0	0	
Career Total	1	0	0	0	

Going:	Sf: 0-0 GS: 0-0 Gd: 0-0 GF: - Fm: 0-1
Distance:	2m/2m3: 0-1 2m4-2m7: 0-0 3m+: 0-0
Track:	LH: 0-1 RH: 0-0 Tight: 0-0 Gall: 0-0
Aids:	Bl: 0-1 Vi: 0-0 Tstrap: 0-0 Ckp: 0-0

Emencee
85   66

7-y-o b g Lucky Wednesday-Nattfari (Tyrnavos)
A Bailey Morris Nicholson Cartwright Ltd

Placings:0/64003					(1987)
2003/04: 16FGF, 16⁴GF, 16⁹G, 16⁹G, 16³GF,					
	Starts	1st	2nd	3rd	Win & Pl
NH Flat	3	0	0	0	0
Hurdles	2	0	0	1	385
Career Total	6	0	0	1	385

Going:	Sf: 0-0 GS: 0-0 Gd: 0-2 GF: - Fm: 0-3
Distance:	2m/2m3: 0-5 2m4-2m7: 0-0 3m+: 0-0
Track:	LH: 0-4 RH: 0-1 Tight: 0-1 Gall: 0-0
Aids:	Bl: 0-0 Vi: 0-0 Tstrap: 0-0 Ckp: 0-0
Best Rating:	91 6/03 Hexm 2m110y gd-fm NHF

Disappointing type; best effort to date when third at Uttoxeter on good to firm in November 2003; stays 2m4f; acts on most ground.

Emerald Express
106f   99f

5-y-o b m Bigstone (IRE)-Nashkara (Shirley Heights)
P R Webber Economic Security

Placings:3030					(4328)
2003/04: 17³G, 17⁹GS, 17³GS, 16⁹S,					
	Starts	1st	2nd	3rd	Win & Pl
NH Flat	4	0	0	2	618
Career Total	4	0	0	2	618

Going:	Sf: 0-1 GS: 0-2 Gd: 0-1 GF: - Fm: 0-0
Distance:	2m/2m3: 0-4 2m4-2m7: 0-0 3m+: 0-0
Track:	LH: 0-1 RH: 0-2 Tight: 0-2 Gall: 0-0
Aids:	Bl: 0-0 Vi: 0-0 Tstrap: 0-0 Ckp: 0-0
Best Rating:	99 10/03 Bang 2m1f good NHF

Half-sister to Flat winner; promising debut when third in Bangor bumper October 2003 despite getting loose prior to the start, disappointing next time, but again ran better at Taunton last time; should stay further over hurdles; acts on easy going.

Emerald Green (GER)
51   39

5-y-o br g Goofalik (USA)-Elaine (GER) (Alkalde (GER))
M J Gingell B M Gray

Placings:04PP					(4435)
2003/04: 16⁶G, 16⁴S, 16FS, 16PGS,					
	Starts	1st	2nd	3rd	Win & Pl
Hurdles	4	0	0	0	356
Career Total	4	0	0	0	356

Going:	Sf: 0-2 GS: 0-1 Gd: 0-1 GF: - Fm: 0-0
Distance:	2m/2m3: 0-4 2m4-2m7: 0-0 3m+: 0-0
Track:	LH: 0-3 RH: 0-1 Tight: 0-3 Gall: 0-0
Aids:	Bl: 0-0 Vi: 0-1 Tstrap: 0-0 Ckp: 0-0
Best Rating:	38 11/03 Fknm 2m good Hdl

Emerald Mist (IRE)
92   68

5-y-o b m Sacrament-Jade's Gem (Sulaafah (USA))
G B Balding Baldings (training) Ltd

Placings:5066O-000					(0884)
2003/04: 19⁹G, 21⁹GF, 20⁹G,					
	Starts	1st	2nd	3rd	Win & Pl
Hurdles	3	0	0	0	
Career Total	8	0	0	0	0

Going:	Sf: 0-0 GS: 0-0 Gd: 0-2 GF: - Fm: 0-1
Distance:	2m/2m3: 0-2 2m4-2m7: 0-3 3m+: 0-0
Track:	LH: 0-1 RH: 0-2 Tight: 0-0 Gall: 0-1
Aids:	Bl: 0-0 Vi: 0-0 Tstrap: 0-0 Ckp: 0-0
Best Rating:	68 4/03 Plum 2m5f gd-fm Hdl

Emerging Star (IRE)
100   103

4-y-o b g Desert Style (IRE)-Feather Star (Soviet Star (USA))
G M Moore Arthur, Chris and Geoff Peacock

Placings:32F325					(3821)
2003/04: 16³G, 16²GS, 16FGS, 19³G, 16²S, 16⁵S,					
	Starts	1st	2nd	3rd	Win & Pl
Hurdles	6	0	2	2	5834
Career Total	6	0	2	2	5834

Going:	Sf: 0-2 GS: 0-2 Gd: 0-2 GF: - Fm: 0-0
Distance:	2m/2m3: 0-5 2m4-2m7: 0-1 3m+: 0-0
Track:	LH: 0-6 RH: 0-0 Tight: 0-0 Gall: 0-1
Aids:	Bl: 0-0 Vi: 0-0 Tstrap: 0-0 Ckp: 0-0
Best Rating:	100 1/04 Donc 2m110y soft Hdl

Moderate juvenile hurdler; middle-distance winner on the Flat; stays two and a half miles; acts on fast ground and with cut.

Emily Dee
73   44

5-y-o b m Classic Cliche (IRE)-Alpi Dora (Valiyar)
J M Bradley K C Trotman

Placings:6P					(1698)
2003/04: 16⁶GF, 16PGF,					
	Starts	1st	2nd	3rd	Win & Pl
Hurdles	2	0	0	0	0
Career Total	2	0	0	0	0

Going:	Sf: 0-0 GS: 0-0 Gd: 0-0 GF: - Fm: 0-2
Distance:	2m/2m3: 0-2 2m4-2m7: 0-0 3m+: 0-0
Track:	LH: 0-2 RH: 0-0 Tight: 0-2 Gall: 0-0
Aids:	Bl: 0-0 Vi: 0-0 Tstrap: 0-0 Ckp: 0-0
Best Rating:	44 9/03 Plum 2m gd-fm Hdl

Emma's Dream
73f   46f

5-y-o ch m Karinga Bay-Some Dream (Vitiges (FR))
P F Nicholls J P Blakeney

Placings:0					(4739)
2003/04: 17⁹G,					
	Starts	1st	2nd	3rd	Win & Pl
NH Flat	1	0	0	0	
Career Total	1	0	0	0	

Going:	Sf: 0-0 GS: 0-0 Gd: 0-0 GF: - Fm: 0-0
Distance:	2m/2m3: 0-1 2m4-2m7: 0-0 3m+: 0-0
Track:	LH: 0-1 RH: 0-0 Tight: 0-1 Gall: 0-0
Aids:	Bl: 0-0 Vi: 0-0 Tstrap: 0-0 Ckp: 0-0

Best Rating: 46   4/04   NAbb   2m1f   good   NHF

Emotional Moment (IRE)

117(112c)   (136+c)143

7-y-o b g Religiously (USA)-Rosceen Bui (IRE) (Phardante (FR))
T J Taaffe Watercork Syndicate

Placings:0606611136/1114144-51F1U550   (4643)
2003/04: 22⁵G, 16¹G, 24⁴FYS, 21¹S, 24⁴US, 16⁵YS, 21⁵G, 24⁴G,

	Starts	1st	2nd	3rd	Win & Pl
Hurdles	3	0	0	0	1875
Chases	5	2	0	0	28264
Career Total	25	9	0	1	121403

136	1/04	Leop	2m5f	Ch	SFT	£22887
131	12/03	Thur	2m	Ch	GD	£5376
143	2/03	Navn	3m	Hdl	Y-S	£21103
126	12/02	Navn	3m	HHdl	Y-S	£11963
117	11/02	DRoy	2m	(0-135)HHdl	HVY	£25920
110	10/02	Wxfd	2m	(74-102)HHdl	Y-S	£5291
98	1/02	Gowr	2m1f	(0-116)HHdl	HVY	£7619
100	1/02	DRoy	2m	(60-88)HHdl	SFT	£3809
82	12/01	Limk	2m	(0-102)HHdl	SFT	£6120
				Total win prize-money £110093

Going: Sf: 1-2 GS: 0-0 Gd: 1-3 GF: - Fm: 0-0
Distance: 2m/2m3: 1-2 2m4-2m7: 1-3 3m+: 0-3
Track: LH: 1-5 RH: 0-0 Tight: 0-1 Gall: 0-1
Aids: Bl: 0-0 Vi: 0-0 Tstrap: 0-0 Ckp: 0-1
Best Rating: 143   2/03   Navn   3m   yld-sft   Hdl

Very useful hurdler/novice chaser; acts well on a soft surface; goes well over two miles but landed a Grade Three at Navan when stepped up to three miles; seemed to handle faster conditions in the 2003 Coral Cup when fourth; has not looked a natural over fences to date, despite winning a Grade Three contest at Leopardstown in January.

Emperor Roscoe

9-y-o b g Roscoe Blake-Royal Celt (Celtic Cone)
A A Day A A Day

Placings:P   (0506)
2003/04: 24ᴾGS,

	Starts	1st	2nd	3rd	Win & Pl
Chases	1	0	0	0	
Career Total	1	0	0	0	

Going: Sf: 0-0 GS: 0-1 Gd: 0-0 GF: - Fm: 0-0
Distance: 2m/2m3: 0-0 2m4-2m7: 0-0 3m+: 0-1
Track: LH: 0-1 RH: 0-0 Tight: 0-1 Gall: 0-0
Aids: Bl: 0-0 Vi: 0-0 Tstrap: 0-0 Ckp: 0-0

Emperor Ross (IRE)

101(112c)   (132c)111

9-y-o b/br g Roselier (FR)-Gilded Empress (Menelek)
N G Richards James Callow & David Wesley Yates

Placings:30/33/111F1P2-1313   (1025)
2003/04: 20¹G, 24³G, 24¹G, 24³GF,

	Starts	1st	2nd	3rd	Win & Pl
Hurdles	3	2	0	1	8222
Chases	1	0	0	1	3464
Career Total	15	6	1	5	35833

91	7/03	Prth	3m110y	E Hdl	GD	£4017
111	5/03	Hexm	2m4f110yE(0-105)HHdl	GD	£3479
129	7/02	Sedg	3m3f	D Ch	G-F	£4693

132	6/02	Hexm	2m4f110yE Ch	G-F	£3237
127	6/02	Prth	3m	D(0-115)HCh	G-S	£6711
112	5/02	Hexm	3m1f	E Ch	G-S	£3185
				Total win prize-money £25322

Going: Sf: 0-0 GS: 0-0 Gd: 2-3 GF: - Fm: 0-1
Distance: 2m/2m3: 2-2 2m4-2m7: 1-1 3m+: 1-3
Track: LH: 1-1 RH: 1-3 Tight: 0-1 Gall: 0-1
Aids: Bl: 0-0 Vi: 0-0 Tstrap: 2-4 Ckp: 0-0
Best Rating: 132   4/03   Prth   2m4f110y   good   Ch

Modest sort in points, over hurdles and over fences; reportedly had breathing problems; stays three and a half miles and acts on any ground.

Emperor's Magic (IRE)

104   123

13-y-o ch g Over The River (FR)-Sengirrefcha (Reformed Character)
R C Guest N B Mason

Placings:63/2/33523/512404/1U13421F3/F61431235-021
                                             (0377)
2003/04: 22⁰G, 25²GS, 24¹S,

	Starts	1st	2nd	3rd	Win & Pl
Chases	3	1	1	0	7229
Career Total	35	7	6	8	53329

124	5/03	Bang	3m110y	D(0-120)HCh	SFT	£5508
112	3/03	MRas	2m4f	E(0-110)HCh	G-S	£4371
115	11/02	Newc	3m	D(0-125)HCh	SFT	£5720
111	3/02	MRas	2m6f110yD(0-120)HCh	SFT	£4771
110	12/01	Catt	3m1f110yF(0-110)HCh	SFT	£4290
98	11/01	Carl	2m4f	E(0-115)HCh	SFT	£6955
97	2/01	Carl	2m4f110yF(0-105)HCh	SFT	£3575
				Total win prize-money £35191

Going: Sf: 1-1 GS: 0-1 Gd: 0-1 GF: - Fm: 0-0
Distance: 2m/2m3: 0-0 2m4-2m7: 0-1 3m+: 1-2
Track: LH: 1-3 RH: 0-0 Tight: 1-3 Gall: 0-0
Aids: Bl: 0-0 Vi: 1-2 Tstrap: 1-2 Ckp: 0-1
Best Rating: 124   5/03   Bang   3m110y   soft   Ch

Fair chaser; stays three miles one furlong but effective over shorter; acts on soft ground; has worn a tongue tie.

Emperor's Monarch

92f   91f

5-y-o ch g Emperor Fountain-Shalta (FR) (Targowice (USA))
J Wade John Wade

Placings:200   (4277)
2003/04: 16²G, 17⁰G, 17⁰G,

	Starts	1st	2nd	3rd	Win & Pl
NH Flat	3	0	1	0	548
Career Total	3	0	1	0	548

Going: Sf: 0-0 GS: 0-0 Gd: 0-3 GF: - Fm: 0-0
Distance: 2m/2m3: 0-3 2m4-2m7: 0-0 3m+: 0-0
Track: LH: 0-1 RH: 0-2 Tight: 0-0 Gall: 0-0
Aids: Bl: 0-0 Vi: 0-0 Tstrap: 0-0 Ckp: 0-0
Best Rating: 95   9/03   Prth   2m110y   good   NHF

Emperors Guest

110(106h)   (110h)140

6-y-o b g Emperor Jones (USA)-Intimate Guest (Be My Guest (USA))
P Mullins Mrs Paul Duffin

Placings:P132010/05F000-1U2254515   (4645)

En El Em Flyer

96(102h)   (70h)73+

9-y-o b g Seymour Hicks (FR)-Sound 'N' Rhythm (Tudor Rhythm)
R Curtis Keith J Bradley/gordon Houldsworth

Placings:60000P/023-5146P   (3872)

2003/04: 17¹Y, 20ᵁF, 17²G, 16²S, 18⁵GY, 16⁴S, 20⁵Y, 16¹Y, 16⁵G,

	Starts	1st	2nd	3rd	Win & Pl
Chases	9	2	2	0	28647
Career Total	22	4	3	1	51299

137	3/04	Naas	2m	Ch	YLD	£11461
118	8/03	Gway	2m1f	Ch	YLD	£8288
120	3/02	Limk	2m	HHdl	SFT	£12760
116	10/01	Tipp	2m	Hdl	HVY	£5564
				Total win prize-money £38076

Going: Sf: 0-2 GS: 0-0 Gd: 0-2 GF: - Fm: 0-1
Distance: 2m/2m3: 2-7 2m4-2m7: 0-2 3m+: 0-0
Track: LH: 1-4 RH: 1-3 Tight: 0-1 Gall: 0-0
Aids: Bl: 0-0 Vi: 0-0 Tstrap: 0-0 Ckp: 0-0
Best Rating: 140   4/04   Aint   2m   good   Ch

Fair Irish chaser; best at around two miles; acts well on soft ground.

Emphatic (IRE)

106   110

9-y-o ch g Ela-Mana-Mou-Sally Rose (Sallust)
J G Portman Hockham Racing

Placings:00352/1401000/02015/234125-F212503   (4870)
2003/04: 24⁵FG, 26²GS, 24¹G, 24²G, 24⁵G, 26⁹G, 24³GS,

	Starts	1st	2nd	3rd	Win & Pl
Hurdles	7	1	2	1	7222
Career Total	30	5	6	3	26973

110	12/03	Tntn	3m110y	D(0-120)HHdl	GD	£3861
109	3/03	Hntg	3m2f	E(0-110)HHdl	GD	£3458
113	3/01	Font	2m6f110yF(0-100)HHdl	HVY	£2457
113	1/00	Sand	2m6f	D(0-110)HHdl	SFT	£5278
109	11/99	Newb	3m110y	D(0-110)HHdl	G-F	£3496
				Total win prize-money £18550

Going: Sf: 0-0 GS: 0-2 Gd: 1-5 GF: - Fm: 0-0
Distance: 2m/2m3: 0-0 2m4-2m7: 0-0 3m+: 1-7
Track: LH: 0-2 RH: 1-5 Tight: 1-2 Gall: 0-3
Aids: Bl: 1-7 Vi: 0-0 Tstrap: 0-0 Ckp: 0-0
Best Rating: 113   1/04   Ludl   3m   good   Hdl

Modest staying handicap hurdler, well suited by testing ground; usually wears blinkers or a visor; front runner.

Empress Of China (IRE)

55f   8f

5-y-o br m Anshan-Suggia (Alzao (USA))
Miss Suzy Smith Robin Smith

Placings:00   (2367)
2003/04: 18⁰G, 16⁰GF,

	Starts	1st	2nd	3rd	Win & Pl
NH Flat	2	0	0	0	
Career Total	2	0	0	0	

Going: Sf: 0-0 GS: 0-0 Gd: 0-1 GF: - Fm: 0-1
Distance: 2m/2m3: 0-2 2m4-2m7: 0-0 3m+: 0-0
Track: LH: 0-1 RH: 0-1 Tight: 0-0 Gall: 0-0
Aids: Bl: 0-0 Vi: 0-0 Tstrap: 0-0 Ckp: 0-0
Best Rating: 8   11/03   Plum   2m2f   good   NHF

2003/04: 19⁵G, 25¹GF, 26⁴S, 24⁶GS, 25⁶GS,

	Starts	1st	2nd	3rd	Win & Pl
Hurdles	1	0	0	0	
Chases	4	1	0	0	3319
Career Total	14	1	1	1	4543
73 11/03 Folk	3m1f	F(0-95)HCh		G-F	£3319
			Total win prize-money		£3319

Going:	Sf: 0-1 GS: 0-2 Gd: 0-1 GF: - Fm: 1-1
Distance:	2m/2m3: 0-0 2m4-2m7: 0-1 3m+: 1-4
Track:	LH: 0-2 RH: 1-2 Tight: 1-3 Gall: 0-0
Aids:	Bl: 0-0 Vi: 0-0 Tstrap: 0-0 Ckp: 0-0
Best Rating:	81 6/01 Worc 2m gd-fm NHF

Plating-class chaser; suited three miles; won weak race on his chase debut.

Encore Cadoudal (FR)

104   **115**

6-y-o b g Cadoudal (FR)-Maousse (FR) (Labus (FR))
P Monteith   P Monteith

Placings: 20/6305-4214   (3676)
2003/04: 16⁴S, 16²S, 16¹S, 16⁴HY,

	Starts	1st	2nd	3rd	Win & Pl
Hurdles	4	1	1	0	5049
Career Total	10	1	2	1	6486
103 1/04 Kels	2m110y	E Hdl		SFT	£3666
			Total win prize-money		£3666

Going:	Sf: 1-4 GS: 0-0 Gd: 0-0 GF: - Fm: 0-0
Distance:	2m/2m3: 1-4 2m4-2m7: 0-0 3m+: 0-0
Track:	LH: 1-4 RH: 0-0 Tight: 1-3 Gall: 0-0
Aids:	Bl: 0-0 Vi: 0-0 Tstrap: 0-0 Ckp: 0-0
Best Rating:	115 12/03 Ayr 2m soft Hdl

Modest hurdler; best around two miles; acts on soft.

End Of An Error

109   **99+**

5-y-o b m Charmer-Needwood Poppy (Rolfe (USA))
Mrs E Slack (M C Chapman 6/7) A Slack

Placings: 004-6601412160130F0   (4605)
2003/04: 23⁶GF, 23²GF, 17⁹GF, 24¹G, 17⁴GF, 21¹GF, 24²GF, 24¹G, 24⁶GF, 24⁰G, 20¹G, 25³GF, 27⁰GS, 26⁶G, 22⁰G,

	Starts	1st	2nd	3rd	Win & Pl
Hurdles	15	4	1	1	11284
Career Total	18	4	1	1	11284
93 9/03 Prth	3m110y	D(0-115)HHdl		GD	£4173
90 7/03 Sedg	2m5f110y	F(0-95)HHdl		G-F	£2639
79 7/03 MRas	3m	G(0-95)HHdl		GD	£2401
			Total win prize-money		£9213

Going:	Sf: 0-0 GS: 0-1 Gd: 3-6 GF: - Fm: 1-8
Distance:	2m/2m3: 0-2 2m4-2m7: 2-3 3m+: 2-10
Track:	LH: 2-8 RH: 2-6 Tight: 2-9 Gall: 1-2
Aids:	Bl: 0-0 Vi: 0-0 Tstrap: 0-0 Ckp: 0-0
Best Rating:	99 11/03 Newc 2m4f good Hdl

Moderate hurdler; changed hands after a wide margin success at Market Rasen in July and has done well for new connections since; suited by three miles; goes well for Owyn Nelmes.

Enhancer

111+f

6-y-o b g Zafonic (USA)-Ypha (USA) (Lyphard (USA))
Mrs L C Jewell   Gallagher Equine Ltd

Placings: 1/11-0   (4649)

2003/04: 17⁹G,

	Starts	1st	2nd	3rd	Win & Pl
NH Flat	1	0	0	0	
Career Total	4	3	0	0	5632
111 3/03 Weth	2m	H NHF		G-F	£1932
103 9/02 Hexm	2m110y	H NHF		G-F	£1834
99 2/02 Muss	2m	H NHF		SFT	£1865
			Total win prize-money		£5632

Going:	Sf: 0-0 GS: 0-0 Gd: 0-1 GF: - Fm: 0-0
Distance:	2m/2m3: 0-1 2m4-2m7: 0-0 3m+: 0-0
Track:	LH: 0-0 RH: 0-0 Tight: 0-0 Gall: 0-0
Aids:	Bl: 0-0 Vi: 0-0 Tstrap: 0-0 Ckp: 0-0
Best Rating:	111 3/03 Weth 2m gd-fm NHF

A half-brother to useful jumper Redemption, he won a weak bumper on his debut at Musselburgh and followed up at Hexham last year; back in action after a six month break when a wide margin winner at Wetherby in March 2003; acts on fast and soft.

Enitsag (FR)

5-y-o ch g Pistolet Bleu (IRE)-Rosala (FR) (Lashkari)
S Flook (M C Pipe 10/9) Glyn Byard

Placings: 1116012-25631F14   (4775)
2003/04: 17²S, 16²GF, 16⁵G, 17⁶GF, 18³GF, 17¹GF, 21⁵GS, 21¹GS, 21⁴G,

	Starts	1st	2nd	3rd	Win & Pl
Hurdles	6	1	2	1	4689
Chases	3	1	0	0	2707
Career Total	15	6	2	1	21888
93 3/04 Fknm	2m5f110y	H CH		G-S	£2444
104 9/03 Hrfd	2m1f	G Hdl		G-F	£1862
102 4/03 NAbb	2m1f	D(0-115)HHdl		G-F	£4912
97 2/03 Bang	2m1f	E Hdl		G-S	£3822
100 12/02 Extr	1m5f	H NHF		SFT	£2733
100 11/02 Newb	1m4f110y	H NHF		G-S	£3024
			Total win prize-money		£18799

Going:	Sf: 0-1 GS: 1-2 Gd: 0-2 GF: - Fm: 1-4
Distance:	2m/2m3: 1-6 2m4-2m7: 1-3 3m+: 0-0
Track:	LH: 1-7 RH: 1-2 Tight: 1-7 Gall: 0-0
Aids:	Bl: 1-1 Vi: 0-1 Tstrap: 0-0 Ckp: 0-1
Best Rating:	104 9/03 Hrfd 2m1f gd-fm Hdl

Modest hurdler; dual bumper winner at less than two miles; sold out of M. Pipe's yard after winning seller September 2003; has become a fair hunter chaser; acts on soft and fast ground; has worn a visor and cheekpieces.

Ennel Boy (IRE)

109(103h)   **(113h)116**

11-y-o ch g Torus-Golden Symphony (Le Moss)
N M Babbage   Provex Products Ltd

Placings: 0/0/PP04/312/23P5-2120   (2150)
2003/04: 17²G, 21¹GS, 21²GF, 25⁰G,

	Starts	1st	2nd	3rd	Win & Pl
Hurdles	1	0	0	0	0
Chases	3	1	2	2	10192
Career Total	17	2	4	2	19778
112 5/03 Strf	2m5f110y	D(0-110)HCh		G-S	£5473
100 5/01 Hntg	3m2f	E(0-105)HHdl		G-F	£2565
			Total win prize-money		£8039

Going:	Sf: 0-0 GS: 1-1 Gd: 0-2 GF: - Fm: 0-1
Distance:	2m/2m3: 0-1 2m4-2m7: 1-2 3m+: 0-1
Track:	LH: 1-4 RH: 0-0 Tight: 1-3 Gall: 0-1
Aids:	Bl: 0-0 Vi: 0-0 Tstrap: 0-0 Ckp: 0-1
Best Rating:	116 6/03 NAbb 2m5f110y gd-fm Ch

Modest hurdler/moderate chaser; won two miles five novices handicap chase at Stratford May 2003; seemed to find the same trip on the short side at Newton Abbot next time; stays 3m plus; acts on fast ground; lightly raced in recent seasons; has worn cheekpieces.

Enrique (GER)

108(106h)   **(127+h)151**

9-y-o ch g Niniski (USA)-Eicidora (GER) (Surumu (GER))
P J Hobbs   Sir Robert Ogden

Placings: 1220113/5211F/4P125/P-1P6211P   (2152)
2003/04: 25¹GF, 32²GF, 24⁶GF, 24²GF, 24¹GF, 24¹G, 27⁶G,

	Starts	1st	2nd	3rd	Win & Pl
Hurdles	3	1	1	0	7375
Chases	4	2	0	0	23166
Career Total	25	9	5	1	82685
151 10/03 Carl	3m	C(0-135)HCh		GD	£13812
127 9/03 Uttx	3m110y	D(0-125)HHdl		G-F	£5070
149 5/03 Ludl	3m1f110y	C(0-130)HCh		G-F	£9353
141 12/01 Winc	3m1f110y	D(0-125)HCh		GD	£9148
141 11/00 Ludl	3m			GD	£4446
128 11/00 Ludl	2m4f	E Ch		GD	£3552
137 3/00 Ling	2m3f110y	C(0-135)HHdl		G-F	£14885
133 3/00 Sand	2m110y	E(0-115)HHdl		GD	£4212
113 11/99 NAbb	2m1f	E Hdl		SFT	£2422
			Total win prize-money		£66904

Going:	Sf: 0-0 GS: 0-0 Gd: 1-2 GF: - Fm: 2-5
Distance:	2m/2m3: 0-0 2m4-2m7: 0-0 3m+: 3-7
Track:	LH: 1-3 RH: 1-2 Tight: 0-1 Gall: 0-1
Aids:	Bl: 0-0 Vi: 0-0 Tstrap: 0-0 Ckp: 0-0
Best Rating:	151 10/03 Carl 3m good Ch

Smart handicap chaser/useful hurdler, won over hurdles at Uttoxeter in September 2003 and over fences at Carlisle following month; stays 3m 1f; best on fast ground, but acts on soft.

Ensemble

4-y-o b g Polish Precedent (USA)-Full Orchestra (Shirley Heights)
M W Easterby   David Sugars & Bob Parker

Placings: P   (0919)
2003/04: 17⁶GF,

	Starts	1st	2nd	3rd	Win & Pl
Hurdles	1	0	0	0	
Career Total	1	0	0	0	

Going:	Sf: 0-0 GS: 0-0 Gd: 0-0 GF: - Fm: 0-1
Distance:	2m/2m3: 0-1 2m4-2m7: 0-0 3m+: 0-1
Track:	LH: 0-0 RH: 0-1 Tight: 0-1 Gall: 0-0
Aids:	Bl: 0-0 Vi: 0-0 Tstrap: 0-0 Ckp: 0-0

Entertainer (IRE)

109(86c)   **(75c)106**

8-y-o b g Be My Guest (USA)-Green Wings (General Assembly (USA))
A R Dicken   Ron Affleck

Placings: 22/1F2401/001/0052646-3003000   (4942)
2003/04: 22³G, 22⁰G, 22⁰S, 20³G, 22⁰GS, 20⁰G, 20⁰GS,

	Starts	1st	2nd	3rd	Win & Pl
Hurdles	7	0	0	2	3663
Career Total	25	3	4	2	20250
135 6/01 Worc	2m4f	C(0-135)HHdl		GD	£5519
126 4/01 Winc	2m	E Hdl		SFT	£3493
126 5/00 Font	2m2f110y	E Hdl		GD	£2450
			Total win prize-money		£11463

Going:	Sf: 0-1 GS: 0-2 Gd: 0-4 GF: - Fm: 0-0
Distance:	2m2/m3: 0-0 2m4-2m7: 0-7 3m+: 0-0
Track:	LH: 0-4 RH: 0-3 Tight: 0-3 Gall: 0-0
Aids:	Bl: 0-0 Vi: 0-0 Tstrap: 0-0 Ckp: 0-0
Best Rating:	135 6/01 Worc 2m4f good Hdl

Fair hurdler, now on the downgrade; best at around two and a half miles; acts on good but has won on softer.

Entree (FR)
90f   85f

5-y-o b m Ela-Mana-Mou-Easter Baby (Derrylin)
P D Cundell Mrs Sara Wickins

Placings:62-3   (0372)
2003/04: 16³G,

	Starts	1st	2nd	3rd	Win & Pl
NH Flat	1	0	0	1	269
Career Total	3	0	1	1	841

Going:	Sf: 0-0 GS: 0-0 Gd: 0-0 GF: - Fm: 0-0
Distance:	2m/2m3: 0-0 2m4-2m7: 0-0 3m+: 0-0
Track:	LH: 0-0 RH: 0-0 Tight: 0-0 Gall: 0-0
Aids:	Bl: 0-0 Vi: 0-0 Tstrap: 0-0 Ckp: 0-0
Best Rating:	90 5/03 Worc 2m good NHF

Twice placed in bumpers; wore blinkers third start.

Envious
109   81+

5-y-o ch g Hernando (FR)-Prima Verde (Leading Counsel (USA))
R Allan Mrs Rita Cioffi

Placings:600-0432261   (1368)
2003/04: 16⁵G, 20⁴G, 20³G, 17²GF, 21²GF, 16⁶GF, 16¹F,

	Starts	1st	2nd	3rd	Win & Pl
Hurdles	7	1	2	1	5044
Career Total	10	1	2	1	5044
81	9/03 Hexm 2m110y E(0-100)HHdl FRM £2331
	Total win prize-money £2331

Going:	Sf: 0-0 GS: 0-0 Gd: 0-3 GF: - Fm: 1-4
Distance:	2m/2m3: 1-4 2m4-2m7: 0-3 3m+: 0-0
Track:	LH: 1-4 RH: 0-3 Tight: 0-3 Gall: 0-0
Aids:	Bl: 0-0 Vi: 0-0 Tstrap: 0-0 Ckp: 1-4
Best Rating:	82 7/03 Sedg 2m5f110y gd-fm Hdl

Moderate novice; best efforts when runner-up at Cartmel in July and Sedgefield a week later.

Environment Audit
76   93

5-y-o ch g Kris-Bold And Beautiful (Bold Lad (IRE))
J R Jenkins Humphrey Solomons

Placings:0442064-0   (4339)
2003/04: 16⁶G,

	Starts	1st	2nd	3rd	Win & Pl
Hurdles	1	0	0	0	
Career Total	8	0	1	0	2591

Going:	Sf: 0-0 GS: 0-0 Gd: 0-0 GF: 0-1 GF: - Fm: 0-0
Distance:	2m/2m3: 0-1 2m4-2m7: 0-0 3m+: 0-0
Track:	LH: 0-1 RH: 0-0 Tight: 0-0 Gall: 0-0
Aids:	Bl: 0-0 Vi: 0-0 Tstrap: 0-0 Ckp: 0-0
Best Rating:	95 12/02 Sand 2m110y soft Hdl

Enzo De Baune (FR)
113   124

7-y-o b g En Calcat (FR)-Pure Moon (FR) (Pure Flight (USA))
G A Harker Lord Bolton

Placings:5403F/06P4444U21-435F41122   (4953)
2003/04: 22⁴G, 16³GF, 22⁵GS, 20⁵GS, 20⁴GF, 16¹G, 20¹F, 18²G, 20²G,

	Starts	1st	2nd	3rd	Win & Pl
Chases	9	2	2	1	19282
Career Total	24	3	3	2	28257
118	2/04	Muss	2m4f	D(0-115)HCh	FRM	£6682
113	1/04	Leic	2m	F(0-100)HCh	GD	£3445
106	4/03	Carl	2m	E(0-100)HCh	G-F	£4485
				Total win prize-money £14612

Going:	Sf: 0-0 GS: 0-2 Gd: 1-4 GF: - Fm: 1-3
Distance:	2m/2m3: 1-3 2m4-2m7: 1-6 3m+: 0-0
Track:	LH: 0-4 RH: 2-5 Tight: 1-5 Gall: 0-2
Aids:	Bl: 0-0 Vi: 0-0 Tstrap: 0-0 Ckp: 0-0
Best Rating:	124 4/04 Sand 2m4f110y good Ch

Modest chaser; acts on a sound surface; has worn blinkers; best going right-handed and making the running.

Epicure (FR)
101   92

7-y-o b/br g Northern Crystal-L'Epicurienne (FR) (Rex Magna (FR))
M C Pipe Mrs Belinda Harvey

Placings:0000/1112P500PP-5405   (1473)
2003/04: 20⁵HG, 16⁴G, 21⁰G, 17⁵F,

	Starts	1st	2nd	3rd	Win & Pl
Hurdles	4	0	0	0	919
Career Total	18	3	1	0	13396
117	8/02	Bang	2m4f	D(0-115)HHdl	SFT	£4868
117	6/02	NAbb	2m1f	E(0-105)HHdl	G-F	£3031
112	5/02	NAbb	2m1f	D Hdl	SFT	£3419
				Total win prize-money £11319

Going:	Sf: 0-1 GS: 0-0 Gd: 0-2 GF: - Fm: 0-1
Distance:	2m/2m3: 0-2 2m4-2m7: 0-2 3m+: 0-0
Track:	LH: 0-2 RH: 0-2 Tight: 0-0 Gall: 0-0
Aids:	Bl: 0-0 Vi: 0-3 Tstrap: 0-0 Ckp: 0-0
Best Rating:	117 8/02 NAbb 2m1f gd-fm Hdl

Epitre (FR)
75

7-y-o b g Common Grounds-Epistolienne (Law Society (USA))
M F Harris Let's Live Racing

Placings:60P-4   (4762)
2003/04: 19⁴S,

	Starts	1st	2nd	3rd	Win & Pl
Hurdles	1	0	0	0	0
Career Total	4	0	0	0	600

Going:	Sf: 0-1 GS: 0-0 Gd: 0-0 GF: - Fm: 0-0
Distance:	2m/2m3: 0-0 2m4-2m7: 0-1 3m+: 0-0
Track:	LH: 0-0 RH: 0-0 Tight: 0-0 Gall: 0-0
Aids:	Bl: 0-0 Vi: 0-0 Tstrap: 0-0 Ckp: 0-0
Best Rating:	107 1/03 Hayd 2m gd-sft Hdl

Epsilo De La Ronce (FR)

12-y-o b/br g Le Riverain (FR)-India Rosa (FR) (Carnaval)
Major General C A Ramsay (S Flook 31/5) Will Ramsay

Placings:61440PF250/4/56210/215F2P40P/11262154-312430   (4626)
2003/04: 21³G, 20¹GF, 20²GF, 24⁴G, 24³G, 21⁰G,

	Starts	1st	2nd	3rd	Win & Pl
Chases	6	1	1	2	3629
Career Total	39	7	7	2	28122
107	5/03	Wwck	2m4f110yH Ch	G-F	£1561
107	3/03	Ludl	2m4f	H Ch	G-F	£3167
103	5/02	Wwck	2m4f110yH Ch	FRM	£1260
109	5/02	Chel	2m5f	H Ch	G-F	£3902
109	5/01	Strf	3m	H Ch	G-S	£3523
109	4/01	Asct	2m3f110yH Ch	SFT	£3227
	9/98	Prnnl	2m2f110y Ch	GD	£2727
				Total win prize-money £19369

Going:	Sf: 0-0 GS: 0-0 Gd: 0-0 GF: - Fm: 1-2
Distance:	2m/2m3: 0-0 2m4-2m7: 1-4 3m+: 0-2
Track:	LH: 1-4 RH: 0-2 Tight: 0-4 Gall: 0-1
Aids:	Bl: 0-0 Vi: 0-0 Tstrap: 0-0 Ckp: 0-0
Best Rating:	109 5/02 Chel 2m5f gd-fm Ch

Fair hunter chaser; stays three miles, although possibly better at shorter; acts on fast and yielding ground.

Equal Balance
27

6-y-o ch g Pivotal-Thatcher's Era (IRE) (Never So Bold)
C J Hemsley Keith McKay

Placings:F00-P   (2383)
2003/04: 19²G,

	Starts	1st	2nd	3rd	Win & Pl
Hurdles	1	0	0	0	
Career Total	4	0	0	0	

Going:	Sf: 0-0 GS: 0-0 Gd: 0-0 GF: - Fm: 0-0
Distance:	2m/2m3: 0-1 2m4-2m7: 0-0 3m+: 0-0
Track:	LH: 0-0 RH: 0-0 Tight: 0-0 Gall: 0-0
Aids:	Bl: 0-0 Vi: 0-0 Tstrap: 0-0 Ckp: 0-0
Best Rating:	27 9/02 Plum 2m good Hdl

Ercon (IRE)

6-y-o ch g Thatching-Certain Impression (USA) (Forli (ARG))
L Waring Mrs J Waring

Placings:06PP-P   (0990)
2003/04: 22²G,

	Starts	1st	2nd	3rd	Win & Pl
Hurdles	1	0	0	0	
Career Total	5	0	0	0	0

Going:	Sf: 0-0 GS: 0-0 Gd: 0-0 GF: - Fm: 0-0
Distance:	2m/2m3: 0-0 2m4-2m7: 0-0 3m+: 0-0
Track:	LH: 0-1 RH: 0-0 Tight: 0-1 Gall: 0-0
Aids:	Bl: 0-0 Vi: 0-0 Tstrap: 0-0 Ckp: 0-0
Best Rating:	72 6/02 Hrfd 2m1f gd-fm NHF

Eric's Charm (FR)
114   147

6-y-o b g Nikos-Ladoun (FR) (Kaldoun (FR))

O Sherwood M St Quinton & P Deal

Placings:115-1132124   (4641)
2003/04: 19¹G, 19¹GS, 16³G, 21²GS, 21¹G, 20²S, 24⁴G,

	Starts	1st	2nd	3rd	Win & Pl
Hurdles	7	3	2	1	41982
Career Total	10	5	2	1	46680

140	2/04	Kemp	2m5f	C Hdl	GD	£6220
139	12/03	Hrfd	2m3f110yD Hdl		G-S	£3809
121	11/03	Ling	2m3f110yD Hdl		GD	£4303
113	3/03	Hntg	2m110y H NHF		GD	£2009
110	2/03	Font	2m2f110yH NHF		G-S	£1939

Total win prize-money £18280

Going:	Sf: 0-1 GS: 1-2 Gd: 2-4 GF: - Fm: 0-0
Distance:	2m/2m3: 0-1 **2m4-2m7: 3-5** 3m+: 0-1
Track:	LH: 1-3 RH: **2-4** Tight: 1-2 Gall: 0-0
Aids:	Bl: 0-0 Vi: 0-0 Tstrap: 0-0 Ckp: 0-0
Best Rating:	**146** 3/04 Sand 2m4f110y soft Hdl

Smart novice hurdler; half-brother to Monkerhostin; has won five of his ten outings in both bumpers and hurdles, but beaten on each occasion he has run in a Class A race; best going right-handed; acts on good and good to soft ground; consistent.

Erin Alley (IRE)
106(80h)   81
11-y-o ch g Be My Native (USA)-Cousin Flo (True Song)
D J Wintle Lavender Hill Stud L L C

Placings:55005/P3P/022F1P/553-P44   (4446)
2003/04: 20⁵S, 16⁴HY, 16⁴GS,

	Starts	1st	2nd	3rd	Win & Pl
Chases	3	0	0	0	326
Career Total	21	1	2	2	5802

85	1/02	Plum	2m4f	F(0-90)HCh	HVY	£2847

Total win prize-money £2847

Going:	Sf: 0-2 GS: 0-1 Gd: 0-0 GF: - Fm: 0-0
Distance:	2m/2m3: 0-2 2m4-2m7: 0-1 3m+: 0-0
Track:	LH: 0-2 RH: 0-1 Tight: 0-1 Gall: 0-0
Aids:	Bl: 0-0 Vi: 0-0 Tstrap: 0-0 Ckp: 0-0
Best Rating:	**104** 12/97 Towc 2m soft NHF

Modest chaser, stays two and a half miles and acts in the mud.

Erins Lass (IRE)
102   98
7-y-o b m Erin's Isle-Amative (Beau Charmeur (FR))
R Dickin Stratford Members Club

Placings:00P6/02206-30120142U50   (4651)
2003/04: 16³GF, 20⁴G, 17¹GF, 17²G, 19⁹G, 17¹GF, 17⁴GF, 16²F, 16ᵁGF, 16⁵G, 17⁰G,

	Starts	1st	2nd	3rd	Win & Pl
Hurdles	11	2	2	1	10620
Career Total	20	2	4	1	12748

94	8/03	MRas	2m1f110yE Hdl		G-F	£3474
84	6/03	MRas	2m1f110yE(0-100)HHdl		G-F	£3668

Total win prize-money £7142

Going:	Sf: 0-0 GS: 0-0 Gd: 0-5 GF: - Fm: 2-6
Distance:	**2m/2m3: 2-10** 2m4-2m7: 0-1 3m+: 0-0
Track:	LH: 0-5 **RH: 2-6** Tight: 2-6 Gall: 0-0
Aids:	Bl: 0-0 Vi: 0-0 Tstrap: 0-0 Ckp: 0-1
Best Rating:	**96** 10/03 Towc 2m firm Hdl

Plating-class hurdler; successful in novices' handicap at Market Rasen in June 2003; took a weak mares' only novices' event at same track in August; best suited by two miles; acts on fast ground.

Eriskay (IRE)
95   107
8-y-o b g Montelimar (USA)-Little Peach (Ragapan)
L Lungo Colonel D C Greig

Placings:0UPU12/0P   (3520)
2003/04: 21⁰GS, 20⁰S,

	Starts	1st	2nd	3rd	Win & Pl
Hurdles	2	0	0	0	
Career Total	8	1	1	0	3659

107	3/02	Kels	2m6f110yE Hdl		SFT	£2723

Total win prize-money £2723

Going:	Sf: 0-1 GS: 0-1 Gd: 0-0 GF: - Fm: 0-0
Distance:	2m/2m3: 0-0 2m4-2m7: 0-2 3m+: 0-0
Track:	LH: 0-2 RH: 0-0 Tight: 0-1 Gall: 0-0
Aids:	Bl: 0-0 Vi: 0-0 Tstrap: 0-0 Ckp: 0-0
Best Rating:	**107** 3/02 Kels 2m6f110y soft Hdl

Ernest William (IRE)
89(96c)   (102c)108
12-y-o b/br g Phardante (FR)-Minerstown (IRE) (Miners Lamp)
J A Supple Geoff Hubbard Racing

Placings:0/0F450/11F141/1/52311U/P3PP4462-02P   (1374)
2003/04: 21⁰GF, 21²GF, 24⁸GF,

	Starts	1st	2nd	3rd	Win & Pl
Hurdles	3	0	1	0	964
Career Total	30	7	3	2	35698

117	4/02	MRas	2m6f110yD(0-120)HCh		GD	£6890
95	4/02	MRas	2m1f110yD Ch		GD	£4088
115	4/01	Prth	2m4f110yC(0-130)HHdl		HVY	£5882
117	3/98	Ling	2m3f110yC(0-135)HHdl		GF	£4889
115	2/98	Hntg	2m5f110yE(0-110)HHdl		GD	£2652
100	12/97	Hntg	2m5f110yD(0-100)HHdl		G-S	£2244
93	12/97	Wwck	2m3f	E(0-100)HHdl	GD	£2640

Total win prize-money £29290

Going:	Sf: 0-0 GS: 0-0 Gd: 0-0 GF: - Fm: 0-0
Distance:	2m/2m3: 0-0 2m4-2m7: 0-2 3m+: 0-1
Track:	LH: 0-2 RH: 0-1 Tight: 0-0 Gall: 0-1
Aids:	Bl: 0-0 Vi: 0-0 Tstrap: 0-0 Ckp: 0-0
Best Rating:	**117** 4/02 MRas 2m6f110y good Ch

Moderate chaser; stays two and three-quarter miles; acts on a sound surface but handles heavy.

Erris Express (IRE)
91(100h)   (91h)84
6-y-o ch g Definite Article-Postie (Sharpo)
J R Jenkins Erris Boys

Placings:000-0P6F03P3   (4759)
2003/04: 17⁰GS, 16⁵S, 20⁵GS, 24⁵F, 20⁰G, 24³G, 20⁴GS, 16⁵S,

	Starts	1st	2nd	3rd	Win & Pl
Hurdles	2	0	0	0	0
Chases	6	0	0	2	1552
Career Total	11	0	0	2	1552

Going:	Sf: 0-2 GS: 0-3 Gd: 0-3 GF: - Fm: 0-0
Distance:	2m/2m3: 0-3 2m4-2m7: 0-3 3m+: 0-2
Track:	LH: 0-2 RH: 0-1 Tight: 0-2 Gall: 0-1
Aids:	Bl: 0-0 Vi: 0-0 Tstrap: 0-0 Ckp: 0-0
Best Rating:	**91** 1/03 Donc 2m110y gd-sft Hdl

Erro Codigo
95   59
9-y-o b g Formidable (USA)-Home Wrecker (DEN)

(Affiliation Order (USA))
F P Murtagh Mrs Anna Kenny

Placings:0500660/26/0550F04P0-04506F   (1204)
2003/04: 16⁰G, 17⁴G, 20⁵GF, 17⁰GF, 17⁶GF, 17⁷GF,

	Starts	1st	2nd	3rd	Win & Pl
Hurdles	6	0	0	0	
Career Total	24	0	1	0	576

Going:	Sf: 0-0 GS: 0-0 Gd: 0-3 GF: - Fm: 0-3
Distance:	2m/2m3: 0-5 2m4-2m7: 0-1 3m+: 0-3
Track:	LH: 0-6 RH: 0-0 Tight: 0-4 Gall: 0-0
Aids:	Bl: 0-0 Vi: 0-0 Tstrap: 0-0 Ckp: 0-0
Best Rating:	**76** 6/02 Hexm 2m110y gd-fm Hdl

Errol
91   82+
5-y-o ch g Dancing Spree (USA)-Primo Panache (Primo Dominie)
J F Coupland J F Coupland

Placings:600   (3523)
2003/04: 16⁶GS, 16⁹GS, 16⁸S,

	Starts	1st	2nd	3rd	Win & Pl
Hurdles	3	0	0	0	0
Career Total	3	0	0	0	0

Going:	Sf: 0-1 GS: 0-2 Gd: 0-0 GF: - Fm: 0-0
Distance:	2m/2m3: 0-3 2m4-2m7: 0-0 3m+: 0-0
Track:	LH: 0-3 RH: 0-0 Tight: 0-1 Gall: 0-0
Aids:	Bl: 0-0 Vi: 0-0 Tstrap: 0-0 Ckp: 0-0
Best Rating:	**82** 1/04 Catt 2m gd-sft Hdl

Escort
89   53
8-y-o b g Most Welcome-Benazir (High Top)
W Clay The Escort Partnership

Placings:2P4/06512533/303P/004464-00   (4603)
2003/04: 16⁰G, 17⁰G,

	Starts	1st	2nd	3rd	Win & Pl
Hurdles	2	0	0	0	
Career Total	23	1	2	4	6541

94	12/00	Weth	2m4f110yD(0-110)HHdl		SFT	£3250

Total win prize-money £3250

Going:	Sf: 0-0 GS: 0-0 Gd: 0-2 GF: - Fm: 0-0
Distance:	2m/2m3: 0-2 2m4-2m7: 0-0 3m+: 0-0
Track:	LH: 0-1 RH: 0-1 Tight: 0-1 Gall: 0-0
Aids:	Bl: 0-0 Vi: 0-0 Tstrap: 0-0 Ckp: 0-0
Best Rating:	**100** 5/01 Sthl 3m110y firm Hdl

Esendi
104(74h)   (98h)99
9-y-o b g Buckley-Cagaleena (Cagirama)
Miss Venetia Williams T England

Placings:0/P445/U0-3   (1816)
2003/04: 24³G,

	Starts	1st	2nd	3rd	Win & Pl
Chases	1	0	0	1	550
Career Total	8	0	0	1	925

Going:	Sf: 0-0 GS: 0-0 Gd: 0-1 GF: - Fm: 0-0
Distance:	2m/2m3: 0-0 2m4-2m7: 0-0 3m+: 0-1
Track:	LH: 0-1 RH: 0-0 Tight: 0-1 Gall: 0-0
Aids:	Bl: 0-0 Vi: 0-0 Tstrap: 0-0 Ckp: 0-0

Best Rating: 101 10/03 Bang 3m110y good Ch

Moderate form in bumpers, novice hurdles and chases.

Esenin

5-y-o b g Danehill (USA)-Boojum (Mujtahid (USA))
D G Bridgwater D G Bridgwater

Placings:P				(0680)

2003/04: 16PGF,

	Starts	1st	2nd	3rd	Win & Pl
Hurdles	1	0	0	0	
Career Total	1	0	0	0	

Going:	Sf: 0-0 GS: 0-0 Gd: 0-0 GF: 0-0 Fm: 0-1
Distance:	2m/2m3: 0-1 2m4-2m7: 0-0 3m+: 0-0
Track:	LH: 0-1 RH: 0-0 Tight: 0-0 Gall: 0-0
Aids:	Bl: 0-0 Vi: 0-0 Tstrap: 0-0 Ckp: 0-0

Esh Bran Girl (IRE)
105f   75f

4-y-o b f Shahrastani (USA)-Logstown (IRE) (Keen)
D W Thompson P J Harle

Placings:01R0				(4264)

2003/04: 13QGF, 161GF, 16RG, 16QGF,

	Starts	1st	2nd	3rd	Win & Pl
NH Flat	4	1	0	0	2954
Career Total	4	1	0	0	2954
75	1/04	Muss	2m	H NHF	G-F £2954

Total win prize-money £2954

Going:	Sf: 0-0 GS: 0-0 Gd: 0-1 GF: - Fm: 1-3
Distance:	2m/2m3: 1-3 2m4-2m7: 0-1 3m+: 0-0
Track:	LH: 0-2 RH: 1-1 Tight: 1-3 Gall: 0-0
Aids:	Bl: 0-0 Vi: 0-0 Tstrap: 0-0 Ckp: 0-0
Best Rating:	75 1/04 Muss 2m gd-fm NHF

Winner on second start in a bumper at Musselburgh; got left at the start latest after getting caught on the rail next time; will stay further over hurdles; acts well on a sound surface.

Eshbran Lad
96   88

7-y-o b g Golden Lahab (USA)-Lansdowne Lady (Orange Bay)
N J Henderson P J Harle

Placings:50-3				(2262)

2003/04: 19QG,

	Starts	1st	2nd	3rd	Win & Pl
Hurdles	1	0	0	1	542
Career Total	3	0	0	1	542

Going:	Sf: 0-0 GS: 0-0 Gd: 0-1 GF: - Fm: 0-0
Distance:	2m/2m3: 0-0 2m4-2m7: 0-1 3m+: 0-0
Track:	LH: 0-0 RH: 0-1 Tight: 0-1 Gall: 0-0
Aids:	Bl: 0-0 Vi: 0-0 Tstrap: 0-0 Ckp: 0-0
Best Rating:	94 11/03 MRas 2m3f110y good Hdl

Made a pleasing debut when staying on fifth in bumper at Wetherby in March 2003; well beaten third on hurdling debut at Market Rasen in November; suited by two and a half miles.

Esher Common (IRE)
84

6-y-o b g Common Grounds-Alsahah (IRE) (Unfuwain (USA))
A E Price Leahall Lodge Racing 1

Placings:00-P				(0084)

2003/04: 16PGS,

	Starts	1st	2nd	3rd	Win & Pl
Hurdles	1	0	0	0	
Career Total	3	0	0	0	

Going:	Sf: 0-0 GS: 0-1 Gd: 0-0 GF: - Fm: 0-0
Distance:	2m/2m3: 0-1 2m4-2m7: 0-0 3m+: 0-0
Track:	LH: 0-1 RH: 0-0 Tight: 0-0 Gall: 0-0
Aids:	Bl: 0-0 Vi: 0-0 Tstrap: 0-0 Ckp: 0-0
Best Rating:	84 12/02 Newb 2m110y heavy Hdl

Eskimo Pie (IRE)
91f   104f

5-y-o ch g Glacial Storm (USA)-Arctic Verb (Proverb)
C C Bealby Irvin S Naylor

Placings:25				(4179)

2003/04: 172GS, 165G,

	Starts	1st	2nd	3rd	Win & Pl
NH Flat	2	0	1	0	534
Career Total	2	0	1	0	534

Going:	Sf: 0-0 GS: 0-1 Gd: 0-1 GF: - Fm: 0-0
Distance:	2m/2m3: 0-2 2m4-2m7: 0-0 3m+: 0-0
Track:	LH: 0-1 RH: 0-1 Tight: 0-1 Gall: 0-1
Aids:	Bl: 0-0 Vi: 0-0 Tstrap: 0-0 Ckp: 0-0
Best Rating:	104 2/04 Folk 2m1f110y gd-sft NHF

Eskleybrook
98   (88h)153

11-y-o b g Arzanni-Crystal Run Vii (Damsire Unregistered)
V Y Gethin (N A Twiston-Davies 13/12) V Y Gethin

Placings:00/P54PP111/1132/11F/4F30U6/11P-50P0000P				(4964)

2003/04: 165GF, 16QG, 20PGS, 19QGS, 19QG, 16RG, 16QG, 16PGF,

	Starts	1st	2nd	3rd	Win & Pl
Chases	8	0	0	0	0
Career Total	34	9	1	2	67543
153	2/03	Kemp	2m	B Ch	GD £12435
153	2/03	Sand	2m	B HCh	HVY £12483
149	2/01	Sand	2m	C(0-135)HCh	SFT £8580
139	1/01	Kemp	2m	D(0-120)HCh	SFT £5668
123	10/99	Extr	2m1f	C(0-115)HCh	GD £4143
119	5/99	Strf	2m1f110yC(0-130)HCh	GD £5725
111	4/99	Bang	2m1f110yF(0-100)HCh	G-S £4260
134	4/99	Wwck	2m	C(0-115)HCh	SFT £3028
99	4/99	Hrfd	2m	F(0-110)HCh	G-F £3550

Total win prize-money £59873

Going:	Sf: 0-0 GS: 0-2 Gd: 0-4 GF: - Fm: 0-2
Distance:	2m/2m3: 0-5 2m4-2m7: 0-3 3m+: 0-0
Track:	LH: 0-4 RH: 0-4 Tight: 0-0 Gall: 0-3
Aids:	Bl: 0-0 Vi: 0-0 Tstrap: 0-0 Ckp: 0-3
Best Rating:	153 2/03 Kemp 2m good Ch

Very useful front-running chaser; caused a surprise when winning a good race at 50/1 at Sandown in February 2003; followed up in conditions event at Kempton; has not come close to reproducing that form subsequently; suited by two

miles; looks especially suited by soft conditions but acts on good ground too; has been tried in cheekpieces; does not always jump off on terms.

Esp Hill

6-y-o ch m Moscow Society (USA)-Heatheridge (IRE) (Carlingford Castle)
L Lungo The Timbertops

Placings:563-4PP				(3213)

2003/04: 16QG, 16RG, 24PGS, 16PGS,

	Starts	1st	2nd	3rd	Win & Pl
NH Flat	1	0	0	1	268
Hurdles	3	0	0	0	0
Career Total	6	0	0	1	268

Going:	Sf: 0-0 GS: 0-2 Gd: 0-2 GF: - Fm: 0-0
Distance:	2m/2m3: 0-3 2m4-2m7: 0-0 3m+: 0-1
Track:	LH: 0-4 RH: 0-0 Tight: 0-0 Gall: 0-0
Aids:	Bl: 0-0 Vi: 0-0 Tstrap: 0-0 Ckp: 0-0
Best Rating:	72 3/03 Carl 2m1f good NHF

Esperado (IRE)
99   91

8-y-o br m Un Desperado (FR)-Latin Guest (Be My Guest (USA))
T R George (D Dorgan 11/5) T R George

Placings:0000000/0/655-11				(0602)

2003/04: 221GF, 221G,

	Starts	1st	2nd	3rd	Win & Pl
Hurdles	2	2	0	0	9533
Career Total	13	2	0	0	9533
93	6/03	NAbb	2m6f	E(0-105)HHdl	GD £3399
91	6/03	NAbb	2m6f	E(0-105)HHdl	G-F £6133

Total win prize-money £9533

Going:	Sf: 0-0 GS: 0-0 Gd: 1-1 GF: - Fm: 1-1
Distance:	2m/2m3: 0-0 2m4-2m7: 2-2 3m+: 0-0
Track:	LH: 2-2 RH: 0-0 Tight: 2-2 Gall: 0-0
Aids:	Bl: 0-0 Vi: 0-0 Tstrap: 0-0 Ckp: 0-0
Best Rating:	94 5/00 Klny 2m1f gd-fm NHF

Plating-class performer; won last three points in Ireland; well backed when making successful British debut in 2m 6f novices handicap hurdle at Newton Abbot June 2003; followed up over course and distance next time; stays two mile six well; acts on a sound surface.

Espere D'Or
66   16

7-y-o b g Golden Heights-Drummer's Dream (IRE) (Drumalis)
M Wellings (T Wall 8/8) Snax Catering Services Limited

Placings:PO00U0				(2418)

2003/04: 17PGS, 16QGF, 16QGF, 16UGF, 16QGS,

	Starts	1st	2nd	3rd	Win & Pl
Hurdles	6	0	0	0	
Career Total	6	0	0	0	

Going:	Sf: 0-0 GS: 0-2 Gd: 0-0 GF: - Fm: 0-4
Distance:	2m/2m3: 0-6 2m4-2m7: 0-0 3m+: 0-0
Track:	LH: 0-5 RH: 0-1 Tight: 0-2 Gall: 0-0
Aids:	Bl: 0-0 Vi: 0-0 Tstrap: 0-0 Ckp: 0-0
Best Rating:	15 10/03 Ludl 2m gd-fm Hdl

Esprit De Cotte (FR)

12-y-o b g Lute Antique (FR)-Rafale De Cotte (FR) (Italic (FR))
R Gurney Mrs J M Newsome & Mrs A A Gurney

Placings:1/123/1/3321/2FPP40FP/P06U/450-P0 (3898)
2003/04: 24^PG, 20^QG,

	Starts	1st	2nd	3rd	Win & Pl
Chases	2	0	0	0	
Career Total	26	4	3	3	62757
113 4/99 Strf	2m6f110yE Hdl			G-S	£2178
2/98 Autl	2m6f Ch			VS	£10101
5/96 Autl	2m1f110y Ch			VS	£15810
1/96 Pau	2m1f Ch			HVY	£6588
			Total win prize-money £34677		

Going: Sf: 0-0 GS: 0-0 Gd: 0-2 GF: - Fm: 0-0
Distance: 2m/2m3: 0-2 2m4-2m7: 0-1 3m+: 0-1
Track: LH: 0-1 RH: 0-1 Tight: 0-1 Gall: 0-0
Aids: Bl: 0-0 Vi: 0-0 Tstrap: 0-0 Ckp: 0-0
Best Rating: 145 11/99 Worc 2m7f110y gd-sft Ch

Former ex-French chaser, now pointing and hunter/chasing; seems best on easy ground; sometimes wears blinkers.

Essay Baby (FR)

91   **76**

4-y-o b f Saumarez-Easter Baby (Derrylin)
P D Cundell P D Cundell

Placings:0 (3806)
2003/04: 16^QG,

	Starts	1st	2nd	3rd	Win & Pl
Hurdles	1	0	0	0	
Career Total	1	0	0	0	

Going: Sf: 0-0 GS: 0-0 Gd: 0-1 GF: 0-0 Fm: 0-0
Distance: 2m/2m3: 0-1 2m4-2m7: 0-1 3m+: 0-0
Track: LH: 0-0 RH: 0-1 Tight: 0-0 Gall: 0-0
Aids: Bl: 0-0 Vi: 0-0 Tstrap: 0-0 Ckp: 0-0
Best Rating: 76 2/04 Kemp 2m good Hdl

Essex Bird

79   **49**

5-y-o b m Primitive Rising (USA)-L'Hawaienne (USA) (Hawaii)
Mrs S D Williams Berry Racing

Placings:600 (4736)
2003/04: 17^PG, 22^QGS, 17^QG,

	Starts	1st	2nd	3rd	Win & Pl
NH Flat	1	0	0	0	
Hurdles	2	0	0	0	
Career Total	3	0	0	0	

Going: Sf: 0-0 GS: 0-1 Gd: 0-2 GF: - Fm: 0-0
Distance: 2m/2m3: 0-2 2m4-2m7: 0-1 3m+: 0-0
Track: LH: 0-2 RH: 0-1 Tight: 0-2 Gall: 0-0
Aids: Bl: 0-0 Vi: 0-0 Tstrap: 0-0 Ckp: 0-0
Best Rating: 70 11/03 NAbb 2m1f good NHF

Esters Boy

                                                      74

6-y-o b g Sure Blade (USA)-Moheli (Ardross)
P G Murphy J Cooper

Placings:000-UP (4931)

2003/04: 20^UGF, 22^PG,

	Starts	1st	2nd	3rd	Win & Pl
Hurdles	2	0	0	0	
Career Total	5	0	0	0	

Going: Sf: 0-0 GS: 0-0 Gd: 0-1 GF: - Fm: 0-1
Distance: 2m/2m3: 0-0 2m4-2m7: 0-2 3m+: 0-0
Track: LH: 0-2 RH: 0-0 Tight: 0-1 Gall: 0-0
Aids: Bl: 0-0 Vi: 0-0 Tstrap: 0-0 Ckp: 0-0
Best Rating: 76 9/02 Worc 2m good NHF

Eternal Night (FR)

(95h)   (111h) **116**

8-y-o b g Night Shift (USA)-Echoes Of Eternity (USA) (Cougar (CHI))
C J Mann Martin Myers

Placings:16003/0402003F/0002F3022F60/45-PP0P (4493)
2003/04: 20^PG, 20^PGS, 16^QG, 16^PG,

	Starts	1st	2nd	3rd	Win & Pl
Hurdles	2	0	0	0	0
Chases	2	0	0	0	0
Career Total	31	1	4	3	13012
114 1/00 Naas	2m Hdl			SH	£4416
			Total win prize-money £4416		

Going: Sf: 0-0 GS: 0-1 Gd: 0-3 GF: - Fm: 0-0
Distance: 2m/2m3: 0-2 2m4-2m7: 0-2 3m+: 0-0
Track: LH: 0-1 RH: 0-3 Tight: 0-2 Gall: 0-0
Aids: Bl: 0-1 Vi: 0-0 Tstrap: 0-0 Ckp: 0-0
Best Rating: 121 12/00 Fair 2m2f yld-sft Hdl

Ethan Snowflake

94   **74**

5-y-o b g Weld-Snow Child (Mandrake Major)
John Berry John Berry

Placings:P3 (4120)
2003/04: 16^PGS, 17^QG,

	Starts	1st	2nd	3rd	Win & Pl
Hurdles	2	0	0	1	374
Career Total	2	0	0	1	374

Going: Sf: 0-0 GS: 0-1 Gd: 0-1 GF: - Fm: 0-0
Distance: 2m/2m3: 0-2 2m4-2m7: 0-0 3m+: 0-0
Track: LH: 0-0 RH: 0-2 Tight: 0-1 Gall: 0-1
Aids: Bl: 0-0 Vi: 0-0 Tstrap: 0-0 Ckp: 0-0
Best Rating: 79 3/04 Folk 2m1f110y good Hdl

Euradream (IRE)

99   **107+**

6-y-o ch g Eurobus-Its All A Dream (Le Moss)
N A Gaselee Lady Eliza Mays-Smith

Placings:44021 (4762)
2003/04: 18^HY, 17^HY, 16^QG, 16^QGS, 19^1S,

	Starts	1st	2nd	3rd	Win & Pl
Hurdles	5	1	1	0	4611
Career Total	5	1	1	0	4611
107 4/04 Towc	2m3f110yF Hdl			SFT	£3087
			Total win prize-money £3087		

Going: Sf: 1-3 GS: 0-1 Gd: 0-1 GF: - Fm: 0-0
Distance: 2m/2m3: 0-4 2m4-2m7: 1-1 3m+: 0-0
Track: LH: 0-1 RH: 0-3 Tight: 0-1 Gall: 0-0
Aids: Bl: 0-0 Vi: 0-0 Tstrap: 0-0 Ckp: 0-0
Best Rating: 107 4/04 Towc 2m3f110y soft Hdl

Ran green on debut in novice hurdle at Fontwell in January on heavy ground, staying on late; similar run next time; entitled to improve for a sound surface.

Euro American (GER)

4-y-o br g Snurge-Egyptale (Crystal Glitters (USA))
Mario Hofer Stall Jenny

Placings:6P (3288)
2003/04: 16^6S, 16^PGS,

	Starts	1st	2nd	3rd	Win & Pl
Hurdles	2	0	0	0	
Career Total	2	0	0	0	

Going: Sf: 0-1 GS: 0-1 Gd: 0-0 GF: - Fm: 0-0
Distance: 2m/2m3: 0-2 2m4-2m7: 0-0 3m+: 0-0
Track: LH: 0-1 RH: 0-0 Tight: 0-0 Gall: 0-0
Aids: Bl: 0-0 Vi: 0-0 Tstrap: 0-0 Ckp: 0-0

German-trained hurdler; well beaten on soft ground in Italy on hurdles debut.

Euro Bleu (FR)

105   **112**

6-y-o b g Franc Bleu Argent (USA)-Princess Card (FR) (Gift Card (FR))
Mrs L Wadham Hebomapa

Placings:0510-23 (0363)
2003/04: 20^2S, 20^3S,

	Starts	1st	2nd	3rd	Win & Pl
Hurdles	2	0	1	1	4602
Career Total	6	1	1	1	12443
1/03 Pau	2m1f110y Hdl			VS	£7169
			Total win prize-money £7169		

Going: Sf: 0-2 GS: 0-0 Gd: 0-0 GF: - Fm: 0-0
Distance: 2m/2m3: 0-0 2m4-2m7: 0-2 3m+: 0-0
Track: LH: 0-2 RH: 0-0 Tight: 0-0 Gall: 0-0
Aids: Bl: 0-0 Vi: 0-0 Tstrap: 0-0 Ckp: 0-0
Best Rating: 112 5/03 Uttx 2m4f110y soft Hdl

Winning hurdler in France; runner-up on second outing here at Uttoxeter in April; suited by soft ground and will stay three miles.

Euro Falcon

100   **89**

7-y-o b h Polar Falcon (USA)-Sarabah (IRE) (Ela-Mana-Mou)
C Von Der Recke P Cnockaert

Placings:26 (3652)
2003/04: 20^2GF, 17^6S,

	Starts	1st	2nd	3rd	Win & Pl
Hurdles	2	0	1	0	872
Career Total	2	0	1	0	872

Going: Sf: 0-1 GS: 0-0 Gd: 0-0 GF: - Fm: 0-1
Distance: 2m/2m3: 0-1 2m4-2m7: 0-1 3m+: 0-0
Track: LH: 0-1 RH: 0-1 Tight: 0-1 Gall: 0-0
Aids: Bl: 0-0 Vi: 0-0 Tstrap: 0-0 Ckp: 0-0
Best Rating: 89 2/04 Tntn 2m1f soft Hdl

11 times a winner on the Flat in Europe at distances varying between seven furlongs and a mile and a half; second on hurdling debut to the useful Wintertide over 2m 4f at Worcester August 2003; handles fastr and soft.

Euro Import

82   **77**

6-y-o ch g Imp Society (USA)-Upper Club (IRE) (Taufan (USA))
P D Niven Exors of the late W G Swiers

Placings:6   (2402)
2003/04: 17⁵HY,

	Starts	1st	2nd	3rd	Win & Pl
Hurdles	1	0	0	0	0
Career Total	**1**	**0**	**0**	**0**	**0**

Going:	Sf: 0-1 GS: 0-0 Gd: 0-0 GF: - Fm: 0-0
Distance:	2m/2m3: 0-1 2m4-2m7: 0-0 3m+: 0-0
Track:	LH: 0-0 RH: 0-1 Tight: 0-0 Gall: 0-0
Aids:	Bl: 0-0 Vi: 0-0 Tstrap: 0-0 Ckp: 0-0
Best Rating:	77 11/03 Carl 2m1f heavy Hdl

Euro Leader (IRE)

107   **119**

6-y-o b g Supreme Leader-Noreaster (IRE) (Nordance (USA))
W P Mullins John Cox

Placings:1151220S   (4803a)
2003/04: 20¹G, 16¹GF, 17⁵G, 16¹Y, 18²HY, 16²HY, 16⁰G, 20⁵Y,

	Starts	1st	2nd	3rd	Win & Pl
NH Flat	3	2	0	0	13890
Hurdles	5	1	2	0	14764
Career Total	**8**	**3**	**2**	**0**	**28654**
112	12/03	Cork	2m	Hdl	YLD	£5376
117	10/03	Tipp	2m	NHF	G-F	£8064
117	9/03	List	2m4f	NHF	GD	£5824
				Total win prize-money £19267

Going:	Sf: 0-2 GS: 0-0 Gd: 1-3 GF: - Fm: 1-1
Distance:	2m/2m3: 2-6 2m4-2m7: 1-2 3m+: 0-0
Track:	LH: 0-1 RH: 0-2 Tight: 0-0 Gall: 0-0
Aids:	Bl: 0-0 Vi: 0-0 Tstrap: 0-0 Ckp: 0-0
Best Rating:	119 2/04 Punc 2m heavy Hdl

Irish bumper winner; fifth under penalty at Aintree in November; has been consistent in novice hurdles without really fulfilling potential; acts on soft, but has won twice on good ground; best at around two miles.

Euroallstar (IRE)

                                      23

6-y-o gr g Roselier (FR)-Pharleng (IRE) (Phardante (FR))
C A McBratney R Acheson

Placings:0000   (4747a)
2003/04: 16⁰S, 16⁰HY, 20⁰Y, 16⁰Y,

	Starts	1st	2nd	3rd	Win & Pl
NH Flat	2	0	0	0	0
Hurdles	2	0	0	0	0
Career Total	**4**	**0**	**0**	**0**	0

Going:	Sf: 0-2 GS: 0-0 Gd: 0-0 GF: - Fm: 0-0
Distance:	2m/2m3: 0-3 2m4-2m7: 0-1 3m+: 0-0
Track:	LH: 0-1 RH: 0-1 Tight: 0-0 Gall: 0-0
Aids:	Bl: 0-0 Vi: 0-0 Tstrap: 0-0 Ckp: 0-0
Best Rating:	46 1/04 Ayr 2m heavy NHF

Europa

99(84h)   (79h) **150**

8-y-o b g Jupiter Island-Dublin Ferry (Celtic Cone)
T P Tate B T Stewart-Brown

Placings:15/1112/1312FP2/1131F-3P0   (4559)
2003/04: 16³S, 20⁶G, 16⁶GS,

	Starts	1st	2nd	3rd	Win & Pl
Hurdles	1	0	0	0	0
Chases	2	0	0	1	2098
Career Total	**21**	**9**	**3**	**3**	**52349**
150	3/03	Donc	2m3f	C(0-135)HCh	GD	£10101
142	12/02	Donc	2m3f	C(0-135)HCh	G-S	£8096
119	5/02	Prth	2m	D Ch	G-F	£5330
137	1/02	Catt	2m3f	D Ch	G-S	£6279
120	12/01	Hexm	2m110y	E Ch	SFT	£3003
131	2/01	Bang	2m1f	E Hdl	HVY	£2744
143	1/01	Donc	2m4f	D Hdl	GD	£4007
112	11/00	Wwck	2m	H NHF	HVY	£1575
119	3/00	Donc	2m110y	H NHF	GD	£1631
				Total win prize-money £42767

Going:	Sf: 0-1 GS: 0-1 Gd: 0-1 GF: - Fm: 0-0
Distance:	2m/2m3: 0-2 2m4-2m7: 0-1 3m+: 0-0
Track:	LH: 0-3 RH: 0-0 Tight: 0-0 Gall: 0-3
Aids:	Bl: 0-0 Vi: 0-0 Tstrap: 0-0 Ckp: 0-0
Best Rating:	150 3/03 Donc 2m3f good Ch

Useful hurdler/very useful chaser; lightly raced in 2003/4; stays two and half miles; handles any going but prefers decent ground.

Euryalus (IRE)

76   **73**

6-y-o ch g Presenting-New Talent (The Parson)
R F Fisher Great Head House Estates Limited

Placings:0600   (4612)
2003/04: 16⁵HY, 17⁵G, 20⁰G, 21⁰G,

	Starts	1st	2nd	3rd	Win & Pl
NH Flat	2	0	0	0	0
Hurdles	2	0	0	0	0
Career Total	**4**	**0**	**0**	**0**	0

Going:	Sf: 0-1 GS: 0-0 Gd: 0-3 GF: - Fm: 0-0
Distance:	2m/2m3: 0-2 2m4-2m7: 0-2 3m+: 0-0
Track:	LH: 0-2 RH: 0-2 Tight: 0-1 Gall: 0-0
Aids:	Bl: 0-0 Vi: 0-0 Tstrap: 0-0 Ckp: 0-0
Best Rating:	89 2/04 Carl 2m1f good NHF

Eva So Charming

103   **118+**

6-y-o ch g Karinga Bay-Charming Gale (Strong Gale)
Miss H C Knight Eva So Charming Partnership

Placings:32312P3   (4712)
2003/04: 21³GF, 21²S, 22³GS, 23¹GS, 24²S, 24⁰G, 24³G,

	Starts	1st	2nd	3rd	Win & Pl
Hurdles	7	1	2	3	12434
Career Total	**7**	**1**	**2**	**3**	**12434**
118	1/04	Fknm	2m7f110yF Hdl	G-S	£2618
				Total win prize-money £2618

Going:	Sf: 0-2 GS: 1-2 Gd: 0-2 GF: - Fm: 0-1
Distance:	2m/2m3: 0-0 2m4-2m7: 0-3 3m+: 1-4
Track:	LH: 1-5 RH: 0-2 Tight: 1-3 Gall: 0-3
Aids:	Bl: 0-0 Vi: 0-0 Tstrap: 0-0 Ckp: 0-0
Best Rating:	118 1/04 Donc 3m110y soft Hdl

Winning pointer; useful novice hurdler; likely to do better over fences; stays 3m.

Even More (IRE)

106   **113**

9-y-o b g Husyan (USA)-Milan Moss (Le Moss)

R H Alner G Keirle

Placings:02P33-4U11256622   (4820)
2003/04: 25⁴GF, 23⁰GF, 24¹GF, 24¹GF, 23²F, 25⁵S, 24⁶G, 30⁶G, 25²GS, 25²GF,

	Starts	1st	2nd	3rd	Win & Pl
Chases	10	2	3	0	16956
Career Total	**15**	**2**	**4**	**2**	**21339**
113	11/03	Kemp	3m	D Ch	G-F	£4968
113	11/03	Kemp	3m	D(0-110)HCh	G-F	£4980
				Total win prize-money £9948

Going:	Sf: 0-1 GS: 0-1 Gd: 0-2 GF: - Fm: 2-6
Distance:	2m/2m3: 0-0 2m4-2m7: 0-0 3m+: 2-10
Track:	LH: 0-0 RH: 2-10 Tight: 0-0 Gall: 0-0
Aids:	Bl: 0-1 Vi: 0-0 Tstrap: 0-0 Ckp: 0-0
Best Rating:	113 4/04 Extr 3m1f110y gd-fm Ch

Modest chaser; stays and jumps well; acts on good ground; handles tight tracks well for a big horse.

Evening Chorus (USA)

9-y-o b g Shadeed (USA)-Evening Air (USA) (J O Tobin (USA))
P Wegmann P Wegmann

Placings:36/P4102635/010111343600F0/542210540300/PPP   (2258)
2003/04: 24⁰GF, 21⁰GF, 22⁰G,

	Starts	1st	2nd	3rd	Win & Pl
Hurdles	3	0	0	0	0
Career Total	**39**	**6**	**3**	**5**	**17186**
101	6/01	NAbb	2m6f	F(0-105)HHdl	G-F	£2401
108	7/00	Worc	3m	D(0-125)HHdl	G-F	£4043
100	7/00	Worc	2m4f	G(0-90)HHdl	G-F	£1519
91	6/00	Hexm	2m4f110yG(0-95)HHdl	G-F	£1951
91	5/00	Towc	2m	G Hdl	G-F	£1533
88	9/99	Worc	2m	G(0-95)HHdl	G-F	£1744
				Total win prize-money £13192

Going:	Sf: 0-0 GS: 0-0 Gd: 0-1 GF: - Fm: 0-2
Distance:	2m/2m3: 0-0 2m4-2m7: 0-2 3m+: 0-1
Track:	LH: 0-1 RH: 0-1 Tight: 0-0 Gall: 0-0
Aids:	Bl: 0-2 Vi: 0-1 Tstrap: 0-0 Ckp: 0-0
Best Rating:	108 7/00 Worc 3m gd-fm Hdl

Ever Present (IRE)

106   **122**

6-y-o ch g Presenting-My Grand Rose (IRE) (Executive Perk)
A King Ramsay Donald Brown

Placings:51245-5   (1883)
2003/04: 20⁵G,

	Starts	1st	2nd	3rd	Win & Pl
Hurdles	1	0	0	0	0
Career Total	**6**	**1**	**1**	**0**	**5046**
109	11/02	Bang	2m1f	E Hdl	SFT	£3178
				Total win prize-money £3178

Going:	Sf: 0-0 GS: 0-0 Gd: 0-1 GF: - Fm: 0-0
Distance:	2m/2m3: 0-0 2m4-2m7: 0-1 3m+: 0-0
Track:	LH: 0-1 RH: 0-0 Tight: 0-0 Gall: 0-0
Aids:	Bl: 0-0 Vi: 0-0 Tstrap: 0-0 Ckp: 0-0
Best Rating:	118 1/03 Chel 2m1f gd-sft Hdl

Fair hurdler; best at around two miles; suited by soft ground

Everready

91   **99+**

6-y-o b g Afzal-Sister Shot (Celtic Cone)
M G Quinlan (P J Hobbs 2/2) Ms C Hehir

Placings:0/43-06P0F   (3642)
2003/04: 16⁰GS, 17⁵GS, 16⁹GS, 21⁹G, 19⁹FS,

	Starts	1st	2nd	3rd	Win & Pl
Hurdles	5	0	0	0	0
Career Total	8	0	0	1	542

Going:	Sf: 0-1 GS: 0-3 Gd: 0-1 GF: - Fm: 0-0
Distance:	2m/2m3: 0-4 2m4-2m7: 0-1 3m+: 0-0
Track:	LH: 0-2 RH: 0-3 Tight: 0-2 Gall: 0-0
Aids:	Bl: 0-0 Vi: 0-0 Tstrap: 0-0 Ckp: 0-0
Best Rating:	99 3/03 Strf 2m110y gd-sft NHF

Eviyrn (IRE)

93   **78+**

8-y-o b g In The Wings-Evrana (USA) (Nureyev (USA))
J R Jenkins S C Finance Limited

Placings:65056/0143500P/32FP/00P-2403   (4278)
2003/04: 16²G, 16⁴GS, 21⁰S, 19³GS,

	Starts	1st	2nd	3rd	Win & Pl
Hurdles	4	0	1	1	1176
Career Total	24	1	2	3	5673
86	10/00 Plum 2m		E(0-105)HHdl	SFT	£2576

Total win prize-money £2576

Going:	Sf: 0-1 GS: 0-2 Gd: 0-1 GF: - Fm: 0-0
Distance:	2m/2m3: 0-2 2m4-2m7: 0-2 3m+: 0-0
Track:	LH: 0-1 RH: 0-2 Tight: 0-0 Gall: 0-1
Aids:	Bl: 0-0 Vi: 0-1 Tstrap: 0-0 Ckp: 0-3
Best Rating:	90 12/00 Donc 2m110y heavy Hdl

Fair hurdler over the minimum trip; hHas looked a bit quirky in the past; suited by soft ground.

Evolution (IRE)

77   **54**

7-y-o b m Phardante (FR)-Cape Breeze (IRE) (Strong Gale)
M J Gingell The Equus Club

Placings:56/40034/6066050-40PP   (0625)
2003/04: 26⁴GF, 20⁹GF, 23⁹GF, 16⁹GF,

	Starts	1st	2nd	3rd	Win & Pl
Hurdles	4	0	0	0	0
Career Total	18	0	0	1	636

Going:	Sf: 0-0 GS: 0-0 Gd: 0-0 GF: - Fm: 0-4
Distance:	2m/2m3: 0-1 2m4-2m7: 0-1 3m+: 0-2
Track:	LH: 0-3 RH: 0-1 Tight: 0-2 Gall: 0-1
Aids:	Bl: 0-0 Vi: 0-0 Tstrap: 0-0 Ckp: 0-0
Best Rating:	79 2/01 Wwck 2m soft NHF

Ewe Beauty (FR)

92f   **63f**

4-y-o b f Phantom Breeze-Baie De Chalamont (FR)
(Balsamo (FR))
Ferdy Murphy Mr And Mrs Neil Iveson

Placings:00   (4663)
2003/04: 16⁹GF, 16⁹S,

	Starts	1st	2nd	3rd	Win & Pl
NH Flat	2	0	0	0	
Career Total	2	0	0	0	

Exact (FR)

12-y-o ch g Beyssac (FR)-Valse De Sienne (FR) (Petit Montmorency (USA))
Mrs R L Elliot Miss V A Russell

Placings:PPP4/U655034/1/P35/5-4   (0044)
2003/04: 25⁴G,

	Starts	1st	2nd	3rd	Win & Pl
Chases	1	0	0	0	0
Career Total	17	1	0	2	3971
103	5/99 Chep 3m		E(0-115)HHdl	GD	£2542

Total win prize-money £2542

Going:	Sf: 0-0 GS: 0-0 Gd: 0-1 GF: - Fm: 0-0
Distance:	2m/2m3: 0-0 2m4-2m7: 0-0 3m+: 0-1
Track:	LH: 0-1 RH: 0-2 Tight: 0-0 Gall: 0-0
Aids:	Bl: 0-0 Vi: 0-0 Tstrap: 0-0 Ckp: 0-0
Best Rating:	106 4/99 Uttx 2m4f gd-sft Ch

Modest pointer/hunter chaser; suited by good ground or faster and front-running tactics; wears blinkers and has worn a tongue tie.

Excellent Vibes (IRE)

107   **93+**

6-y-o b g Doyoun-Hawait Al Barr (Green Desert (USA))
N A Twiston-Davies Thomas D Goodman

Placings:060-051P52211366   (2288)
2003/04: 19⁰G, 19⁵GF, 24¹GF, 24²GF, 24⁵G, 26²GF, 26²GF, 24¹GF, 22¹F, 21³GF, 23⁶GF, 24⁶G,

	Starts	1st	2nd	3rd	Win & Pl
Hurdles	12	3	2	1	9915
Career Total	15	3	2	1	9915
93	9/03 Extr	2m6f110yF(0-100)HHdl	FRM	£2331
86	9/03 Worc	3m	F(0-100)HHdl	G-F	£2289
74	6/03 Uttx	3m110y	F(0-100)HHdl	G-F	£3388

Total win prize-money £8008

Going:	Sf: 0-0 GS: 0-0 Gd: 0-3 GF: - Fm: 3-9
Distance:	2m/2m3: 0-0 2m4-2m7: 1-5 3m+: 2-7
Track:	LH: 2-5 RH: 1-7 Tight: 0-1 Gall: 0-1
Aids:	Bl: 0-0 Vi: 0-0 Tstrap: 0-0 Ckp: 0-0
Best Rating:	93 9/03 Extr 2m6f110y firm Hdl

Modest staying handicap hurdler; appreciated step up to 3m when winning Uttoxeter handicap in June 2003; inclined to lose his position when twice runner-up prior to beating a big field at Worcester in September; followed up at Exeter next time; tends to sweat heavily before and during his races; stays very well; acts on good to firm.

Executive Decision (IRE)

102(108h)   (121h)**127**

10-y-o ch g Classic Music (USA)-Bengala (FR) (Hard To Beat)
Mrs L Wadham Ms K J Austin

Placings:116/2055150/14/F/6U26/PP263133-P25456U340   (4843)
2003/04: 20⁰G, 16²GS, 17⁵GS, 16⁴GS, 16⁵HY, 16⁶G, 16⁰U, 16³GS, 18⁴G, 16⁰G,

Exact (cont.)

	Starts	1st	2nd	3rd	Win & Pl
Hurdles	2	0	1	0	1504
Chases	8	0	0	1	2347
Career Total	35	5	4	4	36592
127	2/03 Hntg	2m110y	D(0-120)HCh	GD	£6630
129	11/99 NAbb	2m110y	E Ch	SFT	£3156
133	3/99 Chep	2m110y	C(0-130)HHdl	HVY	£4417
117	2/98 Navn	2m	Hdl	SFT	£5956
119	12/97 Leop	2m	Hdl	HVY	£4069

Total win prize-money £24230

Going:	Sf: 0-2 GS: 0-3 Gd: 0-5 GF: - Fm: 0-0
Distance:	2m/2m3: 0-9 2m4-2m7: 0-1 3m+: 0-0
Track:	LH: 0-6 RH: 0-4 Tight: 0-3 Gall: 0-3
Aids:	Bl: 0-0 Vi: 0-10 Tstrap: 0-0 Ckp: 0-0
Best Rating:	133 3/99 Chel 2m1f gd-sft Hdl

Fair hurdler, decent chaser; best over two miles; acts on ground ranging from good to heavy; has worn blinkers and a visor.

Executive Director (IRE)

101   (109h)**109**

8-y-o ch g Executive Perk-What Side (General Ironside)
Miss Venetia Williams (Michael Cullen 19/10) Mrs O Marchant

Placings:4200/52426-05F3013F   (3589)
2003/04: 16⁰YS, 24⁵S, 18⁴F, 18³F, 22⁰G, 17¹GF, 20³F, 24⁵S,

	Starts	1st	2nd	3rd	Win & Pl
Chases	8	1	0	2	9756
Career Total	17	1	3	2	14521
109	10/03 Gowr	2m1f	Ch	G-F	£7392

Total win prize-money £7393

Going:	Sf: 0-2 GS: 0-0 Gd: 0-1 GF: - Fm: 1-4
Distance:	2m/2m3: 1-4 2m4-2m7: 0-2 3m+: 0-2
Track:	LH: 0-0 RH: 0-5 Tight: 0-0 Gall: 0-0
Aids:	Bl: 0-0 Vi: 0-0 Tstrap: 0-4 Ckp: 0-0
Best Rating:	109 10/03 Gowr 2m1f gd-fm Ch

Moderate chaser; ex-Irish; best around two miles; acts on fast ground.

Executive Games (IRE)

101   (78h)**88**

7-y-o b/br m Executive Perk-Scrahans Touch (Skyliner)
Paul John Gilligan Savoy Shower Syndicate

Placings:00000P0P05/0P3F5-0056045   (1875)
2003/04: 17⁰F, 20⁴GY, 22⁵Y, 16⁶F, 22⁰G, 25⁴F, 22⁵G,

	Starts	1st	2nd	3rd	Win & Pl
Chases	7	0	0	0	309
Career Total	22	0	0	1	1413

Going:	Sf: 0-0 GS: 0-0 Gd: 0-2 GF: - Fm: 0-3
Distance:	2m/2m3: 0-2 2m4-2m7: 0-4 3m+: 0-1
Track:	LH: 0-3 RH: 0-2 Tight: 0-2 Gall: 0-0
Aids:	Bl: 0-0 Vi: 0-0 Tstrap: 0-3 Ckp: 0-0
Best Rating:	88 10/03 Kels 3m1f firm Ch

Plating-class Irish-trained mare, stays three miles; acts on fast ground.

Executive Office (IRE)

91

11-y-o bl g Executive Perk-Lilly's Pride (IRE) (Long Pond)

S T Lewis Simon T Lewis

Placings:0000/6/5230435/PPF/P114P-PPP   (3963)
2003/04: 26^PGF, 24^PG, 24^PGS,

	Starts	1st	2nd	3rd	Win & Pl
Hurdles	1	0	0	0	0
Chases	2	0	0	0	0
Career Total	23	2	1	2	10872
91	2/03	Leic	2m4f110yE(0-105)HCh	SFT	£4927
81	1/03	Wwck	2m4f110yF(0-90)HCh	SFT	£3542

Total win prize-money £8469

Going: Sf: 0-0 GS: 0-1 Gd: 0-1 GF: - Fm: 0-1
Distance: 2m/2m3: 0-0 2m4-2m7: 0-3 3m+: 0-3
Track: LH: 0-1 RH: 0-2 Tight: 0-0 Gall: 0-1
Aids: Bl: 0-0 Vi: 0-0 Tstrap: 0-0 Ckp: 0-0
Best Rating: 93 10/00 Extr 2m7f110y good Ch

Executive Park (IRE)

8-y-o br g Executive Perk-Brave Park (Brave Invader (USA))
C R Egerton Christy Kilgour

Placings:1F   (0294)
2003/04: 24^1S, 20^FGS,

	Starts	1st	2nd	3rd	Win & Pl
Chases	2	1	0	0	1866
Career Total	2	1	0	0	1866
108	5/03	Bang	3m110y H Ch	SFT	£1865

Total win prize-money £1866

Going: Sf: 1-1 GS: 0-1 Gd: 0-0 GF: - Fm: 0-0
Distance: 2m/2m3: 0-0 2m4-2m7: 0-1 3m+: 1-1
Track: LH: 1-2 RH: 0-0 Tight: 1-2 Gall: 0-0
Aids: Bl: 0-0 Vi: 0-0 Tstrap: 0-0 Ckp: 0-0
Best Rating: 108 5/03 Bang 3m110y soft Ch

Ex-Irish pointer; made impressive debut when winning 3m hunter chase at Bangor May 2003; looked set to follow-up when falling two out at Stratford a fortnight later; acts on soft ground.

Executive Roseann (IRE)

8-y-o ch m Executive Perk-Dazzling Roseann (Black Minstrel)
B G Powell Anthony Ward-Thomas

Placings:0-P   (3045)
2003/04: 21^PGS,

	Starts	1st	2nd	3rd	Win & Pl
Hurdles	1	0	0	0	0
Career Total	2	0	0	0	0

Going: Sf: 0-0 GS: 0-1 Gd: 0-0 GF: - Fm: 0-0
Distance: 2m/2m3: 0-0 2m4-2m7: 0-1 3m+: 0-0
Track: LH: 0-1 RH: 0-0 Tight: 0-0 Gall: 0-1
Aids: Bl: 0-0 Vi: 0-0 Tstrap: 0-0 Ckp: 0-0
Best Rating: 52 6/02 Cork 2m4f soft NHF

Exhibit (IRE)
79   57
6-y-o b g Royal Academy (USA)-Juno Madonna (IRE) (Sadler's Wells (USA))
N J Hawke Truscotts (Barnstaple) Ltd - Peugeot

Placings:P-605   (0970)

2003/04: 17^6GF, 17^0GF, 17^5GS,

	Starts	1st	2nd	3rd	Win & Pl
Hurdles	3	0	0	0	0
Career Total	4	0	0	0	0

Going: Sf: 0-0 GS: 0-1 Gd: 0-0 GF: - Fm: 0-2
Distance: 2m/2m3: 0-3 2m4-2m7: 0-0 3m+: 0-0
Track: LH: 0-3 RH: 0-0 Tight: 0-3 Gall: 0-0
Aids: Bl: 0-0 Vi: 0-0 Tstrap: 0-0 Ckp: 0-0
Best Rating: 57 7/03 NAbb 2m1f gd-sft Hdl

Existential (FR)
101(100h)   (97h)120
9-y-o b g Exit To Nowhere (USA)-Lyceana (USA) (Super Concorde (USA))
P F Nicholls H B Geddes

Placings:5/32P3P/2/4/135215-346P436   (4101)
2003/04: 25^3G, 22^4GS, 22^6S, 24^PS, 24^4S, 24^3GS, 26^6G,

	Starts	1st	2nd	3rd	Win & Pl
Hurdles	4	0	0	1	981
Chases	3	0	0	1	872
Career Total	21	2	3	5	14936
117	2/03	Kemp	3m E(0-115)HCh	G-S	£4329
114	10/02	Fknm	2m5f110yF(0-100)HCh	G-S	£3779

Total win prize-money £8109

Going: Sf: 0-3 GS: 0-2 Gd: 0-2 GF: - Fm: 0-0
Distance: 2m/2m3: 0-0 2m4-2m7: 0-2 3m+: 0-0
Track: LH: 0-2 RH: 0-5 Tight: 0-3 Gall: 0-0
Aids: Bl: 0-3 Vi: 0-0 Tstrap: 0-0 Ckp: 0-0
Best Rating: 117 2/03 Kemp 3m gd-sft Ch

Fair handicap chaser; suited by trips of around two and a half miles to three miles; acts on a soft surface.

Exit Swinger (FR)
106   (139h)150
9-y-o b g Exit To Nowhere (USA)-Morganella (FR) (D'Arras (FR))
P F Nicholls Sandicroft Stud I

Placings:26/5F306431221051/263F/316420/U0403-262210   (4196)
2003/04: 21^2F, 20^6G, 16^2S, 21^2G, 25^1G, 20^0G,

	Starts	1st	2nd	3rd	Win & Pl
Chases	6	1	3	0	46386
Career Total	37	5	8	5	160835
137	2/04	Winc	3m1f110yA Ch	GD	£29000
155	12/01	Newb	2m1f C(0-135)HCh	SFT	£9510
136	4/00	Sand	2m4f110yC HCh	SFT	£17517
136	2/00	Chep	2m4f D Hdl	SFT	£3334
	12/99	Autl	2m1f110y Ch	HLD	£6997

Total win prize-money £66360

Going: Sf: 0-1 GS: 0-0 Gd: 1-4 GF: - Fm: 0-1
Distance: 2m/2m3: 0-1 2m4-2m7: 0-4 3m+: 1-1
Track: LH: 0-3 RH: 1-3 Tight: 0-0 Gall: 0-3
Aids: Bl: 0-0 Vi: 0-0 Tstrap: 0-0 Ckp: 0-0
Best Rating: 155 3/02 Chel 2m110y good Ch

Smart chaser; just kept missing out in decent handicap chases before winning Country Gentlemen's Association (Jim Ford) Chase at Wincanton in February 2004; slightly disappointing next time; stays 3m 1f; but effective at shorter and acts on most types of ground.

Exit To Wave (FR)
114   146
8-y-o ch g Exit To Nowhere (USA)-Hereke (Blakeney)
P F Nicholls Malcolm Pearce & Gerry Mizel Ii

Placings:11111P344/P1F1P142U/440/4320PUP-35336P0   (4861)
2003/04: 24^3S, 25^5G, 24^3G, 24^3S, 28^6G, 36^PG, 33^0GS,

	Starts	1st	2nd	3rd	Win & Pl
Chases	7	0	0	3	13274
Career Total	35	8	2	5	101541
148	3/01	Wwck	2m110y B HCh	HVY	£10717
136	1/01	Asct	2m A Ch	G-S	£15000
125	11/00	Wwck	2m110y D Ch	HVY	£4039
	12/99	Cagn	2m2f Hdl	SFT	£7685
	12/99	Bord	2m2f Hdl	GD	£3842
	11/99	Bord	2m2f Hdl	VS	£3445
	10/99	Bord	2m110y Hdl	HVY	£3767
	10/99	Mtbn	2m1f110y Hdl	SFT	£2368

Total win prize-money £50863

Going: Sf: 0-2 GS: 0-1 Gd: 0-4 GF: - Fm: 0-0
Distance: 2m/2m3: 0-0 2m4-2m7: 0-0 3m+: 0-7
Track: LH: 0-4 RH: 0-3 Tight: 0-1 Gall: 0-1
Aids: Bl: 0-0 Vi: 0-0 Tstrap: 0-2 Ckp: 0-0
Best Rating: 150 11/01 Weth 2m4f110y good Ch

Smart handicap chaser; best on a soft surface; stays three miles, but has never won beyond two; has worn a tongue tie and blinkers; hard to win with.

Exodous (ARG)
102   97
8-y-o ch g Equalize (USA)-Empire Glory (ARG) (Good Manners (USA))
J A B Old W E Sturt

Placings:65/303-12452   (4697)
2003/04: 20^1GF, 24^2GF, 21^4G, 16^5G, 17^2G,

	Starts	1st	2nd	3rd	Win & Pl
Hurdles	5	1	2	0	5366
Career Total	10	1	2	2	6609
90	8/03	Uttx	2m4f110yE Hdl	G-F	£3711

Total win prize-money £3712

Going: Sf: 0-0 GS: 0-0 Gd: 0-3 GF: - Fm: 1-2
Distance: 2m/2m3: 0-2 2m4-2m7: 1-2 3m+: 0-1
Track: LH: 1-1 RH: 0-4 Tight: 0-0 Gall: 0-0
Aids: Bl: 0-0 Vi: 0-0 Tstrap: 0-0 Ckp: 0-0
Best Rating: 97 3/03 Asct 2m110y good Hdl

Won six times on the Flat in Argentina at up to a mile and a half. Now with Jim Old, has only shown moderate form over hurdles.

Expensive Folly (IRE)
77f   50f
6-y-o b g Satco (FR)-Tarasandy (IRE) (Arapahos (FR))
Mrs A J Hamilton-Fairley Hamilton-Fairley Racing

Placings:00   (4199)
2003/04: 16^PGS, 16^0G,

	Starts	1st	2nd	3rd	Win & Pl
NH Flat	2	0	0	0	0
Career Total	2	0	0	0	0

Going: Sf: 0-0 GS: 0-1 Gd: 0-1 GF: - Fm: 0-0
Distance: 2m/2m3: 0-2 2m4-2m7: 0-0 3m+: 0-0
Track: LH: 0-1 RH: 0-1 Tight: 0-0 Gall: 0-1
Aids: Bl: 0-0 Vi: 0-0 Tstrap: 0-0 Ckp: 0-0
Best Rating: 50 3/04 Newb 2m110y good NHF

Explode

7-y-o b g Zafonic (USA)-Didicoy (USA) (Danzig (USA))
Miss L C Siddall Lynn Siddall Racing II

Placings:P					(4577)
2003/04: 16^PG,					

	Starts	1st	2nd	3rd	Win & Pl
Hurdles	1	0	0	0	
Career Total	1	0	0	0	

Going:	Sf: 0-0 GS: 0-0 Gd: 0-1 GF: - Fm: 0-0
Distance:	2m/2m3: 0-1 2m4-2m7: 0-0 3m+: 0-0
Track:	LH: 0-1 RH: 0-0 Tight: 0-0 Gall: 0-1
Aids:	Bl: 0-0 Vi: 0-0 Tstrap: 0-0 Ckp: 0-0

Express Lily
54f   34f

5-y-o b m Environment Friend-Jaydeeglen (Bay Express)
G A Harker A P Muir

Placings:00					(1985)
2003/04: 16⁰F, 16⁰GF,					

	Starts	1st	2nd	3rd	Win & Pl
NH Flat	2	0	0	0	
Career Total	2	0	0	0	

Going:	Sf: 0-0 GS: 0-0 Gd: 0-0 GF: - Fm: 0-2
Distance:	2m/2m3: 0-2 2m4-2m7: 0-0 3m+: 0-0
Track:	LH: 0-2 RH: 0-0 Tight: 0-0 Gall: 0-0
Aids:	Bl: 0-0 Vi: 0-0 Tstrap: 0-0 Ckp: 0-0
Best Rating:	34 11/03 Hexm 2m110y gd-fm NHF

Exstoto
100(106h)   (114h)120

7-y-o b g Mtoto-Stoproveritate (Scorpio (FR))
R A Fahey J D Clark And Partners

Placings:4/107313F241/523P263-F212					(4162)
2003/04: 20^FG, 24²G, 24¹G, 24²G,					

	Starts	1st	2nd	3rd	Win & Pl
Hurdles	2	0	1	0	1490
Chases	2	1	1	0	6201
Career Total	22	5	5	4	30378
105	11/03	Newc	3m	D Ch		GD	£4992
108	4/02	Weth	2m4f110yB(0-145)HHdl		GD	£5109
113	10/01	MRas	2m3f110yD Hdl		G-S	£3430
97	7/01	Sedg	2m1f	H NHF		G-F	£1536
97	5/01	Sthl	2m	H NHF		G-F	£1564
				Total win prize-money £16633			

Going:	Sf: 0-0 GS: 0-0 Gd: 1-4 GF: - Fm: 0-0
Distance:	2m/2m3: 0-0 2m4-2m7: 0-1 3m+: 1-3
Track:	LH: 1-4 RH: 0-0 Tight: 0-0 Gall: 1-2
Aids:	Bl: 0-0 Vi: 0-0 Tstrap: 0-0 Ckp: 0-0
Best Rating:	119 3/04 Donc 3m good Ch

Fair hurdler; dual bumper winner on fast ground; pleasing chasing debut when successful at Newcastle in November 2003; just held at Doncaster in March; stays three miles and effective on good or softer ground; should improve again over fences.

Extra Cache (NZ)
99   (121h)117

11-y-o br g Cache Of Gold (USA)-Gizmo (NZ) (Jubilee Wine (USA))

O Brennan Lady Anne Bentinck

Placings:3/1432/114643/42U14211-0600204					(4778)
2003/04: 20⁰G, 20⁶S, 20⁰G, 19⁰G, 21²GS, 20⁰GS, 21⁴G,					

	Starts	1st	2nd	3rd	Win & Pl
Chases	7	0	1	0	2643
Career Total	26	6	4	3	29875
110	4/03	Hntg	2m4f110yE Ch		G-F	£4158
114	3/03	Hntg	2m4f110yE Ch		GD	£3900
117	12/02	Donc	2m3f	D Ch		G-S	£4918
121	5/01	Weth	2m	E(0-115)HHdl		FRM	£2562
114	5/01	Weth	2m	E(0-115)HHdl		GD	£2632
108	5/00	Towc	2m	E Hdl		G-F	£2534
				Total win prize-money £20705			

Going:	Sf: 0-1 GS: 0-2 Gd: 0-4 GF: - Fm: 0-0
Distance:	2m/2m3: 0-1 2m4-2m7: 0-4 3m+: 0-0
Track:	LH: 0-5 RH: 0-2 Tight: 0-5 Gall: 0-0
Aids:	Bl: 0-0 Vi: 0-0 Tstrap: 0-0 Ckp: 0-1
Best Rating:	121 5/01 Weth 2m firm Hdl

Fair chaser; winner three times over hurdles; stays two and a half miles; acts on most types of ground.

Extra Jack (FR)
109(79h)   (89h)139

12-y-o b g Neustrien (FR)-Union Jack Iii (FR) (Mister Jack (FR))
P F Nicholls Sir Robert Ogden

Placings:511/P/0450/12061011031231/0PF1/511420/5425					
550-1					(0072)
2003/04: 20¹S,					

	Starts	1st	2nd	3rd	Win & Pl
Chases	1	1	0	0	8307
Career Total	40	12	4	2	144132
133	5/03	Bang	2m4f110yC(0-130)HCh		SFT	£8307
151	1/01	Chep	2m3f110yC(0-135)HCh		G-S	£10270
147	11/01	Chep	2m3f110yD(0-130)HCh		SFT	£7322
144	4/01	Prth	2m	B(0-150)HCh		HVY	£9818
123	4/00	Strf	2m6f110yE Hdl		GD	£2646
	12/99	Cagn	2m5f110y Hdl		GD	£6459
	11/99	Autl	2m3f	Ch		HLD	£6997
	10/99	Autl	2m3f	Ch		HVY	£6997
	9/99	Autl	2m2f110y Ch		VS	£6997
	6/99	Autl	2m2f110y Ch		VS	£6997
	4/97	Autl	2m5f110y HCh		VS	£22447
	3/97	Autl	2m6f	Ch		VS	£11223
				Total win prize-money £106482			

Going:	Sf: 1-1 GS: 0-0 Gd: 0-0 GF: - Fm: 0-0
Distance:	2m/2m3: 0-0 2m4-2m7: 1-1 3m+: 0-0
Track:	LH: 1-1 RH: 0-0 Tight: 1-1 Gall: 0-0
Aids:	Bl: 1-1 Vi: 0-0 Tstrap: 0-0 Ckp: 0-0
Best Rating:	151 3/02 Donc 2m3f110y gd-sft Ch

Very useful handicap chaser; probably best at around two and a half miles these days; goes well in testing conditions and usually wears blinkers.

Extra Proud
104(93h)   (96h)108

10-y-o ch g Dancing High-Spring Onion (King Sitric)
W Amos W Amos

Placings:6F62/60/2PF102/U1U14322-005240					(2787)
2003/04: 22⁰G, 22⁰G, 21⁵GF, 22²GF, 22⁴G, 20⁰GF,					

	Starts	1st	2nd	3rd	Win & Pl
Hurdles	1	0	1	0	1060
Chases	5	0	0	0	375
Career Total	26	3	6	1	19800
108	7/02	Strf	2m5f110yE(0-105)HCh		G-F	£4290
97	5/02	Kels	2m6f110yD Ch		G-F	£4176
95	12/01	Muss	2m4f	E Hdl		GD	£3052

Going:	Sf: 0-0 GS: 0-0 Gd: 0-3 GF: - Fm: 0-3
Distance:	2m/2m3: 0-0 2m4-2m7: 0-6 3m+: 0-0
Track:	LH: 0-4 RH: 0-2 Tight: 0-6 Gall: 0-0
Aids:	Bl: 0-0 Vi: 0-0 Tstrap: 0-6 Ckp: 0-0
Best Rating:	108 4/03 Carl 2m4f gd-fm Ch

Fair chaser; suited by around two and a half miles; acts on a sound surface; not the most fluent of jumpers; wears tongue tie.

Extremist (USA)
99   100

5-y-o b g Dynaformer (USA)-Strumming (IRE) (Ballad Rock)
K C Bailey Be Lucky Partnership

Placings:333PP					(4762)
2003/04: 17³G, 16³GS, 19³GS, 19^PGS, 19^PS,					

	Starts	1st	2nd	3rd	Win & Pl
Hurdles	5	0	0	3	1562
Career Total	5	0	0	3	1562

Going:	Sf: 0-1 GS: 0-3 Gd: 0-1 GF: - Fm: 0-0
Distance:	2m/2m3: 0-2 2m4-2m7: 0-3 3m+: 0-0
Track:	LH: 0-2 RH: 0-2 Tight: 0-1 Gall: 0-0
Aids:	Bl: 0-0 Vi: 0-0 Tstrap: 0-0 Ckp: 0-0
Best Rating:	100 11/03 Uttx 2m gd-sft Hdl

Moderate hurdler; suited by cut in the ground.

Eye Of The Tiger (IRE)
109(106h)   (101h)118

8-y-o ch g Regular Guy-Banner Lady (Milan)
S A Kirk K J Martin

Placings:51/0403000-P2F35FF					(4293)
2003/04: 24^PGY, 21²GY, 21^FYS, 17³S, 16⁵S, 24^FS, 20^FGF,					

	Starts	1st	2nd	3rd	Win & Pl
Chases	7	0	1	1	2451
Career Total	16	1	1	2	8235
105	3/02	DRoy		Hdl		SFT	£3809
				Total win prize-money £3810			

Going:	Sf: 0-3 GS: 0-0 Gd: 0-0 GF: - Fm: 0-1
Distance:	2m/2m3: 0-2 2m4-2m7: 0-3 3m+: 0-2
Track:	LH: 0-4 RH: 0-1 Tight: 0-0 Gall: 0-0
Aids:	Bl: 0-0 Vi: 0-0 Tstrap: 0-0 Ckp: 0-0
Best Rating:	118 1/04 Fair 2m1f soft Ch

Eyes To The Right (IRE)
91   62

5-y-o ch g Eagle Eyed (USA)-Capable Kate (IRE) (Alzao (USA))
A J Chamberlain Lord Goldicote

Placings:6P0645U-0P64006					(1756)
2003/04: 16⁰G, 16^PGF, 17⁶GF, 18⁴GF, 17⁰GF, 16⁰GF, 16⁰G,					

	Starts	1st	2nd	3rd	Win & Pl
Hurdles	7	0	0	0	0
Career Total	14	0	0	0	0

Going:	Sf: 0-0 GS: 0-0 Gd: 0-2 GF: - Fm: 0-5
Distance:	2m/2m3: 0-7 2m4-2m7: 0-0 3m+: 0-0
Track:	LH: 0-5 RH: 0-2 Tight: 0-4 Gall: 0-0
Aids:	Bl: 0-0 Vi: 0-0 Tstrap: 0-0 Ckp: 0-0
Best Rating:	71 3/03 Hntg 2m110y good Hdl

Plating-class gelding; best at around two miles; acts on good ground.

Eyze (IRE)

101(110h) (95h)**117**
8-y-o b g Lord Americo-Another Raheen (IRE) (Sandalay)
B Mactaggart Stoneage Paving

Placings:0/U6P6FP0-232223101UPF (4861)
2003/04: 22²G, 22³G, 22²F, 22²GF, 24²GF, 22³G, 25¹G, 20⁰GS, 20¹GF, 25⁴UG, 24²G, 33³GS,

	Starts	1st	2nd	3rd	Win & Pl
Hurdles	6	0	4	2	6282
Chases	6	2	0	0	11724
Career Total	20	2	4	2	18006
113 12/03 Muss	2m4f		E Ch	G-F	£3484
100 11/03 Kels	3m1f		D Ch	GD	£8240
			Total win prize-money £11724		

Going:	Sf: 0-0 GS: 0-2 Gd: 1-6 GF: - Fm: 1-4
Distance:	2m/2m3: 0-0 2m4-2m7: 1-7 3m+: 1-5
Track:	LH: 1-9 RH: 1-3 Tight: 2-8 Gall: 0-0
Aids:	Bl: 0-0 Vi: 0-0 Tstrap: 0-0 Ckp: 0-0
Best Rating:	117 11/03 Ayr 2m4f gd-sft Ch

Modest ex-Irish chaser; improved for the switch to fences; off the mark at Kelso in November and even better effort when scoring again at Musselburgh the following month; stays three miles; acts best on good or fast ground but handles cut.

Ezz Elkheil

5-y-o b g Bering-Numidie (FR) (Baillamont (USA))
J R Jenkins (J W Payne 24/9) Kevin Hudson

Placings:U (4207)
2003/04: 16ᵁG,

	Starts	1st	2nd	3rd	Win & Pl
Hurdles	1	0	0	0	
Career Total	1	0	0	0	

Going:	Sf: 0-0 GS: 0-0 Gd: 0-0 GF: - Fm: 0-0
Distance:	2m/2m3: 0-1 2m4-2m7: 0-0 3m+: 0-0
Track:	LH: 0-0 RH: 0-1 Tight: 0-0 Gall: 0-0
Aids:	Bl: 0-0 Vi: 0-0 Tstrap: 0-0 Ckp: 0-0

Fabled Historian (IRE)

4-y-o b g Titus Livius (FR)-Princess Raisa (Indian King (USA))
M J Coombe (Miss I T Oakes 30/5) J Coombe

Placings:PP (3465)
2003/04: 16ᴾGS, 16ᴾS,

	Starts	1st	2nd	3rd	Win & Pl
Hurdles	2	0	0	0	
Career Total	2	0	0	0	

Going:	Sf: 0-1 GS: 0-1 Gd: 0-0 GF: - Fm: 0-0
Distance:	2m/2m3: 0-2 2m4-2m7: 0-0 3m+: 0-0
Track:	LH: 0-1 RH: 0-1 Tight: 0-0 Gall: 0-0
Aids:	Bl: 0-0 Vi: 0-0 Tstrap: 0-0 Ckp: 0-0

Fabrezan (FR)

108 **118+**
5-y-o b g Nikos-Fabulous Secret (FR) (Fabulous Dancer (USA))

B J Llewellyn (Nick Williams 7/1) B W Parren

Placings:P3633P-41P2321110 (4307)
2003/04: 17⁴G, 20¹G, 22ᴾGF, 22²GF, 19³GF, 24²G, 26¹GS, 21¹S, 21¹S, 22⁰G,

	Starts	1st	2nd	3rd	Win & Pl
Hurdles	10	4	2	1	21404
Career Total	16	4	2	4	22798
118 2/04 Plum	2m5f		D(0-115)HHdl	SFT	£6857
103 1/04 Plum	2m5f		D(0-125)HHdl	SFT	£5557
99 1/04 Hrfd	3m2f		F Hdl	G-S	£2674
85 7/03 Worc	2m4f		E Hdl	GD	£3514
			Total win prize-money £18604		

Going:	Sf: 2-2 GS: 1-1 Gd: 1-3 GF: - Fm: 0-4
Distance:	2m/2m3: 0-2 2m4-2m7: 3-6 3m+: 1-2
Track:	LH: 3-5 RH: 1-5 Tight: 2-4 Gall: 0-0
Aids:	Bl: 0-0 Vi: 0-0 Tstrap: 0-0 Ckp: 0-0
Best Rating:	118 2/04 Plum 2m5f soft Hdl

Fair hurdler; in good form in early 2004; stays 3m2f; handles fast, but considered best with some cut in the ground.

Face The Limelight (IRE)

65 **29**
5-y-o b g Quest For Fame-Miss Boniface (Tap On Wood)
Jedd O'Keeffe (H Morrison 20/10) Highbeck Racing

Placings:F0 (3335)
2003/04: 16ᶠGF, 16⁰GS,

	Starts	1st	2nd	3rd	Win & Pl
Hurdles	2	0	0	0	
Career Total	2	0	0	0	

Going:	Sf: 0-0 GS: 0-1 Gd: 0-0 GF: - Fm: 0-1
Distance:	2m/2m3: 0-2 2m4-2m7: 0-0 3m+: 0-0
Track:	LH: 0-1 RH: 0-1 Tight: 0-2 Gall: 0-0
Aids:	Bl: 0-0 Vi: 0-0 Tstrap: 0-0 Ckp: 0-0
Best Rating:	29 1/04 Catt 2m gd-sft Hdl

Factor Fifteen

(109h) (107+h)
5-y-o gr g Hector Protector (USA)-Catch The Sun (Kalaglow)
J Howard Johnson (E A L Dunlop 4/10) Andrea & Graham Wylie

Placings:2022U (4261)
2003/04: 16²GF, 16⁰S, 16²GF, 16²F, 16ᵁGF,

	Starts	1st	2nd	3rd	Win & Pl
Hurdles	4	0	3	0	3888
Chases	1	0	0	0	0
Career Total	5	0	3	0	3888

Going:	Sf: 0-1 GS: 0-0 Gd: 0-0 GF: - Fm: 0-4
Distance:	2m/2m3: 0-5 2m4-2m7: 0-0 3m+: 0-0
Track:	LH: 0-2 RH: 0-3 Tight: 0-5 Gall: 0-0
Aids:	Bl: 0-0 Vi: 0-0 Tstrap: 0-0 Ckp: 0-1
Best Rating:	107 12/03 Muss 2m gd-fm Hdl

Useful handicapper on the Flat; expensive purchase, finished runner-up twice in novices' hurdles; early casualty on chase debut.

Fadalko (FR)

(97h) (113h)**161**
11-y-o b g Cadoudal (FR)-Kalliste (FR) (Calicot (FR))
M Todhunter Sir Robert Ogden

Placings:2111/25P6210/11512U2F/122112/33620314/5250 U6-4 (3596)
2003/04: 20⁴HY,

	Starts	1st	2nd	3rd	Win & Pl
Hurdles	1	0	0	0	731
Career Total	40	11	10	3	351147
163 4/02 Chel	2m5f	A Ch		G-F	£24562
168 4/01 Aint	2m4f	A Ch		SFT	£74400
161 12/00 Winc	2m5f	B Ch		G-S	£9642
157 10/00 Winc	2m5f	A HCh		G-S	£21000
162 2/00 Uttx	2m	C HCh		SFT	£7020
145 11/99 Chel	2m	A Ch		GD	£13100
140 10/99 Bang	2m1f110y D Ch			SFT	£4130
145 4/99 Ayr	2m	A HHdl		SFT	£15385
3/98 Autl	2m2f	Hdl		VS	£30303
12/97 Autl	2m1f110y Hdl			HLD	£16835
11/97 Autl	2m1f110y Hdl			VS	£11223
			Total win prize-money £227602		

Going:	Sf: 0-1 GS: 0-0 Gd: 0-0 GF: - Fm: 0-0
Distance:	2m/2m3: 0-0 2m4-2m7: 0-1 3m+: 0-0
Track:	LH: 0-1 RH: 0-0 Tight: 0-0 Gall: 0-0
Aids:	Bl: 0-0 Vi: 0-0 Tstrap: 0-0 Ckp: 0-0
Best Rating:	168 4/01 Aint 2m4f soft Ch

Smart chaser; best at two to two and a half miles; a genuine sort, handles all grounds; has shown his best form in the spring; below best after break on first run for Martin Todhunter on first hurdles outing since 1999 on testing ground at Ayr in January.

Faddad (USA)

95 **85**
8-y-o b g Irish River (FR)-Miss Mistletoes (IRE) (The Minstrel (CAN))
D C O'Brien Mrs V O'Brien

Placings:0/0/50P-0040 (4123)
2003/04: 16⁰S, 22⁰G, 16⁴S, 17⁰G,

	Starts	1st	2nd	3rd	Win & Pl
Hurdles	4	0	0	0	0
Career Total	9	0	0	0	0

Going:	Sf: 0-2 GS: 0-0 Gd: 0-0 GF: - Fm: 0-0
Distance:	2m/2m3: 0-3 2m4-2m7: 0-1 3m+: 0-0
Track:	LH: 0-3 RH: 0-1 Tight: 0-4 Gall: 0-0
Aids:	Bl: 0-0 Vi: 0-0 Tstrap: 0-0 Ckp: 0-0
Best Rating:	85 5/02 Folk 2m1f110y good Hdl

Fadoudal Du Cochet (FR)

113(101h) (140h)**149**
11-y-o b g Cadoudal (FR)-Eau De Vie (FR) (Dhaudevi (FR))
A L T Moore Sir Anthony O'Reilly

Placings:002/2131134/14312/0115/321133/3302P-03F1 (4769a)

2003/04: 16⁰S, 16³HY, 16ᶠG, 17¹Y,

	Starts	1st	2nd	3rd	Win & Pl
Hurdles	1	0	0	0	
Chases	3	1	0	1	34627
Career Total	35	10	5	10	170090
149 4/04 Fair	2m1f	HCh		YLD	£32091
143 3/02 Chel	2m110y A HCh			GD	£39000
140 2/02 Gowr	2m	Hdl		SFT	£23926
143 1/01 Navn	2m1f	(0-123)HCh		SFT	£6677
128 12/00 Punc	2m	(0-123)HCh		SH	£6072
125 2/00 Punc	2m	Ch		SFT	£10400
110 10/99 Navn	2m1f	Ch		Y-S	£4312
134 1/99 Naas	2m	Hdl		HVY	£6138
134 1/99 Thur	2m	Hdl		HVY	£4296

106 11/98 Cork 2m   Hdl   SFT £2391
Total win prize-money £135306

Going:	Sf: 0-2 GS: 0-0 Gd: 0-1 GF: - Fm: 0-0
Distance:	2m/2m3: 1-4 2m4-2m7: 0-0 3m+: 0-0
Track:	LH: 0-2 RH: 1-2 Tight: 0-0 Gall: 0-1
Aids:	Bl: 0-0 Vi: 0-0 Tstrap: 0-0 Ckp: 0-1
Best Rating:	149 4/04 Fair 2m1f yield Ch

Smart hurdler/chaser; Irish trained; game win in the Grand Annual Chase at the 2002 Cheltenham Festival career highlight; best at two miles; acts well in soft ground.

Failte (IRE)
62

6-y-o b g Most Welcome-Esh Sham (USA) (Damascus (USA))
L A Dace J J Smith

Placings:F   (3449)
2003/04: 17^{F}GS,

	Starts	1st	2nd	3rd	Win & Pl
Hurdles	1	0	0	0	
Career Total	1	0	0	0	

Going:	Sf: 0-0 GS: 0-1 Gd: 0-0 GF: - Fm: 0-0
Distance:	2m/2m3: 0-1 2m4-2m7: 0-0 3m+: 0-0
Track:	LH: 0-0 RH: 0-1 Tight: 0-1 Gall: 0-0
Aids:	Bl: 0-0 Vi: 0-0 Tstrap: 0-0 Ckp: 0-0
Best Rating:	62 1/04 Tntn 2m1f gd-sft Hdl

Fair Charmeur (IRE)

10-y-o ch m Buckskin (FR)-Beau Croft Lass (Beau Charmeur (FR))
R R Smedley R R Smedley

Placings:4   (4815)
2003/04: 24^{4}G,

	Starts	1st	2nd	3rd	Win & Pl
Chases	1	0	0	0	259
Career Total	1	0	0	0	259

Going:	Sf: 0-0 GS: 0-0 Gd: 0-1 GF: - Fm: 0-0
Distance:	2m/2m3: 0-0 2m4-2m7: 0-0 3m+: 0-1
Track:	LH: 0-1 RH: 0-0 Tight: 0-0 Gall: 0-0
Aids:	Bl: 0-0 Vi: 0-0 Tstrap: 0-0 Ckp: 0-0
Best Rating:	76 4/04 Chep 3m good Ch

Winner of three points; inclined to get let down by her jumping.

Fair Enough (IRE)
91   (0c)83

9-y-o b m Phardante (FR)-Woodford Princess (Menelek)
R Rowe Mr & Mrs Robin Lamb

Placings:4400600/6003-4PP0303   (4118)
2003/04: 23^{4}GF, 24^{P}GF, 23^{P}G, 21^{0}GS, 22^{3}G, 22^{0}G, 22^{3}G,

	Starts	1st	2nd	3rd	Win & Pl
Hurdles	4	0	0	2	892
Chases	3	0	0	0	371
Career Total	18	0	0	3	2867

Going:	Sf: 0-0 GS: 0-1 Gd: 0-4 GF: - Fm: 0-2
Distance:	2m/2m3: 0-0 2m4-2m7: 0-4 3m+: 0-3
Track:	LH: 0-4 RH: 0-3 Tight: 0-3 Gall: 0-2
Aids:	Bl: 0-0 Vi: 0-0 Tstrap: 0-0 Ckp: 0-0
Best Rating:	89 5/01 Tipp 2m2f heavy NHF

Plating-class hurdler; stays three miles-three; best on a sound surface.

Fair Prospect
99(102h)   (116h)116+

8-y-o b g Sir Harry Lewis (USA)-Fair Sara (Mcindoe)
P F Nicholls Fourstar Partners

Placings:15/F41-1331   (2654)
2003/04: 23^{1}G, 25^{3}G, 24^{3}GS, 22^{1}G,

	Starts	1st	2nd	3rd	Win & Pl
Hurdles	3	1	0	2	6286
Chases	1	1	0	0	4037
Career Total	9	4	0	2	16181
116	12/03 Font	2m6f	E Ch		GD £4036
104	5/03 Weth	2m7f	D Hdl		GD £4761
106	4/03 Uttx	2m4f110yE Hdl		GD £3864
102	6/01 Hexm	2m	H NHF		G-S £1610
					Total win prize-money £14272

Going:	Sf: 0-0 GS: 0-1 Gd: 2-3 GF: - Fm: 0-0
Distance:	2m/2m3: 0-0 2m4-2m7: 2-2 3m+: 0-2
Track:	LH: 1-3 RH: 0-0 Tight: 1-1 Gall: 0-0
Aids:	Bl: 0-0 Vi: 0-0 Tstrap: 0-0 Ckp: 0-0
Best Rating:	116 12/03 Font 2m6f good Ch

Fair novice hurdler; nice winner on chasing debut; stays well; suited by decent ground.

Fair Question (IRE)
106   117+

6-y-o b g Rainbow Quest (USA)-Fair Of The Furze (Ela-Mana-Mou)
Miss Venetia Williams The MerseyClyde Partnership

Placings:P642-51   (4588)
2003/04: 16^{6}GS, 21^{1}G,

	Starts	1st	2nd	3rd	Win & Pl
Hurdles	2	1	0	0	3536
Career Total	6	1	1	0	4741
117	3/04 Hntg	2m5f110yE Hdl		GD £3536
				Total win prize-money £3536

Going:	Sf: 0-0 GS: 0-1 Gd: 1-1 GF: - Fm: 0-0
Distance:	2m/2m3: 0-1 2m4-2m7: 1-1 3m+: 0-0
Track:	LH: 0-0 RH: 1-2 Tight: 0-0 Gall: 1-1
Aids:	Bl: 0-0 Vi: 0-0 Tstrap: 0-0 Ckp: 0-0
Best Rating:	117 3/04 Hntg 2m5f110y good Hdl

Fair hurdler; tends to race a bit freely; has shown form on most types of ground.

Fair Wind (IRE)

12-y-o b g Strong Gale-Corcomroe (Busted)
Mrs H Bartlett Mrs H Bartlett

Placings:31/P164/2PRP-51   (4761)
2003/04: 25^{5}GF, 21^{1}S,

	Starts	1st	2nd	3rd	Win & Pl
Chases	2	1	0	0	2282
Career Total	12	3	1	1	8455
101	4/04 Towc	3m1f	H Ch	SFT £2282
115	2/02 Wwck	3m2f	H Ch	HVY £1330
115	4/01 Extr	2m7f110yH Ch	SFT £2271
				Total win prize-money £5884

Going:	Sf: 1-1 GS: 0-0 Gd: 0-0 GF: - Fm: 0-1
Distance:	2m/2m3: 0-0 2m4-2m7: 0-0 3m+: 1-2
Track:	LH: 0-0 RH: 1-2 Tight: 0-0 Gall: 0-0
Aids:	Bl: 0-0 Vi: 0-0 Tstrap: 0-0 Ckp: 0-0
Best Rating:	117 3/02 Chel 3m2f110y good Ch

Fair Wizard (IRE)

5-y-o b/br g Distinctly North (USA)-Richmond Lillie (Fairbairn)
R Nixon G R S Nixon

Placings:P   (2145)
2003/04: 16^{P}G,

	Starts	1st	2nd	3rd	Win & Pl
Hurdles	1	0	0	0	
Career Total	1	0	0	0	

Going:	Sf: 0-0 GS: 0-0 Gd: 0-1 GF: - Fm: 0-0
Distance:	2m/2m3: 0-1 2m4-2m7: 0-0 3m+: 0-0
Track:	LH: 0-1 RH: 0-0 Tight: 0-0 Gall: 0-0
Aids:	Bl: 0-0 Vi: 0-0 Tstrap: 0-0 Ckp: 0-0

Fairfields Lad (IRE)

5-y-o b g Norwich-Fahoora (IRE) (Orchestra)
J Howard Johnson J R McAleese

Placings:PP   (4881)
2003/04: 24^{P}G, 17^{P}GS,

	Starts	1st	2nd	3rd	Win & Pl
Hurdles	2	0	0	0	
Career Total	2	0	0	0	

Going:	Sf: 0-0 GS: 0-1 Gd: 0-1 GF: - Fm: 0-0
Distance:	2m/2m3: 0-1 2m4-2m7: 0-0 3m+: 0-1
Track:	LH: 0-0 RH: 0-2 Tight: 0-0 Gall: 0-0
Aids:	Bl: 0-0 Vi: 0-0 Tstrap: 0-0 Ckp: 0-0

Fairland (IRE)
79

5-y-o b g Blues Traveller (IRE)-Massive Powder (Caerleon (USA))
S Dow (Joseph Crowley 7/1) S Dow

Placings:606P000P   (4750)
2003/04: 16^{6}S, 16^{0}GF, 20^{6}GF, 16^{P}GY, 16^{0}F, 17^{0}G, 16^{0}S, 21^{P}G,

	Starts	1st	2nd	3rd	Win & Pl
Hurdles	8	0	0	0	
Career Total	8	0	0	0	

Going:	Sf: 0-2 GS: 0-0 Gd: 0-2 GF: - Fm: 0-3
Distance:	2m/2m3: 0-6 2m4-2m7: 0-2 3m+: 0-0
Track:	LH: 0-1 RH: 0-2 Tight: 0-1 Gall: 0-0
Aids:	Bl: 0-1 Vi: 0-0 Tstrap: 0-1 Ckp: 0-0
Best Rating:	87 7/03 Rosc 2m4f gd-fm Hdl

Fairly Smart
82   47

5-y-o b m Good Thyne (USA)-Smart Chick (True Song)
M F Harris C J Courage

Placings:00   (4650)
2003/04: 17^{0}G, 19^{0}G,

	Starts	1st	2nd	3rd	Win & Pl
Hurdles	2	0	0	0	
Career Total	2	0	0	0	

Going:	Sf: 0-0 GS: 0-0 Gd: 0-2 GF: - Fm: 0-0
Distance:	2m/2m3: 0-1 2m4-2m7: 0-1 3m+: 0-0
Track:	LH: 0-1 RH: 0-1 Tight: 0-1 Gall: 0-0

Aids: Bl: 0-0 Vi: 0-0 Tstrap: 0-0 Ckp: 0-0
Best Rating: 49 4/04 Hrfd 2m3f110y good Hdl

Fairmorning (IRE)

98   84

5-y-o b g Ridgewood Ben-The Bratpack (IRE) (Mister Majestic)
J W Unett T Morning

Placings: 4B0   (2542)
2003/04: 20⁴GF, 16ᴮGF, 16⁹G,

	Starts	1st	2nd	3rd	Win & Pl
Hurdles	3	0	0	0	0
Career Total	3	0	0	0	0

Going:	Sf: 0-0 GS: 0-0 Gd: 0-0 GF: - Fm: 0-2
Distance:	2m/2m3: 0-2 2m4-2m7: 0-1 3m+: 0-0
Track:	LH: 0-2 RH: 0-1 Tight: 0-0 Gall: 0-0
Aids:	Bl: 0-0 Vi: 0-0 Tstrap: 0-0 Ckp: 0-0
Best Rating:	84 12/03 Leic 2m good Hdl

Fairtoto

96(109h)   (94dh)81

8-y-o b g Mtoto-Fairy Feet (Sadler's Wells (USA))
D J Wintle John W Egan

Placings: 650/51222/22203/060-005320126P00   (4115)
2003/04: 21⁹G, 24⁵GF, 22⁵GF, 21³F, 22²G, 21⁹G, 20¹G, 21²GS, 19⁶GS, 24⁷G, 19⁹GS, 20⁶GF,

	Starts	1st	2nd	3rd	Win & Pl
Hurdles	8	1	2	1	3852
Chases	4	0	0	0	0
Career Total	28	2	8	2	12891
88	12/03	Leic	2m4f110y	Gd(0-90)	HHdl	GD	£2324
106	7/00	Strf	2m6f110y	D Hdl		G-F	£3266

Total win prize-money £5590

Going:	Sf: 0-0 GS: 0-3 Gd: 1-5 GF: - Fm: 0-4
Distance:	2m/2m3: 0-2 2m4-2m7: 1-8 3m+: 0-2
Track:	LH: 0-4 RH: 1-8 Tight: 0-3 Gall: 0-2
Aids:	Bl: 1-7 Vi: 0-0 Tstrap: 0-2 Ckp: 0-0
Best Rating:	110 5/01 NAbb 2m6f gd-fm Hdl

Plating-class dual-purpose stayer; stays two miles-six, appreciates fast ground and a sharp track.

Fairwood Present (IRE)

109   137

6-y-o ch g Presenting-Ladys Wager (Girandole)
P J Rothwell R J Bagnall

Placings: 411-00133512253   (4768a)
2003/04: 16⁸G, 20⁵S, 20¹GF, 20³Y, 16³GF, 16⁵GF, 20¹G, 20²GF, 21²G, 20⁵S, 20³Y,

	Starts	1st	2nd	3rd	Win & Pl
NH Flat	1	0	0	0	0
Hurdles	10	2	2	3	19349
Career Total	14	4	2	3	27047
130	10/03	Bang	2m4f	E Hdl		GD	£2446
90	5/03	Tram	2m4f	Hdl		G-F	£4704
109	8/02	Rosc	2m	NHF		YLD	£4233
87	8/02	Slig	2m	NHF		HVY	£3386

Total win prize-money £14772

Going:	Sf: 0-2 GS: 0-0 Gd: 1-3 GF: - Fm: 1-4
Distance:	2m/2m3: 0-3 2m4-2m7: 2-8 3m+: 0-0
Track:	LH: 1-3 RH: 0-3 Tight: 1-1 Gall: 0-1
Aids:	Bl: 0-0 Vi: 0-0 Tstrap: 0-0 Ckp: 0-0

Best Rating: 137 11/03 Chel 2m5f good Hdl

Fair novice Irish-trained hurdler; a winner on the Flat in Ireland; won 2m 4f maiden hurdle at Tramore May 2003; followed up over same distance at Bangor in October; seems to act on most types of ground.

Fairy House (FR)

85   68

8-y-o b g Tel Quel (FR)-Ceiling (Thatch (USA))
S McParlan (A J Martin 18/5) S McParlan

Placings: 0000/F0/0/003   (0849a)
2003/04: 16⁹G, 16⁹F, 16³F,

	Starts	1st	2nd	3rd	Win & Pl
Hurdles	3	0	0	1	500
Career Total	10	0	0	1	500

Going:	Sf: 0-0 GS: 0-0 Gd: 0-1 GF: - Fm: 0-0
Distance:	2m/2m3: 0-3 2m4-2m7: 0-0 3m+: 0-0
Track:	LH: 0-1 RH: 0-0 Tight: 0-0 Gall: 0-0
Aids:	Bl: 0-0 Vi: 0-0 Tstrap: 0-0 Ckp: 0-0
Best Rating:	(85) 7/00 Kbgn 2m gd-fm Hdl

Fairy Loch

75   30

5-y-o b m Sure Blade (USA)-Tremloch (Tremblant)
J W Mullins Mrs Kathy Blackman

Placings: 00   (1698)
2003/04: 18⁰G, 16⁹GF,

	Starts	1st	2nd	3rd	Win & Pl
Hurdles	2	0	0	0	
Career Total	2	0	0	0	

Going:	Sf: 0-0 GS: 0-0 Gd: 0-0 GF: - Fm: 0-1
Distance:	2m/2m3: 0-2 2m4-2m7: 0-0 3m+: 0-0
Track:	LH: 0-2 RH: 0-0 Tight: 0-0 Gall: 0-0
Aids:	Bl: 0-0 Vi: 0-0 Tstrap: 0-0 Ckp: 0-0
Best Rating:	30 10/03 Font 2m2f110y good Hdl

Fairy Skin Maker (IRE)

103   99+

6-y-o ch g Nomadic Way (USA)-Malvern Madam (Reesh)
G A Harker The Four S

Placings: 224100001016   (4911)
2003/04: 17²G, 17²G, 16⁴G, 16¹S, 20⁹GS, 16⁹G, 16⁹HY, 20⁹GS, 17¹G, 20⁰HY, 16¹G, 16⁶S,

	Starts	1st	2nd	3rd	Win & Pl
NH Flat	4	1	2	0	3234
Hurdles	8	2	0	0	7690
Career Total	12	3	2	0	10924
99	4/04	Kels	2m110y	E(0-105)	HHdl	GD	£4329
97	3/04	Sedg	2m1f	E(0-105)	HHdl	GD	£3360
109	11/03	Ayr	2m	H NHF		SFT	£2352

Total win prize-money £10042

Going:	Sf: 1-4 GS: 0-2 Gd: 2-6 GF: - Fm: 0-0
Distance:	2m/2m3: 3-9 2m4-2m7: 0-3 3m+: 0-0
Track:	LH: 3-11 RH: 0-1 Tight: 2-5 Gall: 0-3
Aids:	Bl: 0-0 Vi: 0-0 Tstrap: 0-0 Ckp: 0-0
Best Rating:	109 11/03 Ayr 2m soft NHF

Moderate performer; bumper winner; suited by easy ground and front-running; best at around two miles; acts on good ground or softer; improving.

Falchion

109(101c)   (110c)110

9-y-o b g Broadsword (USA)-Fastlass (Celtic Cone)
J R Bewley R Bewley

Placings: 6/56025/1352/3233F2U-PFU2240F6   (4617)
2003/04: 20⁹GS, 21⁵FS, 25ᵁS, 20²S, 23⁶S, 20⁴G, 20⁰G, 24⁴HY, 27⁶G,

	Starts	1st	2nd	3rd	Win & Pl
Hurdles	4	0	2	0	3454
Chases	5	0	0	0	0
Career Total	26	1	6	4	15223
106	11/01	Ayr	2m6f	E Hdl		G-S	£2597

Total win prize-money £2597

Going:	Sf: 0-5 GS: 0-1 Gd: 0-3 GF: - Fm: 0-0
Distance:	2m/2m3: 0-0 2m4-2m7: 0-6 3m+: 0-3
Track:	LH: 0-6 RH: 0-3 Tight: 0-3 Gall: 0-0
Aids:	Bl: 0-0 Vi: 0-0 Tstrap: 0-9 Ckp: 0-0
Best Rating:	112 12/03 Ayr 2m5f110y soft Ch

Modest chaser/hurdler; yet to win over fences, but chancy jumper and often placed; stays well; usually wears a tongue tie.

Falcon Du Coteau (FR)

102(88h)   (67h)119

11-y-o b/br g Apeldoorn (FR)-Ifrika (FR) (Bamako Iii)
C J Mann The Whitcoombe Partnership

Placings: 000460/102/60/03131213F/0000050-443P (2315)
2003/04: 24⁴GF, 34⁴GF, 20⁹G, 30⁶GS,

	Starts	1st	2nd	3rd	Win & Pl
Chases	4	0	0	1	7108
Career Total	31	4	2	4	44692
115	1/02	Leop	2m3f	(0-130)	HCh	HVY	£13957
110	12/01	Punc	2m	(0-116)	HCh	SFT	£7862
101	11/01	Clon	2m1f	(0-102)	HCh	YLD	£5008
87	5/99	Gowr	2m	(0-102)	HHdl	GD	£3069

Total win prize-money £29857

Going:	Sf: 0-0 GS: 0-1 Gd: 0-1 GF: - Fm: 0-2
Distance:	2m/2m3: 0-0 2m4-2m7: 0-1 3m+: 0-3
Track:	LH: 0-3 RH: 0-1 Tight: 0-2 Gall: 0-1
Aids:	Bl: 0-0 Vi: 0-0 Tstrap: 0-0 Ckp: 0-0
Best Rating:	119 4/03 Aint 2m5f110y good Ch

Modest ex-Irish handicap chaser; best over two and a half to three miles, stays further; acts well with cut in the ground; likes to make the running; has worn blinkers.

Famfoni (FR)

(98h)   (96h)119

11-y-o b g Pamponi (FR)-India Rosa (FR) (Carnaval)
K C Bailey The Propelers Partnership

Placings: 322/424/43452/2/15/341-PPP   (4525)
2003/04: 24⁰G, 24⁵S, 24⁰GS,

	Starts	1st	2nd	3rd	Win & Pl
Chases	3	0	0	0	0
Career Total	20	2	5	3	39519
119	11/02	Chel	3m7f	B Ch		G-S	£19314
110	3/02	Ludl	3m	D Ch		G-S	£4036

Total win prize-money £23351

Going:	Sf: 0-1 GS: 0-1 Gd: 0-1 GF: - Fm: 0-0
Distance:	2m/2m3: 0-0 2m4-2m7: 0-0 3m+: 0-3
Track:	LH: 0-1 RH: 0-2 Tight: 0-1 Gall: 0-0
Aids:	Bl: 0-1 Vi: 0-0 Tstrap: 0-0 Ckp: 0-1
Best Rating:	119 11/02 Chel 3m7f gd-sft Ch

Modest staying chaser; won a cross country chase at Cheltenham in November 2002; absent for 14 months afterwards; acts on any ground.

Familie Footsteps

(93h)   (106h)
10-y-o b g Primitive Rising (USA)-Ramilie (Rambah)
G A Swinbank   Miss A H Sykes

Placings:*0l*4/3500/311F2/5-P   (0782)
2003/04: 16⁶G,

	Starts	1st	2nd	3rd	Win & Pl
Chases	1	0	0		
Career Total	13	2	1	2	7444
102 8/01	Sedg	2m1f	D Hdl		G-F £3265
94 7/01	Sedg	2m1f	E Hdl		G-F £2523

Total win prize-money £5790

Going:	Sf: 0-0 GS: 0-0 Gd: 0-1 GF: - Fm: 0-0
Distance:	2m/2m3: 0-1 2m4-2m7: 0-0 3m+: 0-0
Track:	LH: 0-0 RH: 0-1 Tight: 0-0 Gall: 0-0
Aids:	Bl: 0-0 Vi: 0-0 Tstrap: 0-0 Ckp: 0-0
Best Rating:	106 9/01 Sedg 2m1f good Hdl

Family Venture (IRE)

105(110h)   (107h)111+
7-y-o br g Montelimar (USA)-Well Honey (Al Sirat)
Ferdy Murphy   The Family Venture Partnership

Placings:036132-1314   (2789)
2003/04: 21¹G, 21³G, 21¹G, 24⁴GF,

	Starts	1st	2nd	3rd	Win & Pl
Chases	4	2	0	1	9343
Career Total	10	3	1	3	16137
117 11/03	Ayr	2m5f110yD(0-110)HCh		GD	£5421
119 10/03	Sedg	2m5f	E Ch	GD	£3094
101 1/03	Muss	3m	E(0-105)HHdl	GD	£4163

Total win prize-money £12678

Going:	Sf: 0-0 GS: 0-0 Gd: 2-3 GF: - Fm: 0-0
Distance:	2m/2m3: 0-0 2m4-2m7: 2-3 3m+: 0-1
Track:	LH: 2-3 RH: 0-0 Tight: 1-3 Gall: 0-0
Aids:	Bl: 0-0 Vi: 0-0 Tstrap: 2-4 Ckp: 0-0
Best Rating:	119 10/03 Sedg 2m5f good Ch

Modest hurdler/useful novice chaser; Irish point winner; stays three miles and best on good ground; sometimes wears a tongue-tie.

Famous Grouse

101   97+
4-y-o b g Selkirk (USA)-Shoot Clear (Bay Express)
C J Mann (M Charlton 4/10) Martin Myers

Placings:020   (4788)
2003/04: 16⁶G, 16²G, 16⁶G,

	Starts	1st	2nd	3rd	Win & Pl
Hurdles	3	0	1	0	1060
Career Total	3	0	1	0	1060

Going:	Sf: 0-0 GS: 0-0 Gd: 0-3 GF: - Fm: 0-0
Distance:	2m/2m3: 0-3 2m4-2m7: 0-0 3m+: 0-0
Track:	LH: 0-3 RH: 0-0 Tight: 0-0 Gall: 0-1
Aids:	Bl: 0-0 Vi: 0-0 Tstrap: 0-0 Ckp: 0-0
Best Rating:	97 3/04 Strf 2m110y good Hdl

Moderate hurdler; handles most types of ground.

Fandango De Chassy (FR)

90(102c)   (96c)106
11-y-o b g Brezzo (FR)-Laita De Mercurey (FR) (Dom Luc (FR))
Mrs L Wadham   C J Hays

Placings:0000/35**FU052/211122211P6/PPP/3451110321/P**
2520P34P-5   (0132)
2003/04: 26⁵GF,

	Starts	1st	2nd	3rd	Win & Pl
Hurdles	1	0	0	0	0
Career Total	45	9	8	4	55196
107 3/02	Towc	3m1f	F(0-100)HCh	G-S	£3559
113 12/01	Towc	3m	E(0-115)HHdl	HVY	£5248
110 11/01	Towc	3m	D(0-120)HHdl	SFT	£5362
108 11/01	Towc	3m	F(0-90)Hdl	SFT	£2362
100 11/01	Naas	3m	(0-116)HCh	SH	£6072
95 1/00	Fair	3m1f	(0-123)HCh	SFT	£8320
103 6/99	Prth	3m110y	F(0-110)HHdl	SFT	£2879
91 6/99	Prth	2m4f110y	F(0-95)HCh	G-S	£3582
109 5/99	DRoy	3m	Hdl	SFT	£3069

Total win prize-money £40458

Going:	Sf: 0-0 GS: 0-0 Gd: 0-0 GF: - Fm: 0-1
Distance:	2m/2m3: 0-0 2m4-2m7: 0-0 3m+: 0-1
Track:	LH: 0-0 RH: 0-0 Tight: 0-0 Gall: 0-1
Aids:	Bl: 0-0 Vi: 0-0 Tstrap: 0-0 Ckp: 0-0
Best Rating:	116 1/02 Wwck 3m1f heavy Hdl

Modest handicap chaser, a real stayer; suited by soft ground and a stiff track.

Fanion De Nourry (FR)

11-y-o ch g Bad Conduct (USA)-Ottomane (FR) (Quart De Vin (FR))
E Haddock   Miss H M Newell

Placings:4FF/OP040O/0P5/12P0/00P/F6P-PP3   (4761)
2003/04: 25⁵PGS, 25⁵GS, 25³S,

	Starts	1st	2nd	3rd	Win & Pl
Chases	3	0	0	1	326
Career Total	25	1	1	1	2790
101 5/00	Towc	3m1f	H Ch	G-F	£1568

Total win prize-money £1568

Going:	Sf: 0-1 GS: 0-2 Gd: 0-0 GF: - Fm: 0-0
Distance:	2m/2m3: 0-0 2m4-2m7: 0-0 3m+: 0-3
Track:	LH: 0-0 RH: 0-3 Tight: 0-0 Gall: 0-0
Aids:	Bl: 0-0 Vi: 0-0 Tstrap: 0-0 Ckp: 0-0
Best Rating:	108 5/00 Uttx 4m2f gd-fm Ch

Fanny By Gaslight

60f   25f
6-y-o b m Opera Ghost-Highly Inflammable (USA) (Wind And Wuthering (USA))
J W Mullins   P Fry

Placings:0   (0533)
2003/04: 16⁶GF,

	Starts	1st	2nd	3rd	Win & Pl
NH Flat	1	0	0	0	
Career Total	1	0	0	0	

Going:	Sf: 0-0 GS: 0-0 Gd: 0-0 GF: - Fm: 0-0
Distance:	2m/2m3: 0-1 2m4-2m7: 0-0 3m+: 0-0
Track:	LH: 0-1 RH: 0-0 Tight: 0-0 Gall: 0-0
Aids:	Bl: 0-0 Vi: 0-0 Tstrap: 0-0 Ckp: 0-0

Best Rating: 25 6/03 Worc 2m gd-fm NHF

Fantastic Arts (FR)

95   106
4-y-o b g Royal Applause-Magic Arts (IRE) (Fairy King (USA))
Miss Venetia Williams (Mme J Laurent-Joye Rossi 26/10) Knightsbridge Bc

Placings:F426   (3821)
2003/04: 16⁶G, 16⁴S, 16²G, 16⁶S,

	Starts	1st	2nd	3rd	Win & Pl
Hurdles	4	0	1	0	2770
Career Total	4	0	1	0	2770

Going:	Sf: 0-2 GS: 0-0 Gd: 0-2 GF: - Fm: 0-0
Distance:	2m/2m3: 0-4 2m4-2m7: 0-0 3m+: 0-0
Track:	LH: 0-3 RH: 0-1 Tight: 0-1 Gall: 0-0
Aids:	Bl: 0-0 Vi: 0-0 Tstrap: 0-0 Ckp: 0-0
Best Rating:	106 1/04 Kemp 2m good Hdl

Modest juvenile hurdler; just touched off at Kempton in January; winner in France on the level; stayed 1m7f; acts well on soft ground.

Fantastic Champion (IRE)

108   115d
5-y-o b g Entrepreneur-Reine Mathilde (USA) (Vaguely Noble)
Mrs L Wadham   Champion And The Fantastics

Placings:022-4244014   (4931)
2003/04: 16⁴GF, 19²GF, 20⁴G, 20⁴GS, 17⁹GS, 20¹GF, 22⁴G,

	Starts	1st	2nd	3rd	Win & Pl
Hurdles	7	1	1	0	6268
Career Total	10	1	3	0	9432
112 3/04	Font	2m4f	E Hdl	G-F	£3738

Total win prize-money £3738

Going:	Sf: 0-0 GS: 0-0 Gd: 0-2 GF: - Fm: 1-3
Distance:	2m/2m3: 0-3 2m4-2m7: 1-4 3m+: 0-0
Track:	LH: 0-3 RH: 0-0 Tight: 1-3 Gall: 0-2
Aids:	Bl: 0-1 Vi: 0-0 Tstrap: 0-0 Ckp: 0-0
Best Rating:	118 2/03 Kemp 2m gd-sft Hdl

Modest novice hurdler; goes well on good and good to soft ground; effective over two miles.

Fantastico (IRE)

101   77
4-y-o b f Bahhare (USA)-Minatina (IRE) (Ela-Mana-Mou)
Mrs K Walton (S Kirk 16/9) The Suffolk Punch Syndicate

Placings:32000   (4459)
2003/04: 16³GF, 16²G, 16⁹GS, 16⁹G, 20⁹HY,

	Starts	1st	2nd	3rd	Win & Pl
Hurdles	5	0	1	1	1151
Career Total	5	0	1	1	1151

Going:	Sf: 0-1 GS: 0-1 Gd: 0-2 GF: - Fm: 0-1
Distance:	2m/2m3: 0-4 2m4-2m7: 0-1 3m+: 0-0
Track:	LH: 0-4 RH: 0-1 Tight: 0-0 Gall: 0-4
Aids:	Bl: 0-0 Vi: 0-0 Tstrap: 0-0 Ckp: 0-0
Best Rating:	77 11/03 Newc 2m good Hdl

Placed in first two juvenile hurdles; acts on fast ground.

Far Bridge (IRE)

(57h)

9-y-o ch g Phardante (FR)-Droichidin (Good Thyne (USA))
P Wegmann P Wegmann

Placings:6/00P/6P-F   (0206)
2003/04: 16FGF,

	Starts	1st	2nd	3rd	Win & Pl
Chases	1	0	0	0	
Career Total	7	0	0	0	0

Going:	Sf: 0-0 GS: 0-0 Gd: 0-0 GF: - Fm: 0-1
Distance:	2m/2m3: 0-1 2m4-2m7: 0-0 3m+: 0-0
Track:	LH: 0-1 RH: 0-0 Tight: 0-0 Gall: 0-0
Aids:	Bl: 0-0 Vi: 0-0 Tstrap: 0-0 Ckp: 0-0
Best Rating:	59 3/01 Extr 2m3f heavy Hdl

Far Dawn (USA)
109

11-y-o b g Sunshine Forever (USA)-Dawn's Reality (USA)
(In Reality)
J Gallagher John L Marriott

Placings:11422/230002P/34061/5/32/61P2-FP6 (1028)
2003/04: 24FGF, 24PG, 25FGF,

	Starts	1st	2nd	3rd	Win & Pl
Chases	3	0	0	0	0
Career Total	27	4	6	3	40478
101	3/03	Sthl	3m110y	E Chs	G-F	£3841
123	4/99	Chel	3m	B(0-140)HHdl	GD	£10845
118	12/96	Sand	2m110y	D Hdl	GD	£2905
87	11/96	Wind	2m	E Hdl	GD	£2687

Total win prize-money £20280

Going:	Sf: 0-0 GS: 0-0 Gd: 0-1 GF: - Fm: 0-2
Distance:	2m/2m3: 0-0 2m4-2m7: 0-0 3m+: 0-3
Track:	LH: 0-2 RH: 0-1 Tight: 0-3 Gall: 0-0
Aids:	Bl: 0-0 Vi: 0-0 Tstrap: 0-0 Ckp: 0-0
Best Rating:	132 10/97 Chep 2m110y gd-fm Hdl

Modest chaser; stays three miles; suited by a sound surface.

Far Glen (IRE)

9-y-o b g Phardante (FR)-Asigh Glen (Furry Glen)
P H Morris W Puddifer

Placings:FPP/553P50063/2F2-P   (4257)
2003/04: 24PG,

	Starts	1st	2nd	3rd	Win & Pl
Chases	1	0	0	0	
Career Total	16	0	2	2	2678

Going:	Sf: 0-0 GS: 0-0 Gd: 0-1 GF: - Fm: 0-0
Distance:	2m/2m3: 0-0 2m4-2m7: 0-0 3m+: 0-1
Track:	LH: 0-1 RH: 0-0 Tight: 0-1 Gall: 0-0
Aids:	Bl: 0-0 Vi: 0-0 Tstrap: 0-0 Ckp: 0-0
Best Rating:	97 4/03 Ayr 3m3f110y good Ch

Far Horizon (IRE)
103(109h)   (130 h)103+

10-y-o b g Phardante (FR)-Polly Puttens (Pollerton)
N J Henderson Lady Tennant

Placings:12/222/213P-5   (3316)
2003/04: 16SG,

	Starts	1st	2nd	3rd	Win & Pl
Chases	1	0	0	0	0

Career Total		10	2	5	1	18698
129	12/02	Asct	2m4f	C Hdl	SFT	£7133
122	5/99	Hrfd	2m1f	H NHF	G-S	£1651

Total win prize-money £8785

Going:	Sf: 0-0 GS: 0-0 Gd: 0-0 GF: - Fm: 0-0
Distance:	2m/2m3: 0-1 2m4-2m7: 0-0 3m+: 0-0
Track:	LH: 0-0 RH: 0-1 Tight: 0-0 Gall: 0-0
Aids:	Bl: 0-0 Vi: 0-0 Tstrap: 0-0 Ckp: 0-0
Best Rating:	129 1/03 Kemp 2m5f good Hdl

Decent novice hurdler; suited by two and a half miles and soft ground.

Far Pavilions
107   131

5-y-o b g Halling (USA)-Flambera (FR) (Akarad (FR))
G A Swinbank J David Abell

Placings:1111P-1   (0164)
2003/04: 16SG,

	Starts	1st	2nd	3rd	Win & Pl
Hurdles	1	1	0	0	9451
Career Total	6	5	0	0	34499
118	5/03	Kels	2m110y	B Hdl	GD	£9451
131	3/03	Hayd	2m	B Hdl	GD	£10166
117	2/03	Muss	2m	D Hdl	GD	£5525
121	12/02	Muss	2m	D Hdl	G-S	£5538
107	12/02	Catt	2m	D Hdl	G-S	£3818

Total win prize-money £34499

Going:	Sf: 0-0 GS: 0-0 Gd: 1-1 GF: - Fm: 0-0
Distance:	2m/2m3: 1-1 2m4-2m7: 0-0 3m+: 0-0
Track:	LH: 1-1 RH: 0-0 Tight: 1-1 Gall: 0-0
Aids:	Bl: 0-0 Vi: 0-0 Tstrap: 0-0 Ckp: 0-0
Best Rating:	131 3/03 Hayd 2m good Hdl

Useful hurdler; best over two miles and acts on good or easy ground.

Far To Fall (IRE)
105   108

6-y-o br g Phardante (FR)-Fall About (Comedy Star (USA))
H D Daly Vicky Jeyes Helen Plumbly Jane Trafford

Placings:05   (4197)
2003/04: 20PS, 24SG,

	Starts	1st	2nd	3rd	Win & Pl
Hurdles	2	0	0	0	0
Career Total	2	0	0	0	0

Going:	Sf: 0-1 GS: 0-0 Gd: 0-0 GF: - Fm: 0-0
Distance:	2m/2m3: 0-0 2m4-2m7: 0-1 3m+: 0-1
Track:	LH: 0-2 RH: 0-0 Tight: 0-0 Gall: 0-1
Aids:	Bl: 0-0 Vi: 0-0 Tstrap: 0-0 Ckp: 0-0
Best Rating:	107 3/04 Newb 3m110y good Hdl

Far Two Friendly
73f   45f

5-y-o ch m Environment Friend-Four Friends (Quayside)
Ms Deborah J Evans Paul Green (Oaklea)

Placings:0   (4144)
2003/04: 16SG,

	Starts	1st	2nd	3rd	Win & Pl
NH Flat	1	0	0	0	0
Career Total	1	0	0	0	0

Going:	Sf: 0-0 GS: 0-0 Gd: 0-1 GF: - Fm: 0-0
Distance:	2m/2m3: 0-1 2m4-2m7: 0-0 3m+: 0-0

Track:	LH: 0-0 RH: 0-1 Tight: 0-0 Gall: 0-0
Aids:	Bl: 0-0 Vi: 0-0 Tstrap: 0-0 Ckp: 0-0
Best Rating:	45 3/04 Ludl 2m good NHF

Faraway John (IRE)

6-y-o b g Farhaan-Indiana Dancer (Hallgate)
G P Enright Exors of the late Neil Kenworthy

Placings:P-P   (1921)
2003/04: 16PG,

	Starts	1st	2nd	3rd	Win & Pl
Hurdles	1	0	0	0	
Career Total	2	0	0	0	

Going:	Sf: 0-0 GS: 0-0 Gd: 0-1 GF: - Fm: 0-0
Distance:	2m/2m3: 0-1 2m4-2m7: 0-0 3m+: 0-0
Track:	LH: 0-1 RH: 0-0 Tight: 0-1 Gall: 0-0
Aids:	Bl: 0-0 Vi: 0-0 Tstrap: 0-0 Ckp: 0-0

Farceur (FR)

(80h)   (70h)

5-y-o b/br g Anabaa (USA)-Fabulous Account (USA)
(Private Account)
M C Pipe (J Bertran De Balanda 10/6) M C Pipe

Placings:0040036-26   (1675)
2003/04: 19PVS, 16PF,

	Starts	1st	2nd	3rd	Win & Pl
Hurdles	2	0	1	0	3896
Career Total	9	0	1	1	7708

Going:	Sf: 0-0 GS: 0-0 Gd: 0-0 GF: - Fm: 0-1
Distance:	2m/2m3: 0-1 2m4-2m7: 0-1 3m+: 0-0
Track:	LH: 0-1 RH: 0-1 Tight: 0-0 Gall: 0-0
Aids:	Bl: 0-0 Vi: 0-0 Tstrap: 0-0 Ckp: 0-0
Best Rating:	70 10/03 Towc 2m firm Hdl

Placed on soft ground over hurdles in France; finished lame on fast ground on British debut.

Fard Du Moulin Mas (FR)
107(95c)   (99c)103+

11-y-o b/br g Morespeed-Soiree D'Ex (FR) (Kashtan (FR))
M E D Francis Mrs Merrick Francis Iii

Placings:13/1P3P/0054PP6/6325116F/0PP/4P50/F5P-
000P4P   (4693)
2003/04: 22PGS, 20PG, 23PGS, 24PG, 22PG, 22PG,

	Starts	1st	2nd	3rd	Win & Pl
Hurdles	6	0	0	0	650
Career Total	37	4	1	3	71714
136	11/99	Sand	2m4f110y	C(0-130)HCh	GD	£7002
137	10/99	Worc	2m4f	C(0-135)HHdl	G-F	£5084
9/97	Autl	2m2f	Ch	SFT	£13468
3/97	Autl	2m1f110y	Hdl	VS	£11223

Total win prize-money £36778

Going:	Sf: 0-0 GS: 0-2 Gd: 0-4 GF: - Fm: 0-0
Distance:	2m/2m3: 0-0 2m4-2m7: 0-4 3m+: 0-2
Track:	LH: 0-2 RH: 0-4 Tight: 0-0 Gall: 0-1
Aids:	Bl: 0-0 Vi: 0-0 Tstrap: 0-0 Ckp: 0-0
Best Rating:	137 10/99 Worc 2m4f gd-fm Hdl

Moderate hurdler these days; one-time decent chaser; stays 3m; acts in soft ground.

Fare Dealing (IRE)

(106h)   (97h)**95**
11-y-o b g Tremblant-Charming Whisper (Deep Run)
M J Gingell Fare Dealing Partnership

Placings:34B450/FF/4312P0321/05622003-520F   (2579)
2003/04: 22⁵G, 21²G, 20⁰G, 16^FGF,

	Starts	1st	2nd	3rd	Win & Pl
Hurdles	2	0	0	0	0
Chases	2	0	1	0	830
Career Total	29	2	5	4	12649
102 4/02 Plum	2m5f		E(0-110)HHdl		GD £2499
97 12/01 Sthl	2m4f110yE(0-105)HHdl				GD £2478
				Total win prize-money £4977	

Going:	Sf: 0-0 GS: 0-0 Gd: 0-3 GF: - Fm: 0-1
Distance:	2m/2m3: 0-1 2m4-2m7: 0-3 3m+: 0-0
Track:	LH: 0-3 RH: 0-1 Tight: 0-4 Gall: 0-0
Aids:	Bl: 0-0 Vi: 0-0 Tstrap: 0-0 Ckp: 0-0
Best Rating:	102 4/02 Plum 2m5f good Hdl

Modest hurdler/chaser; suited by good ground; front runner.

Farewell Child

7-y-o b m Afzal-Bye Bye Baby (FR) (Baby Turk)
Miss Suzy Smith John Young

Placings:P5   (2582)
2003/04: 21^PGS, 24⁵GF,

	Starts	1st	2nd	3rd	Win & Pl
Hurdles	2	0	0	0	0
Career Total	2	0	0	0	0

Going:	Sf: 0-0 GS: 0-1 Gd: 0-0 GF: - Fm: 0-1
Distance:	2m/2m3: 0-0 2m4-2m7: 0-1 3m+: 0-1
Track:	LH: 0-1 RH: 0-1 Tight: 0-1 Gall: 0-0
Aids:	Bl: 0-0 Vi: 0-0 Tstrap: 0-0 Ckp: 0-0

Farington Lodge (IRE)

101   86
6-y-o b g Simply Great (FR)-Lodge Party (IRE) (Strong Gale)
C Grant Trevor Hemmings

Placings:0-554PP   (4913)
2003/04: 20⁵GS, 23⁵G, 20⁴S, 24^PGF, 24^PS,

	Starts	1st	2nd	3rd	Win & Pl
Hurdles	5	0	0	0	448
Career Total	6	0	0	0	448

Going:	Sf: 0-2 GS: 0-1 Gd: 0-1 GF: - Fm: 0-1
Distance:	2m/2m3: 0-0 2m4-2m7: 0-3 3m+: 0-2
Track:	LH: 0-3 RH: 0-2 Tight: 0-0 Gall: 0-0
Aids:	Bl: 0-0 Vi: 0-0 Tstrap: 0-0 Ckp: 0-0
Best Rating:	86 11/03 Carl 2m4f gd-sft Hdl

Modest form in bumpers but disappointing so far over hurdles; should stay well; likely chaser.

Farlington

102   109
7-y-o b g Alflora (IRE)-Annapurna (Rakaposhi King)
J Howard Johnson John Smart

Placings:2223   (3733)
2003/04: 21²GF, 21²G, 19²GS, 24³G,

	Starts	1st	2nd	3rd	Win & Pl
Chases	4	0	3	1	3740
Career Total	4	0	3	1	3740

Going:	Sf: 0-0 GS: 0-1 Gd: 0-2 GF: - Fm: 0-1
Distance:	2m/2m3: 0-1 2m4-2m7: 0-2 3m+: 0-1
Track:	LH: 0-3 RH: 0-1 Tight: 0-4 Gall: 0-0
Aids:	Bl: 0-0 Vi: 0-0 Tstrap: 0-0 Ckp: 0-0
Best Rating:	109 1/04 Catt 2m3f gd-sft Ch

Winning pointer; runner-up in two novice chases at Sedgefield and one at Catterick; third at Musselburgh in February; suited by three miles; acts on fast and easy ground.

Farmer Jack

106   (135h)**154**
8-y-o b g Alflora (IRE)-Cheryls Pet (IRE) (General Ironside)
P J Hobbs Peter Partridge

Placings:1/4511420/4111243-P0100   (4399)
2003/04: 19^PS, 16⁰GS, 16¹S, 20⁰G, 20⁰G,

	Starts	1st	2nd	3rd	Win & Pl
Chases	5	1	0	0	12023
Career Total	20	7	2	1	85589
151 2/04 Sand	2m	B HCh		SFT £12023
154 1/03 Kemp	2m	B Ch		GD £15446
146 12/02 Hayd	2m	C Ch		GD £9187
130 11/02 Tntn	2m3f	D Ch		G-S £6352
135 1/02 Asct	2m4f	C Hdl		G-S £5304
110 12/01 Extr	2m3f	E Hdl		GD £2922
105 4/01 Tntn	2m1f	H NHF		G-F £1568
				Total win prize-money £52804

Going:	Sf: 1-2 GS: 0-1 Gd: 0-2 GF: - Fm: 0-0
Distance:	2m/2m3: 1-2 2m4-2m7: 0-3 3m+: 0-0
Track:	LH: 0-2 RH: 1-3 Tight: 0-0 Gall: 0-2
Aids:	Bl: 0-0 Vi: 0-0 Tstrap: 0-0 Ckp: 0-0
Best Rating:	154 1/03 Kemp 2m good Ch

Smart chaser; was a very decent novice chaser; suited by two miles, but gets further on decent ground; generally jumps well.

Farmer Josh

91   (0c)**68**
10-y-o b g Dancing High-Millie Duffer (Furry Glen)
Miss L V Davis Miss Louise Davis

Placings:000P/50405PP/P/00-UU53   (1929)
2003/04: 21^UG, 22^UGF, 20⁵GF, 25³GF,

	Starts	1st	2nd	3rd	Win & Pl
Hurdles	3	0	0	1	439
Chases	1	0	0	0	0
Career Total	18	0	0	1	439

Going:	Sf: 0-0 GS: 0-0 Gd: 0-1 GF: - Fm: 0-3
Distance:	2m/2m3: 0-0 2m4-2m7: 0-3 3m+: 0-1
Track:	LH: 0-2 RH: 0-2 Tight: 0-1 Gall: 0-0
Aids:	Bl: 0-0 Vi: 0-0 Tstrap: 0-0 Ckp: 0-0
Best Rating:	73 4/99 MRas 2m3f110y good Hdl

Farnaheezview (IRE)

105   111
6-y-o b g Naheez (USA)-Sweet View (King's Ride)
O Sherwood J Ledwidge and J McCarthy

Placings:24423   (4445)

2003/04: 18²S, 22⁴GS, 24⁴G, 24²G, 25³S,

	Starts	1st	2nd	3rd	Win & Pl
NH Flat	1	0	1	0	669
Hurdles	4	0	1	1	3410
Career Total	5	0	2	1	4079

Going:	Sf: 0-2 GS: 0-1 Gd: 0-2 GF: - Fm: 0-0
Distance:	2m/2m3: 0-1 2m4-2m7: 0-1 3m+: 0-3
Track:	LH: 0-4 RH: 0-1 Tight: 0-1 Gall: 0-1
Aids:	Bl: 0-0 Vi: 0-0 Tstrap: 0-0 Ckp: 0-0
Best Rating:	111 3/04 Newb 3m110y good Hdl

Runner-up in a Plumpton bumper on his racecourse debut; placed over hurdles; won his only start in an Irish point; likely to do better over fences; stays three miles.

Farnando (IRE)

10-y-o b g Zaffaran (USA)-Kasperova (He Loves Me)
S G Parkyn (J F O'Shea 25/5) Des Davies

Placings:6P404F2/6UP4241PU5/P0/F   (4626)
2003/04: 21^FG,

	Starts	1st	2nd	3rd	Win & Pl
Chases	1	0	0	0	
Career Total	20	1	2	0	6728
				Total win prize-money £4416

Going:	Sf: 0-0 GS: 0-0 Gd: 0-1 GF: - Fm: 0-0
Distance:	2m/2m3: 0-0 2m4-2m7: 0-1 3m+: 0-0
Track:	LH: 0-1 RH: 0-1 Tight: 0-1 Gall: 0-0
Aids:	Bl: 0-0 Vi: 0-0 Tstrap: 0-0 Ckp: 0-0
Best Rating:	105 12/99 Punc 2m4f soft Ch

Farne Isle

97   92+
5-y-o ch m Midnight Legend-Biloela (Nicholas Bill)
G A Harker M F Spence

Placings:1650-4446453   (4799)
2003/04: 16⁴G, 16⁴G, 19⁴GF, 16^FGS, 16⁴HY, 16⁵G, 17³G,

	Starts	1st	2nd	3rd	Win & Pl
Hurdles	7	0	1	2105
Career Total	11	1	0	1	3960
98 1/03 Sedg 2m1f	H NHF		HVY £1855
			Total win prize-money £1855

Going:	Sf: 0-1 GS: 0-1 Gd: 0-4 GF: - Fm: 0-1
Distance:	2m/2m3: 0-7 2m4-2m7: 0-0 3m+: 0-0
Track:	LH: 0-6 RH: 0-1 Tight: 0-2 Gall: 0-1
Aids:	Bl: 0-0 Vi: 0-0 Tstrap: 0-1 Ckp: 0-1
Best Rating:	98 1/03 Sedg 2m1f heavy NHF

Winning bumper horse; has shown ability over hurdles; raced only around two miles to date; acts on most ground.

Farouk (IRE)

71f   59f
6-y-o b g Fourstars Allstar (USA)-Clontinty Queen (Laurence O)
Mrs S D Williams Berry Racing

Placings:0   (4529)
2003/04: 16⁰GS,

	Starts	1st	2nd	3rd	Win & Pl
NH Flat	1	0	0	0	
Career Total	1	0	0	0	

Going:	Sf: 0-0 GS: 0-1 Gd: 0-0 GF: - Fm: 0-0

Distance: 2m/2m3: 0-1 2m4-2m7: 0-0 3m+: 0-0
Track: LH: 0-1 RH: 0-0 Tight: 0-0 Gall: 0-0
Aids: Bl: 0-0 Vi: 0-0 Tstrap: 0-0 Ckp: 0-0
Best Rating: 59 3/04 Chep 2m110y   gd-sft NHF

Fasgo (IRE)

108   (110h)**133+**

9-y-o b g Montelimar (USA)-Action Plan (Creative Plan (USA))
P F Nicholls F A Smith

Placings:1P31P0/2F235-1222P0   (4965)
2003/04: 26¹G, 29²S, 29²G, 33³G, 33P0G, 29P0GF,

	Starts	1st	2nd	3rd	Win & Pl
Chases	6	1	3	0	26440
Career Total	17	3	5	2	42049
133	11/03 NAbb	3m2f110yD(0-120)HCh	GD	£4725
118	2/02 Sand	3m110y D(0-115)HCh	SFT	£5005
110	11/01 Chep	3m F Hdl	G-S	£1918

Total win prize-money £11649

Going: Sf: 0-1 GS: 0-0 Gd: 1-4 GF: - Fm: 0-1
Distance: 2m/2m3: 0-0 2m4-2m7: 0-0 3m+: 1-6
Track: LH: 1-4 RH: 0-2 Tight: 1-2 Gall: 0-0
Aids: Bl: 0-0 Vi: 0-0 Tstrap: 0-0 Ckp: 0-0
Best Rating: 133 1/04 Chel 4m1f   good   Ch

Useful handicap chaser; stays well; likes soft ground; has been tried blinkered as he can race lazily; has become consistent after a wind operation in 2003.

Fashion House

100(85h)   92

8-y-o b m Homo Sapien-High Heels (IRE) (Supreme Leader)
S Pike Stewart Pike

Placings:50/0552-P4153   (4139)
2003/04: 21PG, 264GF, 241GF, 235G, 203G,

	Starts	1st	2nd	3rd	Win & Pl
Chases	5	1	0	1	7087
Career Total	11	1	1	1	7935
84	10/03 Ludl	3m	D(0-110)HCh	G-F	£5780

Total win prize-money £5780

Going: Sf: 0-0 GS: 0-0 Gd: 0-3 GF: - Fm: 1-2
Distance: 2m/2m3: 0-0 2m4-2m7: 0-0 3m+: 1-3
Track: LH: 0-2 RH: 1-3 Tight: 1-2 Gall: 0-0
Aids: Bl: 0-0 Vi: 0-0 Tstrap: 0-0 Ckp: 0-0
Best Rating: 92 4/03 Ludl 3m   good   Ch

Won two points in March 2003; a shade unlucky not to complete a hat-trick in modest hunter chase at Ludlow next month; jumped badly left when winning a match at the same venue in October; stays three miles; effective on fast ground.

Fashions Monty (IRE)

103(92h)   (97h)**100+**

8-y-o ch m Montelimar (USA)-Fashions Side (Quayside)
Ferdy Murphy Brian Mulholland

Placings:40/605050224/3P4106U03-PP01452   (4757)
2003/04: 25PGS, 27PGS, 25P0GS, 271GS, 25⁴G, 24⁵S, 25²S,

	Starts	1st	2nd	3rd	Win & Pl
Chases	7	1	1	0	6370
Career Total	27	2	3	2	17567
100	2/04 Sedg	3m3f	E(0-110)HCh	G-S	£5099
95	12/02 Limk	3m	(67-109)HHdl	HVY	£6773

Total win prize-money £11872

Going: Sf: 0-2 GS: 1-4 Gd: 0-1 GF: - Fm: 0-0
Distance: 2m/2m3: 0-0 2m4-2m7: 0-0 **3m+: 1-7**
Track: **LH: 1-5** RH: 0-2 **Tight: 1-4** Gall: 0-1
Aids: Bl: 0-0 Vi: 0-2 Tstrap: 0-0 Ckp: 0-0
Best Rating: 100 2/04 Sedg 3m3f   gd-sft   Ch

Moderate Irish-trained staying hurdler/chaser; runaway winner of handicap chase at Sedgefield in February; stays exceptionally well; suited by soft ground.

Fashions Mystique (IRE)

6-y-o b m Religiously (USA)-Fashions Side (Quayside)
Ferdy Murphy Miss J V Morgan

Placings:00   (4323)
2003/04: 16⁰G, 16⁰S,

	Starts	1st	2nd	3rd	Win & Pl
NH Flat	2	0	0	0	
Career Total	2	0	0	0	

Going: Sf: 0-1 GS: 0-0 Gd: 0-1 GF: - Fm: 0-0
Distance: 2m/2m3: 0-2 2m4-2m7: 0-0 3m+: 0-0
Track: LH: 0-2 RH: 0-1 Tight: 0-0 Gall: 0-0
Aids: Bl: 0-0 Vi: 0-0 Tstrap: 0-0 Ckp: 0-0

Fast King (FR)

(0c)**101**

6-y-o b g Housamix (FR)-Fast Girl (FR) (Gay Minstrel (FR))
Dr P Pritchard (P J Hobbs 1/5) Docs'R'Us

Placings:3105/05100F-43P   (1222)
2003/04: 19⁴GS, 20³GF, 17PGF,

	Starts	1st	2nd	3rd	Win & Pl
Hurdles	2	0	0	1	718
Chases	1	0	0	0	346
Career Total	13	2	0	2	8847
96	12/02 Tntn	2m3f110y	D(0-120)HHdl	G-S	£4342
90	11/01 Bang	2m1f	E Hdl	G-S	£2691

Total win prize-money £7034

Going: Sf: 0-0 GS: 0-1 Gd: 0-0 GF: - Fm: 0-2
Distance: 2m/2m3: 0-2 2m4-2m7: 0-1 3m+: 0-0
Track: LH: 0-2 RH: 0-1 Tight: 0-1 Gall: 0-0
Aids: Bl: 0-0 Vi: 0-0 Tstrap: 0-0 Ckp: 0-0
Best Rating: 101 11/01 Asct 2m110y   good   Hdl

Modest ex-French hurdler, suited by soft ground.

Fast Mix (FR)

101   118

5-y-o gr g Linamix (FR)-Fascinating Hill (FR) (Danehill (USA))
M C Pipe Jim Weeden

Placings:1P2F2-P0421F0P2   (4859)
2003/04: 16PG, 17⁰G, 17⁴G, 19²GS, 16¹G, 19FG, 16⁰GS, 17PG, 19²GF,

	Starts	1st	2nd	3rd	Win & Pl
Hurdles	9	1	2	0	8758
Career Total	14	2	4	0	15201
117	3/04 Plum	2m	D(0-115)HHdl	GD	£5488
103	11/02 Newb	2m110y	D Hdl	G-S	£4101

Total win prize-money £9590

Going: Sf: 0-0 GS: 0-2 Gd: 1-6 GF: - Fm: 0-1
Distance: **2m/2m3: 1-7** 2m4-2m7: 0-0 3m+: 0-0
Track: **LH: 1-2** RH: 0-7 **Tight: 1-5** Gall: 0-0

Aids: Bl: 0-0 Vi: **1-6** Tstrap: 0-0 Ckp: 0-0
Best Rating: 117 4/04 Tntn   2m3f110y   gd-fm Hdl

Modest hurdler; has ability, but is hard to win with; seems to handle any ground; has worn visor; likes to force the pace.

Fast Track (IRE)

85

7-y-o b/br g Doyoun-Manntika (Kalamoun)
N R Mitchell Mccourt Fine Meats Ltd & D J Rushen

Placings:006/F   (0139)
2003/04: 16FG,

	Starts	1st	2nd	3rd	Win & Pl
Hurdles	1	0	0	0	
Career Total	4	0	0	0	0

Going: Sf: 0-0 GS: 0-0 Gd: 0-1 GF: - Fm: 0-0
Distance: 2m/2m3: 0-1 2m4-2m7: 0-0 3m+: 0-0
Track: LH: 0-0 RH: 0-1 Tight: 0-0 Gall: 0-0
Aids: Bl: 0-0 Vi: 0-0 Tstrap: 0-0 Ckp: 0-0
Best Rating: 85 12/01 Hayd 2m   soft   Hdl

Faster Sweep (IRE)

7-y-o ch g Phardante (FR)-Sweeping Brush (IRE) (Brush Aside (USA))
W T Reed The Hot Chestnuts Club

Placings:2   (0044)
2003/04: 25²G,

	Starts	1st	2nd	3rd	Win & Pl
Chases	1	0	1	0	852
Career Total	1	0	1	0	852

Going: Sf: 0-0 GS: 0-0 Gd: 0-1 GF: - Fm: 0-0
Distance: 2m/2m3: 0-0 2m4-2m7: 0-0 3m+: 0-1
Track: LH: 0-1 RH: 0-0 Tight: 0-1 Gall: 0-0
Aids: Bl: 0-0 Vi: 0-0 Tstrap: 0-0 Ckp: 0-0
Best Rating: 84 4/03 Kels 3m1f   good   Ch

Fataliste (FR)

90(94h)   (73h)**73**

10-y-o b g Nikos-Faracha (FR) (Kenmare (FR))
B A Pearce Dennis Cook

Placings:501144211/50/F/P/00600623   (1172)
2003/04: 16⁰GF, 16⁰G, 16⁶GF, 16⁰GF, 16⁰G, 16⁶G, 20²GF, 20³GF,

	Starts	1st	2nd	3rd	Win & Pl
Hurdles	6	0	0	0	159
Chases	2	0	1	1	2290
Career Total	21	4	2	1	39067
138	4/98 Aint	2m110y	A Hdl	GD	£17180
138	2/98 Kemp	2m	A Hdl	G-F	£9509
118	9/97 Strf	2m110y	E Hdl	GD	£2176
	9/97 Autl	1m7f	Hdl	SFT	£6295

Total win prize-money £35161

Going: Sf: 0-0 GS: 0-0 Gd: 0-2 GF: - Fm: 0-6
Distance: 2m/2m3: 0-6 2m4-2m7: 0-2 3m+: 0-0
Track: LH: 0-4 RH: 0-3 Tight: 0-3 Gall: 0-1
Aids: Bl: 0-0 Vi: 0-1 Tstrap: 0-0 Ckp: 0-4
Best Rating: 138 2/99 Winc 2m   gd-sft   Hdl

Once a useful hurdler when with Martin Pipe, but moderate now.

Fatehalkhair (IRE)

(102h)   (125h)**128**
12-y-o ch g Kris-Midway Lady (USA) (Alleged (USA))
B Ellison   R Wagner

Placings:3232/11021134F1F/163301P0/04/011**F521464**/01
0P5421/1304P5-6   (4799)
2003/04: 17⁶G,

	Starts	1st	2nd	3rd	Win & Pl
Hurdles	1	0	0	0	
Career Total	50	13	5	6	84179
123 7/02 Sedg	2m5f110yD(0-120)HHdl		G-F		£3740
135 4/02 Sedg	3m4f	D(0-125)HCh	G-F		£14105
125 11/01 Sedg	2m5f110yB HHdl		SFT		£8438
125 12/00 Sedg	2m5f	E Ch	SFT		£3168
125 8/00 Sedg	2m110y E Ch		GD		£3042
106 7/00 Sedg	2m110y E Ch		FRM		£3168
131 2/99 Sedg	2m1f	D(0-125)HHdl	GD		£5836
120 7/98 Sedg	2m5f110yD(0-120)HHdl		G-F		£2843
117 2/98 Sedg	2m1f	D(0-125)HHdl	GD		£2952
105 10/97 Sedg	2m5f110yD(0-125)HHdl		G-F		£3685
106 9/97 Sedg	2m1f	E Hdl	G-F		£2320
101 5/97 Sedg	2m1f	F(0-100)HHdl	G-F		£2248
96 5/97 Sedg	2m1f	E Hdl	G-F		£2320
		Total win prize-money £57870			

Going:	Sf: 0-0 GS: 0-0 Gd: 0-1 GF: - Fm: 0-0
Distance:	2m/2m3: 0-1 2m4-2m7: 0-0 3m+: 0-0
Track:	LH: 0-1 RH: 0-0 Tight: 0-1 Gall: 0-0
Aids:	Bl: 0-0 Vi: 0-0 Tstrap: 0-0 Ckp: 0-0
Best Rating:	135 4/02 Sedg 3m4f gd-fm Ch

Useful chaser/fair hurdler; versatile performer; difficult to beat at Sedgefield where he has gained all of his jumps wins; stays three and a half miles; suited by a sound surface.

Father Abraham (IRE)

98(106h)   (103h)**97**
6-y-o b g Idris (IRE)-Mothers Blessing (Wolver Hollow)
J Akehurst (Noel Meade 4/5)   A D Spence

Placings:03452O-156PP06   (4305)
2003/04: 20¹S, 21⁵G, 20⁶GS, 20⁶G, 22⁵S, 16⁹G, 20⁶G,

	Starts	1st	2nd	3rd	Win & Pl
Hurdles	4	1	0	0	5528
Chases	3	0	0	0	0
Career Total	13	1	1	1	7730
103 5/03 Gowr	2m4f	Hdl	SFT	£5152
		Total win prize-money £5153

Going:	Sf: 1-2 GS: 0-1 Gd: 0-4 GF: - Fm: 0-0
Distance:	2m/2m3: 0-1 2m4-2m7: 1-6 3m+: 0-0
Track:	LH: 0-1 RH: 0-4 Tight: 0-1 Gall: 0-1
Aids:	Bl: 0-3 Vi: 0-0 Tstrap: 0-0 Ckp: 0-0
Best Rating:	107 2/03 Gowr 2m yield Hdl

Ex-Irish; winner over hurdles; pulled up on chase debut in first-time blinkers.

Father Andy (IRE)

11-y-o ch g Executive Perk-Twinkle Sunset (Deep Run)
R A Wernham   Philip Newton

Placings:526/0035F5/3312212F/6025/F22/F   (4626)
2003/04: 21⁵G,

	Starts	1st	2nd	3rd	Win & Pl
Chases	1	0	0	0	
Career Total	25	2	7	3	17541
93 3/00 Gowr	3m	Ch	YLD	£5520

---

89 2/00 Clon	3m	Ch	SH	£3036
		Total win prize-money £8556

Going:	Sf: 0-0 GS: 0-0 Gd: 0-1 GF: 0-0 Fm: 0-0
Distance:	2m/2m3: 0-0 2m4-2m7: 0-1 3m+: 0-0
Track:	LH: 0-1 RH: 0-0 Tight: 0-1 Gall: 0-0
Aids:	Bl: 0-0 Vi: 0-0 Tstrap: 0-1 Ckp: 0-0
Best Rating:	127 4/00 Aint 3m1f good Ch

Father Bob

7-y-o gr g Bold Fox-Annie Bee (Rusticaro (FR))
P D Niven (B S Rothwell 6/7)   R N Forman

Placings:PPFP   (3691)
2003/04: 19⁵G, 17⁹GS, 19⁴GS, 19⁶G,

	Starts	1st	2nd	3rd	Win & Pl
Hurdles	3	0	0	0	0
Chases	1	0	0	0	0
Career Total	4	0	0	0	

Going:	Sf: 0-0 GS: 0-2 Gd: 0-2 GF: - Fm: 0-0
Distance:	2m/2m3: 0-3 2m4-2m7: 0-1 3m+: 0-0
Track:	LH: 0-2 RH: 0-2 Tight: 0-4 Gall: 0-0
Aids:	Bl: 0-0 Vi: 0-0 Tstrap: 0-0 Ckp: 0-0

Father D (IRE)

(101h)   (97dh)
9-y-o b g Mister Lord (USA)-Abrahams Cross (IRE) (Bustomi)
R H Buckler   C T & A Samways

Placings:03P2401/F00014-000F   (4576)
2003/04: 18⁰G, 24⁰GF, 20⁰GF, 18⁷G,

	Starts	1st	2nd	3rd	Win & Pl
Hurdles	3	0	0	0	0
Chases	1	0	0	0	0
Career Total	17	2	1	1	7657
97 4/03 Extr	2m3f	F(0-90)HHdl	G-F	£3835
100 4/02 Uttx	2m	E Hdl	GD	£2702
		Total win prize-money £6537

Going:	Sf: 0-0 GS: 0-0 Gd: 0-2 GF: - Fm: 0-2
Distance:	2m/2m3: 0-2 2m4-2m7: 0-1 3m+: 0-1
Track:	LH: 0-2 RH: 0-1 Tight: 0-0 Gall: 0-1
Aids:	Bl: 0-0 Vi: 0-0 Tstrap: 0-0 Ckp: 0-0
Best Rating:	105 12/01 NAbb 2m1f heavy NHF

Moderate hurdler; keen front-running sort; won over two miles at Uttoxeter in April 2002; returned to form when winning at Exeter April 2003; acts on ground good and faster.

Father Mulcahy

87   **78**
8-y-o b g Safawan-Constant Delight (Never So Bold)
D McCain   D McCain

Placings:43/3020/P034P-P25P14P   (2944)
2003/04: 20⁰G, 23⁴HY, 16⁵GF, 16⁸GF, 22¹GF, 22⁴GS, 20⁸S,

	Starts	1st	2nd	3rd	Win & Pl
Hurdles	1	0	0	0	0
Chases	6	1	1	0	5501
Career Total	18	1	2	3	9090
78 11/03 Hayd	2m6f	E Ch	G-F	£3605
		Total win prize-money £3605

Going:	Sf: 0-2 GS: 0-1 Gd: 0-1 GF: - Fm: 1-3
Distance:	2m/2m3: 0-2 2m4-2m7: 1-5 3m+: 0-0
Track:	LH: 1-6 RH: 0-1 Tight: 0-1 Gall: 0-0
Aids:	Bl: 0-1 Vi: 1-3 Tstrap: 0-0 Ckp: 0-1

Best Rating: 100 3/02 Uttx   2m4f110y   heavy   Hdl

Novicechaser/hurdler; returned from 684 days off to run a creditable third at Towcester in January 2002; gained first carerr win in modest novice chase at Haydock on good to firm in November 2003; suited by heavy ground; stays 2m7f.

Father Paddy

102(102h)   (104h)**97**
9-y-o ch g Minster Son-Sister Claire (Quayside)
T J Fitzgerald   P McMahon

Placings:321/6/5063/32-2   (4794)
2003/04: 21²G,

	Starts	1st	2nd	3rd	Win & Pl
Chases	1	0	1	0	1381
Career Total	11	1	3	3	9051
107 3/00 Carl	2m1f	H NHF	G-S	£4446
		Total win prize-money £4446

Going:	Sf: 0-0 GS: 0-0 Gd: 0-1 GF: - Fm: 0-0
Distance:	2m/2m3: 0-0 2m4-2m7: 0-1 3m+: 0-0
Track:	LH: 0-1 RH: 0-0 Tight: 0-1 Gall: 0-0
Aids:	Bl: 0-0 Vi: 0-0 Tstrap: 0-0 Ckp: 0-0
Best Rating:	107 3/00 Carl 2m1f gd-sft NHF

Lightly-raced bumper winner who has shown only moderate form over hurdles and fences.

Father Rector (IRE)

15-y-o b g The Parson-Mwanamio (Sole Mio (USA))
Mrs F E Needham   William Lamarque

Placings:05/5056f12U350/504303P/64263211461016/13F/
111P/240141550/5/41043/116F-34   (0416)
2003/04: 25³GF, 22⁴G,

	Starts	1st	2nd	3rd	Win & Pl
Chases	2	0	1	0	207
Career Total	62	15	4	7	62239
104 6/02 MRas	2m6f110yH Ch		G-F	£1757
105 5/02 Weth	3m1f	H Ch	G-F	£1547
113 5/01 MRas	2m6f110yH Ch		G-F	£2460
126 10/99 Strf	2m5f110yC(0-135)HCh		G-F	£8008
125 6/99 Worc	2m4f110yD(0-120)HCh		G-F	£3923
124 10/98 Winc	2m5f	E(0-115)HCh	G-F	£4580
123 10/98 MRas	2m6f110yH Ch		G-F	£2052
117 5/98 Hrfd	2m3f	H Ch	GD	£1830
122 2/98 Hntg	3m	H Ch	GD	£1213
104 3/97 Thur	3m	Ch	GD	£2712
117 9/96 List	3m	HHdl	G-F	£7371
117 8/96 Tram	2m4f	(0-109)HHdl	GD	£2824
110 8/96 Gway	2m5f190y HHdl		G-F	£9974
114 11/94 Clon	3m	Hdl	HVY	£2120
11/94 Clon	2m	NHF	Y-S	£2446
		Total win prize-money £54822

Going:	Sf: 0-0 GS: 0-0 Gd: 0-1 GF: - Fm: 0-1
Distance:	2m/2m3: 0-0 2m4-2m7: 0-1 3m+: 0-1
Track:	LH: 0-1 RH: 0-1 Tight: 0-1 Gall: 0-1
Aids:	Bl: 0-0 Vi: 0-0 Tstrap: 0-0 Ckp: 0-0
Best Rating:	129 5/99 Uttx 2m4f gd-fm Ch

Veteran pointer/hunter chaser, suited by fast ground; stays three miles plus, but looks better at shorter.

Fathom

6-y-o ch g Zafonic (USA)-River Lullaby (USA) (Riverman (USA))
Mrs L B Normile   K J Fehilly

Placings:00-P   (0557)

2003/04: 16PGF,

	Starts	1st	2nd	3rd	Win & Pl
Hurdles	1	0	0	0	
Career Total	3	0	0	0	

Going: Sf: 0-0 GS: 0-0 Gd: 0-0 GF: - Fm: 0-1
Distance: 2m/2m3: 0-1 2m4-2m7: 0-0 3m+: 0-0
Track: LH: 0-0 RH: 0-1 Tight: 0-0 Gall: 0-0
Aids: Bl: 0-0 Vi: 0-0 Tstrap: 0-0 Ckp: 0-0
Best Rating: 70 4/03 Prth 2m110y good NHF

Fattaan (IRE)
94   73+
4-y-o b g Danehill (USA)-Bintalshaati (Kris)
J G M O'Shea (P J Hobbs 16/10) Gary Roberts

Placings:514 (1673)
2003/04: 17¹GF, 17¹F, 16⁴F,

	Starts	1st	2nd	3rd	Win & Pl
Hurdles	3	1	0	0	3341
Career Total	3	1	0	0	3341
70	9/03 Extr	2m1f	E Hdl	FRM	£3341
				Total win prize-money	£3341

Going: Sf: 0-0 GS: 0-0 Gd: 0-0 GF: - Fm: 1-3
Distance: 2m/2m3: 1-3 2m4-2m7: 0-0 3m+: 0-0
Track: LH: 0-1 RH: 1-2 Tight: 0-1 Gall: 0-0
Aids: Bl: 0-0 Vi: 0-0 Tstrap: 0-0 Ckp: 0-0
Best Rating: 73 10/03 Towc 2m firm Hdl

Very moderate hurdler; acts on firm.

Fauntleroy (IRE)
83   60
5-y-o b g Lord Americo-Ballyroe Ann (IRE) (Over The River (FR))
J A Supple A W K Merriam

Placings:00000 (3916)
2003/04: 17⁹GS, 16⁹GS, 16⁹S, 19⁰G, 20⁰G,

	Starts	1st	2nd	3rd	Win & Pl
NH Flat	2	0	0	0	0
Hurdles	3	0	0	0	0
Career Total	5	0	0	0	0

Going: Sf: 0-1 GS: 0-2 Gd: 0-2 GF: - Fm: 0-0
Distance: 2m/2m3: 0-4 2m4-2m7: 0-1 3m+: 0-0
Track: LH: 0-2 RH: 0-3 Tight: 0-3 Gall: 0-2
Aids: Bl: 0-0 Vi: 0-0 Tstrap: 0-0 Ckp: 0-0
Best Rating: 60 1/04 Hntg 2m110y soft Hdl

Favoured Option (IRE)
105   (20h)122
9-y-o ch g Glacial Storm (USA)-Hot House Flower (Derring Rose)
Ian Williams K A Cosby

Placings:006/P20351/0F634321P/U52222211-2354 (2464)
2003/04: 25²GF, 23³GF, 24⁵GF, 22⁴S,

	Starts	1st	2nd	3rd	Win & Pl
Chases	4	0	1	1	2773
Career Total	31	4	8	4	43940
122	4/03 Carl	3m	D(0-125)HCh	G-F	£13975
122	4/03 Hrfd	3m1f110y	E(0-110)HCh	G-F	£6097
106	4/02 Carl	3m2f	D(0-115)HCh	G-F	£7003
97	2/01 Folk	2m6f110y	E Hdl	HVY	£2544
				Total win prize-money	£29621

Going: Sf: 0-1 GS: 0-0 Gd: 0-0 GF: - Fm: 0-3
Distance: 2m/2m3: 0-2 2m4-2m7: 0-1 3m+: 0-3
Track: LH: 0-1 RH: 0-3 Tight: 0-0 Gall: 0-0
Aids: Bl: 0-0 Vi: 0-0 Tstrap: 0-0 Ckp: 0-0
Best Rating: 122 5/03 Winc 3m1f110y gd-fm Ch

Fair chaser; ended a frustrating run of seconds when winning a weakly contested extended three mile handicap at Hereford in April 2003 and followed up at Carlisle two weeks later; seems weighted up to the hilt now; stays three and a half miles; suited by fast ground, but effective with cut.

Fayrway Rhythm (IRE)
103(79h)   (36h)99+
7-y-o b g Fayruz-The Way She Moves (North Stoke)
Ian Emmerson Ms Josie Swinburn

Placings:06/3446031230/06-6532 (4880)
2003/04: 16⁶G, 17⁵GS, 16³S, 20²GS,

	Starts	1st	2nd	3rd	Win & Pl
Chases	4	0	1	1	1997
Career Total	18	1	2	4	6551
103	11/01 Tntn	2m1f	G(0-90)HHdl	GD	£1732
				Total win prize-money	£1733

Going: Sf: 0-1 GS: 0-2 Gd: 0-1 GF: - Fm: 0-0
Distance: 2m/2m3: 0-3 2m4-2m7: 0-1 3m+: 0-0
Track: LH: 0-2 RH: 0-2 Tight: 0-1 Gall: 0-0
Aids: Bl: 0-0 Vi: 0-4 Tstrap: 0-0 Ckp: 0-0
Best Rating: 103 11/01 Carl 2m1f heavy Hdl

Moderate chaser; best around two and a half miles; acts on good or soft.

Fays Two (IRE)
83f   53f
6-y-o b m Binary Star (USA)-Claudette (Claude Monet (USA))
A Robson A Robson

Placings:00 (4885)
2003/04: 16⁹GF, 17⁰GS,

	Starts	1st	2nd	3rd	Win & Pl
NH Flat	2	0	0	0	0
Career Total	2	0	0	0	

Going: Sf: 0-0 GS: 0-1 Gd: 0-0 GF: - Fm: 0-1
Distance: 2m/2m3: 0-2 2m4-2m7: 0-0 3m+: 0-0
Track: LH: 0-0 RH: 0-2 Tight: 0-1 Gall: 0-0
Aids: Bl: 0-0 Vi: 0-0 Tstrap: 0-0 Ckp: 0-0
Best Rating: 53 12/03 Muss 2m gd-fm NHF

Feanor
107   (0c)101
6-y-o b m Presidium-Nouvelle Cuisine (Yawa)
Mrs S A Watt Mrs S A Watt

Placings:5F653P133/UPPP0-250131254P00 (3885)
2003/04: 16²GF, 16⁵GF, 17⁰GF, 17¹GF, 16³GF, 17¹GF, 17²GS, 17⁵G, 16⁴S, 20²GF, 16⁹G, 16⁸G,

	Starts	1st	2nd	3rd	Win & Pl
Hurdles	11	2	2	1	12044
Chases	1	0	0	0	0
Career Total	26	3	2	4	16415
98	7/03 Sthl	2m1f	D(0-125)HHdl	G-F	£5434
91	6/03 Sthl	2m1f	E(0-110)HHdl	G-F	£3423
95	1/02 Catt	2m	E Hdl	SFT	£2723
				Total win prize-money	£11580

Going: Sf: 0-1 GS: 0-1 Gd: 0-3 GF: - Fm: 2-7
Distance: 2m/2m3: 2-11 2m4-2m7: 0-1 3m+: 0-0
Track: LH: 2-9 RH: 0-3 Tight: 0-7 Gall: 0-0
Aids: Bl: 0-0 Vi: 0-0 Tstrap: 0-0 Ckp: 0-0
Best Rating: 101 12/03 Hexm 2m110y soft Hdl

Modest hurdler; in good form in the summer of 2003; pulled up on chase debut; effective at 2m; seems to handle all types of ground.

Fear Siuil (IRE)
108   123
11-y-o b g Strong Gale-Astral River (Over The River (FR))
Nick Williams Mrs Jane Williams

Placings:0P0/54P/P/P1FPP3/4212P34-P03P111030 (4889)
2003/04: 16⁶G, 20⁰GF, 20³GF, 21⁵GS, 21¹GF, 24¹GF, 20¹GF, 24⁵GF, 20³GF, 20⁰GF,

	Starts	1st	2nd	3rd	Win & Pl
Chases	10	3	0	2	19878
Career Total	30	5	2	4	39032
123	10/03 Strf	2m4f	D(0-125)HCh	G-F	£4745
123	9/03 Strf	3m	D(0-125)HCh	G-F	£7273
122	8/03 NAbb	2m5f110y	D(0-120)HCh	G-F	£5369
110	7/02 Strf	2m4f	D(0-125)HCh	G-F	£8190
110	11/01 Catt	2m3f	E(0-115)HCh	G-F	£5027
				Total win prize-money	£30605

Going: Sf: 0-0 GS: 0-1 Gd: 0-1 GF: - Fm: 3-8
Distance: 2m/2m3: 0-1 2m4-2m7: 2-7 3m+: 1-2
Track: LH: 3-8 RH: 0-3 Tight: 3-7 Gall: 0-0
Aids: Bl: 0-0 Vi: 0-0 Tstrap: 3-10 Ckp: 0-0
Best Rating: 123 10/03 Strf 2m4f gd-fm Ch

Fair chaser; in good form in the autumn of 2003, landing a hat-trick despite a rise of 18lb; stays 3m, but effective at shorter; suited by a sharp track; best on a sound surface; has worn a tongue tie.

Feel The Pride (IRE)
110   131+
6-y-o b m Persian Bold-Nordic Pride (Horage)
Jonjo O'Neill Mrs M Liston

Placings:3-111311P201U (4963)
2003/04: 16¹GF, 16¹G, 17¹GF, 16³GF, 16¹GS, 16¹S, 16⁶GS, 16²G, 18⁹GS, 16¹GS, 20ᵁG,

	Starts	1st	2nd	3rd	Win & Pl
Hurdles	11	6	1	1	61186
Career Total	12	6	1	2	62025
128	4/04 Ayr	2m	B HHdl	G-S	£17664
129	11/03 Ayr	2m	B HHdl	SFT	£14841
124	11/03 Hayd	2m	C(0-130)HHdl	G-S	£11924
112	7/03 MRas	2m1f110y	D Hdl	G-F	£5492
112	6/03 Strf	2m110y	E Hdl	GD	£4212
93	6/03 Uttx	2m	E Hdl	G-F	£3490
				Total win prize-money	£57626

Going: Sf: 1-1 GS: 2-4 Gd: 1-3 GF: - Fm: 2-3
Distance: 2m/2m3: 6-10 2m4-2m7: 0-1 3m+: 0-0
Track: LH: 5-7 RH: 1-4 Tight: 2-3 Gall: 0-0
Aids: Bl: 3-7 Vi: 0-0 Tstrap: 0-0 Ckp: 0-0
Best Rating: 129 11/03 Ayr 2m soft Hdl

Useful hurdler; completed a hat-trick in novice hurdles in the summer of 2003; improved for easy ground and the application of blinkers when scoring twice in valuable mares' races in November; best around two miles; acts on any ground.

Feeling Fizzical
86   29
6-y-o b g Feelings (FR)-Stepdaughter (Relkino)

Mrs J C McGregor Mrs Dorothy Thomson

Placings:PP-0 (1763)
2003/04: 24⁰GF,

	Starts	1st	2nd	3rd	Win & Pl
Hurdles	1	0	0	0	
Career Total	3	0	0	0	

Going:	Sf: 0-0 GS: 0-0 Gd: 0-0 GF: - Fm: 0-0
Distance:	2m/2m3: 0-0 2m4-2m7: 0-0 3m+: 0-1
Track:	LH: 0-0 RH: 0-1 Tight: 0-0 Gall: 0-0
Aids:	Bl: 0-0 Vi: 0-0 Tstrap: 0-0 Ckp: 0-0
Best Rating:	32 10/03 Carl 3m110y gd-fm Hdl

Feeling Grand (IRE)

12-y-o b/br g Naheez (USA)-Tourneys Girl (Yankee Gold)
Mrs Richard Arthur Mrs Richard Arthur

Placings:0/0360/00F6FP12/130651/15U524131/50P/P
(0255)
2003/04: 16²G,

	Starts	1st	2nd	3rd	Win & Pl
Chases	1	0	0	0	
Career Total	32	6	2	3	49662
132	4/01	Leop	2m1f	(0-127)HCh	SH	£10483
130	1/01	Leop	2m3f	HCh	SFT	£13104
118	5/00	Punc	2m	(0-127)HCh	G-F	£7800
114	4/00	Gowr	2m2f	(0-116)HCh	G-Y	£4416
111	11/99	Naas	2m3f	(0-130)HCh	Y-S	£4928
94	4/99	Cork	2m		Y-S	£4296
				Total win prize-money £45031

Going:	Sf: 0-0 GS: 0-0 Gd: 0-1 GF: - Fm: 0-0
Distance:	2m/2m3: 0-1 2m4-2m7: 0-0 3m+: 0-0
Track:	LH: 0-0 RH: 0-1 Tight: 0-0 Gall: 0-0
Aids:	Bl: 0-0 Vi: 0-0 Tstrap: 0-0 Ckp: 0-0
Best Rating:	132 4/01 Leop 2m1f sft-hvy Ch

Feizor (IRE)

80   42

4-y-o ch f Titus Livius (FR)-Blues Queen (Lahib (USA))
R F Fisher Great Head House Estates Limited

Placings:4 (1133)
2003/04: 17⁴G,

	Starts	1st	2nd	3rd	Win & Pl
Hurdles	1	0	0	0	264
Career Total	1	0	0	0	264

Going:	Sf: 0-0 GS: 0-0 Gd: 0-1 GF: - Fm: 0-0
Distance:	2m/2m3: 0-1 2m4-2m7: 0-0 3m+: 0-0
Track:	LH: 0-1 RH: 0-0 Tight: 0-1 Gall: 0-0
Aids:	Bl: 0-0 Vi: 0-0 Tstrap: 0-0 Ckp: 0-0
Best Rating:	42 8/03 Bang 2m1f good Hdl

Felix (IRE)

97(78c)   (44c)86

8-y-o b g Religiously (USA)-Knock Bantiama (Abednego)
Miss K M George The Entrepreneurs

Placings:P2P3624460P0 (4148)
2003/04: 23⁵GF, 22²GF, 26⁶G, 22³GF, 22⁶GF, 24²GF, 22⁴G, 22⁴G, 22⁶G, 19⁰G, 24⁴G, 19⁰G,

	Starts	1st	2nd	3rd	Win & Pl
Hurdles	9	0	2	1	2405
Chases	3	0	0	0	0
Career Total	12	0	2	1	2405

Going:	Sf: 0-0 GS: 0-0 Gd: 0-7 GF: - Fm: 0-5
Distance:	2m/2m3: 0-1 2m4-2m7: 0-7 3m+: 0-4
Track:	LH: 0-5 RH: 0-6 Tight: 0-6 Gall: 0-0
Aids:	Bl: 0-8 Vi: 0-0 Tstrap: 0-0 Ckp: 0-3
Best Rating:	86 9/03 Worc 3m gd-fm Hdl

Plating-class hurdler; modest form in Irish points; has had his limitations exposed at up to 3m over hurdles; has worn blinkers and cheekpieces;

Felix Darby (IRE)

99(94h)   (73 h)94+

9-y-o b g Buckskin (FR)-Cool Anne (Orchardist)
Mrs G Harvey Ms Pat Treacy

Placings:44542-PR24431 (4817)
2003/04: 25⁵GF, 23³HY, 24²GF, 25⁴S, 26⁴GS, 24³GS, 24¹G,

	Starts	1st	2nd	3rd	Win & Pl
Chases	7	1	1		6503
Career Total	12	1	2	1	8432
94	4/04	Chep	3m	E(0-110)HCh	GD	£4585
				Total win prize-money £4586

Going:	Sf: 0-2 GS: 0-2 Gd: 1-1 GF: - Fm: 0-2
Distance:	2m/2m3: 0-0 2m4-2m7: 0-2 3m+: 1-6
Track:	LH: 1-5 RH: 0-2 Tight: 0-1 Gall: 0-0
Aids:	Bl: 0-0 Vi: 0-0 Tstrap: 0-0 Ckp: 0-0
Best Rating:	94 4/04 Chep 3m good Ch

Moderate chaser stays well; acts on fast ground.

Felixrdotcom

96   106

8-y-o ch g Gran Alba (USA)-Golden Curd (FR) (Nice Havrais (USA))
N J Gifford Felix Rosenstiel's Widow & Son

Placings:6/5P42/P04 (4777)
2003/04: 16⁶HY, 18⁹G, 23⁴G,

	Starts	1st	2nd	3rd	Win & Pl
Hurdles	3	0	0	0	548
Career Total	8	0	1	0	1556

Going:	Sf: 0-1 GS: 0-0 Gd: 0-2 GF: - Fm: 0-0
Distance:	2m/2m3: 0-2 2m4-2m7: 0-0 3m+: 0-1
Track:	LH: 0-2 RH: 0-1 Tight: 0-2 Gall: 0-0
Aids:	Bl: 0-0 Vi: 0-0 Tstrap: 0-0 Ckp: 0-0
Best Rating:	106 3/02 Font 2m2f110y soft Hdl

Moderate hurdler; best at around two miles; acts on soft ground.

Fellow Ship

76   90+

4-y-o b g Elmaamul (USA)-Genoa (Zafonic (USA))
P Butler (G A Butler 11/9) E H Whatmough

Placings:F00 (3511)
2003/04: 16⁶GF, 16⁹G, 18⁹G,

	Starts	1st	2nd	3rd	Win & Pl
Hurdles	3	0	0	0	
Career Total	3	0	0	0	

Going:	Sf: 0-0 GS: 0-0 Gd: 0-2 GF: - Fm: 0-1
Distance:	2m/2m3: 0-3 2m4-2m7: 0-0 3m+: 0-0
Track:	LH: 0-1 RH: 0-2 Tight: 0-1 Gall: 0-0
Aids:	Bl: 0-0 Vi: 0-0 Tstrap: 0-2 Ckp: 0-0
Best Rating:	80 10/03 Kemp 2m gd-fm Hdl

Felony (IRE)

90   66

9-y-o ch g Pharly (FR)-Scales Of Justice (Final Straw)
L P Grassick Baskerville Racing Club

Placings:P0063/1/P/00PP45-4P000 (4441)
2003/04: 16⁴GS, 24⁵G, 19⁰G, 16⁹GF, 21⁰S,

	Starts	1st	2nd	3rd	Win & Pl
Hurdles	5	0	0	0	0
Career Total	18	1	0	1	1865
82	5/99	Hrfd	2m3f110yG	Hdl	G-S	£1658
				Total win prize-money £1658

Going:	Sf: 0-1 GS: 0-1 Gd: 0-2 GF: - Fm: 0-1
Distance:	2m/2m3: 0-2 2m4-2m7: 0-2 3m+: 0-1
Track:	LH: 0-3 RH: 0-2 Tight: 0-2 Gall: 0-0
Aids:	Bl: 0-0 Vi: 0-0 Tstrap: 0-4 Ckp: 0-1
Best Rating:	82 5/99 Hrfd 2m3f110y gd-sft Hdl

Fen Gypsy

60

6-y-o b g Nashwan (USA)-Didicoy (USA) (Danzig (USA))
P D Evans P D Evans

Placings:00-P (2154)
2003/04: 16⁵GS,

	Starts	1st	2nd	3rd	Win & Pl
Hurdles	1	0	0	0	
Career Total	3	0	0	0	

Going:	Sf: 0-0 GS: 0-1 Gd: 0-0 GF: - Fm: 0-0
Distance:	2m/2m3: 0-0 2m4-2m7: 0-0 3m+: 0-0
Track:	LH: 0-1 RH: 0-0 Tight: 0-0 Gall: 0-0
Aids:	Bl: 0-0 Vi: 0-0 Tstrap: 0-0 Ckp: 0-0
Best Rating:	60 12/02 Ludl 2m good Hdl

Fencote (IRE)

103   86

7-y-o b g Norwich-Primrose Forest (Menelek)
P Beaumont Mrs H M Richardson

Placings:FU04 (4685)
2003/04: 18⁶S, 19¹⁰G, 20⁹GS, 16⁴G,

	Starts	1st	2nd	3rd	Win & Pl
Hurdles	4	0	0	0	283
Career Total	4	0	0	0	283

Going:	Sf: 0-1 GS: 0-1 Gd: 0-2 GF: - Fm: 0-0
Distance:	2m/2m3: 0-3 2m4-2m7: 0-1 3m+: 0-0
Track:	LH: 0-4 RH: 0-0 Tight: 0-3 Gall: 0-1
Aids:	Bl: 0-0 Vi: 0-0 Tstrap: 0-0 Ckp: 0-0
Best Rating:	88 4/04 Kels 2m110y good Hdl

Fencote Gold

92f   74f

4-y-o ch g Bob's Return (IRE)-Goldaw (Gala Performance (ZIM))
P Beaumont Mrs H M Richardson

Placings:6 (3738)
2003/04: 16⁶G,

	Starts	1st	2nd	3rd	Win & Pl
NH Flat	1	0	0	0	0
Career Total	1	0	0	0	0

Going:	Sf: 0-0 GS: 0-0 Gd: 0-1 GF: - Fm: 0-0

Distance:	2m/2m3: 0-1 2m4-2m7: 0-0 3m+: 0-0
Track:	LH: 0-0 RH: 0-0 Tight: 0-1 Gall: 0-0
Aids:	Bl: 0-0 Vi: 0-0 Tstrap: 0-0 Ckp: 0-0
Best Rating:	74 2/04 Muss 2m good NHF

Fenix (GER)
113   129
5-y-o b g Lavirco (GER)-Frille (FR) (Shareef Dancer (USA))
Mrs L Wadham (P Rau 18/10) P A Philipps,T S Redman &
J S Redman

Placings:441322   (4874)
2003/04: 16⁴GS, 16⁴HY, 17¹GS, 16³S, 16²GS, 20²GS,

	Starts	1st	2nd	3rd	Win & Pl
Hurdles	6	1	2	1	15338
Career Total	6	1	2	1	15338
110 2/04 Folk 2m1f110yE Hdl				G-S	£3584
			Total win prize-money £3584		

Going:	Sf: 0-2 GS: 1-4 Gd: 0-0 GF: - Fm: 0-0
Distance:	2m/2m3: 1-5 2m4-2m7: 0-1 3m+: 0-0
Track:	LH: 0-2 RH: 1-4 Tight: 1-2 Gall: 0-1
Aids:	Bl: 0-0 Vi: 0-0 Tstrap: 0-0 Ckp: 0-0
Best Rating:	129 3/04 Newb 2m110y gd-sft Hdl

Fair hurdler; useful Flat performer in Germany; well held on British debut over hurdles in January, but much improved latest when scoring at Folkestone in February; suited by two miles; best on good ground; has worn blinkers.

Fenney Spring
98f   90f
4-y-o b f Polish Precedent (USA)-Sliiprail (USA) (Our Native (USA))
W Jenks Michael Stoddart

Placings:421   (4345)
2003/04: 16⁴G, 16²G, 16¹GS,

	Starts	1st	2nd	3rd	Win & Pl
NH Flat	3	1	1	0	2733
Career Total	3	1	1	0	2733
90 3/04 Wwck 2m			H NHF	G-S	£1995
			Total win prize-money £1995		

Going:	Sf: 0-0 GS: 1-1 Gd: 0-2 GF: - Fm: 0-0
Distance:	2m/2m3: 1-3 2m4-2m7: 0-0 3m+: 0-0
Track:	LH: 1-2 RH: 0-1 Tight: 0-1 Gall: 0-0
Aids:	Bl: 0-0 Vi: 0-0 Tstrap: 0-0 Ckp: 0-0
Best Rating:	90 3/04 Wwck 2m gd-sft NHF

Modest form in bumper company; acts on good ground.

Fergal The Piler
67   8
5-y-o b g Jendali (USA)-Dorado Beach (Lugana Beach)
N G Richards Taranto De Pol

Placings:00   (4908)
2003/04: 16⁵G, 20²S,

	Starts	1st	2nd	3rd	Win & Pl
Hurdles	2	0	0	0	
Career Total	2	0	0	0	

Going:	Sf: 0-1 GS: 0-0 Gd: 0-1 GF: - Fm: 0-0
Distance:	2m/2m3: 0-1 2m4-2m7: 0-1 3m+: 0-0
Track:	LH: 0-1 RH: 0-1 Tight: 0-1 Gall: 0-0
Aids:	Bl: 0-0 Vi: 0-0 Tstrap: 0-0 Ckp: 0-0
Best Rating:	10 4/04 Kels 2m110y good Hdl

Ferimon
99f   99+f
5-y-o br g Terimon-Rhyming Moppet (Rymer)
H D Daly Strachan Myddleton Gabb Stoddart Lawson

Placings:1   (3354)
2003/04: 16¹S,

	Starts	1st	2nd	3rd	Win & Pl
NH Flat	1	1	0	0	1950
Career Total	1	1	0	0	1950
99 1/04 Hntg 2m110y H NHF				SFT	£1949
			Total win prize-money £1950		

Going:	Sf: 1-1 GS: 0-0 Gd: 0-0 GF: - Fm: 0-0
Distance:	2m/2m3: 1-1 2m4-2m7: 0-0 3m+: 0-0
Track:	LH: 0-0 RH: 1-1 Tight: 0-0 Gall: 1-1
Aids:	Bl: 0-0 Vi: 0-0 Tstrap: 0-0 Ckp: 0-0
Best Rating:	99 1/04 Hntg 2m110y soft NHF

Won despite greeness when winning soft ground bumper on debut at Huntingdon in January; will stay a trip in time.

Fern Lord (IRE)
98(96h)   (114+h)104
7-y-o ch h Mister Lord (USA)-Deep Fern (Deep Run)
Jonjo O'Neill Mrs L Busteed

Placings:051-3PFF   (4048)
2003/04: 22³S, 22⁵S, 25⁶GS, 22⁶FG,

	Starts	1st	2nd	3rd	Win & Pl
Chases	4	0	0	1	529
Career Total	7	1	0	1	6096
114 3/03 Newb 3m110y D Hdl				SFT	£5271
			Total win prize-money £5272		

Going:	Sf: 0-2 GS: 0-1 Gd: 0-1 GF: - Fm: 0-0
Distance:	2m/2m3: 0-0 2m4-2m7: 0-3 3m+: 0-1
Track:	LH: 0-2 RH: 0-2 Tight: 0-0 Gall: 0-1
Aids:	Bl: 0-0 Vi: 0-0 Tstrap: 0-0 Ckp: 0-0
Best Rating:	114 3/03 Newb 3m110y soft Hdl

Winning hurdler; promise on chase debut but pulled up next time; stays three miles plus; effective in soft ground.

Fidalus (IRE)
65   73
11-y-o b g Mandalus-Fifi L'Amour (Fair Turn)
R C Guest Miss S Howell

Placings:054/460022505203 1/1010234F05341/14450/4000
F44/0/F50P   (4814)
2003/04: 24⁴GS, 22⁵GS, 20⁹HY, 19⁶FG,

	Starts	1st	2nd	3rd	Win & Pl
Chases	4	0	0	0	
Career Total	46	5	4	3	30889
119 1/00 Tram 2m4f Ch				SH	£6900
110 4/99 Punc 3m (0-120)HHdl				GD	£6752
103 7/98 Limk 2m5f (0-109)HHdl				YLD	£3586
105 6/98 Tram 2m4f (0-95)HHdl				G-Y	£2382
105 4/98 Cork 2m4f NHF				SH	£2978
		Total win prize-money £22600			

Going:	Sf: 0-1 GS: 0-2 Gd: 0-1 GF: - Fm: 0-0
Distance:	2m/2m3: 0-0 2m4-2m7: 0-3 3m+: 0-1
Track:	LH: 0-2 RH: 0-2 Tight: 0-1 Gall: 0-0
Aids:	Bl: 0-1 Vi: 0-0 Tstrap: 0-0 Ckp: 0-0
Best Rating:	119 1/00 Tram 2m4f sft-hvy Ch

Fiddlers Creek (IRE)
95   85
5-y-o b g Danehill (USA)-Mythical Creek (USA) (Pleasant

Tap (USA))
R Allan I Flannigan, R Allan & A Grant

Placings:55   (4073)
2003/04: 17⁵GS, 16⁵F,

	Starts	1st	2nd	3rd	Win & Pl
Hurdles	2	0	0	0	0
Career Total	2	0	0	0	0

Going:	Sf: 0-0 GS: 0-1 Gd: 0-0 GF: - Fm: 0-1
Distance:	2m/2m3: 0-2 2m4-2m7: 0-0 3m+: 0-0
Track:	LH: 0-1 RH: 0-1 Tight: 0-2 Gall: 0-0
Aids:	Bl: 0-0 Vi: 0-0 Tstrap: 0-0 Ckp: 0-0
Best Rating:	85 2/04 Muss 2m firm Hdl

Field Of Blue
5-y-o b g Shambo-Flashing Silks (Kind Of Hush)
P Winkworth A G Russell

Placings:00P   (4664)
2003/04: 16⁵S, 16⁹G, 19³GS,

	Starts	1st	2nd	3rd	Win & Pl
NH Flat	2	0	0	0	0
Hurdles	1	0	0	0	0
Career Total	3	0	0	0	0

Going:	Sf: 0-1 GS: 0-1 Gd: 0-1 GF: - Fm: 0-0
Distance:	2m/2m3: 0-2 2m4-2m7: 0-1 3m+: 0-0
Track:	LH: 0-1 RH: 0-2 Tight: 0-1 Gall: 0-1
Aids:	Bl: 0-0 Vi: 0-0 Tstrap: 0-0 Ckp: 0-0
Best Rating:	72 3/04 Hntg 2m110y good NHF

Fielding's Hay (IRE)
104(92h)   (85h)93
8-y-o b m Supreme Leader-Kates Fling (USA) (Quiet Fling (USA))
Mrs J Candlish Greencard Golfers

Placings:0/134U55/0P0642-114P   (4941)
2003/04: 24¹GF, 22¹GS, 25⁴G, 31³GS,

	Starts	1st	2nd	3rd	Win & Pl
Chases	4	2	0	0	7537
Career Total	17	3	1	1	11329
93 3/04 Towc 2m6f F(0-100)HCh				G-S	£3202
93 5/03 Hntg 3m F(0-90)HCh				G-F	£3776
108 5/01 Sthl 2m H NHF				G-F	£1561
			Total win prize-money £8558		

Going:	Sf: 0-0 GS: 1-2 Gd: 0-1 GF: - Fm: 1-1
Distance:	2m/2m3: 0-0 2m4-2m7: 1-1 3m+: 1-3
Track:	LH: 0-0 RH: 2-3 Tight: 0-0 Gall: 1-1
Aids:	Bl: 0-0 Vi: 0-0 Tstrap: 0-0 Ckp: 0-0
Best Rating:	108 5/01 Sthl 2m gd-fm NHF

Moderate chaser; stays beyond three miles; acts on fast and easy ground.

Fieldings Society (IRE)
88f   65f
5-y-o ch g Moscow Society (USA)-Lone Trail (IRE) (Strong Gale)
Mrs J Candlish Martin Jump

Placings:0   (1605)
2003/04: 17⁰GF,

	Starts	1st	2nd	3rd	Win & Pl
NH Flat	1	0	0	0	
Career Total	1	0	0	0	

Going:	Sf: 0-0 GS: 0-0 Gd: 0-0 GF: - Fm: 0-1
Distance:	2m2/m3: 0-1 1m4-2m7: 0-0 3m+: 0-0
Track:	LH: 0-0 RH: 0-1 Tight: 0-0 Gall: 0-0
Aids:	Bl: 0-0 Vi: 0-0 Tstrap: 0-0 Ckp: 0-0
Best Rating:	65 10/03 Carl 2m1f gd-fm NHF

Fields Of Home (IRE)

105　　　　　116+

6-y-o b m Synefos (USA)-Homefield Girl (IRE) (Rahotep (FR))
J Howard Johnson　Mrs Lucy Forbes

Placings:21F　　　　　(4910)
2003/04: 22²S, 21¹GS, 24²S,

	Starts	1st	2nd	3rd	Win & Pl
Chases	3	1	1	0	7168
Career Total	3	1	1	0	7168
118 2/04 Sedg 2m5f D Ch				G-S	£5720

Total win prize-money £5720

Going:	Sf: 0-2 GS: 1-1 Gd: 0-0 GF: - Fm: 0-0
Distance:	2m2/m3: 0-0 **2m4-2m7: 1-2** 3m+: 0-1
Track:	**LH: 1-2** RH: 0-1 **Tight: 1-2** Gall: 0-0
Aids:	Bl: 0-0 Vi: 0-0 Tstrap: 0-0 Ckp: 0-0
Best Rating:	118 2/04 Sedg 2m5f gd-sft Ch

Won sole start in Irish points; successful by a wide margin in mares' only novices' chase at Sedgefield in February; will be suited by three miles.

Fier Goumier (FR)

98　　　　　104

9-y-o b g Chef De Clan Ii (FR)-Azilal (FR) (Rex Magna (FR))
Jonjo O'Neill　John P McManus

Placings:6S2/61405/211P34/006-62PP　　　　　(1631)
2003/04: 16⁶GF, 21²GF, 24⁴PG, 21⁵GF,

	Starts	1st	2nd	3rd	Win & Pl
Chases	4	0	1	0	1984
Career Total	21	3	3	1	31109
114 7/01 Tipp 2m4f HCh				GD	£13104
105 6/01 Kbgn 2m4f (0-116)HCh				GD	£7862
73 6/00 Kbgn 2m4f Ch				G-F	£3450

Total win prize-money £24418

Going:	Sf: 0-0 GS: 0-0 Gd: 0-1 GF: - Fm: 0-3
Distance:	2m2/m3: 0-1 2m4-2m7: 0-2 3m+: 0-1
Track:	LH: 0-3 RH: 0-1 Tight: 0-1 Gall: 0-0
Aids:	Bl: 0-1 Vi: 0-0 Tstrap: 0-2 Ckp: 0-1
Best Rating:	114 7/01 Tipp 2m4f good Ch

Moderate ex-Irish chaser; now with Jonjo O'Neill; won three times over two miles four over fences on good ground; has been tongue tied; has been tried in blinkers.

Fiery Creek

98　　　　　69

7-y-o ch m Moscow Society (USA)-Deep Creek (Deep Run)
D J Wintle　John W Egan

Placings:30/000-P040　　　　　(3352)
2003/04: 21⁵PS, 22⁰GS, 17⁴HY, 16⁰S,

	Starts	1st	2nd	3rd	Win & Pl
Hurdles	4	0	0	0	0
Career Total	9	0	0	1	271

Going:	Sf: 0-3 GS: 0-1 Gd: 0-0 GF: - Fm: 0-0
Distance:	2m2/m3: 0-2 2m4-2m7: 0-2 3m+: 0-6
Track:	LH: 0-0 RH: 0-4 Tight: 0-2 Gall: 0-1
Aids:	Bl: 0-0 Vi: 0-0 Tstrap: 0-0 Ckp: 0-0
Best Rating:	89 2/02 Wwck 2m heavy NHF

Plating-class hurdler; acts on heavy ground.

Fiery Peace

110(101h)　　　(97h)115+

7-y-o ch g Tina's Pet-Burning Mirage (Pamroy)
H D Daly　R M Kirkland

Placings:5P0/65F0-23423211　　　　　(4593)
2003/04: 19²GF, 16³GF, 16⁴G, 17²GF, 16³GF, 16²GF, 16¹GF, 16¹G,

	Starts	1st	2nd	3rd	Win & Pl
Hurdles	3	0	1	1	1634
Chases	5	2	2	1	13315
Career Total	15	2	3	2	14949
112 3/04 Hntg 2m110y E(0-105)HCh				GD	£4056
110 12/03 Ludl 2m D(0-115)HCh				G-F	£6630

Total win prize-money £10686

Going:	Sf: 0-0 GS: 0-0 Gd: 1-2 GF: - Fm: 1-6
Distance:	**2m2/m3: 2-7** 2m4-2m7: 0-1 3m+: 0-0
Track:	LH: 0-3 **RH: 2-5** Tight: 1-2 Gall: 1-1
Aids:	Bl: 0-0 Vi: 0-0 Tstrap: 0-0 Ckp: 0-0
Best Rating:	112 3/04 Hntg 2m110y good Ch

Fair chaser; best at 2m; acts on fast ground.

Fiery Ring (IRE)

109　　　　(121h)129

9-y-o b g Torus-Kakemona (Kambalda)
J R H Fowler　S P Tindall

Placings:00/61F46/63350/6P00043F50/313133525-2002404326130　　　　　(4769a)
2003/04: 16²YS, 20⁰YS, 20⁹GF, 17²GF, 16⁴F, 19⁹GY, 16⁴GF, 17³S, 19²YS, 16⁶HY, 17¹GY, 16⁸S, 17⁰Y,

	Starts	1st	2nd	3rd	Win & Pl
Chases	13	1	3	2	25660
Career Total	44	4	4	9	61471
129 2/04 Fair 2m1f (0-135)HCh				G-Y	£9169
128 10/02 Limk 2m1f Ch				GD	£9969
107 6/02 Limk 2m1f Ch				G-Y	£7619
108 1/00 Fair 2m Hdl				SFT	£3312

Total win prize-money £30070

Going:	Sf: 0-3 GS: 0-0 Gd: 0-0 GF: - Fm: 0-4
Distance:	**2m2/m3: 1-11** 2m4-2m7: 0-2 3m+: 0-0
Track:	LH: 0-4 **RH: 1-7** Tight: 0-1 Gall: 0-0
Aids:	Bl: 0-0 Vi: 0-0 Tstrap: 0-0 Ckp: 0-0
Best Rating:	129 3/04 Punc 2m soft Ch

Useful chaser; Irish trained; best at around two miles on good or easy ground.

Fifteen Reds

100(71c)　　　(51c)84

9-y-o b g Jumbo Hirt (USA)-Dominance (Dominion)
J C Haynes　J C Haynes

Placings:20/56/460/60635/2553O1550-5300600　　　　　(3235)
2003/04: 24⁵GS, 27³S, 24⁰G, 26⁰GF, 21⁶GF, 24⁰S, 24⁰GF,

	Starts	1st	2nd	3rd	Win & Pl
Hurdles	6	0	0	1	491
Chases	1	0	0	0	0
Career Total	28	1	2	3	4675
87 10/02 Hexm 3m F(0-100)HHdl				GD	£2170

Total win prize-money £2170

Fifth Generation (IRE)

96　　　　(95c)110

14-y-o b g Bulldozer-Fragrant's Last (Little Buskins)
Dr P Pritchard　Mrs T Pritchard

Placings:40/24U4/633.5F/01111/30F/6U00026F00/P544254010/05P524P0U2131O443035/3602103040020-604U5450555066　　　　　(4774)
2003/04: 16⁶G, 19⁰G, 22⁴GS, 20⁰GF, 19⁵GF, 16⁴GF, 20⁵G, 16⁰GS, 16⁵G, 16⁵S, 16⁰G, 18⁶G, 16⁶G,

	Starts	1st	2nd	3rd	Win & Pl
Hurdles	14	0	0	0	4538
Career Total	86	8	7	8	42141
94 7/02 Strf 2m110y E(0-110)HHdl				G-F	£4056
96 1/02 Uttx 2m F(0-90)Hdl				HVY	£1946
90 12/01 Leic 2m4f110yG(0-90)HHdl				HVY	£1988
96 4/01 NAbb 2m6f E(0-105)HHdl				SFT	£3136
114 12/97 Limk 2m4f (0-123)HCh				HVY	£3391
107 12/97 Clon 2m4f (0-102)HCh				HVY	£3899
95 12/97 Thur 2m4f (0-109)HCh				SFT	£2204
93 11/97 Clon 2m4f (0-109)HCh				HVY	£3391

Total win prize-money £24012

Going:	Sf: 0-1 GS: 0-2 Gd: 0-8 GF: - Fm: 0-3
Distance:	2m2/m3: 0-11 2m4-2m7: 0-3 3m+: 0-0
Track:	LH: 0-9 RH: 0-5 Tight: 0-6 Gall: 0-0
Aids:	Bl: 0-0 Vi: 0-0 Tstrap: 0-0 Ckp: 0-0
Best Rating:	114 12/97 Limk 2m4f heavy Ch

Plating-class hurdler; probably best over two miles; likes to make the running.

Fifty Franks (IRE)

100　　　　　77

5-y-o b h Oscar (IRE)-Deny's Run (IRE) (Commanche Run)
M D Hammond　Frank Hanson

Placings:54204　　　　　(4731)
2003/04: 16⁵GS, 16⁴G, 16²S, 22⁰G, 20⁴G,

	Starts	1st	2nd	3rd	Win & Pl
NH Flat	3	0	1	0	570
Hurdles	2	0	0	0	309
Career Total	5	0	1	0	879

Going:	Sf: 0-1 GS: 0-1 Gd: 0-3 GF: - Fm: 0-0
Distance:	2m2/m3: 0-3 2m4-2m7: 0-2 3m+: 0-0
Track:	LH: 0-3 RH: 0-1 Tight: 0-1 Gall: 0-0
Aids:	Bl: 0-0 Vi: 0-0 Tstrap: 0-0 Ckp: 0-0
Best Rating:	91 2/04 Weth 2m soft NHF

Has shown some ability in bumpers; should stay well.

Figaro Du Rocher (FR)

106　　　　　97

4-y-o ch g Beyssac (FR)-Fabinou (FR) (Cavan)
M C Pipe　Simon Roberts

Placings:120220005225　　　　　(4818)
2003/04: 17¹G, 17²GF, 16⁰G, 16²GF, 16²GF, 16⁰G, 17⁰G, 19⁰GS, 17⁵G, 17²G, 17²GS, 17⁵GF,

	Starts	1st	2nd	3rd	Win & Pl
Hurdles	12	1	5	0	8785

Career Total	12	1	5	0		8785
6/03	Vire	2m1f	Hdl		GD	£2805

Total win prize-money £2805

Going:	Sf: 0-0 GS: 0-2 Gd: 1-6 GF: - Fm: 0-4
Distance:	**2m/2m3: 1-11** 2m4-2m7: 0-1 3m+: 0-0
Track:	LH: 0-5 RH: 0-6 Tight: 0-6 Gall: 0-1
Aids:	Bl: 1-1 Vi: 0-9 Tstrap: 0-2 Ckp: 0-0
Best Rating:	99 3/04 Extr 2m1f gd-sft Hdl

Modest hurdler; winner over hurdles in France; runner-up three of his first four starts; has not progressed including in a visor; keen sort.

Figawin

101   91+

9-y-o b g Rudimentary (USA)-Dear Person (Rainbow Quest (USA))
P A Blockley C A Walton

Placings:5540066/625F3453/230U060363F1/52/50-1
                                                              (3917)
2003/04: 24[1]G,

	Starts	1st	2nd	3rd	Win & Pl
Chases	1	1	0	0	4440
Career Total	32	2	3	5	13535
93	2/04	Fknm	3m110y	F(0-100)HCh	GD	£4439
90	4/01	Fknm	2m5f110yF(0-110)HCh	G-S	£4231

Total win prize-money £8672

Going:	Sf: 0-0 GS: 0-0 Gd: 1-1 GF: - Fm: 0-0
Distance:	2m/2m3: 0-0 2m4-2m7: 0-0 **3m+: 1-1**
Track:	LH: 1-1 RH: 0-0 **Tight: 1-1** Gall: 0-0
Aids:	Bl: 0-0 Vi: 0-0 Tstrap: 0-0 Ckp: 0-0
Best Rating:	93 2/04 Fknm 3m110y good Ch

Plating-class chaser, suited by good and soft ground; stays well; goes well at Fakenham.

Fighting Chance (IRE)

108f   97f

4-y-o b g Germany (USA)-Una Juna (IRE) (Good Thyne (USA))
R H Alner Peter Bonner

Placings:3   (4578)
2003/04: 16[3]G,

	Starts	1st	2nd	3rd	Win & Pl
NH Flat	1	0	0	1	474
Career Total	1	0	0	1	474

Going:	Sf: 0-0 GS: 0-0 Gd: 0-1 GF: - Fm: 0-0
Distance:	2m/2m3: 0-1 2m4-2m7: 0-0 3m+: 0-0
Track:	LH: 0-1 RH: 0-0 Tight: 0-0 Gall: 0-1
Aids:	Bl: 0-0 Vi: 0-0 Tstrap: 0-0 Ckp: 0-0
Best Rating:	97 3/04 Newb 2m110y good NHF

Fighting Times

                                                              (42h)

12-y-o b g Good Times (ITY)-Duellist (Town Crier)
Miss K Marks Nick Shutts

Placings:06012/021043/2050F/0/P   (0456)
2003/04: 21[P]HY,

	Starts	1st	2nd	3rd	Win & Pl
Chases	1	0	0	0	
Career Total	18	2	3	1	6592
81	2/99	NAbb	2m110y	E Ch	HVY	£2697
78	2/98	Tntn	2m1f	G(0-95)HHdl	G-F	£1495

Total win prize-money £4192

Going:	Sf: 0-1 GS: 0-0 Gd: 0-0 GF: - Fm: 0-0
Distance:	2m/2m3: 0-0 2m4-2m7: 0-1 3m+: 0-0
Track:	LH: 0-1 RH: 0-0 Tight: 0-0 Gall: 0-0
Aids:	Bl: 0-0 Vi: 0-1 Tstrap: 0-0 Ckp: 0-0
Best Rating:	88 6/99 Worc 2m gd-fm Hdl

Fille Detente

70f   69f

4-y-o ch f Double Trigger (IRE)-Matoaka (Be My Chief (USA))
Mrs P Sly David L Bayliss

Placings:004   (3920)
2003/04: 12[0]GF, 12[0]GF, 16[4]G,

	Starts	1st	2nd	3rd	Win & Pl
NH Flat	3	0	0	0	0
Career Total	3	0	0	0	0

Going:	Sf: 0-0 GS: 0-0 Gd: 0-1 GF: - Fm: 0-2
Distance:	2m/2m3: 0-1 2m4-2m7: 0-0 3m+: 0-0
Track:	LH: 0-3 RH: 0-0 Tight: 0-1 Gall: 0-0
Aids:	Bl: 0-0 Vi: 0-0 Tstrap: 0-0 Ckp: 0-0
Best Rating:	69 2/04 Fknm 2m good NHF

Fils A Papa (FR)

90   82

5-y-o b g Double Bed (FR)-Syvanie (FR) (Sicyos (USA))
F Doumen M Charlton

Placings:2-10300   (2919)
2003/04: 18[1]HO, 18[0]VS, 19[3]VS, 18[0]VS, 21[0]G,

	Starts	1st	2nd	3rd	Win & Pl
Hurdles	5	1	0	1	21156
Career Total	6	1	1	1	27046
10/03	Engh	2m2f	Hdl		HLD	£14338

Total win prize-money £14338

Going:	Sf: 0-0 GS: 0-0 Gd: 0-1 GF: - Fm: 0-0
Distance:	2m/2m3: 1-3 2m4-2m7: 0-2 3m+: 0-0
Track:	LH: 0-1 RH: 0-1 Tight: 0-0 Gall: 0-0
Aids:	Bl: 0-0 Vi: 0-0 Tstrap: 0-0 Ckp: 0-0
Best Rating:	82 12/03 Kemp 2m5f good Hdl

French hurdler; stays 2m 5f; acts in soft ground.

Filscot

12-y-o b g Scottish Reel-Fillilode (Mossberry)
Mrs S S Harbour P J Morgan

Placings:261/F443/31400124/2542224023/5F21244303P/5
030P34/12436144P2-53   (4717)
2003/04: 23[5]G, 24[3]G,

	Starts	1st	2nd	3rd	Win & Pl
Chases	2	0	0	1	415
Career Total	55	6	11	9	39789
100	7/02	Strf	3m	D(0-115)HCh	GD	£6942
100	5/02	Hrfd	3m1f110yF(0-95)HCh	GD	£3926
113	10/00	Ludl	2m4f	E Ch	G-F	£3081
105	2/99	Kemp	2m5f	D(0-120)HHdl	GD	£3680
108	5/98	Hntg	2m4f110yE Hdl	G-F	£2530
103	4/97	NAbb	2m1f	H NHF	FRM	£1278

Total win prize-money £21437

Going:	Sf: 0-0 GS: 0-0 Gd: 0-2 GF: - Fm: 0-0
Distance:	2m/2m3: 0-0 2m4-2m7: 0-0 3m+: 0-2
Track:	LH: 0-0 RH: 0-2 Tight: 0-1 Gall: 0-0
Aids:	Bl: 0-0 Vi: 0-0 Tstrap: 0-0 Ckp: 0-0
Best Rating:	116 11/99 Leic 2m7f110y gd-fm Ch

Modest hunter chaser; best on a sound surface; stays three miles.

Fin Bec (FR)

108   121

11-y-o b g Tip Moss (FR)-Tourbrune (FR) (Pamponi (FR))
A P Jones P Newell

Placings:30/235332/3411PU/35125621UP/35P24046/3UP
PP1541-11P   (3041)
2003/04: 22[1]G, 28[1]G, 24[P]GS,

	Starts	1st	2nd	3rd	Win & Pl
Chases	3	2	0	0	5900
Career Total	44	8	5	8	43262
121	11/03	MRas	3m4f110yD(0-120)HCh	GD	£3653
121	11/03	Towc	2m6f	E(0-105)HCh	GD	£2247
120	4/03	MRas	3m1f	F(0-95)Ch	GD	£3720
104	1/03	Leic	2m4f110yE(0-105)HCh	SFT	£5512
106	1/01	Folk	3m2f	F(0-100)HCh	HVY	£2520
111	1/00	Sthl	3m110y	E Hdl	HVY	£2710
106	3/00	Sand	3m110y	D(0-115)HCh	GD	£5027
106	2/00	Leic	2m4f110yF(0-95)HCh	SFT	£3526

Total win prize-money £28918

Going:	Sf: 0-0 GS: 0-1 Gd: 2-2 GF: - Fm: 0-0
Distance:	2m/2m3: 0-0 2m4-2m7: 1-1 3m+: 1-2
Track:	LH: 0-1 **RH: 2-2** Tight: 1-1 Gall: 0-1
Aids:	**Bl: 2-3** Vi: 0-0 Tstrap: 0-0 Ckp: 0-0
Best Rating:	121 11/03 MRas 3m4f110y good Ch

Modest chaser; likes to front run; has won last three chases; stays three miles plus but effective over shorter; suited by soft ground; usually wears blinkers and has worn sheepskin cheekpieces.

Final Command

72   48

7-y-o ch g Gildoran-Fine Fettle (Final Straw)
J C Tuck The Fine Gild Racing Partnership

Placings:2[/]P0   (4691)
2003/04: 20[P]S, 17[0]G,

	Starts	1st	2nd	3rd	Win & Pl
Hurdles	2	0	0	0	
Career Total	3	0	1	0	492

Going:	Sf: 0-1 GS: 0-0 Gd: 0-1 GF: - Fm: 0-0
Distance:	2m/2m3: 0-1 2m4-2m7: 0-1 3m+: 0-0
Track:	LH: 0-0 RH: 0-2 Tight: 0-0 Gall: 0-0
Aids:	Bl: 0-0 Vi: 0-0 Tstrap: 0-0 Ckp: 0-0
Best Rating:	101 4/02 Towc 2m good NHF

Final Dancer

75   53

9-y-o b g Ski Dancer-Final Flirtation (Clear Run)
N A Twiston-Davies The Yes - No - Wait Sorries

Placings:0   (1013)
2003/04: 20[0]GF,

	Starts	1st	2nd	3rd	Win & Pl
Hurdles	1	0	0	0	
Career Total	1	0	0	0	

Going:	Sf: 0-0 GS: 0-0 Gd: 0-0 GF: - Fm: 0-1
Distance:	2m/2m3: 0-0 2m4-2m7: 0-1 3m+: 0-0
Track:	LH: 0-1 RH: 0-0 Tight: 0-0 Gall: 0-0
Aids:	Bl: 0-0 Vi: 0-0 Tstrap: 0-0 Ckp: 0-0
Best Rating:	59 8/03 Worc 2m4f gd-fm Hdl

Final Deal (IRE)

5-y-o b g Rashar (USA)-Cute Boro (IRE) (Borovoe)
C J Down P Holland

Placings:U (3779)
2003/04: 21^UG,

	Starts	1st	2nd	3rd	Win & Pl
Hurdles	1	0	0	0	
Career Total	1	0	0	0	

Going: Sf: 0-0 GS: 0-0 Gd: 0-1 GF: - Fm: 0-0
Distance: 2m/2m3: 0-0 2m4-2m7: 0-1 3m+: 0-0
Track: LH: 0-0 RH: 0-1 Tight: 0-0 Gall: 0-0
Aids: Bl: 0-0 Vi: 0-0 Tstrap: 0-0 Ckp: 0-0

Final Lap
88   68

8-y-o b g Batshoof-Lap Of Honour (Final Straw)
S T Lewis Simon T Lewis

Placings:0PP/6U000P040/600P15P023335000-000PPP0P00 (3081)
2003/04: 17^UGS, 16⁰G, 17⁰GF, 20^PG, 16^PG, 22^PGF, 16⁰GF, 22^PG, 16⁰GS, 16⁰GS,

	Starts	1st	2nd	3rd	Win & Pl
Hurdles	10	0	0	0	
Career Total	38	1	1	3	3802
72 8/02 Strf 2m110y G Hdl				SFT	£2254

Total win prize-money £2254

Going: Sf: 0-0 GS: 0-3 Gd: 0-4 GF: - Fm: 0-3
Distance: 2m/2m3: 0-7 2m4-2m7: 0-3 3m+: 0-0
Track: LH: 0-6 RH: 0-3 Tight: 0-5 Gall: 0-1
Aids: Bl: 0-0 Vi: 0-0 Tstrap: 0-0 Ckp: 0-0
Best Rating: 78   11/02   Hrfd   2m1f   good   Hdl

Final Project (IRE)

12-y-o ch g Project Manager-Tower Belle (Tower Walk)
Mrs G Drury Mrs G Drury

Placings:0064312/50/015U21F0F0006F/20/P (0354)
2003/04: 21^PGF,

	Starts	1st	2nd	3rd	Win & Pl
Chases	1	0	0	0	
Career Total	26	3	3	1	10538
112 7/98 Klny 2m6f Ch				G-F	£2989
127 5/98 Clon 2m4f (0-102)HHdl				G-F	£2382
105 4/96 Tipp 2m Hdl				SFT	£2824

Total win prize-money £8197

Going: Sf: 0-0 GS: 0-0 Gd: 0-0 GF: - Fm: 0-1
Distance: 2m/2m3: 0-0 2m4-2m7: 0-1 3m+: 0-0
Track: LH: 0-0 RH: 0-1 Tight: 0-1 Gall: 0-0
Aids: Bl: 0-0 Vi: 0-0 Tstrap: 0-0 Ckp: 0-0
Best Rating: 127   5/98   Clon   2m4f   gd-fm   Hdl

Final View (FR)

5-y-o b g Distant View (USA)-Unafurtivalagrima (USA)
(Quest For Fame)
N P Littmoden V And J Properties

Placings:0-P (2030)
2003/04: 26^PG,

	Starts	1st	2nd	3rd	Win & Pl
Hurdles	1	0	0	0	

Career Total   2   0   0   0

Going: Sf: 0-0 GS: 0-0 Gd: 0-1 GF: - Fm: 0-0
Distance: 2m/2m3: 0-0 2m4-2m7: 0-0 3m+: 0-1
Track: LH: 0-1 RH: 0-0 Tight: 0-0 Gall: 0-0
Aids: Bl: 0-0 Vi: 0-0 Tstrap: 0-0 Ckp: 0-0

Finbar's Law
98   93

7-y-o b g Contract Law (USA)-De Valera (Faustus (USA))
R Johnson Mrs June Quinn

Placings:P/O6/P04P01-205F40 (4760)
2003/04: 20²G, 20⁰G, 24⁴GS, 16^FHY, 17⁴HY, 16⁰S,

	Starts	1st	2nd	3rd	Win & Pl
Hurdles	5	0	1	0	1775
Chases	1	0	0	0	
Career Total	15	1	1	0	5693
89 3/03 Hexm 2m110y E Hdl				GD	£3657

Total win prize-money £3658

Going: Sf: 0-3 GS: 0-0 Gd: 0-3 GF: - Fm: 0-0
Distance: 2m/2m3: 0-3 2m4-2m7: 0-2 3m+: 0-1
Track: LH: 0-3 RH: 0-3 Tight: 0-0 Gall: 0-0
Aids: Bl: 0-0 Vi: 0-0 Tstrap: 0-6 Ckp: 0-0
Best Rating: 93   5/03   Hexm   2m4f110y   good   Hdl

Finbar's Revenge
106   111+

9-y-o b g Gildoran-Grotto Princess (Pollerton)
S E H Sherwood K A Price

Placings:3251/F05652/PF1P (4916)
2003/04: 24^PGS, 24^FG, 24¹GS, 23^PGS,

	Starts	1st	2nd	3rd	Win & Pl
Chases	4	1	0	0	4466
Career Total	14	2	2	1	10555
111 3/04 Strf 3m E(0-110)HCh				G-S	£4466
105 4/01 Hrfd 2m3f110yE(0-105)HHdl				GD	£3514

Total win prize-money £7980

Going: Sf: 0-0 GS: 1-3 Gd: 0-1 GF: - Fm: 0-0
Distance: 2m/2m3: 0-0 2m4-2m7: 0-0 3m+: 1-4
Track: LH: 1-2 RH: 0-2 Tight: 1-1 Gall: 0-1
Aids: Bl: 1-3 Vi: 0-0 Tstrap: 0-0 Ckp: 0-0
Best Rating: 111   3/04   Strf   3m   gd-sft   Ch

Moderate chaser; lightly-raced; stays 3m; acts on yielding ground; has been successful in blinkers.

Finches Lane (IRE)
67

10-y-o b g Le Bavard (FR)-Alice Mann (Mandalus)
Miss Victoria Roberts D C Roberts

Placings:0/56/0P (4897)
2003/04: 19⁰GS, 22^PG,

	Starts	1st	2nd	3rd	Win & Pl
Hurdles	2	0	0	0	
Career Total	5	0	0	0	0

Going: Sf: 0-0 GS: 0-1 Gd: 0-1 GF: - Fm: 0-0
Distance: 2m/2m3: 0-0 2m4-2m7: 0-2 3m+: 0-0
Track: LH: 0-1 RH: 0-1 Tight: 0-1 Gall: 0-0
Aids: Bl: 0-0 Vi: 0-0 Tstrap: 0-0 Ckp: 0-0
Best Rating: 99   9/00   Fair   2m   gd-fm   NHF

Find Me Another (IRE)

8-y-o b g Shardari-Naujwan Too (Kafu)
Mrs Caroline Bailey Charles Dixey

Placings:2 (4302)
2003/04: 20²G,

	Starts	1st	2nd	3rd	Win & Pl
Chases	1	0	1	0	686
Career Total	1	0	1	0	686

Going: Sf: 0-0 GS: 0-0 Gd: 0-1 GF: - Fm: 0-0
Distance: 2m/2m3: 0-0 2m4-2m7: 0-1 3m+: 0-0
Track: LH: 0-0 RH: 0-1 Tight: 0-0 Gall: 0-0
Aids: Bl: 0-0 Vi: 0-0 Tstrap: 0-0 Ckp: 0-0
Best Rating: 88   3/04   Leic   2m4f110y   good   Ch

Fine And Dandy (IRE)

8-y-o b g Roselier (FR)-Hawthorn Dandy (Deep Run)
J M Turner J M Turner

Placings:0/P4P/2 (0350)
2003/04: 21²GF,

	Starts	1st	2nd	3rd	Win & Pl
Chases	1	0	1	0	651
Career Total	5	0	1	0	651

Going: Sf: 0-0 GS: 0-0 Gd: 0-0 GF: - Fm: 0-1
Distance: 2m/2m3: 0-0 2m4-2m7: 0-1 3m+: 0-0
Track: LH: 0-0 RH: 0-1 Tight: 0-1 Gall: 0-0
Aids: Bl: 0-0 Vi: 0-0 Tstrap: 0-0 Ckp: 0-0
Best Rating: 88   5/03   Folk   2m5f   gd-fm   Ch

Fine Frenzy (IRE)
88   73

4-y-o b f Great Commotion (USA)-Fine Project (IRE)
(Project Manager)
Miss S J Wilton (J W Hills 14/10) John Pointon And Sons

Placings:3UP (2839)
2003/04: 16³GF, 16^UGF, 16^PGS,

	Starts	1st	2nd	3rd	Win & Pl
Hurdles	3	0	0	1	322
Career Total	3	0	0	1	322

Going: Sf: 0-0 GS: 0-1 Gd: 0-0 GF: - Fm: 0-2
Distance: 2m/2m3: 0-3 2m4-2m7: 0-0 3m+: 0-0
Track: LH: 0-1 RH: 0-2 Tight: 0-0 Gall: 0-0
Aids: Bl: 0-0 Vi: 0-0 Tstrap: 0-0 Ckp: 0-0
Best Rating: 73   11/03   Leic   2m   gd-fm   Hdl

Fine Times

10-y-o b g Timeless Times (USA)-Marfen (Lochnager)
Milson Robinson Milson Robinson

Placings:0P/0P/1/5-F (0160)
2003/04: 24^FGF,

	Starts	1st	2nd	3rd	Win & Pl
Chases	1	0	0	0	
Career Total	7	1	0	0	1091

87	4/02	MRas	3m1f	H Ch	GD	£1090

Total win prize-money £1091

Going:	Sf: 0-0 GS: 0-0 Gd: 0-0 GF: 0-0 Fm: 0-1
Distance:	2m/2m3: 0-0 2m4-2m7: 0-0 3m+: 0-1
Track:	LH: 0-1 RH: 0-0 Tight: 0-1 Gall: 0-0
Aids:	Bl: 0-0 Vi: 0-0 Tstrap: 0-1 Ckp: 0-0
Best Rating:	87 4/02 MRas 3m1f good Ch

Finely Tuned (IRE)
105f   103f

5-y-o g g Lord Americo-Gusserane Princess (Paddy's Stream)
M Pitman Malcolm C Denmark

Placings:305   (4213)
2003/04: 16³GS, 16⁰G, 16⁵G,

	Starts	1st	2nd	3rd	Win & Pl
NH Flat	3	0	0	1	378
Career Total	3	0	0	1	378

Going:	Sf: 0-0 GS: 0-1 Gd: 0-2 GF: - Fm: 0-0
Distance:	2m/2m3: 0-3 2m4-2m7: 0-0 3m+: 0-0
Track:	LH: 0-2 RH: 0-1 Tight: 0-0 Gall: 0-2
Aids:	Bl: 0-0 Vi: 0-0 Tstrap: 0-0 Ckp: 0-0
Best Rating:	103 12/03 Newb 2m110y gd-sft NHF

Made a pleasing debut at Newbury in hot bumper in December when third and running green; held subsequently.

Finzi (IRE)
98   99

6-y-o b g Zaffaran (USA)-Sporting Talent (IRE) (Seymour Hicks (FR))
M Scudamore The Meld Partnership

Placings:00-535305   (4508)
2003/04: 21⁵GF, 26³GS, 24⁵HY, 23³S, 24⁰G, 26⁵GS,

	Starts	1st	2nd	3rd	Win & Pl
Hurdles	6	0	0	2	1223
Career Total	8	0	0	2	1223

Going:	Sf: 0-2 GS: 0-2 Gd: 0-1 GF: - Fm: 0-1
Distance:	2m/2m3: 0-0 2m4-2m7: 0-2 3m+: 0-4
Track:	LH: 0-3 RH: 0-3 Tight: 0-1 Gall: 0-2
Aids:	Bl: 0-0 Vi: 0-0 Tstrap: 0-0 Ckp: 0-0
Best Rating:	99 12/03 Hntg 3m2f gd-sft Hdl

Moderate form in bumpers/novice hurdles; seems to stay well.

Fiolino (FR)
(102h)   (74h)

11-y-o b g Bayolidaan (FR)-Vellea (FR) (Cap Martin (FR))
M W Easterby Mrs M E Curtis

Placings:0440/04062/P61P55323/PFP0-3PP   (0414)
2003/04: 24³G, 22²G, 25²G,

	Starts	1st	2nd	3rd	Win & Pl
Hurdles	1	0	0	1	390
Chases	2	0	0	0	0
Career Total	25	1	2	3	6171
95	12/01	Uttx	3m	E(0-105)HCh	SFT	£3159

Total win prize-money £3159

Going:	Sf: 0-0 GS: 0-0 Gd: 0-3 GF: - Fm: 0-0
Distance:	2m/2m3: 0-0 2m4-2m7: 0-1 3m+: 0-2
Track:	LH: 0-3 RH: 0-0 Tight: 0-1 Gall: 0-0
Aids:	Bl: 0-1 Vi: 0-0 Tstrap: 0-0 Ckp: 0-0
Best Rating:	99 3/02 Hexm 4m heavy Ch

Moderate staying chaser/plating-class hurdler; acts on soft ground; tends to make mistakes over fences; best held up; stays well.

Fionn Mac Cumaill (IRE)

5-y-o ch g Sabrehill (USA)-North Gale (Oats)
J J Quinn Miss K J Watson

Placings:0   (4179)
2003/04: 16⁰G,

	Starts	1st	2nd	3rd	Win & Pl
NH Flat	1	0	0	0	
Career Total	1	0	0	0	

Going:	Sf: 0-0 GS: 0-0 Gd: 0-1 GF: - Fm: 0-0
Distance:	2m/2m3: 0-1 2m4-2m7: 0-0 3m+: 0-0
Track:	LH: 0-1 RH: 0-0 Tight: 0-0 Gall: 0-1
Aids:	Bl: 0-0 Vi: 0-0 Tstrap: 0-0 Ckp: 0-0

Fionnula's Rainbow (IRE)
(84c)   (68c)81

9-y-o ch m Rainbows For Life (CAN)-Bon Retour (Sallust)
S T Lewis Simon T Lewis

Placings:052526631/2202/14435/2141140P3P4/6P643006 205-PP   (1012)
2003/04: 16⁰G, 24⁰G,

	Starts	1st	2nd	3rd	Win & Pl
Hurdles	2	0	0	0	
Career Total	42	5	7	4	27636
125	12/01	Hntg	2m4f110yD Ch	G-S	£3987
125	11/01	Fknm	2m5f110yD Ch	SFT	£3767
113	9/01	Hntg	2m4f110yD(0-120)HHdl	GD	£4134
113	11/00	Winc	2m	E(0-115)HHdl	SFT	£3698
92	4/99	Wxfd	2m	Hdl	Y-S	£2455

Total win prize-money £18043

Going:	Sf: 0-0 GS: 0-0 Gd: 0-2 GF: - Fm: 0-0
Distance:	2m/2m3: 0-1 2m4-2m7: 0-3 3m+: 0-1
Track:	LH: 0-2 RH: 0-0 Tight: 0-1 Gall: 0-0
Aids:	Bl: 0-0 Vi: 0-0 Tstrap: 0-0 Ckp: 0-0
Best Rating:	125 12/01 Hntg 2m4f110y gd-sft Ch

Fiori
113   (134h)126

8-y-o b g Anshan-Fen Princess (IRE) (Trojan Fen)
P C Haslam Wilson Imports I

Placings:2/13211/40061610/10023F-12   (0702)
2003/04: 16¹GF, 20²GF,

	Starts	1st	2nd	3rd	Win & Pl
Chases	2	1	1	0	9667
Career Total	22	7	4	2	33396
119	6/03	Hexm	2m110y	D(0-125)HCh	G-F	£5434
102	10/02	Kels	2m1f	D Ch	GD	£4680
130	11/01	Carl	2m1f	D(0-120)HHdl	HVY	£3311
130	3/01	MRas	2m1f110yD Hdl	G-S	£3822
122	2/01	Uttx	2m	D Hdl	SFT	£2859
134	12/00	Hayd	2m	D Hdl	HVY	£3250

Total win prize-money £23357

Going:	Sf: 0-0 GS: 0-0 Gd: 0-0 GF: - Fm: 1-2
Distance:	2m/2m3: 1-1 2m4-2m7: 0-1 3m+: 0-1
Track:	LH: 1-1 RH: 0-1 Tight: 0-1 Gall: 0-0
Aids:	Bl: 0-0 Vi: 0-0 Tstrap: 0-0 Ckp: 0-0
Best Rating:	134 2/02 Wwck 2m soft Hdl

Fair hurdler/chaser; goes well in testing ground but acts on faster; best at around two miles although stays two and a half.

Fire Mountain
83f   63f

6-y-o b g North Col-Emma Wright (Skyliner)
C L Tizzard R E Dimond

Placings:00   (4934)
2003/04: 16⁰G, 18⁰G,

	Starts	1st	2nd	3rd	Win & Pl
NH Flat	2	0	0	0	
Career Total	2	0	0	0	

Going:	Sf: 0-0 GS: 0-0 Gd: 0-2 GF: - Fm: 0-0
Distance:	2m/2m3: 0-2 2m4-2m7: 0-0 3m+: 0-0
Track:	LH: 0-1 RH: 0-1 Tight: 0-1 Gall: 0-0
Aids:	Bl: 0-0 Vi: 0-0 Tstrap: 0-0 Ckp: 0-0
Best Rating:	63 4/04 Font 2m2f110y good NHF

Fire Ranger
97   84+

8-y-o ch m Presidium-Regal Flame (Royalty)
J D Frost P A Tylor

Placings:52445-466304   (4239)
2003/04: 17⁴G, 19⁶GS, 16⁶S, 19³HY, 17⁰GS, 19⁴G,

	Starts	1st	2nd	3rd	Win & Pl
Hurdles	6	0	0	1	1086
Career Total	11	0	1	1	2132

Going:	Sf: 0-2 GS: 0-2 Gd: 0-2 GF: - Fm: 0-0
Distance:	2m/2m3: 0-5 2m4-2m7: 0-1 3m+: 0-0
Track:	LH: 0-1 RH: 0-5 Tight: 0-0 Gall: 0-0
Aids:	Bl: 0-0 Vi: 0-0 Tstrap: 0-0 Ckp: 0-0
Best Rating:	88 7/02 NAbb 2m1f gd-fm NHF

Fireaway
81(97h)   (117h)104

10-y-o b g Infantry-Handymouse (Nearly A Hand)
O Brennan Mrs Pat Brennan

Placings:1132/12362/4-U3   (4604)
2003/04: 20¹⁰, 17³GS,

	Starts	1st	2nd	3rd	Win & Pl
Chases	2	0	0	1	1034
Career Total	12	3	3	3	13780
104	12/01	Donc	2m110y	E Hdl	GD	£3236
126	12/00	Donc	2m110y	H NHF	HVY	£1736
114	5/00	Chep	2m110y	H NHF	FRM	£1662

Total win prize-money £6675

Going:	Sf: 0-0 GS: 0-1 Gd: 0-1 GF: - Fm: 0-0
Distance:	2m/2m3: 0-1 2m4-2m7: 0-1 3m+: 0-0
Track:	LH: 0-0 RH: 0-2 Tight: 0-1 Gall: 0-1
Aids:	Bl: 0-0 Vi: 0-0 Tstrap: 0-0 Ckp: 0-0
Best Rating:	126 12/00 Chep 2m110y soft NHF

Moderate chaser; formerly useful hurdler; est sround two miles; acts on any ground.

Fireball Macnamara (IRE)
(99h)   (113h)124

8-y-o b g Lord Americo-Glint Of Baron (Glint Of Gold)

M Pitman J C Hitchins

Placings:56/4/01421024100/**22212**PP-0   **(0760)**
2003/04: 20⁰G,

	Starts	1st	2nd	3rd	Win & Pl
Hurdles	1	0	0	0	
Career Total	22	4	6	0	34181
124	1/03	Donc	2m3f	D Ch	GD	£6987
113	11/01	Chel	2m110y	A Hdl	GD	£15000
112	8/01	Sthl	2m	E Hdl	G-F	£2450
103	5/01	Hntg	2m110y	E Hdl	G-F	£2429
			Total win prize-money £26867		

Going:	Sf: 0-0 GS: 0-0 Gd: 0-1 GF: - Fm: 0-0
Distance:	2m/2m3: 0-0 2m4-2m7: 0-1 3m+: 0-0
Track:	LH: 0-1 RH: 0-0 Tight: 0-0 Gall: 0-0
Aids:	Bl: 0-0 Vi: 0-0 Tstrap: 0-0 Ckp: 0-0
Best Rating:	**124** 1/03 Donc 2m3f good Ch

Fair chaser, seemingly better on a sound surface but does act well enough on soft; stays two miles three.

Fireside Legend (IRE)

62

5-y-o b g College Chapel-Miss Sandman (Manacle)
Miss M P Bryant Miss M Bryant

Placings:005O44650B-0   **(0125)**
2003/04: 20⁰G,

	Starts	1st	2nd	3rd	Win & Pl
Hurdles	1	0	0	0	
Career Total	11	0	0	0	0

Going:	Sf: 0-0 GS: 0-0 Gd: 0-1 GF: - Fm: 0-0
Distance:	2m/2m3: 0-0 2m4-2m7: 0-1 3m+: 0-0
Track:	LH: 0-0 RH: 0-0 Tight: 0-1 Gall: 0-0
Aids:	Bl: 0-1 Vi: 0-0 Tstrap: 0-0 Ckp: 0-0
Best Rating:	**72** 12/02 Winc 2m gd-sft Hdl

Firestone (GER)

99   101

7-y-o b g Dictator's Song (USA)-Fatinizza (IRE) (Niniski (USA))
A W Carroll K Marshall

Placings:50P24131/50036242-320   **(0715)**
2003/04: 16³G, 16²G, 16⁰G,

	Starts	1st	2nd	3rd	Win & Pl
Hurdles	3	0	1	1	1792
Career Total	19	2	4	3	16456
103	3/02	Chep	2m110y	C(0-130)HHdl	G-S	£6825
88	2/02	Plum	2m	F(0-90)HHdl	HVY	£1949
			Total win prize-money £8775		

Going:	Sf: 0-0 GS: 0-0 Gd: 0-3 GF: - Fm: 0-0
Distance:	2m/2m3: 0-3 2m4-2m7: 0-0 3m+: 0-0
Track:	LH: 0-1 RH: 0-2 Tight: 0-0 Gall: 0-0
Aids:	Bl: 0-0 Vi: 0-0 Tstrap: 0-1 Ckp: 0-0
Best Rating:	**103** 3/02 Chep 2m110y gd-sft Hdl

Moderate hurdler; suited by soft ground; likes to be held up; best at two miles; has had bleeding and breathing problems; has worn a tongue tie.

Firozi

80   84

5-y-o b m Forzando-Lambast (Relkino)
R A Fahey Galaxy Racing

Placings:230   **(3213)**
2003/04: 16²G, 16³GF, 16⁰GS,

	Starts	1st	2nd	3rd	Win & Pl
Hurdles	3	0	1	1	2580
Career Total	3	0	1	1	2580

Going:	Sf: 0-0 GS: 0-1 Gd: 0-1 GF: - Fm: 0-1
Distance:	2m/2m3: 0-3 2m4-2m7: 0-0 3m+: 0-0
Track:	LH: 0-3 RH: 0-0 Tight: 0-0 Gall: 0-0
Aids:	Bl: 0-0 Vi: 0-0 Tstrap: 0-0 Ckp: 0-0
Best Rating:	**84** 11/03 Weth 2m good Hdl

Plating-class hurdler; acts on a sound surface.

First Adare (IRE)

39   21

4-y-o ch g Un Desperado (FR)-First Mistake (Posse (USA))
Miss Lucinda V Russell Mrs C G Greig

Placings:0P0   **(4597)**
2003/04: 16⁰G, 16²S, 16⁰G,

	Starts	1st	2nd	3rd	Win & Pl
NH Flat	1	0	0	0	0
Hurdles	2	0	0	0	
Career Total	3	0	0	0	

Going:	Sf: 0-1 GS: 0-0 Gd: 0-2 GF: - Fm: 0-0
Distance:	2m/2m3: 0-3 2m4-2m7: 0-0 3m+: 0-0
Track:	LH: 0-2 RH: 0-1 Tight: 0-2 Gall: 0-1
Aids:	Bl: 0-0 Vi: 0-0 Tstrap: 0-0 Ckp: 0-0
Best Rating:	**65** 2/04 Muss 2m good NHF

First Ballot (IRE)

110   135

8-y-o br g Perugino (USA)-Election Special (Chief Singer)
D R C Elsworth J C Smith

Placings:61P/300/23   **(1669)**
2003/04: 16²G, 16³F,

	Starts	1st	2nd	3rd	Win & Pl
Hurdles	2	0	1	1	6274
Career Total	8	1	1	2	18460
140	2/01	Kemp	2m5f	C Hdl	G-S	£6136
			Total win prize-money £6136		

Going:	Sf: 0-0 GS: 0-0 Gd: 0-1 GF: - Fm: 0-0
Distance:	2m/2m3: 0-2 2m4-2m7: 0-0 3m+: 0-0
Track:	LH: 0-2 RH: 0-0 Tight: 0-1 Gall: 0-0
Aids:	Bl: 0-0 Vi: 0-0 Tstrap: 0-0 Ckp: 0-0
Best Rating:	**140** 2/01 Kemp 2m5f gd-sft Hdl

Useful hurdler; better known as a smart stayer on the Flat, stays 2m 5f and suited by a sound surface; has faced some stiff tasks over timber; likes to race prominently.

First Base

75   77

5-y-o ch g First Trump-Rose Music (Luthier)
R E Barr Malcolm O'Hair

Placings:0P3-0   **(0432)**
2003/04: 17⁰G,

	Starts	1st	2nd	3rd	Win & Pl
Hurdles	1	0	0	0	
Career Total	4	0	0	1	506

Going:	Sf: 0-0 GS: 0-0 Gd: 0-1 GF: - Fm: -
Distance:	2m/2m3: 0-1 2m4-2m7: 0-0 3m+: 0-0
Track:	LH: 0-1 RH: 0-0 Tight: 0-1 Gall: 0-0

Aids: Bl: 0-0 Vi: 0-0 Tstrap: 0-0 Ckp: 0-1
Best Rating: **77**   4/03   Sedg   2m1f   good   Hdl

Plating-class novice hurdler; best effort when third in a poor contest at Sedgefield in April 2003; may do better when stepped up in trip; has worn cheekpieces.

First Boy (GER)

102   99

5-y-o b h Bering-First Smile (Surumu (GER))
D J Wintle Lavender Hill Stud L L C

Placings:2   **(4524)**
2003/04: 16²GS,

	Starts	1st	2nd	3rd	Win & Pl
Hurdles	1	0	1	0	1096
Career Total	1	0	1	0	1096

Going:	Sf: 0-0 GS: 0-1 Gd: 0-0 GF: - Fm: 0-0
Distance:	2m/2m3: 0-1 2m4-2m7: 0-0 3m+: 0-0
Track:	LH: 0-1 RH: 0-0 Tight: 0-0 Gall: 0-0
Aids:	Bl: 0-0 Vi: 0-0 Tstrap: 0-0 Ckp: 0-0
Best Rating:	**99** 3/04 Chep 2m110y gd-sft Hdl

Dual ten furlong winner in Germany; highly promising second on debut in 2m novice hurdle at Chepstow March 2004, but well held on next start; acts on good ground.

First Dynasty (USA)

97   93

4-y-o b/br c Danzig (USA)-Willow Runner (USA) (Alydar (USA))
Miss S J Wilton (A P O'Brien 25/10) John Pointon And Sons

Placings:3   **(2669)**
2003/04: 16³GF,

	Starts	1st	2nd	3rd	Win & Pl
Hurdles	1	0	0	1	781
Career Total	1	0	0	1	781

Going:	Sf: 0-0 GS: 0-0 Gd: 0-0 GF: - Fm: 0-1
Distance:	2m/2m3: 0-1 2m4-2m7: 0-0 3m+: 0-0
Track:	LH: 0-1 RH: 0-0 Tight: 0-0 Gall: 0-1
Aids:	Bl: 0-0 Vi: 0-0 Tstrap: 0-0 Ckp: 0-0
Best Rating:	**93** 12/03 Newb 2m110y gd-fm Hdl

First Flight

103   (114h)**121+**

8-y-o br g Neltino-The Beginning (Goldhill)
K C Bailey Major Basil Heaton

Placings:3/4220/FP-323   **(3645)**
2003/04: 20³GS, 22²S, 24³GS,

	Starts	1st	2nd	3rd	Win & Pl
Chases	3	0	1	2	3698
Career Total	10	0	3	3	6781

Going:	Sf: 0-1 GS: 0-2 Gd: 0-0 GF: - Fm: 0-0
Distance:	2m/2m3: 0-0 2m4-2m7: 0-2 3m+: 0-1
Track:	LH: 0-2 RH: 0-1 Tight: 0-1 Gall: 0-1
Aids:	Bl: 0-0 Vi: 0-0 Tstrap: 0-0 Ckp: 0-0
Best Rating:	**121** 2/04 Kemp 3m gd-sft Ch

Has shown ability in novice chases; acts on soft ground; stays three miles.

First Gold (FR)

120   (151h) **170**

11-y-o b g Shafoun (FR)-Nuit D'Or li (FR) (Pot D'Or (FR))
F Doumen John P McManus

Placings:6242111F/1/F2/32111121U/534/303P1-15352
(4624)

2003/04: 25¹G, 19⁵HY, 24³G, 26⁶G, 25⁰G,

	Starts	1st	2nd	3rd	Win & Pl
Hurdles	1	0	0	0	1052
Chases	4	1	1	1	121688
Career Total	33	11	6	5	816001
170	4/03	Punc	3m1f	Ch		GD	£62337
174	4/03	Aint	3m1f	A Ch		GD	£87000
178	4/01	Aint	3m1f	A Ch		SFT	£71400
178	12/00	Kemp	3m	A Ch		G-S	£87000
170	11/00	Autl	3m3f110y	Ch		HVY	£84534
	10/00	Autl	2m6f	Ch		VS	£38425
	9/00	Autl	2m4f110y	Hdl		VS	£10567
	5/98	Autl	3m5f	Ch		SFT	£121212
	3/98	Autl	2m5f110y	HCh		VS	£35353
	2/98	Autl	2m2f110y	Ch		VS	£10101
	1/98	Pau	2m4f110y	Ch		SFT	£5051

Total win prize-money £612981

Going: Sf: 0-1 GS: 0-0 Gd: 1-4 GF: - Fm: 0-0
Distance: 2m/2m3: 0-0 2m4-2m7: 0-1 3m+: 1-4
Track: LH: 0-3 RH: 1-2 Tight: 0-0 Gall: 0-1
Aids: Bl: 1-4 Vi: 0-0 Tstrap: 0-0 Ckp: 0-0
Best Rating: 178   4/01   Aint   3m1f   soft   Ch

High-class French chaser; hugely impressive winner of the King George VI Chase and the Martell Cup in 2000/01; injured after and lost form, but bounced back with a runaway success at Aintree race in the Martell Cup of 2003 when blinkered for the first time; followed up at Punchestown in the Grade One Heineken Gold Cup; third in the 2003 King George; not disgraced in the Gold Cup and runner-up at Aintree; suited by a sharp three miles; best form with cut in the ground, but has won on good ground; sometimes blinkered.

First Grey

94   **72**

5-y-o gr m Environment Friend-Myrtilla (Beldale Flutter (USA))
E W Tuer Nigel E M Jones

Placings:0420-00000
(4459)

2003/04: 16⁹G, 16⁰GS, 16⁶HY, 20⁰G, 20⁰HY,

	Starts	1st	2nd	3rd	Win & Pl
Hurdles	5	0	0	0	
Career Total	9	0	1	0	576

Going: Sf: 0-2 GS: 0-1 Gd: 0-2 GF: - Fm: 0-0
Distance: 2m/2m3: 0-3 2m4-2m7: 0-2 3m+: 0-0
Track: LH: 0-4 RH: 0-1 Tight: 0-1 Gall: 0-2
Aids: Bl: 0-0 Vi: 0-0 Tstrap: 0-0 Ckp: 0-0
Best Rating: 87   3/03   Carl   2m1f   gd-sft   NHF

First Harmony

107f   **109f**

5-y-o ch m First Trump-Enchanting Melody (Chief Singer)
M Brittain Mel Brittain

Placings:11360
(4649)

2003/04: 16¹F, 16¹GS, 16³G, 16⁶S, 17⁰G,

	Starts	1st	2nd	3rd	Win & Pl
NH Flat	5	2	0	1	4877
Career Total	5	2	0	1	4877
99	11/03	Weth	2m	H NHF		G-S	£2366

| 86 | 9/03 | Hexm | 2m110y | H NHF | | FRM | £1638 |

Total win prize-money £4004

Going: Sf: 0-1 GS: 1-1 Gd: 0-2 GF: - Fm: 1-1
Distance: 2m/2m3: 2-5 2m4-2m7: 0-0 3m+: 0-0
Track: LH: 2-2 RH: 0-2 Tight: 0-0 Gall: 0-0
Aids: Bl: 0-0 Vi: 0-0 Tstrap: 0-0 Ckp: 0-0
Best Rating: 109   3/04   Sand   2m110y   soft   NHF

Winner on debut at Hexham and defied a penalty at Wetherby; should stay further than two miles over hurdles; acts on most ground.

First Love

107   (138h) **138**

8-y-o br g Bustino-First Romance (Royalty)
N J Henderson The Queen

Placings:2121/1221/2212-1PP
(4327)

2003/04: 24¹G, 19⁰GS, 24⁰PGS,

	Starts	1st	2nd	3rd	Win & Pl
Chases	3	1	0	0	6747
Career Total	15	6	7	0	35766
131	5/03	Prth	3m	D Ch		GD	£6747
138	2/03	Folk	2m5f	E Ch		SFT	£4046
116	3/02	Sand	2m110y	D Hdl		G-S	£4524
138	12/01	Sand	2m110y	D Hdl		SFT	£4524
128	4/01	Asct	2m110y	H NHF		HVY	£2583
123	2/01	Towc	2m	H NHF		HVY	£1575

Total win prize-money £23999

Going: Sf: 0-0 GS: 0-2 Gd: 1-1 GF: - Fm: 0-0
Distance: 2m/2m3: 0-0 2m4-2m7: 0-1 3m+: 1-2
Track: LH: 0-0 RH: 1-3 Tight: 0-0 Gall: 0-0
Aids: Bl: 0-0 Vi: 0-0 Tstrap: 0-0 Ckp: 0-0
Best Rating: 138   2/03   Folk   2m5f   soft   Ch

Useful chaser/hurdler; jumps well; got off the mark at Folkestone in February 2003, and won at Perth in May; pulled up in handicaps since; stays three miles and appears to appreciate cut in the ground; all his wins have been on right-handed tracks.

First Officer (USA)

(94h)   (93h) **93**

7-y-o b g Lear Fan (USA)-Trampoli (USA) (Trempolino (USA))
C C Bealby K McGeorge & T Radford

Placings:0/6505P32-1PF2PPP
(4265)

2003/04: 26¹GF, 24²F, 26⁶GF, 25²G, 24⁶G, 25⁰GS, 26⁶GF,

	Starts	1st	2nd	3rd	Win & Pl
Chases	7	1	1	0	4483
Career Total	15	1	2	1	6495
93	5/03	Sthl	3m2f	F(0-90)HCh		G-F	£3523

Total win prize-money £3523

Going: Sf: 0-0 GS: 0-1 Gd: 0-3 GF: - Fm: 1-3
Distance: 2m/2m3: 0-0 2m4-2m7: 0-0 3m+: 1-7
Track: LH: 1-3 RH: 0-4 Tight: 0-3 Gall: 0-1
Aids: Bl: 1-6 Vi: 0-0 Tstrap: 0-0 Ckp: 0-1
Best Rating: 93   5/03   Sthl   3m2f   gd-fm   Ch

Plating-class chaser; fair stayer on the Flat, limited ability over hurdles; off the mark over fences at Southwell in May; stays well; acts on good to soft and good to firm; has worn blinkers.

First Thought

91   **69**

6-y-o b m Primitive Rising (USA)-Precis (Pitpan)
O J Carter O J Carter

[First Thought continued right column]

Placings:0000PP06
(4544)

2003/04: 16⁰GF, 17⁰GF, 16⁰G, 21⁰S, 24⁰PHY, 19⁰S, 19⁰G, 22⁶GS,

	Starts	1st	2nd	3rd	Win & Pl
NH Flat	3	0	0	0	0
Hurdles	5	0	0	0	0
Career Total	8	0	0	0	0

Going: Sf: 0-3 GS: 0-1 Gd: 0-2 GF: - Fm: 0-2
Distance: 2m/2m3: 0-5 2m4-2m7: 0-2 3m+: 0-1
Track: LH: 0-2 RH: 0-6 Tight: 0-1 Gall: 0-0
Aids: Bl: 0-0 Vi: 0-0 Tstrap: 0-0 Ckp: 0-0
Best Rating: 69   3/04   Extr   2m3f   good   Hdl

First Truth

94   **93**

7-y-o b g Rudimentary (USA)-Pursuit Of Truth (USA) (Irish River (FR))
Mrs H Dalton Ray Bailey

Placings:20063/31-0
(0576)

2003/04: 16⁰G,

	Starts	1st	2nd	3rd	Win & Pl
Hurdles	1	0	0	0	
Career Total	8	1	1	2	6337
111	5/02	Bang	2m1f	D(0-120)HHdl		SFT	£4407

Total win prize-money £4407

Going: Sf: 0-0 GS: 0-0 Gd: 0-1 GF: - Fm: 0-0
Distance: 2m/2m3: 0-2 2m4-2m7: 0-3 3m+: 0-0
Track: LH: 0-0 RH: 0-1 Tight: 0-0 Gall: 0-0
Aids: Bl: 0-0 Vi: 0-0 Tstrap: 0-0 Ckp: 0-0
Best Rating: 111   5/02   Bang   2m1f   soft   Hdl

Firstflor

98f   **92f**

5-y-o b m Alflora (IRE)-First Crack (Scallywag)
F Jordan F Jordan

Placings:1335
(4407)

2003/04: 16¹F, 16³GS, 16³GS, 16⁵G,

	Starts	1st	2nd	3rd	Win & Pl
NH Flat	4	1	0	2	2287
Career Total	4	1	0	2	2287
76	10/03	Towc	2m	H NHF		FRM	£1720

Total win prize-money £1720

Going: Sf: 0-0 GS: 0-1 Gd: 0-1 GF: - Fm: 1-2
Distance: 2m/2m3: 1-4 2m4-2m7: 0-0 3m+: 0-0
Track: LH: 0-1 RH: 1-3 Tight: 0-0 Gall: 0-2
Aids: Bl: 0-0 Vi: 0-0 Tstrap: 0-0 Ckp: 0-0
Best Rating: 92   3/04   Hntg   2m110y   good   NHF

Readily beat odds-on favourite in Towcester bumper where only two finished; held since; acts on a sound surface.

Fisherman Jack

9-y-o b g Carlingford Castle-Troublewithjack (Sulaafah (USA))
John Burton John Burton

Placings:4P
(4283)

2003/04: 24⁴S, 25⁰G,

	Starts	1st	2nd	3rd	Win & Pl
Chases	2	0	0	0	108
Career Total	2	0	0	0	108

Going: Sf: 0-1 GS: 0-0 Gd: 0-1 GF: - Fm: 0-0
Distance: 2m/2m3: 0-0 2m4-2m7: 0-0 3m+: 0-2

Track:	LH: 0-0 RH: 0-2 Tight: 0-0 Gall: 0-1
Aids:	Bl: 0-0 Vi: 0-0 Tstrap: 0-0 Ckp: 0-0
Best Rating:	44 2/04 Hntg 3m soft Ch

Fishki's Lad

107 **105**

9-y-o b g Casteddu-Fishki (Niniski (USA))
E W Tuer Far Distant Partnership

Placings:3310/2061512/04432/00P0P/213024-651565
(2799)
2003/04: 24⁶GF, 24⁵GF, 23¹GF, 22⁵G, 25⁶GF, 24⁵S,

	Starts	1st	2nd	3rd	Win & Pl
Hurdles	6	1	0	0	3536
Career Total	33	5	5	4	19482
103	10/03	Hayd	2m7f110yD(0-115)HHdl	G-F	£3536
102	6/02	Hexm	3m	F(0-100)HHdl	GD	£2320
103	4/00	Hexm	2m4f110yD(0-125)HHdl	GD	£3172
102	2/00	Muss	3m	E Hdl	GD	£2450
97	3/99	Hexm	2m	H NHF	G-S	£1556
			Total win prize-money £13036		

Going:	Sf: 0-1 GS: 0-0 Gd: 0-1 GF: - Fm: 1-4
Distance:	2m/2m3: 0-0 2m4-2m7: 0-1 3m+: 1-5
Track:	LH: 1-5 RH: 0-1 Tight: 0-2 Gall: 0-0
Aids:	Bl: 0-0 Vi: 0-0 Tstrap: 0-0 Ckp: 1-3
Best Rating:	107 1/01 Muss 3m gd-sft Hdl

Modest handicap hurdler; acts on good ground and stays three miles; likes to lead; has worn blinkers/cheekpieces.

Fittleworth (IRE)

4-y-o gr f Bijou D'Inde-Remany (Bellypha)
W G M Turner Mrs Lesley Smith

Placings:0
(1770)
2003/04: 16⁰GF,

	Starts	1st	2nd	3rd	Win & Pl
Hurdles	1	0	0	0	
Career Total	1	0	0	0	

Going:	Sf: 0-0 GS: 0-0 Gd: 0-0 GF: - Fm: 0-1
Distance:	2m/2m3: 0-1 2m4-2m7: 0-0 3m+: 0-0
Track:	LH: 0-0 RH: 0-1 Tight: 0-0 Gall: 0-0
Aids:	Bl: 0-0 Vi: 0-0 Tstrap: 0-0 Ckp: 0-0

Fitz The Bill (IRE)

72 **29**

4-y-o b f Mon Tresor-In The Sky (IRE) (Imp Society (USA))
N B King The Greyhound Partnership

Placings:F0P
(4440)
2003/04: 16²GS, 16⁹S, 16⁸GS,

	Starts	1st	2nd	3rd	Win & Pl
Hurdles	3	0	0	0	
Career Total	3	0	0	0	

Going:	Sf: 0-1 GS: 0-2 Gd: 0-0 GF: - Fm: 0-0
Distance:	2m/2m3: 0-3 2m4-2m7: 0-0 3m+: 0-0
Track:	LH: 0-3 RH: 0-0 Tight: 0-3 Gall: 0-0
Aids:	Bl: 0-0 Vi: 0-0 Tstrap: 0-0 Ckp: 0-0
Best Rating:	29 2/04 Plum 2m soft Hdl

Five Pence

92 **89+**

8-y-o b g Henbit (USA)-Le Saule D'Or (Sonnen Gold)

R T Phillips Bill Naylor

Placings:00-2200
(4676)
2003/04: 16²GS, 20²GS, 20⁰GS, 22⁴G,

	Starts	1st	2nd	3rd	Win & Pl
Hurdles	4	0	2	0	1941
Career Total	6	0	2	0	1941

Going:	Sf: 0-0 GS: 0-3 Gd: 0-1 GF: - Fm: 0-0
Distance:	2m/2m3: 0-1 2m4-2m7: 0-3 3m+: 0-0
Track:	LH: 0-2 RH: 0-2 Tight: 0-0 Gall: 0-0
Aids:	Bl: 0-0 Vi: 0-0 Tstrap: 0-0 Ckp: 0-0
Best Rating:	89 12/03 Hayd 2m4f gd-sft Hdl

Lightly raced novice hurdler; promising run after lay-off in November 2003; acts in soft ground.

Fizzy Pop

91f **58f**

5-y-o b m Robellino (USA)-Maria Isabella (FR) (Young Generation)
W S Cunningham Ann And David Bell

Placings:000
(4323)
2003/04: 17⁰GF, 16⁰G, 16⁰S,

	Starts	1st	2nd	3rd	Win & Pl
NH Flat	3	0	0	0	
Career Total	3	0	0	0	

Going:	Sf: 0-1 GS: 0-0 Gd: 0-1 GF: - Fm: 0-1
Distance:	2m/2m3: 0-3 2m4-2m7: 0-0 3m+: 0-0
Track:	LH: 0-2 RH: 0-1 Tight: 0-0 Gall: 0-0
Aids:	Bl: 0-0 Vi: 0-0 Tstrap: 0-0 Ckp: 0-1
Best Rating:	58 10/03 MRas 2m1f110y gd-fm NHF

Flagship Uberalles (IRE)

115 **166**

10-y-o br g Accordion-Fourth Degree (Oats)
P J Hobbs John P McManus

Placings:113/22121111/11213PP/1244/112/4P51-322P
(4639)
2003/04: 16¹GY, 16³G, 16²G, 16²G, 20⁰G,

	Starts	1st	2nd	3rd	Win & Pl
Chases	5	1	2	1	125481
Career Total	33	14	8	3	623106
160	4/03	Punc	2m	Ch	G-Y	£48480
170	3/02	Chel	2m	A Ch	G-S	£127600
170	12/01	Sand	2m	A Ch	G-S	£46400
173	12/00	Chel	2m110y	A Ch	SFT	£31900
167	2/00	Newb	2m1f	A Ch	G-S	£25350
166	12/99	Sand	2m	A Ch	GD	£38700
158	11/99	Extr	2m1f	A HCh	G-S	£19050
151	4/99	Aint	2m	A Ch	G-S	£32725
157	3/99	Chel	2m	A Ch	G-S	£57300
144	2/99	Wwck	2m	A Ch	G-S	£16224
131	1/99	Kemp	2m	D Ch	SFT	£4810
131	12/98	Extr	2m1f110yC Ch	GD	£5114
99	3/98	Limk	2m	Hdl	YLD	£3573
113	3/98	Navn	2m	Hdl	Y-S	£2680
			Total win prize-money £459909		

Going:	Sf: 0-0 GS: 0-0 Gd: 0-4 GF: - Fm: 0-0
Distance:	2m/2m3: 1-4 2m4-2m7: 0-1 3m+: 0-0
Track:	LH: 0-3 RH: 1-2 Tight: 0-1 Gall: 0-1
Aids:	Bl: 0-0 Vi: 0-0 Tstrap: 0-0 Ckp: 0-1
Best Rating:	173 12/00 Chel 2m110y soft Ch

High-class two-mile chaser; winner of the 1999 Arkle and 2002 Champion Chase at the Cheltenham Festival; also

---

three time winner of the Tingle Creek, all for different trainers; below form in the 2002/03 season until winning a Grade One at Punchestown; good effort in the 2003 Tingle Creek on return, but disappointed when beaten by Kadarann at Wetherby on Boxing Day before finishing runner-up at Cheltenham in Queen Mother; suited by some cut in the ground and all best form around 2m; not the greatest jumper among the top 2m chasers and has a history of back problems; goes very well fresh; has been tried blinkered.

Flahive's First

112(96h) **(65 h)115**

10-y-o ch g Interrex (CAN)-Striking Image (IRE) (Flash Of Steel)
D Burchell Don Gould

Placings:F043206/000020331410040336F44U0255/34130 P/P502P/PF0420/2223525311404UP0360464-21223313422244PF0P
(4938)
2003/04: 16²GS, 17¹GS, 16²GF, 20²GF, 21³GS, 16³G, 17¹G, 16³GF, 20⁴GF, 19²GF, 16²GF, 16⁴GF, 19⁴GS, 16⁶G, 16⁶S, 16⁰G, 16⁰GS,

	Starts	1st	2nd	3rd	Win & Pl
Hurdles	1	0	0	0	
Chases	17	2	6	3	25219
Career Total	90	7	15	13	54972
115	8/03	Ctml	2m1f110yD(0-115)HCh	GD	£6240
108	5/03	Ctml	2m1f110yD(0-125)HCh	G-S	£6812
95	8/02	Ctml	2m1f110yD(0-115)HCh	GD	£5590
92	8/02	Ctml	2m1f110yF(0-95)HCh	GD	£3484
87	6/99	Worc	2m	F(0-105)HHdl	G-S	£1957
84	8/98	Ctml	2m1f110yG(0-90)HHdl	G-F	£2432
80	8/98	Worc	2m	G Hdl	GD	£1520
			Total win prize-money £28036		

Going:	Sf: 0-1 GS: 1-5 Gd: 1-4 GF: - Fm: 0-8
Distance:	2m/2m3: 2-13 2m4-2m7: 0-5 3m+: 0-0
Track:	LH: 2-15 RH: 0-3 Tight: 2-7 Gall: 0-0
Aids:	Bl: 0-0 Vi: 0-0 Tstrap: 0-0 Ckp: 0-0
Best Rating:	115 11/03 Chep 2m110y gd-fm Ch

Modest chaser; has scored five times over the extended two miles at Cartmel; in fine form in 2003 with two wins at his favourite track; stays two miles four furlongs; best on good or faster ground; prefers a decent pace.

Flake

103 **102+**

4-y-o ch g Zilzal (USA)-Impatiente (USA) (Vaguely Noble)
Mrs S J Smith (G M Moore 17/5) Keith Nicholson

Placings:32250
(4452)
2003/04: 16³GF, 17²G, 16²GS, 16⁵S, 16⁹GS,

	Starts	1st	2nd	3rd	Win & Pl
Hurdles	5	0	2	1	3778
Career Total	5	0	2	1	3778

Going:	Sf: 0-1 GS: 0-2 Gd: 0-1 GF: - Fm: 0-1
Distance:	2m/2m3: 0-5 2m4-2m7: 0-0 3m+: 0-0
Track:	LH: 0-4 RH: 0-1 Tight: 0-1 Gall: 0-0
Aids:	Bl: 0-0 Vi: 0-0 Tstrap: 0-0 Ckp: 0-0
Best Rating:	102 1/04 Wwck 2m gd-sft Hdl

Decent juvenile hurdler; effective at two miles; acts on most ground.

Flame Creek (IRE)

114(105c) **(125c)159**

8-y-o b g Shardari-Sheila's Pet (IRE) (Welsh Term)
Noel T Chance Martin Wesson Partners

Placings:f/21/1110P-111436
(3507a)

2003/04: 17¹S, 20¹G, 16¹GF, 16⁴GS, 16²Y, 16⁶Y,

	Starts	1st	2nd	3rd	Win & Pl
Hurdles	3	0	0	1	8425
Chases	3	3	0	0	16320
Career Total	14	8	1	1	83031

113	10/03	Kels	2m110y	D Ch	G-F	£5040
106	5/03	Weth	2m4f110y	D Ch	GD	£5852
116	5/03	Bang	2m1f110y	D Ch	SFT	£5427
158	1/03	Hayd	2m	A Hdl	G-S	£23200
147	1/03	Chel	2m1f	B(0-150)HHdl	HVY	£15300
136	5/02	Kels	2m110y	B Hdl	GD	£8320
138	4/02	Chel	2m1f	B Hdl	GD	£9009
119	4/01	Winc	2m	H NHF	SFT	£1673

Total win prize-money £73822

Going:	Sf: 1-1 GS: 0-1 Gd: 1-1 GF: -: Fm: 1-1
Distance:	2m/2m3: 2-5 2m4-2m7: 1-1 3m+: 0-0
Track:	LH: 2-5 RH: 0-0 Tight: 1-1 Gall: 0-0
Aids:	Bl: 0-0 Vi: 0-0 Tstrap: 0-0 Ckp: 0-0
Best Rating:	159 12/03 Leop 2m yield Hdl

High-class hurdler; impressive in a decent handicap at Cheltenham at the start of 2003 and again won well in muddling Grade 2 Champion Hurdle Trial at Haydock; well beaten in Champion Hurdle; did not jump well in the Scottish Champion Hurdle; landed his first three starts over fences, but did not impress with his jumping; sent back over hurdles and was fourth in the Bula before a fine third at Leopardstown in a Grade One (may have been second but for jockey dropping his hands); disappointed in the Irish Champion Hurdle; suited by 2m; effective on heavy ground but ideally suited by a sound surface.

Flame Phoenix (USA)
93   111
5-y-o b/br g Quest For Fame-Kingscote (King's Lake (USA))
P R Webber The Chamberlain Addiscott Partnership

Placings: 1005 (4207)
2003/04: 16¹G, 16⁰G, 17⁰S, 16⁵G,

	Starts	1st	2nd	3rd	Win & Pl
NH Flat	1	1	0	0	2776
Hurdles	3	0	0	0	0
Career Total	4	1	0	0	2776
103 5/03 Ludl 2m	H NHF			GD	£2776

Total win prize-money £2776

Going:	Sf: 0-1 GS: 0-0 Gd: 1-3 GF: -: Fm: 0-0
Distance:	2m/2m3: 1-4 2m4-2m7: 0-0 3m+: 0-0
Track:	LH: 0-0 RH: 1-4 Tight: 0-1 Gall: 0-0
Aids:	Bl: 0-0 Vi: 0-0 Tstrap: 0-0 Ckp: 0-0
Best Rating:	111 3/04 Kemp 2m good Hdl

Well-bred gelding; winner of a Ludlow bumper; well beaten since.

Flamenca (USA)
93   61
5-y-o b m Diesis-Highland Ceilidh (IRE) (Scottish Reel)
Mrs L B Normile (R Allan 14/6) Allan A Grant

Placings: 0326P06543-03060P (3468)
2003/04: 16⁹G, 16³G, 16⁹G, 20⁶GF, 21⁰GS, 20⁰GF,

	Starts	1st	2nd	3rd	Win & Pl
Hurdles	6	0	0	1	524
Career Total	16	0	1	3	3030

Going:	Sf: 0-0 GS: 0-1 Gd: 0-3 GF: -: Fm: 0-2
Distance:	2m/2m3: 0-3 2m4-2m7: 0-3 3m+: 0-0
Track:	LH: 0-4 RH: 0-2 Tight: 0-2 Gall: 0-1
Aids:	Bl: 0-0 Vi: 0-0 Tstrap: 0-1 Ckp: 0-1
Best Rating:	81 3/03 Hexm 2m110y good Hdl

Plating-class hurdler; moody sort; acts on a sound surface.

Flaming Cheek
105   90
6-y-o b g Blushing Flame (USA)-Rueful Lady (Streetfighter)
A G Blackmore A G Blackmore

Placings: 40456-03516330 (4833)
2003/04: 16⁰GS, 17⁹GF, 16⁵GF, 16¹G, 20⁶G, 16³GS, 16³GS, 21⁹GF,

	Starts	1st	2nd	3rd	Win & Pl
Hurdles	8	1	0	3	4814
Career Total	13	1	0	3	4814
85 11/03 Fknm 2m	E(0-105)HHdl			GD	£2576

Total win prize-money £2576

Going:	Sf: 0-0 GS: 0-3 Gd: 1-2 GF: -: Fm: 0-3
Distance:	2m/2m3: 1-6 2m4-2m7: 0-2 3m+: 0-0
Track:	LH: 1-5 RH: 0-2 Tight: 0-1 Gall: 0-2
Aids:	Bl: 0-0 Vi: 0-0 Tstrap: 0-0 Ckp: 0-0
Best Rating:	93 2/04 Towc 2m gd-sft Hdl

Moderate hurdler; effective at two miles, should stay farther.

Flaming Heck
99   90+
7-y-o b g Dancing High-Heckley Spark (Electric)
Mrs L B Normile D A Whitaker

Placings: 3/0P403 (4937)
2003/04: 20⁰S, 18⁵S, 20⁴HY, 20⁹GS, 16⁹GS,

	Starts	1st	2nd	3rd	Win & Pl
Hurdles	5	0	0	1	1160
Career Total	6	0	0	2	1392

Going:	Sf: 0-3 GS: 0-2 Gd: 0-0 GF: -: Fm: 0-0
Distance:	2m/2m3: 0-2 2m4-2m7: 0-3 3m+: 0-0
Track:	LH: 0-4 RH: 0-1 Tight: 0-1 Gall: 0-1
Aids:	Bl: 0-0 Vi: 0-0 Tstrap: 0-0 Ckp: 0-0
Best Rating:	90 4/04 Prth 2m110y gd-sft Hdl

Flaminion Way (IRE)
92   55
8-y-o br g Good Thyne (USA)-Rose Fointin Vii (Damsire Unregistered)
Miss Venetia Williams Ms Francesca Baring

Placings: 6 (3462)
2003/04: 24⁶S,

	Starts	1st	2nd	3rd	Win & Pl
Hurdles	1	0	0	0	0
Career Total	1	0	0	0	0

Going:	Sf: 0-1 GS: 0-0 Gd: 0-0 GF: -: Fm: 0-0
Distance:	2m/2m3: 0-0 2m4-2m7: 0-0 3m+: 0-1
Track:	LH: 0-1 RH: 0-0 Tight: 0-0 Gall: 0-0
Aids:	Bl: 0-0 Vi: 0-0 Tstrap: 0-0 Ckp: 0-0
Best Rating:	66 1/04 Chep 3m soft Hdl

Did not shape too badly when sixth at Chepstow on debut; should be capable of better.

Flash Gordon
111   109
10-y-o ch g Gildoran-Florence May (Grange Melody)
Mrs S Richardson R G Fairbarns

Placings: 0/1/51/FPU-0123P (0855)
2003/04: 16⁹G, 20¹G, 19²GF, 20³GF, 20⁹GF,

	Starts	1st	2nd	3rd	Win & Pl
Chases	5	1	1	1	10531
Career Total	12	3	1	1	18201

109	5/03	Bang	2m4f110y	D(0-120)HCh	GD	£7098
109	3/02	Hrfd	2m	D(0-115)HCh	GD	£4524
99	4/01	Tntn	2m3f	E Ch	G-F	£3146

Total win prize-money £14768

Going:	Sf: 0-0 GS: 0-0 Gd: 1-2 GF: -: Fm: 0-3
Distance:	2m/2m3: 0-2 2m4-2m7: 1-3 3m+: 0-0
Track:	LH: 1-3 RH: 0-2 Tight: 1-3 Gall: 0-0
Aids:	Bl: 0-0 Vi: 0-0 Tstrap: 0-0 Ckp: 0-0
Best Rating:	109 6/03 MRas 2m4f gd-fm Ch

Modest chaser; likes to front run; effective at up to 2m 4f; sometimes gives problems at the start; lightly raced.

Flash Henry
7-y-o b g Executive Perk-Running Valley (Buckskin (FR))
J L Needham J L Needham

Placings: 0P (3698)
2003/04: 16⁰S, 17⁰HY,

	Starts	1st	2nd	3rd	Win & Pl
NH Flat	1	0	0	0	0
Hurdles	1	0	0	0	0
Career Total	2	0	0	0	0

Going:	Sf: 0-2 GS: 0-0 Gd: 0-0 GF: -: Fm: 0-0
Distance:	2m/2m3: 0-2 2m4-2m7: 0-0 3m+: 0-0
Track:	LH: 0-1 RH: 0-2 Tight: 0-0 Gall: 0-0
Aids:	Bl: 0-0 Vi: 0-0 Tstrap: 0-0 Ckp: 0-0

Flashant
93(87h)   (48h)58
9-y-o ch g Henbit (USA)-La Furze (Winden)
A W Carroll A Bayman

Placings: 000/4001/P0/00/P54-5P (4916)
2003/04: 24⁵G, 23³GS,

	Starts	1st	2nd	3rd	Win & Pl
Chases	2	0	0	0	0
Career Total	16	1	0	0	2562
84 3/00 Sedg 2m1f	E(0-105)HHdl			G-F	£2282

Total win prize-money £2282

Going:	Sf: 0-0 GS: 0-1 Gd: 0-1 GF: -: Fm: 0-0
Distance:	2m/2m3: 0-2 2m4-2m7: 0-0 3m+: 0-2
Track:	LH: 0-1 RH: 0-0 Tight: 0-0 Gall: 0-0
Aids:	Bl: 0-0 Vi: 0-0 Tstrap: 0-0 Ckp: 0-0
Best Rating:	84 3/00 Sedg 2m1f gd-fm Hdl

Flat Stanley
72   27
5-y-o b g Celtic Swing-Cool Grey (Absalom)
R Bastiman John Endersby

Placings: P-0 (0432)
2003/04: 17⁰G,

	Starts	1st	2nd	3rd	Win & Pl
Hurdles	1	0	0	0	0
Career Total	2	0	0	0	0

Going:	Sf: 0-0 GS: 0-0 Gd: 0-1 GF: -: Fm: 0-0
Distance:	2m/2m3: 0-1 2m4-2m7: 0-0 3m+: 0-0
Track:	LH: 0-1 RH: 0-0 Tight: 0-1 Gall: 0-0

Aids: BI: 0-0 Vi: 0-0 Tstrap: 0-0 Ckp: 0-0
Best Rating: 41   5/03   Ctml   2m1f110y   good   Hdl

Flat Top

13-y-o b g Blakeney-New Edition (Great Nephew)
David M Easterby   Lord Manton

Placings:21F4/P6200P/F4P042P4/2P5F2P1113/U2134431
12/P353/12253302FP/522P0313/5UU0-P24   (4798)
2003/04: 24PG, 252GS, 274G,

					Starts	1st	2nd	3rd	Win & Pl
Chases					3	0	1	0	437
Career Total					69	9	13	9	71899
117	3/02	Newb	3m		C(0-135)HCh	G-S	£15636		
113	10/00	Hexm	2m4f110yE(0-115)HCh			HVY	£2847		
121	3/99	Newc	3m		E(0-115)HCh	GD	£2788		
121	3/99	Newc	3m		D(0-125)HCh	SFT	£8609		
110	12/98	Catt	3m1f110yE(0-115)HHdl			GD	£2486		
125	4/98	Hexm	3m1f		E Ch	HVY	£3154		
125	4/98	Chel	2m5f		D(0-115)HCh	HVY	£5402		
113	4/98	Weth	2m4f110yD Ch			G-S	£3684		
	3/95	Hexm	3m		E Hdl	HVY	£2304		

         Total win prize-money £46912

Going: Sf: 0-0 GS: 0-1 Gd: 0-2 GF: - Fm: 0-0
Distance: 2m/2m3: 0-0 2m4-2m7: 0-0 3m+: 0-3
Track: LH: 0-1 RH: 0-2 Tight: 0-2 Gall: 0-0
Aids: BI: 0-0 Vi: 0-0 Tstrap: 0-0 Ckp: 0-0
Best Rating: 125   4/98   Sand   2m4f110y   gd-sft   Ch

Fair chaser, stays three miles and suited by soft ground.

Flecthefawna (IRE)

102(91h)   (82h)89

8-y-o b g Glacial Storm (USA)-Lady Sperrin (Abednego)
L A Dace   Churchfields Partnership

Placings:004-66U4   (3926)
2003/04: 246S, 256GS, 24UG, 244G,

	Starts	1st	2nd	3rd	Win & Pl
Chases	4	0	0	0	913
Career Total	7	0	0	0	1348

Going: Sf: 0-1 GS: 0-1 Gd: 0-2 GF: - Fm: 0-0
Distance: 2m/2m3: 0-0 2m4-2m7: 0-0 3m+: 0-4
Track: LH: 0-2 RH: 0-2 Tight: 0-0 Gall: 0-1
Aids: BI: 0-0 Vi: 0-0 Tstrap: 0-0 Ckp: 0-0
Best Rating: 87   1/03   Kemp   2m5f   gd-sft   Hdl

Modest performer, yet to really find a trip; seemingly acts on soft ground.

Fleet Street

111   145

5-y-o ch g Wolfhound (USA)-Farmer's Pet (Sharrood (USA))
N J Henderson   W H Ponsonby

Placings:13133   (4638)
2003/04: 161GF, 163GS, 171GS, 163G, 163G,

				Starts	1st	2nd	3rd	Win & Pl
Hurdles				5	2	0	3	28342
Career Total				5	2	0	3	28342
118	1/04	Tntn	2m1f	E Hdl		G-S	£4238	
115	10/03	Strf	2m110y	D Hdl		G-F	£5239	

         Total win prize-money £9477

Going: Sf: 0-0 GS: 1-2 Gd: 0-2 GF: - Fm: 1-1
Distance: 2m/2m3: 2-5 2m4-2m7: 0-0 3m+: 0-0
Track: LH: 1-4 RH: 1-0 Tight: 2-3 Gall: 0-1
Aids: BI: 0-0 Vi: 0-0 Tstrap: 0-0 Ckp: 0-0

Very useful novice hurdler; Flat winner in Germany; won novice hurdles at Stratford and Taunton and finished fine third in the 2004 Supreme Novices; good third in Grade 2 at Aintree; acts on fast and soft ground, but does not want it too testing; still has scope.

Fleetwood Forest

96f   91f

4-y-o b g Fleetwood (IRE)-Louise Moillon (Mansingh (USA))
A King   A King A R Bromley D Veysey & J Winchester

Placings:30   (4454)
2003/04: 163G, 169GS,

	Starts	1st	2nd	3rd	Win & Pl
NH Flat	2	0	0	1	349
Career Total	2	0	0	1	349

Going: Sf: 0-0 GS: 0-1 Gd: 0-1 GF: - Fm: 0-0
Distance: 2m/2m3: 0-2 2m4-2m7: 0-0 3m+: 0-1
Track: LH: 0-0 RH: 0-2 Tight: 0-0 Gall: 0-0
Aids: BI: 0-0 Vi: 0-0 Tstrap: 0-0 Ckp: 0-0
Best Rating: 91   2/04   Winc   2m   good   NHF

Flemming (USA)

87   60

7-y-o ch g Green Dancer (USA)-La Groupie (FR) (Groom Dancer (USA))
A G Juckes   Ten Out Of Ten Racing Partnership

Placings:P66-000   (3226)
2003/04: 20PS, 21PGF, 26PGS,

	Starts	1st	2nd	3rd	Win & Pl
Hurdles	3	0	0	0	0
Career Total	6	0	0	0	0

Going: Sf: 0-1 GS: 0-1 Gd: 0-0 GF: - Fm: 0-1
Distance: 2m/2m3: 0-2 2m4-2m7: 0-2 3m+: 0-1
Track: LH: 0-1 RH: 0-2 Tight: 0-0 Gall: 0-1
Aids: BI: 0-1 Vi: 0-0 Tstrap: 0-1 Ckp: 0-1
Best Rating: 60   8/02   Worc   2m4f   gd-fm   Hdl

Fleurenka

65f   24f

6-y-o br m Alflora (IRE)-Tochenka (Fine Blue)
D G Bridgwater   Anita & Relton Minton

Placings:00   (4920)
2003/04: 160GS, 169GS,

	Starts	1st	2nd	3rd	Win & Pl
NH Flat	2	0	0	0	
Career Total	2	0	0	0	

Going: Sf: 0-0 GS: 0-2 Gd: 0-0 GF: - Fm: 0-0
Distance: 2m/2m3: 0-2 2m4-2m7: 0-0 3m+: 0-0
Track: LH: 0-1 RH: 0-1 Tight: 0-0 Gall: 0-0
Aids: BI: 0-0 Vi: 0-0 Tstrap: 0-0 Ckp: 0-0
Best Rating: 24   4/04   Worc   2m   gd-sft   NHF

Flick Em Off

66f   34f

4-y-o b f Turtle Island (IRE)-Spark (IRE) (Flash Of Steel)
J M Bradley (J A Pickering 15/12)   Miss F Fenley

Placings:00   (4920)
2003/04: 130S, 169GS,

	Starts	1st	2nd	3rd	Win & Pl
NH Flat	2	0	0	0	
Career Total	2	0	0	0	

Going: Sf: 0-1 GS: 0-1 Gd: 0-0 GF: - Fm: 0-0
Distance: 2m/2m3: 0-1 2m4-2m7: 0-0 3m+: 0-0
Track: LH: 0-1 RH: 0-1 Tight: 0-0 Gall: 0-0
Aids: BI: 0-0 Vi: 0-0 Tstrap: 0-0 Ckp: 0-0
Best Rating: 16   4/04   Worc   2m   gd-sft   NHF

Flight Command

100   100+

6-y-o ch g Gunner B-Wing On (Quayside)
P Beaumont   N W A Bannister

Placings:1-634522   (4868)
2003/04: 166GS, 183S, 204HY, 205GS, 222GS, 202GS,

		Starts	1st	2nd	3rd	Win & Pl
NH Flat		1	0	0	0	
Hurdles		5	0	2	1	3091
Career Total		7	1	2	1	6633
102	4/03	Prth	2m110y	H NHF	GD	£3542

         Total win prize-money £3542

Going: Sf: 0-2 GS: 0-4 Gd: 0-0 GF: - Fm: 0-0
Distance: 2m/2m3: 0-2 2m4-2m7: 0-4 3m+: 0-0
Track: LH: 0-6 RH: 0-0 Tight: 0-3 Gall: 0-2
Aids: BI: 0-0 Vi: 0-0 Tstrap: 0-0 Ckp: 0-0
Best Rating: 102   4/03   Prth   2m110y   good   NHF

Bred to be a chaser; made successful debut in a Perth bumper in 2003; placed in novice hurdles; stays well.

Flight To Tuscany

88   60

6-y-o b m Bonny Scot (IRE)-Tuscan Butterfly (Beldale Flutter (USA))
J M Bradley   J M Bradley

Placings:0-056   (1415)
2003/04: 160GF, 205GF, 186GF,

	Starts	1st	2nd	3rd	Win & Pl
Hurdles	3	0	0	0	0
Career Total	4	0	0	0	0

Going: Sf: 0-0 GS: 0-0 Gd: 0-0 GF: - Fm: 0-3
Distance: 2m/2m3: 0-2 2m4-2m7: 0-1 3m+: 0-0
Track: LH: 0-3 RH: 0-0 Tight: 0-1 Gall: 0-0
Aids: BI: 0-1 Vi: 0-0 Tstrap: 0-0 Ckp: 0-2
Best Rating: 60   9/03   Worc   2m   gd-fm   Hdl

Flight West (IRE)

90f   83f

5-y-o gr g Norwich-Bee In The Rose (IRE) (Roselier (FR))
J Wade   John Wade

Placings:O00   (3766)
2003/04: 160GS, 169S, 179GS,

	Starts	1st	2nd	3rd	Win & Pl
NH Flat	3	0	0	0	
Career Total	3	0	0	0	

Going: Sf: 0-1 GS: 0-2 Gd: 0-0 GF: - Fm: 0-0
Distance: 2m/2m3: 0-3 2m4-2m7: 0-0 3m+: 0-0
Track: LH: 0-3 RH: 0-0 Tight: 0-2 Gall: 0-0
Aids: BI: 0-0 Vi: 0-0 Tstrap: 0-0 Ckp: 0-0

Best Rating: 83   1/04   Weth   2m   soft   NHF

Flighty Leader (IRE)
96   66
12-y-o b g Supreme Leader-Flighty Ann (The Parson)
P Spottiswood   P Spottiswood

Placings:033044/140533/46423F5/30600/040P-054 **(0689)**
2003/04: 24⁴GF, 24⁰G, 20⁵G, 20⁴GF,

	Starts	1st	2nd	3rd	Win & Pl
Hurdles	4	0	0	0	
Career Total	31	1	1	6	5789
101 10/99 Kels	2m6f110yG Hdl		GD	£1954
			Total win prize-money £1954

Going:	Sf: 0-0 GS: 0-0 Gd: 0-2 GF: - Fm: 0-2
Distance:	2m/2m3: 0-0 2m4-2m7: 0-2 3m+: 0-2
Track:	LH: 0-4 RH: 0-0 Tight: 0-0 Gall: 0-1
Aids:	Bl: 0-0 Vi: 0-4 Tstrap: 0-0 Ckp: 0-0
Best Rating:	101 10/99 Kels 2m6f110y good Hdl

Poor selling hurdler; stays two mile six.

Flinders
109   (81h)91
9-y-o b m Henbit (USA)-Stupid Cupid (Idiots Delight)
R Rowe   Leith Hill Chasers

Placings:363/4300/3054550/5102P-P4413FP01 **(4933)**
2003/04: 25⁶GF, 24⁴G, 25⁴GF, 24¹G, 25³GF, 26⁴HY, 25⁴GS, 25⁰G, 26¹G,

	Starts	1st	2nd	3rd	Win & Pl
Chases	9	2	0	1	7597
Career Total	28	3	1	5	13996
91 4/04 Font	3m2f110yF(0-100)HCh	GD	£3393
91 11/03 Fknm	3m110y E(0-105)HCh	GD	£3731
80 11/02 Folk	3m1f F(0-95)HCh	GD	£4199
		Total win prize-money £11323

Going:	Sf: 0-1 GS: 0-1 Gd: 2-4 GF: - Fm: 0-3
Distance:	2m/2m3: 0-0 2m4-2m7: 0-0 3m+: 2-9
Track:	LH: 1-1 RH: 0-6 Tight: 2-7 Gall: 0-1
Aids:	Bl: 0-0 Vi: 0-0 Tstrap: 0-0 Ckp: 0-0
Best Rating:	97 1/00 Folk 2m1f110y soft NHF

Moderate chaser; stays three miles plus; acts on ground good or faster.

Flinders Chase
105   124
9-y-o gr g Terimon-Proverbial Rose (Proverb)
C J Mann   P M Warren

Placings:41/3U/3333223U-132U41P4 **(4640)**
2003/04: 17¹G, 18³GS, 20²GS, 18⁰S, 21⁴GS, 20¹G, 16²GS, 21⁴G,

	Starts	1st	2nd	3rd	Win & Pl
Chases	8	2	1	1	18228
Career Total	20	3	3	7	29785
122 2/04 Sand	2m4f110yD Ch	GD	£7262
123 11/03 Extr	2m1f110yE(0-105)HCh	GD	£3211
113 11/00 MRas	2m1f110yD Hdl	SFT	£3225
		Total win prize-money £13699

Going:	Sf: 0-1 GS: 0-4 Gd: 2-3 GF: - Fm: 0-0
Distance:	2m/2m3: 1-4 2m4-2m7: 1-4 3m+: 0-0
Track:	LH: 0-4 RH: 2-4 Tight: 0-1 Gall: 0-4
Aids:	Bl: 0-0 Vi: 0-0 Tstrap: 0-0 Ckp: 0-0
Best Rating:	123 4/04 Aint 2m5f110y good Ch

Fair chaser; frustrating type; stays three miles; suited by ease in the ground.

Flite Of Araby
91   (0c)50
7-y-o b g Green Desert (USA)-Allegedly Blue (USA) (Alleged (USA))
R J Price (N J Hawke 21/6)   E J Whilding

Placings:P0-PR0 **(1485)**
2003/04: 16⁶PG, 16⁸GF, 17⁰GF,

	Starts	1st	2nd	3rd	Win & Pl
Hurdles	2	0	0	0	0
Chases	1	0	0	0	0
Career Total	5	0	0	0	

Going:	Sf: 0-0 GS: 0-0 Gd: 0-1 GF: - Fm: 0-2
Distance:	2m/2m3: 0-2 2m4-2m7: 0-0 3m+: 0-0
Track:	LH: 0-2 RH: 0-1 Tight: 0-1 Gall: 0-0
Aids:	Bl: 0-0 Vi: 0-0 Tstrap: 0-0 Ckp: 0-0
Best Rating:	50 10/03 Hrfd 2m1f gd-fm Hdl

Flood's Fancy
11-y-o gr m Then Again-Port Na Blath (On Your Mark)
B R Foster   Michael Brownrigg

Placings:025/0/30P/P065F/P-P **(0071)**
2003/04: 24⁴PS,

	Starts	1st	2nd	3rd	Win & Pl
Hurdles	1	0	0	0	
Career Total	14	0	1	1	1016

Going:	Sf: 0-1 GS: 0-0 Gd: 0-0 GF: - Fm: 0-0
Distance:	2m/2m3: 0-0 2m4-2m7: 0-0 3m+: 0-1
Track:	LH: 0-1 RH: 0-0 Tight: 0-0 Gall: 0-0
Aids:	Bl: 0-0 Vi: 0-0 Tstrap: 0-0 Ckp: 0-0
Best Rating:	80 10/96 Worc 2m gd-fm Hdl

Flora Muck
102(96h)   (82h)84
8-y-o b m Alflora (IRE)-Muckertoo (Sagaro)
N A Twiston-Davies   The Yes - No - Wait   Sorries

Placings:46060/123FU5-3123F3U **(4757)**
2003/04: 25³GF, 26¹GF, 25²F, 24³GF, 25²FS, 22³GS, 25⁰S,

	Starts	1st	2nd	3rd	Win & Pl
Chases	7	1	1	3	3886
Career Total	18	2	2	4	7613
84 10/03 Uttx	3m2f F(0-100)HCh	G-F	£2555
82 5/02 Towc	3m F(0-100)HHdl	G-S	£2278
		Total win prize-money £4834

Going:	Sf: 0-2 GS: 0-1 Gd: 0-0 GF: - Fm: 1-4
Distance:	2m/2m3: 0-0 2m4-2m7: 0-0 3m+: 1-6
Track:	LH: 1-1 RH: 0-6 Tight: 0-0 Gall: 0-1
Aids:	Bl: 0-0 Vi: 0-0 Tstrap: 0-0 Ckp: 0-0
Best Rating:	88 10/01 Bang 2m1f good NHF

Modest hurdle/ chaser; off the mark over fences at Uttoxeter in October; jumps well; stays really well.

Flora Poste
(77h)   (30h)
8-y-o ch m Alflora (IRE)-Preachers Popsy (The Parson)
J C Tuck   Piers F Dibben

Placings:6/40/050-PCU6 **(4855)**
2003/04: 22⁵PS, 20ᶜGF, 25⁵UG, 24⁸GF,

	Starts	1st	2nd	3rd	Win & Pl
Hurdles	1	0	0	0	0

Chases	3	0	0	0	0
Career Total	10	0	0	0	0

Going:	Sf: 0-1 GS: 0-0 Gd: 0-1 GF: - Fm: 0-2
Distance:	2m/2m3: 0-2 2m4-2m7: 0-2 3m+: 0-2
Track:	LH: 0-0 RH: 0-4 Tight: 0-1 Gall: 0-0
Aids:	Bl: 0-0 Vi: 0-0 Tstrap: 0-0 Ckp: 0-0
Best Rating:	77 3/01 Newb 2m110y heavy NHF

Floranz
86   74
8-y-o br m Afzal-Tuesday Member (New Member)
Mrs M Evans   W J Evans

Placings:0/P3P34 **(1524)**
2003/04: 20⁵S, 22³GF, 22⁰GF, 19³GF, 22⁴G,

	Starts	1st	2nd	3rd	Win & Pl
Hurdles	5	0	0	2	966
Career Total	6	0	0	2	966

Going:	Sf: 0-1 GS: 0-0 Gd: 0-1 GF: - Fm: 0-3
Distance:	2m/2m3: 0-1 2m4-2m7: 0-4 3m+: 0-0
Track:	LH: 0-4 RH: 0-0 Tight: 0-4 Gall: 0-0
Aids:	Bl: 0-0 Vi: 0-0 Tstrap: 0-0 Ckp: 0-0
Best Rating:	76 9/03 NAbb 2m3f gd-fm Hdl

Modest form in novice hurdles at up to 2m 6f.

Florenzar (IRE)
95   69
6-y-o b m Inzar (USA)-Nurse Tyra (USA) (Dr Blum (USA))
P D Evans (Miss Sheena West 28/8)   D Healy

Placings:6-3UP6P **(4714)**
2003/04: 16³GF, 16ᵁG, 16⁶PGS, 19⁶GF, 16⁰PG,

	Starts	1st	2nd	3rd	Win & Pl
Hurdles	5	0	0	1	332
Career Total	6	0	0	1	332

Going:	Sf: 0-0 GS: 0-1 Gd: 0-2 GF: - Fm: 0-2
Distance:	2m/2m3: 0-5 2m4-2m7: 0-0 3m+: 0-0
Track:	LH: 0-1 RH: 0-4 Tight: 0-1 Gall: 0-0
Aids:	Bl: 0-0 Vi: 0-4 Tstrap: 0-0 Ckp: 0-0
Best Rating:	73 11/03 Ludl 2m gd-fm Hdl

Florida (IRE)
95   63
6-y-o b m Sri Pekan (USA)-Florinda (CAN) (Vice Regent (CAN))
I A Wood   Neardown Stables

Placings:P5/P-42 **(1676)**
2003/04: 21⁴GF, 19²F,

	Starts	1st	2nd	3rd	Win & Pl
Hurdles	2	0	1	0	526
Career Total	5	0	1	0	526

Going:	Sf: 0-0 GS: 0-0 Gd: 0-0 GF: - Fm: 0-2
Distance:	2m/2m3: 0-2 2m4-2m7: 0-2 3m+: 0-0
Track:	LH: 0-1 RH: 0-0 Tight: 0-1 Gall: 0-0
Aids:	Bl: 0-0 Vi: 0-0 Tstrap: 0-0 Ckp: 0-0
Best Rating:	63 10/03 Towc 2m3f110y firm Hdl

Plating class maiden over hurdles; looked a very difficult ride when runner-up in poor Towcester seller October 2003; needs distances in excess of 2m.

Florida Dream (IRE)

99   **84**

5-y-o b g Florida Son-Ice Pearl (Flatbush)
Ms Bridget Nicholls D J & S A Goodman & T Puffett

Placings:0000   (4691)
2003/04: 16⁶GS, 16⁶GS, 16⁶G, 17⁰G,

	Starts	1st	2nd	3rd	Win & Pl
NH Flat	2	0	0	0	0
Hurdles	2	0	0	0	0
Career Total	**4**	**0**	**0**	**0**	

Going:	Sf: 0-0 GS: 0-2 Gd: 0-2 GF: - Fm: 0-0
Distance:	2m2m3: 0-4 2m4-2m7: 0-0 3m+: 0-0
Track:	LH: 0-4 RH: 0-3 Tight: 0-0 Gall: 0-2
Aids:	Bl: 0-0 Vi: 0-0 Tstrap: 0-0 Ckp: 0-0
Best Rating:	86 3/04 Hntg 2m110y good Hdl

Florida Rain (IRE)

91   **97+**

8-y-o b g Florida Son-Ameretto (Stetchworth (USA))
Mrs M Reveley Andy Peake

Placings:00/34/01-6   (2608)
2003/04: 16⁶G,

	Starts	1st	2nd	3rd	Win & Pl
Hurdles	1	0	0	0	0
Career Total	**7**	**1**	**0**	**1**	**3271**
101 12/02 Catt	2m3f	E Hdl		G-S	£3024

Total win prize-money £3024

Going:	Sf: 0-0 GS: 0-0 Gd: 0-1 GF: - Fm: 0-0
Distance:	2m2m3: 0-1 2m4-2m7: 0-0 3m+: 0-0
Track:	LH: 0-1 RH: 0-0 Tight: 0-0 Gall: 0-0
Aids:	Bl: 0-0 Vi: 0-0 Tstrap: 0-0 Ckp: 0-0
Best Rating:	101 12/02 Catt 2m3f gd-sft Hdl

Modest hurdler; a chaser in the making; showed promise in bumpers; finished lame on return to action at Wetherby in December.

Florries Son

105(108h)   (121 h)**125**

9-y-o b g Minster Son-Florrie Palmer (Deadly Nightshade)
M Todhunter Mrs F M Gray

Placings:2/1113121-F2F154   (4659)
2003/04: 20¹G, 25⁵G, 24²GF, 25⁵G, 20¹HY, 20⁵S, 16⁴S,

	Starts	1st	2nd	3rd	Win & Pl
Chases	7	2	1	0	12222
Career Total	**14**	**6**	**3**	**1**	**30627**
118 2/04 Newc	2m4f	E Ch		HVY	£4410
125 4/03 Hexm	2m4f110yD Ch			GD	£5408
120 3/03 Weth	3m1f	E Hdl		G-F	£3425
119 11/02 Weth	2m7f	F(0-100)HHdl		GD	£2362
90 10/02 Kels	2m6f110yE Hdl			GD	£3809
85 10/02 Hexm	3m	E Hdl		G-F	£2835

Total win prize-money £22251

Going:	Sf: 1-3 GS: 0-0 Gd: 1-3 GF: - Fm: 0-1
Distance:	2m2m3: 0-1 **2m4-2m7: 2-3** 3m+: 0-3
Track:	**LH: 2-6** RH: 0-1 Tight: 0-0 **Gall: 1-2**
Aids:	Bl: 0-0 Vi: 0-0 Tstrap: 0-0 Ckp: 0-0
Best Rating:	125 4/03 Hexm 2m4f110y good Ch

Fair novice chaser; progressive novice hurdler winning four times in 2002/2003; successful on chasing debut and should prove useful in that sphere; stays three miles; acts on a sound surface.

Flower Breeze (USA)

93   **66**

4-y-o ch f Rahy (USA)-Now Showing (USA) (Golden Act (USA))
M W Easterby John Southway

Placings:6   (1071)
2003/04: 17⁵GF,

	Starts	1st	2nd	3rd	Win & Pl
Hurdles	1	0	0	0	0
Career Total	**1**	**0**	**0**	**0**	

Going:	Sf: 0-0 GS: 0-0 Gd: 0-0 GF: - Fm: 0-0
Distance:	2m2m3: 0-1 2m4-2m7: 0-0 3m+: 0-0
Track:	LH: 0-1 RH: 0-0 Tight: 0-1 Gall: 0-0
Aids:	Bl: 0-0 Vi: 0-0 Tstrap: 0-0 Ckp: 0-0
Best Rating:	70 8/03 Sedg 2m1f gd-fm Hdl

Flower Of Pitcur

104   **105+**

7-y-o b g Alflora (IRE)-Coire Vannich (Celtic Cone)
T R George Mrs Strachan,L-Palmer,Parkinson,J Morris

Placings:1P0-P64104   (4546)
2003/04: 20⁵GS, 19⁶GS, 19⁴S, 17¹GS, 19⁰G, 16⁴GS,

	Starts	1st	2nd	3rd	Win & Pl
Hurdles	6	1	0	0	3638
Career Total	**9**	**2**	**0**	**0**	**5717**
105 2/04 Hrfd	2m1f	F(0-95)HHdl		G-S	£3346
96 3/03 Hntg	2m110y	H NHF		GD	£2079

Total win prize-money £5425

Going:	Sf: 0-1 GS: 1-4 Gd: 0-1 GF: - Fm: 0-0
Distance:	**2m2m3: 1-4** 2m4-2m7: 0-2 3m+: 0-0
Track:	LH: 0-2 **RH: 1-4** Tight: 0-0 Gall: 0-1
Aids:	Bl: 0-0 Vi: 0-0 Tstrap: 0-0 Ckp: 0-0
Best Rating:	105 2/04 Hrfd 2m1f gd-sft Hdl

Disappointing in bumpers after making winning debut on good ground at Huntingdon March 2003; won novices' handicap hurdle at Hereford February 2004; effective at 2m.

Flowing River (IRE)

70f   **79f**

6-y-o ch g Over The River (FR)-Minature Miss (Move Off)
D Eddy Mrs H Scotto

Placings:60   (3737)
2003/04: 16⁶GS, 16⁶G,

	Starts	1st	2nd	3rd	Win & Pl
NH Flat	2	0	0	0	0
Career Total	**2**	**0**	**0**	**0**	

Going:	Sf: 0-0 GS: 0-1 Gd: 0-1 GF: - Fm: 0-0
Distance:	2m2m3: 0-2 2m4-2m7: 0-0 3m+: 0-0
Track:	LH: 0-1 RH: 0-1 Tight: 0-2 Gall: 0-0
Aids:	Bl: 0-0 Vi: 0-0 Tstrap: 0-0 Ckp: 0-0
Best Rating:	79 1/04 Catt 2m gd-sft NHF

Flownaway

94   **123+**

5-y-o b g Polar Falcon (USA)-No More Rosies (Warpath)
J Howard Johnson (W Jarvis 18/10) Andrea & Graham Wylie

Placings:F1   (4732)

2003/04: 16⁵GF, 17¹G,

	Starts	1st	2nd	3rd	Win & Pl
Hurdles	2	1	0	0	3689
Career Total	**2**	**1**	**0**	**0**	**3689**
123 4/04 Carl	2m1f	E Hdl		GD	£3688

Total win prize-money £3689

Going:	Sf: 0-0 GS: 0-0 Gd: 1-1 GF: - Fm: 0-1
Distance:	**2m2m3: 1-2** 2m4-2m7: 0-0 3m+: 0-0
Track:	LH: 0-0 **RH: 1-2** Tight: 0-0 Gall: 0-0
Aids:	Bl: 0-0 Vi: 0-0 Tstrap: 0-0 Ckp: 0-0
Best Rating:	123 4/04 Carl 2m1f good Hdl

Very useful stayer on the Flat, winner of six races; suited by a sound surface; jumped right-handed, but clear when falling two out on hurdling debut at Musselburgh in January.

Fluff 'N' Puff

105   (66h)**101**

10-y-o ch g Nicholas Bill-Puff Puff (All Systems Go)
J S King Dajam Ltd

Placings:003/062/0PF32F53/3124P2235-44422134 (4379)
2003/04: 16⁴G, 21⁴G, 21⁴G, 24²G, 20²G, 20¹S, 24²G, 24⁴G,

	Starts	1st	2nd	3rd	Win & Pl
Chases	8	1	2	1	9235
Career Total	**31**	**2**	**7**	**6**	**27174**
101 2/04 Hntg	2m4f110yF(0-95)HCh			SFT	£3388
97 11/02 Ludl	3m	E(0-110)HCh		GD	£5473

Total win prize-money £8861

Going:	Sf: 1-1 GS: 0-0 Gd: 0-7 GF: - Fm: 0-0
Distance:	2m2m3: 0-1 **2m4-2m7: 1-4** 3m+: 0-3
Track:	LH: 0-1 **RH: 1-7** Tight: 0-5 **Gall: 1-1**
Aids:	Bl: 0-0 Vi: 0-0 Tstrap: 0-0 **Ckp: 1-4**
Best Rating:	103 2/01 Ludl 2m gd-sft Hdl

Plating-class chaser; best on a decent surface; stays three miles but possibly best suited by shorter.

Flur Na H Alba

79   **49**

5-y-o b g Atraf-Tyrian Belle (Enchantment)
J M Jefferson (I Semple 12/10) The Mathieson Partnership

Placings:0   (4260)
2003/04: 16⁰GF,

	Starts	1st	2nd	3rd	Win & Pl
Hurdles	1	0	0	0	
Career Total	**1**	**0**	**0**	**0**	

Going:	Sf: 0-0 GS: 0-0 Gd: 0-0 GF: - Fm: 0-1
Distance:	2m2m3: 0-1 2m4-2m7: 0-0 3m+: 0-0
Track:	LH: 0-1 RH: 0-0 Tight: 0-1 Gall: 0-0
Aids:	Bl: 0-0 Vi: 0-0 Tstrap: 0-0 Ckp: 0-0
Best Rating:	49 3/04 Catt 2m gd-fm Hdl

Flurry

89f   **59f**

5-y-o gr m Terimon-Queen's Favourite (Sunyboy)
C J Down J Selby

Placings:0   (4213)
2003/04: 16⁶G,

	Starts	1st	2nd	3rd	Win & Pl
NH Flat	1	0	0	0	
Career Total	**1**	**0**	**0**	**0**	

Going:	Sf: 0-0 GS: 0-0 Gd: 0-0 GF: - Fm: 0-0
Distance:	2m2m3: 0-1 2m4-2m7: 0-0 3m+: 0-0

Track: LH: 0-0 RH: 0-1 Tight: 0-0 Gall: 0-0
Aids: Bl: 0-0 Vi: 0-0 Tstrap: 0-0 Ckp: 0-0
Best Rating: 59 3/04 Kemp 2m   good NHF

Fly Kicker

103   102

7-y-o ch g High Kicker (USA)-Double Birthday (Cavo Doro)
W Storey M D Townson

Placings:300P300-2023204115   (2378)
2003/04: 16³G, 16²G, 16⁰G, 16²GF, 17³G, 16²F, 16⁰G, 17⁴G,
16¹GF, 16¹G, 17⁵GF,

	Starts	1st	2nd	3rd	Win & Pl
Hurdles	11	2	3	1	9582
Career Total	17	2	3	3	10398
102	11/03 Weth	2m	E(0-100)HHdl		£3423
97	10/03 Weth	2m	E(0-110)HHdl		£2936
			Total win prize-money £6360

Going: Sf: 0-0 GS: 0-0 Gd: 1-6 GF: - Fm: 1-5
Distance: 2m/2m3: 2-11 2m4-2m7: 0-0 3m+: 0-0
Track: LH: 2-9 RH: 0-2 Tight: 0-4 Gall: 0-1
Aids: Bl: 0-0 Vi: 0-0 Tstrap: 0-0 Ckp: 2-9
Best Rating: 102 11/03 Weth 2m   good Hdl

Moderate hurdler; consistent in his grade; successful twice at Wetherby in November; yet to prove he stays further than two miles one; acts on good ground.

Flyaway Rose

77f   36f

4-y-o b f Busy Flight-Flaming Rose (IRE) (Roselier (FR))
Miss I E Craig Mrs M L Luck

Placings:0   (4936)
2003/04: 18⁰G,

	Starts	1st	2nd	3rd	Win & Pl
NH Flat	1	0	0	0	
Career Total	1	0	0	0	

Going: Sf: 0-0 GS: 0-0 Gd: 0-1 GF: - Fm: 0-0
Distance: 2m/2m3: 0-1 2m4-2m7: 0-0 3m+: 0-0
Track: LH: 0-1 RH: 0-0 Tight: 0-1 Gall: 0-0
Aids: Bl: 0-0 Vi: 0-0 Tstrap: 0-0 Ckp: 0-0
Best Rating: 36 4/04 Font 2m2f110y good NHF

Flying Bold (IRE)

78   90

9-y-o ch g Persian Bold-Princess Reema (USA) (Affirmed (USA))
N G Ayliffe Mrs M A Barrett

Placings:0/33103120/0530/304000/640150-0   (0487)
2003/04: 22⁰GF,

	Starts	1st	2nd	3rd	Win & Pl
Hurdles	1	0	0	0	
Career Total	26	3	1	5	8134
90	8/02 NAbb	2m6f	G(0-95)HHdl	G-F	£2198
89	1/00 Catt	2m3f	G(0-90)HHdl	GD	£1620
86	10/99 Kels	2m110y	G Hdl	GD	£2010
			Total win prize-money £5829

Going: Sf: 0-0 GS: 0-0 Gd: 0-0 GF: - Fm: 0-1
Distance: 2m/2m3: 0-0 2m4-2m7: 0-1 3m+: 0-0
Track: LH: 0-1 RH: 0-0 Tight: 0-1 Gall: 0-0
Aids: Bl: 0-0 Vi: 0-0 Tstrap: 0-0 Ckp: 0-0
Best Rating: 94 2/00 Catt 2m3f   good Hdl

Selling hurdler, stays two miles six furlongs on a sound surface.

Flying Druid (FR)

101f   87f

4-y-o b g Celtic Swing-Sky Bibi (FR) (Sky Lawyer (FR))
Evan Williams Mr and Mrs Glynne Clay

Placings:3   (4447)
2003/04: 16³S,

	Starts	1st	2nd	3rd	Win & Pl
NH Flat	1	0	0	1	329
Career Total	1	0	0	1	329

Going: Sf: 0-1 GS: 0-0 Gd: 0-0 GF: - Fm: 0-0
Distance: 2m/2m3: 0-1 2m4-2m7: 0-0 3m+: 0-0
Track: LH: 0-1 RH: 0-0 Tight: 0-0 Gall: 0-0
Aids: Bl: 0-0 Vi: 0-0 Tstrap: 0-0 Ckp: 0-0
Best Rating: 87 3/04 Wwck 2m   soft NHF

Half-brother to French hurdles and chase winner Sky Warrior; promising third when 66/1 on bumper debut.

Flying Falcon

97f   115+f

5-y-o b g Polar Falcon (USA)-Lemon Balm (High Top)
Miss Venetia Williams Peter Diamond

Placings:36110   (4649)
2003/04: 17³G, 16⁶GS, 16¹G, 14¹GS, 17⁰G,

	Starts	1st	2nd	3rd	Win & Pl
NH Flat	5	2	0	1	4213
Career Total	5	2	0	1	4213
115	3/04 Hrfd	1m6f	H NHF	G-S	£1988
104	3/04 Winc	2m	H NHF	GD	£2009
			Total win prize-money £3997

Going: Sf: 0-0 GS: 1-2 Gd: 1-3 GF: - Fm: 0-0
Distance: 2m/2m3: 1-4 2m4-2m7: 0-0 3m+: 0-0
Track: LH: 0-0 RH: 1-2 Tight: 0-1 Gall: 0-0
Aids: Bl: 0-0 Vi: 0-0 Tstrap: 0-0 Ckp: 0-0
Best Rating: 115 3/04 Hrfd 1m6f   gd-sft NHF

Flying Fiddler (IRE)

(92c)

13-y-o ch g Orchestra-Rambling Ivy (Mandalus)
Mrs L P Baker Mrs L P Baker

Placings:5044/3244126/130/5/405/2/P   (0203)
2003/04: 21³GF,

	Starts	1st	2nd	3rd	Win & Pl
Hurdles	1	0	0	0	
Career Total	20	2	3	2	10975
110	10/97 Kemp	2m5f	C(0-135)HHdl	GD	£3517
106	2/97 Asct	2m4f	E(0-120)HHdl	G-F	£3533
			Total win prize-money £7052

Going: Sf: 0-0 GS: 0-0 Gd: 0-0 GF: - Fm: 0-1
Distance: 2m/2m3: 0-0 2m4-2m7: 0-1 3m+: 0-0
Track: LH: 0-0 RH: 0-0 Tight: 0-0 Gall: 0-1
Aids: Bl: 0-1 Vi: 0-0 Tstrap: 0-0 Ckp: 0-0
Best Rating: 110 10/97 Kemp 2m5f   good Hdl

Flying First (IRE)

87   51

9-y-o b g Executive Perk-Rule The Waves (Deep Run)
T D McCarthy A D Spence

Placings:020/PP-P0   (0445)
2003/04: 16⁰GF, 16⁰G,

	Starts	1st	2nd	3rd	Win & Pl
Hurdles	2	0	0	0	

Career Total   7   0   1   0   490

Going: Sf: 0-0 GS: 0-0 Gd: 0-1 GF: - Fm: 0-1
Distance: 2m/2m3: 0-2 2m4-2m7: 0-0 3m+: 0-0
Track: LH: 0-0 RH: 0-2 Tight: 0-0 Gall: 0-2
Aids: Bl: 0-0 Vi: 0-0 Tstrap: 0-0 Ckp: 0-0
Best Rating: 100 3/00 Folk 2m1f110y gd-fm NHF

Flying Fuselier

71f   26f

5-y-o ch g Gunner B-Wing On (Quayside)
P J Hobbs Mrs Z S Clark

Placings:0   (4578)
2003/04: 16⁰G,

	Starts	1st	2nd	3rd	Win & Pl
NH Flat	1	0	0	0	
Career Total	1	0	0	0	

Going: Sf: 0-0 GS: 0-0 Gd: 0-1 GF: - Fm: 0-0
Distance: 2m/2m3: 0-1 2m4-2m7: 0-0 3m+: 0-0
Track: LH: 0-1 RH: 0-0 Tight: 0-0 Gall: 0-1
Aids: Bl: 0-0 Vi: 0-0 Tstrap: 0-0 Ckp: 0-0
Best Rating: 26 3/04 Newb 2m110y   good NHF

Flying Instructor

113   140

14-y-o gr g Neltino-Flying Mistress (Lear Jet)
P R Webber Mrs John Webber

Placings:60/301611/P03143F3/1326143525/135101/64142
32/455P104P/16046521P3/5P31   (1080)
2003/04: 20⁵G, 23³GF, 26⁵GF, 23¹GF,

	Starts	1st	2nd	3rd	Win & Pl
Chases	4	1	0	1	7937
Career Total	61	14	5	10	196922
140	8/03 Worc	2m7f110yD(0-125)HCh	G-F	£6695
142	3/02 Donc	2m3f110yB(0-140)HCh	G-S	£10842
148	5/01 Weth	3m1f	B(0-145)HCh	FRM	£9083
150	2/01 Hayd	2m4f	B HCh	SFT	£14170
153	12/99 Weth	2m4f110yB HCh	G-S	£10338
153	4/99 Aint	2m	A HCh	GD	£26775
157	2/99 Newb	2m4f	B(0-145)HCh	G-S	£10934
156	12/98 Chel	2m110y	B HCh	GD	£8563
154	1/98 Hayd	2m	B HCh	SFT	£7067
118	5/97 Bang	2m1f110yD Ch	GD	£3355
132	2/97 Hayd	2m	C Ch	GD	£4485
130	4/96 Asct	2m110y	C(0-135)HHdl	G-F	£5152
126	3/96 Uttx	2m	C Hdl	G-S	£3891
90	11/95 Nott	2m	D Hdl	G-F	£3202
			Total win prize-money £124555

Going: Sf: 0-0 GS: 0-0 Gd: 0-1 GF: - Fm: 1-3
Distance: 2m/2m3: 0-0 2m4-2m7: 0-1 3m+: 1-3
Track: LH: 0-4 RH: 0-0 Tight: 0-1 Gall: 0-0
Aids: Bl: 0-0 Vi: 0-0 Tstrap: 0-0 Ckp: 0-0
Best Rating: 157 2/99 Newb 2m4f   gd-sft Ch

Useful handicap chaser at up to 3m in his heyday; acts on most types of ground; now in the veteran stage but showed he is no back number when winning four-runner 3m handicap at Worcester August 2003.

Flying Lyric (IRE)

99   97

6-y-o b g Definite Article-Lyric Junction (IRE) (Classic Secret (USA))
A King Nigel Bunter

Placings:U430   **(3483)**
2003/04: 19^{U}GS, 20^{4}GS, 16^{3}GS, 17^{9}GS,

	Starts	1st	2nd	3rd	Win & Pl
Hurdles	4	0	0	1	520
Career Total	4	0	0	1	520

Going:	Sf: 0-0 GS: 0-4 Gd: 0-0 GF: - Fm: 0-0
Distance:	2m/2m3: 0-2 2m4-2m7: 0-2 3m+: 0-0
Track:	LH: 0-2 RH: 0-0 Tight: 0-0 Gall: 0-1
Aids:	Bl: 0-0 Vi: 0-0 Tstrap: 0-0 Ckp: 0-0
Best Rating:	97 1/04 Winc 2m gd-sft Hdl

Moderate hurdler; acts on easy ground.

Flying Spirit (IRE)
105   116
5-y-o b g Flying Spur (AUS)-All Laughter (Vision (USA))
G L Moore (M H Tompkins 14/5) Richard Green (fine Paintings)

Placings:56-12U12   **(1833)**
2003/04: 18^{1}GF, 19^{2}GF, 18^{U}GF, 16^{1}GF, 16^{2}GF,

	Starts	1st	2nd	3rd	Win & Pl
Hurdles	5	2	2	0	11365
Career Total	7	2	2	0	11365
106	9/03	Plum	2m	E Hdl	G-F	£3094
110	8/03	Font	2m2f110yE Hdl		G-F	£3360

Total win prize-money £6455

Going:	Sf: 0-0 GS: 0-0 Gd: 0-0 GF: - Fm: 2-5
Distance:	2m/2m3: 2-4 2m4-2m7: 0-1 3m+: 0-0
Track:	LH: 2-4 RH: 0-1 Tight: 2-3 Gall: 0-0
Aids:	Bl: 0-0 Vi: 0-0 Tstrap: 0-0 Ckp: 0-0
Best Rating:	116 10/03 Chel 2m110y gd-fm Hdl

Moderate novice hurdler; stays beyond two miles and acts on fast ground.

Flying Trix (IRE)
107   113
8-y-o b g Lord Americo-Bannow Drive (IRE) (Miners Lamp)
M Pitman Patrick Bancroft

Placings:35/43113PP/00643/P0511   **(4834)**
2003/04: 22^{P}S, 20^{3}GS, 23^{5}G, 24^{1}G, 26^{1}GF,

	Starts	1st	2nd	3rd	Win & Pl
Chases	5	2	0	0	16012
Career Total	19	4	0	4	26097
109	4/04	Chel	3m2f110yC(0-135)HCh	G-F	£11663
113	3/04	Kemp	3m	E(0-105)HCh	G-F	£4348
113	1/01	Uttx	3m110y	D Hdl	HVY	£3612
119	12/00	Towc	2m5f	D Hdl	HVY	£3055

Total win prize-money £22680

Going:	Sf: 0-1 GS: 0-1 Gd: 1-2 GF: - Fm: 1-1
Distance:	2m/2m3: 0-0 2m4-2m7: 0-2 3m+: 2-3
Track:	LH: 1-1 RH: 1-4 Tight: 0-0 Gall: 1-2
Aids:	Bl: 0-0 Vi: 0-0 Tstrap: 0-0 Ckp: 0-0
Best Rating:	126 2/01 Asct 3m heavy Hdl

Moderate chaser; stays three miles; acts on most types of ground.

Flying Wanda
96   78+
4-y-o b f Alzao (USA)-Royal York (Bustino)
P F Nicholls (J Noseda 29/10) Sir Robert Ogden

Placings:4U0   **(4166)**
2003/04: 16^{4}S, 16^{U}G, 16^{9}G,

	Starts	1st	2nd	3rd	Win & Pl
Hurdles	3	0	0	0	267

	Starts	1st	2nd	3rd	Win & Pl
Career Total	3	0	0	0	267

Going:	Sf: 0-1 GS: 0-0 Gd: 0-2 GF: - Fm: 0-0
Distance:	2m/2m3: 0-3 2m4-2m7: 0-0 3m+: 0-0
Track:	LH: 0-2 RH: 0-1 Tight: 0-1 Gall: 0-1
Aids:	Bl: 0-0 Vi: 0-0 Tstrap: 0-0 Ckp: 0-0
Best Rating:	78 2/04 Plum 2m soft Hdl

Listed-class on the Flat; disappointed on hurdling bow at Plumpton in February when pulling hard in testing conditions; best on good ground.

Flyoff (IRE)
103   75+
7-y-o b g Mtoto-Flyleaf (FR) (Persian Bold)
K A Morgan Harmer Personal Care Ltd

Placings:6/60-404060P   **(3915)**
2003/04: 16^{4}GF, 16^{9}G, 16^{4}GS, 20^{0}G, 16^{6}S, 16^{0}G, 16^{P}G,

	Starts	1st	2nd	3rd	Win & Pl
Hurdles	7	0	0	0	0
Career Total	10	0	0	0	0

Going:	Sf: 0-1 GS: 0-1 Gd: 0-4 GF: - Fm: 0-1
Distance:	2m/2m3: 0-0 2m4-2m7: 0-0 3m+: 0-0
Track:	LH: 0-5 RH: 0-2 Tight: 0-3 Gall: 0-2
Aids:	Bl: 0-0 Vi: 0-0 Tstrap: 0-0 Ckp: 0-0
Best Rating:	75 11/03 Uttx 2m gd-sft Hdl

Plating-class hurdler; Flat winner; seems to handle any ground; has worn an eyeshield and a visor.

Flyover
99   73
7-y-o b m Presidium-Flash-By (Ilium)
J C Fox Miss Sarah-Jane Durman

Placings:00056-446   **(0833)**
2003/04: 16^{4}G, 16^{4}GF, 24^{6}GF,

	Starts	1st	2nd	3rd	Win & Pl
Hurdles	3	0	0	0	0
Career Total	8	0	0	0	0

Going:	Sf: 0-0 GS: 0-0 Gd: 0-1 GF: - Fm: 0-2
Distance:	2m/2m3: 0-2 2m4-2m7: 0-0 3m+: 0-1
Track:	LH: 0-3 RH: 0-0 Tight: 0-1 Gall: 0-0
Aids:	Bl: 0-0 Vi: 0-0 Tstrap: 0-0 Ckp: 0-0
Best Rating:	73 5/03 Strf 2m110y good Hdl

Plating-class hurdler; well-beaten in a seller on her handicap debut, and again since.

Follow The Bear
107f   102f
6-y-o ch g Weld-Run Lady Run (General Ironside)
D R Gandolfo D R Gandolfo Ltd

Placings:05   **(4578)**
2003/04: 16^{9}G, 16^{5}G,

	Starts	1st	2nd	3rd	Win & Pl
NH Flat	2	0	0	0	0
Career Total	2	0	0	0	0

Going:	Sf: 0-0 GS: 0-0 Gd: 0-2 GF: - Fm: 0-0
Distance:	2m/2m3: 0-2 2m4-2m7: 0-0 3m+: 0-0
Track:	LH: 0-2 RH: 0-0 Tight: 0-0 Gall: 0-2
Aids:	Bl: 0-0 Vi: 0-0 Tstrap: 0-0 Ckp: 0-0
Best Rating:	102 3/04 Newb 2m110y good NHF

Follow The Flow (IRE)
102   90
8-y-o ch g Over The River (FR)-October Lady (Lucifer (USA))
P A Pritchard Woodland Generators

Placings:4P3P004-5324000U62U5   **(4792)**
2003/04: 26^{5}HY, 26^{3}HY, 26^{2}G, 25^{4}GS, 25^{9}S, 25^{0}GS, 26^{9}S, 25^{U}HY, 29^{9}GS, 25^{2}GS, 25^{U}G, 26^{5}G,

	Starts	1st	2nd	3rd	Win & Pl
Chases	12	0	2	1	3556
Career Total	19	0	2	2	4905

Going:	Sf: 0-6 GS: 0-4 Gd: 0-2 GF: - Fm: 0-0
Distance:	2m/2m3: 0-0 2m4-2m7: 0-0 3m+: 0-12
Track:	LH: 0-6 RH: 0-6 Tight: 0-2 Gall: 0-0
Aids:	Bl: 0-0 Vi: 0-0 Tstrap: 0-0 Ckp: 0-0
Best Rating:	87 12/03 Hrfd 3m1f110y gd-sft Ch

Plating-class chaser; stays three miles plus; effective on good ground.

Follow The Trend (IRE)
100(88h)   (67h)103
10-y-o br g Beau Sher-Newgate Princess (Prince Regent (FR))
Miss A M Newton-Smith Brighton Racing Club

Placings:503405/63U1U1UF/P5544112P/641044- **PP23P34P**   **(4792)**
2003/04: 20^{0}PS, 20^{P}S, 21^{2}GS, 21^{3}S, 25^{P}GS, 24^{3}G, 19^{4}GS, 26^{P}G,

	Starts	1st	2nd	3rd	Win & Pl
Chases	8	0	1	2	2078
Career Total	37	5	2	4	18877
103	1/03	Leic	2m4f110yF(0-95)HCh	SFT	£3503
98	2/02	Hntg	2m4f110yF(0-95)HCh	SFT	£2688
89	1/02	Folk	2m5f	F(0-95)HCh	SFT	£3376
89	2/01	Folk	2m5f	F(0-90)HCh	SFT	£2520
88	1/01	Folk	2m5f	G(0-90)HCh	SFT	£1929

Total win prize-money £14018

Going:	Sf: 0-2 GS: 0-4 Gd: 0-2 GF: - Fm: 0-0
Distance:	2m/2m3: 0-0 2m4-2m7: 0-5 3m+: 0-3
Track:	LH: 0-2 RH: 0-5 Tight: 0-6 Gall: 0-1
Aids:	Bl: 0-0 Vi: 0-0 Tstrap: 0-0 Ckp: 0-5
Best Rating:	103 1/03 Leic 2m4f110y soft Ch

Modest handicap chaser; goes well at Folkestone; suited by two miles five and best on soft ground; wears sheepskin sidebuns due to lack of concentration, according to his trainer; usually hits form at the beginning of the year.

Folly Road (IRE)
101
14-y-o b g Mister Lord (USA)-Lady Can (Cantab)
D L Williams Miss L Horner

Placings:541015FF/0/23115/P353U13412/404PPP202P0/0 **S4240P4U513/44620-0**   **(4443)**
2003/04: 29^{0}GS,

	Starts	1st	2nd	3rd	Win & Pl
Chases	1	0	0	0	
Career Total	53	7	6	5	71313
114	3/02	Sand	3m110y	E Ch	GD	£7182
118	4/00	Chep	3m	E(0-115)HCh	SFT	£3324
118	2/00	MRas	3m4f110yD(0-120)HCh	G-S	£4192
122	12/98	Folk	3m2f	D(0-125)HCh	G-S	£7580
118	11/98	Wwck	3m2f	C(0-130)HCh	SFT	£4926
118	1/97	Punc	3m	Ch	YLD	£3051

99   11/96 Naas   2m4f   Hdl   YLD   £3177
                                Total win prize-money £33437

Going:	Sf: 0-0 GS: 0-1 Gd: 0-0 GF: - Fm: 0-0
Distance:	2m/2m3: 0-0 2m4-2m7: 0-0 3m+: 0-1
Track:	LH: 0-1 RH: 0-0 Tight: 0-0 Gall: 0-0
Aids:	Bl: 0-0 Vi: 0-0 Tstrap: 0-0 Ckp: 0-0
Best Rating:	**122** 12/98 Folk 3m2f gd-sft Ch

Formerly a useful staying chaser, but now a modest performer in hunter chases; lacks pace and requires extreme distances.

Foly Pleasant (FR)

111(116c)   (164c)**134+**

10-y-o ch g Vaguely Pleasant (FR)-Jeffologie (FR)
(Jefferson)
Miss H C Knight Jim Lewis & Friends

Placings:1/111P1/122/22/1210P/4220-P3010   (4397)
2003/04: 20PGS, 213G, 20HY, 201S, 21OG,

	Starts	1st	2nd	3rd	Win & Pl
Hurdles	3	1	0	0	7339
Chases	2	0	1	0	4400
Career Total	25	9	7	1	163699
134	2/04	Hayd	2m4f	C(0-130)HHdl	SFT	£7338
164	1/02	Chel	2m5f	A HCh	HVY	£32500
145	10/01	Strf	2m5f110yC(0-135)HCh		G-S	£6838
	5/99	Dax	2m1f110y Hdl		SFT	£4306
	4/99	Pau	2m4f110y Hdl		VS	£4306
	1/99	Pau	2m2f	Hdl	VS	£15070
	1/99	Pau	2m2f	Hdl	HVY	£7535
	12/98	Pau	2m2f110y Ch		SFT	£5382
	4/98	Pau	2m1f110y Ch		SFT	£4
				Total win prize-money £83280		

Going:	Sf: 1-2 GS: 0-1 Gd: 0-2 GF: - Fm: 0-0
Distance:	2m/2m3: 0-0 **2m4-2m7: 1-5** 3m+: 0-0
Track:	**LH: 1-4** RH: 0-0 Tight: 0-0 Gall: 0-3
Aids:	Bl: 0-0 Vi: 0-0 Tstrap: 1-5 Ckp: 0-0
Best Rating:	**164** 12/02 Chel 2m5f good Ch

Smart chaser/useful hurdler; good efforts at Cheltenham in 2002/3, in the frame in the Thomas Pink, the Tripleprint and the Pillar Chase; reverted to hurdles from a lenient mark and successful at Haydock in February; effective between 2m 4f and 3m 1f; acts on a sound surface, but prefers an easy one; wears a tongue tie.

Fondmort (FR)

115   **165**

8-y-o b g Cyborg (FR)-Hansie (FR) (Sukawa (FR))
N J Henderson W J Brown

Placings:30/214132P/1P1153/31F022-14534F   (4835)
2003/04: 201G, 244G, 195S, 203G, 254G, 21FGF,

	Starts	1st	2nd	3rd	Win & Pl
Chases	6	1	0	1	90050
Career Total	27	7	4	5	263962
165	11/03	Chel	2m4f110yA HCh		GD	£63800
158	12/02	Chel	2m5f	A HCh	GD	£58000
146	12/01	Kemp	2m	B Ch	GD	£11287
150	12/01	Sand	2m	A Ch	G-S	£18000
140	10/01	Kemp	2m	D Ch	G-S	£4914
130	12/00	Kemp	2m	B Hdl	G-S	£7215
	9/00	Autl	2m2f	Hdl	VS	£14409
				Total win prize-money £177626		

Going:	Sf: 0-1 GS: 0-0 Gd: 1-4 GF: - Fm: 0-1
Distance:	2m/2m3: 0-0 **2m4-2m7: 1-4** 3m+: 0-2
Track:	**LH: 1-4** RH: 0-0 Tight: 0-1 Gall: 1-3
Aids:	Bl: 0-0 Vi: 0-0 Tstrap: 0-0 Ckp: 0-0
Best Rating:	**165** 3/04 Chel 2m4f110y good Ch

High-class chaser; won the Tripleprint Gold Cup at Cheltenham in December 2002 and Paddy Power Gold Cup at the same track in November 2003, struggles to stay three miles; best on good ground.

Fontanesi (IRE)

106   **104**

4-y-o b g Sadler's Wells (USA)-Northern Script (USA) (Arts And Letters (USA))
M C Pipe (A P O'Brien 5/10) D A Johnson

Placings:13011   (4854)
2003/04: 171GS, 163G, 21OG, 181G, 171GF,

	Starts	1st	2nd	3rd	Win & Pl
Hurdles	5	3	0	1	13865
Career Total	5	3	0	1	13865
104	4/04	Tntn	2m1f	E Hdl	G-F	£4602
104	4/04	Font	2m2f110yE Hdl		GD	£3563
91	2/04	Tntn	2m1f	D Hdl	G-S	£5096
				Total win prize-money £13261		

Going:	Sf: 0-0 GS: 1-1 Gd: 1-3 GF: - Fm: 1-1
Distance:	**2m/2m3: 3-4** 2m4-2m7: 0-1 3m+: 0-0
Track:	LH: 1-3 RH: **2-2** Tight: 3-3 Gall: 0-2
Aids:	Bl: 0-0 **Vi: 1-1** Tstrap: 0-0 Ckp: 0-0
Best Rating:	**104** 4/04 Tntn 2m1f gd-fm Hdl

Fair novice hurdler; winner for Aidan O'Brien on the Flat; hung badly left when winning novice hurdle at Fontwell in April 2004 and fitted with a visor when following up at Taunton next time; stays 2m 2f; acts on good ground; disappointing when tried in decent company.

Fool On The Hill

111   **136**

7-y-o b g Reprimand-Stock Hill Lass (Air Trooper)
P J Hobbs (L G Cottrell 6/10) Louisville Syndicate

Placings:225124   (4638)
2003/04: 162GS, 162S, 175S, 161G, 162G, 164G,

	Starts	1st	2nd	3rd	Win & Pl
Hurdles	6	1	3	0	15518
Career Total	6	1	3	0	15518
123	2/04	Winc	2m	D Hdl	GD	£5044
				Total win prize-money £5044		

Going:	Sf: 0-2 GS: 0-1 Gd: 1-3 GF: - Fm: 0-0
Distance:	**2m/2m3: 1-6** 2m4-2m7: 0-0 3m+: 0-0
Track:	**LH: 0-2** RH: 1-4 Tight: 0-2 Gall: 0-1
Aids:	Bl: 0-0 Vi: 0-0 Tstrap: 0-0 Ckp: 0-0
Best Rating:	**136** 4/04 Aint 2m110y good Hdl

Useful novice hurdler; winner at Wincanton in February; good fourth in Grade Two at Aintree; suited by two miles and ground good or softer.

Football Crazy (IRE)

104   **110**

5-y-o b g Mujadil (USA)-Schonbein (IRE) (Persian Heights)
P Bowen (S Gollings 29/10) KB Construction & The Galloping Punters

Placings:5-24424   (4822)
2003/04: 162GS, 175S, 164G, 192GF, 194GF,

	Starts	1st	2nd	3rd	Win & Pl
Hurdles	5	0	2	0	3891
Career Total	6	0	2	0	3891

Going:	Sf: 0-1 GS: 0-1 Gd: 0-1 GF: - Fm: 0-2
Distance:	2m/2m3: 0-4 2m4-2m7: 0-1 3m+: 0-0
Track:	LH: 0-0 RH: 0-5 Tight: 0-1 Gall: 0-0
Aids:	Bl: 0-1 Vi: 0-0 Tstrap: 0-0 Ckp: 0-3

For Your Ears Only (IRE)

102   **84**

8-y-o b g Be My Native (USA)-Sister Ida (Bustino)
A Parker Mr & Mrs Raymond Anderson Green

Placings:3/00/30-3032433   (4950)
2003/04: 163G, 170GS, 163HY, 172HY, 164GF, 163G, 203GS,

	Starts	1st	2nd	3rd	Win & Pl
Hurdles	6	0	1	3	3746
Chases	1	0	0	1	834
Career Total	12	0	1	6	5313

Going:	Sf: 0-2 GS: 0-2 Gd: 0-2 GF: - Fm: 0-1
Distance:	2m/2m3: 0-6 2m4-2m7: 0-1 3m+: 0-0
Track:	LH: 0-5 RH: 0-2 Tight: 0-0 Gall: 0-1
Aids:	Bl: 0-0 Vi: 0-0 Tstrap: 0-0 Ckp: 0-0
Best Rating:	**96** 10/02 Hexm 2m110y gd-fm NHF

Modest efforts over hurdles around two miles; acts on fast and soft ground; worth a try over further.

Forager

88f   **94f**

5-y-o ch g Faustus (USA)-Jolimo (Fortissimo)
M J Ryan Joseph Curran

Placings:1   (0451)
2003/04: 161GF,

	Starts	1st	2nd	3rd	Win & Pl
NH Flat	1	1	0	0	1866
Career Total	1	1	0	0	1866
94	5/03	Hntg	2m110y H NHF		G-F	£1865
				Total win prize-money £1866		

Going:	Sf: 0-0 GS: 0-0 Gd: 0-0 GF: - Fm: 1-1
Distance:	2m/2m3: 1-1 2m4-2m7: 0-0 3m+: 0-0
Track:	LH: 0-0 **RH: 1-1** Tight: 0-0 **Gall: 1-1**
Aids:	Bl: 0-0 Vi: 0-0 Tstrap: 0-0 Ckp: 0-0
Best Rating:	**94** 5/03 Hntg 2m110y gd-fm NHF

Winner of a modest bumper on debut.

Forbearing (IRE)

102   **110**

7-y-o b g Bering-For Example (USA) (Northern Baby (CAN))
M C Pipe (Sir Mark Prescott 5/8) A J Lomas

Placings:34P1401100   (4859)
2003/04: 163GS, 164GS, 25PGS, 171G, 164GS, 170GS, 161S, 161GF, 164GF, 190GF,

	Starts	1st	2nd	3rd	Win & Pl
Hurdles	10	3	0	1	15194
Career Total	10	3	0	1	15194
109	3/04	Chep	2m110y	D(0-120)HHdl	G-F	£5200
109	2/04	Leic	2m	E(0-105)HHdl	SFT	£4270
102	12/03	Tntn	2m1f	D(0-115)HHdl	GD	£4501
				Total win prize-money £13972		

Going:	Sf: 1-1 GS: 0-5 Gd: 1-1 GF: - Fm: 1-3
Distance:	**2m/2m3: 3-8** 2m4-2m7: 0-1 3m+: 0-1
Track:	LH: 1-7 **RH: 2-3** Tight: 1-3 Gall: 0-2
Aids:	Bl: 0-0 **Vi: 2-5** Tstrap: 0-0 Ckp: 0-0
Best Rating:	**110** 1/04 Wwck 2m gd-sft Hdl

Moderate novice hurdler; won three middle-distance

claimers for Sir Mark Prescott; got off the mark on handicap debut at Taunton in December 2003; handled soft ground when winning Class E handicap at Leicester February 2004; hung and jumped left under pressure when following up in weak event at Chepstow next time; acts on a sound surface; has won a visor.

Force Twelve (IRE)
105(84h)   (62+h)**80**

6-y-o b g Magical Wonder (USA)-Gale Force Nine (Strong Gale)
P R Hedger Mrs A Trigg

Placings:00630523   (3100)
2003/04: 16⁵GS, 22⁰GF, 22⁶G, 20³GF, 18⁰G, 21⁵GF, 20²G, 26³G,

	Starts	1st	2nd	3rd	Win & Pl
Hurdles	5	0	0	1	390
Chases	3	0	1	1	1469
Career Total	8	0	1	2	1859

Going:	Sf: 0-0 GS: 0-1 Gd: 0-4 GF: - Fm: 0-3
Distance:	2m/2m3: 0-2 2m4-2m7: 0-5 3m+: 0-1
Track:	LH: 0-4 RH: 0-1 Tight: 0-7 Gall: 0-0
Aids:	Bl: 0-0 Vi: 0-0 Tstrap: 0-0 Ckp: 0-1
Best Rating:	80 12/03 Font 3m2f110y good Ch

Plating-class hurdler/chaser.

Fordingbridge (USA)
102f   **94f**

4-y-o b g Diesis-Souffle (Zafonic (USA))
P J Hobbs Colin Brown Racing IV

Placings:60   (4578)
2003/04: 16⁶G, 16⁰G,

	Starts	1st	2nd	3rd	Win & Pl
NH Flat	2	0	0	0	0
Career Total	2	0	0	0	0

Going:	Sf: 0-0 GS: 0-0 Gd: 0-2 GF: - Fm: 0-0
Distance:	2m/2m3: 0-2 2m4-2m7: 0-0 3m+: 0-0
Track:	LH: 0-2 RH: 0-0 Tight: 0-0 Gall: 0-2
Aids:	Bl: 0-0 Vi: 0-0 Tstrap: 0-0 Ckp: 0-0
Best Rating:	94 3/04 Newb 2m110y good NHF

Foreman (GER)
113   **159+**

6-y-o ch g Monsun (GER)-Fleurie (GER) (Dashing Blade)
T Doumen John P McManus

Placings:1132323141-1F4140   (4646)
2003/04: 18¹VS, 19⁶HO, 16⁴G, 16¹Y, 16⁴G, 20⁰G,

			Starts	1st	2nd	3rd	Win & Pl
Hurdles			6	2	0	0	100634
Career Total			16	6	2	3	196345
155	1/04	Leop	2m		Hdl	YLD	£63556
	11/03	Engh	2m2f		Hdl	VS	£18078
	4/03	Engh	2m3f		Hdl	VS	£20260
147	2/03	Kemp	2m4f	C Hdl		GD	£6844
	5/02	Badn	2m110y	Hdl		GD	£6748
98	5/02	Folk	2m1f110yE Hdl			GD	£2870

Total win prize-money £118356

Going:	Sf: 0-0 GS: 0-0 Gd: 0-3 GF: - Fm: 0-0
Distance:	2m/2m3: 2-5 2m4-2m7: 0-1 3m+: 0-0
Track:	LH: 1-3 RH: 0-1 Tight: 0-1 Gall: 0-0
Aids:	Bl: 1-4 Vi: 0-0 Tstrap: 0-0 Ckp: 0-0
Best Rating:	159 3/04 Chel 2m110y good Hdl

Smart French-trained hurdler; won the AIG Europe

Champion Hurdle at Leopardstown in January 2004; good fourth in the Champion Hurdle at Cheltenham; effective at around 2m, but stays 2m 5f; handles soft ground, but best on good; likes to be held up; has worn blinkers; improving.

Forest Bell (IRE)
77   **45**

6-y-o b m Glacial Storm (USA)-Tiverton Castle (IRE) (Supreme Leader)
J G M O'Shea K W Bell & Son Ltd

Placings:000   (4736)
2003/04: 16⁰S, 16⁰HY, 17⁰G,

	Starts	1st	2nd	3rd	Win & Pl
NH Flat	2	0	0	0	0
Hurdles	1	0	0	0	0
Career Total	3	0	0	0	0

Going:	Sf: 0-2 GS: 0-0 Gd: 0-1 GF: - Fm: 0-0
Distance:	2m/2m3: 0-3 2m4-2m7: 0-0 3m+: 0-0
Track:	LH: 0-3 RH: 0-0 Tight: 0-0 Gall: 0-0
Aids:	Bl: 0-0 Vi: 0-0 Tstrap: 0-0 Ckp: 0-0
Best Rating:	50 4/04 NAbb 2m1f good Hdl

Forest Dante (IRE)
103   **108+**

11-y-o ch g Phardante (FR)-Mossy Mistress (IRE) (Le Moss)
F Kirby Fred Kirby

Placings:6000F/602F1043/S1131PF/435231FP2/U630P5U
4-21   (2578)
2003/04: 26²G, 24¹TG,

			Starts	1st	2nd	3rd	Win & Pl
Chases			2	1	1	0	4593
Career Total			39	6	4	5	40917
105	12/03	Sthl	3m110y	E(0-110)HCh	G-F	£3328
112	1/02	Catt	2m3f	D(0-120)HCh	SFT	£4062
109	11/00	Catt	2m3f	E(0-115)HCh	GD	£5005
112	10/00	Sthl	2m4f110yD(0-120)HCh	HVY	£6808
105	9/00	MRas	2m4f	F(0-110)HCh	G-F	£4251
87	1/00	Catt	2m	E(0-105)HCh	GD	£4264

Total win prize-money £27721

Going:	Sf: 0-0 GS: 0-0 Gd: 0-1 GF: - Fm: 1-1
Distance:	2m/2m3: 0-0 2m4-2m7: 0-0 3m+: 1-2
Track:	LH: 1-2 RH: 0-0 Tight: 1-2 Gall: 0-0
Aids:	Bl: 0-0 Vi: 0-0 Tstrap: 0-0 Ckp: 1-1
Best Rating:	112 3/02 MRas 2m6f110y soft Ch

Moderate chaser; a big, able jumper at his best; stays beyond three miles but highly effective over much shorter; acts on any ground; goes well at Catterick; has worn cheekpieces.

Forest Green Flyer
92   **60**

8-y-o b m Syrtos-Bolton Flyer (Aragon)
O O'Neill K G Boulton

Placings:60000/046/406255P0P/05100025P-P004 (4700)
2003/04: 17⁰GS, 16⁰GF, 17⁰G, 20⁴G,

			Starts	1st	2nd	3rd	Win & Pl
Hurdles			4	0	0	0	0
Career Total			30	1	2	0	3375
73	11/02	Tntn	2m1f	G(0-90)HHdl	G-S	£2019

Total win prize-money £2020

Going:	Sf: 0-0 GS: 0-1 Gd: 0-2 GF: - Fm: 0-1
Distance:	2m/2m3: 0-3 2m4-2m7: 0-0 3m+: 0-0
Track:	LH: 0-1 RH: 0-2 Tight: 0-2 Gall: 0-0
Aids:	Bl: 0-0 Vi: 0-0 Tstrap: 0-0 Ckp: 0-0

Best Rating: 80   2/02   Ludl   2m   soft   Hdl

Selling-class hurdler; acts on fast and easy ground.

Forest Gunner
96   (123h)**136+**

10-y-o ch g Gunner B-Gouly Duff (Party Mink)
R Ford John Gilsenan

Placings:40/36/1213125/112-315   (4951)
2003/04: 26³G, 21¹G, 24⁵GS,

			Starts	1st	2nd	3rd	Win & Pl
Chases			3	1	0	1	20833
Career Total			17	6	3	3	43246
136	4/04	Aint	2m5f110yB Ch			GD	£19430
132	11/02	Fknm	2m5f110yD Ch			G-S	£5096
112	10/02	Sedg	2m5f	E Ch		GD	£4147
123	1/02	Weth	2m7f	E Hdl		G-S	£2681
123	11/01	MRas	2m5f110yF Hdl			G-S	£2254
120	5/01	Aint	2m4f	D Hdl		GD	£3584

Total win prize-money £37192

Going:	Sf: 0-0 GS: 0-1 Gd: 1-2 GF: - Fm: 0-0
Distance:	2m/2m3: 0-0 2m4-2m7: 1-1 3m+: 0-2
Track:	LH: 1-1 RH: 0-1 Tight: 1-2 Gall: 0-0
Aids:	Bl: 0-0 Vi: 0-0 Tstrap: 0-0 Ckp: 0-0
Best Rating:	136 4/04 Aint 2m5f110y good Ch

Formerly very useful hurdler/novice chaser; evidently had problems; ran for first time since December 2002 when third at Fontwell on hunter chase debut; jumped really well in front when taking the Fox Hunters' at Aintree; capable of even better; stays three miles; acts well with a little cut in the ground.

Forest Heath (IRE)
94   **82**

7-y-o gr g Common Grounds-Caroline Lady (JPN) (Caro)
H J Collingridge Group 1 Racing (1994) Ltd

Placings:5/056-5   (0367)
2003/04: 16⁵G,

	Starts	1st	2nd	3rd	Win & Pl
Hurdles	1	0	0	0	0
Career Total	5	0	0	0	0

Going:	Sf: 0-0 GS: 0-0 Gd: 0-1 GF: - Fm: 0-0
Distance:	2m/2m3: 0-1 2m4-2m7: 0-0 3m+: 0-0
Track:	LH: 0-1 RH: 0-0 Tight: 0-0 Gall: 0-0
Aids:	Bl: 0-0 Vi: 0-0 Tstrap: 0-0 Ckp: 0-0
Best Rating:	85 4/03 Strf 2m110y gd-fm Hdl

Forest Ivory (NZ)
103   **93**

13-y-o ch g Ivory Hunter (USA)-Fair And Square (NZ) (Crown Lease)
Dr P Pritchard Lady Maria Coventry

Placings:1220/11241/F112/4333460/53235/30/00P3600/00
2450056-343343P046440250   (4840)
2003/04: 26³GF, 27⁴G, 24³G, 27³G, 24⁴GF, 22³G, 24⁰GF, 24⁰G, 24⁴GS, 24⁶G, 19⁴HY, 24¹G, 20⁰G, 22²G, 26⁵G, 24⁰G,

			Starts	1st	2nd	3rd	Win & Pl
Hurdles			16	0	1	4	4710
Career Total			59	6	7	11	100965
141	11/97	Bang	3m110y	D Ch		SFT	£3842
115	11/97	Weth	3m1f	D Ch		G-S	£3600
144	4/97	Aint	3m110y	A Hdl		GD	£21532
122	12/96	Worc	2m4f	E Hdl		G-S	£2915
119	11/96	Towc	2m5f	F Hdl		GD	£1849
121	11/95	Worc	2m	H NHF		SFT	£1455

Total win prize-money £35194

Going:	Sf: 0-1 GS: 0-1 Gd: 0-11 GF: - Fm: 0-3
Distance:	2m/2m3: 0-0 2m4-2m7: 0-4 3m+: 0-12
Track:	LH: 0-13 RH: 0-2 Tight: 0-6 Gall: 0-4
Aids:	Bl: 0-0 Vi: 0-0 Tstrap: 0-0 Ckp: 0-0
Best Rating:	145 12/97 Kemp 3m soft Ch

Plating-class hurdler; a Grade One winner as a novice, but only selling class now; stays really well; suited by testing conditions.

Forest Maze

95   78

8-y-o b m Arzanni-Forest Nymph (NZ) (Oak Ridge (FR))
A J Whiting A J Whiting

Placings:06/0400P					(4914)
2003/04: 21⁰G, 22⁴G, 19⁰G, 23⁰GS, 24⁰GS,					

	Starts	1st	2nd	3rd	Win & Pl
Hurdles	5	0	0	0	0
Career Total	7	0	0	0	0

Going:	Sf: 0-0 GS: 0-2 Gd: 0-3 GF: - Fm: 0-0
Distance:	2m/2m3: 0-0 2m4-2m7: 0-4 3m+: 0-1
Track:	LH: 0-2 RH: 0-3 Tight: 0-3 Gall: 0-0
Aids:	Bl: 0-0 Vi: 0-0 Tstrap: 0-0 Ckp: 0-0
Best Rating:	78 3/04 Tntn 2m3f110y good Hdl

Forest Tune (IRE)

103   114

6-y-o b g Charnwood Forest (IRE)-Swift Chorus (Music Boy)
B Hanbury The Acorn Partnership

Placings:20212-44030					(4883)
2003/04: 16⁴GS, 16⁴G, 16⁰S, 17³GS, 17⁰GS,					

	Starts	1st	2nd	3rd	Win & Pl
Hurdles	5	0	0	1	1809
Career Total	10	1	3	1	9989
118 3/03 Ludl 2m		E(0-105)HHdl	G-F		£4940
Total win prize-money £4940					

Going:	Sf: 0-1 GS: 0-3 Gd: 0-1 GF: - Fm: 0-0
Distance:	2m/2m3: 0-5 2m4-2m7: 0-0 3m+: 0-0
Track:	LH: 0-1 RH: 0-4 Tight: 0-1 Gall: 0-1
Aids:	Bl: 0-0 Vi: 0-0 Tstrap: 0-0 Ckp: 0-0
Best Rating:	118 3/03 Ludl 2m gd-fm Hdl

Modest hurdler; acts on most types of ground; effective over two miles.

Forever Dream

108   116

6-y-o b g Afzal-Quadrapol (Pollerton)
P J Hobbs W McKibbin & A Stevens

Placings:6251-1260312					(4718)
2003/04: 16¹G, 19²GF, 17⁶G, 17⁰GS, 16³G, 16¹GS, 16²G,					

	Starts	1st	2nd	3rd	Win & Pl
Hurdles	7	2	2	1	16025
Career Total	11	3	3	1	19040
112 3/04 Winc 2m		D(0-125)HHdl	G-S		£6812
106 11/03 Kemp 2m		D Hdl	GD		£3437
98 3/03 Winc 2m		H NHF	G-F		£2331
Total win prize-money £12580					

Going:	Sf: 0-0 GS: 1-2 Gd: 1-4 GF: - Fm: 0-1
Distance:	2m/2m3: 2-7 2m4-2m7: 0-0 3m+: 0-1
Track:	LH: 0-3 RH: 2-4 Tight: 0-0 Gall: 0-3
Aids:	Bl: 0-0 Vi: 0-0 Tstrap: 0-0 Ckp: 0-0
Best Rating:	116 4/04 Ludl 2m good Hdl

Fair novice hurdler; stays trips of around two and a half miles and acts on most types of ground; likely to make a chaser in time.

Forever Eyesofblue

101   87

7-y-o b g Leading Counsel (USA)-Forever Silver (IRE) (Roselier (FR))
A Parker Mrs Wilma Wright

Placings:503001					(4913)
2003/04: 20⁵S, 18⁰S, 25³G, 22⁰GS, 24⁰HY, 24¹S,					

	Starts	1st	2nd	3rd	Win & Pl
Hurdles	6	1	0	1	6229
Career Total	6	1	0	1	6229
87 4/04 Prth 3m110y		E(0-105)HHdl	SFT		£5681
Total win prize-money £5681					

Going:	Sf: 1-4 GS: 0-1 Gd: 0-1 GF: - Fm: 0-0
Distance:	2m/2m3: 0-1 2m4-2m7: 0-2 3m+: 1-3
Track:	LH: 0-4 RH: 1-2 Tight: 0-0 Gall: 0-0
Aids:	Bl: 0-0 Vi: 0-0 Tstrap: 0-0 Ckp: 0-0
Best Rating:	87 4/04 Prth 3m110y soft Hdl

Modest novice hurdler; stays three miles; acts on soft.

Forever My Lord

95   90+

6-y-o g g Be My Chief (USA)-In Love Again (IRE) (Prince Rupert (FR))
J R Best Steve Cook

Placings:550					(4589)
2003/04: 16⁵G, 16⁵G, 16⁰G,					

	Starts	1st	2nd	3rd	Win & Pl
Hurdles	3	0	0	0	0
Career Total	3	0	0	0	0

Going:	Sf: 0-0 GS: 0-0 Gd: 0-3 GF: - Fm: 0-0
Distance:	2m/2m3: 0-3 2m4-2m7: 0-0 3m+: 0-0
Track:	LH: 0-1 RH: 0-2 Tight: 0-1 Gall: 0-1
Aids:	Bl: 0-0 Vi: 0-0 Tstrap: 0-0 Ckp: 0-0
Best Rating:	90 3/04 Hntg 2m110y good Hdl

Forever Noble (IRE)

82

11-y-o b g Forzando-Pagan Queen (Vaguely Noble)
R Allan Mrs Florence C Ratter

Placings:32/620/1P222241/F352U3/1/6505/0-4P4P					(0786)
2003/04: 25⁴G, 22⁰PG, 20⁴GF, 24⁰PG,					

	Starts	1st	2nd	3rd	Win & Pl
Hurdles	2	0	0	0	423
Chases	2	0	0	0	630
Career Total	29	3	7	3	20169
125 10/00 Fknm 3m110y		F(0-110)HCh	QD		£4602
116 4/99 Weth 2m4f110yD Hdl			G-F		£3436
103 11/98 Hntg 2m110y		E Hdl	G-S		£2110
Total win prize-money £10148					

Going:	Sf: 0-0 GS: 0-0 Gd: 0-3 GF: - Fm: 0-1
Distance:	2m/2m3: 0-0 2m4-2m7: 0-2 3m+: 0-2
Track:	LH: 0-2 RH: 0-2 Tight: 0-2 Gall: 0-0
Aids:	Bl: 0-0 Vi: 0-0 Tstrap: 0-0 Ckp: 0-2
Best Rating:	125 10/00 Fknm 3m110y good Ch

Plating-class hurdler/chaser; stays three miles; acts on good/good to soft ground.

Forever Posh

80f   49f

7-y-o b m Rakaposhi King-B Final (Gunner B)
Mrs S M Johnson P J Allen

Placings:0-0					(1622)
2003/04: 17⁰G,					

	Starts	1st	2nd	3rd	Win & Pl
NH Flat	1	0	0	0	
Career Total	2	0	0	0	

Going:	Sf: 0-0 GS: 0-0 Gd: 0-1 GF: - Fm: 0-0
Distance:	2m/2m3: 0-1 2m4-2m7: 0-0 3m+: 0-0
Track:	LH: 0-1 RH: 0-0 Tight: 0-1 Gall: 0-0
Aids:	Bl: 0-0 Vi: 0-0 Tstrap: 0-0 Ckp: 0-0
Best Rating:	49 2/03 Ludl 2m good NHF

Forever Waywood

43f   6f

5-y-o ch g Rakaposhi King-I'm Fine (Fitzwilliam (USA))
P Beaumont Wood Racing

Placings:0					(4885)
2003/04: 17⁰GS,					

	Starts	1st	2nd	3rd	Win & Pl
NH Flat	1	0	0	0	
Career Total	1	0	0	0	

Going:	Sf: 0-0 GS: 0-1 Gd: 0-0 GF: - Fm: 0-0
Distance:	2m/2m3: 0-1 2m4-2m7: 0-0 3m+: 0-0
Track:	LH: 0-0 RH: 0-1 Tight: 0-0 Gall: 0-0
Aids:	Bl: 0-0 Vi: 0-0 Tstrap: 0-0 Ckp: 0-0
Best Rating:	6 4/04 Carl 2m1f gd-sft NHF

Fork Lightning (IRE)

116(107h)   (120h)152+

8-y-o gr g Roselier (FR)-Park Breeze (IRE) (Strong Gale)
A King Mr & Mrs F C Welch

Placings:441321-31U211					(4384)
2003/04: 23³G, 25¹GS, 24U⁴GS, 24²G, 25¹G, 24¹G,					

	Starts	1st	2nd	3rd	Win & Pl
Chases	6	3	1	1	58222
Career Total	12	5	2	2	77271
152 3/04 Chel 3m110y A HCh			GD		£46400
134 2/04 Winc 3m1f110yD Ch			GD		£5525
130 12/03 Hrfd 3m1f110yE Ch			G-S		£2899
120 4/03 Chei 3m		D(0-120)HHdl	GD		£10483
115 1/03 Kemp 2m5f		D Hdl	G-S		£5664
Total win prize-money £70972					

Going:	Sf: 0-0 GS: 1-2 Gd: 2-4 GF: - Fm: 0-0
Distance:	2m/2m3: 0-0 2m4-2m7: 0-0 3m+: 3-6
Track:	LH: 1-2 RH: 2-4 Tight: 0-1 Gall: 1-1
Aids:	Bl: 0-0 Vi: 0-0 Tstrap: 0-0 Ckp: 0-0
Best Rating:	152 3/04 Chel 3m110y good Ch

Smart novice chaser; winner of novice chases at Hereford and Wincanton in 2003/4 and would have won at Stratford but for falling two out; ran well against Lord Sam at Kempton; gave his trainer his first winner at the Festival when taking the National Hunt Handicap Chase; stays well; acts on good and yielding ground.

Forlorn Hope

7-y-o b g Tragic Role (USA)-Rum N Raisin (Rakaposhi King)
B D Leavy A J McMullan

Placings:P0-F   (0137)
2003/04: 16^FG,

	Starts	1st	2nd	3rd	Win & Pl
Hurdles	1	0	0	0	
Career Total	3	0	0	0	

Going:	Sf: 0-0 GS: 0-0 Gd: 0-1 GF: - Fm: 0-0
Distance:	2m/2m3: 0-1 2m4-2m7: 0-0 3m+: 0-0
Track:	LH: 0-0 RH: 0-1 Tight: 0-0 Gall: 0-0
Aids:	Bl: 0-0 Vi: 0-0 Tstrap: 0-1 Ckp: 0-0

Formal Bid (USA)
96(110h)   (123h)104+
7-y-o b/br g Dynaformer (USA)-Fantastic Bid (USA) (Auction Ring (USA))
C C Bealby   Michael Hill

Placings:2522P3/313012233-2F   (2189)
2003/04: 20³GY, 16²G, 22^FGS,

	Starts	1st	2nd	3rd	Win & Pl
Hurdles	1	0	0	1	2045
Chases	2	0	1	0	784
Career Total	17	2	6	5	25357
110 12/02	Leic	2m4f110yD Hdl		HVY	£4940
118 10/02	MRas	2m3f110yE Hdl		GD	£3710
		Total win prize-money £8650			

Going:	Sf: 0-0 GS: 0-1 Gd: 0-1 GF: - Fm: 0-0
Distance:	2m/2m3: 0-1 2m4-2m7: 0-2 3m+: 0-0
Track:	LH: 0-1 RH: 0-2 Tight: 0-0 Gall: 0-0
Aids:	Bl: 0-0 Vi: 0-0 Tstrap: 0-0 Ckp: 0-0
Best Rating:	123 4/03 Punc 2m4f gd-yld Hdl

Decent hurdler/novice chaser; acts on good ground or softer; effective at around two and a half miles; consistent.

Formal Cliche
74f   73f
5-y-o b g Classic Cliche (IRE)-Formal Affair (Rousillon (USA))
Mrs M Reveley   Mr And Mrs J D Cotton

Placings:00   (4867)
2003/04: 16⁰GS, 16⁰S,

	Starts	1st	2nd	3rd	Win & Pl
NH Flat	2	0	0	0	
Career Total	2	0	0	0	

Going:	Sf: 0-1 GS: 0-1 Gd: 0-0 GF: 0-0 Fm: 0-0
Distance:	2m/2m3: 0-2 2m4-2m7: 0-0 3m+: 0-0
Track:	LH: 0-2 RH: 0-0 Tight: 0-0 Gall: 0-0
Aids:	Bl: 0-0 Vi: 0-0 Tstrap: 0-0 Ckp: 0-0
Best Rating:	67 3/04 Weth 2m gd-sft NHF

Foronlymo
80   51
5-y-o b g Forzando-Polish Descent (IRE) (Danehill (USA))
P Beaumont   Commander David Wilmot-Smith

Placings:P0   (4260)
2003/04: 17^PHY, 16⁰GF,

	Starts	1st	2nd	3rd	Win & Pl
Hurdles	2	0	0	0	
Career Total	2	0	0	0	

Going:	Sf: 0-1 GS: 0-0 Gd: 0-0 GF: - Fm: 0-1
Distance:	2m/2m3: 0-2 2m4-2m7: 0-0 3m+: 0-0

Track:	LH: 0-1 RH: 0-1 Tight: 0-1 Gall: 0-0
Aids:	Bl: 0-0 Vi: 0-0 Tstrap: 0-0 Ckp: 0-0
Best Rating:	51 3/04 Catt 2m gd-fm Hdl

Forrest Tribe (IRE)
99   98
11-y-o b/br g Be My Native (USA)-Island Bridge (Mandalus)
W Jenks   Mrs Douglas Graham

Placings:0644/140/234143P4/55020PF/500636232/3-004F   (4505)
2003/04: 24⁹G, 20⁰S, 24⁴G, 25^FG,

	Starts	1st	2nd	3rd	Win & Pl
Chases	4	0	0	0	0
Career Total	36	2	4	5	19325
112 2/00	Kels	2m6f110yC(0-130)HCh	G-S	£7621
115 3/99	Ayr	2m4f E Ch	SFT	£2898
		Total win prize-money £10519		

Going:	Sf: 0-1 GS: 0-0 Gd: 0-3 GF: - Fm: 0-0
Distance:	2m/2m3: 0-0 2m4-2m7: 0-1 3m+: 0-3
Track:	LH: 0-0 RH: 0-4 Tight: 0-1 Gall: 0-2
Aids:	Bl: 0-4 Vi: 0-0 Tstrap: 0-0 Ckp: 0-0
Best Rating:	115 3/99 Ayr 2m4f soft Ch

Moderate ex-Irish chaser, effective over three miles and best with a bit of cut.

Forrestfield (IRE)
110   (97h)112+
10-y-o b g Toca Madera-Interj (Salmon Leap (USA))
J E Mulhern   J C Savage

Placings:3432/230/4520/654/2-3505112560   (4830a)
2003/04: 18³YS, 17⁵HY, 16⁰YS, 19⁵GY, 18¹F, 16¹GF, 16²GF, 16⁵G, 17⁶GY, 17⁰Y,

	Starts	1st	2nd	3rd	Win & Pl
Hurdles	1	0	0	0	0
Chases	9	2	1	1	19034
Career Total	25	2	5	4	27157
111 10/03	Punc	2m (0-130)HCh	G-F	£7840
109 9/03	Punc	2m2f Ch	FRM	£7168
		Total win prize-money £15010		

Going:	Sf: 0-1 GS: 0-0 Gd: 0-1 GF: - Fm: 2-3
Distance:	2m/2m3: 2-10 2m4-2m7: 0-0 3m+: 0-0
Track:	LH: 0-2 RH: 2-6 Tight: 0-0 Gall: 0-1
Aids:	Bl: 0-0 Vi: 0-0 Tstrap: 0-0 Ckp: 0-0
Best Rating:	121 1/01 Leop 2m soft Hdl

Modest Irish chaser; best at around two miles; acts well on fast ground; improving.

Fort Saumarez
62   58
5-y-o b g Magic Ring (IRE)-Rocquaine Bay (Morston (FR))
G L Moore (Mrs L Richards 29/6)   The Warrenwood Racing Partnership

Placings:P0   (4207)
2003/04: 17^PGS, 16⁰G,

	Starts	1st	2nd	3rd	Win & Pl
Hurdles	2	0	0	0	
Career Total	2	0	0	0	

Going:	Sf: 0-0 GS: 0-1 Gd: 0-1 GF: - Fm: 0-0
Distance:	2m/2m3: 0-2 2m4-2m7: 0-0 3m+: 0-0
Track:	LH: 0-0 RH: 0-2 Tight: 0-1 Gall: 0-0
Aids:	Bl: 0-1 Vi: 0-0 Tstrap: 0-0 Ckp: 0-0
Best Rating:	58 3/04 Kemp 2m good Hdl

Fortunate Dave (USA)
108   107
5-y-o b g Lear Fan (USA)-Lady Ameriflora (USA) (Lord Avie (USA))
Ian Williams   M N Dennis

Placings:10232420-30P2   (4180)
2003/04: 20³GF, 20⁰GS, 24^PGS, 20²G,

	Starts	1st	2nd	3rd	Win & Pl
Hurdles	4	0	1	1	1141
Career Total	12	1	4	2	10083
102 11/02	Wwck	2m D Hdl	GD	£4013
		Total win prize-money £4014		

Going:	Sf: 0-0 GS: 0-2 Gd: 0-1 GF: - Fm: 0-1
Distance:	2m/2m3: 0-0 2m4-2m7: 0-3 3m+: 0-1
Track:	LH: 0-3 RH: 0-1 Tight: 0-1 Gall: 0-2
Aids:	Bl: 0-0 Vi: 0-0 Tstrap: 0-0 Ckp: 0-0
Best Rating:	105 11/03 Hayd 2m4f gd-fm Hdl

Modest hurdler; handles good ground or softer; effective at up to two and a half miles.

Fortune Island (IRE)
98   116+
5-y-o b g Turtle Island (IRE)-Blue Kestrel (IRE) (Bluebird (USA))
M C Pipe   J M Brown & M J Blackburn

Placings:P10-P006   (4243)
2003/04: 16^PGS, 21⁰G, 19⁰G, 19⁶G,

	Starts	1st	2nd	3rd	Win & Pl
Hurdles	4	0	0	0	0
Career Total	7	1	0	0	3523
113 2/03	Extr	2m1f E Hdl	G-S	£3523
		Total win prize-money £3523		

Going:	Sf: 0-0 GS: 0-1 Gd: 0-3 GF: - Fm: 0-0
Distance:	2m/2m3: 0-3 2m4-2m7: 0-1 3m+: 0-0
Track:	LH: 0-0 RH: 0-4 Tight: 0-0 Gall: 0-0
Aids:	Bl: 0-0 Vi: 0-4 Tstrap: 0-0 Ckp: 0-0
Best Rating:	116 3/03 Chel 2m1f good Hdl

Fair hurdler; effective over two miles but should stay further; acts on most ground; has been tried in a visor.

Fortune Point (IRE)
98   104
6-y-o ch g Cadeaux Genereux-Mountains Of Mist (IRE) (Shirley Heights)
A W Carroll (M C Pipe 12/6)   The T J Racing Partnership

Placings:6505/353P   (2770)
2003/04: 16³G, 16⁵G, 16³S, 16^PS,

	Starts	1st	2nd	3rd	Win & Pl
Hurdles	4	0	0	2	697
Career Total	8	0	0	2	697

Going:	Sf: 0-2 GS: 0-0 Gd: 0-2 GF: - Fm: 0-0
Distance:	2m/2m3: 0-4 2m4-2m7: 0-0 3m+: 0-0
Track:	LH: 0-2 RH: 0-2 Tight: 0-2 Gall: 0-0
Aids:	Bl: 0-0 Vi: 0-0 Tstrap: 0-0 Ckp: 0-0
Best Rating:	104 11/03 Plum 2m good Hdl

Moderate hurdler; acts on good ground or softer.

Fortune's Fool
93   70
5-y-o b g Zilzal (USA)-Peryllys (Warning)

I A Brown I A Brown

Placings:P604-6   (2087)
2003/04: 17⁵GF,

	Starts	1st	2nd	3rd	Win & Pl
Hurdles	1	0	0	0	0
Career Total	5	0	0	0	0

Going:	Sf: 0-0 GS: 0-0 Gd: 0-0 GF: - Fm: 0-1
Distance:	2m/2m3: 0-1 2m4-2m7: 0-0 3m+: 0-0
Track:	LH: 0-1 RH: 0-0 Tight: 0-1 Gall: 0-0
Aids:	Bl: 0-0 Vi: 0-0 Tstrap: 0-0 Ckp: 0-0
Best Rating:	72 11/03 Sedg 2m1f gd-fm Hdl

Plating-class novice hurdler.

Forum Chris (IRE)

86(101h)   (119+h)93
7-y-o ch g Trempolino (USA)-Memory Green (USA) (Green
Forest (USA))
Mrs S J Smith Mrs Jacqueline Conroy

Placings:111-03F   (3519)
2003/04: 20⁹GF, 16⁹GS, 16⁵S,

	Starts	1st	2nd	3rd	Win & Pl
Hurdles	1	0	0	0	0
Chases	2	0	0	1	843
Career Total	6	3	0	1	9813
115 7/02 Worc	2m4f	E Hdl		G-F	£2877
119 6/02 Hexm	2m4f110yE Hdl		G-F	£2583
97 6/02 Ctml	2m6f	D Hdl		HVY	£3510
			Total win prize-money £8970

Going:	Sf: 0-1 GS: 0-1 Gd: 0-0 GF: - Fm: 0-1
Distance:	2m/2m3: 0-2 2m4-2m7: 0-0 3m+: 0-0
Track:	LH: 0-3 RH: 0-0 Tight: 0-1 Gall: 0-0
Aids:	Bl: 0-0 Vi: 0-0 Tstrap: 0-0 Ckp: 0-0
Best Rating:	119 6/02 Hexm 2m4f110y gd-fm Hdl

Modest hurdler; acts on any ground.

Forza Glory

98   88
5-y-o ch m Forzando-Glory Isle (Hittite Glory)
Miss B Sanders Mrs J Laycock & A C Verdie

Placings:3054-3   (1170)
2003/04: 18³GF,

	Starts	1st	2nd	3rd	Win & Pl
Hurdles	1	0	0	1	517
Career Total	5	0	0	2	1226

Going:	Sf: 0-0 GS: 0-0 Gd: 0-0 GF: - Fm: 0-1
Distance:	2m/2m3: 0-1 2m4-2m7: 0-0 3m+: 0-0
Track:	LH: 0-1 RH: 0-0 Tight: 0-1 Gall: 0-0
Aids:	Bl: 0-0 Vi: 0-0 Tstrap: 0-0 Ckp: 0-0
Best Rating:	84 8/03 Font 2m2f110y gd-fm Hdl

Modest novice hurdler on soft ground.

Forzacurity

106   103+
5-y-o ch g Forzando-Nice Lady (Connaught)
D Burchell (J L Spearing 13/11) Don Gould, Mervyn
Phillips & Jeff Smith

Placings:65-123005316   (3966)
2003/04: 17¹G, 16²GF, 16³S, 17⁰G, 16⁹GS, 17⁵GS, 16³HY, 17¹GS,
16⁶GS,

	Starts	1st	2nd	3rd	Win & Pl
Hurdles	9	2	1	2	9536

Career Total   11   2   1   2   9536
103 2/04 Hrfd   2m1f   E(0-110)HHdl   G-S   £4595
86 11/03 NAbb   2m1f   G Hdl   GD   £2898
                        Total win prize-money £7494

Going:	Sf: 0-2 GS: 1-4 Gd: 1-2 GF: - Fm: 0-1
Distance:	2m/2m3: 2-9 2m4-2m7: 0-0 3m+: 0-0
Track:	LH: 1-4 RH: 1-5 Tight: 1-3 Gall: 0-0
Aids:	Bl: 0-0 Vi: 0-0 Tstrap: 0-0 Ckp: 0-0
Best Rating:	103 2/04 Hrfd 2m1f gd-sft Hdl

Plating-class hurdler; won second start over jumps in selling
hurdle at Newton Abbot in November 2003; has run well
since and landed a Hereford handicap in February; best
around two miles; acts on most ground.

Fosforito (FR)

90   80
6-y-o b g Zieten (USA)-Bardouine (USA) (Northern Baby
(CAN))
G L Moore (R C Guest 5/6) N J Jones

Placings:55   (0557)
2003/04: 17⁵G, 16⁵GF,

	Starts	1st	2nd	3rd	Win & Pl
Hurdles	2	0	0	0	0
Career Total	2	0	0	0	0

Going:	Sf: 0-0 GS: 0-0 Gd: 0-1 GF: - Fm: 0-1
Distance:	2m/2m3: 0-2 2m4-2m7: 0-0 3m+: 0-0
Track:	LH: 0-1 RH: 0-1 Tight: 0-1 Gall: 0-0
Aids:	Bl: 0-0 Vi: 0-0 Tstrap: 0-0 Ckp: 0-1
Best Rating:	80 6/03 Prth 2m110y gd-fm Hdl

Novice hurdler; hinted at ability first two starts over hurdles;
has worn cheekpieces.

Fota Island (IRE)

111   (117c)156+
8-y-o b g Supreme Leader-Mary Kate Finn (Saher)
M F Morris John P McManus

Placings:11/U24322113-F336   (4383)
2003/04: 16³GY, 20⁵S, 16³GY, 16²Y, 16⁶G,

	Starts	1st	2nd	3rd	Win & Pl
Hurdles	5	0	0	3	19426
Career Total	15	4	3	4	53431
130 3/03 Punc	2m	Hdl	YLD	£8441
132 3/03 Leop	2m	Hdl	HVY	£7168
111 4/02 Cork	2m	NHF	G-Y	£5291
131 3/02 Navn	2m	NHF	HVY	£4444
			Total win prize-money £25347

Going:	Sf: 0-1 GS: 0-0 Gd: 0-1 GF: - Fm: 0-0
Distance:	2m/2m3: 0-4 2m4-2m7: 0-1 3m+: 0-0
Track:	LH: 0-2 RH: 0-3 Tight: 0-0 Gall: 0-0
Aids:	Bl: 0-0 Vi: 0-0 Tstrap: 0-0 Ckp: 0-0
Best Rating:	156 3/04 Chel 2m110y good Hdl

Smart Irish-trained hurdler; excellent efforts when third in the
Irish Champion Hurdle and sixth in the Champion Hurdle at
Cheltenham; has placed form over fences; stays 2m 4f;
effective in soft ground.

Fountain Bank (IRE)

100(106c)   (0c)102+
11-y-o b g Lafontaine (USA)-Clogrecon Lass (Raise You
Ten)
M J Gingell T Alexander And G S Plastow

Placings:30/4046/P3F/21112441P4660/U561340PPP3-
P5140P   (1173)

2003/04: 21⁸GF, 21⁵GF, 22¹GF, 22⁴GF, 24⁰GF, 22⁸GF,

	Starts	1st	2nd	3rd	Win & Pl
Hurdles	5	1	0	0	2777
Chases	1	0	0	0	0
Career Total	39	6	2	4	21977
102 6/03 Uttx	2m6f110yG(0-90)HHdl		G-F	£2499
104 8/02 Worc	2m7f110yE Ch		GD	£4036
109 9/01 Font	2m6f110yF(0-110)HHdl		G-F	£2688
108 6/01 Strf	2m6f110yF(0-95)HHdl		G-F	£2443
101 6/01 Worc	2m4f	F(0-110)HHdl		G-F	£2562
95 6/01 Fknm	2m7f110yF(0-100)HHdl		G-F	£3003
			Total win prize-money £17232

Going:	Sf: 0-0 GS: 0-0 Gd: 0-0 GF: - Fm: 1-6
Distance:	2m/2m3: 0-0 2m4-2m7: 1-5 3m+: 0-1
Track:	LH: 1-5 RH: 0-1 Tight: 0-3 Gall: 0-1
Aids:	Bl: 0-0 Vi: 0-0 Tstrap: 0-0 Ckp: 1-5
Best Rating:	109 9/01 Font 2m6f110y gd-fm Hdl

Plating-class hurdler/chaser; acts on decent ground; stays
three miles.

Fountain Hill (IRE)

110   128
5-y-o b g King's Theatre (IRE)-Highest Land (FR) (Highest
Honor (FR))
P F Nicholls The Fountains Partnership

Placings:13212   (4561)
2003/04: 17¹GF, 17⁹G, 17²GS, 21¹G, 24²GS,

	Starts	1st	2nd	3rd	Win & Pl
NH Flat	2	1	0	1	2816
Hurdles	3	1	2	0	9030
Career Total	5	2	2	1	11846
116 3/04 Newb	2m5f	D Hdl	GD	£6051
88 5/03 Extr	2m1f	H NHF	G-F	£2394
			Total win prize-money £8446

Going:	Sf: 0-0 GS: 0-2 Gd: 1-2 GF: - Fm: 1-1
Distance:	2m/2m3: 1-3 2m4-2m7: 1-1 3m+: 0-1
Track:	LH: 1-3 RH: 1-2 Tight: 0-2 Gall: 1-2
Aids:	Bl: 0-0 Vi: 0-0 Tstrap: 0-0 Ckp: 0-0
Best Rating:	132 3/04 Newb 3m110y gd-sft Hdl

Useful novice hurdler; bumper winner; stays two miles five
and acts on a sound surface; progressive.

Fountain Street (IRE)

11-y-o b g Sharp Charter-Maylands (Windjammer (USA))
Mrs T R Kinsey (T R Kinsey 3/8) Mrs T R Kinsey

Placings:60/64P3PP   (4542)
2003/04: 16⁸GF, 20⁴G, 24⁶GF, 20³GS, 25⁸GS, 20⁸GS,

	Starts	1st	2nd	3rd	Win & Pl
Chases	6	0	0	1	1154
Career Total	8	0	0	1	1154

Going:	Sf: 0-0 GS: 0-2 Gd: 0-1 GF: - Fm: 0-3
Distance:	2m/2m3: 0-1 2m4-2m7: 0-3 3m+: 0-2
Track:	LH: 0-1 RH: 0-5 Tight: 0-5 Gall: 0-0
Aids:	Bl: 0-0 Vi: 0-0 Tstrap: 0-0 Ckp: 0-0
Best Rating:	88 7/03 MRas 2m4f good Ch

Four Candles

4-y-o b f Perpendicular-Skyers Tryer (Lugana Beach)
B P J Baugh J H Chrimes

Placings:P   **(1590)**
2003/04: 16PGF,

	Starts	1st	2nd	3rd	Win & Pl
Hurdles	1	0	0	0	
Career Total	1	0	0	0	

Going:	Sf: 0-0 GS: 0-0 Gd: 0-0 GF: - Fm: 0-1
Distance:	2m/2m3: 0-1 2m4-2m7: 0-0 3m+: 0-0
Track:	LH: 0-0 RH: 0-1 Tight: 0-0 Gall: 0-0
Aids:	Bl: 0-0 Vi: 0-0 Tstrap: 0-0 Ckp: 0-0

Four To Win (IRE)
91   (88h)95
8-y-o b g Tremblant-Ballybeg Rose (IRE) (Roselier (FR))
Miss Jacqueline S Doyle   Cover Point Racing

Placings:0460P/FPF-53F   **(0448)**
2003/04: 19GS, 16QGF, 16FGF,

	Starts	1st	2nd	3rd	Win & Pl
Chases	3	0	0	1	628
Career Total	11	0	0	1	628

Going:	Sf: 0-0 GS: 0-1 Gd: 0-0 GF: - Fm: 0-2
Distance:	2m/2m3: 0-3 2m4-2m7: 0-0 3m+: 0-0
Track:	LH: 0-1 RH: 0-2 Tight: 0-0 Gall: 0-1
Aids:	Bl: 0-2 Vi: 0-1 Tstrap: 0-0 Ckp: 0-0
Best Rating:	95 5/03 Wwck 2m110y gd-fm Ch

Fourboystoy (IRE)
68f   92f
5-y-o ch g Roselier (FR)-Little Twig (IRE) (Good Thyne (USA))
C C Bealby   Farmers, Foresters & Financiers

Placings:00   **(4517)**
2003/04: 16QG, 16QGS,

	Starts	1st	2nd	3rd	Win & Pl
NH Flat	2	0	0	0	
Career Total	2	0	0	0	

Going:	Sf: 0-0 GS: 0-0 Gd: 0-1 GF: - Fm: 0-0
Distance:	2m/2m3: 0-2 2m4-2m7: 0-0 3m+: 0-0
Track:	LH: 0-1 RH: 0-1 Tight: 0-0 Gall: 0-0
Aids:	Bl: 0-0 Vi: 0-0 Tstrap: 0-0 Ckp: 0-0
Best Rating:	92 2/04 Asct 2m110y good NHF

Fox In The Box
100(104h)   (106 h)124+
7-y-o gr g Supreme Leader-Charlotte Gray (Rolfe (USA))
R H Alner   Peter Bonner

Placings:046/41P5-11   **(4811)**
2003/04: 24TGF, 24IG,

	Starts	1st	2nd	3rd	Win & Pl
Chases	2	2	0	0	7582
Career Total	9	3	0	0	11010
124 4/04	Chep	3m	E Ch		GD £4163
111 11/03	Uttx	3m	E Ch		G-F £3419
102 12/02	Chep	2m4f	E Hdl		SFT £2919
			Total win prize-money £10501		

Going:	Sf: 0-0 GS: 0-0 Gd: 1-1 GF: - Fm: 1-1
Distance:	2m/2m3: 0-0 2m4-2m7: 0-0 3m+: 2-2
Track:	LH: 2-2 RH: 0-0 Tight: 0-0 Gall: 0-0
Aids:	Bl: 0-0 Vi: 0-0 Tstrap: 0-0 Ckp: 0-0
Best Rating:	124 4/04 Chep 3m good Ch

Won 2m 4f novice hurdle on soft ground at Chepstow December 2002; always considered three mile chaser in the making and duly scored over that trip in novice events at Uttoxeter November 2003 and Chepstow April 2004; stays well; seems to act on most types of ground.

Fox John
92f   86f
5-y-o b g Ballet Royal (USA)-Muskerry Miss (IRE) (Bishop Of Orange)
H J Manners   H J Manners

Placings:5426   **(4934)**
2003/04: 16SG, 17HG, 17QG, 18QG,

	Starts	1st	2nd	3rd	Win & Pl
NH Flat	4	0	1	0	850
Career Total	4	0	1	0	850

Going:	Sf: 0-0 GS: 0-0 Gd: 0-4 GF: - Fm: 0-0
Distance:	2m/2m3: 0-4 2m4-2m7: 0-0 3m+: 0-0
Track:	LH: 0-2 RH: 0-0 Tight: 0-2 Gall: 0-0
Aids:	Bl: 0-0 Vi: 0-0 Tstrap: 0-0 Ckp: 0-0
Best Rating:	86 4/04 NAbb 2m1f good NHF

Foxes Fandango
79   58
7-y-o br g Munjarid-The Pride Of Pokey (Uncle Pokey)
N A Gaselee   Dean Woodley & Mark Fiander

Placings:00-0   **(2671)**
2003/04: 16QGF,

	Starts	1st	2nd	3rd	Win & Pl
Hurdles	1	0	0	0	
Career Total	3	0	0	0	

Going:	Sf: 0-0 GS: 0-0 Gd: 0-0 GF: - Fm: 0-1
Distance:	2m/2m3: 0-1 2m4-2m7: 0-0 3m+: 0-0
Track:	LH: 0-1 RH: 0-0 Tight: 0-0 Gall: 0-1
Aids:	Bl: 0-0 Vi: 0-0 Tstrap: 0-0 Ckp: 0-0
Best Rating:	93 2/03 Winc 2m gd-sft NHF

Foxhall Lady
37
7-y-o gr m Lyphento (USA)-Carmel (Malaspina)
J C Tuck   Robert House

Placings:000-PP   **(4519)**
2003/04: 16PS, 22PGS,

	Starts	1st	2nd	3rd	Win & Pl
Hurdles	2	0	0	0	
Career Total	5	0	0	0	

Going:	Sf: 0-1 GS: 0-1 Gd: 0-0 GF: - Fm: 0-0
Distance:	2m/2m3: 0-1 2m4-2m7: 0-1 3m+: 0-0
Track:	LH: 0-0 RH: 0-2 Tight: 0-0 Gall: 0-0
Aids:	Bl: 0-0 Vi: 0-0 Tstrap: 0-0 Ckp: 0-0
Best Rating:	38 2/03 Extr 2m3f gd-sft Hdl

Foxies Lad
101(78h)   80
13-y-o b g Then Again-Arctic Sands (Riboboy (USA))
C J Gray   P Popham, F D Popham, T Bartlett

Placings:4/34002323/4P/22230/3510P6/05U06U-50 **(0236)**
2003/04: 19SG, 25UGF,

	Starts	1st	2nd	3rd	Win & Pl
Chases	2	0	0	0	0
Career Total	30	1	5	5	13369
100 2/01	Winc	2m	C Ch		GD £6077
			Total win prize-money £6078		

Going:	Sf: 0-0 GS: 0-0 Gd: 0-1 GF: - Fm: 0-1
Distance:	2m/2m3: 0-0 2m4-2m7: 0-1 3m+: 0-1
Track:	LH: 0-0 RH: 0-2 Tight: 0-0 Gall: 0-0
Aids:	Bl: 0-1 Vi: 0-0 Tstrap: 0-0 Ckp: 0-0
Best Rating:	110 3/97 Newb 2m5f good Hdl

Won Class C 2m novice chase at Wincanton February 2001; has often been let down by his jumping since.

Foxmeade Dancer
(95h)   (72+h)
6-y-o b g Lyphento (USA)-Georgian Quickstep (Dubassoff (USA))
P C Ritchens   Mrs A E Morton

Placings:0PP6F-561PP4PPP   **(4814)**
2003/04: 19SGF, 17RG, 22TG, 22PG, 19PGS, 224HY, 16PS, 22PGF, 19PG,

	Starts	1st	2nd	3rd	Win & Pl
Hurdles	7	1	0	0	2191
Chases	2	0	0	0	
Career Total	14	1	0	0	2191
72 11/03	Folk	2m6f110yG(0-95)HHdl		GD £2191
			Total win prize-money £2191		

Going:	Sf: 0-2 GS: 0-1 Gd: 1-3 GF: - Fm: 0-3
Distance:	2m/2m3: 0-4 2m4-2m7: 1-5 3m+: 0-0
Track:	LH: 0-2 RH: 1-6 Tight: 1-4 Gall: 0-0
Aids:	Bl: 0-1 Vi: 0-0 Tstrap: 0-0 Ckp: 0-0
Best Rating:	72 11/03 Folk 2m6f110y good Hdl

Plating-class hurdler; stays two mile six and likes fast ground.

Foxton Brook (IRE)
102f   95+f
5-y-o br g Presenting-Martins Times (IRE) (Bulldozer)
N J Henderson   Lynn Wilson

Placings:6   **(4213)**
2003/04: 16QG,

	Starts	1st	2nd	3rd	Win & Pl
NH Flat	1	0	0	0	0
Career Total	1	0	0	0	0

Going:	Sf: 0-0 GS: 0-0 Gd: 0-1 GF: - Fm: 0-0
Distance:	2m/2m3: 0-1 2m4-2m7: 0-0 3m+: 0-0
Track:	LH: 0-0 RH: 0-1 Tight: 0-0 Gall: 0-0
Aids:	Bl: 0-0 Vi: 0-0 Tstrap: 0-0 Ckp: 0-0
Best Rating:	95 3/04 Kemp 2m good NHF

Foxtrotromeoyankee
4-y-o b g Tragic Role (USA)-Hope Chest (Kris)
L A Dace (M D I Usher 29/5)   Bryan Fry

Placings:P4P   **(3329)**
2003/04: 17PG, 18AG, 16PS,

	Starts	1st	2nd	3rd	Win & Pl
Hurdles	3	0	0	0	0
Career Total	3	0	0	0	0

Going:	Sf: 0-1 GS: 0-0 Gd: 0-2 GF: - Fm: 0-0
Distance:	2m/2m3: 0-3 2m4-2m7: 0-0 3m+: 0-0

Track: LH: 0-2 RH: 0-1 Tight: 0-2 Gall: 0-1
Aids: Bl: 0-0 Vi: 0-0 Tstrap: 0-0 Ckp: 0-0

Well beaten in juvenile hurdles; very keen sort who does not get home.

Foxy Royale

8-y-o b g Bold Fox-Celtic Royale (Celtic Cone)
Mrs A Price Mrs A Price

Placings:00/F					(4510)
2003/04: 19FGS,					
	Starts	1st	2nd	3rd	Win & Pl
Chases	1	0	0	0	
Career Total	3	0	0	0	

Going: Sf: 0-0 GS: 0-1 Gd: 0-0 GF: 0-0 Fm: 0-0
Distance: 2m/2m3: 0-1 2m4-2m7: 0-0 3m+: 0-0
Track: LH: 0-0 RH: 0-1 Tight: 0-0 Gall: 0-0
Aids: Bl: 0-0 Vi: 0-0 Tstrap: 0-0 Ckp: 0-0
Best Rating: 42 5/01 Bang 2m1f gd-sft Hdl

Foxy Trix

67f   **21f**

5-y-o b/br m Mind Games-Hill Vixen (Goldhill)
J W Unett (T R George 11/12) Mrs A D Williams

Placings:00					(2697)
2003/04: 17DGS, 16DG,					
	Starts	1st	2nd	3rd	Win & Pl
NH Flat	2	0	0	0	
Career Total	2	0	0	0	

Going: Sf: 0-0 GS: 0-1 Gd: 0-1 GF: - Fm: 0-0
Distance: 2m/2m3: 0-2 2m4-2m7: 0-0 3m+: 0-0
Track: LH: 0-0 RH: 0-2 Tight: 0-1 Gall: 0-0
Aids: Bl: 0-0 Vi: 0-0 Tstrap: 0-0 Ckp: 0-0
Best Rating: 21 12/03 Ludl 2m good NHF

Fragrant Rose

70(83c)   **(92+c)110**

8-y-o b m Alflora (IRE)-Levantine Rose (Levanter)
Miss H C Knight David Jenks

Placings:1316/113621-3606					(4248)
2003/04: 20³GS, 19FGS, 16FG, 19FGF,					
	Starts	1st	2nd	3rd	Win & Pl
Hurdles	2	0	0	0	0
Chases	2	0	0	1	836
Career Total	14	5	1	3	20895
108	4/03	Uttx	2m4f110yE Hdl	GD	£3535
109	11/02	Tntn	2m3f110yC Hdl	G-S	£6110
97	11/02	Hrfd	2m1f E Hdl	GD	£3445
116	1/02	Tntn	H NHF	SFT	£2114
110	11/01	Hrfd	2m1f H NHF	GD	£1631
			Total win prize-money £16835		

Going: Sf: 0-0 GS: 0-2 Gd: 0-1 GF: - Fm: 0-1
Distance: 2m/2m3: 0-2 2m4-2m7: 0-2 3m+: 0-0
Track: LH: 0-0 RH: 0-4 Tight: 0-0 Gall: 0-1
Aids: Bl: 0-0 Vi: 0-0 Tstrap: 0-0 Ckp: 0-0
Best Rating: 116 1/02 Tntn 2m1f soft NHF

Modest hurdler; novice chaser; stays two miles three; acts on good and soft ground.

Framlingham

91   **50**

9-y-o gr g Out Of Hand-Sugar Hall (Weatherbird)
B J Llewellyn Crouch Morgan Partnership

Placings:0P00					(4171)
2003/04: 20³S, 26PGS, 24DS, 19DG,					
	Starts	1st	2nd	3rd	Win & Pl
Hurdles	4	0	0	0	
Career Total	4	0	0	0	

Going: Sf: 0-2 GS: 0-1 Gd: 0-0 GF: - Fm: 0-0
Distance: 2m/2m3: 0-1 2m4-2m7: 0-1 3m+: 0-2
Track: LH: 0-3 RH: 0-1 Tight: 0-0 Gall: 0-1
Aids: Bl: 0-0 Vi: 0-0 Tstrap: 0-0 Ckp: 0-0
Best Rating: 50 1/04 Chep 3m soft Hdl

Francies Fancy (IRE)

98   **110**

7-y-o b g Imperial Frontier (USA)-Cheeky Maid (IRE) (Bob Back (USA))
J J Lambe Mike Futter

Placings:00412/6400/5					(1143)
2003/04: 20⁵GF,					
	Starts	1st	2nd	3rd	Win & Pl
Hurdles	1	0	0	0	0
Career Total	10	1	1	0	12288
126	12/00	Fair	2m	Hdl	Y-S	£7800
			Total win prize-money £7800		

Going: Sf: 0-0 GS: 0-0 Gd: 0-0 GF: - Fm: 0-1
Distance: 2m/2m3: 0-0 2m4-2m7: 0-1 3m+: 0-0
Track: LH: 0-0 RH: 0-1 Tight: 0-0 Gall: 0-0
Aids: Bl: 0-0 Vi: 0-0 Tstrap: 0-0 Ckp: 0-0
Best Rating: 128 12/00 Leop 2m sft-hvy Hdl

Modest hurdler; surprised connections when coming good in a Grade Three event at Fairyhouse but showed that to be no fluke when chasing home Pittsburgh Phil on his next start; acts on soft ground.

Francis Bay (USA)

(96h)   **(96h)**

9-y-o b g Alleged (USA)-Montage (USA) (Alydar (USA))
Mrs S J Smith M Magowan & T Sinnamon

Placings:3123/153016/0110106/440P00/0					(4047)
2003/04: 20DG,					
	Starts	1st	2nd	3rd	Win & Pl
Hurdles	1	0	0	0	0
Career Total	24	6	1	3	33508
125	8/00	Gway	2m1f	HCh	GD	£8560
112	7/00	Klny	2m1f	(0-123)HCh	GF	£4416
105	6/00	Baln	2m1f	(0-102)HCh	GD	£4002
81	3/00	DRoy	2m	Ch	G-Y	£3312
115	7/99	Gway	2m	Hdl	GD	£4296
96	2/99	Naas	2m	Hdl	SFT	£3069
			Total win prize-money £27656		

Going: Sf: 0-0 GS: 0-0 Gd: 0-1 GF: - Fm: 0-0
Distance: 2m/2m3: 0-0 2m4-2m7: 0-1 3m+: 0-0
Track: LH: 0-1 RH: 0-0 Tight: 0-0 Gall: 0-0
Aids: Bl: 0-0 Vi: 0-0 Tstrap: 0-0 Ckp: 0-0
Best Rating: 135 9/01 Gway 2m gd-fm Hdl

Francken (ITY)

87   **65**

5-y-o ro g Petit Loup (USA)-Filicaia (Sallust)
Lady Susan Watson Lady Susan Watson

Placings:P4					(4618)
2003/04: 19PG, 214G,					
	Starts	1st	2nd	3rd	Win & Pl
Hurdles	2	0	0	0	260
Career Total	2	0	0	0	260

Going: Sf: 0-0 GS: 0-0 Gd: 0-2 GF: - Fm: 0-0
Distance: 2m/2m3: 0-0 2m4-2m7: 0-2 3m+: 0-0
Track: LH: 0-2 RH: 0-0 Tight: 0-1 Gall: 0-0
Aids: Bl: 0-0 Vi: 0-0 Tstrap: 0-0 Ckp: 0-0
Best Rating: 65 3/04 Sedg 2m5f110y good Hdl

Francolino (FR)

98(71h)   **(10h)73**

11-y-o b g Useful (FR)-Quintefeuille Ii (FR) (Kashtan (FR))
N A Gaselee Barry Marsden

Placings:4321350/45314/2P442/2541512/41PP04P/P040/0					
P53-P6342					(1545)
2003/04: 24PGF, 23⁶GF, 23³G, 26⁴GF, 26²GF,					
	Starts	1st	2nd	3rd	Win & Pl
Hurdles	1	0	0	0	0
Chases	4	0	1	1	1703
Career Total	44	5	6	5	62014
130	10/00	Plum	2m4f	D(0-125)HCh	SFT	£4480
4/00	Pmnl	2m3f	Ch	SFT	£2882
2/00	Pau	2m3f	Ch	SFT	£3842
11/97	Ange	2m5f	Ch	VS	£9540
1/97	Pau	2m2f110y	Ch	VS	£5612
			Total win prize-money £26356		

Going: Sf: 0-0 GS: 0-0 Gd: 0-0 GF: - Fm: 0-4
Distance: 2m/2m3: 0-0 2m4-2m7: 0-0 3m+: 0-5
Track: LH: 0-5 RH: 0-0 Tight: 0-2 Gall: 0-0
Aids: Bl: 0-0 Vi: 0-0 Tstrap: 0-0 Ckp: 0-5
Best Rating: 130 10/00 Plum 2m4f soft Ch

Plating-class hurdler/chaser; poor form since returning to the course after more than a year off; usually wears cheek-pieces; has been tried in blinkers; does not appear to stay 3m.

Frankie Anson

89(103h)   **(90h)56**

7-y-o b g Anshan-Smilingatstrangers (Macmillion)
M D Hammond Frank Hanson

Placings:50/41040041-400P					(0937)
2003/04: 24⁴G, 25DGF, 24DGF, 27PGF,					
	Starts	1st	2nd	3rd	Win & Pl
Hurdles	2	0	0	0	0
Chases	2	0	0	0	0
Career Total	14	2	0	0	4719
90	4/03	Weth	2m7f	G(0-90)HHdl	G-F	£2422
102	10/02	MRas	2m1f110yH NHF	G-F	£2030
			Total win prize-money £4452		

Going: Sf: 0-0 GS: 0-0 Gd: 0-1 GF: - Fm: 0-3
Distance: 2m/2m3: 0-0 2m4-2m7: 0-0 3m+: 0-2
Track: LH: 0-4 RH: 0-0 Tight: 0-1 Gall: 0-0
Aids: Bl: 0-0 Vi: 0-0 Tstrap: 0-0 Ckp: 0-0
Best Rating: 102 10/02 MRas 2m1f110y gd-fm NHF

Moderate hurdler; suited by a sound surface; fatally injured on chase debut in July. (DEAD)

Frankincense (IRE)

99   **92**

8-y-o gr g Paris House-Mistral Wood (USA) (Far North (CAN))
A J Lockwood Chester Bosomworth

Placings:6230/05616PP-5034P30   (4796)
2003/04: 16⁵GS, 21⁰G, 19³G, 27⁴GS, 24⁴G, 27³G, 21⁰G,

	Starts	1st	2nd	3rd	Win & Pl
Hurdles	7	0	0	2	1299
Career Total	18	1	1	3	4969
92	1/03	Sedg	2m5f110yG(0-90)HHdl	HVY	£2373
			Total win prize-money £2373		

Going:	Sf: 0-0 GS: 0-2 Gd: 0-5 GF: - Fm: 0-0
Distance:	2m/2m3: 0-2 2m4-2m7: 0-2 3m+: 0-3
Track:	LH: 0-7 RH: 0-0 Tight: 0-6 Gall: 0-0
Aids:	Bl: 0-0 Vi: 0-0 Tstrap: 0-0 Ckp: 0-0
Best Rating:	92 1/03 Sedg 2m5f110y heavy Hdl

Plating-class hurdler; winner on the Flat in Germany, best over trips of around two and a half miles and suited by soft ground.

Frazers Fortune

4-y-o ch g Environment Friend-Safidar (Roan Rocket)
G Brown M Faulkner And A King

Placings:P   (1673)
2003/04: 16⁰F,

	Starts	1st	2nd	3rd	Win & Pl
Hurdles	1	0	0	0	
Career Total	1	0	0	0	

Going:	Sf: 0-0 GS: 0-0 Gd: 0-0 GF: - Fm: 0-1
Distance:	2m/2m3: 0-1 2m4-2m7: 0-0 3m+: 0-0
Track:	LH: 0-0 RH: 0-1 Tight: 0-0 Gall: 0-0
Aids:	Bl: 0-0 Vi: 0-0 Tstrap: 0-0 Ckp: 0-0

Fred's In The Know

103(105h)   (121h)**123**

9-y-o ch g Interrex (CAN)-Lady Vynz (Whitstead)
N Waggott N Waggott

Placings:52/23213300/54222P/2421U1-54F3UPP0 (4662)
2003/04: 20⁵S, 16⁴S, 20⁵S, 19³G, 20⁰GS, 17⁰GS, 24⁴HY, 20⁰S,

	Starts	1st	2nd	3rd	Win & Pl
Hurdles	4	0	0	0	544
Chases	4	0	0	1	840
Career Total	30	3	9	3	26815
114	3/03	Hexm	2m110y E Ch	SFT	£3861
110	2/03	Weth	2m E Ch	GD	£4111
131	12/00	Leic	2m4f110yD Hdl	HVY	£3848
			Total win prize-money £11820		

Going:	Sf: 0-5 GS: 0-2 Gd: 0-1 GF: - Fm: 0-0
Distance:	2m/2m3: 0-3 2m4-2m7: 0-4 3m+: 0-1
Track:	LH: 0-7 RH: 0-1 Tight: 0-2 Gall: 0-1
Aids:	Bl: 0-0 Vi: 0-0 Tstrap: 0-0 Ckp: 0-0
Best Rating:	131 1/01 Newc 2m4f soft Hdl

Fair handicap hurdler/chaser; stays two and a half miles and suited by ground good or softer; likes to come from off the pace.

Freddy Crystal (FR)

5-y-o b g Northern Crystal-Native Times (FR) (Faraway Times (USA))

P J Hobbs Terry Warner

Placings:05635P23-F   (2566)
2003/04: 17⁵G,

	Starts	1st	2nd	3rd	Win & Pl
Chases	1	0	0	0	
Career Total	9	0	1	2	15952

Going:	Sf: 0-0 GS: 0-0 Gd: 0-1 GF: - Fm: 0-0
Distance:	2m/2m3: 0-1 2m4-2m7: 0-0 3m+: 0-0
Track:	LH: 0-0 RH: 0-1 Tight: 0-0 Gall: 0-0
Aids:	Bl: 0-0 Vi: 0-0 Tstrap: 0-0 Ckp: 0-0
Best Rating:	108 4/03 Autl 2m1f110y v soft Ch

Placed over hurdles and fences in France; fell on British chasing debut.

Frederic Forever (IRE)

96(104h)   (119h)**86+**

6-y-o b g Exit To Nowhere (USA)-Sarooh's Love (USA) (Nureyev (USA))
P J Hobbs Mrs D A Winton

Placings:11215225/22-505004   (4855)
2003/04: 16⁵G, 17⁰G, 20⁵G, 19⁰G, 20⁴G, 24⁴GF,

	Starts	1st	2nd	3rd	Win & Pl
Hurdles	2	0	0	0	0
Chases	4	0	0	0	713
Career Total	16	3	5	0	18485
107	10/01	Chep	2m110y D Hdl	GD	£3464
108	9/01	NAbb	2m1f E Hdl	G-F	£2863
96	8/01	Font	2m2f110yE Hdl	G-F	£2324
			Total win prize-money £8652		

Going:	Sf: 0-0 GS: 0-0 Gd: 0-5 GF: - Fm: 0-1
Distance:	2m/2m3: 0-2 2m4-2m7: 0-3 3m+: 0-1
Track:	LH: 0-1 RH: 0-4 Tight: 0-3 Gall: 0-0
Aids:	Bl: 0-0 Vi: 0-0 Tstrap: 0-0 Ckp: 0-0
Best Rating:	119 10/02 Chep 2m110y gd-fm Hdl

Fair hurdler; useful juvenile form shown in 2001; has some decent placed form in handicaps; best at around two miles; prefers a fast surface, but has been placed on softer; not seen since 2002.

Free Return (IRE)

(103h)   (111h)**102**

9-y-o ch g Magical Wonder (USA)-Free Reserve (USA) (Tom Rolfe)
Noel T Chance Mrs Jill Cox

Placings:2133/050/331515335-P4   (2097)
2003/04: 16⁰G, 19⁴GF,

	Starts	1st	2nd	3rd	Win & Pl
Hurdles	1	0	0	0	545
Chases	1	0	0	0	
Career Total	18	3	1	6	12912
111	12/02	Hrfd	2m1f E(0-105)HHdl	GD	£2940
103	10/02	Font	2m6f110yD(0-120)HHdl	GD	£4309
95	8/00	NAbb	2m1f H NHF	GD	£1491
			Total win prize-money £8741		

Going:	Sf: 0-0 GS: 0-0 Gd: 0-1 GF: - Fm: 0-1
Distance:	2m/2m3: 0-2 2m4-2m7: 0-0 3m+: 0-0
Track:	LH: 0-2 RH: 0-0 Tight: 0-0 Gall: 0-1
Aids:	Bl: 0-0 Vi: 0-0 Tstrap: 0-0 Ckp: 0-0
Best Rating:	111 12/02 Hrfd 2m1f good Hdl

Modest chaser/hurdler; successful at trips between two miles one and two miles six over hurdles.

Free Strike (NZ)

82   **98**

7-y-o ch g Straight Strike (USA)-Ansellia (NZ) (Nassipour (USA))
P Mitchell R Cheetham

Placings:0P0   (4207)
2003/04: 20⁰G, 21ᴾGS, 16⁰G,

	Starts	1st	2nd	3rd	Win & Pl
Hurdles	3	0	0	0	
Career Total	3	0	0	0	

Going:	Sf: 0-0 GS: 0-1 Gd: 0-2 GF: - Fm: 0-0
Distance:	2m/2m3: 0-1 2m4-2m7: 0-2 3m+: 0-0
Track:	LH: 0-0 RH: 0-2 Tight: 0-1 Gall: 0-0
Aids:	Bl: 0-0 Vi: 0-0 Tstrap: 0-0 Ckp: 0-0
Best Rating:	98 3/04 Kemp 2m good Hdl

Free To Run (IRE)

107   (43h)**117**

10-y-o b g Satco (FR)-Lady Oats (Oats)
Mrs S J Smith Keith Nicholson

Placings:00040/100/40030044F/0045344/4121323134123-3P223324351   (4615)
2003/04: 23⁵G, 24ᴾGF, 24²GF, 23ᴾGF, 24³G, 28³G, 24²GF, 25⁴GS, 25³GS, 26⁵G, 28¹G,

	Starts	1st	2nd	3rd	Win & Pl
Hurdles	1	0	0	0	0
Chases	10	1	3	4	13874
Career Total	48	6	6	10	41397
111	3/04	Sedg	3m4f	E(0-110)HCh	GD	£5148
106	11/02	Hayd	2m6f	E(0-105)HCh	SFT	£3614
112	8/02	Ctml	3m2f	E Ch	GD	£4192
103	6/02	Hexm	3m1f	E(0-105)HCh	G-F	£3133
112	6/02	Ctml	2m5f110yE Ch	HVY	£3374
80	5/99	Dpat	2m1f172y NHF	GD	£1994
			Total win prize-money £21457		

Going:	Sf: 0-0 GS: 0-2 Gd: 1-5 GF: - Fm: 0-4
Distance:	2m/2m3: 0-0 2m4-2m7: 0-0 3m+: 1-11
Track:	LH: 1-8 RH: 0-3 Tight: 1-3 Gall: 0-0
Aids:	Bl: 0-0 Vi: 0-0 Tstrap: 0-0 Ckp: 0-0
Best Rating:	116 8/03 Uttx 3m gd-fm Ch

Moderate ex-Irish chaser; consistent sort; best at around 3m; jumps well.

Free Willie (IRE)

76   **37**

4-y-o b g Ridgewood Ben-Dance In The Wings (In The Wings)
M C Pipe D A Johnson

Placings:P00   (3376)
2003/04: 16ᴾGS, 17⁰GS, 16⁰S,

	Starts	1st	2nd	3rd	Win & Pl
Hurdles	3	0	0	0	
Career Total	3	0	0	0	

Going:	Sf: 0-1 GS: 0-2 Gd: 0-0 GF: - Fm: 0-0
Distance:	2m/2m3: 0-3 2m4-2m7: 0-0 3m+: 0-0
Track:	LH: 0-1 RH: 0-2 Tight: 0-0 Gall: 0-0
Aids:	Bl: 0-0 Vi: 0-3 Tstrap: 0-0 Ckp: 0-0
Best Rating:	37 1/04 Winc 2m soft Hdl

Freedom Bay

85   **83+**

4-y-o b g Slip Anchor-Bobbie Dee (Blakeney)
Mrs P N Dutfield Simon Dutfield

Placings:3   (2253)
2003/04: 17³GF,

	Starts	1st	2nd	3rd	Win & Pl
Hurdles	1	0	0	1	349
Career Total	1	0	0	1	349

Going: Sf: 0-0 GS: 0-0 Gd: 0-0 GF: - Fm: 0-1
Distance: 2m/2m3: 0-1 2m4-2m7: 0-0 3m+: 0-0
Track: LH: 0-1 RH: 0-1 Tight: 0-0 Gall: 0-0
Aids: Bl: 0-0 Vi: 0-0 Tstrap: 0-0 Ckp: 0-0
Best Rating: 83 11/03 Hrfd 2m1f   gd-fm Hdl

Well-beaten in third on hurdles debut.

Freedom Fighter

13-y-o b g Fearless Action (USA)-Zuleika Hill (Yellow River)
Mrs Rosemary Gasson Mrs Rosemary Gasson

Placings:1PF2P/P303P/52PP43C/PPP-4   (4283)
2003/04: 25⁴G,

	Starts	1st	2nd	3rd	Win & Pl
Chases	1	0	0	0	0
Career Total	21	1	2	3	5792
90 5/99 Strf 3m H Ch			G-S	£3184
Total win prize-money £3184

Going: Sf: 0-0 GS: 0-0 Gd: 0-1 GF: - Fm: 0-0
Distance: 2m/2m3: 0-0 2m4-2m7: 0-0 3m+: 0-1
Track: LH: 0-0 RH: 0-1 Tight: 0-0 Gall: 0-0
Aids: Bl: 0-0 Vi: 0-0 Tstrap: 0-0 Ckp: 0-0
Best Rating: 97 5/00 Strf 3m   gd-fm Ch

Winning pointer, prefers a sound surface.

Freedom Now (IRE)

93   **102**

6-y-o b g Sadler's Wells (USA)-Free At Last (Shirley Heights)
M D Hammond (J W Hills 17/10) Frank Hanson

Placings:0F5   (3720)
2003/04: 16⁹G, 25²G, 16⁵S,

	Starts	1st	2nd	3rd	Win & Pl
Hurdles	3	0	0	0	750
Career Total	3	0	0	0	750

Going: Sf: 0-1 GS: 0-0 Gd: 0-2 GF: - Fm: 0-0
Distance: 2m/2m3: 0-2 2m4-2m7: 0-0 3m+: 0-1
Track: LH: 0-3 RH: 0-0 Tight: 0-1 Gall: 0-0
Aids: Bl: 0-0 Vi: 0-0 Tstrap: 0-0 Ckp: 0-0
Best Rating: 100 1/04 Catt 3m1f110y good Hdl

Useful handicapper on the Flat; just in front when falling two out in three mile novices' hurdle at Catterick in January.

Freestyler (IRE)

12-y-o b/br g Phardante (FR)-Financial Burden (Mandalus)
B P J Baugh Mrs B L Shaw

Placings:40000/0/00/UP/5/R   (1008)
2003/04: 20ᴿG,

	Starts	1st	2nd	3rd	Win & Pl
Chases	1	0	0	0	

| Career Total | 14 | 0 | 0 | 0 | 139 |

Going: Sf: 0-0 GS: 0-0 Gd: 0-1 GF: - Fm: 0-0
Distance: 2m/2m3: 0-0 2m4-2m7: 0-1 3m+: 0-0
Track: LH: 0-1 RH: 0-0 Tight: 0-1 Gall: 0-0
Aids: Bl: 0-0 Vi: 0-0 Tstrap: 0-1 Ckp: 0-0
Best Rating: 91 11/97 Navn 2m   heavy NHF

Freetown (IRE)

88   **107**

8-y-o b g Shirley Heights-Pageantry (Welsh Pageant)
L Lungo Miss S Blumberg & R Nairn

Placings:32/111123/34113/0-P40   (4386)
2003/04: 25ᴾGS, 23⁴HY, 25⁰G,

	Starts	1st	2nd	3rd	Win & Pl
Hurdles	3	0	0	0	1040
Career Total	17	6	2	4	65883
154 3/02 Chel 3m1f110yA HHdl		G-S	£32500
113 2/02 Ayr 2m4f C Ch		HVY	£8807
136 12/00 Weth 2m7f D Hdl		SFT	£3250
114 11/00 Carl 3m110y E Hdl		HVY	£2396
121 11/00 Carl 3m110y E Hdl		SFT	£2475
120 6/00 Prth 3m110y E Hdl		SFT	£2933
Total win prize-money £52363

Going: Sf: 0-1 GS: 0-1 Gd: 0-1 GF: - Fm: 0-0
Distance: 2m/2m3: 0-0 2m4-2m7: 0-0 3m+: 0-3
Track: LH: 0-0 RH: 0-0 Tight: 0-0 Gall: 0-0
Aids: Bl: 0-0 Vi: 0-0 Tstrap: 0-0 Ckp: 0-0
Best Rating: 154 4/02 Aint 3m110y good Hdl

Smart hurdler; has also won over fences; successful in the Pertemps Final at the Cheltenham Festival in March 2002; held since; stays well; effective with cut in the ground.

Freindlypersuasion

30f

4-y-o b c Shambo-Sea Sky (Oats)
Mrs A Duffield Billy Maguire

Placings:00   (4886)
2003/04: 13⁰GF, 17⁰GS,

	Starts	1st	2nd	3rd	Win & Pl
NH Flat	2	0	0	0	
Career Total	2	0	0	0	

Going: Sf: 0-0 GS: 0-1 Gd: 0-0 GF: - Fm: 0-1
Distance: 2m/2m3: 0-2 2m4-2m7: 0-0 3m+: 0-0
Track: LH: 0-0 RH: 0-1 Tight: 0-0 Gall: 0-0
Aids: Bl: 0-0 Vi: 0-0 Tstrap: 0-0 Ckp: 0-0
Best Rating: 33 11/03 Donc 1m5f   gd-fm NHF

French Direction (IRE)

92   **89+**

5-y-o ch g John French-Shelikesitstraight (IRE) (Rising)
R Rowe Mrs R A Proctor

Placings:40050U   (4859)
2003/04: 21⁴GF, 16⁰G, 16⁸GF, 16⁰GS, 19ᵁGF,

	Starts	1st	2nd	3rd	Win & Pl
Hurdles	6	0	0	0	0
Career Total	6	0	0	0	0

Going: Sf: 0-0 GS: 0-1 Gd: 0-2 GF: - Fm: 0-3
Distance: 2m/2m3: 0-4 2m4-2m7: 0-2 3m+: 0-0

Track: LH: 0-3 RH: 0-3 Tight: 0-3 Gall: 0-1
Aids: Bl: 0-0 Vi: 0-0 Tstrap: 0-0 Ckp: 0-0
Best Rating: 89 12/03 Newb 2m110y   gd-fm Hdl

French Envoy (FR)

97f   **93f**

5-y-o bl g Cadoudal (FR)-Miss Merry (FR) (Pedege (FR))
Ian Williams Sir Robert Ogden

Placings:43   (4920)
2003/04: 16⁴GF, 16³GS,

	Starts	1st	2nd	3rd	Win & Pl
NH Flat	2	0	0	1	601
Career Total	2	0	0	1	601

Going: Sf: 0-0 GS: 0-1 Gd: 0-0 GF: - Fm: 0-1
Distance: 2m/2m3: 0-2 2m4-2m7: 0-0 3m+: 0-0
Track: LH: 0-1 RH: 0-0 Tight: 0-0 Gall: 0-0
Aids: Bl: 0-0 Vi: 0-0 Tstrap: 0-0 Ckp: 0-0
Best Rating: 93 4/04 Worc 2m   gd-sft NHF

Has shown ability in bumpers.

French Executive (IRE)

104   **(109h)122**

9-y-o br g Beau Sher-Executive Move (IRE) (Executive Perk)
P F Nicholls T Chappell,R Eddy,Mrs Jackson,Mrs Solman

Placings:43/223216332/143P322-P135P10   (4834)
2003/04: 24ᴾS, 28¹G, 24³GF, 25⁵G, 28ᴾG, 26¹G, 26⁰GF,

	Starts	1st	2nd	3rd	Win & Pl
Chases	7	2	0	1	11836
Career Total	25	4	6	7	32513
122 3/04 Plum 3m2f E(0-115)Ch	GD	£5174
122 10/03 Strf 3m4f D(0-125)HCh	GD	£4305
122 11/02 Plum 3m2f D(0-110)HCh	G-S	£5443
109 1/02 Tntn 2m3f110yE(0-105)HHdl	SFT	£2870
Total win prize-money £17793

Going: Sf: 0-1 GS: 0-0 Gd: 2-4 GF: - Fm: 0-2
Distance: 2m/2m3: 0-0 2m4-2m7: 0-0 3m+: 2-7
Track: LH: 2-5 RH: 0-1 Tight: 2-3 Gall: 0-2
Aids: Bl: 0-0 Vi: 0-0 Tstrap: 0-1 Ckp: 0-0
Best Rating: 122 3/04 Plum 3m2f   good Ch

Fair chaser; stays well but lacks a turn of foot; acts on fast and soft ground; has been tried in tongue tie.

French Horn

83   **50**

7-y-o b g Fraam-Runcina (Runnett)
M Wigham (M J Ryan 7/1) D Hassan

Placings:0   (2777)
2003/04: 17⁰GS,

	Starts	1st	2nd	3rd	Win & Pl
Hurdles	1	0	0	0	
Career Total	1	0	0	0	

Going: Sf: 0-0 GS: 0-1 Gd: 0-0 GF: - Fm: 0-0
Distance: 2m/2m3: 0-1 2m4-2m7: 0-0 3m+: 0-0
Track: LH: 0-0 RH: 0-1 Tight: 0-1 Gall: 0-0
Aids: Bl: 0-0 Vi: 0-0 Tstrap: 0-0 Ckp: 0-0
Best Rating: 50 12/03 Folk 2m1f110y gd-sft Hdl

French Mannequin (IRE)

107   **100**

5-y-o b/br m Key Of Luck (USA)-Paris Model (IRE) (Thatching)
Mrs A J Hamilton-Fairley Runs In The Family

Placings:63110-463340224315   (4163)
2003/04: 18⁴G, 16⁶GF, 17³GF, 17³GF, 16⁴G, 16⁹GF, 16²GF, 16²GF, 19⁴GS, 17³GS, 16¹G, 16⁵G,

	Starts	1st	2nd	3rd	Win & Pl
Hurdles	12	1	2	3	9243
Career Total	**17**	**3**	**2**	**4**	**16462**
100	2/04	Ludl	2m	D(0-115)HHdl	GD £4745
91	3/03	Plum	2m	E Hdl	G-F £3513
91	3/03	Folk	2m1f110yF Hdl		GD £3083

Total win prize-money £11342

Going:	Sf: 0-0 GS: 0-2 Gd: 1-4 GF: - Fm: 0-6
Distance:	**2m/2m3:** 1-11 2m4-2m7: 0-1 3m+: 0-0
Track:	LH: 0-7 RH: **1-5** Tight: 0-4 Gall: 0-2
Aids:	Bl: 0-0 Vi: 0-0 Tstrap: 0-0 Ckp: 0-0
Best Rating:	**100** 2/04 Ludl 2m good Hdl

Moderate hurdler; front-runner; acts on soft ground but suited by fast; suited to a sharp track.

French Tune (FR)

101   **95**

6-y-o ch g Green Tune (USA)-Guerre De Troie (Risk Me (FR))
Miss S E Hall C Platts

Placings:40-36   (1208)
2003/04: 17³GF, 17⁶G,

	Starts	1st	2nd	3rd	Win & Pl
Hurdles	2	0	0	1	494
Career Total	**4**	**0**	**0**	**1**	**757**

Going:	Sf: 0-0 GS: 0-0 Gd: 0-1 GF: 0-1 Fm: 0-1
Distance:	2m/2m3: 0-2 2m4-2m7: 0-0 3m+: 0-0
Track:	LH: 0-2 RH: 0-0 Tight: 0-2 Gall: 0-0
Aids:	Bl: 0-0 Vi: 0-0 Tstrap: 0-0 Ckp: 0-0
Best Rating:	**95** 8/03 Sedg 2m1f gd-fm Hdl

French-flat winner but looks to have lost his way; best effort over hurdles when third at Sedgefield in August.

Frentzen

102(100h)   (84h)**89**

7-y-o b g Golden Heights-Milly Black (IRE) (Double Schwartz)
Miss E C Lavelle J Spence

Placings:FP63U2-0302   (0836)
2003/04: 24⁰GF, 26³GF, 27⁰GF, 23²GF,

	Starts	1st	2nd	3rd	Win & Pl
Hurdles	3	0	0	1	494
Chases	1	0	1	0	1099
Career Total	**10**	**0**	**2**	**2**	**4238**

Going:	Sf: 0-0 GS: 0-0 Gd: 0-0 GF: - Fm: 0-4
Distance:	2m/2m3: 0-0 2m4-2m7: 0-0 3m+: 0-4
Track:	LH: 0-2 RH: 0-2 Tight: 0-1 Gall: 0-1
Aids:	Bl: 0-0 Vi: 0-0 Tstrap: 0-0 Ckp: 0-0
Best Rating:	**89** 7/03 Worc 2m7f110y gd-fm Chm

Plating-class maiden hurdler; good second to Maidstone Monument on chasing debut in 3m Worcester handicap July 2003; stays 3m 3f; acts on fast ground.

Fresh Run (FR)

5-y-o b g Kadalko (FR)-Tatifly (FR) (Saumon (FR))
A Ennis A T A Wates

Placings:00P   (3956)
2003/04: 16⁰GS, 20⁰GS, 22⁰G,

	Starts	1st	2nd	3rd	Win & Pl
Hurdles	3	0	0	0	
Career Total	**3**	**0**	**0**	**0**	

Going:	Sf: 0-0 GS: 0-2 Gd: 0-0 GF: - Fm: 0-0
Distance:	2m/2m3: 0-1 2m4-2m7: 0-2 3m+: 0-0
Track:	LH: 0-1 RH: 0-2 Tight: 0-1 Gall: 0-0
Aids:	Bl: 0-0 Vi: 0-0 Tstrap: 0-0 Ckp: 0-0

Freteval (FR)

100   **106**

7-y-o b g Valanjou (FR)-La Beaumont (FR) (Hellios (USA))
S J Gilmore (Mrs K J Gilmore 16/5) Mrs Diane Gane

Placings:064FFP/P26/1-3P52U063220   (4606)
2003/04: 24³S, 20⁶GS, 20⁵GS, 20²G, 21⁴UGS, 23⁰G, 23⁶G, 19³GS, 19²G, 20²GS, 20⁰GS,

	Starts	1st	2nd	3rd	Win & Pl
Chases	11	0	3	2	4628
Career Total	**21**	**1**	**4**	**2**	**11104**
106	3/03	Leic	2m4f110yH Ch	G-S £2171

Total win prize-money £2171

Going:	Sf: 0-1 GS: 0-6 Gd: 0-4 GF: - Fm: 0-0
Distance:	2m/2m3: 0-2 2m4-2m7: 0-6 3m+: 0-3
Track:	LH: 0-4 RH: 0-7 Tight: 0-5 Gall: 0-1
Aids:	Bl: 0-0 Vi: 0-0 Tstrap: 0-0 Ckp: 0-0
Best Rating:	**106** 3/03 Leic 2m4f110y gd-sft Ch

Plating-class chaser; effective at 2m 4f; acts on soft ground.

Freya Alex

99   **87+**

5-y-o b m Makbul-Crissem (IRE) (Thatching)
G M Moore Keith Nicholson

Placings:16   (0646)
2003/04: 17¹GS, 16⁶GF,

	Starts	1st	2nd	3rd	Win & Pl
Hurdles	2	1	0	0	2650
Career Total	**2**	**1**	**0**	**0**	**2650**
88	5/03	Ctml	2m1f110yG Hdl	G-S £2649

Total win prize-money £2650

Going:	Sf: 0-0 GS: 1-1 Gd: 0-0 GF: - Fm: 0-1
Distance:	**2m/2m3:** 1-2 2m4-2m7: 0-0 3m+: 0-0
Track:	**LH: 1-2** RH: 0-0 **Tight: 1-1** Gall: 0-0
Aids:	Bl: 0-0 Vi: 0-0 Tstrap: 0-0 Ckp: 0-0
Best Rating:	**88** 5/03 Ctml 2m1f110y gd-sft Hdl

Moderate novice hurdler; made winning hurdles debut in a weak selling hurdle at Cartmel.

Freydis (IRE)

97f   **84f**

6-y-o b m Supreme Leader-Lulu Buck (Buckskin (FR))
S Gollings The Highfield House Partnership

Placings:0-56   (3426)
2003/04: 16⁵GF, 17⁶HY,

	Starts	1st	2nd	3rd	Win & Pl
NH Flat	2	0	0	0	0
Career Total	**3**	**0**	**0**	**0**	**0**

Going:	Sf: 0-1 GS: 0-0 Gd: 0-0 GF: - Fm: 0-1
Distance:	2m/2m3: 0-2 2m4-2m7: 0-0 3m+: 0-0
Track:	LH: 0-1 RH: 0-1 Tight: 0-1 Gall: 0-0
Aids:	Bl: 0-0 Vi: 0-0 Tstrap: 0-0 Ckp: 0-0
Best Rating:	84 3/03 MRas 2m1f110y good NHF

Friar Peter

7-y-o b g Petoski-Misty Lough (Deep Run)
B G Powell M J Howard

Placings:PPPUC   (4146)
2003/04: 16⁶G, 22⁶GS, 24⁴PS, 24⁴UGS, 24⁰G,

	Starts	1st	2nd	3rd	Win & Pl
NH Flat	1	0	0	0	0
Hurdles	2	0	0	0	0
Chases	2	0	0	0	0
Career Total	**5**	**0**	**0**	**0**	

Going:	Sf: 0-1 GS: 0-2 Gd: 0-2 GF: - Fm: 0-0
Distance:	2m/2m3: 0-1 2m4-2m7: 0-1 3m+: 0-3
Track:	LH: 0-1 RH: 0-4 Tight: 0-3 Gall: 0-0
Aids:	Bl: 0-0 Vi: 0-0 Tstrap: 0-0 Ckp: 0-0

Friar Waddon

11-y-o b g Pablond-Looking Swell (Simbir)
K Cumings P J Clarke

Placings:F6P3/3FP-P   (0028)
2003/04: 21⁸G,

	Starts	1st	2nd	3rd	Win & Pl
Chases	1	0	0	0	
Career Total	**8**	**0**	**0**	**2**	**705**

Going:	Sf: 0-0 GS: 0-0 Gd: 0-1 GF: - Fm: 0-0
Distance:	2m/2m3: 0-0 2m4-2m7: 0-1 3m+: 0-0
Track:	LH: 0-1 RH: 0-0 Tight: 0-0 Gall: 0-1
Aids:	Bl: 0-0 Vi: 0-0 Tstrap: 0-0 Ckp: 0-0
Best Rating:	**101** 5/02 Chel 2m5f gd-fm Ch

Fair pointer/hunter, handles any ground.

Friedhelmo (GER)

105(106c)   (125c)**114**

8-y-o ch g Dashing Blade-Fox For Gold (Glint Of Gold)
R A Fahey G H Leatham

Placings:03/1/0/0041UP55-441P   (4326)
2003/04: 17⁴G, 16⁴G, 16¹G, 16⁸S,

	Starts	1st	2nd	3rd	Win & Pl
Hurdles	4	1	0	0	7393
Career Total	**16**	**3**	**0**	**1**	**14149**
117	2/04	Muss	2m	D(0-120)HHdl	GD £6864
125	12/02	Sthl	2m	E(0-110)HCh	G-S £3571
109	5/00	Worc	2m	E Hdl	G-F £2401

Total win prize-money £12837

Going:	Sf: 0-1 GS: 0-0 Gd: 1-3 GF: - Fm: 0-0
Distance:	**2m/2m3:** 1-4 2m4-2m7: 0-0 3m+: 0-0
Track:	LH: 0-2 RH: **1-2** Tight: **1-3** Gall: 0-0
Aids:	Bl: 0-0 Vi: 0-0 Tstrap: 0-0 Ckp: 0-0
Best Rating:	**125** 12/02 Sthl 2m gd-sft Ch

Fair hurdler; winning chaser; best suited by two miles; effective on fast and easy ground; sometimes tongue tied.

Friendly Fellow

97   **88**

5-y-o gr g Environment Friend-Good Fetch (Siberian Express (USA))
M C Pipe D A Johnson

Placings:546305   (4733)
2003/04: 16⁵G, 16⁴S, 17⁶G, 19³G, 17⁹G, 22⁵G,

	Starts	1st	2nd	3rd	Win & Pl
NH Flat	1	0	0	0	422
Hurdles	5	0	0	1	602
Career Total	**6**	**0**	**0**	**1**	**1024**

Going:	Sf: 0-1 GS: 0-0 Gd: 0-5 GF: - Fm: 0-0
Distance:	2m/2m3: 0-5 2m4-2m7: 0-1 3m+: 0-0
Track:	LH: 0-3 RH: 0-3 Tight: 0-4 Gall: 0-0
Aids:	Bl: 0-0 Vi: 0-0 Tstrap: 0-0 Ckp: 0-0
Best Rating:	99 11/03 Chel 2m110y good NHF

Friendly Request

91   **83**

5-y-o b/br m Environment Friend-Who Tells Jan (Royal Fountain)
Mrs P Ford W E Donohue

Placings:00-06P0P   (4716)
2003/04: 19⁰GS, 16⁶G, 17⁷PG, 16⁰GS, 21ᴾG,

	Starts	1st	2nd	3rd	Win & Pl
Hurdles	5	0	0	0	0
Career Total	**7**	**0**	**0**	**0**	**0**

Going:	Sf: 0-0 GS: 0-2 Gd: 0-3 GF: - Fm: 0-0
Distance:	2m/2m3: 0-3 2m4-2m7: 0-2 3m+: 0-0
Track:	LH: 0-1 RH: 0-4 Tight: 0-1 Gall: 0-0
Aids:	Bl: 0-0 Vi: 0-0 Tstrap: 0-0 Ckp: 0-0
Best Rating:	83 2/04 Ludl 2m good Hdl

Frightening Fred

7-y-o ch g Almoojid-Very Bold (Never So Bold)
W M Brisbourne John E Oldknow

Placings:4   (2122)
2003/04: 16⁴GF,

	Starts	1st	2nd	3rd	Win & Pl
NH Flat	1	0	0	0	0
Career Total	**1**	**0**	**0**	**0**	**0**

Going:	Sf: 0-0 GS: 0-0 Gd: 0-0 GF: - Fm: 0-1
Distance:	2m/2m3: 0-1 2m4-2m7: 0-0 3m+: 0-0
Track:	LH: 0-0 RH: 0-1 Tight: 0-0 Gall: 0-0
Aids:	Bl: 0-0 Vi: 0-0 Tstrap: 0-0 Ckp: 0-0

Frileux Royal (FR)

(87h)

11-y-o br g Sarpedon (FR)-La Frileuse (FR) (El Toro (FR))
B N Pollock S G B Morrison

Placings:F/12411PU0/443RPP/2R0RR0120P/0-R (0627)
2003/04: 24ᴿGF,

	Starts	1st	2nd	3rd	Win & Pl
Chases	1	0	0	0	0
Career Total	**27**	**4**	**3**	**1**	**23621**

96	2/02	Ludl	3m2f110yE(0-110)HHdl	G-S	£3688
	12/99	Seic	3m110y	Ch	SFT	£6459
	11/99	Agtn	2m6f110y	Ch	HVY	£3445

9/99	Chag	2m6f110y	Ch		SFT	£2153

Total win prize-money £15746

Going:	Sf: 0-0 GS: 0-0 Gd: 0-0 GF: - Fm: 0-1
Distance:	2m/2m3: 0-0 2m4-2m7: 0-0 3m+: 0-1
Track:	LH: 0-1 RH: 0-0 Tight: 0-0 Gall: 0-0
Aids:	Bl: 0-0 Vi: 0-0 Tstrap: 0-0 Ckp: 0-0
Best Rating:	129 11/00 Chel 3m7f soft Ch

Frixos (IRE)

83   **77**

4-y-o ch g Barathea (IRE)-Local Lass (Local Suitor (USA))
M Scudamore (P F I Cole 11/9) The Yes - No - Wait Sorries

Placings:5P05P   (2819)
2003/04: 16⁵GF, 16⁷ᴾF, 16⁹GF, 16⁵GF, 16ᴾGF,

	Starts	1st	2nd	3rd	Win & Pl
Hurdles	5	0	0	0	0
Career Total	**5**	**0**	**0**	**0**	**0**

Going:	Sf: 0-0 GS: 0-0 Gd: 0-0 GF: - Fm: 0-5
Distance:	2m/2m3: 0-5 2m4-2m7: 0-0 3m+: 0-0
Track:	LH: 0-1 RH: 0-4 Tight: 0-0 Gall: 0-1
Aids:	Bl: 0-0 Vi: 0-0 Tstrap: 0-0 Ckp: 0-0
Best Rating:	77 10/03 Hntg 2m110y gd-fm Hdl

From Dawn To Dusk

101f   **108+f**

5-y-o b g Afzal-Herald The Dawn (Dubassoff (USA))
P J Hobbs C G M Lloyd-Baker

Placings:1   (4816)
2003/04: 16¹G,

	Starts	1st	2nd	3rd	Win & Pl
NH Flat	1	1	0	0	2051
Career Total	**1**	**1**	**0**	**0**	**2051**

108	4/04	Chep	2m110y	H NHF		GD	£2051

Total win prize-money £2051

Going:	Sf: 0-0 GS: 0-0 Gd: 1-1 GF: - Fm: 0-0
Distance:	2m/2m3: 1-1 2m4-2m7: 0-0 3m+: 0-0
Track:	LH: 1-1 RH: 0-0 Tight: 0-0 Gall: 0-0
Aids:	Bl: 0-0 Vi: 0-0 Tstrap: 0-0 Ckp: 0-0
Best Rating:	108 4/04 Chep 2m110y good NHF

Half-brother to three mile hurdle winner King Of Arms; showed that stamina is likely to be his forte when making a winning debut in Chepstow bumper April 2004.

From This Moment (IRE)

6-y-o b g Parthian Springs-Swatter (IRE) (Over The River (FR))
P F Nicholls Mick Coburn

Placings:PP   (4561)
2003/04: 22ᴾG, 24ᴾGS,

	Starts	1st	2nd	3rd	Win & Pl
Hurdles	2	0	0	0	0
Career Total	**2**	**0**	**0**	**0**	**0**

Going:	Sf: 0-0 GS: 0-1 Gd: 0-1 GF: - Fm: 0-0
Distance:	2m/2m3: 0-0 2m4-2m7: 0-1 3m+: 0-0
Track:	LH: 0-2 RH: 0-0 Tight: 0-0 Gall: 0-1
Aids:	Bl: 0-0 Vi: 0-0 Tstrap: 0-0 Ckp: 0-0

Fromragstoriches (IRE)

106   **106+**

8-y-o b g Supreme Leader-Family Birthday (Sandalay)
Mrs S J Smith Mrs S Smith

Placings:2224   (4660)
2003/04: 20²GS, 20²G, 24²G, 24⁴S,

	Starts	1st	2nd	3rd	Win & Pl
Hurdles	4	0	3	0	3207
Career Total	**4**	**0**	**3**	**0**	**3207**

Going:	Sf: 0-1 GS: 0-1 Gd: 0-2 GF: - Fm: 0-0
Distance:	2m/2m3: 0-0 2m4-2m7: 0-2 3m+: 0-2
Track:	LH: 0-1 RH: 0-3 Tight: 0-0 Gall: 0-0
Aids:	Bl: 0-0 Vi: 0-0 Tstrap: 0-0 Ckp: 0-0
Best Rating:	109 3/04 Carl 3m110y good Hdl

Novice hurdler; stays three miles; acts on good ground.

Front Rank (IRE)

92   **90**

4-y-o b c Sadler's Wells (USA)-Alignment (IRE) (Alzao (USA))
K C Bailey (Sir Michael Stoute 26/9) Off The Bridle Partnership

Placings:005   (4103)
2003/04: 16⁰G, 16⁰GS, 16⁵G,

	Starts	1st	2nd	3rd	Win & Pl
Hurdles	3	0	0	0	0
Career Total	**3**	**0**	**0**	**0**	**0**

Going:	Sf: 0-0 GS: 0-1 Gd: 0-2 GF: - Fm: 0-0
Distance:	2m/2m3: 0-3 2m4-2m7: 0-0 3m+: 0-0
Track:	LH: 0-1 RH: 0-2 Tight: 0-1 Gall: 0-1
Aids:	Bl: 0-2 Vi: 0-0 Tstrap: 0-0 Ckp: 0-0
Best Rating:	90 2/04 Hntg 2m110y gd-sft Hdl

Modest hurdler; placed in middle-distance maidens on Fibresand on the Flat at up to 12 furlongs; has worn blinkers.

Frontier

100   **108+**

7-y-o b g Indian Ridge-Adatiya (IRE) (Shardari)
B J Llewellyn F Jeffers

Placings:423B   (4372)
2003/04: 17⁴G, 16²S, 17³S, 16ᴮGF,

	Starts	1st	2nd	3rd	Win & Pl
Hurdles	4	0	1	1	2588
Career Total	**4**	**0**	**1**	**1**	**2588**

Going:	Sf: 0-2 GS: 0-0 Gd: 0-1 GF: - Fm: 0-1
Distance:	2m/2m3: 0-4 2m4-2m7: 0-0 3m+: 0-0
Track:	LH: 0-1 RH: 0-3 Tight: 0-3 Gall: 0-0
Aids:	Bl: 0-0 Vi: 0-0 Tstrap: 0-4 Ckp: 0-0
Best Rating:	108 2/04 Tntn 2m1f soft Hdl

Fair middle-distance Flat handicapper; has shown promise over timber without winning; acted on fast and easy ground on the Flat; now qualified for handicaps.

Frontis

101(77h)   (63h)**79**

7-y-o ch g Be My Chief (USA)-Heavy Rock (IRE) (Ballad Rock)

T J Fitzgerald Marquesa De Moratalla

Placings: *0/*3300/5P2   (3882)
2003/04: 20⁵G, 21ᴾGS, 24²G,

	Starts	1st	2nd	3rd	Win & Pl
Hurdles	1	0	0	0	0
Chases	2	0	1	0	1038
Career Total	8	0	1	2	1541

Going: Sf: 0-0 GS: 0-1 Gd: 0-2 GF: - Fm: 0-0
Distance: 2m/2m3: 0-0 2m4-2m7: 0-2 3m+: 0-1
Track: LH: 0-2 RH: 0-1 Tight: 0-2 Gall: 0-0
Aids: Bl: 0-0 Vi: 0-1 Tstrap: 0-0 Ckp: 0-0
Best Rating: 91   11/01   Uttx   2m   soft   NHF

Plating-class chaser; has worn a visor.

Frosty Jak
87   **59**

6-y-o b g Morpeth-Allied Newcastle (Crooner)
J D Frost Jack Joseph

Placings: *00000*   (4232)
2003/04: 16⁵S, 16⁹GS, 24⁹GS, 17⁰HY, 20⁹GF,

	Starts	1st	2nd	3rd	Win & Pl
NH Flat	2	0	0	0	0
Hurdles	3	0	0	0	0
Career Total	5	0	0	0	0

Going: Sf: 0-2 GS: 0-2 Gd: 0-0 GF: - Fm: 0-1
Distance: 2m/2m3: 0-3 2m4-2m7: 0-1 3m+: 0-1
Track: LH: 0-1 RH: 0-3 Tight: 0-1 Gall: 0-0
Aids: Bl: 0-0 Vi: 0-0 Tstrap: 0-0 Ckp: 0-0
Best Rating: 86   1/04   Ludl   2m   gd-sft   NHF

Frosty Run (IRE)
99   **94**

6-y-o b g Commanche Run-Here To-Day (King's Equity)
Mrs H Dalton C B Compton

Placings: *6-*24P0   (3900)
2003/04: 16²GF, 19⁴G, 23ᴾGS, 17⁰GS,

	Starts	1st	2nd	3rd	Win & Pl
NH Flat	1	0	1	0	472
Hurdles	3	0	0	0	0
Career Total	5	0	1	0	472

Going: Sf: 0-0 GS: 0-2 Gd: 0-1 GF: 0-0 Fm: 0-1
Distance: 2m/2m3: 0-2 2m4-2m7: 0-1 3m+: 0-1
Track: LH: 0-2 RH: 0-2 Tight: 0-3 Gall: 0-0
Aids: Bl: 0-0 Vi: 0-0 Tstrap: 0-0 Ckp: 0-0
Best Rating: 93   12/03   MRas   2m3f110y   good   Hdl

Frozen Assets (IRE)
74   **70**

7-y-o br g Shardari-Frost Bound (Hawaiian Return (USA))
M Pitman The Nicky Watts Partnership

Placings: 5/*0000*   (3916)
2003/04: 17⁰GS, 20⁹G, 21⁰GS, 20⁹G,

	Starts	1st	2nd	3rd	Win & Pl
NH Flat	1	0	0	0	0
Hurdles	3	0	0	0	0
Career Total	5	0	0	0	0

Going: Sf: 0-0 GS: 0-2 Gd: 0-2 GF: - Fm: 0-0
Distance: 2m/2m3: 0-1 2m4-2m7: 0-3 3m+: 0-0

Track: LH: 0-1 RH: 0-3 Tight: 0-2 Gall: 0-0
Aids: Bl: 0-0 Vi: 0-0 Tstrap: 0-0 Ckp: 0-0
Best Rating: 90   4/02   Font   2m2f110y   gd-fm   NHF

Some ability on his bumper debut.

Fruit Defendu (FR)
93   **95**

7-y-o b g Exit To Nowhere (USA)-Pauvresse (FR) (Home
Guard (USA))
P F Nicholls Mrs Monica Hackett

Placings: 1420/41F66F06/6P202   (4526)
2003/04: 17⁶G, 16ᴾGS, 19⁴HY, 17⁰GS, 16²GS,

	Starts	1st	2nd	3rd	Win & Pl
Hurdles	5	0	2	0	1394
Career Total	17	2	3	0	12795
118	11/01	Cork	2m		Hdl	Y-S	£5564
130	12/00	Fair	2m		Hdl	SFT	£3312
					Total win prize-money £8877

Going: Sf: 0-1 GS: 0-3 Gd: 0-1 GF: - Fm: 0-0
Distance: 2m/2m3: 0-4 2m4-2m7: 0-1 3m+: 0-0
Track: LH: 0-3 RH: 0-2 Tight: 0-3 Gall: 0-0
Aids: Bl: 0-4 Vi: 0-0 Tstrap: 0-5 Ckp: 0-0
Best Rating: 130   12/00   Fair   2m   soft   Hdl

Ex-Irish; disappointing performer; beaten in selling hurdles;
acts on soft ground; best at two miles.

Frys No Fool

14-y-o b g Idiots Delight-Scotch And Ice (Balinger)
Mrs J Butler Mrs J Butler

Placings: *13/*5U/30613/F/6P/0   (0031)
2003/04: 21⁰G,

	Starts	1st	2nd	3rd	Win & Pl
Chases	1	0	0	0	
Career Total	13	2	0	3	6034
110	3/98	Chep	2m3f110yE(0-100)HCh	GD	£2996
110	12/95	Towc	2m	H NHF	G-S	£1785
				Total win prize-money £4781

Going: Sf: 0-0 GS: 0-0 Gd: 0-1 GF: - Fm: 0-0
Distance: 2m/2m3: 0-0 2m4-2m7: 0-1 3m+: 0-0
Track: LH: 0-1 RH: 0-0 Tight: 0-0 Gall: 0-1
Aids: Bl: 0-0 Vi: 0-0 Tstrap: 0-0 Ckp: 0-0
Best Rating: 110   3/98   Chep   2m3f110y   good   Ch

Fryup Booster

7-y-o ch g Bollin William-Comedy Imp (Import)
P T Midgley A Dimmock

Placings: PP0-F   (1690)
2003/04: 17ᶠGF,

	Starts	1st	2nd	3rd	Win & Pl
Hurdles	1	0	0	0	
Career Total	4	0	0	0	

Going: Sf: 0-0 GS: 0-0 Gd: 0-0 GF: - Fm: 0-1
Distance: 2m/2m3: 0-1 2m4-2m7: 0-0 3m+: 0-0
Track: LH: 0-0 RH: 0-1 Tight: 0-1 Gall: 0-0
Aids: Bl: 0-0 Vi: 0-0 Tstrap: 0-0 Ckp: 0-0

Fryup Satellite

13-y-o br g Leading Star-Comedy Imp (Import)

J S Swindells J S Swindells

Placings: 002050556/61033225/322432/005603/2-54
     (0475)
2003/04: 24⁵G, 26⁴GS,

	Starts	1st	2nd	3rd	Win & Pl
Chases	2	0	0	0	0
Career Total	32	1	7	5	9744
84	12/96	Catt	2m3f	F(0-100)HHdl	GD	£2120
				Total win prize-money £2120

Going: Sf: 0-0 GS: 0-1 Gd: 0-1 GF: - Fm: 0-0
Distance: 2m/2m3: 0-2 2m4-2m7: 0-0 3m+: 0-2
Track: LH: 0-2 RH: 0-0 Tight: 0-2 Gall: 0-0
Aids: Bl: 0-0 Vi: 0-0 Tstrap: 0-0 Ckp: 0-0
Best Rating: 103   11/97   Catt   2m   good   Ch

Pointer/hunter chaser; one-time fair handicap hurdler; on the
downgrade now.

Fulgere (IRE)
81   **72**

6-y-o b g Old Vic-Moppet's Last (Pitpan)
K C Bailey The Shine On Partnership

Placings: 54   (3277)
2003/04: 16⁵S, 20⁴G,

	Starts	1st	2nd	3rd	Win & Pl
NH Flat	1	0	0	0	0
Hurdles	1	0	0	0	393
Career Total	2	0	0	0	393

Going: Sf: 0-1 GS: 0-0 Gd: 0-1 GF: - Fm: 0-0
Distance: 2m/2m3: 0-1 2m4-2m7: 0-1 3m+: 0-0
Track: LH: 0-1 RH: 0-1 Tight: 0-0 Gall: 0-0
Aids: Bl: 0-0 Vi: 0-0 Tstrap: 0-0 Ckp: 0-0
Best Rating: 75   12/03   Towc   2m   soft   NHF

Full English

5-y-o b m Perugino (USA)-Grown At Rowan (Gabitat)
A P Jones T G N Burrage

Placings: 0U   (3314)
2003/04: 16⁰GF, 16ᵁS,

	Starts	1st	2nd	3rd	Win & Pl
NH Flat	1	0	0	0	0
Hurdles	1	0	0	0	0
Career Total	2	0	0	0	0

Going: Sf: 0-1 GS: 0-0 Gd: 0-0 GF: - Fm: 0-1
Distance: 2m/2m3: 0-2 2m4-2m7: 0-0 3m+: 0-0
Track: LH: 0-1 RH: 0-1 Tight: 0-0 Gall: 0-0
Aids: Bl: 0-0 Vi: 0-0 Tstrap: 0-0 Ckp: 0-0

Full House (IRE)
110   **127**

5-y-o br g King's Theatre (IRE)-Nirvavita (FR) (Highest
Honor (FR))
P R Webber The Chamberlain Addiscott Partnership

Placings: 636133   (4844)
2003/04: 16⁶S, 16³G, 21⁶G, 16¹G, 16³G, 17³G,

	Starts	1st	2nd	3rd	Win & Pl
Hurdles	6	1	0	3	9393
Career Total	6	1	0	3	9393
115	2/04	Asct	2m110y	D(0-120)HHdl	GD	£4771
				Total win prize-money £4771

Going:	Sf: 0-1 GS: 0-0 Gd: 1-5 GF: - Fm: 0-0
Distance:	2m/2m3: 1-5 2m4-2m7: 0-1 3m+: 0-0
Track:	LH: 0-2 RH: 1-4 Tight: 0-0 Gall: 0-2
Aids:	Bl: 0-0 Vi: 0-0 Tstrap: 0-0 Ckp: 0-0
Best Rating:	127 4/04 Chel 2m1f good Hdl

Promising novice hurdler; wide margin eased down winner of a handicap at Ascot in February; best suited by two miles; acts on good.

Full Irish (IRE)

116(114h)   (139 h) **141**

8-y-o ch g Rashar (USA)-Ross Gale (Strong Gale)
L Lungo D Stronach

Placings:2/11F111/1200-12F21   (4940)
2003/04: 16¹S, 20²G, 20⁶GS, 16²GS, 16¹GS,

	Starts	1st	2nd	3rd	Win & Pl
Chases	5	2	2	0	19755
Career Total	16	8	4	0	48704
120	4/04	Prth	2m	D Ch		G-S	£7228
134	12/03	Hexm	2m110y	E Ch		SFT	£2912
139	11/02	Sedg	2m5f110yB	HHdl		SFT	£8897
127	4/02	Prth	2m	D Hdl		GD	£3874
137	3/02	Donc	2m4f	C Hdl		G-S	£5648
115	1/02	Sedg	2m1f	D Hdl		HVY	£3464
121	11/01	Hayd	2m	H NHF		SFT	£2170
120	10/01	Sedg	2m1f	H NHF		GD	£1575
						Total win prize-money £35770

Going:	Sf: 1-1 GS: 1-3 Gd: 0-1 GF: - Fm: 0-0
Distance:	2m/2m3: 2-3 2m4-2m7: 0-2 3m+: 0-0
Track:	LH: 1-4 RH: 1-1 Tight: 0-0 Gall: 0-0
Aids:	Bl: 0-0 Vi: 0-0 Tstrap: 0-0 Ckp: 0-0
Best Rating:	141 4/04 Ayr 2m gd-sft Ch

Smart novice chaser/useful handicap hurdler; made a winning chasing debut in average event at Hexham, and chased a decent sort home at Haydock next time; poised to challenge when coming to grief at Ayr in February; runner-up at the same track next time; stays two miles five furlongs; acts on ground ranging from good to heavy.

Full Minty

108   (121h) **117**

9-y-o br g Phardante (FR)-Jouvencelle (Rusticaro (FR))
N A Twiston-Davies H R Mould

Placings:30/F1P1/P2-12   (2189)
2003/04: 20¹G, 22²GS,

	Starts	1st	2nd	3rd	Win & Pl
Chases	2	1	1	0	6588
Career Total	10	3	2	1	15502
117	9/03	Bang	2m4f110yE	Ch		GD	£4069
121	4/01	Kemp	2m5f	D(0-115)HHdl		GD	£3822
120	1/01	Ludl	2m5f	E Hdl		SFT	£2912
						Total win prize-money £10803

Going:	Sf: 0-0 GS: 0-1 Gd: 1-1 GF: - Fm: 0-0
Distance:	2m/2m3: 0-0 2m4-2m7: 1-2 3m+: 0-0
Track:	LH: 1-2 RH: 0-0 Tight: 0-1 Gall: 0-0
Aids:	Bl: 0-0 Vi: 0-0 Tstrap: 0-0 Ckp: 0-0
Best Rating:	121 4/01 Kemp 2m5f good Hdl

Fair novice chaser; decisive winner at Bangor in September; effective over two miles four but will be suited by three miles; suited by cut in the ground.

Full Of Michel (FR)

(91h)   (92h)

5-y-o gr g Michel Georges-Quinte Royale (FR) (Kaldoun (FR))
N J Henderson Roa Dawn Run Partnership

Placings:0P1-3   (2203)
2003/04: 17³G,

	Starts	1st	2nd	3rd	Win & Pl
Hurdles	1	0	0	1	430
Career Total	4	1	0	1	6614
10/02	Autl	2m1f110y		HVY	£6184
				Total win prize-money £6184

Going:	Sf: 0-0 GS: 0-0 Gd: 0-1 GF: - Fm: 0-0
Distance:	2m/2m3: 0-1 2m4-2m7: 0-0 3m+: 0-0
Track:	LH: 0-0 RH: 0-1 Tight: 0-1 Gall: 0-0
Aids:	Bl: 0-0 Vi: 0-0 Tstrap: 0-0 Ckp: 0-0
Best Rating:	92 11/03 Folk 2m1f110y good Hdl

Winner over fences in France; third in novice hurdle on hurdles debut; acts in heavy ground.

Full On

104(102h)   (96 h) **107**

7-y-o b g Le Moss-Flighty Dove (Cruise Missile)
A M Hales Coach House Racing

Placings:0/42PP-4223   (4305)
2003/04: 21⁴S, 22²GS, 19²GS, 20³G,

	Starts	1st	2nd	3rd	Win & Pl
Hurdles	1	0	0	0	287
Chases	3	0	2	1	4869
Career Total	9	0	3	1	6085

Going:	Sf: 0-1 GS: 0-2 Gd: 0-1 GF: - Fm: 0-0
Distance:	2m/2m3: 0-1 2m4-2m7: 0-3 3m+: 0-0
Track:	LH: 0-2 RH: 0-2 Tight: 0-1 Gall: 0-1
Aids:	Bl: 0-0 Vi: 0-0 Tstrap: 0-0 Ckp: 0-0
Best Rating:	105 3/04 Sand 2m4f110y good Ch

Moderate novice chaser; stays two miles six; acts on soft ground.

Full Time (IRE)

73   **55**

5-y-o b g Bigstone (IRE)-Oiche Mhaith (Night Shift (USA))
G A Swinbank Mrs Michele Rutter

Placings:0   (2508)
2003/04: 16⁰S,

	Starts	1st	2nd	3rd	Win & Pl
Hurdles	1	0	0	0	0
Career Total	1	0	0	0	0

Going:	Sf: 0-1 GS: 0-0 Gd: 0-0 GF: - Fm: 0-0
Distance:	2m/2m3: 0-1 2m4-2m7: 0-0 3m+: 0-0
Track:	LH: 0-1 RH: 0-0 Tight: 0-1 Gall: 0-0
Aids:	Bl: 0-0 Vi: 0-0 Tstrap: 0-0 Ckp: 0-0
Best Rating:	66 12/03 Kels 2m110y soft Hdl

Fullards

113   **109+**

6-y-o b g Alderbrook-Milly Kelly (Murrayfield)
Mrs P Sly M S Smith

Placings:0P-00P2153210   (4777)
2003/04: 22⁶S, 20⁰G, 21⁵PS, 19²GS, 22¹G, 21⁵S, 22³G, 23²G, 26¹G, 23⁹G,

	Starts	1st	2nd	3rd	Win & Pl
Hurdles	10	2	2	1	11961
Career Total	12	2	2	1	11961
106	3/04	Hntg	3m2f	E(0-110)HHdl		GD	£3535
109	1/04	Hayd	2m6f	D(0-110)HHdl		GD	£5213
						Total win prize-money £8748

Going:	Sf: 0-3 GS: 0-1 Gd: 2-6 GF: - Fm: 0-0
Distance:	2m/2m3: 0-1 2m4-2m7: 1-6 3m+: 1-3
Track:	LH: 1-7 RH: 1-2 Tight: 0-4 Gall: 1-1
Aids:	Bl: 0-0 Vi: 0-0 Tstrap: 0-0 Ckp: 0-0
Best Rating:	109 1/04 Hayd 2m6f good Hdl

Moderate hurdler; stays well; acts on good ground.

Fullopep

10-y-o g g Dunbeath (USA)-Suggia (Alzao (USA))
Paul Morris P B R Abrasives (w'Ton) Ltd

Placings:112/1155/PP/113350/P-4   (0483)
2003/04: 24⁴GF,

	Starts	1st	2nd	3rd	Win & Pl
Chases	1	0	0	0	0
Career Total	17	6	1	2	27515
134	5/01	Newc	2m110y	C(0-125)HCh		G-F	£4696
125	5/01	Weth	2m	E(0-115)HCh		GD	£3346
125	11/99	Sedg	2m5f	C Ch		GD	£6937
122	10/99	Sedg	2m5f	E Ch		GD	£3436
118	9/98	Sedg	2m1f	E Hdl		GD	£2687
104	9/98	Sedg	2m1f	E Hdl		G-F	£2337
						Total win prize-money £23442

Going:	Sf: 0-0 GS: 0-0 Gd: 0-0 GF: - Fm: 0-1
Distance:	2m/2m3: 0-0 2m4-2m7: 0-0 3m+: 0-1
Track:	LH: 0-0 RH: 0-1 Tight: 0-0 Gall: 0-1
Aids:	Bl: 0-0 Vi: 0-0 Tstrap: 0-0 Ckp: 0-0
Best Rating:	134 10/01 Weth 2m4f110y good Ch

Fair hunter chaser; formerly useful hurdler; stays three miles; likes good to firm.

Fulwell Hill

85f   **85f**

6-y-o b m Anshan-Finkin (Fine Blue)
Ian Williams J Tredwell

Placings:0-6   (0309)
2003/04: 17⁶G,

	Starts	1st	2nd	3rd	Win & Pl
NH Flat	1	0	0	0	0
Career Total	2	0	0	0	0

Going:	Sf: 0-0 GS: 0-0 Gd: 0-0 GF: - Fm: 0-0
Distance:	2m/2m3: 0-1 2m4-2m7: 0-0 3m+: 0-0
Track:	LH: 0-1 RH: 0-0 Tight: 0-1 Gall: 0-0
Aids:	Bl: 0-0 Vi: 0-0 Tstrap: 0-0 Ckp: 0-0
Best Rating:	85 5/03 Bang 2m1f good NHF

Fundamental

108   **132**

5-y-o ch g Rudimentary (USA)-I'Ll Try (Try My Best (USA))
Jonjo O'Neill D N Green

Placings:3214-024112   (4644)
2003/04: 16⁰GF, 16²GF, 16⁴GF, 20¹S, 16¹G, 16²G,

	Starts	1st	2nd	3rd	Win & Pl
Hurdles	6	2	2	0	23681
Career Total	10	3	3	1	29231
125	3/04	Newb	2m110y	C(0-130)HHdl		GD	£9233
121	1/04	Leic	2m4f110yE(0-110)HHdl		SFT	£3575
103	2/03	Ayr	2m	E Hdl		G-S	£3610
						Total win prize-money £16420

Going:	Sf: 1-1 GS: 0-0 Gd: 1-2 GF: - Fm: 0-3
Distance:	2m/2m3: 1-5 2m4-2m7: 1-1 3m+: 0-0
Track:	LH: 1-4 RH: 1-2 Tight: 0-1 Gall: 1-2

Aids: Bl: 0-0 Vi: 0-0 Tstrap: 0-0 Ckp: 0-0
Best Rating: 132 4/04 Aint 2m110y good Hdl

Useful hurdler; progressive; prefers to race prominently; stays 2m4f; acts on easy and good ground.

Fundamentalist (IRE)

115   157+

6-y-o b g Supreme Leader-Run For Shelter (Strong Gale)
N A Twiston-Davies Gripen

Placings: 121   (4394)
2003/04: 24[1]G, 23[2]G, 21[1]G,

	Starts	1st	2nd	3rd	Win & Pl
Hurdles	3	2	1	0	69553
Career Total	3	2	1	0	69553

157	3/04	Chel	2m5f	A Hdl	GD £58000
128	2/04	Kemp	3m110y	D Hdl	GD £4953

Total win prize-money £62953

Going: Sf: 0-0 GS: 0-0 Gd: 2-3 GF: - Fm: 0-0
Distance: 2m/2m3: 0-0 2m4-2m7: 1-1 3m+: 1-2
Track: LH: 1-2 RH: 1-1 Tight: 0-0 Gall: 1-1
Aids: Bl: 0-0 Vi: 0-0 Tstrap: 0-0 Ckp: 0-0
Best Rating: 157 3/04 Chel 2m5f good Hdl

Smart novice hurdler; very promising son of Supreme Leader who won three points in Ireland before easily scoring on his hurdles debut at Kempton in February; narrowly beaten by Royal Rosa at Haydock next time before winning the Royal & SunAlliance Hurdle at Cheltenham; stays three miles but might be suited by shorter; acts on fast ground; future chaser.

Funny Genie (FR)

                  (0c)

11-y-o b g Genereux Genie-Sauteuse De Retz (FR) (Funny Hobby)
Miss H M Irving Miss H M Irving

Placings: P/P0PP11/P62331P/P/5U4/P-P00   (0565)
2003/04: 16[P]G, 16[0]GF, 16[6]GS,

	Starts	1st	2nd	3rd	Win & Pl
Hurdles	1	0	0	0	0
Chases	2	0	0	0	0
Career Total	22	3	1	2	9148

93	3/00	Folk	2m	F(0-90)HCh	G-F £2452
88	2/98	Folk	2m1f110y	F(0-95)HHdl	G-F £2136
90	2/98	Hrfd	2m1f	F(0-90)HHdl	GD £2570

Total win prize-money £7159

Going: Sf: 0-0 GS: 0-0 Gd: 0-1 GF: - Fm: 0-2
Distance: 2m/2m3: 0-3 2m4-2m7: 0-0 3m+: 0-0
Track: LH: 0-2 RH: 0-1 Tight: 0-0 Gall: 0-1
Aids: Bl: 0-3 Vi: 0-0 Tstrap: 0-0 Ckp: 0-0
Best Rating: 93 3/00 Folk 2m gd-fm Ch

Fusion Of Tunes

69   36

6-y-o b m Mr Confusion (IRE)-Daleria (Darshaan)
Mrs K Walton Jeff McCarthy

Placings: 400   (4881)
2003/04: 16[4]G, 16[0]GS, 17[0]GS,

	Starts	1st	2nd	3rd	Win & Pl
NH Flat	2	0	0	0	0
Hurdles	1	0	0	0	0
Career Total	3	0	0	0	

Going: Sf: 0-0 GS: 0-2 Gd: 0-1 GF: - Fm: 0-0
Distance: 2m/2m3: 0-3 2m4-2m7: 0-0 3m+: 0-0
Track: LH: 0-1 RH: 0-2 Tight: 0-0 Gall: 0-1
Aids: Bl: 0-0 Vi: 0-0 Tstrap: 0-0 Ckp: 0-0
Best Rating: 84 11/03 Newc 2m good NHF

G V A Ireland (IRE)

111   128

6-y-o b g Beneficial-Dippers Daughter (Strong Gale)
F Flood Donal O'Buachalla

Placings: 0340/0312200-025131225   (4768a)
2003/04: 20[0]S, 20[2]GY, 20[5]Y, 24[1]S, 24[3]S, 20[1]S, 24[2]S, 25[2]G, 20[5]Y,

	Starts	1st	2nd	3rd	Win & Pl
Hurdles	9	2	3	1	41211
Career Total	20	3	5	3	51964

125	12/03	Punc	2m4f	HHdl	SFT £11607
113	12/03	Navn	3m	(0-130)HHdl	SFT £8441
114	12/02	Fair	2m	NHF	SH £4444

Total win prize-money £24494

Going: Sf: 2-5 GS: 0-0 Gd: 0-1 GF: - Fm: 0-0
Distance: 2m/2m3: 0-0 2m4-2m7: 1-5 3m+: 1-4
Track: LH: 1-4 RH: 1-4 Tight: 0-0 Gall: 0-1
Aids: Bl: 0-0 Vi: 0-0 Tstrap: 0-0 Ckp: 0-0
Best Rating: 129 3/04 Chel 3m1f110y good Hdl

Useful Irish hurdler; much improved this season and has become most consistent; runner-up in Pertemps Final at Cheltenham in March; has won over three miles, but also effective over shorter; acts on good, but best on soft ground; progressive.

Gabla (NZ)

101(93c)   (92c)106

8-y-o b g Prince Of Praise (NZ)-Dynataine (NZ) (Centaine (AUS))
R C Guest T N Siviter

Placings: 3322313060   (4718)
2003/04: 16[3]G, 16[3]G, 17[2]GF, 17[2]G, 16[3]G, 17[1]GF, 20[3]F, 16[0]GF, 16[6]G, 16[0]G,

	Starts	1st	2nd	3rd	Win & Pl
Hurdles	9	1	2	4	8618
Chases	1	0	0	0	0
Career Total	10	1	2	4	8618

106	10/03	Carl	2m1f	E(0-115)HHdl	G-F £3080

Total win prize-money £3080

Going: Sf: 0-0 GS: 0-0 Gd: 0-6 GF: - Fm: 1-4
Distance: 2m/2m3: 1-9 2m4-2m7: 0-0 3m+: 0-0
Track: LH: 0-4 RH: 1-6 Tight: 0-2 Gall: 0-0
Aids: Bl: 0-0 Vi: 0-0 Tstrap: 0-0 Ckp: 1-4
Best Rating: 106 10/03 Carl 2m1f gd-fm Hdl

Moderate hurdler; multiple Flat winner in New Zealand; acts on a sound surface; effective at around two miles.

Gablesea

10-y-o b g Beveled (USA)-Me Spede (Valiyar)
B P J Baugh Messrs Chrimes, Winn & Wilson

Placings: P/0/000/P   (0285)
2003/04: 16[P]GS,

	Starts	1st	2nd	3rd	Win & Pl
Hurdles	1	0	0	0	
Career Total	6	0	0	0	

Going: Sf: 0-0 GS: 0-1 Gd: 0-0 GF: - Fm: 0-0
Distance: 2m/2m3: 0-1 2m4-2m7: 0-0 3m+: 0-0
Track: LH: 0-1 RH: 0-0 Tight: 0-1 Gall: 0-0

Aids: Bl: 0-0 Vi: 0-1 Tstrap: 0-0 Ckp: 0-0
Best Rating: 53 10/01 Aint 2m110y good Hdl

Gabor

102   111

5-y-o b g Danzig Connection (USA)-Kiorni (Niniski (USA))
G L Moore Leydens Farm Stud

Placings: 122P-5416   (2313)
2003/04: 18[5]G, 16[4]GF, 16[1]GF, 16[6]GS,

	Starts	1st	2nd	3rd	Win & Pl
Hurdles	4	1	0	0	5290
Career Total	8	2	2	0	14206

111	11/03	Hntg	2m110y	D(0-115)HHdl	G-F £4361
106	9/02	Plum	2m	D Hdl	GF £5073

Total win prize-money £9435

Going: Sf: 0-0 GS: 0-1 Gd: 0-1 GF: - Fm: 1-2
Distance: 2m/2m3: 1-4 2m4-2m7: 0-0 3m+: 0-0
Track: LH: 0-2 RH: 1-2 Tight: 0-1 Gall: 1-2
Aids: Bl: 1-2 Vi: 0-0 Tstrap: 0-0 Ckp: 0-0
Best Rating: 111 11/03 Hntg 2m110y gd-fm Hdl

Modest hurdler; fair middle-distance handicapper on the Flat; acts on a sound surface; usually wears headgear.

Gaelic Flight (IRE)

87f   100+f

6-y-o b/br g Norwich-Ash-Dame (IRE) (Strong Gale)
Noel T Chance Top Flight Racing 3

Placings: 01   (4374)
2003/04: 16[6]S, 16[1]GF,

	Starts	1st	2nd	3rd	Win & Pl
NH Flat	2	1	0	0	3816
Career Total	2	1	0	0	3816

100	3/04	Strf	2m110y	H NHF	G-F £3815

Total win prize-money £3816

Going: Sf: 0-1 GS: 0-0 Gd: 0-0 GF: - Fm: 1-1
Distance: 2m/2m3: 1-2 2m4-2m7: 0-0 3m+: 0-0
Track: LH: 0-0 RH: 0-1 Tight: 0-0 Gall: 0-0
Aids: Bl: 0-0 Vi: 0-0 Tstrap: 0-0 Ckp: 0-0
Best Rating: 100 3/04 Strf 2m110y gd-fm NHF

Bumper winner; acts on fast ground.

Gaelic Lord (IRE)

9-y-o b g Mister Lord (USA)-Mum's Eyes (Al Sirat)
D R C Elsworth Godfrey Wilson

Placings: 00P/P0   (4146)
2003/04: 21[P]GS, 24[0]G,

	Starts	1st	2nd	3rd	Win & Pl
Chases	2	0	0	0	
Career Total	5	0	0	0	

Going: Sf: 0-0 GS: 0-1 Gd: 0-1 GF: - Fm: 0-0
Distance: 2m/2m3: 0-0 2m4-2m7: 0-1 3m+: 0-0
Track: LH: 0-0 RH: 0-2 Tight: 0-2 Gall: 0-0
Aids: Bl: 0-0 Vi: 0-0 Tstrap: 0-0 Ckp: 0-1
Best Rating: 87 11/00 Ludl 2m good NHF

Gaelic Music (IRE)

75f   108+f

5-y-o b g Accordion-Cuilin Bui (IRE) (Kemal (FR))
M Bradstock P J Constable

Placings:1					(4824)
2003/04: 17^{1}GF,					

	Starts	1st	2nd	3rd	Win & Pl
NH Flat	1	1	0	0	2772
Career Total	**1**	**1**	**0**	**0**	**2772**
108 4/04 Extr 2m1f H NHF				G-F	£2772

Total win prize-money £2772

Going:	Sf: 0-0 GS: 0-0 Gd: 0-0 GF: - Fm: 1-1
Distance:	2m/2m3: 0-0 2m4-2m7: 0-0 3m+: 0-0
Track:	LH: 0-0 RH: 1-1 Tight: 0-0 Gall: 0-0
Aids:	Bl: 0-0 Vi: 0-0 Tstrap: 0-0 Ckp: 0-0
Best Rating:	108 4/04 Extr 2m1f gd-fm NHF

Bumper winner; acts on fast ground.

Gaelic Probe (IRE)
93   (0c)65
10-y-o b g Roi Danzig (USA)-Scottish Gaelic (USA)
(Highland Park (USA))
R M H Cowell A Dunmore

Placings:652/3306400/03/4P/PP5P4					(2921)
2003/04: 17^{P}G, 24^{P}GF, 20^{5}G, 17^{P}GS, 17^{4}G,					

	Starts	1st	2nd	3rd	Win & Pl
Hurdles	4	0	0	0	0
Chases	1	0	0	0	0
Career Total	**19**	**0**	**1**	**3**	**1535**

Going:	Sf: 0-0 GS: 0-1 Gd: 0-3 GF: - Fm: 0-1
Distance:	2m/2m3: 0-3 2m4-2m7: 0-1 3m+: 0-1
Track:	LH: 0-1 RH: 0-4 Tight: 0-3 Gall: 0-1
Aids:	Bl: 0-0 Vi: 0-1 Tstrap: 0-0 Ckp: 0-0
Best Rating:	103 2/98 Naas 2m yield Hdl

Gala Du Moulin Mas (FR)
(75h)   (66h)80
10-y-o b g Le Riverain (FR)-Soiree D'Ex (FR) (Kashtan
(FR))
M E D Francis Mrs Merrick Francis Iii

Placings:12/344P/PP43/20U044PP-PR					(0888)
2003/04: 16^{P}G, 24^{R}G,					

	Starts	1st	2nd	3rd	Win & Pl
Hurdles	1	0	0	0	0
Chases	1	0	0	0	0
Career Total	**20**	**1**	**2**	**2**	**10959**
7/98 Diep 2m1f110y Ch				SFT	£3535

Total win prize-money £3535

Going:	Sf: 0-0 GS: 0-0 Gd: 0-1 GF: - Fm: 0-1
Distance:	2m/2m3: 0-1 2m4-2m7: 0-0 3m+: 0-0
Track:	LH: 0-2 RH: 0-0 Tight: 0-1 Gall: 0-0
Aids:	Bl: 0-0 Vi: 0-0 Tstrap: 0-0 Ckp: 0-0
Best Rating:	84 5/02 Worc 2m gd-fm Ch

Gala Festival (IRE)
88f   80f
5-y-o b m Supreme Leader-Noon Performance (Strong
Gale)
Mrs P N Dutfield Mrs Caren Walsh

Placings:0040					(4739)
2003/04: 17^{0}GF, 16^{0}GS, 16^{4}G, 17^{0}G,					

	Starts	1st	2nd	3rd	Win & Pl
NH Flat	4	0	0	0	0
Career Total	**4**	**0**	**0**	**0**	**0**

Gala Performance (USA)
101
6-y-o b g Theatrical-Claxton's Slew (USA) (Seattle Slew
(USA))
Jonjo O'Neill Russell McAllister

Placings:30554-U					(1009)
2003/04: 17^{U}G,					

	Starts	1st	2nd	3rd	Win & Pl
Hurdles	1	0	0	0	0
Career Total	**6**	**0**	**0**	**1**	**718**

Going:	Sf: 0-0 GS: 0-0 Gd: 0-1 GF: - Fm: 0-0
Distance:	2m/2m3: 0-1 2m4-2m7: 0-0 3m+: 0-0
Track:	LH: 0-1 RH: 0-0 Tight: 0-1 Gall: 0-0
Aids:	Bl: 0-0 Vi: 0-0 Tstrap: 0-0 Ckp: 0-0
Best Rating:	101 12/02 Hayd 2m good Hdl

Formerly trained by Aidan O'Brien; has shown just fair form
in novice hurdles; banned for 30-days for schooling in public
at Haydock on his third start; disappointing.

Galant Eye (IRE)
94   93
5-y-o ch g Eagle Eyed (USA)-Galandria (Sharpo)
R J Baker Richard Palmer

Placings:343365P-P0110					(4634)
2003/04: 20^{P}GF, 20^{0}GF, 19^{1}GS, 19^{1}G, 19^{0}G,					

	Starts	1st	2nd	3rd	Win & Pl
Hurdles	5	2	0	0	6388
Career Total	**12**	**2**	**0**	**3**	**8856**
93 12/03 Extr 2m3f D Hdl			GD	£3913
92 12/03 Extr 2m3f F(0-95)HHdl			G-S	£2474

Total win prize-money £6388

Going:	Sf: 0-0 GS: 1-1 Gd: 1-2 GF: - Fm: 0-2
Distance:	2m/2m3: 2-2 2m4-2m7: 0-3 3m+: 0-0
Track:	LH: 0-1 RH: 2-4 Tight: 0-1 Gall: 0-0
Aids:	Bl: 0-0 Vi: 0-0 Tstrap: 0-0 Ckp: 0-0
Best Rating:	93 12/03 Extr 2m3f good Hdl

Modest novice hurdler; stays two and a half miles and handles cut, but best on fast ground.

Galapiat Du Mesnil (FR)
10-y-o b g Sarpedon (FR)-Polka De Montrin (FR) (Danoso)
R T Phillips (P F Nicholls 1/5) Mel Fordham

Placings:3210/4131513/31F25/102412210/1600P-22					(3873)
2003/04: 33^{2}G, 25^{2}GS,					

	Starts	1st	2nd	3rd	Win & Pl
Chases	2	0	2	0	3407
Career Total	**32**	**9**	**7**	**4**	**94617**
140 5/02 Chep 3m B(0-145)HCh			G-F	£10120
136 3/02 Chep 2m3f110yC(0-135)HCh			G-S	£10029
136 10/01 Chep 2m3f110yC(0-130)HCh			SFT	£9150
130 5/01 Strf 3m C(0-135)HCh			G-S	£6942
130 9/00 Worc 2m7f110yC(0-135)HCh			G-F	£8127
108 3/00 Fknm 3m110y D Ch			GD	£3906

130 11/99 Asct 3m110y C HCh		GD	£6840
123 10/99 Worc 2m7f110yD Ch		G-F	£4109
112 1/99 Plum 2m4f E Hdl		HVY	£2215

Total win prize-money £61441

Going:	Sf: 0-0 GS: 0-1 Gd: 0-1 GF: - Fm: 0-0
Distance:	2m/2m3: 0-0 2m4-2m7: 0-0 3m+: 0-2
Track:	LH: 0-2 RH: 0-2 Tight: 0-1 Gall: 0-0
Aids:	Bl: 0-0 Vi: 0-0 Tstrap: 0-0 Ckp: 0-0
Best Rating:	140 5/02 Chep 3m gd-fm Ch

Very useful chaser; versatile when it comes to trip, stays 3m
7f; especially suited by soft ground.

Galaxy Fallon
6-y-o b m Dancing Spree (USA)-No Comebacks (Last
Tycoon)
M Dods Mrs Stella Barclay

Placings:P					(4159)
2003/04: 19^{P}G,					

	Starts	1st	2nd	3rd	Win & Pl
Hurdles	1	0	0	0	0
Career Total	**1**	**0**	**0**	**0**	**0**

Going:	Sf: 0-0 GS: 0-0 Gd: 0-1 GF: - Fm: 0-0
Distance:	2m/2m3: 0-0 2m4-2m7: 0-1 3m+: 0-0
Track:	LH: 0-1 RH: 0-0 Tight: 0-0 Gall: 0-0
Aids:	Bl: 0-0 Vi: 0-0 Tstrap: 0-0 Ckp: 0-0

Galaxy Sam (USA)
101   108+
5-y-o ch g Royal Academy (USA)-Istiska (FR) (Irish River
(FR))
N J Gifford S Munir

Placings:00P0-106					(4561)
2003/04: 22^{1}G, 22^{0}G, 24^{6}GS,					

	Starts	1st	2nd	3rd	Win & Pl
Hurdles	3	1	0	0	2744
Career Total	**7**	**1**	**0**	**0**	**2744**
108 1/04 Font 2m6f110yF(0-90)HHdl			GD	£2744

Total win prize-money £2744

Going:	Sf: 0-0 GS: 0-1 Gd: 1-2 GF: - Fm: 0-0
Distance:	2m/2m3: 0-0 2m4-2m7: 1-2 3m+: 0-1
Track:	LH: 1-3 RH: 0-0 Tight: 1-2 Gall: 0-1
Aids:	Bl: 0-0 Vi: 0-0 Tstrap: 0-0 Ckp: 0-0
Best Rating:	108 1/04 Font 2m6f110y good Hdl

Moderate hurdler; stays two miles six; acts on easy ground.

Galeaway (IRE)
89   84
10-y-o b g Strong Gale-Geeaway (Gala Performance (ZIM))
Mrs D M Grissell Major J R D Barnard

Placings:0/415/PF4/PP43-0U					(4306)
2003/04: 24^{8}G, 24^{U}G,					

	Starts	1st	2nd	3rd	Win & Pl
Chases	2	0	0	0	0
Career Total	**13**	**1**	**0**	**1**	**2628**
85 5/00 Folk 3m2f H Ch			GD	£1456

Total win prize-money £1456

Going:	Sf: 0-0 GS: 0-0 Gd: 0-2 GF: - Fm: 0-0
Distance:	2m/2m3: 0-0 2m4-2m7: 0-0 3m+: 0-2
Track:	LH: 0-1 RH: 0-1 Tight: 0-0 Gall: 0-1
Aids:	Bl: 0-0 Vi: 0-0 Tstrap: 0-0 Ckp: 0-0
Best Rating:	85 5/00 Folk 3m2f good Ch

Plating-class chaser; stays three miles-two; acts on a sound surface.

Galen (IRE)

101(89h)   (44h)88

13-y-o br g Roselier (FR)-Gaye Le Moss (Le Moss)
Mrs S J Smith   David Campbell

Placings:440/45063/25140153/53P011P0/P611431164/065
64P32/151232/03F0033   (4457)
2003/04: 20⁰HY, 24³GF, 25ᶠGS, 24⁰HY, 20⁰HY, 25³G, 24³HY,

	Starts	1st	2nd	3rd	Win & Pl
Hurdles	1	0	0	0	0
Chases	6	0	0	3	1793
Career Total	55	10	4	9	53573
103 6/01 Worc	2m7f110yF(0-110)HCh		GD		£4761
99 5/01 Sthl	3m110y F(0-110)HCh		FRM		£3805
113 1/00 Towc	2m6f	D(0-120)HCh		HVY	£7020
113 12/99 Uttx	3m	D(0-120)HCh		SFT	£5408
113 11/99 Towc	2m6f	D(0-125)HCh		G-S	£4655
101 10/99 Sthl	2m4f110yF(0-110)HCh		G-S		£3485
102 2/99 Catt	3m6f	C(0-130)HCh		GD	£6937
102 1/99 Catt	3m1f	D(0-120)HCh		SFT	£2840
101 11/97 Sedg	3m3f110yE Hdl		GD		£2285
		Total win prize-money £41199			

Going:	Sf: 0-4 GS: 0-1 Gd: 0-1 GF: - Fm: 0-1
Distance:	2m/2m3: 0-0 2m4-2m7: 0-2 3m+: 0-5
Track:	LH: 0-4 RH: 0-0 Tight: 0-2 Gall: 0-2
Aids:	Bl: 0-0 Vi: 0-0 Tstrap: 0-0 Ckp: 0-0
Best Rating:	113 3/00 Towc 3m1f good Ch

Poor handicap chaser at around three miles; has won on fast ground and softer.

Galey River (USA)

102   90

5-y-o ch g Irish River (FR)-Carefree Kate (USA) (Lyphard (USA))
J J Sheehan (G L Moore 7/7) D J Dowling

Placings:4   (4402)
2003/04: 16⁴G,

	Starts	1st	2nd	3rd	Win & Pl
Hurdles	1	0	0	0	0
Career Total	1	0	0	0	0

Going:	Sf: 0-0 GS: 0-0 Gd: 0-0 GF: - Fm: 0-0
Distance:	2m/2m3: 0-1 2m4-2m7: 0-0 3m+: 0-0
Track:	LH: 0-0 RH: 0-1 Tight: 0-0 Gall: 0-1
Aids:	Bl: 0-0 Vi: 0-0 Tstrap: 0-0 Ckp: 0-0
Best Rating:	92 3/04 Hntg 2m110y good Hdl

Showed a little ability on hurdling debut.

Galileo (POL)

111   136

8-y-o b g Jape (USA)-Goldika (POL) (Dakota)
T R George   Mrs S Nelson,Allan Stennett,Terry Warner

Placings:11/06-0060   (4840)
2003/04: 20⁰G, 21⁰G, 24⁶G, 24⁰G,

	Starts	1st	2nd	3rd	Win & Pl
Hurdles	4	0	0	0	600
Career Total	8	2	0	0	61070
154 3/02 Chel	2m5f	A Hdl		G-S	£52200
142 2/02 Kemp	2m5f	C Hdl		GD	£7670
		Total win prize-money £59870			

Going:	Sf: 0-0 GS: 0-0 Gd: 0-4 GF: - Fm: 0-0
Distance:	2m/2m3: 0-0 2m4-2m7: 0-2 3m+: 0-2

Track:	LH: 0-4 RH: 0-0 Tight: 0-1 Gall: 0-2
Aids:	Bl: 0-1 Vi: 0-1 Tstrap: 0-0 Ckp: 0-0
Best Rating:	154 3/02 Chel 2m5f gd-sft Hdl

Very useful hurdler; winner of the Polish St Leger and Listed placed on the Flat in Germany; bolted up on his hurdling debut at Kempton in February 2002 and followed up in the Royal & SunAlliance Hurdle the following month; lightly raced and below that level since; stays 2m 5f; seems to act on any ground; has worn visor.

Gallant Boy (IRE)

81   65

5-y-o ch g Grand Lodge (USA)-Damerela (IRE) (Alzao (USA))
P D Evans   M W Lawrence

Placings:4   (1082)
2003/04: 16⁴GF,

	Starts	1st	2nd	3rd	Win & Pl
Hurdles	1	0	0	0	0
Career Total	1	0	0	0	0

Going:	Sf: 0-0 GS: 0-0 Gd: 0-0 GF: - Fm: 0-0
Distance:	2m/2m3: 0-1 2m4-2m7: 0-0 3m+: 0-0
Track:	LH: 0-1 RH: 0-0 Tight: 0-0 Gall: 0-0
Aids:	Bl: 0-0 Vi: 0-0 Tstrap: 0-1 Ckp: 0-0
Best Rating:	65 8/03 Worc 2m gd-fm Hdl

Three times a winner at up to 10f; did not prove he stays on his hurdling debut.

Gallant Hero

100   110+

5-y-o b g Rainbow Quest (USA)-Gay Gallanta (USA) (Woodman (USA))
P J Hobbs (Sir Michael Stoute 25/8) Mrs David Thompson

Placings:4F   (2409)
2003/04: 16⁴G, 17ᶠGF,

	Starts	1st	2nd	3rd	Win & Pl
Hurdles	2	0	0	0	289
Career Total	2	0	0	0	289

Going:	Sf: 0-0 GS: 0-0 Gd: 0-1 GF: - Fm: 0-1
Distance:	2m/2m3: 0-2 2m4-2m7: 0-0 3m+: 0-0
Track:	LH: 0-1 RH: 0-1 Tight: 0-2 Gall: 0-0
Aids:	Bl: 0-0 Vi: 0-0 Tstrap: 0-0 Ckp: 0-0
Best Rating:	110 11/03 Tntn 2m1f gd-fm Hdl

Smart Flat performer; showed ability on hurdles debut.

Gallik Dawn

89   78

6-y-o ch g Anshan-Sticky Money (Relkino)
A Hollingsworth   Perry Adams

Placings:0-030PP020   (4716)
2003/04: 16⁰G, 24³G, 20⁰G, 25ᴾS, 26ᴾGS, 16⁰G, 19²GS, 21⁰G,

	Starts	1st	2nd	3rd	Win & Pl
NH Flat	1	0	0	0	0
Hurdles	7	0	1	1	1281
Career Total	9	0	1	1	1281

Going:	Sf: 0-1 GS: 0-2 Gd: 0-4 GF: - Fm: 0-1
Distance:	2m/2m3: 0-2 2m4-2m7: 0-3 3m+: 0-3
Track:	LH: 0-4 RH: 0-3 Tight: 0-0 Gall: 0-0
Aids:	Bl: 0-0 Vi: 0-0 Tstrap: 0-0 Ckp: 0-0
Best Rating:	78 3/04 Towc 2m3f110y gd-sft Hdl

Gallium

(66h)   (49h)

7-y-o gr m Terimon-Genie Spirit (Nishapour (FR))
M Scudamore   Mrs J D Kington

Placings:654-0PF   (4139)
2003/04: 16⁰GS, 19⁵HY, 20ᶠG,

	Starts	1st	2nd	3rd	Win & Pl
Hurdles	2	0	0	0	0
Chases	1	0	0	0	0
Career Total	6	0	0	0	394

Going:	Sf: 0-1 GS: 0-1 Gd: 0-1 GF: - Fm: 0-0
Distance:	2m/2m3: 0-1 2m4-2m7: 0-2 3m+: 0-0
Track:	LH: 0-1 RH: 0-2 Tight: 0-1 Gall: 0-0
Aids:	Bl: 0-0 Vi: 0-0 Tstrap: 0-0 Ckp: 0-0
Best Rating:	65 12/02 Ludl 2m good NHF

Galtee View (IRE)

99   92

6-y-o b g Namaqualand (USA)-Miss Dolly (IRE) (Alzao (USA))
C Roche   Mrs Noeleen Roche

Placings:33331314460500   (3400a)
2003/04: 16³G, 16³GF, 18³F, 16³G, 16¹F, 20³GF, 16¹GF, 17⁴GF, 24⁴G, 16⁶G, 16⁰YS, 20⁵S, 16⁰Y, 20⁶S,

	Starts	1st	2nd	3rd	Win & Pl
NH Flat	5	1	0	4	5623
Hurdles	9	1	0	1	6134
Career Total	14	2	0	5	11757
100 9/03 Clon	2m	Hdl		G-F	£4480
103 8/03 Tram	2m	NHF		FRM	£4032
		Total win prize-money £8513			

Going:	Sf: 0-2 GS: 0-0 Gd: 0-3 GF: - Fm: 2-7
Distance:	2m/2m3: 2-10 2m4-2m7: 0-3 3m+: 0-1
Track:	LH: 0-2 RH: 0-2 Tight: 0-0 Gall: 0-0
Aids:	Bl: 0-0 Vi: 0-0 Tstrap: 0-0 Ckp: 0-0
Best Rating:	105 6/03 Clon 2m firm NHF

Moderate Irish-trained hurdler; winner of a bumper; acts well on fast ground; stays three miles.

Galwaybay Stan (IRE)

101   93

6-y-o b g Safety Catch (USA)-Crook Lady (Croghan Hill)
L Wells   Paul Zetter

Placings:34-PP31   (3261)
2003/04: 24ᴾS, 22ᴾGS, 22³HY, 24¹HY,

	Starts	1st	2nd	3rd	Win & Pl
Hurdles	4	1	0	1	4710
Career Total	6	1	0	2	5266
92 1/04 Towc	3m	E Hdl		HVY	£4202
		Total win prize-money £4202			

Going:	Sf: 1-3 GS: 0-1 Gd: 0-0 GF: - Fm: 0-0
Distance:	2m/2m3: 0-0 2m4-2m7: 0-2 3m+: 1-2
Track:	LH: 0-1 RH: 1-3 Tight: 0-3 Gall: 0-0
Aids:	Bl: 0-0 Vi: 0-0 Tstrap: 1-1 Ckp: 0-0
Best Rating:	99 2/03 Extr 2m1f gd-sft NHF

Fair hurdler; ex-Irish; stays three miles and suited by soft ground.

Gamblers Dream (IRE)

72   **66**

7-y-o b g Executive Perk-Tinkers Lady (Sheer Grit)
P J Hobbs Mrs L R Lovell

Placings:05-P0   (4812)
2003/04: 16^6G, 16^9G,

	Starts	1st	2nd	3rd	Win & Pl
Hurdles	2	0	0	0	
Career Total	4	0	0	0	

Going: Sf: 0-0 GS: 0-0 Gd: 0-0 GF: - Fm: 0-0
Distance: 2m/2m3: 0-2 2m4-2m7: 0-0 3m+: 0-0
Track: LH: 0-1 RH: 0-1 Tight: 0-0 Gall: 0-0
Aids: Bl: 0-0 Vi: 0-0 Tstrap: 0-0 Ckp: 0-0
Best Rating: 85 4/03 Gowr 2m   gd-fm NHF

Game Gunner

12-y-o b g Gunner B-The Waiting Game (Cruise Missile)
Miss B Lewis Miss B Lewis

Placings:14U4P2/P-11P   (4425)
2003/04: 25^1G, 24^1G, 26^6G,

	Starts	1st	2nd	3rd	Win & Pl
Chases	3	2	0	0	7674
Career Total	10	3	1	0	12901

102 2/04 Ludl 3m   H Ch   GD £3423
102 4/03 Chel 3m1f110yH Ch   GD £4251
95 6/01 Strf 3m   H Ch   G-F £3705
Total win prize-money £11379

Going: Sf: 0-0 GS: 0-0 Gd: 2-3 GF: - Fm: 0-0
Distance: 2m/2m3: 0-0 2m4-2m7: 0-0 3m+: 2-3
Track: LH: 1-2 RH: 1-1 Tight: 1-1 Gall: 1-2
Aids: Bl: 0-0 Vi: 0-0 Tstrap: 0-0 Ckp: 0-0
Best Rating: 102 2/04 Ludl 3m   good Ch

Winning hunter chaser; likes fast ground; big strong sort who generally jumps well; has few miles on the clock for his age; stays three miles.

Game On (IRE)

107   (90h)**98**

8-y-o b g Terimon-Nun So Game (The Parson)
B N Pollock Mrs S Platt

Placings:2P24P/U6-24322   (1544)
2003/04: 16^2GF, 17^4GF, 17^3GF, 17^2GF, 20^2GF,

	Starts	1st	2nd	3rd	Win & Pl
Chases	5	0	3	1	3863
Career Total	12	0	5	1	5221

Going: Sf: 0-0 GS: 0-0 Gd: 0-0 GF: - Fm: 0-5
Distance: 2m/2m3: 0-4 2m4-2m7: 0-1 3m+: 0-0
Track: LH: 0-3 RH: 0-2 Tight: 0-3 Gall: 0-1
Aids: Bl: 0-0 Vi: 0-0 Tstrap: 0-0 Ckp: 0-0
Best Rating: 109 5/01 Folk 2m1f110y gd-sft NHF

Plating-class novice chaser; former pointer; yet to get off the mark in either sphere.

Gan Eagla (IRE)

107   **98**

5-y-o b g Paris House-Mafiosa (Miami Springs)
Miss Venetia Williams (J S Bolger 5/7) T Hywel Jones

Placings:3043P   (4892)
2003/04: 16^4GF, 17^0S, 17^4GS, 17^3G, 16^9GF,

	Starts	1st	2nd	3rd	Win & Pl
Hurdles	5	0	0	2	1319
Career Total	5	0	0	2	1319

Going: Sf: 0-1 GS: 0-1 Gd: 0-1 GF: - Fm: 0-2
Distance: 2m/2m3: 0-5 2m4-2m7: 0-0 3m+: 0-0
Track: LH: 0-1 RH: 0-4 Tight: 0-4 Gall: 0-1
Aids: Bl: 0-0 Vi: 0-0 Tstrap: 0-0 Ckp: 0-0
Best Rating: 98 3/04 MRas 2m1f110y good Hdl

Modest hurdler; proving expensive to follow over hurdles, still a maiden after several good chances; barely stays two miles; suited by decent ground.

Gandon

103   **83**

7-y-o ch g Hernando (FR)-Severine (USA) (Trempolino (USA))
A E Jones (P G Murphy 14/10) Amos Eaton

Placings:00000/0650004-50330   (4339)
2003/04: 19^5G, 17^0GF, 20^3G, 21^3G, 16^9G,

	Starts	1st	2nd	3rd	Win & Pl
Hurdles	5	0	0	2	761
Career Total	17	0	0	2	761

Going: Sf: 0-0 GS: 0-0 Gd: 0-4 GF: - Fm: 0-1
Distance: 2m/2m3: 0-2 2m4-2m7: 0-3 3m+: 0-0
Track: LH: 0-4 RH: 0-1 Tight: 0-2 Gall: 0-0
Aids: Bl: 0-0 Vi: 0-0 Tstrap: 0-0 Ckp: 0-0
Best Rating: 83 10/03 Sedg 2m5f110y good Hdl

Plating-class; stays 2m4f; likes a sound surface; tends to find little off the bridle.

Gangsters R Us (IRE)

106(101h)   (102+h)**109+**

8-y-o br g Treasure Hunter-Our Mare Mick (Choral Society)
A Parker J B Purefoy

Placings:P/536/6310-2041110   (4726)
2003/04: 16^2GF, 25^5S, 21^4GS, 20^1GF, 24^1G, 24^1F, 24^0G,

	Starts	1st	2nd	3rd	Win & Pl
Chases	7	3	1	0	13300
Career Total	15	4	1	2	17535

109 2/04 Muss 3m   F(0-95)HCh   FRM £4252
104 2/04 Muss 3m   F(0-95)HCh   GD £3373
98 1/04 Muss 2m4f E(0-110)HCh G-F £4680
102 2/03 Ayr 2m4f F(0-95)HHdl HVY £3150
Total win prize-money £15456

Going: Sf: 0-1 GS: 0-1 Gd: 1-2 GF: - Fm: 2-3
Distance: 2m/2m3: 0-1 2m4-2m7: 1-2 3m+: 2-4
Track: LH: 0-3 RH: 3-4 Tight: 3-4 Gall: 0-0
Aids: Bl: 0-0 Vi: 0-0 Tstrap: 0-0 Ckp: 0-0
Best Rating: 109 2/04 Muss 3m   firm Ch

Modest chaser; completed a hat-trick at Musselburgh in early 2004; stays three miles; appears to go on any ground; usually held up.

Gaora Bridge (IRE)

105   **104**

6-y-o b g Warcraft (USA)-Miss Good Night (Buckskin (FR))
C J Mann Robert Tompkins & Mrs Lynda Lovell

Placings:0432   (4671)

2003/04: 20^0GS, 16^4GS, 16^9G, 16^2G,

	Starts	1st	2nd	3rd	Win & Pl
Hurdles	4	0	1	1	2047
Career Total	4	0	1	1	2047

Going: Sf: 0-0 GS: 0-2 Gd: 0-2 GF: - Fm: 0-0
Distance: 2m/2m3: 0-3 2m4-2m7: 0-1 3m+: 0-0
Track: LH: 0-2 RH: 0-2 Tight: 0-1 Gall: 0-0
Aids: Bl: 0-0 Vi: 0-0 Tstrap: 0-0 Ckp: 0-0
Best Rating: 104 2/04 Ludl 2m   good Hdl

Moderate novice hurdler; won only start in Irish point; has shown promise over hurdles, but has not been seeing his races out.

Garde Bien

98   **101+**

7-y-o br g Afzal-May Lady (Deep Run)
Ferdy Murphy Mrs M B Scholey

Placings:P2P4F6   (4613)
2003/04: 20^0S, 16^2G, 19^0GS, 16^4G, 19^2G, 16^0G,

	Starts	1st	2nd	3rd	Win & Pl
Chases	6	0	1	0	1355
Career Total	6	0	1	0	1355

Going: Sf: 0-0 GS: 0-1 Gd: 0-4 GF: - Fm: 0-0
Distance: 2m/2m3: 0-5 2m4-2m7: 0-1 3m+: 0-0
Track: LH: 0-4 RH: 0-2 Tight: 0-2 Gall: 0-1
Aids: Bl: 0-0 Vi: 0-0 Tstrap: 0-0 Ckp: 0-0
Best Rating: 98 12/03 Donc 2m110y   good Ch

Moderate novice chaser; runner-up in maiden point; narrowly outpointed in weak novices' chase at Doncaster in December; stays two miles four; acts on a sound surface.

Garde Champetre (FR)

113   **146**

5-y-o b g Garde Royale-Clementine Fleurie (FR) (Lionel (FR))
P F Nicholls Million In Mind Partnership

Placings:212251   (4629)
2003/04: 16^2S, 17^1TGS, 16^2S, 16^2S, 16^5G, 20^1G,

	Starts	1st	2nd	3rd	Win & Pl
Hurdles	6	2	3	0	52586
Career Total	6	2	3	0	52586

141 4/04 Aint 2m4f   A Hdl   GD £29000
112 12/03 Bang 2m1f E Hdl   G-S £4030
Total win prize-money £33030

Going: Sf: 0-2 GS: 1-2 Gd: 1-2 GF: - Fm: 0-0
Distance: 2m/2m3: 1-5 2m4-2m7: 1-1 3m+: 0-0
Track: LH: 2-4 RH: 0-2 Tight: 2-3 Gall: 0-0
Aids: Bl: 0-0 Vi: 0-0 Tstrap: 0-0 Ckp: 0-0
Best Rating: 146 2/04 Sand 2m110y   soft Hdl

Smart novice hurdler; ex-French; runner-up in the Grade One Tolworth Hurdle in 2004 and filled the same position in the Agfa next time; took a Grade Two at Aintree; suited by two and a half miles; acts on good ground or softer; consistent sort who should make into a useful chaser.

Garden Feature

93   **86**

6-y-o b m Minster Son-Super Fountain (Royal Fountain)
J B Walton Messrs F T Walton

Placings:5650-05P015   (4612)

2003/04: 27⁰G, 21⁵GS, 24ᴾHY, 24⁰GS, 21¹G, 21⁵G,

	Starts	1st	2nd	3rd	Win & Pl
Hurdles	6	1	0	0	3341
Career Total	10	1	0	0	3341

86　3/04　Sedg　2m5f110yE Hdl　　　　　GD　£3341
Total win prize-money £3341

Going:	Sf: 0-1 GS: 0-2 Gd: 1-3 GF: - Fm: 0-0
Distance:	2m/2m3: 0-0 2m4-2m7: 1-3 3m+: 0-0
Track:	LH: 1-6 RH: 0-0 Tight: 1-4 Gall: 0-1
Aids:	Bl: 0-0 Vi: 0-0 Tstrap: 0-0 Ckp: 0-0
Best Rating:	86　3/04　Sedg　2m5f110y　good　Hdl

Modest novice hurdler; much improved when taking a mares' only event at Sedgefield in March by a wide margin; suited by soft ground; will stay three miles.

Garden Party II (FR)
103　　　　　　90

10-y-o br g Argument (FR)-Betty Royale (FR) (Royal Charter (FR))
Mrs J C McGregor Discounted Cashflow

Placings:2604/0060F0/0P62F50/30032454/33456443-2544P4544405　　　　(4940)
2003/04: 20²GS, 16⁵GF, 21⁴G, 20⁴GS, 21ᴾS, 24⁴GF, 24⁵GF, 24⁴G, 17⁴GS, 16⁴GF, 16⁰G, 16⁵GS,

	Starts	1st	2nd	3rd	Win & Pl
Chases	12	0	1	0	3192
Career Total	45	0	4	5	10774

Going:	Sf: 0-1 GS: 0-4 Gd: 0-3 GF: - Fm: 0-4
Distance:	2m/2m3: 0-5 2m4-2m7: 0-4 3m+: 0-3
Track:	LH: 0-6 RH: 0-6 Tight: 0-5 Gall: 0-0
Aids:	Bl: 0-0 Vi: 0-0 Tstrap: 0-0 Ckp: 0-0
Best Rating:	104　3/99　Ludl　2m　　good　NHF

Plating-class maiden chaser; has run well on varying ground; lacks a turn of foot.

Gardor (FR)
101　　　　　　97

6-y-o b g Kendor (FR)-Garboesque (Priolo (USA))
T J Fitzgerald Mrs Anne M Halewood

Placings:452/0500-2FP　　　　　　(0820)
2003/04: 16²G, 16ᶠG, 17ᴾG,

	Starts	1st	2nd	3rd	Win & Pl
Hurdles	3	0	1	0	1728
Career Total	10	0	2	0	2858

Going:	Sf: 0-0 GS: 0-0 Gd: 0-3 GF: - Fm: 0-0
Distance:	2m/2m3: 0-3 2m4-2m7: 0-0 3m+: 0-0
Track:	LH: 0-2 RH: 0-1 Tight: 0-2 Gall: 0-0
Aids:	Bl: 0-0 Vi: 0-0 Tstrap: 0-3 Ckp: 0-0
Best Rating:	99　3/02　MRas　2m1f110y　gd-sft　Hdl

Moderate maiden hurdler; narrowly beaten in seller at Kelso in May and would have finished runner-up in a better race at Wetherby a week later but for falling at the last; best at two miles; acts on any ground; has worn a tongue tie.

Garethson (IRE)

13-y-o b g Cataldi-Tartan Sash (Crofter (USA))
O W King A King

Placings:3233/30613/1U40FP5/2U/133/3P-P　　(0018)
2003/04: 21ᴾS,

	Starts	1st	2nd	3rd	Win & Pl
Chases	1	0	0	0	

Career Total | 24 | 3 | 2 | 8 | 14930

98　2/02　Donc　2m3f110yH Ch　　　SFT　£1596
128　5/98　Towc　2m6f　　E Ch　　　GD　£3065
127　3/98　Extr　2m3f110yD Ch　　　SFT　£3906
Total win prize-money £8568

Going:	Sf: 0-1 GS: 0-0 Gd: 0-0 GF: - Fm: 0-0
Distance:	2m/2m3: 0-0 2m4-2m7: 0-1 3m+: 0-0
Track:	LH: 0-1 RH: 0-0 Tight: 0-1 Gall: 0-0
Aids:	Bl: 0-0 Vi: 0-0 Tstrap: 0-0 Ckp: 0-0
Best Rating:	128　5/98　Towc　2m6f　　good　Ch

Gargoyle Girl
105　　　　　　91+

7-y-o b m Be My Chief (USA)-May Hills Legacy (IRE) (Be My Guest (USA))
J S Goldie Mrs C Brown

Placings:0502/214-244415　　　　　(4294)
2003/04: 16²G, 16⁴GF, 18⁴S, 16⁴S, 19¹G, 22⁵GF,

	Starts	1st	2nd	3rd	Win & Pl
Hurdles	6	1	1	0	4966
Career Total	13	2	3	0	10216

95　1/04　Donc　2m3f110yE(0-110)HHdl　GD　£3701
95　6/02　Prth　2m110y　F(0-90)HHdl　G-S　£2957
Total win prize-money £6660

Going:	Sf: 0-2 GS: 0-0 Gd: 1-2 GF: - Fm: 0-2
Distance:	2m/2m3: 0-2 2m4-2m7: 1-2 3m+: 0-0
Track:	LH: 1-5 RH: 0-1 Tight: 0-0 Gall: 0-0
Aids:	Bl: 0-0 Vi: 0-1 Tstrap: 0-0 Ckp: 1-2
Best Rating:	95　1/04　Donc　2m3f110y　good　Hdl

Moderate hurdler; improved effort when winning easing down at Doncaster in January; stays two and a half miles; best suited by a sound surface; has worn a visor and cheekpieces.

Garolsa (FR)
105　　　　　　110+

10-y-o b g Rivelago (FR)-Rols Du Chatelier (FR) (Diaghilev)
C L Tizzard R G And C L Tizzard

Placings:02/1/2P4/P2P/026PP/22U4U4P-155UP6142　(4894)
2003/04: 26¹S, 24⁵S, 29⁵S, 24ᵁS, 25ᴾHY, 24²RG, 24¹GS, 24⁴S, 25²G,

	Starts	1st	2nd	3rd	Win & Pl
Chases	9	2	1	0	11098
Career Total	30	3	7	0	28308

108　3/04　Chep　3m　F(0-100)HCh　G-S　£3438
110　11/03　Plum　3m2f　　D Ch　　SFT　£5460
105　3/99　Chep　2m4f110yD Hdl　　SFT　£2996
Total win prize-money £11895

Going:	Sf: 1-6 GS: 1-1 Gd: 0-2 GF: - Fm: 0-0
Distance:	2m/2m3: 0-0 2m4-2m7: 0-3 3m+: 2-9
Track:	LH: 2-6 RH: 0-3 Tight: 1-4 Gall: 0-0
Aids:	Bl: 0-0 Vi: 0-1 Tstrap: 1-6 Ckp: 0-0
Best Rating:	111　4/00　Asct　3m110y　soft　Ch

Modest handicap chaser; took advantage of an 11lb drop in the ratings when winning 3m Class F handicap chase at Chepstow March 2004; stays well; acts on soft ground.

Garraheen Princess (IRE)
89　　　　　　74

6-y-o b m Shernazar-Money Incinerator (Laurence O)
B J Llewellyn G Halnon

Placings:00-50　　　　　　　(2288)
2003/04: 16⁵GF, 22⁰G,

	Starts	1st	2nd	3rd	Win & Pl
Hurdles	2	0	0	0	0
Career Total	4	0	0	0	0

Going:	Sf: 0-0 GS: 0-0 Gd: 0-1 GF: - Fm: 0-1
Distance:	2m/2m3: 0-1 2m4-2m7: 0-1 3m+: 0-0
Track:	LH: 0-1 RH: 0-1 Tight: 0-1 Gall: 0-0
Aids:	Bl: 0-0 Vi: 0-1 Tstrap: 0-0 Ckp: 0-1
Best Rating:	74　6/03　Worc　2m　　gd-fm　Hdl

Garruth (IRE)

10-y-o gr g Good Thyne (USA)-Lady Sipash (Erin's Hope)
R Barber Richard Barber

Placings:6/405331/00113221141/14363251/5P02P-04　(4522)
2003/04: 25⁰G, 25⁵GS,

	Starts	1st	2nd	3rd	Win & Pl
Chases	2	0	0	0	280
Career Total	33	8	4	5	81785

102　4/02　Sedg　3m3f　　D Ch　　G-F　£4378
108　11/01　Plum　3m2f　　D Ch　　GD　£4322
150　4/01　Aint　3m110y A Hdl　　SFT　£29000
135　1/01　Uttx　3m110y　C(0-135)HHdl　HVY　£5239
127　12/00　Chel　3m　　A Hdl　　SFT　£12000
126　10/00　Kels　2m6f110yE Hdl　　G-S　£2422
104　9/00　Sedg　2m5f110yE Hdl　　SFT　£2716
91　4/00　List　2m4f　　NHF　　SH　£3588
Total win prize-money £63667

Going:	Sf: 0-0 GS: 0-1 Gd: 0-1 GF: - Fm: 0-0
Distance:	2m/2m3: 0-0 2m4-2m7: 0-0 3m+: 0-2
Track:	LH: 0-0 RH: 0-2 Tight: 0-0 Gall: 0-0
Aids:	Bl: 0-0 Vi: 0-0 Tstrap: 0-0 Ckp: 0-0
Best Rating:	150　4/01　Aint　3m110y　soft　Hdl

Moderate hunter chaser; acts on any ground.

Garryspillane (IRE)

12-y-o b g Royal Fountain-Lucylet (Kinglet)
P Jones M Mann

Placings:00/35/3233/4　　　　　(0073)
2003/04: 24⁴S,

	Starts	1st	2nd	3rd	Win & Pl
Chases	1	0	0	0	144
Career Total	9	0	1	4	5606

Going:	Sf: 0-1 GS: 0-0 Gd: 0-0 GF: - Fm: 0-0
Distance:	2m/2m3: 0-2 2m4-2m7: 0-0 3m+: 0-1
Track:	LH: 0-1 RH: 0-0 Tight: 0-1 Gall: 0-0
Aids:	Bl: 0-0 Vi: 0-0 Tstrap: 0-0 Ckp: 0-0
Best Rating:	112　4/02　Aint　3m1f　　good　Ch

Garw Valley
102　　　　　　86+

5-y-o b m Mtoto-Morgannwg (IRE) (Simply Great (FR))
Miss J Feilden Steven Rees

Placings:UU34P445　　　　　　(2516)
2003/04: 16ᵁGF, 17ᵁGF, 16³GF, 16⁴GF, 16ᴾGF, 16⁴GF, 16⁴GF, 17⁵GS,

	Starts	1st	2nd	3rd	Win & Pl
Hurdles	8	0	0	1	275

| Career Total | 8 | 0 | 0 | 1 | 275 |

Going:	Sf: 0-0 GS: 0-1 Gd: 0-0 GF: - Fm: 0-7
Distance:	2m/2m3: 0-8 2m4-2m7: 0-0 3m+: 0-0
Track:	LH: 0-4 RH: 0-4 Tight: 0-4 Gall: 0-0
Aids:	Bl: 0-0 Vi: 0-0 Tstrap: 0-0 Ckp: 0-0
Best Rating:	86 10/03 Plum 2m gd-fm Hdl

Plating-class hurdler; best effort to date in selling company at Uttoxeter in September 2003.

Gary's Pimpernel
103   94

5-y-o b g Shaddad (USA)-Pennine Star (IRE) (Pennine Walk)
M W Easterby Lord Daresbury

Placings: 12-2235   (4946)
2003/04: 16²GS, 16²GS, 16³HY, 16⁵GS,

	Starts	1st	2nd	3rd	Win & Pl
NH Flat	2	0	2	0	1052
Hurdles	2	0	0	1	543
Career Total	6	1	3	1	4116
90 3/03 Catt 2m		H NHF		SFT	£1939
			Total win prize-money £1939

Going:	Sf: 0-1 GS: 0-3 Gd: 0-0 GF: - Fm: 0-0
Distance:	2m/2m3: 0-4 2m4-2m7: 0-0 3m+: 0-0
Track:	LH: 0-3 RH: 0-1 Tight: 0-1 Gall: 0-1
Aids:	Bl: 0-0 Vi: 0-0 Tstrap: 0-0 Ckp: 0-0
Best Rating:	103 1/04 Catt 2m gd-sft NHF

Made a successful bow in low-grade bumper at Catterick in March 2003; ran well when runner-up under a penalty at Wetherby two weeks later; narrowly held at Catterick in January; acts on soft ground; handles fast.

Gastornis
113+

6-y-o ch g Primitive Rising (USA)-Meggies Dene (Apollo Eight)
M W Easterby Lord Daresbury

Placings: 5/212121-P   (1782)
2003/04: 24⁰G,

	Starts	1st	2nd	3rd	Win & Pl
Hurdles	1	0	0	0	0
Career Total	8	3	3	0	11302
119 4/03 Weth 2m4f110yE Hdl			G-F	£3724
104 3/03 Weth 2m4f110yF Hdl			G-F	£3167
98 10/02 Hexm 2m110y H NHF			G-F	£1827
			Total win prize-money £8719

Going:	Sf: 0-0 GS: 0-0 Gd: 0-1 GF: - Fm: 0-0
Distance:	2m/2m3: 0-0 2m4-2m7: 0-0 3m+: 0-1
Track:	LH: 0-1 RH: 0-0 Tight: 0-1 Gall: 0-0
Aids:	Bl: 0-0 Vi: 0-0 Tstrap: 0-0 Ckp: 0-0
Best Rating:	119 4/03 Weth 2m4f110y gd-fm Hdl

Fair hurdler; effective up to two miles four furlongs; acts on decent ground; usually wears a tongue tie.

Gate Expectations
85   70

6-y-o b m Alflora (IRE)-Dorazine (Kalaglow)
R J Price Englands Gate Limited

Placings: 0/060600-4   (1309)
2003/04: 16⁴GF,

	Starts	1st	2nd	3rd	Win & Pl
Hurdles	1	0	0	0	0
Career Total	8	0	0	0	0

Going:	Sf: 0-0 GS: 0-0 Gd: 0-0 GF: - Fm: 0-1
Distance:	2m/2m3: 0-1 2m4-2m7: 0-0 3m+: 0-0
Track:	LH: 0-1 RH: 0-0 Tight: 0-0 Gall: 0-0
Aids:	Bl: 0-0 Vi: 0-0 Tstrap: 0-0 Ckp: 0-0
Best Rating:	80 9/03 Worc 2m gd-fm Hdl

Plating-class hurdler.

Gatejumper (IRE)
92   95

6-y-o b g Zaffaran (USA)-Nelly Don (Shackleton)
R H Alner Pell-Mell Partners

Placings: 0-31000   (4897)
2003/04: 20³GS, 21¹S, 20⁰GS, 21⁰GS, 22⁰G,

	Starts	1st	2nd	3rd	Win & Pl
Hurdles	5	1	0	1	3837
Career Total	6	1	0	1	3837
95 1/04 Plum 2m5f		E Hdl		SFT	£3503
			Total win prize-money £3504

Going:	Sf: 1-1 GS: 0-3 Gd: 0-1 GF: - Fm: 0-0
Distance:	2m/2m3: 0-0 2m4-2m7: 1-5 3m+: 0-0
Track:	LH: 1-2 RH: 0-3 Tight: 1-2 Gall: 0-0
Aids:	Bl: 0-0 Vi: 0-0 Tstrap: 0-0 Ckp: 0-0
Best Rating:	95 1/04 Plum 2m5f soft Hdl

Gathering Storm (IRE)
93   60

6-y-o ch g Roselier (FR)-Queen Of The Rock (IRE) (The Parson)
P R Hedger Howard Spooner

Placings: 0-2300   (4197)
2003/04: 17⁰S, 16²GS, 16³S, 20⁰GS, 24⁰G,

	Starts	1st	2nd	3rd	Win & Pl
NH Flat	3	0	1	1	747
Hurdles	2	0	0	0	0
Career Total	5	0	1	1	747

Going:	Sf: 0-2 GS: 0-2 Gd: 0-1 GF: - Fm: 0-0
Distance:	2m/2m3: 0-3 2m4-2m7: 0-1 3m+: 0-1
Track:	LH: 0-2 RH: 0-3 Tight: 0-2 Gall: 0-3
Aids:	Bl: 0-0 Vi: 0-0 Tstrap: 0-0 Ckp: 0-0
Best Rating:	93 1/04 Hntg 2m110y soft NHF

Gatorade (NZ)
102(102h)   (107h)110

12-y-o ch g Dahar (USA)-Ribena (NZ) (Battle-Waggon)
R C Guest (N H Oliver 29/4) The Cider Sauce Partnership

Placings: 046/0112201212P/421245P/1245202P-11 (0979)
2003/04: 21¹GF, 21¹GF,

	Starts	1st	2nd	3rd	Win & Pl
Chases	2	2	0	0	7725
Career Total	31	8	9	0	47135
108 7/03 Sedg 2m5f E(0-110)HCh			G-F	£4332
110 7/03 Sthl 2m5f110yF(0-95)HCh			G-F	£3393
115 6/02 Worc 2m4f110yC(0-130)HCh			GD	£6760
112 7/01 Strf 2m1f110yE Ch			GD	£3055
121 9/00 Uttx 2m4f110yB(0-140)HHdl			G-S	£6721
104 8/00 NAbb 2m1f D Hdl			GD	£2879
113 6/00 Worc 2m4f F(0-110)HHdl			GF	£2348
105 6/00 Uttx 2m4f110yD Hdl			G-F	£3237
			Total win prize-money £32727

Going:	Sf: 0-0 GS: 0-0 Gd: 0-0 GF: - Fm: 2-2

Distance:	2m/2m3: 0-0 2m4-2m7: 2-2 3m+: 0-0
Track:	LH: 2-2 RH: 0-0 Tight: 1-1 Gall: 0-0
Aids:	Bl: 0-0 Vi: 0-0 Tstrap: 0-0 Ckp: 2-2
Best Rating:	121 10/00 Chel 2m5f good Hdl

Fair chaser/hurdler in his time; won extended 2m5f handicap chase at Southwell July 2003 on first outing for Richard Guest; followed up in facile fashion at Sedgefield a week later; acts on most types of ground.

Gatsby (IRE)

8-y-o gr g Roselier (FR)-Burren Gale (IRE) (Strong Gale)
J Groucott Mrs J K Powell

Placings: 630/21   (3785)
2003/04: 24²GF, 24¹S,

	Starts	1st	2nd	3rd	Win & Pl
Chases	2	1	1	0	1855
Career Total	5	1	1	1	2569
99 2/04 Hntg 3m		H Ch		SFT	£1407
			Total win prize-money £1407

Going:	Sf: 1-1 GS: 0-0 Gd: 0-0 GF: - Fm: 0-1
Distance:	2m/2m3: 0-0 2m4-2m7: 0-0 3m+: 1-2
Track:	LH: 0-1 RH: 1-1 Tight: 0-0 Gall: 1-1
Aids:	Bl: 0-0 Vi: 0-0 Tstrap: 0-0 Ckp: 0-0
Best Rating:	99 2/04 Hntg 3m soft Ch

Moderate hunter chaser; stepped up on his point form when runner-up to Cherry Gold in novice hunter at Chepstow May 2003; won on next outing in novice hunter chase at Huntingdon in February over three miles; acts on soft ground.

Gaucho
107   (30h)100

7-y-o b g Rambo Dancer (CAN)-Sioux Be It (Warpath)
Miss T Jackson H L Thompson

Placings: 460/00PP/U22052   (4613)
2003/04: 19ᵁGS, 16²HY, 16²S, 16⁰HY, 16⁵G, 16²G,

	Starts	1st	2nd	3rd	Win & Pl
Chases	6	0	3	0	3815
Career Total	13	0	3	0	3815

Going:	Sf: 0-3 GS: 0-1 Gd: 0-2 GF: - Fm: 0-0
Distance:	2m/2m3: 0-6 2m4-2m7: 0-0 3m+: 0-0
Track:	LH: 0-6 RH: 0-0 Tight: 0-2 Gall: 0-2
Aids:	Bl: 0-0 Vi: 0-0 Tstrap: 0-0 Ckp: 0-6
Best Rating:	100 1/04 Newc 2m110y heavy Ch

Modest novice chaser; should be suited by more than two miles; handles testing conditions; wears cheekpieces.

Gaultier Gale (IRE)

10-y-o b g Ajraas (USA)-David's Pleasure (Welsh Saint)
Ms J M Findlay Ms J M Findlay

Placings: 15060/500/00B0351206P44/342014144F0/10P50 PPP/6U-4P   (4078)
2003/04: 24⁴G, 24ᴾF,

	Starts	1st	2nd	3rd	Win & Pl
Chases	2	0	0	0	0
Career Total	44	5	2	2	19111
94 5/01 Fknm 2m5f110yF(0-90)HCh			G-F	£2536
94 8/00 Sthl 2m4f110yF(0-105)HCh			GD	£3406
85 7/00 Sthl 2m4f110yF(0-95)HCh			G-F	£2808
79 9/99 Dpat 2m2f (0-95)HCh			GD	£2464
113 12/97 Clon 2m Hdl			HVY	£2712
			Total win prize-money £13928

Going:	Sf: 0-0 GS: 0-0 Gd: 0-1 GF: - Fm: 0-1
Distance:	2m/2m3: 0-0 2m4-2m7: 0-0 3m+: 0-2
Track:	LH: 0-0 RH: 0-2 Tight: 0-2 Gall: 0-0
Aids:	Bl: 0-0 Vi: 0-0 Tstrap: 0-0 Ckp: 0-0
Best Rating:	113 12/97 Clon 2m heavy Hdl

Gay Clown

10-y-o b m Petoski-Gay Edition (New Member)
P J Hobbs A L Hobbs

Placings:0/550/F   (0589)
2003/04: 20[F]GF,

	Starts	1st	2nd	3rd	Win & Pl
Chases	1	0	0	0	
Career Total	5	0	0	0	0

Going:	Sf: 0-0 GS: 0-0 Gd: 0-0 GF: - Fm: 0-1
Distance:	2m/2m3: 0-0 2m4-2m7: 0-1 3m+: 0-0
Track:	LH: 0-1 RH: 0-0 Tight: 0-2 Gall: 0-0
Aids:	Bl: 0-0 Vi: 0-0 Tstrap: 0-0 Ckp: 0-0
Best Rating:	67 3/00 Tntn 2m3f110y good Hdl

Gay Kindersley (IRE)

80   **23**

6-y-o ch g Roselier (FR)-Ramble Bramble (Random Shot)
Mrs M Reveley W J Smith And M D Dudley

Placings:400   (4319)
2003/04: 16[4]GS, 16[0]G, 20[P]S,

	Starts	1st	2nd	3rd	Win & Pl
NH Flat	2	0	0	0	0
Hurdles	1	0	0	0	0
Career Total	3	0	0	0	0

Going:	Sf: 0-1 GS: 0-1 Gd: 0-1 GF: - Fm: 0-0
Distance:	2m/2m3: 0-2 2m4-2m7: 0-1 3m+: 0-0
Track:	LH: 0-3 RH: 0-0 Tight: 0-0 Gall: 0-2
Aids:	Bl: 0-0 Vi: 0-0 Tstrap: 0-0 Ckp: 0-0
Best Rating:	101 12/03 Newb 2m110y gd-sft NHF

Related to useful staying chaser Seven Towers; good debut in hot bumper at Newbury in December on good to soft; held subsequently.

Gay Oscar (IRE)

88f   **101f**

5-y-o b/br g Oscar (IRE)-Deep Inthought (IRE) (Warcraft (USA))
Mrs K Walton Percy Vere Partnership

Placings:24   (4885)
2003/04: 16[2]GS, 17[4]GS,

	Starts	1st	2nd	3rd	Win & Pl
NH Flat	2	0	1	0	582
Career Total	2	0	1	0	582

Going:	Sf: 0-0 GS: 0-2 Gd: 0-0 GF: - Fm: 0-0
Distance:	2m/2m3: 0-2 2m4-2m7: 0-0 3m+: 0-0
Track:	LH: 0-1 RH: 0-1 Tight: 0-0 Gall: 0-0
Aids:	Bl: 0-0 Vi: 0-0 Tstrap: 0-0 Ckp: 0-0
Best Rating:	95 3/04 Weth 2m gd-sft NHF

Jump bred; runner-up to wide margin winner on debut in bumper at Wetherby in March.

Gaye Dream

93   **88**

6-y-o b g Gildoran-Gaye Fame (Ardross)
M Scudamore Mrs S Tainton

Placings:50-FP6400   (4339)
2003/04: 20[F]GS, 20[P]G, 16[6]GF, 21[4]S, 17[9]GS, 16[6]G,

	Starts	1st	2nd	3rd	Win & Pl
Hurdles	6	0	0	0	0
Career Total	8	0	0	0	0

Going:	Sf: 0-1 GS: 0-2 Gd: 0-2 GF: - Fm: 0-1
Distance:	2m/2m3: 0-3 2m4-2m7: 0-3 3m+: 0-0
Track:	LH: 0-4 RH: 0-2 Tight: 0-0 Gall: 0-1
Aids:	Bl: 0-0 Vi: 0-0 Tstrap: 0-0 Ckp: 0-0
Best Rating:	102 12/02 Wwck 2m soft NHF

Gaye Trigger

98   **95**

6-y-o ch g Karinga Bay-Gaye Memory (Buckskin (FR))
J L Spearing (Miss H C Knight 18/11) Mrs Mercy Rimell

Placings:633   (4868)
2003/04: 17[6]G, 19[3]G, 20[3]GS,

	Starts	1st	2nd	3rd	Win & Pl
Hurdles	3	0	0	2	1239
Career Total	3	0	0	2	1239

Going:	Sf: 0-0 GS: 0-1 Gd: 0-2 GF: - Fm: 0-0
Distance:	2m/2m3: 0-1 2m4-2m7: 0-2 3m+: 0-0
Track:	LH: 0-2 RH: 0-1 Tight: 0-2 Gall: 0-0
Aids:	Bl: 0-0 Vi: 0-0 Tstrap: 0-0 Ckp: 0-0
Best Rating:	95 4/04 Bang 2m4f gd-sft Hdl

From a fine jumping family; has shown ability in novice hurdles; will stay 3m in time.

Gayle Abated (IRE)

105f   **117f**

5-y-o b g Moscow Society (USA)-Hurricane Girl (IRE) (Strong Gale)
W P Mullins Sean Dunne

Placings:10   (4400)
2003/04: 16[1]S, 16[0]G,

	Starts	1st	2nd	3rd	Win & Pl
NH Flat	2	1	0	0	4859
Career Total	2	1	0	0	4859
109 1/04 Fair	2m	NHF		SFT	£4859

Total win prize-money £4859

Going:	Sf: 1-1 GS: 0-0 Gd: 0-1 GF: - Fm: 0-0
Distance:	2m/2m3: 1-2 2m4-2m7: 0-0 3m+: 0-0
Track:	LH: 0-1 RH: 1-1 Tight: 0-0 Gall: 0-0
Aids:	Bl: 0-0 Vi: 0-0 Tstrap: 0-0 Ckp: 0-0
Best Rating:	117 3/04 Chel 2m110y good NHF

Future chasing type; won on debut in soft ground bumper at Fairyhouse in January.

Gazeila

75   **59**

5-y-o b m Makbul-Liberatrice (FR) (Assert)
J J Bridger The Hop-Pickers Partnership

Placings:006-0   (0207)
2003/04: 16[0]GF,

	Starts	1st	2nd	3rd	Win & Pl
Hurdles	1	0	0	0	
Career Total	4	0	0	0	0

Going:	Sf: 0-0 GS: 0-0 Gd: 0-0 GF: - Fm: 0-1
Distance:	2m/2m3: 0-1 2m4-2m7: 0-0 3m+: 0-0
Track:	LH: 0-1 RH: 0-0 Tight: 0-0 Gall: 0-0
Aids:	Bl: 0-0 Vi: 0-0 Tstrap: 0-0 Ckp: 0-0
Best Rating:	59 12/02 Winc 2m gd-sft Hdl

Gazump (FR)

101   **81**

6-y-o b g Iris Noir (FR)-Viva Sacree (FR) (Maiymad)
N A Twiston-Davies H R Mould

Placings:300-0005   (4716)
2003/04: 17[0]G, 19[0]S, 20[P]S, 21[5]G,

	Starts	1st	2nd	3rd	Win & Pl
Hurdles	4	0	0	0	0
Career Total	7	0	0	1	480

Going:	Sf: 0-2 GS: 0-1 Gd: 0-1 GF: - Fm: 0-0
Distance:	2m/2m3: 0-2 2m4-2m7: 0-2 3m+: 0-0
Track:	LH: 0-1 RH: 0-3 Tight: 0-0 Gall: 0-0
Aids:	Bl: 0-0 Vi: 0-0 Tstrap: 0-0 Ckp: 0-0
Best Rating:	95 11/02 Aint 2m1f good NHF

Gebora (FR)

106   **104**

5-y-o ch g Villez (USA)-Sitapanoki (FR) (Houston (FR))
M C Pipe Neil J Edwards

Placings:162-1U24461005064   (4859)
2003/04: 17[1]GF, 17[U]S, 17[2]GF, 16[4]G, 20[4]G, 21[6]G, 19[1]GF, 25[0]G, 18[0]G, 18[0]GS, 19[0]GS, 19[6]G, 19[4]G,

	Starts	1st	2nd	3rd	Win & Pl
Hurdles	13	2	1	0	9990
Career Total	16	3	2	0	13179
104 11/03 Tntn	2m3f110yD(0-120)HHdl		HHdl	G-F	£3809
98 5/03 Extr	2m1f	E Hdl		G-F	£3978
91 2/03 Folk	2m1f110yH	NHF		HVY	£2093

Total win prize-money £9880

Going:	Sf: 0-1 GS: 0-2 Gd: 0-6 GF: - Fm: 2-4
Distance:	2m/2m3: 1-6 2m4-2m7: 1-6 3m+: 0-1
Track:	LH: 0-7 RH: 2-6 Tight: 1-8 Gall: 0-2
Aids:	Bl: 0-0 Vi: 0-5 Tstrap: 0-0 Ckp: 0-0
Best Rating:	106 3/03 Plum 2m2f gd-fm NHF

Modest performer; seems to act on all types of ground; effective at around two and a half miles.

Gee Aker Malayo (IRE)

90   **68**

8-y-o b g Phardante (FR)-Flying Silver (Master Buck)
R T Phillips Darren Bloom & Matthew Miller

Placings:530/4P5   (4512)
2003/04: 24[4]G, 20[P]S, 20[S]GS,

	Starts	1st	2nd	3rd	Win & Pl
Hurdles	3	0	0	0	317
Career Total	6	0	0	1	552

Going:	Sf: 0-1 GS: 0-1 Gd: 0-1 GF: - Fm: 0-0
Distance:	2m/2m3: 0-0 2m4-2m7: 0-2 3m+: 0-1
Track:	LH: 0-2 RH: 0-1 Tight: 0-0 Gall: 0-0
Aids:	Bl: 0-0 Vi: 0-0 Tstrap: 0-0 Ckp: 0-0
Best Rating:	103 3/02 Chep 2m110y soft NHF

Gee Bee Boy

(73c)**55**

10-y-o ch g Beveled (USA)-Blue And White (Busted)
G F Bridgwater Woodnorton Hall - Evesham

Placings:23/361U4PP020/323413106/0U045034600040/00
000-P   (1362)
2003/04: 16PGF,

	Starts	1st	2nd	3rd	Win & Pl
Hurdles	1	0	0	0	
Career Total	41	3	3	6	12620
100 10/00 Strf	2m110y F(0-100)HHdl		SFT	£2310
100 8/00 Worc	2m G Hdl			G-F	£1498
105 6/99 Uttx	2m D Hdl			G-S	£3793

Total win prize-money £7602

Going: Sf: 0-0 GS: 0-0 Gd: 0-0 GF: - Fm: 0-1
Distance: 2m/2m3: 0-1 2m4-2m7: 0-0 3m+: 0-0
Track: LH: 0-1 RH: 0-0 Tight: 0-0 Gall: 0-0
Aids: Bl: 0-0 Vi: 0-0 Tstrap: 0-0 Ckp: 0-0
Best Rating: 105 6/99 Uttx 2m gd-sft Hdl

Gemi Bed (FR)

99(99h)   (85h)**98**

9-y-o b g Double Bed (FR)-Gemia (FR) (King Of Macedon)
G L Moore B Lennard

Placings:6/2003-03014   (4754)
2003/04: 17PG, 163GF, 16PG, 171G, 204G,

	Starts	1st	2nd	3rd	Win & Pl
Hurdles	1	0	0	0	0
Chases	4	1	0	1	3936
Career Total	10	1	1	2	5004
98 3/04 Plum	2m1f F(0-90)HCh			GD	£3318

Total win prize-money £3318

Going: Sf: 0-0 GS: 0-0 Gd: 1-4 GF: - Fm: 0-1
Distance: 2m/2m3: 1-4 2m4-2m7: 0-1 3m+: 0-0
Track: LH: 1-3 RH: 0-2 Tight: 1-4 Gall: 0-0
Aids: Bl: 1-5 Vi: 0-0 Tstrap: 0-0 Ckp: 0-0
Best Rating: 98 3/04 Plum 2m1f good Ch

Moderate chaser/hurdler; French import; wears blinkers;
acts on good.

Gemineye Lord (IRE)

90   82

7-y-o b g Mister Lord (USA)-Mum's Eyes (Al Sirat)
Mrs S J Smith The Kalleys

Placings:00P-P0F6   (3481)
2003/04: 20PGS, 20PHY, 24FGF, 256G,

	Starts	1st	2nd	3rd	Win & Pl
Hurdles	4	0	0	0	0
Career Total	7	0	0	0	0

Going: Sf: 0-1 GS: 0-1 Gd: 0-1 GF: - Fm: 0-1
Distance: 2m/2m3: 0-0 2m4-2m7: 0-2 3m+: 0-2
Track: LH: 0-3 RH: 0-1 Tight: 0-2 Gall: 0-0
Aids: Bl: 0-0 Vi: 0-0 Tstrap: 0-0 Ckp: 0-0
Best Rating: 82 12/03 Sthl 2m110y gd-fm Hdl

Gemini Dancer

91   71+

5-y-o b g Glory Of Dancer-Lamloum (IRE) (Vacarme (USA))
C L Tizzard R G Tizzard

Placings:005   (4893)
2003/04: 16PG, 16PGS, 16PG,

	Starts	1st	2nd	3rd	Win & Pl
NH Flat	2	0	0	0	0
Hurdles	1	0	0	0	0
Career Total	3	0	0	0	0

Going: Sf: 0-0 GS: 0-1 Gd: 0-2 GF: - Fm: 0-0
Distance: 2m/2m3: 0-3 2m4-2m7: 0-0 3m+: 0-0
Track: LH: 0-0 RH: 0-3 Tight: 0-3 Gall: 0-0
Aids: Bl: 0-0 Vi: 0-0 Tstrap: 0-0 Ckp: 0-0
Best Rating: 75 3/04 Winc 2m gd-sft NHF

Gemster

106   59

6-y-o b m Alflora (IRE)-Gemmabel (True Song)
A Hollingsworth Kombined Motor Services Ltd

Placings:00P64   (3904)
2003/04: 16PG, 16PGS, 25FS, 246S, 244GS,

	Starts	1st	2nd	3rd	Win & Pl
NH Flat	1	0	0	0	0
Hurdles	4	0	0	0	0
Career Total	5	0	0	0	0

Going: Sf: 0-2 GS: 0-2 Gd: 0-1 GF: - Fm: 0-0
Distance: 2m/2m3: 0-2 2m4-2m7: 0-0 3m+: 0-3
Track: LH: 0-4 RH: 0-1 Tight: 0-1 Gall: 0-0
Aids: Bl: 0-0 Vi: 0-0 Tstrap: 0-0 Ckp: 0-0
Best Rating: 59 2/04 Tntn 3m110y gd-sft Hdl

General

100(113h)   (116 h)**110**

7-y-o b g Cadeaux Genereux-Bareilly (USA) (Lyphard
(USA))
N P Littmoden (Mrs N Smith 5/3) Nigel Shields

Placings:05/301151/501505-P2424   (3965)
2003/04: 17PS, 162S, 174S, 162HY, 194GS,

	Starts	1st	2nd	3rd	Win & Pl
Chases	5	0	2	0	3554
Career Total	19	4	2	1	17405
123 12/02 Chep	2m110y D(0-120)HHdl		HVY	£3786
123 3/02 Plum	2m E Hdl			G-S	£2457
120 1/02 Leic	2m E Hdl			SFT	£3451
115 12/01 Towc	2m E Hdl			HVY	£3073

Total win prize-money £12767

Going: Sf: 0-4 GS: 0-1 Gd: 0-0 GF: - Fm: 0-0
Distance: 2m/2m3: 0-4 2m4-2m7: 0-1 3m+: 0-0
Track: LH: 0-3 RH: 0-1 Tight: 0-2 Gall: 0-0
Aids: Bl: 0-4 Vi: 0-0 Tstrap: 0-0 Ckp: 0-0
Best Rating: 123 12/02 Chep 2m110y heavy Hdl

Fair chaser; suited by 2m and soft/heavy ground; a little
quirky.

General Claremont (IRE)

11-y-o gr g Strong Gale-Kasam (General Ironside)
P F Nicholls K G Manley

Placings:0/300305/2F1F0/51243/P1224U4/22165U4U-
3242313B   (4626)
2003/04: 243GF, 282GS, 324GF, 242GF, 263GF, 261GF, 253GF,
21BG,

	Starts	1st	2nd	3rd	Win & Pl
Hurdles	2	1	0	1	3182
Chases	6	0	2	2	9573
Career Total	40	5	8	6	56424
107 10/03 Sthl	3m2f E Hdl			G-F	£2562
128 8/02 Worc	2m7H110yC(0-130)HCh		SFT	£8855
126 6/01 NAbb	3m2f110yD(0-120)HCh		GD	£4124
120 11/00 Tntn	3m F(0-105)HCh			GD	£2925
112 1/00 Leic	2m4f110yE Ch			GD	£3042

Total win prize-money £21508

Going: Sf: 0-0 GS: 0-1 Gd: 0-1 GF: - Fm: 1-6
Distance: 2m/2m3: 0-2 2m4-2m7: 0-1 3m+: 1-7
Track: LH: 1-6 RH: 0-0 Tight: 0-4 Gall: 0-0
Aids: Bl: 0-0 Vi: 0-0 Tstrap: 0-0 Ckp: 0-0
Best Rating: 128 9/03 Strf 3m gd-fm Ch

Fair staying chaser; best on good ground or faster, but also
handles cut in the ground; often let down by his jumping;
stays extreme distances.

General Custer (IRE)

(99h)   (80h)

10-y-o b g Buckskin (FR)-Cottage Theme (Brave Invader
(USA))
F M Barton (Evan Williams 7/1) F M Barton

Placings:04523/F2P505/0/F325P   (4888)
2003/04: 25FS, 263GS, 252G, 263G, 244GF,

	Starts	1st	2nd	3rd	Win & Pl
Hurdles	3	0	1	1	1478
Chases	2	0	0	0	0
Career Total	17	0	3	2	4074

Going: Sf: 0-1 GS: 0-1 Gd: 0-2 GF: - Fm: 0-1
Distance: 2m/2m3: 0-0 2m4-2m7: 0-0 3m+: 0-5
Track: LH: 0-2 RH: 0-3 Tight: 0-2 Gall: 0-0
Aids: Bl: 0-0 Vi: 0-0 Tstrap: 0-0 Ckp: 0-0
Best Rating: 103 11/00 Kels 2m6f110y soft Ch

Plating-class novice hurdler; stays well.

General Duroc (IRE)

105   122

8-y-o ch g Un Desperado (FR)-Satula (Deep Run)
R T Phillips Graeme Love

Placings:26/604111-P4310   (4948)
2003/04: 243GS, 204GS, 243G, 241HY, 270GS,

	Starts	1st	2nd	3rd	Win & Pl
Hurdles	5	1	0	1	7095
Career Total	13	4	1	1	21432
118 3/04 Newc	3m D(0-125)HHdl		HVY	£5902
122 3/03 Kels	2m6f110yE Hdl		GD	£4368
109 3/03 Ayr	3m110y D(0-115)HHdl		SFT	£5492
113 2/03 Newc	3m E Hdl			SFT	£3445

Total win prize-money £19208

Going: Sf: 1-1 GS: 0-2 Gd: 0-2 GF: - Fm: 0-0
Distance: 2m/2m3: 0-0 2m4-2m7: 0-1 3m+: 1-4
Track: LH: 1-2 RH: 0-2 Tight: 0-2 Gall: 1-1
Aids: Bl: 0-0 Vi: 0-0 Tstrap: 0-0 Ckp: 0-0
Best Rating: 122 3/03 Kels 2m6f110y good Hdl

Fair but progressive hurdler; stays three miles; completed a
hat trick at the start of 2003 and back to winning ways at
Newcastle in March 2004; acts on any ground; suited by a
thorough test of stamina..

General Gossip (IRE)

100   104+

8-y-o b/br g Supreme Leader-Sno-Sleigh (Bargello)
R T Phillips The Early Birds

Placings:052/FPP-P0U0   (4183)
2003/04: 22²GS, 25¹GS, 24ᵁS, 26⁰G,

	Starts	1st	2nd	3rd	Win & Pl
Hurdles	3	1	1	0	3913
Chases	1	0	0	0	
Career Total	10	1	2	0	5305
104 12/03 Weth	3m1f		F(0-95)HHdl	G-S	£2838
			Total win prize-money £2839

Going:	Sf: 0-1 GS: 1-2 Gd: 0-1 GF: - Fm: 0-0
Distance:	2m/2m3: 0-0 2m4-2m7: 0-1 3m+: 1-3
Track:	LH: 1-2 RH: 0-2 Tight: 0-0 Gall: 0-1
Aids:	Bl: 0-0 Vi: 0-0 Tstrap: 0-0 Ckp: 0-0
Best Rating:	113 2/02 Asct 2m110y soft NHF

Moderate hurdler; messy on chasing debut latest; looks improved since returning from a year off having had a wind operation; stays three miles; suited by good to soft ground; has worn tongue tie.

General Tantrum (IRE)

(81h)   (67h)

7-y-o b g Ilium-Barna Havna (Crash Course)
A Ennis J G M Wates

Placings:P00P-P   (4341)
2003/04: 20ᴾGS,

	Starts	1st	2nd	3rd	Win & Pl
Chases	1	0	0	0	
Career Total	5	0	0	0	

Going:	Sf: 0-0 GS: 0-1 Gd: 0-0 GF: - Fm: 0-0
Distance:	2m/2m3: 0-0 2m4-2m7: 0-1 3m+: 0-0
Track:	LH: 0-1 RH: 0-0 Tight: 0-0 Gall: 0-0
Aids:	Bl: 0-0 Vi: 0-0 Tstrap: 0-0 Ckp: 0-1
Best Rating:	67 12/02 Newb 2m110y good Hdl

General Wolfe

15-y-o ch g Rolfe (USA)-Pillbox (Spartan General)
T W Dennis Mark Gichero

Placings:6/4141/U411/211F2/140/261/1F60P/24B5/521/2-2
            (0457)
2003/04: 23²HY,

	Starts	1st	2nd	3rd	Win & Pl
Chases	1	0	1	0	862
Career Total	34	10	7	0	130362
125 4/02 Prth	3m7f	H Ch		GD	£4186
166 1/99 Hayd	3m	A HCh		SFT	£25300
152 1/98 Hayd	3m	A HCh		SFT	£25408
152 2/97 Hayd	3m	C(0-135)HCh	G-S	£4531
147 2/96 Hayd	3m	C(0-135)HCh	G-S	£4508
127 1/96 Carl	3m	B(0-140)HCh	G-S	£7185
118 3/95 Worc	2m7f	F(0-110)HCh	G-S	£3315
120 1/95 Leic	3m	E(0-110)HCh	G-S	£3522
126 2/94 Folk	2m6f110y	Hdl	HVY	£1896
106 12/93 Towc	2m5f	Hdl	SFT	£2041
			Total win prize-money £81895

Going:	Sf: 0-1 GS: 0-0 Gd: 0-0 GF: - Fm: 0-0
Distance:	2m/2m3: 0-0 2m4-2m7: 0-1 3m+: 0-0
Track:	LH: 0-1 RH: 0-0 Tight: 0-0 Gall: 0-0

Aids:	Bl: 0-0 Vi: 0-0 Tstrap: 0-0 Ckp: 0-0
Best Rating:	166 1/99 Hayd 3m soft Ch

Very useful staying chaser at his best but now in the veteran stage; very lightly raced in recent years and now competes in hunter chases, runner-up in the Foxhunters' at Aintree in April 2003; best when fresh; stays extreme distances; suited by an easy surface.

Generosity

94   90

9-y-o ch h Generous (IRE)-Pageantry (Welsh Pageant)
Dr P Pritchard Steven R Hanney

Placings:0/30   (0628)
2003/04: 16³GS, 16⁰GF,

	Starts	1st	2nd	3rd	Win & Pl
Hurdles	2	0	0	1	742
Career Total	3	0	0	1	742

Going:	Sf: 0-0 GS: 0-1 Gd: 0-0 GF: - Fm: 0-1
Distance:	2m/2m3: 0-2 2m4-2m7: 0-1 3m+: 0-0
Track:	LH: 0-2 RH: 0-0 Tight: 0-1 Gall: 0-0
Aids:	Bl: 0-0 Vi: 0-0 Tstrap: 0-0 Ckp: 0-0
Best Rating:	90 5/03 Aint 2m110y gd-sft Hdl

One-time decent stayer on the Flat; third in weak novice hurdle May 2003 after lengthy absence.

Generous Ways

101(102c)   (79c)93

9-y-o ch g Generous (IRE)-Clara Bow (USA) (Coastal (USA))
R Lee Mrs C Lee

Placings:PP021-PP0300030   (4523)
2003/04: 16ᴾGF, 17ᴾG, 16⁰G, 16³GF, 16⁰G, 16⁰G, 17⁰G, 17⁰GS,

	Starts	1st	2nd	3rd	Win & Pl
Hurdles	7	0	0	2	1249
Chases	2	0	0	0	0
Career Total	14	1	1	2	6487
93 4/03 Extr	2m1f	E(0-105)HHdl	G-F	£3718
			Total win prize-money £3718

Going:	Sf: 0-0 GS: 0-0 Gd: 0-6 GF: - Fm: 0-2
Distance:	2m/2m3: 0-9 2m4-2m7: 0-0 3m+: 0-0
Track:	LH: 0-2 RH: 0-7 Tight: 0-0 Gall: 0-0
Aids:	Bl: 0-0 Vi: 0-0 Tstrap: 0-9 Ckp: 0-0
Best Rating:	93 4/03 Extr 2m1f gd-fm Hdl

Plating-class hurdler; staying handicapper on the Flat; improved form to win extended two mile novices' handicap on fast ground at Exeter April 2003; well held since.

Genscher

(92h)   (95h)81

8-y-o b g Cadeaux Genereux-Marienbad (FR) (Darshaan)
R Allan Robert Miller-Bakewell

Placings:145P44/3S/04144605/0FPPFP0   (4688)
2003/04: 18⁰G, 17⁰S, 20ᴾGF, 16ᴾGF, 16ᴾG, 22ᴾGS, 16⁰G,

	Starts	1st	2nd	3rd	Win & Pl
Hurdles	3	0	0	0	0
Chases	4	0	0	0	0
Career Total	23	2	0	1	7448
95 6/01 Prth	2m110y	E(0-115)HHdl	G-F	£4225
84 11/99 Ayr	2m	E Hdl	GD	£2355
			Total win prize-money £6580

Going:	Sf: 0-1 GS: 0-1 Gd: 0-3 GF: - Fm: 0-2
Distance:	2m/2m3: 0-5 2m4-2m7: 0-2 3m+: 0-0

Track:	LH: 0-4 RH: 0-3 Tight: 0-7 Gall: 0-0
Aids:	Bl: 0-0 Vi: 0-0 Tstrap: 0-3 Ckp: 0-1
Best Rating:	95 6/01 Prth 2m110y gd-fm Hdl

Gentle Beau

101   113+

6-y-o b g Homo Sapien-Tapua Taranata (IRE) (Mandalus)
P J Hobbs Rod Hamilton

Placings:24-2F6615   (4243)
2003/04: 17⁴S, 17²GF, 17ᶠG, 21⁶S, 16⁶S, 16¹G, 19⁵G,

	Starts	1st	2nd	3rd	Win & Pl
NH Flat	2	0	1	0	684
Hurdles	5	1	0	0	3552
Career Total	8	1	2	0	4824
101 2/04 Ludl	2m	E Hdl	GD	£3552
			Total win prize-money £3552

Going:	Sf: 0-3 GS: 0-0 Gd: 1-3 GF: - Fm: 0-1
Distance:	2m/2m3: 1-6 2m4-2m7: 0-1 3m+: 0-0
Track:	LH: 0-2 RH: 1-5 Tight: 0-2 Gall: 0-0
Aids:	Bl: 0-0 Vi: 0-0 Tstrap: 0-0 Ckp: 0-0
Best Rating:	113 11/03 Extr 2m1f good Hdl

Modest novice hurdler; placed in all three starts in bumpers; seems effective on all ground; should stay further than two miles.

Genuine Article (IRE)

96   106

8-y-o ch g Insan (USA)-Rosemount Rose (Ashmore (FR))
M Pitman Malcolm C Denmark

Placings:10/34400/3311/21UPF   (3602)
2003/04: 17²GF, 19¹GF, 19ᵁS, 20ᴾG, 19ᶠS,

	Starts	1st	2nd	3rd	Win & Pl
Chases	5	1	1	0	7036
Career Total	16	4	1	3	16633
106 11/03 Asct	2m3f110yD Ch		G-F	£5796
106 7/01 Strf	2m110y	D(0-125)HHdl	G-F	£3393
104 7/01 Strf	2m110y	E(0-105)HHdl	G-F	£2471
91 2/00 Wrwck	2m	H NHF	SFT	£1956
			Total win prize-money £13617

Going:	Sf: 0-2 GS: 0-0 Gd: 0-1 GF: - Fm: 1-2
Distance:	2m/2m3: 0-2 2m4-2m7: 1-3 3m+: 0-0
Track:	LH: 0-2 RH: 1-3 Tight: 0-1 Gall: 0-0
Aids:	Bl: 0-0 Vi: 0-0 Tstrap: 0-0 Ckp: 0-0
Best Rating:	106 11/03 Asct 2m3f110y gd-fm Ch

Novice chaser; lightly raced; wide-margin winner at Ascot November 2003; failed to complete next three starts; stays 2m 4f; acts on fast ground.

Geography (IRE)

81   69

4-y-o ch g Definite Article-Classic Ring (IRE) (Auction Ring (USA))
P Butler (P F I Cole 4/7) Homewoodgate Racing Club

Placings:4660   (2205)
2003/04: 16⁴GS, 16⁶F, 16⁶GF, 17⁰G,

	Starts	1st	2nd	3rd	Win & Pl
Hurdles	4	0	0	0	265
Career Total	4	0	0	0	265

Going:	Sf: 0-0 GS: 0-0 Gd: 0-1 GF: - Fm: 0-3
Distance:	2m/2m3: 0-4 2m4-2m7: 0-0 3m+: 0-0
Track:	LH: 0-1 RH: 0-3 Tight: 0-2 Gall: 0-1

Aids: Bl: 0-0 Vi: 0-2 Tstrap: 0-1 Ckp: 0-2
Best Rating: 69 10/03 Towc 2m   firm   Hdl

Moderate juvenile hurdler; modest maiden on the Flat, often in cheekpieces.

Geordies Express

12-y-o b g Tina's Pet-Maestroes Beauty (Music Maestro)
G T Bewley G T Bewley

Placings:5/33U261/5PU1-44U20   (4689)
2003/04: 22⁴S, 24⁴F, 26ᵁG, 25ⁿG,

	Starts	1st	2nd	3rd	Win & Pl
Chases	5	0	1	0	1350
Career Total	16	2	2	2	7954
113 4/03 Kels 3m1f H Ch				GD	£3038
99 4/02 Kels 3m1f H Ch				G-F	£2587
				Total win prize-money	£5625

Going: Sf: 0-1 GS: 0-0 Gd: 0-3 GF: - Fm: 0-1
Distance: 2m/2m3: 0-0 2m4-2m7: 0-1 3m+: 0-4
Track: LH: 0-4 RH: 0-1 Tight: 0-3 Gall: 0-1
Aids: Bl: 0-0 Vi: 0-0 Tstrap: 0-0 Ckp: 0-0
Best Rating: 113 4/03 Kels 3m1f   good   Ch

Fair hunter chaser/pointer; not the greatest of jumpers; stays three miles one; suited by a sound surface, although has won on softer.

George Blest
81f   71f

6-y-o ch g Safawan-Praise The Lord (Lord Gayle (USA))
P Winkworth Miss Katie Powell

Placings:00   (3861)
2003/04: 18ᵁHY, 18ᵁS,

	Starts	1st	2nd	3rd	Win & Pl
NH Flat	2	0	0	0	
Career Total	2	0	0	0	

Going: Sf: 0-2 GS: 0-0 Gd: 0-0 GF: - Fm: 0-0
Distance: 2m/2m3: 0-2 2m4-2m7: 0-0 3m+: 0-0
Track: LH: 0-2 RH: 0-0 Tight: 0-1 Gall: 0-0
Aids: Bl: 0-0 Vi: 0-0 Tstrap: 0-0 Ckp: 0-0
Best Rating: 71 2/04 Plum 2m2f   soft   NHF

George Romney (USA)

5-y-o b g Distant View (USA)-Polish Socialite (USA) (Polish Navy (USA))
Miss L J Sheen Mrs P J Sheen

Placings:0   (4097)
2003/04: 16⁰G,

	Starts	1st	2nd	3rd	Win & Pl
Hurdles	1	0	0	0	
Career Total	1	0	0	0	

Going: Sf: 0-0 GS: 0-0 Gd: 0-1 GF: - Fm: 0-0
Distance: 2m/2m3: 0-1 2m4-2m7: 0-0 3m+: 0-0
Track: LH: 0-1 RH: 0-0 Tight: 0-1 Gall: 0-0
Aids: Bl: 0-0 Vi: 0-0 Tstrap: 0-1 Ckp: 0-0

George Street (IRE)

6-y-o b g Danehill (USA)-Sweet Justice (Law Society (USA))

M C Pipe W F Frewen & M C Pipe

Placings:0P0P-0   (1077)
2003/04: 20⁰GF,

	Starts	1st	2nd	3rd	Win & Pl
Hurdles	1	0	0	0	
Career Total	5	0	0	0	

Going: Sf: 0-0 GS: 0-0 Gd: 0-0 GF: - Fm: 0-1
Distance: 2m/2m3: 0-0 2m4-2m7: 0-0 3m+: 0-0
Track: LH: 0-1 RH: 0-0 Tight: 0-0 Gall: 0-0
Aids: Bl: 0-0 Vi: 0-0 Tstrap: 0-0 Ckp: 0-0

Georgias Gift

9-y-o b g Genuine Gift (CAN)-Georgias Fancy (Montreal Boy)
A M Crow A M Crow

Placings:P-PP   (4275)
2003/04: 16ᴾG, 20ᴾG,

	Starts	1st	2nd	3rd	Win & Pl
Hurdles	2	0	0	0	
Career Total	3	0	0	0	

Going: Sf: 0-0 GS: 0-0 Gd: 0-0 GF: - Fm: 0-1
Distance: 2m/2m3: 0-1 2m4-2m7: 0-1 3m+: 0-0
Track: LH: 0-0 RH: 0-2 Tight: 0-1 Gall: 0-0
Aids: Bl: 0-0 Vi: 0-0 Tstrap: 0-1 Ckp: 0-0

Georgic Blaze
95   (0c)69

10-y-o b g Petoski-Pooka (Dominion)
G A Ham E Simmons

Placings:60P/000/P1PU0U0F/U000U3-24   (0152)
2003/04: 20²S, 20⁴GF,

	Starts	1st	2nd	3rd	Win & Pl
Hurdles	2	0	1	0	726
Career Total	22	1	1	1	3455
91 11/01 NAbb 2m1f			G Hdl	SFT	£2289
				Total win prize-money	£2289

Going: Sf: 0-1 GS: 0-0 Gd: 0-0 GF: - Fm: 0-1
Distance: 2m/2m3: 0-0 2m4-2m7: 0-2 3m+: 0-0
Track: LH: 0-2 RH: 0-0 Tight: 0-0 Gall: 0-0
Aids: Bl: 0-0 Vi: 0-0 Tstrap: 0-0 Ckp: 0-0
Best Rating: 91 11/01 NAbb 2m1f   soft   Hdl

Plating-class hurdler; runner-up in the mud at Uttoxeter in April 2003; ran well on ground faster than he prefers at Chepstow next time.

Geos (FR)
123(112c)   (159c)162

9-y-o b/br g Pistolet Bleu (IRE)-Kaprika (FR) (Cadoudal (FR))
N J Henderson Thurloe Finsbury

Placings:12111/063132102/31132/264P/3312405-21P0   (4954)
2003/04: 16²G, 16¹G, 16ᴾG, 16⁰G,

	Starts	1st	2nd	3rd	Win & Pl
Hurdles	4	1	1	0	82400
Career Total	34	10	7	6	383812
156 2/04 Newb 2m110y A HHdl				GD	£72500
159 12/02 Weth 2m A Ch				HVY	£26800
154 12/00 Kemp 2m A Hdl				G-S	£29000
167 12/00 Chel 2m1f A Hdl				SFT	£24000
164 2/00 Newb 2m110y A HHdl				G-S	£58000
135 11/99 Leic 2m C(0-130)HHdl				G-S	£7200
3/99 Lyrh 2m1f Ch				HLD	£4306
12/98 Engh 2m1f110y Hdl				HLD	£11111
12/98 Engh 2m1f110y Hdl				VS	£10101
6/98 Vitr 1m7f Hdl				SFT	£2626
				Total win prize-money	£245644

Going: Sf: 0-0 GS: 0-0 Gd: 1-4 GF: - Fm: 0-0
Distance: 2m/2m3: 1-4 2m4-2m7: 0-0 3m+: 0-0
Track: LH: 1-3 RH: 0-1 Tight: 0-0 Gall: 1-2
Aids: Bl: 0-0 Vi: 0-0 Tstrap: 0-0 Ckp: 0-0
Best Rating: 167 4/01 Sand 2m110y   soft   Hdl

High-class hurdler/chaser; good fourth in the 2003 Champion Chase; beat Rooster Booster to land Tote Gold Trophy at Newbury in 2004, a race he also won in 2000; pulled up in Champion Hurdle; best at two miles, but effective at further; has good form on heavy ground, but reportedly prefers a sound surface.

Geraldo (IRE)
87

7-y-o b g Lycius (USA)-Floralia (Auction Ring (USA))
Noel T Chance (Sean Gannon 26/5) Mrs M Chance

Placings:000/0P/0P40-P0PP   (0946)
2003/04: 24ᴾG, 25⁰YS, 17ᴾG, 23ᴾG,

	Starts	1st	2nd	3rd	Win & Pl
Hurdles	1	0	0	0	0
Chases	3	0	0	0	0
Career Total	13	0	0	0	208

Going: Sf: 0-0 GS: 0-0 Gd: 0-3 GF: - Fm: 0-0
Distance: 2m/2m3: 0-1 2m4-2m7: 0-0 3m+: 0-3
Track: LH: 0-1 RH: 0-1 Tight: 0-1 Gall: 0-0
Aids: Bl: 0-0 Vi: 0-0 Tstrap: 0-0 Ckp: 0-0
Best Rating: 89 12/00 Fair 2m   soft   Hdl

Geri Roulette
103   96+

6-y-o b m Perpendicular-Clashfern (Smackover)
M Todhunter (E J Alston 21/11) Ellison Racing

Placings:0P1PU   (4727)
2003/04: 16⁰GS, 21ᴾGS, 16¹HY, 20ᴾGS, 17ᵁG,

	Starts	1st	2nd	3rd	Win & Pl
Hurdles	5	1	0	0	3484
Career Total	5	1	0	0	3484
96 1/04 Newc 2m		E Hdl		HVY	£3484
				Total win prize-money	£3484

Going: Sf: 1-1 GS: 0-3 Gd: 0-1 GF: - Fm: 0-0
Distance: 2m/2m3: 1-3 2m4-2m7: 0-2 3m+: 0-0
Track: LH: 1-4 RH: 0-1 Tight: 0-1 Gall: 1-1
Aids: Bl: 0-0 Vi: 0-0 Tstrap: 0-0 Ckp: 0-0
Best Rating: 96 1/04 Newc 2m   heavy   Hdl

Surprise winner of novice hurdle at Newcastle in January but failed by long chalk to reproduce that at Ayr following month when upped to two and a half miles (beaten before stamina became an issue); acts in testing ground.

Gerrard (IRE)
84   61

6-y-o b g Jurado (USA)-Vienna Waltz (IRE) (Orchestra)
Mrs A Barclay Mrs Althea Barclay

Placings:004P0   (4560)
2003/04: 16⁰GS, 16⁰GS, 17⁴GS, 21ᴾG, 21⁰GS,

	Starts	1st	2nd	3rd	Win & Pl
NH Flat	3	0	0	0	

Hurdles	2	0	0	0	0
Career Total	5	0	0	0	0

Going:	Sf: 0-0 GS: 0-4 Gd: 0-1 GF: - Fm: 0-0
Distance:	2m/2m3: 0-3 2m4-2m7: 0-2 3m+: 0-0
Track:	LH: 0-2 RH: 0-3 Tight: 0-0 Gall: 0-3
Aids:	Bl: 0-0 Vi: 0-0 Tstrap: 0-0 Ckp: 0-3
Best Rating:	89 1/04 Extr 2m1f gd-sft NHF

Get The Point

103   102+

10-y-o b g Sadler's Wells (USA)-Tolmi (Great Nephew)
G Brown (R M Stronge 5/5) M D Killick

Placings:631P01335/6610016664/046/2056-P15312 (4957)
2003/04: 16⁶GF, 161GS, 16⁵G, 223HY, 21¹S, 172GS,

	Starts	1st	2nd	3rd	Win & Pl
Chases	6	2	1	1	8101
Career Total	32	6	2	4	26748
102 1/04	Folk	2m5f	F(0-95)HCh	SFT	£3493
95 11/03	Towc	2m110y	E(0-105)HCh	SFT	£2905
125 2/00	Donc	2m110y	C(0-135)HHdl	GD	£6955
120 1/00	Leic	2m	F(0-110)HHdl	SFT	£2422
122 3/99	Towc	2m	D(0-120)HHdl	SFT	£2784
118 2/99	Towc	2m	E Hdl	SFT	£2512
			Total win prize-money £21074		

Going:	Sf: 1-2 GS: 1-2 Gd: 0-1 GF: - Fm: 0-1
Distance:	2m/2m3: 1-4 2m4-2m7: 1-2 3m+: 0-0
Track:	LH: 0-0 RH: 2-5 Tight: 1-4 Gall: 0-1
Aids:	Bl: 0-0 Vi: 0-0 Tstrap: 0-1 Ckp: 1-2
Best Rating:	125 2/00 Donc 2m110y good Hdl

Very modest handicap chaser; stays two miles five; acts on soft ground; has worn cheekpieces.

Get Up And Go Go (IRE)

86   91

7-y-o ch g Mister Lord (USA)-Monadante (IRE) (Phardante (FR))
K C Bailey Graham And Alison Jelley

Placings:0-0 (4783)
2003/04: 210G,

	Starts	1st	2nd	3rd	Win & Pl
Hurdles	1	0	0	0	
Career Total	2	0	0	0	

Going:	Sf: 0-0 GS: 0-0 Gd: 0-1 GF: - Fm: 0-0
Distance:	2m/2m3: 0-0 2m4-2m7: 0-1 3m+: 0-0
Track:	LH: 0-0 RH: 0-1 Tight: 0-0 Gall: 0-1
Aids:	Bl: 0-0 Vi: 0-0 Tstrap: 0-0 Ckp: 0-0
Best Rating:	91 4/04 Hntg 2m5f110y good Hdl

Getaway Girl

6-y-o b m Perpendicular-Viowen (IRE) (Denel (FR))
O Brennan Mrs Pat Brennan

Placings:0 (4780)
2003/04: 16⁰S,

	Starts	1st	2nd	3rd	Win & Pl
NH Flat	1	0	0	0	
Career Total	1	0	0	0	

Going:	Sf: 0-1 GS: 0-0 Gd: 0-0 GF: - Fm: 0-0

Distance:	2m/2m3: 0-1 2m4-2m7: 0-0 3m+: 0-0
Track:	LH: 0-1 RH: 0-0 Tight: 0-0 Gall: 0-0
Aids:	Bl: 0-0 Vi: 0-0 Tstrap: 0-0 Ckp: 0-0

Getinbybutonlyjust

85   71

5-y-o b g King's Ride-Madame President (IRE) (Supreme Leader)
Mrs Dianne Sayer Andrew Sayer

Placings:660 (3664)
2003/04: 16⁶G, 20⁶S, 20⁰HY,

	Starts	1st	2nd	3rd	Win & Pl
NH Flat	1	0	0	0	0
Hurdles	2	0	0	0	0
Career Total	3	0	0	0	0

Going:	Sf: 0-2 GS: 0-0 Gd: 0-1 GF: - Fm: 0-0
Distance:	2m/2m3: 0-1 2m4-2m7: 0-2 3m+: 0-0
Track:	LH: 0-3 RH: 0-0 Tight: 0-0 Gall: 0-1
Aids:	Bl: 0-0 Vi: 0-0 Tstrap: 0-0 Ckp: 0-0
Best Rating:	70 12/03 Ayr 2m4f soft Hdl

Ghadames (FR)

102(87h)   (107+h)114

10-y-o b g Synefos (USA)-Ouargla (FR) (Armos)
M Todhunter (W M Brisbourne 18/6) Mrs J Mandle

Placings:50/0P12/6152/11/1F0P-62PF15 (3772)
2003/04: 20⁵GF, 21²G, 20⁰GF, 20⁰GF, 20¹HY, 175HY,

	Starts	1st	2nd	3rd	Win & Pl
Hurdles	2	1	0	0	2366
Chases	4	0	1	0	978
Career Total	22	6	3	0	21959
107 1/04	Newc	2m4f	G(0-95)HHdl	HVY	£2366
120 5/02	Sthl	2m4f110y	E(0-110)HCh	G-S	£4202
120 8/01	Bang	2m4f110y	F(0-105)HCh	GD	£2996
108 5/01	Hexm	2m4f110y	F(0-105)HCh	FRM	£2814
112 10/00	Ludl	2m5f	E(0-105)HHdl	G-F	£2695
92 3/00	Bang	2m1f110y	D Ch	GD	£3867
			Total win prize-money £18942		

Going:	Sf: 1-2 GS: 0-0 Gd: 0-1 GF: - Fm: 0-3
Distance:	2m/2m3: 0-1 2m4-2m7: 1-5 3m+: 0-0
Track:	LH: 1-4 RH: 0-2 Tight: 0-2 Gall: 1-1
Aids:	Bl: 0-0 Vi: 0-0 Tstrap: 0-0 Ckp: 0-0
Best Rating:	120 5/02 Sthl 2m4f110y gd-sft Ch

Modest chaser/plating-class hurdler; effective at two and a half miles; appears to act on most types of ground; needs a decent pace.

Ghost Moon

76

9-y-o b g Cadeaux Genereux-Sickle Moon (Shirley Heights)
R J Hodges Mrs J B Jenkins

Placings:30/F02/PP00/0/0525FU00-U (0589)
2003/04: 20⁰GF,

	Starts	1st	2nd	3rd	Win & Pl
Chases	1	0	0	0	
Career Total	19	0	2	1	2296

Going:	Sf: 0-0 GS: 0-0 Gd: 0-0 GF: - Fm: 0-1
Distance:	2m/2m3: 0-0 2m4-2m7: 0-1 3m+: 0-0
Track:	LH: 0-1 RH: 0-0 Tight: 0-0 Gall: 0-0
Aids:	Bl: 0-0 Vi: 0-0 Tstrap: 0-0 Ckp: 0-0
Best Rating:	79 1/99 MRas 1m5f110y soft NHF

Ghost Rider (IRE)

97   101

7-y-o br g Good Thyne (USA)-Pit Runner (Deep Run)
L Lungo The Border Reivers

Placings:40420 (3935)
2003/04: 16⁴G, 20⁵S, 18⁴S, 16⁹HY, 16⁹GS,

	Starts	1st	2nd	3rd	Win & Pl
NH Flat	1	0	0	0	
Hurdles	4	0	1	0	1468
Career Total	5	0	1	0	1468

Going:	Sf: 0-3 GS: 0-1 Gd: 0-1 GF: - Fm: 0-0
Distance:	2m/2m3: 0-4 2m4-2m7: 0-1 3m+: 0-0
Track:	LH: 0-4 RH: 0-1 Tight: 0-2 Gall: 0-1
Aids:	Bl: 0-0 Vi: 0-0 Tstrap: 0-0 Ckp: 0-0
Best Rating:	101 2/04 Kels 2m110y heavy Hdl

Ghutah

97(107c)   (94c)69

10-y-o ch g Lycius (USA)-Barada (USA) (Damascus (USA))
Mrs A M Thorpe Three A's Caravans

Placings:0F0PP/U23046P/6F1115450433/515P46F0134F-44FP550 (1081)
2003/04: 16⁴GF, 16⁴GF, 16⁶G, 175G, 16⁵GF, 16⁹GF,

	Starts	1st	2nd	3rd	Win & Pl
Hurdles	3	0	0	0	0
Chases	3	0	0	0	565
Career Total	42	5	1	4	15501
95 10/02	Extr	2m1f	G(0-95)HHdl	FRM	£2324
100 6/02	Hntg	2m110y	E(0-105)HCh	G-F	£3248
88 9/01	Sedg	2m1f	G(0-95)HHdl	G-F	£2033
83 8/01	Uttx	2m	G(0-95)HHdl	G-F	£2009
83 8/01	Sedg	2m1f	G(0-90)HHdl	G-F	£1981
			Total win prize-money £11596		

Going:	Sf: 0-0 GS: 0-0 Gd: 0-2 GF: - Fm: 0-4
Distance:	2m/2m3: 0-6 2m4-2m7: 0-0 3m+: 0-0
Track:	LH: 0-4 RH: 0-2 Tight: 0-1 Gall: 0-2
Aids:	Bl: 0-0 Vi: 0-0 Tstrap: 0-0 Ckp: 0-0
Best Rating:	100 6/02 Hntg 2m110y gd-fm Ch

Easily won handicap chase at Huntingdon June 2002. Useful selling plater over hurdles. At his best when held up. Acts on fast ground.

Gideon Putnam (IRE)

98   87+

6-y-o b/br g Good Thyne (USA)-Penthouse Pearl (Green Shoon)
Jonjo O'Neill Mrs Susan Granger

Placings:12654 (2993)
2003/04: 16¹GS, 16²GS, 24⁶GF, 20⁵GS, 20⁴GS,

	Starts	1st	2nd	3rd	Win & Pl
NH Flat	2	1	1	0	2656
Hurdles	3	0	0	0	274
Career Total	5	1	1	0	2930
91 10/03	Chep	2m110y	H NHF	G-F	£1526
			Total win prize-money £1526		

Going:	Sf: 0-0 GS: 0-2 Gd: 0-0 GF: - Fm: 1-3
Distance:	2m/2m3: 1-2 2m4-2m7: 0-2 3m+: 1-0
Track:	LH: 1-4 RH: 0-1 Tight: 0-1 Gall: 0-0
Aids:	Bl: 0-0 Vi: 0-0 Tstrap: 0-0 Ckp: 0-0
Best Rating:	114 10/03 Chel 2m110y gd-fm NHF

All out to win 6-runner fast ground Chepstow bumper in

October on debut; jumped poorly on first try over hurdles but shaped better second start at Uttoxeter in December; considered a stayer.

Gielgud

99(104h)   (100+h)**113**
7-y-o b g Faustus (USA)-Shirl (Shirley Heights)
P R Webber Mrs J K Powell

Placings:20632/0002-132P3PFP   (4385)
2003/04: 20¹GF, 21³GF, 22²GF, 24²PGS, 20³G, 24²PG, 22²FG, 24²PG,

	Starts	1st	2nd	3rd	Win & Pl
Hurdles	2	1	0	1	6257
Chases	6	0	1	1	3408
Career Total	17	1	4	3	12927
98	5/03	Weth	2m4f110yD Hdl	G-F	£5425

Total win prize-money £5425

Going:	Sf: 0-0 GS: 0-1 Gd: 0-4 GF: - Fm: 1-3
Distance:	2m/2m3: 0-1 2m4-2m7: 1-5 3m+: 0-3
Track:	LH: 1-7 RH: 0-1 Tight: 0-0 Gall: 0-4
Aids:	Bl: 0-0 Vi: 0-0 Tstrap: 1-7 Ckp: 0-0
Best Rating:	113 12/03 Kemp 2m4f110y good Ch

Modest novice chaser; stays two miles six; acts on fast ground; usually wears a tongue strap.

Giftneyev (FR)

85
5-y-o b/br g Goldneyev (USA)-Girl's Gift (FR) (Gairloch)
C P Morlock Pell-Mell Partners

Placings:5-F   (0123)
2003/04: 18⁶G,

	Starts	1st	2nd	3rd	Win & Pl
Hurdles	1	0	0	0	
Career Total	2	0	0	0	0

Going:	Sf: 0-0 GS: 0-0 Gd: 0-1 GF: - Fm: 0-0
Distance:	2m/2m3: 0-1 2m4-2m7: 0-0 3m+: 0-0
Track:	LH: 0-1 RH: 0-0 Tight: 0-1 Gall: 0-0
Aids:	Bl: 0-0 Vi: 0-0 Tstrap: 0-1 Ckp: 0-0
Best Rating:	86 5/03 Font 2m2f110y good Hdl

Gigs Bounty

100   **111+**
6-y-o ch g Weld-City's Sister (Maystreak)
M Pitman J Barson

Placings:44-61120   (2717)
2003/04: 16⁶G, 16¹GF, 21¹G, 20²G, 21⁰GS,

	Starts	1st	2nd	3rd	Win & Pl
NH Flat	1	0	0	0	
Hurdles	4	2	1	0	7234
Career Total	7	2	1	0	7234
111	11/03	Plum	2m5f	E Hdl	GD	£3136
95	10/03	Uttx	2m	E Hdl	G-F	£3332

Total win prize-money £6468

Going:	Sf: 0-0 GS: 0-1 Gd: 1-3 GF: - Fm: 1-1
Distance:	2m/2m3: 1-2 2m4-2m7: 1-3 3m+: 0-0
Track:	LH: 2-5 RH: 0-0 Tight: 1-1 Gall: 0-1
Aids:	Bl: 0-0 Vi: 0-0 Tstrap: 0-0 Ckp: 0-0
Best Rating:	111 11/03 Chep 2m4f good Hdl

Fair novice hurdler; half-brother to Better Times Ahead; stays 2m5f; acts on good ground or faster.

Gigs Gambit (IRE)

110(94h)   (92h)**106**
7-y-o ch g Hubbly Bubbly (USA)-Music Slipper (Orchestra)
M Pitman J Barson

Placings:350/255F-113PP   (3100)
2003/04: 26¹GF, 22¹G, 26³GF, 24²G, 26²PG,

	Starts	1st	2nd	3rd	Win & Pl
Chases	5	2	0	1	7047
Career Total	12	2	1	2	8549
107	10/03	Font	2m6f	F(0-95)HCh	GD	£3029
105	9/03	Font	3m2f110yE(0-105)HCh	G-F	£3290

Total win prize-money £6319

Going:	Sf: 0-0 GS: 0-0 Gd: 1-3 GF: - Fm: 1-2
Distance:	2m/2m3: 0-0 2m4-2m7: 1-1 3m+: 1-4
Track:	LH: 0-1 RH: 0-1 Tight: 2-4 Gall: 0-0
Aids:	Bl: 0-0 Vi: 0-0 Tstrap: 0-0 Ckp: 0-1
Best Rating:	107 10/03 Font 2m6f good Ch

Fair novice chaser; won back-to-back races at Fontwell in the autumn of 2003; stays beyond three miles, but also effective over shorter; acts on good ground.

Gilbert White

93   **73**
11-y-o ch g Little Wolf-Caribs Love (Caliban)
R Lee Mrs G Rowan-Hamilton

Placings:4P/P3/0/00F/4P5-6P   (0676)
2003/04: 16⁶GF, 16²PG,

	Starts	1st	2nd	3rd	Win & Pl
Hurdles	2	0	0	0	0
Career Total	13	0	0	1	772

Going:	Sf: 0-0 GS: 0-0 Gd: 0-0 GF: - Fm: 0-2
Distance:	2m/2m3: 0-2 2m4-2m7: 0-0 3m+: 0-0
Track:	LH: 0-1 RH: 0-1 Tight: 0-0 Gall: 0-1
Aids:	Bl: 0-0 Vi: 0-0 Tstrap: 0-0 Ckp: 0-0
Best Rating:	99 3/99 Chep 2m110y gd-sft NHF

Poor selling hurdler; lightly raced in recent seasons.

Gilded Ally

81f   **62f**
4-y-o b g Gildoran-Allyfair (Scallywag)
Mrs S Gardner Graham Brown

Placings:00   (4636)
2003/04: 16⁶G, 17⁰G,

	Starts	1st	2nd	3rd	Win & Pl
NH Flat	2	0	0	0	
Career Total	2	0	0	0	

Going:	Sf: 0-0 GS: 0-0 Gd: 0-2 GF: - Fm: 0-0
Distance:	2m/2m3: 0-2 2m4-2m7: 0-0 3m+: 0-0
Track:	LH: 0-0 RH: 0-1 Tight: 0-0 Gall: 0-0
Aids:	Bl: 0-0 Vi: 0-0 Tstrap: 0-0 Ckp: 0-0
Best Rating:	62 3/04 Winc 2m good NHF

Gilfoot Breeze (IRE)

99   **83**
7-y-o b g Forest Wind (USA)-Ma Bella Luna (Jalmood (USA))
A Robson A Robson

Placings:3006/0600/4543-3534233   (3435)
2003/04: 16³GF, 16³G, 17⁵G, 16³GF, 17⁴G, 18²S, 16³GS, 20³HY,

	Starts	1st	2nd	3rd	Win & Pl
Hurdles	8	0	1	5	2725

Career Total	19	0	1	6	3815

Going:	Sf: 0-2 GS: 0-1 Gd: 0-3 GF: - Fm: 0-2
Distance:	2m/2m3: 0-7 2m4-2m7: 0-1 3m+: 0-0
Track:	LH: 0-7 RH: 0-0 Tight: 0-3 Gall: 0-3
Aids:	Bl: 0-0 Vi: 0-0 Tstrap: 0-1 Ckp: 0-0
Best Rating:	86 11/00 MRas 2m1f110y soft Hdl

Plating-class hurdler; yet to prove he stays two and a half miles; acts on any ground.

Gill The Till (IRE)

88   **52**
5-y-o ch m Anshan-Bilander (High Line)
R J Baker Graham Brown

Placings:5F500-05   (1957)
2003/04: 22²GF, 22⁵G,

	Starts	1st	2nd	3rd	Win & Pl
Hurdles	2	0	0	0	0
Career Total	7	0	0	0	0

Going:	Sf: 0-0 GS: 0-0 Gd: 0-1 GF: - Fm: 0-1
Distance:	2m/2m3: 0-0 2m4-2m7: 0-2 3m+: 0-0
Track:	LH: 0-2 RH: 0-0 Tight: 0-2 Gall: 0-0
Aids:	Bl: 0-0 Vi: 0-0 Tstrap: 0-0 Ckp: 0-0
Best Rating:	58 11/03 NAbb 2m6f good Hdl

Gillespie (IRE)

5-y-o b g Persian Bold-Share The Vision (Vision (USA))
D G Bridgwater The Rule Racing Syndicate

Placings:055   (1572)
2003/04: 16⁹GF, 17⁵GF, 21⁵F,

	Starts	1st	2nd	3rd	Win & Pl
NH Flat	2	0	0	0	0
Hurdles	1	0	0	0	0
Career Total	3	0	0	0	0

Going:	Sf: 0-0 GS: 0-0 Gd: 0-0 GF: - Fm: 0-3
Distance:	2m/2m3: 0-2 2m4-2m7: 0-1 3m+: 0-0
Track:	LH: 0-1 RH: 0-2 Tight: 0-0 Gall: 0-0
Aids:	Bl: 0-0 Vi: 0-0 Tstrap: 0-0 Ckp: 0-0
Best Rating:	76 9/03 Worc 2m gd-fm NHF

Gilou

103   **95+**
8-y-o b m Midyan (USA)-Lunagraphe (USA) (Time For A Change (USA))
C W Fairhurst P Richmond & Partners

Placings:05/32/220-35110   (4688)
2003/04: 21³GF, 22⁵GF, 20¹F, 16¹GF, 16⁰G,

	Starts	1st	2nd	3rd	Win & Pl
Hurdles	5	2	0	1	4994
Career Total	12	2	3	2	7547
100	10/03	Hexm	2m110y	E Hdl	G-F	£2278
86	9/03	Hexm	2m4f110yF(0-95)HHdl	FRM	£2338

Total win prize-money £4617

Going:	Sf: 0-0 GS: 0-0 Gd: 0-1 GF: - Fm: 2-4
Distance:	2m/2m3: 1-2 2m4-2m7: 1-3 3m+: 0-0
Track:	LH: 2-4 RH: 0-0 Tight: 0-2 Gall: 0-0
Aids:	Bl: 0-0 Vi: 0-0 Tstrap: 0-0 Ckp: 0-0
Best Rating:	100 10/03 Hexm 2m110y gd-fm Hdl

Modest novice hurdler and has won twice at Hexham at up to two and a half miles; acts on fast ground and stays well.

Gimme Shelter (IRE)

97(104h)　　　　　　　　(82 h)104
10-y-o ch m Glacial Storm (USA)-Glen Dieu (Furry Glen)
S J Marshall　S J Marshall

Placings:004042P/4/F/P3140P44212-0FP06P4　　(4432)
2003/04: 20⁹G, 30⁵GS, 27⁹GS, 24⁰HY, 28⁶G, 26⁹G, 32⁴G,

	Starts	1st	2nd	3rd	Win & Pl
Hurdles	2	0	0	0	0
Chases	5	0	0	0	296
Career Total	**27**	**2**	**3**	**1**	**18213**
100	3/03	Hexm	4m	F(0-100)HCh	SFT £3805
82	11/02	Kels	3m3f	E(0-110)HHdl	SFT £5096
				Total win prize-money £8902

Going:	Sf: 0-1 GS: 0-2 Gd: 0-4 GF: - Fm: 0-0
Distance:	2m/2m3: 0-0 2m4-2m7: 0-1 3m+: 0-6
Track:	LH: 0-5 RH: 0-2 Tight: 0-2 Gall: 0-2
Aids:	Bl: 0-0 Vi: 0-0 Tstrap: 0-0 Ckp: 0-0
Best Rating:	100 4/03 Prth 3m7f good Ch

Modest form over hurdles and fences; runaway winner of a long distance handicap chase run in bad ground at Hexham in March 2003; effective on a sound surface but best on soft ground.

Gimmick (FR)

112(104c)　　　　　　　(114c)122+
10-y-o b g Chamberlin (FR)-Jaida (FR) (Alfaro)
Jonjo O'Neill　The Risky Partnership

Placings:12/111/0F26F20P2-2100　　(2486)
2003/04: 20²GF, 16¹F, 16⁹GF, 16⁹GS,

	Starts	1st	2nd	3rd	Win & Pl
Hurdles	4	1	1	0	14918
Career Total	**18**	**5**	**5**	**0**	**31970**
122	10/03	Weth	2m	B(0-140)HHdl	FRM £13673
125	8/00	MRas	2m3f110yE Hdl	G-F	£2834
116	7/00	MRas	2m3f110yD Hdl	GD	£3721
111	6/00	Worc	2m	E Hdl	G-F	£2642
111	4/00	Tntn	2m1f	E Hdl	G-S	£2478
				Total win prize-money £25349

Going:	Sf: 0-0 GS: 0-1 Gd: 0-0 GF: - Fm: 1-3
Distance:	**2m/2m3: 1-3** 2m4-2m7: 0-1 3m+: 0-0
Track:	**LH: 1-3** RH: 0-1 Tight: 0-0 Gall: 0-1
Aids:	Bl: 0-0 Vi: 0-0 Tstrap: 0-0 Ckp: 0-0
Best Rating:	125 8/00 MRas 2m3f110y gd-fm Hdl

Fair hurdler; showed ability in novice chases in 2002/3; returned to hurdles in 2003 winning at Wetherby; stays two miles three; acts on ground ranging from firm to heavy; has been tried unsuccessfully in blinkers.

Gin

67　　　　　　　　　9
4-y-o b f Abou Zouz (USA)-Skedaddle (Formidable (USA))
J Wade　John Wade

Placings:0P　　(1429)
2003/04: 17⁰GF, 16⁶G,

	Starts	1st	2nd	3rd	Win & Pl
Hurdles	2	0	0	0	0
Career Total	**2**	**0**	**0**	**0**	**0**

Going:	Sf: 0-0 GS: 0-0 Gd: 0-1 GF: - Fm: 0-0
Distance:	2m/2m3: 0-2 2m4-2m7: 0-0 3m+: 0-0
Track:	LH: 0-1 RH: 0-1 Tight: 0-1 Gall: 0-0
Aids:	Bl: 0-0 Vi: 0-0 Tstrap: 0-0 Ckp: 0-0
Best Rating:	13 8/03 Sedg 2m1f gd-fm Hdl

Gin And Terimonic

84f　　　　　　　　73f
6-y-o gr m Terimon-Genie Spirit (Nishapour (FR))
P Winkworth　Mrs Gillian Hayward

Placings:4-4　　(1924)
2003/04: 18⁴G,

	Starts	1st	2nd	3rd	Win & Pl
NH Flat	1	0	0	0	0
Career Total	**2**	**0**	**0**	**0**	**0**

Going:	Sf: 0-0 GS: 0-0 Gd: 0-1 GF: - Fm: 0-0
Distance:	2m/2m3: 0-1 2m4-2m7: 0-0 3m+: 0-0
Track:	LH: 0-1 RH: 0-0 Tight: 0-0 Gall: 0-0
Aids:	Bl: 0-0 Vi: 0-0 Tstrap: 0-0 Ckp: 0-0
Best Rating:	73 11/03 Plum 2m2f good NHF

Some promise in a bumpers.

Gin Palace (IRE)

110　　　　　　　　134+
6-y-o gr m King's Theatre (IRE)-Ikala (Lashkari)
G L Moore　Mrs Patricia Gilmore

Placings:42/26511-1503　　(4963)
2003/04: 21¹G, 16⁵S, 20⁹G, 20³G,

	Starts	1st	2nd	3rd	Win & Pl
Hurdles	4	1	0	1	21672
Career Total	**11**	**3**	**2**	**1**	**47553**
134	2/04	Kemp	2m5f	C(0-130)HHdl	GD	£17400
122	3/03	Newb	2m110y	B(0-140)HHdl	GD	£18513
120	2/03	Plum	2m	F Hdl	SFT	£3094
				Total win prize-money £39008

Going:	Sf: 0-1 GS: 0-0 Gd: 1-3 GF: - Fm: 0-0
Distance:	2m/2m3: 1-2 **2m4-2m7: 1-3** 3m+: 0-0
Track:	LH: 0-0 **RH: 1-3** Tight: 0-1 Gall: 0-0
Aids:	Bl: 0-0 Vi: 0-0 Tstrap: 0-0 Ckp: 0-0
Best Rating:	134 3/04 Sand 2m110y soft Hdl

Useful hurdler; acts on any ground; suited by two miles; needs a strong pace.

Ginger Folly (IRE)

6-y-o ch m General Monash (USA)-Lapland Lights (USA) (Northern Prospect (USA))
P Butler　Mrs Gill Oakley

Placings:6　　(1498)
2003/04: 16⁶GF,

	Starts	1st	2nd	3rd	Win & Pl
NH Flat	1	0	0	0	0
Career Total	**1**	**0**	**0**	**0**	**0**

Going:	Sf: 0-0 GS: 0-0 Gd: 0-0 GF: - Fm: 0-1
Distance:	2m/2m3: 0-1 2m4-2m7: 0-0 3m+: 0-0
Track:	LH: 0-1 RH: 0-0 Tight: 0-0 Gall: 0-0
Aids:	Bl: 0-0 Vi: 0-0 Tstrap: 0-0 Ckp: 0-0

Gingerbread House (IRE)

107　　　　　　　　121+
6-y-o b g Old Vic-Furun (IRE) (Deep Run)
R T Phillips　Mrs J Stewart

Placings:14　　(4852)
2003/04: 20¹GS, 20⁴GS,

	Starts	1st	2nd	3rd	Win & Pl
Hurdles	2	1	0	0	3348
Career Total	**2**	**1**	**0**	**0**	**3348**
115	3/04	Weth	2m4f110yF Hdl	G-S	£2754
			Total win prize-money £2755

Going:	Sf: 0-0 GS: 1-2 Gd: 0-0 GF: - Fm: 0-0
Distance:	2m/2m3: 0-0 **2m4-2m7: 1-2** 3m+: 0-0
Track:	LH: **1-2** RH: 0-0 Tight: 0-0 Gall: 0-0
Aids:	Bl: 0-0 Vi: 0-0 Tstrap: 0-0 Ckp: 0-0
Best Rating:	121 4/04 Ayr 2m4f gd-sft Hdl

Winnner of two points in Ireland in 2003; made a successful hurdling bow at Wetherby in March, making most and coming clear; suited by two and a half miles and will stay further.

Gingerbread Man

9-y-o ch g Derrylin-Red Rambler (Rymer)
J A Moore　Mrs J M Moore

Placings:000/PP/P-P　　(0195)
2003/04: 16⁶G,

	Starts	1st	2nd	3rd	Win & Pl
Chases	1	0	0	0	
Career Total	**7**	**0**	**0**	**0**	

Going:	Sf: 0-0 GS: 0-0 Gd: 0-1 GF: - Fm: 0-0
Distance:	2m/2m3: 0-1 2m4-2m7: 0-0 3m+: 0-0
Track:	LH: 0-1 RH: 0-0 Tight: 0-0 Gall: 0-0
Aids:	Bl: 0-0 Vi: 0-0 Tstrap: 0-0 Ckp: 0-0
Best Rating:	68 7/00 Worc 2m good NHF

Gingerslookingreat (IRE)

76f
5-y-o ch g Ashkalani (IRE)-Just An Illusion (IRE) (Shemazar)
O Brennan　G F Sheridan

Placings:4　　(0334)
2003/04: 17⁴GF,

	Starts	1st	2nd	3rd	Win & Pl
NH Flat	1	0	0	0	0
Career Total	**1**	**0**	**0**	**0**	**0**

Going:	Sf: 0-0 GS: 0-0 Gd: 0-0 GF: - Fm: 0-1
Distance:	2m/2m3: 0-1 2m4-2m7: 0-0 3m+: 0-0
Track:	LH: 0-1 RH: 0-0 Tight: 0-0 Gall: 0-0
Aids:	Bl: 0-0 Vi: 0-0 Tstrap: 0-1 Ckp: 0-0
Best Rating:	76 5/03 Sthl 2m1f gd-fm NHF

Gingko

89　　　　　　　　92
7-y-o b g Pursuit of Love-Arboretum (IRE) (Green Desert (USA))
P R Webber　Four Counties Partnership

Placings:0P34-03　　(2866)
2003/04: 17⁰GS, 16³GS,

	Starts	1st	2nd	3rd	Win & Pl
Hurdles	2	0	0	1	348
Career Total	**6**	**0**	**0**	**2**	**951**

Going:	Sf: 0-0 GS: 0-2 Gd: 0-0 GF: - Fm: 0-0
Distance:	2m/2m3: 0-2 2m4-2m7: 0-0 3m+: 0-0
Track:	LH: 0-1 RH: 0-1 Tight: 0-0 Gall: 0-0

Aids: Bl: 0-0 Vi: 0-0 Tstrap: 0-0 Ckp: 0-0
Best Rating: 94 12/03 Wwck 2m   gd-sft Hdl

Novice hurdler; acts on a sound surface.

Ginner Morris

82   80

9-y-o b g Emarati (USA)-Just Run (IRE) (Runnett)
J Hetherton Mrs C A Brown

Placings: UP5F/33/P256F-03   (2526)
2003/04: 16⁶GS, 16⁹GS,

	Starts	1st	2nd	3rd	Win & Pl
Hurdles	2	0	0	1	272
Career Total	13	0	1	3	2090

Going: Sf: 0-0 GS: 0-2 Gd: 0-0 GF: - Fm: 0-0
Distance: 2m/2m3: 0-2 2m4-2m7: 0-0 3m+: 0-0
Track: LH: 0-2 RH: 0-0 Tight: 0-1 Gall: 0-0
Aids: Bl: 0-0 Vi: 0-0 Tstrap: 0-0 Ckp: 0-0
Best Rating: 86 5/00 Ctml 2m1f110y gd-fm Hdl

Plating-class hurdler; in the frame in selling hurdles; suited by soft ground.

Ginski

55

8-y-o ch g Petoski-Upham Lass (Sula Bula)
C J Drewe C J Drewe

Placings: 0/0000/0006-PPP   (4656)
2003/04: 22⁸G, 21⁸GS, 26⁹G,

	Starts	1st	2nd	3rd	Win & Pl
Hurdles	3	0	0	0	0
Career Total	12	0	0	0	0

Going: Sf: 0-0 GS: 0-1 Gd: 0-2 GF: - Fm: 0-0
Distance: 2m/2m3: 0-0 2m4-2m7: 0-2 3m+: 0-1
Track: LH: 0-1 RH: 0-2 Tight: 0-0 Gall: 0-0
Aids: Bl: 0-0 Vi: 0-0 Tstrap: 0-1 Ckp: 0-0
Best Rating: 55 4/03 Strf 2m6f110y gd-fm Hdl

Giocomo (IRE)

109(107h)   (132dh)126+

6-y-o ch g Indian Ridge-Karri Valley (USA) (Storm Bird (CAN))
R A Fahey (P Monteith 4/5) Mugsrus

Placings: 4311P0/061P00-1U1P   (3597)
2003/04: 16¹G, 17ᵁGS, 19¹G, 20ᴾHY,

	Starts	1st	2nd	3rd	Win & Pl
Chases	4	2	0	0	7749
Career Total	16	5	0	1	44782
126	1/04	Catt	2m3f	D Ch	GD £5508
119	11/03	Hexm	2m110y	F Ch	GD £2240
132	12/02	Chep	2m4f	B(0-140)HHdl	SFT £15274
127	2/02	Kemp	2m	A Hdl	GD £12000
117	2/02	Hntg	2m110y	B Hdl	SFT £8671

Total win prize-money £43694

Going: Sf: 0-1 GS: 0-1 Gd: 2-2 GF: - Fm: 0-0
Distance: 2m/2m3: 2-3 2m4-2m7: 0-1 3m+: 0-0
Track: LH: 2-3 RH: 0-1 Tight: 1-2 Gall: 0-0
Aids: Bl: 0-0 Vi: 0-0 Tstrap: 0-0 Ckp: 0-0
Best Rating: 132 12/02 Chep 2m4f soft Hdl

Very useful hurdler; useful novice chaser; stays two and a half miles, but effective over shorter; acts on good ground, but prefers softer.

Giorgio (IRE)

94   87+

6-y-o b g Presenting-Billys Pet (Le Moss)
P J Hobbs Sir Robert Ogden

Placings: 4P   (2851)
2003/04: 17⁴G, 19ᴾGS,

	Starts	1st	2nd	3rd	Win & Pl
Hurdles	2	0	0	0	0
Career Total	2	0	0	0	0

Going: Sf: 0-0 GS: 0-1 Gd: 0-1 GF: - Fm: 0-0
Distance: 2m/2m3: 0-1 2m4-2m7: 0-1 3m+: 0-0
Track: LH: 0-1 RH: 0-1 Tight: 0-1 Gall: 0-0
Aids: Bl: 0-0 Vi: 0-0 Tstrap: 0-0 Ckp: 0-0
Best Rating: 87 11/03 NAbb 2m1f good Hdl

Gipsy Cricketer

93   (51h)80

8-y-o b g Anshan-Tinkers Fairy (Myjinski (USA))
D J Caro The Yes - No - Wait Sorries

Placings: 006P/53003600/0P/6421PP-55   (0448)
2003/04: 16⁵G, 16⁵GF,

	Starts	1st	2nd	3rd	Win & Pl
Chases	2	0	0	0	0
Career Total	22	1	1	2	4410
86	7/02	Worc	2m	F(0-95)HCh	G-F £2736

Total win prize-money £2737

Going: Sf: 0-0 GS: 0-0 Gd: 0-1 GF: - Fm: 0-1
Distance: 2m/2m3: 0-2 2m4-2m7: 0-0 3m+: 0-0
Track: LH: 0-1 RH: 0-1 Tight: 0-0 Gall: 0-1
Aids: Bl: 0-0 Vi: 0-0 Tstrap: 0-0 Ckp: 0-0
Best Rating: 86 7/02 Worc 2m gd-fm Ch

A useful pointer; made all when winning 2m handicap at Worcester July 2002;held since; acts on fast.

Gipsy Wood

75   52

8-y-o gr m Rakaposhi King-Silva Linda (Precipice Wood)
P Beaumont Mrs Sue Plowright

Placings: 6-060P   (0644)
2003/04: 16⁰GF, 17⁶G, 20⁰G, 20ᴾGF,

	Starts	1st	2nd	3rd	Win & Pl
Hurdles	4	0	0	0	0
Career Total	5	0	0	0	0

Going: Sf: 0-0 GS: 0-0 Gd: 0-2 GF: - Fm: 0-2
Distance: 2m/2m3: 0-2 2m4-2m7: 0-2 3m+: 0-0
Track: LH: 0-3 RH: 0-1 Tight: 0-1 Gall: 0-0
Aids: Bl: 0-0 Vi: 0-0 Tstrap: 0-0 Ckp: 0-0
Best Rating: 53 3/03 Weth 2m4f110y good Hdl

Giuliani

101   76

4-y-o b c Sadler's Wells (USA)-Anka Germania (Malinowski (USA))
J Howard Johnson (L M Cumani 7/7) J R McAleese

Placings: 06   (4271)
2003/04: 16⁰G, 20⁶G,

	Starts	1st	2nd	3rd	Win & Pl
Hurdles	2	0	0	0	0
Career Total	2	0	0	0	0

Going: Sf: 0-0 GS: 0-0 Gd: 0-2 GF: - Fm: 0-0
Distance: 2m/2m3: 0-1 2m4-2m7: 0-1 3m+: 0-0
Track: LH: 0-0 RH: 0-2 Tight: 0-1 Gall: 0-0
Aids: Bl: 0-0 Vi: 0-0 Tstrap: 0-0 Ckp: 0-0
Best Rating: 76 3/04 Carl 2m4f good Hdl

Giust In Temp (IRE)

97   83

5-y-o b h Polish Precedent (USA)-Blue Stricks (Bluebird (USA))
P W Hiatt River Side Partnership

Placings: 0420   (1849)
2003/04: 16⁰GF, 16⁴GF, 16²GF, 16⁰G,

	Starts	1st	2nd	3rd	Win & Pl
Hurdles	4	0	1	0	658
Career Total	4	0	1	0	658

Going: Sf: 0-0 GS: 0-0 Gd: 0-1 GF: - Fm: 0-3
Distance: 2m/2m3: 0-4 2m4-2m7: 0-0 3m+: 0-0
Track: LH: 0-4 RH: 0-0 Tight: 0-2 Gall: 0-0
Aids: Bl: 0-0 Vi: 0-0 Tstrap: 0-0 Ckp: 0-0
Best Rating: 81 10/03 Strf 2m110y gd-fm Hdl

Poor maiden on the Flat; best effort over hurdles when well beaten second in Stratford seller October 2003.

Giverny (GER)

82   52

6-y-o b m Sternkoenig (IRE)-Georgia O'Keeffe (GER) (Helikon (GER))
Frau A Bertram W Renggli

Placings: 6320   (2778)
2003/04: 15⁶G, 15³G, 16²HY, 17⁰GS,

	Starts	1st	2nd	3rd	Win & Pl
Hurdles	4	0	1	1	3344
Career Total	4	0	1	1	3344

Going: Sf: 0-1 GS: 0-1 Gd: 0-2 GF: - Fm: 0-0
Distance: 2m/2m3: 0-2 2m4-2m7: 0-0 3m+: 0-0
Track: LH: 0-0 RH: 0-1 Tight: 0-1 Gall: 0-0
Aids: Bl: 0-0 Vi: 0-0 Tstrap: 0-0 Ckp: 0-0
Best Rating: 52 12/03 Folk 2m1f110y gd-sft Hdl

Glacial Dancer (IRE)

11-y-o b g Glacial Storm (USA)-Castleblagh (General Ironside)
Mrs E J Clark (S B Clark 18/5) S B Clark

Placings: 6234421/13/P/323/P4U   (4607)
2003/04: 26ᴾGF, 21⁴GS, 25ᵁGS,

	Starts	1st	2nd	3rd	Win & Pl
Chases	3	0	0	0	117
Career Total	16	2	3	4	10383
112	1/00	Ayr	3m110y	D(0-110)HHdl	SFT £3152
99	5/99	Hexm	3m	F(0-100)HHdl	GD £2220

Total win prize-money £5374

Going: Sf: 0-0 GS: 0-2 Gd: 0-0 GF: - Fm: 0-0
Distance: 2m/2m3: 0-0 2m4-2m7: 0-1 3m+: 0-2
Track: LH: 0-2 RH: 0-1 Tight: 0-2 Gall: 0-0
Aids: Bl: 0-0 Vi: 0-0 Tstrap: 0-0 Ckp: 0-0
Best Rating: 112 1/00 Ayr 3m110y soft Hdl

Glacial Delight (IRE)

69f   **95f**

5-y-o b g Glacial Storm (USA)-Annagh Delight (Saint Denys)
Miss E C Lavelle The Friday Night Racing Club

Placings:0   (4824)
2003/04: 17⁰GF,

	Starts	1st	2nd	3rd	Win & Pl
NH Flat	1	0	0	0	
Career Total	1	0	0	0	

Going:	Sf: 0-0 GS: 0-0 Gd: 0-0 GF: - Fm: 0-1
Distance:	2m/2m3: 0-1 2m4-2m7: 0-0 3m+: 0-1
Track:	LH: 0-0 RH: 0-1 Tight: 0-0 Gall: 0-0
Aids:	Bl: 0-0 Vi: 0-0 Tstrap: 0-0 Ckp: 0-0
Best Rating:	95 4/04 Extr 2m1f gd-fm NHF

Glacial Evening (IRE)

109   **110+**

8-y-o b g Glacial Storm (USA)-Cold Evening (IRE) (Strong Gale)
R H Buckler The Deadly Sins Partnership

Placings:5/00P-43224110   (3942)
2003/04: 20⁴GF, 17³GF, 20²GF, 22²G, 22⁴S, 24¹S, 23¹S, 22²G,

	Starts	1st	2nd	3rd	Win & Pl
Hurdles	8	2	2	1	11472
Career Total	12	2	2	1	11472
110 2/04 Weth	2m7f		D(0-115)HHdl	SFT	£4956
98 1/04 Newb	3m110y	E(0-110)HHdl	SFT	£3794
			Total win prize-money £8750		

Going:	Sf: 2-3 GS: 0-0 Gd: 0-2 GF: - Fm: 0-3
Distance:	2m/2m3: 0-1 2m4-2m7: 1-6 3m+: 1-1
Track:	LH: 2-3 RH: 0-5 Tight: 0-0 Gall: 1-1
Aids:	Bl: 0-0 Vi: 0-0 Tstrap: 0-0 Ckp: 0-0
Best Rating:	110 2/04 Weth 2m7f soft Hdl

Modest hurdler; winner at Newbury in January; easily followed up at Wetherby the following month and is on the upgrade; stays three miles; suited to soft ground.

Glacial River (IRE)

           (85h) **98**

11-y-o ch g Glacial Storm (USA)-Lucky Trout (Beau Charmeur (FR))
D J Caro D J Caro

Placings:60/603U/6350/3/22/P223P-PP   (4888)
2003/04: 24³S, 27⁴GF,

	Starts	1st	2nd	3rd	Win & Pl
Chases	2	0	0	0	
Career Total	20	0	4	4	8562

Going:	Sf: 0-1 GS: 0-0 Gd: 0-0 GF: - Fm: 0-1
Distance:	2m/2m3: 0-0 2m4-2m7: 0-4 3m+: 0-2
Track:	LH: 0-2 RH: 0-0 Tight: 0-2 Gall: 0-0
Aids:	Bl: 0-0 Vi: 0-0 Tstrap: 0-0 Ckp: 0-0
Best Rating:	98 12/02 Wwck 3m5f gd-sft Ch

Glacial Sunset (IRE)

104   **125+**

9-y-o ch g Glacial Storm (USA)-Twinkle Sunset (Deep Run)
C Tinkler George Ward

Placings:4/10/34/12114-B00   (4963)
2003/04: 21⁸G, 24⁰G, 20⁰G,

	Starts	1st	2nd	3rd	Win & Pl
Hurdles	3	0	0	0	
Career Total	13	4	1	1	21032
123 12/02 Chel	3m	B HHdl	GD	£9448
123 6/02 Hrfd	3m2f	E Hdl	G-F	£2968
116 5/02 Winc	2m6f	F(0-100)HHdl	G-F	£3150
111 5/00 Font	2m2f110yH HNF		£1736
		Total win prize-money £17302	

Going:	Sf: 0-0 GS: 0-0 Gd: 0-3 GF: - Fm: 0-0
Distance:	2m/2m3: 0-0 2m4-2m7: 0-2 3m+: 0-1
Track:	LH: 0-1 RH: 0-2 Tight: 0-1 Gall: 0-0
Aids:	Bl: 0-0 Vi: 0-0 Tstrap: 0-0 Ckp: 0-0
Best Rating:	125 4/04 Sand 2m4f110y good Hdl

Useful hurdler; lightly raced in recent seasons; has improved with step up to three miles; appreciates a sound surface.

Glacial Trial (IRE)

11-y-o b m Glacial Storm (USA)-Protrial (Proverb)
P Jones M J Parr

Placings:0/1-14   (0519)
2003/04: 24¹G, 28⁴G,

	Starts	1st	2nd	3rd	Win & Pl
Chases	2	1	0	0	5784
Career Total	4	2	0	0	8826
92 5/03 Bang	3m110y H Ch		GD	£4212
99 5/02 Strf	3m	H Ch	GD	£3041
		Total win prize-money £7254	

Going:	Sf: 0-0 GS: 0-0 Gd: 1-2 GF: - Fm: 0-0
Distance:	2m/2m3: 0-0 2m4-2m7: 0-0 **3m+:** 1-2
Track:	**LH:** 1-2 RH: 0-0 Tight: 1-2 Gall: 0-0
Aids:	Bl: 0-0 Vi: 0-0 Tstrap: 0-0 Ckp: 0-0
Best Rating:	101 5/03 Strf 3m4f good Ch

Fair pointer/hunter chaser; needs to go left-handed.

Gladiatorial (IRE)

12-y-o b g Mazaad-Arena (Sallust)
Mrs Frances Bishop Mrs Frances Bishop

Placings:020/21134/F2F0/P0P0F/**P2F2P44U64303/P**   (4696)
2003/04: 19⁰G,

	Starts	1st	2nd	3rd	Win & Pl
Chases	1	0	0	0	
Career Total	31	2	5	3	13182
105 8/96 Tral	2m1f	Hdl	G-Y	£3530
100 8/96 Slig	2m	NHF	HVY	£2295
		Total win prize-money £5826	

Going:	Sf: 0-0 GS: 0-0 Gd: 0-1 GF: - Fm: 0-0
Distance:	2m/2m3: 0-0 2m4-2m7: 0-1 3m+: 0-0
Track:	LH: 0-0 RH: 0-1 Tight: 0-0 Gall: 0-0
Aids:	Bl: 0-0 Vi: 0-0 Tstrap: 0-0 Ckp: 0-0
Best Rating:	115 8/97 Slig 2m4f yld-sft Hdl

Gladie

76   **51**

9-y-o ch m Arzanni-Palm Lady (Palm Track)
Mrs S M Johnson G J Powell

Placings:6   (1013)
2003/04: 20⁶GF,

	Starts	1st	2nd	3rd	Win & Pl
Hurdles	1	0	0	0	0
Career Total	1	0	0	0	0

Going:	Sf: 0-0 GS: 0-0 Gd: 0-0 GF: - Fm: 0-0
Distance:	2m/2m3: 0-0 2m4-2m7: 0-1 3m+: 0-0
Track:	LH: 0-1 RH: 0-0 Tight: 0-0 Gall: 0-0
Aids:	Bl: 0-0 Vi: 0-0 Tstrap: 0-0 Ckp: 0-0
Best Rating:	57 8/03 Worc 2m4f gd-fm Hdl

Gladstone Spirit (IRE)

93   **67**

4-y-o b g Woodborough (USA)-Alpencrocus (IRE) (Waajib)
G M Moore Mrs Susan Moore

Placings:30UF   (4614)
2003/04: 16³GS, 16⁰GF, 16⁰G, 17⁰G,

	Starts	1st	2nd	3rd	Win & Pl
Hurdles	4	0	0	1	340
Career Total	4	0	0	1	340

Going:	Sf: 0-0 GS: 0-1 Gd: 0-2 GF: - Fm: 0-1
Distance:	2m/2m3: 0-4 2m4-2m7: 0-0 3m+: 0-0
Track:	LH: 0-3 RH: 0-1 Tight: 0-4 Gall: 0-0
Aids:	Bl: 0-0 Vi: 0-0 Tstrap: 0-0 Ckp: 0-0
Best Rating:	67 1/04 Catt 2m gd-sft Hdl

Gladtoknowyou (IRE)

98   **114+**

11-y-o ch g Over The River (FR)-Jonsemma (IRE) (Denel (FR))
R Rowe W Packham

Placings:34/2/15-16P   (3946)
2003/04: 21¹S, 24⁶GS, 21⁶G,

	Starts	1st	2nd	3rd	Win & Pl
Chases	3	1	0	0	5668
Career Total	8	2	1	1	12837
114 1/04 Winc	2m5f	D(0-120)HCh	SFT	£5427
104 1/03 Kemp	2m4f110yD(0-115)HCh	G-S	£5798
		Total win prize-money £11226	

Going:	Sf: 1-1 GS: 0-1 Gd: 0-1 GF: - Fm: 0-0
Distance:	2m/2m3: 0-0 **2m4-2m7:** 1-2 3m+: 0-1
Track:	LH: 0-0 RH: 1-3 Tight: 0-0 Gall: 0-0
Aids:	Bl: 0-0 Vi: 0-0 Tstrap: 0-0 Ckp: 0-0
Best Rating:	114 1/04 Winc 2m5f soft Ch

Moderate chaser; fragile and very lightly raced; both wins have come after lenghty absences; stays 2m7f; acts on soft ground.

Gladys Aylward

66   **18**

4-y-o b f Polar Falcon (USA)-Versami (USA) (Riverman (USA))
A Crook (T D Easterby 6/6) Leeds Plywood And Doors Ltd

Placings:0   (2302)
2003/04: 16⁰GF,

	Starts	1st	2nd	3rd	Win & Pl
Hurdles	1	0	0	0	
Career Total	1	0	0	0	

Going:	Sf: 0-0 GS: 0-0 Gd: 0-0 GF: - Fm: 0-1

Distance: 2m/2m3: 0-1 2m4-2m7: 0-0 3m+: 0-0
Track: LH: 0-1 RH: 0-0 Tight: 0-1 Gall: 0-0
Aids: Bl: 0-1 Vi: 0-0 Tstrap: 0-0 Ckp: 0-0
Best Rating: 18 11/03 Catt 2m   gd-fm Hdl

Glamour Girl

86   **49**

8-y-o b m Lord Americo-Money Galore (IRE) (Monksfield)
F Jordan Mrs S G Davies

Placings:0/000/0040P6-0   (0487)
2003/04: 22⁰GF,

	Starts	1st	2nd	3rd	Win & Pl
Hurdles	1	0	0	0	
Career Total	11	0	0	0	268

Going: Sf: 0-0 GS: 0-0 Gd: 0-0 GF: - Fm: 0-1
Distance: 2m/2m3: 0-0 2m4-2m7: 0-1 3m+: 0-0
Track: LH: 0-1 RH: 0-0 Tight: 0-1 Gall: 0-0
Aids: Bl: 0-0 Vi: 0-0 Tstrap: 0-0 Ckp: 0-0
Best Rating: 74 2/02 Hntg 2m110y   soft Hdl

Glandore Moon

53f   **16f**

5-y-o br g Presenting-My Gonny (IRE) (Mandalus)
N J Gifford Chris Keeley

Placings:0   (4454)
2003/04: 16⁰GS,

	Starts	1st	2nd	3rd	Win & Pl
NH Flat	1	0	0	0	
Career Total	1	0	0	0	

Going: Sf: 0-0 GS: 0-1 Gd: 0-0 GF: - Fm: 0-0
Distance: 2m/2m3: 0-1 2m4-2m7: 0-0 3m+: 0-0
Track: LH: 0-1 RH: 0-1 Tight: 0-0 Gall: 0-0
Aids: Bl: 0-0 Vi: 0-0 Tstrap: 0-0 Ckp: 0-0
Best Rating: 16 3/04 Asct 2m110y gd-sft NHF

Glanmerin (IRE)

100   **96**

13-y-o b g Lomond (USA)-Abalvina (FR) (Abdos)
R Lee Rex Norton

Placings:113/0/5024/02P/U2114/503/U624P01/P30P262-
6UPU3F3PP   (4737)
2003/04: 20⁶G, 21⁰UG, 21PGF, 24UG, 25³S, 19FS, 20³S, 24PG,
21PG,

	Starts	1st	2nd	3rd	Win & Pl
Chases	9	0	2	2	802
Career Total	42	5	6	5	28965
102	3/02	Sthl	2m4f110yF(0-90)HCh	HVY	£3119
123	3/00	Hntg	2m110y D(0-125)HCh	SFT	£4396
123	2/00	Hntg	2m110y D(0-125)HCh	SFT	£4420
113	3/95	Worc	2m E Hdl	G-S	£2320
106	2/95	Nott	2m D Hdl	G-S	£3662
			Total win prize-money £17918		

Going: Sf: 0-3 GS: 0-0 Gd: 0-0 GF: - Fm: 0-1
Distance: 2m/2m3: 0-0 2m4-2m7: 0-6 3m+: 0-3
Track: LH: 0-5 RH: 0-3 Tight: 0-2 Gall: 0-2
Aids: Bl: 0-0 Vi: 0-0 Tstrap: 0-1 Ckp: 0-0
Best Rating: 124 2/97 Hntg 2m110y good Hdl

Plating-class chaser; effective at around two and a half miles in the mud.

Glashedy Rock (IRE)

91

7-y-o b g Shernazar-Classical Lady (IRE) (Orchestra)
Miss H C Knight Flora Lane & Gwen meacham

Placings:4F64-P   (1846)
2003/04: 22PG,

	Starts	1st	2nd	3rd	Win & Pl
Hurdles	1	0	0	0	
Career Total	5	0	0	0	624

Going: Sf: 0-0 GS: 0-0 Gd: 0-1 GF: - Fm: 0-0
Distance: 2m/2m3: 0-0 2m4-2m7: 0-1 3m+: 0-0
Track: LH: 0-1 RH: 0-0 Tight: 0-1 Gall: 0-0
Aids: Bl: 0-0 Vi: 0-0 Tstrap: 0-0 Ckp: 0-0
Best Rating: 91 4/03 Extr 2m6f110y gd-fm Hdl

Moderate hurdler; Irish point winner; showed some promise on hurdling bow at Doncaster in January 2003 but disappointing since; stays at least two and a half miles; may do better when switching to fences.

Glass Breaker

10-y-o b g Infantry-Bottle Basher (Le Soleil)
Mrs Debby Ewing Mrs Debby Ewing

Placings:P-P   (0202)
2003/04: 30PGF,

	Starts	1st	2nd	3rd	Win & Pl
Chases	1	0	0	0	
Career Total	2	0	0	0	

Going: Sf: 0-0 GS: 0-0 Gd: 0-0 GF: - Fm: 0-1
Distance: 2m/2m3: 0-0 2m4-2m7: 0-0 3m+: 0-1
Track: LH: 0-0 RH: 0-0 Tight: 0-0 Gall: 0-1
Aids: Bl: 0-0 Vi: 0-0 Tstrap: 0-0 Ckp: 0-0

Glass Note (IRE)

90   **60**

6-y-o b m Spectrum (IRE)-Alice En Ballade (Tap On Wood)
S T Lewis Simon T Lewis

Placings:PP06PPO63FU60PP   (4868)
2003/04: 19PGS, 17PGF, 20PGF, 17⁶GF, 21PGF, 16PGF, 16⁰GF,
16⁶GF, 20³GF, 16FS, 16UHY, 16⁶S, 19⁹S, 16PGS, 20PGS,

	Starts	1st	2nd	3rd	Win & Pl
Hurdles	15	0	0	1	535
Career Total	15	0	0	1	535

Going: Sf: 0-4 GS: 0-3 Gd: 0-0 GF: - Fm: 0-8
Distance: 2m/2m3: 0-10 2m4-2m7: 0-5 3m+: 0-0
Track: LH: 0-5 RH: 0-10 Tight: 0-3 Gall: 0-1
Aids: Bl: 0-2 Vi: 0-0 Tstrap: 0-1 Ckp: 0-0
Best Rating: 60 11/03 Leic 2m4f110y gd-fm Hdl

Glasson House (IRE)

97f   **79+f**

5-y-o b m Supreme Leader-Nasowas (IRE) (Cardinal Flower)
P D Evans Supreme Corner Gang

Placings:24   (1019)

2003/04: 16²G, 16⁴GF,

	Starts	1st	2nd	3rd	Win & Pl
NH Flat	2	0	1	0	537
Career Total	2	0	1	0	537

Going: Sf: 0-0 GS: 0-0 Gd: 0-1 GF: - Fm: 0-1
Distance: 2m/2m3: 0-2 2m4-2m7: 0-0 3m+: 0-0
Track: LH: 0-2 RH: 0-0 Tight: 0-0 Gall: 0-0
Aids: Bl: 0-0 Vi: 0-0 Tstrap: 0-0 Ckp: 0-0
Best Rating: 82 7/03 Worc 2m   good NHF

Could not overcome greenness when runner-up on bumper debut at Worcester July 2003; fourth in similar event at the same venue next time.

Glen Warrior

111   **125**

8-y-o b g Michelozzo (USA)-Mascara Vii (Damsire Unregistered)
J S Smith Donald Smith

Placings:0U/3022131-20312   (4567)
2003/04: 22¹S, 24²G, 22⁰GS, 21³S, 24¹G, 24²GS,

	Starts	1st	2nd	3rd	Win & Pl
Hurdles	6	2	2	1	16568
Career Total	14	3	4	3	23554
114	3/04	Bang	3m	D(0-125)HHdl	GD	£5193
111	4/03	NAbb	2m6f	D(0-120)HHdl	SFT	£6388
97	1/03	Tntn	3m110y	E(0-110)HHdl	SFT	£3770
				Total win prize-money £15352	

Going: Sf: 1-2 GS: 0-2 Gd: 1-2 GF: - Fm: 0-0
Distance: 2m/2m3: 0-2 2m4-2m7: 1-3 3m+: 1-3
Track: LH: 2-4 RH: 0-2 Tight: 2-4 Gall: 0-0
Aids: Bl: 0-0 Vi: 0-0 Tstrap: 0-0 Ckp: 0-0
Best Rating: 125 3/04 Bang 3m   gd-sft Hdl

Modest hurdler; usually held up; acts on good and soft ground; stays three miles.

Glenburn (IRE)

88   **72**

6-y-o br g Dr Devious (IRE)-Edwina (IRE) (Caerleon (USA))
Miss Lucinda V Russell Mrs Ann Rutherford

Placings:PP0P-0550O0   (3885)
2003/04: 16⁰G, 16⁵G, 16⁵G, 16⁰G, 17⁰S, 16⁰G,

	Starts	1st	2nd	3rd	Win & Pl
Hurdles	5	0	0	0	0
Chases	1	0	0	0	0
Career Total	10	0	0	0	0

Going: Sf: 0-1 GS: 0-0 Gd: 0-5 GF: - Fm: 0-0
Distance: 2m/2m3: 0-6 2m4-2m7: 0-0 3m+: 0-0
Track: LH: 0-3 RH: 0-3 Tight: 0-4 Gall: 0-0
Aids: Bl: 0-0 Vi: 0-0 Tstrap: 0-6 Ckp: 0-0
Best Rating: 72 5/03 Kels 2m110y good Hdl

Glencoyle (IRE)

105   **106**

4-y-o b g In The Wings-Lucky State (USA) (State Dinner (USA))
N J Henderson (A C Stewart 13/10) Raymond Tooth

Placings:212   (4573)
2003/04: 16²G, 16¹G, 19²G,

	Starts	1st	2nd	3rd	Win & Pl
Hurdles	3	1	2	0	6212
Career Total	3	1	2	0	6212
101	3/04	Plum	2m	F Hdl	GD	£3115

Total win prize-money £3115

Going:	Sf: 0-0 GS: 0-0 Gd: 1-3 GF: Fm: 0-0
Distance:	**2m/2m3:** 1-3 2m4-2m7: 0-0 3m+: 0-0
Track:	**LH:** 1-2 RH: 0-0 **Tight:** 1-1 Gall: 0-1
Aids:	Bl: 0-0 Vi: 0-0 Tstrap: 0-0 Ckp: 0-0
Best Rating:	**105** 3/04 Newb 2m3f good Hdl

Modest hurdler; acts on good ground.

Glendamah (IRE)
101   **87**

7-y-o b g Mukaddamah (USA)-Sea Glen (IRE) (Glenstal (USA))
J R Weymes White Rose Poultry Ltd

Placings:650026/1124-56   (0412)
2003/04: 17⁵S, 20⁶G,

	Starts	1st	2nd	3rd	Win & Pl
Hurdles	2	0	0	0	
Career Total	12	2	2	0	5440
87	5/02	Hexm	2m110y	G(0-95)HHdl	GD £2478
85	5/02	Hexm	2m110y	G Hdl	G-S £1841

Total win prize-money £4319

Going:	Sf: 0-1 GS: 0-0 Gd: 0-0 GF: 0-0 Fm: 0-0
Distance:	2m/2m3: 0-1 2m4-2m7: 0-1 3m+: 0-0
Track:	LH: 0-2 RH: 0-0 Tight: 0-0 Gall: 0-0
Aids:	Bl: 0-0 Vi: 0-0 Tstrap: 0-0 Ckp: 0-0
Best Rating:	**87** 6/02 Hexm 2m110y good Hdl

Plating-class hurdler; winner of two sellers at Hexham in May 2002; suited by a sound surface.

Glendevon Grey

5-y-o gr g Karinga Bay-Sandy Etna (IRE) (Sandalay)
G M Moore Mrs J M Gray

Placings:000   (3814)
2003/04: 17⁰GS, 16⁹GS, 24⁰GS,

	Starts	1st	2nd	3rd	Win & Pl
NH Flat	2	0	0	0	
Hurdles	1	0	0	0	0
Career Total	3	0	0	0	

Going:	Sf: 0-3 GS: 0-3 Gd: 0-0 GF: 0-0 Fm: 0-0
Distance:	2m/2m3: 0-2 2m4-2m7: 0-0 3m+: 0-1
Track:	LH: 0-3 RH: 0-0 Tight: 0-1 Gall: 0-0
Aids:	Bl: 0-0 Vi: 0-0 Tstrap: 0-0 Ckp: 0-0
Best Rating:	**48** 1/04 Weth 2m gd-sft NHF

Glenelly Gale (IRE)
115(101h)   (109h)**150**

10-y-o b/br g Strong Gale-Smart Fashion (Carlburg)
A L T Moore F Bradley

Placings:0/2F140/5124U13/5035103/4F3104-3032126300   (4964)
2003/04: 17³GF, 17⁰YS, 20³F, 24²GF, 24¹F, 16²GF, 16⁶YS, 18³Y, 25⁹G, 16⁰GF,

	Starts	1st	2nd	3rd	Win & Pl
Hurdles	1	0	0	0	
Chases	9	1	2	3	79458
Career Total	36	6	4	7	145976
145	11/03	DRoy	3m		Ch	FRM £59090
132	3/03	Limk	2m1f	HCh	SFT £12662
119	1/02	Thur	2m		Y-S £7831
122	2/01	Fair	2m100y	Ch	HVY £18346
119	10/00	Gowr	2m1f	Ch	SFT £4692
123	1/00	Punc	2m	Hdl	SFT £3312

Total win prize-money £105935

Going:	Sf: 0-0 GS: 0-0 Gd: 0-1 GF: - Fm: 1-6
Distance:	2m/2m3: 0-6 2m4-2m7: 0-1 **3m+:** 1-3
Track:	LH: 0-3 RH: 0-4 Tight: 0-1 Gall: 0-0
Aids:	Bl: 0-0 Vi: 0-0 Tstrap: 0-0 Ckp: 0-0
Best Rating:	**150** 3/04 Thur 2m2f yield Ch

Smart Irish chaser; effective at around two miles but won a Grade One at Down Royal over three miles; acts on soft/heavy ground.

Glenfarclas Boy (IRE)
101   (78h)**112**

8-y-o b g Montelimar (USA)-Fairy Blaze (IRE) (Good Thyne (USA))
Miss Lucinda V Russell Mrs Ishbel Grant

Placings:600F/0F4P46/U1PP2F5233P-0151P0F2F (4912)
2003/04: 24⁰G, 20¹GS, 20⁵GF, 20¹S, 20⁵PHY, 16⁵HY, 20²GF, 20²G, 20⁵FS,

	Starts	1st	2nd	3rd	Win & Pl
Chases	9	2	1	0	8110
Career Total	30	3	3	2	18518
108	12/03	Ayr	2m4f	F(0-95)Ch	SFT £3445
95	5/03	Prth	2m4f110yF(0-90)Ch	G-S £3255
112	6/02	Prth	2m	D Ch	G-S £5012

Total win prize-money £11712

Going:	Sf: 1-4 GS: 1-1 Gd: 0-2 GF: - Fm: 0-2
Distance:	2m/2m3: 0-1 **2m4-2m7:** 2-7 3m+: 0-1
Track:	LH: 1-3 RH: 1-6 Tight: 0-0 Gall: 0-1
Aids:	Bl: 0-0 Vi: 0-0 Tstrap: 0-0 Ckp: 0-3
Best Rating:	**112** 3/04 Ayr 2m4f gd-fm Ch

Moderate and inconsistent chaser; stays 2m 5f; acts on soft ground; has worn cheekpieces; races prominently.

Glengarra (IRE)
(88h)   (89h)

7-y-o ch g Phardante (FR)-Glengarra Princess (Cardinal Flower)
D R Gandolfo T J Whitley

Placings:035P0   (4733)
2003/04: 20⁰GS, 20³GS, 16⁵HY, 18⁰G, 22⁰G,

	Starts	1st	2nd	3rd	Win & Pl
Hurdles	5	0	0	1	589
Career Total	5	0	0	1	589

Going:	Sf: 0-1 GS: 0-2 Gd: 0-2 GF: - Fm: 0-0
Distance:	2m/2m3: 0-2 2m4-2m7: 0-3 3m+: 0-0
Track:	LH: 0-4 RH: 0-1 Tight: 0-2 Gall: 0-0
Aids:	Bl: 0-0 Vi: 0-0 Tstrap: 0-0 Ckp: 0-0
Best Rating:	**89** 12/03 Hayd 2m4f gd-sft Hdl

Ex-pointer; has shown ability over hurdles.

Glenhaven Boy (IRE)

6-y-o br g Satco (FR)-Dunabell Lady (Garda's Revenge (USA))
K C Bailey P J Vogt

Placings:P   (2277)
2003/04: 24⁰G,

	Starts	1st	2nd	3rd	Win & Pl
Hurdles	1	0	0	0	
Career Total	1	0	0	0	

Going:	Sf: 0-0 GS: 0-0 Gd: 0-1 GF: - Fm: 0-0
Distance:	2m/2m3: 0-0 2m4-2m7: 0-0 3m+: 0-1
Track:	LH: 0-0 RH: 0-1 Tight: 0-0 Gall: 0-0
Aids:	Bl: 0-0 Vi: 0-0 Tstrap: 0-0 Ckp: 0-0

Glenmoss Tara (IRE)
108   **130+**

6-y-o b m Zaffaran (USA)-Majestic Run (Deep Run)
N G Richards West Coast Fiddlers

Placings:112/1112-25   (2717)
2003/04: 16²S, 21⁵GS,

	Starts	1st	2nd	3rd	Win & Pl
Hurdles	2	0	1	0	6152
Career Total	9	5	3	0	36252
104	1/03	Muss	2m4f	D Hdl	GD £6077
115	12/02	Ayr	2m4f	E Hdl	SFT £3052
105	11/02	Catt	2m3f	F Hdl	GD £2394
98	2/02	Donc	2m110y	H NHF	SFT £2002

Total win prize-money £13526

Going:	Sf: 0-1 GS: 0-1 Gd: 0-0 GF: - Fm: 0-0
Distance:	2m/2m3: 0-1 2m4-2m7: 0-1 3m+: 0-0
Track:	LH: 0-2 RH: 0-0 Tight: 0-0 Gall: 0-1
Aids:	Bl: 0-0 Vi: 0-0 Tstrap: 0-0 Ckp: 0-0
Best Rating:	**130** 3/03 Newb 2m5f good Hdl

Useful hurdler; very progressive form throughout novice season; stays two miles five and acts on good ground or softer; a tough mare who should jump a fence in time.

Glenogue (IRE)
108   **102**

6-y-o b m Hushang (IRE)-Glenamal (Kemal (FR))
K C Bailey Big Hitters Racing Partnership

Placings:433242   (4909)
2003/04: 16⁴S, 22³GS, 16⁵HY, 19²GS, 21⁴G, 24²S,

	Starts	1st	2nd	3rd	Win & Pl
Hurdles	6	0	2	2	6899
Career Total	6	0	2	2	6899

Going:	Sf: 0-3 GS: 0-2 Gd: 0-1 GF: - Fm: 0-0
Distance:	2m/2m3: 0-2 2m4-2m7: 0-3 3m+: 0-1
Track:	LH: 0-2 RH: 0-4 Tight: 0-1 Gall: 0-1
Aids:	Bl: 0-0 Vi: 0-0 Tstrap: 0-0 Ckp: 0-0
Best Rating:	**102** 3/04 Newb 2m5f good Hdl

Big mare; Irish point winner; placed but well held in mares' only novices' hurdles; should stay well.

Glimpse Of Glory
86   **52**

4-y-o b g Makbul-Bright-One (Electric)
C W Thornton The Challengers

Placings:00   (2136)
2003/04: 16⁰GF, 16⁰G,

	Starts	1st	2nd	3rd	Win & Pl
Hurdles	2	0	0	0	
Career Total	2	0	0	0	

Going:	Sf: 0-0 GS: 0-0 Gd: 0-1 GF: - Fm: 0-1
Distance:	2m/2m3: 0-2 2m4-2m7: 0-0 3m+: 0-0
Track:	LH: 0-2 RH: 0-0 Tight: 0-0 Gall: 0-1
Aids:	Bl: 0-0 Vi: 0-0 Tstrap: 0-0 Ckp: 0-0
Best Rating:	**52** 11/03 Newc 2m good Hdl

Glinger (IRE)

110(96h)   (91h)112

11-y-o b g Remainder Man-Harilla (Sir Herbert)
N G Richards James Westoll

Placings:6650/FP/4422/3113-221   (1141)
2003/04: 20²G, 22²GF, 20¹GF,

	Starts	1st	2nd	3rd	Win & Pl
Hurdles	2	0	2	0	2296
Chases	1	1	0	0	7963
Career Total	17	3	4	2	27186
112 8/03 Prth	2m4f110yD(0-125)HCh		G-F	£7962
112 10/02 Carl	2m4f	D Ch		G-F	£5668
99 8/02 MRas	2m4f	D(0-120)HCh		G-F	£5109

Total win prize-money £18740

Going:	Sf: 0-0 GS: 0-0 Gd: 0-1 GF: - Fm: 1-2
Distance:	2m/2m3: 0-0 2m4-2m7: 1-3 3m+: 0-0
Track:	LH: 0-1 RH: 1-2 Tight: 0-1 Gall: 0-0
Aids:	Bl: 0-0 Vi: 0-0 Tstrap: 0-0 Ckp: 0-0
Best Rating:	112 8/03 Prth 2m4f110y gd-fm Ch

Moderate chaser; won two fast-ground events over two and a half miles in the autumn of 2002; runner-up twice over hurdles in July; should continue to win his share of modest events over fences.

Gloaming

79   55

6-y-o b m Celtic Swing-Kandavu (Safawan)
J Gallagher www.network-racing.com

Placings:5P   (1702)
2003/04: 17⁵GF, 16ᴾGF,

	Starts	1st	2nd	3rd	Win & Pl
Hurdles	2	0	0	0	0
Career Total	2	0	0	0	0

Going:	Sf: 0-0 GS: 0-0 Gd: 0-0 GF: - Fm: 0-2
Distance:	2m/2m3: 0-0 2m4-2m7: 0-0 3m+: 0-0
Track:	LH: 0-2 RH: 0-0 Tight: 0-2 Gall: 0-0
Aids:	Bl: 0-0 Vi: 0-0 Tstrap: 0-0 Ckp: 0-0
Best Rating:	55 7/03 Sedg 2m1f gd-fm Hdl

Global Challenge (IRE)

98   107

5-y-o b g Sadler's Wells (USA)-Middle Prospect (USA) (Mr Prospector (USA))
Jonjo O'Neill (Sir Michael Stoute 12/9) Mrs Jonjo O'Neill

Placings:330054   (4783)
2003/04: 16⁵S, 20³S, 16⁰HY, 20⁴GS, 25⁵S, 21⁴G,

	Starts	1st	2nd	3rd	Win & Pl
Hurdles	6	0	0	2	1568
Career Total	6	0	0	2	1568

Going:	Sf: 0-4 GS: 0-1 Gd: 0-1 GF: - Fm: 0-0
Distance:	2m/2m3: 0-2 2m4-2m7: 0-3 3m+: 0-1
Track:	LH: 0-2 RH: 0-4 Tight: 0-0 Gall: 0-1
Aids:	Bl: 0-1 Vi: 0-0 Tstrap: 0-2 Ckp: 0-1
Best Rating:	107 1/04 Leic 2m4f110y soft Hdl

Modest hurdler; stays two miles-four; acts on good ground or softer.

Globe Star (IRE)

47f   74f

5-y-o b m Germany (USA)-Chaparette (Chaparly (FR))

F P Murtagh E Chapman

Placings:00   (4952)
2003/04: 16⁰GF, 16⁰GS,

	Starts	1st	2nd	3rd	Win & Pl
NH Flat	2	0	0	0	
Career Total	2	0	0	0	

Going:	Sf: 0-0 GS: 0-1 Gd: 0-0 GF: - Fm: 0-1
Distance:	2m/2m3: 0-2 2m4-2m7: 0-0 3m+: 0-0
Track:	LH: 0-1 RH: 0-1 Tight: 0-0 Gall: 0-0
Aids:	Bl: 0-0 Vi: 0-0 Tstrap: 0-0 Ckp: 0-0
Best Rating:	74 3/04 Ayr 2m gd-fm NHF

Glorious Welcome

72   38

6-y-o b g Past Glories-Rest And Welcome (Town And Country)
Jane Southcombe Mrs V H Nicholas

Placings:004P/P06P-00PP   (4790)
2003/04: 24⁰S, 19⁰S, 26ᴾG, 21ᴾG,

	Starts	1st	2nd	3rd	Win & Pl
Hurdles	4	0	0	0	
Career Total	12	0	0	0	0

Going:	Sf: 0-2 GS: 0-0 Gd: 0-2 GF: - Fm: 0-0
Distance:	2m/2m3: 0-1 2m4-2m7: 0-1 3m+: 0-2
Track:	LH: 0-2 RH: 0-2 Tight: 0-1 Gall: 0-0
Aids:	Bl: 0-0 Vi: 0-4 Tstrap: 0-0 Ckp: 0-0
Best Rating:	53 12/01 Plum 2m good Hdl

Plating-class hurdler; well beaten in all starts over hurdles.

Glory Of Love

75

9-y-o b g Belmez (USA)-Princess Lieven (Royal Palace)
J A Supple Miss Lorna Preston

Placings:5P/2/0   (1942)
2003/04: 22⁰G,

	Starts	1st	2nd	3rd	Win & Pl
Hurdles	1	0	0	0	
Career Total	4	0	1	0	541

Going:	Sf: 0-0 GS: 0-0 Gd: 0-0 GF: - Fm: 0-0
Distance:	2m/2m3: 0-0 2m4-2m7: 0-1 3m+: 0-0
Track:	LH: 0-0 RH: 0-1 Tight: 0-1 Gall: 0-0
Aids:	Bl: 0-0 Vi: 0-0 Tstrap: 0-0 Ckp: 0-0
Best Rating:	75 5/01 Hexm 2m soft Hdl

Glory Storey (IRE)

(82h)

10-y-o b g Tremblant-Boule De Soie (The Parson)
B J Llewellyn Richards & Thomas

Placings:403/0U455213/1P-P   (3049)
2003/04: 24ᴾG,

	Starts	1st	2nd	3rd	Win & Pl
Hurdles	1	0	0	0	
Career Total	14	2	1	2	10547
104 6/02 Hntg	3m	F(0-100)HCh		G-F	£3300
104 4/02 Ludl	3m	D(0-110)HCh		G-F	£4498

Total win prize-money £7799

Going:	Sf: 0-0 GS: 0-0 Gd: 0-0 GF: - Fm: 0-0
Distance:	2m/2m3: 0-0 2m4-2m7: 0-0 3m+: 0-1
Track:	LH: 0-0 RH: 0-1 Tight: 0-1 Gall: 0-0

Aids:	Bl: 0-0 Vi: 0-0 Tstrap: 0-0 Ckp: 0-0
Best Rating:	104 6/02 Hntg 3m gd-fm Ch

Glory Trail (IRE)

10-y-o b g Supreme Leader-Death Or Glory (Hasdrubal)
Mrs D M Grissell Richard Griffiths

Placings:00/6/4-F   (0349)
2003/04: 26ᶠGF,

	Starts	1st	2nd	3rd	Win & Pl
Chases	1	0	0	0	
Career Total	5	0	0	0	219

Going:	Sf: 0-0 GS: 0-0 Gd: 0-0 GF: - Fm: 0-1
Distance:	2m/2m3: 0-0 2m4-2m7: 0-0 3m+: 0-1
Track:	LH: 0-0 RH: 0-1 Tight: 0-1 Gall: 0-0
Aids:	Bl: 0-0 Vi: 0-0 Tstrap: 0-0 Ckp: 0-0
Best Rating:	76 6/01 Strf 2m6f110y gd-fm Hdl

Gloster Gunner

5-y-o ch g Gunner B-Blue Empress (Blue Cashmere)
Dr P Pritchard Four For Fun

Placings:0-06   (4173)
2003/04: 17⁰S, 16⁰HY, 19⁶G,

	Starts	1st	2nd	3rd	Win & Pl
NH Flat	1	0	0	0	0
Hurdles	2	0	0	0	0
Career Total	3	0	0	0	0

Going:	Sf: 0-2 GS: 0-0 Gd: 0-1 GF: - Fm: 0-0
Distance:	2m/2m3: 0-2 2m4-2m7: 0-1 3m+: 0-0
Track:	LH: 0-3 RH: 0-0 Tight: 0-1 Gall: 0-0
Aids:	Bl: 0-0 Vi: 0-0 Tstrap: 0-0 Ckp: 0-0
Best Rating:	0 3/04 MRas 2m6f good Hdl

Glowing Ember

45f

4-y-o b f Blushing Flame (USA)-California Dreamin (Slip Anchor)
T Wall D Bunn

Placings:0   (2101)
2003/04: 12⁰GF,

	Starts	1st	2nd	3rd	Win & Pl
NH Flat	1	0	0	0	
Career Total	1	0	0	0	

Going:	Sf: 0-0 GS: 0-0 Gd: 0-0 GF: - Fm: 0-1
Distance:	2m/2m3: 0-0 2m4-2m7: 0-0 3m+: 0-0
Track:	LH: 0-1 RH: 0-0 Tight: 0-0 Gall: 0-0
Aids:	Bl: 0-0 Vi: 0-0 Tstrap: 0-0 Ckp: 0-0
Best Rating:	45 11/03 Newb 1m4f110y gd-fm NHF

Glynn Dingle (IRE)

109(101h)   (95h)112

11-y-o b g Millfontaine-Banner Lady (Milan)
A J Martin Patrick McCaughey

Placings:0/FF0602P51-11F32U4000   (4803a)
2003/04: 24¹G, 20¹YS, 24²G, 22³Y, 20²GF, 24ᵁG, 24⁴GF, 18⁰GY, 24⁰GY, 20⁰Y,

	Starts	1st	2nd	3rd	Win & Pl
Hurdles	1	0	0	0	0
Chases	9	2	1	1	37197
Career Total	**20**	**3**	**2**	**1**	**47904**
119 5/03 Punc	2m4f		(0-135)HCh	Y-S	£7392
112 5/03 DRoy	3m		(0-123)HCh	GD	£16883
106 4/03 Prth	2m4f110yD(0-115)HCh			GD	£8287
			Total win prize-money £32564		

Going:	Sf: 0-0 GS: 0-0 Gd: 1-3 GF: - Fm: 0-2
Distance:	2m/2m3: 0-1 2m4-2m7: 1-4 3m+: 1-5
Track:	LH: 0-2 RH: 1-7 Tight: 0-0 Gall: 0-0
Aids:	Bl: 0-0 Vi: 0-0 Tstrap: 0-0 Ckp: 0-0
Best Rating:	136 8/03 Prth 2m4f110y gd-fm Ch

Moderate chaser; ex-Irish; acts on good and soft ground; stays two and a half miles.

Go For Bust

98f   97+f

5-y-o b g Sabrehill (USA)-Butsova (Formidable (USA))
N J Henderson Mrs E Roberts & Nick Roberts

Placings:06					(4824)
2003/04: 16⁶G, 17⁵GF,					

	Starts	1st	2nd	3rd	Win & Pl
NH Flat	2	0	0	0	0
Career Total	**2**	**0**	**0**	**0**	**0**

Going:	Sf: 0-0 GS: 0-0 Gd: 0-1 GF: - Fm: 0-1
Distance:	2m/2m3: 0-2 2m4-2m7: 0-0 3m+: 0-0
Track:	LH: 0-1 RH: 0-1 Tight: 0-0 Gall: 0-1
Aids:	Bl: 0-0 Vi: 0-0 Tstrap: 0-0 Ckp: 0-0
Best Rating:	97 4/04 Extr 2m1f gd-fm NHF

Go Nomadic

10-y-o br g Nomadic Way (USA)-Dreamago (Sir Mago)
D G Atkinson D G Atkinson

Placings:210/332321-32323					(4949)
2003/04: 25³G, 27²G, 25³G, 27²G, 26³GS,					

	Starts	1st	2nd	3rd	Win & Pl
Chases	5	0	2	3	2143
Career Total	**14**	**2**	**5**	**6**	**11652**
105 4/03 Prth	3m7f	H Ch		GD	£4069
105 3/02 Kels	3m1f	H Ch		HVY	£2691
			Total win prize-money £6761		

Going:	Sf: 0-0 GS: 0-1 Gd: 0-4 GF: - Fm: 0-0
Distance:	2m/2m3: 0-0 2m4-2m7: 0-0 3m+: 0-5
Track:	LH: 0-4 RH: 0-0 Tight: 0-3 Gall: 0-0
Aids:	Bl: 0-0 Vi: 0-0 Tstrap: 0-4 Ckp: 0-0
Best Rating:	105 4/04 Sedg 3m3f good Ch

Fair hunter chaser; acts on a good and soft surface; stays three miles-seven; usually wears a tongue strap.

Go On Jack

88f   82f

6-y-o ch g Saint Keyne-Swift Messenger (Giolla Mear)
G Fierro G Fierro

Placings:0040					(0947)
2003/04: 16⁰G, 17⁵G, 17⁴GF, 16⁰G,					

	Starts	1st	2nd	3rd	Win & Pl
NH Flat	4	0	0	0	0
Career Total	**4**	**0**	**0**	**0**	**0**

Going:	Sf: 0-0 GS: 0-0 Gd: 0-3 GF: - Fm: 0-1

Distance:	2m/2m3: 0-4 2m4-2m7: 0-0 3m+: 0-0
Track:	LH: 0-4 RH: 0-0 Tight: 0-1 Gall: 0-0
Aids:	Bl: 0-0 Vi: 0-0 Tstrap: 0-0 Ckp: 0-0
Best Rating:	82 6/03 Sthl 2m1f gd-fm NHF

Go White Lightning (IRE)

103   (91h) 115

9-y-o gr g Zaffaran (USA)-Rosy Posy (IRE) (Roselier (FR))
M Bradstock J Macleod

Placings:U1/1/0U/3P234-P230					(4398)
2003/04: 26⁶HY, 22²G, 26³GS, 32⁰G,					

	Starts	1st	2nd	3rd	Win & Pl
Chases	4	0	1	1	2381
Career Total	**14**	**2**	**2**	**3**	**8952**
107 5/00 Hrfd	2m1f	H NHF		GD	£1841
107 4/00 MRas	2m1f110yH NHF			SFT	£1582
			Total win prize-money £3423		

Going:	Sf: 0-1 GS: 0-1 Gd: 0-2 GF: - Fm: 0-0
Distance:	2m/2m3: 0-0 2m4-2m7: 0-1 3m+: 0-3
Track:	LH: 0-3 RH: 0-0 Tight: 0-2 Gall: 0-0
Aids:	Bl: 0-0 Vi: 0-0 Tstrap: 0-0 Ckp: 0-0
Best Rating:	115 1/03 Donc 3m good Ch

Modest chaser; stays three miles; acts on most ground; without a win since bumper days.

Goblet Of Fire (USA)

111   116+

5-y-o b g Green Desert (USA)-Laurentine (USA) (Private Account (USA))
P F Nicholls (B J Meehan 4/10) Mrs Susan Roy

Placings:3553					(3593)
2003/04: 16³S, 16⁵GF, 17⁵GS, 16³HY,					

	Starts	1st	2nd	3rd	Win & Pl
Hurdles	4	0	0	2	2925
Career Total	**4**	**0**	**0**	**2**	**2925**

Going:	Sf: 0-2 GS: 0-1 Gd: 0-0 GF: - Fm: 0-1
Distance:	2m/2m3: 0-4 2m4-2m7: 0-0 3m+: 0-0
Track:	LH: 0-1 RH: 0-3 Tight: 0-1 Gall: 0-1
Aids:	Bl: 0-1 Vi: 0-0 Tstrap: 0-0 Ckp: 0-0
Best Rating:	116 1/03 Asct 2m110y soft Hdl

Very useful performer on the Flat; suited by ten furlongs and fast ground; appreciates a strong gallop; usually wears blinkers.

Godfather (IRE)

6-y-o ch g Insan (USA)-Lady Letitia (Le Bavard (FR))
M Pitman Malcolm C Denmark

Placings:00-0P					(2237)
2003/04: 16⁰G, 16⁸PG,					

	Starts	1st	2nd	3rd	Win & Pl
NH Flat	1	0	0	0	0
Hurdles	1	0	0	0	0
Career Total	**4**	**0**	**0**	**0**	

Going:	Sf: 0-0 GS: 0-0 Gd: 0-2 GF: - Fm: 0-0
Distance:	2m/2m3: 0-2 2m4-2m7: 0-0 3m+: 0-0
Track:	LH: 0-0 RH: 0-2 Tight: 0-0 Gall: 0-0
Aids:	Bl: 0-0 Vi: 0-0 Tstrap: 0-0 Ckp: 0-0
Best Rating:	85 11/03 Sand 2m110y good NHF

Gods Token

111   120+

6-y-o gr g Gods Solution-Pro-Token (Proverb)
Miss Venetia Williams The Silver Cod Partnership

Placings:612-2144					(4793)
2003/04: 16²GS, 16¹GS, 16⁴G, 16⁴G,					

	Starts	1st	2nd	3rd	Win & Pl
Hurdles	4	1	1	0	6223
Career Total	**7**	**2**	**2**	**0**	**8352**
118 2/04 Sand	2m110y D Hdl			G-S	£5109
95 6/02 MRas	2m1f110yH NHF			G-F	£1561
			Total win prize-money £6670		

Going:	Sf: 0-0 GS: 1-2 Gd: 0-2 GF: - Fm: 0-0
Distance:	2m/2m3: 1-4 2m4-2m7: 0-0 3m+: 0-0
Track:	LH: 0-1 RH: 1-3 Tight: 0-1 Gall: 0-1
Aids:	Bl: 0-0 Vi: 0-0 Tstrap: 0-0 Ckp: 0-0
Best Rating:	120 12/03 Sand 2m110y gd-sft Hdl

Fair novice hurdler; bumper winner; effective at two miles; acts on most type of ground; tough sort.

Gofagold

107 (102h)   (88h) 91+

9-y-o ch g Tina's Pet-Golden Della (Glint Of Gold)
A C Whillans Mrs L M Whillans

Placings:40/53/0432/222F-45053336					(4730)
2003/04: 20⁴G, 16⁵S, 16⁵G, 16⁵HY, 16³HY, 16³G, 16³HP, 20⁶G,					

	Starts	1st	2nd	3rd	Win & Pl
Hurdles	2	0	0	0	372
Chases	6	0	0	3	2049
Career Total	**20**	**0**	**4**	**5**	**7838**

Going:	Sf: 0-4 GS: 0-4 Gd: 0-4 GF: - Fm: 0-0
Distance:	2m/2m3: 0-2 2m4-2m7: 0-2 3m+: 0-0
Track:	LH: 0-5 RH: 0-3 Tight: 0-1 Gall: 0-1
Aids:	Bl: 0-0 Vi: 0-0 Tstrap: 0-0 Ckp: 0-0
Best Rating:	91 3/04 Carl 2m good Ch

Modest hurdler/chaser; yet to win a race; stays two and a quarter miles, but yet to convince over further; suited by ground good or softer.

Gohh

(96h)   (97h) 102

8-y-o ch g Afflora (IRE)-Lavenham's Last (Rymer)
M W Easterby Mrs P A H Hartley

Placings:45/1021P/0303F-FPP					(4957)
2003/04: 16⁶G, 17⁵S, 17⁵GS,					

	Starts	1st	2nd	3rd	Win & Pl
Chases	3	0	0	0	
Career Total	**15**	**2**	**1**	**2**	**7117**
97 12/01 MRas	2m1f110yD Hdl			SFT	£3444
97 10/01 MRas	2m1f110yH NHF			G-S	£1582
			Total win prize-money £5026		

Going:	Sf: 0-1 GS: 0-1 Gd: 0-1 GF: - Fm: 0-0
Distance:	2m/2m3: 0-3 2m4-2m7: 0-0 3m+: 0-0
Track:	LH: 0-2 RH: 0-1 Tight: 0-0 Gall: 0-1
Aids:	Bl: 0-0 Vi: 0-0 Tstrap: 0-0 Ckp: 0-0
Best Rating:	102 2/03 Weth 2m good Ch

Going Global (IRE)

109   121

7-y-o ch g Bob Back (USA)-Ukraine Girl (Targowice (USA))
G L Moore Allen House Partnership

Placings:000/3310/66-22320   (3409)
2003/04: 16²G, 18²G, 20³G, 20²HY, 21⁰S,

	Starts	1st	2nd	3rd	Win & Pl
Hurdles	5	0	3	1	8286
Career Total	14	1	3	3	12482
112 2/02 Plum 2m5f	E Hdl			HVY	£2604
			Total win prize-money		£2604

Going:	Sf: 0-2 GS: 0-0 Gd: 0-3 GF: - Fm: 0-0
Distance:	2m/2m3: 0-2 2m4-2m7: 0-3 3m+: 0-0
Track:	LH: 0-2 RH: 0-2 Tight: 0-3 Gall: 0-0
Aids:	Bl: 0-0 Vi: 0-0 Tstrap: 0-0 Ckp: 0-1
Best Rating:	121 1/04 Font 2m4f heavy Hdl

Modest hurdler; formerly useful on the Flat; stays trip of around two and a half miles and suited by ground good or softer; has been tongue-tied in the past.

Going Solo

8-y-o ch m Sula Bula-Little Beaver (Privy Seal)
Mrs S Gardner D V Gardner

Placings:00/0P6-P   (0530)
2003/04: 20PGF,

	Starts	1st	2nd	3rd	Win & Pl
Hurdles	1	0	0	0	
Career Total	6	0	0	0	0

Going:	Sf: 0-0 GS: 0-0 Gd: 0-0 GF: - Fm: 0-1
Distance:	2m/2m3: 0-0 2m4-2m7: 0-0 3m+: 0-0
Track:	LH: 0-1 RH: 0-0 Tight: 0-0 Gall: 0-0
Aids:	Bl: 0-1 Vi: 0-0 Tstrap: 0-0 Ckp: 0-0
Best Rating:	73 5/02 Extr 2m1f good NHF

Gola Cher (IRE)
97   140

10-y-o ch g Beau Sher-Owen Money (Master Owen)
A King Mr & Mrs F C Welch

Placings:11212/1210/2F3-3   (2445)
2003/04: 28³S,

	Starts	1st	2nd	3rd	Win & Pl
Chases	1	0	0	1	1090
Career Total	13	5	4	2	61200
118 1/02 Kemp 3m	D Ch			SFT	£4114
131 11/01 Chep 2m3f110yA Ch				G-S	£15000
126 2/01 Sand 2m6f	B Hdl			HVY	£7182
132 11/00 Asct 3m	C Hdl			SFT	£4836
113 10/00 Strf 2m6f110yE Hdl				G-S	£2681
			Total win prize-money		£33815

Going:	Sf: 0-1 GS: 0-0 Gd: 0-0 GF: - Fm: 0-0
Distance:	2m/2m3: 0-0 2m4-2m7: 0-0 3m+: 0-1
Track:	LH: 0-1 RH: 0-0 Tight: 0-0 Gall: 0-0
Aids:	Bl: 0-0 Vi: 0-0 Tstrap: 0-0 Ckp: 0-0
Best Rating:	140 11/02 Winc 3m1f110y Ch

Useful handicap chaser; stays beyond three miles and effective on soft ground; has been tried in blinkers and cheekpieces.

Gola Supreme (IRE)
100(103c)   (116c)116+

9-y-o gr g Supreme Leader-Coal Burn (King Sitric)
R Lee James P Smith

Placings:1P/2UP-P1PP   (4693)
2003/04: 22PGS, 24¹S, 24PGS, 22PG,

	Starts	1st	2nd	3rd	Win & Pl
Hurdles	3	1	0	0	3948
Chases	1	0	0	0	0
Career Total	9	2	1	0	10336
117 2/04 Tntn 3m110y	E(0-110)HHdl			SFT	£3948
103 11/01 Asct 3m	C Hdl			GD	£4888
			Total win prize-money		£8836

Going:	Sf: 1-1 GS: 0-2 Gd: 0-1 GF: - Fm: 0-0
Distance:	2m/2m3: 0-0 2m4-2m7: 0-2 3m+: 1-2
Track:	LH: 0-1 RH: 1-3 Tight: 1-1 Gall: 0-1
Aids:	Bl: 0-0 Vi: 0-0 Tstrap: 0-0 Ckp: 0-0
Best Rating:	117 2/04 Tntn 3m110y soft Hdl

Fair performer; won on rules debut at Ascot but pulled up next time in only other hurdle; promising chasing debut when second at Bangor; disappointing since, but relished the return to hurdles when winning at Taunton in February; stays three miles; acts on an easy surface.

Gold Again (IRE)
95f   83f

6-y-o b g Old Vic-Thomastown Girl (Tekoah)
Noel T Chance Dan Jim Partnership

Placings:05   (4739)
2003/04: 16⁰GS, 17⁵G,

	Starts	1st	2nd	3rd	Win & Pl
NH Flat	2	0	0	0	0
Career Total	2	0	0	0	0

Going:	Sf: 0-0 GS: 0-1 Gd: 0-1 GF: - Fm: 0-0
Distance:	2m/2m3: 0-2 2m4-2m7: 0-0 3m+: 0-0
Track:	LH: 0-1 RH: 0-1 Tight: 0-1 Gall: 0-1
Aids:	Bl: 0-0 Vi: 0-0 Tstrap: 0-0 Ckp: 0-0
Best Rating:	83 12/03 Hntg 2m10y gd-sft NHF

Gold Menelek (IRE)
99   68

5-y-o ch g Goldmark (USA)-Newlands Cross (Mandalus)
T P McGovern Lewes Racing

Placings:0-0024   (1846)
2003/04: 16⁰G, 16⁰GF, 21²GF, 22⁴G,

	Starts	1st	2nd	3rd	Win & Pl
NH Flat	2	0	0	0	0
Hurdles	2	0	1	0	1067
Career Total	5	0	1	0	1067

Going:	Sf: 0-0 GS: 0-0 Gd: 0-2 GF: - Fm: 0-2
Distance:	2m/2m3: 0-2 2m4-2m7: 0-0 3m+: 0-0
Track:	LH: 0-4 RH: 0-0 Tight: 0-2 Gall: 0-0
Aids:	Bl: 0-0 Vi: 0-0 Tstrap: 0-0 Ckp: 0-0
Best Rating:	71 9/03 Worc 2m gd-fm NHF

Novice hurdler; well-beaten second on hurdles debut.

Gold Native (IRE)
99   71

6-y-o br g Be My Native (USA)-Goldiyana (FR) (Glint Of Gold)
B Ellison K M Everitt

Placings:43-005   (4660)
2003/04: 17⁰GS, 20⁰S, 24⁴S,

	Starts	1st	2nd	3rd	Win & Pl
Hurdles	3	0	0	0	0
Career Total	5	0	0	1	425

Going:	Sf: 0-2 GS: 0-1 Gd: 0-0 GF: - Fm: 0-0
Distance:	2m/2m3: 0-1 2m4-2m7: 0-0 3m+: 0-1
Track:	LH: 0-3 RH: 0-0 Tight: 0-1 Gall: 0-1
Aids:	Bl: 0-0 Vi: 0-0 Tstrap: 0-0 Ckp: 0-0
Best Rating:	95 1/03 Muss 2m good NHF

Improved on initial effort when third in a bumper at Musselburgh in January.

Gold Summerland (HOL)
79   48

6-y-o b m Learn By Heart (USA)-Sabara Raaphorst (HOL) (Glint Of Gold)
C J Mann The Dunnkirk Partnership

Placings:0   (2663)
2003/04: 16⁰G,

	Starts	1st	2nd	3rd	Win & Pl
Hurdles	1	0	0	0	
Career Total	1	0	0	0	

Going:	Sf: 0-0 GS: 0-0 Gd: 0-1 GF: - Fm: 0-0
Distance:	2m/2m3: 0-1 2m4-2m7: 0-0 3m+: 0-0
Track:	LH: 0-0 RH: 0-1 Tight: 0-0 Gall: 0-0
Aids:	Bl: 0-0 Vi: 0-0 Tstrap: 0-0 Ckp: 0-0
Best Rating:	48 12/03 Leic 2m good Hdl

Goldamie (IRE)
84   60

5-y-o ch m Zaffaran (USA)-Keeping Company (Kings Company)
M Scudamore Mrs S Tainton

Placings:6400   (4668)
2003/04: 16⁰GS, 17⁴HY, 19⁰GS, 23⁰GS,

	Starts	1st	2nd	3rd	Win & Pl
NH Flat	2	0	0	0	0
Hurdles	2	0	0	0	0
Career Total	4	0	0	0	0

Going:	Sf: 0-1 GS: 0-3 Gd: 0-0 GF: - Fm: 0-0
Distance:	2m/2m3: 0-2 2m4-2m7: 0-2 3m+: 0-0
Track:	LH: 0-1 RH: 0-3 Tight: 0-2 Gall: 0-1
Aids:	Bl: 0-0 Vi: 0-0 Tstrap: 0-0 Ckp: 0-0
Best Rating:	78 1/04 Folk 2m1f110y heavy NHF

Full-sister to Browjoshy; has shown signs of ability in bumpers.

Goldbrook
113   128

6-y-o b g Alderbrook-Miss Marigold (Norwick (USA))
R J Hodges John & Greer Norman

Placings:23342-31131040   (4559)
2003/04: 16⁰GS, 16¹GF, 17¹G, 20³S, 16¹S, 16⁰G, 16⁴S, 16⁰GS,

	Starts	1st	2nd	3rd	Win & Pl
Hurdles	8	3	0	2	31400
Career Total	13	3	2	4	35218
120 1/04 Winc 2m	D(0-125)HHdl			SFT	£9065
112 12/03 Extr 2m1f	D(0-120)HHdl			GD	£13975
101 5/03 Winc 2m	E Hdl			G-F	£3752
			Total win prize-money		£26792

Going:	Sf: 1-3 GS: 0-2 Gd: 1-2 GF: - Fm: 1-1
Distance:	2m/2m3: 3-7 2m4-2m7: 0-1 3m+: 0-0
Track:	LH: 0-3 RH: 3-5 Tight: 0-0 Gall: 0-2
Aids:	Bl: 0-0 Vi: 0-0 Tstrap: 0-0 Ckp: 0-0
Best Rating:	128 2/04 Newb 2m110y good Hdl

Fair hurdler; stays two and a half miles and acts on most types of ground, suited by racing prominently; progressive.

Golden Alpha (IRE)

112(96h)   (137h)156

10-y-o b g Alphabatim (USA)-Gina's Love (Golden Love)

M C Pipe D A Johnson

Placings:1/120/131064/11112U24F1-50203   (4864)
2003/04: 16⁵GF, 16⁹G, 16²G, 16⁹G, 16³S,

	Starts	1st	2nd	3rd	Win & Pl
Hurdles	1	0	0	0	0
Chases	4	0	1	1	9154
Career Total	25	9	4	2	100210

156	4/03	Aint	2m	A HCh	GD	£40600
120	7/02	Wolv	2m	E Ch	GD	£3497
133	6/02	NAbb	2m110y	D Ch	G-F	£3991
146	5/02	NAbb	2m110y	E Ch	SFT	£3435
115	5/02	Wwck	2m110y	E Ch	FRM	£3094
120	1/02	Winc	2m	E Hdl	G-S	£3136
128	12/01	Chep	2m110y	D Hdl	SFT	£3412
128	2/99	Newb	2m110y	H NHF	GD	£2931
121	4/98	Punc	2m	NHF	HVY	£5956

Total win prize-money £70055

Going:	Sf: 0-1 GS: 0-0 Gd: 0-3 GF: - Fm: 0-1
Distance:	2m/2m3: 0-5 2m4-2m7: 0-0 3m+: 0-0
Track:	LH: 0-3 RH: 0-2 Tight: 0-1 Gall: 0-0
Aids:	Bl: 0-0 Vi: 0-0 Tstrap: 0-0 Ckp: 0-0
Best Rating:	156 4/03 Aint 2m good Ch

Former useful hurdler/very useful novice chaser in 2002/3; every chance when fell in 2003 Grand Annual Handicap at Cheltenham; ran away with competitive handicap at Aintree; held off higher marks in 2003/4; all form around 2m; acts on any ground but best on fast; very much suited by forcing tactics; has worn a visor.

Golden Amber (IRE)

60   58

5-y-o b g Glacial Storm (USA)-Rigton Angle (Sit In The Corner (USA))

John R Upson The Peter Partnership

Placings:P5   (4762)
2003/04: 16⁹S, 19⁵S,

	Starts	1st	2nd	3rd	Win & Pl
Hurdles	2	0	0	0	0
Career Total	2	0	0	0	0

Going:	Sf: 0-2 GS: 0-0 Gd: 0-0 GF: - Fm: 0-0
Distance:	2m/2m3: 0-1 2m4-2m7: 0-1 3m+: 0-0
Track:	LH: 0-0 RH: 0-1 Tight: 0-0 Gall: 0-0
Aids:	Bl: 0-0 Vi: 0-0 Tstrap: 0-0 Ckp: 0-0
Best Rating:	58 4/04 Towc 2m3f110y soft Hdl

Golden Aruba

5-y-o ch g Golden Lahab (USA)-Clover Girl (Spin Of A Coin)

B Ellison Mrs Claire Ellison

Placings:FP   (2712)
2003/04: 21⁵GF, 16²GS,

	Starts	1st	2nd	3rd	Win & Pl
Hurdles	2	0	0	0	
Career Total	2	0	0	0	

Going:	Sf: 0-0 GS: 0-1 Gd: 0-0 GF: - Fm: 0-0
Distance:	2m/2m3: 0-1 2m4-2m7: 0-0 3m+: 0-0
Track:	LH: 0-2 RH: 0-0 Tight: 0-1 Gall: 0-1

Aids: Bl: 0-0 Vi: 0-0 Tstrap: 0-0 Ckp: 0-1

Golden Bay

99f   100f

5-y-o ch m Karinga Bay-Goldenswift (IRE) (Meneval (USA))

G B Balding Goldie's Friends

Placings:4210   (4328)
2003/04: 16⁴GF, 17²GS, 18¹S, 16⁹S,

	Starts	1st	2nd	3rd	Win & Pl
NH Flat	4	1	1	0	3046
Career Total	4	1	1	0	3046
100	2/04	Plum	2m2f	H NHF	SFT	£2289

Total win prize-money £2289

Going:	Sf: 1-2 GS: 0-1 Gd: 0-0 GF: - Fm: 0-1
Distance:	2m/2m3: 1-4 2m4-2m7: 0-0 3m+: 0-0
Track:	LH: 1-1 RH: 0-2 Tight: 0-0 Gall: 0-0
Aids:	Bl: 0-0 Vi: 0-0 Tstrap: 0-0 Ckp: 0-0
Best Rating:	100 2/04 Plum 2m2f soft NHF

Tough daughter of Karinga Bay; has improved with each bumper outing to date, winning latest at Plumpton in February over 2m 2f in testing ground; should stay further in time; acts on most ground.

Golden Chimes (USA)

9-y-o ch g Woodman (USA)-Russian Ballet (USA) (Nijinsky (CAN))

G Tuer G Tuer

Placings:P222/1000/14/4-1   (4263)
2003/04: 25¹GF,

	Starts	1st	2nd	3rd	Win & Pl
Chases	1	1	0	0	1095
Career Total	12	3	3	0	9237
110	3/04	Catt	3m1f110y	H Ch	G-F	£1095
116	7/01	Sedg	2m5f110y	D(0-120) HHdl	G-F	£3255
114	5/00	Sedg	2m5f110y	E Hdl	G-F	£2646

Total win prize-money £6996

Going:	Sf: 0-0 GS: 0-0 Gd: 0-0 GF: - Fm: 1-1
Distance:	2m/2m3: 0-0 2m4-2m7: 0-0 3m+: 1-1
Track:	LH: 1-1 RH: 0-0 Tight: 1-1 Gall: 0-0
Aids:	Bl: 0-0 Vi: 0-0 Tstrap: 0-0 Ckp: 0-0
Best Rating:	116 7/01 Sedg 2m5f110y gd-fm Hdl

Handicap hurdler, now hunter chaser; easy winner of a novices' event at Catterick in March; suited by fast ground.

Golden Coin

97   84

8-y-o ch g St Ninian-Legal Coin (Official)

W M Brisbourne Bob Moseley

Placings:6/114533U-3   (2939)
2003/04: 20³GS,

	Starts	1st	2nd	3rd	Win & Pl
Hurdles	1	0	0	1	496
Career Total	9	2	0	3	5739
116	5/02	Sthl	2m	H NHF	G-S	£1677
105	5/02	Uttx	2m	H NHF	GD	£2198

Total win prize-money £3875

Going:	Sf: 0-0 GS: 0-1 Gd: 0-0 GF: - Fm: 0-0
Distance:	2m/2m3: 0-0 2m4-2m7: 0-1 3m+: 0-0
Track:	LH: 0-1 RH: 0-0 Tight: 0-0 Gall: 0-0
Aids:	Bl: 0-0 Vi: 0-0 Tstrap: 0-0 Ckp: 0-0
Best Rating:	116 5/02 Sthl 2m gd-sft NHF

Dual bumper winner but has struggled so far over hurdles.

Golden Cross (IRE)

117   155

5-y-o b g Goldmark (USA)-Fordes Cross (Ya Zaman (USA))

M Halford Exors of the late Mrs H Johnson

Placings:16213-3100   (4383)
2003/04: 16³GY, 16¹Y, 16⁰Y, 16⁹G,

	Starts	1st	2nd	3rd	Win & Pl
Hurdles	4	1	0	1	40195
Career Total	9	3	1	2	84827
155	12/03	Leop	2m	Hdl	YLD	£33766
136	2/03	Fair	2m	Hdl	Y-S	£13506
121	11/02	Fair	2m	Hdl	SFT	£13957

Total win prize-money £61229

Going:	Sf: 0-0 GS: 0-0 Gd: 0-1 GF: - Fm: 0-0
Distance:	2m/2m3: 1-4 2m4-2m7: 0-0 3m+: 0-0
Track:	LH: 1-3 RH: 0-1 Tight: 0-0 Gall: 0-0
Aids:	Bl: 0-0 Vi: 0-0 Tstrap: 0-0 Ckp: 1-3
Best Rating:	155 12/03 Leop 2m yield Hdl

Smart hurdler; third in the Triumph Hurdle in 2003; surprise winner of the Grade One December Festival Hurdle at Leopardstown; disappointing next time; stayed on into seventh in Champion Hurdle; best at two miles; effective on soft ground; has worn cheekpieces of late.

Golden Crusader

106   108

7-y-o b g Gildoran-Pusey Street (Native Bazaar)

J W Mullins First Impressions Racing Group

Placings:00/305P00/0O4343-2   (0135)
2003/04: 16²G,

	Starts	1st	2nd	3rd	Win & Pl
Hurdles	1	0	1	0	1300
Career Total	15	0	1	3	3296

Going:	Sf: 0-0 GS: 0-0 Gd: 0-1 GF: - Fm: 0-0
Distance:	2m/2m3: 0-1 2m4-2m7: 0-0 3m+: 0-0
Track:	LH: 0-0 RH: 0-1 Tight: 0-0 Gall: 0-0
Aids:	Bl: 0-0 Vi: 0-0 Tstrap: 0-0 Ckp: 0-0
Best Rating:	108 5/03 Ludl 2m good Hdl

Modest novice hurdler; inclined to be headstrong and often makes the running; let down by his jumping when fourth in a handicap at Exeter February 2003.

Golden Dawn

(77h)   (69h)

7-y-o gr g Gran Alba (USA)-Golden Curd (FR) (Nice Havrais (USA))

B D Leavy Mrs Alurie O'Sullivan

Placings:00P40/06-P   (1303)
2003/04: 16⁰GF,

	Starts	1st	2nd	3rd	Win & Pl
Chases	1	0	0	0	0
Career Total	8	0	0	0	0

Going:	Sf: 0-0 GS: 0-0 Gd: 0-0 GF: - Fm: 0-1
Distance:	2m/2m3: 0-1 2m4-2m7: 0-0 3m+: 0-0
Track:	LH: 0-1 RH: 0-0 Tight: 0-0 Gall: 0-0
Aids:	Bl: 0-0 Vi: 0-0 Tstrap: 0-0 Ckp: 0-0
Best Rating:	69 4/02 Hexm 2m110y gd-fm Hdl

Modest hurdle form.

Golden Fields (IRE)
97   84

4-y-o b f Definite Article-Quickstep Queen (FR) (Pampabird)
A P Jones (A P Jarvis 10/7) Mrs K T Pilkington

Placings:60030   (3732)
2003/04: 16⁶G, 16⁶GF, 16⁰G, 20³HY, 16⁸G,

	Starts	1st	2nd	3rd	Win & Pl
Hurdles	5	0	0	1	357
Career Total	5	0	0	1	357

Going:	Sf: 0-1 GS: 0-0 Gd: 0-3 GF: - Fm: 0-1
Distance:	2m/2m3: 0-4 2m4-2m7: 0-1 3m+: 0-0
Track:	LH: 0-2 RH: 0-3 Tight: 0-1 Gall: 0-0
Aids:	Bl: 0-0 Vi: 0-1 Tstrap: 0-0 Ckp: 0-0
Best Rating:	80 12/03 Kemp 2m good Hdl

Plating-class novice hurdler; probably best suited by two miles.

Golden Flight (FR)

(104h)   (114h)

5-y-o b g Saint Cyrien (FR)-Sunday Flight (FR) (Johnny O'Day (USA))
G Macaire J D Cotton

Placings:2/1523-2111U   (3134)
2003/04: 17²S, 17¹VS, 20¹VS, 20¹VS, 21⁰G,

	Starts	1st	2nd	3rd	Win & Pl
Chases	5	3	1	0	67676
Career Total	10	4	3	1	92489
11/03	Autl	2m4f110y Ch			VS £32143
11/03	Autl	2m4f110y Ch			VS £20260
9/03	Autl	2m1f110y Ch			VS £13091
104 5/02	Autl	2m1f110y Hdl			VS £11779
			Total win prize-money £77273		

Going:	Sf: 0-1 GS: 0-0 Gd: 0-1 GF: - Fm: 0-0
Distance:	2m/2m3: 1-2 2m4-2m7: 2-3 3m+: 0-0
Track:	LH: 0-1 RH: 0-0 Tight: 0-0 Gall: 0-1
Aids:	Bl: 0-0 Vi: 0-0 Tstrap: 0-0 Ckp: 0-0
Best Rating:	120 3/03 Strf 2m110y gd-sft Hdl

Useful French-trained chaser; best around two and a half miles; acts on soft ground.

Golden Haze
84   29

7-y-o ch m Safawan-Hazel Hill (Abednego)
J R Bewley R Bewley

Placings:00-352R0   (0644)
2003/04: 21³S, 21⁵S, 24²GS, 24ᴿGF, 20⁰GF,

	Starts	1st	2nd	3rd	Win & Pl
Hurdles	5	0	1	1	1937
Career Total	7	0	1	1	1937

Going:	Sf: 0-2 GS: 0-1 Gd: 0-0 GF: - Fm: 0-2
Distance:	2m/2m3: 0-0 2m4-2m7: 0-3 3m+: 0-2
Track:	LH: 0-3 RH: 0-2 Tight: 0-2 Gall: 0-0
Aids:	Bl: 0-0 Vi: 0-0 Tstrap: 0-0 Ckp: 0-0
Best Rating:	64 5/03 Prth 3m110y gd-sft Hdl

Golden Host

10-y-o ch g Roman Warrior-Prominent Princess (Prominer)
R J Smith Con Rutledge

Placings:400P/P/P   (1190)

2003/04: 20⁰GF,

	Starts	1st	2nd	3rd	Win & Pl
Hurdles	1	0	0	0	
Career Total	6	0	0	0	0

Going:	Sf: 0-0 GS: 0-0 Gd: 0-0 GF: - Fm: 0-1
Distance:	2m/2m3: 0-0 2m4-2m7: 0-1 3m+: 0-0
Track:	LH: 0-1 RH: 0-0 Tight: 0-0 Gall: 0-0
Aids:	Bl: 0-0 Vi: 0-0 Tstrap: 0-0 Ckp: 0-0
Best Rating:	75 5/99 Worc 2m gd-sft NHF

Golden Law
93f   86f

6-y-o b m Gildoran-Sister-In-Law (Legal Tender)
P R Webber Mrs P Scott-Dunn

Placings:30   (4608)
2003/04: 16⁹G, 17⁰G,

	Starts	1st	2nd	3rd	Win & Pl
NH Flat	2	0	0	1	383
Career Total	2	0	0	1	383

Going:	Sf: 0-0 GS: 0-0 Gd: 0-2 GF: - Fm: 0-0
Distance:	2m/2m3: 0-2 2m4-2m7: 0-0 3m+: 0-0
Track:	LH: 0-0 RH: 0-2 Tight: 0-1 Gall: 0-0
Aids:	Bl: 0-0 Vi: 0-0 Tstrap: 0-0 Ckp: 0-0
Best Rating:	86 3/04 Ludl 2m good NHF

Golden Legend (IRE)

7-y-o b g Last Tycoon-Adjalisa (IRE) (Darshaan)
R J Price E G Bevan

Placings:PP/PP-P   (0445)
2003/04: 16⁶G,

	Starts	1st	2nd	3rd	Win & Pl
Hurdles	1	0	0	0	
Career Total	5	0	0	0	

Going:	Sf: 0-0 GS: 0-0 Gd: 0-0 GF: - Fm: 0-0
Distance:	2m/2m3: 0-1 2m4-2m7: 0-0 3m+: 0-0
Track:	LH: 0-0 RH: 0-1 Tight: 0-0 Gall: 0-1
Aids:	Bl: 0-0 Vi: 0-0 Tstrap: 0-0 Ckp: 0-0

Golden Measure
93f

4-y-o b g Rainbow Quest (USA)-Dawna (Polish Precedent (USA))
G A Swinbank R H Hall

Placings:2   (2387)
2003/04: 14²G,

	Starts	1st	2nd	3rd	Win & Pl
NH Flat	1	0	1	0	781
Career Total	1	0	1	0	781

Going:	Sf: 0-0 GS: 0-0 Gd: 0-1 GF: - Fm: 0-0
Distance:	2m/2m3: 0-1 2m4-2m7: 0-0 3m+: 0-0
Track:	LH: 0-1 RH: 0-0 Tight: 0-0 Gall: 0-0
Aids:	Bl: 0-0 Vi: 0-0 Tstrap: 0-0 Ckp: 0-0
Best Rating:	93 11/03 Wwck 1m6f good NHF

Supported in the market when runner-up on debut in a bumper; effective over a mile six; acts on good ground.

Golden Oak (IRE)
91f   100f

4-y-o b g Goldmark (USA)-Embroidery (Lords (USA))
R A Fahey Mrs Jane Dwyer

Placings:2   (4481)
2003/04: 17²HY,

	Starts	1st	2nd	3rd	Win & Pl
NH Flat	1	0	1	0	550
Career Total	1	0	1	0	550

Going:	Sf: 0-1 GS: 0-0 Gd: 0-0 GF: - Fm: 0-0
Distance:	2m/2m3: 0-1 2m4-2m7: 0-0 3m+: 0-0
Track:	LH: 0-0 RH: 0-1 Tight: 0-0 Gall: 0-0
Aids:	Bl: 0-0 Vi: 0-0 Tstrap: 0-0 Ckp: 0-0
Best Rating:	105 3/04 Carl 2m1f heavy NHF

Golden Odyssey (IRE)
97f   106+f

4-y-o ch f Barathea (IRE)-Opus One (Slip Anchor)
Mrs M Reveley Sir Robert Ogden

Placings:1211   (4846)
2003/04: 13¹G, 16²G, 17¹G, 17¹G,

	Starts	1st	2nd	3rd	Win & Pl
NH Flat	4	3	1	0	9664
Career Total	4	3	1	0	9664
104 4/04	Chel	2m1f	H NHF		GD £3867
108 3/04	MRas	2m1f110yH NHF			GD £1858
89 11/03	Donc	1m5f	H NHF		G-F £3085
			Total win prize-money £8813		

Going:	Sf: 0-0 GS: 0-0 Gd: 2-3 GF: - Fm: 1-1
Distance:	2m/2m3: 2-3 2m4-2m7: 0-0 3m+: 0-0
Track:	LH: 1-1 RH: 1-2 Tight: 1-2 Gall: 1-1
Aids:	Bl: 0-0 Vi: 0-0 Tstrap: 0-0 Ckp: 0-0
Best Rating:	108 3/04 MRas 2m1f110y good NHF

Dam 1m7f Flat winner; won three out of four bumper outings in 2003/04; will get further when sent hurdling; acts on fast ground; interesting prospect.

Golden Oldie (IRE)
36f   46f

6-y-o b g Old Vic-Misty Gold (Arizona Duke)
D Flood A M McArdle - Pamela McArdle

Placings:00   (4058)
2003/04: 16⁰G, 16⁹G,

	Starts	1st	2nd	3rd	Win & Pl
NH Flat	2	0	0	0	
Career Total	2	0	0	0	

Going:	Sf: 0-0 GS: 0-1 Gd: 0-1 GF: - Fm: 0-0
Distance:	2m/2m3: 0-2 2m4-2m7: 0-0 3m+: 0-0
Track:	LH: 0-1 RH: 0-1 Tight: 0-1 Gall: 0-0
Aids:	Bl: 0-0 Vi: 0-0 Tstrap: 0-0 Ckp: 0-0
Best Rating:	46 1/04 Catt 2m gd-sft NHF

Golden Orion (IRE)
89   93+

9-y-o ch g Phardante (FR)-Raise The Bells (Belfalas)
Mrs J C McGregor Discounted Cashflow

Placings:65606233550/P-5   (1874)
2003/04: 22⁵G,

	Starts	1st	2nd	3rd	Win & Pl
Hurdles	1	0	0	0	0
Career Total	13	0	1	2	1752

Going: Sf: 0-0 GS: 0-0 Gd: 0-1 GF: - Fm: 0-0
Distance: 2m2/2m3: 0-0 2m4-2m7: 0-1 3m+: 0-0
Track: LH: 0-1 RH: 0-0 Tight: 0-0 Gall: 0-0
Aids: Bl: 0-0 Vi: 0-0 Tstrap: 0-0 Ckp: 0-0
Best Rating: 93   9/02   Prth   3m110y   gd-fm   Hdl

Modest novice hurdler, stays two and a half miles.

Golden Rambler (IRE)

94   **108+**

8-y-o br g Roselier (FR)-Goldiyana (FR) (Glint Of Gold)
Jonjo O'Neill   J C, J R And S R Hitchins

Placings: 5/24211/000   (4628)
2003/04: 20⁰G, 24⁰GS, 20⁰G,

	Starts	1st	2nd	3rd	Win & Pl
Hurdles	3	0	0	0	
Career Total	9	2	2	0	8959
129	1/02	Hayd	2m4f	E Hdl	SFT £3500
115	12/01	Hayd	2m4f	D Hdl	HVY £3848

Total win prize-money £7348

Going: Sf: 0-0 GS: 0-1 Gd: 0-2 GF: - Fm: 0-0
Distance: 2m2/2m3: 0-0 2m4-2m7: 0-2 3m+: 0-1
Track: LH: 0-3 RH: 0-0 Tight: 0-2 Gall: 0-0
Aids: Bl: 0-0 Vi: 0-0 Tstrap: 0-0 Ckp: 0-0
Best Rating: 129   1/02   Hayd   2m4f   soft   Hdl

Former fair hurdler; returned from a long absence in February 2004; acts on heavy ground; stays two miles four furlongs.

Golden Reward (SAF)

98   **102+**

6-y-o ro g Goldmark (SAF)-Enticement (SAF) (Capture Him (USA))
Miss Venetia Williams   P A Deal

Placings: 4   (3651)
2003/04: 17⁴S,

	Starts	1st	2nd	3rd	Win & Pl
Hurdles	1	0	0	0	331
Career Total	1	0	0	0	331

Going: Sf: 0-1 GS: 0-0 Gd: 0-0 GF: - Fm: 0-0
Distance: 2m/2m3: 0-1 2m4-2m7: 0-0 3m+: 0-0
Track: LH: 0-0 RH: 0-1 Tight: 0-1 Gall: 0-0
Aids: Bl: 0-0 Vi: 0-0 Tstrap: 0-0 Ckp: 0-0
Best Rating: 102   2/04   Tntn   2m1f   soft   Hdl

Golden Rod

101(105h)   (86h)**82**

7-y-o ch g Rainbows For Life (CAN)-Noble Form (Double Form)
K C Bailey   Neil Rodway & Carol Cope

Placings: 5000051-333445CP   (3428)
2003/04: 21³G, 23³GF, 21³GF, 24⁴G, 24⁴GF, 16²G, 21⁰G, 21⁰GS,

	Starts	1st	2nd	3rd	Win & Pl
Hurdles	3	0	0	2	1172
Chases	5	0	0	1	835
Career Total	15	1	0	3	5374
86	4/03	Uttx	2m4f110yF(0-100)HHdl	GD	£3367

Total win prize-money £3367

Going: Sf: 0-0 GS: 0-1 Gd: 0-4 GF: - Fm: 0-3
Distance: 2m/2m3: 0-1 2m4-2m7: 0-3 3m+: 0-3
Track: LH: 0-5 RH: 0-3 Tight: 0-4 Gall: 0-1
Aids: Bl: 0-0 Vi: 0-0 Tstrap: 0-0 Ckp: 0-6
Best Rating: 87   5/03   Ludl   2m5f   good   Hdl

Poor hurdler/chaser; best at distances short of three miles; suited by decent ground.

Golden Snoopy (IRE)

100f   **80f**

7-y-o ch g Insan (USA)-Lovely Snoopy (IRE) (Phardante (FR))
H D Daly   Stephen Tomkinson

Placings: 5   (1195)
2003/04: 16⁵GF,

	Starts	1st	2nd	3rd	Win & Pl
NH Flat	1	0	0	0	0
Career Total	1	0	0	0	0

Going: Sf: 0-0 GS: 0-0 Gd: 0-0 GF: - Fm: 0-1
Distance: 2m2/2m3: 0-1 2m4-2m7: 0-0 3m+: 0-0
Track: LH: 0-1 RH: 0-0 Tight: 0-0 Gall: 0-0
Aids: Bl: 0-0 Vi: 0-0 Tstrap: 0-0 Ckp: 0-0
Best Rating: 80   8/03   Worc   2m   gd-fm   NHF

A half-brother to a couple of bumper winners who both went on to score over obstacles; unable to sustain effort when well beaten fifth in Worcester bumper August 2003.

Golden Tamesis

88   **63**

7-y-o b g Golden Heights-Escribana (Main Reef)
R Dickin   Tamesis & Partners

Placings: 0000   (4887)
2003/04: 16⁰G, 21⁰G, 25⁰S, 22⁰GF,

	Starts	1st	2nd	3rd	Win & Pl
NH Flat	1	0	0	0	0
Hurdles	3	0	0	0	
Career Total	4	0	0	0	

Going: Sf: 0-1 GS: 0-0 Gd: 0-2 GF: - Fm: 0-1
Distance: 2m/2m3: 0-2 2m4-2m7: 0-2 3m+: 0-0
Track: LH: 0-3 RH: 0-1 Tight: 0-1 Gall: 0-0
Aids: Bl: 0-0 Vi: 0-0 Tstrap: 0-0 Ckp: 0-0
Best Rating: 63   3/04   Wwck   3m1f   soft   Hdl

Golden Thunderbolt (FR)

101   (105c)**87+**

11-y-o b g Persian Bold-Carmita (Caerleon (USA))
H Alexander   Lever, Alexander, Dallas

Placings: 2205/34523232/35244533/3624226P2415/5520P PP0123144/40352600336-0P5UPP21   (4774)
2003/04: 17⁰G, 22⁰GF, 19⁵GS, 16⁴G, 19⁰G, 20⁰S, 17²G, 16¹G,

	Starts	1st	2nd	3rd	Win & Pl
Hurdles	8	1	1	0	3419
Career Total	65	4	14	11	26010
87	4/04	Fknm	2m	G(0-85)HHdl	GD £2723
103	4/02	Fknm	2m4f	E(0-105)HHdl	GD £3003
95	1/02	Catt	2m3f	G(0-90)HHdl	SFT £1904
100	2/01	Fknm	2m	G(0-90)HHdl	SFT £1877

Total win prize-money £9507

Going: Sf: 0-1 GS: 0-1 Gd: 1-5 GF: - Fm: 0-1
Distance: 2m2/2m3: 1-6 2m4-2m7: 0-2 3m+: 0-0
Track: LH: 1-8 RH: 1-7 Gall: 0-1
Aids: Bl: 0-0 Vi: 0-0 Tstrap: 0-0 Ckp: 0-1
Best Rating: 103   4/02   Fknm   2m4f   good   Hdl

Plating-class front-running hurdler; acts on good and soft ground; effective at up to two miles three furlongs and likes a sharp track, particularly Fakenham.

Golden Thyne (IRE)

           53

10-y-o ch g Alphabatim (USA)-Droichidin (Good Thyne (USA))
Ms A E Embiricos   Mrs S N J Embiricos

Placings: 6/0-P   (0158)
2003/04: 23⁰GF,

	Starts	1st	2nd	3rd	Win & Pl
Hurdles	1	0	0	0	
Career Total	3	0	0	0	0

Going: Sf: 0-0 GS: 0-0 Gd: 0-0 GF: - Fm: 0-1
Distance: 2m/2m3: 0-0 2m4-2m7: 0-0 3m+: 0-1
Track: LH: 0-1 RH: 0-0 Tight: 0-1 Gall: 0-0
Aids: Bl: 0-0 Vi: 0-0 Tstrap: 0-0 Ckp: 0-0
Best Rating: 79   5/00   Folk   2m1f110y   good   NHF

Golders Green

7-y-o b g Gildoran-Mayfair Minx (St Columbus)
M G Rimell   Mrs M D W Wilson

Placings: 0/04PPP   (4762)
2003/04: 18⁰S, 17⁴GS, 25⁰GS, 23⁰GS, 19⁰S,

	Starts	1st	2nd	3rd	Win & Pl
NH Flat	2	0	0	0	
Hurdles	3	0	0	0	
Career Total	6	0	0	0	

Going: Sf: 0-2 GS: 0-3 Gd: 0-0 GF: - Fm: 0-0
Distance: 2m/2m3: 0-2 2m4-2m7: 0-1 3m+: 0-2
Track: LH: 0-3 RH: 0-1 Tight: 0-1 Gall: 0-0
Aids: Bl: 0-1 Vi: 0-0 Tstrap: 0-0 Ckp: 0-0
Best Rating: 66   12/03   Hrfd   2m1f   gd-sft   NHF

Poor form so far.

Goldhorn (IRE)

74   **60**

9-y-o b g Little Bighorn-Stylish Gold (IRE) (Tumble Gold)
O Brennan   O Brennan

Placings: 100/0   (4165)
2003/04: 19⁰G,

	Starts	1st	2nd	3rd	Win & Pl
Hurdles	1	0	0	0	
Career Total	4	1	0	0	1701
108	1/00	Donc	2m110y	H NHF	G-F £1701

Total win prize-money £1701

Going: Sf: 0-0 GS: 0-0 Gd: 0-1 GF: - Fm: 0-0
Distance: 2m/2m3: 0-0 2m4-2m7: 0-1 3m+: 0-0
Track: LH: 0-1 RH: 0-0 Tight: 0-0 Gall: 0-0
Aids: Bl: 0-0 Vi: 0-0 Tstrap: 0-0 Ckp: 0-0
Best Rating: 108   1/00   Donc   2m110y   gd-fm   NHF

Goldseam (GER)

5-y-o gr g Neshad (USA)-Goldkatze (GER) (Czaravich (USA))
C J Mann M Rowland, B Beacham

Placings:0/P   (3244)
2003/04: 16PGS,

	Starts	1st	2nd	3rd	Win & Pl
Hurdles	1	0	0	0	
Career Total	2	0	0	0	

Going:	Sf: 0-0 GS: 0-1 Gd: 0-0 GF: - Fm: 0-0
Distance:	2m/2m3: 0-1 2m4-2m7: 0-0 3m+: 0-0
Track:	LH: 0-0 RH: 0-1 Tight: 0-0 Gall: 0-0
Aids:	Bl: 0-0 Vi: 0-0 Tstrap: 0-0 Ckp: 0-0

Goldstreet (IRE)

112(110h)   (122h)132
7-y-o b g Dolphin Street (FR)-Up To You (Sallust)
Joseph Crowley (Miss F M Crowley 29/5) Crock Of Gold Syndicate

Placings:2352/4C102/314455252-422240   (0995a)
2003/04: 184GY, 202YS, 242F, 232GF, 204GF, 220Y,

	Starts	1st	2nd	3rd	Win & Pl
Hurdles	1	0	1	0	1818
Chases	5	0	2	0	9091
Career Total	24	2	8	2	36459
126 11/02 Navn 2m1f		Ch.		Y-S	£6773
115 7/01 Bell 2m1f		Hdl		G-F	£5286
				Total win prize-money £12059	

Going:	Sf: 0-0 GS: 0-0 Gd: 0-0 GF: - Fm: 0-3
Distance:	2m/2m3: 0-1 2m4-2m7: 0-4 3m+: 0-1
Track:	LH: 0-0 RH: 0-4 Tight: 0-1 Gall: 0-0
Aids:	Bl: 0-4 Vi: 0-0 Tstrap: 0-0 Ckp: 0-0
Best Rating:	137 2/01 Gowr 2m heavy Hdl

Useful chaser; Irish trained; got off the mark over fences when scoring at Navan in November 2002; effective at up to two miles seven; acts on a sound surface, but goes on soft; has worn blinkers.

Golfagent

100   102
6-y-o b g Kris-Alusha (Soviet Star (USA))
Miss K Marks Nick Shutts

Placings:PF212325002633L1-300220P11P   (4735)
2003/04: 243GF, 270G, 210G, 242GF, 242GF, 220GS, 19PGS, 171GS, 191G, 17PG,

	Starts	1st	2nd	3rd	Win & Pl
Hurdles	10	2	2	1	9397
Career Total	26	4	6	4	25297
102 3/04 Tntn	2m3f110yE(0-105)HHdl	GD	£4030
99 2/04 Tntn	2m1f	G Hdl	G-S	£2450
102 4/03 Uttx	3m110y E(0-100)HHdl	GD	£3689
81 8/02 Strf	2m3f	D Hdl	SFT	£4225
			Total win prize-money £14394	

Going:	Sf: 0-0 GS: 1-3 Gd: 1-4 GF: - Fm: 0-3
Distance:	2m/2m3: 1-2 2m4-2m7: 1-4 3m+: 0-4
Track:	LH: 0-7 RH: 2-3 Tight: 2-4 Gall: 0-4
Aids:	Bl: 0-0 Vi: 0-1 Tstrap: 2-10 Ckp: 0-0
Best Rating:	102 3/04 Tntn 2m3f110y good Hdl

Moderate hurdler; stays three miles; acts on most types of ground; wears a tongue tie.

Gollinger

8-y-o b g St Ninian-Edith Rose (Cheval)
R D E Woodhouse R D E Woodhouse

Placings:2/53P   (0430)
2003/04: 215S, 203G, 26PG,

	Starts	1st	2nd	3rd	Win & Pl
Chases	3	0	0	1	515
Career Total	4	0	1	1	948

Going:	Sf: 0-1 GS: 0-0 Gd: 0-2 GF: - Fm: 0-0
Distance:	2m/2m3: 0-0 2m4-2m7: 0-2 3m+: 0-1
Track:	LH: 0-2 RH: 0-1 Tight: 0-2 Gall: 0-0
Aids:	Bl: 0-0 Vi: 0-0 Tstrap: 0-0 Ckp: 0-0
Best Rating:	86 5/00 Worc 2m gd-fm NHF

Golly (IRE)

109(89h)   (97+h)113
8-y-o b g Toulon-Tor-Na-Grena (Torus)
D L Williams Reliance Car Hire Services Ltd

Placings:U-3124P323U1   (4857)
2003/04: 163GF, 221GF, 172GF, 214G, 23PG, 203GF, 162G, 183G, 20UG, 191GF,

	Starts	1st	2nd	3rd	Win & Pl
Hurdles	1	0	1	0	1648
Chases	9	2	1	3	11957
Career Total	11	2	2	3	13605
105 4/04 Tntn	2m3f	E(0-105)HCh	G-F	£4127
99 10/03 MRas	2m6f110yE Ch	G-F	£3049
			Total win prize-money £7178	

Going:	Sf: 0-0 GS: 0-0 Gd: 0-5 GF: - Fm: 2-5
Distance:	2m/2m3: 1-5 2m4-2m7: 1-4 3m+: 0-1
Track:	LH: 0-3 RH: 2-6 Tight: 2-6 Gall: 0-1
Aids:	Bl: 0-0 Vi: 0-0 Tstrap: 0-0 Ckp: 0-0
Best Rating:	107 10/03 Fknm 2m5f110y good Ch

Moderate chaser/hurdler; winner and placed in first three chases in autumn 2003; won modest 2m 3f handicap chase at Taunton April 2004; stays two miles six; acts on a sound surface.

Gollyhott (IRE)

(72h)   (75h)
9-y-o gr g Roselier (FR)-Liffey Lady (Camden Town)
M F Harris Let's Live Racing

Placings:02P/0/5P   (4256)
2003/04: 215S, 20PG,

	Starts	1st	2nd	3rd	Win & Pl
Hurdles	1	0	0	0	0
Chases	1	0	0	0	0
Career Total	6	0	1	0	424

Going:	Sf: 0-1 GS: 0-0 Gd: 0-1 GF: - Fm: 0-0
Distance:	2m/2m3: 0-0 2m4-2m7: 0-2 3m+: 0-0
Track:	LH: 0-2 RH: 0-0 Tight: 0-2 Gall: 0-0
Aids:	Bl: 0-1 Vi: 0-0 Tstrap: 0-0 Ckp: 0-0
Best Rating:	107 1/01 Chep 2m110y gd-sft NHF

Gondola (AUS)

95   91
8-y-o b g Air De France (USA)-Idyllic (AUS) (Clear Choice (USA))
S E H Sherwood T N Siviter

Placings:2F   (1309)
2003/04: 162GF, 16FGF,

	Starts	1st	2nd	3rd	Win & Pl
Hurdles	2	0	1	0	1021
Career Total	2	0	1	0	1021

Going:	Sf: 0-0 GS: 0-0 Gd: 0-0 GF: - Fm: 0-2
Distance:	2m/2m3: 0-2 2m4-2m7: 0-0 3m+: 0-0
Track:	LH: 0-2 RH: 0-0 Tight: 0-0 Gall: 0-0
Aids:	Bl: 0-0 Vi: 0-0 Tstrap: 0-0 Ckp: 0-0
Best Rating:	91 8/03 Worc 2m gd-fm Hdl

Three times a winner at around nine furlongs in Australia; good second on hurdling debut August 2003; fell and broke leg next time. (DEAD)

Gone Bonkers (IRE)

9-y-o b g Lord Americo-Lady Harrier (Some Hawk)
Mark Campion The Gone Bonkers Partnership

Placings:000-PP   (3408)
2003/04: 21PGF, 16PG,

	Starts	1st	2nd	3rd	Win & Pl
Hurdles	2	0	0	0	
Career Total	5	0	0	0	

Going:	Sf: 0-0 GS: 0-0 Gd: 0-1 GF: - Fm: 0-1
Distance:	2m/2m3: 0-1 2m4-2m7: 0-1 3m+: 0-0
Track:	LH: 0-2 RH: 0-0 Tight: 0-1 Gall: 0-1
Aids:	Bl: 0-0 Vi: 0-0 Tstrap: 0-0 Ckp: 0-0

Gone Far (USA)

102   127
7-y-o b g Gone West (USA)-Vallee Dansante (USA) (Lyphard (USA))
M C Pipe Matt Archer & Miss Jean Broadhurst

Placings:134/5-F002P00   (4836)
2003/04: 16FG, 170G, 170GS, 162G, 16PS, 20PG, 210GF,

	Starts	1st	2nd	3rd	Win & Pl
Hurdles	7	0	1	0	3502
Career Total	11	1	1	1	9011
119 1/02 Tntn	2m1f	E Hdl	SFT	£2643
			Total win prize-money £2643	

Going:	Sf: 0-1 GS: 0-1 Gd: 0-4 GF: - Fm: 0-1
Distance:	2m/2m3: 0-5 2m4-2m7: 0-3 3m+: 0-0
Track:	LH: 0-6 RH: 0-1 Tight: 0-1 Gall: 0-4
Aids:	Bl: 0-0 Vi: 0-5 Tstrap: 0-0 Ckp: 0-0
Best Rating:	127 3/04 Newb 2m110y good Hdl

Useful hurdler; effective at two miles; acts on soft ground; has worn visor; hard to win with.

Gone Too Far

101   122
6-y-o b g Reprimand-Blue Nile (IRE) (Bluebird (USA))
M C Pipe (M Dods 22/7) D A Johnson

Placings:2202/5122110356   (3780)
2003/04: 205G, 161G, 162GF, 162G, 171GF, 161G, 160GS, 193G, 205GF, 166GS,

	Starts	1st	2nd	3rd	Win & Pl
Hurdles	10	3	2	1	22270
Career Total	14	3	5	1	24860
119 11/03 Chel	2m110y D(0-110)HHdl	GD	£13456
105 7/03 Sedg	2m1f	E(0-105)HHdl	G-F	£3493
97 5/03 Hexm	2m110y F(0-95)HHdl	GD	£2695
			Total win prize-money £19644	

Going: Sf: 0-0 GS: 0-2 Gd: 2-5 GF: - Fm: 1-3
Distance: 2m/2m3: 3-7 2m4-2m7: 0-3 3m+: 0-0
Track: LH: 3-5 RH: 0-5 **Tight: 1-3** Gall: 0-2
Aids: Bl: 2-4 Vi: 1-5 Tstrap: 0-0 Ckp: 0-0
Best Rating: 119 11/03 Chel 2m110y good Hdl

Fair handicap hurdler; on the downgrade and beaten in a claiming hurdle; effective at around two miles and suited by a sound surface; often blinkered or visored.

Good Bone (FR)
100   90+
7-y-o b g Perrault-Bone Crasher (FR) (Cadoudal (FR))
L Wells L Wells

Placings:3235216   (4792)
2003/04: 21³GF, 23²F, 20³HY, 18⁵G, 25²GS, 25¹G, 26⁶G,

	Starts	1st	2nd	3rd	Win & Pl
Chases	7	1	2	2	7289
Career Total	7	1	2	2	7289
90	3/04	Folk	3m1f	F(0-85)HCh	GD £3727

Total win prize-money £3728

Going: Sf: 0-1 GS: 0-1 Gd: 1-3 GF: - Fm: 0-2
Distance: 2m/2m3: 0-1 2m4-2m7: 0-2 **3m+: 1-4**
Track: LH: 0-1 **RH: 1-4 Tight: 1-6** Gall: 0-0
Aids: Bl: 0-0 Vi: 0-0 Tstrap: 0-0 Ckp: 0-0
Best Rating: 90 3/04 Folk 3m1f good Ch

Ex-Irish pointer; placed, but well beat in all three starts over fences to date; stays 2m7f; acts on soft ground.

Good Book (IRE)

6-y-o b g Good Thyne (USA)-Book Of Rules (IRE)
(Phardante (FR))
M Bradstock The Silver Cloud Partnership

Placings:5B0   (4147)
2003/04: 16⁵G, 21³BG, 24⁰G,

	Starts	1st	2nd	3rd	Win & Pl
NH Flat	1	0	0	0	0
Hurdles	2	0	0	0	0
Career Total	3	0	0	0	0

Going: Sf: 0-0 GS: 0-0 Gd: 0-3 GF: - Fm: 0-0
Distance: 2m/2m3: 0-1 2m4-2m7: 0-1 3m+: 0-1
Track: LH: 0-2 RH: 0-1 Tight: 0-1 Gall: 0-0
Aids: Bl: 0-0 Vi: 0-0 Tstrap: 0-0 Ckp: 0-1
Best Rating: 85 5/03 Worc 2m good NHF

Half-brother to Irish 3m chase and hurdle winner Rule Supreme;modest form so far.

Good Boy (FR)

10-y-o b g Cadoudal (FR)-Cazeres (FR) (Goodland (FR))
R S Elwell M H D Barlow

Placings:05434615FF/P116066P6/0162003030P00/04050
36300646006640/05402113656600/2105502425-51 (0483)
2003/04: 21⁵G, 24¹GF,

	Starts	1st	2nd	3rd	Win & Pl
Chases	2	1	0	0	1572
Career Total	76	8	5	6	103942
92	5/03	Hntg	3m	H Ch	G-F £1571
	5/02	Frau	2m5f	Ch	GD £4959
	9/01	Diel	2m5f110y	Ch	GD £8000
	8/01	Chat	2m4f110y	HHdl	GD £7274
	6/99	Pari	2m3f	HHdl	VS £11841
	10/98	Nanc	2m3f	Hdl	VS £4040

10/98	Comp	2m1f110y	Hdl	VS £3535
11/97	Autl	2m1f110y	Ch	HLD £13468

Total win prize-money £54689

Going: Sf: 0-0 GS: 0-0 Gd: 0-1 GF: - Fm: 1-1
Distance: 2m/2m3: 0-0 2m4-2m7: 0-1 **3m+: 1-1**
Track: LH: 0-1 **RH: 1-1** Tight: 0-0 **Gall: 1-2**
Aids: Bl: 0-0 Vi: 0-0 Tstrap: 0-0 Ckp: 0-0
Best Rating: 92 5/03 Hntg 3m gd-fm Ch

Fair hunter-chaser; got off the mark under rules in this country when winning at Huntingdon in May; stays three miles well; likes fast ground.

Good Debate (IRE)
87   74
6-y-o b g Glacial Storm (USA)-Drachma (IRE) (Netherkelly)
Paul John Gilligan E Gilligan

Placings:00003020F   (4347a)
2003/04: 20⁶G, 22⁰G, 16⁰Y, 20⁵S, 16³HY, 16⁰SH, 19²S, 20⁰S,
24²S,

	Starts	1st	2nd	3rd	Win & Pl
NH Flat	1	0	0	0	0
Hurdles	8	0	1	1	1960
Career Total	9	0	1	1	1960

Going: Sf: 0-5 GS: 0-0 Gd: 0-2 GF: - Fm: 0-0
Distance: 2m/2m3: 0-4 2m4-2m7: 0-4 3m+: 0-1
Track: LH: 0-3 RH: 0-1 Tight: 0-1 Gall: 0-0
Aids: Bl: 0-3 Vi: 0-0 Tstrap: 0-0 Ckp: 0-0
Best Rating: 74 2/04 Naas 2m3f soft Hdl

Good Evans Above

7-y-o br m Tragic Role (USA)-Dark Amber (Formidable (USA))
Mrs S M Johnson David F Evans

Placings:PP   (1300)
2003/04: 16⁰GF, 16⁰GF,

	Starts	1st	2nd	3rd	Win & Pl
Hurdles	2	0	0	0	
Career Total	2	0	0	0	

Going: Sf: 0-0 GS: 0-0 Gd: 0-0 GF: - Fm: 0-2
Distance: 2m/2m3: 0-2 2m4-2m7: 0-0 3m+: 0-0
Track: LH: 0-2 RH: 0-0 Tight: 0-0 Gall: 0-0
Aids: Bl: 0-0 Vi: 0-0 Tstrap: 0-0 Ckp: 0-0

Good Form (IRE)

4-y-o b g Danetime (IRE)-Faapette (Runnett)
Miss K M George A B Parr

Placings:UP   (1355)
2003/04: 17⁰GF, 17⁰G,

	Starts	1st	2nd	3rd	Win & Pl
Hurdles	2	0	0	0	
Career Total	2	0	0	0	

Going: Sf: 0-0 GS: 0-0 Gd: 0-1 GF: - Fm: 0-1
Distance: 2m/2m3: 0-2 2m4-2m7: 0-0 3m+: 0-0
Track: LH: 0-2 RH: 0-0 Tight: 0-0 Gall: 0-0
Aids: Bl: 0-0 Vi: 0-0 Tstrap: 0-0 Ckp: 0-0

Good Heart (IRE)
88(86c)   (75c)70
9-y-o ch g Be My Native (USA)-Johnstown Love (IRE)
(Golden Love)
T H Caldwell M J Caldwell

Placings:1/06/43/06/0F4-0P6   (0405)
2003/04: 26⁰GS, 21²GF, 22⁶G,

	Starts	1st	2nd	3rd	Win & Pl
Hurdles	3	0	0	0	
Career Total	13	1	0	1	2588
119	2/99	Hayd	2m	H NHF	SFT £1495

Total win prize-money £1495

Going: Sf: 0-0 GS: 0-1 Gd: 0-1 GF: - Fm: 0-1
Distance: 2m/2m3: 0-2 2m4-2m7: 0-2 3m+: 0-1
Track: LH: 0-2 RH: 0-1 Tight: 0-1 Gall: 0-0
Aids: Bl: 0-0 Vi: 0-0 Tstrap: 0-0 Ckp: 0-1
Best Rating: 119 2/99 Hayd 2m soft NHF

Good Lord Louis (IRE)
98   93
6-y-o br g Presenting-Ash Queen (IRE) (Altountash)
P J Hobbs The Country Side

Placings:2560P0   (4716)
2003/04: 17²G, 16⁵S, 19⁶G, 19⁰GS, 21⁰G, 21⁰G,

	Starts	1st	2nd	3rd	Win & Pl
Hurdles	6	0	1	0	974
Career Total	6	0	1	0	974

Going: Sf: 0-1 GS: 0-1 Gd: 0-4 GF: - Fm: 0-0
Distance: 2m/2m3: 0-2 2m4-2m7: 0-4 3m+: 0-0
Track: LH: 0-1 RH: 0-5 Tight: 0-3 Gall: 0-0
Aids: Bl: 0-0 Vi: 0-0 Tstrap: 0-0 Ckp: 0-0
Best Rating: 95 2/04 Tntn 2m3f110y gd-sft Hdl

Moderate form in novice hurdles.

Good Lord Murphy (IRE)
102(92c)   (88c)99
12-y-o br g Montelimar (USA)-Semiwild (USA) (Rumbo (USA))
Dr P Pritchard Mrs T Pritchard

Placings:2/0211214/P50P/1212/10P/30/06F06R4-
P00050602500   (4890)
2003/04: 26⁶GF, 25⁰G, 24⁰GS, 23⁰G, 24⁵S, 16⁰S, 26⁶HY, 30⁰G,
26²GS, 24⁵G, 21⁰GF, 19⁰GF,

	Starts	1st	2nd	3rd	Win & Pl
Hurdles	9	0	1	0	1060
Chases	3	0	0	0	0
Career Total	40	6	6	1	46411
140	11/00	Asct	3m110y	B(0-150)HCh	SFT £10296
135	12/99	Hrfd	3m1f110yE	Ch	HVY £4340
128	11/99	Towc	3m1f	D Ch	GD £4086
127	3/98	Sand	2m6f	D Hdl	SFT £3663
127	2/98	Sand	2m6f	D Hdl	GD £3598
108	1/98	Wwck	2m4f110yE	Hdl	SFT £3352

Total win prize-money £29338

Going: Sf: 0-3 GS: 0-2 Gd: 0-4 GF: - Fm: 0-3
Distance: 2m/2m3: 0-2 2m4-2m7: 0-1 3m+: 0-9
Track: LH: 0-9 RH: 0-3 Tight: 0-2 Gall: 0-3
Aids: Bl: 0-0 Vi: 0-0 Tstrap: 0-0 Ckp: 0-3
Best Rating: 140 11/00 Asct 3m110y soft Ch

Moderate hurdler/fair chaser; very useful in his time, but on

the way down at a fair rate these days; his attitude is also in question; best on easy ground; stays well.

Good Outlook (IRE)

106(86h)   (76 h)119

5-y-o b g Lord Americo-I'Ll Say She Is (Ashmore (FR))
M C Pipe D A Johnson

Placings:F60FF12PF   (4857)
2003/04: 17FG, 16PS, 19QG, 22FG, 24FGS, 20¹GF, 24²G, 20PGS, 19FGF,

	Starts	1st	2nd	3rd	Win & Pl
Hurdles	3	0	0	0	0
Chases	6	1	1	0	5076
Career Total	9	1	1	0	5076
119 3/04 Leic	2m4f110y			F(0-95)HCh	
G-F £3737					

Total win prize-money £3738

Going:	Sf: 0-1 GS: 0-2 Gd: 0-4 GF: - Fm: 1-2
Distance:	2m/2m3: 0-2 2m4-2m7: 1-4 3m+: 0-2
Track:	LH: 0-4 RH: 1-7 Tight: 0-6 Gall: 0-0
Aids:	Bl: 0-0 Vi: 0-0 Tstrap: 0-0 Ckp: 0-0
Best Rating:	119 3/04 Leic 2m4f110y gd-fm Ch

Modest chaser; got his act together when winning 2m 4f novices' handicap chase at Leicester March 2004; subsequently has twice broken blood vessels; probably stays three miles; acts on good to firm.

Good Potential (IRE)

98   (64c)95+

8-y-o b g Petardia-Steel Duchess (IRE) (Yashgan)
D J Wintle Brigadier Racing 2000

Placings:00400446/5246126P0/P331/P40P00-03410P310
                                                (4339)
2003/04: 16QGS, 22³G, 26⁴GF, 22¹GF, 20⁴G, 21PGS, 22³GF, 20¹G, 16QG,

	Starts	1st	2nd	3rd	Win & Pl
Hurdles	9	2	0	2	7978
Career Total	36	4	2	4	16531
94 9/03 Bang	2m4f	E(0-110)HHdl		GD	£3549
95 6/03 NAbb	2m6f	E(0-105)HHdl		G-F	£3511
90 3/02 Font	2m6f110yF(0-100)HHdl			SFT	£2509
96 1/01 Sthl	2m	F(0-95)HHdl		HVY	£2443

Total win prize-money £12014

Going:	Sf: 0-0 GS: 0-2 Gd: 1-4 GF: - Fm: 1-3
Distance:	2m/2m3: 2-6 2m4-2m7: 2-6 3m+: 0-1
Track:	LH: 2-9 RH: 0-0 Tight: 2-4 Gall: 0-0
Aids:	Bl: 0-0 Vi: 0-0 Tstrap: 2-8 Ckp: 0-0
Best Rating:	96 2/01 Carl 2m1f heavy Hdl

Moderate handicap hurdler; raised 11lb after easy win in 2m 6f Class E handicap at Newton Abbot June 2003; disappointing next time and is inconsistent; fortunate winner at Bangor in September; stays at least 2m 6f; acts on soft and fast ground.

Good Samaritan (IRE)

99f   96f

5-y-o ch g Insan (USA)-Ballymave (IRE) (Jareer (USA))
M Pitman Malcolm C Denmark

Placings:0   (2850)
2003/04: 16QS,

	Starts	1st	2nd	3rd	Win & Pl
NH Flat	1	0	0	0	
Career Total	1	0	0	0	

Going:	Sf: 0-1 GS: 0-0 Gd: 0-0 GF: - Fm: 0-0
Distance:	2m/2m3: 0-1 2m4-2m7: 0-0 3m+: 0-0
Track:	LH: 0-0 RH: 0-1 Tight: 0-6 Gall: 0-0
Aids:	Bl: 0-0 Vi: 0-0 Tstrap: 0-0 Ckp: 0-0
Best Rating:	96 12/03 Asct 2m110y soft NHF

Good Sante

83f   67f

5-y-o b m Deploy-Kumzar (Hotfoot)
M Scudamore F J Mills & W Mills

Placings:00   (4144)
2003/04: 16QGS, 16QG,

	Starts	1st	2nd	3rd	Win & Pl
NH Flat	2	0	0	0	
Career Total	2	0	0	0	

Going:	Sf: 0-0 GS: 0-1 Gd: 0-1 GF: - Fm: 0-0
Distance:	2m/2m3: 0-2 2m4-2m7: 0-0 3m+: 0-0
Track:	LH: 0-0 RH: 0-2 Tight: 0-0 Gall: 0-0
Aids:	Bl: 0-0 Vi: 0-0 Tstrap: 0-0 Ckp: 0-0
Best Rating:	67 3/04 Ludl 2m good NHF

Good Shuil (IRE)

(86h)   (136h)138

9-y-o b g Good Thyne (USA)-Shuil Run (Deep Run)
C J Mann R Newsholme D Gorton F Wilson & B Walsh

Placings:0002114/3F43U132PP/054300P-P   (2326)
2003/04: 27QG,

	Starts	1st	2nd	3rd	Win & Pl
Chases	1	0	0	0	
Career Total	25	3	2	4	47941
122 1/02 Punc	2m5f	Ch		SH	£7831
130 2/01 Fair	3m	HHdl		Y-S	£15725
109 1/01 DRoy	2m4f	Hdl		YLD	£6120

Total win prize-money £29678

Going:	Sf: 0-0 GS: 0-0 Gd: 0-1 GF: - Fm: 0-0
Distance:	2m/2m3: 0-0 2m4-2m7: 0-0 3m+: 0-1
Track:	LH: 0-1 RH: 0-0 Tight: 0-1 Gall: 0-0
Aids:	Bl: 0-0 Vi: 0-0 Tstrap: 0-0 Ckp: 0-0
Best Rating:	138 11/02 Chel 3m3f110y gd-sft Ch

Useful Irish-trained chaser; stays beyond three miles and acts on a soft surface.

Good Thyne Guy (IRE)

101   (106c)94+

9-y-o b g Good Thyne (USA)-Mourne Trix (Golden Love)
C L Tizzard The Wakehill Partnership

Placings:23010/F0/P260PF   (4669)
2003/04: 24PS, 22²G, 19PS, 24PS, 22PG, 23FGS,

	Starts	1st	2nd	3rd	Win & Pl
Hurdles	5	0	1	0	746
Chases	1	0	0	0	0
Career Total	13	1	2	1	4438
103 3/01 Font	2m2f110yD Hdl			HVY	£2982

Total win prize-money £2982

Going:	Sf: 0-3 GS: 0-1 Gd: 0-2 GF: - Fm: 0-0
Distance:	2m/2m3: 0-1 2m4-2m7: 0-3 3m+: 0-2
Track:	LH: 0-2 RH: 0-3 Tight: 0-2 Gall: 0-1
Aids:	Bl: 0-0 Vi: 0-0 Tstrap: 0-1 Ckp: 0-0
Best Rating:	103 3/01 Font 2m2f110y heavy Hdl

Lightly-raced, he has won on heavy ground over two miles two furlongs but has shown nothing since being switched to fences.

Good Thyne Johnny (IRE)

96   96

10-y-o b g Good Thyne (USA)-Wiasma (Ashmore (FR))
Mrs J Candlish N M Wynne

Placings:00014034/P003PP/00/0120P2U25P-50003 (4781)
2003/04: 24⁵GS, 21QS, 22QG, 20QGS, 16³G,

	Starts	1st	2nd	3rd	Win & Pl
Hurdles	5	0	0	1	344
Career Total	31	2	3	3	9435
96 5/02 Uttx	3m110y	E(0-105)HHdl		GD	£2786
90 3/00 Dpat	2m1f172y Hdl			SFT	£2760

Total win prize-money £5546

Going:	Sf: 0-1 GS: 0-2 Gd: 0-2 GF: - Fm: 0-0
Distance:	2m/2m3: 0-1 2m4-2m7: 0-3 3m+: 0-1
Track:	LH: 0-2 RH: 0-2 Tight: 0-0 Gall: 0-2
Aids:	Bl: 0-0 Vi: 0-0 Tstrap: 0-0 Ckp: 0-0
Best Rating:	96 8/02 Bang 3m soft Hdl

Ex-Irish hurdler, surprise winner at Uttoxeter in May 2002 under a positive ride and those look the ideal tactics for him; suited by fast ground and stays well.

Good Time Bobby

81   61

7-y-o b g Primitive Rising (USA)-Goodreda (Good Times (ITY))
G A Swinbank Mrs K Morrell

Placings:0/00PU3/0-0   (0012)
2003/04: 20QGF,

	Starts	1st	2nd	3rd	Win & Pl
Hurdles	1	0	0	0	
Career Total	8	0	0	1	386

Going:	Sf: 0-0 GS: 0-0 Gd: 0-0 GF: - Fm: 0-1
Distance:	2m/2m3: 0-0 2m4-2m7: 0-1 3m+: 0-0
Track:	LH: 0-1 RH: 0-0 Tight: 0-0 Gall: 0-1
Aids:	Bl: 0-0 Vi: 0-0 Tstrap: 0-0 Ckp: 0-0
Best Rating:	87 4/01 MRas 1m5f110y gd-sft NHF

Modest hurdler, seems better on a sound surface.

Good Time Melody (IRE)

11-y-o b g Good Thyne (USA)-Raashideah (Dancer's Image (USA))
J W Mullins R I Webb-Bowen

Placings:2/22400/22121P/14005P/301   (4703)
2003/04: 25³G, 20QG, 26¹G,

	Starts	1st	2nd	3rd	Win & Pl
Chases	3	1	0	1	1749
Career Total	21	4	6	1	26801
114 4/04 Font	3m2f110yH Ch			GD	£1526
135 5/01 Extr	2m7f110yC(0-135)HCh			G-S	£6571
129 1/01 Sthl	3m110y E Ch			HVY	£3182
130 11/00 Winc	3m1f110yD(0-120)HCh			SFT	£5206

Total win prize-money £16487

Going:	Sf: 0-0 GS: 0-0 Gd: 1-3 GF: - Fm: 0-0
Distance:	2m/2m3: 0-0 2m4-2m7: 0-1 3m+: 1-2
Track:	LH: 0-0 RH: 0-2 Tight: 1-1 Gall: 0-0
Aids:	Bl: 0-0 Vi: 0-0 Tstrap: 0-0 Ckp: 0-0

Best Rating: 135 5/01   Extr   2m7f110y   gd-sft   Ch

Fair hunter; stays beyond three miles and suited by soft ground.

Good Timing

90   **64**

6-y-o gr g Timeless Times (USA)-Fort Vally (Belfort (FR))
J Hetherton   Mrs C A Brown

Placings:0-0P66   (2921)
2003/04: 16⁰G, 16P GS, 16⁰G, 17⁶G,

	Starts	1st	2nd	3rd	Win & Pl
Hurdles	4	0	0	0	0
Career Total	5	0	0	0	0

Going:	Sf: 0-0 GS: 0-1 Gd: 0-3 GF: - Fm: 0-0
Distance:	2m/2m3: 0-4 2m4-2m7: 0-0 3m+: 0-0
Track:	LH: 0-0 RH: 0-2 Tight: 0-2 Gall: 0-0
Aids:	Bl: 0-0 Vi: 0-0 Tstrap: 0-0 Ckp: 0-0
Best Rating: 63	12/03 Leic 2m good Hdl

Good Vintage (IRE)

107   (121h)**122**

9-y-o b g Lashkari-Furry Hope (Furry Glen)
Noel Meade   Kieran McGinn

Placings:2U24 12F20/5532U0245/222152R20-030P12PPR
                  (4805a)
2003/04: 25⁰G, 25³GF, 22⁰G, 24P GF, 22¹F, 28²G, 27⁰G, 28P YS, 29R Y,

	Starts	1st	2nd	3rd	Win & Pl
Chases	9	1	1	1	15130
Career Total	36	3	12	3	43281
117 10/03 Cork	2m6f		(0-116)HCh	FRM	£7616
115 10/02 Gowr	2m6f		Ch	Y-S	£6773
113 10/00 Leop	2m4f		NHF	HVY	£3588
			Total win prize-money £17978		

Going:	Sf: 0-0 GS: 0-0 Gd: 0-4 GF: - Fm: 1-3
Distance:	2m/2m3: 0-0 **2m4-2m7: 1-2** 3m+: 0-7
Track:	LH: 0-1 RH: 0-4 Tight: 0-1 Gall: 0-0
Aids:	Bl: 0-0 Vi: 0-0 Tstrap: 0-0 Ckp: 0-1
Best Rating: 122	11/03 Cork 3m4f good Ch

Fair Irish chaser; stays three miles and acts on most types of ground.

Goodandplenty

77   **42**

6-y-o b g Sovereign Water (FR)-Our Wilma (Master Willie)
Mrs J C McGregor   The Kelsae Selection

Placings:0400   (4595)
2003/04: 16⁰G, 16⁴HY, 16⁰G, 22⁰G,

	Starts	1st	2nd	3rd	Win & Pl
NH Flat	3	0	0	0	0
Hurdles	1	0	0	0	0
Career Total	4	0	0	0	0

Going:	Sf: 0-1 GS: 0-1 Gd: 0-2 GF: - Fm: 0-0
Distance:	2m/2m3: 0-3 2m4-2m7: 0-1 3m+: 0-0
Track:	LH: 0-4 RH: 0-0 Tight: 0-1 Gall: 0-0
Aids:	Bl: 0-0 Vi: 0-0 Tstrap: 0-0 Ckp: 0-0
Best Rating: 92	11/03 Ayr 2m good NHF

Has shown ability in bumpers but looks type to be seen to best advantage when sent hurdling over further in due course.

Goodbye Goldstone

                 69

8-y-o b g Mtoto-Shareehan (Dancing Brave (USA))
B Ellison (T P McGovern 2/6) Ashley Carr

Placings:04/00-F   (1838)
2003/04: 17F G,

	Starts	1st	2nd	3rd	Win & Pl
Hurdles	1	0	0	0	
Career Total	5	0	0	0	0

Going:	Sf: 0-0 GS: 0-0 Gd: 0-1 GF: - Fm: 0-0
Distance:	2m/2m3: 0-1 2m4-2m7: 0-0 3m+: 0-0
Track:	LH: 0-1 RH: 0-0 Tight: 0-1 Gall: 0-0
Aids:	Bl: 0-0 Vi: 0-0 Tstrap: 0-0 Ckp: 0-0
Best Rating: 69	1/03 Plum 2m heavy Hdl

Goodbye Mrs Chips

91   **69+**

5-y-o ch m Zilzal (USA)-Happydrome (Ahonoora)
Mrs L B Normile   Robert Gibbons

Placings:PP-50   (4297)
2003/04: 16⁵GF, 16⁰GF,

	Starts	1st	2nd	3rd	Win & Pl
Hurdles	2	0	0	0	0
Career Total	4	0	0	0	0

Going:	Sf: 0-0 GS: 0-0 Gd: 0-0 GF: - Fm: 0-2
Distance:	2m/2m3: 0-2 2m4-2m7: 0-0 3m+: 0-0
Track:	LH: 0-1 RH: 0-1 Tight: 0-1 Gall: 0-0
Aids:	Bl: 0-0 Vi: 0-0 Tstrap: 0-2 Ckp: 0-0
Best Rating: 69	12/03 Muss 2m gd-fm Hdl

Poor novice hurdler, pulled up first two starts.

Goodenough Star

4-y-o b f Stronz (IRE)-Goodenough Girl (Mac's Imp (USA))
A P Jones (J S King 27/11) Miss K J Webster

Placings:P   (2410)
2003/04: 17P GF,

	Starts	1st	2nd	3rd	Win & Pl
Hurdles	1	0	0	0	
Career Total	1	0	0	0	

Going:	Sf: 0-0 GS: 0-0 Gd: 0-0 GF: - Fm: 0-1
Distance:	2m/2m3: 0-1 2m4-2m7: 0-0 3m+: 0-0
Track:	LH: 0-0 RH: 0-1 Tight: 0-1 Gall: 0-0
Aids:	Bl: 0-0 Vi: 0-0 Tstrap: 0-0 Ckp: 0-0

Goodly News (IRE)

85   (0c)**55**

8-y-o b g Project Manager-Nordic Relation (IRE) (Nordico (USA))
A W Carroll   The Bartley Syndicate

Placings:0000/0/0/0PP0   (0996)
2003/04: 16⁰G, 16P G, 20P GF, 16⁰G,

	Starts	1st	2nd	3rd	Win & Pl
Hurdles	3	0	0	0	0
Chases	1	0	0	0	0
Career Total	9	0	0	0	0

Going:	Sf: 0-0 GS: 0-0 Gd: 0-3 GF: - Fm: 0-1

Goodbye Goldstone details (right column continued)

Distance:	2m/2m3: 0-3 2m4-2m7: 0-1 3m+: 0-0
Track:	LH: 0-3 RH: 0-1 Tight: 0-1 Gall: 0-1
Aids:	Bl: 0-0 Vi: 0-1 Tstrap: 0-1 Ckp: 0-0
Best Rating: 85	6/01 Clon 2m gd-fm Hdl

Goodtime George (IRE)

100   **118+**

11-y-o b g Strong Gale-Game Sunset (Menelek)
M Pitman   Mrs M J Bone

Placings:32550/22110/13/F/6-1P   (2704)
2003/04: 22¹GF, 25P G,

	Starts	1st	2nd	3rd	Win & Pl
Chases	2	1	0	0	5538
Career Total	16	4	3	2	18172
118 11/03 Newb	2m6f110yD Ch			G-F	£5538
137 5/99 Uttx	3m110y E Hdl			G-F	£2442
131 1/99 Donc	3m110y D Hdl			GD	£3330
135 12/98 Strf	2m6f110yE Hdl			SFT	£2250
			Total win prize-money £13561		

Going:	Sf: 0-0 GS: 0-0 Gd: 0-1 GF: - Fm: 1-1
Distance:	2m/2m3: 0-0 **2m4-2m7: 1-1** 3m+: 0-1
Track:	**LH: 1-2** RH: 0-0 Tight: 0-0 **Gall: 1-2**
Aids:	Bl: 0-0 Vi: 0-0 Tstrap: 0-0 Ckp: 0-0
Best Rating: 137	5/99 Uttx 3m110y gd-fm Hdl

Novice chaser; smart staying novice hurdler back in 1998/9; very lightly raced since; stays three miles; acts on most types of ground.

Goodtimelady (IRE)

110   **100**

10-y-o b/br m Good Thyne (USA)-Peppardstownlady (Gleason (USA))
D G Bridgwater   Cheltenham Racing Ltd

Placings:00400/666211/03/62PP   (4932)
2003/04: 19⁴HY, 24²GS, 26P GS, 27P G,

	Starts	1st	2nd	3rd	Win & Pl
Hurdles	4	0	1	0	851
Career Total	17	2	2	1	7495
100 4/01 Plum	3m1f110yE(0-105)HHdl			SFT	£2523
91 4/01 Plum	2m5f		G(0-90)HHdl	HVY	£2180
			Total win prize-money £4705		

Going:	Sf: 0-1 GS: 0-2 Gd: 0-1 GF: - Fm: 0-0
Distance:	2m/2m3: 0-0 2m4-2m7: 0-1 3m+: 0-3
Track:	LH: 0-0 RH: 0-3 Tight: 0-2 Gall: 0-0
Aids:	Bl: 0-0 Vi: 0-0 Tstrap: 0-0 Ckp: 0-0
Best Rating: 100	4/01 Plum 3m1f110y soft Hdl

Scored a Plumpton double on her first two starts over hurdles, but very well held since then.

Goodwood Promise

61   **6**

5-y-o b g Primo Dominie-Noble Destiny (Dancing Brave (USA))
N E Berry (J M Bradley 21/6) Leeway Group Limited

Placings:0   (2361)
2003/04: 16⁰GG,

	Starts	1st	2nd	3rd	Win & Pl
Hurdles	1	0	0	0	
Career Total	1	0	0	0	

Going:	Sf: 0-0 GS: 0-0 Gd: 0-0 GF: - Fm: 0-1
Distance:	2m/2m3: 0-1 2m4-2m7: 0-0 3m+: 0-1

Track: LH: 0-0 RH: 0-1 Tight: 0-0 Gall: 0-0
Aids: Bl: 0-0 Vi: 0-0 Tstrap: 0-0 Ckp: 0-0
Best Rating: 10 11/03 Ludl 2m   gd-fm Hdl

Goodys (IRE)

85f   55f

5-y-o ch g Good Thyne (USA)-Katie Baggage (IRE) (Brush Aside (USA))
G Prodromou Mrs B Macalister

Placings:5   (1537)
2003/04: 17⁵GF,

	Starts	1st	2nd	3rd	Win & Pl
NH Flat	1	0	0	0	0
Career Total	1	0	0	0	0

Going: Sf: 0-0 GS: 0-0 Gd: 0-0 GF: - Fm: 0-1
Distance: 2m/2m3: 0-0 2m4-2m7: 0-0 3m+: 0-0
Track: LH: 0-0 RH: 0-0 Tight: 0-1 Gall: 0-0
Aids: Bl: 0-0 Vi: 0-0 Tstrap: 0-0 Ckp: 0-0
Best Rating: 57 10/03 MRas 2m1f110y gd-fm NHF

Gordon Highlander

5-y-o ch m Master Willie-No Chili (Glint Of Gold)
Mrs P Robeson T E Short

Placings:060-PP   (2688)
2003/04: 20⁶G, 20⁸GS,

	Starts	1st	2nd	3rd	Win & Pl
Hurdles	2	0	0	0	
Career Total	5	0	0	0	0

Going: Sf: 0-0 GS: 0-1 Gd: 0-1 GF: - Fm: 0-0
Distance: 2m/2m3: 0-0 2m4-2m7: 0-2 3m+: 0-0
Track: LH: 0-1 RH: 0-1 Tight: 0-1 Gall: 0-1
Aids: Bl: 0-0 Vi: 0-0 Tstrap: 0-0 Ckp: 0-0
Best Rating: 82 4/03 Asct 2m110y good NHF

Gordons Friend

6-y-o ch g Clantime-Auntie Fay (IRE) (Fayruz)
B S Rothwell S P Hudson

Placings:0   (0897)
2003/04: 17⁰GF,

	Starts	1st	2nd	3rd	Win & Pl
Hurdles	1	0	0	0	
Career Total	1	0	0	0	0

Going: Sf: 0-0 GS: 0-0 Gd: 0-0 GF: - Fm: 0-1
Distance: 2m/2m3: 0-0 2m4-2m7: 0-0 3m+: 0-0
Track: LH: 0-1 RH: 0-0 Tight: 0-0 Gall: 0-0
Aids: Bl: 0-0 Vi: 0-0 Tstrap: 0-0 Ckp: 0-0

Gordy's Joy

72   31

4-y-o b f Cloudings (IRE)-Beatle Song (Song)
G A Ham Sally & Tom Dalley

Placings:000000   (4898)
2003/04: 17⁰GF, 16⁰G, 16⁰GS, 16⁹S, 17⁰GS, 16⁰G,

	Starts	1st	2nd	3rd	Win & Pl
Hurdles	6	0	0	0	

Career Total   6   0   0   0

Going: Sf: 0-1 GS: 0-2 Gd: 0-0 GF: - Fm: 0-1
Distance: 2m/2m3: 0-6 2m4-2m7: 0-0 3m+: 0-0
Track: LH: 0-2 RH: 0-4 Tight: 0-0 Gall: 0-0
Aids: Bl: 0-2 Vi: 0-0 Tstrap: 0-0 Ckp: 0-0
Best Rating: 31 4/04 Winc 2m   good Hdl

Tailed off on hurdling debut.

Gortmore Mews (IRE)

98   (113h) 103

10-y-o b g Persian Mews-Flat Out (Random Shot)
Ferdy Murphy John McMullen W F-Clennell Susan Sample

Placings:51/152010/02103/U550143P/0-34F   (3340)
2003/04: 20³GF, 20⁴G, 25⁶GS,

	Starts	1st	2nd	3rd	Win & Pl
Chases	3	0	0	1	797
Career Total	25	5	2	3	19900
111 12/01	Hrfd	2m3f	F(0-105)HCh	GD	£3349
6/00	Tral	2m	Ch	Y-S	£3312
99 3/00	Leop	2m	Hdl	GD	£3588
119 3/99	Gowr	2m	NHF	YLD	£3069
106 3/99	Wxfd	2m2f	NHF	Y-S	£2608
			Total win prize-money £15928		

Going: Sf: 0-0 GS: 0-1 Gd: 0-1 GF: - Fm: 0-0
Distance: 2m/2m3: 0-0 2m4-2m7: 0-2 3m+: 0-1
Track: LH: 0-3 RH: 0-0 Tight: 0-2 Gall: 0-0
Aids: Bl: 0-0 Vi: 0-0 Tstrap: 0-0 Ckp: 0-0
Best Rating: 119 5/99 Gowr 2m   yield NHF

Moderate chaser; formerly trained in Ireland; suited by two miles to two miles-three and good or softer ground.

Gospel Song

104   92

12-y-o ch g King Among Kings-Market Blues (Porto Bello)
A C Whillans Chas N Whillans

Placings:432/023/416415/2453415/6025/02620005/P0003/131P550-6530P126   (3674)
2003/04: 16⁶G, 16⁵G, 20³G, 16⁰GF, 19⁰HY, 16¹S, 16²HY, 18⁶HY,

	Starts	1st	2nd	3rd	Win & Pl
Hurdles	8	1	1	1	5166
Career Total	51	6	7	6	26980
92 1/04	Weth	2m	E(0-105)HHdl	SFT	£3598
92 6/02	Hexm	2m110y	E(0-105)HHdl	GD	£2562
92 6/02	Cttml	2m1f110yG(0-90)HHdl	HVY	£3290
114 3/99	Ayr	2m4f	C(0-130)HHdl	SFT	£2804
111 3/98	Ayr	2m	E(0-110)HHdl	SFT	£2910
109 1/98	Muss	2m	F Hdl	G-S	£2185
			Total win prize-money £17349		

Going: Sf: 1-4 GS: 0-0 Gd: 0-3 GF: - Fm: 0-1
Distance: 2m/2m3: 1-6 2m4-2m7: 0-2 3m+: 0-0
Track: LH: 1-6 RH: 0-1 Tight: 0-1 Gall: 0-1
Aids: Bl: 0-0 Vi: 0-0 Tstrap: 0-0 Ckp: 0-0
Best Rating: 114 11/00 Newc 2m   soft Hdl

Plating-class hurdler; recorded sixth career success at Wetherby in January; best at two miles but stays further; ideally suited by soft ground.

Goss Hawk (NZ)

70f   69f

4-y-o b r g Senor Pete (USA)-Stapleton Row (NZ) (Long Row)
W Jenks W Jenks

Placings:0   (4543)
2003/04: 16⁰GS,

	Starts	1st	2nd	3rd	Win & Pl
NH Flat	1	0	0	0	
Career Total	1	0	0	0	

Going: Sf: 0-0 GS: 0-1 Gd: 0-0 GF: - Fm: 0-0
Distance: 2m/2m3: 0-1 2m4-2m7: 0-0 3m+: 0-0
Track: LH: 0-0 RH: 0-1 Tight: 0-0 Gall: 0-0
Aids: Bl: 0-0 Vi: 0-0 Tstrap: 0-0 Ckp: 0-0
Best Rating: 69 3/04 Ludl 2m   gd-sft NHF

Got Alot On (USA)

95   80

6-y-o b/br g Charnwood Forest (IRE)-Fleety Belle (GER) (Assert)
Miss M Bragg G Gout, R Watts, G Standing

Placings:0/0450-6PP   (0975)
2003/04: 17⁶G, 17⁰GF, 17⁰GS,

	Starts	1st	2nd	3rd	Win & Pl
Hurdles	3	0	0	0	0
Career Total	8	0	0	0	383

Going: Sf: 0-0 GS: 0-1 Gd: 0-1 GF: - Fm: 0-1
Distance: 2m/2m3: 0-3 2m4-2m7: 0-0 3m+: 0-0
Track: LH: 0-3 RH: 0-0 Tight: 0-3 Gall: 0-0
Aids: Bl: 0-0 Vi: 0-0 Tstrap: 0-0 Ckp: 0-0
Best Rating: 80 1/03 Tntn 2m1f   soft Hdl

Got One Too (FR)

117   (148h) 156+

7-y-o ch g Green Tune (USA)-Gloria Mundi (FR) (Saint Cyrien (FR))
N J Henderson Sir Eric Parker & Mary Anne Parker

Placings:202/1115140/12U10-15303   (4964)
2003/04: 16¹GS, 16⁵S, 16³GGS, 16⁰G, 16³GF,

	Starts	1st	2nd	3rd	Win & Pl
Chases	5	1	0	2	39325
Career Total	20	7	3	4	101071
153 12/03	Chel	2m	B(0-145)HCh	G-S	£13875
142 3/03	Newb	2m2f110yC Ch	SFT	£8890
140 11/02	Leic	2m	D Ch	GD	£4784
148 1/02	Asct	2m110y	B HHdl	G-S	£10179
147 12/01	Newb	2m110y	A(0-145)HHdl	SFT	£15500
120 11/01	Newb	2m3f	D Hdl	GD	£3952
125 5/01	Hrfd	2m1f	E Hdl	GD	£3272
			Total win prize-money £60453		

Going: Sf: 0-1 GS: 1-2 Gd: 0-1 GF: - Fm: 0-1
Distance: 2m/2m3: 1-5 2m4-2m7: 0-0 3m+: 0-0
Track: LH: 1-2 RH: 0-3 Tight: 0-0 Gall: 1-2
Aids: Bl: 0-0 Vi: 0-0 Tstrap: 0-0 Ckp: 0-0
Best Rating: 153 4/04 Sand 2m   gd-fm Ch

Smart chaser; suited by two miles, probably stays 2m 3f; acts on ground good or softer; suited by forcing tactics.

Gotaknockonthehead (IRE)

61   89

6-y-o b m Accordion-Graphic Lady (IRE) (Phardante (FR))
Michael Aherne (P J Rothwell 8/12) Mrs Monica Aherne

Placings:201-256S50   (4202a)
2003/04: 17²G, 16⁵GF, 16⁸GF, 24⁸YS, 16⁵GY, 20⁰YS,

	Starts	1st	2nd	3rd	Win & Pl
NH Flat	1	0	1	0	478
Hurdles	5	0	0	0	0
Career Total	**9**	**1**	**2**	**0**	**4894**
104 4/03 Slig 2m		NHF		GD	£3584

Total win prize-money £3584

Going:	Sf: 0-0 GS: 0-0 Gd: 0-0 GF: - Fm: 0-2
Distance:	2m/2m3: 0-4 2m4-2m7: 0-1 3m+: 0-1
Track:	LH: 0-2 RH: 0-0 Tight: 0-1 Gall: 0-0
Aids:	Bl: 0-1 Vi: 0-0 Tstrap: 0-0 Ckp: 0-1
Best Rating:	108 10/03 Bang 2m1f good NHF

Won Sligo bumper April 2003; not disgraced under penalty when runner-up to the well backed Refinement at Bangor in October; acts on good ground.

Gotham (IRE)
98(101h)   (106+h)115+
7-y-o gr g Gothland (FR)-Inchriver (IRE) (Over The River (FR))
R H Alner Pell-Mell Partners

Placings:00/12-4   (2840)
2003/04: 16⁴GS,

	Starts	1st	2nd	3rd	Win & Pl
Chases	1	0	0	0	264
Career Total	**5**	**1**	**1**	**0**	**4458**
106 10/02 Plum 2m		E Hdl		G-F	£2989

Total win prize-money £2989

Going:	Sf: 0-0 GS: 0-1 Gd: 0-0 GF: - Fm: 0-0
Distance:	2m/2m3: 0-1 2m4-2m7: 0-0 3m+: 0-0
Track:	LH: 0-1 RH: 0-0 Tight: 0-0 Gall: 0-0
Aids:	Bl: 0-0 Vi: 0-0 Tstrap: 0-0 Ckp: 0-0
Best Rating:	115 12/03 Uttx 2m gd-sft Ch

Showed improved form to win a novice hurdle at Plumpton in October 2002; showed promise when fourth on debut over fences at Uttoxeter in December.

Gotham Abbey (IRE)
94   70
7-y-o gr m Gothland (FR)-Abbeyside (Paddy's Stream)
Mrs D A Hamer (B Llewellyn 16/5) H M Thomas

Placings:00/00PPF-306   (1120)
2003/04: 17³G, 16⁹G, 19⁵GF,

	Starts	1st	2nd	3rd	Win & Pl
Hurdles	3	0	0	1	532
Career Total	**10**	**0**	**0**	**1**	**532**

Going:	Sf: 0-0 GS: 0-0 Gd: 0-2 GF: - Fm: 0-1
Distance:	2m/2m3: 0-3 2m4-2m7: 0-0 3m+: 0-0
Track:	LH: 0-1 RH: 0-1 Tight: 0-1 Gall: 0-0
Aids:	Bl: 0-0 Vi: 0-0 Tstrap: 0-0 Ckp: 0-0
Best Rating:	70 4/03 Extr 2m1f good Hdl

Gothic Bay
69   37
4-y-o b g Gothenberg (IRE)-Greyhill Lady (Grey Desire)
M W Easterby Mrs C M Haigh

Placings:0   (1958)
2003/04: 16⁰GF,

	Starts	1st	2nd	3rd	Win & Pl
Hurdles	1	0	0	0	
Career Total	**1**	**0**	**0**	**0**	

Going:	Sf: 0-0 GS: 0-0 Gd: 0-0 GF: - Fm: 0-1

Distance:	2m/2m3: 0-1 2m4-2m7: 0-0 3m+: 0-0
Track:	LH: 0-1 RH: 0-1 Tight: 0-0 Gall: 0-0
Aids:	Bl: 0-0 Vi: 0-0 Tstrap: 0-0 Ckp: 0-0
Best Rating:	37 11/03 Hayd 2m gd-fm Hdl

Gottabe
111   (115h)124
11-y-o ch g Gunner B-Topsy Bee (Be Friendly)
Mrs S J Smith Keith Nicholson

Placings:02U46134/2600153430/1211345F4-443313   (3606)
2003/04: 24⁴HY, 20⁴G, 26³G, 23³G, 24¹G, 24³S,

	Starts	1st	2nd	3rd	Win & Pl
Chases	6	1	0	3	17110
Career Total	**33**	**6**	**3**	**7**	**48943**
124 1/04 Donc 3m		C(0-130)HCh		GD	£8361
124 11/02 Weth 3m1f		D(0-120)HCh		HVY	£7294
115 6/02 Worc 2m7f110yD Ch				GD	£4153
102 5/02 Weth 2m4f110yD(0-110)HCh				G-F	£4108
115 12/01 Sthl 2m4f110yD(0-125)HHdl				SFT	£3464
108 2/01 Sedg 2m5f110yE Hdl				SFT	£2548

Total win prize-money £29931

Going:	Sf: 0-2 GS: 0-0 Gd: 1-4 GF: - Fm: 0-0
Distance:	2m/2m3: 0-0 2m4-2m7: 0-1 3m+: 1-5
Track:	LH: 1-5 RH: 0-0 Tight: 0-0 Gall: 1-2
Aids:	Bl: 0-0 Vi: 0-0 Tstrap: 0-0 Ckp: 0-0
Best Rating:	124 1/04 Donc 3m good Ch

Fair chaser; career-best effort when wide-margin winner at Doncaster in January 2004; stays three miles plus and acts on any ground; likes to race prominently.

Governor Daniel
108(102c)   (110c)112
13-y-o b g Governor General-Princess Semele (Imperial Fling (USA))
Ian Williams Dsm Demolition Limited

Placings:2/0306/1U44/4P50/42131/11PF111P/P5P0/31114 113312-1P12223111   (2684)
2003/04: 17¹GF, 19⁵GF, 16¹G, 17²GF, 20²GF, 18²GF, 16³GF, 16¹GF, 18¹GF, 21¹GS,

	Starts	1st	2nd	3rd	Win & Pl
Hurdles	9	5	3	1	14632
Chases	1	0	0	0	0
Career Total	**51**	**19**	**6**	**6**	**65288**
101 12/03 Hntg 2m5f110yF Hdl				G-S	£2247
96 11/03 Font 2m2f110yF Hdl				G-F	£1855
106 10/03 Towc 2m		F(0-100)HHdl		G-F	£1844
101 6/03 Worc 2m				GD	£2653
105 6/03 NAbb 2m1f		F Hdl		G-F	£3410
110 4/03 NAbb 2m5f110yG(0-95)HCh				G-F	£3024
112 11/02 Ludl 2m		G Hdl		GD	£2765
105 11/02 Ludl 2m		G Hdl		G-S	£2712
99 9/02 Font 2m4f		E(0-105)HCh		G-F	£4134
99 8/02 MRas 2m1f		G Hdl		G-F	£2058
99 8/02 Hntg 2m4f110yG Hdl				G-F	£1903
115 9/00 Plum 2m5f		D(0-125)HHdl		G-F	£3103
115 9/00 Hrfd 2m3f110yF(0-100)HHdl				G-F	£2877
115 8/00 Sthl 2m4f110yF(0-110)HHdl				GD	£2891
112 6/00 MRas 2m4f		C(0-135)HCh		G-F	£10481
115 6/00 NAbb 2m110y F(0-105)HCh				G-F	£3454
102 9/99 Sedg 2m6f		E Ch		G-F	£3254
95 8/99 MRas 2m1f110yG(0-95)HHdl				G-F	£1679
105 5/96 Sthl 2m2f		E Hdl		G-F	£2658

Total win prize-money £59007

Going:	Sf: 0-0 GS: 1-1 Gd: 1-1 GF: - Fm: 3-8
Distance:	2m/2m3: 4-8 2m4-2m7: 1-2 3m+: 0-0
Track:	LH: 3-7 RH: 2-3 Tight: 2-5 Gall: 1-1
Aids:	Bl: 0-0 Vi: 0-0 Tstrap: 0-0 Ckp: 0-0

Best Rating:	115 9/00 Plum 2m5f gd-fm Hdl

Modest chaser/hurdler; has a superb record in selling grade; likes fast ground, best at around two miles, but stays two and a half.

Graceful Dancer
104(94c)   (80c)96
7-y-o b m Old Vic-Its My Turn (Palm Track)
C P Morlock The Fairway Connection

Placings:20/55601212-0003P5   (3904)
2003/04: 24⁵S, 26⁶GS, 24⁰S, 24³S, 25⁵PHY, 24⁵GS,

	Starts	1st	2nd	3rd	Win & Pl
Hurdles	4	0	0	0	0
Chases	2	0	0	1	653
Career Total	**16**	**2**	**3**	**1**	**9766**
92 3/03 Hrfd 3m2f		F(0-95)HHdl		SFT	£3045
92 2/03 Tntn 3m110y		F(0-100)HHdl		SFT	£3454

Total win prize-money £6500

Going:	Sf: 0-4 GS: 0-2 Gd: 0-0 GF: - Fm: 0-0
Distance:	2m/2m3: 0-0 2m4-2m7: 0-0 3m+: 0-6
Track:	LH: 0-2 RH: 0-4 Tight: 0-1 Gall: 0-2
Aids:	Bl: 0-0 Vi: 0-0 Tstrap: 0-0 Ckp: 0-0
Best Rating:	98 3/02 Donc 2m110y soft NHF

Moderate handicap hurdler; improved since being fitted with a visor and stepped up in distance; loves the mud and stamina is her forte.

Gracilis (IRE)
101   110+
7-y-o b g Caerleon (USA)-Grace Note (FR) (Top Ville)
G A Swinbank Michael H Watt

Placings:51   (4783)
2003/04: 17⁵GS, 21¹G,

	Starts	1st	2nd	3rd	Win & Pl
Hurdles	2	1	0	0	3738
Career Total	**2**	**1**	**0**	**0**	**3738**
110 4/04 Hntg 2m5f110yE Hdl				GD	£3738

Total win prize-money £3738

Going:	Sf: 0-0 GS: 0-1 Gd: 1-1 GF: - Fm: 0-0
Distance:	2m/2m3: 0-0 2m4-2m7: 1-1 3m+: 0-0
Track:	LH: 0-1 RH: 1-1 Tight: 0-1 Gall: 1-1
Aids:	Bl: 0-0 Vi: 0-0 Tstrap: 0-0 Ckp: 0-0
Best Rating:	110 4/04 Hntg 2m5f110y good Hdl

Useful staying handicapper on the Flat; opened account over hurdles with clear-cut success at Huntingdon in April; will be suited by three miles.

Grady
82   61
5-y-o ch g Bluegrass Prince (IRE)-Lady Sabina (Bairn (USA))
W M Brisbourne (Miss Jacqueline S Doyle 30/10) Mark Brisbourne

Placings:P-06   (1844)
2003/04: 16⁰G, 16⁶G,

	Starts	1st	2nd	3rd	Win & Pl
Hurdles	2	0	0	0	0
Career Total	**3**	**0**	**0**	**0**	**0**

Going:	Sf: 0-0 GS: 0-0 Gd: 0-1 GF: - Fm: 0-1
Distance:	2m/2m3: 0-2 2m4-2m7: 0-0 3m+: 0-0
Track:	LH: 0-2 RH: 0-0 Tight: 0-2 Gall: 0-0
Aids:	Bl: 0-0 Vi: 0-0 Tstrap: 0-0 Ckp: 0-1
Best Rating:	61 10/03 Strf 2m110y good Hdl

Gralmano (IRE)

111(101c)   (117c)**148**

9-y-o b g Scenic-Llangollen (IRE) (Caerleon (USA))
K A Ryan Coleorton Moor Racing

Placings:111/2P1102-4160   (4423)
2003/04: 16⁴GS, 25¹G, 25⁶G, 24⁹G,

	Starts	1st	2nd	3rd	Win & Pl
Hurdles	4	1	0	0	21500
Career Total	13	6	2	0	63543
148	11/03	Weth	3m1f	A Hdl	GD	£17400
106	12/02	Muss	2m4f	D Ch	G-F	£5434
117	11/02	Catt	2m	D Ch	GD	£4790
122	12/01	Weth	2m	C(0-135)HHdl	SFT	£5343
126	11/01	Kels	2m110y	E Hdl	G-S	£3125
122	10/01	Kels	2m110y	E Hdl	GD	£2450

Total win prize-money £38544

Going:	Sf: 0-0 GS: 0-1 Gd: 1-3 GF: - Fm: 0-0
Distance:	2m/2m3: 0-1 2m4-2m7: 0-0 3m+: 1-3
Track:	LH: 1-4 RH: 0-0 Tight: 0-0 Gall: 0-2
Aids:	Bl: 0-0 Vi: 0-0 Tstrap: 0-0 Ckp: 0-0
Best Rating:	148 11/03 Weth 3m1f good Hdl

Smart hurdler; useful handicapper on the Flat, stays three miles well; goes very well on fast ground.

Grand Ambition (USA)

8-y-o b g Lear Fan (USA)-Longing To Dance (USA)
(Nureyev (USA))
Mrs P Sly Mrs P M Sly

Placings:0/30063P0P3/4F00001-FP0003   (3919)
2003/04: 21⁷PGF, 21⁹PGF, 17⁹G, 16⁹GF, 16⁸G, 21³G,

	Starts	1st	2nd	3rd	Win & Pl
Hurdles	3	0	0	0	0
Chases	3	0	0	1	370
Career Total	23	1	0	4	4100
77	4/03	Fknm	2m5f110yH Ch	GD	£2048

Total win prize-money £2049

Going:	Sf: 0-0 GS: 0-0 Gd: 0-3 GF: - Fm: 0-3
Distance:	2m/2m3: 0-3 2m4-2m7: 0-3 3m+: 0-0
Track:	LH: 0-5 RH: 0-1 Tight: 0-5 Gall: 0-0
Aids:	Bl: 0-0 Vi: 0-0 Tstrap: 0-0 Ckp: 0-0
Best Rating:	94 5/01 Hntg 2m110y gd-fm Hdl

Ex-Irish hunter chaser; won at Fakenham in April; suited by fast ground.

Grand Canyon (IRE)

11-y-o b g Gallic Heir-Kay Kelly (Pitskelly)
Mrs J Shirley Mrs J Shirley

Placings:0/2PPP4/4/P/P   (0028)
2003/04: 21⁸G,

	Starts	1st	2nd	3rd	Win & Pl
Chases	1	0	0	0	
Career Total	9	0	1	0	848

Going:	Sf: 0-0 GS: 0-0 Gd: 0-1 GF: - Fm: 0-0
Distance:	2m/2m3: 0-0 2m4-2m7: 0-1 3m+: 0-0
Track:	LH: 0-1 RH: 0-0 Tight: 0-0 Gall: 0-1
Aids:	Bl: 0-0 Vi: 0-0 Tstrap: 0-0 Ckp: 0-0
Best Rating:	87 10/98 Hntg 2m4f110y good Hdl

Grand Finale (IRE)

104   **127+**

7-y-o b h Sadler's Wells (USA)-Final Figure (USA) (Super Concorde (USA))
Miss Venetia Williams Leinster Bar

Placings:P4-131105   (4559)
2003/04: 16¹GS, 17³GF, 16¹GS, 16¹GS, 16⁹S, 16⁵GS,

	Starts	1st	2nd	3rd	Win & Pl
Hurdles	6	3	0	1	11978
Career Total	8	3	0	1	12416
127	2/04	Sand	2m110y	E(0-115)HHdl	G-S	£4221
115	11/03	Uttx	2m	E Hdl	G-S	£2737
117	5/03	Worc	2m	E Hdl	G-S	£3619

Total win prize-money £10578

Going:	Sf: 0-1 GS: 3-4 Gd: 0-0 GF: - Fm: 0-1
Distance:	2m/2m3: 3-6 2m4-2m7: 0-0 3m+: 0-0
Track:	LH: 2-4 RH: 1-2 Tight: 0-1 Gall: 0-1
Aids:	Bl: 0-0 Vi: 0-0 Tstrap: 0-0 Ckp: 0-0
Best Rating:	127 2/04 Sand 2m110y gd-sft Hdl

Fair hurdler; ex-Irish; very useful on the Flat, the only horse ever to beat Sinndar; ready winner of 2m maiden hurdle at Worcester in May 2003; possibly found the ground on the fast side next time, but has won twice since; disappointing in the Imperial Cup latest, but better than he showed their; acts on good and soft ground; has had breathing problems.

Grand Gousier (FR)

10-y-o b g Perrault-Tartifume Ii (FR) (Mistigri)
G C Evans M P Wiggin

Placings:22/P0/P25P421P/01214/2435-P   (3778)
2003/04: 24⁸G,

	Starts	1st	2nd	3rd	Win & Pl
Chases	1	0	0	0	
Career Total	22	3	6	1	20710
112	1/01	Sthl	2m4f110yE(0-115)HCh	HVY	£3469
109	11/00	Leic	2m4f110yE(0-115)HCh	G-S	£3510
105	3/00	Wwck	2m4f	D(0-110)HCh	SFT	£5668

Total win prize-money £12647

Going:	Sf: 0-0 GS: 0-0 Gd: 0-1 GF: - Fm: 0-0
Distance:	2m/2m3: 0-0 2m4-2m7: 0-3 3m+: 0-1
Track:	LH: 0-0 RH: 0-1 Tight: 0-1 Gall: 0-0
Aids:	Bl: 0-0 Vi: 0-0 Tstrap: 0-0 Ckp: 0-0
Best Rating:	112 1/01 Sthl 2m4f110y heavy Ch

Fair chaser at up to two and a half miles. Ran well when second in October 2002, his first run for more than eighteen months.

Grand Lass (IRE)

5-y-o b m Grand Lodge (USA)-Siskin (IRE) (Royal Academy (USA))
A Sadik (T D Barron 9/2) A Sadik

Placings:0   (4569)
2003/04: 17⁰GS,

	Starts	1st	2nd	3rd	Win & Pl
Hurdles	1	0	0	0	
Career Total	1	0	0	0	

Going:	Sf: 0-0 GS: 0-1 Gd: 0-0 GF: - Fm: 0-0
Distance:	2m/2m3: 0-1 2m4-2m7: 0-0 3m+: 0-0
Track:	LH: 0-1 RH: 0-0 Tight: 0-1 Gall: 0-0
Aids:	Bl: 0-0 Vi: 0-0 Tstrap: 0-0 Ckp: 0-1

Grand Opinion (IRE)

99f   **91f**

5-y-o b g Grand Plaisir (IRE)-Cousin Rose (Track Spare)
B W Duke The G S M Group

Placings:00   (3948)
2003/04: 16⁹G, 16⁹G,

	Starts	1st	2nd	3rd	Win & Pl
NH Flat	2	0	0	0	
Career Total	2	0	0	0	

Going:	Sf: 0-0 GS: 0-0 Gd: 0-2 GF: - Fm: 0-0
Distance:	2m/2m3: 0-2 2m4-2m7: 0-0 3m+: 0-0
Track:	LH: 0-1 RH: 0-1 Tight: 0-0 Gall: 0-1
Aids:	Bl: 0-0 Vi: 0-0 Tstrap: 0-0 Ckp: 0-0
Best Rating:	94 2/04 Newb 2m110y good NHF

Grand Prairie (SWE)

106   **102+**

8-y-o b g Prairie-Platonica (ITY) (Primo Dominie)
G L Moore (R C Guest 5/5) N J Jones

Placings:5U/P-521F65   (4793)
2003/04: 16⁵S, 16²S, 17¹G, 16⁵G, 19⁵GS, 16⁵G,

	Starts	1st	2nd	3rd	Win & Pl
Hurdles	6	1	1	0	3945
Career Total	9	1	1	0	3945
100	3/04	Folk	2m1f110yF(0-90)HHdl	GD	£3101

Total win prize-money £3101

Going:	Sf: 0-2 GS: 0-1 Gd: 1-3 GF: - Fm: 0-0
Distance:	2m/2m3: 1-6 2m4-2m7: 0-0 3m+: 0-0
Track:	LH: 0-4 RH: 1-2 Tight: 1-3 Gall: 0-3
Aids:	Bl: 0-0 Vi: 0-0 Tstrap: 0-0 Ckp: 0-0
Best Rating:	100 3/04 Folk 2m1f110y good Hdl

Moderate hurdler; multiple scorer on the Flat in Sweden and in Spain; has shown a fair level of ability over hurdles in Britain; acts on good and soft ground.

Grand Prompt

102   **96**

5-y-o ch g Grand Lodge (USA)-Prompting (Primo Dominie)
Miss L J Sheen (B R Johnson 1/12) Mrs P J Sheen

Placings:3P06-510534PP   (3319)
2003/04: 16⁵GS, 20¹GF, 19⁹G, 21⁵GF, 19³G, 20⁴GF, 22⁸GS, 20⁸S,

	Starts	1st	2nd	3rd	Win & Pl
Hurdles	8	1	0	1	4526
Career Total	12	1	0	2	5222
95	5/03	Fknm	2m4f	E Hdl	G-F	£3544

Total win prize-money £3544

Going:	Sf: 0-1 GS: 0-2 Gd: 0-2 GF: - Fm: 1-3
Distance:	2m/2m3: 0-3 2m4-2m7: 1-5 3m+: 0-0
Track:	LH: 1-5 RH: 0-3 Tight: 1-4 Gall: 0-0
Aids:	Bl: 0-1 Vi: 1-5 Tstrap: 0-0 Ckp: 0-1
Best Rating:	96 11/03 Asct 2m4f gd-fm Hdl

Moderate hurdler; relished fast ground and sharp track when winning modest 2m 4f novice hurdle at Fakenham May 2003; often visored.

Grand Slam (IRE)

97(87h)   (104h)**94**

9-y-o b g Second Set (IRE)-Lady In The Park (IRE) (Last Tycoon)
A C Whillans 7 Up Partnership

Placings:00/312/120045P0/P0025-63   (4880)

2003/04: 16⁶S, 20³GS,

	Starts	1st	2nd	3rd	Win & Pl
Chases	2	0	0	1	690
Career Total	20	2	3	2	9325
98	5/01 Ayr 2m E Hdl			G-F	£2999
88	1/01 Muss 2m E Hdl			G-S	£2254
			Total win prize-money £5254		

Going:	Sf: 0-1 GS: 0-1 Gd: 0-0 GF: - Fm: 0-0	
Distance:	2m/2m3: 0-1 2m4-2m7: 0-0 3m+: 0-0	
Track:	LH: 0-1 RH: 0-1 Tight: 0-0 Gall: 0-0	
Aids:	Bl: 0-0 Vi: 0-0 Tstrap: 0-0 Ckp: 0-0	
Best Rating:	104 5/01 MRas 2m1f110y good	Hdl

Some ability over fences, but is not the most reliable of sorts.

Grande Bretagne (FR)

5-y-o b g Legend Of France (USA)-L'Epicurienne (FR) (Rex Magna (FR))
Ian Williams Sir Robert Ogden

Placings:00P (4589)
2003/04: 16⁶G, 16⁰G, 16⁶G,

	Starts	1st	2nd	3rd	Win & Pl
NH Flat	1	0	0	0	0
Hurdles	2	0	0	0	0
Career Total	3	0	0	0	

Going:	Sf: 0-0 GS: 0-1 Gd: 0-2 GF: - Fm: 0-0	
Distance:	2m/2m3: 0-3 2m4-2m7: 0-0 3m+: 0-0	
Track:	LH: 0-2 RH: 0-1 Tight: 0-0 Gall: 0-1	
Aids:	Bl: 0-0 Vi: 0-0 Tstrap: 0-0 Ckp: 0-0	
Best Rating:	72 11/03 Weth 2m good	NHF

Grande Creole (FR)

93f   93f

5-y-o b g Byzantium (FR)-Sclos (FR) (Direct Flight)
P F Nicholls Sir Robert Ogden

Placings:43 (4636)
2003/04: 18⁴GS, 17³G,

	Starts	1st	2nd	3rd	Win & Pl
NH Flat	2	0	0	1	271
Career Total	2	0	0	1	271

Going:	Sf: 0-0 GS: 0-1 Gd: 0-1 GF: - Fm: 0-0	
Distance:	2m/2m3: 0-2 2m4-2m7: 0-0 3m+: 0-0	
Track:	LH: 0-1 RH: 0-0 Tight: 0-0 Gall: 0-0	
Aids:	Bl: 0-0 Vi: 0-0 Tstrap: 0-0 Ckp: 0-0	
Best Rating:	93 2/04 Font 2m2f110y gd-sft	NHF

Ran green on debut when fourth in a Fontwell bumper in February; should come on plenty for the experience.

Grande Jete (SAF)

104   122+

7-y-o ch g Jallad (USA)-Corps De Ballet (SAF) (Truely Nureyev (USA))
N J Henderson L Westwood A Chandler J J Hindley

Placings:315 (3593)
2003/04: 17³GS, 16¹GS, 16⁵HY,

	Starts	1st	2nd	3rd	Win & Pl
Hurdles	3	1	0	1	4257
Career Total	3	1	0	1	4257
122	1/04 Winc 2m E Hdl			G-S	£3636

Total win prize-money £3637

Going:	Sf: 0-1 GS: 1-2 Gd: 0-0 GF: - Fm: 0-0	
Distance:	2m/2m3: 1-3 2m4-2m7: 0-0 3m+: 0-0	
Track:	LH: 0-1 RH: 1-2 Tight: 0-1 Gall: 0-0	
Aids:	Bl: 0-0 Vi: 0-0 Tstrap: 0-0 Ckp: 0-0	
Best Rating:	122 1/04 Winc 2m gd-sft	Hdl

Useful novice hurdler; formerly South African Group One winner; suited by two miles and does not want the ground too soft.

Grandee Line

99   (95h)98

9-y-o gr g Gran Alba (USA)-Judys Line (Capricorn Line)
R H Alner Cliff Gaylard

Placings:0/¹P/34FP (4667)
2003/04: 16⁵HY, 22⁴G, 21⁵GS, 24⁵S,

	Starts	1st	2nd	3rd	Win & Pl
Chases	4	0	0	1	1375
Career Total	7	1	0	1	4056
95	4/02 Chep 2m4f E Hdl			G-F	£2681
			Total win prize-money £2681		

Going:	Sf: 0-2 GS: 0-1 Gd: 0-1 GF: - Fm: 0-0	
Distance:	2m/2m3: 0-1 2m4-2m7: 0-2 3m+: 0-1	
Track:	LH: 0-4 RH: 0-0 Tight: 0-2 Gall: 0-1	
Aids:	Bl: 0-0 Vi: 0-0 Tstrap: 0-0 Ckp: 0-0	
Best Rating:	100 2/04 Chep 2m10y heavy	Ch

Won 2m4f novice hurdle at Chepstow on good to firm April 2002; pulled up later that month and was not seen until finishing a well beaten third in 2m novice chase on heavy ground at the same venue February 2004; held subsequently.

Grangewick Flight

94   109

10-y-o b g Lighter-Feathery (Le Coq D'Or)
N Wilson Mrs H D Marks

Placings:F4463/POP222F01UU233-32P5043334BU (4961)
2003/04: 24⁵G, 20²G, 20⁶G, 21⁵GS, 20⁹G, 20⁴G, 22³G, 20³G, 20³G, 20⁴GS, 21⁸G, 20⁰GS,

	Starts	1st	2nd	3rd	Win & Pl
Chases	12	0	1	4	6595
Career Total	31	1	5	7	18875
99	2/03 Newc 2m4f F(0-100)HCh			SFT	£3399
			Total win prize-money £3400		

Going:	Sf: 0-0 GS: 0-3 Gd: 0-9 GF: - Fm: 0-0	
Distance:	2m/2m3: 0-0 2m4-2m7: 0-11 3m+: 0-1	
Track:	LH: 0-6 RH: 0-6 Tight: 0-5 Gall: 0-0	
Aids:	Bl: 0-3 Vi: 0-0 Tstrap: 0-0 Ckp: 0-1	
Best Rating:	109 4/03 Prth 2m4f110y good	Ch

Moderate chaser; stays three miles, but effective at shorter; acts on soft ground; not the most fluent jumper.

Granit D'Estruval (FR)

117   (120h)137+

10-y-o b g Quart De Vin (FR)-Jalousie (FR) (Blockhaus)
Ferdy Murphy W J Gott

Placings:5/2/211F/12P1/P-UP341F (4861)
2003/04: 27⁵U, 28⁶S, 30³G, 33⁴G, 29¹Y, 33⁶GS,

	Starts	1st	2nd	3rd	Win & Pl
Chases	6	3	0	1	84545
Career Total	17	5	3	1	105545
137	4/04 Fair 3m5f HCh			YLD	£79450
120	2/02 Uttx 3m11y D Hdl			HVY	£3649
143	11/01 Carl 3m2f C(0-130)HCh			SFT	£6922
120	12/00 Newc 3m E Ch			SFT	£3120
104	11/00 Carl 3m2f F Ch			SFT	£2353
			Total win prize-money £95497		

Going:	Sf: 0-1 GS: 0-1 Gd: 0-3 GF: - Fm: 0-0	
Distance:	2m/2m3: 0-0 2m4-2m7: 0-0 3m+: 1-6	
Track:	LH: 0-5 RH: 1-1 Tight: 0-2 Gall: 0-1	
Aids:	Bl: 0-0 Vi: 0-0 Tstrap: 0-0 Ckp: 0-0	
Best Rating:	143 11/01 Carl 3m2f soft	Ch

Fair chaser; winner over hurdles at Uttoxeter in February 2002; absent for over a year subsequently; won the Irish Grand National at Fairyhouse in April 2004; stays four miles and effective on soft ground.

Granite Steps

(106h)   (112+h)97

8-y-o gr g Gran Alba (USA)-Pablena (Pablond)
N G Richards Mrs T H Barclay/Mrs F D McInnes Skinner

Placings:0/22231/FU3P-12 (4729)
2003/04: 20¹HY, 20²G,

	Starts	1st	2nd	3rd	Win & Pl
Hurdles	2	1	1	0	6163
Career Total	12	2	4	2	11956
112	3/04 Carl 2m4f E(0-110)HHdl			HVY	£3802
103	3/02 Towc 2m5f F Hdl			G-S	£1953
			Total win prize-money £5756		

Going:	Sf: 1-1 GS: 0-0 Gd: 0-1 GF: - Fm: 0-0	
Distance:	2m/2m3: 0-0 2m4-2m7: 1-2 3m+: 0-0	
Track:	LH: 0-0 RH: 1-2 Tight: 0-0 Gall: 0-0	
Aids:	Bl: 0-0 Vi: 0-0 Tstrap: 0-0 Ckp: 0-0	
Best Rating:	112 4/04 Carl 2m4f good	Hdl

Moderate hurdler/chaser; best around two miles-four on soft ground.

Granny Annie

5-y-o b m Minster Son-Castle Fountain (Royal Fountain)
W Amos W G Macmillan

Placings:U (4731)
2003/04: 20¹U,

	Starts	1st	2nd	3rd	Win & Pl
Hurdles	1	0	0	0	
Career Total	1	0	0	0	

Going:	Sf: 0-0 GS: 0-0 Gd: 0-1 GF: - Fm: 0-0	
Distance:	2m/2m3: 0-0 2m4-2m7: 0-1 3m+: 0-0	
Track:	LH: 0-0 RH: 0-1 Tight: 0-0 Gall: 0-0	
Aids:	Bl: 0-0 Vi: 0-0 Tstrap: 0-0 Ckp: 0-0	

Granny Kellys Tart (IRE)

118f

6-y-o ch g Old Vic-Le Idol (Le Bavard (FR))
W P Mullins Patrick J Fahy

Placings:5-120 (4400)
2003/04: 18¹F, 16²YS, 16⁰G,

	Starts	1st	2nd	3rd	Win & Pl
NH Flat	3	1	1	0	5280
Career Total	4	1	1	0	5280
107	7/03 Wxfd 2m2f NHF			FRM	£4032
			Total win prize-money £4032		

Going: Sf: 0-0 GS: 0-0 Gd: 0-1 GF: - Fm: 1-1
Distance: 2m/2m3: 1-3 2m4-2m7: 0-0 3m+: 0-0
Track: LH: 0-1 RH: 0-0 Tight: 0-0 Gall: 0-0
Aids: Bl: 0-0 Vi: 0-0 Tstrap: 0-0 Ckp: 0-0
Best Rating: 118 3/04 Navn 2m   yld-sft NHF

Granrich

4-y-o ch f Alflora (IRE)-Weareagrandmother (Prince Tenderfoot (USA))
P M Rich P M Rich

Placings:60F (3641)
2003/04: 12⁶S, 13⁹GS, 17ᶠS,

	Starts	1st	2nd	3rd	Win & Pl
NH Flat	2	0	0	0	0
Hurdles	1	0	0	0	0
Career Total	3	0	0	0	0

Going: Sf: 0-2 GS: 0-1 Gd: 0-0 GF: - Fm: 0-0
Distance: 2m/2m3: 0-2 2m4-2m7: 0-0 3m+: 0-0
Track: LH: 0-0 RH: 0-2 Tight: 0-0 Gall: 0-0
Aids: Bl: 0-0 Vi: 0-0 Tstrap: 0-0 Ckp: 0-0
Best Rating: 46 11/03 Asct 1m4f   soft NHF

Grantie Boy (IRE)
69f   33f

5-y-o b g Nashwan (USA)-Radiant (USA) (Foolish Pleasure (USA))
W M Brisbourne M Stewkesbury

Placings:00 (1019)
2003/04: 17⁹GF, 16⁹GF,

	Starts	1st	2nd	3rd	Win & Pl
NH Flat	2	0	0	0	0
Career Total	2	0	0	0	0

Going: Sf: 0-0 GS: 0-0 Gd: 0-0 GF: - Fm: 0-2
Distance: 2m/2m3: 0-2 2m4-2m7: 0-0 3m+: 0-0
Track: LH: 0-2 RH: 0-0 Tight: 0-1 Gall: 0-0
Aids: Bl: 0-0 Vi: 0-0 Tstrap: 0-0 Ckp: 0-0
Best Rating: 33 8/03 Worc 2m   gd-fm NHF

Graphic Approach (IRE)
111   123

6-y-o b g King's Ride-Sharp Approach (Crash Course)
C R Egerton Mr & Mrs Peter Orton

Placings:53-11F3 (3897)
2003/04: 17¹GS, 20¹GS, 19ᶠGS, 16³GS,

	Starts	1st	2nd	3rd	Win & Pl
NH Flat	1	1	0	0	1694
Hurdles	3	1	0	2	5232
Career Total	6	2	0	2	7517
123	1/04	Weth	2m4f110yE Hdl	G-S	£4446
115	12/03	Hrfd	2m1f	H NHF	G-S	£1694

Total win prize-money £6140

Going: Sf: 0-0 GS: 2-4 Gd: 0-0 GF: - Fm: 0-0
Distance: 2m/2m3: 2-6 2m4-2m7: 1-2 3m+: 0-0
Track: LH: 1-1 RH: 1-3 Tight: 0-1 Gall: 0-0
Aids: Bl: 0-0 Vi: 0-0 Tstrap: 0-0 Ckp: 0-0
Best Rating: 123 1/04 Tntn   2m3f110y gd-sft Hdl

Irish import who had decent form in a couple of soft ground Leopardstown bumpers; impressive winner of Hereford

---

bumper for new connections in December; made a winning hurdling bow at Wetherby the following month; appears to have a bright future.

Graphic Designer (IRE)

15-y-o b g Sheer Grit-Kates Princess (Pitpan)
J J Hazeltine J J Hazeltine

Placings:20FPP/5 (0353)
2003/04: 21⁵GF,

	Starts	1st	2nd	3rd	Win & Pl
Chases	1	0	0	0	0
Career Total	6	0	1	0	1085

Going: Sf: 0-0 GS: 0-0 Gd: 0-0 GF: - Fm: 0-1
Distance: 2m/2m3: 0-0 2m4-2m7: 0-1 3m+: 0-0
Track: LH: 0-0 RH: 0-1 Tight: 0-1 Gall: 0-0
Aids: Bl: 0-0 Vi: 0-0 Tstrap: 0-0 Ckp: 0-0
Best Rating: 95 11/95 Asct 3m   good Hdl

Grate Deel (IRE)
103   108

14-y-o ch g The Parson-Cahernane Girl (Bargello)
Mrs S J Smith Mrs M Ashby

Placings:6/05014/5632/4224P/3P0P11622P/36550/343514 10/0P5/114141P-0P631 (1280)
2003/04: 30⁹G, 26ᴾGF, 26⁶GF, 25³GF, 27¹GF,

	Starts	1st	2nd	3rd	Win & Pl
Chases	5	1	0	1	3969
Career Total	53	10	5	6	54333
106	9/03	Sedg	3m3f	E(0-105)HCh	G-F	£3341
108	10/02	Uttx	3m2f	E(0-110)HCh	G-F	£4230
108	8/02	MRas	3m1f	E(0-110)HCh	G-S	£4891
108	6/02	Ctml	3m6f	D(0-130)HCh	GD	£6825
95	5/02	Weth	3m1f	E(0-110)HCh	GS	£3388
104	10/00	MRas	3m4f110yF(0-110)HCh	GD	£3667
104	8/00	MRas	3m1f	F(0-110)HCh	G-F	£7377
111	11/98	Hayd	2m4f	D Ch	SFT	£4335
108	10/98	Weth	3m4f	E(0-105)HCh	GD	£3493
93	2/96	Sedg	2m5f110yE Hdl	GD	£2407

Total win prize-money £43956

Going: Sf: 0-0 GS: 0-0 Gd: 0-1 GF: - Fm: 1-4
Distance: 2m/2m3: 0-0 2m4-2m7: 0-0 3m+: 1-5
Track: LH: 1-3 RH: 0-1 Tight: 1-3 Gall: 0-0
Aids: Bl: 0-0 Vi: 0-0 Tstrap: 0-0 Ckp: 0-0
Best Rating: 108 10/02 Uttx 3m2f   gd-fm Ch

Moderate handicap chaser; now a veteran; effective beyond three miles; acts on fast and easy ground; likes to race up with the pace.

Gratomi (IRE)

14-y-o b g Bustomi-Granny Grumble (Politico (USA))
Mrs A E Lee W J Lee

Placings:S/P/21662F112221/3FU224212/30304304/06650 3F503/31006/43 (0483)
2003/04: 20⁴GF, 24³GF,

	Starts	1st	2nd	3rd	Win & Pl
Chases	2	0	0	1	225
Career Total	48	6	9	8	35543
96	5/01	Hntg	2m110y	F(0-105)HCh	G-F	£2912
117	4/99	Ludl	2m4f	D(0-125)HCh	GD	£4143
104	4/98	Extr	2m3f110yD(0-125)HCh	SFT	£3818
101	2/98	Folk	2m	F(0-100)HCh	G-F	£2691

91	2/98	Hrfd	2m3f	E(0-100)HCh	GD	£3009
100	6/97	Worc	2m4f	E Hdl	GD	£2617

Total win prize-money £19191

Going: Sf: 0-0 GS: 0-0 Gd: 0-0 GF: - Fm: 0-2
Distance: 2m/2m3: 0-0 2m4-2m7: 0-1 3m+: 0-1
Track: LH: 0-1 RH: 0-1 Tight: 0-0 Gall: 0-1
Aids: Bl: 0-0 Vi: 0-0 Tstrap: 0-0 Ckp: 0-0
Best Rating: 121 3/99 Extr 2m3f   good Ch

Fair hunter chaser; stays three miles; likes good to firm.

Grattan Lodge (IRE)
101 (106h)   (118+h) 123+

7-y-o gr g Roselier (FR)-Shallow Run (Deep Run)
J Howard Johnson W M G Black

Placings:P0P/601111-1F141 (4728)
2003/04: 21¹GS, 20ᶠHY, 24¹HY, 25⁴G, 24¹G,

	Starts	1st	2nd	3rd	Win & Pl
Chases	5	3	0	0	18194
Career Total	14	7	0	0	32639
123	4/04	Carl	3m	D Ch	GD	£7630
115	2/04	Carl	3m	D Ch	HVY	£5642
115	1/04	Sedg	2m5f	E Ch	G-S	£4498
118	3/03	Carl	3m110y	D(0-125)HHdl	G-S	£5460
105	1/03	Sedg	3m3f110yE(0-105)HHdl	HVY	£3412
90	11/02	Carl	2m4f	E(0-105)HHdl	HVY	£2919
90	11/02	Newc	2m4f	F(0-90)HHdl	SFT	£2653

Total win prize-money £32215

Going: Sf: 1-2 GS: 1-1 Gd: 1-2 GF: - Fm: 0-0
Distance: 2m/2m3: 0-2 2m4-2m7: 1-2 3m+: 2-3
Track: LH: 1-3 RH: 2-2 Tight: 1-2 Gall: 0-1
Aids: Bl: 0-0 Vi: 0-0 Tstrap: 0-0 Ckp: 0-0
Best Rating: 123 4/04 Carl 3m   good Ch

Fair chaser/hurdler; in great form in 2002/2003, completing a four-timer; won three times over fences in 2004; stays three and a half miles and suited by soft ground.

Grave Doubts
110   132

8-y-o ch g Karinga Bay-Redgrave Girl (Deep Run)
K Bishop Bill Davies & Bernard Tottle

Placings:1302/03061111PF-0130 (4428)
2003/04: 20⁰G, 16¹G, 16³G, 17⁰G,

	Starts	1st	2nd	3rd	Win & Pl
Hurdles	4	1	0	1	11306
Career Total	18	6	1	3	36196
132	2/04	Winc	2m	D(0-125)HHdl	GD	£4706
129	10/02	Chel	2m110y B HHdl	GD	£10938
116	10/02	Hrfd	2m1f	E Hdl	GD	£3633
110	10/02	Extr	2m1f	E Hdl	FRM	£3430
103	9/02	Plum	2m	E Hdl	GD	£3220
110	6/01	NAbb	2m1f	H NHF	GD	£2282

Total win prize-money £28211

Going: Sf: 0-1 GS: 0-0 Gd: 1-3 GF: - Fm: 0-0
Distance: 2m/2m3: 1-3 2m4-2m7: 0-1 3m+: 0-0
Track: LH: 0-1 RH: 1-3 Tight: 0-0 Gall: 0-1
Aids: Bl: 0-0 Vi: 0-0 Tstrap: 1-4 Ckp: 0-0
Best Rating: 132 2/04 Winc 2m   good Hdl

Fair hurdler; likes a sound surface; effective at around two miles.

Gray's Eulogy
103   85

6-y-o b g Presenting-Gray's Ellergy (Oats)
D R Gandolfo M A Dore

Placings:0-6UPP5   **(4183)**
2003/04: 21⁶G, 21ᵁS, 21ᴾS, 24ᴾS, 26⁶G,

	Starts	1st	2nd	3rd	Win & Pl
Hurdles	5	0	0	0	0
Career Total	6	0	0	0	0

Going:	Sf: 0-3 GS: 0-0 Gd: 0-2 GF: - Fm: 0-0
Distance:	2m/2m3: 0-0 2m4-2m7: 0-3 3m+: 0-2
Track:	LH: 0-3 RH: 0-2 Tight: 0-0 Gall: 0-2
Aids:	Bl: 0-0 Vi: 0-0 Tstrap: 0-0 Ckp: 0-0
Best Rating:	85 11/02 Aint 2m110y good Hdl

Poor form in novice hurdles.

Grayslake (IRE)

106(101h)   (92h)102+
8-y-o b g King's Ride-Castlegrace (IRE) (Kemal (FR))
K C Bailey   Prof D B A & Mrs H E Silk, D J Coldman

Placings:003-4U   **(3359)**
2003/04: 20⁴GS, 25ᵁS,

	Starts	1st	2nd	3rd	Win & Pl
Chases	2	0	0	0	380
Career Total	5	0	0	1	906

Going:	Sf: 0-1 GS: 0-1 Gd: 0-0 GF: - Fm: 0-0
Distance:	2m/2m3: 0-0 2m4-2m7: 0-1 3m+: 0-1
Track:	LH: 0-2 RH: 0-0 Tight: 0-1 Gall: 0-0
Aids:	Bl: 0-0 Vi: 0-0 Tstrap: 0-0 Ckp: 0-1
Best Rating:	104 12/03 Uttx 2m4f gd-sft Ch

Maiden chaser; fourth under a stiff task in handicap company at Uttoxeter in December.

Great As Gold (IRE)

111   121
5-y-o b g Goldmark (USA)-Great Land (USA) (Friend's Choice (USA))
B Ellison   Keith Middleton

Placings:523-111200   **(3937)**
2003/04: 16¹G, 24¹G, 23¹G, 24²GS, 25⁰GS, 20⁰GS,

	Starts	1st	2nd	3rd	Win & Pl
Hurdles	6	3	1	0	13752
Career Total	9	3	2	1	15228
119	12/03	Weth	2m7f	D Hdl	GD £4371
109	11/03	Newc	3m	E Hdl	GD £4017
98	5/03	Hexm	2m110y	E Hdl	GD £3668
			Total win prize-money £12056		

Going:	Sf: 0-0 GS: 0-3 Gd: 3-3 GF: - Fm: 0-0
Distance:	2m/2m3: 1-1 2m4-2m7: 1-2 3m+: 1-3
Track:	LH: 3-6 RH: 0-0 Tight: 0-0 Gall: 1-3
Aids:	Bl: 0-0 Vi: 0-0 Tstrap: 0-0 Ckp: 3-6
Best Rating:	121 12/03 Newc 3m gd-sft Hdl

Fair novice hurdler; recorded third win at Wetherby in December 2003; stays three miles well; acts on good ground; usually wears cheekpieces.

Great Benefit (IRE)

                              38f
5-y-o ch g Beneficial-That's Lucy (IRE) (Henbit (USA))
Miss H C Knight   Senate Racing Partnership

Placings:0   **(4495)**
2003/04: 16⁰G,

	Starts	1st	2nd	3rd	Win & Pl
NH Flat	1	0	0	0	
Career Total	1	0	0	0	

Going:	Sf: 0-0 GS: 0-0 Gd: 0-1 GF: - Fm: 0-0
Distance:	2m/2m3: 0-1 2m4-2m7: 0-0 3m+: 0-0
Track:	LH: 0-0 RH: 0-0 Tight: 0-0 Gall: 0-0
Aids:	Bl: 0-0 Vi: 0-0 Tstrap: 0-0 Ckp: 0-0
Best Rating:	38 3/04 Strf 2m110y good NHF

Great Crusader

100(98c)   (92c)117
12-y-o ch g Deploy-Shannon Princess (Connaught)
M J Hogan   Mrs Barbara Hogan

Placings:32/44P3FP/3114516114-52FP06560 **(4932)**
2003/04: 27⁵G, 25²G, 24ᶠGF, 24ᴾS, 24⁶S, 22⁶G, 22⁵G, 26⁶G, 27⁶G,

	Starts	1st	2nd	3rd	Win & Pl
Hurdles	7	0	0	0	0
Chases	2	0	1	0	1355
Career Total	27	5	2	3	24228
117	4/03	Prth	3m110y	E(0-105)HHdl	GD £5876
106	3/03	Folk	3m4f	F(0-100)HHdl	GD £3425
106	2/03	Folk	2m6f110yF(0-95)HHdl		HVY £3129
92	12/02	Tntn	3m110y	G(0-90)HHdl	SFT £2058
88	12/02	Folk	2m1f110yG(0-95)HHdl		HVY £2268
			Total win prize-money £16757		

Going:	Sf: 0-2 GS: 0-0 Gd: 0-6 GF: - Fm: 0-0
Distance:	2m/2m3: 0-0 2m4-2m7: 0-2 3m+: 0-7
Track:	LH: 0-4 RH: 0-4 Tight: 0-4 Gall: 0-2
Aids:	Bl: 0-0 Vi: 0-0 Tstrap: 0-0 Ckp: 0-0
Best Rating:	133 1/99 Sand 2m110y soft Hdl

Modest staying hurdler/novice chaser; stays further than three miles and best on soft ground, but handles faster; yet to win on a left-handed course.

Great Hopper

                             56
9-y-o b m Rock Hopper-Spun Gold (Thatch (USA))
F Watson   F Watson

Placings:4/0   **(0796)**
2003/04: 16⁰G,

	Starts	1st	2nd	3rd	Win & Pl
Hurdles	1	0	0	0	
Career Total	2	0	0	0	0

Going:	Sf: 0-0 GS: 0-0 Gd: 0-1 GF: - Fm: 0-0
Distance:	2m/2m3: 0-1 2m4-2m7: 0-0 3m+: 0-0
Track:	LH: 0-0 RH: 0-1 Tight: 0-0 Gall: 0-0
Aids:	Bl: 0-0 Vi: 0-0 Tstrap: 0-0 Ckp: 0-0
Best Rating:	56 10/01 Sedg 2m1f gd-sft Hdl

Great Jubilee (IRE)

100   93+
6-y-o ch g Beneficial-Red Donna (Don)
M C Pipe   D A Johnson

Placings:3   **(1729)**
2003/04: 20³GF,

	Starts	1st	2nd	3rd	Win & Pl
Hurdles	1	0	0	1	370
Career Total	1	0	0	1	370

Going:	Sf: 0-0 GS: 0-0 Gd: 0-0 GF: - Fm: 0-0
Distance:	2m/2m3: 0-0 2m4-2m7: 0-0 3m+: 0-0
Track:	LH: 0-1 RH: 0-0 Tight: 0-0 Gall: 0-0
Aids:	Bl: 0-0 Vi: 0-0 Tstrap: 0-0 Ckp: 0-0
Best Rating:	93 10/03 Chep 2m4f gd-fm Hdl

Impressive winner of maiden point March 2003; run out of it and rather let down by his jumping when third in 2m 4f novices' hurdle at Chepstow in October.

Great Oaks

96(85c)   (77c)84
10-y-o b g Sylvan Express-Springdale Hall (USA) (Bates Motel (USA))
Miss Z C Davison (J M Jefferson 19/7) The Secret Circle

Placings:043/3/446-363P440P   **(4697)**
2003/04: 20³G, 20⁶G, 16³GF, 17⁶G, 20⁴GF, 16⁴G, 20⁰G, 17⁰G,

	Starts	1st	2nd	3rd	Win & Pl
Hurdles	6	0	0	2	887
Chases	2	0	0	0	518
Career Total	15	0	0	4	2862

Going:	Sf: 0-0 GS: 0-0 Gd: 0-6 GF: - Fm: 0-2
Distance:	2m/2m3: 0-4 2m4-2m7: 0-4 3m+: 0-0
Track:	LH: 0-3 RH: 0-5 Tight: 0-2 Gall: 0-0
Aids:	Bl: 0-0 Vi: 0-0 Tstrap: 0-0 Ckp: 0-0
Best Rating:	84 5/03 Hexm 2m4f110y good Hdl

Plating-class hurdler; effective on good ground; stays two miles four and should stay further.

Great Ovation (FR)

93   85
5-y-o ch m Boston Two Step (USA)-Baldiloa (No Lute (FR))
R T Phillips   Ladbrokes Staff Racing Partnership

Placings:050-60   **(2866)**
2003/04: 16⁶G, 16⁰GS,

	Starts	1st	2nd	3rd	Win & Pl
Hurdles	2	0	0	0	0
Career Total	5	0	0	0	0

Going:	Sf: 0-0 GS: 0-1 Gd: 0-1 GF: - Fm: 0-0
Distance:	2m/2m3: 0-2 2m4-2m7: 0-0 3m+: 0-0
Track:	LH: 0-2 RH: 0-0 Tight: 0-0 Gall: 0-0
Aids:	Bl: 0-0 Vi: 0-0 Tstrap: 0-0 Ckp: 0-0
Best Rating:	85 12/03 Wwck 2m good Hdl

Great Risk

8-y-o b m Risk Me (FR)-Vaisigano (USA) (Vaguely Noble)
G R Pewter   N J Pewter

Placings:F   **(4782)**
2003/04: 24ᶠG,

	Starts	1st	2nd	3rd	Win & Pl
Chases	1	0	0	0	
Career Total	1	0	0	0	

Going:	Sf: 0-0 GS: 0-0 Gd: 0-1 GF: - Fm: 0-0
Distance:	2m/2m3: 0-0 2m4-2m7: 0-0 3m+: 0-1
Track:	LH: 0-0 RH: 0-1 Tight: 0-0 Gall: 0-1
Aids:	Bl: 0-0 Vi: 0-0 Tstrap: 0-0 Ckp: 0-0

Great Travel (FR)

107(88h)   (96h)115+
5-y-o b g Great Palm (USA)-Travel Free (Be My Guest (USA))
P F Nicholls   Mrs J Stewart

Placings:21-23F311244   **(4699)**

2003/04: 17²GF, 16³G, 16FGF, 16³GF, 16¹S, 16¹G, 16²G, 16⁴GS, 18⁴G,

	Starts	1st	2nd	3rd	Win & Pl
Hurdles	2	0	1	1	1726
Chases	7	2	1	1	20059
Career Total	**11**	**3**	**3**	**2**	**38616**
115 2/04 Sand 2m	C(0-135)HCh		GD		£12035
114 1/04 Folk 2m	E(0-105)HCh		SFT		£4056
4/03 Nanc 2m1f	Hdl		SFT		£11221

Total win prize-money £27312

Going: Sf: 1-1 GS: 0-1 Gd: 1-4 GF: - Fm: 0-3
Distance: 2m/2m3: 2-9 2m4-2m7: 0-0 3m+: 0-0
Track: LH: 0-4 RH: 2-4 Tight: 1-4 Gall: 0-2
Aids: Bl: 0-0 Vi: 0-0 Tstrap: 0-0 Ckp: 0-0
Best Rating: 115 4/04 Font 2m2f good Ch

Fair chaser; best around two miles; handles fast ground but better on soft; has question marks over his attitude.

Grecian Star

12-y-o b g Crested Lark-Grecian Lace (Spartan General)
G J Tarry R John White

Placings:512/32P6-1U (0352)
2003/04: 30¹GF, 31UGF,

	Starts	1st	2nd	3rd	Win & Pl
Chases	2	1	0	0	2184
Career Total	**9**	**2**	**2**	**1**	**8228**
105 5/03 Hntg 3m6f110yH Ch			G-F		£2184
105 3/02 Towc 2m6f H Ch			G-F		£2226

Total win prize-money £4410

Going: Sf: 0-0 GS: 0-0 Gd: 0-0 GF: - Fm: 1-0
Distance: 2m/2m3: 0-0 2m4-2m7: 0-0 3m+: 1-2
Track: LH: 0-0 RH: 1-2 Tight: 0-1 Gall: 1-1
Aids: Bl: 0-0 Vi: 0-0 Tstrap: 0-0 Ckp: 0-0
Best Rating: 105 5/03 Hntg 3m6f110y gd-fm Ch

Hunter chaser; headstrong sort; good jumper; stays very well; appears to act on all types of ground.

Green 'N' Gold

91　　82
4-y-o b f Cloudings (IRE)-Fishki (Niniski (USA))
M D Hammond E Whalley

Placings:053 (4612)
2003/04: 17⁰GS, 17⁵G, 21³G,

	Starts	1st	2nd	3rd	Win & Pl
Hurdles	3	0	0	1	520
Career Total	**3**	**0**	**0**	**1**	**520**

Going: Sf: 0-0 GS: 0-1 Gd: 0-2 GF: - Fm: 0-0
Distance: 2m/2m3: 0-2 2m4-2m7: 0-1 3m+: 0-0
Track: LH: 0-2 RH: 0-1 Tight: 0-3 Gall: 0-0
Aids: Bl: 0-0 Vi: 0-0 Tstrap: 0-0 Ckp: 0-0
Best Rating: 82 3/04 Sedg 2m5f110y good Hdl

Moderate form over hurdles so far; suited by a test of stamina.

Green Admiral

92　　73
5-y-o b g Slip Anchor-Jade Mistress (Damister (USA))
J J Quinn Mrs C T Bletsoe

Placings:60-00505 (4393)
2003/04: 16⁰GS, 17⁰GS, 19⁵G, 22⁰GS, 17⁵G,

	Starts	1st	2nd	3rd	Win & Pl
Hurdles	5	0	0	0	

	Career Total	7	0	0	0	0

Going: Sf: 0-0 GS: 0-2 Gd: 0-3 GF: - Fm: 0-0
Distance: 2m/2m3: 0-3 2m4-2m7: 0-2 3m+: 0-0
Track: LH: 0-3 RH: 0-0 Tight: 0-3 Gall: 0-0
Aids: Bl: 0-0 Vi: 0-0 Tstrap: 0-0 Ckp: 0-0
Best Rating: 82 1/03 Hayd 2m gd-sft NHF

Green Belt Flyer (IRE)

113　　124
6-y-o b g Leading Counsel (USA)-Current Liability (Caribo)
Mrs John Harrington Green Belters Syndicate

Placings:6123516314 (4826a)
2003/04: 20⁶S, 16¹SH, 16²GF, 16³GF, 20⁵GS, 16¹Y, 16⁶S, 16³HY, 16¹Y, 16⁴Y,

	Starts	1st	2nd	3rd	Win & Pl
Hurdles	10	3	1	2	29275
Career Total	**10**	**3**	**1**	**2**	**29275**
124 2/04 Naas 2m	(88-130)HHdl		YLD		£9169
121 12/03 Gowr 2m	Hdl		YLD		£6272
105 6/03 Baln 2m	Hdl		SH		£4704

Total win prize-money £20147

Going: Sf: 0-3 GS: 0-1 Gd: 0-0 GF: - Fm: 0-2
Distance: 2m/2m3: 3-8 2m4-2m7: 0-2 3m+: 0-0
Track: LH: 1-4 RH: 0-3 Tight: 0-0 Gall: 0-0
Aids: Bl: 0-0 Vi: 0-0 Tstrap: 0-0 Ckp: 0-0
Best Rating: 124 4/04 Fair 2m yield Hdl

Green Gamble

97　　74
4-y-o gr g Environment Friend-Gemma's Wager (IRE) (Phardante (FR))
D B Feek Barry & Baroness Noakes

Placings:00640 (4752)
2003/04: 12⁰GF, 18⁰HY, 16⁶S, 18⁴G, 16⁰G,

	Starts	1st	2nd	3rd	Win & Pl
NH Flat	1	0	0	0	0
Hurdles	4	0	0	0	269
Career Total	**5**	**0**	**0**	**0**	**269**

Going: Sf: 0-2 GS: 0-0 Gd: 0-2 GF: - Fm: 0-1
Distance: 2m/2m3: 0-4 2m4-2m7: 0-2 3m+: 0-1
Track: LH: 0-5 RH: 0-0 Tight: 0-4 Gall: 0-0
Aids: Bl: 0-0 Vi: 0-0 Tstrap: 0-0 Ckp: 0-0
Best Rating: 74 3/04 Font 2m2f110y good Hdl

Green Go (GER)

101(102h)　　(99h)98
6-y-o ch g Secret 'n Classy (CAN)-Green Fee (GER) (Windwurf (GER))
A Sadik A Sadik

Placings:51364P-2P045311FPP (1880)
2003/04: 19⁰G, 20PGF, 22⁰GF, 20⁴G, 17⁵GS, 20³G, 21¹G, 26¹G, 24FGF, 20PGF, 20PG,

	Starts	1st	2nd	3rd	Win & Pl
Hurdles	6	0	1	1	2051
Chases	5	2	0	0	8759
Career Total	**17**	**3**	**1**	**2**	**15286**
98 8/03 Ctml 3m2f	E Ch		GD		£4338
98 8/03 Ctml 2m5f110yE Ch			GD		£4420
91 7/02 Uttx 2m4f110yD Hdl			G-F		£4056

Total win prize-money £12815

Going: Sf: 0-0 GS: 0-1 Gd: 2-6 GF: - Fm: 0-4
Distance: 2m/2m3: 0-2 2m4-2m7: 1-7 3m+: 1-2
Track: LH: 2-11 RH: 0-0 Tight: 2-7 Gall: 0-0
Aids: Bl: 0-0 Vi: 0-0 Tstrap: 0-0 Ckp: 0-0
Best Rating: 98 9/03 Strf 3m gd-fm Ch

Winner on the Flat in the Czech Republic; moderate hurdler; easy winner on second start over fences at Cartmel in August; followed up at the same track two days later; stays 3m 3f; quick jumper; acts on fast ground.

Green Iceni

92　　85
5-y-o br g Greensmith-Boadicea's Chariot (Commanche Run)
J R Best Paul Hudson

Placings:04-103 (3350)
2003/04: 17¹GS, 19⁰GS, 16³S,

	Starts	1st	2nd	3rd	Win & Pl
NH Flat	1	1	0	0	1638
Hurdles	2	0	0	1	753
Career Total	**5**	**1**	**0**	**1**	**2391**
102 11/03 Folk 2m1f110yH Hdl			G-S		£1638

Total win prize-money £1638

Going: Sf: 0-1 GS: 1-2 Gd: 0-0 GF: - Fm: 0-0
Distance: 2m/2m3: 1-2 2m4-2m7: 0-1 3m+: 0-0
Track: LH: 0-0 RH: 1-3 Tight: 1-1 Gall: 0-1
Aids: Bl: 0-0 Vi: 0-0 Tstrap: 0-0 Ckp: 0-0
Best Rating: 102 11/03 Folk 2m1f110y gd-sft NHF

Half-brother to Aggrippina out of a winning middle distance/hurdles performer; showed ability in bumpers, winning at Folkestone on third start.

Green Ideal

104(111h)　　(129h)120
6-y-o b g Mark Of Esteem (IRE)-Emerald (USA) (El Gran Senor (USA))
Ferdy Murphy (N J Henderson 17/5) Mrs J Morgan

Placings:1P0/024-F42U32PP (4938)
2003/04: 20FGF, 17⁴GS, 16²GS, 21UGS, 16³HY, 16²G, 20PG, 16PGS,

	Starts	1st	2nd	3rd	Win & Pl
Chases	8	0	2	1	3313
Career Total	**14**	**1**	**3**	**1**	**9751**
121 12/01 Newb 2m110y D Hdl			G-S		£4426

Total win prize-money £4427

Going: Sf: 0-2 GS: 0-3 Gd: 0-2 GF: - Fm: 0-1
Distance: 2m/2m3: 0-5 2m4-2m7: 0-3 3m+: 0-0
Track: LH: 0-4 RH: 0-4 Tight: 0-1 Gall: 0-2
Aids: Bl: 0-0 Vi: 0-0 Tstrap: 0-0 Ckp: 0-0
Best Rating: 129 2/03 Winc 2m gd-sft Hdl

Useful hurdler; best effort over fences when runner-up in a potentially very useful newcomer at Uttoxeter in December; effective at two miles but should stay further; acts on any ground bar extremes.

Green Smoke

(82h)90
8-y-o gr g Green Adventure (USA)-Smoke (Rusticaro (FR))
J M Jefferson Mrs J U Hales

Placings:U000/20325/332-PP (0622)
2003/04: 20PG, 22PG,

	Starts	1st	2nd	3rd	Win & Pl
Chases	2	0	0	0	
Career Total	**14**	**0**	**3**	**3**	**4487**

Going: Sf: 0-0 GS: 0-0 Gd: 0-2 GF: - Fm: 0-0
Distance: 2m/2m3: 0-0 2m4-2m7: 0-2 3m+: 0-0
Track: LH: 0-1 RH: 0-1 Tight: 0-1 Gall: 0-0
Aids: Bl: 0-0 Vi: 0-0 Tstrap: 0-0 Ckp: 0-2
Best Rating: 90 2/03 Newc 2m4f   soft   Ch

Moderate maiden over hurdles and fences.

Green Tango
102   127+
5-y-o br g Greensmith-Furry Dance (USA) (Nureyev (USA))
H D Daly Mrs Strachan,Gabb,Lady Barlow & Harford

Placings:3121101   (4915)
2003/04: 16³GS, 16¹GS, 16²GF, 16¹S, 16¹G, 16⁹G, 16¹GS,

	Starts	1st	2nd	3rd	Win & Pl
NH Flat	3	1	1	1	2692
Hurdles	4	3	0	0	13207
Career Total	7	4	1	1	15899

115	4/04	Worc	2m	E Hdl	G-S	£3948
127	3/04	Ludl	2m	E Hdl	GD	£4368
115	1/04	Hntg	2m110y	D Hdl	SFT	£4891
118	11/03	Uttx	2m	H NHF	G-S	£1596
				Total win prize-money £14803		

Going: Sf: 1-1 GS: 2-3 Gd: 1-2 GF: - Fm: 0-1
Distance: 2m/2m3: 4-7 2m4-2m7: 0-0 3m+: 0-0
Track: LH: 2-4 RH: 2-3 Tight: 0-1 Gall: 1-1
Aids: Bl: 0-0 Vi: 0-0 Tstrap: 0-0 Ckp: 0-0
Best Rating: 127 3/04 Ludl 2m   good   Hdl

Useful novice hurdler; former bumper winner; winner three
times over hurdles; held in Grade Two at Aintree; suited by
two miles and acts on most types of ground.

Greenacres Boy
(93h)   (70h)
9-y-o b g Roscoe Blake-Deep Goddess (Deep Run)
M Mullineaux Geoffrey Arthur Probin

Placings:6-PP0000PFUP   (2440)
2003/04: 20⁹G, 20⁹GF, 16⁶GF, 17⁰GF, 17⁰G, 16⁹GF, 17⁵G, 17⁵G,
20ᵁF, 17⁵GS,

	Starts	1st	2nd	3rd	Win & Pl
Hurdles	7	0	0	0	0
Chases	3	0	0	0	0
Career Total	11	0	0	0	0

Going: Sf: 0-0 GS: 0-1 Gd: 0-4 GF: - Fm: 0-5
Distance: 2m/2m3: 0-7 2m4-2m7: 0-3 3m+: 0-0
Track: LH: 0-8 RH: 0-2 Tight: 0-5 Gall: 0-0
Aids: Bl: 0-3 Vi: 0-0 Tstrap: 0-0 Ckp: 0-3
Best Rating: 70 10/03 Bang 2m1f   good   Hdl

Greenback (BEL)
85   79
13-y-o b g Absalom-Batalya (BEL) (Boulou)
J Joseph Jack Joseph

Placings:U2112122111100/1/23F1113313/504005443/233
110/1340-005P6   (2684)
2003/04: 20⁰GF, 22⁰G, 18⁵GF, 26⁸GS, 21⁶GS,

	Starts	1st	2nd	3rd	Win & Pl
Hurdles	5	0	0	0	0
Career Total	49	15	6	8	71511

102	6/02	Hrfd	2m3f110yG Hdl	GD	£2128
100	11/01	Ludl	2m G Hdl	G-F	£2107
90	11/01	Ludl	2m G Hdl	G-F	£2096
130	4/97	Asct	2m3f110yC Ch	G-F	£5654
130	12/96	Kemp	2m4f110yB Ch	G-F	£10308

121	12/96	Folk	2m	E Ch	G-S	£3305
115	11/96	Tntn	2m3f	C Ch	G-F	£4531
124	5/95	Towc	2m	D(0-125)HHdl	G-F	£2883
124	2/95	Kemp	2m	A Hdl	HVY	£9780
104	12/94	Sand	2m110y	Hdl	GD	£3129
118	11/94	Kemp	2m	Hdl	GD	£2448
112	11/94	Kemp	2m	Hdl	SFT	£3192
104	9/94	Tntn	2m1f	Hdl	G-F	£1733
81	8/94	Extr	2m1f110y	Hdl	FRM	£2263
91	8/94	NAbb	2m1f	Hdl	G-S	£1818
				Total win prize-money £57382		

Going: Sf: 0-0 GS: 0-2 Gd: 0-1 GF: - Fm: 0-2
Distance: 2m/2m3: 0-1 2m4-2m7: 0-3 3m+: 0-1
Track: LH: 0-3 RH: 0-2 Tight: 0-2 Gall: 0-2
Aids: Bl: 0-0 Vi: 0-0 Tstrap: 0-0 Ckp: 0-0
Best Rating: 130 4/97 Asct 2m3f110y gd-fm Ch

Moderate hurdler nowadays; likes fast ground and stays 2m
4f; front-runner; genuine sort.

Greenborough (IRE)
90   59
6-y-o b g Dr Devious (IRE)-Port Isaac (USA) (Seattle Song
(USA))
Mrs P Ford W E Donohue

Placings:0-PP065   (4506)
2003/04: 20⁰GS, 19⁷HY, 21⁹G, 17⁶GF, 19⁵GS,

	Starts	1st	2nd	3rd	Win & Pl
Hurdles	5	0	0	0	0
Career Total	6	0	0	0	0

Going: Sf: 0-1 GS: 0-2 Gd: 0-1 GF: - Fm: 0-1
Distance: 2m/2m3: 0-1 2m4-2m7: 0-4 3m+: 0-0
Track: LH: 0-1 RH: 0-4 Tight: 0-0 Gall: 0-0
Aids: Bl: 0-0 Vi: 0-0 Tstrap: 0-0 Ckp: 0-3
Best Rating: 59 3/04 Hrfd 2m1f   gd-fm   Hdl

Greenfield (IRE)
100   114+
6-y-o ch g Pleasant Tap (USA)-No Review (USA) (Nodouble
(USA))
R T Phillips Mrs S J Harvey

Placings:33-034401   (4890)
2003/04: 16⁰GS, 19³GS, 20⁴S, 16⁴G, 21⁹GS, 19¹GF,

	Starts	1st	2nd	3rd	Win & Pl
Hurdles	6	1	0	1	8262
Career Total	8	1	0	3	9588

| 110 | 4/04 | Strf | 2m3f | D(0-120)HHdl | G-F | £7260 |
| | | | | Total win prize-money £7261 | | |

Going: Sf: 0-1 GS: 0-3 Gd: 0-1 GF: - Fm: 1-1
Distance: 2m/2m3: 1-3 2m4-2m7: 0-3 3m+: 0-0
Track: LH: 1-3 RH: 0-3 Tight: 1-1 Gall: 0-0
Aids: Bl: 1-3 Vi: 0-0 Tstrap: 0-0 Ckp: 0-0
Best Rating: 114 12/03 Hrfd 2m3f110y gd-sft Hdl

Fair hurdler; stays two miles-three; acts on fast.

Greenfire (FR)
79   29
6-y-o ch g Ashkalani (IRE)-Greenvera (USA) (Riverman
(USA))
Mrs Dianne Sayer Andrew Sayer

Placings:0/00-3065   (1689)
2003/04: 16³G, 16⁰G, 22⁶F, 22⁵GF,

	Starts	1st	2nd	3rd	Win & Pl
NH Flat	1	0	0	1	311

| Hurdles | 3 | 0 | 0 | 0 | 0 |
| Career Total | 7 | 0 | 0 | 1 | 311 |

Going: Sf: 0-0 GS: 0-0 Gd: 0-2 GF: - Fm: 0-2
Distance: 2m/2m3: 0-2 2m4-2m7: 0-2 3m+: 0-0
Track: LH: 0-2 RH: 0-2 Tight: 0-2 Gall: 0-0
Aids: Bl: 0-0 Vi: 0-0 Tstrap: 0-0 Ckp: 0-0
Best Rating: 97 7/03 Prth 2m110y   good   NHF

Greenhope (IRE)
111   134
6-y-o b g Definite Article-Unbidden Melody (USA) (Chieftain)
N J Henderson Lynn Wilson Giles Wilson Martin Landau

Placings:1110/0-1304   (4644)
2003/04: 16¹G, 16³G, 17⁰G, 16⁴G,

	Starts	1st	2nd	3rd	Win & Pl
Hurdles	4	1	0	1	13956
Career Total	9	4	0	1	34503

134	12/03	Kemp		D(0-125)HHdl	GD	£6206
118	12/01	Kemp	2m	B Hdl	GD	£7052
118	11/01	Chel	2m110y	B Hdl	GD	£8619
118	11/01	Asct	2m110y	C Hdl	GD	£4875
				Total win prize-money £26753		

Going: Sf: 0-0 GS: 0-0 Gd: 1-4 GF: - Fm: 0-0
Distance: 2m/2m3: 1-4 2m4-2m7: 0-0 3m+: 0-0
Track: LH: 0-2 RH: 1-2 Tight: 0-1 Gall: 0-1
Aids: Bl: 0-0 Vi: 0-0 Tstrap: 0-0 Ckp: 0-0
Best Rating: 134 4/04 Aint 2m110y   good   Hdl

Useful hurdler; best at two miles; does not want the ground
too soft and is seen to best effect when making the running.

Greenkeys (AUS)
91(88h)   (67h)64
10-y-o b g Bonhomie (USA)-Cindy Doll (AUS) (Cindy's Son)
R C Guest George and Doris Racing

Placings:6000/0/5-FU0444F66   (1040)
2003/04: 17⁵S, 21ᵁGF, 17⁰GF, 20⁴G, 20⁴G, 21⁴GF, 24²G, 20⁶G,
26⁶GF,

	Starts	1st	2nd	3rd	Win & Pl
Hurdles	4	0	0	0	314
Chases	5	0	0	0	0
Career Total	15	0	0	0	314

Going: Sf: 0-1 GS: 0-0 Gd: 0-4 GF: - Fm: 0-4
Distance: 2m/2m3: 0-2 2m4-2m7: 0-5 3m+: 0-2
Track: LH: 0-7 RH: 0-2 Tight: 0-5 Gall: 0-0
Aids: Bl: 0-0 Vi: 0-2 Tstrap: 0-0 Ckp: 0-9
Best Rating: 71 3/00 Uttx 2m4f110y good   Hdl

Greensmith Lane
107   104+
8-y-o br g Greensmith-Handy Lane (Nearly A Hand)
G B Balding (Mrs L C Jewell 23/11) Leon Best

Placings:26F/465P020-0650111510   (4859)
2003/04: 20⁹G, 17⁶GF, 19⁵GF, 17⁰GF, 18¹GF, 20¹G, 16¹G, 16⁵G,
16¹G, 19⁰GF,

	Starts	1st	2nd	3rd	Win & Pl
Hurdles	10	4	0	0	9113
Career Total	20	4	2	0	11025

106	4/04	Winc	2m	E(0-110)HHdl	GD	£3513
93	11/03	Plum	2m	F Hdl	GD	£1876
93	10/03	Font	2m4f	F Hdl	GD	£1883
88	9/03	Font	2m2f110yG(0-95)HHdl	G-F	£1841
				Total win prize-money £9113		

Going: Sf: 0-0 GS: 0-0 Gd: 3-5 GF: - Fm: 1-5
Distance: 2m/2m3: 3-7 2m4-2m7: 1-3 3m+: 0-0
Track: LH: 2-5 RH: 1-3 Tight: 3-7 Gall: 0-0
Aids: Bl: 0-0 Vi: 0-0 Tstrap: 0-0 Ckp: 4-7
Best Rating: 106 4/04 Winc 2m   good   Hdl

Plating-class hurdler; much improved by cheekpieces recently when winning a seller and following up in a claimer in October; stays further than two miles and acts on fast ground.

Greenwich
99   113

10-y-o br g Handsome Sailor-Praise The Lord (Lord Gayle (USA))
M Scudamore Mrs Marilyn Scudamore

Placings:60/2045540/634PF/2B35/P3   (3872)
2003/04: 26³S, 25³GS,

	Starts	1st	2nd	3rd	Win & Pl
Chases	2	0	0	1	547
Career Total	20	0	2	3	3753

Going: Sf: 0-1 GS: 0-1 Gd: 0-0 GF: - Fm: 0-0
Distance: 2m/2m3: 0-0 2m4-2m7: 0-0 3m+: 0-2
Track: LH: 0-1 RH: 0-1 Tight: 0-2 Gall: 0-0
Aids: Bl: 0-0 Vi: 0-0 Tstrap: 0-0 Ckp: 0-0
Best Rating: 103 6/01 Strf 3m4f   gd-fm   Ch

Modest maiden hurdler/hunter. Capable of winning a hunter chase when things go his way.

Gregorian (IRE)
104   (0c) 106

7-y-o b g Foxhound (USA)-East River (FR) (Arctic Tern (USA))
R Flint (J G M O'Shea 24/3) R Flint

Placings:510400/4F015P55-1P53P341130   (4714)
2003/04: 16¹G, 19⁰G, 17⁵GF, 17⁷GF, 16⁶G, 16³GF, 16⁴GF, 16¹GS, 16¹GS, 16³GS, 16⁹G,

	Starts	1st	2nd	3rd	Win & Pl
Hurdles	11	3	0	3	9152
Career Total	25	5	0	3	19368
103	1/04	Ludl	2m	G Hdl		G-S	£2569
103	12/03	Leic	2m	G Hdl		G-S	£2310
95	5/03	Ludl	2m	G Hdl		GD	£2926
101	8/02	Tram		Ch		G-F	£5503
106	11/01	Tram	2m	Hdl		YLD	£4173
				Total win prize-money £17481			

Going: Sf: 0-0 GS: 2-3 Gd: 1-4 GF: - Fm: 0-4
Distance: 2m/2m3: 3-10 2m4-2m7: 0-1 3m+: 0-0
Track: LH: 0-5 RH: 3-6 Tight: 0-4 Gall: 0-1
Aids: Bl: 0-0 Vi: 0-0 Tstrap: 0-0 Ckp: 0-0
Best Rating: 106 6/03 NAbb 2m1f   gd-fm   Hdl

Plating-class hurdler, ex-Irish; won back-to-back sellers around the turn of the year 2004; yet to prove he acts on really soft going; best at 2m; has been inclined to race too freely.

Gregory Peckory (IRE)
83   76

6-y-o b g Teamster-Vill Alba (IRE) (Cataldi)
N A Twiston-Davies Mrs R Mackness

Placings:204   (1675)
2003/04: 16²G, 17⁰G, 16⁴F,

	Starts	1st	2nd	3rd	Win & Pl
NH Flat	2	0	1	0	537
Hurdles	1	0	0	0	0
Career Total	3	0	1	0	537

Going: Sf: 0-0 GS: 0-0 Gd: 0-2 GF: - Fm: 0-1
Distance: 2m/2m3: 0-3 2m4-2m7: 0-0 3m+: 0-0
Track: LH: 0-2 RH: 0-1 Tight: 0-1 Gall: 0-0
Aids: Bl: 0-0 Vi: 0-0 Tstrap: 0-0 Ckp: 0-0
Best Rating: 98 5/03 Worc 2m   good   NHF

Not disgraced when 20/1 second to Mister Flint in Worcester bumper May 2003; failed to get home on hurdling debut at Towcester in October.

Grey Abbey (IRE)
113(114h)   (121 h) 165+

10-y-o gr g Nestor-Tacovaon (Avocat)
J Howard Johnson Ken Roper,Elinor M Roper,Norman Furness

Placings:50/P0P11153/4F62F11121/51F4P0314/453P-6111   (4861)
2003/04: 20⁶GS, 25¹G, 24¹G, 33¹GS,

	Starts	1st	2nd	3rd	Win & Pl
Hurdles	2	1	0	0	7816
Chases	2	2	0	0	87176
Career Total	37	12	2	3	167217
165	4/04	Ayr	4m1f	A HCh		G-S	£69600
159	3/04	Donc	3m	B(0-145)HCh		GD	£17576
121	2/04	Catt	3m1f110yD(0-120)HHdl			GD	£7065
155	4/02	Weth	3m	B(0-150)HCh		GD	£10962
144	11/01	Ayr	3m1f	C(0-135)HCh		G-S	£6812
135	4/01	Ayr	2m4f	A Ch		G-F	£15600
133	2/01	Kels	2m	D Ch		SFT	£3867
125	1/01	Ayr	2m	D Ch		SFT	£4134
129	1/01	Ayr	2m5f110yD Ch			SFT	£4108
116	2/00	Newc	2m4f	F(0-90)HHdl		SFT	£1974
108	2/00	Newc	2m	F(0-100)HHdl		SFT	£1939
85	12/99	Ayr	2m	E(0-105)HHdl		HVY	£2654
				Total win prize-money £146293			

Going: Sf: 0-0 GS: 1-2 Gd: 2-2 GF: - Fm: 0-0
Distance: 2m/2m3: 0-0 2m4-2m7: 0-1 3m+: 3-3
Track: LH: 3-4 RH: 0-0 Tight: 1-1 Gall: 1-2
Aids: Bl: 0-0 Vi: 0-0 Tstrap: 0-0 Ckp: 0-0
Best Rating: 165 4/04 Ayr 4m1f   gd-sft   Ch

Very useful chaser/fair hurdler; at his best when forcing the pace; seems to act on any ground; stays beyond four miles; goes very well at Ayr and turned in career best effort when winning Scottish National in April 2004; superb jumper at best and is a most tough and genuine sort.

Grey Brother
103   113

6-y-o gr g Morpeth-Pigeon Loft (IRE) (Bellypha)
J D Frost Christine And Aubrey Loze

Placings:03231-3   (4243)
2003/04: 19³G,

	Starts	1st	2nd	3rd	Win & Pl
Hurdles	1	0	0	1	793
Career Total	6	1	1	3	5990
110	2/03	Extr	2m6f110yE Hdl		G-S	£3737
			Total win prize-money £3738		

Going: Sf: 0-0 GS: 0-0 Gd: 0-1 GF: - Fm: 0-0
Distance: 2m/2m3: 0-2 2m4-2m7: 0-0 3m+: 0-0
Track: LH: 0-0 RH: 0-1 Tight: 0-0 Gall: 0-0
Aids: Bl: 0-0 Vi: 0-0 Tstrap: 0-0 Ckp: 0-0
Best Rating: 113 3/04 Extr 2m3f   good   Hdl

Got off the mark over hurdles when winning over two miles six on good to soft ground; looks a real stayer.

Grey Ciseaux (IRE)
100(97h)   (80+h) 97

9-y-o gr g Mujtahid (USA)-Inisfail (Persian Bold)
A E Jones John Spence

Placings:P030/51P63326/5/3656PP-222P22140   (4259)
2003/04: 21²GF, 22²GF, 21²GF, 25⁷GF, 27²GF, 21²GF, 24¹GF, 25⁴F, 25⁰GF,

	Starts	1st	2nd	3rd	Win & Pl
Hurdles	3	0	3	0	1900
Chases	6	1	2	0	7611
Career Total	28	2	6	4	13731
97	10/03	Strf	3m	D Ch	G-F	£4758
84	6/99	Kbgn	2m	Hdl	GD	£2455
			Total win prize-money £7213		

Going: Sf: 0-0 GS: 0-0 Gd: 0-0 GF: - Fm: 1-9
Distance: 2m/2m3: 0-0 2m4-2m7: 0-4 3m+: 1-5
Track: LH: 1-5 RH: 0-3 Tight: 1-6 Gall: 0-0
Aids: Bl: 0-1 Vi: 0-0 Tstrap: 0-0 Ckp: 1-5
Best Rating: 97 10/03 Strf 3m   gd-fm   Ch

Moderate chaser; winning pointer; plating-class hurdler; finally got off the mark in this country when winning four-runner 3m beginners chase at Stratford October 2003; suited by a sound surface.

Grey Report (IRE)
115   151+

7-y-o gr g Roselier (FR)-Busters Lodge (Antwerp City)
P J Hobbs Mrs D A La Trobe

Placings:S40-113112322   (4833)
2003/04: 16¹GS, 16¹G, 21³GS, 18¹HY, 21¹S, 21²G, 21³G, 24²G, 21²GF,

	Starts	1st	2nd	3rd	Win & Pl
Hurdles	9	4	3	2	68819
Career Total	12	4	3	2	69040
136	1/04	Plum	2m5f	D Hdl	SFT	£5492
142	1/04	Font	2m2f110yE Hdl	HVY	£3562
131	12/03	Chel	2m110y B Hdl	GD	£10695
124	11/03	Newb	2m110y D Hdl	G-S	£8157
			Total win prize-money £27908		

Going: Sf: 2-2 GS: 1-2 Gd: 1-4 GF: - Fm: 0-1
Distance: 2m/2m3: 3-3 2m4-2m7: 1-5 3m+: 0-1
Track: LH: 4-9 RH: 0-0 Tight: 2-3 Gall: 1-5
Aids: Bl: 0-0 Vi: 0-0 Tstrap: 0-0 Ckp: 0-0
Best Rating: 151 3/04 Chel 2m5f   good   Hdl

Smart novice hurdler; ex-Irish point winner; four-time hurdle winner; third in a hot Grade One hurdle at Newbury in December 2003 and in the Royal & SunAlliance Hurdle at Cheltenham; runner-up in a Grade One novices' contest at Aintree; stays 3m; acts on most ground; likes to front run; tough and genuine.

Grey Samurai
88f   66f

4-y-o gr g Gothenberg (IRE)-Royal Rebeka (Grey Desire)
P T Midgley Robert E Cook

Placings:0   (4962)
2003/04: 17⁰G,

	Starts	1st	2nd	3rd	Win & Pl
NH Flat	1	0	0	0	
Career Total	1	0	0	0	

Going: Sf: 0-0 GS: 0-0 Gd: 0-1 GF: - Fm: 0-0

Distance: 2m/2m3: 0-1 2m4-2m7: 0-0 3m+: 0-0
Track: LH: 0-0 RH: 0-1 Tight: 0-1 Gall: 0-0
Aids: Bl: 0-0 Vi: 0-0 Tstrap: 0-0 Ckp: 0-0
Best Rating: 66   4/04   MRas   2m1f110y   good   NHF

Grey Shark (IRE)
93   81
5-y-o gr g Roselier (FR)-Sharkezan (IRE) (Double Schwartz)
D P Keane   R M Fear

Placings:0000   (4565)
2003/04: 16⁰GS, 16⁰S, 16⁰HY, 17⁰GS,

	Starts	1st	2nd	3rd	Win & Pl
NH Flat	1	0	0	0	0
Hurdles	3	0	0	0	0
Career Total	4	0	0	0	

Going: Sf: 0-2 GS: 0-2 Gd: 0-0 GF: - Fm: 0-0
Distance: 2m/2m3: 0-4 2m4-2m7: 0-0 3m+: 0-0
Track: LH: 0-4 RH: 0-0 Tight: 0-2 Gall: 0-0
Aids: Bl: 0-0 Vi: 0-0 Tstrap: 0-0 Ckp: 0-0
Best Rating: 81   3/04   Bang   2m1f   gd-sft   Hdl

Greyton (IRE)

11-y-o gr g Zaffaran (USA)-Rosy Posy (IRE) (Roselier (FR))
L A Dace   Brendan Laverty

Placings:352045/34154/2/4-P   (3811)
2003/04: 24⁰G,

	Starts	1st	2nd	3rd	Win & Pl
Chases	1	0	0	0	
Career Total	14	1	2	2	7541
98 1/01 Winc 3m1f110yE(0-115)HCht SFT £4173

Total win prize-money £4173

Going: Sf: 0-0 GS: 0-0 Gd: 0-1 GF: - Fm: 0-0
Distance: 2m/2m3: 0-0 2m4-2m7: 0-0 3m+: 0-1
Track: LH: 0-0 RH: 0-1 Tight: 0-0 Gall: 0-0
Aids: Bl: 0-0 Vi: 0-0 Tstrap: 0-0 Ckp: 0-0
Best Rating: 98   5/01   Hntg   3m   gd-fm   Ch

Griffens Brook
72f   62f
4-y-o b g Alderbrook-Ima Delight (Idiots Delight)
Mrs P Sly   Mrs P M Sly

Placings:0   (4517)
2003/04: 16⁰GS,

	Starts	1st	2nd	3rd	Win & Pl
NH Flat	1	0	0	0	
Career Total	1	0	0	0	

Going: Sf: 0-0 GS: 0-1 Gd: 0-0 GF: - Fm: 0-0
Distance: 2m/2m3: 0-1 2m4-2m7: 0-0 3m+: 0-0
Track: LH: 0-1 RH: 0-0 Tight: 0-0 Gall: 0-0
Aids: Bl: 0-0 Vi: 0-0 Tstrap: 0-0 Ckp: 0-0
Best Rating: 56   3/04   Weth   2m   gd-sft   NHF

Griffin's Legacy

5-y-o b g Wace (USA)-Griffin's Girl (Bairn (USA))
N G Ayliffe   Mrs M A Barrett

Placings:0   (3312)

2003/04: 18⁰HY,

	Starts	1st	2nd	3rd	Win & Pl
NH Flat	1	0	0	0	
Career Total	1	0	0	0	

Going: Sf: 0-1 GS: 0-0 Gd: 0-0 GF: - Fm: 0-0
Distance: 2m/2m3: 0-1 2m4-2m7: 0-0 3m+: 0-0
Track: LH: 0-1 RH: 0-0 Tight: 0-1 Gall: 0-0
Aids: Bl: 0-0 Vi: 0-0 Tstrap: 0-0 Ckp: 0-0

Grimshaw (USA)
100   (66c) 105
9-y-o ch g St Jovite (USA)-Loa (USA) (Hawaii)
Mrs D A Hamer   John Cole

Placings:050/4103054FU1300/0350454533/260650/06000-41F5FFP0   (3773)
2003/04: 20⁴GF, 19¹GF, 19⁶GF, 20⁵GF, 16⁶GS, 19⁶G, 16⁶PG,

	Starts	1st	2nd	3rd	Win & Pl
Hurdles	6	1	0	0	2023
Chases	1	0	0	0	0
Career Total	44	3	1	5	14521
93	9/03	Hrfd	2m3f110yF(0-100)HHdl	G-F	£2023
117	10/99	Wxfd	2m4f	(0-109)HHdl	SFT	£3696
98	5/99	Clon	2m	Hdl	GD	£3069

Total win prize-money £8788

Going: Sf: 0-0 GS: 0-1 Gd: 0-2 GF: - Fm: 1-4
Distance: 2m/2m3: 0-3 2m4-2m7: 1-4 3m+: 0-0
Track: LH: 0-3 RH: 1-4 Tight: 0-1 Gall: 0-0
Aids: Bl: 0-0 Vi: 0-0 Tstrap: 0-0 Ckp: 0-1
Best Rating: 119   6/00   Tral   2m4f   sft-hvy   Hdl

Grizzly Activewear (IRE)
98   97
10-y-o ch g Camden Town-Boro Cent (Little Buskins)
B D Leavy   Mrs Alurie O'Sullivan

Placings:0/00323110406/6306   (4605)
2003/04: 22⁶G, 22³GS, 21⁰G, 22⁶G,

	Starts	1st	2nd	3rd	Win & Pl
Hurdles	4	0	0	1	696
Career Total	16	2	1	3	7997
104	10/01	Sedg	3m3f110yE Hdl	G-S	£2565
104	9/01	Prth	3m110y E Hdl	GD	£2968

Total win prize-money £5534

Going: Sf: 0-0 GS: 0-1 Gd: 0-3 GF: - Fm: 0-0
Distance: 2m/2m3: 0-0 2m4-2m7: 0-4 3m+: 0-0
Track: LH: 0-3 RH: 0-0 Tight: 0-2 Gall: 0-0
Aids: Bl: 0-0 Vi: 0-0 Tstrap: 0-0 Ckp: 0-0
Best Rating: 104   10/01   Sedg   3m3f110y   gd-sft   Hdl

Modest staying hurdler; stays three miles plus; suited by good ground or slightly softer.

Grizzly Golfwear (IRE)

10-y-o b g Commanche Run-Dunwellan (Tekoah)
Mrs S E Hughes   Mrs S E Hughes

Placings:FP/5P500/P06/23F-33P   (3778)
2003/04: 24³GF, 28³GS, 24⁶G,

	Starts	1st	2nd	3rd	Win & Pl
Chases	3	0	0	2	2094
Career Total	16	0	1	3	3523

Going: Sf: 0-0 GS: 0-1 Gd: 0-1 GF: - Fm: 0-1
Distance: 2m/2m3: 0-0 2m4-2m7: 0-0 3m+: 0-3
Track: LH: 0-2 RH: 0-1 Tight: 0-2 Gall: 0-0
Aids: Bl: 0-0 Vi: 0-0 Tstrap: 0-0 Ckp: 0-0
Best Rating: 85   5/03   Strf   3m4f   gd-sft   Ch

Hunter chaser; dual winning pointer; effective on good.

Groovejet

5-y-o b g Emperor Jones (USA)-Sir Hollow (USA) (Sir Ivor (USA))
J R Jenkins   R M Ellis

Placings:P-P   (0433)
2003/04: 18⁰GF,

	Starts	1st	2nd	3rd	Win & Pl
Hurdles	1	0	0	0	
Career Total	2	0	0	0	

Going: Sf: 0-0 GS: 0-0 Gd: 0-0 GF: - Fm: 0-1
Distance: 2m/2m3: 0-1 2m4-2m7: 0-0 3m+: 0-0
Track: LH: 0-1 RH: 0-0 Tight: 0-1 Gall: 0-0
Aids: Bl: 0-0 Vi: 0-1 Tstrap: 0-0 Ckp: 0-0

Ground Ball (IRE)
114(114h)   (124h) 144
7-y-o b/br g Bob's Return (IRE)-Bettyhill (Ardross)
C F Swan   John P McManus

Placings:1/42105/F2123F2-2313F120   (4627)
2003/04: 18²GY, 20³G, 16¹GY, 16³GY, 22F SH, 18¹GY, 16²G, 16⁰G,

	Starts	1st	2nd	3rd	Win & Pl
Hurdles	2	1	0	1	7506
Chases	6	1	2	1	31226
Career Total	21	5	6	3	73939
136	1/04	Thur	2m2f	Ch	G-Y	£9154
122	11/03	Punc	2m	Hdl	G-Y	£7168
135	12/02	Navn	2m4f	Ch	SFT	£6773
121	1/02	Navn	2m	Hdl	Y-S	£8009
123	4/01	Cork	2m	NHF	Y-S	£4173

Total win prize-money £35279

Going: Sf: 0-0 GS: 0-0 Gd: 0-3 GF: - Fm: 0-0
Distance: 2m/2m3: 2-6 2m4-2m7: 0-2 3m+: 0-0
Track: LH: 0-3 RH: 2-4 Tight: 0-1 Gall: 0-1
Aids: Bl: 0-0 Vi: 0-0 Tstrap: 0-0 Ckp: 0-0
Best Rating: 144   3/04   Chel   2m110y   good   Ch

Useful chaser/hurdler; runner-up in Grand Annual at Cheltenham festival of 2004; stays two and a half miles; acts on soft ground.

Ground Breaker
98f   91f
4-y-o b g Emperor Jones (USA)-Startino (Bustino)
M W Easterby   The Woodford Group Limited

Placings:45   (4962)
2003/04: 16⁴G, 17⁵G,

	Starts	1st	2nd	3rd	Win & Pl
NH Flat	2	0	0	0	0
Career Total	2	0	0	0	0

Going: Sf: 0-0 GS: 0-0 Gd: 0-2 GF: - Fm: 0-0
Distance: 2m/2m3: 0-2 2m4-2m7: 0-0 3m+: 0-0
Track: LH: 0-1 RH: 0-1 Tight: 0-1 Gall: 0-1
Aids: Bl: 0-0 Vi: 0-0 Tstrap: 0-0 Ckp: 0-0
Best Rating: 91   3/04   Donc   2m110y   good   NHF

Group One's Hope

35

8-y-o b m Absalom-Hopeful Waters (Forlorn River)
A W Carroll Group 1 Racing (1994) Ltd

Placings:*0/0/P0FP-0PP4UP*　(1967)
2003/04: 16⁰GF, 17⁵GF, 16⁵GF, 19⁴F, 17ᵁG, 16⁵G,

	Starts	1st	2nd	3rd	Win & Pl
Hurdles	4	0	0	0	0
Chases	2	0	0	0	0
Career Total	12	0	0	0	0

Going:	Sf: 0-0 GS: 0-0 Gd: 0-2 GF: - Fm: 0-4
Distance:	2m/2m3: 0-5 2m4-2m7: 0-1 3m+: 0-0
Track:	LH: 0-4 RH: 0-1 Tight: 0-0 Gall: 0-0
Aids:	Bl: 0-0 Vi: 0-2 Tstrap: 0-0 Ckp: 0-0
Best Rating:	35　10/03　Towc　2m3f110y　firm　Hdl

Grouse Hall

84　　89

10-y-o ch g Primitive Rising (USA)-Em-Kay-Em (Slim Jim)
M Todhunter P E Sowerby

Placings:*10/6U0026/4/4/32-2*　(1664)
2003/04: 20²GF,

	Starts	1st	2nd	3rd	Win & Pl
Chases	1	0	1	0	1026
Career Total	13	1	3	1	5746
103	3/99	Ayr	2m	H NHF	SFT £1346

Total win prize-money £1347

Going:	Sf: 0-0 GS: 0-0 Gd: 0-0 GF: - Fm: 0-1
Distance:	2m/2m3: 0-0 2m4-2m7: 0-0 3m+: 0-0
Track:	LH: 0-1 RH: 0-0 Tight: 0-0 Gall: 0-0
Aids:	Bl: 0-0 Vi: 0-0 Tstrap: 0-0 Ckp: 0-0
Best Rating:	103　3/99　Ayr　2m　soft　NHF

Plating-class chaser; won a bumper in the soft; has had leg problems and lightly raced since.

Grouse Moor (USA)

91　　79+

5-y-o b g Distant View (USA)-Caithness (USA) (Roberto (USA))
P Winkworth Tweenhills Racing (Cleeve Hill)

Placings:*40-5550P*　(4123)
2003/04: 17⁵GS, 16⁵GS, 16⁵S, 18⁰GS, 17⁶G,

	Starts	1st	2nd	3rd	Win & Pl
NH Flat	1	0	0	0	0
Hurdles	4	0	0	0	0
Career Total	7	0	0	0	0

Going:	Sf: 0-1 GS: 0-3 Gd: 0-1 GF: - Fm: 0-0
Distance:	2m/2m3: 0-5 2m4-2m7: 0-0 3m+: 0-0
Track:	LH: 0-1 RH: 0-4 Tight: 0-0 Gall: 0-0
Aids:	Bl: 0-0 Vi: 0-0 Tstrap: 0-0 Ckp: 0-0
Best Rating:	86　1/04　Winc　2m　gd-sft　Hdl

Grove Juliet (IRE)

5-y-o ch m Moscow Society (USA)-Cloona Lady (IRE) (Duky)
B G Powell P H Betts

Placings:*0*　(4495)
2003/04: 16⁰G,

	Starts	1st	2nd	3rd	Win & Pl
NH Flat	1	0	0	0	

Career Total　　1　　0　　0　　0

Going:	Sf: 0-0 GS: 0-0 Gd: 0-1 GF: - Fm: 0-0
Distance:	2m/2m3: 0-1 2m4-2m7: 0-0 3m+: 0-0
Track:	LH: 0-0 RH: 0-0 Tight: 0-0 Gall: 0-0
Aids:	Bl: 0-0 Vi: 0-0 Tstrap: 0-0 Ckp: 0-0
Best Rating:	0　3/04　Strf　2m110y　good　NHF

Guard Duty

105(107h)　　(128h)117

7-y-o b g Deploy-Hymne D'Amour (USA) (Dixieland Band (USA))
M C Pipe Neil Edwards And Malcolm Jones

Placings:*211114/2000/50F350-2132P66*　(4930)
2003/04: 20²S, 24¹GF, 26⁵GS, 24²G, 32⁶G, 24⁶G, 22⁶G,

	Starts	1st	2nd	3rd	Win & Pl
Chases		7	1	2	1	7543
Career Total	23	5	4	2	27087
112	12/03	Tntn	3m	D Ch	G-F £4452
131	2/01	Wwck	2m5f	E(0-115)HHdl	SFT £3818
125	2/01	Tntn	2m3f110yF(0-110)HHdl	HVY £3540
134	1/01	Tntn	2m3f110yF(0-100)HHdl	HVY £2381
112	1/01	Tntn	2m1f	G Hdl	SFT £1631

Total win prize-money £15824

Going:	Sf: 0-1 GS: 0-1 Gd: 0-4 GF: - Fm: 1-1
Distance:	2m/2m3: 0-2 2m4-2m7: 0-2 3m+: 1-5
Track:	LH: 0-2 RH: 1-3 Tight: 1-6 Gall: 0-1
Aids:	Bl: 0-0 Vi: 0-4 Tstrap: 1-7 Ckp: 0-0
Best Rating:	134　1/01　Tntn　2m3f110y　heavy　Hdl

Novice chaser/fair hurdler; ran into a useful sort on his chasing debut; acts well on a soft surface; suited by trips around two miles five furlongs, but just stays three; usually tongue tied these days; is not a natural chaser.

Guarded Secret

99　　104+

7-y-o gr g Mystiko (USA)-Fen Dance (IRE) (Trojan Fen)
J Mackie Peter McMahon

Placings:*1454*　(3523)
2003/04: 16¹GS, 17⁴GS, 16⁵S, 16⁴S,

	Starts	1st	2nd	3rd	Win & Pl
Hurdles	4	1	0	0	2984
Career Total	4	1	0	0	2984
104	11/03	Uttx	2m	E Hdl	G-S £2674

Total win prize-money £2674

Going:	Sf: 0-2 GS: 1-2 Gd: 0-0 GF: - Fm: 0-0
Distance:	2m/2m3: 1-4 2m4-2m7: 0-0 3m+: 0-0
Track:	LH: 1-3 RH: 0-1 Tight: 0-1 Gall: 0-0
Aids:	Bl: 0-0 Vi: 0-0 Tstrap: 0-0 Ckp: 0-0
Best Rating:	110　1/04　Weth　2m　soft　Hdl

Novice hurdler; winner on debut at Uttoxeter in November; far from disgraced since; suited by soft ground.

Gudlage (USA)

95　　(111c)109+

8-y-o b g Gulch (USA)-Triple Kiss (Shareef Dancer (USA))
M W Easterby Lord Daresbury

Placings:*0/1P3003/12-0*　(1017)
2003/04: 16⁰GF,

	Starts	1st	2nd	3rd	Win & Pl
Hurdles	1	0	0	0	
Career Total	10	2	1	2	10546
109	11/02	Newc	2m	E(0-110)HHdl	G-S £3259
96	10/01	Aint	2m110y	E Hdl	GD £3248

Going:	Sf: 0-0 GS: 0-0 Gd: 0-0 GF: - Fm: 0-1
Distance:	2m/2m3: 0-1 2m4-2m7: 0-0 3m+: 0-0
Track:	LH: 0-1 RH: 0-0 Tight: 0-0 Gall: 0-0
Aids:	Bl: 0-0 Vi: 0-0 Tstrap: 0-0 Ckp: 0-0
Best Rating:	109　3/03　MRas　2m1f110y　good　Hdl

Fair hurdler; best over two miles; winner at Newcastle in November and runner-up at Market Rasen in March; goes well fresh; usually tongue tied.

Gue Au Loup (FR)

95　　99

10-y-o gr g Royal Charter (FR)-Arche D'Alliance (FR) (Pamponi (FR))
B Ellison C E Sherry

Placings:*2552/F5/2/12/05U346-1*　(0920)
2003/04: 17¹GF,

	Starts	1st	2nd	3rd	Win & Pl
Chases	1	1	0	0	8190
Career Total	16	2	4	1	23785
99	7/03	MRas	2m1f110yD(0-115)HCh	GF £8190
109	5/01	Bang	2m1f110yF(0-100)HCh	G-S £4485

Total win prize-money £12675

Going:	Sf: 0-0 GS: 0-0 Gd: 0-0 GF: - Fm: 1-1
Distance:	2m/2m3: 1-1 2m4-2m7: 0-0 3m+: 0-0
Track:	LH: 0-0 RH: 1-1 Tight: 1-1 Gall: 0-0
Aids:	Bl: 0-0 Vi: 0-0 Tstrap: 0-1 Ckp: 0-0
Best Rating:	120　5/01　Bang　2m4f110y　good　Ch

Ex-French; moderate chaser; effective at around two and a half miles; acts on fast ground.

Guignol Du Cochet (FR)

10-y-o ch g Secret Of Success-Pasquita (FR) (Bourbon (FR))
S Flook (Mrs L Richards 2/5) S Flook

Placings:*P14P4P0/4403251322240/221340/0224F-4522451*　(4717)
2003/04: 16⁴GS, 22⁵S, 20²G, 20²G, 19⁴GS, 20⁵GS, 24¹G,

	Starts	1st	2nd	3rd	Win & Pl
Chases		7	1	2	0	4455
Career Total	38	4	10	3	26368
102	4/04	Ludl	3m	H Ch	GD £2905
102	12/00	Folk	2m	F(0-100)HCh	SFT £2359
99	11/99	Worc	2m	F(0-100)HCh	GD £2530
	5/98	Fntb	2m3f	Ch	GD £2322

Total win prize-money £11026

Going:	Sf: 0-1 GS: 0-3 Gd: 1-3 GF: - Fm: 0-0
Distance:	2m/2m3: 0-1 2m4-2m7: 0-5 3m+: 1-1
Track:	LH: 0-2 RH: 1-5 Tight: 1-3 Gall: 0-0
Aids:	Bl: 0-0 Vi: 0-0 Tstrap: 0-0 Ckp: 0-0
Best Rating:	102　4/04　Ludl　3m　good　Ch

Hunter chaser; moderate two-mile handicapper at best under Rules; stays 2m4f; acts on good ground.

Guilsborough Gorse

105　　100

9-y-o b g Past Glories-Buckby Folly (Netherkelly)
T D Walford Peter Crafts

Placings:*32P3/525F31/22P1053343-350212*　(4300)
2003/04: 24³GF, 25³G, 22⁵G, 23⁰GF, 24²G, 24¹F, 20²G,

	Starts	1st	2nd	3rd	Win & Pl
Chases	7	1	2	2	5726
Career Total	26	3	6	7	20976

93	2/04	Muss	3m	H Ch	FRM	£2240
100	10/02	Hexm	2m4f110yD(0-115)HCh		GD	£4550
96	4/02	Weth	2m4f110yE Ch		G-F	£3503

Total win prize-money £10294

Going:	Sf: 0-0 GS: 0-0 Gd: 0-4 GF: - Fm: 1-3
Distance:	2m/2m3: 0-0 2m4-2m7: 0-2 3m+: 1-5
Track:	LH: 0-3 RH: 1-4 Tight: 1-3 Gall: 0-1
Aids:	Bl: 0-1 Vi: 0-0 Tstrap: 0-0 Ckp: 0-2
Best Rating:	100 3/04 Leic 2m4f110y good Ch

Won a point-to-point in Febuary 2000, he has shown moderate form over fences and eventually broke his duck in a modest event at Wetherby in April 2002; scored at Hexham in October.

Guilt
96   **111+**

4-y-o b c Mark Of Esteem (IRE)-Guillem (USA) (Nijinsky (CAN))
D T Hughes (P Bary 6/6) T C D D Syndicate

Placings:0105   (3739a)
2003/04: 16OS, 16¹S, 17OGS, 16⁵S,

	Starts	1st	2nd	3rd	Win & Pl
Hurdles	4	1	0	0	8442
Career Total	4	1	0	0	8442

110	12/03	Leop	2m	Hdl	SFT	£8441

Total win prize-money £8442

Going:	Sf: 1-3 GS: 0-1 Gd: 0-0 GF: - Fm: 0-0
Distance:	2m/2m3: 1-4 2m4-2m7: 0-0 3m+: 0-0
Track:	LH: 1-3 RH: 0-1 Tight: 0-0 Gall: 0-1
Aids:	Bl: 0-0 Vi: 0-0 Tstrap: 1-3 Ckp: 0-0
Best Rating:	111 2/04 Leop 2m soft Hdl

Modest novice hurdler; placed on the Flat in both France and Ireland; acts on good and soft ground; effective over two miles.

Gulabill
86f   **85f**

5-y-o b g Safawan-Gulsha (Glint Of Gold)
N A Twiston-Davies Mrs J K Powell

Placings:0   (4454)
2003/04: 16OGS,

	Starts	1st	2nd	3rd	Win & Pl
NH Flat	1	0	0	0	
Career Total	1	0	0	0	

Going:	Sf: 0-0 GS: 0-1 Gd: 0-0 GF: - Fm: 0-0
Distance:	2m/2m3: 0-1 2m4-2m7: 0-0 3m+: 0-0
Track:	LH: 0-0 RH: 0-1 Tight: 0-0 Gall: 0-0
Aids:	Bl: 0-0 Vi: 0-0 Tstrap: 0-0 Ckp: 0-0
Best Rating:	85 3/04 Asct 2m110y gd-sft NHF

Gullible Guy

12-y-o b g Domynsky-Halmaseta (Lochnager)
George R Moscrop George R Moscrop

Placings:53/1P2246/0/34/0-   (0008)
2003/04: 20OGF,

	Starts	1st	2nd	3rd	Win & Pl
Chases	1	0	0	0	
Career Total	12	1	2	2	4727

107	5/98	Chep	2m110y H NHF	G-F	£1570

Total win prize-money £1571

Going:	Sf: 0-0 GS: 0-0 Gd: 0-0 GF: - Fm: 0-1
Distance:	2m/2m3: 0-0 2m4-2m7: 0-1 3m+: 0-0
Track:	LH: 0-1 RH: 0-0 Tight: 0-0 Gall: 0-1
Aids:	Bl: 0-0 Vi: 0-0 Tstrap: 0-0 Ckp: 0-0
Best Rating:	107 5/98 Chep 2m110y gd-fm NHF

Gullivers Travels
79f   **45f**

5-y-o ch g Un Desperado (FR)-Drivers Bureau (Proverb)
G L Moore Juniper Stud Racing

Placings:00   (4578)
2003/04: 16OG, 16OG,

	Starts	1st	2nd	3rd	Win & Pl
NH Flat	2	0	0	0	
Career Total	2	0	0	0	

Going:	Sf: 0-0 GS: 0-0 Gd: 0-2 GF: - Fm: 0-0
Distance:	2m/2m3: 0-2 2m4-2m7: 0-0 3m+: 0-0
Track:	LH: 0-1 RH: 0-1 Tight: 0-0 Gall: 0-1
Aids:	Bl: 0-0 Vi: 0-0 Tstrap: 0-0 Ckp: 0-0
Best Rating:	45 3/04 Kemp 2m good NHF

Gumley Gale
102   **101**

9-y-o b g Greensmith-Clodaigh Gale (Strong Gale)
K Bishop Portcullis Racing

Placings:34/0/2631F512/14065-004045   (4897)
2003/04: 19OG, 17OG, 22⁴S, 24OGS, 19⁴G, 22⁵G,

	Starts	1st	2nd	3rd	Win & Pl
Hurdles	6	0	0	0	778
Career Total	22	3	2	2	22232

121	5/02	Uttx	2m4f110yB(0-140)HHdl	GD	£10478
121	11/01	NAbb	2m6f D(0-125)HHdl	GD	£3267
110	7/01	Worc	2m4f E(0-115)HHdl	SFT	£3510

Total win prize-money £17256

Going:	Sf: 0-1 GS: 0-1 Gd: 0-4 GF: - Fm: 0-0
Distance:	2m/2m3: 0-2 2m4-2m7: 0-3 3m+: 0-1
Track:	LH: 0-0 RH: 0-6 Tight: 0-2 Gall: 0-0
Aids:	Bl: 0-0 Vi: 0-0 Tstrap: 0-0 Ckp: 0-0
Best Rating:	121 5/02 Uttx 2m4f110y good Hdl

Fair handicap hurdler, handles any ground and stays two miles six.

Gumption
93   **105**

6-y-o b g Muhtarram (USA)-Dancing Spirit (IRE) (Ahonoora)
K C Bailey Sir David Sieff

Placings:2-P4P   (2006)
2003/04: 24PS, 20⁴G, 20PG,

	Starts	1st	2nd	3rd	Win & Pl
Hurdles	3	0	0	0	328
Career Total	4	0	1	0	1698

Going:	Sf: 0-1 GS: 0-0 Gd: 0-2 GF: - Fm: 0-0
Distance:	2m/2m3: 0-0 2m4-2m7: 0-2 3m+: 0-1
Track:	LH: 0-1 RH: 0-0 Tight: 0-1 Gall: 0-0
Aids:	Bl: 0-0 Vi: 0-0 Tstrap: 0-0 Ckp: 0-0
Best Rating:	105 2/03 Tntn 3m110y gd-sft Hdl

Fair maiden on the Flat; promising over hurdles.

Gun'n Roses II (FR)

10-y-o gr g Royal Charter (FR)-Offenbach Ii (FR) (Ermitage (FR))
D P Keane Lady Clarke

Placings:11P32/12P0/3P/1P11P/3F516F/P1P6-13   (4626)
2003/04: 22¹S, 21³G,

	Starts	1st	2nd	3rd	Win & Pl
Chases	2	1	0	1	12655
Career Total	28	9	2	4	75517

133	2/04	Hayd	2m6f H Ch		SFT	£8970
143	12/02	Weth	2m4f110yB(0-145)HCh		G-S	£10907
145	1/02	Donc	2m3f110yC(0-130)HCh		SFT	£6376
134	3/01	Hayd	2m6f D Ch		HVY	£5671
145	2/01	Wwck	2m4f110yC(0-130)HCh		SFT	£6695
138	12/00	Chep	2m3f110yD(0-125)HCh		SFT	£6776
116	5/98	Uttx	2m E Hdl		G-S	£2263
	1/98	Pau	2m2f	Hdl	SFT	£6061
	12/97	Pau	2m110y	Hdl	VS	£6734

Total win prize-money £60455

Going:	Sf: 1-1 GS: 0-0 Gd: 0-1 GF: - Fm: 0-0
Distance:	2m/2m3: 0-0 2m4-2m7: 1-2 3m+: 0-0
Track:	LH: 1-2 RH: 0-0 Tight: 0-1 Gall: 0-0
Aids:	Bl: 1-2 Vi: 0-0 Tstrap: 0-0 Ckp: 0-0
Best Rating:	145 1/02 Donc 2m3f110y soft Ch

Very useful chaser in his prime; has been around a few yards; successfull on first outing for present handler in hunter chase at Haydock in February; third in the Fox Hunters at Aintree; has won at up to two miles six; suited by cut in the ground; best in blinkers nowadays.

Gunna Be King

10-y-o b g Rakaposhi King-Gunna Be Precious (Gunner B)
Mrs S Robinson Mrs S Robinson

Placings:PP/P/F   (0103)
2003/04: 25FG,

	Starts	1st	2nd	3rd	Win & Pl
Chases	1	0	0	0	
Career Total	4	0	0	0	

Going:	Sf: 0-0 GS: 0-0 Gd: 0-1 GF: - Fm: 0-0
Distance:	2m/2m3: 0-0 2m4-2m7: 0-0 3m+: 0-1
Track:	LH: 0-1 RH: 0-0 Tight: 0-0 Gall: 0-0
Aids:	Bl: 0-0 Vi: 0-0 Tstrap: 0-0 Ckp: 0-0

Gunner Dream
79   **75**

8-y-o b g Gunner B-Star Route (Owen Dudley)
C Grant The Hon Mrs M Faulkner

Placings:543-P03P   (3770)
2003/04: 25PS, 25OS, 25³G, 24PHY,

	Starts	1st	2nd	3rd	Win & Pl
Chases	4	0	0	1	480
Career Total	7	0	0	2	2053

Going:	Sf: 0-2 GS: 0-0 Gd: 0-2 GF: - Fm: 0-0
Distance:	2m/2m3: 0-0 2m4-2m7: 0-0 3m+: 0-4
Track:	LH: 0-2 RH: 0-2 Tight: 0-1 Gall: 0-0
Aids:	Bl: 0-0 Vi: 0-0 Tstrap: 0-0 Ckp: 0-0
Best Rating:	75 1/03 Newc 2m4f heavy Ch

Runner-up in maiden points but struggling under Rules.

Gunner Royal

89   **80**

6-y-o b g Gunner B-Loadplan Lass (Nicholas Bill)
J Wade John Wade

Placings:50P   (4319)
2003/04: 17⁵HY, 24⁰S, 20⁰S,

	Starts	1st	2nd	3rd	Win & Pl
Hurdles	3	0	0	0	0
Career Total	3	0	0	0	0

Going:	Sf: 0-3 GS: 0-0 Gd: 0-0 GF: - Fm: 0-0
Distance:	2m/2m3: 0-1 2m4-2m7: 0-1 3m+: 0-1
Track:	LH: 0-2 RH: 0-1 Tight: 0-1 Gall: 0-1
Aids:	Bl: 0-0 Vi: 0-0 Tstrap: 0-0 Ckp: 0-0
Best Rating:	80 11/03 Carl 2m1f heavy Hdl

Gunner Welburn

118   **148+**

12-y-o ch g Gunner B-Vedra (IRE) (Carlingford Castle)
A M Balding W A Ritson/D H Hall/R D Ellis

Placings:1/111/F121/5122/13014-P1P1P   (4647)
2003/04: 20⁵PGS, 25¹GS, 29⁵GS, 24¹G, 36⁵PG,

	Starts	1st	2nd	3rd	Win & Pl
Chases	5	2	0		24578
Career Total	22	11	3	1	139158
133	2/04	Sand	3m110y	E Ch		GD	£6727
148	12/03	Weth	3m1f	A HCh		G-S	£17850
144	3/03	Newb	3m	C(0-130)HCh		SFT	£9966
138	12/02	Chep	3m	C(0-130)HCh		SFT	£7884
119	2/02	Hayd	2m6f	H Ch		HVY	£6890
144	4/01	Aint	2m5f110yB Ch		SFT	£18460
140	2/01	Hayd	3m	H Ch		HVY	£6857
128	4/00	Bang	3m1f	H Ch		G-S	£1715
128	2/00	Font	3m2f110yH Ch		SFT	£3591
110	2/00	Wwck	3m1f110yH Ch		GD	£1270
105	4/99	Chel	3m1f110yH Ch		G-S	£2775

Total win prize-money £83989

Going:	Sf: 0-0 GS: 1-3 Gd: 1-2 GF: - Fm: 0-0
Distance:	2m/2m3: 0-0 2m4-2m7: 0-1 **3m+: 2-4**
Track:	LH: 1-4 RH: 1-1 Tight: 0-1 Gall: 0-1
Aids:	Bl: 0-0 Vi: 0-0 Tstrap: 0-0 Ckp: 0-0
Best Rating:	148 12/03 Weth 3m1f gd-sft Ch

Smart chaser; formerly a top hunter; made much of the running when fourth in the 2003 Grand National; successful twice in 2003-04; revels in the mud; both stays and jumps well.

Gunnerbe Posh

95(91h)   (84h)**66**

10-y-o ch g Rakaposhi King-Triggered (Gunner B)
B G Powell Mrs S Maxse & J Maxse

Placings:23/P00240/00-440   (0704)
2003/04: 23⁴G, 21⁴GF, 22⁰GF,

	Starts	1st	2nd	3rd	Win & Pl
Chases	3	0	0	0	683
Career Total	13	0	2	1	2090

Going:	Sf: 0-0 GS: 0-0 Gd: 0-1 GF: - Fm: 0-2
Distance:	2m/2m3: 0-0 2m4-2m7: 0-2 3m+: 0-1
Track:	LH: 0-2 RH: 0-0 Tight: 0-2 Gall: 0-0
Aids:	Bl: 0-0 Vi: 0-0 Tstrap: 0-0 Ckp: 0-0
Best Rating:	105 3/99 Newb 2m110y soft NHF

Gunson Hight

86   **85+**

7-y-o b g Be My Chief (USA)-Glas Y Dorlan (Sexton Blake)
M Todhunter Lord Cavendish And Bill Parkinson

Placings:00-100   (3816)
2003/04: 16¹G, 19⁰GS, 20⁰GS,

	Starts	1st	2nd	3rd	Win & Pl
Hurdles	3	1	0	0	2576
Career Total	5	1	0	0	2576
80	11/03	Hexm	2m110y	E Hdl		GD	£2576

Total win prize-money £2576

Going:	Sf: 0-0 GS: 0-2 Gd: 1-1 GF: - Fm: 0-0
Distance:	**2m/2m3: 1-2** 2m4-2m7: 0-1 3m+: 0-0
Track:	LH: 1-3 RH: 0-0 Tight: 0-0 Gall: 0-0
Aids:	Bl: 0-0 Vi: 0-0 **Tstrap: 1-2** Ckp: 0-0
Best Rating:	80 11/03 Hexm 2m110y good Hdl

Plating-class hurdler; surprise winner of a poor race on hurdling debut; well beaten next time; acts on good ground; has worn a tongue tie.

Gunther McBride (IRE)

120   (117h)**146**

9-y-o b g Glacial Storm (USA)-What Side (General Ironside)
P J Hobbs M J Tuckey

Placings:1/3P1/12221163/1652U3-2P425   (4637)
2003/04: 25²GF, 26⁶GS, 26⁴G, 24²G, 25⁵G,

	Starts	1st	2nd	3rd	Win & Pl
Chases	5	1	2	0	35344
Career Total	23	6	6	3	171267
120	11/02	Kemp	3m1f	D(0-120)HHdl		HVY	£4309
144	2/02	Kemp	3m	A HCh		GD	£52200
125	1/02	Kemp	3m	D(0-125)HCh		SFT	£7215
117	10/01	Extr	2m6f110yE Hdl		GD	£2716
106	4/01	Leop	3m	Ch		SH	£5564
78	4/00	Cork	3m	Ch		Y-S	£3588

Total win prize-money £75594

Going:	Sf: 0-0 GS: 0-1 Gd: 0-3 GF: - Fm: 0-1
Distance:	2m/2m3: 0-0 2m4-2m7: 0-0 3m+: 0-5
Track:	LH: 0-3 RH: 0-2 Tight: 0-1 Gall: 0-2
Aids:	Bl: 0-0 Vi: 0-0 Tstrap: 0-0 Ckp: 0-0
Best Rating:	144 2/04 Kemp 3m good Ch

Useful handicap chaser; keen sort; won the Racing Post Chase at Kempton in 2002 and runner-up in 2003 and 2004; effective at three miles, but stays four; best on good ground; likes a right-handed track and goes well at Kempton.

Guru

108   **115**

6-y-o b g Slip Anchor-Ower (IRE) (Lomond (USA))
G L Moore Will Bennett

Placings:164/3P0011-5   (2486)
2003/04: 16⁵GS,

	Starts	1st	2nd	3rd	Win & Pl
Hurdles	1	0	0	0	554
Career Total	10	3	0	1	14093
108	3/03	Font	2m2f110yD(0-115)HHdl		GD	£5079
108	2/03	Plum	2m	D(0-115)HHdl		SFT	£4823
101	12/01	Folk	2m1f110yE Hdl		SFT	£2894

Total win prize-money £12798

Going:	Sf: 0-0 GS: 0-1 Gd: 0-0 GF: - Fm: 0-0
Distance:	2m/2m3: 0-1 2m4-2m7: 0-0 3m+: 0-0
Track:	LH: 0-1 RH: 0-0 Tight: 0-0 Gall: 0-1
Aids:	Bl: 0-0 Vi: 0-0 Tstrap: 0-0 Ckp: 0-0

Best Rating: 115   11/03   Newb   2m110y   gd-sft   Hdl

Modest hurdler; acts on good and soft ground; is effective at around two miles.

Gus Berry (IRE)

11-y-o ch g Montelimar (USA)-Eurolink Sea Baby (Deep Run)
Mrs Alison Christmas J Kilner

Placings:10P/P2520/FPP145/6P11P/U4240/35-4   (4392)
2003/04: 27⁴G,

	Starts	1st	2nd	3rd	Win & Pl
Chases	1	0	0	0	0
Career Total	27	4	3	1	17929
96	2/01	Sedg	3m3f	F(0-110)HCh		G-S	£4026
103	12/00	Sedg	3m3f	F(0-95)HCh		SFT	£3978
106	2/00	Sedg	3m3f110yF(0-110)HHdl		G-S	£5239
84	12/97	Catt	2m	H NHF		G-S	£1213

Total win prize-money £14458

Going:	Sf: 0-0 GS: 0-0 Gd: 0-1 GF: - Fm: 0-0
Distance:	2m/2m3: 0-0 2m4-2m7: 0-0 3m+: 0-1
Track:	LH: 0-1 RH: 0-0 Tight: 0-1 Gall: 0-0
Aids:	Bl: 0-0 Vi: 0-0 Tstrap: 0-0 Ckp: 0-0
Best Rating:	106 2/00 Sedg 3m3f110y gd-sft Hdl

Hunter chaser; likes Sedgefield; stays well; best with give in the ground.

Gus Des Bois (FR)

105   **118**

10-y-o ch g Lampon (FR)-Fiacina (FR) (Fiasco)
R H Alner The Cd Partnership

Placings:F61/53512/F0F2010/254/F4/UP4213P-U03523346   (4817)
2003/04: 19⁰G, 19⁰GS, 20⁰S, 17⁵S, 18²GS, 19³GS, 19³GF, 24⁴G, 24⁶G,

	Starts	1st	2nd	3rd	Win & Pl
Chases	9	0	1	3	3887
Career Total	36	4	5	4	40635
111	2/03	Plum	2m4f	D(0-125)HCh		HVY	£5395
4/00	Drtl	2m6f110y	Ch		SFT	£3074
8/98	LE L	2m4f	Ch		SFT	£7071
4/98	Ange	2m2f110y	Ch		HVY	£3030

Total win prize-money £18570

Going:	Sf: 0-2 GS: 0-4 Gd: 0-2 GF: - Fm: 0-1
Distance:	2m/2m3: 0-3 2m4-2m7: 0-4 3m+: 0-2
Track:	LH: 0-5 RH: 0-2 Tight: 0-4 Gall: 0-0
Aids:	Bl: 0-4 Vi: 0-5 Tstrap: 0-0 Ckp: 0-0
Best Rating:	111 2/03 Chep 2m3f110y gd-sft Ch

Winning chaser in France at up to two miles six furlongs; won at Plumpton in January 2003 when fitted with blinkers; acts on a soft surface; best going left-handed.

Guthrie (IRE)

91f   **88f**

6-y-o ch g Mister Lord (USA)-Nephin Far (IRE) (Phardante (FR))
A King Mrs J K Powell

Placings:03   (4739)
2003/04: 16⁶G, 17³G,

	Starts	1st	2nd	3rd	Win & Pl
NH Flat	2	0	0	1	424
Career Total	2	0	0	1	424

Going:	Sf: 0-0 GS: 0-0 Gd: 0-2 GF: - Fm: 0-0

Distance: 2m/2m3: 0-2 2m4-2m7: 0-0 3m+: 0-0
Track: LH: 0-2 RH: 0-0 Tight: 0-1 Gall: 0-0
Aids: Bl: 0-0 Vi: 0-0 Tstrap: 0-0 Ckp: 0-0
Best Rating: 88   4/04   NAbb   2m1f   good   NHF

Gwen

5-y-o ch m Beveled (USA)-Taffidale (Welsh Pageant)
B L Lay B L Lay

Placings:*0-0*   (4345)
2003/04: 16⁰GS,

	Starts	1st	2nd	3rd	Win & Pl
NH Flat	1	0	0	0	0
Career Total	2	0	0	0	0

Going: Sf: 0-0 GS: 0-1 Gd: 0-0 GF: - Fm: 0-0
Distance: 2m/2m3: 0-1 2m4-2m7: 0-0 3m+: 0-0
Track: LH: 0-1 RH: 0-0 Tight: 0-0 Gall: 0-0
Aids: Bl: 0-0 Vi: 0-0 Tstrap: 0-0 Ckp: 0-0

Gwens Girl

22f

4-y-o b f Wizard King-Russian Project (IRE) (Project Manager)
M Wellings J C Bradbury

Placings:*000*   (3215)
2003/04: 14⁰G, 13⁰S, 16⁰GS,

	Starts	1st	2nd	3rd	Win & Pl
NH Flat	3	0	0	0	0
Career Total	3	0	0	0	0

Going: Sf: 0-1 GS: 0-1 Gd: 0-1 GF: - Fm: 0-0
Distance: 2m/2m3: 0-1 2m4-2m7: 0-0 3m+: 0-0
Track: LH: 0-2 RH: 0-0 Tight: 0-0 Gall: 0-0
Aids: Bl: 0-0 Vi: 0-0 Tstrap: 0-0 Ckp: 0-0
Best Rating: 22   11/03   Wwck   1m6f   good   NHF

Gwylan

9-y-o b g Crested Lark-Flopsy Mopsy (Full Of Hope)
J S King W J Lee

Placings:*0*FP0FP   (4856)
2003/04: 16⁰S, 21⁰GS, 18⁰HY, 20⁰G, 19⁰GF,

	Starts	1st	2nd	3rd	Win & Pl
Hurdles	4	0	0	0	0
Chases	1	0	0	0	0
Career Total	6	0	0	0	0

Going: Sf: 0-2 GS: 0-1 Gd: 0-1 GF: - Fm: 0-1
Distance: 2m/2m3: 0-2 2m4-2m7: 0-0 3m+: 0-0
Track: LH: 0-1 RH: 0-4 Tight: 0-2 Gall: 0-1
Aids: Bl: 0-0 Vi: 0-0 Tstrap: 0-0 Ckp: 0-0
Best Rating: 63   12/01   Ludl   2m   good   NHF

Ha Ha Ha

6-y-o b g Sure Blade (USA)-Crownego (Abednego)
K F Clutterbuck (J R Jenkins 12/9) K F Clutterbuck

Placings:*550P*   (1788)
2003/04: 17⁵GF, 20⁵GF, 17⁰GF, 24ᵖGF,

	Starts	1st	2nd	3rd	Win & Pl
NH Flat	1	0	0	0	0
Hurdles	3	0	0	0	0
Career Total	4	0	0	0	0

Going: Sf: 0-0 GS: 0-0 Gd: 0-0 GF: - Fm: 0-4
Distance: 2m/2m3: 0-2 2m4-2m7: 0-1 3m+: 0-1
Track: LH: 0-3 RH: 0-1 Tight: 0-0 Gall: 0-0
Aids: Bl: 0-0 Vi: 0-0 Tstrap: 0-0 Ckp: 0-1
Best Rating: 81   6/03   Sthl   2m1f   gd-fm   NHF

Haafel (USA)

96(98h)   (104h)**104**

7-y-o ch g Diesis-Dish Dash (Bustino)
G L Moore D R Hunnisett

Placings:*0/1P66P/U2-32*   (1210)
2003/04: 20³GF, 18²GF,

	Starts	1st	2nd	3rd	Win & Pl
Chases	2	0	1	1	1863
Career Total	10	1	2	1	5346
111	11/01	Font	2m4f		E Hdl

					G-S	£2387
					Total win prize-money £2387

Going: Sf: 0-0 GS: 0-0 Gd: 0-0 GF: - Fm: 0-2
Distance: 2m/2m3: 0-1 2m4-2m7: 0-1 3m+: 0-0
Track: LH: 0-0 RH: 0-0 Tight: 0-2 Gall: 0-0
Aids: Bl: 0-1 Vi: 0-0 Tstrap: 0-0 Ckp: 0-0
Best Rating: 111   11/01   Font   2m4f   gd-sft   Hdl

Plating-class hurdler/novice chaser; acts in soft and fast ground; stays two miles five; has worn blinkers.

Hackballs Cross (IRE)

94f   **73f**

5-y-o b m Ashkalani (IRE)-Masalika (IRE) (Kahyasi)
O Brennan G F Sheridan

Placings:*0600*   (1450)
2003/04: 17⁰G, 17⁶GF, 16⁰G, 17⁰GF,

	Starts	1st	2nd	3rd	Win & Pl
NH Flat	4	0	0	0	0
Career Total	4	0	0	0	0

Going: Sf: 0-0 GS: 0-0 Gd: 0-2 GF: - Fm: 0-2
Distance: 2m/2m3: 0-4 2m4-2m7: 0-0 3m+: 0-0
Track: LH: 0-2 RH: 0-2 Tight: 0-3 Gall: 0-0
Aids: Bl: 0-0 Vi: 0-0 Tstrap: 0-0 Ckp: 0-0
Best Rating: 73   6/03   MRas   2m1f110y   gd-fm   NHF

Hadath (IRE)

86

7-y-o br g Mujtahid (USA)-Al Sylah (Nureyev (USA))
B G Powell (R J Osborne 17/8) Seamus Mannion

Placings:*0000/5*   (2034)
2003/04: 16⁵GF,

	Starts	1st	2nd	3rd	Win & Pl
Hurdles	1	0	0	0	0
Career Total	5	0	0	0	0

Going: Sf: 0-0 GS: 0-0 Gd: 0-0 GF: - Fm: 0-0
Distance: 2m/2m3: 0-1 2m4-2m7: 0-0 3m+: 0-0
Track: LH: 0-1 RH: 0-0 Tight: 0-0 Gall: 0-0
Aids: Bl: 0-0 Vi: 0-0 Tstrap: 0-0 Ckp: 0-0
Best Rating: 86   12/01   Leop   2m   yield   Hdl

Hadaway Lad

12-y-o ch g Meadowbrook-Little Swinburn (Apollo Eight)
K Waters K Waters

Placings:*0/65P0/0-F5*   (0415)
2003/04: 25⁶G, 20⁵G,

	Starts	1st	2nd	3rd	Win & Pl
Chases	2	0	0	0	0
Career Total	8	0	0	0	0

Going: Sf: 0-0 GS: 0-0 Gd: 0-2 GF: - Fm: 0-0
Distance: 2m/2m3: 0-0 2m4-2m7: 0-1 3m+: 0-1
Track: LH: 0-2 RH: 0-0 Tight: 0-0 Gall: 0-0
Aids: Bl: 0-0 Vi: 0-0 Tstrap: 0-0 Ckp: 0-0
Best Rating: 61   5/03   Hexm   2m4f110y   good   Ch

Hadeqa

8-y-o ch g Hadeer-Heavenly Queen (Scottish Reel)
M J Brown M J Brown

Placings:*13P0/P000/0400/U*   (0269)
2003/04: 20ᵁG,

	Starts	1st	2nd	3rd	Win & Pl
Chases	1	0	0	0	0
Career Total	13	1	0	1	3183
82	7/99	MRas	2m1f110yE Hdl		G-F	£2765

					Total win prize-money £2765

Going: Sf: 0-0 GS: 0-0 Gd: 0-0 GF: - Fm: 0-0
Distance: 2m/2m3: 0-0 2m4-2m7: 0-1 3m+: 0-0
Track: LH: 0-0 RH: 0-1 Tight: 0-0 Gall: 0-0
Aids: Bl: 0-0 Vi: 0-0 Tstrap: 0-0 Ckp: 0-0
Best Rating: 82   8/99   NAbb   2m1f   gd-sft   Hdl

Hades De Sienne (FR)

106   (76h)**105**

9-y-o b g Concorde Jr (USA)-Aube De Sienne (FR) (Cupids Dew)
A Parker Mr & Mrs Raymond Anderson Green

Placings:PF454/22P13/4232F2/6P022-0P2U3033   (4432)
2003/04: 22⁰G, 24ᵖG, 28²G, 30⁴G, 25³S, 20ᴾHY, 28³G, 32³G,

	Starts	1st	2nd	3rd	Win & Pl
Chases	8	0	1	3	3987
Career Total	29	1	8	5	27444
94	1/01	Ayr	3m1f	E(0-105)HCh	SFT	£3256

					Total win prize-money £3257

Going: Sf: 0-2 GS: 0-0 Gd: 0-6 GF: - Fm: 0-0
Distance: 2m/2m3: 0-0 2m4-2m7: 0-2 3m+: 0-6
Track: LH: 0-5 RH: 0-3 Tight: 0-3 Gall: 0-1
Aids: Bl: 0-0 Vi: 0-0 Tstrap: 0-0 Ckp: 0-3
Best Rating: 105   2/04   Carl   3m4f   good   Ch

Modest, consistent handicap chaser; stays four miles; acts on good and soft ground.

Haditovski

104(114h)   (131h)**116**

8-y-o b g Hatim (USA)-Grand Occasion (Great Nephew)
J Mackie Mrs Sue Adams

Placings:U641005662/20111140303126/220153206/52405-61P1F4   (4568)
2003/04: 16⁶GS, 17¹G, 16ᴾHY, 16¹G, 16ᶠGS, 20⁴GS,

	Starts	1st	2nd	3rd	Win & Pl
Chases	6	2	0	0	10380
Career Total	44	9	7	3	57731
80	3/04	Hntg	2m110y	D HCh		GD	£5768
114	12/03	MRas	2m1f110yE	Ch		GD	£3799
131	12/01	Uttx	2m	C(0-130)HHdl		SFT	£4992
122	3/01	Newb	2m110y	C(0-130)HHdl		HVY	£5902
129	11/00	Uttx	2m110y	D(0-120)HHdl		G-S	£7117
120	11/00	Weth	2m	D(0-125)HHdl		HVY	£3601
110	11/00	Uttx	2m	F(0-100)HHdl		HVY	£2324
115	10/00	Sthl	2m	F(0-105)HHdl		SFT	£1808
111	11/99	Uttx	2m	E Hdl		SFT	£2337
				Total win prize-money £37650			

Going: Sf: 0-1 GS: 0-3 Gd: 2-2 GF: - Fm: 0-0
Distance: 2m/2m3: 2-5 2m4-2m7: 0-1 3m+: 0-0
Track: LH: 0-4 RH: 2-2 Tight: 1-2 Gall: 1-1
Aids: Bl: 0-0 Vi: 2-6 Tstrap: 0-0 Ckp: 0-0
Best Rating: 131 3/02 Newb 2m110y soft Hdl

Fair novice chaser/useful handicap hurdler; jumped well to win his second start over fences at Market Rasen in December; suited by around two miles and a soft surface; usually races prominently; regularly visored.

Haikal

(101h)   (84h)
7-y-o b g Owington-Magic Milly (Simply Great (FR))
R H Buckler (E W Tuer 2/5) The Crop Circle

Placings:P45/52430021P/44600-0224P422330   (4790)
2003/04: 17⁰G, 19²G, 22²GF, 24⁴GF, 22⁶F, 19⁴GF, 22²GF, 16²S, 17³GS, 24³G, 21⁰G,

	Starts	1st	2nd	3rd	Win & Pl
Hurdles	11	0	4	2	4274
Career Total	28	1	6	3	9628
88	4/02	Carl	2m4f	E(0-110)HHdl	GD	£2982
				Total win prize-money £2982		

Going: Sf: 0-1 GS: 0-1 Gd: 0-2 GF: - Fm: 0-7
Distance: 2m/2m3: 0-5 2m4-2m7: 0-4 3m+: 0-2
Track: LH: 0-6 RH: 0-4 Tight: 0-6 Gall: 0-0
Aids: Bl: 0-0 Vi: 0-0 Tstrap: 0-0 Ckp: 0-0
Best Rating: 93 2/01 Muss 2m good Hdl

Plating-class hurdler; stays 2m 4f but does not seem to quite get 3m; acts on any ground.

Hail Stone (IRE)

9-y-o b g Glacial Storm (USA)-Rockmount (IRE) (Cidrax (FR))
Miss K A Williams Miss K A Williams

Placings:0000P0/00-F   (4815)
2003/04: 24⁴G,

	Starts	1st	2nd	3rd	Win & Pl
Chases	1	0	0	0	
Career Total	9	0	0	0	

Going: Sf: 0-0 GS: 0-0 Gd: 0-1 GF: - Fm: 0-0
Distance: 2m/2m3: 0-0 2m4-2m7: 0-0 3m+: 0-1
Track: LH: 0-1 RH: 0-0 Tight: 0-0 Gall: 0-0
Aids: Bl: 0-0 Vi: 0-0 Tstrap: 0-0 Ckp: 0-1
Best Rating: 85 12/00 Thur 2m sft-hvy Hdl

Hail The King (USA)
99   95
4-y-o gr g Allied Forces (USA)-Hail Kris (USA) (Kris S (USA))
R M Carson (R M Beckett 9/10) Mrs P Carson

Placings:40P03   (4788)
2003/04: 16⁴GF, 16⁰G, 16ᴾG, 16⁰G, 16³G,

	Starts	1st	2nd	3rd	Win & Pl
Hurdles	5	0	0	1	524
Career Total	5	0	0	1	524

Going: Sf: 0-0 GS: 0-0 Gd: 0-4 GF: - Fm: 0-1
Distance: 2m/2m3: 0-5 2m4-2m7: 0-0 3m+: 0-0
Track: LH: 0-2 RH: 0-3 Tight: 0-1 Gall: 0-1
Aids: Bl: 0-0 Vi: 0-0 Tstrap: 0-0 Ckp: 0-0
Best Rating: 95 4/04 Plum 2m good Hdl

Moderate hurdler; finished up wearing headgear on the Flat; modest form to date over hurdles on good/good to firm.

Haile Selassie
95   97+
4-y-o b g Awesome-Lady Of The Realm (Prince Daniel (USA))
W Jenks (B W Hills 22/9) Michael Stoddart

Placings:064   (4504)
2003/04: 16⁰G, 17⁵G, 17⁴G,

	Starts	1st	2nd	3rd	Win & Pl
Hurdles	3	0	0	0	267
Career Total	3	0	0	0	267

Going: Sf: 0-1 GS: 0-0 Gd: 0-0 GF: - Fm: 0-0
Distance: 2m/2m3: 0-3 2m4-2m7: 0-0 3m+: 0-0
Track: LH: 0-2 RH: 0-1 Tight: 0-1 Gall: 0-1
Aids: Bl: 0-0 Vi: 0-0 Tstrap: 0-0 Ckp: 0-0
Best Rating: 97 3/04 Hrfd 2m1f good Hdl

Modest hurdler; moderate performer on the Flat; stayed a mile and a half; acts on good ground.

Hailstorm (IRE)
98   91
11-y-o ch g Glacial Storm (USA)-Sindys Gale (Strong Gale)
Miss Lucinda V Russell Peter K Dale Ltd

Placings:064222100/4/6422/6P02143/1UFPP60/03232C6P 060-3UP   (1028)
2003/04: 25⁰G, 25³G, 23ᵁG, 25ᴾGF,

	Starts	1st	2nd	3rd	Win & Pl
Chases	4	0	0	1	497
Career Total	42	3	8	4	21043
95	9/01	MRas	2m4f	D(0-120)HCh	G-F	£4478
98	12/00	Ayr	2m5f110yD(0-110)HCh		SFT	£4046
111	2/98	Ludl	2m5f110yE Hdl		GD	£2500
				Total win prize-money £11025		

Going: Sf: 0-0 GS: 0-0 Gd: 3 GF: - Fm: 0-1
Distance: 2m/2m3: 0-0 2m4-2m7: 0-0 3m+: 0-4
Track: LH: 0-3 RH: 0-1 Tight: 0-1 Gall: 0-0
Aids: Bl: 0-0 Vi: 0-0 Tstrap: 0-0 Ckp: 0-0
Best Rating: 119 12/97 Strf 2m110y soft Hdl

Plating-chaser; suited by a sound surface; probably needs further than two and a half miles.

Hakam (USA)
78   57
5-y-o ch g Woodman (USA)-Haniya (IRE) (Caerleon (USA))
John Berry The Premier Cru 2

Placings:0   (0680)
2003/04: 16⁰GF,

	Starts	1st	2nd	3rd	Win & Pl
Hurdles	1	0	0	0	

Career Total	1	0	0	0

Going: Sf: 0-0 GS: 0-0 Gd: 0-0 GF: - Fm: 0-1
Distance: 2m/2m3: 0-1 2m4-2m7: 0-0 3m+: 0-0
Track: LH: 0-1 RH: 0-0 Tight: 0-0 Gall: 0-0
Aids: Bl: 0-0 Vi: 0-0 Tstrap: 0-0 Ckp: 0-0
Best Rating: 63 6/03 Worc 2m gd-fm Hdl

Hakim (NZ)
100(107h)   (98h)98
10-y-o ch g Half Iced (USA)-Topitup (NZ) (Little Brown Jug (NZ))
J L Spearing T N Siviter

Placings:2/P350235-31   (1105)
2003/04: 20³G, 17¹GS,

	Starts	1st	2nd	3rd	Win & Pl
Chases	2	1	1	0	4455
Career Total	10	1	2	3	7499
98	8/03	Sthl	2m1f	E(0-100)HCh	G-S	£3822
				Total win prize-money £3822		

Going: Sf: 0-0 GS: 1-1 Gd: 0-1 GF: - Fm: 0-0
Distance: 2m/2m3: 1-1 2m4-2m7: 0-1 3m+: 0-0
Track: LH: 1-2 RH: 0-0 Tight: 0-0 Gall: 0-0
Aids: Bl: 0-0 Vi: 0-0 Tstrap: 0-0 Ckp: 0-0
Best Rating: 98 8/03 Sthl 2m1f gd-sft Ch

Modest chaser; Flat winner in New Zealand; keen sort; effective at 2m; acts on soft.

Hale Bopp (GER)
82   117+
7-y-o b h Monsun (GER)-Heatherland (FR) (Be My Guest (USA))
Frau E Mader G K Stadtwald

Placings:F412-30   (2486)
2003/04: 21³S, 16⁰GS,

	Starts	1st	2nd	3rd	Win & Pl
Hurdles	2	0	0	1	1948
Career Total	6	1	1	1	7224
117	2/03	Folk	2m1f110yE Hdl	HVY	£3612
				Total win prize-money £3612		

Going: Sf: 0-1 GS: 0-1 Gd: 0-0 GF: - Fm: 0-0
Distance: 2m/2m3: 0-1 2m4-2m7: 0-1 3m+: 0-0
Track: LH: 0-1 RH: 0-0 Tight: 0-0 Gall: 0-1
Aids: Bl: 0-0 Vi: 0-0 Tstrap: 0-0 Ckp: 0-0
Best Rating: 117 2/03 Folk 2m1f110y heavy Hdl

Fair German-trained hurdler; acts in heavy ground; effective at around two miles.

Halexy (FR)
105   133
9-y-o b g Iron Duke (FR)-Tartifume Ii (FR) (Mistigri)
Jonjo O'Neill Sir Robert Ogden

Placings:10116/4144/P/11U0-5   (1885)
2003/04: 20⁵G,

	Starts	1st	2nd	3rd	Win & Pl
Chases	1	0	0	0	0
Career Total	15	6	0	0	33041
133	11/02	Chel	2m4f110yD(0-125)HCh	G-S	£12876
129	10/02	Chep	2m3f110yD(0-125)HCh	GD	£6711
128	12/00	Sthl	3m110y	E Ch	SFT	£2866
119	2/00	MRas	2m3f110yD Hdl	G-S	£3282
128	1/00	Hayd	2m	D Hdl	SFT	£3266
110	11/99	NAbb	2m1f	H NHF	SFT	£1565
				Total win prize-money £30568		

Career Total 1 0 0 0

Going: Sf: 0-0 GS: 0-0 Gd: 0-1 GF: - Fm: 0-0
Distance: 2m/2m3: 0-0 2m4-2m7: 0-1 3m+: 0-0
Track: LH: 0-1 RH: 0-0 Tight: 0-0 Gall: 0-0
Aids: Bl: 0-0 Vi: 0-0 Tstrap: 0-0 Ckp: 0-0
Best Rating: 133 11/02 Chel 2m4f110y gd-sft Ch

Useful handicap chaser; bounced back from injury with an easy win at Chepstow in October 2002; but lightly raced in 2003 and has obviously had his problems; can go well fresh; acts well on soft, but handles good; stays three miles, but better at shorter.

Half An Hour

83(103h)   (109h)**86**
7-y-o b g Alflora (IRE)-Country Mistress (Town And Country)
A King C W Lane

Placings:136/04410-P00   (3318)
2003/04: 20⁵GS, 22⁵GS, 23⁶G,

	Starts	1st	2nd	3rd	Win & Pl
Chases	3	0	0	0	
Career Total	11	2	0	1	9788
109	3/03	Hayd	2m6f	D Hdl		G-F	£5031
114	1/02	Hayd	2m	H NHF		SFT	£2338
				Total win prize-money £7369			

Going: Sf: 0-0 GS: 0-2 Gd: 0-1 GF: - Fm: 0-0
Distance: 2m/2m3: 0-0 2m4-2m7: 0-2 3m+: 0-1
Track: LH: 0-2 RH: 0-1 Tight: 0-0 Gall: 0-2
Aids: Bl: 0-0 Vi: 0-0 Tstrap: 0-0 Ckp: 0-0
Best Rating: 114 2/02 Wwck 2m soft NHF

Hall's Mill (IRE)

15-y-o ch g Buckskin (FR)-Grainne Geal (General Ironside)
Miss S Waugh Rupert C Irving

Placings:6/U/U23/456/1/F/3-1   (0031)
2003/04: 21¹G,

	Starts	1st	2nd	3rd	Win & Pl
Chases	1	1	0	0	3851
Career Total	12	2	1	2	7383
101	4/03	Chel	2m5f	H Ch		GD	£3851
101	5/00	Chel	2m5f	H Ch		GD	£2262
				Total win prize-money £6113			

Going: Sf: 0-0 GS: 0-0 Gd: 1-1 GF: - Fm: 0-0
Distance: 2m/2m3: 0-0 2m4-2m7: 1-1 3m+: 0-0
Track: LH: 1-1 RH: 0-0 Tight: 0-0 Gall: 1-1
Aids: Bl: 0-0 Vi: 0-0 Tstrap: 0-0 Ckp: 0-0
Best Rating: 109 5/98 Chep 3m good Ch

Winning pointer/hunter chaser, acted on most ground bar extremes of going; reportedly retired.

Halland

86   **98**
6-y-o ch g Halling (USA)-Northshiel (Northfields (USA))
N P Littmoden The Headquarters Partnership Ltd

Placings:2   (4630)
2003/04: 17²G,

	Starts	1st	2nd	3rd	Win & Pl
Hurdles	1	0	1	0	1144
Career Total	1	0	1	0	1144

Going: Sf: 0-0 GS: 0-0 Gd: 0-1 GF: - Fm: 0-0
Distance: 2m/2m3: 0-1 2m4-2m7: 0-0 3m+: 0-0
Track: LH: 0-0 RH: 0-1 Tight: 0-0 Gall: 0-0
Aids: Bl: 0-0 Vi: 0-0 Tstrap: 0-0 Ckp: 0-0

Best Rating: 98 4/04 Tntn 2m1f good Hdl

Fair effort on his hurdling debut.

Hallem Hall

7-y-o ch g Little Wolf-Oneninefive (Sayyaf)
Mrs E B Scott Mrs E B Scott

Placings:0   (2984)
2003/04: 16⁰S,

	Starts	1st	2nd	3rd	Win & Pl
NH Flat	1	0	0	0	
Career Total	1	0	0	0	

Going: Sf: 0-1 GS: 0-0 Gd: 0-0 GF: - Fm: 0-0
Distance: 2m/2m3: 0-1 2m4-2m7: 0-0 3m+: 0-0
Track: LH: 0-1 RH: 0-0 Tight: 0-0 Gall: 0-0
Aids: Bl: 0-0 Vi: 0-0 Tstrap: 0-0 Ckp: 0-0

Hallrule (IRE)

101   **83+**
10-y-o ch g Be My Native (USA)-Phantom Thistle (Deep Run)
Miss P Robson (Mrs J K M Oliver 5/6) Raymond Anderson Green

Placings:F0P/04/5/P-PP11   (4882)
2003/04: 16⁶G, 25⁹G, 24⁴GF, 25¹S, 26¹GS,

	Starts	1st	2nd	3rd	Win & Pl
Chases	5	2	0	0	7181
Career Total	11	2	0	0	7443
83	4/04	Carl	3m2f	F(0-95)HCh		G-S	£4563
76	4/04	Hexm	3m1f	G(0-90)HCh		SFT	£2618
				Total win prize-money £7181			

Going: Sf: 1-1 GS: 1-1 Gd: 0-2 GF: - Fm: 0-1
Distance: 2m/2m3: 0-1 2m4-2m7: 0-0 3m+: 2-4
Track: LH: 1-3 RH: 1-2 Tight: 0-0 Gall: 0-0
Aids: Bl: 0-0 Vi: 2-2 Tstrap: 0-0 Ckp: 0-0
Best Rating: 83 4/04 Carl 3m2f gd-sft Ch

Winning pointer who opened account wearing first time visor in selling handicap chase over three miles and one furlong at Hexham on soft ground in April 2004 followed up at Carlisle later in month; does not look entirely straightforward.

Hallyards Gael (IRE)

105(111h)   (116+h)**130**
10-y-o br g Strong Gale-Secret Ocean (Most Secret)
L Lungo G M Mair

Placings:4/411/32323/31P311-U1213   (2142)
2003/04: 25¹⁰G, 24¹G, 24²G, 22¹G, 20³G,

	Starts	1st	2nd	3rd	Win & Pl
Hurdles	2	1	1	0	4625
Chases	3	1	0	1	9155
Career Total	20	7	3	6	48281
116	11/03	Kels	2m6f110yD(0-125)HHdl		GD	£3360
130	5/03	Prth	3m	D(0-115)HCh		GD	£8320
	4/03	Carl	3m	D Ch		G-F	£10800
124	3/03	Carl	2m4f	D Ch		GD	£7085
116	5/02	Weth	2m4f110yD Ch		G-S	£4256
116	10/00	Kels	2m110y E Hdl		G-S	£2506
96	6/00	Prth	2m110y D Hdl		GD	£3435
				Total win prize-money £39762			

Going: Sf: 0-0 GS: 0-0 Gd: 2-5 GF: - Fm: 0-0
Distance: 2m/2m3: 0-0 2m4-2m7: 1-2 3m+: 1-3
Track: LH: 1-3 RH: 1-2 Tight: 1-2 Gall: 0-0

Aids: Bl: 0-0 Vi: 0-0 Tstrap: 0-0 Ckp: 2-4
Best Rating: 130 5/03 Prth 3m good Ch

Fair chaser/hurdler; has had various problems; stays three miles; acts on good ground.

Ham Stone

76   **52**
6-y-o b g Picea-Blushing Belle (Local Suitor (USA))
B J M Ryall B J M Ryall

Placings:0/00   (3053)
2003/04: 19³G, 19⁰G,

	Starts	1st	2nd	3rd	Win & Pl
Hurdles	2	0	0	0	
Career Total	3	0	0	0	

Going: Sf: 0-0 GS: 0-0 Gd: 0-2 GF: - Fm: 0-0
Distance: 2m/2m3: 0-1 2m4-2m7: 0-1 3m+: 0-0
Track: LH: 0-0 RH: 0-2 Tight: 0-1 Gall: 0-0
Aids: Bl: 0-0 Vi: 0-0 Tstrap: 0-0 Ckp: 0-0
Best Rating: 52 12/03 Extr 2m3f good Hdl

Hamadeenah

105   **99**
6-y-o ch m Alhijaz-Mahbob Dancer (FR) (Groom Dancer (USA))
D McCain Mrs N L Spence

Placings:5416/55514152-4244   (1171)
2003/04: 16⁶G, 17²GF, 174⁵GS, 18⁴GF,

	Starts	1st	2nd	3rd	Win & Pl
Hurdles	4	0	1	0	1700
Career Total	16	3	2	0	11609
87	3/03	Ludl	2m	F Hdl		G-F	£3010
83	9/02	Uttx	2m	G Hdl		GD	£2058
93	3/02	Hntg	2m110y	E Hdl		G-F	£2758
				Total win prize-money £7826			

Going: Sf: 0-0 GS: 0-1 Gd: 0-1 GF: - Fm: 0-2
Distance: 2m/2m3: 0-4 2m4-2m7: 0-0 3m+: 0-0
Track: LH: 0-3 RH: 0-1 Tight: 0-1 Gall: 0-0
Aids: Bl: 0-0 Vi: 0-0 Tstrap: 0-0 Ckp: 0-0
Best Rating: 99 4/03 Sedg 2m1f gd-fm Hdl

Plating-class hurdler; effective at around two miles and acts on a sound surface; likes to race prominently.

Hambleton Jo

69   **49**
4-y-o ch g Bijou D'Inde-Elegant Rose (Noalto)
F P Murtagh Three J's Racing

Placings:60P00   (4795)
2003/04: 16⁶G, 16⁰G, 20⁰G, 17⁰G, 17⁰G,

	Starts	1st	2nd	3rd	Win & Pl
Hurdles	5	0	0	0	
Career Total	5	0	0	0	

Going: Sf: 0-0 GS: 0-0 Gd: 0-5 GF: - Fm: 0-0
Distance: 2m/2m3: 0-4 2m4-2m7: 0-1 3m+: 0-0
Track: LH: 0-2 RH: 0-3 Tight: 0-3 Gall: 0-0
Aids: Bl: 0-0 Vi: 0-0 Tstrap: 0-0 Ckp: 0-0
Best Rating: 47 4/04 Carl 2m1f good Hdl

Hamish G

90   **70**
7-y-o ch g Sure Blade (USA)-Horton Line (High Line)

John Berry W Ginzel

Placings:06					(0234)
2003/04: 16ᴰGS, 17ᴿGF,					

	Starts	1st	2nd	3rd	Win & Pl
Hurdles	2	0	0	0	0
Career Total	2	0	0	0	0

Going:	Sf: 0-0 GS: 0-1 Gd: 0-0 GF: - Fm: 0-1
Distance:	2m/2m3: 0-2 2m4-2m7: 0-0 3m+: 0-0
Track:	LH: 0-1 RH: 0-1 Tight: 0-0 Gall: 0-0
Aids:	Bl: 0-0 Vi: 0-0 Tstrap: 0-0 Ckp: 0-0
Best Rating:	70 5/03 Hrfd 2m1f gd-fm Hdl

Hammock (IRE)
60

6-y-o b/br g Hamas (IRE)-Sure Victory (IRE) (Stalker)
M J Gingell A White

Placings:P00-P					(1676)
2003/04: 19ᴾF,					

	Starts	1st	2nd	3rd	Win & Pl
Hurdles	1	0	0	0	
Career Total	4	0	0	0	

Going:	Sf: 0-0 GS: 0-0 Gd: 0-0 GF: - Fm: 0-1
Distance:	2m/2m3: 0-0 2m4-2m7: 0-1 3m+: 0-0
Track:	LH: 0-0 RH: 0-0 Tight: 0-0 Gall: 0-0
Aids:	Bl: 0-0 Vi: 0-0 Tstrap: 0-0 Ckp: 0-1
Best Rating:	60 3/03 Fknm 2m good Hdl

Hanbrin Rose
95(99h)   (80h)**79**

7-y-o gr m Lancastrian-Rymolbreese (Rymer)
R Dickin John Hanley John Brindley

Placings:03-0300065P5					(4855)
2003/04: 22ᴰG, 20ᴿGF, 17ᴰG, 19ᴰG, 16ᴰGS, 16ᴿG, 20ᴿGF, 20ᴾGS, 24⁵GF,					

	Starts	1st	2nd	3rd	Win & Pl
Hurdles	5	0	0	1	595
Chases	4	0	0	0	0
Career Total	11	0	0	2	1025

Going:	Sf: 0-0 GS: 0-2 Gd: 0-4 GF: - Fm: 0-3
Distance:	2m/2m3: 0-4 2m4-2m7: 0-4 3m+: 0-1
Track:	LH: 0-6 RH: 0-0 Tight: 0-2 Gall: 0-0
Aids:	Bl: 0-0 Vi: 0-0 Tstrap: 0-0 Ckp: 0-0
Best Rating:	80 4/03 Strf 2m3f gd-fm Hdl

Modest third in low grade 2m 3f maiden on hurdling debut at Stratford April 2003.

Hand Inn Hand
112(110h)   (136+h)**165**

8-y-o b g Alflora (IRE)-Deep Line (Deep Run)
H D Daly Patrick Burling Developments Ltd

Placings:141/015:311115-3B2F143					(4624)
2003/04: 20³GS, 20ᴮGS, 20²G, 21ᶠGS, 19¹S, 20⁴G, 25³G,					

	Starts	1st	2nd	3rd	Win & Pl
Hurdles	1	0	0	1	1980
Chases	6	1	1	1	84769
Career Total	19	8	1	3	149690
165	1/04	Asct	2m3f110yA Ch		SFT £59500
152	2/03	Kemp	2m4f110yA Ch		GD £20300
153	2/03	Uttx	2m	C Ch	HVY £10251
145	12/02	Hayd	2m4f	C Ch	SFT £7722

133	12/02	Chep	2m3f110yD Ch	SFT	£4784
133	2/02	Asct	2m110y D(0-120)HHdl	SFT	£4836
124	3/01	MRas	2m1f110yD Hdl	G-S	£3822
118	1/01	Tntn	2m3f110yD Hdl	SFT	£3626
			Total win prize-money		£114841

Going:	Sf: 1-1 GS: 0-3 Gd: 0-3 GF: - Fm: 0-0
Distance:	2m/2m3: 0-0 2m4-2m7: 1-6 3m+: 0-1
Track:	LH: 0-5 RH: 1-2 Tight: 0-2 Gall: 0-3
Aids:	Bl: 0-0 Vi: 0-0 Tstrap: 0-0 Ckp: 0-0
Best Rating:	165 4/04 Aint 3m1f good Ch

High-class chaser; winner of the Grade One Ascot Chase in 2004; has been let down by his jumping on occasions; effective from 2 to 3m but possibly best over two and a half; third in the Martell Cup over three miles at Aintree; suited by cut in the ground, but handles good; usually held up.

Handa Island (USA)
62

5-y-o br g Pleasant Colony (USA)-Remote (USA) (Seattle Slew (USA))
C J Mann Lee Bolingbroke & Partners I

Placings:5					(2715)
2003/04: 19⁵GS,					

	Starts	1st	2nd	3rd	Win & Pl
Hurdles	1	0	0	0	0
Career Total	1	0	0	0	0

Going:	Sf: 0-0 GS: 0-1 Gd: 0-0 GF: - Fm: 0-0
Distance:	2m/2m3: 0-0 2m4-2m7: 0-1 3m+: 0-0
Track:	LH: 0-1 RH: 0-0 Tight: 0-0 Gall: 0-0
Aids:	Bl: 0-0 Vi: 0-0 Tstrap: 0-0 Ckp: 0-0
Best Rating:	62 12/03 Donc 2m3f110y gd-sft Hdl

Handshake
85   **50**

4-y-o ch g Most Welcome-Lady Day (FR) (Lightning (FR))
W McKeown Christy Partnership

Placings:0P					(2460)
2003/04: 16ᴰG, 16ᴾG,					

	Starts	1st	2nd	3rd	Win & Pl
Hurdles	2	0	0	0	
Career Total	2	0	0	0	

Going:	Sf: 0-0 GS: 0-0 Gd: 0-2 GF: - Fm: 0-0
Distance:	2m/2m3: 0-2 2m4-2m7: 0-0 3m+: 0-0
Track:	LH: 0-2 RH: 0-0 Tight: 0-0 Gall: 0-0
Aids:	Bl: 0-0 Vi: 0-0 Tstrap: 0-0 Ckp: 0-0
Best Rating:	50 11/03 Newc 2m good Hdl

Handy Boy

9-y-o b g Arzanni-Handymouse (Nearly A Hand)
M J Jackson R M Phillips

Placings:6/F					(3785)
2003/04: 24ᶠS,					

	Starts	1st	2nd	3rd	Win & Pl
Chases	1	0	0	0	
Career Total	2	0	0	0	0

Going:	Sf: 0-1 GS: 0-0 Gd: 0-0 GF: - Fm: 0-0
Distance:	2m/2m3: 0-0 2m4-2m7: 0-0 3m+: 0-1
Track:	LH: 0-0 RH: 0-1 Tight: 0-0 Gall: 0-1
Aids:	Bl: 0-0 Vi: 0-0 Tstrap: 0-0 Ckp: 0-0

Best Rating:	90 6/01 NAbb 2m1f good NHF

Handy Money
101   **122+**

7-y-o b g Imperial Frontier (USA)-Cryptic Gold (Glint Of Gold)
M J Ryan William Dixon

Placings:000/4325214-10					(1868)
2003/04: 19¹G, 16ᴰGF,					

	Starts	1st	2nd	3rd	Win & Pl
Hurdles	2	1	0	0	7670
Career Total	12	2	2	1	17408
122	5/03	MRas	2m3f110yC(0-135)HHdl	GD	£7670
103	2/03	Donc	2m3f110yE Hdl	G-S	£3718
			Total win prize-money		£11388

Going:	Sf: 0-0 GS: 0-0 Gd: 1-1 GF: - Fm: 0-1
Distance:	2m/2m3: 0-0 2m4-2m7: 1-1 3m+: 0-0
Track:	LH: 0-0 RH: 1-2 Tight: 1-1 Gall: 0-0
Aids:	Bl: 0-0 Vi: 0-0 Tstrap: 0-0 Ckp: 0-0
Best Rating:	122 5/03 MRas 2m3f110y good Hdl

Fair hurdler; finally got off the mark at Doncaster in February 2003; acts on soft; stays nearly two and a half miles.

Handyman (IRE)
102   **128**

10-y-o b g Hollow Hand-Shady Ahan (Mon Capitaine)
P J Hobbs Elizabeth Hodgson And Denise Winton

Placings:2/2421/U12P36/126U22/12F3P3-230					(2814)
2003/04: 23²G, 22³GS, 25ᴿG,					

	Starts	1st	2nd	3rd	Win & Pl
Chases	3	0	1	1	3489
Career Total	26	4	9	4	39206
123	5/02	Extr	2m7f110yC(0-135)HCh	GD	£6916
127	10/01	Extr	3m1f110yF(0-105)HCh	G-S	£3024
127	11/00	Uttx	3m	D Ch	HVY	£3740
106	3/00	NAbb	2m6f	E Hdl	GD	£2359
			Total win prize-money		£16040

Going:	Sf: 0-0 GS: 0-1 Gd: 0-2 GF: - Fm: 0-0
Distance:	2m/2m3: 0-0 2m4-2m7: 0-1 3m+: 0-2
Track:	LH: 0-1 RH: 0-2 Tight: 0-0 Gall: 0-1
Aids:	Bl: 0-0 Vi: 0-0 Tstrap: 0-0 Ckp: 0-0
Best Rating:	128 11/03 Extr 2m7f110y good Ch

Useful handicap chaser; suited by three miles plus; acts on good and soft ground.

Hank Dandy

7-y-o ch m Bandmaster (USA)-Junior Lancaster (Dubassoff (USA))
Mrs G Harvey Brian Hurst

Placings:5P					(2228)
2003/04: 16⁵GF, 21ᴾGS,					

	Starts	1st	2nd	3rd	Win & Pl
NH Flat	1	0	0	0	0
Hurdles	1	0	0	0	0
Career Total	2	0	0	0	0

Going:	Sf: 0-0 GS: 0-1 Gd: 0-0 GF: - Fm: 0-1
Distance:	2m/2m3: 0-1 2m4-2m7: 0-1 3m+: 0-0
Track:	LH: 0-1 RH: 0-1 Tight: 0-0 Gall: 0-0
Aids:	Bl: 0-0 Vi: 0-0 Tstrap: 0-0 Ckp: 0-0

Hanley (IRE)

86

8-y-o b g Lashkari-Midnight Gale (IRE) (Tumble Wind (USA))
B N Pollock (D T Hughes 3/6) Mrs K Lloyd Mrs L Pollock L Stilwell

Placings:*0/305600-0PP*   (1215)
2003/04: 16⁰HY, 22²GF, 20⁰GF,

	Starts	1st	2nd	3rd	Win & Pl
NH Flat	1	0	0	0	0
Hurdles	2	0	0	0	0
Career Total	10	0	0	1	344

Going:	Sf: 0-1 GS: 0-0 Gd: 0-0 GF: - Fm: 0-2
Distance:	2m/2m3: 0-2 2m4-2m7: 0-2 3m+: 0-0
Track:	LH: 0-1 RH: 0-1 Tight: 0-1 Gall: 0-1
Aids:	Bl: 0-0 Vi: 0-0 Tstrap: 0-1 Ckp: 0-0
Best Rating:	91 7/02 Wxfd 2m gd-fm NHF

Hanover Square

102(104c)   (106c)**93**

8-y-o b g Le Moss-Hilly-Down Lass (Deep Run)
N A Twiston-Davies The Oriental Partnership Iii

Placings:*60/U20P/253P44-U5PP*333102   (4592)
2003/04: 24ᵁG, 25⁵GF, 28PGS, 25PG, 24⁹GS, 24⁹S, 26¹GS, 24⁰GS, 26²G,

	Starts	1st	2nd	3rd	Win & Pl
Hurdles	6	1	1	3	6467
Chases	4	0	0	0	0
Career Total	22	1	3	4	11812
93 2/04 Hntg 3m2f		E(0-110)HHdl G-S			£4258

Total win prize-money £4259

Going:	Sf: 0-1 GS: 1-5 Gd: 0-3 GF: - Fm: 0-1
Distance:	2m/2m3: 0-0 2m4-2m7: 0-0 3m+: 1-10
Track:	LH: 0-3 RH: 1-7 Tight: 0-2 Gall: 1-3
Aids:	Bl: 0-0 Vi: 0-0 Tstrap: 0-0 Ckp: 0-0
Best Rating:	106 11/02 Tntn 3m3f gd-sft Ch

Moderate hurdler/chaser; acts on good to soft; stays three miles.

Happicat (IRE)

(107h)   (119h)**81+**

9-y-o gr g Cataldi-Gladonia (Godswalk (USA))
P R Webber D A Beaumont

Placings:*O6/0P00/23552/122120/0660-PP*   (0746)
2003/04: 19PG, 16PG,

	Starts	1st	2nd	3rd	Win & Pl
Hurdles	2	0	0	0	
Career Total	23	2	5	1	12598
115 7/01 Strf	2m110y	C(0-130)HHdl	G-F		£4888
99 5/01 Hrfd	2m1f	D(0-110)HHdl	GD		£3150

Total win prize-money £8038

Going:	Sf: 0-0 GS: 0-0 Gd: 0-2 GF: - Fm: 0-0
Distance:	2m/2m3: 0-1 2m4-2m7: 0-1 3m+: 0-0
Track:	LH: 0-1 RH: 0-1 Tight: 0-2 Gall: 0-0
Aids:	Bl: 0-0 Vi: 0-0 Tstrap: 0-0 Ckp: 0-0
Best Rating:	119 5/02 Hayd 2m good Hdl

Fair hurdler who goes well on fast ground and a tight track. Has won on a right-handed track but apparently prefers to go in the other direction.

Happy Change (GER)

104   (86h)**93**

10-y-o ch g Surumu (GER)-Happy Gini (USA) (Ginistrelli (USA))
Ian Williams Favourites Racing

Placings:*1/0/0/332PP-26P0*   (0819)
2003/04: 19²G, 21⁶GF, 21PGS, 22⁹G,

	Starts	1st	2nd	3rd	Win & Pl
Chases	4	0	1	0	1056
Career Total	12	1	2	2	7833
117 10/99 Uttx	2m	D Hdl	G-S		£3631

Total win prize-money £3631

Going:	Sf: 0-0 GS: 0-1 Gd: 0-2 GF: - Fm: 0-1
Distance:	2m/2m3: 0-0 2m4-2m7: 0-4 3m+: 0-0
Track:	LH: 0-2 RH: 0-2 Tight: 0-3 Gall: 0-0
Aids:	Bl: 0-0 Vi: 0-0 Tstrap: 0-0 Ckp: 0-0
Best Rating:	117 10/99 Uttx 2m gd-sft Hdl

Moderate novice chaser; placed in a Group One on the Flat; has been a long way off that form in recent years; possibly unsuited by really soft ground.

Happy Days

90   **83**

9-y-o b g Primitive Rising (USA)-Miami Dolphin (Derrylin)
James Moffatt C Lewis

Placings:*050F333/30/45/64005/40PB22-40*   (1184)
2003/04: 20²G, 22⁴G, 22⁰G,

	Starts	1st	2nd	3rd	Win & Pl
Hurdles	3	0	1	0	732
Career Total	24	0	2	4	2896

Going:	Sf: 0-0 GS: 0-0 Gd: 0-3 GF: - Fm: 0-0
Distance:	2m/2m3: 0-0 2m4-2m7: 0-3 3m+: 0-0
Track:	LH: 0-3 RH: 0-0 Tight: 0-2 Gall: 0-0
Aids:	Bl: 0-0 Vi: 0-0 Tstrap: 0-0 Ckp: 0-0
Best Rating:	92 3/99 Kels 2m110y soft Hdl

Plating-class novice hurdler.

Happy Hussar (IRE)

112(89c)   (88c)**95**

11-y-o b g Balinger-Merry Mirth (Menelek)
Dr P Pritchard Dr J J Kabler

Placings:*f30P/U03PBP/02P5U/2401343546604/33P*22031 254-6652P10003300   (4749)
2003/04: 27⁶G, 27⁶GF, 16⁵GF, 26²GF, 26PGF, 19¹GF, 24⁰G, 24⁰GS, 25⁰G, 22³G, 19³S, 20⁰G, 25⁰G,

	Starts	1st	2nd	3rd	Win & Pl
Hurdles	13	1	1	2	6292
Career Total	52	4	6	9	25593
95 10/03 Extr	2m3f	D(0-125)HHdl	G-F	£4109
94 12/02 Extr	2m6f110yF(0-100)HHdl	G-S	£2828
88 10/01 Hrfd	3m1f110yE	Ch	GD	£3100
101 12/98 Ludl	2m	H NHF	G-S	£1350

Total win prize-money £11388

Going:	Sf: 0-1 GS: 0-1 Gd: 0-6 GF: - Fm: 1-5
Distance:	2m/2m3: 1-3 2m4-2m7: 0-3 3m+: 0-8
Track:	LH: 0-7 RH: 1-5 Tight: 0-3 Gall: 0-2
Aids:	Bl: 0-0 Vi: 0-0 Tstrap: 0-0 Ckp: 0-0
Best Rating:	101 12/98 Ludl 2m gd-sft NHF

Moderate handicap chaser/hurdler; stays extreme distances, but effective at shorter; acts on most ground.

Harapour (FR)

102   **124+**

6-y-o b g Valanour (IRE)-Haratiyna (Top Ville)
P F Nicholls Mrs Jan Smith

Placings:*3P/02102*   (4528)
2003/04: 17⁰GS, 22²HY, 19¹S, 20⁰HY, 20²GS,

	Starts	1st	2nd	3rd	Win & Pl
Hurdles	5	1	2	0	6338
Career Total	7	1	2	1	7034
110 2/04 Extr	2m3f	E Hdl	SFT	£3692

Total win prize-money £3692

Going:	Sf: 1-3 GS: 0-2 Gd: 0-0 GF: - Fm: 0-0
Distance:	2m/2m3: 1-2 2m4-2m7: 0-3 3m+: 0-0
Track:	LH: 0-3 RH: 1-2 Tight: 0-2 Gall: 0-0
Aids:	Bl: 0-0 Vi: 0-0 Tstrap: 0-0 Ckp: 0-0
Best Rating:	124 3/04 Chep 2m4f gd-sft Hdl

Fair hurdler; a middle-distance winner on the Flat in France; has had training problems; won 2m 3f novice hurdle at Exeter February 2004; found race coming too soon when pulled up next time; stays 2m 6f; acts on soft ground.

Harben (FR)

92f   **73f**

5-y-o ch g Luchiroverte (IRE)-Dixia (FR) (Altayan)
M Todhunter D M Proos

Placings:*00*   (1605)
2003/04: 16⁰G, 17⁰GF,

	Starts	1st	2nd	3rd	Win & Pl
NH Flat	2	0	0	0	
Career Total	2	0	0	0	

Going:	Sf: 0-0 GS: 0-0 Gd: 0-1 GF: - Fm: 0-1
Distance:	2m/2m3: 0-2 2m4-2m7: 0-0 3m+: 0-0
Track:	LH: 0-0 RH: 0-2 Tight: 0-0 Gall: 0-0
Aids:	Bl: 0-0 Vi: 0-0 Tstrap: 0-0 Ckp: 0-0
Best Rating:	73 10/03 Carl 2m1f gd-fm NHF

Harbour Pilot (IRE)

116(105h)   (128h)**170**

9-y-o b g Be My Native (USA)-Las-Cancellas (Monksfield)
Noel Meade Kays Syndicate

Placings:*110/*2S11534/1161U2/2333-0U3   (4424)
2003/04: 24⁰GY, 24ᵁYS, 26³G,

	Starts	1st	2nd	3rd	Win & Pl
Hurdles	1	0	0	0	0
Chases	2	0	0	1	38500
Career Total	23	7	3	5	240358
154 2/02 Leop	2m5f	Ch	HVY	£43865
141 12/01 Fair	2m4f	Ch	YLD	£31451
144 10/01 Gway	2m6f	Ch	SH	£8125
141 12/00 Navn	2m3f	Hdl	HVY	£13000
127 11/00 Naas	2m3f	Hdl	SH	£4416
111 3/00 Navn	2m	NHF	Y-S	£3588
97 1/00 Naas	2m	NHF	SH	£3312

Total win prize-money £107758

Going:	Sf: 0-0 GS: 0-0 Gd: 0-1 GF: - Fm: 0-0
Distance:	2m/2m3: 0-0 2m4-2m7: 0-0 3m+: 0-3
Track:	LH: 0-3 RH: 0-0 Tight: 0-0 Gall: 0-1
Aids:	Bl: 0-2 Vi: 0-0 Tstrap: 0-0 Ckp: 0-0
Best Rating:	170 3/04 Chel 3m2f110y good Ch

High-class chaser; good form in novice company in 2001/2; often let down by his jumping; third to Best Mate in the Cheltenham Gold Cup in 2003 and 2004; stays three miles two; has won on soft, acts on heavy.

Harbour Point (IRE)
98   **89+**

8-y-o b g Glacial Storm (USA)-Forest Jem (Croghan Hill)
D J Caro   Eddie Moss

Placings: *0/1*36B3-022   (2155)
2003/04: 21⁰G, 20²G, 20²GS,

	Starts	1st	2nd	3rd	Win & Pl
Hurdles	3	0	2	0	1858
Career Total	9	1	2	2	4793
101	10/02 Fknm	2m		H NHF	G-S £1776

Total win prize-money £1777

Going:	Sf: 0-0 GS: 0-1 Gd: 0-2 GF: - Fm: 0-0
Distance:	2m/2m3: 0-0 2m4-2m7: 0-3 3m+: 0-0
Track:	LH: 0-2 RH: 0-0 Tight: 0-1 Gall: 0-0
Aids:	Bl: 0-0 Vi: 0-0 Tstrap: 0-0 Ckp: 0-0
Best Rating:	101 10/02 Fknm 2m gd-sft NHF

Moderate hurdler; got off the mark in a bumper at Fakenham in October 2002; well beaten over hurdles to date and appears to have stamina limitations.

Harbour Rock (IRE)
100f   **95+f**

5-y-o b g Midhish-Annie's Glen (IRE) (Glenstal (USA))
D J Wintle   Mrs B Grainger

Placings: *00*   (3446)
2003/04: 16⁹G, 16⁸G,

	Starts	1st	2nd	3rd	Win & Pl
NH Flat	2	0	0	0	
Career Total	2	0	0	0	

Going:	Sf: 0-0 GS: 0-1 Gd: 0-1 GF: - Fm: 0-0
Distance:	2m/2m3: 0-2 2m4-2m7: 0-0 3m+: 0-0
Track:	LH: 0-0 RH: 0-2 Tight: 0-0 Gall: 0-1
Aids:	Bl: 0-0 Vi: 0-0 Tstrap: 0-0 Ckp: 0-0
Best Rating:	95 12/03 Hntg 2m110y gd-sft NHF

Harchibald (FR)
117   **138+**

5-y-o b g Perugino (USA)-Dame D'Harvard (USA) (Quest For Fame)
Noel Meade   D P Sharkey

Placings: 1403252-1415   (4428)
2003/04: 16¹G, 16⁴GF, 16¹G, 17⁵G,

	Starts	1st	2nd	3rd	Win & Pl
Hurdles	4	2	0	0	25266
Career Total	11	3	2	1	40540
132	2/04 Leop	2m	(0-135)HHdl	GD	£10085
119	4/03 Punc	2m	Hdl	GD	£11607
125	12/02 Fair	2m	Hdl	SFT	£5503

Total win prize-money £27196

Going:	Sf: 0-0 GS: 0-0 Gd: 2-3 GF: - Fm: 0-1
Distance:	2m/2m3: 2-4 2m4-2m7: 0-0 3m+: 0-0
Track:	LH: 1-2 RH: 1-1 Tight: 0-0 Gall: 0-1
Aids:	Bl: 0-0 Vi: 0-0 Tstrap: 1-1 Ckp: 0-0
Best Rating:	138 3/04 Chel 2m1f good Hdl

Fair Irish hurdler; posted a decent display when winning at Leopardstown in February; effective in soft ground, but has looked best on good; has worn a tongue tie; prospered from a successful wind operation in 2003.

Hardi De Chalamont (FR)
90(93c)   (72c)**85**

9-y-o gr g Royal Charter (FR)-Naita Ii (FR) (Dom Luc (FR))
Mrs J Candlish (A Parker 14/5)   N Heath

Placings: 14/1FP2/F3P/554234F0-354F0   (2940)
2003/04: 16³G, 24⁵GF, 24⁴GS, 22⁶G, 24⁰GS,

	Starts	1st	2nd	3rd	Win & Pl
Hurdles	3	0	0	1	529
Chases	2	0	0	0	0
Career Total	22	2	2	3	14563
5/00	Fntb	2m3f	Ch	GD	£3074
1/00	Pau	2m2f	Hdl	SFT	£5764

Total win prize-money £8838

Going:	Sf: 0-0 GS: 0-2 Gd: 0-2 GF: - Fm: 0-1
Distance:	2m/2m3: 0-1 2m4-2m7: 0-1 3m+: 0-3
Track:	LH: 0-3 RH: 0-1 Tight: 0-1 Gall: 0-0
Aids:	Bl: 0-0 Vi: 0-0 Tstrap: 0-0 Ckp: 0-1
Best Rating:	111 4/01 Ayr 2m good Ch

Hardiman (IRE)
102   **108**

11-y-o ch h Phardante (FR)-Mention Of Money (Le Bavard (FR))
Jonjo O'Neill   John P McManus

Placings: *0/10/*3500F13/0650F46/1205/1331P03P/00-43P5PP   (4342)
2003/04: 24⁴G, 26³G, 29⁵S, 32⁵G, 24⁷GS, 29⁶GS,

	Starts	1st	2nd	3rd	Win & Pl
Chases	6	0	0	1	1002
Career Total	37	5	1	6	40635
111	7/01 Gway	2m6f	Ch	G-Y	£10483
109	6/01 Gowr	2m4f	(0-102)HCh	G-F	£6677
117	6/00 Navn	2m4f	Hdl	YLD	£4140
107	4/99 Fair	2m2f	Ch	YLD	£6752
90	11/97 Naas	2m	NHF	Y-S	£2712

Total win prize-money £30766

Going:	Sf: 0-1 GS: 0-2 Gd: 0-3 GF: - Fm: 0-0
Distance:	2m/2m3: 0-0 2m4-2m7: 0-0 3m+: 0-6
Track:	LH: 0-5 RH: 0-1 Tight: 0-3 Gall: 0-1
Aids:	Bl: 0-0 Vi: 0-0 Tstrap: 0-0 Ckp: 0-2
Best Rating:	126 6/00 Wxfd 2m4f gd-yld Hdl

Modest Ex-Irish chaser; stays over three miles; acts on good and soft ground; on a long losing run, but falling in the weights as a result.

Harding
13-y-o b g Dowsing (USA)-Orange Hill (High Top)
Mrs Jenny Gordon   S P Tindall

Placings: 2452313463/5/513UF/5P/F   (3873)
2003/04: 25⁵GS,

	Starts	1st	2nd	3rd	Win & Pl
Chases	1	0	0	0	
Career Total	19	2	2	4	9919
114	1/99 Folk	2m	F(0-100)HCh	SFT	£3002
119	3/96 Newb	2m5f	D(0-120)HHdl	G-S	£2801

Total win prize-money £5803

Going:	Sf: 0-0 GS: 0-1 Gd: 0-0 GF: - Fm: 0-0
Distance:	2m/2m3: 0-0 2m4-2m7: 0-0 3m+: 0-1
Track:	LH: 0-0 RH: 0-0 Tight: 0-1 Gall: 0-0
Aids:	Bl: 0-0 Vi: 0-0 Tstrap: 0-0 Ckp: 0-0
Best Rating:	119 3/96 Newb 2m5f gd-sft Hdl

Hardy Breeze (IRE)
(55h)

13-y-o b g Henbit (USA)-Chake-Chake (Goldhill)
Miss A M Newton-Smith   Mrs John Grist

Placings: P5606/5P656/02P30051/56P25/000552/33-P   (1545)
2003/04: 26⁷GF,

	Starts	1st	2nd	3rd	Win & Pl
Chases	1	0	0	0	
Career Total	32	1	3	3	6638
83	4/00 Plum	3m2f	F(0-90)HCh	GD	£2898

Total win prize-money £2898

Going:	Sf: 0-0 GS: 0-0 Gd: 0-0 GF: - Fm: 0-1
Distance:	2m/2m3: 0-0 2m4-2m7: 0-0 3m+: 0-1
Track:	LH: 0-1 RH: 0-0 Tight: 0-1 Gall: 0-0
Aids:	Bl: 0-0 Vi: 0-0 Tstrap: 0-0 Ckp: 0-0
Best Rating:	85 12/96 Folk 2m6f110y gd-sft Hdl

Moderate staying chaser. Seems to handle any ground.

Hardy Eustace (IRE)
126   **169+**

7-y-o b g Archway (IRE)-Stema Star (Corvaro (USA))
D T Hughes   Laurence Byrne

Placings: 516/011215-20221   (4383)
2003/04: 20²G, 16⁶Y, 20²GS, 16²YS, 16¹G,

	Starts	1st	2nd	3rd	Win & Pl
Hurdles	5	1	3	0	199239
Career Total	14	5	4	0	332511
169	3/04 Chel	2m110y	A Hdl	GD	£174000
153	3/03 Chel	2m5f	A Hdl	GD	£58000
144	12/02 Leop	2m4f	Hdl	HVY	£11963
144	12/02 Fair	2m	Hdl	SH	£27914
120	4/02 Fair	2m	NHF	YLD	£24141

Total win prize-money £296018

Going:	Sf: 0-0 GS: 0-1 Gd: 1-1 GF: - Fm: 0-1
Distance:	2m/2m3: 1-3 2m4-2m7: 0-2 3m+: 0-0
Track:	LH: 1-4 RH: 0-0 Tight: 0-0 Gall: 0-1
Aids:	Bl: 1-1 Vi: 0-0 Tstrap: 0-0 Ckp: 0-0
Best Rating:	169 3/04 Chel 2m110y good Hdl

Top-class Irish hurdler; winner of the Royal & SunAlliance Novices' Hurdle at the 2003 Festival; ran some fair races in defeat in 2003/4 before leaving that form behind when making all in the Champion Hurdle at Cheltenham, beating Rooster Booster by five lengths; effective at two miles, but stays 2m 5f; acts on most ground; blinkered for the first time in the Champion Hurdle.

Harem Scarem (IRE)
94   (64h)**69+**

13-y-o b g Lord Americo-River Rescue (Over The River (FR))
Mrs L Williamson   Halewood International Ltd

Placings: *014/*06PB30F6/O003410622120F2/0P535136P52/224-645630P3   (4789)
2003/04: 16⁶GF, 20⁴G, 20⁵S, 24⁶G, 19³G, 20⁰G, 16⁶GS, 17³G,

	Starts	1st	2nd	3rd	Win & Pl
Hurdles	1	0	0	0	0
Chases	7	0	0	2	874
Career Total	48	4	7	6	22024
86	2/02 Hrfd	2m	F(0-100)HCh	HVY	£3848
84	3/01 Ling	2m	F(0-95)HCh	HVY	£2947
83	1/01 Leic	2m	G(0-90)HHdl	HVY	£1932
102	8/97 Tral	2m1f	NHF	SFT	£3391

Total win prize-money £12118

Going:	Sf: 0-1 GS: 0-1 Gd: 0-5 GF: - Fm: 0-1
Distance:	2m/2m3: 0-4 2m4-2m7: 0-3 3m+: 0-1
Track:	LH: 0-7 RH: 0-1 Tight: 0-2 Gall: 0-1
Aids:	Bl: 0-0 Vi: 0-0 Tstrap: 0-0 Ckp: 0-0
Best Rating:	102 8/97 Tral 2m1f soft NHF

Very modest veteran chaser; likes to front run; stays two miles three; effective in testing ground.

Harewood End

72   **54**

6-y-o b g Bin Ajwaad (IRE)-Tasseled (USA) (Tate Gallery (USA))
A Crook John Sinclair (haulage) Ltd

Placings:00U00				(2526)

2003/04: 16⁰GF, 16⁰GF, 17⁰G, 17⁰GF, 16⁰GS,

	Starts	1st	2nd	3rd	Win & Pl
Hurdles	5	0	0	0	
Career Total	5	0	0	0	

Going:	Sf: 0-0 GS: 0-1 Gd: 0-1 GF: - Fm: 0-3
Distance:	2m/2m3: 0-5 2m4-2m7: 0-0 3m+: 0-0
Track:	LH: 0-4 RH: 0-1 Tight: 0-3 Gall: 0-0
Aids:	Bl: 0-0 Vi: 0-0 Tstrap: 0-0 Ckp: 0-3
Best Rating:	54 5/03 Weth 2m gd-fm Hdl

Harfdecent

13-y-o b g Primitive Rising (USA)-Grand Queen (Grand Conde (FR))
A G Hobbs Miss Joanne Tremain

Placings:0/030P413/453112/F314P/332112P/P0/3P26F/66FU2-P				(0592)

2003/04: 20⁰GF,

	Starts	1st	2nd	3rd	Win & Pl
Chases	1	0	0	0	
Career Total	39	6	5	7	35048
124	1/00	Donc	2m3f110yC(0-130)HCh	G-F	£5993
114	1/00	Muss	3m	E(0-115)HCh	SFT	£3575
113	2/99	Donc	2m3f110yE(0-115)HCh	G-F	£2960
108	4/98	Sedg	2m5f	E(0-115)HCh	G-S	£4055
108	3/98	Catt	2m3f	D Ch	SFT	£3574
88	3/97	Sedg	2m5f110yE Hdl	G-F	£2253
			Total win prize-money		£22410

Going:	Sf: 0-0 GS: 0-0 Gd: 0-0 GF: - Fm: 0-1
Distance:	2m/2m3: 0-0 2m4-2m7: 0-1 3m+: 0-0
Track:	LH: 0-1 RH: 0-0 Tight: 0-0 Gall: 0-0
Aids:	Bl: 0-0 Vi: 0-0 Tstrap: 0-0 Ckp: 0-0
Best Rating:	127 1/02 Catt 2m3f soft Ch

Fair chaser; stays three miles but possibly most effective at shorter; handles soft ground but probably best on a sound surface.

Harik

102   **117**

10-y-o ch g Persian Bold-Yaqut (USA) (Northern Dancer)
G L Moore The Best Beech Partnership

Placings:P/32F36331/53436/21136/306212P23P/23442114-466622410U02				(4935)

2003/04: 21⁴G, 20⁶GF, 17⁵G, 20⁶GF, 16²GF, 17²G, 16⁴G, 18¹GS, 16⁹G, 16⁴G, 16⁰G, 18²G,

	Starts	1st	2nd	3rd	Win & Pl
Chases	12	3	1	0	9798
Career Total	49	7	10	10	45019
115	2/04	Font	2m2f	E(0-105)HCh	G-S	£4046

117	3/03	Plum	2m4f	E(0-110)HCh	G-F	£5616
113	3/03	Tntn	2m3f	E(0-105)HCh	FRM	£3932
109	9/01	Font	2m4f	F(0-105)HCh	G-F	£3167
105	5/00	Font	2m4f	F Ch	GD	£2843
105	5/00	Hntg	2m110y	E Ch	G-F	£2880
113	4/99	Font	2m2f110yE Hdl		GD	£2215
			Total win prize-money		£24702

Going:	Sf: 0-0 GS: 1-1 Gd: 0-7 GF: - Fm: 0-4
Distance:	2m/2m3: 1-9 2m4-2m7: 0-3 3m+: 0-0
Track:	LH: 0-3 RH: 0-7 Tight: 1-7 Gall: 0-2
Aids:	Bl: 1-11 Vi: 0-0 Tstrap: 1-12 Ckp: 0-0
Best Rating:	117 3/03 Plum 2m4f gd-fm Ch

Modest chaser; very versatile performer; splits his time between racing on sand and over fences and is successful under both codes; has found things tougher since being raised over a stone after winning two chases in March 2003; suited by fast ground over fences; stays 2m 4f; has worn a tongue tie, visor and blinkers.

Harley

81   **58**

6-y-o ch g Alderbrook-Chichell's Hurst (Oats)
Mrs P Sly P J Turner

Placings:0F0P0				(4512)

2003/04: 16⁰GS, 20⁰FGS, 16⁰GS, 19⁰G, 20⁰GS,

	Starts	1st	2nd	3rd	Win & Pl
NH Flat	1	0	0	0	0
Hurdles	4	0	0	0	0
Career Total	5	0	0	0	0

Going:	Sf: 0-0 GS: 0-4 Gd: 0-1 GF: - Fm: 0-0
Distance:	2m/2m3: 0-2 2m4-2m7: 0-3 3m+: 0-0
Track:	LH: 0-3 RH: 0-2 Tight: 0-0 Gall: 0-0
Aids:	Bl: 0-0 Vi: 0-0 Tstrap: 0-0 Ckp: 0-0
Best Rating:	68 5/03 Worc 2m gd-sft NHF

Harlov (FR)

104   (104h)**114+**

9-y-o ch g Garde Royale-Paulownia (FR) (Montevideo)
A Parker Mr & Mrs Raymond Anderson Green

Placings:00/3030313/2F22/F26602131/12-215				(3938)

2003/04: 30²GS, 30¹G, 33⁵G,

	Starts	1st	2nd	3rd	Win & Pl
Chases	3	1	1	0	13822
Career Total	27	5	7	5	40508
114	1/04	Catt	3m6f	C(0-130)HCh	GD	£10364
103	11/02	Carl	2m4f	D(0-115)HCh	HVY	£4595
104	4/02	Hexm	3m1f	E Ch	GD	£3672
95	3/02	Carl	3m2f	D Ch	G-S	£4868
91	3/00	Ayr	3m110y	D(0-115)HHdl	HVY	£3614
			Total win prize-money		£27116

Going:	Sf: 0-0 GS: 0-1 Gd: 1-2 GF: - Fm: 0-0
Distance:	2m/2m3: 0-0 2m4-2m7: 0-0 3m+: 1-3
Track:	LH: 1-3 RH: 0-0 Tight: 1-2 Gall: 0-1
Aids:	Bl: 0-0 Vi: 0-0 Tstrap: 0-0 Ckp: 1-3
Best Rating:	114 1/04 Catt 3m6f good Ch

Modest chaser; stays three miles six; acts on most types of ground; has worn cheekpieces.

Harmony Hall

102   **111+**

10-y-o ch g Music Boy-Fleeting Affair (Hotfoot)
J M Bradley E A Hayward

Placings:3F0/3/1154/5-1100				(1376)

2003/04:	16¹GF, 16¹GF, 16⁰GF, 16⁰GF,

	Starts	1st	2nd	3rd	Win & Pl
Hurdles	4	2	0	0	6523
Career Total	13	4	0	2	15555
110	8/03	Worc	2m	E(0-110)HHdl	G-F	£3513
111	7/03	Worc	2m	F(0-100)HHdl	GD	£3010
127	10/99	Asct	2m110y	C Hdl	GD	£5083
114	10/99	Strf	2m110y	E Hdl	G-F	£3002
			Total win prize-money		£14610

Going:	Sf: 0-0 GS: 0-0 Gd: 1-1 GF: - Fm: 1-3
Distance:	2m/2m3: 2-4 2m4-2m7: 0-0 3m+: 0-0
Track:	LH: 2-4 RH: 0-0 Tight: 0-0 Gall: 0-0
Aids:	Bl: 0-0 Vi: 0-0 Tstrap: 0-0 Ckp: 0-0
Best Rating:	127 10/99 Asct 2m110y good Hdl

Modest hurdler; very lightly raced over hurdles since back-to-back victories in October 1999; fit from the Flat when gaining successive wins at Worcester in the summer of 2003; acts on good ground and faster; best at 2m.

Harnage (IRE)

(76h)

9-y-o b g Mujadil (USA)-Wilderness (Martinmas)
Jean-Rene Auvray R T Grant

Placings:F006/P				(1121)

2003/04: 21³GF,

	Starts	1st	2nd	3rd	Win & Pl
Chases	1	0	0	0	
Career Total	5	0	0	0	0

Going:	Sf: 0-0 GS: 0-0 Gd: 0-0 GF: - Fm: 0-1
Distance:	2m/2m3: 0-0 2m4-2m7: 0-1 3m+: 0-0
Track:	LH: 0-1 RH: 0-0 Tight: 0-1 Gall: 0-0
Aids:	Bl: 0-0 Vi: 0-0 Tstrap: 0-0 Ckp: 0-0
Best Rating:	76 4/01 Hntg 2m110y soft Hdl

Harpoon Harry (IRE)

111   **99**

7-y-o ch g Alphabatim (USA)-Procastrian (IRE) (Lancastrian)
K C Bailey This Horse Is For Sale Partnership

Placings:4				(4319)

2003/04: 20⁴S,

	Starts	1st	2nd	3rd	Win & Pl
Hurdles	1	0	0	0	273
Career Total	1	0	0	0	273

Going:	Sf: 0-1 GS: 0-0 Gd: 0-0 GF: - Fm: 0-0
Distance:	2m/2m3: 0-0 2m4-2m7: 0-1 3m+: 0-0
Track:	LH: 0-1 RH: 0-0 Tight: 0-0 Gall: 0-1
Aids:	Bl: 0-0 Vi: 0-0 Tstrap: 0-0 Ckp: 0-0
Best Rating:	99 3/04 Newc 2m4f soft Hdl

Showed some ability when fourth on belated debut at Newcastle in March; will get three miles in time; acts on soft ground.

Harringay

81f   **85+f**

4-y-o b f Sir Harry Lewis (USA)-Tamergale (IRE) (Strong Gale)
Miss H C Knight Mrs R Vaughan

Placings:1				(4186)

2003/04: 16¹G,

	Starts	1st	2nd	3rd	Win & Pl
NH Flat	1	1	0	0	1897

Career Total	1	1	0	0	1897
85 3/04 Hntg	2m110y	H NHF		GD	£1897

Total win prize-money £1897

Going:	Sf: 0-0 GS: 0-0 Gd: 1-1 GF: - Fm: 0-0
Distance:	2m/2m3: 1-1 2m4-2m7: 0-0 3m+: 0-0
Track:	LH: 0-0 RH: 1-1 Tight: 0-0 Gall: 1-1
Aids:	Bl: 0-0 Vi: 0-0 Tstrap: 0-0 Ckp: 0-0
Best Rating:	85 3/04 Hntg 2m110y good NHF

Bumper winner on debut; acts on good.

Harris Bay

96f   105f

5-y-o b g Karinga Bay-Harristown Lady (Muscatite)
Miss H C Knight Mrs G M Sturges & H Stephen Smith

Placings:13					(3650)
2003/04: 16¹GS, 16³GS,					

	Starts	1st	2nd	3rd	Win & Pl
NH Flat	2	1	0	1	3076
Career Total	2	1	0	1	3076
105 1/04 Ludl	2m	H NHF		G-S	£2723

Total win prize-money £2723

Going:	Sf: 0-0 GS: 1-2 Gd: 0-0 GF: - Fm: 0-0
Distance:	2m/2m3: 1-2 2m4-2m7: 0-0 3m+: 0-0
Track:	LH: 0-0 RH: 1-2 Tight: 0-0 Gall: 0-0
Aids:	Bl: 0-0 Vi: 0-0 Tstrap: 0-0 Ckp: 0-0
Best Rating:	109 2/04 Kemp 2m gd-sft NHF

Won a Ludlow bumper on his debut and third in a a better race under his penalty.

Harrovian

91   102

7-y-o b g Deploy-Homeoftheclassics (Tate Gallery (USA))
Miss P Robson Major & Mrs Ivan Straker

Placings:2/54-3					(4595)
2003/04: 22³G,					

	Starts	1st	2nd	3rd	Win & Pl
Hurdles	1	0	0	1	546
Career Total	4	0	1	1	4271

Going:	Sf: 0-0 GS: 0-0 Gd: 0-1 GF: 0-0 Fm: 0-0
Distance:	2m/2m3: 0-0 2m4-2m7: 0-1 3m+: 0-0
Track:	LH: 0-1 RH: 0-0 Tight: 0-1 Gall: 0-0
Aids:	Bl: 0-0 Vi: 0-0 Tstrap: 0-0 Ckp: 0-0
Best Rating:	107 2/02 Newb 2m110y soft NHF

Promising debut in a Newbury bumper; disappointing after until changing stables and third in novices' hurdle at Kelso in March; headstrong but stays well.

Harry B

93   95

5-y-o b g Midyan (USA)-Vilcabamba (USA) (Green Dancer (USA))
R J Price Fox And Cub Partnership

Placings:33-PP3					(3841)
2003/04: 17³GS, 24³G, 19³GS,					

	Starts	1st	2nd	3rd	Win & Pl
Hurdles	3	0	0	1	432
Career Total	5	0	0	3	1592

Going:	Sf: 0-0 GS: 0-2 Gd: 0-1 GF: - Fm: 0-0
Distance:	2m/2m3: 0-1 2m4-2m7: 0-1 3m+: 0-1
Track:	LH: 0-1 RH: 0-2 Tight: 0-1 Gall: 0-0
Aids:	Bl: 0-0 Vi: 0-0 Tstrap: 0-0 Ckp: 0-1

Best Rating:	94 11/02 Wwck 2m good Hdl

Plating-class hurdler; stays 2m 4f; has worn cheekpieces.

Harry Bridges

63f   60f

5-y-o ch g Weld-Northern Quay (Quayside)
R Lee Mrs R M McFarlane

Placings:0					(4050)
2003/04: 16⁹G,					

	Starts	1st	2nd	3rd	Win & Pl
NH Flat	1	0	0	0	
Career Total	1	0	0	0	

Going:	Sf: 0-0 GS: 0-0 Gd: 0-1 GF: - Fm: 0-0
Distance:	2m/2m3: 0-1 2m4-2m7: 0-0 3m+: 0-0
Track:	LH: 0-1 RH: 0-0 Tight: 0-0 Gall: 0-0
Aids:	Bl: 0-0 Vi: 0-0 Tstrap: 0-0 Ckp: 0-0
Best Rating:	59 2/04 Hayd 2m good NHF

Harry Collins

101   92

6-y-o ch g Sir Harry Lewis (USA)-Run Fast For Gold (Deep Run)
B I Case B I Case

Placings:000-4322					(4956)
2003/04: 20⁴GS, 24³HY, 22²GS, 22²G,					

	Starts	1st	2nd	3rd	Win & Pl
Hurdles	4	0	2	1	2295
Career Total	7	0	2	1	2295

Going:	Sf: 0-1 GS: 0-2 Gd: 0-1 GF: - Fm: 0-0
Distance:	2m/2m3: 0-0 2m4-2m7: 0-3 3m+: 0-1
Track:	LH: 0-1 RH: 0-2 Tight: 0-1 Gall: 0-0
Aids:	Bl: 0-0 Vi: 0-0 Tstrap: 0-1 Ckp: 0-0
Best Rating:	92 4/04 MRas 2m6f good Hdl

Modest placed form in novice hurdles.

Harry Hotspur (IRE)

11-y-o gr g Celio Rufo-Midsummer Blends (IRE) (Duky)
G C Evans M M E H Dearden

Placings:0040/5023P/PP31/P					(4143)
2003/04: 25⁹G,					

	Starts	1st	2nd	3rd	Win & Pl
Chases	1	0	0	0	
Career Total	14	1	1	2	4613
81 3/02 Hntg	3m		F(0-95)HCh	G-F	£2674

Total win prize-money £2674

Going:	Sf: 0-0 GS: 0-0 Gd: 0-1 GF: - Fm: 0-0
Distance:	2m/2m3: 0-0 2m4-2m7: 0-1 3m+: 0-1
Track:	LH: 0-0 RH: 0-0 Tight: 0-0 Gall: 0-0
Aids:	Bl: 0-0 Vi: 0-0 Tstrap: 0-0 Ckp: 0-0
Best Rating:	81 3/02 Hntg 3m gd-fm Ch

Harry The Hoover (IRE)

4-y-o b g Fayruz-Mitsubishi Style (Try My Best (USA))
M J Gingell (M D Hammond 16/5) W Stanger, P Whittall and G Plastow

---

Placings:P0					(2331)
2003/04: 16⁹GF, 16⁹G,					

	Starts	1st	2nd	3rd	Win & Pl
Hurdles	2	0	0	0	
Career Total	2	0	0	0	

Going:	Sf: 0-0 GS: 0-0 Gd: 0-1 GF: - Fm: 0-1
Distance:	2m/2m3: 0-2 2m4-2m7: 0-0 3m+: 0-0
Track:	LH: 0-2 RH: 0-0 Tight: 0-1 Gall: 0-1
Aids:	Bl: 0-0 Vi: 0-0 Tstrap: 0-0 Ckp: 0-0

Harry The Horse

79   64

6-y-o b g Sir Harry Lewis (USA)-Miss Optimist (Relkino)
Miss E C Lavelle Club Ten

Placings:P-P0					(4691)
2003/04: 24⁹G, 17⁹G,					

	Starts	1st	2nd	3rd	Win & Pl
Hurdles	2	0	0	0	
Career Total	3	0	0	0	

Going:	Sf: 0-0 GS: 0-0 Gd: 0-2 GF: - Fm: 0-0
Distance:	2m/2m3: 0-1 2m4-2m7: 0-0 3m+: 0-0
Track:	LH: 0-1 RH: 0-1 Tight: 0-0 Gall: 0-1
Aids:	Bl: 0-0 Vi: 0-0 Tstrap: 0-0 Ckp: 0-0
Best Rating:	63 4/04 Extr 2m1f good Hdl

Harry's Ace

6-y-o b g Phountzi (USA)-Throw In Your Hand (Niniski (USA))
Mrs Merrita Jones Mrs D J Hughes

Placings:00-30					(0832)
2003/04: 17³GF, 20⁰GF,					

	Starts	1st	2nd	3rd	Win & Pl
NH Flat	1	0	0	1	342
Hurdles	1	0	0	0	0
Career Total	4	0	0	1	342

Going:	Sf: 0-0 GS: 0-0 Gd: 0-0 GF: - Fm: 0-2
Distance:	2m/2m3: 0-1 2m4-2m7: 0-1 3m+: 0-0
Track:	LH: 0-1 RH: 0-1 Tight: 0-0 Gall: 0-0
Aids:	Bl: 0-0 Vi: 0-0 Tstrap: 0-0 Ckp: 0-0
Best Rating:	87 5/03 Extr 2m1f gd-fm NHF

Showed improvement on faster ground third start in bumpers.

Harry's Dream

93(103h)   (98h)114+

7-y-o b g Alflora (IRE)-Cheryls Pet (IRE) (General Ironside)
P J Hobbs Peter Partridge

Placings:P5P040-314210					(4694)
2003/04: 20³GS, 21¹G, 20⁴G, 21²S, 22¹G, 23⁹G,					

	Starts	1st	2nd	3rd	Win & Pl
Hurdles	1	0	0	1	381
Chases	5	2	1	0	12887
Career Total	12	2	1	1	13552
114 3/04 Newb	2m6f110yD(0-120)HCh			GD	£6987
112 12/03 Winc	2m5f		E(0-105)HCh	GD	£3454

Total win prize-money £10443

Going:	Sf: 0-1 GS: 0-1 Gd: 2-4 GF: - Fm: 0-0
Distance:	2m/2m3: 0-0 2m4-2m7: 2-5 3m+: 0-1
Track:	LH: 1-2 RH: 1-4 Tight: 0-0 Gall: 1-1

Aids: Bl: 0-0 Vi: 0-0 Tstrap: 0-0 Ckp: 0-0
Best Rating: 114 3/04 Newb 2m6f110y good Ch

Modest novice chaser; brother to smart chaser Farmer Jack; winner of a point-to-point over three miles; won under rules at Wincanton over 2m5f in December 2003; best on good ground.

Harry's Game

92   74

7-y-o gr g Emperor Jones (USA)-Lady Shikari (Kala Shikari)
A P Jones T G N Burrage

Placings: 0/6   (0367)
2003/04: 16⁶G,

	Starts	1st	2nd	3rd	Win & Pl
Hurdles	1	0	0	0	0
Career Total	2	0	0	0	0

Going: Sf: 0-0 GS: 0-0 Gd: 0-1 GF: - Fm: 0-0
Distance: 2m/2m3: 0-1 2m4-2m7: 0-0 3m+: 0-0
Track: LH: 0-1 RH: 0-0 Tight: 0-0 Gall: 0-0
Aids: Bl: 0-0 Vi: 0-0 Tstrap: 0-0 Ckp: 0-0
Best Rating: 74 5/03 Worc 2m good Hdl

Harrycone Lewis

98(98h)   (91h)113+

6-y-o b g Sir Harry Lewis (USA)-Rosie Cone (Celtic Cone)
Mrs P Sly The Craftsmen

Placings: 60-05601P13   (4562)
2003/04: 22⁵S, 21¹S, 25⁶S, 25⁹GS, 24¹GS, 24⁵, 24¹G, 22³G,

	Starts	1st	2nd	3rd	Win & Pl
Hurdles	4	0	0	0	0
Chases	4	2	0	1	11072
Career Total	10	2	0	1	11072
107 2/04	Fknm	3m110y E Ch		GD	£4576
109 1/04	Fknm	3m110y D Ch		G-S	£5421
			Total win prize-money £9997		

Going: Sf: 0-4 GS: 1-2 Gd: 1-2 GF: - Fm: 0-0
Distance: 2m/2m3: 0-0 2m4-2m7: 0-3 3m+: 2-5
Track: LH: 2-6 RH: 0-2 Tight: 2-2 Gall: 0-2
Aids: Bl: 0-0 Vi: 0-0 Tstrap: 0-0 Ckp: 0-0
Best Rating: 113 3/04 Newb 2m6f110y good Ch

Modest chaser; stays three miles miles; acts on good ground; connections feel a galloping track suits best.

Hartest Rose

5-y-o b m Komaite (USA)-Plough Hill (North Briton)
D E Cantillon J W Orbell

Placings: 01-306   (0692)
2003/04: 16³G, 16⁰GF, 16⁶GF,

	Starts	1st	2nd	3rd	Win & Pl
NH Flat	2	0	0	1	397
Hurdles	1	0	0	0	0
Career Total	5	1	0	1	3319
93 4/03	Ludl	2m	H NHF	GD	£2922
			Total win prize-money £2923		

Going: Sf: 0-0 GS: 0-0 Gd: 0-1 GF: - Fm: 0-2
Distance: 2m/2m3: 0-3 2m4-2m7: 0-0 3m+: 0-0
Track: LH: 0-1 RH: 0-2 Tight: 0-0 Gall: 0-1
Aids: Bl: 0-0 Vi: 0-1 Tstrap: 0-0 Ckp: 0-0
Best Rating: 99 5/03 Ludl 2m good NHF

Appreciated the fast ground when ready winner of modest bumper at Ludlow in April; poor efforts so far over hurdles.

Harvis (FR)

103(103h)   (121h)130

9-y-o b g Djarvis (FR)-Tirana (FR) (Over)
G B Balding (Miss Venetia Williams 2/5) Peter Richardson

Placings: 6302233/4111FF0/12422/F3226106-P55P363055   (4540)
2003/04: 20⁵S, 22⁵GS, 19⁵G, 24⁵GS, 18³S, 16⁶S, 16³G, 20⁴G, 16⁵GS, 20⁵GS,

	Starts	1st	2nd	3rd	Win & Pl
Chases	10	0	0	2	3860
Career Total	37	5	7	6	79357
130 2/03	Sand	2m	C(0-135)HCh	SFT	£12209
129 12/01	Hayd	2m4f	C Ch	HVY	£6435
136 12/00	Chep	2m110y	D(0-120)HHdl	SFT	£10400
130 11/00	Leic	2m4f110yD Hdl		HVY	£3367
110 11/00	Towc	2m	E Hdl	SFT	£2324
			Total win prize-money £34735		

Going: Sf: 0-3 GS: 0-4 Gd: 0-3 GF: - Fm: 0-0
Distance: 2m/2m3: 0-4 2m4-2m7: 0-5 3m+: 0-1
Track: LH: 0-4 RH: 0-6 Tight: 0-2 Gall: 0-2
Aids: Bl: 0-0 Vi: 0-0 Tstrap: 0-0 Ckp: 0-0
Best Rating: 136 12/00 Chep 2m110y soft Hdl

Fair chaser; ex-French; effective from two to three miles; acts on soft ground.

Has Scored (IRE)

6-y-o b g Sadler's Wells (USA)-City Ex (Ardross)
Ferdy Murphy The Has Scored Partnership

Placings: 0   (2838)
2003/04: 20⁰GS,

	Starts	1st	2nd	3rd	Win & Pl
Hurdles	1	0	0	0	
Career Total	1	0	0	0	

Going: Sf: 0-0 GS: 0-1 Gd: 0-0 GF: - Fm: 0-0
Distance: 2m/2m3: 0-0 2m4-2m7: 0-0 3m+: 0-0
Track: LH: 0-1 RH: 0-0 Tight: 0-0 Gall: 0-0
Aids: Bl: 0-0 Vi: 0-0 Tstrap: 0-0 Ckp: 0-0

Hasanpour (IRE)

71   102

4-y-o b g Dr Devious (IRE)-Hasainiya (IRE) (Top Ville)
C F Swan (Sir Michael Stoute 29/9) Mrs G Smith

Placings: 10P   (4422)
2003/04: 16¹S, 16⁵G, 17⁷G,

	Starts	1st	2nd	3rd	Win & Pl
Hurdles	3	1	0	0	7775
Career Total	3	1	0	0	7775
102 1/04	Cork	2m	Hdl	SFT	£7774
			Total win prize-money £7775		

Going: Sf: 1-2 GS: 0-0 Gd: 0-1 GF: - Fm: 0-0
Distance: 2m/2m3: 1-3 2m4-2m7: 0-0 3m+: 0-0
Track: LH: 0-2 RH: 0-0 Tight: 0-0 Gall: 0-1
Aids: Bl: 0-0 Vi: 0-0 Tstrap: 0-0 Ckp: 0-0
Best Rating: 102 1/04 Cork 2m soft Hdl

Lightly-raced on the Flat in Britain, but useful; impressive winner of hurdle debut at Cork in January on soft ground; suffered breathing problems on next start when unplaced in Graded event at Leopardstown.

Hastate

9-y-o b g Persian Bold-Gisame (USA) (Diesis)
N M Lampard The Red Lion Racing Club

Placings: 536U23213/2/P43/P   (4172)
2003/04: 24⁶G,

	Starts	1st	2nd	3rd	Win & Pl
Chases	1	0	0	0	
Career Total	14	1	3	4	9611
106 3/00	Newb	2m3f	E(0-110)HHdl	G-F	£3981
			Total win prize-money £3981		

Going: Sf: 0-0 GS: 0-0 Gd: 0-1 GF: - Fm: 0-0
Distance: 2m/2m3: 0-0 2m4-2m7: 0-0 3m+: 0-1
Track: LH: 0-1 RH: 0-0 Tight: 0-0 Gall: 0-1
Aids: Bl: 0-0 Vi: 0-0 Tstrap: 0-0 Ckp: 0-0
Best Rating: 106 3/02 Newb 2m6f110y gd-sft Ch

Hastener

10-y-o ch m Crested Lark-Spartella (Spartan General)
J L Barnett J L Barnett

Placings: P   (0032)
2003/04: 25⁰G,

	Starts	1st	2nd	3rd	Win & Pl
Chases	1	0	0	0	
Career Total	1	0	0	0	

Going: Sf: 0-0 GS: 0-0 Gd: 0-1 GF: - Fm: 0-0
Distance: 2m/2m3: 0-0 2m4-2m7: 0-0 3m+: 0-1
Track: LH: 0-1 RH: 0-0 Tight: 0-0 Gall: 0-1
Aids: Bl: 0-0 Vi: 0-0 Tstrap: 0-0 Ckp: 0-0

Hasty Prince

116   159+

6-y-o ch g Halling (USA)-Sister Sophie (USA) (Effervescing (USA))
Jonjo O'Neill F F Racing Services Partnership III

Placings: 21B1-13320051   (4954)
2003/04: 20¹GF, 16³G, 16³GS, 16²G, 16⁹G, 16⁰G, 24⁵G, 16¹G,

	Starts	1st	2nd	3rd	Win & Pl
Hurdles	8	2	1	2	81800
Career Total	12	4	2	2	93192
159 4/04	Sand	2m110y	B Hdl	GD	£40600
154 11/03	Chep	2m4f	B HHdl	G-F	£17400
134 3/03	Donc	2m3f110yC Hdl		G-S	£6753
121 1/03	Hntg	2m110y E Hdl		SFT	£3668
			Total win prize-money £68422		

Going: Sf: 0-0 GS: 1-0 Gd: 1-6 GF: - Fm: 1-1
Distance: 2m/2m3: 1-6 2m4-2m7: 1-1 3m+: 0-1
Track: LH: 1-7 RH: 1-1 Tight: 0-1 Gall: 0-1
Aids: Bl: 0-0 Vi: 0-0 Tstrap: 0-0 Ckp: 0-0
Best Rating: 159 4/04 Sand 2m110y good Hdl

Smart hurdler; easy winner of the Tote Silver Trophy at Chepstow on his reappearance in November 2003; placed in better company since, including in the Bula and Haydock Champion Hurdle Trial, but held in the real thing; picked up valuable hurdle at Sandown in April 2004; failed to stay three miles, but stays two and a half miles and effective at two; acts on fast and soft ground; regularly held up.

Hatch Gate

11-y-o gr g Lighter-Yankee Silver (Yankee Gold)

P York Mrs K H York

Total win prize-money £18225

Placings:4-1P   (0509)
2003/04: 24^IGF, 28^PGS,

	Starts	1st	2nd	3rd	Win & Pl
Chases	2	1	0	0	1398
Career Total	3	1	0	0	1561
80 5/03 Hntg	3m		H Ch	G-F	£1397

Total win prize-money £1398

Going:	Sf: 0-0 GS: 0-1 Gd: 0-0 GF: - Fm: 1-1
Distance:	2m/2m3: 0-0 2m4-2m7: 0-0 **3m+: 1-2**
Track:	LH: 0-1 **RH: 1-1** Tight: 0-1 **Gall: 1-1**
Aids:	Bl: 0-0 Vi: 0-0 Tstrap: 0-0 Ckp: 0-0
Best Rating:	80 5/03 Hntg 3m gd-fm Ch

Novice hunter chaser; prolific winner between the flags; likes fast ground; stays three miles well.

Hatsnall

100   (69c)**87**

6-y-o b g Mtoto-Anna Of Brunswick (Rainbow Quest (USA))
Miss C J E Caroe M P Bass

Placings:460F0/P043504-60045   (4785)
2003/04: 22⁶S, 19^OG, 16⁹G, 21⁴G, 21⁵G,

	Starts	1st	2nd	3rd	Win & Pl
Hurdles	5	0	0	0	272
Career Total	17	0	0	1	1736

Going:	Sf: 0-1 GS: 0-0 Gd: 0-4 GF: - Fm: 0-0
Distance:	2m/2m3: 0-1 2m4-2m7: 0-0 3m+: 0-0
Track:	LH: 0-2 RH: 0-3 Tight: 0-1 Gall: 0-2
Aids:	Bl: 0-0 Vi: 0-0 Tstrap: 0-0 Ckp: 0-0
Best Rating:	90 3/02 Navn 2m sft-hvy Hdl

Hatteras (FR)

98   **90**

5-y-o b g Octagonal (NZ)-Hylandra (USA) (Bering)
P F Nicholls (Y Fouin 4/5) Neil Smith

Placings:60-245   (4698)
2003/04: 17²VS, 17⁴G, 18⁵G,

	Starts	1st	2nd	3rd	Win & Pl
Hurdles	3	0	1	0	2555
Career Total	5	0	1	0	2555

Going:	Sf: 0-0 GS: 0-0 Gd: 0-2 GF: - Fm: 0-0
Distance:	2m/2m3: 0-3 2m4-2m7: 0-0 3m+: 0-0
Track:	LH: 0-2 RH: 0-0 Tight: 0-2 Gall: 0-0
Aids:	Bl: 0-0 Vi: 0-0 Tstrap: 0-0 Ckp: 0-0
Best Rating:	91 6/03 NAbb 2m1f good Hdl

Ran better than finishing position suggested on British debut.

Haut Cercy (FR)

110   **148+**

9-y-o b g Roi De Rome (USA)-Mamoussia (FR) (Laniste)
H D Daly The Wiggin Partnership

Placings:3/213221/2/3325F/143132-20P   (4965)
2003/04: 25²G, 24⁰G, 29^PGF,

	Starts	1st	2nd	3rd	Win & Pl
Chases	3	0	1	0	8800
Career Total	22	4	7	6	59137
135 1/03 Winc	3m1f110yC(0-135)HCh		G-S	£8775
127 10/02 Chep	3m	D Ch		GD	£4784
120 3/00 Tntn	3m110y E Hdl		GD	£2459
119 12/99 Hrfd	2m3f110yE Hdl		SFT	£2206

Havantadoubt (IRE)

72   **30**

4-y-o ch f Desert King (IRE)-Batiba (USA) (Time For A Change (USA))
M R Bosley (J G Portman 12/10) Bayard Racing

Placings:0   (3432)
2003/04: 16⁹GS,

	Starts	1st	2nd	3rd	Win & Pl
Hurdles	1	0	0	0	
Career Total	1	0	0	0	

Going:	Sf: 0-0 GS: 0-1 Gd: 0-0 GF: - Fm: 0-0
Distance:	2m/2m3: 0-1 2m4-2m7: 0-0 3m+: 0-0
Track:	LH: 0-1 RH: 0-0 Tight: 0-1 Gall: 0-0
Aids:	Bl: 0-0 Vi: 0-0 Tstrap: 0-0 Ckp: 0-0
Best Rating:	30 1/04 Fknm 2m gd-sft Hdl

Have-No-Doubt (IRE)

61   (100c)

10-y-o b g Glacial Storm (USA)-Lady Kas (Pollerton)
L A Dace D Newman

Placings:F5/2/60PP   (3784)
2003/04: 20⁶GS, 22⁰GS, 19^PG, 26^PGS,

	Starts	1st	2nd	3rd	Win & Pl
Hurdles	4	0	0	0	
Career Total	7	0	1	0	332

Going:	Sf: 0-0 GS: 0-3 Gd: 0-1 GF: - Fm: 0-0
Distance:	2m/2m3: 0-0 2m4-2m7: 0-3 3m+: 0-1
Track:	LH: 0-1 RH: 0-0 Tight: 0-2 Gall: 0-1
Aids:	Bl: 0-0 Vi: 0-0 Tstrap: 0-0 Ckp: 0-0
Best Rating:	99 2/02 Folk 2m5f soft Ch

Havetwotaketwo (IRE)

10-y-o b g Phardante (FR)-Arctic Tartan (Deep Run)
Michael Smith Michael Smith

Placings:000/PU/UPF   (4687)
2003/04: 25^UGS, 27^PG, 25^FG,

	Starts	1st	2nd	3rd	Win & Pl
Chases	3	0	0	0	
Career Total	8	0	0	0	

Going:	Sf: 0-0 GS: 0-1 Gd: 0-2 GF: - Fm: 0-0
Distance:	2m/2m3: 0-0 2m4-2m7: 0-0 3m+: 0-0
Track:	LH: 0-3 RH: 0-0 Tight: 0-3 Gall: 0-0
Aids:	Bl: 0-0 Vi: 0-0 Tstrap: 0-0 Ckp: 0-0
Best Rating:	74 4/02 Newc 2m4f good Ch

Having A Party

108f   **98f**

6-y-o b m Dancing High-Lady Manello (Mandrake Major)
J Mackie Mrs Linda Court

Placings:4310   (4328)
2003/04: 16⁴GS, 16³HY, 16¹HY, 16⁰S,

	Starts	1st	2nd	3rd	Win & Pl
NH Flat	4	1	0	1	2309
Career Total	4	1	0	1	2309
98 2/04 Chep	2m110y H NHF		HVY	£2016

Total win prize-money £2016

Going:	Sf: 1-3 GS: 0-1 Gd: 0-0 GF: - Fm: 0-0
Distance:	2m/2m3: 1-4 2m4-2m7: 0-0 3m+: 0-0
Track:	LH: 1-3 RH: 0-1 Tight: 0-0 Gall: 0-0
Aids:	Bl: 0-0 Vi: 0-0 Tstrap: 0-0 Ckp: 0-0
Best Rating:	98 2/04 Chep 2m110y heavy NHF

All out to win weak mares' only bumper in heavy ground at Chepstow February 2004; has slowly been getting better with experience; will stay further over hurdles; acts well on soft ground.

Hawaadej (IRE)

77(74h)   (74h)**63**

7-y-o b g Barathea (IRE)-Lover's Rose (King Emperor (USA))
N F Glynn N F Glynn

Placings:0060500004U0P   (2978a)
2003/04: 18^PY, 16⁶G, 17⁶F, 20⁹GF, 16⁵GF, 16⁰Y, 16⁹F, 20⁹GF, 20⁵S, 21⁴G, 20^UG, 24⁹G, 22^PS,

	Starts	1st	2nd	3rd	Win & Pl
NH Flat	2	0	0	0	0
Hurdles	4	0	0	0	0
Chases	7	0	0	0	0
Career Total	13	0	0	0	0

Going:	Sf: 0-2 GS: 0-0 Gd: 0-4 GF: - Fm: 0-5
Distance:	2m/2m3: 0-6 2m4-2m7: 0-6 3m+: 0-1
Track:	LH: 0-3 RH: 0-3 Tight: 0-1 Gall: 0-0
Aids:	Bl: 0-0 Vi: 0-0 Tstrap: 0-0 Ckp: 0-0
Best Rating:	74 8/03 Gway 2m yield Hdl

Hawadeth

118   **139**

9-y-o ch g Machiavellian (USA)-Ghzaalh (USA) (Northern Dancer)
V R A Dartnall Nick Viney

Placings:30234/24121612/325320B0-025320   (4963)
2003/04: 20⁰GF, 16²G, 16⁵G, 16³G, 17²G, 20⁹G,

	Starts	1st	2nd	3rd	Win & Pl
Hurdles	6	0	2	1	19655
Career Total	27	3	8	5	59507
121 3/02 NAbb	2m1f	D(0-115)HHdl		GD	£5720
119 1/02 Plum	2m	E Hdl		SFT	£2688
109 12/01 NAbb	2m1f	D Hdl		HVY	£3519

Total win prize-money £11928

Going:	Sf: 0-0 GS: 0-0 Gd: 0-5 GF: - Fm: 0-1
Distance:	2m/2m3: 0-4 2m4-2m7: 0-2 3m+: 0-0
Track:	LH: 0-3 RH: 0-3 Tight: 0-0 Gall: 0-2
Aids:	Bl: 0-0 Vi: 0-0 Tstrap: 0-0 Ckp: 0-2
Best Rating:	139 3/04 Chel 2m1f good Hdl

Very useful handicap hurdler; effective at around two miles; acts on soft, but prefers good ground; consistent performer who needs a fast pace to be seen at his best; has been tried in cheekpieces.

Smart chaser; good reappearance when chasing home Kingscliff at Cheltenham in December; disappointing in the William Hill National Hunt Chase at Cheltenham, a race in which he had been second in 2003; stays 3m 1f; effective on good and soft ground.

Hawick

7-y-o b g Toulon-Slave's Bangle (Prince Rheingold)
D W Whillans Chas N Whillans

Placings:*23-25U*   **(2900)**
2003/04: 16²G, 16⁵G, 20ᵁS,

	Starts	1st	2nd	3rd	Win & Pl
NH Flat	2	0	1	0	860
Hurdles	1	0	0	0	0
Career Total	5	0	2	1	1718

Going:	Sf: 0-1 GS: 0-0 Gd: 0-2 GF: - Fm: 0-0
Distance:	2m/2m3: 0-2 2m4-2m7: 0-1 3m+: 0-0
Track:	LH: 0-1 RH: 0-1 Tight: 0-0 Gall: 0-0
Aids:	Bl: 0-0 Vi: 0-0 Tstrap: 0-0 Ckp: 0-0
Best Rating:	110 2/03 Ayr 2m heavy NHF

Useful form in bumpers but is looking exposed; effective at two miles; acts on a sound surface.

Hawk's Landing (IRE)

112(106h)   (116+h)**128+**
7-y-o gr g Peacock (FR)-Lady Cheyenne (Stanford)
Jonjo O'Neill John P McManus

Placings:*214-1222F1F*   **(4398)**
2003/04: 21²G, 21²S, 21²GS, 19²S, 16FS, 21¹GS, 32FG,

	Starts	1st	2nd	3rd	Win & Pl
Hurdles	4	1	3	0	7391
Chases	3	1	0	0	4183
Career Total	10	3	4	0	14742
128	2/04	Folk	2m5f	E Ch	G-S	£4182
112	10/03	Strf	2m6f110yD Hdl	GD	£4260
111	1/03	Kemp	2m	H NHF	G-S	£2383

Total win prize-money £10828

Going:	Sf: 0-3 GS: 1-2 Gd: 1-2 GF: - Fm: 0-0
Distance:	2m/2m3: 0-2 **2m4-2m7: 2-4** 3m+: 0-1
Track:	LH: 1-4 RH: 1-3 **Tight: 2-5** Gall: 0-0
Aids:	Bl: 0-0 Vi: 0-0 Tstrap: 0-0 Ckp: 0-0
Best Rating:	128 2/04 Folk 2m5f gd-sft Ch

Fair hurdler; stays two miles six; acts in soft ground.

Hawkes Run

104   **116**
6-y-o b g Hernando (FR)-Wise Speculation (USA) (Mr Prospector (USA))
C J Mann The Baron Rouge Partnership

Placings:*11213P0/5C5-3506*   **(0924)**
2003/04: 24³G, 22⁵G, 20ᴾG, 22ᴾGF,

	Starts	1st	2nd	3rd	Win & Pl
Hurdles	4	0	0	1	1746
Career Total	14	3	1	2	22435
116	11/01	Hntg	2m110y B Hdl	GD	£8190
94	8/01	Strf	2m110y E Hdl	GD	£2989
95	7/01	MRas	2m1f110yD Hdl	G-S	£3835

Total win prize-money £15014

Going:	Sf: 0-0 GS: 0-0 Gd: 0-2 GF: - Fm: 0-2
Distance:	2m/2m3: 0-0 2m4-2m7: 0-3 3m+: 0-1
Track:	LH: 0-3 RH: 0-0 Tight: 0-1 Gall: 0-0
Aids:	Bl: 0-0 Vi: 0-0 Tstrap: 0-0 Ckp: 0-4
Best Rating:	129 12/01 Chep 2m110y gd-sft Hdl

Useful juvenile hurdler in 2001/2 winning three times; lightly-raced and not as good since; acts on good ground or slightly softer; has been tried in blinkers and cheekpieces.

Hawthorn

8-y-o ch g Primo Dominie-Starr Danias (USA) (Sensitive Prince (USA))
B J Clarke Clock House Racing

Placings:*36/0/0/5P-F*   **(4563)**
2003/04: 22FG,

	Starts	1st	2nd	3rd	Win & Pl
Chases	1	0	0	0	
Career Total	7	0	0	1	243

Going:	Sf: 0-0 GS: 0-0 Gd: 0-1 GF: - Fm: 0-0
Distance:	2m/2m3: 0-0 2m4-2m7: 0-1 3m+: 0-0
Track:	LH: 0-1 RH: 0-0 Tight: 0-0 Gall: 0-1
Aids:	Bl: 0-0 Vi: 0-0 Tstrap: 0-0 Ckp: 0-0
Best Rating:	95 4/00 Ayr 2m good NHF

Hawthorn Prince (IRE)

101   **114**
9-y-o ch g Black Monday-Goose Loose (Dual)
Mrs P Sly Messrs G A Libson,D L Bayliss & G Taylor

Placings:*00000/0PUU30-11P35*   **(2581)**
2003/04: 23¹GF, 23¹GF, 22ᴾGF, 24³G, 20⁵GF,

	Starts	1st	2nd	3rd	Win & Pl
Hurdles	5	2	0	1	8093
Career Total	16	2	0	2	8630
114	5/03	Fknm	2m7f110yE(0-100)HHdl	G-F	£3393
98	5/03	Fknm	2m7f110yE Hdl	G-F	£3926

Total win prize-money £7319

Going:	Sf: 0-0 GS: 0-0 Gd: 0-1 GF: - Fm: 2-4
Distance:	2m/2m3: 0-0 2m4-2m7: 0-2 **3m+: 2-3**
Track:	**LH: 2-5** RH: 0-0 **Tight: 2-4** Gall: 0-0
Aids:	Bl: 0-0 Vi: 0-0 Tstrap: 0-0 Ckp: 0-0
Best Rating:	114 5/03 Fknm 2m7f110y gd-fm Hdl

Won back-to-back points spring 2002; completed four-timer with two clear-cut victories in 3m novice hurdles at Fakenham in May; acts on good to firm.

Hay Dance

13-y-o b g Shareef Dancer (USA)-Hay Reef (Mill Reef (USA))
J Ibbott Mrs S J Ruddle

Placings:*000/021431231531/F/F35/F/3P-P*   **(0198)**
2003/04: 20ᴾGF,

	Starts	1st	2nd	3rd	Win & Pl
Chases	1	0	0	0	
Career Total	23	5	2	4	18566
119	4/97	NAbb	2m1f	D(0-125)HHdl	FRM	£2735
121	1/97	Winc	2m	D(0-125)HHdl	G-F	£3183
109	12/96	Hrfd	2m1f	D(0-120)HHdl	G-S	£2857
96	11/96	Tntn	2m1f	C HHdl	G-F	£3533
87	7/96	Baln	2m	Hdl	G-F	£2295

Total win prize-money £14605

Going:	Sf: 0-0 GS: 0-0 Gd: 0-0 GF: - Fm: 0-1
Distance:	2m/2m3: 0-0 2m4-2m7: 0-1 3m+: 0-0
Track:	LH: 0-0 RH: 0-1 Tight: 0-0 Gall: 0-1
Aids:	Bl: 0-0 Vi: 0-0 Tstrap: 0-0 Ckp: 0-0
Best Rating:	122 12/98 Tntn 2m1f good Hdl

Modest hunter chaser/pointer, suited by fast ground.

Hayaain

100   **95**
11-y-o b g Shirley Heights-Littlefield (Bay Express)
N W Alexander Jamie Alexander

Placings:*1451/1024400/0050B2112P0/0252-2P000* **(4948)**
2003/04: 24²GS, 24ᴾGS, 24ᵁGF, 18ᵁHY, 27ᵁGS,

	Starts	1st	2nd	3rd	Win & Pl
Hurdles	5	0	1	0	830
Career Total	31	5	6	0	35737
110	12/01	Muss	3m	D(0-125)HHdl	GD	£8465
107	12/01	Muss	3m	D(0-125)HHdl	G-F	£4891
132	9/99	Hntg	2m4f110yD(0-125)HHdl	GD	£7002
97	3/97	Uttx	2m4f110yE Hdl	G-F	£2200
108	2/97	Sand	2m110y C Hdl	G-F	£3517

Total win prize-money £26078

Going:	Sf: 0-1 GS: 0-3 Gd: 0-0 GF: - Fm: 0-1
Distance:	2m/2m3: 0-1 2m4-2m7: 0-0 3m+: 0-4
Track:	LH: 0-3 RH: 0-0 Tight: 0-1 Gall: 0-1
Aids:	Bl: 0-0 Vi: 0-0 Tstrap: 0-0 Ckp: 0-0
Best Rating:	132 11/99 Asct 3m good Hdl

Moderate hurdler; front-runner; lost his way until a change of stable jolted him back to winning form for his new trainer Jim Barclay, scoring twice at Musselburgh in December 2001; looks to need three miles and a sound surface although does handle some cut.

Hayburn Vaults

68   **28**
6-y-o b m Bettergeton-Agdistis (Petoski)
Mrs S J Smith Mrs A E Astall

Placings:*0-00*   **(4253)**
2003/04: 17ᴾGS, 17ᴾGS,

	Starts	1st	2nd	3rd	Win & Pl
NH Flat	1	0	0	0	0
Hurdles	1	0	0	0	0
Career Total	3	0	0	0	

Going:	Sf: 0-0 GS: 0-1 Gd: 0-1 GF: - Fm: 0-0
Distance:	2m/2m3: 0-2 2m4-2m7: 0-0 3m+: 0-0
Track:	LH: 0-2 RH: 0-0 Tight: 0-2 Gall: 0-0
Aids:	Bl: 0-0 Vi: 0-0 Tstrap: 0-0 Ckp: 0-0
Best Rating:	48 2/04 Sedg 2m1f gd-sft NHF

Haydens Field

106   **127**
10-y-o b g Bedford (USA)-Releta (Relkino)
P M Rich Miss H Lewis

Placings:*63623/21/111PP26-10*   **(2325)**
2003/04: 20¹S, 20ᴾGS,

	Starts	1st	2nd	3rd	Win & Pl
Hurdles	2	1	0	0	9344
Career Total	16	5	3	2	28216
127	5/03	Uttx	2m4f110yB(0-140)HHdl	SFT	£9343
137	5/02	Weth	3m1f	D Hdl	G-S	£3332
123	5/02	NAbb	2m6f	E Hdl	G-S	£3073
123	5/02	Bang	3m	E Hdl	GD	£3122
120	4/02	Chep	2m4f	E Hdl	GS	£2961

Total win prize-money £21832

Going:	Sf: 1-1 GS: 0-1 Gd: 0-0 GF: - Fm: 0-0
Distance:	2m/2m3: 0-0 **2m4-2m7: 1-2** 3m+: 0-0
Track:	**LH: 1-2** RH: 0-0 Tight: 0-1 Gall: 0-0
Aids:	Bl: 0-0 Vi: 0-0 Tstrap: 0-0 Ckp: 0-0
Best Rating:	137 5/02 Weth 3m1f gd-sft Hdl

Useful hurdler; completed a four-timer of front-running victo-

ries in the spring of 2002; back to that sort of form when resuming his winning ways at Uttoxeter in April 2003; stays three miles and suited by soft ground.

Hayley's Pearl

5-y-o b m Nomadic Way (USA)-Pacific Girl (IRE) (Emmson)
Mrs P Ford Paul Martin

Placings:000P0   (4654)
2003/04: 16⁰S, 17⁰GS, 16⁰GS, 22ᴾGS, 17⁰G,

	Starts	1st	2nd	3rd	Win & Pl
NH Flat	3	0	0	0	0
Hurdles	2	0	0	0	0
Career Total	**5**	**0**	**0**	**0**	

Going:	Sf: 0-1 GS: 0-3 Gd: 0-1 GF: - Fm: 0-0
Distance:	2m/2m3: 0-4 2m4-2m7: 0-1 3m+: 0-0
Track:	LH: 0-2 RH: 0-3 Tight: 0-0 Gall: 0-0
Aids:	Bl: 0-0 Vi: 0-0 Tstrap: 0-0 Ckp: 0-0
Best Rating:	21 12/03 Hrfd 2m1f gd-sft NHF

Haystacks (IRE)
105   105+

8-y-o b g Contract Law (USA)-Florissa (FR) (Persepolis (FR))
James Moffatt Mr & Mrs A G Milligan

Placings:0225F14/413050/05634/1516   (2862)
2003/04: 22¹GS, 22²GF, 25¹GF, 24⁸GS,

	Starts	1st	2nd	3rd	Win & Pl
Hurdles	4	2	0	0	10013
Career Total	**22**	**4**	**2**	**2**	**19436**
105	11/03	Catt	3m1f110yD(0-115)HHdl		G-F	£4147
102	5/03	Ctml	2m6f	D(0-120)HHdl	G-S	£5866
104	5/00	Ctml	2m6f	D(0-120)HHdl	G-F	£3721
97	3/00	Kels	2m2f	E Hdl	G-S	£2366
			Total win prize-money £16100

Going:	Sf: 0-0 GS: 1-2 Gd: 0-0 GF: - Fm: 1-2
Distance:	2m/2m3: 0-0 2m4-2m7: 0-2 3m+: 1-2
Track:	LH: 2-3 RH: 0-0 Tight: 2-2 Gall: 0-1
Aids:	Bl: 0-0 Vi: 1-2 Tstrap: 0-0 Ckp: 1-2
Best Rating:	105 11/03 Catt 3m1f110y gd-fm Hdl

Moderate staying hurdler, lightly raced over jumps in recent seasons; lame when winning at Catterick in November; stays well; handles any ground.

Hayton Boy

10-y-o ch g Gypsy Castle-Young Christine Vii (Damsire Unregistered)
S G Chadwick S Chadwick

Placings:UPF-P   (4431)
2003/04: 24ᶠG,

	Starts	1st	2nd	3rd	Win & Pl
Hurdles	1	0	0	0	
Career Total	**4**	**0**	**0**	**0**	

Going:	Sf: 0-0 GS: 0-0 Gd: 0-1 GF: - Fm: 0-0
Distance:	2m/2m3: 0-0 2m4-2m7: 0-0 3m+: 0-1
Track:	LH: 0-1 RH: 0-0 Tight: 0-0 Gall: 0-0
Aids:	Bl: 0-0 Vi: 0-0 Tstrap: 0-0 Ckp: 0-0

Hazel Flight
85f   61f

4-y-o ch f Hazaaf (USA)-Sapphire Flight (Scallywag)
Miss M Bragg Mrs J M Whitley

Placings:0   (4738)
2003/04: 17⁰G,

	Starts	1st	2nd	3rd	Win & Pl
NH Flat	1	0	0	0	
Career Total	**1**	**0**	**0**	**0**	

Going:	Sf: 0-0 GS: 0-0 Gd: 0-1 GF: - Fm: 0-0
Distance:	2m/2m3: 0-1 2m4-2m7: 0-0 3m+: 0-0
Track:	LH: 0-1 RH: 0-0 Tight: 0-1 Gall: 0-0
Aids:	Bl: 0-0 Vi: 0-0 Tstrap: 0-0 Ckp: 0-0
Best Rating:	61 4/04 NAbb 2m1f good NHF

Hazel Reilly (IRE)

13-y-o b m Mister Lord (USA)-Vickies Gold (Golden Love)
Mrs Sarah L Dent John Mackley

Placings:6243/3422/P11242-2   (0172)
2003/04: 25²GF,

	Starts	1st	2nd	3rd	Win & Pl
Chases	1	0	1	0	414
Career Total	**15**	**2**	**6**	**2**	**9694**
78	3/03	Kels	3m1f	H Ch		G-S	£2479
99	2/03	Catt	3m4f110yH Ch		GD	£1491
			Total win prize-money £3971

Going:	Sf: 0-0 GS: 0-0 Gd: 0-0 GF: - Fm: 0-1
Distance:	2m/2m3: 0-0 2m4-2m7: 0-0 3m+: 0-1
Track:	LH: 0-1 RH: 0-0 Tight: 0-0 Gall: 0-0
Aids:	Bl: 0-0 Vi: 0-0 Tstrap: 0-0 Ckp: 0-0
Best Rating:	99 4/03 Prth 3m7f good Ch

Modest hunter chaser; out-and-out stayer; acts on any ground.

Hazeljack
105(83h)   (96h)110

9-y-o b g Sula Bula-Hazelwain (Hard Fact)
A J Whiting A J Whiting

Placings:0/065F4/004U60P34   (4427)
2003/04: 20⁴G, 21³G, 26⁴S, 20ᴜG, 20⁶GS, 21⁰G, 25ᴾS, 20³G, 21⁴G,

	Starts	1st	2nd	3rd	Win & Pl
Hurdles	2	0	0	0	0
Chases	7	0	0	1	6257
Career Total	**15**	**0**	**0**	**1**	**6257**

Going:	Sf: 0-2 GS: 0-1 Gd: 0-6 GF: - Fm: 0-0
Distance:	2m/2m3: 0-0 2m4-2m7: 0-7 3m+: 0-2
Track:	LH: 0-5 RH: 0-3 Tight: 0-5 Gall: 0-2
Aids:	Bl: 0-0 Vi: 0-0 Tstrap: 0-0 Ckp: 0-0
Best Rating:	110 3/04 Chel 2m5f good Ch

Moderate chaser; unlucky at Ludlow in December; ran well when remote fourth in Cathcart at Cheltenham; stays 2m 5f.

Hazy Morn

5-y-o gr m Cyrano De Bergerac-Hazy Kay (IRE) (Treasure Kay)
R J Hodges R J Hart

Placings:FP   (2409)

2003/04: 16ᶠG, 17ᴾGF,

	Starts	1st	2nd	3rd	Win & Pl
Hurdles	2	0	0	0	
Career Total	**2**	**0**	**0**	**0**	

Going:	Sf: 0-0 GS: 0-0 Gd: 0-1 GF: - Fm: 0-1
Distance:	2m/2m3: 0-2 2m4-2m7: 0-0 3m+: 0-0
Track:	LH: 0-1 RH: 0-1 Tight: 0-2 Gall: 0-0
Aids:	Bl: 0-0 Vi: 0-0 Tstrap: 0-0 Ckp: 0-0

He's A Leader (IRE)
82   63

5-y-o b g Supreme Leader-Raise The Bells (Belfalas)
M C Pipe Matt Archer & Miss Jean Broadhurst

Placings:0P05   (4756)
2003/04: 16⁹GS, 22ᴾGS, 24⁰G, 19⁵S,

	Starts	1st	2nd	3rd	Win & Pl
NH Flat	1	0	0	0	0
Hurdles	3	0	0	0	0
Career Total	**4**	**0**	**0**	**0**	**0**

Going:	Sf: 0-1 GS: 0-2 Gd: 0-1 GF: - Fm: 0-0
Distance:	2m/2m3: 0-1 2m4-2m7: 0-2 3m+: 0-1
Track:	LH: 0-2 RH: 0-1 Tight: 0-1 Gall: 0-1
Aids:	Bl: 0-0 Vi: 0-0 Tstrap: 0-0 Ckp: 0-0
Best Rating:	71 11/03 Newb 2m110y gd-sft NHF

Plating-class hurdler; has shown promise; capable of better once handicapped.

He's My Uncle

9-y-o ch g Phardante (FR)-Red Dusk (Deep Run)
Mrs J K M Oliver Mrs J K M Oliver

Placings:0P/P-5P   (0413)
2003/04: 22⁵G, 20ᴾG,

	Starts	1st	2nd	3rd	Win & Pl
Hurdles	2	0	0	0	0
Career Total	**5**	**0**	**0**	**0**	**0**

Going:	Sf: 0-0 GS: 0-0 Gd: 0-2 GF: - Fm: 0-0
Distance:	2m/2m3: 0-0 2m4-2m7: 0-2 3m+: 0-0
Track:	LH: 0-2 RH: 0-0 Tight: 0-1 Gall: 0-0
Aids:	Bl: 0-0 Vi: 0-0 Tstrap: 0-0 Ckp: 0-0
Best Rating:	63 11/01 Carl 2m1f soft NHF

He's The Biz (FR)
101   93+

5-y-o b g Nikos-Irun (FR) (Son Of Silver)
Nick Williams Mrs Jane Williams

Placings:0065P-P1314PP   (4492)
2003/04: 17ᴾGS, 20¹GF, 22³G, 24¹GF, 24⁴G, 24ᴾG, 22ᴾG,

	Starts	1st	2nd	3rd	Win & Pl
Hurdles	7	2	0	1	6696
Career Total	**12**	**2**	**0**	**1**	**7596**
93	11/03	Worc	3m	E(0-110)HHdl	G-F	£2954
80	8/03	Worc	2m4f	F(0-95)HHdl	G-F	£2975
			Total win prize-money £5929

Going:	Sf: 0-0 GS: 0-1 Gd: 0-4 GF: - Fm: 2-2
Distance:	2m/2m3: 0-1 2m4-2m7: 1-3 3m+: 1-3
Track:	LH: 2-5 RH: 0-2 Tight: 0-4 Gall: 0-0
Aids:	Bl: 0-0 Vi: 0-0 Tstrap: 0-0 Ckp: 0-0
Best Rating:	93 11/03 Worc 3m gd-fm Hdl

Appreciated the combination of a longer trip and a sounder surface when winning weak 2m 4f amateur riders' novices' handicap hurdle at Worcester August 2003.

He's The Boss (IRE)
100   121

7-y-o b g Supreme Leader-Attykee (IRE) (Le Moss)
R H Buckler M J Hallett

Placings:01/260-1F35   (3825)
2003/04: 20¹G, 21FS, 21³GS, 20⁵S,

	Starts	1st	2nd	3rd	Win & Pl
Hurdles	4	1	0	1	8530
Career Total	9	2	1	1	15611
115 11/03 Asct	2m4f	D Hdl		GD	£4680
109 3/02 Strf	2m110y	H NHF		G-S	£3101
			Total win prize-money £7781		

Going:	Sf: 0-2 GS: 0-1 Gd: 1-1 GF: - Fm: 0-0
Distance:	2m/2m3: 0-0 2m4-2m7: 1-4 3m+: 0-0
Track:	LH: 0-3 RH: 1-1 Tight: 0-1 Gall: 0-0
Aids:	Bl: 0-0 Vi: 0-0 Tstrap: 0-0 Ckp: 0-0
Best Rating:	127 3/03 Chel 2m110y good NHF

Fair hurdler; formerly useful in bumpers; successful on his hurdling debut at Ascot in Novemebr 2003; stays two and a half miles and acts on ground good or softer; well beaten and ran as if something was amiss at Haydock in February.

He's The Guv'nor (IRE)
61

5-y-o b g Supreme Leader-Love The Lord (IRE) (Mister Lord (USA))
R H Buckler M J Hallett

Placings:0064   (4664)
2003/04: 16⁰GS, 16⁰G, 16⁶GF, 19⁴GS,

	Starts	1st	2nd	3rd	Win & Pl
NH Flat	3	0	0	0	0
Hurdles	1	0	0	0	290
Career Total	4	0	0	0	290

Going:	Sf: 0-0 GS: 0-2 Gd: 0-1 GF: - Fm: 0-1
Distance:	2m/2m3: 0-3 2m4-2m7: 0-1 3m+: 0-0
Track:	LH: 0-2 RH: 0-1 Tight: 0-1 Gall: 0-1
Aids:	Bl: 0-0 Vi: 0-0 Tstrap: 0-0 Ckp: 0-0
Best Rating:	100 2/04 Newb 2m110y good NHF

Heart Midoltian (FR)
117(106h)   (127?h)137

7-y-o gr g Royal Charter (FR)-Pride Of Queen (FR) (Saint Henri)
Seamus Neville Mrs S Neville

Placings:5306306/1225144PF11-3P650UF   (4805a)
2003/04: 20¹GY, 20³GF, 22PY, 20⁶F, 25⁵Y, 21⁰G, 21ᵁG, 29FY,

	Starts	1st	2nd	3rd	Win & Pl
Hurdles	2	0	0	1	727
Chases	6	1	0		16883
Career Total	25	4	2	3	43032
137 4/03 Punc	2m4f	Ch		G-Y	£16883
127 4/03 Fair	2m6f100y Ch			G-F	£8064
111 8/02 Cork	2m4f	Hdl		GD	£7831
95 5/02 Navn	2m2f	Hdl		SFT	£5503
			Total win prize-money £38282		

Going:	Sf: 0-0 GS: 0-0 Gd: 0-2 GF: - Fm: 0-2
Distance:	2m/2m3: 0-0 2m4-2m7: 1-6 3m+: 0-2
Track:	LH: 0-3 RH: 1-5 Tight: 0-1 Gall: 0-0

Aids:
Bl: 0-0 Vi: 0-0 Tstrap: 1-7 Ckp: 0-0
Best Rating: 137 4/03 Punc 2m4f   gd-yld   Ch

Useful Irish performer; stays just short of two mile seven; acts on most ground; usually wears a tongue-tie.

Heartache
104(83h)   (73h)98

7-y-o b g Jurado (USA)-Heresy (IRE) (Black Minstrel)
R Mathew Robin Mathew

Placings:P/3O0-062F   (4759)
2003/04: 19⁰S, 19⁶GS, 17²GS, 16FS,

	Starts	1st	2nd	3rd	Win & Pl
Hurdles	2	0	0	0	0
Chases	2	0	1	0	1665
Career Total	8	0	1	1	2436

Going:	Sf: 0-2 GS: 0-2 Gd: 0-0 GF: - Fm: 0-0
Distance:	2m/2m3: 0-3 2m4-2m7: 0-1 3m+: 0-0
Track:	LH: 0-1 RH: 0-2 Tight: 0-1 Gall: 0-0
Aids:	Bl: 0-0 Vi: 0-0 Tstrap: 0-0 Ckp: 0-1
Best Rating:	98 3/04 Bang 2m1f110y gd-sft Ch

Heartbreaker (IRE)
95   74

4-y-o b g In Command (IRE)-No Hard Feelings (IRE) (Alzao (USA))
M W Easterby E A Brook

Placings:5   (1071)
2003/04: 17⁵GF,

	Starts	1st	2nd	3rd	Win & Pl
Hurdles	1	0	0	0	0
Career Total	1	0	0	0	0

Going:	Sf: 0-0 GS: 0-0 Gd: 0-0 GF: - Fm: 0-1
Distance:	2m/2m3: 0-1 2m4-2m7: 0-0 3m+: 0-0
Track:	LH: 0-1 RH: 0-0 Tight: 0-1 Gall: 0-0
Aids:	Bl: 0-0 Vi: 0-0 Tstrap: 0-0 Ckp: 0-0
Best Rating:	78 8/03 Sedg 2m1f gd-fm Hdl

Heartofmidlothian (IRE)
89f   75f

5-y-o ch g Anshan-Random Wind (Random Shot)
K C Bailey L Haugh

Placings:0   (4594)
2003/04: 16⁰G,

	Starts	1st	2nd	3rd	Win & Pl
NH Flat	1	0	0	0	
Career Total	1	0	0	0	

Going:	Sf: 0-0 GS: 0-0 Gd: 0-0 GF: - Fm: 0-0
Distance:	2m/2m3: 0-1 2m4-2m7: 0-0 3m+: 0-0
Track:	LH: 0-0 RH: 0-1 Tight: 0-0 Gall: 0-1
Aids:	Bl: 0-0 Vi: 0-0 Tstrap: 0-0 Ckp: 0-0
Best Rating:	75 3/04 Hntg 2m110y good NHF

Heatherjack
62   25

7-y-o b m Nalchik (USA)-Healaughs Pride (Healaugh Fox)
B Mactaggart J Jack

Placings:0-0   (0380)
2003/04: 16⁰G,

	Starts	1st	2nd	3rd	Win & Pl
Hurdles	1	0	0	0	
Career Total	2	0	0	0	

Going:	Sf: 0-0 GS: 0-0 Gd: 0-1 GF: - Fm: 0-0
Distance:	2m/2m3: 0-1 2m4-2m7: 0-0 3m+: 0-0
Track:	LH: 0-1 RH: 0-0 Tight: 0-1 Gall: 0-0
Aids:	Bl: 0-0 Vi: 0-0 Tstrap: 0-0 Ckp: 0-0
Best Rating:	25 5/03 Kels 2m110y good Hdl

Heathy Gore

5-y-o ch m Environment Friend-Hazel Hill (Abednego)
J K Cresswell J K S Cresswell

Placings:0   (2844)
2003/04: 16⁰GS,

	Starts	1st	2nd	3rd	Win & Pl
NH Flat	1	0	0	0	
Career Total	1	0	0	0	

Going:	Sf: 0-0 GS: 0-1 Gd: 0-0 GF: - Fm: 0-0
Distance:	2m/2m3: 0-1 2m4-2m7: 0-0 3m+: 0-0
Track:	LH: 0-1 RH: 0-0 Tight: 0-0 Gall: 0-0
Aids:	Bl: 0-0 Vi: 0-0 Tstrap: 0-0 Ckp: 0-0

Heathyards Friend
91   75

5-y-o b g Forest Wind (USA)-Heathyards Lady (USA) (Mining (USA))
R Hollinshead L A Morgan

Placings:2100-00   (1300)
2003/04: 16⁰G, 16⁰GS,

	Starts	1st	2nd	3rd	Win & Pl
Hurdles	2	0	0	0	
Career Total	6	1	1	0	3927
71 12/02 Donc	2m110y	G Hdl		GD	£3026
			Total win prize-money £3027		

Going:	Sf: 0-0 GS: 0-0 Gd: 0-1 GF: - Fm: 0-1
Distance:	2m/2m3: 0-2 2m4-2m7: 0-0 3m+: 0-0
Track:	LH: 0-2 RH: 0-0 Tight: 0-1 Gall: 0-0
Aids:	Bl: 0-0 Vi: 0-0 Tstrap: 0-0 Ckp: 0-0
Best Rating:	75 8/02 Bang 2m1f soft Hdl

Clera-cut winner of a selling hurdle at Doncaster in December.

Heathyards Guest (IRE)
81   80

6-y-o ch g Be My Guest (USA)-Noble Nadia (Thatching)
Mrs K Walton G M Marshall

Placings:04/3406-0   (0011)
2003/04: 16⁰GF,

	Starts	1st	2nd	3rd	Win & Pl
Hurdles	1	0	0	0	
Career Total	7	0	0	1	366

Going:	Sf: 0-0 GS: 0-0 Gd: 0-0 GF: - Fm: 0-1
Distance:	2m/2m3: 0-1 2m4-2m7: 0-0 3m+: 0-0
Track:	LH: 0-1 RH: 0-0 Tight: 0-0 Gall: 0-1
Aids:	Bl: 0-1 Vi: 0-0 Tstrap: 0-0 Ckp: 0-0

Best Rating: 84 4/02 Sedg 2m1f   gd-fm Hdl

Heathyards Swing
94 | **85**

6-y-o b g Celtic Swing-Butsova (Formidable (USA))
James Moffatt (R Hollinshead 25/6) WRR Syndicate

Placings:64000   (4688)
2003/04: 16^{6}S, 16^{4}GS, 16^{9}HY, 22^{0}GF, 16^{0}G,

	Starts	1st	2nd	3rd	Win & Pl
Hurdles	5	0	0	0	0
Career Total	5	0	0	0	0

Going:	Sf: 0-2 GS: 0-1 Gd: 0-1 GF: - Fm: 0-1
Distance:	2m/2m3: 0-4 2m4-2m7: 0-1 3m+: 0-0
Track:	LH: 0-5 RH: 0-0 Tight: 0-4 Gall: 0-0
Aids:	Bl: 0-0 Vi: 0-0 Tstrap: 0-0 Ckp: 0-5
Best Rating:	85 1/04 Catt 2m gd-sft Hdl

Temperamental plater on the Flat; showed ability when fourth on second start over hurdles at Catterick in January.

Heaven Is Above (IRE)

9-y-o b g Hymns On High-Great Supper (Slippered)
Mrs S J Hickman Mrs Diana Rowell

Placings:00/0060P/1-P   (4150)
2003/04: 24^{0}G,

	Starts	1st	2nd	3rd	Win & Pl
Chases	1	0	0	0	
Career Total	9	1	0	0	5153
113 4/03 Cork 3m			Ch	G-F	£5152

Total win prize-money £5153

Going:	Sf: 0-0 GS: 0-0 Gd: 0-1 GF: - Fm: 0-0
Distance:	2m/2m3: 0-0 2m4-2m7: 0-0 3m+: 0-1
Track:	LH: 0-0 RH: 0-1 Tight: 0-1 Gall: 0-0
Aids:	Bl: 0-0 Vi: 0-0 Tstrap: 0-0 Ckp: 0-0
Best Rating:	113 4/03 Cork 3m gd-fm Ch

Heavenly Hill
72 | **27**

7-y-o b m Nomadic Way (USA)-Tees Gazette Girl (Kalaglow)
M J Gingell Gentlemen Don't Work On Mondays

Placings:0/30-05   (0531)
2003/04: 20^{0}GF, 20^{5}GF,

	Starts	1st	2nd	3rd	Win & Pl
Hurdles	2	0	0	0	0
Career Total	5	0	0	1	425

Going:	Sf: 0-0 GS: 0-0 Gd: 0-0 GF: - Fm: 0-2
Distance:	2m/2m3: 0-0 2m4-2m7: 0-2 3m+: 0-0
Track:	LH: 0-2 RH: 0-0 Tight: 0-1 Gall: 0-0
Aids:	Bl: 0-0 Vi: 0-0 Tstrap: 0-0 Ckp: 0-0
Best Rating:	94 2/03 Muss 2m good NHF

Moderate form in bumper company; acts on good ground; effective over two miles.

Heavenly King
98 | **80**

6-y-o b g Homo Sapien-Chapel Hill (IRE) (The Parson)
P Bowen Eamonn O'Malley

Placings:6PPP-20   (0681)
2003/04: 19^{2}GF, 24^{0}GF,

	Starts	1st	2nd	3rd	Win & Pl
Hurdles	2	0	1	0	1060
Career Total	6	0	1	0	1060

Going:	Sf: 0-0 GS: 0-0 Gd: 0-0 GF: - Fm: 0-2
Distance:	2m/2m3: 0-1 2m4-2m7: 0-0 3m+: 0-1
Track:	LH: 0-1 RH: 0-1 Tight: 0-0 Gall: 0-1
Aids:	Bl: 0-2 Vi: 0-0 Tstrap: 0-0 Ckp: 0-0
Best Rating:	80 5/03 Extr 2m3f gd-fm Hdl

Pulled up in soft ground on first three starts over hurdles; second on fast ground to the progressive Anzal at Exeter May 2003.

Heavenly Pleasure (IRE)
94f | **84f**

5-y-o b m Presenting-Galynn (IRE) (Strong Gale)
C Roberts W S Rogers

Placings:06   (4920)
2003/04: 16^{9}G, 16^{6}GS,

	Starts	1st	2nd	3rd	Win & Pl
NH Flat	2	0	0	0	0
Career Total	2	0	0	0	0

Going:	Sf: 0-0 GS: 0-1 Gd: 0-1 GF: - Fm: 0-0
Distance:	2m/2m3: 0-2 2m4-2m7: 0-0 3m+: 0-0
Track:	LH: 0-1 RH: 0-1 Tight: 0-0 Gall: 0-0
Aids:	Bl: 0-0 Vi: 0-0 Tstrap: 0-0 Ckp: 0-0
Best Rating:	84 4/04 Worc 2m gd-sft NHF

Heckley Clare Glen
97f | **103+f**

6-y-o b m Dancing High-Heckley Spark (Electric)
N G Richards James Callow & David Wesley Yates

Placings:10   (3438)
2003/04: 16^{1}G, 16^{0}HY,

	Starts	1st	2nd	3rd	Win & Pl
NH Flat	2	1	0	0	1477
Career Total	2	1	0	0	1477
103 11/03 Newc 2m			H NHF	GD	£1477

Total win prize-money £1477

Going:	Sf: 0-1 GS: 0-0 Gd: 1-1 GF: - Fm: 0-0
Distance:	2m/2m3: 1-2 2m4-2m7: 0-0 3m+: 0-0
Track:	LH: 1-2 RH: 0-0 Tight: 0-0 Gall: 0-0
Aids:	Bl: 0-0 Vi: 0-0 Tstrap: 0-0 Ckp: 0-0
Best Rating:	103 11/03 Newc 2m good NHF

Won weak bumper on debut.

Hedgehunter (IRE)
115 | **(126h)150+**

8-y-o b g Montelimar (USA)-Aberedw (IRE) (Caerwent)
W P Mullins Trevor Hemmings

Placings:22/2224.2621/22310-2431F   (4647)
2003/04: 25^{2}G, 26^{4}GS, 29^{3}S, 24^{1}S, 24^{2}F,

	Starts	1st	2nd	3rd	Win & Pl
Chases	5	1	1	1	59735
Career Total	20	3	10	2	90532
156 1/04 Gowr 3m		HCh		SFT	£34330
132 2/03 Punc 3m4f		HCh		SH	£13506
125 1/02 Clon 3m		Hdl		HVY	£4868

Going:	Sf: 1-2 GS: 0-1 Gd: 0-2 GF: - Fm: 0-0
Distance:	2m/2m3: 0-0 2m4-2m7: 0-0 3m+: 1-5
Track:	LH: 0-3 RH: 1-2 Tight: 0-1 Gall: 0-1
Aids:	Bl: 0-0 Vi: 0-0 Tstrap: 0-0 Ckp: 0-0
Best Rating:	156 1/04 Gowr 3m soft Ch

Useful chaser; took well to fences in 2002/03, winning the Punchestown Grand National Trial on his handicap debut; every chance when blundered two out in National Hunt Challenge Cup at Cheltenham; ran well when fourth in Hennessy at Newbury on reappearance; third in the Welsh National before winning the Thyestes at Gowran; booked for third spot when falling at the last in the Grand National; stays very well and acts on testing ground.

Hee's A Dancer

12-y-o b g Rambo Dancer (CAN)-Heemee (On Your Mark)
R W J Willcox R W J Willcox

Placings:1F41/6402F5/2/F1/U63/26P5P/P/P   (0262)
2003/04: 20^{0}GF,

	Starts	1st	2nd	3rd	Win & Pl
Chases	1	0	0	0	
Career Total	23	3	3	1	8148
100 4/99 Ludl 2m4f		H Ch		GD	£1725
98 11/95 Catt 2m		G Hdl		G-F	£1856
98 9/95 Kels 2m110y		E Hdl		FRM	£1716

Total win prize-money £5297

Going:	Sf: 0-0 GS: 0-0 Gd: 0-0 GF: - Fm: 0-0
Distance:	2m/2m3: 0-0 2m4-2m7: 0-1 3m+: 0-0
Track:	LH: 0-0 RH: 0-1 Tight: 0-1 Gall: 0-0
Aids:	Bl: 0-0 Vi: 0-0 Tstrap: 0-0 Ckp: 0-0
Best Rating:	102 2/97 Muss 2m gd-fm Ch

Hehasalife (IRE)
100(59h) | **(102h)118**

7-y-o b g Safety Catch (USA)-America River (IRE) (Lord Americo)
Mrs H Dalton (Michael Hourigan 27/10) Norton House Racing

Placings:3/660000-02322106126243U4   (4960)
2003/04: 20^{0}YS, 24^{2}G, 24^{3}F, 24^{2}GF, 20^{2}GF, 20^{1}G, 20^{0}Y, 17^{6}GF, 22^{1}G, 20^{2}S, 20^{6}GF, 20^{2}F, 20^{4}GF, 20^{3}G, 20^{0}UG, 20^{4}GS,

	Starts	1st	2nd	3rd	Win & Pl
Hurdles	10	1	4	1	12724
Chases	6	1	1	1	12967
Career Total	23	2	5	3	26422
100 9/03 Gway 2m6f		Ch		GD	£7840
89 7/03 Limk 2m4f		Hdl		GD	£5600

Total win prize-money £13442

Going:	Sf: 0-1 GS: 0-1 Gd: 2-5 GF: - Fm: 0-7
Distance:	2m/2m3: 0-1 2m4-2m7: 2-12 3m+: 0-3
Track:	LH: 2-2 RH: 2-8 Tight: 0-2 Gall: 0-0
Aids:	Bl: 1-4 Vi: 0-0 Tstrap: 0-0 Ckp: 0-0
Best Rating:	116 3/04 Kemp 2m4f110y good Ch

Heidi III (FR)

9-y-o b g Bayolidaan (FR)-Irlandaise (FR) (Or De Chine)
Mrs L Williamson Turner Technology Ltd

Placings:01/21/11222110/52PP2/602-234   (4872)
2003/04: 24^{2}G, 20^{3}GS, 24^{4}S,

	Starts	1st	2nd	3rd	Win & Pl
Chases	3	0	1	1	2282

Career Total	23	6	8	1	77855
138	2/01	Newc	2m4f	B(0-140)HCh	HVY	£8684
138	1/01	Donc	3m	B(0-145)HCh	GD	£31850
128	6/00	Prth	2m4f110y	E Hdl	HVY	£2691
113	5/00	Weth	2m	E Hdl	G-F	£2772
117	4/00	Carl	2m1f	E Hdl	SFT	£2786
	1/99	Pau	2m1f	Ch	HLD	£5382
				Total win prize-money		£54166

Going: Sf: 0-1 GS: 0-1 Gd: 0-1 GF: - Fm: 0-0
Distance: 2m/2m3: 0-0 2m4-2m7: 0-1 3m+: 0-2
Track: LH: 0-3 RH: 0-0 Tight: 0-3 Gall: 0-0
Aids: Bl: 0-0 Vi: 0-0 Tstrap: 0-0 Ckp: 0-3
Best Rating: 138 2/01 Newc 2m4f   heavy   Ch

Hunter Chaser these days; stays three miles; acts on good ground; has worn cheekpieces.

Hektikos

61   35

4-y-o ch g Hector Protector (USA)-Green Danube (USA) (Irish River (FR))
S Dow S Dow

Placings: 0U   (4363)
2003/04: 16⁰G, 16⁰GS,

	Starts	1st	2nd	3rd	Win & Pl
Hurdles	2	0	0	0	
Career Total	2	0	0	0	

Going: Sf: 0-0 GS: 0-0 Gd: 0-1 GF: - Fm: 0-0
Distance: 2m/2m3: 0-2 2m4-2m7: 0-0 3m+: 0-0
Track: LH: 0-2 RH: 0-0 Tight: 0-2 Gall: 0-0
Aids: Bl: 0-0 Vi: 0-0 Tstrap: 0-0 Ckp: 0-0
Best Rating: 38 3/04 Plum 2m   good   Hdl

Helderberg (USA)

64   39

4-y-o b f Diesis-Banissa (USA) (Lear Fan (USA))
B S Rothwell (C E Brittain 7/11) D Coles, J King, J Broughton

Placings: 000   (4368)
2003/04: 16⁰S, 16⁰G, 16⁰GF,

	Starts	1st	2nd	3rd	Win & Pl
Hurdles	3	0	0	0	
Career Total	3	0	0	0	

Going: Sf: 0-1 GS: 0-0 Gd: 0-1 GF: - Fm: 0-1
Distance: 2m/2m3: 0-3 2m4-2m7: 0-0 3m+: 0-0
Track: LH: 0-3 RH: 0-0 Tight: 0-2 Gall: 0-1
Aids: Bl: 0-0 Vi: 0-0 Tstrap: 0-0 Ckp: 0-0
Best Rating: 48 2/04 Catt 2m   good   Hdl

Helixir Du Theil (FR)

103(99h)   (107h) 108+

9-y-o ch g Aelan Hapi (USA)-Manolette (FR) (Signani (FR))
R H Buckler The Manolettes

Placings: 0/4P/0400222/4342-31P   (2567)
2003/04: 19³GF, 26¹G, 32⁶G,

	Starts	1st	2nd	3rd	Win & Pl
Chases	3	1	0	1	3857
Career Total	11	1	4	2	9679
105	11/03	NAbb	3m2f110y		E(0-105)HCh
GD	£3029				
				Total win prize-money	£3029

Going: Sf: 0-0 GS: 0-0 Gd: 1-2 GF: - Fm: 0-1

Distance: 2m/2m3: 0-0 2m4-2m7: 0-1 **3m+: 1-2**
Track: **LH: 1-1** RH: 0-2 **Tight: 1-1** Gall: 0-1
Aids: Bl: 0-0 Vi: 0-0 Tstrap: 0-0 **Ckp: 1-3**
Best Rating: 111 4/02 Bang 3m   good   Hdl

Modest hurdler/chaser; stays beyond three miles; still lightly raced.

Hell Of A Time (IRE)

7-y-o b g Phardante (FR)-Ticking Over (IRE) (Decent Fellow)
Mrs N S Sharpe Islwyn Thomas

Placings: 5-05P   (2005)
2003/04: 16⁰GF, 16⁵GF, 24ᵖGF,

	Starts	1st	2nd	3rd	Win & Pl
NH Flat	2	0	0	0	0
Hurdles	1	0	0	0	0
Career Total	4	0	0	0	0

Going: Sf: 0-0 GS: 0-0 Gd: 0-0 GF: - Fm: 0-3
Distance: 2m/2m3: 0-2 2m4-2m7: 0-0 3m+: 0-1
Track: LH: 0-3 RH: 0-0 Tight: 0-0 Gall: 0-0
Aids: Bl: 0-0 Vi: 0-0 Tstrap: 0-0 Ckp: 0-0
Best Rating: 81 .10/03 Chep 2m110y   gd-fm   NHF

Hell-Of-A-Shindy (IRE)

95(102h)   (84+h) 114

10-y-o b g Phardante (FR)-Tonto's Girl (Strong Gale)
Jonjo O'Neill John P McManus

Placings: 4F/F3/P15324/125PP-53   (1519)
2003/04: 24⁵GF, 20³G,

	Starts	1st	2nd	3rd	Win & Pl
Hurdles	1	0	0	1	269
Chases	1	0	0	0	314
Career Total	17	2	2	3	18844
114	11/02	Winc	2m5f	D(0-115)HCh	GD	£7525
95	6/01	Clon	3m	Ch	FRM	£3895
				Total win prize-money	£11420

Going: Sf: 0-0 GS: 0-0 Gd: 0-1 GF: - Fm: 0-0
Distance: 2m/2m3: 0-0 2m4-2m7: 0-1 3m+: 0-1
Track: LH: 0-1 RH: 0-0 Tight: 0-2 Gall: 0-0
Aids: Bl: 0-0 Vi: 0-0 Tstrap: 0-0 Ckp: 0-0
Best Rating: 114 11/02 Winc 2m5f   good   Ch

Fair handicap chaser/Moderate hurdler; won a Wincanton handicap chase in November 2002; stays three miles; acts on a sound surface; has looked less then willing in the past.

Hello Baby

102f   88f

4-y-o b g Jumbo Hirt (USA)-Silver Flyer (Silver Season)
A C Whillans Miss J Gibson

Placings: 6325   (4886)
2003/04: 16⁶G, 16³G, 17²G, 17⁵GS,

	Starts	1st	2nd	3rd	Win & Pl
NH Flat	4	0	1	1	995
Career Total	4	0	1	1	995

Going: Sf: 0-0 GS: 0-1 Gd: 0-2 GF: - Fm: 0-1
Distance: 2m/2m3: 0-4 2m4-2m7: 0-0 3m+: 0-0
Track: LH: 0-0 RH: 0-4 Tight: 0-2 Gall: 0-0
Aids: Bl: 0-0 Vi: 0-0 Tstrap: 0-0 Ckp: 0-0
Best Rating: 88 3/04 Carl 2m1f   good   NHF

Hello Dee

82   79

6-y-o b m Alflora (IRE)-Donna Farina (Little Buskins)
Jonjo O'Neill Mrs R H Thompson

Placings: 32-3P   (1507)
2003/04: 20³GF, 22ᴾGF,

	Starts	1st	2nd	3rd	Win & Pl
Hurdles	2	0	0	1	370
Career Total	4	0	1	2	1179

Going: Sf: 0-0 GS: 0-0 Gd: 0-0 GF: - Fm: 0-2
Distance: 2m/2m3: 0-0 2m4-2m7: 0-2 3m+: 0-0
Track: LH: 0-2 RH: 0-0 Tight: 0-0 Gall: 0-0
Aids: Bl: 0-0 Vi: 0-0 Tstrap: 0-0 Ckp: 0-0
Best Rating: 92 3/03 MRas 2m1f110y   good   NHF

Good third on bumper debut and just touched off next time; easy to back when third behind favourite and stable mate Music To My Ears on hurdling debut at Worcester in September; pulled up the following month; will stay well.

Hello Mrs

61f   16f

6-y-o b m Sir Harry Lewis (USA)-Five And Four (IRE) (Green Desert (USA))
Mrs S J Smith A P Russell

Placings: 000   (4663)
2003/04: 16⁰GS, 16⁰HY, 16⁰S,

	Starts	1st	2nd	3rd	Win & Pl
NH Flat	3	0	0	0	
Career Total	3	0	0	0	

Going: Sf: 0-2 GS: 0-1 Gd: 0-0 GF: - Fm: 0-0
Distance: 2m/2m3: 0-3 2m4-2m7: 0-0 3m+: 0-0
Track: LH: 0-3 RH: 0-0 Tight: 0-0 Gall: 0-0
Aids: Bl: 0-0 Vi: 0-0 Tstrap: 0-0 Ckp: 0-0
Best Rating: 16 1/04 Newc 2m   heavy   NHF

Help Yourself (IRE)

99   74

8-y-o gr m Roselier (FR)-Sweet Run (Deep Run)
L Lungo Alistair Duncan

Placings: 16/00500-030FO35   (3470)
2003/04: 16⁰G, 24³G, 20⁹GF, 20ᶠGS, 16⁰GF, 22³S, 24⁴GF,

	Starts	1st	2nd	3rd	Win & Pl
Hurdles	7	0	0	2	777
Career Total	14	1	0	2	2303
98	11/01	Weth	2m	H NHF	GD	£1526
				Total win prize-money	£1526

Going: Sf: 0-1 GS: 0-1 Gd: 0-2 GF: - Fm: 0-3
Distance: 2m/2m3: 0-2 2m4-2m7: 0-3 3m+: 0-2
Track: LH: 0-5 RH: 0-1 Tight: 0-2 Gall: 0-0
Aids: Bl: 0-0 Vi: 0-0 Tstrap: 0-0 Ckp: 0-0
Best Rating: 98 11/01 Weth 2m   good   NHF

Bumper winner; plating-class hurdler; stays 2m 4f.

Helvetius

102(87h)   (99h) 113

8-y-o b g In The Wings-Hejraan (USA) (Alydar (USA))
P C Ritchens John Pearl

Placings: 0/44221324420/512542PP3-05P4P5130 (4817)
2003/04: 25⁰GS, 22⁵GF, 25ᴾGF, 24⁵GS, 21ᴾG, 22⁵G, 23¹GF, 26³GF, 24⁰G,

	Starts	1st	2nd	3rd	Win & Pl
Hurdles	1	0	0	0	0
Chases	8	1	0	1	6305
Career Total	30	3	6	3	22790

100 3/04 Leic 2m7f110yD(0-115)HCh G-F £5629
101 7/02 NAbb 2m5f110yD Ch G-F £4690
82 8/01 NAbb 2m6f D Hdl GD £3210
Total win prize-money £13530

Going: Sf: 0-2 GS: 0-2 Gd: 0-3 GF: - Fm: 1-4
Distance: 2m/2m3: 0-0 2m4-2m7: 0-3 3m+: 1-6
Track: LH: 0-2 RH: 1-5 Tight: 0-4 Gall: 0-0
Aids: Bl: 0-2 Vi: 0-0 Tstrap: 0-0 Ckp: 0-3
Best Rating: 113 12/02 Newb 2m6f110y soft Ch

Moderate chaser; suited by two and three-quarter miles and a sound surface; has worn cheekpieces and blinkers.

Hemsworthy
99   94
9-y-o ch g North Col-Look Back (Country Retreat)
Miss M Bragg W H Whitley

Placings:035/03-0   (0602)
2003/04: 27^3S, 22^0G,

	Starts	1st	2nd	3rd	Win & Pl
Hurdles	2	0	0	1	544
Career Total	6	0	0	2	771

Going: Sf: 0-1 GS: 0-0 Gd: 0-1 GF: - Fm: 0-0
Distance: 2m/2m3: 0-0 2m4-2m7: 0-1 3m+: 0-1
Track: LH: 0-2 RH: 0-0 Tight: 0-2 Gall: 0-0
Aids: Bl: 0-0 Vi: 0-0 Tstrap: 0-0 Ckp: 0-0
Best Rating: 94 4/03 NAbb 3m3f soft Hdl

Henbridge
108   68
8-y-o ch m Henbit (USA)-Celtic Bridge (Celtic Cone)
Mrs S M Johnson I K Johnson

Placings:000/P500P0/6F-03P303   (1077)
2003/04: 16^0GS, 17^3GF, 17^0GF, 20^3G, 16^0G, 20^3GF,

	Starts	1st	2nd	3rd	Win & Pl
Hurdles	6	0	0	3	1227
Career Total	17	0	0	3	1227

Going: Sf: 0-0 GS: 0-1 Gd: 0-2 GF: - Fm: 0-3
Distance: 2m/2m3: 0-4 2m4-2m7: 0-2 3m+: 0-0
Track: LH: 0-6 RH: 0-0 Tight: 0-3 Gall: 0-0
Aids: Bl: 0-0 Vi: 0-0 Tstrap: 0-0 Ckp: 0-0
Best Rating: 69 8/03 Worc 2m4f gd-fm Hdl

Selling hurdler; best effort to date when close third from 10lb 'wrong' at Newton Abbot June 2003; acts on good to firm; yet to prove she can be effective at 2m 4f.

Henrianjames
106(66h)   (90+h)118+
9-y-o b g Tina's Pet-Real Claire (Dreams To Reality (USA))
Mrs M Reveley K Benson

Placings:0/00616/2F4003S123-1F0201430   (4915)
2003/04: 16^1GF, 17^2GF, 17^0GF, 17^2G, 16^9GF, 17^1G, 16^4G, 16^3GF, 16^0GS,

	Starts	1st	2nd	3rd	Win & Pl
Hurdles	1	0	0	0	0
Chases	8	2	1	1	12237
Career Total	25	4	3	3	25746

118 11/03 MRas 2m1f110yD(0-115)HCh GD £3925
116 5/03 Weth 2m D(0-115)HCh G-F £5668

103 9/02 Prth 2m D Ch G-F £6727
94 4/02 Newc 2m110y E Ch FRM £3328
Total win prize-money £19651

Going: Sf: 0-0 GS: 0-1 Gd: 1-3 GF: - Fm: 1-5
Distance: 2m/2m3: 2-9 2m4-2m7: 0-0 3m+: 0-0
Track: LH: 1-7 RH: 1-2 Tight: 1-3 Gall: 0-1
Aids: Bl: 0-0 Vi: 0-0 Tstrap: 0-0 Ckp: 0-0
Best Rating: 118 11/03 MRas 2m1f110y good Ch

Modest chaser; comfortable winner at Wetherby May; scored again at Market Rasen in November; best on a sound surface, but handles good to soft; suited by around two miles.

Henrietta (IRE)
105   103+
6-y-o b m Hushang (IRE)-Jennie's First (Idiots Delight)
M C Pipe B A Kilpatrick

Placings:113010   (4574)
2003/04: 16^1G, 21^1GS, 16^3G, 21^0GS, 19^1G, 21^0G,

	Starts	1st	2nd	3rd	Win & Pl
Hurdles	6	3	0	1	9781
Career Total	6	3	0	1	9781

99 3/04 Extr 2m3f D Hdl GD £5135
103 11/03 Towc 2m5f E Hdl G-S £2079
107 11/03 Towc 2m E Hdl GD £2219
Total win prize-money £9433

Going: Sf: 0-0 GS: 1-2 Gd: 2-4 GF: - Fm: 0-0
Distance: 2m/2m3: 2-3 2m4-2m7: 1-3 3m+: 0-0
Track: LH: 0-2 RH: 3-4 Tight: 0-0 Gall: 0-2
Aids: Bl: 0-0 Vi: 0-0 Tstrap: 0-0 Ckp: 0-0
Best Rating: 107 11/03 Towc 2m good Hdl

Lightly-raced hurdler; half-sister to useful chaser Horus; former winning pointer; made winning debut under Rules at Towcester in November 2003 and has won two out of four since; effective over two miles five; appreciates soft ground, but has won on good.

Henry Pearson (USA)
100   86+
6-y-o ch g Distant View (USA)-Lady Ellen (USA) (Explosive Bid (USA))
H P Hogarth Hogarth Racing

Placings:0/0-60P33   (3760)
2003/04: 20^6G, 17^0GF, 25^5PGS, 17^3GS, 17^9GS,

	Starts	1st	2nd	3rd	Win & Pl
Hurdles	5	0	0	2	732
Career Total	7	0	0	2	732

Going: Sf: 0-0 GS: 0-3 Gd: 0-1 GF: - Fm: 0-1
Distance: 2m/2m3: 0-3 2m4-2m7: 0-1 3m+: 0-0
Track: LH: 0-5 RH: 0-0 Tight: 0-3 Gall: 0-1
Aids: Bl: 0-2 Vi: 0-0 Tstrap: 0-0 Ckp: 0-0
Best Rating: 86 12/02 Muss 2m gd-fm Hdl

Erratic maiden on the Flat; finished fast when distant third in selling handicap hurdle at Sedgefield in January; will be suited by two and a half miles.

Henry The Great (IRE)
5-y-o b g Alderbrook-Country Style (Town And Country)
N A Twiston-Davies The Lodgers

Placings:P   (2867)
2003/04: 25^5Ps,

	Starts	1st	2nd	3rd	Win & Pl
Hurdles	1	0	0	0	
Career Total	1	0	0	0	

Going: Sf: 0-1 GS: 0-0 Gd: 0-0 GF: - Fm: 0-0
Distance: 2m/2m3: 0-0 2m4-2m7: 0-0 3m+: 0-1
Track: LH: 0-1 RH: 0-0 Tight: 0-0 Gall: 0-0
Aids: Bl: 0-0 Vi: 0-0 Tstrap: 0-0 Ckp: 0-0

Henry's Happiness
92   74
5-y-o b m Bob's Return (IRE)-Irish Mint (Dusky Boy)
C P Morlock W R Morlock

Placings:000020   (4873)
2003/04: 17^9GS, 16^9GS, 16^0S, 18^0GGS, 22^2G, 20^0GS,

	Starts	1st	2nd	3rd	Win & Pl
NH Flat	1	0	0	0	0
Hurdles	5	0	1	0	858
Career Total	6	0	1	0	858

Going: Sf: 0-1 GS: 0-4 Gd: 0-1 GF: - Fm: 0-0
Distance: 2m/2m3: 0-4 2m4-2m7: 0-2 3m+: 0-0
Track: LH: 0-3 RH: 0-3 Tight: 0-4 Gall: 0-1
Aids: Bl: 0-0 Vi: 0-0 Tstrap: 0-0 Ckp: 0-0
Best Rating: 74 3/04 Winc 2m6f good Hdl

Her Royal Highness
70f   77f
7-y-o b/br m Rock City-Dutch Princess (Royalty)
P S McEntee Peter P Scott

Placings:0/0   (2912)
2003/04: 16^0GS,

	Starts	1st	2nd	3rd	Win & Pl
NH Flat	1	0	0	0	
Career Total	2	0	0	0	

Going: Sf: 0-0 GS: 0-1 Gd: 0-0 GF: - Fm: 0-0
Distance: 2m/2m3: 0-1 2m4-2m7: 0-0 3m+: 0-0
Track: LH: 0-0 RH: 0-1 Tight: 0-0 Gall: 0-1
Aids: Bl: 0-0 Vi: 0-0 Tstrap: 0-0 Ckp: 0-0
Best Rating: 76 2/02 Sand 2m110y soft NHF

Heracles
102(103h)   (120h)120
8-y-o b g Unfuwain (USA)-La Masse (High Top)
R H Buckler Mrs D A La Trobe

Placings:022/1135/524P/31511334-0P6   (4834)
2003/04: 22^0G, 22^2G, 26^6GF,

	Starts	1st	2nd	3rd	Win & Pl
Hurdles	2	0	0	0	0
Chases	1	0	0	0	302
Career Total	22	5	3	4	26785

120 7/02 Worc 2m7f110yE Ch G-F £3506
106 6/02 NAbb 2m4f110yE Ch G-F £4153
120 5/02 Sthl 2m4f110yE Ch G-S £3149
116 1/01 Kemp 2m5f D Hdl SFT £3851
125 1/01 Kemp 2m D Hdl SFT £4738
Total win prize-money £19400

Going: Sf: 0-0 GS: 0-0 Gd: 0-2 GF: - Fm: 0-1
Distance: 2m/2m3: 0-0 2m4-2m7: 0-2 3m+: 0-1
Track: LH: 0-1 RH: 0-2 Tight: 0-0 Gall: 0-1

Aids: Bl: 0-1 Vi: 0-0 Tstrap: 0-0 Ckp: 0-0
Best Rating: 127 2/01 Kemp 2m5f   gd-sft Hdl

Modest hurdler/chaser; stays two and a half miles plus, acts on most types of ground; suited by a flat, right-handed track.

Heraclitean Fire (IRE)

105(103h)   (99 h)111
7-y-o b g Norwich-Mazovia (FR) (Taufan (USA))
J J Lambe Seamus O'Farrell

Placings:000065504-20P036F5164   (2971a)
2003/04: 22²Y, 19⁰YS, 20⁰G, 17⁹GF, 17³Y, 16⁶F, 17⁷G, 17⁵G, 16¹G, 18⁶G, 17⁴S,

	Starts	1st	2nd	3rd	Win & Pl
Hurdles	4	0	1	0	1039
Chases	7	1	0	1	8055
Career Total	20	1	1	1	9863
106	11/03 DRoy	2m		(0-109)HCh	GD £6720

Total win prize-money £6721

Going:	Sf: 0-1 GS: 0-0 Gd: 1-5 GF: - Fm: 0-2	
Distance:	2m/2m3: 1-9 2m4-2m7: 0-2 3m+: 0-0	
Track:	LH: 0-4 RH: 0-2 Tight: 0-3 Gall: 0-0	
Aids:	Bl: 0-1 Vi: 0-0 Tstrap: 0-0 Ckp: 0-0	
Best Rating:	111 8/03 Gway 2m1f	yield Ch

Moderate chaser; booked for second spot when falling at the last at Cartmel in August.

Hercules Morse (IRE)

96(82h)   (69h)93+
8-y-o b g Spanish Place (USA)-Pragownia (Pragmatic)
D B Feek D M Grissell

Placings:5F023U   (4855)
2003/04: 20⁵GS, 25⁶GS, 22⁰GS, 25²G, 26³G, 24⁰GF,

	Starts	1st	2nd	3rd	Win & Pl
Hurdles	2	0	0	0	
Chases	4	0	1	1	1774
Career Total	6	0	1	1	1774

Going:	Sf: 0-0 GS: 0-3 Gd: 0-2 GF: 0-1 Fm: 0-1	
Distance:	2m/2m3: 0-2 2m4-2m7: 0-2 3m+: 0-4	
Track:	LH: 0-2 RH: 0-4 Tight: 0-6 Gall: 0-0	
Aids:	Bl: 0-0 Vi: 0-0 Tstrap: 0-0 Ckp: 0-0	
Best Rating:	93 3/04 Folk 3m1f	good Ch

Here Comes Harry

86   76+
8-y-o ch g Sunley Builds-Coole Dolly Day (Arctic Lord)
C J Down Miss Claire Howarth

Placings:4PP13   (2696)
2003/04: 22⁴G, 19⁰GF, 22⁰GF, 22¹G, 21³G,

	Starts	1st	2nd	3rd	Win & Pl
Hurdles	5	1	0	1	3388
Career Total	5	1	0	1	3388
76	12/03 Winc	2m6f	E(0-100)HHdl	GD £2443

Total win prize-money £2443

Going:	Sf: 0-0 GS: 0-0 Gd: 1-3 GF: - Fm: 0-2	
Distance:	2m/2m3: 0-1 2m4-2m7: 1-4 3m+: 0-0	
Track:	LH: 0-1 RH: 1-3 Tight: 0-1 Gall: 0-0	
Aids:	Bl: 0-0 Vi: 0-0 Tstrap: 0-0 Ckp: 0-0	
Best Rating:	76 12/03 Winc 2m6f	good Hdl

Here Comes Henry

103   113
10-y-o ch g Dortino-Epryana (English Prince)
R H Alner A D & Mrs S A Old

Placings:136/P/522U023P4-530P   (3654)
2003/04: 24⁵GS, 26³GS, 29⁰S, 24³S,

	Starts	1st	2nd	3rd	Win & Pl
Hurdles	1	0	0	0	0
Chases	3	0	0	1	583
Career Total	17	1	3	3	9410
127	3/01 Strf	3m	H Ch	SFT £2249

Total win prize-money £2249

Going:	Sf: 0-2 GS: 0-2 Gd: 0-0 GF: - Fm: 0-0	
Distance:	2m/2m3: 0-0 2m4-2m7: 0-0 3m+: 0-4	
Track:	LH: 0-3 RH: 0-1 Tight: 0-3 Gall: 0-0	
Aids:	Bl: 0-0 Vi: 0-0 Tstrap: 0-0 Ckp: 0-1	
Best Rating:	127 3/01 Strf 3m	soft Ch

Modest chaser; stays well; acts on a sound surface.

Here's Johnny (IRE)

102f   113f
5-y-o ch g Presenting-Treble Base (IRE) (Orchestra)
V R A Dartnall The Big Boys Toys Partnership

Placings:321   (4407)
2003/04: 16³GS, 16²GS, 16¹G,

	Starts	1st	2nd	3rd	Win & Pl
NH Flat	3	1	1	1	3766
Career Total	3	1	1	1	3766
110	3/04 Hntg	2m110y	H NHF	GD £1904

Total win prize-money £1904

Going:	Sf: 0-0 GS: 0-2 Gd: 1-1 GF: - Fm: 0-0	
Distance:	2m/2m3: 1-3 2m4-2m7: 0-0 3m+: 0-0	
Track:	LH: 0-1 RH: 1-2 Tight: 0-0 Gall: 1-2	
Aids:	Bl: 0-0 Vi: 0-0 Tstrap: 0-0 Ckp: 0-0	
Best Rating:	113 2/04 Sand 2m110y	gd-sft NHF

Bumper winner; acts on easy ground.

Herecomespapin (IRE)

96   79
7-y-o b m Naheez (USA)-Bold Kim (King's Ride)
D J Wintle Mick Coulson, John Bull, John Gent

Placings:20456   (4630)
2003/04: 17²GF, 16⁹G, 20⁴G, 19⁰G, 17⁶G,

	Starts	1st	2nd	3rd	Win & Pl
NH Flat	2	0	1	0	550
Hurdles	3	0	0	0	
Career Total	5	0	1	0	550

Going:	Sf: 0-0 GS: 0-0 Gd: 0-0 GF: 0-4 Fm: 0-0	
Distance:	2m/2m3: 0-3 2m4-2m7: 0-2 3m+: 0-0	
Track:	LH: 0-3 RH: 0-2 Tight: 0-2 Gall: 0-0	
Aids:	Bl: 0-0 Vi: 0-0 Tstrap: 0-0 Ckp: 0-0	
Best Rating:	96 6/03 Sthl 2m1f	gd-fm NHF

Supported in the market when well beaten second on debut in Southwell bumper June 2003; disappointing at Worcester next time; ran better on hurdling debut at the same course the following month.

Herecomestanley

5-y-o b g Missed Flight-Moonspell (Batshoof)

M F Harris The Paddysaurus Coming Partnership

Placings:0-30P   (3079)
2003/04: 18³GF, 17⁰GS, 16ᴾGS,

	Starts	1st	2nd	3rd	Win & Pl
NH Flat	2	0	0	1	321
Hurdles	1	0	0	0	0
Career Total	4	0	0	1	321

Going:	Sf: 0-0 GS: 0-2 Gd: 0-0 GF: - Fm: 0-1	
Distance:	2m/2m3: 0-3 2m4-2m7: 0-0 3m+: 0-0	
Track:	LH: 0-2 RH: 0-1 Tight: 0-1 Gall: 0-0	
Aids:	Bl: 0-0 Vi: 0-0 Tstrap: 0-0 Ckp: 0-0	
Best Rating:	61 12/03 Hrld 2m1f	gd-sft NHF

Heres Harry

4-y-o b c Most Welcome-Nahla (Wassl)
Miss Jacqueline S Doyle The Safe Six

Placings:0   (4374)
2003/04: 16⁰GF,

	Starts	1st	2nd	3rd	Win & Pl
NH Flat	1	0	0	0	
Career Total	1	0	0	0	

Going:	Sf: 0-0 GS: 0-0 Gd: 0-0 GF: - Fm: 0-1	
Distance:	2m/2m3: 0-1 2m4-2m7: 0-0 3m+: 0-0	
Track:	LH: 0-0 RH: 0-0 Tight: 0-0 Gall: 0-0	
Aids:	Bl: 0-0 Vi: 0-0 Tstrap: 0-0 Ckp: 0-0	

Hermes III (FR)

9-y-o b g Quart De Vin (FR)-Queenly (FR) (Pot D'Or (FR))
M W Easterby (N J Henderson 3/5) The Grand National Racing Club Limited

Placings:1/52/1113P-32B1   (4949)
2003/04: 24³HY, 20²G, 21⁸G, 26¹GS,

	Starts	1st	2nd	3rd	Win & Pl
Chases	4	1	1	1	7130
Career Total	12	5	2	2	32066
117	4/04 Prth	3m2f110yH Ch	G-S £4186
144	12/02 Sand	2m4f110yC(0-135)HCh	SFT £9820
116	6/02 Prth	2m4f110yE Hdl	G-S £2884
123	5/02 Weth	2m4f110yD Hdl	G-S £3360
	4/00 Fntb	2m1f110y Ch	SFT £3074

Total win prize-money £23324

Going:	Sf: 0-1 GS: 1-1 Gd: 0-2 GF: - Fm: 0-0	
Distance:	2m/2m3: 0-0 2m4-2m7: 0-2 3m+: 1-2	
Track:	LH: 0-2 RH: 0-1 Tight: 0-1 Gall: 0-0	
Aids:	Bl: 0-0 Vi: 0-0 Tstrap: 0-0 Ckp: 0-0	
Best Rating:	144 5/03 Uttx 3m	heavy Ch

Useful chaser; finished second in a hunter chase in February on first start for new yard, formerly with Nicky Henderson; stays three and a quarter miles; acts on most types of ground.

Hernandita

99   100
6-y-o b m Hernando (FR)-Dara Dee (Dara Monarch)
Miss E C Lavelle P Clarke

Placings:1145/00P-454   (4548)
2003/04: 18⁴GS, 16⁵G, 16⁴GS,

	Starts	1st	2nd	3rd	Win & Pl
Hurdles	3	0	0	0	845

Career Total	10	2	0	0	6252
110 1/02 Sthl 2m	E Hdl			G-S	£2464
113 12/01 Winc 2m	E Hdl			GD	£2569

Total win prize-money £5033

Going: Sf: 0-0 GS: 0-2 Gd: 0-1 GF: - Fm: 0-0
Distance: 2m/2m3: 0-2 2m4-2m7: 0-0 3m+: 0-0
Track: LH: 0-1 RH: 0-2 Tight: 0-1 Gall: 0-0
Aids: Bl: 0-0 Vi: 0-0 Tstrap: 0-0 Ckp: 0-0
Best Rating: 113 12/01 Winc 2m good Hdl

Moderate hurdler; suited by two miles and has won on good and heavy ground.

Heroicus (NZ)
87(80h)   (63h)45
7-y-o ch g Heroicity (AUS)-Glenford (NZ) (Sackford (USA))
F Kirby Fred Kirby

Placings:04FPPP/6PP000-0F   (1367)
2003/04: 16⁰G, 16FF,

	Starts	1st	2nd	3rd	Win & Pl
Chases	2	0	0	0	
Career Total	14	0	0	0	0

Going: Sf: 0-0 GS: 0-0 Gd: 0-1 GF: - Fm: 0-1
Distance: 2m/2m3: 0-2 2m4-2m7: 0-0 3m+: 0-0
Track: LH: 0-2 RH: 0-0 Tight: 0-0 Gall: 0-0
Aids: Bl: 0-0 Vi: 0-0 Tstrap: 0-0 Ckp: 0-0
Best Rating: 76 11/01 Ludl 2m gd-fm NHF

Heron's Ghyll (IRE)
105   115
7-y-o b g Simply Great (FR)-Leisure Centre (IRE) (Tanfirion)
Miss Venetia Williams Mrs Vida Bingham

Placings:2510-525120210   (4449)
2003/04: 17⁰S, 20⁵G, 17²G, 21⁵G, 17¹G, 16²S, 17⁰GS, 20²GS, 19¹G, 20⁰GS,

	Starts	1st	2nd	3rd	Win & Pl
NH Flat	1	0	0	0	0
Hurdles	9	2	3	0	20136
Career Total	13	3	4	0	22883
113 3/04 Tntn 2m3f110yD Hdl				GD	£6656
104 12/03 Chel 2m1f D(0-120)HHdl				GD	£9831
101 2/03 Hrfd 2m1f H NHF				GD	£2051

Total win prize-money £18538

Going: Sf: 0-2 GS: 0-3 Gd: 2-5 GF: - Fm: 0-0
Distance: 2m/2m3: 1-5 2m4-2m7: 1-5 3m+: 0-0
Track: LH: 1-5 RH: 1-5 Tight: 1-4 Gall: 1-2
Aids: Bl: 0-0 Vi: 0-0 Tstrap: 0-0 Ckp: 0-0
Best Rating: 115 2/04 Sand 2m4f110y gd-sft Hdl

Modest hurdler; stays two and a half miles and is suited by good ground.

Hersov (IRE)
107(103h)   (129h)131
8-y-o gr g Roselier (FR)-Higher Again (IRE) (Strong Gale)
N J Henderson Michael H Watt

Placings:352/114-140P   (4861)
2003/04: 22¹GS, 33⁴G, 24⁰S, 33PGS,

	Starts	1st	2nd	3rd	Win & Pl
Hurdles	1	1	0	0	5512
Chases	3	0	0	0	1083
Career Total	10	3	1	1	22263
129 12/03 Sand 2m6f C(0-130)HHdl				G-S	£5512
124 1/03 Kemp 3m D Ch				G-S	£7910
124 12/02 Leic 2m7f110yE Ch				GD	£4124

Total win prize-money £17546

Going: Sf: 0-1 GS: 1-2 Gd: 0-1 GF: - Fm: 0-0
Distance: 2m/2m3: 0-0 2m4-2m7: 1-1 3m+: 0-3
Track: LH: 0-2 RH: 1-2 Tight: 0-0 Gall: 0-1
Aids: Bl: 0-1 Vi: 0-0 Tstrap: 0-0 Ckp: 0-0
Best Rating: 130 1/04 Chel 4m1f good Ch

Fair hurdler/chaser; stays four miles, effective at three; acts on good and soft ground.

Hescondido (FR)
95   105
9-y-o gr g Dadarissime (FR)-Vahine De Prairie (FR) (Brezzo (FR))
Miss Venetia Williams Mrs C A T Swire

Placings:311413321/6236P/F21146/5U6P   (4327)
2003/04: 20⁵G, 20Uᴸˢ, 20⁶G, 24PGS,

	Starts	1st	2nd	3rd	Win & Pl
Chases	4	0	0	0	709
Career Total	24	6	3	4	45912
149 2/02 Kemp 2m4f110yC(0-135)HCh				SFT	£7182
135 12/01 Newb 2m4f110yC(0-130)HCh				GD	£6786
125 4/00 Weth 2m4f110yD Ch				SFT	£4134
8/99 Mesl 2m1f110y Ch				SFT	£6997
6/99 Segr 2m3f Ch				GD	£2906
6/99 Stma 2m1f Ch				GD	£3229

Total win prize-money £31235

Going: Sf: 0-1 GS: 0-1 Gd: 0-2 GF: - Fm: 0-0
Distance: 2m/2m3: 0-0 2m4-2m7: 0-3 3m+: 0-1
Track: LH: 0-1 RH: 0-3 Tight: 0-0 Gall: 0-0
Aids: Bl: 0-0 Vi: 0-0 Tstrap: 0-0 Ckp: 0-0
Best Rating: 149 2/02 Kemp 2m4f110y soft Ch

Fair chaser; stays three miles; has had his jumping problems; suited by soft ground, lightly raced since the 2001/2 season; has been tried in blinkers; dropping in the weights.

Hessac (FR)
9-y-o b g Beyssac (FR)-Chic Lilie (FR) (Olmeto)
Ernie Fenwick Ernie Fenwick

Placings:5   (0430)
2003/04: 26⁵G,

	Starts	1st	2nd	3rd	Win & Pl
Chases	1	0	0	0	0
Career Total	1	0	0	0	0

Going: Sf: 0-0 GS: 0-0 Gd: 0-1 GF: - Fm: 0-0
Distance: 2m/2m3: 0-0 2m4-2m7: 0-0 3m+: 0-1
Track: LH: 0-1 RH: 0-0 Tight: 0-1 Gall: 0-0
Aids: Bl: 0-0 Vi: 0-0 Tstrap: 0-0 Ckp: 0-0
Best Rating: 70 5/03 Ctml 3m2f good Ch

Hetland Hill
73   29
8-y-o ch g Secret Appeal-Mohibbah (USA) (Conquistador Cielo (USA))
L Lungo Mrs Barbara Lungo

Placings:36-P0P   (2262)
2003/04: 16PGF, 17⁰GF, 19PG,

	Starts	1st	2nd	3rd	Win & Pl
Hurdles	3	0	0	0	
Career Total	5	0	0	1	324

Going: Sf: 0-0 GS: 0-0 Gd: 0-1 GF: - Fm: 0-2

Hever Golf Glory
101   75
10-y-o b g Efisio-Zaius (Artaius (USA))
C N Kellett D H & Mrs R E Muir

Placings:600/05/0-40064P   (0909)
2003/04: 16⁴GF, 16⁰G, 19⁰G, 17⁶GF, 22⁴GF, 21PGF,

	Starts	1st	2nd	3rd	Win & Pl
Hurdles	6	0	0	0	0
Career Total	12	0	0	0	0

Going: Sf: 0-0 GS: 0-0 Gd: 0-2 GF: - Fm: 0-4
Distance: 2m/2m3: 0-3 2m4-2m7: 0-3 3m+: 0-0
Track: LH: 0-0 RH: 0-4 Tight: 0-2 Gall: 0-2
Aids: Bl: 0-0 Vi: 0-0 Tstrap: 0-0 Ckp: 0-0
Best Rating: 75 5/03 Hntg 2m110y gd-fm Hdl

Plating-class hurdler; limited promise so far.

Hevergolf Princess (IRE)
75   36
9-y-o ch m Petardia-High Profile (High Top)
B Bousfield Mrs D A Bousfield

Placings:P0P   (4727)
2003/04: 17PGF, 17⁰GF, 17PG,

	Starts	1st	2nd	3rd	Win & Pl
Hurdles	3	0	0	0	
Career Total	3	0	0	0	

Going: Sf: 0-0 GS: 0-0 Gd: 0-1 GF: - Fm: 0-2
Distance: 2m/2m3: 0-3 2m4-2m7: 0-0 3m+: 0-0
Track: LH: 0-2 RH: 0-1 Tight: 0-2 Gall: 0-0
Aids: Bl: 0-0 Vi: 0-0 Tstrap: 0-0 Ckp: 0-0
Best Rating: 36 8/03 Sedg 2m1f gd-fm Hdl

Hey Boy (IRE)
91f   95f
5-y-o b g Courtship-Make Me An Island (Creative Plan (USA))
C J Mann J E Brown

Placings:3   (4454)
2003/04: 16⁰GS,

	Starts	1st	2nd	3rd	Win & Pl
NH Flat	1	0	0	1	359
Career Total	1	0	0	1	359

Going: Sf: 0-0 GS: 0-1 Gd: 0-0 GF: - Fm: 0-0
Distance: 2m/2m3: 0-1 2m4-2m7: 0-0 3m+: 0-0
Track: LH: 0-0 RH: 0-1 Tight: 0-0 Gall: 0-0
Aids: Bl: 0-0 Vi: 0-0 Tstrap: 0-0 Ckp: 0-0
Best Rating: 95 3/04 Asct 2m110y gd-sft NHF

Former Irish pointer; placed on numper debut uner Rules; looks to need further than two miles.

Hey Ref (IRE)
100(101c)   (120c)120+
7-y-o b g King's Ride-Jeanarie (Reformed Character)

Jonjo O'Neill John P McManus

Placings:0/f41-3U6P   (4729)
2003/04: 16⁹GS, 16ᵁS, 20⁶G, 20⁹G,

	Starts	1st	2nd	3rd	Win & Pl
Hurdles	2	0	0	0	404
Chases	2	0	0	1	527
Career Total	8	2	0	1	8588
120	2/03	Hayd	2m	D Hdl	G-S £5216
111	10/02	Carl	2m1f	H NHF	SFT £2049
					Total win prize-money £7266

Going: Sf: 0-1 GS: 0-1 Gd: 0-2 GF: - Fm: 0-0
Distance: 2m/2m3: 0-2 2m4-2m7: 0-2 3m+: 0-0
Track: LH: 0-3 RH: 0-1 Tight: 0-0 Gall: 0-0
Aids: Bl: 0-0 Vi: 0-0 Tstrap: 0-0 Ckp: 0-0
Best Rating: 120 12/03 Uttx 2m gd-sft Ch

Fair hurdler; won over hurdles at Haydock in February 2003; finished well when good third on chasing debut at Uttoxeter in December; should be suited by two and a half miles.

Heynestown Pride (IRE)
91   75

7-y-o ch m Zaffaran (USA)-Mayobridge (Our Mirage)
N G Richards Mrs O E Matthews

Placings:0/000056-02P   (3433)
2003/04: 21⁰S, 16²GF, 18⁶HY,

	Starts	1st	2nd	3rd	Win & Pl
Hurdles	3	0	1	0	994
Career Total	10	0	1	0	994

Going: Sf: 0-2 GS: 0-0 Gd: 0-0 GF: - Fm: 0-1
Distance: 2m/2m3: 0-2 2m4-2m7: 0-1 3m+: 0-0
Track: LH: 0-3 RH: 0-0 Tight: 0-1 Gall: 0-1
Aids: Bl: 0-0 Vi: 0-0 Tstrap: 0-0 Ckp: 0-0
Best Rating: 79 6/03 Hexm 2m1y10y gd-fm Hdl

Hi Fi
108   111+

6-y-o b g Homo Sapien-Baroness Orkzy (Baron Blakeney)
Ian Williams Mrs Rosemary Paterson

Placings:044065-320F116   (4776)
2003/04: 20³GS, 19²GS, 20⁰GS, 19⁶G, 17¹GS, 17¹G, 20⁶G,

	Starts	1st	2nd	3rd	Win & Pl
Hurdles	7	2	1	1	8871
Career Total	13	2	1	1	8871
114	4/04	Extr	2m1f	F(0-100)HHdl	GD £3192
98	3/04	Extr	2m1f	E(0-105)HHdl	G-S £4316
					Total win prize-money £7508

Going: Sf: 0-0 GS: 1-4 Gd: 1-3 GF: - Fm: 0-0
Distance: 2m/2m3: 2-4 2m4-2m7: 0-3 3m+: 0-0
Track: LH: 0-3 RH: 2-4 Tight: 0-2 Gall: 0-2
Aids: Bl: 0-0 Vi: 0-0 Tstrap: 0-0 Ckp: 0-0
Best Rating: 114 4/04 Extr 2m1f good Hdl

Moderate hurdler; effective up to two miles three; acts with cut in the ground.

Hi Lily
94(100h)   (94h)94

8-y-o b m Jupiter Island-By Line (High Line)
Miss Z C Davison (C C Bealby 7/5) Richard Antony Jones

Placings:0/05/P223P22P00P2-300   (4929)
2003/04: 21³GF, 16⁰G, 18⁰G,

	Starts	1st	2nd	3rd	Win & Pl
Hurdles	2	0	0	0	0
Chases	1	0	0	1	575
Career Total	18	0	5	2	6710

Going: Sf: 0-0 GS: 0-0 Gd: 0-2 GF: - Fm: 0-1
Distance: 2m/2m3: 0-2 2m4-2m7: 0-1 3m+: 0-0
Track: LH: 0-3 RH: 0-0 Tight: 0-3 Gall: 0-0
Aids: Bl: 0-0 Vi: 0-0 Tstrap: 0-0 Ckp: 0-0
Best Rating: 94 12/02 Hntg 2m4f110y gd-sft Ch

Moderate chaser; suited by fast ground; effective at two and a half miles.

Hi Pal (IRE)

7-y-o b g Phardante (FR)-Bright Princess (IRE) (Deep Run)
C C Bealby Ady Boughen

Placings:P   (4436)
2003/04: 24⁵GS,

	Starts	1st	2nd	3rd	Win & Pl
Chases	1	0	0	0	0
Career Total	1	0	0	0	0

Going: Sf: 0-0 GS: 0-1 Gd: 0-0 GF: - Fm: 0-0
Distance: 2m/2m3: 0-2 2m4-2m7: 0-0 3m+: 0-1
Track: LH: 0-1 RH: 0-0 Tight: 0-1 Gall: 0-0
Aids: Bl: 0-0 Vi: 0-0 Tstrap: 0-0 Ckp: 0-0

Hi Rudolf
99   (76h)88

9-y-o b g Ballet Royal (USA)-Hi Darlin' (Prince De Galles)
H J Manners H J Manners

Placings:053P/0P/P/53P3/535FPP1F-P34   (4935)
2003/04: 25⁸GS, 24³G, 18⁴G,

	Starts	1st	2nd	3rd	Win & Pl
Chases	3	0	0	1	850
Career Total	22	1	0	5	6717
88	3/03	Font	2m4f	E Ch	SFT £4357
					Total win prize-money £4358

Going: Sf: 0-0 GS: 0-1 Gd: 0-2 GF: - Fm: 0-0
Distance: 2m/2m3: 0-2 2m4-2m7: 0-0 3m+: 0-2
Track: LH: 0-0 RH: 0-2 Tight: 0-2 Gall: 0-1
Aids: Bl: 0-0 Vi: 0-0 Tstrap: 0-0 Ckp: 0-0
Best Rating: 88 3/03 Font 2m4f soft Ch

Modest hunter/novice chaser; best at around two and a half miles; acts on soft ground.

Hi Tech
97   89

5-y-o b g Polar Falcon (USA)-Just Speculation (IRE) (Ahonoora)
Dr P Pritchard Mrs T Pritchard

Placings:0P654P-5540   (4892)
2003/04: 16⁵GS, 24⁵G, 24⁴GF, 16⁰GF,

	Starts	1st	2nd	3rd	Win & Pl
Hurdles	4	0	0	0	556
Career Total	10	0	0	0	802

Going: Sf: 0-0 GS: 0-1 Gd: 0-1 GF: - Fm: 0-2
Distance: 2m/2m3: 0-2 2m4-2m7: 0-0 3m+: 0-2
Track: LH: 0-2 RH: 0-2 Tight: 0-1 Gall: 0-0
Aids: Bl: 0-0 Vi: 0-0 Tstrap: 0-0 Ckp: 0-0
Best Rating: 92 3/04 Chep 3m gd-fm Hdl

Poor novice hurdler at up to 3m.

Hickerthriftcastle
57   52

5-y-o ch g Carlingford Castle-Sun Sprite (Morston (FR))
C C Bealby Ady Boughen

Placings:000   (4654)
2003/04: 16⁶G, 20⁰G, 17⁰G,

	Starts	1st	2nd	3rd	Win & Pl
NH Flat	1	0	0	0	0
Hurdles	2	0	0	0	0
Career Total	3	0	0	0	

Going: Sf: 0-0 GS: 0-0 Gd: 0-3 GF: - Fm: 0-0
Distance: 2m/2m3: 0-2 2m4-2m7: 0-1 3m+: 0-0
Track: LH: 0-2 RH: 0-1 Tight: 0-2 Gall: 0-0
Aids: Bl: 0-0 Vi: 0-0 Tstrap: 0-0 Ckp: 0-0
Best Rating: 73 1/04 Catt 2m good NHF

Hickleton Club
72   40

6-y-o b g Aragon-Honest Opinion (Free State)
R M Clark Michael Clark

Placings:0-0000   (4292)
2003/04: 16⁰GF, 16⁰G, 16⁰F, 16⁰GF,

	Starts	1st	2nd	3rd	Win & Pl
NH Flat	2	0	0	0	0
Hurdles	2	0	0	0	0
Career Total	5	0	0	0	

Going: Sf: 0-0 GS: 0-0 Gd: 0-1 GF: - Fm: 0-3
Distance: 2m/2m3: 0-4 2m4-2m7: 0-0 3m+: 0-0
Track: LH: 0-1 RH: 0-3 Tight: 0-0 Gall: 0-0
Aids: Bl: 0-0 Vi: 0-0 Tstrap: 0-0 Ckp: 0-0
Best Rating: 59 12/02 Muss 2m gd-sft NHF

Hickleton Dream
100   84

7-y-o b m Rambo Dancer (CAN)-Elegant Approach (Prince Ragusa)
G A Swinbank D Leech

Placings:33   (2303)
2003/04: 16⁰GF, 19³GF,

	Starts	1st	2nd	3rd	Win & Pl
Hurdles	2	0	0	2	681
Career Total	2	0	0	2	681

Going: Sf: 0-0 GS: 0-0 Gd: 0-0 GF: - Fm: 0-2
Distance: 2m/2m3: 0-2 2m4-2m7: 0-0 3m+: 0-0
Track: LH: 0-2 RH: 0-0 Tight: 0-1 Gall: 0-0
Aids: Bl: 0-0 Vi: 0-0 Tstrap: 0-0 Ckp: 0-0
Best Rating: 84 10/03 Hexm 2m1f10y gd-fm Hdl

Maiden plater on the Flat; well beaten third in modest novices' hurdles.

Hidden Bounty (IRE)
117   122+

8-y-o b g Generous (IRE)-Sought Out (IRE) (Rainbow Quest (USA))
Mrs M Reveley M E Foxton

Placings:006121/311F1P   (4386)
2003/04: 20³G, 24¹G, 22¹S, 23⁶S, 20¹GS, 25⁶G,

	Starts	1st	2nd	3rd	Win & Pl
Hurdles	6	3	0	1	17788

Career Total	12	5	1	1	30134
122 2/04 Newc	2m4f	C(0-135)HHdl		G-S	£6124
121 11/03 Hayd	2m6f	C(0-135)HHdl		SFT	£5736
106 11/03 Ayr	3m110y	D(0-125)HHdl		GD	£4842
104 4/02 Chel	3m	D(0-120)HHdl		G-F	£9243
109 2/02 Hntg	2m4f110yF(0-95)HHdl			SFT	£2063
			Total win prize-money £28011		

Going:	Sf: 1-2 GS: 1-1 Gd: 1-3 GF: - Fm: 0-0		
Distance:	2m/2m3: 0-0 **2m4-2m7:** 2-3 3m+: 1-3		
Track:	**LH:** 3-6 RH: 0-0 Tight: 0-0 **Gall:** 1-2		
Aids:	Bl: 0-0 Vi: 0-0 Tstrap: 0-0 Ckp: 0-0		
Best Rating: 122 2/04 Newc 2m4f		gd-sft	Hdl

Fair hurdler; winner at Ayr and Haydock in November 2003 and best effort at Newcastle in February 2004; stays three miles and acts on most types of ground; good strike-rate and may be capable of better.

Hidden Depth

5-y-o b g Classic Cliche (IRE)-Rochestown Lass (Deep Run)
P T Dalton Miss Charlotte A I Perkins

Placings:00　　　　　　　　　　　(3354)
2003/04: 16⁰S, 16⁰S,

	Starts	1st	2nd	3rd	Win & Pl
NH Flat	2	0	0	0	
Career Total	**2**	**0**	**0**	**0**	

Going:	Sf: 0-2 GS: 0-0 Gd: 0-0 GF: - Fm: 0-0
Distance:	2m/2m3: 0-0 2m4-2m7: 0-0 3m+: 0-0
Track:	LH: 0-0 RH: 0-2 Tight: 0-0 Gall: 0-1
Aids:	Bl: 0-0 Vi: 0-0 Tstrap: 0-0 Ckp: 0-0

Hidden Exit

95　　　　　　　　　　　　75

8-y-o b m Landyap (USA)-Queen Of The Nile (Hittite Glory)
Mrs L Williamson The Castle Bend Syndicate

Placings:000/453456-0020　　　　(1134)
2003/04: 17⁰G, 17⁰G, 20²GF, 20⁴G,

	Starts	1st	2nd	3rd	Win & Pl
Hurdles	4	0	1	0	850
Career Total	**13**	**0**	**1**	**1**	**1438**

Going:	Sf: 0-0 GS: 0-0 Gd: 0-2 GF: - Fm: 0-2		
Distance:	2m/2m3: 0-2 2m4-2m7: 0-2 3m+: 0-0		
Track:	LH: 0-4 RH: 0-0 Tight: 0-2 Gall: 0-0		
Aids:	Bl: 0-0 Vi: 0-0 Tstrap: 0-0 Ckp: 0-0		
Best Rating: 75 10/02 Bang 2m1f		gd-sft	Hdl

Poor novice hurdler.

Hidden Pearl (IRE)

8-y-o b g Posen (USA)-Cockney Miss (Camden Town)
R A Mills (J A Supple 29/5) Ciaran J Mooney

Placings:P0P05/56300-64P5　　　(4263)
2003/04: 21⁶GF, 16⁴GF, 20⁷GF, 25⁵GF,

	Starts	1st	2nd	3rd	Win & Pl
Chases	4	0	0	0	294
Career Total	**14**	**0**	**0**	**1**	**612**

Going:	Sf: 0-0 GS: 0-0 Gd: 0-0 GF: - Fm: 0-4
Distance:	2m/2m3: 0-1 2m4-2m7: 0-2 3m+: 0-1
Track:	LH: 0-3 RH: 0-1 Tight: 0-3 Gall: 0-1
Aids:	Bl: 0-1 Vi: 0-0 Tstrap: 0-0 Ckp: 0-2

Best Rating: 73 5/03 Fknm 2m110y		gd-fm	Ch

First worthwhile form when well beaten third in a selling handicap hurdle at Market Rasen in December.

Hidden Smile (USA)

105　　　　　　　　　　79

7-y-o b m Twilight Agenda (USA)-Smooth Edge (USA)
(Meadowlake (USA))
F Jordan The Bhiss Partnership

Placings:0P-462020　　　　　　　(4654)
2003/04: 16⁴GF, 16⁹G, 16²GF, 17⁰GF, 16²GF, 17⁰G,

	Starts	1st	2nd	3rd	Win & Pl
Hurdles	6	0	2	0	1212
Career Total	**8**	**0**	**2**	**0**	**1212**

Going:	Sf: 0-0 GS: 0-0 Gd: 0-2 GF: - Fm: 0-4		
Distance:	2m/2m3: 0-6 2m4-2m7: 0-0 3m+: 0-0		
Track:	LH: 0-4 RH: 0-2 Tight: 0-2 Gall: 0-0		
Aids:	Bl: 0-0 Vi: 0-0 Tstrap: 0-0 Ckp: 0-0		
Best Rating: 79 9/03 Worc 2m		gd-fm	Hdl

Poor novice hurdler; just denied in Uttoxeter selling handicap July 2003; disappointing next time but well held in second at Worcester in September.

Hidden Valley

102　　　　　(127h)111

12-y-o b g St Columbus-Leven Valley (Ragstone)
J D Frost G G A Gregson

Placings:0/0/05112F62/011F11/544024/P622P-23 (1123)
2003/04: 21²GS, 21³GF,

	Starts	1st	2nd	3rd	Win & Pl
Chases	2	0	1	1	2686
Career Total	**29**	**6**	**6**	**1**	**33948**
127 4/01 Extr	2m3f	D(0-125)HHdl		SFT	£3969
127 3/01 Extr	2m6f110yD(0-125)HHdl		HVY	£3656
109 1/01 Extr	2m1f110yF(0-100)HCh		HVY	£3132
103 11/00 NAbb	2m5f110yD(0-110)HCh		HVY	£5404
80 11/99 Extr	2m6f	E(0-105)HHdl		G-S	£2921
90 8/99 NAbb	2m1f	F(0-100)HHdl		G-F	£2862
			Total win prize-money £21945		

Going:	Sf: 0-0 GS: 0-1 Gd: 0-0 GF: - Fm: 0-1		
Distance:	2m/2m3: 0-0 2m4-2m7: 0-2 3m+: 0-0		
Track:	LH: 0-2 RH: 0-0 Tight: 0-2 Gall: 0-0		
Aids:	Bl: 0-0 Vi: 0-0 Tstrap: 0-0 Ckp: 0-0		
Best Rating: 127 4/01 Extr 2m3f		soft	Hdl

Modest handicapper over both hurdles and fences; stays 2m 7f; goes well in the mud; has a good record at Exeter.

Hiers De Brouage (FR)

107　　　　　　　　114+

9-y-o b g Neustrien (FR)-Thalandrezienne (FR) (Le Correzien (FR))
J G Portman Seddon - Brown Partnership

Placings:0300/PP16/310P1-332P330　　(4817)
2003/04: 20³GF, 19³GS, 21²G, 24⁶S, 21³G, 21³GF, 24⁰G,

	Starts	1st	2nd	3rd	Win & Pl
Chases	7	0	1	4	6601
Career Total	**20**	**3**	**1**	**6**	**23367**
109 3/03 Extr	2m3f110yD(0-115)HCh		GD	£5739
107 12/02 Winc	2m5f	E(0-105)HCh		G-S	£4257
107 3/02 Chep	2m3f110yD Ch		G-S	£3997
			Total win prize-money £13996		

Going:	Sf: 0-1 GS: 0-1 Gd: 0-3 GF: - Fm: 0-2		
Distance:	2m/2m3: 0-0 2m4-2m7: 0-5 3m+: 0-2		
Track:	LH: 0-4 RH: 0-3 Tight: 0-0 Gall: 0-1		
Aids:	Bl: 0-0 Vi: 0-0 Tstrap: 0-0 Ckp: 0-3		
Best Rating: 112 12/03 Winc 2m5f		good	Ch

Modest ex-French chaser; stays two miles five; unsuited by extremes of going; has been wearing cheekpieces of late.

High Action (USA)

80　　　　　　　　　　79

4-y-o ch g Theatrical-Secret Imperatrice (USA) (Secretariat (USA))
Ian Williams (Sir Michael Stoute 14/9) C N Barnes

Placings:000　　　　　　　　　　(3329)
2003/04: 16⁰GS, 16⁰GS, 16⁰S,

	Starts	1st	2nd	3rd	Win & Pl
Hurdles	3	0	0	0	
Career Total	**3**	**0**	**0**	**0**	

Going:	Sf: 0-1 GS: 0-2 Gd: 0-0 GF: - Fm: 0-0		
Distance:	2m/2m3: 0-2 2m4-2m7: 0-0 3m+: 0-0		
Track:	LH: 0-3 RH: 0-0 Tight: 0-0 Gall: 0-1		
Aids:	Bl: 0-0 Vi: 0-0 Tstrap: 0-0 Ckp: 0-0		
Best Rating: 79 12/03 Chel 2m110y		gd-sft	Hdl

Middle-distance winner on the Flat on fast ground; well beaten over hurdles.

High Bird Humphrey

91f　　　　　　　　81+f

5-y-o ch g Nomadic Way (USA)-Miss Kewmill (Billion (USA))
P R Webber Paul Webber

Placings:60　　　　　　　　　　　(4571)
2003/04: 18⁶S, 17⁰GS,

	Starts	1st	2nd	3rd	Win & Pl
NH Flat	2	0	0	0	0
Career Total	**2**	**0**	**0**	**0**	**0**

Going:	Sf: 0-1 GS: 0-1 Gd: 0-0 GF: - Fm: 0-0		
Distance:	2m/2m3: 0-2 2m4-2m7: 0-0 3m+: 0-0		
Track:	LH: 0-2 RH: 0-0 Tight: 0-1 Gall: 0-0		
Aids:	Bl: 0-0 Vi: 0-0 Tstrap: 0-0 Ckp: 0-0		
Best Rating: 81 3/04 Bang 2m1f		gd-sft	NHF

Half-brother to two winning pointers; showed ability before tiring on debut in fair bumper at Plumpton.

High Class Pet

75f　　　　　　　　　47f

4-y-o b f Petong-What A Pet (Mummy's Pet)
F P Murtagh R Millican

Placings:00　　　　　　　　　　　(3887)
2003/04: 16⁰HY, 16⁰G,

	Starts	1st	2nd	3rd	Win & Pl
NH Flat	2	0	0	0	
Career Total	**2**	**0**	**0**	**0**	

Going:	Sf: 0-1 GS: 0-0 Gd: 0-1 GF: - Fm: 0-0		
Distance:	2m/2m3: 0-2 2m4-2m7: 0-0 3m+: 0-0		
Track:	LH: 0-1 RH: 0-1 Tight: 0-1 Gall: 0-0		
Aids:	Bl: 0-0 Vi: 0-0 Tstrap: 0-0 Ckp: 0-0		
Best Rating: 51 2/04 Muss 2m		good	NHF

High Cotton (IRE)

95   **121+**

9-y-o gr g Ala Hounak-Planalife (Beau Charmeur (FR))
Mrs M Reveley (D R C Elsworth 30/11) R Burridge, H
Burridge, J H W Lloyd

Placings:62522/243543/244244P-3P422F   (4865)
2003/04: 22³GF, 24PGS, 25⁴HY, 28²G, 20²G, 25FS,

	Starts	1st	2nd	3rd	Win & Pl
Chases	6	0	2	1	6172
Career Total	24	0	8	3	31378

Going:	Sf: 0-2 GS: 0-1 Gd: 0-2 GF: - Fm: 0-1
Distance:	2m/2m3: 0-0 2m4-2m7: 0-2 3m+: 0-4
Track:	LH: 0-4 RH: 0-2 Tight: 0-1 Gall: 0-2
Aids:	Bl: 0-0 Vi: 0-0 Tstrap: 0-0 Ckp: 0-0
Best Rating:	132 12/01 Kemp 3m good Ch

Modest hurdler/decent chaser; seems to stay up to four
miles; acts on good ground but appreciates very soft
ground; once tried in blinkers; ery hard to win with.

High Diva

5-y-o b m Piccolo-Gifted (Shareef Dancer (USA))
J R Best (B R Johnson 15/1) D S Nevison

Placings:P   (2777)
2003/04: 17PGS,

	Starts	1st	2nd	3rd	Win & Pl
Hurdles	1	0	0	0	
Career Total	1	0	0	0	

Going:	Sf: 0-0 GS: 0-1 Gd: 0-0 GF: - Fm: 0-0
Distance:	2m/2m3: 0-1 2m4-2m7: 0-0 3m+: 0-0
Track:	LH: 0-0 RH: 0-1 Tight: 0-1 Gall: 0-0
Aids:	Bl: 0-0 Vi: 0-0 Tstrap: 0-0 Ckp: 0-0

High Drama

110   **106**

7-y-o b/br g In The Wings-Maestrale (Top Ville)
P Bowen   T W Raymond

Placings:332PP01-1P   (0261)
2003/04: 22¹G, 24PGF,

	Starts	1st	2nd	3rd	Win & Pl
Hurdles	2	1	0	0	4992
Career Total	9	2	1	2	10447
107 4/03	Extr	2m6f110yD(0-115)HHdl		GD	£4992
106 3/03	Sedg	2m5f110yE Hdl		GD	£3535
		Total win prize-money £8527			

Going:	Sf: 0-0 GS: 0-0 Gd: 1-1 GF: - Fm: 0-1
Distance:	2m/2m3: 0-0 2m4-2m7: 1-1 3m+: 0-1
Track:	LH: 0-0 RH: 1-2 Tight: 0-0 Gall: 0-0
Aids:	Bl: 0-0 Vi: 0-0 Tstrap: 0-0 Ckp: 0-0
Best Rating:	107 4/03 Extr 2m6f110y good Hdl

Modest novice hurdler; runaway winner at Sedgefield in
March 2003; followed-up in 2m 6f handicap at Exeter the following month; needs the ground good or faster; reported to
have schooled well over fences.

High Expectations (IRE)

92   **87**

9-y-o ch g Over The River (FR)-Andy's Fancy (IRE)
(Andretti)

J S Haldane   John & Mary Stenhouse

Placings:0/U/04-P42PPP   (4880)
2003/04: 25PG, 19⁴G, 25²GF, 25PG, 25PG, 20PGS,

	Starts	1st	2nd	3rd	Win & Pl
Chases	6	0	1	0	1811
Career Total	10	0	1	0	2030

Going:	Sf: 0-0 GS: 0-1 Gd: 0-4 GF: - Fm: 0-1
Distance:	2m/2m3: 0-1 2m4-2m7: 0-1 3m+: 0-4
Track:	LH: 0-5 RH: 0-1 Tight: 0-3 Gall: 0-0
Aids:	Bl: 0-0 Vi: 0-0 Tstrap: 0-0 Ckp: 0-0
Best Rating:	85 4/04 Kels 3m1f good Ch

Moderate pointer/hunter chaser; multiple winner between
the flags in his time; stays three miles plus; suited by cut in
the ground.

High Jinks

96   **77+**

9-y-o b g High Estate-Waffling (Lomond (USA))
R N Bevis   R N Bevis

Placings:5/4   (3226)
2003/04: 26⁴GS,

	Starts	1st	2nd	3rd	Win & Pl
Hurdles	1	0	0	0	0
Career Total	2	0	0	0	0

Going:	Sf: 0-0 GS: 0-1 Gd: 0-0 GF: - Fm: 0-0
Distance:	2m/2m3: 0-0 2m4-2m7: 0-0 3m+: 0-1
Track:	LH: 0-0 RH: 0-1 Tight: 0-0 Gall: 0-0
Aids:	Bl: 0-0 Vi: 0-0 Tstrap: 0-0 Ckp: 0-0
Best Rating:	80 1/04 Hrfd 3m2f gd-sft Hdl

High Paddy

102   **99+**

5-y-o b g Master Willie-Ivy Edith (Blakeney)
R Ingram   Glen Antill

Placings:4-43   (4365)
2003/04: 16⁴G, 16³GS,

	Starts	1st	2nd	3rd	Win & Pl
Hurdles	2	0	0	1	772
Career Total	3	0	0	1	1612

Going:	Sf: 0-0 GS: 0-1 Gd: 0-1 GF: - Fm: 0-0
Distance:	2m/2m3: 0-2 2m4-2m7: 0-0 3m+: 0-0
Track:	LH: 0-2 RH: 0-0 Tight: 0-2 Gall: 0-0
Aids:	Bl: 0-0 Vi: 0-0 Tstrap: 0-0 Ckp: 0-0
Best Rating:	99 3/04 Plum 2m gd-sft Hdl

Moderate form in novice hurdles.

High Powered (GER)

5-y-o br m So Factual (USA)-High Habit (Slip Anchor)
D W Thompson (J A Moore 18/5) Mrs J M Moore

Placings:P   (0327)
2003/04: 20PGF,

	Starts	1st	2nd	3rd	Win & Pl
Hurdles	1	0	0	0	
Career Total	1	0	0	0	

Going:	Sf: 0-0 GS: 0-0 Gd: 0-0 GF: - Fm: 0-1

Distance:	2m/2m3: 0-0 2m4-2m7: 0-1 3m+: 0-0
Track:	LH: 0-1 RH: 0-0 Tight: 0-1 Gall: 0-0
Aids:	Bl: 0-0 Vi: 0-0 Tstrap: 0-0 Ckp: 0-0

High Rank

106   **108+**

5-y-o b g Emperor Jones (USA)-Hotel Street (USA) (Alleged
(USA))
J Mackie (R J Osborne 5/5) Trying To Buy Fun Partnership

Placings:06-042006325   (4492)
2003/04: 16⁰G, 16⁴GF, 21²G, 19⁰GS, 20⁰S, 20⁰GS, 22³G, 21²GS,
22⁵G,

	Starts	1st	2nd	3rd	Win & Pl
NH Flat	1	0	0	0	0
Hurdles	8	0	2	1	2723
Career Total	11	0	2	1	2723

Going:	Sf: 0-1 GS: 0-3 Gd: 0-4 GF: - Fm: 0-1
Distance:	2m/2m3: 0-2 2m4-2m7: 0-7 3m+: 0-0
Track:	LH: 0-4 RH: 0-3 Tight: 0-1 Gall: 0-0
Aids:	Bl: 0-0 Vi: 0-0 Tstrap: 0-3 Ckp: 0-0
Best Rating:	108 3/04 Wwck 2m5f gd-sft Hdl

Ex-Irish maiden hurdler; stays 2m 6f; seems to go on any
ground.

High Rocker

86   **46**

6-y-o b g First Trump-Wild Abandon (USA) (Graustark)
M C Pipe   Lucayan Stud

Placings:00-PP00P   (0910)
2003/04: 16PGF, 22PGF, 19⁰GF, 22⁰GF, 26PGF,

	Starts	1st	2nd	3rd	Win & Pl
Hurdles	5	0	0	0	
Career Total	7	0	0	0	

Going:	Sf: 0-0 GS: 0-0 Gd: 0-0 GF: - Fm: 0-5
Distance:	2m/2m3: 0-1 2m4-2m7: 0-3 3m+: 0-0
Track:	LH: 0-3 RH: 0-2 Tight: 0-2 Gall: 0-0
Aids:	Bl: 0-0 Vi: 0-0 Tstrap: 0-1 Ckp: 0-0
Best Rating:	103 2/03 Winc 2m gd-sft NHF

High Sun

77   **56**

8-y-o b g High Estate-Clyde Goddess (IRE) (Scottish Reel)
Mrs A M Thorpe   M V Morgan

Placings:00/P-F0P   (0449)
2003/04: 24FS, 19⁰G, 20PGF,

	Starts	1st	2nd	3rd	Win & Pl
Hurdles	3	0	0	0	
Career Total	6	0	0	0	

Going:	Sf: 0-1 GS: 0-0 Gd: 0-1 GF: - Fm: 0-1
Distance:	2m/2m3: 0-0 2m4-2m7: 0-2 3m+: 0-1
Track:	LH: 0-1 RH: 0-2 Tight: 0-1 Gall: 0-1
Aids:	Bl: 0-0 Vi: 0-0 Tstrap: 0-0 Ckp: 0-0
Best Rating:	57 5/03 Hrfd 2m3f110y good Hdl

High Tower

(96h)   (99h)**102**

7-y-o b g Lycius (USA)-Sedova (USA) (Nijinsky (CAN))
A M Hales (M J P O'Brien 11/6) The Cornish 'Crac'
Partnership

Placings:660/6100654F-0455F   (3407)
2003/04: 18⁰G, 20⁴YS, 16⁵G, 16⁵S, 16⁶G,

	Starts	1st	2nd	3rd	Win & Pl
Hurdles	3	0	0	0	0
Chases	2	0	0	0	390
Career Total	**16**	**1**	**0**	**0**	**4680**
93 5/02 Kbgn 2m3f	Hdl			Y-S	£3809

Total win prize-money £3810

Going:	Sf: 0-1 GS: 0-0 Gd: 0-3 GF: - Fm: 0-0
Distance:	2m/2m3: 0-4 2m4-2m7: 0-1 3m+: 0-0
Track:	LH: 0-3 RH: 0-0 Tight: 0-1 Gall: 0-0
Aids:	Bl: 0-1 Vi: 0-0 Tstrap: 0-1 Ckp: 0-0
Best Rating:	102 6/03 Kbgn 2m4f yld-sft Ch

Irish hurdles winner; handles cut in the ground; stays two-and-a-half miles.

Highbank

90   94

12-y-o b g Puissance-Highland Daisy (He Loves Me)
Mrs M Reveley D H & C Thrower

Placings:03114412/522/0P300/010P/0032301002212/2415
/04061040B30/000003103-00   (0618)
2003/04: 16⁰G, 19⁰G,

	Starts	1st	2nd	3rd	Win & Pl
Hurdles	2	0	0	0	
Career Total	**59**	**9**	**8**	**7**	**31075**
95 3/03 MRas 2m1ff110y	G(0-95)HHdl			GD	£2464
103 12/01 Donc 2m4f	E(0-115)HHdl			GD	£3178
114 12/00 Newc 2m	F(0-105)HHdl			SFT	£2380
93 12/99 Muss 2m	G(0-95)HHdl			G-S	£2668
93 8/99 Hntg 2m4f110y	G(0-90)HHdl			G-F	£1618
80 5/98 Hexm 2m110y	E Ch			G-F	£2310
110 4/96 Newb 2m	G(0-100)HHdl			GD	£2547
97 1/96 Newc 2m	G Hdl			GD	£2099
99 12/95 Donc 2m110y	G Hdl			G-F	£2176

Total win prize-money £21442

Going:	Sf: 0-0 GS: 0-0 Gd: 0-2 GF: - Fm: 0-0
Distance:	2m/2m3: 0-1 2m4-2m7: 0-1 3m+: 0-0
Track:	LH: 0-1 RH: 0-1 Tight: 0-1 Gall: 0-0
Aids:	Bl: 0-2 Vi: 0-0 Tstrap: 0-0 Ckp: 0-0
Best Rating:	114 12/00 Newc 2m soft Hdl

Plating-class hurdler; has been around a bit, but is still effective in selling hurdle company and added another victory in that grade at Market Rasen in March 2003; best at up to two and a half miles on good to soft ground.

Highcroft Boy

(93h)   (95 h)

9-y-o gr g Silver Owl-Caroline Ranger (Pony Express)
P J Hobbs Mrs Ann Weston

Placings:2/122-PP   (0546)
2003/04: 25⁵GF, 21⁵GF,

	Starts	1st	2nd	3rd	Win & Pl
Chases	2	0	0	0	
Career Total	**6**	**1**	**3**	**0**	**5422**
110 5/02 Winc 2m6f	E Hdl			G-F	£2618

Total win prize-money £2618

Going:	Sf: 0-0 GS: 0-0 Gd: 0-0 GF: - Fm: 0-2
Distance:	2m/2m3: 0-0 2m4-2m7: 0-0 3m+: 0-1
Track:	LH: 0-1 RH: 0-1 Tight: 0-1 Gall: 0-0
Aids:	Bl: 0-0 Vi: 0-0 Tstrap: 0-0 Ckp: 0-0
Best Rating:	110 5/02 Winc 2m6f gd-fm Hdl

Modest hurdler; lightly-raced over fences; stays two miles six; acts on decent ground.

Highest Offer

70f   85f

5-y-o b g Puissance-Scoffera (Scottish Reel)
W S Coltherd The Lighthouse Racing Syndicate

Placings:000   (4885)
2003/04: 16⁰GF, 16⁰S, 17⁰GS,

	Starts	1st	2nd	3rd	Win & Pl
NH Flat	3	0	0	0	
Career Total	**3**	**0**	**0**	**0**	

Going:	Sf: 0-1 GS: 0-1 Gd: 0-0 GF: - Fm: 0-1
Distance:	2m/2m3: 0-3 2m4-2m7: 0-0 3m+: 0-0
Track:	LH: 0-2 RH: 0-1 Tight: 0-0 Gall: 0-0
Aids:	Bl: 0-0 Vi: 0-0 Tstrap: 0-0 Ckp: 0-0
Best Rating:	85 3/04 Ayr 2m gd-fm NHF

Highfield's Clover

5-y-o b g Petoski-Dipped In Clover (Golden Dipper)
Mrs Jenny Gordon S P Tindall

Placings:P   (4122)
2003/04: 21⁵PG,

	Starts	1st	2nd	3rd	Win & Pl
Chases	1	0	0	0	
Career Total	**1**	**0**	**0**	**0**	

Going:	Sf: 0-0 GS: 0-0 Gd: 0-0 GF: - Fm: 0-0
Distance:	2m/2m3: 0-0 2m4-2m7: 0-1 3m+: 0-0
Track:	LH: 0-0 RH: 0-0 Tight: 0-1 Gall: 0-0
Aids:	Bl: 0-0 Vi: 0-0 Tstrap: 0-0 Ckp: 0-0

Highland Brig

8-y-o b g Homo Sapien-Birniebrig (New Brig)
Tim Butt W Hamilton, T Butt & D J Amos

Placings:5   (4687)
2003/04: 25⁵G,

	Starts	1st	2nd	3rd	Win & Pl
Chases	1	0	0	0	0
Career Total	**1**	**0**	**0**	**0**	**0**

Going:	Sf: 0-0 GS: 0-0 Gd: 0-0 GF: 0-1 Fm: 0-0
Distance:	2m/2m3: 0-0 2m4-2m7: 0-0 3m+: 0-0
Track:	LH: 0-1 RH: 0-0 Tight: 0-1 Gall: 0-0
Aids:	Bl: 0-0 Vi: 0-0 Tstrap: 0-0 Ckp: 0-0
Best Rating:	70 4/04 Kels 3m1f good Ch

Highland Island

(97h)   (79h)60

8-y-o b m Jupiter Island-Close Call (Nearly A Hand)
Mrs R L Elliot Mrs Patrick Campbell Fraser

Placings:30PPP   (3882)
2003/04: 27³GF, 16⁰S, 27⁶G, 27⁶GS, 24⁶PG,

	Starts	1st	2nd	3rd	Win & Pl
Hurdles	2	0	0	1	354
Chases	3	0	0	0	0
Career Total	**5**	**0**	**0**	**1**	**354**

Going:	Sf: 0-1 GS: 0-1 Gd: 0-2 GF: - Fm: 0-1
Distance:	2m/2m3: 0-1 2m4-2m7: 0-0 3m+: 0-4
Track:	LH: 0-4 RH: 0-1 Tight: 0-4 Gall: 0-0
Aids:	Bl: 0-0 Vi: 0-0 Tstrap: 0-5 Ckp: 0-0
Best Rating:	79 11/03 Sedg 3m3f110y gd-fm Hdl

Highland Reel

99   91+

7-y-o ch g Selkirk (USA)-Taj Victory (Final Straw)
D R C Elsworth Sir Gordon Brunton

Placings:40   (3047)
2003/04: 17⁴G, 17⁰G,

	Starts	1st	2nd	3rd	Win & Pl
Hurdles	2	0	0	0	433
Career Total	**2**	**0**	**0**	**0**	**433**

Going:	Sf: 0-0 GS: 0-0 Gd: 0-2 GF: - Fm: 0-0
Distance:	2m/2m3: 0-2 2m4-2m7: 0-0 3m+: 0-0
Track:	LH: 0-0 RH: 0-2 Tight: 0-2 Gall: 0-0
Aids:	Bl: 0-0 Vi: 0-0 Tstrap: 0-0 Ckp: 0-0
Best Rating:	97 12/03 Tntn 2m1f good Hdl

Ex-Flat handicapper; has shown ability over hurdles but needs to jump more fluently.

Highland Rose (IRE)

99   (0c)95d

8-y-o b m Roselier (FR)-Carrick Grinder (Sheer Grit)
Ms A E Embiricos S N J Embiricos

Placings:0010/PF00-52   (0458)
2003/04: 20⁵GF, 16⁸HY,

	Starts	1st	2nd	3rd	Win & Pl
Hurdles	2	0	1	0	1275
Career Total	**10**	**1**	**1**	**0**	**3921**
90 3/02 Hntg 2m110y	E Hdl			SFT	£2646

Total win prize-money £2646

Going:	Sf: 0-1 GS: 0-0 Gd: 0-0 GF: - Fm: 0-1
Distance:	2m/2m3: 0-1 2m4-2m7: 0-1 3m+: 0-0
Track:	LH: 0-2 RH: 0-0 Tight: 0-1 Gall: 0-0
Aids:	Bl: 0-0 Vi: 0-0 Tstrap: 0-0 Ckp: 0-0
Best Rating:	90 11/02 Wwck 2m3f gd-sft Hdl

Won 2m soft ground novice hurdle at Huntingdon March 2002; has since been tried over a variety of distances and is struggling to find her best trip.

Highland Tracker (IRE)

(101h)   (92h)92

9-y-o ch g Indian Ridge-Track Twenty Nine (IRE) (Standaan (FR))
Miss M E Rowland J Taqvi

Placings:63563/3052/62/16   (2477)
2003/04: 21¹G, 24⁶GF,

	Starts	1st	2nd	3rd	Win & Pl
Hurdles	2	1	0	0	2996
Career Total	**13**	**1**	**2**	**3**	**6199**
92 10/03 Sedg 2m5f110y	E(0-105)HHdl			GD	£2996

Total win prize-money £2996

Going:	Sf: 0-0 GS: 0-0 Gd: 1-1 GF: - Fm: 0-1
Distance:	2m/2m3: 0-0 2m4-2m7: 1-1 3m+: 0-1
Track:	LH: 1-2 RH: 0-0 Tight: 1-1 Gall: 0-1
Aids:	Bl: 0-0 Vi: 0-0 Tstrap: 0-0 Ckp: 0-0
Best Rating:	97 5/01 Hexm 2m4f110y gd-fm Ch

Highway Robbery

87(97h)   (97h)**93+**

7-y-o b g Un Desperado (FR)-Drivers Bureau (Proverb)
Mrs J Candlish (Miss E C Lavelle 2/1) Martin Jump

Placings:6FP-56506F   (4888)
2003/04: 16⁵GF, 22⁶GS, 25⁵GS, 24⁰G, 21⁶G, 24⁶GF,

	Starts	1st	2nd	3rd	Win & Pl
Hurdles	4	0	0	0	
Chases	2	0	0	0	
Career Total	9	0	0	0	0

Going:	Sf: 0-0 GS: 0-2 Gd: 0-2 GF: - Fm: 0-2
Distance:	2m/2m3: 0-1 2m4-2m7: 0-2 3m+: 0-3
Track:	LH: 0-1 RH: 0-5 Tight: 0-3 Gall: 0-0
Aids:	Bl: 0-0 Vi: 0-0 Tstrap: 0-0 Ckp: 0-0
Best Rating:	97 11/03 Asct 2m110y gd-fm Hdl

Modest hurdler; showed some promise on chasing debut.

Hill Charm

87   **56**

6-y-o ch m Minster Son-Snarry Hill (Vitiges (FR))
Mrs S J Smith Roy Robinson

Placings:60/P-000   (3209)
2003/04: 17⁰HY, 19⁰G, 25⁰GS,

	Starts	1st	2nd	3rd	Win & Pl
Hurdles	3	0	0	0	
Career Total	6	0	0	0	0

Going:	Sf: 0-1 GS: 0-1 Gd: 0-1 GF: - Fm: 0-0
Distance:	2m/2m3: 0-1 2m4-2m7: 0-1 3m+: 0-1
Track:	LH: 0-1 RH: 0-2 Tight: 0-1 Gall: 0-1
Aids:	Bl: 0-0 Vi: 0-0 Tstrap: 0-0 Ckp: 0-0
Best Rating:	61 4/02 Newc 2m firm NHF

Hill Farm Classic

4-y-o ch g Meqdaam (USA)-Wing Of Freedom (Troy)
M Wellings Dennis Newton

Placings:PP   (2819)
2003/04: 17⁶GF, 16⁶GF,

	Starts	1st	2nd	3rd	Win & Pl
Hurdles	2	0	0	0	
Career Total	2	0	0	0	

Going:	Sf: 0-0 GS: 0-0 Gd: 0-1 GF: - Fm: 0-1
Distance:	2m/2m3: 0-2 2m4-2m7: 0-0 3m+: 0-0
Track:	LH: 0-1 RH: 0-1 Tight: 0-1 Gall: 0-0
Aids:	Bl: 0-1 Vi: 0-0 Tstrap: 0-0 Ckp: 0-0

Hill Forts Henry

90   **82**

6-y-o ch g Karinga Bay-Maggie Tee (Lepanto (GER))
J W Mullins Mrs J C Scorgie

Placings:50/F0-60225   (2555)
2003/04: 22⁶G, 24⁰GF, 22²F, 22²G, 22⁵G,

	Starts	1st	2nd	3rd	Win & Pl
Hurdles	5	0	2	0	1826
Career Total	9	0	2	0	1826

Going:	Sf: 0-0 GS: 0-0 Gd: 0-3 GF: - Fm: 0-2
Distance:	2m/2m3: 0-0 2m4-2m7: 0-4 3m+: 0-1

Hill Port (IRE)

105   **117**

7-y-o ch g Port Lucaya-Minstrels Daughter (IRE) (Magical
Wonder (USA))
J J Lambe Stephen McConville

Placings:332220/2153355P32/F3-003613   (3743a)
2003/04: 24⁰Y, 20⁰YS, 16⁴YS, 20⁶GF, 27¹GF, 16³S,

	Starts	1st	2nd	3rd	Win & Pl
Hurdles	6	1	0	2	6341
Career Total	24	2	5	8	33811
114	7/03	Sedg	3m3f110yE(0-110)HHdl		G-F	£3437
114	10/01	Gowr	2m1f	Hdl		GD	£5842
				Total win prize-money £9280

Going:	Sf: 0-1 GS: 0-0 Gd: 0-0 GF: - Fm: 1-2
Distance:	2m/2m3: 0-2 2m4-2m7: 0-2 3m+: 1-2
Track:	LH: 1-4 RH: 0-1 Tight: 1-1 Gall: 0-0
Aids:	Bl: 0-0 Vi: 0-0 Tstrap: 0-0 Ckp: 0-0
Best Rating:	123 4/02 Punc 3m yield Hdl

Moderate staying hurdler; successfull over a marathon trip
at Sedgefield in July.

Hill Track

(102h)   (73h)

10-y-o b g Royal Match-Win Green Hill (National Trust)
R Johnson (C J Teague 13/1) B Batey

Placings:0/P/P0PP1P   (4794)
2003/04: 22⁵GS, 20⁰GS, 21⁶GS, 17⁶GS, 17¹G, 21⁶G,

	Starts	1st	2nd	3rd	Win & Pl
Hurdles	3	1	0	0	2436
Chases	3	0	0	0	0
Career Total	8	1	0	0	2436
73	3/04	Sedg	2m1f	G(0-90)HHdl		GD	£2436
				Total win prize-money £2436

Going:	Sf: 0-1 GS: 0-2 Gd: 1-3 GF: - Fm: 0-0
Distance:	2m/2m3: 1-2 2m4-2m7: 0-4 3m+: 0-0
Track:	LH: 1-6 RH: 0-0 Tight: 1-5 Gall: 0-0
Aids:	Bl: 0-0 Vi: 0-0 Tstrap: 0-0 Ckp: 0-1
Best Rating:	73 3/04 Sedg 2m1f good Hdl

No form before causing a 100/1 shock in a Sedgefield seller
in March 2004; acts on good ground.

Hill Trail

9-y-o ch g Royal Match-Win Green Hill (National Trust)
R K Bliss R K Bliss

Placings:0/PF/P   (4510)
2003/04: 19⁰GS,

	Starts	1st	2nd	3rd	Win & Pl
Chases	1	0	0	0	
Career Total	4	0	0	0	

Going:	Sf: 0-0 GS: 0-1 Gd: 0-0 GF: - Fm: 0-0
Distance:	2m/2m3: 0-1 2m4-2m7: 0-0 3m+: 0-0
Track:	LH: 0-0 RH: 0-1 Tight: 0-0 Gall: 0-0
Aids:	Bl: 0-0 Vi: 0-0 Tstrap: 0-1 Ckp: 0-0
Best Rating:	78 4/00 Font 2m2f110y good NHF

Hills Of Rakaposhi

5-y-o ch m Rakaposhi King-Hilly Path (Brave Invader (USA))
R Fielder R Fielder

Placings:060F0   (4929)
2003/04: 16⁶GS, 16⁶GS, 16⁶GS, 20⁶G, 18⁰G,

	Starts	1st	2nd	3rd	Win & Pl
NH Flat	3	0	0	0	0
Hurdles	2	0	0	0	0
Career Total	5	0	0	0	0

Going:	Sf: 0-0 GS: 0-3 Gd: 0-2 GF: - Fm: 0-0
Distance:	2m/2m3: 0-4 2m4-2m7: 0-1 3m+: 0-0
Track:	LH: 0-2 RH: 0-2 Tight: 0-0 Gall: 0-0
Aids:	Bl: 0-0 Vi: 0-0 Tstrap: 0-0 Ckp: 0-0
Best Rating:	45 3/04 Wwck 2m gd-sft NHF

Hills Of View

87   **60**

6-y-o b g Sea Raven (IRE)-Hardwick Sun (Dieu Soleil)
J M Jefferson R G Marshall

Placings:000   (4946)
2003/04: 16⁰HY, 20⁰G, 16⁰GS,

	Starts	1st	2nd	3rd	Win & Pl
NH Flat	1	0	0	0	0
Hurdles	2	0	0	0	0
Career Total	3	0	0	0	0

Going:	Sf: 0-1 GS: 0-1 Gd: 0-1 GF: - Fm: 0-0
Distance:	2m/2m3: 0-2 2m4-2m7: 0-1 3m+: 0-0
Track:	LH: 0-1 RH: 0-2 Tight: 0-0 Gall: 0-0
Aids:	Bl: 0-0 Vi: 0-0 Tstrap: 0-0 Ckp: 0-0
Best Rating:	60 4/04 Prth 2m110y gd-sft Hdl

Hilltime (IRE)

100   **96**

4-y-o b g Danetime (IRE)-Ceannanas (IRE) (Magical
Wonder (USA))
J J Quinn Mrs S Quinn

Placings:121   (1293)
2003/04: 17¹GF, 17²G, 16¹GF,

	Starts	1st	2nd	3rd	Win & Pl
Hurdles	3	2	1	0	8781
Career Total	3	2	1	0	8781
94	9/03	Strf	2m110y	D Hdl		G-F	£4104
91	8/03	Sedg	2m1f	E Hdl		G-F	£3500
				Total win prize-money £7605

Going:	Sf: 0-0 GS: 0-0 Gd: 0-1 GF: - Fm: 2-2
Distance:	2m/2m3: 2-3 2m4-2m7: 0-0 3m+: 0-0
Track:	LH: 2-3 RH: 0-0 Tight: 2-3 Gall: 0-0
Aids:	Bl: 0-0 Vi: 0-0 Tstrap: 0-0 Ckp: 0-0
Best Rating:	96 8/03 Ctml 2m1f110y good Hdl

Maiden sprint plater on the Flat; jumped well and just held
on after taking a clear advantage when successful on debut
over hurdles at Sedgefield in August 2003; just edged out
under a penalty at Cartmel two weeks later; lucky winner at
Stratford in September; barely stays 2m.

Hilltop Harry (IRE)

78   **81**

7-y-o b g Commanche Run-What's In A Name (IRE) (Le
Moss)
Lady Connell Sir Michael Connell

Placings:553-0					(4783)

2003/04: 21⁰G,

	Starts	1st	2nd	3rd	Win & Pl
Hurdles	1	0	0	0	
Career Total	4	0	0	1	534

Going:	Sf: 0-0 GS: 0-0 Gd: 0-1 GF: - Fm: 0-0
Distance:	2m/2m3: 0-0 2m4-2m7: 0-1 3m+: 0-0
Track:	LH: 0-0 RH: 0-1 Tight: 0-0 Gall: 0-1
Aids:	Bl: 0-0 Vi: 0-0 Tstrap: 0-0 Ckp: 0-0
Best Rating:	94 12/02 Uttx 2m soft NHF

Irish point winner; modest form in long distance novice hurdles.

Him Of Distinction
98   94+

5-y-o br g Rainbow Quest (USA)-Air Of Distinction (IRE) (Distinctly North (USA))
R T Phillips Nicholas Cooper

Placings:63					(4588)

2003/04: 17⁶S, 21³G,

	Starts	1st	2nd	3rd	Win & Pl
Hurdles	2	0	0	1	544
Career Total	2	0	0	1	544

Going:	Sf: 0-1 GS: 0-0 Gd: 0-1 GF: - Fm: 0-0
Distance:	2m/2m3: 0-0 2m4-2m7: 0-1 3m+: 0-0
Track:	LH: 0-0 RH: 0-2 Tight: 0-1 Gall: 0-1
Aids:	Bl: 0-0 Vi: 0-0 Tstrap: 0-0 Ckp: 0-0
Best Rating:	94 3/04 Hntg 2m5f110y good Hdl

Himalayan Heights

9-y-o ch g North Col-Chestertons Choice (Country Retreat)
Mrs J Marles J P Thorne

Placings:P					(0294)

2003/04: 20ᴾG,

	Starts	1st	2nd	3rd	Win & Pl
Chases	1	0	0	0	
Career Total	1	0	0	0	

Going:	Sf: 0-0 GS: 0-1 Gd: 0-0 GF: - Fm: 0-0
Distance:	2m/2m3: 0-0 2m4-2m7: 0-1 3m+: 0-0
Track:	LH: 0-1 RH: 0-0 Tight: 0-1 Gall: 0-0
Aids:	Bl: 0-0 Vi: 0-0 Tstrap: 0-0 Ckp: 0-0

Hint Of Magic
70   69

7-y-o b g Magic Ring (IRE)-Thames Glow (Kalaglow)
H W Lavis Bob And Mrs Vicky Burks

Placings:P/P640-0					(0676)

2003/04: 16⁰GF,

	Starts	1st	2nd	3rd	Win & Pl
Hurdles	1	0	0	0	
Career Total	6	0	0	0	0

Going:	Sf: 0-0 GS: 0-0 Gd: 0-0 GF: - Fm: 0-1
Distance:	2m/2m3: 0-1 2m4-2m7: 0-0 3m+: 0-0
Track:	LH: 0-1 RH: 0-0 Tight: 0-0 Gall: 0-0
Aids:	Bl: 0-0 Vi: 0-0 Tstrap: 0-0 Ckp: 0-0
Best Rating:	69 12/02 Hrfd 2m1f soft Hdl

Hirapour (IRE)
96   135+

8-y-o b g Kahyasi-Himaya (IRE) (Mouktar)
Ian Williams C N Barnes And M Murphy

Placings:423111-11					(0357)

2003/04: 20¹GS, 22¹G,

	Starts	1st	2nd	3rd	Win & Pl
Hurdles	2	2	0	0	18715
Career Total	8	5	1	1	37782
135	5/03	Kels	2m6f110yB Hdl		GD	£13775
114	5/03	Aint	2m4f D Hdl		G-S	£4940
135	4/03	Prth	2m4f110yD(0-130)HHdl		GD	£8401
139	4/03	Extr	2m1f F(0-100)HHdl		G-F	£3556
124	4/03	Ludl	2m5f E(0-105)HHdl		GD	£4875
			Total win prize-money			£35547

Going:	Sf: 0-0 GS: 1-1 Gd: 1-1 GF: - Fm: 0-0
Distance:	2m/2m3: 0-0 2m4-2m7: 2-2 3m+: 0-0
Track:	LH: 2-2 RH: 0-0 Tight: 2-2 Gall: 0-0
Aids:	Bl: 0-0 Vi: 0-0 Tstrap: 0-0 Ckp: 0-0
Best Rating:	139 4/03 Extr 2m1f gd-fm Hdl

Useful hurdler; progressive this season, completing a five-timer in the spring of 2003; effective on good to soft and fast ground; stays at least 2m 6f and likely to get further.

Hirayna

5-y-o b m Doyoun-Himaya (IRE) (Mouktar)
W M Brisbourne Preece Haden Partnership

Placings:0-1244					(1625)

2003/04: 16¹G, 17²GF, 16⁴G, 16⁴GF,

	Starts	1st	2nd	3rd	Win & Pl
NH Flat	3	1	1	0	2697
Hurdles	1	0	0	0	0
Career Total	5	1	1	0	2697
97	7/03	Prth	2m110y H NHF		GD	£2177
			Total win prize-money			£2177

Going:	Sf: 0-0 GS: 0-0 Gd: 1-2 GF: - Fm: 0-2
Distance:	2m/2m3: 1-4 2m4-2m7: 0-0 3m+: 0-0
Track:	LH: 0-2 RH: 1-2 Tight: 0-0 Gall: 0-0
Aids:	Bl: 0-0 Vi: 0-0 Tstrap: 0-0 Ckp: 0-0
Best Rating:	97 7/03 Prth 2m110y good NHF

Has shown ability in bumpers but failed to match that form on hurdles debut; acts on good to firm ground.

Hired Gun (IRE)
77f   58f

5-y-o b g Needle Gun (IRE)-Monahullen Rose (IRE) (Fayruz)
V R A Dartnall The Hired Gun Partnership

Placings:00					(4739)

2003/04: 14⁰GS, 17⁰G,

	Starts	1st	2nd	3rd	Win & Pl
NH Flat	2	0	0	0	
Career Total	2	0	0	0	

Going:	Sf: 0-0 GS: 0-1 Gd: 0-1 GF: - Fm: 0-0
Distance:	2m/2m3: 0-1 2m4-2m7: 0-0 3m+: 0-0
Track:	LH: 0-1 RH: 0-0 Tight: 0-1 Gall: 0-0
Aids:	Bl: 0-0 Vi: 0-0 Tstrap: 0-0 Ckp: 0-0
Best Rating:	58 4/04 NAbb 2m1f good NHF

Hirt Lodge
(100h)   (92dh)48

13-y-o ch g Jumbo Hirt (USA)-Holly Lodge (Rubor)
J E Dixon Mrs S F Dixon

Placings:6026/30626/30416P0-P0					(2802)

2003/04: 26ᴾG, 16⁰S,

	Starts	1st	2nd	3rd	Win & Pl
Hurdles	1	0	0	0	0
Chases	1	0	0	0	0
Career Total	18	1	2	2	5511
92	11/02	Kels	2m6f110yF(0-100)HHdl		SFT	£3471
			Total win prize-money			£3471

Going:	Sf: 0-1 GS: 0-0 Gd: 0-1 GF: - Fm: 0-0
Distance:	2m/2m3: 0-1 2m4-2m7: 0-0 3m+: 0-1
Track:	LH: 0-2 RH: 0-0 Tight: 0-1 Gall: 0-0
Aids:	Bl: 0-0 Vi: 0-0 Tstrap: 0-0 Ckp: 0-1
Best Rating:	92 11/02 Kels 2m6f110y soft Hdl

Hirvine (FR)
106   127+

6-y-o ch g Snurge-Guadanella (FR) (Guadanini (FR))
P Bowen (T P Tate 7/10) B A Crumbley

Placings:3F1-11U1					(3644)

2003/04: 16¹G, 17¹S, 22¹GS, 25ᵁGS, 24¹G,

	Starts	1st	2nd	3rd	Win & Pl
Hurdles	5	4	0	1	14974
Career Total	7	4	0	1	15450
134	2/04	Kemp	3m110y D(0-120)HHdl		G-S	£4992
126	12/03	Folk	2m6f110yE(0-105)HHdl		G-S	£3094
85	5/03	Sedg	2m1f E Hdl		SFT	£3521
94	4/03	Hexm	2m110y E Hdl		GD	£3367
			Total win prize-money			£14974

Going:	Sf: 1-1 GS: 2-3 Gd: 1-1 GF: - Fm: 0-0
Distance:	2m/2m3: 2-2 2m4-2m7: 1-1 3m+: 1-2
Track:	LH: 2-3 RH: 2-2 Tight: 2-2 Gall: 0-0
Aids:	Bl: 0-0 Vi: 0-0 Tstrap: 0-0 Ckp: 0-0
Best Rating:	134 2/04 Kemp 3m110y gd-sft Hdl

Fair hurdler; will make a chaser in time; stays three miles; acts on good ground or softer; has worn blinkers on the Flat.

His Nibs (IRE)
111   (0c)137+

7-y-o b g Afflora (IRE)-Mrs Jennifer (River Knight (FR))
Miss Venetia Williams John Galvanoni

Placings:150/133P-R114242541					(4643)

2003/04: 25ᴿG, 23¹G, 22¹G, 25⁴G, 25²G, 25⁴GS, 23²HY, 22⁵G, 25⁴G, 24¹G,

	Starts	1st	2nd	3rd	Win & Pl
Hurdles	9	3	2	0	54435
Chases	1	0	0	0	0
Career Total	17	5	2	2	62075
137	4/04	Aint	3m110y A HHdl		GD	£23200
128	11/03	MRas	2m6f B HHdl		GD	£9412
127	11/03	Ling	2m7f D(0-115)HHdl		GD	£6792
119	12/02	Folk	2m1f110yE Hdl		HVY	£3073
105	5/01	Folk	2m1f110yH NHF		G-S	£1904
			Total win prize-money			£44382

Going:	Sf: 0-1 GS: 1-0 Gd: 3-8 GF: - Fm: 0-0
Distance:	2m/2m3: 0-0 2m4-2m7: 2-3 3m+: 1-7
Track:	LH: 2-7 RH: 0-0 Tight: 2-2 Gall: 0-2
Aids:	Bl: 0-0 Vi: 0-0 Tstrap: 0-0 Ckp: 0-0
Best Rating:	137 4/04 Aint 3m110y good Hdl

Useful hurdler; landed a competitive handicap at Aintree; best on soft ground but acts on good, stays three miles two.

His Song (IRE)

(108h)   (131 h)
11-y-o ch g Accordion-Pampered Finch Vii (Damsire Unregistered)
N J Henderson David Lloyd

Placings:111221/**112115U**/32341P0/6P/4000/024-0505P
                                              (4784)
2003/04: 22²GS, 24²S, 21⁰G, 20⁵GS, 24⁸G,

		Starts	1st	2nd	3rd	Win & Pl
Hurdles		4	0	0	0	0
Chases		1	0	0	0	0
Career Total		34	9	5	2	147934
133	2/00	Naas	2m	Ch	SFT	£15600
144	1/99	Leop	2m1f	Ch	HVY	£16187
145	12/98	Leop	2m1f	Ch	SFT	£22608
132	10/98	Punc	2m	Ch	SFT	£3586
126	10/98	Tipp	2m	SH		£3586
146	4/98	Punc	2m	Hdl	HVY	£22826
136	12/97	Leop	2m	Hdl	HVY	£9579
120	11/97	Fair	2m2f	Hdl	Y-S	£3391
109	11/97	Naas	2m	Hdl	Y-S	£3730
			Total win prize-money £101097			

Going:	Sf: 0-1 GS: 0-2 Gd: 0-2 GF: - Fm: 0-0
Distance:	2m/2m3: 0-0 2m4-2m7: 0-3 3m+: 0-2
Track:	LH: 0-1 RH: 0-4 Tight: 0-0 Gall: 0-1
Aids:	Bl: 0-0 Vi: 0-0 Tstrap: 0-0 Ckp: 0-0
Best Rating:	147 3/98 Chel 2m110y good Hdl

Fair hurdler; lacks a turn of foot; suited by soft ground; stays three miles.

Hisar (IRE)

100   76
11-y-o br g Doyoun-Himaya (IRE) (Mouktar)
P C Ritchens R Catton

Placings:002/21U2/53P2301/**3122226212**/3600/**422111115**
40/33043-0P550P423P545U6   (2911)
2003/04: 16⁹G, 16⁸GF, 16⁵GF, 16⁸GF, 17⁸G, 17⁴G, 18²GF, 20³GF,
19⁸GF, 20⁵GF, 17⁴GF, 16⁵GS, 16⁸UGF, 16⁶GS,

		Starts	1st	2nd	3rd	Win & Pl
Chases		14	0	1	1	2178
Career Total		58	9	13	8	59373
124	9/01	Worc	2m	C(0-135)HCh	G-F	£6679
128	8/01	Strf	2m1f110yD(0-125)HCh	GD	£5434
128	8/01	NAbb	2m110y	D(0-125)HCh	GD	£3721
117	7/01	Wolv	2m	C(0-135)HCh	G-S	£8080
114	6/01	NAbb	2m110y	F(0-105)HCh	G-F	£2947
122	11/99	Wwck	2m	D(0-125)HCh	GD	£3822
108	5/99	Hrfd	2m	E Ch	GD	£3257
112	4/99	Hrfd	2m1f	E(0-115)HHdl	G-F	£2931
103	10/97	Uttx	2m	E Hdl	GD	£2337
			Total win prize-money £39212			

Going:	Sf: 0-0 GS: 0-2 Gd: 0-3 GF: - Fm: 0-9
Distance:	2m/2m3: 0-12 2m4-2m7: 0-2 3m+: 0-0
Track:	LH: 0-7 RH: 0-4 Tight: 0-7 Gall: 0-2
Aids:	Bl: 0-0 Vi: 0-0 Tstrap: 0-7 Ckp: 0-0
Best Rating:	128 8/01 Strf 2m1f110y good Ch

Plating-class chaser; best forcing the pace; completed a fine five-timer over fences in the summer of 2001; generally out of form and has plummeted down weights since; best at around two miles on fast ground.

Historic (IRE)

106   (157h) 127+
8-y-o b g Sadler's Wells (USA)-Urjwan (USA) (Seattle Slew (USA))
T R George Mrs R E R Rumboll

Placings:3312/3F15650/**P2151**   (4782)
2003/04: 19⁸GS, 19²GS, 23¹S, 24⁵G, 24¹G,

		Starts	1st	2nd	3rd	Win & Pl
Chases		5	2	1	0	13799
Career Total		16	4	2	3	58920
121	4/04	Hntg	3m	E Ch	GD	£3939
127	2/04	Extr	2m7f110yE Ch	SFT	£4900
157	12/01	Newb	3m110y	A Hdl	SFT	£14500
142	2/01	Hayd	2m7f110yA Hdl	SFT	£15000
			Total win prize-money £38339			

Going:	Sf: 1-1 GS: 0-2 Gd: 1-2 GF: - Fm: 0-0
Distance:	2m/2m3: 0-1 2m4-2m7: 0-1 3m+: 2-3
Track:	LH: 0-2 RH: 2-3 Tight: 0-0 Gall: 1-2
Aids:	Bl: 0-0 Vi: 0-0 Tstrap: 0-0 Ckp: 0-0
Best Rating:	157 12/01 Newb 3m110y soft Hdl

Very useful novice chaser; smart staying hurdler back in 2002; recorded second success over fences at Huntingdon in April; stays three miles; acts on soft ground; likes to race prominently; has been tried in blinkers; still has time to go on to better things.

Historic Place (USA)

94f   106f
4-y-o b g Dynaformer (USA)-Captive Island (Northfields (USA))
G B Balding Miss Georgina Bishop

Placings:2315   (4649)
2003/04: 13²GS, 12³G, 16¹HY, 17⁵G,

		Starts	1st	2nd	3rd	Win & Pl
NH Flat		4	1	1	1	5038
Career Total		4	1	1	1	5038
101	1/04	Asct	2m110y	H NHF	HVY	£2509
			Total win prize-money £2510			

Going:	Sf: 1-1 GS: 0-1 Gd: 0-2 GF: - Fm: 0-0
Distance:	2m/2m3: 1-2 2m4-2m7: 0-0 3m+: 0-0
Track:	LH: 0-0 RH: 1-2 Tight: 0-0 Gall: 0-0
Aids:	Bl: 0-0 Vi: 0-0 Tstrap: 0-0 Ckp: 0-0
Best Rating:	101 4/04 Aint 2m1f good NHF

Promising efforts in juvenile bumpers.

Hit And Run (FR)

88   135
9-y-o ch g River Mist (USA)-La Dunanerie (FR) (Guadanini (FR))
M C Pipe Gerry Scanlon & Miss J Kirk

Placings:1112351/5230/0243P/**1130**/315P-B0   (4843)
2003/04: 16⁸G, 16⁰G,

		Starts	1st	2nd	3rd	Win & Pl
Chases		2	0	0	0	
Career Total		27	8	3	5	62352
125	6/02	Hrfd	2m	E Ch	GD	£3409
135	1/02	Donc	2m110y	D Ch	SFT	£4452
128	11/01	Plum	2m1f	F Ch	GD	£2990
143	4/99	Wwck	2m	C(0-135)HHdl	GF	£4789
128	12/98	Sand	2m110y	D Hdl	GD	£2775
119	10/98	Chel	2m110y	C Hdl	GD	£4260
122	9/98	Sedg	2m1f	E Hdl	G-F	£2390
100	9/98	NAbb	2m1f	E Hdl	G-F	£2130
			Total win prize-money £27196			

Going:	Sf: 0-0 GS: 0-0 Gd: 0-2 GF: - Fm: 0-0
Distance:	2m/2m3: 0-2 2m4-2m7: 0-0 3m+: 0-0
Track:	LH: 0-2 RH: 0-0 Tight: 0-0 Gall: 0-2
Aids:	Bl: 0-0 Vi: 0-0 Tstrap: 0-0 Ckp: 0-0
Best Rating:	158 2/01 Newb 2m110y soft Hdl

A smart front-running handicap hurdler in his prime; winning

chaser; ran a shocker when pulled up in a claiming hurdle at Fontwell when last seen in August 2002; best at two miles; has won on fast ground but seems better on a yielding surface; has clearly experienced problems; has been tried in blinkers and visor.

Hit Royal (FR)

105   (95h) 116
9-y-o ch g Montorselli-Valse Royale (FR) (Cap Martin (FR))
P R Webber David Czarnetzki

Placings:066/515P/**241F32F6**/1145-1626   (4784)
2003/04: 20¹GF, 20⁶G, 19²G, 24⁶G,

		Starts	1st	2nd	3rd	Win & Pl
Chases		4	1	1	0	9179
Career Total		23	5	3	1	29160
114	9/03	Hntg	2m4f110yC(0-135)HCh	G-F	£6760
110	9/02	MRas	2m1f110yD(0-120)HCh	G-F	£6857
102	8/02	Hntg	2m110y	F(0-100)HCh	G-F	£2940
110	11/01	Ludl	2m	E(0-105)HCh	G-F	£3760
103	8/00	Worc	3m	F(0-95)HHdl	G-F	£1799
			Total win prize-money £22117			

Going:	Sf: 0-0 GS: 0-0 Gd: 0-3 GF: - Fm: 1-1
Distance:	2m/2m3: 0-1 2m4-2m7: 1-2 3m+: 0-1
Track:	LH: 0-2 RH: 1-2 Tight: 0-0 Gall: 1-3
Aids:	Bl: 0-0 Vi: 0-0 Tstrap: 0-0 Ckp: 0-0
Best Rating:	114 9/03 Hntg 2m4f110y gd-fm Ch

Modest chaser, effective at two miles and best on good ground.

Hitchhiker

82
10-y-o b g Picea-Lady Lax (Henbit (USA))
R Ford Miss J M Slater

Placings:0000000/6022144320/240122P1P/F5/UPF6/P245
U0F-P   (0479)
2003/04: 21⁸GF,

		Starts	1st	2nd	3rd	Win & Pl
Hurdles		1	0	0	0	
Career Total		40	3	7	1	19495
108	3/00	Newc	3m	E(0-115)HCh	GD	£5421
102	12/99	Hntg	3m	E(0-105)HCh	GD	£3446
90	10/98	Weth	3m1f	E(0-105)HHdl	GD	£2903
			Total win prize-money £11771			

Going:	Sf: 0-0 GS: 0-0 Gd: 0-0 GF: - Fm: 0-1
Distance:	2m/2m3: 0-0 2m4-2m7: 0-1 3m+: 0-0
Track:	LH: 0-0 RH: 0-1 Tight: 0-0 Gall: 0-1
Aids:	Bl: 0-1 Vi: 0-0 Tstrap: 0-0 Ckp: 0-0
Best Rating:	108 3/00 Newc 3m good Ch

Moderate handicap chaser; acts on good.

Ho Pang Yau

103   64
6-y-o b/br g Pivotal-La Cabrilla (Carwhite)
Mrs R L Elliot (Miss L A Perratt 5/2) Alan Guthrie

Placings:00P00   (4614)
2003/04: 16⁶G, 16⁰S, 16⁵HY, 16⁶GF, 17⁰G,

		Starts	1st	2nd	3rd	Win & Pl
Hurdles		5	0	0	0	
Career Total		5	0	0	0	

Going:	Sf: 0-2 GS: 0-0 Gd: 0-1 GF: - Fm: 0-2
Distance:	2m/2m3: 0-5 2m4-2m7: 0-0 3m+: 0-0
Track:	LH: 0-4 RH: 0-1 Tight: 0-5 Gall: 0-0
Aids:	Bl: 0-0 Vi: 0-0 Tstrap: 0-0 Ckp: 0-0
Best Rating:	64 3/04 Catt 2m gd-fm Hdl

Moderate novice hurdler; first worthwhile form when 50/1 winner at Wetherby in April; unlikely to stay beyond two miles; suited by decent ground.

Hobart Junction (IRE)

89   **74**

9-y-o ch g Classic Secret (USA)-Art Duo (Artaius (USA))
J A T De Giles J A T De Giles

Placings: PU/002540/04325/14305065000/03P2U-0600   **(0768)**
2003/04: 17⁹GS, 22⁶GF, 21⁰GF, 22⁹GF,

	Starts	1st	2nd	3rd	Win & Pl
Hurdles	4	0	0	0	0
Career Total	33	1	3	3	5403
84 6/01 NAbb 2m1f	G(0-95)HHdl		GD		£2380
				Total win prize-money £2380

Going:	Sf: 0-0 GS: 0-1 Gd: 0-0 GF: - Fm: 0-3
Distance:	2m/2m3: 1-2 2m4-2m7: 0-3 3m+: 0-0
Track:	LH: 0-1 RH: 0-3 Tight: 0-0 Gall: 0-1
Aids:	Bl: 0-0 Vi: 0-0 Tstrap: 0-0 Ckp: 0-0
Best Rating:	84 8/01 Strf 2m110y good Hdl

Hobgoblin

61   **51**

11-y-o ch g Fearless Action (USA)-Swallow This (Town Crier)
H H G Owen H H G Owen

Placings: 04   **(0258)**
2003/04: 16⁹GF, 16⁴GF,

	Starts	1st	2nd	3rd	Win & Pl
Hurdles	2	0	0	0	311
Career Total	2	0	0	0	311

Going:	Sf: 0-0 GS: 0-0 Gd: 0-0 GF: - Fm: 0-2
Distance:	2m/2m3: 0-2 2m4-2m7: 0-0 3m+: 0-0
Track:	LH: 0-0 RH: 0-2 Tight: 0-0 Gall: 0-1
Aids:	Bl: 0-0 Vi: 0-0 Tstrap: 0-0 Ckp: 0-0
Best Rating:	51 5/03 Ludl 2m gd-fm Hdl

Hodgson's Choice (IRE)

5-y-o b m Fourstars Allstar (USA)-Waterland Lady (Strong Gale)
M J Ryan William Dixon

Placings: 5P   **(4402)**
2003/04: 16⁵G, 16⁶G,

	Starts	1st	2nd	3rd	Win & Pl
NH Flat	1	0	0	0	0
Hurdles	1	0	0	0	0
Career Total	2	0	0	0	0

Going:	Sf: 0-0 GS: 0-0 Gd: 0-2 GF: - Fm: 0-0
Distance:	2m/2m3: 0-2 2m4-2m7: 0-0 3m+: 0-0
Track:	LH: 0-0 RH: 0-2 Tight: 0-0 Gall: 0-0
Aids:	Bl: 0-0 Vi: 0-0 Tstrap: 0-0 Ckp: 0-0
Best Rating:	87 3/04 Hntg 2m110y good NHF

Hoh Invader (IRE)

81(84c)   (85c)**100d**

12-y-o b g Accordion-Newgate Fairy (Flair Path)

Mrs A Duffield Exors Of The Late N Midgley

Placings: 501/112142040/1322PP/212024/0P1500-0 (0196)
2003/04: 16⁶G,

	Starts	1st	2nd	3rd	Win & Pl
Hurdles	1	0	0	0	
Career Total	31	7	7	1	42696
96 1/03 Muss 2m4f	G Hdl		GD		£2947
123 6/00 Strf	2m1f110yC(0-135)HCh		GD		£6142
88 8/99 Prth 2m	D Ch		G-F		£4104
128 11/98 Chel	2m110y A Hdl		GD		£9002
108 9/98 Worc 2m	E Hdl		G-F		£2302
114 5/98 Worc 2m	H NHF		G-F		£1560
95 9/97 Gway 2m	NHF		Y-S		£3391
				Total win prize-money £29450

Going:	Sf: 0-0 GS: 0-0 Gd: 0-1 GF: - Fm: 0-0
Distance:	2m/2m3: 0-1 2m4-2m7: 0-0 3m+: 0-0
Track:	LH: 0-1 RH: 0-0 Tight: 0-0 Gall: 0-1
Aids:	Bl: 0-0 Vi: 0-0 Tstrap: 0-1 Ckp: 0-0
Best Rating:	134 12/98 Asct 2m110y soft Hdl

One-time useful chaser, but looks just modest these days, including over hurdles; acts on decent ground; effective at up to two and a half miles.

Hoh Tel (IRE)

10-y-o ch g Montelimar (USA)-Party Dancer (Be My Guest (USA))
G F White F V White

Placings: 0/230620/FU4U6P0/5-2   **(0101)**
2003/04: 25²G,

	Starts	1st	2nd	3rd	Win & Pl
Chases	1	0	1	0	766
Career Total	16	0	3	1	3019

Going:	Sf: 0-0 GS: 0-0 Gd: 0-1 GF: - Fm: 0-0
Distance:	2m/2m3: 0-0 2m4-2m7: 0-0 3m+: 0-1
Track:	LH: 0-1 RH: 0-0 Tight: 0-0 Gall: 0-0
Aids:	Bl: 0-0 Vi: 0-0 Tstrap: 0-0 Ckp: 0-1
Best Rating:	112 5/99 Hrfd 2m1f gd-sft NHF

Moderate pointer/hunter chaser; dual winner between the flags; stays three miles one; usually wears a visor.

Hoh Viss

106   **107+**

4-y-o b g Rudimentary (USA)-Now And Forever (IRE) (Kris)
C J Mann (S Kirk 17/12) D F Allport

Placings: 023   **(3894)**
2003/04: 16⁶S, 18²G, 16³GS,

	Starts	1st	2nd	3rd	Win & Pl
Hurdles	3	0	1	1	1774
Career Total	3	0	1	1	1774

Going:	Sf: 0-1 GS: 0-1 Gd: 0-1 GF: - Fm: 0-0
Distance:	2m/2m3: 0-3 2m4-2m7: 0-0 3m+: 0-0
Track:	LH: 0-2 RH: 0-1 Tight: 0-0 Gall: 0-1
Aids:	Bl: 0-0 Vi: 0-0 Tstrap: 0-0 Ckp: 0-0
Best Rating:	114 2/04 Sand 2m110y gd-sft Hdl

Novice hurdler; stays two miles two.

Holland Park (IRE)

108   **125+**

7-y-o gr g Roselier (FR)-Bluebell Avenue (Boreen Beag)
Mrs S D Williams B M Yin

Placings: 323-1232   **(4870)**
2003/04: 19¹S, 18²GS, 20³S, 24²GS,

	Starts	1st	2nd	3rd	Win & Pl
Hurdles	4	1	2	1	13127
Career Total	7	1	3	3	15345
111 1/04 Extr 2m3f	E Hdl		SFT		£3809
				Total win prize-money £3809

Fair novice hurdler; stays three miles, but effective at shorter; best on a soft surface.

Holloa Away (IRE)

91   **74**

12-y-o b g Red Sunset-Lili Bengam (Welsh Saint)
J A T De Giles J A T De Giles

Placings: 140/354P/0/04163000/6-P55   **(0884)**
2003/04: 22⁰GF, 22⁵GF, 20⁹G,

	Starts	1st	2nd	3rd	Win & Pl
Hurdles	3	0	0	0	0
Career Total	20	2	0	2	4068
70 9/01 Strf	2m6f110yG(0-95)HHdl		G-F		£1946
101 5/97 Worc 2m	H NHF		G-S		£1402
				Total win prize-money £3349

Going:	Sf: 0-0 GS: 0-0 Gd: 0-1 GF: - Fm: 0-2
Distance:	2m/2m3: 0-0 2m4-2m7: 0-3 3m+: 0-0
Track:	LH: 0-3 RH: 0-0 Tight: 0-1 Gall: 0-0
Aids:	Bl: 0-0 Vi: 0-0 Tstrap: 0-0 Ckp: 0-0
Best Rating:	101 5/97 Worc 2m gd-sft NHF

Hollows Mill

108   **97+**

8-y-o b g Rudimentary (USA)-Strawberry Song (Final Straw)
F P Murtagh The Great Expectations Sporting Club

Placings: 0004/45365512-636035F322100FP4   **(4883)**
2003/04: 16²G, 16⁶G, 16³G, 16⁶G, 17⁰GF, 16³GF, 16⁵F, 17⁵GF, 17³GS, 17²GS, 17²HY, 20¹GF, 16⁵S, 16⁶F, 20⁶HY, 17⁴GS,

	Starts	1st	2nd	3rd	Win & Pl
Hurdles	17	1	3	3	12046
Career Total	28	2	3	4	16215
99 12/03 Muss 2m4f	D(0-125)HHdl		G-F		£6760
90 4/03 Carl 2m1f	E Hdl		G-F		£3458
				Total win prize-money £10218

Going:	Sf: 0-3 GS: 0-3 Gd: 0-6 GF: - Fm: 1-5
Distance:	2m/2m3: 0-15 2m4-2m7: 1-2 3m+: 0-0
Track:	LH: 0-6 RH: 1-11 Tight: 1-4 Gall: 0-0
Aids:	Bl: 0-0 Vi: 0-0 Tstrap: 0-0 Ckp: 0-0
Best Rating:	103 11/03 Carl 2m1f heavy Hdl

Moderate hurdler; keen sort; suited by hold-up tactics; stays two and a half miles.

Hollows Mist

100   **94**

6-y-o b g Missed Flight-Joyfulness (FR) (Cure The Blues (USA))
F P Murtagh The Great Expectations Sporting Club 2

Placings: 3P6626   **(4685)**
2003/04: 17³G, 16⁹S, 16⁶HY, 17⁶GS, 16²GF, 16⁶G,

	Starts	1st	2nd	3rd	Win & Pl
NH Flat	1	0	0	1	217
Hurdles	5	0	1	0	932

Career Total   6   0   1   1   1149

Going:	Sf: 0-2 GS: 0-1 Gd: 0-2 GF: - Fm: 0-1
Distance:	2m2/2m3: 0-6 2m4-2m7: 0-3 3m+: 0-0
Track:	LH: 0-6 RH: 0-0 Tight: 0-4 Gall: 0-0
Aids:	Bl: 0-0 Vi: 0-0 Tstrap: 0-3 Ckp: 0-0
Best Rating:	94 3/04 Ayr 2m gd-fm Hdl

Showed promise on his bumper debut on good ground and best effort over hurdles came on a sound surface; should stay further than two miles.

Holly Rose

79   **35**

5-y-o b m Charnwood Forest (IRE)-Divina Luna (Dowsing (USA))
D E Cantillon Mrs Catherine Reed

Placings:0   (1217)
2003/04: 16⁰GF,

	Starts	1st	2nd	3rd	Win & Pl
Hurdles	1	0	0	0	
Career Total	1	0	0	0	

Going:	Sf: 0-0 GS: 0-0 Gd: 0-0 GF: - Fm: 0-1
Distance:	2m2/2m3: 0-1 2m4-2m7: 0-0 3m+: 0-0
Track:	LH: 0-0 RH: 0-1 Tight: 0-1 Gall: 0-0
Aids:	Bl: 0-0 Vi: 0-0 Tstrap: 0-0 Ckp: 0-1
Best Rating:	46 8/03 Hntg 2m110y gd-fm Hdl

Hollywest (FR)

97   **81+**

4-y-o ch g Sillery (USA)-Hollywood Trick (USA) (Caro)
M E Sowersby (R M Beckett 3/7) The Southwold Set

Placings:50303443   (4758)
2003/04: 16⁵F, 16⁰GF, 16³G, 16⁹G, 16³S, 19⁴G, 17⁴G, 16³S,

	Starts	1st	2nd	3rd	Win & Pl
Hurdles	8	0	0	3	2786
Career Total	8	0	0	3	2786

Going:	Sf: 0-2 GS: 0-0 Gd: 0-4 GF: - Fm: 0-2
Distance:	2m2/2m3: 0-7 2m4-2m7: 0-1 3m+: 0-0
Track:	LH: 0-5 RH: 0-3 Tight: 0-1 Gall: 0-2
Aids:	Bl: 0-1 Vi: 0-0 Tstrap: 0-0 Ckp: 0-0
Best Rating:	81 4/04 Towc 2m soft Hdl

Modest form in juvenile hurdles.

Holy Orders (IRE)

122   **153**

7-y-o b h Unblest-Shadowglow (Shaadi (USA))
W P Mullins A McLuckie

Placings:611/3/0000-10056   (4623)
2003/04: 24¹GY, 20¹⁰VS, 20⁵G, 24⁵G, 24⁶G,

	Starts	1st	2nd	3rd	Win & Pl
Hurdles	5	1	0	0	44510
Career Total	13	3	0	1	93469
153	5/03	Punc	3m		Hdl	G-Y £40259
133	4/01	Fair	2m		Hdl	Y-S £42500
121	2/01	Gowr	2m		Hdl	HVY £5008

Total win prize-money £87768

Going:	Sf: 0-1 GS: 0-0 Gd: 0-2 GF: - Fm: 0-0
Distance:	2m2/2m3: 0-0 2m4-2m7: 0-0 3m+: 1-3
Track:	LH: 0-3 RH: 1-2 Tight: 0-1 Gall: 0-1
Aids:	Bl: 1-5 Vi: 0-0 Tstrap: 0-0 Ckp: 0-0
Best Rating:	153 4/04 Aint 3m110y good Hdl

Smart handicap hurdler; stays three miles; appreciates cut in the ground; usually wears blinkers; has shown temperament in the past.

Hombre

106   **95**

9-y-o ch g Shernazar-Delray Jet (USA) (Northjet)
M D Hammond R D Bickerson

Placings:F05P/245601P/0PP005/13243P-45625   (4458)
2003/04: 22⁴G, 20⁵GS, 21⁶GS, 16²GS, 16⁵HY,

	Starts	1st	2nd	3rd	Win & Pl
Chases	5	0	1	0	1863
Career Total	28	2	3	2	13099
85	12/02	Sedg	2m5f	E(0-105)HCh	SFT £4075
95	1/01	Weth	2m4f110yE(0-105)HCh	HVY £3133

Total win prize-money £7209

Going:	Sf: 0-1 GS: 0-3 Gd: 0-1 GF: - Fm: 0-0
Distance:	2m2/2m3: 0-2 2m4-2m7: 0-4 3m+: 0-0
Track:	LH: 0-5 RH: 0-0 Tight: 0-3 Gall: 0-1
Aids:	Bl: 0-0 Vi: 0-0 Tstrap: 0-0 Ckp: 0-0
Best Rating:	103 5/00 Sedg 2m5f110y gd-fm Hdl

Plating-class handicap chaser; best around two and a half miles; suited by soft ground.

Home Again (IRE)

10-y-o b g Homo Sapien-Texarkana (IRE) (Furry Glen)
E W Morris E W Morris

Placings:3P   (4510)
2003/04: 25³GF, 19⁹GS,

	Starts	1st	2nd	3rd	Win & Pl
Chases	2	0	0	1	223
Career Total	2	0	0	1	223

Going:	Sf: 0-0 GS: 0-1 Gd: 0-0 GF: - Fm: 0-1
Distance:	2m2/2m3: 0-1 2m4-2m7: 0-0 3m+: 0-1
Track:	LH: 0-0 RH: 0-2 Tight: 0-0 Gall: 0-0
Aids:	Bl: 0-0 Vi: 0-0 Tstrap: 0-0 Ckp: 0-0
Best Rating:	86 3/04 Hrfd 3m1f110y gd-fm Ch

Home James (IRE)

93   **120**

7-y-o b g Commanche Run-Take Me Home (Amoristic (USA))
A King Mrs Stewart Catherwood

Placings:1/3211-6   (2793)
2003/04: 24⁶GS,

	Starts	1st	2nd	3rd	Win & Pl
Hurdles	1	0	0	0	0
Career Total	6	3	1	1	12384
119	4/03	MRas	2m3f110yD Hdl	GD £5232
120	2/03	Hrfd	2m3f110yE Hdl	GD £3844
103	3/02	Sthl	2m	H NHF	HVY £1771

Total win prize-money £10849

Going:	Sf: 0-0 GS: 0-1 Gd: 0-0 GF: - Fm: 0-0
Distance:	2m2/2m3: 0-0 2m4-2m7: 0-0 3m+: 0-1
Track:	LH: 0-1 RH: 0-0 Tight: 0-1 Gall: 0-0
Aids:	Bl: 0-0 Vi: 0-0 Tstrap: 0-0 Ckp: 0-0
Best Rating:	120 2/03 Hrfd 2m3f110y good Hdl

Fair hurdler; successful debut in a bumper; most decisive winner of a novices' hurdle at Hereford in February 2003; followed up at Market Rasen in April; should make an even better chaser.

Home Made

96   **92**

6-y-o b g Homo Sapien-Inch Maid (Le Moss)
S A Brookshaw S A Brookshaw

Placings:0/0-432PF24P   (4538)
2003/04: 20⁴GF, 22³GF, 24²GF, 20⁹GS, 24⁴G, 20²G, 24⁴G, 24⁴GS,

	Starts	1st	2nd	3rd	Win & Pl
Hurdles	1	0	0	0	0
Chases	7	0	2	1	3850
Career Total	10	0	2	1	3850

Going:	Sf: 0-0 GS: 0-2 Gd: 0-3 GF: - Fm: 0-3
Distance:	2m2/2m3: 0-0 2m4-2m7: 0-4 3m+: 0-4
Track:	LH: 0-4 RH: 0-4 Tight: 0-4 Gall: 0-1
Aids:	Bl: 0-0 Vi: 0-0 Tstrap: 0-0 Ckp: 0-0
Best Rating:	92 11/03 Ludl 3m gd-fm Ch

Former dual point-to-point winner, stays 2m6f; best on good/good to firm.

Homebred Buddy

5-y-o ch g Environment Friend-Royal Brush (King Of Spain)
G P Enright Homebred Racing

Placings:00PP   (4755)
2003/04: 16⁸GS, 18⁰HY, 16⁸G, 21⁷G,

	Starts	1st	2nd	3rd	Win & Pl
NH Flat	1	0	0	0	0
Hurdles	3	0	0	0	0
Career Total	4	0	0	0	

Going:	Sf: 0-1 GS: 0-1 Gd: 0-2 GF: - Fm: 0-0
Distance:	2m2/2m3: 0-3 2m4-2m7: 0-1 3m+: 0-0
Track:	LH: 0-3 RH: 0-1 Tight: 0-2 Gall: 0-1
Aids:	Bl: 0-0 Vi: 0-0 Tstrap: 0-0 Ckp: 0-0
Best Rating:	29 11/03 Newb 2m110y gd-sft NHF

Homeleigh Mooncoin

100   **121+**

9-y-o ch g Jamesmead-Super Sol (Rolfe (USA))
Mrs L Wadham Miss S Wilson

Placings:61114-42P0   (4386)
2003/04: 24⁴GS, 22²G, 24⁴PGS, 25⁰G,

	Starts	1st	2nd	3rd	Win & Pl
Hurdles	4	0	1	0	3447
Career Total	9	3	1	0	12639
121	10/02	Sthl	3m2f	E Hdl	GD £2961
121	9/02	Sthl	2m5f110yE Hdl	GD £2996
110	8/02	Worc	2m4f	E Hdl	G-F £2940

Total win prize-money £8897

Going:	Sf: 0-0 GS: 0-2 Gd: 0-2 GF: - Fm: 0-0
Distance:	2m2/2m3: 0-2 2m4-2m7: 0-1 3m+: 0-3
Track:	LH: 0-2 RH: 0-2 Tight: 0-0 Gall: 0-1
Aids:	Bl: 0-0 Vi: 0-0 Tstrap: 0-0 Ckp: 0-0
Best Rating:	121 10/02 Sthl 3m2f good Hdl

Fair hurdler; stays three miles-two; acts well on a sound surface.

Homer (IRE)

96   **108**

7-y-o b g Sadler's Wells (USA)-Gravieres (FR) (Saint Estephe (FR))

M C Pipe V J Tickel

Placings:6001002220/P020-P6   (0545)
2003/04: 18⁸GF, 17⁵GF,

	Starts	1st	2nd	3rd	Win & Pl
Hurdles	2	0	0	0	0
Career Total	**16**	**1**	**4**	**0**	**10545**
114 7/01 Naas 2m3f Hdl		GD		£6677	

Total win prize-money £6677

Going: Sf: 0-0 GS: 0-0 Gd: 0-0 GF: - Fm: 0-2
Distance: 2m/2m3: 0-2 2m4-2m7: 0-0 3m+: 0-0
Track: LH: 0-2 RH: 0-0 Tight: 0-2 Gall: 0-0
Aids: Bl: 0-0 Vi: 0-0 Tstrap: 0-0 Ckp: 0-0
Best Rating: 114 12/01 Donc 2m4f   good   Hdl

Homme De Fer

12-y-o b g Arctic Lord-Florence May (Grange Melody)
N M Bloom (K C Bailey 15/5) Countess Cathcart

Placings:66/623/1211045/2113/4022/01124P/516023-443
                                                    (4301)
2003/04: 25⁵GF, 21⁴G, 23³G,

	Starts	1st	2nd	3rd	Win & Pl
Chases	3	0	0	1	1776
Career Total	**35**	**8**	**7**	**4**	**42892**
117 11/02 Ludl 3m	D(0-115)HCh	GD		£5736	
114 11/01 Ludl 3m	F(0-110)HCh	G-F		£3672	
107 11/01 Winc 2m5f	E(0-115)HCh	GD		£5323	
111 7/99 NAbb 2m5f110yE Ch		G-F		£3403	
111 6/99 NAbb 2m5f110yE Ch		GD		£3156	
119 1/99 Font 2m2f110yD Hdl		SFT		£3062	
121 12/98 Hrfd 2m3f110yE Hdl		SFT		£3060	
118 10/98 Plum 2m4f E Hdl		G-F		£2302	

Total win prize-money £29719

Going: Sf: 0-0 GS: 0-0 Gd: 0-2 GF: - Fm: 0-1
Distance: 2m/2m3: 0-0 2m4-2m7: 0-1 3m+: 0-2
Track: LH: 0-1 RH: 0-1 Tight: 0-1 Gall: 0-0
Aids: Bl: 0-0 Vi: 0-0 Tstrap: 0-0 Ckp: 0-0
Best Rating: 121 12/98 Hrfd 2m3f110y soft   Hdl

Modest chaser; stays three miles; prefers a sound surface.

Honan (IRE)

99f   **105+f**

5-y-o b g College Chapel-Medical Times (IRE) (Auction Ring (USA))
M C Pipe (John Joseph Murphy 25/1) M C Pipe

Placings:061   (4739)
2003/04: 16⁰G, 16⁸Y, 17¹G,

	Starts	1st	2nd	3rd	Win & Pl
NH Flat	3	1	0	0	2968
Career Total	**3**	**1**	**0**	**0**	**2968**
105 4/04 NAbb 2m1f H NHF		GD		£2968	

Total win prize-money £2968

Going: Sf: 0-0 GS: 0-0 Gd: 1-2 GF: - Fm: 0-0
Distance: 2m/2m3: 1-3 2m4-2m7: 0-0 3m+: 0-0
Track: LH: 1-1 RH: 0-0 Tight: 1-1 Gall: 0-0
Aids: Bl: 0-0 Vi: 0-0 Tstrap: 0-0 Ckp: 0-0
Best Rating: 105 4/04 NAbb 2m1f   good   NHF

Honest Endeavour

95f   **72f**

5-y-o b g Alflora (IRE)-Isabeau (Law Society (USA))
J M Jefferson Warren Butterworth & Terry Pryke

Placings:500   (4264)

2003/04: 16⁵GS, 16⁹GF, 16⁹GF,

	Starts	1st	2nd	3rd	Win & Pl
NH Flat	3	0	0	0	0
Career Total	**3**	**0**	**0**	**0**	**0**

Going: Sf: 0-0 GS: 0-1 Gd: 0-0 GF: - Fm: 0-2
Distance: 2m/2m3: 0-3 2m4-2m7: 0-0 3m+: 0-0
Track: LH: 0-2 RH: 0-1 Tight: 0-2 Gall: 0-0
Aids: Bl: 0-0 Vi: 0-0 Tstrap: 0-0 Ckp: 0-0
Best Rating: 72 12/03 Newc 2m   gd-sft NHF

Half-brother to yard's modest Bellefleur; hinted at ability on debut in Newcastle bumper on good to soft; should improve.

Honest Yer Honour (IRE)

108   **124**

8-y-o b g Witness Box (USA)-Castle Duchess (Abednego)
R J Osborne Sean P Burke

Placings:00156/30-521F43   (4803a)
2003/04: 16⁵GF, 20²S, 18¹S, 19⁵S, 20⁴Y, 20³Y,

	Starts	1st	2nd	3rd	Win & Pl
Hurdles	6	1	1	1	11683
Career Total	**13**	**2**	**1**	**2**	**17006**
124 12/03 Leop 2m2f	(74-116)HHdl	SFT		£8064	
107 3/02 Punc 2m	NHF	SFT		£4868	

Total win prize-money £12933

Going: Sf: 1-3 GS: 0-0 Gd: 0-0 GF: - Fm: 0-1
Distance: 2m/2m3: 1-3 2m4-2m7: 0-3 3m+: 0-0
Track: LH: 1-3 RH: 0-3 Tight: 0-0 Gall: 0-0
Aids: Bl: 0-0 Vi: 0-0 Tstrap: 0-0 Ckp: 0-0
Best Rating: 124 2/04 Fair 2m4f   yield   Hdl

Bumper winner in Ireland; acts on soft ground.

Honey's Gift

101   **86**

5-y-o b g Terimon-Honeycroft (Crofter (USA))
G G Margarson Russell Evans

Placings:U0U35-3632032P   (4760)
2003/04: 16³S, 16⁶S, 18³G, 16²S, 20⁹GS, 16³G, 16²GS, 16⁸S,

	Starts	1st	2nd	3rd	Win & Pl
Hurdles	8	0	2	3	3030
Career Total	**13**	**0**	**2**	**4**	**3781**

Going: Sf: 0-3 GS: 0-2 Gd: 0-3 GF: - Fm: 0-0
Distance: 2m/2m3: 0-2 2m4-2m7: 0-1 3m+: 0-0
Track: LH: 0-4 RH: 0-4 Tight: 0-2 Gall: 0-1
Aids: Bl: 0-0 Vi: 0-0 Tstrap: 0-0 Ckp: 0-0
Best Rating: 86 3/04 Fknm 2m   gd-sft Hdl

Middle-distance maiden on the Flat; has only shown plating-class form to date over hurdles.

Honeybourne

76f   **53f**

5-y-o b m Sri Pekan (USA)-Peetsie (IRE) (Fairy King (USA))
Mrs Mary Hambro Richard Hambro

Placings:0   (0533)
2003/04: 16⁰GF,

	Starts	1st	2nd	3rd	Win & Pl
NH Flat	1	0	0	0	0
Career Total	**1**	**0**	**0**	**0**	**0**

Going: Sf: 0-0 GS: 0-0 Gd: 0-0 GF: - Fm: 0-1

Distance: 2m/2m3: 0-1 2m4-2m7: 0-0 3m+: 0-0
Track: LH: 0-1 RH: 0-0 Tight: 0-0 Gall: 0-0
Aids: Bl: 0-0 Vi: 0-0 Tstrap: 0-0 Ckp: 0-0
Best Rating: 53 6/03 Worc 2m   gd-fm NHF

Honeystreet (IRE)

85   **77**

4-y-o b f Woodborough (USA)-Ring Of Kerry (IRE) (Kenmare (FR))
J D Frost (J S Moore 12/10) W A Edgington

Placings:4   (2253)
2003/04: 17⁴GF,

	Starts	1st	2nd	3rd	Win & Pl
Hurdles	1	0	0	0	0
Career Total	**1**	**0**	**0**	**0**	**0**

Going: Sf: 0-0 GS: 0-0 Gd: 0-0 GF: - Fm: 0-1
Distance: 2m/2m3: 0-1 2m4-2m7: 0-0 3m+: 0-0
Track: LH: 0-0 RH: 0-1 Tight: 0-0 Gall: 0-0
Aids: Bl: 0-0 Vi: 0-0 Tstrap: 0-0 Ckp: 0-0
Best Rating: 77 11/03 Hrfd 2m1f   gd-fm Hdl

Flat winner at a mile; showed a little ability on hurdles debut.

Honneur Fontenail (FR)

92(80h)   (44h)**80+**

5-y-o ch g Tel Quel (FR)-Fontanalia (FR) (Rex Magna (FR))
N J Hawke Wags To Riches Partnership

Placings:00-5PU01S   (4855)
2003/04: 19⁵G, 21⁹S, 20⁰G, 19⁰GS, 22¹GF, 24⁵GF,

	Starts	1st	2nd	3rd	Win & Pl
Hurdles	2	0	0	0	0
Chases	4	1	0	0	4326
Career Total	**8**	**1**	**0**	**0**	**4326**
80 3/04 Font 2m6f E Ch		G-F		£4326	

Total win prize-money £4326

Going: Sf: 0-1 GS: 0-1 Gd: 0-1 GF: - Fm: 1-3
Distance: 2m/2m3: 0-2 2m4-2m7: 1-3 3m+: 0-0
Track: LH: 0-2 RH: 0-3 Tight: 1-4 Gall: 0-1
Aids: Bl: 0-0 Vi: 0-0 Tstrap: 0-0 Ckp: 0-0
Best Rating: 80 3/04 Font 2m6f   gd-fm Ch

Plating-class novice chaser; inclined to make mistakes; did not achieve much when winning 2m 6f novice chase at Fontwell March 2004; bang in contention when slipping up after the fourth last at Taunton next time; acts on fast ground.

Hopbine

105   **119+**

8-y-o ch m Gildoran-Haraka Sasa (Town And Country)
J L Spearing Miss S Howell

Placings:50/025511225/060020-4106   (4219)
2003/04: 19⁴G, 22¹S, 20⁰HY, 24⁶G,

	Starts	1st	2nd	3rd	Win & Pl
Hurdles	4	1	0	0	5292
Career Total	**21**	**3**	**4**	**0**	**32847**
116 1/04 Winc 2m6f	D(0-115)HHdl	SFT		£4966	
105 2/02 Wwck 2m5f	D Hdl	HVY		£4077	
99 1/02 Sthl	2m4f110yE(0-105)HHdl	G-S		£2534	

Total win prize-money £11578

Going: Sf: 1-2 GS: 0-0 Gd: 0-2 GF: - Fm: 0-0
Distance: 2m/2m3: 0-1 2m4-2m7: 1-2 3m+: 0-1
Track: LH: 0-1 RH: 1-3 Tight: 0-1 Gall: 0-0

Aids: Bl: 0-0 Vi: 0-0 Tstrap: 0-0 Ckp: 0-0
Best Rating: 118 3/02 Newb 2m5f gd-sft Hdl

Fair hurdler; stays 2m 6f; effective in soft ground but does handle faster conditions.

Hope Diamond (IRE)
101 (0c)69
6-y-o ch g Bigstone (IRE)-Mujtahida (IRE) (Mujtahid (USA))
Mrs J Candlish (Cathal McCarthy 10/6) N M Wynne

Placings:0000-00306 (1601)
2003/04: 16⁰YS, 17⁰GF, 20³GF, 16⁶GF, 20⁶GF,

	Starts	1st	2nd	3rd	Win & Pl
Hurdles	4	0	0	0	0
Chases	1	0	0	1	587
Career Total	9	0	0	1	587

Going: Sf: 0-0 GS: 0-0 Gd: 0-0 GF: - Fm: 0-4
Distance: 2m2/2m3: 0-3 2m4-2m7: 0-2 3m+: 0-0
Track: LH: 0-3 RH: 0-2 Tight: 0-1 Gall: 0-0
Aids: Bl: 0-0 Vi: 0-1 Tstrap: 0-0 Ckp: 0-0
Best Rating: 69 11/02 Navn 2m soft Hdl

Hope Sound (IRE)
102 92
4-y-o b g Turtle Island (IRE)-Lucky Pick (Auction Ring (USA))
B Ellison (J Noseda 21/7) R Wagner

Placings:234054 (4795)
2003/04: 16²G, 16³S, 16⁴S, 16⁹GS, 16⁹HY, 17⁴G,

	Starts	1st	2nd	3rd	Win & Pl
Hurdles	6	0	1	1	4406
Career Total	6	0	1	1	4406

Going: Sf: 0-3 GS: 0-1 Gd: 0-2 GF: - Fm: 0-0
Distance: 2m/2m3: 0-6 2m4-2m7: 0-0 3m+: 0-0
Track: LH: 0-6 RH: 0-0 Tight: 0-3 Gall: 0-3
Aids: Bl: 0-0 Vi: 0-0 Tstrap: 0-0 Ckp: 0-0
Best Rating: 97 11/03 Newc 2m good Hdl

Modest form in juvenile hurdles on good and soft ground; open to improvement.

Hopeful Chance (IRE)
102(98h) (92h)81
7-y-o b g Machiavellian (USA)-Don't Rush (USA) (Alleged (USA))
J R Turner J Lee

Placings:2/0000012P/501P0P40 (4794)
2003/04: 18⁵G, 18⁰S, 16¹GS, 21⁵GS, 16⁰HY, 16⁸G, 16⁴G, 21⁰G,

	Starts	1st	2nd	3rd	Win & Pl
Hurdles	5	1	0	0	2674
Chases	3	0	0	0	340
Career Total	17	2	2	0	7548
92 12/03 Newc 2m	E(0-100)HHdl		G-S	£2674	
90 1/02 Muss 2m4f	E(0-100)HHdl		GD	£3262	
			Total win prize-money	£5936	

Going: Sf: 0-2 GS: 1-2 Gd: 0-4 GF: - Fm: 0-0
Distance: 2m/2m3: 1-6 2m4-2m7: 0-2 3m+: 0-0
Track: LH: 1-8 RH: 0-0 Tight: 0-5 Gall: 1-2
Aids: Bl: 0-0 Vi: 0-0 Tstrap: 1-6 Ckp: 0-0
Best Rating: 114 3/01 Hayd 2m heavy NHF

Modest hurdler; effective at two and a half miles; acts on good ground or softer; has had breathing problems; has worn a tongue tie.

Hopesarising
95 79
5-y-o b g Primitive Rising (USA)-Super Brush (IRE) (Brush Aside (USA))
P R Johnson P Johnson

Placings:00045 (4887)
2003/04: 16⁰GS, 16⁰HY, 19⁴G, 22⁵GF,

	Starts	1st	2nd	3rd	Win & Pl
NH Flat	2	0	0	0	0
Hurdles	3	0	0	0	331
Career Total	5	0	0	0	331

Going: Sf: 0-1 GS: 0-1 Gd: 0-2 GF: - Fm: 0-1
Distance: 2m/2m3: 0-3 2m4-2m7: 0-2 3m+: 0-0
Track: LH: 0-3 RH: 0-2 Tight: 0-1 Gall: 0-0
Aids: Bl: 0-0 Vi: 0-0 Tstrap: 0-0 Ckp: 0-0
Best Rating: 79 4/04 Strf 2m6f110y gd-fm Hdl

Hoping
98 74
6-y-o b m Kris-Shimmering (IRE) (Royal Academy (USA))
A W Carroll Mrs D Brown

Placings:000/0P654 (1253)
2003/04: 20⁰GF, 16⁰HY, 16⁶G, 19⁵G, 22⁴GF,

	Starts	1st	2nd	3rd	Win & Pl
Hurdles	5	0	0	0	0
Career Total	8	0	0	0	0

Going: Sf: 0-1 GS: 0-0 Gd: 0-2 GF: - Fm: 0-2
Distance: 2m/2m3: 0-3 2m4-2m7: 0-2 3m+: 0-0
Track: LH: 0-4 RH: 0-0 Tight: 0-1 Gall: 0-0
Aids: Bl: 0-0 Vi: 0-0 Tstrap: 0-0 Ckp: 0-0
Best Rating: 74 8/03 MRas 2m6f gd-fm Hdl

Poor novice hurdler; suited by two mile six.

Hoppertree
8-y-o b g Rock Hopper-Snow Tree (Welsh Pageant)
R S Brookhouse R S Brookhouse

Placings:5/04F/U-PFU (3774)
2003/04: 17⁸G, 22²G, 24⁰G,

	Starts	1st	2nd	3rd	Win & Pl
Hurdles	1	0	0	0	0
Chases	2	0	0	0	0
Career Total	8	0	0	0	0

Going: Sf: 0-0 GS: 0-0 Gd: 0-3 GF: - Fm: 0-0
Distance: 2m/2m3: 0-1 2m4-2m7: 0-1 3m+: 0-1
Track: LH: 0-1 RH: 0-1 Tight: 0-3 Gall: 0-0
Aids: Bl: 0-0 Vi: 0-0 Tstrap: 0-0 Ckp: 0-0
Best Rating: 105 1/02 Font 2m2f110y good NHF

Horcott Bay
4-y-o b f Thowra (FR)-Armagnac Messenger (Pony Express)
M G Rimell The Posties Partnership

Placings:0 (4738)
2003/04: 17⁰G,

	Starts	1st	2nd	3rd	Win & Pl
NH Flat	1	0	0	0	
Career Total	1	0	0	0	

Going: Sf: 0-0 GS: 0-0 Gd: 0-1 GF: - Fm: 0-0
Distance: 2m/2m3: 0-1 2m4-2m7: 0-0 3m+: 0-0
Track: LH: 0-1 RH: 0-0 Tight: 0-0 Gall: 0-0
Aids: Bl: 0-0 Vi: 0-0 Tstrap: 0-0 Ckp: 0-0

Horizon (FR)
7-y-o ch g Arctic Tern (USA)-Furtchella (FR) (Dancing Spree (USA))
P C Ritchens John Pearl

Placings:00042540/000151P0/4P-P0PP (4789)
2003/04: 17⁰GS, 20⁰GF, 20⁰S, 17⁰G,

	Starts	1st	2nd	3rd	Win & Pl
Hurdles	2	0	0	0	0
Chases	2	0	0	0	0
Career Total	22	2	1	0	20011
10/01 Saum 2m4f	Ch		G-S	£3104	
10/01 LePe 2m2f110y	Ch		HLD	£2910	
			Total win prize-money	£6014	

Going: Sf: 0-1 GS: 0-1 Gd: 0-1 GF: - Fm: 0-1
Distance: 2m/2m3: 0-2 2m4-2m7: 0-2 3m+: 0-0
Track: LH: 0-3 RH: 0-1 Tight: 0-2 Gall: 0-0
Aids: Bl: 0-0 Vi: 0-0 Tstrap: 0-0 Ckp: 0-0

Hornbill
(93h) (62h)
6-y-o b g Sir Harry Lewis (USA)-Tangara (Town Crier)
Mrs P Robeson Mrs P Robeson

Placings:0P-6600PP (4112)
2003/04: 16⁶G, 19⁶G, 22⁰G, 16⁰GS, 20⁰S, 20⁰GF,

	Starts	1st	2nd	3rd	Win & Pl
Hurdles	4	0	0	0	0
Chases	2	0	0	0	0
Career Total	8	0	0	0	0

Going: Sf: 0-1 GS: 0-1 Gd: 0-3 GF: - Fm: 0-1
Distance: 2m/2m3: 0-3 2m4-2m7: 0-3 3m+: 0-0
Track: LH: 0-2 RH: 0-4 Tight: 0-0 Gall: 0-1
Aids: Bl: 0-0 Vi: 0-0 Tstrap: 0-0 Ckp: 0-0
Best Rating: 62 1/04 Weth 2m gd-sft Hdl

Horrified
10-y-o b g Deltic (USA)-Parlet (Kinglet)
Mrs Janet Ackner Mrs Janet Ackner

Placings:P (4373)
2003/04: 24⁰G,

	Starts	1st	2nd	3rd	Win & Pl
Chases	1	0	0	0	0
Career Total	1	0	0	0	0

Going: Sf: 0-0 GS: 0-0 Gd: 0-1 GF: - Fm: 0-0
Distance: 2m/2m3: 0-0 2m4-2m7: 0-0 3m+: 0-1
Track: LH: 0-1 RH: 0-0 Tight: 0-1 Gall: 0-0
Aids: Bl: 0-1 Vi: 0-0 Tstrap: 0-0 Ckp: 0-0

Hors Concours (NZ)

6-y-o b g Starjo (NZ)-Lana (NZ) (Tristram's Heritage (NZ))
R C Guest N Brookes

Placings:0					(0373)
2003/04: 16⁰G,					

	Starts	1st	2nd	3rd	Win & Pl
NH Flat	1	0	0	0	
Career Total	1	0	0	0	

Going:	Sf: 0-0 GS: 0-0 Gd: 0-1 GF: - Fm: 0-0
Distance:	2m/2m3: 0-1 2m4-2m7: 0-0 3m+: 0-0
Track:	LH: 0-1 RH: 0-0 Tight: 0-0 Gall: 0-0
Aids:	Bl: 0-0 Vi: 0-0 Tstrap: 0-0

Hors La Loi (FR)

115(105c)   (109c) **119**
8-y-o ch g Exit To Nowhere (USA)-Kernia (IRE) (Raise A
Cup (USA))
Ian Williams The Not So Risky Partnership

Placings:30/411430/0032-20310010					(4718)
2003/04: 16²GS, 16⁰G, 16³G, 16¹GF, 17⁰GF, 16⁹GF, 17¹GF, 16⁰G,					

	Starts	1st	2nd	3rd	Win & Pl
Hurdles	7	1	1	1	12750
Chases	1	1	0	0	4017
Career Total	20	4	2	4	27889
109 10/03 Strf	2m1f110yD Ch			G-F	£4017
119 7/03 Strf	2m110y D(0-125)HHdl			G-F	£6831
119 12/00 Tntn	2m1f E(0-115)HHdl			SFT	£3883
107 12/00 Donc	2m110y F(0-100)HHdl			HVY	£2457
	Total win prize-money £17190				

Going:	Sf: 0-0 GS: 0-0 Gd: 0-3 GF: - Fm: 2-4
Distance:	**2m/2m3: 2-8** 2m4-2m7: 0-0 3m+: 0-0
Track:	**LH: 2-5** RH: 0-3 **Tight: 2-6** Gall: 0-0
Aids:	Bl: 0-0 Vi: 0-0 Tstrap: 0-0 Ckp: 0-0
Best Rating:	119 7/03 Strf 2m110y gd-fm Hdl

Modest hurdler/novice chaser; won easily in minor novice
chase on debut at Stratford in October; effective at around
two miles; acts well on a soft surface, but effective on faster.

Horus (IRE)

114   **153+**
9-y-o b g Teenoso (USA)-Jennie's First (Idiots Delight)
M C Pipe B A Kilpatrick

Placings:1P/13111406P-21U65UP					(4385)
2003/04: 24²S, 24¹S, 24ᵁG, 21⁶GS, 24⁵G, 24ᵁG, 24ᴾG,					

	Starts	1st	2nd	3rd	Win & Pl
Chases	7	1	1	0	35566
Career Total	18	6	1	1	102151
150 12/03 Asct	3m110y A HCh			SFT	£29000
144 12/02 Chel	3m1f110yB HCh			GD	£25589
143 11/02 Newb	2m4f B(0-145)HCh			G-S	£24000
133 6/02 Strf	3m D(0-125)HCh			G-F	£10400
120 5/02 Chel	3m2f110yH Ch			G-F	£5395
132 2/02 Winc	3m1f110yH Ch			SFT	£1352
	Total win prize-money £92037				

Going:	Sf: 1-2 GS: 0-1 Gd: 0-4 GF: - Fm: 0-0
Distance:	2m/2m3: 0-0 2m4-2m7: 0-1 **3m+: 1-6**
Track:	LH: 0-4 **RH: 1-3** Tight: 0-0 Gall: 0-3
Aids:	Bl: 0-0 Vi: 0-0 Tstrap: 0-0 Ckp: 0-0
Best Rating:	153 2/04 Kemp 3m good Ch

Smart chaser; stays further than three miles; likes to be produced late; acts on any ground, but particularly effective with
cut.

Hot Air (IRE)

89f   **89+f**
6-y-o b g Air Display (USA)-Lyraisa (Tumble Wind (USA))
J I A Charlton J I A Charlton

Placings:005					(4517)
2003/04: 16⁹G, 17⁰G, 16⁵GS,					

	Starts	1st	2nd	3rd	Win & Pl
NH Flat	3	0	0	0	0
Career Total	3	0	0	0	0

Going:	Sf: 0-0 GS: 0-1 Gd: 0-2 GF: - Fm: 0-0
Distance:	2m/2m3: 0-3 2m4-2m7: 0-0 3m+: 0-0
Track:	LH: 0-2 RH: 0-1 Tight: 0-0 Gall: 0-0
Aids:	Bl: 0-0 Vi: 0-0 Tstrap: 0-1 Ckp: 0-0
Best Rating:	83 3/04 Weth 2m gd-sft NHF

Hot Girl

91f   **78f**
6-y-o b m State Diplomacy (USA)-Hundred Islands (Hotfoot)
S P Griffiths M Grant

Placings:060					(3215)
2003/04: 17⁰GF, 16⁶G, 16⁰GS,					

	Starts	1st	2nd	3rd	Win & Pl
NH Flat	3	0	0	0	0
Career Total	3	0	0	0	0

Going:	Sf: 0-0 GS: 0-1 Gd: 0-1 GF: - Fm: 0-1
Distance:	2m/2m3: 0-3 2m4-2m7: 0-0 3m+: 0-0
Track:	LH: 0-2 RH: 0-1 Tight: 0-1 Gall: 0-0
Aids:	Bl: 0-0 Vi: 0-0 Tstrap: 0-0 Ckp: 0-0
Best Rating:	78 5/03 MRas 2m1f110y gd-fm NHF

Hot Plunge

8-y-o b g Bustino-Royal Seal (Privy Seal)
Mrs J P Lomax Mrs J P Lomax

Placings:1/244/0346					(4696)
2003/04: 20⁰G, 20³G, 16⁴G, 19⁶G,					

	Starts	1st	2nd	3rd	Win & Pl
Chases	4	0	0	1	392
Career Total	8	1	1	1	2294
100 6/00 Worc	2m H NHF			GD	£1463
	Total win prize-money £1463				

Going:	Sf: 0-0 GS: 0-0 Gd: 0-4 GF: - Fm: 0-0
Distance:	2m/2m3: 0-1 2m4-2m7: 0-3 3m+: 0-0
Track:	LH: 0-0 RH: 0-4 Tight: 0-1 Gall: 0-0
Aids:	Bl: 0-0 Vi: 0-0 Tstrap: 0-0 Ckp: 0-0
Best Rating:	109 6/01 Worc 2m good NHF

Hot Produxion (USA)

110   **108**
5-y-o ch g Tabasco Cat (USA)-Princess Harriet (USA) (Mt.
Livermore (USA))
J Mackie A J Winterton

Placings:02332-0320200					(4343)
2003/04: 20⁰G, 20³GF, 20²GF, 22⁰S, 20²G, 21⁰G, 21⁰GS,					

	Starts	1st	2nd	3rd	Win & Pl
Hurdles	7	0	2	1	3214
Career Total	12	0	4	3	6888

Hot Shots (FR)

119(110h)   (138+h)**146**
9-y-o b g Passing Sale (FR)-Uguette Iv (FR) (Chamberlin
(FR))
M Pitman Mrs Jill Eynon & Robin Eynon

Placings:343210/6300/213416220P/P50UU12P-					
021215105					(4964)
2003/04: 16⁰G, 16²GF, 16¹GF, 16²G, 16¹S, 16⁵GS, 16¹G, 16⁶S, 16⁵GF,					

	Starts	1st	2nd	3rd	Win & Pl
Hurdles	4	1	1	0	10633
Chases	5	2	1	0	59667
Career Total	37	7	7	4	99830
138 3/04 Winc	2m D(0-125)HHdl			GD	£8961
150 12/03 Asct	2m B HCh			SFT	£29750
135 11/03 Asct	2m A(0-150)HCh			G-F	£20825
128 3/03 Winc	2m D(0-125)HHdl			G-F	£4771
116 9/01 Worc	2m D Ch			G-F	£3926
108 6/01 Baln	2m1f Ch			GD	£5564
110 2/00 Punc	2m Hdl			Y-S	£4140
	Total win prize-money £77938				

Going:	Sf: 1-2 GS: 0-1 Gd: 1-3 GF: - Fm: 1-3
Distance:	**2m/2m3: 3-9** 2m4-2m7: 0-0 3m+: 0-0
Track:	LH: 0-1 **RH: 3-8** Tight: 0-0 Gall: 0-1
Aids:	Bl: 0-0 Vi: 0-0 Tstrap: 0-0 Ckp: 0-0
Best Rating:	150 12/03 Asct 2m soft Ch

Smart chaser/fair hurdler; suited by two miles; acts well on
decent ground, but does appear effective with a bit of cut;
goes well at Ascot.

Hot Weld

89   **99**
5-y-o b g Weld-Deb's Ball (Glenstal (USA))
Ferdy Murphy S Hubbard Rodwell

Placings:2-4B5					(4783)
2003/04: 23⁴GS, 23⁸G, 21⁵G,					

	Starts	1st	2nd	3rd	Win & Pl
Hurdles	3	0	0	0	0
Career Total	4	0	1	0	574

Going:	Sf: 0-0 GS: 0-0 Gd: 0-3 GF: - Fm: 0-0
Distance:	2m/2m3: 0-0 2m4-2m7: 0-3 3m+: 0-0
Track:	LH: 0-2 RH: 0-1 Tight: 0-1 Gall: 0-1
Aids:	Bl: 0-0 Vi: 0-0 Tstrap: 0-0 Ckp: 0-0
Best Rating:	99 4/04 Hntg 2m5f110y good Hdl

Dam prolific winner over hurdles; bumper winner; has
shown limited abilty in novices; hurdles; will be suited by
three miles.

Hoteliers' Dream

74   **54**
6-y-o b m Reprimand-Pride Of Britain (CAN) (Linkage
(USA))
W S Kittow Reg Gifford

Placings:FP0-00					(0996)
2003/04: 16⁰GS, 16⁰G,					

	Starts	1st	2nd	3rd	Win & Pl
Hurdles	2	0	0	0	

| Career Total | 5 | 0 | 0 | 0 |

Going:	Sf: 0-0 GS: 0-1 Gd: 0-1 GF: - Fm: 0-0
Distance:	2m/2m3: 0-2 2m4-2m7: 0-0 3m+: 0-0
Track:	LH: 0-2 RH: 0-0 Tight: 0-1 Gall: 0-0
Aids:	Bl: 0-0 Vi: 0-1 Tstrap: 0-0 Ckp: 0-0
Best Rating:	54 3/03 Extr 2m1f good Hdl

Hotters (IRE)

72(96h)   (64h)91

9-y-o b g Be My Native (USA)-Siul Currach (Deep Run)
J R Norton Reddal Racing

Placings:0/100554/004UF505-5UPP   (4796)
2003/04: 21⁵GS, 25ᵁGS, 32ᴾG, 21ᴾG,

	Starts	1st	2nd	3rd	Win & Pl
Hurdles	1	0	0	0	
Chases	3	0	0	0	
Career Total	19	1	0	0	2175
82	10/01	Hntg	2m110y	H NHF	GD	£1452

Total win prize-money £1453

Going:	Sf: 0-0 GS: 0-2 Gd: 0-2 GF: - Fm: 0-0
Distance:	2m/2m3: 0-0 2m4-2m7: 0-2 3m+: 0-2
Track:	LH: 0-3 RH: 0-1 Tight: 0-2 Gall: 0-0
Aids:	Bl: 0-0 Vi: 0-2 Tstrap: 0-0 Ckp: 0-1
Best Rating:	98 1/02 Font 2m2f110y good Hdl

Moderate hurdler; on the downgrade.

Houghton Bay (IRE)

99(106h)   (108h)111

9-y-o b g Camden Town-Royal Bavard (Le Bavard (FR))
J G Portman Mrs William Hall

Placings:533203/10133504/1153000/3306   (4307)
2003/04: 19³GS, 24³G, 24⁰G, 22⁶G,

	Starts	1st	2nd	3rd	Win & Pl
Hurdles	1	0	0	0	
Chases	3	0	0	2	1368
Career Total	25	4	1	8	17394
120	10/01	Chep	2m4f	D(0-120)HHdl	SFT	£3391
110	10/01	Hrfd	2m3f110yF(0-110)HHdl	GD	£3062
120	11/00	NAbb	2m1f	D Hdl	HVY	£3347
117	10/00	Bang	2m4f	E Hdl	SFT	£2348

Total win prize-money £12152

Going:	Sf: 0-0 GS: 0-1 Gd: 0-3 GF: - Fm: 0-0
Distance:	2m/2m3: 0-0 2m4-2m7: 0-2 3m+: 0-2
Track:	LH: 0-1 RH: 0-3 Tight: 0-4 Gall: 0-0
Aids:	Bl: 0-0 Vi: 0-0 Tstrap: 0-0 Ckp: 0-1
Best Rating:	125 12/01 Sand 2m6f soft Hdl

Fair hurdler; back-to-back wins in 2m 4f handicaps October 2001; promising chasing debut when third in 2m 4f Beginners' chase at Chepstow December 2003; acts on soft ground; will be suited by 3m.

Houlihans Choice

89   69+

7-y-o ch g Norton Challenger-Model Lady (Le Bavard (FR))
B G Powell Paddy O'Donnell

Placings:0/0-00060   (3415)
2003/04: 17⁰GS, 19⁶S, 26⁶GS, 21⁶S, 24⁰GS,

	Starts	1st	2nd	3rd	Win & Pl
NH Flat	1	0	0	0	0
Hurdles	4	0	0	0	0
Career Total	7	0	0	0	0

Going:	Sf: 0-2 GS: 0-3 Gd: 0-0 GF: - Fm: 0-0
Distance:	2m/2m3: 0-1 2m4-2m7: 0-2 3m+: 0-2
Track:	LH: 0-2 RH: 0-1 Tight: 0-3 Gall: 0-1
Aids:	Bl: 0-0 Vi: 0-2 Tstrap: 0-1 Ckp: 0-0
Best Rating:	85 3/02 Hayd 2m good NHF

House Warmer (IRE)

5-y-o ch g Carroll House-Under The Duvet (IRE) (Brush Aside (USA))
A Ennis A T A Wates

Placings:P0P   (4702)
2003/04: 19ᴾS, 24⁰G, 20ᴾG,

	Starts	1st	2nd	3rd	Win & Pl
Hurdles	3	0	0	0	
Career Total	3	0	0	0	

Going:	Sf: 0-1 GS: 0-0 Gd: 0-2 GF: - Fm: 0-0
Distance:	2m/2m3: 0-1 2m4-2m7: 0-1 3m+: 0-1
Track:	LH: 0-1 RH: 0-1 Tight: 0-1 Gall: 0-1
Aids:	Bl: 0-0 Vi: 0-0 Tstrap: 0-1 Ckp: 0-0

Houseparty (IRE)

98   109

6-y-o b/br g Grand Lodge (USA)-Special Display (Welsh Pageant)
J A B Old W E Sturt

Placings:F-320P   (2741)
2003/04: 16³GF, 16²F, 16⁰G, 16⁶S,

	Starts	1st	2nd	3rd	Win & Pl
Hurdles	4	0	1	1	1536
Career Total	5	0	1	1	1536

Going:	Sf: 0-1 GS: 0-0 Gd: 0-1 GF: - Fm: 0-2
Distance:	2m/2m3: 0-4 2m4-2m7: 0-0 3m+: 0-0
Track:	LH: 0-3 RH: 0-1 Tight: 0-1 Gall: 0-0
Aids:	Bl: 0-0 Vi: 0-0 Tstrap: 0-0 Ckp: 0-0
Best Rating:	109 10/03 Chep 2m110y gd-fm Hdl

Modest hurdler; collapsed in soft ground on his hurdling debut March 2003; effective over two miles.

How Burn

11-y-o b g Meadowbrook-Kinkell (Netherkelly)
Mrs V S Jackson Mrs V Jackson

Placings:P   (4884)
2003/04: 24ᴾGS,

	Starts	1st	2nd	3rd	Win & Pl
Chases	1	0	0	0	
Career Total	1	0	0	0	

Going:	Sf: 0-0 GS: 0-1 Gd: 0-0 GF: - Fm: 0-0
Distance:	2m/2m3: 0-0 2m4-2m7: 0-0 3m+: 0-1
Track:	LH: 0-0 RH: 0-1 Tight: 0-0 Gall: 0-0
Aids:	Bl: 0-0 Vi: 0-0 Tstrap: 0-0 Ckp: 0-0

How Great Thou Art

99   82

8-y-o b g Almoojid-Mamamere (Tres Gate)
R J Baker D R Walsh

Placings:0/03/66005-42   (0635)
2003/04: 22⁴GF, 22²GF,

	Starts	1st	2nd	3rd	Win & Pl
Hurdles	2	0	1	0	1078
Career Total	10	0	1	1	1292

Going:	Sf: 0-0 GS: 0-0 Gd: 0-0 GF: - Fm: 0-2
Distance:	2m/2m3: 0-0 2m4-2m7: 0-2 3m+: 0-0
Track:	LH: 0-1 RH: 0-1 Tight: 0-1 Gall: 0-0
Aids:	Bl: 0-0 Vi: 0-0 Tstrap: 0-0 Ckp: 0-0
Best Rating:	92 10/02 Extr 2m1f good NHF

Modest novice hurdler; improved form since being stepped up in distance; no match for Dun An Doras in 2m 6f maiden hurdle at Newton Abbot June 2003.

How Is The Lord (IRE)

99   66

8-y-o b/br g Lord Americo-Joaney How (Crash Course)
C J Down G Waterman

Placings:2   (0832)
2003/04: 20²GF,

	Starts	1st	2nd	3rd	Win & Pl
Hurdles	1	0	1	0	998
Career Total	1	0	1	0	998

Going:	Sf: 0-0 GS: 0-0 Gd: 0-0 GF: - Fm: 0-1
Distance:	2m/2m3: 0-0 2m4-2m7: 0-1 3m+: 0-0
Track:	LH: 0-1 RH: 0-0 Tight: 0-0 Gall: 0-0
Aids:	Bl: 0-0 Vi: 0-0 Tstrap: 0-0 Ckp: 0-0
Best Rating:	71 7/03 Worc 2m4f gd-fm Hdl

Irish point winner; shaped as though he needs further when runner-up in 2m 4f Worcester novice hurdle July 2003.

How Ran On (IRE)

102   84

13-y-o b/br g Mandalus-Kelly's Bridge (Netherkelly)
Mrs L Williamson Halewood International Ltd

Placings:41/20010/F0F0254P22/P115F3/0P0/0O51026523
400/42634521103-64P12P3565   (1925)
2003/04: 16⁶GF, 17⁴GF, 16⁶GF, 16¹GF, 16²GF, 18ᴾGF, 16³GF, 16⁵GF, 19⁶GF, 16⁵GF,

	Starts	1st	2nd	3rd	Win & Pl
Chases	10	1	1	1	5868
Career Total	60	8	9	5	38995
84	6/03	NAbb	2m110y	E(0-105)HCh	G-F	£4046
81	11/02	Wwck	2m110y	F(0-100)HCh	GD	£3038
80	10/02	Ludl	2m	G(0-95)HCh	FRM	£3406
99	6/01	NAbb	2m110y	F(0-100)HCh	GD	£2982
116	6/99	Gowr	2m5f	(0-109)HCh	GF	£4296
109	5/99	Wxfd	2m4f	(0-109)HCh	Y-S	£3376
99	4/98	Navn	2m	Hdl	SH	£2680
109	4/97	List	2m4f	NHF	G-Y	£3391

Total win prize-money £27216

Going:	Sf: 0-0 GS: 0-0 Gd: 0-0 GF: - Fm: 1-10
Distance:	2m/2m3: 1-10 2m4-2m7: 0-0 3m+: 0-0
Track:	LH: 1-6 RH: 0-3 Tight: 1-4 Gall: 0-2
Aids:	Bl: 0-0 Vi: 0-0 Tstrap: 0-0 Ckp: 0-2
Best Rating:	116 6/99 Gowr 2m5f good Ch

Plating-class handicap chaser; best at around two miles; appears to act on all types of ground.

Howaboys Quest (USA)

98(91c)   (68c)84

7-y-o b g Quest For Fame-Doctor Black (USA) (Family

Doctor (USA))
Ferdy Murphy Winlow Brothers

Placings:0345044/640-151223P   (3235)
2003/04: 22^1GF, 22^5G, 22^1GF, 20^2F, 25^2F, 27^3G, 24^PGF,

	Starts	1st	2nd	3rd	Win & Pl
Hurdles	6	2	1	1	6270
Chases	1	0	1	0	668
Career Total	17	2	2	2	7351
82	8/03	MRas	2m6f	F(0-95)HHdl	G-F	£2634
81	7/03	Ctml	2m6f	G(0-90)HHdl	G-F	£2691

Total win prize-money £5327

Going:	Sf: 0-0 GS: 0-0 Gd: 0-2 GF: - Fm: 2-5
Distance:	2m/2m3: 0-0 **2m4-2m7: 2-4** 3m+: 0-3
Track:	**LH: 1-5** RH: 0-0 **Tight: 1-3** Gall: 0-0
Aids:	Bl: 0-1 Vi: 0-0 Tstrap: 0-0 **Ckp: 2-5**
Best Rating:	84 9/03 Hexm 2m4f110y firm Hdl

Moderate hurdler; took a selling handicap hurdle in smooth style at Cartmel in July; scored again in novices' handicap at Market Rasen the following month; suited by two mile six; acts well on fast ground; has worn cheekpieces.

Howdydoody (IRE)
106(108h)   (110h)**125+**
8-y-o b g Hawkstone (IRE)-Larry's Law (IRE) (Law Society (USA))
P F Nicholls B L Blinman

Placings:0/33131-0210   (3380)
2003/04: 22^0G, 25^2GS, 25^1S, 25^0S,

	Starts	1st	2nd	3rd	Win & Pl
Hurdles	1	0	0	0	0
Chases	3	1	1	0	6450
Career Total	10	3	1	3	18114
125	1/04	Winc	3m1f110yD(0-125)HCh	SFT	£5557
110	3/03	Font	3m3f	D(0-120)HHdl	G-F	£4920
103	1/03	Tntn	3m110y	E Hdl	SFT	£4478

Total win prize-money £14958

Going:	Sf: 1-2 GS: 0-1 Gd: 0-1 GF: - Fm: 0-0
Distance:	2m/2m3: 0-0 2m4-2m7: 0-1 **3m+: 1-3**
Track:	LH: 0-1 **RH: 1-3** Tight: 0-0 Gall: 0-0
Aids:	Bl: 0-1 Vi: 0-0 Tstrap: 1-4 Ckp: 0-0
Best Rating:	125 1/04 Winc 3m1f110y soft Ch

Modest hurdler/chaser; not disgraced when runner-up to Fork Lightning on chasing debut at Hereford December 2003 and went one better on next outing; stays 3m 3f; acts on both fast and soft ground; usually wears a tongue tie; looks tricky.

Howle Hill (IRE)
111   **132**
4-y-o b g Ali-Royal (IRE)-Grandeur And Grace (USA) (Septieme Ciel (USA))
A King J E Brown,R Benton,R Devereux,R A Lucas

Placings:121450   (4625)
2003/04: 16^1G, 16^2GS, 16^1GS, 17^4GS, 17^5G, 16^0G,

	Starts	1st	2nd	3rd	Win & Pl
Hurdles	6	2	1	0	24787
Career Total	6	2	1	0	24787
119	1/04	Winc	2m	E Hdl	G-S	£3636
120	11/03	Weth	2m	A Hdl	GD	£13000

Total win prize-money £16637

Going:	Sf: 0-0 GS: 1-3 Gd: 1-3 GF: - Fm: 0-0
Distance:	**2m/2m3: 2-6** 2m4-2m7: 0-0 3m+: 0-0
Track:	LH: 1-4 RH: 1-2 Tight: 0-1 Gall: 0-0
Aids:	Bl: 0-0 Vi: 0-0 Tstrap: 0-0 Ckp: 0-0
Best Rating:	132 3/04 Chel 2m1f good Hdl

Useful juvenile hurdler; smart performer on the Flat; easy winner of Class A juvenile hurdle on debut at Wetherby in November; held since; suited by flat tracks; effective over two miles; acts on good and soft ground.

Howrwenow (IRE)
105(105h)   (116h)**116+**
6-y-o b g Commanche Run-Maythefifth (Hard Boy)
Miss H C Knight Toby Cole

Placings:624-1F2223   (4939)
2003/04: 24^1S, 23^2G, 26^2G, 24^2GS, 24^2G, 24^3GS,

	Starts	1st	2nd	3rd	Win & Pl
Hurdles	3	1	1	1	6658
Chases	3	0	2	0	2576
Career Total	9	1	4	1	10782
96	5/03	Bang	3m	E Hdl	SFT	£3731

Total win prize-money £3731

Going:	Sf: 1-1 GS: 0-2 Gd: 0-3 GF: - Fm: 0-0
Distance:	2m/2m3: 0-0 2m4-2m7: 0-0 **3m+: 1-6**
Track:	**LH: 1-3** RH: 0-3 **Tight: 1-2** Gall: 0-0
Aids:	Bl: 0-0 Vi: 0-0 Tstrap: 0-0 Ckp: 0-0
Best Rating:	119 2/04 Kemp 3m110y good Hdl

Won maiden Irish point on debut in 2002; won 3m novice hurdle at Bangor May 2003; going well when falling on chasing debut; solid efforts when runner-up next two starts; acts on good and soft ground; stays 3m.

Howsham Lad
66f   **66f**
5-y-o b g Perpendicular-Sherwood Hope (Eborneezer)
G P Kelly Stephen Fox

Placings:0   (4050)
2003/04: 16^0G,

	Starts	1st	2nd	3rd	Win & Pl
NH Flat	1	0	0	0	
Career Total	1	0	0	0	

Going:	Sf: 0-0 GS: 0-0 Gd: 0-1 GF: - Fm: 0-0
Distance:	2m/2m3: 0-1 2m4-2m7: 0-0 3m+: 0-0
Track:	LH: 0-1 RH: 0-0 Tight: 0-0 Gall: 0-0
Aids:	Bl: 0-0 Vi: 0-0 Tstrap: 0-0 Ckp: 0-0
Best Rating:	65 2/04 Hayd 2m good NHF

Howya Matey (IRE)
89   **45**
7-y-o ch g Treasure Hunter-Clonaslee Baby (Konigssee)
M C Pipe P J Finn

Placings:005   (0854)
2003/04: 24^0G, 20^0GF, 22^5GF,

	Starts	1st	2nd	3rd	Win & Pl
Hurdles	3	0	0	0	0
Career Total	3	0	0	0	0

Going:	Sf: 0-0 GS: 0-0 Gd: 0-1 GF: - Fm: 0-2
Distance:	2m/2m3: 0-0 2m4-2m7: 0-0 3m+: 0-1
Track:	LH: 0-3 RH: 0-0 Tight: 0-1 Gall: 0-0
Aids:	Bl: 0-0 Vi: 0-0 Tstrap: 0-0 Ckp: 0-0
Best Rating:	47 7/03 Strf 2m6f110y gd-fm Hdl

Huge Heart (NZ)
(57h)   (73h)
8-y-o b g T V Heart Throb (USA)-Christmas Lady (NZ)

(Palm Beach (FR))
W M Brisbourne (Miss Lucinda V Russell 20/6) Raymond McNeill

Placings:P0PU0-PU   (0691)
2003/04: 20^PS, 20^UGF,

	Starts	1st	2nd	3rd	Win & Pl
Hurdles	1	0	0	0	0
Chases	1	0	0	0	0
Career Total	7	0	0	0	0

Going:	Sf: 0-1 GS: 0-0 Gd: 0-0 GF: - Fm: 0-1
Distance:	2m/2m3: 0-0 2m4-2m7: 0-2 3m+: 0-0
Track:	LH: 0-2 RH: 0-0 Tight: 0-1 Gall: 0-0
Aids:	Bl: 0-0 Vi: 0-0 Tstrap: 0-0 Ckp: 0-0
Best Rating:	73 1/03 Hntg 2m110y soft Hdl

Hughie
9-y-o ch g Super Sunrise-Clarilaw (White Speck)
J S Haldane Mrs Hugh Fraser

Placings:U   (4296)
2003/04: 21^UGF,

	Starts	1st	2nd	3rd	Win & Pl
Chases	1	0	0	0	
Career Total	1	0	0	0	

Going:	Sf: 0-0 GS: 0-0 Gd: 0-0 GF: - Fm: 0-1
Distance:	2m/2m3: 0-0 2m4-2m7: 0-0 3m+: 0-0
Track:	LH: 0-1 RH: 0-0 Tight: 0-0 Gall: 0-0
Aids:	Bl: 0-0 Vi: 0-0 Tstrap: 0-0 Ckp: 0-0

Hugo
8-y-o b h Golden Heights-Just Lynn (Legend Of France (USA))
D J Caro Mrs V Stockdale

Placings:6   (0440)
2003/04: 17^6GF,

	Starts	1st	2nd	3rd	Win & Pl
Hurdles	1	0	0	0	0
Career Total	1	0	0	0	0

Going:	Sf: 0-0 GS: 0-0 Gd: 0-0 GF: - Fm: 0-1
Distance:	2m/2m3: 0-1 2m4-2m7: 0-0 3m+: 0-0
Track:	LH: 0-0 RH: 0-1 Tight: 0-0 Gall: 0-0
Aids:	Bl: 0-0 Vi: 0-0 Tstrap: 0-0 Ckp: 0-0

Hugo De Grez (FR)
101(107h)   (96+h)**141**
9-y-o b g Useful (FR)-Piqua Des Gres (FR) (Waylay)
A Parker Mr & Mrs Raymond Anderson Green

Placings:01P0/223111/1240/21P5/U11205-45PP   (4951)
2003/04: 25^4S, 25^5GS, 25^PG, 24^PGS,

	Starts	1st	2nd	3rd	Win & Pl
Chases	4	0	0	0	1778
Career Total	28	8	5	1	74250
138	12/02	Kels	3m1f	B(0-145)HCh	HVY	£13325
134	11/02	Carl	3m2f	C(0-130)HCh	HVY	£7800
127	11/01	Carl	3m2f	C(0-130)HCh	HVY	£6890
127	11/00	Carl	3m2f	C(0-130)HCh	SFT	£7020
112	4/00	Carl	3m2f	E Ch	SFT	£3542
117	3/00	Carl	3m2f	D(0-115)HCh	G-S	£14495
102	2/00	Carl	2m4f110y			F(0-105)HCh

HVY £3558

72	2/99	Ayr	3m110y	E Hdl			SFT	£2670	

Total win prize-money £59302

Going:	Sf: 0-1 GS: 0-2 Gd: 0-1 GF: - Fm: 0-0
Distance:	2m/2m3: 0-0 2m4-2m7: 0-0 3m+: 0-4
Track:	LH: 0-3 RH: 0-1 Tight: 0-2 Gall: 0-0
Aids:	Bl: 0-0 Vi: 0-0 Tstrap: 0-0 Ckp: 0-0
Best Rating:	141 2/03 Ayr 2m4f soft Ch

Very useful handicap chaser; stays three miles two; effective on heavy ground; goes well at Carlisle; has worn a tongue tie.

Hugo De Perro (FR)
109 (0c)131

9-y-o b g Perrault-Fontaine Aux Faons (FR) (Nadjar (FR))
P Monteith J W D Campbell

Placings:52501414/5304/**1F**36432/313R155P12-31R5R0F614R (4853)
2003/04: 23³GS, 22¹G, 20ᴿG, 24⁵G, 20ᴿS, 16⁰S, 25ᶠS, 20ᴿGS, 20¹G, 20⁴S, 22ᴿGS,

		Starts	1st	2nd	3rd	Win & Pl
Hurdles		10	2	0	1	21182
Chases		1	0	0	0	0
Career Total		40	8	3	6	55266
114	3/04	Carl	2m4f		F Hdl		GD	£2733
131	5/03	Kels	2m6f110yB(0-140)HHdl			GD	£15051
110	3/03	Carl	2m4f		F Hdl		SFT	£3066
129	12/02	Kels	2m6f110yD(0-125)HHdl			HVY	£4069
113	5/01	MRas	2m4f		D Ch		GD	£5096
136	2/00	Wwck	2m4f110yE(0-115)HHdl			SFT	£2632
124	1/00	Leic	2m		E Hdl		SFT	£3042

Total win prize-money £39486

Going:	Sf: 0-4 GS: 0-3 Gd: 2-4 GF: - Fm: 0-0
Distance:	2m/2m3: 0-1 2m4-2m7: 2-7 3m+: 0-3
Track:	LH: 1-10 RH: 1-1 Tight: 1-3 Gall: 0-1
Aids:	Bl: 0-0 Vi: 0-0 Tstrap: 0-0 Ckp: 0-0
Best Rating:	136 2/00 Wwck 2m4f110y soft Hdl

Useful handicap hurdler/fair chaser; acts on any ground; stays three miles; has refused to race on occasions.

Huic Holloa (IRE)
80 54

8-y-o b g Denel (FR)-Buckalgo (IRE) (Buckskin (FR))
J A T De Giles V W H Hunt Partnership

Placings:0/036/05-066 (0764)
2003/04: 26⁰GS, 20ᴿGF, 20ᴿGF,

		Starts	1st	2nd	3rd	Win & Pl
Hurdles		3	0	0	0	0
Career Total		9	0	0	1	341

Going:	Sf: 0-0 GS: 0-1 Gd: 0-0 GF: - Fm: 0-2
Distance:	2m/2m3: 0-0 2m4-2m7: 0-2 3m+: 0-1
Track:	LH: 0-2 RH: 0-1 Tight: 0-0 Gall: 0-0
Aids:	Bl: 0-0 Vi: 0-0 Tstrap: 0-0 Ckp: 0-0
Best Rating:	86 12/01 Wwck 2m soft NHF

Unplaced in two bumpers in the spring, he was staying on strongly in a Taunton bumper in November on good ground.

Huish (IRE)

13-y-o br g Orchestra-Lysanders Lady (Saulingo)
Mrs N Macauley W Murdoch

Placings:U/0/006P/06604/3/P-PP (0618)

2003/04: 21ᴾGF, 19ᴾG,

	Starts	1st	2nd	3rd	Win & Pl
Hurdles	2	0	0	0	
Career Total	15	0	0	1	319

Going:	Sf: 0-0 GS: 0-0 Gd: 0-0 GF: - Fm: 0-1
Distance:	2m/2m3: 0-0 2m4-2m7: 0-2 3m+: 0-0
Track:	LH: 0-0 RH: 0-2 Tight: 0-1 Gall: 0-1
Aids:	Bl: 0-0 Vi: 0-0 Tstrap: 0-0 Ckp: 0-0
Best Rating:	81 3/97 Sand 2m110y good Hdl

Huka Lodge (IRE)
95 100

7-y-o gr g Roselier (FR)-Derrella (Derrylin)
L Lungo Mrs J M Jones

Placings:0530-6FU12P (4950)
2003/04: 20⁶GS, 23ᶠGS, 25ᵁGS, 24¹GS, 20²HY, 20ᴾGS,

		Starts	1st	2nd	3rd	Win & Pl
Hurdles		6	1	1	0	4006
Career Total		10	1	1	1	4537
99	2/04	Newc	3m	F(0-100)HHdl	G-S	£2765

Total win prize-money £2765

Going:	Sf: 0-1 GS: 1-5 Gd: 0-0 GF: - Fm: 0-0
Distance:	2m/2m3: 0-0 2m4-2m7: 0-4 3m+: 1-2
Track:	LH: 1-4 RH: 0-2 Tight: 0-0 Gall: 1-2
Aids:	Bl: 0-0 Vi: 0-0 Tstrap: 0-0 Ckp: 0-0
Best Rating:	103 3/04 Newc 2m4f heavy Hdl

Modest hurdler who turned in an improved effort when winning over 3m at Newcastle in February 2004; in good hands and the type to improve again.

Hulysse Royal (FR)
101 131

9-y-o ch g Garde Royale-Ulysse Moriniere (FR) (Mbaiki (FR))
O Sherwood R K Carvill

Placings:1F2/1203P/5/00P00 (4963)
2003/04: 20⁰HY, 20⁰S, 20ᴾG, 24⁰GS, 20ᴾGS,

		Starts	1st	2nd	3rd	Win & Pl
Hurdles		5	0	0	0	
Career Total		14	2	2	1	41845
144	11/00	Chel	2m110y	B HHdl	G-S	£32500
111	11/99	Wwck	2m	E Hdl	GD	£2805

Total win prize-money £35305

Going:	Sf: 0-2 GS: 0-1 Gd: 0-2 GF: - Fm: 0-0
Distance:	2m/2m3: 0-0 2m4-2m7: 0-4 3m+: 0-1
Track:	LH: 0-2 RH: 0-3 Tight: 0-0 Gall: 0-0
Aids:	Bl: 0-0 Vi: 0-0 Tstrap: 0-0 Ckp: 0-0
Best Rating:	146 2/01 Font 2m4f gd-sft Hdl

Useful hurdler; showed very useful form in 2000/1; off the course for more than two years subsequently and has struggled to regain his form since his return; stays two and a half miles; acts on good ground or softer; has worn cheekpieces.

Humid Climate
93 91

4-y-o ch g Desert King (IRE)-Pontoon (Zafonic (USA))
R A Fahey (Mrs A J Perrett 10/9) J E M Hawkins Ltd

Placings:022P (4625)
2003/04: 16⁰S, 16²G, 16²G, 16ᴾG,

	Starts	1st	2nd	3rd	Win & Pl
Hurdles	4	0	2	0	2469
Career Total	4	0	2	0	2469

Going:	Sf: 0-1 GS: 0-0 Gd: 0-3 GF: - Fm: 0-0
Distance:	2m/2m3: 0-4 2m4-2m7: 0-0 3m+: 0-0
Track:	LH: 0-3 RH: 0-1 Tight: 0-3 Gall: 0-1
Aids:	Bl: 0-0 Vi: 0-0 Tstrap: 0-0 Ckp: 0-0
Best Rating:	100 2/04 Catt 2m good Hdl

Juvenile hurdler; useful on the Flat at around ten furlongs; not straightforward.

Humming
92 85+

7-y-o b g Bluebird (USA)-Risanda (Kris)
Miss M E Rowland Miss M E Rowland

Placings:0/50/P2-5 (0941)
2003/04: 20⁶G,

	Starts	1st	2nd	3rd	Win & Pl
Hurdles	1	0	0	0	0
Career Total	6	0	1	0	674

Going:	Sf: 0-0 GS: 0-0 Gd: 0-1 GF: - Fm: 0-0
Distance:	2m/2m3: 0-0 2m4-2m7: 0-1 3m+: 0-0
Track:	LH: 0-1 RH: 0-0 Tight: 0-0 Gall: 0-0
Aids:	Bl: 0-0 Vi: 0-0 Tstrap: 0-1 Ckp: 0-0
Best Rating:	85 3/03 Hrfd 2m3f110y gd-fm Hdl

Huncheon Siss (IRE)
101

7-y-o b m Phardante (FR)-Parsons Term (IRE) (The Parson)
J Howard Johnson J R McAleese

Placings:03/02022/P (4273)
2003/04: 24²G,

	Starts	1st	2nd	3rd	Win & Pl
Hurdles	1	0	0	0	
Career Total	8	0	3	1	3095

Going:	Sf: 0-0 GS: 0-0 Gd: 0-1 GF: - Fm: 0-0
Distance:	2m/2m3: 0-0 2m4-2m7: 0-0 3m+: 0-1
Track:	LH: 0-0 RH: 0-0 Tight: 0-0 Gall: 0-0
Aids:	Bl: 0-0 Vi: 0-0 Tstrap: 0-0 Ckp: 0-0
Best Rating:	101 3/02 Dpat 2m4f110y soft Hdl

Hunters Creek (IRE)
97(108h) (101 h)118+

10-y-o b g Persian Mews-Creek's Sister (King's Ride)
Mrs M Reveley Bewley's Hotels, Glasgow (bsh Ltd)

Placings:20/33F1213F/532621-53F550 (4175)
2003/04: 20⁵G, 20³G, 19ᶠGF, 20⁵G, 19⁵G, 19⁰G,

		Starts	1st	2nd	3rd	Win & Pl
Hurdles		1	0	0	1	617
Chases		5	0	0	0	
Career Total		22	3	4	5	19832
110	4/03	Sedg	2m5f	E(0-110)HCh	G-F	£4390
120	1/02	Catt	2m3f	D Ch	SFT	£4179
116	12/01	Catt	2m3f	F Ch	GD	£2886

Total win prize-money £11457

Going:	Sf: 0-0 GS: 0-0 Gd: 0-5 GF: - Fm: 0-0
Distance:	2m/2m3: 0-3 2m4-2m7: 0-3 3m+: 0-0
Track:	LH: 0-6 RH: 0-0 Tight: 0-3 Gall: 0-2
Aids:	Bl: 0-0 Vi: 0-0 Tstrap: 0-0 Ckp: 0-0
Best Rating:	120 11/03 Catt 2m3f gd-fm Ch

Fair chaser/modest hurdler; effective at up to two miles five; goes well on a sharp track like Catterick; acts on any ground.

Hunters Tweed

113 (134h) **149**

8-y-o ch g Nashwan (USA)-Zorette (USA) (Zilzal (USA))
P Beaumont Trevor Hemmings

Placings:113022/03634000/**1233321U1-6121PP0** (4637)
2003/04: 25⁶G, 20¹G, 20²G, 21¹¹GS, 24⁴G, 20⁶G, 25⁶G,

	Starts	1st	2nd	3rd	Win & Pl
Chases	7	2	1	0	29845
Career Total	**30**	**7**	**5**	**6**	**87655**
147 1/04 Chel	2m5f	A HCh		G-S	£23200
133 12/03 Weth	2m4f110yD(0-125)HCh		GD	£4485
133 4/03 Prth	2m4f110yD(0-125)HCh		GD	£12504
134 3/03 Hayd	2m4f	D(0-120)HCh	GD	£5395
117 5/02 Prth	3m	D Ch		G-F	£5499
134 2/01 Kels	2m110y	D Hdl		SFT	£4013
126 12/00 Weth	2m	D Hdl		SFT	£3679
			Total win prize-money £58777

Going: Sf: 0-0 GS: 1-1 Gd: 1-6 GF: - Fm: 0-0
Distance: 2m/2m3: 0-0 2m4-2m7: 2-4 3m+: 0-3
Track: LH: 2-6 RH: 0-1 Tight: 0-1 Gall: 1-2
Aids: Bl: 0-0 Vi: 0-0 Tstrap: 0-0 Ckp: 0-0
Best Rating: 147 1/04 Chel 2m5f   gd-sft   Ch

Smart chaser; very consistent sort; won valuable handicap at Cheltenham in January; stays three miles, but also effective at shorter; seems best on decent ground.

Hunters Wood (IRE)

9-y-o gr g Wood Chanter-Barnmeen Lass (IRE) (Floriferous)
R J Baker David Heath

Placings:P/5/4-PP (0613)
2003/04: 23⁸G, 25⁸GF,

	Starts	1st	2nd	3rd	Win & Pl
Chases	2	0	0	0	
Career Total	**5**	**0**	**0**	**0**	**317**

Going: Sf: 0-0 GS: 0-0 Gd: 0-1 GF: - Fm: 0-1
Distance: 2m/2m3: 0-0 2m4-2m7: 0-0 3m+: 0-2
Track: LH: 0-1 RH: 0-1 Tight: 0-0 Gall: 0-0
Aids: Bl: 0-1 Vi: 0-0 Tstrap: 0-0 Ckp: 0-0

Hunting Yuppie (IRE)

101 **112+**

7-y-o ch g Treasure Hunter-Super Yuppie (Belfalas)
N A Twiston-Davies E T Clarke

Placings:614 (4868)
2003/04: 20⁶S, 21¹GS, 20⁴GS,

	Starts	1st	2nd	3rd	Win & Pl
Hurdles	3	1	0	0	4530
Career Total	**3**	**1**	**0**	**0**	**4530**
112 3/04 Ludl	2m5f	E Hdl		G-S	£4241
			Total win prize-money £4241

Going: Sf: 0-1 GS: 1-2 Gd: 0-0 GF: - Fm: 0-0
Distance: 2m/2m3: 0-0 2m4-2m7: 1-3 3m+: 0-0
Track: LH: 0-1 RH: 1-2 Tight: 0-1 Gall: 0-0
Aids: Bl: 0-0 Vi: 0-0 Tstrap: 0-0 Ckp: 0-0
Best Rating: 112 3/04 Ludl 2m5f   gd-sft   Hdl

Modest novice hurdler; showed promise in Irish points; hampered when sixth on debut; won next time over 2m5f at Ludlow, but sure to stay further; looks sure to do better as a chaser; should appreciate soft ground.

Hurlers Cross (IRE)

103(99h) (72+h)**87+**

6-y-o b g Jurado (USA)-Maid Of Music (IRE) (Orchestra)
M Appleby (Jonjo O'Neill 5/10) P J Hughes Developments Ltd

Placings:4340541P (4590)
2003/04: 24⁴G, 22³GF, 24⁴GF, 22⁰G, 26⁵G, 26⁴GF, 26¹G, 24⁴PG,

	Starts	1st	2nd	3rd	Win & Pl
Hurdles	5	0	0	0	
Chases	3	1	0	1	4545
Career Total	**8**	**1**	**0**	**1**	**4545**
87 3/04 Plum	3m2f	E(0-105)HCh	GD	£4075
			Total win prize-money £4076

Going: Sf: 0-0 GS: 0-0 Gd: 1-5 GF: - Fm: 0-3
Distance: 2m/2m3: 0-0 2m4-2m7: 0-2 3m+: 1-6
Track: LH: 1-3 RH: 0-5 Tight: 1-4 Gall: 0-1
Aids: Bl: 0-1 Vi: 0-0 Tstrap: 0-0 Ckp: 0-0
Best Rating: 87 3/04 Plum 3m2f   good   Ch

Hurricane Bay

109(96h) (79h)**87**

8-y-o ch g Karinga Bay-Clodagh Gale (Strong Gale)
P D Niven (Jonjo O'Neill 7/9) Ian G M Dalgleish

Placings:5006/2530-414420524P4 (2234)
2003/04: 24⁴GF, 25¹G, 26⁴GF, 25⁴GF, 23²GF, 23⁰GF, 25⁵GF, 25²F, 20⁴GF, 28⁸G, 25⁴G,

	Starts	1st	2nd	3rd	Win & Pl
Hurdles	2	0	1	0	632
Chases	9	1	1	0	6016
Career Total	**19**	**1**	**3**	**1**	**7809**
86 5/03 Weth	3m1f	F(0-100)HCh	GD	£3640
			Total win prize-money £3640

Going: Sf: 0-0 GS: 0-0 Gd: 1-3 GF: - Fm: 0-8
Distance: 2m/2m3: 0-0 2m4-2m7: 0-0 3m+: 1-10
Track: LH: 1-8 RH: 0-3 Tight: 0-3 Gall: 0-1
Aids: Bl: 0-2 Vi: 0-0 Tstrap: 0-3 Ckp: 0-0
Best Rating: 87 8/03 Worc 2m7f110y   gd-fm   Ch

Moderate chaser; opened his account in a 3m 1f handicap chase at Wetherby in May 2003; unreliable since and has changed stables; runner-up over hurdles in October; stays well and handles quick ground.

Hurricane Dipper (IRE)

82 **75**

6-y-o b g Glacial Storm (USA)-Minnies Dipper (Royal Captive)
Miss A M Newton-Smith Mrs John Grist

Placings:00-54300 (4361)
2003/04: 19⁵G, 17⁴GS, 17³GS, 16⁹GS, 21⁰GS,

	Starts	1st	2nd	3rd	Win & Pl
Hurdles	5	0	0	1	318
Career Total	**7**	**0**	**0**	**1**	**318**

Going: Sf: 0-0 GS: 0-4 Gd: 0-1 GF: - Fm: 0-0
Distance: 2m/2m3: 0-3 2m4-2m7: 0-2 3m+: 0-0
Track: LH: 0-2 RH: 0-3 Tight: 0-4 Gall: 0-0
Aids: Bl: 0-0 Vi: 0-0 Tstrap: 0-0 Ckp: 0-0
Best Rating: 75 2/04 Sand 2m110y   gd-sft   Hdl

Hurricane Katie

5-y-o ch m Dolphin Street (FR)-Hurricane Dancer (IRE) (Nabeel Dancer (USA))
N Wilson Steven Downes

Placings:44 (1494)
2003/04: 17⁴GF, 24⁴GF,

	Starts	1st	2nd	3rd	Win & Pl
NH Flat	1	0	0	0	0
Hurdles	1	0	0	0	0
Career Total	**2**	**0**	**0**	**0**	**0**

Going: Sf: 0-0 GS: 0-0 Gd: 0-0 GF: - Fm: 0-2
Distance: 2m/2m3: 0-1 2m4-2m7: 0-0 3m+: 0-1
Track: LH: 0-2 RH: 0-0 Tight: 0-1 Gall: 0-0
Aids: Bl: 0-0 Vi: 0-0 Tstrap: 0-0 Ckp: 0-0

Hurricane Lamp

101 **144**

13-y-o b g Derrylin-Lampstone (Ragstone)
A King Mr & Mrs F C Welch & Alan King

Placings:16/112F/6U1230/126143F/12523/144F0/4133411 PP0/22212P042-460 (4784)
2003/04: 25⁴G, 25⁶G, 24⁰G,

	Starts	1st	2nd	3rd	Win & Pl
Chases	3	0	0	0	
Career Total	**51**	**12**	**10**	**5**	**120661**
144 11/02 Kemp	2m4f110yB(0-140)HCh	GD	£11128
144 12/01 Sand	2m4f110yC(0-135)HCh	G-S	£6955
142 11/01 Hntg	2m4f110yC(0-130)HCh	GD	£6776
144 5/01 Wwck	2m4f110yC(0-135)HCh	GD	£8684
144 5/00 Wwck	2m	B Ch	G-F	£8743
140 10/99 Weth	2m	C(0-135)HCh	GD	£5735
134 1/99 Sand	2m	B HCh	G-S	£8130
122 5/98 Uttx	2m	D Ch	G-S	£3533
127 1/98 Ludl	2m	E Ch	SFT	£3004
121 12/96 Sand	2m110y	D Hdl	GD	£2970
110 11/96 Wwck	2m	E Hdl	GD	£2721
114 2/96 Sand	2m110y	H NHF	SFT	£2304
			Total win prize-money £70685

Going: Sf: 0-0 GS: 0-0 Gd: 0-3 GF: - Fm: 0-0
Distance: 2m/2m3: 0-0 2m4-2m7: 0-0 3m+: 0-3
Track: LH: 0-0 RH: 0-2 Tight: 0-0 Gall: 0-1
Aids: Bl: 0-0 Vi: 0-0 Tstrap: 0-0 Ckp: 0-0
Best Rating: 144 12/02 Donc 2m3f   gd-sft   Ch

Useful handicap chaser; acted on most types of ground; effective from two to three miles; at the veteran stage and reportedly retired after sustaining an injury at Cheltenham in April 2003.

Husky (POL)

94 **86**

6-y-o b g Special Power-Hallo Bambina (POL) (Neman (POL))
R M H Cowell Mrs J M Penney

Placings:2640F20 (2334)
2003/04: 16²GF, 16⁶G, 17⁴GS, 17⁰GF, 16⁶GF, 16²G, 16⁰G,

	Starts	1st	2nd	3rd	Win & Pl
Hurdles	7	0	2	0	1378
Career Total	**7**	**0**	**2**	**0**	**1378**

Going: Sf: 0-0 GS: 0-1 Gd: 0-3 GF: - Fm: 0-3
Distance: 2m/2m3: 0-7 2m4-2m7: 0-0 3m+: 0-0
Track: LH: 0-5 RH: 0-2 Tight: 0-5 Gall: 0-1
Aids: Bl: 0-0 Vi: 0-0 Tstrap: 0-0 Ckp: 0-7

Best Rating:	83	10/03	Fknm	2m	good Hdl

Plating-class hurdler; has worn cheekpieces; acts on fast ground; likes to front-run.

Hussard (FR)

9-y-o b g Concorde Jr (USA)-Cerise De Totes (FR) (Champ Libre (FR))
O Sherwood H M Heyman

Placings:061/26P/0U1PP6/P   (2737)
2003/04: 24PS,

	Starts	1st	2nd	3rd	Win & Pl
Chases	1	0	0	0	
Career Total	13	2	1	0	6287
98	12/01	Hntg	3m	E(0-105)HCh	£3107
92	4/00	Font	2m2f110yE Hdl	GD	£2226
			Total win prize-money £5333		

Going:	Sf: 0-1 GS: 0-0 Gd: 0-0 GF: - Fm: 0-0
Distance:	2m/2m3: 0-0 2m4-2m7: 0-0 3m+: 0-1
Track:	LH: 0-1 RH: 0-1 Tight: 0-1 Gall: 0-0
Aids:	Bl: 0-0 Vi: 0-0 Tstrap: 0-0 Ckp: 0-0
Best Rating:	100 2/00 Newb 2m110y gd-sft NHF

Hussard Collonges (FR)

103   (122h)**168**
9-y-o b g Video Rock (FR)-Ariane Collonges (FR) (Quart De Vin (FR))
P Beaumont N W A Bannister

Placings:00012/21F21/242P-F23F   (3004)
2003/04: 25FG, 242GS, 24³S, 25FGS,

	Starts	1st	2nd	3rd	Win & Pl
Chases	4	0	1	1	18100
Career Total	18	3	6	1	134295
156	3/02	Chel	3m110y A Ch	G-S	£72500
141	12/01	Weth	2m4f110yD(0-110)HCh	G-S	£4446
122	4/01	Weth	2m4f110yD Hdl	G-S	£3395
			Total win prize-money £80341		

Going:	Sf: 0-1 GS: 0-2 Gd: 0-1 GF: - Fm: 0-0
Distance:	2m/2m3: 0-2 2m4-2m7: 0-0 3m+: 0-4
Track:	LH: 0-3 RH: 0-1 Tight: 0-0 Gall: 0-0
Aids:	Bl: 0-0 Vi: 0-0 Tstrap: 0-0 Ckp: 0-0
Best Rating:	168 1/03 Hayd 3m gd-sft Ch

Smart chaser; a leading novice in 2001/2, running much his best race when a game winner of the Royal & SunAlliance Chase at Cheltenham; running really well in defeat in top company throughout 2002/03, but found to have sore throat after pulling up in Cheltenham Gold Cup; encouraging efforts at Haydock in November and December; jumps well; suited by forcing tactics; acts on yielding and soft ground; stays 3m 2f; tough.

Hutch

104   103
6-y-o b g Rock Hopper-Polly's Teahouse (Shack (USA))
P Beaumont Robert Gibbons

Placings:PP36   (4937)
2003/04: 17PGS, 20PGS, 17³GS, 16PGS,

	Starts	1st	2nd	3rd	Win & Pl
Hurdles	4	0	0	1	630
Career Total	4	0	0	1	630

Going:	Sf: 0-0 GS: 0-4 Gd: 0-0 GF: - Fm: 0-0

Distance:	2m/2m3: 0-3 2m4-2m7: 0-1 3m+: 0-0				
Track:	LH: 0-3 RH: 0-1 Tight: 0-2 Gall: 0-0				
Aids:	Bl: 0-0 Vi: 0-0 Tstrap: 0-0 Ckp: 0-0				
Best Rating:	103	3/04	Bang	2m1f	gd-sft Hdl

Huw The News

5-y-o b g Primo Dominie-Martha Stevens (USA) (Super Concorde (USA))
C L Popham H J W Davies

Placings:00PP   (3140)
2003/04: 16ºGF, 17ºGF, 17ºG, 19ºS,

	Starts	1st	2nd	3rd	Win & Pl
NH Flat	2	0	0	0	0
Hurdles	2	0	0	0	0
Career Total	4	0	0	0	0

Going:	Sf: 0-1 GS: 0-0 Gd: 0-0 GF: - Fm: 0-2
Distance:	2m/2m3: 0-4 2m4-2m7: 0-0 3m+: 0-0
Track:	LH: 0-1 RH: 0-3 Tight: 0-1 Gall: 0-0
Aids:	Bl: 0-0 Vi: 0-0 Tstrap: 0-0 Ckp: 0-0
Best Rating:	43 6/03 Worc 2m gd-fm NHF

Huxley (IRE)

96   88
5-y-o b g Danehill Dancer (IRE)-Biddy Mulligan (Ballad Rock)
M G Quinlan (P J Hobbs 19/2) Liam Mulryan

Placings:0   (3901)
2003/04: 17ºGS,

	Starts	1st	2nd	3rd	Win & Pl
Hurdles	1	0	0	0	
Career Total	1	0	0	0	

Going:	Sf: 0-0 GS: 0-1 Gd: 0-0 GF: - Fm: 0-0
Distance:	2m/2m3: 0-1 2m4-2m7: 0-0 3m+: 0-0
Track:	LH: 0-0 RH: 0-1 Tight: 0-1 Gall: 0-0
Aids:	Bl: 0-0 Vi: 0-0 Tstrap: 0-0 Ckp: 0-0
Best Rating:	89 2/04 Tntn 2m1f gd-sft Hdl

Former useful Irish-trained Flat horse; unplaced on British debut over timber at Taunton when second favourite on good ground; has to prove he will stay two miles.

Hylia

98   85
5-y-o ch m Sir Harry Lewis (USA)-Lady Stock (Crofter (USA))
Mrs P Robeson Mrs P Robeson

Placings:6051P   (3229)
2003/04: 16ºG, 17ºG, 21⁵G, 21¹GF, 19ºS,

	Starts	1st	2nd	3rd	Win & Pl
NH Flat	2	0	0	0	0
Hurdles	3	1	0	0	4105
Career Total	5	1	0	0	4105
88	12/03	Ludl	D Hdl	G-F	£4104
			Total win prize-money £4105		

Going:	Sf: 0-0 GS: 0-1 Gd: 0-3 GF: - Fm: 1-1
Distance:	2m/2m3: 0-0 2m4-2m7: 1-3 3m+: 0-0
Track:	LH: 0-3 RH: 1-2 Tight: 0-1 Gall: 0-0
Aids:	Bl: 0-0 Vi: 0-0 Tstrap: 0-0 Ckp: 0-0
Best Rating:	88 12/03 Ludl 2m5f gd-fm Hdl

Winning novice hurdler; stays 2m 4f.

Hypothesis (IRE)

62
7-y-o b g Sadler's Wells (USA)-Surmise (USA) (Alleged (USA))
Ian Williams G Ferrigno

Placings:0/630P0P/0   (1059)
2003/04: 20ºGF,

	Starts	1st	2nd	3rd	Win & Pl
Hurdles	1	0	0	0	
Career Total	8	0	0	1	386

Going:	Sf: 0-0 GS: 0-0 Gd: 0-0 GF: - Fm: 0-1
Distance:	2m/2m3: 0-0 2m4-2m7: 0-1 3m+: 0-0
Track:	LH: 0-1 RH: 0-0 Tight: 0-0 Gall: 0-0
Aids:	Bl: 0-0 Vi: 0-0 Tstrap: 0-0 Ckp: 0-0
Best Rating:	82 11/01 Kels 2m110y good Hdl

Modest hurdler.

I D Technology (IRE)

101   109+
8-y-o ch g Commanche Run-Lady Geeno (IRE) (Cheval)
G L Moore T Keogh

Placings:0000/0U1   (4793)
2003/04: 16ºG, 18ºG, 16¹G,

	Starts	1st	2nd	3rd	Win & Pl
Hurdles	3	1	0	0	3595
Career Total	7	1	0	0	3595
109	4/04	Plum	2m	E Hdl	GD	£3594
			Total win prize-money £3595		

Going:	Sf: 0-0 GS: 0-0 Gd: 1-3 GF: - Fm: 0-0
Distance:	2m/2m3: 1-3 2m4-2m7: 0-0 3m+: 0-0
Track:	LH: 1-2 RH: 0-1 Tight: 1-2 Gall: 0-0
Aids:	Bl: 0-0 Vi: 0-0 Tstrap: 0-0 Ckp: 0-0
Best Rating:	109 4/04 Plum 2m good Hdl

Modest novice hurdler; surprise winner of a Plumpton novice hurdle in April 2004; acts on good ground.

I Got Rhythm

110   104+
6-y-o gr m Lycius (USA)-Eurythmic (Pharly (FR))
Mrs M Reveley G Thomson

Placings:516/4F023-524306   (3722)
2003/04: 17⁵G, 16²GS, 16⁴S, 16³GS, 19ºG, 16⁶S,

	Starts	1st	2nd	3rd	Win & Pl
Hurdles	6	0	1	1	6640
Career Total	14	1	2	2	13894
102	11/01	Weth	2m	D Hdl	GD	£3696
			Total win prize-money £3696		

Going:	Sf: 0-2 GS: 0-2 Gd: 0-2 GF: - Fm: 0-0
Distance:	2m/2m3: 0-5 2m4-2m7: 0-1 3m+: 0-0
Track:	LH: 0-6 RH: 0-0 Tight: 0-1 Gall: 0-0
Aids:	Bl: 0-0 Vi: 0-0 Tstrap: 0-0 Ckp: 0-0
Best Rating:	104 12/03 Weth 2m gd-sft Hdl

Moderate hurdler; best at around two miles; suited by good ground or faster.

I Hear Thunder (IRE)

93(97c)   (105+c)**91**
6-y-o b g Montelimar (USA)-Carrigeen Gala (Strong Gale)

R H Buckler Nick Elliott

Placings:00-053020   (4733)
2003/04: 19⁰S, 20⁵G, 19³S, 20⁰S, 20²G, 22⁹G,

	Starts	1st	2nd	3rd	Win & Pl
Hurdles	5	0	0	1	560
Chases	1	0	1	0	1712
Career Total	**8**	**0**	**1**	**1**	**2272**

Going:	Sf: 0-3 GS: 0-0 Gd: 0-3 GF: - Fm: 0-0
Distance:	2m/2m3: 0-1 2m4-2m7: 0-0 3m+: 0-0
Track:	LH: 0-4 RH: 0-1 Tight: 0-4 Gall: 0-1
Aids:	Bl: 0-0 Vi: 0-0 Tstrap: 0-0 Ckp: 0-0
Best Rating:	105 3/04 Strf 2m4f good Ch

Modest form in novice hurdles; stays 2m 4f; acts in soft ground.

I Move Earth

7-y-o b m Bandmaster (USA)-Lady Of Milton (Old Jocus)
C J Down Fred Champion

Placings:0/45P/P   (4819)
2003/04: 22⁰GF,

	Starts	1st	2nd	3rd	Win & Pl
Hurdles	1	0	0	0	
Career Total	**5**	**0**	**0**	**0**	**0**

Going:	Sf: 0-0 GS: 0-0 Gd: 0-0 GF: - Fm: 0-1
Distance:	2m/2m3: 0-0 2m4-2m7: 0-1 3m+: 0-0
Track:	LH: 0-0 RH: 0-1 Tight: 0-0 Gall: 0-0
Aids:	Bl: 0-0 Vi: 0-0 Tstrap: 0-0 Ckp: 0-0
Best Rating:	89 10/01 Chep 2m110y good NHF

I Tina

95   76+

8-y-o b m Lycius (USA)-Tintomara (IRE) (Niniski (USA))
A G Juckes Mrs K C Price

Placings:004-4030631400   (4569)
2003/04: 16⁴GS, 16⁰G, 16³GF, 17⁰F, 17⁶GF, 16³G, 16¹GS, 16⁴GS, 16⁹G, 17⁰GS,

	Starts	1st	2nd	3rd	Win & Pl
Hurdles	10	1	0	2	2584
Career Total	**13**	**1**	**0**	**2**	**2861**
80 11/03 Chep 2m110y G Hdl				G-S	£1918

Total win prize-money £1918

Going:	Sf: 0-0 GS: 1-4 Gd: 0-3 GF: - Fm: 0-3
Distance:	2m/2m3: 1-10 2m4-2m7: 0-0 3m+: 0-0
Track:	LH: 1-7 RH: 0-3 Tight: 0-2 Gall: 0-0
Aids:	Bl: 0-1 Vi: 1-9 Tstrap: 0-0 Ckp: 0-0
Best Rating:	80 11/03 Chep 2m110y gd-sft Hdl

Plating-class; finally got off the mark when landing poor seller at Chepstow November 2003; best at around 2m; effective with cut in the ground.

I'll Fly

101   81

4-y-o ch g Polar Falcon (USA)-I'Ll Try (Try My Best (USA))
J R Fanshawe Mrs K Fraser Mrs D Strauss Mrs R Hambro

Placings:P5   (4402)
2003/04: 16⁵S, 16⁵G,

	Starts	1st	2nd	3rd	Win & Pl
Hurdles	2	0	0	0	0
Career Total	**2**	**0**	**0**	**0**	**0**

Going:	Sf: 0-1 GS: 0-0 Gd: 0-1 GF: - Fm: 0-0
Distance:	2m/2m3: 0-2 2m4-2m7: 0-0 3m+: 0-0
Track:	LH: 0-1 RH: 0-1 Tight: 0-0 Gall: 0-1
Aids:	Bl: 0-0 Vi: 0-0 Tstrap: 0-0 Ckp: 0-0
Best Rating:	83 3/04 Hntg 2m110y good Hdl

Showed a little abilty on second run over hurdles.

I'lleveit Tou (IRE)

101   91

8-y-o b g King Luthier-Shady Jumbo (Callernish)
R Rowe Thomas Thompson

Placings:2/040F04U6   (4592)
2003/04: 20⁰G, 22⁴HY, 21⁰G, 24⁴GS, 20⁹GS, 22⁴G, 26⁰G, 26⁶G,

	Starts	1st	2nd	3rd	Win & Pl
Hurdles	8	0	0	0	0
Career Total	**9**	**0**	**1**	**0**	**488**

Going:	Sf: 0-1 GS: 0-2 Gd: 0-5 GF: - Fm: 0-0
Distance:	2m/2m3: 0-0 2m4-2m7: 0-5 3m+: 0-3
Track:	LH: 0-0 RH: 0-7 Tight: 0-3 Gall: 0-2
Aids:	Bl: 0-0 Vi: 0-0 Tstrap: 0-0 Ckp: 0-0
Best Rating:	89 1/04 Folk 2m6f110y heavy Hdl

I'm Dreaming (IRE)

10-y-o ch g White Christmas-Suffolk Bells (London Bells (CAN))
Andrew J Martin Andrew J Martin

Placings:0240/P00PP/0P/3P546-5PP   (4373)
2003/04: 21⁵G, 24²GF, 24³G,

	Starts	1st	2nd	3rd	Win & Pl
Chases	3	0	0	0	0
Career Total	**19**	**0**	**1**	**1**	**1363**

Going:	Sf: 0-0 GS: 0-0 Gd: 0-2 GF: - Fm: 0-1
Distance:	2m/2m3: 0-0 2m4-2m7: 0-1 3m+: 0-2
Track:	LH: 0-3 RH: 0-0 Tight: 0-1 Gall: 0-1
Aids:	Bl: 0-0 Vi: 0-0 Tstrap: 0-0 Ckp: 0-0
Best Rating:	89 4/03 Chel 2m5f good Ch

I'm For Waiting

94   84

8-y-o ch g Democratic (USA)-Faustelerie (Faustus (USA))
John Allen Hobson's Choice Partnership

Placings:0550006P6/060145/430/2-2442003   (4956)
2003/04: 19²G, 19⁴GS, 21⁴GS, 22⁸HY, 22⁹GS, 21⁰S, 22³G,

	Starts	1st	2nd	3rd	Win & Pl
Hurdles	7	0	2	1	1720
Career Total	**26**	**1**	**3**	**2**	**4310**
76 11/00 MRas 2m3f110yG(0-90)HHdl				G-S	£1498

Total win prize-money £1498

Going:	Sf: 0-2 GS: 0-3 Gd: 0-2 GF: - Fm: 0-0
Distance:	2m/2m3: 0-1 2m4-2m7: 0-6 3m+: 0-0
Track:	LH: 0-2 RH: 0-4 Tight: 0-3 Gall: 0-1
Aids:	Bl: 0-0 Vi: 0-0 Tstrap: 0-0 Ckp: 0-0
Best Rating:	84 4/04 MRas 2m6f good Hdl

Plating-class; very lightly-raced in recent years; trips of around two and a half miles suit; acts on good ground.

I'm The Man

13-y-o ro g Say Primula-Vinovia (Ribston)
Mrs S H Shirley-Beavan Marco Syndicate

Placings:60/05403/434143/1220U21F5053130/PP01311/4
313F/45P0P3P63F01/23-0   (4689)
2003/04: 25⁰G,

	Starts	1st	2nd	3rd	Win & Pl
Chases	1	0	0	0	0
Career Total	**55**	**9**	**4**	**11**	**47787**
96	2/02	Muss	3m	F(0-95)HCh	SFT	£3220
111	5/00	Ctml	3m6f	C(0-130)HCh	G-S	£7117
110	4/00	Carl	3m2f	F(0-95)HCh	G-S	£3851
103	4/00	Carl	2m4f110yF(0-110)HCh		SFT	£3328
111	3/00	Muss	3m	E(0-115)HCh	G-F	£3657
97	2/99	Muss	3m	E(0-115)HHdl	GD	£2827
104	10/98	Sedg	3m3f	E(0-110)HCh	G-S	£4320
87	5/98	Hexm	3m1f	E(0-115)HCh	G-F	£2490
90	3/98	Hexm	2m4f110y			F(0-100)HCh
SFT	£3288					

Total win prize-money £34101

Going:	Sf: 0-0 GS: 0-0 Gd: 0-1 GF: - Fm: 0-0
Distance:	2m/2m3: 0-0 2m4-2m7: 0-0 3m+: 0-1
Track:	LH: 0-1 RH: 0-0 Tight: 0-1 Gall: 0-0
Aids:	Bl: 0-0 Vi: 0-0 Tstrap: 0-0 Ckp: 0-0
Best Rating:	111 6/00 Prth 3m good Ch

Hunter chaser; stays 3m 4f; effective in soft ground; races prominently; excellent third in the Foxhunters' at Aintree in April.

I'm Thinking So (IRE)

(90h)   (87h)

6-y-o b g Roselier (FR)-Arctic Alice (Brave Invader (USA))
P J Hobbs Seamus Ross

Placings:0-0600P   (4520)
2003/04: 19⁰G, 16⁶GS, 16⁰S, 20⁰GS, 23⁶GS,

	Starts	1st	2nd	3rd	Win & Pl
Hurdles	4	0	0	0	0
Chases	1	0	0	0	0
Career Total	**6**	**0**	**0**	**0**	**0**

Going:	Sf: 0-1 GS: 0-3 Gd: 0-1 GF: - Fm: 0-0
Distance:	2m/2m3: 0-2 2m4-2m7: 0-3 3m+: 0-1
Track:	LH: 0-0 RH: 0-5 Tight: 0-1 Gall: 0-0
Aids:	Bl: 0-1 Vi: 0-0 Tstrap: 0-0 Ckp: 0-0
Best Rating:	91 4/03 Fair 2m good NHF

I'm Your Man

89f   71f

5-y-o gr g Bigstone (IRE)-Snowgirl (IRE) (Mazaad)
Mrs Dianne Sayer A Slack

Placings:55   (2790)
2003/04: 16⁵G, 16⁵GF,

	Starts	1st	2nd	3rd	Win & Pl
NH Flat	2	0	0	0	0
Career Total	**2**	**0**	**0**	**0**	**0**

Going:	Sf: 0-0 GS: 0-0 Gd: 0-1 GF: - Fm: 0-1
Distance:	2m/2m3: 0-2 2m4-2m7: 0-0 3m+: 0-0
Track:	LH: 0-1 RH: 0-1 Tight: 0-1 Gall: 0-0
Aids:	Bl: 0-0 Vi: 0-0 Tstrap: 0-0 Ckp: 0-0
Best Rating:	71 12/03 Muss 2m gd-fm NHF

I've No Say (IRE)

99(91h)   (60h)96

11-y-o ch g Rising-Mon Democrat (Tanfirion)
Mrs P Sly   Messrs G A Libson,D L Bayliss & G Taylor

Placings:400/106022U4/03P44155150/024   (0946)
2003/04: 20⁰GF, 22²G, 23⁴G,

	Starts	1st	2nd	3rd	Win & Pl
Hurdles	1	0	0	0	0
Chases	2	0	1	0	1574
Career Total	25	3	3	1	14094
105	1/02	Fknm	2m5f110yE(0-100)HCh	SFT	£2970
105	11/01	Hntg	2m4f110yF(0-110)HCh	G-S	£3003
111	5/00	Strf	2m6f110yD Hdl	G-F	£3428

Total win prize-money £9403

Going:	Sf: 0-0 GS: 0-0 Gd: 0-2 GF: - Fm: 0-1
Distance:	2m/2m3: 0-0 2m4-2m7: 0-2 3m+: 0-1
Track:	LH: 0-2 RH: 0-1 Tight: 0-1 Gall: 0-0
Aids:	Bl: 0-0 Vi: 0-0 Tstrap: 0-0 Ckp: 0-0
Best Rating:	111 5/00 Strf 2m6f110y gd-fm Hdl

Moderate chaser; does not appear to stay 3m; acts on most types of ground; suited by positive tactics.

Iacacia (FR)

102(97h)   (91h)102

8-y-o b/br g Silver Rainbow-Palencia (FR) (Taj Dewan)
E Haddock (Miss Venetia Williams 27/10) Miss H M Newell

Placings:B4/U54/2/0-54423300   (3847)
2003/04: 22⁵G, 20⁴GF, 17⁴G, 21²GF, 16³GF, 17³GF, 20⁰G, 16⁰GS,

	Starts	1st	2nd	3rd	Win & Pl
Hurdles	3	0	0	0	544
Chases	5	0	1	2	3398
Career Total	15	0	2	2	12423

Going:	Sf: 0-0 GS: 0-1 Gd: 0-3 GF: - Fm: 0-4
Distance:	2m/2m3: 0-4 2m4-2m7: 0-4 3m+: 0-0
Track:	LH: 0-5 RH: 0-3 Tight: 0-5 Gall: 0-0
Aids:	Bl: 0-0 Vi: 0-0 Tstrap: 0-0 Ckp: 0-0
Best Rating:	102 7/03 Uttx 2m5f gd-fm Ch

Ex-French plating-class chaser; has not impressed with his attitude; effective in soft and fast ground; stays two miles six.

Iadora

(83h)   (89h)74

9-y-o br m Gildoran-Combe Hill (Crozier)
J A B Old   Mrs J A Fowler/the Kentish Men

Placings:20/U330/0P4-P   (0110)
2003/04: 20⁰HY,

	Starts	1st	2nd	3rd	Win & Pl
Chases	1	0	0	0	
Career Total	10	0	1	2	1667

Going:	Sf: 0-1 GS: 0-0 Gd: 0-0 GF: - Fm: 0-0
Distance:	2m/2m3: 0-0 2m4-2m7: 0-1 3m+: 0-0
Track:	LH: 0-1 RH: 0-0 Tight: 0-0 Gall: 0-0
Aids:	Bl: 0-0 Vi: 0-0 Tstrap: 0-0 Ckp: 0-0
Best Rating:	100 11/00 Folk 2m1f110y heavy NHF

Moderate hurdler/chaser; suited by easy ground.

Iambe De La See (FR)

97   106

8-y-o b m Useful (FR)-Reine Mati (SWI) (Matahawk)

N J Henderson   Elite Racing Club

Placings:412/1/306401   (4569)
2003/04: 17³G, 16⁰GS, 16⁵HY, 16⁴G, 16⁰G, 17¹GS,

	Starts	1st	2nd	3rd	Win & Pl
Hurdles	6	1	0	1	3438
Career Total	10	3	1	1	10757
94	3/04	Bang	2m1f	F Hdl	G-S	£2649
119	5/01	Hrfd	2m1f	E Hdl	GD	£2765
109	4/01	NAbb	2m1f	E Hdl	SFT	£3192

Total win prize-money £8607

Going:	Sf: 0-1 GS: 1-2 Gd: 0-3 GF: - Fm: 0-0
Distance:	2m/2m3: 1-6 2m4-2m7: 0-0 3m+: 0-0
Track:	LH: 1-3 RH: 0-3 Tight: 1-2 Gall: 0-1
Aids:	Bl: 0-0 Vi: 0-0 Tstrap: 0-0 Ckp: 0-0
Best Rating:	119 5/01 Hrfd 2m1f good Hdl

Modest hurdler; scored twice in the spring of 2001 but absent for two and a half years subsequently; returned to form in March 2004; acts on good ground or softer.

Ibal (FR)

91   (144dh)145d

8-y-o b g Balsamo (FR)-Quart D'Hekla (FR) (Quart De Vin (FR))
Mrs N Smith   Tony Hayward And Barry Fulton

Placings:3335/0F21312/24020P/31111-405P   (4426)
2003/04: 19⁴S, 16⁰G, 16⁵S, 16⁶G,

	Starts	1st	2nd	3rd	Win & Pl
Chases	4	0	0	0	3518
Career Total	26	6	4	5	76494
145	3/03	Sand	2m	D Ch	SFT	£7157
129	1/03	Plum	3m2f	D Ch	HVY	£7245
133	12/02	Chep	2m3f110yD Ch	HVY	£5215
124	12/02	Plum	2m4f	E Ch	HVY	£4522
144	3/01	Sand	2m110y	B HHdl	HVY	£23200
125	1/01	Leic	2m	E Hdl	HVY	£3209

Total win prize-money £50550

Going:	Sf: 0-2 GS: 0-0 Gd: 0-2 GF: - Fm: 0-0
Distance:	2m/2m3: 0-3 2m4-2m7: 0-1 3m+: 0-0
Track:	LH: 0-1 RH: 0-3 Tight: 0-0 Gall: 0-1
Aids:	Bl: 0-0 Vi: 0-0 Tstrap: 0-0 Ckp: 0-0
Best Rating:	145 3/03 Sand 2m soft Ch

Useful chaser/hurdler; stays three miles plus, but effective at shorter; best on very soft ground.

Iberus (GER)

77   113+

6-y-o b g Monsun (GER)-Iberica (GER) (Green Dancer (USA))
S Gollings (M C Pipe 28/6) D A Johnson

Placings:3F6-0P   (4438)
2003/04: 16⁰G, 16⁷GS,

	Starts	1st	2nd	3rd	Win & Pl
Hurdles	2	0	0	0	
Career Total	5	0	0	1	442

Going:	Sf: 0-0 GS: 0-1 Gd: 0-1 GF: - Fm: 0-0
Distance:	2m/2m3: 0-2 2m4-2m7: 0-0 3m+: 0-0
Track:	LH: 0-2 RH: 0-0 Tight: 0-1 Gall: 0-0
Aids:	Bl: 0-0 Vi: 0-0 Tstrap: 0-0 Ckp: 0-0
Best Rating:	113 2/03 Plum 2m soft Hdl

Modest hurdler; suited by ground good or softer; has worn a visor.

Ibin St James

102   (90h)103

10-y-o b g Salse (USA)-St James's Antigua (IRE) (Law Society (USA))
M Bradstock   Dave Breakspear

Placings:04/P11301001/P0P0P/P04P/4101-2   (2548)
2003/04: 28²GS,

	Starts	1st	2nd	3rd	Win & Pl
Chases	1	0	1	0	934
Career Total	25	6	1	1	20689
103	2/03	Hntg	3m	F(0-90)HCh	GD	£3469
103	11/02	Fknm	3m5f110yF(0-100)HCh	G-S	£4706
117	3/00	Hntg	3m2f	E(0-115)HHdl	SFT	£2887
115	12/99	Towc	3m	E(0-115)HHdl	GD	£2547
109	9/99	Hrfd	3m2f	E(0-115)HHdl	GD	£3113
93	8/99	Worc	3m	F(0-95)HHdl	SFT	£2045

Total win prize-money £18769

Going:	Sf: 0-0 GS: 0-1 Gd: 0-0 GF: - Fm: 0-0
Distance:	2m/2m3: 0-0 2m4-2m7: 0-0 3m+: 0-1
Track:	LH: 0-0 RH: 0-1 Tight: 0-1 Gall: 0-0
Aids:	Bl: 0-1 Vi: 0-0 Tstrap: 0-0 Ckp: 0-0
Best Rating:	117 3/00 Hntg 3m2f soft Hdl

Moderate chaser; stays very well; acts on good and soft ground.

Ibis Rochelais (FR)

105   (115h)129

8-y-o b g Passing Sale (FR)-Ta Rochelaise (FR) (Carmont (FR))
A Ennis   A T A Wates

Placings:F2/3P/134252F/232212P-33   (4385)
2003/04: 24³G, 24³G,

	Starts	1st	2nd	3rd	Win & Pl
Chases	2	0	0	2	7785
Career Total	20	2	7	5	52460
129	2/03	Sand	3m110y	B(0-140)HCh	SFT	£12678
115	5/01	Folk	2m1f110yE Hdl	G-S	£3080

Total win prize-money £15759

Going:	Sf: 0-0 GS: 0-0 Gd: 0-2 GF: - Fm: 0-0
Distance:	2m/2m3: 0-0 2m4-2m7: 0-0 3m+: 0-0
Track:	LH: 0-1 RH: 0-1 Tight: 0-0 Gall: 0-1
Aids:	Bl: 0-0 Vi: 0-0 Tstrap: 0-0 Ckp: 0-0
Best Rating:	129 2/03 Sand 3m110y soft Ch

Fair chaser; runner-up in the 2003 Kim Muir chase at Cheltenham and third in the same race in 2004; stays three miles; acts on good and soft ground; tough and consistent.

Icare D'Oudairies (FR)

104   108

8-y-o ch g Port Etienne (FR)-Vellea (FR) (Cap Martin (FR))
C L Tizzard   Anthony Knott

Placings:100/2400/1500/0-1220550   (3921)
2003/04: 21¹G, 24²S, 24²G, 20⁰G, 16⁵S, 20⁵HY, 16⁰GS,

	Starts	1st	2nd	3rd	Win & Pl
Hurdles	7	1	2	0	17321
Career Total	19	3	3	0	23036
105	11/03	Chel	2m5f	E(0-115)HHdl	GD	£10788
108	12/01	Weth	2m4f110yE(0-105)HHdl	SFT	£2926
102	1/00	Hayd	2m	H NHF	SFT	£1771

Total win prize-money £15485

Going:	Sf: 0-3 GS: 0-1 Gd: 1-3 GF: - Fm: 0-0
Distance:	2m/2m3: 0-2 2m4-2m7: 1-3 3m+: 0-2
Track:	LH: 1-2 RH: 0-5 Tight: 0-1 Gall: 1-1

Aids: Bl: 0-0 Vi: 0-1 Tstrap: 0-0 Ckp: 0-0
Best Rating: 108 12/03 Tntn 3m110y good Hdl

Modest hurdler; best caught fresh; stays three miles; suited by cut in the ground.

Ice And Fire

96   84

5-y-o b g Cadeaux Genereux-Tanz (IRE) (Sadler's Wells (USA))
B D Leavy (G Barnett 30/7) J T Stimpson & B Trubshaw

Placings: U00   (4565)
2003/04: 16^{U}GS, 16^{0}G, 17^{0}GS,

	Starts	1st	2nd	3rd	Win & Pl
Hurdles	3	0	0	0	
Career Total	3	0	0	0	

Going: Sf: 0-0 GS: 0-2 Gd: 0-1 GF: - Fm: 0-0
Distance: 2m/2m3: 0-2 2m4-2m7: 0-0 3m+: 0-0
Track: LH: 0-2 RH: 0-1 Tight: 0-1 Gall: 0-1
Aids: Bl: 0-0 Vi: 0-0 Tstrap: 0-0 Ckp: 0-0
Best Rating: 84 3/04 Bang 2m1f gd-sft Hdl

Ice Cool Lad (IRE)

103   94+

10-y-o b g Glacial Storm (USA)-My Serena (No Argument)
R Rowe The Reality Partnership

Placings: 0/065PP/15PP/032FP10/635P015-25222P (4933)
2003/04: 26^{2}GF, 28^{5}GS, 24^{2}GS, 24^{2}G, 28^{2}G, 26^{P}G,

	Starts	1st	2nd	3rd	Win & Pl
Chases	6	0	4	0	6299
Career Total	30	3	5	2	19082
82 3/03	Font	3m4f	E(0-105)HCh	GD	£4361
94 2/02	Font	2m2f	E(0-105)HCh	HVY	£3234
94 12/00	Font	3m4f	E(0-100)HCh	SFT	£3172
			Total win prize-money £10768		

Going: Sf: 0-0 GS: 0-2 Gd: 0-3 GF: - Fm: 0-1
Distance: 2m/2m3: 0-0 2m4-2m7: 0-0 3m+: 0-6
Track: LH: 0-0 RH: 0-3 Tight: 0-3 Gall: 0-0
Aids: Bl: 0-0 Vi: 0-0 Tstrap: 0-0 Ckp: 0-0
Best Rating: 94 3/04 Font 3m4f good Ch

Plating-class chaser; stays three miles four, but effective at shorter; acts on both good and soft ground.

Ice Crystal

78   115

7-y-o b g Slip Anchor-Crystal Fountain (Great Nephew)
S Woodman Fortune Racing

Placings: R42411/2PP/P1-060   (3409)
2003/04: 20^{0}G, 20^{6}HY, 21^{0}S,

	Starts	1st	2nd	3rd	Win & Pl
Hurdles	3	0	0	0	
Career Total	14	3	2	0	15152
113 1/03	Font	2m4f	D(0-125)HHdl	HVY	£6078
109 4/01	Font	2m6f110y	E Hdl	GD	£2639
96 4/01	Plum	2m5f	E Hdl	HVY	£3528
			Total win prize-money £12245		

Going: Sf: 0-2 GS: 0-0 Gd: 0-1 GF: - Fm: 0-0
Distance: 2m/2m3: 0-2 2m4-2m7: 0-3 3m+: 0-0
Track: LH: 0-1 RH: 0-0 Tight: 0-3 Gall: 0-0
Aids: Bl: 0-0 Vi: 0-0 Tstrap: 0-0 Ckp: 0-0
Best Rating: 115 10/01 Kemp 2m5f gd-sft Hdl

Fair hurdler; suited by a tight track and has a good record at Fontwell; needs trips of at least two and a half miles; goes well in testing ground.

Ice Cube

(99h)   (67 h)63

8-y-o b g Rakaposhi King-Arctic Flymes (Rymer)
Mrs L Williamson Mrs Lisa Williamson

Placings: F000302003250/300530P/00350100/00406400-0F50FP   (3917)
2003/04: 19^{0}G, 24^{F}GS, 25^{5}GF, 26^{0}GS, 25^{F}HY, 24^{P}G,

	Starts	1st	2nd	3rd	Win & Pl
Hurdles	2	0	0	0	0
Chases	4	0	0	0	0
Career Total	42	1	2	5	7039
76 2/02	Tntn	2m110y	E(0-100)HCh	SFT	£3428
			Total win prize-money £3429		

Going: Sf: 0-1 GS: 0-2 Gd: 0-2 GF: - Fm: 0-1
Distance: 2m/2m3: 0-0 2m4-2m7: 0-1 3m+: 0-5
Track: LH: 0-3 RH: 0-2 Tight: 0-0 Gall: 0-0
Aids: Bl: 0-0 Vi: 0-0 Tstrap: 0-0 Ckp: 0-0
Best Rating: 86 4/01 Plum 2m5f heavy Hdl

Ice Green Pearl

65f   30f

6-y-o b m Green Ruby (USA)-Ice Moon (Ballymoss)
M G Rimell Mrs M R T Rimell

Placings: 0   (3446)
2003/04: 16^{0}G,

	Starts	1st	2nd	3rd	Win & Pl
NH Flat	1	0	0	0	
Career Total	1	0	0	0	

Going: Sf: 0-0 GS: 0-0 Gd: 0-1 GF: - Fm: 0-0
Distance: 2m/2m3: 0-1 2m4-2m7: 0-0 3m+: 0-0
Track: LH: 0-0 RH: 0-1 Tight: 0-0 Gall: 0-0
Aids: Bl: 0-0 Vi: 0-0 Tstrap: 0-0 Ckp: 0-0
Best Rating: 34 1/04 Ludl 2m good NHF

Ice Rain (IRE)

64f   38f

4-y-o g g Zaffaran (USA)-Turbet Lass (IRE) (Carlingford Castle)
T P Tate T P Tate

Placings: 00   (4886)
2003/04: 16^{0}GS, 17^{0}GS,

	Starts	1st	2nd	3rd	Win & Pl
NH Flat	2	0	0	0	
Career Total	2	0	0	0	

Going: Sf: 0-0 GS: 0-2 Gd: 0-0 GF: - Fm: 0-0
Distance: 2m/2m3: 0-2 2m4-2m7: 0-0 3m+: 0-0
Track: LH: 0-1 RH: 0-1 Tight: 0-0 Gall: 0-0
Aids: Bl: 0-0 Vi: 0-0 Tstrap: 0-0 Ckp: 0-0
Best Rating: 37 4/04 Carl 2m1f gd-sft NHF

Ice Saint

(102h)   (91 h)

9-y-o gr g Ballacashtal (CAN)-Sylvan Song (Song)
M J Gingell C N & Mrs A V Roberts

Placings: 0566P/3402/1O14300-U   (4233)
2003/04: 22^{U}GF,

	Starts	1st	2nd	3rd	Win & Pl
Chases	1	0	0	0	
Career Total	17	2	1	2	10221
91 7/02	Strf	2m6f110y	D Hdl	G-F	£4858

| 86 6/02 | Strf | 2m6f110yF(0-95)HHdl | G-F | £3272 |
| | | Total win prize-money £8132 | | |

Going: Sf: 0-0 GS: 0-0 Gd: 0-0 GF: - Fm: 0-1
Distance: 2m/2m3: 0-0 2m4-2m7: 0-1 3m+: 0-0
Track: LH: 0-0 RH: 0-0 Tight: 0-1 Gall: 0-0
Aids: Bl: 0-0 Vi: 0-0 Tstrap: 0-0 Ckp: 0-0
Best Rating: 91 7/02 Strf 2m6f110y gd-fm Hdl

Modest pointer, winner twice over hurdles at Stratford in the summer of 2002; lightly raced since.

Icelandic Spring

12-y-o ch g Derrylin-Snow Time (Deep Run)
J E Brockbank J E Brockbank

Placings: P/0633-43   (0430)
2003/04: 25^{4}G, 26^{3}G,

	Starts	1st	2nd	3rd	Win & Pl
Chases	2	0	0	1	336
Career Total	7	0	0	3	996

Going: Sf: 0-0 GS: 0-0 Gd: 0-2 GF: - Fm: 0-0
Distance: 2m/2m3: 0-0 2m4-2m7: 0-0 3m+: 0-2
Track: LH: 0-2 RH: 0-0 Tight: 0-0 Gall: 0-0
Aids: Bl: 0-2 Vi: 0-0 Tstrap: 0-0 Ckp: 0-0
Best Rating: 80 4/03 Kels 3m1f good Ch

Moderate pointer/hunter chaser; handles a sound surface; has won blinkers.

Ichi Beau (IRE)

104(105h)   (113h)133

10-y-o b g Convinced-May As Well (Kemal (FR))
A J Martin (Ferdy Murphy 13/12) Mrs Fiona Butterly

Placings: 0000/504/11F52312/351233264/56P222-432211B44031U060   (4828a)
2003/04: 20^{4}YS, 16^{3}G, 17^{2}G, 20^{2}G, 20^{1}GF, 17^{1}G, 20^{B}GF, 17^{4}G, 20^{4}GF, 20^{0}G, 16^{3}G, 16^{1}G, 16^{U}GF, 16^{8}G, 16^{6}S, 16^{0}Y,

	Starts	1st	2nd	3rd	Win & Pl
Hurdles	7	2	2	0	9503
Chases	9	1	0	2	9163
Career Total	47	7	9	6	82879
129 11/03	Aint	2m	D(0-125)HCh	GD	£5378
116 7/03	Sthl	2m1f	E Hdl	GD	£3479
101 6/03	Hexm	2m4f110yE Hdl	G-F	£3447
144 12/01	Donc	2m110y	C(0-135)HCh	GD	£6097
128 4/01	Ayr	2m	C Ch	GD	£6301
121 11/00	Aint	2m	D(0-115)HCh	G-S	£10383
118 10/00	Carl	2m	F(0-100)HCh	G-S	£2886
			Total win prize-money £37975		

Going: Sf: 0-1 GS: 0-0 Gd: 2-9 GF: - Fm: 1-4
Distance: 2m/2m3: 2-10 2m4-2m7: 1-6 3m+: 0-0
Track: LH: 3-11 RH: 0-1 Tight: 1-5 Gall: 0-2
Aids: Bl: 0-0 Vi: 0-0 Tstrap: 3-13 Ckp: 0-0
Best Rating: 144 2/02 Kemp 2m good Ch

Useful chaser/fair hurdler; consistent sort; best over two miles and effective on a sound surface; suited by a flat, left-handed track; regularly tongue tied and has been tried in cheekpieces; made the most of simple opportunities in novices' hurdles in the summer of 2003.

Ickford Okey

12-y-o b g Broadsword (USA)-Running Kiss (Deep Run)
Mrs S S Harbour P J Morgan

Placings: 00/50U/2P6/52U-UP   (0240)

2003/04: 21UG, 25PG,

	Starts	1st	2nd	3rd	Win & Pl
Chases	2	0	0	0	
Career Total	13	0	2	0	1290

Going:	Sf: 0-0 GS: 0-0 Gd: 0-0 GF: - Fm: 0-0
Distance:	2m/2m3: 0-0 2m4-2m7: 0-1 3m+: 0-1
Track:	LH: 0-1 RH: 0-1 Tight: 0-0 Gall: 0-1
Aids:	Bl: 0-0 Vi: 0-0 Tstrap: 0-0 Ckp: 0-1
Best Rating:	101 3/02 Strf 3m gd-sft Ch

Iconic

10-y-o b g Reprimand-Miami Melody (Miami Springs)
Trevor Crawford Darren Page

Placings:0/64/0206P/4/P/5-P   (4122)
2003/04: 21PG,

	Starts	1st	2nd	3rd	Win & Pl
Chases	1	0	0	0	
Career Total	12	0	1	0	1068

Going:	Sf: 0-0 GS: 0-0 Gd: 0-1 GF: - Fm: 0-0
Distance:	2m/2m3: 0-0 2m4-2m7: 0-1 3m+: 0-0
Track:	LH: 0-0 RH: 0-1 Tight: 0-1 Gall: 0-0
Aids:	Bl: 0-0 Vi: 0-0 Tstrap: 0-0 Ckp: 0-0
Best Rating:	79 7/99 Sedg 2m110y gd-fm Ch

Icy Blast (IRE)

104f   103+f

5-y-o b g Glacial Storm (USA)-Fair Lisselan (IRE) (Kemal (FR))
P R Webber Mrs P Sherwood

Placings:16   (4578)
2003/04: 16¹G, 16⁶G,

	Starts	1st	2nd	3rd	Win & Pl
NH Flat	2	1	0	0	1995
Career Total	2	1	0	0	1995
103 2/04	Weth	2m		H NHF	SFT £1995

Total win prize-money £1995

Going:	Sf: 1-1 GS: 0-0 Gd: 0-0 GF: - Fm: 0-0
Distance:	2m/2m3: 1-2 2m4-2m7: 0-0 3m+: 0-0
Track:	LH: 1-2 RH: 0-0 Tight: 0-0 Gall: 0-1
Aids:	Bl: 0-0 Vi: 0-0 Tstrap: 0-0 Ckp: 0-0
Best Rating:	103 3/04 Newb 2m110y good NHF

Rangy type; came right away to take a bumper on debut at Wetherby in February; should stay well; handles testing conditions.

Icy River (IRE)

110   95+

7-y-o ch g Over The River (FR)-Icy Lou (Blue Rullah)
Mrs M Reveley Andy Peake

Placings:5606-231P   (2951)
2003/04: 20²G, 20³GF, 20¹GS, 20PG,

	Starts	1st	2nd	3rd	Win & Pl
Hurdles	4	1	1	1	4620
Career Total	8	1	1	1	4620
95 11/03	Carl	2m4f	E(0-100)HHdl	G-S	£2688

Total win prize-money £2688

Going:	Sf: 0-0 GS: 1-1 Gd: 0-1 GF: - Fm: 0-2
Distance:	2m/2m3: 0-0 2m4-2m7: 1-4 3m+: 0-0
Track:	LH: 0-2 RH: 1-2 Tight: 0-0 Gall: 0-0
Aids:	Bl: 0-0 Vi: 0-0 Tstrap: 0-0 Ckp: 0-0

Best Rating: 95   11/03   Carl   2m4f   gd-sft   Hdl

Moderate novice hurdler; winner at Carlisle in November; ran badly next time; effective at around two mile four; acts on yielding ground.

Idaho D'Ox (FR)

106(104c)   (130c)133

8-y-o b/br g Bad Conduct (USA)-Queseda (FR) (Quart De Vin (FR))
M C Pipe The Dionysius Partnership

Placings:4F00F462F66/O413123200120/P0020005-1111P006100P55   (4963)
2003/04: 17¹G, 17¹G, 16¹GF, 17¹G, 20PG, 16⁹G, 17⁹G, 16⁶G, 17¹GS, 16PS, 17⁰G, 16PG, 16⁵G, 20⁵G,

	Starts	1st	2nd	3rd	Win & Pl
Hurdles	9	1	0	0	14255
Chases	5	4	0	0	21530
Career Total	46	8	5	2	94948
126 1/04	Chel	2m1f	B(0-145)HHdl	G-S	£12818
130 7/03	Sthl	2m1f	D(0-125)HCh	GD	£6695
105 6/03	NAbb	2m110y	D Ch	G-F	£5894
104 5/03	Bang	2m1f110yE Ch		GD	£4176
119 4/03	Extr	2m1f110yE Ch		GD	£4764
125 4/02	Winc	2m	E Hdl	GD	£2884
120 12/01	Sand	2m110y	D(0-110)HHdl	SFT	£7117
93 10/01	Extr	2m6f110yE Hdl		G-F	£2450

Total win prize-money £46800

Going:	Sf: 0-1 GS: 1-1 Gd: 3-11 GF: - Fm: 1-1
Distance:	**2m/2m3: 5-12** 2m4-2m7: 0-2 3m+: 0-0
Track:	**LH: 4-10** RH: 1-4 Tight: 2-4 Gall: 1-3
Aids:	Bl: 0-0 Vi: 0-0 Tstrap: 0-0 Ckp: 0-0
Best Rating:	138 4/02 Aint 2m110y good Hdl

Useful handicap hurdler; also useful over fences; stays 2m 6f over hurdles but effective at shorter trips; seems to handle any ground; has worn a visor.

Idbury (IRE)

66   63+

6-y-o b g Zaffaran (USA)-Delcarrow (Roi Guillaume (FR))
N A Twiston-Davies H R Mould

Placings:005-4   (2277)
2003/04: 24⁴G,

	Starts	1st	2nd	3rd	Win & Pl
Hurdles	1	0	0	0	355
Career Total	4	0	0	0	355

Going:	Sf: 0-0 GS: 0-0 Gd: 0-1 GF: - Fm: 0-0
Distance:	2m/2m3: 0-0 2m4-2m7: 0-0 3m+: 0-1
Track:	LH: 0-0 RH: 0-1 Tight: 0-0 Gall: 0-0
Aids:	Bl: 0-0 Vi: 0-0 Tstrap: 0-0 Ckp: 0-0
Best Rating:	89 3/03 Hayd 2m good NHF

Ideal De L'Ile (FR)

78   (73h)89

8-y-o ch g Aelan Hapi (USA)-Ad Vitam Eternam (FR) (Cap Martin (FR))
R T Phillips Stephen Lambert

Placings:5P/50   (3255)
2003/04: 25⁵G, 24⁰G,

	Starts	1st	2nd	3rd	Win & Pl
Chases	2	0	0	0	0
Career Total	4	0	0	0	0

Going:	Sf: 0-0 GS: 0-0 Gd: 0-0 GF: - Fm: 0-0

Distance:	2m/2m3: 0-0 2m4-2m7: 0-0 3m+: 0-2
Track:	LH: 0-0 RH: 0-2 Tight: 0-2 Gall: 0-0
Aids:	Bl: 0-0 Vi: 0-0 Tstrap: 0-2 Ckp: 0-0
Best Rating:	89 12/03 Folk 3m1f good Ch

Ideal Du Bois Beury (FR)

101(102c)   (110c)112

8-y-o b/br g Useful (FR)-Pampa Star (FR) (Pampabird)
P Monteith G M Cowan

Placings:5/132110P/224P000-4253660046   (4314)
2003/04: 20⁴G, 17²G, 16⁵G, 20³GS, 25⁶S, 16⁶GF, 20⁰HY, 16⁶G, 16⁴F, 20⁶GF,

	Starts	1st	2nd	3rd	Win & Pl
Hurdles	4	0	0	0	771
Chases	6	0	1	1	2421
Career Total	25	3	4	2	41742
134 2/02	Asct	2m4f	B(0-150)HHdl	SFT	£18087
116 1/02	Leic	2m4f110yE(0-110)HHdl		SFT	£5648
120 12/01	Newb	2m110y	B Hdl	SFT	£7410

Total win prize-money £31146

Going:	Sf: 0-2 GS: 0-1 Gd: 0-4 GF: - Fm: 0-3
Distance:	2m/2m3: 0-5 2m4-2m7: 0-4 3m+: 0-1
Track:	LH: 0-5 RH: 0-5 Tight: 0-4 Gall: 0-0
Aids:	Bl: 0-0 Vi: 0-0 Tstrap: 0-0 Ckp: 0-0
Best Rating:	134 2/02 Asct 2m4f soft Hdl

Fair hurdler/modest novice chaser; effective over two and a half miles; goes well in soft ground; has worn a visor.

Idealko (FR)

105(97h)   (100h)108

8-y-o b g Kadalko (FR)-Belfaster (FR) (Royal Charter (FR))
Ian Williams Mrs Maggie Bull

Placings:62/4/1111/0/42PU133-22426   (4889)
2003/04: 20²G, 18²GF, 20⁴G, 20²GF, 20⁶GF,

	Starts	1st	2nd	3rd	Win & Pl
Chases	5	0	3	0	5657
Career Total	20	5	5	2	25721
106 3/03	Ludl	2m4f	F(0-100)HCh	GD	£3523
4/01	Lrsy	2m1f	Ch	GD	£3201
6/00	Diep	2m1f110y Ch		GD	£2882
6/00	Roya	2m2f	Ch	GD	£2690
6/00	Gemz	2m3f	Ch	GD	£1537

Total win prize-money £13833

Going:	Sf: 0-0 GS: 0-0 Gd: 0-2 GF: - Fm: 0-3
Distance:	2m/2m3: 0-2 2m4-2m7: 0-4 3m+: 0-0
Track:	LH: 0-4 RH: 0-1 Tight: 0-2 Gall: 0-1
Aids:	Bl: 0-0 Vi: 0-0 Tstrap: 0-0 Ckp: 0-0
Best Rating:	106 3/04 Leic 2m4f110y gd-fm Ch

Moderate performer; won four chases in France; he showed ability over hurdles in this country before winning a two and a half mile chase in March 2003; effective over two and a half miles; suited by good ground; has shown a tendency to jump left handed.

Ideas Man (IRE)

97(68h)   (36h)70

8-y-o b g Executive Perk-Emmodee (Bowling Pin)
D McCain B Dunn

Placings:50/R544FP-5P   (0669)
2003/04: 17⁵GF, 17PGF,

	Starts	1st	2nd	3rd	Win & Pl
Chases	2	0	0	0	
Career Total	10	0	0	0	891

Going: Sf: 0-0 GS: 0-0 Gd: 0-0 GF: - Fm: 0-2
Distance: 2m/2m3: 0-2 2m4-2m7: 0-0 3m+: 0-0
Track: LH: 0-1 RH: 0-1 Tight: 0-1 Gall: 0-0
Aids: Bl: 0-0 Vi: 0-0 Tstrap: 0-0 Ckp: 0-0
Best Rating: 81 12/01 Ludl 2m   good NHF

Idiome (FR)
108   (121h) 126
8-y-o b g Djarvis (FR)-Asterie L'Ermitage (FR) (Hamster (FR))
Mrs L C Taylor Mrs L C Taylor

Placings:43/P32/2062F2416333/212334   (4865)
2003/04: 19²GS, 16¹HY, 17²GS, 19³GS, 19³G, 25⁴S,

	Starts	1st	2nd	3rd	Win & Pl
Chases	6	1	2	2	11207
Career Total	23	2	6	7	30183
121 2/04	Hrld	2m	E Ch		HVY £4488
121 2/02	Font	2m2f110yD(0-115)HHdl		HVY £5352
		Total win prize-money £9841

Going: Sf: 1-2 GS: 0-3 Gd: 0-1 GF: - Fm: 0-0
Distance: 2m/2m3: 1-4 2m4-2m7: 0-1 3m+: 0-1
Track: LH: 0-2 RH: 1-4 Tight: 0-1 Gall: 0-0
Aids: Bl: 0-0 Vi: 0-0 Tstrap: 0-0 Ckp: 0-0
Best Rating: 123 3/04 Extr 2m3f110y gd-sft Ch

Fair novice chaser; effective on soft ground; should stay 2m 4f.

Idlewild (IRE)
(0c) 66
9-y-o br g Phardante (FR)-Delia Murphy (Golden Love)
M J Polglase P J Parsons

Placings:P/5PP-RP   (0332)
2003/04: 16⁸GF, 26⁶GF,

	Starts	1st	2nd	3rd	Win & Pl
Hurdles	1	0	0	0	0
Chases	1	0	0	0	0
Career Total	6	0	0	0	0

Going: Sf: 0-0 GS: 0-0 Gd: 0-0 GF: - Fm: 0-2
Distance: 2m/2m3: 0-1 2m4-2m7: 0-0 3m+: 0-1
Track: LH: 0-1 RH: 0-1 Tight: 0-0 Gall: 0-1
Aids: Bl: 0-0 Vi: 0-0 Tstrap: 0-0 Ckp: 0-0
Best Rating: 66 3/03 Sthl 2m4f110y gd-fm Hdl

Maiden pointer; no form so far under Rules.

Idole First (IRE)
100   120+
5-y-o b g Flemensfirth (USA)-Sharon Doll (IRE) (Shahrastani (USA))
Miss Venetia Williams Direct Sales UK Ltd

Placings:1321   (4959)
2003/04: 19¹G, 20³G, 20²GS, 19¹G,

	Starts	1st	2nd	3rd	Win & Pl
Hurdles	4	2	1	1	11435
Career Total	4	2	1	1	11435
120 4/04	MRas	2m3f110yD Hdl		GD £5037
114 7/03	Strf	2m3f	D Hdl	GD £5382
		Total win prize-money £10420

Going: Sf: 0-0 GS: 0-1 Gd: 2-3 GF: - Fm: 0-0
Distance: 2m/2m3: 1-1 2m4-2m7: 1-3 3m+: 0-0
Track: LH: 1-2 RH: 1-2 Tight: 2-4 Gall: 0-0
Aids: Bl: 0-0 Vi: 0-0 Tstrap: 0-0 Ckp: 0-0
Best Rating: 120 4/04 MRas 2m3f110y good Hdl

Fair ex-French novice hurdler; won on soft ground in France and wore blinkers there; stays two miles three; acts on good ground.

Ifni Du Luc (FR)
101   (120h) 145
8-y-o b/br m Chamberlin (FR)-Acca Du Luc (FR) (Djarvis (FR))
N J Henderson Mary-Anne Parker,Sir Eric Parker,P White

Placings:1224/10200/2121P/2F40U6-10   (4572)
2003/04: 20¹G, 24⁰G,

	Starts	1st	2nd	3rd	Win & Pl
Chases	2	1	0	0	8151
Career Total	22	5	6	0	50076
134 3/04	Kemp	2m4f110yD(0-125)HCh	GD	£8151
137 1/02	Hayd	2m6f	B Ch	SFT £10185
104 12/01	Winc	2m	D Ch	GD £4095
121 12/00	Font	2m2f110yC(0-130)HHdl	SFT £7046
109 12/99	Sand	2m110y	D Hdl	G-S £3046
		Total win prize-money £32523

Going: Sf: 0-0 GS: 0-0 Gd: 1-2 GF: - Fm: 0-0
Distance: 2m/2m3: 0-0 2m4-2m7: 1-1 3m+: 0-1
Track: LH: 0-1 RH: 1-1 Tight: 0-0 Gall: 0-1
Aids: Bl: 0-0 Vi: 0-0 Tstrap: 0-0 Ckp: 0-0
Best Rating: 145 11/02 Leic 2m4f110y good Ch

Useful handicap chaser; stays two miles six; acts on good and soft ground; first run for 11 months when winning at Kempton in March 2004.

Ifrane Balima (FR)
95 (105h)   (104dh) 101
8-y-o ch g Video Rock (FR)-Balima Des Saccart (FR) (Quart De Vin (FR))
J C Tuck The Kermit Klub

Placings:000F00/3114600-P0P30   (4507)
2003/04: 17⁶G, 19⁰GS, 19⁵S, 16³GF, 16⁰GS,

	Starts	1st	2nd	3rd	Win & Pl
Hurdles	3	0	0	0	0
Chases	2	0	0	1	618
Career Total	18	2	0	2	11272
104 11/02	Leic	2m	D(0-120)HHdl	HVY £6870
92 11/02	Uttx	2m	F(0-100)HHdl	HVY £2702
		Total win prize-money £9573

Going: Sf: 0-1 GS: 0-2 Gd: 0-1 GF: - Fm: 0-1
Distance: 2m/2m3: 0-2 2m4-2m7: 0-1 3m+: 0-1
Track: LH: 0-1 RH: 0-4 Tight: 0-1 Gall: 0-0
Aids: Bl: 0-0 Vi: 0-1 Tstrap: 0-0 Ckp: 0-0
Best Rating: 104 11/02 Leic 2m heavy Hdl

Moderate hurdler/chaser; suited by two miles and handles plenty of cut.

Iftikhar (USA)
91f   97f
5-y-o b g Storm Cat (USA)-Muhbubh (USA) (Blushing Groom (FR))
W M Brisbourne L R Owen

Placings:2-004   (0797)
2003/04: 16⁰G, 17⁰GF, 16⁴G,

	Starts	1st	2nd	3rd	Win & Pl
NH Flat	3	0	0	0	0
Career Total	4	0	1	0	560

Going: Sf: 0-0 GS: 0-0 Gd: 0-2 GF: - Fm: 0-1
Distance: 2m/2m3: 0-3 2m4-2m7: 0-0 3m+: 0-0

Track: LH: 0-1 RH: 0-2 Tight: 0-0 Gall: 0-0
Aids: Bl: 0-0 Vi: 0-0 Tstrap: 0-1 Ckp: 0-0
Best Rating: 97 3/03 Ludl 2m   good NHF

Igloo D'Estruval (FR)
99 (103h)   (96h) 123+
8-y-o br g Garde Royale-Jalousie (FR) (Blockhaus)
Mrs L C Taylor Mrs L C Taylor

Placings:0/01P21U/F3454044P/331F505   (4694)
2003/04: 23³G, 22³GS, 28¹G, 27⁴GS, 24⁴S, 30⁴G, 23⁵G,

	Starts	1st	2nd	3rd	Win & Pl
Hurdles	3	0	0	2	2513
Chases	4	1	0	0	9471
Career Total	23	3	1	3	31130
123 12/03	Font	3m4f	D(0-125)HHCh	GD	£9470
104 1/01	Donc	3m	D Ch	GD	£4420
6/00	Autl	2m1f110y	Ch	HLD £11527
		Total win prize-money £25418

Going: Sf: 0-1 GS: 0-2 Gd: 1-4 GF: - Fm: 0-0
Distance: 2m/2m3: 0-2 2m4-2m7: 0-2 3m+: 1-5
Track: LH: 0-2 RH: 0-4 Tight: 0-2 Gall: 0-1
Aids: Bl: 0-0 Vi: 1-7 Tstrap: 0-0 Ckp: 0-0
Best Rating: 123 12/03 Font 3m4f   good Ch

Modest chaser/hurdler, ex-French; has had jumping problems since and has mixed chasing and hurdling; won valuable handicap chase at Fontwell in December 2003; stays three and a half miles and looks best suited by soft ground; has worn a visor.

Ijika (FR)
(82h)   (55h) 40
8-y-o ch g Aelan Hapi (USA)-Belle Des Airs (FR) (Saumon (FR))
H D Daly Roy Van Gelder & Brian Luby

Placings:00/26033/0PPP-0   (0368)
2003/04: 20⁰G,

	Starts	1st	2nd	3rd	Win & Pl
Hurdles	1	0	0	0	
Career Total	12	0	1	2	2383

Going: Sf: 0-0 GS: 0-0 Gd: 0-1 GF: - Fm: 0-0
Distance: 2m/2m3: 0-0 2m4-2m7: 0-1 3m+: 0-0
Track: LH: 0-1 RH: 0-0 Tight: 0-0 Gall: 0-0
Aids: Bl: 0-0 Vi: 0-0 Tstrap: 0-0 Ckp: 0-0
Best Rating: 100 4/02 Strf 2m110y   good Hdl

Ikrenel Royal (FR)
87   126
8-y-o b g Bricassar (USA)-Kreneldore (FR) (Trenel)
N J Henderson Lynn Wilson

Placings:630111/P6-P4   (2706)
2003/04: 24⁵GS, 20⁴G,

	Starts	1st	2nd	3rd	Win & Pl
Chases	2	0	0	0	848
Career Total	10	3	0	1	41830
146 4/01	Sand	2m4f110yB Ch	G-S £17225
12/00	Autl	2m2f	Hdl	HVY £9606
11/00	Engh	2m3f	Ch	HLD £10567
		Total win prize-money £37398

Going: Sf: 0-0 GS: 0-1 Gd: 0-1 GF: - Fm: 0-0
Distance: 2m/2m3: 0-0 2m4-2m7: 0-1 3m+: 0-0
Track: LH: 0-2 RH: 0-0 Tight: 0-1 Gall: 0-1

Aids: Bl: 0-0 Vi: 0-0 Tstrap: 0-0 Ckp: 0-0
Best Rating: 146 4/01 Sand 2m4f110y gd-sft Ch

Fair ex-French chaser; looked a classy prospect when winning at Sandown in April of 2001, but subsequently injured and has not looked the same horse since; effective over two and a half miles; acts on soft ground.

Il Capitano

113(106h)   (128h)130
7-y-o ch g Be My Chief (USA)-Taza (Persian Bold)
P F Nicholls Terry Evans

Placings:25/152363621/11311112131-13F3   (0922)
2003/04: 24¹GF, 21³G, 20FGF, 20³GF,

	Starts	1st	2nd	3rd	Win & Pl
Hurdles	1	1	0	0	7175
Chases	3	0	0	2	9504
Career Total	**26**	**11**	**4**	**6**	**85302**
128	5/03	Ludl	3m	C(0-130)HHdl	G-F	£7175
130	4/03	Sand	2m4f110yB HCh		G-F	£15812
110	4/03	Tntn	2m3f	D Ch	FRM	£5564
117	10/02	Tntn	2m3f	D Ch	FRM	£5443
127	10/02	Extr	2m3f	D(0-125)HHdl	FRM	£4602
119	10/02	Chep	2m4f	D(0-120)HHdl	G-F	£4134
122	10/02	Extr	3m110y	D(0-125)HHdl	FRM	£5005
106	5/02	Font	2m4f	E Ch	G-F	£3081
127	5/02	Font	3m2f110yE Ch		G-F	£3071
116	4/02	Font	3m3f	D(0-125)HHdl	G-F	£3482
95	10/01	Tntn	2m1f	E Hdl	FRM	£3276
				Total win prize-money £60648

Going: Sf: 0-0 GS: 0-0 Gd: 0-1 GF: - Fm: 1-3
Distance: 2m/2m3: 0-0 2m4-2m7: 0-3 3m+: 1-1
Track: LH: 0-1 RH: 1-3 Tight: 0-3 Gall: 0-0
Aids: Bl: 0-0 Vi: 0-0 Tstrap: 0-0 Ckp: 0-0
Best Rating: 130 4/03 Sand 2m4f110y gd-fm Ch

Useful hurdler/chaser; in sparkling form in 2002/2003 with eight wins, five over fences; won at Ludlow on first run of 2003/4 season; stays two and a half miles; fast-ground specialist; suited by a right-handed track.

Il Cavaliere

104   127
9-y-o b g Mtoto-Kalmia (Miller's Mate)
Mrs M Reveley The Thoughtful Partnership

Placings:15214/322/2211F-P362U060   (4449)
2003/04: 24PG, 22³G, 22⁶GS, 21²G, 21UG, 21⁰G, 24⁶G, 20⁹GS,

	Starts	1st	2nd	3rd	Win & Pl
Hurdles	8	0	1	1	3786
Career Total	**21**	**4**	**6**	**2**	**24266**
124	1/03	Kemp	2m5f	C(0-130)HHdl	GD	£6554
124	12/02	Muss	2m4f	D Hdl	G-S	£4202
117	10/99	Sedg	2m1f	H NHF	GD	£1647
115	6/99	MRas	1m5f110yH NHF		G-F	£1493
				Total win prize-money £13898

Going: Sf: 0-0 GS: 0-2 Gd: 0-6 GF: - Fm: 0-0
Distance: 2m/2m3: 0-0 2m4-2m7: 0-6 3m+: 0-2
Track: LH: 0-2 RH: 0-5 Tight: 0-1 Gall: 0-1
Aids: Bl: 0-0 Vi: 0-0 Tstrap: 0-0 Ckp: 0-0
Best Rating: 126 4/00 Aint 2m110y good NHF

Fair handicap hurdler; effective at around two and a half miles; acts on good and soft ground; suited by a flat track.

Il'Athou (FR)

(88h)   (102h)147
8-y-o b g Lute Antique (FR)-Va Thou Line (FR) (El Badr)
S E H Sherwood Lady Thompson

Placings:2/011P0/111P/F2P13-P60F   (4871)
2003/04: 20PGS, 20⁶G, 21⁹G, 24FS,

	Starts	1st	2nd	3rd	Win & Pl
Hurdles	1	0	0	0	0
Chases	3	0	0	0	0
Career Total	**19**	**6**	**2**	**1**	**50460**
147	2/03	Weth	2m4f110yB HCh		G-S	£13481
140	1/02	Asct	2m	A Ch	GD	£16750
133	11/01	Hntg	2m4f110yD Ch		GD	£4280
135	10/01	Bang	2m1f110yD Ch		SFT	£4134
116	1/01	Folk	2m1f110yF(0-105)HHdl		HVY	£2226
109	12/00	Folk	2m1f110yE Hdl		HVY	£3042
				Total win prize-money £43913

Going: Sf: 0-1 GS: 0-1 Gd: 0-2 GF: - Fm: 0-0
Distance: 2m/2m3: 0-2 2m4-2m7: 0-3 3m+: 0-1
Track: LH: 0-3 RH: 0-1 Tight: 0-2 Gall: 0-1
Aids: Bl: 0-0 Vi: 0-0 Tstrap: 0-0 Ckp: 0-0
Best Rating: 147 2/03 Weth 2m4f110y gd-sft Ch

Very useful chaser; suited by two and a half miles; best on soft ground; suited by forcing tactics; jumps well.

Ilabon (FR)

103   119
8-y-o ch g Secret Haunt (USA)-Ahuille (FR) (Haltea (FR))
M C Pipe Beau Girls

Placings:4532-20014   (4915)
2003/04: 20²S, 16⁶S, 24⁰G, 16¹G, 16⁴GS,

	Starts	1st	2nd	3rd	Win & Pl
Hurdles	5	1	1	0	5165
Career Total	**9**	**1**	**2**	**1**	**9529**
111	4/04	Chep	2m110y	E Hdl	GD	£3601
				Total win prize-money £3601

Going: Sf: 0-2 GS: 0-1 Gd: 1-2 GF: - Fm: 0-0
Distance: 2m/2m3: 1-3 2m4-2m7: 0-1 3m+: 0-1
Track: LH: 1-3 RH: 0-2 Tight: 0-0 Gall: 0-0
Aids: Bl: 0-0 Vi: 1-2 Tstrap: 0-0 Ckp: 0-0
Best Rating: 119 1/04 Leic 2m4f110y soft Hdl

Fair novice hurdler, ex-French; appreciated a drop in class when justifying odds of 1/3 in first-time visor at Chepstow April 2004; stays two and a half miles; acts on good ground and soft.

Ile De Librate

100(89h)   (69h)101
10-y-o b g Librate-Little Missile (Ile De Bourbon (USA))
R J O'Sullivan Skampcargo Racing Partnership

Placings:222F02214/4360/22/5/421212/000U-3   (0508)
2003/04: 28³GS,

	Starts	1st	2nd	3rd	Win & Pl
Chases	1	0	0	1	1069
Career Total	**27**	**3**	**10**	**2**	**20770**
101	9/01	Worc	2m7f110yD Ch		G-F	£3900
101	7/01	Strf	3m	D Ch	GD	£4338
98	3/98	Plum	2m4f	E Hdl	GD	£2763
				Total win prize-money £11002

Going: Sf: 0-0 GS: 0-1 Gd: 0-0 GF: - Fm: 0-0
Distance: 2m/2m3: 0-0 2m4-2m7: 0-0 3m+: 0-1
Track: LH: 0-1 RH: 0-0 Tight: 0-1 Gall: 0-0
Aids: Bl: 0-0 Vi: 0-0 Tstrap: 0-1 Ckp: 0-0
Best Rating: 101 5/03 Strf 3m4f gd-sft Ch

Moderate staying hurdler/chaser; acts on a sound surface.

Ile De Paris (FR)

97   99
5-y-o b g Cadoudal (FR)-Sweet Beauty (FR)(Tip Moss (FR))

P J Hobbs Sir Robert Ogden

Placings:220   (4242)
2003/04: 17²G, 19²S, 24⁰G,

	Starts	1st	2nd	3rd	Win & Pl
Hurdles	3	0	2	0	2453
Career Total	**3**	**0**	**2**	**0**	**2453**

Going: Sf: 0-1 GS: 0-0 Gd: 0-2 GF: - Fm: 0-0
Distance: 2m/2m3: 0-2 2m4-2m7: 0-0 3m+: 0-1
Track: LH: 0-1 RH: 0-2 Tight: 0-1 Gall: 0-0
Aids: Bl: 0-0 Vi: 0-0 Tstrap: 0-0 Ckp: 0-0
Best Rating: 99 2/04 Extr 2m3f soft Hdl

Promise on his hurdling debut and next outing, but disappointed when odds-on and failing to get home over three miles latest; embryonic chaser.

Ile De Re (IRE)

7-y-o gr m Roselier (FR)-Kam Slave (Kambalda)
B G Powell John Studd

Placings:P   (0485)
2003/04: 22PGF,

	Starts	1st	2nd	3rd	Win & Pl
Hurdles	1	0	0	0	
Career Total	**1**	**0**	**0**	**0**	

Going: Sf: 0-0 GS: 0-0 Gd: 0-0 GF: - Fm: 0-1
Distance: 2m/2m3: 0-0 2m4-2m7: 0-1 3m+: 0-0
Track: LH: 0-1 RH: 0-0 Tight: 0-1 Gall: 0-0
Aids: Bl: 0-0 Vi: 0-0 Tstrap: 0-0 Ckp: 0-0

Ile Distinct (IRE)

96(92h)   (41h)79
10-y-o b g Dancing Dissident (USA)-Golden Sunlight (Ile De Bourbon (USA))
K R Pearce Keith R Pearce

Placings:2/40/FF0454/P6-P500043   (1419)
2003/04: 24PG, 25⁵G, 24⁰GF, 24⁰GF, 16⁶GS, 17⁴GF, 18³GF,

	Starts	1st	2nd	3rd	Win & Pl
Hurdles	2	0	0	0	0
Chases	5	0	0	1	621
Career Total	**18**	**0**	**1**	**1**	**1289**

Going: Sf: 0-0 GS: 0-1 Gd: 0-2 GF: - Fm: 0-4
Distance: 2m/2m3: 0-3 2m4-2m7: 0-0 3m+: 0-4
Track: LH: 0-4 RH: 0-2 Tight: 0-3 Gall: 0-0
Aids: Bl: 0-0 Vi: 0-0 Tstrap: 0-0 Ckp: 0-0
Best Rating: 96 9/99 Kels 2m2f gd-fm Hdl

Plating-class hurdler/chaser; does not stay three miles.

Ile Michel

107   106
7-y-o b g Machiavellian (USA)-Circe's Isle (Be My Guest (USA))
J G M O'Shea (M C Pipe 11/2) Bill Tyler

Placings:20302   (3773)
2003/04: 16²GF, 16⁰G, 19³GF, 16⁰GS, 16²G,

	Starts	1st	2nd	3rd	Win & Pl
Hurdles	5	0	2	1	3190
Career Total	**5**	**0**	**2**	**1**	**3190**

Going: Sf: 0-0 GS: 0-1 Gd: 0-2 GF: - Fm: 0-2

Distance:	2m/2m3: 0-5 2m4-2m7: 0-0 3m+: 0-0
Track:	LH: 0-3 RH: 0-2 Tight: 0-2 Gall: 0-1
Aids:	Bl: 0-0 Vi: 0-0 Tstrap: 0-0 Ckp: 0-0
Best Rating:	106 10/03 Strf 2m110y gd-fm Hdl

Modest hurdler; beaten in a seller and has become disappointing; just about gets two miles; acts on fast ground.

Illicium (IRE)

101f   92f

5-y-o b m Fourstars Allstar (USA)-Sweet Mignonette (Tina's Pet)
Mrs M Reveley Mr & Mrs W J Williams

Placings:6034   (4608)
2003/04: 16⁶GS, 16⁹G, 16³G, 17⁴G,

	Starts	1st	2nd	3rd	Win & Pl
NH Flat	4	0	0	1	271
Career Total	4	0	0	1	271

Going:	Sf: 0-0 GS: 0-1 Gd: 0-3 GF: - Fm: 0-0
Distance:	2m/2m3: 0-4 2m4-2m7: 0-0 3m+: 0-0
Track:	LH: 0-0 RH: 0-4 Tight: 0-2 Gall: 0-2
Aids:	Bl: 0-0 Vi: 0-0 Tstrap: 0-0 Ckp: 0-0
Best Rating:	92 3/04 MRas 2m1f110y good NHF

Placed in a bumper; acts on good.

Illineylad (IRE)

95   (83h)74

10-y-o b g Whitehall Bridge-Illiney Girl (Lochnager)
Mrs N S Sharpe The Illiney Group

Placings:064/60/PF03443P/P2P3-021P   (1356)
2003/04: 22⁰G, 23²G, 23¹GF, 24⁴PG,

	Starts	1st	2nd	3rd	Win & Pl
Chases	4	1	1	0	5241
Career Total	21	1	2	3	8003
74 8/03 Worc	2m7f110yE(0-105)HCh		G-F		£4056
		Total win prize-money £4056

Going:	Sf: 0-0 GS: 0-0 Gd: 0-2 GF: - Fm: 1-2
Distance:	2m/2m3: 0-0 2m4-2m7: 0-1 3m+: 1-3
Track:	LH: 1-3 RH: 0-1 Tight: 0-2 Gall: 0-0
Aids:	Bl: 0-0 Vi: 0-0 Tstrap: 0-0 Ckp: 0-0
Best Rating:	83 9/01 Worc 3m gd-fm Hdl

Former point winner; sometimes let down by his jumping; overcame bad mistake at last ditch to land Class E novices' handicap at Worcester August 2003; stays 3m; best on a sound surface.

Iloveturtle (IRE)

100   87

4-y-o b g Turtle Island (IRE)-Gan Ainm (IRE) (Mujadil (USA))
M C Chapman (M Johnston 30/6) Coverscope Ductwork & Reedkleen Supplies

Placings:0662   (4602)
2003/04: 16⁰S, 16⁶S, 17⁶G, 17²G,

	Starts	1st	2nd	3rd	Win & Pl
Hurdles	4	0	1	0	1496
Career Total	4	0	1	0	1496

Going:	Sf: 0-2 GS: 0-0 Gd: 0-2 GF: - Fm: 0-0
Distance:	2m/2m3: 0-4 2m4-2m7: 0-0 3m+: 0-0
Track:	LH: 0-0 RH: 0-4 Tight: 0-2 Gall: 0-0
Aids:	Bl: 0-0 Vi: 0-0 Tstrap: 0-0 Ckp: 0-0
Best Rating:	87 3/04 MRas 2m1f110y good Hdl

Imaginaire (USA)

104   111

9-y-o b g Quest For Fame-Hail The Dancer (USA) (Green Dancer (USA))
Miss Venetia Williams Miss J Davies,L Jakeman,W Fenn

Placings:P66/00243406P/02200125/33214F/43B34-4200
                                              (4575)
2003/04: 17⁴S, 16²S, 19⁰G, 18⁰G,

	Starts	1st	2nd	3rd	Win & Pl
Chases	4	0	1	0	2168
Career Total	35	2	6	5	68127
129 3/02 Strf	2m4f	D Ch		G-S	£5284
120 1/01 Folk	2m6f110yE Hdl		HVY		£2744
		Total win prize-money £8029

Going:	Sf: 0-2 GS: 0-0 Gd: 0-2 GF: - Fm: 0-0
Distance:	2m/2m3: 0-0 2m4-2m7: 0-0 3m+: 0-0
Track:	LH: 0-4 RH: 0-0 Tight: 0-2 Gall: 0-1
Aids:	Bl: 0-0 Vi: 0-0 Tstrap: 0-0 Ckp: 0-0
Best Rating:	129 3/02 Strf 2m4f gd-sft Ch

Modest chaser; stays two and a half miles; acts on soft ground.

Imago II (FR)

87   (102h)98

8-y-o b g Chamberlin (FR)-Pensee D'Amour (FR) (Porto Rafti (FR))
Jonjo O'Neill Tony Eaves

Placings:1/340/P06-6   (0589)
2003/04: 20⁶GF,

	Starts	1st	2nd	3rd	Win & Pl
Chases	1	0	0	0	
Career Total	8	1	0	1	2754
110 2/01 Hayd	2m	H NHF		SFT	£2159
		Total win prize-money £2160

Going:	Sf: 0-0 GS: 0-0 Gd: 0-0 GF: - Fm: 0-1
Distance:	2m/2m3: 0-0 2m4-2m7: 0-1 3m+: 0-0
Track:	LH: 0-1 RH: 0-0 Tight: 0-0 Gall: 0-0
Aids:	Bl: 0-1 Vi: 0-0 Tstrap: 0-0 Ckp: 0-0
Best Rating:	110 2/01 Hayd 2m soft NHF

Moderate hurdler/chaser; showed only moderate form over hurdles and has been let down by his jumping over fences so far; acts on soft.

Immola (FR)

100+

8-y-o b/br g Quart De Vin (FR)-Jessica (FR) (Laniste)
Miss E C Lavelle Mrs Sarah Stevens

Placings:0451-PP   (3823)
2003/04: 20²PS, 20²PS,

	Starts	1st	2nd	3rd	Win & Pl
Hurdles	2	0	0	0	
Career Total	6	1	0	0	4908
115 3/03 Sand	2m110y	D Hdl		HVY	£4907
		Total win prize-money £4908

Going:	Sf: 0-2 GS: 0-0 Gd: 0-0 GF: - Fm: 0-0
Distance:	2m/2m3: 0-0 2m4-2m7: 0-2 3m+: 0-0
Track:	LH: 0-1 RH: 0-1 Tight: 0-0 Gall: 0-0
Aids:	Bl: 0-0 Vi: 0-0 Tstrap: 0-0 Ckp: 0-0
Best Rating:	115 3/03 Sand 2m110y heavy Hdl

Moderate hurdler; suited by testing ground; effective over two miles; keen sort.

Impek (FR)

119   (153h)161+

8-y-o b g Lute Antique (FR)-Attualita (FR) (Master Thatch)
Miss H C Knight Jim Lewis

Placings:2150/24423/11123-215U232   (4964)
2003/04: 16²GY, 24¹G, 24⁵S, 21ᵁGS, 19²S, 21³G, 16²GF,

	Starts	1st	2nd	3rd	Win & Pl
Chases	7	3	1	3	73294
Career Total	21	5	7	3	171295
161 12/03 Sand	3m110y	B Ch		GD	£8757
160 12/02 Sand	2m	A Ch		SFT	£20100
148 11/02 Hrfd	2m	E Ch		GD	£4199
128 5/02 Hntg	2m110y	E Ch		GD	£3055
131 2/01 Ludl	2m	E Hdl		G-S	£3006
		Total win prize-money £39118

Going:	Sf: 0-2 GS: 0-1 Gd: 1-2 GF: - Fm: 0-1
Distance:	2m/2m3: 0-2 2m4-2m7: 0-3 3m+: 1-2
Track:	LH: 0-2 RH: 1-5 Tight: 0-1 Gall: 0-2
Aids:	Bl: 0-0 Vi: 0-0 Tstrap: 0-0 Ckp: 0-0
Best Rating:	161 1/04 Asct 2m3f110y soft Ch

Smart chaser; runner-up to Azertyuiop in Arkle at Cheltenham in 2003; easy winner at Sandown when stepped up to the three miles in December 2003; effective over a strongly-run two miles, though gets three miles; acts on good and soft ground; often led at the start and generally reported to be not that straightforward; dislikes being crowded in big fields.

Imperative (USA)

100   92

4-y-o ch c Woodman (USA)-Wandesta (Nashwan (USA))
Miss Gay Kelleway (Ian Williams 16/2) Webtack Racing

Placings:20P4   (3254)
2003/04: 16²GF, 16⁰GF, 17⁶G, 16⁴GS,

	Starts	1st	2nd	3rd	Win & Pl
Hurdles	4	0	1	0	1081
Career Total	4	0	1	0	1081

Going:	Sf: 0-0 GS: 0-1 Gd: 0-1 GF: - Fm: 0-2
Distance:	2m/2m3: 0-4 2m4-2m7: 0-0 3m+: 0-0
Track:	LH: 0-1 RH: 0-3 Tight: 0-1 Gall: 0-2
Aids:	Bl: 0-0 Vi: 0-0 Tstrap: 0-0 Ckp: 0-0
Best Rating:	92 11/03 Hntg 2m110y gd-fm Hdl

Runner-up on hurdles bow, running green; held since.

Imperial De Thaix (FR)

104(116h)   (125h)125

8-y-o b g Roi De Rome (USA)-Soiree D'Ete (FR) (Prove It Baby (USA))
M C Pipe J S Lammiman

Placings:16411PF/F1/032P000P-002203002P0   (4965)
2003/04: 23⁹G, 22⁰GS, 25²G, 26²G, 24⁹S, 26³G, 25⁰G, 24⁰G, 26²G, 26²GF, 29⁰GF,

	Starts	1st	2nd	3rd	Win & Pl
Hurdles	3	0	1	0	4380
Chases	8	0	2	1	8429
Career Total	28	4	4	2	39065
125 4/02 Chel	2m5f110yB HHdl		G-F	£10452
120 1/01 Chep	3m	E Ch		G-S	£2960
141 12/00 Chep	2m3f110yD Ch		SFT	£3838
10/00 Nant	2m1f110y Hdl		HVY	£3362
		Total win prize-money £20613

| Going: | Sf: 0-1 GS: 0-1 Gd: 0-7 GF: - Fm: 0-2 |

Distance: 2m/2m3: 0-0 2m4-2m7: 0-1 3m+: 0-10
Track: LH: 0-7 RH: 0-4 Tight: 0-2 Gall: 0-5
Aids: Bl: 0-0 Vi: 0-4 Tstrap: 0-10 Ckp: 0-5
Best Rating: 141 12/00 Chep 2m3f110y soft   Ch

Modest chaser/modest hurdler, inconsistent; stays beyond three miles; acts on any ground; often wears a tongue tie; has been visored.

Imperial Dream (IRE)

93   92

6-y-o b g Roselier (FR)-Royal Nora (IRE) (Dromod Hill)
Miss H C Knight Hogarth Racing

Placings:22-U2P3   (4676)
2003/04: 17^UG, 19²G, 22^PGS, 22³G,

	Starts	1st	2nd	3rd	Win & Pl
Hurdles	4	0	1	1	1730
Career Total	6	0	3	1	2904

Going: Sf: 0-0 GS: 0-1 Gd: 0-3 GF: - Fm: 0-0
Distance: 2m/2m3: 0-2 2m4-2m7: 0-2 3m+: 0-0
Track: LH: 0-1 RH: 0-3 Tight: 0-1 Gall: 0-0
Aids: Bl: 0-0 Vi: 0-0 Tstrap: 0-0 Ckp: 0-0
Best Rating: 95 3/03 Bang 2m1f   good   NHF

Imperial Island (FR)

70f   67f

5-y-o b g Exit To Nowhere (USA)-Imperial Prospect (USA) (Imperial Falcon (CAN))
J J Sheehan Mrs Eileen Sheehan

Placings:0   (3594)
2003/04: 16⁰HY,

	Starts	1st	2nd	3rd	Win & Pl
NH Flat	1	0	0	0	
Career Total	1	0	0	0	

Going: Sf: 0-1 GS: 0-0 Gd: 0-0 GF: - Fm: 0-0
Distance: 2m/2m3: 0-1 2m4-2m7: 0-0 3m+: 0-0
Track: LH: 0-0 RH: 0-1 Tight: 0-0 Gall: 0-0
Aids: Bl: 0-0 Vi: 0-0 Tstrap: 0-0 Ckp: 0-0
Best Rating: 62 1/04 Asct 2m110y   heavy   NHF

Imperial Line (IRE)

10-y-o ch g Mac's Imp (USA)-Ellaline (Corvaro (USA))
H L Thompson Mrs P A Cowey

Placings:00/062-P0   (4626)
2003/04: 25^PGS, 21⁰G,

	Starts	1st	2nd	3rd	Win & Pl
Chases	2	0	0	0	
Career Total	7	0	1	0	708

Going: Sf: 0-0 GS: 0-1 Gd: 0-1 GF: - Fm: 0-0
Distance: 2m/2m3: 0-0 2m4-2m7: 0-1 3m+: 0-1
Track: LH: 0-1 RH: 0-1 Tight: 0-2 Gall: 0-0
Aids: Bl: 0-0 Vi: 0-0 Tstrap: 0-2 Ckp: 0-0
Best Rating: 77 6/02 Ctml 3m2f   good   Ch

Imperial Man (IRE)

(70c)
9-y-o b g Mandalus-The Foalicule (Imperial Fling (USA))

R Johnson (P Spottiswood 28/4) Robert Johnson

Placings:3/0000000450/060060F45F05P/0P-U44   (2137)
2003/04: 20^PG, 17^UG, 20⁴GF, 24⁴G,

	Starts	1st	2nd	3rd	Win & Pl
Hurdles	4	0	0	0	
Career Total	29	0	0	1	440

Going: Sf: 0-0 GS: 0-0 Gd: 0-3 GF: - Fm: 0-1
Distance: 2m/2m3: 0-1 2m4-2m7: 0-2 3m+: 0-1
Track: LH: 0-4 RH: 0-0 Tight: 0-1 Gall: 0-1
Aids: Bl: 0-1 Vi: 0-0 Tstrap: 0-0 Ckp: 0-0
Best Rating: 92 12/00 Clon 2m   sft-hvy   NHF

Imperial Rocket (USA)

102   94

7-y-o b/br g Northern Flagship (USA)-Starsawhirl (USA) (Star De Naskra (USA))
Mrs A L M King Lynda Lovell And Aiden Murphy

Placings:05/1/5P623   (0999)
2003/04: 16⁵G, 18⁷GF, 16⁶GF, 16²G, 16³G,

	Starts	1st	2nd	3rd	Win & Pl
Hurdles	5	0	1	1	1688
Career Total	8	1	1	1	4327
120	5/01	Font	2m2f110yE Hdl		G-F £2639
				Total win prize-money £2639

Going: Sf: 0-0 GS: 0-0 Gd: 0-3 GF: - Fm: 0-2
Distance: 2m/2m3: 0-5 2m4-2m7: 0-0 3m+: 0-0
Track: LH: 0-5 RH: 0-0 Tight: 0-2 Gall: 0-0
Aids: Bl: 0-0 Vi: 0-0 Tstrap: 0-0 Ckp: 0-1
Best Rating: 120 5/01 Font 2m2f110y   gd-fm   Hdl

Moderate hurdler; lightly raced since winning a Fontwell novice hurdle in May 2001; shaped as though he needed a bit further when runner-up in Class F 2m handicap at Worcester July 2003 and looked unlucky next time; acts on a sound surface; has worn blinkers and cheekpieces.

Imperial Sho

74   34

5-y-o ch g Royal Abjar (USA)-Magnetic Point (USA) (Bering)
J R Weymes White Rose Poultry Ltd

Placings:0-0   (4074)
2003/04: 20⁰F,

	Starts	1st	2nd	3rd	Win & Pl
Hurdles	1	0	0	0	
Career Total	2	0	0	0	

Going: Sf: 0-0 GS: 0-0 Gd: 0-0 GF: - Fm: 0-1
Distance: 2m/2m3: 0-0 2m4-2m7: 0-1 3m+: 0-0
Track: LH: 0-0 RH: 0-1 Tight: 0-1 Gall: 0-0
Aids: Bl: 0-0 Vi: 0-0 Tstrap: 0-0 Ckp: 0-0
Best Rating: 33 2/04 Muss 2m4f   firm   Hdl

Imperious Way (GR)

8-y-o b g Wadood (USA)-Pringipessa (GR) (Flash N Thunder (USA))
P R Chamings Mrs Alexandra J Chandris

Placings:P5   (1170)
2003/04: 16^PG, 18⁵GF,

	Starts	1st	2nd	3rd	Win & Pl
Hurdles	2	0	0	0	

Career Total   2   0   0   0   0

Going: Sf: 0-0 GS: 0-0 Gd: 0-0 GF: 0-1 GF: - Fm: 0-1
Distance: 2m/2m3: 0-2 2m4-2m7: 0-0 3m+: 0-0
Track: LH: 0-2 RH: 0-0 Tight: 0-2 Gall: 0-0
Aids: Bl: 0-0 Vi: 0-0 Tstrap: 0-0 Ckp: 0-0

Impero

91   69

6-y-o b g Emperor Jones (USA)-Fight Right (FR) (Crystal Glitters (USA))
W Clay (R J Armson 3/8) B Donkin

Placings:565P0/PPP-00504020   (4441)
2003/04: 16³GF, 16⁰G, 21⁵GF, 24⁰GF, 25⁴F, 16⁰G, 22²G, 21⁰S,

	Starts	1st	2nd	3rd	Win & Pl
Hurdles	8	0	1	0	517
Career Total	16	0	1	0	517

Going: Sf: 0-1 GS: 0-0 Gd: 0-3 GF: - Fm: 0-4
Distance: 2m/2m3: 0-3 2m4-2m7: 0-3 3m+: 0-2
Track: LH: 0-5 RH: 0-2 Tight: 0-1 Gall: 0-1
Aids: Bl: 0-0 Vi: 0-2 Tstrap: 0-0 Ckp: 0-0
Best Rating: 69 11/03 Towc 2m   good   Hdl

Plating-class hurdler; stays two mile six.

Impertio

101   108

10-y-o b g Primitive Rising (USA)-Silly Beggar (Silly Prices)
P Beaumont Mrs S Sunter

Placings:4542/36632633233/422F22331/0322U31U20P/44 03323P-3434   (3878)
2003/04: 25³GS, 24⁴HY, 22³HY, 23⁴G,

	Starts	1st	2nd	3rd	Win & Pl
Chases	4	0	0	2	3121
Career Total	47	2	11	15	36237
114	2/02	Leic	2m7f110yD(0-125)HCh	SFT	£7150
114	4/01	Prth	2m	D Ch	HVY	£3698
				Total win prize-money £10849

Going: Sf: 0-2 GS: 0-1 Gd: 0-1 GF: - Fm: 0-0
Distance: 2m/2m3: 0-0 2m4-2m7: 0-1 3m+: 0-3
Track: LH: 0-3 RH: 0-1 Tight: 0-2 Gall: 0-0
Aids: Bl: 0-0 Vi: 0-0 Tstrap: 0-0 Ckp: 0-0
Best Rating: 114 3/02 Sthl 3m110y   heavy   Ch

Modest chaser; stays three miles; suited by soft ground; does not win very often; likes to be held up.

Impinda (IRE)

98   88

5-y-o b m Idris (IRE)-Last Finale (USA) (Stop The Music (USA))
P Monteith Mrs A F Tullie

Placings:300-243B   (3233)
2003/04: 16²G, 16⁴S, 16³GF, 20^BGF,

	Starts	1st	2nd	3rd	Win & Pl
Hurdles	4	0	1	1	1559
Career Total	7	0	1	2	1937

Going: Sf: 0-1 GS: 0-0 Gd: 0-1 GF: - Fm: 0-2
Distance: 2m/2m3: 0-3 2m4-2m7: 0-1 3m+: 0-0
Track: LH: 0-2 RH: 0-2 Tight: 0-4 Gall: 0-0
Aids: Bl: 0-0 Vi: 0-0 Tstrap: 0-1 Ckp: 0-0
Best Rating: 90 11/03 Kels 2m110y   good   Hdl

Modest form in bumpers; achieved little so far over hurdles despite being placed twice.

Impish Jude

104   **100**

6-y-o b m Imp Society (USA)-Miss Nanna (Vayrann)
J Mackie J W H Fryer

Placings:031020-512462F6   (4883)
2003/04: 16⁵G, 16¹G, 16²S, 16⁴GS, 20⁶S, 16²G, 18ᶠG, 17⁶GS,

	Starts	1st	2nd	3rd	Win & Pl
Hurdles	8	1	2	0	8012
Career Total	14	2	3	1	11449
94 12/03 Leic	2m	E(0-105)HHdl		GD	£3024
100 12/02 Hrfd	2m1f	G Hdl		SFT	£2065

Total win prize-money £5089

Going:	Sf: 0-2 GS: 0-2 Gd: 1-4 GF: - Fm: 0-0
Distance:	2m/2m3: 1-7 2m4-2m7: 0-1 3m+: 0-0
Track:	LH: 0-5 RH: 1-3 Tight: 0-1 Gall: 0-1
Aids:	Bl: 0-0 Vi: 0-0 Tstrap: 0-0 Ckp: 0-1
Best Rating:	100 3/04 Donc 2m110y good Hdl

Moderate hurdler; in good form in late 2003; effective at two miles; handles good and heavy ground.

Important Boy (ARG)

86   **74**

7-y-o ch g Equalize (USA)-Important Girl (ARG) (Candy Stripes (USA))
D D Scott Mrs D D Scott

Placings:0603P-P30P0P0   (4893)
2003/04: 16ᴾGF, 17³GF, 17⁰G, 17ᴾGF, 16⁰GF, 17ᴾS, 16⁰G,

	Starts	1st	2nd	3rd	Win & Pl
Hurdles	7	0	0	1	864
Career Total	12	0	0	2	1298

Going:	Sf: 0-0 GS: 0-0 Gd: 0-3 GF: - Fm: 0-4
Distance:	2m/2m3: 0-7 2m4-2m7: 0-0 3m+: 0-0
Track:	LH: 0-4 RH: 0-3 Tight: 0-3 Gall: 0-0
Aids:	Bl: 0-0 Vi: 0-5 Tstrap: 0-0 Ckp: 0-0
Best Rating:	77 10/02 Winc 2m firm Hdl

Imps Way

9-y-o br m Nomadic Way (USA)-Dalton's Delight (Wonderful Surprise)
Mrs T Corrigan-Clark Mrs T Corrigan-Clark

Placings:P0P/3U3   (4607)
2003/04: 24³S, 25ᵁGF, 25³GS,

	Starts	1st	2nd	3rd	Win & Pl
Chases	3	0	0	2	435
Career Total	6	0	0	2	435

Going:	Sf: 0-1 GS: 0-1 Gd: 0-0 GF: - Fm: 0-1
Distance:	2m/2m3: 0-0 2m4-2m7: 0-0 3m+: 0-3
Track:	LH: 0-1 RH: 0-2 Tight: 0-2 Gall: 0-1
Aids:	Bl: 0-0 Vi: 0-0 Tstrap: 0-0 Ckp: 0-0
Best Rating:	72 2/04 Hntg 3m soft Ch

Modest pointer; well held in novice chases.

Imtihan (IRE)

105   **120**

5-y-o ch h Unfuwain (USA)-Azyaa (Kris)

S C Burrough Mrs Christine Priest

Placings:0051115   (4862)
2003/04: 20⁹GS, 16⁹GS, 16⁵G, 17¹G, 16¹GS, 22¹G, 16⁵GS,

	Starts	1st	2nd	3rd	Win & Pl
Hurdles	7	3	0	0	15859
Career Total	7	3	0	0	15859
116 3/04 Strf	2m6f110yD(0-120)HHdl		GD	£6873
105 3/04 Towc	2m	E(0-110)HHdl	G-S	£3581
102 3/04 Tntn	2m1f	E(0-105)HHdl	GD	£4403

Total win prize-money £14860

Going:	Sf: 0-0 GS: 1-4 Gd: 2-3 GF: - Fm: 0-0
Distance:	2m/2m3: 2-5 2m4-2m7: 1-2 3m+: 0-0
Track:	LH: 1-3 RH: 2-4 Tight: 2-2 Gall: 0-0
Aids:	Bl: 0-0 Vi: 0-0 Tstrap: 0-0 Ckp: 0-0
Best Rating:	120 4/04 Ayr 2m gd-sft Hdl

Modest hurdler; completed a hat-trick in March 2004; stays two miles six and suited by good ground; suited by patient tactics.

In Accord

84f   **100f**

5-y-o ch g Accordion-Henry's True Love (Random Shot)
H D Daly T F F Nixon

Placings:5   (4050)
2003/04: 16⁵G,

	Starts	1st	2nd	3rd	Win & Pl
NH Flat	1	0	0	0	0
Career Total	1	0	0	0	0

Going:	Sf: 0-0 GS: 0-0 Gd: 0-1 GF: - Fm: 0-0
Distance:	2m/2m3: 0-1 2m4-2m7: 0-0 3m+: 0-0
Track:	LH: 0-1 RH: 0-0 Tight: 0-0 Gall: 0-0
Aids:	Bl: 0-0 Vi: 0-0 Tstrap: 0-0 Ckp: 0-0
Best Rating:	99 2/04 Hayd 2m good NHF

Showed ability when fifth on debut in bumper at Haydock in February.

In Contrast (IRE)

111   (0c) **154**

8-y-o b/br g Be My Native (USA)-Ballinamona Lady (IRE) (Le Bavard (FR))
P J Hobbs Tony Staple

Placings:2/2110/211F311/3F3461-3P505   (4644)
2003/04: 16³GS, 17⁵GS, 20⁵G, 17⁹G, 16⁵G,

	Starts	1st	2nd	3rd	Win & Pl
Hurdles	4	0	0	1	10075
Chases	1	0	0	0	0
Career Total	23	7	3	4	138596
153 4/03 Ayr	2m	A HHdl	GD	£24800
144 4/02 Chel	2m5f110yB Hdl		G-F	£19500
151 4/02 Aint	2m110y A Hdl		GD	£29000
137 12/01 Newb	2m110y D Hdl		GD	£4914
117 12/01 Chel	2m1f	B Hdl	GD	£8697
142 11/00 Chel	2m110y B NHF		G-S	£7670
113 10/00 Chel	2m110y H NHF		GD	£2964

Total win prize-money £97545

Going:	Sf: 0-0 GS: 0-2 Gd: 0-3 GF: - Fm: 0-0
Distance:	2m/2m3: 0-4 2m4-2m7: 0-1 3m+: 0-0
Track:	LH: 0-4 RH: 0-0 Tight: 0-3 Gall: 0-1
Aids:	Bl: 0-0 Vi: 0-0 Tstrap: 0-0 Ckp: 0-0
Best Rating:	154 5/03 Hayd 2m gd-sft Hdl

Smart hurdler; a high-class novice in 2001/2 but only win since came in the 2003 Scottish Champion Hurdle at Ayr; effective from 2m to 2m 5f; suffering from hip injury when pulled up after the first on his chasing debut; ran well at

---

Aintree in the spring; does not want the ground too soft; tends to hang left and needs a left-handed track.

In Demand

13-y-o b g Nomination-Romantic Saga (Prince Tenderfoot (USA))
Alan Balmer Alan Balmer

Placings:P/451/P/0-   (0008)
2003/04: 20⁰GF,

	Starts	1st	2nd	3rd	Win & Pl
Chases	1	0	0	0	0
Career Total	6	1	0	0	2160
94 6/99 Hexm	2m4f110yF Hdl		G-F	£2009

Total win prize-money £2010

Going:	Sf: 0-0 GS: 0-0 Gd: 0-0 GF: - Fm: 0-1
Distance:	2m/2m3: 0-0 2m4-2m7: 0-1 3m+: 0-0
Track:	LH: 0-1 RH: 0-0 Tight: 0-0 Gall: 0-1
Aids:	Bl: 0-0 Vi: 0-0 Tstrap: 0-0 Ckp: 0-0
Best Rating:	94 6/99 Hexm 2m4f110y gd-fm Hdl

In Extremis II (FR)

95(105h)   (95h)**80**

8-y-o b g Useful (FR)-Princesa Real (FR) (Garde Royale)
G M Moore Mrs I I Plumb

Placings:25/540P/5P6P0F2/125323220-P2P00P434P   (1604)
2003/04: 25⁵G, 20²G, 20ᴾGF, 27⁰GF, 16⁰G, 20ᴾG, 21⁴G, 21³GF, 21⁴G, 17ᴾGF,

	Starts	1st	2nd	3rd	Win & Pl
Hurdles	2	0	0	0	298
Chases	8	0	1	1	2479
Career Total	32	1	7	3	11326
95 5/02 Sedg	2m5f110yE(0-100)HHdl		G-F	£2632

Total win prize-money £2632

Going:	Sf: 0-0 GS: 0-0 Gd: 0-5 GF: - Fm: 0-5
Distance:	2m/2m3: 0-2 2m4-2m7: 0-6 3m+: 0-2
Track:	LH: 0-9 RH: 0-1 Tight: 0-6 Gall: 0-0
Aids:	Bl: 0-3 Vi: 0-3 Tstrap: 0-0 Ckp: 0-3
Best Rating:	95 10/02 Carl 2m4f gd-fm Hdl

Modest hurdler, stays three miles; best on fast ground.

In For The Craic (IRE)

5-y-o b g Our Emblem (USA)-Lucky State (USA) (State Dinner (USA))
P Butler E H Whatmough

Placings:F   (0433)
2003/04: 18ᶠGF,

	Starts	1st	2nd	3rd	Win & Pl
Hurdles	1	0	0	0	
Career Total	1	0	0	0	

Going:	Sf: 0-0 GS: 0-0 Gd: 0-0 GF: - Fm: 0-1
Distance:	2m/2m3: 0-1 2m4-2m7: 0-0 3m+: 0-0
Track:	LH: 0-1 RH: 0-0 Tight: 0-1 Gall: 0-0
Aids:	Bl: 0-0 Vi: 0-0 Tstrap: 0-0 Ckp: 0-0

In Good Faith

103(98c)   (72c)**91**

12-y-o b g Beveled (USA)-Dulcidene (Behistoun)

R E Barr P Cartmell

Placings:02240/4F/41P5/4110/2323651433116525 64/4351115125P0/055045440650-6153042416445320000 **(4796)**
2003/04: 17⁶S, 17¹G, 16⁵GF, 16³GF, 17⁰G, 22⁴GF, 17²GF, 17⁴GF, 21¹GF, 21⁸G, 20⁴G, 17⁴GF, 21⁵S, 19³GS, 16²G, 19⁰G, 19⁰GF, 17⁰G, 21⁰G,

			Starts	1st	2nd	3rd	Win & Pl
Hurdles			19	2	2	2	7204
Career Total			76	12	8	7	45859

85	9/03	Sedg	2m5f110yF(0-95)HHdl		G-F		£1925
79	5/03	Ctml	2m1f110yG(0-90)HHdl		GD		£2828
129	8/00	Sthl	2m C(0-130)HHdl		G-F		£4793
125	7/00	Uttx	2m C(0-130)HHdl		G-F		£5044
119	6/00	Hexm	2m E(0-115)HHdl		G-F		£2363
117	6/00	Hexm	2m F(0-105)HHdl		G-F		£2187
110	12/99	Hexm	2m D(0-125)HHdl		HVY		£3106
110	11/99	Newc	2m E(0-130)HHdl		GD		£2872
110	10/99	Sthl	2m F(0-110)HHdl		G-S		£2284
104	4/99	Hexm	2m E(0-115)HHdl		G-F		£2586
93	4/99	Sedg	2m1f E(0-115)HHdl		FRM		£2337
95	5/97	Ctml	2m1f110yE Hdl		G-F		£2318
				Total win prize-money			£34649

Going: Sf: 0-1 GS: 0-1 Gd: 1-9 GF: -- Fm: 1-8
Distance: 2m/2m3: 1-13 2m4-2m7: 1-6 3m+: 0-0
Track: LH: 2-19 RH: 0-0 Tight: 2-14 Gall: 0-1
Aids: Bl: 0-0 Vi: 0-0 Tstrap: 0-0 Ckp: 0-0
Best Rating: 129 8/00 Uttx 2m gd-fm Hdl

Plating-class veteran hurdler; stays two miles five but effective over much shorter; has won on heavy but best suited nowadays by fast ground.

In Good Time
73 66
5-y-o b g Classic Cliche (IRE)-Primum Tempus (Primo Dominie)
Mrs S J Smith Billy McCullough

Placings:4P **(2804)**
2003/04: 17⁴GF, 16ᴾS,

	Starts	1st	2nd	3rd	Win & Pl
Hurdles	2	0	0	0	0
Career Total	2	0	0	0	0

Going: Sf: 0-1 GS: 0-0 Gd: 0-0 GF: -- Fm: 0-1
Distance: 2m/2m3: 0-2 2m4-2m7: 0-0 3m+: 0-0
Track: LH: 0-1 RH: 0-1 Tight: 0-0 Gall: 0-0
Aids: Bl: 0-0 Vi: 0-0 Tstrap: 0-0 Ckp: 0-0
Best Rating: 66 10/03 Carl 2m1f gd-fm Hdl

In The Clouds
4-y-o gr g Cloudings (IRE)-Tread Carefully (Sharpo)
T D Easterby Mrs Ian Wills

Placings:P **(2871)**
2003/04: 16ᴾS,

	Starts	1st	2nd	3rd	Win & Pl
Hurdles	1	0	0	0	0
Career Total	1	0	0	0	0

Going: Sf: 0-0 GS: 0-0 Gd: 0-0 GF: -- Fm: 0-0
Distance: 2m/2m3: 0-1 2m4-2m7: 0-0 3m+: 0-0
Track: LH: 0-1 RH: 0-0 Tight: 0-0 Gall: 0-0
Aids: Bl: 0-0 Vi: 0-0 Tstrap: 0-0 Ckp: 0-0

Plating-class maiden on the Flat.

In The Frame (IRE)
112 117+
5-y-o b g Definite Article-Victorian Flower (Tate Gallery (USA))
P J Hobbs The Gascoigne Brookes Partnership

Placings:FP23061 **(4893)**
2003/04: 16⁶G, 16ᴾGF, 17²GS, 16³G, 16⁰G, 17⁶G, 16¹G,

			Starts	1st	2nd	3rd	Win & Pl
Hurdles			7	1	1	1	5171
Career Total			7	1	1	1	5171
117	4/04	Winc	2m	E Hdl		GD	£3563
				Total win prize-money			£3563

Going: Sf: 0-0 GS: 0-1 Gd: 1-5 GF: -- Fm: 0-1
Distance: 2m/2m3: 1-7 2m4-2m7: 0-0 3m+: 0-0
Track: LH: 1-2 RH: 1-5 Tight: 0-0 Gall: 0-1
Aids: Bl: 0-0 Vi: 0-0 Tstrap: 0-0 Ckp: 0-0
Best Rating: 117 4/04 Winc 2m good Hdl

Fair novice hurdler; acts on a sound and easy surface; unlikely to stay beyond two miles.

In The Park (IRE)
7-y-o gr g Roselier (FR)-Gay Seeker (Status Seeker)
Jonjo O'Neill (Miss F M Crowley 13/5) John P McManus

Placings:1P **(3084)**
2003/04: 17¹HY, 22ᴾGS,

			Starts	1st	2nd	3rd	Win & Pl
NH Flat			1	1	0	0	4032
Hurdles			1	0	0	0	0
Career Total			2	1	0	0	4032
108	5/03	Klny	2m1f	NHF		HVY	£4032
				Total win prize-money			£4032

Going: Sf: 1-1 GS: 0-1 Gd: 0-0 GF: -- Fm: 0-0
Distance: 2m/2m3: 1-1 2m4-2m7: 0-1 3m+: 0-0
Track: LH: 0-1 RH: 0-0 Tight: 0-1 Gall: 0-0
Aids: Bl: 0-0 Vi: 0-0 Tstrap: 0-0 Ckp: 0-0
Best Rating: 108 5/03 Klny 2m1f heavy NHF

Won heavy ground bumper at Killarney May 2003; favourite when pulled up in 2m 6f maiden hurdle at Stratford in December.

In The Rough (IRE)
104(103h) 101
13-y-o b g Strong Gale-Cherry Dawn (Pollerton)
J A B Old Mrs L R Lovell

Placings:1/4/0U/214/1531F/13U62/20-5 **(0105)**
2003/04: 24⁵HY,

			Starts	1st	2nd	3rd	Win & Pl
Chases			1	0	0	0	518
Career Total			20	5	3	2	27488
117	11/01	NAbb	3m2f110yC(0-130)HCh		GD		£5944
112	2/01	Weth	3m1f C(0-130)HHdl		SFT		£5411
103	5/00	Towc	3m D Hdl		SFT		£3009
124	3/00	Chep	2m3f110yD Ch		G-S		£3737
93	3/96	Ludl	2m H NHF		GD		£1346
				Total win prize-money			£19451

Going: Sf: 0-1 GS: 0-0 Gd: 0-0 GF: -- Fm: 0-0
Distance: 2m/2m3: 0-0 2m4-2m7: 0-0 3m+: 0-1
Track: LH: 0-1 RH: 0-0 Tight: 0-0 Gall: 0-0
Aids: Bl: 0-0 Vi: 0-0 Tstrap: 0-0 Ckp: 0-0
Best Rating: 124 3/00 Chep 2m3f110y gd-sft Ch

Moderate chaser; stays three and a quarter miles; acts on soft ground, but handles good.

In The Stars (IRE)
96(97h) (95h)87+
6-y-o ch g Definite Article-Astronomer Lady (IRE) (Montekin)
P R Webber The Fancy Colours Partnership

Placings:425643 **(4751)**
2003/04: 16⁴GS, 17²GF, 17⁵GS, 16⁶G, 16⁴GS, 17³G,

	Starts	1st	2nd	3rd	Win & Pl
Hurdles	4	0	1	0	1372
Chases	2	0	0	1	965
Career Total	6	0	1	1	2337

Going: Sf: 0-0 GS: 0-3 Gd: 0-2 GF: -- Fm: 0-1
Distance: 2m/2m3: 0-6 2m4-2m7: 0-0 3m+: 0-0
Track: LH: 0-3 RH: 0-3 Tight: 0-4 Gall: 0-0
Aids: Bl: 0-0 Vi: 0-1 Tstrap: 0-0 Ckp: 0-2
Best Rating: 95 11/03 Uttx 2m gd-sft Hdl

Plating-class chaser/hurdler; acts on any ground.

In Tune
4-y-o b g Distinctly North (USA)-Lingering (Kind Of Hush)
S C Burrough Hill, Kemp and Hill

Placings:P **(4440)**
2003/04: 16ᴾGS,

	Starts	1st	2nd	3rd	Win & Pl
Hurdles	1	0	0	0	0
Career Total	1	0	0	0	0

Going: Sf: 0-0 GS: 0-1 Gd: 0-0 GF: -- Fm: 0-0
Distance: 2m/2m3: 0-1 2m4-2m7: 0-0 3m+: 0-0
Track: LH: 0-1 RH: 0-0 Tight: 0-1 Gall: 0-0
Aids: Bl: 0-0 Vi: 0-0 Tstrap: 0-0 Ckp: 0-0

Inagh Road (IRE)
88 75
9-y-o b g Broken Hearted-Fiodoir (Weavers Hall)
B N Pollock Oasby Racing

Placings:500/0-0U3P60 **(1309)**
2003/04: 17⁰G, 16ᵁGF, 16³G, 16ᴾGF, 17⁶GF, 16⁰GF,

	Starts	1st	2nd	3rd	Win & Pl
Hurdles	6	0	0	1	524
Career Total	10	0	0	1	524

Going: Sf: 0-0 GS: 0-0 Gd: 0-2 GF: -- Fm: 0-4
Distance: 2m/2m3: 0-6 2m4-2m7: 0-0 3m+: 0-0
Track: LH: 0-5 RH: 0-1 Tight: 0-1 Gall: 0-0
Aids: Bl: 0-1 Vi: 0-0 Tstrap: 0-0 Ckp: 0-3
Best Rating: 102 1/00 Kemp 2m good NHF

Plating-class hurdler; showed marked improvement when 50/1 third in 2m novice hurdle at Worcester on first run in cheekpieces July 2003.

Inaki (FR)
100 113+
7-y-o b g Dounba (FR)-Incredue (FR) (Concertino (FR))
P Winkworth Robert Scott & Partners

Placings:P0P046F13F00F/005F43444/561522-31 **(3201)**
2003/04: 20³S, 17¹S,

			Starts	1st	2nd	3rd	Win & Pl
Chases			2	1	0	1	6036
Career Total			30	3	2	3	24760
113	1/04	Plum	2m1f	D(0-120)HCh		SFT	£5411

105	1/03	Plum	2m4f	E(0-105)HCh	SFT	£4065
	1/01	Pau	2m1f	Ch	HLD	£3880
				Total win prize-money £13357		

Going:	Sf: 1-2 GS: 0-0 Gd: 0-0 GF: - Fm: 0-0
Distance:	2m/2m3: 1-1 2m4-2m7: 0-0 3m+: 0-0
Track:	LH: 1-2 RH: 0-0 Tight: 1-2 Gall: 0-0
Aids:	Bl: 0-0 Vi: 1-1 Tstrap: 0-0 Ckp: 0-0
Best Rating:	113 1/04 Plum 2m1f soft Ch

Moderate chaser; effective around two and a half miles; acts on soft ground; has worn visor.

Inca Moon

4-y-o b f Sheikh Albadou-Incatinka (Inca Chief (USA))
R Brotherton The Joiners Arms Racing Club Quarndon

Placings: P   (1926)
2003/04: 16PGF,

	Starts	1st	2nd	3rd	Win & Pl
Hurdles	1	0	0	0	
Career Total	1	0	0	0	

Going:	Sf: 0-0 GS: 0-0 Gd: 0-0 GF: - Fm: 0-1
Distance:	2m/2m3: 0-1 2m4-2m7: 0-0 3m+: 0-0
Track:	LH: 0-1 RH: 0-0 Tight: 0-0 Gall: 0-0
Aids:	Bl: 0-0 Vi: 0-0 Tstrap: 0-0 Ckp: 0-0

Inca Trail (IRE)

107(102c)   (111c)**138+**
8-y-o br g Un Desperado (FR)-Katday (FR) (Miller's Mate)
Miss H C Knight Philip F Myerscough

Placings: 1/3210P-2P100   (4628)
2003/04: 16PGF, 20PGS, 22 1G, 21 0G, 20 0G,

	Starts	1st	2nd	3rd	Win & Pl
Hurdles	3	1	0	0	19018
Chases	2	0	1	0	1351
Career Total	11	3	2	1	31705
139	2/04	Winc	2m6f	C(0-135)HHdl	GD	£19018
115	1/03	Ludl	2m5f	E Hdl	SFT	£3737
120	1/02	Naas	2m	NHF	YLD	£3809
				Total win prize-money £26566		

Going:	Sf: 0-0 GS: 0-1 Gd: 1-3 GF: - Fm: 0-0
Distance:	2m/2m3: 0-1 2m4-2m7: 1-1 3m+: 0-0
Track:	LH: 0-2 RH: 1-3 Tight: 0-0 Gall: 0-3
Aids:	Bl: 0-0 Vi: 0-0 Tstrap: 1-3 Ckp: 0-0
Best Rating:	139 2/04 Winc 2m6f good Hdl

Full brother to Best Mate; useful bumper and hurdles winner, but disappointed over fences; bounced back to form when winning at Wincanton; stays 2m 6f; acts on good ground but also effective with some cut.

Inch Island (IRE)

95   **87**
4-y-o b g Turtle Island (IRE)-Persian Light (IRE) (Persian Heights)
J J Quinn Birdstown Syndicate

Placings: F02P   (4187)
2003/04: 16FG, 16 0GS, 16 2S, 16 PGS,

	Starts	1st	2nd	3rd	Win & Pl
Hurdles	4	0	1	0	1128
Career Total	4	0	1	0	1128

| **Going:** | Sf: 0-1 GS: 0-2 Gd: 0-1 GF: - Fm: 0-0 |
| **Distance:** | 2m/2m3: 0-4 2m4-2m7: 0-0 3m+: 0-0 |

Track:	LH: 0-4 RH: 0-0 Tight: 0-3 Gall: 0-0
Aids:	Bl: 0-0 Vi: 0-0 Tstrap: 0-0 Ckp: 0-0
Best Rating:	87 1/04 Kels 2m110y soft Hdl

Has shown ability over hurdles but there is plenty of room for improvement in his jumping technique and he will have to settle better if he is to progress in this sphere.

Inch'Allah (FR)

95   **98**
8-y-o b g Royal Charter (FR)-Cadoudaline (FR) (Cadoudal (FR))
Mrs J Candlish N M Wynne

Placings: 6/54P6   (2943)
2003/04: 17 5G, 20 4GS, 20 PS, 16 PGS,

	Starts	1st	2nd	3rd	Win & Pl
Hurdles	4	0	0	0	281
Career Total	5	0	0	0	281

Going:	Sf: 0-1 GS: 0-2 Gd: 0-1 GF: - Fm: 0-0
Distance:	2m/2m3: 0-2 2m4-2m7: 0-1 3m+: 0-0
Track:	LH: 0-4 RH: 0-0 Tight: 0-1 Gall: 0-0
Aids:	Bl: 0-0 Vi: 0-0 Tstrap: 0-0 Ckp: 0-0
Best Rating:	99 12/01 Leop 2m yield NHF

Inching Closer

97(111h)   (149h)**127+**
7-y-o b g Inchinor-Maiyaasah (Kris)
J Howard Johnson (Jonjo O'Neill 18/11) Andrea & Graham Wylie

Placings: 6/14010/110-21P00   (4386)
2003/04: 22 2GS, 24 1GS, 23 PS, 23 0S, 25 0G,

	Starts	1st	2nd	3rd	Win & Pl
Hurdles	2	0	0	0	0
Chases	3	1	1	0	3728
Career Total	14	5	1	0	51337
115	12/03	Newc	3m	E Ch	G-S	£2886
149	3/03	Chel	3m1f110yA HHdl	GD	£34800
140	2/03	Hayd	2m4f	C(0-130)HHdl	G-S	£6890
129	3/02	Sedg	3m3f110yD(0-130)HHdl	SFT	£3265
117	11/01	Uttx	2m6f110yE Hdl	SFT	£2653
				Total win prize-money £50495		

Going:	Sf: 0-2 GS: 1-2 Gd: 0-1 GF: - Fm: 0-0
Distance:	2m/2m3: 0-0 2m4-2m7: 0-1 3m+: 1-4
Track:	LH: 1-3 RH: 0-1 Tight: 0-0 Gall: 1-2
Aids:	Bl: 1-3 Vi: 0-0 Tstrap: 0m1f110y 0-0
Best Rating:	149 3/03 Chel 3m1f110y good Hdl

Useful novice chaser; very useful hurdler; narrow winner of the Pertemps Final at the Cheltenham Festival in March 2003; opened account over fences at the second time of asking at Newcastle in December 2003 wearing first-time blinkers; found nothing and pulled up next time; effective from two miles four to three miles one; acts on good ground or softer.

Inchinnan

100   **97**
7-y-o b m Inchinor-Westering (Auction Ring (USA))
C Weedon Bill Hinge

Placings: 043U/43035   (3791)
2003/04: 16 4GF, 16 2GF, 16 0G, 16 3S, 16 0G,

	Starts	1st	2nd	3rd	Win & Pl
Hurdles	5	0	0	2	1099
Career Total	9	0	0	3	1468

Going:	Sf: 0-1 GS: 0-0 Gd: 0-2 GF: - Fm: 0-2
Distance:	2m/2m3: 0-2 2m4-2m7: 0-0 3m+: 0-0
Track:	LH: 0-2 RH: 0-3 Tight: 0-0 Gall: 0-1
Aids:	Bl: 0-0 Vi: 0-0 Tstrap: 0-0 Ckp: 0-0
Best Rating:	99 1/02 Tntn 2m1f soft Hdl

Moderate hurdler; lightly raced; suited by soft ground; best at two miles.

Indeed (IRE)

105(103c)   (121c)**116+**
9-y-o ch g Camden Town-Pamrina (Pamroy)
N J Gifford Pell-Mell Partners

Placings: 4F1/0F22-FF006   (4963)
2003/04: 25 FGS, 24 FS, 22 2G, 22 0G, 20 6G,

	Starts	1st	2nd	3rd	Win & Pl
Hurdles	3	0	0	0	412
Chases	2	0	0	0	0
Career Total	12	1	2	0	8692
109	3/02	Sand	2m4f110yD Hdl	G-S	£4309
				Total win prize-money £4310		

Going:	Sf: 0-1 GS: 0-1 Gd: 0-3 GF: - Fm: 0-0
Distance:	2m/2m3: 0-2 2m4-2m7: 0-3 3m+: 0-2
Track:	LH: 0-0 RH: 0-5 Tight: 0-1 Gall: 0-1
Aids:	Bl: 0-0 Vi: 0-0 Tstrap: 0-1 Ckp: 0-0
Best Rating:	121 2/03 Kemp 2m4f110y gd-sft Ch

Fair hurdler/chaser; effective at around two and a half miles; acts on easy ground.

Indeed To Goodness (IRE)

104(106h)   (108+h)**119**
9-y-o b m Welsh Term-Clare's Sheen (Choral Society)
J W Mullins Ian M McGready

Placings: 0/433P43/013U3106/321UF3P-234056   (4715)
2003/04: 22 2S, 24 3S, 24 4S, 24 0S, 26 5G, 20 6G,

	Starts	1st	2nd	3rd	Win & Pl
Hurdles	1	0	0	1	864
Chases	5	0	0	1	1484
Career Total	28	3	2	8	22830
110	11/02	Plum	3m2f	D Ch	SFT	£5476
105	2/02	Kemp	2m5f	B HHdl	SFT	£6955
102	10/01	Font	2m6f110yE Hdl	G-S	£2513
				Total win prize-money £14944		

Going:	Sf: 0-4 GS: 0-0 Gd: 0-2 GF: - Fm: 0-0
Distance:	2m/2m3: 0-0 2m4-2m7: 0-2 3m+: 0-4
Track:	LH: 0-4 RH: 0-2 Tight: 0-2 Gall: 0-1
Aids:	Bl: 0-0 Vi: 0-0 Tstrap: 0-0 Ckp: 0-0
Best Rating:	119 11/03 Towc 2m6f soft Ch

Fair hurdler/novice chaser; stays three miles two; acts on soft ground; seemingly lost confidence over fences due to jumping errors.

Indestructible (FR)

90   **72+**
5-y-o b g Hero's Honor (USA)-Money Bag (FR) (Badayoun)
M Bradstock The United Front Partnership

Placings: FP0   (4145)
2003/04: 16 FGS, 22 PHY, 19 0G,

	Starts	1st	2nd	3rd	Win & Pl
NH Flat	1	0	0	0	0
Hurdles	2	0	0	0	0
Career Total	3	0	0	0	

Going: Sf: 0-1 GS: 0-1 Gd: 0-1 GF: - Fm: 0-0
Distance: 2m/2m3: 0-1 2m4-2m7: 0-2 3m+: 0-0
Track: LH: 0-2 RH: 0-1 Tight: 0-1 Gall: 0-0
Aids: Bl: 0-0 Vi: 0-0 Tstrap: 0-0 Ckp: 0-0
Best Rating: 72　3/04　Tntn　2m3f110y　good　Hdl

Indian Beat

105　　　　　　　　　　76

7-y-o ch g Indian Ridge-Rappa Tap Tap (FR) (Tap On Wood)
C L Popham　Mrs C R Hayton

Placings:0/5P-5P04340325　　　　　　　(2699)
2003/04: 17⁵GF, 16⁵G, 16⁰GF, 16⁴GF, 17³F, 19⁴GF, 19⁰G, 21³GF, 19²GF, 19⁵G,

	Starts	1st	2nd	3rd	Win & Pl
Hurdles	10	0	1	2	2077
Career Total	13	0	1	2	2077

Going: Sf: 0-0 GS: 0-0 Gd: 0-3 GF: - Fm: 0-7
Distance: 2m/2m3: 0-6 2m4-2m7: 0-4 3m+: 0-0
Track: LH: 0-4 RH: 0-5 Tight: 0-4 Gall: 0-0
Aids: Bl: 0-1 Vi: 0-0 Tstrap: 0-0 Ckp: 0-0
Best Rating: 76　12/03　Tntn　2m3f110y　good　Hdl

Plating-class maiden hurdler; stays 2m4f; acts on good ground.

Indian Chance

107　　　　　　　　　　123

10-y-o b g Teenoso (USA)-Icy Miss (Random Shot)
Dr J R J Naylor　Chris And Stella Watson And Jock Cullen

Placings:00/3F61311/P46-411　　　　　(2956)
2003/04: 24⁴S, 25¹G, 25¹G,

	Starts	1st	2nd	3rd	Win & Pl
Chases	3	2	0	0	13515
Career Total	15	5	0	2	29073
123	12/03	Winc	3m1f110yD(0-125)HCh	GD	£6968
123	12/03	Winc	3m1f110yD(0-120)HCh	GD	£5492
120	4/02	Towc	3m1f	D(0-115)HCh	G-S	£4221
115	3/02	Winc	3m1f110yE(0-110)HCh	SFT	£5375
106	2/02	Leic	2m7f110yE(0-105)HCh	SFT	£3263
			Total win prize-money		£25322

Going: Sf: 0-1 GS: 0-0 Gd: 2-2 GF: - Fm: 0-0
Distance: 2m/2m3: 0-0 2m4-2m7: 0-0 3m+: 2-3
Track: LH: 0-0 RH: 2-3 Tight: 0-0 Gall: 0-0
Aids: Bl: 0-0 Vi: 0-0 Tstrap: 0-0 Ckp: 0-0
Best Rating: 123　12/03　Winc　3m1f110y　good　Ch

Modest staying chaser; gets beyond three miles; acts on good and soft ground.

Indian Chase

87　　　　　　　　　　33

7-y-o b g Terimon-Icy Gunner (Gunner B)
Dr J R J Naylor　The Indian Chase Partnership

Placings:0023PPPFR0　　　　　　　　(4234)
2003/04: 17⁰GF, 16⁰GF, 18²GF, 17³GF, 17⁶G, 21⁵S, 22⁰GS, 23⁶G, 20⁶GF, 22⁰GF,

	Starts	1st	2nd	3rd	Win & Pl
NH Flat	4	0	1	1	947
Hurdles	4	0	0	0	0
Chases	2	0	0	0	0
Career Total	10	0	1	1	947

Going: Sf: 0-1 GS: 0-1 Gd: 0-2 GF: - Fm: 0-6
Distance: 2m/2m3: 0-5 2m4-2m7: 0-4 3m+: 0-1

Track: LH: 0-6 RH: 0-4 Tight: 0-6 Gall: 0-0
Aids: Bl: 0-0 Vi: 0-0 Tstrap: 0-0 Ckp: 0-0
Best Rating: 80　9/03　NAbb　2m1f　gd-fm　NHF

Indian Laburnum (IRE)

97　　　　　　　　　　88+

7-y-o b g Alphabatim (USA)-St.Cristoph (The Parson)
C C Bealby　Mrs Joan Martin

Placings:P54424　　　　　　　　　(4757)
2003/04: 21⁸S, 24⁵G, 24⁴S, 25⁴GS, 25²GS, 25⁴S,

	Starts	1st	2nd	3rd	Win & Pl
Hurdles	1	0	0	0	0
Chases	5	0	1	0	1855
Career Total	6	0	1	0	1855

Going: Sf: 0-3 GS: 0-2 Gd: 0-1 GF: - Fm: 0-0
Distance: 2m/2m3: 0-0 2m4-2m7: 0-1 3m+: 0-5
Track: LH: 0-2 RH: 0-4 Tight: 0-5 Gall: 0-1
Aids: Bl: 0-0 Vi: 0-0 Tstrap: 0-0 Ckp: 0-0
Best Rating: 88　3/04　Weth　3m1f　gd-sft　Ch

Moderate novice chaser; best effort when runner-up at Wetherby in March; stays three miles.

Indian Scout (IRE)

108　　　　　　　　　　136

9-y-o b g Phardante (FR)-Kemchee (Kemal (FR))
B De Haan　Indian Scout Partnership

Placings:51U11P/12F-3FP　　　　　(4568)
2003/04: 25³G, 20⁶GS, 20⁶GS,

	Starts	1st	2nd	3rd	Win & Pl
Chases	3	0	0	1	1080
Career Total	12	4	1	1	36556
136	11/02	Hayd	2m4f	B Ch	GD	£16477
131	2/01	Uttx	2m4f110yA Hdl	HVY	£12000
131	1/01	Leic	2m4f110yE Hdl	HVY	£3272
109	12/00	Extr	2m1f	E Hdl	HVY	£2275
			Total win prize-money		£34026

Going: Sf: 0-0 GS: 0-2 Gd: 0-1 GF: - Fm: 0-0
Distance: 2m/2m3: 0-0 2m4-2m7: 0-2 3m+: 0-1
Track: LH: 0-3 RH: 0-0 Tight: 0-0 Gall: 0-1
Aids: Bl: 0-0 Vi: 0-0 Tstrap: 0-0 Ckp: 0-0
Best Rating: 136　11/02　Hayd　2m4f　good　Ch

Useful chaser; formerly very useful novice hurdler; in front when taking a heavy fall in the 2003 Tripleprint Gold Cup; best over two and a half miles, but stays further; acts on good ground, but effective on softer; likes to race prominently.

Indian Solitaire (IRE)

101　　　　　　　　　　95

5-y-o b g Bigstone (IRE)-Terrama Sioux (Relkino)
R A Fahey　P D Smith Holdings Ltd

Placings:535042　　　　　　　　　(3760)
2003/04: 16⁵GS, 17³HY, 16⁵G, 16⁰GS, 16⁴HY, 17²GS,

	Starts	1st	2nd	3rd	Win & Pl
Hurdles	6	0	1	1	1443
Career Total	6	0	1	1	1443

Going: Sf: 0-2 GS: 0-3 Gd: 0-1 GF: - Fm: 0-0
Distance: 2m/2m3: 0-6 2m4-2m7: 0-0 3m+: 0-0
Track: LH: 0-5 RH: 0-1 Tight: 0-1 Gall: 0-1

Aids: Bl: 0-0 Vi: 0-0 Tstrap: 0-0 Ckp: 0-0
Best Rating: 95　2/04　Sedg　2m1f　gd-sft　Hdl

Moderate novice hurdler; fair on the Flat; ordinary form so far; will be suited by two and a half miles; acts in heavy ground.

Indian Star (GER)

103　　　　　　　　　　87+

6-y-o br g Sternkoenig (IRE)-Indian Night (GER) (Windwurf (GER))
J C Tuck　D J Neale

Placings:001-036000　　　　　　　(3050)
2003/04: 19⁹G, 17³GF, 17⁶GF, 17⁰G, 16⁹GF, 17⁰G,

	Starts	1st	2nd	3rd	Win & Pl
Hurdles	6	0	0	1	625
Career Total	9	1	0	1	3635
87	4/03	Strf	2m3f	F Hdl	G-F	£3010
			Total win prize-money		£3010

Going: Sf: 0-0 GS: 0-0 Gd: 0-3 GF: - Fm: 0-3
Distance: 2m/2m3: 0-6 2m4-2m7: 0-0 3m+: 0-0
Track: LH: 0-4 RH: 0-2 Tight: 0-4 Gall: 0-0
Aids: Bl: 0-0 Vi: 0-0 Tstrap: 0-0 Ckp: 0-0
Best Rating: 87　8/03　NAbb　2m1f　gd-fm　Hdl

Plating-class hurdler; fortunate winner at Stratford in April 2003; acts on fast ground; stays two miles three.

Indian Sun

105　　　　　　　　　　102

7-y-o ch g Indian Ridge-Star Tulip (Night Shift (USA))
Mrs A M Thorpe (R L Brown 24/3)　Mrs A M Thorpe

Placings:0/00P25F1-0060P22555110　　(4890)
2003/04: 17⁰GS, 19⁹GS, 16⁶GF, 16⁹G, 22⁸GF, 16²GS, 16²GS, 16⁵G, 19⁵HY, 16⁵GF, 16¹GS, 17¹G, 19⁰GF,

	Starts	1st	2nd	3rd	Win & Pl
Hurdles	13	2	2	0	8847
Career Total	21	3	3	0	12681
102	4/04	NAbb	2m1f	D(0-115)HHdl	GD	£4901
102	3/04	Chep	2m110y	G Hdl	G-S	£2352
77	4/03	Ludl	2m	G Hdl	GD	£3250
			Total win prize-money		£10503

Going: Sf: 0-1 GS: 1-4 Gd: 1-4 GF: - Fm: 0-4
Distance: 2m/2m3: 2-10 2m4-2m7: 0-3 3m+: 0-0
Track: LH: 2-8 RH: 0-5 Tight: 1-4 Gall: 0-0
Aids: Bl: 0-1 Vi: 0-0 Tstrap: 1-12 Ckp: 0-0
Best Rating: 102　4/04　NAbb　2m1f　good　Hdl

Moderate hurdler; won his first race for some time when scoring at Ludlow April 2003; gained due reward for some sound efforts when winning twice in spring 2004; acts on ground good and softer.

Indian Venture (IRE)

102　　　　　　　(116h)118

10-y-o b g Commanche Run-Believe It Or Not (Quayside)
N G Richards　Dr K S Fraser & Ashleybank Investments

Placings:10/0/31102321/4F42511-2　　(0255)
2003/04: 16²G,

	Starts	1st	2nd	3rd	Win & Pl
Chases	1	0	0	0	2490
Career Total	19	6	4	2	30523
110	4/03	MRas	2m1f110yD Ch	GD	£5414
110	3/03	Sedg	2m110y E Ch	GD	£4046
116	4/02	Prth	2m110y D(0-120)HHdl	GD	£5746
105	11/01	Kels	2m2f	F(0-110)HHdl	GD	£2257

96	10/01	Carl	2m1f	E Hdl		G-S	£2654
105	12/99	Muss	2m	H NHF		G-S	£1576

Total win prize-money £21695

Going: Sf: 0-0 GS: 0-0 Gd: 0-1 GF: - Fm: 0-0
Distance: 2m/2m3: 0-1 2m4-2m7: 0-0 3m+: 0-0
Track: LH: 0-0 RH: 0-1 Tight: 0-0 Gall: 0-0
Aids: Bl: 0-0 Vi: 0-0 Tstrap: 0-0 Ckp: 0-0
Best Rating: 118 5/03 Prth 2m good Ch

Fair chaser/hurdler; has done well in modest handicap hurdles in the north; struggling to make an impact over fences so far; suited by two miles and the ground good or slightly softer.

Indian Viceroy

11-y-o b g Lord Bud-Poppadom (Rapid River)
R T Phillips Bill Naylor

Placings:0600000/04600/036/213/RU5/P0P-FP (2515)
2003/04: 16FGS, 19PGS,

	Starts	1st	2nd	3rd	Win & Pl
Chases	2	0	0	0	
Career Total	26	1	1	2	4759
90	11/00	Hntg	2m4f110yF(0-110)HCh	G-S	£2834

Total win prize-money £2834

Going: Sf: 0-0 GS: 0-2 Gd: 0-0 GF: - Fm: 0-0
Distance: 2m/2m3: 0-1 2m4-2m7: 0-0 3m+: 0-0
Track: LH: 0-0 RH: 0-2 Tight: 0-0 Gall: 0-0
Aids: Bl: 0-0 Vi: 0-0 Tstrap: 0-0 Ckp: 0-0
Best Rating: 90 11/00 Hntg 2m4f110y gd-sft Ch

Indien Du Boulay (FR)

8-y-o ch g Chef De Clan Ii (FR)-Radesgirl (FR) (Radetzky Marsch (USA))
Major General C A Ramsay (P Monteith 15/5) Major General C A Ramsay

Placings:6/21112F3/4F3410P-PP534 (4689)
2003/04: 22PG, 24PG, 24SF, 24³G, 25⁴G,

	Starts	1st	2nd	3rd	Win & Pl
Chases	5	0	0	1	840
Career Total	20	4	2	3	26009
116	12/02	Muss	3m	D(0-120)HCh	G-S	£10036
114	11/01	Ayr	2m	D Ch	GD	£4127
102	5/01	Newc	2m4f	E Hdl	G-F	£2894
100	5/01	Prth	2m4f110yE Hdl	G-S	£3241

Total win prize-money £20300

Going: Sf: 0-0 GS: 0-0 Gd: 0-4 GF: - Fm: 0-1
Distance: 2m/2m3: 0-0 2m4-2m7: 0-1 3m+: 0-4
Track: LH: 0-2 RH: 0-3 Tight: 0-3 Gall: 0-0
Aids: Bl: 0-1 Vi: 0-0 Tstrap: 0-0 Ckp: 0-1
Best Rating: 116 12/02 Muss 3m gd-sft Ch

Hunter chaser, stays two and a half miles and is suited by a sound surface; has worn blinkers.

Indigo Beach (IRE) 93

8-y-o b g Rainbows For Life (CAN)-Sandy Maid (Sandy Creek)
G J Smith Graham Smith

Placings:P224/303004/0155/011-PP (1844)
2003/04: 17PG, 16PG,

	Starts	1st	2nd	3rd	Win & Pl
Hurdles	2	0	0	0	
Career Total	19	3	2	2	7616
93	5/02	Fknm	2m	G(0-90)HHdl	GD	£1971
92	5/02	Fknm	2m	G Hdl	GD	£1615
70	4/02	Fknm	2m	G(0-90)HHdl	GD	£1887

Total win prize-money £5475

Going: Sf: 0-0 GS: 0-0 Gd: 0-1 GF: - Fm: 0-1
Distance: 2m/2m3: 0-1 2m4-2m7: 0-0 3m+: 0-0
Track: LH: 0-1 RH: 0-0 Tight: 0-2 Gall: 0-0
Aids: Bl: 0-1 Vi: 0-0 Tstrap: 0-1 Ckp: 0-0
Best Rating: 103 10/00 Font 2m4f good Hdl

Selling grade hurdler; acts on a sound surface and is effective at around two miles.

Indiscret (FR) 109 81

8-y-o b g Garde Royale-Please (FR) (Le Pontet (FR))
F Jordan Tony Cocum, Mark Doyle, Stephen Green

Placings:60P4/F6FF3U01-52 (2382)
2003/04: 21⁵GF, 26²GF,

	Starts	1st	2nd	3rd	Win & Pl
Chases	2	0	1	0	860
Career Total	14	1	1	4	5535
81	3/03	Wwck	3m110y F(0-95)HCh	G-F	£3630

Total win prize-money £3630

Going: Sf: 0-0 GS: 0-0 Gd: 0-0 GF: - Fm: 0-2
Distance: 2m/2m3: 0-0 2m4-2m7: 0-1 3m+: 0-1
Track: LH: 0-2 RH: 0-0 Tight: 0-1 Gall: 0-0
Aids: Bl: 0-0 Vi: 0-0 Tstrap: 0-0 Ckp: 0-0
Best Rating: 81 11/03 Wwck 3m2f gd-fm Ch

Plating-class chaser; stays three miles two; effective on good and fast ground.

Indoux (FR) 92 (81c) (78c) 94

8-y-o b g Useful (FR)-Pin'Hup (FR) (Signani (FR))
R J Hodges Frank E Crumpler

Placings:300/5/6010016P-FP4506PPF (4290)
2003/04: 26⁶G, 23⁰G, 19⁴G, 25⁵GS, 26⁰S, 24⁶S, 24PG, 19⁰G, 22⁰G,

	Starts	1st	2nd	3rd	Win & Pl
Hurdles	4	0	0	0	0
Chases	5	0	0	0	220
Career Total	21	2	0	1	8536
94	2/03	Sand	2m4f110yD(0-110)HHdl	HVY	£5346
94	12/02	Extr	2m3f	F(0-95)HHdl	SFT	£2754

Total win prize-money £8101

Going: Sf: 0-2 GS: 0-2 Gd: 0-5 GF: - Fm: 0-0
Distance: 2m/2m3: 0-2 2m4-2m7: 0-1 3m+: 0-6
Track: LH: 0-2 RH: 0-7 Tight: 0-4 Gall: 0-0
Aids: Bl: 0-3 Vi: 0-0 Tstrap: 0-0 Ckp: 0-0
Best Rating: 94 2/03 Sand 2m4f110y heavy Hdl

Modest hurdler/chaser; has twice won this season at double figure odds; stays two and a half miles; acts well in soft ground.

Indulgent Way (IRE) 79 48

13-y-o gr g Roselier (FR)-Glenmore Lady (Stetchworth (USA))
A P Jones Mrs T Lewis

Placings:000F/0P/50235/0/600 (3753)
2003/04: 26⁶S, 21⁰GS, 22⁰GS,

	Starts	1st	2nd	3rd	Win & Pl
Chases	3	0	0	0	0
Career Total	15	0	1	1	1690

Going: Sf: 0-1 GS: 0-2 Gd: 0-0 GF: - Fm: 0-0
Distance: 2m/2m3: 0-0 2m4-2m7: 0-2 3m+: 0-1
Track: LH: 0-1 RH: 0-1 Tight: 0-3 Gall: 0-0
Aids: Bl: 0-1 Vi: 0-0 Tstrap: 0-0 Ckp: 0-0
Best Rating: 78 10/97 Navn 2m gd-yld Hdl

Indy Mood 97f 95f

5-y-o ch g Endoli (USA)-Amanta (IRE) (Electric)
Mrs H O Graham R D Graham

Placings:0516 (3495)
2003/04: 16⁰G, 16⁵S, 16¹GS, 16⁰HY,

	Starts	1st	2nd	3rd	Win & Pl
NH Flat	4	1	0	0	1659
Career Total	4	1	0	0	1659
95	12/03	Newc	2m	H NHF	G-S	£1659

Total win prize-money £1659

Going: Sf: 0-2 GS: 1-1 Gd: 0-1 GF: - Fm: 0-0
Distance: 2m/2m3: 1-4 2m4-2m7: 0-0 3m+: 0-0
Track: LH: 1-4 RH: 0-0 Tight: 0-0 Gall: 0-0
Aids: Bl: 0-0 Vi: 0-0 Tstrap: 0-0 Ckp: 0-0
Best Rating: 95 12/03 Newc 2m gd-sft NHF

Progressive form in bumpers and opened account at Newcastle in December; will be suited by a good test over hurdles.

Infamelia

8-y-o b m Infantry-Incamelia (St Columbus)
Miss Tessa Clark Miss Tessa Clark

Placings:0000P/0-P (4373)
2003/04: 24PG,

	Starts	1st	2nd	3rd	Win & Pl
Chases	1	0	0	0	
Career Total	7	0	0	0	

Going: Sf: 0-0 GS: 0-0 Gd: 0-1 GF: - Fm: 0-0
Distance: 2m/2m3: 0-0 2m4-2m7: 0-0 3m+: 0-1
Track: LH: 0-1 RH: 0-0 Tight: 0-1 Gall: 0-0
Aids: Bl: 0-0 Vi: 0-1 Tstrap: 0-0 Ckp: 0-0
Best Rating: 88 5/01 Folk 2m1f110y gd-sft NHF

Infinite Risk 85 71

5-y-o gr g Vettori (IRE)-Dolly Bevan (Another Realm)
N J Hawke Mrs D Horton

Placings:0065P-50P (0545)
2003/04: 16⁵GS, 16⁰GF, 17PGF,

	Starts	1st	2nd	3rd	Win & Pl
Hurdles	3	0	0	0	0
Career Total	8	0	0	0	0

Going: Sf: 0-0 GS: 0-0 Gd: 0-1 GF: - Fm: 0-2
Distance: 2m/2m3: 0-2 2m4-2m7: 0-1 3m+: 0-0
Track: LH: 0-1 RH: 0-2 Tight: 0-1 Gall: 0-0
Aids: Bl: 0-0 Vi: 0-0 Tstrap: 0-0 Ckp: 0-2
Best Rating: 71 5/03 Ludl 2m good Hdl

Influence Pedler

82(80h) (25h)91

11-y-o b g Keen-La Vie En Primrose (Henbit (USA))

Miss K M George Stableline

Placings:61203/3253063/213P14411PP/033121242/P4052 223422P1/233346-60 (4632)

2003/04: 24^{6}GF, 24^{0}G,

	Starts	1st	2nd	3rd	Win & Pl
Hurdles	1	0	0	0	0
Chases	1	0	0	0	0
Career Total	**53**	**8**	**12**	**11**	**57187**

99	4/02	Extr	3m1f110yD(0-115)HCh		FRM	£5193
105	9/99	Sedg	3m3f	E(0-115)HCh	G-F	£3470
105	8/99	Strf	3m	F(0-105)HCh	GD	£3018
109	12/98	Hrfd	2m3f	E(0-110)HCh	GD	£3430
108	11/98	Ludl	2m4f	D Ch	GD	£3972
91	8/98	MRas	2m4f	D Ch	GD	£3418
88	6/98	MRas	2m1f110yD Ch		G-F	£4176
114	2/97	Wwck	2m4f110yB Hdl		GD	£7100

Total win prize-money £33781

Going: Sf: 0-0 GS: 0-0 Gd: 0-1 GF: - Fm: 0-1
Distance: 2m/2m3: 0-0 2m4-2m7: 0-0 3m+: 0-2
Track: LH: 0-1 RH: 0-1 Tight: 0-1 Gall: 0-0
Aids: Bl: 0-0 Vi: 0-0 Tstrap: 0-0 Ckp: 0-0
Best Rating: **121** 11/97 NAbb 2m6f gd-fm Hdl

Plating-class chaser; stays three miles-three; likes ground conditions good or faster; consistent and often makes the frame.

Infrasonique (FR)

108 133

8-y-o b g Teresio-Quatalina Iii (FR) (Chateau Du Diable (FR))

Mrs L C Taylor Miss M Talbot

Placings:43225/2412324204221/5206345-564446 (4652)

2003/04: 24^{5}S, 24^{6}S, 24^{4}G, 24^{4}G, 24^{4}GS, 25^{6}G,

	Starts	1st	2nd	3rd	Win & Pl
Chases	6	0	0	0	3101
Career Total	**31**	**2**	**9**	**3**	**63780**

133	4/02	Ayr	3m1f	B HCh	GD	£21450
	6/01	Autl	2m4f110y	Ch	SFT	£12124

Total win prize-money £33574

Going: Sf: 0-2 GS: 0-1 Gd: 0-3 GF: - Fm: 0-0
Distance: 2m/2m3: 0-0 2m4-2m7: 0-0 3m+: 0-6
Track: LH: 0-1 RH: 0-5 Tight: 0-0 Gall: 0-1
Aids: Bl: 0-0 Vi: 0-2 Tstrap: 0-0 Ckp: 0-1
Best Rating: **133** 11/02 Asct 3m110y gd-sft Ch

Modest handicap chaser; winless since April 2002, but often in the frame; stays three miles; acts on good and soft ground.

Ingenu (FR)

97(107h) (109h)95

8-y-o b g Royal Charter (FR)-Una Volta (FR) (Toujours Pret (USA))

R H Alner G L Porter

Placings:403/1423522/352P6/014405-00 (0247)

2003/04: 23^{0}G, 25^{0}GF,

	Starts	1st	2nd	3rd	Win & Pl
Chases	2	0	0	0	0
Career Total	**23**	**2**	**4**	**3**	**26773**

108	11/02	Hayd	2m4f	D Hdl	SFT	£3913
	8/00	Diep	2m1f110y	Ch	SFT	£3362

Total win prize-money £7275

Going: Sf: 0-0 GS: 0-0 Gd: 0-1 GF: - Fm: 0-1

Distance: 2m/2m3: 0-0 2m4-2m7: 0-0 3m+: 0-2
Track: LH: 0-0 RH: 0-2 Tight: 0-0 Gall: 0-0
Aids: Bl: 0-0 Vi: 0-0 Tstrap: 0-0 Ckp: 0-0
Best Rating: **115** 12/01 Plum 2m4f soft Ch

Ex-French chaser; won over hurdles at Haydock in November 2002; likes soft ground; stays two and a half miles.

Inglewood

95 79+

4-y-o ch g Fleetwood (IRE)-Preening (Persian Bold)

C W Thornton G B Turnbull Ltd

Placings:410P000 (4796)

2003/04: 17^{4}GF, 17^{1}G, 16^{0}S, 18^{P}HY, 19^{0}GF, 27^{0}G, 21^{0}G,

	Starts	1st	2nd	3rd	Win & Pl
Hurdles	7	1	0	0	3432
Career Total	**7**	**1**	**0**	**0**	**3432**

79	8/03	Bang	2m1f	E Hdl	GD	£3432

Total win prize-money £3432

Going: Sf: 0-2 GS: 0-0 Gd: 1-3 GF: - Fm: 0-2
Distance: **2m/2m3: 1-5** 2m4-2m7: 0-1 3m+: 0-1
Track: **LH: 1-7** RH: 0-0 **Tight: 1-7** Gall: 0-0
Aids: Bl: 0-0 Vi: 0-0 Tstrap: 0-0 Ckp: 0-0
Best Rating: **79** 8/03 Bang 2m1f good Hdl

Plating-class performer; scored on second start over hurdles at Bangor in August 2003.

Inglis Drever

115 157+

5-y-o b g In The Wings-Cormorant Creek (Gorytus (USA))

J Howard Johnson (Sir Mark Prescott 18/10) Andrea & Graham Wylie

Placings:11124 (4629)

2003/04: 20^{1}G, 20^{1}GS, 21^{1}GS, 21^{2}G, 20^{4}G,

	Starts	1st	2nd	3rd	Win & Pl
Hurdles	5	3	1	0	67727
Career Total	**5**	**3**	**1**	**0**	**67727**

157	1/04	Wwck	2m5f	A Hdl	G-S	£21700
152	12/03	Sand	2m4f110yA Hdl		G-S	£14500
140	11/03	Aint	2m4f	C Hdl	GD	£7026

Total win prize-money £43227

Going: Sf: 0-0 GS: 2-2 Gd: 1-3 GF: - Fm: 0-0
Distance: 2m/2m3: 0-0 **2m4-2m7: 3-5** 3m+: 0-0
Track: **LH: 2-4** RH: 1-1 **Tight: 1-2** Gall: 0-1
Aids: Bl: 0-0 Vi: 0-0 Tstrap: 0-0 Ckp: 0-0
Best Rating: **157** 3/04 Chel 2m5f good Hdl

Smart novice hurdler; sold out of Sir Mark Prescott's yard for 110,000gns; impressive winner of first three starts over hurdles including a couple of Grade Two events; lost a shoe when runner-up in the Royal & Sun Alliance Hurdle; had a poor run when good fourth in Grade Two at Aintree; effective over 2m 4f; acts on easy ground.

Inigo Jones (IRE)

107(105h) (101 h)108+

8-y-o b g Alzao (USA)-Kindjal (Kris)

G Brown M D Killick

Placings:3U15/4P34-534111 (4896)

2003/04: 16^{5}G, 16^{3}S, 16^{4}G, 16^{1}GS, 16^{1}G, 16^{1}G,

	Starts	1st	2nd	3rd	Win & Pl
Hurdles	2	0	0	1	551
Chases	4	3	0	0	18527
Career Total	**14**	**4**	**0**	**3**	**23318**

108	4/04	Winc	2m	D(0-115)HCh	GD	£6812
108	4/04	Winc	2m	D(0-110)HCh	GD	£6753
110	3/04	Hrfd	2m	E(0-100)HCh	G-S	£4696
120	4/02	Sedg	2m1f	E Hdl	G-F	£2702

Total win prize-money £20964

Going: Sf: 0-1 GS: 1-1 Gd: 2-4 GF: - Fm: 0-0
Distance: **2m/2m3: 3-6** 2m4-2m7: 0-0 3m+: 0-0
Track: LH: 0-0 **RH: 3-6** Tight: 0-1 Gall: 0-0
Aids: Bl: 0-1 Vi: 0-0 Tstrap: 0-0 Ckp: 0-0
Best Rating: **120** 4/02 Sedg 2m1f gd-fm Hdl

Modest chaser; free-running novice hurdler; has improved since learning to settle and completed a hat-trick in the spring of 2004; suited by fast but handles easy ground; has worn blinkers.

Inis Cara (IRE)

12-y-o b g Carlingford Castle-Good Sailing (Scorpio (FR))

G W Thomas G W Thomas

Placings: 1/026051161106/113F1232264/023310664/34350 F/04P/55P-P (4815)

2003/04: 24^{P}G,

	Starts	1st	2nd	3rd	Win & Pl
Chases	1	0	0	0	
Career Total	**46**	**9**	**5**	**6**	**126593**

132	12/99	Leop	3m	(0-140)HCh	SFT	£63616
123	1/99	Tram	2m4f	Ch	HVY	£4296
127	11/98	Fair	2m5f110y	Ch	Y-S	£3586
132	10/98	Gowr	2m6f	Ch	SH	£4782
133	2/98	Clon	2m4f	(0-116)HHdl	Y-S	£2680
122	1/98	Leop	2m6f	(0-130)HHdl	Y-S	£3573
112	12/97	Thur	2m6f110y	Hdl	SFT	£2204
111	11/97	Dpat	2m6f	Hdl	SH	£2712
106	4/97	Slig	2m	NHF	HVY	£2204

Total win prize-money £89658

Going: Sf: 0-0 GS: 0-0 Gd: 0-1 GF: - Fm: 0-0
Distance: 2m/2m3: 0-0 2m4-2m7: 0-0 3m+: 0-1
Track: LH: 0-1 RH: 0-0 Tight: 0-0 Gall: 0-0
Aids: Bl: 0-0 Vi: 0-0 Tstrap: 0-0 Ckp: 0-0
Best Rating: **140** 11/00 DRoy 3m gd-yld Ch

Initiate

95f 79f

6-y-o ch g North Col-Silver Fig (True Song)

J L Spearing Mrs B Graham

Placings:3 (1487)

2003/04: 17^{3}GF,

	Starts	1st	2nd	3rd	Win & Pl
NH Flat	1	0	0	1	217
Career Total	**1**	**0**	**0**	**1**	**217**

Going: Sf: 0-0 GS: 0-0 Gd: 0-0 GF: - Fm: 0-1
Distance: 2m/2m3: 0-1 2m4-2m7: 0-0 3m+: 0-0
Track: LH: 0-0 RH: 0-1 Tight: 0-0 Gall: 0-0
Aids: Bl: 0-0 Vi: 0-0 Tstrap: 0-0 Ckp: 0-0
Best Rating: **79** 10/03 Hrfd 2m1f gd-fm NHF

Third in modest bumper in October.

Initiative

101(105h) (99h)95

8-y-o ch g Arazi (USA)-Dance Quest (FR) (Green Dancer (USA))

J Hetherton Frank Reay

Placings:0/451P23341500-0P33 (1425)

2003/04: 16^{0}GF, 21^{P}GF, 16^{3}GF, 16^{3}G,

	Starts	1st	2nd	3rd	Win & Pl
Hurdles	1	0	0	0	0

Chases	3	0	0	2	1447
Career Total	**17**	**2**	**1**	**4**	**9122**
99 12/02 Sedg	2m1f	E(0-100)HHdl		SFT	£3304
95 9/02 Sedg	2m1f	G(0-95)HHdl		G-F	£2009

Total win prize-money £5313

Going:	Sf: 0-0 GS: 0-0 Gd: 0-1 GF: - Fm: 0-3
Distance:	2m/2m3: 0-3 2m4-2m7: 0-1 3m+: 0-0
Track:	LH: 0-3 RH: 0-1 Tight: 0-2 Gall: 0-0
Aids:	Bl: 0-0 Vi: 0-0 Tstrap: 0-0 Ckp: 0-0
Best Rating:	99 12/02 Sedg 2m1f soft Hdl

Moderate hurdler/novice chaser; much better effort over fences when third at Sedgefield in August; acts on any ground; best at around two miles.

Injun

81   **83**

5-y-o ch g Efisio-Lassoo (Caerleon (USA))
Miss A M Newton-Smith Julian Smith

Placings:0000-5P4   (4120)
2003/04: 22⁵HY, 16⁵S, 17⁴G,

	Starts	1st	2nd	3rd	Win & Pl
Hurdles	3	0	0	0	0
Career Total	**7**	**0**	**0**	**0**	**0**

Going:	Sf: 0-2 GS: 0-0 Gd: 0-1 GF: - Fm: 0-0
Distance:	2m/2m3: 0-2 2m4-2m7: 0-1 3m+: 0-0
Track:	LH: 0-1 RH: 0-2 Tight: 0-3 Gall: 0-0
Aids:	Bl: 0-0 Vi: 0-0 Tstrap: 0-1 Ckp: 0-2
Best Rating:	83 10/02 Kemp 2m good Hdl

Injunear (IRE)

68   **82**

6-y-o ch g Executive Perk-Chancy Gale (IRE) (Strong Gale)
T P McGovern Lewes Racing

Placings:4   (4755)
2003/04: 21⁴G,

	Starts	1st	2nd	3rd	Win & Pl
Hurdles	1	0	0	0	0
Career Total	**1**	**0**	**0**	**0**	**0**

Going:	Sf: 0-0 GS: 0-0 Gd: 0-1 GF: - Fm: 0-0
Distance:	2m/2m3: 0-0 2m4-2m7: 0-1 3m+: 0-0
Track:	LH: 0-1 RH: 0-0 Tight: 0-1 Gall: 0-0
Aids:	Bl: 0-0 Vi: 0-0 Tstrap: 0-0 Ckp: 0-0
Best Rating:	82 4/04 Plum 2m5f good Hdl

Inland Run (IRE)

83   **81**

8-y-o b g Insan (USA)-Anns Run (Deep Run)
R T Phillips A Beard, B Beard, P Doble, T Pearce

Placings:05/0   (3646)
2003/04: 21⁰GS,

	Starts	1st	2nd	3rd	Win & Pl
Hurdles	1	0	0	0	0
Career Total	**3**	**0**	**0**	**0**	**0**

Going:	Sf: 0-0 GS: 0-1 Gd: 0-0 GF: - Fm: 0-0
Distance:	2m/2m3: 0-0 2m4-2m7: 0-0 3m+: 0-0
Track:	LH: 0-0 RH: 0-1 Tight: 0-0 Gall: 0-0
Aids:	Bl: 0-0 Vi: 0-0 Tstrap: 0-0 Ckp: 0-0
Best Rating:	89 6/01 Naas 2m good NHF

Inn Antique (FR)

112(106h)   (121 h)**134+**

8-y-o b g Lute Antique (FR)-Taghera (FR) (Toujours Pret (USA))
Ferdy Murphy W J Gott

Placings:0P1P1FP/4P2F/1421210-P050   (4399)
2003/04: 20⁰GS, 16⁵S, 20⁵GS, 20⁰G,

	Starts	1st	2nd	3rd	Win & Pl
Hurdles	2	0	0	0	0
Chases	2	0	0	0	0
Career Total	**22**	**5**	**3**	**0**	**31445**
121 1/03 Sedg	2m1f	E Hdl		HVY	£4527
121 11/02 Sedg	2m1f	D Hdl		SFT	£4316
115 5/02 Winc	2m	E Hdl		G-F	£2688
116 1/01 Kemp	2m	D Ch		SFT	£4290
9/00 Autl	2m2f	Ch		VS	£11527

Total win prize-money £27348

Going:	Sf: 0-1 GS: 0-2 Gd: 0-1 GF: - Fm: 0-0
Distance:	2m/2m3: 0-1 2m4-2m7: 0-3 3m+: 0-0
Track:	LH: 0-4 RH: 0-0 Tight: 0-1 Gall: 0-1
Aids:	Bl: 0-0 Vi: 0-0 Tstrap: 0-0 Ckp: 0-0
Best Rating:	134 3/04 Chel 2m4f110y good Ch

Fair hurdler; won twice over fences, but suffered jumping problems; effective at around two miles; acts on any ground; goes well at Sedgefield.

Inn From The Cold (IRE)

82   **59**

8-y-o ch g Glacial Storm (USA)-Silver Apollo (General Ironside)
L Lungo Mrs Barbara Lungo

Placings:0/P0P060-0   (2506)
2003/04: 22⁰S,

	Starts	1st	2nd	3rd	Win & Pl
Hurdles	1	0	0	0	0
Career Total	**8**	**0**	**0**	**0**	**0**

Going:	Sf: 0-1 GS: 0-0 Gd: 0-0 GF: - Fm: 0-0
Distance:	2m/2m3: 0-0 2m4-2m7: 0-1 3m+: 0-0
Track:	LH: 0-1 RH: 0-0 Tight: 0-1 Gall: 0-0
Aids:	Bl: 0-0 Vi: 0-0 Tstrap: 0-0 Ckp: 0-0
Best Rating:	60 1/03 Newc 2m heavy Hdl

Inner Sanctum (IRE)

85

7-y-o ch g Bob's Return (IRE)-Princess Wager (Pollerton)
Miss Venetia Williams P Ryan

Placings:304-FP6   (4702)
2003/04: 21⁵FG, 24⁸G, 20⁶G,

	Starts	1st	2nd	3rd	Win & Pl
Hurdles	3	0	0	0	0
Career Total	**6**	**0**	**0**	**1**	**564**

Going:	Sf: 0-0 GS: 0-0 Gd: 0-3 GF: - Fm: 0-0
Distance:	2m/2m3: 0-0 2m4-2m7: 0-2 3m+: 0-1
Track:	LH: 0-0 RH: 0-2 Tight: 0-1 Gall: 0-0
Aids:	Bl: 0-0 Vi: 0-0 Tstrap: 0-0 Ckp: 0-0
Best Rating:	93 1/03 Font 2m2f110y heavy NHF

Innocent Bystander

69f   **14f**

5-y-o ch g Rudimentary (USA)-Right To The Top (Nashwan (USA))

J M Jefferson Ashleybank Investments Limited

Placings:0   (1843)
2003/04: 17⁰G,

	Starts	1st	2nd	3rd	Win & Pl
NH Flat	1	0	0	0	
Career Total	**1**	**0**	**0**	**0**	

Going:	Sf: 0-0 GS: 0-0 Gd: 0-1 GF: - Fm: 0-0
Distance:	2m/2m3: 0-1 2m4-2m7: 0-0 3m+: 0-0
Track:	LH: 0-1 RH: 0-0 Tight: 0-1 Gall: 0-0
Aids:	Bl: 0-0 Vi: 0-0 Tstrap: 0-0 Ckp: 0-0
Best Rating:	19 10/03 Sedg 2m1f good NHF

Innovate (IRE)

89   **73**

12-y-o b m Posen (USA)-Innate (Be My Native (USA))
Miss Lucinda V Russell Peter K Dale

Placings:00P350/5PPF02/5144P/6113P/P4/23P3-0   (0414)
2003/04: 25⁰G,

	Starts	1st	2nd	3rd	Win & Pl
Chases	1	0	0	0	
Career Total	**29**	**3**	**2**	**4**	**14173**
91 10/00 Towc	3m4f	F(0-90)HCh		G-F	£2821
91 8/00 Uttx	3m	F(0-100)HCh		G-F	£2710
92 6/99 Hexm	2m4f110yF Ch			G-F	£2909

Total win prize-money £8442

Going:	Sf: 0-0 GS: 0-0 Gd: 0-1 GF: - Fm: 0-0
Distance:	2m/2m3: 0-0 2m4-2m7: 0-3 3m+: 0-1
Track:	LH: 0-1 RH: 0-0 Tight: 0-0 Gall: 0-1
Aids:	Bl: 0-0 Vi: 0-0 Tstrap: 0-0 Ckp: 0-1
Best Rating:	95 10/00 Aint 3m1f good Ch

Plating-class staying chaser; lightly raced since winning extended three miles handicap chase at Towcester October 2000; stays three miles-two; likes fast ground.

Innox (FR)

109   **139+**

8-y-o b g Lute Antique (FR)-Savane Iii (FR) (Quart De Vin (FR))
F Doumen Marquesa De Moratalla

Placings:0F/324F/62512F321P2/04344P50-P032FF   (4385)
2003/04: 19⁵VS, 21⁵VS, 23³VS, 24²G, 24⁸G, 23⁷HO,

	Starts	1st	2nd	3rd	Win & Pl
Chases	6	0	1	1	19342
Career Total	**31**	**2**	**6**	**4**	**169066**
134 2/02 Wwck	3m2f	C Ch		SFT	£6812
9/01 Autl	2m5f110y HCh			VS	£10699

Total win prize-money £17511

Going:	Sf: 0-0 GS: 0-0 Gd: 0-2 GF: - Fm: 0-0
Distance:	2m/2m3: 0-1 2m4-2m7: 0-1 3m+: 0-4
Track:	LH: 0-1 RH: 0-1 Tight: 0-0 Gall: 0-1
Aids:	Bl: 0-3 Vi: 0-0 Tstrap: 0-0 Ckp: 0-0
Best Rating:	139 2/04 Sand 3m110y good Ch

Very useful French chaser; stays three miles; likes soft ground.

Insharann (FR)

5-y-o b g Sheyrann-My Last Chance (FR) (Tiffauges)
N J Henderson W H Ponsonby

Placings:P-0   (4374)
2003/04: 16⁰GF,

	Starts	1st	2nd	3rd	Win & Pl
NH Flat	1	0	0	0	
Career Total	2	0	0	0	

Going:	Sf: 0-0 GS: 0-0 Gd: 0-0 GF: - Fm: 0-1
Distance:	2m/2m3: 0-1 2m4-2m7: 0-0 3m+: 0-0
Track:	LH: 0-0 RH: 0-0 Tight: 0-0 Gall: 0-0
Aids:	Bl: 0-0 Vi: 0-0 Tstrap: 0-0 Ckp: 0-0

Insurrection (IRE)

90   **76**

7-y-o b g Un Desperado (FR)-Ballycahan Girl (Bargello)
J D Frost (K J Burke 1/7) Mrs J McCormack

Placings:0000   (4819)
2003/04: 16⁰GY, 20⁰GF, 16⁰G, 22⁰GF,

	Starts	1st	2nd	3rd	Win & Pl
NH Flat	1	0	0	0	0
Hurdles	3	0	0	0	0
Career Total	4	0	0	0	

Going:	Sf: 0-0 GS: 0-0 Gd: 0-1 GF: - Fm: 0-2
Distance:	2m/2m3: 0-2 2m4-2m7: 0-2 3m+: 0-0
Track:	LH: 0-1 RH: 0-1 Tight: 0-2 Gall: 0-0
Aids:	Bl: 0-0 Vi: 0-0 Tstrap: 0-0 Ckp: 0-0
Best Rating:	76 3/04 Strf 2m110y good Hdl

Intelligent (IRE)

(127h)**153**

8-y-o b g Religiously (USA)-Culkeern (Master Buck)
Mrs John Harrington Norman Moore

Placings:6¹12⁄502313430/2P1216321-0F   (2575)
2003/04: 20⁰YS, 24⁰G,

	Starts	1st	2nd	3rd	Win & Pl
Chases	2	0	0	0	
Career Total	23	5	5	4	110184
153	3/03	Uttx	4m2f	A HCh	SFT £58000
147	12/02	Limk	2m4f	Ch	SFT £17944
126	11/02	DRoy	2m4f	Ch	HVY £6984
117	2/02	Thur	2m6f	Hdl	HVY £3809
105	10/00	Punc	2m	NHF	G-Y £3588

Total win prize-money £90328

Going:	Sf: 0-0 GS: 0-0 Gd: 0-1 GF: - Fm: 0-0
Distance:	2m/2m3: 0-0 2m4-2m7: 0-1 3m+: 0-1
Track:	LH: 0-0 RH: 0-2 Tight: 0-0 Gall: 0-0
Aids:	Bl: 0-0 Vi: 0-0 Tstrap: 0-0 Ckp: 0-0
Best Rating:	153 3/03 Uttx 4m2f soft Ch

Smart Irish chaser, stayed 3m; was suited by soft ground; (DEAD)

Intensity

87   **98+**

8-y-o b g Bigstone (IRE)-Brillante (FR) (Green Dancer (USA))
P A Blockley (R J Osborne 11/10) Bill Cahill

Placings:00P/0511   (2582)
2003/04: 16⁰Y, 16⁵F, 21¹G, 24¹GF,

	Starts	1st	2nd	3rd	Win & Pl
Hurdles	4	2	0	0	6321
Career Total	7	2	0	0	6321
98	12/03	Sthl	3m110y	E Hdl	G-F £2730
100	11/03	Sthl	2m5f110yE(0-105)HHdl	GD	£3591

Total win prize-money £6321

Going:	Sf: 0-0 GS: 0-0 Gd: 1-1 GF: - Fm: 1-2

Distance:	2m/2m3: 0-2 2m4-2m7: 1-1 3m+: 1-1
Track:	LH: 2-2 RH: 0-1 Tight: 1-1 Gall: 0-0
Aids:	Bl: 0-0 Vi: 0-0 Tstrap: 0-0 Ckp: 0-0
Best Rating:	100 11/03 Sthl 2m5f110y good Hdl

Poor form in novices' hurdles in Ireland; back here took a handicap at Southwell in late 2003 stays three miles; acts on a sound surface.

Interdit (FR)

108(106h)   (107h)**120+**

8-y-o b/br g Shafoun (FR)-Solaine (FR) (Pot D'Or (FR))
Mrs B K Thomson Mrs B K Thomson

Placings:4120/F55426/212F233122245136225-3PP11F03051604P   (4726)
2003/04: 25³G, 28²GS, 25⁵G, 28¹G, 25¹G, 24⁴S, 30⁰GS, 25³GS, 21⁹GS, 30⁵G, 22¹HY, 25⁶GS, 30⁰G, 32⁴G, 24⁴PG,

	Starts	1st	2nd	3rd	Win & Pl
Hurdles	1	0	0	0	0
Chases	14	3	0	2	23556
Career Total	44	7	10	5	72757
120	2/04	Kels	2m6f110yC(0-130)HCh	HVY	£8170
116	11/03	Ayr	3m1f	D(0-120)HCh	GD	£5862
106	11/03	Kels	3m4f	E(0-110)HCh	GD	£5026
109	2/03	Ayr	3m1f	D(0-120)HCh	HVY	£6890
116	10/02	Ludl	3m	D(0-110)HCh	FRM	£5638
112	5/02	Extr	3m1f110yD(0-115)HCh	GD	£5018
100	12/00	Extr	2m1f	E Hdl	HVY	£2275

Total win prize-money £38882

Going:	Sf: 1-2 GS: 0-5 Gd: 2-8 GF: - Fm: 0-0
Distance:	2m/2m3: 0-0 2m4-2m7: 1-2 3m+: 2-13
Track:	LH: 3-12 RH: 0-3 Tight: 2-9 Gall: 0-0
Aids:	Bl: 0-1 Vi: 0-0 Tstrap: 0-0 Ckp: 0-0
Best Rating:	120 2/04 Kels 2m6f110y heavy Ch

Modest chaser, stays three and a half miles and acts on any ground; best when able to dominate; has worn blinkers.

Intersky Falcon

116   **164**

7-y-o ch g Polar Falcon (USA)-I'LI Try (Try My Best (USA))
Jonjo O'Neill Interskyracing.com & Mrs Jonjo O'Neill

Placings:32/2312111612/11115-1312345   (4954)
2003/04: 16¹GF, 16³G, 16¹G, 16²G, 16⁹G, 20⁴G, 16⁵G,

	Starts	1st	2nd	3rd	Win & Pl
Hurdles	7	2	1	2	149008
Career Total	24	11	5	4	347336
146	12/03	Kemp	2m	A Hdl	GD £46400
151	10/03	Tipp	2m	Hdl	G-F £42207
160	12/02	Kemp	2m	A Hdl	SFT £43500
160	11/02	Newc	2m	A Hdl	G-S £29000
154	10/02	Tipp	2m	Hdl	G-F £31901
159	5/02	Hayd	2m	A HHdl	GD £31900
149	4/02	Aint	2m110y	A HHdl	GD £23200
124	2/02	Donc	2m110y	C(0-130)HHdl	SFT £5876
108	11/01	Sedg	2m1f	D Hdl	GD £3328
121	9/01	Sedg	2m1f	Hdl	GD £2380
102	8/01	MRas	2m3f110yE Hdl	G-F £3104

Total win prize-money £262800

Going:	Sf: 0-0 GS: 0-0 Gd: 1-6 GF: - Fm: 1-1
Distance:	2m/2m3: 2-6 2m4-2m7: 0-1 3m+: 0-0
Track:	LH: 0-3 RH: 1-3 Tight: 0-1 Gall: 0-1
Aids:	Bl: 2-7 Vi: 0-0 Tstrap: 0-3 Ckp: 0-0
Best Rating:	160 12/02 Kemp 2m soft Hdl

High-class hurdler; started off 2003/2004 with a repeat victory at Tipperary; disappointing third in the Fighting Fifth next time but bounced back at Kempton in the Christmas Hurdle when held up for a change; disappointing at Wincanton when no match for Rigmarole; fair third in the Champion

---

Hurdle and good fourth at Aintree; stays two and a half miles but possibly best at two miles; acts on good ground or faster, but has won on soft; much improved since being fitted with blinkers; has worn tongue-tie; travels well; tough.

Intersky Native (IRE)

105(86c)   (46c)**87**

8-y-o ch g Be My Native (USA)-Creative Music (Creative Plan (USA))
J Howard Johnson (N G Richards 5/6) interskyracing.com

Placings:25/6042-042   (4879)
2003/04: 24²GF, 25⁰G, 24⁴GF, 20²GS,

	Starts	1st	2nd	3rd	Win & Pl
Hurdles	3	0	2	0	2286
Chases	1	0	0	0	0
Career Total	9	0	3	0	3049

Going:	Sf: 0-0 GS: 0-0 Gd: 0-1 GF: - Fm: 0-2
Distance:	2m/2m3: 0-0 2m4-2m7: 0-0 3m+: 0-3
Track:	LH: 0-2 RH: 0-2 Tight: 0-1 Gall: 0-1
Aids:	Bl: 0-0 Vi: 0-0 Tstrap: 0-0 Ckp: 0-1
Best Rating:	106 12/01 Bang 2m1f gd-sft NHF

Modest novice hurdler; first outing for new stable and improved effort when runner-up at Carlisle in April; stays three miles; acts on fast and soft ground.

Intersky Sovereign (IRE)

74   **64+**

6-y-o b g Aristocracy-Queen's Prize (Random Shot)
J Howard Johnson interskyracing.com

Placings:0-3P   (3209)
2003/04: 24³G, 25⁰GS,

	Starts	1st	2nd	3rd	Win & Pl
Hurdles	2	0	0	1	618
Career Total	3	0	0	1	618

Going:	Sf: 0-0 GS: 0-1 Gd: 0-1 GF: - Fm: 0-0
Distance:	2m/2m3: 0-0 2m4-2m7: 0-0 3m+: 0-2
Track:	LH: 0-2 RH: 0-0 Tight: 0-0 Gall: 0-1
Aids:	Bl: 0-0 Vi: 0-0 Tstrap: 0-0 Ckp: 0-0
Best Rating:	66 11/03 Newc 3m good Hdl

Modest form in novice hurdles.

Into Battle

89   **84**

10-y-o b g Daring March-Mischievous Miss (Niniski (USA))
J J Quinn Lady Anne Bentinck

Placings:20/5P003/2P/041/0F   (4262)
2003/04: 17⁰GS, 19⁵GF,

	Starts	1st	2nd	3rd	Win & Pl
Hurdles	2	0	0	0	
Career Total	14	1	2	1	4106
83	12/01	Donc	2m110y	F(0-100)HHdl	GD £2425

Total win prize-money £2426

Going:	Sf: 0-0 GS: 0-1 Gd: 0-0 GF: - Fm: 0-1
Distance:	2m/2m3: 0-2 2m4-2m7: 0-0 3m+: 0-0
Track:	LH: 0-2 RH: 0-0 Tight: 0-2 Gall: 0-0
Aids:	Bl: 0-0 Vi: 0-0 Tstrap: 0-0 Ckp: 0-0
Best Rating:	96 2/98 Wwck 2m good NHF

Into The Black (IRE)

13-y-o ch g Over The River (FR)-Legal Fortune (Cash And Courage)
S Lloyd J Huckle

Placings:*321/0015/22P/P3P/P2/P*					(0032)
2003/04: 25PG,					
	Starts	1st	2nd	3rd	Win & Pl
Chases	1	0	0	0	
Career Total	16	2	4	2	8665
87	3/98	Sedg	3m3f110yF Hdl	G-S	£1996
103	3/97	Hexm	2m	H NHF	SFT £1350
			Total win prize-money £3346		

Going:	Sf: 0-0 GS: 0-0 Gd: 0-1 GF: - Fm: 0-0
Distance:	2m/2m3: 0-2 2m4-2m7: 0-0 3m+: 0-1
Track:	LH: 0-1 RH: 0-0 Tight: 0-0 Gall: 0-1
Aids:	Bl: 0-0 Vi: 0-0 Tstrap: 0-0 Ckp: 0-0
Best Rating:	111 11/98 Sedg 2m5f gd-sft Ch

Into The Shadows

100f   **101f**

4-y-o ch f Safawan-Shadows Of Silver (Carwhite)
Mrs M Reveley R C Mayall

Placings:*2252*					(4787)
2003/04: 12²GF, 12²GF, 12⁵G, 16²G,					
	Starts	1st	2nd	3rd	Win & Pl
NH Flat	4	0	3	0	2149
Career Total	4	0	3	0	2149

Going:	Sf: 0-0 GS: 0-0 Gd: 0-0 GF: - Fm: 0-2
Distance:	2m/2m3: 0-1 2m4-2m7: 0-0 3m+: 0-0
Track:	LH: 0-2 RH: 0-1 Tight: 0-0 Gall: 0-1
Aids:	Bl: 0-0 Vi: 0-0 Tstrap: 0-0 Ckp: 0-0
Best Rating:	101 4/04 Hntg 2m110y good NHF

Runner-up in three bumpers to date over 12 furlongs at Newbury and two miles at Huntingdon.

Intox III (FR)

100(88c)   (67c)**112+**

8-y-o ch g Garde Royale-Naftane (FR) (Trac)
M C Pipe Stef Stefanou

Placings:*10/2156P0P/15611F3/54B04P00-135400*					(1588)
2003/04: 17¹GF, 16³G, 16⁵GF, 16⁴GF, 16⁶GF, 16⁰GF,					
	Starts	1st	2nd	3rd	Win & Pl
Hurdles	4	1	0	1	4250
Chases	2	0	0	0	412
Career Total	30	6	1	2	18602
112	6/03	NAbb	2m1f	E(0-105)HHdl	G-F £3393
120	9/01	NAbb	2m1f	G(0-115)HHdl	G-F £2639
115	8/01	NAbb	2m1f	F(0-100)HHdl	G-F £2667
108	5/01	MRas	2m1f110yF(0-105)HHdl	GD £2138
108	7/00	NAbb	2m1f	D Hdl	G-F £3088
99	1/00	Towc	2m	H NHF	HVY £1641
			Total win prize-money £15570		

Going:	Sf: 0-0 GS: 0-0 Gd: 0-1 GF: - Fm: 1-5
Distance:	2m/2m3: 1-6 2m4-2m7: 0-0 3m+: 0-0
Track:	LH: 1-5 RH: 0-1 Tight: 1-4 Gall: 0-0
Aids:	Bl: 0-0 Vi: 1-6 Tstrap: 0-0 Ckp: 0-0
Best Rating:	125 1/02 Tntn 2m1f soft Hdl

Modest handicap hurdler, fitted with a tongue tie and got his own way out in front when scoring for the fourth time over the extended 2m at Newton Abbot June 2003; folded up tamely on chasing debut at the same course in August; acts on most types of ground; effective over 2m.

Intrepid Mogal

103(99h)   (91h)**111+**

7-y-o b g Terimon-Padrigal (Paddy's Stream)
N J Pomfret J N Cheatle

Placings:*00P53/PP2226-241604PP0*					(4652)
2003/04: 26²HY, 24⁴GF, 26¹GF, 25⁶G, 23⁰G, 25⁴S, 26PHY, 32PG, 25⁰G,					
	Starts	1st	2nd	3rd	Win & Pl
Chases	9	1	1	0	11037
Career Total	20	1	4	1	14211
107	11/03	Donc	3m2f	C Ch	G-F £8620
			Total win prize-money £8621		

Going:	Sf: 0-3 GS: 0-0 Gd: 0-4 GF: - Fm: 1-2
Distance:	2m/2m3: 0-0 2m4-2m7: 0-0 3m+: 1-9
Track:	LH: 1-7 RH: 0-2 Tight: 0-0 Gall: 1-4
Aids:	Bl: 0-0 Vi: 0-0 Tstrap: 0-0 Ckp: 0-0
Best Rating:	107 11/03 Donc 3m2f gd-fm Ch

Moderate hurdler/chaser; stays well; probably best on an easy surface.

Intymcginty (IRE)

100   **101**

7-y-o b g Port Lucaya-Mother Tongue (Montelimar (USA))
Noel T Chance Let's Get Ready To Rumble Partnership

Placings:*56/5320-350*					(4561)
2003/04: 21³G, 21⁵G, 24⁰GS,					
	Starts	1st	2nd	3rd	Win & Pl
Hurdles	3	0	0	1	1001
Career Total	9	0	1	2	3477

Going:	Sf: 0-0 GS: 0-1 Gd: 0-2 GF: - Fm: 0-0
Distance:	2m/2m3: 0-0 2m4-2m7: 0-2 3m+: 0-1
Track:	LH: 0-3 RH: 0-0 Tight: 0-0 Gall: 0-2
Aids:	Bl: 0-0 Vi: 0-0 Tstrap: 0-0 Ckp: 0-0
Best Rating:	109 12/01 Newb 2m110y good NHF

Modest performer; stays two and a half miles plus; acts on most ground.

Investment Force (IRE)

96   **87+**

6-y-o b g Imperial Frontier (USA)-Superb Investment (IRE) (Hatim (USA))
C J Mann (M Johnston 5/8) The Whitcoombe Partnership

Placings:*210U*					(2153)
2003/04: 16²GF, 17¹GF, 16⁶GF, 16⁰G,					
	Starts	1st	2nd	3rd	Win & Pl
Hurdles	4	1	1	0	4279
Career Total	4	1	1	0	4279
93	9/03	Sthl	2m1f	E Hdl	G-F £3521
			Total win prize-money £3521		

Going:	Sf: 0-0 GS: 0-0 Gd: 0-1 GF: - Fm: 1-3
Distance:	2m/2m3: 1-4 2m4-2m7: 0-0 3m+: 0-0
Track:	LH: 1-2 RH: 0-2 Tight: 0-0 Gall: 0-1
Aids:	Bl: 0-0 Vi: 0-0 Tstrap: 0-0 Ckp: 0-0
Best Rating:	93 9/03 Sthl 2m1f gd-fm Hdl

Moderate hurdler; mile winner on the Flat; ridden for speed when scoring at Southwell on his second outing over hurdles; acts on a sound surface; wore a visor on the Flat, but left off over hurdles.

Investor Relations (IRE)

(102h)   (96h)

6-y-o b g Goldmark (USA)-Debach Delight (Great Nephew)
N J Hawke N J McMullan And N R Packer

Placings:*4453/03132520-P5605F*					(2028)
2003/04: 17PGF, 16⁵GF, 16⁶GF, 17⁰G, 16⁵F, 17⁰FG,					
	Starts	1st	2nd	3rd	Win & Pl
Hurdles	5	0	0	0	317
Chases	1	0	0	0	0
Career Total	18	1	2	3	5013
89	6/02	NAbb	2m1f	G(0-95)HHdl	GD £2268
			Total win prize-money £2268		

Going:	Sf: 0-0 GS: 0-0 Gd: 0-2 GF: - Fm: 0-4
Distance:	2m/2m3: 0-6 2m4-2m7: 0-0 3m+: 0-0
Track:	LH: 0-5 RH: 0-1 Tight: 0-3 Gall: 0-0
Aids:	Bl: 0-0 Vi: 0-0 Tstrap: 0-0 Ckp: 0-0
Best Rating:	96 9/03 Plum 2m gd-fm Hdl

Moderate hurdler; barely stays two miles; acts on a sound surface.

Inviramental

93

8-y-o b g Pursuit Of Love-Corn Futures (Nomination)
R Williams R Williams

Placings:*360U/24/PP*					(4813)
2003/04: 24PG, 16PG,					
	Starts	1st	2nd	3rd	Win & Pl
Hurdles	2	0	0	0	
Career Total	8	0	1	1	1161

Going:	Sf: 0-0 GS: 0-0 Gd: 0-2 GF: - Fm: 0-0
Distance:	2m/2m3: 0-1 2m4-2m7: 0-0 3m+: 0-1
Track:	LH: 0-1 RH: 0-1 Tight: 0-0 Gall: 0-0
Aids:	Bl: 0-0 Vi: 0-0 Tstrap: 0-0 Ckp: 0-0
Best Rating:	93 5/01 Hntg 2m110y good Hdl

Invitado (IRE)

101   **74**

5-y-o ch g Be My Guest (USA)-Lady Dulcinea (ARG) (General (FR))
T J Fitzgerald A Huddlestone

Placings:*5-6604304*					(1690)
2003/04: 16⁶GF, 20⁶G, 17⁰GF, 17⁴GF, 17³GF, 17⁰GF, 17⁴GF,					
	Starts	1st	2nd	3rd	Win & Pl
Hurdles	7	0	0	1	443
Career Total	8	0	0	1	443

Going:	Sf: 0-0 GS: 0-0 Gd: 0-1 GF: - Fm: 0-6
Distance:	2m/2m3: 0-6 2m4-2m7: 0-1 3m+: 0-0
Track:	LH: 0-4 RH: 0-3 Tight: 0-4 Gall: 0-0
Aids:	Bl: 0-0 Vi: 0-1 Tstrap: 0-5 Ckp: 0-0
Best Rating:	74 5/03 Weth 2m gd-fm Hdl

Plating-class maiden hurdler; suited by two and a half miles; handles fast ground.

Invitation

90   **94**

6-y-o b g Bin Ajwaad (IRE)-On Request (IRE) (Be My Guest (USA))
A Charlton Woodhaven Racing Syndicate

Placings:6005   **(4198)**
2003/04: 16⁰GS, 17⁰GS, 16⁰G, 16⁵G,

	Starts	1st	2nd	3rd	Win & Pl
Hurdles	4	0	0	0	171
Career Total	4	0	0	0	171

Going:	Sf: 0-0 GS: 0-2 Gd: 0-2 GF: - Fm: 0-0
Distance:	2m/2m3: 0-4 2m4-2m7: 0-0 3m+: 0-0
Track:	LH: 0-3 RH: 0-1 Tight: 0-1 Gall: 0-3
Aids:	Bl: 0-0 Vi: 0-0 Tstrap: 0-0 Ckp: 0-0
Best Rating:	93 3/04 Newb 2m110y good Hdl

Ioga (FR)

93(97h)   (87h)76+

8-y-o b/br g Video Rock (FR)-Valentia (FR) (Brezzo (FR))
John Allen   John Allen

Placings:P00/5/06-056   **(4811)**
2003/04: 21⁰GS, 21⁵GS, 24⁸G,

	Starts	1st	2nd	3rd	Win & Pl
Chases	3	0	0	0	0
Career Total	9	0	0	0	0

Going:	Sf: 0-0 GS: 0-2 Gd: 0-1 GF: - Fm: 0-0
Distance:	2m/2m3: 0-0 2m4-2m7: 0-2 3m+: 0-1
Track:	LH: 0-2 RH: 0-1 Tight: 0-2 Gall: 0-0
Aids:	Bl: 0-0 Vi: 0-0 Tstrap: 0-0 Ckp: 0-0
Best Rating:	87 5/01 Aint 2m4f good Hdl

Iorana (FR)

105(108c)   (121c)115

8-y-o ch g Marignan (USA)-Fareham (FR) (Fast Topaze (USA))
Miss K Marks (M C Pipe 13/5)   Nick Shutts

Placings:3/F111502/14121U5/PP4/33111143452-2145   **(0568)**
2003/04: 16²GS, 19¹G, 20⁴G, 20⁵GF,

	Starts	1st	2nd	3rd	Win & Pl
Hurdles	4	1	1	0	3539
Career Total	33	11	4	4	51431
114	5/03	Hrfd	2m3f110yG Hdl		GD	£2422
121	10/02	Hrfd	2m E(0-110)HCh		GD	£4030
103	10/02	Ludl	2m G Hdl		FRM	£3062
99	10/02	Uttx	2m G Hdl		G-F	£1820
108	8/02	Worc	2m D(0-115)HHdl		GD	£4036
105	2/01	Uttx	2m D Ch		SFT	£3718
130	9/00	Chep	2m110y B HHdl		GD	£9821
130	8/00	Uttx	2m4f110yD(0-125)HHdl		G-F	£3090
115	9/99	Font	2m2f110yE Hdl		GD	£2232
105	8/99	Worc	2m E Hdl		G-S	£2355
	6/99	Autl	1m7f Hdl		VS	£6997

Total win prize-money £43588

Going:	Sf: 0-0 GS: 0-1 Gd: 1-2 GF: - Fm: 0-1
Distance:	2m/2m3: 0-1 2m4-2m7: 1-3 3m+: 0-0
Track:	LH: 0-3 RH: 1-1 Tight: 0-0 Gall: 0-0
Aids:	Bl: 0-0 Vi: 0-0 Tstrap: 0-0 Ckp: 0-0
Best Rating:	130 9/00 Chep 2m110y good Hdl

Fair hurdler/chaser, career total stands at nine; effective at around two miles; has won in the soft but is probably better on a sounder surface; below par since being claimed out of Martin Pipe's yard.

Iranoo (IRE)

96   66

7-y-o b g Persian Bold-Rose Of Summer (IRE) (Taufan (USA))
R Allan   The Banana Bunch

Placings:06/25/0005   **(4614)**
2003/04: 16⁰G, 17⁰GS, 16⁹GF, 17⁵G,

	Starts	1st	2nd	3rd	Win & Pl
Hurdles	4	0	0	0	171
Career Total	8	0	1	0	858

Going:	Sf: 0-0 GS: 0-1 Gd: 0-2 GF: - Fm: 0-1
Distance:	2m/2m3: 0-4 2m4-2m7: 0-0 3m+: 0-0
Track:	LH: 0-4 RH: 0-0 Tight: 0-3 Gall: 0-0
Aids:	Bl: 0-0 Vi: 0-0 Tstrap: 0-4 Ckp: 0-0
Best Rating:	74 6/01 Prth 2m110y gd-fm Hdl

Irbee

12-y-o b g Gunner B-Cupids Bower (Owen Dudley)
P F Nicholls   Mrs Bunty Millard

Placings:5/11PF21123/2233115/1F/43523044/221341-43656F   **(4626)**
2003/04: 21¹S, 16⁴G, 23⁹HY, 26⁶GF, 20⁵G, 26⁶G, 21⁵G,

	Starts	1st	2nd	3rd	Win & Pl
Chases	7	1	0	1	13761
Career Total	39	9	7	7	103913
111	4/03	NAbb	2m5f110yB HCh	SFT	£12470
99	3/03	Plum	3m2f H Ch	SFT	£1820
108	10/00	Chep	2m110y D Hdl	G-S	£2996
148	2/00	Kemp	2m B Ch	SFT	£10042
145	1/00	Hayd	2m D(0-145)HCh	SFT	£8649
144	3/99	Uttx	2m5f C(0-135)HCh	G-S	£7132
148	3/99	Chep	2m3f110yD Ch	SFT	£4030
134	11/98	Chep	2m3f110yA(0-115)Ch	GD	£12680
130	10/98	Worc	2m4f110yD Ch	SFT	£3738

Total win prize-money £63561

Going:	Sf: 1-2 GS: 0-0 Gd: 0-4 GF: - Fm: 0-1
Distance:	2m/2m3: 0-1 2m4-2m7: 1-4 3m+: 0-2
Track:	LH: 1-6 RH: 0-1 Tight: 1-3 Gall: 0-1
Aids:	Bl: 1-7 Vi: 0-0 Tstrap: 0-0 Ckp: 0-0
Best Rating:	148 2/00 Kemp 2m soft Ch

Formerly a useful chaser; also a winner in hunter chase company; has developed a questionable attitude; stays three miles two but effective at shorter; probably best on good ground or softer; usually wears blinkers.

Ireland's Eye (IRE)

109   101

9-y-o b g Shareef Dancer (USA)-So Romantic (IRE) (Teenoso (USA))
J R Norton   Ejam Connection

Placings:1214/651431/4044-1U0003   **(4662)**
2003/04: 20¹G, 23⁵US, 20⁹S, 24⁰G, 20⁰HY, 20⁹S,

	Starts	1st	2nd	3rd	Win & Pl
Hurdles	6	1	0	1	5674
Career Total	20	6	1	1	17714
101	5/03	Hexm	2m4f110yD(0-125)HHdl	GD	£4888
113	3/02	Newc	2m4f E Hdl	HVY	£2702
96	12/01	Hexm	2m D Hdl	SFT	£3705
113	3/99	Newc	2m H NHF	SFT	£1710
99	1/99	Catt	2m H NHF	SFT	£1842

Total win prize-money £14848

Going:	Sf: 0-4 GS: 0-0 Gd: 1-2 GF: - Fm: 0-0
Distance:	2m/2m3: 0-0 2m4-2m7: 1-5 3m+: 0-1
Track:	LH: 1-4 RH: 0-2 Tight: 0-1 Gall: 0-0
Aids:	Bl: 0-0 Vi: 0-0 Tstrap: 0-0 Ckp: 0-0
Best Rating:	118 4/99 Ayr 2m soft NHF

Moderate hurdler, stays two and a half miles; acts on good ground or softer.

Irene Kate

76f   49f

5-y-o b m Bob's Return (IRE)-Shean Deas (Le Moss)
P R Webber   Raymond Anderson Green

Placings:0   **(2504)**
2003/04: 17⁰GS,

	Starts	1st	2nd	3rd	Win & Pl
NH Flat	1	0	0	0	
Career Total	1	0	0	0	

Going:	Sf: 0-0 GS: 0-1 Gd: 0-0 GF: - Fm: 0-0
Distance:	2m/2m3: 0-1 2m4-2m7: 0-0 3m+: 0-0
Track:	LH: 0-0 RH: 0-1 Tight: 0-1 Gall: 0-0
Aids:	Bl: 0-0 Vi: 0-0 Tstrap: 0-0 Ckp: 0-0
Best Rating:	49 12/03 Folk 2m1f110y gd-sft NHF

Irilut (FR)

8-y-o br g Lute Antique (FR)-Patchourie (FR) (Taj Dewan)
R Waley-Cohen   Robert Waley-Cohen

Placings:P   **(3785)**
2003/04: 24⁰S,

	Starts	1st	2nd	3rd	Win & Pl
Chases	1	0	0	0	
Career Total	1	0	0	0	

Going:	Sf: 0-1 GS: 0-0 Gd: 0-0 GF: - Fm: 0-0
Distance:	2m/2m3: 0-0 2m4-2m7: 0-0 3m+: 0-1
Track:	LH: 0-0 RH: 0-1 Tight: 0-0 Gall: 0-1
Aids:	Bl: 0-0 Vi: 0-0 Tstrap: 0-0 Ckp: 0-1

Iris Royal (FR)

118   (136h)153+

8-y-o b g Garde Royale-Tchela (FR) (Le Nain Jaune (FR))
N J Henderson   Sir Robert Ogden

Placings:41521/1PPP/231022/211PP2-111P2   **(4427)**
2003/04: 20¹GF, 19¹S, 21⁰GS, 21⁰G, 21²G,

	Starts	1st	2nd	3rd	Win & Pl
Chases	5	3	1	0	117868
Career Total	26	9	7	1	200142
153	12/03	Chel	2m4f110yA HCh	G-S	£58000
144	11/03	Asct	2m3f110yA HCh	SFT	£37200
136	11/03	Sand	2m4f110yC(0-135)HCh	G-F	£5068
136	2/03	Donc	3m E Ch	GD	£4776
131	12/02	Newb	3m C Ch	GD	£8450
131	2/02	Sand	2m6f A HHdl	SFT	£29000
129	1/01	Font	2m4f C(0-135)HHdl	SFT	£5382
121	4/00	Ayr	2m4f C HHdl	GD	£4881
119	1/00	Wwck	2m D Hdl	SFT	£4543

Total win prize-money £157302

Going:	Sf: 1-1 GS: 1-1 Gd: 0-2 GF: - Fm: 1-1
Distance:	2m/2m3: 0-0 2m4-2m7: 3-5 3m+: 0-0
Track:	LH: 1-3 RH: 2-2 Tight: 0-0 Gall: 1-3
Aids:	Bl: 0-0 Vi: 0-0 Tstrap: 0-0 Ckp: 0-0
Best Rating:	153 12/03 Chel 2m4f110y gd-sft Ch

Smart chaser; winner of the 2003 First National Gold Cup at Ascot and Tripleprint Gold Cup at Cheltenham; pulled up next time; good second in the Cathcart at Cheltenham; effective from two and a half to three miles; acts on most types of ground.

Iris's Gift

116   **176**

7-y-o gr g Gunner B-Shirley's Gift (Scallywag)
Jonjo O'Neill Robert Lester

Placings: *11152*/1111121-211   (4623)
2003/04: 23²S, 24¹G, 24¹G,

	Starts	1st	2nd	3rd	Win & Pl
Hurdles	3	2	1	0	114160
Career Total	15	11	3	0	274468

165 4/04	Aint	3m110y	A Hdl	GD	£29000
176 3/04	Chel	3m	A Hdl	GD	£81200
169 4/03	Aint	3m110y	A Hdl	GD	£46040
160 3/03	Hayd	2m7f110y	A Hdl	GD	£17850
160 2/03	Uttx	2m4f110y	A Hdl	HVY	£20100
150 12/02	Chel	3m	A Hdl	GD	£14500
139 10/02	Chel	3m1f110y	C Hdl	G-F	£7113
127 10/02	Bang	2m4f	E Hdl	G-S	£3094
116 2/02	Newb	2m110y	A NHF	SFT	£9000
102 9/01	Worc	2m	H NHF	G-F	£1515
95 8/01	Worc	2m	H NHF	G-F	£1494

Total win prize-money £231269

Going: Sf: 0-1 GS: 0-0 Gd: 2-2 GF: - Fm: 0-0
Distance: 2m/2m3: 0-0 2m4-2m7: 0-0 3m+: 2-3
Track: LH: 2-3 RH: 0-0 Tight: 1-1 Gall: 1-1
Aids: Bl: 0-0 Vi: 0-0 Tstrap: 0-0 Ckp: 0-0
Best Rating: 176 3/04 Chel 3m good Hdl

Top-class hurdler; a winner of three bumpers and unbeaten over hurdles until high-class second to Baracouda in Stayers' Hurdle at Cheltenham; clear-cut winner of Grade One novices' event at Aintree; good effort when runner-up under a big weight on return at Haydock in February 2004 and produced personal best to reverse form with Baracouda when winning Stayers' Hurdle on next outing; also landed a Grade Two at Aintree; acts on any ground, but better with cut; stays three miles one; very tough and an excellent long-term chase prospect.

Irish Blessing (USA)

95   **74+**

7-y-o b g Ghazi (USA)-Win For Leah (USA) (His Majesty (USA))
F Jordan The Bhiss Partnership

Placings: 05P0/0-P0P43   (4401)
2003/04: 23⁹GF, 20⁰HY, 20⁶GS, 20⁴G, 21³G,

	Starts	1st	2nd	3rd	Win & Pl
Hurdles	5	0	0	1	349
Career Total	9	0	0	1	349

Going: Sf: 0-1 GS: 0-1 Gd: 0-2 GF: - Fm: 0-1
Distance: 2m/2m3: 0-0 2m4-2m7: 0-4 3m+: 0-1
Track: LH: 0-3 RH: 0-2 Tight: 0-2 Gall: 0-2
Aids: Bl: 0-0 Vi: 0-0 Tstrap: 0-0 Ckp: 0-2
Best Rating: 74 3/04 Hntg 2m5f110y good Hdl

Irish Distinction (IRE)

108   **109**

6-y-o b g Distinctly North (USA)-Shane's Girl (IRE) (Marktingo)
T R George Ryder Racing Ltd

Placings: F003-311124203   (4651)
2003/04: 17³GS, 16¹GF, 16¹GF, 16¹G, 17²G, 16⁴GF, 16²GF, 16⁰G, 17³G,

	Starts	1st	2nd	3rd	Win & Pl
Hurdles	9	3	2	2	13354

Career Total	13	3	2	3	13874
104 5/03	Weth	2m	F(0-100)HHdl	GD	£2660
90 5/03	Winc	2m	E(0-110)HHdl	G-F	£3454
87 5/03	Chep	2m110y	E(0-105)HHdl	G-F	£3484

Total win prize-money £9599

Going: Sf: 0-1 GS: 0-0 Gd: 1-4 GF: - Fm: 2-4
Distance: 2m/2m3: 3-9 2m4-2m7: 0-0 3m+: 0-0
Track: LH: 2-7 RH: 1-2 Tight: 0-2 Gall: 0-0
Aids: Bl: 0-0 Vi: 0-0 Tstrap: 0-0 Ckp: 0-0
Best Rating: 109 6/03 NAbb 2m1f good Hdl

Moderate handicap hurdler; on the upgrade and completed a hat-trick with a wide-margin success at Wetherby in May 2003; may have been unsuited by the ground next time; likes a strong gallop; effective at around two miles; acts on fast ground.

Irish Fashion (USA)

(90c)   (80c) **113**

9-y-o ch g Nashwan (USA)-L'Irlandaise (USA) (Irish River (FR))
A J Whiting A J Whiting

Placings: 4030531/000/60312120634/5-P   (1504)
2003/04: 20⁰GF,

	Starts	1st	2nd	3rd	Win & Pl
Hurdles	1	0	0	0	
Career Total	23	3	2	4	11979

106 12/01	Plum	2m	F(0-110)HHdl	GD	£3542
103 12/01	Wwck	2m	F(0-100)HHdl	SFT	£2000
113 4/00	Plum	2m	F(0-90)Hdl	HVY	£2394

Total win prize-money £7938

Going: Sf: 0-0 GS: 0-0 Gd: 0-0 GF: 0-0 Fm: 0-1
Distance: 2m/2m3: 0-0 2m4-2m7: 0-1 3m+: 0-0
Track: LH: 0-1 RH: 0-0 Tight: 0-0 Gall: 0-0
Aids: Bl: 0-0 Vi: 0-0 Tstrap: 0-0 Ckp: 0-0
Best Rating: 113 2/02 Asct 2m110y soft Hdl

Irish Flight (IRE)

104   **98**

7-y-o ch g Duky-Arewehavingfunyet (Green Shoon)
Noel T Chance Court Jesters Partnership 2

Placings: 402   (3414)
2003/04: 16⁴GS, 16⁰S, 16²S,

	Starts	1st	2nd	3rd	Win & Pl
NH Flat	2	0	0	0	
Hurdles	1	0	1	0	1536
Career Total	3	0	1	0	1536

Going: Sf: 0-2 GS: 0-1 Gd: 0-0 GF: - Fm: 0-0
Distance: 2m/2m3: 0-3 2m4-2m7: 0-0 3m+: 0-0
Track: LH: 0-3 RH: 0-0 Tight: 0-1 Gall: 0-0
Aids: Bl: 0-0 Vi: 0-0 Tstrap: 0-0 Ckp: 0-0
Best Rating: 98 1/04 Plum 2m soft Hdl

Moderate hurdler; acts on soft.

Irish Gold (IRE)

81 (62h)   (48h) **89**

9-y-o b g Good Thyne (USA)-Ardfallon (IRE) (Supreme Leader)
P Winkworth R R A Eadie

Placings: 0/5-5P   (3141)
2003/04: 16⁵S, 19⁵PS,

	Starts	1st	2nd	3rd	Win & Pl
Chases	2	0	0	0	0
Career Total	4	0	0	0	0

Irish Grouse (IRE)

5-y-o b g Anshan-Another Grouse (Pragmatic)
Miss H C Knight Mrs R A Humphries

Placings: 0   (2797)
2003/04: 17⁰GS,

	Starts	1st	2nd	3rd	Win & Pl
NH Flat	1	0	0	0	
Career Total	1	0	0	0	

Going: Sf: 0-0 GS: 0-1 Gd: 0-0 GF: - Fm: 0-0
Distance: 2m/2m3: 0-1 2m4-2m7: 0-0 3m+: 0-0
Track: LH: 0-1 RH: 0-0 Tight: 0-1 Gall: 0-0
Aids: Bl: 0-0 Vi: 0-0 Tstrap: 0-0 Ckp: 0-0

Irish Hussar (IRE)

107   (141h) **161**

8-y-o b g Supreme Leader-Shuil Ard (Quayside)
N J Henderson Major Christopher Hanbury

Placings: 1/210/1F121-P2P   (4424)
2003/04: 26³G, 24²G, 26⁶P,

	Starts	1st	2nd	3rd	Win & Pl
Chases	3	0	1	0	15400
Career Total	12	5	3	0	98485

143 4/03	Aint	3m1f	A Ch	GD	£44625
127 2/03	Leic	2m7f110y	D Ch	G-S	£5590
134 12/02	Winc	2m5f	D Ch	G-S	£5561
125 3/02	Newb	3m3f	D Hdl	SFT	£4953
127 3/01	Sand	2m110y	H NHF	HVY	£2803

Total win prize-money £63534

Going: Sf: 0-0 GS: 0-1 Gd: 0-2 GF: - Fm: 0-0
Distance: 2m/2m3: 0-0 2m4-2m7: 0-0 3m+: 0-3
Track: LH: 0-3 RH: 0-0 Tight: 0-0 Gall: 0-3
Aids: Bl: 0-0 Vi: 0-0 Tstrap: 0-0 Ckp: 0-0
Best Rating: 161 2/04 Newb 3m good Ch

High-class chaser; runner-up in 2003 Cathcart Chase at the Festival and comfortable winner of Grade Two at Aintree; pulled up in the Hennessy on return and fine second in the 2004 Aon Chase; pulled up in the Gold Cup; stays three miles; acts on soft ground, but best form to date is on good; has suffered from sore shins.

Irish Pleasure (IRE)

91   **97**

8-y-o b/br g Grand Plaisir (IRE)-Killegney (Reformed Character)
P Monteith J Stephenson

Placings: 30035/P4   (1527)
2003/04: 20⁰G, 22⁴F,

	Starts	1st	2nd	3rd	Win & Pl
Hurdles	2	0	0	0	0
Career Total	7	0	0	2	621

Going: Sf: 0-0 GS: 0-0 Gd: 0-1 GF: - Fm: 0-1
Distance: 2m/2m3: 0-0 2m4-2m7: 0-2 3m+: 0-0
Track: LH: 0-1 RH: 0-1 Tight: 0-1 Gall: 0-0
Aids: Bl: 0-0 Vi: 0-0 Tstrap: 0-0 Ckp: 0-0

Best Rating: 97 3/02 Hrfd 2m3f110y good Hdl

Moderate, lightly raced hurdler; seems best on a sound surface.

Irish Prince (IRE)

91 76

8-y-o b g Fresh Breeze (USA)-Killvarig (Crozier)
J G M O'Shea (D Shaw 24/1) Owen Lutchmaya

Placings:0P2P-026P0P (4234)
2003/04: 21³G, 16²GS, 16⁶G, 16⁶GS, 16⁰G, 22PGF,

	Starts	1st	2nd	3rd	Win & Pl
Hurdles	6	0	1	0	844
Career Total	10	0	2	0	1872

Going:	Sf: 0-0 GS: 0-2 Gd: 0-3 GF: - Fm: 0-1
Distance:	2m/2m3: 0-4 2m4-2m7: 0-2 3m+: 0-0
Track:	LH: 0-6 RH: 0-0 Tight: 0-3 Gall: 0-0
Aids:	Bl: 0-0 Vi: 0-5 Tstrap: 0-0 Ckp: 0-0
Best Rating:	82 5/02 Hrfd 2m1f good NHF

Irish Raider (NZ)

82 64

10-y-o b g Epidaurus (USA)-On The Move (AUS) (Bending Away (USA))
J L Spearing T N Siviter

Placings:0/00 (0417)
2003/04: 16⁹GS, 17⁰G,

	Starts	1st	2nd	3rd	Win & Pl
Hurdles	2	0	0	0	
Career Total	3	0	0	0	

Going:	Sf: 0-0 GS: 0-1 Gd: 0-1 GF: - Fm: 0-0
Distance:	2m/2m3: 0-2 2m4-2m7: 0-0 3m+: 0-0
Track:	LH: 0-1 RH: 0-1 Tight: 0-1 Gall: 0-0
Aids:	Bl: 0-0 Vi: 0-0 Tstrap: 0-0 Ckp: 0-0
Best Rating:	62 5/03 MRas 2m1f110y good Hdl

Irish Sea (USA)

105(95c) (96c)**90+**

11-y-o b g Zilzal (USA)-Dunkellin (USA) (Irish River (FR))
A E Price (S Flook 31/5) Glyn Byard

Placings:050P/6622F10U556011/B12/P/3P13/F334-
F6PP30 (1232)
2003/04: 21⁴GS, 16⁶G, 24⁶G, 20⁰G, 21⁰G, 20³GF, 21⁰GF,

	Starts	1st	2nd	3rd	Win & Pl
Hurdles	2	0	0	1	425
Chases	5	0	0	0	1075
Career Total	36	5	3	5	13856
90	4/02	Uttx	2m7f	H Ch	G-F	£1631
71	7/99	Worc	2m2f	E(0-115)HHdl	G-F	£2372
85	4/99	Folk	2m1f110yG(0-95)HHdl	G-F	£1660
74	4/99	Tntn	2m3f110yG(0-90)HHdl	G-S	£1509
84	10/98	MRas	2m1f110yG(0-95)HHdl	SFT	£1576
			Total win prize-money £8749

Going:	Sf: 0-1 GS: 0-0 Gd: 0-4 GF: - Fm: 0-2
Distance:	2m/2m3: 0-1 2m4-2m7: 0-5 3m+: 0-1
Track:	LH: 0-7 RH: 0-0 Tight: 0-4 Gall: 0-0
Aids:	Bl: 0-0 Vi: 0-0 Tstrap: 0-0 Ckp: 0-2
Best Rating:	96 4/03 Asct 2m3f110y good Ch

Plating-class chaser/hurdler; seems to have lost his way over fences and did not jump the French style hurdles at Worcester in August 2003 very well.

Irishkawa Bellevue (FR)

104 **101+**

6-y-o b/br g Irish Prospector (FR)-Strakawa (FR) (Sukawa (FR))
Jean-Rene Auvray The Magpie Partnership

Placings:64505-3553122P11 (4897)
2003/04: 20³GF, 22²G, 27⁵G, 27³GF, 22¹GF, 20²G, 22²G, 22PS, 22¹G, 22¹G,

	Starts	1st	2nd	3rd	Win & Pl
Hurdles	10	3	2	2	11582
Career Total	15	3	2	2	11582
101	4/04	Winc	2m6f	E(0-105)HHdl	GD	£3752
93	3/04	Font	2m6f110yF(0-100)HHdl	GD	£2821
81	9/03	Font	2m6f110yE(0-110)HHdl	G-F	£2590
			Total win prize-money £9163

Going:	Sf: 0-1 GS: 0-0 Gd: 2-6 GF: - Fm: 1-3
Distance:	2m/2m3: 0-0 2m4-2m7: 3-8 3m+: 0-3
Track:	LH: 2-6 RH: 1-3 Tight: 2-6 Gall: 0-0
Aids:	Bl: 3-8 Vi: 0-0 Tstrap: 0-0 Ckp: 0-1
Best Rating:	101 4/04 Winc 2m6f good Hdl

Moderate hurdler; front-runner; suited by trip just short of three miles and fast ground; has worn blinkers.

Irishman (IRE)

105(64h) (29h)**82**

10-y-o b g Bob Back (USA)-Future Tense (USA) (Pretense)
Miss I E Craig Miss I E L Craig

Placings:0/0005003F0.0P/P/6320.4401F2P/031UF303P5-
F34P1 (3526)
2003/04: 24PGF, 21³GF, 24⁴GS, 26PGF, 23¹G,

	Starts	1st	2nd	3rd	Win & Pl
Chases	5	1	0	1	4680
Career Total	39	3	2	6	21727
83	1/04	Leic	2m7f110yF(0-95)HCh	GD	£4260
94	7/02	Wxfd	3m	(0-88)HCh	G-F	£4868
86	8/01	Tram	2m4f	(0-95)HCh	G-Y	£5842
			Total win prize-money £14972

Going:	Sf: 0-0 GS: 0-1 Gd: 1-1 GF: - Fm: 0-3
Distance:	2m/2m3: 0-0 2m4-2m7: 0-1 3m+: 1-4
Track:	LH: 0-2 RH: 1-3 Tight: 0-1 Gall: 0-1
Aids:	Bl: 0-1 Vi: 0-0 Tstrap: 0-0 Ckp: 0-0
Best Rating:	107 5/01 Dund 2m135y firm NHF

Plating-class chaser; stays 3m; acts on a sound surface; has worn blinkers.

Irishtown Leader (IRE)

6-y-o b g Supreme Leader-Glamorous Gale (Strong Gale)
Miss M E Rowland The Christie Partnership

Placings:PP (3209)
2003/04: 21PS, 25PGS,

	Starts	1st	2nd	3rd	Win & Pl
Hurdles	2	0	0	0	
Career Total	2	0	0	0	

Going:	Sf: 0-1 GS: 0-1 Gd: 0-0 GF: - Fm: 0-0
Distance:	2m/2m3: 0-0 2m4-2m7: 0-1 3m+: 0-1
Track:	LH: 0-1 RH: 0-1 Tight: 0-0 Gall: 0-0
Aids:	Bl: 0-0 Vi: 0-0 Tstrap: 0-0 Ckp: 0-0

Iro Origny (FR)

94(99h) (88h)**78**

8-y-o b g Saint Cyrien (FR)-Coralline (FR) (Iron Duke (FR))
Miss Venetia Williams M J Morris

Placings:6/6F205043/P6434RR-56 (1303)
2003/04: 20⁵GF, 16⁶GF,

	Starts	1st	2nd	3rd	Win & Pl
Chases	2	0	0	0	0
Career Total	18	0	1	2	4917

Going:	Sf: 0-0 GS: 0-0 Gd: 0-0 GF: - Fm: 0-2
Distance:	2m/2m3: 0-1 2m4-2m7: 0-1 3m+: 0-0
Track:	LH: 0-2 RH: 0-0 Tight: 0-0 Gall: 0-0
Aids:	Bl: 0-0 Vi: 0-0 Tstrap: 0-2 Ckp: 0-0
Best Rating:	88 4/01 Tntn 2m3f110y gd-fm Hdl

Iron Buck

78 25

11-y-o gr g Buckley-Rusty To Reign (General Ironside)
W Davies Bill Davies

Placings:5PPPPP3R0 (4814)
2003/04: 25⁵GS, 25⁵GS, 22PS, 25PHY, 26PS, 24PHY, 22³G, 22RGS, 19⁰G,

	Starts	1st	2nd	3rd	Win & Pl
Chases	9	0	0	1	942
Career Total	9	0	0	1	942

Going:	Sf: 0-4 GS: 0-3 Gd: 0-2 GF: - Fm: 0-0
Distance:	2m/2m3: 0-0 2m4-2m7: 0-4 3m+: 0-5
Track:	LH: 0-3 RH: 0-6 Tight: 0-0 Gall: 0-0
Aids:	Bl: 0-0 Vi: 0-0 Tstrap: 0-0 Ckp: 0-0
Best Rating:	25 4/04 Chep 2m3f110y good Ch

Iron Express

108 (82h)**104**

8-y-o b g Teenoso (USA)-Sylvia Beach (The Parson)
G M Moore David Parker

Placings:30/433210/P/33553431-3PP22P3PF2P150 (4941)
2003/04: 25¹G, 25³G, 28PGS, 26PGF, 26²GF, 21²GF, 25PGF, 26³G, 24PG, 24PGS, 25²S, 22PG, 32¹G, 28⁵G, 31⁰GS,

	Starts	1st	2nd	3rd	Win & Pl
Chases	15	2	3	2	15057
Career Total	31	3	4	9	21597
102	3/04	Hexm	4m	F(0-100)HCh	GD	£3848
102	4/03	Hexm	3m1f	D(0-115)HCh	GD	£5525
90	1/01	Donc	2m4f	E Hdl	GD	£2254
			Total win prize-money £11627

Going:	Sf: 0-1 GS: 0-3 Gd: 2-7 GF: - Fm: 0-4
Distance:	2m/2m3: 0-0 2m4-2m7: 0-2 3m+: 2-13
Track:	LH: 2-13 RH: 0-1 Tight: 0-7 Gall: 0-0
Aids:	Bl: 0-1 Vi: 0-0 Tstrap: 0-0 Ckp: 0-0
Best Rating:	102 3/04 Hexm 4m good Ch

Moderate chaser; stays four miles; suited by good or softer; not the most consistent.

Iron N Gold

79 94

12-y-o b g Heights Of Gold-Southern Dynasty (Gunner B)
B G Powell D C T Partnership

Placings:023/12P03145/5/22235/2425311/P0P-1 (0456)
2003/04: 21¹HY,

	Starts	1st	2nd	3rd	Win & Pl
Chases	1	1	0	0	3521

Career Total	28	5	7	4	24127
94	5/03	Uttx	2m5f	F(0-90)HCh	HVY	£3521
103	11/01	Uttx	2m4f	F(0-110)HCh	HVY	£3400
93	11/01	Uttx	2m4f	E(0-105)HCh	SFT	£3120
99	3/97	Hntg	2m1f10y	E(0-110)HHdl	G-F	£2267
94	10/96	Strf	2m1f10y	E Hdl	GD	£2757

Total win prize-money £15067

Going:	Sf: 1-1 GS: 0-0 Gd: 0-0 GF: - Fm: 0-0
Distance:	2m/2m3: 0-0 **2m4-2m7: 1-1** 3m+: 0-0
Track:	**LH: 1-1** RH: 0-0 Tight: 0-0 Gall: 0-0
Aids:	Bl: 0-0 Vi: 0-0 Tstrap: 0-0 Ckp: 0-0
Best Rating:	103 11/01 Uttx 2m4f heavy Ch

Plating-class chaser, absent for a year when pulled up on return; also pulled up in selling handicap at Chepstow April 2003; has been breaking blood vessels and was promptly retired after landing 2m 5f handicap chase at Uttoxeter the following month.

Iron Warrior (IRE)

4-y-o b g Lear Fan (USA)-Robalana (USA) (Wild Again (USA))
G M Moore David Parker

Placings:U				(2136)

2003/04: 16UG,

	Starts	1st	2nd	3rd	Win & Pl
Hurdles	1	0	0	0	
Career Total	1	0	0	0	

Going:	Sf: 0-0 GS: 0-0 Gd: 0-1 GF: - Fm: 0-0
Distance:	2m/2m3: 0-1 2m4-2m7: 0-0 3m+: 0-0
Track:	LH: 0-1 RH: 0-0 Tight: 0-0 Gall: 0-1
Aids:	Bl: 0-0 Vi: 0-0 Tstrap: 0-0 Ckp: 0-0

Ironbridge

9-y-o gr g Scallywag-Bahama (Bali Dancer)
M Mullineaux (G L Edwards 16/5) John R Wilson

Placings:0/P/FP				(0614)

2003/04: 20FGS, 16PGF,

	Starts	1st	2nd	3rd	Win & Pl
Chases	2	0	0	0	
Career Total	4	0	0	0	

Going:	Sf: 0-0 GS: 0-1 Gd: 0-0 GF: - Fm: 0-1
Distance:	2m/2m3: 0-1 2m4-2m7: 0-0 3m+: 0-0
Track:	LH: 0-0 RH: 0-1 Tight: 0-1 Gall: 0-0
Aids:	Bl: 0-0 Vi: 0-0 Tstrap: 0-0 Ckp: 0-0
Best Rating:	46 4/01 MRas 2m1f110y heavy NHF

Isam Top (FR)

96(105c)   (95c)105

8-y-o b g Siam (USA)-Miss Sic Top (FR) (Mister Sic Top (FR))
M J Hogan Mrs Barbara Hogan

Placings:60/P6022246P0/422300324/5FP0P01243-				
606PF2202				(4898)

2003/04: 16⁶G, 18⁰G, 16⁶S, 18⁷G, 18⁷GS, 16²G, 17²G, 16⁸G, 16²G,

	Starts	1st	2nd	3rd	Win & Pl
Hurdles	6	0	1	0	1258
Chases	3	0	2	0	2008
Career Total	40	1	10	3	18195
105	8/02	Font	2m2f110yD(0-115)HHdl	GD	£3786

Total win prize-money £3786

Going:	Sf: 0-1 GS: 0-1 Gd: 0-7 GF: - Fm: 0-0
Distance:	2m/2m3: 0-9 2m4-2m7: 0-0 3m+: 0-0
Track:	LH: 0-5 RH: 0-4 Tight: 0-7 Gall: 0-0
Aids:	Bl: 0-0 Vi: 0-0 Tstrap: 0-0 Ckp: 0-0
Best Rating:	106 10/00 Kemp 2m gd-sft Hdl

Moderate hurdler/chaser, front runner; suited by a sound surface.

Isard Du Buard (FR)

73   59

8-y-o b g April Night (FR)-Upsala Du Buard (FR) (Un Numide (FR))
E L James Lady Thompson

Placings:1/2/0P				(4539)

2003/04: 16⁶GS, 21PGS,

	Starts	1st	2nd	3rd	Win & Pl
Hurdles	2	0	0	0	
Career Total	4	1	1	0	1932
108	1/01	Fknm	2m	H NHF	SFT	£1470

Total win prize-money £1470

Going:	Sf: 0-0 GS: 0-2 Gd: 0-0 GF: - Fm: 0-0
Distance:	2m/2m3: 0-1 2m4-2m7: 0-1 3m+: 0-0
Track:	LH: 0-0 RH: 0-2 Tight: 0-0 Gall: 0-0
Aids:	Bl: 0-0 Vi: 0-0 Tstrap: 0-0 Ckp: 0-0
Best Rating:	108 10/01 Chep 2m110y good NHF

Isard III (FR)

104(110h)   (132+h)125+

8-y-o gr g Royal Charter (FR)-Aurore D'Ex (FR) (Mont Basile (FR))
M C Pipe C M , B J & R F Batterham Ii

Placings:1/F1-624				(4840)

2003/04: 24⁵GS, 20²GS, 24⁴G,

	Starts	1st	2nd	3rd	Win & Pl
Hurdles	1	0	0	0	1036
Chases	2	0	1	0	11000
Career Total	6	2	1	0	18960
132	4/03	Asct	2m4f	D Hdl	GD	£5174
111	4/01	Newb	2m110y	H NHF	SFT	£1750

Total win prize-money £6924

Going:	Sf: 0-0 GS: 0-2 Gd: 0-1 GF: - Fm: 0-0
Distance:	2m/2m3: 0-0 2m4-2m7: 0-1 3m+: 0-0
Track:	LH: 0-3 RH: 0-0 Tight: 0-1 Gall: 0-2
Aids:	Bl: 0-0 Vi: 0-0 Tstrap: 0-0 Ckp: 0-0
Best Rating:	132 4/03 Asct 2m4f good Hdl

Useful performer; landed a bumper at Newbury first time up, before winning a point-to-point in February 2002; fell on chasing debut at Newbury; off track for a while after that until returning over hurdles to win at Ascot in 2003; has run well over fences twice since without winning; stays three miles; acts well on soft ground.

Isca Maiden

93(80c)   (75c)79+

10-y-o b m Full Extent (USA)-Sharp N' Easy (Swing Easy (USA))
G Brown Mrs C A Davies

Placings:660P00/01B306/46565P/P100P/630P-451P				(2773)

2003/04: 18⁴GF, 16²S, 19¹GS, 16⁸S,

	Starts	1st	2nd	3rd	Win & Pl
Hurdles	4	1	0	0	1834
Career Total	31	3	0	2	8733

79	12/03	MRas	2m3f110y	G(0-95)HdlG-S	£1834
80	10/01	Towc	2m	F(0-100)HHdl	SFT	£4407
87	12/99	Towc	2m	G(0-95)HHdl	SFT	£1660

Total win prize-money £7901

Going:	Sf: 0-2 GS: 1-1 Gd: 0-0 GF: - Fm: 0-1
Distance:	2m/2m3: 0-3 **2m4-2m7: 1-1** 3m+: 0-0
Track:	LH: 0-2 RH: **1-3** Gall: 0-0
Aids:	Bl: 0-0 Vi: 0-0 Tstrap: 0-0 Ckp: 0-0
Best Rating:	87 5/00 Towc 2m gd-fm Hdl

Very moderate hurdler/chaser; took a selling handicap hurdle at Market Rasen in December; stays two and a half miles.

Ishandraz (GER)

92   92

7-y-o gr g Mondrian (GER)-Isla Limpia (GER) (Limbo (GER))
M C Pipe Roger Stanley & Yvonne Reynolds

Placings:50012-2P				(0487)

2003/04: 22²G, 22PGF,

	Starts	1st	2nd	3rd	Win & Pl
Hurdles	2	0	1	0	1082
Career Total	7	1	2	0	5808
90	3/03	Plum	3m1f110yF(0-95)HHdl	G-F	£2901

Total win prize-money £2902

Going:	Sf: 0-0 GS: 0-0 Gd: 0-1 GF: - Fm: 0-1
Distance:	2m/2m3: 0-0 2m4-2m7: 0-2 3m+: 0-1
Track:	LH: 0-2 RH: 0-0 Tight: 0-2 Gall: 0-0
Aids:	Bl: 0-0 Vi: 0-2 Tstrap: 0-0 Ckp: 0-0
Best Rating:	92 5/03 Font 2m6f110y good Hdl

Plating-class hurdler; got off the mark over hurdles in Britain on handicap debut at Plumpton in March 2003; acts well on a fast surface; stays three miles plus well.

Isio (FR)

122(111h)   (135h)167+

8-y-o b g Silver Rainbow-Swifty (FR) (Le Riverain (FR))
N J Henderson Sir Peter and Lady Gibbings

Placings:221211/1113-5112				(4639)

2003/04: 16⁵GS, 16¹GS, 20¹G, 20²G,

	Starts	1st	2nd	3rd	Win & Pl
Hurdles	1	0	0	0	1250
Chases	3	2	1	0	163802
Career Total	14	8	4	1	214752
165	3/04	Newb	2m4f	B HCh	GD	£61201
157	1/04	Asct	2m	A HCh	G-S	£69600
141	2/03	Hntg	2m110y	D Ch	GD	£5434
138	1/03	Donc	2m110y	E Ch	GD	£4169
138	11/02	Kemp	2m	D Ch	GD	£5027
135	4/02	Ayr	2m	C Hdl	GD	£5183
133	3/02	Newb	2m110y	D Hdl	GD	£4504
123	2/02	Ludl	2m	E Hdl	SFT	£3003

Total win prize-money £158125

Going:	Sf: 0-0 GS: 1-2 Gd: 1-2 GF: - Fm: 0-0
Distance:	2m/2m3: 1-2 2m4-2m7: 1-2 3m+: 0-0
Track:	LH: 1-2 RH: 1-2 Tight: 0-1 **Gall: 1-1**
Aids:	Bl: 0-0 Vi: 0-0 Tstrap: 0-0 Ckp: 0-0
Best Rating:	167 4/04 Aint 2m4f good Ch

Smart chaser; easy winner of three minor novice chases in 2002/3, and third to Azertyuiop in Arkle at Cheltenham; beat Azertyuiop (who was conceding 19lb) in the Victor Chandler Chase at Ascot in January 2004; won the valuable Vodafone Gold Cup at Newbury on first try at two and a half miles; runner-up in Melling Chase at Aintree; acts on ground good or softer; neat jumper; still open to improvement.

Island Faith (IRE)

103(106h)   (106 h)123+

7-y-o b g Turtle Island (IRE)-Keep The Faith (Furry Glen)
Ferdy Murphy K Lee

Placings:10/623102-125P3   (4318)
2003/04: 16¹G, 16²G, 20⁵G, 16⁶G, 16³S,

	Starts	1st	2nd	3rd	Win & Pl
Chases	5	1	1		8107
Career Total	13	3	3	2	16304
120	11/03	Carl	2m	D Ch		GD £4576
104	1/03	Newc	2m4f	E Hdl		HVY £3445
119	4/02	Carl	2m1f	H NHF		GD £1834

Total win prize-money £9855

Going: Sf: 0-1 GS: 0-0 Gd: 1-4 GF: - Fm: 0-0
Distance: **2m/2m3: 1-4** 2m4-2m7: 0-1 3m+: 0-0
Track: LH: 0-3 **RH: 1-2** Tight: 0-1 Gall: 0-1
Aids: Bl: 0-0 Vi: 0-0 Tstrap: 0-0 Ckp: 0-0
Best Rating: 123 11/03 Aint 2m   good   Ch

Fair novice chaser; won on his chasing debut at Carlisle; no match for Santenay next time; stays two and a half miles, but effective at shorter; has won on heavy and good ground.

Island Fortress

97(94h)   (80h)85

5-y-o ch m Infantry-Misty Fort (Menelek)
H D Daly J B Sumner

Placings:55-5P53535   (4674)
2003/04: 16⁵G, 16⁹S, 16⁵GS, 16³G, 17⁵GS, 17³G, 16⁵G,

	Starts	1st	2nd	3rd	Win & Pl
Hurdles	5	0	0	1	730
Chases	2	0	0	1	824
Career Total	9	0	0	2	1554

Going: Sf: 0-1 GS: 0-2 Gd: 0-4 GF: - Fm: 0-0
Distance: 2m/2m3: 0-7 2m4-2m7: 0-0 3m+: 0-0
Track: LH: 0-2 RH: 0-5 Tight: 0-2 Gall: 0-0
Aids: Bl: 0-0 Vi: 0-0 Tstrap: 0-0 Ckp: 0-0
Best Rating: 85 3/04 Bang 2m1f110y good   Ch

Island Sound

98(107h)   (126h)120

7-y-o b g Turtle Island (IRE)-Ballet (Sharrood (USA))
D R C Elsworth Mrs Michael Meredith

Placings:412P5/U32U-1P2   (1296)
2003/04: 17¹GS, 16⁵GF, 16²GF,

	Starts	1st	2nd	3rd	Win & Pl
Hurdles	1	0	1	0	1448
Chases	2	1	0	0	5460
Career Total	12	3	3	1	17997
108	5/03	Strf	2m1f110yD Ch		G-S £5460
125	12/01	Tntn	2m1f	C Hdl		G-S £5853

Total win prize-money £11313

Going: Sf: 0-0 GS: 1-1 Gd: 0-0 GF: - Fm: 0-2
Distance: **2m/2m3: 1-3** 2m4-2m7: 0-0 3m+: 0-0
Track: **LH: 1-3** RH: 0-0 **Tight: 1-3** Gall: 0-0
Aids: Bl: 0-0 Vi: 0-0 Tstrap: 0-0 Ckp: 0-0
Best Rating: 126 12/01 Kemp 2m   good   Hdl

Useful front-running hurdler/chaser; won weakly contested extended 2m novice chase at Stratford May 2003; has been let down by his jumping; best suited by 2m and decent ground.

Island Star (IRE)

66   35+

4-y-o b g Turtle Island (IRE)-Orthorising (Aragon)
G P Enright (S Dow 21/1) R Gurney

Placings:05   (4363)
2003/04: 16⁵S, 16⁵GS,

	Starts	1st	2nd	3rd	Win & Pl
Hurdles	2	0	0	0	0
Career Total	2	0	0	0	0

Going: Sf: 0-1 GS: 0-1 Gd: 0-0 GF: - Fm: 0-0
Distance: 2m/2m3: 0-2 2m4-2m7: 0-0 3m+: 0-0
Track: LH: 0-2 RH: 0-0 Tight: 0-2 Gall: 0-0
Aids: Bl: 0-0 Vi: 0-0 Tstrap: 0-0 Ckp: 0-0
Best Rating: 35 3/04 Plum 2m   gd-sft   Hdl

Island Stream (IRE)

110   113

5-y-o b g Turtle Island (IRE)-Tilbrook (IRE) (Don't Forget Me)
J R Jenkins Mark Apps

Placings:0404-36PP0211U500UP5   (4776)
2003/04: 16³G, 16⁶GS, 20⁶GF, 16²GF, 16⁹GF, 16²G, 16¹GF, 16¹G, 16∪G, 16⁵GS, 16⁹GS, 17⁶GS, 19∪G, 16⁹G, 20⁵G,

	Starts	1st	2nd	3rd	Win & Pl
Hurdles	15	2	1	1	6786
Career Total	19	2	1	1	7197
113	11/03	Kemp	2m	E(0-100)HHdl	GD £2933
108	11/03	Uttx	2m	F(0-100)HHdl	G-F £2282

Total win prize-money £5215

Going: Sf: 0-0 GS: 0-3 Gd: 1-7 GF: - Fm: 1-5
Distance: **2m/2m3: 2-13** 2m4-2m7: 0-2 3m+: 0-0
Track: LH: 1-11 RH: 1-4 Tight: 0-2 Gall: 0-4
Aids: Bl: 0-0 Vi: 0-0 Tstrap: 0-0 Ckp: 0-0
Best Rating: 113 11/03 Kemp 2m   good   Hdl

Modest hurdler; suited by two miles; wants good ground; goes well for Tim Bailey.

Islands Thorns

5-y-o b g Thowra (FR)-Holly Hatch (Sulaafah (USA))
R H Alner Mrs U Wainwright

Placings:00P   (4664)
2003/04: 18⁰HY, 17⁰GS, 19⁰GS,

	Starts	1st	2nd	3rd	Win & Pl
NH Flat	2	0	0	0	0
Hurdles	1	0	0	0	0
Career Total	3	0	0	0	0

Going: Sf: 0-1 GS: 0-2 Gd: 0-0 GF: - Fm: 0-0
Distance: 2m/2m3: 0-2 2m4-2m7: 0-1 3m+: 0-0
Track: LH: 0-2 RH: 0-1 Tight: 0-3 Gall: 0-0
Aids: Bl: 0-0 Vi: 0-0 Tstrap: 0-0 Ckp: 0-0
Best Rating: 72 2/04 Folk 2m1f110y gd-sft NHF

Isle Be Lord (NZ)

12-y-o b g Isle Of Man (NZ)-Hi Pico (NZ) (Minnamour)
B P J Baugh M W & A N Harris

Placings:25243PP2/PPFPP/P   (0442)
2003/04: 19⁰GF,

	Starts	1st	2nd	3rd	Win & Pl
Hurdles	1	0	0	0	

Career Total	14	0	3	1	3813

Going: Sf: 0-0 GS: 0-0 Gd: 0-0 GF: - Fm: 0-1
Distance: 2m/2m3: 0-0 2m4-2m7: 0-1 3m+: 0-0
Track: LH: 0-0 RH: 0-1 Tight: 0-0 Gall: 0-0
Aids: Bl: 0-0 Vi: 0-0 Tstrap: 0-0 Ckp: 0-0
Best Rating: 105 3/00 Newc 3m   good   Hdl

Ismahaan

70f   72f

5-y-o ch m Unfuwain (USA)-River Divine (USA) (Irish River (FR))
M J Wallace Mrs Solna Thomson Jones

Placings:05   (4780)
2003/04: 16⁰G, 16⁵S,

	Starts	1st	2nd	3rd	Win & Pl
NH Flat	2	0	0	0	0
Career Total	2	0	0	0	0

Going: Sf: 0-1 GS: 0-0 Gd: 0-1 GF: - Fm: 0-0
Distance: 2m/2m3: 0-2 2m4-2m7: 0-0 3m+: 0-0
Track: LH: 0-1 RH: 0-1 Tight: 0-2 Gall: 0-0
Aids: Bl: 0-0 Vi: 0-0 Tstrap: 0-0 Ckp: 0-0
Best Rating: 72 2/04 Muss 2m   good   NHF

Isotop (FR)

103   (95h)104

8-y-o b g Port Etienne (FR)-Clorane (FR) (Rahotep (FR))
John Allen Avon Estates Ltd

Placings:4/0024400/F3243   (4888)
2003/04: 24²GS, 24³GS, 24²GS, 24⁴S, 24³GF,

	Starts	1st	2nd	3rd	Win & Pl
Hurdles	1	0	0	0	0
Chases	4	0	1	2	3349
Career Total	13	0	2	2	4221

Going: Sf: 0-1 GS: 0-2 Gd: 0-1 GF: - Fm: 0-0
Distance: 2m/2m3: 0-0 2m4-2m7: 0-0 3m+: 0-5
Track: **LH: 0-2** RH: 0-3 Tight: 0-4 Gall: 0-0
Aids: Bl: 0-0 Vi: 0-0 Tstrap: 0-0 Ckp: 0-0
Best Rating: 103 3/04 Ludl 3m   gd-sft   Ch

Modest chaser; returned from a long break to run well twice at Ludlow in 2004; stays three miles.

Istanbul (IRE)

87   92+

5-y-o b g Revoque (IRE)-Song Of The Glens (Horage)
C J Mann The Second Scrubbers Partnership

Placings:0R500   (4577)
2003/04: 16⁰G, 16ᴿGF, 16⁵GS, 16⁰G, 16⁰G,

	Starts	1st	2nd	3rd	Win & Pl
Hurdles	5	0	0	0	285
Career Total	5	0	0	0	285

Going: Sf: 0-0 GS: 0-1 Gd: 0-3 GF: - Fm: 0-1
Distance: 2m/2m3: 0-5 2m4-2m7: 0-0 3m+: 0-0
Track: LH: 0-4 RH: 0-1 Tight: 0-0 Gall: 0-4
Aids: Bl: 0-0 Vi: 0-0 Tstrap: 0-0 Ckp: 0-0
Best Rating: 92 11/03 Newb 2m110y gd-sft   Hdl

It Takes Time (IRE)
107(110h)   (163h)**154**
10-y-o b g Montelimar (USA)-Dysart Lady (King's Ride)
M C Pipe D A Johnson

Placings:*2110/111/1113331/32162-F5P*   (2917)
2003/04: 20FG, 20SGS, 24PG,

	Starts	1st	2nd	3rd	Win & Pl
Chases	3	0	0	0	2500
Career Total	22	10	3	4	170372

155	1/03	Hayd	2m6f	B Ch		G-S	£16640
151	4/02	Sand	3m	B Hdl		GD	£29000
149	12/01	Chel	3m	B HHdl		GD	£8572
139	11/01	Chel	3m1f110y	B HHdl		GD	£27716
138	11/01	NAbb	2m6f	C(0-130)	HHdl	SFT	£4820
134	2/01	Font	2m6f110y	D(0-125)	HHdl	G-S	£5489
123	1/01	Donc	3m110y	D Hdl		GD	£3752
104	10/00	Extr	2m3f	D Hdl		SFT	£3445
128	1/00	Leop	2m2f	NHF		YLD	£3588
120	12/99	Leop	2m	NHF		SH	£4312

Total win prize-money £107335

Going:	Sf: 0-0 GS: 0-1 Gd: 0-2 GF: - Fm: 0-0
Distance:	2m/2m3: 0-0 2m4-2m7: 0-0 3m+: 0-1
Track:	LH: 0-2 RH: 0-1 Tight: 0-0 Gall: 0-2
Aids:	Bl: 0-0 Vi: 0-0 Tstrap: 0-0 Ckp: 0-0
Best Rating:	163 11/02 Chel 3m1f110y gd-sft Hdl

Smart chaser; former high-class staying hurdler, a good third in both the Cheltenham Stayers' and the Martell Aintree Hurdle in 2002; won decent novice chase at Haydock on second start over fences in impressive fashion; runner-up in Grade 2 at Aintree; fell when still in contention on reappearance at Cheltenham but disappointed on a return to that track; stays at least 3m 1f; has won on good ground and soft.

It's A Wizard
68   **33**
4-y-o b g Wizard King-Axed Again (Then Again)
M A Barnes D Maloney

Placings:*0*   (1958)
2003/04: 16QGF,

	Starts	1st	2nd	3rd	Win & Pl
Hurdles	1	0	0	0	
Career Total	1	0	0	0	

Going:	Sf: 0-0 GS: 0-0 Gd: 0-0 GF: - Fm: 0-1
Distance:	2m/2m3: 0-1 2m4-2m7: 0-0 3m+: 0-0
Track:	LH: 0-1 RH: 0-0 Tight: 0-0 Gall: 0-0
Aids:	Bl: 0-0 Vi: 0-0 Tstrap: 0-0 Ckp: 0-0
Best Rating:	33 11/03 Hayd 2m gd-fm Hdl

It's A Wrap (IRE)
79   **89**
6-y-o b m Carroll House-Wraparound Sue (Touch Paper)
Miss K Marks Nick Shutts

Placings:*02*   (2941)
2003/04: 16QGF, 16²GS,

	Starts	1st	2nd	3rd	Win & Pl
NH Flat	1	0	0	0	0
Hurdles	1	0	1	0	582
Career Total	2	0	1	0	582

Going:	Sf: 0-0 GS: 0-1 Gd: 0-0 GF: - Fm: 0-1
Distance:	2m/2m3: 0-2 2m4-2m7: 0-0 3m+: 0-0
Track:	LH: 0-2 RH: 0-0 Tight: 0-0 Gall: 0-0
Aids:	Bl: 0-0 Vi: 0-0 Tstrap: 0-0 Ckp: 0-0

Best Rating: 89 12/03 Uttx 2m gd-sft Hdl

Pulled up in both starts in points; flattered by proximity to winner when 40/1 second in Uttoxeter seller Boxing Day 2003.

It's Beyond Belief (IRE)
98   **120**
10-y-o b g Supreme Leader-Rossacurra (Deep Run)
P F Nicholls J G Crumpler

Placings:*22/1-24P*   (4694)
2003/04: 26²HY, 26⁴HY, 23PG,

	Starts	1st	2nd	3rd	Win & Pl
Chases	3	0	1	0	1897
Career Total	6	1	3	0	11014

120	3/03	Plum	3m2f	E Ch	SFT	£7189

Total win prize-money £7189

Going:	Sf: 0-2 GS: 0-0 Gd: 0-1 GF: - Fm: 0-0
Distance:	2m/2m3: 0-0 2m4-2m7: 0-0 3m+: 0-3
Track:	LH: 0-2 RH: 0-1 Tight: 0-0 Gall: 0-0
Aids:	Bl: 0-1 Vi: 0-0 Tstrap: 0-0 Ckp: 0-0
Best Rating:	120 3/03 Plum 3m2f soft Ch

Winning pointer, modest haser; returned from a 15-month break to win at Plumpton in March 2003; lightly raced since; stays 3m 2f; acts on soft ground; goes well when fresh.

It's Definite (IRE)

5-y-o b g Definite Article-Taoveret (IRE) (Flash Of Steel)
P Bowen (A P Jarvis 30/7) R Owen

Placings:*P*   (2512)
2003/04: 19PGS,

	Starts	1st	2nd	3rd	Win & Pl
Hurdles	1	0	0	0	
Career Total	1	0	0	0	

Going:	Sf: 0-0 GS: 0-1 Gd: 0-0 GF: - Fm: 0-0
Distance:	2m/2m3: 0-0 2m4-2m7: 0-1 3m+: 0-0
Track:	LH: 0-0 RH: 0-1 Tight: 0-0 Gall: 0-0
Aids:	Bl: 0-0 Vi: 0-0 Tstrap: 0-0 Ckp: 0-0

It's Ej
101f   **91f**
6-y-o b g Karinga Bay-Merry Marigold (Sonnen Gold)
Mrs S J Smith Keith Nicholson

Placings:*606*   (4481)
2003/04: 16⁶GS, 16⁰GS, 17⁶HY,

	Starts	1st	2nd	3rd	Win & Pl
NH Flat	3	0	0	0	
Career Total	3	0	0	0	

Going:	Sf: 0-1 GS: 0-2 Gd: 0-0 GF: - Fm: 0-0
Distance:	2m/2m3: 0-3 2m4-2m7: 0-0 3m+: 0-0
Track:	LH: 0-2 RH: 0-0 Tight: 0-0 Gall: 0-0
Aids:	Bl: 0-0 Vi: 0-0 Tstrap: 0-0 Ckp: 0-0
Best Rating:	91 1/04 Weth 2m gd-sft NHF

Showed limited ability in bumper at Wetherby in January.

It's Got Buckleys
77f   **71f**
5-y-o b g El Conquistador-Saucey Pup (The Parson)

J W Mullins Ms Christina Storey

Placings:*00*   (3874)
2003/04: 16⁰GS, 17⁰GS,

	Starts	1st	2nd	3rd	Win & Pl
NH Flat	2	0	0	0	
Career Total	2	0	0	0	

Going:	Sf: 0-0 GS: 0-2 Gd: 0-0 GF: - Fm: 0-0
Distance:	2m/2m3: 0-2 2m4-2m7: 0-0 3m+: 0-0
Track:	LH: 0-1 RH: 0-1 Tight: 0-1 Gall: 0-1
Aids:	Bl: 0-0 Vi: 0-0 Tstrap: 0-0 Ckp: 0-0
Best Rating:	71 2/04 Folk 2m1f110y gd-sft NHF

It's Harry
105   **96+**
6-y-o b g Aragon-Andbracket (Import)
Mrs S J Smith Keith Nicholson

Placings:*24-3433300*   (4879)
2003/04: 16³GF, 17⁴G, 16³GF, 20³S, 20³G, 20⁰S, 20⁰GS,

	Starts	1st	2nd	3rd	Win & Pl
NH Flat	1	0	0	1	267
Hurdles	6	0	0	3	2101
Career Total	9	0	1	4	2813

Going:	Sf: 0-2 GS: 0-1 Gd: 0-2 GF: - Fm: 0-2
Distance:	2m/2m3: 0-3 2m4-2m7: 0-4 3m+: 0-0
Track:	LH: 0-6 RH: 0-1 Tight: 0-1 Gall: 0-0
Aids:	Bl: 0-0 Vi: 0-0 Tstrap: 0-0 Ckp: 0-0
Best Rating:	100 12/03 Weth 2m4f110y good Hdl

Modest form in summer bumpers; improved effort when third in novices' hurdle at Haydock in November; stays two and a half miles well.

It's Just Harry
95   **102**
7-y-o b g Tragic Role (USA)-Nipotina (Simply Great (FR))
C R Egerton James Blackshaw

Placings:*3/3*   (4309)
2003/04: 16³G,

	Starts	1st	2nd	3rd	Win & Pl
Hurdles	1	0	0	1	772
Career Total	2	0	0	2	1140

Going:	Sf: 0-0 GS: 0-0 Gd: 0-1 GF: - Fm: 0-0
Distance:	2m/2m3: 0-1 2m4-2m7: 0-0 3m+: 0-0
Track:	LH: 0-0 RH: 0-1 Tight: 0-0 Gall: 0-0
Aids:	Bl: 0-0 Vi: 0-0 Tstrap: 0-0 Ckp: 0-0
Best Rating:	109 3/02 Newb 2m110y gd-sft NHF

Moderate novice hurdler; promising third in a Newbury bumper behind Lord Sam on his debut but off the course for two years after; third on hurdles debut behind two useful prospects; acts on easy ground.

It's Music (IRE)
91(92h)   (94+h)**103+**
5-y-o b g Accordion-Leadon Lady (Monksfield)
M C Pipe D A Johnson

Placings:*52626*   (4048)
2003/04: 16⁵G, 19²G, 18⁶HY, 25²S, 22⁶G,

	Starts	1st	2nd	3rd	Win & Pl
Hurdles	3	0	1	0	787
Chases	2	0	1	0	1580
Career Total	5	0	2	0	2367

Going: Sf: 0-2 GS: 0-0 Gd: 0-3 GF: - Fm: 0-0
Distance: 2m/2m3: 0-2 2m4-2m7: 0-2 3m+: 0-1
Track: LH: 0-2 RH: 0-3 Tight: 0-2 Gall: 0-0
Aids: Bl: 0-0 Vi: 0-0 Tstrap: 0-0 Ckp: 0-0
Best Rating: 103 2/04   Extr   3m1f110y   soft   Ch

Modest efforts over hurdles so far, but improved for chase debut latest at Exeter when upped to three miles; should be capable of better in time.

It's Norman

8-y-o b g Vantastic-Arrogant Daughter (Aragon)
Mrs L Pomfret R P Brett

Placings:4/P   (4303)
2003/04: 16PG,

	Starts	1st	2nd	3rd	Win & Pl
Chases	1	0	0	0	
Career Total	2	0	0	0	0

Going: Sf: 0-0 GS: 0-0 Gd: 0-1 GF: - Fm: 0-0
Distance: 2m/2m3: 0-1 2m4-2m7: 0-0 3m+: 0-0
Track: LH: 0-0 RH: 0-1 Tight: 0-0 Gall: 0-0
Aids: Bl: 0-0 Vi: 0-0 Tstrap: 0-0 Ckp: 0-0
Best Rating: 31   7/99   Bang   2m1f   gd-fm   Hdl

It's Rumoured

97   81

4-y-o ch g Fleetwood (IRE)-Etourdie (USA) (Arctic Tern (USA))
Jean-Rene Auvray The Simpsons Partnership

Placings:313   (1559)
2003/04: 16SG, 161GF, 163GF,

	Starts	1st	2nd	3rd	Win & Pl
Hurdles	3	1	0	2	7018
Career Total	3	1	0	2	7018

81   8/03   Strf   2m110y   D Hdl   G-F   £5538
Total win prize-money £5538

Going: Sf: 0-0 GS: 0-0 Gd: 0-1 GF: - Fm: 1-2
Distance: 2m/2m3: 1-3 2m4-2m7: 0-0 3m+: 0-0
Track: LH: 1-3 RH: 0-0 Tight: 1-3 Gall: 0-0
Aids: Bl: 0-0 Vi: 0-0 Tstrap: 0-0 Ckp: 0-0
Best Rating: 81   10/03   Strf   2m110y   gd-fm   Hdl

Moderate juvenile hurdler; showed signs of ability on the Flat prior to finishing third on hurdling debut at Stratford July 2003 and scored at the same track the following month; suited by a sound surface.

It's Wallace

109   103

11-y-o b g Bedford (USA)-Rua Batric (Energist)
Miss Sheena West Grand Day Out Partnership

Placings:45P2301/P50F2146611/61126/2330/5FP05/P020
616   (4441)
2003/04: 24PS, 24QS, 212S, 20QS, 216S, 201G, 216S,

	Starts	1st	2nd	3rd	Win & Pl
Hurdles	7	1	1	0	4202
Career Total	39	7	5	3	28684

103	3/04	Hntg	2m4f110yG Hdl		GD	£2492
126	1/00	Plum	2m	E(0-115)HHdl	HVY	£2811
122	12/99	Plum	2m	F(0-110)HHdl	HVY	£2867
112	3/99	Plum	2m1f	B HHdl	HVY	£5714
108	2/99	Plum	2m4f	F(0-105)HHdl	G-S	£2425
104	11/98	Plum	2m4f	F(0-100)HHdl	SFT	£2792
91	12/97	Extr	2m2f	F(0-105)HHdl	SFT	£2176

Total win prize-money £21279

Going: Sf: 0-6 GS: 0-0 Gd: 1-1 GF: - Fm: 0-0
Distance: 2m/2m3: 0-0 2m4-2m7: 1-5 3m+: 0-2
Track: LH: 0-4 RH: 1-3 Tight: 0-2 Gall: 1-2
Aids: Bl: 0-0 Vi: 0-0 Tstrap: 0-0 Ckp: 0-2
Best Rating: 130 4/01   Sand   3m   gd-sft   Hdl

Moderate hurdler; acts on good or softer; runs his best races when racing prominently at distances up to two and a half miles.

Italian Clover

71   (0c)44

8-y-o b g Michelozzo (USA)-National Clover (National Trust)
Mrs H Dalton Michael H Ings

Placings:PP0   (1013)
2003/04: 24PG, 26PGF, 20QGF,

	Starts	1st	2nd	3rd	Win & Pl
Hurdles	1	0	0	0	0
Chases	2	0	0	0	0
Career Total	3	0	0	0	0

Going: Sf: 0-0 GS: 0-0 Gd: 0-1 GF: - Fm: 0-2
Distance: 2m/2m3: 0-0 2m4-2m7: 0-1 3m+: 0-0
Track: LH: 0-3 RH: 0-0 Tight: 0-1 Gall: 0-0
Aids: Bl: 0-1 Vi: 0-0 Tstrap: 0-0 Ckp: 0-0
Best Rating: 50   8/03   Worc   2m4f   gd-fm   Hdl

Italian Counsel (IRE)

116(97c)   (93c)117

7-y-o b g Leading Counsel (USA)-Mullaghroe (Tarboosh (USA))
L A Dace B V Ward & C Feeney

Placings:00000000/50123P03265P-U16111000   (4644)
2003/04: 16UG, 161GF, 16PG, 161GF, 171GF, 191GF, 16PG, 16PS, 16QG,

	Starts	1st	2nd	3rd	Win & Pl
Hurdles	9	4	0	0	36093
Career Total	29	5	2	2	41397

120	8/03	MRas	2m3f110yC(0-130)HHdl	G-F	£6739
117	7/03	MRas	2m110yB(0-140)HHdl	G-F	£23200
106	7/03	Worc	2m	E(0-110)HHdl	G-F	£3396
107	6/03	Worc	2m	G(0-90)HHdl	G-F	£2758
83	8/02	MRas	2m1f110yG(0-95)HHdl	G-S	£2023

Total win prize-money £38116

Going: Sf: 0-1 GS: 0-0 Gd: 0-4 GF: - Fm: 4-4
Distance: 2m/2m3: 3-8 2m4-2m7: 1-1 3m+: 0-0
Track: LH: 2-5 RH: 2-4 Tight: 2-4 Gall: 0-2
Aids: Bl: 0-0 Vi: 0-0 Tstrap: 0-0 Ckp: 0-0
Best Rating: 120 8/03   MRas   2m3f110y   gd-fm   Hdl

Useful hurdler; not as good over fences; four-time winner in the summer of 2003 including when a surprise winner of valuable handicap hurdle at Market Rasen; suited by two miles, but further; acts on most types of ground, though probably best on a fast surface.

Italian Mist (FR)

5-y-o b g Forzando-Digamist Girl (IRE) (Digamist (USA))
Julian Poulton S P Shore

Placings:P0   (0484)
2003/04: 16PGS, 16QGF,

	Starts	1st	2nd	3rd	Win & Pl
Hurdles	2	0	0	0	
Career Total	2	0	0	0	

Going: Sf: 0-0 GS: 0-1 Gd: 0-0 GF: - Fm: 0-1
Distance: 2m/2m3: 0-2 2m4-2m7: 0-0 3m+: 0-0
Track: LH: 0-1 RH: 0-1 Tight: 0-0 Gall: 0-1
Aids: Bl: 0-0 Vi: 0-0 Tstrap: 0-0 Ckp: 0-0

Itcanbedone Again (IRE)

103   90+

5-y-o b g Sri Pekan (USA)-Maradata (IRE) (Shardari)
Ian Williams David J Dunne

Placings:60-P1P   (0908)
2003/04: 18PG, 161GF, 17PGF,

	Starts	1st	2nd	3rd	Win & Pl
Hurdles	3	1	0	0	4173
Career Total	5	1	0	0	4173

90   6/03   Uttx   2m   E(0-105)HHdl   G-F   £4173
Total win prize-money £4173

Going: Sf: 0-0 GS: 0-0 Gd: 0-1 GF: - Fm: 1-2
Distance: 2m/2m3: 1-3 2m4-2m7: 0-0 3m+: 0-0
Track: LH: 1-3 RH: 0-0 Tight: 0-1 Gall: 0-0
Aids: Bl: 0-0 Vi: 0-0 Tstrap: 0-0 Ckp: 0-0
Best Rating: 90   6/03   Uttx   2m   gd-fm   Hdl

Plating-class hurdler; unlikely to stay beyond two miles; acts on fast ground.

Itch

102   64

9-y-o b g Puissance-Panienka (POL) (Dom Racine (FR))
R Bastiman Mrs P Bastiman

Placings:P4P0-46   (0322)
2003/04: 16PGF, 164G, 16PGF,

	Starts	1st	2nd	3rd	Win & Pl
Hurdles	3	0	0	0	0
Career Total	6	0	0	0	0

Going: Sf: 0-0 GS: 0-0 Gd: 0-1 GF: - Fm: 0-2
Distance: 2m/2m3: 0-3 2m4-2m7: 0-0 3m+: 0-0
Track: LH: 0-3 RH: 0-0 Tight: 0-1 Gall: 0-1
Aids: Bl: 0-0 Vi: 0-0 Tstrap: 0-0 Ckp: 0-0
Best Rating: 70   2/03   Uttx   2m   heavy   Hdl

Itchen Mill

86   66

7-y-o b m Afflora (IRE)-Treble Chance (Balinger)
R H Alner Roger and Victoria Harrison

Placings:5-556   (0709)
2003/04: 17QG, 16SHY, 176GF,

	Starts	1st	2nd	3rd	Win & Pl
Hurdles	3	0	0	0	0
Career Total	4	0	0	0	0

Going: Sf: 0-1 GS: 0-0 Gd: 0-1 GF: - Fm: 0-1
Distance: 2m/2m3: 0-3 2m4-2m7: 0-0 3m+: 0-0
Track: LH: 0-2 RH: 0-1 Tight: 0-0 Gall: 0-0
Aids: Bl: 0-0 Vi: 0-0 Tstrap: 0-0 Ckp: 0-0
Best Rating: 79   4/03   Extr   2m1f   gd-fm   NHF

Itchintogo (IRE)
53

6-y-o b g Namaqualand (USA)-Lamp Of Phoebus (USA)
(Sunshine Forever (USA))
L A Dace Miss S L O'Neill

Placings:0-504 (2067)
2003/04: 16⁵GF, 21¹⁰G, 20⁴GF,

	Starts	1st	2nd	3rd	Win & Pl
NH Flat	1	0	0	0	0
Hurdles	2	0	0	0	0
Career Total	4	0	0	0	0

Going:	Sf: 0-0 GS: 0-0 Gd: 0-1 GF: - Fm: 0-2
Distance:	2m/2m3: 0-1 2m4-2m7: 0-2 3m+: 0-0
Track:	LH: 0-1 RH: 0-1 Tight: 0-2 Gall: 0-1
Aids:	Bl: 0-0 Vi: 0-0 Tstrap: 0-0 Ckp: 0-0
Best Rating:	72 10/03 Hntg 2m110y gd-fm NHF

Its A Mystery (IRE)
90   70

5-y-o b m Idris (IRE)-Blue Infanta (Chief Singer)
R T Phillips Richard Phillips

Placings:500U (3254)
2003/04: 16⁵GS, 16⁹G, 16⁹S, 16ᵁGS,

	Starts	1st	2nd	3rd	Win & Pl
Hurdles	4	0	0	0	0
Career Total	4	0	0	0	0

Going:	Sf: 0-1 GS: 0-2 Gd: 0-1 GF: - Fm: 0-0
Distance:	2m/2m3: 0-4 2m4-2m7: 0-0 3m+: 0-0
Track:	LH: 0-3 RH: 0-1 Tight: 0-0 Gall: 0-0
Aids:	Bl: 0-0 Vi: 0-0 Tstrap: 0-0 Ckp: 0-0
Best Rating:	70 11/03 Wwck 2m good Hdl

Its Gotta Be Alfie (IRE)
93   78+

9-y-o ch g Zaffaran (USA)-Nimbi (Orchestra)
M Scudamore Mrs S Tainton

Placings:0/0P0/053/F34F (4505)
2003/04: 24⁵GS, 25⁵GS, 25⁴G, 25⁵FG,

	Starts	1st	2nd	3rd	Win & Pl
Chases	4	0	0	1	877
Career Total	11	0	0	2	1263

Going:	Sf: 0-0 GS: 0-2 Gd: 0-2 GF: - Fm: 0-0
Distance:	2m/2m3: 0-0 2m4-2m7: 0-0 3m+: 0-4
Track:	LH: 0-1 RH: 0-3 Tight: 0-0 Gall: 0-0
Aids:	Bl: 0-0 Vi: 0-0 Tstrap: 0-0 Ckp: 0-0
Best Rating:	82 3/02 Plum 3m2f good Ch

Lightly-raced, has shown a glimmer of ability over both hurdles and fences.

Its Only Polite (IRE)
97   (108h)111

8-y-o b g Roselier (FR)-Decent Debbie (Decent Fellow)
C Tinkler Bonusprint

Placings:0/4433/215-1 (4667)
2003/04: 24¹S,

	Starts	1st	2nd	3rd	Win & Pl
Chases	1	1	0	0	4862

Career Total   9   2   1   2   12372
111 4/04 Ling 3m   E(0-110)HCh SFT £4862
91 12/02 Hrfd 3m1f110y   E Ch   SFT
£4585
                        Total win prize-money £9448

Going:	Sf: 1-1 GS: 0-0 Gd: 0-0 GF: - Fm: 0-0
Distance:	2m/2m3: 0-0 2m4-2m7: 0-0 3m+: 1-1
Track:	LH: 1-1 RH: 1-1 Tight: 1-1 Gall: 0-0
Aids:	Bl: 0-0 Vi: 0-0 Tstrap: 0-0 Ckp: 0-0
Best Rating:	111 4/04 Ling 3m soft Ch

Modest chaser; stays three miles plus; acts on fast.

Its Sunny
92   81

10-y-o ch m Sunley Builds-Free To Go (Free State)
Mrs S J Smith Mrs S Smith

Placings:0253 (4569)
2003/04: 19⁹GF, 16²GF, 175G, 173GS,

	Starts	1st	2nd	3rd	Win & Pl
Hurdles	4	0	1	1	1139
Career Total	4	0	1	1	1139

Going:	Sf: 0-0 GS: 0-1 Gd: 0-1 GF: - Fm: 0-2
Distance:	2m/2m3: 0-4 2m4-2m7: 0-0 3m+: 0-0
Track:	LH: 0-4 RH: 0-0 Tight: 0-4 Gall: 0-0
Aids:	Bl: 0-0 Vi: 0-0 Tstrap: 0-0 Ckp: 0-0
Best Rating:	81 3/04 Bang 2m1f good Hdl

Novice hurdler; shaped with promise on second start.

Its Wallace Jnr
103   111

5-y-o b g Bedford (USA)-Built In Heaven (Sunley Builds)
Miss Sheena West Michael Moriarty

Placings:1300-1300 (4054)
2003/04: 18¹G, 21³G, 20⁹HY, 21⁹G,

	Starts	1st	2nd	3rd	Win & Pl
Hurdles	4	1	0	1	4961
Career Total	8	2	0	2	9013
111 10/03 Font	2m2f110yD(0-125)HHdl	GD			£3786
96 12/02 Winc	2m	E Hdl		G-S	£3192
		Total win prize-money £6978			

Going:	Sf: 0-1 GS: 0-0 Gd: 1-3 GF: - Fm: 0-0
Distance:	2m/2m3: 1-1 2m4-2m7: 0-3 3m+: 0-0
Track:	LH: 1-1 RH: 0-3 Tight: 1-1 Gall: 0-0
Aids:	Bl: 0-0 Vi: 0-0 Tstrap: 0-0 Ckp: 0-0
Best Rating:	111 1/04 Kemp 2m5f good Hdl

Modest hurdler; acts on yielding ground; effective at up to two miles-five.

Itsa Legend
109f   125f

5-y-o b g Midnight Legend-Onawing Andaprayer (Energist)
A King The We're A Legend Partnership

Placings:120 (4400)
2003/04: 16¹GS, 16²G, 16⁹G,

	Starts	1st	2nd	3rd	Win & Pl
NH Flat	3	1	1	0	3230
Career Total	3	1	1	0	3230
105 2/04 Kemp	2m	H NHF		G-S	£2467
		Total win prize-money £2468			

Going:	Sf: 0-0 GS: 1-1 Gd: 0-2 GF: - Fm: 0-0
Distance:	2m/2m3: 1-3 2m4-2m7: 0-0 3m+: 0-0
Track:	LH: 0-2 RH: 1-1 Tight: 0-0 Gall: 0-1

Aids:	Bl: 0-0 Vi: 0-0 Tstrap: 0-0 Ckp: 0-0
Best Rating:	125 3/04 Chel 2m110y good NHF

Stayed on late to land a Kempton bumper on his debut and also finished well when runner-up at Newbury next time.

Itsaboy

4-y-o b g Wizard King-French Project (IRE) (Project Manager)
L A Dace (J R Boyle 15/6) Brian McAtavey

Placings:4PP (4664)
2003/04: 22⁴GF, 16²GS, 19³GS,

	Starts	1st	2nd	3rd	Win & Pl
Hurdles	3	0	0	0	0
Career Total	3	0	0	0	0

Going:	Sf: 0-0 GS: 0-2 Gd: 0-0 GF: - Fm: 0-1
Distance:	2m/2m3: 0-1 2m4-2m7: 0-2 3m+: 0-0
Track:	LH: 0-3 RH: 0-0 Tight: 0-3 Gall: 0-0
Aids:	Bl: 0-0 Vi: 0-0 Tstrap: 0-0 Ckp: 0-0

Itsalf

6-y-o ch g Afzal-Sail On Sunday (Sunyboy)
J Rudge D H Morgan

Placings:066-00 (4524)
2003/04: 16⁹G, 16⁹GS,

	Starts	1st	2nd	3rd	Win & Pl
NH Flat	1	0	0	0	0
Hurdles	1	0	0	0	0
Career Total	5	0	0	0	0

Going:	Sf: 0-0 GS: 0-1 Gd: 0-1 GF: - Fm: 0-0
Distance:	2m/2m3: 0-2 2m4-2m7: 0-0 3m+: 0-0
Track:	LH: 0-2 RH: 0-0 Tight: 0-0 Gall: 0-1
Aids:	Bl: 0-0 Vi: 0-0 Tstrap: 0-0 Ckp: 0-0
Best Rating:	86 2/03 Winc 2m gd-sft NHF

Itsallgoingon
79f   88f

5-y-o b g Slip Anchor-Miss Springtime (Bluebird (USA))
N Wilson Mrs N C Wilson

Placings:0 (4179)
2003/04: 16⁹G,

	Starts	1st	2nd	3rd	Win & Pl
NH Flat	1	0	0	0	
Career Total	1	0	0	0	

Going:	Sf: 0-0 GS: 0-0 Gd: 0-1 GF: - Fm: 0-0
Distance:	2m/2m3: 0-1 2m4-2m7: 0-0 3m+: 0-0
Track:	LH: 0-1 RH: 0-0 Tight: 0-0 Gall: 0-1
Aids:	Bl: 0-0 Vi: 0-0 Tstrap: 0-0 Ckp: 0-0
Best Rating:	88 3/04 Donc 2m110y good NHF

Itsasurething
78   59

4-y-o b g Sure Blade (USA)-Ginka (Petoski)
J W Mullins M Jenkins

Placings:0006 (4664)
2003/04: 17⁹GS, 16⁹G, 16⁹GS, 19⁹GS,

	Starts	1st	2nd	3rd	Win & Pl
NH Flat	2	0	0	0	0
Hurdles	2	0	0	0	0
Career Total	**4**	**0**	**0**	**0**	**0**

Going:	Sf: 0-0 GS: 0-3 Gd: 0-1 GF: - Fm: 0-0
Distance:	2m/2m3: 0-3 2m4-2m7: 0-1 3m+: 0-0
Track:	LH: 0-2 RH: 0-2 Tight: 0-1 Gall: 0-0
Aids:	Bl: 0-0 Vi: 0-0 Tstrap: 0-0 Ckp: 0-0
Best Rating:	73 2/04 Kemp 2m good NHF

Itsdedfast (IRE)
96   **85**

8-y-o ch g Lashkari-Amazing Silks (Furry Glen)
L Lungo Mrs Barbara Lungo

Placings:1P-5500 (1838)
2003/04: 17⁵GF, 16⁵GF, 17⁹G, 17⁹G,

	Starts	1st	2nd	3rd	Win & Pl
Hurdles	4	0	0	0	0
Career Total	**6**	**1**	**0**	**0**	**2268**
107	10/02 Sedg 2m1f H NHF GD £2268				
				Total win prize-money	£2268

Going:	Sf: 0-0 GS: 0-0 Gd: 0-2 GF: - Fm: 0-2
Distance:	2m/2m3: 0-4 2m4-2m7: 0-0 3m+: 0-0
Track:	LH: 0-3 RH: 0-1 Tight: 0-3 Gall: 0-0
Aids:	Bl: 0-0 Vi: 0-0 Tstrap: 0-0 Ckp: 0-0
Best Rating:	107 10/02 Sedg 2m1f good NHF

Bumper winner; too keen and disappointing over hurdles so far.

Itsgottabdun (IRE)
71   **58**

7-y-o b g Foxhound (USA)-Lady Ingrid (Taufan (USA))
Miss M Bragg W H Whitley

Placings:000P0 (2699)
2003/04: 16⁹G, 17⁹GF, 17⁹G, 19⁹GS, 19⁹G,

	Starts	1st	2nd	3rd	Win & Pl
Hurdles	5	0	0	0	
Career Total	**5**	**0**	**0**	**0**	

Going:	Sf: 0-0 GS: 0-2 Gd: 0-2 GF: - Fm: 0-1
Distance:	2m/2m3: 0-4 2m4-2m7: 0-1 3m+: 0-0
Track:	LH: 0-3 RH: 0-2 Tight: 0-3 Gall: 0-0
Aids:	Bl: 0-0 Vi: 0-0 Tstrap: 0-0 Ckp: 0-0
Best Rating:	59 6/03 NAbb 2m1f good Hdl

Itsmyboy (IRE)
104f   **109+f**

4-y-o br g Frimaire-Hawkfield Lass (IRE) (The Parson)
M C Pipe D A Johnson

Placings:1 (4934)
2003/04: 18¹G,

	Starts	1st	2nd	3rd	Win & Pl
NH Flat	1	1	0	0	1918
Career Total	**1**	**1**	**0**	**0**	**1918**
109	4/04 Font 2m2f110yH NHF GD £1918				
				Total win prize-money	£1918

Going:	Sf: 0-0 GS: 0-0 Gd: 1-1 GF: - Fm: 0-0
Distance:	2m/2m3: 1-1 2m4-2m7: 0-0 3m+: 0-0
Track:	LH: 1-1 RH: 0-0 Tight: 1-1 Gall: 0-0
Aids:	Bl: 0-0 Vi: 0-0 Tstrap: 0-0 Ckp: 0-0
Best Rating:	109 4/04 Font 2m2f110y good NHF

Modest bumper performer; won on debut; acts on good.

Itsmyturnnow (IRE)

9-y-o b g Glacial Storm (USA)-Snuggle (Music Boy)
M J Roberts Mike Roberts

Placings:65-3160 (4626)
2003/04: 30³GF, 26¹GF, 23⁶GF, 21⁰G,

	Starts	1st	2nd	3rd	Win & Pl
Chases	4	1	0	1	1723
Career Total	**6**	**1**	**0**	**1**	**1723**
95	5/03 Folk 3m2f H Ch G-F £1410				
				Total win prize-money	£1411

Going:	Sf: 0-0 GS: 0-0 Gd: 0-1 GF: - Fm: 1-3
Distance:	2m/2m3: 0-0 2m4-2m7: 0-1 3m+: 1-3
Track:	LH: 0-2 RH: 1-2 Tight: 1-2 Gall: 0-1
Aids:	Bl: 0-0 Vi: 0-0 Tstrap: 0-0 Ckp: 0-0
Best Rating:	95 5/03 Folk 3m2f gd-fm Ch

Hunter chaser; dual winning pointer; suited by good/fast ground; stays three miles two, but yet to prove he gets further.

Itsonlyagame
80   **76**

4-y-o b c Ali-Royal (IRE)-Mena (Blakeney)
R Ingram Mrs Gina Brown

Placings:6 (2483)
2003/04: 16⁶GS,

	Starts	1st	2nd	3rd	Win & Pl
Hurdles	1	0	0	0	0
Career Total	**1**	**0**	**0**	**0**	**0**

Going:	Sf: 0-0 GS: 0-1 Gd: 0-0 GF: - Fm: 0-0
Distance:	2m/2m3: 0-1 2m4-2m7: 0-0 3m+: 0-0
Track:	LH: 0-1 RH: 0-0 Tight: 0-0 Gall: 0-1
Aids:	Bl: 0-0 Vi: 0-0 Tstrap: 0-0 Ckp: 0-0
Best Rating:	76 11/03 Newb 2m110y gd-sft Hdl

Modest performer; held but not disgraced on hurdling debut at Newbury.

Itsonlyme (IRE)
110   **135+**

11-y-o b g Broken Hearted-Over The Arctic (Over The River (FR))
Miss Venetia Williams Mel Davies

Placings:13110¹11561/P/F21/13FPP-2131P266PPP (4834)
2003/04: 25⁵GY, 20²G, 20¹G, 20³G, 24¹GF, 20⁵GS, 24²G, 26⁶G, 25⁶S, 24⁷S, 24⁶G, 26⁷GF,

	Starts	1st	2nd	3rd	Win & Pl
Chases	12	2	2	1	31606
Career Total	**30**	**10**	**3**	**3**	**62932**
135	11/03 Chel 3m110y E(0-135)HCh G-F £12426				
131	5/03 Weth 2m4f110yD Ch GD £5810				
126	5/02 Towc 2m6f D Ch G-S £4745				
126	4/02 Towc 2m4f D Ch G-S £5369				
126	4/00 Font 2m6f110yE Hdl GD £2702				
126	11/99 Bang 2m1f E Hdl SFT £2752				
118	11/99 Wwck 2m2f110yD Hdl GD £4198				
116	3/99 Hntg 2m110y H NHF G-S £1462				
116	1/99 Folk 2m1f110yH NHF HVY £1457				
107	11/98 Aint 2m110y H NHF G-S £2029				
				Total win prize-money	£42951

Going:	Sf: 0-2 GS: 0-1 Gd: 1-6 GF: - Fm: 1-2
Distance:	2m/2m3: 0-0 2m4-2m7: 1-4 3m+: 1-8
Track:	LH: 2-8 RH: 0-4 Tight: 0-1 Gall: 1-4
Aids:	Bl: 0-0 Vi: 0-0 Tstrap: 0-0 Ckp: 0-0
Best Rating:	135 12/03 Kemp 3m good Ch

Ivanoph (FR)
109(97h)   (111h)**133+**

8-y-o b g Roi De Rome (USA)-Veronique Iv (FR) (Mont Basile (FR))
P F Nicholls Neil Smith

Placings:06F/62142/F132F3P/214022-6U203F1 (4871)
2003/04: 17⁶GS, 17⁰GS, 17²GS, 16⁶HY, 19³G, 20⁶GS, 24¹S,

	Starts	1st	2nd	3rd	Win & Pl
Chases	7	1	1	1	13072
Career Total	**28**	**4**	**7**	**3**	**60471**
133	4/04 Bang 3m110y C(0-135)HCh SFT £9490				
125	11/02 Winc 2m D(0-120)HCh G-S £4754				
111	10/01 Chep 2m110y D Hdl SFT £3454				
	10/00 Autl 2m1f110y Ch HLD £11527				
				Total win prize-money	£29227

Going:	Sf: 1-2 GS: 0-4 Gd: 0-1 GF: - Fm: 0-0
Distance:	2m/2m3: 0-5 2m4-2m7: 0-1 3m+: 1-1
Track:	LH: 1-7 RH: 0-0 Tight: 1-4 Gall: 0-1
Aids:	Bl: 0-0 Vi: 0-0 Tstrap: 0-0 Ckp: 0-0
Best Rating:	133 4/04 Bang 3m110y soft Ch

Useful handicap chaser; goes well with cut in the ground; has shown a tendency to jump to his left; has done most of his racing at 2m, but stepped up successfully to 3m at Bangor in April.

Iverain (FR)
105   (136h)**132+**

8-y-o b g Le Riverain (FR)-Ursala (FR) (Toujours Pret (USA))
Sir John Barlow Bt (P F Nicholls 4/10) Sir John & Lady Barlow

Placings:0004/11P/124341-204106R (3037)
2003/04: 25²G, 24⁰G, 20⁴G, 20¹GF, 21⁰GS, 20⁶G, 24⁶GS,

	Starts	1st	2nd	3rd	Win & Pl
Chases	7	1	1	0	11711
Career Total	**20**	**5**	**2**	**1**	**42952**
132	11/03 Hayd 2m4f D(0-125)HCh G-F £3347				
116	4/03 Chep 3m E Ch G-F £5028				
119	10/02 Winc 3m1f110yD Ch GD £4800				
136	2/02 Winc 2m6f C(0-135)HHdl G-S £8463				
112	11/01 Chep 2m4f D Hdl SFT £3484				
				Total win prize-money	£25123

Going:	Sf: 0-0 GS: 0-2 Gd: 0-3 GF: - Fm: 1-2
Distance:	2m/2m3: 0-2 2m4-2m7: 1-4 3m+: 0-3
Track:	LH: 1-7 RH: 0-0 Tight: 0-3 Gall: 0-1
Aids:	Bl: 0-0 Vi: 0-0 Tstrap: 0-0 Ckp: 0-0
Best Rating:	136 2/02 Winc 2m6f gd-sft Hdl

Useful chaser; lightly raced when trained in France, stays beyond three miles and handles most types of ground; has worn blinkers; likes to race prominently.

Ivorsagoodun
97   **86**

5-y-o b m Piccolo-Malibasta (Auction Ring (USA))
N R Mitchell (M C Pipe 3/6) K L Dare

Placings:544636-620 (4818)
2003/04: 24⁶GF, 22²GF, 17⁰GF,

	Starts	1st	2nd	3rd	Win & Pl
Hurdles	3	0	1	0	2327
Career Total	**9**	**0**	**1**	**1**	**3487**

Going:	Sf: 0-0 GS: 0-0 Gd: 0-0 GF: - Fm: 0-3

Distance: 2m/2m3: 0-1 2m4-2m7: 0-1 3m+: 0-1
Track: LH: 0-1 RH: 0-2 Tight: 0-1 Gall: 0-0
Aids: Bl: 0-0 Vi: 0-0 Tstrap: 0-0 Ckp: 0-0
Best Rating: 87 6/03 NAbb 2m6f   gd-fm Hdl

Plating-class hurdler at up to 3m; acts on soft ground.

Ivory Bay

5-y-o b g Piccolo-Fantasy Racing (IRE) (Tirol)
J Hetherton K C West

Placings:6   (2089)
2003/04: 16⁶G,

	Starts	1st	2nd	3rd	Win & Pl
Hurdles	1	0	0	0	0
Career Total	1	0	0	0	0

Going: Sf: 0-0 GS: 0-0 Gd: 0-1 GF: - Fm: 0-0
Distance: 2m/2m3: 0-1 2m4-2m7: 0-0 3m+: 0-0
Track: LH: 0-1 RH: 0-0 Tight: 0-1 Gall: 0-0
Aids: Bl: 0-0 Vi: 0-0 Tstrap: 0-0 Ckp: 0-0

Ivory Fort

83f   65f

4-y-o ch g Bold Fort-Ivory Girl (IRE) (Sharp Victor (USA))
R Williams (M F Harris 22/3) R Williams

Placings:00   (4816)
2003/04: 14⁰GS, 16⁰G,

	Starts	1st	2nd	3rd	Win & Pl
NH Flat	2	0	0	0	
Career Total	2	0	0	0	

Going: Sf: 0-0 GS: 0-1 Gd: 0-1 GF: - Fm: 0-0
Distance: 2m/2m3: 0-1 2m4-2m7: 0-0 3m+: 0-0
Track: LH: 0-1 RH: 0-0 Tight: 0-0 Gall: 0-0
Aids: Bl: 0-0 Vi: 0-0 Tstrap: 0-0 Ckp: 0-0
Best Rating: 65 4/04 Chep 2m11y   good NHF

Ivory Girl (IRE)

9-y-o ch m Sharp Victor (USA)-Nordic Dance (USA)
(Graustark)
R Williams R Williams

Placings:PO   (0136)
2003/04: 19⁰GS, 20⁰G,

	Starts	1st	2nd	3rd	Win & Pl
Hurdles	1	0	0	0	0
Chases	1	0	0	0	0
Career Total	2	0	0	0	0

Going: Sf: 0-0 GS: 0-1 Gd: 0-1 GF: - Fm: 0-0
Distance: 2m/2m3: 0-0 2m4-2m7: 0-2 3m+: 0-0
Track: LH: 0-0 RH: 0-2 Tight: 0-1 Gall: 0-0
Aids: Bl: 0-0 Vi: 0-0 Tstrap: 0-0 Ckp: 0-0

Ivory Venture

4-y-o b f Reprimand-Julietta Mia (USA) (Woodman (USA))
I R Brown (D K Ivory 23/2) I R Brown

Placings:P   (4504)
2003/04: 17⁰G,

	Starts	1st	2nd	3rd	Win & Pl
Hurdles	1	0	0	0	
Career Total	1	0	0	0	

Going: Sf: 0-0 GS: 0-0 Gd: 0-1 GF: - Fm: 0-0
Distance: 2m/2m3: 0-1 2m4-2m7: 0-0 3m+: 0-0
Track: LH: 0-0 RH: 0-1 Tight: 0-0 Gall: 0-0
Aids: Bl: 0-0 Vi: 0-0 Tstrap: 0-0 Ckp: 0-0

Ivy House Lad (IRE)

4-y-o b g Presidium-Nice Spice (IRE) (Common Grounds)
I W McInnes Ivy House Racing

Placings:0   (3724)
2003/04: 16⁰S,

	Starts	1st	2nd	3rd	Win & Pl
NH Flat	1	0	0	0	
Career Total	1	0	0	0	

Going: Sf: 0-1 GS: 0-0 Gd: 0-0 GF: - Fm: 0-0
Distance: 2m/2m3: 0-1 2m4-2m7: 0-0 3m+: 0-0
Track: LH: 0-1 RH: 0-0 Tight: 0-0 Gall: 0-0
Aids: Bl: 0-0 Vi: 0-0 Tstrap: 0-0 Ckp: 0-0

Iznogoud (FR)

120   (70h)149

8-y-o b/br g Shafoun (FR)-Vancia (FR) (Top Dancer (FR))
M C Pipe County Stores-Avalon Surfacing

Placings:21140/312F/P5U05-00P132F6   (4965)
2003/04: 25⁰VS, 26⁰GS, 24⁸S, 20¹G, 24³G, 20²G, 21⁶G, 29⁶GF,

	Starts	1st	2nd	3rd	Win & Pl
Hurdles	1	0	0	0	0
Chases	7	1	1	1	38984
Career Total	22	4	3	2	100965
143	2/04	Kemp	2m4f110yC(0-135)HCh	GD	£9233
149	2/02	Asct	2m3f110yB Ch	G-S	£10808
144	1/01	Asct	2m110y A Hdl	SFT	£12000
117	12/00	Chep	2m110y D Hdl	HVY	£3383
			Total win prize-money		£35425

Going: Sf: 0-1 GS: 0-1 Gd: 1-4 GF: - Fm: 0-1
Distance: 2m/2m3: 0-0 2m4-2m7: 1-3 3m+: 0-5
Track: LH: 0-4 RH: 1-4 Tight: 0-1 Gall: 0-0
Aids: Bl: 0-0 Vi: 0-0 Tstrap: 0-0 Ckp: 0-0
Best Rating: 154 3/02 Chel 3m110y   gd-sft Ch

Very useful chaser; second to Hussard Collonges in the Royal & SunAlliance Chase in 2002; best run of 2002/3 when fifth in Attheraces Gold Cup; won handicap at Kempton in February 2004; good second in the Mildmay of Flete at Cheltenham; fell heavily at Becher's in the Topham Trophy at Aintree; stays three mile five; effective in yielding ground; has worn a visor.

Izzykeen

98f   96+f

5-y-o b g Keen-Washita (Valiyar)
Mrs S J Smith A A Thomason

Placings:3   (4962)
2003/04: 17³G,

	Starts	1st	2nd	3rd	Win & Pl
NH Flat	1	0	0	1	311
Career Total	1	0	0	1	311

Going: Sf: 0-0 GS: 0-0 Gd: 0-0 GF: - Fm: 0-0

Distance: 2m/2m3: 0-1 2m4-2m7: 0-0 3m+: 0-0
Track: LH: 0-0 RH: 0-1 Tight: 0-1 Gall: 0-0
Aids: Bl: 0-0 Vi: 0-0 Tstrap: 0-0 Ckp: 0-0
Best Rating: 96 4/04 MRas 2m1f110y good NHF

J J Baboo (IRE)

85   85

11-y-o b g Be My Guest (USA)-Maricica (Ahonoora)
Jedd O'Keeffe Roland Roper

Placings:5442/622245302/43065/32131/2P03P/0031PP-04
                                               (1654)
2003/04: 21⁰G, 27⁴S,

	Starts	1st	2nd	3rd	Win & Pl
Chases	2	0	0	0	
Career Total	36	3	7	6	24137
85	3/03	Weth	3m1f	F(0-100)HCh	GD	£4160
99	4/00	Sedg	2m5f	D Ch	GD	£3984
96	3/00	Catt	2m	D Ch	G-F	£4290
			Total win prize-money		£12435

Going: Sf: 0-0 GS: 0-0 Gd: 0-2 GF: - Fm: 0-0
Distance: 2m/2m3: 0-0 2m4-2m7: 0-1 3m+: 0-1
Track: LH: 0-2 RH: 0-0 Tight: 0-2 Gall: 0-0
Aids: Bl: 0-0 Vi: 0-1 Tstrap: 0-0 Ckp: 0-0
Best Rating: 105 11/00 Catt 2m3f   good Ch

Plating-class chaser; stays three miles; off the track for nearly two years through injury after December 2000; emerged from the wilderness with a narrow win at Wetherby in March 2003.

Jabiru (IRE)

11-y-o b/br g Lafontaine (USA)-Country Glen (Furry Glen)
Mrs K M Sanderson Mrs K M Sanderson

Placings:200/335F6/P/1/21230114-01P323   (4858)
2003/04: 25⁰GF, 26¹GF, 25⁸G, 24³G, 22²G, 24³GF,

	Starts	1st	2nd	3rd	Win & Pl
Chases	6	1	1	2	4856
Career Total	24	5	4	5	23201
97	5/03	NAbb	3m2f110yH Ch	G-F	£3672
89	4/03	Tntn	3m	H Ch	FRM	£2681
99	3/03	Tntn	3m	H Ch	FRM	£3094
101	5/02	NAbb	3m2f110yH Ch	G-S	£2212
97	4/02	Extr	2m7f110yH Ch	FRM	£1761
			Total win prize-money		£13422

Going: Sf: 0-0 GS: 0-0 Gd: 0-3 GF: - Fm: 1-3
Distance: 2m/2m3: 0-0 2m4-2m7: 0-1 3m+: 1-5
Track: LH: 1-2 RH: 0-4 Tight: 1-3 Gall: 0-1
Aids: Bl: 1-4 Vi: 0-0 Tstrap: 0-0 Ckp: 0-0
Best Rating: 123 6/02 Strf 3m4f   gd-fm Ch

Useful pointer/hunter chaser; stays three miles and handles any ground; probably best going right-handed.

Jaboune (FR)

113(108c)   (125+c)135

7-y-o ch g Johann Quatz (FR)-Seasonal Pleasure (USA)
(Graustark)
A King Mrs R J Skan

Placings:2323/2111P122032050-112445460   (4853)
2003/04: 19¹GS, 16¹GF, 21²GF, 16⁴GF, 16⁴G, 16⁵G, 20⁴GS, 16⁶G, 22⁸GS,

	Starts	1st	2nd	3rd	Win & Pl
Hurdles	4	0	0	0	5175
Chases	5	2	1	0	11371
Career Total	27	6	7	3	64586
111	5/03	Fknm	2m110y E Ch	G-F	£3822

124	5/03	Hrfd	2m3f	E Ch		G-S	£4498
123	11/02	Weth	2m	C Hdl		G-S	£6805
131	6/02	MRas	2m1f110yC(0-130)HHdl		G-F	£7150
119	6/02	NAbb	2m1f	D Hdl		GD	£3469
108	6/02	Hrfd	2m1f	E Hdl		GD	£2765

Total win prize-money £28511

Going:	Sf: 0-0 GS: 1-3 Gd: 0-3 GF: - Fm: 1-3
Distance:	2m/2m3: 2-6 2m4-2m7: 0-3 3m+: 0-0
Track:	LH: 1-6 RH: 1-3 Tight: 1-4 Gall: 0-0
Aids:	Bl: 0-0 Vi: 0-0 Tstrap: 0-0 Ckp: 0-0
Best Rating:	137 11/03 Chel 2m110y good Hdl

Useful hurdler/chaser; effective up to two and a half miles; acts on most types of ground; has worn a tongue-tie; likes to race prominently; tough.

Jabulani (IRE)

98   82

5-y-o b g Marju (IRE)-Houwara (IRE) (Darshaan)
G M Moore   Keith Nicholson

Placings:3   (0473)
2003/04: 17³GS,

	Starts	1st	2nd	3rd	Win & Pl
Hurdles	1	0	0	1	596
Career Total	1	0	0	1	596

Going:	Sf: 0-0 GS: 0-1 Gd: 0-0 GF: - Fm: 0-0
Distance:	2m/2m3: 0-1 2m4-2m7: 0-0 3m+: 0-0
Track:	LH: 0-1 RH: 0-0 Tight: 0-1 Gall: 0-0
Aids:	Bl: 0-0 Vi: 0-0 Tstrap: 0-0 Ckp: 0-0
Best Rating:	82 5/03 Crtml 2m1f110y gd-sft Hdl

Novice hurdler; made satisfactory hurdles debut at Cartmel.

Jac An Ree (IRE)

94   89

8-y-o b g Supreme Leader-Nic An Ree (IRE) (King's Ride)
A King   C Newport, J Draper & T Edmonds

Placings:2/65-00   (4560)
2003/04: 21⁰G, 21⁰GS,

	Starts	1st	2nd	3rd	Win & Pl
Hurdles	2	0	0	0	
Career Total	5	0	1	0	415

Going:	Sf: 0-0 GS: 0-1 Gd: 0-1 GF: - Fm: 0-0
Distance:	2m/2m3: 0-4 2m4-2m7: 0-2 3m+: 0-0
Track:	LH: 0-2 RH: 0-0 Tight: 0-0 Gall: 0-2
Aids:	Bl: 0-0 Vi: 0-0 Tstrap: 0-0 Ckp: 0-0
Best Rating:	101 12/02 Wwck 2m soft NHF

Has shown promise in bumpers and novice hurdles; will be capable of better in time.

Jacarado (IRE)

89   67

6-y-o b g Jurado (USA)-Lady Mearba (IRE) (Le Bavard (FR))
R Dickin   R G & R A Whitehead

Placings:000P   (4445)
2003/04: 16⁰G, 22⁰GS, 19⁰G, 25²S,

	Starts	1st	2nd	3rd	Win & Pl
NH Flat	1	0	0	0	0
Hurdles	3	0	0	0	0
Career Total	4	0	0	0	0

Going:	Sf: 0-1 GS: 0-1 Gd: 0-2 GF: - Fm: 0-0

Distance:	2m/2m3: 0-1 2m4-2m7: 0-2 3m+: 0-1
Track:	LH: 0-3 RH: 0-1 Tight: 0-2 Gall: 0-0
Aids:	Bl: 0-0 Vi: 0-0 Tstrap: 0-0 Ckp: 0-0
Best Rating:	70 12/03 Wwck 2m good NHF

Has shown very little over hurdles.

Jaccout (FR)

104(76c)   (49c)85

6-y-o b g Sheyrann-Jacottiere (FR) (Dom Racine (FR))
R Johnson (P C Ritchens 2/8)   Robert Johnson

Placings:0/05511FF43324F/6P312122000P-P000046000
         (4883)
2003/04: 20PGF, 16⁰GF, 22⁰G, 20⁰G, 16⁰GS, 20⁴S, 17⁶GS, 20⁰HY, 20⁰S, 17⁰GS,

	Starts	1st	2nd	3rd	Win & Pl
Hurdles	8	0	0	0	
Chases	2	0	0	0	
Career Total	36	4	4	3	40347

8/02	Stma	2m1f	Hdl	GD	£3828
7/02	Autl	2m1f110y	Ch	VS	£6184
12/01	Ange	2m2f110y	Ch	G-S	£4090
11/01	Mchl	2m2f	Ch	GD	£2910

Total win prize-money £17012

Going:	Sf: 0-3 GS: 0-3 Gd: 0-2 GF: - Fm: 0-2
Distance:	2m/2m3: 0-4 2m4-2m7: 0-6 3m+: 0-0
Track:	LH: 0-7 RH: 0-3 Tight: 0-3 Gall: 0-0
Aids:	Bl: 0-0 Vi: 0-0 Tstrap: 0-3 Ckp: 0-0
Best Rating:	85 11/03 Kels 2m6f110y good Hdl

Ex-French moderate hurdler/chaser; suited by trips around two miles.

Jacdor (IRE)

108(115h)   (127 h)118+

10-y-o b g Be My Native (USA)-Bellalma (Belfalas)
R Dickin   Jackie Matthews & Doreen Evans

Placings:45220/3016P/153FFP/PF41305414/12612-
60204511   (3905)
2003/04: 20⁶S, 20⁰GF, 24²GS, 30⁰GS, 20⁴GS, 25⁵S, 24¹G, 24¹GS,

	Starts	1st	2nd	3rd	Win & Pl
Hurdles	2	0	0	0	242
Chases	6	2	1	0	12832
Career Total	39	8	5	3	49117

127	2/04	Tntn	3m	D(0-115)HCh	G-S	£5668
114	2/04	Kemp	3m	E(0-115)HCh	GD	£4221
127	1/03	Wwck	3m1f	D(0-120)HHdl	HVY	£5167
117	10/02	Chel	2m110y	E(0-135)HHdl	GD	£6954
111	3/02	Towc	2m	E(0-110)HHdl	SFT	£2628
105	11/01	Bang	2m1f	F(0-110)HHdl	G-S	£3558
119	11/00	Wwck	2m110y	D(0-125)HCh	SFT	£4192
125	3/00	Bang	2m1f110yE Ch		SFT	£3412

Total win prize-money £35806

Going:	Sf: 0-2 GS: 1-4 Gd: 1-1 GF: - Fm: 0-1
Distance:	2m/2m3: 0-2 2m4-2m7: 0-3 3m+: 2-5
Track:	LH: 0-6 RH: 2-2 Tight: 1-3 Gall: 0-0
Aids:	Bl: 2-5 Vi: 0-3 Tstrap: 0-0 Ckp: 0-0
Best Rating:	127 2/04 Tntn 3m gd-sft Ch

Moderate hurdler/chaser; suited by three miles plus; best on soft but is effective on good; has worn blinkers and a visor.

Jack Dash (IRE)

6-y-o b g Teamster-Gathering Moss (Le Moss)
Miss H C Knight   Philip Newton

Placings:5P   (3956)
2003/04: 16⁵GF, 22PG,

	Starts	1st	2nd	3rd	Win & Pl
NH Flat	1	0	0	0	0
Hurdles	1	0	0	0	0
Career Total	2	0	0	0	0

Going:	Sf: 0-0 GS: 0-0 Gd: 0-1 GF: - Fm: 0-1
Distance:	2m/2m3: 0-1 2m4-2m7: 0-1 3m+: 0-0
Track:	LH: 0-1 RH: 0-0 Tight: 0-1 Gall: 0-0
Aids:	Bl: 0-0 Vi: 0-0 Tstrap: 0-0 Ckp: 0-0
Best Rating:	77 12/03 Ludl 2m gd-fm NHF

Jack Dawson (IRE)

106   128+

7-y-o b g Persian Bold-Dream Of Jenny (Caerleon (USA))
John Berry   The Premier Cru

Placings:P/12-3   (4644)
2003/04: 16³G,

	Starts	1st	2nd	3rd	Win & Pl
Hurdles	1	0	0	1	4950
Career Total	4	1	1	1	8765

117 9/02 Sthl 2m1f E Hdl GD £2961

Total win prize-money £2961

Going:	Sf: 0-0 GS: 0-0 Gd: 0-1 GF: - Fm: 0-0
Distance:	2m/2m3: 0-1 2m4-2m7: 0-0 3m+: 0-0
Track:	LH: 0-1 RH: 0-0 Tight: 0-1 Gall: 0-0
Aids:	Bl: 0-0 Vi: 0-0 Tstrap: 0-0 Ckp: 0-0
Best Rating:	128 4/04 Aint 2m110y good Hdl

Useful hurdler, best at two miles; acts well on fast ground.

Jack Doran

85f   58f

4-y-o ch g Gildoran-Faustelerie (Faustus (USA))
J R Jenkins   Nolan's Bar Racing Syndicate

Placings:000   (4213)
2003/04: 12⁰GF, 14⁰G, 16⁰G,

	Starts	1st	2nd	3rd	Win & Pl
NH Flat	3	0	0	0	
Career Total	3	0	0	0	

Going:	Sf: 0-0 GS: 0-0 Gd: 0-2 GF: - Fm: 0-1
Distance:	2m/2m3: 0-1 2m4-2m7: 0-0 3m+: 0-0
Track:	LH: 0-2 RH: 0-1 Tight: 0-0 Gall: 0-0
Aids:	Bl: 0-0 Vi: 0-0 Tstrap: 0-0 Ckp: 0-0
Best Rating:	58 11/03 Newb 1m4f110y gd-fm NHF

Jack Durrance (IRE)

81   49

4-y-o b g Polish Precedent (USA)-Atlantic Desire (IRE) (Ela-Mana-Mou)
G A Ham (M Johnston 29/9)   Jack Durrance Partnership

Placings:0000   (4444)
2003/04: 16⁰GS, 18⁰G, 16⁰G, 16⁰S,

	Starts	1st	2nd	3rd	Win & Pl
Hurdles	4	0	0	0	
Career Total	4	0	0	0	

Going:	Sf: 0-1 GS: 0-1 Gd: 0-2 GF: - Fm: 0-0
Distance:	2m/2m3: 0-4 2m4-2m7: 0-0 3m+: 0-0
Track:	LH: 0-2 RH: 0-2 Tight: 0-1 Gall: 0-0
Aids:	Bl: 0-0 Vi: 0-0 Tstrap: 0-0 Ckp: 0-0
Best Rating:	49 2/04 Kemp 2m good Hdl

Jack Flush (IRE)

89   **85**

10-y-o b g Broken Hearted-Clubhouse Turn (IRE) (King Of Clubs)
M E Sowersby B Walker (Hull)

Placings:015300P/33345612/440P63/005000   (4614)
2003/04: 17⁰GS, 17⁹GS, 16⁵G, 19⁹G, 16⁹GF, 17⁰G,

	Starts	1st	2nd	3rd	Win & Pl
Hurdles	6	0	0	0	0
Career Total	27	2	1	5	5699
84 2/01 Catt	2m3f	G(0-90)HHdl		SFT	£1939
92 12/98 Catt	2m3f	G Hdl		GD	£1495

Total win prize-money £3434

Going:	Sf: 0-0 GS: 0-1 Gd: 0-4 GF: - Fm: 0-1
Distance:	2m/2m3: 0-6 2m4-2m7: 0-0 3m+: 0-0
Track:	LH: 0-5 RH: 0-1 Tight: 0-6 Gall: 0-0
Aids:	Bl: 0-4 Vi: 0-1 Tstrap: 0-5 Ckp: 0-0
Best Rating:	92 12/98 Catt 2m3f good Hdl

Jack Fuller (IRE)

106(98h)   (87h)**104**

7-y-o b g Be My Native (USA)-Jacks Sister (IRE) (Entitled)
P R Hedger The Brightling Club 1997

Placings:304003-033213   (4593)
2003/04: 20⁰GS, 16³G, 16⁹GS, 16²S, 16¹G, 16³G,

	Starts	1st	2nd	3rd	Win & Pl
Hurdles	1	0	0	0	0
Chases	5	1	1	3	7042
Career Total	12	1	1	5	7828
104 3/04 Tntn	2m110y E(0-100)HCh		£4111		

Total win prize-money £4111

Going:	Sf: 0-1 GS: 0-2 Gd: 1-3 GF: - Fm: 0-0
Distance:	2m/2m3: 1-5 2m4-2m7: 0-0 3m+: 0-0
Track:	LH: 0-1 RH: 1-5 Tight: 1-5 Gall: 0-1
Aids:	Bl: 1-2 Vi: 0-1 Tstrap: 0-0 Ckp: 0-1
Best Rating:	104 3/04 Tntn 2m110y good Ch

Very moderate chaser; best over two miles and a sound surface; suited by forcing tactics; has worn headgear.

Jack Mack

8-y-o b g Solway Beleef-Maybella (Quiet Fling (USA))
M A Barnes Brian McNichol

Placings:P   (0557)
2003/04: 16ᴾGF,

	Starts	1st	2nd	3rd	Win & Pl
Hurdles	1	0	0	0	0
Career Total	1	0	0	0	0

Going:	Sf: 0-0 GS: 0-0 Gd: 0-0 GF: - Fm: 0-1
Distance:	2m/2m3: 0-1 2m4-2m7: 0-0 3m+: 0-0
Track:	LH: 0-0 RH: 0-1 Tight: 0-0 Gall: 0-0
Aids:	Bl: 0-0 Vi: 0-0 Tstrap: 0-1 Ckp: 0-0

Jack Martin (IRE)

109   **127**

7-y-o ch g Erin's Isle-Rolling Penny (IRE) (Le Moss)
S Gollings J B Webb

Placings:34-43F32123   (4852)
2003/04: 17⁴GS, 16³S, 20ᶠHY, 21³GS, 19²G, 20¹HY, 20²G, 20³GS,

	Starts	1st	2nd	3rd	Win & Pl
NH Flat	2	0	0	1	298

Hurdles	6	1	2	2	7833
Career Total	10	1	2	4	9354
112 3/04 Newc	2m4f	E(0-105)HHdl		HVY	£4033

Total win prize-money £4033

Going:	Sf: 1-3 GS: 0-3 Gd: 0-2 GF: - Fm: 0-0
Distance:	2m/2m3: 0-2 2m4-2m7: 1-6 3m+: 0-0
Track:	LH: 1-6 RH: 0-1 Tight: 0-3 Gall: 1-1
Aids:	Bl: 0-0 Vi: 0-0 Tstrap: 0-0 Ckp: 0-0
Best Rating:	127 4/04 Ayr 2m4f gd-sft Hdl

Fair hurdler; stays two and a half miles; acts on good and heavy ground; consistent sort who is sure to win more races.

Jack Of Kilcash (IRE)

10-y-o br g Glacial Storm (USA)-Candora (Cantab)
Nigel Benstead Nigel Benstead

Placings:6   (0350)
2003/04: 21⁶GF,

	Starts	1st	2nd	3rd	Win & Pl
Chases	1	0	0	0	0
Career Total	1	0	0	0	0

Going:	Sf: 0-0 GS: 0-0 Gd: 0-0 GF: - Fm: 0-1
Distance:	2m/2m3: 0-0 2m4-2m7: 0-1 3m+: 0-0
Track:	LH: 0-0 RH: 0-1 Tight: 0-1 Gall: 0-0
Aids:	Bl: 0-0 Vi: 0-0 Tstrap: 0-0 Ckp: 0-0
Best Rating:	51 5/03 Folk 2m5f gd-fm Ch

Jack Of Spades (IRE)

90   **98**

8-y-o b g Mister Lord (USA)-Dooney's Daughter (The Parson)
R Dickin E R Clifford Beech

Placings:0P   (3225)
2003/04: 16⁶GS, 19ᴾGS,

	Starts	1st	2nd	3rd	Win & Pl
Chases	2	0	0	0	0
Career Total	2	0	0	0	0

Going:	Sf: 0-0 GS: 0-2 Gd: 0-0 GF: - Fm: 0-0
Distance:	2m/2m3: 0-2 2m4-2m7: 0-0 3m+: 0-0
Track:	LH: 0-1 RH: 0-1 Tight: 0-0 Gall: 0-0
Aids:	Bl: 0-0 Vi: 0-0 Tstrap: 0-0 Ckp: 0-0
Best Rating:	98 12/03 Uttx 2m gd-sft Ch

Jack Pot II (FR)

104   **95+**

7-y-o ch g Luchiroverte (IRE)-Roxane Ii (FR) (Signani (FR))
L Lungo Ashleybank Investments Limited

Placings:364-444531   (3518)
2003/04: 24⁴G, 21⁴S, 20⁴HY, 20⁵G, 24³S, 23¹S,

	Starts	1st	2nd	3rd	Win & Pl
Hurdles	6	1	0	1	3821
Career Total	9	1	0	2	4094
95 1/04 Weth	2m7f	E Hdl		SFT	£3542

Total win prize-money £3542

Going:	Sf: 1-4 GS: 0-0 Gd: 0-2 GF: - Fm: 0-0
Distance:	2m/2m3: 0-0 2m4-2m7: 1-4 3m+: 0-2
Track:	LH: 1-5 RH: 0-1 Tight: 0-1 Gall: 0-0

| Aids: | Bl: 0-0 Vi: 0-0 Tstrap: 0-0 Ckp: 0-0 |
| Best Rating: | 107 1/03 Ayr 2m   heavy   NHF |

Lightly-raced novice hurdler; improved form when taking a modest event over three miles at Wetherby in January; needs to brush up jumping.

Jack Weighell

94   **84**

5-y-o b g Accordion-Magic Bloom (Full Of Hope)
J M Jefferson P Nelson

Placings:0-500000   (4879)
2003/04: 17⁵G, 16⁹GS, 16⁹GS, 20⁹G, 21⁹G, 20⁹GS,

	Starts	1st	2nd	3rd	Win & Pl
NH Flat	2	0	0	0	0
Hurdles	4	0	0	0	0
Career Total	7	0	0	0	0

Going:	Sf: 0-0 GS: 0-3 Gd: 0-3 GF: - Fm: 0-0
Distance:	2m/2m3: 0-3 2m4-2m7: 0-3 3m+: 0-0
Track:	LH: 0-3 RH: 0-3 Tight: 0-0 Gall: 0-1
Aids:	Bl: 0-0 Vi: 0-0 Tstrap: 0-0 Ckp: 0-0
Best Rating:	84 3/04 Carl 2m4f good Hdl

Jackem (IRE)

(103h)   (106 h)**101**

10-y-o b/br g Lord Americo-Laurence Lady (Laurence O)
Ian Williams The Duck Racing Partnership

Placings:U41BFP0/UF5363505O/134334022-P   (0362)
2003/04: 26ᴾHY,

	Starts	1st	2nd	3rd	Win & Pl
Chases	1	0	0	0	0
Career Total	27	2	2	5	11008
106 5/02 Fknm	2m7f110yE Hdl		GD	£2373
108 11/00 Tram	2m	NHF		HVY	£2760

Total win prize-money £5133

Going:	Sf: 0-1 GS: 0-0 Gd: 0-0 GF: - Fm: 0-0
Distance:	2m/2m3: 0-0 2m4-2m7: 0-0 3m+: 0-1
Track:	LH: 0-1 RH: 0-0 Tight: 0-0 Gall: 0-0
Aids:	Bl: 0-0 Vi: 0-0 Tstrap: 0-0 Ckp: 0-0
Best Rating:	108 11/00 Tram 2m heavy NHF

Modest chaser: stays three miles; acts on good or softer.

Jackie Jarvis (IRE)

7-y-o b m Alphabatim (USA)-Miss Brantridge (Riboboy (USA))
J S Swindells Mrs Jan Wood

Placings:00/R/U1-5   (4303)
2003/04: 16⁵G,

	Starts	1st	2nd	3rd	Win & Pl
Chases	1	0	0	0	0
Career Total	6	1	0	0	2085
107 3/03 Fknm	2m5f110yH Ch		GD	£2085

Total win prize-money £2085

Going:	Sf: 0-0 GS: 0-0 Gd: 0-1 GF: - Fm: 0-0
Distance:	2m/2m3: 0-1 2m4-2m7: 0-0 3m+: 0-0
Track:	LH: 0-0 RH: 0-1 Tight: 0-0 Gall: 0-0
Aids:	Bl: 0-0 Vi: 0-0 Tstrap: 0-0 Ckp: 0-0
Best Rating:	107 3/03 Fknm 2m5f110y good Ch

Jackofalltrades (IRE)

6-y-o b g Lord Americo-Wind Chimes (The Parson)
A C Whillans Robert Robinson

Placings:50P-P   (0252)
2003/04: 20PG,

	Starts	1st	2nd	3rd	Win & Pl
Hurdles	1	0	0	0	
Career Total	4	0	0	0	0

Going:	Sf: 0-0 GS: 0-0 Gd: 0-1 GF: - Fm: 0-0
Distance:	2m/2m3: 0-0 2m4-2m7: 0-1 3m+: 0-0
Track:	LH: 0-0 RH: 0-1 Tight: 0-0 Gall: 0-0
Aids:	Bl: 0-0 Vi: 0-0 Tstrap: 0-0 Ckp: 0-0
Best Rating:	53 2/03 Ayr 2m heavy NHF

Jacks Birthday (IRE)

60

6-y-o b g Mukaddamah (USA)-High Concept (IRE) (Thatching)
J Joseph Jack Joseph

Placings:53/0P0-PP   (1013)
2003/04: 20PG, 20PGF,

	Starts	1st	2nd	3rd	Win & Pl
Hurdles	2	0	0	0	
Career Total	7	0	0	1	469

Going:	Sf: 0-0 GS: 0-0 Gd: 0-1 GF: - Fm: 0-1
Distance:	2m/2m3: 0-0 2m4-2m7: 0-2 3m+: 0-0
Track:	LH: 0-2 RH: 0-0 Tight: 0-0 Gall: 0-0
Aids:	Bl: 0-0 Vi: 0-0 Tstrap: 0-0 Ckp: 0-0
Best Rating:	81 10/01 Winc 2m gd-fm Hdl

Jacks Craic (IRE)

101   **95**

5-y-o b g Lord Americo-Boleree (IRE) (Mandalus)
J L Spearing Bbb Computer Services

Placings:0-20F36   (3775)
2003/04: 162GF, 16RG, 21FS, 163G, 16RG,

	Starts	1st	2nd	3rd	Win & Pl
NH Flat	2	0	1	0	632
Hurdles	3	0	1	1	529
Career Total	6	0	1	1	1161

Going:	Sf: 0-1 GS: 0-1 Gd: 0-2 GF: - Fm: 0-1
Distance:	2m/2m3: 0-4 2m4-2m7: 0-1 3m+: 0-0
Track:	LH: 0-4 RH: 0-1 Tight: 0-1 Gall: 0-2
Aids:	Bl: 0-0 Vi: 0-0 Tstrap: 0-0 Ckp: 0-0
Best Rating:	101 1/04 Donc 2m110y good Hdl

Moderate novice hurdler; respectable third at Doncaster in January.

Jacks Jewel (IRE)

97   **89+**

7-y-o b g Welsh Term-September Daydream (IRE) (Phardante (FR))
C J Down Ken Field

Placings:40-0P3P   (3415)

2003/04: 17RG, 21PG, 213S, 24PGS,

	Starts	1st	2nd	3rd	Win & Pl
NH Flat	1	0	0	0	0
Hurdles	3	0	0	1	539
Career Total	6	0	0	1	539

Going:	Sf: 0-1 GS: 0-1 Gd: 0-2 GF: - Fm: 0-0
Distance:	2m/2m3: 0-1 2m4-2m7: 0-2 3m+: 0-1
Track:	LH: 0-3 RH: 0-1 Tight: 0-2 Gall: 0-0
Aids:	Bl: 0-0 Vi: 0-0 Tstrap: 0-0 Ckp: 0-0
Best Rating:	89 1/04 Plum 2m5f soft Hdl

Jackson (FR)

7-y-o b g Passing Sale (FR)-Tynia (FR) (Djarvis (FR))
A N Dalton C B Brookes

Placings:0/0/005-U   (4218)
2003/04: 25UGS,

	Starts	1st	2nd	3rd	Win & Pl
Chases	1	0	0	0	
Career Total	6	0	0	0	0

Going:	Sf: 0-0 GS: 0-1 Gd: 0-0 GF: - Fm: 0-0
Distance:	2m/2m3: 0-0 2m4-2m7: 0-0 3m+: 0-1
Track:	LH: 0-0 RH: 0-1 Tight: 0-1 Gall: 0-0
Aids:	Bl: 0-0 Vi: 0-0 Tstrap: 0-0 Ckp: 0-0
Best Rating:	77 2/03 Bang 2m1f gd-sft Hdl

Jacksonville (FR)

107(90h)   (102h)**101+**

7-y-o b g Petit Montmorency (USA)-Quinine Des Aulnes (FR) (Air Du Nord (USA))
A Parker Mr & Mrs Raymond Anderson Green

Placings:0/0223P/2-P5551   (4947)
2003/04: 25PG, 20RS, 24RHY, 245HY, 201GS,

	Starts	1st	2nd	3rd	Win & Pl
Hurdles	1	0	0	0	0
Chases	4	1	0	0	8483
Career Total	12	1	3	1	12185
101 4/04 Prth	2m4f110yD(0-115)HCh	G-S	£8482		

Total win prize-money £8483

Going:	Sf: 0-3 GS: 1-1 Gd: 0-1 GF: - Fm: 0-0
Distance:	2m/2m3: 0-0 2m4-2m7: 1-2 3m+: 0-3
Track:	LH: 0-3 RH: 1-2 Tight: 0-0 Gall: 0-0
Aids:	Bl: 0-0 Vi: 0-0 Tstrap: 0-0 Ckp: 0-0
Best Rating:	102 2/02 Ayr 2m4f heavy Hdl

Moderate hurdler/novice chaser, stays three miles, suited by soft ground.

Jacob's Wife

14-y-o gr m Baron Blakeney-Vido (Vimadee)
G L Edwards D Pugh

Placings:003414/3115/FP4F/15PP34/P2/4/4-43   (0262)
2003/04: 254GS, 203GF,

	Starts	1st	2nd	3rd	Win & Pl
Chases	2	0	0	1	442
Career Total	26	4	1	4	18165
117 5/97 Bang	2m4f110yD(0-120)HCh	GD	£4182		
115 3/96 Wwck	2m	D Ch	GD	£3834	
88 12/95 Uttx	2m	D Ch	G-F	£3623	
104 4/95 Worc	2m	E Hdl	GD	£2757	

Total win prize-money £14398

Jade's Treasure

84f   **66f**

5-y-o b m Zamindar (USA)-Jade Venture (Never So Bold)
T Keddy Mrs S Green

Placings:6   (1611)
2003/04: 16RGF,

	Starts	1st	2nd	3rd	Win & Pl
NH Flat	1	0	0	0	0
Career Total	1	0	0	0	0

Going:	Sf: 0-0 GS: 0-0 Gd: 0-0 GF: - Fm: 0-1
Distance:	2m/2m3: 0-1 2m4-2m7: 0-0 3m+: 0-0
Track:	LH: 0-0 RH: 0-1 Tight: 0-0 Gall: 0-1
Aids:	Bl: 0-0 Vi: 0-0 Tstrap: 0-0 Ckp: 0-0
Best Rating:	66 10/03 Hntg 2m110y gd-fm NHF

Jaffa

89   **120**

12-y-o ch g Kind Of Hush-Sip Of Orange (Celtic Cone)
Miss J Wormall Mrs R Wormall

Placings:00/4P5/FF/P121/15   (4606)
2003/04: 201G, 205GS,

	Starts	1st	2nd	3rd	Win & Pl
Chases	2	1	0	0	4037
Career Total	13	3	1	0	12600
112 3/04 Leic	2m4f110yE(0-110)HCh	GD	£4036		
114 4/02 MRas	2m4f	D Ch	G-F	£4982	
102 3/02 Leic	2m4f110yH Ch	SFT	£2112		

Total win prize-money £11132

Going:	Sf: 0-0 GS: 0-1 Gd: 1-1 GF: - Fm: 0-0
Distance:	2m/2m3: 0-0 2m4-2m7: 1-2 3m+: 0-0
Track:	LH: 0-0 RH: 1-2 Tight: 0-1 Gall: 0-0
Aids:	Bl: 0-0 Vi: 0-0 Tstrap: 0-0 Ckp: 0-0
Best Rating:	114 4/02 MRas 2m4f gd-fm Ch

Fair chaser; best around two and a half miles; acts on any ground.

Jahangir

5-y-o b g Zamindar (USA)-Imperial Jade (Lochnager)
B R Johnson (W J Musson 19/5) A A Lyons

Placings:P   (2295)
2003/04: 16PS,

	Starts	1st	2nd	3rd	Win & Pl
Hurdles	1	0	0	0	
Career Total	1	0	0	0	

Going:	Sf: 0-1 GS: 0-0 Gd: 0-0 GF: - Fm: 0-0
Distance:	2m/2m3: 0-1 2m4-2m7: 0-0 3m+: 0-0
Track:	LH: 0-0 RH: 0-1 Tight: 0-0 Gall: 0-0
Aids:	Bl: 0-0 Vi: 0-0 Tstrap: 0-0 Ckp: 0-0

Fair hunter chaser.

Jahash

110(112h)   (123h)**136+**

6-y-o ch g Hernando (FR)-Jalsun (Jalmood (USA))

(Note: the "Going: Sf: 0-0 GS: 0-1 Gd: 0-0 GF: - Fm: 0-1 / Distance: 2m/2m3: 0-0 2m4-2m7: 0-1 3m+: -0-1 / Track: LH: 0-0 RH: 0-2 Tight: 0-1 Gall: 0-0 / Aids: Bl: 0-0 Vi: 0-0 Tstrap: 0-0 Ckp: 0-0 / Best Rating: 118 11/95 Chep 2m110y gd-sft Ch" block appears at top of third column above "Fair hunter chaser.")

Going:	Sf: 0-0 GS: 0-1 Gd: 0-0 GF: - Fm: 0-1
Distance:	2m/2m3: 0-0 2m4-2m7: 0-1 3m+: 0-1
Track:	LH: 0-0 RH: 0-2 Tight: 0-1 Gall: 0-0
Aids:	Bl: 0-0 Vi: 0-0 Tstrap: 0-0 Ckp: 0-0
Best Rating:	118 11/95 Chep 2m110y gd-sft Ch

A King (P J Hobbs 22/11) J Hawkins

Placings:12231-0313242452 (4955)
2003/04: 24⁰YS, 20³GF, 17¹F, 19³S, 16²GS, 16⁴S, 16²G, 16⁴G, 20⁵GS, 20²G,

	Starts	1st	2nd	3rd	Win & Pl
Hurdles	2	0	0	1	623
Chases	8	1	3	1	26496
Career Total	15	3	5	3	40982
100	10/03 Extr	2m1f110yD Ch		FRM	£5726
108	4/03 Ludl	3m E Hdl		GD	£3770
104	11/02 Tntn	2m1f D Hdl		G-S	£4316
			Total win prize-money		£13812

Going: Sf: 0-2 GS: 0-2 Gd: 0-3 GF: - Fm: 1-2
Distance: 2m/2m3: 1-5 2m4-2m7: 0-4 3m+: 0-1
Track: LH: 0-4 RH: 1-6 Tight: 0-1 Gall: 0-1
Aids: Bl: 0-0 Vi: 0-0 Tstrap: 0-0 Ckp: 0-0
Best Rating: 136 4/04 Sand 2m4f110y good Ch

Fair hurdler/chaser; fourth in the Arkle at Cheltenham in 2004; stays three miles but effective over shorter; acts on fast and soft ground.

Jahia (NZ)

5-y-o br m Jahafil-Lana (NZ) (Tristram's Heritage (NZ))
R C Guest DDB Racing

Placings:0P00 (1587)
2003/04: 16⁹G, 19²G, 16⁹GF, 16⁹GF,

	Starts	1st	2nd	3rd	Win & Pl
Hurdles	4	0	0	0	
Career Total	4	0	0	0	

Going: Sf: 0-0 GS: 0-0 Gd: 0-0 GF: - Fm: 0-2
Distance: 2m/2m3: 0-3 2m4-2m7: 0-1 3m+: 0-0
Track: LH: 0-2 RH: 0-2 Tight: 0-0 Gall: 0-1
Aids: Bl: 0-0 Vi: 0-0 Tstrap: 0-1 Ckp: 0-0

Jair Du Cochet (FR)
123 (165h)170+
7-y-o b g Rahotep (FR)-Dilaure (FR) (Rose Laurel)
G Macaire Mrs F Montauban

Placings:C111211/41302/1111U2-211P1 (3487)
2003/04: 20²GS, 18¹G, 20¹GS, 24⁶G, 25¹GS,

	Starts	1st	2nd	3rd	Win & Pl
Hurdles	2	1	1	0	4221
Chases	3	2	0	0	91400
Career Total	23	13	4	1	268020
170	1/04 Chel	3m1f110yA Ch		G-S	£62400
166	11/03 Hntg	2m4f110yA Ch		G-S	£29000
	11/03 Chep	2m2f110y Hdl		GD	£4221
158	12/02 Kemp	3m A Ch		SFT	£29000
149	11/02 Newb	2m4f A Ch		G-S	£10846
127	11/02 Folk	2m E Ch		G-F	£3731
	5/02 LE L	2m1f Ch		SFT	£10012
165	1/02 Hayd	2m7f110yA Hdl		SFT	£15080
165	1/01 Chel	2m1f A Hdl		SFT	£12000
156	12/00 Chep	2m110y A Hdl		SFT	£17400
	11/00 Engh	2m110y Hdl		HVY	£9606
	10/00 Engh	2m110y Hdl		HLD	£9606
	10/00 Comp	2m Hdl		VS	£3362
			Total win prize-money		£216264

Going: Sf: 0-0 GS: 2-3 Gd: 1-2 GF: - Fm: 0-0
Distance: 2m/2m3: 1-1 2m4-2m7: 1-2 3m+: 1-2
Track: LH: 1-1 RH: 1-2 Tight: 0-0 Gall: 2-2
Aids: Bl: 0-0 Vi: 0-0 Tstrap: 0-0 Ckp: 0-0
Best Rating: 170 1/04 Chel 3m1f110y gd-sft Ch

Top-class French-trained chaser; won his first four starts over fences and finished a good second in the 2003 Royal & SunAlliance Chase; had a couple of warm ups over hurdles before taking Best Mate's scalp in the Peterborough Chase later the same year; never travelling and eventually pulled up in King George; bounced back with easy victory in Pillar Property Chase at Cheltenham in January; acted on any ground, but is well suited by soft; stayed three miles; arguably best in small fields.(DEAD)

Jakari (FR)
116(95h) (107h)150+
7-y-o b g Apeldoorn (FR)-Tartifume Ii (FR) (Mistigri)
H D Daly The Earl Cadogan

Placings:5/1/32311P-115103 (4835)
2003/04: 20¹G, 19¹G, 21⁵G, 20¹GS, 20⁰G, 21³GF,

	Starts	1st	2nd	3rd	Win & Pl
Chases	6	3	0	1	45976
Career Total	14	6	1	3	61532
150	2/04 Ayr	2m4f B(0-145)HCh		G-S	£12265
146	12/03 Asct	2m3f110yD(0-135)HCh		GD	£13812
137	11/03 Chel	2m4f110yD(0-125)HCh		GD	£13398
131	3/03 Strf	2m4f D Ch		G-S	£4790
119	2/03 Hrfd	2m3f E Ch		GD	£4182
107	11/01 Uttx	2m E Hdl		SFT	£2688
			Total win prize-money		£51860

Going: Sf: 0-0 GS: 1-1 Gd: 2-4 GF: - Fm: 0-1
Distance: 2m/2m3: 0-0 2m4-2m7: 3-6 3m+: 0-0
Track: LH: 2-5 RH: 1-1 Tight: 0-0 Gall: 1-4
Aids: Bl: 0-0 Vi: 0-0 Tstrap: 0-0 Ckp: 0-0
Best Rating: 150 2/04 Ayr 2m4f gd-sft Ch

Smart and progressive chaser; suited by two and a half miles and acts on any ground; suited by forcing tactics.

Jake Black (IRE)
102 95+
4-y-o b g Definite Article-Tirhala (IRE) (Chief Singer)
J J Quinn G A Lucas

Placings:1442 (4178)
2003/04: 16¹G, 16⁴GS, 20⁴G, 16²G,

	Starts	1st	2nd	3rd	Win & Pl
Hurdles	4	1	1	0	4410
Career Total	4	1	1	0	4410
84	11/03 Newc	2m E Hdl		GD	£2653
			Total win prize-money		£2653

Going: Sf: 0-0 GS: 0-1 Gd: 1-3 GF: - Fm: 0-0
Distance: 2m/2m3: 1-3 2m4-2m7: 0-1 3m+: 0-0
Track: LH: 1-4 RH: 0-0 Tight: 0-0 Gall: 1-2
Aids: Bl: 0-0 Vi: 0-0 Tstrap: 0-0 Ckp: 0-0
Best Rating: 92 3/04 Donc 2m110y good Hdl

Moderate juvenile hurdler; got up on line to win on hurdles debut at Newcastle; suited by good ground.

Jake The Jumper (IRE)
101 102
7-y-o b g Jolly Jake (NZ)-Princess Tino (IRE) (Rontino)
Mrs G Harvey Mrs Rosalinde Elsbury

Placings:5045/2P-62 (4405)
2003/04: 24⁶G, 26²G,

	Starts	1st	2nd	3rd	Win & Pl
Hurdles	2	0	1	0	1010
Career Total	8	0	2	0	2137

Going: Sf: 0-0 GS: 0-0 Gd: 0-2 GF: - Fm: 0-0
Distance: 2m/2m3: 0-0 2m4-2m7: 0-0 3m+: 0-2
Track: LH: 0-0 RH: 0-2 Tight: 0-0 Gall: 0-1
Aids: Bl: 0-0 Vi: 0-0 Tstrap: 0-0 Ckp: 0-0
Best Rating: 102 3/04 Hntg 3m2f good Hdl

Lightly-raced individual, with only moderate form to date in novice hurdles; runner up at Huntingdon in March; suited by three miles; acts on soft and firm ground.

Jakeal (IRE)

5-y-o b g Eagle Eyed (USA)-Karoi (IRE) (Kafu)
R M Whitaker James Marshall & Mrs Susan Marshall

Placings:P (4220)
2003/04: 17⁵G,

	Starts	1st	2nd	3rd	Win & Pl
Hurdles	1	0	0	0	
Career Total	1	0	0	0	

Going: Sf: 0-0 GS: 0-0 Gd: 0-1 GF: - Fm: 0-0
Distance: 2m/2m3: 0-1 2m4-2m7: 0-0 3m+: 0-0
Track: LH: 0-0 RH: 0-1 Tight: 0-0 Gall: 0-0
Aids: Bl: 0-0 Vi: 0-0 Tstrap: 0-0 Ckp: 0-0

Jallastep (FR)
110 101+
7-y-o b g Boston Two Step (USA)-Balladine (FR) (Rivelago (FR))
J S Goldie Mr & Mrs Raymond Anderson Green

Placings:60P510/32101-0030255 (4913)
2003/04: 16⁵S, 16⁰S, 17³HY, 22⁰GS, 20²GF, 22⁵G, 24⁵S,

	Starts	1st	2nd	3rd	Win & Pl
Hurdles	7	0	1	1	2098
Career Total	18	3	2	2	13871
101	12/02 Ayr	2m4f E(0-105)HHdl		G-S	£3066
85	10/02 Kels	2m6f110yF(0-100)HHdl		GD	£4199
77	4/02 Hexm	2m110y G(0-105)HHdl		G-F	£2772
			Total win prize-money		£10037

Going: Sf: 0-4 GS: 0-1 Gd: 0-1 GF: - Fm: 0-1
Distance: 2m/2m3: 0-3 2m4-2m7: 0-3 3m+: 0-1
Track: LH: 0-5 RH: 0-2 Tight: 0-3 Gall: 0-0
Aids: Bl: 0-0 Vi: 0-0 Tstrap: 0-0 Ckp: 0-0
Best Rating: 101 12/02 Ayr 2m4f gd-sft Hdl

Moderate hurdler, acts on a fast surface and stays two miles-six plus; tends to idle in front.

Jalons Star (IRE)
95(91h) (92h)92
6-y-o b g Eagle Eyed (USA)-Regina St Cyr (IRE) (Doulab (USA))
M Quinn J G Dooley

Placings:4435204012/00605-452443 (0961)
2003/04: 17⁴GS, 19⁵GF, 21²GF, 16⁴G, 16⁴GF, 17³GS,

	Starts	1st	2nd	3rd	Win & Pl
Chases	6	0	1	1	3084
Career Total	21	1	3	2	11893
107	3/02 Sedg	2m1f D(0-115)HHdl		SFT	£3297
			Total win prize-money		£3297

Going: Sf: 0-0 GS: 0-2 Gd: 0-1 GF: - Fm: 0-3
Distance: 2m/2m3: 0-5 2m4-2m7: 0-1 3m+: 0-0
Track: LH: 0-5 RH: 0-1 Tight: 0-2 Gall: 0-0
Aids: Bl: 0-0 Vi: 0-0 Tstrap: 0-0 Ckp: 0-0
Best Rating: 107 3/02 Newb 2m110y gd-sft Hdl

Moderate hurdler; best effort over fences when runner-up in four horse race at Uttoxeter June 2003; stays 2m 4f, probably better over shorter; acts on soft ground.

Jaloux D'Estruval (FR)

102(105c)   (131c)116+

7-y-o b g Kadalko (FR)-Pommette Iii (FR) (Trac)

Mrs L C Taylor Mrs W Morrell

Placings:05/40P/1F3F-41FU3F16   (4870)

2003/04: 24⁴S, 23¹S, 24⁴S, 24ᵁS, 24³GS, 24⁴FG, 23¹GS, 24⁶GS,

	Starts	1st	2nd	3rd	Win & Pl
Hurdles	3	1	0	1	4241
Chases	5	1	0	0	6118
Career Total	17	3	0	2	15153
116	4/04	Ling	2m7f	F(0-100)HHdl	G-S £3669
131	1/04	Extr	2m7f110yD(0-120)HCh	SFT	£5687
122	12/02	Hrfd	3m1f110yE Ch	GD	£4130
				Total win prize-money £13491

Going:	Sf: 1-4 GS: 1-3 Gd: 0-1 GF: - Fm: 0-0
Distance:	2m/2m3: 0-0 2m4-2m7: 1-1 3m+: 1-7
Track:	LH: 1-5 RH: 1-3 Tight: 1-3 Gall: 0-2
Aids:	Bl: 0-0 Vi: 0-0 Tstrap: 0-0 Ckp: 0-0
Best Rating:	131 1/04 Extr 2m7f110y soft Ch

Fair chaser/modest hurdler; not always the best of jumpers; regularly held up; stays three miles well; effective in good and soft ground.

Jamaican Flight (USA)

103   116

11-y-o b h Sunshine Forever (USA)-Kalamona (USA) (Hawaii)

Mrs S Lamyman P Lamyman

Placings:UO52/11111326/31213400/62P24/50F/44604/41P P5-32   (1691)

2003/04: 19³GF, 22²GF,

	Starts	1st	2nd	3rd	Win & Pl
Hurdles	2	0	1	1	2270
Career Total	40	8	6	4	41569
116	9/02	MRas	2m3f110yE(0-110)HHdl	G-F	£3486
132	11/98	MRas	2m5f110yB HHdl	HVY	£6716
131	10/98	MRas	2m3f110yC(0-130)HHdl	GD	£4445
128	9/97	MRas	2m3f110yD(0-120)HHdl	GD	£2745
105	7/97	MRas	2m3f110yD Hdl	GD	£2882
113	6/97	MRas	2m3f110yD Hdl	GD	£2872
109	5/97	MRas	2m3f110yD(0-120)HHdl	G-F	£2951
102	5/97	Towc	2m E Hdl	GD	£2407
				Total win prize-money £28508

Going:	Sf: 0-0 GS: 0-0 Gd: 0-0 GF: - Fm: 0-2
Distance:	2m/2m3: 0-0 2m4-2m7: 0-2 3m+: 0-0
Track:	LH: 0-0 RH: 0-1 Tight: 0-1 Gall: 0-0
Aids:	Bl: 0-0 Vi: 0-0 Tstrap: 0-0 Ckp: 0-0
Best Rating:	132 12/99 MRas 2m3f110y good Hdl

Modest hurdler; natural front-runner, this smashing dual-purpose horse has given his connections tremendous value for money on the Flat and over hurdles; stays two miles five; acts on any ground; goes particularly well at Market Rasen.

Jamerosier (FR)

103   (109h)111+

7-y-o b g The Wonder (FR)-Teuphaine (FR) (Barbotan (FR))

Mrs L C Taylor Mrs L C Taylor

Placings:5326/23   (3330)

2003/04: 22²S, 22³S,

	Starts	1st	2nd	3rd	Win & Pl
Chases	2	0	1	1	1987
Career Total	6	0	2	2	3779

Going:	Sf: 0-2 GS: 0-0 Gd: 0-0 GF: - Fm: 0-0
Distance:	2m/2m3: 0-0 2m4-2m7: 0-2 3m+: 0-0
Track:	LH: 0-1 RH: 0-1 Tight: 0-0 Gall: 0-1
Aids:	Bl: 0-0 Vi: 0-0 Tstrap: 0-0 Ckp: 0-0
Best Rating:	116 1/04 Newb 2m6f110y soft Ch

Fair chaser; half-brother to his trainer's Scottish National winner Gingembre; returned from a lengthy absence to finish placed in novice chases; stays three miles; acts in soft ground.

Jamie Browne (IRE)

7-y-o ch g Sayaarr (USA)-Glowing Embers (Nebbiolo)

W G Young W G Young

Placings:0-   (0008)

2003/04: 20⁰GF,

	Starts	1st	2nd	3rd	Win & Pl
Chases	1	0	0	0	
Career Total	1	0	0	0	

Going:	Sf: 0-0 GS: 0-0 Gd: 0-0 GF: - Fm: 0-1
Distance:	2m/2m3: 0-0 2m4-2m7: 0-0 3m+: 0-0
Track:	LH: 0-1 RH: 0-0 Tight: 0-0 Gall: 0-1
Aids:	Bl: 0-0 Vi: 0-0 Tstrap: 0-1 Ckp: 0-0
Best Rating:	16 4/03 Newc 2m4f gd-fm Hdl

Jamorin Dancer

104(97h)   (68h)89

9-y-o b g Charmer-Geryea (USA) (Desert Wine (USA))

S G Chadwick (R C Guest 1/8) S Chadwick

Placings:0P0V40/5/0003426005/033306036P004015-422225043U   (1303)

2003/04: 16⁵G, 16⁴G, 17²GF, 16²GF, 17²GF, 16²G, 16⁵G, 17⁹GF, 17⁴G, 17³G, 16ᵁGF,

	Starts	1st	2nd	3rd	Win & Pl
Chases	11	0	4	1	7406
Career Total	43	1	5	6	15117
89	4/03	MRas	2m1f110y	E(0-105)HCh	
GD	£4438				
				Total win prize-money £4438

Going:	Sf: 0-0 GS: 0-0 Gd: 0-6 GF: - Fm: 0-5
Distance:	2m/2m3: 0-11 2m4-2m7: 0-0 3m+: 0-0
Track:	LH: 0-7 RH: 0-4 Tight: 0-4 Gall: 0-0
Aids:	Bl: 0-0 Vi: 0-0 Tstrap: 0-0 Ckp: 0-11
Best Rating:	89 6/03 Sthl 2m1f gd-fm Ch

Modest novice chaser; runner-up four times on the trot in the summer of 2003; best at around 2m; effective on good ground; usually wears cheekpieces.

Jan's Dream (IRE)

79   47

10-y-o ch m Executive Perk-Aunty Babs (Sexton Blake)

P R Webber Mrs J A Chenery

Placings:46/01/300/4PUR205/P42-UUPUP0   (2781)

2003/04: 17ᵁS, 16ᵁGF, 17PG, 16ᵁGS, 17PGS, 16⁹G,

	Starts	1st	2nd	3rd	Win & Pl
Chases	6	0	0	0	
Career Total	23	1	3	1	7120
100	4/00	NAbb	2m1f	E Hdl	HVY £2555
				Total win prize-money £2555

Going:	Sf: 0-1 GS: 0-2 Gd: 0-2 GF: - Fm: 0-1
Distance:	2m/2m3: 0-6 2m4-2m7: 0-0 3m+: 0-0
Track:	LH: 0-3 RH: 0-3 Tight: 0-5 Gall: 0-0
Aids:	Bl: 0-0 Vi: 0-0 Tstrap: 0-6 Ckp: 0-0
Best Rating:	100 3/03 Folk 2m good Ch

Janbre (IRE)

106f   109f

5-y-o br g Zaffaran (USA)-Black Gayle (IRE) (Strong Gale)

M Scudamore Granite By Design Ltd

Placings:256   (4936)

2003/04: 16²S, 17⁵GS, 18⁶G,

	Starts	1st	2nd	3rd	Win & Pl
NH Flat	3	0	1	0	596
Career Total	3	0	1	0	596

Going:	Sf: 0-1 GS: 0-1 Gd: 0-1 GF: - Fm: 0-0
Distance:	2m/2m3: 0-3 2m4-2m7: 0-0 3m+: 0-0
Track:	LH: 0-1 RH: 0-2 Tight: 0-2 Gall: 0-0
Aids:	Bl: 0-0 Vi: 0-0 Tstrap: 0-0 Ckp: 0-0
Best Rating:	104 12/03 Towc 2m soft NHF

Jandal

86   80

10-y-o ch g Arazi (USA)-Littlefield (Bay Express)

B Scriven B Scriven

Placings:0054/60F/0/4P042/0-0   (4818)

2003/04: 17⁰GF,

	Starts	1st	2nd	3rd	Win & Pl
Hurdles	1	0	0	0	
Career Total	15	0	1	0	602

Going:	Sf: 0-0 GS: 0-0 Gd: 0-0 GF: - Fm: 0-1
Distance:	2m/2m3: 0-1 2m4-2m7: 0-0 3m+: 0-0
Track:	LH: 0-0 RH: 0-1 Tight: 0-0 Gall: 0-0
Aids:	Bl: 0-0 Vi: 0-0 Tstrap: 0-0 Ckp: 0-0
Best Rating:	80 4/02 Hrfd 2m1f gd-fm Hdl

Janidou (FR)

92(108h)   (123h)113

8-y-o b g Cadoudal (FR)-Majathen (FR) (Carmarthen (FR))

A L T Moore John P McManus

Placings:6/621/0P630/000300-110533   (2290)

2003/04: 17¹S, 16¹S, 16⁹Y, 17⁵G, 17³GF, 16³G,

	Starts	1st	2nd	3rd	Win & Pl
Hurdles	1	0	0	0	
Chases	5	2	0	2	15358
Career Total	21	3	1	4	31241
104	6/03	Rosc	2m	Ch	SFT £5824
106	5/03	Klny	2m1f	Ch	SFT £6720
130	1/01	Tram	2m	Hdl	SH £5564
				Total win prize-money £18111

Going:	Sf: 2-2 GS: 0-0 Gd: 0-2 GF: - Fm: 0-1
Distance:	2m/2m3: 2-6 2m4-2m7: 0-0 3m+: 0-0
Track:	LH: 0-1 RH: 0-2 Tight: 0-1 Gall: 0-0
Aids:	Bl: 0-0 Vi: 0-0 Tstrap: 0-0 Ckp: 0-0
Best Rating:	130 1/01 Tram 2m sft-hvy Hdl

Fair Irish novice chaser/hurdler; effective over two miles; acts on a soft surface.

Janiture (FR)

103   (112h)**135**

7-y-o gr m Turgeon (USA)-Majaway (FR) (Timmy's Way (FR))

P F Nicholls Malcolm Pearce & Gerry Mizel

Placings:46P111/P23/51F311-P2550   (4843)
2003/04: 20⁰G, 20²GF, 19⁴GS, 16⁵G, 16⁸G,

	Starts	1st	2nd	3rd	Win & Pl
Chases	5	0	1	0	2484
Career Total	20	6	2	2	31307
133	4/03	Winc	2m	D(0-115)HCh	FRM £5726
124	4/03	Plum	2m1f	E Ch	G-F £4410
128	11/02	Tntn	2m3f	E(0-105)HCh	G-S £5460
	4/01	Nant	2m1f110y	Hdl		VS £3492
	4/01	Loud	2m1f	Hdl		VS £2716
	3/01	Seno	1m7f	Hdl		HVY £2716

Total win prize-money £24520

Going:	Sf: 0-0 GS: 0-1 Gd: 0-3 GF: - Fm: 0-1
Distance:	2m/2m3: 0-2 2m4-2m7: 0-3 3m+: 0-1
Track:	LH: 0-3 RH: 0-2 Tight: 0-0 Gall: 0-1
Aids:	Bl: 0-0 Vi: 0-0 Tstrap: 0-3 Ckp: 0-0
Best Rating:	133 11/03 Kemp 2m4f110y gd-fm Ch

Useful chaser; successful three times over hurdles in France; stays 2m 5f but may be more effective over shorter trips; acts on soft and firm ground; improving.

Janoramic (FR)

80   **98**

7-y-o g Panoramic-Victoire V (FR) (Nellio (FR))

T J Fitzgerald Richard Brown

Placings:332U22/P0   (4892)
2003/04: 20⁵S, 16⁶GF,

	Starts	1st	2nd	3rd	Win & Pl
Hurdles	1	0	0	0	0
Chases	1	0	0	0	0
Career Total	8	0	3	2	3065

Going:	Sf: 0-1 GS: 0-0 Gd: 0-0 GF: - Fm: 0-1
Distance:	2m/2m3: 0-1 2m4-2m7: 0-1 3m+: 0-0
Track:	LH: 0-2 RH: 0-0 Tight: 0-1 Gall: 0-1
Aids:	Bl: 0-0 Vi: 0-0 Tstrap: 0-0 Ckp: 0-0
Best Rating:	101 3/02 Catt 2m gd-sft Hdl

Modest novice hurdler at around two and a half miles.

Janoueix (IRE)

5-y-o b g Desert King (IRE)-Miniver (IRE) (Mujtahid (USA))

C R Egerton Andy J Smith, Nigel R Smith

Placings:P   (0234)
2003/04: 17⁵GF,

	Starts	1st	2nd	3rd	Win & Pl
Hurdles	1	0	0	0	
Career Total	1	0	0	0	

Going:	Sf: 0-0 GS: 0-0 Gd: 0-0 GF: - Fm: 0-1
Distance:	2m/2m3: 0-1 2m4-2m7: 0-0 3m+: 0-0
Track:	LH: 0-0 RH: 0-1 Tight: 0-0 Gall: 0-1
Aids:	Bl: 0-0 Vi: 0-0 Tstrap: 0-0 Ckp: 0-0

Janus Du Cochet (FR)

111   (149h)**134**

7-y-o b g Rahotep (FR)-Qualite Du Cochet (FR) (Illustrator (FR))

M C Pipe Terry Neill

Placings:121424/42/214   (3820)
2003/04: 21²G, 23¹GS, 22⁴S,

	Starts	1st	2nd	3rd	Win & Pl
Chases	3	1	1	0	6098
Career Total	11	3	4	0	70185
134	1/04	Extr	2m7f110y	E Ch		G-S £4273
	11/00	Autl	2m2f	HHdl		HVY £33622
	10/00	Autl	1m7f	Hdl		HLD £13449

Total win prize-money £51345

Going:	Sf: 0-1 GS: 1-1 Gd: 0-1 GF: - Fm: 0-0
Distance:	2m/2m3: 0-0 2m4-2m7: 0-2 3m+: 1-1
Track:	LH: 0-1 RH: 1-2 Tight: 0-0 Gall: 0-0
Aids:	Bl: 0-0 Vi: 0-0 Tstrap: 0-0 Ckp: 0-0
Best Rating:	143 12/01 Chel 3m good Hdl

Very useful ex-French and dual hurdles winner at Auteuil; improved for step up to three miles over hurdles; off for two years before beginning a chasing career; successful on his second start over fences at Exeter in January; well beaten and finished lame next time; handles mud; stays well.

Jaoka Du Gord (FR)

7-y-o b g Concorde Jr (USA)-Theorie Du Cochet (FR) (Franc Ryk)

P R Webber R W Barnett

Placings:440P   (3774)
2003/04: 16⁴S, 16⁴GS, 19⁰GS, 24⁹PG,

	Starts	1st	2nd	3rd	Win & Pl
NH Flat	2	0	0	0	0
Chases	2	0	0	0	0
Career Total	4	0	0	0	0

Going:	Sf: 0-1 GS: 0-2 Gd: 0-1 GF: - Fm: 0-0
Distance:	2m/2m3: 0-3 2m4-2m7: 0-0 3m+: 0-1
Track:	LH: 0-2 RH: 0-2 Tight: 0-1 Gall: 0-0
Aids:	Bl: 0-0 Vi: 0-0 Tstrap: 0-0 Ckp: 0-0
Best Rating:	94 11/03 Chep 2m110y gd-sft NHF

Jardin De Beaulieu (FR)

109   **130+**

7-y-o ch g Rough Magic (FR)-Emblem (FR) (Siberian Express (USA))

Ian Williams Mr & Mrs John Poynton

Placings:2/2P3F/P245-02113PP   (4648)
2003/04: 20⁹G, 18²GS, 20¹G, 20¹GS, 20³GS, 24⁴G, 20⁸G,

	Starts	1st	2nd	3rd	Win & Pl
Chases	7	2	1	2	22886
Career Total	16	2	4	2	30134
130	1/04	Wwck	2m4f110yC(0-135)HCh	G-S £8482
124	12/03	Kemp	2m4f110yC(0-130)HCh	GD £9216

Total win prize-money £17700

Going:	Sf: 0-0 GS: 1-3 Gd: 1-4 GF: - Fm: 0-0
Distance:	2m/2m3: 0-1 2m4-2m7: 2-5 3m+: 0-1
Track:	LH: 1-6 RH: 1-1 Tight: 0-1 Gall: 0-3
Aids:	Bl: 0-2 Vi: 0-0 Tstrap: 0-0 Ckp: 1-2
Best Rating:	130 1/04 Wwck 2m4f110y gd-sft Ch

Fair chaser; overcame mistakes to get off the mark in novice chase at Kempton Boxing Day 2003; followed up in Class C handicap at Warwick in first-time cheekpieces; blinkered next time; stays 2m 4f; acts on soft ground; likes to race prominently.

Jardin Fleuri (FR)

(99h)   (88+h)

7-y-o ch g Cyborg (FR)-Merry Durgan (FR) (Le Nain Jaune (FR))

M C Pipe M C Pipe

Placings:03/PP05UB021P   (4814)
2003/04: 17⁵GF, 22⁸GF, 22⁰G, 19⁵GF, 21⁰UG, 19⁸GF, 19⁰GS, 22²GS, 21¹G, 19⁸G,

	Starts	1st	2nd	3rd	Win & Pl
Hurdles	9	1	1	0	3390
Chases	1	0	0	0	0
Career Total	12	1	1	1	5281
81	2/04	Ludl	2m5f	G Hdl		GD £2691

Total win prize-money £2692

Going:	Sf: 0-0 GS: 0-2 Gd: 1-4 GF: - Fm: 0-4
Distance:	2m/2m3: 0-3 2m4-2m7: 1-7 3m+: 0-0
Track:	LH: 0-6 RH: 1-4 Tight: 0-6 Gall: 0-0
Aids:	Bl: 0-0 Vi: 0-0 Tstrap: 0-0 Ckp: 0-0
Best Rating:	91 2/04 Font 2m6f110y gd-sft Hdl

Plating-class hurdler; ex-French; scrambled home in a weak seller at Ludlow in February; acts on fast ground; stays 2m5f.

Jarod (FR)

95   **80**

6-y-o b g Scribe (IRE)-Somnambula (IRE) (Petoski)

P J Hobbs Network Training

Placings:0600P   (4914)
2003/04: 16⁰GS, 19⁶G, 20⁵S, 21⁹GS, 24⁷GS,

	Starts	1st	2nd	3rd	Win & Pl
NH Flat	1	0	0	0	0
Hurdles	4	0	0	0	0
Career Total	5	0	0	0	0

Going:	Sf: 0-1 GS: 0-3 Gd: 0-1 GF: - Fm: 0-0
Distance:	2m/2m3: 0-1 2m4-2m7: 0-3 3m+: 0-1
Track:	LH: 0-2 RH: 0-3 Tight: 0-1 Gall: 0-1
Aids:	Bl: 0-1 Vi: 0-0 Tstrap: 0-0 Ckp: 0-0
Best Rating:	87 2/04 Kemp 2m gd-sft NHF

Jarro (FR)

128

8-y-o b g Pistolet Bleu (IRE)-Junta (FR) (Cariellor (FR))

Miss Venetia Williams Mrs P A H Hartley

Placings:1PF135/5/31513/F241P25-U   (2078)
2003/04: 16⁰G,

	Starts	1st	2nd	3rd	Win & Pl
Chases	1	0	0	0	
Career Total	20	5	2	3	61484
128	12/02	Uttx	2m	C(0-130)HCh	SFT £11625
113	3/02	Plum	2m1f	E Ch		GD £3120
123	1/02	Tntn	2m110y	D Ch	SFT £4823
	1/00	Pau	2m2f	Hdl		GD £13449
	10/99	Autl	1m7f	Hdl		HLD £7535

Total win prize-money £40552

Going:	Sf: 0-0 GS: 0-0 Gd: 0-1 GF: - Fm: 0-0
Distance:	2m/2m3: 0-1 2m4-2m7: 0-0 3m+: 0-0
Track:	LH: 0-1 RH: 0-0 Tight: 0-1 Gall: 0-0
Aids:	Bl: 0-0 Vi: 0-0 Tstrap: 0-0 Ckp: 0-0
Best Rating:	128 3/03 Sand 2m soft Ch

Fair handicap chaser, likes soft ground and best at two miles.

Jaseur (USA)

106(87c)   (47c)**113**

11-y-o b g Lear Fan (USA)-Spur Wing (USA) (Storm Bird (CAN))
S T Lewis (G Barnett 5/7) J C Bradbury

Placings:2U220/2456/4605316513-350P4P   (4870)
2003/04: 26³GF, 26⁵G, 24⁹GF, 25⁹G, 24⁴GS, 24ᴾGS,

	Starts	1st	2nd	3rd	Win & Pl
Hurdles	5	0	0	1	1612
Chases	1	0	0	0	0
Career Total	25	2	4	3	19988
110 2/03 Bang	2m4f	E(0-105)HHdl		G-S	£4855
111 12/02 Weth	2m4f110yE(0-105)HHdl		G-S	£3178

Total win prize-money £8034

Going:	Sf: 0-0 GS: 0-2 Gd: 0-2 GF: - Fm: 0-2
Distance:	2m/2m3: 0-0 2m4-2m7: 0-0 3m+: 0-6
Track:	LH: 0-4 RH: 0-2 Tight: 0-4 Gall: 0-1
Aids:	Bl: 0-5 Vi: 0-0 Tstrap: 0-0 Ckp: 0-0
Best Rating:	125 12/00 Asct 2m110y heavy Hdl

Modest hurdler; best at two and a half miles; likes the mud, but is effective on decent ground; usually wears a visor or blinkers; suffered a career threatening leg injury at Market Rasen in November 2003.

Jasmin D'Oudairies (FR)

102   (118h)**124**

7-y-o b g Apeldoorn (FR)-Vellea (FR) (Cap Martin (FR))
W P Mullins Decies & Dubs Syndicate

Placings:03152B12/6051-03F32   (4876a)
2003/04: 19⁰YS, 20³S, 24²G, 20³YS, 20²HY,

	Starts	1st	2nd	3rd	Win & Pl
Chases	5	0	1	2	4351
Career Total	17	3	3	3	23870
124 3/03 Navn	2m1f	Ch		G-Y	£8288
118 11/01 Thur	2m	Hdl		Y-S	£3895
114 7/01 Klny	2m1f	NHF		GD	£3895

Total win prize-money £16079

Going:	Sf: 0-2 GS: 0-0 Gd: 0-1 GF: - Fm: 0-0
Distance:	2m/2m3: 0-1 2m4-2m7: 0-3 3m+: 0-1
Track:	LH: 0-4 RH: 0-0 Tight: 0-0 Gall: 0-1
Aids:	Bl: 0-0 Vi: 0-0 Tstrap: 0-0 Ckp: 0-0
Best Rating:	124 4/04 List 2m4f heavy Ch

Fair chaser; best at two miles; acts on good ground or softer.

Jasmin Guichois (FR)

101(90h)   (90+h)**125+**

7-y-o ch g Dom Alco (FR)-Lady Belle (FR) (Or De Chine)
Miss Venetia Williams Seasons Holidays

Placings:4/FP/01033F-3115P5   (4960)
2003/04: 20³G, 20¹G, 21¹G, 24⁵G, 25ᴾS, 20⁵GS,

	Starts	1st	2nd	3rd	Win & Pl
Chases	6	2	0	1	24221
Career Total	15	5	0	3	30176
125 2/04 Winc	2m5f	D(0-120)HCh		GD	£12191
115 12/03 Chel	2m4f110yE(0-125)HCh		GD	£9831
90 12/02 Folk	2m4f110yF Hdl		HVY	£2261

Total win prize-money £24284

Going:	Sf: 0-1 GS: 0-1 Gd: 2-4 GF: - Fm: 0-0
Distance:	2m/2m3: 0-0 2m4-2m7: 2-4 3m+: 0-2
Track:	LH: 1-4 RH: 1-2 Tight: 0-4 Gall: 1-2
Aids:	Bl: 0-0 Vi: 0-0 Tstrap: 0-0 Ckp: 0-0

Best Rating: **125** 2/04 Winc 2m5f good Ch

Fair chaser, ex-French; stays three miles, but best over shorter; acts on good but handles testing ground.

Jasper Rooney

74f   **56f**

5-y-o b g Riverwise (USA)-Miss Secret (El Conquistador)
C W Mitchell C W Mitchell

Placings:0   (4550)
2003/04: 16⁰GS,

	Starts	1st	2nd	3rd	Win & Pl
NH Flat	1	0	0	0	
Career Total	1	0	0	0	

Going:	Sf: 0-0 GS: 0-1 Gd: 0-0 GF: - Fm: 0-0
Distance:	2m/2m3: 0-1 2m4-2m7: 0-0 3m+: 0-0
Track:	LH: 0-0 RH: 0-1 Tight: 0-0 Gall: 0-0
Aids:	Bl: 0-0 Vi: 0-0 Tstrap: 0-0 Ckp: 0-0
Best Rating:	56 3/04 Winc 2m gd-sft NHF

Jaunty Times

94f   **88f**

4-y-o b g Luso-Jaunty June (Primitive Rising (USA))
B J Eckley Brian Eckley

Placings:5   (4816)
2003/04: 16⁵G,

	Starts	1st	2nd	3rd	Win & Pl
NH Flat	1	0	0	0	0
Career Total	1	0	0	0	0

Going:	Sf: 0-0 GS: 0-0 Gd: 0-1 GF: - Fm: 0-0
Distance:	2m/2m3: 0-1 2m4-2m7: 0-0 3m+: 0-0
Track:	LH: 0-1 RH: 0-0 Tight: 0-0 Gall: 0-0
Aids:	Bl: 0-0 Vi: 0-0 Tstrap: 0-0 Ckp: 0-0
Best Rating:	88 4/04 Chep 2m110y good NHF

Java Sea

82   (111h)**99**

8-y-o br g Warning-Sarah Siddons (FR) (Le Levanstell)
Jonjo O'Neill John B Sunley & A K Collins

Placings:34/034P6/02111/40P   (3522)
2003/04: 25⁴G, 22⁰GS, 25ᴾS,

	Starts	1st	2nd	3rd	Win & Pl
Chases	3	0	0	0	240
Career Total	15	3	1	2	12570
111 3/02 Bang	2m4f	D(0-110)HHdl		SFT	£5187
99 1/02 Weth	2m4f110yE(0-105)HHdl		G-S	£2898
91 11/01 Uttx	2m4f110yE(0-105)HHdl		SFT	£2646

Total win prize-money £10731

Going:	Sf: 0-1 GS: 0-1 Gd: 0-1 GF: - Fm: 0-0
Distance:	2m/2m3: 0-0 2m4-2m7: 0-1 3m+: 0-2
Track:	LH: 0-2 RH: 0-1 Tight: 0-1 Gall: 0-1
Aids:	Bl: 0-0 Vi: 0-0 Tstrap: 0-0 Ckp: 0-0
Best Rating:	111 3/02 Bang 2m4f soft Hdl

Javelin

111(78c)   (88c)**115**

8-y-o ch g Generous (IRE)-Moss (Alzao (USA))
Ian Williams Cockbury Court Partnership

Placings:006F111225/4F3126P   (2919)

2003/04: 16⁴GF, 19ᶠGF, 19³GF, 20¹G, 19²GF, 20⁶GS, 21ᴾG,

	Starts	1st	2nd	3rd	Win & Pl
Hurdles	5	1	1	1	10496
Chases	2	0	0	0	233
Career Total	17	4	3	1	22611
115 11/03 Weth	2m4f110yC(0-130)HHdl		GD	£7046
115 8/01 Worc	2m E(0-115)HHdl		G-F	£3415
109 8/01 NAbb	2m1f D(0-100)HHdl		GD	£2940
107 7/01 Worc	2m F(0-110)HHdl		GD	£1869

Total win prize-money £15271

Going:	Sf: 0-0 GS: 0-1 Gd: 1-2 GF: - Fm: 0-4
Distance:	2m/2m3: 0-3 2m4-2m7: 1-4 3m+: 0-0
Track:	LH: 1-5 RH: 0-2 Tight: 0-1 Gall: 0-0
Aids:	Bl: 0-0 Vi: 0-0 Tstrap: 0-0 Ckp: 0-0
Best Rating:	115 11/03 Donc 2m3f110y gd-fm Hdl

Modest novice chaser/hurdler; effective at around 2m 4f; seemingly best on a sound surface.

Javelot D'Or (FR)

82   **80+**

7-y-o b/br g Useful (FR)-Flika D'Or (FR) (Pot D'Or (FR))
Miss Venetia Williams John Nicholls (banbury) Ltd

Placings:10/4111/P-FPP65P   (4536)
2003/04: 20ᶠS, 17ᴾGS, 18ᴾS, 18⁶GS, 17⁵GS, 19ᴾGS,

	Starts	1st	2nd	3rd	Win & Pl
Chases	6	0	0	0	0
Career Total	13	4	0	0	13386
6/01 Diep	2m1f110y Ch		GD	£3686
6/01 Sbri	2m2f Ch		G-S	£3104
5/01 LE L	2m4f Ch		GD	£3880
3/01 Seno	1m7f Hdl		HVY	£2716

Total win prize-money £13386

Going:	Sf: 0-2 GS: 0-4 Gd: 0-0 GF: - Fm: 0-0
Distance:	2m/2m3: 0-4 2m4-2m7: 0-2 3m+: 0-0
Track:	LH: 0-3 RH: 0-1 Tight: 0-0 Gall: 0-1
Aids:	Bl: 0-0 Vi: 0-0 Tstrap: 0-0 Ckp: 0-0
Best Rating:	80 2/04 Font 2m2f gd-sft Ch

Ex-French chaser; poor form in Britain; acts on good ground or softer.

Jawah (IRE)

75   **35**

10-y-o br g In The Wings-Saving Mercy (Lord Gayle (USA))
H J Manners H J Manners

Placings:P050/53P/PP0   (1520)
2003/04: 24ᴾGF, 20ᴾGF, 18⁰G,

	Starts	1st	2nd	3rd	Win & Pl
Hurdles	3	0	0	0	
Career Total	10	0	0	1	328

Going:	Sf: 0-0 GS: 0-0 Gd: 0-1 GF: - Fm: 0-2
Distance:	2m/2m3: 0-1 2m4-2m7: 0-1 3m+: 0-1
Track:	LH: 0-2 RH: 0-1 Tight: 0-1 Gall: 0-1
Aids:	Bl: 0-0 Vi: 0-1 Tstrap: 0-0 Ckp: 0-0
Best Rating:	107 2/00 Sand 2m110y soft Hdl

Jawwala (USA)

102   **91**

5-y-o b m Green Dancer (USA)-Fetch N Carry (USA) (Alleged (USA))
J R Jenkins Skullduggery

Placings:032P63-2232P3R043   (4756)
2003/04: 16²HY, 21²GF, 20³GF, 20²G, 17ᶠG, 19³GF, 17ᴿHY, 16⁶S, 19⁴GS, 19³S,

	Starts	1st	2nd	3rd	Win & Pl
Hurdles	10	0	3	3	4985
Career Total	16	0	4	5	7526

Going:	Sf: 0-4 GS: 0-1 Gd: 0-2 GF: - Fm: 0-3
Distance:	2m/2m3: 0-5 2m4-2m7: 0-5 3m+: 0-0
Track:	LH: 0-5 RH: 0-4 Tight: 0-3 Gall: 0-3
Aids:	Bl: 0-0 Vi: 0-0 Tstrap: 0-0 Ckp: 0-7
Best Rating:	91 3/04 Newb 2m3f 　　gd-sft Hdl

Modest form over hurdles so far; has shown plenty of temperament and virtually refused to race on one occasion; stays two and a half miles; acts on fast and easy ground; has worn various headgear.

Jay Bee Ell

92　　　　　　　　　　　　**91**

7-y-o b g Pursuit Of Love-On Request (IRE) (Be My Guest (USA))
A King J M & A L Longman

Placings:	405/14-00				(4693)
2003/04: 21⁰GS, 22⁰G,

	Starts	1st	2nd	3rd	Win & Pl
Hurdles	2	0	0	0	
Career Total	7	1	0	0	4483
90 5/02 Strf 2m6f110yD Hdl				G-F	£4147
			Total win prize-money £4147		

Going:	Sf: 0-0 GS: 0-1 Gd: 0-1 GF: - Fm: 0-0
Distance:	2m/2m3: 0-0 2m4-2m7: 0-2 3m+: 0-0
Track:	LH: 0-1 RH: 0-1 Tight: 0-0 Gall: 0-0
Aids:	Bl: 0-0 Vi: 0-0 Tstrap: 0-0 Ckp: 0-0
Best Rating:	110 12/01 Newb 2m110y 　good NHF

Jay Jay Lass

4-y-o b f Bold Fort-Suelizelle (Carnival Dancer)
R Williams (D Burchell 28/6) R Williams

Placings:	P				(1502)
2003/04: 16ᴾGF,

	Starts	1st	2nd	3rd	Win & Pl
Hurdles	1	0	0	0	
Career Total	1	0	0	0	

Going:	Sf: 0-0 GS: 0-0 Gd: 0-0 GF: - Fm: 0-1
Distance:	2m/2m3: 0-1 2m4-2m7: 0-0 3m+: 0-0
Track:	LH: 0-1 RH: 0-0 Tight: 0-0 Gall: 0-0
Aids:	Bl: 0-0 Vi: 0-0 Tstrap: 0-0 Ckp: 0-0

Jay Man (IRE)

14-y-o ch g Remainder Man-Pas-De-Jay (Pas De Seul)
Joss Saville Joss Saville

Placings:	100/0323F51320/UU				(4600)
2003/04: 16ᵁG, 25ᵁG,

	Starts	1st	2nd	3rd	Win & Pl
Chases	2	0	0	0	
Career Total	15	2	2	3	6746
118 12/96 Thur 2m Hdl				Y-S	£2295
111 5/95 Limk 2m NHF				Y-S	£2712
			Total win prize-money £5008		

Going:	Sf: 0-0 GS: 0-0 Gd: 0-2 GF: - Fm: 0-0
Distance:	2m/2m3: 0-1 2m4-2m7: 0-0 3m+: 0-1
Track:	LH: 0-1 RH: 0-1 Tight: 0-1 Gall: 0-0
Aids:	Bl: 0-0 Vi: 0-0 Tstrap: 0-0 Ckp: 0-0

Best Rating: 118 12/96 Thur 2m 　　yld-sft Hdl

Jaybeedee

99(87c)　　　　　　　　　(71c)**92+**

8-y-o b g Rudimentary (USA)-Meavy (Kalaglow)
K C Bailey Mrs C A T Swire & G D W Swire

Placings:	36/3230514/4-0003P050				(4760)
2003/04: 22⁰GS, 20⁰G, 16⁰S, 16³HY, 18ᴾGS, 17⁰G, 20⁵G, 16⁰S,

	Starts	1st	2nd	3rd	Win & Pl
Hurdles	6	0	0	1	742
Chases	2	0	0	0	0
Career Total	18	1	1	4	6770
111 3/02 Uttx 2m D Hdl				HVY	£3552
			Total win prize-money £3552		

Going:	Sf: 0-3 GS: 0-2 Gd: 0-3 GF: - Fm: 0-0
Distance:	2m/2m3: 0-3 2m4-2m7: 0-0 3m+: 0-0
Track:	LH: 0-3 RH: 0-5 Tight: 0-2 Gall: 0-0
Aids:	Bl: 0-0 Vi: 0-0 Tstrap: 0-0 Ckp: 0-1
Best Rating:	111 3/02 Uttx 2m 　heavy Hdl

Jaybejay (NZ)

95(93h)　　　　　　　(126h)**126**

9-y-o b g High Ice (USA)-Galaxy Light (NZ) (Balios)
M C Pipe Lady Clarke

Placings:	310/0315P330-452				(3417)
2003/04: 19⁴GS, 25⁵G, 19²GS,

	Starts	1st	2nd	3rd	Win & Pl
Chases	3	0	1	0	
Career Total	14	2	1	4	15026
126 1/03 Winc 2m5f D Ch				G-S	£5928
116 2/02 Winc 2m D Hdl				G-S	£3990
			Total win prize-money £9918		

Going:	Sf: 0-0 GS: 0-2 Gd: 0-1 GF: - Fm: 0-0
Distance:	2m/2m3: 0-0 2m4-2m7: 0-2 3m+: 0-1
Track:	LH: 0-1 RH: 0-2 Tight: 0-0 Gall: 0-0
Aids:	Bl: 0-0 Vi: 0-1 Tstrap: 0-0 Ckp: 0-0
Best Rating:	126 3/03 Winc 2m5f 　soft Ch

Fair chaser; won 2m 5f novice chase at Wincanton January 2003; clear when falling at the last and remounting to finish third over same course and distance in March; subsequently disappointing; stays 2m 5f, effective on good to soft ground; keen sort.

Jayed (IRE)

94　　　　　　　　　　　　**88**

6-y-o b/br g Marju (IRE)-Taqreem (IRE) (Nashwan (USA))
M Bradstock Miss J C Blackwell

Placings:	3540-02156440				(3081)
2003/04: 16⁰GJ, 16²G, 16¹GF, 16⁵GF, 17⁶GF, 16⁴GF, 16⁴G,

	Starts	1st	2nd	3rd	Win & Pl
Hurdles	8	1	1	0	4292
Career Total	12	1	1	1	5152
88 8/03 Worc 2m E Hdl				G-F	£3533
			Total win prize-money £3534		

Going:	Sf: 0-0 GS: 0-1 Gd: 0-3 GF: - Fm: 1-4
Distance:	2m/2m3: 1-8 2m4-2m7: 0-0 3m+: 0-0
Track:	LH: 1-6 RH: 0-2 Tight: 0-4 Gall: 0-0
Aids:	Bl: 0-0 Vi: 0-0 Tstrap: 0-0 Ckp: 0-0
Best Rating:	88 10/03 Plum 2m 　gd-fm Hdl

Best effort when narrowly beaten by Governor Daniel in Worcester seller June 2003; had things his own way and showed his old headstrong tendencies when making all in a maiden at the same course in August; acts on fast ground.

Jayneybee

6-y-o b m Sovereign Water (FR)-Day Return (Electric)
R D E Woodhouse Mrs Jayne E Benn

Placings:	0-				(0007)
2003/04: 16⁰G,

	Starts	1st	2nd	3rd	Win & Pl
NH Flat	1	0	0	0	
Career Total	1	0	0	0	

Going:	Sf: 0-0 GS: 0-0 Gd: 0-1 GF: - Fm: 0-0
Distance:	2m/2m3: 0-1 2m4-2m7: 0-0 3m+: 0-0
Track:	LH: 0-1 RH: 0-0 Tight: 0-0 Gall: 0-0
Aids:	Bl: 0-0 Vi: 0-0 Tstrap: 0-0 Ckp: 0-0

Jazz D'Estruval (FR)

112　　　　　　　　　　　**133+**

7-y-o gr g Bayolidaan (FR)-Caro D'Estruval (FR) (Caramo (FR))
N G Richards Ashleybank Investments Limited

Placings:	1/123				(2949)
2003/04: 24¹G, 22²S, 25³G,

	Starts	1st	2nd	3rd	Win & Pl
Hurdles	3	1	1	1	9396
Career Total	4	2	1	1	12210
134 5/03 Prth 3m110y D(0-120)HHdl				GD	£5470
123 4/01 Prth 2m4f110yD Hdl				HVY	£2814
			Total win prize-money £8284		

Going:	Sf: 0-1 GS: 0-0 Gd: 1-2 GF: - Fm: 0-0
Distance:	2m/2m3: 0-0 2m4-2m7: 0-1 3m+: 1-2
Track:	LH: 0-2 RH: 1-1 Tight: 0-0 Gall: 0-0
Aids:	Bl: 0-0 Vi: 0-0 Tstrap: 0-0 Ckp: 0-0
Best Rating:	134 12/03 Weth 3m1f 　good Hdl

Useful hurdler; won first two starts; narrowly denied on return to action at Haydock in November 2003; stays three miles; acts on heavy and good ground.

Jazz Du Forez (FR)

102(100h)　　　　　　(65h)**89+**

7-y-o b g Video Rock (FR)-Ophyr Du Forez (FR) (Fin Bon)
John Allen Devey, Hawkins and Allen Partnership

Placings:	00000/P3B23663-05445034444				(4888)
2003/04: 23⁰GS, 21⁵GF, 26⁴G, 23⁴GF, 24⁵GS, 25⁰GS, 21³S, 24⁴G, 27⁴G, 25⁴S, 24⁴GF,

	Starts	1st	2nd	3rd	Win & Pl
Hurdles	2	0	0	1	400
Chases	9	0	0	0	1422
Career Total	24	0	1	4	3767

Going:	Sf: 0-2 GS: 0-3 Gd: 0-3 GF: - Fm: 0-3
Distance:	2m/2m3: 0-0 2m4-2m7: 0-2 3m+: 0-9
Track:	LH: 0-9 RH: 0-2 Tight: 0-4 Gall: 0-0
Aids:	Bl: 0-1 Vi: 0-0 Tstrap: 0-0 Ckp: 0-0
Best Rating:	89 4/04 Strf 3m 　gd-fm Ch

Jazz Duke

98　　　　　　　　　　　　**85**

11-y-o ch g Rising-Gone (Whistling Wind)
M J Weeden M J Weeden

Placings:	0/320PP/F16P04/3344230/2543U/230-3351				(3413)

2003/04: 26³G, 26³S, 26⁵G, 26¹S,

	Starts	1st	2nd	3rd	Win & Pl
Chases	4	1	0	2	4173
Career Total	31	2	4	8	18179

85 1/04 Plum 3m2f F(0-90)HCh SFT £3339
110 12/99 Tntn 3m110y D(0-120)HHdl G-S £3631
Total win prize-money £6970

Going:	Sf: 1-2 GS: 0-0 Gd: 0-2 GF: - Fm: 0-0
Distance:	2m/2m3: 0-0 2m4-2m7: 0-0 3m+: 1-4
Track:	LH: 1-3 RH: 0-0 Tight: 1-4 Gall: -
Aids:	Bl: 0-0 Vi: 0-0 Tstrap: 0-0 Ckp: 1-1
Best Rating:	110 12/99 Tntn 3m110y gd-sft Hdl

Plating-class chaser; without a win since 1999; stays three miles; suited to cut in the ground.

Jazz Night

7-y-o b g Alhijaz-Hen Night (Mummy's Game)
Shaun Lycett The Berryman Lycett Experience

Placings:6/200-P621 (4655)
2003/04: 20PG, 21⁶G, 16²G, 16¹G,

	Starts	1st	2nd	3rd	Win & Pl
Chases	4	1	1	0	2845
Career Total	8	1	2	0	3697

89 4/04 Hrfd 2m H Ch GD £2205
Total win prize-money £2205

Going:	Sf: 0-0 GS: 0-0 Gd: 1-4 GF: - Fm: 0-0
Distance:	2m/2m3: 1-2 2m4-2m7: 0-2 3m+: 0-0
Track:	LH: 0-0 RH: 1-4 Tight: 0-1 Gall: 0-0
Aids:	Bl: 0-0 Vi: 0-0 Tstrap: 0-0 Ckp: 0-0
Best Rating:	89 4/04 Hrfd 2m good Ch

Moderate hurdler/chaser; best at two miles.

Jazzaam

94　　75

5-y-o ch m Fraam-Aldwick Colonnade (Kind Of Hush)
M D I Usher Midweek Racing

Placings:4465 (4100)
2003/04: 16⁴HY, 19⁴HY, 16⁶S, 21⁵G,

	Starts	1st	2nd	3rd	Win & Pl
Hurdles	4	0	0	0	320
Career Total	4	0	0	0	320

Going:	Sf: 0-3 GS: 0-0 Gd: 0-1 GF: - Fm: 0-0
Distance:	2m/2m3: 0-2 2m4-2m7: 0-2 3m+: 0-0
Track:	LH: 0-1 RH: 0-3 Tight: 0-1 Gall: 0-0
Aids:	Bl: 0-0 Vi: 0-0 Tstrap: 0-0 Ckp: 0-0
Best Rating:	75 2/04 Hrfd 2m3f110y heavy Hdl

Jballingall

5-y-o b g Overbury (IRE)-Sister Delaney (Deep Run)
N Wilson W R S

Placings:0P (4319)
2003/04: 17⁰G, 20⁶S,

	Starts	1st	2nd	3rd	Win & Pl
NH Flat	1	0	0	0	0
Hurdles	1	0	0	0	0
Career Total	2	0	0	0	0

Going:	Sf: 0-1 GS: 0-0 Gd: 0-1 GF: - Fm: 0-0
Distance:	2m/2m3: 0-1 2m4-2m7: 0-1 3m+: 0-0
Track:	LH: 0-1 RH: 0-1 Tight: 0-0 Gall: 0-1
Aids:	Bl: 0-0 Vi: 0-0 Tstrap: 0-0 Ckp: 0-0

Best Rating: 58 2/04 Carl 2m1f good NHF

Je Suis (IRE)

60

8-y-o b m Le Bavard (FR)-La Tortue (Lafontaine (USA))
B J Eckley Brian Eckley

Placings:0/00/0-0 (0869)
2003/04: 22⁰GF,

	Starts	1st	2nd	3rd	Win & Pl
Hurdles	1	0	0	0	
Career Total	5	0	0	0	

Going:	Sf: 0-0 GS: 0-0 Gd: 0-0 GF: - Fm: 0-1
Distance:	2m/2m3: 0-0 2m4-2m7: 0-1 3m+: 0-0
Track:	LH: 0-1 RH: 0-0 Tight: 0-1 Gall: 0-0
Aids:	Bl: 0-0 Vi: 0-0 Tstrap: 0-0 Ckp: 0-0
Best Rating:	33 2/02 Ludl 2m good NHF

Jeanie's Last

70f　　46f

5-y-o b m Primitive Rising (USA)-Jean Jeanie (Roman Warrior)
C C Bealby Tony Evans

Placings:P0P (4780)
2003/04: 16PG, 16⁰GS, 16PS,

	Starts	1st	2nd	3rd	Win & Pl
NH Flat	3	0	0	0	
Career Total	3	0	0	0	

Going:	Sf: 0-1 GS: 0-1 Gd: 0-1 GF: - Fm: 0-0
Distance:	2m/2m3: 0-3 2m4-2m7: 0-0 3m+: 0-0
Track:	LH: 0-3 RH: 0-0 Tight: 0-2 Gall: 0-0
Aids:	Bl: 0-0 Vi: 0-0 Tstrap: 0-0 Ckp: 0-0
Best Rating:	46 3/04 Wwck 2m gd-sft NHF

Jeepers Creepers

4-y-o b g Wizard King-Dark Amber (Formidable (USA))
Mrs A M Thorpe Mrs A M Thorpe

Placings:0 (2301)
2003/04: 12⁰S,

	Starts	1st	2nd	3rd	Win & Pl
NH Flat	1	0	0	0	
Career Total	1	0	0	0	

Going:	Sf: 0-1 GS: 0-0 Gd: 0-0 GF: - Fm: 0-0
Distance:	2m/2m3: 0-0 2m4-2m7: 0-0 3m+: 0-0
Track:	LH: 0-0 RH: 0-0 Tight: 0-0 Gall: 0-0
Aids:	Bl: 0-0 Vi: 0-0 Tstrap: 0-0 Ckp: 0-0

Jefertiti (FR)

106(98h)　　(100h)106

7-y-o ch g Le Nain Jaune (FR)-Nefertiti (FR) (Tourangeau (FR))
Miss H C Knight Jim Lewis

Placings:3526-223 (1988)
2003/04: 19²GF, 20²GF, 20³GF,

	Starts	1st	2nd	3rd	Win & Pl
Chases	3	0	2	1	2484
Career Total	7	0	3	2	8008

Going:	Sf: 0-0 GS: 0-0 Gd: 0-0 GF: - Fm: 0-3
Distance:	2m/2m3: 0-1 2m4-2m7: 0-2 3m+: 0-0
Track:	LH: 0-1 RH: 0-2 Tight: 0-0 Gall: 0-1
Aids:	Bl: 0-0 Vi: 0-0 Tstrap: 0-0 Ckp: 0-0
Best Rating:	106 10/03 Hntg 2m4f110y gd-fm Ch

Showed ability over fences in France; placed in novice chases in this country; suited by fast ground; stays 2m 4f.

Jem's Law

5-y-o b m Contract Law (USA)-Alnasr Jewel (USA) (Al Nasr (FR))
J R Jenkins Mrs P J Rowland

Placings:000 (4495)
2003/04: 16⁰S, 16⁰GS, 16⁰G,

	Starts	1st	2nd	3rd	Win & Pl
NH Flat	3	0	0	0	
Career Total	3	0	0	0	

Going:	Sf: 0-1 GS: 0-1 Gd: 0-1 GF: - Fm: 0-0
Distance:	2m/2m3: 0-3 2m4-2m7: 0-0 3m+: 0-0
Track:	LH: 0-1 RH: 0-1 Tight: 0-0 Gall: 0-1
Aids:	Bl: 0-0 Vi: 0-0 Tstrap: 0-0 Ckp: 0-0

Jemaro (IRE)

13-y-o b g Tidaro (USA)-Jeremique (Sunny Way)
Mrs C J Robinson Jeremy Beasley

Placings:00P/PPF5453F1/151U152FP/3114360/5UP606/3 31P-F5 (4143)
2003/04: 24⁶FG, 25⁵G,

	Starts	1st	2nd	3rd	Win & Pl
Chases	2	0	0	0	0
Career Total	40	7	1	5	31196

105 4/03 Ludl 3m H Ch GD £3250
116 12/99 Hayd 3m D(0-125)HCh SFT £6481
113 11/99 Hayd 3m E(0-115)HCh G-S £3241
116 12/98 Ludl 2m4f E(0-115)HCh GD £3126
115 11/98 Hayd 2m4f E(0-115)HCh HVY £2879
95 5/98 Ludl 3m E(0-100)HCh G-F £3412
87 4/98 Ludl 3m D(0-110)HCh GD £3200
Total win prize-money £25589

Going:	Sf: 0-0 GS: 0-0 Gd: 0-2 GF: - Fm: 0-0
Distance:	2m/2m3: 0-0 2m4-2m7: 0-0 3m+: 0-2
Track:	LH: 0-1 RH: 0-0 Tight: 0-1 Gall: 0-0
Aids:	Bl: 0-0 Vi: 0-0 Tstrap: 0-0 Ckp: 0-0
Best Rating:	117 3/99 Ludl 3m good Ch

Fair hunter chaser these days; acts on good ground; stays three miles, but effective at shorter; goes well at Ludlow and Haydock.

Jenavive

97　　68+

4-y-o b f Danzig Connection (USA)-Promise Fulfilled (USA) (Bet Twice (USA))
N J Hawke (T D Easterby 14/11) Trevor Heayns

Placings:0560 (3467)
2003/04: 16⁰GF, 16⁵G, 16⁶GS, 16⁰S,

	Starts	1st	2nd	3rd	Win & Pl
Hurdles	4	0	0	0	0
Career Total	4	0	0	0	0

Going:	Sf: 0-1 GS: 0-1 Gd: 0-1 GF: - Fm: 0-1

Distance:	2m/2m3: 0-4 2m4-2m7: 0-0 3m+: 0-0
Track:	LH: 0-4 RH: 0-0 Tight: 0-0 Gall: 0-1
Aids:	Bl: 0-0 Vi: 0-0 Tstrap: 0-0 Ckp: 0-0
Best Rating:	68 11/03 Newc 2m good Hdl

Has shown a little ability in juvenile hurdles.

Jenga

82(102h)   (90+h)**116+**

7-y-o ro m Minster Son-Maybe Daisy (Nicholas Bill)
K C Bailey John Loudon

Placings:11-P15P   (3782)
2003/04: 24⁵GS, 25¹GS, 22⁵S, 24⁵S,

	Starts	1st	2nd	3rd	Win & Pl
Hurdles	1	0	0	0	0
Chases	3	1	0	0	3320
Career Total	6	3	0	0	12462
116	12/03	Hrfd	3m1f110yE(0-110)HCh	G-S	£3320
90	3/03	Extr	2m3f	SFT	£5245
90	1/03	Ludl	2m5f	E Hdl	SFT	£3896

Total win prize-money £12463

Going:	Sf: 0-2 GS: 1-2 Gd: 0-0 GF: - Fm: 0-0
Distance:	2m/2m3: 0-0 2m4-2m7: 0-1 3m+: 1-3
Track:	LH: 0-1 RH: 1-3 Tight: 0-1 Gall: 0-1
Aids:	Bl: 0-0 Vi: 0-0 Tstrap: 0-0 Ckp: 0-0
Best Rating:	116 12/03 Hrfd 3m1f110y gd-sft Ch

Placed in a point before winning a mares' maiden hurdle at Ludlow in January 2003; followed up in a similar event at Exeter March 2003; made successful chasing debut in yet another mares' only event over 3m1f at Hereford in December; stays well; likes soft ground.

Jeremy Spider

104   **126+**

11-y-o b g Nearly A Hand-Lucibella (Comedy Star (USA))
C L Tizzard R G Tizzard

Placings:4152U221/4/P22P1/3105-1PF   (3249)
2003/04: 25⁵GY, 29¹S, 29⁵S, 25⁵S,

	Starts	1st	2nd	3rd	Win & Pl
Chases	4	1	0	0	19064
Career Total	21	5	5	1	42338
126	11/03	Plum	3m5f	C(0-130)HCh	SFT	£19063
124	2/03	Leic	2m7f110yD(0-115)HCh	G-S	£7007
115	2/02	Tntn	3m	E Ch	SFT	£3656
110	4/00	Extr	2m7f	E Hdl	HVY	£2254
110	12/99	Plum	2m5f	E Hdl	HVY	£2040

Total win prize-money £34022

Going:	Sf: 1-3 GS: 0-0 Gd: 0-0 GF: - Fm: 0-0
Distance:	2m/2m3: 0-0 2m4-2m7: 0-0 3m+: 1-4
Track:	LH: 1-2 RH: 0-2 Tight: 1-1 Gall: 0-0
Aids:	Bl: 0-0 Vi: 0-0 Tstrap: 0-0 Ckp: 0-0
Best Rating:	126 11/03 Plum 3m5f soft Ch

Useful chaser; winner of the 2003 Sussex National at Plumpton in very testing ground; acts well with cut in the ground; stays 3m 5f; front-runner.

Jericho III (FR)

105   **115**

7-y-o b g Lute Antique (FR)-La Salamandre (FR) (Pot D'Or (FR))
R C Guest (M Todhunter 18/6) Sir Robert Ogden

Placings:141P/F1F4-P0PPP33   (4730)
2003/04: 16⁶G, 16⁶GF, 17⁶GF, 20⁶G, 21⁶G, 20⁶G, 20⁶G,

	Starts	1st	2nd	3rd	Win & Pl
Hurdles	1	0	0	0	0
Chases	6	0	0	2	2274

Career Total	15	3	0	2	13333
114	1/03	Leic	2m	E Ch	SFT	£4771
106	1/02	Hntg	2m110y	D Hdl	G-S	£3643
97	11/01	Winc	2m	H NHF	GD	£1610

Total win prize-money £10025

Going:	Sf: 0-0 GS: 0-0 Gd: 0-5 GF: - Fm: 0-2
Distance:	2m/2m3: 0-3 2m4-2m7: 0-4 3m+: 0-0
Track:	LH: 0-4 RH: 0-3 Tight: 0-2 Gall: 0-0
Aids:	Bl: 0-2 Vi: 0-0 Tstrap: 0-2 Ckp: 0-0
Best Rating:	115 11/02 Tntn 2m3f gd-sft Ch

Modeste chaser; formerly fair hurdler; best over two miles; suited by soft ground; does not look an easy ride; suited by forcing tactics, but his jumping has let him down on more than one occasion and appears to have lost his confidence over fences; has been tried in tongue tie and blinkers.

Jerom De Vindecy (FR)

7-y-o ch g Roi De Rome (USA)-Preves Du Forez (FR) (Quart De Vin (FR))
A R Dicken Ron Affleck

Placings:P6224/640/P   (3767)
2003/04: 17⁵HY,

	Starts	1st	2nd	3rd	Win & Pl
Hurdles	1	0	0	0	0
Career Total	9	0	2	0	8729

Going:	Sf: 0-1 GS: 0-0 Gd: 0-0 GF: - Fm: 0-0
Distance:	2m/2m3: 0-1 2m4-2m7: 0-0 3m+: 0-0
Track:	LH: 0-0 RH: 0-1 Tight: 0-0 Gall: 0-0
Aids:	Bl: 0-0 Vi: 0-0 Tstrap: 0-0 Ckp: 0-0

Jeropino (IRE)

94   **97+**

6-y-o b g Norwich-Guillig Lady (IRE) (Hatim (USA))
J Mackie J White

Placings:40P   (3825)
2003/04: 20⁴S, 16⁶GS, 20⁶S,

	Starts	1st	2nd	3rd	Win & Pl
Hurdles	3	0	0	0	304
Career Total	3	0	0	0	304

Going:	Sf: 0-2 GS: 0-1 Gd: 0-0 GF: - Fm: 0-0
Distance:	2m/2m3: 0-2 2m4-2m7: 0-0 3m+: 0-0
Track:	LH: 0-3 RH: 0-0 Tight: 0-0 Gall: 0-0
Aids:	Bl: 0-0 Vi: 0-0 Tstrap: 0-0 Ckp: 0-0
Best Rating:	97 12/03 Hayd 2m4f soft Hdl

Novice hurdler; acts in soft ground; front runner; probably stays 2m 4f.

Jeruflo (IRE)

88   (109h)**92**

9-y-o b m Glacial Storm (USA)-Martiness (Martiness)
P R Webber Raymond Anderson Green

Placings:310/PP1/1/P53-44P   (2937)
2003/04: 21⁴GF, 20⁴S, 25⁶S,

	Starts	1st	2nd	3rd	Win & Pl
Chases	3	0	0	0	525
Career Total	13	3	0	2	11097
109	5/01	Hexm	2m4f110yE Hdl		G-F	£1900
97	4/01	Plum	2m	D Hdl	SFT	£3500
103	3/00	Towc	2m	H NHF	SFT	£1652

Total win prize-money £7053

Going:	Sf: 0-2 GS: 0-0 Gd: 0-0 GF: - Fm: 0-1
Distance:	2m/2m3: 0-0 2m4-2m7: 0-2 3m+: 0-1
Track:	LH: 0-1 RH: 0-2 Tight: 0-2 Gall: 0-0
Aids:	Bl: 0-0 Vi: 0-0 Tstrap: 0-3 Ckp: 0-0
Best Rating:	109 5/01 Hexm 2m4f110y gd-fm Hdl

Decent hurdler; has shown ability over fences; stays 2m 5f; acts on fast and soft ground.

Jesper (FR)

96   **88+**

7-y-o b g Video Rock (FR)-Belle Des Airs (FR) (Saumon (FR))
R T Phillips Mrs R J Skan

Placings:4   (0234)
2003/04: 17⁴GF,

	Starts	1st	2nd	3rd	Win & Pl
Hurdles	1	0	0	0	268
Career Total	1	0	0	0	268

Going:	Sf: 0-0 GS: 0-0 Gd: 0-0 GF: - Fm: 0-1
Distance:	2m/2m3: 0-1 2m4-2m7: 0-0 3m+: 0-0
Track:	LH: 0-0 RH: 0-1 Tight: 0-0 Gall: 0-0
Aids:	Bl: 0-0 Vi: 0-0 Tstrap: 0-0 Ckp: 0-0
Best Rating:	88 5/03 Hrfd 2m1f gd-fm Hdl

Jessie Macdougall

83   **89**

4-y-o br f Overbury (IRE)-Miss Crusty (Belfort (FR))
Dr P Pritchard (P D Evans 4/10) Four For Fun

Placings:465   (2716)
2003/04: 16⁴GF, 16⁶GS, 16⁶GS,

	Starts	1st	2nd	3rd	Win & Pl
Hurdles	3	0	0	0	751
Career Total	3	0	0	0	751

Going:	Sf: 0-0 GS: 0-2 Gd: 0-0 GF: - Fm: 0-1
Distance:	2m/2m3: 0-3 2m4-2m7: 0-0 3m+: 0-0
Track:	LH: 0-2 RH: 0-1 Tight: 0-0 Gall: 0-0
Aids:	Bl: 0-0 Vi: 0-0 Tstrap: 0-0 Ckp: 0-0
Best Rating:	89 12/03 Chel 2m110y gd-sft Hdl

Jetowa Du Bois Hue (FR)

108   (103h)**116+**

7-y-o b g Kadrou (FR)-Vaika (FR) (Cosmopolitan (FR))
T R George B A Kilpatrick

Placings:260/3414-1331   (2266)
2003/04: 16¹GF, 16³GF, 17³G, 16¹GF,

	Starts	1st	2nd	3rd	Win & Pl
Chases	4	2	0	2	8934
Career Total	11	3	1	3	15532
116	11/03	Winc	2m	D(0-120)HCh	G-F	£4004
108	5/03	Hntg	2m110y	F(0-100)HCh	G-F	£3513
102	3/03	Hrfd	2m	E(0-100)HCh	G-F	£4410

Total win prize-money £11927

Going:	Sf: 0-0 GS: 0-0 Gd: 0-1 GF: - Fm: 2-3
Distance:	2m/2m3: 2-4 2m4-2m7: 0-0 3m+: 0-0
Track:	LH: 0-1 RH: 2-3 Tight: 0-1 Gall: 1-2
Aids:	Bl: 0-0 Vi: 0-0 Tstrap: 0-0 Ckp: 0-0
Best Rating:	116 11/03 Winc 2m gd-fm Ch

Modest chaser; winless in three outings over hurdles, has looked much better over fences; best at around two miles; likes fast ground, but handles good to soft.

Jewel Fighter

85(97h)   (67h)57

10-y-o br m Good Times (ITY)-Duellist (Town Crier)
Dr P Pritchard Juro Antiques

Placings:0/0/P02F/P5-626**C5**   (0879)
2003/04: 16⁶G, 20²GF, 16⁸GF, 16⁶GF, 16⁵GF,

	Starts	1st	2nd	3rd	Win & Pl
Hurdles	3	0	1	0	1190
Chases	2	0	0	0	0
Career Total	13	0	2	0	1685

Going:	Sf: 0-0 GS: 0-0 Gd: 0-1 GF: - Fm: 0-4
Distance:	2m/2m3: 0-4 2m4-2m7: 0-1 3m+: 0-0
Track:	LH: 0-5 RH: 0-0 Tight: 0-1 Gall: 0-0
Aids:	Bl: 0-0 Vi: 0-0 Tstrap: 0-0 Ckp: 0-0
Best Rating:	67 6/03 Uttx 2m4f110y gd-fm Hdl

Plating-class hurdler; acts on fast.

Jewel Of India

100   108+

5-y-o ch g Bijou D'Inde-Low Hill (Rousillon (USA))
Mrs A L M King (P J Hobbs 20/10) Touchwood Racing

Placings:4-3161   (1717)
2003/04: 16³GF, 16¹GF, 16⁶GF, 16¹GF,

	Starts	1st	2nd	3rd	Win & Pl
Hurdles	4	2	0	1	6178
Career Total	5	2	0	1	6178
109	10/03 Plum	2m	E(0-100)HHdl	G-F	£3020
96	8/03 Hntg	2m110y F Hdl	G-F	£2653
			Total win prize-money £5674		

Going:	Sf: 0-0 GS: 0-0 Gd: 0-0 GF: - Fm: 2-4
Distance:	2m/2m3: 2-4 2m4-2m7: 0-0 3m+: 0-0
Track:	LH: 1-3 RH: 1-1 Tight: 1-2 Gall: 1-1
Aids:	Bl: 0-0 Vi: 0-0 Tstrap: 0-0 Ckp: 0-0
Best Rating:	109 10/03 Plum 2m gd-fm Hdl

Moderate hurdler; best on fast ground.

Jidiya (IRE)

96   86

5-y-o b g Lahib (USA)-Yaqatha (IRE) (Sadler's Wells (USA))
S Gollings (John E Kiely 27/10) Holmes Court Securities Ltd

Placings:1P600   (4716)
2003/04: 16¹G, 19⁶G, 24⁶G, 17⁹G, 21⁰G,

	Starts	1st	2nd	3rd	Win & Pl
NH Flat	1	1	0	0	3808
Hurdles	4	0	0	0	0
Career Total	5	1	0	0	3808
101	9/03 Rosc	2m	NHF	GD	£3808
			Total win prize-money £3808		

Going:	Sf: 0-0 GS: 0-1 Gd: 1-4 GF: - Fm: 0-0
Distance:	2m/2m3: 1-2 2m4-2m7: 0-2 3m+: 0-1
Track:	LH: 0-2 RH: 0-2 Tight: 0-1 Gall: 0-0
Aids:	Bl: 0-0 Vi: 0-0 Tstrap: 0-0 Ckp: 0-0
Best Rating:	101 9/03 Rosc 2m good NHF

Jim Bell (IRE)

73   109+

9-y-o br g Supreme Leader-Mightyatom (Black Minstrel)

J G M O'Shea K W Bell

Placings:4/0030P6/33121-0   (3036)
2003/04: 23⁹GS,

	Starts	1st	2nd	3rd	Win & Pl
Hurdles	1	0	0	0	
Career Total	13	2	1	3	8789
107	3/03 Hexm	3m	F(0-100)HHdl	SFT	£2646
107	2/03 Catt	3m1f110yE(0-105)HHdl	GD	£3454
			Total win prize-money £6101		

Going:	Sf: 0-0 GS: 0-1 Gd: 0-0 GF: - Fm: 0-0
Distance:	2m/2m3: 0-0 2m4-2m7: 0-0 3m+: 0-1
Track:	LH: 0-1 RH: 0-0 Tight: 0-0 Gall: 0-0
Aids:	Bl: 0-0 Vi: 0-0 Tstrap: 0-0 Ckp: 0-0
Best Rating:	109 2/03 Catt 3m1f110y good Hdl

Moderate hurdler; stays 3m; acts in soft ground.

Jim Dore (IRE)

9-y-o b/br g Mac's Imp (USA)-Secret Assignment (Vitiges (FR))
R Williams R Williams

Placings:0/P   (4915)
2003/04: 16ᴾGS,

	Starts	1st	2nd	3rd	Win & Pl
Hurdles	1	0	0	0	
Career Total	2	0	0	0	

Going:	Sf: 0-0 GS: 0-1 Gd: 0-0 GF: - Fm: 0-0
Distance:	2m/2m3: 0-1 2m4-2m7: 0-0 3m+: 0-0
Track:	LH: 0-1 RH: 0-0 Tight: 0-0 Gall: 0-0
Aids:	Bl: 0-0 Vi: 0-0 Tstrap: 0-0 Ckp: 0-0
Best Rating:	38 5/00 Cork 2m gd-yld Hdl

Jim Jam Joey (IRE)

106   108

11-y-o ch g Big Sink Hope (USA)-Ascot Princess (Prince Hansel)
Miss Suzy Smith Miss Suzy Smith

Placings:2315226/6**F**123/3/4420/2000-P200   (4451)
2003/04: 24ᴾS, 24²S, 24⁶GS,

	Starts	1st	2nd	3rd	Win & Pl
Hurdles	4	0	1	0	1084
Career Total	25	2	7	3	16257
125	2/00 Folk	2m6f110yF(0-110)HHdl	SFT	£2395
105	12/98 Font	2m6f110yE Hdl	SFT	£2775
			Total win prize-money £5170		

Going:	Sf: 0-3 GS: 0-1 Gd: 0-0 GF: - Fm: 0-0
Distance:	2m/2m3: 0-0 2m4-2m7: 0-0 3m+: 0-4
Track:	LH: 0-1 RH: 0-3 Tight: 0-1 Gall: 0-1
Aids:	Bl: 0-3 Vi: 0-0 Tstrap: 0-0 Ckp: 0-0
Best Rating:	125 4/00 Chel 3m soft Hdl

Moderate hurdler; acts on soft ground; effective at around two miles six furlongs; has worn blinkers.

Jim Lad

94   72

4-y-o b g Young Em-Anne's Bank (IRE) (Burslem)
Dr J R J Naylor Chris And Stella Watson

Placings:40520625   (4758)
2003/04: 16⁴GF, 16⁰G, 16⁵S, 16²S, 17⁰GS, 22⁵GF, 17²GS, 16⁵S,

	Starts	1st	2nd	3rd	Win & Pl
Hurdles	8	0	2	0	1957
Career Total	8	0	2	0	1957

Going:	Sf: 0-3 GS: 0-2 Gd: 0-1 GF: - Fm: 0-2
Distance:	2m/2m3: 0-7 2m4-2m7: 0-1 3m+: 0-0
Track:	LH: 0-3 RH: 0-5 Tight: 0-3 Gall: 0-0
Aids:	Bl: 0-1 Vi: 0-4 Tstrap: 0-0 Ckp: 0-0
Best Rating:	75 1/04 Chep 2m110y soft Hdl

Plating-class on the Flat; held so far over hurdles.

Jimal

87   55

7-y-o b g Reprimand-Into The Fire (Dominion)
J W Mullins Mrs Sally Mullins

Placings:000/4604/0056   (4237)
2003/04: 21⁰G, 19⁰GS, 16⁵GS, 18⁶GF,

	Starts	1st	2nd	3rd	Win & Pl
Hurdles	4	0	0	0	0
Career Total	11	0	0	0	0

Going:	Sf: 0-0 GS: 0-2 Gd: 0-1 GF: - Fm: 0-1
Distance:	2m/2m3: 0-3 2m4-2m7: 0-1 3m+: 0-0
Track:	LH: 0-2 RH: 0-2 Tight: 0-1 Gall: 0-0
Aids:	Bl: 0-0 Vi: 0-0 Tstrap: 0-0 Ckp: 0-0
Best Rating:	80 4/01 Kemp 2m good Hdl

Jimjo

66f   68f

5-y-o ch g Up And At 'Em-Ushimado (IRE) (Ela-Mana-Mou)
W M Brisbourne Preece Haden Partnership

Placings:00   (4543)
2003/04: 16⁹G, 16⁸GS,

	Starts	1st	2nd	3rd	Win & Pl
NH Flat	2	0	0	0	
Career Total	2	0	0	0	

Going:	Sf: 0-0 GS: 0-1 Gd: 0-1 GF: - Fm: 0-0
Distance:	2m/2m3: 0-2 2m4-2m7: 0-0 3m+: 0-0
Track:	LH: 0-1 RH: 0-1 Tight: 0-0 Gall: 0-1
Aids:	Bl: 0-0 Vi: 0-0 Tstrap: 0-0 Ckp: 0-0
Best Rating:	68 3/04 Ludl 2m gd-sft NHF

Jimmy Blues

94   (86h)68

9-y-o b g Durgam (USA)-Tibbi Blues (Cure The Blues (USA))
Ferdy Murphy Miss Barbara Spittal

Placings:4/00/46066P/0645-30P   (1842)
2003/04: 21³G, 20⁰F, 27⁶G,

	Starts	1st	2nd	3rd	Win & Pl
Chases	3	0	0	1	680
Career Total	16	0	0	1	1003

Going:	Sf: 0-0 GS: 0-0 Gd: 0-2 GF: - Fm: 0-1
Distance:	2m/2m3: 0-0 2m4-2m7: 0-2 3m+: 0-1
Track:	LH: 0-3 RH: 0-0 Tight: 0-2 Gall: 0-0
Aids:	Bl: 0-0 Vi: 0-0 Tstrap: 0-0 Ckp: 0-1
Best Rating:	86 5/01 Ayr 2m gd-fm Hdl

Poor novice chaser.

Jimmy Bond

90   81

5-y-o b g Primitive Rising (USA)-Miss Moneypenny (Silly Prices)

Jedd O'Keeffe The Odd Jobs

Placings:006004   (4873)
2003/04: 16⁶G, 20⁹GS, 20⁶G, 19⁹G, 22⁵GS, 20⁴GS,

	Starts	1st	2nd	3rd	Win & Pl
NH Flat	1	0	0	0	0
Hurdles	5	0	0	0	360
Career Total	6	0	0	0	360

Going:	Sf: 0-0 GS: 0-3 Gd: 0-3 GF: - Fm: 0-0	
Distance:	2m/2m3: 0-1 2m4-2m7: 0-5 3m+: 0-0	
Track:	LH: 0-4 RH: 0-1 Tight: 0-3 Gall: 0-0	
Aids:	Bl: 0-0 Vi: 0-0 Tstrap: 0-0 Ckp: 0-0	
Best Rating:	81 4/04 Bang 2m4f gd-sft Hdl	

Jimmy Jumbo (IRE)

11-y-o ch g Dragon Palace (USA)-Sail On Lady (New Member)
J S Swindells J S Swindells

Placings:0/06P/P0-6   (0430)
2003/04: 26⁶G,

	Starts	1st	2nd	3rd	Win & Pl
Chases	1	0	0	0	0
Career Total	7	0	0	0	0

Going:	Sf: 0-0 GS: 0-0 Gd: 0-1 GF: - Fm: 0-0	
Distance:	2m/2m3: 0-0 2m4-2m7: 0-0 3m+: 0-1	
Track:	LH: 0-1 RH: 0-0 Tight: 0-1 Gall: 0-0	
Aids:	Bl: 0-0 Vi: 0-0 Tstrap: 0-0 Ckp: 0-0	
Best Rating:	69 5/03 Ctml 3m2f good Ch	

Jimmy Tennis (FR)
112   141

7-y-o b/br g Video Rock (FR)-Via Tennise (FR) (Brezzo (FR))
Miss Venetia Williams Derek And Jean Clee

Placings:35/2131PP/U5-U22F16   (4055)
2003/04: 19ᵁGS, 19²S, 24²G, 24⁴S, 23¹G, 24⁶G,

	Starts	1st	2nd	3rd	Win & Pl
Chases	6	1	2	0	16728
Career Total	16	3	3	2	64547
141 2/04 Leic	2m7f110yD(0-125)HCh			GD	£6929
131 2/02 Asct	3m110y A Ch			G-S	£20825
6/01 Autl	2m1f110y Ch			VS	£12124
				Total win prize-money £39878	

Going:	Sf: 0-2 GS: 0-1 Gd: 1-3 GF: - Fm: 0-0	
Distance:	2m/2m3: 0-0 2m4-2m7: 0-2 3m+: 1-4	
Track:	LH: 0-3 RH: 1-3 Tight: 0-0 Gall: 0-1	
Aids:	Bl: 0-0 Vi: 0-0 Tstrap: 0-0 Ckp: 0-0	
Best Rating:	141 2/04 Leic 2m7f110y good Ch	

Useful chaser; ex-French; fair efforts in the winter of 2003/4; suited by soft ground; stays three miles, although effctive at shorter.

Jimmys Duky (IRE)
81   59

6-y-o b g Duky-Harvey's Cream (IRE) (Mandalus)
D M Forster D M Forster

Placings:0P00   (3940)
2003/04: 20⁵HY, 27⁶G, 19⁹G, 24⁵GS,

	Starts	1st	2nd	3rd	Win & Pl
Hurdles	4	0	0	0	0
Career Total	4	0	0	0	0

Going:	Sf: 0-1 GS: 0-1 Gd: 0-2 GF: - Fm: 0-0	
Distance:	2m/2m3: 0-1 2m4-2m7: 0-1 3m+: 0-2	
Track:	LH: 0-3 RH: 0-1 Tight: 0-2 Gall: 0-1	
Aids:	Bl: 0-0 Vi: 0-0 Tstrap: 0-0 Ckp: 0-0	
Best Rating:	61 11/03 Carl 2m4f heavy Hdl	

Jimsue

13-y-o gr g Afzal-Gentian (Roan Rocket)
B L Lay B L Lay

Placings:0/P   (0130)
2003/04: 16⁶GF,

	Starts	1st	2nd	3rd	Win & Pl
Hurdles	1	0	0	0	
Career Total	2	0	0	0	

Going:	Sf: 0-0 GS: 0-0 Gd: 0-0 GF: - Fm: 0-1	
Distance:	2m/2m3: 0-1 2m4-2m7: 0-0 3m+: 0-1	
Track:	LH: 0-0 RH: 0-1 Tight: 0-0 Gall: 0-1	
Aids:	Bl: 0-0 Vi: 0-0 Tstrap: 0-0 Ckp: 0-1	

Jinful Du Grand Val (FR)

7-y-o b g Useful (FR)-Marine (FR) (African Joy)
N W Alexander (A L T Moore 26/8) Jamie Alexander

Placings:6U   (4191)
2003/04: 20⁶F, 25ᵁGS,

	Starts	1st	2nd	3rd	Win & Pl
Chases	2	0	0	0	
Career Total	2	0	0	0	

Going:	Sf: 0-0 GS: 0-1 Gd: 0-0 GF: - Fm: 0-1	
Distance:	2m/2m3: 0-0 2m4-2m7: 0-1 3m+: 0-1	
Track:	LH: 0-1 RH: 0-0 Tight: 0-1 Gall: 0-0	
Aids:	Bl: 0-0 Vi: 0-0 Tstrap: 0-1 Ckp: 0-0	
Best Rating:	41 8/03 Tral 2m4f firm Ch	

Jivaros (FR)
102   (106h)113

7-y-o br g Video Rock (FR)-Rives (FR) (Reasonable Choice (USA)
H D Daly Mrs G Leigh

Placings:001/6P1-FPP45   (4784)
2003/04: 28⁶G, 22⁵PS, 24⁸GF, 25⁴GS, 24⁵G,

	Starts	1st	2nd	3rd	Win & Pl
Chases	5	0	0	0	532
Career Total	11	2	0	0	8648
113 3/03 Hntg	3m	D(0-110)HCh		GD	£5512
106 3/02 Wwck	3m1f	E Hdl		G-S	£2604
				Total win prize-money £8116	

Going:	Sf: 0-1 GS: 0-1 Gd: 0-2 GF: - Fm: 0-1	
Distance:	2m/2m3: 0-0 2m4-2m7: 0-1 3m+: 0-4	
Track:	LH: 0-1 RH: 0-4 Tight: 0-2 Gall: 0-1	
Aids:	Bl: 0-0 Vi: 0-0 Tstrap: 0-0 Ckp: 0-0	
Best Rating:	113 3/03 Hntg 3m good Ch	

Modest chaser; stays three miles; acts on good ground.

Jivaty (FR)
100   111

7-y-o b g Quart De Vin (FR)-Tenacity (FR) (Prove It Baby (USA))

M C Pipe D A Johnson

Placings:212   (4539)
2003/04: 22²G, 21¹GS, 21²GS,

	Starts	1st	2nd	3rd	Win & Pl
Hurdles	3	1	2	0	6225
Career Total	3	1	2	0	6225
109 3/04 Plum	2m5f	E Hdl		G-S	£3581
				Total win prize-money £3582	

Going:	Sf: 0-0 GS: 1-2 Gd: 0-1 GF: - Fm: 0-0	
Distance:	2m/2m3: 0-0 2m4-2m7: 1-3 3m+: 0-0	
Track:	LH: 1-2 RH: 0-1 Tight: 1-2 Gall: 0-0	
Aids:	Bl: 0-0 Vi: 0-0 Tstrap: 0-0 Ckp: 0-0	
Best Rating:	111 3/04 Ludl 2m5f gd-sft Hdl	

Modest novice hurdler; given a fine ride when winner of a weak Plumpton event; beaten at odds-on next time; lacks scope; acts on easy ground.

Jiver (IRE)
88f   87f

5-y-o b g Flemensfirth (USA)-Choice Brush (IRE) (Brush Aside (USA))
M Scudamore Mrs S Tainton

Placings:04   (4543)
2003/04: 16⁶GS, 16⁴GS,

	Starts	1st	2nd	3rd	Win & Pl
NH Flat	2	0	0	0	0
Career Total	2	0	0	0	0

Going:	Sf: 0-0 GS: 0-2 Gd: 0-0 GF: - Fm: 0-0	
Distance:	2m/2m3: 0-2 2m4-2m7: 0-0 3m+: 0-0	
Track:	LH: 0-0 RH: 0-2 Tight: 0-0 Gall: 0-0	
Aids:	Bl: 0-0 Vi: 0-0 Tstrap: 0-0 Ckp: 0-0	
Best Rating:	87 3/04 Ludl 2m gd-sft NHF	

Jocker Du Sapin (FR)
99   97

7-y-o br g Franc Parler-Nymphe Rose (FR) (Rose Laurel)
A J Whitehead A J Whitehead

Placings:0/0050P/4562   (4530)
2003/04: 16⁴HY, 16⁵G, 17⁶G, 16²GS,

	Starts	1st	2nd	3rd	Win & Pl
Chases	4	0	1	0	1373
Career Total	10	0	1	0	2440

Going:	Sf: 0-1 GS: 0-1 Gd: 0-2 GF: - Fm: 0-0	
Distance:	2m/2m3: 0-4 2m4-2m7: 0-0 3m+: 0-0	
Track:	LH: 0-3 RH: 0-1 Tight: 0-1 Gall: 0-0	
Aids:	Bl: 0-0 Vi: 0-0 Tstrap: 0-0 Ckp: 0-0	
Best Rating:	97 3/04 Chep 2m110y gd-sft Ch	

Ex-French; showed significant improvement when trying to concede a stone to the well handicapped Barton Nic in Class F 2m handicap chase at Chepstow March 2004.

Jockie Wells
82   62

6-y-o b g Primitive Rising (USA)-Princess Maxine (IRE) (Horage)
Miss Lucinda V Russell Miss G Joughin

Placings:600-6   (0467)
2003/04: 16⁶G,

	Starts	1st	2nd	3rd	Win & Pl
Hurdles	1	0	0	0	0

Career Total   4   0   0   0   0

Going:	Sf: 0-0 GS: 0-0 Gd: 0-1 GF: - Fm: 0-0
Distance:	2m/2m3: 0-1 2m4-2m7: 0-0 3m+: 0-0
Track:	LH: 0-1 RH: 0-0 Tight: 0-0 Gall: 0-0
Aids:	Bl: 0-0 Vi: 0-0 Tstrap: 0-0 Ckp: 0-0
Best Rating:	64 2/03 Ayr 2m gd-sft NHF

Jodante (IRE)

106(96h)   (89h)103

7-y-o ch g Phardante (FR)-Crashtown Lucy (Crash Course)
P Beaumont Trevor Hemmings

Placings:0/54-UP20202   (4659)
2003/04: 20UG, 20PS, 19²GS, 20⁰GS, 16²HY, 16⁵GS, 16²S,

	Starts	1st	2nd	3rd	Win & Pl
Hurdles	6	0	2	0	1906
Chases	1	0	1	0	1233
Career Total	10	0	3	0	3502

Going:	Sf: 0-3 GS: 0-3 Gd: 0-1 GF: - Fm: 0-0
Distance:	2m/2m3: 0-3 2m4-2m7: 0-4 3m+: 0-0
Track:	LH: 0-7 RH: 0-0 Tight: 0-0 Gall: 0-2
Aids:	Bl: 0-0 Vi: 0-0 Tstrap: 0-0 Ckp: 0-0
Best Rating:	103 4/04 Hexm 2m110y soft Ch

Out of a sister to Gold Cup winner Jodami; bettered pick of modest hurdles form over two miles on chasing debut at Hexham in April; sure to win races over fences.

Joe Blake (IRE)

106   142+

9-y-o b g Jurado (USA)-I'Ve No Idea (Nishapour (FR))
L Lungo R A Bartlett

Placings:F141F/31-12P4   (4327)
2003/04: 23¹G, 19²GS, 28⁶G, 24⁴GS,

	Starts	1st	2nd	3rd	Win & Pl
Chases	4	1	1	0	8894
Career Total	11	4	1	1	33224
135 11/03 Weth	2m7f110yD(0-125)HCh		GD		£4485
135 4/03 Gowr	3m	Ch	G-F		£10551
121 4/02 Fair	3m1f	Ch	YLD		£6349
106 2/02 Fair	3m1f	Ch	SFT		£4656

Total win prize-money £26043

Going:	Sf: 0-0 GS: 0-2 Gd: 1-2 GF: - Fm: 0-0
Distance:	2m/2m3: 0-0 2m4-2m7: 0-0 3m+: 1-3
Track:	LH: 0-2 RH: 0-1 Tight: 0-0 Gall: 0-0
Aids:	Bl: 0-0 Vi: 0-0 Tstrap: 0-0 Ckp: 0-0
Best Rating:	142 2/04 Ayr 2m4f gd-sft Ch

Useful chaser; ex-Irish hunter; won four of his six starts in point-to-points and good efforts in hunter chases early in 2002, suffered problems in 2003, but won on first start for Len Lungo at Wetherby in November; back to form when successful there again in April; stays three miles and acts on all ground, especially soft.

Joe Cooley (IRE)

87f   82f

4-y-o b g Accordion-My Miss Molly (IRE) (Entitled)
K A Ryan I Bray

Placings:4   (4866)
2003/04: 16⁴S,

	Starts	1st	2nd	3rd	Win & Pl
NH Flat	1	0	0	0	273
Career Total	1	0	0	0	273

Going:	Sf: 0-1 GS: 0-0 Gd: 0-0 GF: - Fm: 0-0
Distance:	2m/2m3: 0-1 2m4-2m7: 0-0 3m+: 0-0
Track:	LH: 0-1 RH: 0-0 Tight: 0-0 Gall: 0-0
Aids:	Bl: 0-0 Vi: 0-0 Tstrap: 0-0 Ckp: 0-0
Best Rating:	82 4/04 Ayr 2m soft NHF

Attracted support and showed ability before getting tired on testing ground in bumper at Ayr on debut in April 2004; may be capable of better.

Joe Cullen (IRE)

100(108h)   (123 h)110

9-y-o ch g River Falls-Moycullen (Le Moss)
Ian Williams Mark F Sheasby

Placings:11/13/42105000/300-2F162   (1790)
2003/04: 17²GF, 16⁶G, 20¹GF, 17⁶G, 16²GF,

	Starts	1st	2nd	3rd	Win & Pl
Hurdles	1	0	0	0	0
Chases	4	1	2	0	8108
Career Total	20	5	3	2	52898
96 8/03 MRas	2m4f	D Ch	G-F		£5434
137 11/01 Punc	2m	Hdl	SFT		£7233
137 2/01 Fair	2m	Hdl	HVY		£5008
149 3/00 Chel	2m110y	A NHF	GD		£18000
118 6/99 Tral	2m	NHF	GD		£3222

Total win prize-money £38899

Going:	Sf: 0-0 GS: 0-0 Gd: 0-2 GF: - Fm: 1-3
Distance:	2m/2m3: 0-4 2m4-2m7: 1-1 3m+: 0-0
Track:	LH: 0-1 RH: 1-4 Tight: 1-3 Gall: 0-0
Aids:	Bl: 0-0 Vi: 0-0 Tstrap: 0-0 Ckp: 0-0
Best Rating:	149 3/00 Chel 2m110y good NHF

Ex-Irish hurdler/chaser; former Cheltenham Festival bumper winner; not as good these days despite winning a novice chase in August 2003; suited by soft ground.

Joe Deane (IRE)

103(93h)   (92+h)108+

8-y-o ch g Alphabatim (USA)-Craic Go Leor (Deep Run)
T R George Mr & Mrs D A Gamble

Placings:632P-21243   (4494)
2003/04: 19²S, 20¹S, 24²S, 22⁴G, 24³GS,

	Starts	1st	2nd	3rd	Win & Pl
Chases	5	1	2	1	7721
Career Total	9	1	3	2	9540
106 1/04 Plum	2m4f	E(0-105)HCh	SFT		£4069

Total win prize-money £4069

Going:	Sf: 1-3 GS: 0-1 Gd: 0-1 GF: - Fm: 0-0
Distance:	2m/2m3: 0-0 2m4-2m7: 1-3 3m+: 0-2
Track:	LH: 1-3 RH: 0-1 Tight: 1-2 Gall: 0-0
Aids:	Bl: 0-0 Vi: 0-0 Tstrap: 0-0 Ckp: 0-0
Best Rating:	108 1/04 Asct 3m110y soft Ch

Moderate chaser; stays three miles-two but possibly better at around two and a half miles; acts on soft ground.

Joe Di Capo (IRE)

105   (94h)94

9-y-o b g Phardante (FR)-Supreme Glen (IRE) (Supreme Leader)
A Crook Joe Buzzeo

Placings:432P/01PP/422F2F2445-P35264   (3437)
2003/04: 24⁵GF, 25²G, 30³G, 25⁵S, 24²GS, 24⁶GF, 24⁴HY,

	Starts	1st	2nd	3rd	Win & Pl
Chases	7	0	1	1	1614
Career Total	24	1	6	2	13302
94 11/01 Newc	2m4f	E Hdl	GD		£2618

Total win prize-money £2618

Going:	Sf: 0-2 GS: 0-1 Gd: 0-2 GF: - Fm: 0-2
Distance:	2m/2m3: 0-0 2m4-2m7: 0-0 3m+: 0-7
Track:	LH: 0-6 RH: 0-1 Tight: 0-2 Gall: 0-4
Aids:	Bl: 0-4 Vi: 0-1 Tstrap: 0-0 Ckp: 0-0
Best Rating:	106 12/00 Newc 3m soft Hdl

Moderate chaser; stays three miles; likes to be ridden prominently; yet to win over fences; has worn blinkers and cheekpieces.

Joe Malone (IRE)

89f   84f

5-y-o br g Rashar (USA)-Bucktina (Buckskin (FR))
C C Bealby Foreneish Racing

Placings:00   (4454)
2003/04: 16⁵GS, 16⁰GS,

	Starts	1st	2nd	3rd	Win & Pl
NH Flat	2	0	0	0	
Career Total	2	0	0	0	

Going:	Sf: 0-0 GS: 0-2 Gd: 0-0 GF: - Fm: 0-0
Distance:	2m/2m3: 0-2 2m4-2m7: 0-0 3m+: 0-0
Track:	LH: 0-0 RH: 0-2 Tight: 0-0 Gall: 0-0
Aids:	Bl: 0-0 Vi: 0-0 Tstrap: 0-0 Ckp: 0-0
Best Rating:	88 2/04 Kemp 2m gd-sft NHF

Joe Public (IRE)

6-y-o b g Actinium (FR)-Cool Boreen (Boreen (FR))
T P McGovern (Ferdy Murphy 28/2) Anthony O'Gorman

Placings:0P   (4895)
2003/04: 16⁰G, 22P⁰G,

	Starts	1st	2nd	3rd	Win & Pl
NH Flat	1	0	0	0	0
Hurdles	1	0	0	0	0
Career Total	2	0	0	0	

Going:	Sf: 0-0 GS: 0-0 Gd: 0-2 GF: - Fm: 0-0
Distance:	2m/2m3: 0-1 2m4-2m7: 0-1 3m+: 0-0
Track:	LH: 0-1 RH: 0-1 Tight: 0-0 Gall: 0-0
Aids:	Bl: 0-0 Vi: 0-0 Tstrap: 0-0 Ckp: 0-0
Best Rating:	36 2/04 Hayd 2m good NHF

Joebriggs

58f   68f

6-y-o b g Hatim (USA)-Meadow Brig (Meadowbrook)
A C Whillans Mrs Anne Taylor

Placings:0   (2181)
2003/04: 16⁰G,

	Starts	1st	2nd	3rd	Win & Pl
NH Flat	1	0	0	0	
Career Total	1	0	0	0	

Going:	Sf: 0-0 GS: 0-0 Gd: 0-1 GF: - Fm: 0-0
Distance:	2m/2m3: 0-1 2m4-2m7: 0-0 3m+: 0-0
Track:	LH: 0-1 RH: 0-0 Tight: 0-0 Gall: 0-0
Aids:	Bl: 0-0 Vi: 0-0 Tstrap: 0-0 Ckp: 0-0
Best Rating:	68 11/03 Ayr 2m good NHF

Joely Green

79   98

7-y-o b g Binary Star (USA)-Comedy Lady (Comedy Star (USA))

N P Littmoden Paul J Dixon

Placings:0/1P-0   (0211)
2003/04: 16^5G,

	Starts	1st	2nd	3rd	Win & Pl
Hurdles	1	0	0	0	
Career Total	4	1	0	0	2218
98	8/02	Hntg	2m110y F Hdl	G-F	£2217
			Total win prize-money		£2218

Going:	Sf: 0-0 GS: 0-0 Gd: 0-1 GF: - Fm: 0-0
Distance:	2m/2m3: 0-1 2m4-2m7: 0-0 3m+: 0-0
Track:	LH: 0-1 RH: 0-0 Tight: 0-0 Gall: 0-0
Aids:	Bl: 0-1 Vi: 0-0 Tstrap: 0-0
Best Rating:	98 8/02 Hntg 2m110y gd-fm Hdl

Made a winning hurdles debut in August 2002; acts on fast ground; lightly raced since.

Joes Edge (IRE)
105   **115+**
7-y-o b/br g Supreme Leader-Right Dark (Buckskin (FR))
Ferdy Murphy (Miss Venetia Williams 13/3) Chemipetro Limited

Placings:10/221010   (4325)
2003/04: 17^2G, 20^2GS, 20^1S, 20^5HY, 20^1G, 20^5S,

	Starts	1st	2nd	3rd	Win & Pl
Hurdles	6	2	2	0	11381
Career Total	8	3	2	0	13880
115	2/04	Carl	2m4f	E Hdl	GD £3932
115	1/04	Asct	2m4f	D Hdl	SFT £5460
103	3/03	Carl	2m1f	H NHF	GD £2499
			Total win prize-money		£11892

Going:	Sf: 1-3 GS: 0-1 Gd: 1-2 GF: - Fm: 0-0
Distance:	2m/2m3: 0-1 2m4-2m7: 2-5 3m+: 0-0
Track:	LH: 0-2 RH: 2-4 Tight: 0-1 Gall: 0-0
Aids:	Bl: 0-0 Vi: 0-0 Tstrap: 0-0 Ckp: 0-0
Best Rating:	115 2/04 Carl 2m4f good Hdl

Fair novice hurdler; stays 2m 4f; effective in soft ground, but acts on good; progressive.

Joey Tribbiani (IRE)
95(94h)   (81h)**113**
7-y-o b g Foxhound (USA)-Mardi Gras Belle (USA) (Masked Dancer (USA))
Ian Williams newmarketconnections.com

Placings:PP/0/63356212312-146   (1465)
2003/04: 16^1GS, 17^4G, 20^6GF,

	Starts	1st	2nd	3rd	Win & Pl
Chases	3	1	0	0	6086
Career Total	17	3	3	3	21347
113	5/03	Aint	2m	D(0-125)HCh	G-S £5460
105	3/03	Hntg	2m110y	D(0-115)HCh	S £5356
95	2/03	Hrfd	2m	F(0-100)HCh	GD £3360
			Total win prize-money		£14177

Going:	Sf: 0-0 GS: 1-1 Gd: 0-1 GF: - Fm: 0-1
Distance:	2m/2m3: 1-2 2m4-2m7: 0-1 3m+: 0-0
Track:	LH: 1-2 RH: 0-1 Tight: 1-2 Gall: 0-1
Aids:	Bl: 0-0 Vi: 0-0 Tstrap: 0-0 Ckp: 0-0
Best Rating:	113 5/03 Aint 2m gd-sft Ch

Modest chaser; on the upgrade; keen sort; effective on good ground; best at around two miles.

Jofi (IRE)
71f   **55f**
5-y-o b g Shemazar-Giolla Donn (Giolla Mear)
Miss Lucinda V Russell J R Adam

Placings:0   (4866)
2003/04: 16^9S,

	Starts	1st	2nd	3rd	Win & Pl
NH Flat	1	0	0	0	
Career Total	1	0	0	0	

Going:	Sf: 0-1 GS: 0-0 Gd: 0-0 GF: 0-0 Fm: 0-0
Distance:	2m/2m3: 0-1 2m4-2m7: 0-0 3m+: 0-0
Track:	LH: 0-1 RH: 0-0 Tight: 0-0 Gall: 0-0
Aids:	Bl: 0-0 Vi: 0-0 Tstrap: 0-0 Ckp: 0-0
Best Rating:	55 4/04 Ayr 2m soft NHF

Johann De Vonnas (FR)
93   **81**
7-y-o b g Cadoudal (FR)-Diana De Vonnas (FR) (El Badr)
N J Henderson B T M Racing

Placings:0/3-P30   (4931)
2003/04: 20^5S, 20^3G, 22^0G,

	Starts	1st	2nd	3rd	Win & Pl
Hurdles	3	0	0	1	513
Career Total	5	0	0	2	763

Going:	Sf: 0-1 GS: 0-0 Gd: 0-2 GF: - Fm: 0-0
Distance:	2m/2m3: 0-0 2m4-2m7: 0-3 3m+: 0-0
Track:	LH: 0-1 RH: 0-1 Tight: 0-2 Gall: 0-0
Aids:	Bl: 0-0 Vi: 0-0 Tstrap: 0-0 Ckp: 0-0
Best Rating:	100 5/02 Font 2m2f110y gd-fm NHF

Very moderate hurdler/bumper performer; acts on varying ground.

John James (IRE)
108(105h)   (97h)**128?**
8-y-o b g Bravefoot-Glitter Grey (Nishapour (FR))
J H Scott Mrs Monica Cogan

Placings:5/0235/220414340/014560-0FF3165   (4827a)
2003/04: 20^0S, 18^4S, 17^4S, 24^3S, 18^1YS, 16^6G, 20^5Y,

	Starts	1st	2nd	3rd	Win & Pl
Hurdles	1	0	0	0	
Chases	6	1	0	1	13372
Career Total	27	3	3	3	28787
128	2/04	Gowr	2m2f	Ch	Y-S £7785
99	5/02	Naas	2m3f	Hdl	GD £4656
103	9/01	List	2m	NHF	G-F £5564
			Total win prize-money		£18007

Going:	Sf: 0-4 GS: 0-0 Gd: 0-0 GF: - Fm: 0-0
Distance:	2m/2m3: 1-4 2m4-2m7: 0-2 3m+: 0-1
Track:	LH: 0-2 RH: 1-4 Tight: 0-0 Gall: 0-1
Aids:	Bl: 0-0 Vi: 0-0 Tstrap: 0-0 Ckp: 0-1
Best Rating:	128 4/04 Fair 2m4f yield Ch

Irish novice chaser; stays 2m 4f; effective in soft ground.

John Jorrocks (FR)
79f   **56f**
5-y-o br g Chamberlin (FR)-Caryatide (FR) (Maiymad)
J C Tuck The Cat & Custard Pot

Placings:60   (4374)
2003/04: 16^6GF, 16^9GF,

	Starts	1st	2nd	3rd	Win & Pl
NH Flat	2	0	0	0	0
Career Total	2	0	0	0	0

Going:	Sf: 0-0 GS: 0-0 Gd: 0-0 GF: - Fm: 0-2
Distance:	2m/2m3: 0-2 2m4-2m7: 0-0 3m+: 0-0
Track:	LH: 0-0 RH: 0-1 Tight: 0-0 Gall: 0-0
Aids:	Bl: 0-0 Vi: 0-0 Tstrap: 0-0 Ckp: 0-0
Best Rating:	63 11/03 Ludl 2m gd-fm NHF

John Oliver (IRE)
91   **112+**
6-y-o gr g Lure (USA)-Glitter Grey (Nishapour (FR))
E J O'Grady P F Lehane

Placings:0/110-5100   (4804a)
2003/04: 16^5YS, 16^1Y, 16^0G, 16^6Y,

	Starts	1st	2nd	3rd	Win & Pl
Hurdles	4	1	0	0	8261
Career Total	8	3	0	0	19014
112	1/04	Leop	2m	Hdl	YLD £8260
123	3/03	Navn	2m	NHF	HVY £4928
110	2/03	Naas	2m	NHF	YLD £5824
			Total win prize-money		£19015

Going:	Sf: 0-0 GS: 0-0 Gd: 0-1 GF: - Fm: 0-0
Distance:	2m/2m3: 1-4 2m4-2m7: 0-0 3m+: 0-0
Track:	LH: 1-3 RH: 0-1 Tight: 0-0 Gall: 0-0
Aids:	Bl: 0-0 Vi: 0-0 Tstrap: 0-0 Ckp: 0-0
Best Rating:	123 3/03 Navn 2m heavy NHF

Modest hurdler/ bumper winner; off the mark over timber on second outing at Leopardstown in January; raced mainly at two miles; acts on soft ground.

John Rich
(101c)   (80c)
8-y-o b g Mesleh-South Lodge (Current Magic)
M E Sowersby C N Richardson

Placings:4222RPOP   (4762)
2003/04: 22^4GF, 22^2GF, 25^2G, 24^2G, 25^8S, 25^8GS, 21^0G, 19^9S,

	Starts	1st	2nd	3rd	Win & Pl
Hurdles	2	0	0	0	0
Chases	6	0	3	0	3727
Career Total	8	0	3	0	3727

Going:	Sf: 0-2 GS: 0-1 Gd: 0-3 GF: - Fm: 0-2
Distance:	2m/2m3: 0-0 2m4-2m7: 0-4 3m+: 0-0
Track:	LH: 0-4 RH: 0-3 Tight: 0-4 Gall: 0-1
Aids:	Bl: 0-0 Vi: 0-0 Tstrap: 0-0 Ckp: 0-0
Best Rating:	80 11/03 Newc 3m good Ch

Novice chaser; winning pointer; stays three miles; acts on good ground.

John Steed (IRE)
86   (0c)**75**
7-y-o b g Thatching-Trinity Hall (Hallgate)
Mrs A C Tate Richard Tate

Placings:P2004/0106P-000P   (1015)
2003/04: 19^0GS, 20^0G, 16^0G, 20^8GF,

	Starts	1st	2nd	3rd	Win & Pl
Hurdles	3	0	0	0	0
Chases					
Career Total	14	1	1	0	2584
75	10/02	Hrfd	2m3f110yG Hdl	GD	£1918
			Total win prize-money		£1918

Going:	Sf: 0-0 GS: 0-1 Gd: 0-2 GF: - Fm: 0-1
Distance:	2m/2m3: 0-2 2m4-2m7: 0-2 3m+: 0-0
Track:	LH: 0-3 RH: 0-1 Tight: 0-0 Gall: 0-0
Aids:	Bl: 0-0 Vi: 0-1 Tstrap: 0-0 Ckp: 0-0
Best Rating:	83 11/01 Plum 2m gd-sft Hdl

John The Mole (IRE)

87(92h)   (86h)41

6-y-o ch g Glacial Storm (USA)-City Dame (Golden Love)
M D Hammond M T McCarthy and L Ibbotson

Placings:430/3500300-0P0P6   (4882)
2003/04: 20⁰G, 25⁵GS, 19⁹GS, 25⁵GF, 26⁶GS,

	Starts	1st	2nd	3rd	Win & Pl
Hurdles	2	0	0	0	0
Chases	3	0	0	0	0
Career Total	15	0	0	3	1174

Going:	Sf: 0-0 GS: 0-3 Gd: 0-1 GF: - Fm: 0-1
Distance:	2m/2m3: 0-1 2m4-2m7: 0-1 3m+: 0-3
Track:	LH: 0-4 RH: 0-1 Tight: 0-2 Gall: 0-0
Aids:	Bl: 0-0 Vi: 0-0 Tstrap: 0-0 Ckp: 0-2
Best Rating:	98 3/02 MRas 2m1f110y gd-sft NHF

John's Treasure (IRE)

80   42

4-y-o b g Entrepreneur-Misallah (IRE) (Shirley Heights)
M A Barnes J Millican

Placings:0   (1071)
2003/04: 17⁰GF,

	Starts	1st	2nd	3rd	Win & Pl
Hurdles	1	0	0	0	
Career Total	1	0	0	0	

Going:	Sf: 0-0 GS: 0-0 Gd: 0-0 GF: - Fm: 0-1
Distance:	2m/2m3: 0-1 2m4-2m7: 0-0 3m+: 0-0
Track:	LH: 0-1 RH: 0-0 Tight: 0-1 Gall: 0-0
Aids:	Bl: 0-0 Vi: 0-0 Tstrap: 0-0
Best Rating:	46 8/03 Sedg 2m1f gd-fm Hdl

Johnjoe's Express (IRE)

105   115

7-y-o gr g Moscow Society (USA)-Abigail's Dream (Kalaglow)
Michael Hourigan T J Doran

Placings:005/2542-2125035040   (4828a)
2003/04: 16²GS, 16¹S, 18²Y, 16⁵G, 16⁹GF, 16³G, 22⁵S, 20⁹HY, 18⁴YS, 16⁰Y,

	Starts	1st	2nd	3rd	Win & Pl
NH Flat	1	0	1	0	1039
Hurdles	9	1	1	1	16715
Career Total	17	1	4	1	20183
98 7/03 Gway 2m		(81-123)HHdl		SFT	£8737

Total win prize-money £8737

Going:	Sf: 1-3 GS: 0-0 Gd: 0-2 GF: - Fm: 0-2
Distance:	2m/2m3: 1-8 2m4-2m7: 0-2 3m+: 0-0
Track:	LH: 0-2 RH: 1-4 Tight: 0-0 Gall: 0-0
Aids:	Bl: 0-0 Vi: 0-0 Tstrap: 0-0 Ckp: 0-0
Best Rating:	112 11/03 Chel 2m110y good Hdl

Moderate Irish hurdler; best at two miles; acts on good/good to soft; often well-backed.

Johnlegood

(91h)   (112h)112

8-y-o ch g Karinga Bay-Dancing Years (USA) (Fred Astaire (USA))

G L Moore Bryan Pennick

Placings:004/4F43P13/24FR52520-P   (2311)
2003/04: 20⁰GS,

	Starts	1st	2nd	3rd	Win & Pl
Chases	1	0	0	0	
Career Total	20	1	3	2	9044
112 3/02 Font	2m2f110yD Hdl			SFT	£3528

Total win prize-money £3528

Going:	Sf: 0-0 GS: 0-1 Gd: 0-0 GF: - Fm: 0-0
Distance:	2m/2m3: 0-0 2m4-2m7: 0-1 3m+: 0-0
Track:	LH: 0-0 RH: 0-1 Tight: 0-0 Gall: 0-1
Aids:	Bl: 0-0 Vi: 0-0 Tstrap: 0-0 Ckp: 0-0
Best Rating:	113 5/02 Folk 2m1f110y good Hdl

Modest chaser; effective at around two and a half miles; acts on decent and soft ground.

Johnny Oscar

101   93

7-y-o b g Belmez (USA)-Short Rations (Lorenzaccio)
Miss Venetia Williams F F Racing Services Partnership VI

Placings:32P   (0897)
2003/04: 17³GF, 17²GS, 17⁰GF,

	Starts	1st	2nd	3rd	Win & Pl
Hurdles	3	0	1	1	1804
Career Total	3	0	1	1	1804

Going:	Sf: 0-0 GS: 0-1 Gd: 0-0 GF: - Fm: 0-2
Distance:	2m/2m3: 0-3 2m4-2m7: 0-0 3m+: 0-0
Track:	LH: 0-2 RH: 0-1 Tight: 0-2 Gall: 0-0
Aids:	Bl: 0-0 Vi: 0-0 Tstrap: 0-0 Ckp: 0-0
Best Rating:	93 5/03 Ctml 2m1f110y gd-sft Hdl

Novice hurdler; extended 14 furlong winner on the Flat; placed on first two starts over two miles one. (DEAD)

Johnny Reb

93   75

6-y-o b g Danehill (USA)-Dixie Eyes Blazing (USA) (Gone West (USA))
Mrs S J Smith Richard Longley

Placings:0O36   (4958)
2003/04: 16⁶GF, 17⁰S, 17³G, 17⁶G,

	Starts	1st	2nd	3rd	Win & Pl
Hurdles	4	0	0	1	575
Career Total	4	0	0	1	575

Going:	Sf: 0-1 GS: 0-0 Gd: 0-2 GF: - Fm: 0-1
Distance:	2m/2m3: 0-4 2m4-2m7: 0-0 3m+: 0-0
Track:	LH: 0-2 RH: 0-2 Tight: 0-3 Gall: 0-0
Aids:	Bl: 0-0 Vi: 0-0 Tstrap: 0-3 Ckp: 0-0
Best Rating:	75 6/03 MRas 2m1f110y good Hdl

Clear leader when running out on second start; third in weak novices hurdle at Market Rasen in June.

Johns Legacy

9-y-o gr g Almoojid-Flying Joker (Kalaglow)
Miss S E Robinson Brian Robinson

Placings:F   (4823)
2003/04: 23⁰GF,

	Starts	1st	2nd	3rd	Win & Pl
Chases	1	0	0	0	
Career Total	1	0	0	0	

Going:	Sf: 0-0 GS: 0-0 Gd: 0-0 GF: - Fm: 0-1
Distance:	2m/2m3: 0-0 2m4-2m7: 0-0 3m+: 0-1
Track:	LH: 0-0 RH: 0-1 Tight: 0-0 Gall: 0-0
Aids:	Bl: 0-0 Vi: 0-0 Tstrap: 0-0 Ckp: 0-0
Best Rating:	97 4/04 Extr 2m7f110y gd-fm Ch

Johnston's Art (IRE)

107   105+

11-y-o b g Law Society (USA)-Mirror Of Flowers (Artaius (USA))
Mrs J C McGregor The Bold And Old

Placings:350/13312/P3FPP5/100300/P45052061P40/2131 20P44P0P00-0S12245006   (2788)
2003/04: 24⁵G, 20⁵GF, 24¹G, 24²GF, 27²GF, 20⁴GF, 24⁵G, 22⁰F, 27⁰G, 20⁶GF,

	Starts	1st	2nd	3rd	Win & Pl
Hurdles	10	1	2	0	7777
Career Total	56	7	6	8	33836
101 7/03	Prth	3m110y	E(0-110)HHdl	GD	£5345
105 6/02	Prth	3m110y	E(0-110)HHdl	G-S	£2933
103 5/02	Prth	3m110y	D(0-120)HHdl	G-F	£4124
103 1/02	Muss	3m	E(0-110)HHdl	SFT	£3388
116 10/00	Font	2m6f110yD(0-120)HHdl		GD	£3168
115 3/99	Plum	2m4f	E Hdl	SFT	£2285
114 1/99	Ling	2m110y	H NHF	HVY	£1327

Total win prize-money £22572

Going:	Sf: 0-0 GS: 0-0 Gd: 1-4 GF: - Fm: 0-6
Distance:	2m/2m3: 0-0 2m4-2m7: 0-4 3m+: 1-6
Track:	LH: 0-4 RH: 1-6 Tight: 0-4 Gall: 0-0
Aids:	Bl: 1-10 Vi: 0-0 Tstrap: 0-0 Ckp: 0-0
Best Rating:	120 4/99 Plum 2m4f gd-sft Hdl

Modest hurdler; stays three miles plus; acts on any ground; not the most resolute.

Johnston's Ville (IRE)

11-y-o b g Commanche Run-Slavesville (Charlottesvilles Flyer)
Mrs M B Stephens Mrs M B Stephens

Placings:255/0502/2354/34/6   (0240)
2003/04: 25⁶G,

	Starts	1st	2nd	3rd	Win & Pl
Chases	1	0	0	0	0
Career Total	14	0	3	2	3199

Going:	Sf: 0-0 GS: 0-0 Gd: 0-1 GF: - Fm: 0-0
Distance:	2m/2m3: 0-0 2m4-2m7: 0-0 3m+: 0-1
Track:	LH: 0-0 RH: 0-1 Tight: 0-0 Gall: 0-0
Aids:	Bl: 0-0 Vi: 0-0 Tstrap: 0-0 Ckp: 0-0
Best Rating:	105 12/97 Thur 2m sft-hvy NHF

Joint Account

119

14-y-o ch g Sayyaf-Dancing Clara (Billion (USA))
R Tate K Needham

Placings:00/U/14221/132PF1/24/15U3FP11/125235P-F6   (0508)

2003/04: 24⁶G, 28⁶GS,

	Starts	1st	2nd	3rd	Win & Pl
Chases	2	0	0	0	0
Career Total	33	8	6	3	35897
135 5/02	Weth	3m1f	B(0-145)HCh	GD	£9236
124 4/02	Weth	2m7f110yD(0-120)HCh		G-F	£5492

116	3/02	MRas	2m4f	E(0-110)HCh	G-S	£3388
115	5/01	Weth	3m1f	H Ch	GD	£2030
102	4/00	Sedg	3m3f	H Ch	GD	£1578
109	5/99	MRas	3m1f	H Ch	G-F	£1062
116	4/99	Hntg	3m	H Ch	GD	£1623
105	5/98	Uttx	2m5f	H Ch	G-F	£1127
				Total win prize-money		£25541

Going:	Sf: 0-0 GS: 0-1 Gd: 0-1 GF: - Fm: 0-0
Distance:	2m/2m3: 0-0 2m4-2m7: 0-0 3m+: 0-2
Track:	LH: 0-2 RH: 0-0 Tight: 0-1 Gall: 0-0
Aids:	Bl: 0-0 Vi: 0-0 Tstrap: 0-0 Ckp: 0-0
Best Rating:	135 6/02 Worc 2m7f110y soft Ch

Modest hunter chaser these days; suited by three miles and a sound surface.

Joint Authority (IRE)

106(100h)   (95h)119+

9-y-o b g Religiously (USA)-Highway's Last (Royal Highway)
L Lungo Mrs Barbara Lungo

Placings:P04423-6212212U   (4295)
2003/04: 20⁶G, 18²G, 21¹¹GF, 16²GF, 16²G, 20¹GF, 20²GF, 20⁴GF,

	Starts	1st	2nd	3rd	Win & Pl
Hurdles	1	0	1	0	1084
Chases	7	2	3	0	10908
Career Total	14	2	5	1	14417

115	1/04	Muss	2m4f	E(0-110)HCh	G-F	£4810
109	11/03	Sedg	2m5f	E Ch	G-F	£2938
				Total win prize-money		£7748

Going:	Sf: 0-0 GS: 0-0 Gd: 0-3 GF: - Fm: 2-5
Distance:	2m/2m3: 0-3 **2m4-2m7: 2-5** 3m+: 0-0
Track:	LH: 1-6 RH: 1-2 **Tight: 2-6** Gall: 0-0
Aids:	Bl: 0-0 Vi: 0-0 Tstrap: 0-0 Ckp: 0-0
Best Rating:	121 1/04 Muss 2m4f gd-fm Ch

Moderate chaser; stays two miles-five; acts on any ground.

Joizel (FR)

93   74

7-y-o b g Fill My Hopes (FR)-Anne De Boizel (FR) (Dhausli (FR))
R H Alner Mrs Lynsey Le Cornu

Placings:P/00U0   (4733)
2003/04: 20⁰GS, 24⁰G, 24ᵁG, 22⁰G,

	Starts	1st	2nd	3rd	Win & Pl
Hurdles	4	0	0	0	
Career Total	5	0	0	0	

Going:	Sf: 0-0 GS: 0-1 Gd: 0-3 GF: - Fm: 0-0
Distance:	2m/2m3: 0-0 2m4-2m7: 0-2 3m+: 0-2
Track:	LH: 0-1 RH: 0-3 Tight: 0-1 Gall: 0-0
Aids:	Bl: 0-0 Vi: 0-0 Tstrap: 0-0 Ckp: 0-0
Best Rating:	77 2/04 Kemp 3m110y good Hdl

Jojo (FR)

87   (0c)51

7-y-o ch g Dadarissime (FR)-Belle Mome (FR) (Grand Tresor (FR))
Miss Lucinda V Russell (N W Alexander 15/5) Jamie Alexander

Placings:00024/503FP305-5UP3P   (0783)
2003/04: 16⁵G, 20ᵁG, 20⁹G, 16³GF, 20⁵G,

	Starts	1st	2nd	3rd	Win & Pl
Hurdles	4	0	0	1	486

Chases	1	0	0	0		0
Career Total	18	0	1	3		3820

Going:	Sf: 0-0 GS: 0-0 Gd: 0-4 GF: - Fm: 0-1
Distance:	2m/2m3: 0-2 2m4-2m7: 0-3 3m+: 0-0
Track:	LH: 0-2 RH: 0-2 Tight: 0-1 Gall: 0-0
Aids:	Bl: 0-0 Vi: 0-0 Tstrap: 0-0 Ckp: 0-0
Best Rating:	76 4/03 Prth 2m4f110y good Hdl

Ex-French; a bitter disapointment here.

Jokers Charm

94   100

13-y-o b g Idiots Delight-By The Lake (Tyrant (USA))
R C Guest N B Mason

Placings:50P/05303/53100042253301440/4136651130442 206/35245/P6P1-P14PP   (2084)
2003/04: 16⁶PGF, 21¹¹GF, 16⁴G, 24⁵PG, 16⁶GF,

	Starts	1st	2nd	3rd	Win & Pl
Chases	5	1	0	0	4673
Career Total	55	7	5	8	37255

97	10/03	Uttx	2m5f	E(0-105)HCh	G-F	£4389
100	10/02	Sedg	2m110y	D(0-115)HCh	G-F	£4979
109	12/00	Muss	2m	F(0-95)HCh	GD	£2821
109	12/00	Fknm	2m110y	F(0-100)HCh	G-S	£4072
109	9/00	Sedg	2m5f	D(0-120)HCh	GD	£3851
103	11/99	Hexm	2m110y	F(0-95)HCh	GD	£2748
94	7/99	Sedg	2m110y	E Ch	G-F	£3285
				Total win prize-money		£26146

Going:	Sf: 0-0 GS: 0-0 Gd: 0-2 GF: - Fm: 1-3
Distance:	2m/2m3: 0-3 2m4-2m7: 1-1 3m+: 0-1
Track:	LH: 1-5 RH: 0-0 Tight: 0-1 Gall: 0-0
Aids:	Bl: 1-5 Vi: 0-0 Tstrap: 1-5 Ckp: 0-0
Best Rating:	109 2/01 Sedg 2m110y soft Ch

Moderate chaser; fortunate winner at Sedgefield in October 2002; took a weak event at Uttoxeter in October 2003; stays two miles five; handles most types of ground; wears blinkers and a tongue tie.

Jokesmith (IRE)

73

6-y-o b g Mujadil (USA)-Grinning (IRE) (Bellypha)
K A Ryan Uncle Jacks Pub

Placings:P-P   (1476)
2003/04: 17⁰G,

	Starts	1st	2nd	3rd	Win & Pl
Hurdles	1	0	0	0	
Career Total	2	0	0	0	

Going:	Sf: 0-0 GS: 0-0 Gd: 0-1 GF: - Fm: 0-0
Distance:	2m/2m3: 0-1 2m4-2m7: 0-0 3m+: 0-0
Track:	LH: 0-1 RH: 0-0 Tight: 0-0 Gall: 0-0
Aids:	Bl: 0-0 Vi: 0-0 Tstrap: 0-0 Ckp: 0-0
Best Rating:	76 1/03 Ayr 2m heavy Hdl

A useful handicapper on the Flat, he showed some promise in testing ground on hurdling debut.

Jolewis

79f   58f

6-y-o ch m Sir Harry Lewis (USA)-Askwood (IRE) (Gunner B)
E W Tuer Tagwood Syndicate

Placings:0   (1436)
2003/04: 16⁰G,

	Starts	1st	2nd	3rd	Win & Pl
NH Flat	1	0	0	0	

	Starts	1st	2nd	3rd	Win & Pl
Career Total	1	0	0	0	

Going:	Sf: 0-0 GS: 0-0 Gd: 0-1 GF: - Fm: 0-0
Distance:	2m/2m3: 0-1 2m4-2m7: 0-0 3m+: 0-0
Track:	LH: 0-0 RH: 0-1 Tight: 0-0 Gall: 0-0
Aids:	Bl: 0-0 Vi: 0-0 Tstrap: 0-0 Ckp: 0-0
Best Rating:	62 9/03 Prth 2m110y good NHF

Joli Posh

68   28

7-y-o ch m Rakaposhi King-Nunswalk (The Parson)
R J Hodges Joli Racing

Placings:00-0   (0039)
2003/04: 17⁰G,

	Starts	1st	2nd	3rd	Win & Pl
Hurdles	1	0	0	0	
Career Total	3	0	0	0	

Going:	Sf: 0-0 GS: 0-0 Gd: 0-1 GF: - Fm: 0-0
Distance:	2m/2m3: 0-2 2m4-2m7: 0-0 3m+: 0-0
Track:	LH: 0-0 RH: 0-1 Tight: 0-0 Gall: 0-0
Aids:	Bl: 0-0 Vi: 0-0 Tstrap: 0-0 Ckp: 0-0
Best Rating:	56 1/03 Tntn 2m1f soft NHF

Joli Saddlers

(90h)   (95h)

8-y-o b m Saddlers' Hall (IRE)-Vitality (Young Generation)
P F Nicholls Joli Racing

Placings:2/1/P66F   (4916)
2003/04: 24⁵GS, 21⁶G, 21⁶G, 23⁷GS,

	Starts	1st	2nd	3rd	Win & Pl
Hurdles	3	0	0	0	0
Chases	1	0	0	0	0
Career Total	6	1	1	0	3806

85	6/01	NAbb	2m6f	E Hdl	GD	£3052
				Total win prize-money		£3052

Going:	Sf: 0-0 GS: 0-2 Gd: 0-2 GF: - Fm: 0-0
Distance:	2m/2m3: 0-0 2m4-2m7: 0-2 3m+: 0-2
Track:	LH: 0-3 RH: 0-1 Tight: 0-3 Gall: 0-0
Aids:	Bl: 0-0 Vi: 0-0 Tstrap: 0-3 Ckp: 0-0
Best Rating:	95 4/01 Font 2m6f110y good Hdl

Jolika (FR)

102   101

7-y-o b m Grand Tresor (FR)-Unika Ii (FR) (Rolling Bowl (FR))
L Lungo Dr Kenneth S Fraser

Placings:4/13/2-1414P   (4879)
2003/04: 16¹G, 16⁴S, 20¹GS, 16⁴G, 20⁵GS,

	Starts	1st	2nd	3rd	Win & Pl
Hurdles	5	2	0	0	7909
Career Total	9	3	1	1	10981

101	2/04	Ayr	2m4f	F(0-95)HHdl	G-S	£3542
79	5/03	Prth	2m110y	E Hdl	GD	£4095
100	5/01	Prth	2m110y	H NHF	SFT	£2289
				Total win prize-money		£9926

Going:	Sf: 0-1 GS: 1-2 Gd: 1-2 GF: - Fm: 0-0
Distance:	2m/2m3: 1-3 2m4-2m7: 1-2 3m+: 0-0
Track:	LH: 1-3 RH: 1-2 Tight: 0-0 Gall: 0-0
Aids:	Bl: 0-0 Vi: 0-0 Tstrap: 0-0 Ckp: 0-0
Best Rating:	102 1/03 Sedg 2m1f heavy NHF

Moderate hurdler; landed a farcical bumper at Perth in May 2002 and won modest event on hurdles debut at same

course a year later; confirmed reappearance promise when winning ordinary handicap at Ayr in February 2004; stays two and a half miles and acts on soft ground.

Jolirose

90   **51**

9-y-o b m Joligeneration-Rose Red City (Relkino)
Miss V A Stephens   D G Stephens

Placings:0/P0P4   (1470)
2003/04: 22PGF, 22QGF, 22PGF, 19QF,

	Starts	1st	2nd	3rd	Win & Pl
Hurdles	4	0	0	0	0
Career Total	5	0	0	0	0

Going: Sf: 0-0 GS: 0-0 Gd: 0-0 GF: - Fm: 0-4
Distance: 2m/2m3: 0-1 2m4-2m7: 0-3 3m+: 0-0
Track: LH: 0-3 RH: 0-1 Tight: 0-3 Gall: 0-0
Aids: Bl: 0-0 Vi: 0-0 Tstrap: 0-0 Ckp: 0-0
Best Rating: 59   7/01   Worc   2m   good   NHF

Jolitan

9-y-o b g Joligeneration-Tanber Lass (New Member)
P Greenwood   Mrs P A Wilkins

Placings:P   (0249)
2003/04: 19PGF,

	Starts	1st	2nd	3rd	Win & Pl
Chases	1	0	0	0	0
Career Total	1	0	0	0	0

Going: Sf: 0-0 GS: 0-0 Gd: 0-0 GF: - Fm: 0-1
Distance: 2m/2m3: 0-0 2m4-2m7: 0-1 3m+: 0-0
Track: LH: 0-0 RH: 0-1 Tight: 0-0 Gall: 0-0
Aids: Bl: 0-1 Vi: 0-0 Tstrap: 0-0 Ckp: 0-0

Jolly Giant (IRE)

101   **109**

8-y-o b g Jolly Jake (NZ)-Reve Clair (Deep Run)
P F Nicholls   Derek Millard

Placings:4P/F31PF1U-24P4   (4525)
2003/04: 24²GS, 30⁴GS, 26²HY, 24⁴GS,

	Starts	1st	2nd	3rd	Win & Pl
Chases	4	0	1	0	1880
Career Total	13	2	1	1	12961
109	1/03	Extr	3m1f110yE(0-105)HCh		G-S	£5785
101	11/02	Chep	3m	E(0-110)HCh	SFT	£4134
			Total win prize-money £9919

Going: Sf: 0-1 GS: 0-3 Gd: 0-0 GF: - Fm: 0-0
Distance: 2m/2m3: 0-0 2m4-2m7: 0-0 3m+: 0-4
Track: LH: 0-2 RH: 0-1 Tight: 0-2 Gall: 0-0
Aids: Bl: 0-4 Vi: 0-0 Tstrap: 0-0 Ckp: 0-0
Best Rating: 109   3/04   Chep   3m   gd-sft   Ch

Modest chaser; stays an extended three miles one; acts on soft ground; has worn blinkers.

Jolly Jake

10-y-o br g Vital Season-Sols Joker (Comedy Star (USA))
Miss E J Baker   Miss E J Baker

Placings:6   (4302)
2003/04: 20⁶G,

	Starts	1st	2nd	3rd	Win & Pl
Chases	1	0	0	0	0
Career Total	1	0	0	0	0

Going: Sf: 0-0 GS: 0-0 Gd: 0-0 GF: - Fm: - 0-0
Distance: 2m/2m3: 0-0 2m4-2m7: 0-0
Track: LH: 0-0 RH: 0-1 Tight: 0-0 Gall: 0-0
Aids: Bl: 0-0 Vi: 0-0 Tstrap: 0-0 Ckp: 0-0
Best Rating: 62   3/04   Leic   2m4f110y   good   Ch

Jolly Joe (IRE)

7-y-o b g Jolly Jake (NZ)-The Bread Robber (Mandalus)
S T Lewis   Simon T Lewis

Placings:6/P5P   (4837)
2003/04: 24⁵PS, 19⁵G, 25⁵PGF,

	Starts	1st	2nd	3rd	Win & Pl
Hurdles	1	0	0	0	0
Chases	2	0	0	0	0
Career Total	4	0	0	0	0

Going: Sf: 0-1 GS: 0-0 Gd: 0-1 GF: - Fm: 0-1
Distance: 2m/2m3: 0-1 2m4-2m7: 0-0 3m+: 0-2
Track: LH: 0-1 RH: 0-2 Tight: 0-2 Gall: 0-1
Aids: Bl: 0-0 Vi: 0-0 Tstrap: 0-0 Ckp: 0-1
Best Rating: 69   4/02   Towc   2m   good   NHF

Jolly John (IRE)

95   **80**

13-y-o b g Jolly Jake (NZ)-Golden Seekers (Manado)
C J Mann   Mrs C J Mann

Placings:00/440U/B50303/603042P6/0P1UF0/065365/443 3235P/34234-64P   (4913)
2003/04: 22⁶GS, 21⁴G, 24⁵PS,

	Starts	1st	2nd	3rd	Win & Pl
Hurdles	3	0	0	0	0
Career Total	48	1	3	9	10187
93	11/99	Thur	2m2f	Ch	Y-S	£3850
			Total win prize-money £3850

Going: Sf: 0-1 GS: 0-1 Gd: 0-1 GF: - Fm: 0-0
Distance: 2m/2m3: 0-0 2m4-2m7: 0-0 3m+: 0-1
Track: LH: 0-0 RH: 0-3 Tight: 0-1 Gall: 0-1
Aids: Bl: 0-0 Vi: 0-0 Tstrap: 0-0 Ckp: 0-0
Best Rating: 105   10/97   Gowr   2m2f   gd-fm   Ch

Jolly Red (FR)

7-y-o ch g Cyborg (FR)-Orne Ii (FR) (Beau Fixe)
M C Pipe   Terry Neill

Placings:0/P   (0563)
2003/04: 24PGF,

	Starts	1st	2nd	3rd	Win & Pl
Hurdles	1	0	0	0	0
Career Total	2	0	0	0	0

Going: Sf: 0-0 GS: 0-0 Gd: 0-0 GF: - Fm: 0-1
Distance: 2m/2m3: 0-0 2m4-2m7: 0-0 3m+: 0-1
Track: LH: 0-1 RH: 0-0 Tight: 0-0 Gall: 0-0
Aids: Bl: 0-0 Vi: 0-0 Tstrap: 0-0 Ckp: 0-0
Best Rating: 83   11/01   Tntn   2m1f   good   NHF

Jolly Side (IRE)

83(99h)   (96 h)**101**

11-y-o b g Jolly Jake (NZ)-South Quay Lady (Quayside)
Dr P Pritchard   Mrs T Pritchard

Placings:410/4664522004P0/6212P22P236F14F/31/63P43 0-0U   (1093)
2003/04: 16⁹GF, 17⁰G,

	Starts	1st	2nd	3rd	Win & Pl
Chases	2	0	0	0	0
Career Total	40	4	7	4	27128
121	5/00	Cork	2m	Ch	GD	£5032
121	3/00	Wxfd	2m	Ch	YLD	£5520
90	6/99	Cork	2m1f	Ch	G-F	£4296
113	1/98	Gowr	2m	NHF	YLD	£2382
			Total win prize-money £17232

Going: Sf: 0-0 GS: 0-0 Gd: 0-1 GF: - Fm: 0-1
Distance: 2m/2m3: 0-2 2m4-2m7: 0-0 3m+: 0-0
Track: LH: 0-2 RH: 0-0 Tight: 0-2 Gall: 0-0
Aids: Bl: 0-0 Vi: 0-0 Tstrap: 0-0 Ckp: 0-0
Best Rating: 123   4/00   Gowr   2m2f   gd-yld   Ch

Jollyolly

111   **140**

5-y-o gr g Environment Friend-Off The Air (IRE) (Taufan (USA))
P Bowen   Eamonn O'Malley

Placings:002-121101112P   (3958)
2003/04: 18¹G, 18²GF, 19¹GF, 19¹G, 20⁰Y, 20¹GF, 21¹GF, 21¹G, 22²G, 20PG,

	Starts	1st	2nd	3rd	Win & Pl
Hurdles	10	6	2	0	44142
Career Total	13	6	3	0	45662
140	11/03	Chel	2m5f	B Hdl	GD	£12818
134	10/03	Chel	2m5f	(0-145)HHdl	G-F	£9352
127	10/03	Uttx	2m4f110yC(0-130)HHdl	G-F	£6373
109	7/03	MRas	3m1f110yD Hdl	GD	£5265
102	6/03	Hrfd	2m3f110yE Hdl	G-F	£3472
99	5/03	Font	2m2f110yE Hdl	GD	£3412
			Total win prize-money £40694

Going: Sf: 0-0 GS: 0-0 Gd: 3-5 GF: - Fm: 3-4
Distance: 2m/2m3: 1-2 **2m4-2m7: 5-8** 3m+: 0-0
Track: **LH: 4-5** RH: 2-4 Tight: 2-4 Gall: 2-2
Aids: Bl: 0-0 Vi: 0-0 Tstrap: 0-0 **Ckp: 4-7**
Best Rating: 140   11/03   Chel   2m5f   good   Hdl

Useful novice hurdler; won six races in 2003; stays at least two and a half miles well and best on good or faster ground; wears cheekpieces; a progressive sort.

Jollyshau (IRE)

92   **85**

6-y-o b g Jolly Jake (NZ)-Escheat (Torus)
Miss A M Newton-Smith   Michael Coates

Placings:040-05P055   (4790)
2003/04: 21⁰G, 22⁵G, 19PS, 16⁰G, 16⁵G, 21⁵G,

	Starts	1st	2nd	3rd	Win & Pl
Hurdles	6	0	0	0	0
Career Total	9	0	0	0	267

Going: Sf: 0-1 GS: 0-1 Gd: 0-4 GF: - Fm: 0-0
Distance: 2m/2m3: 0-3 2m4-2m7: 0-3 3m+: 0-0
Track: LH: 0-3 RH: 0-3 Tight: 0-2 Gall: 0-1
Aids: Bl: 0-0 Vi: 0-0 Tstrap: 0-0 Ckp: 0-0
Best Rating: 85   4/04   Plum   2m5f   good   Hdl

Plating-class novice hurdler; stays two miles five; acts on good ground.

Joly Bey (FR)

115(114h)   (138+h)**146**

7-y-o ch g Beyssac (FR)-Rivolie (FR) (Mistigri)

N J Gifford (P F Nicholls 29/4) David Dunsdon

Placings:0532/152123111232-515F   **(4640)**
2003/04: 20²GY, 19⁵S, 24¹G, 20⁵G, 21⁶G,

	Starts	1st	2nd	3rd	Win & Pl
Hurdles	1	1	0	0	6403
Chases	4	0	1	0	9268
Career Total	20	6	5	3	84132
138	2/04	Newb	3m10y	C(0-130)HHdl	GD	£6403
128	2/03	Chep	3m	E Hdl	G-S	£3552
150	2/03	Sand	2m4f110yD Ch		SFT	£7525
140	1/03	Fknm	3m110y D Ch		SFT	£5782
135	11/02	NAbb	2m5f110yC Ch		HVY	£7568
	5/02	Autl	2m4f110y Ch		VS	£12368

Total win prize-money £43199

Going: Sf: 0-1 GS: 0-0 Gd: 1-3 GF: - Fm: 0-0
Distance: 2m/2m3: 0-1 2m4-2m7: 0-3 3m+: 1-1
Track: LH: 1-3 RH: 0-1 Tight: 0-1 Gall: 1-2
Aids: Bl: 0-0 Vi: 0-0 Tstrap: 0-0 Ckp: 0-0
Best Rating: 150 2/03 Sand 2m4f110y soft Ch

Smart chaser/hurdler; previously trained by Paul Nicholls; suited by trips of up to three miles; acts on soft ground; handles a sharp track.

Jonaem (IRE)

97(102c)   (78c)**79**

14-y-o b g Mazaad-Priors Mistress (Sallust)

Mrs Dianne Sayer Mrs Evelyn Slack

Placings:00P0/25000236/55412600063/F502/P11/F006/3/
P00/3300421P33041P5P104-25606   **(0980)**
2003/04: 27²S, 27⁵S, 24⁶G, 22⁰GF, 27⁶GF,

	Starts	1st	2nd	3rd	Win & Pl
Hurdles	4	0	0	0	0
Chases	1	0	1	0	1362
Career Total	62	6	6	7	25900
79	3/03	Sedg	3m3f110yE(0-110)HHdl	GD	£3479
79	11/02	Sedg	3m3f110yG(0-90)HHdl	SFT	£1890
73	8/02	Sedg	2m5f110yG(0-95)HHdl	GD	£1960
98	4/99	Sedg	3m3f	F(0-110)HCh	G-F	£3852
93	4/99	Sedg	3m3f	D Ch	G-S	£3606
84	10/96	Carl	2m4f110yE(0-100)HHdl	FRM	£2332

Total win prize-money £17120

Going: Sf: 0-2 GS: 0-0 Gd: 0-1 GF: - Fm: 0-2
Distance: 2m/2m3: 0-4 2m4-2m7: 0-1 3m+: 0-4
Track: LH: 0-4 RH: 0-1 Tight: 0-4 Gall: 0-0
Aids: Bl: 0-0 Vi: 0-0 Tstrap: 0-0 Ckp: 0-0
Best Rating: 98 4/99 Sedg 3m3f gd-fm Ch

Plating-class hurdler/chaser, stays three miles three, acts on any ground and has gained most of his wins at Sedgefield.

Jonalton (IRE)

105   **104**

5-y-o b g Perugino (USA)-Vago Pequeno (IRE) (Posen (USA))

C R Dore T Crowson

Placings:120313P0F0200P   **(4777)**
2003/04: 21¹GF, 22²G, 20⁰GF, 19³GF, 20¹GF, 24³GF, 21⁶GF, 21⁰G, 22⁶G, 20⁰S, 24²GS, 26⁶G, 22⁰G, 23⁶G,

	Starts	1st	2nd	3rd	Win & Pl
Hurdles	14	2	2	2	10223
Career Total	14	2	2	2	10223
104	9/03	Hntg	2m4f110yD(0-120)HHdl	G-F	£3762
104	7/03	Sthl	2m5f110yG Hdl	G-F	£2604

Total win prize-money £6366

Jonanaud

108   **108**

5-y-o b g Ballet Royal (USA)-Margaret Modes (Thatching)

H J Manners H J Manners

Placings:002-0353P21221   **(4524)**
2003/04: 16⁵GF, 16³GF, 20⁵G, 16³S, 24⁴PHY, 24²S, 20¹HY, 22²G, 21²GS, 16¹GS,

	Starts	1st	2nd	3rd	Win & Pl
NH Flat	1	0	0	0	0
Hurdles	9	2	3	2	12403
Career Total	13	2	4	2	12985
108	3/04	Chep	2m110y E Hdl	G-S	£3562
108	2/04	Chep	2m4f	D(0-125)HHdl	HVY	£4962

Total win prize-money £8525

Going: Sf: 1-4 GS: 1-2 Gd: 0-2 GF: - Fm: 0-2
Distance: 2m/2m3: 1-4 2m4-2m7: 1-4 3m+: 0-2
Track: LH: 2-6 RH: 0-4 Tight: 0-2 Gall: 0-0
Aids: Bl: 0-0 Vi: 0-0 Tstrap: 0-0 Ckp: 0-0
Best Rating: 108 3/04 Chep 2m110y gd-sft Hdl

Improving novice hurdler; caused 40/1 shock when winning Class D 2m4f handicap hurdle in heavy ground at Chepstow February 2004; overcame a drop back to 2m when scoring again at the same venue in March; stays three miles; acts on most ground, but best with cut.

Jongleur Collonges (FR)

94(101h)   (104 h)**106**

7-y-o gr g Royal Charter (FR)-Soubrette Collonge (FR) (Saumon (FR))

R H Alner Andrew Wiles

Placings:345/3465-2   **(2076)**
2003/04: 24²G,

	Starts	1st	2nd	3rd	Win & Pl
Chases	1	0	1	0	1056
Career Total	8	0	1	2	2951

Going: Sf: 0-0 GS: 0-0 Gd: 0-1 GF: - Fm: 0-0
Distance: 2m/2m3: 0-0 2m4-2m7: 0-0 3m+: 0-1
Track: LH: 0-1 RH: 0-0 Tight: 0-1 Gall: 0-0
Aids: Bl: 0-0 Vi: 0-0 Tstrap: 0-0 Ckp: 0-0
Best Rating: 106 11/03 Ling 3m good Ch

Modest hurdler/chaser; stays three miles; looks suited by soft ground.

Jonny's Kick

102f   **72f**

4-y-o b g Revoque (IRE)-Prudence (Grundy)

T D Easterby Seven Up Partnership

Placings:03   **(3669)**
2003/04: 16⁶S, 16³HY,

	Starts	1st	2nd	3rd	Win & Pl
NH Flat	2	0	0	1	288

Jordan's Ridge (IRE)

101(113c)   (136c)**104**

8-y-o b/br g Indian Ridge-Sadie Jordan (USA) (Hail The Pirates (USA))

P Monteith Melville/Stewart

Placings:0/05002442200/33525341/41242-114111F24630   **(4478)**
2003/04: 16¹G, 20¹G, 20⁴GF, 20¹GF, 22¹G, 25¹G, 25⁵S, 21²GS, 20⁴HY, 20⁶GS, 22³GF, 20⁰HY,

	Starts	1st	2nd	3rd	Win & Pl
Hurdles	3	0	1	1	1867
Chases	9	5	0	0	26445
Career Total	37	7	7	4	40573
136	11/03	Kels	3m1f	C(0-130)HCh	GD	10056
133	11/03	Kels	2m6f110yD(0-120)HCh	GD	£4875
123	10/03	Hexm	2m4f110yE(0-110)HCh	G-F	2576
120	5/03	Hexm	2m4f110yE(0-105)HCh	GD	£3939
109	5/03	Hexm	2m110y F(0-95)HCh	GD	£3433
99	6/02	Hexm	2m110y E Ch	GD	£3055
102	4/02	Newc	2m4f	G(0-95)HHdl	FRM	£1792

Total win prize-money £29727

Going: Sf: 0-3 GS: 0-2 Gd: 4-4 GF: - Fm: 1-3
Distance: 2m/2m3: 1-1 2m4-2m7: 3-9 3m+: 1-2
Track: LH: 5-10 RH: 0-2 Tight: 2-4 Gall: 0-0
Aids: Bl: 0-0 Vi: 0-0 Tstrap: 0-0 Ckp: 0-0
Best Rating: 136 11/03 Kels 3m1f good Ch

Useful chaser; improved dramatically for switch to fences; has a good strike rate; appears to like Hexham; stays three miles plus and very effective on good ground.

Jorn Du Soleil (FR)

(95h)**101**

7-y-o ch g Murmure (FR)-Ina Du Soleil (FR) (Or De Chine)

Mrs J C McGregor Capt Ben Coutts

Placings:200/B43-6   **(1435)**
2003/04: 20⁶G,

	Starts	1st	2nd	3rd	Win & Pl
Chases	1	0	0	0	0
Career Total	7	0	1	1	3085

Going: Sf: 0-0 GS: 0-0 Gd: 0-1 GF: - Fm: 0-0
Distance: 2m/2m3: 0-0 2m4-2m7: 0-1 3m+: 0-0
Track: LH: 0-0 RH: 0-1 Tight: 0-0 Gall: 0-0
Aids: Bl: 0-0 Vi: 0-0 Tstrap: 0-0 Ckp: 0-0
Best Rating: 101 2/03 Weth 2m good Ch

Jorodama King

101   **82**

10-y-o b g Lighter-Princess Hecate (Autre Prince)

R J Price (O Sherwood 14/5) R J Price

Placings:200U/56PF/P20U01/504033330PUP-532   **(1575)**
2003/04: 25⁵GF, 26³GF, 25²F,

	Starts	1st	2nd	3rd	Win & Pl
Chases	3	0	1	1	365

Career Total   2   0   0   1   288

Going: Sf: 0-2 GS: 0-0 Gd: 0-0 GF: - Fm: 0-0
Distance: 2m/2m3: 0-2 2m4-2m7: 0-0 3m+: 0-0
Track: LH: 0-2 RH: 0-1 Tight: 0-0 Gall: 0-0
Aids: Bl: 0-0 Vi: 0-0 Tstrap: 0-0 Ckp: 0-0
Best Rating: 80 2/04 Newc 2m heavy NHF

Moderate hurdler; annihilated the opposition when making successful hurdling debut in 2m5f seller at Southwell; won at Huntingdon in 2m4f handicap on good to firm in September; will stay three miles.

Career Total		29	1	3	5	9247
83	4/02	Plum	3m2f	E Ch	GD	£3640

Total win prize-money £3640

Going:	Sf: 0-0 GS: 0-0 Gd: 0-0 GF: - Fm: 0-3
Distance:	2m/2m3: 0-0 2m4-2m7: 0-0 3m+: 0-3
Track:	LH: 0-1 RH: 0-2 Tight: 0-0 Gall: 0-0
Aids:	Bl: 0-0 Vi: 0-0 Tstrap: 0-0 Ckp: 0-0
Best Rating:	93 11/99 Ludl 2m good NHF

Plating-class chaser; stays well; acts on a sound surface.

Joshua's Bay

106   115+

6-y-o b g Karinga Bay-Bonita Blakeney (Baron Blakeney)
J R Jenkins Mr & Mrs Leon Shack

Placings:2/000U60322414-24131F24100   (4890)
2003/04: 16²G, 16⁴G, 21¹GS, 21³GF, 21¹GF, 21²GF, 23²G, 20⁴GF, 18¹G, 21²G, 19⁹GF,

	Starts	1st	2nd	3rd	Win & Pl
Hurdles	11	3	2	1	15434
Career Total	24	4	5	2	22351
115	1/04	Font	2m2f110yD(0-120)HHdl	GD	£5089
114	10/03	Plum	2m5f	E(0-110)HHdl	G-F	£2915
104	8/03	Sthl	2m5f110yE(0-110)HHdl	G-S	£3388
86	3/03	Sedg	2m1f	E(0-105)HHdl	SFT	£3486

Total win prize-money £14880

Going:	Sf: 0-0 GS: 1-1 Gd: 1-5 GF: - Fm: 1-5
Distance:	2m/2m3: 1-4 2m4-2m7: 2-7 3m+: 0-0
Track:	LH: 3-11 RH: 0-0 Tight: 2-5 Gall: 0-2
Aids:	Bl: 0-0 Vi: 0-0 Tstrap: 0-0 Ckp: 0-0
Best Rating:	115 1/04 Font 2m2f110y good Hdl

Fair hurdler; stays two-miles five furlongs, but effective at shorter; has shown form on decent ground, but also acts on a soft surface; regularly held up.

Joshua's Vision (IRE)

13-y-o b g Vision (USA)-Perle's Fashion (Sallust)
Lady Susan Brooke Lady Susan Brooke

Placings:25/32P02/02/FF/0566P3/P404523F/5/PP-P   (4872)
2003/04: 24ᴾS,

	Starts	1st	2nd	3rd	Win & Pl
Chases	1	0	0	0	
Career Total	29	0	5	3	4249

Going:	Sf: 0-1 GS: 0-0 Gd: 0-0 GF: - Fm: 0-0
Distance:	2m/2m3: 0-0 2m4-2m7: 0-0 3m+: 0-1
Track:	LH: 0-1 RH: 0-0 Tight: 0-1 Gall: 0-0
Aids:	Bl: 0-0 Vi: 0-0 Tstrap: 0-0 Ckp: 0-0
Best Rating:	102 4/96 Worc 2m gd-fm Hdl

Joss Naylor (IRE)

115   (148h)151

9-y-o b g Be My Native (USA)-Sister Ida (Bustino)
Jonjo O'Neill Darren C Mercer

Placings:15/1351125/1110-2P   (4647)
2003/04: 26²GS, 36ᴾG,

	Starts	1st	2nd	3rd	Win & Pl
Chases	2	0	1	0	24200
Career Total	15	7	2	1	84783
151	1/03	Chel	2m5f	B Ch	SFT	£13206
151	12/02	Bang	2m4f110yD Ch		SFT	£5486

124	11/02	Uttx	3m	D Ch	SFT	£6304
148	2/02	Wwck	2m5f	B Hdl	SFT	£10497
125	1/02	Donc	2m4f	D Hdl	SFT	£3727
119	10/01	Carl	2m1f	H NHF	G-S	£1687
117	10/00	Chep	2m110y	H NHF	G-S	£1589

Total win prize-money £42498

Going:	Sf: 0-0 GS: 0-1 Gd: 0-1 GF: - Fm: 0-0
Distance:	2m/2m3: 0-0 2m4-2m7: 0-0 3m+: 0-2
Track:	LH: 0-2 RH: 0-0 Tight: 0-1 Gall: 0-1
Aids:	Bl: 0-0 Vi: 0-0 Tstrap: 0-0 Ckp: 0-0
Best Rating:	151 1/03 Chel 2m5f soft Ch

Smart chaser; talented novice hurdler in 2001/02; easy winner of his first two novice chases in 2002/3 and then just came out best in a thrilling battle with Tarxien at Cheltenham; disappointed in a hot handicap on fourth start; runner-up to Strong Flow in Hennessy on reappearance in November; never going when pulled up in the Grand National; stays 3m 2f; effective in soft ground; can continue to progress.

Journey

11-y-o ch g Tina's Pet-Lady Vynz (Whitstead)
Mrs Sarah L Dent Miss J A Sawney

Placings:6000/00/00/6-0   (0416)
2003/04: 22⁰G,

	Starts	1st	2nd	3rd	Win & Pl
Chases	1	0	0	0	
Career Total	9	0	0	0	0

Going:	Sf: 0-0 GS: 0-0 Gd: 0-0 GF: - Fm: 0-0
Distance:	2m/2m3: 0-0 2m4-2m7: 0-1 3m+: 0-0
Track:	LH: 0-0 RH: 0-1 Tight: 0-1 Gall: 0-0
Aids:	Bl: 0-0 Vi: 0-0 Tstrap: 0-0 Ckp: 0-0
Best Rating:	77 2/98 Naas 2m soft Hdl

Joy Box

69f   58f

4-y-o ch g Unfuwain (USA)-El Jazirah (Kris)
T D Easterby M H Easterby

Placings:0   (4179)
2003/04: 16⁰G,

	Starts	1st	2nd	3rd	Win & Pl
NH Flat	1	0	0	0	
Career Total	1	0	0	0	

Going:	Sf: 0-0 GS: 0-0 Gd: 0-1 GF: - Fm: 0-0
Distance:	2m/2m3: 0-1 2m4-2m7: 0-0 3m+: 0-0
Track:	LH: 0-1 RH: 0-0 Tight: 0-0 Gall: 0-1
Aids:	Bl: 0-0 Vi: 0-0 Tstrap: 0-0 Ckp: 0-0
Best Rating:	58 3/04 Donc 2m110y good NHF

Joyce Bel (FR)

81(86h)   (49h)87

11-y-o br g Rose Laurel-Jeanne De Laval (FR) (Gairloch)
Mrs H Dalton A N Dalton

Placings:0/P000600/00P0224004U/621F020/551F6/0PF24
6U-0   (0819)
2003/04: 22⁰G,

	Starts	1st	2nd	3rd	Win & Pl
Chases	1	0	0	0	
Career Total	39	2	5	0	13181
101	9/01	Dpat	2m2f	(0-95)HCh	G-F	£4729
86	7/00	Wxfd	2m4f	Ch	FRM	£3588

Total win prize-money £8318

Going:	Sf: 0-0 GS: 0-0 Gd: 0-1 GF: - Fm: 0-0
Distance:	2m/2m3: 0-0 2m4-2m7: 0-1 3m+: 0-0
Track:	LH: 0-0 RH: 0-1 Tight: 0-1 Gall: 0-1
Aids:	Bl: 0-5 Vi: 0-0 Tstrap: 0-0 Ckp: 0-1
Best Rating:	101 9/01 Dpat 2m2f gd-fm Ch

Joye Des Iles (FR)

98   76+

7-y-o b g Mont Basile (FR)-Titjana (FR) (Quart De Vin (FR))
B G Powell John Studd

Placings:PP5-3465P   (3872)
2003/04: 22³GS, 26⁴G, 24⁶G, 26⁵HY, 25⁹GS,

	Starts	1st	2nd	3rd	Win & Pl
Chases	5	0	0	1	689
Career Total	8	0	0	1	1849

Going:	Sf: 0-1 GS: 0-2 Gd: 0-2 GF: - Fm: 0-0
Distance:	2m/2m3: 0-0 2m4-2m7: 0-1 3m+: 0-4
Track:	LH: 0-2 RH: 0-2 Tight: 0-2 Gall: 0-0
Aids:	Bl: 0-5 Vi: 0-0 Tstrap: 0-0 Ckp: 0-0
Best Rating:	83 12/03 Wwck 3m2f good Ch

Ex-French; winning pointer; has shown little in chases at Towcester and Warwick; stays three miles; acts on good ground; has worn blinkers.

Joyeux Royal (FR)

108(104c)   (121c)111+

7-y-o b g Cyborg (FR)-Samba Du Cochet (FR) (Tanlas (FR))
P F Nicholls Barry Fulton, Liam Brady, Tony Hayward

Placings:40/02125/21FPP6-P0100   (4932)
2003/04: 20ᴾGS, 16⁰G, 24¹S, 24⁹GS, 27⁰G,

	Starts	1st	2nd	3rd	Win & Pl
Hurdles	4	1	0	0	5616
Chases	1	0	0	0	0
Career Total	18	3	3	0	17067
111	12/03	Chep	3m	C(0-135)HHdl	SFT	£5616
121	11/02	Plum	2m1f	E(0-110)HCh	G-S	£4043
106	12/01	Winc	2m	F(0-95)HHdl	GD	£2709

Total win prize-money £12368

Going:	Sf: 1-1 GS: 0-2 Gd: 0-2 GF: - Fm: 0-0
Distance:	2m/2m3: 0-1 2m4-2m7: 0-0 3m+: 1-3
Track:	LH: 1-2 RH: 0-2 Tight: 0-2 Gall: 0-1
Aids:	Bl: 0-1 Vi: 0-0 Tstrap: 0-0 Ckp: 0-0
Best Rating:	121 11/02 Winc 2m5f good Ch

Modest hurdler/chaser; stays three miles, but has won over two; best with cut in the ground; has worn blinkers and a tongue tie.

Joyful Princess

4-y-o b f Gildoran-Joyful Pabs (Pablond)
C J Down Mike Rowe

Placings:00P   (3641)
2003/04: 13⁰GS, 12⁰G, 17ᴾS,

	Starts	1st	2nd	3rd	Win & Pl
NH Flat	2	0	0	0	0
Hurdles	1	0	0	0	0
Career Total	3	0	0	0	0

Going:	Sf: 0-1 GS: 0-1 Gd: 0-1 GF: - Fm: 0-0
Distance:	2m/2m3: 0-1 2m4-2m7: 0-0 3m+: 0-0
Track:	LH: 0-0 RH: 0-2 Tight: 0-0 Gall: 0-0
Aids:	Bl: 0-0 Vi: 0-0 Tstrap: 0-0 Ckp: 0-0

Best Rating: 56 1/04 Chel 1m4f   good   NHF

Jr-Kay (IRE)

14-y-o ch g Tremblant-Promising Very Vii (Damsire Unregistered)
Miss A Armitage N W A Bannister

Placings:1/4P/1   (0389)
2003/04: 25¹G,

	Starts	1st	2nd	3rd	Win & Pl
Chases	1	1	0	0	3484
Career Total	4	2	0	0	5735
104 5/03	Weth	3m1f	H Ch	GD	£3484
89 5/96	Ctml	3m2f	H Ch	G-F	£2008
			Total win prize-money £5492

Going:	Sf: 0-0 GS: 0-0 Gd: 1-1 GF: - Fm: 0-0
Distance:	2m/2m3: 0-0 2m4-2m7: 0-0 3m+: 1-1
Track:	LH: 1-1 RH: 0-0 Tight: 0-0 Gall: 0-0
Aids:	Bl: 0-0 Vi: 0-0 Tstrap: 0-0 Ckp: 0-0
Best Rating:	**104** 5/03 Weth 3m1f good Ch

Winning pointer; landed a lady riders' hunter chase at Wetherby in May.

Jubba's Jester (USA)

5-y-o b g St Jovite (USA)-Wisecrack (USA) (Secretariat (USA))
B G Powell J R Vail & P D Vail

Placings:0PP   (2907)
2003/04: 16⁹GS, 19⁹S, 26⁹GS,

	Starts	1st	2nd	3rd	Win & Pl
NH Flat	1	0	0	0	0
Hurdles	2	0	0	0	0
Career Total	3	0	0	0	

Going:	Sf: 0-1 GS: 0-2 Gd: 0-0 GF: - Fm: 0-0
Distance:	2m/2m3: 0-1 2m4-2m7: 0-1 3m+: 0-1
Track:	LH: 0-2 RH: 0-1 Tight: 0-1 Gall: 0-2
Aids:	Bl: 0-0 Vi: 0-0 Tstrap: 0-0 Ckp: 0-0
Best Rating:	**43** 11/03 Newb 2m110y gd-sft NHF

Judaic Ways

(72h)**106**

10-y-o b g Rudimentary (USA)-Judeah (Great Nephew)
H D Daly D Sandells & T Broderick

Placings:604/5004F0P0/6FF14/P1P12PP0/30133P-PF   (2363)

2003/04: 23ᴾGF, 24ᶠGF,

	Starts	1st	2nd	3rd	Win & Pl
Chases	2	0	0	0	
Career Total	32	4	1	3	26109
102 1/03	Ludl	3m	E(0-105)HCh	G-S	£6812
105 11/01	Ludl	3m	E(0-115)HCh	G-F	£4810
96 7/01	Worc	2m7h110yF(0-100)HCh	GD	£3209
94 2/01	Ludl	3m	F(0-95)HCh	GD	£4634
			Total win prize-money £19467

Going:	Sf: 0-0 GS: 0-0 Gd: 0-1 GF: - Fm: 0-0
Distance:	2m/2m3: 0-0 2m4-2m7: 0-0 3m+: 0-2
Track:	LH: 0-1 RH: 0-1 Tight: 0-1 Gall: 0-0
Aids:	Bl: 0-0 Vi: 0-0 Tstrap: 0-0 Ckp: 0-0
Best Rating:	**106** 12/01 Ludl 3m3f110y good Ch

Modest handicap chaser; suited by fast ground but has won on good to soft; Ludlow specialist.

Judes Law

6-y-o gr m Contract Law (USA)-Linen Thread (Broxted)
P R Rodford (S C Burrough 7/8) P R Rodford

Placings:0-0P   (3448)
2003/04: 17⁹G, 17ᴾGS,

	Starts	1st	2nd	3rd	Win & Pl
NH Flat	1	0	0	0	0
Hurdles	1	0	0	0	0
Career Total	3	0	0	0	

Going:	Sf: 0-0 GS: 0-1 Gd: 0-1 GF: - Fm: 0-0
Distance:	2m/2m3: 0-2 2m4-2m7: 0-0 3m+: 0-0
Track:	LH: 0-1 RH: 0-1 Tight: 0-2 Gall: 0-0
Aids:	Bl: 0-0 Vi: 0-0 Tstrap: 0-0 Ckp: 0-0
Best Rating:	**46** 6/03 NAbb 2m1f good NHF

Judge Jim

77   57

7-y-o b g Contract Law (USA)-My Moody Girl (IRE) (Alzao (USA))
Mrs S D Williams Bideford Tool Ltd

Placings:0/050   (0757)
2003/04: 16⁰GF, 17⁵GF, 20⁹G,

	Starts	1st	2nd	3rd	Win & Pl
Hurdles	3	0	0	0	0
Career Total	4	0	0	0	

Going:	Sf: 0-0 GS: 0-0 Gd: 0-1 GF: - Fm: 0-2
Distance:	2m/2m3: 0-2 2m4-2m7: 0-1 3m+: 0-0
Track:	LH: 0-2 RH: 0-1 Tight: 0-1 Gall: 0-0
Aids:	Bl: 0-1 Vi: 0-0 Tstrap: 0-0 Ckp: 0-0
Best Rating:	**57** 5/03 NAbb 2m1f gd-fm Hdl

Judicious Norman (IRE)

13-y-o br g Strong Gale-Smart Fashion (Carlburg)
Miss Katherine Self Miss Katherine Self

Placings:60/U05P/F3F35/5P4/P0/F40/33   (0353)
2003/04: 24³GF, 21³GF,

	Starts	1st	2nd	3rd	Win & Pl
Chases	2	0	0	2	433
Career Total	21	0	0	4	1652

Going:	Sf: 0-0 GS: 0-0 Gd: 0-0 GF: - Fm: 0-2
Distance:	2m/2m3: 0-0 2m4-2m7: 0-1 3m+: 0-1
Track:	LH: 0-0 RH: 0-2 Tight: 0-1 Gall: 0-1
Aids:	Bl: 0-0 Vi: 0-0 Tstrap: 0-0 Ckp: 0-0
Best Rating:	**96** 3/96 Newb 2m110y gd-sft Hdl

Hunter chaser; winning pointer; stays three miles; effective on good ground.

Judy Gale (IRE)

6-y-o br m Glacial Storm (USA)-Gale Choice (IRE) (Strong Gale)
J Gallagher Miss K Mundy

Placings:0P-6   (4118)
2003/04: 22⁶G,

	Starts	1st	2nd	3rd	Win & Pl
Hurdles	1	0	0	0	0
Career Total	3	0	0	0	0

Going:	Sf: 0-0 GS: 0-0 Gd: 0-1 GF: - Fm: 0-0
Distance:	2m/2m3: 0-0 2m4-2m7: 0-1 3m+: 0-0
Track:	LH: 0-0 RH: 0-1 Tight: 0-1 Gall: 0-0
Aids:	Bl: 0-0 Vi: 0-0 Tstrap: 0-0 Ckp: 0-0
Best Rating:	**46** 12/02 Folk 2m1f110y heavy NHF

Jug Of Punch (IRE)

101   78

5-y-o ch g In The Wings-Mysistra (FR) (Machiavellian (USA))
S T Lewis (S J Treacy 13/6) Simon T Lewis

Placings:0303   (4716)
2003/04: 16⁰YS, 16⁰G, 16⁰GF, 21³G,

	Starts	1st	2nd	3rd	Win & Pl
Hurdles	4	0	0	2	1717
Career Total	4	0	0	2	1717

Going:	Sf: 0-0 GS: 0-0 Gd: 0-2 GF: - Fm: 0-1
Distance:	2m/2m3: 0-3 2m4-2m7: 0-1 3m+: 0-0
Track:	LH: 0-0 RH: 0-2 Tight: 0-0 Gall: 0-0
Aids:	Bl: 0-0 Vi: 0-0 Tstrap: 0-0 Ckp: 0-0
Best Rating:	**78** 4/04 Ludl 2m5f good Hdl

Julandi

89f   77f

5-y-o ch m Southern Music-Dull'Un (True Song)
B N Doran B N Doran

Placings:406   (2038)
2003/04: 16⁴GF, 16⁰GF, 16ᴾGF,

	Starts	1st	2nd	3rd	Win & Pl
NH Flat	3	0	0	0	0
Career Total	3	0	0	0	0

Going:	Sf: 0-0 GS: 0-0 Gd: 0-0 GF: - Fm: 0-3
Distance:	2m/2m3: 0-3 2m4-2m7: 0-0 3m+: 0-0
Track:	LH: 0-3 RH: 0-0 Tight: 0-0 Gall: 0-0
Aids:	Bl: 0-0 Vi: 0-0 Tstrap: 0-0 Ckp: 0-0
Best Rating:	**80** 9/03 Worc 2m gd-fm NHF

Julia's Choice

99   79

5-y-o ch m Elmaamul (USA)-Daarat Alayaam (IRE) (Reference Point)
J R Jenkins M Ng

Placings:05033-P623P   (2907)
2003/04: 16⁶GF, 16⁶GF, 16²GF, 23³G, 26ᴾGS,

	Starts	1st	2nd	3rd	Win & Pl
Hurdles	5	0	1	1	1264
Career Total	10	0	1	3	2223

Going:	Sf: 0-0 GS: 0-1 Gd: 0-1 GF: - Fm: 0-3
Distance:	2m/2m3: 0-3 2m4-2m7: 0-1 3m+: 0-1
Track:	LH: 0-2 RH: 0-3 Tight: 0-2 Gall: 0-2
Aids:	Bl: 0-0 Vi: 0-0 Tstrap: 0-0 Ckp: 0-0
Best Rating:	**79** 11/03 Ling 2m7f good Hdl

Modest novice hurdler; acts on a sound surface.

Julie's Leader (IRE)

103(103h)   (113h)**115**

10-y-o b g Supreme Leader-Parkavooreen (Deep Run)
P F Nicholls   T Curry

Placings:0/U4F14/1U33/32041/F4PP11-121   **(0755)**
2003/04: 24¹GF, 27²G, 26¹GF,

	Starts	1st	2nd	3rd	Win & Pl
Hurdles	2	1	1	0	5247
Chases	1	1	0	0	4076
Career Total	24	7	2	3	31402
115 6/03	NAbb	3m2f110yE(0-110)HCh		G-F	£4075
104 5/03	Chep	3m	E(0-115)HHdl	G-F	£3591
100 4/03	NAbb	3m3f	F Hdl	G-F	£2947
92 3/03	Font	2m4f	G Hdl	G-F	£2359
87 4/02	Ludl	3m	D Ch	GD	£5200
125 1/01	Tntn	3m110y	F(0-110)HHdl	HVY	£3262
105 3/00	Tntn	3m110y	E Hdl	GD	£2472
			Total win prize-money £23907		

Going:	Sf: 0-0 GS: 0-0 Gd: 0-1 GF: - Fm: 2-2
Distance:	2m/2m3: 0-0 2m4-2m7: 0-0 3m+: 2-3
Track:	LH: 2-3 RH: 1-2 Gall: 0-0
Aids:	Bl: 0-0 Vi: 0-0 Tstrap: 0-0 Ckp: 0-0
Best Rating:	125 11/01 Chep 3m gd-sft Hdl

Fair hurdler/chaser; completed a hat-trick over hurdles and scored over fences in the spring of 2003; effective at up to 3m 3f; acts on most types of ground; needs a break between his races.

Julies Boy (IRE)

89(103c)   (99c)**72+**

7-y-o b g Toulon-Chickmo (IRE) (Seclude (USA))
T R George   R P Foden

Placings:02P0-PP5P20   **(4592)**
2003/04: 22ᴾGF, 24ᴾGS, 19⁵G, 26ᴾGS, 24²G, 26⁹G,

	Starts	1st	2nd	3rd	Win & Pl
Hurdles	4	0	0	0	0
Chases	2	0	1	0	980
Career Total	10	0	2	0	2109

Going:	Sf: 0-0 GS: 0-2 Gd: 0-3 GF: - Fm: 0-1
Distance:	2m/2m3: 0-1 2m4-2m7: 0-1 3m+: 0-4
Track:	LH: 0-1 RH: 0-5 Tight: 0-2 Gall: 0-1
Aids:	Bl: 0-0 Vi: 0-0 Tstrap: 0-0 Ckp: 0-1
Best Rating:	106 12/02 Thur 2m yield Hdl

Ex-Irish novice hurdler; highly-tried and let down by his jumping so far here.

Jumbo's Dream

105(99h)   (56h)**83**

13-y-o b g Jumbo Hirt (USA)-Joyful Star (Rubor)
J E Dixon   Mrs E M Dixon

Placings:00/23065/10000/421000/006336/000P0/6F0-0603345F212P4P3   **(4882)**
2003/04: 24⁰GF, 24⁰G, 24⁶G, 24⁰G, 20³GF, 26³GF, 26⁴G, 27⁵GF, 20ᴾGF, 25²G, 27¹GF, 27²G, 26⁵G, 20⁴G, 28ᴾG, 26²GS,

	Starts	1st	2nd	3rd	Win & Pl
Hurdles	4	0	0	0	0
Chases	12	1	2	3	6302
Career Total	47	3	4	6	13752
82 11/03	Sedg	3m3f	F(0-100)HCh	G-F	£2520
88 6/99	Hexm	3m	F(0-105)HHdl	G-F	£2658
78 10/98	Hexm	3m	E Hdl	GD	£2238
			Total win prize-money £7416		

Going:	Sf: 0-0 GS: 0-1 Gd: 0-9 GF: - Fm: 1-6
Distance:	2m/2m3: 0-0 2m4-2m7: 0-3 3m+: 1-13

Track:	LH: 1-13 RH: 0-3 Tight: 1-6 Gall: 0-1
Aids:	Bl: 0-0 Vi: 0-0 Tstrap: 0-1 Ckp: 1-15
Best Rating:	89 5/99 Ctml 3m2f gd-fm Hdl

Plating-class chaser; acts on fast ground; stays three miles three.

Jumpty Dumpty (FR)

90   **90**

7-y-o b/br g Chamberlin (FR)-Caryatide (FR) (Maiymad)
J C Tuck   M Tuck

Placings:0/3323160P/144006-P0P   **(3747)**
2003/04: 22ᴾGS, 19⁴GS, 18ᴾGS,

	Starts	1st	2nd	3rd	Win & Pl
Hurdles	3	0	0	0	0
Career Total	18	2	1	3	12139
90 5/02	Extr	2m6f110yE(0-100)HHdl	GD	£3255
10/01	Pina	2m4f110y Ch	SFT	£3395
		Total win prize-money £6650	

Going:	Sf: 0-0 GS: 0-3 Gd: 0-0 GF: - Fm: 0-0
Distance:	2m/2m3: 0-1 2m4-2m7: 0-2 3m+: 0-0
Track:	LH: 0-2 RH: 0-1 Tight: 0-1 Gall: 0-0
Aids:	Bl: 0-0 Vi: 0-0 Tstrap: 0-0 Ckp: 0-0
Best Rating:	90 9/02 Bang 2m4f good Hdl

A

June's River (IRE)

104(91h)   (73h)**114**

11-y-o ch g Over The River (FR)-June Bug (Welsh Saint)
Mrs M Reveley   A Flannigan

Placings:002/444011/F/F251U210/U4/P23PP6-44F02446   **(3981)**
2003/04: 20⁴GS, 20⁴G, 20⁶G, 17⁰S, 20⁰HY, 16⁴G, 20⁴HY, 20⁶G,

	Starts	1st	2nd	3rd	Win & Pl
Hurdles	1	0	0	0	0
Chases	7	0	1	0	2243
Career Total	34	4	5	1	22200
112 2/01	Carl	2m	F(0-105)HCh	HVY	£3477
106 12/00	Hntg	2m110y	F(0-110)HCh	SFT	£2616
110 3/99	Carl	2m	F(0-110)HCh	SFT	£2723
98 2/99	Carl	2m	E(0-105)HCh	HVY	£2931
			Total win prize-money £11749		

Going:	Sf: 0-3 GS: 0-1 Gd: 0-4 GF: - Fm: 0-0
Distance:	2m/2m3: 0-2 2m4-2m7: 0-6 3m+: 0-0
Track:	LH: 0-3 RH: 0-5 Tight: 0-1 Gall: 0-2
Aids:	Bl: 0-0 Vi: 0-0 Tstrap: 0-0 Ckp: 0-0
Best Rating:	116 3/02 Newc 2m110y heavy Ch

Moderate chaser; best over two miles and suited by soft ground; not always the best of jumpers; likes to be held up.

Jungle Fresh

11-y-o b g Rambo Dancer (CAN)-Report 'Em (USA) (Staff Writer (USA))
M Rodda   P Senter

Placings:PP/P/5   **(0204)**
2003/04: 20⁵GF,

	Starts	1st	2nd	3rd	Win & Pl
Chases	1	0	0	0	0
Career Total	4	0	0	0	0

Going:	Sf: 0-0 GS: 0-0 Gd: 0-0 GF: - Fm: 0-1
Distance:	2m/2m3: 0-0 2m4-2m7: 0-1 3m+: 0-0
Track:	LH: 0-1 RH: 0-0 Tight: 0-0 Gall: 0-0

Aids:	Bl: 0-0 Vi: 0-0 Tstrap: 0-1 Ckp: 0-0

Jungle Jinks (IRE)

116   (120h)**135**

9-y-o b g Proud Panther (FR)-Three Ladies (Menelek)
G M Moore   Mrs Mary And Miss Susan Hatfield

Placings:6114/11121-B4PP3245   **(4598)**
2003/04: 25⁸G, 25⁴G, 26ᴾGS, 25ᴾGS, 25⁵S, 24²S, 28⁴G, 32⁵G,

	Starts	1st	2nd	3rd	Win & Pl
Chases	8	0	1	1	10103
Career Total	17	6	2	1	52493
135 2/03	Weth	3m1f	C Ch	GD	£8841
135 12/02	Weth	3m1f	D Ch	SFT	£6041
135 11/02	Sedg	2m5f	C Ch	SFT	£8375
122 11/02	Weth	3m1f	D Ch	GD	£4803
101 4/02	Carl	2m4f	E Hdl	GD	£3143
115 3/02	Ayr	3m110y	E Hdl	SFT	£2712
			Total win prize-money £33917		

Going:	Sf: 0-2 GS: 0-2 Gd: 0-4 GF: - Fm: 0-0
Distance:	2m/2m3: 0-0 2m4-2m7: 0-0 3m+: 0-8
Track:	LH: 0-6 RH: 0-2 Tight: 0-1 Gall: 0-1
Aids:	Bl: 0-0 Vi: 0-0 Tstrap: 0-0 Ckp: 0-0
Best Rating:	135 2/03 Weth 3m1f good Ch

Fair chaser; won four times as a novice; back to his best when runner-up at Haydock in February, but disappointing since; stays three miles, handles good or softer ground; suited by forcing tactics.

Jungle Rumbler

67

5-y-o b m Charnwood Forest (IRE)-Blueberry Walk (Green Desert (USA))
P Winkworth   Mrs Tessa Winkworth

Placings:PF0-6F   **(2596)**
2003/04: 17⁶G, 16⁶FG,

	Starts	1st	2nd	3rd	Win & Pl
Hurdles	2	0	0	0	0
Career Total	5	0	0	0	0

Going:	Sf: 0-0 GS: 0-0 Gd: 0-2 GF: - Fm: 0-0
Distance:	2m/2m3: 0-2 2m4-2m7: 0-0 3m+: 0-0
Track:	LH: 0-1 RH: 0-1 Tight: 0-1 Gall: 0-0
Aids:	Bl: 0-0 Vi: 0-1 Tstrap: 0-0 Ckp: 0-0
Best Rating:	67 12/03 Wwck 2m good Hdl

Flat winner in France; no promise so far over hurdles.

Jungli (IRE)

97   (132h)**111**

11-y-o b g Be My Native (USA)-Simple Mind (Decent Fellow)
P R Webber   Mrs P Starkey

Placings:243/312410/1213311/1221U6/563324/F-F0   **(4843)**
2003/04: 16⁵G, 16⁰G,

	Starts	1st	2nd	3rd	Win & Pl
Chases	2	0	0	0	
Career Total	31	4	6	5	95865
151 1/01	Donc	2m110y	B(0-150)HCh	GD	£10413
140 10/00	Weth	2m	C(0-135)HCh	GD	£6405
140 4/00	Aint	2m	A HCh	GD	£30000
140 3/00	Newb	2m1f	C(0-135)HCh	SFT	£6244
130 12/99	Wwck	2m	D Ch	SFT	£4816
116 10/99	Weth	2m	E Ch	GD	£2908
130 3/99	Uttx	2m4f110yC Hdl		G-S	£5537
130 12/98	Uttx	2m	E Hdl	SFT	£2431

Total win prize-money £68756

Going:	Sf: 0-0 GS: 0-0 Gd: 0-2 GF: - Fm: 0-0
Distance:	2m/2m3: 0-2 2m4-2m7: 0-0 3m+: 0-0
Track:	LH: 0-2 RH: 0-0 Tight: 0-0 Gall: 0-2
Aids:	Bl: 0-0 Vi: 0-0 Tstrap: 0-0 Ckp: 0-0
Best Rating:	151 12/01 Weth 2m gd-sft Ch

Useful handicap chaser; very useful in his day; lightly raced of late; best at two miles, although stays two and a half miles; acts well on good ground.

Jupiter's Fancy

9-y-o ch m Jupiter Island-Joe's Fancy (Apollo Eight)
M V Coglan (D W Barker 11/8) M V Coglan

Placings: 4300P/P3-0046   (3987)
2003/04: 20³GF, 17⁰GF, 21⁶GF, 26⁴G, 21⁶GS,

	Starts	1st	2nd	3rd	Win & Pl
Hurdles	1	0	0	0	0
Chases	4	0	0	1	536
Career Total	11	0	0	2	769

Going:	Sf: 0-0 GS: 0-1 Gd: 0-1 GF: - Fm: 0-3
Distance:	2m/2m3: 0-1 2m4-2m7: 0-3 3m+: 0-1
Track:	LH: 0-5 RH: 0-0 Tight: 0-3 Gall: 0-1
Aids:	Bl: 0-0 Vi: 0-0 Tstrap: 0-0 Ckp: 0-0
Best Rating:	82 12/01 Catt 2m good NHF

Modest hunter chaser; best on fast ground.

Jupon Vert (FR)

105(98h)   (101h)101+
7-y-o g Lights Out (FR)-Danse Verte (FR) (Brezzo (FR))
R J Hodges (P F Nicholls 9/6) Mrs J B Jenkins

Placings: P5/2P42/546120143F3-002124242322   (4896)
2003/04: 19⁰G, 16⁶G, 16²GF, 16¹GF, 19²GF, 16⁴GS, 16²GS, 16⁴G, 20²G, 20³GS, 19²GF, 16²G,

	Starts	1st	2nd	3rd	Win & Pl
Hurdles	1	0	0	0	0
Chases	11	0	0	1	13470
Career Total	29	3	9	3	25708
101 11/03 Wwck 2m110y E(0-110)HCh	G-F				£3255
95 2/03 Tntn 2m110y E(0-100)HCh	G-S				£4290
86 12/02 Tntn 2m3f110yG Hdl	G-S				£1988

Total win prize-money £9533

Going:	Sf: 0-0 GS: 0-3 Gd: 0-5 GF: - Fm: 1-4
Distance:	2m/2m3: 1-10 2m4-2m7: 0-2 3m+: 0-0
Track:	LH: 1-4 RH: 0-8 Tight: 0-7 Gall: 0-1
Aids:	Bl: 0-0 Vi: 0-0 Tstrap: 1-6 Ckp: 0-0
Best Rating:	101 4/04 Winc 2m good Ch

Moderate hurdler/chaser; effective on most types of ground; stays two and a half miles.

Jurado Express (IRE)

105(109h)   (101h)139
8-y-o b g Jurado (USA)-Express Film (Ashmore (FR))
A L T Moore Miss Susan Traynor

Placings: 0032U/0223311155P-542F20   (4627)
2003/04: 16⁵GY, 17⁴Y, 18²GY, 20⁵S, 16²S, 16⁰G,

	Starts	1st	2nd	3rd	Win & Pl
Chases	6	0	2	0	8273
Career Total	22	3	5	3	32319
139 12/02 Cork 2m	Ch			SFT	£7975
139 12/02 Thur 2m	Ch			SFT	£4868

| 102 11/02 Cork 2m | Hdl | | | SFT | £6773 |

Total win prize-money £19616

Going:	Sf: 0-2 GS: 0-0 Gd: 0-1 GF: - Fm: 0-0
Distance:	2m/2m3: 0-5 2m4-2m7: 0-1 3m+: 0-0
Track:	LH: 0-2 RH: 0-3 Tight: 0-1 Gall: 0-0
Aids:	Bl: 0-0 Vi: 0-0 Tstrap: 0-0 Ckp: 0-0
Best Rating:	139 12/02 Cork 2m soft Ch

Modest Irish-trained hurdler but shown better form over fences; stays two miles; suited by soft ground.

Juralan (IRE)

109(102h)   (105+h)134+
9-y-o b g Jurado (USA)-Boylan (Buckskin (FR))
H P Hogarth Hogarth Racing

Placings: 624/511P/PPP3-25124   (4850)
2003/04: 16²G, 20⁵S, 19¹G, 20²GS, 20⁴GS,

	Starts	1st	2nd	3rd	Win & Pl
Hurdles	2	1	1	0	4650
Chases	3	0	1	0	4826
Career Total	16	3	3	1	23545
105 3/04 Donc 2m3f110yE Hdl	GD				£3592
131 1/02 Winc 2m5f	D Ch		GD		£4602
124 11/01 Tntn 2m3f	C Ch		G-S		£6756

Total win prize-money £14951

Going:	Sf: 0-1 GS: 0-2 Gd: 1-2 GF: - Fm: 0-0
Distance:	2m/2m3: 0-1 2m4-2m7: 1-4 3m+: 0-0
Track:	LH: 1-5 RH: 0-0 Tight: 0-1 Gall: 0-1
Aids:	Bl: 0-0 Vi: 0-0 Tstrap: 0-0 Ckp: 0-0
Best Rating:	134 3/04 Bang 2m4f110y gd-sft Ch

Very useful chaser at his best; jumps well; changed stables and back to form when narrowly held in novices' hurdle at Doncaster in January; went one better there in March; stays two miles five and acts on a sound surface.

Jurancon II (FR)

110(112h)   (126+h)157
7-y-o g Scooter Bleu (IRE)-Volniste (FR) (Olmeto)
M C Pipe D A Johnson

Placings: 456011P/1P13-14521F   (4647)
2003/04: 32¹GF, 29⁴S, 29⁶S, 29²GS, 28¹G, 36⁶G,

	Starts	1st	2nd	3rd	Win & Pl
Chases	6	2	1	0	132202
Career Total	17	6	1	1	166896
152 2/04 Hayd 3m4f110yA HCh	GD				£69600
139 6/03 Uttx 4m110y B(0-140)HCh	G-F				£34800
126 12/02 Uttx 2m5f	D Ch		G-F		£4715
126 11/02 Chel 2m5f	E(0-115)HHdl		GD		£11005
109 2/02 Plum 2m5f	D(0-115)HHdl		HVY		£5330
112 2/02 MRas 2m5f110yE(0-110)HHdl	G-S				£2642

Total win prize-money £128094

Going:	Sf: 0-2 GS: 0-1 Gd: 1-2 GF: - Fm: 1-1
Distance:	2m/2m3: 0-0 2m4-2m7: 0-0 3m+: 2-6
Track:	LH: 1-5 RH: 0-0 Tight: 0-2 Gall: 0-0
Aids:	Bl: 0-0 Vi: 0-0 Tstrap: 0-0 Ckp: 0-0
Best Rating:	152 2/04 Hayd 3m4f110y good Ch

Smart chaser; winner of the Summer National at Uttoxeter in 2003; bounced back to form when good second in Tote Classic Chase at Warwick January; ran away with another valuable prize at Haydock the following month; fell in the National when sent off co-favourite; stays extreme distances; acts on most types of ground but ideally suited by quick conditions; still has the scope for further improvement.

Just A Touch

88(106h)   (96 h)92+
8-y-o ch g Rakaposhi King-Minim (Rymer)
P Winkworth R N Scott, R G Robinson, Peter Broste

Placings: 000/F014/P11524-3P35F1   (4446)
2003/04: 16³GS, 16⁶GS, 17³HY, 16⁵S, 16⁶GS, 16¹GS,

	Starts	1st	2nd	3rd	Win & Pl
Hurdles	1	0	0	1	491
Chases	5	1	0	1	4003
Career Total	19	4	1	2	14497
92 3/04 Wwck 2m110y F(0-95)HHdl	G-S				£3542
96 12/02 Wwck 2m E(0-110)HHdl	SFT				£3013
79 11/02 Wwck 2m3f F(0-100)HHdl	G-S				£2488
82 2/02 Folk 2m1f110yF(0-90)HHdl	SFT				£2688

Total win prize-money £11733

Going:	Sf: 0-2 GS: 1-4 Gd: 0-0 GF: - Fm: 0-0
Distance:	2m/2m3: 1-6 2m4-2m7: 0-0 3m+: 0-0
Track:	LH: 1-3 RH: 0-3 Tight: 0-2 Gall: 0-0
Aids:	Bl: 0-0 Vi: 0-0 Tstrap: 0-0 Ckp: 0-0
Best Rating:	96 1/04 Folk 2m1f110y heavy Hdl

Moderate hurdler/novice chaser; twice a winner over hurdles at Warwick again showed his liking for the course when landing Class F handicap chase March 2004; stays two miles three; acts in soft ground.

Just Anvil (IRE)

87   71
6-y-o ch g Baron Blakeney-Amy Just (IRE) (Bustomi)
L Wells David Cox

Placings: 4430   (3753)
2003/04: 20⁴S, 22⁴G, 20³S, 22⁰GS,

	Starts	1st	2nd	3rd	Win & Pl
Chases	4	0	0	1	1647
Career Total	4	0	0	1	1647

Going:	Sf: 0-2 GS: 0-1 Gd: 0-1 GF: - Fm: 0-0
Distance:	2m/2m3: 0-0 2m4-2m7: 0-3 3m+: 0-0
Track:	LH: 0-2 RH: 0-0 Tight: 0-4 Gall: 0-0
Aids:	Bl: 0-0 Vi: 0-0 Tstrap: 0-0 Ckp: 0-0
Best Rating:	76 1/04 Plum 2m4f soft Ch

Just Aretha

                                                          13
8-y-o b m Weld-Just Something (Good Times (ITY))
G J Smith G L Edwards

Placings: 0P   (0909)
2003/04: 21⁰GY, 21⁸GF,

	Starts	1st	2nd	3rd	Win & Pl
Hurdles	2	0	0	0	
Career Total	2	0	0	0	

Going:	Sf: 0-0 GS: 0-0 Gd: 0-0 GF: - Fm: 0-2
Distance:	2m/2m3: 0-2 2m4-2m7: 0-2 3m+: 0-0
Track:	LH: 0-2 RH: 0-0 Tight: 0-0 Gall: 0-0
Aids:	Bl: 0-0 Vi: 0-0 Tstrap: 0-0 Ckp: 0-0
Best Rating:	18 6/03 Sthl 2m5f110y gd-fm Hdl

Just Barney Boy

85   (48h)62
7-y-o b g Past Glories-Pablena (Pablond)
R Nixon G R S Nixon

Placings: 44005F/PPPC-4UP   (0795)

2003/04: 24⁴GF, 20ᵁGF, 24ᴾG,

	Starts	1st	2nd	3rd	Win & Pl
Chases	3	0	0	0	524
Career Total	13	0	0	0	524

Going:	Sf: 0-0 GS: 0-0 Gd: 0-1 GF: - Fm: 0-2
Distance:	2m/2m3: 0-0 2m4-2m7: 0-1 3m+: 0-2
Track:	LH: 0-1 RH: 0-2 Tight: 0-0 Gall: 0-0
Aids:	Bl: 0-1 Vi: 0-0 Tstrap: 0-0 Ckp: 0-0
Best Rating:	62 6/03 Prth 3m gd-fm Ch

Plating-class chaser; rattled up a hat-trick of points in spring 2003; has found life much tougher under Rules; stays three miles; effective on decent ground.

Just Beth
99   **86**

8-y-o ch m Carlingford Castle-One For The Road (Warpath)
G Fierro   G Fierro

Placings: 00440/05/P20-000120522P0P2   (4914)
2003/04: 24⁰GS, 27⁰G, 20⁰HY, 24¹G, 21²GF, 22⁰G, 20⁵GF, 24²GF, 17²GS, 25ᴾGS, 16⁰GS, 17ᴾGS, 24ᴾGS,

	Starts	1st	2nd	3rd	Win & Pl
Hurdles	13	1	4	0	7491
Career Total	23	1	5	0	8249
81 6/03 MRas 3m		E Hdl		GD	3526

Total win prize-money £3526

Going:	Sf: 0-1 GS: 0-5 Gd: 1-4 GF: - Fm: 0-3
Distance:	2m/2m3: 0-3 2m4-2m7: 0-4 3m+: 1-6
Track:	LH: 0-11 RH: 1-2 Tight: 1-5 Gall: 0-1
Aids:	Bl: 0-2 Vi: 0-0 Tstrap: 0-0 Ckp: 0-0
Best Rating:	98 3/01 Hntg 2m110y soft NHF

Small mare, novice hurdler; acts on any ground; stays three miles.

Just Bryan
64f   **35f**

5-y-o ch g Southern Music-Prospect Of Whitby (True Song)
P A Pritchard   P A Pritchard

Placings: 0   (4787)
2003/04: 16⁰G,

	Starts	1st	2nd	3rd	Win & Pl
NH Flat	1	0	0	0	
Career Total	1	0	0	0	

Going:	Sf: 0-0 GS: 0-0 Gd: 0-1 GF: - Fm: 0-0
Distance:	2m/2m3: 0-1 2m4-2m7: 0-0 3m+: 0-0
Track:	LH: 0-0 RH: 0-1 Tight: 0-0 Gall: 0-1
Aids:	Bl: 0-0 Vi: 0-0 Tstrap: 0-0 Ckp: 0-0
Best Rating:	35 4/04 Hntg 2m110y good NHF

Just Classic
102f   **103+f**

4-y-o gr g Classic Cliche (IRE)-Misty View (Absalom)
M C Pipe   D A Johnson

Placings: 1   (4936)
2003/04: 18¹G,

	Starts	1st	2nd	3rd	Win & Pl
NH Flat	1	1	0	0	1918
Career Total	1	1	0	0	1918
103 4/04 Font 2m2f110yH NHF				GD	£1918

Total win prize-money £1918

Going:	Sf: 0-0 GS: 0-0 Gd: 1-1 GF: - Fm: 0-0
Distance:	2m/2m3: 1-1 2m4-2m7: 0-0 3m+: 0-0

Track:	LH: 1-1 RH: 0-0 Tight: 1-1 Gall: 0-0
Aids:	Bl: 0-0 Vi: 0-0 Tstrap: 0-0 Ckp: 0-0
Best Rating:	103 4/04 Font 2m2f110y good NHF

Made winning debut in Fontwell bumper on good.

Just Flora

8-y-o ch m Democratic (USA)-Figrant (USA) (L'Emigrant (USA))
Miss K M George   Stableline

Placings: 0   (0628)
2003/04: 16⁰GF,

	Starts	1st	2nd	3rd	Win & Pl
Hurdles	1	0	0	0	
Career Total	1	0	0	0	

Going:	Sf: 0-0 GS: 0-0 Gd: 0-0 GF: - Fm: 0-1
Distance:	2m/2m3: 0-1 2m4-2m7: 0-0 3m+: 0-0
Track:	LH: 0-1 RH: 0-0 Tight: 0-0 Gall: 0-0
Aids:	Bl: 0-0 Vi: 0-0 Tstrap: 0-0 Ckp: 0-0

Just For Fun (IRE)
97   **79**

6-y-o br g Kahyasi-Copper Breeze (IRE) (Strong Gale)
Ferdy Murphy   Northumberland Jumpers

Placings: 0-20030   (4690)
2003/04: 20²GF, 16⁰S, 24⁰S, 24³G, 22⁰G,

	Starts	1st	2nd	3rd	Win & Pl
Hurdles	5	0	1	1	1135
Career Total	6	0	1	1	1135

Going:	Sf: 0-2 GS: 0-0 Gd: 0-2 GF: - Fm: 0-1
Distance:	2m/2m3: 0-1 2m4-2m7: 0-3 3m+: 0-2
Track:	LH: 0-5 RH: 0-0 Tight: 0-2 Gall: 0-0
Aids:	Bl: 0-0 Vi: 0-0 Tstrap: 0-0 Ckp: 0-0
Best Rating:	87 3/03 Hayd 2m good NHF

Has shown ability in novice events on a sound surface at up to three miles; likely to do better in ordinary handicap company in due course.

Just For Ger (IRE)
99(97h)   (85+h)**103**

10-y-o b g Beau Sher-Reasonar (Reasonable (FR))
J S Goldie   Strathayr Publishing Ltd

Placings: 000/100000/53U334132/00144-PP16   (3816)
2003/04: 20ᴾS, 17ᴾS, 16¹HY, 20⁶GS,

	Starts	1st	2nd	3rd	Win & Pl
Hurdles	1	0	0	0	
Chases	3	1	0	0	5434
Career Total	27	4	1	4	21294
103 1/04 Ayr 2m	D(0-115)HCh	HVY	£5434
101 3/03 Ayr 2m	F(0-95)HCh	SFT	£4225
103 1/02 Muss 2m4f	E(0-110)HCh	SFT	£4192
86 5/00 Dpat 2m1f172y	Hdl	SFT	£2345

Total win prize-money £16198

Going:	Sf: 1-3 GS: 0-1 Gd: 0-0 GF: - Fm: 0-0
Distance:	2m/2m3: 1-2 2m4-2m7: 0-2 3m+: 0-0
Track:	LH: 1-4 RH: 0-0 Tight: 0-1 Gall: 0-0
Aids:	Bl: 0-0 Vi: 0-0 Tstrap: 0-0 Ckp: 0-0
Best Rating:	103 1/04 Ayr 2m heavy Ch

Moderate hurdler/chaser; effective from two to two and a half miles and notched second win over two miles at Ayr in January 2004; likes soft ground.

Just Good Fun (IRE)
(92h)   (96 h)

10-y-o br g Good Thyne (USA)-Killonerry (Croghan Hill)
M Pitman   Just Good Fun Club

Placings: 40223/2113221/2P/05P   (0819)
2003/04: 20⁰S, 22⁵G, 22ᴾG,

	Starts	1st	2nd	3rd	Win & Pl
Hurdles	2	0	0	0	0
Chases	1	0	0	0	0
Career Total	17	3	6	2	25544
128 1/00 Asct 3m	B(0-140)HHdl	G-S	£10335
126 10/99 Chep 2m4f	D HHdl	SFT	£3420
104 8/99 Uttx 2m4f110yD Hdl		G-F	£2963

Total win prize-money £16719

Going:	Sf: 0-1 GS: 0-0 Gd: 0-2 GF: - Fm: 0-0
Distance:	2m/2m3: 0-0 2m4-2m7: 0-3 3m+: 0-0
Track:	LH: 0-2 RH: 0-1 Tight: 0-2 Gall: 0-0
Aids:	Bl: 0-0 Vi: 0-0 Tstrap: 0-0 Ckp: 0-0
Best Rating:	128 1/00 Asct 3m gd-sft Hdl

Just In Debt (IRE)
107   (113h)**140**

8-y-o b/br g Montelimar (USA)-No Debt (Oats)
M Todhunter (P M J Doyle 17/9)   J W Hazeldean

Placings: 4/02326F/231F56-03122035P1UP   (4861)
2003/04: 25⁰G, 20³GY, 24¹F, 20²GF, 23²G, 22⁰F, 24³G, 20⁵GS, 28ᴾG, 25¹GF, 36ᵁG, 33ᴾGS,

	Starts	1st	2nd	3rd	Win & Pl
Hurdles	4	1	1	1	7974
Chases	8	1	1	1	21199
Career Total	25	3	5	4	41697
133 3/04 Ayr 3m1f	D(0-125)HCh	G-F	£6020
98 6/03 Kbgn 3m	Hdl	FRM	£5824
129 11/02 Cork 2m6f	Ch	SFT	£7975

Total win prize-money £19820

Going:	Sf: 0-0 GS: 0-2 Gd: 0-5 GF: - Fm: 2-4
Distance:	2m/2m3: 0-0 2m4-2m7: 0-5 3m+: 2-7
Track:	LH: 1-6 RH: 0-1 Tight: 0-1 Gall: 0-0
Aids:	Bl: 0-0 Vi: 0-0 Tstrap: 0-0 Ckp: 0-0
Best Rating:	140 7/03 Kbgn 2m7f good Ch

Useful ex-Irish chaser; won on third start for Martin Todhunter at Ayr in March; stays three miles; effective on fast and soft ground.

Just In Time
111(103c)   (120c)**127**

9-y-o b g Night Shift (USA)-Future Past (USA) (Super Concorde (USA))
P J Hobbs   B K Peppiatt

Placings: 130/113043/1113F-U2126404   (4836)
2003/04: 20¹GF, 19²GF, 19¹GF, 21²GF, 20⁶GF, 19⁴GF, 20⁰G, 21⁴GF,

	Starts	1st	2nd	3rd	Win & Pl
Hurdles	7	1	2	0	14004
Chases	1	0	0	0	0
Career Total	22	7	2	4	48861
127 10/03 Strf 2m3f	C(0-135)HHdl	G-F	£7294
120 9/02 Prth 2m4f110yD Ch		G-F	£6760
116 5/02 Strf 2m1f110yD Ch		G-F	£4858
109 5/02 Extr 2m1f110yE Ch		GD	£3737
132 5/01 Prth 2m110y D Hdl		G-F	£3432
128 5/01 Extr 2m1f	D Hdl	GD	£3836
118 12/00 Tntn 2m1f	D Hdl	SFT	£5211

Total win prize-money £35131

Going:	Sf: 0-0 GS: 0-0 Gd: 0-1 GF: - Fm: 1-7

Distance: 2m/2m3: 1-2 2m4-2m7: 0-6 3m+: 0-0
Track: LH: 1-6 RH: 0-2 Tight: 1-2 Gall: 0-3
Aids: Bl: 0-0 Vi: 0-0 Tstrap: 0-0 Ckp: 0-0
Best Rating: 134 6/01 Worc 2m   gd-fm   Hdl

Useful hurdler/fair chaser; won his first three starts over fences in the middle of 2002; let down by jumping since; won weakly contested 2m 3f hurdle at Stratford in October 2003; effective at up to 2m 4f; acts well on a decent surface.

Just Jasmine

98   140

12-y-o ch m Nicholas Bill-Linguistic (Porto Bello)
K Bishop   Mrs E K Ellis

Placings:*64/354/3301F4334/35022111/162/5153P/543232 3/2120U-60*   (4843)
2003/04: 19⁶GS, 16⁰G,

	Starts	1st	2nd	3rd	Win & Pl
Chases	2	0	0	0	0
Career Total	44	7	7	10	101701
140	11/02	Chel	2m	B HCh	GD	£14811
140	1/01	Tntn	2m3f	D(0-125)HCh	HVY	£6987
130	1/00	Tntn	2m3f	D(0-125)HCh	SFT	£6987
121	4/99	Extr	2m1f110yD(0-120)HCh	SFT	£4138
119	3/99	Uttx	2m5f	C HCh	G-S	£18156
110	2/99	Uttx	2m4f	D Ch	HVY	£5558
94	12/97	Worc	2m	E Hdl	SFT	£2425

Total win prize-money £59065

Going: Sf: 0-0 GS: 0-1 Gd: 0-1 GF: - Fm: 0-0
Distance: 2m/2m3: 0-1 2m4-2m7: 0-1 3m+: 0-0
Track: LH: 0-1 RH: 0-1 Tight: 0-0 Gall: 0-1
Aids: Bl: 0-0 Vi: 0-0 Tstrap: 0-0 Ckp: 0-1
Best Rating: 140 11/02 Asct 2m   heavy   Ch

Very useful chaser; best at two miles, though does stay further; suited by soft ground and is usually held up.

Just Jed

5-y-o b g Presidium-Carrapateira (Gunner B)
R Shiels   R Shiels

Placings:*000P*   (4601)
2003/04: 16⁰G, 16⁰GF, 16⁰GS, 22⁰GS,

	Starts	1st	2nd	3rd	Win & Pl
NH Flat	3	0	0	0	0
Hurdles	1	0	0	0	0
Career Total	4	0	0	0	

Going: Sf: 0-0 GS: 0-2 Gd: 0-1 GF: - Fm: 0-1
Distance: 2m/2m3: 0-3 2m4-2m7: 0-1 3m+: 0-0
Track: LH: 0-3 RH: 0-1 Tight: 0-2 Gall: 0-0
Aids: Bl: 0-0 Vi: 0-0 Tstrap: 0-0 Ckp: 0-0
Best Rating: 48 11/03 Ayr 2m   good   NHF

Just Kate

103   84+

5-y-o b m Bob's Return (IRE)-M I Babe (Celtic Cone)
Mrs H Dalton   C B Brookes

Placings:*3P451*   (4716)
2003/04: 16³GF, 16⁶G, 16⁴GF, 20⁵GS, 21¹G,

	Starts	1st	2nd	3rd	Win & Pl
NH Flat	1	0	0	1	283
Hurdles	4	1	0	0	5694
Career Total	5	1	0	1	5977
84	4/04	Ludl	2m5f	E(0-105)HHdl	GD	£5694

Total win prize-money £5694

Going: Sf: 0-0 GS: 0-1 Gd: 1-2 GF: - Fm: 0-2
Distance: 2m/2m3: 0-3 2m4-2m7: 1-2 3m+: 0-0
Track: LH: 0-2 RH: 1-3 Tight: 0-1 Gall: 0-0
Aids: Bl: 0-0 Vi: 0-0 Tstrap: 0-0 Ckp: 0-0
Best Rating: 93 6/03 Worc 2m   gd-fm   NHF

Plating-class hurdler; stays two miles-five; acts on a sound surface.

Just Lambrini

5-y-o br m Overbury (IRE)-Lambrini (IRE) (Buckskin (FR))
D McCain   D McCain

Placings:*6PO*   (2665)
2003/04: 16⁶GF, 16⁶GF, 16⁰G,

	Starts	1st	2nd	3rd	Win & Pl
NH Flat	1	0	0	0	0
Hurdles	2	0	0	0	0
Career Total	3	0	0	0	0

Going: Sf: 0-0 GS: 0-0 Gd: 0-1 GF: - Fm: 0-2
Distance: 2m/2m3: 0-3 2m4-2m7: 0-0 3m+: 0-0
Track: LH: 0-1 RH: 0-2 Tight: 0-0 Gall: 0-0
Aids: Bl: 0-0 Vi: 0-0 Tstrap: 0-0 Ckp: 0-0
Best Rating: 68 10/03 Uttx 2m   gd-fm   NHF

Just Maybe (IRE)

113(107c)   (131c)106+

10-y-o b g Glacial Storm (USA)-Purlace (Realm)
Miss Venetia Williams   W E Prichard

Placings:*0/0U40P/5F022/4355111P-P023*   (3694)
2003/04: 26²HY, 24⁰G, 26²G, 25³G,

	Starts	1st	2nd	3rd	Win & Pl
Hurdles	3	0	1	1	1939
Chases	1	0	0	0	0
Career Total	23	3	3	2	31854
131	2/03	Uttx	3m2f	B HCh	HVY	£12810
125	1/03	Tntn	3m3f	C(0-130)HCh	SFT	£8151
119	12/02	Bang	3m6f	D(0-120)HCh	SFT	£5434

Total win prize-money £26395

Going: Sf: 0-1 GS: 0-0 Gd: 0-3 GF: - Fm: 0-0
Distance: 2m/2m3: 0-0 2m4-2m7: 0-0 3m+: 0-4
Track: LH: 0-4 RH: 0-0 Tight: 0-2 Gall: 0-0
Aids: Bl: 0-4 Vi: 0-0 Tstrap: 0-0 Ckp: 0-0
Best Rating: 131 2/03 Uttx 3m2f   heavy   Ch

Fair staying chaser/moderate hurdler; stays three miles six; best in blinkers; acts on soft ground.

Just Midas

106   83

6-y-o b g Merdon Melody-Thabeh (Shareef Dancer (USA))
M C Pipe (N A Smith 29/5)   D G & D J Robinson

Placings:*06/00-011206*   (1333)
2003/04: 22⁰GF, 16¹GF, 16¹GF, 18²GF, 17⁹GF, 19⁶GF,

	Starts	1st	2nd	3rd	Win & Pl
Hurdles	6	2	1	0	6178
Career Total	10	2	1	0	6178
83	8/03	Worc	2m	G(0-90)HHdl	G-F	£2646
74	7/03	Uttx	2m	G(0-95)HHdl	G-F	£2387

Total win prize-money £5033

Going: Sf: 0-0 GS: 0-0 Gd: 0-0 GF: - Fm: 2-6
Distance: 2m/2m3: 2-4 2m4-2m7: 0-2 3m+: 0-0
Track: LH: 2-5 RH: 0-1 Tight: 0-3 Gall: 0-0
Aids: Bl: 0-0 Vi: 0-0 Tstrap: 0-0 Ckp: 0-0
Best Rating: 83 8/03 Font 2m2f110y gd-fm Hdl

Improving selling hurdler; narrow winner at Uttoxeter in July 2003 on first outing for Martin Pipe; confirmed he has benefited from his trainer's golden touch when following up off a 7lb higher mark at Worcester in August; acts on fast.

Just Muckin Around (IRE)

103(102h)   (70h)95+

8-y-o gr g Celio Rufo-Cousin Muck (IRE) (Henbit (USA))
R H Buckler   Twentyman

Placings:*05PP/46BFP42-F26142253*   (4099)
2003/04: 21⁵GF, 21²G, 25⁸GF, 17¹S, 19⁴GF, 17²S, 20²S, 18⁵GS, 20³G,

	Starts	1st	2nd	3rd	Win & Pl
Chases	9	1	3	1	10820
Career Total	20	1	4	1	11559
95	11/03	Plum	2m1f	E Ch	SFT	£4592

Total win prize-money £4592

Going: Sf: 1-3 GS: 0-1 Gd: 0-2 GF: - Fm: 0-3
Distance: 2m/2m3: 1-4 2m4-2m7: 0-4 3m+: 0-1
Track: LH: 1-6 RH: 0-2 Tight: 1-7 Gall: 0-0
Aids: Bl: 0-0 Vi: 0-0 Tstrap: 0-0 Ckp: 0-0
Best Rating: 95 3/04 Plum 2m4f   good   Ch

Plating-class chaser/hurdler; won bad novice chase at Plumpton in November 2003; stays 2m 6f; acts in most types of ground.

Just Murphy (IRE)

105(104h)   (126 h)120

6-y-o b g Namaqualand (USA)-Bui-Doi (IRE) (Dance Of Life (USA))
N J Henderson   Raymond Tooth

Placings:*4513/23350-121*   (0834)
2003/04: 17¹G, 16²GF, 16¹GF,

	Starts	1st	2nd	3rd	Win & Pl
Chases	3	2	1	0	10728
Career Total	12	3	2	3	19965
120	7/03	Worc	2m	E Ch	G-F	£4065
120	5/03	Kels	2m1f	D Ch	GD	£5447
126	3/02	Hrfd	2m1f	D Hdl	SFT	£3575

Total win prize-money £13088

Going: Sf: 0-0 GS: 0-0 Gd: 1-1 GF: - Fm: 1-2
Distance: 2m/2m3: 2-3 2m4-2m7: 0-0 3m+: 0-0
Track: LH: 2-3 RH: 0-0 Tight: 1-1 Gall: 0-0
Aids: Bl: 0-0 Vi: 0-0 Tstrap: 0-0 Ckp: 0-0
Best Rating: 126 1/03 Winc 2m   gd-sft   Hdl

Decent handicap hurdler; made a promising chase debut when winning at Kelso in May 2003; eventually a well beaten second under a penalty by Brother Joe at Worcester next time; narrow winner when faced with an easier task at the same venue the following month. acts on both fast and soft ground; effective over two miles.

Just Reuben (IRE)

107   97

9-y-o gr g Roselier (FR)-Sharp Mama Vii (Damsire Unregistered)
C L Tizzard   Alvin Trowbridge

Placings:*F04P2345/F25453-65404312132163534*   (4236)
2003/04: 21⁶GF, 18⁵GF, 26⁴G, 25⁹GF, 21⁴G, 22⁹GF, 20¹GF, 20²GF, 20¹GF, 20⁹GF, 21²GF, 20¹G, 21⁶G, 26³HY, 21⁵G, 26³G, 26⁴GF,

	Starts	1st	2nd	3rd	Win & Pl
Chases	17	3	2	4	17294

Career Total	31	3	4	6		23039
97	12/03 Font	2m4f	E(0-100)HCh	GD	£3360
97	9/03 Font	2m4f	E(0-105)HCh	G-F	£3347
68	8/03 Font	2m4f	F(0-90)HCh	G-F	£3360
			Total win prize-money £10070

Going:	Sf: 0-1 GS: 0-0 Gd: 1-6 GF: - Fm: 2-10
Distance:	2m/2m3: 0-1 2m4-2m7: 3-11 3m+: 0-5
Track:	LH: 0-4 RH: 0-5 Tight: 3-11 Gall: 0-1
Aids:	Bl: 0-1 Vi: 0-3 Tstrap: 0-0 Ckp: 0-1
Best Rating:	97 12/03 Font 2m4f good Ch

Plating-class chaser; stays three miles plus and effective on good ground.

Just Riva (IRE)

66   **68**

6-y-o ch m Roaring Riva-Yankee Trader (Stanford)
C A McBratney Peter McGleenon

Placings:000/06P200F   (4745a)
2003/04: 17OGY, 20⁶S, 24³HY, 20²Y, 20⁰VdS, 20⁰Y, 20⁰FY,

	Starts	1st	2nd	3rd	Win & Pl
Hurdles	7	0	1	0	1134
Career Total	10	0	1	0	1134

Going:	Sf: 0-2 GS: 0-0 Gd: 0-0 GF: - Fm: 0-0
Distance:	2m/2m3: 0-1 2m4-2m7: 0-5 3m+: 0-1
Track:	LH: 0-2 RH: 0-1 Tight: 0-0 Gall: 0-0
Aids:	Bl: 0-4 Vi: 0-0 Tstrap: 0-0 Ckp: 0-2
Best Rating:	68 2/04 DRoy 2m4f yield Hdl

Just Sal

108   **91**

8-y-o b m Silly Prices-Hanim (IRE) (Hatim (USA))
R Nixon G R S Nixon

Placings:5030P006/4P0234501P6-204P060003012 (4688)
2003/04: 16²G, 16⁹GS, 16⁴GF, 20⁶G, 17⁰GS, 17⁶GS, 18⁰S, 16⁰S, 18⁰HY, 20³GS, 20⁰G, 16¹G, 16²G,

	Starts	1st	2nd	3rd	Win & Pl
Hurdles	13	1	2	1	6219
Career Total	32	2	3	3	11450
91	3/04 Hexm	2m110y	E(0-110)HHdl	GD	£3402
82	3/03 Hexm	2m110y	E(0-110)HHdl	SFT	£3395
			Total win prize-money £6797

Going:	Sf: 0-3 GS: 0-3 Gd: 1-6 GF: - Fm: 0-1
Distance:	2m/2m3: 1-10 2m4-2m7: 0-3 3m+: 0-0
Track:	LH: 1-8 RH: 0-5 Tight: 0-3 Gall: 0-0
Aids:	Bl: 0-1 Vi: 0-0 Tstrap: 0-0 Ckp: 0-1
Best Rating:	91 4/04 Kels 2m110y good Hdl

Plating-class hurdler; stays two and a half miles; easy winner at Hexham in March 2004; acts on good and soft ground.

Just Serenade

77   **79+**

5-y-o ch m Factual (USA)-Thimbalina (Salmon Leap (USA))
M J Ryan Andy Beard

Placings:1-P   (1907)
2003/04: 16⁵GF,

	Starts	1st	2nd	3rd	Win & Pl
Hurdles	1	0	0	0	
Career Total	2	1	0	0	4238
79	9/02 Strf	2m110y	D Hdl	G-F	£4238
			Total win prize-money £4238

Going:	Sf: 0-0 GS: 0-0 Gd: 0-0 GF: - Fm: 0-1

Just Sooty

107(95h)   (92h)**112+**

9-y-o br g Be My Native (USA)-March Fly (Sousa)
N G Richards David Wesley Yates

Placings:0/3/62F5/5-21   (4794)
2003/04: 20²S, 21¹G,

	Starts	1st	2nd	3rd	Win & Pl
Chases	2	1	1	0	5548
Career Total	9	1	2	1	6618
112	4/04 Sedg	2m5f	E Ch	GD	£4488
			Total win prize-money £4488

Going:	Sf: 0-1 GS: 0-0 Gd: 1-1 GF: - Fm: 0-0
Distance:	2m/2m3: 0-0 2m4-2m7: 1-2 3m+: 0-0
Track:	LH: 1-2 RH: 0-0 Tight: 1-1 Gall: 0-0
Aids:	Bl: 0-0 Vi: 0-0 Tstrap: 0-0 Ckp: 0-0
Best Rating:	112 4/04 Sedg 2m5f good Ch

Lightly-raced plating-class hurdler/chaser, usually held up.

Just Strong (IRE)

99   **91**

11-y-o b/br g Strong Gale-Just Dont Know (Buckskin (FR))
Mrs A M Naughton Miss J M Thompson

Placings:301/P/44PPP14/264535-P3F6541F05 (4882)
2003/04: 25PG, 26³GF, 21FG, 216GF, 20⁵F, 25⁴GF, 27¹G, 25FGS, 25⁰G, 26⁵GS,

	Starts	1st	2nd	3rd	Win & Pl
Chases	10	1	0	1	3230
Career Total	27	3	1	3	14272
78	10/03 Sedg	3m3f	F(0-90)HCh	GD	£2604
94	4/02 Carl	2m4f	E(0-110)HCh	G-F	£3542
78	4/00 MRas	3m1f	D Ch	G-F	£4371
			Total win prize-money £10518

Going:	Sf: 0-0 GS: 0-2 Gd: 1-4 GF: - Fm: 0-4
Distance:	2m/2m3: 0-0 2m4-2m7: 0-3 3m+: 1-7
Track:	LH: 1-8 RH: 0-2 Tight: 1-3 Gall: 0-0
Aids:	Bl: 0-1 Vi: 0-0 Tstrap: 0-0 Ckp: 0-0
Best Rating:	97 5/02 Weth 3m1f gd-sft Ch

Modest and inconsistent chaser, stays three miles, best on fast ground.

Just Superb

107   **100**

5-y-o ch g Superlative-Just Greenwich (Chilibang)
P A Pritchard D R Pritchard

Placings:0P0-12051202   (4890)
2003/04: 16¹GS, 16²GS, 17⁰GS, 16⁵S, 16¹G, 16²G, 16⁰G, 19²GF,

	Starts	1st	2nd	3rd	Win & Pl
Hurdles	8	2	3	0	11133
Career Total	11	2	3	0	11133
100	3/04 Wwck	2m	F(0-100)HHdl	GD	£3090
92	12/03 Wwck	2m	F(0-100)HHdl	G-S	£2436
			Total win prize-money £5527

Going:	Sf: 0-1 GS: 1-3 Gd: 1-3 GF: - Fm: 0-1
Distance:	2m/2m3: 2-8 2m4-2m7: 0-0 3m+: 0-0
Track:	LH: 2-7 RH: 0-1 Tight: 0-2 Gall: 0-1
Aids:	Bl: 0-0 Vi: 0-0 Tstrap: 0-0 Ckp: 0-0
Best Rating:	100 4/04 Strf 2m3f gd-fm Hdl

Plating-class hurdler; showed marked improvement when

---

causing 100/1 shock from 8lb out of the handicap in Class F 2m Warwick handicap hurdle in December 2003; good second at the same venue off 13lb higher mark next time; acts on soft ground.

Just The Jobe

(99h)   (110h)

6-y-o gr g Roselier (FR)-Radical Lady (Radical)
R C Guest N B Mason

Placings:264-10F326F100   (4729)
2003/04: 16¹S, 16⁹GS, 21FGS, 19³G, 19²S, 23⁶S, 22FG, 22¹GF, 24⁰GS, 20⁰G,

	Starts	1st	2nd	3rd	Win & Pl
Hurdles	10	2	1	1	8241
Career Total	13	2	2	1	8780
110	3/04 Ayr	2m6f	E(0-110)HHdl	G-F	£3692
101	12/03 Hexm	2m110y	E Hdl	SFT	£1876
			Total win prize-money £5568

Going:	Sf: 1-3 GS: 0-3 Gd: 0-3 GF: - Fm: 1-1
Distance:	2m/2m3: 1-2 2m4-2m7: 1-7 3m+: 0-1
Track:	LH: 2-8 RH: 0-1 Tight: 0-2 Gall: 0-0
Aids:	Bl: 0-0 Vi: 0-0 Tstrap: 0-0 Ckp: 1-4
Best Rating:	110 3/04 Ayr 2m6f gd-fm Hdl

Moderate hurdler; won a novices' event at Hexham in December and handicap over two miles and six at Ayr in March; stays three miles.; acts on any ground.

Just Whiskey (IRE)

11-y-o b g Satco (FR)-Illinois Belle (Le Bavard (FR))
N A Twiston-Davies Mrs R Vaughan

Placings:0/3/0P/44/21/PP-P   (0133)
2003/04: 24FGF,

	Starts	1st	2nd	3rd	Win & Pl
Chases	1	0	0	0	
Career Total	11	1	1	1	5834
100	10/01 Plum	3m2f	D(0-110)HCh	SFT	£4095
			Total win prize-money £4095

Going:	Sf: 0-0 GS: 0-0 Gd: 0-0 GF: - Fm: 0-1
Distance:	2m/2m3: 0-0 2m4-2m7: 0-0 3m+: 0-1
Track:	LH: 0-0 RH: 0-1 Tight: 0-0 Gall: 0-1
Aids:	Bl: 0-0 Vi: 0-0 Tstrap: 0-0 Ckp: 0-0
Best Rating:	115 4/99 Ayr 2m soft NHF

Justafancy

70   **26**

6-y-o b g Green Desert (USA)-Justsayno (USA) (Dr Blum (USA))
Miss J Feilden Miss J Feilden

Placings:0   (0156)
2003/04: 16⁰GF,

	Starts	1st	2nd	3rd	Win & Pl
Hurdles	1	0	0	0	
Career Total	1	0	0	0	

Going:	Sf: 0-0 GS: 0-0 Gd: 0-0 GF: - Fm: 0-1
Distance:	2m/2m3: 0-1 2m4-2m7: 0-0 3m+: 0-0
Track:	LH: 0-1 RH: 0-0 Tight: 0-1 Gall: 0-0
Aids:	Bl: 0-0 Vi: 0-0 Tstrap: 0-0 Ckp: 0-0
Best Rating:	26 5/03 Fknm 2m gd-fm Hdl

Justin Mac (IRE)

85   **77**

13-y-o br g Satco (FR)-Quantas (Roan Rocket)
Mrs H Dalton Mrs Caroline Shaw

Placings:121143/P14350P/512F4P0/**1RP/6U1P/**415205-R0P   (0759)
2003/04: 26RG, 22ºG, 23PG,

	Starts	1st	2nd	3rd	Win & Pl
Chases	3	0	0		
Career Total	36	8	3	2	34321
110 5/02	NAbb	2m5f110yB HCh		SFT	£10067
105 3/02	Leic	2m	H Ch	SFT	£2198
100 2/01	Fknm	2m5f110yH Ch		SFT	£2256
118 11/99	Carl	2m1f	F(0-110)HHdl	SFT	£5281
132 11/98	Kels	2m110y	D(0-125)HHdl	SFT	£2731
114 12/97	Weth	2m	D Hdl	SFT	£3323
113 11/97	Aint	2m110y	H NHF	G-S	£1987
113 10/97	Sedg	2m1f	H NHF	G-F	£1213

Total win prize-money £29059

Going:	Sf: 0-0 GS: 0-0 Gd: 0-3 GF: - Fm: 0-0
Distance:	2m/2m3: 0-0 2m4-2m7: 0-1 3m+: 0-2
Track:	LH: 0-2 RH: 0-1 Tight: 0-1 Gall: 0-1
Aids:	Bl: 0-0 Vi: 0-0 Tstrap: 0-0 Ckp: 0-0
Best Rating:	132 11/98 Kels 2m110y soft Hdl

Plating-class chaser; appears to go on any ground; won the 21 furlong handicap hunter chase on soft ground at Newton Abbot May 2002; does not quite get three miles.

Justino

91   **82**

6-y-o b g Bustino-Jupiter's Message (Jupiter Island)
G B Balding Argent Racing

Placings:00006   (4676)
2003/04: 19ºGS, 18ºHY, 16ºGS, 19ºG, 22ºG,

	Starts	1st	2nd	3rd	Win & Pl
Hurdles	5	0	0	0	0
Career Total	5	0	0	0	0

Going:	Sf: 0-1 GS: 0-2 Gd: 0-2 GF: - Fm: 0-0
Distance:	2m/2m3: 0-3 2m4-2m7: 0-2 3m+: 0-0
Track:	LH: 0-2 RH: 0-3 Tight: 0-1 Gall: 0-0
Aids:	Bl: 0-0 Vi: 0-0 Tstrap: 0-0 Ckp: 0-0
Best Rating:	82 2/04 Sand 2m110y gd-sft Hdl

Justjim

12-y-o b g Derring Rose-Crystal Run Vii (Damsire Unregistered)
Mrs C Gethin E T Clarke

Placings:000/P0650/6/1411/62012B6PF2P/23P4PP/4PPP-P556   (4717)
2003/04: 25PGS, 20ºG, 24ºG, 24ºG,

	Starts	1st	2nd	3rd	Win & Pl
Chases	4	0	0	0	
Career Total	38	4	4	1	23123
110 8/00	Bang	3m110y	D(0-125)HCh	GD	£4914
106 8/99	Worc	2m7f110yE(0-105)HCh		SFT	£2966
85 8/99	Bang	2m4f110yF(0-100)HCh		GD	£4338
87 7/99	Worc	2m	F(0-100)HCh	G-F	£2672

Total win prize-money £14891

Going:	Sf: 0-0 GS: 0-1 Gd: 0-3 GF: - Fm: 0-0
Distance:	2m/2m3: 0-0 2m4-2m7: 0-1 3m+: 0-3
Track:	LH: 0-1 RH: 0-3 Tight: 0-3 Gall: 0-0
Aids:	Bl: 0-0 Vi: 0-0 Tstrap: 0-0 Ckp: 0-1
Best Rating:	113 11/01 Newb 2m4f good Ch

Justupyourstreet (IRE)

105   **119**

8-y-o b g Dolphin Street (FR)-Sure Flyer (IRE) (Sure Blade (USA))
Ms Liz Harrison David Alan Harrison

Placings:224F41/P1650   (1897)
2003/04: 20PGF, 16¹G, 16RG, 16ºG, 17ºGS,

	Starts	1st	2nd	3rd	Win & Pl
Hurdles	5	1	0	0	5413
Career Total	11	2	2	0	10730
119 6/03	Prth	2m110y	D(0-115)HHdl	GD	£4737
110 3/02	Carl	2m1f	E Hdl	G-S	£3094

Total win prize-money £7831

Going:	Sf: 0-0 GS: 0-1 Gd: 1-3 GF: - Fm: 0-1
Distance:	2m/2m3: 1-4 2m4-2m7: 0-1 3m+: 0-0
Track:	LH: 0-0 RH: 1-5 Tight: 0-0 Gall: 0-0
Aids:	Bl: 0-0 Vi: 0-0 Tstrap: 0-0 Ckp: 0-0
Best Rating:	119 6/03 Prth 2m110y good Hdl

Modest hurdler; best at two miles, but stays further; effective with cut in the ground.

Kabeer

78f   **95f**

6-y-o ch g Unfuwain (USA)-Ta Rib (USA) (Mr Prospector (USA))
P S McEntee Placida Racing

Placings:2-0   (4787)
2003/04: 16ºG,

	Starts	1st	2nd	3rd	Win & Pl
NH Flat	1	0	0	0	
Career Total	2	0	1	0	552

Going:	Sf: 0-0 GS: 0-0 Gd: 0-1 GF: - Fm: 0-0
Distance:	2m/2m3: 0-1 2m4-2m7: 0-0 3m+: 0-0
Track:	LH: 0-0 RH: 0-1 Tight: 0-0 Gall: 0-1
Aids:	Bl: 0-0 Vi: 0-0 Tstrap: 0-0 Ckp: 0-0
Best Rating:	95 4/03 Hntg 2m110y gd-fm NHF

Classically-bred but sold cheaply; runner-up behind clear cut winner in weak bumper on debut at Huntingdon in April; well beaten subsequently.

Kadam (IRE)

88   **68**

4-y-o b g Night Shift (USA)-Kadassa (IRE) (Shardari)
P F Nicholls (A De Royer-Dupre 3/5) Notalottery

Placings:5   (4489)
2003/04: 16ºG,

	Starts	1st	2nd	3rd	Win & Pl
Hurdles	1	0	0	0	0
Career Total	1	0	0	0	0

Going:	Sf: 0-0 GS: 0-0 Gd: 0-1 GF: - Fm: 0-0
Distance:	2m/2m3: 0-1 2m4-2m7: 0-0 3m+: 0-0
Track:	LH: 0-1 RH: 0-0 Tight: 0-0 Gall: 0-0
Aids:	Bl: 0-0 Vi: 0-0 Tstrap: 0-1 Ckp: 0-0
Best Rating:	68 3/04 Strf 2m110y good Hdl

Kadara (IRE)

108   **131**

5-y-o b m Slip Anchor-Kadassa (IRE) (Shardari)
R H Alner Mrs Norma Kelly

Placings:16P-02120500   (4963)
2003/04: 20ºGS, 24²G, 16¹GS, 20ºHY, 23ºS, 24ºG, 20ºGS, 20ºG,

	Starts	1st	2nd	3rd	Win & Pl
Hurdles	8	1	2	0	33571
Career Total	11	2	2	0	40633
125 1/04	Sand	2m110y	B HHdl	G-S	£18072
111 12/02	Kemp	2m	C Hdl	SFT	£6612

Total win prize-money £24685

Going:	Sf: 0-2 GS: 1-3 Gd: 0-3 GF: - Fm: 0-0
Distance:	2m/2m3: 1-1 2m4-2m7: 1-1 3m+: 0-3
Track:	LH: 0-2 RH: 1-6 Tight: 0-0 Gall: 0-0
Aids:	Bl: 0-0 Vi: 0-0 Tstrap: 0-0 Ckp: 0-0
Best Rating:	131 2/04 Kemp 3m110y good Hdl

Useful hurdler; winner of a valuable mares-only race at Sandown in January 2004; stays three miles but fully effective at shorter; suited by testing conditions.

Kadarann (IRE)

114   **166**

7-y-o b g Bigstone (IRE)-Kadassa (IRE) (Shardari)
P F Nicholls Notalottery

Placings:121P/1101211/U2110313-3214P   (4196)
2003/04: 17ºG, 16²GF, 16¹G, 17⁴G, 20ºG,

	Starts	1st	2nd	3rd	Win & Pl
Chases	5	1	1	1	47511
Career Total	24	11	4	3	180194
166 12/03	Weth	2m	A Ch	GD	£33500
145 4/03	Ayr	2m4f	B HCh	GD	£13491
166 2/03	Newb	2m1f	A Ch	GD	£31000
158 12/02	Chel	2m110y	B(0-145)HCh	GD	£14101
147 4/02	Prth	2m	C Ch	GD	£7124
145 4/02	Ayr	2m	B HCh	GD	£13403
145 3/02	Winc	2m	D Ch	SFT	£4134
136 2/02	Winc	2m	C Ch	G-S	£6288
132 11/01	Wwck	2m110y	C Ch	GD	£6753
128 12/00	Fknm	2m	E Hdl	G-S	£2257
120 10/00	Chel	2m	C Hdl	GD	£5486

Total win prize-money £137541

Going:	Sf: 0-0 GS: 0-0 Gd: 1-4 GF: - Fm: 0-1
Distance:	2m/2m3: 1-4 2m4-2m7: 0-1 3m+: 0-0
Track:	LH: 1-4 RH: 0-1 Tight: 0-0 Gall: 0-3
Aids:	Bl: 0-0 Vi: 0-0 Tstrap: 0-0 Ckp: 0-0
Best Rating:	166 12/03 Weth 2m good Ch

High-class chaser; landed the Game Spirit Chase and Castleford Chase in 2003; has sometimes looked reluctant to start; travels well; best form over two miles and ideally suited by a sound surface; seems to like a left-handed flat track.

Kadlass (FR)

105   **96**

9-y-o b g Kadounor (FR)-Brave Lass (Ridan)
Mrs D A Hamer J L Flint

Placings:6525/21-20   (0150)
2003/04: 17²GS, 16ºGF,

	Starts	1st	2nd	3rd	Win & Pl
Hurdles	2	0	1	0	712
Career Total	8	1	3	0	4769
89 4/03	Hrfd	2m1f	G Hdl	G-F	£2625

Total win prize-money £2625

Going:	Sf: 0-0 GS: 0-1 Gd: 0-0 GF: - Fm: 0-1
Distance:	2m/2m3: 0-2 2m4-2m7: 0-0 3m+: 0-0
Track:	LH: 0-1 RH: 0-1 Tight: 0-0 Gall: 0-0
Aids:	Bl: 0-0 Vi: 0-0 Tstrap: 0-0 Ckp: 0-0
Best Rating:	105 12/99 Kemp 2m soft Hdl

Plating-class hurdler; ex-pointer; won extended two mile seller at Hereford on good to firm ground April 2003; acts in soft ground.

Kadouko (FR)

99   102

11-y-o b g Cadoudal (FR)-Perle Bleue (FR) (Iron Duke (FR))
J R Cornwall J R Cornwall

Placings:33/33160/26F25/11545/365453P/531-44P5020 (4961)
2003/04: 16⁴GS, 20⁴S, 25⁵S, 16⁵HY, 16⁰GS, 20²GS, 20⁰GS,

	Starts	1st	2nd	3rd	Win & Pl
Chases	7	0	1	0	1459
Career Total	34	4	3	7	24632
102	3/03	Carl		E(0-105)HCh	SFT	£4556
118	12/00	Thur	2m2f	(0-109)HCh	HVY	£5520
114	11/00	Thur	2m2f	Ch	HVY	£4140
104	1/99	Fair	2m2f	Hdl	HVY	£3069
				Total win prize-money £17286		

Going: Sf: 0-3 GS: 0-4 Gd: 0-0 GF: - Fm: 0-0
Distance: 2m/2m3: 0-3 2m4-2m7: 0-3 3m+: 0-1
Track: LH: 0-2 RH: 0-5 Tight: 0-2 Gall: 0-2
Aids: Bl: 0-0 Vi: 0-0 Tstrap: 0-0 Ckp: 0-0
Best Rating: 118 12/00 Thur 2m2f heavy Ch

Moderate chaser; suited by heavy ground and is possibly best going right-handed.

Kadoun (FR)

102   (0c)106+

5-y-o gr g Sleeping Car (FR)-Dea De Chalamont (FR) (Royal Charter (FR))
H D Daly (H Billot 14/6) Million In Mind Partnership

Placings:FF6002364P101-10331 (4868)
2003/04: 17¹HO, 17¹VS, 17⁰HY, 19³G, 16³G, 20¹GS,

	Starts	1st	2nd	3rd	Win & Pl
Hurdles	4	1	0	2	5637
Chases	2	2	0	0	33351
Career Total	18	4	1	3	51291
106	4/04	Bang	2m4f	E Hdl	G-S	£3753
	6/03	Autl	2m1f110y	HCh	VS	£20260
	4/03	Engh	2m1f	HCh	HLD	£13091
	11/02	Engh	2m1f	Ch	HVY	£6184
				Total win prize-money £43289		

Going: Sf: 0-1 GS: 1-1 Gd: 0-2 GF: - Fm: 0-0
Distance: 2m/2m3: 2-4 2m4-2m7: 1-2 3m+: 0-0
Track: LH: 1-3 RH: 0-1 Tight: 1-1 Gall: 0-1
Aids: Bl: 0-0 Vi: 0-0 Tstrap: 1-4 Ckp: 0-0
Best Rating: 108 3/04 Newb 2m110y good Hdl

Winner over fences in France; well beaten in this country prior to making all in Bangor novices' hurdle; stays 2m 4f; likes soft ground.

Kadoun (IRE)

110(108h)   (143h)148

7-y-o b h Doyoun-Kumta (IRE) (Priolo (USA))
M J P O'Brien John P McManus

Placings:213/33322152134/346452111-F21010 (4805a)
2003/04: 25⁵G, 22²Y, 16¹GY, 20⁰GS, 20¹Y, 29⁰Y,

	Starts	1st	2nd	3rd	Win & Pl
Hurdles	1	1	0	0	9169
Chases	5	1	1	0	32256
Career Total	29	8	6	6	150398
143	2/04	Fair	2m4f	(0-140)HHdl	YLD	£9169
148	11/03	Naas	2m	Ch	G-Y	£13506
133	4/03	Cork	3m	Ch	G-F	£16883
148	3/03	Leop	2m5f	Ch	HVY	£10974

118	2/03	Limk	2m6f	Ch	SFT	£8064
141	3/02	Leop	2m	HHdl	HVY	£15950
126	12/01	Limk	2m4f	Hdl	SFT	£7862
126	1/01	DRoy	2m	Hdl	YLD	£13104
				Total win prize-money £95516		

Going: Sf: 0-0 GS: 0-1 Gd: 0-1 GF: - Fm: 0-0
Distance: 2m/2m3: 1-1 2m4-2m7: 1-3 3m+: 0-2
Track: LH: 1-2 RH: 1-4 Tight: 0-0 Gall: 0-1
Aids: Bl: 0-1 Vi: 0-1 Tstrap: 0-0 Ckp: 0-1
Best Rating: 148 11/03 Naas 2m gd-yld Ch

Smart Irish-trained chaser/very useful hurdler; effective from two to three miles; has been tried in blinkers, a visor and cheekpieces.

Kadoun (FR)

102   106+

5-y-o gr g Sleeping Car (FR)-Dea De Chalamont (FR) (Royal Charter (FR))
H D Daly (H Billot 14/6) Million In Mind Partnership

Placings:FF6002364P101-10331 (4868)
2003/04: 17¹HO, 17¹VS, 17⁰HY, 19³G, 16³G, 20¹GS,

	Starts	1st	2nd	3rd	Win & Pl
Hurdles	4	1	0	2	5637
Chases	2	2	0	0	33351
Career Total	18	4	1	3	51291
106	4/04	Bang	2m4f	E Hdl	G-S	£3753
	6/03	Autl	2m1f110y	HCh	VS	£20260
	4/03	Engh	2m1f	HCh	HLD	£13091
	11/02	Engh	2m1f	Ch	HVY	£6184
				Total win prize-money £43289		

Going: Sf: 0-1 GS: 1-1 Gd: 0-2 GF: - Fm: 0-0
Distance: 2m/2m3: 2-4 2m4-2m7: 1-2 3m+: 0-0
Track: LH: 1-3 RH: 0-1 Tight: 1-1 Gall: 0-1
Aids: Bl: 0-0 Vi: 0-0 Tstrap: 1-4 Ckp: 0-0
Best Rating: 108 3/04 Newb 2m110y good Hdl

Winner over fences in France; well beaten in this country prior to making all in Bangor novices' hurdle; stays 2m 4f; likes soft ground.

Kadount (FR)

105   126

6-y-o b g Our Account (USA)-Une De Lann (FR) (Spoleto)
A King (X-L Le Stang 11/9) Elite Racing Club

Placings:1110P (4326)
2003/04: 16¹GS, 16¹S, 16¹GS, 16⁰G, 16⁰PS,

	Starts	1st	2nd	3rd	Win & Pl
Hurdles	5	3	0	0	18015
Career Total	5	3	0	0	18015
134	12/03	Leic	2m	C(0-130)HHdl	G-S	£11206
114	12/03	Plum	2m	E Hdl	SFT	£2999
109	11/03	Hayd	2m	D Hdl	G-S	£3809
				Total win prize-money £18015		

Going: Sf: 1-2 GS: 2-2 Gd: 0-1 GF: - Fm: 0-0
Distance: 2m/2m3: 3-5 2m4-2m7: 0-0 3m+: 0-0
Track: LH: 2-2 RH: 1-3 Tight: 1-1 Gall: 0-0
Aids: Bl: 0-0 Vi: 0-0 Tstrap: 0-0 Ckp: 0-0
Best Rating: 134 12/03 Leic 2m gd-sft Hdl

Useful novice hurdler; slightly fortunate to win on his hurdles debut, but went on to complete a hat-trick; disappointed in the Lanzarote Hurdle at Kempton on unsuitably good ground; should stay two miles four; acts on soft ground.

Kafri D'Airy (FR)

                                 78

6-y-o b m Sheyrann-Afrika D'Airy (FR) (Marasali)

R T Phillips Mrs Claire Smith

Placings:322P/466-F (4793)
2003/04: 16⁶G,

	Starts	1st	2nd	3rd	Win & Pl
Hurdles	1	0	0	0	
Career Total	8	0	2	1	12060

Going: Sf: 0-0 GS: 0-0 Gd: 0-1 GF: - Fm: 0-0
Distance: 2m/2m3: 0-1 2m4-2m7: 0-0 3m+: 0-0
Track: LH: 0-1 RH: 0-0 Tight: 0-1 Gall: 0-0
Aids: Bl: 0-0 Vi: 0-0 Tstrap: 0-0 Ckp: 0-0
Best Rating: 81 3/03 Font 2m4f soft Hdl

Kaid (IRE)

94(101h)   (99 h)90

9-y-o b g Alzao (USA)-Very Charming (USA) (Vaguely Noble)
R Lee Richard Lee

Placings:6/452/021264/004526P0/3022P160-5346P3 (4491)
2003/04: 20⁵S, 20³GF, 20⁴G, 16⁶GS, 20⁰GF, 21³GS,

	Starts	1st	2nd	3rd	Win & Pl
Hurdles	1	0	0	0	
Chases	5	0	0	2	1591
Career Total	32	2	6	3	13282
99	11/02	Hrfd	2m1f	G(0-95)HHdl	SFT	£2044
106	11/00	Hrfd	2m1f	E(0-105)HHdl	SFT	£2607
				Total win prize-money £4652		

Going: Sf: 0-1 GS: 0-2 Gd: 0-1 GF: - Fm: 0-0
Distance: 2m/2m3: 0-1 2m4-2m7: 0-5 3m+: 0-0
Track: LH: 0-4 RH: 0-2 Tight: 0-4 Gall: 0-0
Aids: Bl: 0-1 Vi: 0-0 Tstrap: 0-0 Ckp: 0-0
Best Rating: 112 11/00 Weth 2m heavy Hdl

Plating-class hurdler/chaser; acts on soft and fast ground; best at 2m 4f.

Kaikovra (IRE)

107   99

8-y-o ch g Toulon-Drefflane Supreme (Rusticaro (FR))
M F Harris (Noel T Chance 2/5) The Eight Bells Inn Partnership

Placings:02134/P6265F6/403222-04504253210 (1832)
2003/04: 16⁰GS, 16⁴G, 19⁵G, 16⁰GF, 17⁴GS, 16²GF, 17⁵G, 16³GF, 16²GF, 19¹GF, 16⁰GF,

	Starts	1st	2nd	3rd	Win & Pl
Hurdles	11	1	2	1	5238
Career Total	29	2	7	3	15928
99	10/03	Hrfd	2m3f110yE Hdl		G-F	£2380
103	10/00	Fknm	2m	N NHF	GD	£1463
				Total win prize-money £3843		

Going: Sf: 0-0 GS: 0-2 Gd: 0-3 GF: - Fm: 1-6
Distance: 2m/2m3: 0-9 2m4-2m7: 1-2 3m+: 0-0
Track: LH: 0-9 RH: 1-2 Tight: 0-6 Gall: 0-0
Aids: Bl: 0-0 Vi: 0-0 Tstrap: 0-0 Ckp: 0-0
Best Rating: 105 11/01 Chel 2m110y good Hdl

Plating-class hurdler; free-running sort; moderate hurdler; broke duck at Hereford in October 2003; suited by fast ground; stays 2m 3f.

Kaiser (IRE)

4-y-o b g Barathea (IRE)-Emerald Waters (King's Lake (USA))
R T Phillips (J R Fanshawe 2/7) Paul Green

Placings:P0   (3465)
2003/04: 16PGS, 16OS,

	Starts	1st	2nd	3rd	Win & Pl
Hurdles	2	0	0	0	
Career Total	2	0	0	0	

Going:	Sf: 0-1 GS: 0-1 Gd: 0-0 GF: - Fm: 0-0
Distance:	2m/2m3: 0-2 2m4-2m7: 0-0 3m+: 0-0
Track:	LH: 0-2 RH: 0-0 Tight: 0-1 Gall: 0-0
Aids:	Bl: 0-0 Vi: 0-1 Tstrap: 0-0 Ckp: 0-0

Kaki Crazy (FR)

109(109h)   (128h)130

9-y-o b g Passing Sale (FR)-Radiante Rose (FR) (Akarad (FR))
E Retter (J D Frost 22/6) Edward Retter

Placings:15P311F1034P/V515526FP104/64P54F0/412PU
4503/P5-112P1   (1230)
2003/04: 20¹G, 21¹GF, 24²G, 20PGF, 26¹GF,

	Starts	1st	2nd	3rd	Win & Pl
Hurdles	2	2	0	0	6019
Chases	3	1	1	0	12389
Career Total	47	10	3	3	103805
128 8/03	Sthl	3m2f	F Hdl	G-F	£3380
130 5/03	NAbb	2m5f110yD(0-120)HCh	G-F	£5460
128 5/03	Weth	2m4f110yF Hdl	GD	£2639
127 5/01	Bang	3m6f	D(0-125)HCh	GD	£5551
2/00	Autl	2m5f	HCh	HVY	£14409
7/99	Claf	2m1f	HCh	HVY	£5920
12/98	Autl	2m2f	Hdl	HVY	£6566
11/98	Autl	2m2f	Hdl	HVY	£6566
10/98	Autl	2m2f	Hdl	HLD	£6566
8/98	Claf	2m	Hdl	VS	£4040
				Total win prize-money £61097	

Going:	Sf: 0-0 GS: 0-0 Gd: 0-0 GF: 1-2 Fm: 2-3
Distance:	2m/2m3: 0-2 2m4-2m7: 2-3 3m+: 1-2
Track:	LH: 3-3 RH: 0-2 Tight: 1-2 Gall: 0-0
Aids:	Bl: 3-5 Vi: 0-0 Tstrap: 0-0 Ckp: 0-0
Best Rating:	136 6/01 Strf 3m4f gd-fm Ch

Useful ex-French chaser;is one of the few to have improved since leaving Martin Pipe; ran away with a claiming hurdle at Wetherby in May 2003; followed up with easy win in 2m 5f chase at Newton Abbot next time; seems best on good ground or faster; usually wears a visor or blinkers; suited by forcing tactics.

Kalambari (IRE)

5-y-o b g Kahyasi-Kalamba (IRE) (Green Dancer (USA))
J Joseph Jack Joseph

Placings:UUPU   (4756)
2003/04: 24UG, 16UG, 16PGS, 19US,

	Starts	1st	2nd	3rd	Win & Pl
Hurdles	4	0	0	0	
Career Total	4	0	0	0	

Going:	Sf: 0-1 GS: 0-1 Gd: 0-2 GF: - Fm: 0-0
Distance:	2m/2m3: 0-2 2m4-2m7: 0-1 3m+: 0-1
Track:	LH: 0-1 RH: 0-2 Tight: 0-1 Gall: 0-0
Aids:	Bl: 0-1 Vi: 0-1 Tstrap: 0-0 Ckp: 0-0

Kalasara (IRE)

97   90

6-y-o b g Darshaan-Kumta (IRE) (Priolo (USA))

C J Mann Mrs Susan Roy

Placings:1/0   (2576)
2003/04: 16OGS,

	Starts	1st	2nd	3rd	Win & Pl
Hurdles	1	0	0	0	
Career Total	2	1	0	0	2153
93 4/02	Wwck	2m	H NHF	G-F	£2152
				Total win prize-money £2153	

Going:	Sf: 0-0 GS: 0-1 Gd: 0-0 GF: - Fm: 0-0
Distance:	2m/2m3: 0-1 2m4-2m7: 0-0 3m+: 0-0
Track:	LH: 0-0 RH: 0-1 Tight: 0-0 Gall: 0-0
Aids:	Bl: 0-0 Vi: 0-0 Tstrap: 0-0 Ckp: 0-0
Best Rating:	93 4/02 Wwck 2m gd-fm NHF

Kalca Mome (FR)

109(109h)   (130+h)139

6-y-o b g En Calcat (FR)-Belle Mome (FR) (Grand Tresor (FR))
P J Hobbs Miss I D Du Pre

Placings:210151-12141310   (4645)
2003/04: 16¹G, 16²GS, 16¹GS, 20⁴G, 16¹HY, 16³G, 16¹GS, 16⁰G,

	Starts	1st	2nd	3rd	Win & Pl
Chases	8	4	1	1	29608
Career Total	14	7	2	1	52441
131 3/04	Sand	2m	C Ch	G-S	£10008
139 1/04	Hayd	2m	C Ch	HVY	£10003
136 12/03	Hrfd	2m	E Ch	G-S	£2587
118 11/03	NAbb	2m110y	E Ch	GD	£2990
130 3/03	Winc	2m	D(0-125)HHdl	SFT	£12557
117 1/03	Tntn	2m1f	E Hdl	SFT	£4530
100 11/02	Hayd	2m	D Hdl	GD	£4381
				Total win prize-money £47058	

Going:	Sf: 1-1 GS: 2-3 Gd: 1-4 GF: - Fm: 0-0
Distance:	2m/2m3: 4-7 2m4-2m7: 0-1 3m+: 0-0
Track:	LH: 2-5 RH: 2-3 Tight: 1-2 Gall: 0-0
Aids:	Bl: 0-0 Vi: 0-0 Tstrap: 0-0 Ckp: 0-0
Best Rating:	139 1/04 Hayd 2m heavy Ch

Very useful and progressive chaser; has won four times this season; does not get home over 2m4f; acts on any ground.

Kali Des Obeaux (FR)

102   107

6-y-o b m Panoramic-Alpaga (FR) (Le Pontet (FR))
Mrs L C Taylor Miss M Talbot

Placings:1131232002-PP435   (4917)
2003/04: 25PGS, 21PS, 22⁴G, 29³GS, 20⁵GS,

	Starts	1st	2nd	3rd	Win & Pl
Hurdles	3	0	0	1	1078
Chases	2	0	0	0	
Career Total	15	3	3	3	27355
6/02	Autl	2m4f110y	Ch	VS	£13252
5/02	Csma	2m1f	Ch	GD	£2650
5/02	Roya	2m2f	Ch	GD	£2945
				Total win prize-money £18847	

Going:	Sf: 0-1 GS: 0-3 Gd: 0-1 GF: - Fm: 0-0
Distance:	2m/2m3: 0-0 2m4-2m7: 0-4 3m+: 0-1
Track:	LH: 0-3 RH: 0-2 Tight: 0-2 Gall: 0-0
Aids:	Bl: 0-0 Vi: 0-0 Tstrap: 0-0 Ckp: 0-0
Best Rating:	108 11/02 Wwck 2m gd-sft Hdl

Moderate chaser/hurdler; winner three times over fences in France; probably stays three miles.

Kalic D'Alm (FR)

64   4

6-y-o b g Passing Sale (FR)-Bekaa II (FR) (Djarvis (FR))
Miss Suzy Smith Robin Smith

Placings:5P-P0   (2736)
2003/04: 21PS, 19OS,

	Starts	1st	2nd	3rd	Win & Pl
Hurdles	2	0	0	0	
Career Total	4	0	0	0	0

Going:	Sf: 0-2 GS: 0-0 Gd: 0-0 GF: - Fm: 0-0
Distance:	2m/2m3: 0-0 2m4-2m7: 0-2 3m+: 0-0
Track:	LH: 0-2 RH: 0-0 Tight: 0-2 Gall: 0-0
Aids:	Bl: 0-1 Vi: 0-0 Tstrap: 0-0 Ckp: 0-0
Best Rating:	79 11/02 Folk 2m1f110y soft NHF

Kalin De Thaix (FR)

6-y-o ch g Agent Bleu (FR)-Une Amie (FR) (Prove It Baby (USA))
R T Phillips Million In Mind Partnership

Placings:P   (3523)
2003/04: 16PS,

	Starts	1st	2nd	3rd	Win & Pl
Hurdles	1	0	0	0	
Career Total	1	0	0	0	

Going:	Sf: 0-1 GS: 0-0 Gd: 0-0 GF: - Fm: 0-0
Distance:	2m/2m3: 0-1 2m4-2m7: 0-0 3m+: 0-0
Track:	LH: 0-1 RH: 0-0 Tight: 0-0 Gall: 0-0
Aids:	Bl: 0-0 Vi: 0-0 Tstrap: 0-0 Ckp: 0-0

Kalisko (FR)

106   (14h)72+

14-y-o b g Cadoudal (FR)-Mista (FR) (Misti Iv)
Miss L V Davis Miss Louise Davis

Placings:5U5000/05/1/P3/045/1PP/0U35/30P   (2841)
2003/04: 24³GS, 24⁰GS, 20PGS,

	Starts	1st	2nd	3rd	Win & Pl
Chases	3	0	0	1	431
Career Total	24	2	0	3	8437
70 11/00	Uttx	2m4f	E(0-105)HCh	HVY	£4485
95 1/97	Muss	2m4f	E(0-100)HHdl	G-F	£2637
				Total win prize-money £7122	

Going:	Sf: 0-0 GS: 0-3 Gd: 0-0 GF: - Fm: 0-0
Distance:	2m/2m3: 0-0 2m4-2m7: 0-1 3m+: 0-2
Track:	LH: 0-3 RH: 0-0 Tight: 0-0 Gall: 0-0
Aids:	Bl: 0-0 Vi: 0-0 Tstrap: 0-0 Ckp: 0-0
Best Rating:	95 1/97 Muss 2m4f gd-fm Hdl

Kalko Du Charmil (FR)

7-y-o b g Kadalko (FR)-Licada (FR) (A Tempo (FR))
Ian Williams (Mrs M Reveley 9/6) Mr And Mrs J D Cotton

Placings:00F6/U6F-6FP   (0854)
2003/04: 20⁶GS, 20⁰F, 22PGF,

	Starts	1st	2nd	3rd	Win & Pl
Hurdles	1	0	0	0	0
Chases	2	0	0	0	0
Career Total	10	0	0	0	0

Going: Sf: 0-0 GS: 0-1 Gd: 0-1 GF: - Fm: 0-1
Distance: 2m/2m3: 0-0 2m4-2m7: 0-3 3m+: 0-0
Track: LH: 0-1 RH: 0-0 Tight: 0-1 Gall: 0-0
Aids: Bl: 0-0 Vi: 0-0 Tstrap: 0-0 Ckp: 0-0
Best Rating: 96 10/01 Chel 2m110y good NHF

Kallassor (FR)

(0c)77
6-y-o b g Assessor (IRE)-Balladine (FR) (Rivelago (FR))
P C Ritchens Alan Kidd And Mr Andrew Johnson

Placings:05/0U34P-PP (0479)
2003/04: 21^{P}GF, 21^{P}GF,

	Starts	1st	2nd	3rd	Win & Pl
Hurdles	1	0	0	0	0
Chases	1	0	0	0	0
Career Total	**9**	**0**	**0**	**1**	**423**

Going: Sf: 0-0 GS: 0-0 Gd: 0-0 GF: - Fm: 0-2
Distance: 2m/2m3: 0-0 2m4-2m7: 0-2 3m+: 0-0
Track: LH: 0-0 RH: 0-2 Tight: 0-0 Gall: 0-1
Aids: Bl: 0-1 Vi: 0-0 Tstrap: 0-0 Ckp: 0-0
Best Rating: 77 6/02 NAbb 2m6f good Hdl

Kalou (GER)

98 78
6-y-o br g Law Society (USA)-Kompetenz (IRE) (Be My Guest (USA))
B J Curley P Byrne

Placings:600-46 (3210)
2003/04: 16^{4}GS, 16^{6}GS,

	Starts	1st	2nd	3rd	Win & Pl
Hurdles	2	0	0	0	0
Career Total	**5**	**0**	**0**	**0**	**0**

Going: Sf: 0-0 GS: 0-2 Gd: 0-0 GF: - Fm: 0-0
Distance: 2m/2m3: 0-2 2m4-2m7: 0-0 3m+: 0-0
Track: LH: 0-2 RH: 0-0 Tight: 0-0 Gall: 0-0
Aids: Bl: 0-0 Vi: 0-0 Tstrap: 0-0 Ckp: 0-0
Best Rating: 78 1/03 Hntg 2m110y soft Hdl

Flat winner in Germany; very moderate form over hurdles here so far.

Kaluana Court

82
8-y-o b m Batshoof-Fairfields Cone (Celtic Cone)
R J Price Derek & Cheryl Holder

Placings:P0P/F (0744)
2003/04: 22^{F}G,

	Starts	1st	2nd	3rd	Win & Pl
Hurdles	1	0	0	0	
Career Total	**4**	**0**	**0**	**0**	

Going: Sf: 0-0 GS: 0-0 Gd: 0-1 GF: - Fm: 0-0
Distance: 2m/2m3: 0-0 2m4-2m7: 0-1 3m+: 0-0
Track: LH: 0-1 RH: 0-0 Tight: 0-1 Gall: 0-0
Aids: Bl: 0-0 Vi: 0-0 Tstrap: 0-0 Ckp: 0-0
Best Rating: 89 6/03 Strf 2m6f110y good Hdl

Kaluga (IRE)

91(95h) (82h)82
6-y-o ch m Tagula (IRE)-Another Baileys (Deploy)
S C Burrough Mrs Christine Priest

Placings:600053/00-060F4 (4631)
2003/04: 22^{0}G, 21^{6}G, 21^{0}G, 20^{F}HY, 19^{4}G,

	Starts	1st	2nd	3rd	Win & Pl
Hurdles	1	0	0	0	0
Chases	4	0	0	0	423
Career Total	**13**	**0**	**0**	**1**	**815**

Going: Sf: 0-1 GS: 0-0 Gd: 0-4 GF: - Fm: 0-0
Distance: 2m/2m3: 0-1 2m4-2m7: 0-4 3m+: 0-0
Track: LH: 0-3 RH: 0-2 Tight: 0-3 Gall: 0-0
Aids: Bl: 0-0 Vi: 0-0 Tstrap: 0-0 Ckp: 0-0
Best Rating: 82 4/04 Tntn 2m3f good Ch

Kandjar D'Allier (FR)

92(95h) (99+h)99
6-y-o gr g Royal Charter (FR)-Miss Akarad (FR) (Akarad (FR))
M F Harris (J Bertran De Balanda 4/5) Let's Live Racing

Placings:600F221/F40020F1335-1440FP500 (4889)
2003/04: 21^{1}VS, 21^{4}GF, 20^{4}GF, 20^{0}G, 16^{F}GS, 16^{P}S, 16^{5}S, 16^{0}G, 20^{0}GF,

	Starts	1st	2nd	3rd	Win & Pl
Hurdles	4	0	0	0	2048
Chases	5	1	0	0	29610
Career Total	**26**	**3**	**3**	**2**	**79308**

5/03	Autl	2m5f110y HCh		VS	£29610
11/02	Autl	2m1f110y Ch		HVY	£13546
4/02	Autl	2m1f110y Ch		VS	£12368

Total win prize-money £55524

Going: Sf: 0-2 GS: 0-1 Gd: 0-2 GF: - Fm: 0-3
Distance: 2m/2m3: 0-4 **2m4-2m7: 1-5** 3m+: 0-0
Track: LH: 0-7 RH: 0-1 Tight: 0-3 Gall: 0-3
Aids: Bl: 0-0 Vi: 0-0 Tstrap: 0-0 Ckp: 0-0
Best Rating: 99 4/04 Strf 2m4f gd-fm Ch

Useful hurdler/useful chaser; ex-French; stays two miles five plus; acts on testing ground; front-runner.

Kandy Four (NZ)

93 109
9-y-o ch g Zeditave (AUS)-Executive Suite (NZ) (Western Symphony (USA))
P F Nicholls D J & F A Jackson

Placings:3/0324032/23P2362F/2211F2-0 (0171)
2003/04: 16^{0}GF,

	Starts	1st	2nd	3rd	Win & Pl
Chases	1	0	0	0	
Career Total	**23**	**2**	**8**	**5**	**25317**

114	8/02	Prth	2m4f110yD(0-115)HCh	G-S	£8131
114	7/02	MRas	2m4f E Ch	G-S	£4375

Total win prize-money £12507

Going: Sf: 0-0 GS: 0-0 Gd: 0-0 GF: - Fm: 0-1
Distance: 2m/2m3: 0-1 2m4-2m7: 0-0 3m+: 0-0
Track: LH: 0-1 RH: 0-0 Tight: 0-0 Gall: 0-0
Aids: Bl: 0-0 Vi: 0-0 Tstrap: 0-0 Ckp: 0-0
Best Rating: 114 8/02 Prth 2m4f110y gd-sft Ch

Modest chaser; stays two miles-five; acts on good to firm and good to soft ground; lacks a turn of foot.

Kansas City (FR)

84(86h) (73h)89
6-y-o b/br m Lute Antique (FR)-Tenacity (FR) (Prove It Baby (USA))
M F Harris Let's Live Racing III

Placings:1056433F3PP-3PU0P (4666)
2003/04: 20^{3}GF, 24^{P}G, 19^{U}G, 16^{0}GS, 20^{P}S,

	Starts	1st	2nd	3rd	Win & Pl
Hurdles	2	0	0	1	342
Chases	3	0	0	0	0
Career Total	**16**	**1**	**0**	**4**	**6874**

5/02	Clun	2m2f	Ch	GD	£2945

Total win prize-money £2945

Going: Sf: 0-1 GS: 0-1 Gd: 0-2 GF: - Fm: 0-1
Distance: 2m/2m3: 0-2 2m4-2m7: 0-2 3m+: 0-1
Track: LH: 0-3 RH: 0-2 Tight: 0-2 Gall: 0-0
Aids: Bl: 0-0 Vi: 0-0 Tstrap: 0-2 Ckp: 0-0
Best Rating: 89 11/02 Wwck 2m110y good Ch

Kaolin De Perche (FR)

(91h) (87+h)
6-y-o b g Luchiroverte (IRE)-Craven Ii (FR) (Rhapsodien)
C P Morlock Pell-Mell Partners

Placings:0F-P50P (4505)
2003/04: 21^{P}S, 26^{5}GS, 24^{0}S, 25^{P}G,

	Starts	1st	2nd	3rd	Win & Pl
Hurdles	3	0	0	0	0
Chases	1	0	0	0	0
Career Total	**6**	**0**	**0**	**0**	**0**

Going: Sf: 0-2 GS: 0-1 Gd: 0-1 GF: - Fm: 0-0
Distance: 2m/2m3: 0-0 2m4-2m7: 0-1 3m+: 0-3
Track: LH: 0-0 RH: 0-4 Tight: 0-1 Gall: 0-1
Aids: Bl: 0-0 Vi: 0-0 Tstrap: 0-0 Ckp: 0-0
Best Rating: 87 3/03 Wwck 3m1f soft Hdl

Kaparolo (USA)

105 116+
5-y-o ch g El Prado (IRE)-Parliament House (USA) (General Assembly (USA))
Mrs A J Perrett John Connolly

Placings:21233210 (4704)
2003/04: 16^{2}GF, 18^{1}G, 21^{2}GF, 16^{3}GF, 17^{3}GS, 22^{2}GF, 18^{1}G, 18^{0}G,

	Starts	1st	2nd	3rd	Win & Pl
Hurdles	8	2	3	2	11790
Career Total	**8**	**2**	**3**	**2**	**11790**

118	3/04	Font	2m2f110yD(0-115)HHdl	GD	£5187
105	10/03	Font	2m2f110yE Hdl	GD	£2695

Total win prize-money £7882

Going: Sf: 0-0 GS: 0-1 Gd: 2-3 GF: - Fm: 0-4
Distance: **2m/2m3: 2-6** 2m4-2m7: 0-2 3m+: 0-0
Track: **LH: 2-6** RH: 0-2 **Tight: 2-6** Gall: 0-0
Aids: Bl: 0-0 Vi: 0-0 Tstrap: 0-0 Ckp: 0-0
Best Rating: 118 3/04 Font 2m2f110y good Hdl

Fair hurdler; fair stayer on the Flat; stays an extended two miles and acts on fast ground.

Kappelhoff (IRE)

75 70d
7-y-o b g Mukaddamah (USA)-Miss Penguin (General Assembly (USA))
Mrs L Richards Mrs Lydia Richards

Placings:*000*/U000U-00 (0833)
2003/04: 22^{0}G, 24^{0}GF,

	Starts	1st	2nd	3rd	Win & Pl
Hurdles	2	0	0	0	
Career Total	10	0	0	0	

Going:	Sf: 0-0 GS: 0-0 Gd: 0-1 GF: - Fm: 0-1
Distance:	2m/2m3: 0-0 2m4-2m7: 0-1 3m+: 0-1
Track:	LH: 0-2 RH: 0-0 Tight: 0-1 Gall: 0-0
Aids:	Bl: 0-0 Vi: 0-0 Tstrap: 0-0 Ckp: 0-0
Best Rating:	88 5/01 Font 2m2f110y gd-fm NHF

Kappillan (IRE)

5-y-o b g Flemensfirth (USA)-Snuggle (Music Boy)
C Grant J Henderson (co Durham)

Placings:000   (3941)
2003/04: 16⁴HY, 16⁹HY, 20⁰GS,

	Starts	1st	2nd	3rd	Win & Pl
NH Flat	2	0	0	0	0
Hurdles	1	0	0	0	0
Career Total	3	0	0	0	

Going:	Sf: 0-2 GS: 0-1 Gd: 0-0 GF: - Fm: 0-0
Distance:	2m/2m3: 0-2 2m4-2m7: 0-1 3m+: 0-0
Track:	LH: 0-3 RH: 0-0 Tight: 0-0 Gall: 0-1
Aids:	Bl: 0-0 Vi: 0-0 Tstrap: 0-0 Ckp: 0-0
Best Rating:	65 1/04 Uttx 2m heavy NHF

Kapska (FR)

63   **39**

6-y-o b g Silver Rainbow-Chapska (FR) (Le Pontet (FR))
M J Roberts Mike Roberts

Placings:P0-00   (4749)
2003/04: 21⁰GS, 25⁰G,

	Starts	1st	2nd	3rd	Win & Pl
Hurdles	2	0	0	0	
Career Total	4	0	0	0	

Going:	Sf: 0-0 GS: 0-1 Gd: 0-1 GF: - Fm: 0-0
Distance:	2m/2m3: 0-0 2m4-2m7: 0-1 3m+: 0-1
Track:	LH: 0-1 RH: 0-0 Tight: 0-1 Gall: 0-0
Aids:	Bl: 0-0 Vi: 0-0 Tstrap: 0-0 Ckp: 0-0
Best Rating:	39 3/04 Plum 2m5f gd-sft Hdl

Karajan (IRE)

101   (102h)**105**

7-y-o b g Fairy King (USA)-Dernier Cri (Slip Anchor)
G M Moore J R F (management consultants) Ltd

Placings:5434241222550/235-544223P05   (4947)
2003/04: 20⁵G, 21⁴G, 24⁴GF, 20²GF, 24²GF, 20³GF, 24⁴G, 20⁰G, 20⁵GS,

	Starts	1st	2nd	3rd	Win & Pl
Chases	9	0	2	1	3543
Career Total	25	1	7	3	13047
102 9/01 Prth	2m4f110yE Hdl			GD	£3157
	Total win prize-money £3157				

Going:	Sf: 0-0 GS: 0-0 Gd: 0-4 GF: - Fm: 0-4
Distance:	2m/2m3: 0-0 2m4-2m7: 0-6 3m+: 0-3
Track:	LH: 0-1 RH: 0-8 Tight: 0-5 Gall: 0-0
Aids:	Bl: 0-0 Vi: 0-0 Tstrap: 0-0 Ckp: 0-0
Best Rating:	105 12/03 Muss 2m4f gd-fm Ch

Modest hurdler, runner-up in novice chases at Musselburgh in December and again the following month; stays three miles; suited by fast ground but handles soft.

Karakum

96   **75**

5-y-o b g Mtoto-Magongo (Be My Chief (USA))
A J Chamberlain A J Chamberlain

Placings:056-P0202433   (2116)
2003/04: 22⁰G, 16⁹GF, 17²GF, 17⁹GF, 16²GF, 16⁴GF, 16³G, 16³GF,

	Starts	1st	2nd	3rd	Win & Pl
Hurdles	8	0	2	2	1825
Career Total	11	0	2	2	1825

Going:	Sf: 0-0 GS: 0-0 Gd: 0-0 GF: - Fm: 0-6
Distance:	2m/2m3: 0-7 2m4-2m7: 0-1 3m+: 0-0
Track:	LH: 0-4 RH: 0-4 Tight: 0-3 Gall: 0-0
Aids:	Bl: 0-0 Vi: 0-0 Tstrap: 0-0 Ckp: 0-0
Best Rating:	77 11/03 Ludl 2m gd-fm Hdl

Plating-class hurdler; acts on fast ground; barely stays two miles.

Karatchi (FR)

101   **105+**

6-y-o b/br g Iris Noir (FR)-Eclipse Royale II (FR) (Brezzo (FR))
L Lungo R A Bartlett

Placings:1P   (4515)
2003/04: 24¹GS, 25ᴾGS,

	Starts	1st	2nd	3rd	Win & Pl
Hurdles	2	1	0	0	3021
Career Total	2	1	0	0	3021
105 11/03 Ayr	3m110y E Hdl			G-S	£3020
	Total win prize-money £3021				

Going:	Sf: 0-0 GS: 1-2 Gd: 0-0 GF: - Fm: 0-0
Distance:	2m/2m3: 0-0 2m4-2m7: 0-0 **3m+: 1-2**
Track:	**LH: 1-2** RH: 0-0 Tight: 0-0 Gall: 0-0
Aids:	Bl: 0-0 Vi: 0-0 Tstrap: 0-0 Ckp: 0-0
Best Rating:	105 11/03 Ayr 3m110y gd-sft Hdl

French-bred gelding; got off the mark on hurdling debut at Ayr in November; pulled up lame next time; stays three miles; acts on easy ground.

Kariba Dream

9-y-o ch m Hatim (USA)-Noss Head (New Brig)
W S Coltherd S Coltherd

Placings:P   (0194)
2003/04: 20⁰G,

	Starts	1st	2nd	3rd	Win & Pl
Hurdles	1	0	0	0	
Career Total	1	0	0	0	

Going:	Sf: 0-0 GS: 0-0 Gd: 0-1 GF: - Fm: 0-0
Distance:	2m/2m3: 0-0 2m4-2m7: 0-1 3m+: 0-0
Track:	LH: 0-1 RH: 0-0 Tight: 0-0 Gall: 0-0
Aids:	Bl: 0-0 Vi: 0-0 Tstrap: 0-0 Ckp: 0-0

Karibee

55

4-y-o b f Karinga Bay-Jaydeebee (Buckley)
M Madgwick J D Brownrigg

Placings:060P   (4702)
2003/04: 18⁰HY, 20⁶HY, 16⁰S, 20ᴾG,

	Starts	1st	2nd	3rd	Win & Pl
NH Flat	1	0	0	0	0

	Starts	1st	2nd	3rd	Win & Pl
Hurdles	3	0	0	0	0
Career Total	4	0	0	0	0

Going:	Sf: 0-3 GS: 0-0 Gd: 0-1 GF: - Fm: 0-0
Distance:	2m/2m3: 0-2 2m4-2m7: 0-2 3m+: 0-0
Track:	LH: 0-3 RH: 0-0 Tight: 0-3 Gall: 0-0
Aids:	Bl: 0-0 Vi: 0-0 Tstrap: 0-0 Ckp: 0-0

Kariblue

86f   **73f**

6-y-o ch m Imp Society (USA)-Kadastra (FR) (Stradavinsky)
R Dickin A P Paton

Placings:0   (2255)
2003/04: 17⁰GF,

	Starts	1st	2nd	3rd	Win & Pl
NH Flat	1	0	0	0	
Career Total	1	0	0	0	

Going:	Sf: 0-0 GS: 0-0 Gd: 0-0 GF: - Fm: 0-1
Distance:	2m/2m3: 0-1 2m4-2m7: 0-0 3m+: 0-0
Track:	LH: 0-0 RH: 0-1 Tight: 0-0 Gall: 0-0
Aids:	Bl: 0-0 Vi: 0-0 Tstrap: 0-0 Ckp: 0-0
Best Rating:	73 11/03 Hrfd 2m1f gd-fm NHF

Karing Kenda

5-y-o ch m Karinga Bay-Song Of Kenda (Rolfe (USA))
K Bishop Michael Wingfield Digby

Placings:UP   (4544)
2003/04: 19ᵁG, 22ᴾGS,

	Starts	1st	2nd	3rd	Win & Pl
Hurdles	2	0	0	0	
Career Total	2	0	0	0	

Going:	Sf: 0-0 GS: 0-1 Gd: 0-1 GF: - Fm: 0-0
Distance:	2m/2m3: 0-1 2m4-2m7: 0-1 3m+: 0-0
Track:	LH: 0-0 RH: 0-2 Tight: 0-0 Gall: 0-0
Aids:	Bl: 0-0 Vi: 0-0 Tstrap: 0-0 Ckp: 0-0

Karinga City

100   **108**

7-y-o ch g Karinga Bay-Panicaly (Rock City)
E Retter Edward Retter

Placings:3605P/50   (4833)
2003/04: 17⁵G, 21⁰GF,

	Starts	1st	2nd	3rd	Win & Pl
Hurdles	2	0	0	0	
Career Total	7	0	0	1	1725

Going:	Sf: 0-0 GS: 0-0 Gd: 0-1 GF: - Fm: 0-1
Distance:	2m/2m3: 0-1 2m4-2m7: 0-1 3m+: 0-0
Track:	LH: 0-1 RH: 0-1 Tight: 0-0 Gall: 0-1
Aids:	Bl: 0-0 Vi: 0-0 Tstrap: 0-0 Ckp: 0-0
Best Rating:	108 4/04 Chel 2m5f110y gd-fm Hdl

Modest novice hurdler; lightly raced since bumper days, placed in point-to-points, stays three miles; acts on fast ground.

Karinga Coin

94   **78**

6-y-o ch g Karinga Bay-Coinridge (Charlie's Pal)

C J Down Edward Darke

Placings: 0P5PP   (4242)
2003/04: 17⁰GF, 22⁸GS, 19⁵S, 22²G, 24⁸G,

	Starts	1st	2nd	3rd	Win & Pl
NH Flat	1	0	0	0	0
Hurdles	4	0	0	0	0
Career Total	5	0	0	0	0

Going:	Sf: 0-1 GS: 0-1 Gd: 0-2 GF: - Fm: 0-1	
Distance:	2m/2m3: 0-2 2m4-2m7: 0-2 3m+: 0-1	
Track:	LH: 0-2 RH: 0-3 Tight: 0-2 Gall: 0-0	
Aids:	Bl: 0-0 Vi: 0-0 Tstrap: 0-0 Ckp: 0-0	
Best Rating:	78 2/04 Extr 2m3f soft Hdl	

Karisaban

5-y-o b g Hatim (USA)-Swiss Beauty (Ballacashtal (CAN))
R Johnson K Eichler

Placings: 00-P5   (0692)
2003/04: 17⁵G, 16⁵G,

	Starts	1st	2nd	3rd	Win & Pl
Hurdles	2	0	0	0	0
Career Total	4	0	0	0	0

Going:	Sf: 0-0 GS: 0-1 Gd: 0-0 GF: - Fm: 0-1	
Distance:	2m/2m3: 0-2 2m4-2m7: 0-0 3m+: 0-1	
Track:	LH: 0-2 RH: 0-0 Tight: 0-1 Gall: 0-0	
Aids:	Bl: 0-0 Vi: 0-0 Tstrap: 0-0 Ckp: 0-0	
Best Rating:	30 3/03 Carl 2m1f gd-sft NHF	

Karju (IRE)

100   **103**

5-y-o b g Marju (IRE)-Karmisymixa (FR) (Linamix (FR))
M Todhunter B Batey

Placings: 0023-211   (0796)
2003/04: 16³G, 17²G, 20¹G, 16¹G,

	Starts	1st	2nd	3rd	Win & Pl
Hurdles	4	2	1	1	9130
Career Total	7	2	2	1	10377
108 7/03	Prth	2m110y E Hdl		GD	£3445
101 6/03	Prth	2m4f110yE Hdl		GD	£4095

Total win prize-money £7540

Going:	Sf: 0-0 GS: 0-0 Gd: 2-4 GF: - Fm: 0-0	
Distance:	2m/2m3: 1-3 2m4-2m7: 1-1 3m+: 0-0	
Track:	LH: 0-2 RH: 2-2 Tight: 0-1 Gall: 0-0	
Aids:	Bl: 0-0 Vi: 0-0 Tstrap: 0-0 Ckp: 0-0	
Best Rating:	108 7/03 Prth 2m110y good Hdl	

Ex-Irish novice hurdler; changed hands cheaply; got off the mark over two and a half miles at Perth in June and followed up the next month over two; acts on good ground.

Karo De Vindecy (FR)

100(93h)   (72h)**73+**

6-y-o b g Mollicone Junior (FR)-Preves Du Forez (FR) (Quart De Vin (FR))
M D Hammond Racing Management & Training Ltd

Placings: 46000-154444   (4880)
2003/04: 17¹G, 17⁵GF, 20⁴G, 21⁴G, 16⁴GF, 20⁴GS,

	Starts	1st	2nd	3rd	Win & Pl
Chases	6	1	0	0	5809
Career Total	11	1	0	0	6567

69	5/03	Ctml	2m1f110yE(0-100)HCh	GD	£4810

Total win prize-money £4810

Going:	Sf: 0-0 GS: 0-1 Gd: 1-3 GF: - Fm: 0-2	
Distance:	2m/2m3: 1-3 2m4-2m7: 0-3 3m+: 0-0	
Track:	LH: 1-5 RH: 0-1 Tight: 1-2 Gall: 0-0	
Aids:	Bl: 0-0 Vi: 0-0 Tstrap: 1-6 Ckp: 0-0	
Best Rating:	73 4/04 Carl 2m4f gd-sft Ch	

Had shown ability in France but ran poorly over hurdles here; took a very modest event on his debut over fences at Cartmel May 2003; best at around two miles.

Karoo

85f   **75f**

6-y-o b g Karinga Bay-Cupids Bower (Owen Dudley)
P F Nicholls R D Cox

Placings: 0   (4739)
2003/04: 17⁰G,

	Starts	1st	2nd	3rd	Win & Pl
NH Flat	1	0	0	0	
Career Total	1	0	0	0	

Going:	Sf: 0-0 GS: 0-0 Gd: 0-1 GF: - Fm: 0-0	
Distance:	2m/2m3: 0-1 2m4-2m7: 0-0 3m+: 0-0	
Track:	LH: 0-1 RH: 0-0 Tight: 0-1 Gall: 0-0	
Aids:	Bl: 0-0 Vi: 0-0 Tstrap: 0-0 Ckp: 0-0	
Best Rating:	75 4/04 NAbb 2m1f good NHF	

Karyon (IRE)

94   **63**

4-y-o b f Presidium-Stealthy (Kind Of Hush)
Miss Kate Milligan (P C Haslam 13/10) S Ward

Placings: P61P00   (4958)
2003/04: 16⁸GS, 16⁶GS, 16¹GS, 17⁰GS, 16⁹GF, 17⁰G,

	Starts	1st	2nd	3rd	Win & Pl
Hurdles	6	1	0	0	2380
Career Total	6	1	0	0	2380
63 1/04	Catt	2m	G Hdl	G-S	£2380

Total win prize-money £2380

Going:	Sf: 0-0 GS: 1-4 Gd: 0-1 GF: - Fm: 0-1	
Distance:	2m/2m3: 1-6 2m4-2m7: 0-0 3m+: 0-0	
Track:	LH: 1-5 RH: 0-1 Tight: 1-5 Gall: 0-1	
Aids:	Bl: 0-0 Vi: 0-0 Tstrap: 0-0 Ckp: 0-0	
Best Rating:	63 1/04 Catt 2m gd-sft Hdl	

Karzhang

12-y-o b g Rakaposhi King-Smokey Baby (Sagaro)
Mrs C J Robinson Jeremy Beasley

Placings: 000/5P0/3040/24/F/6-P   (0262)
2003/04: 20⁰GF,

	Starts	1st	2nd	3rd	Win & Pl
Chases	1	0	0	0	
Career Total	15	0	1	1	1474

Going:	Sf: 0-0 GS: 0-0 Gd: 0-0 GF: - Fm: 0-1	
Distance:	2m/2m3: 0-0 2m4-2m7: 0-1 3m+: 0-0	
Track:	LH: 0-0 RH: 0-0 Tight: 0-1 Gall: 0-0	
Aids:	Bl: 0-0 Vi: 0-0 Tstrap: 0-0 Ckp: 0-0	
Best Rating:	88 5/00 Bang 2m1f good Hdl	

Kashimo (GER)

94   **91+**

5-y-o b h Lomitas-Kardia (Mister Rock'S (GER))
G L Moore Gillespie Brothers

Placings: 4   (4577)
2003/04: 16⁴G,

	Starts	1st	2nd	3rd	Win & Pl
Hurdles	1	0	0	0	404
Career Total	1	0	0	0	404

Going:	Sf: 0-0 GS: 0-0 Gd: 0-1 GF: - Fm: 0-0	
Distance:	2m/2m3: 0-1 2m4-2m7: 0-0 3m+: 0-0	
Track:	LH: 0-1 RH: 0-0 Tight: 0-0 Gall: 0-1	
Aids:	Bl: 0-0 Vi: 0-0 Tstrap: 0-0 Ckp: 0-0	
Best Rating:	96 3/04 Newb 2m110y good Hdl	

Kasilia (FR)

6-y-o b g Silver Rainbow-Basilia (FR) (Mont Basile (FR))
Tim Brown (Mme I Pacault 5/10) Tim Brown

Placings: 406/023305FFP223F0P-P32   (4775)
2003/04: 21⁸PS, 21³GS, 21²G,

	Starts	1st	2nd	3rd	Win & Pl
Chases	3	0	1	1	1429
Career Total	21	0	4	4	15915

Going:	Sf: 0-1 GS: 0-1 Gd: 0-1 GF: - Fm: 0-0	
Distance:	2m/2m3: 0-0 2m4-2m7: 0-3 3m+: 0-0	
Track:	LH: 0-2 RH: 0-0 Tight: 0-2 Gall: 0-0	
Aids:	Bl: 0-1 Vi: 0-0 Tstrap: 0-0 Ckp: 0-0	
Best Rating:	87 4/04 Fknm 2m5f110y good Ch	

Kassel (USA)

4-y-o ch g Swain (IRE)-Gretel (Hansel (USA))
Ian Williams Patrick Kelly

Placings: 04   (3754)
2003/04: 13⁰S, 17⁴G,

	Starts	1st	2nd	3rd	Win & Pl
NH Flat	1	0	0	0	0
Hurdles	1	0	0	0	358
Career Total	2	0	0	0	358

Going:	Sf: 0-1 GS: 0-0 Gd: 0-1 GF: - Fm: 0-0	
Distance:	2m/2m3: 0-1 2m4-2m7: 0-0 3m+: 0-0	
Track:	LH: 0-0 RH: 0-1 Tight: 0-1 Gall: 0-0	
Aids:	Bl: 0-0 Vi: 0-0 Tstrap: 0-0 Ckp: 0-0	

Kasthari (IRE)

114   **120+**

5-y-o gr g Vettori (IRE)-Karliyka (IRE) (Last Tycoon)
J Howard Johnson (Sir Michael Stoute 18/10) Elliott Brothers

Placings: 311P   (4641)
2003/04: 16³GS, 20¹GS, 20¹S, 24⁸G,

	Starts	1st	2nd	3rd	Win & Pl
Hurdles	4	2	0	1	7532
Career Total	4	2	0	1	7532
119 3/04	Newc	2m4f	E Hdl	SFT	£3542
120 2/04	Newc	2m4f	E Hdl	G-S	£3555

Total win prize-money £7099

Going:	Sf: 1-1 GS: 1-2 Gd: 0-1 GF: - Fm: 0-0
Distance:	2m/2m3: 0-1 2m4-2m7: 2-2 3m+: 0-1
Track:	LH: 2-4 RH: 0-0 Tight: 0-1 Gall: 2-3
Aids:	Bl: 0-0 Vi: 0-0 Tstrap: 0-0 Ckp: 0-0
Best Rating:	120 2/04 Newc 2m4f gd-sft Hdl

Former smart stayer on the Flat, placed at Group level; bettered form of hurdles debut when upped to two and a half miles at Newcastle (successful) in February; repeated the dose on return visit there the following month; suited by 2m 4f; acts on most ground.

Kastina

57

5-y-o b m Lancastrian-Kit (Green Ruby (USA))
M J Gingell Mrs B T Joyce

| Placings:03P | (1190) |

2003/04: 16⁶G, 22³GF, 20⁸GF,

	Starts	1st	2nd	3rd	Win & Pl
Hurdles	3	0	0	1	826
Career Total	3	0	0	1	826

Going:	Sf: 0-0 GS: 0-0 Gd: 0-1 GF: - Fm: 0-2
Distance:	2m/2m3: 0-1 2m4-2m7: 0-2 3m+: 0-0
Track:	LH: 0-3 RH: 0-0 Tight: 0-1 Gall: 0-0
Aids:	Bl: 0-0 Vi: 0-0 Tstrap: 0-0 Ckp: 0-0

Kathakali (IRE)

104   103

7-y-o b g Dancing Dissident (USA)-She's A Dancer (IRE) (Alzao (USA))
C J Bennett C J Bennett

| Placings:000P-0150 | (1376) |

2003/04: 17⁹GF, 16¹G, 16⁵GF, 16⁶GF,

	Starts	1st	2nd	3rd	Win & Pl
Hurdles	4	1	0	0	3556
Career Total	8	1	0	0	3556
103 7/03 Worc 2m	E Hdl			GD	3556
			Total win prize-money £3556

Going:	Sf: 0-0 GS: 0-0 Gd: 1-1 GF: - Fm: 0-3
Distance:	2m/2m3: 1-4 2m4-2m7: 0-0 3m+: 0-0
Track:	LH: 1-4 RH: 0-0 Tight: 0-1 Gall: 0-0
Aids:	Bl: 1-4 Vi: 0-0 Tstrap: 0-0 Ckp: 0-0
Best Rating:	103 8/03 Worc 2m gd-fm Hdl

Finally lived up to his Flat form when causing 66/1 shock when readily winning 2m maiden hurdle at Worcester July 2003; raised no less than 33lb when fifth in a competitive handicap at the same course next time; unsuited by soft ground.

Kathella (IRE)

101   59+

7-y-o b m Fourstars Allstar (USA)-Niat Supreme (IRE) (Supreme Leader)
N G Ayliffe R Allatt

| Placings:00/0000PP-34P | (1272) |

2003/04: 22³GF, 24⁴GF, 22⁸GF,

	Starts	1st	2nd	3rd	Win & Pl
Hurdles	3	0	0	1	836
Career Total	11	0	0	1	836

Going:	Sf: 0-0 GS: 0-0 Gd: 0-0 GF: - Fm: 0-3
Distance:	2m/2m3: 0-0 2m4-2m7: 0-2 3m+: 0-1
Track:	LH: 0-3 RH: 0-0 Tight: 0-2 Gall: 0-0
Aids:	Bl: 0-0 Vi: 0-0 Tstrap: 0-0 Ckp: 0-0

| Best Rating: | 72 6/02 NAbb 2m1f good Hdl |

Invariably well beaten when completing over hurdles; does not appear to stay 2m 6f.

Katie Buckers (IRE)

89   83

10-y-o ch m Yashgan-Glenkins (Furry Glen)
K C Bailey K C Bailey

| Placings:103PP/43411/144P0P-3 | (0110) |

2003/04: 20³HY,

	Starts	1st	2nd	3rd	Win & Pl
Chases	1	0	0	1	682
Career Total	17	4	0	3	15455
104 5/02 Uttx	2m4f	E(0-105)HCh	GD	£3328
104 3/02 Uttx	3m2f	E(0-105)HCh	HVY	£4095
96 3/02 Hrfd	3m1f110yE Ch	GD	£3357
100 11/00 Chep	2m110y H NHF	HVY	£1505
		Total win prize-money £12286

Going:	Sf: 0-1 GS: 0-0 Gd: 0-0 GF: - Fm: 0-0
Distance:	2m/2m3: 0-0 2m4-2m7: 0-1 3m+: 0-0
Track:	LH: 0-1 RH: 0-0 Tight: 0-0 Gall: 0-0
Aids:	Bl: 0-0 Vi: 0-0 Tstrap: 0-0 Ckp: 0-1
Best Rating:	104 5/02 Uttx 2m4f good Ch

Fair form in novice chases. completed a hat-trick in the spring of 2002; bang out of form of late; stays three and a quarter miles; acts on heavy ground.

Katie Savage

81   46

4-y-o b f Emperor Jones (USA)-Coax Me Molly (USA) (L'Enjoleur (CAN))
J Mackie A League Of 4 English Gentlemen

| Placings:P06U | (4569) |

2003/04: 16⁶S, 16⁹GS, 16⁶S, 17⁰UGS,

	Starts	1st	2nd	3rd	Win & Pl
Hurdles	4	0	0	0	0
Career Total	4	0	0	0	0

Going:	Sf: 0-1 GS: 0-2 Gd: 0-1 GF: - Fm: 0-0
Distance:	2m/2m3: 0-4 2m4-2m7: 0-0 3m+: 0-0
Track:	LH: 0-3 RH: 0-1 Tight: 0-1 Gall: 0-1
Aids:	Bl: 0-0 Vi: 0-0 Tstrap: 0-0 Ckp: 0-0
Best Rating:	51 1/04 Chep 2m110y soft Hdl

Katies Dolphin (IRE)

87   82

6-y-o ch m Dolphin Street (FR)-Kuwah (IRE) (Be My Guest (USA))
R Johnson Foster Watson

| Placings:600436-6F0P06F | (4958) |

2003/04: 21⁶GF, 16⁶FS, 16⁹G, 21⁸GS, 19⁰G, 21⁶G, 17⁷G,

	Starts	1st	2nd	3rd	Win & Pl
Hurdles	6	0	0	0	0
Chases	1	0	0	0	0
Career Total	13	0	0	1	504

Going:	Sf: 0-1 GS: 0-1 Gd: 0-4 GF: - Fm: 0-1
Distance:	2m/2m3: 0-3 2m4-2m7: 0-4 3m+: 0-0
Track:	LH: 0-6 RH: 0-1 Tight: 0-6 Gall: 0-0
Aids:	Bl: 0-0 Vi: 0-0 Tstrap: 0-0 Ckp: 0-5
Best Rating:	82 3/03 Sedg 2m5f110y soft Hdl

Plating-class hurdler; acts on soft; has worn tongue tie.

Katies Hero

97   93+

6-y-o b g Pontevecchio Notte-Kindly Lady (Kind Of Hush)
J D Frost D C & Mrs T M Fisher

| Placings:00-56P506 | (4818) |

2003/04: 17⁵G, 20⁶G, 16⁸S, 16⁵G, 17⁹G, 17⁸GF,

	Starts	1st	2nd	3rd	Win & Pl
Hurdles	6	0	0	0	0
Career Total	8	0	0	0	0

Going:	Sf: 0-1 GS: 0-1 Gd: 0-4 GF: - Fm: 0-1
Distance:	2m/2m3: 0-5 2m4-2m7: 0-1 3m+: 0-0
Track:	LH: 0-1 RH: 0-4 Tight: 0-3 Gall: 0-0
Aids:	Bl: 0-0 Vi: 0-0 Tstrap: 0-0 Ckp: 0-0
Best Rating:	93 2/04 Ludl 2m good Hdl

Katies Tight Jeans

10-y-o b m Green Adventure (USA)-Haraka Sasa (Town And Country)
R E Peacock M F Harris

| Placings:05/0/00/P6/PP-0 | (0752) |

2003/04: 17⁰GS,

	Starts	1st	2nd	3rd	Win & Pl
Hurdles	1	0	0	0	0
Career Total	10	0	0	0	0

Going:	Sf: 0-0 GS: 0-0 Gd: 0-0 GF: - Fm: 0-1
Distance:	2m/2m3: 0-1 2m4-2m7: 0-0 3m+: 0-0
Track:	LH: 0-1 RH: 0-0 Tight: 0-1 Gall: 0-0
Aids:	Bl: 0-0 Vi: 0-0 Tstrap: 0-0 Ckp: 0-0
Best Rating:	65 5/00 Worc 2m gd-fm NHF

Katinka

91   49

11-y-o b m Rymer-Millymeeta (New Brig)
A M Thomson A M Thomson

| Placings:F4/06P/P0 | (0718) |

2003/04: 16⁶G, 20⁸G,

	Starts	1st	2nd	3rd	Win & Pl
Hurdles	2	0	0	0	
Career Total	7	0	0	0	450

Going:	Sf: 0-0 GS: 0-0 Gd: 0-2 GF: - Fm: 0-0
Distance:	2m/2m3: 0-1 2m4-2m7: 0-1 3m+: 0-0
Track:	LH: 0-0 RH: 0-2 Tight: 0-0 Gall: 0-0
Aids:	Bl: 0-0 Vi: 0-0 Tstrap: 0-0 Ckp: 0-0
Best Rating:	49 6/03 Prth 2m4f110y good Hdl

Katmandu

101   110+

5-y-o b g Sadler's Wells (USA)-Kithanga (IRE) (Darshaan)
J Howard Johnson (L M Cumani 8/9) Ada Partnership

| Placings:3241 | (4618) |

2003/04: 16⁹S, 20²HY, 20⁴G, 21¹G,

	Starts	1st	2nd	3rd	Win & Pl
Hurdles	4	1	1	1	5321
Career Total	4	1	1	1	5321
110 3/04 Sedg	2m5f110yE Hdl		GD	£3373
		Total win prize-money £3374

| Going: | Sf: 0-2 GS: 0-0 Gd: 1-2 GF: - Fm: 0-0 |

Distance:	2m/2m3: 0-1 **2m4-2m7:** 1-3 3m+: 0-0
Track:	**LH:** 1-3 RH: 0-1 **Tight:** 1-2 Gall: 0-1
Aids:	**Bl:** 1-1 Vi: 0-0 Tstrap: 0-0 Ckp: 0-1
Best Rating:	110 3/04 Sedg 2m5f110y good Hdl

Moderate hurdler; off the mark at Sedgefield in March; good runner-up at Wetherby the following month; stays two miles-five; acts on any ground; has worn blinkers and cheekpieces.

Katoof (USA)

6-y-o b g Silver Hawk (USA)-The Caretaker (Caerleon (USA))
J A B Old W E Sturt

Placings:0   (2012)
2003/04: 16⁰G,

	Starts	1st	2nd	3rd	Win & Pl
NH Flat	1	0	0		
Career Total	**1**	**0**	**0**		

Going:	Sf: 0-0 GS: 0-0 Gd: 0-1 GF: - Fm: 0-0
Distance:	2m/2m3: 0-1 2m4-2m7: 0-0 3m+: 0-0
Track:	LH: 0-0 RH: 0-1 Tight: 0-0 Gall: 0-0
Aids:	Bl: 0-0 Vi: 0-0 Tstrap: 0-0 Ckp: 0-0

Kattegat

95   105

8-y-o b g Slip Anchor-Kirsten (Kris)
Mrs H M Bridges Mrs H M Bridges

Placings:220/04/100**353P**/33534F-P04000U0661 (4932)
2003/04: 22⁰G, 22⁰G, 16⁴S, 20⁰G, 16⁰S, 24⁰S, 21¹¹S, 19⁰G, 22⁶G, 25⁵G, 27¹G,

	Starts	1st	2nd	3rd	Win & Pl
Hurdles	11	1	0		4362
Career Total	**29**	**2**	**2**	**5**	**17493**
105 4/04	Font	3m3f	E(0-110)HHdl	GD	£4095
112 11/01	Leic	2m	C(0-130)HHdl	G-S	£5395
			Total win prize-money £9490		

Going:	Sf: 0-4 GS: 0-0 Gd: 1-7 GF: - Fm: 0-0
Distance:	2m/2m3: 0-2 2m4-2m7: 0-6 **3m+:** 1-3
Track:	LH: 0-4 RH: 0-5 **Tight:** 1-7 Gall: 0-0
Aids:	**Bl:** 1-4 Vi: 0-0 Tstrap: 0-0 Ckp: 0-2
Best Rating:	115 2/00 Hntg 2m4f110y soft Hdl

Fair hurdler; stays three miles-three; goes well on a good and soft surface.

Katy The Duck (IRE)

81   78

9-y-o br m Over The River (FR)-Zagliarelle (FR) (Rose Laurel)
R J Price R J Price

Placings:0P6/0U0/250106-F040 (4700)
2003/04: 16⁶G, 21⁰G, 17⁴GS, 20⁰G,

	Starts	1st	2nd	3rd	Win & Pl
Hurdles	4	0	0	0	
Career Total	**16**	**1**	**1**	**0**	**3318**
78 3/03	Bang	2m1f	F Hdl	GD	£2618
			Total win prize-money £2618		

Going:	Sf: 0-0 GS: 0-1 Gd: 0-3 GF: - Fm: 0-0
Distance:	2m/2m3: 0-2 2m4-2m7: 0-2 3m+: 0-0
Track:	LH: 0-1 RH: 0-2 Tight: 0-2 Gall: 0-1
Aids:	Bl: 0-0 Vi: 0-0 Tstrap: 0-0 Ckp: 0-0

| Best Rating: | 78 3/03 Bang 2m1f good Hdl |

Kausse De Thaix (FR)

79   64

6-y-o ch g Iris Noir (FR)-Etoile De Thaix (FR) (Lute Antique (FR))
P M Phelan Andrew L Cohen

Placings:40-54   (3807)
2003/04: 21⁵G, 20⁴G,

	Starts	1st	2nd	3rd	Win & Pl
Chases	2	0	0	0	528
Career Total	**4**	**0**	**0**	**0**	**528**

Going:	Sf: 0-0 GS: 0-0 Gd: 0-2 GF: - Fm: 0-0
Distance:	2m/2m3: 0-0 2m4-2m7: 0-2 3m+: 0-0
Track:	LH: 0-0 RH: 0-2 Tight: 0-0 Gall: 0-0
Aids:	Bl: 0-0 Vi: 0-0 Tstrap: 0-0 Ckp: 0-0
Best Rating:	96 1/03 Kemp 2m gd-sft NHF

Kavi (IRE)

100   91

4-y-o ch g Perugino (USA)-Premier Leap (IRE) (Salmon Leap (USA))
Simon Earle (P C Haslam 27/9) Natural Racing

Placings:21523   (1448)
2003/04: 16²G, 17¹G, 16⁵GF, 16²GF, 17⁹GF,

	Starts	1st	2nd	3rd	Win & Pl
Hurdles	5	1	2	1	6741
Career Total	**5**	**1**	**2**	**1**	**6741**
91 8/03	Bang	2m1f	E Hdl	GD	£3536
			Total win prize-money £3536		

Going:	Sf: 0-0 GS: 0-0 Gd: 1-2 GF: - Fm: 0-3
Distance:	**2m/2m3:** 1-5 2m4-2m7: 0-0 3m+: 0-0
Track:	**LH:** 1-4 RH: 0-1 **Tight:** 1-5 Gall: 0-0
Aids:	Bl: 0-1 Vi: 0-0 Tstrap: 0-0 Ckp: 0-0
Best Rating:	91 9/03 Strf 2m110y gd-fm Hdl

Plating-class juvenile hurdler; suited by a sound surface; not the most fluent of jumpers; has been tried in blinkers.

Kay Bee Venture

5-y-o ch m Karinga Bay-Take The Veil (Monksfield)
G F H Charles-Jones Okebrooke Racing

Placings:000PUPP   (3226)
2003/04: 17⁰GF, 17⁰GF, 17⁰GF, 19⁰GF, 17⁰GS, 19⁰G, 26⁰GS,

	Starts	1st	2nd	3rd	Win & Pl
NH Flat	3	0	0	0	0
Hurdles	4	0	0	0	0
Career Total	**7**	**0**	**0**	**0**	**0**

Going:	Sf: 0-0 GS: 0-2 Gd: 0-1 GF: - Fm: 0-4
Distance:	2m/2m3: 0-4 2m4-2m7: 0-2 3m+: 0-1
Track:	LH: 0-1 RH: 0-6 Tight: 0-3 Gall: 0-0
Aids:	Bl: 0-0 Vi: 0-0 Tstrap: 0-0 Ckp: 0-0
Best Rating:	38 11/03 Hrfd 2m1f gd-fm NHF

Kaysa (GER)

63   16

5-y-o b m Second Set (IRE)-Kaytiggy (Busted)
Dr P Pritchard A J Whiting

Placings:P4F   (0749)
2003/04: 19⁰GS, 17⁴S, 16²G,

	Starts	1st	2nd	3rd	Win & Pl
Hurdles	3	0	0	0	272
Career Total	**3**	**0**	**0**	**0**	**272**

Going:	Sf: 0-1 GS: 0-1 Gd: 0-1 GF: - Fm: 0-0
Distance:	2m/2m3: 0-2 2m4-2m7: 0-1 3m+: 0-0
Track:	LH: 0-2 RH: 0-1 Tight: 0-2 Gall: 0-0
Aids:	Bl: 0-0 Vi: 0-0 Tstrap: 0-1 Ckp: 0-0
Best Rating:	18 5/03 Bang 2m1f soft Hdl

Kaytash

94   72

5-y-o b m Silverdale Knight-Lady Swift (Jalmood (USA))
K W Hogg K W Hogg

Placings:5P0-0   (1653)
2003/04: 17⁰G,

	Starts	1st	2nd	3rd	Win & Pl
Hurdles	1	0	0	0	
Career Total	**4**	**0**	**0**	**0**	**0**

Going:	Sf: 0-0 GS: 0-0 Gd: 0-1 GF: - Fm: 0-0
Distance:	2m/2m3: 0-1 2m4-2m7: 0-3 3m+: 0-0
Track:	LH: 0-1 RH: 0-0 Tight: 0-1 Gall: 0-0
Aids:	Bl: 0-0 Vi: 0-0 Tstrap: 0-0 Ckp: 0-0
Best Rating:	76 10/03 Sedg 2m1f good Hdl

Kedge Anchor Man

100   96

13-y-o b g Bustino-Jenny Mere (Brigadier Gerard)
N A Gaselee Anthony M Green

Placings:3/F/2265/6U2F4/02115/20355-0 (0035)
2003/04: 22⁰G,

	Starts	1st	2nd	3rd	Win & Pl
Hurdles	1	0	0	0	
Career Total	**22**	**2**	**5**	**2**	**12454**
106 2/02	Sand	2m4f110yD(0-110)HHdl	HVY	£4446
100 1/02	Hntg	2m4f110yF(0-95)HHdl	G-S	£2024
			Total win prize-money £6470		

Going:	Sf: 0-0 GS: 0-0 Gd: 0-1 GF: - Fm: 0-0
Distance:	2m/2m3: 0-0 2m4-2m7: 0-1 3m+: 0-0
Track:	LH: 0-0 RH: 0-1 Tight: 0-0 Gall: 0-0
Aids:	Bl: 0-0 Vi: 0-0 Tstrap: 0-0 Ckp: 0-0
Best Rating:	109 12/99 Extr 2m7f110y gd-sft Ch

Moderate hurdler; stays two and a half miles, effective on testing ground.

Keen And Able

81f   72f

4-y-o ch f Keen-Four Thyme (Idiots Delight)
N G Richards E Briggs

Placings:00   (4663)
2003/04: 16⁹G, 16⁰S,

	Starts	1st	2nd	3rd	Win & Pl
NH Flat	2	0	0	0	
Career Total	**2**	**0**	**0**	**0**	

Going:	Sf: 0-1 GS: 0-0 Gd: 0-1 GF: - Fm: 0-0
Distance:	2m/2m3: 0-2 2m4-2m7: 0-0 3m+: 0-0
Track:	LH: 0-2 RH: 0-0 Tight: 0-0 Gall: 0-0
Aids:	Bl: 0-0 Vi: 0-0 Tstrap: 0-0 Ckp: 0-0

Best Rating: 57 1/04 Hayd 2m   good NHF

Keen Leader (IRE)
107 (154h)**170**
8-y-o b g Supreme Leader-Keen Gale (IRE) (Strong Gale)
Jonjo O'Neill Mrs Stewart Catherwood

Placings:1/111F/F1115-U136 (4424)
2003/04: 26^UGS, 24^1S, 24^3G, 26^RG,

	Starts	1st	2nd	3rd	Win & Pl
Chases	4	1	0	1	44750
Career Total	14	8	0	1	132347
170	12/03	Hayd	3m	A Ch	SFT £34800
157	2/03	Asct	3m110y	A Ch	G-S £27300
154	2/03	Weth	3m1f	A Ch	G-S £20825
150	11/02	Hayd	2m6f	C Ch	SFT £10885
154	2/02	Uttx	2m4f110yA Hdl		HVY £12000
126	1/02	Leic	2m4f110yE Hdl		SFT £3052
114	12/01	Towc	2m5f	D Hdl	HVY £4192
124	4/01	Prth	2m110y	H NHF	HVY £2842

Total win prize-money £115897

Going: Sf: 1-1 GS: 0-1 Gd: 0-2 GF: - Fm: 0-0
Distance: 2m/2m3: 0-0 2m4-2m7: 0-0 3m+: 1-4
Track: LH: 1-4 RH: 0-0 Tight: 0-0 Gall: 0-2
Aids: Bl: 0-0 Vi: 0-0 Tstrap: 0-0 Ckp: 0-0
Best Rating: 170 12/03 Hayd 3m soft Ch

High-class chaser; unseated on his seasonal reappearance, but impressive winner of the Tommy Whittle at Haydock; below par in the Aon Chase at Newbury on fast ground; has never shown his best at Cheltenham and was well beaten in the Gold Cup; handles soft conditions well, unproven on faster, stays at least 3m 1f; suited by small fields.

Keen To The Last (FR)
107 (102h)**112+**
12-y-o ch g Keen-Derniere Danse (Gay Mecene (USA))
Mrs S J Smith D E Allen & S Balmer

Placings:03223/13442/2122/P44514/22/12F22641P/12-613321 (2547)
2003/04: 21^6GS, 21^1G, 24^3GF, 22^3GF, 20^2G, 22^1GS,

	Starts	1st	2nd	3rd	Win & Pl
Hurdles	1	0	0	0	0
Chases	5	2	1	2	11753
Career Total	39	8	13	5	48891
112	12/03	MRas	2m6f110yD(0-120)HCh		G-S £3731
112	8/03	Ctml	2m5f110yE(0-105)HCh		GD £4387
109	5/02	Sthl	3m110y E(0-110)HCh		GD £3718
106	3/02	Sedg	2m5f	D(0-115)HCh	SFT £4284
102	10/01	Sthl	2m4f110yE(0-115)HHdl		GD £2562
107	3/00	MRas	2m4f	F(0-110)HCh	G-F £3581
113	3/99	Newc	2m4f	E Ch	SFT £4195
97	10/96	Weth	2m4f110yE Hdl		GD £2075

Total win prize-money £28535

Going: Sf: 0-0 GS: 1-2 Gd: 1-3 GF: - Fm: 0-1
Distance: 2m/2m3: 0-0 2m4-2m7: 2-5 3m+: 0-1
Track: LH: 1-4 RH: 1-2 Tight: 2-3 Gall: 0-0
Aids: Bl: 0-0 Vi: 0-0 Tstrap: 0-0 Ckp: 0-0
Best Rating: 113 4/99 Weth 2m4f110y good Ch

Modest chaser; effective at around two and a half miles; needs the top of the ground to stay three miles but handles all types of going; sound jumper.

Keep On Running (FR)
(106h) (116dh)
6-y-o ch g Beyssac (FR)-Kiruna V (a.Arab) (FR) (Thalian)
A King Paul Green

Placings:10P-P (0214)
2003/04: 16^PG,

	Starts	1st	2nd	3rd	Win & Pl
Chases	1	0	0	0	
Career Total	4	1	0	0	3605
116	12/02	Hrfd	2m3f110yE Hdl	SFT	£3605

Total win prize-money £3605

Going: Sf: 0-0 GS: 0-0 Gd: 0-1 GF: - Fm: 0-0
Distance: 2m/2m3: 0-1 2m4-2m7: 0-0 3m+: 0-0
Track: LH: 0-1 RH: 0-0 Tight: 0-0 Gall: 0-0
Aids: Bl: 0-0 Vi: 0-0 Tstrap: 0-0 Ckp: 0-0
Best Rating: 116 12/02 Hrfd 2m3f110y soft Hdl

Keep Smiling (IRE)
(91h) (96+h)**115**
8-y-o b g Broken Hearted-Laugh Away (Furry Glen)
Miss Venetia Williams Mrs Kathy Stuart

Placings:64P/F1UUP-333F (4715)
2003/04: 22^3G, 19^3GS, 22^3S, 20^FG,

	Starts	1st	2nd	3rd	Win & Pl
Hurdles	3	0	0	3	1330
Chases	1	0	0	0	
Career Total	12	1	0	3	7399
115	10/02	Bang	2m4f110yD Ch	G-S	£5796

Total win prize-money £5796

Going: Sf: 0-1 GS: 0-1 Gd: 0-2 GF: - Fm: 0-0
Distance: 2m/2m3: 0-1 2m4-2m7: 0-3 3m+: 0-0
Track: LH: 0-0 RH: 0-4 Tight: 0-1 Gall: 0-0
Aids: Bl: 0-0 Vi: 0-0 Tstrap: 0-0 Ckp: 0-0
Best Rating: 115 10/02 Bang 2m4f110y gd-sft Ch

Fair chaser; moderate hurdler; seemingly best over two and a half miles, but sometimes does not get home in his races; may prefer decent ground.

Keep The Peace (IRE)
70 **36**
6-y-o br g Petardia-Eiras Mood (Jalmood (USA))
D J Wintle D J Wintle

Placings:0 (0528)
2003/04: 16^0GF,

	Starts	1st	2nd	3rd	Win & Pl
Hurdles	1	0	0	0	
Career Total	1	0	0	0	

Going: Sf: 0-0 GS: 0-0 Gd: 0-0 GF: - Fm: 0-1
Distance: 2m/2m3: 0-1 2m4-2m7: 0-0 3m+: 0-0
Track: LH: 0-1 RH: 0-0 Tight: 0-0 Gall: 0-0
Aids: Bl: 0-0 Vi: 0-0 Tstrap: 0-0 Ckp: 0-0
Best Rating: 41 6/03 Worc 2m gd-fm Hdl

Keepatem (IRE)
109 **130**
8-y-o ch g Be My Native (USA)-Ariannrun (Deep Run)
M F Morris John P McManus

Placings:0/0B1/00051413-302 (4643)
2003/04: 24^3S, 25^UG, 24^2G,

	Starts	1st	2nd	3rd	Win & Pl
Hurdles	3	0	1	1	11018
Career Total	15	3	1	2	49821
123	2/03	Punc	3m	HHdl	SH £12678
113	1/03	Leop	3m	HHdl	SFT £16883
114	2/01	Thur	2m	Hdl	Y-S £4451

Total win prize-money £34014

Going: Sf: 0-1 GS: 0-1 Gd: 0-2 GF: - Fm: 0-0
Distance: 2m/2m3: 0-0 2m4-2m7: 0-0 3m+: 0-3
Track: LH: 0-3 RH: 0-0 Tight: 0-1 Gall: 0-1
Aids: Bl: 0-0 Vi: 0-0 Tstrap: 0-0 Ckp: 0-0
Best Rating: 130 4/04 Aint 3m110y good Hdl

Useful Irish hurdler; effective at two miles, but seemingly better suited by three; goes well on soft ground; open to further improvement.

Keeper's Call (IRE)
12-y-o b g Mandalus-Thistletopper (Le Bavard (FR))
Mrs V J Makin R G Makin

Placings:12/4/P/56/5-F (0103)
2003/04: 25^FG,

	Starts	1st	2nd	3rd	Win & Pl
Chases	1	0	0	0	
Career Total	8	1	1	0	2433
102	4/99	Carl	3m2f	H Ch	GD £1155

Total win prize-money £1155

Going: Sf: 0-0 GS: 0-0 Gd: 0-1 GF: - Fm: 0-0
Distance: 2m/2m3: 0-0 2m4-2m7: 0-0 3m+: 0-1
Track: LH: 0-1 RH: 0-0 Tight: 0-0 Gall: 0-0
Aids: Bl: 0-0 Vi: 0-0 Tstrap: 0-0 Ckp: 0-0
Best Rating: 107 4/99 Chel 3m1f110y gd-sft Ch

Keepers Mead (IRE)
104 **108+**
6-y-o ch g Aahsaylad-Runaway Pilot (Cheval)
R H Alner J C Browne

Placings:6F6P-216356 (4819)
2003/04: 24^2GF, 24^1G, 25^6GS, 24^3GS, 24^5G, 22^6GF,

	Starts	1st	2nd	3rd	Win & Pl
Hurdles	6	1	1	1	6162
Career Total	10	1	1	1	6162
108	11/03	Asct	3m	D Hdl	GD £4615

Total win prize-money £4615

Going: Sf: 0-0 GS: 0-2 Gd: 1-2 GF: - Fm: 0-2
Distance: 2m/2m3: 0-0 2m4-2m7: 0-1 3m+: 1-5
Track: LH: 0-2 RH: 1-4 Tight: 0-0 Gall: 0-1
Aids: Bl: 0-0 Vi: 0-0 Tstrap: 0-0 Ckp: 0-1
Best Rating: 108 2/04 Kemp 3m110y good Hdl

Modest hurdler; stays three miles and probably best with some cut.

Keepthedreamalive
104 **103**
6-y-o gr g Roselier (FR)-Nicklup (Netherkelly)
R H Buckler Twentyman

Placings:5532 (4098)
2003/04: 16^5S, 17^5GS, 18^3GS, 21^2G,

	Starts	1st	2nd	3rd	Win & Pl
NH Flat	3	0	0	1	282
Hurdles	1	0	1	0	1840
Career Total	4	0	1	1	2122

Going: Sf: 0-1 GS: 0-2 Gd: 0-1 GF: - Fm: 0-0
Distance: 2m/2m3: 0-3 2m4-2m7: 0-1 3m+: 0-0
Track: LH: 0-3 RH: 0-1 Tight: 0-2 Gall: 0-0
Aids: Bl: 0-0 Vi: 0-0 Tstrap: 0-0 Ckp: 0-0
Best Rating: 110 3/04 Plum 2m5f good Hdl

Fifth of 14 in Grade Two bumper on debut at Chepstow, but disappointed next time at Exter; beaten a length on latest effort in average bumper at Fontwell latest on good to soft.

Keetchy (IRE)
71   **86**
5-y-o b g Darshaan-Ezana (Ela-Mana-Mou)
J D Frost The Tuesday Syndicate

Placings:5-P0   (3251)
2003/04: 19PS, 16QGS,

	Starts	1st	2nd	3rd	Win & Pl
Hurdles	2	0	0	0	
Career Total	3	0	0	0	0

Going: Sf: 0-1 GS: 0-1 Gd: 0-0 GF: - Fm: 0-0
Distance: 2m/2m3: 0-1 2m4-2m7: 0-1 3m+: 0-0
Track: LH: 0-1 RH: 0-1 Tight: 0-1 Gall: 0-0
Aids: Bl: 0-0 Vi: 0-0 Tstrap: 0-0 Ckp: 0-0
Best Rating: 92 3/03 Strf 2m110y gd-sft Hdl

Keimar
5-y-o b g Syrtos-Crimson Sol (Crimson Beau)
D G Bridgwater Mrs Mary Bridgwater

Placings:00P   (1270)
2003/04: 16QG, 16QG, 19PGF,

	Starts	1st	2nd	3rd	Win & Pl
NH Flat	2	0	0	0	0
Hurdles	1	0	0	0	0
Career Total	3	0	0	0	

Going: Sf: 0-0 GS: 0-0 Gd: 0-2 GF: - Fm: 0-1
Distance: 2m/2m3: 0-3 2m4-2m7: 0-0 3m+: 0-0
Track: LH: 0-2 RH: 0-0 Tight: 0-0 Gall: 0-0
Aids: Bl: 0-0 Vi: 0-0 Tstrap: 0-0 Ckp: 0-0
Best Rating: 69 7/03 Worc 2m good NHF

Keiran (IRE)
109(104h)   (101h)**130**
10-y-o b g Be My Native (USA)-Myra Gaye (Buckskin (FR))
H P Hogarth Hogarth Racing

Placings:60/241400/261213P412-1F41   (3374)
2003/04: 251G, 28FS, 284G, 251S,

	Starts	1st	2nd	3rd	Win & Pl
Chases	4	2	0	0	19051
Career Total	22	6	4	1	50703

130 1/04 Weth 3m1f B(0-150)HCh SFT £11492
127 11/03 Weth 3m1f C(0-130)HCh GD £7020
124 3/03 Newc 3m D(0-115)HCh G-S £6747
117 11/02 Newc 3m D Ch G-S £6711
117 10/02 Sedg 2m5f E Ch GD £4030
101 11/01 Catt 2m F(0-100)HHdl G-F £2607
Total win prize-money £38608

Going: Sf: 1-2 GS: 0-0 Gd: 1-2 GF: - Fm: 0-0
Distance: 2m/2m3: 0-3 2m4-2m7: 0-0 3m+: 2-4
Track: LH: 2-3 RH: 0-1 Tight: 0-1 Gall: 0-0
Aids: Bl: 1-2 Vi: 0-0 Tstrap: 0-0 Ckp: 0-0
Best Rating: 130 1/04 Weth 3m1f soft Ch

Fair chaser; recorded fourth career success on return to action at Wetherby in November 2003; on the mark again there in January; best at three miles; effective on soft ground; has been tried in blinkers.

Keitho (IRE)
(99h)   (82h)
9-y-o b g Niels-Swift Charmer (Beau Charmeur (FR))
P F Nicholls John Honeyball

Placings:00P/P43   (0870)
2003/04: 26PG, 224GF, 213GF,

	Starts	1st	2nd	3rd	Win & Pl
Hurdles	1	0	0	0	376
Chases	2	0	0	1	828
Career Total	6	0	0	1	1204

Going: Sf: 0-0 GS: 0-0 Gd: 0-1 GF: - Fm: 0-2
Distance: 2m/2m3: 0-0 2m4-2m7: 0-2 3m+: 0-1
Track: LH: 0-3 RH: 0-0 Tight: 0-3 Gall: 0-0
Aids: Bl: 0-1 Vi: 0-0 Tstrap: 0-0 Ckp: 0-0
Best Rating: 82 6/03 NAbb 2m6f gd-fm Hdl

Joined the Nicholls yard after doing well in points; disappointed on chase debut; stays three miles; acts on good ground.

Kelami (FR)
110   (120h)**140+**
6-y-o b g Lute Antique (FR)-Voltige De Nievre (FR) (Brezzo (FR))
F Doumen Halewood International Ltd

Placings:22P/4302315-36514B0   (4647)
2003/04: 213VS, 216VS, 215VS, 241G, 244G, 36QG, 230HO,

	Starts	1st	2nd	3rd	Win & Pl
Chases	7	1	0	1	39553
Career Total	17	2	3	6	91818

140 12/03 Kemp 3m C(0-135)HCh GD £23200
3/03 Autl 2m1f110y HCh VS £23377
Total win prize-money £46577

Going: Sf: 0-0 GS: 0-0 Gd: 1-3 GF: - Fm: 0-0
Distance: 2m/2m3: 0-0 2m4-2m7: 0-3 3m+: 1-4
Track: LH: 0-2 RH: 1-1 Tight: 0-1 Gall: 0-1
Aids: Bl: 0-0 Vi: 0-0 Tstrap: 0-1 Ckp: 0-0
Best Rating: 140 12/03 Kemp 3m good Ch

Useful chaser; French trained; impressive winner at Kempton on his British debut in December 2003; fourth in good handicap at the Cheltenham Festival; stays three miles and acts on most types of ground.

Kelantan
104(85h)   (100h)**119**
7-y-o b g Kris-Surf Bird (Shareef Dancer (USA))
K C Bailey Have Fun Racing Partnership

Placings:0/6-U14414324   (4941)
2003/04: 20US, 201G, 164GS, 184GS, 241GS, 234G, 203S, 222G, 314GS,

	Starts	1st	2nd	3rd	Win & Pl
Hurdles	2	1	0	0	5173
Chases	7	1	1	1	9254
Career Total	11	2	1	1	14427

114 12/03 Hntg 3m E(0-110)HCh G-S £3920
100 5/03 Weth 2m4f110yD Hdl GD £5173
Total win prize-money £9093

Going: Sf: 0-2 GS: 1-4 Gd: 1-3 GF: - Fm: 0-0
Distance: 2m/2m3: 0-2 2m4-2m7: 1-4 3m+: 1-3
Track: LH: 1-5 RH: 1-3 Tight: 0-0 Gall: 1-4

Aids: Bl: 0-0 Vi: 0-0 Tstrap: 0-0 Ckp: 0-2
Best Rating: 114 12/03 Hntg 3m gd-sft Ch

No form in two bumpers; upset a long odds-on shot on second outing over hurdles at Wetherby in May; has shown a little ability over hurdles; moderate chaser so far; stays three miles and seems to handle most types of ground.

Kelly (SAF)
98   **109**
7-y-o b g Ethique (ARG)-Dancing Flower (SAF) (Dancing Champ (USA))
Miss Venetia Williams P A Deal

Placings:35   (1503)
2003/04: 173GF, 165GF,

	Starts	1st	2nd	3rd	Win & Pl
Hurdles	2	0	0	1	503
Career Total	2	0	0	1	503

Going: Sf: 0-0 GS: 0-0 Gd: 0-0 GF: - Fm: 0-2
Distance: 2m/2m3: 0-2 2m4-2m7: 0-0 3m+: 0-0
Track: LH: 0-2 RH: 0-0 Tight: 0-0 Gall: 0-0
Aids: Bl: 0-0 Vi: 0-0 Tstrap: 0-0 Ckp: 0-0
Best Rating: 109 10/03 Chep 2m110y gd-fm Hdl

Ex-South African gelding; showed promise in an above average Southwell hurdle on his debut; disappointing when a springer next time.

Kelly Pride
83(99h)   (86h)**51**
7-y-o b g Afflora (IRE)-Pearly-B (IRE) (Gunner B)
Mrs S J Smith J Townson, A Thomason, P Chapman

Placings:000/P503-226530   (3325)
2003/04: 262GS, 202GF, 206S, 245S, 253GS, 210GS,

	Starts	1st	2nd	3rd	Win & Pl
Hurdles	5	0	2	1	2568
Chases	1	0	0	0	0
Career Total	13	0	2	2	3088

Going: Sf: 0-2 GS: 0-3 Gd: 0-0 GF: - Fm: 0-1
Distance: 2m/2m3: 0-0 2m4-2m7: 0-3 3m+: 0-3
Track: LH: 0-6 RH: 0-0 Tight: 0-2 Gall: 0-0
Aids: Bl: 0-0 Vi: 0-0 Tstrap: 0-0 Ckp: 0-0
Best Rating: 86 12/03 Weth 3m1f gd-sft Hdl

Very limited ability over hurdles to date.

Kellys Fable
85f   **70f**
4-y-o b g Thowra (FR)-Kellys Special (Netherkelly)
J W Mullins F G Matthews

Placings:6   (4739)
2003/04: 176G,

	Starts	1st	2nd	3rd	Win & Pl
NH Flat	1	0	0	0	0
Career Total	1	0	0	0	0

Going: Sf: 0-0 GS: 0-0 Gd: 0-1 GF: - Fm: 0-0
Distance: 2m/2m3: 0-1 2m4-2m7: 0-0 3m+: 0-0
Track: LH: 0-1 RH: 0-0 Tight: 0-1 Gall: 0-0
Aids: Bl: 0-0 Vi: 0-0 Tstrap: 0-0 Ckp: 0-0
Best Rating: 70 4/04 NAbb 2m1f good NHF

Kelnik Glory

102   **75**

8-y-o b g Nalchik (USA)-Areal (IRE) (Roselier (FR))
Mrs S M Johnson G Button

Placings:000062/P/50-433					(0833)
2003/04: 20⁴GF, 22³GF, 24³GF,					

	Starts	1st	2nd	3rd	Win & Pl
Hurdles	3	0	0	2	933
Career Total	12	0	1	2	1556

Going:	Sf: 0-0 GS: 0-0 Gd: 0-0 GF: - Fm: 0-3
Distance:	2m/2m3: 0-0 2m4-2m7: 0-2 3m+: 0-1
Track:	LH: 0-3 RH: 0-0 Tight: 0-1 Gall: 0-0
Aids:	Bl: 0-0 Vi: 0-0 Tstrap: 0-0 Ckp: 0-0
Best Rating:	81 6/03 NAbb 2m6f gd-fm Hdl

Modest maiden hurdler at up to 2m 6f.

Kelrev (FR)

114(101h)   (116+h)**141**

6-y-o ch g Video Rock (FR)-Belliile II (FR) (Brezzo (FR))
Miss Venetia Williams Len Jakeman, Flintham, King & Roberts

Placings:21F111333-3412204					(4399)
2003/04: 16²GS, 16⁴G, 16¹HY, 21²GS, 21²S, 20⁶G, 20⁴G,					

	Starts	1st	2nd	3rd	Win & Pl
Hurdles	1	0	1	0	2110
Chases	6	1	1	1	25751
Career Total	16	5	3	4	57718
140	1/04	Uttx	2m	C(0-130)HCh	HVY £11948
	11/02	Engh	2m3f	Ch	HVY £12368
	10/02	Pina	2m2f110y	Ch	GD £3534
	9/02	Comp	2m1f110y	Ch	SFT £4417
	8/02	Vich	2m110y	Hdl	GD £3828
				Total win prize-money £36095

Going:	Sf: 1-3 GS: 0-1 Gd: 0-3 GF: - Fm: 0-0
Distance:	2m/2m3: 1-3 2m4-2m7: 0-4 3m+: 0-0
Track:	LH: 1-5 RH: 0-2 Tight: 0-1 Gall: 0-3
Aids:	Bl: 0-0 Vi: 0-0 Tstrap: 0-0 Ckp: 0-0
Best Rating:	140 1/04 Chel 2m5f gd-sft Ch

Fair hurdler/useful chaser; winning hurdler/chaser in France; has won over two miles over hurdles and two miles three over fences; suited by heavy ground.

Keltic Bard

114(108h)   (139+h)**149+**

7-y-o b g Emperor Jones (USA)-Broughton Singer (IRE) (Common Grounds)
C J Mann M Rowland, M Collins & P Cox

Placings:4/63245/1021F4-2512011					(4860)
2003/04: 17²G, 16⁵GS, 16¹G, 16²S, 16⁹G, 20¹G, 20¹GS,					

	Starts	1st	2nd	3rd	Win & Pl
Chases	7	3	2	0	50707
Career Total	19	5	4	1	75952
145	4/04	Ayr	2m4f	A Ch	G-S £20825
149	4/04	Aint	2m4f	B HCh	GD £19256
132	1/04	Leic	2m	E Ch	GD £4836
125	1/03	Chel	2m1f	D(0-120)HHdl	G-S £10483
124	11/02	Newb	2m110y	C Hdl	SFT £6815
				Total win prize-money £62215

Going:	Sf: 0-1 GS: 1-2 Gd: 2-4 GF: - Fm: 0-0
Distance:	2m/2m3: 1-5 2m4-2m7: 2-2 3m+: 0-0
Track:	LH: 2-4 RH: 1-3 Tight: 1-1 Gall: 0-1
Aids:	Bl: 0-0 Vi: 0-0 Tstrap: 0-0 Ckp: 0-0
Best Rating:	149 4/04 Aint 2m4f good Ch

Smart novice chaser; very disappointing in the Arkle at Cheltenham, always behind and never getting involved; bounced back to win an amateur riders' chase at Aintree; fortunate winner at Ayr in April; stays 2m4f; best on top of the ground; suited by coming late off a strong pace.

Keltic Blue (IRE)

51   **16**

5-y-o b g Blues Traveller (IRE)-White Cap'S (Shirley Heights)
R Dickin The Alscot Blue Group

Placings:0					(3697)
2003/04: 17⁰HY,					

	Starts	1st	2nd	3rd	Win & Pl
Hurdles	1	0	0	0	
Career Total	1	0	0	0	

Going:	Sf: 0-1 GS: 0-0 Gd: 0-0 GF: - Fm: 0-0
Distance:	2m/2m3: 0-1 2m4-2m7: 0-0 3m+: 0-0
Track:	LH: 0-0 RH: 0-1 Tight: 0-0 Gall: 0-0
Aids:	Bl: 0-0 Vi: 0-0 Tstrap: 0-0 Ckp: 0-0
Best Rating:	10 2/04 Hrld 2m1f heavy Hdl

Keltic Heritage (IRE)

102(104h)   (97h)**124**

10-y-o gr g Roselier (FR)-Peek-A-Step (IRE) (Step Together (USA))
L A Dace Danny O'Sullivan

Placings:5P0/06P/32311202/41F634211P-42065					(4327)
2003/04: 26⁴GF, 28²G, 24⁰GS, 24⁶G, 24⁵GS,					

	Starts	1st	2nd	3rd	Win & Pl
Hurdles	1	0	0	0	0
Chases	4	0	1	0	1230
Career Total	29	5	5	3	38318
120	4/03	Chel	3m1f110yB Ch	GD £13030
124	3/03	MRas	3m1f	D Ch	GD £6760
114	10/02	Hrfd	3m1f110yE Ch	GD £4134
91	1/02	Font	2m6f110yF(0-90)HHdl	SFT £2324
83	1/02	Hntg	2m5f110yF(0-95)HHdl	G-S £2058
				Total win prize-money £28307

Going:	Sf: 0-0 GS: 0-2 Gd: 0-2 GF: - Fm: 0-1
Distance:	2m/2m3: 0-0 2m4-2m7: 0-0 3m+: 0-5
Track:	LH: 0-3 RH: 0-2 Tight: 0-1 Gall: 0-3
Aids:	Bl: 0-0 Vi: 0-0 Tstrap: 0-4 Ckp: 0-0
Best Rating:	124 10/03 Strf 3m4f good Ch

Modest chaser; stays three miles one; front-runner; jumps soundly and likes fast ground; wears a tongue tie.

Keltic Lord

8-y-o b g Arctic Lord-Scarlet Dymond (Rymer)
Miss S Waugh The Last to Leave Racing Partnership

Placings:00/0/00/FPP					(4858)
2003/04: 24⁵G, 19⁰PG, 24⁰GF,					

	Starts	1st	2nd	3rd	Win & Pl
Chases	3	0	0	0	
Career Total	8	0	0	0	

Going:	Sf: 0-0 GS: 0-0 Gd: 0-2 GF: - Fm: 0-1
Distance:	2m/2m3: 0-0 2m4-2m7: 0-1 3m+: 0-2
Track:	LH: 0-1 RH: 0-2 Tight: 0-2 Gall: 0-0
Aids:	Bl: 0-0 Vi: 0-0 Tstrap: 0-0 Ckp: 0-0
Best Rating:	60 2/00 Winc 2m good NHF

Keltic Rock

90f   **80f**

5-y-o ch g Bigstone (IRE)-Sibley (Northfields (USA))
G B Balding D J Erwin Bloodstock & Tony Geake

Placings:00					(3354)
2003/04: 16⁰S, 16⁰S,					

	Starts	1st	2nd	3rd	Win & Pl
NH Flat	2	0	0	0	
Career Total	2	0	0	0	

Going:	Sf: 0-2 GS: 0-0 Gd: 0-0 GF: - Fm: 0-0
Distance:	2m/2m3: 0-2 2m4-2m7: 0-0 3m+: 0-0
Track:	LH: 0-0 RH: 0-2 Tight: 0-0 Gall: 0-1
Aids:	Bl: 0-0 Vi: 0-0 Tstrap: 0-0 Ckp: 0-0
Best Rating:	80 1/04 Hntg 2m10y soft NHF

Kemal's Council (IRE)

94   (113h)**121**

8-y-o gr g Leading Counsel (USA)-Kemal's Princess (Kemal (FR))
Jonjo O'Neill Bateman, Gilruth, Milward & Singleton

Placings:403/1222P/11FP-F5FP					(3214)
2003/04: 24⁵GS, 25⁵G, 29⁵S, 25⁶GS,					

	Starts	1st	2nd	3rd	Win & Pl
Chases	4	0	0	0	0
Career Total	16	3	3	1	15340
120	12/02	Fknm	3m110y	E Ch	G-S £4424
120	11/02	Weth	3m1f	D Ch	G-S £4745
113	5/01	Hexm	3m	E Hdl	SFT £2688
				Total win prize-money £11857

Going:	Sf: 0-2 GS: 0-1 Gd: 0-1 GF: - Fm: 0-0
Distance:	2m/2m3: 0-0 2m4-2m7: 0-0 3m+: 0-4
Track:	LH: 0-3 RH: 0-1 Tight: 0-0 Gall: 0-0
Aids:	Bl: 0-2 Vi: 0-0 Tstrap: 0-0 Ckp: 0-0
Best Rating:	120 12/02 Fknm 3m110y gd-sft Ch

Fair chaser/hurdler, made a good start over fences in late 2002, but disappointing since; stays 3m 1f; acts well in soft ground.

Kempski

86f   **68f**

4-y-o b g Petoski-Little Katrina (Little Buskins)
R Nixon G R S Nixon

Placings:500					(4663)
2003/04: 16⁵GS, 16⁰S, 16⁰S,					

	Starts	1st	2nd	3rd	Win & Pl
NH Flat	3	0	0	0	0
Career Total	3	0	0	0	0

Going:	Sf: 0-2 GS: 0-1 Gd: 0-0 GF: - Fm: 0-0
Distance:	2m/2m3: 0-3 2m4-2m7: 0-0 3m+: 0-0
Track:	LH: 0-3 RH: 0-0 Tight: 0-0 Gall: 0-0
Aids:	Bl: 0-0 Vi: 0-0 Tstrap: 0-0 Ckp: 0-0
Best Rating:	68 2/04 Ayr 2m gd-sft NHF

Half-brother to a couple of winning jumpers and not disgraced in bumper at Ayr in February 2004 on debut; may do better.

Ken Scott (FR)

101   **112+**

6-y-o b g Kendor (FR)-Scottish Bride (FR) (Owen Dudley)

P Winkworth Help-Yourself

Placings:1642-35663P **(4651)**
2003/04: 16²S, 16⁵S, 16⁶G, 21⁶G, 18³G, 17⁸G,

	Starts	1st	2nd	3rd	Win & Pl
Hurdles	6	0	0	2	2391
Career Total	10	1	1	2	7381

108 11/02 Hntg 2m110y E Hdl G-S £3003
Total win prize-money £3003

Going: Sf: 0-2 GS: 0-0 Gd: 0-4 GF: - Fm: 0-0
Distance: 2m/2m3: 0-5 2m4-2m7: 0-1 3m+: 0-0
Track: LH: 0-2 RH: 0-0 Tight: 0-2 Gall: 0-0
Aids: Bl: 0-0 Vi: 0-0 Tstrap: 0-0 Ckp: 0-0
Best Rating: 112 2/03 Font 2m2f110y soft Hdl

Modest hurdler; a winner on the level in France; acts on soft ground; best at around two miles.

Ken'tucky (FR)
109   115+
6-y-o b g Video Rock (FR)-La Salamandre (FR) (Pot D'Or (FR))
N J Henderson Sir Robert Ogden

Placings:343-44011P **(4838)**
2003/04: 16⁴G, 21⁴S, 22⁹GS, 24¹G, 26¹G, 24⁸GF,

	Starts	1st	2nd	3rd	Win & Pl
Hurdles	6	2	0	0	9507
Career Total	9	2	0	2	10398

115 2/04 Ludl 3m2f110yE(0-110)HHdl GD £4124
100 1/04 Ludl 3m D(0-115)HHdl GD £4832
Total win prize-money £8957

Going: Sf: 0-1 GS: 0-1 Gd: 2-3 GF: - Fm: 0-1
Distance: 2m/2m3: 0-1 2m4-2m7: 0-2 3m+: 2-3
Track: LH: 0-2 RH: 2-4 Tight: 0-1 Gall: 0-1
Aids: Bl: 0-0 Vi: 0-0 Tstrap: 0-0 Ckp: 0-0
Best Rating: 115 2/04 Ludl 3m2f110y good Hdl

Moderate hurdler; twice a Ludlow winer in 2004; acts on good ground.

Kendra (GER)
91   75+
5-y-o b m Goofalik (USA)-Keniana (IRE) (Sharpo)
Frau E Mader Mader Trainingsbetrieb GmbH

Placings:0540 **(3859)**
2003/04: 15⁰G, 15⁵G, 21⁴S, 16⁰S,

	Starts	1st	2nd	3rd	Win & Pl
Hurdles	4	0	0	0	162
Career Total	4	0	0	0	162

Going: Sf: 0-2 GS: 0-0 Gd: 0-2 GF: - Fm: 0-0
Distance: 2m/2m3: 0-1 2m4-2m7: 0-1 3m+: 0-0
Track: LH: 0-2 RH: 0-0 Tight: 0-2 Gall: 0-0
Aids: Bl: 0-0 Vi: 0-0 Tstrap: 0-0 Ckp: 0-0
Best Rating: 75 12/03 Plum 2m5f soft Hdl

Kent
77   46
9-y-o b g Kylian (USA)-Precious Caroline (IRE) (The Noble Player (USA))
P D Cundell Miss M C Fraser

Placings:5 **(0289)**
2003/04: 20⁵GS,

	Starts	1st	2nd	3rd	Win & Pl
Hurdles	1	0	0	0	0
Career Total	1	0	0	0	0

Going: Sf: 0-0 GS: 0-1 Gd: 0-0 GF: - Fm: 0-0
Distance: 2m/2m3: 0-0 2m4-2m7: 0-1 3m+: 0-0
Track: LH: 0-1 RH: 0-0 Tight: 0-0 Gall: 0-0
Aids: Bl: 0-0 Vi: 0-1 Tstrap: 0-0 Ckp: 0-0
Best Rating: 57 5/03 Aint 2m4f gd-sft Hdl

Kentford Busy B

10-y-o b m Petoski-Busy Mittens (Nearly A Hand)
Miss S A Loggin K Rolls

Placings:3245/526P5/6P1350/6-U **(4761)**
2003/04: 25⁵U,

	Starts	1st	2nd	3rd	Win & Pl
Chases	1	0	0	0	
Career Total	17	1	2	2	5182

100 10/00 Extr 2m6f110yE(0-105)HHdl SFT £3071
Total win prize-money £3071

Going: Sf: 0-1 GS: 0-0 Gd: 0-0 GF: - Fm: 0-0
Distance: 2m/2m3: 0-0 2m4-2m7: 0-0 3m+: 0-1
Track: LH: 0-0 RH: 0-1 Tight: 0-0 Gall: 0-0
Aids: Bl: 0-0 Vi: 0-0 Tstrap: 0-0 Ckp: 0-0
Best Rating: 100 11/00 Extr 2m6f110y gd-sft Hdl

Kentford Grebe
109   111
5-y-o b m Teenoso (USA)-Notinhand (Nearly A Hand)
J W Mullins D I Bare

Placings:600U3-114013 **(4842)**
2003/04: 20¹G, 21¹G, 17⁴G, 20⁹GS, 21¹G, 21³G,

	Starts	1st	2nd	3rd	Win & Pl
Hurdles	6	3	0	1	39727
Career Total	11	3	0	2	40248

108 3/04 Newb 2m5f A HHdl GD £29000
98 11/03 Wwck 2m5f E Hdl GD £3391
90 10/03 Bang 2m4f D Hdl GD £3737
Total win prize-money £36130

Going: Sf: 0-0 GS: 0-1 Gd: 3-5 GF: - Fm: 0-0
Distance: 2m/2m3: 0-1 2m4-2m7: 3-5 3m+: 0-0
Track: LH: 3-5 RH: 0-1 Tight: 1-1 Gall: 1-3
Aids: Bl: 0-0 Vi: 0-0 Tstrap: 0-0 Ckp: 0-0
Best Rating: 111 4/04 Chel 2m5f110y good Hdl

Modest hurdler; stays two and a half miles; acts on good ground.

Kentish Warrior (IRE)

6-y-o b g Warcraft (USA)-Garden County (Ragapan)
B I Case Lady Jane Grosvenor

Placings:0-P0P **(3170)**
2003/04: 21⁸S, 20⁹GS, 22⁸HY,

	Starts	1st	2nd	3rd	Win & Pl
Hurdles	3	0	0	0	
Career Total	4	0	0	0	

Going: Sf: 0-1 GS: 0-1 Gd: 0-0 GF: - Fm: 0-0
Distance: 2m/2m3: 0-0 2m4-2m7: 0-3 3m+: 0-0
Track: LH: 0-2 RH: 0-1 Tight: 0-2 Gall: 0-0
Aids: Bl: 0-0 Vi: 0-0 Tstrap: 0-3 Ckp: 0-0
Best Rating: 46 3/03 Newb 2m110y good NHF

Kentucky Blue (IRE)
101   115
4-y-o b g Revoque (IRE)-Delta Town (USA) (Sanglamore (USA))
T D Easterby C H Stevens

Placings:1F145 **(4190)**
2003/04: 16¹GS, 16⁶GS, 16¹G, 16⁴S, 18⁵GS,

	Starts	1st	2nd	3rd	Win & Pl
Hurdles	5	2	0	0	8603
Career Total	5	2	0	0	8603

111 2/04 Catt 2m E Hdl GD £3489
104 11/03 Weth 2m D Hdl G-S £3576
Total win prize-money £7065

Going: Sf: 0-1 GS: 1-3 Gd: 1-1 GF: - Fm: 0-0
Distance: 2m/2m3: 2-5 2m4-2m7: 0-0 3m+: 0-0
Track: LH: 2-5 RH: 0-0 Tight: 1-2 Gall: 0-0
Aids: Bl: 0-0 Vi: 0-0 Tstrap: 0-0 Ckp: 0-0
Best Rating: 115 2/04 Hayd 2m soft Hdl

Fair juvenile hurdler; useful on the Flat; winner of novice events at Wetherby and Catterick in February so far; suited by two miles; suited by soft ground.

Kepi De Kerfellec (FR)
91   59
6-y-o b g Valanjou (FR)-Ulfica (FR) (Quart De Vin (FR))
M D Hammond Mike Newbould

Placings:P60 **(3767)**
2003/04: 24⁸HY, 23⁶S, 17⁰HY,

	Starts	1st	2nd	3rd	Win & Pl
Hurdles	3	0	0	0	0
Career Total	3	0	0	0	0

Going: Sf: 0-3 GS: 0-0 Gd: 0-0 GF: - Fm: 0-0
Distance: 2m/2m3: 0-1 2m4-2m7: 0-1 3m+: 0-1
Track: LH: 0-1 RH: 0-2 Tight: 0-0 Gall: 0-0
Aids: Bl: 0-0 Vi: 0-0 Tstrap: 0-0 Ckp: 0-0
Best Rating: 59 1/04 Weth 2m7f soft Hdl

Kercabellec (FR)
105   108
6-y-o b/br g Useful (FR)-Marie De Geneve (FR) (Nishapour (FR))
N J Henderson Sir Peter and Lady Gibbings

Placings:2/5-1PF6 **(4589)**
2003/04: 16¹GS, 16⁸GS, 16⁶G, 16⁶G,

	Starts	1st	2nd	3rd	Win & Pl
Hurdles	4	1	0	0	3399
Career Total	6	1	1	0	5313

104 11/03 Wwck 2m E Hdl GD £3398
Total win prize-money £3399

Going: Sf: 0-0 GS: 0-1 Gd: 1-3 GF: - Fm: 0-0
Distance: 2m/2m3: 1-4 2m4-2m7: 0-0 3m+: 0-0
Track: LH: 1-1 RH: 0-3 Tight: 0-0 Gall: 0-1
Aids: Bl: 0-0 Vi: 0-0 Tstrap: 0-2 Ckp: 0-0
Best Rating: 108 12/02 Newb 2m110y heavy Hdl

Modest novice hurdler; effective over two miles; acts on any ground.

Kerrigand (FR)
105(110h)   (121h)135
6-y-o gr g April Night (FR)-Gouerie (FR) (Cadoudal (FR))

M C Pipe Mrs Sarah Ling

Placings:52400/3521250-1115   (0716)
2003/04: 23^{1}G, 23^{1}G, 24^{1}GF, 24^{5}G,

	Starts	1st	2nd	3rd	Win & Pl
Chases	4	3	0	0	15914
Career Total	16	4	3	1	46091
127 6/03 Uttx	3m	E Ch		G-F	£5464
135 5/03 Worc	2m7f110y	E Ch		GD	£3958
132 5/03 Worc	2m7f110y	D Ch		GD	£5703
116 12/02 Tntn	2m1f	D Hdl		SFT	£4972
				Total win prize-money	£20100

Going:	Sf: 0-0 GS: 0-0 Gd: 2-3 GF: - Fm: 1-1
Distance:	2m/2m3: 0-0 2m4-2m7: 0-0 3m+: 3-4
Track:	LH: 3-3 RH: 0-1 Tight: 0-0 Gall: 0-0
Aids:	Bl: 0-0 Vi: 0-0 Tstrap: 0-0 Ckp: 0-0
Best Rating:	135 5/03 Worc 2m7f110y good Ch

Ex-French; decent novice hurdler; won 3m novice chases at Worcester May 2003 on first two starts over fences; acts on most types of ground; has worn blinkers; looks the type to run up a sequence in novice chases and won a match by a wide margin at Uttoxeter in June.

Kerry Lads (IRE)
105(110h)   (113+h)129
9-y-o ch g Mister Lord (USA)-Minstrel Top (Black Minstrel)
Miss Lucinda V Russell Mrs C G Greig

Placings:340/30F3312132/3F321F4-2PF5P12   (4861)
2003/04: 24^{2}S, 26^{6}G, 20^{5}HY, 28^{5}G, 24^{5}S, 24^{1}HY, 33^{2}GS,

	Starts	1st	2nd	3rd	Win & Pl
Hurdles	1	1	0	0	3868
Chases	6	0	2	0	29112
Career Total	27	4	5	7	74354
113 3/04 Carl	3m110y	E(0-105)HHdl		HVY	£3867
129 2/03 Ayr	3m1f	D(0-125)HCh		G-S	£6812
114 3/02 Ayr	3m1f	D Ch		HVY	£4452
101 1/02 Carl	3m2f	D Ch		HVY	£4959
				Total win prize-money	£20092

Going:	Sf: 1-4 GS: 0-1 Gd: 0-2 GF: - Fm: 0-0
Distance:	2m/2m3: 0-0 2m4-2m7: 0-1 3m+: 1-6
Track:	LH: 0-4 RH: 1-3 Tight: 0-0 Gall: 0-2
Aids:	Bl: 0-0 Vi: 0-0 Tstrap: 0-0 Ckp: 0-1
Best Rating:	129 11/03 Carl 3m soft Ch

Useful chaser; consistent sort; fourth in the 2003 Scottish National and second in 2004 renewal; won over hurdles at Carlisle in March 2004; stays well; effective in testing ground but tendency to make mistakes has held him back to a certain degree.

Kerry Soldier Blue

15-y-o gr g Blue Flag-Kerry Maid (Maestoso)
D O Stephens D O Stephens

Placings:P3/P2/24P/62430F/0-P   (0240)
2003/04: 25^{5}G,

	Starts	1st	2nd	3rd	Win & Pl
Chases	1	0	0	0	
Career Total	15	0	3	2	3922

Going:	Sf: 0-0 GS: 0-0 Gd: 0-1 GF: - Fm: 0-0
Distance:	2m/2m3: 0-0 2m4-2m7: 0-0 3m+: 0-1
Track:	LH: 0-0 RH: 0-1 Tight: 0-0 Gall: 0-0
Aids:	Bl: 0-0 Vi: 0-0 Tstrap: 0-0 Ckp: 0-0
Best Rating:	100 4/00 Chep 3m soft Ch

Kestick
9-y-o b g Roscoe Blake-Hop The Twig (Full Of Hope)
M Biddick C J Rush

Placings:3211   (4635)
2003/04: 21^{3}G, 19^{2}GF, 24^{1}G, 24^{1}G,

	Starts	1st	2nd	3rd	Win & Pl
Chases	4	2	1	1	5798
Career Total	4	2	1	1	5798
113 4/04 Tntn	3m	H Ch		GD	£2404
100 3/04 Tntn	3m	H Ch		GD	£2027
				Total win prize-money	£4432

Going:	Sf: 0-0 GS: 0-0 Gd: 2-3 GF: - Fm: 0-1
Distance:	2m/2m3: 0-2 2m4-2m7: 0-0 3m+: 2-2
Track:	LH: 0-1 RH: 2-3 Tight: 2-2 Gall: 0-1
Aids:	Bl: 0-0 Vi: 0-0 Tstrap: 0-0 Ckp: 0-0
Best Rating:	113 4/04 Tntn 3m good Ch

Useful hunter/pointer; stays three miles and suited by good ground; goes well at Taunton.

Kettong (IRE)
4-y-o b f Among Men (USA)-Kettenblume (Cagliostro (GER))
D W Barker J J Crosier

Placings:000   (4663)
2003/04: 16^{9}GS, 17^{0}G, 16^{9}S,

	Starts	1st	2nd	3rd	Win & Pl
NH Flat	3	0	0	0	
Career Total	3	0	0	0	

Going:	Sf: 0-1 GS: 0-1 Gd: 0-1 GF: - Fm: 0-0
Distance:	2m/2m3: 0-3 2m4-2m7: 0-0 3m+: 0-0
Track:	LH: 0-2 RH: 0-1 Tight: 0-0 Gall: 0-0
Aids:	Bl: 0-0 Vi: 0-0 Tstrap: 0-0 Ckp: 0-0

Kety Star (FR)
108(102h)   (94 h)134+
6-y-o b g Bojador (FR)-Danystar (FR) (Alycos (FR))
Miss Venetia Williams Mrs S A J Kinsella-Hurley

Placings:3F06-453114211   (2672)
2003/04: 16^{4}GF, 22^{2}⁵GF, 16^{3}GF, 16^{1}GF, 17^{1}G, 16^{4}GF, 16^{2}GF, 16^{1}GF, 18^{1}GF,

	Starts	1st	2nd	3rd	Win & Pl
Hurdles	2	0	0	0	532
Chases	7	4	1	1	23572
Career Total	13	4	1	2	24484
134 12/03 Newb	2m2f110y	D(0-120)HCh		G-F	£5852
130 11/03 Donc	2m110y	D(0-125)HCh		G-F	£7210
116 7/03 Strf	2m1f110y	E(0-105)HCh		GD	£4793
106 7/03 NAbb	2m110y	F(0-100)HCh		G-F	£3385
				Total win prize-money	£21241

Going:	Sf: 0-0 GS: 0-0 Gd: 1-1 GF: - Fm: 3-8
Distance:	2m/2m3: 4-8 2m4-2m7: 0-1 3m+: 0-0
Track:	LH: 4-9 RH: 0-0 Tight: 2-5 Gall: 2-2
Aids:	Bl: 0-0 Vi: 0-0 Tstrap: 0-0 Ckp: 0-0
Best Rating:	134 12/03 Newb 2m2f110y gd-fm Ch

Useful chaser; keen sort; best at around two miles; acts on a sound surface; progressive.

Kew
3
5-y-o b g Royal Applause-Cutleaf (Kris)

C L Popham (J J Bridger 14/5) C L Popham

Placings:P0F-P   (0970)
2003/04: 17^{0}GS,

	Starts	1st	2nd	3rd	Win & Pl
Hurdles	1	0	0	0	
Career Total	4	0	0	0	

Going:	Sf: 0-0 GS: 0-1 Gd: 0-0 GF: - Fm: 0-0
Distance:	2m/2m3: 0-1 2m4-2m7: 0-0 3m+: 0-0
Track:	LH: 0-1 RH: 0-0 Tight: 0-1 Gall: 0-0
Aids:	Bl: 0-0 Vi: 0-0 Tstrap: 0-0 Ckp: 0-0
Best Rating:	6 11/02 Newb 2m110y soft Hdl

Kew Jumper (IRE)
96   88
5-y-o b g Mister Lord (USA)-Pharisee (IRE) (Phardante (FR))
Andrew Turnell Robinson Webster (holdings) Ltd

Placings:S05   (4181)
2003/04: 16^{5}S, 20^{0}GS, 16^{5}G,

	Starts	1st	2nd	3rd	Win & Pl
Hurdles	3	0	0	0	0
Career Total	3	0	0	0	0

Going:	Sf: 0-1 GS: 0-1 Gd: 0-1 GF: - Fm: 0-0
Distance:	2m/2m3: 0-2 2m4-2m7: 0-1 3m+: 0-0
Track:	LH: 0-2 RH: 0-1 Tight: 0-0 Gall: 0-1
Aids:	Bl: 0-0 Vi: 0-0 Tstrap: 0-0 Ckp: 0-0
Best Rating:	88 3/04 Hntg 2m110y good Hdl

Showed promise third outing over timber.

Kewlake Lane
59f   10f
6-y-o b m Afzal-Sheer Impulse (IRE) (Montelimar (USA))
R H Alner Mrs U Wainwright

Placings:0   (2504)
2003/04: 17^{0}GS,

	Starts	1st	2nd	3rd	Win & Pl
NH Flat	1	0	0	0	
Career Total	1	0	0	0	

Going:	Sf: 0-0 GS: 0-1 Gd: 0-0 GF: - Fm: 0-0
Distance:	2m/2m3: 0-0 2m4-2m7: 0-0 3m+: 0-0
Track:	LH: 0-0 RH: 0-1 Tight: 0-1 Gall: 0-0
Aids:	Bl: 0-0 Vi: 0-0 Tstrap: 0-0 Ckp: 0-0
Best Rating:	10 12/03 Folk 2m1f110y gd-sft NHF

Kez
94   93
8-y-o b g Polar Falcon (USA)-Briggsmaid (Elegant Air)
P R Webber Dennis Yardy

Placings:0/5-4   (0182)
2003/04: 16^{4}GF,

	Starts	1st	2nd	3rd	Win & Pl
Hurdles	1	0	0	0	0
Career Total	3	0	0	0	0

Going:	Sf: 0-0 GS: 0-0 Gd: 0-0 GF: - Fm: 0-1
Distance:	2m/2m3: 0-1 2m4-2m7: 0-0 3m+: 0-0
Track:	LH: 0-0 RH: 0-1 Tight: 0-0 Gall: 0-0
Aids:	Bl: 0-0 Vi: 0-0 Tstrap: 0-0 Ckp: 0-0
Best Rating:	93 5/03 Winc 2m gd-fm Hdl

Moderate novice hurdler; winner seven times on the Flat; yet to translate that form to hurdles; yet to prove he stays two miles; acts on a sound surface.

Khaladjistan (IRE)

97(105h) (89h)**89**

6-y-o gr g Tirol-Khaladja (IRE) (Akarad (FR))
Miss S J Wilton (P F Nicholls 9/3) John Pointon And Sons

Placings:4535/64-P5P31P41 (4919)
2003/04: 19PGS, 225HY, 19PHY, 213G, 171GF, 16PGS, 174G, 201GS,

	Starts	1st	2nd	3rd	Win & Pl
Hurdles	4	1	0	1	2800
Chases	4	1	0	0	3669
Career Total	14	2	0	2	7191
89	4/04	Worc	2m4f110yF(0-100)HCh		GD-S £3669
89	3/04	Hrfd	2m1f	G Hdl	G-F £2415

Total win prize-money £6084

Going:	Sf: 0-2 GS: 1-3 Gd: 0-2 GF: - Fm: 1-1
Distance:	2m/2m3: 1-4 2m4-2m7: 1-4 3m+: 0-0
Track:	LH: 1-2 RH: 1-5 Tight: 0-0 Gall: 0-0
Aids:	Bl: 1-3 Vi: 0-0 Tstrap: 1-5 Ckp: 1-2
Best Rating:	97 1/02 Hayd 2m soft NHF

Plating-class hurdler/chaser; some ability in bumpers; won weak handicap chase at Worcester in April; effective at 2m 4f; has worn a tongue tie and blinkers.

Khan Kicker (IRE)

101(99h) (118h)**118**

8-y-o b g Husyan (USA)-Orient Conquest (Dual)
N G Richards E H Birkbeck,A Stewart,Sir David Landale

Placings:422/0F21412/0003-22 (2232)
2003/04: 212G, 162G,

	Starts	1st	2nd	3rd	Win & Pl
Chases	2	0	2	0	1592
Career Total	16	2	6	1	14603
116	4/02	Kels	2m110y	E Hdl	G-F £3010
120	1/02	Muss	2m	E Hdl	SFT £2814

Total win prize-money £5824

Going:	Sf: 0-0 GS: 0-0 Gd: 0-2 GF: - Fm: 0-0
Distance:	2m/2m3: 0-1 2m4-2m7: 0-1 3m+: 0-0
Track:	LH: 0-2 RH: 0-0 Tight: 0-1 Gall: 0-0
Aids:	Bl: 0-0 Vi: 0-0 Tstrap: 0-0 Ckp: 0-0
Best Rating:	132 4/02 Ayr 2m good Hdl

Decent hurdler/modest novice chaser; effective at two miles; acts on most types of ground.

Kharak (FR)

112 **114+**

5-y-o gr g Danehill (USA)-Khariyda (FR) (Shakapour)
Mrs S C Bradburne Hardie, Robb, Copland & Steel

Placings:1324-6024421325 (4942)
2003/04: 166G, 179GS, 162S, 164GS, 164S, 182HY, 201G, 209GF, 242HY, 205GS,

	Starts	1st	2nd	3rd	Win & Pl
Hurdles	10	1	3	1	12486
Career Total	14	2	4	2	19477
115	2/04	Carl	2m4f	D(0-125)HHdl	GD £5255
97	3/03	Ayr	2m	E Hdl	SFT £3510

Total win prize-money £8765

Going:	Sf: 0-4 GS: 0-3 Gd: 1-2 GF: - Fm: 0-1
Distance:	2m/2m3: 0-6 2m4-2m7: 1-3 3m+: 0-1
Track:	LH: 0-6 RH: 1-4 Tight: 0-2 Gall: 0-1
Aids:	Bl: 0-0 Vi: 0-1 Tstrap: 0-0 Ckp: 0-0
Best Rating:	115 2/04 Carl 2m4f good Hdl

Moderate ex-French hurdler; suited by two miles, but should get further; has worn a visor and cheekpieces; consistent.

Khatani (IRE)

97 (100h)**105**

9-y-o b g Kahyasi-Khanata (USA) (Riverman (USA))
D R Gandolfo R E Brinkworth

Placings:35351/111144/13235/1346-0P (0532)
2003/04: 239G, 23PGF,

	Starts	1st	2nd	3rd	Win & Pl
Chases	2	0	0	0	
Career Total	22	7	1	5	40346
126	5/02	Bang	2m4f110yC(0-130)HCh	GD	£6734
119	5/01	Hrfd	2m3f	D Ch	GD	£4875
126	7/00	Worc	2m4f	C(0-135)HHdl	GD	£5395
123	6/00	Worc	2m4f	C(0-135)HHdl	GD	£4875
120	5/00	Worc	2m	D(0-120)HHdl	GD	£3497
119	5/00	Bang	2m1f	D(0-120)HHdl	GD	£4348
115	4/00	Font	2m2f110yE Hdl	GD	£2240

Total win prize-money £31965

Going:	Sf: 0-0 GS: 0-0 Gd: 0-1 GF: - Fm: 0-1
Distance:	2m/2m3: 0-0 2m4-2m7: 0-0 3m+: 0-2
Track:	LH: 0-1 RH: 0-1 Tight: 0-0 Gall: 0-0
Aids:	Bl: 0-0 Vi: 0-0 Tstrap: 0-0 Ckp: 0-0
Best Rating:	129 6/01 Strf 2m5f110y gd-fm Ch

Fair handicap chaser when the ground rides fast but has looked quirky on occasion; back to winning form at Bangor in May 2002 over an extended two and a half miles.

Khayal (USA)

102 **82**

10-y-o b g Green Dancer (USA)-Look Who's Dancing (USA) (Affirmed (USA))
C J Down (R J Down 29/5) D Cossey

Placings:2P430/05/4403/6-62425 (1040)
2003/04: 19PGF, 262GF, 264GF, 242G, 265GF,

	Starts	1st	2nd	3rd	Win & Pl
Hurdles	1	0	1	0	982
Chases	4	0	1	0	1309
Career Total	17	0	3	2	3724

Going:	Sf: 0-0 GS: 0-0 Gd: 0-1 GF: - Fm: 0-4
Distance:	2m/2m3: 0-0 2m4-2m7: 0-1 3m+: 0-4
Track:	LH: 0-4 RH: 0-1 Tight: 0-3 Gall: 0-0
Aids:	Bl: 0-0 Vi: 0-0 Tstrap: 0-0 Ckp: 0-0
Best Rating:	84 8/97 NAbb 2m1f gd-fm Hdl

One-time decent pointer, his jumping lacks fluency under Rules.

Khaysar (IRE)

104 **106**

6-y-o br g Pennekamp (USA)-Khaytada (IRE) (Doyoun)
N B King (Mrs L Wadham 12/2) St Gatien Racing Club

Placings:2FP033214/0-063PP3542 (4776)
2003/04: 166GF, 166GF, 163G, 19PGS, 19PG, 163GS, 165G, 174G, 202G,

	Starts	1st	2nd	3rd	Win & Pl
Hurdles	9	0	1	2	2893
Career Total	19	1	3	4	10890
106	4/02	MRas	2m1f110yD(0-115)HHdl	GD	£5362

Total win prize-money £5363

Going:	Sf: 0-0 GS: 0-2 Gd: 0-5 GF: - Fm: 0-2
Distance:	2m/2m3: 0-6 2m4-2m7: 0-3 3m+: 0-0
Track:	LH: 0-4 RH: 0-5 Tight: 0-2 Gall: 0-2
Aids:	Bl: 0-0 Vi: 0-0 Tstrap: 0-0 Ckp: 0-0
Best Rating:	106 4/02 MRas 2m1f110y good Hdl

Moderate hurdler; effective over two miles; acts on good ground.

Khayyam (USA)

93 **80**

6-y-o b g Affirmed (USA)-True Celebrity (USA) (Lyphard (USA))
S Gollings W Hobson,J King,G King,P Winfrow

Placings:030 (0761)
2003/04: 16PGF, 163GF, 16PG,

	Starts	1st	2nd	3rd	Win & Pl
Hurdles	3	0	0	1	388
Career Total	3	0	0	1	388

Going:	Sf: 0-0 GS: 0-0 Gd: 0-1 GF: - Fm: 0-2
Distance:	2m/2m3: 0-3 2m4-2m7: 0-0 3m+: 0-0
Track:	LH: 0-3 RH: 0-0 Tight: 0-1 Gall: 0-0
Aids:	Bl: 0-1 Vi: 0-0 Tstrap: 0-0 Ckp: 0-0
Best Rating:	86 6/03 Worc 2m gd-fm Hdl

Kicasso

97f **91f**

5-y-o b g Environment Friend-Merry Jane (Rymer)
Miss H C Knight D J Smith and D J Ellis

Placings:00 (4199)
2003/04: 16PHY, 16PG,

	Starts	1st	2nd	3rd	Win & Pl
NH Flat	2	0	0	0	
Career Total	2	0	0	0	

Going:	Sf: 0-1 GS: 0-0 Gd: 0-1 GF: - Fm: 0-0
Distance:	2m/2m3: 0-2 2m4-2m7: 0-0 3m+: 0-0
Track:	LH: 0-1 RH: 0-1 Tight: 0-0 Gall: 0-1
Aids:	Bl: 0-0 Vi: 0-0 Tstrap: 0-0 Ckp: 0-0
Best Rating:	91 3/04 Newb 2m110y good NHF

Kick For Touch (IRE)

104 (93h)**128+**

7-y-o ch g Insan (USA)-Anns Run (Deep Run)
Miss H C Knight Trevor Hemmings

Placings:64/F32211-2F (3406)
2003/04: 262G, 24FG,

	Starts	1st	2nd	3rd	Win & Pl
Chases	2	0	1	0	1454
Career Total	10	2	3	1	14777
115	4/03	Strf	3m	D Ch	GD	£5655
100	3/03	Hntg	3m	E Ch	G-F	£4163

Total win prize-money £9818

Going:	Sf: 0-0 GS: 0-0 Gd: 0-2 GF: - Fm: 0-0
Distance:	2m/2m3: 0-0 2m4-2m7: 0-0 3m+: 0-2
Track:	LH: 0-2 RH: 0-0 Tight: 0-1 Gall: 0-1
Aids:	Bl: 0-0 Vi: 0-0 Tstrap: 0-0 Ckp: 0-0
Best Rating:	128 11/03 NAbb 3m2f110y good Ch

Modest chaser; successful over fences at Huntingdon in March 2003 and followed up at Stratford; stays 3m; acts on fast and soft ground.

Kickback

85   56

4-y-o b g High Kicker (USA)-Moniques Venture (Midyan (USA))
B A Pearce Martin J Gibbs

Placings:P6   (1293)
2003/04: 16^{P}G, 16^{6}GF,

	Starts	1st	2nd	3rd	Win & Pl
Hurdles	2	0	0	0	0
Career Total	2	0	0	0	0

Going:	Sf: 0-0 GS: 0-0 Gd: 0-1 GF: - Fm: 0-1
Distance:	2m/2m3: 0-2 2m4-2m7: 0-0 3m+: 0-0
Track:	LH: 0-2 RH: 0-0 Tight: 0-2 Gall: 0-0
Aids:	Bl: 0-0 Vi: 0-0 Tstrap: 0-0 Ckp: 0-0
Best Rating:	56 9/03 Strf 2m110y gd-fm Hdl

Juvenile hurdler; showed little in first two starts; plating-class maiden on the Flat.

Kicking Bear (IRE)

80   53

6-y-o b g Little Bighorn-Rongo (IRE) (Tumble Gold)
R T Phillips The Brightling Club 1998

Placings:O50-0   (4181)
2003/04: 16^{5}G,

	Starts	1st	2nd	3rd	Win & Pl
Hurdles	1	0	0	0	0
Career Total	4	0	0	0	0

Going:	Sf: 0-0 GS: 0-0 Gd: 0-1 GF: 0-0 Fm: 0-0
Distance:	2m/2m3: 0-1 2m4-2m7: 0-0 3m+: 0-0
Track:	LH: 0-0 RH: 0-1 Tight: 0-0 Gall: 0-1
Aids:	Bl: 0-0 Vi: 0-0 Tstrap: 0-0 Ckp: 0-0
Best Rating:	87 2/03 Folk 2m1f110y heavy NHF

Kicking King (IRE)

120(122h)   (145h)152+

6-y-o b g Old Vic-Fairy Blaze (IRE) (Good Thyne (USA))
T J Taaffe Conor Clarkson

Placings:13^{3}12112-5F1122   (4827a)
2003/04: 16^{5}GY, 17^{F}S, 16^{1}S, 17^{1}YS, 16^{2}G, 20^{2}Y,

	Starts	1st	2nd	3rd	Win & Pl
Chases	6	2	2	0	88617
Career Total	13	6	4	1	158820
150	1/04	Leop	2m1f		Ch	Y-S	£36619
145	1/04	Punc	2m		Ch	SFT	£9154
142	2/03	Punc	2m		Hdl	SH	£21103
131	1/03	Cork	2m2f		Hdl	SFT	£8288
122	11/02	Naas	2m		Hdl	SFT	£7196
105	1/02	Leop	2m		NHF	Y-S	£5291

Total win prize-money £87655

Going:	Sf: 1-2 GS: 0-0 Gd: 0-1 GF: - Fm: 0-0
Distance:	2m/2m3: 2-5 2m4-2m7: 0-1 3m+: 0-0
Track:	LH: 1-3 RH: 1-3 Tight: 0-0 Gall: 0-1
Aids:	Bl: 0-0 Vi: 0-0 Tstrap: 0-0 Ckp: 0-0
Best Rating:	155 3/04 Chel 2m good Ch

Irish-trained novice chaser/former useful hurdler; runner-up in the Supreme Novices' at Cheltenham in 2003; won the Grade 1 Arkle Perpetual Challenge Cup Chase at Leopardstown in January 2004; runner-up to Well Chief in Arkle at Cheltenham and to Hi Cloy in Grade 1 at Fairyhouse; effective from 2m to 2m 4f; acts on good and soft ground; likes to race prominently.

Kidithou (FR)

104   120+

6-y-o b g Royal Charter (FR)-De Thou (FR) (Trebrook (FR))
L Lungo Roman Wall Racing

Placings:23P46-114222   (4431)
2003/04: 16^{1}G, 20^{1}G, 20^{4}G, 27^{2}G, 20^{2}G, 24^{2}G,

	Starts	1st	2nd	3rd	Win & Pl
Hurdles	6	2	3	0	10278
Career Total	11	2	4	1	11790
115	5/03	Hexm	2m4f110yE Hdl		GD	£3458
101	5/03	Hexm	2m110y E Hdl		GD	£3489

Total win prize-money £6948

Going:	Sf: 0-0 GS: 0-0 Gd: 2-6 GF: - Fm: 0-0
Distance:	2m/2m3: 1-1 2m4-2m7: 1-3 3m+: 0-2
Track:	LH: 2-5 RH: 0-1 Tight: 0-1 Gall: 0-0
Aids:	Bl: 0-0 Vi: 0-0 Tstrap: 0-0 Ckp: 0-0
Best Rating:	115 5/03 Hexm 2m4f110y good Hdl

Fair novice hurdler; effective at up to three miles and three furlongs; acts on heavy ground and a sound surface; may be capable of better in handicaps.

Kids Inheritance (IRE)

99   103+

6-y-o b g Presenting-Princess Tino (IRE) (Rontino)
J M Jefferson Mr & Mrs J M Davenport

Placings:3520-42541   (4297)
2003/04: 20^{4}G, 16^{2}GF, 19^{5}G, 17^{4}GS, 16^{1}GF,

	Starts	1st	2nd	3rd	Win & Pl
Hurdles	5	1	1	0	6411
Career Total	9	1	2	1	7276
103	3/04	Ayr	2m		E(0-105)HHdl	G-F	£5102

Total win prize-money £5103

Going:	Sf: 0-0 GS: 0-1 Gd: 0-2 GF: - Fm: 1-2
Distance:	2m/2m3: 1-4 2m4-2m7: 0-1 3m+: 0-0
Track:	LH: 1-3 RH: 0-0 Tight: 0-3 Gall: 0-0
Aids:	Bl: 0-0 Vi: 0-0 Tstrap: 0-0 Ckp: 0-0
Best Rating:	103 3/04 Ayr 2m gd-fm Hdl

Moderate novice hurdler; showed promise in bumpers; won handicap over two miles at Ayr in February; seems best suited by two miles; acts on fast ground and heavy.

Kiev (IRE)

67f   79f

4-y-o b g Bahhare (USA)-Badrah (USA) (Private Account (USA))
D G Bridgwater Terry & Sarah Amos

Placings:60   (4374)
2003/04: 16^{6}G, 16^{9}GF,

	Starts	1st	2nd	3rd	Win & Pl
NH Flat	2	0	0	0	0
Career Total	2	0	0	0	0

Going:	Sf: 0-0 GS: 0-0 Gd: 0-1 GF: - Fm: 0-1
Distance:	2m/2m3: 0-2 2m4-2m7: 0-0 3m+: 0-0
Track:	LH: 0-0 RH: 0-1 Tight: 0-0 Gall: 0-0
Aids:	Bl: 0-0 Vi: 0-0 Tstrap: 0-0 Ckp: 0-0
Best Rating:	79 2/04 Kemp 2m good NHF

Kilcaskin Gold (IRE)

9-y-o ch g Ore-Maypole Gayle (Strong Gale)

Kilcreggan

R A Ross The Pavillion Syndicate

73   45

10-y-o b g Landyap (USA)-Lehmans Lot (Oats)
Mrs Barbara Waring B W Parren

Placings:463/6/6304106/40PPP   (3915)
2003/04: 22^{4}GF, 16^{9}GS, 20^{P}HY, 19^{P}G, 16^{P}G,

	Starts	1st	2nd	3rd	Win & Pl
Hurdles	5	0	0	0	269
Career Total	16	1	0	2	2602
95	10/01	Sthl	2m		G(0-95)HHdl	GD	£1939

Total win prize-money £1939

Going:	Sf: 0-1 GS: 0-1 Gd: 0-2 GF: - Fm: 0-1
Distance:	2m/2m3: 0-2 2m4-2m7: 0-3 3m+: 0-0
Track:	LH: 0-5 RH: 0-0 Tight: 0-2 Gall: 0-0
Aids:	Bl: 0-0 Vi: 0-0 Tstrap: 0-0 Ckp: 0-0
Best Rating:	100 10/98 Hntg 2m110y good NHF

Kildare Chiller (IRE)

91   102

10-y-o ch g Shahrastani (USA)-Ballycuirke (Taufan (USA))
P R Hedger Bill Broomfield

Placings:0500/101000/210F55/65222361/6650350426-453   (4237)
2003/04: 20^{4}S, 22^{5}GF, 18^{3}GF,

	Starts	1st	2nd	3rd	Win & Pl
Hurdles	3	0	0	1	493
Career Total	37	4	5	3	21850
107	3/02	Font	2m2f110yD(0-115)HHdl		SFT	£5382
117	10/00	Font	2m2f110yD(0-120)HHdl		G-S	£3168
106	11/98	Thur	2m2f	(0-102)HHdl		SFT	£2301
	5/98	Dpat	2m1f172y Hdl		G-F	£1489

Total win prize-money £12342

Going:	Sf: 0-1 GS: 0-0 Gd: 0-0 GF: - Fm: 0-2
Distance:	2m/2m3: 0-1 2m4-2m7: 0-2 3m+: 0-0
Track:	LH: 0-3 RH: 0-0 Tight: 0-2 Gall: 0-0
Aids:	Bl: 0-0 Vi: 0-0 Tstrap: 0-0 Ckp: 0-1
Best Rating:	117 1/01 Plum 2m heavy Hdl

Modest hurdler; best at around two and a quarter miles; suited by easy ground.

Kildee Lass

100   93

5-y-o gr m Morpeth-Pigeon Loft (IRE) (Bellypha)
J D Frost J F O'Donovan

Placings:4000-5515043   (4735)
2003/04: 17^{5}G, 16^{6}G, 16^{1}G, 17^{5}GS, 19^{0}G, 16^{4}G, 17^{3}G,

	Starts	1st	2nd	3rd	Win & Pl
Hurdles	7	1	0	1	3455
Career Total	11	1	0	1	3455

93   12/03 Winc   2m   E Hdl   GD   £2436
Total win prize-money £2436

Going: Sf: 0-0 GS: 0-1 Gd: 1-6 GF: - Fm: 0-0
Distance: 2m/2m3: 1-7 2m4-2m7: 0-0 3m+: 0-0
Track: LH: 0-3 RH: 1-4 Tight: 0-3 Gall: 0-0
Aids: Bl: 0-0 Vi: 0-0 Tstrap: 0-0 Ckp: 0-0
Best Rating: 93   12/03   Winc   2m   good   Hdl

Winner of a weak novice hurdle in December on good ground.

Kildorragh (IRE)
90   122
10-y-o b g Glacial Storm (USA)-Take A Dare (Pragmatic)
L Wells   Mrs Carrie Zetter-Wells

Placings:*0002045/12/3PU1U1/P22P-P2RP0340*   (4933)
2003/04: 24PS, 28²G, 24RS, 24PHY, 24⁹G, 25⁵GS, 26⁹G,

	Starts	1st	2nd	3rd	Win & Pl
Chases	8	0	1	1	3858
Career Total	27	3	5	2	40643
123 12/01 Chep	3m2f110yC(0-130)HCh			SFT	£10166
123 11/01 Font	3m2f110yD(0-125)HCh			G-S	£3818
121 2/01 Font	3m2f110yH Ch			G-S	£7345

Total win prize-money £21330

Going: Sf: 0-3 GS: 0-1 Gd: 0-4 GF: - Fm: 0-0
Distance: 2m/2m3: 0-0 2m4-2m7: 0-0 3m+: 0-8
Track: LH: 0-5 RH: 0-1 Tight: 0-2 Gall: 0-0
Aids: Bl: 0-6 Vi: 0-0 Tstrap: 0-0 Ckp: 0-0
Best Rating: 123   12/01   Chep   3m2f110y   soft   Ch

Moderate handicap chaser; acts on soft ground; handles a fast surface; stays 3m2f; usually blinkered.

Killala Bay (IRE)
9-y-o b m Executive Perk-Killinure Point (Smooth Stepper)
K C Bailey   Mrs J Way

Placings:*40/6P-3*   (0136)
2003/04: 20³G,

	Starts	1st	2nd	3rd	Win & Pl
Chases	1	0	0	1	828
Career Total	5	0	0	1	828

Going: Sf: 0-0 GS: 0-0 Gd: 0-1 GF: - Fm: 0-0
Distance: 2m/2m3: 0-0 2m4-2m7: 0-1 3m+: 0-0
Track: LH: 0-0 RH: 0-1 Tight: 0-1 Gall: 0-0
Aids: Bl: 0-0 Vi: 0-0 Tstrap: 0-0 Ckp: 0-0
Best Rating: 88   10/00   Sthl   2m   soft   NHF

Killalongford (IRE)
100   84
7-y-o b g Tenby-Queen Crab (Private Walk)
Mrs S M Johnson   Mrs M E Mason

Placings:*00630/00P02244-0242*   (2696)
2003/04: 20⁹GF, 24²GF, 24⁴GF, 21²G,

	Starts	1st	2nd	3rd	Win & Pl
Hurdles	4	0	2	0	2365
Career Total	17	0	4	1	5143

Going: Sf: 0-0 GS: 0-0 Gd: 0-1 GF: - Fm: 0-3
Distance: 2m/2m3: 0-0 2m4-2m7: 0-2 3m+: 0-2
Track: LH: 0-2 RH: 0-2 Tight: 0-0 Gall: 0-0
Aids: Bl: 0-0 Vi: 0-0 Tstrap: 0-0 Ckp: 0-0
Best Rating: 100   12/01   Navn   2m   yld-sft   Hdl

Plating-class hurdler; effective over two miles, but needs further; acts on a soft surface.

Killarney
85   72
6-y-o gr m Pursuit Of Love-Laune (AUS) (Kenmare (FR))
Miss Kate Milligan   E Whalley

Placings:*0P0/30240-0*   (0473)
2003/04: 17⁹GS,

	Starts	1st	2nd	3rd	Win & Pl
Hurdles	1	0	0	0	
Career Total	9	0	1	1	763

Going: Sf: 0-0 GS: 0-1 Gd: 0-0 GF: - Fm: 0-0
Distance: 2m/2m3: 0-1 2m4-2m7: 0-0 3m+: 0-0
Track: LH: 0-1 RH: 0-0 Tight: 0-1 Gall: 0-0
Aids: Bl: 0-0 Vi: 0-0 Tstrap: 0-0 Ckp: 0-0
Best Rating: 72   6/02   MRas   2m1f110y   gd-fm   Hdl

Selling hurdler, best at around two miles.

Killarney Prince (IRE)
92f   80f
5-y-o b g Lord Americo-Henry Woman (IRE) (Mandalus)
Mrs J M Mann   Mrs J M Mann

Placings:*350*   (3657)
2003/04: 16³GF, 16⁵GS, 17⁰S,

	Starts	1st	2nd	3rd	Win & Pl
NH Flat	3	0	0	1	262
Career Total	3	0	0	1	262

Going: Sf: 0-1 GS: 0-1 Gd: 0-0 GF: - Fm: 0-1
Distance: 2m/2m3: 0-3 2m4-2m7: 0-0 3m+: 0-0
Track: LH: 0-1 RH: 0-1 Tight: 0-0 Gall: 0-0
Aids: Bl: 0-0 Vi: 0-0 Tstrap: 0-0 Ckp: 0-0
Best Rating: 80   2/04   Tntn   2m1f   soft   NHF

Killers Fury (IRE)
100   103+
5-y-o br g Topanoora-Ellen Gail (IRE) (Strong Gale)
M C Pipe   D A Johnson

Placings:*FP3*   (4212)
2003/04: 24⁶GS, 24PG, 24³G,

	Starts	1st	2nd	3rd	Win & Pl
Hurdles	2	0	0	1	782
Chases	1	0	0	0	0
Career Total	3	0	0	1	782

Going: Sf: 0-0 GS: 0-1 Gd: 0-2 GF: - Fm: 0-0
Distance: 2m/2m3: 0-0 2m4-2m7: 0-0 3m+: 0-3
Track: LH: 0-0 RH: 0-3 Tight: 0-0 Gall: 0-0
Aids: Bl: 0-0 Vi: 0-0 Tstrap: 0-0 Ckp: 0-0
Best Rating: 106   3/04   Kemp   3m110y   good   Hdl

Fell in decent novice chase on racecourse debut; placed over hurdles since; stays three miles.

Killoughter (IRE)
6-y-o b g Magical Wonder (USA)-Miss Bobby Bennett (King's Lake (USA))
M C Pipe   B A Kilpatrick

Placings:*P*   (0485)
2003/04: 22PGF,

	Starts	1st	2nd	3rd	Win & Pl
Hurdles	1	0	0	0	
Career Total	1	0	0	0	

Going: Sf: 0-0 GS: 0-0 Gd: 0-0 GF: - Fm: 0-1
Distance: 2m/2m3: 0-0 2m4-2m7: 0-1 3m+: 0-0
Track: LH: 0-1 RH: 0-0 Tight: 0-1 Gall: 0-0
Aids: Bl: 0-0 Vi: 0-1 Tstrap: 0-0 Ckp: 0-0

Killultagh Dawn (IRE)
95   102?
6-y-o b m Phardante (FR)-Rostrevor Lady (Kemal (FR))
J Howard Johnson (Michael Hourigan 26/12) Mrs Rose Boyd

Placings:*000466-006306P0*   (4429)
2003/04: 16⁰F, 18⁰GF, 19⁶GY, 16³GY, 18⁰S, 18⁶S, 17PGS, 16⁰G,

	Starts	1st	2nd	3rd	Win & Pl
NH Flat	2	0	0	0	0
Hurdles	6	0	0	1	773
Career Total	14	0	0	1	1188

Going: Sf: 0-2 GS: 0-1 Gd: 0-1 GF: - Fm: 0-2
Distance: 2m/2m3: 0-8 2m4-2m7: 0-0 3m+: 0-0
Track: LH: 0-5 RH: 0-0 Tight: 0-1 Gall: 0-0
Aids: Bl: 0-0 Vi: 0-0 Tstrap: 0-0 Ckp: 0-1
Best Rating: 102   3/03   Leop   2m   heavy   Hdl

Killultagh Storm (IRE)
108   (113h) 150
10-y-o b g Mandalus-Rostrevor Lady (Kemal (FR))
W P Mullins   Mrs Rose Boyd

Placings:*00/60.33301332211/133320124/2U130536622/P5* *0546413-5655134400*   (4769a)
2003/04: 16³GY, 20⁵YS, 16⁶S, 17⁵YS, 24⁵G, 19¹S, 20³GF, 16⁴YS, 17⁴S, 16⁹GS, 17⁰Y,

	Starts	1st	2nd	3rd	Win & Pl
Hurdles	1	0	0	0	0
Chases	10	1	0	2	23279
Career Total	54	8	7	12	172536
150 9/03 List	2m3f	Ch		SFT	£9496
143 4/03 Fair	2m1f	HCh		G-F	£25324
142 11/01 DRoy	2m2f	Ch		Y-S	£20967
124 2/01 Naas	2m	Ch		SH	£6120
135 5/00 Punc	2m	(0-135)HHdl		GD	£8320
130 4/00 Fair	2m	HHdl		SFT	£39000
123 3/00 Leop	2m	(0-116)HHdl		GD	£5520
105 11/99 Fair	2m	(0-109)HHdl		SFT	£5236

Total win prize-money £119988

Going: Sf: 1-3 GS: 0-1 Gd: 0-1 GF: - Fm: 0-1
Distance: 2m/2m3: 1-8 2m4-2m7: 0-2 3m+: 0-1
Track: LH: 0-2 RH: 0-6 Tight: 0-0 Gall: 0-0
Aids: Bl: 0-1 Vi: 0-0 Tstrap: 0-0 Ckp: 1-7
Best Rating: 150   9/03   List   2m3f   soft   Ch

Smart Irish chaser; acts on good and soft ground; effective from 2m to 2m 4f.

Killwillie (IRE)
51f   92f
5-y-o b g Carroll House-Home In The Glen (Furry Glen)
J I A Charlton   J I A Charlton

Placings:5   (4316)
2003/04: 16⁵GF,

	Starts	1st	2nd	3rd	Win & Pl
NH Flat	1	0	0	0	0
Career Total	1	0	0	0	0

Going: Sf: 0-0 GS: 0-0 Gd: 0-0 GF: - Fm: 0-1
Distance: 2m/2m3: 0-1 2m4-2m7: 0-0 3m+: 0-0
Track: LH: 0-1 RH: 0-0 Tight: 0-0 Gall: 0-0
Aids: Bl: 0-0 Vi: 0-0 Tstrap: 0-0 Ckp: 0-0
Best Rating: 92 3/04 Ayr 2m gd-fm NHF

Related to bumper winner and to fair hurdler Tana River; attracted support and showed ability on debut over two miles in slowly run Ayr bumper in March 2004; type to improve.

Killy Beach

93(87h)   (73h)**73+**

6-y-o b g Kuwait Beach (USA)-Spiritual Lily (Brianston Zipper)
J W Mullins J A G Meaden

Placings:000/44-P65P3   (4814)
2003/04: 21PG, 16⁶GS, 21⁵S, 25PG, 19³G,

	Starts	1st	2nd	3rd	Win & Pl
Chases	5	0	0	1	384
Career Total	10	0	0	1	384

Going: Sf: 0-1 GS: 0-1 Gd: 0-3 GF: - Fm: 0-0
Distance: 2m/2m3: 0-1 2m4-2m7: 0-3 3m+: 0-1
Track: LH: 0-1 RH: 0-4 Tight: 0-2 Gall: 0-0
Aids: Bl: 0-0 Vi: 0-0 Tstrap: 0-0 Ckp: 0-0
Best Rating: 73 4/04 Chep 2m3f110y good Ch

Best effort over fences when modest third in 2m 4f selling handicap chase at Chepstow April 2004.

Kilmore King (IRE)

94   **69**

7-y-o b g Big Sink Hope (USA)-Le Dawn (Le Bavard (FR))
N Wilson J McKinnon

Placings:442P   (3327)
2003/04: 16⁴G, 21⁴GF, 21²G, 21³GS,

	Starts	1st	2nd	3rd	Win & Pl
Chases	4	0	1	0	2071
Career Total	4	0	1	0	2071

Going: Sf: 0-0 GS: 0-1 Gd: 0-2 GF: - Fm: 0-1
Distance: 2m/2m3: 0-1 2m4-2m7: 0-3 3m+: 0-0
Track: LH: 0-3 RH: 0-1 Tight: 0-3 Gall: 0-0
Aids: Bl: 0-0 Vi: 0-0 Tstrap: 0-3 Ckp: 0-0
Best Rating: 69 8/03 Ctml 2m5f110y good Ch

Irish point winner; best effort over fences here when distant second at Cartmel in August.

Kilmore Quay (IRE)

100   **93**

9-y-o ch g Over The River (FR)-Sustenance (Torus)
G B Balding (Dermot Day 21/9) Stan Miller,Max Aitken,Bill & John Craig

Placings:PP-1F   (4209)
2003/04: 25¹G, 24FG,

	Starts	1st	2nd	3rd	Win & Pl
Chases	2	1	0	0	4404
Career Total	4	1	0	0	4404

---

93   10/03 Towc   3m1f   D Ch   GD   £4403
              Total win prize-money £4404

Going: Sf: 0-0 GS: 0-0 Gd: 1-2 GF: - Fm: 0-0
Distance: 2m/2m3: 0-2 2m4-2m7: 0-0 **3m+: 1-2**
Track: LH: 0-0 **RH: 1-2** Tight: 0-0 Gall: 0-0
Aids: Bl: 0-0 Vi: 0-0 Tstrap: 0-0 Ckp: 0-0
Best Rating: 93 10/03 Towc 3m1f good Ch

Modest novice chaser; stays an extended three miles; suited by forcing tactics; does have some scope.

Kiltulaa Lad (IRE)

102   (124c)**91+**

11-y-o ch g Phardante (FR)-Galway Shawl (Cure The Blues (USA))
J F Panvert (D L Williams 18/5) J F Panvert

Placings:4314/2321/PF45/2013U5U/5P00026   (4697)
2003/04: 21⁵GF, 21PGF, 22⁶S, 16⁶GS, 17⁹GS, 17²G, 17⁶G,

	Starts	1st	2nd	3rd	Win & Pl
Hurdles	7	0	1	0	702
Career Total	26	3	4	3	12618

114   10/01 Towc   2m110y   E Ch   GD   £3851
112   3/00 Chep   2m110y   D(0-125)HHdl   HVY   £2918
100   11/98 Ludl   2m   H NHF   GD   £1276
             Total win prize-money £8047

Going: Sf: 0-1 GS: 0-2 Gd: 0-2 GF: - Fm: 0-2
Distance: 2m/2m3: 0-4 2m4-2m7: 0-3 3m+: 0-0
Track: LH: 0-1 RH: 0-6 Tight: 0-1 Gall: 0-1
Aids: Bl: 0-0 Vi: 0-0 Tstrap: 0-0 Ckp: 0-0
Best Rating: 114 11/01 Kemp 2m good Ch

Kim Fontenail (FR)

106   **99+**

4-y-o b f Kaldounevees (FR)-Fontanalia (FR) (Rex Magna (FR))
N J Hawke Bryan Fry

Placings:53316   (4574)
2003/04: 13⁵GS, 17³GS, 17³HY, 19¹GS, 21⁶G,

	Starts	1st	2nd	3rd	Win & Pl
NH Flat	1	0	0	0	0
Hurdles	4	1	0	2	7442
Career Total	5	1	0	2	7442

101   2/04   Hrfd   2m3f110yD Hdl   G-S   £5642
             Total win prize-money £5642

Going: Sf: 0-1 GS: 1-3 Gd: 0-1 GF: - Fm: 0-0
Distance: 2m/2m3: 0-2 **2m4-2m7: 1-2** 3m+: 0-0
Track: LH: 0-1 **RH: 1-4** Tight: 0-0 Gall: 0-1
Aids: Bl: 0-0 Vi: 0-0 Tstrap: 0-0 Ckp: 0-0
Best Rating: 101 2/04 Hrfd 2m3f110y gd-sft Hdl

Winning novice hurdler; stays 2m 4f; acts on soft ground.

Kimbambo (FR)

101   **116+**

6-y-o gr h Genereux Genie-Contessina (FR) (Mistigri)
N M L Ewart N M L Ewart

Placings:1625   (3935)
2003/04: 16¹S, 16⁶S, 16²S, 16⁵GS,

	Starts	1st	2nd	3rd	Win & Pl
Hurdles	4	1	1	0	4686
Career Total	4	1	1	0	4686

93   12/03 Kels   2m110y   E Hdl   SFT   £3164
             Total win prize-money £3164

Going: Sf: 1-3 GS: 0-1 Gd: 0-0 GF: - Fm: 0-0
Distance: 2m/2m3: 1-4 2m4-2m7: 0-0 3m+: 0-0

Track: LH: 1-4 RH: 0-0 **Tight: 1-2** Gall: 0-1
Aids: Bl: 0-0 Vi: 0-0 Tstrap: 0-0 Ckp: 0-0
Best Rating: 116 2/04 Newc 2m gd-sft Hdl

Maiden hurdle winner on debut at Kelso in December and ran well there behind subsequent winner Paddy The Piper in January; didn't find as much as seemed likely off the bridle on handicap debut at Newcastle following month.

Kimberley

107   (125c)**126+**

9-y-o b g Shareef Dancer (USA)-Willowbank (Gay Fandango (USA))
J G M O'Shea K W Bell & Son Ltd

Placings:433/22111U/5050**B**00**F**05231250P/06614-020   (3292)
2003/04: 24⁰GS, 24²S, 25⁰GS,

	Starts	1st	2nd	3rd	Win & Pl
Hurdles	3	0	1	0	1728
Career Total	34	5	5	3	44595

125   2/03 Uttx   2m6f110yC(0-135)HHdl   HVY   £8106
108   4/02 Fair   2m6f100y Ch   G-Y   £7831
131   10/00 Naas   2m4f   HHdl   YLD   £7800
126   10/00 Cork   2m4f   Hdl   SFT   £6072
117   9/00 List   2m4f   Hdl   HVY   £4416
             Total win prize-money £34226

Going: Sf: 0-1 GS: 0-2 Gd: 0-0 GF: - Fm: 0-0
Distance: 2m/2m3: 0-0 2m4-2m7: 0-0 3m+: 0-3
Track: LH: 0-3 RH: 0-0 Tight: 0-1 Gall: 0-0
Aids: Bl: 0-0 Vi: 0-2 Tstrap: 0-0 Ckp: 0-0
Best Rating: 135 5/01 Fair 2m4f gd-yld Hdl

Useful hurdler; acts well on a soft surface; effective at up to three miles, but may be better over slightly shorter; successful in a visor.

Kimbo Lady

6-y-o ch m Husyan (USA)-Fair Cruise (Cruise Missile)
R J Smith A Harris, R Wealthy, R G Wareing

Placings:0   (3453)
2003/04: 17⁰GS,

	Starts	1st	2nd	3rd	Win & Pl
NH Flat	1	0	0	0	
Career Total	1	0	0	0	

Going: Sf: 0-0 GS: 0-1 Gd: 0-0 GF: - Fm: 0-0
Distance: 2m/2m3: 0-1 2m4-2m7: 0-0 3m+: 0-0
Track: LH: 0-0 RH: 0-0 Tight: 0-0 Gall: 0-0
Aids: Bl: 0-0 Vi: 0-0 Tstrap: 0-0 Ckp: 0-0

Kimdaloo (IRE)

103(86h)   (56h)**98**

12-y-o b g Mandalus-Kimin (Kibenka)
M A Barnes J G Graham

Placings:0/560/5P/4560**F**10/U25/33**P**22223566/253000PB 411242500-13P   (0470)
2003/04: 16¹G, 16³G, 20PG,

	Starts	1st	2nd	3rd	Win & Pl
Chases	3	1	0	1	4482
Career Total	47	4	8	5	26723

98   5/03 Hexm   2m110y   E(0-105)HCh   GD   £3991
98   10/02 Hexm   2m110y   F(0-90)Ch   GD   £2863
98   10/02 Hexm   2m110y   F(0-100)HCh   G-F   £3080
68   2/00 Newc   2m110y   E(0-105)HCh   SFT   £3143
             Total win prize-money £13077

Going:	Sf: 0-0 GS: 0-0 Gd: 1-3 GF: - Fm: 0-0
Distance:	2m/2m3: 1-2 2m4-2m7: 0-1 3m+: 0-0
Track:	LH: 1-3 RH: 0-0 Tight: 0-0 Gall: 0-0
Aids:	Bl: 0-0 Vi: 0-0 Tstrap: 1-3 Ckp: 0-0
Best Rating:	98 5/03 Hexm 2m110y good Ch

Moderate chaser; suited by two miles; best with cut in the ground; goes well at Hexham; wears tongue tie.

Kimmeridge Bay

67   **12**

6-y-o b m Karinga Bay-Chanelle (The Parson)
J W Mullins Mrs J M Bailey

Placings:000   (4239)
2003/04: 17⁰HY, 16⁰HY, 19⁰G,

	Starts	1st	2nd	3rd	Win & Pl
NH Flat	2	0	0	0	0
Hurdles	1	0	0	0	
Career Total	3	0	0	0	

Going:	Sf: 0-2 GS: 0-0 Gd: 0-1 GF: - Fm: 0-0
Distance:	2m/2m3: 0-3 2m4-2m7: 0-0 3m+: 0-0
Track:	LH: 0-1 RH: 0-2 Tight: 0-0 Gall: 0-0
Aids:	Bl: 0-0 Vi: 0-0 Tstrap: 0-0 Ckp: 0-0
Best Rating:	66 1/04 Folk 2m1f110y heavy NHF

Kimoe Warrior

106   **88**

6-y-o ch g Royal Abjar (USA)-Thewaari (USA) (Eskimo (USA))
M Mullineaux David Ashbrook

Placings:F004354PP6/P63053-F515PP   (4380)
2003/04: 16⁶G, 21⁵GF, 17¹GF, 20⁵GF, 17⁵GF, 19⁵G,

	Starts	1st	2nd	3rd	Win & Pl
Hurdles	6	1	0	0	3170
Career Total	22	1	0	3	4804
88	5/03	MRas 2m1f110yF(0-100)HHdl	G-F	£3169	

Total win prize-money £3170

Going:	Sf: 0-0 GS: 0-0 Gd: 0-2 GF: - Fm: 1-4
Distance:	2m/2m3: 1-3 2m4-2m7: 0-3 3m+: 0-0
Track:	LH: 0-1 RH: 1-5 Tight: 1-2 Gall: 0-0
Aids:	Bl: 1-5 Vi: 0-0 Tstrap: 0-0 Ckp: 0-0
Best Rating:	88 5/03 MRas 2m1f110y gd-fm Hdl

Poor hurdler; effective around two and a half miles; acts on soft but best on fast ground; has worn blinkers and cheekpieces.

Kimono Royal (FR)

108f   **110f**

6-y-o b/br g Garde Royale-Alizane (FR) (Mourtazam)
A King Nigel Bunter

Placings:14   (4578)
2003/04: 16¹G, 16⁴G,

	Starts	1st	2nd	3rd	Win & Pl
NH Flat	2	1	0	0	3660
Career Total	2	1	0	0	3660
95	2/04	Kemp 2m	H NHF	GD	£3659

Total win prize-money £3660

Going:	Sf: 0-0 GS: 0-0 Gd: 1-2 GF: - Fm: 0-0
Distance:	2m/2m3: 1-2 2m4-2m7: 0-0 3m+: 0-0
Track:	LH: 0-1 RH: 1-1 Tight: 0-0 Gall: 0-1
Aids:	Bl: 0-0 Vi: 0-0 Tstrap: 0-0 Ckp: 0-0
Best Rating:	110 3/04 Newb 2m110y good NHF

Modest bumper winner on good ground.

Kims Pearl (IRE)

82f

6-y-o b m Jurado (USA)-Blushing Pearl (Monksfield)
D Burchell John Richards

Placings:4   (4495)
2003/04: 16⁴G,

	Starts	1st	2nd	3rd	Win & Pl
NH Flat	1	0	0	0	0
Career Total	1	0	0	0	0

Going:	Sf: 0-0 GS: 0-0 Gd: 0-0 GF: - Fm: 0-0
Distance:	2m/2m3: 0-1 2m4-2m7: 0-0 3m+: 0-0
Track:	LH: 0-0 RH: 0-0 Tight: 0-0 Gall: 0-0
Aids:	Bl: 0-0 Vi: 0-0 Tstrap: 0-0 Ckp: 0-0
Best Rating:	82 3/04 Strf 2m110y good NHF

Kinburn (IRE)

85   **66**

5-y-o gr g Roselier (FR)-Leadaro (IRE) (Supreme Leader)
J Howard Johnson W M G Black

Placings:04   (4601)
2003/04: 20⁹GS, 22⁴GS,

	Starts	1st	2nd	3rd	Win & Pl
Hurdles	2	0	0	0	273
Career Total	2	0	0	0	273

Going:	Sf: 0-0 GS: 0-2 Gd: 0-0 GF: - Fm: 0-0
Distance:	2m/2m3: 0-0 2m4-2m7: 0-2 3m+: 0-0
Track:	LH: 0-2 RH: 0-0 Tight: 0-1 Gall: 0-1
Aids:	Bl: 0-0 Vi: 0-0 Tstrap: 0-0 Ckp: 0-0
Best Rating:	66 3/04 Kels 2m6f110y gd-sft Hdl

Kincora (IRE)

13-y-o b g King Persian-Miss Noora (Ahonoora)
Ms Lisa Stock Ms Lisa Stock

Placings:000000/454/454P/U66/3-4   (0349)
2003/04: 26⁴GF,

	Starts	1st	2nd	3rd	Win & Pl
Chases	1	0	0	0	109
Career Total	18	0	0	1	890

Going:	Sf: 0-0 GS: 0-0 Gd: 0-0 GF: - Fm: 0-1
Distance:	2m/2m3: 0-0 2m4-2m7: 0-0 3m+: 0-1
Track:	LH: 0-0 RH: 0-1 Tight: 0-1 Gall: 0-0
Aids:	Bl: 0-0 Vi: 0-0 Tstrap: 0-0 Ckp: 0-0
Best Rating:	92 5/99 Folk 2m5f gd-fm Ch

Kind Sir

108   **(96h)117**

8-y-o b g Generous (IRE)-Noble Conquest (USA) (Vaguely Noble)
A W Carroll Layton T Cheshire

Placings:23206/60P204/0023P3/P4321F111U2P-33P46522121   (4935)
2003/04: 20³GF, 19³GS, 20⁵G, 16⁴S, 16⁶G, 16⁵GS, 16²GF, 16²GF, 20¹GS, 20²G, 18¹G,

	Starts	1st	2nd	3rd	Win & Pl
Chases	11	2	3	2	18554
Career Total	40	6	9	6	44894
111	4/04	Font	2m2f	E(0-110)HCh	GD	£4657
102	3/04	Ludl	2m4f	D(0-115)HCh	G-S	£6656

117	1/03	Catt	2m	E(0-105)HCh	GD	£3870
117	1/03	Leic	2m	F(0-90)HCh	SFT	£3357
117	12/02	Hrfd	2m3f	D(0-110)HCh	SFT	£5928
105	12/02	Hrfd	2m	F(0-95)HCh	GD	£3799

Total win prize-money £28268

Going:	Sf: 0-1 GS: 1-3 Gd: 1-4 GF: - Fm: 0-3
Distance:	2m/2m3: 1-7 2m4-2m7: 1-4 3m+: 0-0
Track:	LH: 0-2 RH: 1-8 Tight: 2-3 Gall: 0-1
Aids:	Bl: 0-0 Vi: 0-0 Tstrap: 0-0 Ckp: 0-0
Best Rating:	117 1/03 Catt 2m good Ch

Moderate chaser; best at two miles, but has won at two miles four; acts on good and soft ground.

Kind Word (IRE)

106   **(0c)69**

11-y-o b/br m Yashgan-Lucifer's Way (Lucifer (USA))
C A Wilkinson C Wilkinson

Placings:050000/000100P/603453/PFF0-45502P   (1245a)
2003/04: 21⁴GF, 24⁵S, 20⁵GY, 16⁰GF, 20²GY, 20⁰F,

	Starts	1st	2nd	3rd	Win & Pl
Hurdles	6	0	1	0	1263
Career Total	29	1	1	2	5228
96	10/00	Gowr	2m	NHF	SFT	£2760

Total win prize-money £2760

Going:	Sf: 0-1 GS: 0-0 Gd: 0-0 GF: - Fm: 0-3
Distance:	2m/2m3: 0-1 2m4-2m7: 0-4 3m+: 0-1
Track:	LH: 0-2 RH: 0-1 Tight: 0-0 Gall: 0-0
Aids:	Bl: 0-1 Vi: 0-0 Tstrap: 0-6 Ckp: 0-0
Best Rating:	96 10/00 Gowr 2m soft NHF

Moderate handicap hurdler; stays well.

Kinda Crazy

83+

4-y-o b g Petoski-Margaret Modes (Thatching)
H J Manners H J Manners

Placings:000003P   (4918)
2003/04: 16⁵G, 17⁰S, 16⁰G, 16⁹G, 17⁰G, 19³S, 20⁰GS,

	Starts	1st	2nd	3rd	Win & Pl
NH Flat	4	0	0	0	0
Hurdles	3	0	0	1	441
Career Total	7	0	0	1	441

Going:	Sf: 0-2 GS: 0-1 Gd: 0-4 GF: - Fm: 0-0
Distance:	2m/2m3: 0-5 2m4-2m7: 0-2 3m+: 0-0
Track:	LH: 0-1 RH: 0-3 Tight: 0-0 Gall: 0-0
Aids:	Bl: 0-0 Vi: 0-0 Tstrap: 0-0 Ckp: 0-0
Best Rating:	83 4/04 Towc 2m3f110y soft Hdl

Kindle Ball (FR)

96   **92**

6-y-o gr m Kaldounevees (FR)-Scala Iv (FR) (Quart De Vin (FR))
Miss Venetia Williams Miss V M Williams

Placings:3-533131352   (4387)
2003/04: 17⁵G, 20³GF, 16³GF, 17¹G, 21³G, 16¹GF, 20⁵HY, 19⁵G, 21²G,

	Starts	1st	2nd	3rd	Win & Pl
NH Flat	1	0	0	0	0
Hurdles	8	2	1	4	9513
Career Total	10	2	1	5	9941
91	12/03	Sthl	2m	E Hdl	G-F	£2660
91	11/03	Sthl	2m1f	D Hdl	GD	£3471

Total win prize-money £6131

Going: Sf: 0-1 GS: 0-1 Gd: 1-4 GF: - Fm: 1-3
Distance: 2m/2m3: 2-4 2m4-2m7: 0-5 3m+: 0-0
Track: LH: 2-8 RH: 0-1 Tight: 1-3 Gall: 0-0
Aids: Bl: 0-0 Vi: 0-0 Tstrap: 0-0 Ckp: 0-0
Best Rating: 92 3/04 Sedg 2m5f110y good Hdl

Won a couple of modest novice hurdles over 2m at Southwell but stays further; goes on fast ground; should make a chaser in time.

King Bee (IRE)

106(110h)   (104+h)114+
7-y-o b g Supreme Leader-Honey Come Back (Master Owen)
H D Daly Trevor Hemmings

Placings:305/16645-323U1   (4590)
2003/04: 23³G, 24²GS, 24³S, 24ᵁHY, 24¹G,

	Starts	1st	2nd	3rd	Win & Pl
Chases	5	1	1	2	6970
Career Total	13	2	1	3	12029
120 3/04 Hntg	3m		E(0-105)HCh		GD £4212
102 11/02 Asct	2m4f		E(0-105)Hdl		G-S £4290
				Total win prize-money	£8502

Going: Sf: 0-2 GS: 0-1 Gd: 1-2 GF: - Fm: 0-0
Distance: 2m/2m3: 0-2 2m4-2m7: 0-0 3m+: 1-5
Track: LH: 0-1 RH: 1-4 Tight: 0-0 Gall: 1-1
Aids: Bl: 0-0 Vi: 0-0 Tstrap: 0-0 Ckp: 0-0
Best Rating: 120 3/04 Hntg 3m good Ch

Moderate novice chaser; stays 3m; acts on good to soft ground.

King Coal (IRE)

91   90
5-y-o b/br g Anshan-Lucky Trout (Beau Charmeur (FR))
R Rowe Anthony D Kerman

Placings:P0   (3042)
2003/04: 17²GS, 16⁰GS,

	Starts	1st	2nd	3rd	Win & Pl
Hurdles	2	0	0	0	
Career Total	2	0	0	0	

Going: Sf: 0-0 GS: 0-2 Gd: 0-0 GF: - Fm: 0-0
Distance: 2m/2m3: 0-2 2m4-2m7: 0-0 3m+: 0-0
Track: LH: 0-1 RH: 0-1 Tight: 0-1 Gall: 0-1
Aids: Bl: 0-0 Vi: 0-0 Tstrap: 0-0 Ckp: 0-0
Best Rating: 99 12/03 Newb 2m110y gd-sft Hdl

King Creole

5-y-o b g Slip Anchor-Myrrh (Salse (USA))
Ian Williams G R Phillips

Placings:0   (1506)
2003/04: 16⁰GF,

	Starts	1st	2nd	3rd	Win & Pl
Hurdles	1	0	0	0	
Career Total	1	0	0	0	

Going: Sf: 0-0 GS: 0-0 Gd: 0-0 GF: - Fm: 0-1
Distance: 2m/2m3: 0-1 2m4-2m7: 0-0 3m+: 0-0
Track: LH: 0-1 RH: 0-0 Tight: 0-0 Gall: 0-0
Aids: Bl: 0-0 Vi: 0-0 Tstrap: 0-0 Ckp: 0-0

King Darshaan

4-y-o b g Darshaan-Urchin (IRE) (Fairy King (USA))
P R Hedger J J Whelan

Placings:5   (2008)
2003/04: 16⁵G,

	Starts	1st	2nd	3rd	Win & Pl
Hurdles	1	0	0	0	386
Career Total	1	0	0	0	386

Going: Sf: 0-0 GS: 0-0 Gd: 0-0 GF: - Fm: 0-0
Distance: 2m/2m3: 0-1 2m4-2m7: 0-0 3m+: 0-0
Track: LH: 0-0 RH: 0-1 Tight: 0-0 Gall: 0-0
Aids: Bl: 0-0 Vi: 0-0 Tstrap: 0-0 Ckp: 0-0

King Eider

99   111
5-y-o b/br g Mtoto-Hen Harrier (Polar Falcon (USA))
N J Henderson (J L Dunlop 24/10) Mr & Mrs Peter Orton

Placings:463102   (4937)
2003/04: 17⁴GS, 19⁶G, 16³G, 16¹G, 16⁰GS, 16²GS,

	Starts	1st	2nd	3rd	Win & Pl
Hurdles	6	1	1	1	6523
Career Total	6	1	1	1	6523
99 3/04 Winc	2m		E Hdl		GD £3591
				Total win prize-money	£3591

Going: Sf: 0-0 GS: 0-3 Gd: 1-3 GF: - Fm: 0-0
Distance: 2m/2m3: 1-5 2m4-2m7: 0-1 3m+: 0-0
Track: LH: 0-3 RH: 1-3 Tight: 0-1 Gall: 0-2
Aids: Bl: 0-0 Vi: 0-0 Tstrap: 0-0 Ckp: 0-0
Best Rating: 114 2/04 Newb 2m110y good Hdl

Fair hurdler; got off the mark for the first time when winning at Wincanton; effective at two miles; needed fast ground on the level.

King Georges (FR)

98   110+
6-y-o b g Kadalko (FR)-Djoumi (FR) (Brezzo (FR))
J C Tuck The Try-Line Partnership

Placings:F0/P015416-010F   (4451)
2003/04: 22⁰G, 25¹G, 24⁰GS, 24ᶠGS,

	Starts	1st	2nd	3rd	Win & Pl
Hurdles	4	1	0	0	4046
Career Total	13	3	0	0	10507
108 11/03 Kemp	3m1f		D(0-120)HHdl		GD £4046
96 2/03 Extr	2m1f		F(0-90)HHdl		G-S £3059
82 12/02 Winc	2m		F(0-95)HHdl		G-S £3402
				Total win prize-money	£10507

Going: Sf: 0-0 GS: 0-2 Gd: 1-2 GF: - Fm: 0-0
Distance: 2m/2m3: 0-2 2m4-2m7: 0-1 3m+: 1-3
Track: LH: 0-0 RH: 1-4 Tight: 0-0 Gall: 0-0
Aids: Bl: 0-0 Vi: 0-0 Tstrap: 0-0 Ckp: 0-0
Best Rating: 108 11/03 Kemp 3m1f good Hdl

Moderate hurdler; stays three miles one; acts on good to soft ground; inconsistent; should make a chaser.

King James

24

7-y-o b g Homo Sapien-Bowling Fort (Bowling Pin)
J Mackie A J Wall

Placings:0600B/PP   (4511)
2003/04: 19⁰G, 20⁰GS,

	Starts	1st	2nd	3rd	Win & Pl
Hurdles	2	0	0	0	
Career Total	7	0	0	0	0

Going: Sf: 0-0 GS: 0-1 Gd: 0-1 GF: - Fm: 0-0
Distance: 2m/2m3: 0-0 2m4-2m7: 0-2 3m+: 0-0
Track: LH: 0-2 RH: 0-0 Tight: 0-0 Gall: 0-0
Aids: Bl: 0-0 Vi: 0-0 Tstrap: 0-2 Ckp: 0-0
Best Rating: 68 10/01 Hntg 2m110y good NHF

King Of Arms

105(98c)   (76c)81+
6-y-o b g Rakaposhi King-Herald The Dawn (Dubassoff (USA))
J Howard Johnson M McKernan

Placings:00P0P-14P44   (4796)
2003/04: 24¹S, 24⁴HY, 24ᴾG, 21⁴G, 21⁴G,

	Starts	1st	2nd	3rd	Win & Pl
Hurdles	4	1	0	0	2327
Chases	1	0	0	0	269
Career Total	10	1	0	0	2596
81 12/03 Hexm	3m		E(0-105)HHdl		SFT £1953
				Total win prize-money	£1953

Going: Sf: 1-2 GS: 0-0 Gd: 0-3 GF: - Fm: 0-0
Distance: 2m/2m3: 0-0 2m4-2m7: 0-2 3m+: 1-3
Track: LH: 1-4 RH: 0-0 Tight: 0-2 Gall: 0-0
Aids: Bl: 0-0 Vi: 0-0 Tstrap: 0-0 Ckp: 0-0
Best Rating: 81 12/03 Hexm 3m soft Hdl

Plating-class hurdler/chaser; first worthwhile form when winning three-mile amateur riders' handicap hurdle on soft ground at Hexham in December 2003; fair chasing debut in March 2004.

King Of Barbury (IRE)

99   110+
7-y-o b g Moscow Society (USA)-Aine's Alice (IRE) (Drumalis)
A King Miss J M Bodycote

Placings:42/343P-1043   (4634)
2003/04: 17¹GS, 16⁰GS, 16⁴G, 19³G,

	Starts	1st	2nd	3rd	Win & Pl
Hurdles	4	1	0	1	3821
Career Total	10	1	1	3	6126
110 12/03 Bang	2m1f		F(0-100)HHdl		G-S £2712
				Total win prize-money	£2713

Going: Sf: 0-0 GS: 1-2 Gd: 0-2 GF: - Fm: 0-0
Distance: 2m/2m3: 1-3 2m4-2m7: 0-1 3m+: 0-0
Track: LH: 1-3 RH: 0-1 Tight: 1-2 Gall: 0-1
Aids: Bl: 0-0 Vi: 0-0 Tstrap: 0-0 Ckp: 0-0
Best Rating: 110 12/03 Bang 2m1f gd-sft Hdl

He has shown ability in bumpers and novice hurdles; acts on easy ground.

King Of Gothland (IRE)

104f   101f
5-y-o b/br g Gothland (FR)-Rose Deer (Whistling Deer)
K C Bailey The Norfolk Neighbours

Placings:044   (4050)
2003/04: 16⁰GS, 16⁴GS, 16⁴G,

	Starts	1st	2nd	3rd	Win & Pl
NH Flat	3	0	0	0	0

| Career Total | 3 | 0 | 0 | 0 | 0 |

Going: Sf: 0-0 GS: 0-2 Gd: 0-1 GF: 0-0 - Fm: 0-0
Distance: 2m/2m3: 0-3 2m4-2m7: 0-0 3m+: 0-0
Track: LH: 0-2 RH: 0-1 Tight: 0-0 Gall: 0-2
Aids: Bl: 0-0 Vi: 0-0 Tstrap: 0-0 Ckp: 0-0
Best Rating: 100 2/04 Hayd 2m   good NHF

Showed promise when staying on fourth on debut in bumper at Haydock in February.

King Of Mommur (IRE)

93(93h)   (98h)105

9-y-o b g Fairy King (USA)-Monoglow (Kalaglow)
B G Powell The Three Bears Racing

Placings:6135/0P0/1155/5114-5P   (1301)
2003/04: 20⁵G, 21ᴾGF,

	Starts	1st	2nd	3rd	Win & Pl
Chases	2	0	0	0	
Career Total	17	5	0	1	19228
105 3/03	Font	2m2f	D(0-115)HCh	G-F	£5655
103 2/03	Leic	2m	F(0-95)Ch	G-S	£4153
105 5/01	Font	2m4f	F Ch	G-F	£2973
109 5/01	Sthl	2m	F(0-110)HCh	G-F	£2968
115 3/00	Extr	2m3f110yE Hdl		G-S	£2556
			Total win prize-money £18307		

Going: Sf: 0-0 GS: 0-0 Gd: 0-1 GF: - Fm: 0-1
Distance: 2m/2m3: 0-0 2m4-2m7: 0-2 3m+: 0-1
Track: LH: 0-1 RH: 0-0 Tight: 0-0 Gall: 0-0
Aids: Bl: 0-0 Vi: 0-0 Tstrap: 0-0 Ckp: 0-0
Best Rating: 115 3/00 Chep 2m110y   good Hdl

Fair chaser; well-placed to win third chase in five starts at Leicester in February; followed up at Fontwell in March; has worn blinkers and cheek-pieces; stays two and a half miles; acts well on decent ground.

King Of The Arctic (IRE)

106   101+

6-y-o b g Arctic Lord-Ye Little Daisy (Prince Tenderfoot (USA)
J Wade (D K Weld 31/5) John Wade

Placings:350-0021424   (4911)
2003/04: 16⁶G, 20⁰YS, 20²GF, 16¹S, 20⁴GS, 16²G, 16⁴S,

	Starts	1st	2nd	3rd	Win & Pl
NH Flat	1	0	0	0	
Hurdles	6	1	2	0	4991
Career Total	10	1	2	1	5593
104 12/03	Hexm	2m110y E Hdl		SFT	£1883
			Total win prize-money £1883		

Going: Sf: 1-2 GS: 0-1 Gd: 0-2 GF: - Fm: 0-1
Distance: 2m/2m3: 1-4 2m4-2m7: 0-3 3m+: 0-0
Track: LH: 1-3 RH: 0-2 Tight: 0-1 Gall: 0-0
Aids: Bl: 0-0 Vi: 0-0 Tstrap: 0-0 Ckp: 0-0
Best Rating: 104 12/03 Hexm 2m110y   soft Hdl

Modest form in Irish bumpers and hurdle; improved effort on first run for John Wade when winning novice at Hexham in December, but held since; stays two and a half miles and acts on fast and soft ground.

King Of The Castle (IRE)

94(96h)   (109h)95

9-y-o b g Cataldi-Monashuna (Boreen (FR))

B Mactaggart The Potassium Partnership

Placings:11/F0PP1/2023100/3-34   (4860)
2003/04: 20³S, 20⁴GS,

	Starts	1st	2nd	3rd	Win & Pl
Chases	2	0	0	0	2638
Career Total	17	4	2	3	25741
109 10/01	Extr	2m3f	E(0-115)HHdl	G-S	£3290
103 4/01	Tntn	2m1f	F(0-95)HHdl	GD	£2415
128 4/99	Aint	2m110y	A NHF	GD	£13200
109 3/99	Folk	2m1f110y		H NHF	G-S £1577
			Total win prize-money £20483		

Going: Sf: 0-1 GS: 0-1 Gd: 0-0 GF: - Fm: 0-0
Distance: 2m/2m3: 0-0 2m4-2m7: 0-2 3m+: 0-0
Track: LH: 0-1 RH: 0-1 Tight: 0-0 Gall: 0-0
Aids: Bl: 0-0 Vi: 0-0 Tstrap: 0-0 Ckp: 0-0
Best Rating: 128 4/99 Aint 2m110y   good NHF

Useful handicap hurdler; well beaten on chase debut; stays just short of two and a half miles; acts on most ground.

King Of The Dawn

13-y-o b/br g Rakaposhi King-Dawn Encounter (Rymer)
Mrs Georgina Worsley (P R Hedger 5/5) Mrs Georgina Worsley

Placings:14/11206/03/03424P/32P03/U6321360P0/12-0UU   (4563)
2003/04: 20⁰G, 20ᵁG, 22ᵁG,

	Starts	1st	2nd	3rd	Win & Pl
Chases	3	0	0	0	
Career Total	35	5	5	6	24526
96 1/03	Font	2m6f	F(0-90)HCh	HVY	£3339
103 10/01	Font	2m6f	F(0-95)HCh	SFT	£2899
116 11/97	Extr	2m1f110yE Hdl		G-S	£2679
109 8/97	Tram		Hdl	GD	£2712
100 9/96	Clon	2m	NHF	GD	£2471
			Total win prize-money £14102		

Going: Sf: 0-0 GS: 0-0 Gd: 0-3 GF: - Fm: 0-0
Distance: 2m/2m3: 0-0 2m4-2m7: 0-3 3m+: 0-0
Track: LH: 0-0 RH: 0-0 Tight: 0-2 Gall: 0-1
Aids: Bl: 0-0 Vi: 0-0 Tstrap: 0-0 Ckp: 0-0
Best Rating: 116 11/97 Extr 2m1f110y gd-sft Hdl

Modest hunter; handles most types of ground; suited by trips at around two and a half miles.

King Of The Forest (IRE)

91   98

9-y-o b g Good Thyne (USA)-Coolbawn Lady (Laurence O)
Miss S E Forster A G & Mrs E J Bell

Placings:5/0/2420-F   (0097)
2003/04: 25⁰G, 25⁶G,

	Starts	1st	2nd	3rd	Win & Pl
Chases	2	0	0	0	
Career Total	7	0	2	0	2815

Going: Sf: 0-0 GS: 0-0 Gd: 0-2 GF: - Fm: 0-0
Distance: 2m/2m3: 0-0 2m4-2m7: 0-0 3m+: 0-2
Track: LH: 0-2 RH: 0-0 Tight: 0-0 Gall: 0-1
Aids: Bl: 0-0 Vi: 0-0 Tstrap: 0-0 Ckp: 0-1
Best Rating: 98 1/03 Ayr 3m1f   soft Ch

King Of The Naul (IRE)

11-y-o b g King's Ride-Glenastar Vii (Damsire Unregistered)
C L Tizzard Mrs J E Purdie

Placings:6061/0/P   (0434)
2003/04: 20ᴾGF,

	Starts	1st	2nd	3rd	Win & Pl
Chases	1	0	0	0	
Career Total	6	1	0	0	2455
110 3/99	DRoy	2m	NHF	G-Y	£2455
			Total win prize-money £2455		

Going: Sf: 0-0 GS: 0-0 Gd: 0-0 GF: - Fm: 0-1
Distance: 2m/2m3: 0-0 2m4-2m7: 0-1 3m+: 0-0
Track: LH: 0-0 RH: 0-0 Tight: 0-1 Gall: 0-0
Aids: Bl: 0-0 Vi: 0-0 Tstrap: 0-0 Ckp: 0-0
Best Rating: 110 3/99 DRoy 2m   gd-yld NHF

King On The Run (IRE)

99   110

11-y-o b g King's Ride-Fly Run (Deep Run)
Miss Venetia Williams Lady Harris

Placings:31166/1U3/113/1/5   (4057)
2003/04: 20⁵G,

	Starts	1st	2nd	3rd	Win & Pl
Chases	1	0	0	0	520
Career Total	13	6	0	3	44337
141 1/02	Kemp	2m4f110yB(0-140)HCh	GD	£13910
127 11/00	Kemp	2m4f110yB(0-140)HCh	SFT	£9178
132 11/00	Newb	2m4f	D(0-125)HCh	SFT	£5642
123 11/98	Wwck	2m4f110yD Ch		GD	£3834
131 1/98	Kemp	2m5f	D Hdl	G-S	£3074
131 12/97	Strf	2m6f110yE Hdl		SFT	£2500
			Total win prize-money £38138		

Going: Sf: 0-0 GS: 0-0 Gd: 0-1 GF: - Fm: 0-0
Distance: 2m/2m3: 0-0 2m4-2m7: 0-1 3m+: 0-0
Track: LH: 0-0 RH: 0-1 Tight: 0-0 Gall: 0-0
Aids: Bl: 0-0 Vi: 0-0 Tstrap: 0-0 Ckp: 0-0
Best Rating: 141 1/02 Kemp 2m4f110y good Ch

Fair chaser; has been lightly raced due to injuries; stays three miles; goes well fresh; has won on good and soft ground; great record at Kempton.

King Plato (IRE)

100(108h)   (85 h)85

7-y-o b g King's Ride-You Are A Lady (IRE) (Lord Americo)
M D Hammond Jay Dee Bloodstock Limited

Placings:6406/501153-464F03   (4961)
2003/04: 16⁴S, 20⁶GS, 25⁴HY, 20⁴S, 20⁰G, 20³GS,

	Starts	1st	2nd	3rd	Win & Pl
Chases	6	0	0	1	1096
Career Total	16	2	0	2	7149
83 8/02	Worc	2m4f	E(0-100)HHdl	SFT	£3122
93 8/02	Bang	3m	F(0-95)HHdl	SFT	£2404
			Total win prize-money £5527		

Going: Sf: 0-3 GS: 0-2 Gd: 0-1 GF: - Fm: 0-0
Distance: 2m/2m3: 0-1 2m4-2m7: 0-4 3m+: 0-1
Track: LH: 0-4 RH: 0-2 Tight: 0-2 Gall: 0-1
Aids: Bl: 0-0 Vi: 0-0 Tstrap: 0-0 Ckp: 0-0
Best Rating: 93 12/03 Hexm 2m110y   soft Ch

Plating-class hurdler/moderate chaser; won first two starts in

handicap hurdles off 77 in August 2002, but struggled after; has a high knee action and appreciates soft ground.

King Player (IRE)

7-y-o b g King's Ride-West Along (Crash Course)
N J Henderson Trevor Hemmings

Placings:2-P				(2488)
2003/04: 16PGS,				

	Starts	1st	2nd	3rd	Win & Pl
Hurdles	1	0	0	0	
Career Total	2	0	1	0	756

Going:	Sf: 0-0 GS: 0-1 Gd: 0-0 GF: - Fm: 0-0
Distance:	2m/2m3: 0-1 2m4-2m7: 0-0 3m+: 0-0
Track:	LH: 0-1 RH: 0-0 Tight: 0-0 Gall: 0-1
Aids:	Bl: 0-0 Vi: 0-0 Tstrap: 0-0 Ckp: 0-0
Best Rating:	110 12/02 Newb 2m110y heavy NHF

Runner-up in a bumper December 2002; pulled up lame on hurdles debut 11 months later.

King Revo (IRE)
108   125

4-y-o b g Revoque (IRE)-Tycoon Aly (IRE) (Last Tycoon)
P C Haslam Dick Renwick & Mrs C Barclay

Placings:11116				(4625)
2003/04: 16¹GS, 16¹GS, 16¹S, 16¹S, 16⁶G,				

	Starts	1st	2nd	3rd	Win & Pl
Hurdles	5	4	0	0	33502
Career Total	5	4	0	0	33502
123	2/04	Hayd	2m	B Hdl		SFT	£10244
125	1/04	Weth	2m	E Hdl		SFT	£3892
113	12/03	Weth	2m	B Hdl		G-S	£14183
113	12/03	Catt	2m	D Hdl		G-S	£3532
				Total win prize-money £31852

Going:	Sf: 2-2 GS: 2-2 Gd: 0-1 GF: - Fm: 0-0
Distance:	2m/2m3: 4-5 2m4-2m7: 0-0 3m+: 0-0
Track:	LH: 4-5 RH: 0-0 Tight: 1-2 Gall: 0-0
Aids:	Bl: 0-0 Vi: 0-0 Tstrap: 0-0 Ckp: 0-0
Best Rating:	125 4/04 Aint 2m110y good Hdl

Highly progressive juvenile hurdler; fair Flat performer; winner of first four starts over hurdles; handles most types of ground.

King Silca
89   58

7-y-o b g Emarati (USA)-Silca-Cisa (Hallgate)
R Williams R Williams

Placings:0560				(0635)
2003/04: 16⁰G, 17⁵GF, 16⁶GF, 22⁰GF,				

	Starts	1st	2nd	3rd	Win & Pl
Hurdles	4	0	0	0	0
Career Total	4	0	0	0	0

Going:	Sf: 0-0 GS: 0-0 Gd: 0-1 GF: 0-3
Distance:	2m/2m3: 0-3 2m4-2m7: 0-1 3m+: 0-0
Track:	LH: 0-2 RH: 0-2 Tight: 0-1 Gall: 0-0
Aids:	Bl: 0-0 Vi: 0-0 Tstrap: 0-0 Ckp: 0-0
Best Rating:	60 5/03 Extr 2m1f gd-fm Hdl

King Solomon (FR)
108   123+

5-y-o gr h Simon Du Desert (FR)-All Square (FR) (Holst (USA))

Miss Venetia Williams Seasons Holidays

Placings:200-3126201B				(4644)
2003/04: 16³G, 16¹GS, 17²G, 20⁶HY, 16²G, 21⁰G, 17¹GS, 16⁸G,				

	Starts	1st	2nd	3rd	Win & Pl
Hurdles	8	2	2	1	11414
Career Total	11	2	3	1	12498
121	3/04	Bang	2m1f	E Hdl		G-S	£4095
111	12/03	Chep	2m110y	D Hdl		G-S	£3399
				Total win prize-money £7495

Going:	Sf: 0-1 GS: 2-2 Gd: 0-5 GF: - Fm: 0-0
Distance:	2m/2m3: 2-6 2m4-2m7: 0-2 3m+: 0-0
Track:	LH: 2-5 RH: 0-3 Tight: 1-3 Gall: 0-1
Aids:	Bl: 0-0 Vi: 0-0 Tstrap: 1-3 Ckp: 0-0
Best Rating:	123 3/04 Ludl 2m good Hdl

Fair novice hurdler; smart on the Flat; made all to win uncompetitive maiden hurdle at Chepstow in December 2003; unable to add to that success since; effective over 2m; acts on good ground; tried in tongue-tie latest.

King Summerland
93   81+

7-y-o b h Minshaanshu Amad (USA)-Alaskan Princess (IRE) (Prince Rupert (FR))
C J Mann The Safest Syndicate

Placings:P000				(3430)
2003/04: 16⁵PS, 16⁰GF, 16⁰GS, 16⁰GS,				

	Starts	1st	2nd	3rd	Win & Pl
Hurdles	4	0	0	0	
Career Total	4	0	0	0	

Going:	Sf: 0-1 GS: 0-2 Gd: 0-0 GF: - Fm: 0-1
Distance:	2m/2m3: 0-4 2m4-2m7: 0-0 3m+: 0-0
Track:	LH: 0-2 RH: 0-2 Tight: 0-1 Gall: 0-1
Aids:	Bl: 0-0 Vi: 0-0 Tstrap: 0-0 Ckp: 0-0
Best Rating:	81 12/03 Newb 2m110y gd-fm Hdl

King's Bounty
109(91h)   (112h)108

8-y-o b g Le Moss-Fit For A King (Royalty)
T D Easterby C H Stevens

Placings:003/542123/03F0B322114-0U0223				(4615)
2003/04: 25⁰G, 25⁰UGS, 27⁰GS, 22²GS, 24²S, 28³G,				

	Starts	1st	2nd	3rd	Win & Pl
Chases	6	0	2	1	5414
Career Total	26	3	6	5	24310
108	4/03	Kels	3m1f	D Ch		GD	£5395
103	3/03	Weth	2m4f110yE Ch		G-F	£4075
109	2/02	Newc	2m4f	E Hdl		SFT	£2555
				Total win prize-money £12026

Going:	Sf: 0-1 GS: 0-3 Gd: 0-2 GF: - Fm: 0-0
Distance:	2m/2m3: 0-0 2m4-2m7: 0-1 3m+: 0-0
Track:	LH: 0-6 RH: 0-0 Tight: 0-4 Gall: 0-1
Aids:	Bl: 0-0 Vi: 0-0 Tstrap: 0-0 Ckp: 0-0
Best Rating:	112 3/02 Donc 2m4f soft Hdl

Modest chaser; suited by three miles; jumps well; likes a sound surface; returned to form at Kelso in March 2004 and will be suited by the return to three miles.

King's Champion (IRE)
92   90

8-y-o br g King's Ride-Decent Slave (Decent Fellow)
Mrs Merrita Jones Speed 2911 Ltd

Placings:0⁰5				(2279)
2003/04: 20⁵G,				

	Starts	1st	2nd	3rd	Win & Pl
Hurdles	1	0	0	0	0
Career Total	2	0	0	0	0

Going:	Sf: 0-0 GS: 0-0 Gd: 0-1 GF: - Fm: 0-0
Distance:	2m/2m3: 0-0 2m4-2m7: 0-1 3m+: 0-0
Track:	LH: 0-0 RH: 0-1 Tight: 0-0 Gall: 0-0
Aids:	Bl: 0-0 Vi: 0-0 Tstrap: 0-0 Ckp: 0-0
Best Rating:	90 11/03 Asct 2m4f good Hdl

King's Crest
96   91+

6-y-o b g Deploy-Classic Beauty (IRE) (Fairy King (USA))
R A Fahey Seamus Farrey & Partners

Placings:235				(3767)
2003/04: 16²GS, 16³GS, 17⁵HY,				

	Starts	1st	2nd	3rd	Win & Pl
Hurdles	3	0	1	1	1687
Career Total	3	0	1	1	1687

Going:	Sf: 0-2 GS: 0-1 Gd: 0-0 GF: - Fm: 0-0
Distance:	2m/2m3: 0-3 2m4-2m7: 0-0 3m+: 0-0
Track:	LH: 0-2 RH: 0-1 Tight: 0-1 Gall: 0-0
Aids:	Bl: 0-0 Vi: 0-0 Tstrap: 0-0 Ckp: 0-0
Best Rating:	92 11/03 Hayd 2m soft Hdl

Modest handicapper on the Flat winning eight times; runner-up on hurdling debut at Haydock in November; well beaten third at Catterick two months later; finds little under pressure.

King's Echo
58   83

6-y-o b g Rakaposhi King-Welgenco (Welsh Saint)
S Gollings J B Webb

Placings:44-43206P				(3272)
2003/04: 16⁴G, 16⁰GF, 23²G, 20⁰GS, 20⁶GS, 22⁰G,				

	Starts	1st	2nd	3rd	Win & Pl
NH Flat	2	0	0	1	236
Hurdles	4	0	1	0	626
Career Total	8	0	1	1	862

Going:	Sf: 0-0 GS: 0-2 Gd: 0-3 GF: - Fm: 0-1
Distance:	2m/2m3: 0-2 2m4-2m7: 0-3 3m+: 0-1
Track:	LH: 0-6 RH: 0-0 Tight: 0-2 Gall: 0-0
Aids:	Bl: 0-0 Vi: 0-0 Tstrap: 0-0 Ckp: 0-0
Best Rating:	83 11/03 Fknm 2m7f110y good Hdl

Modest form in bumpers on varying ground; looks likely to stay further.

King's Envoy (USA)
52

5-y-o b g Royal Academy (USA)-Island Of Silver (USA) (Forty Niner (USA))
Mrs J C McGregor Mrs Dorothy Thomson

Placings:0PP-P				(2508)
2003/04: 16PS,				

	Starts	1st	2nd	3rd	Win & Pl
Hurdles	1	0	0	0	
Career Total	4	0	0	0	

Going: Sf: 0-1 GS: 0-0 Gd: 0-0 GF: - Fm: 0-0
Distance: 2m/2m3: 0-1 2m4-2m7: 0-0 3m+: 0-0
Track: LH: 0-1 RH: 0-0 Tight: 0-1 Gall: 0-0
Aids: Bl: 0-0 Vi: 0-0 Tstrap: 0-0 Ckp: 0-0
Best Rating: 52 11/02 Ayr 2m soft Hdl

King's Mill (IRE)
80   111

7-y-o b g Doyoun-Adarika (King's Lake (USA))
N A Graham First Millennium Racing

Placings:520-0   (1424)
2003/04: 20⁰G,

	Starts	1st	2nd	3rd	Win & Pl
Hurdles	1	0	0	0	
Career Total	4	0	1	0	1458

Going: Sf: 0-0 GS: 0-0 Gd: 0-1 GF: - Fm: 0-0
Distance: 2m/2m3: 0-0 2m4-2m7: 0-1 3m+: 0-0
Track: LH: 0-0 RH: 0-1 Tight: 0-0 Gall: 0-0
Aids: Bl: 0-0 Vi: 0-0 Tstrap: 0-0 Ckp: 0-0
Best Rating: 111 12/02 Newb 2m110y good Hdl

Decent on the Flat, he was all but brought down on his hurdling debut but showed what he can do when runner-up at Newbury next time; held since.

King's Reign (IRE)
83   86

8-y-o b g King's Ride-Lena's Reign (Quayside)
N A Twiston-Davies Mrs Lorna Berryman

Placings:00P/0000-5P   (0706)
2003/04: 26⁵GF, 22⁷GF,

	Starts	1st	2nd	3rd	Win & Pl
Hurdles	2	0	0	0	0
Career Total	9	0	0	0	0

Going: Sf: 0-0 GS: 0-0 Gd: 0-0 GF: - Fm: 0-2
Distance: 2m/2m3: 0-0 2m4-2m7: 0-1 3m+: 0-1
Track: LH: 0-1 RH: 0-1 Tight: 0-1 Gall: 0-1
Aids: Bl: 0-0 Vi: 0-0 Tstrap: 0-0 Ckp: 0-0
Best Rating: 86 11/02 Newb 2m3f gd-sft Hdl

Plating-class hurdler; best at just short of three miles; acts on fast and soft ground.

King's Travel (FR)
91(99h)   (87 h)89

8-y-o gr g Balleroy (USA)-Travel Free (Be My Guest (USA))
J D Frost C Johnston

Placings:P/0/50601-612   (2834)
2003/04: 17⁶GF, 17¹GS, 16²G,

	Starts	1st	2nd	3rd	Win & Pl
Hurdles	1	0	0	0	0
Chases	2	1	1	0	4894
Career Total	10	2	1	0	7974
89	11/03 Bang	2m1f110yE(0-105)HCh		G-S	£2834
87	4/03 NAbb	2m1f	G(0-95)HHdl	GD	£3080

Total win prize-money £5914

Going: Sf: 0-0 GS: 1-1 Gd: 0-1 GF: - Fm: 0-1
Distance: 2m/2m3: 1-3 2m4-2m7: 0-0 3m+: 0-0
Track: LH: 1-2 RH: 0-1 Tight: 1-2 Gall: 0-0
Aids: Bl: 0-0 Vi: 0-0 Tstrap: 0-0 Ckp: 0-0
Best Rating: 89 12/03 Asct 2m good Ch

Plating-class hurdler, successful in weak event at Newton Abbot in April 2003.

King-For-Life (IRE)
70   41

6-y-o ch g Rainbows For Life (CAN)-Fair Song (Pitskelly)
R Ford T D Williams

Placings:0622P-0   (1787)
2003/04: 20⁰G,

	Starts	1st	2nd	3rd	Win & Pl
Hurdles	1	0	0	0	
Career Total	6	0	2	0	1142

Going: Sf: 0-0 GS: 0-0 Gd: 0-1 GF: - Fm: 0-0
Distance: 2m/2m3: 0-0 2m4-2m7: 0-1 3m+: 0-0
Track: LH: 0-1 RH: 0-0 Tight: 0-1 Gall: 0-0
Aids: Bl: 0-0 Vi: 0-0 Tstrap: 0-0 Ckp: 0-0
Best Rating: 98 2/03 Catt 2m good NHF

Kingfisher Eve (IRE)
95   75

6-y-o b m Hamas (IRE)-Houwara (IRE) (Darshaan)
C Grant Henry Bell

Placings:33   (2137)
2003/04: 20³GF, 24³G,

	Starts	1st	2nd	3rd	Win & Pl
Hurdles	2	0	0	2	672
Career Total	2	0	0	2	672

Going: Sf: 0-0 GS: 0-0 Gd: 0-1 GF: - Fm: 0-1
Distance: 2m/2m3: 0-0 2m4-2m7: 0-1 3m+: 0-1
Track: LH: 0-1 RH: 0-1 Tight: 0-0 Gall: 0-1
Aids: Bl: 0-0 Vi: 0-0 Tstrap: 0-0 Ckp: 0-0
Best Rating: 75 11/03 Newc 3m good Hdl

Kingfisher Star

9-y-o ch g Derrylin-Legata (IRE) (Orchestra)
S R Andrews D Morgan

Placings:63-P   (0349)
2003/04: 26PGF,

	Starts	1st	2nd	3rd	Win & Pl
Chases	1	0	0	0	
Career Total	3	0	0	1	327

Going: Sf: 0-0 GS: 0-0 Gd: 0-0 GF: - Fm: 0-1
Distance: 2m/2m3: 0-0 2m4-2m7: 0-0 3m+: 0-1
Track: LH: 0-0 RH: 0-1 Tight: 0-0 Gall: 0-0
Aids: Bl: 0-1 Vi: 0-0 Tstrap: 0-0 Ckp: 0-0
Best Rating: 49 5/02 Folk 2m5f good Ch

Kingfisher Sunset

8-y-o b g Afflora (IRE)-Jack It In (Derrylin)
J G M O'Shea K A Ayres

Placings:0450-U   (2194)
2003/04: 20UGS,

	Starts	1st	2nd	3rd	Win & Pl
Hurdles	1	0	0	0	
Career Total	5	0	0	0	0

Going: Sf: 0-0 GS: 0-0 Gd: 0-0 GF: - Fm: 0-0
Distance: 2m/2m3: 0-0 2m4-2m7: 0-1 3m+: 0-0
Track: LH: 0-1 RH: 0-0 Tight: 0-0 Gall: 0-0

Aids: Bl: 0-0 Vi: 0-0 Tstrap: 0-0 Ckp: 0-0
Best Rating: 65 10/02 Chep 2m110y gd-fm NHF

Kingkohler (IRE)
103   98+

5-y-o b g King's Theatre (IRE)-Legit (IRE) (Runnett)
K A Morgan Jo Champion, H Morgan, E Barlow

Placings:3-21   (3230)
2003/04: 16²S, 16¹GF,

	Starts	1st	2nd	3rd	Win & Pl
Hurdles	2	1	1	0	3923
Career Total	3	1	1	1	4667
104	1/04 Muss	2m	E Hdl	G-F	£3386

Total win prize-money £3387

Going: Sf: 0-1 GS: 0-0 Gd: 0-0 GF: - Fm: 1-1
Distance: 2m/2m3: 1-2 2m4-2m7: 0-0 3m+: 0-0
Track: LH: 0-1 RH: 1-1 Tight: 0-0 Gall: 0-0
Aids: Bl: 0-0 Vi: 0-0 Tstrap: 0-0 Ckp: 0-0
Best Rating: 104 1/04 Muss 2m gd-fm Hdl

Middle-distance winner on the Flat; keen-type and suited by sharp tracks; off the mark with a decisive win in modest company at Musselburgh in January.

Kings Boy (IRE)

10-y-o ch g Be My Native (USA)-Love-In-A-Mist (Paddy's Stream)
David M Easterby Lord Daresbury

Placings:311/6P/4P/P/2   (0031)
2003/04: 21²G,

	Starts	1st	2nd	3rd	Win & Pl
Chases	1	0	1	0	1185
Career Total	9	2	1	1	8065
115	4/99 Asct	2m4f	D Hdl	G-F	£3728
130	1/99 Donc	2m4f	E Hdl	G-S	£2477

Total win prize-money £6207

Going: Sf: 0-0 GS: 0-0 Gd: 0-1 GF: - Fm: 0-0
Distance: 2m/2m3: 0-0 2m4-2m7: 0-1 3m+: 0-0
Track: LH: 0-1 RH: 0-0 Tight: 0-0 Gall: 0-1
Aids: Bl: 0-0 Vi: 0-0 Tstrap: 0-1 Ckp: 0-0
Best Rating: 130 1/99 Donc 2m4f gd-sft Hdl

One-time useful hurdler; now a decent hunter chaser; not easy to train.

Kings Brook
87   77

4-y-o br g Alderbrook-Kins Token (Relkino)
Nick Williams Tony Gale

Placings:064P   (4671)
2003/04: 12⁰G, 17⁶S, 16⁴G, 16⁶G,

	Starts	1st	2nd	3rd	Win & Pl
NH Flat	2	0	0	0	0
Hurdles	2	0	0	0	276
Career Total	4	0	0	0	276

Going: Sf: 0-1 GS: 0-0 Gd: 0-3 GF: - Fm: 0-0
Distance: 2m/2m3: 0-3 2m4-2m7: 0-0 3m+: 0-0
Track: LH: 0-0 RH: 0-2 Tight: 0-0 Gall: 0-0
Aids: Bl: 0-0 Vi: 0-0 Tstrap: 0-0 Ckp: 0-0
Best Rating: 80 3/04 Winc 2m good Hdl

Kings Castle (IRE)

(100c)   (111c)143

9-y-o b g King's Ride-Kilmana (IRE) (Castle Keep)
R J Hodges Fieldspring Racing

Placings: 112/4116100/2PFP   (4449)
2003/04: 21²G, 24PG, 22FG, 20PGS,

	Starts	1st	2nd	3rd	Win & Pl
Hurdles	2	0	0	0	0
Chases	2	0	1	0	1481
Career Total	14	5	2	0	30804
143	1/02	Wwck	3m1f		B HHdl	SFT £8892
138	11/01	Aint	2m4f	C(0-130)HHdl	G-S £10822
122	11/01	Winc	2m6f	E(0-115)HHdl	GD £4212
113	2/00	Font	2m6f110yE Hdl	G-S £2590
122	2/00	Font	2m2f110yH NHF	SFT £1704

Total win prize-money £28222

Going:	Sf: 0-0 GS: 0-1 Gd: 0-3 GF: - Fm: 0-0
Distance:	2m2m3: 0-0 2m4-2m7: 0-3 3m+: 0-1
Track:	LH: 0-1 RH: 0-3 Tight: 0-1 Gall: 0-0
Aids:	Bl: 0-0 Vi: 0-0 Tstrap: 0-0 Ckp: 0-0
Best Rating:	143 1/02 Wwck 3m1f soft Hdl

Useful hurdler/novice chaser; stays three miles one; best in soft ground.

Kings Command

72   63

7-y-o b g Henbit (USA)-Country Festival (Town And Country)
A King Miss Janet Menzies

Placings: 04-P4   (0271)
2003/04: 16PGS, 164GF,

	Starts	1st	2nd	3rd	Win & Pl
Hurdles	2	0	0	0	0
Career Total	4	0	0	0	0

Going:	Sf: 0-0 GS: 0-1 Gd: 0-0 GF: - Fm: 0-1
Distance:	2m2m3: 0-2 2m4-2m7: 0-0 3m+: 0-0
Track:	LH: 0-1 RH: 0-1 Tight: 0-0 Gall: 0-0
Aids:	Bl: 0-0 Vi: 0-0 Tstrap: 0-0 Ckp: 0-0
Best Rating:	102 2/03 Winc 2m gd-sft NHF

Kings Hill Leader (IRE)

93f   75f

5-y-o b g Supreme Leader-Mary Kate Finn (Saher)
J Howard Johnson J R McAleese

Placings: 0   (3601)
2003/04: 16ºHY,

	Starts	1st	2nd	3rd	Win & Pl
NH Flat	1	0	0	0	
Career Total	1	0	0	0	

Going:	Sf: 0-1 GS: 0-0 Gd: 0-0 GF: - Fm: 0-0
Distance:	2m2m3: 0-1 2m4-2m7: 0-0 3m+: 0-0
Track:	LH: 0-1 RH: 0-0 Tight: 0-0 Gall: 0-0
Aids:	Bl: 0-0 Vi: 0-0 Tstrap: 0-0 Ckp: 0-0
Best Rating:	75 1/04 Ayr 2m heavy NHF

Full-brother to dual bumper/hurdles winner Fota Island; only a modicum of promise on debut at Ayr in January 2004; may well be capable of better.

Kings Linen (IRE)

86   81

8-y-o b g Persian Mews-Kings Princess (King's Ride)
B I Case Dudley C Moore

Placings: 0/0/030F636-23   (0910)
2003/04: 26²GF, 26³GF,

	Starts	1st	2nd	3rd	Win & Pl
Hurdles	2	0	1	1	1485
Career Total	11	0	1	3	2357

Going:	Sf: 0-0 GS: 0-0 Gd: 0-0 GF: - Fm: 0-2
Distance:	2m2m3: 0-0 2m4-2m7: 0-0 3m+: 0-2
Track:	LH: 0-1 RH: 0-1 Tight: 0-0 Gall: 0-1
Aids:	Bl: 0-0 Vi: 0-0 Tstrap: 0-0 Ckp: 0-0
Best Rating:	81 4/03 Hrfd 3m2f gd-fm Hdl

Plating-class; stays well; likes fast ground.

Kings Mistral (IRE)

114   135

11-y-o b g Strong Gale-Mrs Simpson (Kinglet)
P R Chamings R V Shaw

Placings: 024/02/00/12/3P160/1141-1F3124   (4965)
2003/04: 29¹G, 29⁵S, 24³HY, 24³S, 24²G, 29⁴GF,

	Starts	1st	2nd	3rd	Win & Pl
Chases	6	2	1	1	66752
Career Total	24	7	4	2	104890
134	2/04	Sand	3m110y B(0-145)HCh	SFT £29000
128	12/03	Sand	3m5f110yA(0-145)HCh	GD £26100
117	3/03	Sand	3m110y E Ch	SFT £8151
127	12/02	Sand	3m110y D(0-120)HCh	G-S £6987
114	11/02	Asct	3m110y D(0-115)HCh	HVY £5590
112	2/02	Sand	3m110y E Ch	SFT £5564
116	3/01	Sand	3m110y E Ch	SFT £7117

Total win prize-money £88511

Going:	Sf: 1-3 GS: 0-0 Gd: 1-2 GF: - Fm: 0-1
Distance:	2m2m3: 0-0 2m4-2m7: 0-0 3m+: 2-6
Track:	LH: 0-2 RH: 2-4 Tight: 0-0 Gall: 0-0
Aids:	Bl: 0-0 Vi: 0-0 Tstrap: 0-0 Ckp: 0-0
Best Rating:	134 2/04 Sand 3m110y soft Ch

Useful handicap chaser; dual winner of the Grand Military Gold Cup at Sandown; jumps well; stays three miles one; acts on soft ground; loves Sandown.

Kings Square

91   62

4-y-o b g Bal Harbour-Prime Property (IRE) (Tirol)
M W Easterby A G Black & J E H Quickfall

Placings: 00P0P   (4433)
2003/04: 16ºG, 16ºGS, 16PS, 16ºG, 24PG,

	Starts	1st	2nd	3rd	Win & Pl
Hurdles	5	0	0	0	
Career Total	5	0	0	0	

Going:	Sf: 0-1 GS: 0-1 Gd: 0-3 GF: - Fm: 0-0
Distance:	2m2m3: 0-4 2m4-2m7: 0-0 3m+: 0-1
Track:	LH: 0-5 RH: 0-0 Tight: 0-0 Gall: 0-2
Aids:	Bl: 0-1 Vi: 0-0 Tstrap: 0-0 Ckp: 0-0
Best Rating:	62 11/03 Newc 2m good Hdl

Kingsbay

107f   121+f

5-y-o ch m Beveled (USA)-Storm Of Plenty (Billion (USA))
H Morrison P J Doherty

(page right column)

Placings: 122   (4328)
2003/04: 17¹GS, 18²G, 16²S,

	Starts	1st	2nd	3rd	Win & Pl
NH Flat	3	1	2	0	7916
Career Total	3	1	2	0	7916
121	12/03	Folk	2m1f110yH NHF	G-S £1568

Total win prize-money £1568

Going:	Sf: 0-1 GS: 1-1 Gd: 0-1 GF: - Fm: 0-0
Distance:	2m2m3: 1-3 2m4-2m7: 0-0 3m+: 0-0
Track:	LH: 0-1 RH: 1-2 Tight: 1-2 Gall: 0-0
Aids:	Bl: 0-1 Vi: 0-0 Tstrap: 0-0 Ckp: 0-0
Best Rating:	121 12/03 Folk 2m1f110y gd-sft NHF

Won a bumper on her debut in good style at Folkestone in a mares' only race and was very well backed to do so; failed narrowly under a penalty at Fontwell last time; runner-up in the big Mares' bumper at Sandown; has size and scope and looks a promising filly; should get two and a half miles over hurdles; acts on good and easy going; not straightforward.

Kingsbridge (IRE)

97   (68h)75

10-y-o b g Cataldi-Rockport Rosa (IRE) (Roselier (FR))
M C Pipe M C Pipe

Placings: 0/P06304/P35-455   (1132)
2003/04: 16⁴GF, 26⁶GF, 20⁵G,

	Starts	1st	2nd	3rd	Win & Pl
Chases	3	0	0	0	311
Career Total	13	0	0	2	1481

Going:	Sf: 0-0 GS: 0-0 Gd: 0-1 GF: - Fm: 0-2
Distance:	2m2m3: 0-1 2m4-2m7: 0-0 3m+: 0-1
Track:	LH: 0-3 RH: 0-0 Tight: 0-2 Gall: 0-0
Aids:	Bl: 0-0 Vi: 0-0 Tstrap: 0-0 Ckp: 0-0
Best Rating:	82 7/02 NAbb 2m110y gd-fm Ch

Winning pointer; plating-class chaser under Rules; acts on fast ground.

Kingscliff (IRE)

120   168+

7-y-o b g Toulon-Pixies Glen (Furry Glen)
R H Alner A J Sendell

Placings: 11-112   (3274)
2003/04: 24¹S, 25¹G, 24²G,

	Starts	1st	2nd	3rd	Win & Pl
Chases	3	2	1	0	50102
Career Total	5	4	1	0	74814
168	12/03	Chel	3m1f110yB HCh	GD £23200
168	11/03	Asct	3m110y B(0-140)HCh	SFT £13702
140	3/03	Chel	3m2f110yB Ch	GD £23200
143	2/03	Winc	3m1f110yH Ch	G-S £1512

Total win prize-money £61614

Going:	Sf: 1-1 GS: 0-0 Gd: 1-2 GF: - Fm: 0-0
Distance:	2m2m3: 0-0 2m4-2m7: 0-0 3m+: 2-3
Track:	LH: 1-2 RH: 1-1 Tight: 0-0 Gall: 1-1
Aids:	Bl: 0-0 Vi: 0-0 Tstrap: 0-0 Ckp: 0-0
Best Rating:	168 1/04 Hayd 3m good Ch

High-class chaser; highly promising recruit from the pointing field; impressive winner of the 2003 Christie's Foxhunter Chase at Cheltenham; joined Robert Alner and most impressive on his handicap debut at Ascot; followed-up at Cheltenham, and was suffering from a muscular problem when beaten at Haydock subsequently; stays an extended 3m 2f; acts on good ground or softer; remains an exciting prospect.

Kingscote Thunder (IRE)

7-y-o b g Montelimar (USA)-Sweet Thunder (Le Bavard (FR))
Noel T Chance Pulse Racing & Mrs S Rowley-Williams

Placings:0/01-2P   (1270)
2003/04: 17²G, 19P°GF,

	Starts	1st	2nd	3rd	Win & Pl
NH Flat	1	0	1	0	574
Hurdles	1	0	0	0	0
Career Total	**5**	**1**	**1**	**0**	**2590**
105	4/03 Chep 2m110y H NHF			G-F	£2016

Total win prize-money £2016

Going: Sf: 0-0 GS: 0-0 Gd: 0-1 GF: - Fm: 0-1
Distance: 2m/2m3: 0-2 2m4-2m7: 0-0 3m+: 0-0
Track: LH: 0-0 RH: 0-1 Tight: 0-0 Gall: 0-0
Aids: Bl: 0-0 Vi: 0-0 Tstrap: 0-0 Ckp: 0-0
Best Rating: 107 5/03 Hrfd 2m1f   good   NHF

Highly tried on good to soft ground in his first two bumpers; did not beat much when winning on a fast surface at Chepstow April 2003; fair run in defeat next time.

Kingsdown Trix (IRE)

97(81c)   (45c)**89**
10-y-o b g Contract Law (USA)-Three Of Trumps (Tyrnavos)
R Dickin The Invincibles

Placings:0414P000/545115/056/316/03020/5035P0040-5P
(0442)
2003/04: 21⁵GF, 19P°GF,

	Starts	1st	2nd	3rd	Win & Pl
Hurdles	2	0	0	0	0
Career Total	**36**	**4**	**1**	**3**	**14699**
104	4/01 Fknm 2m4f	F(0-105)HHdl		G-S	£3108
97	4/99 Fknm 2m4f	F(0-110)HHdl		GD	£3310
98	3/99 Font	2m6f110yE(0-115)HHdl		G-F	£2477
93	12/97 Font	2m2f110yE Hdl		SFT	£2532

Total win prize-money £11428

Going: Sf: 0-0 GS: 0-0 Gd: 0-0 GF: - Fm: 0-2
Distance: 2m/2m3: 0-0 2m4-2m7: 0-2 3m+: 0-0
Track: LH: 0-1 RH: 0-1 Tight: 0-0 Gall: 0-0
Aids: Bl: 0-0 Vi: 0-0 Tstrap: 0-0 Ckp: 0-0
Best Rating: 104 4/02 Chep 2m4f   gd-sft   Hdl

Kingsfold Freddie

(98h)   (79h)
6-y-o ch g Rock City-Kingsfold Flame (No Loiterer)
P R Webber Mrs Ann Shaw

Placings:03000-20PR4   (4751)
2003/04: 21²GF, 19°GS, 20P°GF, 21R°GS, 17⁴G,

	Starts	1st	2nd	3rd	Win & Pl
Hurdles	2	0	1	0	1105
Chases	3	0	0	0	302
Career Total	**10**	**0**	**1**	**1**	**1811**

Going: Sf: 0-0 GS: 0-2 Gd: 0-1 GF: - Fm: 0-0
Distance: 2m/2m3: 0-2 2m4-2m7: 0-3 3m+: 0-0
Track: LH: 0-4 RH: 0-1 Tight: 0-2 Gall: 0-0
Aids: Bl: 0-0 Vi: 0-4 Tstrap: 0-0 Ckp: 0-1
Best Rating: 94 2/03 Winc 2m   gd-sft   NHF

Plating-class on the form he has shown so far over both hurdles and fences; stays 2m 5f; raced mainly on fast ground; has worn visor.

Kingsland Taverner

13-y-o ch g True Song-Princess Hecate (Autre Prince)
A W Carroll (M Harris 21/5) E O Steward

Placings:3/22/4PF5F/3/P6P44/0P/P3F-P4F   (0853)
2003/04: 25P°GF, 24⁴G, 24F°GF,

	Starts	1st	2nd	3rd	Win & Pl
Chases	3	0	0	0	311
Career Total	**22**	**0**	**2**	**3**	**2757**

Going: Sf: 0-0 GS: 0-0 Gd: 0-1 GF: - Fm: 0-2
Distance: 2m/2m3: 0-0 2m4-2m7: 0-0 3m+: 0-3
Track: LH: 0-2 RH: 0-1 Tight: 0-3 Gall: 0-0
Aids: Bl: 0-0 Vi: 0-0 Tstrap: 0-0 Ckp: 0-0
Best Rating: 96 5/96 Hrfd 2m1f   firm   NHF

Moderate hunter chaser, suited by a sound surface.

Kingsmark (IRE)

94   **166**
11-y-o gr g Roselier (FR)-Gaye Le Moss (Le Moss)
M Todhunter Sir Robert Ogden

Placings:3/111120/51F1322/11160310/124/13-360 (4647)
2003/04: 24³GS, 24⁶S, 36⁹G,

	Starts	1st	2nd	3rd	Win & Pl
Chases	3	0	0	1	6650
Career Total	**30**	**12**	**4**	**5**	**206790**
166	11/02 Hayd	3m	A HCh	SFT	£30000
166	11/01 Hayd	3m	A HCh	GD	£27000
158	4/01 Aint	3m1f	B HCh	SFT	£26000
158	11/00 Hayd	3m	A HCh	SFT	£25200
140	10/00 MRas	3m1f	C(0-130)HCh	GD	£9178
141	10/00 Kels	3m1f	D(0-125)HCh	GD	£3887
131	1/00 Folk	3m2f	E Ch	SFT	£3510
137	11/99 Bang	3m110y	D Ch	SFT	£4842
137	1/99 Kemp	3m2f	D Hdl	HVY	£3793
121	12/98 Folk	2m6f110yE Hdl		SFT	£2650
131	11/98 Folk	2m6f110yE Hdl		SFT	£2008
116	10/98 Strf	2m6f110yE Hdl		G-S	£2075

Total win prize-money £140146

Going: Sf: 0-1 GS: 0-1 Gd: 0-1 GF: - Fm: 0-0
Distance: 2m/2m3: 0-0 2m4-2m7: 0-0 3m+: 0-3
Track: LH: 0-3 RH: 0-0 Tight: 0-1 Gall: 0-0
Aids: Bl: 0-0 Vi: 0-0 Tstrap: 0-0 Ckp: 0-0
Best Rating: 166 11/02 Hayd 3m   soft   Ch

Smart handicap chaser; well suited by a flat, left-handed track and three miles; suffered an over-reach when a distant fourth in the Grand National in 2002, but came back to complete a hat-trick in the Edward Hanmer at Haydock in November 2002; lightly raced and held since; goes on good ground but is better with give.

Kingsmoor

106   (88h)**96+**
8-y-o b g Regal Embers (IRE)-Cupids Bower (Owen Dudley)
K Bishop R D Cox

Placings:0/6/F-PP1P0   (4919)
2003/04: 25P°GS, 24P°G, 20¹GF, 25P°GS, 20⁹GS,

	Starts	1st	2nd	3rd	Win & Pl
Chases	5	1	0	0	4290
Career Total	**8**	**1**	**0**	**0**	**4290**
96	3/04 Leic	2m4f110yE(0-105)HCh		G-F	£4290

Total win prize-money £4290

Going: Sf: 0-0 GS: 0-3 Gd: 0-1 GF: - Fm: 1-1
Distance: 2m/2m3: 0-0 **2m4-2m7: 1-2** 3m+: 0-3
Track: LH: 0-1 RH: **1-4** Tight: 0-1 Gall: 0-0

Aids: Bl: 0-0 Vi: 0-0 Tstrap: 0-0 Ckp: 0-0
Best Rating: 96 3/04 Leic 2m4f110y gd-fm Ch

Moderate chaser; stays 2m 4f; effective on fast ground.

Kingston Game

5-y-o b g Mind Games-Valmaranda (USA) (Sir Ivor)
Miss K M George Stableline

Placings:PPP-P   (0137)
2003/04: 16P°G,

	Starts	1st	2nd	3rd	Win & Pl
Hurdles	1	0	0	0	
Career Total	**4**	**0**	**0**	**0**	

Going: Sf: 0-0 GS: 0-0 Gd: 0-1 GF: - Fm: 0-0
Distance: 2m/2m3: 0-1 2m4-2m7: 0-0 3m+: 0-0
Track: LH: 0-0 RH: 0-1 Tight: 0-0 Gall: 0-0
Aids: Bl: 0-0 Vi: 0-1 Tstrap: 0-0 Ckp: 0-0

Kingston-Banker

8-y-o b g Teamster-Happy Manda (Mandamus)
Mrs S Alner H Wellstead

Placings:60/332/523P2F-111   (4823)
2003/04: 24¹G, 25¹G, 23¹GF,

	Starts	1st	2nd	3rd	Win & Pl
Chases	3	3	0	0	8418
Career Total	**14**	**3**	**3**	**3**	**15731**
114	4/04 Extr	2m7f110yH Ch		G-F	£2782
113	4/04 Winc	3m1f110yH Ch		GD	£2054
101	3/04 Strf	3m	H Ch	GD	£3581

Total win prize-money £8418

Going: Sf: 0-0 GS: 0-0 Gd: 2-2 GF: - Fm: 1-1
Distance: 2m/2m3: 0-0 2m4-2m7: 0-0 **3m+: 3-3**
Track: LH: 1-1 RH: **2-2** Tight: **1-1** Gall: 0-0
Aids: Bl: 0-0 Vi: 0-0 Tstrap: 0-0 Ckp: 0-0
Best Rating: 117 3/03 Chep 2m3f110y good Ch

Winning hunter chaser; acts on soft ground; stays three miles.

Kingswood Fox

9-y-o b g Bold Fox-Teye (Mummy's Pet)
Mrs A M Thorpe Mrs M E Nolan

Placings:P   (0764)
2003/04: 20P°GF,

	Starts	1st	2nd	3rd	Win & Pl
Hurdles	1	0	0	0	
Career Total	**1**	**0**	**0**	**0**	

Going: Sf: 0-0 GS: 0-0 Gd: 0-0 GF: - Fm: 0-1
Distance: 2m/2m3: 0-0 2m4-2m7: 0-1 3m+: 0-0
Track: LH: 0-1 RH: 0-0 Tight: 0-0 Gall: 0-0
Aids: Bl: 0-0 Vi: 0-0 Tstrap: 0-0 Ckp: 0-0

Kinnescash (IRE)

99   **103**
11-y-o ch g Persian Heights-Gayla Orchestra (Lord Gayle (USA))
P Bowen D R James

Placings:302211/4131125P3/P0212030143310/64000/022
2/P/P60PF (1291)
2003/04: 24PG, 20⁶S, 20⁹GF, 20PGF, 22FGF,

	Starts	1st	2nd	3rd	Win & Pl
Hurdles	5	0	0	0	0
Career Total	44	8	8	6	80564
141 4/99 Aint 2m110y B HHdl				GD	£19350
141 11/98 Aint 2m110y C(0-135)HHdl				G-S	£10406
128 9/98 Hntg 2m4f110yD(0-125)HHdl				G-F	£6840
117 6/97 MRas 2m1f110yC(0-130)HHdl				GD	£8637
115 5/97 Hrfd 2m110yD(0-120)HHdl				GD	£2864
125 5/97 Worc 2m E Hdl				G-S	£2302
105 4/97 Chep 2m110y E Hdl				FRM	£2808
105 3/97 Plum 2m1f E Hdl				G-F	£2490
				Total win prize-money £55698	

Going: Sf: 0-1 GS: 0-0 Gd: 0-1 GF: - Fm: 0-3
Distance: 2m/2m3: 0-0 2m4-2m7: 0-4 3m+: 0-1
Track: LH: 0-5 RH: 0-0 Tight: 0-1 Gall: 0-0
Aids: Bl: 0-0 Vi: 0-0 Tstrap: 0-0 Ckp: 0-0
Best Rating: 141 4/99 Aint 2m110y good Hdl

Moderate hurdler nowadays, but has been a fine servant to his connections over the years; stays 2m 4f; effective on fast ground.

Kinnino

93　　　　　　　　76

10-y-o b g Polish Precedent (USA)-On Tiptoes (Shareef Dancer (USA))
G L Moore Exors Of The Late Mr A Moore

Placings:55/F0/050PP-5 (0200)
2003/04: 16⁵GF,

	Starts	1st	2nd	3rd	Win & Pl
Hurdles	1	0	0	0	0
Career Total	10	0	0	0	0

Going: Sf: 0-0 GS: 0-0 Gd: 0-0 GF: - Fm: 0-1
Distance: 2m/2m3: 0-1 2m4-2m7: 0-0 3m+: 0-0
Track: LH: 0-0 RH: 0-1 Tight: 0-0 Gall: 0-1
Aids: Bl: 0-0 Vi: 0-0 Tstrap: 0-0 Ckp: 0-0
Best Rating: 76 5/03 Hntg 2m110y gd-fm Hdl

Kiora Bay

7-y-o b g Karinga Bay-Equasion (IRE) (Cyrano De Bergerac)
P D Niven C D Carr

Placings:0-0P (3371)
2003/04: 16⁰GS, 20PS,

	Starts	1st	2nd	3rd	Win & Pl
NH Flat	1	0	0	0	0
Hurdles	1	0	0	0	0
Career Total	3	0	0	0	0

Going: Sf: 0-1 GS: 0-1 Gd: 0-0 GF: - Fm: 0-0
Distance: 2m/2m3: 0-1 2m4-2m7: 0-1 3m+: 0-0
Track: LH: 0-2 RH: 0-0 Tight: 0-0 Gall: 0-0
Aids: Bl: 0-0 Vi: 0-0 Tstrap: 0-0 Ckp: 0-0
Best Rating: 65 12/03 Newc 2m gd-sft NHF

Kipling

85

8-y-o b g Rudimentary (USA)-Sharmood (USA) (Sharpen Up)
Miss Sheena West Graham Flight

Placings:653P3-P (2536)
2003/04: 25PS,

	Starts	1st	2nd	3rd	Win & Pl
Hurdles	1	0	0	0	
Career Total	6	0	0	2	1231

Going: Sf: 0-1 GS: 0-0 Gd: 0-0 GF: - Fm: 0-0
Distance: 2m/2m3: 0-0 2m4-2m7: 0-0 3m+: 0-1
Track: LH: 0-0 RH: 0-0 Tight: 0-0 Gall: 0-0
Aids: Bl: 0-0 Vi: 0-0 Tstrap: 0-0 Ckp: 0-0
Best Rating: 85 3/03 Font 3m3f soft Hdl

Modest novice hurdler; stays three miles three.

Kippanour (USA)

109　　　　　　　(68c)101

12-y-o b g Alleged (USA)-Innsbruck (General Assembly (USA))
A G Hobbs Furnish With Abbey

Placings:12323/33020005/P6543365P/P6/16310P214406/
56123016000/351P0633055-P55444511P (2309)
2003/04: 27PG, 27⁵GF, 24⁵G, 27⁴G, 26⁴GS, 26⁴GF, 26⁵GF, 26¹GF,
27¹G, 26PGS,

	Starts	1st	2nd	3rd	Win & Pl
Hurdles	10	2	0	0	4724
Career Total	68	9	5	11	31007
101 10/03 Sedg 3m3f110yF(0-100)HHdl				GD	£1932
93 9/03 Hntg 3m2f F(0-90)HHdl				G-F	£2219
96 5/02 NAbb 3m3f E(0-110)HHdl				SFT	£2933
101 1/02 Hntg 3m2f F(0-90)HHdl				SFT	£2765
93 9/01 Hrfd 3m2f F(0-90)HHdl				GD	£2044
89 11/00 Hntg 3m2f G(0-95)HHdl				GD	£1951
92 7/00 Worc 2m7f110yF(0-100)HCh				G-F	£2970
92 5/00 Uttx 3m2f F(0-90)HCh				GD	£2960
93 9/95 Slig 2m Hdl					£2204
				Total win prize-money £21981	

Going: Sf: 0-0 GS: 0-2 Gd: 1-4 GF: - Fm: 1-4
Distance: 2m/2m3: 0-0 2m4-2m7: 0-0 3m+: 2-10
Track: LH: 1-6 RH: 1-4 Tight: 1-5 Gall: 1-2
Aids: Bl: 0-5 Vi: 2-5 Tstrap: 0-0 Ckp: 0-0
Best Rating: 120 12/95 Chel 2m1f good Hdl

Moderate handicap hurdler; out-and-out stayer who finds soft ground helping bring his stamina into play.

Kirisnippa

101　　　　　　　71

9-y-o b g Beveled (USA)-Kiri Te (Liboi (USA))
W G M Turner D A Drake

Placings:P/P/P-4340 (1855)
2003/04: 18⁴GF, 19³GF, 22⁴GF, 19⁰G,

	Starts	1st	2nd	3rd	Win & Pl
Hurdles	4	0	0	1	340
Career Total	7	0	0	1	340

Going: Sf: 0-0 GS: 0-0 Gd: 0-1 GF: - Fm: 0-3
Distance: 2m/2m3: 0-1 2m4-2m7: 0-3 3m+: 0-0
Track: LH: 0-1 RH: 0-2 Tight: 0-1 Gall: 0-0
Aids: Bl: 0-3 Vi: 0-0 Tstrap: 0-0 Ckp: 0-0
Best Rating: 71 10/03 Hrfd 2m3f110y gd-fm Hdl

Modest hurdler; seems best at up to two and a half miles.

Kismet

80　　　　　　　59

6-y-o b m Tirol-Belamcanda (Belmez (USA))
Lady Susan Watson Lady Susan Watson

Placings:PP0 (4612)
2003/04: 21PGS, 17PG, 21⁰G,

	Starts	1st	2nd	3rd	Win & Pl
Hurdles	3	0	0	0	
Career Total	3	0	0	0	

Going: Sf: 0-0 GS: 0-1 Gd: 0-2 GF: - Fm: 0-0
Distance: 2m/2m3: 0-1 2m4-2m7: 0-2 3m+: 0-0
Track: LH: 0-2 RH: 0-1 Tight: 0-3 Gall: 0-0
Aids: Bl: 0-0 Vi: 0-0 Tstrap: 0-0 Ckp: 0-0
Best Rating: 59 3/04 Sedg 2m5f110y good Hdl

Kiss Me Kate

86　　　　　　　78

8-y-o b m Aragon-Ingerence (FR) (Akarad (FR))
Mrs P Robeson The Royal George Racing Partnership

Placings:44115F/4005/2-40 (2909)
2003/04: 23⁴GS, 21⁰GS,

	Starts	1st	2nd	3rd	Win & Pl
Hurdles	2	0	0	0	0
Career Total	13	2	1	0	5935
109 3/00 Plum 2m F(0-110)HHdl				GD	£2226
111 2/00 Hntg 2m110y E Hdl				SFT	£2730
				Total win prize-money £4956	

Going: Sf: 0-0 GS: 0-2 Gd: 0-0 GF: - Fm: 0-0
Distance: 2m/2m3: 0-0 2m4-2m7: 0-2 3m+: 0-0
Track: LH: 0-1 RH: 0-1 Tight: 0-0 Gall: 0-1
Aids: Bl: 0-0 Vi: 0-0 Tstrap: 0-0 Ckp: 0-0
Best Rating: 111 6/00 Uttx 2m4f110y gd-fm Hdl

Plating-class hurdler; best on soft ground; yet to prove she stays further than 2m 3f.

Kitale (FR)

6-y-o ch g Phantom Breeze-Indjaren (FR) (Argument (FR))
Ferdy Murphy Miss J V Morgan

Placings:P-R (0098)
2003/04: 20PG, 16PG,

	Starts	1st	2nd	3rd	Win & Pl
Hurdles	2	0	0	0	
Career Total	2	0	0	0	

Going: Sf: 0-0 GS: 0-0 Gd: 0-2 GF: - Fm: 0-0
Distance: 2m/2m3: 0-1 2m4-2m7: 0-1 3m+: 0-0
Track: LH: 0-2 RH: 0-0 Tight: 0-0 Gall: 0-0
Aids: Bl: 0-0 Vi: 0-0 Tstrap: 0-0 Ckp: 0-0

Kitimat

100(85h)　　　　(89h)84

7-y-o b g Then Again-Quago (New Member)
R H Buckler The Eight Optimists

Placings:06/P40560P46-036461346P2 (4531)
2003/04: 20⁰GF, 25³GF, 21⁶G, 20⁴G, 17⁶S, 22¹HY, 18³G, 22⁴GS,
20⁶GF, 19PGF, 16²GS,

	Starts	1st	2nd	3rd	Win & Pl
Chases	11	1	1	2	5601
Career Total	22	1	1	2	5918
84 1/04 Font 2m6f F(0-90)HCh				HVY	£3406
				Total win prize-money £3406	

Going: Sf: 1-2 GS: 0-2 Gd: 0-3 GF: - Fm: 0-4
Distance: 2m/2m3: 0-3 2m4-2m7: 1-7 3m+: 0-1
Track: LH: 0-3 RH: 0-4 Tight: 1-5 Gall: 0-1
Aids: Bl: 0-0 Vi: 0-0 Tstrap: 0-0 Ckp: 0-0

Best Rating: 89   6/02   Hrfd   2m3f110y   gd-fm   Hdl

Plating-class chaser; says three miles, but only win came over 2m 6f; acts on soft ground.

Kitski (FR)

102f   111f

6-y-o b g Perrault-Macyrienne (FR) (Saint Cyrien (FR))
S Gollings   J B Webb

Placings: *1-02*   (4962)
2003/04: 16⁰G, 17²G,

	Starts	1st	2nd	3rd	Win & Pl
NH Flat	2	0	1	0	622
Career Total	3	1	1	0	5551
97 3/03 Cork 2m2f	NHF		G-Y	£4928	

Total win prize-money £4929

Going: Sf: 0-0 GS: 0-0 Gd: 0-0 GF: - Fm: 0-0
Distance: 2m/2m3: 0-2 2m4-2m7: 0-0 3m+: 0-0
Track: LH: 0-1 RH: 0-0 Tight: 0-1 Gall: 0-1
Aids: Bl: 0-0 Vi: 0-0 Tstrap: 0-0 Ckp: 0-0
Best Rating: 111 4/04   MRas   2m1f110y   good   NHF

Kitte Ou Double (FR)

98   (0c)111

6-y-o b g Agent Bleu (FR)-Briffault (FR) (Olmeto)
F Jordan (G Cherel 4/5) Le Tricolore

Placings: 0P0351F331-50331   (3759)
2003/04: 21⁵VS, 20⁹G, 16³S, 21³S, 22¹G,

	Starts	1st	2nd	3rd	Win & Pl
Hurdles	4	1	0	2	4929
Chases	1	0	0	0	2776
Career Total	15	3	0	5	39356
113 2/04 MRas 2m6f	E(0-110)HHdl		GD	£3477	
4/03 Autl 2m6f	Ch		VS	£13091	
2/03 Pau	2m3f110y	Ch		HVY	£8103

Total win prize-money £24673

Going: Sf: 0-2 GS: 0-0 Gd: 1-2 GF: - Fm: 0-0
Distance: 2m/2m3: 0-1 2m4-2m7: 1-3 3m+: 0-0
Track: LH: 0-2 RH: 0-1 Tight: 0-1 Gall: 0-1
Aids: Bl: 0-0 Vi: 0-0 Tstrap: 0-0 Ckp: 0-0
Best Rating: 113 2/04   MRas   2m6f   good   Hdl

Ex-French chaser/hurdler; won on first outing in handicap company over hurdles at Market Rasen in February; effective on testing ground; stays two miles-six.

Kittenkat

102   (111h)101

10-y-o b m Riverwise (USA)-Cut Above The Rest (Indiaro)
N R Mitchell   Piers Butler

Placings: 60/02033P3P1/462411003P3P/34450460/3533F5
U54206-6423PU36P4U   (4734)
2003/04: 26⁶G, 26⁴G, 32²G, 30⁵GS, 33⁵G, 25ᵁS, 23³S, 26⁶GS, 30⁶G, 23⁴G, 26ᵁG,

	Starts	1st	2nd	3rd	Win & Pl
Chases	11	0	1	2	5561
Career Total	54	3	4	11	37381
123 12/00 Winc 2m6f	B HHdl		G-S	£8424	
106 12/00 Folk	2m4f110yC(2-130)HHdl		HVY	£6773	
95 4/00 Extr	2m7f	E Hdl		HVY	£2254

Total win prize-money £17452

Going: Sf: 0-2 GS: 0-2 Gd: 0-7 GF: - Fm: 0-0
Distance: 2m/2m3: 0-0 2m4-2m7: 0-0 3m+: 0-11
Track: LH: 0-5 RH: 0-5 Tight: 0-6 Gall: 0-5

Aids: Bl: 0-0 Vi: 0-0 Tstrap: 0-0 Ckp: 0-0
Best Rating: 123 4/01   Extr   2m6f110y   gd-sft   Hdl

Moderate chaser; stays very well; acts in the mud; yet to win over fences.

Kitty John (IRE)

95   85

7-y-o gr m Safety Catch (USA)-La Baladina (Modern Dancer)
J L Spearing   Masonaires

Placings: 0050504-1   (2032)
2003/04: 20¹GF,

	Starts	1st	2nd	3rd	Win & Pl
Hurdles	1	1	0	0	3367
Career Total	8	1	0	0	3601
80 11/03 Worc 2m4f	E Hdl		G-F	£3367	

Total win prize-money £3367

Going: Sf: 0-0 GS: 0-0 Gd: 0-0 GF: - Fm: 1-1
Distance: 2m/2m3: 0-0 2m4-2m7: 1-1 3m+: 0-0
Track: LH: 1-1 RH: 0-0 Tight: 0-0 Gall: 0-0
Aids: Bl: 0-0 Vi: 0-0 Tstrap: 0-0 Ckp: 0-0
Best Rating: 82 5/02   Wxfd   2m   soft   NHF

Kittylee

89   71

5-y-o b m Bal Harbour-Courtesy Call (Northfields (USA))
M A Buckley   Fair Price Racing

Placings: 5256050   (4180)
2003/04: 16⁵F, 16²G, 16⁵G, 17⁶GF, 16⁰GS, 16⁵GS, 20⁰G,

	Starts	1st	2nd	3rd	Win & Pl
Hurdles	7	0	1	0	642
Career Total	7	0	1	0	642

Going: Sf: 0-0 GS: 0-2 Gd: 0-3 GF: - Fm: 0-2
Distance: 2m/2m3: 0-6 2m4-2m7: 0-1 3m+: 0-0
Track: LH: 0-4 RH: 0-3 Tight: 0-2 Gall: 0-2
Aids: Bl: 0-0 Vi: 0-0 Tstrap: 0-0 Ckp: 0-0
Best Rating: 70 10/03   Strf   2m110y   good   Hdl

Kituhwa (USA)

66   23

4-y-o br g Cherokee Run (USA)-Ruhnke (USA) (Cox's Ridge (USA))
R Shiels (J H M Gosden 16/8) R Shiels

Placings: 0   (4795)
2003/04: 17⁰G,

	Starts	1st	2nd	3rd	Win & Pl
Hurdles	1	0	0	0	
Career Total	1	0	0	0	

Going: Sf: 0-0 GS: 0-0 Gd: 0-0 GF: 0-1 Fm: - 0-0
Distance: 2m/2m3: 0-1 2m4-2m7: 0-0 3m+: 0-0
Track: LH: 0-1 RH: 0-0 Tight: 0-1 Gall: 0-0
Aids: Bl: 0-0 Vi: 0-0 Tstrap: 0-0 Ckp: 0-0
Best Rating: 23 4/04   Sedg   2m1f   good   Hdl

Kivotos (USA)

114   121

6-y-o gr g Trempolino (USA)-Authorized Staff (USA) (Relaunch (USA))
A C Whillans   C Bird

Placings: 01P32-21424231   (4853)
2003/04: 20²G, 22¹G, 20⁴GS, 24²GS, 25⁴G, 20²S, 20³GS, 22¹GS,

	Starts	1st	2nd	3rd	Win & Pl
Hurdles	8	2	3	1	27689
Career Total	13	3	4	2	33483
121 4/04 Ayr 2m6f	B HHdl		G-S	£10332	
109 5/03 Kels	2m6f110yD(0-115)HHdl		GD	£5564	
105 1/03 Ayr	2m	E Hdl		HVY	£3451

Total win prize-money £19348

Going: Sf: 0-1 GS: 1-4 Gd: 1-3 GF: - Fm: 0-0
Distance: 2m/2m3: 0-0 2m4-2m7: 2-6 3m+: 0-2
Track: LH: 2-7 RH: 0-1 Tight: 1-3 Gall: 0-1
Aids: Bl: 0-0 Vi: 0-0 Tstrap: 0-0 Ckp: 0-0
Best Rating: 121 4/04   Ayr   2m6f   gd-sft   Hdl

Fair hurdler; stays three miles; acts on any ground; likes to race prominently; tough and consistent.

Kiwi Babe

95   101

5-y-o b m Karinga Bay-Sunshine Gal (Alto Volante)
P F Nicholls   David Chown

Placings: 216   (4239)
2003/04: 17²HY, 22¹G, 19⁶G,

	Starts	1st	2nd	3rd	Win & Pl
NH Flat	1	0	1	0	548
Hurdles	2	1	0	0	4823
Career Total	3	1	1	0	5371
103 2/04 Winc 2m6f	D Hdl		GD	£4823	

Total win prize-money £4823

Going: Sf: 0-1 GS: 0-0 Gd: 1-2 GF: - Fm: 0-0
Distance: 2m/2m3: 0-2 2m4-2m7: 1-1 3m+: 0-0
Track: LH: 0-0 RH: 1-3 Tight: 0-1 Gall: 0-0
Aids: Bl: 0-0 Vi: 0-0 Tstrap: 0-0 Ckp: 0-0
Best Rating: 103 2/04   Winc   2m6f   good   Hdl

Moderate novice hurdler; cheaply-bought daughter of a hurdles winner; ran with promise on bumper debut; won a mares' only contest at Wincanton on her hurdling debut.

Kiwi Riverman

81f   63f

4-y-o b g Alderbrook-Kiwi Velocity (NZ) (Veloso (NZ))
C L Tizzard   M L Stoddart

Placings: 00   (4291)
2003/04: 16⁰G, 16⁰G,

	Starts	1st	2nd	3rd	Win & Pl
NH Flat	2	0	0	0	
Career Total	2	0	0	0	

Going: Sf: 0-0 GS: 0-1 Gd: 0-1 GF: - Fm: 0-0
Distance: 2m/2m3: 0-2 2m4-2m7: 0-0 3m+: 0-0
Track: LH: 0-0 RH: 0-2 Tight: 0-0 Gall: 0-0
Aids: Bl: 0-0 Vi: 0-0 Tstrap: 0-0 Ckp: 0-0
Best Rating: 63 3/04   Winc   2m   good   NHF

Kjetil (USA)

99   104

4-y-o b g King Of Kings (IRE)-I Wich (FR) (Kris)
P F Nicholls (C Laffon-Parias 30/9) Clive D Smith

Placings: 560   (4053)
2003/04: 16⁵GS, 16⁶S, 16⁰G,

	Starts	1st	2nd	3rd	Win & Pl
Hurdles	3	0	0	0	161
Career Total	3	0	0	0	161

Going:	Sf: 0-1 GS: 0-1 Gd: 0-1 GF: - Fm: 0-0
Distance:	2m/2m3: 0-3 2m4-2m7: 0-0 3m+: 0-0
Track:	LH: 0-0 RH: 0-3 Tight: 0-0 Gall: 0-0
Aids:	Bl: 0-0 Vi: 0-0 Tstrap: 0-0 Ckp: 0-0
Best Rating:	104 2/04 Kemp 2m good Hdl

Ex-French juvenile hurdler; won twice on the Flat over ten to 12 furlongs; disappointing so far over hurdles in Britain; acts on good and soft ground.

Klondike Charger (USA)

106   **111**

10-y-o b g Crafty Prospector (USA)-Forever Waving (USA) (Hoist The Flag (USA))
Dr P Pritchard David & Lesley Byrne

Placings:0333/1P26/**1212**/5PP/3PP2P522520-
500211336333   **(2068)**
2003/04: 17⁵G, 22⁹G, 26⁹GF, 24²G, 26¹GF, 22¹GF, 26³GF, 22³G,
21⁶GF, 25³F, 28⁹G, 18³GF,

	Starts	1st	2nd	3rd	Win & Pl
Chases	12	2	1	5	13742
Career Total	38	5	8	9	36162
105	8/03	Font	2m6f	E(0-110)HCh	G-F	£4322
101	8/03	Font	3m2f110yE(0-110)HCh	G-F	£4943
114	9/00	NAbb	3m2f110yE Ch	G-F	£3234
114	5/00	Font	3m2f110yE Ch	GD	£3580
100	10/99	Weth	3m1f	(0-105)HHdl	G-F	£2304

Total win prize-money £18384

Going:	Sf: 0-0 GS: 0-0 Gd: 0-5 GF: - Fm: 2-7
Distance:	2m/2m3: 0-2 2m4-2m7: 1-4 3m+: 1-6
Track:	LH: 0-6 RH: 0-2 Tight: 2-10 Gall: 0-0
Aids:	Bl: 0-0 Vi: 0-0 Tstrap: 0-0 Ckp: 0-0
Best Rating:	114 9/00 NAbb 3m2f110y gd-fm Ch

Moderate staying chaser; inconsistent; stays three miles; best on fast ground; likes to race prominently; not one to trust.

Knight General Mac

60   **39**

5-y-o b g Presidium-Agnes Jane (Sweet Monday)
N Bycroft N Bycroft

Placings:0   **(1599)**
2003/04: 17⁰GF,

	Starts	1st	2nd	3rd	Win & Pl
Hurdles	1	0	0	0	
Career Total	1	0	0	0	

Going:	Sf: 0-0 GS: 0-0 Gd: 0-0 GF: - Fm: 0-1
Distance:	2m/2m3: 0-1 2m4-2m7: 0-0 3m+: 0-0
Track:	LH: 0-0 RH: 0-1 Tight: 0-0 Gall: 0-0
Aids:	Bl: 0-0 Vi: 0-0 Tstrap: 0-0 Ckp: 0-0
Best Rating:	39 10/03 Carl 2m1f gd-fm Hdl

Knight Of Silver

82(101h)   (74h)**61**

7-y-o gr g Presidium-Misty Rocket (Roan Rocket)
J D Frost (R Williams 25/8) C Johnston

Placings:P00P/U//00402PP323P02-00155   **(1363)**
2003/04: 17⁰GF, 19⁰GF, 17¹GF, 16⁵GF, 16⁵GF,

	Starts	1st	2nd	3rd	Win & Pl
Hurdles	3	1	0	0	3478
Chases	2	0	0	0	0
Career Total	23	1	3	2	6651

77	8/03	NAbb	2m1f	F Hdl	G-F	£3478

Total win prize-money £3478

Going:	Sf: 0-0 GS: 0-0 Gd: 0-0 GF: - Fm: 1-5
Distance:	2m/2m3: 1-4 2m4-2m7: 0-1 3m+: 0-0
Track:	LH: 1-3 RH: 0-2 Tight: 1-2 Gall: 0-0
Aids:	Bl: 0-0 Vi: 0-0 Tstrap: 0-0 Ckp: 0-0
Best Rating:	77 8/03 NAbb 2m1f gd-fm Hdl

Nervous type who benefitted from having travelled to the course the previous day when causing 40/1 shock in 2m 1f Newton Abbot claimer August 2003; subsequently claimed for £5,000.

Knights Croft

11-y-o b g Henbit (USA)-Bright Tiger-Moth (Funny Man)
S T Lewis Simon T Lewis

Placings:U   **(4566)**
2003/04: 17ᵁGS,

	Starts	1st	2nd	3rd	Win & Pl
Chases	1	0	0	0	
Career Total	1	0	0	0	

Going:	Sf: 0-0 GS: 0-0 Gd: 0-0 GF: - Fm: 0-0
Distance:	2m/2m3: 0-1 2m4-2m7: 0-0 3m+: 0-0
Track:	LH: 0-1 RH: 0-0 Tight: 0-1 Gall: 0-0
Aids:	Bl: 0-0 Vi: 0-0 Tstrap: 0-0 Ckp: 0-0

Knightsbridge King

105   **101**

8-y-o ch g Michelozzo (USA)-Shahdjat (IRE) (Vayrann)
John Allen (A King 1/5) John Allen

Placings:20040/20345212-3P36216604   **(4890)**
2003/04: 17³GS, 22²GF, 16³GS, 17⁶GS, 16²GS, 16¹GS, 17⁵GS,
19⁶G, 21⁰GS, 19⁴GF,

	Starts	1st	2nd	3rd	Win & Pl
Hurdles	10	1	1	2	4895
Career Total	23	2	5	3	11115
103	12/03	Strf	2m110y	G(0-95)HHdl	G-S	£3010
96	3/03	Hrfd	2m1f	G Hdl	SFT	£2492

Total win prize-money £5502

Going:	Sf: 0-0 GS: 1-7 Gd: 0-1 GF: - Fm: 0-2
Distance:	2m/2m3: 2-9 2m4-2m7: 0-3 3m+: 0-0
Track:	LH: 1-7 RH: 0-3 Tight: 1-4 Gall: 0-0
Aids:	Bl: 0-0 Vi: 0-0 Tstrap: 0-0 Ckp: 0-1
Best Rating:	103 12/03 Strf 2m110y gd-sft Hdl

Selling hurdler; well ridden by 10lb claimer when landing handicap seller at Stratford December 2003; effective at 2m; acts in soft ground; difficult to win with.

Knock Star (IRE)

13-y-o gr g Celio Rufo-Star Of Monroe (Derring Rose)
S J Partridge Miss E A Baverstock

Placings:P0/55FPP0360P4/60F050/23FP/34   **(0509)**
2003/04: 25³GF, 28⁴GS,

	Starts	1st	2nd	3rd	Win & Pl
Chases	2	0	0	1	1459
Career Total	25	0	1	3	2539

Going:	Sf: 0-0 GS: 0-1 Gd: 0-0 GF: - Fm: 0-1
Distance:	2m/2m3: 0-0 2m4-2m7: 0-1 3m+: 0-2
Track:	LH: 0-1 RH: 0-1 Tight: 0-1 Gall: 0-0
Aids:	Bl: 0-0 Vi: 0-0 Tstrap: 0-0 Ckp: 0-0

Best Rating:	93 12/97 Sthl 2m4f110y good Hdl

Knockanard (IRE)

12-y-o br g Executive Perk-Trianqo (Tarqogan)
M J Gingell J M Valdes-Scott

Placings:P/F/P5F60/PP   **(4778)**
2003/04: 24ᴾGS, 21ᴾG,

	Starts	1st	2nd	3rd	Win & Pl
Chases	2	0	0	0	
Career Total	9	0	0	0	0

Going:	Sf: 0-0 GS: 0-1 Gd: 0-1 GF: - Fm: 0-0
Distance:	2m/2m3: 0-2 2m4-2m7: 0-1 3m+: 0-1
Track:	LH: 0-2 RH: 0-0 Tight: 0-2 Gall: 0-0
Aids:	Bl: 0-0 Vi: 0-0 Tstrap: 0-0 Ckp: 0-0
Best Rating:	71 3/00 Winc 2m5f gd-sft Ch

Knockdoo (IRE)

107(56c)**112**

11-y-o ch g Be My Native (USA)-Ashken (Artaius (USA))
J S Goldie Mrs D I Goldie

Placings:00/0000/241562/00515/3031016023/352**U**54/304
2-622   **(1134)**
2003/04: 24⁶G, 20²G, 20²G,

	Starts	1st	2nd	3rd	Win & Pl
Hurdles	3	0	2	0	2144
Career Total	40	4	7	5	24747
116	11/00	Carl	2m1f	F(0-110)HHdl	HVY	£2588
98	9/00	Gway	2m	(0-102)HHdl	YLD	£4416
81	9/99	Gway	2m	(0-102)HHdl	HVY	£3696
80	9/98	List	2m	(0-102)HHdl	Y-S	£4184

Total win prize-money £14886

Going:	Sf: 0-0 GS: 0-0 Gd: 0-3 GF: - Fm: 0-0
Distance:	2m/2m3: 0-0 2m4-2m7: 0-2 3m+: 0-1
Track:	LH: 0-1 RH: 0-2 Tight: 0-1 Gall: 0-0
Aids:	Bl: 0-0 Vi: 0-0 Tstrap: 0-0 Ckp: 0-0
Best Rating:	116 11/00 Carl 2m1f heavy Hdl

Modest hurdler; best on testing ground.

Knocknabooly (IRE)

111f   **131f**

5-y-o ch g John French-Valiyist (IRE) (Valiyar)
W P Mullins Mrs Margaret O'Rourke

Placings:16   **(4400)**
2003/04: 17¹YS, 16⁶G,

	Starts	1st	2nd	3rd	Win & Pl
NH Flat	2	1	0	0	5466
Career Total	2	1	0	0	5466
113	2/04	Gowr	2m1f	NHF	Y-S	£4866

Total win prize-money £4866

Going:	Sf: 0-0 GS: 0-0 Gd: 0-1 GF: - Fm: 0-0
Distance:	2m/2m3: 1-2 2m4-2m7: 0-0 3m+: 0-0
Track:	LH: 0-1 RH: 0-0 Tight: 0-0 Gall: 0-0
Aids:	Bl: 0-0 Vi: 0-0 Tstrap: 0-0 Ckp: 0-0
Best Rating:	131 3/04 Chel 2m110y good NHF

Impressive winner of a decent looking bumper at Gowran Park in February over 2m 1f before running well in the Festival bumper; acts on soft ground; promising.

Knockrigg (IRE)

100   (98c)**88**

10-y-o ch g Commanche Run-Gaiety Lass (Le Moss)
Dr P Pritchard The Shooting Stars

Placings:000/0632201/254342136/4223F5200/666022552-
022   **(4270)**
2003/04: 17OGF, 162GS, 162GF,

	Starts	1st	2nd	3rd	Win & Pl
Hurdles	3	0	2	0	2312
Career Total	40	2	12	4	21756
96 2/01 Leic	2m		F(0-110)HCh	SFT	£3370
85 4/00 Cork	2m		(0-102)HHdl	G-Y	£4140
			Total win prize-money £7511

Going:	Sf: 0-0 GS: 0-1 Gd: 0-0 GF: - Fm: 0-2
Distance:	2m/2m3: 0-3 2m4-2m7: 0-0 3m+: 0-0
Track:	LH: 0-2 RH: 0-1 Tight: 0-1 Gall: 0-0
Aids:	Bl: 0-0 Vi: 0-0 Tstrap: 0-0 Ckp: 0-0
Best Rating:	98 7/01 Worc 2m4f110y soft Ch

Plating-class performer; lost his way over fences, and is a
frustrating type, finishing in the frame quite often but rarely
winning; suited by two miles on soft ground.

Knocktopher Abbey

96   **102**

7-y-o ch g Pursuit Of Love-Kukri (Kris)
B R Millman (Miss Venetia Williams 27/1) Seasons
Holidays

Placings:3/341-004PPP   **(4380)**
2003/04: 20OGF, 16OG, 194GF, 20PG, 20PS, 19OG,

	Starts	1st	2nd	3rd	Win & Pl
Hurdles	6	0	0	0	293
Career Total	10	1	0	2	6068
102 4/03 Chep	2m110y E Hdl			G-F	£3549
			Total win prize-money £3549

Going:	Sf: 0-1 GS: 0-0 Gd: 0-3 GF: - Fm: 0-2
Distance:	2m/2m3: 0-1 2m4-2m7: 0-5 3m+: 0-0
Track:	LH: 0-1 RH: 0-4 Tight: 0-3 Gall: 0-0
Aids:	Bl: 0-2 Vi: 0-1 Tstrap: 0-0 Ckp: 0-0
Best Rating:	105 11/01 Tntn 2m1f good Hdl

Won strongly-run 2m maiden hurdle at Chepstow April 2003;
disappointing since; has worn blinkers; acts on fast ground;
likely to prove best at 2m.

Know Thyne (IRE)

78

10-y-o ch g Good Thyne (USA)-Bail Out (Quayside)
P T Dalton Mrs R Gabb & The Hon Mrs A H Todd

Placings:/P/P00P-P   **(0170)**
2003/04: 20PGF,

	Starts	1st	2nd	3rd	Win & Pl
Hurdles	1	0	0	0	
Career Total	7	1	0	0	3895
122 5/01 Tipp	2m4f		NHF	G-F	£3895
			Total win prize-money £3895

Going:	Sf: 0-0 GS: 0-0 Gd: 0-0 GF: - Fm: 0-1
Distance:	2m/2m3: 0-0 2m4-2m7: 0-1 3m+: 0-0
Track:	LH: 0-1 RH: 0-0 Tight: 0-0 Gall: 0-0
Aids:	Bl: 0-0 Vi: 0-0 Tstrap: 0-0 Ckp: 0-0
Best Rating:	122 5/01 Tipp 2m4f gd-fm NHF

Known Maneuver (USA)

88   **64**

6-y-o b g Known Fact (USA)-Northernmaneuver (USA) (Al
Nasr (FR))
M C Chapman David Fravigar,Alan Mann,David Marshall

Placings:6P00   **(4512)**
2003/04: 19OG, 20PGS, 19OG, 20OGS,

	Starts	1st	2nd	3rd	Win & Pl
Hurdles	4	0	0	0	0
Career Total	4	0	0	0	0

Going:	Sf: 0-0 GS: 0-2 Gd: 0-2 GF: - Fm: 0-0
Distance:	2m/2m3: 0-0 2m4-2m7: 0-4 3m+: 0-0
Track:	LH: 0-3 RH: 0-1 Tight: 0-1 Gall: 0-0
Aids:	Bl: 0-1 Vi: 0-0 Tstrap: 0-0 Ckp: 0-0
Best Rating:	64 12/03 MRas 2m3f110y good Hdl

Kobyla

6-y-o ch m Moscow Society (USA)-Jalmaid (Jalmood (USA))
H Alexander Atkinson Baillie Gill

Placings:00003P   **(4660)**
2003/04: 16OGS, 16OG, 16OG, 21OG, 253GS, 24PS,

	Starts	1st	2nd	3rd	Win & Pl
NH Flat	3	0	0	0	0
Hurdles	3	0	0	1	496
Career Total	6	0	0	1	496

Going:	Sf: 0-1 GS: 0-2 Gd: 0-3 GF: - Fm: 0-0
Distance:	2m/2m3: 0-3 2m4-2m7: 0-1 3m+: 0-2
Track:	LH: 0-5 RH: 0-1 Tight: 0-3 Gall: 0-0
Aids:	Bl: 0-0 Vi: 0-0 Tstrap: 0-0 Ckp: 0-0
Best Rating:	69 1/04 Catt 2m good NHF

Kock De La Vesvre (FR)

106   **136+**

6-y-o b g Sassanian (USA)-Csardas (FR) (Maiymad)
Miss Venetia Williams O P Dakin

Placings:42252622/610231F21-1302501PU1   **(4951)**
2003/04: 161G, 203G, 20OG, 192G, 215G, 20OG, 191GS, 19PG,
24US, 241GS,

	Starts	1st	2nd	3rd	Win & Pl
Chases	10	3	1	1	37894
Career Total	27	6	8	2	90564
135 4/04 Prth	3m	B HCh		G-S	£18047
136 2/04 Towc	2m3f110yD(0-125)HCh		G-S	£5434
114 5/03 Prth	2m	D Ch		GD	£6682
120 4/03 Prth	2m	C Ch		GD	£8268
136 3/03 Bang	2m1f110yD Ch		SFT	£5343
5/02 Autl	2m1f110y Ch		VS	£12368
			Total win prize-money £56142

Going:	Sf: 0-1 GS: 2-2 Gd: 1-7 GF: - Fm: 0-0
Distance:	2m/2m3: 1-2 2m4-2m7: 1-6 3m+: 1-2
Track:	LH: 0-5 RH: 2-4 Tight: 0-2 Gall: 0-2
Aids:	Bl: 0-0 Vi: 0-0 Tstrap: 0-0 Ckp: 0-0
Best Rating:	136 2/04 Towc 2m3f110y gd-sft Ch

Useful chaser; ex-French; effective from two to three miles;
best on soft ground but handles faster.

Kohinor

96f   **99f**

5-y-o b m Supreme Leader-Always Shining (Tug Of War)
O Sherwood R J Bassett

Placings:352   **(4345)**
2003/04: 163G, 185GS, 162GS,

	Starts	1st	2nd	3rd	Win & Pl
NH Flat	3	0	1	1	864
Career Total	3	0	1	1	864

Going:	Sf: 0-0 GS: 0-2 Gd: 0-1 GF: - Fm: 0-0
Distance:	2m/2m3: 0-3 2m4-2m7: 0-0 3m+: 0-0
Track:	LH: 0-3 RH: 0-0 Tight: 0-1 Gall: 0-0
Aids:	Bl: 0-0 Vi: 0-0 Tstrap: 0-0 Ckp: 0-0
Best Rating:	98 3/04 Wwck 2m gd-sft NHF

Promising debut in mares' bumper, but well held next outing
at Fontwell.

Koloma (FR)

6-y-o b/br m Useful (FR)-Cadoudaline (FR) (Cadoudal (FR))
Miss Kate Milligan Racing Management & Training Ltd

Placings:00P   **(2580)**
2003/04: 17OG, 17OG, 16PGF,

	Starts	1st	2nd	3rd	Win & Pl
NH Flat	2	0	0	0	0
Hurdles	1	0	0	0	0
Career Total	3	0	0	0	0

Going:	Sf: 0-0 GS: 0-0 Gd: 0-2 GF: - Fm: 0-1
Distance:	2m/2m3: 0-3 2m4-2m7: 0-0 3m+: 0-0
Track:	LH: 0-3 RH: 0-0 Tight: 0-3 Gall: 0-0
Aids:	Bl: 0-0 Vi: 0-0 Tstrap: 0-0 Ckp: 0-0
Best Rating:	53 10/03 Sedg 2m1f good NHF

Kombinacja (POL)

108   **114**

6-y-o ch m Jape (USA)-Komancza (POL) (Dakota)
T R George C Davies,S Nelson,A Stennett,T Warner

Placings:04-114402   **(4842)**
2003/04: 161G, 171G, 164GF, 164GS, 17OGS, 212G,

	Starts	1st	2nd	3rd	Win & Pl
Hurdles	6	2	1	0	19202
Career Total	8	2	1	0	19792
104 6/03 NAbb	2m1f	C Hdl		GD	£6133
112 5/03 Strf	2m110y D Hdl		GD	£5590
			Total win prize-money £11723

Going:	Sf: 0-0 GS: 0-2 Gd: 2-3 GF: - Fm: 0-1
Distance:	2m/2m3: 2-5 2m4-2m7: 0-1 3m+: 0-0
Track:	LH: 2-6 RH: 0-0 Tight: 2-2 Gall: 0-2
Aids:	Bl: 0-0 Vi: 0-0 Tstrap: 0-0 Ckp: 0-0
Best Rating:	114 11/03 Hayd 2m gd-sft Hdl

High-class mare on the Flat in Poland; modest novice hurdler; best at two miles; needs a sound surface.

Konfuzius (GER)

84   **67**

6-y-o b g Motley (USA)-Katrina (GER) (Windwurf (GER))
P Monteith Oriental Mist Partnership

Placings:60F604P-0   **(0428)**
2003/04: 17OG,

	Starts	1st	2nd	3rd	Win & Pl
Hurdles	1	0	0	0	

	Starts	1st	2nd	3rd	Win & Pl
Career Total	8	0	0	0	0

Going: Sf: 0-0 GS: 0-0 Gd: 0-1 GF: - Fm: 0-0
Distance: 2m/2m3: 0-1 2m4-2m7: 0-0 3m+: 0-0
Track: LH: 0-1 RH: 0-0 Tight: 0-1 Gall: 0-0
Aids: Bl: 0-1 Vi: 0-0 Tstrap: 0-0 Ckp: 0-0
Best Rating: 68 12/02 Kels 2m10y heavy Hdl

Konker

101(105h)   (125+h)102
9-y-o ch g Selkirk (USA)-Helens Dreamgirl (Caerleon (USA))
Mrs M Reveley J & M Leisure / Unos Restaurant

Placings:5040/11315/66405004/2-40102   (3693)
2003/04: 16^4G, 17^0HY, 16^1G, 16^0S, 19^2G,

	Starts	1st	2nd	3rd	Win & Pl
Hurdles	4	1	0	0	7886
Chases	1	0	0	0	1188
Career Total	23	4	2	1	21710

125 12/03 Weth 2m	C(0-135)HHdl	GD	£7098
133 1/01 Weth 2m	C(0-130)HHdl	G-S	£5382
122 11/00 Newc 2m	E(0-115)HHdl	SFT	£2541
122 11/00 Weth 2m	E(0-105)HHdl	HVY	£2925

Total win prize-money £17946

Going: Sf: 0-2 GS: 0-0 Gd: 1-3 GF: - Fm: 0-0
Distance: 2m/2m3: 1-5 2m4-2m7: 0-0 3m+: 0-0
Track: LH: 1-4 RH: 0-1 Tight: 0-2 Gall: 0-0
Aids: Bl: 0-0 Vi: 0-0 Tstrap: 0-0 Ckp: 0-0
Best Rating: 133 1/01 Weth 2m gd-sft Hdl

Fair handicap hurdler/novice chaser, best suited by two miles and soft ground.

Koquelicot (FR)

107(96h)   (84h)123+
6-y-o ch g Video Rock (FR)-Ixia Des Saccarts (FR) (Laniste)
P J Hobbs Alan Peterson

Placings:635F4P/060P5FP240-530111615   (4871)
2003/04: 20^5G, 21^3S, 16^0S, 20^1S, 21^1S, 20^1GS, 24^6G, 24^1G, 24^5S,

	Starts	1st	2nd	3rd	Win & Pl
Hurdles	3	0	0	1	427
Chases	6	4	0	0	27696
Career Total	25	5	4	1	2	45180

126 4/04 Tntn 3m	D(0-120)HCh		£6581
123 2/04 Kemp 2m4f110y	D(0-115)HCh	G-S	£5421
120 1/04 Winc 2m5f	D(0-125)HCh	SFT	£10205
109 12/03 Uttx 2m4f	E(0-105)HCh	SFT	£5177

Total win prize-money £27384

Going: Sf: 2-5 GS: 1-2 Gd: 1-2 GF: 0-0
Distance: 2m/2m3: 0-1 2m4-2m7: 3-5 3m+: 1-3
Track: LH: 1-4 RH: 3-5 Tight: 1-2 Gall: 0-0
Aids: Bl: 0-0 Vi: 0-0 Tstrap: 0-0 Ckp: 0-0
Best Rating: 126 4/04 Tntn 3m good Ch

Fair novice chaser; progressive; stays three miles and acts on most types of ground.

Korakor (FR)

104   143
10-y-o ch g Nikos-Aniflore (FR) (Satingo)
Ian Williams Mr And Mrs J D Cotton

Placings:1/31/331P/516434/PP4P1/051232/PP203012-33F040F   (4640)
2003/04: 20^3G, 21^3GF, 20^0G, 17^0GS, 21^4G, 16^0G, 21^3FG,

	Starts	1st	2nd	3rd	Win & Pl
Chases	7	0	0	2	4092

	Starts	1st	2nd	3rd	Win & Pl
Career Total	39	7	4	8	151994

142 4/03 Ayr 2m	B HCh	GD	£15680
139 12/01 Donc 2m3f110yC(0-135)HCh		GD	£7130
141 4/01 Ayr 2m4f	B HCh	GD	£10787
11/98 Autl 2m4f110y Ch		HVY	£21529
11/98 Autl 2m4f110y Ch		VS	£12121
9/97 Autl 2m2f Hdl		SFT	£22447
4/97 Autl 1m7f Hdl		VS	£13468

Total win prize-money £103163

Going: Sf: 0-0 GS: 0-1 Gd: 0-5 GF: - Fm: 0-1
Distance: 2m/2m3: 0-2 2m4-2m7: 0-5 3m+: 0-0
Track: LH: 0-7 RH: 0-0 Tight: 0-2 Gall: 0-3
Aids: Bl: 0-0 Vi: 0-0 Tstrap: 0-0 Ckp: 0-0
Best Rating: 143 4/02 Ayr 2m4f good Ch

Useful chaser; best at up to two and a half miles and effective on good ground; goes well fresh.

Korelo (FR)

116(110c)   (127c)146
6-y-o b g Cadoudal (FR)-Lora Du Charmil (FR) (Panoramic)
M C Pipe D A Johnson

Placings:63325/2505314115P-4336P0031   (4963)
2003/04: 17^4G, 20^3GF, 16^3G, 16^5S, 18^6G, 21^0G, 20^0G, 21^3GF, 20^1G,

	Starts	1st	2nd	3rd	Win & Pl
Hurdles	4	1	0	1	18170
Chases	5	0	0	2	2094
Career Total	25	4	2	6	112951

143 4/04 Sand 2m4f110yB(0-140)HHdl		GD	£15935
146 3/03 Sand 2m110y B(0-150)HHdl		HVY	£29000
136 2/03 Asct 2m4f	B(0-140)HHdl	SFT	£29000
107 12/02 Tntn 2m1f	D Hdl	SFT	£4972

Total win prize-money £78908

Going: Sf: 0-1 GS: 0-0 Gd: 1-6 GF: - Fm: 0-2
Distance: 2m/2m3: 0-4 2m4-2m7: 1-5 3m+: 0-0
Track: LH: 0-5 RH: 1-4 Tight: 0-3 Gall: 0-4
Aids: Bl: 0-0 Vi: 0-2 Tstrap: 0-0 Ckp: 0-0
Best Rating: 146 3/03 Sand 2m110y heavy Hdl

Very useful hurdler; won Imperial Cup at Sandown in 2003 on heavy ground; good efforts in Coral Cups of 2003 and 2004; won a competitive handicap on his return to Sandown in April 2004; modest novice chaser on evidence so far, showing a tendency to jump left; stays two miles five very well; relishes soft ground; has been tried in visor over hurdles and fences.

Kosmic Lady

87   70
7-y-o b m Cosmonaut-Ktolo (Tolomeo)
P W Hiatt P J Morgan

Placings:040/640-0   (1362)
2003/04: 16^0GF,

	Starts	1st	2nd	3rd	Win & Pl
Hurdles	1	0	0	0	
Career Total	7	0	0	0	0

Going: Sf: 0-0 GS: 0-0 Gd: 0-0 GF: - Fm: 0-0
Distance: 2m/2m3: 0-1 2m4-2m7: 0-0 3m+: 0-0
Track: LH: 0-1 RH: 0-0 Tight: 0-0 Gall: 0-0
Aids: Bl: 0-0 Vi: 0-0 Tstrap: 0-0 Ckp: 0-0
Best Rating: 70 12/02 Hrfd 2m1f good Hdl

Kosmos Bleu (FR)

98   105+
6-y-o ch g Franc Bleu Argent (USA)-Fee Du Lac (FR)

(Cimon)
R H Alner P M De Wilde

Placings:P-2UP5   (4051)
2003/04: 19^2G, 19^4G, 20^5GS, 21^5G,

	Starts	1st	2nd	3rd	Win & Pl
Hurdles	4	0	1	0	1568
Career Total	5	0	1	0	1568

Going: Sf: 0-0 GS: 0-2 Gd: 0-2 GF: - Fm: 0-0
Distance: 2m/2m3: 0-1 2m4-2m7: 0-3 3m+: 0-0
Track: LH: 0-1 RH: 0-3 Tight: 0-0 Gall: 0-0
Aids: Bl: 0-0 Vi: 0-0 Tstrap: 0-0 Ckp: 0-0
Best Rating: 105 11/03 Extr 2m3f good Hdl

Fair hurdler; ex-French; stays two miles three; acts on good ground.

Koumba (FR)

94   77
6-y-o b g Luchiroverte (IRE)-Agenore (FR) (Le Riverain (FR))
B N Pollock Mrs Nicola Pollock

Placings:50-036   (0455)
2003/04: 16^0GF, 16^3G, 20^6HY,

	Starts	1st	2nd	3rd	Win & Pl
Hurdles	3	0	0	1	600
Career Total	5	0	0	1	600

Going: Sf: 0-1 GS: 0-0 Gd: 0-1 GF: - Fm: 0-1
Distance: 2m/2m3: 0-2 2m4-2m7: 0-1 3m+: 0-0
Track: LH: 0-2 RH: 0-1 Tight: 0-0 Gall: 0-0
Aids: Bl: 0-0 Vi: 0-0 Tstrap: 0-0 Ckp: 0-0
Best Rating: 77 5/03 Uttx 2m good Hdl

Kouros Des Obeaux (FR)

99   105
6-y-o b g Grand Tresor (FR)-Valse Des Obeaux (FR) (Pot D'Or (FR))
M C Pipe (Jack Barbe 18/5) D J Ayres

Placings:052006-126F230   (4520)
2003/04: 19^1S, 19^2G, 20^6G, 26^6GS, 26^2G, 25^3G, 23^9GS,

	Starts	1st	2nd	3rd	Win & Pl
Chases	7	1	2	1	9005
Career Total	13	1	3	1	15300

105 5/03 Ange 2m3f	Ch	SFT	£4987

Total win prize-money £4987

Going: Sf: 1-1 GS: 0-2 Gd: 0-3 GF: - Fm: 0-1
Distance: 2m/2m3: 1-1 2m4-2m7: 0-2 3m+: 0-4
Track: LH: 0-1 RH: 0-2 Tight: 0-0 Gall: 0-0
Aids: Bl: 0-0 Vi: 0-4 Tstrap: 0-0 Ckp: 0-0
Best Rating: 105 5/03 Ange 2m3f soft Ch

Won 2m 3f chase in soft ground in French Provinces May 2003; beaten a distance when second on British debut on fast ground at Towcester in October.

Koyaanisqatsi

72   49+
4-y-o ch g Selkirk (USA)-Bogus John (CAN) (Blushing John (USA))
Jamie Poulton Ormonde Racing

Placings:002P   (4750)
2003/04: 16^0G, 16^0S, 16^2G, 21^0G,

	Starts	1st	2nd	3rd	Win & Pl
Hurdles	4	0	1	0	728
Career Total	4	0	1	0	728

Going:	Sf: 0-1 GS: 0-1 Gd: 0-2 GF: - Fm: 0-0
Distance:	2m/2m3: 0-3 2m4-2m7: 0-1 3m+: 0-0
Track:	LH: 0-3 RH: 0-1 Tight: 0-3 Gall: 0-0
Aids:	Bl: 0-0 Vi: 0-0 Tstrap: 0-0 Ckp: 0-0
Best Rating:	49 3/04 Plum 2m gd-sft Hdl

Krach (FR)

81 **121+**

6-y-o b g Lute Antique (FR)-Voilette (FR) (Brezzo (FR))
F Doumen John P McManus

Placings:2/2-1 (2845)
2003/04: 24¹S,

	Starts	1st	2nd	3rd	Win & Pl
Hurdles	1	1	0	0	6906
Career Total	3	1	2	0	13813
121	12/03	Asct	3m	C Hdl	SFT £6906

Total win prize-money £6906

Going:	Sf: 1-1 GS: 0-0 Gd: 0-0 GF: - Fm: 0-0
Distance:	2m/2m3: 0-0 2m4-2m7: 0-0 3m+: 1-1
Track:	LH: 0-0 RH: 1-1 Tight: 0-0 Gall: 0-0
Aids:	Bl: 0-0 Vi: 0-0 Tstrap: 0-0 Ckp: 0-0
Best Rating:	121 12/03 Asct 3m soft Hdl

Krack De L'Isle (FR)

92 **116**

6-y-o b g Kadalko (FR)-Ceres De L'Isle (FR) (Bad Conduct (USA))
A C Whillans John J Elliot

Placings:44/5413U-0 (3819)
2003/04: 23⁰S,

	Starts	1st	2nd	3rd	Win & Pl
Hurdles	1	0	0	0	
Career Total	8	1	0	1	4126
116	1/03	Ayr	2m6f	E Hdl	HVY £3542

Total win prize-money £3542

Going:	Sf: 0-1 GS: 0-0 Gd: 0-0 GF: - Fm: 0-0
Distance:	2m/2m3: 0-0 2m4-2m7: 0-0 3m+: 0-1
Track:	LH: 0-1 RH: 0-0 Tight: 0-0 Gall: 0-0
Aids:	Bl: 0-0 Vi: 0-0 Tstrap: 0-0 Ckp: 0-0
Best Rating:	116 1/03 Ayr 2m6f heavy Hdl

Fair hurdler; looked much improved for the switch to hurdles and step up in trip in early 2003; stays two miles six; acts on soft ground.

Kristal Forest (IRE)

66

5-y-o b g Charnwood Forest (IRE)-Kristal's Paradise (IRE) (Bluebird (USA))
Mrs S Lamyman The Underlaws

Placings:3 (0673)
2003/04: 17³GF,

	Starts	1st	2nd	3rd	Win & Pl
Hurdles	1	0	0	1	518
Career Total	1	0	0	1	518

Going:	Sf: 0-0 GS: 0-0 Gd: 0-0 GF: - Fm: 0-1
Distance:	2m/2m3: 0-1 2m4-2m7: 0-0 3m+: 0-0
Track:	LH: 0-1 RH: 0-0 Tight: 0-0 Gall: 0-0
Aids:	Bl: 0-0 Vi: 0-0 Tstrap: 0-0 Ckp: 0-0

| Best Rating: | 66   6/03   Sthl   2m1f   gd-fm   Hdl |

Kristineau

95 **98**

6-y-o ch m Cadeaux Genereux-Kantikoy (Alzao (USA))
Mrs E Slack A Slack

Placings:6-435 (4908)
2003/04: 20⁴GS, 17³G, 20⁵S,

	Starts	1st	2nd	3rd	Win & Pl
Hurdles	3	0	0	1	568
Career Total	4	0	0	1	568

Going:	Sf: 0-1 GS: 0-1 Gd: 0-1 GF: - Fm: 0-0
Distance:	2m/2m3: 0-1 2m4-2m7: 0-2 3m+: 0-0
Track:	LH: 0-1 RH: 0-2 Tight: 0-0 Gall: 0-0
Aids:	Bl: 0-0 Vi: 0-0 Tstrap: 0-2 Ckp: 0-0
Best Rating:	97 4/04 Carl 2m1f good Hdl

Moderate novice hurdler; first worthwhile form when fourth at Wetherby in March; suited by two and a half miles.

Kristoffersen

105 **111**

4-y-o ch g Kris-Towaahi (IRE) (Caerleon (USA))
R M Stronge (G A Butler 27/10) Mrs Bernice Stronge

Placings:30U0F (4378)
2003/04: 16³G, 16⁶GS, 16ᵁG, 16⁰GS, 17ᶠG,

	Starts	1st	2nd	3rd	Win & Pl
Hurdles	5	0	0	1	1227
Career Total	5	0	0	1	1227

Going:	Sf: 0-0 GS: 0-2 Gd: 0-3 GF: - Fm: 0-0
Distance:	2m/2m3: 0-5 2m4-2m7: 0-0 3m+: 0-0
Track:	LH: 0-1 RH: 0-4 Tight: 0-2 Gall: 0-1
Aids:	Bl: 0-0 Vi: 0-0 Tstrap: 0-0 Ckp: 0-0
Best Rating:	107 12/03 Kemp 2m good Hdl

Fair performer at up to a mile and a half on the Flat; third on hurdles debut, well held since; possibly best on a sound surface.

Kroisos (IRE)

107(100h) (76h)**95+**

6-y-o b g Kris-Lydia Maria (Dancing Brave (USA))
R Curtis Mrs R A Smith

Placings:60642-446PP0212 (4933)
2003/04: 21⁴S, 25⁴S, 22⁶S, 26⁵S, 24ᴾHY, 24⁰G, 24²G, 26¹G, 26²G,

	Starts	1st	2nd	3rd	Win & Pl
Hurdles	3	0	0	0	
Chases	6	1	2	0	5742
Career Total	14	1	3	0	6909
95	4/04	Plum	3m2f	F(0-90)HCh	GD £3402

Total win prize-money £3402

Going:	Sf: 0-3 GS: 0-0 Gd: 1-6 GF: - Fm: 0-0
Distance:	2m/2m3: 0-0 2m4-2m7: 0-2 3m+: 1-7
Track:	LH: 1-4 RH: 0-3 Tight: 1-4 Gall: 0-2
Aids:	Bl: 1-4 Vi: 0-0 Tstrap: 0-0 Ckp: 0-0
Best Rating:	95 4/04 Plum 3m2f good Ch

Plating-class chaser; stays three miles two; acts on testing ground, but possibly better on good.

Kung Hei Fat Choi (IRE)

106 **105**

9-y-o b g Roselier (FR)-Gallant Blade (Fine Blade (USA))
J S Goldie Strathayr Publishing Ltd

Placings:0506/341404/3631422P-P12P3P (2904)
2003/04: 25ᴾGS, 24¹GS, 24²G, 24ᴾG, 24³G, 25ᴾS,

	Starts	1st	2nd	3rd	Win & Pl
Chases	6	1	1	1	7678
Career Total	24	3	3	4	18761
105	5/03	Prth	3m	E(0-105)HCh	G-S £4158
93	1/03	Catt	3m1f110yF(0-100)HCh	GD	£3474
98	3/02	Ayr	2m5f110yH Ch	HVY	£1589

Total win prize-money £9221

Going:	Sf: 0-1 GS: 1-2 Gd: 0-3 GF: - Fm: 0-0
Distance:	2m/2m3: 0-0 2m4-2m7: 0-0 3m+: 1-6
Track:	LH: 0-2 RH: 1-4 Tight: 0-0 Gall: 0-0
Aids:	Bl: 0-0 Vi: 0-0 Tstrap: 0-0 Ckp: 0-0
Best Rating:	105 6/03 Prth 3m good Ch

Moderate staying chaser; acts on good or softer; stays 3m plus.

Kustom Kit Grizzly (IRE)

9-y-o br g Be My Native (USA)-Bridgetown Girl (Al Sirat)
Mrs F Kehoe M Kehoe

Placings:3/06/0040P/5 (4298)
2003/04: 23⁵G,

	Starts	1st	2nd	3rd	Win & Pl
Chases	1	0	0	0	0
Career Total	9	0	0	1	236

Going:	Sf: 0-0 GS: 0-0 Gd: 0-1 GF: - Fm: 0-0
Distance:	2m/2m3: 0-0 2m4-2m7: 0-0 3m+: 0-1
Track:	LH: 0-0 RH: 0-1 Tight: 0-0 Gall: 0-0
Aids:	Bl: 0-0 Vi: 0-1 Tstrap: 0-0 Ckp: 0-0
Best Rating:	77 6/01 MRas 3m gd-fm Hdl

Kwaheri

65 **20**

6-y-o b m Efisio-Fleeting Affair (Hotfoot)
Mrs P N Dutfield Simon Dutfield

Placings:0 (4736)
2003/04: 17⁰G,

	Starts	1st	2nd	3rd	Win & Pl
Hurdles	1	0	0	0	
Career Total	1	0	0	0	

Going:	Sf: 0-0 GS: 0-0 Gd: 0-1 GF: - Fm: 0-0
Distance:	2m/2m3: 0-1 2m4-2m7: 0-0 3m+: 0-0
Track:	LH: 0-1 RH: 0-0 Tight: 0-1 Gall: 0-0
Aids:	Bl: 0-0 Vi: 0-0 Tstrap: 0-0 Ckp: 0-0
Best Rating:	25 4/04 NAbb 2m1f good Hdl

Kylie Time (IRE)

104 **96**

7-y-o ch g Good Thyne (USA)-Miss Kylogue (IRE) (Lancastrian)
P Beaumont Mr & Mrs Raymond Anderson Green

Aids: Bl: 0-0 **Vi:** 1-2 Tstrap: 0-0 Ckp: 0-0
Best Rating: 109 6/03 Worc 2m4f gd-fm Hdl

Placings:000P-0P3   (4946)
2003/04: 19⁰G, 17ᴾG, 16³GS,

	Starts	1st	2nd	3rd	Win & Pl
Hurdles	3	0	0	1	872
Career Total	7	0	0	1	872

Moderate hurdler; acted on fast ground; stayed 2m 4f; (DEAD).

Going: Sf: 0-0 GS: 0-1 Gd: 0-2 GF: - Fm: 0-0
Distance: 2m/2m3: 0-2 2m4-2m7: 0-1 3m+: 0-0
Track: LH: 0-0 RH: 0-3 Tight: 0-2 Gall: 0-0
Aids: Bl: 0-0 Vi: 0-0 Tstrap: 0-0 Ckp: 0-0
Best Rating: 96 4/04 Prth 2m10y gd-sft Hdl

Kylkenny
92   83+
9-y-o b g Kylian (USA)-Fashion Flow (Balidar)
H Morrison H Morrison

Placings:56/0-0   (2553)
2003/04: 16⁵G,

	Starts	1st	2nd	3rd	Win & Pl
Hurdles	1	0	0	0	0
Career Total	4	0	0	0	0

Going: Sf: 0-0 GS: 0-0 Gd: 0-1 GF: - Fm: 0-0
Distance: 2m/2m3: 0-1 2m4-2m7: 0-0 3m+: 0-0
Track: LH: 0-0 RH: 0-1 Tight: 0-0 Gall: 0-0
Aids: Bl: 0-0 Vi: 0-0 Tstrap: 0-1 Ckp: 0-0
Best Rating: 86 11/00 Wwck 2m heavy Hdl

Winning handicapper on the Flat; yet to show much over hurdles.

Kymani Prince (IRE)
85   101+
8-y-o b g Shemazar-Best Of British (Young Generation)
L Lungo D Stronach & R Buck

Placings:3/2-5F   (2505)
2003/04: 16⁵GF, 16²S,

	Starts	1st	2nd	3rd	Win & Pl
Hurdles	2	0	0	0	0
Career Total	4	0	1	1	2036

Going: Sf: 0-1 GS: 0-0 Gd: 0-0 GF: - Fm: 0-1
Distance: 2m/2m3: 0-2 2m4-2m7: 0-0 3m+: 0-0
Track: LH: 0-2 RH: 0-0 Tight: 0-1 Gall: 0-0
Aids: Bl: 0-0 Vi: 0-0 Tstrap: 0-0 Ckp: 0-0
Best Rating: 102 3/02 Donc 2m10y gd-sft NHF

Lightly-raced individual; modest form in a bumper and hurdle races; possibly best on a sound surface.

Kymberlya (FR)
108   105
6-y-o ch g Esteem Ball (FR)-Catty Douce (FR) (Cadoudal (FR))
M C Pipe P A Deal & J S Dale

Placings:FP3-41F   (0678)
2003/04: 16⁴HY, 20¹GF, 20⁶GF,

	Starts	1st	2nd	3rd	Win & Pl
Hurdles	3	1	0	1	3763
Career Total	6	1	0	1	4513
109 6/03 Worc 2m4f	E Hdl			G-F	£3444
				Total win prize-money	£3444

Going: Sf: 0-1 GS: 0-0 Gd: 0-0 GF: - Fm: 1-2
Distance: 2m/2m3: 0-1 2m4-2m7: 1-2 3m+: 0-0
Track: LH: 1-3 RH: 0-0 Tight: 0-0 Gall: 0-0

Kynance Cove
82   47
5-y-o b g Karinga Bay-Excelled (IRE) (Treasure Kay)
C P Morlock Mrs Jenny Melbourne

Placings:000P00   (4898)
2003/04: 16⁰GF, 16⁰GF, 17⁰G, 21ᴾG, 20⁰GF, 16⁰G,

	Starts	1st	2nd	3rd	Win & Pl
NH Flat	2	0	0	0	0
Hurdles	4	0	0	0	0
Career Total	6	0	0	0	0

Going: Sf: 0-0 GS: 0-0 Gd: 0-3 GF: - Fm: 0-3
Distance: 2m/2m3: 0-4 2m4-2m7: 0-2 3m+: 0-0
Track: LH: 0-2 RH: 0-3 Tight: 0-2 Gall: 0-0
Aids: Bl: 0-0 Vi: 0-0 Tstrap: 0-0 Ckp: 0-0
Best Rating: 55 6/03 Worc 2m gd-fm NHF

L For Leisure
5-y-o ch g Cosmonaut-York Street (USA) (Diamond Shoal)
Julian Poulton Tony Taylor

Placings:P   (3314)
2003/04: 16ᴾS,

	Starts	1st	2nd	3rd	Win & Pl
Hurdles	1	0	0	0	0
Career Total	1	0	0	0	0

Going: Sf: 0-1 GS: 0-0 Gd: 0-0 GF: - Fm: 0-0
Distance: 2m/2m3: 0-1 2m4-2m7: 0-0 3m+: 0-0
Track: LH: 0-0 RH: 0-1 Tight: 0-0 Gall: 0-0
Aids: Bl: 0-0 Vi: 0-0 Tstrap: 0-0 Ckp: 0-0

L'Ange Au Ciel (FR)
112   119
5-y-o b g Agent Bleu (FR)-Epopee II (FR) (Comrade In Arms)
P F Nicholls B C Marshall

Placings:1-1   (2566)
2003/04: 17¹G,

	Starts	1st	2nd	3rd	Win & Pl
Chases	1	1	0	0	10725
Career Total	2	2	0	0	17894
119 12/03 Extr	2m1f110yC Ch			GD	£10725
1/03 Pau	2m110y Hdl			HVY	£7169
				Total win prize-money	£17894

Going: Sf: 0-0 GS: 0-0 Gd: 0-0 GF: - Fm: 0-0
Distance: 2m/2m3: 1-1 2m4-2m7: 0-0 3m+: 0-0
Track: LH: 0-0 RH: 1-1 Tight: 0-0 Gall: 0-0
Aids: Bl: 0-0 Vi: 0-0 Tstrap: 0-0 Ckp: 0-0
Best Rating: 119 12/03 Extr 2m1f110y good Ch

Promising novice chaser; ex-French; winner of a decent contest at Exeter on his British chasing debut; suited by two miles and good ground; should go on to better things.

L'Archer
79   61
6-y-o b g Lancastrian-Sailors Joy (Handsome Sailor)

A E Jessop A Jessop

Placings:600P0   (4959)
2003/04: 18⁶G, 17⁰GS, 16⁰S, 16²G, 19⁰G,

	Starts	1st	2nd	3rd	Win & Pl
NH Flat	2	0	0	0	0
Hurdles	3	0	0	0	0
Career Total	5	0	0	0	0

Going: Sf: 0-1 GS: 0-1 Gd: 0-3 GF: - Fm: 0-0
Distance: 2m/2m3: 0-4 2m4-2m7: 0-1 3m+: 0-0
Track: LH: 0-2 RH: 0-3 Tight: 0-3 Gall: 0-1
Aids: Bl: 0-0 Vi: 0-0 Tstrap: 0-3 Ckp: 0-0
Best Rating: 71 11/03 Plum 2m2f good NHF

L'Artiste Bellevue (FR)
81f   46f
5-y-o b g Start Fast (FR)-Enus Du Manoir (FR) (Le Nain Jaune (FR))
Jean-Rene Auvray Lambourn Racing

Placings:0   (4578)
2003/04: 16⁰G,

	Starts	1st	2nd	3rd	Win & Pl
NH Flat	1	0	0	0	0
Career Total	1	0	0	0	0

Going: Sf: 0-0 GS: 0-0 Gd: 0-0 GF: - Fm: 0-0
Distance: 2m/2m3: 0-1 2m4-2m7: 0-0 3m+: 0-0
Track: LH: 0-1 RH: 0-0 Tight: 0-0 Gall: 0-1
Aids: Bl: 0-0 Vi: 0-0 Tstrap: 0-0 Ckp: 0-0
Best Rating: 46 3/04 Newb 2m110y good NHF

L'Aventure (FR)
108   133
5-y-o b m Cyborg (FR)-Amphitrite (FR) (Lazer (FR))
P F Nicholls (Y-M Porzier 25/11) C J Harriman

Placings:334116-P122222F112422   (4837)
2003/04: 18ᴾVS, 18¹VS, 18²S, 17²VS, 17²VS, 19²VS, 16²GF, 16⁶G, 20¹G, 19¹S, 20²S, 24⁴G, 25²G, 25²GF,

	Starts	1st	2nd	3rd	Win & Pl
Hurdles	3	1	1	0	8883
Chases	11	2	7	0	68756
Career Total	20	5	8	2	94751
130 1/04 Donc	2m3f	D Ch		SFT	£6890
94 1/04 Ludl	2m4f	E Ch		GD	£4420
6/03 Autl	2m2f	Hdl		VS	£6545
3/03 Engh	2m	Hdl		VS	£6545
3/03 Engh	2m	Hdl		HVY	£6545
				Total win prize-money	£30945

Going: Sf: 1-3 GS: 0-0 Gd: 1-4 GF: - Fm: 0-2
Distance: 2m/2m3: 2-9 2m4-2m7: 1-2 3m+: 0-3
Track: LH: 1-5 RH: 1-3 **Tight:** 1-2 Gall: 0-2
Aids: Bl: 2-8 Vi: 0-0 Tstrap: 2-8 Ckp: 0-0
Best Rating: 130 1/04 Donc 2m3f soft Ch

Useful novice chaser; ex-French; runner-up in a Grade Two at Aintree; stays three miles one; acts on most types of ground; usually wears blinkers and a tongue tie; very consistent to date.

L'Etang Bleu (FR)
100 (101h)   (99 h) 99
6-y-o gr g Graveron (FR)-Strawberry Jam (FR) (Fill My Hopes (FR))

P Butler (M C Pipe 10/11) Mrs E Lucey-Butler

Placings:P4/632222332/35600020S1-FP3U62332326P00P24 (4957)

2003/04: 16FGS, 16PG, 16³GF, 20UG, 16⁶GF, 17²F, 19³GF, 16³GF, 17²G, 18³GF, 17²S, 20⁶F, 17PGS, 16⁶S, 22⁰G, 16⁶G, 17²G, 17⁴GS,

	Starts	1st	2nd	3rd	Win & Pl
Hurdles	8	0	2	3	2317
Chases	10	0	2	1	3449
Career Total	39	1	10	8	20300
99 4/03 Uttx 2m G(0-90)HHdl GD £2471					
Total win prize-money £2471					

Going:	Sf: 0-2 GS: 0-3 Gd: 0-6 GF: - Fm: 0-7
Distance:	2m/2m3: 0-15 2m4-2m7: 0-3 3m+: 0-0
Track:	LH: 0-13 RH: 0-5 Tight: 0-13 Gall: 0-0
Aids:	Bl: 0-0 Vi: 0-2 Tstrap: 0-11 Ckp: 0-4
Best Rating:	99 5/03 Worc 2m gd-sft Ch

Plating-class hurdler; got off the mark in his 16th hurdle race in a poor seller at Uttoxeter in April 2003; looked unlucky not to make a winning debut over fences when falling at the last at Worcester; disappointing since; handles any ground; has worn a tongue tie.

L'Oiseau (FR)

82   95

5-y-o br g Video Rock (FR)-Roseraie (FR) (Quart De Vin (FR))

L Lungo Ashleybank Investments Limited

Placings:20003P2 (4727)

2003/04: 16²G, 17⁰G, 17⁹G, 16⁰GS, 20³G, 17PGS, 17²G,

	Starts	1st	2nd	3rd	Win & Pl
NH Flat	3	0	1	0	1060
Hurdles	4	0	1	1	1763
Career Total	7	0	2	1	2823

Going:	Sf: 0-0 GS: 0-2 Gd: 0-5 GF: - Fm: 0-0
Distance:	2m/2m3: 0-6 2m4-2m7: 0-1 3m+: 0-0
Track:	LH: 0-3 RH: 0-2 Tight: 0-3 Gall: 0-0
Aids:	Bl: 0-0 Vi: 0-0 Tstrap: 0-0 Ckp: 0-0
Best Rating:	96 11/03 Aint 2m1f good NHF

Moderate novice hurdler; acts on good ground; effective over two miles.

L'Orage Lady (IRE)

101   86+

6-y-o ch m Glacial Storm (USA)-Commanche Glen (IRE) (Commanche Run)

Mrs H Dalton Simpson, Shirley and Dalton

Placings:343160 (2951)

2003/04: 16³G, 16⁴GF, 16³GF, 19¹GF, 16⁶G, 20⁰G,

	Starts	1st	2nd	3rd	Win & Pl
NH Flat	3	0	0	2	651
Hurdles	3	1	0	0	2212
Career Total	6	1	0	2	2863
86 11/03 Catt 2m3f F Hdl G-F £2212					
Total win prize-money £2212					

Going:	Sf: 0-0 GS: 0-0 Gd: 0-3 GF: - Fm: 1-3
Distance:	2m/2m3: 1-5 2m4-2m7: 0-1 3m+: 0-0
Track:	LH: 1-4 RH: 0-2 Tight: 1-1 Gall: 0-1
Aids:	Bl: 0-0 Vi: 0-0 Tstrap: 0-0 Ckp: 0-0
Best Rating:	96 6/03 Worc 2m good NHF

Modest form in bumpers; narrow winner of poor mares' only novices' event at Catterick in November on first try over hurdles; acts on fast.

L'Orphelin

104(93h)   (78h)90+

9-y-o ch g Gildoran-Balula (Balinger)

C L Tizzard Mrs John Pope And Friends

Placings:310/P04P-U2U444U (4753)

2003/04: 21PS, 24UGF, 19²GS, 19UHY, 19⁴GS, 16⁴G, 19⁴GS, 26UG,

	Starts	1st	2nd	3rd	Win & Pl
Chases	8	0	1	0	2889
Career Total	14	1	1	1	4813
107 12/00 Ludl 2m H NHF SFT £1680					
Total win prize-money £1680					

Going:	Sf: 0-2 GS: 0-3 Gd: 0-2 GF: - Fm: 0-1
Distance:	2m/2m3: 0-4 2m4-2m7: 0-2 3m+: 0-2
Track:	LH: 0-3 RH: 0-5 Tight: 0-4 Gall: 0-1
Aids:	Bl: 0-0 Vi: 0-1 Tstrap: 0-0 Ckp: 0-0
Best Rating:	107 12/00 Ludl 2m soft NHF

Very moderate novice chaser; has been let down by his jumping; acts on soft ground; probably stays 3m.

La Folichonne (FR)

87f   66f

5-y-o b m Useful (FR)-Allure Folle (FR) (Kenmare (FR))

M C Banks Mrs M C Banks

Placings:03 (4780)

2003/04: 16⁰G, 16³S,

	Starts	1st	2nd	3rd	Win & Pl
NH Flat	2	0	0	1	328
Career Total	2	0	0	1	328

Going:	Sf: 0-1 GS: 0-0 Gd: 0-1 GF: - Fm: 0-0
Distance:	2m/2m3: 0-2 2m4-2m7: 0-0 3m+: 0-0
Track:	LH: 0-1 RH: 0-1 Tight: 0-1 Gall: 0-1
Aids:	Bl: 0-0 Vi: 0-0 Tstrap: 0-0 Ckp: 0-0
Best Rating:	66 3/04 Hntg 2m110y good NHF

La Ganadora

5-y-o b m El Conquistador-Discipline (Roman Warrior)

J White Mrs P A White

Placings:0 (3453)

2003/04: 17⁰GS,

	Starts	1st	2nd	3rd	Win & Pl
NH Flat	1	0	0	0	
Career Total	1	0	0	0	

Going:	Sf: 0-0 GS: 0-1 Gd: 0-0 GF: - Fm: 0-0
Distance:	2m/2m3: 0-1 2m4-2m7: 0-0 3m+: 0-0
Track:	LH: 0-0 RH: 0-0 Tight: 0-0 Gall: 0-0
Aids:	Bl: 0-0 Vi: 0-0 Tstrap: 0-0 Ckp: 0-0

La Landiere (FR)

109   (122h)161

9-y-o b/br m Synefos (USA)-As You Are (FR) (Saint Estephe (FR))

R T Phillips Mrs R J Skan

Placings:42112104/0200/5400/21111111-4636 (4427)

2003/04: 20⁴GS, 24⁶G, 21³GS, 21⁶G,

	Starts	1st	2nd	3rd	Win & Pl
Chases	4	0	0	1	10500
Career Total	28	10	4	1	179002
151 3/03 Chel 2m5f A Ch GD £46400					

159 2/03 Kemp 3m A HCh GD £58000
160 1/03 Chel 2m5f B HCh G-S £12818
153 12/02 Kemp 2m4f110yC(0-130)HCh G-S £13392
145 11/02 Winc 2m5f D Ch G-S £5218
127 10/02 Chep 2m3f110yC Ch G-F £10114
97 6/02 MRas 2m4f D Ch G-F £4173
120 2/00 Sand 2m110y D Hdl SFT £3753
129 12/99 Uttx 2m E Hdl SFT £2473
126 12/99 Tntn 2m1f C Hdl G-S £5158
Total win prize-money £161503

Going:	Sf: 0-0 GS: 0-2 Gd: 0-2 GF: - Fm: 0-0
Distance:	2m/2m3: 0-2 2m4-2m7: 0-3 3m+: 0-1
Track:	LH: 0-2 RH: 0-2 Tight: 0-2 Gall: 0-3
Aids:	Bl: 0-0 Vi: 0-0 Tstrap: 0-0 Ckp: 0-0
Best Rating:	160 1/03 Chel 2m5f gd-sft Ch

Smart chaser; rattled up a seven-timer in the 2002/03 season culminating in the Racing Post Chase and Cathcart Chase victories; well beaten at Huntingdon on her reappearance and in the King George, but better run in Cheltenham handicap next time; well beaten in 2004 Cathcart; stays three miles but very effective at shorter; acts on soft and fast ground. Reportedly retired.

La Luna (IRE)

107   95+

7-y-o b m Gothland (FR)-Diane's Glen (Furry Glen)

Noel T Chance Mrs S Rowley-Williams

Placings:0/6|2-103155 (2207)

2003/04: 17¹GF, 17⁰GF, 19³F, 22¹GF, 22⁵GF, 20⁵GS,

	Starts	1st	2nd	3rd	Win & Pl
NH Flat	1	1	0	0	1918
Hurdles	5	1	0	1	4204
Career Total	9	2	1	1	6748
100 10/03 Kels 2m6f110yE Hdl G-F £2968					
84 6/03 MRas 2m1f110yH NHF G-F £1918					
Total win prize-money £4886					

Going:	Sf: 0-0 GS: 0-1 Gd: 0-0 GF: - Fm: 2-5
Distance:	2m/2m3: 1-3 2m4-2m7: 1-3 3m+: 0-0
Track:	LH: 1-1 RH: 1-5 Tight: 2-4 Gall: 0-0
Aids:	Bl: 0-0 Vi: 0-0 Tstrap: 0-0 Ckp: 0-0
Best Rating:	100 10/03 Kels 2m6f110y gd-fm Hdl

Modest hurdler bumper performer; scored at Market Rasen June and over hurdles at Kelso in October 2003; acts on a sound surface.

La Mago

53f   30f

4-y-o b f Wizard King-Dancing Dancer (Niniski (USA))

F P Murtagh Petroman Partnership

Placings:00 (4482)

2003/04: 16⁰G, 17⁰HY,

	Starts	1st	2nd	3rd	Win & Pl
NH Flat	2	0	0	0	
Career Total	2	0	0	0	

Going:	Sf: 0-1 GS: 0-0 Gd: 0-1 GF: - Fm: 0-0
Distance:	2m/2m3: 0-2 2m4-2m7: 0-0 3m+: 0-0
Track:	LH: 0-0 RH: 0-2 Tight: 0-1 Gall: 0-0
Aids:	Bl: 0-0 Vi: 0-0 Tstrap: 0-0 Ckp: 0-0
Best Rating:	30 2/04 Muss 2m good NHF

La Marette

101   85

6-y-o ch m Karinga Bay-Persistent Gunner (Gunner B)

John Allen (R J Hodges 22/2) John Allen

Placings:*0006/5555P5413-004410* (4890)
2003/04: 19^9GF, 16^0G, 16^4G, 19^4HY, 16^1GS, 19^9GF,

	Starts	1st	2nd	3rd	Win & Pl
Hurdles	6	1	0	0	2492
Career Total	19	2	0	1	6888

85	2/04	Towc	2m	G(0-95)HHdl	G-S	£2492
73	4/03	NAbb	2m1f	E Hdl	G-F	£3596

Total win prize-money £6088

Going:	Sf: 0-1 GS: 1-1 Gd: 0-2 GF: - Fm: 0-2
Distance:	2m/2m3: 1-5 2m4-2m7: 0-1 3m+: 0-0
Track:	LH: 0-1 RH: 1-5 Tight: 0-1 Gall: 0-0
Aids:	Bl: 0-0 Vi: 0-0 Tstrap: 0-0 Ckp: 0-0
Best Rating:	85 2/04 Towc 2m gd-sft Hdl

Plating-class novice hurdler; no promise in two starts before lucky winner of maiden hurdle at Newton Abbot in April 2003; stays two miles five; seems to go on most types of ground.

La Muette (IRE)
92   72
4-y-o b f Charnwood Forest (IRE)-Elton Grove (IRE) (Astronef)
M Appleby (Mrs A J Perrett 31/10) Clovers

Placings:PP50 (4251)
2003/04: 16^PHY, 16^PS, 16^5S, 17^0G,

	Starts	1st	2nd	3rd	Win & Pl
Hurdles	4	0	0	0	0
Career Total	4	0	0	0	0

Going:	Sf: 0-3 GS: 0-0 Gd: 0-1 GF: - Fm: 0-0
Distance:	2m/2m3: 0-4 2m4-2m7: 0-0 3m+: 0-0
Track:	LH: 0-4 RH: 0-0 Tight: 0-2 Gall: 0-1
Aids:	Bl: 0-0 Vi: 0-0 Tstrap: 0-0 Ckp: 0-0
Best Rating:	72 3/04 Bang 2m1f good Hdl

La Perrotine (FR)
88f   91f
4-y-o b f Northern Crystal-Haratiyna (Top Ville)
J Howard Johnson Mrs M W Bird

Placings:*26* (4608)
2003/04: 16^2G, 17^6G,

	Starts	1st	2nd	3rd	Win & Pl
NH Flat	2	0	1	0	602
Career Total	2	0	1	0	602

Going:	Sf: 0-0 GS: 0-0 Gd: 0-2 GF: - Fm: 0-0
Distance:	2m/2m3: 0-2 2m4-2m7: 0-0 3m+: 0-0
Track:	LH: 0-1 RH: 0-1 Tight: 0-1 Gall: 0-1
Aids:	Bl: 0-0 Vi: 0-0 Tstrap: 0-0 Ckp: 0-0
Best Rating:	91 3/04 Donc 2m110y good NHF

La Rose
94   72
4-y-o b f Among Men (USA)-Marie La Rose (FR) (Night Shift (USA))
J W Unett V And J Properties

Placings:*2525* (4569)
2003/04: 16^2GF, 16^5G, 16^2GF, 17^5GS,

	Starts	1st	2nd	3rd	Win & Pl
Hurdles	4	0	2	0	1682
Career Total	4	0	2	0	1682

Going:	Sf: 0-0 GS: 0-1 Gd: 0-1 GF: - Fm: 0-2
Distance:	2m/2m3: 0-4 2m4-2m7: 0-0 3m+: 0-0
Track:	LH: 0-2 RH: 0-2 Tight: 0-1 Gall: 0-0
Aids:	Bl: 0-0 Vi: 0-0 Tstrap: 0-0 Ckp: 0-0
Best Rating:	70 11/03 Wwck 2m gd-fm Hdl

Modest form over hurdles so far; acts on a sound surface.

La Vita E Bella (FR)
66   8
5-y-o b m Le Nain Jaune (FR)-Fontaine Aux Faons (FR) (Nadjar (FR))
G F H Charles-Jones (M C Pipe 9/10) Okebrooke Racing

Placings:*40* (4518)
2003/04: 16^4GF, 17^0GS,

	Starts	1st	2nd	3rd	Win & Pl
NH Flat	1	0	0	0	0
Hurdles	1	0	0	0	0
Career Total	2	0	0	0	0

Going:	Sf: 0-0 GS: 0-1 Gd: 0-0 GF: - Fm: 0-1
Distance:	2m/2m3: 0-2 2m4-2m7: 0-0 3m+: 0-0
Track:	LH: 0-0 RH: 0-2 Tight: 0-0 Gall: 0-0
Aids:	Bl: 0-0 Vi: 0-0 Tstrap: 0-0 Ckp: 0-0
Best Rating:	14 3/04 Extr 2m1f gd-sft Hdl

Laazim Afooz
94(99h)   (91 h)92
11-y-o b g Mtoto-Balwa (USA) (Danzig (USA))
R T Phillips Nut Club Partnership

Placings:023/0003121/002/01112F4P/4333433564/332231 560-035 (1842)
2003/04: 27^0GF, 26^3GF, 27^5G,

	Starts	1st	2nd	3rd	Win & Pl
Chases	3	0	0	1	414
Career Total	43	6	6	11	28031

92	10/02	Sedg	3m3f	F(0-100)HCh	GD	£3367
115	8/00	Strf	3m	F(0-105)HCh	G-F	£2941
110	6/00	Worc	2m7f110yE Ch		G-F	£2938
120	6/00	Folk	3m2f	F(0-95)HCh	GD	£2486
104	9/98	NAbb	2m6f	E Hdl	G-F	£2088
99	8/98	NAbb	2m6f	D Hdl	G-F	£2805

Total win prize-money £16627

Going:	Sf: 0-0 GS: 0-0 Gd: 0-1 GF: - Fm: 0-2
Distance:	2m/2m3: 0-0 2m4-2m7: 0-0 3m+: 0-3
Track:	LH: 0-3 RH: 0-0 Tight: 0-0 Gall: 0-0
Aids:	Bl: 0-0 Vi: 0-0 Tstrap: 0-0 Ckp: 0-3
Best Rating:	120 6/00 Folk 3m2f good Ch

Fairly consistent chaser at a low level; suited by three miles and fast ground.

Labelthou (FR)
101   101
5-y-o b m Saint Preuil (FR)-Suzy De Thou (FR) (Toujours Pret (USA))
F Jordan (G Cherel 17/9) Le Tricolore

Placings:*40426* (3265)
2003/04: 19^4VS, 18^0S, 18^4VS, 16^2G, 16^6S,

	Starts	1st	2nd	3rd	Win & Pl
Hurdles	5	0	1	0	6006
Career Total	5	0	1	0	6006

Going:	Sf: 0-2 GS: 0-0 Gd: 0-1 GF: - Fm: 0-0
Distance:	2m/2m3: 0-4 2m4-2m7: 0-0 3m+: 0-0
Track:	LH: 0-1 RH: 0-2 Tight: 0-0 Gall: 0-0
Aids:	Bl: 0-0 Vi: 0-0 Tstrap: 0-0 Ckp: 0-0
Best Rating:	100 1/04 Asct 2m110y soft Hdl

Moderate novice hurdler; effective over two miles; acts on good ground.

Labula Bay
103   114+
10-y-o b g Sula Bula-Lady Barunbe (Deep Run)
B G Powell Richard Cook Limited

Placings:*00PP0/16/3-20331F1* (4820)
2003/04: 25^2GS, 23^9G, 24^3G, 23^3GF, 26^1GF, 28^6G, 25^1GF,

	Starts	1st	2nd	3rd	Win & Pl
Chases	7	2	1	2	12933
Career Total	15	3	1	3	15177

114	4/04	Extr	3m1f110yD(0-115)HCh	G-F	£5785
109	3/04	Font	3m2f110yE(0-110)HCh	G-F	£4390
112	3/02	Fknm	2m5f110yH Ch	GD	£2022

Total win prize-money £12199

Going:	Sf: 0-0 GS: 0-1 Gd: 0-3 GF: - Fm: 2-3
Distance:	2m/2m3: 0-2 2m4-2m7: 0-0 3m+: 2-7
Track:	LH: 0-1 RH: 1-4 Tight: 1-2 Gall: 0-0
Aids:	Bl: 0-0 Vi: 0-0 Tstrap: 0-0 Ckp: 0-0
Best Rating:	114 4/04 Extr 3m1f110y gd-fm Ch

Moderate chaser; former winning pointer; suited by good ground.

Lacdoudal (FR)
104   130
5-y-o gr g Cadoudal (FR)-Belfaster (FR) (Royal Charter (FR))
P J Hobbs (F Nicolle 21/12) Mrs R J Skan

Placings:*3-F11024* (4844)
2003/04: 17^FVS, 16^1HY, 16^1G, 16^9G, 17^2G, 17^4G,

	Starts	1st	2nd	3rd	Win & Pl
Hurdles	6	2	1	0	15103
Career Total	7	2	1	1	16285

130	3/04	Kemp	2m	D Hdl	GD	£5434
	12/03	Pau	2m110y	Hdl	HVY	£7481

Total win prize-money £12915

Going:	Sf: 1-1 GS: 0-0 Gd: 1-4 GF: - Fm: 0-0
Distance:	2m/2m3: 2-6 2m4-2m7: 0-0 3m+: 0-0
Track:	LH: 0-2 RH: 1-2 Tight: 0-0 Gall: 0-1
Aids:	Bl: 0-0 Vi: 0-0 Tstrap: 0-0 Ckp: 0-0
Best Rating:	130 4/04 Extr 2m1f good Hdl

Heavy ground winner of four-year-old hurdle in France in Decmber 2003; good winner on British debut at Kempton in March; effective at two miles, but should stay further; acts on most ground.

Ladalko (FR)
112   118+
5-y-o b g Kadalko (FR)-Debandade (FR) (Le Pontet (FR))
P F Nicholls Paul K Barber & Mrs M Findlay

Placings:*2-1F22* (4545)
2003/04: 16^1GS, 20^2S, 16^2G, 16^2GS,

	Starts	1st	2nd	3rd	Win & Pl
Chases	4	1	2	0	7383
Career Total	5	1	3	0	12993

118	1/04	Folk	2m	F Ch	G-S	£4085

Total win prize-money £4085

Going:	Sf: 0-1 GS: 1-2 Gd: 0-1 GF: - Fm: 0-0
Distance:	2m/2m3: 1-3 2m4-2m7: 0-1 3m+: 0-0
Track:	LH: 0-0 RH: 1-4 Tight: 1-1 Gall: 0-1
Aids:	Bl: 0-0 Vi: 0-0 Tstrap: 0-0 Ckp: 0-0

Best Rating: 118 3/04 Winc 2m gd-sft Ch

Fair novice chaser; ex-French; jumped well when winning on his British debut; took a heavy fall next time; suited by two miles and good ground; should stay 2m 4f; likely to go on to better things.

Ladies From Leeds
66f   26f

5-y-o b m Primitive Rising (USA)-Keldholme (Derek H)
A Crook Stef Stefanou

Placings:00   (3724)
2003/04: 16⁰GS, 16⁰S,

	Starts	1st	2nd	3rd	Win & Pl
NH Flat	2	0	0	0	
Career Total	2	0	0	0	

Going:	Sf: 0-1 GS: 0-1 Gd: 0-0 GF: - Fm: 0-0
Distance:	2m/2m3: 0-2 2m4-2m7: 0-0 3m+: 0-0
Track:	LH: 0-2 RH: 0-0 Tight: 0-0 Gall: 0-0
Aids:	Bl: 0-0 Vi: 0-0 Tstrap: 0-0 Ckp: 0-0
Best Rating:	26 12/03 Newc 2m gd-sft NHF

Lady Alderbrook (IRE)
95f   64f

4-y-o b f Alderbrook-Madame President (IRE) (Supreme Leader)
C J Down Clear Racing

Placings:0   (4213)
2003/04: 16⁰G,

	Starts	1st	2nd	3rd	Win & Pl
NH Flat	1	0	0	0	
Career Total	1	0	0	0	

Going:	Sf: 0-0 GS: 0-0 Gd: 0-1 GF: - Fm: 0-0
Distance:	2m/2m3: 0-1 2m4-2m7: 0-0 3m+: 0-0
Track:	LH: 0-0 RH: 0-1 Tight: 0-0 Gall: 0-0
Aids:	Bl: 0-0 Vi: 0-0 Tstrap: 0-0 Ckp: 0-0
Best Rating:	64 3/04 Kemp 2m good NHF

Lady Arnica

(90h)   (75h)

5-y-o b m Ezzoud (IRE)-Brand (Shareef Dancer (USA))
A W Carroll Roger Clarke

Placings:3002-PPP   (4782)
2003/04: 26⁰GF, 22⁰G, 24⁰G,

	Starts	1st	2nd	3rd	Win & Pl
Hurdles	1	0	0	0	0
Chases	2	0	0	0	0
Career Total	7	0	1	1	1641

Going:	Sf: 0-0 GS: 0-0 Gd: 0-2 GF: - Fm: 0-1
Distance:	2m/2m3: 0-0 2m4-2m7: 0-1 3m+: 0-2
Track:	LH: 0-0 RH: 0-2 Tight: 0-1 Gall: 0-2
Aids:	Bl: 0-0 Vi: 0-0 Tstrap: 0-0 Ckp: 0-0
Best Rating:	75 4/03 Uttx 2m4f110y good Hdl

Plating-class; placed on a couple of occasions; stays two and a half miles; acts on good ground.

Lady At Leisure (IRE)

4-y-o ch f Dolphin Street (FR)-In A Hurry (FR) (In Fijar (USA))
M J Ryan (Julian Poulton 23/3) The Aldora Partnership

Placings:PP   (3511)
2003/04: 16ᴾHY, 18ᴾG,

	Starts	1st	2nd	3rd	Win & Pl
Hurdles	2	0	0	0	
Career Total	2	0	0	0	

Going:	Sf: 0-1 GS: 0-0 Gd: 0-1 GF: - Fm: 0-0
Distance:	2m/2m3: 0-2 2m4-2m7: 0-0 3m+: 0-0
Track:	LH: 0-2 RH: 0-0 Tight: 0-1 Gall: 0-0
Aids:	Bl: 0-0 Vi: 0-0 Tstrap: 0-0 Ckp: 0-0

Lady Baronette

7-y-o b m Baron Blakeney-Rueful Lady (Streetfighter)
Andrew J Martin Mrs David Plunkett

Placings:R   (4823)
2003/04: 23ᴿGF,

	Starts	1st	2nd	3rd	Win & Pl
Chases	1	0	0	0	
Career Total	1	0	0	0	

Going:	Sf: 0-0 GS: 0-0 Gd: 0-0 GF: - Fm: 0-1
Distance:	2m/2m3: 0-0 2m4-2m7: 0-0 3m+: 0-1
Track:	LH: 0-0 RH: 0-1 Tight: 0-0 Gall: 0-0
Aids:	Bl: 0-0 Vi: 0-0 Tstrap: 0-0 Ckp: 0-0

Lady Blaze
58f   33f

5-y-o ch m Alflora (IRE)-Lady Elle (IRE) (Persian Mews)
Mrs G Harvey Ms Pat Treacy

Placings:0   (4407)
2003/04: 16⁰G,

	Starts	1st	2nd	3rd	Win & Pl
NH Flat	1	0	0	0	
Career Total	1	0	0	0	

Going:	Sf: 0-0 GS: 0-0 Gd: 0-1 GF: - Fm: 0-0
Distance:	2m/2m3: 0-1 2m4-2m7: 0-0 3m+: 0-0
Track:	LH: 0-0 RH: 0-0 Tight: 0-0 Gall: 0-1
Aids:	Bl: 0-0 Vi: 0-0 Tstrap: 0-0 Ckp: 0-0
Best Rating:	33 3/04 Hntg 2m110y good NHF

Lady Bob Back
97(96h)   (83h)79

7-y-o br m Bob Back (USA)-Whimbrel (Dara Monarch)
M A Barnes John Wills

Placings:60540/5P25603-64PUF005   (4794)
2003/04: 20ᴿG, 21⁴GS, 24ᴾHY, 20ᴜG, 21ᶠGS, 24⁰GF, 17⁰G, 21⁵G,

	Starts	1st	2nd	3rd	Win & Pl
Hurdles	5	0	0	0	259
Chases	3	0	0	0	0
Career Total	20	0	1	1	2146

Going:	Sf: 0-1 GS: 0-2 Gd: 0-4 GF: - Fm: 0-1

Lady Bouncer

6-y-o b m Milieu-Superior Maid (Gay Fandango (USA))
G F Bridgwater (C Grant 14/6) Mrs Gail Bridgwater

Placings:P0   (4345)
2003/04: 16ᴾGF, 16⁰GS,

	Starts	1st	2nd	3rd	Win & Pl
NH Flat	2	0	0	0	
Career Total	2	0	0	0	

Going:	Sf: 0-0 GS: 0-1 Gd: 0-0 GF: - Fm: 0-1
Distance:	2m/2m3: 0-2 2m4-2m7: 0-0 3m+: 0-0
Track:	LH: 0-2 RH: 0-0 Tight: 0-0 Gall: 0-0
Aids:	Bl: 0-0 Vi: 0-0 Tstrap: 0-0 Ckp: 0-0

Lady Busted

9-y-o b m Almoojid-Sindos (Busted)
D Burchell R A Hughes

Placings:30/P   (3966)
2003/04: 16ᴾGS,

	Starts	1st	2nd	3rd	Win & Pl
Hurdles	1	0	0	0	
Career Total	3	0	0	1	211

Going:	Sf: 0-0 GS: 0-1 Gd: 0-0 GF: - Fm: 0-0
Distance:	2m/2m3: 0-1 2m4-2m7: 0-0 3m+: 0-0
Track:	LH: 0-0 RH: 0-1 Tight: 0-0 Gall: 0-0
Aids:	Bl: 0-0 Vi: 0-0 Tstrap: 0-0 Ckp: 0-0
Best Rating:	80 3/99 Newc 2m soft NHF

Lady Dynamite
92f   87f

4-y-o b f Glacial Storm (USA)-Lady Elle (IRE) (Persian Mews)
H D Daly C G Johnson

Placings:20   (4846)
2003/04: 16²GS, 17⁰G,

	Starts	1st	2nd	3rd	Win & Pl
NH Flat	2	0	1	0	558
Career Total	2	0	1	0	558

Going:	Sf: 0-0 GS: 0-1 Gd: 0-1 GF: - Fm: 0-0
Distance:	2m/2m3: 0-2 2m4-2m7: 0-0 3m+: 0-0
Track:	LH: 0-1 RH: 0-1 Tight: 0-0 Gall: 0-1
Aids:	Bl: 0-0 Vi: 0-0 Tstrap: 0-0 Ckp: 0-0
Best Rating:	87 4/04 Chel 2m1f good NHF

Lady Felix
96(93h)   (120h)97

9-y-o br m Batshoof-Volcalmeh (Lidhame)
R H Alner J P M & J W Cook

Placings:455B41/1132201/42-4   (0212)
2003/04: 23⁴G,

	Starts	1st	2nd	3rd	Win & Pl
Chases	1	0	0	0	439
Career Total	16	4	3	1	22327
120 4/01 Kemp 3m110y C(0-130)HHdl				GD	£7441
112 6/00 MRas 3m E Hdl				G-S	£2455
110 5/00 MRas 3m D Hdl				G-F	£3096
99 4/00 Ludl 3m E Hdl				G-S	£2796
				Total win prize-money	£15791

Going:	Sf: 0-0 GS: 0-0 Gd: 0-0 GF: 0-1 GF: - Fm: 0-0
Distance:	2m/2m3: 0-2 2m4-2m7: 0-0 3m+: 0-0
Track:	LH: 0-1 RH: 0-0 Tight: 0-0 Gall: 0-0
Aids:	Bl: 0-0 Vi: 0-0 Tstrap: 0-0 Ckp: 0-0
Best Rating:	120 4/01 Kemp 3m110y good Hdl

Fair hurdler/novice chaser; runner-up on chase debut at Stratford in April 2003; stays well; seems to go on all types of ground.

Lady Glyde

4-y-o b f Inchinor-Happy And Blessed (IRE) (Prince Sabo)
A D Smith David M Williams

Placings:P (1673)
2003/04: 16PF,

	Starts	1st	2nd	3rd	Win & Pl
Hurdles	1	0	0	0	
Career Total	1	0	0	0	

Going:	Sf: 0-0 GS: 0-0 Gd: 0-0 GF: - Fm: 0-1
Distance:	2m/2m3: 0-1 2m4-2m7: 0-0 3m+: 0-0
Track:	LH: 0-0 RH: 0-0 Tight: 0-0 Gall: 0-0
Aids:	Bl: 0-0 Vi: 0-0 Tstrap: 0-0 Ckp: 0-0

Lady Godson
77f   65f
5-y-o ch m Bold Arrangement-Dreamy Desire (Palm Track)
B Mactaggart B Mactaggart

Placings:00 (4886)
2003/04: 16OS, 17OGS,

	Starts	1st	2nd	3rd	Win & Pl
NH Flat	2	0	0	0	
Career Total	2	0	0	0	

Going:	Sf: 0-1 GS: 0-1 Gd: 0-0 GF: - Fm: 0-0
Distance:	2m/2m3: 0-2 2m4-2m7: 0-0 3m+: 0-0
Track:	LH: 0-1 RH: 0-1 Tight: 0-0 Gall: 0-0
Aids:	Bl: 0-0 Vi: 0-0 Tstrap: 0-0 Ckp: 0-0
Best Rating:	65 11/03 Ayr 2m soft NHF

Lady Harriet
101   92+
5-y-o b m Sir Harry Lewis (USA)-Forever Together (Hawaiian Return (USA))
N J Gifford The Brabourne Partnership

Placings:0010P0 (4892)
2003/04: 16OS, 16OS, 16IS, 16OG, 16PGS, 16OGF,

	Starts	1st	2nd	3rd	Win & Pl
NH Flat	2	0	0	0	0
Hurdles	4	1	0	0	3474
Career Total	6	1	0	0	3474
92 2/04 Plum 2m E Hdl				SFT	£3474
				Total win prize-money	£3474

Going:	Sf: 1-3 GS: 0-1 Gd: 0-1 GF: - Fm: 0-1
Distance:	2m/2m3: 1-6 2m4-2m7: 0-0 3m+: 0-0
Track:	LH: 1-2 RH: 0-4 Tight: 1-2 Gall: 0-1
Aids:	Bl: 0-0 Vi: 0-0 Tstrap: 0-0 Ckp: 0-0
Best Rating:	92 2/04 Plum 2m soft Hdl

Plating-class hurdler; acts on soft.

Lady Heccles
57f   37f
5-y-o b m Sayaarr (USA)-Rae Un Soleil (Rushmere)
M R Hoad Phil Collins

Placings:0 (3426)
2003/04: 17OHY,

	Starts	1st	2nd	3rd	Win & Pl
NH Flat	1	0	0	0	
Career Total	1	0	0	0	

Going:	Sf: 0-1 GS: 0-0 Gd: 0-0 GF: - Fm: 0-0
Distance:	2m/2m3: 0-1 2m4-2m7: 0-0 3m+: 0-0
Track:	LH: 0-0 RH: 0-1 Tight: 0-1 Gall: 0-0
Aids:	Bl: 0-0 Vi: 0-0 Tstrap: 0-0 Ckp: 0-0
Best Rating:	37 1/04 Folk 2m1f110y heavy NHF

Lady In Command (IRE)

4-y-o b f In Command (IRE)-Harmer (IRE) (Alzao (USA))
Mrs J Candlish (R M Beckett 30/7) Mrs J M Phillips

Placings:PP (1603)
2003/04: 17OGF, 17PGF,

	Starts	1st	2nd	3rd	Win & Pl
Hurdles	2	0	0	0	
Career Total	2	0	0	0	

Going:	Sf: 0-0 GS: 0-0 Gd: 0-0 GF: - Fm: 0-2
Distance:	2m/2m3: 0-2 2m4-2m7: 0-0 3m+: 0-0
Track:	LH: 0-0 RH: 0-2 Tight: 0-1 Gall: 0-0
Aids:	Bl: 0-0 Vi: 0-0 Tstrap: 0-0 Ckp: 0-0

Lady Inch
37
6-y-o b m Inchinor-Head Turner (My Dad Tom (USA))
J A Supple The Dyball Partnership

Placings:60/PPP-P (1756)
2003/04: 16PG,

	Starts	1st	2nd	3rd	Win & Pl
Hurdles	1	0	0	0	
Career Total	6	0	0	0	0

Going:	Sf: 0-0 GS: 0-0 Gd: 0-0 GF: 0-1 GF: - Fm: 0-0
Distance:	2m/2m3: 0-1 2m4-2m7: 0-0 3m+: 0-0
Track:	LH: 0-1 RH: 0-0 Tight: 0-1 Gall: 0-0
Aids:	Bl: 0-0 Vi: 0-0 Tstrap: 0-0 Ckp: 0-1
Best Rating:	37 8/01 Strf 2m110y good Hdl

Lady Janal
96   76
6-y-o gr m Sir Harry Lewis (USA)-Mrs Dawson (Sharrood (USA))
Miss S E Forster A G & Mrs E J Bell

Placings:4-0066F35030 (4612)
2003/04: 16AG, 16OG, 16OGF, 20OG, 22OS, 24FS, 21OGS, 20OHY, 24OGS, 21OG, 21OG,

	Starts	1st	2nd	3rd	Win & Pl
NH Flat	1	0	0	0	0
Hurdles	10	0	0	2	1032
Career Total	11	0	0	2	1032

Going:	Sf: 0-3 GS: 0-2 Gd: 0-5 GF: - Fm: 0-1
Distance:	2m/2m3: 0-3 2m4-2m7: 0-6 3m+: 0-2
Track:	LH: 0-9 RH: 0-2 Tight: 0-5 Gall: 0-1
Aids:	Bl: 0-0 Vi: 0-0 Tstrap: 0-0 Ckp: 0-0
Best Rating:	76 2/04 Newc 2m4f heavy Hdl

Poor form in bumpers and novices' hurdles; stays two miles six; handles heavy ground.

Lady Lambrini
52f
4-y-o b f Overbury (IRE)-Miss Lambrini (Henbit (USA))
Mrs L Williamson Halewood International Ltd

Placings:0 (2387)
2003/04: 14OG,

	Starts	1st	2nd	3rd	Win & Pl
NH Flat	1	0	0	0	
Career Total	1	0	0	0	

Going:	Sf: 0-0 GS: 0-0 Gd: 0-0 GF: - Fm: 0-0
Distance:	2m/2m3: 0-0 2m4-2m7: 0-0 3m+: 0-0
Track:	LH: 0-0 RH: 0-0 Tight: 0-0 Gall: 0-0
Aids:	Bl: 0-0 Vi: 0-0 Tstrap: 0-0 Ckp: 0-0
Best Rating:	52 11/03 Wwck 1m6f good NHF

Well in rear in bumper on debut.

Lady Lap Dancer
87   90+
6-y-o b m Shareef Dancer (USA)-Jelabna (Jalmood (USA))
R C Harper R C Harper

Placings:4361P23-5P (1572)
2003/04: 20SF, 21PF,

	Starts	1st	2nd	3rd	Win & Pl
Hurdles	2	0	0	0	
Career Total	9	1	1	2	4526
90 11/02 Kels 2m110y G Hdl				SFT	£2257
				Total win prize-money	£2258

Going:	Sf: 0-0 GS: 0-0 Gd: 0-0 GF: - Fm: 0-2
Distance:	2m/2m3: 0-0 2m4-2m7: 0-2 3m+: 0-0
Track:	LH: 0-1 RH: 0-1 Tight: 0-0 Gall: 0-0
Aids:	Bl: 0-0 Vi: 0-0 Tstrap: 0-0 Ckp: 0-0
Best Rating:	90 3/03 Hexm 2m4f110y good Hdl

Moderate hurdler; got off the mark in a a seller over two miles at Kelso; showed improved form over further when placed at Hexham and Kelso; acts on good and soft.

Lady Laureate
89   83d
6-y-o b m Sir Harry Lewis (USA)-Cyrillic (Rock City)
G C Bravery Blackfoot Bloodstock

Placings:64/043PP-232 (1694)
2003/04: 22OG, 21OGF, 19OGF,

	Starts	1st	2nd	3rd	Win & Pl
Hurdles	3	0	2	1	3037
Career Total	10	0	2	2	13137

Going:	Sf: 0-0 GS: 0-0 Gd: 0-0 GF: - Fm: 0-3
Distance:	2m/2m3: 0-0 2m4-2m7: 0-3 3m+: 0-0

Track: LH: 0-2 RH: 0-1 Tight: 0-2 Gall: 0-0
Aids: Bl: 0-0 Vi: 0-0 Tstrap: 0-0 Ckp: 0-0
Best Rating: 120 4/02 Aint 2m110y good Hdl

Moderate hurdler; four times a winner on the level; has been highly tried at times and still looking for her first win; seems best suited by a sound surface; stays 2m 5f; one to have doubts about.

Lady Lighthouse
87f   67f
6-y-o b m Alhijaz-Fairfield's Breeze (Buckskin (FR))
R J Price Derek & Cheryl Holder

Placings:0-0P   (2697)
2003/04: 16⁰GF, 16⁰G,

	Starts	1st	2nd	3rd	Win & Pl
NH Flat	2	0	0	0	
Career Total	3	0	0	0	

Going: Sf: 0-0 GS: 0-0 Gd: 0-1 GF: - Fm: 0-1
Distance: 2m/2m3: 0-2 2m4-2m7: 0-0 3m+: 0-0
Track: LH: 0-1 RH: 0-1 Tight: 0-0 Gall: 0-0
Aids: Bl: 0-0 Vi: 0-0 Tstrap: 0-0 Ckp: 0-0
Best Rating: 67 11/03 Worc 2m gd-fm NHF

Lady Lola (IRE)
87f   77+f
6-y-o b m Supreme Leader-Regents Prancer (Prince Regent (FR))
C J Mann Simon Moyes & Charlie Mann

Placings:406   (4780)
2003/04: 17⁴GS, 16⁰GS, 16⁶S,

	Starts	1st	2nd	3rd	Win & Pl
NH Flat	3	0	0	0	0
Career Total	3	0	0	0	0

Going: Sf: 0-1 GS: 0-2 Gd: 0-0 GF: - Fm: 0-0
Distance: 2m/2m3: 0-3 2m4-2m7: 0-0 3m+: 0-0
Track: LH: 0-2 RH: 0-1 Tight: 0-2 Gall: 0-0
Aids: Bl: 0-0 Vi: 0-0 Tstrap: 0-0 Ckp: 0-0
Best Rating: 77 12/03 Folk 2m1f110y gd-sft NHF

Lady Maranzi
94   75
5-y-o b m Teenoso (USA)-Maranzi (Jimmy Reppin)
Mrs D A Hamer Mrs D A Hamer

Placings:60   (3843)
2003/04: 16⁶G, 19⁰GS,

	Starts	1st	2nd	3rd	Win & Pl
Hurdles	2	0	0	0	0
Career Total	2	0	0	0	0

Going: Sf: 0-0 GS: 0-1 Gd: 0-1 GF: - Fm: 0-0
Distance: 2m/2m3: 0-1 2m4-2m7: 0-1 3m+: 0-0
Track: LH: 0-0 RH: 0-2 Tight: 0-0 Gall: 0-0
Aids: Bl: 0-0 Vi: 0-0 Tstrap: 0-0 Ckp: 0-0
Best Rating: 75 11/03 Towc 2m good Hdl

Lady Matador
71f   57f
5-y-o b m El Conquistador-Slashing (Broadsword (USA))
Mrs Jane Galpin G S Moore

Placings:5   (3264)
2003/04: 16⁵HY,

	Starts	1st	2nd	3rd	Win & Pl
NH Flat	1	0	0	0	0
Career Total	1	0	0	0	0

Going: Sf: 0-1 GS: 0-0 Gd: 0-0 GF: - Fm: 0-0
Distance: 2m/2m3: 0-1 2m4-2m7: 0-0 3m+: 0-0
Track: LH: 0-0 RH: 0-1 Tight: 0-0 Gall: 0-0
Aids: Bl: 0-0 Vi: 0-0 Tstrap: 0-0 Ckp: 0-0
Best Rating: 57 1/04 Towc 2m heavy NHF

Lady Mercury
86   66
6-y-o b m Rock Hopper-Bellezza (Ardross)
S C Burrough Allen And Bowler

Placings:PPP0P-460P0   (3467)
2003/04: 16⁴G, 16⁶GF, 19⁰G, 16⁰G, 16⁰S,

	Starts	1st	2nd	3rd	Win & Pl
Hurdles	5	0	0	0	0
Career Total	10	0	0	0	0

Going: Sf: 0-1 GS: 0-0 Gd: 0-0 GF: - Fm: 0-1
Distance: 2m/2m3: 0-4 2m4-2m7: 0-1 3m+: 0-0
Track: LH: 0-2 RH: 0-3 Tight: 0-2 Gall: 0-0
Aids: Bl: 0-1 Vi: 0-0 Tstrap: 0-1 Ckp: 0-0
Best Rating: 65 10/03 Strf 2m110y good Hdl

Lady Netbetsports (IRE)
99   69
5-y-o b m In The Wings-Auntie Maureen (IRE) (Roi Danzig (USA))
B S Rothwell Paul Moorhouse

Placings:6F-100   (3233)
2003/04: 19¹GF, 20⁰G, 20⁰GF,

	Starts	1st	2nd	3rd	Win & Pl
Hurdles	3	1	0	0	
Career Total	5	1	0	0	0

Going: Sf: 0-0 GS: 0-0 Gd: 0-0 GF: - Fm: 1-2
Distance: 2m/2m3: 1-1 2m4-2m7: 0-2 3m+: 0-0
Track: LH: 1-2 RH: 0-1 Tight: 1-2 Gall: 0-0
Aids: Bl: 0-0 Vi: 0-0 Tstrap: 0-0 Ckp: 0-0
Best Rating: 75 11/03 Catt 2m3f gd-fm Hdl

Plating-class hurdler; dead-heated in poor mares' only novices' hurdle at Catterick in November; suited by two and a half miles.

Lady Of Fortune (IRE)
100f   108+f
5-y-o b m Sovereign Water (FR)-Needwood Fortune (Tycoon Ii)
N J Henderson Gary Stewart

Placings:10   (4328)
2003/04: 17¹GS, 16⁰S,

	Starts	1st	2nd	3rd	Win & Pl
NH Flat	2	1	0	0	2650
Career Total	2	1	0	0	2650
108 1/04 Tntn 2m1f H NHF				G-S	£2649
Total win prize-money £2650					

Going: Sf: 0-1 GS: 1-1 Gd: 0-0 GF: - Fm: 0-0
Distance: 2m/2m3: 1-2 2m4-2m7: 0-0 3m+: 0-0
Track: LH: 0-0 RH: 0-1 Tight: 0-0 Gall: 0-0
Aids: Bl: 0-0 Vi: 0-0 Tstrap: 0-0 Ckp: 0-0
Best Rating: 108 1/04 Tntn 2m1f gd-sft NHF

A half-sister to top-class stayer Lady Rebecca; did it nicely when winning on her debut at Taunton and can only improve; will obviously get further over hurdles; acts on easy going.

Lady Of The Isle (IRE)
54   28
6-y-o b m Aristocracy-Smurfette (Baptism)
B D Leavy (G B Balding 21/5) Mrs Alurie O'Sullivan

Placings:0060   (4630)
2003/04: 16⁶G, 16⁰S, 16⁶S, 17⁹G,

	Starts	1st	2nd	3rd	Win & Pl
NH Flat	3	0	0	0	0
Hurdles	1	0	0	0	0
Career Total	4	0	0	0	0

Going: Sf: 0-2 GS: 0-0 Gd: 0-2 GF: - Fm: 0-0
Distance: 2m/2m3: 0-4 2m4-2m7: 0-0 3m+: 0-0
Track: LH: 0-3 RH: 0-1 Tight: 0-1 Gall: 0-0
Aids: Bl: 0-0 Vi: 0-0 Tstrap: 0-0 Ckp: 0-0
Best Rating: 78 1/04 Weth 2m soft NHF

Lady Racquet (IRE)
98f   95f
5-y-o b m Glacial Storm (USA)-Kindly Light (IRE) (Supreme Leader)
Mrs A J Bowlby The Norman Partnership

Placings:0-305   (4846)
2003/04: 17³S, 16⁰S, 17⁵G,

	Starts	1st	2nd	3rd	Win & Pl
NH Flat	3	0	0	1	372
Career Total	4	0	0	1	372

Going: Sf: 0-2 GS: 0-0 Gd: 0-1 GF: - Fm: 0-0
Distance: 2m/2m3: 0-3 2m4-2m7: 0-0 3m+: 0-0
Track: LH: 0-1 RH: 0-1 Tight: 0-0 Gall: 0-1
Aids: Bl: 0-0 Vi: 0-0 Tstrap: 0-0 Ckp: 0-0
Best Rating: 95 4/04 Chel 2m1f good NHF

Improved on debut effort when third at Taunton; will stay further over hurdles; acts on most ground.

Lady Shanan (IRE)
60f   44f
4-y-o b f Anshan-Cothill Lady (IRE) (Orchestra)
D A Rees D A Rees & P Harris

Placings:0   (4543)
2003/04: 16⁰GS,

	Starts	1st	2nd	3rd	Win & Pl
NH Flat	1	0	0	0	
Career Total	1	0	0	0	

Going: Sf: 0-0 GS: 0-1 Gd: 0-0 GF: - Fm: 0-0
Distance: 2m/2m3: 0-1 2m4-2m7: 0-0 3m+: 0-0
Track: LH: 0-0 RH: 0-1 Tight: 0-0 Gall: 0-0
Aids: Bl: 0-0 Vi: 0-0 Tstrap: 0-0 Ckp: 0-0
Best Rating: 44 3/04 Ludl 2m gd-sft NHF

Lady Solrski

(19h)

7-y-o b m Petoski-Flaxen Tina (Beau Tudor)
A C Whillans Solway Racing Syndicate

Placings:600/PPP-P   (0410)
2003/04: 20³G,

	Starts	1st	2nd	3rd	Win & Pl
Chases	1	0	0	0	
Career Total	7	0	0	0	0

Going:	Sf: 0-0 GS: 0-0 Gd: 0-1 GF: - Fm: 0-0
Distance:	2m/2m3: 0-0 2m4-2m7: 0-1 3m+: 0-0
Track:	LH: 0-1 RH: 0-0 Tight: 0-1 Gall: 0-0
Aids:	Bl: 0-0 Vi: 0-0 Tstrap: 0-0 Ckp: 0-0
Best Rating:	88 3/02 Ayr 2m heavy NHF

Lady Stratagem

95   73

5-y-o gr m Mark Of Esteem (IRE)-Grey Angel (Kenmare (FR))
E W Tuer E Tuer

Placings:1P00P-P5654065   (3691)
2003/04: 20⁵F, 16⁵F, 16⁶GF, 16⁵GS, 16⁴GS, 16⁰GS, 16⁶G, 19⁵G,

	Starts	1st	2nd	3rd	Win & Pl
Hurdles	8	0	0	0	0
Career Total	13	1	0	0	3874
82 10/02 Kels	2m110y D Hdl		G-F		£3874
			Total win prize-money £3874		

Going:	Sf: 0-0 GS: 0-2 Gd: 0-2 GF: - Fm: 0-4
Distance:	2m/2m3: 0-7 2m4-2m7: 0-1 3m+: 0-0
Track:	LH: 0-7 RH: 0-0 Tight: 0-3 Gall: 0-0
Aids:	Bl: 0-0 Vi: 0-0 Tstrap: 0-0 Ckp: 0-0
Best Rating:	82 10/02 Kels 2m110y gd-fm Hdl

Plating-class hurdler; acts on fast.

Lady Ward (IRE)

109   82

6-y-o b m Mujadil (USA)-Sans Ceriph (IRE) (Thatching)
P R Rodford (S C Burrough 21/6) Les Trott

Placings:51/322332206040-41P00P   (2817)
2003/04: 17⁴G, 17¹GF, 17⁰GF, 16⁹GS, 19⁰G, 22⁰G,

	Starts	1st	2nd	3rd	Win & Pl
Hurdles	6	1	0	0	3010
Career Total	20	2	4	3	9333
82 6/03 NAbb	2m1f	G(0-95)HHdl	G-F		£3010
71 4/02 Hrfd	2m1f	G Hdl	G-F		£2107
			Total win prize-money £5117		

Going:	Sf: 0-0 GS: 0-1 Gd: 0-3 GF: - Fm: 1-2
Distance:	2m/2m3: 1-4 2m4-2m7: 0-2 3m+: 0-0
Track:	LH: 1-4 RH: 0-0 Tight: 1-4 Gall: 0-0
Aids:	Bl: 0-1 Vi: 0-0 Tstrap: 0-0 Ckp: 0-0
Best Rating:	82 6/03 NAbb 2m1f gd-fm Hdl

Plating class hurdler; won amateur riders seller at Newton Abbot June 2003; suited to waiting tactics; best at around 2m; likes good to firm ground.

Lady West

4-y-o b f The West (USA)-Just Run (IRE) (Runnett)
Dr J R J Naylor Dr J R J Naylor

Placings:P   (4489)
2003/04: 16⁰G,

	Starts	1st	2nd	3rd	Win & Pl
Hurdles	1	0	0	0	
Career Total	1	0	0	0	

Going:	Sf: 0-0 GS: 0-0 Gd: 0-1 GF: - Fm: 0-0
Distance:	2m/2m3: 0-1 2m4-2m7: 0-0 3m+: 0-0
Track:	LH: 0-1 RH: 0-0 Tight: 0-1 Gall: 0-0
Aids:	Bl: 0-0 Vi: 0-0 Tstrap: 0-1 Ckp: 0-0

Lady Wurzel

5-y-o b m Dilum (USA)-Fly The Wind (Windjammer (USA))
W S Kittow Mrs Pam Pengelly

Placings:0P   (2691)
2003/04: 17⁹GF, 16⁵G,

	Starts	1st	2nd	3rd	Win & Pl
NH Flat	1	0	0	0	0
Hurdles	1	0	0	0	0
Career Total	2	0	0	0	

Going:	Sf: 0-0 GS: 0-0 Gd: 0-1 GF: - Fm: 0-1
Distance:	2m/2m3: 0-2 2m4-2m7: 0-0 3m+: 0-0
Track:	LH: 0-1 RH: 0-0 Tight: 0-1 Gall: 0-0
Aids:	Bl: 0-0 Vi: 0-0 Tstrap: 0-0 Ckp: 0-0
Best Rating:	12 9/03 NAbb 2m1f gd-fm NHF

Lady Zephyr (IRE)

100f   110+f

6-y-o b m Toulon-Sorimak Gale (IRE) (Strong Gale)
N A Twiston-Davies N A Twiston-Davies

Placings:31   (4780)
2003/04: 17³G, 16¹S,

	Starts	1st	2nd	3rd	Win & Pl
NH Flat	2	1	0	1	2562
Career Total	2	1	0	1	2562
110 4/04 Fknm	2m	H NHF	SFT		£2296
			Total win prize-money £2296		

Going:	Sf: 1-1 GS: 0-0 Gd: 0-1 GF: - Fm: 0-0
Distance:	2m/2m3: 1-2 2m4-2m7: 0-0 3m+: 0-0
Track:	LH: 1-1 RH: 0-0 Tight: 1-2 Gall: 0-0
Aids:	Bl: 0-0 Vi: 0-0 Tstrap: 0-0 Ckp: 0-0
Best Rating:	110 4/04 Fknm 2m soft NHF

Bumper winner; winning pointer in Ireland; handles soft ground; has a bright future.

Ladyalder

6-y-o br m Alderbrook-Ina's Farewell (Random Shot)
L J Williams L J Williams

Placings:P   (0239)
2003/04: 17⁰G,

	Starts	1st	2nd	3rd	Win & Pl
NH Flat	1	0	0	0	
Career Total	1	0	0	0	

Going:	Sf: 0-0 GS: 0-0 Gd: 0-1 GF: - Fm: 0-0
Distance:	2m/2m3: 0-1 2m4-2m7: 0-0 3m+: 0-0
Track:	LH: 0-0 RH: 0-1 Tight: 0-0 Gall: 0-0
Aids:	Bl: 0-0 Vi: 0-0 Tstrap: 0-0 Ckp: 0-0

Laganside (IRE)

11-y-o b g Montelimar (USA)-Ruby Girl (Crash Course)
J F W Muir J F W Muir

Placings:106313/1P4/266451P/P-64P   (4949)
2003/04: 25⁶G, 25⁴G, 26⁰GS,

	Starts	1st	2nd	3rd	Win & Pl
Chases	3	0	1	2	
Career Total	20	4	1	2	20090
112 12/01 Muss	3m	D(0-120)HCh	GD		£6126
120 5/00 Prth	2m4f110yE(0-115)HCh		GD		£4940
109 12/99 Muss	2m4f	E Ch	G-S		£4221
82 5/99 Dpat	2m1f172y Hdl		G-F		£1994
			Total win prize-money £17282		

Going:	Sf: 0-0 GS: 0-1 Gd: 0-2 GF: - Fm: 0-0
Distance:	2m/2m3: 0-0 2m4-2m7: 0-0 3m+: 0-3
Track:	LH: 0-2 RH: 0-0 Tight: 0-2 Gall: 0-0
Aids:	Bl: 0-0 Vi: 0-0 Tstrap: 0-0 Ckp: 0-0
Best Rating:	120 5/01 Prth 2m4f110y gd-sft Ch

Former fair chaser, winning pointer in 2003; stays three miles and seems to handle most ground; suited by a sharp, right-handed track.

Lager Dash

62f   8f

6-y-o b g Suave Dancer (USA)-Padelia (Thatching)
R J Price E G Bevan

Placings:P-0   (1817)
2003/04: 17⁰G,

	Starts	1st	2nd	3rd	Win & Pl
NH Flat	1	0	0	0	
Career Total	2	0	0	0	

Going:	Sf: 0-0 GS: 0-0 Gd: 0-0 GF: - Fm: 0-0
Distance:	2m/2m3: 0-1 2m4-2m7: 0-0 3m+: 0-0
Track:	LH: 0-1 RH: 0-0 Tight: 0-1 Gall: 0-0
Aids:	Bl: 0-0 Vi: 0-0 Tstrap: 0-0 Ckp: 0-0
Best Rating:	9 10/03 Bang 2m1f good NHF

Laggan Bay (IRE)

88   75

4-y-o b g Alzao (USA)-Green Lucia (Green Dancer (USA))
J C Fox (R Hannon 14/7) Mitchell Block

Placings:0   (2669)
2003/04: 16⁰GF,

	Starts	1st	2nd	3rd	Win & Pl
Hurdles	1	0	0	0	
Career Total	1	0	0	0	

Going:	Sf: 0-0 GS: 0-0 Gd: 0-0 GF: - Fm: 0-1
Distance:	2m/2m3: 0-1 2m4-2m7: 0-0 3m+: 0-0
Track:	LH: 0-1 RH: 0-0 Tight: 0-0 Gall: 0-1
Aids:	Bl: 0-0 Vi: 0-0 Tstrap: 0-0 Ckp: 0-0
Best Rating:	75 12/03 Newb 2m110y gd-fm Hdl

Laggan Minstrel (IRE)

6-y-o b g Mark Of Esteem (IRE)-Next Episode (USA) (Nijinsky (CAN))
B Llewellyn (P A Blockley 3/2) Mrs M Llewellyn

Placings:PP (4714)
2003/04: 17²G, 16²G,

	Starts	1st	2nd	3rd	Win & Pl
Hurdles	2	0	0	0	
Career Total	2	0	0	0	

Going: Sf: 0-0 GS: 0-0 Gd: 0-2 GF: - Fm: 0-0
Distance: 2m/2m3: 0-2 2m4-2m7: 0-0 3m+: 0-0
Track: LH: 0-0 RH: 0-2 Tight: 0-0 Gall: 0-0
Aids: Bl: 0-0 Vi: 0-0 Tstrap: 0-0 Ckp: 0-0

Lago
102   90
6-y-o b g Maelstrom Lake-Jugendliebe (IRE) (Persian Bold)
James Moffatt Bernard Bargh, Jeff Hamer, Steve Henshaw

Placings:6B0603/04262 (4690)
2003/04: 16⁶S, 17⁴GS, 22²GS, 24⁴HY, 22²G,

	Starts	1st	2nd	3rd	Win & Pl
Hurdles	5	0	2	0	2476
Career Total	11	0	2	1	2947

Going: Sf: 0-2 GS: 0-2 Gd: 0-1 GF: - Fm: 0-0
Distance: 2m/2m3: 0-2 2m4-2m7: 0-2 3m+: 0-1
Track: LH: 0-3 RH: 0-2 Tight: 0-3 Gall: 0-0
Aids: Bl: 0-0 Vi: 0-1 Tstrap: 0-0 Ckp: 0-3
Best Rating: 92 3/04 Kels 2m6f110y gd-sft Hdl

Plating-class hurdler; turned in improved effort over hurdles (looked unlucky) when upped in trip to 2m6f at Kelso in March 2004; acts on good or easy ground.

Lago D'Oro
98f   79f
4-y-o b f Slip Anchor-Salala (Connaught)
Miss J A Camacho Mrs S Camacho

Placings:423 (4663)
2003/04: 13⁴GF, 17²GS, 16³S,

	Starts	1st	2nd	3rd	Win & Pl
NH Flat	3	0	1	1	851
Career Total	3	0	1	1	851

Going: Sf: 0-1 GS: 0-1 Gd: 0-0 GF: - Fm: 0-0
Distance: 2m/2m3: 0-2 2m4-2m7: 0-0 3m+: 0-0
Track: LH: 0-2 RH: 0-0 Tight: 0-1 Gall: 0-0
Aids: Bl: 0-0 Vi: 0-1 Tstrap: 0-0 Ckp: 0-0
Best Rating: 77 4/04 Hexm 2m110y soft NHF

Half-sister to winning hurdler Mindanao; promising fourth on bumper debut and ran well in defeat at Sedgefield and Hexham; likely to be suited by further than two miles when sent over hurdles.

Lago Nam (FR)
5-y-o gr g Cardoun (FR)-Rivalago (FR) (Grey Dawn Ii)
M C Pipe D A Johnson

Placings:00P (3377)
2003/04: 19⁰G, 19⁰G, 16⁶S,

	Starts	1st	2nd	3rd	Win & Pl
Hurdles	3	0	0	0	
Career Total	3	0	0	0	

Going: Sf: 0-1 GS: 0-0 Gd: 0-2 GF: - Fm: 0-0
Distance: 2m/2m3: 0-2 2m4-2m7: 0-0 3m+: 0-0
Track: LH: 0-0 RH: 0-3 Tight: 0-1 Gall: 0-0

Aids: Bl: 0-0 Vi: 0-0 Tstrap: 0-0 Ckp: 0-0

Lagosta (SAF)
94   81
4-y-o ch g Fort Wood (USA)-Rose Wine (Chilibang)
G M Moore (W J Haggas 26/7) Mrs A Roddis

Placings:352342 (1904)
2003/04: 17³G, 17⁵G, 16²G, 16³F, 17⁴GF, 16²GF,

	Starts	1st	2nd	3rd	Win & Pl
Hurdles	6	0	2	2	2646
Career Total	6	0	2	2	2646

Going: Sf: 0-0 GS: 0-0 Gd: 0-3 GF: - Fm: 0-3
Distance: 2m/2m3: 0-6 2m4-2m7: 0-0 3m+: 0-0
Track: LH: 0-2 RH: 0-3 Tight: 0-1 Gall: 0-1
Aids: Bl: 0-0 Vi: 0-0 Tstrap: 0-0 Ckp: 0-0
Best Rating: 84 10/03 Carl 2m1f gd-fm Hdl

Plating-class juvenile hurdler; acts on a sound surface; exposed.

Laird Dara Mac
86   64
4-y-o b c Presidium-Nishara (Nishapour (FR))
N Bycroft N Bycroft

Placings:65P (4795)
2003/04: 17⁶GF, 16⁵GF, 17⁶G,

	Starts	1st	2nd	3rd	Win & Pl
Hurdles	3	0	0	0	0
Career Total	3	0	0	0	0

Going: Sf: 0-0 GS: 0-0 Gd: 0-1 GF: - Fm: 0-2
Distance: 2m/2m3: 0-3 2m4-2m7: 0-0 3m+: 0-0
Track: LH: 0-1 RH: 0-2 Tight: 0-1 Gall: 0-1
Aids: Bl: 0-0 Vi: 0-0 Tstrap: 0-0 Ckp: 0-0
Best Rating: 64 11/03 Hntg 2m110y gd-fm Hdl

Lake 'O' Gold
90   71
5-y-o ch m Karinga Bay-Ginka (Petoski)
D W Thompson (J W Mullins 10/7) D Morland

Placings:5656 (4914)
2003/04: 20⁵GS, 19⁶GF, 20⁵GF, 24⁶GS,

	Starts	1st	2nd	3rd	Win & Pl
Hurdles	4	0	0	0	0
Career Total	4	0	0	0	0

Going: Sf: 0-0 GS: 0-2 Gd: 0-0 GF: - Fm: 0-2
Distance: 2m/2m3: 0-1 2m4-2m7: 0-2 3m+: 0-1
Track: LH: 0-2 RH: 0-2 Tight: 0-2 Gall: 0-0
Aids: Bl: 0-0 Vi: 0-0 Tstrap: 0-0 Ckp: 0-0
Best Rating: 71 12/03 Muss 2m4f gd-fm Hdl

Lakeside Lad
104   76
12-y-o b g St Columbus-Beyond The Trimm (Trimmingham)
P A Blockley Mrs Joanna Hughes

Placings:0L/PB24/UU322PUF33/U4P/5F400P2/12P-P53 (1040)
2003/04: 23³GF, 21⁵GF, 26³GF,

	Starts	1st	2nd	3rd	Win & Pl
Chases	3	0	0	1	522
Career Total	32	1	5	4	10842

98 5/02 Fknm 3m110y E Ch GD £3616
Total win prize-money £3617

Going: Sf: 0-0 GS: 0-0 Gd: 0-1 GF: - Fm: 0-2
Distance: 2m/2m3: 0-0 2m4-2m7: 0-1 3m+: 0-2
Track: LH: 0-3 RH: 0-0 Tight: 0-1 Gall: 0-0
Aids: Bl: 0-0 Vi: 0-0 Tstrap: 0-0 Ckp: 0-0
Best Rating: 98 5/02 Uttx 3m2f good Ch

Lalagune (FR)
102   116
5-y-o b m Kadalko (FR)-Donatella II (FR) (Brezzo (FR))
A King Mrs A J Davies

Placings:3512F3 (4544)
2003/04: 16³GS, 17⁵GS, 16¹HY, 16²GS, 16⁶G, 22³GS,

	Starts	1st	2nd	3rd	Win & Pl
Hurdles	6	1	1	2	5583
Career Total	6	1	1	2	5583

94 1/04 Uttx 2m E Hdl HVY £3555
Total win prize-money £3556

Going: Sf: 1-2 GS: 0-3 Gd: 0-1 GF: - Fm: 0-0
Distance: 2m/2m3: 1-5 2m4-2m7: 0-1 3m+: 0-0
Track: LH: 1-3 RH: 0-3 Tight: 0-1 Gall: 0-0
Aids: Bl: 0-0 Vi: 0-0 Tstrap: 0-0 Ckp: 0-0
Best Rating: 116 2/04 Asct 2m110y good Hdl

Much improved effort on third start when wide margin winner of mares' only novices' hurdle at Uttoxeter in January; upsides when falling at the final flight at Ascot the following month; handles testing conditions.

Lambhill Stakes (IRE)
103   91+
6-y-o gr g King's Ride-Summerhill Express (IRE) (Roselier (FR))
J M Jefferson Ashleybank Investments Limited

Placings:0/4225-402456 (4777)
2003/04: 20⁴G, 25⁰G, 24²G, 24⁴HY, 20⁵S, 23⁶G,

	Starts	1st	2nd	3rd	Win & Pl
Hurdles	6	0	1	0	1746
Career Total	11	0	3	0	3996

Going: Sf: 0-2 GS: 0-0 Gd: 0-4 GF: - Fm: 0-0
Distance: 2m/2m3: 0-0 2m4-2m7: 0-2 3m+: 0-4
Track: LH: 0-4 RH: 0-1 Tight: 0-3 Gall: 0-0
Aids: Bl: 0-0 Vi: 0-0 Tstrap: 0-0 Ckp: 0-0
Best Rating: 91 4/04 Hexm 2m4f110y soft Hdl

Moderate hurdler; stays three miles; should make a better chaser.

Lambrini Bianco (IRE)
(84h)   (48h)
6-y-o br g Roselier (FR)-Darjoy (Darantus)
Mrs L Williamson Halewood International Ltd

Placings:10/00-P05 (4566)
2003/04: 20³HY, 24⁰G, 17⁵GS,

	Starts	1st	2nd	3rd	Win & Pl
Hurdles	2	0	0	0	0
Chases	1	0	0	0	0
Career Total	7	1	0	0	1729

89 3/02 Bang 2m1f H NHF SFT £1729
Total win prize-money £1729

Going:	Sf: 0-1 GS: 0-1 Gd: 0-1 GF: - Fm: 0-0
Distance:	2m/2m3: 0-1 2m4-2m7: 0-1 3m+: 0-1
Track:	LH: 0-2 RH: 0-1 Tight: 0-1 Gall: 0-0
Aids:	Bl: 0-0 Vi: 0-0 Tstrap: 0-0 Ckp: 0-0
Best Rating:	91 11/02 Hayd 2m good NHF

Lambrini Gold
105

10-y-o b g Gildoran-Fille De Soleil (Sunyboy)
D McCain Halewood International Ltd

Placings:443211/1P/4P2P-PPPP   (4254)
2003/04: 21PS, 20PS, 16PHY, 24PG,

	Starts	1st	2nd	3rd	Win & Pl
Hurdles	1	0	0	0	0
Chases	3	0	0	0	0
Career Total	16	3	2	1	16383
122 11/00 Hayd 2m	D(0-125)HCh		HVY	£5983	
110 4/00 Hexm 2m4f110yE Ch			GD	£3373	
110 3/00 Hexm 2m110y E Ch			SFT	£3003	

Total win prize-money £12360

Going:	Sf: 0-3 GS: 0-0 Gd: 0-1 GF: - Fm: 0-0
Distance:	2m/2m3: 0-1 2m4-2m7: 0-3 3m+: 0-1
Track:	LH: 0-2 RH: 0-3 Tight: 0-1 Gall: 0-1
Aids:	Bl: 0-1 Vi: 0-0 Tstrap: 0-2 Ckp: 0-0
Best Rating:	122 11/00 Hayd 2m heavy Ch

Lambrini Mist

6-y-o gr g Terimon-Miss Fern (Cruise Missile)
Mrs L Williamson Halewood International Ltd

Placings:3/00-P   (0718)
2003/04: 20PG,

	Starts	1st	2nd	3rd	Win & Pl
Hurdles	1	0	0	0	
Career Total	4	0	0	1	245

Going:	Sf: 0-0 GS: 0-0 Gd: 0-1 GF: - Fm: 0-0
Distance:	2m/2m3: 0-0 2m4-2m7: 0-1 3m+: 0-0
Track:	LH: 0-0 RH: 0-1 Tight: 0-0 Gall: 0-0
Aids:	Bl: 0-0 Vi: 0-0 Tstrap: 0-0 Ckp: 0-1
Best Rating:	69 4/02 Plum 2m2f gd-fm NHF

Lambrini Prince
84   **42**

10-y-o b g Derrylin-Flying Faith (Rymer)
Mrs L Williamson Halewood International Ltd

Placings:000/P2/3F22U323/50PPF   (4753)
2003/04: 22PS, 24PG, 32PG, 24PGS, 26PG,

	Starts	1st	2nd	3rd	Win & Pl
Chases	5	0	0	0	0
Career Total	18	0	0	4	7929

Going:	Sf: 0-1 GS: 0-1 Gd: 0-3 GF: - Fm: 0-0
Distance:	2m/2m3: 0-0 2m4-2m7: 0-1 3m+: 0-4
Track:	LH: 0-4 RH: 0-1 Tight: 0-2 Gall: 0-0
Aids:	Bl: 0-1 Vi: 0-0 Tstrap: 0-0 Ckp: 0-0
Best Rating:	94 3/02 Bang 3m110y soft Ch

Lamp's Return
94f   **96f**

5-y-o ch m Bob's Return (IRE)-Lampstone (Ragstone)

A King Mr & Mrs F C Welch

Placings:3   (3961)
2003/04: 18¹³G,

	Starts	1st	2nd	3rd	Win & Pl
NH Flat	1	0	0	1	424
Career Total	1	0	0	1	424

Going:	Sf: 0-0 GS: 0-0 Gd: 0-1 GF: - Fm: 0-0
Distance:	2m/2m3: 0-1 2m4-2m7: 0-0 3m+: 0-0
Track:	LH: 0-1 RH: 0-0 Tight: 0-1 Gall: 0-0
Aids:	Bl: 0-0 Vi: 0-0 Tstrap: 0-0 Ckp: 0-0
Best Rating:	96 2/04 Font 2m2f110y good NHF

Lamzig
75   **40**

5-y-o b g Danzig Connection (USA)-Lamsonetti (Never So Bold)
M Todhunter Mrs Kate Hall

Placings:0   (1075)
2003/04: 17PGF,

	Starts	1st	2nd	3rd	Win & Pl
Hurdles	1	0	0	0	
Career Total	1	0	0	0	

Going:	Sf: 0-0 GS: 0-0 Gd: 0-0 GF: - Fm: 0-1
Distance:	2m/2m3: 0-1 2m4-2m7: 0-0 3m+: 0-0
Track:	LH: 0-1 RH: 0-0 Tight: 0-1 Gall: 0-0
Aids:	Bl: 0-0 Vi: 0-0 Tstrap: 0-0 Ckp: 0-0
Best Rating:	40 8/03 Sedg 2m1f gd-fm Hdl

Lancashire Lass
71 (101h)   (78h) **78**

8-y-o b m Lancastrian-Chanelle (The Parson)
J S King Mrs R M Hill

Placings:00600/6/200P036-2F06U3604   (4139)
2003/04: 22PGF, 22PGF, 22PG, 22PG, 21UGF, 24PGF, 22PG, 24PG, 20PG,

	Starts	1st	2nd	3rd	Win & Pl
Hurdles	8	0	1	1	2183
Chases	1	0	0	0	513
Career Total	22	0	2	2	4320

Going:	Sf: 0-0 GS: 0-0 Gd: 0-4 GF: - Fm: 0-5
Distance:	2m/2m3: 0-0 2m4-2m7: 0-7 3m+: 0-5
Track:	LH: 0-4 RH: 0-5 Tight: 0-8 Gall: 0-0
Aids:	Bl: 0-2 Vi: 0-0 Tstrap: 0-0 Ckp: 0-0
Best Rating:	78 3/04 Ludl 2m4f good Ch

Modest novice hurdler at up 2m 6f; best effort when narrowly beaten after pecking at the last in 2m 6f mares' only event at Newton Abbot July 2003; acts on fast ground.

Lancastrian Jet (IRE)

13-y-o b g Lancastrian-Kilmurray Jet (Le Bavard (FR))
H D Daly The Hon Mrs A E Heber-Percy

Placings:0/2211/41252/121U5P/5535P/2133/2206-111U   (4761)
2003/04: 25PGS, 25PG, 25PGS, 25US,

	Starts	1st	2nd	3rd	Win & Pl
Chases	4	3	0	0	5499
Career Total	34	9	8	3	66911

---

119 3/04 MRas 3m1f	H Ch	G-S	£1529
107 3/04 Towc 3m1f	H Ch	GD	£2149
118 2/04 Hrfd 3m1f110yH Ch		G-S	£1820
127 12/01 Extr 4m	D(0-125)HCh	G-S	£8255
131 1/00 Sand 3m5f110yB HCh		SFT	£20800
131 10/99 Towc 3m1f	E(0-115)HCh	GD	£3142
130 12/98 Towc 3m1f	C(0-130)HCh	SFT	£4926
127 4/98 Uttx 3m2f	E Ch	SFT	£3801
124 3/98 Tntn 3m	E Ch	G-S	£2918

Total win prize-money £49341

Going:	Sf: 0-1 GS: 2-2 Gd: 1-1 GF: - Fm: 0-0
Distance:	2m/2m3: 0-0 2m4-2m7: 0-0 3m+: 3-4
Track:	LH: 0-0 RH: 3-4 Tight: 1-1 Gall: 0-0
Aids:	Bl: 0-0 Vi: 0-0 Tstrap: 0-0 Ckp: 0-0
Best Rating:	131 1/00 Sand 3m5f110y soft Ch

Veteran staying chaser, best going right-handed on soft ground; won hunter chase at Hereford in February; stays four miles.

Lancier D'Estruval (FR)
75   **57**

5-y-o ch g Epervier Bleu-Pommette lii (FR) (Trac)
J C Tuck Lord Huffington-Smythe Racing

Placings:1000P   (4539)
2003/04: 16PGS, 17PGS, 16PGS, 16PG, 21PGS,

	Starts	1st	2nd	3rd	Win & Pl
NH Flat	2	1	0	0	1638
Hurdles	3	0	0	0	0
Career Total	5	1	0	0	1638
85 10/03 Uttx 2m	H NHF	G-F	£1638

Total win prize-money £1638

Going:	Sf: 0-0 GS: 0-3 Gd: 0-1 GF: - Fm: 1-1
Distance:	2m/2m3: 1-4 2m4-2m7: 0-1 3m+: 0-0
Track:	LH: 1-2 RH: 0-3 Tight: 0-2 Gall: 0-0
Aids:	Bl: 0-0 Vi: 0-0 Tstrap: 0-0 Ckp: 0-0
Best Rating:	85 10/03 Uttx 2m gd-fm NHF

Half-brother to winning chaser Jaloux D'Estruval; won a weak Uttoxeter bumper on his debut; well beaten since; looks a chaser.

Land Rover Lad
83   **85**

6-y-o ch g Alflora (IRE)-Fililode (Mossberry)
C P Morlock Mc Coy's Neighbours

Placings:000P4P   (4669)
2003/04: 17PGS, 17PGS, 21PG, 24PG, 21PGS, 23PGS,

	Starts	1st	2nd	3rd	Win & Pl
NH Flat	2	0	0	0	0
Hurdles	4	0	0	0	276
Career Total	6	0	0	0	276

Going:	Sf: 0-0 GS: 0-0 Gd: 0-4 GF: 0-2 Fm: 0-0
Distance:	2m/2m3: 0-2 2m4-2m7: 0-3 3m+: 0-1
Track:	LH: 0-2 RH: 0-4 Tight: 0-2 Gall: 0-0
Aids:	Bl: 0-0 Vi: 0-0 Tstrap: 0-0 Ckp: 0-0
Best Rating:	85 3/04 Plum 2m5f gd-sft Hdl

Landescent (IRE)
97   **69**

4-y-o b g Grand Lodge (USA)-Traumerei (GER) (Surumu (GER))
Miss K M George (M Quinn 13/2) Stableline

Placings:4 (4854)
2003/04: 17⁴GF,

	Starts	1st	2nd	3rd	Win & Pl
Hurdles	1	0	0	0	354
Career Total	1	0	0	0	354

Going:	Sf: 0-0 GS: 0-0 Gd: 0-0 GF: - Fm: 0-1
Distance:	2m/2m3: 0-1 2m4-2m7: 0-0 3m+: 0-0
Track:	LH: 0-0 RH: 0-1 Tight: 0-1 Gall: 0-0
Aids:	Bl: 0-0 Vi: 0-0 Tstrap: 0-0 Ckp: 0-0
Best Rating:	69 4/04 Tntn 2m1f gd-fm Hdl

Langcourt Jester

6-y-o ch m Royal Vulcan-Singing Clown (True Song)
S J Gilmore R A Jeffery

Placings:00-00 (2384)
2003/04: 16⁰GF, 21⁰G,

	Starts	1st	2nd	3rd	Win & Pl
NH Flat	1	0	0	0	0
Hurdles	1	0	0	0	0
Career Total	4	0	0	0	0

Going:	Sf: 0-0 GS: 0-0 Gd: 0-1 GF: - Fm: 0-1
Distance:	2m/2m3: 0-1 2m4-2m7: 0-0 3m+: 0-0
Track:	LH: 0-2 RH: 0-0 Tight: 0-0 Gall: 0-0
Aids:	Bl: 0-0 Vi: 0-0 Tstrap: 0-0 Ckp: 0-0
Best Rating:	76 11/03 Wwck 2m gd-fm NHF

Langham Lake
96   68
7-y-o b g Endoli (USA)-Birbrook Girl (Henricus (AUT))
K Bishop R H Stevens

Placings:FO0 (4147)
2003/04: 19⁶S, 17⁰GS, 24⁶G,

	Starts	1st	2nd	3rd	Win & Pl
Hurdles	3	0	0	0	
Career Total	3	0	0	0	

Going:	Sf: 0-1 GS: 0-1 Gd: 0-1 GF: 0-0 Fm: 0-0
Distance:	2m/2m3: 0-2 2m4-2m7: 0-0 3m+: 0-1
Track:	LH: 0-0 RH: 0-3 Tight: 0-2 Gall: 0-0
Aids:	Bl: 0-0 Vi: 0-0 Tstrap: 0-0 Ckp: 0-0
Best Rating:	68 3/04 Tntn 3m110y good Hdl

Lanhel (FR)
100f   89f
5-y-o ch g Boston Two Step (USA)-Umbrella (FR) (Down The River (FR))
J Wade John Wade

Placings:00 (3482)
2003/04: 16⁰GS, 16⁰G,

	Starts	1st	2nd	3rd	Win & Pl
NH Flat	2	0	0	0	
Career Total	2	0	0	0	

Going:	Sf: 0-0 GS: 0-1 Gd: 0-1 GF: - Fm: 0-0
Distance:	2m/2m3: 0-2 2m4-2m7: 0-0 3m+: 0-0
Track:	LH: 0-0 RH: 0-0 Tight: 0-0 Gall: 0-0
Aids:	Bl: 0-0 Vi: 0-0 Tstrap: 0-0 Ckp: 0-0
Best Rating:	89 1/04 Weth 2m gd-sft NHF

Lanicene (FR)
73f   49f
5-y-o b g Moon Madness-Ocylla (FR) (Medford (FR))
Ferdy Murphy Network Training

Placings:0 (4323)
2003/04: 16⁰S,

	Starts	1st	2nd	3rd	Win & Pl
NH Flat	1	0	0	0	
Career Total	1	0	0	0	

Going:	Sf: 0-1 GS: 0-0 Gd: 0-0 GF: - Fm: 0-0
Distance:	2m/2m3: 0-1 2m4-2m7: 0-0 3m+: 0-0
Track:	LH: 0-1 RH: 0-0 Tight: 0-0 Gall: 0-0
Aids:	Bl: 0-0 Vi: 0-0 Tstrap: 0-0 Ckp: 0-0
Best Rating:	52 3/04 Newc 2m soft NHF

Lanmire Tower (IRE)
100   129
10-y-o b g Celio Rufo-Lanigans Tower (The Parson)
S Gollings Mrs D Dukes

Placings:00/F050R/501134/2035/12P1F13/431440542-5PPP (4784)
2003/04: 24⁵GS, 32⁸PG, 24⁸G, 24⁸G,

	Starts	1st	2nd	3rd	Win & Pl
Chases	4	0	0	0	0
Career Total	37	6	3	4	43985
129	4/02	Chel	3m1f110yB Ch	GD	£15008
129	2/02	Ludl	3m E Ch	GD	£3425
85	10/01	Hntg	3m E Ch	GD	£3626
107	10/99	Weth	3m1f F(0-100)HHdl	GD	£1835
100	10/99	Carl	2m4f110yE(0-105)HHdl	GD	£2332
			Total win prize-money £26227		

Going:	Sf: 0-0 GS: 0-1 Gd: 0-2 GF: - Fm: 0-1
Distance:	2m/2m3: 0-0 2m4-2m7: 0-0 3m+: 0-4
Track:	LH: 0-2 RH: 0-1 Tight: 0-1 Gall: 0-2
Aids:	Bl: 0-4 Vi: 0-0 Tstrap: 0-0 Ckp: 0-0
Best Rating:	129 12/02 Ludl 3m3f110y good Ch

Fair handicap chaser; stays 4m; best on a sound surface; wears blinkers.

Lannkaran (IRE)
103   112
11-y-o b g Shardari-Lankarana (Auction Ring (USA))
H D Daly The Hon Simon Sainsbury

Placings:0211/05/313411/643P1/P3FP0214/6-0344P (4667)
2003/04: 24⁶G, 21³S, 24⁴GS, 24⁴G, 24⁸PS,

	Starts	1st	2nd	3rd	Win & Pl
Chases	5	0	0	1	2445
Career Total	31	7	2	5	36804
125	4/02	Towc	2m6f D(0-125)HCh	GD	£5252
117	4/01	Hntg	3m D(0-120)HCh	SFT	£4855
134	4/00	Strf	3m D Ch	GD	£4374
124	3/00	Towc	2m6f E Ch	SFT	£3198
115	12/99	Towc	3m D Ch	SFT	£4574
131	4/98	Chel	2m1f D Hdl	HVY	£3680
124	3/98	Chep	2m110y E Hdl	GD	£2444
			Total win prize-money £28380		

Going:	Sf: 0-2 GS: 0-1 Gd: 0-2 GF: - Fm: 0-0
Distance:	2m/2m3: 0-0 2m4-2m7: 0-1 3m+: 0-4
Track:	LH: 0-2 RH: 0-3 Tight: 0-2 Gall: 0-0
Aids:	Bl: 0-4 Vi: 0-0 Tstrap: 0-0 Ckp: 0-0
Best Rating:	134 4/00 Strf 3m good Ch

Fair handicap chaser; effective at two and a half to three miles; best on soft ground; appreciates forcing tactics; prone to jumping errors.

Lanos (POL)
90   89
6-y-o ch g Special Power-Lubeka (POL) (Milione (FR))
Miss Sheena West (R Ford 24/2) D W Watson

Placings:03/406-2 (4752)
2003/04: 16²G,

	Starts	1st	2nd	3rd	Win & Pl
Hurdles	1	0	1	0	796
Career Total	6	0	1	1	1611

Going:	Sf: 0-0 GS: 0-0 Gd: 0-1 GF: - Fm: 0-0
Distance:	2m/2m3: 0-1 2m4-2m7: 0-0 3m+: 0-0
Track:	LH: 0-1 RH: 0-0 Tight: 0-1 Gall: 0-0
Aids:	Bl: 0-0 Vi: 0-0 Tstrap: 0-0 Ckp: 0-0
Best Rating:	87 4/04 Plum 2m good Hdl

Prolific winner on the Flat in his native Poland but struggling to make his mark over hurdles here.

Lantern Lad (IRE)
(83h)
8-y-o b g Yashgan-Lantern Lass (Monksfield)
R Ford Tarporley Turf Club

Placings:0/00000P40200/00-5 (2533)
2003/04: 26⁵S,

	Starts	1st	2nd	3rd	Win & Pl
Chases	1	0	0	0	
Career Total	15	0	1	0	1840

Going:	Sf: 0-1 GS: 0-0 Gd: 0-0 GF: - Fm: 0-0
Distance:	2m/2m3: 0-0 2m4-2m7: 0-0 3m+: 0-1
Track:	LH: 0-1 RH: 0-0 Tight: 0-1 Gall: 0-0
Aids:	Bl: 0-0 Vi: 0-0 Tstrap: 0-0 Ckp: 0-0
Best Rating:	83 3/02 Limk 2m soft Hdl

Lantern Leader (IRE)
97(103h)   (119h)98
9-y-o b g Supreme Leader-Lantern Line (The Parson)
Miss Lucinda V Russell (Michael Hourigan 12/9) Mrs L R Joughin

Placings:0000/400034/332212125103/431120U3000P-450P201P535060 (4599)
2003/04: 23⁴F, 22⁵SH, 24⁰GY, 24⁴PY, 25²F, 18⁰GF, 24¹GS, 24⁸PGS, 24³GF, 24⁵G, 27⁰GS, 32⁸G, 18⁰G,

	Starts	1st	2nd	3rd	Win & Pl
Hurdles	4	1	0	0	2905
Chases	10	0	1	1	2286
Career Total	50	6	6	7	59023
110	11/03	Ayr	3m110y F Hdl	G-S	£2905
116	8/02	Gway	3m (0-130)HHdl	Y-S	£9570
107	7/02	Klny	2m6f HHdl	GD	£9969
103	10/01	Naas	2m4f HHdl	Y-S	£13104
103	9/01	Tral	2m4f (0-95)HHdl	GD	£4729
87	7/01	Bell	2m4f (0-95)HHdl	G-F	£4312
			Total win prize-money £44593		

Going:	Sf: 0-0 GS: 1-3 Gd: 0-3 GF: - Fm: 0-5
Distance:	2m/2m3: 0-2 2m4-2m7: 0-2 3m+: 1-10
Track:	LH: 1-5 RH: 0-5 Tight: 0-5 Gall: 0-1
Aids:	Bl: 0-4 Vi: 0-0 Tstrap: 0-0 Ckp: 0-4

Best Rating: 119 9/02 List 2m4f firm Hdl

Fair ex-Irish hurdler; placed over fences in Ireland; made a winning debut for new connections at Ayr in November; stays three miles; acts on any ground but well suited by soft.

Lanty Slee (IRE)
85f   **75f**

5-y-o b g Supreme Leader-Tell A Tale (Le Bavard (FR))
N G Richards Greystoke Stables Ltd

Placings:5 (1436)
2003/04: 16^5G,

	Starts	1st	2nd	3rd	Win & Pl
NH Flat	1	0	0	0	0
Career Total	1	0	0	0	0

Going:	Sf: 0-0 GS: 0-0 Gd: 0-1 GF: - Fm: 0-0
Distance:	2m/2m3: 0-1 2m4-2m7: 0-0 3m+: 0-0
Track:	LH: 0-0 RH: 0-1 Tight: 0-0 Gall: 0-0
Aids:	Bl: 0-0 Vi: 0-0 Tstrap: 0-0 Ckp: 0-0
Best Rating:	79 9/03 Prth 2m110y good NHF

Lanzlo (FR)
107   **96**

7-y-o b/br g Le Balafre (FR)-L'Eternite (FR) (Cariellor (FR))
James Moffatt The Sheroot Partnership

Placings:120F23/115500/2203P454-320614 (3980)
2003/04: 17^3G, 19^2G, 16^6G, 17^6GF, 20^1GF, 17^4G,

	Starts	1st	2nd	3rd	Win & Pl
Hurdles	6	1	1	1	8068
Career Total	26	4	5	3	23516

95	8/03 Prth	2m4f110yD(0-115)HHdl	G-F	£5343
113	9/01 Strf	2m110y D(0-125)HHdl	G-F	£3458
115	7/01 Strf	2m110y F(0-110)HHdl	GD	£3020
115	9/00 Chep	2m110y D Hdl	GD	£3347

Total win prize-money £15170

Going:	Sf: 0-0 GS: 0-0 Gd: 0-4 GF: - Fm: 1-2
Distance:	2m/2m3: 0-4 2m4-2m7: 1-2 3m+: 0-0
Track:	LH: 0-2 RH: 1-4 Tight: 0-3 Gall: 0-0
Aids:	Bl: 0-0 Vi: 0-0 Tstrap: 0-0 Ckp: 0-0
Best Rating:	115 7/01 Strf 2m110y good Hdl

Moderate handicap hurdler; stays two and a half miles; effective on a sound surface; suited by a sharp track.

Laouen (FR)
109   **134**

6-y-o br g Funny Baby (FR)-Olive Noire (FR) (Cadoudal (FR))
L Lungo Ashley Bank Investments & Dr K Fraser

Placings:12/21111-01 (0382)
2003/04: 16^0GS, 18^1G,

	Starts	1st	2nd	3rd	Win & Pl
Hurdles	2	1	0	0	9048
Career Total	9	6	2	0	35838

122	5/03 Kels	2m2f B Hdl	GD	£9048
134	4/03 Prth	2m110y D Hdl	GD	£5785
126	4/03 Ayr	2m C Hdl	GD	£7410
122	1/03 Muss	2m C Hdl	GD	£7182
112	12/02 Donc	2m110y E Hdl	SFT	£3094
106	3/02 Ayr	2m H NHF	HVY	£1788

Total win prize-money £34309

Going:	Sf: 0-0 GS: 0-1 Gd: 1-1 GF: - Fm: 0-0
Distance:	2m/2m3: 1-2 2m4-2m7: 0-0 3m+: 0-0
Track:	LH: 1-2 RH: 0-0 Tight: 1-1 Gall: 0-0
Aids:	Bl: 0-0 Vi: 0-0 Tstrap: 0-0 Ckp: 0-0

Best Rating: 134 4/03 Prth 2m110y good Hdl

Useful hurdler; has a tremendous strike rate; best over two miles; acts on good ground or softer; likes to be held up; progressive.

Lapadar (IRE)
61

5-y-o b/br m Woodborough (USA)-Indescent Blue (Bluebird (USA))
J R Weymes J Weymes

Placings:30P (3322)
2003/04: 19^3GS, 19^0G, 21^PGS,

	Starts	1st	2nd	3rd	Win & Pl
Hurdles	3	0	0	1	435
Career Total	3	0	0	1	435

Going:	Sf: 0-0 GS: 0-2 Gd: 0-1 GF: - Fm: 0-0
Distance:	2m/2m3: 0-0 2m4-2m7: 0-3 3m+: 0-0
Track:	LH: 0-2 RH: 0-1 Tight: 0-2 Gall: 0-0
Aids:	Bl: 0-0 Vi: 0-0 Tstrap: 0-0 Ckp: 0-0
Best Rating:	61 12/03 Donc 2m3f110y gd-sft Hdl

Larssarto (GER)
98   **94+**

6-y-o b h Lomitas-Lady Shepard (GER) (Shepard (GER))
C Von Der Recke (H Hiller 19/10) P Cnockaert

Placings:40 (3654)
2003/04: 16^4GS, 24^0S,

	Starts	1st	2nd	3rd	Win & Pl
Hurdles	2	0	0	0	313
Career Total	2	0	0	0	313

Going:	Sf: 0-1 GS: 0-1 Gd: 0-0 GF: - Fm: 0-0
Distance:	2m/2m3: 0-1 2m4-2m7: 0-0 3m+: 0-1
Track:	LH: 0-1 RH: 0-1 Tight: 0-0 Gall: 0-0
Aids:	Bl: 0-0 Vi: 0-0 Tstrap: 0-0 Ckp: 0-0
Best Rating:	94 11/03 Weth 2m gd-sft Hdl

Novice hurdler; prolific winner on the Flat in Germany; did not jump well on his hurdles debut at Wetherby.

Lascar De Ferbet (FR)
94f   **92f**

5-y-o br g Sleeping Car (FR)-Belle De Ferbet (FR) (Brezzo (FR))
L Lungo Ashleybank Investments Limited

Placings:530 (4571)
2003/04: 17^5GS, 16^3GF, 17^0GS,

	Starts	1st	2nd	3rd	Win & Pl
NH Flat	3	0	0	1	298
Career Total	3	0	0	1	298

Going:	Sf: 0-0 GS: 0-2 Gd: 0-0 GF: - Fm: 0-1
Distance:	2m/2m3: 0-2 2m4-2m7: 0-0 3m+: 0-1
Track:	LH: 0-3 RH: 0-0 Tight: 0-2 Gall: 0-0
Aids:	Bl: 0-0 Vi: 0-0 Tstrap: 0-0 Ckp: 0-0
Best Rating:	92 3/04 Ayr 2m gd-fm NHF

Half-brother to winning hurdler Hakim de Ferbet; has run promisingly on both starts in bumpers and will be suited by a decent test of stamina when sent over hurdles; appeals strongly as the type to win races over obstacles.

Laskari (FR)
92   **92**

5-y-o b g Great Palm (USA)-Hatzarie (FR) (Cyborg (FR))
Mrs L C Taylor (E Lecoiffier 11/9) Mrs L C Taylor

Placings:0 (3042)
2003/04: 16^0GS,

	Starts	1st	2nd	3rd	Win & Pl
Hurdles	1	0	0	0	
Career Total	1	0	0	0	

Going:	Sf: 0-0 GS: 0-1 Gd: 0-0 GF: - Fm: 0-0
Distance:	2m/2m3: 0-1 2m4-2m7: 0-0 3m+: 0-0
Track:	LH: 0-1 RH: 0-0 Tight: 0-0 Gall: 0-1
Aids:	Bl: 0-0 Vi: 0-0 Tstrap: 0-0 Ckp: 0-0
Best Rating:	101 12/03 Newb 2m110y gd-sft Hdl

Last Of The Gales (IRE)

10-y-o b m Strong Gale-Red Celtic (Celtic Cone)
Mrs Caroline Keevil Miss Janet Menzies

Placings:4P62P/2 (0186)
2003/04: 25^2GF,

	Starts	1st	2nd	3rd	Win & Pl
Chases	1	0	1	0	1048
Career Total	6	0	2	0	1720

Going:	Sf: 0-0 GS: 0-0 Gd: 0-0 GF: - Fm: 0-1
Distance:	2m/2m3: 0-0 2m4-2m7: 0-0 3m+: 0-1
Track:	LH: 0-0 RH: 0-0 Tight: 0-0 Gall: 0-0
Aids:	Bl: 0-0 Vi: 0-0 Tstrap: 0-0 Ckp: 0-0
Best Rating:	86 12/99 Muss 2m gd-sft NHF

Hunter chaser; winning pointer; stays three miles one.

Last Rebel (IRE)
62   **73**

5-y-o b g Danehill (USA)-La Curamalal (IRE) (Rainbow Quest (USA))
R T Phillips Coral & Graham Russell

Placings:60-0P (4752)
2003/04: 16^0G, 16^PG,

	Starts	1st	2nd	3rd	Win & Pl
Hurdles	2	0	0	0	
Career Total	4	0	0	0	0

Going:	Sf: 0-0 GS: 0-0 Gd: 0-2 GF: - Fm: 0-0
Distance:	2m/2m3: 0-2 2m4-2m7: 0-0 3m+: 0-0
Track:	LH: 0-2 RH: 0-0 Tight: 0-1 Gall: 0-0
Aids:	Bl: 0-0 Vi: 0-0 Tstrap: 0-0 Ckp: 0-0
Best Rating:	73 1/03 Kemp 2m good Hdl

Plating-class novice hurdler; little worthwhile form so far.

Latalomne (USA)
107(113h)   (133h)**150**

10-y-o ch g Zilzal (USA)-Sanctuary (Welsh Pageant)
M C Pipe (B Ellison 13/12) Alderclad Roofing/k M Everitt

Placings:13/0111/15F6/550F4-2534P000 (4627)
2003/04: 16^4GY, 16^2GF, 17^5GF, 16^3GF, 16^4G, 16^PGS, 16^0G, 16^0G,

	Starts	1st	2nd	3rd	Win & Pl
Hurdles	3	0	0	0	3250

Chases		6	0	1	1	9518
Career Total		**23**	**5**	**1**	**2**	**50983**
158	11/01	Chel	2m	B(0-145)HCh	GD	£14218
133	2/01	Sedg	2m5f	E Ch	G-S	£3103
125	1/01	Muss	2m	E Ch	G-S	£3393
124	1/01	Muss	2m	D Ch	GD	£4270
119	2/00	Catt	2m	E Hdl	GD	£3103
				Total win prize-money £28091		

Going:	Sf: 0-0 GS: 0-1 Gd: 0-4 GF: - Fm: 0-3
Distance:	2m/2m3: 0-9 2m4-2m7: 0-0 3m+: 0-0
Track:	LH: 0-7 RH: 0-2 Tight: 0-2 Gall: 0-5
Aids:	Bl: 0-0 Vi: 0-0 Tstrap: 0-0 Ckp: 0-0
Best Rating:	165 3/02 Chel 2m gd-sft Ch

Useful hurdler/smart chaser; disputing the lead when falling at the second last in the Queen Mother Champion Chase in both 2002 and 2003; now with Martin Pipe, but has had a disappointing season; suited by two miles and a sound surface, though he does stay farther; has worn blinkers; capable of top-class form on his day.

Late Claim (USA)

100   **99+**

4-y-o ch g King Of Kings (IRE)-Irish Flare (USA) (Irish River (FR))

N J Henderson (Ian Williams 13/2) Pertemps Group Limited

Placings:05140	(4591)

2003/04: 16⁰G, 16⁵GS, 16¹G, 16⁴GF, 16⁰G,

	Starts	1st	2nd	3rd	Win & Pl
Hurdles	5	1	0	0	5429
Career Total	**5**	**1**	**0**	**0**	**5429**
98	2/04	Kemp	2m	D Hdl	GD	£4992
				Total win prize-money £4992		

Going:	Sf: 0-0 GS: 0-1 Gd: 1-3 GF: - Fm: 0-1
Distance:	**2m/2m3:** 1-5 2m4-2m7: 0-0 3m+: 0-0
Track:	LH: 0-2 RH: 1-3 Tight: 0-0 Gall: 0-1
Aids:	Bl: 0-0 Vi: 0-0 Tstrap: 0-0 Ckp: 0-0
Best Rating:	99 3/04 Strf 2m110y gd-fm Hdl

Moderate hurdler; acts on a sound surface.

Latefa (IRE)

62f

4-y-o ch f Among Men (USA)-Kraemer (USA) (Lyphard (USA))

Mrs L C Taylor Mrs D Barnett

Placings:0	(4578)

2003/04: 16⁰G,

	Starts	1st	2nd	3rd	Win & Pl
NH Flat	1	0	0	0	
Career Total	**1**	**0**	**0**	**0**	

Going:	Sf: 0-0 GS: 0-0 Gd: 0-1 GF: - Fm: 0-0
Distance:	2m/2m3: 0-1 2m4-2m7: 0-0 3m+: 0-0
Track:	LH: 0-1 RH: 0-0 Tight: 0-0 Gall: 0-1
Aids:	Bl: 0-0 Vi: 0-0 Tstrap: 0-0 Ckp: 0-0

Latensaani

101(97h)   **(120+h)97**

6-y-o b g Shaamit (IRE)-Intoxication (Great Nephew)

G M Moore Keith Nicholson

Placings:U1112P-1	(0469)

2003/04: 16¹G,

	Starts	1st	2nd	3rd	Win & Pl
Chases	1	1	0	0	3890

Career Total		7	4	1	0	16230
97	5/03	Hexm	2m110y	E Ch	GD	£3890
120	10/02	Weth	2m4f110yD Hdl		G-F	£3916
113	10/02	Sedg	2m5f110yE Hdl		G-F	£2884
100	9/02	Hexm	2m4f110yE Hdl		G-F	£2950
				Total win prize-money £13641		

Going:	Sf: 0-0 GS: 0-0 Gd: 1-1 GF: - Fm: 0-0
Distance:	**2m/2m3:** 1-1 2m4-2m7: 0-0 3m+: 0-0
Track:	LH: 1-1 RH: 0-0 Tight: 0-0 Gall: 0-0
Aids:	Bl: 0-0 Vi: 0-0 Tstrap: 0-0 Ckp: 0-0
Best Rating:	120 10/02 Weth 2m4f110y gd-fm Hdl

Moderate chaser/fair hurdler; stays two miles five furlongs; acts on good/fast ground.

Latitude (FR)

107   **111+**

5-y-o b m Kadalko (FR)-Diyala Iii (FR) (Quart De Vin (FR))

M C Pipe (T Civel 9/11) Neil J Edwards

Placings:13F03-513F611	(4485)

2003/04: 18⁵VS, 20¹VS, 20³S, 22⁵VS, 20⁶VS, 19¹G, 22¹G,

	Starts	1st	2nd	3rd	Win & Pl
Chases	7	3	0	1	27160
Career Total	**12**	**4**	**0**	**3**	**49726**
118	3/04	Font	2m6f	E Ch	GD	£4007
118	3/04	Extr	2m3f110yE Ch	GD	£4290
	6/03	Autl	2m4f110y	Ch	VS	£13091
	9/02	Autl	2m2f	Hdl	SFT	£15313
				Total win prize-money £36701		

Going:	Sf: 0-1 GS: 0-0 Gd: 2-2 GF: - Fm: 0-0
Distance:	2m/2m3: 0-1 **2m4-2m7:** 3-2 3m+: 0-0
Track:	LH: 0-0 **RH:** 1-1 Tight: 1-1 Gall: 0-0
Aids:	Bl: 0-1 Vi: 0-0 Tstrap: 0-0 Ckp: 0-0
Best Rating:	118 3/04 Font 2m6f good Ch

Ex-French novice chaser; boasted some decent form in France; won nicely on British debut in weak novices' chase at Exeter in March on good ground and followed up later that month over 2m 6f; ran mostly on testing ground in France; has worn blinkers.

Laudamus

82f   **68f**

6-y-o ch g Anshan-Faint Praise (Lepanto (GER))

R H Alner Lady Cobham

Placings:6	(3312)

2003/04: 18⁶HY,

	Starts	1st	2nd	3rd	Win & Pl
NH Flat	1	0	0	0	0
Career Total	**1**	**0**	**0**	**0**	**0**

Going:	Sf: 0-1 GS: 0-0 Gd: 0-0 GF: - Fm: 0-0
Distance:	2m/2m3: 0-1 2m4-2m7: 0-0 3m+: 0-0
Track:	LH: 0-1 RH: 0-0 Tight: 0-1 Gall: 0-0
Aids:	Bl: 0-0 Vi: 0-0 Tstrap: 0-0 Ckp: 0-0
Best Rating:	68 1/04 Font 2m2f110y heavy NHF

Lauderdale

109   (81h)**114**

8-y-o b g Sula Bula-Miss Tullulah (Hubble Bubble)

Miss Lucinda V Russell Kelso Members Lowflyers Club

Placings:206P5P/550001P60/16FFPF21253305-352342240P	(4941)

2003/04: 17³G, 17⁵GS, 22²G, 20³GF, 20⁴G, 17²S, 22⁴HY, 22⁴GS, 24⁰G, 31³PGS,

	Starts	1st	2nd	3rd	Win & Pl
Chases	10	0	3	2	9269

Career Total		39	3	6	4	26122
110	11/02	Kels	2m1f	E(0-105)HCh	HVY	£3978
99	5/02	Kels	2m1f	D Ch	G-S	£4387
81	2/02	Ayr	3m110y	E Hdl	HVY	£3080
				Total win prize-money £11446		

Going:	Sf: 0-2 GS: 0-3 Gd: 0-4 GF: - Fm: 0-1
Distance:	2m/2m3: 0-3 2m4-2m7: 0-5 3m+: 0-2
Track:	LH: 0-8 RH: 0-1 Tight: 0-6 Gall: 0-1
Aids:	Bl: 0-0 Vi: 0-0 Tstrap: 0-0 Ckp: 0-0
Best Rating:	114 3/03 Kels 2m1f gd-sft Ch

Moderate chaser; has won over three miles over hurdles, but effective at two miles; suited by give in the ground; likes to race prominently.

Laundmower

93   **85**

8-y-o br g Perpendicular-Sound Work (Workboy)

Mrs S J Smith John Endersby

Placings:3/5-P22	(0413)

2003/04: 21³PS, 20²G, 20²G,

	Starts	1st	2nd	3rd	Win & Pl
Hurdles	3	0	2	0	1774
Career Total	**5**	**0**	**2**	**1**	**2020**

Going:	Sf: 0-1 GS: 0-0 Gd: 0-2 GF: - Fm: 0-0
Distance:	2m/2m3: 0-0 2m4-2m7: 0-0 3m+: 0-0
Track:	LH: 0-3 RH: 0-0 Tight: 0-1 Gall: 0-0
Aids:	Bl: 0-0 Vi: 0-0 Tstrap: 0-0 Ckp: 0-0
Best Rating:	96 3/02 Catt 2m gd-sft NHF

Plating-class maiden hurdler; effective at around two and a half miles.

Lauras Girl

63f   **30f**

6-y-o b m Sir Harry Lewis (USA)-Starlight Wonder (Star Appeal)

O O'Neill K G Boulton

Placings:0	(4608)

2003/04: 17⁰G,

	Starts	1st	2nd	3rd	Win & Pl
NH Flat	1	0	0	0	
Career Total	**1**	**0**	**0**	**0**	

Going:	Sf: 0-0 GS: 0-0 Gd: 0-1 GF: - Fm: 0-0
Distance:	2m/2m3: 0-0 2m4-2m7: 0-0 3m+: 0-0
Track:	LH: 0-0 RH: 0-1 Tight: 0-1 Gall: 0-0
Aids:	Bl: 0-0 Vi: 0-0 Tstrap: 0-0 Ckp: 0-0
Best Rating:	32 3/04 MRas 2m1f110y good NHF

Laurier D'Estruval (FR)

5-y-o ch g Ragmar (FR)-Grive D'Estruval (FR) (Quart De Vin (FR))

S E H Sherwood (G Macaire 19/10) T N Siviter

Placings:2-23P	(4340)

2003/04: 18²VS, 18³G, 25⁶PG,

	Starts	1st	2nd	3rd	Win & Pl
Hurdles	2	0	1	0	5610
Chases	1	0	0	1	1091
Career Total	**4**	**0**	**2**	**1**	**8883**

Going: Sf: 0-0 GS: 0-0 Gd: 0-2 GF: - Fm: 0-0
Distance: 2m/2m3: 0-2 2m4-2m7: 0-0 3m+: 0-1
Track: LH: 0-0 RH: 0-0 Tight: 0-0 Gall: 0-0
Aids: Bl: 0-0 Vi: 0-0 Tstrap: 0-0 Ckp: 0-0

Law Unto Himself

(70h)   (42h)
6-y-o b g Contract Law (USA)-Malacanang (Riboboy (USA))
N J Hawke The Fairway Boys

Placings:50/P00-0F   (3141)
2003/04: 19^0G, 19^FS,

	Starts	1st	2nd	3rd	Win & Pl
Hurdles	1	0	0	0	0
Chases	1	0	0	0	0
Career Total	7	0	0	0	0

Going: Sf: 0-1 GS: 0-0 Gd: 0-0 GF: - Fm: 0-0
Distance: 2m/2m3: 0-0 2m4-2m7: 0-2 3m+: 0-0
Track: LH: 0-0 RH: 0-2 Tight: 0-1 Gall: 0-0
Aids: Bl: 0-0 Vi: 0-0 Tstrap: 0-0 Ckp: 0-1
Best Rating: 77 3/02 Winc 2m soft NHF

Lawahik

10-y-o b g Lahib (USA)-Lightning Legacy (USA) (Super Concorde (USA))
T H Caldwell T H Caldwell

Placings:14323134/25/50/PP-U   (0069)
2003/04: 20US,

	Starts	1st	2nd	3rd	Win & Pl
Hurdles	1	0	0	0	
Career Total	15	2	2	3	12187
119	3/99	Bang	2m1f	E Hdl	G-S £3004
122	12/98	Hayd	2m	D Hdl	SFT £2871

Total win prize-money £5875

Going: Sf: 0-1 GS: 0-0 Gd: 0-0 GF: - Fm: 0-0
Distance: 2m/2m3: 0-0 2m4-2m7: 0-0 3m+: 0-0
Track: LH: 0-1 RH: 0-0 Tight: 0-1 Gall: 0-0
Aids: Bl: 0-0 Vi: 0-0 Tstrap: 0-0 Ckp: 0-0
Best Rating: 134 11/99 Chel 2m110y good Hdl

Lawbound (IRE)
65f   32f
6-y-o b g Topanoora-Balela (African Sky)
P J Hobbs M F Barraclough

Placings:0   (0837)
2003/04: 16^0GF,

	Starts	1st	2nd	3rd	Win & Pl
NH Flat	1	0	0	0	
Career Total	1	0	0	0	

Going: Sf: 0-0 GS: 0-0 Gd: 0-0 GF: - Fm: 0-1
Distance: 2m/2m3: 0-1 2m4-2m7: 0-0 3m+: 0-0
Track: LH: 0-1 RH: 0-0 Tight: 0-0 Gall: 0-0
Aids: Bl: 0-0 Vi: 0-0 Tstrap: 0-0 Ckp: 0-0
Best Rating: 32 7/03 Worc 2m gd-fm NHF

Lawman
73f   82f
6-y-o b/br g Afzal-Discipline (Roman Warrior)
J White Mrs P A White

Placings:00   (2856)
2003/04: 16^0G, 17^0GS,

	Starts	1st	2nd	3rd	Win & Pl
NH Flat	2	0	0	0	
Career Total	2	0	0	0	

Going: Sf: 0-0 GS: 0-1 Gd: 0-1 GF: - Fm: 0-0
Distance: 2m/2m3: 0-2 2m4-2m7: 0-0 3m+: 0-0
Track: LH: 0-1 RH: 0-1 Tight: 0-0 Gall: 0-0
Aids: Bl: 0-0 Vi: 0-0 Tstrap: 0-0 Ckp: 0-0
Best Rating: 82 5/03 Worc 2m good NHF

Layasar
89f   93f
4-y-o br g Wizard King-Rasayel (USA) (Bering)
W M Brisbourne Mrs B Penton

Placings:230   (3495)
2003/04: 13^2S, 16^3GS, 16^0HY,

	Starts	1st	2nd	3rd	Win & Pl
NH Flat	3	0	1	1	957
Career Total	3	0	1	1	957

Going: Sf: 0-2 GS: 0-1 Gd: 0-0 GF: - Fm: 0-0
Distance: 2m/2m3: 0-2 2m4-2m7: 0-0 3m+: 0-0
Track: LH: 0-1 RH: 0-1 Tight: 0-0 Gall: 0-0
Aids: Bl: 0-0 Vi: 0-0 Tstrap: 0-0 Ckp: 0-0
Best Rating: 93 12/03 Towc 1m5f110y soft NHF

Lazerito (IRE)
104   111+
6-y-o b g Shernazar-Nemova (IRE) (Cataldi)
Miss Venetia Williams A Butler

Placings:112   (4340)
2003/04: 16^1S, 20^1GS, 25^2G,

	Starts	1st	2nd	3rd	Win & Pl
NH Flat	1	1	0	0	2086
Hurdles	2	1	1	0	4696
Career Total	3	2	1	0	6782
110	2/04	Folk	2m4f110yF Hdl	G-S	£3612
105	12/03	Towc	2m H NHF	SFT	£2086

Total win prize-money £5698

Going: Sf: 1-1 GS: 1-1 Gd: 0-1 GF: - Fm: 0-0
Distance: 2m/2m3: 1-1 2m4-2m7: 1-1 3m+: 0-1
Track: LH: 0-1 RH: 2-2 Tight: 1-1 Gall: 0-0
Aids: Bl: 0-0 Vi: 0-0 Tstrap: 0-0 Ckp: 0-0
Best Rating: 111 3/04 Wwck 3m1f good Hdl

Lazy But Lively (IRE)
99(105h)   (125h)107
8-y-o br g Supreme Leader-Oriel Dream (Oats)
R F Fisher S P Marsh

Placings:00662/53FF10115/23P-60124534FU   (4941)
2003/04: 22^6S, 24^0GS, 21^1G, 20^2HY, 20^4GF, 25^5HY, 21^3G, 20^4HY, 25^FG, 31^UGS,

	Starts	1st	2nd	3rd	Win & Pl
Hurdles	2	0	0	0	
Chases	8	1	1	1	6278
Career Total	27	4	3	3	18457
113	12/03	Sedg	2m5f	E Ch	GD £3191
118	3/02	Hexm	3m	E Hdl	HVY £2551
118	3/02	Ayr	3m110y	D(0-115)HHdl	HVY £3601

| 108 | 11/01 | Carl | 2m4f | E Hdl | HVY £3094 |

Total win prize-money £12439

Going: Sf: 0-4 GS: 0-2 Gd: 1-3 GF: - Fm: 0-1
Distance: 2m/2m3: 0-2 2m4-2m7: 1-6 3m+: 0-4
Track: LH: 1-7 RH: 0-2 Tight: 1-6 Gall: 0-0
Aids: Bl: 0-0 Vi: 0-0 Tstrap: 0-0 Ckp: 0-0
Best Rating: 121 11/02 Kels 2m6f110y soft Hdl

Fair hurdler; made a successful chasing debut at Sedgefield in December 2003; effective at up to 3m; goes well in testing ground.

Lazzaz
105   90
6-y-o b g Muhtarram (USA)-Astern (USA) (Polish Navy (USA))
P W Hiatt Phil Kelly

Placings:4/036F6-3   (0060)
2003/04: 17^3GS,

	Starts	1st	2nd	3rd	Win & Pl
Hurdles	1	0	0	1	535
Career Total	7	0	0	2	1200

Going: Sf: 0-0 GS: 0-1 Gd: 0-0 GF: - Fm: 0-0
Distance: 2m/2m3: 0-1 2m4-2m7: 0-0 3m+: 0-0
Track: LH: 0-0 RH: 0-1 Tight: 0-0 Gall: 0-0
Aids: Bl: 0-0 Vi: 0-0 Tstrap: 0-0 Ckp: 0-0
Best Rating: 92 5/03 Hrfd 2m1f gd-sft Hdl

Le Biassais (FR)
110f   108+f
5-y-o b g Passing Sale (FR)-Petite Fanfan (FR) (Black Beauty Ii (FR))
L Lungo Ashleybank Investments Limited

Placings:010   (3982)
2003/04: 16^0GS, 16^1HY, 17^0G,

	Starts	1st	2nd	3rd	Win & Pl
NH Flat	3	1	0	0	1918
Career Total	3	1	0	0	1918
108	1/04	Ayr	2m	H NHF	HVY £1918

Total win prize-money £1918

Going: Sf: 1-1 GS: 0-1 Gd: 0-1 GF: - Fm: 0-0
Distance: 2m/2m3: 1-3 2m4-2m7: 0-0 3m+: 0-0
Track: LH: 1-2 RH: 0-1 Tight: 0-0 Gall: 0-0
Aids: Bl: 0-0 Vi: 0-0 Tstrap: 0-0 Ckp: 0-0
Best Rating: 108 1/04 Ayr 2m heavy NHF

Bettered debut effort when winning heavy-ground bumper at Ayr in January 2004; staying type who looks sure to win races over obstacles in due course.

Le Coudray (FR)
116   167
10-y-o b g Phantom Breeze-Mos Lie (FR) (Tip Moss (FR))
C Roche John P McManus

Placings:13/111112P/12/F111F4-422F   (4647)
2003/04: 20^4Y, 24^2YS, 24^2YS, 36^FG,

	Starts	1st	2nd	3rd	Win & Pl
Chases	4	2	0	2	41739
Career Total	21	10	4	1	375309
151	12/02	Leop	2m1f	Ch	HVY £39877
151	12/02	Fair	2m4f	Ch	SH £29907
137	11/02	Naas	2m	Ch	SFT £6773
173	10/99	Navn	2m4f	Hdl	Y-S £13058
169	1/99	Naas	2m4f	Hdl	HVY £4910
	11/98	Autl	2m4f110y	Hdl	HLD £60606

10/98	Autl	2m3f110y Hdl		SFT	£30303
10/98	Autl	2m2f Hdl		VS	£30303
6/98	Autl	2m3f110y Hdl		VS	£50505
11/97	Autl	2m2f HHdl		HVY	£39282
		Total win prize-money £305526			

Going: Sf: 0-0 GS: 0-0 Gd: 0-1 GF: - Fm: 0-0
Distance: 2m/2m3: 0-0 2m4-2m7: 0-1 3m+: 0-3
Track: LH: 0-3 RH: 0-1 Tight: 0-1 Gall: 0-0
Aids: Bl: 0-0 Vi: 0-0 Tstrap: 0-4 Ckp: 0-0
Best Rating: 173 10/99 Navn 2m4f   yld-sft   Hdl

High-class chaser, ex-French; formerly a high-class hurdler, runner-up to Anzum in the Stayers' at Cheltenham in 1999; injured later that year and absent for three years; high-class novice chaser in 2002/3, successful in Grade Ones at Fairyhouse and Leopardstown in December; fair efforts in top company in 2003/4; stays 3m but effective at shorter; acts best on soft ground; has worn a tongue tie.

Le Diamont (FR)
98   99

5-y-o ch g Broadway Flyer (USA)-Lady Diamond (FR) (Diamond Prospect (USA))
C P Morlock Pell-Mell Partners

Placings:500-04P   (3368)
2003/04: 16⁶G, 16⁴GF, 21⁶G,

	Starts	1st	2nd	3rd	Win & Pl
Hurdles	3	0	0	0	409
Career Total	6	0	0	0	409

Going: Sf: 0-0 GS: 0-0 Gd: 0-2 GF: - Fm: 0-1
Distance: 2m/2m3: 0-2 2m4-2m7: 0-1 3m+: 0-0
Track: LH: 0-2 RH: 0-1 Tight: 0-0 Gall: 0-1
Aids: Bl: 0-0 Vi: 0-0 Tstrap: 0-1 Ckp: 0-0
Best Rating: 99 12/03 Newb 2m110y   gd-fm   Hdl

Le Duc (FR)
113(118h)   (136h)140+

5-y-o b g Villez (USA)-Beberova (FR) (Synefos (USA))
P F Nicholls Mrs J Stewart

Placings:2224F461-14F2013P4   (4848)
2003/04: 16¹GF, 16⁴G, 19⁵S, 16²G, 16⁶G, 17¹GS, 16³G, 20⁶G, 16⁴GS,

	Starts	1st	2nd	3rd	Win & Pl
Hurdles	1	0	0	0	
Chases	8	2	1	1	28916
Career Total	17	3	4	1	107902
110	3/04	Kels	2m1f	D Ch	G-S £5531
115	10/03	Weth	2m	E Ch	G-F £3990
132	4/03	Aint	2m110y	A Hdl	GD £63800
			Total win prize-money £73322		

Going: Sf: 0-1 GS: 1-2 Gd: 0-5 GF: - Fm: 1-1
Distance: 2m/2m3: 2-7 2m4-2m7: 0-2 3m+: 0-0
Track: LH: 2-8 RH: 0-1 Tight: 1-3 Gall: 0-3
Aids: Bl: 0-0 Vi: 0-0 Tstrap: 0-0 Ckp: 0-0
Best Rating: 143 3/04 Chel 2m   good   Ch

Very useful novice chaser; juvenile hurdler in 2002/3; ex-French; surprise winner of Grade Two race at Aintree in April 2003; ran best race to date over fences when third in the 2004 Arkle; carries an awkward head carriage; has bags of potential, but is tricky; best going left-handed; best at two miles; acts well on a sound surface.

Le Forezien (FR)

5-y-o b g Gunboat Diplomacy (FR)-Diane Du Forez (FR) (Quart De Vin (FR))

C J Gray (T Civel 20/6) S C Botham

Placings:2340-F21P   (3252)
2003/04: 17⁰HO, 17⁵VS, 17²G, 17¹VS, 16⁶G,

	Starts	1st	2nd	3rd	Win & Pl
Chases	5	1	1	0	8571
Career Total	8	1	2	1	16957
6/03	Autl	2m1f110y Ch		VS	£6545
		Total win prize-money £6545			

Going: Sf: 0-0 GS: 0-0 Gd: 0-2 GF: - Fm: 0-0
Distance: 2m/2m3: 1-5 2m4-2m7: 0-0 3m+: 0-0
Track: LH: 0-0 RH: 0-1 Tight: 0-1 Gall: 0-0
Aids: Bl: 0-0 Vi: 0-0 Tstrap: 0-0 Ckp: 0-0

Le Gallois

7-y-o b g Deltic (USA)-Safety First (Wassl)
D Brace David Brace

Placings:0   (1836)
2003/04: 16⁹GF,

	Starts	1st	2nd	3rd	Win & Pl
NH Flat	1	0	0	0	
Career Total	1	0	0	0	

Going: Sf: 0-0 GS: 0-0 Gd: 0-0 GF: - Fm: 0-1
Distance: 2m/2m3: 0-1 2m4-2m7: 0-0 3m+: 0-0
Track: LH: 0-1 RH: 0-0 Tight: 0-0 Gall: 0-0
Aids: Bl: 0-0 Vi: 0-0 Tstrap: 0-1 Ckp: 0-0

Le Grand Rocher
72   28

7-y-o ch g Factual (USA)-Honey Bridge (Crepello)
Jonjo O'Neill The Swinging Richards

Placings:2-0   (2289)
2003/04: 20⁰G,

	Starts	1st	2nd	3rd	Win & Pl
Hurdles	1	0	0	0	
Career Total	2	0	1	0	434

Going: Sf: 0-0 GS: 0-0 Gd: 0-1 GF: - Fm: 0-0
Distance: 2m/2m3: 0-0 2m4-2m7: 0-1 3m+: 0-0
Track: LH: 0-1 RH: 0-0 Tight: 0-1 Gall: 0-0
Aids: Bl: 0-0 Vi: 0-0 Tstrap: 0-0 Ckp: 0-0
Best Rating: 94 6/02 Worc 2m   soft   NHF

Le Gris (GER)
95   86+

5-y-o gr g Neshad (USA)-Lady Pedomade (GER) (Mondrian (GER))
J S Moore Cistm Racing Club Ltd

Placings:002   (4812)
2003/04: 16⁰G, 16⁰G, 16²G,

	Starts	1st	2nd	3rd	Win & Pl
Hurdles	3	0	1	0	1108
Career Total	3	0	1	0	1108

Going: Sf: 0-0 GS: 0-0 Gd: 0-3 GF: - Fm: 0-0
Distance: 2m/2m3: 0-3 2m4-2m7: 0-0 3m+: 0-0
Track: LH: 0-1 RH: 0-2 Tight: 0-0 Gall: 0-1
Aids: Bl: 0-0 Vi: 0-0 Tstrap: 0-0 Ckp: 0-0
Best Rating: 86 4/04 Chep 2m110y   good   Hdl

Wore blinkers for both his wins on the Flat in Germany; much better effort despite being no match for Ilabon at Chepstow on third start over hurdles.

Le Guvnor
23

9-y-o ch g Le Moss-High Heels (IRE) (Supreme Leader)
G J Smith Mrs A D Aldred

Placings:PPP0PP-P   (4401)
2003/04: 21⁰G,

	Starts	1st	2nd	3rd	Win & Pl
Hurdles	1	0	0	0	
Career Total	7	0	0	0	

Going: Sf: 0-0 GS: 0-0 Gd: 0-1 GF: - Fm: 0-0
Distance: 2m/2m3: 0-0 2m4-2m7: 0-1 3m+: 0-0
Track: LH: 0-0 RH: 0-1 Tight: 0-0 Gall: 0-1
Aids: Bl: 0-0 Vi: 0-0 Tstrap: 0-0 Ckp: 0-0
Best Rating: 23 2/03 Leic 2m   heavy   Hdl

Le Joyeux (FR)
84   86

5-y-o br g Video Rock (FR)-Agra (FR) (Brezzo (FR))
B I Case Dudley C Moore

Placings:00000   (4783)
2003/04: 16⁰GS, 16⁰HY, 22⁰G, 25⁰S, 21⁰G,

	Starts	1st	2nd	3rd	Win & Pl
NH Flat	2	0	0	0	0
Hurdles	3	0	0	0	0
Career Total	5	0	0	0	

Going: Sf: 0-2 GS: 0-1 Gd: 0-2 GF: - Fm: 0-0
Distance: 2m/2m3: 0-2 2m4-2m7: 0-2 3m+: 0-1
Track: LH: 0-2 RH: 0-2 Tight: 0-0 Gall: 0-2
Aids: Bl: 0-0 Vi: 0-0 Tstrap: 0-3 Ckp: 0-0
Best Rating: 88 12/03 Newb 2m110y   gd-sft   NHF

Le Mino (FR)
73   44

5-y-o b g Noblequest (FR)-Minouche (FR) (Fill My Hopes (FR))
Ferdy Murphy G R Orchard

Placings:0P   (3481)
2003/04: 16⁰G, 25⁰G,

	Starts	1st	2nd	3rd	Win & Pl
Hurdles	2	0	0	0	
Career Total	2	0	0	0	

Going: Sf: 0-0 GS: 0-1 Gd: 0-1 GF: - Fm: 0-0
Distance: 2m/2m3: 0-1 2m4-2m7: 0-0 3m+: 0-1
Track: LH: 0-2 RH: 0-0 Tight: 0-2 Gall: 0-0
Aids: Bl: 0-0 Vi: 0-0 Tstrap: 0-0 Ckp: 0-0
Best Rating: 44 1/04 Catt 2m   gd-sft   Hdl

Le Passing (FR)
111   (0c)136

5-y-o b g Passing Sale (FR)-Petite Serenade (FR) (Trac)
P F Nicholls The Hon Mrs Townshend & J R Townshend

Placings:42-211220   (4428)
2003/04: 16²GS, 17¹S, 17¹G, 16²S, 16²S, 17⁰G,

	Starts	1st	2nd	3rd	Win & Pl
Hurdles	6	2	3	0	17413
Career Total	8	2	4	0	22884
133	12/03	Tntn	2m1f	D Hdl	GD £4598
111	5/03	Bang	2m1f	E Hdl	SFT £3536
			Total win prize-money £8135		

Going: Sf: 1-3 GS: 0-1 Gd: 1-2 GF: - Fm: 0-0
Distance: 2m/2m3: 2-6 2m4-2m7: 0-0 3m+: 0-0
Track: LH: 1-4 RH: 1-2 Tight: 2-2 Gall: 0-1
Aids: Bl: 0-0 Vi: 0-0 Tstrap: 0-0 Ckp: 0-0
Best Rating: 135 2/04 Weth 2m soft Hdl

Useful novice hurdler; dual winner, runner-up to two very useful sorts since; effective at two miles and acts on soft ground; consistent.

Le Rochelais (FR)

92   95

5-y-o ch g Goldneyev (USA)-Olympiade De Brion (FR) (Night And Day)
R H Alner Martin Short

Placings:043   (4664)
2003/04: 16⁴HY, 16⁴GS, 19³GS,

	Starts	1st	2nd	3rd	Win & Pl
Hurdles	3	0	0	1	854
Career Total	3	0	0	1	854

Going: Sf: 0-1 GS: 0-2 Gd: 0-0 GF: - Fm: 0-0
Distance: 2m/2m3: 0-2 2m4-2m7: 0-1 3m+: 0-0
Track: LH: 0-3 RH: 0-0 Tight: 0-1 Gall: 0-0
Aids: Bl: 0-0 Vi: 0-0 Tstrap: 0-0 Ckp: 0-0
Best Rating: 95 3/04 Chep 2m110y gd-sft Hdl

Showed ability on the Flat in France; more patiently ridden and stepped up on debut when fourth in 2m Chepstow novice hurdle; should stay further.

Le Roi Miguel (FR)

122   (121h)162

6-y-o b g Point Of No Return (FR)-Loumir (USA) (Bob's Dusty (USA))
P F Nicholls Mrs J Stewart

Placings:6212/22F1-124F4F6   (4835)
2003/04: 16¹GY, 19²S, 16⁴G, 24⁴G, 19⁴S, 20⁴G, 21⁶GF,

	Starts	1st	2nd	3rd	Win & Pl
Chases	7	1	1	0	58171
Career Total	15	3	5	0	155491
147	5/03 Punc	2m	Ch	G-Y	£34220
162	4/03 Aint	2m	A Ch	GD	£67000
116	11/01 Newb	2m110y	C Hdl	GD	£5447

Total win prize-money £106668

Going: Sf: 0-2 GS: 0-0 Gd: 0-3 GF: - Fm: 0-1
Distance: 2m/2m3: 1-2 2m4-2m7: 0-4 3m+: 0-1
Track: LH: 0-2 RH: 1-5 Tight: 0-1 Gall: 0-1
Aids: Bl: 0-0 Vi: 0-0 Tstrap: 0-1 Ckp: 0-0
Best Rating: 162 12/03 Sand 2m good Ch

High-class chaser; ex-French; winner of Grade One novice chases at Aintree and Punchestown in the spring of 2003; good effort on seasonal return over two miles four on soft ground, but held since; effective over two miles, but stays farther; acts on ground good or softer; has worn tongue tie; races enthusiastically.

Le Royal (FR)

105   117+

5-y-o b g Garde Royale-Caucasie (FR) (Djarvis (FR))
Mrs M Reveley Mrs Stephanie Smith

Placings:43113   (4049)
2003/04: 20⁴G, 20³S, 20¹G, 20¹HY, 20³G,

	Starts	1st	2nd	3rd	Win & Pl
Hurdles	5	2	0	2	13393
Career Total	5	2	0	2	13393

117	1/04 Hayd	2m4f	D Hdl	HVY	£5031
117	1/04 Hayd	2m4f	D Hdl	GD	£5109

Total win prize-money £10140

Going: Sf: 1-2 GS: 0-0 Gd: 1-3 GF: - Fm: 0-0
Distance: 2m/2m3: 0-0 2m4-2m7: 2-5 3m+: 0-0
Track: LH: 2-5 RH: 0-0 Tight: 0-1 Gall: 0-0
Aids: Bl: 0-0 Vi: 0-0 Tstrap: 0-0 Ckp: 0-0
Best Rating: 117 2/04 Hayd 2m4f good Hdl

Won in the Flat in France; won at twice at Haydock in January; stays two miles four; best in soft ground.

Le Sauvage (IRE)

85

9-y-o b g Tirol-Cistus (Sun Prince)
D W Barker D W Barker

Placings:00/5534/1126/0P0/0P23540-P   (3691)
2003/04: 19⁵G,

	Starts	1st	2nd	3rd	Win & Pl
Hurdles	1	0	0	0	
Career Total	21	2	2	2	7031
105	10/00 Carl	2m4f110yE(0-105)HHdl		SFT	£2497
102	10/00 Carl	2m4f110yF(0-100)HHdl		G-S	£2289

Total win prize-money £4787

Going: Sf: 0-0 GS: 0-0 Gd: 0-1 GF: - Fm: 0-0
Distance: 2m/2m3: 0-1 2m4-2m7: 0-0 3m+: 0-0
Track: LH: 0-1 RH: 0-0 Tight: 0-1 Gall: 0-0
Aids: Bl: 0-0 Vi: 0-0 Tstrap: 0-0 Ckp: 0-0
Best Rating: 110 11/00 Carl 2m4f110y heavy Hdl

Moderate hurdler; acts on soft ground.

Le Turk (FR)

5-y-o b/br g Baby Turk-Valse De Sienne (FR) (Petit Montmorency (USA))
D P Keane Mrs S Clifford

Placings:0PP   (4167)
2003/04: 16⁰HY, 16⁸PG, 21⁸PG,

	Starts	1st	2nd	3rd	Win & Pl
NH Flat	1	0	0	0	0
Hurdles	2	0	0	0	0
Career Total	3	0	0	0	

Going: Sf: 0-1 GS: 0-0 Gd: 0-2 GF: - Fm: 0-0
Distance: 2m/2m3: 0-2 2m4-2m7: 0-1 3m+: 0-0
Track: LH: 0-1 RH: 0-2 Tight: 0-0 Gall: 0-1
Aids: Bl: 0-0 Vi: 0-0 Tstrap: 0-0 Ckp: 0-0
Best Rating: 33 1/04 Asct 2m110y heavy NHF

Leaburn (IRE)

107   129+

11-y-o b g Tremblant-Conderlea (Scorpio (FR))
P J Hobbs The Guburn Set

Placings:2U20/1F41124/21346/416562/3100   (4575)
2003/04: 17³GS, 16¹G, 19⁰S, 18⁰G,

	Starts	1st	2nd	3rd	Win & Pl
Chases	4	1	0	1	11396
Career Total	26	6	5	2	47554
129	12/03 Winc	2m	C(0-130)HCh	GD	£9646
128	10/01 Strf	2m11f110yD(0-120)HCh		G-S	£4095
130	11/00 Newb	2m1f	(0-135)Ch	HVY	£9374
125	2/00 Winc	2m	C Ch	GD	£5817
130	1/00 Tntn	2m110y	D Ch	G-S	£4192
109	12/99 Wwck	2m2f110yE Hdl		SFT	£3095

Total win prize-money £36223

Lead Story (IRE)

11-y-o br g Lead On Time (USA)-Mashmoon (USA) (Habitat)
G Chambers Mrs M Trueman

Placings:P000/P/21P50/6106/FPP-   (0018)
2003/04: 21⁰S,

	Starts	1st	2nd	3rd	Win & Pl
Chases	1	0	0	0	
Career Total	17	2	1	0	4811
100	5/01 NAbb	3m2f110yH Ch		G-F	£2177
112	6/00 NAbb	3m2f110yH Ch		GD	£2177

Total win prize-money £4354

Going: Sf: 0-1 GS: 0-0 Gd: 0-0 GF: - Fm: 0-0
Distance: 2m/2m3: 0-0 2m4-2m7: 0-1 3m+: 0-0
Track: LH: 0-1 RH: 0-0 Tight: 0-1 Gall: 0-0
Aids: Bl: 0-0 Vi: 0-0 Tstrap: 0-0 Ckp: 0-0
Best Rating: 112 6/00 NAbb 3m2f110y good Ch

Fair chaser; best at two miles; off the track from March 2002 until third at Newbury in November 2003; good winner at Wincanton next time; acts on most types of ground; sometimes tongue tied.

Leadaway

62   45

5-y-o b g Supreme Leader-Annicombe Run (Deep Run)
A Parker Mr & Mrs Raymond Anderson Green

Placings:000   (4292)
2003/04: 16⁰G, 20⁰GS, 16⁰GF,

	Starts	1st	2nd	3rd	Win & Pl
NH Flat	1	0	0	0	0
Hurdles	2	0	0	0	0
Career Total	3	0	0	0	

Going: Sf: 0-0 GS: 0-1 Gd: 0-1 GF: - Fm: 0-1
Distance: 2m/2m3: 0-2 2m4-2m7: 0-1 3m+: 0-0
Track: LH: 0-3 RH: 0-0 Tight: 0-0 Gall: 0-1
Aids: Bl: 0-0 Vi: 0-0 Tstrap: 0-0 Ckp: 0-0
Best Rating: 60 11/03 Hexm 2m110y good NHF

Leader Supreme (IRE)

(70h)   (36h)60

9-y-o b m Supreme Leader-Country Daisy Vii (Damsire Unregistered)
J R Jenkins Humphrey Solomons

Placings:0/F6/00P034F4-P   (0134)
2003/04: 26⁸GF,

	Starts	1st	2nd	3rd	Win & Pl
Hurdles	1	0	0	0	
Career Total	12	0	0	1	1142

Going: Sf: 0-0 GS: 0-0 Gd: 0-0 GF: - Fm: 0-1
Distance: 2m/2m3: 0-0 2m4-2m7: 0-0 3m+: 0-1
Track: LH: 0-0 RH: 0-1 Tight: 0-0 Gall: 0-1
Aids: Bl: 0-0 Vi: 0-1 Tstrap: 0-0 Ckp: 0-0

Best Rating: 92 4/01 Kemp 2m good NHF

Leading Man (IRE)
94f **83f**

4-y-o b g Old Vic-Cudder Or Shudder (IRE) (The Parson)
Ferdy Murphy Mrs C McKeane

						(3818)
Placings:44
2003/04: 16⁴GS, 16⁴GS,

	Starts	1st	2nd	3rd	Win & Pl
NH Flat	2	0	0	0	0
Career Total	2	0	0	0	0

Going:	Sf: 0-0 GS: 0-2 Gd: 0-0 GF: - Fm: 0-0
Distance:	2m/2m3: 0-2 2m4-2m7: 0-0 3m+: 0-0
Track:	LH: 0-2 RH: 0-0 Tight: 0-1 Gall: 0-0
Aids:	Bl: 0-0 Vi: 0-0 Tstrap: 0-0 Ckp: 0-0
Best Rating:	83 2/04 Ayr 2m gd-sft NHF

Promising fourth in ordinary bumper at Catterick in January on debut and shaped well at Ayr the following month in ordinary event; should be capable of better.

Leagues (NZ)
(86h) (96h)**103**

9-y-o b g Kenfair (NZ)-Hidden Depths (NZ) (Beaufort Sea (USA))
M J Gingell T Alexander And G S Plastow

						(0764)
Placings:5000/P4P60-45
2003/04: 17⁴GF, 20⁵GF,

	Starts	1st	2nd	3rd	Win & Pl
Hurdles	2	0	0	0	0
Career Total	11	0	0	0	365

Going:	Sf: 0-0 GS: 0-0 Gd: 0-0 GF: - Fm: 0-2
Distance:	2m/2m3: 0-1 2m4-2m7: 0-1 3m+: 0-0
Track:	LH: 0-0 RH: 0-0 Tight: 0-0 Gall: 0-0
Aids:	Bl: 0-0 Vi: 0-0 Tstrap: 0-0 Ckp: 0-0
Best Rating:	103 12/02 Donc 2m110y good Ch

Big sort, very limited ability over hurdles and fences so far.

Leap Year Lass
95 **78**

4-y-o ch f Fleetwood (IRE)-Lady Phyl (Northiam (USA))
C Grant (John Allen 5/7) Chris Grant

						(4958)
Placings:F5535064U
2003/04: 16⁵GF, 16⁵G, 16⁵GS, 16³GS, 16⁵HY, 16⁹GD, 17⁶GS, 17⁴G, 17⁰G,

	Starts	1st	2nd	3rd	Win & Pl
Hurdles	9	0	0	1	965
Career Total	9	0	0	1	965

Going:	Sf: 0-1 GS: 0-4 Gd: 0-3 GF: - Fm: 0-1
Distance:	2m/2m3: 0-9 2m4-2m7: 0-0 3m+: 0-0
Track:	LH: 0-7 RH: 0-2 Tight: 0-0 Gall: 0-4
Aids:	Bl: 0-0 Vi: 0-0 Tstrap: 0-0 Ckp: 0-0
Best Rating:	78 4/04 Carl 2m1f good Hdl

Plating-class novice hurdler; easily best effort when third in mares' only event at Wetherby in January.

Learn The Lingo
82 **72+**

8-y-o b g Teenoso (USA)-Charlotte Gray (Rolfe (USA))

Mrs H Dalton David M Hughes

						(4266)
Placings:40/P-6P00
2003/04: 16⁶GS, 16⁵PS, 17⁰HY, 16⁰GF,

	Starts	1st	2nd	3rd	Win & Pl
Hurdles	4	0	0	0	0
Career Total	7	0	0	0	0

Going:	Sf: 0-2 GS: 0-1 Gd: 0-0 GF: - Fm: 0-1
Distance:	2m/2m3: 0-4 2m4-2m7: 0-0 3m+: 0-0
Track:	LH: 0-2 RH: 0-2 Tight: 0-0 Gall: 0-0
Aids:	Bl: 0-0 Vi: 0-0 Tstrap: 0-1 Ckp: 0-0
Best Rating:	87 12/01 Ludl 2m good NHF

Learned Lad (FR)
70 **75**

6-y-o ch g Royal Academy (USA)-Blushing Storm (USA) (Blushing Groom (FR))
Jamie Poulton J Wotherspoon

						(4207)
Placings:P-0
2003/04: 16⁰G,

	Starts	1st	2nd	3rd	Win & Pl
Hurdles	1	0	0	0	0
Career Total	2	0	0	0	0

Going:	Sf: 0-0 GS: 0-0 Gd: 0-1 GF: - Fm: 0-0
Distance:	2m/2m3: 0-1 2m4-2m7: 0-0 3m+: 0-0
Track:	LH: 0-0 RH: 0-1 Tight: 0-0 Gall: 0-0
Aids:	Bl: 0-0 Vi: 0-0 Tstrap: 0-0 Ckp: 0-0
Best Rating:	75 3/04 Kemp 2m good Hdl

Lease
106 **105+**

6-y-o ch g Lycius (USA)-Risanda (Kris)
John G Carr (T J Taaffe 11/5) James Hepburn

						(1623)
Placings:06350060-0101F
2003/04: 20⁰G, 16¹GF, 16⁸G, 17¹GF, 20⁰GF,

	Starts	1st	2nd	3rd	Win & Pl
Hurdles	5	2	0	0	6092
Career Total	13	2	0	1	6564
98	10/03	Carl	2m1f	E Hdl		G-F	£2660
98	8/03	Prth	2m110y	G Hdl		G-F	£3432
					Total win prize-money £6092

Going:	Sf: 0-0 GS: 0-0 Gd: 0-2 GF: - Fm: 2-3
Distance:	2m/2m3: 2-3 2m4-2m7: 0-2 3m+: 0-0
Track:	LH: 0-1 RH: 2-3 Tight: 0-0 Gall: 0-0
Aids:	Bl: 0-0 Vi: 0-0 Tstrap: 0-0 Ckp: 0-1
Best Rating:	105 10/03 Hexm 2m4f110y gd-fm Hdl

Moderate hurdler; effective at around two miles; acts on decent ground.

Leche Bottes (FR)
91 **106**

5-y-o b g Sleeping Car (FR)-Gibelotte (FR) (Royal Charter (FR))
M C Pipe (Mme I Pacault 10/6) M C Pipe

						(4629)
Placings:04-50
2003/04: 18⁵VS, 20⁰G,

	Starts	1st	2nd	3rd	Win & Pl
Hurdles	2	0	0	0	1052
Career Total	4	0	0	0	2471

Going:	Sf: 0-0 GS: 0-0 Gd: 0-1 GF: - Fm: 0-0

Distance:	2m/2m3: 0-1 2m4-2m7: 0-1 3m+: 0-0
Track:	LH: 0-1 RH: 0-0 Tight: 0-1 Gall: 0-0
Aids:	Bl: 0-0 Vi: 0-0 Tstrap: 0-0 Ckp: 0-0
Best Rating:	106 4/04 Aint 2m4f good Hdl

Ex-French novice hurdler, now with Martin Pipe; shown some form on testing ground.

Leckampton
28

8-y-o b m Bedford (USA)-I'm Unforgettable (Dublin Taxi)
S E H Sherwood I W Thompson

						(0054)
Placings:0/6-P
2003/04: 26⁵GS,

	Starts	1st	2nd	3rd	Win & Pl
Hurdles	1	0	0	0	0
Career Total	3	0	0	0	0

Going:	Sf: 0-0 GS: 0-1 Gd: 0-0 GF: - Fm: 0-0
Distance:	2m/2m3: 0-0 2m4-2m7: 0-0 3m+: 0-1
Track:	LH: 0-0 RH: 0-1 Tight: 0-0 Gall: 0-0
Aids:	Bl: 0-0 Vi: 0-0 Tstrap: 0-0 Ckp: 0-0
Best Rating:	74 8/01 Worc 2m gd-fm NHF

Lee Anna

6-y-o ch m Karinga Bay-Hachimitsu (Vaigly Great)
R J Baker Graham Brown

						(4147)
Placings:P
2003/04: 24⁵G,

	Starts	1st	2nd	3rd	Win & Pl
Hurdles	1	0	0	0	
Career Total	1	0	0	0	

Going:	Sf: 0-0 GS: 0-0 Gd: 0-1 GF: - Fm: 0-0
Distance:	2m/2m3: 0-0 2m4-2m7: 0-0 3m+: 0-1
Track:	LH: 0-0 RH: 0-1 Tight: 0-1 Gall: 0-0
Aids:	Bl: 0-0 Vi: 0-0 Tstrap: 0-0 Ckp: 0-0

Lee's Rosie (IRE)

9-y-o b m Zaffaran (USA)-Muse Of Fire (Laurence O)
Miss Bianca Dunk Miss Bianca Dunk

						(0509)
Placings:05/0PP/01-UP
2003/04: 25⁵GS, 28⁵GS,

	Starts	1st	2nd	3rd	Win & Pl
Chases	2	0	0	0	
Career Total	9	1	0	0	1456
73	4/03	Hexm	3m1f	H Ch		GD	£1456
					Total win prize-money £1456

Going:	Sf: 0-0 GS: 0-1 Gd: 0-1 GF: - Fm: 0-0
Distance:	2m/2m3: 0-0 2m4-2m7: 0-0 3m+: 0-2
Track:	LH: 0-2 RH: 0-0 Tight: 0-2 Gall: 0-0
Aids:	Bl: 0-0 Vi: 0-0 Tstrap: 0-0 Ckp: 0-0
Best Rating:	79 1/01 Ludl 2m soft NHF

Fair hunter chaser; stays beyond three miles and acts on good ground.

Left Bank (IRE)
104 (77h)**90**

8-y-o ch g Over The River (FR)-My Friend Fashion (Laurence O)

Mrs M Reveley C C Buckley

Placings:00/400260633/3P164U30130-P52F525   (4616)
2003/04: 22^PG, 25^5G, 22^2GF, 22^FGS, 19^5G, 20^5GF, 21^5G,

	Starts	1st	2nd	3rd	Win & Pl
Chases	7	0	2	0	2335
Career Total	29	2	3	5	14124
90 3/03 Weth	3m1f E(0-105)HCh		G-F		£4173
80 10/02 Weth	2m7f110yE(0-105)HCh		G-F		£3786

Total win prize-money £7959

Going:	Sf: 0-0 GS: 0-1 Gd: 0-4 GF: - Fm: 0-2
Distance:	2m/2m3: 0-1 2m4-2m7: 0-5 3m+: 0-1
Track:	LH: 0-7 RH: 0-1 Tight: 0-2 Gall: 0-0
Aids:	Bl: 0-0 Vi: 0-0 Tstrap: 0-0 Ckp: 0-1
Best Rating:	90 10/03 Hayd 2m6f gd-fm Ch

Modest chaser, stays three miles, wears headgear; suited by a sound surface and had conditions in his favour when a fortuitous winner at Wetherby in March.

Legal Lunch (USA)
105 / 121+

9-y-o b g Alleged (USA)-Dinner Surprise (USA) (Lyphard (USA))
W K Goldsworthy Greenacre Racing Partnership Ltd

Placings:02120/124/05P0-P3011214   (4643)
2003/04: 19^PGS, 24^3G, 24^0GS, 22^1GS, 22^1G, 21^2G, 20^1GS, 24^4G,

	Starts	1st	2nd	3rd	Win & Pl
Hurdles	7	3	1	1	17592
Chases	1	0	0	0	
Career Total	20	5	4	1	40209
3/04 Chep	2m4f D(0-125)HHdl		G-S		£5167
109 2/04 Font	2m6f110yE(0-110)HHdl		GD		£5616
107 2/04 Font	2m6f110yG Hdl		G-S		£2443
132 10/01 Sthl	2m4f110yC(0-130)HHdl		G-S		£6890
126 2/01 Font	2m6f110yE Hdl		G-S		£3167

Total win prize-money £23285

Going:	Sf: 0-0 GS: 2-4 Gd: 1-4 GF: - Fm: 0-0
Distance:	2m/2m3: 0-0 **2m4-2m7: 3-5** 3m+: 0-3
Track:	**LH: 3-6** RH: 0-2 **Tight: 2-3** Gall: 0-1
Aids:	Bl: 0-0 Vi: 0-0 Tstrap: 0-0 Ckp: 0-0
Best Rating:	132 10/01 Sthl 2m4f110y good Hdl

Progressive hurdler despite his age; graduated from selling company to win three out of four in February/March 2004; stays three miles; acts on good and good to soft ground; has worn a visor; goes well at Fontwell.

Legal Storm (IRE)

12-y-o gr g Roselier (FR)-Stormy Waters (Typhoon II)
P York R M Green

Placings:2204330/000500U453F3/4200F0/U506/0/5F   (4298)

2003/04: 21^5G, 23^FG,

	Starts	1st	2nd	3rd	Win & Pl
Chases	2	0	0	0	0
Career Total	32	0	3	4	4267

Going:	Sf: 0-0 GS: 0-0 Gd: 0-2 GF: - Fm: 0-0
Distance:	2m/2m3: 0-0 2m4-2m7: 0-3 3m+: 0-1
Track:	LH: 0-0 RH: 0-2 Tight: 0-1 Gall: 0-0
Aids:	Bl: 0-0 Vi: 0-0 Tstrap: 0-0 Ckp: 0-0
Best Rating:	105 2/98 Navn 2m heavy NHF

Legatus (IRE)
97 / 109+

7-y-o ch g Alphabatim (USA)-Take A Guess (IRE)

(Carlingford Castle)
M C Pipe (D Pipe 29/4) B A Kilpatrick

Placings:2-3   (2517)
2003/04: 26^2S, 25^3GS,

	Starts	1st	2nd	3rd	Win & Pl
Chases	2	0	1	1	1274
Career Total	2	0	1	1	1274

Going:	Sf: 0-0 GS: 0-1 Gd: 0-0 GF: - Fm: 0-0
Distance:	2m/2m3: 0-0 2m4-2m7: 0-0 3m+: 0-2
Track:	LH: 0-1 RH: 0-1 Tight: 0-0 Gall: 0-0
Aids:	Bl: 0-0 Vi: 0-2 Tstrap: 0-0 Ckp: 0-0
Best Rating:	109 12/03 Hrfd 3m1f110y gd-sft Ch

Won three points for David Pipe; runner-up in novice hunter chase at Newton Abbot April 2003; found the company too hot when third to Fork Lightning at Hereford in December; stays three miles plus; acts on good and soft ground; usually wears a visor.

Leggies Legacy
83 / 91d

13-y-o b g Jupiter Island-Hit The Line (Saulingo)
J Gallagher A Russell & P B Davis Insurance

Placings:0/P/U143/205/0001300-0   (0152)
2003/04: 22^0S, 20^0GF,

	Starts	1st	2nd	3rd	Win & Pl
Hurdles	2	0	0	0	
Career Total	17	2	1	2	11177
91 1/03 Plum	2m5f D(0-125)HHdl		SFT		£5512
86 3/01 Plum	2m5f E Hdl		HVY		£2618

Total win prize-money £8130

Going:	Sf: 0-1 GS: 0-0 Gd: 0-0 GF: - Fm: 0-1
Distance:	2m/2m3: 0-0 2m4-2m7: 0-2 3m+: 0-0
Track:	LH: 0-2 RH: 0-0 Tight: 0-0 Gall: 0-0
Aids:	Bl: 0-1 Vi: 0-0 Tstrap: 0-0 Ckp: 0-0
Best Rating:	94 2/02 Plum 2m5f heavy Hdl

Moderate hurdler; looks best suited by around two miles five furlongs; acts well on soft and heavy ground.

Leith Hill Star
105 / (0c)102+

8-y-o ch m Comme L'Etoile-Sunnyday (Sunley Builds)
R Rowe Mrs N F Maltby

Placings:40/0404/4F6542-313142100   (4842)
2003/04: 24^3GF, 20^1GS, 22^3GS, 18^1G, 21^4S, 21^2G, 20^1GS, 22^0G, 21^0G,

	Starts	1st	2nd	3rd	Win & Pl
Hurdles	9	3	1	2	15716
Career Total	21	3	2	2	16794
102 2/04 Sand	2m4f110yD(0-120)HHdl		G-S		£5447
83 12/03 Font	2m2f110yH(0-)HHdl		GD		£1876
90 11/03 Folk	2m4f110yD(0-125)HHdl		G-S		£4706

Total win prize-money £12029

Going:	Sf: 0-1 GS: 2-3 Gd: 1-4 GF: - Fm: 0-1
Distance:	2m/2m3: 1-1 **2m4-2m7: 2-7** 3m+: 0-1
Track:	LH: 1-3 **RH: 2-6** Tight: 2-4 Gall: 0-1
Aids:	Bl: 0-1 Vi: 0-0 Tstrap: 0-0 Ckp: 0-0
Best Rating:	102 2/04 Sand 2m4f110y gd-sft Hdl

Plating-class hurdler; stays three miles one; seems to act on any ground.

Leitrim Rock (IRE)
71 / 28

4-y-o b g Barathea (IRE)-Kilshanny (Groom Dancer (USA))

A G Newcombe (D W P Arbuthnot 29/9) J D Simpson-Daniel

Placings:5   (1133)
2003/04: 17^5G,

	Starts	1st	2nd	3rd	Win & Pl
Hurdles	1	0	0	0	0
Career Total	1	0	0	0	0

Going:	Sf: 0-0 GS: 0-0 Gd: 0-1 GF: - Fm: 0-0
Distance:	2m/2m3: 0-1 2m4-2m7: 0-0 3m+: 0-0
Track:	LH: 0-0 RH: 0-0 Tight: 0-1 Gall: 0-0
Aids:	Bl: 0-0 Vi: 0-0 Tstrap: 0-0 Ckp: 0-0
Best Rating:	28 8/03 Bang 2m1f good Hdl

Poor hurdler.

Leophin Dancer (USA)
100 / 88

6-y-o b g Green Dancer (USA)-Happy Gal (FR) (Habitat)
P W Hiatt Clive Roberts

Placings:P60-1302P   (3352)
2003/04: 16^1GF, 16^3F, 16^0G, 16^2G, 16^PS,

	Starts	1st	2nd	3rd	Win & Pl
Hurdles	5	1	1	1	3268
Career Total	8	1	1	1	3268
88 9/03 Worc	2m G(0-90)HHdl		G-F		£1855

Total win prize-money £1855

Going:	Sf: 0-1 GS: 0-0 Gd: 0-2 GF: - Fm: 1-2
Distance:	2m/2m3: 1-5 2m4-2m7: 0-0 3m+: 0-0
Track:	LH: 1-2 RH: 0-3 Tight: 0-1 Gall: 0-1
Aids:	Bl: 0-0 Vi: 0-0 Tstrap: 0-0 Ckp: 0-0
Best Rating:	88 12/03 Ludl 2m good Hdl

Plating-class hurdler; ran out a convincing winner under a confident ride of 2m conditional jockeys' selling handicap at Worcester in September; acts on fast.

Leroy's Sister (FR)
96f / 97f

4-y-o b f Phantom Breeze-Loumir (USA) (Bob's Dusty (USA))
P F Nicholls Mrs J Stewart

Placings:642   (4846)
2003/04: 12^6GS, 18^4G, 17^2G,

	Starts	1st	2nd	3rd	Win & Pl
NH Flat	3	0	1	0	1190
Career Total	3	0	1	0	1190

Going:	Sf: 0-0 GS: 0-0 Gd: 0-2 GF: - Fm: 0-1
Distance:	2m/2m3: 0-2 2m4-2m7: 0-0 3m+: 0-1
Track:	LH: 0-3 RH: 0-0 Tight: 0-1 Gall: 0-1
Aids:	Bl: 0-0 Vi: 0-0 Tstrap: 0-0 Ckp: 0-1
Best Rating:	97 4/04 Chel 2m1f good NHF

A half-sister to the stable's Le Roi Miguel; has shown promise on both starts to date; she will stay further over hurdles; acts on decent going.

Lerubis (FR)
95 / 91

5-y-o b g Ragmar (FR)-Perle De Saisy (FR) (Italic (FR))
F Jordan (G Cherel 30/11) F Jordan

Placings:60004P005   (4874)
2003/04: 18^6HO, 17^0S, 18^0VS, 19^0VS, 17^4HO, 20^PHY, 16^0G, 17^0G, 20^5GS,

	Starts	1st	2nd	3rd	Win & Pl
Hurdles	6	0	0	0	0
Chases	3	0	0	0	1295
Career Total	9	0	0	0	1295

Going:	Sf: 0-2 GS: 0-1 Gd: 0-2 GF: - Fm: 0-0
Distance:	2m/2m3: 0-7 2m4-2m7: 0-2 3m+: 0-0
Track:	LH: 0-1 RH: 0-2 Tight: 0-1 Gall: 0-1
Aids:	Bl: 0-2 Vi: 0-0 Tstrap: 0-0 Ckp: 0-0
Best Rating:	91　3/04　Hntg　2m110y　good　Hdl

Lescer's Lad

89　　　　　　　　　　　　　　　　**75**

7-y-o b g Perpendicular-Grange Gracie (Oats)
J Hetherton　Mrs Josephine Church

Placings: *0*/03-00065　　　　　　　　(4595)
2003/04: 16⁶G, 19⁹G, 20⁹GS, 16⁶GF, 22⁵G,

	Starts	1st	2nd	3rd	Win & Pl
NH Flat	1	0	0	0	0
Hurdles	4	0	0	0	0
Career Total	8	0	0	1	272

Going:	Sf: 0-0 GS: 0-1 Gd: 0-3 GF: - Fm: 0-1
Distance:	2m/2m3: 0-3 2m4-2m7: 0-2 3m+: 0-0
Track:	LH: 0-4 RH: 0-1 Tight: 0-2 Gall: 0-1
Aids:	Bl: 0-0 Vi: 0-0 Tstrap: 0-0 Ckp: 0-0
Best Rating:	96　4/03　Hexm　2m110y　good　NHF

Lesdream

102　　　　　　　　　　　　　　　**111**

7-y-o b g Morpeth-Lesbet (Hotfoot)
J D Frost　Mrs L W Carlson

Placings: *4*/0P/00211-142　　　　　　　(4693)
2003/04: 19¹S, 21⁴S, 22⁶G,

	Starts	1st	2nd	3rd	Win & Pl
Hurdles	3	1	1	0	7098
Career Total	11	3	2	0	15928
102　1/04	Extr	2m3f	D(0-115)HHdl	SFT	£5005
97　2/03	Extr	2m1f	D(0-110)HHdl	G-S	£4823
92　2/03	Hrfd	2m1f	F(0-95)HHdl	GD	£2947
			Total win prize-money £12775		

Going:	Sf: 1-2 GS: 0-0 Gd: 0-1 GF: - Fm: 0-0
Distance:	2m/2m3: 1-1 2m4-2m7: 0-2 3m+: 0-0
Track:	LH: 0-1 RH: 1-2 Tight: 0-0 Gall: 0-0
Aids:	Bl: 0-0 Vi: 0-0 Tstrap: 0-0 Ckp: 0-0
Best Rating:	111　4/04　Extr　2m6f110y　good　Hdl

Moderate handicap hurdler; effective over two miles, but stays further; acts on good and good to soft ground.

Lespride

51　　　　　　　　　　　　　　　　**27**

6-y-o b g Morpeth-Lesbet (Hotfoot)
J D Frost　Mrs L W Carlson

Placings: *600*　　　　　　　　　　　(4630)
2003/04: 17⁶GS, 18⁰GS, 17⁹G,

	Starts	1st	2nd	3rd	Win & Pl
NH Flat	2	0	0	0	0
Hurdles	1	0	0	0	0
Career Total	3	0	0	0	0

Going:	Sf: 0-0 GS: 0-2 Gd: 0-1 GF: - Fm: 0-0
Distance:	2m/2m3: 0-3 2m4-2m7: 0-0 3m+: 0-0
Track:	LH: 0-1 RH: 0-2 Tight: 0-2 Gall: 0-0

Aids:	Bl: 0-0 Vi: 0-0 Tstrap: 0-0 Ckp: 0-0
Best Rating:	55　1/04　Extr　2m1f　gd-sft　NHF

Lesssaidthebetter (IRE)

(98h)　　　　　　　　　　　　　　(106h)
7-y-o ch g Montelimar (USA)-Urdite (FR) (Concertino (FR))
Jonjo O'Neill　John P McManus

Placings: 066300/230*B*-PP　　　　　　(4916)
2003/04: 26⁸GS, 23⁹GS,

	Starts	1st	2nd	3rd	Win & Pl
Chases	2	0	0	0	0
Career Total	12	0	1	2	2957

Going:	Sf: 0-0 GS: 0-2 Gd: 0-0 GF: - Fm: 0-0
Distance:	2m/2m3: 0-0 2m4-2m7: 0-0 3m+: 0-2
Track:	LH: 0-2 RH: 0-0 Tight: 0-1 Gall: 0-0
Aids:	Bl: 0-0 Vi: 0-0 Tstrap: 0-0 Ckp: 0-0
Best Rating:	106　12/02　Punc　2m4f　sft-hvy　Hdl

Lestat (IRE)

10-y-o b g Brush Aside (USA)-Shuilernish (Callernish)
Miss A Nolan　Mrs Vanessa Ramm

Placings: 0　　　　　　　　　　　　(0028)
2003/04: 21⁰G,

	Starts	1st	2nd	3rd	Win & Pl
Chases	1	0	0	0	0
Career Total	1	0	0	0	0

Going:	Sf: 0-0 GS: 0-0 Gd: 0-1 GF: - Fm: 0-0
Distance:	2m/2m3: 0-0 2m4-2m7: 0-1 3m+: 0-0
Track:	LH: 0-1 RH: 0-0 Tight: 0-0 Gall: 0-1
Aids:	Bl: 0-0 Vi: 0-0 Tstrap: 0-0 Ckp: 0-0
Best Rating:	67　4/03　Chel　2m5f　good　Ch

Lester Longfellow

98　　　　　　　　　　　　　　　**81+**

8-y-o b/br g Riverwise (USA)-Cut Above The Rest (Indiaro)
N R Mitchell　Mrs E Mitchell

Placings: *0*/P-P4P　　　　　　　　　(4208)
2003/04: 22⁵G, 19⁴S, 20⁹G,

	Starts	1st	2nd	3rd	Win & Pl
Chases	3	0	0	0	330
Career Total	5	0	0	0	330

Going:	Sf: 0-1 GS: 0-0 Gd: 0-2 GF: - Fm: 0-0
Distance:	2m/2m3: 0-0 2m4-2m7: 0-3 3m+: 0-0
Track:	LH: 0-0 RH: 0-2 Tight: 0-1 Gall: 0-0
Aids:	Bl: 0-0 Vi: 0-0 Tstrap: 0-0 Ckp: 0-0
Best Rating:	81　2/04　Extr　2m3f110y　soft　Ch

Let's Celebrate

90　　　　　　　　　　　　　　　**80**

4-y-o b g Groom Dancer (USA)-Shimmer (Bustino)
F Jordan (C E Brittain 7/8)　F Jordan

Placings: FF005　　　　　　　　　　(3337)
2003/04: 16⁶GF, 16⁶GF, 16⁹GF, 16⁹G, 16⁵GS,

	Starts	1st	2nd	3rd	Win & Pl
Hurdles	5	0	0	0	0

Career Total	5	0	0	0	0

Going:	Sf: 0-0 GS: 0-1 Gd: 0-1 GF: - Fm: 0-3
Distance:	2m/2m3: 0-5 2m4-2m7: 0-0 3m+: 0-0
Track:	LH: 0-2 RH: 0-3 Tight: 0-2 Gall: 0-0
Aids:	Bl: 0-0 Vi: 0-0 Tstrap: 0-0 Ckp: 0-0
Best Rating:	79　10/03　Ludl　2m　gd-fm　Hdl

Fell on both first two starts over hurdles, showing ability second time; well beaten in a better race on third run.

Lethem Air

6-y-o ch g Aragon-Llanddona (Royal Palace)
Tim Butt　Tim Butt

Placings: P　　　　　　　　　　　　(4884)
2003/04: 24⁸PGS,

	Starts	1st	2nd	3rd	Win & Pl
Chases	1	0	0	0	0
Career Total	1	0	0	0	0

Going:	Sf: 0-0 GS: 0-1 Gd: 0-0 GF: - Fm: 0-0
Distance:	2m/2m3: 0-0 2m4-2m7: 0-0 3m+: 0-1
Track:	LH: 0-0 RH: 0-1 Tight: 0-0 Gall: 0-0
Aids:	Bl: 0-0 Vi: 0-0 Tstrap: 0-0 Ckp: 0-0

Letitia's Loss (IRE)

106　　　　　　　　　　　　　　**100**

6-y-o ch m Zaffaran (USA)-Satin Sheen (Abednego)
N G Richards　The Saddleworth Knights

Placings: 41F　　　　　　　　　　　(3490)
2003/04: 24⁴GS, 27¹G, 22⁵HY,

	Starts	1st	2nd	3rd	Win & Pl
Hurdles	3	1	0	0	2562
Career Total	3	1	0	0	2562
100　12/03	Sedg	3m3f110yE Hdl		GD	£2562
		Total win prize-money £2562			

Going:	Sf: 0-1 GS: 0-1 Gd: 1-1 GF: - Fm: 0-0
Distance:	2m/2m3: 0-0 2m4-2m7: 0-1 3m+: 1-2
Track:	LH: 1-2 RH: 0-1 Tight: 1-1 Gall: 0-0
Aids:	Bl: 0-0 Vi: 0-0 Tstrap: 0-0 Ckp: 0-0
Best Rating:	100　12/03　Sedg　3m3f110y　good　Hdl

Irish point winner; got off the mark on second attempt over hurdles; acts on good ground or softer; stays three miles.

Lets Go Dutch

100　　　　　　　　　　　　　　**112**

8-y-o b m Nicholas Bill-Dutch Majesty (Homing)
K Bishop　Mrs E K Ellis

Placings: U2/4351F/6213-0　　　　　　(0035)
2003/04: 22⁰G,

	Starts	1st	2nd	3rd	Win & Pl
Hurdles	1	0	0	0	0
Career Total	12	2	2	2	13134
112　2/03	Extr	3m110y D(0-125)HHdl	G-S	£5720
100　3/02	Tntn	2m3f110yD Hdl	SFT	£3649
		Total win prize-money £9369			

Going:	Sf: 0-0 GS: 0-0 Gd: 0-1 GF: - Fm: 0-0
Distance:	2m/2m3: 0-0 2m4-2m7: 0-1 3m+: 0-0
Track:	LH: 0-0 RH: 0-1 Tight: 0-0 Gall: 0-0
Aids:	Bl: 0-0 Vi: 0-0 Tstrap: 0-0 Ckp: 0-0
Best Rating:	112　3/03　Sand　2m6f　heavy　Hdl

Modest hurdler; stays well; acts in soft ground.

Levallois (IRE)

86   **92**

8-y-o b g Trempolino (USA)-Broken Wave (Bustino)
P Winkworth Tweenhills Racing (Cleeve Hill)

Placings:22/26114424/010051055/FP33400-F00   (4704)
2003/04: 20^FG, 20⁰GS, 18⁰G,

	Starts	1st	2nd	3rd	Win & Pl
Hurdles	1	0	0	0	0
Chases	2	0	0	0	0
Career Total	29	4	4	2	97613
9/01	Engh	2m3f		Ch	HLD £11639
5/01	Autl	2m3f110y	HHdl		SFT £26188
9/00	Engh	2m1f		Ch	VS £11527
7/00	Diep	2m1f		Hdl	VS £10567

Total win prize-money £59921

Going: Sf: 0-0 GS: 0-1 Gd: 0-2 GF: - Fm: 0-0
Distance: 2m/2m3: 0-2 2m4-2m7: 0-2 3m+: 0-0
Track: LH: 0-2 RH: 0-1 Tight: 0-2 Gall: 0-0
Aids: Bl: 0-0 Vi: 0-0 Tstrap: 0-0 Ckp: 0-0
Best Rating: 117 6/01 Autl 3m1f110y v soft Hdl

Useful ex-French hurdler/chaser; successful twice over hurdles and twice over fences in his home country; best between two miles and two miles three; acts on soft ground.

Lewis Island (IRE)

105   **130+**

5-y-o b g Turtle Island (IRE)-Phyllode (Pharly (FR))
N A Twiston-Davies Mr & Mrs Peter Orton

Placings:512320-0U002100   (4942)
2003/04: 16⁰G, 16^UGF, 17⁰G, 17⁰GS, 20²GS, 19¹GF, 20⁰GS, 20⁰GS,

	Starts	1st	2nd	3rd	Win & Pl
Hurdles	7	1	1	0	7364
Chases	1	0	0	0	0
Career Total	14	2	3	1	22640
130	3/04	Hrfd	2m3f110y	D(0-120) HHdl	G-F £5687
124	12/02	Leic	2m	D Hdl	HVY £4836

Total win prize-money £10524

Going: Sf: 0-0 GS: 0-4 Gd: 0-2 GF: - Fm: 1-2
Distance: 2m/2m3: 0-4 2m4-2m7: 1-4 3m+: 0-0
Track: LH: 0-4 RH: 1-4 Tight: 0-0 Gall: 0-2
Aids: Bl: 0-0 Vi: 0-0 Tstrap: 0-0 Ckp: 0-0
Best Rating: 130 3/04 Hrfd 2m3f110y gd-fm Hdl

Fair hurdler; keen sort; unseated on chasing debut; best at two miles; acts on any ground; suited by forcing tactics.

Lews A Lady

35f

6-y-o ch m Sir Harry Lewis (USA)-Pretty Gayle (Midland Gayle)
D Eddy Miss Gwen Gibson

Placings:0   (2858)
2003/04: 16⁰GS,

	Starts	1st	2nd	3rd	Win & Pl
NH Flat	1	0	0	0	
Career Total	1	0	0	0	

Going: Sf: 0-0 GS: 0-1 Gd: 0-0 GF: - Fm: 0-0
Distance: 2m/2m3: 0-1 2m4-2m7: 0-0 3m+: 0-0
Track: LH: 0-1 RH: 0-0 Tight: 0-0 Gall: 0-0
Aids: Bl: 0-0 Vi: 0-0 Tstrap: 0-0 Ckp: 0-0

Leyaaly

85   **64**

5-y-o ch m Night Shift (USA)-Lower The Tone (IRE) (Phone Trick (USA))
B A Pearce Mervyn Merwood

Placings:00P   (4668)
2003/04: 16⁰S, 16⁰G, 23^PGS,

	Starts	1st	2nd	3rd	Win & Pl
Hurdles	3	0	0	0	
Career Total	3	0	0	0	

Going: Sf: 0-0 GS: 0-1 Gd: 0-1 GF: - Fm: 0-0
Distance: 2m/2m3: 0-2 2m4-2m7: 0-1 3m+: 0-0
Track: LH: 0-3 RH: 0-0 Tight: 0-3 Gall: 0-0
Aids: Bl: 0-0 Vi: 0-0 Tstrap: 0-0 Ckp: 0-0
Best Rating: 64 3/04 Plum 2m good Hdl

Leyland Comet (IRE)

86f   **73f**

6-y-o b/br g Roselier (FR)-Firey Comet (IRE) (Buckskin (FR))
Ferdy Murphy Trevor Hemmings

Placings:0   (0270)
2003/04: 16⁰G,

	Starts	1st	2nd	3rd	Win & Pl
NH Flat	1	0	0	0	
Career Total	1	0	0	0	

Going: Sf: 0-0 GS: 0-0 Gd: 0-1 GF: - Fm: 0-0
Distance: 2m/2m3: 0-1 2m4-2m7: 0-0 3m+: 0-0
Track: LH: 0-0 RH: 0-1 Tight: 0-0 Gall: 0-0
Aids: Bl: 0-0 Vi: 0-0 Tstrap: 0-0 Ckp: 0-0
Best Rating: 73 5/03 Prth 2m110y good NHF

Liberman (IRE)

99   **104**

6-y-o br g Standiford (USA)-Hail To You (USA) (Kirtling)
M C Pipe D A Johnson

Placings:21/121-1P45   (3906)
2003/04: 20¹GF, 22^PG, 16⁴HY, 19⁵GS,

	Starts	1st	2nd	3rd	Win & Pl
Hurdles	4	1	0	0	3434
Career Total	9	4	2	0	44934
100	12/03	Muss	2m4f	E Hdl	G-F £3062
142	3/03	Chel	2m110y	A NHF	GD £23200
93	7/02	Bell	2m1f	NHF	YLD £4021
111	4/02	Punc	2m	NHF	YLD £6773

Total win prize-money £37057

Going: Sf: 0-0 GS: 0-1 Gd: 0-1 GF: - Fm: 1-1
Distance: 2m/2m3: 0-1 2m4-2m7: 1-3 3m+: 0-0
Track: LH: 0-1 RH: 1-3 Tight: 1-2 Gall: 0-0
Aids: Bl: 0-0 Vi: 0-0 Tstrap: 0-0 Ckp: 0-0
Best Rating: 142 3/03 Chel 2m110y good NHF

Modest hurdler; winner of two bumpers in Ireland; runner-up on his British debut at Cheltenham before landing the Champion Bumper at the Cheltenham Festival; effective at around two miles and acts on a soft surface; has struggled over hurdles despite winning at Musselburgh in December 2003; stays two miles four, acts on fast and easy ground; disappointing sort.

Liberthine (FR)

101   **108+**

5-y-o b m Chamberlin (FR)-Libertina (FR) (Balsamo (FR))
N J Henderson Robert Waley-Cohen

Placings:6611215-14   (4642)
2003/04: 20¹G, 25⁴G,

	Starts	1st	2nd	3rd	Win & Pl
Chases	2	1	0	0	9314
Career Total	9	4	1	0	55519
108	3/04	Strf	2m4f	D Ch	GD £5564
9/02	Autl	2m2f	Hdl	VS £19141
7/02	Autl	2m1f110y	Hdl	VS £11779
6/02	Diep	1m7f	Hdl	GD £4123

Total win prize-money £40607

Going: Sf: 0-0 GS: 0-0 Gd: 1-2 GF: - Fm: 0-0
Distance: 2m/2m3: 0-0 2m4-2m7: 1-1 3m+: 0-1
Track: LH: 1-2 RH: 0-0 Tight: 0-0 Gall: 0-0
Aids: Bl: 0-0 Vi: 0-0 Tstrap: 0-0 Ckp: 0-0
Best Rating: 108 3/04 Strf 2m4f good Ch

Fair hurdler in France in 2002; best at around two miles; acts well on soft ground. Won poor chase on debut.

Liberty Seeker (FR)

107   **121**

5-y-o ch g Machiavellian (USA)-Samara (IRE) (Polish Patriot (USA))
P D Niven (G A Swinbank 18/2) M Sawers

Placings:11653   (3885)
2003/04: 17¹G, 17¹GF, 16⁶G, 16⁵G, 16³G,

	Starts	1st	2nd	3rd	Win & Pl
Hurdles	5	2	0	1	6537
Career Total	5	2	0	1	6537
111	11/03	Sedg	2m1f	E Hdl	G-F £2576
105	10/03	Sedg	2m1f	E Hdl	GD £2534

Total win prize-money £5110

Going: Sf: 0-0 GS: 0-0 Gd: 1-4 GF: - Fm: 1-1
Distance: 2m/2m3: 2-5 2m4-2m7: 0-0 3m+: 0-0
Track: LH: 2-3 RH: 0-2 Tight: 2-4 Gall: 0-0
Aids: Bl: 0-0 Vi: 0-0 Tstrap: 0-0 Ckp: 0-0
Best Rating: 121 2/04 Muss 2m good Hdl

Fair hurdler; winner of moderate novice events at Sedgefield in autumn 2003; effective over two miles; acts on decent ground.

Libre

82   **63**

4-y-o b g Bahamian Bounty-Premier Blues (FR) (Law Society (USA))
R C Guest (F Jordan 7/10) Willie McKay

Placings:600   (4260)
2003/04: 16⁶GF, 17⁰G, 16⁰GF,

	Starts	1st	2nd	3rd	Win & Pl
Hurdles	3	0	0	0	0
Career Total	3	0	0	0	0

Going: Sf: 0-0 GS: 0-0 Gd: 0-1 GF: - Fm: 0-2
Distance: 2m/2m3: 0-3 2m4-2m7: 0-0 3m+: 0-0
Track: LH: 0-2 RH: 0-1 Tight: 0-3 Gall: 0-0
Aids: Bl: 0-0 Vi: 0-0 Tstrap: 0-1 Ckp: 0-0
Best Rating: 63 10/03 Strf 2m110y gd-fm Hdl

Modest on the Flat; proved a costly failure on hurdles debut when well-backed favourite at Stratford in October 2003; not a natural jumper.

Lies And Phibbs (IRE)

6-y-o gr g Supreme Leader-Rosy Waters (Roselier (FR))
Mrs Barbara Waring John Millington, Nigel Trevithick

Placings:04-00   (3698)
2003/04: 16⁶GS, 17⁰HY,

	Starts	1st	2nd	3rd	Win & Pl
NH Flat	1	0	0	0	0
Hurdles	1	0	0	0	0
Career Total	4	0	0	0	208

Going:	Sf: 0-1 GS: 0-1 Gd: 0-0 GF: - Fm: 0-0
Distance:	2m/2m3: 0-2 2m4-2m7: 0-0 3m+: 0-0
Track:	LH: 0-0 RH: 0-2 Tight: 0-0 Gall: 0-1
Aids:	Bl: 0-0 Vi: 0-0 Tstrap: 0-1 Ckp: 0-0
Best Rating:	88 2/03 DRoy 2m soft NHF

Light Des Mulottes (FR)

94   **99+**

5-y-o gr g Solidoun (FR)-Tango Girl (FR) (Tip Moss (FR))
O Sherwood (Edward U Hales 1/5) R K Carvill

Placings:2-01430   (3775)
2003/04: 16⁰GY, 16¹GF, 16⁴G, 17³G, 16⁶G,

	Starts	1st	2nd	3rd	Win & Pl
NH Flat	2	1	0	0	2212
Hurdles	3	0	0	1	1037
Career Total	6	1	1	1	4288
101 11/03 Worc	2m		H NHF		G-F £2212
				Total win prize-money £2212

Going:	Sf: 0-0 GS: 0-0 Gd: 0-3 GF: - Fm: 1-1
Distance:	2m/2m3: 1-5 2m4-2m7: 0-0 3m+: 0-0
Track:	LH: 1-1 RH: 0-4 Tight: 0-1 Gall: 0-0
Aids:	Bl: 0-0 Vi: 0-0 Tstrap: 0-0 Ckp: 0-0
Best Rating:	101 11/03 Worc 2m gd-fm NHF

Ex-Irish, won a Worcester bumper on his British debut; did not hurdle that well on debut over flights; best form on fast ground.

Light Hearted Lily

95   **78**

5-y-o b m Deploy-Darling Splodge (Elegant Air)
R M Beckett The Foxons Fillies Partnership

Placings:0-536P5P035   (4777)
2003/04: 17⁵GF, 16³G, 17⁶GF, 21⁴PG, 20⁵GS, 21⁵PG, 20⁹G, 22³G, 23⁸G,

	Starts	1st	2nd	3rd	Win & Pl
NH Flat	3	0	0	1	268
Hurdles	6	0	0	1	429
Career Total	10	0	0	2	697

Going:	Sf: 0-0 GS: 0-2 Gd: 0-5 GF: - Fm: 0-2
Distance:	2m/2m3: 0-3 2m4-2m7: 0-5 3m+: 0-1
Track:	LH: 0-3 RH: 0-5 Tight: 0-3 Gall: 0-2
Aids:	Bl: 0-0 Vi: 0-0 Tstrap: 0-0 Ckp: 0-0
Best Rating:	80 9/03 MRas 2m1f110y gd-fm NHF

Light The River (IRE)

10-y-o b/br g Over The River (FR)-Mysterious Light (Strong Gale)

Miss C Metcalfe Miss C Metcalfe

Placings:P50344/PP/PP661305/6   (3723)
2003/04: 25⁶S,

	Starts	1st	2nd	3rd	Win & Pl
Chases	1	0	0	0	0
Career Total	17	1	0	2	5526
83 12/01 Hexm	3m1f		E(0-105)HCh		SFT £3591
				Total win prize-money £3591

Going:	Sf: 0-1 GS: 0-0 Gd: 0-0 GF: - Fm: 0-0
Distance:	2m/2m3: 0-0 2m4-2m7: 0-0 3m+: 0-1
Track:	LH: 0-1 RH: 0-0 Tight: 0-0 Gall: 0-0
Aids:	Bl: 0-1 Vi: 0-0 Tstrap: 0-1 Ckp: 0-0
Best Rating:	88 12/99 Leic 2m good Ch

Lightcliffe

25f

5-y-o ch m Abzu-Iron Lass (Thatch (USA))
J R Norton C R Green

Placings:0   (3968)
2003/04: 16⁰GS,

	Starts	1st	2nd	3rd	Win & Pl
NH Flat	1	0	0	0	
Career Total	1	0	0	0	

Going:	Sf: 0-0 GS: 0-1 Gd: 0-0 GF: - Fm: 0-0
Distance:	2m/2m3: 0-1 2m4-2m7: 0-0 3m+: 0-0
Track:	LH: 0-0 RH: 0-1 Tight: 0-0 Gall: 0-0
Aids:	Bl: 0-0 Vi: 0-0 Tstrap: 0-0 Ckp: 0-0

Lightening Returns

69f   **24f**

5-y-o ch m Bob's Return (IRE)-Sally Smith (Alias Smith (USA))
S A Brookshaw S A Brookshaw

Placings:0   (4447)
2003/04: 16⁹S,

	Starts	1st	2nd	3rd	Win & Pl
NH Flat	1	0	0	0	
Career Total	1	0	0	0	

Going:	Sf: 0-1 GS: 0-0 Gd: 0-0 GF: - Fm: 0-0
Distance:	2m/2m3: 0-1 2m4-2m7: 0-0 3m+: 0-0
Track:	LH: 0-1 RH: 0-0 Tight: 0-0 Gall: 0-0
Aids:	Bl: 0-0 Vi: 0-0 Tstrap: 0-0 Ckp: 0-0
Best Rating:	24 3/04 Wwck 2m soft NHF

Lightin' Jack (IRE)

87   **85**

6-y-o ch g Beneficial-Cillrossanta (IRE) (Mandalus)
Miss E C Lavelle H A Watton

Placings:530-3   (2005)
2003/04: 24³GF,

	Starts	1st	2nd	3rd	Win & Pl
Hurdles	1	0	0	1	291
Career Total	4	0	0	2	291

Going:	Sf: 0-0 GS: 0-0 Gd: 0-0 GF: - Fm: 0-0
Distance:	2m/2m3: 0-0 2m4-2m7: 0-0 3m+: 0-1
Track:	LH: 0-1 RH: 0-0 Tight: 0-0 Gall: 0-0
Aids:	Bl: 0-0 Vi: 0-0 Tstrap: 0-0 Ckp: 0-0
Best Rating:	96 11/03 Chep 3m gd-fm Hdl

Close third in Gowran bumper April 2003; beaten for speed rather than stamina when third in 3m novices hurdle at Chepstow in November.

Lightmoor Lady

10f

6-y-o b m Puget (USA)-Dragon Fire (Dragonara Palace (USA))
Mrs L Williamson R A Hughes

Placings:0-0   (0533)
2003/04: 16⁰GF,

	Starts	1st	2nd	3rd	Win & Pl
NH Flat	1	0	0	0	
Career Total	2	0	0	0	

Going:	Sf: 0-0 GS: 0-0 Gd: 0-0 GF: - Fm: 0-1
Distance:	2m/2m3: 0-1 2m4-2m7: 0-0 3m+: 0-0
Track:	LH: 0-1 RH: 0-0 Tight: 0-0 Gall: 0-0
Aids:	Bl: 0-0 Vi: 0-0 Tstrap: 0-0 Ckp: 0-0
Best Rating:	10 4/03 Fknm 2m good NHF

Lightning Quest (IRE)

(105h)   **(99h)**

13-y-o b g Rainbow Quest (USA)-Rare Roberta (USA) (Roberto (USA))
Mrs S J Smith Mrs S Smith

Placings:0/33530/1025161/6/35014541/4F242FF-04 (0314)
2003/04: 20⁰G, 21⁴S,

	Starts	1st	2nd	3rd	Win & Pl
Hurdles	1	0	0	0	
Chases	1	0	0	0	339
Career Total	31	5	3	4	20603
112 3/00 Donc	2m3f110yD Ch			GD	£3789
112 11/99 Hayd	2m4f	E(0-115)HHdl		GD	£2582
116 3/98 Kels	2m2f	D(0-120)HHdl		GD	£2801
108 8/97 MRas	2m5f110yF(0-95)HHdl			GD	£2108
90 6/97 Strf	2m3f	E Hdl		GD	£2276
				Total win prize-money £13558

Going:	Sf: 0-1 GS: 0-0 Gd: 0-1 GF: - Fm: 0-0
Distance:	2m/2m3: 0-0 2m4-2m7: 0-2 3m+: 0-0
Track:	LH: 0-2 RH: 0-0 Tight: 0-1 Gall: 0-0
Aids:	Bl: 0-0 Vi: 0-0 Tstrap: 0-0 Ckp: 0-0
Best Rating:	116 3/98 Kels 2m2f good Hdl

Lightning Star (USA)

101   **97**

9-y-o b g El Gran Senor (USA)-Cuz's Star (USA) (Galaxy Libra)
G L Moore Phil Collins

Placings:535/02303121233/403321310/P/0P620-063234 (4404)
2003/04: 16⁰GS, 18⁶GS, 16³GS, 17⁰G, 16³GF, 16⁴G,

	Starts	1st	2nd	3rd	Win & Pl
Hurdles	6	0	1	2	1460
Career Total	35	6	4	10	16312
112 2/01 Towc	2m	F(0-110)HHdl		HVY	£1876
114 1/01 Folk	2m1f110yG Hdl			HVY	£1554
101 1/00 Folk	2m1f110yG Hdl			SFT	£1519
100 12/99 Chep	2m4f	G Hdl		G-S	£1679
				Total win prize-money £6628

Going:	Sf: 0-0 GS: 0-3 Gd: 0-2 GF: - Fm: 0-1
Distance:	2m/2m3: 0-6 2m4-2m7: 0-0 3m+: 0-0

Track: LH: 0-3 RH: 0-3 Tight: 0-3 Gall: 0-1
Aids: BI: 0-5 Vi: 0-0 Tstrap: 0-0 Ckp: 0-0
Best Rating: 114 1/01 Folk 2m1f110y heavy Hdl

Plating-class hurdler; effective at two miles.

Lihou Mel

68f   **33f**

7-y-o b m Pursuit Of Love-Lovers Tryst (Castle Keep)
L A Dace Luke Dace

Placings:0   (0263)
2003/04: 16⁰GF,

	Starts	1st	2nd	3rd	Win & Pl
NH Flat	1	0	0	0	
Career Total	1	0	0	0	

Going: Sf: 0-0 GS: 0-0 Gd: 0-0 GF: - Fm: 0-1
Distance: 2m/2m3: 0-1 2m4-2m7: 0-0 3m+: 0-0
Track: LH: 0-0 RH: 0-1 Tight: 0-0 Gall: 0-0
Aids: BI: 0-0 Vi: 0-0 Tstrap: 0-0 Ckp: 0-0
Best Rating: 33 5/03 Ludl 2m gd-fm NHF

Lik Wood Power (NZ)

100   **103+**

7-y-o b g Bigstone (IRE)-Lady Paloma (USA) (Clever Trick (USA))
R C Guest Bache Silk

Placings:3F426   (4117)
2003/04: 16⁹G, 16⁶GF, 21⁴GS, 20⁴GS, 22⁶G,

	Starts	1st	2nd	3rd	Win & Pl
Hurdles	5	0	1	1	3128
Career Total	5	0	1	1	3128

Going: Sf: 0-0 GS: 0-2 Gd: 0-2 GF: - Fm: 0-1
Distance: 2m/2m3: 0-2 2m4-2m7: 0-3 3m+: 0-0
Track: LH: 0-3 RH: 0-2 Tight: 0-2 Gall: 0-1
Aids: BI: 0-0 Vi: 0-0 Tstrap: 0-0 Ckp: 0-0
Best Rating: 103 2/04 Hntg 2m4f110y gd-sft Hdl

Moderate hurdler; Flat winner in New Zealand; acts on a sound surface.

Like A Breeze

101f   **85f**

5-y-o bl m Bob Back (USA)-Whatagale (Strong Gale)
C J Down Geoffrey Rowe

Placings:3S   (3961)
2003/04: 16⁹HY, 18⁵G,

	Starts	1st	2nd	3rd	Win & Pl
NH Flat	2	0	0	1	288
Career Total	2	0	0	1	288

Going: Sf: 0-1 GS: 0-0 Gd: 0-1 GF: - Fm: 0-0
Distance: 2m/2m3: 0-2 2m4-2m7: 0-0 3m+: 0-0
Track: LH: 0-2 RH: 0-0 Tight: 0-1 Gall: 0-0
Aids: BI: 0-0 Vi: 0-0 Tstrap: 0-0 Ckp: 0-0
Best Rating: 85 2/04 Chep 2m110y heavy NHF

Out of a mare who scored at up to 3m 1f over fences; made a satisfactory debut when third in heavy ground bumper at Chepstow February 2004.

Like A Lord (IRE)

98   **93**

6-y-o b/br g Arctic Lord-Likashot (Celtic Cone)
Mrs S J Smith Billy McCullough

Placings:50063   (4160)
2003/04: 17⁵G, 16⁶G, 20⁴G, 20⁶GS, 19³G,

	Starts	1st	2nd	3rd	Win & Pl
NH Flat	2	0	0	0	0
Hurdles	3	0	0	1	514
Career Total	5	0	0	1	514

Going: Sf: 0-0 GS: 0-1 Gd: 0-4 GF: - Fm: 0-0
Distance: 2m/2m3: 0-2 2m4-2m7: 0-3 3m+: 0-0
Track: LH: 0-4 RH: 0-1 Tight: 0-0 Gall: 0-0
Aids: BI: 0-0 Vi: 0-0 Tstrap: 0-0 Ckp: 0-0
Best Rating: 89 3/04 Donc 2m3f110y good Hdl

Plating-class novice hurdler; best effort when moderate third at Doncaster in March; suited by two and a half miles.

Lilac

100   **84**

5-y-o ch m Alhijaz-Fairfield's Breeze (Buckskin (FR))
R J Price Derek & Cheryl Holder

Placings:00014033   (4818)
2003/04: 16⁶GS, 16⁶G, 20⁶S, 16¹GF, 16⁴S, 16⁶G, 16³G, 17³GF,

	Starts	1st	2nd	3rd	Win & Pl
Hurdles	8	1	0	2	4034
Career Total	8	1	0	2	4034
74 6/03 Uttx 2m		F(0-95)HHdl		G-F	£2947
		Total win prize-money £2947			

Going: Sf: 0-2 GS: 0-1 Gd: 0-3 GF: - Fm: 1-2
Distance: 2m/2m3: 1-7 2m4-2m7: 0-1 3m+: 0-0
Track: LH: 1-5 RH: 0-3 Tight: 0-0 Gall: 0-0
Aids: BI: 0-0 Vi: 0-0 Tstrap: 0-0 Ckp: 0-0
Best Rating: 84 4/04 Extr 2m1f gd-fm Hdl

Plating-class hurdler; showed improvement when landing weak Uttoxeter handicap hurdle June 2003; acts on fast ground.

Lilium De Cotte (FR)

95(104c)   (124+c)**131**

5-y-o b g Ragmar (FR)-Vanille De Cotte (FR) (Italic (FR))
N J Henderson John P McManus

Placings:3122414-1P0   (4428)
2003/04: 16¹GS, 19⁵S, 17⁰G,

	Starts	1st	2nd	3rd	Win & Pl
Hurdles	1	0	0	0	0
Chases	2	1	0	0	3829
Career Total	10	3	2	1	27288
114 11/03 Uttx	2m	E Ch		G-S	£3828
120 2/03 Sand	2m110y	D Hdl		HVY	£5346
8/02 Vich	2m110y	Hdl		GD	£4417
		Total win prize-money £13592			

Going: Sf: 0-1 GS: 1-1 Gd: 0-1 GF: - Fm: 0-0
Distance: 2m/2m3: 1-2 2m4-2m7: 0-1 3m+: 0-0
Track: LH: 1-2 RH: 0-1 Tight: 0-0 Gall: 0-1
Aids: BI: 0-0 Vi: 0-0 Tstrap: 0-0 Ckp: 0-0
Best Rating: 132 12/02 Chel 2m1f good Hdl

Useful French-trained hurdler/novice chaser; fourth in the Triumph Hurdle in 2003; made a winning chasing debut in November 2003, but pulled up next time; not seen since; best at two miles; acts on good and heavy ground.

Lillebror (GER)

85   **64**

6-y-o b h Top Waltz (FR)-Lady Soliciti (GER) (Solicitor (FR))
B J Curley Mrs B J Curley

Placings:0P0   (3523)
2003/04: 16⁶G, 20⁶GS, 16⁶S,

	Starts	1st	2nd	3rd	Win & Pl
Hurdles	3	0	0	0	
Career Total	3	0	0	0	

Going: Sf: 0-1 GS: 0-1 Gd: 0-1 GF: - Fm: 0-0
Distance: 2m/2m3: 0-2 2m4-2m7: 0-1 3m+: 0-0
Track: LH: 0-3 RH: 0-0 Tight: 0-0 Gall: 0-0
Aids: BI: 0-0 Vi: 0-0 Tstrap: 0-0 Ckp: 0-0
Best Rating: 64 11/03 Wwck 2m good Hdl

Lily Brown

(92h)   (84h)**85**

9-y-o br m Sula Bula-Lily Mab (FR) (Prince Mab (FR))
D P Keane Conkwell Grange Stud Ltd

Placings:4FPP04-P   (0110)
2003/04: 20⁰HY,

	Starts	1st	2nd	3rd	Win & Pl
Chases	1	0	0	0	
Career Total	7	0	0	0	626

Going: Sf: 0-1 GS: 0-0 Gd: 0-0 GF: - Fm: 0-0
Distance: 2m/2m3: 0-0 2m4-2m7: 0-1 3m+: 0-0
Track: LH: 0-1 RH: 0-0 Tight: 0-0 Gall: 0-0
Aids: BI: 0-0 Vi: 0-0 Tstrap: 0-0 Ckp: 0-0
Best Rating: 85 11/02 Chep 2m110y soft Ch

Lily Saunders

4-y-o b f Piccolo-Saunders Lass (Hillandale)
Mrs N S Sharpe Mrs M Gittings-Watts

Placings:P0   (4144)
2003/04: 17⁰GF, 16⁰G,

	Starts	1st	2nd	3rd	Win & Pl
NH Flat	2	0	0	0	
Career Total	2	0	0	0	

Going: Sf: 0-0 GS: 0-1 Gd: 0-1 GF: - Fm: 0-0
Distance: 2m/2m3: 0-2 2m4-2m7: 0-0 3m+: 0-0
Track: LH: 0-0 RH: 0-1 Tight: 0-0 Gall: 0-0
Aids: BI: 0-0 Vi: 0-0 Tstrap: 0-0 Ckp: 0-0

Lime Stone Lass

7-y-o b m General Gambul-Fids Vii (Damsire Unregistered)
M Appleby Steve Parks

Placings:0P0P   (2500)
2003/04: 16⁰GF, 20⁰F, 19⁰GF, 25⁰GF,

	Starts	1st	2nd	3rd	Win & Pl
NH Flat	1	0	0	0	0
Hurdles	1	0	0	0	0
Chases	2	0	0	0	0
Career Total	4	0	0	0	

Going: Sf: 0-0 GS: 0-0 Gd: 0-0 GF: - Fm: 0-4
Distance: 2m/2m3: 0-2 2m4-2m7: 0-1 3m+: 0-1

Track: LH: 0-2 RH: 0-2 Tight: 0-3 Gall: 0-0
Aids: Bl: 0-0 Vi: 0-0 Tstrap: 0-0 Ckp: 0-0

Limerick Boy (GER)
108   **153**

6-y-o b h Alwuhush (USA)-Limoges (GER) (Konigsstuhl (GER))
Miss Venetia Williams Favourites Racing

Placings:1612-P1U00F   **(4862)**
2003/04: 16²GY, 16⁶GS, 16¹G, 16⁰G, 16⁹G, 16⁰G. 16⁶GS,

	Starts	1st	2nd	3rd	Win & Pl
Hurdles	7	1	1	0	39487
Career Total	10	3	1	0	74033
153 1/04	Kemp 2m	B(0-145)HHdl		GD	£29000
137 4/03	Aint	2m110y A Hdl		GD	£29000
114 3/03	Winc	2m	E Hdl	SFT	£4046
			Total win prize-money £62046		

Going: Sf: 0-0 GS: 0-2 Gd: 1-4 GF: - Fm: 0-0
Distance: 2m/2m3: 1-7 2m4-2m7: 0-0 3m+: 0-0
Track: LH: 0-5 RH: 1-2 Tight: 0-1 Gall: 0-2
Aids: Bl: 0-0 Vi: 0-0 Tstrap: 0-0 Ckp: 0-0
Best Rating: 153 1/04 Kemp 2m good Hdl

Smart hurdler; Group-class performer on the Flat in Germany; a smart novice in 2002/2003, winning a Grade Two at Aintree; bounced back to win the 2004 Lanzarote; unseated at the first in the Tote Gold Trophy and ran moderately at Cheltenham and Aintree; effective over two miles and acts on ground good or softer.

Limerick Leader (IRE)
105   **135**

6-y-o b g Supreme Leader-View Of The Hills (Croghan Hill)
P J Hobbs D R Peppiatt

Placings:002-12234115   **(4939)**
2003/04: 20¹G, 20²G, 20²GS, 22³GS, 20⁴S, 24¹G, 24¹GS, 24⁵GS,

	Starts	1st	2nd	3rd	Win & Pl
Hurdles	8	3	2	1	19397
Career Total	11	3	3	1	20003
135 3/04	Bang 3m	C(0-135)HHdl	G-S	£7306
128 3/04	Kemp	3m110y D Hdl	GD	£5083
109 9/03	Prth	2m4f110yE Hdl	GD	£3220
			Total win prize-money £15609		

Going: Sf: 0-1 GS: 1-4 Gd: 2-3 GF: - Fm: 0-0
Distance: 2m/2m3: 0-0 2m4-2m7: 1-5 3m+: 2-3
Track: LH: 1-1 RH: 2-7 Tight: 1-1 Gall: 0-0
Aids: Bl: 2-4 Vi: 0-0 Tstrap: 0-0 Ckp: 0-0
Best Rating: 135 3/04 Bang 3m gd-sft Hdl

Modest novice hurdler; stays 2m6f; prefers good ground.

Limon (GER)
98   **91**

5-y-o b g Lavirco (GER)-Lohsa (IRE) (Aragon)
Ronald O'Leary Aidan J Ryan

Placings:006650   **(2883a)**
2003/04: 16⁰G, 17⁰G, 17⁶F, 16⁶G, 16⁵GF, 16⁰GY,

	Starts	1st	2nd	3rd	Win & Pl
Hurdles	6	0	0	0	0
Career Total	6	0	0	0	0

Going: Sf: 0-0 GS: 0-0 Gd: 0-3 GF: - Fm: 0-0
Distance: 2m/2m3: 0-6 2m4-2m7: 0-0 3m+: 0-0
Track: LH: 0-3 RH: 0-2 Tight: 0-1 Gall: 0-0

Aids: Bl: 0-0 Vi: 0-0 Tstrap: 0-4 Ckp: 0-0
Best Rating: 91 9/03 List 2m good Hdl

Lin D'Estruval (FR)
96f   **93f**

5-y-o b g Cadoudal (FR)-Recolte D'Estruval (FR) (Kouban (FR))
C P Morlock Pell-Mell Partners

Placings:50   **(4199)**
2003/04: 16⁵GS, 16⁰G,

	Starts	1st	2nd	3rd	Win & Pl
NH Flat	2	0	0	0	0
Career Total	2	0	0	0	0

Going: Sf: 0-0 GS: 0-1 Gd: 0-1 GF: - Fm: 0-0
Distance: 2m/2m3: 0-2 2m4-2m7: 0-0 3m+: 0-0
Track: LH: 0-1 RH: 0-1 Tight: 0-0 Gall: 0-1
Aids: Bl: 0-0 Vi: 0-0 Tstrap: 0-0 Ckp: 0-0
Best Rating: 93 2/04 Kemp 2m gd-sft NHF

Lincoln Cross (IRE)
86

9-y-o b g Lord Americo-Keen Cross (IRE) (Black Minstrel)
O Sherwood I W Harfitt & Partners

Placings:02/0053-F   **(0128)**
2003/04: 22²FG,

	Starts	1st	2nd	3rd	Win & Pl
Hurdles	1	0	0	0	
Career Total	7	0	1	1	1327

Going: Sf: 0-0 GS: 0-0 Gd: 0-1 GF: - Fm: 0-0
Distance: 2m/2m3: 0-0 2m4-2m7: 0-0 3m+: 0-0
Track: LH: 0-1 RH: 0-0 Tight: 0-1 Gall: 0-0
Aids: Bl: 0-0 Vi: 0-0 Tstrap: 0-0 Ckp: 0-0
Best Rating: 100 10/01 Hntg 2m110y good NHF

Moderate novice hurdler; runner-up in a Huntingdon bumper on second start; improved form when stepped up to two miles six to finish third at Newton Abbot.

Lincoln Place (IRE)
104(104h)   (95 h)**115**

9-y-o ch g Be My Native (USA)-Miss Lou (Levanter)
P J Hobbs A J Scrimgeour

Placings:0000/00P/11F423-2F023P   **(2706)**
2003/04: 20²G, 20⁵GF, 20⁴GF, 20²G, 19³GF, 20⁰G,

	Starts	1st	2nd	3rd	Win & Pl
Hurdles	2	0	0	1	586
Chases	4	2	0	0	6545
Career Total	19	2	3	2	17295
103 8/02	Worc	2m4f110yE(0-105)HCh	GD	£3818
97 6/02	Worc	2m	F(0-95)HCh	G-F	£3198
			Total win prize-money £7017		

Going: Sf: 0-0 GS: 0-0 Gd: 0-3 GF: - Fm: 0-3
Distance: 2m/2m3: 0-0 2m4-2m7: 0-6 3m+: 0-0
Track: LH: 0-3 RH: 0-2 Tight: 0-2 Gall: 0-2
Aids: Bl: 0-0 Vi: 0-0 Tstrap: 0-0 Ckp: 0-0
Best Rating: 115 11/03 Chel 2m4f110y good Ch

Modest handicap chaser/hurdler; effective at up to two miles four; acts on a sound surface.

Lindajane (IRE)
99   (67h)**80**

12-y-o b m Erin's Hope-Tempo Rose (Crash Course)
D W Whillans Mrs H M Whillans

Placings:33/6/331040/14030/0054/F312O30P-23P **(2082)**
2003/04: 25²G, 20³GF, 27⁹GF,

	Starts	1st	2nd	3rd	Win & Pl
Chases	3	0	1	1	1609
Career Total	29	3	2	8	14995
77 6/02	Hexm	2m4f110yE(0-105)HChs	GD	£3388
89 5/99	Prth	2m110y E(0-105)HHdl	HVY	£2970
89 2/99	Ayr	2m	E Hdl	SFT	£2705
			Total win prize-money £9063		

Going: Sf: 0-0 GS: 0-0 Gd: 0-1 GF: - Fm: 0-2
Distance: 2m/2m3: 0-2 2m4-2m7: 0-1 3m+: 0-2
Track: LH: 0-3 RH: 0-0 Tight: 0-1 Gall: 0-0
Aids: Bl: 0-0 Vi: 0-0 Tstrap: 0-0 Ckp: 0-0
Best Rating: 89 5/99 Prth 2m110y heavy Hdl

Plating-class chaser; effective at up to three miles; acts on a sound surface.

Lindsay (FR)

5-y-o b g Chamberlin (FR)-Oliday (FR) (Djarvis (FR))
G L Edwards (G Macaire 19/10) John R Wilson

Placings:212112   **(4439)**
2003/04: 18²G, 16¹GS, 16²G, 17¹G, 17¹GS, 21²GS,

	Starts	1st	2nd	3rd	Win & Pl
Hurdles	3	1	2	0	7636
Chases	3	2	1	0	10102
Career Total	6	3	3	0	17738
10/03	Comp	2m1f110y Ch	G-S	£4675
9/03	Comp	2m1f110y Ch	GD	£4675
7/03	Vich	2m110y Hdl	G-S	£4052
			Total win prize-money £13402		

Going: Sf: 0-0 GS: 2-3 Gd: 1-3 GF: - Fm: 0-0
Distance: 2m/2m3: 3-5 2m4-2m7: 0-1 3m+: 0-0
Track: LH: 0-1 RH: 0-0 Tight: 0-1 Gall: 0-0
Aids: Bl: 0-0 Vi: 0-0 Tstrap: 0-0 Ckp: 0-0
Best Rating: 89 3/04 Fknm 2m5f110y gd-sft Ch

Line Apple (FR)
95   **94**

7-y-o ch m Apple Tree (FR)-Cackle (USA) (Crow (FR))
P F Nicholls (J J Boulter 10/5) J J Boulter

Placings:4F1/150P1/211140F5F3-23   **(0437)**
2003/04: 21³S, 20²GF, 22³GF,

	Starts	1st	2nd	3rd	Win & Pl
Chases	3	0	1	2	3500
Career Total	20	6	2	2	50797
8/02	Vitt	2m5f	Ch	GD	£7656
7/02	Vitt	2m5f	Ch	GD	£3534
7/02	Claf	2m1f	HCh	SFT	£6184
10/01	Nime	2m1f	Ch	G-S	£3395
5/01	Autl	2m2f	Hdl	G-S	£14549
4/01	Pau	2m110y	Hdl	VS	£4365
			Total win prize-money £39683		

Going: Sf: 0-1 GS: 0-0 Gd: 0-0 GF: - Fm: 0-2
Distance: 2m/2m3: 0-0 2m4-2m7: 0-3 3m+: 0-0
Track: LH: 0-2 RH: 0-0 Tight: 0-2 Gall: 0-0
Aids: Bl: 0-0 Vi: 0-0 Tstrap: 0-1 Ckp: 0-0
Best Rating: 94 5/03 Wwck 2m4f110y gd-fm Ch

Linens Flame

92   **87**

5-y-o ch g Blushing Flame (USA)-Atlantic Air (Air Trooper)
B G Powell D & J Newell

Placings: 5   (0182)
2003/04: 16⁵GF,

	Starts	1st	2nd	3rd	Win & Pl
Hurdles	1	0	0	0	0
Career Total	1	0	0	0	0

Going:	Sf: 0-0 GS: 0-0 Gd: 0-0 GF: - Fm: 0-1
Distance:	2m/2m3: 0-1 2m4-2m7: 0-0 3m+: 0-0
Track:	LH: 0-0 RH: 0-1 Tight: 0-0 Gall: 0-0
Aids:	Bl: 0-0 Vi: 0-0 Tstrap: 0-0 Ckp: 0-0
Best Rating:	87 5/03 Winc 2m gd-fm Hdl

Novice hurdler; promising debut when fifth at Wincanton.

Lingham Bridesmaid

95   **83**

8-y-o b m Minster Son-Lingham Bride (Deep Run)
Mrs J C McGregor Tillyrie Racing Club

Placings: 6/630003P6PP3/22334024030-3P4P   (0981)
2003/04: 16³G, 16²G, 20⁴G, 21PGF,

	Starts	1st	2nd	3rd	Win & Pl
Hurdles	4	0	0	1	889
Career Total	27	0	3	7	7768

Going:	Sf: 0-0 GS: 0-0 Gd: 0-3 GF: - Fm: 0-1
Distance:	2m/2m3: 0-2 2m4-2m7: 0-2 3m+: 0-0
Track:	LH: 0-0 RH: 0-3 Tight: 0-1 Gall: 0-0
Aids:	Bl: 0-0 Vi: 0-0 Tstrap: 0-0 Ckp: 0-0
Best Rating:	85 1/03 Muss 2m4f good Hdl

Moderate hurdler, has been well beaten in ordinary company; placed nine times but yet to get off the mark; stays two miles four.

Lingo (IRE)

114   **150+**

5-y-o b g Poliglote-Sea Ring (FR) (Bering)
Jonjo O'Neill John P McManus

Placings: 121   (3184)
2003/04: 16¹GY, 16²G, 16¹GS,

	Starts	1st	2nd	3rd	Win & Pl
Hurdles	3	2	1	0	40569
Career Total	3	2	1	0	40569
150	1/04	Sand	2m11y	A Hdl	G-S £27900
105	11/03	Naas	2m	Hdl	G-Y £7168
			Total win prize-money £35069

Going:	Sf: 0-0 GS: 1-1 Gd: 0-1 GF: - Fm: 0-0
Distance:	2m/2m3: 2-3 2m4-2m7: 0-0 3m+: 0-0
Track:	LH: 1-1 RH: 1-2 Tight: 0-0 Gall: 0-0
Aids:	Bl: 0-0 Vi: 0-0 Tstrap: 0-0 Ckp: 0-0
Best Rating:	150 1/04 Sand 2m11y gd-sft Hdl

Smart ex-Flat performer; made a winning hurdling debut in Ireland and ran well at Ascot, before winning the Grade One Tolworth Hurdle at Sandown in January; acts on any ground; open to further improvement.

Link Copper

15-y-o ch g Whistlefield-Letitica (Deep Run)

Mrs E J Taplin Mrs E J Taplin

Placings: 5P/PP/2P/4/3-F   (0186)
2003/04: 25FGF,

	Starts	1st	2nd	3rd	Win & Pl
Chases	1	0	0	0	
Career Total	9	0	1	1	1029

Going:	Sf: 0-0 GS: 0-0 Gd: 0-0 GF: - Fm: 0-1
Distance:	2m/2m3: 0-0 2m4-2m7: 0-0 3m+: 0-1
Track:	LH: 0-0 RH: 0-0 Tight: 0-0 Gall: 0-0
Aids:	Bl: 0-0 Vi: 0-0 Tstrap: 0-0 Ckp: 0-0
Best Rating:	93 5/97 Winc 2m5f firm Ch

Modest hunter chaser.

Linus

104   **98**

6-y-o b g Bin Ajwaad (IRE)-Land Line (High Line)
C J Down G Doel

Placings: R00116-S331P02P   (3655)
2003/04: 19⁵G, 17³G, 22³GF, 22¹GF, 24PF, 19PS, 20²S, 24PS,

	Starts	1st	2nd	3rd	Win & Pl
Hurdles	8	1	1	2	4722
Career Total	14	3	1	2	10434
98	9/03	NAbb	2m6f	G Hdl	G-F £2912
91	3/03	Extr	2m1f	F(0-95)HHdl	SFT £3192
98	2/03	Tntn	2m3f110yG(0-95)HHdl	G-S £2520
			Total win prize-money £8624

Going:	Sf: 0-3 GS: 0-0 Gd: 0-2 GF: - Fm: 1-3
Distance:	2m/2m3: 0-3 2m4-2m7: 1-3 3m+: 0-2
Track:	LH: 1-4 RH: 0-4 Tight: 1-5 Gall: 0-0
Aids:	Bl: 0-0 Vi: 0-0 Tstrap: 0-0 Ckp: 0-0
Best Rating:	98 9/03 NAbb 2m6f gd-fm Hdl

Plating-class hurdler; won 2m 6f selling hurdle at Newton Abbot September 2003; stays 2m 6f; acts on all types of ground but may be best in the soft.

Lion Guest (IRE)

99   **87+**

7-y-o ch g Lion Cavern (USA)-Decrescendo (IRE) (Polish Precedent (USA))
Mrs S C Bradburne Cornelius Lysaght

Placings: 0P6004-54014P   (1143)
2003/04: 16⁵G, 16⁴G, 20⁰GF, 20¹G, 22⁴GF, 20PGF,

	Starts	1st	2nd	3rd	Win & Pl
Hurdles	6	1	0	0	4660
Career Total	12	1	0	0	4660
90	7/03	Prth	2m4f110yE(0-100)HHdl	GD £4075
			Total win prize-money £4076

Going:	Sf: 0-0 GS: 0-0 Gd: 1-3 GF: - Fm: 0-3
Distance:	2m/2m3: 0-2 2m4-2m7: 1-4 3m+: 0-0
Track:	LH: 0-4 RH: 1-2 Tight: 0-3 Gall: 0-0
Aids:	Bl: 0-0 Vi: 0-0 Tstrap: 0-0 Ckp: 0-0
Best Rating:	90 8/03 Prth 2m4f110y gd-fm Hdl

Moderate novice hurdler; winner at Perth in July; does not stay two miles six.

Lirfox (FR)

106(109h)   (127 h)**123**

7-y-o ch m Foxhound (USA)-Lirfa (USA) (Lear Fan (USA))
M C Pipe D A Johnson

Placings: 11032-11132   (2241)
2003/04: 19¹GF, 16¹GF, 17¹GF, 16³G, 16²GF,

	Starts	1st	2nd	3rd	Win & Pl
Chases	5	3	1	1	17322
Career Total	10	5	2	2	44637
120	6/03	MRas	2m1f110yD Ch	G-F £6678
123	6/03	Hrfd	2m E Ch	G-F £4065
115	5/03	Hrfd	2m3f E Ch	G-F £4104
	1/03	Pau	2m3f Hdl	VS £12468
	12/02	Pau	2m1f110y Hdl	SFT £7067
			Total win prize-money £34384

Going:	Sf: 0-0 GS: 0-0 Gd: 0-0 GF: 1 Fm: 3-4
Distance:	2m/2m3: 3-5 2m4-2m7: 0-0 3m+: 0-0
Track:	LH: 0-0 RH: 3-5 Tight: 1-1 Gall: 0-0
Aids:	Bl: 0-0 Vi: 0-0 Tstrap: 0-0 Ckp: 0-0
Best Rating:	127 3/03 Chel 2m110y good Hdl

Useful chaser; easy winner of three novice chases at Hereford May and June 2003; not the best of jumpers; keen sort, best at 2m, acts on most types of ground.

Lirkimalong

11-y-o ch g Lir-Kimberley Ann (St Columbus)
Miss S Young Mrs J Holden-White

Placings: U0/4   (4891)
2003/04: 24⁴GF,

	Starts	1st	2nd	3rd	Win & Pl
Chases	1	0	0	0	0
Career Total	3	0	0	0	0

Going:	Sf: 0-0 GS: 0-0 Gd: 0-0 GF: - Fm: 0-1
Distance:	2m/2m3: 0-0 2m4-2m7: 0-0 3m+: 0-0
Track:	LH: 0-1 RH: 0-0 Tight: 0-1 Gall: 0-0
Aids:	Bl: 0-0 Vi: 0-0 Tstrap: 0-0 Ckp: 0-0
Best Rating:	64 1/02 Tntn 2m1f soft Hdl

Lirsleftover

12-y-o ch g Lir-Full Tan (Dairialatan)
Miss S Young B R J Young

Placings: 605F56/050-5   (4150)
2003/04: 24⁵G,

	Starts	1st	2nd	3rd	Win & Pl
Chases	1	0	0	0	0
Career Total	10	0	0	0	0

Going:	Sf: 0-0 GS: 0-0 Gd: 0-1 GF: - Fm: 0-0
Distance:	2m/2m3: 0-0 2m4-2m7: 0-0 3m+: 0-0
Track:	LH: 0-0 RH: 0-0 Tight: 0-1 Gall: 0-0
Aids:	Bl: 0-0 Vi: 0-0 Tstrap: 0-0 Ckp: 0-0
Best Rating:	80 5/01 Chel 2m5f good Ch

Lirta (FR)

5-y-o gr g Art Francais (USA)-Sirta (FR) (Le Pontet (FR))
P J Hobbs (E Leenders 30/5) P A Newey

Placings: 225F-224   (3094)
2003/04: 17²VS, 17²VS, 16⁴G,

	Starts	1st	2nd	3rd	Win & Pl
Chases	3	0	2	0	14160
Career Total	7	0	4	0	22555

Going:	Sf: 0-0 GS: 0-0 Gd: 0-1 GF: - Fm: 0-0
Distance:	2m/2m3: 0-3 2m4-2m7: 0-0 3m+: 0-0
Track:	LH: 0-1 RH: 0-0 Tight: 0-0 Gall: 0-1

Aids: BI: 0-0 Vi: 0-0 Tstrap: 0-0 Ckp: 0-0
Best Rating: 0   12/03 Chel 2m110y   good   Ch

Novice chaser; well beaten on his British debut; placed in two hurdles and two out of four chase starts in France; acts with cut; best at around two miles; keen sort.

Lisa Du Chenet (FR)
107   107+
5-y-o b m Garde Royale-Tchela (FR) (Le Nain Jaune (FR))
Mrs Susan Nock The Siblings

Placings:460-511P   (4909)
2003/04: 19⁵GS, 20¹G, 23¹GS, 24²S,

	Starts	1st	2nd	3rd	Win & PI
Hurdles	4	2	0	0	6971
Career Total	7	2	0	0	6971
107	4/04 Ling	2m7f	E Hdl		G-S	3571
107	1/04 Font	2m4f	E Hdl		GD	3399

Total win prize-money £6972

Going: Sf: 0-1 GS: 1-2 Gd: 1-1 GF: - Fm: 0-0
Distance: 2m/2m3: 0-0 2m4-2m7: 2-3 3m+: 0-1
Track: LH: 1-1 RH: 0-2 Tight: 2-2 Gall: 0-0
Aids: BI: 0-0 Vi: 0-0 Tstrap: 0-0 Ckp: 0-0
Best Rating: 107   4/04 Ling   2m7f   gd-sft   Hdl

Modest novice hurdler; effective over two and half miles; acts on good ground.

Lisa-B (IRE)
(97h)   (64h)
7-y-o b m Case Law-Nishiki (USA) (Brogan (USA))
D L Williams Thrush Golf Club

Placings:55060/P260P430P02P-0PPP   (0923)
2003/04: 19⁰G, 24⁴P, 26⁶PGF, 20⁰PGF,

	Starts	1st	2nd	3rd	Win & PI
Hurdles	1	0	0	0	0
Chases	3	0	0	0	0
Career Total	21	0	2	1	1355

Going: Sf: 0-0 GS: 0-0 Gd: 0-2 GF: - Fm: 0-2
Distance: 2m/2m3: 0-0 2m4-2m7: 0-2 3m+: 0-2
Track: LH: 0-2 RH: 0-2 Tight: 0-3 Gall: 0-0
Aids: BI: 0-0 Vi: 0-2 Tstrap: 0-0 Ckp: 0-0
Best Rating: 76   5/02 Towc   2m   good   Hdl

Liscannor Lad (IRE)
110(111h)   (124h)124
6-y-o b g Nicolotte-Tinerana Memories (IRE) (Don't Forget Me)
D T Hughes C P O'Brien

Placings:065/11052154-12U3F60   (4830a)
2003/04: 20¹GF, 18²S, 22⁶S, 18³YS, 21²FG, 24⁶G, 17⁰Y,

	Starts	1st	2nd	3rd	Win & PI
Hurdles	1	1	0	0	6721
Chases	6	0	1	1	4562
Career Total	18	4	2	1	27142
116	11/03 Navn	2m	Hdl		G-F	6720
114	1/03 Fair	2m2f	Hdl		SFT	3617
99	8/02 Gway	2m	NHF		G-Y	6349
94	5/02 Naas	2m	NHF		GD	3809

Total win prize-money £20499

Going: Sf: 0-2 GS: 0-0 Gd: 0-2 GF: - Fm: 1-1
Distance: 2m/2m3: 0-3 2m4-2m7: 1-3 3m+: 0-0
Track: LH: 1-3 RH: 0-2 Tight: 0-0 Gall: 0-1
Aids: BI: 0-0 Vi: 0-0 Tstrap: 0-0 Ckp: 0-0
Best Rating: 124   12/03 Fair   2m2f100y   soft   Ch

Irish-trained novice chaser; stays 2m 4f; effective on fast and soft ground.

Lisdante (IRE)
109   123
11-y-o b g Phardante (FR)-Shuil Eile (Deep Run)
Mrs S J Smith Keith Nicholson

Placings:004F3F4/200042P23P231/1P15P/52/11PP42163P-P31P2   (2060)
2003/04: 20⁰PGF, 24³GS, 26¹GF, 24⁶PGF, 26²G,

	Starts	1st	2nd	3rd	Win & PI
Chases	5	1	1		8902
Career Total	42	7	7	5	64037
120	8/03 Sthl	3m2f	E(0-110)HCh	G-F	5083
123	10/02 Carl	3m2f	D(0-120)HCh	SFT	13617
117	5/02 Strf	3m4f	D(0-120)HCh	GD	4793
123	5/02 Aint	3m1f	D(0-120)HCh	GD	5304
104	11/00 Weth	3m1f	D(0-120)HCh	HVY	6608
105	6/00 MRas	3m6f110y(0-105)HCh	G-F	4290
99	4/00 Weth	3m5f	C HCh	SFT	5980

Total win prize-money £45677

Going: Sf: 0-0 GS: 0-1 Gd: 0-1 GF: - Fm: 1-3
Distance: 2m/2m3: 0-0 2m4-2m7: 0-1 3m+: 1-4
Track: LH: 1-3 RH: 0-2 Tight: 0-2 Gall: 0-0
Aids: BI: 0-0 Vi: 0-0 Tstrap: 0-0 Ckp: 0-0
Best Rating: 123   10/02 Carl   3m2f   soft   Ch

Fair chaser, in good form over fences in the early summer of 2002; out of sorts in 2003 until winning at Southwell in August; stays three and a half miles and acts on any ground.

Lislaughtin Abbey
108(94h)   (77h)109
12-y-o ch g Nicholas Bill-Kates Fling (USA) (Quiet Fling (USA))
O Brennan T W R Bayley

Placings:0/P00P/244U53231344/1FP21243121/U225P/P244P316/P02551-1P   (4437)
2003/04: 23¹GF, 21⁰GS,

	Starts	1st	2nd	3rd	Win & PI
Chases	2	1	0	0	7053
Career Total	49	8	9	5	47654
109	6/03 Worc	2m7f110yD(0-125)HCh	G-F	7052
99	4/03 Fknm	2m5f110yE(0-110)HCh	GD	5607
99	4/02 Sedg	2m5f	D(0-115)HCh	GD	3874
116	4/00 Fknm	2m5f110yD(0-110)HCh	GD	4621
116	3/00 Fknm	2m5f110yD(0-120)HCh	GD	3974
109	12/99 Fknm	2m110y F(0-100)HCh	GD	2263
92	5/99 Fknm	2m5f110yE(0-110)HCh	G-F	3989
86	10/98 Sthl	2m4f110yE(0-110)HCh	GD	2997

Total win prize-money £34382

Going: Sf: 0-0 GS: 0-1 Gd: 0-0 GF: - Fm: 1-1
Distance: 2m/2m3: 0-0 2m4-2m7: 0-1 3m+: 1-1
Track: LH: 1-2 RH: 0-0 Tight: 0-1 Gall: 0-0
Aids: BI: 0-0 Vi: 0-0 Tstrap: 0-0 Ckp: 0-0
Best Rating: 116   12/00 Fknm   3m110y   gd-sft   Ch

Moderate handicap chaser; a Fakenham specialist; has won five times at the Norfolk track; in good form when registering back-to-back wins in April and June 2003; best on good ground or faster; stays 3m, but is probably better over shorter.

Lissnabrucka (IRE)
96   70
6-y-o b m Lord Americo-Judy Henry (Orchestra)
Jonjo O'Neill John P McManus

Placings:4P   (3490)
2003/04: 21⁴GS, 22⁵HY,

	Starts	1st	2nd	3rd	Win & PI
Hurdles	2	0	0	0	0
Career Total	2	0	0	0	0

Going: Sf: 0-1 GS: 0-1 Gd: 0-0 GF: - Fm: 0-0
Distance: 2m/2m3: 0-0 2m4-2m7: 0-2 3m+: 0-0
Track: LH: 0-1 RH: 0-1 Tight: 0-0 Gall: 0-0
Aids: BI: 0-0 Vi: 0-0 Tstrap: 0-0 Ckp: 0-0
Best Rating: 70   11/03 Towc   2m5f   gd-sft   Hdl

Former winning Irish Points winner; disappointing on her debut inder rules at Towcester in November 2003; stays two miles five; effective on good/good to soft.

Little Alfie (IRE)
(0c)76
7-y-o b g Shahanndeh-Debbies Scud (IRE) (Roselier (FR))
B S Rothwell John H Price

Placings:00/P40404-P   (2530)
2003/04: 19⁰GS,

	Starts	1st	2nd	3rd	Win & PI
Hurdles	1	0	0	0	
Career Total	9	0	0	0	0

Going: Sf: 0-0 GS: 0-1 Gd: 0-0 GF: - Fm: 0-0
Distance: 2m/2m3: 0-1 2m4-2m7: 0-0 3m+: 0-0
Track: LH: 0-1 RH: 0-0 Tight: 0-1 Gall: 0-0
Aids: BI: 0-0 Vi: 0-0 Tstrap: 0-0 Ckp: 0-0
Best Rating: 76   6/02 Uttx   2m   good   Hdl

Little Big Horse (IRE)
107(105h)   (99h)120+
8-y-o b g Little Bighorn-Little Gort (Roselier (FR))
Mrs S J Smith Paul J Dixon

Placings:2660P/22424523-33161   (4960)
2003/04: 21³S, 23³G, 25¹GS, 25⁶G, 20¹GS,

	Starts	1st	2nd	3rd	Win & PI
Hurdles	1	0	0	1	733
Chases	4	2	0	1	11618
Career Total	18	2	5	3	20540
120	4/04 MRas	2m4f	D Ch		G-S	5434
116	3/04 MRas	3m1f	D Ch		G-S	5564

Total win prize-money £10998

Going: Sf: 0-1 GS: 2-2 Gd: 0-2 GF: - Fm: 0-0
Distance: 2m/2m3: 0-0 2m4-2m7: 1-3 3m+: 1-2
Track: LH: 0-3 RH: 2-2 Tight: 2-4 Gall: 0-0
Aids: BI: 0-0 Vi: 0-0 Tstrap: 0-0 Ckp: 0-0
Best Rating: 120   4/04 MRas   2m4f   gd-sft   Ch

Moderate maiden hurdler; fair chaser; jumped well when ready winner on second outing over fences at Market Rasen in March; scored again at the same course the following month; handles most types of ground; stays three miles.

Little Brown Bear (IRE)
112(93h)   (81+h)107
10-y-o br g Strong Gale-Gladtogetit (Green Shoon)
R Ford G B Barlow

Placings:P/3F3142/13323223-115P3   (4817)
2003/04: 24¹GF, 24¹GF, 24⁵G, 26²PGF, 24³G,

	Starts	1st	2nd	3rd	Win & Pl
Hurdles	2	1	0	0	4072
Chases	3	1	0	1	8142
Career Total	20	4	4	7	32394
81 6/03 Prth 3m110y E Hdl				G-F	£4071
107 5/03 Fknm 3m110y D(0-115)HCh				G-F	£7436
105 5/02 Sedg 3m3f E(0-110)HCh				G-F	£3668
90 2/02 Muss 3m E(0-105)HCh				G-S	£5096
				Total win prize-money	£20272

Going: Sf: 0-0 GS: 0-0 Gd: 0-2 GF: - Fm: 2-3
Distance: 2m/2m3: 0-0 2m4-2m7: 0-0 **3m+: 2-5**
Track: LH: 1-3 RH: 1-2 **Tight: 1-2** Gall: 0-0
Aids: Bl: 0-0 Vi: 0-0 Tstrap: 0-0 Ckp: 0-0
Best Rating: 107 4/04 Chep 3m good Ch

Consistent staying chaser; acts on good to firm ground; best when forcing the pace.

Little Bud
101 ... 100

10-y-o br m Lord Bud-Sindur (Rolfe (USA))
Miss A M Newton-Smith Mrs John Grist

Placings:6/0660P/6020/P030144/154011FP54/633P511-04P002R   (4486)
2003/04: 16⁰GF, 21¹⁴GF, 20⁴GS, 24⁰G, 16⁹GS, 21²G, 18⁸G,

	Starts	1st	2nd	3rd	Win & Pl
Hurdles	7	0	1	0	1081
Career Total	41	6	2	3	20145
100 4/03 Plum 2m5f E(0-105)HHdl				G-F	£3503
95 3/03 Plum 2m5f E(0-110)HHdl				G-F	£3562
95 11/01 Plum 2m F(0-110)HHdl				GD	£3178
95 11/01 Plum 2m5f F(0-90)HHdl				G-S	£2352
89 5/01 Folk 2m1f110yG(0-95)HHdl				G-S	£1666
80 11/00 Plum 2m F Hdl				HVY	£2278
				Total win prize-money	£16541

Going: Sf: 0-0 GS: 0-0 Gd: 0-3 GF: - Fm: 0-2
Distance: 2m/2m3: 0-3 2m4-2m7: 0-3 3m+: 0-1
Track: LH: 0-4 RH: 0-3 Tight: 0-5 Gall: 0-0
Aids: Bl: 0-0 Vi: 0-0 Tstrap: 0-0 Ckp: 0-0
Best Rating: 100 3/04 Plum 2m5f good Hdl

Moderate hurdler; stays two miles five, effective at shorter; acts on fast ground; goes well at Plumpton.

Little Chartridge
76f ... 82f

6-y-o b m Anshan-Auntie Dot (Hallodri (AUT))
P R Webber Mrs John Webber

Placings:00   (4571)
2003/04: 16⁹G, 17⁰GS,

	Starts	1st	2nd	3rd	Win & Pl
NH Flat	2	0	0	0	
Career Total	2	0	0	0	

Going: Sf: 0-0 GS: 0-1 Gd: 0-1 GF: - Fm: 0-0
Distance: 2m/2m3: 0-2 2m4-2m7: 0-0 3m+: 0-0
Track: LH: 0-1 RH: 0-1 Tight: 0-1 Gall: 0-0
Aids: Bl: 0-0 Vi: 0-0 Tstrap: 0-0 Ckp: 0-0
Best Rating: 82 3/04 Hntg 2m110y good NHF

Little Daphne
72 ... 35

6-y-o b m Presenting-Glengarra Princess (Cardinal Flower)
P Bowen A P Davies

Placings:046   (0869)
2003/04: 17⁹GF, 16⁴GF, 22⁶GF,

	Starts	1st	2nd	3rd	Win & Pl
NH Flat	2	0	0	0	0
Hurdles	1	0	0	0	0
Career Total	3	0	0	0	0

Going: Sf: 0-0 GS: 0-0 Gd: 0-0 GF: - Fm: 0-3
Distance: 2m/2m3: 0-2 2m4-2m7: 0-1 3m+: 0-0
Track: LH: 0-2 RH: 0-1 Tight: 0-1 Gall: 0-0
Aids: Bl: 0-0 Vi: 0-0 Tstrap: 0-0 Ckp: 0-0
Best Rating: 76 7/03 Worc 2m gd-fm NHF

Finished third in her only point; signs of ability in first two bumpers.

Little Docker (IRE)
106(105h) ... (106h)98+

7-y-o b g Vettori (IRE)-Fair Maid Of Kent (USA) (Diesis)
T D Easterby C H Stevens

Placings:421/03422F55   (3477)
2003/04: 17⁰GS, 16⁹G, 20⁴S, 16²GS, 16²GS, 16⁶GS, 19⁵GS, 19⁵G,

	Starts	1st	2nd	3rd	Win & Pl
Hurdles	2	0	0	1	1575
Chases	6	0	2	0	3009
Career Total	11	1	3	1	8278
110 12/01 Catt 2m3f E Hdl				GD	£2565
				Total win prize-money	£2566

Going: Sf: 0-1 GS: 0-5 Gd: 0-2 GF: - Fm: 0-0
Distance: 2m/2m3: 0-7 2m4-2m7: 0-1 3m+: 0-0
Track: LH: 0-6 RH: 0-2 Tight: 0-2 Gall: 0-1
Aids: Bl: 0-0 Vi: 0-0 Tstrap: 0-0 Ckp: 0-0
Best Rating: 110 12/01 Catt 2m3f good Hdl

Modest hurdler/chaser; promising efforts in novice hurdles in 2001 including victory at Catterick; off for nearly two years after; has jumped poorly in novice chases on return.

Little Ed
76 ... 68

6-y-o b g Shambo-Edina (IRE) (The Parson)
P R Webber Dennis Yardy

Placings:5B2   (2999)
2003/04: 18⁵GS, 17⁸G, 20²GS,

	Starts	1st	2nd	3rd	Win & Pl
NH Flat	1	0	0	0	0
Hurdles	2	0	1	0	1093
Career Total	3	0	1	0	1093

Going: Sf: 0-0 GS: 0-1 Gd: 0-2 GF: - Fm: 0-0
Distance: 2m/2m3: 0-2 2m4-2m7: 0-1 3m+: 0-0
Track: LH: 0-2 RH: 0-1 Tight: 0-1 Gall: 0-0
Aids: Bl: 0-0 Vi: 0-0 Tstrap: 0-0 Ckp: 0-0
Best Rating: 77 12/03 Leic 2m4f110y gd-sft Hdl

Plating-class novice hurdler; acts on easy ground.

Little Enam (IRE)
... 49

8-y-o gr g Un Desperado (FR)-Black Pheasant (IRE) (Sexton Blake)
C R Egerton R K Carvill

Placings:66-PP   (4365)
2003/04: 16²HY, 16²GS,

	Starts	1st	2nd	3rd	Win & Pl
Hurdles	2	0	0	0	0
Career Total	4	0	0	0	0

Going: Sf: 0-1 GS: 0-1 Gd: 0-0 GF: - Fm: 0-0
Distance: 2m/2m3: 0-2 2m4-2m7: 0-0 3m+: 0-0
Track: LH: 0-1 RH: 0-1 Tight: 0-1 Gall: 0-0
Aids: Bl: 0-0 Vi: 0-0 Tstrap: 0-0 Ckp: 0-0
Best Rating: 81 12/02 Newb 2m110y heavy NHF

Little Farmer

10-y-o b g Little Wolf-Sea Farmer (Cantab)
Mrs D M Grissell Christopher Hall

Placings:P/43/13   (4172)
2003/04: 21¹GF, 24³G,

	Starts	1st	2nd	3rd	Win & Pl
Chases	2	1	0	1	1702
Career Total	5	1	0	2	2066
94 5/03 Folk 2m5f H Ch				G-F	£1417
				Total win prize-money	£1417

Going: Sf: 0-0 GS: 0-0 Gd: 0-1 GF: - Fm: 1-1
Distance: 2m/2m3: 0-2 2m4-2m7: 1-1 3m+: 0-1
Track: LH: 0-1 RH: 1-1 Tight: 1-1 Gall: 0-1
Aids: Bl: 0-0 Vi: 0-0 Tstrap: 0-0 Ckp: 0-0
Best Rating: 114 3/04 Newb 3m good Ch

Little Fella (IRE)

5-y-o b/br g Kahyasi-Copper Breeze (IRE) (Strong Gale)
B G Powell Mrs Jean R Bishop

Placings:0   (3247)
2003/04: 22⁰GS,

	Starts	1st	2nd	3rd	Win & Pl
Hurdles	1	0	0	0	
Career Total	1	0	0	0	

Going: Sf: 0-0 GS: 0-1 Gd: 0-0 GF: - Fm: 0-0
Distance: 2m/2m3: 0-0 2m4-2m7: 0-0 3m+: 0-0
Track: LH: 0-0 RH: 0-1 Tight: 0-0 Gall: 0-0
Aids: Bl: 0-0 Vi: 0-0 Tstrap: 0-0 Ckp: 0-0

Little Flora
94 ... 103

8-y-o ch m Alflora (IRE)-Sister's Choice (Lepanto (GER))
Miss V Scott Mrs A Scott

Placings:0/00P35003/02334312355046101/5535-060   (4429)
2003/04: 20⁰GS, 16⁶G, 16⁹G,

	Starts	1st	2nd	3rd	Win & Pl
Hurdles	3	0	0	0	0
Career Total	33	3	2	7	12261
103 4/02 Sedg 2m5f110yE(0-105)HHdl				G-F	£2618
90 4/02 Hexm 2m110y E Hdl				G-F	£2835
91 7/01 Sedg 2m5f110yE Hdl				G-F	£2471
				Total win prize-money	£7924

Going: Sf: 0-0 GS: 0-1 Gd: 0-2 GF: - Fm: 0-0
Distance: 2m/2m3: 0-2 2m4-2m7: 0-1 3m+: 0-0
Track: LH: 0-3 RH: 0-0 Tight: 0-0 Gall: 0-2
Aids: Bl: 0-0 Vi: 0-0 Tstrap: 0-0 Ckp: 0-0
Best Rating: 103 4/02 Sedg 2m5f110y gd-fm Hdl

Moderate hurdler, best on a sound surface and sharp tracks; well beaten on first run since 2002 at Newcastle in February.

Little Herman (IRE)

103(75h)   (90h)**79**

8-y-o b g Mandalus-Kilbricken Bay (Salluceva)
J A B Old W E Sturt

Placings:060/00-P3310   (4792)
2003/04: 26⁶G, 26³GF, 23³G, 26¹GF, 26⁹G,

	Starts	1st	2nd	3rd	Win & Pl
Chases	5	1	0	2	4563
Career Total	10	1	0	2	4563

79   3/04   Chep   3m2f110yF(0-90)HCh   G-F   £3477
Total win prize-money £3478

Going:	Sf: 0-0 GS: 0-0 Gd: 0-3 GF: - Fm: 1-2
Distance:	2m/2m3: 0-0 2m4-2m7: 0-0 **3m+: 1-5**
Track:	LH: **1-4** RH: 0-1 Tight: 0-2 Gall: 0-0
Aids:	Bl: 0-0 Vi: 0-0 Tstrap: 0-0 Ckp: 0-0
Best Rating:	90 1/02 Asct 2m4f gd-sft Hdl

Plating-class chaser; won weak handicap at Chepstow in March 2004; stays 3m 2f; effective on fast ground.

Little Knowledge

49f

6-y-o b m Terimon-Madam-M (Tina's Pet)
N A Twiston-Davies H R Mould

Placings:0-0   (0675)
2003/04: 17⁰GF,

	Starts	1st	2nd	3rd	Win & Pl
NH Flat	1	0	0	0	
Career Total	2	0	0	0	

Going:	Sf: 0-0 GS: 0-0 Gd: 0-0 GF: - Fm: 0-1
Distance:	2m/2m3: 0-1 2m4-2m7: 0-0 3m+: 0-0
Track:	LH: 0-1 RH: 0-0 Tight: 0-0 Gall: 0-0
Aids:	Bl: 0-0 Vi: 0-0 Tstrap: 0-0 Ckp: 0-0
Best Rating:	49 5/02 Worc 2m good NHF

Little Lil

87   **59**

5-y-o ch m Sula Bula-Sherzine (Gorytus (USA))
J D Frost Singing In The Rain

Placings:0005   (4856)
2003/04: 16⁰GS, 16⁹GS, 17⁰G, 19⁵GF,

	Starts	1st	2nd	3rd	Win & Pl
NH Flat	2	0	0	0	0
Hurdles	2	0	0	0	0
Career Total	4	0	0	0	0

Going:	Sf: 0-0 GS: 0-2 Gd: 0-1 GF: - Fm: 0-1
Distance:	2m/2m3: 0-3 2m4-2m7: 0-1 3m+: 0-0
Track:	LH: 0-1 RH: 0-3 Tight: 0-2 Gall: 0-0
Aids:	Bl: 0-0 Vi: 0-0 Tstrap: 0-0 Ckp: 0-0
Best Rating:	60 1/04 Ludl 2m gd-sft NHF

Little Lord Lewis

5-y-o b g Sir Harry Lewis (USA)-Unspoken Prayer (Inca Chief (USA))
Mrs H O Graham Mrs H O Graham

Placings:50   (1605)
2003/04: 16⁵GF, 17⁹GF,

	Starts	1st	2nd	3rd	Win & Pl
NH Flat	2	0	0	0	0
Career Total	2	0	0	0	0

Little Mick (IRE)

78   **63**

7-y-o br g Mister Lord (USA)-Strong Trump (IRE) (Strong Gale)
J A B Old Mrs J A Fowler/M Lovatt

Placings:0P-05   (1013)
2003/04: 16⁰G, 20⁵GF,

	Starts	1st	2nd	3rd	Win & Pl
Hurdles	2	0	0	0	0
Career Total	4	0	0	0	0

Going:	Sf: 0-0 GS: 0-0 Gd: 0-1 GF: - Fm: 0-1
Distance:	2m/2m3: 0-1 2m4-2m7: 0-1 3m+: 0-0
Track:	LH: 0-2 RH: 0-0 Tight: 0-0 Gall: 0-0
Aids:	Bl: 0-0 Vi: 0-0 Tstrap: 0-0 Ckp: 0-0
Best Rating:	69 8/03 Worc 2m4f gd-fm Hdl

Little Miss Prim

95   **91**

8-y-o b m Gildoran-Laced Up (IRE) (The Parson)
J G O'Neill J G O'Neill

Placings:4/00P5/P0U0   (4561)
2003/04: 16⁸S, 22⁹G, 21⁰UG, 24⁰GS,

	Starts	1st	2nd	3rd	Win & Pl
Hurdles	4	0	0	0	
Career Total	9	0	0	0	0

Going:	Sf: 0-1 GS: 0-1 Gd: 0-2 GF: - Fm: 0-0
Distance:	2m/2m3: 0-1 2m4-2m7: 0-2 3m+: 0-1
Track:	LH: 0-2 RH: 0-2 Tight: 0-1 Gall: 0-1
Aids:	Bl: 0-0 Vi: 0-0 Tstrap: 0-0 Ckp: 0-0
Best Rating:	91 12/01 Chel 2m1f good Hdl

Little Mister

8-y-o ch g Gran Alba (USA)-Chrissytino (Baron Blakeney)
N R Mitchell N J Powell

Placings:00/PP-FP   (0436)
2003/04: 19⁰GF, 22⁰GF,

	Starts	1st	2nd	3rd	Win & Pl
Hurdles	2	0	0	0	
Career Total	6	0	0	0	

Going:	Sf: 0-0 GS: 0-0 Gd: 0-0 GF: - Fm: 0-2
Distance:	2m/2m3: 0-1 2m4-2m7: 0-1 3m+: 0-0
Track:	LH: 0-1 RH: 0-1 Tight: 0-1 Gall: 0-0
Aids:	Bl: 0-2 Vi: 0-0 Tstrap: 0-0 Ckp: 0-0

Little Ora (IRE)

99   **90**

7-y-o ch g Black Monday-Country Melody (IRE) (Orchestra)
P J Rothwell F Mellor

Placings:000005423/1301244005-243336320   (3973a)
2003/04: 16²S, 17⁴G, 16³G, 18³GF, 16⁹S, 16⁶S, 18³S, 16²S, 16⁰Y,

Little Ora (IRE) — right column

	Starts	1st	2nd	3rd	Win & Pl
Hurdles	9	0	2	4	5213
Career Total	28	2	4	6	16725

85   8/02   Slig   2m   (67-102)HHdl   HVY   £3809
75   5/02   Dpat   2m1f172y(60-88)HHdl   Y-S   £4230
Total win prize-money £8043

Going:	Sf: 0-5 GS: 0-0 Gd: 0-2 GF: - Fm: 0-1
Distance:	2m/2m3: 0-9 2m4-2m7: 0-0 3m+: 0-0
Track:	LH: 0-4 RH: 0-2 Tight: 0-1 Gall: 0-0
Aids:	Bl: 0-0 Vi: 0-0 Tstrap: 0-0 Ckp: 0-0
Best Rating:	92 10/03 Wxfd 2m good Hdl

Plating-class Irish hurdler; effective at two miles; acts on soft ground.

Little Person

5-y-o ch m Factual (USA)-Chaleureuse (Final Straw)
G A Harker The Norking Partnership

Placings:0   (0309)
2003/04: 17⁰G,

	Starts	1st	2nd	3rd	Win & Pl
NH Flat	1	0	0	0	
Career Total	1	0	0	0	

Going:	Sf: 0-0 GS: 0-0 Gd: 0-1 GF: - Fm: 0-0
Distance:	2m/2m3: 0-1 2m4-2m7: 0-0 3m+: 0-0
Track:	LH: 0-1 RH: 0-0 Tight: 0-1 Gall: 0-0
Aids:	Bl: 0-0 Vi: 0-0 Tstrap: 0-0 Ckp: 0-0

Little Ross

101(101c)   (87c)**91**

9-y-o b g St Ninian-Little Katrina (Little Buskins)
D B Feek Barry & Baroness Noakes

Placings:0/5/06/3U345P-304034   (4123)
2003/04: 24³G, 26⁸GS, 19⁴S, 20⁰HY, 16³S, 17⁴G,

	Starts	1st	2nd	3rd	Win & Pl
Hurdles	4	0	0	0	738
Chases	2	0	0	0	0
Career Total	16	0	0	4	2102

Going:	Sf: 0-3 GS: 0-1 Gd: 0-2 GF: - Fm: 0-0
Distance:	2m/2m3: 0-2 2m4-2m7: 0-2 3m+: 0-2
Track:	LH: 0-1 RH: 0-3 Tight: 0-3 Gall: 0-1
Aids:	Bl: 0-0 Vi: 0-0 Tstrap: 0-6 Ckp: 0-0
Best Rating:	96 4/00 Hntg 2m110y good NHF

Moderate hurdler, suited by two miles five furlongs and soft ground.

Little Sky

89   **52**

7-y-o gr m Terimon-Brown Coast (Oats)
D Mullarkey Dune Racing

Placings:0/0UP-P0P   (1220)
2003/04: 17⁸G, 16⁰G, 26⁷GF,

	Starts	1st	2nd	3rd	Win & Pl
Hurdles	3	0	0	0	
Career Total	7	0	0	0	

Going:	Sf: 0-0 GS: 0-0 Gd: 0-2 GF: - Fm: 0-1
Distance:	2m/2m3: 0-2 2m4-2m7: 0-0 3m+: 0-1
Track:	LH: 0-2 RH: 0-1 Tight: 0-1 Gall: 0-1
Aids:	Bl: 0-0 Vi: 0-0 Tstrap: 0-0 Ckp: 0-1
Best Rating:	51 7/03 Strf 2m110y good Hdl

Little Task

98(103c)   (101c)89

6-y-o b g Environment Friend-Lucky Thing (Green Desert (USA))
J S Wainwright Keith Jackson

Placings:14340/16056200600-3U1363044   (1468)
2003/04: 17³G, 16⁴G, 16¹G, 16³G, 16⁶GF, 17³GS, 17⁰G, 20⁴F, 26⁴GF,

	Starts	1st	2nd	3rd	Win & Pl
Hurdles	4	0	0	1	772
Chases	5	1	0	2	9684
Career Total	**25**	**3**	**1**	**4**	**21048**
101 6/03 Prth	2m	C Ch		GD	£8043
96 5/02 Weth	2m	D(0-115)HHdl		GD	£6449
83 9/01 Strf	2m110y	E Hdl		G-F	£3041
			Total win prize-money £17536		

Going: Sf: 0-0 GS: 0-1 Gd: 1-5 GF: - Fm: 0-3
Distance: 2m/2m3: 1-7 2m4-2m7: 0-1 3m+: 0-1
Track: LH: 0-6 RH: 1-3 Tight: 0-3 Gall: 0-1
Aids: Bl: 0-0 Vi: 0-0 Tstrap: 0-0 Ckp: 0-0
Best Rating: 101 6/03 Prth 2m good Ch

Modest hurdler, suited by fast ground and is effective at around two miles.

Little Tern (IRE)

5-y-o b m Terimon-Miss Fern (Cruise Missile)
R Dickin R T S Matthews

Placings:6P   (3843)
2003/04: 16⁶HY, 19⁸GS,

	Starts	1st	2nd	3rd	Win & Pl
NH Flat	1	0	0	0	0
Hurdles	1	0	0	0	0
Career Total	**2**	**0**	**0**	**0**	**0**

Going: Sf: 0-1 GS: 0-1 Gd: 0-0 GF: - Fm: 0-0
Distance: 2m/2m3: 0-1 2m4-2m7: 0-1 3m+: 0-0
Track: LH: 0-0 RH: 0-2 Tight: 0-0 Gall: 0-0
Aids: Bl: 0-0 Vi: 0-0 Tstrap: 0-0 Ckp: 0-0

Little Tobias (IRE)

99   93

5-y-o ch g Millkom-Barbara Frietchie (IRE) (Try My Best (USA))
Andrew Turnell Mrs Claire Hollowood

Placings:1-040   (2156)
2003/04: 16⁰GF, 19⁴GF, 16⁰GS,

	Starts	1st	2nd	3rd	Win & Pl
Hurdles	3	0	0	0	407
Career Total	**4**	**1**	**0**	**0**	**4424**
93 10/02 Extr	2m1f	D Hdl		FRM	£4017
		Total win prize-money £4017			

Going: Sf: 0-0 GS: 0-1 Gd: 0-0 GF: - Fm: 0-2
Distance: 2m/2m3: 0-2 2m4-2m7: 0-1 3m+: 0-0
Track: LH: 0-2 RH: 0-1 Tight: 0-1 Gall: 0-0
Aids: Bl: 0-0 Vi: 0-0 Tstrap: 0-0 Ckp: 0-0
Best Rating: 93 8/03 MRas 2m3f110y gd-fm Hdl

Moderate hurdler; made a winning debut when winning a poor juvenile event at Exeter October 2002; lightly-raced since; suited by two and a half miles; best on a sound surface.

Little Tuska (IRE)

(89h)   (82h)60

14-y-o gr g Step Together (USA)-Peek-A-Boo (Bustino)
M J M Evans M J M Evans

Placings:06/P041/6P651/231130630230F0F555/24212/PP 43F026353/6346P4554-0   (0152)
2003/04: 20⁰GF,

	Starts	1st	2nd	3rd	Win & Pl
Hurdles	1	0	0	0	0
Career Total	**55**	**5**	**6**	**8**	**29637**
85 9/00 Plum	2m1f	F(0-110)HCh	G-F	£2908
98 6/99 Hrfd	2m3f	E(0-115)HCh	GD	£4201
102 6/99 Prth	2m	E(0-115)HCh	SFT	£3387
102 4/99 Hexm	2m110y	F(0-100)HCh	GD	£2945
102 4/98 Prth	2m	D Ch	G-S	£4500
			Total win prize-money £17945		

Going: Sf: 0-0 GS: 0-0 Gd: 0-0 GF: - Fm: 0-1
Distance: 2m/2m3: 0-0 2m4-2m7: 0-1 3m+: 0-0
Track: LH: 0-1 RH: 0-0 Tight: 0-0 Gall: 0-0
Aids: Bl: 0-0 Vi: 0-0 Tstrap: 0-1 Ckp: 0-0
Best Rating: 102 6/99 Prth 2m soft Ch

Modest chaser who has had just the one win since the summer of 1999, he is getting on now and is best at around two miles one these days. Acts on most surfaces.

Little Valentine (GER)

91   81

4-y-o b c Gold And Ivory (USA)-Lagoa Feia (GER) (Gimont (GER))
C Von Der Recke Mrs U H Alck

Placings:4   (2572)
2003/04: 16⁴GS,

	Starts	1st	2nd	3rd	Win & Pl
Hurdles	1	0	0	0	263
Career Total	**1**	**0**	**0**	**0**	**263**

Going: Sf: 0-0 GS: 0-1 Gd: 0-0 GF: - Fm: 0-0
Distance: 2m/2m3: 0-1 2m4-2m7: 0-0 3m+: 0-0
Track: LH: 0-0 RH: 0-1 Tight: 0-0 Gall: 0-0
Aids: Bl: 0-0 Vi: 0-0 Tstrap: 0-0 Ckp: 0-0
Best Rating: 83 12/03 Sand 2m110y gd-sft Hdl

Littleton Amethyst (IRE)

87   64

5-y-o ch m Revoque (IRE)-Sept Roses (USA) (Septieme Ciel (USA))
Mrs P Ford W E Donohue

Placings:P0   (2663)
2003/04: 20⁰GF, 16⁰G,

	Starts	1st	2nd	3rd	Win & Pl
Hurdles	2	0	0	0	0
Career Total	**2**	**0**	**0**	**0**	**0**

Going: Sf: 0-0 GS: 0-0 Gd: 0-1 GF: - Fm: 0-1
Distance: 2m/2m3: 0-1 2m4-2m7: 0-1 3m+: 0-0
Track: LH: 0-1 RH: 0-1 Tight: 0-0 Gall: 0-0
Aids: Bl: 0-0 Vi: 0-0 Tstrap: 0-0 Ckp: 0-0
Best Rating: 64 12/03 Leic 2m good Hdl

Littleton Valar (IRE)

92   70

4-y-o ch g Definite Article-Fresh Look (IRE) (Alzao (USA))
J R Weymes (T J Naughton 28/4) Miss K Buckle

Placings:6005P   (4614)
2003/04: 16⁶GS, 16⁹G, 16⁹F, 20⁵S, 17⁹G,

	Starts	1st	2nd	3rd	Win & Pl
Hurdles	5	0	0	0	0
Career Total	**5**	**0**	**0**	**0**	**0**

Going: Sf: 0-1 GS: 0-1 Gd: 0-2 GF: - Fm: 0-1
Distance: 2m/2m3: 0-4 2m4-2m7: 0-1 3m+: 0-0
Track: LH: 0-4 RH: 0-1 Tight: 0-4 Gall: 0-1
Aids: Bl: 0-0 Vi: 0-0 Tstrap: 0-0 Ckp: 0-0
Best Rating: 70 2/04 Muss 2m firm Hdl

Littleton Zeus (IRE)

60

5-y-o ch g Woodborough (USA)-La Fandango (IRE) (Taufan (USA))
W S Cunningham J D T Smith

Placings:00-PU   (0466)
2003/04: 20⁰G, 16⁰G,

	Starts	1st	2nd	3rd	Win & Pl
Hurdles	2	0	0	0	
Career Total	**4**	**0**	**0**	**0**	

Going: Sf: 0-0 GS: 0-0 Gd: 0-2 GF: - Fm: 0-0
Distance: 2m/2m3: 0-1 2m4-2m7: 0-1 3m+: 0-0
Track: LH: 0-2 RH: 0-0 Tight: 0-0 Gall: 0-0
Aids: Bl: 0-0 Vi: 0-0 Tstrap: 0-0 Ckp: 0-2
Best Rating: 58 2/03 Muss 2m good Hdl

Litzinsky

101   84

6-y-o b g Muhtarram (USA)-Boulevard Girl (Nicholas Bill)
C B B Booth Paul Gascoigne

Placings:66   (4319)
2003/04: 20⁶GS, 20⁶S,

	Starts	1st	2nd	3rd	Win & Pl
Hurdles	2	0	0	0	0
Career Total	**2**	**0**	**0**	**0**	**0**

Going: Sf: 0-1 GS: 0-1 Gd: 0-0 GF: - Fm: 0-0
Distance: 2m/2m3: 0-0 2m4-2m7: 0-2 3m+: 0-0
Track: LH: 0-2 RH: 0-0 Tight: 0-0 Gall: 0-2
Aids: Bl: 0-0 Vi: 0-0 Tstrap: 0-0 Ckp: 0-0
Best Rating: 84 2/04 Newc 2m4f gd-sft Hdl

Lively Dessert (IRE)

(86h)   (53h)76

11-y-o b g Be My Native (USA)-Liffey Travel (Le Bavard (FR))
F P Murtagh Mrs M E James

Placings:000/000025632/0F000004P06/01131201/PPP33/ 2PF3PPP5P-4   (0477)
2003/04: 26⁴GS,

	Starts	1st	2nd	3rd	Win & Pl
Hurdles	1	0	0	0	292
Career Total	**46**	**4**	**4**	**5**	**36954**
119 4/01 Prth	3m	C Ch	HVY	£7702
119 12/00 Ayr	3m1f	D(0-125)HCh	SFT	£7231

103	10/00	Aint	3m1f	F(0-105)HCh	GD	£5213
108	10/00	Sthl	3m110y	F(0-100)HCh	HVY	£2723
				Total win prize-money		£22871

Going:	Sf: 0-0 GS: 0-1 Gd: 0-0 GF: - Fm: 0-0
Distance:	2m/2m3: 0-0 2m4-2m7: 0-0 3m+: 0-1
Track:	LH: 0-1 RH: 0-0 Tight: 0-1 Gall: 0-0
Aids:	Bl: 0-0 Vi: 0-0 Tstrap: 0-0 Ckp: 0-0
Best Rating:	119 4/01 Prth 3m heavy Ch

Fair handicap chaser at his best but is very much on the downgrade.

Lively Felix

(58h)

7-y-o b g Presidium-Full Of Life (Wolverlife)
D G Bridgwater (D W P Arbuthnot 19/9) D G Bridgwater

Placings:6P30/000P000/0					(0529)
2003/04: 16⁰GF,					

	Starts	1st	2nd	3rd	Win & Pl
Chases	1	0	0	0	
Career Total	12	0	0	1	359

Going:	Sf: 0-0 GS: 0-0 Gd: 0-0 GF: 0-0 Fm: 0-1
Distance:	2m/2m3: 0-1 2m4-2m7: 0-0 3m+: 0-0
Track:	LH: 0-1 RH: 0-0 Tight: 0-0 Gall: 0-0
Aids:	Bl: 0-0 Vi: 0-0 Tstrap: 0-0 Ckp: 0-0
Best Rating:	74 12/00 Folk 2m1f110y heavy Hdl

Poor hurdling form, best with cut in the ground.

Livret Bleu (FR)

(93h)   (85h)

5-y-o b g Panoramic-Azur Bleue (FR) (Djarvis (FR))
A E Jessop (G Cherel 26/11) Mrs Gloria Jessop

Placings:335-0646636					(3328)
2003/04: 17⁰VS, 18⁶VS, 17⁴VS, 17⁶HO, 18⁶VS, 17³HO, 19⁶S,					

	Starts	1st	2nd	3rd	Win & Pl
Hurdles	1	0	0	0	0
Chases	6	0	0	1	4500
Career Total	10	0	0	3	11636

Going:	Sf: 0-1 GS: 0-0 Gd: 0-0 GF: 0-0 Fm: 0-0
Distance:	2m/2m3: 0-7 2m4-2m7: 0-0 3m+: 0-0
Track:	LH: 0-1 RH: 0-0 Tight: 0-0 Gall: 0-1
Aids:	Bl: 0-0 Vi: 0-0 Tstrap: 0-0 Ckp: 0-0
Best Rating:	86 1/04 Newb 2m3f soft Hdl

Lizzie Bathwick (IRE)

90   73

5-y-o b m Glacial Storm (USA)-Protrial (Proverb)
D P Keane W Clifford

Placings:5					(4736)
2003/04: 17⁵G,					

	Starts	1st	2nd	3rd	Win & Pl
Hurdles	1	0	0	0	0
Career Total	1	0	0	0	0

Going:	Sf: 0-0 GS: 0-0 Gd: 0-0 GF: - Fm: 0-0
Distance:	2m/2m3: 0-1 2m4-2m7: 0-0 3m+: 0-0
Track:	LH: 0-1 RH: 0-0 Tight: 0-1 Gall: 0-0
Aids:	Bl: 0-0 Vi: 0-0 Tstrap: 0-0 Ckp: 0-0
Best Rating:	78 4/04 NAbb 2m1f good Hdl

Lizzy Lamb

93   68+

6-y-o gr m Bustino-Caroline Lamb (Hotfoot)
Miss S E Hall Miss S E Hall

Placings:3-5					(1252)
2003/04: 17⁵GF,					

	Starts	1st	2nd	3rd	Win & Pl
Hurdles	1	0	0	0	0
Career Total	2	0	0	1	263

Going:	Sf: 0-0 GS: 0-0 Gd: 0-0 GF: - Fm: 0-1
Distance:	2m/2m3: 0-1 2m4-2m7: 0-0 3m+: 0-0
Track:	LH: 0-0 RH: 0-1 Tight: 0-1 Gall: 0-0
Aids:	Bl: 0-0 Vi: 0-0 Tstrap: 0-0 Ckp: 0-0
Best Rating:	75 7/02 Sedg 2m1f gd-fm NHF

Third in only start in bumper company; well beaten in weak mares' only event on hurdling debut.

Lizzys First

92(102h)   (101 h)78

12-y-o b g Town And Country-Lizzy Longstocking (Jimsun)
C J Down Stephen Goss

Placings:0P/FU21311455/55264/0UFPP0P0/030/34162015					
-00F					(4241)
2003/04: 24⁰GF, 19⁰GS, 19⁷G,					

	Starts	1st	2nd	3rd	Win & Pl
Hurdles	1	0	0	0	0
Chases	2	0	0	0	0
Career Total	39	5	3	3	18225

101	4/03	Tntn	3m110y G(0-95)HHdl	FRM	£2483
101	12/02	Hrfd	2m3f110yE(0-105)HHdl	SFT	£4033
107	2/99	Tntn	2m3fE(0-115)HHdl	G-S	£2775
107	2/99	Tntn	2m3f110yE(0-105)HHdl	G-S	£2309
92	12/98	Extr	2m1f110yE(0-100)HHdl	SFT	£2532
			Total win prize-money		£14133

Going:	Sf: 0-0 GS: 0-1 Gd: 0-1 GF: - Fm: 0-1
Distance:	2m/2m3: 0-1 2m4-2m7: 0-1 3m+: 0-1
Track:	LH: 0-0 RH: 0-3 Tight: 0-0 Gall: 0-0
Aids:	Bl: 0-0 Vi: 0-0 Tstrap: 0-0 Ckp: 0-0
Best Rating:	109 11/00 NAbb 2m5f110y heavy Ch

Moderate hurdler, ended a long losing run in December 2002; won again in April 2003; stays two and a half miles and suited by soft ground, but has won on fast.

Loaded Gun

76   23

4-y-o ch g Highest Honor (FR)-Woodwardia (USA) (El Gran Senor (USA))
Miss J Feilden J F Thomas

Placings:5					(2331)
2003/04: 16⁵G,					

	Starts	1st	2nd	3rd	Win & Pl
Hurdles	1	0	0	0	0
Career Total	1	0	0	0	0

Going:	Sf: 0-0 GS: 0-0 Gd: 0-1 GF: 0-0 Fm: 0-0
Distance:	2m/2m3: 0-1 2m4-2m7: 0-0 3m+: 0-0
Track:	LH: 0-1 RH: 0-0 Tight: 0-0 Gall: 0-0
Aids:	Bl: 0-0 Vi: 0-0 Tstrap: 0-0 Ckp: 0-0
Best Rating:	23 11/03 Fknm 2m good Hdl

Loblite Leader (IRE)

64   92

7-y-o b g Tirol-Cyrano Beauty (IRE) (Cyrano De Bergerac)
G A Swinbank Mrs V McGee

Placings:53-5					(4727)
2003/04: 17⁵G,					

	Starts	1st	2nd	3rd	Win & Pl
Hurdles	1	0	0	0	0
Career Total	3	0	0	1	569

Going:	Sf: 0-0 GS: 0-0 Gd: 0-1 GF: - Fm: 0-0
Distance:	2m/2m3: 0-1 2m4-2m7: 0-0 3m+: 0-0
Track:	LH: 0-0 RH: 0-1 Tight: 0-0 Gall: 0-0
Aids:	Bl: 0-0 Vi: 0-0 Tstrap: 0-0 Ckp: 0-0
Best Rating:	97 2/03 Catt 2m3f good Hdl

Lobuche (IRE)

(84h)   (62h)46

9-y-o b g Petardia-Lhotse (IRE) (Shernazar)
M C Chapman K D Blanch

Placings:21/360366540240055/16233230/04100521200P0					
354P/66-P					(0322)
2003/04: 16⁹GF,					

	Starts	1st	2nd	3rd	Win & Pl
Hurdles	1	0	0	0	
Career Total	45	4	6	6	20508

97	9/01	MRas	2m3f110yE(0-115)HHdl	G-F	£3332
97	6/01	MRas	2m3f110yF(0-105)HHdl	G-F	£2949
91	5/00	Ctml	2m1f110yG(0-90)HHdl	GD	£3582
99	3/99	MRas	2m1f110yD Hdl	G-S	£3367
			Total win prize-money		£13233

Going:	Sf: 0-0 GS: 0-0 Gd: 0-0 GF: - Fm: 0-0
Distance:	2m/2m3: 0-1 2m4-2m7: 0-0 3m+: 0-0
Track:	LH: 0-1 RH: 0-0 Tight: 0-1 Gall: 0-0
Aids:	Bl: 0-0 Vi: 0-0 Tstrap: 0-0 Ckp: 0-0
Best Rating:	104 3/00 Chel 2m1f gd-fm Hdl

Loch Na Bpeisc (IRE)

90(74h)   (58h)66

7-y-o b g Over The River (FR)-Ballyhire Lady (IRE) (Callernish)
P G Murphy Mrs John Spielman

Placings:00P-PP443P					(3967)
2003/04: 25⁵GS, 24⁵GS, 26⁴G, 25⁴GS, 24³HY, 25⁵PGS,					

	Starts	1st	2nd	3rd	Win & Pl
Chases	6	0	0	1	1050
Career Total	9	0	0	1	1050

Going:	Sf: 0-1 GS: 0-4 Gd: 0-1 GF: - Fm: 0-0
Distance:	2m/2m3: 0-0 2m4-2m7: 0-0 3m+: 0-6
Track:	LH: 0-2 RH: 0-3 Tight: 0-1 Gall: 0-0
Aids:	Bl: 0-0 Vi: 0-0 Tstrap: 0-0 Ckp: 0-0
Best Rating:	66 2/04 Chep 3m heavy Ch

Pulled up in first two starts over fences but has shaped better since in low grade staying handicaps.

Loch Red

5-y-o ch g Primitive Rising (USA)-Lochcross (Lochnager)
Mrs A M Naughton Mrs Jill Murphy

Placings:0   (4179)
2003/04: 16⁰G,

	Starts	1st	2nd	3rd	Win & Pl
NH Flat	1	0	0	0	
Career Total	1	0	0	0	

Going:	Sf: 0-0 GS: 0-0 Gd: 0-1 GF: - Fm: 0-0
Distance:	2m/2m3: 0-1 2m4-2m7: 0-0 3m+: 0-0
Track:	LH: 0-1 RH: 0-0 Tight: 0-0 Gall: 0-1
Aids:	Bl: 0-0 Vi: 0-0 Tstrap: 0-0 Ckp: 0-0

Loch Side

6-y-o gr m Tina's Pet-Sparkling Time (USA) (Olden Times)
M Scudamore Mrs S Tainton

Placings:6PP   (4929)
2003/04: 17⁶GS, 22ᴾG, 18ᴾG,

	Starts	1st	2nd	3rd	Win & Pl
NH Flat	1	0	0	0	0
Hurdles	2	0	0	0	0
Career Total	3	0	0	0	0

Going:	Sf: 0-0 GS: 0-1 Gd: 0-2 GF: - Fm: 0-0
Distance:	2m/2m3: 0-2 2m4-2m7: 0-1 3m+: 0-0
Track:	LH: 0-1 RH: 0-1 Tight: 0-1 Gall: 0-0
Aids:	Bl: 0-0 Vi: 0-0 Tstrap: 0-0 Ckp: 0-0
Best Rating:	91 1/04 Tntn 2m1f gd-sft NHF

Loch Sound

92   90

8-y-o g b g Primitive Rising (USA)-Lochcross (Lochnager)
Mrs A M Naughton Mrs Jill Murphy

Placings:0F0/00/0P0   (4688)
2003/04: 19⁰GF, 16ᴾG, 16⁰G,

	Starts	1st	2nd	3rd	Win & Pl
Hurdles	2	0	0	0	0
Chases	1	0	0	0	0
Career Total	8	0	0	0	0

Going:	Sf: 0-0 GS: 0-0 Gd: 0-2 GF: - Fm: 0-1
Distance:	2m/2m3: 0-3 2m4-2m7: 0-0 3m+: 0-0
Track:	LH: 0-3 RH: 0-0 Tight: 0-2 Gall: 0-0
Aids:	Bl: 0-0 Vi: 0-0 Tstrap: 0-0 Ckp: 0-0
Best Rating:	90 4/01 Ayr 2m good Hdl

Lochbuy Junior (FR)

92(107h)   (113h)85

9-y-o g b g Saumarez-Chalabiah (Akarad) (FR))
M Todhunter The G-Guck Group

Placings:F2/4415P2P5/2PP/1-P4   (3336)
2003/04: 21ᴾG, 19⁴GS,

	Starts	1st	2nd	3rd	Win & Pl
Chases	2	0	0	0	306
Career Total	16	2	3	0	11831
104 3/03	Ayr	2m4f	D(0-125)HHdl	SFT	£4842
115 11/00	Catt	2m3f	F(0-110)HHdl	G-S	£1911
			Total win prize-money £6754		

Going:	Sf: 0-0 GS: 0-1 Gd: 0-1 GF: - Fm: 0-0
Distance:	2m/2m3: 0-1 2m4-2m7: 0-1 3m+: 0-0
Track:	LH: 0-2 RH: 0-0 Tight: 0-2 Gall: 0-0
Aids:	Bl: 0-0 Vi: 0-0 Tstrap: 0-1 Ckp: 0-0
Best Rating:	115 11/00 Catt 2m3f gd-sft Hdl

Moderate hurdler; better effort over fences when well beaten fourth at Catterick in January.

Lochiedubs

100(95h)   (89h)100+

9-y-o br g Cragador-Linn Falls (Royal Fountain)
Mrs L B Normile B Thomson

Placings:3/535034/30-005P63165F   (4912)
2003/04: 20⁹HY, 24⁶S, 27⁵G, 21ᴾGS, 24⁶G, 20³HY, 20¹S, 20⁶GS,
20⁵G, 20ᶠS,

	Starts	1st	2nd	3rd	Win & Pl
Hurdles	3	0	0	0	
Chases	7	1	0	1	6324
Career Total	19	1	0	5	8104
100 3/04	Newc	2m4f	D(0-115)HCh	SFT	£5759
			Total win prize-money £5759		

Going:	Sf: 1-5 GS: 0-2 Gd: 0-3 GF: - Fm: 0-0
Distance:	2m/2m3: 0-0 2m4-2m7: 1-7 3m+: 0-3
Track:	LH: 1-4 RH: 0-6 Tight: 0-4 Gall: 1-1
Aids:	Bl: 0-3 Vi: 0-0 Tstrap: 0-0 Ckp: 0-0
Best Rating:	100 3/04 Newc 2m4f soft Ch

Novice chaser; off the mark with clear cut success at Newcastle in March; suited by two and a half miles; acts in the mud.

Lock Inn

89   81

5-y-o g b g Dolphin Street (FR)-Highest Bid (FR) (Highest Honor (FR))
Miss Z C Davison Paul Leavy & Mrs Susan Emmett-Leavy

Placings:404600   (4749)
2003/04: 20⁴G, 20⁰G, 22⁴HY, 22⁶G, 22⁹G, 25⁰G,

	Starts	1st	2nd	3rd	Win & Pl
Hurdles	6	0	0	0	264
Career Total	6	0	0	0	264

Going:	Sf: 0-1 GS: 0-0 Gd: 0-5 GF: - Fm: 0-0
Distance:	2m/2m3: 0-0 2m4-2m7: 0-5 3m+: 0-1
Track:	LH: 0-3 RH: 0-0 Tight: 0-5 Gall: 0-0
Aids:	Bl: 0-0 Vi: 0-1 Tstrap: 0-0 Ckp: 0-0
Best Rating:	81 12/03 Font 2m4f good Hdl

Next door to useless on the Flat but looks a bit better over hurdles judged on his debut effort.

Locksmith

110   132+

4-y-o b/br g Linamix (FR)-Zenith (Shirley Heights)
M C Pipe D A Johnson

Placings:1441220   (4381)
2003/04: 12¹S, 13⁴GS, 12⁴G, 18¹G, 17²HY, 16²G, 16⁰G,

	Starts	1st	2nd	3rd	Win & Pl
NH Flat	3	1	0	0	3099
Hurdles	4	1	2	0	11018
Career Total	7	2	2	0	14117
124 1/04	Font	2m2f110yE Hdl	GD	£3347
100 11/03	Asct	1m4f	H NHF	SFT	£2534
			Total win prize-money £5882		

Going:	Sf: 1-2 GS: 0-1 Gd: 1-4 GF: - Fm: 0-0
Distance:	2m/2m3: 1-4 2m4-2m7: 0-0 3m+: 0-0
Track:	LH: 1-2 RH: 0-3 Tight: 1-1 Gall: 0-0
Aids:	Bl: 0-0 Vi: 0-0 Tstrap: 0-0 Ckp: 0-0
Best Rating:	132 3/04 Chel 2m110y good Hdl

Very useful novice hurdler; can be quite keen; stays further than two miles and suited by ground good or softer.

Lockstockandbarrel (IRE)

103f   104f

5-y-o b g Needle Gun (IRE)-Quill Project (IRE) (Project Manager)
M C Banks Mrs M C Banks

Placings:1   (4962)
2003/04: 17¹G,

	Starts	1st	2nd	3rd	Win & Pl
NH Flat	1	1	0	0	2177
Career Total	1	1	0	0	2177
104 4/04	MRas	2m1f110yH NHF	GD	£2177
			Total win prize-money £2177	

Going:	Sf: 0-0 GS: 0-0 Gd: 1-1 GF: - Fm: 0-0
Distance:	2m/2m3: 1-1 2m4-2m7: 0-0 3m+: 0-0
Track:	LH: 0-0 RH: 1-1 Tight: 1-1 Gall: 0-0
Aids:	Bl: 0-0 Vi: 0-0 Tstrap: 1-1 Ckp: 0-0
Best Rating:	104 4/04 MRas 2m1f110y good NHF

Made winning debut in bumper in April 2004; acts on good.

Lodestar (IRE)

108(107h)   (114+h)114+

7-y-o br g Good Thyne (USA)-Lets Compromise (No Argument)
Ian Williams Sir Robert Ogden

Placings:0/P4F5212-13424   (2324)
2003/04: 24¹G, 24³G, 20⁴G, 24²GF, 25⁴G,

	Starts	1st	2nd	3rd	Win & Pl
Hurdles	1	1	0	0	7134
Chases	4	0	1	1	4431
Career Total	13	2	3	1	18468
114 5/03	Worc	3m	C(0-135)HHdl	GD	£7133
93 4/03	Strf	2m6f110yE Hdl	G-F	£4260
			Total win prize-money £11395		

Going:	Sf: 0-0 GS: 0-0 Gd: 1-4 GF: - Fm: 0-1
Distance:	2m/2m3: 0-0 2m4-2m7: 0-1 3m+: 1-4
Track:	LH: 1-4 RH: 0-1 Tight: 0-1 Gall: 0-1
Aids:	Bl: 0-0 Vi: 0-0 Tstrap: 0-0 Ckp: 0-0
Best Rating:	114 11/03 Newb 3m gd-fm Ch

Fair hurdler; just moderate over fences; stays further than three miles; acts well on fast ground.

Lofty Leader (IRE)

94f   98f

5-y-o b g Norwich-Slaney Jazz (Orchestra)
W McKeown L H Gilmurray

Placings:0502   (4885)
2003/04: 16⁰GF, 16⁵HY, 16⁰GS, 17²GS,

	Starts	1st	2nd	3rd	Win & Pl
NH Flat	4	0	1	0	594
Career Total	4	0	1	0	594

Going:	Sf: 0-1 GS: 0-2 Gd: 0-0 GF: - Fm: 0-1
Distance:	2m/2m3: 0-4 2m4-2m7: 0-0 3m+: 0-0
Track:	LH: 0-2 RH: 0-2 Tight: 0-1 Gall: 0-0
Aids:	Bl: 0-0 Vi: 0-0 Tstrap: 0-0 Ckp: 0-0
Best Rating:	98 4/04 Carl 2m1f gd-sft NHF

Best effort in bumpers when runner-up in modest event at Carlisle in April.

Log On Intersky (IRE)

106(100h)   (93h)**137+**

8-y-o ch g Insan (USA)-Arctic Mo (IRE) (Mandalus)
J Howard Johnson   interskyracing.com

Placings:*00*/030FP32/315**211414**-3210P2   (4864)
2003/04: 17³GF, 20²G, 16¹G, 16⁶S, 16⁶G, 16²S,

	Starts	1st	2nd	3rd	Win & Pl
Chases	6	1	2	1	17906
Career Total	24	5	4	4	42479
140 11/03 Ayr	2m		C(0-130)HCh	GD	£6795
135 2/03 Catt	2m		D Ch	GD	£5476
129 12/02 Catt	2m		E(0-105)HCh	G-S	£3818
116 10/02 Carl	2m		E(0-100)HCh	SFT	£4348
93 9/02 Sedg	2m5f110yE Hdl			GD	£2891

Total win prize-money £23331

Going:	Sf: 0-2 GS: 0-1 Gd: 1-3 GF: - Fm: 0-1
Distance:	2m/2m3: 1-5 2m4-2m7: 0-1 3m+: 0-1
Track:	LH: 1-4 RH: 0-2 Tight: 0-3 Gall: 0-0
Aids:	Bl: 0-0 Vi: 0-0 Tstrap: 0-0 Ckp: 0-0
Best Rating:	140 11/03 Ayr 2m good Ch

Useful chaser; stayed around two and a half miles over hurdles, but best form over fences over two miles; acts on good or softer; has worn a tongue tie.

Logsdail

93   **80**

4-y-o b g Polish Precedent (USA)-Logic (Slip Anchor)
G L Moore (P J Hobbs 25/10)   D T L Limited

Placings:26   (1770)
2003/04: 17²GF, 16⁶GF,

	Starts	1st	2nd	3rd	Win & Pl
Hurdles	2	0	1	0	1056
Career Total	2	0	1	0	1056

Going:	Sf: 0-0 GS: 0-0 Gd: 0-0 GF: - Fm: 0-2
Distance:	2m/2m3: 0-2 2m4-2m7: 0-0 3m+: 0-0
Track:	LH: 0-1 RH: 0-1 Tight: 0-1 Gall: 0-0
Aids:	Bl: 0-0 Vi: 0-0 Tstrap: 0-0 Ckp: 0-0
Best Rating:	80 9/03 NAbb 2m1f gd-fm Hdl

Plating-class hurdler; had stamina limitations exposed by Downtherefordancin when runner-up on hurdling debut at Newton Abbot September 2003.

Loi De Martiale (IRE)

84   **87**

6-y-o br g Presenting-Thresa-Anita (IRE) (Over The River (FR))
J M Jefferson   R G Marshall

Placings:*20*-3360   (4732)
2003/04: 16³G, 17²GF, 24⁶GS, 17⁰G,

	Starts	1st	2nd	3rd	Win & Pl
NH Flat	2	0	0	2	552
Hurdles	2	0	0	0	0
Career Total	6	0	1	2	1824

Going:	Sf: 0-0 GS: 0-1 Gd: 0-2 GF: - Fm: 0-1
Distance:	2m/2m3: 0-3 2m4-2m7: 0-0 3m+: 0-1
Track:	LH: 0-0 RH: 0-4 Tight: 0-0 Gall: 0-0
Aids:	Bl: 0-0 Vi: 0-0 Tstrap: 0-0 Ckp: 0-0
Best Rating:	96 12/02 Muss 2m gd-sft NHF

Moderate bumper performer.

Lone Soldier (FR)

99   **83**

8-y-o ch g Songlines (FR)-Caring Society (Caerleon (USA))
S B Clark   S B Clark

Placings:22P431/54020/401440/600-32UP001F   (4603)
2003/04: 17³GF, 17²GF, 17⁰U, 16⁸GS, 17⁰G, 16⁶G, 19¹GF, 17⁶G,

	Starts	1st	2nd	3rd	Win & Pl
Hurdles	8	1	1	1	3640
Career Total	28	3	4	2	13445
83 3/04 Catt	2m3f	F(0-100)HHdl	G-F	£2716
108 6/01 Worc	2m	E Ch	G-F	£3260
102 3/00 Tntn	2m1f	F(0-100)HHdl	GD	£2107

Total win prize-money £8083

Going:	Sf: 0-0 GS: 0-1 Gd: 0-4 GF: - Fm: 1-3
Distance:	2m/2m3: 1-8 2m4-2m7: 0-0 3m+: 0-0
Track:	LH: 1-4 RH: 0-4 Tight: 1-8 Gall: 0-0
Aids:	Bl: 0-0 Vi: 0-0 Tstrap: 0-0 Ckp: 0-0
Best Rating:	108 6/01 Worc 2m gd-fm Ch

Plating-class hurdler/chaser; ended a long losing run when taking a handicap hurdle at Catterick in March; suited by two and a half miles; best on fast ground..

Lone Star (IRE)

12-y-o b g Satco (FR)-Masterstown Lucy (Bargello)
Martin Ward   Martin Ward

Placings:P/PP3/360/PUF/P/4-P   (0199)
2003/04: 24³GF,

	Starts	1st	2nd	3rd	Win & Pl
Chases	1	0	0	0	
Career Total	13	0	0	2	980

Going:	Sf: 0-0 GS: 0-0 Gd: 0-0 GF: - Fm: 0-1
Distance:	2m/2m3: 0-0 2m4-2m7: 0-0 3m+: 0-1
Track:	LH: 0-0 RH: 0-1 Tight: 0-0 Gall: 0-1
Aids:	Bl: 0-1 Vi: 0-0 Tstrap: 0-1 Ckp: 0-0
Best Rating:	97 5/99 Hrfd 2m3f good Ch

Lonesome Dealer (IRE)

(87h)   (81h)**85**

8-y-o b/br g Supreme Leader-Slievenaree (IRE) (Lancastrian)
B G Powell   Tweenhills Racing (Cleeve Hill)

Placings:60415000/04P40P-P3   (0238)
2003/04: 16⁶G, 17⁵S, 19³G,

	Starts	1st	2nd	3rd	Win & Pl
Hurdles	1	0	0	1	346
Chases	2	0	0	0	0
Career Total	16	1	0	1	7440
108 12/01 Limk	2m	Hdl	SFT	£6129

Total win prize-money £6129

Going:	Sf: 0-1 GS: 0-0 Gd: 0-2 GF: - Fm: 0-0
Distance:	2m/2m3: 0-2 2m4-2m7: 0-1 3m+: 0-0
Track:	LH: 0-2 RH: 0-1 Tight: 0-1 Gall: 0-0
Aids:	Bl: 0-0 Vi: 0-1 Tstrap: 0-0 Ckp: 0-0
Best Rating:	108 12/01 Limk 2m soft Hdl

Lonesome Man (IRE)

85   **106**

8-y-o ch g Broken Hearted-Carn-Na-Ros (Royal Trip)

R T Phillips   P Docherty

Placings:60/056236-630   (4198)
2003/04: 20⁶GS, 20³G, 16⁶G,

	Starts	1st	2nd	3rd	Win & Pl
Hurdles	3	0	0	1	374
Career Total	11	0	1	2	1958

Going:	Sf: 0-0 GS: 0-1 Gd: 0-2 GF: - Fm: 0-0
Distance:	2m/2m3: 0-1 2m4-2m7: 0-2 3m+: 0-0
Track:	LH: 0-2 RH: 0-0 Tight: 0-1 Gall: 0-1
Aids:	Bl: 0-0 Vi: 0-0 Tstrap: 0-0 Ckp: 0-0
Best Rating:	106 2/03 Punc 2m soft Hdl

Long Shot

105   **108**

7-y-o b m Sir Harry Lewis (USA)-Kovalevskia (Ardross)
N J Henderson   W H Ponsonby

Placings:4210/0143F2-313250   (3418)
2003/04: 24³GF, 16¹GF, 19³GF, 20²GS, 24⁵G, 17⁰GS,

	Starts	1st	2nd	3rd	Win & Pl
Hurdles	6	1	1	2	7502
Career Total	16	3	3	3	16556
108 11/03 Hntg	2m110y E(0-110)HHdl	G-F	£3416
98 11/02 Winc	2m6f	D Hdl	GD	£4309
93 4/02 Fknm	2m	H NHF	GD	£1540

Total win prize-money £9266

Going:	Sf: 0-0 GS: 0-2 Gd: 0-1 GF: - Fm: 1-3
Distance:	2m/2m3: 1-3 2m4-2m7: 0-1 3m+: 0-2
Track:	LH: 0-1 RH: 1-5 Tight: 0-1 Gall: 1-2
Aids:	Bl: 0-0 Vi: 0-0 Tstrap: 0-0 Ckp: 0-0
Best Rating:	108 11/03 Folk 2m4f110y gd-sft Hdl

Modest hurdler; acts on any ground; stays three miles, but has won over two; front-runner.

Long Walk (IRE)

104(94h)   (95+h)**119+**

7-y-o br g King's Ride-Seanaphobal Lady (Kambalda)
H D Daly   The Earl Cadogan

Placings:32252/534131   (4713)
2003/04: 20⁵GS, 20³GS, 21⁴S, 24¹GT, 24³G, 24¹G,

	Starts	1st	2nd	3rd	Win & Pl
Hurdles	1	0	0	0	0
Chases	5	2	0	2	13296
Career Total	11	2	3	3	16947
119 4/04 Ludl	3m	D Ch	GD	£6682
103 2/04 Ludl	3m	E Ch	GD	£4832

Total win prize-money £11515

Going:	Sf: 0-1 GS: 0-2 Gd: 2-3 GF: - Fm: 0-0
Distance:	2m/2m3: 0-0 2m4-2m7: 0-3 3m+: 2-3
Track:	LH: 0-2 RH: 2-4 Tight: 2-2 Gall: 0-2
Aids:	Bl: 0-0 Vi: 0-0 Tstrap: 0-0 Ckp: 0-0
Best Rating:	119 4/04 Ludl 3m good Ch

Moderate novice chaser; off the mark over fences at Ludlow in February; scored again there in April; stays three miles; acts on soft and good ground.

Longmeadows Boy (IRE)

99   **91+**

4-y-o b g Victory Note (USA)-Karoi (IRE) (Kafu)
A Berry   John Wilding Promotions

Placings:1P   (1355)

2003/04: 17¹G, 17ᴾG,

	Starts	1st	2nd	3rd	Win & Pl
Hurdles	2	1	0	0	3822
Career Total	2	1	0	0	3822
91 8/03 Ctml 2m1f110yE Hdl				GD	£3822

Total win prize-money £3822

Going:	Sf: 0-0 GS: 0-0 Gd: 1-2 GF: - Fm: 0-0
Distance:	2m/2m3: 1-2 2m4-2m7: 0-0 3m+: 0-0
Track:	LH: 1-2 RH: 0-0 Tight: 1-2 Gall: 0-0
Aids:	Bl: 0-0 Vi: 0-0 Tstrap: 0-0 Ckp: 0-0
Best Rating:	91 8/03 Ctml 2m1f110y good Hdl

Selling-race winner on the Flat; successfull on hurdling bow at Cartmel in August; ran badly at Bangor the following month.

Longshanks

105(107h)   (104 h)130+

7-y-o b g Broadsword (USA)-Brass Castle (IRE) (Carlingford Castle)
K C Bailey D A Halsall

Placings:402P2-1P11132   (4640)
2003/04: 22¹S, 24ᴾG, 22¹GS, 20¹GS, 24¹GS, 24³GS, 21²G,

	Starts	1st	2nd	3rd	Win & Pl
Hurdles	2	1	0	0	3653
Chases	5	3	1	1	37204
Career Total	12	4	3	1	43834
130 12/03 Hayd 3m D(0-125)HCh				G-S	£10296
122 11/03 Ayr 2m4f D(0-110)HCh				G-S	£6734
122 11/03 Hayd 2m6f E(0-105)HCh				G-S	£3010
104 5/03 Uttx 2m6f110yE Hdl				SFT	£3653

Total win prize-money £23693

Going:	Sf: 1-1 GS: 3-4 Gd: 0-2 GF: - Fm: 0-0
Distance:	2m/2m3: 0-0 2m4-2m7: 3-4 3m+: 1-3
Track:	LH: 4-5 RH: 0-2 Tight: 0-1 Gall: 0-0
Aids:	Bl: 0-0 Vi: 0-0 Tstrap: 0-0 Ckp: 0-0
Best Rating:	130 2/04 Kemp 3m gd-sft Ch

Fair chaser; progressive; landed hat-trick in November/December 2003; narrowly beaten in Topham Chase; stays 3m; suited by soft ground; likes to make the running.

Longship

6-y-o b g Saddlers' Hall (IRE)-Main Sail (Blakeney)
D McCain D McCain

Placings:0P   (0473)
2003/04: 16⁰G, 17ᴾGS,

	Starts	1st	2nd	3rd	Win & Pl
NH Flat	1	0	0	0	0
Hurdles	1	0	0	0	0
Career Total	2	0	0	0	0

Going:	Sf: 0-0 GS: 0-1 Gd: 0-1 GF: - Fm: 0-0
Distance:	2m/2m3: 0-2 2m4-2m7: 0-0 3m+: 0-0
Track:	LH: 0-1 RH: 0-1 Tight: 0-1 Gall: 0-0
Aids:	Bl: 0-0 Vi: 0-0 Tstrap: 0-0 Ckp: 0-0
Best Rating:	60 5/03 Ludl 2m good NHF

Longstone Boy (IRE)

12-y-o br g Mazaad-Inger-Lea (Record Run)
E R Clough E R Clough

Placings:0/P26/23-513   (4635)
2003/04: 24⁵G, 20¹G, 24³G,

	Starts	1st	2nd	3rd	Win & Pl
Chases	3	1	0	1	2573
Career Total	9	1	2	2	4667
91 3/04 Leic 2m4f110yH Ch				GD	£2229

Total win prize-money £2230

Going:	Sf: 0-0 GS: 0-0 Gd: 1-3 GF: - Fm: 0-0
Distance:	2m/2m3: 0-2 2m4-2m7: 1-1 3m+: 0-2
Track:	LH: 0-0 RH: 1-3 Tight: 0-2 Gall: 0-0
Aids:	Bl: 0-0 Vi: 0-0 Tstrap: 0-0 Ckp: 0-0
Best Rating:	91 4/04 Tntn 3m good Ch

French-trained novice chaser; won three-runner race at Warwick in November; fell next time; stays three miles; acts in soft ground.

Longstone Lass

4-y-o b f Wizard King-Kamaress (Kampala)
W McKeown The Northumberland Group Racing Club

Placings:500F4   (4317)
2003/04: 16⁶G, 17⁰GS, 16⁰GS, 16ᶠGF, 16⁴S,

	Starts	1st	2nd	3rd	Win & Pl
NH Flat	2	0	0	0	0
Hurdles	3	0	0	0	255
Career Total	5	0	0	0	255

Going:	Sf: 0-1 GS: 0-2 Gd: 0-1 GF: - Fm: 0-1
Distance:	2m/2m3: 0-5 2m4-2m7: 0-0 3m+: 0-0
Track:	LH: 0-5 RH: 0-0 Tight: 0-0 Gall: 0-1
Aids:	Bl: 0-0 Vi: 0-0 Tstrap: 0-0 Ckp: 0-0
Best Rating:	61 1/04 Hayd 2m good NHF

Longstone Loch (IRE)

98(93h)   (84h)95+

7-y-o b g Executive Perk-Lyre-Na-Gcloc (Le Moss)
C C Bealby Ady Boughen

Placings:0P-661   (4164)
2003/04: 17⁶GS, 19⁶GS, 19¹G,

	Starts	1st	2nd	3rd	Win & Pl
Hurdles	2	0	0	0	0
Chases	1	1	0	0	3476
Career Total	5	1	0	0	3476
95 3/04 Donc 2m3f F(0-100)HCh				GD	£3475

Total win prize-money £3476

Going:	Sf: 0-0 GS: 0-2 Gd: 1-1 GF: - Fm: 0-0
Distance:	2m/2m3: 1-3 2m4-2m7: 0-0 3m+: 0-0
Track:	LH: 1-2 RH: 0-1 Tight: 0-1 Gall: 0-0
Aids:	Bl: 0-0 Vi: 0-0 Tstrap: 0-0 Ckp: 0-0
Best Rating:	95 3/04 Donc 2m3f good Ch

Moderate novice chaser; broke his duck in handicap company at Doncaster in March; effective over two miles three but will be suited by further.

Look Collonges (FR)

104   121

5-y-o gr g Dom Alco (FR)-Tessy Collonges (FR) (El Badr)
G Macaire Claude Cohen

Placings:532-221F21   (3645)
2003/04: 17²VS, 20²VS, 16¹GF, 16ᶠGF, 24²GS, 21¹HO,

	Starts	1st	2nd	3rd	Win & Pl
Chases	6	2	3	0	32486
Career Total	9	2	4	1	42596
3/04 Autl 2m5f110y HCh				HLD	£10141
102 11/03 Wwck 2m110y C Ch				G-F	£7140

Going:	Sf: 0-0 GS: 0-1 Gd: 0-0 GF: - Fm: 1-2
Distance:	2m/2m3: 1-3 2m4-2m7: 1-2 3m+: 0-1
Track:	LH: 1-2 RH: 0-1 Tight: 0-0 Gall: 0-0
Aids:	Bl: 0-0 Vi: 0-0 Tstrap: 0-0 Ckp: 0-0
Best Rating:	123 11/03 Wwck 2m110y gd-fm Ch

Total win prize-money £17281

Look Sharpe

13-y-o b g Looking Glass-Washburn Flyer (Owen Dudley)
T S Sharpe T S Sharpe

Placings:20/P/U5/0402-4   (0199)
2003/04: 20²GF, 24⁴GF,

	Starts	1st	2nd	3rd	Win & Pl
Chases	2	0	1	0	560
Career Total	10	0	2	0	1227

Going:	Sf: 0-0 GS: 0-0 Gd: 0-0 GF: - Fm: 0-2
Distance:	2m/2m3: 0-0 2m4-2m7: 0-1 3m+: 0-1
Track:	LH: 0-1 RH: 0-1 Tight: 0-0 Gall: 0-2
Aids:	Bl: 0-0 Vi: 0-0 Tstrap: 0-0 Ckp: 0-0
Best Rating:	76 4/03 Newc 2m4f gd-fm Ch

Modest hunter chaser.

Look To The Future (IRE)

99(108h)   (106h)96

10-y-o b g Roselier (FR)-Toevarro (Raga Navarro (ITY))
Mrs S J Smith M C V Racing

Placings:50/0002240/0006/P2PP36P3-3303U4   (4794)
2003/04: 22³G, 20³S, 25⁰G, 20³G, 25ᵁS, 21⁴G,

	Starts	1st	2nd	3rd	Win & Pl
Hurdles	3	0	0	2	1565
Chases	3	0	0	1	1010
Career Total	27	0	3	5	7122

Going:	Sf: 0-2 GS: 0-0 Gd: 0-4 GF: - Fm: 0-0
Distance:	2m/2m3: 0-0 2m4-2m7: 0-4 3m+: 0-2
Track:	LH: 0-6 RH: 0-0 Tight: 0-3 Gall: 0-0
Aids:	Bl: 0-0 Vi: 0-0 Tstrap: 0-0 Ckp: 0-0
Best Rating:	106 1/04 Weth 2m4f110y soft Hdl

Moderate maiden over both hurdles and fences at up to three miles.

Looking Deadly

75(88c)   (52c)33

10-y-o b m Neltino-Princess Constanza (Relkino)
F P Murtagh Teddy Bears & Big Bear Syndicate

Placings:00000/2P/0500PP/2045U55P-60   (0472)
2003/04: 17⁶G, 17⁰GS,

	Starts	1st	2nd	3rd	Win & Pl
Hurdles	1	0	0	0	0
Chases	1	0	0	0	0
Career Total	23	0	2	0	1637

Going:	Sf: 0-0 GS: 0-1 Gd: 0-1 GF: - Fm: 0-0
Distance:	2m/2m3: 0-0 2m4-2m7: 0-0 3m+: 0-0
Track:	LH: 0-2 RH: 0-0 Tight: 0-2 Gall: 0-0
Aids:	Bl: 0-0 Vi: 0-0 Tstrap: 0-0 Ckp: 0-0

Best Rating: 85 5/00 Kels 2m110y good Hdl

Looking Forward

109   106
8-y-o br g Primitive Rising (USA)-Gilzie Bank (New Brig)
Ferdy Murphy Mrs G Handley

Placings:P53/4PFU1-1P54151   (4797)
2003/04: 19¹GF, 20⁰S, 20⁵HY, 24⁴G, 21¹G, 20⁵G, 21¹G,

	Starts	1st	2nd	3rd	Win & Pl
Chases	7	3	0	0	14602
Career Total	15	4	0	1	20424
106 4/04	Sedg	2m5f	E(0-110)HCh	GD	£5128
103 3/04	Sedg	2m5f	E(0-110)HCh	GD	£5079
99 11/03	Catt	2m3f	D(0-115)HCh	G-F	£4134
98 4/03	Sedg	2m5f	E(0-110)HCh	GD	£5031

Total win prize-money £19374

Going:	Sf: 0-2 GS: 0-0 Gd: 2-4 GF: - Fm: 0-1
Distance:	2m/2m3: 1-1 **2m4-2m7: 2-5** 3m+: 0-1
Track:	LH: 3-6 RH: 0-1 **Tight: 3-4** Gall: 0-1
Aids:	Bl: 0-0 Vi: 0-0 Tstrap: 0-0 Ckp: 0-0
Best Rating:	106 4/04 Sedg 2m5f good Ch

Moderate chaser; former pointer; put jumping problems behind him when successful at Sedgefield in April; fortunate winner at Catterick in November; scored again at Sedgefield in March; best over two miles five.

Looks Like Value (IRE)

8-y-o gr g Euphemism-Crossdrumrosie (IRE) (Roselier (FR))
K C Bailey Have Fun Racing Partnership

Placings:0PP5-P   (0235)
2003/04: 19⁵GF,

	Starts	1st	2nd	3rd	Win & Pl
Chases	1	0	0	0	
Career Total	5	0	0	0	0

Going:	Sf: 0-0 GS: 0-0 Gd: 0-0 GF: - Fm: 0-1
Distance:	2m/2m3: 0-1 2m4-2m7: 0-0 3m+: 0-0
Track:	LH: 0-0 RH: 0-1 Tight: 0-0 Gall: 0-0
Aids:	Bl: 0-0 Vi: 0-0 Tstrap: 0-0 Ckp: 0-0
Best Rating:	51 11/02 Chel 2m110y gd-sft NHF

Looksharp Lad (IRE)

85   61
6-y-o b g Simply Great (FR)-Merry Madness (Raise You Ten)
Mrs A J Bowlby J Shaw

Placings:6-200   (4160)
2003/04: 17²GS, 16⁶G, 19⁰G,

	Starts	1st	2nd	3rd	Win & Pl
NH Flat	2	0	1	0	596
Hurdles	1	0	0	0	
Career Total	4	0	1	0	596

Going:	Sf: 0-0 GS: 0-1 Gd: 0-2 GF: - Fm: 0-0
Distance:	2m/2m3: 0-2 2m4-2m7: 0-1 3m+: 0-0
Track:	LH: 0-3 RH: 0-0 Tight: 0-1 Gall: 0-1
Aids:	Bl: 0-0 Vi: 0-0 Tstrap: 0-0 Ckp: 0-0
Best Rating:	104 12/03 Bang 2m1f gd-sft NHF

Loop The Loup

109   130
8-y-o b g Petit Loup (USA)-Mithi Al Gamar (USA) (Blushing Groom (FR))
Mrs M Reveley Mr And Mrs J D Cotton

Placings:0/102/3/332B31-020453P   (3135)
2003/04: 16⁸GS, 22²G, 17⁰GF, 20⁴G, 20⁵GS, 20³S, 21⁰G,

	Starts	1st	2nd	3rd	Win & Pl
Hurdles	7	0	1	1	9352
Career Total	18	2	3	3	37185
130 4/03	Weth	2m4f110yB(0-145)HHdl	G-F	£9516
130 12/00	Muss	2m4f	E Hdl	GD	£2840

Total win prize-money £12357

Going:	Sf: 0-1 GS: 0-2 Gd: 0-3 GF: - Fm: 0-1
Distance:	2m/2m3: 0-2 2m4-2m7: 0-3 3m+: 0-0
Track:	LH: 0-6 RH: 0-1 Tight: 0-3 Gall: 0-1
Aids:	Bl: 0-1 Vi: 0-2 Tstrap: 0-0 Ckp: 0-2
Best Rating:	130 11/03 Aint 2m4f gd-sft Hdl

Useful hurdler; fair stayer on the Flat; best over two and a half miles on fast ground; needs a strong pace and a galloping track; usually wears headgear of one sort or another these days.

Loopy Linda (IRE)

78   60
6-y-o b g Simply Great (FR)-Albane (Shirley Heights)
T D Easterby Ron George

Placings:01124-0P   (3692)
2003/04: 16⁶S, 19⁰S,

	Starts	1st	2nd	3rd	Win & Pl
Hurdles	2	0	0	0	
Career Total	7	2	1	0	8105
107 12/02	Muss	2m	H NHF	G-S	£4134
110 12/02	Donc	2m110y	H NHF	G-S	£2698

Total win prize-money £6833

Going:	Sf: 0-1 GS: 0-0 Gd: 0-1 GF: - Fm: 0-0
Distance:	2m/2m3: 0-2 2m4-2m7: 0-0 3m+: 0-0
Track:	LH: 0-2 RH: 0-0 Tight: 0-1 Gall: 0-0
Aids:	Bl: 0-0 Vi: 0-0 Tstrap: 0-0 Ckp: 0-0
Best Rating:	110 1/03 Muss 2m good NHF

Loose Nut

6-y-o b m Alflora (IRE)-Emmabella (True Song)
A Hollingsworth Kombined Motor Services Ltd

Placings:0PP   (3462)
2003/04: 16⁰GF, 20⁰GS, 24⁵S,

	Starts	1st	2nd	3rd	Win & Pl
NH Flat	1	0	0	0	
Hurdles	2	0	0	0	
Career Total	3	0	0	0	

Going:	Sf: 0-1 GS: 0-0 Gd: 0-0 GF: - Fm: 0-0
Distance:	2m/2m3: 0-2 2m4-2m7: 0-0 3m+: 0-1
Track:	LH: 0-3 RH: 0-0 Tight: 0-0 Gall: 0-0
Aids:	Bl: 0-0 Vi: 0-0 Tstrap: 0-0 Ckp: 0-0
Best Rating:	60 6/03 Worc 2m gd-fm NHF

Loramore

7-y-o ch m Alflora (IRE)-Apsimore (Touching Wood (USA))
J C Tuck Mrs Erica Griffiths

Placings:0P-50P   (4238)
2003/04: 16⁶G, 21⁰G, 17⁰G,

	Starts	1st	2nd	3rd	Win & Pl
Hurdles	3	0	0	0	0
Career Total	5	0	0	0	0

Going:	Sf: 0-0 GS: 0-0 Gd: 0-3 GF: - Fm: 0-0
Distance:	2m/2m3: 0-2 2m4-2m7: 0-1 3m+: 0-0
Track:	LH: 0-0 RH: 0-3 Tight: 0-0 Gall: 0-0
Aids:	Bl: 0-0 Vi: 0-0 Tstrap: 0-0 Ckp: 0-0
Best Rating:	80 5/02 Extr 2m1f good NHF

Lord 'N' Master (IRE)

111(105h)   (96h)120
8-y-o b g Lord Americo-Miss Good Night (Buckskin (FR))
R Rowe Dr B Alexander

Placings:565/613413P1P5-452532BF0   (4965)
2003/04: 23⁴G, 20⁵S, 24²G, 24⁵G, 20³G, 24²GS, 24⁸G, 23⁶G, 29⁰GF,

	Starts	1st	2nd	3rd	Win & Pl
Chases	9	0	2	1	8163
Career Total	22	3	2	3	28276
120 3/03	Sand	3m110y	D(0-115)HCh	SFT	£6841
115 12/02	Sand	2m4f110yD(0-110)HCh	G-S	£6994
96 10/02	Extr	2m3f	D(0-115)HHdl	GD	£3978

Total win prize-money £17813

Going:	Sf: 0-0 GS: 0-1 Gd: 0-7 GF: - Fm: 0-1
Distance:	2m/2m3: 0-0 2m4-2m7: 0-3 3m+: 0-0
Track:	LH: 0-2 RH: 0-7 Tight: 0-0 Gall: 0-2
Aids:	Bl: 0-0 Vi: 0-0 Tstrap: 0-0 Ckp: 0-0
Best Rating:	120 3/04 Sand 3m110y gd-sft Ch

Modest chaser; stays three miles; seems best on an easy surface; likes Sandown.

Lord Adpar

87f   65f
7-y-o b g Bold Fox-Emlyn Princess (Julio Mariner)
P Bowen L L Jones and daughter

Placings:0   (0763)
2003/04: 16⁰G,

	Starts	1st	2nd	3rd	Win & Pl
NH Flat	1	0	0	0	
Career Total	1	0	0	0	

Going:	Sf: 0-0 GS: 0-0 Gd: 0-1 GF: - Fm: 0-0
Distance:	2m/2m3: 0-1 2m4-2m7: 0-0 3m+: 0-0
Track:	LH: 0-1 RH: 0-0 Tight: 0-0 Gall: 0-0
Aids:	Bl: 0-0 Vi: 0-0 Tstrap: 0-0 Ckp: 0-0
Best Rating:	65 6/03 Worc 2m good NHF

Lord Alyn (IRE)

90   86+
6-y-o b g Topanoora-Glenstal Priory (Glenstal (USA))
C R Egerton Alan & Linda Bird

Placings:P-651P461BP   (3324)
2003/04: 16⁶G, 17⁵GF, 16¹G, 20⁰GF, 20⁴GF, 16⁶G, 17¹GF, 17⁸GF, 17⁸GS,

	Starts	1st	2nd	3rd	Win & Pl
NH Flat	3	1	0	0	1879
Hurdles	6	1	0	0	1904
Career Total	10	2	0	0	3783
86 11/03	Hrfd	2m1f	G(0-95)HHdl	G-F	£1904

94	7/03	Worc	2m	H NHF	GD	£1878
				Total win prize-money £3783		

Going:	Sf: 0-0 GS: 0-1 Gd: 1-4 GF: - Fm: 1-4
Distance:	**2m/2m3: 2-7** 2m4-2m7: 0-2 3m+: 0-0
Track:	LH: 1-5 RH: 1-3 Tight: 0-5 Gall: 0-0
Aids:	Bl: 0-0 Vi: 0-0 Tstrap: **1-4** Ckp: 0-0
Best Rating:	94 7/03 Worc 2m good NHF

Modest hurdler; had shown gradual improvement in bumpers prior to winning modest Worcester event July 2003; won selling hurdle in November; effective on fast ground.

Lord Atterbury (IRE)
111   143+
8-y-o ch g Mister Lord (USA)-Tammyiris (Arapahos (FR))
M C Pipe (D Pipe 18/3) D A Johnson

Placings:11-1P3   (4647)
2003/04: 33[1]G, 26[P]G, 36[3]G,

	Starts	1st	2nd	3rd	Win & Pl
Chases	3	1	0	1	72464
Career Total	5	3	0	1	86654
143	4/03	Chel	4m1f	H Ch	GD	£6464
143	4/03	Aint	3m1f	B Ch	GD	£12025
121	3/03	Leic	2m7f110y	H Ch	G-S	£2164
				Total win prize-money £20654		

Going:	Sf: 0-0 GS: 0-0 Gd: 1-3 GF: - Fm: 0-0
Distance:	2m/2m3: 0-0 2m4-2m7: 0-0 3m+: 1-3
Track:	LH: 1-3 RH: 0-0 Tight: 0-1 Gall: 1-2
Aids:	Bl: 0-0 Vi: 0-0 Tstrap: 0-0 Ckp: 0-0
Best Rating:	143 4/04 Aint 4m4f good Ch

Very useful chaser; smart hunter chaser; runaway winner of valuable novices' event at Aintree in April 2003; followed up at Cheltenham; disappointing in the Cheltenham Foxhunters' in 2004; excellent third in the Grand National, only beaten on the run-in despite several mistakes; usually jumps soundly; stays really well.

Lord Brex (FR)
98(99c)   (95c)95
8-y-o gr g Saint Estephe (FR)-Light Moon (FR) (Mendez (FR))
J G M O'Shea Gary Roberts

Placings:31451/2/000P/1623-24354253   (1663)
2003/04: 17[2]S, 18[4]G, 17[3]S, 20[5]GF, 17[4]GF, 17[2]GF, 22[5]GF, 20[3]GF,

	Starts	1st	2nd	3rd	Win & Pl
Hurdles	4	0	1	1	1006
Chases	4	0	1	1	2466
Career Total	22	3	4	4	52489
95	2/03	Tntn	2m1f	G Hdl	SFT	£2513
136	4/00	Aint	2m110y	A Hdl	GD	£24000
126	1/00	Sand	2m110y	D Hdl	SFT	£4400
				Total win prize-money £30914		

Going:	Sf: 0-2 GS: 0-0 Gd: 0-1 GF: - Fm: 0-5
Distance:	2m/2m3: 0-5 2m4-2m7: 0-3 3m+: 0-0
Track:	LH: 0-6 RH: 0-1 Tight: 0-5 Gall: 0-1
Aids:	Bl: 0-0 Vi: 0-5 Tstrap: 0-0 Ckp: 0-3
Best Rating:	137 5/00 Punc 2m good Hdl

Useful hurdler at his best; suited by two miles and acts on ground good or softer; very good form as a juvenile in 2000, but has had problems since and is now down to contesting sellers.

Lord Broadway (IRE)
109(76h)   (46 h)120
8-y-o b g Shardari-Country Course (IRE) (Crash Course)
N M Babbage D G & D J Robinson

Placings:50/0PP25/0P4F32224-04103P3P4   (4837)
2003/04: 26[9]GF, 24[4]GF, 25[1]S, 25[9]S, 25[3]G, 30[P]G, 28[3]G, 23[P]G, 25[4]GF,

	Starts	1st	2nd	3rd	Win & Pl
Hurdles	1	0	0	0	
Chases	8	1	0	2	4698
Career Total	25	1	4	3	11421
114	11/03	Towc	3m1f	F(0-100)HCh	SFT	£2226
				Total win prize-money £2226		

Going:	Sf: 1-2 GS: 0-0 Gd: 0-4 GF: - Fm: 0-3
Distance:	2m/2m3: 0-0 2m4-2m7: 0-3 **3m+: 1-9**
Track:	LH: 1-4 RH: 1-7 Tight: 0-0 Gall: 0-3
Aids:	Bl: 0-0 Vi: 0-2 Tstrap: 0-0 Ckp: 0-0
Best Rating:	120 4/04 Chel 3m1f110y gd-fm Ch

Moderate chaser; stays three miles; acts on good but suited by soft ground.

Lord Brock
80f
5-y-o b g Alderbrook-Mariner's Air (Julio Mariner)
N A Twiston-Davies Aiden Murphy

Placings:3   (4509)
2003/04: 14[3]GS,

	Starts	1st	2nd	3rd	Win & Pl
NH Flat	1	0	0	1	284
Career Total	1	0	0	1	284

Going:	Sf: 0-0 GS: 0-1 Gd: 0-0 GF: - Fm: 0-0
Distance:	2m/2m3: 0-0 2m4-2m7: 0-0 3m+: 0-0
Track:	LH: 0-0 RH: 0-0 Tight: 0-0 Gall: 0-0
Aids:	Bl: 0-0 Vi: 0-0 Tstrap: 0-0 Ckp: 0-0
Best Rating:	80 3/04 Hrld 1m6f gd-sft NHF

Lord Buckingham
101   105
6-y-o ch g Carroll House-Lady Buck (Pollerton)
N J Henderson Mrs Hugh Maitland-Jones

Placings:50-344U0   (4818)
2003/04: 16[3]GF, 16[4]G, 19[4]G, 19[U]GS, 17[0]GF,

	Starts	1st	2nd	3rd	Win & Pl
Hurdles	5	0	0	1	1329
Career Total	7	0	0	1	1329

Going:	Sf: 0-0 GS: 0-1 Gd: 0-2 GF: - Fm: 0-2
Distance:	2m/2m3: 0-4 2m4-2m7: 0-1 3m+: 0-0
Track:	LH: 0-3 RH: 0-2 Tight: 0-1 Gall: 0-3
Aids:	Bl: 0-0 Vi: 0-0 Tstrap: 0-0 Ckp: 0-0
Best Rating:	105 12/03 Newb 2m110y gd-fm Hdl

Big type; ability in novice hurdles; will be suited by two and a half miles; acts on a sound surface.

Lord Capitaine (IRE)
102   111
10-y-o b/br g Mister Lord (USA)-Salvation Sue (Mon Capitaine)
J Howard Johnson The Scottish Steeplechasing Partnership

Placings:P311P/645635P/U511/P3411-04322				(4615)
2003/04: 30[0]G, 24[4]HY, 27[3]GS, 26[2]G, 28[2]G,				

	Starts	1st	2nd	3rd	Win & Pl
Chases	5	0	2	1	4147
Career Total	26	6	2	4	28420
111	3/03	Sedg	3m4f	E(0-110)HCh	GD	£5021
110	3/03	Sedg	3m3f	E(0-105)HCh	GD	£4342
113	11/01	Sedg	3m3f	F(0-100)HCh	SFT	£2569
105	10/01	Sedg	3m3f	F(0-100)HCh	GD	£2905
116	2/00	Sedg	3m3f	D Ch	G-S	£3575
106	1/00	Muss	3m4f	E Ch	SFT	£3282
				Total win prize-money £21695		

Going:	Sf: 0-1 GS: 0-1 Gd: 0-3 GF: - Fm: 0-0
Distance:	2m/2m3: 0-0 2m4-2m7: 0-0 3m+: 0-5
Track:	LH: 0-4 RH: 0-1 Tight: 0-3 Gall: 0-0
Aids:	Bl: 0-0 Vi: 0-0 Tstrap: 0-0 Ckp: 0-0
Best Rating:	116 2/00 Sedg 3m3f gd-sft Ch

Moderate chaser; winner five times at Sedgefield; stays 3m 4f; acts on fast and soft ground.

Lord Castle (IRE)
8-y-o ch g Mister Lord (USA)-Amandas Castle (IRE) (Carlingford Castle)
Miss C Herrington (M Wennington 29/5) M Wennington

Placings:0-PUPP   (4872)
2003/04: 21[P]G, 24[U]GF, 24[P]GF, 24[P]S,

	Starts	1st	2nd	3rd	Win & Pl
Chases	4	0	0	0	
Career Total	5	0	0	0	

Going:	Sf: 0-1 GS: 0-0 Gd: 0-1 GF: - Fm: 0-2
Distance:	2m/2m3: 0-0 2m4-2m7: 0-1 3m+: 0-3
Track:	LH: 0-2 RH: 0-2 Tight: 0-1 Gall: 0-3
Aids:	Bl: 0-0 Vi: 0-1 Tstrap: 0-0 Ckp: 0-0
Best Rating:	41 5/02 Limk 2m2f gd-yld Hdl

Lord Code (IRE)
96   91+
6-y-o b g Arctic Lord-Tax Code (Workboy)
R H Alner Mrs Norma Kelly

Placings:05PP0   (4524)
2003/04: 17[0]G, 20[5]GS, 16[P]GS, 24[P]G, 16[0]GS,

	Starts	1st	2nd	3rd	Win & Pl
NH Flat	1	0	0	0	0
Hurdles	4	0	0	0	0
Career Total	5	0	0	0	0

Going:	Sf: 0-0 GS: 0-3 Gd: 0-2 GF: - Fm: 0-0
Distance:	2m/2m3: 0-4 2m4-2m7: 0-1 3m+: 0-0
Track:	LH: 0-4 RH: 0-1 Tight: 0-1 Gall: 0-1
Aids:	Bl: 0-0 Vi: 0-0 Tstrap: 0-0 Ckp: 0-0
Best Rating:	91 12/03 Chep 2m4f gd-sft Hdl

Lord Dal (FR)
103   75+
11-y-o b g Cadoudal (FR)-Lady Corteira (FR) (Carvin II)
A J Whitehead A J Whitehead

Placings:1235/140124/2624/4/UP/000P-50000 (4523)
2003/04: 16[5]GS, 20[5]S, 22[P]GS, 16[P]G, 17[P]GS,

	Starts	1st	2nd	3rd	Win & Pl
Hurdles	5	0	0	0	0
Career Total	26	3	4	1	28461

120	1/99	Tram	2m4f	Ch	SH	£3376
124	11/98	Naas	2m4f	HHdl	YLD	£8445
103	12/97	Leop	2m	Hdl	HVY	£4069
					Total win prize-money £15891

Going:	Sf: 0-1 GS: 0-3 Gd: 0-1 GF: - Fm: 0-0
Distance:	2m/2m3: 0-3 2m4-2m7: 0-2 3m+: 0-0
Track:	LH: 0-2 RH: 0-3 Tight: 0-1 Gall: 0-0
Aids:	Bl: 0-0 Vi: 0-0 Tstrap: 0-0 Ckp: 0-2
Best Rating:	129 11/99 Naas 2m4f yld-sft Hdl

Lord Dilrock (IRE)

89   **68**

8-y-o ch g Lord Americo-Dillrock Damsel (Over The River (FR))
Mrs G Harvey Mrs Rosalinde Elsbury

Placings:P-0   (0367)
2003/04: 16⁰G,

	Starts	1st	2nd	3rd	Win & Pl
Hurdles	1	0	0	0	
Career Total	2	0	0	0	

Going:	Sf: 0-0 GS: 0-0 Gd: 0-1 GF: - Fm: 0-0
Distance:	2m/2m3: 0-1 2m4-2m7: 0-0 3m+: 0-0
Track:	LH: 0-1 RH: 0-0 Tight: 0-0 Gall: 0-0
Aids:	Bl: 0-0 Vi: 0-0 Tstrap: 0-0 Ckp: 0-0
Best Rating:	68 5/03 Worc 2m good Hdl

Lord Dundaniel (IRE)

101   **119**

7-y-o b/br g Arctic Lord-Killoskehan Queen (Bustineto)
B De Haan Willsford Racing Incorporated

Placings:064-23105   (4838)
2003/04: 20²GS, 20³S, 20¹G, 20⁰GS, 24⁵GF,

	Starts	1st	2nd	3rd	Win & Pl
Hurdles	5	1	1	1	16058
Career Total	8	1	1	1	16345
119	2/04	Hayd	2m4f	B HHdl	GD £13676
				Total win prize-money £13676

Going:	Sf: 0-1 GS: 0-2 Gd: 1-1 GF: - Fm: 0-1
Distance:	2m/2m3: 0-0 2m4-2m7: 1-4 3m+: 0-0
Track:	LH: 1-5 RH: 0-0 Tight: 0-0 Gall: 0-1
Aids:	Bl: 0-0 Vi: 0-0 Tstrap: 0-0 Ckp: 0-0
Best Rating:	119 2/04 Hayd 2m4f good Hdl

Fair hurdler; has run well over hurdles this season, eventually getting off the mark at Haydock in February; suited by two and a half miles; acts on fast and soft ground.

Lord Earth (IRE)

96   **83+**

6-y-o b g Mister Lord (USA)-Mizuna (Ballymore)
P F Nicholls R M Penny

Placings:/4553PP   (4897)
2003/04: 16¹G, 24⁴GF, 20⁵S, 24⁵S, 21³G, 20²PG, 22⁰PG,

	Starts	1st	2nd	3rd	Win & Pl
NH Flat	1	1	0	0	2058
Hurdles	6	0	0	1	1070
Career Total	7	1	0	1	3128
101	5/03	Worc	2m	H NHF	GD £2058
				Total win prize-money £2058

| Going: | Sf: 0-2 GS: 0-0 Gd: 1-4 GF: - Fm: 0-1 |
| Distance: | 2m/2m3: 1-1 2m4-2m7: 0-4 3m+: 0-2 |

Track:	LH: 1-4 RH: 0-3 Tight: 0-0 Gall: 0-0
Aids:	Bl: 0-1 Vi: 0-0 Tstrap: 0-0 Ckp: 0-0
Best Rating:	101 5/03 Worc 2m good NHF

Out of a 14f winner; pulled up in only point; sprang 20/1 shock at Worcester in bumper debut May 2003; poor since.

Lord Edwards Army (IRE)

9-y-o b g Warcraft (USA)-Celtic Bombshell (Celtic Cone)
W T Reed (P Mullins 2/8) Guy Willoughby

Placings:/630/000/411654102205/0050002064053-650P04F21   (4851)
2003/04: 18⁶GY, 23⁵F, 23⁹G, 22⁴PY, 21⁰GS, 25⁴GS, 21⁵GF, 25²G, 27¹GS,

	Starts	1st	2nd	3rd	Win & Pl
Chases	9	1	1	0	4219
Career Total	40	4	4	2	27995
98	4/04	Ayr	3m3f110yH Ch	G-S	£3432
115	9/01	List	2m4f	Hdl	G-F	£7862
107	7/01	Bell	2m1f	NHF	G-F	£3895
97	6/01	Kbgn	2m3f	NHF	GD	£3338
				Total win prize-money £18529

Going:	Sf: 0-0 GS: 1-3 Gd: 0-2 GF: - Fm: 0-2
Distance:	2m/2m3: 0-1 2m4-2m7: 0-5 3m+: 1-3
Track:	LH: 1-5 RH: 0-2 Tight: 0-3 Gall: 0-0
Aids:	Bl: 0-0 Vi: 0-0 Tstrap: 0-0 Ckp: 0-0
Best Rating:	120 11/01 Navn 2m yield Hdl

Moderate Hunter chaser; just about stays three miles; acts on good to soft.

Lord Fernando

85   **81**

5-y-o ch g Forzando-Lady Lacey (Kampala)
G B Balding The P J Partnership

Placings:040303414-400   (2222)
2003/04: 16⁴G, 16⁹G, 17⁰G,

	Starts	1st	2nd	3rd	Win & Pl
Hurdles	3	0	0	0	0
Career Total	12	1	0	2	4934
79	3/03	Hntg	2m110y E(0-105)HHdl	GD	£3406
				Total win prize-money £3406

Going:	Sf: 0-0 GS: 0-0 Gd: 0-3 GF: - Fm: 0-0
Distance:	2m/2m3: 0-3 2m4-2m7: 0-0 3m+: 0-0
Track:	LH: 0-1 RH: 0-2 Tight: 0-1 Gall: 0-0
Aids:	Bl: 0-0 Vi: 0-2 Tstrap: 0-0 Ckp: 0-1
Best Rating:	81 10/03 Towc 2m good Hdl

Plating-class hurdler; has shown form at around two miles; acts on a good and a soft surface.

Lord Gale (IRE)

106f   **119f**

6-y-o b g Mister Lord (USA)-Dante Gale (IRE) (Phardante (FR))
N A Twiston-Davies C B Sanderson

Placings:2210   (4400)
2003/04: 16²GS, 16²GS, 16¹G, 16⁹G,

	Starts	1st	2nd	3rd	Win & Pl
NH Flat	4	1	2	0	3433
Career Total	4	1	2	0	3433
106	2/04	Hayd	2m	H NHF	GD	£2184
				Total win prize-money £2184

| Going: | Sf: 0-0 GS: 0-2 Gd: 1-2 GF: - Fm: 0-0 |

Distance:	2m/2m3: 1-4 2m4-2m7: 0-0 3m+: 0-0
Track:	LH: 1-3 RH: 0-1 Tight: 0-0 Gall: 0-0
Aids:	Bl: 0-0 Vi: 0-0 Tstrap: 0-0 Ckp: 0-0
Best Rating:	119 3/04 Chel 2m110y good NHF

Fair hurdler; satisfactory debut when second in Uttoxeter bumper Boxing Day 2003; runner-up again next time; went one better at Haydock in February; acts on good and easy ground.

Lord George

12-y-o ch g Lord Bud-Mini Gazette (London Gazette)
G C Evans N Morgan

Placings:0F0-0   (0521)
2003/04: 24⁰G,

	Starts	1st	2nd	3rd	Win & Pl
Chases	1	0	0	0	
Career Total	4	0	0	0	

Going:	Sf: 0-0 GS: 0-0 Gd: 0-1 GF: - Fm: 0-0
Distance:	2m/2m3: 0-0 2m4-2m7: 0-0 3m+: 0-1
Track:	LH: 0-1 RH: 0-0 Tight: 0-1 Gall: 0-0
Aids:	Bl: 0-0 Vi: 0-0 Tstrap: 0-0 Ckp: 0-0
Best Rating:	48 3/03 Ludl 2m4f gd-fm Ch

Lord Gizzmo

93   **60**

7-y-o ch g Democratic (USA)-Fignant (USA) (L'Emigrant (USA))
P W Hiatt (J Cullinan 22/8) The Paddy Pipers

Placings:5000-0   (0150)
2003/04: 16⁰GF,

	Starts	1st	2nd	3rd	Win & Pl
Hurdles	1	0	0	0	
Career Total	5	0	0	0	0

Going:	Sf: 0-0 GS: 0-0 Gd: 0-0 GF: - Fm: 0-1
Distance:	2m/2m3: 0-1 2m4-2m7: 0-0 3m+: 0-0
Track:	LH: 0-1 RH: 0-0 Tight: 0-0 Gall: 0-0
Aids:	Bl: 0-0 Vi: 0-0 Tstrap: 0-0 Ckp: 0-0
Best Rating:	60 4/03 NAbb 2m6f gd-fm Hdl

Lord Halfnothin (IRE)

108   **123+**

8-y-o b g Mandalus-Midnight Seeker (Status Seeker)
R H Alner H V Perry

Placings:54-1112   (2782)
2003/04: 22¹GF, 21¹GF, 16¹F, 21²G,

	Starts	1st	2nd	3rd	Win & Pl
Chases	4	3	1	0	11767
Career Total	6	3	1	0	12052
117	12/03	Leic	2m	E(0-105)HCh	FRM	£4315
118	11/03	Folk	2m5f	E Ch	G-F	£3484
101	11/03	Font	2m6f	E Ch	G-F	£2891
				Total win prize-money £10691

Going:	Sf: 0-0 GS: 0-0 Gd: 0-1 GF: - Fm: 3-3
Distance:	2m/2m3: 1-1 2m4-2m7: 2-3 3m+: 0-0
Track:	LH: 0-0 RH: 2-3 Tight: 2-3 Gall: 0-0
Aids:	Bl: 0-0 Vi: 0-0 Tstrap: 0-0 Ckp: 0-0
Best Rating:	123 12/03 Folk 2m5f good Ch

Fair novice chaser; stays two miles six, but effective at shorter; acts on good ground; jumps well.

Lord Heccles (IRE)

97f   **103f**

5-y-o b g Supreme Leader-Parsons Law (The Parson)
G L Moore Phil Collins

Placings:500   (4936)
2003/04: 16⁵GS, 16⁶G, 18⁰G,

	Starts	1st	2nd	3rd	Win & Pl
NH Flat	3	0	0	0	0
Career Total	3	0	0	0	0

Going: Sf: 0-0 GS: 0-1 Gd: 0-2 GF: - Fm: 0-0
Distance: 2m/2m3: 0-3 2m4-2m7: 0-0 3m+: 0-0
Track: LH: 0-2 RH: 0-1 Tight: 0-1 Gall: 0-1
Aids: Bl: 0-0 Vi: 0-0 Tstrap: 0-0 Ckp: 0-0
Best Rating: 103 2/04 Sand 2m110y   gd-sft NHF

Showed ability on his bumper debut; held since.

Lord Jack (IRE)

107   (107h) **140**

8-y-o ch g Mister Lord (USA)-Gentle Gill (Pollerton)
N G Richards Trevor Hemmings

Placings:0561120/121130-U26P   (4951)
2003/04: 24ᵁS, 20²HY, 33⁶G, 24ᴾGS,

	Starts	1st	2nd	3rd	Win & Pl
Chases	4	0	1	0	4816
Career Total	17	5	3	1	34554
140	1/03	Ayr	2m4f		D(0-125)HCh	SFT	£6747
111	12/02	Sedg	2m5f		E Ch	SFT	£3799
124	11/02	Sedg	2m5f		E Ch	SFT	£4069
109	2/02	Muss	3m		D(0-110)HHdl	SFT	£3526
109	1/02	Muss	2m5f		E(0-100)HHdl	SFT	£2744

Total win prize-money £20885

Going: Sf: 0-2 GS: 0-1 Gd: 0-1 GF: - Fm: 0-0
Distance: 2m/2m3: 0-0 2m4-2m7: 0-0 3m+: 0-3
Track: LH: 0-2 RH: 0-2 Tight: 0-0 Gall: 0-1
Aids: Bl: 0-0 Vi: 0-0 Tstrap: 0-3 Ckp: 0-1
Best Rating: 140 1/03 Ayr 2m4f   soft Ch

Fair chaser; effective from two and a half to three miles; acts on soft and heavy ground; wears a tongue tie.

Lord Jay Jay (IRE)

66f   **99f**

4-y-o b g Lord Of Appeal-Mesena (Pals Passage)
Miss H C Knight Mrs Jan Johnson

Placings:4   (3934)
2003/04: 16⁴G,

	Starts	1st	2nd	3rd	Win & Pl
NH Flat	1	0	0	0	0
Career Total	1	0	0	0	0

Going: Sf: 0-0 GS: 0-0 Gd: 0-1 GF: - Fm: 0-0
Distance: 2m/2m3: 0-1 2m4-2m7: 0-0 3m+: 0-0
Track: LH: 0-0 RH: 0-1 Tight: 0-0 Gall: 0-0
Aids: Bl: 0-0 Vi: 0-0 Tstrap: 0-0 Ckp: 0-0
Best Rating: 99 2/04 Asct 2m110y   good NHF

Good fourth on debut in bumper at Ascot in February; capable of better.

Lord Killeshanra (IRE)

102f   **101f**

5-y-o br g Mister Lord (USA)-Killeshandra Lass (IRE) (King's Ride)

C L Tizzard G F Gingell

Placings:222   (4739)
2003/04: 16²GS, 17²S, 17²G,

	Starts	1st	2nd	3rd	Win & Pl
NH Flat	3	0	3	0	2370
Career Total	3	0	3	0	2370

Going: Sf: 0-1 GS: 0-1 Gd: 0-1 GF: - Fm: 0-0
Distance: 2m/2m3: 0-3 2m4-2m7: 0-0 3m+: 0-0
Track: LH: 0-1 RH: 0-1 Tight: 0-1 Gall: 0-0
Aids: Bl: 0-0 Vi: 0-0 Tstrap: 0-0 Ckp: 0-0
Best Rating: 101 4/04 NAbb 2m1f   good NHF

Moderate bumper performer; acts on good ground or softer.

Lord Kinsale (IRE)

11-y-o ch g Cidrax (FR)-Wolviston (Wolverlife)
D B Feek Tony Feek

Placings:F/6   (1519)
2003/04: 20⁶G,

	Starts	1st	2nd	3rd	Win & Pl
Hurdles	1	0	0	0	0
Career Total	2	0	0	0	0

Going: Sf: 0-0 GS: 0-0 Gd: 0-1 GF: - Fm: 0-0
Distance: 2m/2m3: 0-0 2m4-2m7: 0-0 3m+: 0-0
Track: LH: 0-0 RH: 0-0 Tight: 0-1 Gall: 0-0
Aids: Bl: 0-0 Vi: 0-0 Tstrap: 0-0 Ckp: 0-0

Lord Lington (FR)

110   **110+**

5-y-o b g Bulington (FR)-Tosca De Bussy (FR) (Le Riverain (FR))
P F Nicholls (G Cherel 5/5) Paul K Barber & Mrs M Findlay

Placings:6165000   (4813)
2003/04: 16⁶G, 17¹GS, 16⁶G, 16⁵G, 16⁰GS, 17⁰G, 16⁰G,

	Starts	1st	2nd	3rd	Win & Pl
Hurdles	7	1	0	0	3218
Career Total	7	1	0	0	3218
110	12/03	Folk	2m1f110yE Hdl		G-S	£3059

Total win prize-money £3059

Going: Sf: 0-0 GS: 1-2 Gd: 0-5 GF: - Fm: 0-0
Distance: 2m/2m3: 1-7 2m4-2m7: 0-0 3m+: 0-0
Track: LH: 0-3 RH: 1-4 Tight: 1-2 Gall: 0-0
Aids: Bl: 0-1 Vi: 0-0 Tstrap: 0-0 Ckp: 0-0
Best Rating: 110 12/03 Folk 2m1f110y   gd-sft Hdl

Modest novice hurdler; winner three times on the level in France; too keen and stopped to nothing when beaten a long way on hurdling bow at Wetherby in November, but made amends at Folkestone next time; held in better races at Kempton and Sandown the last twice; suited by two miles; acts on good and easy going.

Lord Luker (IRE)

93   **75**

8-y-o b g Lord Americo-Canon's Dream (Le Bavard)
Miss H C Knight Luker Bros (removals & Storage) Ltd

Placings:6/00F   (4650)
2003/04: 21⁰GS, 20⁰S, 19⁰G,

	Starts	1st	2nd	3rd	Win & Pl
Hurdles	3	0	0	0	0
Career Total	4	0	0	0	0

Going: Sf: 0-1 GS: 0-1 Gd: 0-1 GF: - Fm: 0-0
Distance: 2m/2m3: 0-0 2m4-2m7: 0-3 3m+: 0-0
Track: LH: 0-0 RH: 0-0 Tight: 0-0 Gall: 0-0
Aids: Bl: 0-0 Vi: 0-0 Tstrap: 0-0 Ckp: 0-0
Best Rating: 91 5/01 Hrfd 2m1f   good NHF

Lord Maizey (IRE)

105   **140+**

7-y-o b g Mister Lord (USA)-My Maizey (Buckskin (FR))
N A Twiston-Davies Mr & Mrs Peter Orton

Placings:141-411   (2982)
2003/04: 26⁴G, 19¹GS, 19¹S,

	Starts	1st	2nd	3rd	Win & Pl
Chases	3	2	0	0	17192
Career Total	6	4	0	0	26198
140	12/03	Chep	2m3f110yC(0-135)		SFT	£8346
131	12/03	Chep	2m3f110yC(0-130)HCh		G-S	£8482
106	2/03	Leic	2m		E Ch	SFT	£4875
109	11/02	Naas	2m		NHF	SFT	£3809

Total win prize-money £25514

Going: Sf: 1-1 GS: 1-1 Gd: 0-1 GF: - Fm: 0-0
Distance: 2m/2m3: 0-0 **2m4-2m7: 2-2** 3m+: 0-1
Track: **LH: 2-3** RH: 0-1 Tight: 0-1 Gall: 0-0
Aids: Bl: 0-0 Vi: 0-0 Tstrap: 0-0 Ckp: 0-0
Best Rating: 140 12/03 Chep 2m3f110y   soft Ch

Lightly-raced useful chaser; former Irish bumper winner; bounced back after disappointing on seasonal debut to make all at Chepstow in December 2003 and followed up over course and distance later that month; stays two and a half miles and is suited by soft ground; still has plenty of scope.

Lord Mistral

86   **78**

5-y-o b g Makbul-South Wind (Tina's Pet)
Mrs N S Sharpe B Owen

Placings:0F04065-06   (0507)
2003/04: 16⁰GF, 16⁶G,

	Starts	1st	2nd	3rd	Win & Pl
Hurdles	2	0	0	0	0
Career Total	9	0	0	0	323

Going: Sf: 0-0 GS: 0-0 Gd: 0-1 GF: - Fm: 0-1
Distance: 2m/2m3: 0-2 2m4-2m7: 0-0 3m+: 0-0
Track: LH: 0-1 RH: 0-1 Tight: 0-1 Gall: 0-0
Aids: Bl: 0-0 Vi: 0-0 Tstrap: 0-0 Ckp: 0-0
Best Rating: 78 5/03 Winc 2m   gd-fm Hdl

Very limited ability so far.

Lord Moose (IRE)

91   **122**

10-y-o b g Mister Lord (USA)-Moose (IRE) (Royal Fountain)
H D Daly The Hon Simon Sainsbury

Placings:PF1/P01/13432-P54   (3817)
2003/04: 21ᴾG, 24⁴S, 25⁴GS,

	Starts	1st	2nd	3rd	Win & Pl
Chases	3	0	0	0	428
Career Total	14	3	1	2	28861
122	11/02	Sand	2m4f110yC(0-135)HCh		G-S	£8463
119	3/02	Newb	2m6f110yD(0-120)HCh		SFT	£9009
116	4/00	Asct	2m4f		C Hdl	SFT	£5135

Total win prize-money £22607

Going: Sf: 0-1 GS: 0-1 Gd: 0-1 GF: - Fm: 0-0
Distance: 3m/2m3: 0-0 2m4-2m7: 0-1 3m+: 0-2

Track: LH: 0-3 RH: 0-0 Tight: 0-0 Gall: 0-1
Aids: BI: 0-0 Vi: 0-0 Tstrap: 0-0 Ckp: 0-0
Best Rating: 122 3/03 Sand 3m110y soft Ch

Fair handicap chaser; stays three miles; acts on a soft surface.

Lord Native (IRE)
57

9-y-o b g Be My Native (USA)-Whakapohane (Kampala)
N J Henderson   Lady Annabel Goldsmith

Placings: 106/02/1/P6-5   (0237)
2003/04: 19⁵G,

	Starts	1st	2nd	3rd	Win & Pl
Hurdles	1	0	0	0	0
Career Total	9	2	1	0	5950
96	6/01	MRas	2m1f110yE Hdl		G-F £2509
92	7/99	Klny	2m1f	NHF	G-F £2915
			Total win prize-money £5426		

Going: Sf: 0-0 GS: 0-0 Gd: 0-1 GF: - Fm: 0-0
Distance: 2m/2m3: 0-2 2m4-2m7: 0-1 3m+: 0-0
Track: LH: 0-0 RH: 0-1 Tight: 0-0 Gall: 0-0
Aids: BI: 0-0 Vi: 0-0 Tstrap: 0-0 Ckp: 0-0
Best Rating: 110 1/01 Fknm 2m soft Hdl

Modest ex-Irish hurdler; effective around two miles; acts on fast ground; absent for 20 months after winning at Market Rasen in June 2001; lightly raced since.

Lord Nellsson
85(108h)   (96h)98

8-y-o b g Arctic Lord-Miss Petronella (Petoski)
J S King   Dajam Ltd

Placings: 3600/2032P0-44FP40   (4285)
2003/04: 20⁴GF, 21⁴S, 20⁰FG, 24⁴S, 16⁴G, 16⁰G,

	Starts	1st	2nd	3rd	Win & Pl
Hurdles	2	0	0	0	273
Chases	4	0	0	0	609
Career Total	16	0	2	2	5172

Going: Sf: 0-1 GS: 0-0 Gd: 0-4 GF: - Fm: 0-1
Distance: 2m/2m3: 0-2 2m4-2m7: 0-3 3m+: 0-1
Track: LH: 0-1 RH: 0-5 Tight: 0-1 Gall: 0-1
Aids: BI: 0-0 Vi: 0-0 Tstrap: 0-0 Ckp: 0-1
Best Rating: 98 1/04 Ludl 2m4f good Ch

Moderate novice hurdler; stays two miles five.

Lord Noelie (IRE)
108   153+

11-y-o b g Lord Americo-Leallen (Le Bavard (FR))
Ms Bridget Nicholls   Executive Racing

Placings: 4/16F14/2121/4U2/F4503/U0P-541P   (4861)
2003/04: 27⁵G, 25⁴G, 26¹G, 33⁵GS,

	Starts	1st	2nd	3rd	Win & Pl
Chases	4	1	0	0	18837
Career Total	25	5	3	1	157932
153	12/03	Chel	3m2f110yB(0-145)HCh	GD	£15587
154	3/00	Chel	3m110y A Ch	GD	£66700
142	11/99	Newb	3m C Ch	GD	£6440
130	2/99	Winc	2m6f B Hdl	G-S	£10755
112	10/98	Strf	2m6f110yD Hdl	GD	£3183
			Total win prize-money £102665		

Going: Sf: 0-0 GS: 0-1 Gd: 1-3 GF: - Fm: 0-0
Distance: 2m/2m3: 0-0 2m4-2m7: 0-0 3m+: 1-4
Track: LH: 1-4 RH: 0-0 Tight: 0-0 Gall: 1-3
Aids: BI: 0-0 Vi: 0-0 Tstrap: 0-0 Ckp: 0-0

Best Rating: 170 12/01 Newb 3m2f110y soft Ch

Smart chaser; winner of the Royal & SunAlliance Chase in 2000 when trained by Henrietta Knight; first win since when scoring at Cheltenham in December; capable of high-class form when conditions are right; has bled; best on fast ground; stays three miles.

Lord North (IRE)
98   108

9-y-o b g Mister Lord (USA)-Mrs Hegarty (Decent Fellow)
P R Webber   D Allen

Placings: 4P/3150/21P1P4FP-04342P   (3999)
2003/04: 20⁰GF, 20⁴G, 20³GF, 21⁴S, 17²G, 16⁰G,

	Starts	1st	2nd	3rd	Win & Pl
Chases	6	0	1	1	3488
Career Total	20	3	2	2	27917
131	12/02	Leic	2m4f110yD(0-125)HCh	G-S	£10595
117	5/02	Bang	2m4f110yD(0-120)HCh	SFT	£7247
95	11/01	Leic	2m E Ch	G-F	£3307
			Total win prize-money £21151		

Going: Sf: 0-1 GS: 0-0 Gd: 0-3 GF: - Fm: 0-2
Distance: 2m/2m3: 0-2 2m4-2m7: 0-4 3m+: 0-0
Track: LH: 0-2 RH: 0-4 Tight: 0-2 Gall: 0-1
Aids: BI: 0-0 Vi: 0-0 Tstrap: 0-6 Ckp: 0-0
Best Rating: 131 12/02 Leic 2m4f110y gd-sft Ch

Modest handicap chaser; acts on fast and soft ground; stays two and a half miles; has worn a tongue strap.

Lord Of Beauty (FR)
105   112+

4-y-o ch g Medaaly-Arctic Beauty (USA) (Arctic Tern (USA))
Noel T Chance (H-A Pantall 28/6)   Warren, Upton & Chenkin & Townson

Placings: F423432   (4788)
2003/04: 16⁵GF, 16⁴G, 16²S, 18³G, 16⁴G, 19³G, 16²G,

	Starts	1st	2nd	3rd	Win & Pl
Hurdles	7	0	2	2	4408
Career Total	7	0	2	2	4408

Going: Sf: 0-1 GS: 0-0 Gd: 0-5 GF: - Fm: 0-1
Distance: 2m/2m3: 0-7 2m4-2m7: 0-0 3m+: 0-0
Track: LH: 0-6 RH: 0-1 Tight: 0-2 Gall: 0-4
Aids: BI: 0-0 Vi: 0-0 Tstrap: 0-0 Ckp: 0-0
Best Rating: 108 3/04 Newb 2m3f good Hdl

Fair novice hurdler; ex-French; acts on soft ground; stays two miles three.

Lord Of Illusion (IRE)
88(104h)   (108h)118

7-y-o b g Mister Lord (USA)-Jellaride (IRE) (King's Ride)
T R George   P J Kennedy

Placings: 00120-U3   (2457)
2003/04: 20⁰G, 24³G,

	Starts	1st	2nd	3rd	Win & Pl
Chases	2	0	0	1	768
Career Total	7	1	1	1	5905
98	2/03	Bang	2m1f	E Hdl	G-S £3822
			Total win prize-money £3822		

Going: Sf: 0-0 GS: 0-0 Gd: 0-2 GF: - Fm: 0-0
Distance: 2m/2m3: 0-2 2m4-2m7: 0-1 3m+: 0-0
Track: LH: 0-2 RH: 0-0 Tight: 0-0 Gall: 0-1
Aids: BI: 0-0 Vi: 0-0 Tstrap: 0-0 Ckp: 0-0

Best Rating: 118 11/03 Weth 2m4f110y good Ch

Fair hurdler/novice chaser; stays two miles six and suited by ground good or softer.

Lord Of The Bride (IRE)
70   (29h)70

7-y-o ch g Mister Lord (USA)-Carrigan Springs (IRE) (Tale Quale)
M C Pipe   M C Pipe

Placings: 06-P42   (1227)
2003/04: 21⁵GF, 21⁴G, 26²GF,

	Starts	1st	2nd	3rd	Win & Pl
Chases	3	0	1	0	1635
Career Total	5	0	1	0	1635

Going: Sf: 0-0 GS: 0-0 Gd: 0-1 GF: - Fm: 0-2
Distance: 2m/2m3: 0-0 2m4-2m7: 0-2 3m+: 0-1
Track: LH: 0-3 RH: 0-0 Tight: 0-0 Gall: 0-0
Aids: BI: 0-0 Vi: 0-0 Tstrap: 0-1 Ckp: 0-0
Best Rating: 70 8/03 Sthl 3m2f gd-fm Ch

Plating-class chaser; ex-Irish; stays three miles plus.

Lord Of The Fens

4-y-o b g Danzig Connection (USA)-Zizi (IRE) (Imp Society (USA))
C N Kellett   D H & Mrs R E Muir

Placings: 0   (4962)
2003/04: 17⁰G,

	Starts	1st	2nd	3rd	Win & Pl
NH Flat	1	0	0	0	
Career Total	1	0	0	0	

Going: Sf: 0-0 GS: 0-0 Gd: 0-1 GF: - Fm: 0-0
Distance: 2m/2m3: 0-1 2m4-2m7: 0-0 3m+: 0-0
Track: LH: 0-0 RH: 0-1 Tight: 0-1 Gall: 0-0
Aids: BI: 0-0 Vi: 0-0 Tstrap: 0-0 Ckp: 0-0

Lord Of The Hill (IRE)
107   96+

9-y-o b g Dromod Hill-Telegram Mear (Giolla Mear)
Mrs H Dalton   Tom Segrue

Placings: 0P0U/F4-P41151135   (3253)
2003/04: 24⁸G, 20⁴G, 19¹GF, 20¹GF, 20⁵GF, 16¹GF, 20¹GF, 16³GS, 20⁵G,

	Starts	1st	2nd	3rd	Win & Pl
Chases	9	4	0	1	13387
Career Total	15	4	0	1	13630
96	11/03	Ludl	2m4f	E(0-105)HCh	G-F £4056
100	11/03	Hrfd	2m	D(0-105)HCh	G-F £2730
82	10/03	Hntg	2m4f110yE(0-105)HCh	G-F	£3464
79	10/03	Hrfd	2m3f	G(0-95)HCh	G-F £2093
			Total win prize-money £12343		

Going: Sf: 0-0 GS: 0-1 Gd: 0-2 GF: - Fm: 4-6
Distance: 2m/2m3: 2-3 2m4-2m7: 2-5 3m+: 0-1
Track: LH: 0-3 RH: 4-6 Tight: 1-3 Gall: 1-2
Aids: BI: 0-0 Vi: 0-0 Tstrap: 4-7 Ckp: 0-0
Best Rating: 100 11/03 Hrfd 2m gd-fm Ch

Plating-class chaser; progressed well in the autumn of 2003; free-running sort; has improved leaps and bounds since being fitted with a tongue strap; acts on a sound surface; best going right-handed stays 2m 4f, effective at 2m.

Lord Of The Land

104(108h)   (94h)**94**

11-y-o b g Lord Bud-Saint Motunde (Tyrant (USA))
Mrs E Slack A Slack

Placings:650/000/61110431130/044UFP0/621/00-
020323F003223P051F   (4796)
2003/04: 24⁰G, 17²G, 24⁰G, 21³GF, 17²GF, 20³GF, 27⁶GF, 20⁶G,
22⁰F, 16³GF, 20²GF, 20²G, 25³GS, 25⁵S, 20⁰GF, 25⁵GS, 17¹G,
21⁶G,

	Starts	1st	2nd	3rd	Win & Pl
Hurdles	10	1	2	2	5756
Chases	8	0	2	2	2291
Career Total	47	7	5	6	25083
89	3/04	MRas	2m1f110yG(0-95)HHdl	GD	£2458
94	5/01	Hexm	3m1f	F(0-95)HCh	G-F	£2716
119	9/99	Sedg	2m5f110yG(0-125)HHdl	GD	£2914
107	9/99	Kels	2m6f110yE(0-105)HHdl	G-F	£2276
119	6/99	Hexm	2m4f110yE Hdl	G-F	£2607
104	5/99	Hexm	2m4f110yE Hdl	G-F	£1716
96	5/99	Kels	2m2f	E Hdl	G-F	£1955
			Total win prize-money £16644		

Going:	Sf: 0-1 GS: 0-2 Gd: 1-7 GF: - Fm: 0-8
Distance:	2m/2m3: 1-4 2m4-2m7: 0-8 3m+: 0-6
Track:	LH: 0-13 RH: 1-5 Tight: 1-10 Gall: 0-0
Aids:	Bl: 0-0 Vi: 0-0 Tstrap: 0-0 Ckp: 0-0
Best Rating:	119 9/99 Sedg 2m5f110y good Hdl

Moderate hurdler/chaser; effective over two miles but stays
really well; best on decent ground.

Lord Of The Loch (IRE)

104   **99**

13-y-o b/br g Lord Americo-Loughamaire (Brave Invader
(USA))
W G Young W G Young

Placings:U243/4/1333/1/5401536320/46446U06-02045401
                                                    (4796)
2003/04: 20⁵HY, 16²GS, 19⁰GS, 20⁴HY, 20⁵G, 20⁴GS, 16⁰G, 21¹G,

	Starts	1st	2nd	3rd	Win & Pl
Hurdles	8	1	1	0	3207
Career Total	36	4	3	6	16542
100	4/04	Sedg	2m5f110yG(0-100)HHdl	GD	£2443
112	2/02	Muss	2m4f	F(0-100)HHdl	SFT	£3038
107	2/01	Carl	2m1f	F(0-105)HHdl	HVY	£2702
101	5/99	Prth	2m4f110yE Hdl	SFT	£2409
			Total win prize-money £10593		

Going:	Sf: 0-2 GS: 0-3 Gd: 1-3 GF: - Fm: 0-0
Distance:	2m/2m3: 0-3 2m4-2m7: 1-5 3m+: 0-0
Track:	LH: 1-6 RH: 0-2 Tight: 1-4 Gall: 0-2
Aids:	Bl: 0-0 Vi: 0-0 Tstrap: 0-0 Ckp: 0-0
Best Rating:	112 2/02 Muss 2m4f soft Hdl

Plating-class veteran hurdler; lightly raced due to leg trouble; likes the mud and stays two and a half miles; in top
form at present.

Lord Of The North (IRE)

76   **74**

7-y-o br g Arctic Lord-Ballyfin Maid (IRE) (Boreen (FR))
M R Hoad Mrs J E Taylor

Placings:0/5P300-0   (0238)
2003/04: 19⁰G,

	Starts	1st	2nd	3rd	Win & Pl
Hurdles	1	0	0	0	0
Career Total	7	0	0	1	337

Going:	Sf: 0-0 GS: 0-0 Gd: 0-1 GF: - Fm: 0-0
Distance:	2m/2m3: 0-0 2m4-2m7: 0-1 3m+: 0-0
Track:	LH: 0-0 RH: 0-1 Tight: 0-0 Gall: 0-0
Aids:	Bl: 0-0 Vi: 0-0 Tstrap: 0-0 Ckp: 0-0
Best Rating:	74 3/03 Font 2m4f gd-fm Hdl

Lord Of The Park (IRE)

78   **69**

7-y-o b g Lord Americo-Wind Chimes (The Parson)
John R Upson Middleham Park Racing V

Placings:0/00F00P   (4790)
2003/04: 17⁰GS, 16⁰S, 17FHY, 17⁰GS, 19⁰GS, 21PG,

	Starts	1st	2nd	3rd	Win & Pl
NH Flat	1	0	0	0	0
Hurdles	5	0	0	0	0
Career Total	7	0	0	0	0

Going:	Sf: 0-2 GS: 0-3 Gd: 0-1 GF: - Fm: 0-0
Distance:	2m/2m3: 0-4 2m4-2m7: 0-2 3m+: 0-0
Track:	LH: 0-1 RH: 0-4 Tight: 0-2 Gall: 0-0
Aids:	Bl: 0-0 Vi: 0-0 Tstrap: 0-0 Ckp: 0-0
Best Rating:	68 1/04 Leic 2m soft Hdl

Lord Of The Realm (IRE)

81   **82**

8-y-o b g Mister Lord (USA)-Traditional Lady (Carlingford
Castle)
K C Bailey Ladies of the Realm

Placings:PP3F   (4442)
2003/04: 22PGS, 25PGS, 19³G, 20FGS,

	Starts	1st	2nd	3rd	Win & Pl
Chases	4	0	0	1	625
Career Total	4	0	0	1	625

Going:	Sf: 0-0 GS: 0-3 Gd: 0-1 GF: - Fm: 0-0
Distance:	2m/2m3: 0-1 2m4-2m7: 0-3 3m+: 0-1
Track:	LH: 0-2 RH: 0-2 Tight: 0-0 Gall: 0-0
Aids:	Bl: 0-0 Vi: 0-0 Tstrap: 0-2 Ckp: 0-0
Best Rating:	82 3/04 Donc 2m3f good Ch

Lord Of The River (IRE)

113   **141+**

12-y-o br g Lord Americo-Well Over (Over The River (FR))
N J Henderson B T Stewart-Brown

Placings:5/11415/1F2112/5U2/65-0211   (4637)
2003/04: 25⁰S, 24²G, 24¹GS, 25¹G,

	Starts	1st	2nd	3rd	Win & Pl
Chases	4	2	1	0	37663
Career Total	21	8	4	0	127531
141	4/04	Aint	3m1f	B HCh	GD	£23200
133	3/04	Asct	3m110y	C(0-130)HCh	G-S	£8238
154	2/99	Asct	3m110y	A Ch	GD	£19050
154	12/98	Kemp	3m	A Ch	G-S	£22715
123	11/98	Extr	2m3f	C Ch	SFT	£5433
123	3/98	Newb	2m5f	D Hdl	HVY	£3308
120	12/97	Uttx	2m4f110yE Hdl	G-S	£1945
107	11/97	Wind	2m4f	D Hdl	GD	£2810
			Total win prize-money £86431		

Going:	Sf: 0-1 GS: 1-1 Gd: 1-2 GF: - Fm: 0-0
Distance:	2m/2m3: 0-0 2m4-2m7: 0-0 3m+: 2-4
Track:	LH: 1-3 RH: 1-1 Tight: 1-1 Gall: 0-1
Aids:	Bl: 0-0 Vi: 0-0 Tstrap: 0-0 Ckp: 0-0
Best Rating:	154 2/99 Asct 3m110y good Ch

Very useful chaser; high-class novice in 1998/9, but off the
track for a long time afterwards; second in handicap at
Newbury in March 2004 before scoring at Ascot; followed up
in good style at Aintree; stays three miles; acts on good and
soft ground.

Lord Of The Track (IRE)

91   **85**

6-y-o b g Eve's Error-Tara's Tribe (IRE) (Good Thyne
(USA))
M C Pipe P J Finn

Placings:06501U   (1189)
2003/04: 17⁰G, 22²GF, 22⁵GF, 22⁰GF, 27¹GF, 24UGF,

	Starts	1st	2nd	3rd	Win & Pl
Hurdles	6	1	0	0	2296
Career Total	6	1	0	0	2296
85	8/03	Font	3m3f	G(0-95)HHdl	G-F	£2296
			Total win prize-money £2296		

Going:	Sf: 0-0 GS: 0-0 Gd: 0-1 GF: - Fm: 1-5
Distance:	2m/2m3: 0-1 2m4-2m7: 0-3 3m+: 1-2
Track:	LH: 0-5 RH: 0-0 Tight: 1-5 Gall: 0-0
Aids:	Bl: 0-0 Vi: 0-0 Tstrap: 0-0 Ckp: 0-0
Best Rating:	85 8/03 Font 3m3f gd-fm Hdl

Lord Olympia (IRE)

105f   **101f**

5-y-o b g Lord Americo-Mooreshill (IRE) (Le Moss)
Miss Venetia Williams Mrs Sally-Anne Ryan

Placings:262   (4284)
2003/04: 17²GS, 16⁶S, 16²GS,

	Starts	1st	2nd	3rd	Win & Pl
NH Flat	3	0	2	0	1060
Career Total	3	0	2	0	1060

Going:	Sf: 0-1 GS: 0-2 Gd: 0-0 GF: - Fm: 0-0
Distance:	2m/2m3: 0-3 2m4-2m7: 0-0 3m+: 0-0
Track:	LH: 0-1 RH: 0-2 Tight: 0-1 Gall: 0-0
Aids:	Bl: 0-0 Vi: 0-0 Tstrap: 0-0 Ckp: 0-0
Best Rating:	101 3/04 Towc 2m gd-sft NHF

Modest form in bumpers on easy ground.

Lord Pat (IRE)

100(89c)   (79c)**79**

13-y-o ch g Mister Lord (USA)-Arianrhod (L'Homme Arme)
Miss Kate Milligan The L P Club

Placings:05/05000/321P1033P/62P00/432/0124666/60F31
P2-5502   (4796)
2003/04: 19⁵GS, 20⁵HY, 20⁰S, 21²G,

	Starts	1st	2nd	3rd	Win & Pl
Hurdles	4	0	1	0	698
Career Total	42	4	6	5	16593
79	12/02	MRas	2m3f110yG(0-95)HHdl	SFT	£2226
90	11/01	Newc	2m4f	F(0-90)HHdl	GD	£2009
91	1/99	Muss	2m1f	F(0-100)HHdl	SFT	£4533
81	11/98	Sedg	2m1f	G(0-95)HHdl	G-S	£1626
			Total win prize-money £10395		

Going:	Sf: 0-2 GS: 0-1 Gd: 0-1 GF: - Fm: 0-0

Distance:	2m/2m3: 0-0 2m4-2m7: 0-4 3m+: 0-0
Track:	LH: 0-3 RH: 0-1 Tight: 0-2 Gall: 0-2
Aids:	Bl: 0-0 Vi: 0-0 Tstrap: 0-0 Ckp: 0-0
Best Rating:	91 11/99 Kels 2m110y good Hdl

Lord Payne (IRE)
90   **102**

6-y-o b g Alphabatim (USA)-Clash Boreen (Arapaho)
M C Pipe (John Joseph Murphy 27/1) D A Johnson

Placings:3   (4783)
2003/04: 21³G,

	Starts	1st	2nd	3rd	Win & Pl
Hurdles	1	0	0	1	534
Career Total	1	0	0	1	534

Going:	Sf: 0-0 GS: 0-0 Gd: 0-1 GF: - Fm: 0-0
Distance:	2m/2m3: 0-0 2m4-2m7: 0-1 3m+: 0-0
Track:	LH: 0-0 RH: 0-1 Tight: 0-0 Gall: 0-1
Aids:	Bl: 0-0 Vi: 0-0 Tstrap: 0-0 Ckp: 0-0
Best Rating:	102 4/04 Hntg 2m5f110y good Hdl

Irish point winner; third in novices' hurdle at Huntingdon in April; stays two miles six.

Lord Perseus (IRE)
90   **69**

7-y-o ch g Mister Lord (USA)-Greek Empress (Royal Buck)
M Pitman   J F Garrett

Placings:30/1-35   (0623)
2003/04: 17³GF, 17⁵G,

	Starts	1st	2nd	3rd	Win & Pl
NH Flat	1	0	0	1	297
Hurdles	1	0	1	0	2517
Career Total	5	1	0	2	2517
103 4/03 Hntg 2m110y H NHF G-F £1932					
				Total win prize-money £1932	

Going:	Sf: 0-0 GS: 0-0 Gd: 0-1 GF: - Fm: 0-0
Distance:	2m/2m3: 0-2 2m4-2m7: 0-0 3m+: 0-0
Track:	LH: 0-1 RH: 0-1 Tight: 0-1 Gall: 0-0
Aids:	Bl: 0-0 Vi: 0-0 Tstrap: 0-0 Ckp: 0-0
Best Rating:	103 4/03 Hntg 2m110y gd-fm NHF

Promising third in a Kempton bumper on his debut; returned after a year off to make all on third career start in a weak bumper on fast ground at Huntingdon in April; well beaten on hurdling bow.

Lord Rochester
95(96c)   (62c)**86**

8-y-o b g Distant Relative-Kentfield (Busted)
K F Clutterbuck   K F Clutterbuck

Placings:523/12132314/03F053114/44F3P66-0PP12
           (1792)
2003/04: 21⁹G, 21²G, 17⁶GF, 19¹F, 16²GF,

	Starts	1st	2nd	3rd	Win & Pl
Hurdles	5	1	1	2	2369
Career Total	32	6	4	6	23138
86 10/03 Towc 2m3f110yG(0-90)HHdl FRM £1842					
121 10/01 Chep 2m4f D(0-125)HHdl GD £3474					
117 9/01 Plum 2m5f D(0-125)HHdl G-F £3342					
123 10/00 Folk 2m2f110yF(0-110)HHdl G-F £1757					
110 5/00 Font 2m2f110yE Hdl GD £2285					
104 5/00 Folk 2m1f110yE Hdl GD £2432					
				Total win prize-money £15135	

| Going: | Sf: 0-0 GS: 0-0 Gd: 0-1 GF: - Fm: 1-4 |
| Distance: | 2m/2m3: 0-2 2m4-2m7: 1-3 3m+: 0-0 |

Track:	LH: 0-2 RH: 0-2 Tight: 0-1 Gall: 0-1
Aids:	Bl: 0-1 Vi: 0-0 Tstrap: 0-0 Ckp: 1-2
Best Rating:	124 10/01 Chel 2m5f good Hdl

Fair hurdler at his best but looks on the downgrade; tried in cheekpieces and received treatment on a muscle in his back prior to winning poor Towcester seller October 2003; effective over 2m 4f; suited by good to firm ground; usually wears blinkers; yet to convince over fences.

Lord Rodney (IRE)
88f   **95f**

5-y-o b g Hatim (USA)-Howcleuch (Buckskin (FR))
P Beaumont   Estio Racing

Placings:3   (4886)
2003/04: 17³GS,

	Starts	1st	2nd	3rd	Win & Pl
NH Flat	1	0	0	1	297
Career Total	1	0	0	1	297

Going:	Sf: 0-0 GS: 0-1 Gd: 0-0 GF: - Fm: 0-0
Distance:	2m/2m3: 0-0 2m4-2m7: 0-0 3m+: 0-0
Track:	LH: 0-0 RH: 0-1 Tight: 0-0 Gall: 0-0
Aids:	Bl: 0-0 Vi: 0-0 Tstrap: 0-0 Ckp: 0-0
Best Rating:	94 4/04 Carl 2m1f gd-sft NHF

Half-brother to a bumper winner and out of a dam that won over three miles and five furlongs over fences; well held in the end but clear signs of ability on debut in Carlisle bumper in Ayr 2004; capable of better.

Lord Sam (IRE)
119(111h)   (150+h)**148+**

8-y-o b g Supreme Leader-Russian Gale (IRE) (Strong Gale)
V R A Dartnall   Plain Peeps

Placings:11/1113-111   (3362)
2003/04: 20¹SG, 24¹S, 24¹G,

	Starts	1st	2nd	3rd	Win & Pl
Chases	3	3	0	0	28049
Career Total	9	8	0	1	68739
152 1/04 Kemp 3m C Ch GD £8736					
151 12/03 Ling 3m A Ch SFT £14500					
145 11/03 Hntg 2m4f110yD Ch G-S £4812					
141 1/03 Kemp 2m5f B Hdl GD £12458					
137 12/02 Kemp 2m C Hdl SFT £6583					
121 12/02 Sand 2m110y D Hdl SFT £5798					
123 3/02 Newb 2m110y H NHF G-S £2576					
120 2/02 Sand 2m110y H NHF SFT £2275					
				Total win prize-money £57739	

Going:	Sf: 1-1 GS: 1-1 Gd: 1-1 GF: - Fm: 0-0
Distance:	2m/2m3: 0-0 2m4-2m7: 0-0 3m+: 2-2
Track:	LH: 1-1 RH: 2-2 Tight: 1-1 Gall: 1-1
Aids:	Bl: 0-0 Vi: 0-0 Tstrap: 0-0 Ckp: 0-0
Best Rating:	152 1/04 Kemp 3m good Ch

High-class novice chaser; unbeaten in two bumpers and three starts over hurdles in his first five starts; finished an unlucky fourth the Royal & SunAlliance Novices' Hurdle at the 2003 Festival;unbeaten in novice chases, the second of them a convincing victory at Lingfield in a Grade Two novice event; stays three miles; has won on good ground, but best on soft.

Lord Seamus
103   (88h)**112**

9-y-o b g Arctic Lord-Erica Superba (Langton Heath)
K C Bailey   I F W Buchan

Placings:0/40/0434F231/5F303-4322F3   (4820)
2003/04: 25⁴GS, 25³GF, 24²GF, 24²F, 25⁴GS, 25³GF,

	Starts	1st	2nd	3rd	Win & Pl
Chases	6	0	2	2	5670
Career Total	22	1	3	6	23017
135 4/02 Asct 3m110y B Ch G-F £10998					
				Total win prize-money £10998	

Going:	Sf: 0-0 GS: 2-2 Gd: 0-0 GF: - Fm: 0-4
Distance:	2m/2m3: 0-0 2m4-2m7: 0-0 3m+: 0-6
Track:	LH: 0-0 RH: 0-6 Tight: 0-1 Gall: 0-0
Aids:	Bl: 0-0 Vi: 0-0 Tstrap: 0-0 Ckp: 0-1
Best Rating:	135 4/02 Asct 3m110y gd-fm Ch

Moderate staying chaser; broke the course record over three miles on fast ground at Ascot in April 2002; has not progressed since; seems to need at least 3m.

Lord Strickland
96(105h)   (109h)**101**

11-y-o b g Strong Gale-Lady Rag (Ragapan)
P J Hobbs   Miss H L Cope

Placings:0660/41450306/1113214/401321454/03331F-63
           (0488)
2003/04: 22⁶G, 21³GF,

	Starts	1st	2nd	3rd	Win & Pl
Hurdles	1	0	0	0	0
Chases	1	0	0	1	840
Career Total	36	8	2	7	33049
115 7/02 NAbb 2m5f110yD(0-120)HCh GF £4541					
117 8/01 NAbb 2m5f110yF(0-105)HCh GF £3654					
110 7/01 Strf 2m6f110yF(0-110)HHdl GF £2572					
108 8/00 Hntg 2m4f110yE Ch GF £3445					
119 6/00 NAbb 2m6f F(0-105)HHdl GF £2988					
116 5/00 Font 2m6f110yE(0-115)HHdl GD £2411					
115 5/00 Winc 2m6f F(0-100)HHdl FRM £3133					
85 5/99 Kbgn 2m3f Hdl GD £2455					
				Total win prize-money £25204	

Going:	Sf: 0-0 GS: 0-0 Gd: 0-0 GF: - Fm: 0-1
Distance:	2m/2m3: 0-0 2m4-2m7: 0-0 3m+: 0-0
Track:	LH: 0-1 RH: 0-1 Tight: 0-1 Gall: 0-0
Aids:	Bl: 0-0 Vi: 0-0 Tstrap: 0-0 Ckp: 0-0
Best Rating:	119 7/00 Worc 3m gd-fm Hdl

Fair staying hurdler/chaser, suited by fast ground; has front run but suited by a sharp track and waiting tactics.

Lord Thomas (IRE)
60f   **29f**

6-y-o b g Grand Lodge (USA)-Noble Rocket (Reprimand)
A J Wilson   Tim Leadbeater

Placings:0-00   (3948)
2003/04: 16⁰GS, 16⁰G,

	Starts	1st	2nd	3rd	Win & Pl
NH Flat	2	0	0	0	
Career Total	3	0	0	0	

Going:	Sf: 0-0 GS: 0-1 Gd: 0-1 GF: - Fm: 0-0
Distance:	2m/2m3: 0-2 2m4-2m7: 0-0 3m+: 0-0
Track:	LH: 0-1 RH: 0-1 Tight: 0-0 Gall: 0-0
Aids:	Bl: 0-0 Vi: 0-0 Tstrap: 0-0 Ckp: 0-0
Best Rating:	29 2/04 Winc 2m good NHF

Lord Transcend (IRE)
110(107h)   (160 h)**129++**

7-y-o gr g Aristocracy-Capincur Lady (Over The River (FR))

J Howard Johnson Transcend (Hair And Beauty) Limited

Placings:1/1115-1   (2430)
2003/04: 25¹GS,

	Starts	1st	2nd	3rd	Win & Pl
Chases	1	1	0	0	3689
Career Total	6	5	0	0	39213
129	11/03	Ayr	3m1f	E Ch	G-S	£3689
156	1/03	Hayd	2m7f110yA Hdl	G-S	£23200
145	11/02	Newc	2m	D(0-115)HHdl	G-S	£3701
120	11/02	Hexm	2m110y	F(0-100)HHdl	HVY	£2212
99	3/02	Newc	2m	E HHdl	HVY	£2660

Total win prize-money £35463

Going:	Sf: 0-0 GS: 1-1 Gd: 0-0 GF: - Fm: 0-0
Distance:	2m/2m3: 0-0 2m4-2m7: 0-0 3m+: 1-1
Track:	LH: 1-1 RH: 0-0 Tight: 0-0 Gall: 0-0
Aids:	Bl: 0-0 Vi: 0-0 Tstrap: 0-0 Ckp: 0-0
Best Rating:	156 1/03 Hayd 2m7f110y gd-sft Hdl

Smart chaser/hurdler; progressing really well and won a Grade Two at Haydock over nearly three miles on only his fourth run; unbeaten three times over two miles prior to that; ran with credit in Grade One at Aintree; made a winning chasing debut at Ayr; injured subsequently and missed rest of season; acts well on a soft surface.

Lord Trix (IRE)
98   98

5-y-o b g Lord Americo-Up To Trix (Over The River (FR))
P W Hiatt K Hutsby

Placings:05F2   (4915)
2003/04: 16⁰G, 16⁵GS, 23⁶FS, 16²GS,

	Starts	1st	2nd	3rd	Win & Pl
NH Flat	2	0	0	0	0
Hurdles	2	0	1	0	1128
Career Total	4	0	1	0	1128

Going:	Sf: 0-1 GS: 0-2 Gd: 0-1 GF: - Fm: 0-0
Distance:	2m/2m3: 0-3 2m4-2m7: 0-1 3m+: 0-0
Track:	LH: 0-3 RH: 0-1 Tight: 0-0 Gall: 0-1
Aids:	Bl: 0-0 Vi: 0-0 Tstrap: 0-0 Ckp: 0-0
Best Rating:	98 4/04 Worc 2m gd-sft Hdl

Moderate novice hurdler; runner-up over two miles at Worcester in April; should stay farther.

Lord Valnic (IRE)

8-y-o b g Mister Lord (USA)-Any Wonder (Hard Boy)
Ms A E Embiricos C J Hays

Placings:F   (3785)
2003/04: 24⁴FS,

	Starts	1st	2nd	3rd	Win & Pl
Chases	1	0	0	0	
Career Total	1	0	0	0	

Going:	Sf: 0-1 GS: 0-0 Gd: 0-0 GF: - Fm: 0-0
Distance:	2m/2m3: 0-0 2m4-2m7: 0-0 3m+: 0-1
Track:	LH: 0-0 RH: 0-1 Tight: 0-0 Gall: 0-1
Aids:	Bl: 0-0 Vi: 0-0 Tstrap: 0-0 Ckp: 0-0

Lord Ville (FR)
105   93

5-y-o b g Useful (FR)-Triaina (Lancastrian)
P J Hobbs Rod Hamilton

Placings:656051-20403   (1473)

2003/04: 16²GF, 16⁰G, 17⁴GF, 17⁹GF, 17³F,

	Starts	1st	2nd	3rd	Win & Pl
Hurdles	5	0	1	1	1979
Career Total	11	1	1	1	5395
89	4/03	Winc	2m	E(0-110)HHdl	FRM	£3416

Total win prize-money £3416

Going:	Sf: 0-0 GS: 0-0 Gd: 0-1 GF: - Fm: 0-4
Distance:	2m/2m3: 0-5 2m4-2m7: 0-0 3m+: 0-0
Track:	LH: 0-3 RH: 0-2 Tight: 0-3 Gall: 0-0
Aids:	Bl: 0-0 Vi: 0-0 Tstrap: 0-0 Ckp: 0-0
Best Rating:	94 9/03 NAbb 2m1f gd-fm Hdl

Plating-class hurdler; goes well on sharp tracks; suited by two miles; acts on fast ground.

Lord Warford
102   (90h)90

9-y-o b g Bustino-Jupiter's Message (Jupiter Island)
C L Popham H J W Davies, Rodney Peacock

Placings:03/0432/160/605/55P44-43   (0505)
2003/04: 21⁴GF, 21³GS,

	Starts	1st	2nd	3rd	Win & Pl
Chases	2	0	0	1	1148
Career Total	19	1	1	3	8314
114	5/00	NAbb	2m6f	C Hdl		£4810

Total win prize-money £4810

Going:	Sf: 0-0 GS: 0-1 Gd: 0-0 GF: - Fm: 0-1
Distance:	2m/2m3: 0-2 2m4-2m7: 0-0 3m+: 0-1
Track:	LH: 0-1 RH: 0-1 Tight: 0-1 Gall: 0-0
Aids:	Bl: 0-0 Vi: 0-0 Tstrap: 0-0 Ckp: 0-0
Best Rating:	114 5/00 NAbb 2m6f gd-fm Hdl

Lord York (IRE)
(106h)   (112h)137

12-y-o b/br g Strong Gale-Bunkilla (Arctic Slave)
Ian Williams David J Dunne

Placings:2013/4560/14112221011/2060/113133323/45P34
103-20   (0517)
2003/04: 20²G, 19⁰G,

	Starts	1st	2nd	3rd	Win & Pl
Hurdles	2	0	1	0	2112
Career Total	42	11	7	8	119404
137	3/03	Asct	2m	C(0-135)HCh	GD	£11948
138	11/01	Asct	2m	A(0-150)HCh	GD	£18119
138	5/01	Hntg	2m110y	C(0-135)HCh	G-F	£6668
138	5/01	Extr	2m1f110yD(0-125)HCh	GD	£4826
138	4/00	Ayr	2m	B HCh	GD	£13312
122	4/00	Ayr	2m	C Ch	GD	£5752
138	3/00	Newb	2m2f110yD(0-125)HCh	G-F	£7247
133	10/99	Towc	2m110y	C(0-115)HCh	GD	£3142
122	10/99	Extr	2m1f	D(0-110)HCh	GD	£3837
107	9/99	MRas	2m6f110yE Ch	G-F	£3286
110	3/98	Donc	2m4f	E Hdl	GD	£2658

Total win prize-money £80799

Going:	Sf: 0-0 GS: 0-0 Gd: 0-2 GF: - Fm: 0-0
Distance:	2m/2m3: 0-1 2m4-2m7: 0-1 3m+: 0-0
Track:	LH: 0-2 RH: 0-0 Tight: 0-1 Gall: 0-0
Aids:	Bl: 0-2 Vi: 0-0 Tstrap: 0-0 Ckp: 0-0
Best Rating:	141 4/02 Aint 2m good Ch

Fair handicap chaser; best at two miles, stays 2m 5f; likes to front-run; effective on a sound surface; has worn blinkers/visor/tongue tie.

Lord Youky (FR)
106   117+

10-y-o b g Cadoudal (FR)-Lady Corteira (FR) (Carvin II)

Ian Williams C N Barnes

Placings:2/43/11FFP25/33P151   (2692)
2003/04: 20³GF, 24³G, 23⁸G, 20¹GF, 24⁵F, 20¹G,

	Starts	1st	2nd	3rd	Win & Pl
Chases	6	2	0	2	10360
Career Total	16	4	2	3	18529
91	12/03	Ludl	2m4f	D(0-120)HCh	GD	£4043
117	11/03	Uttx	2m4f	E(0-105)HCh	G-F	£3705
106	10/01	Sthl	2m4f110yE Hdl	GD	£2569
103	10/01	Hrfd	2m3f110yE Hdl	GD	£2744

Total win prize-money £13061

Going:	Sf: 0-0 GS: 0-0 Gd: 1-3 GF: - Fm: 1-3
Distance:	2m/2m3: 0-0 2m4-2m7: 2-3 3m+: 0-3
Track:	LH: 1-4 RH: 1-2 Tight: 1-3 Gall: 0-0
Aids:	Bl: 0-0 Vi: 0-0 Tstrap: 0-0 Ckp: 0-0
Best Rating:	117 11/03 Uttx 2m4f gd-fm Ch

Lightly raced chaser; stays three miles; acts on fast ground.

Lordberniebouffant (IRE)

11-y-o b g Denel (FR)-Noon Hunting (Green Shoon)
David Parker The Marvellous Partnership

Placings:5324212/33F004/413124/3051F0/5-4   (4703)
2003/04: 26⁴G,

	Starts	1st	2nd	3rd	Win & Pl
Chases	1	0	0	0	
Career Total	27	4	4	5	60433
121	3/02	Newb	3m	C(0-130)HCh	G-S	£9552
121	1/01	Font	3m4f	D(0-125)HCh	SFT	£13650
107	9/00	Hntg	3m	D(0-115)HCh	G-F	£3607
125	3/99	Sand	2m4f110yA HHdl	SFT	£16299

Total win prize-money £43111

Going:	Sf: 0-0 GS: 0-0 Gd: 0-1 GF: - Fm: 0-0
Distance:	2m/2m3: 0-0 2m4-2m7: 0-0 3m+: 0-0
Track:	LH: 0-0 RH: 0-0 Tight: 0-1 Gall: 0-0
Aids:	Bl: 0-0 Vi: 0-0 Tstrap: 0-0 Ckp: 0-0
Best Rating:	132 12/02 Chel 3m good Hdl

Lords Best (IRE)
97(107h)   (129+h)121

8-y-o b g Mister Lord (USA)-Ballinlonig Star (Black Minstrel)
A King Jerry Wright, Peter Smith & Jules Sigler

Placings:34224/11431-51F   (3521)
2003/04: 22⁵S, 25¹GS, 23⁶S,

	Starts	1st	2nd	3rd	Win & Pl
Chases	3	1	0	0	4277
Career Total	13	4	2	2	29089
120	1/04	Folk	3m1f	E Ch	G-S	£4277
129	3/03	Bang	3m	C(0-135)HHdl	GD	£6812
121	11/02	Winc	2m6f	C Hdl	G-S	£6610
114	11/02	Kemp	2m5f	D Hdl	SFT	£4504

Total win prize-money £22205

Going:	Sf: 0-2 GS: 1-1 Gd: 0-0 GF: - Fm: 0-0
Distance:	2m/2m3: 0-0 2m4-2m7: 0-1 3m+: 1-2
Track:	LH: 0-0 RH: 1-2 Tight: 1-1 Gall: 0-0
Aids:	Bl: 0-0 Vi: 0-0 Tstrap: 0-0 Ckp: 0-0
Best Rating:	129 3/03 Bang 3m good Hdl

Decent hurdler/fair chaser; off the mark over fences at Folkestone in January; has hung right-handed; best at around three miles; acts on soft ground but better on a sound surface.

Lordston (IRE)

8-y-o b g Mister Lord (USA)-Dawstown (Golden Love)
B G Powell John Plackett

Placings:*6/0/PP* (4823)
2003/04: 25PGS, 23PGF,

	Starts	1st	2nd	3rd	Win & Pl
Chases	2	0	0	0	
Career Total	**4**	**0**	**0**	**0**	**0**

Going: Sf: 0-0 GS: 0-1 Gd: 0-0 GF: - Fm: 0-1
Distance: 2m/2m3: 0-0 2m4-2m7: 0-0 3m+: 0-2
Track: LH: 0-0 RH: 0-2 Tight: 0-1 Gall: 0-0
Aids: Bl: 0-0 Vi: 0-0 Tstrap: 0-0 Ckp: 0-0
Best Rating: 95 4/01 Asct 2m110y heavy NHF

Lorenzino (IRE)

106(106h) (119h)120

7-y-o ch g Thunder Gulch (USA)-Russian Ballet (USA) (Nijinsky (CAN))
Jonjo O'Neill P Piller

Placings:*12/152110/6F060UP-6331F2PP* (3942)
2003/04: 20PGF, 24PGF, 20PG, 241GF, 24PGF, 202GF, 24PS, 22PG,

	Starts	1st	2nd	3rd	Win & Pl
Hurdles	3	0	0	1	1152
Chases	5	1	1	1	4894
Career Total	**23**	**5**	**3**	**2**	**38079**
120	9/03	Hntg	3m	E Ch	G-F	£3038
130	2/02	Kemp	2m5f	C(0-130)HHdl	GD	£13942
125	11/01	Weth	2m4f110yC(0-130)HHdl		GD	£7020
120	5/01	Bang	2m1f	D(0-120)HHdl	G-S	£4485
120	2/01	Weth	2m	E Hdl	SFT	£2628

Total win prize-money £31115

Going: Sf: 0-1 GS: 0-0 Gd: 0-2 GF: - Fm: 1-5
Distance: 2m/2m3: 0-0 2m4-2m7: 0-4 3m+: 1-4
Track: LH: 0-3 RH: 1-5 Tight: 0-3 Gall: 1-2
Aids: Bl: 0-0 Vi: 0-0 Tstrap: 0-0 Ckp: 0-0
Best Rating: 130 2/02 Kemp 2m5f good Hdl

Fair hurdler/chaser; suited by two and a half miles plus and a sound surface; best racing just off the pace.

Lorgnette

107(101c) (104c)113

10-y-o br m Emperor Fountain-Speckyfoureyes (Blue Cashmere)
R H Alner Alvin Trowbridge

Placings:*316453/513514/40224025323-023210* (4643)
2003/04: 22PS, 242S, 223G, 262G, 241GS, 240G,

	Starts	1st	2nd	3rd	Win & Pl
Hurdles	6	1	2	1	9205
Career Total	**29**	**4**	**9**	**6**	**25930**
113	3/04	Asct	3m	D(0-125)HHdl	G-S	£5057
108	11/01	Plum	2m5f	E Hdl	GD	£2460
96	10/01	Winc	2m6f	F(0-105)HHdl	G-F	£3052
95	10/00	Tntn	2m1f	H NHF	GD	£1536

Total win prize-money £12107

Going: Sf: 0-2 GS: 1-1 Gd: 0-3 GF: - Fm: 0-0
Distance: 2m/2m3: 0-0 2m4-2m7: 0-0 3m+: 1-4
Track: LH: 0-2 RH: 1-4 Tight: 0-3 Gall: 0-1
Aids: Bl: 0-0 Vi: 0-0 Tstrap: 0-0 Ckp: 0-0
Best Rating: 113 3/04 Asct 3m gd-sft Hdl

Fair staying handicap hurdler; needs to come late; acts on fast and easy ground.

Lorient Express (FR)

100 90

5-y-o b g Sleeping Car (FR)-Envie De Chalamont (FR) (Pamponi (FR))
M F Harris Let's Live Racing

Placings:*FP56P0* (3921)
2003/04: 16FGF, 16PGS, 165HY, 166S, 16PS, 16PGS,

	Starts	1st	2nd	3rd	Win & Pl
Hurdles	6	0	0	0	0
Career Total	**6**	**0**	**0**	**0**	**0**

Going: Sf: 0-3 GS: 0-2 Gd: 0-0 GF: - Fm: 0-1
Distance: 2m/2m3: 0-6 2m4-2m7: 0-0 3m+: 0-0
Track: LH: 0-4 RH: 0-2 Tight: 0-2 Gall: 0-0
Aids: Bl: 0-0 Vi: 0-0 Tstrap: 0-0 Ckp: 0-0
Best Rating: 90 1/04 Plum 2m soft Hdl

Lorio Du Misselot (FR)

78f 57f

5-y-o gr g Dom Alco (FR)-Byrsa (FR) (Quart De Vin (FR))
Ferdy Murphy R J V Partnership

Placings:*0* (3375)
2003/04: 16PS,

	Starts	1st	2nd	3rd	Win & Pl
NH Flat	1	0	0	0	
Career Total	**1**	**0**	**0**	**0**	

Going: Sf: 0-1 GS: 0-0 Gd: 0-0 GF: - Fm: 0-0
Distance: 2m/2m3: 0-1 2m4-2m7: 0-0 3m+: 0-0
Track: LH: 0-1 RH: 0-0 Tight: 0-0 Gall: 0-0
Aids: Bl: 0-0 Vi: 0-0 Tstrap: 0-0 Ckp: 0-0
Best Rating: 57 1/04 Weth 2m soft NHF

Los Vados (GER)

98 89

5-y-o b g Dashing Blade-La Vega (GER) (Turfkonig (GER))
Ian Williams Allwood-Vaughan-Harris

Placings:*64U-55060* (2006)
2003/04: 16SG, 16SG, 17PGF, 16SG, 20PG,

	Starts	1st	2nd	3rd	Win & Pl
Hurdles	5	0	0	0	0
Career Total	**8**	**0**	**0**	**0**	**322**

Going: Sf: 0-0 GS: 0-0 Gd: 0-4 GF: - Fm: 0-1
Distance: 2m/2m3: 0-4 2m4-2m7: 0-1 3m+: 0-0
Track: LH: 0-2 RH: 0-3 Tight: 0-3 Gall: 0-0
Aids: Bl: 0-0 Vi: 0-0 Tstrap: 0-0 Ckp: 0-0
Best Rating: 89 5/03 Ludl 2m good Hdl

Modest novice hurdler.

Loscar (FR)

76 59

5-y-o b g General Holme (USA)-Unika Ii (FR) (Rolling Bowl (FR))
L Lungo W J E Scott

Placings:*606* (4881)
2003/04: 16SGS, 17PG, 17SGS,

	Starts	1st	2nd	3rd	Win & Pl
NH Flat	2	0	0	0	0

Hurdles

Hurdles	1	0	0	0	0
Career Total	**3**	**0**	**0**	**0**	**0**

Going: Sf: 0-0 GS: 0-2 Gd: 0-1 GF: - Fm: 0-0
Distance: 2m/2m3: 0-3 2m4-2m7: 0-0 3m+: 0-0
Track: LH: 0-1 RH: 0-2 Tight: 0-0 Gall: 0-0
Aids: Bl: 0-0 Vi: 0-0 Tstrap: 0-0 Ckp: 0-0
Best Rating: 77 2/04 Ayr 2m gd-sft NHF

Lost In Normandy (IRE)

107(73h) (57h)86

7-y-o b g Treasure Hunter-Auntie Honnie (IRE) (Radical)
Mrs L Williamson Please Hold UK

Placings:*500P5-640P2011P30* (4914)
2003/04: 21SGF, 264G, 219GF, 23PGF, 202G, 20PGF, 241G, 261GF, 24PG, 263G, 240GS,

	Starts	1st	2nd	3rd	Win & Pl
Hurdles	4	0	0	0	0
Chases	7	2	1	1	9010
Career Total	**16**	**2**	**1**	**1**	**9010**
86	10/03	Sthl	3m2f	F(0-100)HCh	G-F	£2898
80	9/03	Bang	3m110y	E(0-100)HCh	GD	£4134

Total win prize-money £7032

Going: Sf: 0-0 GS: 0-1 Gd: 1-5 GF: - Fm: 1-5
Distance: 2m/2m3: 0-0 2m4-2m7: 0-5 3m+: 2-6
Track: LH: 2-11 RH: 0-0 Tight: 1-5 Gall: 0-0
Aids: Bl: 2-7 Vi: 0-0 Tstrap: 0-0 Ckp: 0-0
Best Rating: 96 5/02 Hrfd 2m1f good NHF

Poor chaser; improved effort when successful at Bangor in September 2003 and followed up at Southwell the following month; stays three miles well; acts on sound surface.

Lost Soldier Two

4-y-o b g Kris-Hejraan (USA) (Alydar (USA))
R C Guest B V Ward

Placings:*000P* (4187)
2003/04: 13PGS, 16PGS, 16PG, 16PGS,

	Starts	1st	2nd	3rd	Win & Pl
NH Flat	3	0	0	0	0
Hurdles	1	0	0	0	0
Career Total	**4**	**0**	**0**	**0**	

Going: Sf: 0-0 GS: 0-2 Gd: 0-1 GF: - Fm: 0-1
Distance: 2m/2m3: 0-0 2m4-2m7: 0-0 3m+: 0-0
Track: LH: 0-2 RH: 0-1 Tight: 0-2 Gall: 0-0
Aids: Bl: 0-1 Vi: 0-0 Tstrap: 0-0 Ckp: 0-1
Best Rating: 52 1/04 Weth 2m gd-sft NHF

Lost The Plot

99(106h) (104h)107

9-y-o b m Lyphento (USA)-La Comedienne (Comedy Star (USA))
K J Burke (D W P Arbuthnot 3/6) Kieran P O'Driscoll

Placings:*11/3000/226/430542/3112-2F60* (4135a)
2003/04: 20PGF, 21PGF, 20PYS, 18PGY,

	Starts	1st	2nd	3rd	Win & Pl
Chases	4	0	1	0	1254
Career Total	**23**	**4**	**5**	**3**	**28779**
101	9/02	Font	2m6f110yE(0-110)HHdl	G-F	£3052
97	9/02	Sthl	2m5f110yE Hdl	GD	£3001
107	4/99	Chel	2m1f	H NHF	GD	£14070

97 2/99 Font 2m2f110yH NHF   GD £1556
Total win prize-money £21681

Going:	Sf: 0-0 GS: 0-0 Gd: 0-0 GF: - Fm: 0-2
Distance:	2m/2m3: 0-1 2m4-2m7: 0-3 3m+: 0-0
Track:	LH: 0-1 RH: 0-1 Tight: 0-2 Gall: 0-0
Aids:	Bl: 0-0 Vi: 0-0 Tstrap: 0-0 Ckp: 0-0
Best Rating:	107 5/03 Font 2m4f gd-fm Ch

Moderate chaser; winner over hurdles when trained by David Arbuthnot; effective at two and a half miles; suited by fast ground.

Lotier (FR)

101   114

5-y-o b g Dress Parade-Dame D'Onze Heures (FR) (Noble Cake (USA))
Mrs L C Taylor Mrs L C Taylor

Placings:0261F   (4325)
2003/04: 16⁰GS, 19²GS, 16⁸GS, 17¹HY, 20⁴S,

	Starts	1st	2nd	3rd	Win & Pl
NH Flat	1	0	0	0	0
Hurdles	4	1	1	0	4280
Career Total	5	1	1	0	4280
114 2/04 Hrfd 2m1f	E Hdl			HVY	£3477

Total win prize-money £3478

Going:	Sf: 1-2 GS: 0-3 Gd: 0-0 GF: 0-0
Distance:	2m/2m3: 1-3 2m4-2m7: 0-2 3m+: 0-0
Track:	LH: 0-2 RH: 1-3 Tight: 0-1 Gall: 0-1
Aids:	Bl: 0-0 Vi: 0-0 Tstrap: 0-0 Ckp: 0-0
Best Rating:	114 2/04 Hrfd 2m1f heavy Hdl

Fair novice hurdler; from the family of Gingembre; winning novice hurdler; effective at around 2m; acts on soft ground; future chaser.

Lotus Des Pictons (FR)

107   (0c)127+

5-y-o b g Grand Tresor (FR)-Ballaway (FR) (Djarvis (FR))
M C Pipe (B Secly 28/10) Lord Donoughmore & Countess Donoughmore

Placings:PP-0435202131155   (4628)
2003/04: 17⁰VS, 20⁴VS, 18³VS, 17⁵VS, 20²VS, 16⁰GS, 19²G, 24¹S, 24³G, 21¹G, 24¹GF, 20⁵GS, 20⁶G,

	Starts	1st	2nd	3rd	Win & Pl
Hurdles	8	3	1	1	16730
Chases	5	0	1	1	10909
Career Total	15	3	2	2	27639
118 3/04 Chep 3m	G-F				£3562
122 3/04 Ludl 2m5f	D(0-120)HHdl			GD	£6955
110 1/04 Chep 3m	F Hdl			SFT	£2667

Total win prize-money £13184

Going:	Sf: 1-1 GS: 0-2 Gd: 1-4 GF: - Fm: 1-1
Distance:	2m/2m3: 0-4 2m4-2m7: 1-6 3m+: 2-3
Track:	LH: 2-4 RH: 1-4 Tight: 0-2 Gall: 0-1
Aids:	Bl: 0-1 Vi: 0-0 Tstrap: 0-0 Ckp: 0-0
Best Rating:	127 4/04 Aint 2m4f good Hdl

Ex-French chaser; placed over fences in France; progressing over hurdles with two wins in weak events over three miles at Chepstow and has also scored over 21 furlongs at Ludlow; stays three miles; appears to act on all types of ground.

Lou Du Moulin Mas (FR)

106(96h)   (93h)117

5-y-o b g Sassanian (USA)-Houf (FR) (Morespeed)
P F Nicholls (T Trapenard 10/6) The Eight Amigos Racing Syndicate

Placings:02420   (4560)
2003/04: 17⁰HY, 18²VS, 16⁴HY, 20²G, 21⁰GS,

	Starts	1st	2nd	3rd	Win & Pl
Hurdles	3	0	1	0	5610
Chases	2	0	1	0	4019
Career Total	5	0	2	0	9629

Going:	Sf: 0-2 GS: 0-1 Gd: 0-1 GF: - Fm: 0-0
Distance:	2m/2m3: 0-3 2m4-2m7: 0-2 3m+: 0-0
Track:	LH: 0-1 RH: 0-1 Tight: 0-0 Gall: 0-1
Aids:	Bl: 0-0 Vi: 0-0 Tstrap: 0-3 Ckp: 0-0
Best Rating:	121 2/04 Font 2m4f good Ch

Ex-French; fourth in beginners' chase on British debut and finished a fair second next time.

Loudy Rowdy (IRE)

97(92h)   (77h)74+

13-y-o br g Strong Gale-Express Film (Ashmore (FR))
Mrs J K M Oliver The British Beef Partnership

Placings:14/F0/P0/044P5P/5P3-F642P44   (4684)
2003/04: 25⁵G, 25⁶G, 22⁴GF, 25²GF, 25⁵G, 25⁴G,

	Starts	1st	2nd	3rd	Win & Pl
Hurdles	1	0	0	0	0
Chases	6	0	1	0	1369
Career Total	22	1	1	1	5484
108 10/97 Wxfd 2m		NHF		G-F	£3221

Total win prize-money £3222

Going:	Sf: 0-1 GS: 0-0 Gd: 0-4 GF: - Fm: 0-2
Distance:	2m/2m3: 0-0 2m4-2m7: 0-2 3m+: 0-5
Track:	LH: 0-7 RH: 0-0 Tight: 0-3 Gall: 0-0
Aids:	Bl: 0-0 Vi: 0-2 Tstrap: 0-0 Ckp: 0-0
Best Rating:	108 10/97 Wxfd 2m gd-fm NHF

Plating-class hurdler/chaser.

Lough Dante (IRE)

97   105

6-y-o b g Phardante (FR)-Shannon Lough (IRE) (Deep Run)
H D Daly Michael Lowe

Placings:234   (3933)
2003/04: 20²S, 20³G, 24⁴G,

	Starts	1st	2nd	3rd	Win & Pl
Hurdles	3	0	1	1	2383
Career Total	3	0	1	1	2383

Going:	Sf: 0-1 GS: 0-0 Gd: 0-2 GF: - Fm: 0-0
Distance:	2m/2m3: 0-0 2m4-2m7: 0-2 3m+: 0-1
Track:	LH: 0-2 RH: 0-1 Tight: 0-0 Gall: 0-0
Aids:	Bl: 0-0 Vi: 0-0 Tstrap: 0-0 Ckp: 0-0
Best Rating:	105 12/03 Hayd 2m4f soft Hdl

Point-to-point winner; runner-up to a potentially useful sort on debut under Rules; suited by three miles.

Lough Derg (FR)

100   127

4-y-o b g Apple Tree (FR)-Asturias (FR) (Pistolet Bleu (IRE))
M C Pipe W Frewen

Placings:11521   (4839)
2003/04: 16¹GF, 16¹GS, 17⁵GS, 17⁹HY, 17¹GF,

	Starts	1st	2nd	3rd	Win & Pl
Hurdles	5	3	1	0	23923
Career Total	5	3	1	0	23923
127 4/04 Chel 2m1f	B Hdl			G-F	£9772
120 1/04 Wwck 2m	C Hdl			G-S	£7507
121 11/03 Newb 2m110y	D Hdl			G-F	£4823

Total win prize-money £22104

Going:	Sf: 0-1 GS: 1-2 Gd: 0-0 GF: - Fm: 2-2
Distance:	2m/2m3: 3-5 2m4-2m7: 0-0 3m+: 0-0
Track:	LH: 3-4 RH: 0-1 Tight: 0-0 Gall: 2-3
Aids:	Bl: 0-0 Vi: 0-0 Tstrap: 0-0 Ckp: 0-0
Best Rating:	127 4/04 Chel 2m1f gd-fm Hdl

Fair novice hurdler; suited by two miles and probably best on good ground.

Lough Rynn (IRE)

96   82

6-y-o b g Beneficial-Liffey Lady (Camden Town)
Miss H C Knight Carfield/Baxter

Placings:650-0P   (3271)
2003/04: 21⁰GS, 20⁷S,

	Starts	1st	2nd	3rd	Win & Pl
Hurdles	2	0	0	0	0
Career Total	5	0	0	0	0

Going:	Sf: 0-1 GS: 0-0 Gd: 0-1 GF: - Fm: 0-0
Distance:	2m/2m3: 0-0 2m4-2m7: 0-2 3m+: 0-0
Track:	LH: 0-1 RH: 0-1 Tight: 0-0 Gall: 0-0
Aids:	Bl: 0-0 Vi: 0-0 Tstrap: 0-0 Ckp: 0-0
Best Rating:	90 12/02 Hrfd 2m1f soft NHF

Has shown promise, but will be at his best over fences.

Loughcrew (IRE)

92   69

8-y-o ch g Good Thyne (USA)-Marys Course (Crash Course)
L Lungo Mrs Barbara Lungo

Placings:0000/0110P00/P-0000   (4911)
2003/04: 17⁰HY, 18⁰HY, 16⁹G, 16⁰S,

	Starts	1st	2nd	3rd	Win & Pl
Hurdles	4	0	0	0	
Career Total	17	2	0	0	8625
99 9/01 Gowr 3m	(0-109)HHdl			G-F	£4729
95 9/01 Clon 2m4f				G-F	£3895

Total win prize-money £8625

Going:	Sf: 0-3 GS: 0-0 Gd: 0-1 GF: - Fm: 0-0
Distance:	2m/2m3: 0-4 2m4-2m7: 0-0 3m+: 0-0
Track:	LH: 0-2 RH: 0-2 Tight: 0-2 Gall: 0-0
Aids:	Bl: 0-0 Vi: 0-0 Tstrap: 0-0 Ckp: 0-0
Best Rating:	99 9/01 Gowr 3m gd-fm Hdl

Louis Csaszar (IRE)

64   33

6-y-o b g Arctic Lord-Satlan's Treasure (IRE) (Treasure Hunter)
R F Fisher Great Head House Estates Limited

Placings:00   (4881)
2003/04: 17⁰G, 17⁰GS,

	Starts	1st	2nd	3rd	Win & Pl
NH Flat	1	0	0	0	0
Hurdles	1	0	0	0	0
Career Total	2	0	0	0	

Going: Sf: 0-0 GS: 0-1 Gd: 0-1 GF: - Fm: 0-0
Distance: 2m/2m3: 0-2 2m4-2m7: 0-0 3m+: 0-0
Track: LH: 0-0 RH: 0-2 Tight: 0-0 Gall: 0-0
Aids: Bl: 0-0 Vi: 0-0 Tstrap: 0-0 Ckp: 0-0
Best Rating: 28 4/04 Carl 2m1f   gd-sft Hdl

Louises Glory (IRE)

96(99h)   (93h)101

9-y-o ch g Executive Perk-Ring-Em-All (Decent Fellow)
D J Wintle D J Wintle

Placings:040242.0/4005100635/60-653   (3847)
2003/04: 16ᴿGS, 16ˢGS, 16ᴿGS,

	Starts	1st	2nd	3rd	Win & Pl
Chases	3	0	0	1	592
Career Total	22	1	2	2	9002

93 1/02 Punc 2m   (0-102)HHdl Y-S £5503
Total win prize-money £5503

Going: Sf: 0-0 GS: 0-3 Gd: 0-0 GF: - Fm: 0-0
Distance: 2m/2m3: 0-3 2m4-2m7: 0-0 3m+: 0-0
Track: LH: 0-1 RH: 0-2 Tight: 0-0 Gall: 0-1
Aids: Bl: 0-0 Vi: 0-0 Tstrap: 0-0 Ckp: 0-0
Best Rating: 104 11/00 Clon 2m   sft-hvy NHF

Ex-Irish; winning hurdler/plating-class chaser.

Loup (FR)

104   116

5-y-o b g Cyborg (FR)-Quintessence Iii (FR) (El Condor (FR))
J R Fanshawe Paul Green

Placings:20   (2837)
2003/04: 16²GS, 16ºG,

	Starts	1st	2nd	3rd	Win & Pl
Hurdles	2	0	1	0	1172
Career Total	2	0	1	0	1172

Going: Sf: 0-0 GS: 0-1 Gd: 0-1 GF: - Fm: 0-0
Distance: 2m/2m3: 0-2 2m4-2m7: 0-0 3m+: 0-0
Track: LH: 0-1 RH: 0-1 Tight: 0-0 Gall: 0-0
Aids: Bl: 0-0 Vi: 0-0 Tstrap: 0-0 Ckp: 0-0
Best Rating: 116 12/03 Asct 2m110y   good Hdl

Brother to Hors La Loi III; made encouraging debut at Haydock in November 2003 but well held in better grade at Ascot next time; handles easy ground.

Loup Du Sud (FR)

57f   23f

5-y-o b g Loup Solitaire (USA)-Jetty (FR) (Fabulous Dancer (USA))
S Pike Stewart Pike

Placings:00   (4291)
2003/04: 16ºS, 16ºG,

	Starts	1st	2nd	3rd	Win & Pl
NH Flat	2	0	0	0	
Career Total	2	0	0	0	

Going: Sf: 0-1 GS: 0-0 Gd: 0-0 GF: - Fm: 0-0
Distance: 2m/2m3: 0-2 2m4-2m7: 0-0 3m+: 0-0
Track: LH: 0-0 RH: 0-2 Tight: 0-0 Gall: 0-0
Aids: Bl: 0-0 Vi: 0-0 Tstrap: 0-0 Ckp: 0-0
Best Rating: 23 3/04 Winc 2m   good NHF

Love Kiss (IRE)

82

9-y-o b g Brief Truce (USA)-Pendulina (Prince Tenderfoot (USA))
M Dods K Knox

Placings:256501P/34P4P-P   (2376)
2003/04: 17ᴾGF,

	Starts	1st	2nd	3rd	Win & Pl
Hurdles	1	0	0	0	
Career Total	13	1	1	1	3916

89 1/02 Newc 2m   E(0-105)HHdl SFT £2646
Total win prize-money £2646

Going: Sf: 0-0 GS: 0-0 Gd: 0-0 GF: - Fm: 0-1
Distance: 2m/2m3: 0-1 2m4-2m7: 0-0 3m+: 0-0
Track: LH: 0-1 RH: 0-0 Tight: 0-1 Gall: 0-0
Aids: Bl: 0-0 Vi: 0-0 Tstrap: 0-1 Ckp: 0-0
Best Rating: 89 1/02 Newc 2m   soft Hdl

Love Mail

6-y-o b m Pursuit Of Love-Wizardry (Shirley Heights)
Simon Earle A Galvin

Placings:105/PP   (4931)
2003/04: 20ᴾHY, 22ᴾG,

	Starts	1st	2nd	3rd	Win & Pl
Hurdles	2	0	0	0	
Career Total	5	1	0	0	1589

85 1/02 Muss 2m   H NHF GD £1589
Total win prize-money £1589

Going: Sf: 0-1 GS: 0-0 Gd: 0-1 GF: - Fm: 0-0
Distance: 2m/2m3: 0-0 2m4-2m7: 0-2 3m+: 0-0
Track: LH: 0-2 RH: 0-0 Tight: 0-1 Gall: 0-0
Aids: Bl: 0-0 Vi: 0-0 Tstrap: 0-0 Ckp: 0-0
Best Rating: 88 3/02 Hayd 2m   good NHF

Love's Design (IRE)

90   59

7-y-o b/br g Pursuit Of Love-Cephista (Shirley Heights)
Miss S J Wilton John Pointon And Sons

Placings:56   (4537)
2003/04: 17ºGF, 16ºGS,

	Starts	1st	2nd	3rd	Win & Pl
Hurdles	2	0	0	0	0
Career Total	2	0	0	0	0

Going: Sf: 0-0 GS: 0-1 Gd: 0-0 GF: - Fm: 0-1
Distance: 2m/2m3: 0-2 2m4-2m7: 0-0 3m+: 0-0
Track: LH: 0-0 RH: 0-2 Tight: 0-0 Gall: 0-0
Aids: Bl: 0-0 Vi: 0-0 Tstrap: 0-0 Ckp: 0-0
Best Rating: 59 3/04 Hrfd 2m1f   gd-fm Hdl

Lovely Laura (IRE)

6-y-o ch m Port Lucaya-Miss Plum (Ardross)
C N Kellett D H & Mrs R E Muir

Placings:P   (2690)
2003/04: 16ºGS,

	Starts	1st	2nd	3rd	Win & Pl
NH Flat	1	0	0	0	
Career Total	1	0	0	0	

Going: Sf: 0-0 GS: 0-0 Gd: 0-0 GF: - Fm: 0-0
Distance: 2m/2m3: 0-1 2m4-2m7: 0-0 3m+: 0-0
Track: LH: 0-0 RH: 0-1 Tight: 0-0 Gall: 0-1
Aids: Bl: 0-0 Vi: 0-0 Tstrap: 0-0 Ckp: 0-0

Lovely Lulu

6-y-o b m Petrizzo-The Green Girls (USA) (Distinctive Pro (USA))
J C Tuck J C Tuck

Placings:00   (4692)
2003/04: 16ºGS, 17ºG,

	Starts	1st	2nd	3rd	Win & Pl
NH Flat	1	0	0	0	0
Hurdles	1	0	0	0	0
Career Total	2	0	0	0	

Going: Sf: 0-0 GS: 0-1 Gd: 0-1 GF: - Fm: 0-0
Distance: 2m/2m3: 0-2 2m4-2m7: 0-0 3m+: 0-0
Track: LH: 0-0 RH: 0-2 Tight: 0-0 Gall: 0-0
Aids: Bl: 0-0 Vi: 0-0 Tstrap: 0-0 Ckp: 0-0
Best Rating: 23 2/04 Kemp 2m   gd-sft NHF

Lovers Tale

93   78

6-y-o b g Pursuit Of Love-Kintail (Kris)
H M Kavanagh Mrs S Kavanagh

Placings:0/000-524F0   (3447)
2003/04: 16ºG, 20²GF, 16⁴GF, 20ºGF, 19ºGS,

	Starts	1st	2nd	3rd	Win & Pl
Hurdles	4	0	1	0	1270
Chases	1	0	0	0	0
Career Total	9	0	1	0	1270

Going: Sf: 0-0 GS: 0-1 Gd: 0-1 GF: - Fm: 0-3
Distance: 2m/2m3: 0-2 2m4-2m7: 0-3 3m+: 0-0
Track: LH: 0-1 RH: 0-4 Tight: 0-2 Gall: 0-0
Aids: Bl: 0-0 Vi: 0-0 Tstrap: 0-0 Ckp: 0-0
Best Rating: 78 11/03 Worc 2m4f   gd-fm Hdl

Lowe Go

102   94

4-y-o b g First Trump-Hotel California (IRE) (Last Tycoon)
Miss J S Davis (J G Portman 19/12) Miss J Davis

Placings:515002   (4506)
2003/04: 17ºG, 16¹GS, 16⁵GS, 16ºG, 16ºG, 19²GS,

	Starts	1st	2nd	3rd	Win & Pl
Hurdles	6	1	1	0	2629
Career Total	6	1	1	0	2629

88 12/03 Uttx 2m   G Hdl G-S £1967
Total win prize-money £1967

Going: Sf: 0-1 GS: 1-3 Gd: 0-2 GF: - Fm: 0-0
Distance: 2m/2m3: 1-5 2m4-2m7: 0-1 3m+: 0-0
Track: LH: 1-3 RH: 0-3 Tight: 0-1 Gall: 0-0
Aids: Bl: 0-0 Vi: 0-0 Tstrap: 0-0 Ckp: 0-0
Best Rating: 94 11/03 Folk 2m1f110y   good Hdl

Plating-class hurdler; showed ability on hurdles debut; changed hands for 5,800 gns after being all out to take seller at Uttoxeter in December 2003; beaten in handicap company subsequently.

Lowlander

90   **117+**

5-y-o b g Fuji Kiseki (JPN)-Lake Valley (USA) (Mr Prospector (USA))
D K Weld Dr Michael Smurfit

Placings:001116   (2131)
2003/04: 16⁰S, 20⁰Y, 18¹GF, 17¹F, 20¹GF, 16⁶GF,

	Starts	1st	2nd	3rd	Win & Pl
Hurdles	6	3	0	0	18973
Career Total	6	3	0	0	18973
117	10/03	Limk	2m4f		Hdl		G-F	£8441
114	8/03	Tral	2m1f		Hdl		FRM	£5600
100	8/03	Dpat	2m2f110y Hdl			G-F	£4480

Total win prize-money £18524

Going: Sf: 0-1 GS: 0-0 Gd: 0-0 GF: - Fm: 3-4
Distance: 2m/2m3: 2-4 2m4-2m7: 1-2 3m+: 0-0
Track: LH: 1-2 RH: 1-2 Tight: 0-0 Gall: 0-0
Aids: Bl: 3-5 Vi: 0-0 Tstrap: 0-0 Ckp: 0-0
Best Rating: 117 10/03 Limk 2m4f gd-fm Hdl

Progressive handicapper at up to two miles on the Flat in Ireland; progressive over hurdles, winning with ease on fast ground over the summer and autumn; stays two and a half miles; regularly blinkered.

Loy's Lad (IRE)

99(58h)   (64h)**91**

8-y-o b g Glacial Storm (USA)-Missing Note (Rarity)
Miss V Scott Miss Victoria Scott Jnr

Placings:060/00000000-413F2F   (2457)
2003/04: 16⁴G, 25¹GF, 20³GF, 25²G, 24⁴G,

	Starts	1st	2nd	3rd	Win & Pl
Chases	6	1	1	1	5907
Career Total	17	1	1	1	5907
91	10/03	Hexm	3m1f		E Ch		G-F	£2338

Total win prize-money £2338

Going: Sf: 0-0 GS: 0-0 Gd: 0-4 GF: - Fm: 1-2
Distance: 2m/2m3: 0-1 2m4-2m7: 0-1 3m+: 1-4
Track: LH: 1-4 RH: 0-0 Tight: 0-2 Gall: 0-1
Aids: Bl: 0-0 Vi: 0-0 Tstrap: 0-0 Ckp: 0-0
Best Rating: 91 11/03 Kels 3m1f good Ch

Modest form in Ireland but improved effort over three miles one furlong when winning uncompetitive Hexham novice event in October; goes on fast ground.

Loyola

93   **73**

4-y-o ch f New Reputation-Stay With Me Baby (Nicholas Bill)
Simon Earle Miss R Wakeford

Placings:P54446   (4929)
2003/04: 16⁶S, 17⁵GS, 16⁴HY, 21⁴G, 22⁴G, 18⁶G,

	Starts	1st	2nd	3rd	Win & Pl
Hurdles	6	0	0	0	548
Career Total	6	0	0	0	548

Going: Sf: 0-2 GS: 0-1 Gd: 0-3 GF: - Fm: 0-0
Distance: 2m/2m3: 0-4 2m4-2m7: 0-2 3m+: 0-0
Track: LH: 0-2 RH: 0-4 Tight: 0-2 Gall: 0-0
Aids: Bl: 0-0 Vi: 0-0 Tstrap: 0-0 Ckp: 0-0
Best Rating: 73 4/04 Winc 2m6f good Hdl

Poor novice hurdler.

Lozzy Lee (IRE)

94   **100+**

6-y-o b g Zaffaran (USA)-Amazing Lee (IRE) (Amazing Bust)
M Scudamore Mrs S Tainton

Placings:024-3F   (2851)
2003/04: 20³G, 19²GS,

	Starts	1st	2nd	3rd	Win & Pl
Hurdles	2	0	0	1	383
Career Total	5	0	1	1	1061

Going: Sf: 0-0 GS: 0-1 Gd: 0-1 GF: - Fm: 0-0
Distance: 2m/2m3: 0-2 2m4-2m7: 0-2 3m+: 0-0
Track: LH: 0-1 RH: 0-1 Tight: 0-0 Gall: 0-0
Aids: Bl: 0-0 Vi: 0-0 Tstrap: 0-0 Ckp: 0-0
Best Rating: 102 12/02 Plum 2m2f heavy NHF

Moderate novice hurdler; stays two and a half miles; acts on good ground.

Lubinas (IRE)

109   **97**

5-y-o b g Grand Lodge (USA)-Liebesgirl (Konigsstuhl (GER))
F Jordan Paul Ratcliffe

Placings:054F02   (4917)
2003/04: 20⁰GS, 16²S, 19⁴G, 26⁶GS, 21⁰GS, 20²GS,

	Starts	1st	2nd	3rd	Win & Pl
Hurdles	6	0	1	0	1632
Career Total	6	0	1	0	1632

Going: Sf: 0-1 GS: 0-4 Gd: 0-1 GF: - Fm: 0-0
Distance: 2m/2m3: 0-1 2m4-2m7: 0-4 3m+: 0-0
Track: LH: 0-4 RH: 0-2 Tight: 0-0 Gall: 0-1
Aids: Bl: 0-0 Vi: 0-0 Tstrap: 0-0 Ckp: 0-0
Best Rating: 97 4/04 Worc 2m4f gd-sft Hdl

Moderate form in novice hurdles; narrowly beaten in handicap in April; stays two and a half miles.

Lucifer Bleu (FR)

104   **109**

5-y-o b g Kadalko (FR)-Figa Dancer (FR) (Bandinelli (FR))
M C Pipe (G Cherel 10/6) A J White

Placings:U105520   (4838)
2003/04: 17⁰VS, 17¹HY, 18⁰VS, 19⁵G, 17⁵S, 19²G, 24⁰GF,

	Starts	1st	2nd	3rd	Win & Pl
Hurdles	7	1	1	0	13269
Career Total	7	1	1	0	13269
	5/03	Autl	2m1f110y Hdl			HVY	£11221

Total win prize-money £11221

Going: Sf: 1-2 GS: 0-0 Gd: 0-2 GF: - Fm: 0-1
Distance: 2m/2m3: 1-4 2m4-2m7: 0-2 3m+: 0-1
Track: LH: 0-1 RH: 0-3 Tight: 0-3 Gall: 0-1
Aids: Bl: 0-0 Vi: 0-0 Tstrap: 0-0 Ckp: 0-0
Best Rating: 109 3/04 Tntn 2m3f110y good Hdl

Ex-French hurdles winner; stays two and a half miles.

Lucken Howe

5-y-o b g Keen-Gilston Lass (Majestic Streak)
Mrs J K M Oliver Mrs J K M Oliver

Placings:00   (4885)
2003/04: 17⁰G, 17⁰GS,

	Starts	1st	2nd	3rd	Win & Pl
NH Flat	2	0	0	0	
Career Total	2	0	0	0	

Going: Sf: 0-0 GS: 0-1 Gd: 0-1 GF: - Fm: 0-0
Distance: 2m/2m3: 0-2 2m4-2m7: 0-0 3m+: 0-0
Track: LH: 0-0 RH: 0-2 Tight: 0-0 Gall: 0-0
Aids: Bl: 0-0 Vi: 0-0 Tstrap: 0-0 Ckp: 0-0

Lucky Archer

99   **87**

11-y-o b g North Briton-Preobrajenska (Double Form)
Ian Williams Andrew & Philippa Wyer

Placings:43/U60/20/50   (1756)
2003/04: 17⁵GF, 16⁰G,

	Starts	1st	2nd	3rd	Win & Pl
Hurdles	2	0	0	0	0
Career Total	9	0	1	1	1014

Going: Sf: 0-0 GS: 0-0 Gd: 0-0 GF: - Fm: 0-1
Distance: 2m/2m3: 0-2 2m4-2m7: 0-0 3m+: 0-0
Track: LH: 0-1 RH: 0-1 Tight: 0-1 Gall: 0-0
Aids: Bl: 0-0 Vi: 0-0 Tstrap: 0-0 Ckp: 0-0
Best Rating: 88 4/97 Ludl 2m firm Hdl

Lucky Bay (IRE)

108   (119h)**139**

8-y-o b g Convinced-Current Liability (Caribo)
Ms Bridget Nicholls Executive Racing II

Placings:6/512P/F22156P-62U4   (3380)
2003/04: 24⁶GF, 25²G, 29⁴G, 25⁴S,

	Starts	1st	2nd	3rd	Win & Pl
Chases	4	0	1	0	3764
Career Total	16	2	4	0	35610
139	11/02	Newb	3m	A Ch		SFT	£17400
114	11/01	Winc	2m6f	C Hdl		G-F	£5343

Total win prize-money £22743

Going: Sf: 0-1 GS: 0-0 Gd: 0-2 GF: - Fm: 0-1
Distance: 2m/2m3: 0-0 2m4-2m7: 0-0 3m+: 0-4
Track: LH: 0-2 RH: 0-2 Tight: 0-0 Gall: 0-0
Aids: Bl: 0-0 Vi: 0-0 Tstrap: 0-0 Ckp: 0-0
Best Rating: 139 11/02 Newb 3m soft Ch

Useful chaser; unlucky at Cheltenham in November 2002, but won a Grade Two event at Newbury next time; has disappointed since, although seasonal return at Wetherby was a good effort; stays three miles; best on good ground; likes to race prominently.

Lucky Catch (IRE)

6-y-o b g Safety Catch (USA)-Lucky Monday (Lucky Wednesday)
A Crook Lucky Catch Partnership

Placings:0-PPFP   (4259)
2003/04: 23⁰G, 24⁰HY, 16⁶G, 25⁰GF,

	Starts	1st	2nd	3rd	Win & Pl
Hurdles	2	0	0	0	0
Chases	2	0	0	0	0
Career Total	5	0	0	0	

Going: Sf: 0-1 GS: 0-0 Gd: 0-2 GF: - Fm: 0-1
Distance: 2m/2m3: 0-1 2m4-2m7: 0-1 3m+: 0-2
Track: LH: 0-3 RH: 0-1 Tight: 0-1 Gall: 0-1

Aids: Bl: 0-0 Vi: 0-0 Tstrap: 0-0 Ckp: 0-0
Best Rating: 87 3/03 Carl 2m1f gd-sft NHF

Lucky Clover

105   **119**

12-y-o ch g Push On-Winning Clover (Winden)
C L Tizzard Mrs P O Perry

Placings:F0P0P/1P2211221P/P40400-P0PP3142P25

                                                             (3255)
2003/04: 33PG, 25UGF, 26PG, 26FGF, 243GF, 261GF, 26XGF, 262GF, 26PGF, 242GF, 245G,

	Starts	1st	2nd	3rd	Win & Pl
Chases	11	1	2	1	9762
Career Total	32	5	6	1	48865

113 8/03 NAbb	3m2f110yF(0-100)HCh	G-F	£4690
127 11/01 Chel	3m7f	B Ch	GD	£21157
116 8/01 NAbb	3m2f110yE(0-105)HCh	G-F	£3410
120 8/01 NAbb	3m2f110yE Ch	GD	£3376
90 5/01 Extr	3m7f110yE Ch	FRM	£4166
		Total win prize-money £36803

Going:	Sf: 0-0 GS: 0-0 Gd: 0-3 GF: - Fm: 1-8
Distance:	2m/2m3: 0-0 2m4-2m7: 0-0 **3m+:** 1-11
Track:	**LH:** 1-7 RH: 0-4 Tight: 1-6 Gall: 0-0
Aids:	Bl: 0-1 Vi: 0-0 Tstrap: 0-0 Ckp: 0-0
Best Rating:	127 11/01 Chel 3m7f good Ch

Moderate chaser; won the Sporting Index Cross Country Chase at Cheltenham in November 2001; stays three miles two on a conventional track; acts well on fast ground; has worn blinkers.

Lucky Duck

107   **115**

7-y-o ch g Minster Son-Petroc Concert (Tina's Pet)
Mrs A Hamilton Ian Hamilton

Placings:0/0-PP3U11   (4881)
2003/04: 20PGS, 21PGS, 173GS, 17UG, 161G, 171GS,

	Starts	1st	2nd	3rd	Win & Pl
Hurdles	6	2	0	1	7979
Career Total	8	2	0	1	7979

110 4/04 Carl	2m1f	E Hdl	G-S	£3770
100 4/04 Kels	2m110y E Hdl	GD	£3679
		Total win prize-money £7449

Going:	Sf: 0-0 GS: 1-4 Gd: 1-2 GF: - Fm: 0-0
Distance:	**2m/2m3:** 2-4 2m4-2m7: 0-2 3m+: 0-0
Track:	**LH:** 1-5 RH: 1-1 **Tight:** 1-4 Gall: 0-0
Aids:	Bl: 0-0 Vi: 0-0 Tstrap: 0-0 Ckp: 0-0
Best Rating:	110 4/04 Carl 2m1f gd-sft Hdl

Fair novice hurdler; off the mark at Kelso in April 2004; followed up at Carlisle two weeks later; best going right-handed; suited by two miles on good ground.

Lucky Heather (IRE)

96   **66**

7-y-o b m Soviet Lad (USA)-Idrak (Young Generation)
R J Baker Graham Brown

Placings:650P/40540-46P000   (4266)
2003/04: 174G, 16FGF, 16FG, 17GGF, 19UG, 16AGF,

	Starts	1st	2nd	3rd	Win & Pl
Hurdles	6	0	0	0	0
Career Total	15	0	0	0	0

Going:	Sf: 0-0 GS: 0-0 Gd: 0-2 GF: - Fm: 0-4
Distance:	2m/2m3: 0-5 2m4-2m7: 0-1 3m+: 0-0
Track:	LH: 0-3 RH: 0-3 Tight: 0-3 Gall: 0-0

Aids: Bl: 0-1 Vi: 0-0 Tstrap: 0-0 Ckp: 0-0
Best Rating: 82 11/01 Ludl 2m gd-fm Hdl

Moderate maiden over hurdles.

Lucky Joe (IRE)

(83c)   (73c) **73**

11-y-o b g Denel (FR)-Breezy Dawn (Kemal (FR))
J White Nick Quesnel

Placings:P/PP4/36-PP   (2854)
2003/04: 25PGF, 26PGS,

	Starts	1st	2nd	3rd	Win & Pl
Hurdles	1	0	0	0	0
Chases	1	0	0	0	0
Career Total	8	0	0	1	520

Going:	Sf: 0-0 GS: 0-1 Gd: 0-0 GF: - Fm: 0-1
Distance:	2m/2m3: 0-2 2m4-2m7: 0-0 3m+: 0-2
Track:	LH: 0-0 RH: 0-2 Tight: 0-0 Gall: 0-0
Aids:	Bl: 0-0 Vi: 0-0 Tstrap: 0-0 Ckp: 0-0
Best Rating:	73 6/02 Ctml 2m6f heavy Hdl

Lucky Largo (IRE)

93   **87+**

4-y-o b/br g Key Of Luck (USA)-Lingering Melody (IRE) (Nordico (USA))
S Gollings (Kevin Prendergast 25/5) J B Webb

Placings:P6P   (4440)
2003/04: 17PHY, 16FG, 16PGS,

	Starts	1st	2nd	3rd	Win & Pl
Hurdles	3	0	0	0	0
Career Total	3	0	0	0	0

Going:	Sf: 0-1 GS: 0-1 Gd: 0-1 GF: - Fm: 0-0
Distance:	2m/2m3: 0-3 2m4-2m7: 0-0 3m+: 0-0
Track:	LH: 0-1 RH: 0-2 Tight: 0-2 Gall: 0-0
Aids:	Bl: 0-2 Vi: 0-0 Tstrap: 0-0 Ckp: 0-0
Best Rating:	87 2/04 Kemp 2m good Hdl

Modest novice hurdler; maiden on the Flat at around a mile.

Lucky Leader (IRE)

104   **95+**

9-y-o b g Supreme Leader-Lucky House (Pollerton)
N R Mitchell Michael Green

Placings:60/PP23F-1PP3P   (4633)
2003/04: 231G, 23PS, 24PG, 23SGS, 24PG,

	Starts	1st	2nd	3rd	Win & Pl
Chases	5	1	0	1	4809
Career Total	12	1	1	2	7594
95 12/03 Extr	2m7f110yE(0-105)HCh	GD	3916
		Total win prize-money £3916

Going:	Sf: 0-1 GS: 0-1 Gd: 1-3 GF: - Fm: 0-0
Distance:	2m/2m3: 0-0 2m4-2m7: 0-0 **3m+:** 1-5
Track:	**LH:** 0-0 **RH:** 1-5 Tight: 0-0 Gall: 0-0
Aids:	Bl: 0-2 Vi: 0-0 Tstrap: 0-0 Ckp: 0-0
Best Rating:	95 3/04 Extr 2m7f110y gd-sft Ch

Moderate novice chaser; stays three miles; acts on soft ground.

Lucky Leo

67   **55**

4-y-o b g Muhtarram (USA)-Wrong Bride (Reprimand)

Ian Williams (M R Channon 27/5) B and S Vaughan

Placings:6   (0919)
2003/04: 17RGF,

	Starts	1st	2nd	3rd	Win & Pl
Hurdles	1	0	0	0	0
Career Total	1	0	0	0	0

Going:	Sf: 0-0 GS: 0-0 Gd: 0-0 GF: - Fm: 0-0
Distance:	2m/2m3: 0-1 2m4-2m7: 0-0 3m+: 0-1
Track:	LH: 0-0 RH: 0-1 Tight: 0-1 Gall: 0-0
Aids:	Bl: 0-0 Vi: 0-0 Tstrap: 0-0 Ckp: 0-0
Best Rating:	55 7/03 MRas 2m1f110y gd-fm Hdl

Lucky Luk (FR)

82f   **73f**

5-y-o b g Lights Out (FR)-Citronelle II (FR) (Kedellic (FR))
K C Bailey Mrs E A Kellar

Placings:00   (4291)
2003/04: 16SGS, 16PG,

	Starts	1st	2nd	3rd	Win & Pl
NH Flat	2	0	0	0	0
Career Total	2	0	0	0	0

Going:	Sf: 0-0 GS: 0-1 Gd: 0-1 GF: - Fm: 0-0
Distance:	2m/2m3: 0-2 2m4-2m7: 0-0 3m+: 0-0
Track:	LH: 0-1 RH: 0-1 Tight: 0-0 Gall: 0-0
Aids:	Bl: 0-0 Vi: 0-0 Tstrap: 0-0 Ckp: 0-0
Best Rating:	73 3/04 Winc 2m good NHF

Lucky Mosco

87f   **70f**

7-y-o b g Lucky Wednesday-Gouly Duff (Party Mink)
Jonjo O'Neill Mr & Mrs M R M Schofield

Placings:0   (1019)
2003/04: 16RGF,

	Starts	1st	2nd	3rd	Win & Pl
NH Flat	1	0	0	0	0
Career Total	1	0	0	0	0

Going:	Sf: 0-0 GS: 0-0 Gd: 0-0 GF: - Fm: 0-1
Distance:	2m/2m3: 0-1 2m4-2m7: 0-0 3m+: 0-0
Track:	LH: 0-1 RH: 0-0 Tight: 0-0 Gall: 0-0
Aids:	Bl: 0-0 Vi: 0-0 Tstrap: 0-0 Ckp: 0-0
Best Rating:	70 8/03 Worc 2m gd-fm NHF

Lucky Nomad

79   **65+**

8-y-o br g Nomadic Way (USA)-Daleena (Dalesa)
R Ford N Morgan

Placings:P446P-3   (1672)
2003/04: 25GF,

	Starts	1st	2nd	3rd	Win & Pl
Hurdles	1	0	0	1	316
Career Total	6	0	0	1	931

Going:	Sf: 0-0 GS: 0-0 Gd: 0-0 GF: - Fm: 0-1
Distance:	2m/2m3: 0-0 2m4-2m7: 0-0 3m+: 0-1
Track:	LH: 0-1 RH: 0-0 Tight: 0-0 Gall: 0-0
Aids:	Bl: 0-0 Vi: 0-0 Tstrap: 0-0 Ckp: 0-0
Best Rating:	65 10/03 Weth 3m1f firm Hdl

Plating-class hurdler; former pointer; stays 3m.

Lucky Pete

89   **70**

7-y-o b g Lyphento (USA)-Clare's Choice (Pragmatic)
P J Jones P J Jones

Placings:06660100P   (4790)
2003/04: 16⁰G, 22⁶GF, 21⁵GF, 19⁶GF, 24⁰GF, 22¹HY, 22⁰GS, 22⁰G, 21⁵G,

	Starts	1st	2nd	3rd	Win & Pl
NH Flat	1	0	0	0	0
Hurdles	8	1	0	0	2310
Career Total	9	1	0	0	2310
70	1/04	Folk	2m6f110yG(0-90)HHdl	HVY	£2310

Total win prize-money £2310

Going:	Sf: 1-1 GS: 0-1 Gd: 0-3 GF: - Fm: 0-4
Distance:	2m/2m3: 0-2 2m4-2m7: 1-6 3m+: 0-1
Track:	LH: 0-4 RH: 1-5 Tight: 1-4 Gall: 0-3
Aids:	Bl: 0-0 Vi: 0-0 Tstrap: 0-0 Ckp: 0-1
Best Rating:	70 1/04 Folk 2m6f110y heavy Hdl

Plating-class hurdler; stays two mile six and acts with cut in the ground; suited by forcing tactics.

Lucky Sinna (IRE)

102(89h)   (119h)**100+**

8-y-o b g Insan (USA)-Bit Of A Chance (Lord Ha Ha)
B G Powell John Plackett

Placings:3/444/2343F/2-22   (4791)
2003/04: 24²GS, 20²G,

	Starts	1st	2nd	3rd	Win & Pl
Chases	2	0	2	0	2938
Career Total	12	0	4	3	9565

Going:	Sf: 0-0 GS: 0-1 Gd: 0-1 GF: - Fm: 0-0
Distance:	2m/2m3: 0-0 2m4-2m7: 0-1 3m+: 0-0
Track:	LH: 0-2 RH: 0-0 Tight: 0-2 Gall: 0-0
Aids:	Bl: 0-0 Vi: 0-0 Tstrap: 0-0 Ckp: 0-0
Best Rating:	126 4/00 Asct 2m110y soft NHF

Lightly-raced chaser/hurdler; stays three miles; acts on fast and easy ground.

Lucky Uno

(80h)   (47h)

8-y-o b g Rock City-Free Skip (Free State)
John A Harris H G Norman

Placings:PP/P000P   (4960)
2003/04: 16⁵G, 16⁰G, 17⁰G, 20⁰GS, 20⁵GS,

	Starts	1st	2nd	3rd	Win & Pl
Hurdles	4	0	0	0	0
Chases	1	0	0	0	0
Career Total	7	0	0	0	0

Going:	Sf: 0-1 GS: 0-3 Gd: 0-1 GF: - Fm: 0-0
Distance:	2m/2m3: 0-3 2m4-2m7: 0-2 3m+: 0-0
Track:	LH: 0-1 RH: 0-4 Tight: 0-2 Gall: 0-1
Aids:	Bl: 0-0 Vi: 0-0 Tstrap: 0-0 Ckp: 0-0
Best Rating:	47 3/04 MRas 2m1f110y good Hdl

Luckycharm (FR)

71   **53**

5-y-o ch g Villez (USA)-Hitifly (FR) (Murmure (FR))
R Dickin Robin's Rebels

Placings:0P0   (4812)
2003/04: 16⁰GF, 19⁵G, 16⁵G,

	Starts	1st	2nd	3rd	Win & Pl
NH Flat	1	0	0	0	0
Hurdles	2	0	0	0	0
Career Total	3	0	0	0	

Going:	Sf: 0-0 GS: 0-0 Gd: 0-2 GF: - Fm: 0-1
Distance:	2m/2m3: 0-2 2m4-2m7: 0-1 3m+: 0-0
Track:	LH: 0-1 RH: 0-1 Tight: 0-0 Gall: 0-1
Aids:	Bl: 0-0 Vi: 0-0 Tstrap: 0-0 Ckp: 0-0
Best Rating:	53 4/04 Chep 2m110y good Hdl

Lucy Lancaster

72   **58**

9-y-o b m Elegant Monarch-Lancaster Rose (Canadel Ii)
Mrs G Harvey Brian Hurst

Placings:B-5U0   (0681)
2003/04: 16⁵GF, 20ᵁGF, 24⁰GF,

	Starts	1st	2nd	3rd	Win & Pl
Hurdles	3	0	0	0	0
Career Total	4	0	0	0	0

Going:	Sf: 0-0 GS: 0-0 Gd: 0-0 GF: - Fm: 0-3
Distance:	2m/2m3: 0-1 2m4-2m7: 0-1 3m+: 0-1
Track:	LH: 0-2 RH: 0-1 Tight: 0-0 Gall: 0-0
Aids:	Bl: 0-0 Vi: 0-0 Tstrap: 0-0 Ckp: 0-0
Best Rating:	58 5/03 Winc 2m gd-fm Hdl

Ludere (IRE)

93   **98**

9-y-o ch g Desse Zenny (USA)-White Jasmin (Jalmood (USA))
B J Llewellyn B W Parren

Placings:65/16406/430132/2143/056610342P-P33F603   (4750)
2003/04: 24⁵PS, 22³HY, 20³S, 22⁶HY, 21⁶G, 24⁰G, 21³G,

	Starts	1st	2nd	3rd	Win & Pl
Hurdles	7	0	0	3	1114
Career Total	34	4	3	7	14945
98	12/02	Leic	2m4f110yE(0-105)HHdl	HVY	£3474
98	12/01	Tntn	2m3f110yG Hdl	G-S	£1596
97	12/00	Tntn	2m3f110yG Hdl	SFT	£1533
89	7/99	Sedg	2m1f	E Hdl	G-F	£2302

Total win prize-money £8906

Going:	Sf: 0-4 GS: 0-0 Gd: 0-3 GF: - Fm: 0-0
Distance:	2m/2m3: 0-2 2m4-2m7: 0-5 3m+: 0-2
Track:	LH: 0-1 RH: 0-6 Tight: 0-4 Gall: 0-1
Aids:	Bl: 0-2 Vi: 0-0 Tstrap: 0-0 Ckp: 0-1
Best Rating:	98 3/03 Bang 3m soft Hdl

Modest hurdler, stays three miles; acts in soft ground.

Luftikus (GER)

97   **77**

7-y-o ch g Formidable (USA)-La Paz (GER) (Roi Dagobert)
A G Hobbs Furnish With Abbey

Placings:300-062   (1189)
2003/04: 17⁰GS, 24⁶GF, 24²GF,

	Starts	1st	2nd	3rd	Win & Pl
Hurdles	3	0	1	0	838
Career Total	6	0	1	1	1266

Going:	Sf: 0-0 GS: 0-1 Gd: 0-0 GF: - Fm: 0-2
Distance:	2m/2m3: 0-1 2m4-2m7: 0-0 3m+: 0-2
Track:	LH: 0-2 RH: 0-1 Tight: 0-0 Gall: 0-0

Aids:	Bl: 0-0 Vi: 0-0 Tstrap: 0-0 Ckp: 0-0
Best Rating:	83 8/03 Worc 3m gd-fm Hdl

Plating-class hurdler; second to the progressive Wee Danny in 3m Conditional Jockeys' Novices' handicap at Worcester August 2003; acts on fast.

Luke After Me (IRE)

86   **65+**

4-y-o b g Victory Note (USA)-Summit Talk (Head For Heights)
G A Swinbank (N Waggott 3/12) Miss T Waggott

Placings:0000   (3337)
2003/04: 16⁰G, 16⁰GF, 16⁰GS, 16⁰GS,

	Starts	1st	2nd	3rd	Win & Pl
Hurdles	4	0	0	0	0
Career Total	4	0	0	0	0

Going:	Sf: 0-0 GS: 0-2 Gd: 0-1 GF: - Fm: 0-1
Distance:	2m/2m3: 0-4 2m4-2m7: 0-0 3m+: 0-0
Track:	LH: 0-4 RH: 0-0 Tight: 0-3 Gall: 0-0
Aids:	Bl: 0-0 Vi: 0-0 Tstrap: 0-0 Ckp: 0-0
Best Rating:	65 11/03 Catt 2m gd-fm Hdl

Lumaca (IRE)

(85h)   (88h)**70**

9-y-o b g Riberetto-Broken Mirror (Push On)
C Roberts C G Bolton

Placings:046/5602/15P0/6P63-P   (0056)
2003/04: 25⁰GS,

	Starts	1st	2nd	3rd	Win & Pl
Chases	1	0	0	0	
Career Total	16	1	1	1	4231
88	1/02	Tntn	3m110y E(0-110)HHdl	SFT	£2593

Total win prize-money £2594

Going:	Sf: 0-0 GS: 0-1 Gd: 0-0 GF: - Fm: 0-0
Distance:	2m/2m3: 0-0 2m4-2m7: 0-0 3m+: 0-1
Track:	LH: 0-0 RH: 0-1 Tight: 0-0 Gall: 0-0
Aids:	Bl: 0-0 Vi: 0-0 Tstrap: 0-0 Ckp: 0-0
Best Rating:	103 2/00 Kemp 2m soft NHF

Plating-class novice chaser; stays well.

Lumyno (FR)

84f   **76f**

5-y-o b g Lute Antique (FR)-Framboline (FR) (Royal Charter (FR))
S E H Sherwood Mrs Yvonne S Kennedy

Placings:00   (4636)
2003/04: 16⁰GS, 17⁰G,

	Starts	1st	2nd	3rd	Win & Pl
NH Flat	2	0	0	0	
Career Total	2	0	0	0	

Going:	Sf: 0-0 GS: 0-1 Gd: 0-1 GF: - Fm: 0-0
Distance:	2m/2m3: 0-2 2m4-2m7: 0-0 3m+: 0-0
Track:	LH: 0-0 RH: 0-1 Tight: 0-0 Gall: 0-0
Aids:	Bl: 0-0 Vi: 0-0 Tstrap: 0-0 Ckp: 0-0
Best Rating:	76 2/04 Sand 2m110y gd-sft NHF

Lunar Fox

83f   **75f**

5-y-o b m Roselier (FR)-Leinthall Fox (Deep Run)

J L Needham   Miss Joanna Needham

Placings:0   (4846)
2003/04: 17⁰G,

	Starts	1st	2nd	3rd	Win & Pl
NH Flat	1	0	0	0	
Career Total	1	0	0	0	

Going:	Sf: 0-0 GS: 0-0 Gd: 0-1 GF: - Fm: 0-0
Distance:	2m/2m3: 0-1 2m4-2m7: 0-0 3m+: 0-0
Track:	LH: 0-1 RH: 0-0 Tight: 0-1 Gall: 0-1
Aids:	Bl: 0-0 Vi: 0-0 Tstrap: 0-0 Ckp: 0-0
Best Rating:	75 4/04 Chel 2m1f good NHF

Lunar Leader (IRE)

4-y-o b f Mujadil (USA)-Moon River (FR) (Groom Dancer (USA))
M J Gingell (Mrs L Stubbs 19/9) Mrs L Bangs

Placings:P   (3432)
2003/04: 16ᴾGS,

	Starts	1st	2nd	3rd	Win & Pl
Hurdles	1	0	0	0	
Career Total	1	0	0	0	

Going:	Sf: 0-0 GS: 0-1 Gd: 0-0 GF: - Fm: 0-0
Distance:	2m/2m3: 0-1 2m4-2m7: 0-0 3m+: 0-0
Track:	LH: 0-1 RH: 0-0 Tight: 0-1 Gall: 0-0
Aids:	Bl: 0-0 Vi: 0-0 Tstrap: 0-0 Ckp: 0-1

Lunar Lord

95   **101**

8-y-o b g Elmaamul (USA)-Cache (Bustino)
D Burchell Brian Williams

Placings:2515/54/0-035   (4735)
2003/04: 16⁰S, 16³GF, 17⁵G,

	Starts	1st	2nd	3rd	Win & Pl
Hurdles	3	0	0	1	800
Career Total	10	1	0	1	3918
105 1/01 Chep 2m110y E Hdl				G-S	£2555

Total win prize-money £2555

Going:	Sf: 0-1 GS: 0-0 Gd: 0-1 GF: - Fm: 0-1
Distance:	2m/2m3: 0-3 2m4-2m7: 0-0 3m+: 0-0
Track:	LH: 0-1 RH: 0-1 Tight: 0-1 Gall: 0-0
Aids:	Bl: 0-0 Vi: 0-0 Tstrap: 0-0 Ckp: 0-0
Best Rating:	105 1/01 Chep 2m110y gd-sft Hdl

Moderate hurdler; acts on any ground.

Lunar Maxwell

85   **(99h)106**

9-y-o b g Dancing High-Pauper Moon (Pauper)
J I A Charlton J W Robson

Placings:4443/62400/62132/3245-3402   (4075)
2003/04: 23³G, 24⁴G, 24⁰HY, 24²F,

	Starts	1st	2nd	3rd	Win & Pl
Chases	4	0	1	4	2182
Career Total	22	1	5	4	10088
93 11/01 Weth 2m7f F(0-100)HHdl				GD	£2506

Total win prize-money £2506

Going:	Sf: 0-1 GS: 0-0 Gd: 0-2 GF: - Fm: 0-1
Distance:	2m/2m3: 0-0 2m4-2m7: 0-0 3m+: 0-4
Track:	LH: 0-2 RH: 0-1 Tight: 0-1 Gall: 0-2
Aids:	Bl: 0-0 Vi: 0-0 Tstrap: 0-0 Ckp: 0-1

Best Rating: 106   11/02   Weth   3m1f   good   Ch

Moderate novice chaser; probably stays 3m 6f; suited by good ground.

Lunardi (IRE)

94(87h)   **75**

6-y-o b g Indian Ridge-Gold Tear (USA) (Tejano (USA))
D L Williams Miss L Horner

Placings:5421565046/30-34U00   (4306)
2003/04: 20³GF, 21⁴GF, 20ᵁGF, 25⁰G, 24⁰G,

	Starts	1st	2nd	3rd	Win & Pl
Chases	5	0	0	1	519
Career Total	17	1	1	2	5073
102 11/01 Hrfd 2m1f E Hdl				GD	£2471

Total win prize-money £2471

Going:	Sf: 0-0 GS: 0-0 Gd: 0-2 GF: - Fm: 0-3
Distance:	2m/2m3: 0-2 2m4-2m7: 0-1 3m+: 0-2
Track:	LH: 0-0 RH: 0-4 Tight: 0-1 Gall: 0-1
Aids:	Bl: 0-0 Vi: 0-0 Tstrap: 0-0 Ckp: 0-1
Best Rating:	102 11/01 Hrfd 2m1f good Hdl

Moderate hunter chaser/hurdler; best on a sound surface; yet to prove he stays three miles.

Luneray (FR)

105(84h)   **(86h)108+**

5-y-o b m Poplar Bluff-Casandre (FR) (Montorselli)
P F Nicholls (T Civel 10/11) Sandicroft Stud I

Placings:25-1U12212   (4811)
2003/04: 18¹HO, 19ᵁVS, 19¹VS, 16²HY, 22²GS, 19¹G, 24²G,

	Starts	1st	2nd	3rd	Win & Pl
Hurdles	2	1	1	0	24471
Chases	5	2	2	0	20734
Career Total	9	3	4	0	52900
108 4/04 Hrfd 2m3f E Ch				GD	£5128
11/03 Engh 2m3f Ch				VS	£13091
10/03 Autl 2m2f Hdl				HLD	£23377

Total win prize-money £41597

Going:	Sf: 0-1 GS: 0-0 Gd: 1-3 GF: - Fm: 0-0
Distance:	**2m/2m3: 3-5** 2m4-2m7: 0-1 3m+: 0-1
Track:	LH: 0-2 **RH: 1-1** Tight: 0-1 Gall: 0-0
Aids:	Bl: 0-0 Vi: 0-0 Tstrap: 0-0 Ckp: 0-0
Best Rating:	108 4/04 Hrfd 2m3f good Ch

Modest chaser; winner of a hurdle race and a chase in France; well beaten when runner-up in mares' only novices' hurdle on debut here at Uttoxeter in January 2004; won 2m 3f novice chase at Hereford April 2004; did not appear to quite get home when stepped up to three miles next time; acts on good and soft ground.

Lupin (FR)

92   **94**

5-y-o b g Luchiroverte (IRE)-Amarante Ii (FR) (Brezzo (FR))
F Doumen E Puerari

Placings:5016-00P   (3925)
2003/04: 17⁰S, 16⁰G, 20ᴾGS,

	Starts	1st	2nd	3rd	Win & Pl
Hurdles	3	0	0	0	0
Career Total	7	1	0	0	11221
4/03 Engh 2m110y Hdl				VS	£11221

Total win prize-money £11221

Going:	Sf: 0-1 GS: 0-1 Gd: 0-1 GF: - Fm: 0-0
Distance:	2m/2m3: 0-2 2m4-2m7: 0-1 3m+: 0-0
Track:	LH: 0-0 RH: 0-2 Tight: 0-0 Gall: 0-0
Aids:	Bl: 0-0 Vi: 0-0 Tstrap: 0-2 Ckp: 0-0

Best Rating: 97   12/03   Kemp   2m   good   Hdl

Luristan (IRE)

74   **41**

4-y-o b g Pennekamp (USA)-Linnga (IRE) (Shardari)
S T Lewis Simon T Lewis

Placings:60305   (3641)
2003/04: 14⁶G, 12⁰G, 16³HY, 17⁰GS, 17⁵S,

	Starts	1st	2nd	3rd	Win & Pl
NH Flat	4	0	0	1	336
Hurdles	1	0	0	0	0
Career Total	5	0	0	1	336

Going:	Sf: 0-2 GS: 0-1 Gd: 0-2 GF: - Fm: 0-0
Distance:	2m/2m3: 0-3 2m4-2m7: 0-0 3m+: 0-0
Track:	LH: 0-1 RH: 0-3 Tight: 0-0 Gall: 0-0
Aids:	Bl: 0-0 Vi: 0-0 Tstrap: 0-0 Ckp: 0-0
Best Rating:	74 11/03 Wwck 1m6f good NHF

Lustral Du Seuil (FR)

106   **113+**

5-y-o b g Sassanian (USA)-Bella Tennise (FR) (Rhapsodien)
N J Henderson (M Boudot 5/5) W J Brown

Placings:P320   (4324)
2003/04: 16⁶G, 17³S, 16²G, 20⁰S,

	Starts	1st	2nd	3rd	Win & Pl
Hurdles	4	0	1	1	1552
Career Total	4	0	1	1	1552

Going:	Sf: 0-2 GS: 0-0 Gd: 0-2 GF: - Fm: 0-0
Distance:	2m/2m3: 0-3 2m4-2m7: 0-1 3m+: 0-0
Track:	LH: 0-1 RH: 0-3 Tight: 0-2 Gall: 0-0
Aids:	Bl: 0-0 Vi: 0-0 Tstrap: 0-0 Ckp: 0-0
Best Rating:	113 3/04 Plum 2m good Hdl

Modest hurdler; ex-French; acts on good and soft ground.

Luteur Des Pictons (FR)

93   **78**

5-y-o ch g Ragmar (FR)-Ezera (FR) (Chamberlin (FR))
B G Powell (A Ennis 16/1) The A T P Racing Partnership

Placings:05P06P   (4180)
2003/04: 16⁰G, 16⁵S, 17⁰GS, 16⁰S, 22⁶GS, 20ᴾG,

	Starts	1st	2nd	3rd	Win & Pl
Hurdles	6	0	0	0	0
Career Total	6	0	0	0	0

Going:	Sf: 0-2 GS: 0-2 Gd: 0-2 GF: - Fm: 0-0
Distance:	2m/2m3: 0-4 2m4-2m7: 0-2 3m+: 0-0
Track:	LH: 0-2 RH: 0-4 Tight: 0-3 Gall: 0-2
Aids:	Bl: 0-0 Vi: 0-0 Tstrap: 0-0 Ckp: 0-0
Best Rating:	78 12/03 Plum 2m soft Hdl

Luthello (FR)

67f   **85+f**

5-y-o b g Marchand De Sable (USA)-Haudello (FR) (Marignan (USA))
J Howard Johnson Mrs M W Bird

Placings:0   (2181)
2003/04: 16⁰G,

	Starts	1st	2nd	3rd	Win & Pl
NH Flat	1	0	0	0	
Career Total	1	0	0	0	

Going:	Sf: 0-0 GS: 0-0 Gd: 0-1 GF: - Fm: 0-0
Distance:	2m/2m3: 0-1 2m4-2m7: 0-0 3m+: 0-0
Track:	LH: 0-1 RH: 0-0 Tight: 0-1 Gall: 0-0
Aids:	Bl: 0-0 Vi: 0-0 Tstrap: 0-0 Ckp: 0-0
Best Rating:	85 11/03 Ayr 2m good NHF

Luxembourg

91   48

5-y-o b g Bigstone (IRE)-Princess Borghese (USA) (Nijinsky (CAN))
N A Twiston-Davies Mrs Lorna Berryman

Placings:0U0-0046   (4000)
2003/04: 20⁹G, 22⁰S, 22⁴G, 26⁶G,

	Starts	1st	2nd	3rd	Win & Pl
Hurdles	4	0	0	0	0
Career Total	7	0	0	0	0

Going:	Sf: 0-1 GS: 0-0 Gd: 0-3 GF: - Fm: 0-0
Distance:	2m/2m3: 0-0 2m4-2m7: 0-3 3m+: 0-1
Track:	LH: 0-1 RH: 0-3 Tight: 0-1 Gall: 0-0
Aids:	Bl: 0-0 Vi: 0-0 Tstrap: 0-0 Ckp: 0-0
Best Rating:	67 11/02 Newb 1m4f110y gd-sft NHF

Luzcadou (FR)

108   133

11-y-o b g Cadoudal (FR)-Luzenia (FR) (Armos)
Ferdy Murphy A G Chappell

Placings:FF461P40123/36531/F5110P/066P1P/0042UF00/1-0F514BPFP   (4861)
2003/04: 21⁹G, 20⁵F, 20⁵G, 20¹HY, 20⁴GS, 33⁸G, 22⁷GS, 36⁶G, 33⁰GS,

	Starts	1st	2nd	3rd	Win & Pl
Hurdles	1	0	0	0	0
Chases	8	1	0	0	13183
Career Total	46	8	2	3	169434
122	1/04	Ayr	2m4f	B(0-140)HCh	HVY £12239
133	11/02	Ayr	2m4f	D(0-120)HCh	SFT £5425
119	12/00	Newc	2m4f	C(0-135)HHdl	SFT £5187
148	2/00	Ayr	2m4f	B(0-145)HCh	HVY £13065
141	1/00	Ayr	2m4f	B(0-140)HCh	SFT £9197
111	12/97	Carl	2m4f110yE Hdl		SFT £2038
	3/97	Autl	1m7f110y Ch		£35671
				Total win prize-money £98634	

Going:	Sf: 1-2 GS: 0-4 Gd: 0-3 GF: - Fm: 0-0
Distance:	2m/2m3: 0-0 2m4-2m7: 1-6 3m+: 0-3
Track:	LH: 1-9 RH: 0-0 Tight: 0-3 Gall: 0-1
Aids:	Bl: 1-7 Vi: 0-2 Tstrap: 0-0 Ckp: 0-0
Best Rating:	148 2/00 Ayr 2m4f heavy Ch

Fair chaser; effective at two and a half miles, but has yet to really prove he stays three miles; fortunate winner over two and a half miles at Ayr in January 2004; regularly wears blinkers or a visor.

Lydford Castle

10-y-o b g Thornberry (USA)-Our Generator (Starch Reduced)
R Jarman R Jarman, E Jarman & Mrs B Fuller

Placings:P/P   (4635)
2003/04: 24⁰G,

	Starts	1st	2nd	3rd	Win & Pl
Chases	1	0	0	0	
Career Total	2	0	0	0	

Going:	Sf: 0-0 GS: 0-0 Gd: 0-1 GF: - Fm: 0-0
Distance:	2m/2m3: 0-0 2m4-2m7: 0-0 3m+: 0-1
Track:	LH: 0-0 RH: 0-1 Tight: 0-1 Gall: 0-0
Aids:	Bl: 0-1 Vi: 0-0 Tstrap: 0-0 Ckp: 0-0

Lynchahaun (IRE)

90   84

8-y-o b/br g Good Thyne (USA)-Smart Decision (IRE) (Le Moss)
P Monteith P Monteith

Placings:0-044   (0578)
2003/04: 16⁰G, 16⁴GS, 20⁴G,

	Starts	1st	2nd	3rd	Win & Pl
Hurdles	3	0	0	0	677
Career Total	4	0	0	0	677

Going:	Sf: 0-0 GS: 0-1 Gd: 0-2 GF: - Fm: 0-0
Distance:	2m/2m3: 0-2 2m4-2m7: 0-1 3m+: 0-0
Track:	LH: 0-1 RH: 0-2 Tight: 0-0 Gall: 0-0
Aids:	Bl: 0-0 Vi: 0-0 Tstrap: 0-0 Ckp: 0-0
Best Rating:	84 6/03 Prth 2m4f110y good Hdl

Plating-class novice hurdler; limited promise so far; may do better in handicaps.

Lynphord Girl

94   96

13-y-o ch m Lyphento (USA)-Woodlands Angel (Levanter)
Dr J R J Naylor The Cayford Partnership

Placings:0/0/2F024-1235   (2953)
2003/04: 19¹G, 21²GF, 19³G, 21⁵G,

	Starts	1st	2nd	3rd	Win & Pl
Chases	4	1	1	1	6627
Career Total	11	1	3	1	9612
96	10/03	Towc	2m3f110yD Ch	GD	£4468
				Total win prize-money £4469	

Going:	Sf: 0-0 GS: 0-0 Gd: 1-3 GF: - Fm: 0-1
Distance:	2m/2m3: 0-0 2m4-2m7: 1-4 3m+: 0-0
Track:	LH: 0-0 RH: 0-3 Tight: 0-0 Gall: 0-0
Aids:	Bl: 0-0 Vi: 0-0 Tstrap: 0-0 Ckp: 0-0
Best Rating:	96 11/03 Winc 2m5f gd-fm Ch

Modest chaser; winning pointer, landed a novice chase just two months short of her 13th birthday; stays an extended three miles but effective over shorter.

Lynrick Lady (IRE)

103(105h)   (110+h)104

8-y-o b m Un Desperado (FR)-Decent Lady (Decent Fellow)
J G Portman Milady Partnership

Placings:0/0/P5140-104P2   (3857)
2003/04: 24¹GS, 25⁰G, 24⁴S, 26²PS, 26²GS,

	Starts	1st	2nd	3rd	Win & Pl
Hurdles	3	1	0	0	5541
Chases	2	0	1	0	2065
Career Total	12	2	1	0	11957
110	11/03	Chep	3m	C(0-130)HHdl	G-S £5109
98	2/03	Chep	2m4f	E Hdl	HVY £3922
				Total win prize-money £9032	

Going: Sf: 0-2 GS: 1-2 Gd: 0-1 GF: - Fm: 0-0
Distance: 2m/2m3: 0-0 2m4-2m7: 0-0 3m+: 1-5
Track: LH: 1-5 RH: 0-0 Tight: 0-1 Gall: 0-1
Aids: Bl: 0-0 Vi: 0-0 Tstrap: 0-0 Ckp: 0-0
Best Rating: 110 12/03 Chep 3m soft Hdl

Modest hurdler; stays three miles; acts on soft ground.

Lynwood Gold

62   31

5-y-o b g Gold Dust-Beths Wish (Rustingo)
B J Llewellyn Colin M Price

Placings:00   (4003)
2003/04: 18⁰GS, 16⁰G,

	Starts	1st	2nd	3rd	Win & Pl
NH Flat	1	0	0	0	0
Hurdles	1	0	0	0	0
Career Total	2	0	0	0	0

Going:	Sf: 0-0 GS: 0-1 Gd: 0-1 GF: - Fm: 0-0
Distance:	2m/2m3: 0-2 2m4-2m7: 0-0 3m+: 0-0
Track:	LH: 0-1 RH: 0-1 Tight: 0-0 Gall: 0-0
Aids:	Bl: 0-0 Vi: 0-0 Tstrap: 0-0 Ckp: 0-0
Best Rating:	31 2/04 Ludl 2m good Hdl

Lyon

68f   85f

4-y-o ch g Pivotal-French Gift (Cadeaux Genereux)
O Sherwood Raymond Tooth

Placings:0   (4824)
2003/04: 17⁰GF,

	Starts	1st	2nd	3rd	Win & Pl
NH Flat	1	0	0	0	
Career Total	1	0	0	0	

Going:	Sf: 0-0 GS: 0-0 Gd: 0-0 GF: - Fm: 0-1
Distance:	2m/2m3: 0-1 2m4-2m7: 0-0 3m+: 0-0
Track:	LH: 0-0 RH: 0-1 Tight: 0-0 Gall: 0-0
Aids:	Bl: 0-0 Vi: 0-0 Tstrap: 0-0 Ckp: 0-0
Best Rating:	85 4/04 Extr 2m1f gd-fm NHF

Lyphard's Fable (USA)

13-y-o b g Al Nasr (FR)-Affirmative Fable (USA) (Affirmed (USA))
Miss M Bayliss J C England

Placings:0P04/40004233F6F/F064/2FF126263/2423325/50 50/0/6/P-U   (4283)
2003/04: 25⁰U,

	Starts	1st	2nd	3rd	Win & Pl
Chases	1	0	0	0	
Career Total	43	1	7	5	9500
74	12/97	Chep	2m4f110yG Hdl	SFT	£1898
				Total win prize-money £1898	

Going:	Sf: 0-0 GS: 0-0 Gd: 0-1 GF: - Fm: 0-0
Distance:	2m/2m3: 0-0 2m4-2m7: 0-0 3m+: 0-1
Track:	LH: 0-0 RH: 0-1 Tight: 0-0 Gall: 0-0
Aids:	Bl: 0-0 Vi: 0-0 Tstrap: 0-0 Ckp: 0-0
Best Rating:	89 11/98 Plum 2m4f soft Hdl

Lypharita's Risk (FR)

90   70

9-y-o b g Take Risks (FR)-Patissima (FR) (Lightning (FR))
Mrs M Evans (Evan Williams 7/6) W J Evans

Placings:P6/2423344/352P/0PFP2150   (2820)
2003/04: 20⁰GF, 16⁵GF, 20⁵G, 25⁵GF, 19²GF, 16¹F, 16⁵GF,
20⁹GF,

	Starts	1st	2nd	3rd	Win & PI
Hurdles	1	0	0	0	0
Chases	7	1	1	0	7218
Career Total	21	1	4	3	11865
69 11/03 Ludl 2m D(0-115)HCh FRM £6620				
			Total win prize-money £6620			

Going:	Sf: 0-0 GS: 0-0 Gd: 0-1 GF: - Fm: 1-7
Distance:	2m/2m3: 1-4 2m4-2m7: 0-3 3m+: 0-1
Track:	LH: 0-3 RH: 1-5 Tight: 1-3 Gall: 0-0
Aids:	Bl: 0-0 Vi: 0-0 Tstrap: 0-0 Ckp: 0-0
Best Rating:	102 11/00 Kemp 2m soft Hdl

Plating-class chaser; ex-pointer; acts on fast ground, best at 2m.

Lyrical Lily

72f   75f

6-y-o b m Afflora (IRE)-Music Interpreter (Kampala)
Mrs S M Johnson Gethyn Mills

Placings:5   (4543)
2003/04: 16⁵GS,

	Starts	1st	2nd	3rd	Win & PI
NH Flat	1	0	0	0	0
Career Total	1	0	0	0	0

Going:	Sf: 0-0 GS: 0-1 Gd: 0-0 GF: - Fm: 0-0
Distance:	2m/2m3: 0-1 2m4-2m7: 0-0 3m+: 0-0
Track:	LH: 0-0 RH: 0-1 Tight: 0-0 Gall: 0-0
Aids:	Bl: 0-0 Vi: 0-0 Tstrap: 0-0 Ckp: 0-0
Best Rating:	75 3/04 Ludl 2m gd-sft NHF

Lyricist's Dream

65f   30f

5-y-o b m Dreams End-Lyricist (Averof)
R L Brown R L Brown

Placings:00   (3446)
2003/04: 16⁹GS, 16⁹G,

	Starts	1st	2nd	3rd	Win & PI
NH Flat	2	0	0	0	0
Career Total	2	0	0	0	0

Going:	Sf: 0-0 GS: 0-1 Gd: 0-1 GF: - Fm: 0-0
Distance:	2m/2m3: 0-2 2m4-2m7: 0-0 3m+: 0-0
Track:	LH: 0-0 RH: 0-2 Tight: 0-0 Gall: 0-0
Aids:	Bl: 0-0 Vi: 0-0 Tstrap: 0-0 Ckp: 0-0
Best Rating:	34 1/04 Ludl 2m good NHF

M'Lord

86f   85f

6-y-o b g Mister Lord (USA)-Dishcloth (Fury Royal)
G B Balding Dr G Madan Mohan

Placings:000   (4738)
2003/04: 16⁹G, 16⁹G, 17⁰G,

	Starts	1st	2nd	3rd	Win & PI
NH Flat	3	0	0	0	

Career Total   3   0   0   0

Going:	Sf: 0-0 GS: 0-0 Gd: 0-3 GF: - Fm: 0-0
Distance:	2m/2m3: 0-3 2m4-2m7: 0-0 3m+: 0-0
Track:	LH: 0-2 RH: 0-1 Tight: 0-1 Gall: 0-1
Aids:	Bl: 0-0 Vi: 0-0 Tstrap: 0-0 Ckp: 0-0
Best Rating:	85 2/04 Asct 2m110y good NHF

Ma Furie (FR)

83   70

4-y-o gr f Balleroy (USA)-Furie De Carmont (FR) (Carmont (FR))
Miss H C Knight The Hon Mrs Peter Tower

Placings:10   (3806)
2003/04: 16¹VS, 16⁹G,

	Starts	1st	2nd	3rd	Win & PI
Hurdles	2	1	0	0	8113
Career Total	2	1	0	0	8113
1/04 Pau 2m110y Hdl VS £8113				
			Total win prize-money £8113			

Going:	Sf: 0-0 GS: 0-0 Gd: 0-1 GF: - Fm: 0-0
Distance:	2m/2m3: 1-2 2m4-2m7: 0-0 3m+: 0-0
Track:	LH: 0-0 RH: 0-1 Tight: 0-0 Gall: 0-0
Aids:	Bl: 0-0 Vi: 0-0 Tstrap: 0-0 Ckp: 0-0
Best Rating:	70 2/04 Kemp 2m good Hdl

Winning hurdler in France; well beaten on British debut; suited by two miles and soft ground.

Ma's Confusion

6-y-o b m Mr Confusion (IRE)-Spirited Lady Vii (Damsire Unregistered)
N Wilson The Listowel Racers

Placings:P-P   (0705)
2003/04: 17⁰GF,

	Starts	1st	2nd	3rd	Win & PI
NH Flat	1	0	0	0	
Career Total	2	0	0	0	

Going:	Sf: 0-0 GS: 0-0 Gd: 0-0 GF: - Fm: 0-1
Distance:	2m/2m3: 0-1 2m4-2m7: 0-0 3m+: 0-0
Track:	LH: 0-0 RH: 0-1 Tight: 0-0 Gall: 0-0
Aids:	Bl: 0-0 Vi: 0-0 Tstrap: 0-0 Ckp: 0-0

Mac Hine (IRE)

110(100h)   (106h)118+

7-y-o b g Eurobus-Zoe Baird (Aragon)
Jonjo O'Neill John P McManus

Placings:142000-323P165   (4865)
2003/04: 20⁵G, 22²GS, 20³GS, 24²PGS, 22¹GS, 32⁶G, 25⁵S,

	Starts	1st	2nd	3rd	Win & PI
Chases	7	1	1	2	11780
Career Total	13	2	2	2	15655
118 3/04 Kels 2m6fi110yC(0-130)HCh G-S £8248				
106 11/02 Sand 2m110y H NHF SFT £2457				
			Total win prize-money £10706			

Going:	Sf: 0-1 GS: 1-4 Gd: 0-2 GF: - Fm: 0-0
Distance:	2m/2m3: 0-0 2m4-2m7: 1-4 3m+: 0-3
Track:	LH: 1-5 RH: 0-2 Tight: 1-3 Gall: 0-0
Aids:	Bl: 0-0 Vi: 0-0 Tstrap: 0-0 Ckp: 0-0
Best Rating:	118 3/04 Kels 2m6f110y gd-sft Ch

Modest hurdler/novice chaser; has not always looked

straightforward but has plenty of ability and turned in an improved effort at Kelso in March (strongly run race); stays two miles six; acts on good and soft ground; may be capable of better.

Macanillo (GER)

6-y-o gr g Acatenango (GER)-Midday Girl (GER) (Black Tie Affair)
Ian Williams G P Services (UK) Ltd

Placings:PP-0P   (2163)
2003/04: 16⁰G, 16⁶G,

	Starts	1st	2nd	3rd	Win & PI
Hurdles	2	0	0	0	
Career Total	4	0	0	0	

Going:	Sf: 0-0 GS: 0-0 Gd: 0-2 GF: - Fm: 0-0
Distance:	2m/2m3: 0-2 2m4-2m7: 0-0 3m+: 0-0
Track:	LH: 0-2 RH: 0-0 Tight: 0-0 Gall: 0-0
Aids:	Bl: 0-0 Vi: 0-0 Tstrap: 0-0 Ckp: 0-0

Maceo (GER)

103(113h)   (118h)93

10-y-o ch g Acatenango (GER)-Metropolitan Star (USA) (Lyphard (USA))
Mrs M Reveley Les De La Haye

Placings:030/4/02241F/443436-42236365513F   (4684)
2003/04: 17⁴G, 16²GF, 19²GF, 16³GF, 16⁶GS, 16³G, 16⁶S, 16⁶HY,
16⁵S, 20¹GF, 16³GS, 25⁶G,

	Starts	1st	2nd	3rd	Win & PI
Hurdles	8	1	1	3	10117
Chases	4	0	1	0	1640
Career Total	29	3	4	6	29464
115 3/04 Ayr 2m4f D(0-125)HHdl G-F £5053				
117 11/02 Weth 2m C(0-135)HHdl GD £6259				
112 3/02 Newb 2m110y D(0-110)HHdl G-S £4582				
			Total win prize-money £15897			

Going:	Sf: 0-3 GS: 0-2 Gd: 0-3 GF: - Fm: 1-4
Distance:	2m/2m3: 0-10 2m4-2m7: 1-1 3m+: 0-1
Track:	LH: 1-11 RH: 0-1 Tight: 0-3 Gall: 0-4
Aids:	Bl: 1-4 Vi: 0-0 Tstrap: 0-0 Ckp: 0-1
Best Rating:	118 3/04 Weth 2m gd-sft Hdl

Modest handicap hurdler who broke losing run at Ayr in March 2004; has shown ability over fences; effective at around 2m but stays 2m 4f; acts on good and soft ground; has worn blinkers and cheekpieces.

Macgeorge (IRE)

14-y-o b g Mandalus-Colleen Donn (Le Moss)
R Lee Mr & Mrs J H Watson

Placings:443/3215/U5F1122/1U44111/126441/4PU2F/4/43
5163/PP11U2-1P6112   (4845)
2003/04: 25¹GS, 28⁸G, 22⁶S, 26¹GS, 25¹GS, 26²G,

	Starts	1st	2nd	3rd	Win & PI
Chases	6	3	1	0	8379
Career Total	51	15	7	4	140041
135 3/04 Extr 3m1f110yH Ch G-S £3640				
134 3/04 Wwck 3m2f H Ch G-S £1603				
122 5/03 Hrfd 3m1f110yH Ch G-S £1617				
118 3/03 Wwck 3m2f H Ch G-S £1470				
128 2/03 Hrfd 3m1f110yH Ch GD £1624				
141 2/02 Wwck 3m2f C(0-130)HCh SFT £7020				
164 4/99 Aint 3m1f A Ch G-S £38275				
151 11/98 Wwck 3m1f B(0-140)HCh GD £7236				
145 3/98 Newb 3m B HCh G-S £7726				

136	2/98	Leic	2m7f110yC(0-130)HCh	GD	£5390
127	5/97	Worc	2m7f110yE Ch	G-S	£3455
135	2/97	Leic	2m4f110yE(0-115)HCh	G-F	£3179
130	1/97	Weth	2m4f110yD(0-110)HCh	GD	£3480
120	2/96	Hayd	2m6f	D Hdl	HVY	£3263

Total win prize-money £96581

Going:	Sf: 0-1 GS: 3-3 Gd: 0-2 GF: - Fm: 0-0
Distance:	2m/2m3: 0-2 2m4-2m7: 0-1 3m+: 0-0
Track:	LH: 1-4 RH: 2-2 Tight: 0-1 Gall: 0-1
Aids:	Bl: 0-0 Vi: 0-0 Tstrap: 0-0 Ckp: 0-0
Best Rating:	164 4/99 Aint 3m1f gd-sft Ch

Very useful chaser in his prime; won Aintree's Martell Cup in 1999; winning hunter chaser in 2003; stays three and a quarter miles; acts on good and soft ground; sometimes let down by his jumping.

Macgyver (NZ)

8-y-o b g Jahafil-Corazon (NZ) (Pag-Asa (AUS))
M F Loggin M Blackford

Placings:210450P32552-P6P (4510)
2003/04: 24PS, 16PG, 19PGS,

	Starts	1st	2nd	3rd	Win & Pl
Chases	3	0	0	0	0
Career Total	15	1	3	1	4583
6/02	Wang 1m6f	Hdl		SFT	£893

Total win prize-money £893

Going:	Sf: 0-1 GS: 0-1 Gd: 0-1 GF: - Fm: 0-0
Distance:	2m/2m3: 0-2 2m4-2m7: 0-0 3m+: 0-1
Track:	LH: 0-0 RH: 0-3 Tight: 0-0 Gall: 0-1
Aids:	Bl: 0-0 Vi: 0-0 Tstrap: 0-0 Ckp: 0-0
Best Rating:	90 3/03 Hrfd 2m gd-fm Ch

Ex-New Zealand horse, he has ability but is somewhat headstrong.

Mach Four (IRE)
89

6-y-o b g Bob Back (USA)-Tasmania Star (Captain James)
N A Twiston-Davies G M Powell

Placings:000-FP (2389)
2003/04: 21FG, 20PG,

	Starts	1st	2nd	3rd	Win & Pl
Hurdles	2	0	0	0	
Career Total	5	0	0	0	

Going:	Sf: 0-0 GS: 0-0 Gd: 0-2 GF: - Fm: 0-0
Distance:	2m/2m3: 0-0 2m4-2m7: 0-2 3m+: 0-0
Track:	LH: 0-1 RH: 0-1 Tight: 0-1 Gall: 0-0
Aids:	Bl: 0-0 Vi: 0-0 Tstrap: 0-0 Ckp: 0-0
Best Rating:	94 2/03 Kemp 2m good NHF

Machete Man
(0c)

9-y-o b g Broadsword (USA)-Ribo Melody (Riboboy (USA))
J A T De Giles J A T De Giles

Placings:45/F/P-FF (0611)
2003/04: 20FGF, 26FG,

	Starts	1st	2nd	3rd	Win & Pl
Hurdles	2	0	0	0	
Career Total	6	0	0	0	0

Going:	Sf: 0-0 GS: 0-0 Gd: 0-0 GF: - Fm: 0-2
Distance:	2m/2m3: 0-0 2m4-2m7: 0-1 3m+: 0-1

Machrihanish
99   86

4-y-o b g Groom Dancer (USA)-Goodwood Lass (IRE) (Alzao (USA))
S C Burrough (Mrs L B Normile 15/1) Mrs Deborah Potter

Placings:4R4PP0 (4673)
2003/04: 16⁴GS, 16⁶GS, 16⁴GF, 16PGS, 17PG, 16PG,

	Starts	1st	2nd	3rd	Win & Pl
Hurdles	6	0	0	0	532
Career Total	6	0	0	0	532

Going:	Sf: 0-0 GS: 0-3 Gd: 0-2 GF: - Fm: 0-1
Distance:	2m/2m3: 0-6 2m4-2m7: 0-0 3m+: 0-1
Track:	LH: 0-3 RH: 0-3 Tight: 0-3 Gall: 0-1
Aids:	Bl: 0-0 Vi: 0-0 Tstrap: 0-0 Ckp: 0-0
Best Rating:	86 12/03 Catt 2m gd-sft Hdl

Temperamental novice hurdler; easily best effort when close third in very modest event at Musselburgh in January.

Mackenzie (IRE)
82

8-y-o b g Mandalus-Crinkle Lady (Buckskin (FR))
Mrs C J Kerr Mrs C J Kerr

Placings:4435/PP (2901)
2003/04: 22PG, 16PS,

	Starts	1st	2nd	3rd	Win & Pl
Hurdles	2	0	0	0	
Career Total	6	0	0	1	354

Going:	Sf: 0-1 GS: 0-0 Gd: 0-0 GF: - Fm: 0-0
Distance:	2m/2m3: 0-1 2m4-2m7: 0-1 3m+: 0-0
Track:	LH: 0-2 RH: 0-0 Tight: 0-1 Gall: 0-0
Aids:	Bl: 0-0 Vi: 0-0 Tstrap: 0-0 Ckp: 0-0
Best Rating:	96 11/01 Ayr 2m gd-sft NHF

Macmillan

4-y-o b g Machiavellian (USA)-Mill On The Floss (Mill Reef (USA))
C J Mann (B J Meehan 23/7) Mrs Susan Roy

Placings:P (1298)
2003/04: 16PGF,

	Starts	1st	2nd	3rd	Win & Pl
Hurdles	1	0	0	0	
Career Total	1	0	0	0	

Going:	Sf: 0-0 GS: 0-0 Gd: 0-0 GF: - Fm: 0-1
Distance:	2m/2m3: 0-1 2m4-2m7: 0-0 3m+: 0-0
Track:	LH: 0-1 RH: 0-0 Tight: 0-0 Gall: 0-0
Aids:	Bl: 0-0 Vi: 0-0 Tstrap: 0-0 Ckp: 0-0

Macnamarasband (IRE)

15-y-o b g Orchestra-Susan Mc Cann (Furry Glen)
Mrs P Chamings M Clarke

Track:	LH: 0-1 RH: 0-1 Tight: 0-0 Gall: 0-0
Aids:	Bl: 0-0 Vi: 0-0 Tstrap: 0-0 Ckp: 0-0
Best Rating:	93 11/00 Towc 2m soft NHF

Placings:01404000/400/42212605/0P/0PPP33034/54/P (0055)
2003/04: 25PGS,

	Starts	1st	2nd	3rd	Win & Pl
Chases	1	0	0	0	0
Career Total	33	2	3	3	18116
121	11/97	Navn 3m	(0-132)HCh	YLD	£4069
121	10/95	Limk 2m4f	Hdl	GD	£3391

Total win prize-money £7460

Going:	Sf: 0-0 GS: 0-1 Gd: 0-0 GF: - Fm: 0-0
Distance:	2m/2m3: 0-0 2m4-2m7: 0-0 3m+: 0-1
Track:	LH: 0-0 RH: 0-1 Tight: 0-0 Gall: 0-0
Aids:	Bl: 0-0 Vi: 0-0 Tstrap: 0-0 Ckp: 0-0
Best Rating:	121 11/97 Navn 3m heavy Ch

Macnance (IRE)
107   110

8-y-o b m Mandalus-Colleen Donn (Le Moss)
R Lee Mrs Keith Lowry

Placings:26/2212U2-P03514660 (4917)
2003/04: 17PS, 19⁰G, 16³GS, 22⁵GS, 19¹GS, 17⁴GS, 20⁶S, 24⁶G, 20⁰GS,

	Starts	1st	2nd	3rd	Win & Pl
Hurdles	9	1	0	1	6045
Career Total	17	2	5	1	15361
111	1/04	Hrfd	2m3f110yE(0-110)HHdl	G-S	£3425
111	11/02	Leic	2m	D Hdl	SFT	£3867

Total win prize-money £7294

Going:	Sf: 0-2 GS: 1-5 Gd: 0-2 GF: - Fm: 0-0
Distance:	2m/2m3: 0-4 2m4-2m7: 1-4 3m+: 0-1
Track:	LH: 0-6 RH: 1-3 Tight: 0-3 Gall: 0-0
Aids:	Bl: 0-0 Vi: 0-0 Tstrap: 0-0 Ckp: 0-0
Best Rating:	111 1/04 Hrfd 2m3f110y gd-sft Hdl

Modest hurdler; half-sister to Macgeorge; acts on good ground, but does handle the soft; stays two and a half miles.

Maconnor (IRE)
83   111

7-y-o b g Religiously (USA)-Door Belle (Fidel)
H D Daly Daniel O'Connor

Placings:0/F4023-F0 (4959)
2003/04: 16FS, 19PG,

	Starts	1st	2nd	3rd	Win & Pl
Hurdles	1	0	0	0	0
Chases	1	0	0	0	0
Career Total	8	0	1	1	2640

Going:	Sf: 0-1 GS: 0-0 Gd: 0-1 GF: - Fm: 0-0
Distance:	2m/2m3: 0-1 2m4-2m7: 0-1 3m+: 0-0
Track:	LH: 0-0 RH: 0-2 Tight: 0-1 Gall: 0-0
Aids:	Bl: 0-0 Vi: 0-0 Tstrap: 0-0 Ckp: 0-0
Best Rating:	111 2/03 Chep 2m110y heavy Hdl

Modest novice hurdler; acts in soft ground; stays two and a half miles.

Macreater
90   54

6-y-o b m Mazaad-Gold Caste (USA) (Singh (USA))
K A Morgan Nigel Stokes

Placings:04350-663P00P (4592)
2003/04: 20⁶G, 20⁶G, 19³Gd, 21PS, 17PGS, 19PGS, 26PG,

	Starts	1st	2nd	3rd	Win & Pl
Hurdles	7	0	0	1	316
Career Total	12	0	0	2	581

Going:	Sf: 0-0 GS: 0-2 Gd: 0-2 GF: - Fm: 0-2
Distance:	2m/2m3: 0-2 2m4-2m7: 0-4 3m+: 0-1
Track:	LH: 0-3 RH: 0-3 Tight: 0-3 Gall: 0-2
Aids:	Bl: 0-0 Vi: 0-0 Tstrap: 0-0 Ckp: 0-0
Best Rating:	81 1/03 Sedg 2m1f heavy NHF

Modest form in bumpers and novices' hurdles.

Macy (IRE)

11-y-o ch g Sharp Charter-Lumax (Maximilian)
Martin Jones Mrs Jackie Jones

Placings:*1440*/23416P/4P5F4046P/FF3040/3536/60/4
                              (0225)
2003/04: 21⁴G,

	Starts	1st	2nd	3rd	Win & Pl
Chases	1	0	0	0	210
Career Total	32	2	1	4	6551
99 12/97 Wwck 2m3f			E(0-105)HHdl	SFT	£2713
71 2/97 Font 2m2f			H NHF	G-F	£1213
				Total win prize-money	£3927

Going:	Sf: 0-0 GS: 0-0 Gd: 0-1 GF: - Fm: 0-0
Distance:	2m/2m3: 0-0 2m4-2m7: 0-1 3m+: 0-0
Track:	LH: 0-1 RH: 0-0 Tight: 0-0 Gall: 0-0
Aids:	Bl: 0-0 Vi: 0-0 Tstrap: 0-0 Ckp: 0-1
Best Rating:	100 5/98 Chep 2m110y good Hdl

Madalyar (IRE)

83(97h)   (93+h)86
5-y-o b g Darshaan-Madaniyya (USA) (Shahrastani (USA))
Jonjo O'Neill Albert Reynolds

Placings:55F-4050   (4730)
2003/04: 17⁴GF, 17⁰GF, 20⁵HY, 20⁶G,

	Starts	1st	2nd	3rd	Win & Pl
Hurdles	3	0	0	0	259
Chases	1	0	0	0	0
Career Total	7	0	0	0	259

Going:	Sf: 0-1 GS: 0-0 Gd: 0-1 GF: - Fm: 0-2
Distance:	2m/2m3: 0-2 2m4-2m7: 0-2 3m+: 0-0
Track:	LH: 0-2 RH: 0-0 Tight: 0-0 Gall: 0-0
Aids:	Bl: 0-0 Vi: 0-0 Tstrap: 0-0 Ckp: 0-0
Best Rating:	91 12/02 Fknm 2m gd-sft Hdl

Middle-distance winner on the Flat in Ireland; yet to show much over hurdles, banned under non-triers' Rule second start.

Madam Flora

97(105c)   (110+c)110
7-y-o b m Alflora (IRE)-Madam's Choice (New Member)
M J Weeden T J Swaffield

Placings:30/36230/0231321-40230   (4842)
2003/04: 20⁴GS, 16⁹G, 19²S, 16³GS, 21⁹G,

	Starts	1st	2nd	3rd	Win & Pl
Hurdles	4	0	0	1	1410
Chases	1	0	1	0	1375
Career Total	19	2	4	6	15017
102 3/03 Winc 2m6f			E Hdl	G-F	£3510
110 12/02 Winc 2m			E Hdl	G-S	£3010
				Total win prize-money	£6521

Going:	Sf: 0-1 GS: 0-2 Gd: 0-2 GF: - Fm: 0-0
Distance:	2m/2m3: 0-2 2m4-2m7: 0-3 3m+: 0-0
Track:	LH: 0-1 RH: 0-4 Tight: 0-1 Gall: 0-1
Aids:	Bl: 0-0 Vi: 0-0 Tstrap: 0-0 Ckp: 0-0

| Best Rating: | 114   1/04   Extr   2m3f110y   soft   Ch |

Modest novice chaser/modest hurdler; goes well at Wincanton; stays two miles six; acts on soft ground.

Madam Mosso

91(104c)   (109c)101
8-y-o b m Le Moss-Rochestown Lass (Deep Run)
Mrs A M Thorpe Aled R Evans

Placings:0/52144414521-0   (1782)
2003/04: 24⁰G,

	Starts	1st	2nd	3rd	Win & Pl
Hurdles	1	0	0	0	
Career Total	13	3	2	0	13902
109 3/03 Hrfd	3m1f110y	E Ch		SFT	£4017
101 12/02 Extr	2m6f110yD(0-115)HHdl			SFT	£4013
95 6/02 Uttx	3m110y	E Hdl		HVY	£2569
				Total win prize-money	£10600

Going:	Sf: 0-0 GS: 0-0 Gd: 0-1 GF: - Fm: 0-0
Distance:	2m/2m3: 0-0 2m4-2m7: 0-3 3m+: 0-1
Track:	LH: 0-1 RH: 0-0 Tight: 0-1 Gall: 0-0
Aids:	Bl: 0-0 Vi: 0-0 Tstrap: 0-0 Ckp: 0-0
Best Rating:	109 3/03 Hrfd 3m1f110y soft Ch

Modest hurdler; showed her liking for soft ground and a test of stamina when making a successful chasing debut in mares only event at Hereford March 2003; stays beyond three miles; acts well on a soft surface.

Madam's Man

107(111h)   (106h)111
8-y-o b g Sir Harry Lewis (USA)-Madam-M (Tina's Pet)
N A Twiston-Davies H R Mould

Placings:000223/30134-13340   (4398)
2003/04: 21¹G, 29³G, 25³G, 30⁴G, 32⁰G,

	Starts	1st	2nd	3rd	Win & Pl
Chases	5	1	0	2	6611
Career Total	16	2	2	5	12682
111 11/03 NAbb	2m5f110yE(0-105)HCh			GD	£3003
100 6/02 Worc	3m	F(0-100)HHdl		GD	£2345
				Total win prize-money	£5348

Going:	Sf: 0-0 GS: 0-0 Gd: 1-5 GF: - Fm: 0-0
Distance:	2m/2m3: 0-0 2m4-2m7: 1-1 3m+: 0-4
Track:	LH: 1-5 RH: 0-0 Tight: 1-2 Gall: 0-2
Aids:	Bl: 0-0 Vi: 0-0 Tstrap: 0-0 Ckp: 0-0
Best Rating:	111 11/03 NAbb 2m5f110y good Ch

Modest hurdler/novice chaser; reappeared after a year off to win over fences at Newton Abbot in November 2003; still has a lot to learn about jumping fences; stays further than three miles and acts on a sound surface.

Made In Japan (JPN)

115   140+
4-y-o b g Barathea (IRE)-Darrery (Darshaan)
P J Hobbs (M A Magnusson 27/10) Terry Evans

Placings:33112   (4625)
2003/04: 16³GS, 17³GS, 16¹GS, 17¹G, 16²G,

	Starts	1st	2nd	3rd	Win & Pl
Hurdles	5	2	1	2	88195
Career Total	5	2	1	2	88195
140 3/04 Chel	2m1f	A Hdl		GD	£58000
120 2/04 Sand	2m110y	D Hdl		G-S	£4823
				Total win prize-money	£62823

| Going: | Sf: 0-0 GS: 1-3 Gd: 1-2 GF: - Fm: 0-0 |

Distance:	**2m/2m3: 2-5** 2m4-2m7: 0-0 3m+: 0-0
Track:	LH: 1-2 RH: 1-3 Tight: 0-2 **Gall: 1-1**
Aids:	Bl: 0-0 Vi: 0-0 Tstrap: 0-0 Ckp: 0-0
Best Rating:	140 4/04 Aint 2m110y good Hdl

Very useful juvenile hurdler; fair middle distance performer on the level; took the 2004 Triumph; narrowly beaten under a penalty at Aintree; suited by two miles on decent ground.

Mademist Sam

12-y-o b g Lord Bud-Mademist Susie (French Vine)
M J Hill M J Hill

Placings:00/066/000F3255/625/14335032P1/3-P   (4607)
2003/04: 25⁵PS,

	Starts	1st	2nd	3rd	Win & Pl
Chases	1	0	0	0	
Career Total	28	2	3	5	14166
100 9/00 Sedg 2m5f			E Ch	SFT	£3250
100 5/00 Weth 2m4f110yD Ch				G-F	£4160
				Total win prize-money	£7410

Going:	Sf: 0-0 GS: 0-1 Gd: 0-0 GF: - Fm: 0-0
Distance:	2m/2m3: 0-0 2m4-2m7: 0-0 3m+: 0-1
Track:	LH: 0-0 RH: 0-1 Tight: 0-1 Gall: 0-0
Aids:	Bl: 0-0 Vi: 0-0 Tstrap: 0-0 Ckp: 0-0
Best Rating:	102 3/99 MRas 2m4f gd-sft Ch

Madge Carroll (IRE)

90(110h)   (94h)111+
7-y-o b m Hollow Hand-Spindle Tree (Laurence O)
T R George Madge At Slad Partnership

Placings:2160-F211P3   (3904)
2003/04: 20⁶FG, 24²GF, 25¹GF, 20¹GS, 25⁶PG, 24³GS,

	Starts	1st	2nd	3rd	Win & Pl
Hurdles	3	0	1	1	1386
Chases	3	2	0	0	8826
Career Total	10	3	2	1	15163
111 12/03 Hntg 2m4f110yD Ch				G-S	£5434
105 12/03 Folk 3m1f			E Ch	G-F	£3392
93 12/02 Hntg 2m4f110yD Hdl				G-S	£3747
				Total win prize-money	£12573

Going:	Sf: 0-0 GS: 1-2 Gd: 0-2 GF: - Fm: 1-2
Distance:	2m/2m3: 0-0 2m4-2m7: 0-1 3m+: 1-4
Track:	LH: 0-3 **RH: 2-3** Tight: 1-3 Gall: 1-2
Aids:	Bl: 0-0 Vi: 0-0 Tstrap: 0-0 Ckp: 0-0
Best Rating:	111 12/03 Hntg 2m4f110y gd-sft Ch

Modest chaser; stays three miles; acts on soft and fast ground.

Madiba

                       92
5-y-o b g Emperor Jones (USA)-Priluki (Lycius (USA))
P Howling (S Dow 3/7) Eastwell Manor Racing Ltd

Placings:30-P   (2736)
2003/04: 19⁰PS,

	Starts	1st	2nd	3rd	Win & Pl
Hurdles	1	0	0	0	
Career Total	3	0	0	1	682

Going:	Sf: 0-0 GS: 0-0 Gd: 0-0 GF: - Fm: 0-0
Distance:	2m/2m3: 0-0 2m4-2m7: 0-1 3m+: 0-0
Track:	LH: 0-1 RH: 0-0 Tight: 0-1 Gall: 0-0
Aids:	Bl: 0-0 Vi: 0-0 Tstrap: 0-0 Ckp: 0-0
Best Rating:	100 11/02 Asct 2m110y gd-sft Hdl

Madison Avenue (GER)

82   **92**

7-y-o b g Mondrian (GER)-Madly Noble (GER) (Irish River (FR))
T M Jones Richard L Page

Placings:1P452-1   (0125)
2003/04: 20[1]G,

	Starts	1st	2nd	3rd	Win & Pl
Hurdles	1	1	0	0	2779
Career Total	6	2	1	0	6960
98 5/03 Font	2m4f		F Hdl	GD	£2779
108 12/02 Plum	2m5f		F Hdl	HVY	£2978
				Total win prize-money £5758

Going:	Sf: 0-0 GS: 0-0 Gd: 1-1 GF: - Fm: 0-0
Distance:	2m/2m3: 0-0 **2m4-2m7: 1-1** 3m+: 0-0
Track:	LH: 0-0 RH: 0-0 **Tight: 1-1** Gall: 0-0
Aids:	Bl: 0-0 Vi: 0-0 Tstrap: 0-0 Ckp: 0-0
Best Rating:	108 12/02 Plum 2m5f heavy Hdl

Plating-class hurdler; acts on good and soft ground; stays two miles five; has worn blinkers.

Madison De Vonnas (FR)

74f   **50f**

4-y-o b g Epervier Bleu-Carine De Neuvy (FR) (Shelley (FR))
Miss E C Lavelle N Mustoe

Placings:0   (4787)
2003/04: 16[0]G,

	Starts	1st	2nd	3rd	Win & Pl
NH Flat	1	0	0	0	
Career Total	1	0	0	0	

Going:	Sf: 0-0 GS: 0-0 Gd: 0-1 GF: - Fm: 0-0
Distance:	2m/2m3: 0-1 2m4-2m7: 0-0 3m+: 0-0
Track:	LH: 0-0 RH: 0-1 Tight: 0-0 Gall: 0-1
Aids:	Bl: 0-0 Vi: 0-0 Tstrap: 0-0 Ckp: 0-0
Best Rating:	50 4/04 Hntg 2m110y good NHF

Madmidge

9-y-o b/br g Jendali (USA)-No Rejection (Mummy's Pet)
D J Kemp M A Kemp

Placings:0/0/P   (4775)
2003/04: 21[P]G,

	Starts	1st	2nd	3rd	Win & Pl
Chases	1	0	0	0	
Career Total	3	0	0	0	

Going:	Sf: 0-0 GS: 0-0 Gd: 0-1 GF: - Fm: 0-0
Distance:	2m/2m3: 0-0 2m4-2m7: 0-1 3m+: 0-0
Track:	LH: 0-1 RH: 0-0 Tight: 0-1 Gall: 0-0
Aids:	Bl: 0-0 Vi: 0-0 Tstrap: 0-0 Ckp: 0-0
Best Rating:	33 4/01 MRas 2m1f110y heavy NHF

Maestro Please (IRE)

56f   **81f**

5-y-o b g Old Vic-Greek Melody (IRE) (Trojan Fort)
Lady Connell S J Connell

Placings:05   (4374)
2003/04: 16[9]HY, 16[5]GF,

	Starts	1st	2nd	3rd	Win & Pl
NH Flat	2	0	0	0	0
Career Total	2	0	0	0	0

Going:	Sf: 0-0 GS: 0-0 Gd: 0-0 GF: - Fm: 0-1
Distance:	2m/2m3: 0-0 2m4-2m7: 0-0 3m+: 0-0
Track:	LH: 0-0 RH: 0-1 Tight: 0-0 Gall: 0-0
Aids:	Bl: 0-0 Vi: 0-0 Tstrap: 0-0 Ckp: 0-0
Best Rating:	81 3/04 Strf 2m110y gd-fm NHF

Magalina (IRE)

103   **98+**

5-y-o br m Norwich-Pike Review (Dawn Review)
D P Keane Dajam & Damian Burbidge

Placings:4P00P10   (4897)
2003/04: 17[4]G, 16[P]G, 16[0]G, 16[9]S, 24[P]G, 22[0]G,

	Starts	1st	2nd	3rd	Win & Pl
NH Flat	1	0	0	0	
Hurdles	6	1	0	0	4323
Career Total	7	1	0	0	4323
98 3/04 Tntn	2m3f110yE Hdl			GD	£4322
				Total win prize-money £4323

Going:	Sf: 0-1 GS: 0-0 Gd: 1-6 GF: - Fm: 0-0
Distance:	2m/2m3: 0-0 **2m4-2m7: 1-2** 3m+: 0-1
Track:	LH: 0-1 **RH: 1-6** Tight: 1-2 Gall: 0-0
Aids:	Bl: 0-0 Vi: 0-0 Tstrap: 0-0 Ckp: 0-0
Best Rating:	98 3/04 Tntn 2m3f110y good Hdl

Moderate hurdler; made all to win weak hurdle at Taunton March 2004; stays two and a half miles.

Magenko (IRE)

105   **82**

7-y-o ch g Forest Wind (USA)-Bebe Auction (IRE) (Auction Ring (USA))
F P Murtagh R & J Wharton

Placings:604440/3030340401/P0-3325P   (3668)
2003/04: 20[3]G, 20[3]HY, 24[2]S, 24[5]GF, 24[P]HY,

	Starts	1st	2nd	3rd	Win & Pl
Hurdles	5	0	1	2	1259
Career Total	23	1	1	5	11265
88 4/02 Sedg	2m5f110yG HHdl			G-F	£8209
				Total win prize-money £8210

Going:	Sf: 0-3 GS: 0-0 Gd: 0-1 GF: - Fm: 0-1
Distance:	2m/2m3: 0-0 2m4-2m7: 0-2 3m+: 0-1
Track:	LH: 0-3 RH: 0-1 Tight: 0-0 Gall: 0-2
Aids:	Bl: 0-0 Vi: 0-0 Tstrap: 0-0 Ckp: 0-0
Best Rating:	88 4/02 Sedg 2m5f110y gd-fm Hdl

Plating-class hurdler; stays three miles; acts on fast ground.

Magenta Rising (IRE)

103   **75+**

4-y-o ch f College Chapel-Fashion Queen (Chilibang)
D Burchell P S & Mrs N G Pritchard

Placings:00624   (4714)
2003/04: 17[9]GF, 16[0]G, 16[6]GS, 17[2]GF, 16[4]G,

	Starts	1st	2nd	3rd	Win & Pl
Hurdles	5	0	1	0	956
Career Total	5	0	1	0	956

Going:	Sf: 0-0 GS: 0-1 Gd: 0-2 GF: - Fm: 0-2
Distance:	2m/2m3: 0-5 2m4-2m7: 0-0 3m+: 0-0
Track:	LH: 0-1 RH: 0-4 Tight: 0-0 Gall: 0-0
Aids:	Bl: 0-0 Vi: 0-0 Tstrap: 0-0 Ckp: 0-0
Best Rating:	75 3/04 Hrfd 2m1f gd-fm Hdl

Maggie Gray (IRE)

88f   **88+f**

6-y-o b m Erin's Isle-Reenoga (Tug Of War)
P D Niven (G A Swinbank 28/11) M Sawers

Placings:02   (4780)
2003/04: 16[0]S, 16[2]S,

	Starts	1st	2nd	3rd	Win & Pl
NH Flat	2	0	1	0	656
Career Total	2	0	1	0	656

Going:	Sf: 0-2 GS: 0-0 Gd: 0-0 GF: - Fm: 0-0
Distance:	2m/2m3: 0-2 2m4-2m7: 0-0 3m+: 0-0
Track:	LH: 0-2 RH: 0-0 Tight: 0-1 Gall: 0-0
Aids:	Bl: 0-0 Vi: 0-0 Tstrap: 0-0 Ckp: 0-0
Best Rating:	88 11/03 Ayr 2m soft NHF

Maggies Brother

11-y-o b g Brotherly (USA)-Sallisses (Pamroy)
R Shail Mrs G M Shail

Placings:PF/52/1125P6FP-21U455   (4522)
2003/04: 30[2]GF, 34[1]HY, 28[U]G, 25[4]GS, 25[5]G, 25[5]GS,

	Starts	1st	2nd	3rd	Win & Pl
Chases	6	1	1	0	3991
Career Total	18	3	3	0	10318
106 5/03 Uttx	4m2f	H Ch		HVY	£3367
86 5/02 Hntg	3m	H Ch		G-F	£1384
88 5/02 Chel	3m1f110yH Ch			G-F	£3926
				Total win prize-money £8678

Going:	Sf: 1-1 GS: 0-2 Gd: 0-2 GF: - Fm: 0-1
Distance:	2m/2m3: 0-0 2m4-2m7: 0-0 **3m+: 1-6**
Track:	**LH: 1-2** RH: 0-4 Tight: 0-1 Gall: 0-1
Aids:	Bl: 0-0 Vi: 0-0 Tstrap: 0-0 Ckp: 0-0
Best Rating:	106 5/03 Uttx 4m2f heavy Ch

Winning pointer/hunter chaser; stays extreme distances; acts on most types of ground.

Magic Bengie

97   **70+**

5-y-o b g Magic Ring (IRE)-Zinzi (Song)
F Kirby Fred Kirby

Placings:PF-4P01   (3476)
2003/04: 20[4]GF, 17[P]GF, 16[0]GS, 16[1]G,

	Starts	1st	2nd	3rd	Win & Pl
Hurdles	4	1	0	0	2674
Career Total	6	1	0	0	2674
70 1/04 Catt	2m	G(0-90)HHdl		GD	£2674
				Total win prize-money £2674

Going:	Sf: 0-0 GS: 0-1 Gd: 1-1 GF: - Fm: 0-2
Distance:	**2m/2m3: 1-3** 2m4-2m7: 0-1 3m+: 0-0
Track:	**LH: 1-4** RH: 0-0 **Tight: 1-3** Gall: 0-0
Aids:	Bl: 0-0 Vi: 0-0 Tstrap: 1-2 Ckp: 0-0
Best Rating:	70 1/04 Catt 2m good Hdl

First worthwhile form when taking a selling handicap hurdle from out of the handicap at Catterick in January; appeared to finish lame; best suited by two miles.

Magic Box

98   85

6-y-o b g Magic Ring (IRE)-Princess Poquito (Hard Fought)
Miss Kate Milligan R A W Racing

Placings:40304/001550F2-0U00   (1690)
2003/04: 16²GF, 17⁰GF, 17ᵁGF, 17⁰GF, 17⁰GF,

	Starts	1st	2nd	3rd	Win & Pl
Hurdles	5	0	1	0	696
Career Total	17	1	1	1	3927
88 7/02 Sedg 2m1f E(0-105)HHdl G-F £2898

                                    Total win prize-money £2898

Going:	Sf: 0-0 GS: 0-0 Gd: 0-0 GF: - Fm: 0-5
Distance:	2m/2m3: 0-5 2m4-2m7: 0-0 3m+: 0-0
Track:	LH: 0-4 RH: 0-1 Tight: 0-4 Gall: 0-1
Aids:	Bl: 0-0 Vi: 0-0 Tstrap: 0-0 Ckp: 0-3
Best Rating:	88 7/02 Sedg 2m1f gd-fm Hdl

Plating-class hurdler; suited by two miles and fast ground.

Magic Charm

69   43

6-y-o b m Magic Ring (IRE)-Loch Clair (IRE) (Lomond (USA))
A G Newcombe Wetherby Racing Bureau 46

Placings:00-4   (1567)
2003/04: 19⁴GF,

	Starts	1st	2nd	3rd	Win & Pl
Hurdles	1	0	0	0	263
Career Total	3	0	0	0	263

Going:	Sf: 0-0 GS: 0-0 Gd: 0-0 GF: - Fm: 0-1
Distance:	2m/2m3: 0-3 2m4-2m7: 0-0 3m+: 0-0
Track:	LH: 0-0 RH: 0-1 Tight: 0-0 Gall: 0-0
Aids:	Bl: 0-0 Vi: 0-0 Tstrap: 0-0 Ckp: 0-0
Best Rating:	54 10/03 Extr 2m3f gd-fm Hdl

Magic Combination (IRE)

93   106

11-y-o b g Scenic-Etage (Ile De Bourbon (USA))
L Lungo Sw Transport (swindon) Ltd & R J Gilbert

Placings:630/P/1U1/P10/0500/01102005/60001-56P00
                                                         (4729)
2003/04: 16⁵GS, 22⁶G, 20⁹GS, 20⁹G, 20⁰G,

	Starts	1st	2nd	3rd	Win & Pl
Hurdles	5	0	0	0	0
Career Total	32	6	1	1	67000
125 8/02 Prth 2m4f110yD(0-115)HHdl GD £5369
138 7/01 MRas 2m1f110yB(0-140)HHdl G-S £20065
135 5/01 MRas 2m3f110yC(0-130)HHdl GD £5772
129 3/00 Sand 2m110y B HHdl GD £21450
130 2/99 Asct 2m4f E(0-120)HHdl G-S £3550
113 1/99 Kemp 2m5f E(0-110)HHdl SFT £2766

                                    Total win prize-money £58973

Going:	Sf: 0-0 GS: 0-2 Gd: 0-3 GF: - Fm: 0-0
Distance:	2m/2m3: 0-1 2m4-2m7: 0-4 3m+: 0-0
Track:	LH: 0-2 RH: 0-2 Tight: 0-0 Gall: 0-1
Aids:	Bl: 0-0 Vi: 0-0 Tstrap: 0-0 Ckp: 0-1
Best Rating:	138 11/01 DRoy 2m soft Hdl

Fair hurdler; winner of the Imperial Cup in 2000; nowhere near as good these days; stays two and a half miles; best on a sound surface.

Magic Dancer (IRE)

93   89

11-y-o b g Carefree Dancer (USA)-Giveushope (Whistling Deer)
Capt J A George Captain & Mrs J A George

Placings:20206046/66/62110621/222P60/4B53456/02P0P
04-P0   (3526)
2003/04: 27⁰GS, 23⁰G,

	Starts	1st	2nd	3rd	Win & Pl
Chases	2	0	0	0	
Career Total	40	3	8	1	28998
118 4/00 Asct 3m110y B Ch SFT £10946
119 1/00 Hntg 2m5f110yD(0-120)HHdl G-S £3178
118 12/99 Extr 2m3f110yD(0-110)HHdl G-S £3168

                                    Total win prize-money £17293

Going:	Sf: 0-0 GS: 0-1 Gd: 0-1 GF: - Fm: 0-0
Distance:	2m/2m3: 0-2 2m4-2m7: 0-0 3m+: 0-2
Track:	LH: 0-0 RH: 0-2 Tight: 0-1 Gall: 0-0
Aids:	Bl: 0-1 Vi: 0-0 Tstrap: 0-0 Ckp: 0-0
Best Rating:	127 11/00 Kemp 3m soft Ch

Magic Dragon (FR)

85   49

6-y-o ch g Cyborg (FR)-Dix Huit Brumaire (FR) (General Assembly (USA))
Mrs M Reveley Sir Robert Ogden

Placings:4-006P   (3756)
2003/04: 16⁰G, 16⁶GS, 20⁶HY, 19⁹G,

	Starts	1st	2nd	3rd	Win & Pl
NH Flat	2	0	0	0	0
Hurdles	2	0	0	0	0
Career Total	5	0	0	0	275

Going:	Sf: 0-1 GS: 0-0 Gd: 0-2 GF: - Fm: 0-0
Distance:	2m/2m3: 0-2 2m4-2m7: 0-2 3m+: 0-0
Track:	LH: 0-3 RH: 0-1 Tight: 0-1 Gall: 0-0
Aids:	Bl: 0-0 Vi: 0-0 Tstrap: 0-0 Ckp: 0-0
Best Rating:	91 4/03 Ayr 2m good NHF

Magic Hour (IRE)

56f

5-y-o b g Weldnaas (USA)-Montohouse (IRE) (Montelimar (USA))
W McKeown Matheson Green

Placings:0   (1843)
2003/04: 17⁰G,

	Starts	1st	2nd	3rd	Win & Pl
NH Flat	1	0	0	0	
Career Total	1	0	0	0	

Going:	Sf: 0-0 GS: 0-0 Gd: 0-1 GF: - Fm: 0-0
Distance:	2m/2m3: 0-1 2m4-2m7: 0-0 3m+: 0-0
Track:	LH: 0-1 RH: 0-0 Tight: 0-1 Gall: 0-0
Aids:	Bl: 0-0 Vi: 0-0 Tstrap: 0-0 Ckp: 0-0

Magic Mistral

6-y-o b m Thowra (FR)-Festival Of Magic (USA) (Clever Trick (USA))
C C Bealby Maggie and Eric Hemming

Placings:0PP   (3427)
2003/04: 17⁰G, 16ᴾGS, 23ᴾGS,

	Starts	1st	2nd	3rd	Win & Pl
NH Flat	1	0	0	0	0
Hurdles	2	0	0	0	
Career Total	3	0	0	0	

Going:	Sf: 0-0 GS: 0-2 Gd: 0-1 GF: - Fm: 0-0
Distance:	2m/2m3: 0-2 2m4-2m7: 0-0 3m+: 0-1
Track:	LH: 0-3 RH: 0-0 Tight: 0-0 Gall: 0-0
Aids:	Bl: 0-0 Vi: 0-0 Tstrap: 0-0 Ckp: 0-0

Magic Mistress

104   118+

5-y-o b m Magic Ring (IRE)-Sight'n Sound (Chief Singer)
N J Henderson (S C Williams 12/10) Brian Twojohns Partnership

Placings:31   (4736)
2003/04: 19³G, 17¹G,

	Starts	1st	2nd	3rd	Win & Pl
Hurdles	2	1	0	1	4110
Career Total	2	1	0	1	4110
123 4/04 NAbb 2m1f E Hdl GD £3445

                                    Total win prize-money £3445

Going:	Sf: 0-0 GS: 0-0 Gd: 1-2 GF: - Fm: 0-0
Distance:	2m/2m3: 1-1 2m4-2m7: 0-1 3m+: 0-0
Track:	LH: 1-1 RH: 0-1 Tight: 1-2 Gall: 0-0
Aids:	Bl: 0-0 Vi: 0-0 Tstrap: 0-0 Ckp: 0-0
Best Rating:	123 4/04 NAbb 2m1f good Hdl

Fair hurdler; acts on good.

Magic Of Sydney (IRE)

100   126

8-y-o b g Broken Hearted-Chat Her Up (Proverb)
R Rowe Ann & John Symes

Placings:06/1F2-65   (3041)
2003/04: 22⁶GS, 24⁵GS,

	Starts	1st	2nd	3rd	Win & Pl
Chases	2	0	0	0	249
Career Total	7	1	1	0	6452
123 11/02 Folk 2m5f D Ch GD £4693

                                    Total win prize-money £4693

Going:	Sf: 0-0 GS: 0-2 Gd: 0-0 GF: - Fm: 0-0
Distance:	2m/2m3: 0-0 2m4-2m7: 0-1 3m+: 0-1
Track:	LH: 0-2 RH: 0-0 Tight: 0-0 Gall: 0-2
Aids:	Bl: 0-0 Vi: 0-0 Tstrap: 0-0 Ckp: 0-0
Best Rating:	126 12/02 Folk 3m1f soft Ch

Fair front-running chaser; scored on his first attempt over fences at Folkestone in November 2002; limitations exposed subsequently; stays two miles five; acts on good ground or softer.

Magic Red

86   84

4-y-o ch g Magic Ring (IRE)-Jacquelina (USA) (Private Account (USA))
M J Ryan M J Ryan

Placings:626P   (4591)
2003/04: 16⁶GF, 16²GF, 16⁶GS, 16ᴾG,

	Starts	1st	2nd	3rd	Win & Pl
Hurdles	4	0	1	0	838
Career Total	4	0	1	0	838

Going: Sf: 0-0 GS: 0-1 Gd: 0-1 GF: - Fm: 0-2
Distance: 2m/2m3: 0-4 2m4-2m7: 0-0 3m+: 0-0
Track: LH: 0-1 RH: 0-3 Tight: 0-0 Gall: 0-2
Aids: Bl: 0-1 Vi: 0-0 Tstrap: 0-0 Ckp: 0-1
Best Rating: 84 10/03 Hntg 2m110y gd-fm Hdl

Plating-class on the Flat; showed improved form on second start over hurdles at Huntingdon in October; suited by two miles; acts on fast ground.

Magic Route (IRE)

(93c)   (69c)85

7-y-o b g Mr Confusion (IRE)-Another Chapter (Respect)
J Howard Johnson Michael Thompson

Placings:0P/20P5P-P   (1765)
2003/04: 20PGF,

	Starts	1st	2nd	3rd	Win & Pl
Hurdles	1	0	0	0	
Career Total	8	0	1	0	822

Going: Sf: 0-0 GS: 0-0 Gd: 0-0 GF: - Fm: 0-1
Distance: 2m/2m3: 0-0 2m4-2m7: 0-1 3m+: 0-0
Track: LH: 0-0 RH: 0-1 Tight: 0-0 Gall: 0-0
Aids: Bl: 0-0 Vi: 0-0 Tstrap: 0-0 Ckp: 0-0
Best Rating: 85 12/02 Muss 2m gd-fm Hdl

Magic Trick

89   61

5-y-o b g Magic Ring (IRE)-Les Amis (Alzao (USA))
Mrs P N Dutfield Lee Jackson

Placings:50   (1217)
2003/04: 17⁵G, 16⁹GF,

	Starts	1st	2nd	3rd	Win & Pl
Hurdles	2	0	0	0	0
Career Total	2	0	0	0	

Going: Sf: 0-0 GS: 0-0 Gd: 0-1 GF: - Fm: 0-1
Distance: 2m/2m3: 0-2 2m4-2m7: 0-0 3m+: 0-0
Track: LH: 0-1 RH: 0-1 Tight: 0-1 Gall: 0-1
Aids: Bl: 0-0 Vi: 0-0 Tstrap: 0-0 Ckp: 0-0
Best Rating: 72 8/03 Hntg 2m110y gd-fm Hdl

Magical Bailiwick (IRE)

114   (105h)129+

8-y-o ch g Magical Wonder (USA)-Alpine Dance (USA)
(Apalachee (USA))
M C Pipe Islands Racing Connection

Placings:0530P/15P362505/P-F111123F   (4398)
2003/04: 16FGS, 19¹G, 25⁴G, 24¹G, 25¹S, 24²S, 33³G, 32FG,

	Starts	1st	2nd	3rd	Win & Pl
Chases	8	4	1	1	55342
Career Total	23	5	2	3	60120
129	1/04	Winc	3m1f110yC(0-135)HCh	SFT	£15457
123	1/04	Ludl	3m	E(0-105)HCh	GD	£6890
123	12/03	Chel	3m1f110yD(0-120)HCh	GD	£11431
115	12/03	Tntn	2m3f	F(0-95)HCh	GD	£2863
104	11/01	NAbb	2m1f	E Hdl	SFT	£2968
				Total win prize-money £39610

Going: Sf: 1-2 GS: 0-1 Gd: 3-5 GF: - Fm: 0-0
Distance: 2m/2m3: 1-2 2m4-2m7: 0-0 3m+: 3-6
Track: LH: 1-4 RH: 3-4 Tight: 2-2 Gall: 1-4
Aids: Bl: 0-0 Vi: 0-1 Tstrap: 0-0 Ckp: 0-0
Best Rating: 129 2/04 Newc 4m1f good Ch

Fair chaser; much improved for switch to Martin Pipe; won twice in two days over Christmas, and has won twice since; stays four miles and one furlong; acts on soft ground; suited by positive tactics; tough sort.

Magical Day

94   91

5-y-o ch m Halling (USA)-Ahla (Unfuwain (USA))
W G M Turner M J B Racing

Placings:45222422103-F400221003P0   (3700)
2003/04: 20FGF, 18⁴G, 16⁹GF, 16⁹GF, 17²GF, 16²GS, 17¹GS, 19⁹G, 18⁹G, 16³GGS, 22PHY, 19PHY,

	Starts	1st	2nd	3rd	Win & Pl
Hurdles	12	1	2	1	3640
Career Total	23	2	7	2	10324
94	12/03	Hrfd	2m1f	G Hdl	G-S	£1890
83	2/03	Hrfd	2m3f110yF Hdl	GD	£2786
				Total win prize-money £4676

Going: Sf: 0-2 GS: 1-3 Gd: 0-3 GF: - Fm: 0-4
Distance: 2m/2m3: 1-8 2m4-2m7: 0-4 3m+: 0-0
Track: LH: 0-3 RH: 1-9 Tight: 0-4 Gall: 0-7
Aids: Bl: 0-0 Vi: 0-1 Tstrap: 0-0 **Ckp:** 1-7
Best Rating: 94 12/03 Hrfd 2m1f gd-sft Hdl

Plating-class hurdler; effective at around 2m, but stays further; acts on any ground; has worn headgear.

Magical Field

(102h)   (94h)

6-y-o ch m Deploy-Ash Glade (Nashwan (USA))
Mrs M Reveley Lightbody Celebration Cakes Ltd

Placings:4F4-224F   (4261)
2003/04: 19²GGS, 16²GS, 20⁴GF, 16FGF,

	Starts	1st	2nd	3rd	Win & Pl
Hurdles	3	0	2	0	3126
Chases	1	0	0	0	0
Career Total	7	0	2	0	3696

Going: Sf: 0-0 GS: 0-1 Gd: 0-0 GF: - Fm: 0-3
Distance: 2m/2m3: 0-2 2m4-2m7: 0-2 3m+: 0-0
Track: LH: 0-3 RH: 0-1 Tight: 0-2 Gall: 0-0
Aids: Bl: 0-0 Vi: 0-0 Tstrap: 0-0 Ckp: 0-0
Best Rating: 94 1/04 Weth 2m gd-sft Hdl

Ex-French, in front when coming to grief at the last in mares' only novices' hurdle at Catterick in February 2003; runner-up in similar event at Wetherby in January; early casualty on chasing debut..

Magical Liaison (IRE)

82   77

6-y-o b g Mujtahid (USA)-Instant Affair (USA) (Lyphard (USA))
W Jenks The Glazeley Partnership 2

Placings:5226-PP02P   (4539)
2003/04: 16PGS, 20PGS, 16⁹S, 19²GGS, 21PGS,

	Starts	1st	2nd	3rd	Win & Pl
Hurdles	5	0	1	0	1118
Career Total	9	0	3	0	2598

Going: Sf: 0-1 GS: 0-3 Gd: 0-0 GF: - Fm: 0-1
Distance: 2m/2m3: 0-2 2m4-2m7: 0-0 3m+: 0-0
Track: LH: 0-2 RH: 0-3 Tight: 0-0 Gall: 0-1
Aids: Bl: 0-0 Vi: 0-0 Tstrap: 0-0 Ckp: 0-1
Best Rating: 90 1/03 Ludl 2m soft NHF

Magical Wonderland

76   66

5-y-o br m Thowra (FR)-Alice's Mirror (Magic Mirror)
B G Powell R H Kerswell

Placings:1555   (2029)
2003/04: 17¹GF, 16⁵G, 17⁵G, 17⁵G,

	Starts	1st	2nd	3rd	Win & Pl
NH Flat	3	1	0	0	1995
Hurdles	1	0	0	0	0
Career Total	4	1	0	0	1995
88	6/03	Hrfd	2m1f	H NHF	G-F	£1995
				Total win prize-money £1995

Going: Sf: 0-0 GS: 0-0 Gd: 0-3 GF: - Fm: 1-1
Distance: 2m/2m3: 1-4 2m4-2m7: 0-0 3m+: 0-0
Track: LH: 0-3 **RH:** 1-1 Tight: 0-1 Gall: 0-0
Aids: Bl: 0-0 Vi: 0-0 Tstrap: 0-0 Ckp: 0-0
Best Rating: 98 10/03 Bang 2m1f good NHF

Out of a mare who scored six times over hurdles; ready winner of Hereford bumper on debut June 2003; held subsequently.

Magicien (FR)

8-y-o b g Muroto-French Look (FR) (Green River (FR))
Steve Isaac Mrs B L Gibbons

Placings:0P/40/P-P   (4510)
2003/04: 19PGS,

	Starts	1st	2nd	3rd	Win & Pl
Chases	1	0	0	0	
Career Total	6	0	0	0	243

Going: Sf: 0-0 GS: 0-1 Gd: 0-0 GF: - Fm: 0-0
Distance: 2m/2m3: 0-1 2m4-2m7: 0-0 3m+: 0-0
Track: LH: 0-0 RH: 0-1 Tight: 0-0 Gall: 0-0
Aids: Bl: 0-0 Vi: 0-0 Tstrap: 0-0 Ckp: 0-0
Best Rating: 40 5/00 Ctml 2m1f110y good Hdl

Magique Etoile (IRE)

72

8-y-o b m Magical Wonder (USA)-She's A Dancer (IRE)
(Alzao (USA))
N J Hawke Mrs G M S Slater

Placings:05/30/500/040R6P-P   (0630)
2003/04: 17PGF,

	Starts	1st	2nd	3rd	Win & Pl
Hurdles	1	0	0	0	
Career Total	14	0	0	1	344

Going: Sf: 0-0 GS: 0-0 Gd: 0-0 GF: - Fm: 0-1
Distance: 2m/2m3: 0-1 2m4-2m7: 0-0 3m+: 0-0
Track: LH: 0-1 RH: 0-0 Tight: 0-1 Gall: 0-0
Aids: Bl: 0-0 Vi: 0-0 Tstrap: 0-0 Ckp: 0-0
Best Rating: 77 9/00 Plum 2m gd-fm Hdl

Magnemite (IRE)

8-y-o b g Dromod Hill-Rostoonstown Lass (IRE) (Decent Fellow)
N J Dawe C A White

Placings:P (4510)
2003/04: 19^{P}GS,

	Starts	1st	2nd	3rd	Win & Pl
Chases	1	0	0	0	
Career Total	1	0	0	0	

Going:	Sf: 0-0 GS: 0-1 Gd: 0-0 GF: - Fm: 0-0
Distance:	2m/2m3: 0-1 2m4-2m7: 0-0 3m+: 0-0
Track:	LH: 0-0 RH: 0-1 Tight: 0-0 Gall: 0-0
Aids:	Bl: 0-1 Vi: 0-0 Tstrap: 0-0 Ckp: 0-0

Mags Two
98   75

7-y-o b g Jumbo Hirt (USA)-Welsh Diamond (High Top)
Ms Liz Harrison   David Alan Harrison

Placings:00006-6524 (1627)
2003/04: 20^{6}F, 20^{5}G, 20^{2}GF, 24^{4}GF,

	Starts	1st	2nd	3rd	Win & Pl
Hurdles	4	0	1	0	645
Career Total	9	0	1	0	645

Going:	Sf: 0-0 GS: 0-0 Gd: 0-1 GF: - Fm: 0-3
Distance:	2m/2m3: 0-0 2m4-2m7: 0-3 3m+: 0-1
Track:	LH: 0-3 RH: 0-1 Tight: 0-0 Gall: 0-0
Aids:	Bl: 0-0 Vi: 0-0 Tstrap: 0-0 Ckp: 0-0
Best Rating:	75 10/03 Hexm 3m gd-fm Hdl

Exposed modest novice hurdler.

Maharbal (FR)
105   115+

4-y-o b g Assessor (IRE)-Cynthia (FR) (Mont Basile (FR))
N J Henderson   The Pheasant Inn Partnership

Placings:155 (3511)
2003/04: 16^{1}GF, 16^{5}G, 18^{5}G,

	Starts	1st	2nd	3rd	Win & Pl
Hurdles	3	1	0	0	5355
Career Total	3	1	0	0	5355
115 12/03 Newb 2m110y D Hdl				G-F	£5076
				Total win prize-money	£5077

Going:	Sf: 0-0 GS: 0-0 Gd: 0-2 GF: - Fm: 1-1
Distance:	2m/2m3: 1-3 2m4-2m7: 0-0 3m+: 0-0
Track:	LH: 1-2 RH: 0-1 Tight: 0-1 Gall: 1-1
Aids:	Bl: 0-0 Vi: 0-0 Tstrap: 0-0 Ckp: 0-0
Best Rating:	115 12/03 Newb 2m110y gd-fm Hdl

Decent juvenile hurdler; ex-French; held since his winning debut; suited by two miles and fast ground.

Maid For A Monarch

4-y-o b f King's Signet (USA)-Regan (USA) (Lear Fan (USA))
Miss J Feilden (J G Given 30/6)   Steven Rees

Placings:060P (4762)
2003/04: 16^{6}G, 17^{6}G, 17^{9}G, 19^{5}S,

	Starts	1st	2nd	3rd	Win & Pl
Hurdles	4	0	0	0	0
Career Total	4	0	0	0	0

Going:	Sf: 0-1 GS: 0-0 Gd: 0-3 GF: - Fm: 0-0
Distance:	2m/2m3: 0-3 2m4-2m7: 0-1 3m+: 0-0
Track:	LH: 0-1 RH: 0-2 Tight: 0-1 Gall: 0-1
Aids:	Bl: 0-0 Vi: 0-0 Tstrap: 0-0 Ckp: 0-0

Maiden Voyage
108   105+

6-y-o b m Slip Anchor-Elaine Tully (IRE) (Persian Bold)
P R Webber   R J McAlpine

Placings:F02323-0110 (0760)
2003/04: 19^{9}GS, 20^{1}S, 16^{1}GF, 20^{9}G,

	Starts	1st	2nd	3rd	Win & Pl
Hurdles	4	2	0	0	7093
Career Total	10	2	2	2	11014
108 6/03 Hexm 2m110y E Hdl				G-F	£3479
110 5/03 Bang 2m4f E Hdl				SFT	£3614
				Total win prize-money	£7093

Going:	Sf: 1-1 GS: 0-1 Gd: 0-1 GF: - Fm: 1-1
Distance:	2m/2m3: 1-2 2m4-2m7: 1-3 3m+: 0-0
Track:	LH: 2-3 RH: 0-1 Tight: 1-1 Gall: 0-0
Aids:	Bl: 0-0 Vi: 2-4 Tstrap: 0-0 Ckp: 0-0
Best Rating:	110 5/03 Bang 2m4f soft Hdl

Modest hurdler; won twice in the spring of 2003; stays two and a half miles; appears to act on any ground.

Maidstone Majesty
77f

7-y-o b g Teenoso (USA)-Easby Mosella (Le Moss)
Mrs S J Smith   Mrs S Smith

Placings:5 (0334)
2003/04: 17^{5}GF,

	Starts	1st	2nd	3rd	Win & Pl
NH Flat	1	0	0	0	
Career Total	1	0	0	0	

Going:	Sf: 0-0 GS: 0-0 Gd: 0-0 GF: - Fm: 0-1
Distance:	2m/2m3: 0-1 2m4-2m7: 0-0 3m+: 0-0
Track:	LH: 0-1 RH: 0-0 Tight: 0-0 Gall: 0-0
Aids:	Bl: 0-0 Vi: 0-0 Tstrap: 0-0 Ckp: 0-0
Best Rating:	77 5/03 Sthl 2m1f gd-fm NHF

Maidstone Mistral
94   88+

4-y-o b g Slip Anchor-Cayla (Tumble Wind (USA))
M C Pipe   Mrs Judith E Wilson

Placings:03300PP (4752)
2003/04: 12^{6}GF, 12^{3}S, 17^{3}GS, 17^{9}S, 17^{9}GS, 17^{9}G, 16^{6}G,

	Starts	1st	2nd	3rd	Win & Pl
NH Flat	2	0	0	1	362
Hurdles	5	0	0	1	491
Career Total	7	0	0	2	853

Going:	Sf: 0-2 GS: 0-2 Gd: 0-2 GF: - Fm: 0-1
Distance:	2m/2m3: 0-5 2m4-2m7: 0-0 3m+: 0-0
Track:	LH: 0-2 RH: 0-4 Tight: 0-4 Gall: 0-0
Aids:	Bl: 0-0 Vi: 0-0 Tstrap: 0-0 Ckp: 0-0
Best Rating:	88 1/04 Extr 2m1f gd-sft Hdl

Maidstone Monument (IRE)
108(111c)   (113c)96+

9-y-o b g Jurado (USA)-Loreto Lady (Brave Invader (USA))
Mrs A M Thorpe   Don Jenkins

Placings:50/P24153PP0P/06053432P/3P41241P2U4PP-P5123231P1P20P0 (4932)
2003/04: 26^{6}G, 24^{5}G, 23^{1}GF, 23^{2}G, 23^{3}GF, 26^{2}GF, 26^{3}GF, 26^{1}GF, 26^{P}GF, 25^{1}GF, 26^{P}G, 26^{2}GS, 21^{0}G, 26^{P}G, 27^{0}G,

	Starts	1st	2nd	3rd	Win & Pl
Hurdles	3	1	0	0	4340
Chases	12	2	3	2	13193
Career Total	49	6	7	6	37389
96 10/03 Plum 3m1f110yD(0-120)HHdl				G-F	£4340
113 9/03 Plum 3m2f D(0-120)HCh				G-F	£5037
107 7/03 Worc 2m7f110yF(0-100)HCh				G-F	£3571
108 9/02 NAbb 3m2f110yD(0-120)HCh				GD	£4655
106 6/02 NAbb 3m2f110yE(0-110)HCh				G-F	£3309
85 6/00 Hexm 2m D Hdl				G-F	£3143
				Total win prize-money	£24058

Going:	Sf: 0-0 GS: 0-1 Gd: 0-7 GF: - Fm: 3-7
Distance:	2m/2m3: 0-0 2m4-2m7: 0-1 3m+: 3-14
Track:	LH: 2-10 RH: 0-1 Tight: 1-8 Gall: 0-2
Aids:	Bl: 0-0 Vi: 0-1 Tstrap: 0-0 Ckp: 0-0
Best Rating:	113 9/03 Plum 3m2f gd-fm Ch

Moderate front-running handicap chaser; acts on a sound surface; stays three miles two.

Maiful (FR)
89   81

4-y-o b g Useful (FR)-Shailann (FR) (Gaspard De La Nuit (FR))
P F Nicholls   Hill Fuels Limited

Placings:020 (4565)
2003/04: 16^{6}S, 16^{2}G, 17^{9}GS,

	Starts	1st	2nd	3rd	Win & Pl
Hurdles	3	0	1	0	1105
Career Total	3	0	1	0	1105

Going:	Sf: 0-1 GS: 0-1 Gd: 0-1 GF: - Fm: 0-0
Distance:	2m/2m3: 0-3 2m4-2m7: 0-0 3m+: 0-0
Track:	LH: 0-1 RH: 0-2 Tight: 0-1 Gall: 0-0
Aids:	Bl: 0-0 Vi: 0-0 Tstrap: 0-0 Ckp: 0-0
Best Rating:	84 3/04 Winc 2m good Hdl

Maisey Down

7-y-o b m Rakaposhi King-Win Green Hill (National Trust)
J A B Old   J A B Old

Placings:0-56 (3787)
2003/04: 16^{6}GF, 22^{6}G,

	Starts	1st	2nd	3rd	Win & Pl
NH Flat	1	0	0	0	0
Hurdles	1	0	0	0	0
Career Total	3	0	0	0	0

Going:	Sf: 0-0 GS: 0-0 Gd: 0-1 GF: - Fm: 0-1
Distance:	2m/2m3: 0-1 2m4-2m7: 0-1 3m+: 0-0
Track:	LH: 0-1 RH: 0-1 Tight: 0-0 Gall: 0-0
Aids:	Bl: 0-0 Vi: 0-0 Tstrap: 0-0 Ckp: 0-0
Best Rating:	61 5/03 Chep 2m110y gd-fm NHF

Maisiebel
89   66+

6-y-o ch m Be My Native (USA)-High 'B' (Gunner B)
R N Bevis   Ewson Contractors

Placings:00-6 (1813)
2003/04: 20^{6}G,

	Starts	1st	2nd	3rd	Win & Pl
Hurdles	1	0	0	0	0
Career Total	3	0	0	0	0

Maitre De Musique (FR) — Going block

Going:	Sf: 0-0 GS: 0-0 Gd: 0-1 GF: - Fm: 0-0
Distance:	2m/2m3: 0-0 2m4-2m7: 0-1 3m+: 0-0
Track:	LH: 0-1 RH: 0-0 Tight: 0-1 Gall: 0-0
Aids:	Bl: 0-0 Vi: 0-0 Tstrap: 0-0 Ckp: 0-0
Best Rating:	68 10/03 Bang 2m4f good Hdl

Maitre De Musique (FR)

13-y-o ch g Quai Voltaire (USA)-Mativa (FR) (Satingo)
Mrs F E Needham Dr M P Tate

Placings: 10/003430/55420/**1**/**422P23**/P13**P664**/53/63/435-
3P62   (0506)
2003/04: 25³G, 30PGF, 22⁶G, 24²GS,

	Starts	1st	2nd	3rd	Win & Pl
Chases	4	0	1	1	1444
Career Total	38	3	5	8	24707
123	11/99	Newc	2m4f		D(0-125)HCh	GD	£3793
120	12/97	Weth	2m4f110yD Ch			GD	£3756
113	2/95	Kemp	2m		H NHF		HVY	£1996
				Total win prize-money £9546

Going:	Sf: 0-0 GS: 0-1 Gd: 0-2 GF: - Fm: 0-1
Distance:	2m/2m3: 0-0 2m4-2m7: 0-0 3m+: 0-3
Track:	LH: 0-2 RH: 0-2 Tight: 0-3 Gall: 0-1
Aids:	Bl: 0-0 Vi: 0-0 Tstrap: 0-4 Ckp: 0-0
Best Rating:	126 4/99 Aint 2m6f good Ch

Maitre Levy (GER)

88   **89+**

6-y-o b g Monsun (GER)-Meerdunung (GDR) (Tauchsport (GER))
M C Pipe (Mario Hofer 24/5) Favourites Racing

Placings: P640   (4873)
2003/04: 25PG, 16⁶GS, 17⁴G, 20⁰GS,

	Starts	1st	2nd	3rd	Win & Pl
Hurdles	4	0	0	0	334
Career Total	4	0	0	0	334

Going:	Sf: 0-0 GS: 0-2 Gd: 0-2 GF: - Fm: 0-0
Distance:	2m/2m3: 0-2 2m4-2m7: 0-1 3m+: 0-1
Track:	LH: 0-3 RH: 0-1 Tight: 0-1 Gall: 0-1
Aids:	Bl: 0-0 Vi: 0-0 Tstrap: 0-2 Ckp: 0-0
Best Rating:	89 4/04 Extr 2m1f good Hdl

Majariyya (IRE)

67   **70**

7-y-o ch m Lycius (USA)-Madaniyya (USA) (Shahrastani (USA))
J K Magee Michael McGovern

Placings: F50-000   (0695a)
2003/04: 22⁰G, 16⁹GF, 16⁶F,

	Starts	1st	2nd	3rd	Win & Pl
Hurdles	3	0	0	0	
Career Total	6	0	0	0	

Going:	Sf: 0-0 GS: 0-0 Gd: 0-0 GF: - Fm: 0-2
Distance:	2m/2m3: 0-2 2m4-2m7: 0-1 3m+: 0-0
Track:	LH: 0-1 RH: 0-0 Tight: 0-0 Gall: 0-0
Aids:	Bl: 0-0 Vi: 0-0 Tstrap: 0-1 Ckp: 0-0
Best Rating:	70 9/02 DRoy 2m good Hdl

Majed (FR)

104   **117**

8-y-o b g Fijar Tango (FR)-Full Of Passion (USA) (Blushing Groom (FR))
P F Nicholls Sandicroft Stud I

Placings: 46PP050/**62042321111**/1210**F0**/00-2342122P
                                                          (4734)
2003/04: 23²GF, 26³S, 26⁴GS, 25²S, 26¹GS, 24²G, 23²GS, 26PG,

	Starts	1st	2nd	3rd	Win & Pl
Chases	8	1	4	1	11983
Career Total	34	7	8	2	78074
117	2/04	Font	3m2f110y E Ch		G-S	£4114
150	12/01	Winc	2m6f	B HHdl	GD	£8430
139	11/01	Chep	2m4f	B HHdl	G-S	£22750
128	4/01	Ayr	3m110y B HHdl		GD	£7228
127	4/01	Extr	2m1f	E Hdl	G-S	£2153
133	3/01	Strf	2m6f110yD Hdl		SFT	£3965
115	2/01	Plum	2m	E Hdl		SFT	£2075
				Total win prize-money £50718

Going:	Sf: 0-2 GS: 1-3 Gd: 0-2 GF: - Fm: 0-1
Distance:	2m/2m3: 0-0 2m4-2m7: 0-1 3m+: 1-8
Track:	LH: 0-5 RH: 0-2 Tight: 1-6 Gall: 0-0
Aids:	Bl: 1-6 Vi: 0-0 Tstrap: 0-0 Ckp: 0-0
Best Rating:	150 12/01 Winc 2m6f good Hdl

Modest chaser; much better over hurdles; stays really well; acts on soft ground; usually wears headgear.

Majestic Bay (IRE)

(105h)   (110h) **127**

8-y-o b g Unfuwain (USA)-That'Ll Be The Day (IRE) (Thatching)
J A B Old W J Smith And M D Dudley

Placings: 0654/4334231-0   (2296)
2003/04: 24⁰S,

	Starts	1st	2nd	3rd	Win & Pl
Hurdles	1	0	0	0	
Career Total	12	1	1	3	15841
127	4/03	Asct	3m110y C Ch		GD	£10159
				Total win prize-money £10160

Going:	Sf: 0-1 GS: 0-0 Gd: 0-0 GF: - Fm: 0-0
Distance:	2m/2m3: 0-0 2m4-2m7: 0-0 3m+: 0-1
Track:	LH: 0-0 RH: 0-1 Tight: 0-0 Gall: 0-0
Aids:	Bl: 0-0 Vi: 0-0 Tstrap: 0-0 Ckp: 0-0
Best Rating:	127 4/03 Asct 3m110y good Ch

Fair hurdler/chaser; got off the mark over jumps when winning a novice chase at Ascot in April 2003; stays 3m; acts on any ground, but better on a sound surface.

Majestic Moonbeam (IRE)

83(97c)   (94c)**67**

6-y-o b g Supreme Leader-Magic Moonbeam (IRE) (Decent Fellow)
Jonjo O'Neill John P McManus

Placings: 1-0U400   (4915)
2003/04: 22⁰GS, 16ᵁHY, 17⁴G, 17⁰G, 16⁰GS,

	Starts	1st	2nd	3rd	Win & Pl
Hurdles	3	0	0	0	0
Chases	2	0	0	0	412
Career Total	6	1	0	0	2533
107	3/03	Wwck	2m	H NHF	GD	£2121
				Total win prize-money £2121

Going:	Sf: 0-1 GS: 0-2 Gd: 0-2 GF: - Fm: 0-0
Distance:	2m/2m3: 0-4 2m4-2m7: 0-1 3m+: 0-0

Majic Dust

77   **80**

4-y-o b g Wizard King-Fuchu (Jupiter Island)
J A Supple Geoff Hubbard Racing

Placings: PP43500   (3915)
2003/04: 16PGF, 16PGF, 16⁴GS, 16³GS, 16⁵S, 19⁰G, 16⁰G,

	Starts	1st	2nd	3rd	Win & Pl
Hurdles	7	0	0	1	281
Career Total	7	0	0	1	281

Going:	Sf: 0-1 GS: 0-2 Gd: 0-2 GF: - Fm: 0-2
Distance:	2m/2m3: 0-7 2m4-2m7: 0-0 3m+: 0-0
Track:	LH: 0-4 RH: 0-3 Tight: 0-0 Gall: 0-1
Aids:	Bl: 0-1 Vi: 0-0 Tstrap: 0-0 Ckp: 0-0
Best Rating:	80 12/03 Uttx 2m gd-sft Hdl

Best effort when third in poor seller at Uttoxeter in December.

Majlis (IRE)

87   (0c)**104**

7-y-o b g Caerleon (USA)-Ploy (Posse (USA))
R M H Cowell (T R George 17/1) Terry Warner

Placings: 623²/2041110P/F0600P-0   (3367)
2003/04: 16⁰G,

	Starts	1st	2nd	3rd	Win & Pl
Hurdles	1	0	0	0	
Career Total	19	3	2	1	35026
128	1/02	Kemp	2m	B(0-145)HHdl	G-S	£23200
122	1/02	Winc	2m	E Hdl	GD	£2940
120	12/01	Tntn	2m1f	E(0-115)HHdl	G-S	£3948
				Total win prize-money £30089

Going:	Sf: 0-0 GS: 0-0 Gd: 0-0 GF: - Fm: 0-0
Distance:	2m/2m3: 0-1 2m4-2m7: 0-0 3m+: 0-0
Track:	LH: 0-0 RH: 0-1 Tight: 0-0 Gall: 0-0
Aids:	Bl: 0-1 Vi: 0-0 Tstrap: 0-0 Ckp: 0-0
Best Rating:	128 1/02 Kemp 2m gd-sft Hdl

Fair handicap hurdler; acts on good and good to soft ground; effective over two miles; suited by a flat, right-handed track; often wears blinkers.

Major Belle (FR)

(78h)   (88+h)

5-y-o b m Cyborg (FR)-Mistine Major (FR) (Major Petingo (FR))
M C Pipe J J Boulter

Placings: 21/0F31U2-6   (4822)
2003/04: 19⁶GF,

	Starts	1st	2nd	3rd	Win & Pl
Hurdles	1	0	0	0	
Career Total	9	2	2	1	15821
3/03	Toul	2m1f110y Ch		HVY	£4052
4/02	Pau	2m	Hdl		G-S	£4712
				Total win prize-money £8764

Going:	Sf: 0-0 GS: 0-0 Gd: 0-0 GF: - Fm: 0-1
Distance:	2m/2m3: 0-1 2m4-2m7: 0-0 3m+: 0-0
Track:	LH: 0-0 RH: 0-1 Tight: 0-0 Gall: 0-0
Aids:	Bl: 0-0 Vi: 0-0 Tstrap: 0-0 Ckp: 0-0
Best Rating:	88 4/04 Extr 2m3f gd-fm Hdl

Major Benefit (IRE)

103   116

7-y-o b g Executive Perk-Merendas Sister (Pauper)
Miss K Marks (Mrs P Grainger 26/5) Nick Shutts

Placings:3-2P122P   (4398)
2003/04: 24²S, 23PHY, 22¹S, 20²S, 27²GS, 32PG,

	Starts	1st	2nd	3rd	Win & Pl
Chases	6	1	3	0	6957
Career Total	7	1	3	1	7180
116 12/03 Towc	2m6f		E Ch		SFT £3438

Total win prize-money £3439

Going:	Sf: 1-4 GS: 0-1 Gd: 0-1 GF: - Fm: 0-0
Distance:	2m/2m3: 0-0 **2m4-2m7: 1-3** 3m+: 0-3
Track:	LH: 0-5 **RH: 1-1** Tight: 0-2 Gall: 0-1
Aids:	Bl: 0-0 Vi: 0-0 Tstrap: 0-0 Ckp: 0-0
Best Rating:	**116** 2/04 Sedg 3m3f gd-sft Ch

Plenty of promise in hunter chases; sprung 28/1 surprise in 2m 6f novice chase at Towcester December 2003; not disgraced under penalty subsequently; acts on soft ground.

Major Blue

98   92

9-y-o ch g Scallywag-Town Blues (Charlottown)
J G M O'Shea Mrs Ruth Nelmes, C L Dubois, P Smith

Placings:34/0362P-212   (2935)
2003/04: 16²G, 26¹GS, 21²S,

	Starts	1st	2nd	3rd	Win & Pl
Hurdles	3	1	2	0	3682
Career Total	10	1	3	2	5817
92 12/03 Hrfd	3m2f	F(0-95)HHdl		G-S	£1925

Total win prize-money £1925

Going:	Sf: 0-1 GS: 1-1 Gd: 0-1 GF: - Fm: 0-0
Distance:	2m/2m3: 0-1 2m4-2m7: 0-0 **3m+: 1-1**
Track:	LH: 0-1 **RH: 1-2** Tight: 0-0 Gall: 0-0
Aids:	Bl: 0-0 Vi: 0-0 Tstrap: 0-0 Ckp: 0-0
Best Rating:	**97** 10/01 Bang 2m1f soft NHF

Plating-class hurdler; appreciated the combination of soft ground and 3m2f when winning conditional jockeys' novices' handicap hurdle at Hereford December 2003; still showed signs of greenness and further improvement is possible.

Major Bob

5-y-o b/br g Syrtos-Miss Pandy (Pitpan)
G P Enright A O Ashford

Placings:0   (1924)
2003/04: 18⁰G,

	Starts	1st	2nd	3rd	Win & Pl
NH Flat	1	0	0	0	
Career Total	1	0	0	0	

Going:	Sf: 0-0 GS: 0-0 Gd: 0-1 GF: - Fm: 0-0
Distance:	2m/2m3: 0-1 2m4-2m7: 0-0 3m+: 0-0
Track:	LH: 0-1 RH: 0-0 Tight: 0-0 Gall: 0-0
Aids:	Bl: 0-0 Vi: 0-0 Tstrap: 0-0 Ckp: 0-0

Major Catch (IRE)

78   50

5-y-o b g Safety Catch (USA)-Inch Tape (Prince Hansel)
N J Gifford Martin & Valerie Slade

Placings:010   (3750)
2003/04: 16⁰S, 18¹HY, 18⁰GS,

	Starts	1st	2nd	3rd	Win & Pl
NH Flat	2	1	0	0	2023
Hurdles	1	0	0	0	0
Career Total	3	1	0	0	2023
110 1/04 Font	2m2f110yH NHF			HVY	£2023

Total win prize-money £2023

Going:	Sf: 1-2 GS: 0-1 Gd: 0-0 GF: - Fm: 0-0
Distance:	**2m/2m3: 1-3** 2m4-2m7: 0-0 3m+: 0-0
Track:	**LH: 1-2** RH: 0-1 Tight: 1-2 Gall: 0-0
Aids:	Bl: 0-0 Vi: 0-0 Tstrap: 0-0 Ckp: 0-0
Best Rating:	**110** 1/04 Font 2m2f110y heavy NHF

Easily won 2m2f bumper on heavy ground at Fontwell in January on second career outing; promising.

Major Drive (IRE)

105   122

6-y-o b g Sadler's Wells (USA)-Puck's Castle (Shirley Heights)
James Moffatt Woodburn, Gallagher & Friends

Placings:0650/21001-215P   (4729)
2003/04: 21²G, 21¹GS, 23⁵HY, 20PG,

	Starts	1st	2nd	3rd	Win & Pl
Hurdles	4	1	1	0	5516
Career Total	13	3	2	1	13995
121 1/04 Sedg	2m5f110yE(0-110)HHdl		G-S	£4221
111 2/03 Muss	3m	D(0-110)HHdl	GD	£4715
95 10/02 Hexm	2m4f110yE Hdl		G-F	£2915

Total win prize-money £11854

Going:	Sf: 0-1 GS: 1-1 Gd: 0-2 GF: - Fm: 0-0
Distance:	2m/2m3: 0-0 **2m4-2m7:** 1-3 3m+: 0-1
Track:	**LH: 1-3** RH: 0-1 **Tight: 1-2** Gall: 0-0
Aids:	Bl: 0-0 Vi: 0-0 Tstrap: 0-0 Ckp: 0-0
Best Rating:	**121** 1/04 Sedg 2m5f110y gd-sft Hdl

Modest hurdler; recorded third career win at Sedgefield in January 2004; stays three miles; acts on most types of ground.

Major Euro (IRE)

105   114+

7-y-o b g Lord Americo-Gold Bank (Over The River (FR))
S J Gilmore Miss Jumbo Frost

Placings:00-232041F0   (4605)
2003/04: 20²GF, 20³S, 20²GF, 20⁰G, 16⁴S, 20¹GS, 21FG, 22⁰G,

	Starts	1st	2nd	3rd	Win & Pl
Hurdles	8	1	2	1	8609
Career Total	10	1	2	1	8609
114 2/04 Sand	2m4f110yD(0-110)HHdl		G-S	£5096

Total win prize-money £5096

Going:	Sf: 0-2 GS: 1-1 Gd: 0-3 GF: - Fm: 0-2
Distance:	2m/2m3: 0-1 **2m4-2m7:** 1-7 3m+: 0-0
Track:	LH: 0-4 **RH: 1-3** Tight: 0-0 Gall: 0-1
Aids:	Bl: 0-0 Vi: 0-0 Tstrap: 0-0 Ckp: 0-0
Best Rating:	**114** 2/04 Sand 2m4f110y gd-sft Hdl

Modest hurdler; stays two and a half miles; acts on fast and easy ground.

Major Shark (FR)

103   93

6-y-o b g Saint Preuil (FR)-Cindy Cad (FR) (Cadoudal (FR))
Mrs J Candlish Greencard Golfers

Placings:035051P-623P3030   (4956)
2003/04: 16⁶G, 21²G, 23⁵GS, 20PHY, 19³GF, 17⁰G, 21³G, 22⁰G,

	Starts	1st	2nd	3rd	Win & Pl
Hurdles	8	0	1	3	5806

Major Fire *(not present)*

Career info (top column)

Career Total	15	1	1	4	8778
91 3/03 Font	2m4f	F(0-90)HHdl	SFT	£2695

Total win prize-money £2695

Going:	Sf: 0-1 GS: 1-1 Gd: 0-5 GF: - Fm: 0-1
Distance:	2m/2m3: 0-2 2m4-2m7: 0-6 3m+: 0-0
Track:	LH: 0-3 RH: 0-4 Tight: 0-0 Gall: 0-2
Aids:	Bl: 0-0 Vi: 0-0 Tstrap: 0-0 Ckp: 0-8
Best Rating:	**93** 3/04 Hrfd 2m3f110y gd-fm Hdl

Moderate hurdler; best at two and a half miles, but stays further; acts on soft ground; has worn cheekpieces.

Major Speculation (IRE)

95   114

4-y-o b g Spectrum (IRE)-Pacific Grove (Persian Bold)
M C Pipe (G A Butler 1/10) Latona Leisure Limited

Placings:106PB0   (4893)
2003/04: 16¹GS, 17⁰G, 16⁶G, 16PS, 17RG, 16⁰G,

	Starts	1st	2nd	3rd	Win & Pl
Hurdles	6	1	0	0	7150
Career Total	6	1	0	0	7150
114 11/03 Newb	2m110y C Hdl		G-S	£7150

Total win prize-money £7150

Going:	Sf: 0-1 GS: 1-1 Gd: 0-4 GF: - Fm: 0-0
Distance:	**2m/2m3: 1-6** 2m4-2m7: 0-0 3m+: 0-0
Track:	**LH: 1-3** RH: 0-3 Tight: 0-0 **Gall: 1-3**
Aids:	Bl: 0-0 Vi: 0-3 Tstrap: 0-0 Ckp: 0-0
Best Rating:	**114** 11/03 Newb 2m110y gd-sft Hdl

Modest novice hurdler; won well at Newbury on hurdles debut despite racing keenly, but limitations exposed since; may be best suited to flat tracks; acts with cut; has worn a visor.

Major Vernon (IRE)

105f   120+f

5-y-o b g Flemensfirth (USA)-Rainys Run (Deep Run)
W P Mullins B Doyle

Placings:10   (4400)
2003/04: 16¹S, 16⁰G,

	Starts	1st	2nd	3rd	Win & Pl
NH Flat	2	1	0	0	4373
Career Total	2	1	0	0	4373
120 2/04 Thur	2m	NHF	SFT	£4373

Total win prize-money £4373

Going:	Sf: 1-1 GS: 0-0 Gd: 0-1 GF: - Fm: 0-0
Distance:	**2m/2m3: 1-2** 2m4-2m7: 0-0 3m+: 0-0
Track:	LH: 0-1 RH: 0-0 Tight: 0-0 Gall: 0-0
Aids:	Bl: 0-0 Vi: 0-0 Tstrap: 0-0 Ckp: 0-0
Best Rating:	**120** 2/04 Thur 2m soft NHF

Fair bumper winner; acts on soft.

Majority Verdict

110(106h)   (112 h)115+

8-y-o b g Leading Counsel (USA)-Culm Valley (Port Corsair)
H D Daly Gibson, Goddard, Hamer & Hawkes

Placings:21/2/2-211F   (2719)
2003/04: 22²S, 20¹S, 20¹S, 20FGS,

	Starts	1st	2nd	3rd	Win & Pl
Hurdles	2	1	1	0	4729
Chases	2	1	0	0	3752
Career Total	8	3	4	0	15046
120 11/03 Hayd	2m4f	E Ch	SFT	£3752
123 5/03 Uttx	2m4f110y		E Hdl	SFT

£3605

| 124 | 3/01 | Strf | | 2m110y H NHF | | SFT | £3241 |

Total win prize-money £10598

Going:	Sf: 2-3 GS: 0-1 Gd: 0-0 GF: - Fm: 0-0
Distance:	2m/2m3: 0-0 **2m4-2m7: 2-4** 3m+: 0-0
Track:	LH: **2-4** RH: 0-0 Tight: 0-0 Gall: 0-1
Aids:	Bl: 0-0 Vi: 0-0 Tstrap: 0-0 Ckp: 0-0
Best Rating:	**124** 3/01 Strf 2m110y soft NHF

Fair hurdler; had luck on his side when making a winning debut over fences at Haydock in November; fell fatally at Cheltenham in December; stayed beyond two and a half miles and loved soft ground. (DEAD)

Majors Mistress

5-y-o b m Superpower-Polola (Aragon)
J C Fox Lord Mutton Racing Partnership

| Placings:0P | | | | | (0889) |
2003/04: 16⁰GS, 16ᴾG,

	Starts	1st	2nd	3rd	Win & Pl
NH Flat	1	0	0	0	0
Hurdles	1	0	0	0	0
Career Total	2	0	0	0	

Going:	Sf: 0-0 GS: 0-1 Gd: 0-1 GF: - Fm: 0-0
Distance:	2m/2m3: 0-2 2m4-2m7: 0-0 3m+: 0-0
Track:	LH: 0-2 RH: 0-0 Tight: 0-0 Gall: 0-0
Aids:	Bl: 0-0 Vi: 0-0 Tstrap: 0-0 Ckp: 0-0
Best Rating:	24 5/03 Worc 2m gd-sft NHF

Make Haste Slowly
94   101

7-y-o b g Terimon-Henry's True Love (Random Shot)
H D Daly T F F Nixon

| Placings:2-3P | | | | | (3775) |
2003/04: 16⁰GS, 16ᴾG,

	Starts	1st	2nd	3rd	Win & Pl
Hurdles	2	0	0	1	770
Career Total	3	0	1	1	2218

Going:	Sf: 0-0 GS: 0-1 Gd: 0-1 GF: - Fm: 0-0
Distance:	2m/2m3: 0-2 2m4-2m7: 0-0 3m+: 0-0
Track:	LH: 0-1 RH: 0-1 Tight: 0-1 Gall: 0-0
Aids:	Bl: 0-0 Vi: 0-0 Tstrap: 0-0 Ckp: 0-0
Best Rating:	101 11/03 Aint 2m110y gd-sft Hdl

Make It Easy (IRE)
98   (6h)65

8-y-o b/br g Alphabatim (USA)-Mammy's Friend (Miners Lamp)
Mrs L C Jewell O J C Shannon

| Placings:0-P0P00P2 | | | | | (4789) |
2003/04: 20ᴾS, 25⁰G, 26ᴾG, 20⁰G, 25⁴G, 28ᴾG, 17²G,

	Starts	1st	2nd	3rd	Win & Pl
Chases	7	0	1	0	754
Career Total	8	0	1	0	754

Going:	Sf: 0-2 GS: 0-0 Gd: 0-5 GF: - Fm: 0-0
Distance:	2m/2m3: 0-1 2m4-2m7: 0-2 3m+: 0-4
Track:	LH: 0-2 RH: 0-3 Tight: 0-5 Gall: 0-1
Aids:	Bl: 0-0 Vi: 0-1 Tstrap: 0-0 Ckp: 0-4
Best Rating:	65 4/04 Plum 2m1f good Ch

Plating-class chaser; ran best race in first-time visor when dropped to two miles-one; acts on good ground.

Make My Hay
93   87+

5-y-o b g Bluegrass Prince (IRE)-Shashi (IRE) (Shaadi (USA))
J Gallagher (J White 4/2) Mrs Irene Clifford

| Placings:306 | | | | | (4793) |
2003/04: 16⁵GS, 17⁰GS, 16⁶G,

	Starts	1st	2nd	3rd	Win & Pl
Hurdles	3	0	0	1	270
Career Total	3	0	0	1	270

Going:	Sf: 0-0 GS: 0-2 Gd: 0-1 GF: - Fm: 0-0
Distance:	2m/2m3: 0-3 2m4-2m7: 0-0 3m+: 0-0
Track:	LH: 0-2 RH: 0-1 Tight: 0-2 Gall: 0-0
Aids:	Bl: 0-0 Vi: 0-0 Tstrap: 0-0 Ckp: 0-0
Best Rating:	87 4/04 Plum 2m good Hdl

Make The Call
47

7-y-o b m Syrtos-Dawn Call (Rymer)
John Allen T D Galer

| Placings:000/PPF0 | | | | | (4539) |
2003/04: 16ᴾS, 21ᴾS, 17ᶠHY, 21⁰GS,

	Starts	1st	2nd	3rd	Win & Pl
Hurdles	4	0	0	0	
Career Total	7	0	0	0	

Going:	Sf: 0-2 GS: 0-1 Gd: 0-1 GF: - Fm: 0-0
Distance:	2m/2m3: 0-2 2m4-2m7: 0-2 3m+: 0-0
Track:	LH: 0-1 RH: 0-3 Tight: 0-1 Gall: 0-0
Aids:	Bl: 0-0 Vi: 0-0 Tstrap: 0-0 Ckp: 0-0
Best Rating:	48 6/01 Worc 2m gd-fm NHF

Makhpiya Patahn (IRE)

12-y-o gr g Nestor-Our Mare Mick (Choral Society)
J H Young J H Young

| Placings:0P0/55/4425P5/4/0FP-P | | | | | (0349) |
2003/04: 26ᴾS, 26ᶠGF,

	Starts	1st	2nd	3rd	Win & Pl
Chases	2	0	0	0	
Career Total	16	0	1	0	2739

Going:	Sf: 0-1 GS: 0-0 Gd: 0-0 GF: - Fm: 0-0
Distance:	2m/2m3: 0-0 2m4-2m7: 0-0 3m+: 0-0
Track:	LH: 0-1 RH: 0-1 Tight: 0-2 Gall: 0-0
Aids:	Bl: 0-0 Vi: 0-1 Tstrap: 0-0 Ckp: 0-1
Best Rating:	88 11/99 Winc 3m1f110y good Ch

Maks Peril

10-y-o br g Makbul-Pink Peril (Mljet)
J Mackie Mrs J Mackie

| Placings:0/P | | | | | (1215) |
2003/04: 20ᴾGF,

	Starts	1st	2nd	3rd	Win & Pl
Hurdles	1	0	0	0	

| Career Total | 2 | 0 | 0 | 0 | |

Going:	Sf: 0-0 GS: 0-0 Gd: 0-0 GF: - Fm: 0-1
Distance:	2m/2m3: 0-0 2m4-2m7: 0-1 3m+: 0-0
Track:	LH: 0-0 RH: 0-1 Tight: 0-0 Gall: 0-1
Aids:	Bl: 0-0 Vi: 0-0 Tstrap: 0-0 Ckp: 0-0
Best Rating:	76 9/99 Carl 2m1f gd-fm NHF

Malbec (IRE)

7-y-o b g Lord Americo-Key Door (IRE) (Beau Charmeur (FR))
Miss A M Newton-Smith Julian Smith

| Placings:P/P4P-04F | | | | | (3199) |
2003/04: 21⁰G, 21⁴GF, 29ᶠS,

	Starts	1st	2nd	3rd	Win & Pl
Hurdles	1	0	0	0	0
Chases	2	0	0	0	268
Career Total	7	0	0	0	268

Going:	Sf: 0-1 GS: 0-0 Gd: 0-1 GF: - Fm: 0-1
Distance:	2m/2m3: 0-0 2m4-2m7: 0-2 3m+: 0-1
Track:	LH: 0-2 RH: 0-1 Tight: 0-3 Gall: 0-0
Aids:	Bl: 0-1 Vi: 0-0 Tstrap: 0-0 Ckp: 0-0

Maldoun (IRE)
104   103

5-y-o b g Kaldoun (FR)-Marzipan (IRE) (Green Desert (USA))
M C Pipe The Dionysius Partnership

| Placings:3134P620 | | | | | (4859) |
2003/04: 17³GS, 16¹G, 17³G, 16⁴G, 16⁵P, 16⁶GF, 16²GS, 19⁰GF,

	Starts	1st	2nd	3rd	Win & Pl
Hurdles	8	1	1	2	9540
Career Total	8	1	1	2	9540

| 84 | 5/03 | Kels | | 2m110y D Hdl | | GD | £5720 |

Total win prize-money £5720

Going:	Sf: 0-1 GS: 0-1 Gd: 1-3 GF: - Fm: 0-3
Distance:	**2m/2m3: 1-7** 2m4-2m7: 0-1 3m+: 0-0
Track:	LH: 1-3 RH: 0-5 **Tight: 1-4** Gall: 0-0
Aids:	Bl: 0-0 Vi: 0-0 Tstrap: 0-0 Ckp: 0-0
Best Rating:	107 3/04 Ludl 2m gd-sft Hdl

Modest hurdler; middle-distance winner on the Flat in France; won at Kelso second hurdles start; effective at two miles; acts on most types of ground.

Malek (IRE)
104(105h)   (118 h)120+

8-y-o b g Tremblant-Any Offers (Paddy's Stream)
Mrs M Reveley Mrs J W Furness & Lord Zetland

| Placings:3U1/15-33P41P | | | | | (4598) |
2003/04: 24³S, 25³G, 25ᴾS, 25⁴S, 28¹G, 32ᴾG,

	Starts	1st	2nd	3rd	Win & Pl
Chases	6	1	0	2	11615
Career Total	11	3	0	3	19392

120	2/04	Carl		3m4f	C(0-130)HCh	GD	£8482
118	11/02	Hayd		2m4f	D Hdl	SFT	£3835
100	3/02	Sthl		3m110y E Ch		HVY	£3159

Total win prize-money £15477

Going:	Sf: 0-3 GS: 0-0 Gd: 1-3 GF: - Fm: 0-0
Distance:	2m/2m3: 0-0 2m4-2m7: 0-0 **3m+: 1-6**
Track:	LH: 0-4 **RH: 1-2** Tight: 0-1 Gall: 0-0
Aids:	Bl: 0-0 Vi: 0-0 Tstrap: 0-0 Ckp: 0-0

Best Rating: 120 2/04   Carl   3m4f   good   Ch

Modest hurdler/chaser; effective in soft ground; stays three miles.

Maljimar (IRE)

80f   88+f

4-y-o b g Un Desperado (FR)-Marble Miller (IRE) (Mister Lord (USA))
Miss H C Knight   Jim Lewis

Placings:2   (4543)
2003/04: 16²GS,

	Starts	1st	2nd	3rd	Win & Pl
NH Flat	1	0	1	0	732
Career Total	1	0	1	0	732

Going:	Sf: 0-0 GS: 0-1 Gd: 0-0 GF: - Fm: 0-0
Distance:	2m/2m3: 0-1 2m4-2m7: 0-0 3m+: 0-0
Track:	LH: 0-0 RH: 0-1 Tight: 0-0 Gall: 0-0
Aids:	Bl: 0-0 Vi: 0-0 Tstrap: 0-0 Ckp: 0-0
Best Rating:	88 3/04 Ludl 2m gd-sft NHF

Related to a number of winners; creditable second in a Ludlow bumper on his debut.

Mallory

103(101h)   (104h)102

10-y-o b g North Col-Veritate (Roman Warrior)
T R George   D J Price

Placings:120/0P/4P32/P1-12P4F44   (3758)
2003/04: 20¹GF, 22¹GF, 20²G, 24⁹G, 20⁴GS, 25FG, 19⁴GS, 22⁴G,

	Starts	1st	2nd	3rd	Win & Pl
Hurdles	5	2	1	0	7973
Chases	3	0	0	0	752
Career Total	18	3	3	1	11968
100	5/03	Winc	2m6f	E(0-100)HHdl	G-F	£3531
90	4/03	Newc	2m4f	E(0-100)HHdl	G-F	£3419
115	12/99	Hntg	2m110y	H NHF	GD	£1800

Total win prize-money £8751

Going:	Sf: 0-0 GS: 0-2 Gd: 0-4 GF: - Fm: 2-2
Distance:	2m/2m3: 0-1 2m4-2m7: 2-5 3m+: 0-2
Track:	LH: 1-5 RH: 1-3 Tight: 0-3 Gall: 1-1
Aids:	Bl: 0-0 Vi: 0-0 Tstrap: 0-0 Ckp: 0-0
Best Rating:	115 2/00 Folk 2m1f110y soft NHF

Moderate chaser/ hurdler; fell when beaten on chasing debut; lightly raced until winning two novice handicap hurdles in spring 2003; just failed to make it a hat-trick of a stone higher mark; stays 2m 6f; handles fast ground, but probably best on soft.

Malmo Boy (IRE)

80   45

5-y-o gr g Roselier (FR)-Charming Mo (IRE) (Callernish)
Mrs H Dalton   Malcolm B Jones

Placings:0P5   (4918)
2003/04: 16⁰S, 21⁰GS, 20⁵GS,

	Starts	1st	2nd	3rd	Win & Pl
NH Flat	1	0	0	0	0
Hurdles	2	0	0	0	0
Career Total	3	0	0	0	0

Going:	Sf: 0-0 GS: 0-2 Gd: 0-0 GF: - Fm: 0-0
Distance:	2m/2m3: 0-0 2m4-2m7: 0-0 3m+: 0-0
Track:	LH: 0-3 RH: 0-0 Tight: 0-1 Gall: 0-0
Aids:	Bl: 0-0 Vi: 0-0 Tstrap: 0-0 Ckp: 0-0
Best Rating:	73 2/04 Weth 2m soft NHF

Maloy (GER)

63f   19f

4-y-o g g Neshad (USA)-Monalind (GER) (Park Romeo)
P A Blockley   Carl Would

Placings:0   (3446)
2003/04: 16⁰G,

	Starts	1st	2nd	3rd	Win & Pl
NH Flat	1	0	0	0	
Career Total	1	0	0	0	

Going:	Sf: 0-0 GS: 0-0 Gd: 0-1 GF: - Fm: 0-0
Distance:	2m/2m3: 0-1 2m4-2m7: 0-0 3m+: 0-0
Track:	LH: 0-0 RH: 0-1 Tight: 0-0 Gall: 0-0
Aids:	Bl: 0-0 Vi: 0-0 Tstrap: 0-0 Ckp: 0-0
Best Rating:	23 1/04 Ludl 2m good NHF

Mambo (IRE)

105   122

6-y-o b g Ashkalani (IRE)-Bold Tango (FR) (In Fijar (USA))
N J Henderson   Mrs Belinda Harvey

Placings:2/22/F130   (4194)
2003/04: 16FGS, 16¹G, 17³GS, 16⁰G,

	Starts	1st	2nd	3rd	Win & Pl
Hurdles	4	1	0	1	7176
Career Total	7	1	3	1	17854
112	12/03	Weth	2m	D Hdl	GD	£4745

Total win prize-money £4745

Going:	Sf: 0-0 GS: 0-2 Gd: 1-2 GF: - Fm: 0-0
Distance:	2m/2m3: 1-4 2m4-2m7: 0-0 3m+: 0-0
Track:	LH: 1-4 RH: 0-0 Tight: 0-0 Gall: 0-2
Aids:	Bl: 0-0 Vi: 0-0 Tstrap: 0-0 Ckp: 0-0
Best Rating:	122 1/04 Chel 2m1f gd-sft Hdl

Fair novice hurdler; had race won when coming down at the last at Haydock in November; easily made amends at Wetherby on Boxing Day; best over two miles; acts on most going; should go on to better things.

Mamboesque (USA)

106   96+

6-y-o b g Miesque's Son (USA)-Brawl (USA) (Fit To Fight (USA))
J Mackie   F E And Mrs J J Brindley

Placings:333/003300016-22P1   (3786)
2003/04: 20²S, 20²GF, 20PS, 20¹GS,

	Starts	1st	2nd	3rd	Win & Pl
Hurdles	4	1	2	0	5201
Career Total	16	2	2	5	10606
96	2/04	Hntg	2m4f110y	F(0-100)HHdl	G-S	£2800
94	3/03	Catt	2m3f	F(0-100)HHdl	SFT	£2681

Total win prize-money £5481

Going:	Sf: 0-2 GS: 1-1 Gd: 0-0 GF: - Fm: 0-1
Distance:	2m/2m3: 0-0 2m4-2m7: 1-4 3m+: 0-0
Track:	LH: 0-2 RH: 1-2 Tight: 0-1 Gall: 1-1
Aids:	Bl: 1-4 Vi: 0-0 Tstrap: 0-0 Ckp: 0-0
Best Rating:	96 2/04 Hntg 2m4f110y gd-sft Hdl

Plating-class hurdler; best at around two miles four; acts with cut in the ground.

Mamideos (IRE)

105(109h)   (105+h)107+

7-y-o br g Good Thyne (USA)-Heavenly Artist (IRE) (Heavenly Manna)
T R George   Silkword Racing Partnership

Placings:1/3311165P/1111413-050P   (4217)
2003/04: 20PS, 225HY, 20⁹G, 17PGS,

Placings:41/103-F3231P   (4652)
2003/04: 22FGS, 19³S, 24²GS, 24³G, 24¹GS, 25PG,

	Starts	1st	2nd	3rd	Win & Pl
Chases	6	1	1	2	9865
Career Total	11	3	1	3	16518
107	3/04	Fknm	2m110y	D Ch	G-S	£6860
99	10/02	MRas	3m	D Hdl	G-F	£4143
110	3/02	Chep	2m110y	H NHF	SFT	£1640

Total win prize-money £12645

Going:	Sf: 0-1 GS: 1-3 Gd: 0-2 GF: - Fm: 0-0
Distance:	2m/2m3: 0-0 2m4-2m7: 0-2 3m+: 1-4
Track:	LH: 1-3 RH: 0-3 Tight: 1-2 Gall: 0-1
Aids:	Bl: 0-0 Vi: 0-0 Tstrap: 1-6 Ckp: 0-0
Best Rating:	110 3/02 Chep 2m110y soft NHF

Modest novice chaser/modest hurdler;stays three miles; acts on fast and easy ground.

Man From Delcarrow (IRE)

85

7-y-o b g Zaffaran (USA)-Delcarrow (Roi Guillaume (FR))
O Sherwood   Ledwidge Best Fforde

Placings:60-4P   (1090)
2003/04: 19⁴G, 22PGF,

	Starts	1st	2nd	3rd	Win & Pl
Hurdles	2	0	0	0	405
Career Total	4	0	0	0	405

Going:	Sf: 0-0 GS: 0-0 Gd: 0-1 GF: - Fm: 0-1
Distance:	2m/2m3: 0-0 2m4-2m7: 0-0 3m+: 0-0
Track:	LH: 0-1 RH: 0-0 Tight: 0-2 Gall: 0-0
Aids:	Bl: 0-0 Vi: 0-0 Tstrap: 0-0 Ckp: 0-0
Best Rating:	104 12/02 Donc 2m110y gd-sft NHF

Man From Highworth

104   111+

5-y-o b g Ballet Royal (USA)-Cavisoir (Afzal)
H J Manners   H J Manners

Placings:5-4054003610   (4638)
2003/04: 16⁶GF, 16⁰S, 16⁵GS, 16⁴S, 17⁰S, 20⁰GS, 16³G, 16⁰G, 16¹G, 16⁰GS,

	Starts	1st	2nd	3rd	Win & Pl
NH Flat	3	0	0	0	0
Hurdles	7	1	0	1	4402
Career Total	11	1	0	1	4402
111	3/04	Strf	2m110y	E Hdl	GD	£3471

Total win prize-money £3471

Going:	Sf: 0-3 GS: 0-2 Gd: 1-4 GF: - Fm: 0-1
Distance:	2m/2m3: 1-9 2m4-2m7: 0-1 3m+: 0-0
Track:	LH: 1-4 RH: 0-6 Tight: 1-5 Gall: 0-1
Aids:	Bl: 0-0 Vi: 0-0 Tstrap: 0-0 Ckp: 0-0
Best Rating:	111 3/04 Strf 2m110y good Hdl

Moderate novice hurdler; suited by two miles and good ground.

Man Murphy (IRE)

94(86h)   (121h)137

8-y-o b g Euphemism-Been About (IRE) (Remainder Man)
W McKeown   W Manners

	Starts	1st	2nd	3rd	Win & Pl
Hurdles	1	0	0	0	0
Chases	3	0	0	0	0
Career Total	20	9	0	3	43258

106	2/03	Ayr	2m4f	C Ch		HVY	£9685
135	12/02	Newc	2m4f	D Ch		SFT	£5018
137	11/02	Newc	2m4f	E Ch		G-S	£3692
108	11/02	Newc	2m4f	E Ch		SFT	£3770
98	11/02	Kels	2m1f	E Ch		SFT	£4368
121	1/02	Catt	2m3f	D Hdl		SFT	£3377
121	1/02	Carl	2m1f	D Hdl		HVY	£3526
102	11/01	Newc	2m	D Hdl		G-S	£3570
106	1/01	Catt	2m	H NHF		G-S	£1659

Total win prize-money £38666

Going:	Sf: 0-2 GS: 0-1 Gd: 0-1 GF: - Fm: 0-0
Distance:	2m/2m3: 0-1 2m4-2m7: 0-3 3m+: 0-0
Track:	LH: 0-3 RH: 0-1 Tight: 0-2 Gall: 0-1
Aids:	Bl: 0-0 Vi: 0-0 Tstrap: 0-0 Ckp: 0-0
Best Rating:	137 11/02 Newc 2m4f gd-sft Ch

Fair chaser; successful in four of his first five chases; acts well on a soft surface; effective from two miles to two miles four.

Man O'Mystery (USA)

119   139

7-y-o b g Diesis-Eurostorm (USA) (Storm Bird (CAN))
P R Webber B E Nielsen

Placings:212-LP00PP   (4862)
2003/04: 16ᴸGS, 16ᴾS, 16ᴺG, 17ᴺG, 16ᴾG, 16ᴾGS,

	Starts	1st	2nd	3rd	Win & Pl
Hurdles	6	0	0	0	0
Career Total	9	1	2	0	16096

| 120 | 3/03 | MRas | 2m1f110yE Hdl | | G-S | £3486 |

Total win prize-money £3486

Going:	Sf: 0-1 GS: 0-2 Gd: 0-3 GF: - Fm: 0-0
Distance:	2m/2m3: 0-6 2m4-2m7: 0-0 3m+: 0-0
Track:	LH: 0-5 RH: 0-1 Tight: 0-1 Gall: 0-2
Aids:	Bl: 0-0 Vi: 0-0 Tstrap: 0-0 Ckp: 0-0
Best Rating:	139 3/03 Newb 2m110y good Hdl

Useful hurdler; formerly useful on the Flat; runner-up in Grade Two at Aintree in 2003, but out of form since; suited by two miles and probably best on good ground.

Man On The Hill (IRE)

103   117+

10-y-o b g Mandalus-Gipsey Jo (Furry Glen)
Ferdy Murphy D A Johnson

Placings:4/01/21130/34P/1111U43P2/PP025   (4175)
2003/04: 24ᴾS, 25ᴾS, 20ᴾGS, 20ᴾG, 19ᶠG,

	Starts	1st	2nd	3rd	Win & Pl
Chases	5	0	1	0	3150
Career Total	25	7	3	3	52452

141	12/01	Hayd	2m4f	B Ch		SFT	£12480
143	11/01	Sedg	2m5f	C Ch		SFT	£6776
120	11/01	Sedg	2m5f	E Ch		GD	£3168
126	5/01	Sedg	2m5f	E Ch		GD	£3529
148	1/00	Hayd	2m4f	E Hdl		SFT	£2730
138	12/99	Hayd	2m	D Hdl		SFT	£3338
102	12/98	Navn	2m		NHF	HVY	£2391

Total win prize-money £34415

Going:	Sf: 0-2 GS: 0-1 Gd: 0-2 GF: - Fm: 0-0
Distance:	2m/2m3: 0-1 2m4-2m7: 0-0 3m+: 0-2
Track:	LH: 0-4 RH: 0-1 Tight: 0-0 Gall: 0-1
Aids:	Bl: 0-0 Vi: 0-0 Tstrap: 0-0 Ckp: 0-0

Best Rating: 148 1/00 Hayd 2m4f soft Hdl

Useful chaser; useful novice hurdler for Martin Pipe; won first four chases for Ferdy Murphy in 2001; lightly raced in recent seasons; acts well on easy ground and enjoys to front-run; best at around two miles five.

Mana-Mou Bay (IRE)

102   108

7-y-o b g Ela-Mana-Mou-Summerhill (Habitat)
B Ellison R Wagner

Placings:40051-32   (0557)
2003/04: 16³GD, 16²GF,

	Starts	1st	2nd	3rd	Win & Pl
Hurdles	2	0	1	1	1783
Career Total	7	1	1	1	5565

| 108 | 4/03 | Sedg | 2m1f | E Hdl | | G-F | £3451 |

Total win prize-money £3452

Going:	Sf: 0-0 GS: 0-0 Gd: 0-0 GF: - Fm: 0-2
Distance:	2m/2m3: 0-2 2m4-2m7: 0-0 3m+: 0-0
Track:	LH: 0-0 RH: 0-2 Tight: 0-0 Gall: 0-1
Aids:	Bl: 0-0 Vi: 0-0 Tstrap: 0-0 Ckp: 0-0
Best Rating:	108 6/03 Prth 2m110y gd-fm Hdl

Moderate hurdler; effective at two miles; suited by a sound surface; has worn cheekpieces, but left off for only win.

Manawanui

109(102h)   (95+h)119+

6-y-o b g Karinga Bay-Kiwi Velocity (NZ) (Veloso (NZ))
R H Alner J M Dare, T Hamlin, J W Snook

Placings:600-311FF1   (4818)
2003/04: 20³G, 16¹G, 16¹GS, 19ᶠGS, 20ᶠGS, 17¹GF,

	Starts	1st	2nd	3rd	Win & Pl
Hurdles	2	1	0	1	4204
Chases	4	2	0	0	8570
Career Total	9	3	1	2	12774

92	4/04	Extr	2m1f	E(0-105)HHdl	G-F	£3822
111	1/04	Weth	2m	D(0-115)HCh	G-S	£5775
119	12/03	Folk	2m	F(0-90)HCh	GD	£2795

Total win prize-money £12392

Going:	Sf: 0-0 GS: 1-3 Gd: 1-2 GF: - Fm: 1-1
Distance:	2m/2m3: 3-3 2m4-2m7: 0-3 3m+: 0-0
Track:	LH: 1-2 RH: 2-4 Tight: 1-1 Gall: 0-0
Aids:	Bl: 0-0 Vi: 0-0 Tstrap: 0-0 Ckp: 0-0
Best Rating:	119 12/03 Folk 2m good Ch

Useful novice chaser; easy winner at Folkestone in January but had luck on his side when following up at Wetherby; a faller on his next two starts and reverted successfully to hurdles; stays two and a half miles, but effective at shorter; acts on fast and easy ground.

Manbow (IRE)

80

6-y-o b g Mandalus-Treble Base (IRE) (Orchestra)
M D Hammond Hope Springs Eternal

Placings:0-0PP   (4731)
2003/04: 16ᴺGS, 20ᴾHY, 20ᴾG,

	Starts	1st	2nd	3rd	Win & Pl
NH Flat	1	0	0	0	0
Hurdles	2	0	0	0	0
Career Total	4	0	0	0	0

Going:	Sf: 0-1 GS: 0-0 Gd: 0-0 GF: - Fm: 0-0
Distance:	2m/2m3: 0-0 2m4-2m7: 0-2 3m+: 0-0
Track:	LH: 0-2 RH: 0-1 Tight: 0-0 Gall: 0-1

Aids: Bl: 0-0 Vi: 0-0 Tstrap: 0-0 Ckp: 0-0
Best Rating: 86 1/04 Weth 2m gd-sft NHF

Manchester (IRE)

75d

5-y-o b g Danehill Dancer (IRE)-Lils Fairy (Fairy King (USA))
Miss A M Newton-Smith Julian Smith

Placings:P0PP-0   (0057)
2003/04: 17ᵖGS,

	Starts	1st	2nd	3rd	Win & Pl
Hurdles	1	0	0	0	
Career Total	5	0	0	0	

Going:	Sf: 0-0 GS: 0-1 Gd: 0-0 GF: - Fm: 0-0
Distance:	2m/2m3: 0-1 2m4-2m7: 0-0 3m+: 0-0
Track:	LH: 0-0 RH: 0-1 Tight: 0-0 Gall: 0-0
Aids:	Bl: 0-1 Vi: 0-0 Tstrap: 0-1 Ckp: 0-0
Best Rating:	75 2/03 Punc 2m soft Hdl

Mandingo Chief (IRE)

109   104

5-y-o b g Flying Spur (AUS)-Elizabethan Air (Elegant Air)
R T Phillips R S Williams

Placings:66412P   (4658)
2003/04: 16ᴿGS, 20ᴾS, 24⁴S, 22¹GS, 24ᴾHY, 20ᴾS,

	Starts	1st	2nd	3rd	Win & Pl
Hurdles	6	1	1	0	4186
Career Total	6	1	1	0	4186

| 92 | 2/04 | Folk | 2m6f110yF(0-95)HHdl | G-S | £2996 |

Total win prize-money £2996

Going:	Sf: 0-4 GS: 1-2 Gd: 0-0 GF: - Fm: 0-0
Distance:	2m/2m3: 0-1 2m4-2m7: 1-3 3m+: 0-2
Track:	LH: 0-4 RH: 1-2 Tight: 1-1 Gall: 0-0
Aids:	Bl: 0-0 Vi: 0-0 Tstrap: 0-0 Ckp: 0-0
Best Rating:	104 3/04 Carl 3m110y heavy Hdl

Progressive at a modest level in 2003/04 and won over two miles and six on easy ground at Folkestone in February; stays three miles and acts on heavy; may be capable of better.

Mandoob

87   105

7-y-o b g Zafonic (USA)-Thaidah (CAN) (Vice Regent (CAN))
B R Johnson J L Guillambert

Placings:63/3-0   (2768)
2003/04: 16ᴼGS,

	Starts	1st	2nd	3rd	Win & Pl
Hurdles	1	0	0	0	
Career Total	4	0	0	2	1610

Going:	Sf: 0-0 GS: 0-1 Gd: 0-0 GF: - Fm: 0-0
Distance:	2m/2m3: 0-1 2m4-2m7: 0-0 3m+: 0-0
Track:	LH: 0-1 RH: 0-0 Tight: 0-1 Gall: 0-0
Aids:	Bl: 0-0 Vi: 0-0 Tstrap: 0-0 Ckp: 0-0
Best Rating:	98 10/02 Kemp 2m good Hdl

A modest winner on the Flat; moderate maiden over hurdles; handles soft ground.

Mandy's Rose (IRE)

105(82h)   (67h)**78**

8-y-o b/br m Mandalus-Rookery Lady (IRE) (Callernish)
T R George Mr & Mrs D A Gamble

Placings:30P4F-145   (1956)
2003/04: 26†G, 25⁴G, 21⁵G,

	Starts	1st	2nd	3rd	Win & Pl
Hurdles	1	0	0	0	2604
Chases	2	0	0	0	280
Career Total	8	1	0	1	3438
67	5/03	Hntg	3m2f	F(0-100)HHdl	G-F	£2604

Total win prize-money £2604

Going:	Sf: 0-0 GS: 0-0 Gd: 0-2 GF: - Fm: 1-1
Distance:	2m/2m3: 0-0 2m4-2m7: 0-1 3m+: 1-2
Track:	LH: 0-0 RH: 1-1 Tight: 0-1 Gall: 1-1
Aids:	Bl: 0-0 Vi: 0-0 Tstrap: 0-0 Ckp: 0-0
Best Rating:	78 5/03 Weth 3m1f good Ch

Dual point winner; modest novice hurdler; off the mark at
Huntingdon in May; well beaten on debut over regulation
fences at Wetherby next time; suited by three miles plus.

Manhattan Rainbow (IRE)

13-y-o b g Mandalus-Clara Girl (Fine Blade (USA))
Mrs J M Hollands Mrs J M Hollands

Placings:0/P/3S23P32405/P1201/1PP0/P/244-P   (4600)
2003/04: 25PG,

	Starts	1st	2nd	3rd	Win & Pl
Chases	1	0	0	0	0
Career Total	26	3	4	3	11734
107	5/00	Kels	3m1f	H Ch	G-S	£1918
110	4/00	Kels	3m1f	H Ch	SFT	£2247
86	2/00	Kels	3m1f	H Ch	G-S	£2352

Total win prize-money £6517

Going:	Sf: 0-0 GS: 0-0 Gd: 0-1 GF: - Fm: 0-0
Distance:	2m/2m3: 0-0 2m4-2m7: 0-0 3m+: 0-1
Track:	LH: 0-1 RH: 0-0 Tight: 0-1 Gall: 0-0
Aids:	Bl: 0-0 Vi: 0-0 Tstrap: 0-0 Ckp: 0-0
Best Rating:	110 4/00 Kels 3m1f soft Ch

Manhattan View (IRE)

5-y-o b g Kadeed (IRE)-Haunted For Sure (IRE) (Executive Perk)
B J Curley D Donovan

Placings:0P   (3524)
2003/04: 16PG, 20PS,

	Starts	1st	2nd	3rd	Win & Pl
NH Flat	1	0	0	0	0
Hurdles	1	0	0	0	0
Career Total	2	0	0	0	

Going:	Sf: 0-1 GS: 0-0 Gd: 0-1 GF: - Fm: 0-0
Distance:	2m/2m3: 0-1 2m4-2m7: 0-1 3m+: 0-0
Track:	LH: 0-1 RH: 0-1 Tight: 0-0 Gall: 0-0
Aids:	Bl: 0-0 Vi: 0-0 Tstrap: 0-0 Ckp: 0-0
Best Rating:	22 12/03 Wwck 2m good NHF

Manhunter (IRE)

108   **91**

8-y-o b g Mandalus-Pinata (Deep Run)
P Bowen Sean Bryan

Placings:6/0P/P2220F   (3334)
2003/04: 24PGF, 22²GF, 20²GF, 25²GF, 22⁰G, 24FS,

	Starts	1st	2nd	3rd	Win & Pl
Hurdles	6	0	3	0	2448
Career Total	9	0	3	0	2448

Going:	Sf: 0-1 GS: 0-0 Gd: 0-1 GF: - Fm: 0-4
Distance:	2m/2m3: 0-0 2m4-2m7: 0-3 3m+: 0-3
Track:	LH: 0-5 RH: 0-1 Tight: 0-0 Gall: 0-1
Aids:	Bl: 0-0 Vi: 0-0 Tstrap: 0-0 Ckp: 0-0
Best Rating:	96 1/01 Kemp 2m soft NHF

Disappointing bumper horse; improved effort when narrowly
beaten in weak novices' hurdle at Uttoxeter October 2003;
stays two miles six; handles fast ground.

Maniatis

102   **108+**

7-y-o b g Slip Anchor-Tamassos (Dance In Time (CAN))
Mrs J Candlish (M D Hammond 26/12) Racing For You Limited

Placings:20-1PU440   (4892)
2003/04: 16†GS, 16PHY, 16UHY, 16⁴S, 17⁴GS, 16⁰GF,

	Starts	1st	2nd	3rd	Win & Pl
Hurdles	6	1	0	0	2628
Career Total	8	1	1	0	4233
95	12/03	Uttx	2m	G Hdl	G-S	£2037

Total win prize-money £2037

Going:	Sf: 0-3 GS: 1-2 Gd: 0-0 GF: - Fm: 0-1
Distance:	2m/2m3: 1-6 2m4-2m7: 0-0 3m+: 0-0
Track:	LH: 1-5 RH: 0-1 Tight: 0-2 Gall: 0-0
Aids:	Bl: 0-0 Vi: 0-2 Tstrap: 0-0 Ckp: 0-0
Best Rating:	111 2/03 Hayd 2m gd-sft Hdl

Moderate hurdler; formerly useful middle-distance performer
on the Flat; suffers from bad knees and has broken blood
vessels so has therefore been difficult to train; changed
hands for 8,800gns after easy win when dropped into seller
at Uttoxeter Boxing Day 2003; likes soft ground.

Manikato (USA)

78   **70**

10-y-o b g Clever Trick (USA)-Pasampsi (USA) (Crow (FR))
K G Wingrove (R Curtis 23/9) A Bourne

Placings:P/P5/6/0-P0   (4339)
2003/04: 18PGF, 16⁰G,

	Starts	1st	2nd	3rd	Win & Pl
Hurdles	2	0	0	0	0
Career Total	7	0	0	0	0

Going:	Sf: 0-0 GS: 0-0 Gd: 0-1 GF: - Fm: 0-1
Distance:	2m/2m3: 0-2 2m4-2m7: 0-0 3m+: 0-1
Track:	LH: 0-2 RH: 0-0 Tight: 0-1 Gall: 0-0
Aids:	Bl: 0-0 Vi: 0-0 Tstrap: 0-0 Ckp: 0-0
Best Rating:	74 9/00 Worc 2m gd-fm Hdl

Maninga

98   **108**

8-y-o ch m Karinga Bay-Amberush (No Rush)
Mrs L Richards The Maninga Partnership

Manhunter

Placings:5/04411P/5004040-06605P   (4367)
2003/04: 22⁰S, 22⁰G, 24⁶S, 21⁶S, 24⁰GS, 24⁵GS, 25PGS,

	Starts	1st	2nd	3rd	Win & Pl
Hurdles	7	0	0	0	0
Career Total	20	2	0	0	8168
108	3/02	Towc	2m5f	E Hdl	SFT	£3136
108	2/02	Winc	2m6f	D Hdl	SFT	£3640

Total win prize-money £6776

Going:	Sf: 0-3 GS: 0-3 Gd: 0-1 GF: - Fm: 0-0
Distance:	2m/2m3: 0-0 2m4-2m7: 0-3 3m+: 0-4
Track:	LH: 0-4 RH: 0-2 Tight: 0-3 Gall: 0-0
Aids:	Bl: 0-3 Vi: 0-0 Tstrap: 0-0 Ckp: 0-0
Best Rating:	108 1/03 Plum 2m5f soft Hdl

Moderate hurdler; stays three miles; effective on soft
ground.

Mankind

(0c)**98**

13-y-o b g Rakaposhi King-Mandarling (Mandalus)
J A T De Giles J A T De Giles

Placings:00/1/P6PP0/3P0230/10P/1/0R-P   (1291)
2003/04: 22PGF,

	Starts	1st	2nd	3rd	Win & Pl
Hurdles	1	0	0	0	
Career Total	21	3	1	2	7371
98	6/01	NAbb	2m6f	G(0-95)HHdl	G-F	£2415
98	5/99	Hrfd	2m3f110yG Hdl		GD	£1857
100	4/97	Strf	2m5f110yH Ch		GD	£2038

Total win prize-money £6311

Going:	Sf: 0-0 GS: 0-0 Gd: 0-0 GF: - Fm: 0-1
Distance:	2m/2m3: 0-0 2m4-2m7: 0-1 3m+: 0-0
Track:	LH: 0-1 RH: 0-0 Tight: 0-1 Gall: 0-0
Aids:	Bl: 0-0 Vi: 0-0 Tstrap: 0-0 Ckp: 0-0
Best Rating:	100 4/97 Strf 2m5f110y good Ch

Manly Money

105   **115+**

6-y-o b g Homo Sapien-Susie's Money (Seymour Hicks (FR))
P F Nicholls Mrs Susie Chown

Placings:5-213P2   (4822)
2003/04: 17⁵S, 17²GS, 19¹GS, 20³S, 20PS, 19²GF,

	Starts	1st	2nd	3rd	Win & Pl
NH Flat	1	0	0	0	0
Hurdles	5	1	2	1	6273
Career Total	6	1	2	1	6273
115	12/03	Hrfd	2m3f110yE Hdl		G-S	£2807

Total win prize-money £2807

Going:	Sf: 0-3 GS: 1-2 Gd: 0-0 GF: - Fm: 0-1
Distance:	2m/2m3: 0-3 2m4-2m7: 1-3 3m+: 0-0
Track:	LH: 0-1 RH: 1-5 Tight: 0-1 Gall: 0-0
Aids:	Bl: 0-0 Vi: 0-0 Tstrap: 0-0 Ckp: 0-0
Best Rating:	115 4/04 Extr 2m3f gd-fm Hdl

Fair novice hurdler; former dual point-to-point winner; built
on the promise of narrow defeat on hurdling debut when
landing 2m3f soft ground novice hurdle at Hereford
December 2003; held under his penalty latest; stays 2m 4f;
acts on good and soft ground.

Manners (IRE)

83f   **100+f**

6-y-o b g Topanoora-Maneree (Mandalus)
Jonjo O'Neill M Tabor

Placings:1   (1964)

2003/04: 16¹GF,

	Starts	1st	2nd	3rd	Win & Pl
NH Flat	1	1	0	0	1652
Career Total	1	1	0	0	1652
100 11/03 Hayd 2m	H NHF			G-F	£1652
			Total win prize-money £1652		

Going:	Sf: 0-0 GS: 0-0 Gd: 0-0 GF: - Fm: 1-1
Distance:	2m/2m3: 1-1 2m4-2m7: 0-0 3m+: 0-0
Track:	LH: 1-1 RH: 0-0 Tight: 0-0 Gall: 0-0
Aids:	Bl: 0-0 Vi: 0-0 Tstrap: 0-0 Ckp: 0-0
Best Rating:	100 11/03 Hayd 2m gd-fm NHF

Winner of fast ground bumper on only outing.

Manolito (IRE)
101   82

10-y-o b g Mandalus-Las-Cancellas (Monksfield)
B I Case Jeremy Hancock

Placings: 0540/F236/0P/3P6F23F-3361355   (1757)
2003/04: 24³GF, 26³GF, 20⁶GF, 22¹GF, 23³G, 24⁵GF, 24⁵G,

	Starts	1st	2nd	3rd	Win & Pl
Chases	7	1	0	3	5885
Career Total	24	1	2	6	9566
82 6/03 MRas 2m6f110yE(0-105)HCh			G-F	£4231	
			Total win prize-money £4232		

Going:	Sf: 0-0 GS: 0-0 Gd: 0-2 GF: - Fm: 1-5
Distance:	2m/2m3: 0-0 2m4-2m7: 1-2 3m+: 0-5
Track:	LH: 0-3 RH: 1-4 Tight: 1-2 Gall: 0-3
Aids:	Bl: 0-0 Vi: 0-1 Tstrap: 0-0 Ckp: 0-0
Best Rating:	94 11/99 Kemp 2m gd-fm Hdl

Plating-class chaser; finally got off the mark under Rules when landing weak novice 2m 6f handicap chase at Market Rasen June 2003; acts on fast ground.

Manor Down (IRE)

6-y-o b g Moscow Society (USA)-Scalp Hunter (IRE) (Commanche Run)
P J Hobbs Colin W Poore

Placings: 00P-P   (0034)
2003/04: 22PG,

	Starts	1st	2nd	3rd	Win & Pl
Hurdles	1	0	0	0	
Career Total	4	0	0	0	

Going:	Sf: 0-0 GS: 0-0 Gd: 0-1 GF: - Fm: 0-0
Distance:	2m/2m3: 0-0 2m4-2m7: 0-1 3m+: 0-0
Track:	LH: 0-0 RH: 0-1 Tight: 0-0 Gall: 0-0
Aids:	Bl: 0-0 Vi: 0-0 Tstrap: 0-0 Ckp: 0-0
Best Rating:	36 3/03 Winc 2m soft NHF

Manor Star

5-y-o b m Weld-Call Coup (IRE) (Callernish)
B D Leavy Manor Racing Club

Placings: 0-00   (2441)
2003/04: 17⁰G, 17⁰G,

	Starts	1st	2nd	3rd	Win & Pl
NH Flat	1	0	0	0	0
Hurdles	1	0	0	0	0
Career Total	3	0	0	0	

Going:	Sf: 0-0 GS: 0-0 Gd: 0-2 GF: - Fm: 0-0
Distance:	2m/2m3: 0-2 2m4-2m7: 0-0 3m+: 0-0

Track:	LH: 0-2 RH: 0-0 Tight: 0-2 Gall: 0-0
Aids:	Bl: 0-0 Vi: 0-0 Tstrap: 0-0 Ckp: 0-0
Best Rating:	64 5/03 Bang 2m1f good NHF

Manoram (GER)
102   89

5-y-o ch g Zinaad-Mayada (USA) (The Minstrel (CAN))
Ian Williams Willsford Racing Incorporated

Placings: 03-614650   (4492)
2003/04: 16⁶GS, 20¹G, 22⁴GF, 19⁶GF, 24⁵G, 22⁰G,

	Starts	1st	2nd	3rd	Win & Pl
Hurdles	6	1	0	0	4106
Career Total	8	1	0	1	4625
89 5/03 Worc 2m4f	E(0-100)HHdl		GD	£3577	
			Total win prize-money £3577		

Going:	Sf: 0-0 GS: 0-1 Gd: 1-3 GF: - Fm: 0-2
Distance:	2m/2m3: 0-1 2m4-2m7: 1-4 3m+: 0-1
Track:	LH: 1-4 RH: 0-2 Tight: 0-2 Gall: 0-0
Aids:	Bl: 0-0 Vi: 0-0 Tstrap: 0-0 Ckp: 0-0
Best Rating:	89 5/03 Worc 2m4f good Hdl

Plating-class hurdler; needed every yard of longer trip when winning 2m 4f novices handicap hurdle at Worcester May 2003; disappointing since.

Manoubi
89   91

5-y-o b g Doyoun-Manuetti (IRE) (Sadler's Wells (USA))
Jonjo O'Neill (Sir Michael Stoute 1/8) F F Racing Services Partnership XII

Placings: 430   (4524)
2003/04: 20⁴GS, 20³G, 16⁰GS,

	Starts	1st	2nd	3rd	Win & Pl
Hurdles	3	0	0	1	899
Career Total	3	0	0	1	899

Going:	Sf: 0-0 GS: 0-2 Gd: 0-1 GF: - Fm: 0-0
Distance:	2m/2m3: 0-1 2m4-2m7: 0-2 3m+: 0-0
Track:	LH: 0-2 RH: 0-1 Tight: 0-0 Gall: 0-0
Aids:	Bl: 0-0 Vi: 0-0 Tstrap: 0-0 Ckp: 0-0
Best Rating:	91 2/04 Carl 2m4f good Hdl

Useful staying handicapper on the Flat; slightly disappointing so far over hurdles.

Manque Neuf
94   53

5-y-o b g Cadeaux Genereux-Flying Squaw (Be My Chief (USA))
Mrs L Richards B Seal

Placings: 0-45   (0832)
2003/04: 18⁴GF, 20⁵GF,

	Starts	1st	2nd	3rd	Win & Pl
Hurdles	2	0	0	0	0
Career Total	3	0	0	0	0

Going:	Sf: 0-0 GS: 0-0 Gd: 0-0 GF: - Fm: 0-2
Distance:	2m/2m3: 0-1 2m4-2m7: 0-1 3m+: 0-0
Track:	LH: 0-2 RH: 0-0 Tight: 0-1 Gall: 0-0
Aids:	Bl: 0-0 Vi: 0-0 Tstrap: 0-0 Ckp: 0-0
Best Rating:	58 7/03 Worc 2m4f gd-fm Hdl

Mantel Mini

5-y-o b m Reprimand-Foretell (Tirol)
B A Pearce Martin J Gibbs

Placings: 00-0   (2504)
2003/04: 17⁰GS,

	Starts	1st	2nd	3rd	Win & Pl
NH Flat	1	0	0	0	
Career Total	3	0	0	0	

Going:	Sf: 0-0 GS: 0-1 Gd: 0-0 GF: - Fm: 0-0
Distance:	2m/2m3: 0-1 2m4-2m7: 0-0 3m+: 0-0
Track:	LH: 0-0 RH: 0-1 Tight: 0-1 Gall: 0-0
Aids:	Bl: 0-0 Vi: 0-0 Tstrap: 0-0 Ckp: 0-0

Mantilla
105   119

7-y-o b m Son Pardo-Well Tried (IRE) (Thatching)
Ian Williams (J D Frost 2/5) Stephen Goss

Placings: 2F6/0340303-622122111160   (4842)
2003/04: 16⁶GS, 16²G, 16⁶GF, 20¹GF, 22⁴GF, 21²GF, 21¹GF, 19¹GF, 20¹F, 21¹GF, 22⁶GF, 21⁰G,

	Starts	1st	2nd	3rd	Win & Pl
Hurdles	12	5	4	0	24267
Career Total	22	5	5	3	26433
119 10/03 Chel 2m5f	C Hdl		G-F	£6415	
105 10/03 Weth 2m4f110y			D(0-		
120)HHdl FRM £7196					
103 10/03 Extr 2m3f	G(0-95)HHdl		G-F	£2184	
86 9/03 Plum 2m5f	G(0-95)HHdl		G-F	£1855	
78 8/03 Font 2m4f	F(0-90)HHdl		G-F	£2730	
			Total win prize-money £20380		

Going:	Sf: 0-0 GS: 0-1 Gd: 0-2 GF: - Fm: 5-9
Distance:	2m/2m3: 1-4 2m4-2m7: 4-8 3m+: 0-0
Track:	LH: 3-7 RH: 1-3 Tight: 2-3 Gall: 1-2
Aids:	Bl: 2-3 Vi: 1-2 Tstrap: 0-0 Ckp: 0-0
Best Rating:	119 10/03 Chel 2m5f gd-fm Hdl

Fair hurdler; in good form in summer/autumn 2003 in low grade events; stays two miles six; best on a sound surface; effective in a visor and in blinkers.

Mantles Pride
74   60

9-y-o br g Petong-State Romance (Free State)
Dr P Pritchard (M Dods 14/10) Juro Antiques

Placings: 0505   (4844)
2003/04: 16⁰G, 23⁵G, 16⁰G, 17⁵G,

	Starts	1st	2nd	3rd	Win & Pl
Hurdles	4	0	0	0	1174
Career Total	4	0	0	0	1174

Going:	Sf: 0-0 GS: 0-0 Gd: 0-4 GF: - Fm: 0-0
Distance:	2m/2m3: 0-3 2m4-2m7: 0-0 3m+: 0-1
Track:	LH: 0-4 RH: 0-0 Tight: 0-1 Gall: 0-2
Aids:	Bl: 0-0 Vi: 0-0 Tstrap: 0-0 Ckp: 0-0
Best Rating:	67 2/04 Newb 2m110y good Hdl

Mantles Prince

10-y-o ch g Emarati (USA)-Miami Mouse (Miami Springs)
A G Juckes Emlyn Hughes' Cleobury Golfers

Placings: 52/123/5121132/55432643/46621312/2U6-P   (4647)

2003/04: 36^PG,

	Starts	1st	2nd	3rd	Win & Pl
Chases	1	0	0	0	
Career Total	32	6	8	5	163666
124	3/02	Naas	2m		Ch		HVY	£7975
134	1/02	Punc	2m		Ch		Y-S	£6561
155	1/00	Leop	2m		HHdl		SFT	£52240
139	1/00	Fair	2m		HHdl		SFT	£5920
127	11/99	Fair	2m		HHdl		Y-S	£11607
102	5/98	Limk	2m1f				Y-S	£2978
						Total win prize-money £87281

Going: Sf: 0-0 GS: 0-0 Gd: 0-1 GF: - Fm: 0-0
Distance: 2m/2m3: 0-0 2m4-2m7: 0-0 3m+: 0-0
Track: LH: 0-1 RH: 0-0 Tight: 0-1 Gall: 0-0
Aids: Bl: 0-0 Vi: 0-1 Tstrap: 0-0 Ckp: 0-0
Best Rating: 166 4/00 Aint 2m4f good Hdl

Mantusis (IRE)
87 (133h)**94**
9-y-o ch g Pursuit Of Love-Mana (GER) (Windwurf (GER))
P J Hobbs Mrs J F Deithrick

Placings:0/31111112/3 (0834)
2003/04: 16^3GF,

	Starts	1st	2nd	3rd	Win & Pl
Chases	1	0	0	1	626
Career Total	10	6	1	2	27799
133	8/01	NAbb	2m1f	B HHdl		G-F	£8248
117	8/01	Bang	2m1f	D Hdl		GD	£3656
115	7/01	NAbb	2m1f	D Hdl		GD	£3376
120	7/01	NAbb	2m1f	D Hdl		G-F	£3478
109	6/01	NAbb	2m1f	D Hdl		G-F	£3554
117	6/01	NAbb	2m1f	D Hdl		GD	£3511
					Total win prize-money £25826

Going: Sf: 0-0 GS: 0-0 Gd: 0-0 GF: - Fm: 0-1
Distance: 2m/2m3: 0-1 2m4-2m7: 0-0 3m+: 0-0
Track: LH: 0-1 RH: 0-0 Tight: 0-0 Gall: 0-0
Aids: Bl: 0-0 Vi: 0-0 Tstrap: 0-0 Ckp: 0-0
Best Rating: 133 8/01 NAbb 2m1f gd-fm Hdl

Moderate chaser/useful hurdler; ran up a six-timer in novice hurdles at the start of the 2001 season; sidelined with leg trouble from September 2001 until a well beaten third on his chasing debut at Worcester July 2003.

Manx Royal (FR)

5-y-o b g Cyborg (FR)-Badj II (FR) (Tadj (FR))
M C Pipe James and Antoinette Kennedy

Placings:P (4641)
2003/04: 24^PG,

	Starts	1st	2nd	3rd	Win & Pl
Hurdles	1	0	0	0	
Career Total	1	0	0	0	

Going: Sf: 0-0 GS: 0-0 Gd: 0-1 GF: - Fm: 0-0
Distance: 2m/2m3: 0-0 2m4-2m7: 0-0 3m+: 0-1
Track: LH: 0-1 RH: 0-0 Tight: 0-1 Gall: 0-0
Aids: Bl: 0-0 Vi: 0-0 Tstrap: 0-0 Ckp: 0-0

Many Thanks

4-y-o b f Octagonal (NZ)-Answered Prayer (Green Desert (USA))
B S Rothwell (E A L Dunlop 13/10) D J Coles

Placings:UF (4258)

2003/04: 16^UG, 16^FGF,

	Starts	1st	2nd	3rd	Win & Pl
Hurdles	2	0	0	0	
Career Total	2	0	0	0	

Going: Sf: 0-0 GS: 0-0 Gd: 0-1 GF: - Fm: 0-1
Distance: 2m/2m3: 0-2 2m4-2m7: 0-0 3m+: 0-0
Track: LH: 0-2 RH: 0-0 Tight: 0-2 Gall: 0-0
Aids: Bl: 0-0 Vi: 0-1 Tstrap: 0-0 Ckp: 0-0

Mapilut Du Moulin (FR)

4-y-o b g Lute Antique (FR)-Api (FR) (El Badr)
P A Blockley Bell House Racing Limited

Placings:0 (4277)
2003/04: 17^0G,

	Starts	1st	2nd	3rd	Win & Pl
NH Flat	1	0	0	0	
Career Total	1	0	0	0	

Going: Sf: 0-0 GS: 0-0 Gd: 0-1 GF: - Fm: 0-0
Distance: 2m/2m3: 0-1 2m4-2m7: 0-0 3m+: 0-0
Track: LH: 0-0 RH: 0-1 Tight: 0-0 Gall: 0-0
Aids: Bl: 0-0 Vi: 0-0 Tstrap: 0-0 Ckp: 0-0

Marabout (FR)
(82h) (50h)
7-y-o b g Baby Turk-Maria Bethania (FR) (Pharly (FR))
Sir John Barlow Bt Sir John & Lady Barlow

Placings:006/402353/0-F (0163)
2003/04: 17^FG,

	Starts	1st	2nd	3rd	Win & Pl
Chases	1	0	0	0	
Career Total	11	0	1	2	16732

Going: Sf: 0-0 GS: 0-0 Gd: 0-1 GF: - Fm: 0-0
Distance: 2m/2m3: 0-1 2m4-2m7: 0-0 3m+: 0-0
Track: LH: 0-1 RH: 0-0 Tight: 0-0 Gall: 0-0
Aids: Bl: 0-0 Vi: 0-0 Tstrap: 0-0 Ckp: 0-0
Best Rating: 50 3/03 Carl 2m1f gd-sft Hdl

Maragun (GER)
103(105h) (123h)**112**
8-y-o b g General Assembly (USA)-Marcelia (GER) (Priamos (GER))
M C Pipe Emlyn Hughes & Stuart Mercer

Placings:3P/311261304/P26202B05-240P11 (4252)
2003/04: 17^2S, 19^4G, 17^0G, 16^PS, 17^1G, 17^1G,

	Starts	1st	2nd	3rd	Win & Pl
Hurdles	3	1	0	0	2911
Chases	3	1	1	0	7026
Career Total	26	5	5	3	25620
103	3/04	Bang	2m1f110yD	Ch		GD	£5356
103	3/04	Folk	2m1f110yG	Hdl		GD	£2618
120	11/01	Hntg	2m110y E	Hdl		G-F	£2429
119	8/01	Uttx	2m	D Hdl		G-F	£3360
123	6/01	MRas	2m1f110yF(0-100)HHdl		G-F	£2902
					Total win prize-money £16665

Going: Sf: 0-2 GS: 0-0 Gd: 2-4 GF: - Fm: 0-0
Distance: 2m/2m3: 2-5 2m4-2m7: 0-0 3m+: 0-0
Track: LH: 1-4 RH: 1-2 Tight: 2-4 Gall: 0-1

Aids: Bl: 0-0 Vi: 2-2 Tstrap: 2-6 Ckp: 0-0
Best Rating: 126 10/02 Extr 2m3f firm Hdl

Modest hurdler/novice chaser; suited by fast ground; effective over two miles to two miles three; has worn a visor and/or a tongue-strap.

Maraud
109 **95**
10-y-o ch g Midyan (USA)-Peak Squaw (USA) (Icecapade (USA))
L R James (R Hollinshead 14/1) David Dyer

Placings:1313/0560060/513/33F56/4U30512O21446F-P4P14F630 (4948)
2003/04: 24^PG, 26^4G, 26^PGF, 24^1GF, 20^4GF, 25^FGF, 25^6G, 26^3G, 27^9GS,

	Starts	1st	2nd	3rd	Win & Pl
Hurdles	9	1	0	1	5736
Career Total	42	6	2	7	25372
95	10/03	Carl	3m1f110y D(0-120)HHdl	G-F	£4712
96	11/02	Catt	3m1f110yD(0-115)HHdl	GD	£3672
92	7/02	Sedg	3m3f110yE(0-110)HHdl	G-F	£2926
97	7/99	Sedg	3m3f110yE(0-115)HHdl	G-F	£2745
110	2/98	Muss	2m	E Hdl		G-F	£2735
98	12/97	Catt	2m	E Hdl		GD	£1912
					Total win prize-money £18705

Going: Sf: 0-0 GS: 0-1 Gd: 0-4 GF: - Fm: 1-4
Distance: 2m/2m3: 0-0 2m4-2m7: 0-1 3m+: 1-8
Track: LH: 0-6 RH: 1-2 Tight: 0-3 Gall: 0-0
Aids: Bl: 0-0 Vi: 0-0 Tstrap: 0-0 Ckp: 0-0
Best Rating: 110 3/98 Kels 2m110y good Hdl

Moderate hurdler; stays really well; suited by fast ground; has worn cheekpieces.

Marble Arch
(120h) (152h)
8-y-o b g Rock Hopper-Mayfair Minx (St Columbus)
H Morrison M S Wilson, R Sweet, Mrs Mary Wilson

Placings:653/534223411/011P2/3450-P (2241)
2003/04: 16^PGF,

	Starts	1st	2nd	3rd	Win & Pl
Chases	1	0	0	0	
Career Total	22	4	3	4	152344
155	12/01	Asct	2m110y B(0-155)HHdl	GD	£58000
141	11/01	Newb	2m110y C(0-130)HHdl	G-S	£9750
118	4/01	Ayr	2m	C Hdl		GD	£5443
118	3/01	Asct	2m110y D(0-120)HHdl	HVY	£5213
					Total win prize-money £78407

Going: Sf: 0-0 GS: 0-0 Gd: 0-0 GF: - Fm: 0-1
Distance: 2m/2m3: 0-1 2m4-2m7: 0-0 3m+: 0-0
Track: LH: 0-0 RH: 0-1 Tight: 0-0 Gall: 0-0
Aids: Bl: 0-0 Vi: 0-0 Tstrap: 0-0 Ckp: 0-0
Best Rating: 162 3/02 Chel 2m110y gd-sft Hdl

Smart hurdler; won the Ladbroke Hurdle at Ascot in 2001 and 3l second in 2002 Champion Hurdle at Cheltenham; creditable 5 1/4l fourth to Rooster Booster in Bula Hurdle at Cheltenham and the ground was unsuitable when well beaten in the Christmas Hurdle at Kempton; warmed up for his Champion Hurdle bid by winning a maiden on the Lingfield Polytrack; only twelfth at Cheltenham; injured a tendon on his chase debut; suited by 2m and does not want the ground too soft.

March North
98(97h) (92 h)**103**
9-y-o b g Petoski-Coral Delight (Idiots Delight)
Mrs P Robeson Ron Collins

Placings:*435/5631/56164F6/0000623-P1*   (0446)
2003/04: 25P GF, 24¹G,

	Starts	1st	2nd	3rd	Win & Pl
Chases	2	1	0	0	3339
Career Total	23	3	1	3	14501
103 5/03 Hntg	3m	F(0-100)HCh	GD	£3339	
113 11/01 Hntg	2m110y	D(0-120)HHdl	GD	£6873	
106 1/01 Fknm	2m	F(0-110)HHdl	SFT	£1838	
			Total win prize-money £12051		

Going: Sf: 0-0 GS: 0-0 Gd: 1-1 GF: - Fm: 0-1
Distance: 2m/2m3: 0-0 2m4-2m7: 0-0 3m+: 1-2
Track: LH: 0-0 RH: 1-2 Tight: 0-0 Gall: 1-1
Aids: Bl: 0-0 Vi: 1-1 Tstrap: 0-0 Ckp: 0-1
Best Rating: 113 11/01 Hntg 2m110y good Hdl

Moderate handicap hurdler/novice chaser; effective at two miles, stays three; suited by a sharp track; effective on good ground or softer.

Marchensis (IRE)
94f   88f
6-y-o ch g Great Marquess-Trelissick (Electric)
O Sherwood O M C Sherwood

Placings:*51*   (0263)
2003/04: 16⁵GS, 16¹GF,

	Starts	1st	2nd	3rd	Win & Pl
NH Flat	2	1	0	0	2958
Career Total	2	1	0	0	2958
88 5/03 Ludl	2m	H NHF	G-F	£2957	
			Total win prize-money £2958		

Going: Sf: 0-0 GS: 0-1 Gd: 0-0 GF: - Fm: 1-1
Distance: 2m/2m3: 1-2 2m4-2m7: 0-0 3m+: 0-0
Track: LH: 0-1 RH: 1-1 Tight: 0-0 Gall: 0-0
Aids: Bl: 0-0 Vi: 0-0 Tstrap: 0-0 Ckp: 0-0
Best Rating: 88 5/03 Ludl 2m gd-fm NHF

A half-brother to a 10f winner; won Ludlow bumper on fast ground second start.

Marching Premier (IRE)
96f   94f
5-y-o ch g Zaffaran (USA)-The Marching Lady (IRE) (Archway (IRE))
Noel T Chance Premier Chance Racing & Ian Murray

Placings:*36*   (4571)
2003/04: 16³GS, 17⁶GS,

	Starts	1st	2nd	3rd	Win & Pl
NH Flat	2	0	0	1	563
Career Total	2	0	0	1	563

Going: Sf: 0-0 GS: 0-1 Gd: 0-1 GF: - Fm: 0-0
Distance: 2m/2m3: 0-2 2m4-2m7: 0-0 3m+: 0-0
Track: LH: 0-1 RH: 0-1 Tight: 0-1 Gall: 0-0
Aids: Bl: 0-0 Vi: 0-0 Tstrap: 0-0 Ckp: 0-0
Best Rating: 94 2/04 Kemp 2m good NHF

Marcus William (IRE)
80   97
7-y-o ch g Roselier (FR)-River Swell (IRE) (Over The River (FR))
B G Powell P H Betts

Placings:*6U/56153-3*   (0125)

2003/04: 20³G,

	Starts	1st	2nd	3rd	Win & Pl
Hurdles	1	0	0	1	397
Career Total	8	1	0	2	5581
109 1/03 Font	2m2f110yE Hdl		HVY	£3640	
			Total win prize-money £3640		

Going: Sf: 0-0 GS: 0-0 Gd: 0-1 GF: - Fm: 0-0
Distance: 2m/2m3: 0-0 2m4-2m7: 0-1 3m+: 0-0
Track: LH: 0-0 RH: 0-0 Tight: 0-1 Gall: 0-0
Aids: Bl: 0-0 Vi: 0-0 Tstrap: 0-0 Ckp: 0-0
Best Rating: 115 2/03 Font 2m4f gd-sft Hdl

Decent hurdler; stays two and a quarter miles plus; acts on testing ground.

Mardello
91f   103+f
6-y-o b m Supreme Leader-Clonmello (Le Bavard (FR))
N J Henderson R D Chugg

Placings:*0-100*   (4328)
2003/04: 16¹G, 16⁹G, 16⁰S,

	Starts	1st	2nd	3rd	Win & Pl
NH Flat	3	1	0	0	2058
Career Total	4	1	0	0	2058
88 1/04 Hayd	2m	H NHF	GD	£2058	
			Total win prize-money £2058		

Going: Sf: 0-0 GS: 0-0 Gd: 1-2 GF: - Fm: 0-0
Distance: 2m/2m3: 1-3 2m4-2m7: 0-0 3m+: 0-0
Track: LH: 1-2 RH: 0-1 Tight: 0-0 Gall: 0-1
Aids: Bl: 0-0 Vi: 0-0 Tstrap: 0-0 Ckp: 0-0
Best Rating: 88 1/04 Hayd 2m good NHF

Moderate bumper performer; she won on her reappearance at Haydock, but was beaten subsequently; should stay further over hurdles; acts on good ground.

Mardereil (IRE)
7-y-o ch m Moscow Society (USA)-Slap Of The Stick (Weavers Hall)
C J Mann Charlie Mann

Placings:*P*   (4909)
2003/04: 24⁰PS,

	Starts	1st	2nd	3rd	Win & Pl
Hurdles	1	0	0	0	
Career Total	1	0	0	0	

Going: Sf: 0-1 GS: 0-0 Gd: 0-0 GF: - Fm: 0-0
Distance: 2m/2m3: 0-0 2m4-2m7: 0-0 3m+: 0-0
Track: LH: 0-0 RH: 0-0 Tight: 0-0 Gall: 0-0
Aids: Bl: 0-0 Vi: 0-0 Tstrap: 0-0 Ckp: 0-0

Margarets Wish
89   76
4-y-o gr f Cloudings (IRE)-Gentle Gain (Final Straw)
T Wall A H Bennett

Placings:*F36*   (4714)
2003/04: 17⁵F, 16³GF, 16⁶G,

	Starts	1st	2nd	3rd	Win & Pl
Hurdles	3	0	0	1	392
Career Total	3	0	0	1	392

Going: Sf: 0-0 GS: 0-0 Gd: 0-2 GF: - Fm: 0-1
Distance: 2m/2m3: 0-3 2m4-2m7: 0-0 3m+: 0-0
Track: LH: 0-1 RH: 0-2 Tight: 0-1 Gall: 0-0

Aids: Bl: 0-0 Vi: 0-0 Tstrap: 0-0 Ckp: 0-0
Best Rating: 76 11/03 Bang 2m1f good Hdl

Margoulin (FR)
89   90
9-y-o gr g Royal Charter (FR)-Marsaude (FR) (Tourangeau (FR))
Mrs J C McGregor (Mrs H Dalton 18/5) Mrs Dorothy Thomson

Placings:*500/414P/3F140/050F606-36PP0P*   (4616)
2003/04: 17³GF, 16⁶GF, 20⁵S, 16⁶HY, 16⁹GF, 21⁶G,

	Starts	1st	2nd	3rd	Win & Pl
Chases	6	0	0	1	636
Career Total	25	2	0	2	14371
109 1/02 Fair	2m100y	Ch	Y-S	£6773	
101 12/00 Gowr	2m2f	Hdl	HVY	£4692	
			Total win prize-money £11465		

Going: Sf: 0-2 GS: 0-0 Gd: 0-1 GF: - Fm: 0-3
Distance: 2m/2m3: 0-4 2m4-2m7: 0-2 3m+: 0-0
Track: LH: 0-4 RH: 0-1 Tight: 0-1 Gall: 0-0
Aids: Bl: 0-0 Vi: 0-0 Tstrap: 0-0 Ckp: 0-0
Best Rating: 116 12/00 Fair 2m2f yld-sft Hdl

Ex-Irish; modest handicap chaser; best at two miles; acts on soft.

Mariah Rollins (IRE)
115   139
6-y-o b/br m Over The River (FR)-Clonloo Lady (IRE) (Nearly A Nose (USA))
P A Fahy Gone West Racing Syndicate

Placings:*0401-211213U*   (4381)
2003/04: 20²GY, 16¹GF, 16¹GF, 20²S, 16¹S, 18²S, 16⁰UG,

	Starts	1st	2nd	3rd	Win & Pl
NH Flat	1	0	1	0	1403
Hurdles	6	3	1	1	55408
Career Total	11	4	2	1	60681
139 12/03 Leop	2m	Hdl	SFT	£21103	
113 11/03 DRoy	2m	Hdl	G-F	£14772	
97 10/03 Gway	2m	Hdl	G-F	£5824	
98 2/03 Thur	2m	NHF	YLD	£3584	
			Total win prize-money £45286		

Going: Sf: 1-3 GS: 0-0 Gd: 0-1 GF: - Fm: 2-2
Distance: 2m/2m3: 3-6 2m4-2m7: 0-1 3m+: 0-0
Track: LH: 1-3 RH: 1-2 Tight: 0-0 Gall: 0-0
Aids: Bl: 0-0 Vi: 0-0 Tstrap: 0-0 Ckp: 0-0
Best Rating: 139 12/03 Leop 2m soft Hdl

Useful Irish-trained novice hurdler; successful in Grade Two at Leopardstown over Christmas; best over two miles; acts on soft and fast ground.

Marico (IRE)
103   83
11-y-o b g Lord Americo-Gilt Course (Crash Course)
Evan Williams (D Brace 14/5) Mrs J M Hegarty

Placings:*00/050 00/5/562P-425*   (1593)
2003/04: 19⁴GF, 20²G, 21⁵GF,

	Starts	1st	2nd	3rd	Win & Pl
Hurdles	3	0	1	0	538
Career Total	15	0	2	0	1207

Going: Sf: 0-0 GS: 0-0 Gd: 0-1 GF: - Fm: 0-2
Distance: 2m/2m3: 0-0 2m4-2m7: 0-3 3m+: 0-0
Track: LH: 0-0 RH: 0-2 Tight: 0-1 Gall: 0-0
Aids: Bl: 0-0 Vi: 0-1 Tstrap: 0-0 Ckp: 0-0

Best Rating: 92 1/00 Tram 2m   sft-hvy NHF

Plating-class hurdler; winning pointer; does not quite get home over two and a half miles; acts on fast ground.

Marigliano (USA)

88(102c)   (103c)**103**

11-y-o g Riverman (USA)-Mount Holyoke (Golden Fleece (USA))

K A Morgan G S Alcock & B R Jones

Placings:P0/L034/F2113313/11042312/31022U/P0563P/30 12-P3306   **(4280)**

2003/04: 16PS, 173G, 163S, 169GS, 166GS,

	Starts	1st	2nd	3rd	Win & Pl
Hurdles	3	0	0	1	387
Chases	2	0	0	1	826
Career Total	43	8	6	10	51932
103	12/02	Fknm	2m	D(0-120)HHdl	G-S	£5096
114	1/01	Fknm	2m110y	F(0-110)HCh	SFT	£2525
111	3/00	MRas	2m1f110yD Ch		G-F	£5124
128	11/99	Hntg	2m110y	C(0-130)HHdl	G-F	£10365
116	11/99	Worc	2m	C(0-130)HHdl	G-S	£4744
111	2/99	Catt	2m	C(0-130)HHdl	GD	£4770
109	1/99	Catt	2m	D(0-120)HHdl	GD	£2775
119	12/98	Hayd	2m	E(0-120)HHdl	SFT	£2232

Total win prize-money £37632

Going:	Sf: 0-2 GS: 0-2 Gd: 0-1 GF: - Fm: 0-0
Distance:	2m/2m3: 0-5 2m4-2m7: 0-0 3m+: 0-0
Track:	LH: 0-3 RH: 0-2 Tight: 0-3 Gall: 0-1
Aids:	Bl: 0-0 Vi: 0-0 Tstrap: 0-0 Ckp: 0-3
Best Rating:	**128** 11/99 Hntg 2m110y gd-fm Hdl

Moderate but versatile gelding who has won under all codes and goes particularly well on a tight track; handles anything but extremes of ground; effective at around two miles; has worn sheepskin cheekpieces.

Marino West (IRE)

88(86h)   (104h)**88**

9-y-o ch g Phardante (FR)-Seanaphobal Lady (Kambalda)

N M Babbage Provex Products Ltd

Placings:61P/0U-3PPP   **(4757)**

2003/04: 213G, 29PS, 24PG, 25PS,

	Starts	1st	2nd	3rd	Win & Pl
Chases	4	0	0	1	648
Career Total	9	1	0	1	6017
104	4/02	Asct	2m4f	C Hdl	G-F	£5369

Total win prize-money £5369

Going:	Sf: 0-2 GS: 0-0 Gd: 0-2 GF: - Fm: 0-0
Distance:	2m/2m3: 0-0 2m4-2m7: 0-1 3m+: 0-3
Track:	LH: 0-1 RH: 0-3 Tight: 0-0 Gall: 0-0
Aids:	Bl: 0-0 Vi: 0-0 Tstrap: 0-0 Ckp: 0-0
Best Rating:	**104** 4/02 Asct 2m4f gd-fm Hdl

Marjina

103   **106**

5-y-o b m Classic Cliche (IRE)-Cavina (Ardross)

Miss E C Lavelle Paul G Jacobs

Placings:3522   **(4544)**

2003/04: 173GS, 163GS, 222G, 222GS,

	Starts	1st	2nd	3rd	Win & Pl
NH Flat	2	0	0	1	224
Hurdles	2	0	2	0	2574
Career Total	4	0	2	1	2798

Going:	Sf: 0-0 GS: 0-3 Gd: 0-1 GF: - Fm: 0-0

Distance:	2m/2m3: 0-2 2m4-2m7: 0-2 3m+: 0-0
Track:	LH: 0-1 RH: 0-3 Tight: 0-1 Gall: 0-1
Aids:	Bl: 0-0 Vi: 0-0 Tstrap: 0-0 Ckp: 0-0
Best Rating:	**106** 3/04 Winc 2m6f gd-sft Hdl

Moderate novice hurdler; dam related to the top-class Bacchanal; has showed plenty of promise in two good bumpers and novices' hurdles; acts on good to soft; will improve for a trip.

Mark Equal

106   **122**

8-y-o b g Nicholas Bill-Dissolution (Henbit (USA))

M C Pipe Heeru Kirpalani Racing

Placings:5/3104/30PP-2311F34   **(4841)**

2003/04: 162G, 193G, 191GF, 201GS, 18FGS, 214G,

	Starts	1st	2nd	3rd	Win & Pl
Chases	7	2	1	2	11954
Career Total	16	3	1	4	17361
122	3/04	Wwck	2m4f110yE(0-105)HCh	G-S	£4550
122	3/04	Chep	2m3f110yE(0-110)HCh	G-F	£4420
110	1/02	Tntn	2m3f110yD Hdl	SFT	£4130

Total win prize-money £13100

Going:	Sf: 0-0 GS: 1-2 Gd: 0-4 GF: - Fm: 1-1
Distance:	2m/2m3: 0-3 **2m4-2m7: 2-4** 3m+: 0-0
Track:	**LH: 2-4** RH: 0-0 Tight: 0-4 Gall: 0-1
Aids:	Bl: 0-0 Vi: 0-0 Tstrap: 0-0 Ckp: 0-1
Best Rating:	**122** 4/04 Font 2m2f good Ch

Plating-class chaser; improved form when easy winner of weak 2m 4f handicap chase at Chepstow March 2004; effective over 2m but stays 2m 4f; appears to act on all types of ground.

Mark Of Zorro (IRE)

96   **99+**

4-y-o b g Mark Of Esteem (IRE)-Sifaara (IRE) (Caerleon (USA))

O Sherwood (R Hannon 24/10) The Waney Racing Group Inc

Placings:06PP   **(4102)**

2003/04: 169GS, 166GS, 16PS, 16PG,

	Starts	1st	2nd	3rd	Win & Pl
Hurdles	4	0	0	0	0
Career Total	4	0	0	0	0

Going:	Sf: 0-1 GS: 0-2 Gd: 0-1 GF: - Fm: 0-0
Distance:	2m/2m3: 0-4 2m4-2m7: 0-0 3m+: 0-0
Track:	LH: 0-3 RH: 0-1 Tight: 0-1 Gall: 0-0
Aids:	Bl: 0-3 Vi: 0-0 Tstrap: 0-0 Ckp: 0-0
Best Rating:	**99** 1/04 Sand 2m110y gd-sft Hdl

Modest hurdler; fair performer on the Flat at around ten furlongs; often wears headgear.

Marked Man (IRE)

114(113h)   (113+h)**125**

8-y-o b g Grand Plaisir (IRE)-Teazle (Quayside)

R Lee Mr & Mrs C R Elliott

Placings:03040/6155-106641   **(4527)**

2003/04: 171G, 202GS, 196G, 16HY, 194G, 191GS,

	Starts	1st	2nd	3rd	Win & Pl
Hurdles	3	1	0	0	5057
Chases	3	1	0	0	6063
Career Total	15	3	0	1	17255
117	3/04	Chep	2m3f110yD(0-110)HCh	G-S	£5733
110	5/03	Bang	2m1f	D(0-120)HHdl	GD	£5057
95	11/02	Aint	2m4f	E(0-100)HHdl	GD	£4543

Total win prize-money £15334

Going:	Sf: 0-1 GS: 1-2 Gd: 1-3 GF: - Fm: 0-0
Distance:	2m/2m3: 1-2 2m4-2m7: 1-4 3m+: 0-0
Track:	**LH: 2-4** RH: 0-2 **Tight: 1-2** Gall: 0-0
Aids:	Bl: 0-0 Vi: 0-0 Tstrap: 0-0 Ckp: 0-0
Best Rating:	**117** 3/04 Chep 2m3f110y gd-sft Ch

Modest hurdler/chaser; always considered a potential chaser and won weak 2m 4f novices' handicap chase at Chepstow March 2004 despite the ground being on the soft side for him; suited by good ground; stays 2m 4f.

Market Value (IRE)

8-y-o b g Montelimar (USA)-Derring Lass (Derring Rose)

Mrs M Evans W J Evans

Placings:0/P0   **(0752)**

2003/04: 21PGF, 17OGF,

	Starts	1st	2nd	3rd	Win & Pl
Hurdles	2	0	0	0	
Career Total	3	0	0	0	

Going:	Sf: 0-0 GS: 0-0 Gd: 0-0 GF: - Fm: 0-2
Distance:	2m/2m3: 0-1 2m4-2m7: 0-1 3m+: 0-0
Track:	LH: 0-2 RH: 0-0 Tight: 0-1 Gall: 0-0
Aids:	Bl: 0-0 Vi: 0-1 Tstrap: 0-0 Ckp: 0-0
Best Rating:	**17** 5/01 Baln 2m gd-yld NHF

Marlborough (IRE)

123   **166+**

12-y-o br g Strong Gale-Wrekenogan (Tarqogan)

J Bertran De Balanda (N J Henderson 16/3) Sir Robert Ogden

Placings:5213/U111FF/PU1216/111/34F0/102F05-2351PP   **(4384)**

2003/04: 252G, 253G, 245G, 241G, 24PG, 23PVS,

	Starts	1st	2nd	3rd	Win & Pl
Chases	6	1	1	1	79600
Career Total	35	11	4	3	350984
166	2/04	Kemp	3m	A HCh	GD	£58000
160	11/02	Weth	3m1f	A Ch	G-S	£29750
165	4/01	Sand	3m110y	A Ch	G-S	£58000
165	2/01	Winc	3m1f110yB Ch	GD	£16932
166	12/00	Chel	3m1f110yB HCh	SFT	£28678
158	3/00	Chel	3m110y	B HCh	GD	£39000
151	1/00	Kemp	3m	C(0-135)HCh	GD	£6955
135	1/99	Kemp	3m	D Ch	SFT	£4924
132	12/98	Ling	3m	A Ch	SFT	£3326
135	11/98	Worc	2m4f110yE Ch	HVY	£3600
126	3/98	Newb	2m5f	D Hdl	G-S	£3793

Total win prize-money £252961

Going:	Sf: 0-0 GS: 0-0 Gd: 1-5 GF: - Fm: 0-0
Distance:	2m/2m3: 0-0 2m4-2m7: 0-0 **3m+: 1-6**
Track:	LH: 0-3 **RH: 1-2** Tight: 0-0 Gall: 0-2
Aids:	Bl: 0-0 Vi: 0-0 Tstrap: 0-0 Ckp: 0-0
Best Rating:	**170** 12/02 Kemp 3m soft Ch

Smart staying chaser; produced best ever display when just failing to overcome Best Mate in King George at Kempton in 2002; looked held subsequently despite finishing runner-up in 2003 Charlie Hall Chase at Wetherby and dropped in the handicap as a result; returned to best to carry top weight to victory in the 2004 Racing Post Chase at Kempton; stays at least 3m 1f; effective on good and soft ground; ideally suited by being held up off a fast pace; has worn cheekpieces.

Marlborough Sound

81f   **66f**

5-y-o b g Overbury (IRE)-Dark City (Sweet Monday)
N G Richards Ashleybank Investments Limited

Placings:6   (4867)
2003/04: 16⁶S,

	Starts	1st	2nd	3rd	Win & Pl
NH Flat	1	0	0	0	0
Career Total	1	0	0	0	0

Going:	Sf: 0-1 GS: 0-0 Gd: 0-0 GF: - Fm: 0-0
Distance:	2m/2m3: 0-1 2m4-2m7: 0-0 3m+: 0-0
Track:	LH: 0-1 RH: 0-0 Tight: 0-0 Gall: 0-0
Aids:	Bl: 0-0 Vi: 0-0 Tstrap: 0-0 Ckp: 0-0
Best Rating:	66 4/04 Ayr 2m soft NHF

Half brother to winning jumpers Do It On Dani, Jessolle and Eternal City; travelled strongly under restraint for long way on debut in Ayr bumper in April 2004 and not knocked about when clearly held; likely to leave this bare form a long way behind in due course.

Marlmont Lad (IRE)

13-y-o b/br g Homo Sapien-Patricias Choice (Laurence O)
Mrs G Harvey Mrs Rhona Alexander

Placings:005/0/P   (0836)
2003/04: 23⁵GF,

	Starts	1st	2nd	3rd	Win & Pl
Chases	1	0	0	0	
Career Total	5	0	0	0	0

Going:	Sf: 0-0 GS: 0-0 Gd: 0-0 GF: - Fm: 0-1
Distance:	2m/2m3: 0-0 2m4-2m7: 0-0 3m+: 0-1
Track:	LH: 0-1 RH: 0-0 Tight: 0-0 Gall: 0-0
Aids:	Bl: 0-0 Vi: 0-0 Tstrap: 0-0 Ckp: 0-0
Best Rating:	88 4/96 DRoy 3m good Hdl

Marmaduke (IRE)

94   **116**

8-y-o ch g Perugino (USA)-Sympathy (Precocious)
M Pitman Martin Butler

Placings:201220/341646/22-4F   (4718)
2003/04: 16⁴G, 16⁶G,

	Starts	1st	2nd	3rd	Win & Pl
Hurdles	2	0	0	0	773
Career Total	16	2	5	1	14626
116	10/01	Hntg	2m110y	HHdl	GD	£5432
116	12/00	Ludl	2m	F Hdl	SFT	£2436
				Total win prize-money £7868

Going:	Sf: 0-0 GS: 0-0 Gd: 0-2 GF: - Fm: 0-0
Distance:	2m/2m3: 0-2 2m4-2m7: 0-0 3m+: 0-0
Track:	LH: 0-0 RH: 0-2 Tight: 0-0 Gall: 0-0
Aids:	Bl: 0-0 Vi: 0-0 Tstrap: 0-0 Ckp: 0-0
Best Rating:	117 7/02 Sthl 2m1f gd-fm Hdl

Fair hurdler; best at two miles; acts on most ground.

Marmaduke Jinks

91

10-y-o b g Primitive Rising (USA)-Keldholme (Derek H)
Mrs M Reveley Minster Commercials

Placings:1/316F/F/00   (4192)
2003/04: 22⁰G, 22⁰GS,

	Starts	1st	2nd	3rd	Win & Pl
Hurdles	2	0	0	0	
Career Total	8	2	0	1	5756
108	2/01	Hayd	2m	D Hdl	HVY	£3640
111	1/00	Newc	2m	H NHF	SFT	£1736
				Total win prize-money £5376

Going:	Sf: 0-0 GS: 0-1 Gd: 0-1 GF: - Fm: 0-0
Distance:	2m/2m3: 0-2 2m4-2m7: 0-2 3m+: 0-0
Track:	LH: 0-1 RH: 0-1 Tight: 0-1 Gall: 0-0
Aids:	Bl: 0-0 Vi: 0-0 Tstrap: 0-0 Ckp: 0-0
Best Rating:	111 1/00 Newc 2m soft NHF

Marmalade Mountain

88   **59**

9-y-o ch g Lochearnhead (USA)-Lady Seville (Orange Bay)
Mrs A M Thorpe Don Jones

Placings:6PFP   (4505)
2003/04: 24⁶G, 25⁵PGS, 24⁶G, 25⁶PG,

	Starts	1st	2nd	3rd	Win & Pl
Chases	4	0	0	0	0
Career Total	4	0	0	0	0

Going:	Sf: 0-0 GS: 0-1 Gd: 0-3 GF: - Fm: 0-0
Distance:	2m/2m3: 0-0 2m4-2m7: 0-0 3m+: 0-4
Track:	LH: 0-1 RH: 0-3 Tight: 0-1 Gall: 0-1
Aids:	Bl: 0-0 Vi: 0-0 Tstrap: 0-0 Ckp: 0-1
Best Rating:	58 2/04 Ludl 3m good Ch

Maron

7-y-o b g Puissance-Will Be Bold (Bold Lad (IRE))
F Jordan (A Berry 26/7) Gary Gibson

Placings:P   (3315)
2003/04: 16⁰PS,

	Starts	1st	2nd	3rd	Win & Pl
Hurdles	1	0	0	0	
Career Total	1	0	0	0	

Going:	Sf: 0-1 GS: 0-0 Gd: 0-0 GF: - Fm: 0-0
Distance:	2m/2m3: 0-1 2m4-2m7: 0-0 3m+: 0-0
Track:	LH: 0-0 RH: 0-1 Tight: 0-0 Gall: 0-0
Aids:	Bl: 0-0 Vi: 0-0 Tstrap: 0-0 Ckp: 0-0

Marrakech (IRE)

113   **114+**

7-y-o ch m Barathea (IRE)-Nashkara (Shirley Heights)
Mrs N Smith T Hayward, B Fulton, M Charge, D Wallis

Placings:21400   (3859)
2003/04: 17²G, 16¹S, 16⁴GS, 18⁰G, 16⁰S,

	Starts	1st	2nd	3rd	Win & Pl
Hurdles	5	1	1	0	17096
Career Total	5	1	1	0	17096
114	11/03	Asct	2m110y	B Hdl	SFT	£14007
				Total win prize-money £14008

Going:	Sf: 1-2 GS: 0-1 Gd: 0-2 GF: - Fm: 0-0
Distance:	2m/2m3: 1-5 2m4-2m7: 0-0 3m+: 0-0
Track:	LH: 0-2 RH: 1-3 Tight: 0-3 Gall: 0-0
Aids:	Bl: 0-0 Vi: 0-0 Tstrap: 0-0 Ckp: 0-0
Best Rating:	114 11/03 Asct 2m110y soft Hdl

Fair novice hurdler, though progressive; suited by two miles and soft ground.

Marrasit (IRE)

84   **71**

8-y-o b m Zaffaran (USA)-Alligator Crawl (IRE) (Pollerton)
Miss Venetia Williams Blondie Partnership

Placings:654   (3967)
2003/04: 26⁶S, 20⁵G, 25⁴GS,

	Starts	1st	2nd	3rd	Win & Pl
Chases	3	0	0	0	305
Career Total	3	0	0	0	305

Going:	Sf: 0-1 GS: 0-1 Gd: 0-1 GF: - Fm: 0-0
Distance:	2m/2m3: 0-0 2m4-2m7: 0-1 3m+: 0-2
Track:	LH: 0-1 RH: 0-2 Tight: 0-1 Gall: 0-0
Aids:	Bl: 0-0 Vi: 0-0 Tstrap: 0-0 Ckp: 0-0
Best Rating:	71 2/04 MRas 2m4f good Ch

Dual Irish point winner; disappointing here so far.

Marrel

106   **110**

6-y-o b g Shareef Dancer (USA)-Upper Caen (High Top)
D Burchell (S L Keightley 13/5) Don Gould

Placings:645-52111333P006   (4942)
2003/04: 20⁵GD, 19⁴G, 17¹G, 16¹GF, 17¹GF, 20³G, 16³AGF, 22³GS, 20⁵PGS, 17⁰G, 16⁰G, 20⁶GS,

	Starts	1st	2nd	3rd	Win & Pl
Hurdles	12	3	1	3	17102
Career Total	15	3	1	3	17102
101	6/03	NAbb	2m1f	D Hdl	G-F	£5616
101	6/03	Worc	2m	E Hdl	G-F	£3647
101	5/03	Ctml	2m1f110yE Hdl	GD	£3679
				Total win prize-money £12942

Going:	Sf: 0-0 GS: 0-3 Gd: 1-5 GF: - Fm: 2-4
Distance:	2m/2m3: 3-6 2m4-2m7: 0-6 3m+: 0-0
Track:	LH: 3-9 RH: 0-3 Tight: 2-4 Gall: 0-0
Aids:	Bl: 0-0 Vi: 3-10 Tstrap: 0-0 Ckp: 0-0
Best Rating:	110 7/03 NAbb 2m6f gd-sft Hdl

Modest hurdler; completed a hat-trick after being claimed when finishing runner-up at Hereford May 2003; not disgraced subsequently; acts on good ground; seems best at around 2m although has been tried over much farther; often wears a visor.

Marron Prince (FR)

64f   **72f**

4-y-o ch g Cyborg (FR)-Colombine (USA) (Empery (USA))
R Rowe Mrs Celia Rayner

Placings:00   (4936)
2003/04: 16⁰G, 18⁰G,

	Starts	1st	2nd	3rd	Win & Pl
NH Flat	2	0	0	0	
Career Total	2	0	0	0	

Going:	Sf: 0-0 GS: 0-0 Gd: 0-2 GF: - Fm: 0-0
Distance:	2m/2m3: 0-2 2m4-2m7: 0-0 3m+: 0-0
Track:	LH: 0-1 RH: 0-1 Tight: 0-1 Gall: 0-0
Aids:	Bl: 0-0 Vi: 0-0 Tstrap: 0-0 Ckp: 0-0
Best Rating:	72 2/04 Kemp 2m good NHF

Marsh Run

104f   **119+f**

5-y-o b m Presenting-Madam Margeaux (IRE) (Ardross)
M W Easterby Mrs M E Curtis

Placings: *21101*   (4328)
2003/04: 16²F, 17¹GF, 16¹GF, 16⁰GS, 16¹S,

	Starts	1st	2nd	3rd	Win & Pl
NH Flat	5	3	1	0	19504
Career Total	5	3	1	0	19504
119	3/04	Sand	2m110y	A NHF	SFT £14500
88	11/03	Hexm	2m110y	H NHF	G-F £2646
86	10/03	MRas	2m1f110yH NHF		G-F £1890
				Total win prize-money £19036

Going:	Sf: 1-1 GS: 0-1 Gd: 0-0 GF: - Fm: 2-3
Distance:	2m/2m3: 3-5 2m4-2m7: 0-0 3m+: 0-0
Track:	LH: 1-3 RH: 2-2 Tight: 1-1 Gall: 0-0
Aids:	Bl: 0-0 Vi: 0-0 Tstrap: 0-0 Ckp: 0-0
Best Rating:	119 3/04 Sand 2m110y soft NHF

Won a bumper at Market Rasen in October on second attempt; followed up at Hexham the following month before disappointing at Wetherby; bounced back to cause a shock in the big Mares bumper at Sandown; should stay further than two miles over hurdles; handles any ground.

Marshal Bond
69   50
6-y-o b g Celtic Swing-Arminda (Blakeney)
B Smart   R C Bond

Placings: 0   (2402)
2003/04: 17⁰HY,

	Starts	1st	2nd	3rd	Win & Pl
Hurdles	1	0	0	0	
Career Total	1	0	0	0	

Going:	Sf: 0-1 GS: 0-0 Gd: 0-0 GF: - Fm: 0-0
Distance:	2m/2m3: 0-1 2m4-2m7: 0-0 3m+: 0-0
Track:	LH: 0-0 RH: 0-1 Tight: 0-0 Gall: 0-0
Aids:	Bl: 0-0 Vi: 0-0 Tstrap: 0-0 Ckp: 0-0
Best Rating:	50 11/03 Carl 2m1f heavy Hdl

Moderate middle-distance Flat performer; always behind on hurdling debut.

Marshal Murat (IRE)

8-y-o ch g Executive Perk-Magneeto (IRE) (Brush Aside (USA))
C R Egerton   Mrs Evelyn Hankinson

Placings: 4/0-P   (2795)
2003/04: 17°GS,

	Starts	1st	2nd	3rd	Win & Pl
Hurdles	1	0	0	0	
Career Total	3	0	0	0	226

Going:	Sf: 0-0 GS: 0-1 Gd: 0-0 GF: - Fm: 0-0
Distance:	2m/2m3: 0-1 2m4-2m7: 0-0 3m+: 0-0
Track:	LH: 0-1 RH: 0-0 Tight: 0-1 Gall: 0-0
Aids:	Bl: 0-0 Vi: 0-0 Tstrap: 0-0 Ckp: 0-0
Best Rating:	101 2/01 Navn 2m soft NHF

Marshys Mia
101f   89f
7-y-o b m Alflora (IRE)-Woodland Flower (Furry Glen)
D Mullarkey   Tony Marsh

Placings: *265*   (1762)
2003/04: 17²GF, 16⁶G, 16⁵G,

	Starts	1st	2nd	3rd	Win & Pl
NH Flat	3	0	1	0	570
Career Total	3	0	1	0	570

Going:	Sf: 0-0 GS: 0-0 Gd: 0-2 GF: - Fm: 0-1
Distance:	2m/2m3: 0-3 2m4-2m7: 0-0 3m+: 0-0
Track:	LH: 0-2 RH: 0-1 Tight: 0-1 Gall: 0-0
Aids:	Bl: 0-0 Vi: 0-0 Tstrap: 0-0 Ckp: 0-0
Best Rating:	89 6/03 Worc 2m good NHF

Half-sister to the winning hurdler and chaser Stamparland Hill; second in Hereford bumper on debut June 2003; well beaten since.

Marteeny
94   60
9-y-o b m Teenoso (USA)-Marejo (Creetown)
J B Walton   Messrs F T Walton

Placings: *0000/046500/0/6*   (0693)
2003/04: 25⁶GF,

	Starts	1st	2nd	3rd	Win & Pl
Chases	1	0	0	0	0
Career Total	12	0	0	0	0

Going:	Sf: 0-0 GS: 0-0 Gd: 0-0 GF: - Fm: 0-1
Distance:	2m/2m3: 0-0 2m4-2m7: 0-0 3m+: 0-1
Track:	LH: 0-1 RH: 0-0 Tight: 0-0 Gall: 0-0
Aids:	Bl: 0-0 Vi: 0-0 Tstrap: 0-0 Ckp: 0-0
Best Rating:	76 10/00 Kels 2m6f110y good Hdl

Martha Reilly (IRE)
93   91
8-y-o ch m Rainbows For Life (CAN)-Debach Delight (Great Nephew)
Mrs Barbara Waring   B W Parren

Placings: *522215/35F43F-F04*   (4669)
2003/04: 24FGF, 22⁰GS, 23⁴GS,

	Starts	1st	2nd	3rd	Win & Pl
Hurdles	3	0	0	0	282
Career Total	15	1	3	2	7559
89	11/01	Strf	2m6f110yE Hdl		SFT £2628
				Total win prize-money £2629

Going:	Sf: 0-0 GS: 0-2 Gd: 0-0 GF: - Fm: 0-1
Distance:	2m/2m3: 0-0 2m4-2m7: 0-2 3m+: 0-1
Track:	LH: 0-3 RH: 0-0 Tight: 0-1 Gall: 0-0
Aids:	Bl: 0-0 Vi: 0-0 Tstrap: 0-0 Ckp: 0-0
Best Rating:	92 3/03 Sthl 3m110y gd-fm Hdl

Martha's Boy (IRE)

13-y-o b g Supreme Leader-Madame Martha (Carlingford Castle)
Mrs Marion Robinson   Mrs Marion Robinson

Placings: *111/P/P/PP/P*   (4703)
2003/04: 26°G,

	Starts	1st	2nd	3rd	Win & Pl
Chases	1	0	0	0	
Career Total	8	3	0	0	10771
110	4/98	Hntg	3m	H Ch	G-S £1236
132	4/98	Aint	3m1f	C Ch	G-S £7253
121	3/98	Strf	3m	H Ch	GD £2281
				Total win prize-money £10771

Going:	Sf: 0-0 GS: 0-0 Gd: 0-1 GF: - Fm: 0-0
Distance:	2m/2m3: 0-0 2m4-2m7: 0-0 3m+: 0-1
Track:	LH: 0-0 RH: 0-0 Tight: 0-1 Gall: 0-0
Aids:	Bl: 0-0 Vi: 0-0 Tstrap: 0-0 Ckp: 0-0
Best Rating:	132 4/98 Aint 3m1f gd-sft Ch

Martha's Kinsman (IRE)
99f   102+f
5-y-o b g Petoski-Martha's Daughter (Majestic Maharaj)
H D Daly   M Ward-Thomas

Placings: *10*   (4454)
2003/04: 16¹GS, 16⁰GS,

	Starts	1st	2nd	3rd	Win & Pl
NH Flat	2	1	0	0	1638
Career Total	2	1	0	0	1638
102	12/03	Hntg	2m110y	H NHF	G-S £1638
				Total win prize-money £1638

Going:	Sf: 0-0 GS: 1-2 Gd: 0-0 GF: - Fm: 0-0
Distance:	2m/2m3: 1-2 2m4-2m7: 0-0 3m+: 0-0
Track:	LH: 0-0 RH: 1-2 Tight: 0-0 Gall: 1-1
Aids:	Bl: 0-0 Vi: 0-0 Tstrap: 0-0 Ckp: 0-0
Best Rating:	102 12/03 Hntg 2m110y gd-sft NHF

From the same family as high-class two mile chaser Martha's Son; impressive bumper winner on debut; beaten under a penalty in a better race next time.

Martin House (IRE)
88   88
5-y-o b g Mujadil (USA)-Dolcezza (FR) (Lichine (USA))
Mrs K Walton (J D Bethell 9/10)   Mile High Racing

Placings: *03P6*   (4727)
2003/04: 16⁰GS, 16³HY, 17⁶GS, 17⁶G,

	Starts	1st	2nd	3rd	Win & Pl
Hurdles	4	0	0	1	590
Career Total	4	0	0	1	590

Going:	Sf: 0-1 GS: 0-2 Gd: 0-1 GF: - Fm: 0-0
Distance:	2m/2m3: 0-4 2m4-2m7: 0-0 3m+: 0-0
Track:	LH: 0-3 RH: 0-1 Tight: 0-3 Gall: 0-0
Aids:	Bl: 0-0 Vi: 0-0 Tstrap: 0-0 Ckp: 0-0
Best Rating:	88 2/04 Kels 2m110y heavy Hdl

Martin's Sunset

6-y-o ch g Royal Academy (USA)-Mainly Sunset (Red Sunset)
W R Muir   Mrs Barbara Jean Martin

Placings: F   (1520)
2003/04: 18FG,

	Starts	1st	2nd	3rd	Win & Pl
Hurdles	1	0	0	0	
Career Total	1	0	0	0	

Going:	Sf: 0-0 GS: 0-0 Gd: 0-0 GF: - Fm: 0-0
Distance:	2m/2m3: 0-1 2m4-2m7: 0-0 3m+: 0-0
Track:	LH: 0-1 RH: 0-0 Tight: 0-1 Gall: 0-0
Aids:	Bl: 0-0 Vi: 0-0 Tstrap: 0-0 Ckp: 0-0

Martinstown (IRE)
111f   125+f
5-y-o ch g Old Vic-Bella Velutina (Coquelin (USA))
C Roche   John P McManus

Placings: *110*   (4400)
2003/04: 16¹GF, 16¹S, 16⁹G,

	Starts	1st	2nd	3rd	Win & Pl
NH Flat	3	2	0	0	9409

Career Total	3	2	0	0	9409
125 11/03 Fair	2m	NHF		SFT	£5376
110 10/03 Naas	2m	NHF		G-F	£4032
			Total win prize-money		£9409

Going:	Sf: 1-1 GS: 0-0 Gd: 0-1 GF: - Fm: 1-1
Distance:	2m/2m3: 2-3 2m4-2m7: 0-0 3m+: 0-0
Track:	LH: 0-1 RH: 1-1 Tight: 0-0 Gall: 0-0
Aids:	Bl: 0-0 Vi: 0-0 Tstrap: 0-0 Ckp: 0-0
Best Rating:	125 11/03 Fair 2m soft NHF

Dual bumper winner before being a beaten favourite for the Cheltenham bumper; acts on any ground.

Mary's Baby

80   66

4-y-o b f Magic Ring (IRE)-Everdene (Bustino)
Mrs A J Perrett S P Tindall

Placings:0   (2205)
2003/04: 17[0]G,

	Starts	1st	2nd	3rd	Win & Pl
Hurdles	1	0	0	0	
Career Total	1	0	0	0	

Going:	Sf: 0-0 GS: 0-0 Gd: 0-1 GF: - Fm: 0-0
Distance:	2m/2m3: 0-1 2m4-2m7: 0-0 3m+: 0-0
Track:	LH: 0-0 RH: 0-1 Tight: 0-1 Gall: 0-0
Aids:	Bl: 0-0 Vi: 0-0 Tstrap: 0-0 Ckp: 0-0
Best Rating:	66 11/03 Folk 2m1f110y good Hdl

Maryland (IRE)

82f   96f

7-y-o b m Executive Perk-Raven Night (IRE) (Mandalus)
O Brennan O Brennan

Placings:02-10   (4328)
2003/04: 16[1]G, 16[0]S,

	Starts	1st	2nd	3rd	Win & Pl
NH Flat	2	1	0	0	2582
Career Total	4	1	1	0	3126
99 2/04 Fknm	2m	H NHF	GD	£2582	
		Total win prize-money		£2582	

Going:	Sf: 0-1 GS: 0-0 Gd: 1-1 GF: - Fm: 0-0
Distance:	2m/2m3: 1-2 2m4-2m7: 0-0 3m+: 0-0
Track:	LH: 1-1 RH: 0-1 Tight: 1-1 Gall: 0-0
Aids:	Bl: 0-0 Vi: 0-0 Tstrap: 0-0 Ckp: 0-0
Best Rating:	99 2/04 Fknm 2m good NHF

Fair form in bumpers; effective over two miles; acts on good ground.

Masalarian (IRE)

9-y-o b g Doyoun-Masamiyda (Lyphard (USA))
Mrs H M Bridges (A L T Moore 19/9) Mrs H M Bridges

Placings:422414/532214/141252202/044P   (4172)
2003/04: 16[0]S, 22[4]S, 19[4]S, 24[P]G,

	Starts	1st	2nd	3rd	Win & Pl
Hurdles	1	0	0	0	0
Chases	3	0	0	0	1023
Career Total	25	4	8	1	90033
130 10/01 Rosc	2m	Ch		YLD	£9322
134 5/01 Fair	2m	HHdl		GD	£41935
134 12/00 Fair	2m2f	Hdl		Y-S	£5796
117 3/00 Leop	2m	Hdl		GD	£3588
		Total win prize-money			£60642

Going:	Sf: 0-3 GS: 0-0 Gd: 0-1 GF: - Fm: 0-0

Masouri Sana (IRE)

7-y-o br m Broken Hearted-Say Thanks (Thatching)
Miss M E Rowland Paul Mayo

Placings:0-0PP   (3841)
2003/04: 16[0]GS, 16[P]GS, 19[P]GS,

	Starts	1st	2nd	3rd	Win & Pl
NH Flat	1	0	0	0	0
Hurdles	2	0	0	0	0
Career Total	4	0	0	0	

Going:	Sf: 0-0 GS: 0-3 Gd: 0-0 GF: - Fm: 0-0
Distance:	2m/2m3: 0-2 2m4-2m7: 0-1 3m+: 0-0
Track:	LH: 0-2 RH: 0-1 Tight: 0-0 Gall: 0-0
Aids:	Bl: 0-0 Vi: 0-0 Tstrap: 0-0 Ckp: 0-0

Massac (FR)

97   116

5-y-o b g Garde Royale-Mirande (FR) (Tiaia (FR))
G Macaire R Fougedoire

Placings:26-121221223   (3602)
2003/04: 17[1]G, 17[2]S, 20[1]G, 20[2]GS, 17[2]GS, 17[1]HO, 20[2]HY, 21[2]G, 19[3]S,

	Starts	1st	2nd	3rd	Win & Pl
Hurdles	2	0	2	0	5922
Chases	7	3	3	1	40253
Career Total	11	3	6	1	48201
10/03 Autl	2m1f110y	Ch		HLD	£13091
7/03 LE L	2m4f	Ch		GD	£5610
5/03 LE L	2m1f	Ch		GD	£4052
		Total win prize-money			£22753

Going:	Sf: 0-3 GS: 0-2 Gd: 2-3 GF: - Fm: 0-0
Distance:	2m/2m3: 2-5 2m4-2m7: 1-4 3m+: 0-0
Track:	LH: 0-2 RH: 0-0 Tight: 0-0 Gall: 0-1
Aids:	Bl: 0-0 Vi: 0-0 Tstrap: 0-0 Ckp: 0-0
Best Rating:	116 1/04 Chel 2m5f good Ch

French-trained chaser, successful between two miles one and two miles four in his own country; chased home Therealbandit at Cheltenham on British debut; suited by good ground.

Massenet (IRE)

106   96

9-y-o b g Caerleon (USA)-Massawippi (Be My Native (USA))
Lindsay Woods Hugh M Duffy

Placings:3030/1/U-30130665   (3892a)
2003/04: 16[3]GY, 16[P]YS, 18[1]YS, 22[3]S, 20[0]S, 20[6]HY, 20[6]HY, 16[5]Y,

	Starts	1st	2nd	3rd	Win & Pl
Hurdles	8	1	0	2	6961
Career Total	14	2	0	4	10543
100 12/03 Clon	2m2f	(74-109)HHdl	Y-S	£5824	
91 5/01 Bang	2m4f	G(0-95)HHdl	GD	£2604	
		Total win prize-money		£8429	

Going:	Sf: 0-4 GS: 0-0 Gd: 0-0 GF: - Fm: 0-0
Distance:	2m/2m3: 1-4 2m4-2m7: 0-4 3m+: 0-0
Track:	LH: 0-3 RH: 0-1 Tight: 0-0 Gall: 0-0
Aids:	Bl: 0-0 Vi: 0-0 Tstrap: 0-0 Ckp: 0-0
Best Rating:	107 12/03 Navn 2m6f soft Hdl

Modest hurdler; now trained in Ireland; stays two and a half miles and suited by ground good or softer.

Master Albert (IRE)

113f   135f

6-y-o b h Supreme Leader-Mullaun (Deep Run)
David Wachman Mrs John Magnier

Placings:S123   (4400)
2003/04: 16[S]GY, 16[1]GY, 16[2]S, 16[3]G,

	Starts	1st	2nd	3rd	Win & Pl
NH Flat	4	1	1	1	10127
Career Total	4	1	1	1	10127
101 11/03 Fair	2m	NHF	G-Y	£4480	
		Total win prize-money		£4481	

Going:	Sf: 0-1 GS: 0-0 Gd: 0-1 GF: - Fm: 0-0
Distance:	2m/2m3: 1-4 2m4-2m7: 0-0 3m+: 0-0
Track:	LH: 0-1 RH: 1-2 Tight: 0-0 Gall: 0-0
Aids:	Bl: 0-0 Vi: 0-0 Tstrap: 0-0 Ckp: 0-0
Best Rating:	135 3/04 Chel 2m110y good NHF

High-class bumper performer; still an entire; staying on third in the Festival bumper after good efforts in Ireland; acts on good ground or softer.

Master Billyboy (IRE)

104   116

6-y-o b g Old Vic-Clonodfoy (Strong Gale)
Mrs S D Williams William Peto

Placings:0/50122-10034   (4449)
2003/04: 22[1]G, 25[0]G, 20[0]HY, 22[3]G, 20[4]GS,

	Starts	1st	2nd	3rd	Win & Pl
Hurdles	5	1	0	1	9334
Career Total	11	2	2	1	15812
113 11/03 NAbb	2m6f	D(0-125)HHdl	GD	£3727	
105 12/02 Extr	2m3f	E Hdl	G-S	£3584	
		Total win prize-money		£7311	

Going:	Sf: 0-1 GS: 0-1 Gd: 1-3 GF: - Fm: 0-0
Distance:	2m/2m3: 0-0 2m4-2m7: 1-4 3m+: 0-1
Track:	LH: 1-2 RH: 0-3 Tight: 1-1 Gall: 0-1
Aids:	Bl: 0-0 Vi: 0-0 Tstrap: 0-0 Ckp: 0-0
Best Rating:	117 3/04 Asct 2m4f gd-sft Hdl

Fair hurdler; stays two miles six and should get further; likes cut in the ground; suited by forcing tactics.

Master Brew

95(91h)   (72h)79

6-y-o b g Homo Sapien-Edithmead (IRE) (Shardari)
J R Best G J Larby & P J Smith

Placings:00-3050FP3   (4919)
2003/04: 17[3]GS, 16[0]GS, 18[5]HY, 18[0]GS, 20[F]GF, 24[P]G, 20[3]GS,

	Starts	1st	2nd	3rd	Win & Pl
NH Flat	1	0	0	1	234
Hurdles	3	0	0	0	0
Chases	3	0	0	1	565
Career Total	9	0	0	2	799

Going:	Sf: 0-1 GS: 0-4 Gd: 0-1 GF: - Fm: 0-1
Distance:	2m/2m3: 0-2 2m4-2m7: 0-2 3m+: 0-1
Track:	LH: 0-4 RH: 0-3 Tight: 0-4 Gall: 0-0
Aids:	Bl: 0-0 Vi: 0-0 Tstrap: 0-0 Ckp: 0-0
Best Rating:	83 11/03 Folk 2m1f110y gd-sft NHF

Plating-class chaser; stays 2m 4f; acts on soft.

Master Chief (IRE)

10-y-o b/br g Euphemism-Shan's Lass (Mandalus)
Andrew Turnell Andrew Turnell

Placings:43   (0481)
2003/04: 17⁴G, 16³GF,

	Starts	1st	2nd	3rd	Win & Pl
Chases	2	0	0	1	1035
Career Total	2	0	0	1	1035

Going:	Sf: 0-0 GS: 0-0 Gd: 0-1 GF: - Fm: 0-1
Distance:	2m/2m3: 0-2 2m4-2m7: 0-0 3m+: 0-0
Track:	LH: 0-1 RH: 0-1 Tight: 0-1 Gall: 0-1
Aids:	Bl: 0-0 Vi: 0-0 Tstrap: 0-1 Ckp: 0-0

Master Elect (IRE)
79   60

7-y-o ch g Phardante (FR)-Proud Polly (IRE) (Pollerton)
P R Johnson Mrs L V Durnall

Placings:5-00P   (4654)
2003/04: 19⁰GS, 16⁰GS, 17⁵G,

	Starts	1st	2nd	3rd	Win & Pl
Hurdles	3	0	0	0	
Career Total	4	0	0	0	0

Going:	Sf: 0-0 GS: 0-0 Gd: 0-1 GF: - Fm: 0-0
Distance:	2m/2m3: 0-2 2m4-2m7: 0-1 3m+: 0-0
Track:	LH: 0-0 RH: 0-3 Tight: 0-0 Gall: 0-0
Aids:	Bl: 0-0 Vi: 0-0 Tstrap: 0-0 Ckp: 0-0
Best Rating:	88 8/02 Worc 2m good NHF

Master Flash (IRE)

11-y-o ch g The Bart (USA)-Continuity Lass (Continuation)
Andrew Nicholls Andrew Nicholls

Placings:0000P/PU/P   (0415)
2003/04: 20⁵G,

	Starts	1st	2nd	3rd	Win & Pl
Chases	1	0	0	0	
Career Total	8	0	0	0	

Going:	Sf: 0-0 GS: 0-0 Gd: 0-1 GF: - Fm: 0-0
Distance:	2m/2m3: 0-0 2m4-2m7: 0-1 3m+: 0-0
Track:	LH: 0-1 RH: 0-0 Tight: 0-0 Gall: 0-0
Aids:	Bl: 0-0 Vi: 0-0 Tstrap: 0-1 Ckp: 0-0
Best Rating:	72 6/00 Naas 2m3f yield NHF

Master Florian (IRE)
(103h)   (113+h)**105+**

7-y-o gr g Roselier (FR)-Paddy's Well (Paddy's Stream)
P F Nicholls K G Manley

Placings:114-4UPP   (4146)
2003/04: 22⁴GS, 23⁰G, 23⁹S, 24⁰G,

	Starts	1st	2nd	3rd	Win & Pl
Hurdles	1	0	0	0	424
Chases	3	0	0	0	0
Career Total	7	2	0	0	7411
108	12/02	Font	2m4f		E(0-105)HHdl	SFT	£3445
95	11/02	Plum	2m5f		E Hdl		SFT	£3251

Total win prize-money £6697

Going:	Sf: 0-1 GS: 0-1 Gd: 0-2 GF: - Fm: 0-0

Master Gatemaker
104   75

6-y-o b g Tragic Role (USA)-Girl At The Gate (Formidable (USA))
F P Murtagh (R C Guest 25/8) Mrs Anna Kenny

Placings:F0P000-016033F   (1838)
2003/04: 16⁰GF, 17⁰G, 17¹GF, 17⁶G, 17⁰G, 16³G, 17³GF, 17⁵G,

	Starts	1st	2nd	3rd	Win & Pl
Hurdles	8	1	0	2	3198
Career Total	13	1	0	2	3198
63	8/03	MRas	2m1f110yG(0-95)HHdl		G-F	£2401

Total win prize-money £2401

Going:	Sf: 0-0 GS: 0-0 Gd: 0-5 GF: - Fm: 1-3
Distance:	**2m/2m3:** 1-8 2m4-2m7: 0-0 3m+: 0-0
Track:	LH: 0-5 **RH:** 1-3 Tight: 1-5 Gall: 0-1
Aids:	Bl: 0-0 Vi: 0-0 Tstrap: 0-1 **Ckp:** 1-5
Best Rating:	69 10/03 MRas 2m1f110y gd-frm Hdl

Plating-class hurdler; suited by two miles and fast ground.

Master George
98(111h)   (119dh)93

7-y-o b g Mtoto-Topwinder (USA) (Topsider (USA))
P J Hobbs David R Watson & Duncan Lofts

Placings:02P/1F0604-1F0   (4947)
2003/04: 16¹GF, 23⁵GS, 20⁰GS,

	Starts	1st	2nd	3rd	Win & Pl
Chases	3	1	0	0	3367
Career Total	12	2	1	0	3367
93	9/03	NAbb	2m110y	E Ch	G-F	£3367
126	11/02	Asct	2m4f	D Hdl	HVY	£5161

Total win prize-money £8528

Going:	Sf: 0-0 GS: 0-0 Gd: 0-2 GF: - Fm: 1-1
Distance:	**2m/2m3:** 1-1 2m4-2m7: 0-1 3m+: 0-1
Track:	**LH:** 1-1 RH: 0-1 **Tight:** 1-1 Gall: 0-0
Aids:	Bl: 0-0 Vi: 0-0 Tstrap: 0-0 Ckp: 0-0
Best Rating:	126 11/02 Asct 2m4f heavy Hdl

Fair staying novice hurdler; stays 2m 4f, handles fast ground, but is well suited by heavy; has been disappointing since falling at Sandown in December 2002; made a successful switch to fence over a trip short of his best when winning over 2m at Newton Abbot September 2003; he can score again; goes well when fresh.

Master Henry (GER)
102   98

10-y-o b g Mille Balles (FR)-Maribelle (GER) (Windwurf (GER))
Ian Williams Terry Sanders

Placings:6/261206/2322P/31341634   (1701)
2003/04: 16⁹G, 16¹G, 17³G, 16⁹GF, 17¹G, 17⁶GF, 17³GF, 17⁴GF,

	Starts	1st	2nd	3rd	Win & Pl
Chases	8	2	0	3	12954
Career Total	20	3	5	4	20521
98	8/03	Ctml	2m1f110yF(0-95)HCh		GD	£3731
98	7/03	Prth	2m	F(0-95)HCh		GD	£6734
98	8/00	Ctml	2m1f110yE(0-105)HHdl		GD	£2338

Total win prize-money £12803

Master Chief (IRE) — (cont. column 3)

Going:	Sf: 0-0 GS: 0-0 Gd: 2-4 GF: - Fm: 0-4
Distance:	**2m/2m3:** 2-8 2m4-2m7: 0-0 3m+: 0-0
Track:	LH: 1-6 RH: 1-2 **Tight:** 1-7 Gall: 0-0
Aids:	Bl: 0-0 Vi: 0-0 Tstrap: 0-0 Ckp: 0-0
Best Rating:	98 8/03 Ctml 2m1f110y good Ch

Moderate chaser; failed to achieve much when making all at Perth in July 2003; followed up from the front again at Cartmel the following month; yet to race much beyond two miles.

Master Jackson
99   93

5-y-o b g Jendali (USA)-Fardella (ITY) (Molvedo)
T D Walford P Spencer

Placings:04P45P   (4459)
2003/04: 16⁵S, 17⁴GF, 16⁵GF, 17⁴GS, 19⁵G, 20⁰PHY,

	Starts	1st	2nd	3rd	Win & Pl
NH Flat	2	0	0	0	0
Hurdles	4	0	0	0	268
Career Total	6	0	0	0	268

Going:	Sf: 0-2 GS: 0-1 Gd: 0-1 GF: - Fm: 0-2
Distance:	2m/2m3: 0-4 2m4-2m7: 0-2 3m+: 0-0
Track:	LH: 0-3 RH: 0-3 Tight: 0-3 Gall: 0-1
Aids:	Bl: 0-0 Vi: 0-0 Tstrap: 0-0 Ckp: 0-0
Best Rating:	93 12/03 MRas 2m3f110y good Hdl

Very modest efforts in bumpers; well beaten so far over hurdles.

Master Jed (IRE)
98   76

7-y-o br g Bob's Return (IRE)-Evan's Love (Master Owen)
J A B Old W E Sturt

Placings:06-P00   (2673)
2003/04: 17⁵GS, 16⁰GS, 19⁰GF,

	Starts	1st	2nd	3rd	Win & Pl
Hurdles	3	0	0	0	
Career Total	5	0	0	0	0

Going:	Sf: 0-0 GS: 0-2 Gd: 0-0 GF: - Fm: 0-1
Distance:	2m/2m3: 0-3 2m4-2m7: 0-0 3m+: 0-0
Track:	LH: 0-1 RH: 0-2 Tight: 0-3 Gall: 0-1
Aids:	Bl: 0-0 Vi: 0-0 Tstrap: 0-0 Ckp: 0-0
Best Rating:	84 3/03 Winc 2m gd-fm NHF

Master Jock

10-y-o ch g Scottish Reel-Mistress Corrado (New Member)
P Jones P S Burke

Placings:4-421U40   (4626)
2003/04: 21⁴G, 24²G, 24¹GS, 25⁴G, 24⁴G, 21⁰G,

	Starts	1st	2nd	3rd	Win & Pl
Chases	6	1	1	0	5882
Career Total	7	1	1	0	6059
94	5/03	Strf	3m	H Ch	G-S	£3563

Total win prize-money £3563

Going:	Sf: 0-0 GS: 1-2 Gd: 0-4 GF: - Fm: 0-0
Distance:	2m/2m3: 0-0 2m4-2m7: 0-0 **3m+:** 1-4
Track:	**LH:** 1-5 RH: 0-1 **Tight:** 1-3 Gall: 0-1
Aids:	Bl: 0-0 Vi: 0-0 Tstrap: 0-0 Ckp: 0-0
Best Rating:	95 2/04 Hrfd 3m1f110y gd-sft Ch

Winner in points and hunter chases; stays three miles; acts on most ground.

Distance: 2m/2m3: 0-0 2m4-2m7: 0-1 3m+: 0-3
Track: LH: 0-0 RH: 0-4 Tight: 0-1 Gall: 0-0
Aids: Bl: 0-0 Vi: 0-0 Tstrap: 0-0 Ckp: 0-0
Best Rating: 113   12/03   Sand   2m6f   gd-sft   Hdl

Modest performer; effective at around two miles six; effective with cut; has worn a tongue tie.

Master Jubb

75   **54**

6-y-o b g Petrizzo-Ziggy's Pearl (USA) (Ziggy's Boy (USA))
D J Caro Ruggur Racing

Placings:00PP0   (3773)
2003/04: 16⁶G, 17⁰GF, 26⁶GS, 21⁶GS, 16⁶G,

	Starts	1st	2nd	3rd	Win & Pl
NH Flat	2	0	0	0	0
Hurdles	3	0	0	0	0
Career Total	**5**	**0**	**0**	**0**	**0**

Going: Sf: 0-0 GS: 0-2 Gd: 0-1 GF: - Fm: 0-2
Distance: 2m/2m3: 0-3 2m4-2m7: 0-1 3m+: 0-1
Track: LH: 0-1 RH: 0-4 Tight: 0-0 Gall: 0-1
Aids: Bl: 0-2 Vi: 0-0 Tstrap: 0-0 Ckp: 0-1
Best Rating: 69 11/03 Hrfd 2m1f   gd-fm NHF

Master McNair (IRE)

98   **87**

6-y-o br g Glacial Storm (USA)-Pollyville (Pollerton)
P D Cundell Ian M Brown

Placings:60P   (4167)
2003/04: 21⁶G, 24⁰G, 21⁶G,

	Starts	1st	2nd	3rd	Win & Pl
Hurdles	3	0	0	0	0
Career Total	**3**	**0**	**0**	**0**	**0**

Going: Sf: 0-0 GS: 0-0 Gd: 0-3 GF: - Fm: 0-0
Distance: 2m/2m3: 0-0 2m4-2m7: 0-2 3m+: 0-1
Track: LH: 0-2 RH: 0-1 Tight: 0-0 Gall: 0-1
Aids: Bl: 0-0 Vi: 0-0 Tstrap: 0-0 Ckp: 0-0
Best Rating: 91 12/03 Wwck 2m5f   good Hdl

Showed promise in bumper on debut; also shaped with promise on hurdles debut;

Master Of Illusion (IRE)

96   **115**

11-y-o ch g Castle Keep-Galloping Gold Vii (Damsire Unregistered)
R Lee Mrs G Goddard,Ben Hinchliff & Des Murray

Placings:40/03P210320P20P/23524102/2433211/63PP3P/32U201-01P0   (3406)
2003/04: 24⁰GS, 26¹G, 23⁸S, 24⁰G,

	Starts	1st	2nd	3rd	Win & Pl
Chases	4	1	0	0	3685
Career Total	**46**	**6**	**10**	**8**	**51050**
115	11/03	NAbb	3m2f110yD(0-125)HCh	GD	£3684
115	3/03	Strf	3m	D(0-120)HCh	G-S	£10270
115	4/01	NAbb	3m2f110yE(0-115)HCh	SFT	£5538
115	3/01	Strf	3m	D(0-120)HCh	SFT	£7150
115	3/00	Folk	3m2f	E Ch	G-F	£3645
99	11/98	Clon	3m	Hdl	SFT	£3288

Total win prize-money £33577

Going: Sf: 0-1 GS: 0-1 Gd: 1-2 GF: - Fm: 0-0
Distance: 2m/2m3: 0-0 2m4-2m7: 0-0 **3m+:** 1-4
Track: **LH:** 1-3 RH: 0-1 **Tight:** 1-2 Gall: 0-1
Aids: Bl: 0-0 **Vi:** 1-4 Tstrap: 0-0 Ckp: 0-0
Best Rating: 115 11/03 NAbb 3m2f110y good Ch

Fair staying chaser; suited by soft ground and a sharp track; stays in excess of three miles; regularly fitted with a visor.

Master Papa (IRE)

108   **119+**

5-y-o br g Key Of Luck (USA)-Beguine (USA) (Green Dancer (USA))
N A Twiston-Davies The Alchemists 2

Placings:413563-2406F001504   (4718)
2003/04: 16²G, 18⁴G, 16⁰GF, 21⁶G, 16⁶G, 19⁰S, 20⁰HY, 16¹G, 16⁵GF, 16⁰GS, 16⁴G,

	Starts	1st	2nd	3rd	Win & Pl
Hurdles	11	1	1	0	10817
Career Total	**17**	**2**	**1**	**2**	**17954**
119	3/04	Kemp	2m	D(0-115)HHdl	GD	£5694
107	11/02	Thur	2m	Hdl	SFT	£3809

Total win prize-money £9504

Going: Sf: 0-2 GS: 0-1 Gd: 1-6 GF: - Fm: 0-2
Distance: **2m/2m3:** 1-9 2m4-2m7: 0-2 3m+: 0-0
Track: LH: 0-7 **RH:** 1-4 Tight: 0-2 Gall: 0-2
Aids: Bl: 0-0 Vi: 0-0 Tstrap: 0-0 Ckp: 0-0
Best Rating: 119 4/04 Ludl 2m   good Hdl

Fair hurdler; ex-Irish; best at around two miles; acts on all ground bar extremes.

Master Rex

106   **(130h)130+**

9-y-o ch g Interrex (CAN)-Whose Lady (USA) (Master Willie)
B De Haan Miss Louise Challis

Placings:20/2113511/P511F   (4843)
2003/04: 16⁶G, 16⁵S, 16¹GF, 16¹GS, 16⁶G,

	Starts	1st	2nd	3rd	Win & Pl
Chases	5	2	0	0	9909
Career Total	**14**	**6**	**2**	**1**	**29326**
130	3/04	Winc	2m	D Ch	G-S	£5775
124	3/04	Leic	2m	E Ch	G-F	£4134
130	11/01	Asct	2m110y	C(0-135)HHdl	GD	£8170
127	11/01	Kemp	2m	F(0-110)HHdl	GD	£3125
110	6/01	NAbb	2m1f	E Hdl	G-S	£3031
110	5/01	Folk	2m1f110yE Hdl	G-F	£2548

Total win prize-money £26785

Going: Sf: 0-1 GS: 1-1 Gd: 0-2 GF: - Fm: 1-1
Distance: **2m/2m3:** 2-5 2m4-2m7: 0-0 3m+: 0-0
Track: LH: 0-1 **RH:** 2-4 Tight: 0-0 Gall: 0-1
Aids: Bl: 0-0 Vi: 0-0 Tstrap: 0-0 Ckp: 0-0
Best Rating: 130 3/04 Winc 2m   gd-sft Ch

Useful hurdler/novice chaser; winner in novice and handicap company in 2001, but off for two years before pulled up on chasing debut; bounced back to form scoring twice in March 2004; best at around two miles; best on a sound surface, but has won on soft; keen sort; needs a strong pace in his races.

Master Ride (IRE)

100(102c)   **(114c)121**

9-y-o g King's Ride-Cahore (Quayside)
C Tinkler Doubleprint

Placings:4/1P/0/223-1F2P   (4693)
2003/04: 19¹GS, 21⁵S, 20²S, 22⁶G,

	Starts	1st	2nd	3rd	Win & Pl
Hurdles	3	1	1	0	4806
Chases	1	0	0	0	0
Career Total	**11**	**2**	**3**	**1**	**11227**
120	12/03	Hrfd	2m3f110yE(0-110)HHdl	G-S	£2548
114	3/01	Font	2m2f110yD Hdl	HVY	£2996

Total win prize-money £5544

Going: Sf: 0-2 GS: 1-1 Gd: 0-1 GF: - Fm: 0-0
Distance: 2m/2m3: 0-0 **2m4-2m7:** 1-4 3m+: 0-0

Master Sebastian

97f   **98f**

5-y-o ch g Kasakov-Anchor Inn (Be My Guest (USA))
Miss Lucinda V Russell Mrs J M Grimston

Placings:253   (4867)
2003/04: 16²G, 16⁵HY, 16³S,

	Starts	1st	2nd	3rd	Win & Pl
NH Flat	3	0	1	1	1114
Career Total	**3**	**0**	**1**	**1**	**1114**

Going: Sf: 0-2 GS: 0-0 Gd: 0-1 GF: - Fm: 0-0
Distance: 2m/2m3: 0-3 2m4-2m7: 0-0 3m+: 0-0
Track: LH: 0-3 RH: 0-0 Tight: 0-0 Gall: 0-0
Aids: Bl: 0-0 Vi: 0-0 Tstrap: 0-0 Ckp: 0-0
Best Rating: 98 4/04 Ayr 2m   soft NHF

Shaped well at Ayr in bumper on debut in November 2003 on good ground but below that level on much more testing ground only subsequent start in January 2004; may be capable of better.

Master T (USA)

103   **110**

5-y-o b g Trempolino (USA)-Our Little C (USA) (Marquetry (USA))
G L Moore Lancing Racing Syndicate

Placings:12-55242U65U5   (4898)
2003/04: 16⁵G, 17⁵GF, 17²GF, 16⁴G, 18²GF, 16ᵁGF, 16⁶G, 16⁵GF, 16ᵁGF, 16⁵G,

	Starts	1st	2nd	3rd	Win & Pl
Hurdles	10	0	2	0	3874
Career Total	**12**	**1**	**3**	**0**	**9808**
76	3/03	Tntn	2m1f	E Hdl	FRM	£4134

Total win prize-money £4134

Going: Sf: 0-0 GS: 0-0 Gd: 0-3 GF: - Fm: 0-7
Distance: 2m/2m3: 0-10 2m4-2m7: 0-0 3m+: 0-0
Track: LH: 0-7 RH: 0-3 Tight: 0-5 Gall: 0-0
Aids: Bl: 0-0 Vi: 0-0 Tstrap: 0-0 Ckp: 0-0
Best Rating: 110 10/03 Chel 2m110y gd-fm Hdl

Modest hurdler; acts on fast ground; best at around two miles.

Master Tern (USA)

106(98h)   **(144h)146**

9-y-o ch g Generous (IRE)-Young Hostess (FR) (Arctic Tern (USA))
Jonjo O'Neill John P McManus

Placings:232/040111/260/3F113/4P421-000000P6   (4951)
2003/04: 20⁰GS, 25⁶G, 21⁰GS, 24⁰S, 24⁰G, 25⁰G, 24⁶GS,

	Starts	1st	2nd	3rd	Win & Pl
Hurdles	1	0	0	0	0
Chases	7	0	0	0	467
Career Total	**30**	**6**	**4**	**3**	**107567**
146	4/03	Aint	3m1f	B HCh	GD	£26000
108	3/02	Hntg	2m110y	E Ch	SFT	£2992
127	1/02	Leic	2m	E Ch	GD	£3536
140	3/00	Chel	2m1f	A HHdl	G-F	£30000

Track: LH: 0-1 **RH:** 1-3 Tight: 0-0 Gall: 0-0
Aids: Bl: 0-0 Vi: 0-0 Tstrap: 0-0 Ckp: 0-0
Best Rating: 121 2/04 Hayd 2m4f   soft Hdl

Lightly raced hurdler/chaser; slightly disappointing in two starts over fences; made successful reappearance when landing extended 2m3f Class E handicap hurdle at Hereford December 2003; acts on soft ground; stays 3m; goes well when fresh.

143 3/00 Kels 2m2f B Hdl G-S £14365
134 1/00 Chel 2m1f D(0-120)HHdl G-S £7442
Total win prize-money £84337

Going:	Sf: 0-1 GS: 0-3 Gd: 0-4 GF: - Fm: 0-0
Distance:	2m/2m3: 0-0 2m4-2m7: 0-3 3m+: 0-5
Track:	LH: 0-6 RH: 0-2 Tight: 0-1 Gall: 0-4
Aids:	Bl: 0-0 Vi: 0-0 Tstrap: 0-0 Ckp: 0-2
Best Rating:	149 12/00 Hayd 2m4f heavy Hdl

Useful chaser/hurdler; took valuable handicap at Aintree in April 2003 despite at least one bad mistake; well held since; stays three miles, but effective at shorter; effective on good ground; best form tends to be in the spring; has worn cheek-pieces.

Master Trix (IRE)
112   128+
7-y-o b g Lord Americo-Bannow Drive (IRE) (Miners Lamp)
M Pitman Patrick Bancroft

Placings:*16*/1232PU-10   (4643)
2003/04: 20¹G, 24⁹G,

	Starts	1st	2nd	3rd	Win & Pl
Hurdles	2	1	0	0	7118
Career Total	10	3	2	1	15856
128 12/03	Asct	2m4f	D(0-115)HHdl	GD	£7117
121 11/02	Folk	2m1f110yE Hdl		SFT	£2905
118 2/02	Font	2m2f110yH NHF		SFT	£1638
			Total win prize-money £11661

Going:	Sf: 0-0 GS: 0-0 Gd: 1-2 GF: - Fm: 0-0
Distance:	2m/2m3: 0-0 2m4-2m7: 1-1 3m+: 0-1
Track:	LH: 0-1 RH: 1-1 Tight: 0-1 Gall: 0-0
Aids:	Bl: 0-0 Vi: 0-0 Tstrap: 0-0 Ckp: 0-0
Best Rating:	128 12/03 Asct 2m4f good Hdl

Fair novice hurdler; acts on soft ground; stays two miles six.

Master Wood
13-y-o b g Wonderful Surprise-Miss Wood (Precipice Wood)
C Grant Chris Grant

Placings:5600/PP4111FPP326/P1P15104/1F31/PPP/4421
1UP-22065   (4851)
2003/04: 25²G, 25²S, 22⁰S, 20⁶HY, 27⁵GS,

	Starts	1st	2nd	3rd	Win & Pl
Chases	5	0	2	0	1344
Career Total	43	10	4	2	64531
126 3/03	Weth	3m1f	H Ch	GD	£2226
123 2/03	Hayd	2m6f	H Ch	G-S	£8840
132 12/00	Weth	2m4f110yB HCh	SFT	£15008
131 10/00	Kels	2m6f110yD(0-120)HCh	SFT	£4654
130 3/00	Weth	2m4f110yD(0-135)HCh	G-S	£7182
111 10/99	Weth	2m4f110yD(0-125)HCh	SFT	£4177
107 11/99	Weth	3m1f	D(0-125)HCh	GD	£4090
118 11/98	Weth	3m1f	D Ch	GD	£4248
107 10/98	Weth	2m4f110yC HCh	GD	£4739
118 10/98	Carl	2m4f110yE Ch	HVY	£2918
			Total win prize-money £58083

Going:	Sf: 0-3 GS: 0-1 Gd: 0-1 GF: - Fm: 0-0
Distance:	2m/2m3: 0-0 2m4-2m7: 0-2 3m+: 0-3
Track:	LH: 0-4 RH: 0-1 Tight: 0-1 Gall: 0-0
Aids:	Bl: 0-0 Vi: 0-0 Tstrap: 0-0 Ckp: 0-0
Best Rating:	132 12/00 Weth 2m4f110y soft Ch

Decent hunter chaser; beat Torduff Express at Haydock in February 2003 and followed up at Wetherby the following month; best at short of three miles; goes well on soft or heavy ground.

Masterpoint
92   78
4-y-o ch g Mark Of Esteem (IRE)-Baize (Efisio)
R T Phillips (B Smart 26/8) Michael Gates

Placings:660   (3422)
2003/04: 16⁶G, 17⁶GS, 17⁰HY,

	Starts	1st	2nd	3rd	Win & Pl
Hurdles	3	0	0	0	0
Career Total	3	0	0	0	0

Going:	Sf: 0-1 GS: 0-1 Gd: 0-1 GF: - Fm: 0-0
Distance:	2m/2m3: 0-3 2m4-2m7: 0-0 3m+: 0-0
Track:	LH: 0-1 RH: 0-2 Tight: 0-0 Gall: 0-1
Aids:	Bl: 0-0 Vi: 0-0 Tstrap: 0-0 Ckp: 0-0
Best Rating:	74 1/04 Folk 2m1f110y heavy Hdl

Masters Of War (IRE)
100 (101c)   (83c)86+
7-y-o b g Sri Pekan (USA)-Velinowski (Malinowski (USA))
Jonjo O'Neill John P McManus

Placings:000/000/4F402   (4950)
2003/04: 17⁴G, 24⁶GF, 24⁴S, 20⁹G, 20²GS,

	Starts	1st	2nd	3rd	Win & Pl
Hurdles	3	0	1	0	2168
Chases	2	0	0	0	274
Career Total	11	0	1	0	2442

Going:	Sf: 0-1 GS: 0-1 Gd: 0-2 GF: - Fm: 0-1
Distance:	2m/2m3: 0-1 2m4-2m7: 0-2 3m+: 0-2
Track:	LH: 0-2 RH: 0-3 Tight: 0-1 Gall: 0-1
Aids:	Bl: 0-0 Vi: 0-0 Tstrap: 0-0 Ckp: 0-0
Best Rating:	99 12/00 Fair 2m yld-sft Hdl

Plating-class chaser/hurdler; acts on good or easy ground.

Matawa Bellevue (FR)
8-y-o b/br m Mister Mat (FR)-Strakawa (FR) (Sukawa (FR))
Jean-Rene Auvray Jean-Rene Auvray

Placings:P   (0376)
2003/04: 20⁰S,

	Starts	1st	2nd	3rd	Win & Pl
Hurdles	1	0	0	0	
Career Total	1	0	0	0	

Going:	Sf: 0-1 GS: 0-0 Gd: 0-0 GF: - Fm: 0-0
Distance:	2m/2m3: 0-0 2m4-2m7: 0-1 3m+: 0-0
Track:	LH: 0-1 RH: 0-0 Tight: 0-1 Gall: 0-0
Aids:	Bl: 0-0 Vi: 0-0 Tstrap: 0-0 Ckp: 0-0

Matchboard Again (IRE)
53f   76f
6-y-o b m Supreme Leader-Avena (Oats)
C P Morlock Mrs Z S Clark

Placings:*0*   (3934)
2003/04: 16⁰G,

	Starts	1st	2nd	3rd	Win & Pl
NH Flat	1	0	0	0	

Career Total   1   0   0   0

Going:	Sf: 0-0 GS: 0-0 Gd: 0-1 GF: - Fm: 0-0
Distance:	2m/2m3: 0-1 2m4-2m7: 0-0 3m+: 0-0
Track:	LH: 0-0 RH: 0-1 Tight: 0-0 Gall: 0-0
Aids:	Bl: 0-0 Vi: 0-0 Tstrap: 0-0 Ckp: 0-0
Best Rating:	76 2/04 Asct 2m110y good NHF

Material World
108   118+
6-y-o b m Karinga Bay-Material Girl (Busted)
Miss Suzy Smith Southern Bloodstock

Placings:*1*-112243325   (4842)
2003/04: 17¹G, 22¹G, 21²GS, 24²S, 22⁴GS, 24³GS, 22³G, 21²G, 21⁵G,

	Starts	1st	2nd	3rd	Win & Pl
NH Flat	1	1	0	0	2009
Hurdles	8	1	3	2	18444
Career Total	10	3	3	2	22483
95 11/03	Folk	2m6f110yE Hdl	GD	£2590
110 5/03	Hrfd	2m1f	H NHF	GD	£2009
110 4/03	MRas	2m1f110yH NHF	GD	£2030
			Total win prize-money £6629

Going:	Sf: 0-1 GS: 0-3 Gd: 2-5 GF: - Fm: 0-0
Distance:	2m/2m3: 1-1 2m4-2m7: 1-6 3m+: 0-2
Track:	LH: 0-2 RH: 2-7 Tight: 1-1 Gall: 0-2
Aids:	Bl: 0-0 Vi: 0-0 Tstrap: 0-0 Ckp: 0-0
Best Rating:	118 3/04 Newb 2m5f good Hdl

Fair novice hurdler; dual bumper winner; blind in her left eye and wears an eyeshield; stays two miles six and acts on fast ground; tough sort.

Mathmagician
5-y-o ch g Hector Protector (USA)-Inherent Magic (IRE) (Magical Wonder (USA))
R F Marvin Mrs M A Marvin

Placings:P   (0331)
2003/04: 17⁵GF,

	Starts	1st	2nd	3rd	Win & Pl
Hurdles	1	0	0	0	
Career Total	1	0	0	0	

Going:	Sf: 0-0 GS: 0-0 Gd: 0-0 GF: - Fm: 0-1
Distance:	2m/2m3: 0-1 2m4-2m7: 0-0 3m+: 0-0
Track:	LH: 0-1 RH: 0-0 Tight: 0-0 Gall: 0-0
Aids:	Bl: 0-0 Vi: 0-0 Tstrap: 0-0 Ckp: 0-0

Matthew Muroto (IRE)
89f   85f
5-y-o b g Muroto-Glenmore Star (IRE) (Teofane)
C L Tizzard Alvin Trowbridge

Placings:*300*   (4936)
2003/04: 16³G, 16⁰GS, 18⁰G,

	Starts	1st	2nd	3rd	Win & Pl
NH Flat	3	0	0	1	287
Career Total	3	0	0	1	287

Going:	Sf: 0-0 GS: 0-1 Gd: 0-2 GF: - Fm: 0-0
Distance:	2m/2m3: 0-3 2m4-2m7: 0-0 3m+: 0-0
Track:	LH: 0-1 RH: 0-2 Tight: 0-1 Gall: 0-0

Career Total   1   0   0   0

Aids: Bl: 0-0 Vi: 0-0 Tstrap: 0-0 Ckp: 0-0
Best Rating: 85 3/04 Winc 2m   good NHF

Maunby Rocker
98   89

4-y-o ch g Sheikh Albadou-Bullion (Sabrehill (USA))
P C Haslam P A Hill-Walker & Mrs C Barclay

Placings:613F1   (2302)
2003/04: 17⁶G, 16¹GF, 16³G, 23⁹GF, 16¹GF,

	Starts	1st	2nd	3rd	Win & Pl
Hurdles	5	2	0	1	5637
Career Total	5	2	0	1	5637
89	11/03	Catt	2m	G Hdl	G-F	£1904
80	9/03	Uttx	2m	F Hdl	G-F	£3311

Total win prize-money £5215

Going: Sf: 0-0 GS: 0-0 Gd: 0-2 GF: - Fm: 2-3
Distance: 2m/2m3: 2-4 2m4-2m7: 0-1 3m+: 0-0
Track: LH: 2-4 RH: 0-1 Tight: 1-2 Gall: 0-0
Aids: Bl: 0-0 Vi: 0-0 Tstrap: 0-0 Ckp: 0-0
Best Rating: 89 11/03 Catt 2m   gd-fm Hdl

Plating-class juvenile hurdler; winner twice on the level; won suspect event at Uttoxeter in September; followed up in claimer at Catterick in November; acts on a sound surface.

Maunby Roller (IRE)
99   68

5-y-o b g Flying Spur (AUS)-Brown Foam (Horage)
K A Morgan (P A Blockley 8/5) D S Cooper

Placings:PP-0350412PB   (4958)
2003/04: 17⁰GF, 17³GF, 17⁵GF, 17⁰GF, 16⁴G, 20¹G, 19²GS, 21⁰GS, 17⁸G,

	Starts	1st	2nd	3rd	Win & Pl
Hurdles	8	1	1	1	2635
Chases	1	0	0	0	0
Career Total	11	1	1	1	2635
68	11/03	Fknm	2m4f	G(0-95)HHdl	GD	£1845

Total win prize-money £1845

Going: Sf: 0-0 GS: 0-2 Gd: 1-3 GF: - Fm: 0-4
Distance: 2m/2m3: 0-6 2m4-2m7: 1-3 3m+: 0-0
Track: LH: 1-4 RH: 0-5 Tight: 1-7 Gall: 0-0
Aids: Bl: 0-0 Vi: 1-9 Tstrap: 0-0 Ckp: 0-0
Best Rating: 68 12/03 MRas 2m3f110y gd-sft Hdl

Plating-class hurdler; successful at Fakenham in November; stays 2m4f; has been tried in various headgear, but usually visored.

Maunsell's Road (IRE)
99   91

5-y-o b g Desert Style (IRE)-Zara's Birthday (IRE) (Waajib)
L Lungo Clarke Boon

Placings:03-356520   (4879)
2003/04: 24³GS, 16⁵GS, 16⁶GS, 20⁵GF, 24²GF, 20⁰GS,

	Starts	1st	2nd	3rd	Win & Pl
Hurdles	6	0	1	1	1781
Career Total	8	0	1	2	2425

Going: Sf: 0-0 GS: 0-4 Gd: 0-0 GF: - Fm: 0-2
Distance: 2m/2m3: 0-2 2m4-2m7: 0-3 3m+: 0-2
Track: LH: 0-2 RH: 0-3 Tight: 0-1 Gall: 0-1
Aids: Bl: 0-0 Vi: 0-1 Tstrap: 0-0 Ckp: 0-0
Best Rating: 93 1/04 Muss 3m110y gd-fm Hdl

Winner on the Flat; modest form over hurdles; best on fast ground.

Max Pride
(104h)   (106+h)121

9-y-o br g Good Thyne (USA)-An Bothar Dubh (Strong Gale)
R Dickin Mrs J Cumiskey, M Doocey & K Doocey

Placings:05P/241UP/211F344P/14112-1F   (2600)
2003/04: 24¹GS, 29⁶G,

	Starts	1st	2nd	3rd	Win & Pl
Hurdles	1	1	0	0	2576
Chases	1	0	0	0	0
Career Total	23	7	3	1	40334
106	11/03	Towc	3m	E(0-110)HHdl	G-S	£2576
121	2/03	Bang	3m6f	D(0-120)HCh	SFT	£5629
117	12/02	Wwck	3m4f	D(0-120)HCh	G-S	£4680
99	11/02	Extr	2m6f110yE(0-105)HHdl	G-S	£3325
112	11/01	Newb	2m6f110yE(0-115)HCh	GD	£5850
95	10/01	Towc	3m1f	D(0-120)HCh	SFT	£8437
100	2/01	Leic	2m4f110yF(0-95)HCh	SFT	£2931

Total win prize-money £33429

Going: Sf: 0-0 GS: 1-1 Gd: 0-1 GF: - Fm: 0-0
Distance: 2m/2m3: 0-0 2m4-2m7: 0-0 3m+: 1-2
Track: LH: 0-1 RH: 1-1 Tight: 0-0 Gall: 0-0
Aids: Bl: 0-0 Vi: 0-0 Tstrap: 0-0 Ckp: 0-0
Best Rating: 121 3/03 Wwck 3m5f   gd-sft Ch

Fair handicap hurdler/chaser; stays really well and was winning for the third time in his last four starts when scoring in most decisive fashion at Bangor in February 2003; jumps well; acts on easy ground.

Max The Obscure
50f

4-y-o b g Cloudings (IRE)-Princess Maxine (IRE) (Horage)
Miss Lucinda V Russell Miss G Joughin

Placings:0   (4952)
2003/04: 16⁰GS,

	Starts	1st	2nd	3rd	Win & Pl
NH Flat	1	0	0	0	
Career Total	1	0	0	0	

Going: Sf: 0-0 GS: 0-1 Gd: 0-0 GF: - Fm: 0-0
Distance: 2m/2m3: 0-1 2m4-2m7: 0-0 3m+: 0-0
Track: LH: 0-0 RH: 0-1 Tight: 0-0 Gall: 0-0
Aids: Bl: 0-0 Vi: 0-0 Tstrap: 0-0 Ckp: 0-0

Max's Micro (IRE)
88   78

5-y-o b g Inzar (USA)-Guess Who (Be My Guest (USA))
C Grant (John Allen 6/7) Dingley Dell Racing Ltd

Placings:06S50213-P64   (1427)
2003/04: 24⁸PG, 17⁶G, 16⁴G,

	Starts	1st	2nd	3rd	Win & Pl
Hurdles	3	0	0	0	267
Career Total	11	1	1	1	5068
78	1/03	Leic	2m	F Hdl	HVY	£3493

Total win prize-money £3494

Going: Sf: 0-0 GS: 0-0 Gd: 0-3 GF: - Fm: 0-0
Distance: 2m/2m3: 0-2 2m4-2m7: 0-0 3m+: 0-1
Track: LH: 0-1 RH: 0-2 Tight: 0-2 Gall: 0-0
Aids: Bl: 0-0 Vi: 0-0 Tstrap: 0-0 Ckp: 0-0
Best Rating: 78 2/03 Leic 2m   heavy Hdl

Moderate hurdler at around two miles on a soft surface.

Maximinus
87   78

4-y-o b g The West (USA)-Candarela (Damister (USA))
M Madgwick M Madgwick

Placings:003   (4285)
2003/04: 16⁶G, 16⁹G, 16³G,

	Starts	1st	2nd	3rd	Win & Pl
Hurdles	3	0	0	1	553
Career Total	3	0	0	1	553

Going: Sf: 0-0 GS: 0-0 Gd: 0-3 GF: - Fm: 0-0
Distance: 2m/2m3: 0-3 2m4-2m7: 0-0 3m+: 0-0
Track: LH: 0-0 RH: 0-3 Tight: 0-0 Gall: 0-0
Aids: Bl: 0-0 Vi: 0-0 Tstrap: 0-0 Ckp: 0-0
Best Rating: 81 3/04 Winc 2m   good Hdl

Maximize (IRE)
109   (88h)141+

10-y-o b g Mandalus-Lone Run (Kemal (FR))
M C Pipe D A Johnson

Placings:322446/2121162/4404F-42P013   (4861)
2003/04: 25⁴GF, 24²GF, 27⁶G, 33⁰G, 24¹G, 33³GS,

	Starts	1st	2nd	3rd	Win & Pl
Chases	6	1	1		49414
Career Total	24	4	6	2	108318
141	3/04	Chel	3m110y	B(0-140)HCh	GD	£29000
141	12/01	Kemp	3m	A Ch	GD	£29750
124	11/01	Kemp	3m	D Ch	GD	£4153
121	10/01	Winc	3m1f110yD Ch	GD	£4407

Total win prize-money £67311

Going: Sf: 0-0 GS: 0-1 Gd: 1-3 GF: - Fm: 0-2
Distance: 2m/2m3: 0-0 2m4-2m7: 0-0 3m+: 1-6
Track: LH: 1-5 RH: 0-1 Tight: 0-1 Gall: 1-3
Aids: Bl: 0-0 Vi: 0-2 Tstrap: 0-0 Ckp: 0-0
Best Rating: 144 12/02 Sand 3m110y gd-sft Ch

Useful handicap chaser; jumps well; effective on good ground and stays extreme distances, but lacks a turn of foot; joined Martin Pipe in the summer of 2003; best run for him when coming from off the pace to win the Fulke Walwyn Kim Muir at Cheltenham; remote third in Scottish National; has worn a visor.

Maximus (IRE)
73   97

9-y-o br g Un Desperado (FR)-Fais Vite (USA) (Sharpen Up)
C P Morlock Cockerell Cowing Racing

Placings:110/4U000/000230-P00   (4634)
2003/04: 20⁵S, 22⁵G, 19⁰G,

	Starts	1st	2nd	3rd	Win & Pl
Hurdles	3	0	0	0	
Career Total	17	2	1	1	9735
123	2/01	Newb	2m1f10y	C Hdl	SFT	£6045
116	1/01	Plum	2m	E Hdl	SFT	£1918

Total win prize-money £7963

Going: Sf: 0-1 GS: 0-0 Gd: 0-2 GF: - Fm: 0-0
Distance: 2m/2m3: 0-0 2m4-2m7: 0-3 3m+: 0-0
Track: LH: 0-1 RH: 0-2 Tight: 0-0 Gall: 0-0
Aids: Bl: 0-0 Vi: 0-0 Tstrap: 0-1 Ckp: 0-0
Best Rating: 123 10/01 Strf 2m3f   gd-sft Hdl

Modest hurdler these days; best on soft ground; stays three miles.

Mayb-Mayb

96(84h)   **78**

14-y-o ch g Gunner B-Mayotte (Little Buskins)
M Appleby Michael Appleby

Placings:*03*/040/51F111/P2P310223P/4501P0P/000PP/0-2U2P03P   (4484)
2003/04: 34²HY, 26U S, 25²S, 29P S, 26QGS, 22³GF, 28P G,

	Starts	1st	2nd	3rd	Win & Pl
Chases	7	0	2	1	2384
Career Total	41	6	5	4	23989
115 1/01	Winc	2m6f	E(0-115)HHdl	SFT	£3332
115 1/00	Plum	2m5f	D(0-125)HHdl	SFT	£3136
110 4/97	Worc	3m	E(0-100)HHdl	SFT	£2775
99 3/97	Plum	2m4f	F(0-100)HHdl	G-S	£2012
91 2/97	Plum	2m4f	F(0-100)HHdl	SFT	£1941
79 2/97	Plum	2m4f	F(0-105)HHdl	G-S	£2194

Total win prize-money £15391

Going: Sf: 0-4 GS: 0-1 Gd: 0-1 GF: - Fm: 0-1
Distance: 2m/2m3: 0-0 2m4-2m7: 0-1 3m+: 0-6
Track: LH: 0-4 RH: 0-1 Tight: 0-4 Gall: 0-0
Aids: Bl: 0-0 Vi: 0-0 Tstrap: 0-0 Ckp: 0-7
Best Rating: 115 1/01   Winc   2m6f   soft   Hdl

Plating-class chaser; winning hurdler; placed in points; stays extreme distances; acts on soft.

Maybe She Will

95f   **75f**

6-y-o b m Tudor Diver-Blue Mischief (Precocious)
D W Whillans Dr Doreen M Steele

Placings:*6-10*   (3474)
2003/04: 16G G, 16¹GF, 16QGF,

	Starts	1st	2nd	3rd	Win & Pl
NH Flat	3	1	0	0	2261
Career Total	3	1	0	0	2261
74 12/03	Muss	2m	H NHF	G-F	£2261

Total win prize-money £2261

Going: Sf: 0-0 GS: 0-0 Gd: 0-1 GF: - Fm: 1-2
Distance: 2m/2m3: 1-3 2m4-2m7: 0-0 3m+: 0-0
Track: LH: 0-1 RH: 1-2 Tight: 1-2 Gall: 0-0
Aids: Bl: 0-0 Vi: 0-0 Tstrap: 0-0 Ckp: 0-0
Best Rating: 75 1/04   Muss   2m   gd-fm   NHF

Moderate bumper winner in December 2003 on fast; looks a stayer.

Maybelle

      50

9-y-o b m Royal Vulcan-Full Of Love (Full Of Hope)
J S King W J Lee

Placings:*00*/0P/06-P   (0034)
2003/04: 22P G,

	Starts	1st	2nd	3rd	Win & Pl
Hurdles	1	0	0	0	
Career Total	7	0	0	0	0

Going: Sf: 0-0 GS: 0-0 Gd: 0-1 GF: - Fm: 0-0
Distance: 2m/2m3: 0-0 2m4-2m7: 0-1 3m+: 0-0
Track: LH: 0-0 RH: 0-1 Tight: 0-0 Gall: 0-0
Aids: Bl: 0-0 Vi: 0-0 Tstrap: 0-0 Ckp: 0-0
Best Rating: 50 3/03   Sthl   2m4f110y   gd-fm   Hdl

Maybeseven

97   **70**

10-y-o gr g Baron Blakeney-Ninth Of May (Comedy Star (USA))

R Dickin The Diamond Seven Partnership

Placings:00/44613/P04P/**P13P6PPP/43PP-55P23**   (4757)
2003/04: 23⁵GS, 25⁵GS, 24P G, 19²GS, 25³S,

	Starts	1st	2nd	3rd	Win & Pl
Chases	5	0	1	1	1530
Career Total	28	2	1	4	9248
88 10/01	Folk	3m1f	F(0-100)HCh	GD	£3347
96 2/00	Hntg	3m2f	F(0-110)HHdl	SFT	£2296

Total win prize-money £5644

Going: Sf: 0-1 GS: 0-2 Gd: 0-2 GF: - Fm: 0-0
Distance: 2m/2m3: 0-0 2m4-2m7: 0-1 3m+: 0-4
Track: LH: 0-0 RH: 0-4 Tight: 0-1 Gall: 0-1
Aids: Bl: 0-0 Vi: 0-0 Tstrap: 0-0 Ckp: 0-0
Best Rating: 96 2/00   Hntg   3m2f   soft   Hdl

Plating-class stayer, suited by cut in the ground; goes well on a right-handed track.

Mayerling

97   **74**

7-y-o b m Old Vic-Manon Lescaut (Then Again)
P Burgoyne The Moonrakers

Placings:*0*/0F-464250P6   (4632)
2003/04: 16⁴GS, 19⁶G, 16⁴S, 24²G, 26⁵GS, 22QGS, 25P G, 24⁶G,

	Starts	1st	2nd	3rd	Win & Pl
Hurdles	7	0	1	0	536
Chases	1	0	0	0	0
Career Total	11	0	1	0	536

Going: Sf: 0-1 GS: 0-3 Gd: 0-4 GF: - Fm: 0-0
Distance: 2m/2m3: 0-2 2m4-2m7: 0-1 3m+: 0-4
Track: LH: 0-2 RH: 0-6 Tight: 0-5 Gall: 0-0
Aids: Bl: 0-0 Vi: 0-0 Tstrap: 0-0 Ckp: 0-0
Best Rating: 76 12/03   Tntn   3m110y   good   Hdl

Plating-class hurdler; stays three miles; acts best on easy ground.

Maysboyo

6-y-o b g Makbul-Maysimp (IRE) (Mac's Imp (USA))
B P J Baugh J H Chrimes And Mr & Mrs G W Hannam

Placings:UP0   (0628)
2003/04: 17U G, 17P G, 16QGF,

	Starts	1st	2nd	3rd	Win & Pl
Hurdles	3	0	0	0	
Career Total	3	0	0	0	

Going: Sf: 0-0 GS: 0-0 Gd: 0-0 GF: - Fm: 0-1
Distance: 2m/2m3: 0-3 2m4-2m7: 0-0 3m+: 0-0
Track: LH: 0-3 RH: 0-0 Tight: 0-2 Gall: 0-0
Aids: Bl: 0-0 Vi: 0-0 Tstrap: 0-0 Ckp: 0-0

Mazamet (USA)

91   (98c)**79**

11-y-o b g Elmaamul (USA)-Miss Mazepah (USA) (Nijinsky (CAN))
O O'Neill D Teevan

Placings:442/2250/45002/**60625634/000**   (4716)
2003/04: 16QG, 17QG, 21QG,

	Starts	1st	2nd	3rd	Win & Pl
Hurdles	3	0	0	0	
Career Total	23	0	5	1	5723

Going: Sf: 0-0 GS: 0-0 Gd: 0-3 GF: - Fm: 0-0
Distance: 2m/2m3: 0-2 2m4-2m7: 0-1 3m+: 0-0
Track: LH: 0-1 RH: 0-1 Tight: 0-2 Gall: 0-0
Aids: Bl: 0-0 Vi: 0-0 Tstrap: 0-0 Ckp: 0-0
Best Rating: 109 1/97   Chel   2m1f   gd-fm   Hdl

Mazileo

99(80h)   (91h)**132**

11-y-o b g Mazilier (USA)-Embroglio (USA) (Empery (USA))
Ian Williams T J & Mrs H Parrott

Placings:*41*/5P052/1101621/31U31F15F/400/06033F414P/5U1-PP02   (4652)
2003/04: 24P GS, 24P G, 24QG, 25²G,

	Starts	1st	2nd	3rd	Win & Pl
Hurdles	2	0	0	0	0
Chases	2	0	1	0	2160
Career Total	43	10	3	4	57422
132 11/02	Sand	3m110y	C(0-130)HCh	G-S	£8307
121 4/02	Hrfd	3m1f110yE(0-110)HCh	G-F	£7577
123 11/99	Hayd	2m4f	B Ch	G-S	£11265
121 11/99	Ludl	2m4f	E Ch	GD	£3533
122 9/99	Hntg	2m110y	E Ch	GF	£3441
124 4/99	Towc	2m	D(0-125)HHdl	GD	£3829
110 11/98	Ludl	2m	E Hdl	GD	£2948
122 10/98	Hrfd	2m1f	E Hdl	G-F	£2829
116 10/98	NAbb	2m1f	E Hdl	GD	£2583
92 3/97	NAbb	2m1f	H NHF	G-F	£1299

Total win prize-money £47613

Going: Sf: 0-0 GS: 0-1 Gd: 0-3 GF: - Fm: 0-0
Distance: 2m/2m3: 0-0 2m4-2m7: 0-0 3m+: 0-4
Track: LH: 0-1 RH: 0-3 Tight: 0-1 Gall: 0-1
Aids: Bl: 0-0 Vi: 0-0 Tstrap: 0-0 Ckp: 0-0
Best Rating: 132 11/02   Sand   3m110y   gd-sft   Ch

Modest chaser/hurdler; stays 3m; acts on fast and soft ground.

Mazury (USA)

75   **62**

5-y-o b g Langfuhr (CAN)-Assurgent (USA) (Damascus (USA))
Miss J S Davis Miss J Davis

Placings:005P5-00   (1190)
2003/04: 16QG, 20QGF,

	Starts	1st	2nd	3rd	Win & Pl
Hurdles	2	0	0	0	
Career Total	7	0	0	0	0

Going: Sf: 0-0 GS: 0-0 Gd: 0-1 GF: - Fm: 0-1
Distance: 2m/2m3: 0-1 2m4-2m7: 0-1 3m+: 0-0
Track: LH: 0-1 RH: 0-1 Tight: 0-0 Gall: 0-0
Aids: Bl: 0-0 Vi: 0-0 Tstrap: 0-0 Ckp: 0-0
Best Rating: 62 3/03   Tntn   2m1f   firm   Hdl

Mazzareme (IRE)

85f   **101f**

6-y-o b g Supreme Leader-Mazza (Mazilier (USA))
N G Richards Ashleybank Investments Limited

Placings:*3*   (3982)
2003/04: 17³G,

	Starts	1st	2nd	3rd	Win & Pl
NH Flat	1	0	0	1	285
Career Total	1	0	0	1	285

Going: Sf: 0-0 GS: 0-0 Gd: 0-1 GF: - Fm: 0-0

Distance: 2m/2m3: 0-1 2m4-2m7: 0-0 3m+: 0-0
Track: LH: 0-0 RH: 0-1 Tight: 0-0 Gall: 0-0
Aids: Bl: 0-0 Vi: 0-0 Tstrap: 0-0 Ckp: 0-0
Best Rating: 101 2/04 Carl 2m1f   good NHF

Mazzini (IRE)

47   **99**

13-y-o b g Celio Rufo-Dontellvi (The Parson)
R Rowe Richard Rowe

Placings: 04/01210344/43FP/0/254/P3551016-P0   (4932)
2003/04: 22⁶G, 27⁰G,

	Starts	1st	2nd	3rd	Win & Pl
Hurdles	2	0	0	0	
Career Total	28	4	2	3	14007
99	3/03	Font	2m6f110yF(0-100)HHdl	GD	£2765
99	12/02	Font	2m6f110yE(0-105)HHdl	GD	£3010
103	11/96	Winc	2m	E Hdl	GD	£2600
91	10/96	Kemp	2m	D Hdl	G-F	£2840

Total win prize-money £11215

Going: Sf: 0-0 GS: 0-0 Gd: 0-2 GF: - Fm: 0-0
Distance: 2m/2m3: 0-0 2m4-2m7: 0-1 3m+: 0-1
Track: LH: 0-0 RH: 0-1 Tight: 0-0 Gall: 0-0
Aids: Bl: 0-0 Vi: 0-0 Tstrap: 0-0 Ckp: 0-0
Best Rating: 104 11/97 Wind 2m   good Hdl

Moderate hurdler, stays two and three-quarter miles; acts on a sound surface.

Mccracken (IRE)

94(104h)   (107h)**112+**

8-y-o b g Scenic-Sakanda (IRE) (Vayrann)
R Ford (P A Pritchard 12/2) Mark Beavan and Nick Morgan

Placings: 6/221320/435/0015153   (4713)
2003/04: 16⁰GS, 16⁰S, 16¹GS, 16⁰G, 19¹G, 16⁶S, 24³G,

	Starts	1st	2nd	3rd	Win & Pl
Hurdles	4	1	0	0	2772
Chases	3	1	0	1	5092
Career Total	17	3	3	3	14560
112	3/04	Donc	2m3f	E Ch	GD	£4063
107	2/04	Hntg	2m110yF Hdl	G-S	£2772
120	10/00	Thur	2m	Hdl	G-Y	£2840

Total win prize-money £9596

Going: Sf: 0-2 GS: 1-2 Gd: 1-3 GF: - Fm: 0-0
Distance: 2m/2m3: 2-6 2m4-2m7: 0-0 3m+: 0-1
Track: LH: 1-3 RH: 1-4 Tight: 0-2 Gall: 1-2
Aids: Bl: 0-0 Vi: 0-0 Tstrap: 1-2 Ckp: 1-4
Best Rating: 120 5/01 Dund 2m4f153y firm   Hdl

Fair novice chaser/plating-class hurdler; ex-Irish; stays about two and a half miles and acts on most types of ground; has worn a tongue tie.

Mccrinkle (IRE)

83   **51**

7-y-o br g Mandalus-Crinkle Lady (Buckskin (FR))
Mrs C J Kerr Mrs C J Kerr

Placings: 0-0PP00   (4946)
2003/04: 16⁶G, 20¹⁶S, 24¹⁴PG, 22⁴⁰G, 16⁶GS,

	Starts	1st	2nd	3rd	Win & Pl
NH Flat	1	0	0	0	0
Hurdles	4	0	0	0	0
Career Total	6	0	0	0	

Going: Sf: 0-1 GS: 0-1 Gd: 0-3 GF: - Fm: 0-0
Distance: 2m/2m3: 0-2 2m4-2m7: 0-2 3m+: 0-1
Track: LH: 0-2 RH: 0-3 Tight: 0-1 Gall: 0-0

Aids: Bl: 0-0 Vi: 0-0 Tstrap: 0-0 Ckp: 0-0
Best Rating: 51 4/04 Prth 2m110y   gd-sft Hdl

Mcfarline (IRE)

8-y-o b g Ela-Mana-Mou-Highland Ball (Bold Lad (IRE))
N J Hawke N J Hawke

Placings: 0001/03/F0PP-PP   (0857)
2003/04: 16⁰GF, 21⁰GF,

	Starts	1st	2nd	3rd	Win & Pl
Chases	2	0	0	0	
Career Total	12	1	0	1	2579
84	4/00	Plum	2m	E(0-105)HHdl	G-S	£2240

Total win prize-money £2240

Going: Sf: 0-0 GS: 0-0 Gd: 0-0 GF: - Fm: 0-2
Distance: 2m/2m3: 0-1 2m4-2m7: 0-1 3m+: 0-0
Track: LH: 0-2 RH: 0-0 Tight: 0-2 Gall: 0-0
Aids: Bl: 0-0 Vi: 0-0 Tstrap: 0-0 Ckp: 0-0
Best Rating: 84 5/00 Towc 2m   gd-fm Hdl

Mcginty All Stars (IRE)

85f   **65f**

6-y-o b m Fourstars Allstar (USA)-Dowdstown Miss (Wolver Hollow)
R J Price R J Price

Placings: 0-0   (4920)
2003/04: 16⁰GS,

	Starts	1st	2nd	3rd	Win & Pl
NH Flat	1	0	0	0	
Career Total	2	0	0	0	

Going: Sf: 0-0 GS: 0-1 Gd: 0-0 GF: - Fm: 0-0
Distance: 2m/2m3: 0-1 2m4-2m7: 0-0 3m+: 0-0
Track: LH: 0-1 RH: 0-0 Tight: 0-0 Gall: 0-0
Aids: Bl: 0-0 Vi: 0-0 Tstrap: 0-0 Ckp: 0-0
Best Rating: 65 4/04 Worc 2m   gd-sft NHF

Mcmahon's Brook

49f

5-y-o br g Alderbrook-Mcmahons River (Over The River (FR))
Mrs N S Sharpe Mrs M Gittings-Watts

Placings: 0   (4509)
2003/04: 14⁰GS,

	Starts	1st	2nd	3rd	Win & Pl
NH Flat	1	0	0	0	
Career Total	1	0	0	0	

Going: Sf: 0-0 GS: 0-1 Gd: 0-0 GF: - Fm: 0-0
Distance: 2m/2m3: 0-0 2m4-2m7: 0-0 3m+: 0-0
Track: LH: 0-0 RH: 0-0 Tight: 0-0 Gall: 0-0
Aids: Bl: 0-0 Vi: 0-0 Tstrap: 0-0 Ckp: 0-0
Best Rating: 49 3/04 Hrfd 1m6f   gd-sft NHF

Mcsnappy

97(97h)   (104h)**108+**

7-y-o ch g Risk Me (FR)-Nannie Annie (Persian Bold)
J W Mullins Cum-Lake Racing

Placings: 22/3403/23-U3P51351   (4930)

2003/04: 26⁰GS, 24³S, 25⁴S, 26⁶GS, 24¹GF, 19³GS, 24⁶G, 22¹G,

	Starts	1st	2nd	3rd	Win & Pl
Chases	8	2	0	2	11216
Career Total	16	2	3	5	15782
108	4/04	Font	2m6f	E Ch	GD	£4085
104	3/04	Chep	3m	E Ch	G-F	£5536

Total win prize-money £9621

Going: Sf: 0-2 GS: 0-3 Gd: 1-2 GF: - Fm: 1-1
Distance: 2m/2m3: 0-0 2m4-2m7: 1-2 3m+: 1-6
Track: LH: 1-6 RH: 0-1 Tight: 1-4 Gall: 0-0
Aids: Bl: 0-0 Vi: 0-0 Tstrap: 0-0 Ckp: 0-0
Best Rating: 108 4/04 Font 2m6f   good Ch

Modest chaser; stays 3m; handles fast but well suited by soft/heavy ground.

Meadows Prince (IRE)

82f   **59f**

5-y-o b g Alzao (USA)-Anita Via (IRE) (Anita's Prince)
B Palling Richard Edwards

Placings: 0   (1019)
2003/04: 16⁶GF,

	Starts	1st	2nd	3rd	Win & Pl
NH Flat	1	0	0	0	
Career Total	1	0	0	0	

Going: Sf: 0-0 GS: 0-0 Gd: 0-0 GF: - Fm: 0-1
Distance: 2m/2m3: 0-1 2m4-2m7: 0-0 3m+: 0-0
Track: LH: 0-1 RH: 0-0 Tight: 0-0 Gall: 0-0
Aids: Bl: 0-0 Vi: 0-0 Tstrap: 0-0 Ckp: 0-0
Best Rating: 59 8/03 Worc 2m   gd-fm NHF

Meandmrsjones

70f   **46f**

5-y-o ch m Alderbrook-Dunbrody Abbey (Proverb)
J G M O'Shea Mrs M E Jones

Placings: 00   (4345)
2003/04: 16⁰GS, 16⁰GS,

	Starts	1st	2nd	3rd	Win & Pl
NH Flat	2	0	0	0	
Career Total	2	0	0	0	

Going: Sf: 0-0 GS: 0-2 Gd: 0-0 GF: - Fm: 0-0
Distance: 2m/2m3: 0-2 2m4-2m7: 0-0 3m+: 0-0
Track: LH: 0-1 RH: 0-1 Tight: 0-0 Gall: 0-0
Aids: Bl: 0-0 Vi: 0-0 Tstrap: 0-0 Ckp: 0-0
Best Rating: 46 3/04 Wwck 2m   gd-sft NHF

Measure Up

96   **97+**

5-y-o ch g Inchinor-Victoria Blue (Old Vic)
J M Bradley Raymond Tooth

Placings: 1   (1361)
2003/04: 16¹GF,

	Starts	1st	2nd	3rd	Win & Pl
Hurdles	1	1	0	0	2626
Career Total	1	1	0	0	2626
97	9/03	Worc	2m	E Hdl	G-F	£2626

Total win prize-money £2626

Going: Sf: 0-0 GS: 0-0 Gd: 0-0 GF: - Fm: 1-1
Distance: 2m/2m3: 1-1 2m4-2m7: 0-0 3m+: 0-0
Track: LH: 1-1 RH: 0-0 Tight: 0-0 Gall: 0-0

Aids: Bl: 0-0 Vi: 0-0 Tstrap: 0-0 Ckp: 0-0
Best Rating: 97   9/03   Worc   2m   gd-fm   Hdl

Made winning debut in 2m Worcester maiden hurdle September 2003; likely to need fast ground to get the trip.

Mecca Prince (IRE)

9-y-o ch g Shalford (IRE)-Fashion Parade (Mount Hagen (FR))
J W Tudor   J Tudor

Placings:04P5P/P   (0151)
2003/04: 24PGF,

	Starts	1st	2nd	3rd	Win & Pl
Chases	1	0	0	0	
Career Total	**6**	**0**	**0**	**0**	**0**

Going: Sf: 0-0 GS: 0-0 Gd: 0-0 GF: - Fm: 0-1
Distance: 2m/2m3: 0-0 2m4-2m7: 0-0 3m+: 0-1
Track: LH: 0-1 RH: 0-0 Tight: 0-0 Gall: 0-0
Aids: Bl: 0-0 Vi: 0-0 Tstrap: 0-0 Ckp: 0-0
Best Rating: 60   9/98   Sedg   2m1f   gd-fm   Hdl

Medallist

95   **73**

5-y-o b g Danehill (USA)-Obsessive (USA) (Seeking The Gold (USA))
B Ellison   Ashley Young

Placings:0504-45   (0432)
2003/04: 17⁴S, 17⁵G,

	Starts	1st	2nd	3rd	Win & Pl
Hurdles	2	0	0	0	0
Career Total	**6**	**0**	**0**	**0**	**0**

Going: Sf: 0-1 GS: 0-0 Gd: 0-1 GF: - Fm: 0-0
Distance: 2m/2m3: 0-2 2m4-2m7: 0-0 3m+: 0-0
Track: LH: 0-2 RH: 0-0 Tight: 0-2 Gall: 0-0
Aids: Bl: 0-1 Vi: 0-0 Tstrap: 0-0 Ckp: 0-0
Best Rating: 74   3/03   Sedg   2m1f   good   Hdl

Disappointing novice hurdler.

Medelai

73(100h)   (63h)**80+**

8-y-o b m Marju (IRE)-No Islands (Lomond (USA))
A G Juckes   M P Tokley

Placings:U/UP/4P5P3306-641   (2117)
2003/04: 17⁶GF, 16⁴GF, 20¹F,

	Starts	1st	2nd	3rd	Win & Pl
Hurdles	2	0	0	0	0
Chases	1	1	0	0	3653
Career Total	**14**	**1**	**0**	**2**	**4293**
80 11/03 Ludl 2m4f E Ch FRM £3653				
Total win prize-money £3653				

Going: Sf: 0-0 GS: 0-0 Gd: 0-0 GF: - Fm: 1-3
Distance: 2m/2m3: 0-2 **2m4-2m7: 1-1** 3m+: 0-0
Track: LH: 0-1 **RH: 1-2** Tight: **1-1** Gall: 0-0
Aids: Bl: 0-2 Vi: 0-0 Tstrap: 0-0 Ckp: 0-0
Best Rating: 80   11/03   Ludl   2m4f   firm   Ch

Plating-class hurdler; madea winning chasing debut; needs distances in excess of 2m; acts on any ground.

Medici (FR)

78   **60**

6-y-o b/br g Cadoudal (FR)-Marie De Valois (FR) (Moulin)
Jonjo O'Neill   Sir Robert Ogden

Placings:4-60   (2488)
2003/04: 16⁸G, 16⁹GF,

	Starts	1st	2nd	3rd	Win & Pl
NH Flat	1	0	0	0	0
Hurdles	1	0	0	0	0
Career Total	**3**	**0**	**0**	**0**	**0**

Going: Sf: 0-0 GS: 0-1 Gd: 0-1 GF: - Fm: 0-0
Distance: 2m/2m3: 0-2 2m4-2m7: 0-0 3m+: 0-0
Track: LH: 0-1 RH: 0-1 Tight: 0-0 Gall: 0-1
Aids: Bl: 0-0 Vi: 0-0 Tstrap: 0-0 Ckp: 0-0
Best Rating: 104   1/03   Hayd   2m   gd-sft   NHF

Medkhan (IRE)

98   **76**

7-y-o ch g Lahib (USA)-Safayn (USA) (Lyphard (USA))
F Jordan   Miss L M Rochford

Placings:00-504   (1593)
2003/04: 17⁵GF, 20⁰GF, 21⁴GF,

	Starts	1st	2nd	3rd	Win & Pl
Hurdles	3	0	0	0	0
Career Total	**5**	**0**	**0**	**0**	**0**

Going: Sf: 0-0 GS: 0-0 Gd: 0-0 GF: - Fm: 0-3
Distance: 2m/2m3: 0-1 2m4-2m7: 0-2 3m+: 0-0
Track: LH: 0-1 RH: 0-2 Tight: 0-0 Gall: 0-0
Aids: Bl: 0-0 Vi: 0-0 Tstrap: 0-0 Ckp: 0-0
Best Rating: 76   5/03   Hrfd   2m1f   gd-fm   Hdl

Has not lived up to signs of promise when fifth in decent 2m 1f novice event at Hereford May 2003.

Mega Chic (FR)

77   **63**

4-y-o b g Useful (FR)-Pampachic (FR) (Pampabird)
J C Tuck   James R Tuck

Placings:U005   (4504)
2003/04: 17⁰G, 16⁹G, 16⁰G, 17⁵G,

	Starts	1st	2nd	3rd	Win & Pl
Hurdles	4	0	0	0	0
Career Total	**4**	**0**	**0**	**0**	**0**

Going: Sf: 0-0 GS: 0-0 Gd: 0-0 GF: - Fm: 0-1
Distance: 2m/2m3: 0-4 2m4-2m7: 0-3 3m+: 0-0
Track: LH: 0-2 RH: 0-2 Tight: 0-2 Gall: 0-0
Aids: Bl: 0-0 Vi: 0-0 Tstrap: 0-0 Ckp: 0-0
Best Rating: 63   3/04   Ludl   2m   good   Hdl

Megazine

(109h)   (98 h)

10-y-o b g Shaab-Sherzine (Gorytus (USA))
J D Frost (M Hill 29/5)   Fun In The Sun Partnership

Placings:0/0005053/4/0P0/235541551-P0F   (1344)
2003/04: 17⁶GF, 17⁰GF, 17⁰GF,

	Starts	1st	2nd	3rd	Win & Pl
Hurdles	2	0	0	0	0
Chases	1	0	0	0	0
Career Total	**24**	**2**	**1**	**2**	**9298**
98 12/02 Tntn 2m1f D(0-115)HHdl SFT £4923				

96   11/02 NAbb   2m1f   E(0-110)HHdl   HVY £2891
Total win prize-money £7815

Going: Sf: 0-0 GS: 0-0 Gd: 0-0 GF: - Fm: 0-3
Distance: 2m/2m3: 0-3 2m4-2m7: 0-0 3m+: 0-0
Track: LH: 0-3 RH: 0-0 Tight: 0-2 Gall: 0-0
Aids: Bl: 0-0 Vi: 0-0 Tstrap: 0-0 Ckp: 0-0
Best Rating: 98   12/02   Tntn   2m1f   soft   Hdl

Moderate hurdler; impressive winner of extended two mile handicap hurdle in heavy ground at Newton Abbot November 2002; followed up at Taunton; liked soft ground, stayed 22 furlongs; fell fatally in September 2003. (DEAD)

Meggie's Lad (IRE)

107   **98**

7-y-o b g Beau Sher-Kambaya (IRE) (Kambalda)
Miss Venetia Williams   T England

Placings:15-24324   (4216)
2003/04: 16⁶G, 19⁴G, 25³S, 24²S, 22⁴G,

	Starts	1st	2nd	3rd	Win & Pl
Hurdles	5	0	2	1	2596
Career Total	**7**	**1**	**2**	**1**	**4980**
105 11/02 Sthl 2m H NHF G-S £2383				
Total win prize-money £2384				

Going: Sf: 0-2 GS: 0-0 Gd: 0-3 GF: - Fm: 0-0
Distance: 2m/2m3: 0-1 2m4-2m7: 0-2 3m+: 0-2
Track: LH: 0-2 RH: 0-2 Tight: 0-1 Gall: 0-0
Aids: Bl: 0-0 Vi: 0-0 Tstrap: 0-0 Ckp: 0-0
Best Rating: 105   12/03   Wwck   3m1f   soft   Hdl

Moderate novice hurdler; bumper winner; stays three miles; suited by some cut.

Meggies Gamble (IRE)

111   **120+**

7-y-o b g Zaffaran (USA)-Glaskerbeg Lady (IRE) (Radical)
Miss Venetia Williams   T England

Placings:3-62114   (4197)
2003/04: 16⁶GS, 20⁰S, 20¹S, 19¹G, 24⁴G,

	Starts	1st	2nd	3rd	Win & Pl
NH Flat	1	0	0	0	0
Hurdles	4	2	1	0	11352
Career Total	**6**	**2**	**1**	**1**	**11629**
120 2/04 Catt 2m3f E Hdl GD £3987				
120 1/04 Weth 2m4f110yD Hdl SFT £5824				
Total win prize-money £9812				

Going: Sf: 1-2 GS: 0-1 Gd: 1-2 GF: - Fm: 0-0
Distance: 2m/2m3: 1-2 2m4-2m7: 1-2 3m+: 0-1
Track: **LH: 2-5** RH: 0-0 **Tight: 1-1** Gall: 0-1
Aids: Bl: 0-0 Vi: 0-0 Tstrap: 0-0 Ckp: 0-0
Best Rating: 120   3/04   Newb   3m110y   good   Hdl

Useful novice hurdler; keen sort; runaway winner of a couple of novice events early in 2004; stays two and a half miles and acts on good ground or softer; likely to stay farther; most progressive.

Meldrum Meg

97f   **76f**

4-y-o b f Bal Harbour-Strathrusdale (Blazing Saddles (AUS))
M W Easterby   Brig Racing Club

Placings:300   (4608)
2003/04: 16³S, 16⁹GS, 17⁹G,

	Starts	1st	2nd	3rd	Win & Pl
NH Flat	3	0	0	1	285

Career Total   3   0   0   1   285

Going:	Sf: 0-1 GS: 0-1 Gd: 0-1 GF: - Fm: 0-0
Distance:	2m/2m3: 0-3 2m4-2m7: 0-0 3m+: 0-0
Track:	LH: 0-2 RH: 0-1 Tight: 0-1 Gall: 0-0
Aids:	Bl: 0-0 Vi: 0-0 Tstrap: 0-0 Ckp: 0-0
Best Rating:	76 2/04 Weth 2m soft NHF

Showed ability when third in soft ground bumper on debut at Wetherby in February; held subsequently.

Meldrum Star (IRE)
108   **108+**
7-y-o ch g Fourstars Allstar (USA)-Meldrum Lass (Buckskin (FR))
Mrs S J Smith Apb Racing

Placings:61P-42331312   (2923)
2003/04: 22⁴GF, 19²GF, 20³GF, 17³GF, 20¹GF, 21³G, 19¹G, 19²G,

	Starts	1st	2nd	3rd	Win & Pl
Hurdles	8	2	2	3	15797
Career Total	11	3	2	3	19749
113 12/03 Donc	2m3f110yD(0-115)HHdl			GD	£3445
107 10/03 Chep	2m4f D(0-120)HHdl			G-F	£4046
94 10/02 Hayd	2m D Hdl			GD	£3952

Total win prize-money £11443

Going:	Sf: 0-0 GS: 0-0 Gd: 1-3 GF: - Fm: 1-5
Distance:	2m/2m3: 0-1 **2m4-2m7: 2-7** 3m+: 0-0
Track:	LH: 2-5 RH: 0-2 Tight: 0-2 Gall: 0-1
Aids:	Bl: 0-0 Vi: 0-0 Tstrap: 0-0 Ckp: 0-0
Best Rating:	113 12/03 MRas 2m3f110y good Hdl

Modest hurdler; hung left and was disqualified from 2nd place in 2m 4f Worcester handicap in August 2003; appreciated a return to that trip when winning a handicap at Chepstow in October and showed right attitude when winning at Doncaster in December; probably stays 2m 6f; lightly raced; likes fast ground; tough sort.

Melford (IRE)
91   **101**
6-y-o br g Presenting-Echo Creek (IRE) (Strong Gale)
Miss H C Knight John Melville

Placings:60-10P   (4167)
2003/04: 19¹G, 20⁰S, 21ᴾG,

	Starts	1st	2nd	3rd	Win & Pl
Hurdles	3	1	0	0	3900
Career Total	5	1	0	0	3900
100 12/03 Extr	2m3f D Hdl			GD	£3900

Total win prize-money £3900

Going:	Sf: 0-1 GS: 0-0 Gd: 1-2 GF: - Fm: 0-0
Distance:	**2m/2m3: 1-1** 2m4-2m7: 0-2 3m+: 0-0
Track:	LH: 0-1 **RH: 1-2** Tight: 0-0 Gall: 0-1
Aids:	Bl: 0-0 Vi: 0-0 Tstrap: 0-0 Ckp: 0-0
Best Rating:	100 12/03 Extr 2m3f good Hdl

Winning novice hurdler; effective in good ground; stays 2m 4f.

Melitma
72   **44**
9-y-o gr g Gods Solution-Melsil (Silly Prices)
R Nixon G R S Nixon

Placings:PP5P   (4852)
2003/04: 16⁵GF, 24ᴾG, 21⁵S, 20ᴾS,

	Starts	1st	2nd	3rd	Win & Pl
Hurdles	4	0	0	0	0
Career Total	4	0	0	0	0

Going:	Sf: 0-0 GS: 0-1 Gd: 0-2 GF: - Fm: 0-1
Distance:	2m/2m3: 0-1 2m4-2m7: 0-2 3m+: 0-1
Track:	LH: 0-4 RH: 0-0 Tight: 0-1 Gall: 0-0
Aids:	Bl: 0-0 Vi: 0-0 Tstrap: 0-0 Ckp: 0-0
Best Rating:	44 3/04 Sedg 2m5f110y good Hdl

Mellino
82   **50**
4-y-o b f Robellino (USA)-Krista (Kris)
T D Easterby Mrs Jean P Connew

Placings:6   (1007)
2003/04: 17⁶G,

	Starts	1st	2nd	3rd	Win & Pl
Hurdles	1	0	0	0	0
Career Total	1	0	0	0	0

Going:	Sf: 0-0 GS: 0-0 Gd: 0-1 GF: - Fm: 0-0
Distance:	2m/2m3: 0-1 2m4-2m7: 0-0 3m+: 0-0
Track:	LH: 0-1 RH: 0-0 Tight: 0-0 Gall: 0-0
Aids:	Bl: 0-0 Vi: 0-0 Tstrap: 0-0 Ckp: 0-0
Best Rating:	50 8/03 Bang 2m1f good Hdl

Showed little on debut over hurdles.

Melody Princess
11-y-o b m Ardross-Letteressie (Alias Smith (USA))
Miss A Dudley Mrs Charlotte Oram

Placings:40000/5   (0030)
2003/04: 33⁵G,

	Starts	1st	2nd	3rd	Win & Pl
Chases	1	0	0	0	0
Career Total	6	0	0	0	0

Going:	Sf: 0-0 GS: 0-0 Gd: 0-1 GF: - Fm: 0-0
Distance:	2m/2m3: 0-0 2m4-2m7: 0-0 3m+: 0-1
Track:	LH: 0-1 RH: 0-0 Tight: 0-0 Gall: 0-1
Aids:	Bl: 0-0 Vi: 0-0 Tstrap: 0-0 Ckp: 0-0
Best Rating:	83 1/98 Ludl 2m soft NHF

Meltonian
101   **91**
7-y-o ch g Past Glories-Meltonby (Sayf El Arab (USA))
K F Clutterbuck K F Clutterbuck

Placings:4O4P/4056323P-65154   (2415)
2003/04: 20⁶GF, 18⁵G, 16¹GF, 16⁵GF, 16⁴GS,

	Starts	1st	2nd	3rd	Win & Pl
Hurdles	5	1	0	0	2954
Career Total	17	1	1	2	4912
91 10/03 Towc	2m E Hdl			G-F	£2954

Total win prize-money £2954

Going:	Sf: 0-0 GS: 0-1 Gd: 0-1 GF: - Fm: 1-3
Distance:	**2m/2m3: 1-4** 2m4-2m7: 0-1 3m+: 0-0
Track:	LH: 0-2 **RH: 1-3** Tight: 0-1 Gall: 0-2
Aids:	Bl: 0-0 Vi: 0-0 Tstrap: 0-0 Ckp: 0-0
Best Rating:	97 4/02 Hntg 2m110y gd-fm NHF

Modest hurdler at around two and a half miles.

Melusina (IRE)
100   **82**
4-y-o b f Barathea (IRE)-Moon Masquerade (IRE)

(Darshaan)
Mrs A J Perrett The Masqueraders (jdrp)

Placings:3   (1211)
2003/04: 18³GF,

	Starts	1st	2nd	3rd	Win & Pl
Hurdles	1	0	0	1	517
Career Total	1	0	0	1	517

Going:	Sf: 0-0 GS: 0-0 Gd: 0-0 GF: - Fm: 0-1
Distance:	2m/2m3: 0-1 2m4-2m7: 0-0 3m+: 0-0
Track:	LH: 0-0 RH: 0-0 Tight: 0-1 Gall: 0-0
Aids:	Bl: 0-0 Vi: 0-0 Tstrap: 0-0 Ckp: 0-0
Best Rating:	82 8/03 Font 2m2f110y gd-fm Hdl

Juvenile hurdler; became disappointing on the Flat; third on debut at Fontwell.

Members Only
100   **106**
5-y-o b g Kris-Could Have Been (Nomination)
M C Pipe D A Johnson

Placings:2-402   (3651)
2003/04: 16⁴GF, 17⁹G, 17²S,

	Starts	1st	2nd	3rd	Win & Pl
Hurdles	3	0	1	0	2414
Career Total	4	0	2	0	3245

Going:	Sf: 0-1 GS: 0-0 Gd: 0-0 GF: - Fm: 0-1
Distance:	2m/2m3: 0-2 2m4-2m7: 0-0 3m+: 0-0
Track:	LH: 0-1 RH: 0-2 Tight: 0-2 Gall: 0-0
Aids:	Bl: 0-0 Vi: 0-0 Tstrap: 0-0 Ckp: 0-0
Best Rating:	111 2/03 Thur 2m sft-hvy NHF

Moderate novice hurdler; ex-Irish bumper performer; should stay 2m 4f; acts best on soft ground.

Mendip Manor
77   **57**
6-y-o b g Rakaposhi King-Broughton Manor (Dubassoff (USA))
S C Burrough Rob Croker

Placings:U0-P00P   (4895)
2003/04: 20ᴾS, 17⁰S, 16⁰G, 22ᴾG,

	Starts	1st	2nd	3rd	Win & Pl
Hurdles	4	0	0	0	
Career Total	6	0	0	0	

Going:	Sf: 0-2 GS: 0-0 Gd: 0-2 GF: - Fm: 0-0
Distance:	2m/2m3: 0-2 2m4-2m7: 0-2 3m+: 0-0
Track:	LH: 0-1 RH: 0-3 Tight: 0-1 Gall: 0-0
Aids:	Bl: 0-0 Vi: 0-0 Tstrap: 0-0 Ckp: 0-0
Best Rating:	57 2/04 Tntn 2m1f soft Hdl

Mendosino (GER)
102   **103+**
5-y-o b g Acatenango (GER)-Maji (Shareef Dancer (USA))
Miss Venetia Williams (P Schiergen 27/5) Direct Sales UK Ltd

Placings:6301000   (4716)
2003/04: 16⁶GS, 20³G, 21⁹GS, 18¹GS, 20⁰GS, 17⁰GS, 21⁰G,

	Starts	1st	2nd	3rd	Win & Pl
Hurdles	7	1	0	1	4546
Career Total	7	1	0	1	4546
103 2/04 Font	2m2f110yE(0-110)HHdl			G-S	£4173

Total win prize-money £4173

Going: Sf: 0-0 GS: 1-5 Gd: 0-2 GF: - Fm: 0-0
Distance: 2m/2m3: 1-3 2m4-2m7: 0-4 3m+: 0-0
Track: LH: 1-2 RH: 0-4 Tight: 1-2 Gall: 0-1
Aids: Bl: 0-1 Vi: 0-0 Tstrap: 0-0 Ckp: 0-0
Best Rating: 103 2/04 Font 2m2f110y gd-sft Hdl

Former Listed winner on the Flat in Germany; off the mark over hurdles in Britain at the fourth attempt when dropped to 2m 2f at Fontwell in February; acts on good to soft.

Menphis Beury (FR)

98   102

4-y-o b g Art Bleu-Pampa Star (FR) (Pampabird)
H D Daly   R M Kirkland

Placings:03U3   (4504)
2003/04: 17⁰VS, 17³HY, 16ᵁG, 17³G,

	Starts	1st	2nd	3rd	Win & Pl
Hurdles	3	0	0	1	534
Chases	1	0	0	1	2364
Career Total	4	0	0	2	2898

Going: Sf: 0-1 GS: 0-0 Gd: 0-2 GF: - Fm: 0-0
Distance: 2m/2m3: 0-4 2m4-2m7: 0-0 3m+: 0-0
Track: LH: 0-0 RH: 0-2 Tight: 0-0 Gall: 0-0
Aids: Bl: 0-0 Vi: 0-0 Tstrap: 0-0 Ckp: 0-0
Best Rating: 102 3/04 Hrfd 2m1f   good   Hdl

Moderate hurdler; placed over fences in France; acts on testing ground.

Mensch (IRE)

102(70h)   (75h)71

8-y-o ch g Husyan (USA)-Floating Dollar (Master Owen)
Evan Williams (Paul Morgan 12/2) Paul Morgan

Placings:U0/600/24-PP02   (4855)
2003/04: 26ᴾGF, 24ᴾS, 26⁰G, 24²GF,

	Starts	1st	2nd	3rd	Win & Pl
Hurdles	1	0	0	0	0
Chases	3	0	1	0	1180
Career Total	11	0	2	0	2208

Going: Sf: 0-1 GS: 0-0 Gd: 0-1 GF: - Fm: 0-2
Distance: 2m/2m3: 0-2 2m4-2m7: 0-0 3m+: 0-4
Track: LH: 0-1 RH: 0-3 Tight: 0-1 Gall: 0-1
Aids: Bl: 0-0 Vi: 0-0 Tstrap: 0-0 Ckp: 0-3
Best Rating: 71 4/04 Tntn 3m   gd-fm   Ch

Winner of two points in 2004; best effort under Rules when runner-up in modest three mile novices' handicap chase at Taunton April 2004; acts on a sound surface.

Mer Bihan (FR)

52   43

4-y-o b f Port Lyautey (FR)-Unika Ii (FR) (Rolling Bowl (FR))
L Lungo The Hookers

Placings:P05   (4597)
2003/04: 16ᴾGF, 16⁰HY, 16⁵G,

	Starts	1st	2nd	3rd	Win & Pl
Hurdles	3	0	0	0	0
Career Total	3	0	0	0	0

Going: Sf: 0-1 GS: 0-0 Gd: 0-1 GF: - Fm: 0-1
Distance: 2m/2m3: 0-3 2m4-2m7: 0-0 3m+: 0-0
Track: LH: 0-3 RH: 0-0 Tight: 0-1 Gall: 0-1
Aids: Bl: 0-0 Vi: 0-0 Tstrap: 0-0 Ckp: 0-0
Best Rating: 43 3/04 Kels 2m110y   good   Hdl

Mercato (FR)

106(108h)   (125 h)128

8-y-o b g Mansonnien (FR)-Royal Lie (FR) (Garde Royale)
J R Best D S Nevison

Placings:43/21525611F/0P056/43U521055-334231FP
                        (4861)
2003/04: 16³G, 16³GS, 16⁴G, 24²G, 24³G, 24¹G, 25ᶠG, 33ᴾGS,

	Starts	1st	2nd	3rd	Win & Pl
Chases	8	1	1	3	20420
Career Total	33	5	4	5	47519
128 3/04	Sand	3m110y	E Ch		GD	£8820
125 2/03	Plum	2m5f	D(0-115)HHdl		HVY	£6906
117 3/01	MRas	2m1f110yF(0-105)HHdl		G-S	£5356
113 3/01	Font	2m2f110yE(0-115)HHdl		SFT	£2628
100 10/00	Hntg	2m110y	H NHF		G-F	£1561
			Total win prize-money £25273			

Going: Sf: 0-0 GS: 0-2 Gd: 1-6 GF: - Fm: 0-0
Distance: 2m/2m3: 0-2 2m4-2m7: 0-0 3m+: 0-0
Track: LH: 0-4 RH: 1-4 Tight: 0-1 Gall: 0-2
Aids: Bl: 0-0 Vi: 0-0 Tstrap: 0-0 Ckp: 0-0
Best Rating: 128 3/04 Sand 3m110y   good   Ch

Fair novice chaser; fifth in the 2003 Imperial Cup at Sandown over hurdles; landed the 2004 Grand Military Gold Cup at the same track when suited by the way the race was run; stays beyond three miles one; acts on any ground; consistent sort.

Merchants Friend (IRE)

112(104h)   (108h)137+

9-y-o b g Lord Americo-Buck Maid (Buckskin (FR))
C J Mann Magic Moments

Placings:0/002021/014F1P/34PUP365/0301112422-
145F352P   (4637)
2003/04: 24¹HY, 25⁴G, 26⁵GS, 24ᶠG, 25³S, 24⁵S, 24²G, 25ᶠG,

	Starts	1st	2nd	3rd	Win & Pl
Chases	8	1	1	1	30484
Career Total	39	7	6	4	81817
137 5/03	Uttx	3m	B HCh		HVY	£12012
126 11/02	Newb	2m4f	D(0-125)HCh		G-S	£7085
122 11/02	Plum	2m4f	D(0-120)HCh		G-S	£5525
	10/02	Pard	2m4f110y	Hdl		SFT	£2957
112 4/01	List	2m	(0-116)HCh		HVY	£6955
95 11/00	Clon	2m1f	Ch		SFT	£4416
97 4/00	List	3m	Hdl		SH	£3864
			Total win prize-money £42816			

Going: Sf: 1-3 GS: 0-1 Gd: 0-4 GF: - Fm: 0-0
Distance: 2m/2m3: 0-0 2m4-2m7: 0-0 3m+: 1-8
Track: LH: 1-5 RH: 0-3 Tight: 0-1 Gall: 0-2
Aids: Bl: 0-0 Vi: 0-0 Tstrap: 0-0 Ckp: 0-5
Best Rating: 137 3/04 Chel 3m110y   good   Ch

Useful handicap chaser; ex-Irish; a very creditable fifth in the 2003 Hennessy; has performed creditably in cheekpieces without winning since; led everywhere bar the line in the Fulke Walwyn Kim Muir at the Festival; stays three miles plus and goes well on soft ground.

Meritocracy (IRE)

98   74

6-y-o b g Lahib (USA)-Merry Devil (IRE) (Sadler's Wells (USA))
Miss A E Broyd Miss Alison Broyd

Placings:006-0003000   (4818)
2003/04: 17⁰GS, 16⁰GF, 16⁰G, 16³G, 16⁰G, 16⁰G, 17⁰GF,

	Starts	1st	2nd	3rd	Win & Pl
Hurdles	7	0	0	1	356
Career Total	10	0	0	1	356

Going: Sf: 0-0 GS: 0-1 Gd: 0-4 GF: - Fm: 0-2
Distance: 2m/2m3: 0-7 2m4-2m7: 0-0 3m+: 0-0
Track: LH: 0-3 RH: 0-4 Tight: 0-1 Gall: 0-0
Aids: Bl: 0-0 Vi: 0-0 Tstrap: 0-0 Ckp: 0-0
Best Rating: 74 12/03 Winc 2m   good   Hdl

Merlo (IRE)

9-y-o b g Supreme Leader-Playwright (Furry Glen)
Mrs L B Normile The Friar Tuck Racing Club

Placings:0/0056P/PP   (0718)
2003/04: 24ᴾGF, 20ᴾG,

	Starts	1st	2nd	3rd	Win & Pl
Hurdles	2	0	0	0	0
Career Total	8	0	0	0	0

Going: Sf: 0-0 GS: 0-0 Gd: 0-1 GF: - Fm: 0-1
Distance: 2m/2m3: 0-0 2m4-2m7: 0-1 3m+: 0-1
Track: LH: 0-0 RH: 0-2 Tight: 0-0 Gall: 0-0
Aids: Bl: 0-0 Vi: 0-0 Tstrap: 0-0 Ckp: 0-0
Best Rating: 113 2/01 Fair 2m   heavy   NHF

Merry Days (IRE)

25f

4-y-o ch f Superlative-Fleur De Tal (Primitive Rising (USA))
N M Babbage Richard Coates

Placings:00   (2776)
2003/04: 14⁰S, 13⁰S,

	Starts	1st	2nd	3rd	Win & Pl
NH Flat	2	0	0	0	0
Career Total	2	0	0	0	0

Going: Sf: 0-1 GS: 0-0 Gd: 0-1 GF: - Fm: 0-0
Distance: 2m/2m3: 0-0 2m4-2m7: 0-0 3m+: 0-0
Track: LH: 0-1 RH: 0-0 Tight: 0-0 Gall: 0-0
Aids: Bl: 0-0 Vi: 0-0 Tstrap: 0-0 Ckp: 0-0
Best Rating: 25 11/03 Wwck 1m6f   good   NHF

Merry Minstrel (IRE)

106

11-y-o b g Black Minstrel-Merry Lesa (Dalesa)
C J Mann Hugh Villiers

Placings:060/266F/U01311/2P23-PF   (0920)
2003/04: 16ᴾGF, 17ᶠGF,

	Starts	1st	2nd	3rd	Win & Pl
Chases	2	0	0	0	0
Career Total	19	3	3	2	21240
94 9/01	Plum	2m1f	E(0-105)HCh		G-S	£3136
78 7/01	Wxfd	2m	(0-95)HCh		G-Y	£5564
80 6/01	Dpat	2m2f	(0-95)HCh		FRM	£4326
			Total win prize-money £13028			

Going: Sf: 0-0 GS: 0-0 Gd: 0-0 GF: - Fm: 0-0
Distance: 2m/2m3: 0-2 2m4-2m7: 0-0 3m+: 0-0
Track: LH: 0-1 RH: 0-1 Tight: 0-2 Gall: 0-0
Aids: Bl: 0-0 Vi: 0-0 Tstrap: 0-0 Ckp: 0-0
Best Rating: 106 4/03 Ludl 2m4f   good   Ch

Moderate chaser; half-brother to Merry Gale; won two races in Ireland before coming to Britain; seemingly best on good ground; stays two and a half miles.

Merry Tina

99 (44h)**70**

9-y-o b m Tina's Pet-Merry Missus (Bargello)
J B Walton Messrs F T Walton

Placings:*000/04605P26-0053P5* (4659)
2003/04: 16⁹G, 17⁰G, 20⁵G, 17³S, 27ᵖG, 16⁵S,

	Starts	1st	2nd	3rd	Win & Pl
Chases	6	0	0	1	442
Career Total	17	0	1	1	1843

Going: Sf: 0-2 GS: 0-0 Gd: 0-4 GF: - Fm: 0-1
Distance: 2m/2m3: 0-4 2m4-2m7: 0-1 3m+: 0-1
Track: LH: 0-6 RH: 0-0 Tight: 0-3 Gall: 0-0
Aids: Bl: 0-0 Vi: 0-2 Tstrap: 0-0 Ckp: 0-0
Best Rating: 70 4/04 Hexm 2m110y soft Ch

Merrylea-Confused

72 **22**

5-y-o ch m Respect-Merry Mermaid (Bairn (USA))
A M Crow The Ancrum Pointer

Placings:*000* (4595)
2003/04: 16⁰G, 16⁰GS, 22⁰G,

	Starts	1st	2nd	3rd	Win & Pl
NH Flat	2	0	0	0	0
Hurdles	1	0	0	0	0
Career Total	3	0	0	0	0

Going: Sf: 0-0 GS: 0-1 Gd: 0-2 GF: - Fm: 0-0
Distance: 2m/2m3: 0-2 2m4-2m7: 0-1 3m+: 0-0
Track: LH: 0-3 RH: 0-0 Tight: 0-1 Gall: 0-0
Aids: Bl: 0-0 Vi: 0-0 Tstrap: 0-0 Ckp: 0-0
Best Rating: 84 11/03 Ayr 2m good NHF

Merryvale Man

105 **114+**

7-y-o b g Rudimentary (USA)-Salu (Ardross)
Miss Kariana Key Miss Kariana Key

Placings:*204204501U1* (4937)
2003/04: 16²GS, 16⁰GF, 16⁴S, 17²HY, 16⁰G, 17⁴GS, 16⁵GF, 16⁰G, 16¹HY, 17⁰UG, 16¹GS,

	Starts	1st	2nd	3rd	Win & Pl
Hurdles	11	2	2	0	13740
Career Total	11	2	2	0	13740
114	4/04	Prth	2m110y D Hdl	G-S	£5759
114	3/04	Newc	2m	E Hdl	HVY	£3529
			Total win prize-money £9289

Going: Sf: 1-3 GS: 1-3 Gd: 0-3 GF: - Fm: 0-2
Distance: 2m/2m3: 2-11 2m4-2m7: 0-0 3m+: 0-0
Track: LH: 1-6 RH: 1-5 Tight: 0-5 Gall: 1-1
Aids: Bl: 0-0 Vi: 0-0 Tstrap: 0-0 Ckp: 0-0
Best Rating: 114 4/04 Prth 2m110y gd-sft Hdl

Modest hurdler best around two miles; goes well on testing ground.

Mersey Beat

(115h)**115**

10-y-o ch g Rock Hopper-Handy Dancer (Green God)
G L Moore Mrs J Moore

Placings:U26/124112/0025/010242/6P0P5U2/1212-U (2011)

2003/04: 20ᵁGF,

	Starts	1st	2nd	3rd	Win & Pl
Chases	1	0	0	0	
Career Total	31	6	9	0	31995
115	6/02	NAbb	2m110y	E(0-105)HCh	GD	£3334
113	5/02	Font	2m2f	E Ch	G-F	£3888
127	5/00	Towc	2m	D(0-120)HHdl	G-F	£2996
138	11/98	Tntn	2m1f	C HHdl	GD	£3940
126	11/98	Wind	2m	E Hdl	G-S	£2530
104	8/98	Strf	2m110y	E Hdl	G-F	£2010
				Total win prize-money £18700

Going: Sf: 0-0 GS: 0-0 Gd: 0-0 GF: - Fm: 0-1
Distance: 2m/2m3: 0-0 2m4-2m7: 0-1 3m+: 0-0
Track: LH: 0-0 RH: 0-1 Tight: 0-0 Gall: 0-0
Aids: Bl: 0-0 Vi: 0-0 Tstrap: 0-0 Ckp: 0-0
Best Rating: 138 11/98 Tntn 2m1f good Hdl

Fair two-mile plus handicap hurdler/chaser. Suited by fast ground. In good form in the summer of 2002, winning a couple of modest events; lightly raced since.

Mersey Mirage

85 **63**

7-y-o b g King's Signet (USA)-Kirriemuir (Lochnager)
R C Guest The Friar Tuck Racing Club

Placings:*P0F6F* (4435)
2003/04: 16ᵖGS, 16⁰GF, 16ᶠS, 16⁶GF, 16ᶠGS,

	Starts	1st	2nd	3rd	Win & Pl
Hurdles	5	0	0	0	0
Career Total	5	0	0	0	0

Going: Sf: 0-1 GS: 0-2 Gd: 0-0 GF: - Fm: 0-2
Distance: 2m/2m3: 0-5 2m4-2m7: 0-0 3m+: 0-0
Track: LH: 0-4 RH: 0-1 Tight: 0-3 Gall: 0-1
Aids: Bl: 0-0 Vi: 0-0 Tstrap: 0-0 Ckp: 0-0
Best Rating: 67 1/04 Muss 2m gd-fm Hdl

Meryl (FR)

95 **121**

4-y-o ch g Garde Royale-Vindhy (FR) (Yelpana (FR))
G Macaire Claude Cohen

Placings:*3B2230* (3485)
2003/04: 15³HO, 18ᵇVS, 15²VS, 17²G, 17³GS, 18⁰VS,

	Starts	1st	2nd	3rd	Win & Pl
Hurdles	6	0	2	2	17284
Career Total	6	0	2	2	17284

Going: Sf: 0-0 GS: 0-0 Gd: 0-1 GF: - Fm: 0-0
Distance: 2m/2m3: 0-4 2m4-2m7: 0-0 3m+: 0-0
Track: LH: 0-2 RH: 0-0 Tight: 0-0 Gall: 0-2
Aids: Bl: 0-0 Vi: 0-0 Tstrap: 0-0 Ckp: 0-0
Best Rating: 121 1/04 Chel 2m1f gd-sft Hdl

Useful juvenile hurdler; placed in France and Britain; effective on testing ground.

Message Recu (FR)

105 (100h)   (112h)**83+**

8-y-o b g Luth Dancer (USA)-High Steppe (Petoski)
S T Lewis Simon T Lewis

Placings:*0631/100000/00P/61540-1P3PP* (4528)
2003/04: 16¹F, 25ᶠG, 21³G, 20ᵖG, 20ᵖGS,

	Starts	1st	2nd	3rd	Win & Pl
Hurdles	1	0	0	0	0
Chases	4	1	0	1	6692
Career Total	23	4	0	2	31750
82	11/03	Leic	2m	E Ch	FRM	£4315

112	7/02	Limk	2m4f	HHdl	YLD	£13957
110	8/00	Tral	2m	HHdl	SFT	£6072
89	4/00	Cork	2m	Hdl	SFT	£4140
				Total win prize-money £28485

Going: Sf: 0-0 GS: 0-1 Gd: 0-3 GF: - Fm: 1-1
Distance: 2m/2m3: 1-1 2m4-2m7: 0-3 3m+: 0-1
Track: LH: 0-3 RH: 1-2 Tight: 0-1 Gall: 0-2
Aids: Bl: 0-0 Vi: 0-0 Tstrap: 0-0 Ckp: 0-0
Best Rating: 112 10/02 Limk 2m4f good Hdl

Formerly a modest hurdler in Ireland, now trained in Britain; shown modest form over fences so far; seems best at 2m4f; acts on soft ground.

Mestre Sala (FR)

103 **118**

9-y-o b g Al Nasr (FR)-Light Lida (USA) (Alleged (USA))
H D Daly Mrs Strachan, Mrs Gabb & Mrs Graham

Placings:*10/1152/041/3F14P* (1294)
2003/04: 20³G, 20ᶠGF, 20¹G, 21⁴GS, 24ᵖGF,

	Starts	1st	2nd	3rd	Win & Pl
Chases	5	1	0	1	5671
Career Total	14	5	1	1	17754
118	6/03	Strf	2m4f	E(0-110)HCh	GD	£4114
121	11/01	Strf	2m4f	D Ch	SFT	£3965
117	12/99	Extr	2m1f110yE Hdl	G-S	£3248
115	11/99	Uttx	2m	E Hdl	SFT	£2337
105	2/99	Winc	2m	H NHF	G-S	£1474
				Total win prize-money £15139

Going: Sf: 0-0 GS: 0-1 Gd: 1-2 GF: - Fm: 0-2
Distance: 2m/2m3: 0-0 2m4-2m7: 1-4 3m+: 0-1
Track: LH: 1-5 RH: 0-0 Tight: 1-4 Gall: 0-0
Aids: Bl: 0-0 Vi: 0-0 Tstrap: 0-0 Ckp: 0-0
Best Rating: 121 11/01 Strf 2m4f soft Ch

Modest chaser; good return in May 2003 after 18 months off with injury; added to his score at Stratford in June; stays two and a half miles; effective on soft ground.

Metal Detector (IRE)

98(111h)   (122 h)**117**

7-y-o b g Treasure Hunter-Las-Cancellas (Monksfield)
K C Bailey D Allen

Placings:*0230/121015-4P5113P* (4633)
2003/04: 20⁴S, 21ᵖS, 19⁵GS, 24¹G, 23¹GF, 20³G, 24ᵖG,

	Starts	1st	2nd	3rd	Win & Pl
Hurdles	2	0	0	0	806
Chases	5	2	0	1	10913
Career Total	17	5	2	2	28204
101	3/04	Leic	2m7f110yD Ch	G-F	£6006
109	1/04	Donc	3m	E Ch	GD	£4305
120	3/03	Wwck	2m5f	D(0-115)HHdl	SFT	£5115
122	11/02	Tntn	3m110y	D Hdl	G-S	£5931
106	5/02	Uttx	2m6f110yE Hdl	GD	£2849
				Total win prize-money £24207

Going: Sf: 0-2 GS: 0-1 Gd: 1-3 GF: - Fm: 1-1
Distance: 2m/2m3: 0-1 2m4-2m7: 0-3 3m+: 2-3
Track: LH: 1-3 RH: 1-4 Tight: 0-1 Gall: 1-2
Aids: Bl: 0-0 Vi: 0-0 Tstrap: 0-0 Ckp: 0-0
Best Rating: 122 11/02 Tntn 3m110y gd-sft Hdl

Fair hurdler/novice chaser; jumped right when scoring by a wide margin in novices' chase at Doncaster in January; added to that at Leicester; consistent and tough; stays three miles; acts on most ground except heavy; best going right-handed.

Meticulous

75   **39**

6-y-o gr g Eagle Eyed (USA)-Careful (IRE) (Distinctly North (USA))
M C Chapman   Eric Knowles

Placings:P00   (4258)
2003/04: 17FGF, 17OG, 16OGF,

	Starts	1st	2nd	3rd	Win & Pl
Hurdles	3	0	0	0	
Career Total	3	0	0	0	

Going:	Sf: 0-0 GS: 0-0 Gd: 0-1 GF: - Fm: 0-2
Distance:	2m/2m3: 0-3 2m4-2m7: 0-0 3m+: 0-0
Track:	LH: 0-1 RH: 0-2 Tight: 0-3 Gall: 0-0
Aids:	Bl: 0-1 Vi: 0-0 Tstrap: 0-1 Ckp: 0-0
Best Rating:	39 3/04 Catt 2m gd-fm Hdl

Meticulous (USA)

28

6-y-o b g Theatrical-Sha Tha (USA) (Mr Prospector (USA))
Mrs A M Thorpe   The Castle Boys

Placings:00-PP   (0517)
2003/04: 22PS, 19OG,

	Starts	1st	2nd	3rd	Win & Pl
Hurdles	2	0	0	0	
Career Total	4	0	0	0	

Going:	Sf: 0-1 GS: 0-0 Gd: 0-1 GF: - Fm: 0-0
Distance:	2m/2m3: 0-1 2m4-2m7: 0-1 3m+: 0-0
Track:	LH: 0-2 RH: 0-0 Tight: 0-1 Gall: 0-0
Aids:	Bl: 0-0 Vi: 0-0 Tstrap: 0-0 Ckp: 0-0
Best Rating:	28 12/02 Donc 2m110y soft Hdl

Mevagissey (BEL)

7-y-o b/br g Sula Bula-Fowey (Grand Conde (FR))
J R Boyle   Miss V A Cunningham

Placings:0   (2850)
2003/04: 16OS,

	Starts	1st	2nd	3rd	Win & Pl
NH Flat	1	0	0	0	
Career Total	1	0	0	0	

Going:	Sf: 0-1 GS: 0-0 Gd: 0-0 GF: - Fm: 0-0
Distance:	2m/2m3: 0-1 2m4-2m7: 0-0 3m+: 0-0
Track:	LH: 0-0 RH: 0-1 Tight: 0-0 Gall: 0-0
Aids:	Bl: 0-0 Vi: 0-0 Tstrap: 0-0 Ckp: 0-0

Mexican (USA)

100(97h)   (88h)**99+**

5-y-o b h Pine Bluff (USA)-Cuando Quiere (USA) (Affirmed (USA))
M D Hammond   M T McCarthy and L Ibbotson

Placings:440-0F1034P   (4938)
2003/04: 16OGS, 16FGF, 16¹GS, 16OG, 16³HY, 16⁴G, 16PGS,

	Starts	1st	2nd	3rd	Win & Pl
Hurdles	1	0	0	0	0
Chases	6	1	0	1	4810
Career Total	10	1	0	1	5515
99   1/04   Catt   2m   E(0-100)HCh   G-S   £3848

Total win prize-money £3849

Going:	Sf: 0-1 GS: 1-3 Gd: 0-2 GF: - Fm: 0-1
Distance:	2m/2m3: 1-7 2m4-2m7: 0-0 3m+: 0-0
Track:	LH: 1-4 RH: 0-3 Tight: 1-3 Gall: 0-1
Aids:	Bl: 0-0 Vi: 0-0 Tstrap: 0-0 Ckp: 1-6
Best Rating:	99 1/04 Catt 2m gd-sft Ch

Moderate chaser; effective over two miles; acts on easy ground.

Mexican Pete

89   **98+**

4-y-o b g Atraf-Eskimo Nel (IRE) (Shy Groom (USA))
P W Hiatt   First Chance Racing

Placings:14   (1881)
2003/04: 16¹GF, 16⁴G,

	Starts	1st	2nd	3rd	Win & Pl
Hurdles	2	1	0	0	3933
Career Total	2	1	0	0	3933
91   10/03   Hntg   2m110y   E Hdl   G-F   £2933

Total win prize-money £2933

Going:	Sf: 0-0 GS: 0-0 Gd: 0-1 GF: - Fm: 1-1
Distance:	2m/2m3: 1-2 2m4-2m7: 0-0 3m+: 0-0
Track:	LH: 0-1 RH: 1-1 Tight: 0-0 Gall: 1-1
Aids:	Bl: 0-0 Vi: 0-0 Tstrap: 0-0 Ckp: 0-0
Best Rating:	100 11/03 Weth 2m good Hdl

Moderate but improved on the Flat this year; looked fair prospect when winning on jumps debut at Huntingdon in October; well beaten in much stronger juvenile hurdle at Wetherby the following month; acts on fast ground.

Mexican Rock

81   **80**

8-y-o b g Rock City-Pink Mex (Tickled Pink)
N J Henderson   Magno-Pulse Ltd

Placings:00   (4692)
2003/04: 16OG, 17OG,

	Starts	1st	2nd	3rd	Win & Pl
Hurdles	2	0	0	0	
Career Total	2	0	0	0	

Going:	Sf: 0-0 GS: 0-0 Gd: 0-2 GF: - Fm: 0-0
Distance:	2m/2m3: 0-2 2m4-2m7: 0-0 3m+: 0-0
Track:	LH: 0-0 RH: 0-2 Tight: 0-0 Gall: 0-0
Aids:	Bl: 0-0 Vi: 0-0 Tstrap: 0-0 Ckp: 0-0
Best Rating:	80 3/04 Ludl 2m good Hdl

Mezereon

93   **99**

4-y-o b f Alzao (USA)-Blown-Over (Ron's Victory (USA))
D Carroll (J G Given 21/8)   Diamond Racing Ltd

Placings:12P0   (4625)
2003/04: 16¹F, 16²G, 16PGF, 16OG,

	Starts	1st	2nd	3rd	Win & Pl
Hurdles	4	1	1	0	8241
Career Total	4	1	1	0	8241
84   10/03   Weth   2m   D Hdl   FRM   £4241

Total win prize-money £4241

Going:	Sf: 0-0 GS: 0-0 Gd: 0-2 GF: - Fm: 1-2
Distance:	2m/2m3: 1-4 2m4-2m7: 0-0 3m+: 0-0
Track:	LH: 1-4 RH: 0-0 Tight: 0-2 Gall: 0-0
Aids:	Bl: 0-0 Vi: 0-0 Tstrap: 0-0 Ckp: 0-0
Best Rating:	101 11/03 Weth 2m good Hdl

Poor flat winner; made a winning debut over hurdles at Wetherby in October; runner-up to easy winner in much

---

stronger race there the following month before pulling up at Stratford; effective at two miles; acts on fast ground.

Mezzo Princess

12-y-o b m Remezzo-Kam Tsin Princess (Prince Regent (FR))
Mike Lurcock   Mike Lurcock

Placings:P0/PP4PF/640645-3   (0029)
2003/04: 26³G,

	Starts	1st	2nd	3rd	Win & Pl
Chases	1	0	0	1	972
Career Total	14	0	0	1	1174

Going:	Sf: 0-0 GS: 0-0 Gd: 0-1 GF: - Fm: 0-0
Distance:	2m/2m3: 0-0 2m4-2m7: 0-0 3m+: 0-1
Track:	LH: 0-1 RH: 0-0 Tight: 0-0 Gall: 0-1
Aids:	Bl: 0-1 Vi: 0-0 Tstrap: 0-0 Ckp: 0-0
Best Rating:	70 3/03 MRas 3m1f good Ch

Mi Favorita

83   **51**

6-y-o b m Piccolo-Mistook (USA) (Phone Trick (USA))
Miss Kate Milligan   S Ward

Placings:0006P-650   (0978)
2003/04: 17⁶S, 17⁵GS, 17OGF,

	Starts	1st	2nd	3rd	Win & Pl
Hurdles	3	0	0	0	0
Career Total	8	0	0	0	0

Going:	Sf: 0-1 GS: 0-1 Gd: 0-0 GF: - Fm: 0-1
Distance:	2m/2m3: 0-3 2m4-2m7: 0-0 3m+: 0-0
Track:	LH: 0-3 RH: 0-0 Tight: 0-3 Gall: 0-0
Aids:	Bl: 0-0 Vi: 0-0 Tstrap: 0-2 Ckp: 0-0
Best Rating:	59 3/03 Sedg 2m1f good Hdl

Mi Sombrero

5-y-o ch m Factual (USA)-Rose Elegance (Bairn (USA))
Mrs B E Matthews   R V Harraway

Placings:P   (4569)
2003/04: 17PGS,

	Starts	1st	2nd	3rd	Win & Pl
Hurdles	1	0	0	0	
Career Total	1	0	0	0	

Going:	Sf: 0-0 GS: 0-1 Gd: 0-0 GF: - Fm: 0-0
Distance:	2m/2m3: 0-1 2m4-2m7: 0-0 3m+: 0-0
Track:	LH: 0-1 RH: 0-0 Tight: 0-1 Gall: 0-0
Aids:	Bl: 0-0 Vi: 0-0 Tstrap: 0-0 Ckp: 0-0

Mice Design (IRE)

70   **26**

7-y-o b g Presidium-Diplomatist (Dominion)
S B Clark   S B Clark

Placings:51320/P6-P0   (0978)
2003/04: 19OG, 17OGF,

	Starts	1st	2nd	3rd	Win & Pl
Hurdles	2	0	0	0	
Career Total	9	1	1	1	3675
86   10/01   Hntg   2m4f110y E Hdl   GD   £2590

Total win prize-money £2590

Going:	Sf: 0-0 GS: 0-0 Gd: 0-1 GF: - Fm: 0-1
Distance:	2m/2m3: 0-1 2m4-2m7: 0-1 3m+: 0-0
Track:	LH: 0-1 RH: 0-1 Tight: 0-0 Gall: 0-0
Aids:	Bl: 0-1 Vi: 0-0 Tstrap: 0-0 Ckp: 0-0
Best Rating:	100 1/02 Hrfd 2m1f soft Hdl

Michael Finnegan (IRE)

(81h)   (60h)97

11-y-o b/br g Phardante (FR)-Decent Slave (Decent Fellow)
Miss L C Siddall Mrs D J Morris

Placings:040/0360F2140/4313P6663/P056124/002020-00
                                                        (2729)
2003/04: 16⁰G, 16⁰G, 16⁰S,

	Starts	1st	2nd	3rd	Win & Pl
Hurdles	2	0	0	0	0
Chases	1	0	0	0	0
Career Total	36	3	4	4	13626
101 12/01 Leic	2m	F(0-110)HHdl	HVY	£2261
107 12/00 Hayd	2m	F(0-110)HHdl	HVY	£2576
85 2/00 Muss	2m	E(0-105)HHdl	GD	£2769

Total win prize-money £7606

Going:	Sf: 0-1 GS: 0-0 Gd: 0-2 GF: - Fm: 0-0
Distance:	2m/2m3: 0-3 2m4-2m7: 0-0 3m+: 0-0
Track:	LH: 0-3 RH: 0-0 Tight: 0-0 Gall: 0-0
Aids:	Bl: 0-0 Vi: 0-0 Tstrap: 0-0 Ckp: 0-0
Best Rating:	107 12/00 Newc 2m soft Hdl

Modest handicap hurdler/novice chaser; goes well over two miles and suited by heavy ground.

Michaels Dream (IRE)

106   99

5-y-o b g Spectrum (IRE)-Stormswept (USA) (Storm Bird (CAN))
J Hetherton Mrs Michael John Paver

Placings:2224040   (4879)
2003/04: 17²GF, 16²S, 19²G, 174GS, 20⁰GS, 164F, 20⁰GS,

	Starts	1st	2nd	3rd	Win & Pl
Hurdles	7	0	3	0	2674
Career Total	7	0	3	0	2674

Going:	Sf: 0-1 GS: 0-3 Gd: 0-1 GF: - Fm: 0-2
Distance:	2m/2m3: 0-4 2m4-2m7: 0-3 3m+: 0-0
Track:	LH: 0-4 RH: 0-3 Tight: 0-5 Gall: 0-1
Aids:	Bl: 0-0 Vi: 0-0 Tstrap: 0-0 Ckp: 0-0
Best Rating:	99 2/04 Muss 2m firm Hdl

Moderate novice hurdler; runner-up first three starts; best on a sound surface.

Mick Murphy (IRE)

94(87h)   (66+h)78+

7-y-o b g Jurado (USA)-Lee Ford Lady (Kemal (FR))
R Johnson (Mrs E Slack 6/1) A Slack

Placings:00/0-6042500064F   (4616)
2003/04: 17⁶GF, 16⁰G, 174G, 22²G, 23⁵GS, 16⁶GS, 24⁰GF, 20⁶S, 25⁶GF, 164S, 21⁷G,

	Starts	1st	2nd	3rd	Win & Pl
Hurdles	7	0	1	0	1076
Chases	4	0	0	0	334
Career Total	14	0	1	0	1410

Going:	Sf: 0-2 GS: 0-2 Gd: 0-4 GF: - Fm: 0-3
Distance:	2m/2m3: 0-5 2m4-2m7: 0-4 3m+: 0-2
Track:	LH: 0-8 RH: 0-5 Tight: 0-1 Gall: 0-2
Aids:	Bl: 0-0 Vi: 0-0 Tstrap: 0-1 Ckp: 0-2
Best Rating:	78 3/04 Newc 2m110y soft Ch

Plating-class hurdler; still a maiden, but has shown promise; stays two miles six; appreciates a sound surface.

Mickey Croke

102   108+

7-y-o b g Alflora (IRE)-Praise The Lord (Lord Gayle (USA))
C R Egerton Lady Lloyd-Webber

Placings:61-F3FP2   (4783)
2003/04: 20⁶GS, 21³GS, 19⁶S, 23⁶S, 21²G,

	Starts	1st	2nd	3rd	Win & Pl
Hurdles	4	0	1	1	1475
Chases	1	0	0	0	0
Career Total	7	1	1	1	3533
108 12/02 Hrfd	2m1f	H NHF	SFT	£2058

Total win prize-money £2058

Going:	Sf: 0-2 GS: 0-2 Gd: 0-1 GF: - Fm: 0-0
Distance:	2m/2m3: 0-0 2m4-2m7: 0-5 3m+: 0-0
Track:	LH: 0-3 RH: 0-2 Tight: 0-1 Gall: 0-1
Aids:	Bl: 0-0 Vi: 0-0 Tstrap: 0-0 Ckp: 0-0
Best Rating:	108 11/03 Hayd 2m4f gd-sft Hdl

Brave winner of a bumper on his second start; has shown ability in novice hurdles; pulled up with breathing problem at Wetherby in January; much better effort when runner-up at Huntingdon in April on next start; stays two miles six well.

Micklow Minster

97   85

10-y-o ch g Minster Son-Scotto's Regret (Celtic Cone)
C Grant W Raw

Placings:00/0624163150/53P0/5/00-P02   (0937)
2003/04: 24⁰GF, 26²PG, 25⁰GF, 27²GF,

	Starts	1st	2nd	3rd	Win & Pl
Hurdles	2	0	0	0	0
Chases	2	0	1	0	1236
Career Total	22	2	2	2	9107
112 1/00 Catt	3m1f110yE Hdl	GD	£2786
108 11/99 Newc	2m4f	D Hdl	G-S	£2944

Total win prize-money £5730

Going:	Sf: 0-0 GS: 0-0 Gd: 0-1 GF: - Fm: 0-3
Distance:	2m/2m3: 0-0 2m4-2m7: 0-0 3m+: 0-4
Track:	LH: 0-4 RH: 0-0 Tight: 0-2 Gall: 0-1
Aids:	Bl: 0-0 Vi: 0-0 Tstrap: 0-0 Ckp: 0-0
Best Rating:	112 1/00 Catt 3m1f110y good Hdl

Moderate novice chaser; stays 3m 3f.

Mickthecutaway (IRE)

12-y-o b g Rontino-Le-Mu-Co (Varano)
Daniel Skelton Daniel Skelton

Placings:U/3260/3/1/UU1120/212611/4FP-U3   (4891)
2003/04: 25ᵁS, 243GF,

	Starts	1st	2nd	3rd	Win & Pl
Chases	2	0	0	1	418
Career Total	24	6	4	3	31765
126 3/02 Bang	2m4f110yC(0-135)HCh	SFT	£6955
126 3/02 Bang	3m110y D(0-120)HCh	SFT	£5169
118 12/01 Towc	3m1f E(0-115)HCh	HVY	£3445
112 2/01 Sand	3m110y D(0-115)HCh	SFT	£5164

107 1/01 Leic   2m7f110y   F(0-95)HCh
SFT £3251
101 3/00 Leic   2m7f110y   H Ch   G-S
£2249

Total win prize-money £26235

Going:	Sf: 0-1 GS: 0-0 Gd: 0-0 GF: - Fm: 0-1
Distance:	2m/2m3: 0-0 2m4-2m7: 0-0 3m+: 0-2
Track:	LH: 0-1 RH: 0-1 Tight: 0-1 Gall: 0-0
Aids:	Bl: 0-0 Vi: 0-0 Tstrap: 0-0 Ckp: 0-0
Best Rating:	126 3/02 Bang 2m4f110y soft Ch

Fair front-running chaser; stays three miles one but is effective over two and a half miles; jumps well; effective in soft ground.

Micmac

6-y-o br g Be My Native (USA)-Padykin (Bustino)
P Winkworth P Winkworth

Placings:0PP-P   (0623)
2003/04: 17⁰G,

	Starts	1st	2nd	3rd	Win & Pl
Hurdles	1	0	0	0	
Career Total	4	0	0	0	

Going:	Sf: 0-0 GS: 0-0 Gd: 0-1 GF: - Fm: 0-0
Distance:	2m/2m3: 0-1 2m4-2m7: 0-0 3m+: 0-0
Track:	LH: 0-0 RH: 0-1 Tight: 0-1 Gall: 0-0
Aids:	Bl: 0-0 Vi: 0-0 Tstrap: 0-0 Ckp: 0-0
Best Rating:	26 5/02 Folk 2m1f110y good NHF

Mid Summer Lark (IRE)

8-y-o b g Tremblant-Tuney Blade (Fine Blade (USA))
I McMath Mrs A J McMath

Placings:2   (4884)
2003/04: 24²GS,

	Starts	1st	2nd	3rd	Win & Pl
Chases	1	0	1	0	464
Career Total	1	0	1	0	464

Going:	Sf: 0-0 GS: 0-1 Gd: 0-0 GF: - Fm: 0-0
Distance:	2m/2m3: 0-0 2m4-2m7: 0-0 3m+: 0-1
Track:	LH: 0-0 RH: 0-1 Tight: 0-0 Gall: 0-0
Aids:	Bl: 0-0 Vi: 0-1 Tstrap: 0-0 Ckp: 0-0
Best Rating:	82 4/04 Carl 3m gd-sft Ch

Mid Sussex Spirit

94f   95f

5-y-o b g Environment Friend-Ranyah (USA) (Our Native (USA))
G L Moore Saloop

Placings:5   (3650)
2003/04: 16⁵GS,

	Starts	1st	2nd	3rd	Win & Pl
NH Flat	1	0	0	0	0
Career Total	1	0	0	0	0

Going:	Sf: 0-0 GS: 0-1 Gd: 0-0 GF: - Fm: 0-0
Distance:	2m/2m3: 0-1 2m4-2m7: 0-0 3m+: 0-0
Track:	LH: 0-0 RH: 0-1 Tight: 0-0 Gall: 0-0
Aids:	Bl: 0-0 Vi: 0-0 Tstrap: 0-0 Ckp: 0-0

Best Rating: 99 2/04 Kemp 2m   gd-sft NHF

Middleham Park (IRE)

84   80

4-y-o b g Revoque (IRE)-Snap Crackle Pop (IRE) (Statoblest)
P C Haslam Middleham Park Racing VIII & J McCarthy

Placings:35   (4310)
2003/04: 16³G, 16⁵GF,

	Starts	1st	2nd	3rd	Win & Pl
Hurdles	2	0	0	1	499
Career Total	2	0	0	1	499

Going:	Sf: 0-0 GS: 0-0 Gd: 0-1 GF: - Fm: 0-1
Distance:	2m2/2m3: 0-2 2m4-2m7: 0-0 3m+: 0-0
Track:	LH: 0-2 RH: 0-0 Tight: 0-1 Gall: 0-0
Aids:	Bl: 0-0 Vi: 0-0 Tstrap: 0-0 Ckp: 0-0
Best Rating:	80 2/04 Catt 2m good Hdl

Some ability over hurdles.

Middlethorpe

112   117+

7-y-o b g Noble Patriarch-Prime Property (IRE) (Tirol)
M W Easterby J H Quickfall & A G Black

Placings:4224211-4142   (3478)
2003/04: 16⁴G, 16¹GS, 16⁴HY, 16²G,

	Starts	1st	2nd	3rd	Win & Pl
Hurdles	4	1	1	0	8883
Career Total	11	3	4	0	20814
117	12/03 Weth	2m	D(0-115)HHdl	G-S	£5443
108	3/03 Catt	2m	E Hdl	SFT	£3630
114	2/03 Weth	2m	E Hdl	GD	£4088
			Total win prize-money £13162		

Going:	Sf: 0-1 GS: 1-1 Gd: 0-2 GF: - Fm: 0-0
Distance:	2m/2m3: 1-4 2m4-2m7: 0-0 3m+: 0-0
Track:	LH: 1-4 RH: 0-0 Tight: 0-1 Gall: 0-0
Aids:	Bl: 1-4 Vi: 0-0 Tstrap: 0-0 Ckp: 0-0
Best Rating:	117 1/04 Catt 2m good Hdl

Fair hurdler; formerly useful handicapper on the Flat; comfortable winner at Wetherby in December; suited by two miles; handles ground good or softer; usually wears blinkers.

Middleway

96(95h)   (81+h)70

8-y-o b g Milieu-Galway Gal (Proverb)
Miss Kate Milligan Mrs J M L Milligan

Placings:00P0/P20P460-0UP41453P   (4882)
2003/04: 20⁹G, 25ᵁGF, 24²GF, 22⁴S, 24¹GF, 24⁴GF, 24⁵G, 24³G, 26²PGS,

	Starts	1st	2nd	3rd	Win & Pl
Hurdles	4	1	0	0	4350
Chases	5	0	0	1	519
Career Total	20	1	1	1	6041
81	1/04 Muss	3m110y E(0-105)HHdl	G-F	£4085
		Total win prize-money £4085		

Going:	Sf: 0-1 GS: 0-1 Gd: 0-3 GF: - Fm: 1-4
Distance:	2m/2m3: 0-0 2m4-2m7: 0-2 3m+: 1-7
Track:	LH: 0-3 RH: 0-4 Tight: 0-3 Gall: 0-0
Aids:	Bl: 0-0 Vi: 0-0 Tstrap: 0-0 Ckp: 1-3
Best Rating:	81 1/04 Muss 3m110y gd-fm Hdl

Plating-class chaser, stays three miles; acts on fast ground.

Midland Flame (IRE)

110   (118h)139+

9-y-o b g Un Desperado (FR)-Lathanona (Reformed Character)
Miss H C Knight Trevor Hemmings

Placings:23/1123P43/2P231-54012P   (4861)
2003/04: 20⁵GS, 19⁴S, 20⁶G, 24¹G, 25²G, 33³PGS,

	Starts	1st	2nd	3rd	Win & Pl
Chases	6	1	1	0	26850
Career Total	20	4	5	4	74889
139	3/04 Newb	3m	C(0-130)HCh	GD	£16408
134	4/03 Aint	2m4f	B HCh	GD	£24895
109	10/01 Winc	2m	D Hdl	GD	£3250
116	10/01 Bang	2m1f	E Hdl	GD	£3136
			Total win prize-money £47689		

Going:	Sf: 0-1 GS: 0-2 Gd: 1-3 GF: - Fm: 0-0
Distance:	2m/2m3: 0-0 2m4-2m7: 0-3 3m+: 1-3
Track:	LH: 1-5 RH: 0-1 Tight: 0-1 Gall: 1-2
Aids:	Bl: 0-0 Vi: 0-0 Tstrap: 0-0 Ckp: 0-0
Best Rating:	139 3/04 Newb 3m good Ch

Fair chaser; broke his duck over fences on fifth start in valuable novices' handicap at Aintree in April 2003, held since then until winning at Newbury in early March; good effort back at Aintree; best suited by good ground, a strong pace and trips of up to and including three miles.

Midlem Melody

106(94h)   (69h)96

8-y-o b m Syrtos-Singing Hills (Crash Course)
W S Coltherd S Coltherd

Placings:060U64/41504605-02202321312514435421   (4880)
2003/04: 17⁹G, 17²G, 20²F, 20⁰G, 16²GF, 16³G, 16²G, 16¹GF, 21³G, 20¹G, 20⁴GS, 16⁵G, 16¹GF, 17⁴S, 20⁴GF, 16³G, 16⁵GF, 16⁴HY, 17²G, 20¹GS,

	Starts	1st	2nd	3rd	Win & Pl
Hurdles	2	0	0	0	0
Chases	18	4	6	3	25595
Career Total	34	5	6	3	28108
95	4/04 Carl	2m4f	E(0-100)HCh	G-S	£4485
92	1/04 Muss	2m	E(0-100)HCh	G-F	£4056
92	11/03 Hexm	2m4f110yE(0-105)HCh	GD	£2177
83	11/03 Carl	2m	E(0-105)HCh	G-F	£3591
70	12/02 Newc	2m	G(0-95)HHdl	SFT	£2247
			Total win prize-money £16556		

Going:	Sf: 0-2 GS: 1-2 Gd: 1-10 GF: - Fm: 2-6
Distance:	2m/2m3: 2-13 2m4-2m7: 2-7 3m+: 0-0
Track:	LH: 1-13 RH: 3-7 Tight: 1-9 Gall: 0-1
Aids:	Bl: 0-0 Vi: 0-0 Tstrap: 0-0 Ckp: 0-0
Best Rating:	95 4/04 Carl 2m4f gd-sft Ch

Plating-class chaser/hurdler, winner of a selling hurdle at Newcastle in December 2002; running well over fences in 2003/4; stays two and a half miles; acts on any ground but better on a sound surface.

Midnight Coup

94(90c)   (74c)74d

8-y-o br g First Trump-Anhaar (Ela-Mana-Mou)
B G Powell Mark Barrett Racing

Placings:400/0P0/006/50435501-042   (0676)
2003/04: 19⁰G, 16⁴GF, 17²F,

	Starts	1st	2nd	3rd	Win & Pl
Hurdles	3	0	1	0	812
Career Total	20	1	1	1	2752
4/03 LesL	2m		Hdl	FRM	£1260
		Total win prize-money £1260			

Going:	Sf: 0-0 GS: 0-0 Gd: 0-1 GF: - Fm: 0-2
Distance:	2m/2m3: 0-2 2m4-2m7: 0-1 3m+: 0-0
Track:	LH: 0-2 RH: 0-1 Tight: 0-0 Gall: 0-0
Aids:	Bl: 0-0 Vi: 0-0 Tstrap: 0-0 Ckp: 0-1
Best Rating:	84 7/02 NAbb 2m6f gd-fm Hdl

Midnight Creek

111   114+

6-y-o br g Tragic Role (USA)-Greek Night Out (IRE) (Ela-Mana-Mou)
Miss Venetia Williams (G A Swinbank 18/5) A Butler

Placings:153633-2222F   (4567)
2003/04: 22²G, 20²G, 24²G, 22²G, 24⁵GS,

	Starts	1st	2nd	3rd	Win & Pl
Hurdles	5	0	4	0	7799
Career Total	11	1	4	3	13273
103	12/02 Kels	2m110y E Hdl	HVY	£3653
		Total win prize-money £3653			

Going:	Sf: 0-0 GS: 0-1 Gd: 0-4 GF: - Fm: 0-0
Distance:	2m/2m3: 0-0 2m4-2m7: 0-3 3m+: 0-2
Track:	LH: 0-2 RH: 0-3 Tight: 0-2 Gall: 0-0
Aids:	Bl: 0-0 Vi: 0-1 Tstrap: 0-0 Ckp: 0-2
Best Rating:	114 3/04 Sand 2m6f good Hdl

Stayer on the Flat; modest hurdler; acts in heavy ground; stays two and a half miles; does not impress in a finish.

Midnight Gold

92f   68f

4-y-o ch g Midnight Legend-Yamrah (Milford)
L P Grassick Nettleton Harts

Placings:0   (4447)
2003/04: 16⁰S,

	Starts	1st	2nd	3rd	Win & Pl
NH Flat	1	0	0	0	
Career Total	1	0	0	0	

Going:	Sf: 0-1 GS: 0-0 Gd: 0-0 GF: - Fm: 0-0
Distance:	2m/2m3: 0-1 2m4-2m7: 0-0 3m+: 0-0
Track:	LH: 0-1 RH: 0-0 Tight: 0-0 Gall: 0-0
Aids:	Bl: 0-0 Vi: 0-0 Tstrap: 0-0 Ckp: 0-0
Best Rating:	68 3/04 Wwck 2m soft NHF

Midnight Gunner

106   (94h)120

10-y-o b g Gunner B-Light Tonight (Lighter)
A E Price M G Racing

Placings:000P06/226C363/41P2612P/2212141-6552   (4834)
2003/04: 29⁶G, 24⁵G, 29⁵GS, 26²GF,

	Starts	1st	2nd	3rd	Win & Pl
Chases	4	0	1	0	5099
Career Total	32	5	8	2	61714
120	4/03 Chel	3m2f110yC(0-135)HCh	GD	£13166
115	2/03 Ludl	3m	D(0-125)HCh	GD	£13728
106	12/02 Ludl	3m3f110yD(0-125)HCh	GD	£10003
93	2/02 Ludl	2m	E(0-105)HHdl	GD	£4576
92	5/01 Hrfd	2m3f	F Ch	GD	£2990
			Total win prize-money £44464		

Going:	Sf: 0-0 GS: 0-1 Gd: 0-2 GF: - Fm: 0-1
Distance:	2m/2m3: 0-0 2m4-2m7: 0-0 3m+: 0-4
Track:	LH: 0-2 RH: 0-0 Tight: 0-1 Gall: 0-0
Aids:	Bl: 0-0 Vi: 0-0 Tstrap: 0-0 Ckp: 0-0
Best Rating:	120 4/04 Chel 3m2f110y gd-fm Ch

Fair chaser; stays 3m 3f and likes good ground; has a good record at Ludlow; lightly raced since the spring of 2003.

Midnight Jazz (IRE)
87   **73**

14-y-o b g Shardari-Round Midnight (Star Appeal)
J Harriman   John Harriman

Placings:030/000051306**P2**/P5/0U22/0P/0P626/PP3-P0
                    (2116)
2003/04: 17^PGS, 16⁰GF,

	Starts	1st	2nd	3rd	Win & Pl
Hurdles	2	0	0	0	
Career Total	32	1	4	3	6150
111 1/97 Tram 2m	Hdl		Y-S	£2204	
			Total win prize-money £2204		

Going:	Sf: 0-0 GS: 0-1 Gd: 0-0 GF: - Fm: 0-1
Distance:	2m/2m3: 0-2 2m4-2m7: 0-0 3m+: 0-0
Track:	LH: 0-0 RH: 0-2 Tight: 0-0 Gall: 0-0
Aids:	Bl: 0-0 Vi: 0-0 Tstrap: 0-0 Ckp: 0-0
Best Rating:	111 1/97 Tram 2m yld-sft Hdl

Midnight Royal

9-y-o b m Prince Daniel (USA)-Dontella's Girl (Royal Clipper)
G R Pewter   N J Pewter

Placings:P0   **(4402)**
2003/04: 16^PGS, 16⁰G,

	Starts	1st	2nd	3rd	Win & Pl
Hurdles	2	0	0	0	
Career Total	2	0	0	0	

Going:	Sf: 0-0 GS: 0-0 Gd: 0-2 GF: - Fm: 0-0
Distance:	2m/2m3: 0-2 2m4-2m7: 0-0 3m+: 0-0
Track:	LH: 0-0 RH: 0-0 Tight: 0-0 Gall: 0-2
Aids:	Bl: 0-0 Vi: 0-0 Tstrap: 0-0 Ckp: 0-0

Midnight Spirit
71f   **62f**

4-y-o b g Midnight Legend-West-Hatch-Spirit (Forzando)
S C Burrough   Mrs P M Underhill

Placings:00   **(4636)**
2003/04: 14⁰GS, 17⁰G,

	Starts	1st	2nd	3rd	Win & Pl
NH Flat	2	0	0	0	
Career Total	2	0	0	0	

Going:	Sf: 0-0 GS: 0-1 Gd: 0-1 GF: - Fm: 0-0
Distance:	2m/2m3: 0-1 2m4-2m7: 0-0 3m+: 0-0
Track:	LH: 0-0 RH: 0-0 Tight: 0-0 Gall: 0-0
Aids:	Bl: 0-0 Vi: 0-0 Tstrap: 0-0 Ckp: 0-0
Best Rating:	62 4/04 Tntn 2m1f good NHF

Midnight Tango

7-y-o ch m Milieu-Whistle Binkie (Slim Jim)
Mrs H O Graham   R D Graham

Placings:00P-0P   **(1491)**
2003/04: 17⁰G, 16^PGF,

	Starts	1st	2nd	3rd	Win & Pl
Hurdles	2	0	0	0	

Career Total   5   0   0   0

Going:	Sf: 0-0 GS: 0-0 Gd: 0-1 GF: - Fm: 0-1
Distance:	2m/2m3: 0-2 2m4-2m7: 0-0 3m+: 0-0
Track:	LH: 0-2 RH: 0-0 Tight: 0-1 Gall: 0-0
Aids:	Bl: 0-0 Vi: 0-0 Tstrap: 0-0 Ckp: 0-1
Best Rating:	21 9/02 Hexm 2m110y gd-fm NHF

Midy's Risk (FR)

7-y-o gr g Take Risks (FR)-Martine Midy (FR) (Lashkari)
Miss S J Davies   John D N Siviter

Placings:00/235134/442464-P   **(4510)**
2003/04: 19^PGS,

	Starts	1st	2nd	3rd	Win & Pl
Chases	1	0	0	0	
Career Total	15	1	2	2	9113
113 2/02 Plum 2m	E Hdl		HVY	£2761	
			Total win prize-money £2762		

Going:	Sf: 0-0 GS: 0-1 Gd: 0-0 GF: - Fm: 0-0
Distance:	2m/2m3: 0-1 2m4-2m7: 0-0 3m+: 0-0
Track:	LH: 0-0 RH: 0-1 Tight: 0-0 Gall: 0-0
Aids:	Bl: 0-0 Vi: 0-0 Tstrap: 0-0 Ckp: 0-0
Best Rating:	113 2/02 Plum 2m heavy Hdl

Mighty Fine
101(109h)   (94+h)**107**

10-y-o gr g Arzanni-Kate Kimberley (Sparkler)
Mrs E Slack   A Slack

Placings:0/2S40/0/0/304321U1U13-3201   **(1656)**
2003/04: 16³GF, 17²S, 21⁹G, 21¹G,

	Starts	1st	2nd	3rd	Win & Pl
Hurdles	2	1	1	0	4088
Chases	2	0	0	1	872
Career Total	22	4	3	4	19283
94 10/03 Sedg	2m5f110yE(0-110)HHdl		GD	£2898	
108 3/03 Sedg	2m5f	F(0-95)HCh	GD	£3386	
101 12/02 Sedg	2m110y	E(0-105)HCh	SFT	£4056	
87 11/02 Sedg	2m110y	F(0-100)HCh	SFT	£3386	
			Total win prize-money £13728		

Going:	Sf: 0-1 GS: 0-0 Gd: 1-2 GF: - Fm: 0-1
Distance:	2m/2m3: 0-2 2m4-2m7: 1-2 3m+: 0-0
Track:	LH: 1-4 RH: 0-0 Tight: 1-3 Gall: 0-0
Aids:	Bl: 0-0 Vi: 0-0 Tstrap: 0-0 Ckp: 0-0
Best Rating:	108 5/03 Weth 2m gd-fm Ch

Lightly-raced modest chaser/hurdler; goes well at Sedgefield winning four times there in 2002/2003; stays two miles five; handles any ground.

Mighty Glen (IRE)
75   **52**

6-y-o gr g Roselier (FR)-Supreme Glen (IRE) (Supreme Leader)
A W Carroll   T J Plant & Lifting Services Ltd

Placings:PP00   **(4819)**
2003/04: 22^PG, 19^PS, 19⁰G, 22⁰GF,

	Starts	1st	2nd	3rd	Win & Pl
Hurdles	4	0	0	0	
Career Total	4	0	0	0	

Going:	Sf: 0-1 GS: 0-0 Gd: 0-2 GF: - Fm: 0-1
Distance:	2m/2m3: 0-1 2m4-2m7: 0-3 3m+: 0-0
Track:	LH: 0-2 RH: 0-2 Tight: 0-1 Gall: 0-0

Aids:	Bl: 0-0 Vi: 0-0 Tstrap: 0-0 Ckp: 0-0
Best Rating:	52 4/04 Extr 2m6f110y gd-fm Hdl

Mighty Kilcash (IRE)
98(97h)   (94h)**97**

11-y-o ch g Black Minstrel-Any Wonder (Hard Boy)
Jonjo O'Neill   Mrs M C Sweeney

Placings:0/010/52131/3-6PF   **(3705)**
2003/04: 30⁶GS, 28^PG, 26^FHY,

	Starts	1st	2nd	3rd	Win & Pl
Chases	3	0	0	0	
Career Total	13	3	1	2	16351
114 2/01 Uttx	3m2f	D Ch	SFT	£4014	
120 1/01 Donc	3m	D(0-115)HCh	GD	£4225	
112 2/99 Thur	2m	NHF	HVY	£2455	
			Total win prize-money £10695		

Going:	Sf: 0-1 GS: 0-1 Gd: 0-1 GF: - Fm: 0-0
Distance:	2m/2m3: 0-0 2m4-2m7: 0-0 3m+: 0-3
Track:	LH: 0-2 RH: 0-0 Tight: 0-1 Gall: 0-0
Aids:	Bl: 0-0 Vi: 0-0 Tstrap: 0-0 Ckp: 0-0
Best Rating:	120 1/01 Donc 3m good Ch

Modest handicap chaser; jumps soundly; effective in soft ground; stays 3m 2f.

Mighty Man (IRE)

9-y-o b g Mandalus-Mossy Mistress (IRE) (Le Moss)
O Brennan   Lady Anne Bentinck

Placings:0/PP/P-P   **(4512)**
2003/04: 20^PGS,

	Starts	1st	2nd	3rd	Win & Pl
Hurdles	1	0	0	0	
Career Total	5	0	0	0	

Going:	Sf: 0-0 GS: 0-1 Gd: 0-0 GF: - Fm: 0-0
Distance:	2m/2m3: 0-0 2m4-2m7: 0-1 3m+: 0-0
Track:	LH: 0-1 RH: 0-0 Tight: 0-0 Gall: 0-0
Aids:	Bl: 0-0 Vi: 0-0 Tstrap: 0-0 Ckp: 0-0

Mighty Max
80   **71**

6-y-o b g Well Beloved-Jokers High (USA) (Vaguely Noble)
G A Ham   Max Pro Bets

Placings:0P6-00   **(3440)**
2003/04: 16⁰GF, 16⁰G,

	Starts	1st	2nd	3rd	Win & Pl
Hurdles	2	0	0	0	
Career Total	5	0	0	0	0

Going:	Sf: 0-0 GS: 0-0 Gd: 0-1 GF: - Fm: 0-1
Distance:	2m/2m3: 0-2 2m4-2m7: 0-0 3m+: 0-0
Track:	LH: 0-1 RH: 0-1 Tight: 0-0 Gall: 0-0
Aids:	Bl: 0-0 Vi: 0-0 Tstrap: 0-2 Ckp: 0-0
Best Rating:	78 11/02 Tntn 2m1f gd-sft Hdl

Plating-class hurdler; well beaten over hurdles so far; has worn tongue tie.

Mighty Minster
                 82

7-y-o ch m Minster Son-Mighty Fly (Comedy Star (USA))

A E Jones (R C Guest 21/5) John Spence

Placings:*4455440*-FPPPP   (1272)
2003/04: 20⁶G, 20⁸G, 17⁸GF, 17⁸GF, 22⁸GF,

	Starts	1st	2nd	3rd	Win & Pl
Hurdles	5	0	0	0	
Career Total	12	0	0	0	534

Going:	Sf: 0-0 GS: 0-0 Gd: 0-2 GF: - Fm: 0-3
Distance:	2m/2m3: 0-2 2m4-2m7: 0-3 3m+: 0-0
Track:	LH: 0-4 RH: 0-1 Tight: 0-3 Gall: 0-3
Aids:	Bl: 0-0 Vi: 0-0 Tstrap: 0-0 Ckp: 0-3
Best Rating:	83 1/03 Newc 2m heavy Hdl

Mighty Montefalco
105(106h)   (116h)125
8-y-o b g Mtoto-Glendera (Glenstal (USA))
Jonjo O'Neill   Mr & Mrs Peter S Thompson

Placings:*3661/211114*-3540P   (2694)
2003/04: 23³GF, 24⁵G, 20⁴GF, 22⁶S, 31³G,

	Starts	1st	2nd	3rd	Win & Pl
Hurdles	2	0	0	0	0
Chases	3	0	0	1	1285
Career Total	15	5	1	2	31776
121 10/02 Chel	3m110y C Ch			GD	£9858
120 10/02 Strf	3m	D Ch		GD	£6041
116 8/02 Uttx	3m110y G(0-110)HHdl		G-F	£3465
113 8/02 Strf	2m6f110yD Hdl		G-S	£4777
116 4/02 Strf	2m6f110yE Hdl		GD	£3230

Total win prize-money £27373

Going:	Sf: 0-1 GS: 0-0 Gd: 0-2 GF: - Fm: 0-2
Distance:	2m/2m3: 0-0 2m4-2m7: 0-3 3m+: 0-3
Track:	LH: 0-3 RH: 0-1 Tight: 0-1 Gall: 0-1
Aids:	Bl: 0-0 Vi: 0-0 Tstrap: 0-2 Ckp: 0-0
Best Rating:	125 9/03 Worc 2m7f110y gd-fm Ch

Fair hurdler; useful chaser; stays three miles; acts on most types of ground.

Mighty Pip (IRE)
98   81
8-y-o b g Pips Pride-Hard To Stop (Hard Fought)
M R Bosley   Mrs Jean M O'Connor

Placings:00/04200/60/330   (0880)
2003/04: 16³GD, 16⁵G, 16⁶GF,

	Starts	1st	2nd	3rd	Win & Pl
Hurdles	3	0	0	2	732
Career Total	12	0	1	2	1993

Going:	Sf: 0-0 GS: 0-0 Gd: 0-1 GF: - Fm: 0-2
Distance:	2m/2m3: 0-3 2m4-2m7: 0-0 3m+: 0-0
Track:	LH: 0-1 RH: 0-2 Tight: 0-0 Gall: 0-2
Aids:	Bl: 0-0 Vi: 0-0 Tstrap: 0-0 Ckp: 0-0
Best Rating:	89 8/00 Slig 2m gd-yld Hdl

Mighty Strong
110   142
10-y-o b g Strong Gale-Muffet's Spider (Rymer)
N J Henderson   Exors of the Late J R Henderson

Placings:44/510/PP102/F21FF43P-6111P0P   (4953)
2003/04: 20⁶G, 20¹GF, 22¹GS, 22¹GF, 24⁴G, 20⁰G, 20⁰G,

	Starts	1st	2nd	3rd	Win & Pl
Chases	7	3	0	0	25116
Career Total	25	6	2	1	48064
142 12/03 Newb	2m6f110yC(0-130)HCh		G-F	£8385

---

135 11/03 Newb   2m6f110yC(0-130)HCh   G-S   £9613
127 11/03 Newb   2m4f   D(0-125)HCh   G-F   £7117
120 10/02 Sthl   2m5f110yD(0-120)HCh   GD   £6776
111 1/02 Newb   2m1f   D(0-120)HCh   GD   £5590
108 12/00 Donc   2m110y D Ch   HVY   £3867

Total win prize-money £41350

Going:	Sf: 0-0 GS: 1-1 Gd: 0-4 GF: - Fm: 2-2
Distance:	2m/2m3: 0-0 2m4-2m7: 3-6 3m+: 0-1
Track:	LH: 3-4 RH: 0-2 Tight: 0-1 Gall: 3-4
Aids:	Bl: 0-0 Vi: 0-0 Tstrap: 0-0 Ckp: 0-0
Best Rating:	142 12/03 Newb 2m6f110y gd-fm Ch

Useful chaser; effective at up to 2m 6f; acts on any ground; has had his problems, but completed a hat-trick at Newbury in autumn 2003 in good style; held in better company since.

Mighty Willing
7-y-o br g Bollin William-Wild Ling (Mufrij)
Mrs M R Sowersby   Paul Clifton

Placings:24   (4373)
2003/04: 24²S, 24⁴G,

	Starts	1st	2nd	3rd	Win & Pl
Chases	2	0	1	0	709
Career Total	2	0	1	0	709

Going:	Sf: 0-1 GS: 0-0 Gd: 0-1 GF: - Fm: 0-0
Distance:	2m/2m3: 0-0 2m4-2m7: 0-0 3m+: 0-0
Track:	LH: 0-1 RH: 0-1 Tight: 0-1 Gall: 0-1
Aids:	Bl: 0-0 Vi: 0-0 Tstrap: 0-0 Ckp: 0-0
Best Rating:	89 3/04 Strf 3m good Ch

Winning pointer; acts on soft ground.

Migsy Malone
65   21
9-y-o b m Afzal-The Dizzy Mole (IRE) (Salluceva)
Mrs A M Thorpe   R Jukes

Placings:0   (0485)
2003/04: 22⁰GF,

	Starts	1st	2nd	3rd	Win & Pl
Hurdles	1	0	0	0	
Career Total	1	0	0	0	

Going:	Sf: 0-0 GS: 0-0 Gd: 0-0 GF: - Fm: 0-1
Distance:	2m/2m3: 0-0 2m4-2m7: 0-1 3m+: 0-0
Track:	LH: 0-1 RH: 0-0 Tight: 0-1 Gall: 0-0
Aids:	Bl: 0-0 Vi: 0-0 Tstrap: 0-0 Ckp: 0-0
Best Rating:	25 5/03 NAbb 2m6f gd-fm Hdl

Migwell (FR)
95   96
4-y-o b g Assessor (IRE)-Uguette lv (FR) (Chamberlin (FR))
D J Wintle (G Cherel 5/11) DGM Partnership

Placings:3404F   (4166)
2003/04: 18³VS, 16⁴VS, 16⁶GS, 16⁴S, 16⁶G,

	Starts	1st	2nd	3rd	Win & Pl
Hurdles	5	0	0	1	7249
Career Total	5	0	0	1	7249

Going:	Sf: 0-1 GS: 0-1 Gd: 0-1 GF: - Fm: 0-0
Distance:	2m/2m3: 0-5 2m4-2m7: 0-0 3m+: 0-0
Track:	LH: 0-3 RH: 0-1 Tight: 0-0 Gall: 0-2
Aids:	Bl: 0-0 Vi: 0-0 Tstrap: 0-0 Ckp: 0-0
Best Rating:	96 1/04 Newb 2m110y soft Hdl

In the frame over hurdles in France and Britain; acts in soft ground.

Mijico (IRE)
81+
8-y-o b g Lord Americo-Mijette (Pauper)
Ferdy Murphy   Mrs R D Cairns

Placings:265/FP   (4215)
2003/04: 24⁵S, 25⁵GS,

	Starts	1st	2nd	3rd	Win & Pl
Chases	2	0	0	0	
Career Total	5	0	1	0	460

Going:	Sf: 0-1 GS: 0-1 Gd: 0-0 GF: - Fm: 0-0
Distance:	2m/2m3: 0-0 2m4-2m7: 0-0 3m+: 0-2
Track:	LH: 0-0 RH: 0-2 Tight: 0-1 Gall: 0-1
Aids:	Bl: 0-0 Vi: 0-0 Tstrap: 0-0 Ckp: 0-0
Best Rating:	112 11/01 Carl 2m1f soft NHF

Mikasa (IRE)
59
4-y-o b g Victory Note (USA)-Resiusa (ITY) (Niniski (USA))
R F Fisher   Great Head House Estates Limited

Placings:0   (3337)
2003/04: 16⁰GS,

	Starts	1st	2nd	3rd	Win & Pl
Hurdles	1	0	0	0	
Career Total	1	0	0	0	

Going:	Sf: 0-0 GS: 0-1 Gd: 0-0 GF: - Fm: 0-0
Distance:	2m/2m3: 0-1 2m4-2m7: 0-0 3m+: 0-0
Track:	LH: 0-1 RH: 0-0 Tight: 0-1 Gall: 0-0
Aids:	Bl: 0-0 Vi: 0-0 Tstrap: 0-0 Ckp: 0-0

Mike Simmons
99   77
8-y-o b g Ballacashtal (CAN)-Lady Crusty (Golden Dipper)
L P Grassick   L P Grassick

Placings:0014/033531/006/P34P0-4506000   (4873)
2003/04: 24⁴GF, 26⁵GF, 24⁰GF, 22⁶GF, 22⁰G, 22⁰G, 20⁰GS,

	Starts	1st	2nd	3rd	Win & Pl
Hurdles	7	0	0	0	0
Career Total	25	2	0	4	8172
104 4/01 Font	2m4f	F(0-100)HHdl	GD	£2761
83 2/00 Tntn	2m1f	E Hdl	SFT	£2472

Total win prize-money £5234

Going:	Sf: 0-0 GS: 0-1 Gd: 0-2 GF: - Fm: 0-4
Distance:	2m/2m3: 0-0 2m4-2m7: 0-4 3m+: 0-3
Track:	LH: 0-6 RH: 0-0 Tight: 0-3 Gall: 0-0
Aids:	Bl: 0-0 Vi: 0-0 Tstrap: 0-0 Ckp: 0-0
Best Rating:	104 4/01 Font 2m4f good Hdl

Moderate handicap hurdler; best at around 2m 4f; has won on good and soft ground.

Mike Stan (IRE)
95   106
13-y-o b g Rontino-Fair Pirouette (Fair Turn)
L Lungo   J M Crichton

Placings:540/14110U2/4223111/62F11/33F0/P/P-2   (0314)
2003/04: 21²S,

	Starts	1st	2nd	3rd	Win & Pl
Chases	1	0	1	0	1354
Career Total	**29**	**8**	**5**	**3**	**59827**
139 4/00 Carl 3m2f	D(0-125)HCh	SFT	£4426
124 2/00 Muss 2m4f	D(0-120)HCh	G-S	£4891
143 4/99 Ayr 3m1f	C HCh	SFT	£25532
122 3/99 Ayr 3m1f	D Ch	SFT	£4570
128 2/99 Muss 3m	E(0-105)HCh	FRM	£3192
116 1/98 Ayr 2m4f	D Hdl	G-S	£3345
107 12/97 Uttx 3m110y	E(0-100)HHdl	G-S	£2515
96 11/97 Carl	2m4f110yE(0-100)HHdl	FRM	£2388
	Total win prize-money £50863		

Going:	Sf: 0-1 GS: 0-0 Gd: 0-0 GF: - Fm: 0-0
Distance:	2m/2m3: 0-0 2m4-2m7: 0-1 3m+: 0-0
Track:	LH: 0-1 RH: 0-0 Tight: 0-1 Gall: 0-0
Aids:	Bl: 0-0 Vi: 0-0 Tstrap: 0-0 Ckp: 0-0
Best Rating:	143 4/99 Ayr 3m1f soft Ch

Modest chaser; best effort for some time when runner-up at Sedgefield in May 2003.

Milan King (IRE)

102 (90c)79+

11-y-o b g King's Ride-Milan Moss (Le Moss)
A J Lockwood Chester Bosomworth

Placings:5P00F00Q/P040F05F/041051P6P2/20110000/030
P40/50P5303P06P0U-441PPF   (2376)
2003/04: 16⁴G, 19⁴G, 17¹GF, 17⁶GF, 16⁹GF, 17⁸GF,

	Starts	1st	2nd	3rd	Win & Pl
Hurdles	6	1	0	0	2408
Career Total	**59**	**5**	**2**	**3**	**11788**
79 7/03 Sedg 2m1f	G(0-90)HHdl	G-F	£2408
101 9/00 Sedg 2m1f	F(0-105)HHdl	GD	£1855
101 7/00 Sedg 2m1f	F(0-105)HHdl	G-F	£1918
83 2/00 Sedg 2m1f	G-S	£1991
77 12/99 MRas	2m1f110y(0-95)HHdl	GD	£1584
	Total win prize-money £9758		

Going:	Sf: 0-0 GS: 0-0 Gd: 0-0 GF: - Fm: 1-4
Distance:	2m/2m3: 1-5 2m4-2m7: 0-1 3m+: 0-0
Track:	LH: 1-5 RH: 0-1 Tight: 1-4 Gall: 0-0
Aids:	Bl: 0-0 Vi: 0-0 Tstrap: 0-0 Ckp: 0-0
Best Rating:	101 9/00 Sedg 2m1f good Hdl

Selling handicap hurdler; scored three times over the extended two miles at Sedgefield in 2000; returned to form when winning there again in July 2003; acts on fast and heavy; has broken blood vessels.

Milbrig

84   45

8-y-o b m Milieu-Meadow Brig (Meadowbrook)
A C Whillans Mrs Anne Taylor

Placings:P0P-4P   (0264)
2003/04: 22⁴G, 24⁵PG,

	Starts	1st	2nd	3rd	Win & Pl
Hurdles	2	0	0	0	268
Career Total	**5**	**0**	**0**	**0**	**268**

Going:	Sf: 0-0 GS: 0-0 Gd: 0-2 GF: - Fm: 0-0
Distance:	2m/2m3: 0-0 2m4-2m7: 0-1 3m+: 0-1
Track:	LH: 0-1 RH: 0-1 Tight: 0-1 Gall: 0-0
Aids:	Bl: 0-0 Vi: 0-0 Tstrap: 0-0 Ckp: 0-0
Best Rating:	53 5/03 Kels 2m6f110y good Hdl

Mildon (IRE)

107   79

8-y-o ch g Dolphin Street (FR)-Lycia (Targowice (USA))

J R Weymes Don Raper

Placings:050/0P/66-2   (1279)
2003/04: 17²GF,

	Starts	1st	2nd	3rd	Win & Pl
Hurdles	1	0	1	0	528
Career Total	**8**	**0**	**1**	**0**	**528**

Going:	Sf: 0-0 GS: 0-0 Gd: 0-0 GF: - Fm: 0-1
Distance:	2m/2m3: 0-1 2m4-2m7: 0-0 3m+: 0-0
Track:	LH: 0-1 RH: 0-0 Tight: 0-1 Gall: 0-0
Aids:	Bl: 0-0 Vi: 0-0 Tstrap: 0-0 Ckp: 0-0
Best Rating:	79 9/03 Sedg 2m1f gd-fm Hdl

Plating-class hurdler; suited to an easy surface; effective over two miles.

Militaire (FR)

6-y-o ch g Bering-Moon Review (USA) (Irish River (FR))
J M Turner J M Turner

Placings:3526/05251PP-3   (4779)
2003/04: 24³S,

	Starts	1st	2nd	3rd	Win & Pl
Chases	1	0	0	1	512
Career Total	**12**	**1**	**2**	**2**	**19746**
110 2/03 Weth 2m	C(0-135)HHdl	G-S	£6942
	Total win prize-money £6942		

Going:	Sf: 0-1 GS: 0-0 Gd: 0-0 GF: - Fm: 0-0
Distance:	2m/2m3: 0-0 2m4-2m7: 0-0 3m+: 0-1
Track:	LH: 0-1 RH: 0-0 Tight: 0-1 Gall: 0-0
Aids:	Bl: 0-0 Vi: 0-0 Tstrap: 0-0 Ckp: 0-0
Best Rating:	110 2/03 Weth 2m gd-sft Hdl

Modest hurdler; effective from two to two and a half miles; best with cut in the ground

Mill Emerald

101 (64c)   (70c)106

7-y-o b m Old Vic-Milinetta (Milford)
Mrs G Harvey (Mrs M Reveley 26/5) The Mill Emerald Partnership

Placings:04001503/113434-414P00P0   (4441)
2003/04: 22⁴G, 20¹HY, 20⁴GF, 20²GS, 20⁹S, 22⁰GS, 24⁰GS, 21⁰S,

	Starts	1st	2nd	3rd	Win & Pl
Hurdles	8	1	0	0	9862
Career Total	**22**	**4**	**0**	**3**	**26560**
106 5/03 Uttx	2m4f110yG(0-100)HHdl	HVY	£9135
108 6/02 Uttx	2m4f110yG(0-100)HHdl	GD	£10582
105 5/02 Weth	2m4f110yF Hdl	GD	£1995
79 1/02 Newc 2m4f	G(0-95)HHdl	SFT	£1932
	Total win prize-money £23644		

Going:	Sf: 1-3 GS: 0-3 Gd: 0-1 GF: - Fm: 0-1
Distance:	2m/2m3: 0-0 2m4-2m7: 1-7 3m+: 0-1
Track:	LH: 1-5 RH: 0-3 Tight: 0-3 Gall: 0-0
Aids:	Bl: 0-2 Vi: 0-0 Tstrap: 0-0 Ckp: 0-1
Best Rating:	108 6/02 Uttx 2m4f110y good Hdl

Selling hurdler; changed hands for 6,400gns after winning valuable 2m 4f seller at Uttoxeter for the second year in succession; acts on ground good and softer.

Mill Lord (IRE)

92   56

11-y-o b g Aristocracy-Millflower (Millfontaine)
C J Drewe W P Long

Placings:000/04/05PFPP/P3434500P/3P450PP53-06
                                                     (0435)

2003/04: 19⁰G, 18⁶GF,

	Starts	1st	2nd	3rd	Win & Pl
Chases	2	0	0	0	0
Career Total	**31**	**0**	**0**	**4**	**2384**

Going:	Sf: 0-0 GS: 0-0 Gd: 0-1 GF: - Fm: 0-1
Distance:	2m/2m3: 0-1 2m4-2m7: 0-1 3m+: 0-0
Track:	LH: 0-0 RH: 0-1 Tight: 0-1 Gall: 0-0
Aids:	Bl: 0-0 Vi: 0-0 Tstrap: 0-0 Ckp: 0-0
Best Rating:	76 11/01 Extr 2m3f110y gd-fm Ch

Poor chaser; yet to win a race of any description; effective at two miles; suited by a sound surface; has worn blinkers.

Mill Tower

87   74

7-y-o b g Milieu-Tringa (GER) (Kaiseradler)
R Nixon G R S Nixon

Placings:0/0PPP   (4908)
2003/04: 16⁵GF, 20⁵S, 24⁵F, 20⁸S,

	Starts	1st	2nd	3rd	Win & Pl
Hurdles	4	0	0	0	0
Career Total	**5**	**0**	**0**	**0**	**0**

Going:	Sf: 0-3 GS: 0-0 Gd: 0-0 GF: - Fm: 0-1
Distance:	2m/2m3: 0-1 2m4-2m7: 0-2 3m+: 0-1
Track:	LH: 0-2 RH: 0-2 Tight: 0-1 Gall: 0-0
Aids:	Bl: 0-0 Vi: 0-0 Tstrap: 0-0 Ckp: 0-0
Best Rating:	73 6/03 Prth 2m110y gd-fm Hdl

Millcroft Seascape (IRE)

81f   89f

5-y-o b g Good Thyne (USA)-Dante's Ville (IRE) (Phardante (FR))
C J Down John Carter

Placings:040   (4543)
2003/04: 16⁹GS, 16⁴GS, 16⁹GS,

	Starts	1st	2nd	3rd	Win & Pl
NH Flat	3	0	0	0	0
Career Total	**3**	**0**	**0**	**0**	**0**

Going:	Sf: 0-0 GS: 0-2 Gd: 0-1 GF: - Fm: 0-0
Distance:	2m/2m3: 0-3 2m4-2m7: 0-0 3m+: 0-0
Track:	LH: 0-0 RH: 0-3 Tight: 0-0 Gall: 0-0
Aids:	Bl: 0-0 Vi: 0-0 Tstrap: 0-0 Ckp: 0-0
Best Rating:	89 2/04 Asct 2m110y good NHF

Millcroft Seaspray (IRE)

101 (104h)   (118h)121

8-y-o br g Good Thyne (USA)-Bucks Gift (IRE) (Buckley)
C J Down (R H Alner 21/11) John Carter

Placings:40/3122/233-3PPP4PU   (4672)
2003/04: 23³G, 23⁶G, 23⁵S, 24⁶F, 24⁴GS, 24⁰G, 25¹UG,

	Starts	1st	2nd	3rd	Win & Pl
Chases	7	0	0	1	1262
Career Total	**16**	**1**	**3**	**4**	**10462**
110 1/02 Tntn	3m110y D Hdl	SFT	£4139
	Total win prize-money £4139		

Going:	Sf: 0-1 GS: 0-1 Gd: 0-5 GF: - Fm: 0-0
Distance:	2m/2m3: 0-0 2m4-2m7: 0-3 3m+: 0-7
Track:	LH: 0-0 RH: 0-7 Tight: 0-3 Gall: 0-0

Aids: Bl: 0-3 Vi: 0-0 Tstrap: 0-4 Ckp: 0-0
Best Rating: 121 11/03 Extr 2m7f110y good Ch

Fair chaser; has had his problems; stays three miles; responded well to first-time blinkers.

Mille Et Une Nuits (FR)

73f   67f

5-y-o b m Ecologist-Migre (FR) (Le Gregol (FR))
Miss K Marks Nick Shutts

Placings:6-0   (0309)
2003/04: 17⁰G,

	Starts	1st	2nd	3rd	Win & Pl
NH Flat	1	0	0	0	
Career Total	2	0	0	0	0

Going: Sf: 0-0 GS: 0-0 Gd: 0-1 GF: - Fm: 0-0
Distance: 2m/2m3: 0-1 2m4-2m7: 0-0 3m+: 0-0
Track: LH: 0-1 RH: 0-0 Tight: 0-1 Gall: 0-0
Aids: Bl: 0-0 Vi: 0-0 Tstrap: 0-0 Ckp: 0-0
Best Rating: 67 4/03 Extr 2m1f gd-fm NHF

Millenaire (FR)

110f   117+f

5-y-o b/br g Mister Mat (FR)-Mille Perles (FR) (Kashtan (FR))
Jonjo O'Neill The Risky Partnership

Placings:10   (4400)
2003/04: 16¹HY, 16⁹G,

	Starts	1st	2nd	3rd	Win & Pl
NH Flat	2	1	0	0	2051
Career Total	2	1	0	0	2051
117 1/04 Hayd 2m		H NHF		HVY	£2051
			Total win prize-money £2051

Going: Sf: 1-1 GS: 0-0 Gd: 0-1 GF: - Fm: 0-0
Distance: 2m/2m3: 1-2 2m4-2m7: 0-0 3m+: 0-0
Track: LH: 1-2 RH: 0-0 Tight: 0-0 Gall: 0-0
Aids: Bl: 0-0 Vi: 0-0 Tstrap: 0-0 Ckp: 0-0
Best Rating: 117 1/04 Hayd 2m heavy NHF

Fair bumper performer; acts on heavy.

Millenium Way (IRE)

10-y-o ch g Ikdam-Fine Drapes (Le Bavard (FR))
J M Turner J M Turner

Placings:2242330/33P33/PP/4-24   (0353)
2003/04: 24²GF, 21⁴GF,

	Starts	1st	2nd	3rd	Win & Pl
Chases	2	0	1	0	733
Career Total	17	0	4	6	7515

Going: Sf: 0-0 GS: 0-0 Gd: 0-0 GF: - Fm: 0-2
Distance: 2m/2m3: 0-2 2m4-2m7: 0-1 3m+: 0-1
Track: LH: 0-1 RH: 0-1 Tight: 0-2 Gall: 0-0
Aids: Bl: 0-0 Vi: 0-0 Tstrap: 0-0 Ckp: 0-0
Best Rating: 106 1/00 Folk 2m6f110y heavy Hdl

Millennium Gold

9-y-o ch g Be My Chief (USA)-Forbearance (Baim (USA))
M Frieze (B J Llewellyn 14/9) M Frieze

Placings:/0060000/0030/3-33233265   (4891)
2003/04: 22³GF, 21³G, 26²GF, 24³G, 26³GF, 26²GF, 20⁶F, 24⁵GF,

	Starts	1st	2nd	3rd	Win & Pl
Chases	8	0	2	4	5430
Career Total	20	0	2	6	6134

Going: Sf: 0-0 GS: 0-0 Gd: 0-2 GF: - Fm: 0-6
Distance: 2m/2m3: 0-0 2m4-2m7: 0-3 3m+: 0-5
Track: LH: 0-6 RH: 0-1 Tight: 0-5 Gall: 0-0
Aids: Bl: 0-0 Vi: 0-0 Tstrap: 0-0 Ckp: 0-0
Best Rating: 92 9/01 Tral 2m4f good Hdl

Plating-class chaser; winning pointer; consistently placed, but still a maiden under rules; stays well; acts on fast ground.

Millers Mead

79f   71f

6-y-o b g Sir Harry Lewis (USA)-Childhay Millie (Idiots Delight)
P F Nicholls Ridge Racing

Placings:0   (0372)
2003/04: 16⁹G,

	Starts	1st	2nd	3rd	Win & Pl
NH Flat	1	0	0	0	
Career Total	1	0	0	0	

Going: Sf: 0-0 GS: 0-0 Gd: 0-1 GF: - Fm: 0-0
Distance: 2m/2m3: 0-1 2m4-2m7: 0-0 3m+: 0-0
Track: LH: 0-1 RH: 0-0 Tight: 0-0 Gall: 0-0
Aids: Bl: 0-0 Vi: 0-0 Tstrap: 0-0 Ckp: 0-0
Best Rating: 76 5/03 Worc 2m good NHF

Millers Way

(65h)   (18h)

6-y-o b m Nomadic Way (USA)-Keldholme (Derek H)
A Crook Minster Commercials

Placings:060P-0   (3757)
2003/04: 20⁰G,

	Starts	1st	2nd	3rd	Win & Pl
Chases	1	0	0	0	
Career Total	5	0	0	0	0

Going: Sf: 0-0 GS: 0-0 Gd: 0-1 GF: - Fm: 0-0
Distance: 2m/2m3: 0-0 2m4-2m7: 0-1 3m+: 0-0
Track: LH: 0-0 RH: 0-1 Tight: 0-1 Gall: 0-0
Aids: Bl: 0-0 Vi: 0-0 Tstrap: 0-0 Ckp: 0-0
Best Rating: 88 11/02 Weth 2m gd-sft NHF

Millersford

90(107c)   (98c)95

13-y-o b g Meadowbrook-My Seer (Menelek)
N A Gaselee Mrs Derek Fletcher

Placings:/0240/14552/33235U/3531F2345/PF503/611P4P3/20605/12P523PP-6510   (0756)
2003/04: 19⁶G, 22⁵GF, 24¹S, 22⁰GF,

	Starts	1st	2nd	3rd	Win & Pl
Hurdles	3	1	0	0	3500
Chases	1	0	0	0	
Career Total	53	6	7	9	34147
95 5/03 Uttx	3m110y	F(0-100)HHdl		SFT	£3500
101 5/02 Towc	2m4f	F(0-90)Ch		GD	£2800
109 6/00 Uttx	3m	D(0-120)HCh		G-F	£4176
109 5/00 Towc	2m6f	F(0-90)Ch		SFT	£2415

---

104 11/98 Wind	3m	E Ch	G-S	£3549
101 11/96 Kemp	2m5f	E Hdl	GD	£2360
			Total win prize-money £18801

Going: Sf: 1-1 GS: 0-0 Gd: 0-1 GF: - Fm: 0-2
Distance: 2m/2m3: 0-0 2m4-2m7: 0-3 3m+: 1-1
Track: LH: 1-2 RH: 0-2 Tight: 0-1 Gall: 0-0
Aids: Bl: 0-0 Vi: 0-0 Tstrap: 0-0 Ckp: 0-0
Best Rating: 115 3/97 Sand 2m6f good Hdl

Modest chaser these days; landed three-mile handicap hurdle in bad ground at Uttoxeter in May, first success over hurdles for over six years.

Milliesome

79   74

6-y-o b m Milieu-Some Shiela (Remainder Man)
J P Dodds R H T Barber

Placings:00-205   (4292)
2003/04: 16⁹G, 16²GF, 16⁹G, 16⁵GF,

	Starts	1st	2nd	3rd	Win & Pl
NH Flat	3	0	1	0	532
Hurdles	1	0	0	0	
Career Total	5	0	1	0	532

Going: Sf: 0-0 GS: 0-0 Gd: 0-2 GF: - Fm: 0-2
Distance: 2m/2m3: 0-4 2m4-2m7: 0-0 3m+: 0-0
Track: LH: 0-3 RH: 0-1 Tight: 0-1 Gall: 0-0
Aids: Bl: 0-0 Vi: 0-0 Tstrap: 0-0 Ckp: 0-0
Best Rating: 90 6/03 Hexm 2m110y gd-fm NHF

Milligan (FR)

88   146d

9-y-o b g Exit To Nowhere (USA)-Madigan Mill (Mill Reef (USA))
R A Fahey G H Leatham

Placings:01/3103360/12044031/0450-4   (2179)
2003/04: 20⁴G,

	Starts	1st	2nd	3rd	Win & Pl
Hurdles	1	0	0	0	1054
Career Total	22	4	1	4	85804
146 4/02 Ayr	2m	A HHdl	GD	£15600
156 5/01 Hayd	2m	A HHdl	GD	£27000
133 10/00 Weth	2m	C(0-135)HHdl	G-S	£4888
119 3/00 Catt	2m	E Hdl	G-F	£3152
			Total win prize-money £50641

Going: Sf: 0-0 GS: 0-0 Gd: 0-1 GF: - Fm: 0-0
Distance: 2m/2m3: 0-0 2m4-2m7: 0-1 3m+: 0-0
Track: LH: 0-1 RH: 0-0 Tight: 0-0 Gall: 0-0
Aids: Bl: 0-0 Vi: 0-0 Tstrap: 0-0 Ckp: 0-0
Best Rating: 156 12/01 Kemp 2m good Hdl

Very useful handicap hurdler who landed the Scottish Champion Hurdle in April 2002; suited by two miles, decent ground and a flat track; jumps soundly.

Millkom Elegance

101   88

5-y-o b m Millkom-Premier Princess (Hard Fought)
K A Ryan Yorkshire Racing Club Iv

Placings:0-022100   (2526)
2003/04: 16⁸GF, 17²GF, 16²GF, 17¹G, 16⁹G, 16⁰GS,

	Starts	1st	2nd	3rd	Win & Pl
Hurdles	6	1	2	0	3230
Career Total	7	1	2	0	3230
89 10/03 Sedg	2m1f	G(0-90)HHdl	GD	£1883
			Total win prize-money £1883

Going: Sf: 0-0 GS: 0-1 Gd: 1-2 GF: - Fm: 0-3
Distance: 2m/2m3: 1-6 2m4-2m7: 0-0 3m+: 0-0
Track: LH: 1-5 RH: 0-1 Tight: 1-3 Gall: 0-0
Aids: Bl: 1-3 Vi: 0-0 Tstrap: 0-0 Ckp: 0-0
Best Rating: 89   10/03 Sedg   2m1f   good   Hdl

Plating-class hurdler; best suited by two miles; suited by fast ground.

Millyhenry

13-y-o b g White Prince (USA)-Milly's Chance (Miljet)
A J Tizzard A J Tizzard

Placings:P/4061323034/323P641P2/P   (0361)
2003/04: 34PHY,

	Starts	1st	2nd	3rd	Win & Pl
Chases	1	0	0	0	
Career Total	21	2	3	5	17992
107 2/02 Plum	3m2f		D(0-115)Ch	HVY	£4252
113 12/00 Tntn	3m		D Ch	SFT	£4348
				Total win prize-money	£8602

Going: Sf: 0-1 GS: 0-0 Gd: 0-0 GF: - Fm: 0-0
Distance: 2m/2m3: 0-0 2m4-2m7: 0-0 3m+: 0-1
Track: LH: 0-1 RH: 0-0 Tight: 0-0 Gall: 0-0
Aids: Bl: 0-0 Vi: 0-0 Tstrap: 0-0 Ckp: 0-0
Best Rating: 113   12/00 Tntn   3m   soft   Ch

Millys Filly

101   75

6-y-o b m Polish Precedent (USA)-Lemon's Mill (USA)
(Roberto (USA))
Miss K Marks (O Sherwood 2/8) Nick Shutts

Placings:005P-35P0P   (1506)
2003/04: 17QGF, 20SGF, 24PGF, 16PGF, 16PGF,

	Starts	1st	2nd	3rd	Win & Pl
Hurdles	5	0	0	1	539
Career Total	9	0	0	1	539

Going: Sf: 0-0 GS: 0-0 Gd: 0-0 GF: - Fm: 0-5
Distance: 2m/2m3: 0-3 2m4-2m7: 0-1 3m+: 0-1
Track: LH: 0-5 RH: 0-0 Tight: 0-1 Gall: 0-0
Aids: Bl: 0-0 Vi: 0-0 Tstrap: 0-0 Ckp: 0-0
Best Rating: 75   8/03 Worc   2m4f   gd-fm   Hdl

Modest form over hurdles; claimed for £6,000 after finishing fifth in 2m 4f Worcester seller August 2003.

Milner Be Good

81f   42f

6-y-o b m Weld-It Beat All (Laurence O)
Mrs J Candlish Greencard Golfers

Placings:000   (2856)
2003/04: 17QG, 16PGS, 17PGS,

	Starts	1st	2nd	3rd	Win & Pl
NH Flat	3	0	0	0	
Career Total	3	0	0	0	

Going: Sf: 0-0 GS: 0-2 Gd: 0-1 GF: - Fm: 0-0
Distance: 2m/2m3: 0-3 2m4-2m7: 0-0 3m+: 0-0
Track: LH: 0-2 RH: 0-1 Tight: 0-1 Gall: 0-0
Aids: Bl: 0-0 Vi: 0-0 Tstrap: 0-0 Ckp: 0-0
Best Rating: 43   10/03 Bang   2m1f   good   NHF

Milner Be Great

8-y-o b g Weld-Bahama (Bali Dancer)
Mrs J Candlish Greencard Golfers

Placings:P   (3280)
2003/04: 24PHY,

	Starts	1st	2nd	3rd	Win & Pl
Hurdles	1	0	0	0	
Career Total	1	0	0	0	

Going: Sf: 0-1 GS: 0-0 Gd: 0-0 GF: - Fm: 0-0
Distance: 2m/2m3: 0-0 2m4-2m7: 0-0 3m+: 0-1
Track: LH: 0-1 RH: 0-0 Tight: 0-0 Gall: 0-0
Aids: Bl: 0-0 Vi: 0-0 Tstrap: 0-0 Ckp: 0-0

Milord Lescribaa (FR)

105   98+

4-y-o b g Cadoudal (FR)-Mona Lisaa (FR) (Karkour (FR))
M C Pipe Jimmyz Jokers

Placings:41   (3875)
2003/04: 16ᵗS, 16¹S,

	Starts	1st	2nd	3rd	Win & Pl
Hurdles	2	1	0	0	4953
Career Total	2	1	0	0	4953
104 2/04 Leic	2m		D Hdl	SFT	£4953
				Total win prize-money	£4953

Going: Sf: 1-2 GS: 0-0 Gd: 0-0 GF: - Fm: 0-0
Distance: 2m/2m3: 1-2 2m4-2m7: 0-0 3m+: 0-0
Track: LH: 0-0 RH: 1-2 Tight: 0-0 Gall: 0-0
Aids: Bl: 0-0 Vi: 0-0 Tstrap: 0-0 Ckp: 0-0
Best Rating: 104   2/04 Leic   2m   soft   Hdl

Juvenile hurdler; won at Leicester on second start; handles soft ground.

Mindanao

105   131+

8-y-o b m Most Welcome-Salala (Connaught)
L Lungo Bob Slee Toby Noble & J B

Placings:10F023/21-1300   (4599)
2003/04: 22¹G, 20³G, 16PS, 18PG,

	Starts	1st	2nd	3rd	Win & Pl
Hurdles	4	1	0	1	6892
Career Total	12	3	2	2	17325
130 4/03 Kels	2m6f110y	D(0-125)HHdl	GD	£4784
130 3/03 Hexm	2m4f110y	D(0-125)HHdl	GD	£4784
103 1/02 Newc	2m	E Hdl	SFT	£3052
			Total win prize-money	£12620

Going: Sf: 0-1 GS: 0-0 Gd: 0-0 GF: 1-3 Fm: 0-0
Distance: 2m/2m3: 0-2 2m4-2m7: 1-2 3m+: 0-0
Track: LH: 1-4 RH: 0-0 Tight: 1-2 Gall: 0-0
Aids: Bl: 0-0 Vi: 0-0 Tstrap: 0-0 Ckp: 0-0
Best Rating: 130   11/03 Ayr   2m4f   good   Hdl

Useful handicap hurdler; acts on a soft surface; stays two miles six.

Minella Storm (IRE)

12-y-o b g Strong Gale-Maul-More (Deep Run)
Miss L Wilkins C J Williams

Placings:12462120/F60/20263/243444/0241/4440-215   (4815)

2003/04: 25²GS, 25¹GF, 24⁵G,

	Starts	1st	2nd	3rd	Win & Pl
Chases	3	1	1	0	2081
Career Total	33	4	8	2	25815
106 3/04 Hrfd	3m1f110yH Ch		G-F	£1561
95 8/01 Uttx	3m	E Ch	G-F	£3584
121 2/98 Navn	2m2f	Hdl	SFT	£2680
115 5/97 Klny	2m1f	NHF	Y-S	£3391
			Total win prize-money	£11216

Going: Sf: 0-0 GS: 0-1 Gd: 0-1 GF: - Fm: 1-1
Distance: 2m/2m3: 0-0 2m4-2m7: 0-0 3m+: 1-3
Track: LH: 0-1 RH: 1-2 Tight: 0-0 Gall: 0-0
Aids: Bl: 0-0 Vi: 0-0 Tstrap: 0-0 Ckp: 0-0
Best Rating: 124   1/00 Leic   2m4f110y   soft   Hdl

Ex-Irish hurdler/hunter chaser, on the downgrade; has worn blinkers; acts on fast ground and with cut.

Minelly

90   61

4-y-o b f Defacto (USA)-Lady Liza (Air Trooper)
M E Sowersby The Southwold Set

Placings:5PP0   (4602)
2003/04: 17⁵GF, 16PG, 16PS, 17PG,

	Starts	1st	2nd	3rd	Win & Pl
Hurdles	4	0	0	0	0
Career Total	4	0	0	0	0

Going: Sf: 0-1 GS: 0-0 Gd: 0-2 GF: - Fm: 0-1
Distance: 2m/2m3: 0-4 2m4-2m7: 0-0 3m+: 0-0
Track: LH: 0-1 RH: 0-3 Tight: 0-3 Gall: 0-0
Aids: Bl: 0-0 Vi: 0-0 Tstrap: 0-0 Ckp: 0-0
Best Rating: 61   3/04 MRas   2m1f110y   good   Hdl

Miners Dance (IRE)

103   106

11-y-o b g Miners Lamp-Prudent Birdie (Lucifer (USA))
B G Powell John Studd

Placings:2B/U4UF5045P/21114P5/4-641100   (3811)
2003/04: 26⁶GF, 24⁴GF, 30¹GS, 32¹G, 30⁴GS, 24⁰G,

	Starts	1st	2nd	3rd	Win & Pl
Chases	6	2	0	0	18303
Career Total	25	5	2	0	31450
106 12/03 Extr	4m	D(0-125)HCh	GD	£10497
104 11/03 Hntg	3m6f110yD(0-120)HCh	G-S	£6734
120 1/01 Folk	3m1f	E Ch	SFT	£3536
116 12/00 Folk	3m2f	F(0-110)HCh	SFT	£3744
117 11/00 Plum	3m1f110yE(0-105)HHdl	HVY	£2296
			Total win prize-money	£26808

Going: Sf: 0-0 GS: 1-2 Gd: 1-2 GF: - Fm: 0-2
Distance: 2m/2m3: 0-0 2m4-2m7: 0-0 3m+: 2-6
Track: LH: 0-3 RH: 2-3 Tight: 0-1 Gall: 1-2
Aids: Bl: 0-0 Vi: 0-0 Tstrap: 0-0 Ckp: 0-0
Best Rating: 120   1/01 Folk   3m1f   soft   Ch

Modest novice chaser a few years ago; successful in point-to-points since; stays extreme distances; acts on most ground.

Mini Cruise

14-y-o ch g Cruise Missile-Mini Pie (Dike (USA))
Miss J Fisher Miss J Fisher

Placings:0P/000/4050   (4078)
2003/04: 20⁴G, 20⁰G, 24⁵G, 24⁰F,

	Starts	1st	2nd	3rd	Win & Pl
Chases	4	0	0	0	258
Career Total	9	0	0	0	258

Going:	Sf: 0-0 GS: 0-0 Gd: 0-3 GF: - Fm: 0-1
Distance:	2m/2m3: 0-0 2m4-2m7: 0-2 3m+: 0-2
Track:	LH: 0-1 RH: 0-3 Tight: 0-2 Gall: 0-0
Aids:	Bl: 0-0 Vi: 0-0 Tstrap: 0-0 Ckp: 0-0
Best Rating:	56 5/03 Prth 2m4f110y good Ch

Mini Dare

97(103c)   (99+c)**91**

7-y-o b g Derrylin-Minim (Rymer)
O Sherwood Furrows Ltd

Placings:63/46625-2U24244   (4914)
2003/04: 24²G, 24ᵁGS, 26²G, 24⁴G, 26²GS, 254GS, 24⁴GS,

	Starts	1st	2nd	3rd	Win & Pl
Hurdles	3	0	1	0	1310
Chases	4	0	2	0	2385
Career Total	14	0	4	1	6041

Going:	Sf: 0-0 GS: 0-4 Gd: 0-3 GF: - Fm: 0-0
Distance:	2m/2m3: 0-0 2m4-2m7: 0-0 3m+: 0-7
Track:	LH: 0-2 RH: 0-3 Tight: 0-3 Gall: 0-2
Aids:	Bl: 0-0 Vi: 0-0 Tstrap: 0-0 Ckp: 0-1
Best Rating:	99 12/03 Font 3m2f110y good Ch

Moderate hurdler/novice chaser; improved when stepped up to three miles; acts on good ground.

Mini Sensation (IRE)

(93h)   (104h)**155**

11-y-o b g Be My Native (USA)-Minorettes Girl (Strong Gale)
Jonjo O'Neill John P McManus

Placings:361P/0210/11/11203P2/411PP-00P   (4861)
2003/04: 20²GS, 20⁰G, 33ᴾGS,

	Starts	1st	2nd	3rd	Win & Pl
Hurdles	2	0	0	0	0
Chases	1	0	0	0	0
Career Total	25	8	3	2	151671
152	2/03	Uttx	3m4f	A HCh	HVY £47600
148	12/02	Chep	3m5f110y	A HCh	HVY £43500
148	11/01	Bang	3m110y	D Ch	G-S £5537
113	11/01	Weth	3m1f	D Ch	GD £4134
140	11/00	Hayd	2m4f	B(0-140)HHdl	SFT £10257
104	10/00	Weth	2m4f110y	C(0-130)HHdl	SFT £7085
116	2/00	Gowr	2m	(0-130)HHdl	Y-S £5520
105	2/99	Gowr	2m	Hdl	SH £3683
				Total win prize-money £127316

Going:	Sf: 0-0 GS: 0-2 Gd: 0-1 GF: - Fm: 0-0
Distance:	2m/2m3: 0-0 2m4-2m7: 0-2 3m+: 0-1
Track:	LH: 0-3 RH: 0-0 Tight: 0-0 Gall: 0-0
Aids:	Bl: 0-0 Vi: 0-0 Tstrap: 0-0 Ckp: 0-0
Best Rating:	152 2/03 Uttx 3m4f heavy Ch

Very useful staying handicap chaser; useful hurdler; landed a gamble in the Welsh National in December 2002; followed up in the National Trial at Uttoxeter in February; well beaten since; stays extreme distances; suited by soft and heavy ground.

Mini Stir

6-y-o b m Minster Son-Carat Stick (Gold Rod)

J B Walton Messrs F T Walton

Placings:F   (0797)
2003/04: 16ᶠG,

	Starts	1st	2nd	3rd	Win & Pl
NH Flat	1	0	0	0	
Career Total	1	0	0	0	

Going:	Sf: 0-0 GS: 0-0 Gd: 0-1 GF: - Fm: 0-0
Distance:	2m/2m3: 0-1 2m4-2m7: 0-0 3m+: 0-0
Track:	LH: 0-0 RH: 0-1 Tight: 0-0 Gall: 0-0
Aids:	Bl: 0-0 Vi: 0-0 Tstrap: 0-0 Ckp: 0-0

Minivet

106   (111c)**114**

9-y-o b g Midyan (USA)-Bronzewing (Beldale Flutter (USA))
T D Easterby Oakhill Wood Stud

Placings:21211101/PC0/P56F3/0113316-0201   (4159)
2003/04: 22²G, 20²S, 25⁰G, 19¹G,

	Starts	1st	2nd	3rd	Win & Pl
Hurdles	4	1	1	0	3362
Career Total	27	9	3	3	36281
102	3/04	Donc	2m3f110yF Hdl	GD	£2702
112	4/03	Kels	2m6f110yE(0-110)HHdl	GD	£4225
109	2/03	Weth	2m	E(0-110)HHdl	GD	£3752
104	2/03	Catt	2m	G Hdl	GD	£2492
132	4/00	Ayr	2m	C Hdl	GD	£5135
134	1/00	Donc	2m110y	C(0-135)HHdl	GD	£5850
118	1/00	Kels	2m110y	D Hdl	GD	£3201
118	1/00	Muss	2m	E Hdl	GD	£2415
123	12/99	Donc	2m110y	E Hdl	G-S	£1976
				Total win prize-money £31749

Going:	Sf: 0-1 GS: 0-0 Gd: 1-3 GF: - Fm: 0-0
Distance:	2m/2m3: 0-0 2m4-2m7: 1-3 3m+: 0-1
Track:	LH: 1-4 RH: 0-0 Tight: 0-2 Gall: 0-0
Aids:	Bl: 0-0 Vi: 0-0 Tstrap: 0-0 Ckp: 0-0
Best Rating:	134 1/00 Donc 2m110y good Hdl

Fair handicap hurdler att his best; winner of nine hurdle races, latest claimer att Doncaster in March; game; best at distances short of thhree miles; suited by good ground but acts on most types of ground.

Minnie Secret

81   **62**

5-y-o b m Primitive Rising (USA)-Mobile Miss (IRE) (Classic Secret (USA))
B N Pollock Major G W Thompson

Placings:4UP   (4511)
2003/04: 16⁴S, 17ᵁG, 20ᴾGS,

	Starts	1st	2nd	3rd	Win & Pl
Hurdles	3	0	0	0	275
Career Total	3	0	0	0	275

Going:	Sf: 0-1 GS: 0-1 Gd: 0-1 GF: - Fm: 0-0
Distance:	2m/2m3: 0-2 2m4-2m7: 0-1 3m+: 0-0
Track:	LH: 0-2 RH: 0-1 Tight: 0-0 Gall: 0-0
Aids:	Bl: 0-0 Vi: 0-0 Tstrap: 0-0 Ckp: 0-0
Best Rating:	63 1/04 Leic 2m soft Hdl

Minora Blue

89   **65**

6-y-o b m Bob Back (USA)-Minora (IRE) (Cataldi)
Ms Bridget Nicholls Mrs Angela Tincknell

Placings:500P0   (4856)

2003/04: 17⁵GS, 16⁵G, 19⁰G, 18ᴾG, 19⁰GF,

	Starts	1st	2nd	3rd	Win & Pl
NH Flat	2	0	0	0	0
Hurdles	3	0	0	0	0
Career Total	5	0	0	0	0

Going:	Sf: 0-0 GS: 0-1 Gd: 0-3 GF: - Fm: 0-1
Distance:	2m/2m3: 0-0 2m4-2m7: 0-1 3m+: 0-0
Track:	LH: 0-1 RH: 0-3 Tight: 0-2 Gall: 0-0
Aids:	Bl: 0-0 Vi: 0-0 Tstrap: 0-0 Ckp: 0-0
Best Rating:	94 1/04 Tntn 2m1f gd-sft NHF

Minsgill Glen

95(92h)   (76h)**82**

8-y-o b m Minster Son-Gilmanscleuch (IRE) (Mandalus)
Mrs J K M Oliver Miss J S Peat

Placings:000/PP-4040403510   (4882)
2003/04: 16⁴G, 16⁰GF, 20⁴GF, 20⁰GF, 25⁴GF, 24⁰G, 24³G, 25⁵GF, 25¹G, 26⁰GS,

	Starts	1st	2nd	3rd	Win & Pl
Hurdles	4	0	0	0	0
Chases	6	1	0	1	5850
Career Total	15	1	0	1	5850
82	4/04	Kels	3m1f	E Ch	GD	£4771
				Total win prize-money £4771

Going:	Sf: 0-0 GS: 0-1 Gd: 1-4 GF: - Fm: 0-5
Distance:	2m/2m3: 0-2 2m4-2m7: 0-2 3m+: 1-6
Track:	LH: 1-5 RH: 0-5 Tight: 1-2 Gall: 0-0
Aids:	Bl: 0-0 Vi: 0-0 Tstrap: 0-0 Ckp: 0-0
Best Rating:	82 4/04 Kels 3m1f good Ch

Moderate novice hurdler/chaser; finally off the mark in weak beginners' chase at Kelso in April; stays three miles; acts on good ground; has had injury problems.

Minster Abbi

80f   **74f**

4-y-o b f Minster Son-Elitist (Keren)
W Storey David Swan

Placings:05   (4885)
2003/04: 17⁰HY, 17⁵GS,

	Starts	1st	2nd	3rd	Win & Pl
NH Flat	2	0	0	0	0
Career Total	2	0	0	0	0

Going:	Sf: 0-1 GS: 0-0 Gd: 0-0 GF: - Fm: 0-0
Distance:	2m/2m3: 0-2 2m4-2m7: 0-0 3m+: 0-0
Track:	LH: 0-0 RH: 0-2 Tight: 0-0 Gall: 0-0
Aids:	Bl: 0-0 Vi: 0-0 Tstrap: 0-0 Ckp: 0-0
Best Rating:	74 4/04 Carl 2m1f gd-sft NHF

Minster Bay

6-y-o b g Minster Son-Melaura Belle (Meldrum)
W Storey J S Simpson

Placings:220-2P   (3230)
2003/04: 16²G, 16ᴾGF,

	Starts	1st	2nd	3rd	Win & Pl
NH Flat	1	0	1	0	544
Hurdles	1	0	0	0	0
Career Total	5	0	3	0	1758

Going:	Sf: 0-0 GS: 0-0 Gd: 0-1 GF: - Fm: 0-1
Distance:	2m/2m3: 0-2 2m4-2m7: 0-0 3m+: 0-0

Track: LH: 0-1 RH: 0-1 Tight: 0-1 Gall: 0-0
Aids: Bl: 0-0 Vi: 0-0 Tstrap: 0-0 Ckp: 0-0
Best Rating: 98 11/03 Hexm 2m110y good NHF

Moderate form in bumpers on good ground; can race keenly.

Minster Belle

9-y-o ch m Minster Son-Palmahalm (Mandrake Major)
D W Barber D Rees

Placings:00R/P   (4815)
2003/04: 24PG,

	Starts	1st	2nd	3rd	Win & Pl
Chases	1	0	0	0	
Career Total	4	0	0	0	

Going: Sf: 0-0 GS: 0-0 Gd: 0-1 GF: - Fm: 0-0
Distance: 2m/2m3: 0-0 2m4-2m7: 0-0 3m+: 0-1
Track: LH: 0-1 RH: 0-0 Tight: 0-0 Gall: 0-0
Aids: Bl: 0-0 Vi: 0-0 Tstrap: 0-0 Ckp: 0-0
Best Rating: 47 2/00 Winc 2m good NHF

Minster Blue

95   68

6-y-o b m Minster Son-Elitist (Keren)
F P Murtagh J M Elliott

Placings:P4P5   (4731)
2003/04: 21PGS, 204HY, 21PG, 205G,

	Starts	1st	2nd	3rd	Win & Pl
Hurdles	4	0	0	0	0
Career Total	4	0	0	0	0

Going: Sf: 0-1 GS: 0-1 Gd: 0-2 GF: - Fm: 0-0
Distance: 2m/2m3: 0-0 2m4-2m7: 0-4 3m+: 0-0
Track: LH: 0-2 RH: 0-0 Tight: 0-2 Gall: 0-0
Aids: Bl: 0-0 Vi: 0-0 Tstrap: 0-0 Ckp: 0-0
Best Rating: 68 2/04 Carl 2m4f heavy Hdl

Minster Fair

94   88

6-y-o b m Minster Son-Fair Echo (Quality Fair)
A C Whillans E Waugh

Placings:04/434555-40   (2506)
2003/04: 224G, 220S,

	Starts	1st	2nd	3rd	Win & Pl
Hurdles	2	0	0	0	0
Career Total	10	0	0	1	884

Going: Sf: 0-1 GS: 0-0 Gd: 0-1 GF: - Fm: 0-0
Distance: 2m/2m3: 0-0 2m4-2m7: 0-2 3m+: 0-0
Track: LH: 0-2 RH: 0-0 Tight: 0-2 Gall: 0-0
Aids: Bl: 0-0 Vi: 0-0 Tstrap: 0-0 Ckp: 0-0
Best Rating: 96 10/02 Carl 2m1f soft NHF

Limited ability in bumpers, fourth in mares' only novices hurdle at Newcastle in January.

Minster Glory

112(105c)   (119c)111+

13-y-o b g Minster Son-Rapid Glory (Hittite Glory)
M W Easterby Mrs P A H Hartley

Placings:002F/1/331U554/12223232/311F211/20106/4211
2/P42030-46111112660   (4883)

2003/04: 164GF, 176GF, 171G, 161GF, 171GS, 161GF, 161GF,
192GS, 166GS, 176GS, 170GS,

	Starts	1st	2nd	3rd	Win & Pl
Hurdles	6	3	1	0	14976
Chases	5	2	0	0	14102
Career Total	54	15	12	6	82262
103	11/03	Winc	2m	E(0-115)HHdl	G-F	£2401
107	11/03	Leic	2m	D(0-120)HHdl	G-F	£8209
111	11/03	Carl	2m1f	E(0-110)HHdl	G-S	£3396
122	10/03	Weth	2m	C(0-135)HCh	G-F	£10107
112	10/03	Bang	2m1f110yE(0-110)HCh	GD	£3558
135	11/01	MRas	2m2f110yD(0-120)HCh	G-S	£4498
121	11/01	Kels	2m1f	E(0-115)HCh	GD	£3770
125	12/00	Muss	2m	E(0-115)HCh	GD	£2866
119	3/00	Newc	2m110y	E(0-115)HCh	GD	£3074
115	2/00	Catt	2m	E(0-115)HCh	GD	£3503
112	1/00	Newc	2m110y	E(0-115)HCh	SFT	£2983
111	12/99	Catt	2m	F(0-105)HCh	G-F	£2862
99	11/98	Newc	2m110y	E(0-115)HCh	G-F	£2762
95	12/97	Catt	2m	E Ch	GD	£3113
87	5/95	Weth	2m	E Hdl	G-F	£2635

Total win prize-money £59745

Going: Sf: 0-0 GS: 1-5 Gd: 1-1 GF: - Fm: 3-5
Distance: 2m/2m3: 5-11 2m4-2m7: 0-0 3m+: 0-0
Track: LH: 2-4 RH: 3-7 Tight: 1-4 Gall: 0-1
Aids: Bl: 4-8 Vi: 0-0 Tstrap: 0-0 Ckp: 0-0
Best Rating: 139 12/01 Weth 2m gd-sft Ch

Modest chaser/hurdler; completed a fantastic five-timer in 2003 with two wins over fences and three over hurdles; best around two miles; suited to good ground; sometimes wears blinkers.

Minster Madness

9-y-o ch g Minster Son-Spring Garden (Silly Prices)
B Ellison Mrs Claire Ellison

Placings:055/0   (0413)
2003/04: 200G,

	Starts	1st	2nd	3rd	Win & Pl
Hurdles	1	0	0	0	
Career Total	4	0	0	0	0

Going: Sf: 0-0 GS: 0-0 Gd: 0-0 GF: - Fm: 0-0
Distance: 2m/2m3: 0-0 2m4-2m7: 0-1 3m+: 0-0
Track: LH: 0-1 RH: 0-0 Tight: 0-0 Gall: 0-0
Aids: Bl: 0-0 Vi: 0-0 Tstrap: 0-0 Ckp: 0-0
Best Rating: 85 7/00 Sedg 2m1f gd-fm NHF

Minster Meadow

67   40

5-y-o ch g Minster Son-Eddies Well (Torus)
S G Chadwick S Chadwick

Placings:60P0   (4881)
2003/04: 166F, 170GF, 200GS, 170GS,

	Starts	1st	2nd	3rd	Win & Pl
NH Flat	2	0	0	0	
Hurdles	2	0	0	0	
Career Total	4	0	0	0	

Going: Sf: 0-0 GS: 0-2 Gd: 0-0 GF: - Fm: 0-2
Distance: 2m/2m3: 0-3 2m4-2m7: 0-1 3m+: 0-0
Track: LH: 0-2 RH: 0-2 Tight: 0-0 Gall: 0-0
Aids: Bl: 0-0 Vi: 0-0 Tstrap: 0-0 Ckp: 0-0
Best Rating: 78 10/03 Carl 2m1f gd-fm NHF

Minster Missile

98+f

6-y-o b g Minster Son-Manettia (IRE) (Mandalus)
Mrs M Reveley Guy Stevenson

Placings:1   (0386)
2003/04: 161G,

	Starts	1st	2nd	3rd	Win & Pl
NH Flat	1	1	0	0	3445
Career Total	1	1	0	0	3445
98	5/03	Kels	2m110y	H NHF	GD	£3445

Total win prize-money £3445

Going: Sf: 0-0 GS: 0-0 Gd: 1-1 GF: - Fm: 0-0
Distance: 2m/2m3: 1-1 2m4-2m7: 0-0 3m+: 0-0
Track: LH: 0-0 RH: 0-0 Tight: 0-0 Gall: 0-0
Aids: Bl: 0-0 Vi: 0-0 Tstrap: 0-0 Ckp: 0-0
Best Rating: 98 5/03 Kels 2m110y good NHF

Good winner on debut at Kelso in May; effective at two miles; acts well on good ground.

Minster Park

84f   62f

5-y-o b g Minster Son-Go Gipsy (Move Off)
S C Burrough The Three Diamonds Partnership

Placings:0   (1019)
2003/04: 160GF,

	Starts	1st	2nd	3rd	Win & Pl
NH Flat	1	0	0	0	
Career Total	1	0	0	0	

Going: Sf: 0-0 GS: 0-0 Gd: 0-0 GF: - Fm: 0-1
Distance: 2m/2m3: 0-1 2m4-2m7: 0-0 3m+: 0-0
Track: LH: 0-1 RH: 0-0 Tight: 0-0 Gall: 0-0
Aids: Bl: 0-0 Vi: 0-0 Tstrap: 0-0 Ckp: 0-0
Best Rating: 62 8/03 Worc 2m gd-fm NHF

Minster Shadow

97f   95f

5-y-o b g Minster Son-Polar Belle (Arctic Lord)
C Grant Panther Racing Ltd

Placings:343   (4277)
2003/04: 165S, 174G, 173G,

	Starts	1st	2nd	3rd	Win & Pl
NH Flat	3	0	0	2	581
Career Total	3	0	0	2	581

Going: Sf: 0-1 GS: 0-0 Gd: 0-2 GF: - Fm: 0-0
Distance: 2m/2m3: 0-3 2m4-2m7: 0-0 3m+: 0-0
Track: LH: 0-1 RH: 0-2 Tight: 0-0 Gall: 0-0
Aids: Bl: 0-0 Vi: 0-0 Tstrap: 0-0 Ckp: 0-0
Best Rating: 95 3/04 Carl 2m1f good NHF

Third in ordinary bumper run on bad ground on debut at Wetherby in January.

Minster York

106(82h)   (82h)117

10-y-o ch g Minster Son-Another Treat (Derring Do)
M D Hammond The Adbrokes Partnership

Placings:0035000P/45PP/326143430432/1211123456-
05322521543   (2579)
2003/04: 170G, 205G, 213GF, 172G, 172GF, 175GF, 162GF, 161GF,
165GF, 194GF, 163GF,

	Starts	1st	2nd	3rd	Win & Pl
Hurdles	1	0	0	0	0

Chases					
	10	1	3	2	8428
Career Total	45	6	7	8	41283
113 10/03 Towc	2m110y	D(0-125)HCh		G-F	£2688
124 8/02 Bang	2m4f110yD(0-125)HCh			G-F	£6890
115 7/02 Sedg	2m110y	D(0-115)HCh		G-F	£4732
114 7/02 MRas	2m1f110yE(0-110)HCh			G-F	£4257
103 5/02 Hexm	2m110y	F(0-95)HCh		GD	£2754
90 9/01 Sedg	2m110y	E Ch		GD	£3435

Total win prize-money £24758

Going:	Sf: 0-0 GS: 0-0 Gd: 0-3 GF: - Fm: 1-8
Distance:	2m/2m3: 1-9 2m4-2m7: 0-2 3m+: 0-0
Track:	LH: 0-8 RH: 1-3 Tight: 0-7 Gall: 0-0
Aids:	Bl: 0-0 Vi: 0-0 Tstrap: 0-0 Ckp: 1-9
Best Rating:	124 8/02 Uttx 2m5f gd-fm Ch

Moderate chaser; stays two and a half miles; suited by ground good or faster; has worn cheekpieces.

Minstrel Hall
100　　　　93
5-y-o b m Saddlers' Hall (IRE)-Mindomica (Dominion)
P Monteith Melville/Stewart

Placings:044304-U500601305　　　(4849)
2003/04: 17UHY, 16⁵S, 16⁹GS, 16⁹HY, 17⁶GS, 16⁹G, 16¹GF, 16³G, 16⁶G, 16⁵GS,

	Starts	1st	2nd	3rd	Win & Pl
Hurdles	10	1	0	1	3704
Career Total	16	1	0	2	4510
84 3/04 Catt	2m	G Hdl		G-F	£2457

Total win prize-money £2457

Going:	Sf: 0-3 GS: 0-3 Gd: 0-3 GF: - Fm: 1-1
Distance:	2m/2m3: 1-10 2m4-2m7: 0-0 3m+: 0-0
Track:	LH: 1-8 RH: 0-2 Tight: 1-4 Gall: 0-1
Aids:	Bl: 0-0 Vi: 0-0 Tstrap: 0-4 Ckp: 0-0
Best Rating:	93 4/04 Ayr 2m gd-sft Hdl

Plating-class hurdler; improved effort when getting off the mark at Catterick in March; best suited by two miles; handles fast ground.

Mint Approval (USA)

5-y-o gr/ro g With Approval (CAN)-Mint Bell (USA) (Key To The Mint (USA))
Dr P Pritchard Mrs T Pritchard

Placings:0　　　(4664)
2003/04: 19⁹GS,

	Starts	1st	2nd	3rd	Win & Pl
Hurdles	1	0	0	0	
Career Total	1	0	0	0	

Going:	Sf: 0-0 GS: 0-1 Gd: 0-0 GF: - Fm: 0-0
Distance:	2m/2m3: 0-0 2m4-2m7: 0-1 3m+: 0-0
Track:	LH: 0-1 RH: 0-0 Tight: 0-1 Gall: 0-0
Aids:	Bl: 0-0 Vi: 0-0 Tstrap: 0-0 Ckp: 0-0

Mio Caro (FR)
102　　　109
4-y-o ch g Bering-Composition (USA) (Sillery (USA))
Noel T Chance Mike Browne

Placings:2P31　　　(4602)
2003/04: 16²GS, 16⁶P, 16³G, 17¹G,

	Starts	1st	2nd	3rd	Win & Pl
Hurdles	4	1	1	1	7434
Career Total	4	1	1	1	7434
92 3/04 MRas	2m1f110yD Hdl		GD	£4862

Total win prize-money £4862

Going:	Sf: 0-0 GS: 0-1 Gd: 1-3 GF: - Fm: 0-0
Distance:	2m/2m3: 1-4 2m4-2m7: 0-0 3m+: 0-0
Track:	LH: 0-0 RH: 1-4 Tight: 1-1 Gall: 0-0
Aids:	Bl: 0-0 Vi: 0-0 Tstrap: 0-0 Ckp: 0-0
Best Rating:	109 3/04 Kemp 2m good Hdl

Ex-French juvenile hurdler; ran well when second on debut at Sandown; acts on easy ground; wore blinkers when winning on the Flat in France.

Mioche D'Estruval (FR)
101　　　111
4-y-o bl g Lute Antique (FR)-Charme D'Estruval (FR) (Mistigri)
M C Pipe Joe Moran

Placings:1120　　　(4452)
2003/04: 16¹GS, 17¹GS, 16²S, 16⁶GS,

	Starts	1st	2nd	3rd	Win & Pl
Hurdles	4	2	1	0	7462
Career Total	4	2	1	0	7462
98 1/04 Extr	2m1f	E Hdl		G-S	£3437
111 12/03 Plum	2m	E Hdl		G-S	£2744

Total win prize-money £6181

Going:	Sf: 0-1 GS: 2-3 Gd: 0-0 GF: - Fm: 0-0
Distance:	2m/2m3: 2-4 2m4-2m7: 0-0 3m+: 0-0
Track:	LH: 1-2 RH: 1-2 Tight: 1-2 Gall: 0-0
Aids:	Bl: 0-0 Vi: 0-1 Tstrap: 0-0 Ckp: 0-0
Best Rating:	111 12/03 Plum 2m gd-sft Hdl

Modest hurdler; made a winning hurdles debut in a juvenile event at Plumpton; followed up in unimpressive style at Exeter; wore a visor when beaten next time.

Mirabad
81f　　　45f
5-y-o b g Pursuit Of Love-Shemaleyah (Lomond (USA))
J S Haldane J S Haldane

Placings:00　　　(3474)
2003/04: 16⁵S, 16⁹GF,

	Starts	1st	2nd	3rd	Win & Pl
NH Flat	2	0	0	0	
Career Total	2	0	0	0	

Going:	Sf: 0-1 GS: 0-0 Gd: 0-0 GF: - Fm: 0-1
Distance:	2m/2m3: 0-2 2m4-2m7: 0-0 3m+: 0-0
Track:	LH: 0-1 RH: 0-1 Tight: 0-1 Gall: 0-0
Aids:	Bl: 0-0 Vi: 0-0 Tstrap: 0-0 Ckp: 0-0
Best Rating:	45 1/04 Muss 2m gd-fm NHF

Mirant
109　　　118
5-y-o b h Danzig Connection (USA)-Ingerence (FR) (Akarad (FR))
M C Pipe Lucayan Stud

Placings:F23-1124　　　(1060)
2003/04: 17¹G, 18¹GF, 17²GF, 16⁴GF,

	Starts	1st	2nd	3rd	Win & Pl
Hurdles	4	2	1	0	9306
Career Total	7	2	2	1	13092
118 5/03 Font	2m2f110yE Hdl		G-F	£3514
118 5/03 Bang	2m1f	E Hdl		GD	£3802

Total win prize-money £7317

Going:	Sf: 0-0 GS: 0-0 Gd: 1-1 GF: - Fm: 1-3

Distance:	2m/2m3: 2-4 2m4-2m7: 0-0 3m+: 0-0
Track:	LH: 2-4 RH: 0-0 Tight: 2-3 Gall: 0-0
Aids:	Bl: 0-0 Vi: 0-0 Tstrap: 0-0 Ckp: 0-0
Best Rating:	118 5/03 NAbb 2m1f gd-fm Hdl

Fair hurdler; stays two and a ahlf miles; acts on a sound surface.

Mirjan (IRE)
103　　　128
8-y-o b g Tenby-Mirana (IRE) (Ela-Mana-Mou)
L Lungo Mrs Barbara Lungo

Placings:63101/1406500/03100102/54P6012-0P3　　(4853)
2003/04: 16⁰G, 24PGS, 22³GS,

	Starts	1st	2nd	3rd	Win & Pl
Hurdles	3	0	0	1	1590
Career Total	30	6	2	3	61101
127 4/03 Ayr	2m6f	B(0-150)HHdl	GD	£10197
135 11/01 Newc	2m4f	D(0-125)HHdl	G-S	£5018
131 5/01 Weth	2m4f110yD(0-120)HHdl	FRM	£3620
133 5/00 Hayd	2m	A HHdl	GD	£24000
128 4/00 Chel	2m1f	B Hdl	SFT	£6760
109 3/00 Kels	2m110y	E Hdl	G-S	£2478

Total win prize-money £52074

Going:	Sf: 0-0 GS: 0-2 Gd: 0-1 GF: - Fm: 0-0
Distance:	2m/2m3: 0-1 2m4-2m7: 0-1 3m+: 0-1
Track:	LH: 0-3 RH: 0-0 Tight: 0-1 Gall: 0-0
Aids:	Bl: 0-0 Vi: 0-0 Tstrap: 0-0 Ckp: 0-1
Best Rating:	135 11/01 Newc 2m4f gd-sft Hdl

Useful handicap hurdler; suited by hold-up tactics; best at distances short of 3 miles; has won on fast and soft ground; has worn a visor.

Misbehaviour
100　　　78
5-y-o b g Tragic Role (USA)-Exotic Forest (Dominion)
P Butler Homewoodgate Racing Club

Placings:0U10525351-0P6606004　　(4958)
2003/04: 17¹S, 17⁰GF, 18⁶G, 16⁶S, 16⁶G, 16⁹GS, 22⁶HY, 18⁶G, 16⁰G, 17⁴G,

	Starts	1st	2nd	3rd	Win & Pl
Hurdles	10	1	0	0	4056
Career Total	19	2	1	1	7118
78 4/03 NAbb	2m1f	E(0-110)HHdl	SFT	£4056
85 11/02 Tntn	2m1f	G Hdl	G-S	£1939

Total win prize-money £5995

Going:	Sf: 1-3 GS: 0-1 Gd: 0-5 GF: - Fm: 0-1
Distance:	2m/2m3: 1-9 2m4-2m7: 0-1 3m+: 0-1
Track:	LH: 1-6 RH: 0-4 Tight: 1-9 Gall: 0-0
Aids:	Bl: 0-0 Vi: 0-2 Tstrap: 0-0 Ckp: 1-7
Best Rating:	87 2/03 Hrfd 2m1f good Hdl

Sprinter on the Flat; plating-class hurdler; suited by easy ground.

Mishead
103　　　74
6-y-o ch g Unfuwain (USA)-Green Jannat (USA) (Alydar (USA))
M C Chapman N Malbon

Placings:30446/3P4-0P30036F　　(1253)
2003/04: 16⁶GF, 17⁶G, 22³GS, 19⁶G, 17⁰GF, 17³GF, 22⁶GS, 22FGF,

	Starts	1st	2nd	3rd	Win & Pl
Hurdles	8	0	0	2	883
Career Total	16	0	0	4	1934

Going:	Sf: 0-0 GS: 0-0 Gd: 0-4 GF: - Fm: 0-4
Distance:	2m/2m3: 0-4 2m4-2m7: 0-4 3m+: 0-0
Track:	LH: 0-4 RH: 0-3 Tight: 0-7 Gall: 0-0
Aids:	Bl: 0-0 Vi: 0-0 Tstrap: 0-0 Ckp: 0-0
Best Rating:	83 6/02 MRas 2m1f110y gd-fm Hdl

Plating-class hurdler.

Miss Aragont

5-y-o b m Aragon-Uninvited (Be My Guest (USA))
S G Chadwick S Chadwick

Placings:0-PPP (0822)
2003/04: 17PS, 17PGS, 19PG,

	Starts	1st	2nd	3rd	Win & Pl
Hurdles	3	0	0	0	
Career Total	4	0	0	0	

Going:	Sf: 0-1 GS: 0-1 Gd: 0-1 GF: - Fm: 0-0
Distance:	2m/2m3: 0-2 2m4-2m7: 0-1 3m+: 0-0
Track:	LH: 0-2 RH: 0-1 Tight: 0-3 Gall: 0-0
Aids:	Bl: 0-0 Vi: 0-0 Tstrap: 0-3 Ckp: 0-0
Best Rating:	23 3/03 Weth 2m gd-fm NHF

Miss Barton Ridge

7-y-o b m Broadsword (USA)-Yamrah (Milford)
J M Bradley Leeway Group Limited

Placings:6 (0154)
2003/04: 16PGF,

	Starts	1st	2nd	3rd	Win & Pl
NH Flat	1	0	0	0	0
Career Total	1	0	0	0	0

Going:	Sf: 0-0 GS: 0-0 Gd: 0-0 GF: - Fm: 0-1
Distance:	2m/2m3: 0-0 2m4-2m7: 0-0 3m+: 0-0
Track:	LH: 0-1 RH: 0-0 Tight: 0-0 Gall: 0-0
Aids:	Bl: 0-0 Vi: 0-0 Tstrap: 0-0 Ckp: 0-0

Miss Biddy

73   45

9-y-o ch m Sula Bula-Bickfield Approach (Dubassoff (USA))
M S Saunders M S Saunders

Placings:4 (0485)
2003/04: 224GF,

	Starts	1st	2nd	3rd	Win & Pl
Hurdles	1	0	0	0	275
Career Total	1	0	0	0	275

Going:	Sf: 0-0 GS: 0-0 Gd: 0-0 GF: - Fm: 0-1
Distance:	2m/2m3: 0-0 2m4-2m7: 0-1 3m+: 0-0
Track:	LH: 0-1 RH: 0-0 Tight: 0-1 Gall: 0-0
Aids:	Bl: 0-0 Vi: 0-0 Tstrap: 0-0 Ckp: 0-0
Best Rating:	49 5/03 NAbb 2m6f gd-fm Hdl

Miss Chinchilla

104   100+

8-y-o b m Perpendicular-Furry Baby (Furry Glen)
Miss Venetia Williams (O Brennan 11/2) Direct Sales UK Ltd

Placings:0110 (4574)

2003/04: 19OG, 16¹G, 21¹G, 21OG,

	Starts	1st	2nd	3rd	Win & Pl
Hurdles	4	2	0	0	6152
Career Total	4	2	0	0	6152
100 3/04 Sedg	2m5f110yE Hdl			GD	£3334
100 2/04 Ludl	2m G Hdl			GD	£2817
				Total win prize-money	£6153

Going:	Sf: 0-0 GS: 0-0 Gd: 2-4 GF: - Fm: 0-0
Distance:	2m/2m3: 1-1 2m4-2m7: 1-3 3m+: 0-0
Track:	LH: 1-2 RH: 1-2 Tight: 1-2 Gall: 0-1
Aids:	Bl: 0-0 Vi: 0-0 Tstrap: 0-0 Ckp: 0-0
Best Rating:	100 3/04 Newb 2m5f good Hdl

Moderate novice hurdler; caused a massive shock when winning a Ludlow seller on her second start; changed stables and took a mares only event by a wide margin at Sedgefield in March; suited by soft ground; will stay three miles.

Miss Colmesnil (FR)

4-y-o b f Dear Doctor (FR)-Princesse Dolly (FR) (The Wonder (FR))
A E Jessop (E Leenders 28/10) Mrs Gloria Jessop

Placings:3553P (4698)
2003/04: 17³G, 17⁵GS, 15⁵VS, 15³VS, 18PG,

	Starts	1st	2nd	3rd	Win & Pl
Hurdles	5	0	0	2	6299
Career Total	5	0	0	2	6299

Going:	Sf: 0-0 GS: 0-1 Gd: 0-2 GF: - Fm: 0-0
Distance:	2m/2m3: 0-3 2m4-2m7: 0-0 3m+: 0-0
Track:	LH: 0-1 RH: 0-0 Tight: 0-1 Gall: 0-0
Aids:	Bl: 0-0 Vi: 0-0 Tstrap: 0-0 Ckp: 0-0

Miss Cool

88(110h)   (133 h)102

8-y-o b m Jupiter Island-Laurel Diver (Celtic Cone)
M C Pipe N G Mills

Placings:103/13/334013-F210U6F (4139)
2003/04: 21FGF, 21²GF, 21¹G, 25OG, 24⁶G, 20FG,

	Starts	1st	2nd	3rd	Win & Pl
Hurdles	2	0	0	0	314
Chases	5	1	1	0	6999
Career Total	18	4	1	5	34655
90 7/03 NAbb	2m5f110yD Ch			GD	£5343
133 3/03 Hayd	2m6f C(0-135)HHdl			G-F	£10335
126 2/02 Ludl	2m E Hdl			G-S	£2688
107 9/00 Chep	2m110y H NHF			GD	£1617
				Total win prize-money	£19983

Going:	Sf: 0-0 GS: 0-0 Gd: 1-5 GF: - Fm: 0-2
Distance:	2m/2m3: 0-0 2m4-2m7: 1-5 3m+: 0-2
Track:	LH: 1-4 RH: 0-3 Tight: 1-4 Gall: 0-1
Aids:	Bl: 0-0 Vi: 0-3 Tstrap: 0-0 Ckp: 0-0
Best Rating:	133 4/03 Chel 2m5f110y good Hdl

Useful handicap hurdler/modest chaser; acts well on a sound surface, but yet to prove herself on really soft ground; effective at up to two miles six; struggled to land the odds at Newton Abbot in July 2003 and is nowhere near as good over fences; has worn a visor.

Miss Cospector

96   81

5-y-o ch m Emperor Fountain-Gypsy Race (IRE) (Good Thyne (USA))
T H Caldwell R Cabrera-Vargas

Placings:0-04006 (4731)
2003/04: 16OGS, 16⁴HY, 16⁹G, 17⁹GS, 20⁶G,

	Starts	1st	2nd	3rd	Win & Pl
NH Flat	3	0	0	0	0
Hurdles	2	0	0	0	0
Career Total	6	0	0	0	0

Going:	Sf: 0-1 GS: 0-2 Gd: 0-2 GF: - Fm: 0-0
Distance:	2m/2m3: 0-4 2m4-2m7: 0-1 3m+: 0-0
Track:	LH: 0-3 RH: 0-2 Tight: 0-1 Gall: 0-0
Aids:	Bl: 0-0 Vi: 0-0 Tstrap: 0-0 Ckp: 0-0
Best Rating:	86 1/04 Hayd 2m heavy NHF

Miss Egypt (IRE)

99   68

8-y-o br m Alphabatim (USA)-Enchanted Queen (Tender King)
Lindsay Woods Foyle Valley Syndicate

Placings:0/0F000/00-32434000 (2245a)
2003/04: 17³Y, 20²G, 16⁴G, 18³GF, 18⁴GF, 17⁰GF, 17⁰GF, 22⁰G,

	Starts	1st	2nd	3rd	Win & Pl
Hurdles	8	0	1	2	2379
Career Total	16	0	1	2	2379

Going:	Sf: 0-0 GS: 0-0 Gd: 0-3 GF: - Fm: 0-4
Distance:	2m/2m3: 0-6 2m4-2m7: 0-2 3m+: 0-0
Track:	LH: 0-0 RH: 0-5 Tight: 0-0 Gall: 0-0
Aids:	Bl: 0-0 Vi: 0-0 Tstrap: 0-0 Ckp: 0-1
Best Rating:	85 7/03 Prth 2m110y good Hdl

Miss Ellie

76   41

8-y-o b m Elmaamul (USA)-Jussoli (Don)
Mrs C J Kerr Mrs C J Kerr

Placings:560/3P511PU/45P603/PPP-P0P (0311)
2003/04: 16PG, 16OG, 16PS,

	Starts	1st	2nd	3rd	Win & Pl
Hurdles	1	0	0	0	0
Chases	2	0	0	0	0
Career Total	22	2	0	2	8149
105 1/01 Muss	2m4f F(0-100)HHdl			G-S	£3164
95 1/01 Muss	2m4f F(0-100)HHdl			GD	£3780
				Total win prize-money	£6944

Going:	Sf: 0-1 GS: 0-0 Gd: 0-2 GF: - Fm: 0-0
Distance:	2m/2m3: 0-3 2m4-2m7: 0-0 3m+: 0-0
Track:	LH: 0-3 RH: 0-0 Tight: 0-1 Gall: 0-0
Aids:	Bl: 0-0 Vi: 0-0 Tstrap: 0-0 Ckp: 0-2
Best Rating:	105 1/01 Muss 2m4f gd-sft Hdl

Moderate handicapper over hurdles, best at around two and a half miles with cut in the ground.

Miss Fahrenheit (IRE)

100f   94f

5-y-o b m Oscar (IRE)-Gunner B Sharp (Gunner B)
C Roberts C.L.R.S. Associates

Placings:0042 (4920)
2003/04: 16OG, 16OG, 16⁴GS, 16²GS,

	Starts	1st	2nd	3rd	Win & Pl
NH Flat	4	0	1	0	615
Career Total	4	0	1	0	615

Going:	Sf: 0-0 GS: 0-2 Gd: 0-2 GF: - Fm: 0-0
Distance:	2m/2m3: 0-4 2m4-2m7: 0-0 3m+: 0-0
Track:	LH: 0-3 RH: 0-1 Tight: 0-0 Gall: 0-0
Aids:	Bl: 0-0 Vi: 0-0 Tstrap: 0-0 Ckp: 0-0
Best Rating:	94 4/04 Worc 2m gd-sft NHF

Has shown ability in bumpers.

Miss Foss

89f   **88f**

5-y-o b m Primitive Rising (USA)-Crammond Brig (New Brig)
R D E Woodhouse The Rumpole Partnership

Placings:450   (4846)
2003/04: 16⁴G, 17⁵G, 17⁰G,

	Starts	1st	2nd	3rd	Win & Pl
NH Flat	3	0	0	0	0
Career Total	3	0	0	0	0

Going:	Sf: 0-0 GS: 0-0 Gd: 0-3 GF: - Fm: 0-0
Distance:	2m/2m3: 0-3 2m4-2m7: 0-0 3m+: 0-0
Track:	LH: 0-1 RH: 0-2 Tight: 0-0 Gall: 0-2
Aids:	Bl: 0-0 Vi: 0-0 Tstrap: 0-0 Ckp: 0-0
Best Rating:	90 3/04 MRas 2m1f110y good NHF

Miss Janica

79   **72**

6-y-o b m Sir Harry Lewis (USA)-Supreme Wonder (IRE)
(Supreme Leader)
Miss Venetia Williams B Moore & E C Stephens

Placings:6/00U23-4   (1013)
2003/04: 20⁴GF,

	Starts	1st	2nd	3rd	Win & Pl
Hurdles	1	0	0	0	0
Career Total	7	0	1	1	1738

Going:	Sf: 0-0 GS: 0-0 Gd: 0-0 GF: - Fm: 0-1
Distance:	2m/2m3: 0-0 2m4-2m7: 0-0 3m+: 0-0
Track:	LH: 0-1 RH: 0-0 Tight: 0-0 Gall: 0-0
Aids:	Bl: 0-0 Vi: 0-0 Tstrap: 0-0 Ckp: 0-0
Best Rating:	88 4/02 Uttx 2m good NHF

Twice placed over hurdles in August 2002; returned after a year off to finish fourth in 2m 4f novices hurdle at Worcester August 2003; has shown signs of temperament in the past.

Miss Jessica (IRE)

65   **67**

4-y-o b/br f Woodborough (USA)-Sarah Blue (IRE) (Bob
Back (USA))
Miss M E Rowland K Hopkin, S Deeman

Placings:04P   (4783)
2003/04: 17⁰GS, 19⁴GF, 21⁰G,

	Starts	1st	2nd	3rd	Win & Pl
NH Flat	1	0	0	0	0
Hurdles	2	0	0	0	280
Career Total	3	0	0	0	280

Going:	Sf: 0-0 GS: 0-1 Gd: 0-1 GF: - Fm: 0-1
Distance:	2m/2m3: 0-1 2m4-2m7: 0-2 3m+: 0-0
Track:	LH: 0-1 RH: 0-2 Tight: 0-1 Gall: 0-1
Aids:	Bl: 0-0 Vi: 0-0 Tstrap: 0-0 Ckp: 0-0
Best Rating:	67 3/04 Hrfd 2m3f110y gd-fm Hdl

Miss Jojo (IRE)

4-y-o b/br f Darnay-Rose Tint (IRE) (Salse (USA))
B S Rothwell Brian Rothwell

Placings:P   (3337)
2003/04: 16ᴾGS,

	Starts	1st	2nd	3rd	Win & Pl
Hurdles	1	0	0	0	0
Career Total	1	0	0	0	0

Going:	Sf: 0-0 GS: 0-1 Gd: 0-0 GF: - Fm: 0-0
Distance:	2m/2m3: 0-1 2m4-2m7: 0-0 3m+: 0-0
Track:	LH: 0-1 RH: 0-0 Tight: 0-1 Gall: 0-0
Aids:	Bl: 0-0 Vi: 0-0 Tstrap: 0-0 Ckp: 0-0

Miss Koen (IRE)

                   79

5-y-o b m Barathea (IRE)-Fanny Blankers (IRE) (Persian
Heights)
D L Williams Girls On Top Racing 2000

Placings:0PP00P-P   (2865)
2003/04: 19ᴾGS,

	Starts	1st	2nd	3rd	Win & Pl
Hurdles	1	0	0	0	
Career Total	7	0	0	0	

Going:	Sf: 0-0 GS: 0-1 Gd: 0-0 GF: - Fm: 0-0
Distance:	2m/2m3: 0-1 2m4-2m7: 0-0 3m+: 0-0
Track:	LH: 0-1 RH: 0-0 Tight: 0-0 Gall: 0-0
Aids:	Bl: 0-0 Vi: 0-0 Tstrap: 0-0 Ckp: 0-0
Best Rating:	79 2/03 Kemp 2m good Hdl

Miss Lacroix

105   **76**

9-y-o b m Picea-Smartie Lee (Dominion)
R Hollinshead Mrs Norma Harris

Placings:0656/6001/5010041336/02263U04630/03016630
000-26025P06   (1841)
2003/04: 20²GF, 21⁶GF, 22⁰GF, 24²G, 22⁵GF, 19²GF, 24⁰GF,
21⁶G,

	Starts	1st	2nd	3rd	Win & Pl
Hurdles	8	0	2	0	1572
Career Total	48	4	4	6	18498
75	8/02	Font	2m6f110yF(0-100)HHdl		G-F	£3094
87	12/00	Ludl	2m	F(0-110)HHdl	SFT	£3178
84	5/00	MRas	2m1f110yF(0-105)HHdl		G-S	£2074
71	8/99	Bang	2m1f	E(0-105)HHdl	GD	£2931
			Total win prize-money £11279			

Going:	Sf: 0-0 GS: 0-0 Gd: 0-2 GF: - Fm: 0-6
Distance:	2m/2m3: 0-0 2m4-2m7: 0-6 3m+: 0-2
Track:	LH: 0-6 RH: 0-2 Tight: 0-5 Gall: 0-0
Aids:	Bl: 0-0 Vi: 0-0 Tstrap: 0-0 Ckp: 0-8
Best Rating:	87 2/01 Ludl 2m gd-sft Hdl

Plating-class hurdler; best when able to dominate; has run well on fast ground, but is better suited by cut; stays two and three-quarter miles.

Miss Lehman

                54+f

6-y-o ch m Beveled (USA)-Lehmans Lot (Oats)
Mrs M Reveley P A Tylor

Placings:5-   (0007)

2003/04: 16⁵G,

	Starts	1st	2nd	3rd	Win & Pl
NH Flat	1	0	0	0	0
Career Total	1	0	0	0	0

Going:	Sf: 0-0 GS: 0-0 Gd: 0-1 GF: - Fm: 0-0
Distance:	2m/2m3: 0-1 2m4-2m7: 0-0 3m+: 0-0
Track:	LH: 0-1 RH: 0-0 Tight: 0-0 Gall: 0-0
Aids:	Bl: 0-0 Vi: 0-0 Tstrap: 0-0 Ckp: 0-0
Best Rating:	54 4/03 Hexm 2m110y good NHF

Beaten a long way in bumper at Hexham in April on first outing.

Miss Lewis

82   **56**

6-y-o b m Sir Harry Lewis (USA)-Teelyna (Teenoso (USA))
C J Down May & Edwards

Placings:42-00P0   (4736)
2003/04: 17⁰G, 16⁰G, 22ᴾGS, 17⁰G,

	Starts	1st	2nd	3rd	Win & Pl
NH Flat	2	0	0	0	0
Hurdles	2	0	0	0	0
Career Total	6	0	1	0	576

Going:	Sf: 0-0 GS: 0-1 Gd: 0-3 GF: - Fm: 0-0
Distance:	2m/2m3: 0-3 2m4-2m7: 0-1 3m+: 0-0
Track:	LH: 0-2 RH: 0-2 Tight: 0-2 Gall: 0-0
Aids:	Bl: 0-0 Vi: 0-0 Tstrap: 0-3 Ckp: 0-0
Best Rating:	98 4/03 Chep 2m110y gd-fm NHF

Miss Librate

75f   **17f**

6-y-o b m Librate-Hayley's Lass (Royal Boxer)
J M Bradley J M Bradley

Placings:000   (3968)
2003/04: 16⁰GS, 17⁰GS, 16⁰GS,

	Starts	1st	2nd	3rd	Win & Pl
NH Flat	3	0	0	0	0
Career Total	3	0	0	0	0

Going:	Sf: 0-0 GS: 0-3 Gd: 0-0 GF: - Fm: 0-0
Distance:	2m/2m3: 0-3 2m4-2m7: 0-0 3m+: 0-0
Track:	LH: 0-1 RH: 0-2 Tight: 0-0 Gall: 0-0
Aids:	Bl: 0-0 Vi: 0-0 Tstrap: 0-0 Ckp: 0-0
Best Rating:	17 12/03 Hrfd 2m1f gd-sft NHF

Miss Mailmit

99   **91**

7-y-o b m Rakaposhi King-Flora Louisa (Rymer)
J A B Old Peter Guntrip

Placings:6-03F34   (4282)
2003/04: 17⁰G, 16³G, 22ᴾHY, 16³G, 21⁴GS,

	Starts	1st	2nd	3rd	Win & Pl
NH Flat	1	0	0	0	0
Hurdles	4	0	0	2	1316
Career Total	6	0	0	2	1316

Going:	Sf: 0-1 GS: 0-1 Gd: 0-3 GF: - Fm: 0-0
Distance:	2m/2m3: 0-3 2m4-2m7: 0-2 3m+: 0-0
Track:	LH: 0-2 RH: 0-3 Tight: 0-1 Gall: 0-0
Aids:	Bl: 0-0 Vi: 0-0 Tstrap: 0-0 Ckp: 0-0
Best Rating:	91 2/04 Asct 2m110y good Hdl

Showed modest ability in two bumpers and hurdles; acts on good ground; raced only at two miles to date.

Miss Mattie Ross

8-y-o b m Milieu-Mother Machree (Bing li)
S J Marshall S J Marshall

Placings:PP/500P6-0U111F   (4949)
2003/04: 20⁶GF, 16⁹G, 25⁴HG, 25¹GS, 25¹G, 25¹G, 26⁶GS,

	Starts	1st	2nd	3rd	Win & Pl
Hurdles	2	0	0	0	0
Chases	5	3	0	0	6094
Career Total	13	3	0	0	6094
103 4/04	Kels	3m1f	H Ch	GD	£2373
102 3/04	Kels	3m1f	H Ch	GD	£2310
81 3/04	Kels	3m1f	H Ch	G-S	£1410

Total win prize-money £6094

Going:	Sf: 0-1 GS: 1-2 Gd: 2-3 GF: - Fm: 0-1
Distance:	2m/2m3: 0-1 2m4-2m7: 0-1 3m+: 3-5
Track:	LH: 3-5 RH: 0-0 Tight: 3-4 Gall: 0-1
Aids:	Bl: 0-0 Vi: 0-0 Tstrap: 0-0 Ckp: 0-0
Best Rating:	103 4/04 Kels 3m1f good Ch

Progressive hunter chaser; landed a course-and-distance hat-trick to Kelso over 3m 1f in early 2004; acts on good to soft ground.

Miss Mia

4f   14f

4-y-o b f Merit (IRE)-Alisa Bower (Old Lucky)
N Waggott Mrs J Waggott

Placings:0   (4482)
2003/04: 17⁰HY,

	Starts	1st	2nd	3rd	Win & Pl
NH Flat	1	0	0	0	
Career Total	1	0	0	0	

Going:	Sf: 0-1 GS: 0-0 Gd: 0-0 GF: - Fm: 0-0
Distance:	2m/2m3: 0-1 2m4-2m7: 0-0 3m+: 0-0
Track:	LH: 0-0 RH: 0-0 Tight: 0-0 Gall: 0-0
Aids:	Bl: 0-0 Vi: 0-0 Tstrap: 0-0 Ckp: 0-0
Best Rating:	14 3/04 Carl 2m1f heavy NHF

Miss Muffin

75f   33f

4-y-o b f Contract Law (USA)-Charossa (Ardross)
Miss B Sanders Miss Brooke Sanders

Placings:0   (4934)
2003/04: 18⁰G,

	Starts	1st	2nd	3rd	Win & Pl
NH Flat	1	0	0	0	
Career Total	1	0	0	0	

Going:	Sf: 0-0 GS: 0-0 Gd: 0-1 GF: - Fm: 0-0
Distance:	2m/2m3: 0-0 2m4-2m7: 0-0 3m+: 0-0
Track:	LH: 0-1 RH: 0-0 Tight: 0-1 Gall: 0-0
Aids:	Bl: 0-0 Vi: 0-0 Tstrap: 0-0 Ckp: 0-0
Best Rating:	33 4/04 Font 2m2f110y good NHF

Miss O'Grady (IRE)

12-y-o ch m Over The River (FR)-Polar Mistress (IRE) (Strong Gale)

Mrs S Alner Mrs J M Miller

Placings:1/U/P/P2U/4212P-F434   (4635)
2003/04: 21⁵FG, 24⁴G, 19³GS, 24⁴G,

	Starts	1st	2nd	3rd	Win & Pl
Chases	4	0	0	1	310
Career Total	15	2	3	1	6781
92 3/03	Font	2m4f	H Ch	GD	£1834
101 4/99	Chel	2m5f	H Ch	G-S	£2078

Total win prize-money £3912

Going:	Sf: 0-0 GS: 0-1 Gd: 0-3 GF: - Fm: 0-0
Distance:	2m/2m3: 0-2 2m4-2m7: 0-2 3m+: 0-2
Track:	LH: 0-1 RH: 0-3 Tight: 0-2 Gall: 0-1
Aids:	Bl: 0-0 Vi: 0-0 Tstrap: 0-0 Ckp: 0-0
Best Rating:	101 4/99 Chel 2m5f gd-sft Ch

Useful pointer/modest hunter chaser; suited by 3m; acts on any ground.

Miss Parker

61f   47f

6-y-o b m Saddlers' Hall (IRE)-Quivira (Rainbow Quest (USA))
M Wigham Maurice Kirby

Placings:0   (3426)
2003/04: 17⁰HY,

	Starts	1st	2nd	3rd	Win & Pl
NH Flat	1	0	0	0	
Career Total	1	0	0	0	

Going:	Sf: 0-1 GS: 0-0 Gd: 0-0 GF: - Fm: 0-0
Distance:	2m/2m3: 0-1 2m4-2m7: 0-0 3m+: 0-0
Track:	LH: 0-0 RH: 0-1 Tight: 0-1 Gall: 0-0
Aids:	Bl: 0-0 Vi: 0-0 Tstrap: 0-0 Ckp: 0-0
Best Rating:	47 1/04 Folk 2m1f110y heavy NHF

Miss Portcello

11-y-o b m Bybicello-Port Mallaig (Royal Fountain)
Mrs J M Hollands W F Jeffrey

Placings:3U/33531-2P   (0269)
2003/04: 25²G, 20ᴾG,

	Starts	1st	2nd	3rd	Win & Pl
Chases	2	0	1	0	638
Career Total	9	1	1	4	3377
89 4/03	Carl	3m	H Ch	G-F	£1443

Total win prize-money £1443

Going:	Sf: 0-0 GS: 0-0 Gd: 0-0 GF: - Fm: 0-0
Distance:	2m/2m3: 0-0 2m4-2m7: 0-1 3m+: 0-1
Track:	LH: 0-1 RH: 0-0 Tight: 0-0 Gall: 0-0
Aids:	Bl: 0-0 Vi: 0-0 Tstrap: 0-0 Ckp: 0-0
Best Rating:	89 5/03 Hexm 3m1f good Ch

Modest form in ladies' points and hunter chases; scored at Carlisle in April; acts on any ground.

Miss Quickly (IRE)

5-y-o b m Anshan-Shari Owen (IRE) (Shardari)
Miss H C Knight Mrs Nicola Moores

Placings:04P5   (4702)
2003/04: 16⁶GF, 17⁴S, 19⁷G, 20⁵G,

	Starts	1st	2nd	3rd	Win & Pl
NH Flat	2	0	0	0	0
Hurdles	2	0	0	0	0
Career Total	4	0	0	0	0

Going: Sf: 0-1 GS: 0-0 Gd: 0-2 GF: - Fm: 0-1

Distance:	2m/2m3: 0-3 2m4-2m7: 0-1 3m+: 0-0
Track:	LH: 0-1 RH: 0-1 Tight: 0-1 Gall: 0-0
Aids:	Bl: 0-0 Vi: 0-0 Tstrap: 0-0 Ckp: 0-0
Best Rating:	86 2/04 Tntn 2m1f soft NHF

Miss Rideamight

106f   81f

5-y-o b m Overbury (IRE)-Nicolynn (Primitive Rising (USA))
B J Eckley Brian Eckley

Placings:5200   (4846)
2003/04: 16⁵G, 17²GS, 16⁹G, 17⁰G,

	Starts	1st	2nd	3rd	Win & Pl
NH Flat	4	0	1	0	510
Career Total	4	0	1	0	510

Going:	Sf: 0-0 GS: 0-2 Gd: 0-2 GF: - Fm: 0-0
Distance:	2m/2m3: 0-4 2m4-2m7: 0-0 3m+: 0-0
Track:	LH: 0-2 RH: 0-2 Tight: 0-0 Gall: 0-0
Aids:	Bl: 0-0 Vi: 0-0 Tstrap: 0-0 Ckp: 0-0
Best Rating:	81 4/04 Chel 2m1f good NHF

Plating-class bumper performer; should stay further over hurdles; acts on good and easy going.

Miss Royello

7-y-o b m Royal Fountain-Lady Manello (Mandrake Major)
Mrs A Hamilton Ian Hamilton

Placings:5323   (4884)
2003/04: 21⁵GS, 25³GS, 25²G, 24³GS,

	Starts	1st	2nd	3rd	Win & Pl
Chases	4	0	1	2	1094
Career Total	4	0	1	2	1094

Going:	Sf: 0-0 GS: 0-3 Gd: 0-1 GF: - Fm: 0-0
Distance:	2m/2m3: 0-0 2m4-2m7: 0-1 3m+: 0-3
Track:	LH: 0-3 RH: 0-1 Tight: 0-3 Gall: 0-0
Aids:	Bl: 0-0 Vi: 0-0 Tstrap: 0-0 Ckp: 0-0
Best Rating:	80 4/04 Kels 3m1f good Ch

Winning pointer; maiden under rules; stays three miles well; acts on most ground; lightly-raced.

Miss Skippy

92f   82f

5-y-o b m Saddlers' Hall (IRE)-Katie Scarlett (Lochnager)
P D Evans Mike Murray

Placings:30   (4920)
2003/04: 16⁵G, 16⁰GS,

	Starts	1st	2nd	3rd	Win & Pl
NH Flat	2	0	0	1	268
Career Total	2	0	0	1	268

Going:	Sf: 0-0 GS: 0-1 Gd: 0-1 GF: - Fm: 0-0
Distance:	2m/2m3: 0-2 2m4-2m7: 0-0 3m+: 0-0
Track:	LH: 0-1 RH: 0-0 Tight: 0-0 Gall: 0-0
Aids:	Bl: 0-0 Vi: 0-0 Tstrap: 0-0 Ckp: 0-0
Best Rating:	82 3/04 Strf 2m110y good NHF

Miss Sutton

98   60

6-y-o b m Formidable (USA)-Saysana (Sayf El Arab (USA))

G F H Charles-Jones Mrs Jessica Charles-Jones

Placings:0-004000   (0869)
2003/04: 16⁰GF, 17⁰GF, 17⁴GF, 17⁰G, 17⁰GF, 22⁰GF,

	Starts	1st	2nd	3rd	Win & Pl
Hurdles	6	0	0	0	432
Career Total	7	0	0	0	432

Going: Sf: 0-0 GS: 0-0 Gd: 0-1 GF: - Fm: 0-5
Distance: 2m2m3: 0-5 2m4-2m7: 0-1 3m+: 0-0
Track: LH: 0-4 RH: 0-2 Tight: 0-4 Gall: 0-0
Aids: Bl: 0-0 Vi: 0-0 Tstrap: 0-0 Ckp: 0-0
Best Rating: 61   6/03   NAbb 2m1f   good   Hdl

Miss Trooper
86f   86f

4-y-o b f Infantry-Mountain Glen (Lochnager)
F Jordan   Andrew Mobley

Placings:0   (4824)
2003/04: 17⁰GF,

	Starts	1st	2nd	3rd	Win & Pl
NH Flat	1	0	0	0	
Career Total	1	0	0	0	

Going: Sf: 0-0 GS: 0-0 Gd: 0-0 GF: - Fm: 0-1
Distance: 2m2m3: 0-1 2m4-2m7: 0-0 3m+: 0-0
Track: LH: 0-0 RH: 0-1 Tight: 0-0 Gall: 0-0
Aids: Bl: 0-0 Vi: 0-0 Tstrap: 0-0 Ckp: 0-0
Best Rating: 86   4/04   Extr 2m1f   gd-fm   NHF

Miss Vettori
66f   17f

5-y-o b m Vettori (IRE)-Dahlawise (IRE) (Caerleon (USA))
G L Moore   Mrs Eileen Sheehan

Placings:0   (0871)
2003/04: 17⁰GF,

	Starts	1st	2nd	3rd	Win & Pl
NH Flat	1	0	0	0	
Career Total	1	0	0	0	

Going: Sf: 0-0 GS: 0-0 Gd: 0-0 GF: - Fm: 0-1
Distance: 2m2m3: 0-1 2m4-2m7: 0-0 3m+: 0-0
Track: LH: 0-1 RH: 0-0 Tight: 0-1 Gall: 0-0
Aids: Bl: 0-0 Vi: 0-0 Tstrap: 0-0 Ckp: 0-0
Best Rating: 17   7/03   NAbb 2m1f   gd-fm   NHF

Miss Wizadora
99   81+

9-y-o ch m Gildoran-Lizzie The Twig (Precipice Wood)
Simon Earle   Miss Jenny Grant

Placings:5/5500/3P0/3601/203F2   (4754)
2003/04: 20²S, 21⁰GS, 20³G, 19²GS, 20²G,

	Starts	1st	2nd	3rd	Win & Pl
Chases	5	0	2	1	2928
Career Total	17	1	2	3	7189
91	11/01	NAbb	2m5f110yE(0-105)HChs	SFT	£3376

Total win prize-money £3377

Going: Sf: 0-1 GS: 0-2 Gd: 0-2 GF: - Fm: 0-0
Distance: 2m2m3: 0-0 2m4-2m7: 0-5 3m+: 0-0
Track: LH: 0-3 RH: 0-1 Tight: 0-4 Gall: 0-0
Aids: Bl: 0-0 Vi: 0-0 Tstrap: 0-0 Ckp: 0-0
Best Rating: 91   11/01   NAbb 2m5f110y   soft   Ch

Plating-class chaser; acts on good and soft ground

Miss Wizz

4-y-o b f Wizard King-Fyas (Sayf El Arab (USA))
W Storey   Tony McCormick

Placings:P   (2136)
2003/04: 16⁶G,

	Starts	1st	2nd	3rd	Win & Pl
Hurdles	1	0	0	0	
Career Total	1	0	0	0	

Going: Sf: 0-0 GS: 0-0 Gd: 0-0 GF: - Fm: 0-0
Distance: 2m2m3: 0-1 2m4-2m7: 0-0 3m+: 0-0
Track: LH: 0-1 RH: 0-0 Tight: 0-0 Gall: 0-1
Aids: Bl: 0-0 Vi: 0-0 Tstrap: 0-0 Ckp: 0-0

Miss Woodpigeon
95   69

8-y-o b m Landyap (USA)-Pigeon Loft (IRE) (Bellypha)
J D Frost   Christine And Aubrey Loze

Placings:00/41400/000   (4266)
2003/04: 19⁰HY, 16⁰S, 16⁰GF,

	Starts	1st	2nd	3rd	Win & Pl
Hurdles	3	0	0	0	
Career Total	10	1	0	0	2592
101	8/01	NAbb	2m1f	H NHF	G-F	£2177

Total win prize-money £2177

Going: Sf: 0-2 GS: 0-0 Gd: 0-0 GF: - Fm: 0-1
Distance: 2m2m3: 0-2 2m4-2m7: 0-1 3m+: 0-0
Track: LH: 0-2 RH: 0-1 Tight: 0-1 Gall: 0-0
Aids: Bl: 0-0 Vi: 0-0 Tstrap: 0-0 Ckp: 0-0
Best Rating: 101   8/01   NAbb 2m1f   gd-fm   NHF

Missed Edition

6-y-o ch m Missed Flight-Exclusive Edition (IRE) (Bob Back (USA))
M J Gingell   M J Gingell

Placings:0/0PP   (1535)
2003/04: 17⁰GF, 16⁶GF, 19⁰GF,

	Starts	1st	2nd	3rd	Win & Pl
Hurdles	3	0	0	0	
Career Total	4	0	0	0	

Going: Sf: 0-0 GS: 0-0 Gd: 0-0 GF: - Fm: 0-3
Distance: 2m2m3: 0-2 2m4-2m7: 0-1 3m+: 0-0
Track: LH: 0-1 RH: 0-2 Tight: 0-2 Gall: 0-0
Aids: Bl: 0-0 Vi: 0-0 Tstrap: 0-0 Ckp: 0-0

Mission To Be
96   96

5-y-o ch g Elmaamul (USA)-All The Girls (IRE) (Alzao (USA))
Jedd O'Keeffe   John E Lund

Placings:53F3   (4292)
2003/04: 17⁵GS, 16³GS, 19⁰G, 16³GF,

	Starts	1st	2nd	3rd	Win & Pl
NH Flat	1	0	0	0	0
Hurdles	3	0	0	2	1060
Career Total	4	0	0	2	1060

Going: Sf: 0-0 GS: 0-2 Gd: 0-1 GF: - Fm: 0-1

Distance: 2m/2m3: 0-4 2m4-2m7: 0-0 3m+: 0-0
Track: LH: 0-3 RH: 0-1 Tight: 0-1 Gall: 0-0
Aids: Bl: 0-0 Vi: 0-0 Tstrap: 0-0 Ckp: 0-0
Best Rating: 96   12/03   Hayd 2m   gd-sft   Hdl

Moderate form in bumpers and hurdles on varying ground.

Mistanoora
110   144

5-y-o b g Topanoora-Mistinguett (IRE) (Doyoun)
N A Twiston-Davies   A M J Duggan

Placings:463215102-15051420   (4386)
2003/04: 16¹GF, 20⁵GF, 16⁰GS, 21⁵S, 25¹GS, 22⁴S, 24²G, 25⁰G,

	Starts	1st	2nd	3rd	Win & Pl
Hurdles	8	2	1	0	36177
Career Total	17	4	3	1	52306
146	1/04	Wwck	3m1f	B HHdl	G-S	£17160
133	10/03	Chel	2m110y	E(0-135)HHdl	G-F	£6467
128	2/03	Sand	2m110y	C Hdl	HVY	£6467
112	11/02	Weth	2m	D Hdl	G-S	£3835

Total win prize-money £33929

Going: Sf: 0-2 GS: 1-2 Gd: 0-2 GF: - Fm: 1-2
Distance: 2m2m3: 1-2 2m4-2m7: 0-3 3m+: 1-3
Track: LH: 2-5 RH: 0-3 Tight: 0-0 Gall: 0-1
Aids: Bl: 2-8 Vi: 0-0 Tstrap: 0-0 Ckp: 0-0
Best Rating: 146   1/04   Wwck 3m1f   gd-sft   Hdl

Smart handicap hurdler; patiently ridden when landing Pertemps Handicap Hurdle Qualifier on step up to 3m 1f at Warwick January 2004; effective at any trip from two to three miles; acts on all types of ground; wears blinkers.

Mistaway

6-y-o b m Nomadic Way (USA)-Miss Puck (Tepukei)
I A Brown   W Brown

Placings:00-0P   (2305)
2003/04: 16⁰GF, 19⁰GF,

	Starts	1st	2nd	3rd	Win & Pl
NH Flat	1	0	0	0	
Hurdles	1	0	0	0	
Career Total	4	0	0	0	

Going: Sf: 0-0 GS: 0-0 Gd: 0-0 GF: - Fm: 0-2
Distance: 2m2m3: 0-2 2m4-2m7: 0-0 3m+: 0-0
Track: LH: 0-2 RH: 0-0 Tight: 0-1 Gall: 0-0
Aids: Bl: 0-0 Vi: 0-0 Tstrap: 0-0 Ckp: 0-0
Best Rating: 57   11/03   Hexm 2m110y   gd-fm   NHF

Mister Arjay (USA)
103   110+

4-y-o b c Mister Baileys-Crystal Stepper (USA) (Fred Astaire (USA))
B Ellison (G A Butler 22/10)   Keith Middleton

Placings:33114   (4863)
2003/04: 16⁰GS, 16³G, 16¹GS, 16¹S, 16⁴S,

	Starts	1st	2nd	3rd	Win & Pl
Hurdles	5	2	0	2	11063
Career Total	5	2	0	2	11063
110	4/04	Hexm	2m110y	E Hdl	SFT	£3760
94	3/04	Fknm	2m	E Hdl	G-S	£3809

Total win prize-money £7569

Going: Sf: 1-2 GS: 1-2 Gd: 0-1 GF: - Fm: 0-0
Distance: 2m/2m3: 2-5 2m4-2m7: 0-0 3m+: 0-0
Track: LH: 2-4 RH: 0-1 Tight: 1-2 Gall: 0-0
Aids: Bl: 0-0 Vi: 0-0 Tstrap: 0-0 Ckp: 0-0

Best Rating: 110 4/04 Hexm 2m110y soft Hdl

Modest hurdler; mile winner on the Flat who has won at Fakenham and at Hexham over hurdles; acts on soft.

Mister Banjo (FR)
105   131+
8-y-o b g Mister Mat (FR)-Migre (FR) (Le Gregol (FR))
P F Nicholls J Hales

Placings:1110/F12P/13F0P   (4861)
2003/04: 20¹GS, 20³G, 24²FG, 32⁰G, 33ᴾGS,

	Starts	1st	2nd	3rd	Win & Pl
Chases	5	1	0	1	7319
Career Total	13	5	1	1	63824
136	12/03	Bang	2m4f110yD Ch		G-S	£5616
160	12/00	Chel	2m5f110yB Hdl		SFT	£10530
140	1/00	Chel	2m1f	A Hdl	G-S	£12000
150	12/99	Chep	2m110y	A Hdl	HVY	£17250
136	12/99	Chel	2m1f	C Hdl	GD	£5225

Total win prize-money £50621

Going: Sf: 0-0 GS: 1-2 Gd: 0-3 GF: - Fm: 0-0
Distance: 2m/2m3: 0-0 2m4-2m7: 1-2 3m+: 0-3
Track: LH: 1-4 RH: 0-1 Tight: 1-1 Gall: 0-2
Aids: Bl: 0-0 Vi: 0-0 Tstrap: 0-0 Ckp: 0-0
Best Rating: 169 1/01 Chel 2m5f110y soft Hdl

Useful novice chaser; leading juvenile hurdler of 1999/2000, he was sold for a record-breaking 240,000gns at Doncaster in May 2000; absent from April 2001 until making a winning chasing debut in December 2003; unsuited by the track next time; best around two and a half miles; acts on good ground or softer.

Mister Bigtime (IRE)
100   113
10-y-o br g Roselier (FR)-Cnoc An Oir (Goldhill)
B G Powell Mrs Jean R Bishop

Placings:452320/33220/4P3P-54   (3733)
2003/04: 25⁵S, 24⁴G,

	Starts	1st	2nd	3rd	Win & Pl
Chases	2	0	0	0	314
Career Total	17	0	4	4	12033

Going: Sf: 0-1 GS: 0-0 Gd: 0-1 GF: - Fm: 0-0
Distance: 2m/2m3: 0-0 2m4-2m7: 0-0 3m+: 0-2
Track: LH: 0-0 RH: 0-2 Tight: 0-1 Gall: 0-0
Aids: Bl: 0-0 Vi: 0-0 Tstrap: 0-0 Ckp: 0-0
Best Rating: 121 1/02 Newb 3m good Ch

Fair maiden hurdler/chaser; he acts on good ground but handles softer; stays three miles.

Mister Chisum
109   94
8-y-o b g Sabrehill (USA)-Anchor Inn (Be My Guest (USA))
Miss Kariana Key (R Allan 7/5) Mrs Jean Key

Placings:0063020/0/23022U440P111-226P2FP0430440020   (3436)
2003/04: 18²G, 16²G, 16⁶G, 16⁸G, 16²GF, 17⁶G, 16ᴾGF, 16⁰GF, 16⁴F, 17³GF, 16⁰F, 16⁴GF, 16⁴G, 16⁰S, 16⁰S, 16²GS, 16⁰HY,

	Starts	1st	2nd	3rd	Win & Pl
Hurdles	17	0	4	1	7480
Career Total	38	3	8	3	23557
102	4/03	Kels	2m110y	E(0-105)HHdl	GD	£4459
105	4/03	Newc	2m	F Hdl	GD	£2793
91	3/03	Ayr	2m	D(0-110)HHdl	SFT	£5005

Total win prize-money £12257

Going: Sf: 0-3 GS: 0-1 Gd: 0-6 GF: - Fm: 0-7
Distance: 2m/2m3: 0-17 2m4-2m7: 0-0 3m+: 0-0
Track: LH: 0-15 RH: 0-1 Tight: 0-4 Gall: 0-2
Aids: Bl: 0-0 Vi: 0-0 Tstrap: 0-0 Ckp: 0-0
Best Rating: 106 6/03 Uttx 2m gd-fm Hdl

Moderate hurdler; likes to set the pace; adopted more patient tactics when well beaten second to the improving Barton Gate at Uttoxeter Boxing Day 2003; acts on most types of ground; suited by two miles.

Mister Club Royal
89   (63h)78
8-y-o b g Alflora (IRE)-Miss Club Royal (Avocat)
D McCain John Singleton

Placings:0003F/P024P-1P42P   (4256)
2003/04: 20ᴾG, 20¹GF, 27ᴾG, 24⁴GS, 20²F, 20ᴾG,

	Starts	1st	2nd	3rd	Win & Pl
Chases	6	1	1	0	5423
Career Total	15	1	2	1	8067
78	10/03	Uttx	2m4f	E(0-105)HCh	G-F	£4104

Total win prize-money £4104

Going: Sf: 0-0 GS: 0-1 Gd: 0-3 GF: - Fm: 1-2
Distance: 2m/2m3: 0-0 2m4-2m7: 1-4 3m+: 0-2
Track: LH: 1-5 RH: 0-1 Tight: 0-2 Gall: 0-0
Aids: Bl: 0-1 Vi: 0-0 Tstrap: 0-2 Ckp: 0-0
Best Rating: 78 11/03 Leic 2m4f110y firm Ch

Plating-class chaser; stays two and a half miles; acts on any ground.

Mister Dave's (IRE)
105(104h)   (103h)121+
9-y-o ch g Bluffer-Tacovaon (Avocat)
Mrs S J Smith David Campbell

Placings:0605P01/00F224-331FFU3F   (4455)
2003/04: 25⁴G, 23³G, 24³GF, 23¹G, 25²FG, 24²S, 25ᵁS, 23³S, 24ᴾHY,

	Starts	1st	2nd	3rd	Win & Pl
Hurdles	2	0	0	1	763
Chases	7	1	0	2	6717
Career Total	21	2	2	3	12642
121	11/03	Weth	2m7f110yD(0-110)HCh		GD	£5145
94	4/02	Weth	3m1f	F(0-95)HHdl	G-F	£2443

Total win prize-money £7588

Going: Sf: 0-4 GS: 0-0 Gd: 1-4 GF: - Fm: 0-1
Distance: 2m/2m3: 0-0 2m4-2m7: 0-1 3m+: 1-8
Track: LH: 0-6 RH: 0-1 Tight: 0-1 Gall: 0-1
Aids: Bl: 0-0 Vi: 0-0 Tstrap: 0-0 Ckp: 0-0
Best Rating: 121 11/03 Weth 2m7f110y good Ch

Modest hurdler/chaser; off the mark over fences with wide margin win at Wetherby in November; stays well, acts on fast ground.

Mister Ermyn
(84h)   (49h)
11-y-o ch g Minster Son-Rosana Park (Music Boy)
L Montague Hall J Daniels

Placings:310/625/P/O60/1011PUS2UPP/P5P/P46-0PP   (0885)
2003/04: 21⁰GF, 16ᴾG, 16ᴾG,

	Starts	1st	2nd	3rd	Win & Pl
Hurdles	1	0	0	0	0
Chases	2	0	0	0	0
Career Total	30	4	2	1	12273
100	8/00	Worc	2m4f	F(0-100)HHdl	G-F	£1904
92	7/00	Strf	2m3f	E(0-105)HHdl	G-F	£2744

| 83 | 5/00 | Folk | 2m1f110yG(0-95)HHdl | | GD | £1645 |
| 97 | 2/97 | Asct | 2m110y | H NHF | G-F | £2274 |

Total win prize-money £8567

Going: Sf: 0-0 GS: 0-0 Gd: 0-2 GF: - Fm: 0-1
Distance: 2m/2m3: 0-2 2m4-2m7: 0-1 3m+: 0-0
Track: LH: 0-2 RH: 0-1 Tight: 0-0 Gall: 0-1
Aids: Bl: 0-3 Vi: 0-0 Tstrap: 0-0 Ckp: 0-0
Best Rating: 101 11/00 Chel 2m110y gd-sft Hdl

Mister Falcon (FR)
7-y-o b g Passing Sale (FR)-Falcon Crest (FR) (Cadoudal (FR))
S Flook S Flook

Placings:363/122113655P/5P-B5P   (4775)
2003/04: 21ᴮGS, 19⁵GS, 21ᴾG,

	Starts	1st	2nd	3rd	Win & Pl
Chases	3	0	0	0	0
Career Total	18	3	2	3	11935
99	7/01	Strf	2m6f110yD Hdl		G-F	£3666
101	6/01	NAbb	2m6f	D Hdl	G-F	£3241
103	5/01	Sthl	2m4f110yE Hdl		FRM	£2233

Total win prize-money £9141

Going: Sf: 0-0 GS: 0-2 Gd: 0-1 GF: - Fm: 0-0
Distance: 2m/2m3: 0-1 2m4-2m7: 0-2 3m+: 0-0
Track: LH: 0-0 RH: 0-1 Tight: 0-2 Gall: 0-0
Aids: Bl: 0-0 Vi: 0-0 Tstrap: 0-0 Ckp: 0-0
Best Rating: 106 6/01 NAbb 2m6f gd-sft Hdl

Mister Felix (IRE)
103   110+
8-y-o b g Ore-Pixies Glen (Furry Glen)
Mrs Susan Nock Gerard Nock

Placings:f0-2016   (4197)
2003/04: 19²GS, 20⁰GS, 19¹G, 24⁰G,

	Starts	1st	2nd	3rd	Win & Pl
Hurdles	4	1	1	0	5008
Career Total	8	2	1	0	9453
114	1/04	Donc	2m3f110yE Hdl		GD	£3836
110	11/02	DRoy	2m	NHF	HVY	£4444

Total win prize-money £8281

Going: Sf: 0-0 GS: 0-2 Gd: 1-2 GF: - Fm: 0-0
Distance: 2m/2m3: 0-0 2m4-2m7: 1-3 3m+: 0-1
Track: LH: 1-3 RH: 0-1 Tight: 0-0 Gall: 0-1
Aids: Bl: 0-0 Vi: 0-0 Tstrap: 0-0 Ckp: 0-0
Best Rating: 114 1/04 Donc 2m3f110y good Hdl

Modest hurdler; made virtually all in novices' hurdle at Doncaster in January 2004; stays two and a half miles well and will be suited by three; will make a chaser in time.

Mister Flint
107   111+
6-y-o b g Petoski-National Clover (National Trust)
P J Hobbs Alan Peterson

Placings:22-21F4452   (4946)
2003/04: 16²S, 16¹G, 20ᴾGS, 20⁴GS, 24⁴S, 24⁵G, 16²GS,

	Starts	1st	2nd	3rd	Win & Pl
NH Flat	2	1	1	0	2513
Hurdles	5	0	1	0	3525
Career Total	9	1	4	0	7424
111	5/03	Worc	2m	H NHF	GD	£1878

Total win prize-money £1879

Going: Sf: 0-2 GS: 0-3 Gd: 1-2 GF: - Fm: 0-0

Distance: 2m/2m3: 1-3 2m4-2m7: 0-2 3m+: 0-2
Track: LH: 1-3 RH: 0-4 Tight: 0-0 Gall: 0-0
Aids: Bl: 0-0 Vi: 0-0 Tstrap: 0-0 Ckp: 0-0
Best Rating: 111 12/03 Sand 2m4f110y gd-sft Hdl

A half-brother to Go Ballistic; runner-up in first three starts prior to winning Worcester bumper May 2003; held over hurdles; acts on good and easy ground.

Mister Friday (IRE)

103(107h)   (110+h)**116**

7-y-o b/br g Mister Lord (USA)-Rebecca's Storm (IRE) (Strong Gale)
P D Niven   R A Bartlett

Placings: F213F2-5PFP153   (4960)
2003/04: 20⁵GF, 24⁴PG, 19⁵G, 24⁴PG, 20¹G, 25⁵G, 20³GS,

	Starts	1st	2nd	3rd	Win & Pl
Hurdles	2	0	0	0	0
Chases	5	1	0	1	8279
Career Total	13	2	2	2	15943
115 3/04	Carl	2m4f		D Ch	GD £7442
108 2/03	Ayr	2m4f		E Hdl	G-S £3591
				Total win prize-money £11034

Going: Sf: 0-0 GS: 0-1 Gd: 1-5 GF: - Fm: 0-1
Distance: 2m/2m3: 0-1 2m4-2m7: 1-3 3m+: 0-3
Track: LH: 1-4 RH: 1-4 Tight: 0-4 Gall: 0-0
Aids: Bl: 0-0 Vi: 1-3 Tstrap: 0-0 Ckp: 0-0
Best Rating: 116 3/04 Kels 3m1f   good   Ch

Moderate hurdler; Irish point winner; off the mark over fences here at Carlisle in March; stays three miles well; acts on yielding ground.

Mister Graham

91(99c)   (0c)**67**

9-y-o b g Rock Hopper-Celestial Air (Rheingold)
K F Clutterbuck   K F Clutterbuck

Placings: 203/650050/3325/3005P650/245P040500-5504506P6   (3915)
2003/04: 16⁵GF, 20⁵GF, 19⁰G, 26⁴G, 17⁵GF, 17⁰GF, 16⁶GS, 20⁴F, 16⁶G,

	Starts	1st	2nd	3rd	Win & Pl
Hurdles	8	0	0	0	0
Chases	1	0	0	0	0
Career Total	40	0	3	4	4943

Going: Sf: 0-0 GS: 0-1 Gd: 0-3 GF: 0-5 3m+: 0-1
Distance: 2m/2m3: 0-5 2m4-2m7: 0-3 3m+: 0-1
Track: LH: 0-7 RH: 0-2 Tight: 0-6 Gall: 0-0
Aids: Bl: 0-0 Vi: 0-1 Tstrap: 0-1 Ckp: 0-7
Best Rating: 97 11/99 Weth 2m   good   Hdl

Mister Kingston

86   **78**

13-y-o ch g Kinglet-Flaxen Tina (Beau Tudor)
R Dickin   Mrs C M Dickin

Placings: 53642/UP/6BPP33300/P23U   (1575)
2003/04: 25⁵PGF, 24²G, 26³GF, 25¹⁄F,

	Starts	1st	2nd	3rd	Win & Pl
Chases	4	0	1	1	1830
Career Total	20	0	2	5	5327

Going: Sf: 0-0 GS: 0-0 Gd: 0-1 GF: - Fm: 0-3
Distance: 2m/2m3: 0-0 2m4-2m7: 0-3 3m+: 0-4
Track: LH: 0-2 RH: 0-2 Tight: 0-1 Gall: 0-0
Aids: Bl: 0-0 Vi: 0-1 Tstrap: 0-0 Ckp: 0-0

Best Rating: 97 4/00   Towc 3m1f   good   Ch

Modest novice staying chaser now in the veteran stage; lightly raced since 2001; did not achieve much when second at Stratford June 2003.

Mister Magpie

100   (95h)**87+**

8-y-o gr g Neltino-Magic (Sweet Revenge)
T R George   Timothy N Chick

Placings: 035001/PUPP-6633015P   (4919)
2003/04: 20⁶GS, 16⁶GF, 20³G, 21³GS, 19⁰GS, 21¹GS, 16⁵GS, 20⁵GS,

	Starts	1st	2nd	3rd	Win & Pl
Chases	8	1	0	2	6297
Career Total	18	2	0	3	10270
87 3/04	Strf	2m5f110yE(0-100)HCh	G-S £4212
95 4/02	Prth	2m110y D Hdl	GD £3744
		Total win prize-money £7956

Going: Sf: 0-0 GS: 1-6 Gd: 0-1 GF: - Fm: 0-1
Distance: 2m/2m3: 0-3 2m4-2m7: 1-5 3m+: 0-0
Track: LH: 1-5 RH: 0-3 Tight: 1-3 Gall: 0-1
Aids: Bl: 0-0 Vi: 0-0 Tstrap: 0-0 Ckp: 0-0
Best Rating: 100 2/02 Winc 2m   gd-sft NHF

Modest performer; made all in 2m 5f novices' handicap chase at Stratford March 2004; acts on good and good to soft; acts on good ground; tried in blinkers latest.

Mister McGoldrick

117(108h)   (138 h)**150+**

7-y-o b g Sabrehill (USA)-Anchor Inn (Be My Guest (USA))
Mrs S J Smith   Richard Longley

Placings: 00/6001104/10143004-1F63114U31F   (4860)
2003/04: 16¹GF, 16⁶G, 16⁶G, 16³S, 16¹GS, 20¹GS, 16⁴G, 16⁴G, 16³G, 16¹GS, 20⁴GS,

	Starts	1st	2nd	3rd	Win & Pl
Hurdles	2	1	0	0	6226
Chases	9	3	0	2	36765
Career Total	28	8	0	3	66529
148 4/04	Ayr	2m	C Ch	G-S £9647
134 2/04	Ayr	2m4f	C Ch	G-S £8645
120 12/03	Weth	2m	D Ch	G-S £5476
138 10/03	Weth	2m	C(0-135)HHdl	G-F £5551
134 12/02	Weth	2m	C(0-135)HHdl	G-S £6266
134 11/02	Weth	2m	D(0-125)HHdl	HVY £3916
115 3/02	Bang	2m1f	E Hdl	SFT £3262
112 3/02	Donc	2m110y	E(0-105)HHdl	G-S £4062
			Total win prize-money £46826

Going: Sf: 0-1 GS: 3-4 Gd: 0-5 GF: - Fm: 1-1
Distance: 2m/2m3: 3-9 2m4-2m7: 1-2 3m+: 0-0
Track: LH: 4-11 RH: 0-0 Tight: 0-2 Gall: 0-2
Aids: Bl: 0-0 Vi: 0-0 Tstrap: 0-0 Ckp: 0-0
Best Rating: 150 4/04 Ayr   2m4f   gd-sft Ch

Smart hurdler/novice chaser; ran well at Cheltenham and Aintree before winning at Ayr in April; would have followed up the next day at Ayr but for falling; stays two and a half miles, but effective at shorter; handles fast ground but well suited by soft.

Mister Moss (IRE)

103   **89**

11-y-o b g Don Tristan (USA)-Lindas Statement (IRE) (Strong Statement (USA))
B P J Baugh (G D Hanmer 24/5)   D A Malam

Placings: P-335P   (1132)
2003/04: 16³G, 22³G, 17⁵G, 20⁰G,

	Starts	1st	2nd	3rd	Win & Pl
Chases	4	0	0	2	748
Career Total	5	0	0	2	748

Going: Sf: 0-0 GS: 0-0 Gd: 0-4 GF: - Fm: 0-0
Distance: 2m/2m3: 0-2 2m4-2m7: 0-2 3m+: 0-0
Track: LH: 0-3 RH: 0-1 Tight: 0-3 Gall: 0-0
Aids: Bl: 0-0 Vi: 0-0 Tstrap: 0-0 Ckp: 0-0
Best Rating: 89 5/03 MRas 2m6f110y good   Ch

Ex-hunter chaser/pointer; has won on fast surface; should improve from first start back after three months.

Mister Moussac

84   **69+**

5-y-o b g Kasakov-Salu (Ardross)
Miss Kariana Key   Arthur Symons Key

Placings: P565P   (2771)
2003/04: 16²GF, 16⁵G, 17⁶G, 24⁵G, 16⁶S,

	Starts	1st	2nd	3rd	Win & Pl
Hurdles	5	0	0	0	0
Career Total	5	0	0	0	0

Going: Sf: 0-1 GS: 0-0 Gd: 0-3 GF: - Fm: 0-1
Distance: 2m/2m3: 0-4 2m4-2m7: 0-1 3m+: 0-1
Track: LH: 0-3 RH: 0-2 Tight: 0-2 Gall: 0-1
Aids: Bl: 0-0 Vi: 0-0 Tstrap: 0-0 Ckp: 0-0
Best Rating: 69 11/03 MRas 2m1f110y good   Hdl

Mister Muddypaws

14-y-o b g Celtic Cone-Jane's Daughter (Pitpan)
C P Dennis   T W Ellwood

Placings: 2346/4121/P4P4/U3452231/FF433P1P/105P/P1P/4-3   (0167)
2003/04: 25³G,

	Starts	1st	2nd	3rd	Win & Pl
Chases	1	0	0	1	434
Career Total	37	6	4	6	48734
115 4/02	Newc	3m	D(0-120)HCh	FRM £5872
121 5/00	Sedg	3m4f	D(0-125)HCh	G-F £10822
116 3/00	Sedg	3m4f	D(0-120)HCh	G-F £4212
125 4/99	Sedg	3m4f	C(0-130)HCh	G-F £11422
104 11/95	Carl	3m110y	E Hdl	G-F £2136
93 5/95	Hexm	2m4f110y	Hdl	G-F £2469
			Total win prize-money £36935

Going: Sf: 0-0 GS: 0-0 Gd: 0-1 GF: - Fm: 0-0
Distance: 2m/2m3: 0-0 2m4-2m7: 0-3 3m+: 0-1
Track: LH: 0-1 RH: 0-0 Tight: 0-1 Gall: 0-0
Aids: Bl: 0-0 Vi: 0-0 Tstrap: 0-0 Ckp: 0-0
Best Rating: 125 4/99 Sedg 3m4f   gd-sft Ch

A dour stayer, suited by fast ground, he beat his sole opponent at Newcastle in April.

Mister Mustard (IRE)

104   **109**

7-y-o b g Norwich-Monalma (IRE) (Montekin)
Ian Williams   Favourites Racing

Placings: 13-22253   (3947)
2003/04: 20²GS, 20²S, 17²GS, 16⁵S, 16³G,

	Starts	1st	2nd	3rd	Win & Pl
Hurdles	5	0	3	1	4296
Career Total	7	1	3	2	7227

95	2/03	Asct	2m110y H NHF	SFT	£2443
			Total win prize-money		£2443

Going:	Sf: 0-2 GS: 0-2 Gd: 0-1 GF: - Fm: 0-0
Distance:	2m/2m3: 0-3 2m4-2m7: 0-2 3m+: 0-0
Track:	LH: 0-3 RH: 0-0 Tight: 0-1 Gall: 0-0
Aids:	Bl: 0-0 Vi: 0-0 Tstrap: 0-0 Ckp: 0-0
Best Rating:	112 2/04 Winc 2m good Hdl

Decent form in bumpers; runner-up in novice hurdles at Haydock and Bangor; stays two and a half miles; acts on good and soft ground.

Mister One
106   131
13-y-o b/br g Buckley-Miss Redlands (Dubassoff (USA))
C L Tizzard C L Tizzard

Placings:4/113FP33/35012U0/10512/5-P2463400 (4834)
2003/04: 30PGS, 252G, 254G, 236S, 25²G, 304G, 240G, 26⁶GF,

	Starts	1st	2nd	3rd	Win & Pl
Chases	8	0	1	1	8876
Career Total	29	5	3	5	62192

138	3/02	Extr	3m6f110yD(0-125)HCh	GD	£8417
133	1/02	Winc	3m1f110yD(0-125)HCh	GD	£5580
119	2/01	Sand	3m110y E Ch	SFT	£5486
133	12/99	Chel	3m1f110yC Ch	GD	£6905
132	11/99	Chel	3m110y B Ch	GD	£9530
			Total win prize-money		£35920

Going:	Sf: 0-1 GS: 0-1 Gd: 0-5 GF: - Fm: 0-1
Distance:	2m/2m3: 0-0 2m4-2m7: 0-0 3m+: 0-8
Track:	LH: 0-2 RH: 0-6 Tight: 0-0 Gall: 0-3
Aids:	Bl: 0-0 Vi: 0-0 Tstrap: 0-1 Ckp: 0-1
Best Rating:	138 4/02 Chel 3m2f110y gd-fm Ch

Fair chaser; thorough stayer; best on decent ground; goes well fresh; has been tried in cheekpieces.

Mister Pearly
7-y-o ch g Alflora (IRE)-Pearly Dream (Rymer)
J W Mullins Mrs Hilary Pike

Placings:043 (3362)
2003/04: 17⁹GS, 184GS, 243G,

	Starts	1st	2nd	3rd	Win & Pl
NH Flat	1	0	0	0	0
Chases	2	0	0	1	1686
Career Total	3	0	0	1	1686

Going:	Sf: 0-0 GS: 0-2 Gd: 0-1 GF: - Fm: 0-0
Distance:	2m/2m3: 0-2 2m4-2m7: 0-0 3m+: 0-1
Track:	LH: 0-1 RH: 0-2 Tight: 0-0 Gall: 0-1
Aids:	Bl: 0-0 Vi: 0-0 Tstrap: 0-2 Ckp: 0-0
Best Rating:	55 12/03 Hrfd 2m1f gd-sft NHF

Mister Pickwick (IRE)
86   (78c)97+
9-y-o b g Commanche Run-Buckfast Lass (Buckskin (FR))
Mrs J A Ewer (G L Moore 9/2) Mrs J A Ewer

Placings:3036001F/4P02FPP/P46P0304/5151-2536P (4897)

2003/04: 20²G, 215GS, 223HY, 226GS, 22PG,

	Starts	1st	2nd	3rd	Win & Pl
Hurdles	4	0	0	1	367
Chases	1	0	1	0	1030
Career Total	32	3	2	4	11319

97	9/02	Plum	2m5f G(0-95)HHdl	GD	£2226
85	6/02	Font	2m6f110yD(0-115)HHdl	G-F	£3444
102	4/00	Plum	3m1f110yE(0-105)HHdl	G-S	£2660
			Total win prize-money		£8330

Going:	Sf: 0-1 GS: 0-2 Gd: 0-2 GF: - Fm: 0-0
Distance:	2m/2m3: 0-0 2m4-2m7: 0-5 3m+: 0-0
Track:	LH: 0-2 RH: 0-3 Tight: 0-3 Gall: 0-1
Aids:	Bl: 0-4 Vi: 0-0 Tstrap: 0-0 Ckp: 0-1
Best Rating:	102 4/00 Plum 3m1f110y gd-sft Hdl

Moderate, quirky hurdler/chaser; well suited by Fontwell/Plumpton; stays well; seems to handle any ground.

Mister Putt (USA)
98(105h)   (122+h)110+
6-y-o b/br g Mister Baileys-Theresita (GER) (Surumu (GER))
Mrs N Smith Tony Hayward And Barry Fulton

Placings:0432P/00131-0U34 (3860)
2003/04: 16⁶G, 17UGS, 18³GS, 174GS,

	Starts	1st	2nd	3rd	Win & Pl
Hurdles	1	0	0	0	0
Chases	3	0	0	1	1395
Career Total	14	2	1	3	12822

121	3/03	Plum	2m D Hdl	HVY	£5408
103	1/03	Plum	2m E(0-110)HHdl	HVY	£3474
			Total win prize-money		£8882

Going:	Sf: 0-0 GS: 0-3 Gd: 0-1 GF: - Fm: 0-0
Distance:	2m/2m3: 0-2 2m4-2m7: 0-0 3m+: 0-0
Track:	LH: 0-3 RH: 0-1 Tight: 0-2 Gall: 0-1
Aids:	Bl: 0-4 Vi: 0-0 Tstrap: 0-1 Ckp: 0-0
Best Rating:	121 3/03 Plum 2m heavy Hdl

Modest chaser/fair hurdler; goes well at Plumpton; best at two miles; acts on good ground or softer; often wears blinkers; has worn a tongue tie.

Mister Webb
104(87c)   (52c)93+
7-y-o b g Whittingham (IRE)-Ruda (FR) (Free Round (USA))
Dr J R J Naylor Norman E Webb

Placings:34/006P04-435121 (1045)
2003/04: 204G, 20³GF, 23⁶GF, 221GF, 22²GF, 221GF,

	Starts	1st	2nd	3rd	Win & Pl
Hurdles	6	2	1	1	9264
Career Total	14	2	1	2	9965

93	8/03	NAbb	2m6f E(0-110)HHdl	G-F	£4737
93	6/03	NAbb	2m6f F(0-95)HHdl	G-F	£3080
			Total win prize-money		£7817

Going:	Sf: 0-0 GS: 0-0 Gd: 0-0 GF: - Fm: 2-5
Distance:	2m/2m3: 0-0 2m4-2m7: 2-5 3m+: 0-0
Track:	LH: 2-5 RH: 0-0 Tight: 2-5 Gall: 0-0
Aids:	Bl: 0-0 Vi: 2-6 Tstrap: 0-0 Ckp: 0-0
Best Rating:	93 8/03 NAbb 2m6f gd-fm Hdl

Moderate hurdler/chaser; maiden stayer on the Flat; easy winner of 2m 6f Class F handicap hurdle at Newton Abbot June 2003; scored again off 12lb higher mark over the same course and distance in August; usually wears a visor.

Misterllaneous (IRE)
86f
6-y-o b g Mister Lord (USA)-Noras Gale (IRE) (Strong Gale)
R Johnson Mrs Fiona Thompson

Placings:2 (0334)
2003/04: 17²GF,

	Starts	1st	2nd	3rd	Win & Pl
NH Flat	1	0	1	0	594
Career Total	1	0	1	0	594

Going:	Sf: 0-0 GS: 0-0 Gd: 0-0 GF: - Fm: 0-1
Distance:	2m/2m3: 0-0 2m4-2m7: 0-0 3m+: 0-0
Track:	LH: 0-1 RH: 0-0 Tight: 0-0 Gall: 0-0
Aids:	Bl: 0-0 Vi: 0-0 Tstrap: 0-0 Ckp: 0-0
Best Rating:	86 5/03 Sthl 2m1f gd-fm NHF

Big sort; runner-up to a very easy winner on debut at Southwell in May.

Mistress Banjo
86f
4-y-o b f Start Fast (FR)-Temperance (FR) (Beyssac (FR))
A King The Banjo Players

Placings:3 (2675)
2003/04: 123GF,

	Starts	1st	2nd	3rd	Win & Pl
NH Flat	1	0	0	1	383
Career Total	1	0	0	1	383

Going:	Sf: 0-0 GS: 0-0 Gd: 0-0 GF: - Fm: 0-1
Distance:	2m/2m3: 0-0 2m4-2m7: 0-0 3m+: 0-0
Track:	LH: 0-1 RH: 0-0 Tight: 0-0 Gall: 0-0
Aids:	Bl: 0-0 Vi: 0-0 Tstrap: 0-0 Ckp: 0-0
Best Rating:	86 12/03 Newb 1m4f110y gd-fm NHF

Third on debut in 12 furlong junior bumper at Newbury in December 2003 on good to firm.

Mistrio
102   106+
7-y-o gr h Linamix (FR)-Mistreat (Gay Mecene (USA))
K C Bailey Derek J Harding-Jones

Placings:2 (4589)
2003/04: 16²G,

	Starts	1st	2nd	3rd	Win & Pl
Hurdles	1	0	1	0	1088
Career Total	1	0	1	0	1088

Going:	Sf: 0-0 GS: 0-0 Gd: 0-1 GF: - Fm: 0-0
Distance:	2m/2m3: 0-1 2m4-2m7: 0-0 3m+: 0-0
Track:	LH: 0-0 RH: 0-1 Tight: 0-0 Gall: 0-1
Aids:	Bl: 0-0 Vi: 0-0 Tstrap: 0-0 Ckp: 0-0
Best Rating:	106 3/04 Hntg 2m110y good Hdl

Misty Class (IRE)
(98h)   (88h)88
12-y-o gr g Roselier (FR)-Toevarro (Raga Navarro (ITY))
Mrs S J Smith Widdop Wanderers

Placings:4/205600/614325261/1452F23F31U/2C113P04P/14020/0 (3819)
2003/04: 23⁹S,

	Starts	1st	2nd	3rd	Win & Pl
Hurdles	1	0	0	0	
Career Total	42	7	7	4	57230

137	5/01	Sthl	3m110y C(0-130)HHdl	G-F	£5733
137	12/00	Donc	3m2f B(0-140)HCh	G-S	£10773
137	12/00	Weth	3m1f C(0-130)HCh	SFT	£5915
115	3/00	Kels	3m1f D Ch	G-S	£5200
103	5/99	Weth	2m4f110yD Hdl	G-F	£3078
124	4/99	Ayr	2m6f C HHdl	HVY	£7327
98	10/98	Towc	2m5f E(0-100)HHdl	G-S	£2402
			Total win prize-money		£40431

Going:	Sf: 0-1 GS: 0-0 Gd: 0-0 GF: - Fm: 0-0
Distance:	2m/2m3: 0-0 2m4-2m7: 0-0 3m+: 0-1
Track:	LH: 0-1 RH: 0-0 Tight: 0-0 Gall: 0-0
Aids:	Bl: 0-0 Vi: 0-0 Tstrap: 0-0 Ckp: 0-0
Best Rating:	137 5/01 Sthl 3m110y gd-fm Hdl

Fair chaser/hurdler; now in the veteran stage; first start since 2001 when well beaten over hurdles; has won on soft and fast ground; stays three miles.

Misty Dancer
96   98+
5-y-o gr g Vettori (IRE)-Light Fantastic (Deploy)
Miss Venetia Williams Pinks Gym & Leisure Wear Ltd

Placings:16PP   (4651)
2003/04: 17^1GS, 17^6GS, 16^8PG, 17^9G,

	Starts	1st	2nd	3rd	Win & Pl
Hurdles	4	1	0	0	4238
Career Total	4	1	0	0	4238
98	1/04 Tntn	2m1f	E Hdl	G-S	£4238
			Total win prize-money £4238		

Going:	Sf: 0-0 GS: 1-3 Gd: 0-1 GF: - Fm: 0-0
Distance:	**2m/2m3: 1-4** 2m4-2m7: 0-0 3m+: 0-0
Track:	LH: 0-1 **RH: 1-3 Tight: 1-3** Gall: 0-0
Aids:	Bl: 0-0 Vi: 0-0 Tstrap: 0-1 Ckp: 0-0
Best Rating:	98 1/04 Tntn 2m1f gd-sft Ch

Modest hurdler; winner on debut; acts on fast and easy ground.

Misty Future
108(104h)   (94h)130+
6-y-o b g Sanglamore (USA)-Star Of The Future (USA) (El Gran Senor (USA))
Miss Venetia Williams The Mystics

Placings:0642-402142423151122   (2479)
2003/04: 17^4GS, 16^9G, 22^2G, 21^4G, 22^2GF, 19^4GF, 19^2GF, 26^3GF, 25^1GF, 24^5G, 26^1GF, 25^1GF, 25^2G, 26^2GF,

	Starts	1st	2nd	3rd	Win & Pl
Hurdles	7	1	2	0	6606
Chases	8	3	3	1	27948
Career Total	19	4	6	1	35365
130	11/03 Winc	3m1f110yD(0-110)HCh	G-F	£12151
120	10/03 Plum	3m2f D(0-120)HCh	G-F	£4728
102	10/03 Hrfd	3m1f110yE Ch	G-F	£2684
101	6/03 Strf	2m6f110yF(0-95)HHdl	GD	£3571
		Total win prize-money £23137		

Going:	Sf: 0-0 GS: 0-1 Gd: 1-6 GF: - **Fm: 3-8**
Distance:	2m/2m3: 0-3 2m4-2m7: 1-5 **3m+: 3-7**
Track:	LH: 2-9 RH: 2-5 **Tight: 2-9** Gall: 0-1
Aids:	Bl: 0-1 Vi: 0-0 Tstrap: 0-0 Ckp: 0-0
Best Rating:	130 11/03 Aint 3m1f good Ch

Fair chaser; in great form in the autumn of 2003; stays three miles plus and suited by fast ground; best when ridden prominently.

Misty Memory
80   42
5-y-o b m Alderbrook-Misty Sunset (Le Bavard (FR))
R F Knipe Mrs R F Knipe

Placings:*0-000*   (4650)
2003/04: 16^9G, 16^0GS, 19^0G,

	Starts	1st	2nd	3rd	Win & Pl
NH Flat	2	0	0	0	0
Hurdles	1	0	0	0	0
Career Total	4	0	0	0	

Going:	Sf: 0-0 GS: 0-1 Gd: 0-2 GF: - Fm: 0-0
Distance:	2m/2m3: 0-2 2m4-2m7: 0-1 3m+: 0-0
Track:	LH: 0-1 RH: 0-2 Tight: 0-0 Gall: 0-0
Aids:	Bl: 0-0 Vi: 0-0 Tstrap: 0-0 Ckp: 0-0
Best Rating:	72 2/03 Ludl 2m good NHF

Misty Ramble (IRE)
102   95
9-y-o b g Roselier (FR)-Ramble Bramble (Random Shot)
Ferdy Murphy Mrs M B Scholey

Placings:*0*/0420/34352/U52234-2   (0193)
2003/04: 25^2G,

	Starts	1st	2nd	3rd	Win & Pl
Chases	1	0	1	0	1206
Career Total	17	0	5	3	8445

Going:	Sf: 0-0 GS: 0-0 Gd: 0-1 GF: - Fm: 0-0
Distance:	2m/2m3: 0-0 2m4-2m7: 0-0 3m+: 0-1
Track:	LH: 0-1 RH: 0-0 Tight: 0-0 Gall: 0-0
Aids:	Bl: 0-1 Vi: 0-0 Tstrap: 0-1 Ckp: 0-0
Best Rating:	102 11/01 Kels 3m1f gd-sft Ch

Plating-class chaser; often placed, but yet to get off the mark; stays well; best in soft ground; usually wears tongue tie; has worn blinkers.

Misty Ridge (IRE)
92(103c)   (91c)96
9-y-o b g Moscow Society (USA)-Abigail's Dream (Kalaglow)
Mrs S J Smith Widdop Wanderers

Placings:*0*/05/030265U/50213321P-660400   (1362)
2003/04: 19^6G, 22^6G, 21^9G, 21^4GS, 22^0G, 16^0GF,

	Starts	1st	2nd	3rd	Win & Pl
Hurdles	5	0	0	0	0
Chases	1	0	0	0	0
Career Total	25	2	3	3	12808
91	10/02 MRas	2m6f110yE Ch	G-F	£4130
96	6/02 MRas	2m3f110yD(0-120)HHdl	G-F	£4134
		Total win prize-money £8264		

Going:	Sf: 0-0 GS: 0-1 Gd: 0-4 GF: - Fm: 0-1
Distance:	2m/2m3: 0-1 2m4-2m7: 0-5 3m+: 0-0
Track:	LH: 0-4 RH: 0-2 Tight: 0-3 Gall: 0-0
Aids:	Bl: 0-3 Vi: 0-0 Tstrap: 0-0 Ckp: 0-0
Best Rating:	97 8/02 MRas 2m6f110y gd-fm Ch

Very moderate chaser; effective over two and a half miles; acts well on a fast surface, although has gone in soft ground; out of form of late.

Mitey Perk (IRE)
5-y-o b g Executive Perk-More Dash (IRE) (Strong Gale)
J S Haldane Mrs A F Tullie

Placings:*0*   (4881)
2003/04: 17^0GS,

	Starts	1st	2nd	3rd	Win & Pl
Hurdles	1	0	0	0	
Career Total	1	0	0	0	

Going:	Sf: 0-0 GS: 0-0 Gd: 0-0 GF: - Fm: 0-0
Distance:	2m/2m3: 0-1 2m4-2m7: 0-0 3m+: 0-0
Track:	LH: 0-0 RH: 0-1 Tight: 0-0 Gall: 0-0
Aids:	Bl: 0-0 Vi: 0-0 Tstrap: 0-0 Ckp: 0-0

Mithak (USA)
78   24
10-y-o b g Silver Hawk (USA)-Kapalua Butterfly (USA) (Stage Door Johnny (USA))
R T Phillips T Milson C Merson P Nichols R Stokes

Placings:3133/12/065/P40U03/22F112-0PP0   (4870)
2003/04: 20^4G, 20^8S, 24^2PS, 24^8GS,

	Starts	1st	2nd	3rd	Win & Pl
Hurdles	4	0	0	0	
Career Total	25	4	4	4	20487
116	1/03 Ludl	3m D(0-115)HHdl	SFT	£4966
112	12/02 Hayd	2m7f110yE(0-110)HHdl	SFT	£3627
124	5/99 Strf	2m6f110yE Hdl	G-S	£2738
114	1/99 Ludl	2m5f110yF Hdl	SFT	£2255
		Total win prize-money £13586		

Going:	Sf: 0-1 GS: 0-2 Gd: 0-1 GF: - Fm: 0-0
Distance:	2m/2m3: 0-0 2m4-2m7: 0-2 3m+: 0-2
Track:	LH: 0-3 RH: 0-0 Tight: 0-3 Gall: 0-0
Aids:	Bl: 0-0 Vi: 0-0 Tstrap: 0-0 Ckp: 0-0
Best Rating:	131 10/99 Chep 2m4f soft Hdl

Modest handicap hurdler; stays three miles two, effective over shorter; suited by soft ground.

Mixed Marriage (IRE)
87   115
6-y-o ch g Indian Ridge-Marie De Flandre (FR) (Crystal Palace (FR))
Miss Victoria Roberts D C Roberts

Placings:146-0   (4917)
2003/04: 20^9GS,

	Starts	1st	2nd	3rd	Win & Pl
Hurdles	1	0	0	0	
Career Total	4	1	0	0	3510
115	2/03 Plum	2m F Hdl	SFT	£3094
		Total win prize-money £3094		

Going:	Sf: 0-0 GS: 0-1 Gd: 0-0 GF: - Fm: 0-0
Distance:	2m/2m3: 0-2 2m4-2m7: 0-1 3m+: 0-0
Track:	LH: 0-1 RH: 0-0 Tight: 0-0 Gall: 0-0
Aids:	Bl: 0-0 Vi: 0-0 Tstrap: 0-0 Ckp: 0-0
Best Rating:	115 2/03 Plum 2m soft Hdl

Fair novice hurdler; best over two miles and soft ground.

Mixsterthetrixster (USA)
100(111h)   (134dh)109+
8-y-o b g Alleged (USA)-Parliament House (USA) (General Assembly (USA))
Miss T M Ide Miss Tracey Ide

Placings:U12132120/50210F5-3   (4869)
2003/04: 17^3S,

	Starts	1st	2nd	3rd	Win & Pl
Chases	1	0	0	1	857
Career Total	17	4	2	2	37795
134	1/03 Donc	2m110y C(0-130)HHdl	G-S	£7104
123	2/00 Kels	2m2f C Hdl	G-S	£5609
121	11/99 Newc	2m D Hdl	GD	£3028
122	10/99 Weth	2m A Hdl	GD	£9525
		Total win prize-money £25269		

Going:	Sf: 0-1 GS: 0-0 Gd: 0-0 GF: - Fm: 0-0
Distance:	2m/2m3: 0-1 2m4-2m7: 0-0 3m+: 0-0
Track:	LH: 0-1 RH: 0-0 Tight: 0-1 Gall: 0-0
Aids:	Bl: 0-0 Vi: 0-0 Tstrap: 0-0 Ckp: 0-0
Best Rating:	134 1/03 Donc 2m110y gd-sft Hdl

Useful hurdler; well beaten third on chase debut; has won from two to two and a quarter miles; acts on good/good to soft ground.

Mizinky
95 ... **69**

4-y-o b f El Conquistador-Miss Pimpernel (Blakeney)
W G M Turner Bob Chandler

Placings:F054630 (4401)
2003/04: 16^6GF, 16^0GS, 16^5S, 16^4G, 21^6G, 19^3G, 21^0G,

	Starts	1st	2nd	3rd	Win & Pl
Hurdles	7	0	0	1	361
Career Total	7	0	0	1	361

Going:	Sf: 0-1 GS: 0-1 Gd: 0-4 GF: - Fm: 0-1
Distance:	2m/2m3: 0-4 2m4-2m7: 0-3 3m+: 0-0
Track:	LH: 0-2 RH: 0-5 Tight: 0-2 Gall: 0-1
Aids:	Bl: 0-0 Vi: 0-0 Tstrap: 0-0 Ckp: 0-0
Best Rating:	69 3/04 Tntn 2m3f110y good Hdl

Plating-class hurdler; poor form so far.

Mobasher (IRE)
105 ... **119**

5-y-o b g Spectrum (IRE)-Danse Royale (IRE) (Caerleon (USA))
Miss Venetia Williams (D K Weld 19/10) The 1961 Partnership

Placings:101222 (4372)
2003/04: 16^1G, 16^0GS, 16^1HY, 17^2GS, 19^2G, 16^2GF,

	Starts	1st	2nd	3rd	Win & Pl
Hurdles	6	2	3	0	24571
Career Total	6	2	3	0	24571
102 1/04 Towc 2m		E Hdl		HVY	£4153
116 12/03 Donc 2m110y		B Hdl		GD	£14595

Total win prize-money £18749

Going:	Sf: 1-1 GS: 0-2 Gd: 1-2 GF: - Fm: 0-1
Distance:	2m/2m3: 2-5 2m4-2m7: 0-1 3m+: 0-0
Track:	LH: 1-5 RH: 1-1 Tight: 0-2 Gall: 1-2
Aids:	Bl: 0-0 Vi: 0-0 Tstrap: 0-0 Ckp: 0-0
Best Rating:	122 3/04 Strf 2m110y gd-fm Hdl

Fair hurdler; ex-Irish; has done well in early starts over hurdles in this country: suited by two miles and acts on any ground; wore blinkers on the Flat.

Modem (IRE)
100 ... **90**

7-y-o b g Midhish-Holy Water (Monseigneur (USA))
D Shaw Dr J Charlesworth

Placings:U664P24420165 (1989)
2003/04: 17^1G, 17^6G, 16^6G, 17^4G, 17^2G, 17^2GS, 17^4GF, 16^4GF, 17^2GF, 17^0GF, 16^1GF, 16^6GF, 16^5GF,

	Starts	1st	2nd	3rd	Win & Pl
Hurdles	13	1	2	0	3945
Career Total	13	1	2	0	3945
90 10/03 Uttx 2m		G Hdl		G-F	£1925

Total win prize-money £1925

Going:	Sf: 0-0 GS: 0-1 Gd: 0-5 GF: 1-7
Distance:	2m/2m3: 1-12 2m4-2m7: 0-0 3m+: 0-0
Track:	LH: 1-10 RH: 0-1 Tight: 0-5 Gall: 0-0
Aids:	Bl: 0-0 Vi: 0-0 Tstrap: 0-0 Ckp: 0-0
Best Rating:	90 10/03 Uttx 2m gd-fm Hdl

Plating-class hurdler; finally off the mark at Uttoxeter in October; wears a visor, quirky type.

Modem (NZ)
(0c)**120+**

10-y-o br g Omnicorp (NZ)-Replica (NZ) (Creag-An-Sgor)
S E H Sherwood T N Siviter

Placings:121/115/PP-P1P (1306)
2003/04: 16^2GS, 21^1G, 20^0GF,

	Starts	1st	2nd	3rd	Win & Pl
Hurdles	3	1	0	0	3493
Career Total	11	5	1	0	21131
120 7/03 Sthl 2m5f110y	E(0-110)HHdl	GD	£3493
133 5/01 Aint 2m110y	B(0-145)HHdl	GD	£6929
125 5/01 Bang 2m1f	E(0-135)HHdl	GD	£4602
114 10/00 Chel 2m110y	E(0-115)HHdl	GD	£3445
107 9/00 Worc 2m	E Hdl	G-F	£1897

Total win prize-money £20366

Going:	Sf: 0-0 GS: 0-1 Gd: 1-1 GF: - Fm: 0-1
Distance:	2m/2m3: 0-1 **2m4-2m7: 1-2** 3m+: 0-0
Track:	LH: 1-3 RH: 0-0 Tight: 0-1 Gall: 0-0
Aids:	Bl: 0-0 Vi: 0-0 Tstrap: 0-0 Ckp: 0-0
Best Rating:	133 5/01 Aint 2m110y good Hdl

Four times a winner over hurdles in 2000/01, he has clearly had his training problems as he has been very lightly raced since; pulled up on both starts over fences, breaking a blood vessel on the second occasion; bounced back with very impressive win in handicap hurdle at Southwell in June; stays two mile six.

Modulor (FR)
96(100c) ... (106c)**82**

12-y-o gr g Less Ice-Chaumontaise (FR) (Armos)
L R James (M C Pipe 3/6) L R James Limited

Placings:06FF3512102/0132F3P3/064422/14113/21354F4511/3063610/00541301421F/0046P22453B60F-000P040 (4592)
2003/04: 22^0G, 19^0GF, 17^0GF, 22^2PS, 19^0G, 27^4F, 26^0G,

	Starts	1st	2nd	3rd	Win & Pl
Hurdles	7	0	0	0	0
Career Total	80	13	9	10	194534
12/01 Cagn 2m3f	HCh	G-S	£9056
12/01 Cagn 2m2f110y	Ch	VS	£4382
8/01 Mesl 2m5f	Ch	FRM	£2424
10/00 Toul 2m1f110y	Ch	SFT	£2881
4/00 Nant 2m3f110y	Hdl	HVY	£4323
3/00 Toul 2m5f	HCh	SFT	£12488
10/99 Autl 2m2f110y	Ch	VS	£10764
6/98 Toul 2m4f	Hdl	G-S	£3030
6/98 Autl 2m6f	Ch	VS	£12121
5/98 Chol 2m3f	Hdl	VS	£3030
10/96 Autl 2m1f110y	Ch	VS	£10540
3/96 Toul 2m1f110y	Hdl	SFT	£14456
1/96 Pau 2m110y	Hdl	VS	£6588

Total win prize-money £96084

Going:	Sf: 0-1 GS: 0-0 Gd: 0-3 GF: - Fm: 0-3
Distance:	2m/2m3: 0-1 2m4-2m7: 0-4 3m+: 0-2
Track:	LH: 0-3 RH: 0-4 Tight: 0-1 Gall: 0-1
Aids:	Bl: 0-0 Vi: 0-2 Tstrap: 0-0 Ckp: 0-1
Best Rating:	106 3/03 Chel 3m2f110y good Ch

Fair chaser/plating-class hurdler; decent chaser in France; best at around two and a half miles; has worn blinkers and visor.

Moffied (IRE)
64f ... **28f**

4-y-o b g Nashwan (USA)-Del Deya (IRE) (Caerleon (USA))
Mrs L B Normile Fyffees and A K Collins

Placings:0 (4952)

2003/04: 16^0GS,

	Starts	1st	2nd	3rd	Win & Pl
NH Flat	1	0	0	0	
Career Total	1	0	0	0	

Going:	Sf: 0-0 GS: 0-1 Gd: 0-0 GF: - Fm: 0-0
Distance:	2m/2m3: 0-1 2m4-2m7: 0-0 3m+: 0-0
Track:	LH: 0-0 RH: 0-1 Tight: 0-0 Gall: 0-0
Aids:	Bl: 0-0 Vi: 0-0 Tstrap: 0-0 Ckp: 0-0
Best Rating:	28 4/04 Prth 2m110y gd-sft NHF

Mohawk Brave (IRE)
91 ... **92**

6-y-o b g Be My Native (USA)-Aunty Dawn (IRE) (Strong Gale)
K C Bailey Mrs E A Kellar

Placings:04-3U6F (2907)
2003/04: 16^3S, 20^UGS, 17^6GS, 26^FGS,

	Starts	1st	2nd	3rd	Win & Pl
NH Flat	1	0	0	1	317
Hurdles	3	0	0	0	
Career Total	6	0	0	1	317

Going:	Sf: 0-1 GS: 0-3 Gd: 0-0 GF: - Fm: 0-0
Distance:	2m/2m3: 0-2 2m4-2m7: 0-1 3m+: 0-0
Track:	LH: 0-2 RH: 0-2 Tight: 0-0 Gall: 0-1
Aids:	Bl: 0-0 Vi: 0-0 Tstrap: 0-0 Ckp: 0-0
Best Rating:	99 5/03 Uttx 2m soft NHF

Moderate form in bumpers.

Mohera King (IRE)
113

12-y-o br g King's Ride-Kilbrien Star (Goldhill)
Ferdy Murphy Maurice J Barry

Placings:15340/0636153031/25336242/5F0345446P/4436313-P (4912)
2003/04: 20^PS,

	Starts	1st	2nd	3rd	Win & Pl
Chases	1	0	0	0	
Career Total	41	4	3	10	33908
113 3/03 Ayr 2m4f	E(0-110)HCh	SFT	£4127
113 4/00 Fair 2m6f	HHdl	G-Y	£8320
113 1/00 Naas 2m3f	Hdl	SH	£4416
113 11/98 Cork 2m4f	NHF	SFT	£2391

Total win prize-money £19255

Going:	Sf: 0-1 GS: 0-0 Gd: 0-0 GF: - Fm: 0-0
Distance:	2m/2m3: 0-2 2m4-2m7: 0-1 3m+: 0-0
Track:	LH: 0-0 RH: 0-1 Tight: 0-0 Gall: 0-0
Aids:	Bl: 0-0 Vi: 0-0 Tstrap: 0-0 Ckp: 0-0
Best Rating:	113 3/03 Ayr 2m4f soft Ch

Modest novice chaser; took a weak event in the mud at Ayr in March.

Molly Mello (GER)

5-y-o gr m Big Shuffle (USA)-Manitoba (GER) (Surumu (GER))
M F Harris (U Ostmann 9/11) Let's Live Racing

Placings:P0 (3468)
2003/04: 16^0HY, 20^0GF,

	Starts	1st	2nd	3rd	Win & Pl
Hurdles	2	0	0	0	

Career Total	2	0	0	0

Going:	Sf: 0-1 GS: 0-0 Gd: 0-0 GF: 0-1 Fm: 0-1
Distance:	2m/2m3: 0-1 2m4-2m7: 0-1 3m+: 0-0
Track:	LH: 0-1 RH: 0-1 Tight: 0-1 Gall: 0-1
Aids:	Bl: 0-1 Vi: 0-0 Tstrap: 0-0 Ckp: 0-0

Mollycarrsbrekfast

100   89

9-y-o b g Presidium-Imperial Flame (Imperial Lantern)
K Bishop (Miss S E Robinson 31/5) Mrs E M Davis

Placings:50/P46-50414   (1091)
2003/04: 24⁵G, 16⁹G, 23⁴GF, 23¹G, 24⁴G,

	Starts	1st	2nd	3rd	Win & Pl
Chases	5	1	0	0	4053
Career Total	10	1	0	0	4053
89	7/03	Worc	2m7f110yF(0-100)HCh	GD	£3406

Total win prize-money £3406

Going:	Sf: 0-0 GS: 0-0 Gd: 1-4 GF: - Fm: 0-1
Distance:	2m/2m3: 0-1 2m4-2m7: 0-0 3m+: 1-4
Track:	LH: 1-5 RH: 0-0 Tight: 0-2 Gall: 0-0
Aids:	Bl: 0-0 Vi: 0-0 Tstrap: 0-0 Ckp: 0-0
Best Rating:	89 7/03 Worc 2m7f110y good Ch

Plating-class chaser; winner of four points; suited by a return to front-running tactics when winning a handicap at Worcester in July 2003; stays three miles; acts on a sound surface.

Moment Of Madness (IRE)

78

6-y-o ch g Treasure Hunter-Sip Of Orange (Celtic Cone)
T J Fitzgerald Mrs R A G Haggie

Placings:0-40   (4050)
2003/04: 16⁴G, 16⁰G,

	Starts	1st	2nd	3rd	Win & Pl
NH Flat	2	0	0	0	0
Career Total	3	0	0	0	0

Going:	Sf: 0-0 GS: 0-0 Gd: 0-2 GF: - Fm: 0-0
Distance:	2m/2m3: 0-2 2m4-2m7: 0-0 3m+: 0-0
Track:	LH: 0-1 RH: 0-1 Tight: 0-1 Gall: 0-0
Aids:	Bl: 0-0 Vi: 0-0 Tstrap: 0-0 Ckp: 0-0
Best Rating:	88 2/04 Muss 2m good NHF

Momentous Jones

100   (0c)87

7-y-o b g Emperor Jones (USA)-Ivory Moment (USA) (Sir Ivor)
M Madgwick W V Roker

Placings:35F515105/F5454P6/05026P0-06345450 (3855)
2003/04: 22⁹GF, 18⁵GF, 22⁴G, 22⁵G, 18⁴G, 20⁵HY, 16⁸S,

	Starts	1st	2nd	3rd	Win & Pl
Hurdles	8	0	1	0	263
Career Total	31	2	1	2	8668
110	1/01	Font	2m2f110yE Hdl	SFT	£2502
110	12/00	Font	2m2f110yE Hdl	SFT	£2317

Total win prize-money £4820

Going:	Sf: 0-2 GS: 0-0 Gd: 0-3 GF: - Fm: 0-3
Distance:	2m/2m3: 0-4 2m4-2m7: 0-4 3m+: 0-0
Track:	LH: 0-5 RH: 0-3 Tight: 0-7 Gall: 0-0
Aids:	Bl: 0-0 Vi: 0-0 Tstrap: 0-0 Ckp: 0-3

Best Rating: 110 12/01 Font 2m2f110y good Hdl

Modest hurdler; suited by trips just beyond two miles and best form on soft ground.

Mon Arc En Ciel (FR)

97   85

9-y-o b/br g Silver Rainbow-La Bonne Etoile (FR) (Margouillat (FR))
R Mathew Mrs Robin Mathew

Placings:0500/0PPPP/400   (4198)
2003/04: 16⁴G, 16⁰G, 16⁰G,

	Starts	1st	2nd	3rd	Win & Pl
Hurdles	3	0	0	0	0
Career Total	12	0	0	0	0

Going:	Sf: 0-0 GS: 0-0 Gd: 0-3 GF: - Fm: 0-0
Distance:	2m/2m3: 0-3 2m4-2m7: 0-0 3m+: 0-0
Track:	LH: 0-3 RH: 0-0 Tight: 0-1 Gall: 0-1
Aids:	Bl: 0-0 Vi: 0-0 Tstrap: 0-0 Ckp: 0-0
Best Rating:	85 5/03 Worc 2m good Hdl

Mon Petit Diamant

4-y-o b f Hector Protector (USA)-Desert Girl (Green Desert (USA))
M J Polglase (M Wigham 1/8) M J Polglase

Placings:UP   (1007)
2003/04: 16ᵁG, 17²G,

	Starts	1st	2nd	3rd	Win & Pl
Hurdles	2	0	0	0	
Career Total	2	0	0	0	

Going:	Sf: 0-0 GS: 0-0 Gd: 0-2 GF: - Fm: 0-0
Distance:	2m/2m3: 0-2 2m4-2m7: 0-0 3m+: 0-0
Track:	LH: 0-2 RH: 0-0 Tight: 0-2 Gall: 0-0
Aids:	Bl: 0-0 Vi: 0-0 Tstrap: 0-0 Ckp: 0-0

Mon Villez (FR)

110   (0c)142

5-y-o ch g Villez (USA)-Europa (SPA) (Legend Of France (USA))
N J Henderson (T Civel 25/5) Million In Mind Partnership

Placings:33/313153-3115140   (4397)
2003/04: 20⁹VS, 20¹GS, 20¹GS, 21⁵GS, 16¹S, 24⁴G, 21⁹G,

	Starts	1st	2nd	3rd	Win & Pl
Hurdles	6	3	0	0	26388
Chases	1	0	0	1	14773
Career Total	15	5	0	6	113754
133	2/04	Weth	2m A Hdl	SFT	£17850
125	12/03	Uttx	2m4f110yE Hdl	G-S	£3332
117	12/03	Fknm	2m4f110yF Hdl	G-S	£2331
	11/02	Autl	2m1f110y Ch	HLD	£34509
	9/02	Autl	2m1f110y Ch	VS	£12368

Total win prize-money £70390

Going:	Sf: 1-1 GS: 2-3 Gd: 0-2 GF: - Fm: 0-3
Distance:	2m/2m3: 1-1 2m4-2m7: 2-5 3m+: 0-1
Track:	LH: 2-4 RH: 1-2 Tight: 1-1 Gall: 0-2
Aids:	Bl: 0-0 Vi: 0-0 Tstrap: 0-0 Ckp: 0-0
Best Rating:	142 2/04 Kemp 3m110y good Hdl

Very useful hurdler; chase winner in France; disappointing at Cheltenham in the SunAlliance; stays 2m 5f; suited by soft ground.

Monarch's Pursuit

96   125

10-y-o b g Pursuit Of Love-Last Detail (Dara Monarch)
T D Easterby Mrs Jean P Connew

Placings:115/0/F/3253U162/2201F504/3F326-054 (4217)
2003/04: 19⁰G, 20⁵G, 17⁴GS,

	Starts	1st	2nd	3rd	Win & Pl
Chases	3	0	0	0	525
Career Total	29	4	5	4	36696
126	12/01	Uttx	2m	C(0-135)HCh	SFT	£6727
117	2/01	Catt	2m3f	D Ch	SFT	£4212
120	11/97	Weth	2m	A Hdl	G-F	£8955
108	10/97	Weth	2m	D Hdl	G-F	£2810

Total win prize-money £22705

Going:	Sf: 0-0 GS: 0-1 Gd: 0-2 GF: - Fm: 0-0
Distance:	2m/2m3: 0-2 2m4-2m7: 0-1 3m+: 0-0
Track:	LH: 0-2 RH: 0-1 Tight: 0-2 Gall: 0-1
Aids:	Bl: 0-2 Vi: 0-0 Tstrap: 0-0 Ckp: 0-0
Best Rating:	126 12/01 Uttx 2m soft Ch

Modest chaser; stays two and a half miles, but better suited by shorter; acts on soft ground; usually wears blinkers; has worn a tongue tie.

Monbonami (IRE)

110(90h)   (59h)101

7-y-o b g Beau Sher-Hard Riche (Hard Fought)
Miss K Marks (Jonjo O'Neill 21/1) Nick Shutts

Placings:500/P465063/0F504523UP-P0050133214 (4140)
2003/04: 17²HY, 16⁶GF, 16⁰Y, 18⁵F, 16⁰G, 24¹GS, 24³GS, 24³GS, 21²GS, 21¹GS, 21⁴G,

	Starts	1st	2nd	3rd	Win & Pl
Hurdles	4	0	0	0	535
Chases	7	2	1	2	9051
Career Total	31	2	2	4	12167
101	1/04	Fknm	2m5f110yE(0-100)HCh	G-S	£3861
97	11/03	Uttx	3m	F(0-95)HCh	G-S	£3017

Total win prize-money £6878

Going:	Sf: 0-1 GS: 2-5 Gd: 0-2 GF: - Fm: 0-2
Distance:	2m/2m3: 0-5 2m4-2m7: 1-3 3m+: 1-3
Track:	LH: 2-6 RH: 0-0 Tight: 1-3 Gall: 0-0
Aids:	Bl: 0-0 Vi: 0-0 Tstrap: 0-0 Ckp: 0-0
Best Rating:	101 1/04 Fknm 2m5f110y gd-sft Ch

Modest maiden hurdler/chaser; ex-Irish; stays three miles.

Mondeed

102   100

7-y-o b m Terimon-House Deed (Presidium)
N B King (Joseph Crowley 16/10) St Gatien Racing Club

Placings:36003205622U466F1P   (4914)
2003/04: 17³HY, 20⁶GF, 16⁰F, 16⁰F, 16³GF, 19⁴G, 20⁵F, 24⁴S, 20³G, 22²GF, 16ᵁGF, 16³G, 20⁶G, 21²G, 23¹G, 24⁴GS,

	Starts	1st	2nd	3rd	Win & Pl
NH Flat	4	0	0	1	409
Hurdles	14	1	3	1	10826
Career Total	18	1	3	2	11235
100	4/04	Fknm	2m7f110yD(0-110)HHdl	GD	£7118

Total win prize-money £7118

Going:	Sf: 0-2 GS: 0-1 Gd: 1-7 GF: - Fm: 0-8
Distance:	2m/2m3: 0-8 2m4-2m7: 0-7 3m+: 1-3
Track:	LH: 1-7 RH: 0-0 Tight: 1-4 Gall: 0-0
Aids:	Bl: 0-3 Vi: 0-0 Tstrap: 0-0 Ckp: 0-0
Best Rating:	100 4/04 Fknm 2m7f110y good Hdl

Plating-class hurdler; ex-Irish; stays three miles and acts on a sound surface; suited by patient tactics.

Mondial Jack (FR)

114   136

5-y-o ch g Apple Tree (FR)-Cackle (USA) (Crow (FR))
M C Pipe (C Aubert 3/6) C M , B J & R F Batterham Ii

Placings:15-F2P11U1P01   (4953)
2003/04: 17¹HY, 17²S, 19²GF, 19¹GS, 20¹G, 20⁴G, 20¹G, 24²G, 25⁹G, 20¹G,

	Starts	1st	2nd	3rd	Win & Pl
Hurdles	1	0	0	0	0
Chases	9	4	1	0	41137
Career Total	12	5	1	0	50244
136 4/04 Sand	2m4f110yB(0-145)HCh		GD		£15674
125 3/04 Kemp	2m4f110yD Ch		GD		£7315
119 2/04 Kemp	2m4f110yD Ch		GD		£6857
119 1/04 Hrfd	2m3f E Ch		G-S		£4745
2/03 Pau	2m1f110y Hdl		VS		£8727
				Total win prize-money £43319	

Going:	Sf: 0-2 GS: 1-1 Gd: 3-6 GF: - Fm: 0-1	
Distance:	2m/2m3: 1-4 **2m4-2m7: 3-4** 3m+: 0-2	
Track:	LH: 0-3 **RH: 4-4** Tight: 0-3 Gall: 0-1	
Aids:	Bl: 0-0 Vi: 0-0 Tstrap: 0-0 Ckp: 0-0	
Best Rating:	136 4/04 Sand 2m4f110y good Ch	

Useful novice chaser; ex-French; stays trips of around two and a half miles and acts well on good and soft ground.

Mondul (GER)

114   136

4-y-o b c Colon (GER)-Morgenrote (GER) (Aveiro)
M F Harris (C Von Der Recke 30/11) Let's Live Racing

Placings:11215062   (4966a)
2003/04: 16¹S, 16¹S, 16²S, 17¹GS, 16⁵G, 17⁹G, 16⁶S, 19²VS,

	Starts	1st	2nd	3rd	Win & Pl
Hurdles	8	3	2	0	73574
Career Total	8	3	2	0	73574
134 1/04 Chel	2m1f A Hdl		G-S		£17400
136 12/03 Ling	2m110y A Hdl		SFT		£14500
118 12/03 Wwck	2m B Hdl		GD		£10335
				Total win prize-money £42235	

Going:	Sf: 1-3 GS: 1-1 Gd: 1-3 GF: - Fm: 0-0	
Distance:	**2m/2m3: 3-7** 2m4-2m7: 0-1 3m+: 0-0	
Track:	LH: 3-7 RH: 0-0 Tight: 1-1 Gall: 1-2	
Aids:	Bl: 0-0 Vi: 0-0 Tstrap: 0-0 Ckp: 0-0	
Best Rating:	136 12/03 Ling 2m110y soft Hdl	

Very useful juvenile hurdler; 11-furlong winner on the level in Germany; in good form in his first four starts over hurdles in Britain, winning a couple of Grade Twos, but disappointing subsequently; best on soft ground.

Monet's Garden (IRE)

107   140+

6-y-o gr g Roselier (FR)-Royal Remainder (IRE) (Remainder Man)
N G Richards David Wesley Yates

Placings:f-1121   (4939)
2003/04: 22¹G, 20¹G, 20²G, 24¹GS,

	Starts	1st	2nd	3rd	Win & Pl
Hurdles	4	3	1	0	25335
Career Total	4	3	1	0	27351
134 4/04 Prth	3m110y C Hdl		G-S		£7586
117 3/04 Carl	2m4f E Hdl		GD		£4046
114 11/03 Kels	2m6f110yE Hdl		GD		£2702
109 2/03 Ayr	2m H NHF		G-S		£2016
				Total win prize-money £16350	

Going:	Sf: 0-0 GS: 1-1 Gd: 2-3 GF: - Fm: 0-0	
Distance:	2m/2m3: 0-0 **2m4-2m7: 2-3** 3m+: 1-1	
Track:	LH: 1-2 RH: 2-2 Tight: 1-2 Gall: 0-0	
Aids:	Bl: 0-0 Vi: 0-0 Tstrap: 0-0 Ckp: 0-0	
Best Rating:	140 4/04 Aint 2m4f good Hdl	

Very useful novice hurdler; bumper winner; won first two starts over hurdles before excellent second in Grade Two event at Aintree; took a valuable event at Perth in April; stays two and a half miles; acts on good ground; progressive and fine chasing prospect.

Money Crazy (FR)

76   55

5-y-o ch g Green Tune (USA)-Value For Money (FR) (Highest Honor (FR))
Ian Williams Ian Williams

Placings:00660   (4123)
2003/04: 19⁰G, 20⁰G, 16⁶GS, 16⁶GS, 17⁰G,

	Starts	1st	2nd	3rd	Win & Pl
Hurdles	5	0	0	0	0
Career Total	5	0	0	0	0

Going:	Sf: 0-0 GS: 0-2 Gd: 0-3 GF: - Fm: - 0-0	
Distance:	2m/2m3: 0-4 2m4-2m7: 0-1 3m+: 0-0	
Track:	LH: 0-2 RH: 0-3 Tight: 0-1 Gall: 0-0	
Aids:	Bl: 0-2 Vi: 0-0 Tstrap: 0-0 Ckp: 0-0	
Best Rating:	60 12/03 Wwck 2m gd-sft Hdl	

Money Magic

8-y-o ch m Weld-Susie's Money (Seymour Hicks (FR))
Miss S E Broadhurst J R Parrott

Placings:P-P   (0430)
2003/04: 26⁸G,

	Starts	1st	2nd	3rd	Win & Pl
Chases	1	0	0	0	
Career Total	2	0	0	0	

Going:	Sf: 0-0 GS: 0-0 Gd: 0-0 GF: - Fm: 0-0	
Distance:	2m/2m3: 0-0 2m4-2m7: 0-0 3m+: 0-1	
Track:	LH: 0-1 RH: 0-0 Tight: 0-1 Gall: 0-0	
Aids:	Bl: 0-0 Vi: 0-0 Tstrap: 0-0 Ckp: 0-0	

Money Mountain

67   15

7-y-o ch g Rakaposhi King-Black H'Penny (Town And Country)
J A B Old A J Britten

Placings:0-PPP0   (4518)
2003/04: 20⁰S, 16⁰HY, 22⁰G, 17⁰GS,

	Starts	1st	2nd	3rd	Win & Pl
Hurdles	4	0	0	0	
Career Total	5	0	0	0	

Going:	Sf: 0-2 GS: 0-1 Gd: 0-1 GF: - Fm: 0-0	
Distance:	2m/2m3: 0-2 2m4-2m7: 0-2 3m+: 0-0	
Track:	LH: 0-1 RH: 0-3 Tight: 0-0 Gall: 0-0	
Aids:	Bl: 0-0 Vi: 0-0 Tstrap: 0-0 Ckp: 0-1	
Best Rating:	36 2/03 Newb 2m110y good NHF	

Monger Lane

99(100c)   (100+c)120

8-y-o b m Karinga Bay-Grace Moore (Deep Run)
K Bishop Slabs And Lucan

Placings:03/4/0503011/0204-16P   (4451)
2003/04: 22¹HY, 24⁶G, 24⁶GS,

	Starts	1st	2nd	3rd	Win & Pl
Hurdles	2	0	0	0	166
Chases	1	1	0	0	4932
Career Total	17	3	1	2	57205
100 7/04 Towc	2m6f E Ch		HVY		£4932
120 4/02 Chel	2m5f110yA HHdl		GD		£19604
109 3/02 Newb	2m5f A HHdl		G-S		£23200
				Total win prize-money £47736	

Going:	Sf: 1-1 GS: 0-1 Gd: 0-1 GF: - Fm: 0-0	
Distance:	2m/2m3: 0-2 **2m4-2m7: 1-1** 3m+: 0-2	
Track:	LH: 0-1 **RH: 1-2** Tight: 0-0 Gall: 0-1	
Aids:	Bl: 0-0 Vi: 0-0 Tstrap: 0-0 Ckp: 0-0	
Best Rating:	120 12/02 Chel 2m5f110y soft Hdl	

Fair hurdler/chaser; caused a surprise by winning the valuable mares' hurdle final at Newbury in March 2002; won a match on her chasing debut; suited by a strong pace; best at trips just short of three miles; acts on ground good or softer.

Monkerhostin (FR)

122(107c)   (131c)152

7-y-o b g Shining Steel-Ladoun (FR) (Kaldoun (FR))
P J Hobbs M G St Quinton

Placings:3/1235221501/52F13546050-13423116   (4646)
2003/04: 19¹GF, 16³GS, 16⁶S, 21²G, 16³G, 24¹G, 21¹G, 20⁶G,

	Starts	1st	2nd	3rd	Win & Pl
Hurdles	8	3	1	2	106044
Career Total	30	7	5	5	147466
152 3/04 Chel	2m5f A HHdl		GD		£43500
149 2/04 Kemp	3m110y A Hdl		GD		£23200
135 11/03 Newb	2m3f C(0-130)HHdl		G-F		£7085
131 11/03 Wwck	2m110y D Ch		GD		£4693
132 4/02 Strf	2m110y D(0-120)HHdl		GD		£3679
122 2/02 Sedg	2m1f E Hdl		SFT		£2583
5/01 Pari	2m1f Hdl		G-S		£4850
				Total win prize-money £89590	

Going:	Sf: 0-1 GS: 0-1 Gd: 2-5 GF: - Fm: 1-1	
Distance:	2m/2m3: 1-4 2m4-2m7: 1-3 3m+: 1-1	
Track:	**LH: 2-5** RH: 1-3 Tight: 0-1 **Gall: 2-4**	
Aids:	Bl: 0-0 Vi: 0-0 Tstrap: 0-0 Ckp: 0-0	
Best Rating:	152 3/04 Chel 2m5f good Hdl	

Smart hurdler, also pretty decent, but lightly raced over fences; fine effort when third in the 2004 Tote Gold Trophy at Newbury in February and improved on even that to win Rendlesham Hurdle at Kempton and Coral Cup at the Festival; effective from two to three miles and acts on good and soft ground; has worn cheekpieces and a visor; very tough and progressive.

Monksford

103   76

5-y-o b g Minster Son-Mortify (Prince Sabo)
B J Llewellyn B W Parren

Placings:3-000P5F   (4697)
2003/04: 16⁰S, 17⁰GS, 17⁰G, 16⁶G, 17⁵GS, 17⁶G,

	Starts	1st	2nd	3rd	Win & Pl
Hurdles	6	0	0	0	0
Career Total	7	0	0	1	384

Going:	Sf: 0-1 GS: 0-2 Gd: 0-3 GF: - Fm: 0-0

Distance: 2m/2m3: 0-6 2m4-2m7: 0-0 3m+: 0-0
Track: LH: 0-6 RH: 0-6 Tight: 0-2 Gall: 0-1
Aids: Bl: 0-0 Vi: 0-0 Tstrap: 0-0 Ckp: 0-0
Best Rating: 78 3/04 Extr 2m1f   gd-sft Hdl

Monnaie Forte (IRE)

14-y-o b g Strong Gale-Money Run (Deep Run)
C Storey James R Adam

Placings:10/1P1FFF111/P12112312/P56/06042F224/232P
P2/3304P2P/4   (4296)
2003/04: 21⁴GF,

	Starts	1st	2nd	3rd	Win & Pl
Chases	1	0	0	0	0
Career Total	46	10	10	4	93460
128	4/98	Asct	2m110y C(0-135)HHdl	GD	£5015
133	1/98	Ayr	2m4f	B(0-145)HCh	G-S	£12475
137	1/98	Sand	2m	B HCh	G-S	£7139
108	11/97	Ayr	2m	B(0-140)HCh	G-S	£6317
118	4/97	Asct	2m110y	B(0-140)HHdl	G-F	£5622
105	3/97	Carl	2m4f	E(0-115)HHdl	GD	£2213
105	3/97	Kels	2m2f	D(0-120)HHdl	GD	£2827
88	11/96	Ayr	2m4f	D(0-105)HCh	GD	£3616
93	3/95	Hntg	2m110y	E Hdl	SFT	£2635

Total win prize-money £47863

Going: Sf: 0-0 GS: 0-0 Gd: 0-0 GF: - Fm: 0-1
Distance: 2m/2m3: 0-0 2m4-2m7: 0-0 3m+: 0-0
Track: LH: 0-1 RH: 0-0 Tight: 0-0 Gall: 0-0
Aids: Bl: 0-0 Vi: 0-0 Tstrap: 0-0 Ckp: 0-0
Best Rating: 141 4/98 Ayr 2m   good Ch

Monocky

83   53

9-y-o b g Mon Tresor-Solbella (Starch Reduced)
Mrs D A Hamer Treberth Partnership

Placings:/P/4P   (3461)
2003/04: 20⁴GD, 24ᴾS,

	Starts	1st	2nd	3rd	Win & Pl
Hurdles	2	0	0	0	0
Career Total	3	0	0	0	0

Going: Sf: 0-1 GS: 0-0 Gd: 0-0 GF: - Fm: 0-1
Distance: 2m/2m3: 0-0 2m4-2m7: 0-1 3m+: 0-1
Track: LH: 0-2 RH: 0-0 Tight: 0-0 Gall: 0-0
Aids: Bl: 0-0 Vi: 0-0 Tstrap: 0-0 Ckp: 0-0
Best Rating: 53 11/03 Worc 2m4f   gd-fm Hdl

Monolith

110   115+

6-y-o b g Bigstone (IRE)-Ancara (Dancing Brave (USA))
L Lungo Elite Racing Club

Placings:005-11302   (4731)
2003/04: 20¹G, 20¹G, 24³GS, 24⁰G, 20²G,

	Starts	1st	2nd	3rd	Win & Pl
Hurdles	5	2	1	1	9751
Career Total	8	2	1	1	9751
106	5/03	Bang	2m4f	D(0-110)HHdl	GD	£5369
100	5/03	Hexm	2m4f110yF Hdl	GD	£2751

Total win prize-money £8120

Going: Sf: 0-0 GS: 0-1 Gd: 2-4 GF: - Fm: 0-0
Distance: 2m/2m3: 0-0 2m4-2m7: 2-3 3m+: 0-2
Track: LH: 2-3 RH: 0-2 Tight: 1-2 Gall: 0-0
Aids: Bl: 0-0 Vi: 0-0 Tstrap: 0-0 Ckp: 0-0
Best Rating: 115 4/04 Carl 2m4f   good Hdl

Modest hurdler; improved to win twice in May 2003; stays two miles four; effective on good and softer.

Monsal Dale (IRE)

89   72+

5-y-o ch g Desert King (IRE)-Zanella (IRE) (Nordico (USA))
N E Berry (B J Llewellyn 13/1) Terry Reffell

Placings:606510   (3320)
2003/04: 17⁶GF, 16⁹GF, 20⁶G, 22⁵G, 17¹GS, 16⁰S,

	Starts	1st	2nd	3rd	Win & Pl
Hurdles	6	1	0	0	2226
Career Total	6	1	0	0	2226
72	12/03	Folk	2m1f110y		G(0-95)HHdl
G-S £2226					

Total win prize-money £2226

Going: Sf: 0-1 GS: 1-1 Gd: 0-2 GF: - Fm: 0-2
Distance: 2m/2m3: 1-4 2m4-2m7: 0-2 3m+: 0-0
Track: LH: 0-2 RH: 1-3 Tight: 1-3 Gall: 0-0
Aids: Bl: 0-0 Vi: 0-0 Tstrap: 0-0 Ckp: 0-0
Best Rating: 72 12/03 Folk 2m1f110y gd-sft Hdl

Monsieur Delage

99f   76f

4-y-o b g Overbury (IRE)-Sally Ho (Gildoran)
N Wilson G Griffin

Placings:5   (4264)
2003/04: 16⁵GF,

	Starts	1st	2nd	3rd	Win & Pl
NH Flat	1	0	0	0	0
Career Total	1	0	0	0	0

Going: Sf: 0-0 GS: 0-0 Gd: 0-0 GF: - Fm: 0-1
Distance: 2m/2m3: 0-1 2m4-2m7: 0-0 3m+: 0-1
Track: LH: 0-1 RH: 0-0 Tight: 0-0 Gall: 0-0
Aids: Bl: 0-0 Vi: 0-0 Tstrap: 0-0 Ckp: 0-0
Best Rating: 76 3/04 Catt 2m   gd-fm NHF

Monsieur Poirot (IRE)

92(98h)   (83dh)103+

7-y-o b g Lapierre-Mallia Miss (IRE) (Executive Perk)
Mrs S C Bradburne The Hon Thomas Cochrane

Placings:0/34600-0356P302P03   (4940)
2003/04: 24⁰G, 24³G, 20⁵G, 24⁶G, 24ᴾGS, 16³S, 24⁰GF, 26²HY,
16ᴾGF, 20⁰G, 16³GS,

	Starts	1st	2nd	3rd	Win & Pl
Hurdles	6	0	0	2	1179
Chases	5	0	1	1	2584
Career Total	17	0	1	4	4325

Going: Sf: 0-2 GS: 0-2 Gd: 0-5 GF: - Fm: 0-2
Distance: 2m/2m3: 0-4 2m4-2m7: 0-2 3m+: 0-5
Track: LH: 0-5 RH: 0-6 Tight: 0-1 Gall: 0-0
Aids: Bl: 0-0 Vi: 0-5 Tstrap: 0-0 Ckp: 0-0
Best Rating: 103 1/04 Ayr 2m   heavy Ch

Modest chaser/ plating-class staying hurdler; stays three miles; effective at shorter; acts on good ground or softer.

Monsieur Punch (FR)

82   44

5-y-o b g Beyssac (FR)-Ferlia (FR) (Noir Et Or)

P Winkworth P Winkworth

Placings:00   (2598)
2003/04: 18⁰G, 21⁰G,

	Starts	1st	2nd	3rd	Win & Pl
Hurdles	2	0	0	0	
Career Total	2	0	0	0	

Going: Sf: 0-0 GS: 0-0 Gd: 0-2 GF: - Fm: 0-0
Distance: 2m/2m3: 0-1 2m4-2m7: 0-1 3m+: 0-0
Track: LH: 0-2 RH: 0-0 Tight: 0-0 Gall: 0-0
Aids: Bl: 0-0 Vi: 0-0 Tstrap: 0-0 Ckp: 0-0
Best Rating: 48 12/03 Wwck 2m5f   good Hdl

Monsieur Rose (IRE)

91   88

8-y-o gr g Roselier (FR)-Derring Slipper (Derring Rose)
N J Gifford Martin & Valerie Slade

Placings:4/F0033   (4932)
2003/04: 16⁵S, 16⁹GS, 20⁰S, 26³G, 27³G,

	Starts	1st	2nd	3rd	Win & Pl
Hurdles	5	0	0	2	1058
Career Total	6	0	0	2	1058

Going: Sf: 0-2 GS: 0-1 Gd: 0-2 GF: - Fm: 0-0
Distance: 2m/2m3: 0-2 2m4-2m7: 0-1 3m+: 0-0
Track: LH: 0-1 RH: 0-3 Tight: 0-2 Gall: 0-0
Aids: Bl: 0-0 Vi: 0-0 Tstrap: 0-0 Ckp: 0-0
Best Rating: 90 4/01 Hntg 2m110y soft NHF

Lightly raced; would have finished third but for falling on hurdles debut in November.

Monsieur Tagel (FR)

105(101c)   (118c)114

8-y-o b g Tagel (USA)-Miss Zonissa (FR) (Zino)
Ian Williams J Cullen Thermals Ltd

Placings:10442622/511F134F0/501033UF/302FPP-
0460023   (4441)
2003/04: 22⁰G, 20⁴GF, 21⁶GF, 21⁰G, 20⁰G, 19²G, 21³S,

	Starts	1st	2nd	3rd	Win & Pl
Hurdles	6	0	1	1	1713
Chases	1	0	0	0	
Career Total	38	5	5	5	27286
118	11/01	Ludl	2m4f	E Ch	G-F	£3770
127	10/00	Strf	2m6f110yD(0-120)HHdl	G-S	£3068
123	9/00	Chep	2m4f	D(0-125)HHdl	GD	£3415
124	9/00	Hntg	2m4f110yD(0-120)HHdl	G-F	£4348
97	10/99	Worc	2m	E Hdl	GD	£2215

Total win prize-money £16818

Going: Sf: 0-1 GS: 0-0 Gd: 0-4 GF: - Fm: 0-2
Distance: 2m/2m3: 0-0 2m4-2m7: 0-7 3m+: 0-0
Track: LH: 0-4 RH: 0-3 Tight: 0-0 Gall: 0-3
Aids: Bl: 0-0 Vi: 0-0 Tstrap: 0-0 Ckp: 0-0
Best Rating: 127 12/00 MRas 2m3f110y gd-sft Hdl

Fair hurdler/chaser at his best; has won on good and soft but usually raced on a sounder surface; best at trips of around two and a half miles.

Montagnette

102   81d

10-y-o ch m Gildoran-Deep Crevasse (Rolfe (USA))
M R Bosley Girls On Top Racing 2000

Placings:4000/454220/205PF126/06/24PP-P5P4600   (3904)

2003/04: 24⁵PS, 24⁵G, 24⁴PS, 24⁴G, 26⁶GS, 22⁰G, 24⁰GS,

	Starts	1st	2nd	3rd	Win & Pl
Hurdles	7	0	0	0	0
Career Total	31	1	5	0	5473
74 2/01 Towc 2m5f	G(0-90)HHdl				£1694

Total win prize-money £1694

Going: Sf: 0-2 GS: 0-2 Gd: 0-3 GF: - Fm: 0-0
Distance: 2m/2m3: 0-0 2m4-2m7: 0-1 3m+: 0-6
Track: LH: 0-2 RH: 0-5 Tight: 0-3 Gall: 0-0
Aids: Bl: 0-0 Vi: 0-0 Tstrap: 0-0 Ckp: 0-0
Best Rating: 85 11/98 Wwck 2m   soft NHF

Plating-class hurdler; lightly raced in recent years; stays well and acts in the mud.

Montayral (FR)
113(101h)   (127h)137

7-y-o b g Lesotho (USA)-Demi Lune De Mars (FR) (Fast (FR))
P Hughes T Mannion

Placings:2233/4341231211FU/144F-0PP1303363   (4965)

2003/04: 22⁰G, 24⁴PG, 24⁴PG, 28¹G, 27³G, 29⁵S, 20³S, 25³Y, 29⁶Y, 29³GF,

	Starts	1st	2nd	3rd	Win & Pl
Hurdles	1	0	0	1	795
Chases	9	1	0	3	45854
Career Total	30	6	4	8	96872
127 11/03 Cork 3m4f	(0-140)HCh	GD			£21103
127 10/02 Gway 2m4f	Hdl	HVY			£7975
124 4/02 Uttx 3m2f	E Ch	GD			£3445
126 3/02 Plum 3m4f	E Ch	G-S			£3022
115 2/02 Plum 3m4f	E Ch	HVY			£3728
118 12/01 Bang 2m4f110yD	Ch	SFT			£4095

Total win prize-money £43370

Going: Sf: 0-2 GS: 0-0 Gd: 1-5 GF: - Fm: 0-1
Distance: 2m/2m3: 0-0 2m4-2m7: 0-2 3m+: 1-8
Track: LH: 0-2 RH: 0-7 Tight: 0-0 Gall: 0-1
Aids: Bl: 0-0 Vi: 0-0 Tstrap: 0-0 Ckp: 0-0
Best Rating: 137 4/04 Sand 3m5f110y gd-fm Ch

Useful chaser; good form in novice chases for Paul Nicholls in 2001/2; now trained in Ireland; stays three and a half miles; acts well on soft ground.

Monte Cinto (FR)
90   89+

4-y-o br g Bulington (FR)-Algue Rouge (FR) (Perouges (FR))
P F Nicholls Mrs Monica Hackett

Placings:631F0   (4788)

2003/04: 16⁶S, 16⁹VS, 17¹HY, 16⁶GS, 16⁹G,

	Starts	1st	2nd	3rd	Win & Pl
Hurdles	5	1	0	1	10479
Career Total	5	1	0	1	10479
1/04 Pau 2m1f110y	Hdl	HVY			£8113

Total win prize-money £8113

Going: Sf: 1-2 GS: 0-1 Gd: 0-1 GF: - Fm: 0-0
Distance: 2m/2m3: 1-5 2m4-2m7: 0-0 3m+: 0-0
Track: LH: 0-2 RH: 0-0 Tight: 0-1 Gall: 0-0
Aids: Bl: 0-0 Vi: 0-0 Tstrap: 0-0 Ckp: 0-0
Best Rating: 89 3/04 Chep 2m110y gd-sft Hdl

Monte Cristo (FR)
111(109h)   (106h)124

6-y-o ch g Bigstone (IRE)-El Quahirah (FR) (Cadoudal (FR))

Mrs L C Taylor Mrs L C Taylor

Placings:435531P/24U122643223-314P11065   (4889)

2003/04: 18³G, 17¹G, 20⁴GF, 20⁵S, 17¹GS, 16¹GS, 20⁰G, 18⁶G, 20⁵GF,

	Starts	1st	2nd	3rd	Win & Pl
Hurdles	1	0	0	1	583
Chases	8	3	0	0	21857
Career Total	28	5	5	5	51238
125 1/04 Fknm 2m110y	D(0-120)HCh	G-S			£7321
125 12/03 Strf 2m1f110yD(0-120)HCh		G-S			£8209
124 10/03 Strf 2m1f110yD(0-125)HCh		GD			£5369
96 11/02 Plum 2m1f	E Ch	SFT			£3666
106 3/02 Hayd 2m	D Hdl	GD			£4862

Total win prize-money £29429

Going: Sf: 0-1 GS: 2-2 Gd: 1-4 GF: - Fm: 0-2
Distance: 2m/2m3: 3-5 2m4-2m7: 0-4 3m+: 0-0
Track: LH: 3-8 RH: 0-1 Tight: 3-6 Gall: 0-2
Aids: Bl: 0-0 Vi: 3-8 Tstrap: 0-0 Ckp: 0-0
Best Rating: 125 1/04 Fknm 2m110y gd-sft Ch

Modest chaser/moderate hurdler; acts on good and soft ground; effective at around two miles two, but should stay further; usually wears headgear; consistent; twice a winner at Stratford.

Monte Rosa (IRE)
94f   100f

5-y-o b m Supreme Leader-Green Thorn (IRE) (Ovac (ITY))
N G Richards E H Birkbeck and A D Stewart

Placings:2   (4608)

2003/04: 17²G,

	Starts	1st	2nd	3rd	Win & Pl
NH Flat	1	0	1	0	531
Career Total	1	0	1	0	531

Going: Sf: 0-0 GS: 0-0 Gd: 0-1 GF: - Fm: 0-0
Distance: 2m/2m3: 0-1 2m4-2m7: 0-0 3m+: 0-0
Track: LH: 0-0 RH: 0-1 Tight: 0-1 Gall: 0-0
Aids: Bl: 0-0 Vi: 0-0 Tstrap: 0-0 Ckp: 0-0
Best Rating: 102 3/04 MRas 2m1f110y good NHF

Monte Rouge (IRE)
77   78

7-y-o ch g Montelimar (USA)-Drumdeels Star (IRE) (Le Bavard (FR))
Miss L C Siddall The Full Monte

Placings:2/55/6-60   (3209)

2003/04: 20⁶GS, 25⁹GS,

	Starts	1st	2nd	3rd	Win & Pl
Hurdles	2	0	0	0	0
Career Total	6	0	1	0	560

Going: Sf: 0-0 GS: 0-1 Gd: 0-3 GF: - Fm: 1-3
Distance: 2m/2m3: 0-0 2m4-2m7: 0-1 3m+: 0-1
Track: LH: 0-2 RH: 0-0 Tight: 0-0 Gall: 0-1
Aids: Bl: 0-0 Vi: 0-0 Tstrap: 0-0 Ckp: 0-0
Best Rating: 105 1/02 Hayd 2m   soft NHF

Montebank (IRE)
92   70

8-y-o b g Montelimar (USA)-Lady Glenbank (Tarboosh (USA))
R T Phillips Mrs Nicky Gittins

Placings:0R0/43P   (2820)

2003/04: 25⁴G, 25³GF, 20⁰GF,

	Starts	1st	2nd	3rd	Win & Pl
Chases	3	0	0	1	704
Career Total	6	0	0	1	704

Going: Sf: 0-0 GS: 0-0 Gd: 0-1 GF: - Fm: 0-2
Distance: 2m/2m3: 0-0 2m4-2m7: 0-1 3m+: 0-2
Track: LH: 0-1 RH: 0-2 Tight: 0-1 Gall: 0-0
Aids: Bl: 0-0 Vi: 0-0 Tstrap: 0-0 Ckp: 0-0
Best Rating: 70 10/03 Towc 3m1f good Ch

Point winner; poor form under Rules.

Monteforte
109f   117+f

6-y-o b g Alflora (IRE)-Double Dutch (Nicholas Bill)
J A B Old W E Sturt

Placings:12   (3495)

2003/04: 16¹HY, 16²HY,

	Starts	1st	2nd	3rd	Win & Pl
NH Flat	2	1	1	0	2938
Career Total	2	1	1	0	2938
117 1/04 Towc 2m	H NHF	HVY			£2352

Total win prize-money £2352

Going: Sf: 1-2 GS: 0-0 Gd: 0-0 GF: - Fm: 0-0
Distance: 2m/2m3: 1-2 2m4-2m7: 0-0 3m+: 0-0
Track: LH: 0-1 RH: 1-1 Tight: 0-0 Gall: 0-0
Aids: Bl: 0-0 Vi: 0-0 Tstrap: 0-0 Ckp: 0-0
Best Rating: 117 1/04 Hayd 2m   heavy NHF

Easy winner of a heavy-ground bumper on his debut; will need a trip over hurdles; an interesting prospect.

Montel Girl (IRE)
102   94

8-y-o ch m Montelimar (USA)-Grassed (Busted)
T P McGovern The Walking Tall Partnership

Placings:060/63500-12405F6   (4932)

2003/04: 24¹GF, 27²G, 26⁴GF, 24⁰GF, 24⁵GS, 21²FG, 27⁶G,

	Starts	1st	2nd	3rd	Win & Pl
Hurdles	7	1	1	1	4401
Career Total	15	1	1	1	4788
92 6/03 Worc 3m	F(0-95)HHdl	G-F			£3150

Total win prize-money £3150

Going: Sf: 0-0 GS: 0-1 Gd: 0-3 GF: - Fm: 1-3
Distance: 2m/2m3: 0-0 2m4-2m7: 0-1 3m+: 1-6
Track: LH: 1-4 RH: 0-2 Tight: 0-3 Gall: 0-1
Aids: Bl: 0-0 Vi: 0-0 Tstrap: 0-0 Ckp: 0-0
Best Rating: 94 8/03 Hntg 3m2f gd-fm Hdl

Low grade staying hurdler; appreciated step back up to 3m when landing Class F handicap at Worcester June 2003; good effort when second to progressive sort over extra 3f next time; stays well; acts on fast ground.

Montemoss (IRE)
101(109h)   (100h)100

7-y-o ch g Montelimar (USA)-Gaye Le Moss (Le Moss)
M G Rimell Wychwood Racing Partnership

Placings:054-B22U20   (4398)

2003/04: 21⁸S, 23⁹G, 26²GS, 24⁴G, 25²GS, 32⁰G,

	Starts	1st	2nd	3rd	Win & Pl
Hurdles	3	0	2	0	2231
Chases	3	0	1	0	1218
Career Total	9	0	3	0	3712

Going:	Sf: 0-1 GS: 0-2 Gd: 0-3 GF: - Fm: 0-0
Distance:	2m/2m3: 0-0 2m4-2m7: 0-2 3m+: 0-4
Track:	LH: 0-4 RH: 0-2 Tight: 0-1 Gall: 0-3
Aids:	Bl: 0-0 Vi: 0-0 Tstrap: 0-0 Ckp: 0-3
Best Rating:	102 12/03 Weth 2m7f good Hdl

Irish point winner; stayed on to finish runner-up in three mile novices' hurdle at Wetherby in December; lost rider in novices' chase at Doncaster in January; will make a chaser.

Montenegro

67f   55f

6-y-o gr g Terimon-Spartan Sprite (Country Retreat)
Ferdy Murphy Lord Somerleyton

Placings:0   (0451)
2003/04: 16⁰GF,

	Starts	1st	2nd	3rd	Win & Pl
NH Flat	1	0	0	0	
Career Total	1	0	0	0	

Going:	Sf: 0-0 GS: 0-0 Gd: 0-0 GF: - Fm: 0-1
Distance:	2m/2m3: 0-1 2m4-2m7: 0-0 3m+: 0-0
Track:	LH: 0-0 RH: 0-0 Tight: 0-0 Gall: 0-1
Aids:	Bl: 0-0 Vi: 0-0 Tstrap: 0-0 Ckp: 0-1
Best Rating:	55 5/03 Hntg 2m110y gd-fm NHF

Montesino

102   95+

5-y-o b g Bishop Of Cashel-Sutosky (Great Nephew)
R C Guest DDB Racing

Placings:4-000052   (1989)
2003/04: 16⁰G, 17⁰G, 17⁰GS, 16⁰GF, 16⁵G, 16²GF,

	Starts	1st	2nd	3rd	Win & Pl
NH Flat	1	0	0	0	0
Hurdles	5	0	1	0	652
Career Total	7	0	1	0	652

Going:	Sf: 0-0 GS: 0-1 Gd: 0-3 GF: - Fm: 0-2
Distance:	2m/2m3: 0-6 2m4-2m7: 0-0 3m+: 0-0
Track:	LH: 0-3 RH: 0-1 Tight: 0-3 Gall: 0-0
Aids:	Bl: 0-0 Vi: 0-0 Tstrap: 0-0 Ckp: 0-0
Best Rating:	95 11/03 Uttx 2m gd-fm Hdl

Montessori Mio (FR)

80(103h)   (100 h)87

5-y-o b g Robellino (USA)-Child's Play (USA) (Sharpen Up)
R Ford (Mrs M Reveley 28/4) Dantom Production Solutions Ltd

Placings:5345304112-2033P   (3960)
2003/04: 16²G, 21²G, 21⁰G, 21³G, 24³G, 26²PG,

	Starts	1st	2nd	3rd	Win & Pl
Hurdles	2	0	1	0	1036
Chases	4	0	1	2	2028
Career Total	15	2	2	4	12451
95	4/03	Carl	2m1f	E Hdl	G-F	£3794
100	4/03	Sedg	2m1f	E Hdl	GD	£3542
				Total win prize-money £7336

Going:	Sf: 0-0 GS: 0-0 Gd: 0-0 GF: 0-6 GF: - Fm: 0-0
Distance:	2m/2m3: 0-1 2m4-2m7: 0-3 3m+: 0-2
Track:	LH: 0-5 RH: 0-0 Tight: 0-3 Gall: 0-2
Aids:	Bl: 0-0 Vi: 0-1 Tstrap: 0-0 Ckp: 0-5
Best Rating:	100 4/03 Hexm 2m110y good Hdl

Modest hurdler/novice chaser; stays further over fences than hurdles; usually wears cheekpieces, but has worn blinkers; no great battler.

Montevideo

101   95

4-y-o b g Sadler's Wells (USA)-Montessoro (Akarad (FR))
Jonjo O'Neill (John M Oxx 12/10) John P McManus

Placings:043   (4489)
2003/04: 16⁰S, 16⁴S, 16³G,

	Starts	1st	2nd	3rd	Win & Pl
Hurdles	3	0	0	1	911
Career Total	3	0	0	1	911

Going:	Sf: 0-2 GS: 0-0 Gd: 0-1 GF: - Fm: 0-0
Distance:	2m/2m3: 0-3 2m4-2m7: 0-0 3m+: 0-0
Track:	LH: 0-2 RH: 0-1 Tight: 0-0 Gall: 0-1
Aids:	Bl: 0-0 Vi: 0-0 Tstrap: 0-0 Ckp: 0-0
Best Rating:	95 3/04 Strf 2m110y good Hdl

Modesrate chaser; acts on good and soft ground.

Montezuma

69

11-y-o br m Beveled (USA)-Miss Kuwait (The Brianstan)
N A Twiston-Davies A W M Priestley

Placings:0PP/4P3UU0-0   (2865)
2003/04: 19⁰GS,

	Starts	1st	2nd	3rd	Win & Pl
Hurdles	1	0	0	0	
Career Total	10	0	0	1	735

Going:	Sf: 0-0 GS: 0-1 Gd: 0-0 GF: - Fm: 0-0
Distance:	2m/2m3: 0-1 2m4-2m7: 0-0 3m+: 0-0
Track:	LH: 0-1 RH: 0-0 Tight: 0-0 Gall: 0-0
Aids:	Bl: 0-0 Vi: 0-0 Tstrap: 0-0 Ckp: 0-0
Best Rating:	69 8/02 Sthl 2m5f110y gd-fm Ch

Monti Flyer

92   101

6-y-o b g Terimon-Coole Pilate (Celtic Cone)
P F Nicholls B C Marshall

Placings:4P04310   (4656)
2003/04: 16⁴G, 21⁵S, 21⁰GS, 19⁴GS, 23³G, 24¹G, 26⁰G,

	Starts	1st	2nd	3rd	Win & Pl
NH Flat	1	0	0	0	0
Hurdles	6	1	0	1	8351
Career Total	7	1	0	1	8351
101	3/04	Ludl	3m	E(0-110)HHdl	GD	£6864
				Total win prize-money £6864

Going:	Sf: 0-1 GS: 0-2 Gd: 1-4 GF: - Fm: 0-0
Distance:	2m/2m3: 0-1 2m4-2m7: 0-0 3m+: 1-3
Track:	LH: 0-3 RH: 1-4 Tight: 0-3 Gall: 0-0
Aids:	Bl: 0-0 Vi: 0-0 Tstrap: 0-0 Ckp: 0-0
Best Rating:	101 3/04 Ludl 3m good Hdl

Moderate hurdler; brother to staying hurdler Pontius; stays three miles; acts on good ground; embryonic chaser.

Montifault (FR)

89   139

9-y-o ch g Morespeed-Tarde (FR) (Kashtan (FR))
P F Nicholls Mrs A E Fulton

Placings:056/1P13/233121/1P1P/P25P-35P06   (4640)
2003/04: 26³G, 29⁵GS, 24⁵S, 24⁰G, 21⁶G,

	Starts	1st	2nd	3rd	Win & Pl
Chases	5	0	0	1	6756
Career Total	26	6	3	4	100927

134	12/01	Winc	2m5f	B Ch	GD	£11060
152	11/01	Winc	3m1f110yA(0-150)HCh	GD	£26000
127	4/01	Font	2m6f	C Ch	GD	£7410
137	4/01	Asct	3m110y	B Ch	SFT	£10764
115	4/00	Plum	2m5f	E Hdl	HVY	£2674
127	11/99	Worc	2m4f	E Hdl		£2495
				Total win prize-money £60403

Going:	Sf: 0-1 GS: 0-1 Gd: 0-3 GF: - Fm: 0-0
Distance:	2m/2m3: 0-0 2m4-2m7: 0-1 3m+: 0-4
Track:	LH: 0-5 RH: 0-0 Tight: 0-1 Gall: 0-3
Aids:	Bl: 0-0 Vi: 0-0 Tstrap: 0-2 Ckp: 0-0
Best Rating:	152 11/01 Winc 3m1f110y good Ch

Useful chaser; can be a bit in and out; ran well for a long way when fifth in the Grand National in 2003; best effort since probably when running well for a long way in the 2004 Kim Muir at Cheltenham; stays three miles well; acts on any ground; has worn a tongue tie.

Montosari

85   92

5-y-o ch g Persian Bold-Sartigila (Efisio)
P Mitchell Caterham Racing (jdrp)

Placings:200   (3265)
2003/04: 16²S, 16⁰S, 16⁰S,

	Starts	1st	2nd	3rd	Win & Pl
Hurdles	3	0	1	0	606
Career Total	3	0	1	0	606

Going:	Sf: 0-1 GS: 0-0 Gd: 0-2 GF: - Fm: 0-0
Distance:	2m/2m3: 0-3 2m4-2m7: 0-0 3m+: 0-0
Track:	LH: 0-2 RH: 0-1 Tight: 0-0 Gall: 0-0
Aids:	Bl: 0-0 Vi: 0-0 Tstrap: 0-0 Ckp: 0-0
Best Rating:	91 11/03 Fknm 2m good Hdl

Montoya (IRE)

105   100

5-y-o b g Kylian (USA)-Saborinie (Prince Sabo)
P D Cundell Peter Dimmock

Placings:5043-23   (0507)
2003/04: 16²G, 16³G,

	Starts	1st	2nd	3rd	Win & Pl
Hurdles	2	0	1	1	1882
Career Total	6	0	1	2	3009

Going:	Sf: 0-0 GS: 0-0 Gd: 0-0 GF: - Fm: 0-0
Distance:	2m/2m3: 0-2 2m4-2m7: 0-0 3m+: 0-0
Track:	LH: 0-2 RH: 0-0 Tight: 0-1 Gall: 0-0
Aids:	Bl: 0-0 Vi: 0-0 Tstrap: 0-0 Ckp: 0-0
Best Rating:	100 5/03 Strf 2m110y good Hdl

Moderate njovice hurdler; runner-up to long odds-on chance at Worcester next time; acts on good ground.

Montpelier (IRE)

104   132

11-y-o b g Montelimar (USA)-Liscarton (Le Bavard (FR))
N J Henderson The 2020 Droxford Partnership

Placings:40/2F5003/11P0/3112/3-U4402455   (4843)
2003/04: 24⁰GS, 21⁴G, 24⁴G, 24⁰GS, 24²G, 17⁴G, 18⁰G, 16⁵G,

	Starts	1st	2nd	3rd	Win & Pl
Chases	8	0	1	0	4789
Career Total	25	4	3	3	31508
137	12/01	Chel	2m5f	E(0-125)HCh	GD	£8502
130	12/01	Hrfd	2m3f	E(0-115)HCh	SFT	£3523
124	10/00	Chel	2m4f110yD(0-110)HCh	GD	£5642

111	10/00	Hrfd	2m3f	E(0-105)HCh	GD	£3435
				Total win prize-money £21102		

Going:	Sf: 0-0 GS: 0-2 Gd: 0-6 GF: - Fm: 0-0
Distance:	2m/2m3: 0-3 2m4-2m7: 0-1 3m+: 0-4
Track:	LH: 0-6 RH: 0-2 Tight: 0-3 Gall: 0-4
Aids:	Bl: 0-4 Vi: 0-0 Tstrap: 0-0 Ckp: 0-0
Best Rating:	137 12/01 Kemp 2m4f110y good Ch

Fair chaser; disappointing of late; suited by trips of around two and a half miles; acts on any ground.

Montreal (FR)

103   (140h) 135

7-y-o b/br g Chamberlin (FR)-Massada (FR) (Kashtan (FR))
M C Pipe D A Johnson

Placings:3/2123P/611035/1225414U3-F64S6PF4 (4784)
2003/04: 25^{F}G, 20^{G}GF, 224^{G}F, 21^{S}G, 24^{S}S, 24^{P}G, 36^{F}G, 24^{A}G,

	Starts	1st	2nd	3rd	Win & Pl
Chases	8	0	0	0	1833
Career Total	29	5	4	4	69550

133	3/03	Hayd	2m6f	D Ch	G-F	£9440
133	11/02	Extr	2m3f110y	D Ch	GD	£6162
134	12/01	Sand	2m6f	C(0-130)HHdl	SFT	£7410
128	11/01	Asct	3m	B(0-150)HHdl	GD	£8814
115	11/00	Chel	2m110y	B Hdl	G-S	£7052
				Total win prize-money £38879		

Going:	Sf: 0-1 GS: 0-0 Gd: 0-5 GF: - Fm: 0-2
Distance:	2m/2m3: 0-0 2m4-2m7: 0-3 3m+: 0-5
Track:	LH: 0-6 RH: 0-2 Tight: 0-2 Gall: 0-5
Aids:	Bl: 0-0 Vi: 0-2 Tstrap: 0-0 Ckp: 0-0
Best Rating:	140 3/02 Chel 3m1f110y gd-sft Hdl

Fair staying hurdler/chaser; effective from two and a half to three miles; yet to win a handicap over fences; sometimes visored.

Montu

88   86

7-y-o ch g Gunner B-Promitto (Roaring Riva)
Miss K M George Exterior Profiles Ltd

Placings:0/00P-F00P (3786)
2003/04: 17^{F}G, 17°G, 19°G, 20^{P}GS,

	Starts	1st	2nd	3rd	Win & Pl
Hurdles	4	0	0	0	
Career Total	8	0	0	0	

Going:	Sf: 0-0 GS: 0-1 Gd: 0-3 GF: - Fm: 0-0
Distance:	2m/2m3: 0-2 2m4-2m7: 0-2 3m+: 0-0
Track:	LH: 0-1 RH: 0-3 Tight: 0-2 Gall: 0-1
Aids:	Bl: 0-0 Vi: 0-0 Tstrap: 0-0 Ckp: 0-0
Best Rating:	95 10/02 Chep 2m110y good NHF

Monty Be Quick

95   84

8-y-o ch g Mon Tresor-Spartiquick (Spartan General)
J M Castle J M Castle

Placings:600/0003F3-PPF04 (4671)
2003/04: 17^{P}GF, 16^{P}G, 21^{F}S, 20^{P}S, 16^{K}G,

	Starts	1st	2nd	3rd	Win & Pl
Hurdles	5	0	0	0	0
Career Total	14	0	0	2	1172

Going:	Sf: 0-2 GS: 0-0 Gd: 0-2 GF: - Fm: 0-1
Distance:	2m/2m3: 0-3 2m4-2m7: 0-2 3m+: 0-0
Track:	LH: 0-1 RH: 0-4 Tight: 0-0 Gall: 0-1

Aids:	Bl: 0-0 Vi: 0-0 Tstrap: 0-1 Ckp: 0-0
Best Rating:	87 4/02 Hntg 2m110y gd-fm NHF

Some improvement when stepped up to two and a half miles; may be suited by even further.

Monty Flood (IRE)

56

7-y-o b g Camden Town-Clonroche Artic (Pauper)
Ferdy Murphy J Taqvi

Placings:60-P (3280)
2003/04: 24^{P}HY,

	Starts	1st	2nd	3rd	Win & Pl
Hurdles	1	0	0	0	
Career Total	3	0	0	0	0

Going:	Sf: 0-1 GS: 0-0 Gd: 0-0 GF: - Fm: 0-0
Distance:	2m/2m3: 0-0 2m4-2m7: 0-0 3m+: 0-1
Track:	LH: 0-1 RH: 0-0 Tight: 0-0 Gall: 0-0
Aids:	Bl: 0-0 Vi: 0-0 Tstrap: 0-0 Ckp: 0-0
Best Rating:	56 12/02 Hayd 2m soft Hdl

Monty's Double (IRE)

102(100h)   (99h) 104+

7-y-o b g Montelimar (USA)-Macamore Rose (Torus)
O Sherwood W S Watt

Placings:5/4-P34 (4782)
2003/04: 21^{P}GS, 25^{S}GS, 24^{A}G,

	Starts	1st	2nd	3rd	Win & Pl
Chases	3	0	0	1	1159
Career Total	5	0	0	1	1432

Going:	Sf: 0-0 GS: 0-2 Gd: 0-1 GF: - Fm: 0-0
Distance:	2m/2m3: 0-0 2m4-2m7: 0-1 3m+: 0-2
Track:	LH: 0-0 RH: 0-3 Tight: 0-2 Gall: 0-1
Aids:	Bl: 0-0 Vi: 0-0 Tstrap: 0-0 Ckp: 0-0
Best Rating:	104 4/04 Hntg 3m good Ch

Modest maiden hurdler/novice chaser; stays three miles.

Monty's Lass (IRE)

8-y-o b m Montelimar (USA)-Smash N Lass (Crash Course)
Mrs S Prouse Mrs S Prouse

Placings:1- (0020)
2003/04: 26^{1}S,

	Starts	1st	2nd	3rd	Win & Pl
Chases	1	1	0	0	2898
Career Total	1	1	0	0	2898

79	4/03	NAbb	3m2f110yH Ch	SFT	£2898
			Total win prize-money £2898		

Going:	Sf: 1-1 GS: 0-0 Gd: 0-0 GF: - Fm: 0-0
Distance:	2m/2m3: 0-0 2m4-2m7: 0-0 3m+: 1-1
Track:	LH: 1-1 RH: 0-0 Tight: 1-1 Gall: 0-0
Aids:	Bl: 0-0 Vi: 0-0 Tstrap: 0-0 Ckp: 0-0
Best Rating:	79 4/03 NAbb 3m2f110y soft Ch

Monty's Pass (IRE)

105(101h)   (100h) 159

11-y-o b g Montelimar (USA)-Friars Pass (Monksfield)
James Joseph Mangan Dee Racing Syndicate

Placings:21/22460212421/4531323PF03/1326212336552/

23P6313641-50004 (4647)
2003/04: 20^{S}G, 24°G, 20°YS, 16°Y, 36^{K}G,

	Starts	1st	2nd	3rd	Win & Pl
Hurdles	3	0	0	0	0
Chases	2	0	0	0	30000
Career Total	52	8	12	10	541881

162	4/03	Aint	4m4f	A HCh	GD	£348000
142	9/02	List	3m	HCh	FRM	£51748
133	8/01	Tral	2m4f	HCh	GD	£18346
122	5/01	Tipp	2m4f	(0-130)HCh	G-F	£7233
108	6/00	Gowr	2m4f	(0-102)HCh	G-Y	£3588
102	4/00	List	2m4f	(0-95)HCh	SH	£4416
97	12/99	DRoy	2m4f	(0-102)HCh	HVY	£2464
101	4/99	Cork	3m	Ch	SH	£3069
				Total win prize-money £438866		

Going:	Sf: 0-0 GS: 0-0 Gd: 0-3 GF: - Fm: 0-0
Distance:	2m/2m3: 0-1 2m4-2m7: 0-2 3m+: 0-2
Track:	LH: 0-3 RH: 0-0 Tight: 0-1 Gall: 0-0
Aids:	Bl: 0-0 Vi: 0-0 Tstrap: 0-0 Ckp: 0-0
Best Rating:	162 4/03 Aint 4m4f good Ch

Smart Irish chaser; runner-up in the 2002 Topham; returned to land the 2003 Grand National, never putting a foot wrong and coming right away at the end; only fourth in the 2004 renewal; stays exceptionally well; acts on most types of ground.

Monty's Quest (IRE)

106(100h)   (89h) 111

9-y-o b g Montelimar (USA)-A Bit Of Luck (IRE) (Good Thyne (USA))
P Beaumont Graham Frankland

Placings:06/232/0/54F14-20 (4726)
2003/04: 25^{2}G, 24^{0}G,

	Starts	1st	2nd	3rd	Win & Pl
Chases	2	0	1	0	1191
Career Total	13	1	3	1	8033

91	4/03	Hexm	3m1f	E Ch	GD	£4030
				Total win prize-money £4030		

Going:	Sf: 0-0 GS: 0-0 Gd: 0-2 GF: - Fm: 0-0
Distance:	2m/2m3: 0-0 2m4-2m7: 0-0 3m+: 0-2
Track:	LH: 0-1 RH: 0-1 Tight: 0-0 Gall: 0-0
Aids:	Bl: 0-0 Vi: 0-0 Tstrap: 0-0 Ckp: 0-0
Best Rating:	111 5/03 Hexm 3m1f good Ch

Moderate chaser; on the upgrade; stays beyond three miles and acts on any ground.

Monty's Theme (IRE)

92   67

10-y-o b/br g Montelimar (USA)-Theme Music (Tudor Music)
P Wegmann P Wegmann

Placings:3/3F1145P/45650P-2U44PU (3172)
2003/04: 21^{2}GF, 21^{U}G, 20^{4}GF, 19^{4}G, 24^{P}GS, 21^{U}GS,

	Starts	1st	2nd	3rd	Win & Pl
Chases	6	0	1	0	1254
Career Total	20	2	1	2	9784

106	8/01	Font	2m6f	E(0-105)HCh	G-F	£3201
101	7/01	NAbb	2m5f110yE Ch		GD	£3444
			Total win prize-money £6645			

Going:	Sf: 0-0 GS: 0-2 Gd: 0-2 GF: - Fm: 0-2
Distance:	2m/2m3: 0-0 2m4-2m7: 0-0 3m+: 0-1
Track:	LH: 0-4 RH: 0-2 Tight: 0-2 Gall: 0-0
Aids:	Bl: 0-0 Vi: 0-0 Tstrap: 0-0 Ckp: 0-0
Best Rating:	106 8/01 Font 2m6f gd-fm Ch

Very moderate and disappointing chaser; stays two mile six; suited by decent ground.

Moody Blues (IRE)

95(92h)   (79h)**68**

10-y-o ch g Orchestra-Blue Rainbow (Balinger)
A M Hales (Mrs G Harvey 26/5) J Smith

Placings:3PF/5U6PP-56202   (1586)
2003/04: 26⁵GF, 22⁶GF, 22²GF, 22⁰F, 24²GF,

	Starts	1st	2nd	3rd	Win & Pl
Hurdles	2	0	1	0	1042
Chases	3	0	1	0	834
Career Total	13	0	2	1	2363

Going:	Sf: 0-0 GS: 0-0 Gd: 0-0 GF: - Fm: 0-5
Distance:	2m/2m3: 0-0 2m4-2m7: 0-3 3m+: 0-2
Track:	LH: 0-2 RH: 0-2 Tight: 0-2 Gall: 0-1
Aids:	Bl: 0-2 Vi: 0-1 Tstrap: 0-0 Ckp: 0-0
Best Rating:	105 1/02 Hntg 3m gd-sft Ch

Plating-class chaser/hurdler; winning pointer in Ireland; has shown only a little over fences and hurdles so far; has worn blinkers and a visor; stays well.

Moon

83f   **46**f

5-y-o br m Simply Great (FR)-New Broom (IRE) (Brush Aside (USA))
T D Easterby D F Sills

Placings:00   (4264)
2003/04: 16⁹GS, 16⁹GF,

	Starts	1st	2nd	3rd	Win & Pl
NH Flat	2	0	0	0	
Career Total	2	0	0	0	

Going:	Sf: 0-0 GS: 0-1 Gd: 0-0 GF: - Fm: 0-1
Distance:	2m/2m3: 0-2 2m4-2m7: 0-0 3m+: 0-0
Track:	LH: 0-2 RH: 0-0 Tight: 0-1 Gall: 0-0
Aids:	Bl: 0-0 Vi: 0-0 Tstrap: 0-0 Ckp: 0-0
Best Rating:	46 3/04 Catt 2m gd-fm NHF

Moon Colony

103   **93**

11-y-o b g Top Ville-Honeymooning (USA) (Blushing Groom (FR))
A L Forbes Tony Forbes

Placings:0/00235/235/6245U3-1444P   (4890)
2003/04: 16¹HY, 20⁴GF, 17⁴GF, 21⁴G, 19⁹GF,

	Starts	1st	2nd	3rd	Win & Pl
Hurdles	5	1	0	0	5195
Career Total	20	1	3	3	9091
93	5/03	Uttx	2m	E(0-110)HHdl	HVY £4143

Total win prize-money £4144

Going:	Sf: 1-1 GS: 0-0 Gd: 0-1 GF: - Fm: 0-3
Distance:	2m/2m3: 1-3 2m4-2m7: 0-2 3m+: 0-0
Track:	LH: 1-4 RH: 0-1 Tight: 0-2 Gall: 0-0
Aids:	Bl: 0-0 Vi: 0-0 Tstrap: 0-0 Ckp: 0-0
Best Rating:	93 5/03 Uttx 2m heavy Hdl

Moderate handicap hurdler; finally broke his duck when making all in 2m handicap hurdle on heavy ground at Uttoxeter May 2003; acts on ground good and softer; stays 2m 4f.

Moon Emperor

102   **108+**

7-y-o b g Emperor Jones (USA)-Sir Hollow (USA) (Sir Ivor (USA))

J R Jenkins R M Ellis

Placings:100/45   (4170)
2003/04: 16⁴G, 21⁵G,

	Starts	1st	2nd	3rd	Win & Pl
Hurdles	2	0	0	0	367
Career Total	5	1	0	0	3230
114	11/00	Leic	2m	E Hdl	HVY £2863

Total win prize-money £2863

Going:	Sf: 0-0 GS: 0-0 Gd: 0-2 GF: - Fm: 0-0
Distance:	2m/2m3: 0-1 2m4-2m7: 0-1 3m+: 0-0
Track:	LH: 0-1 RH: 0-1 Tight: 0-0 Gall: 0-1
Aids:	Bl: 0-0 Vi: 0-0 Tstrap: 0-0 Ckp: 0-0
Best Rating:	114 11/00 Leic 2m heavy Hdl

Modest hurdler; decent stayer on the Flat; well beaten fourth on return to hurdling in early 2004; will be suited by two and a half miles.

Moon Glow (IRE)

102   (100h)**117**

8-y-o b g Fayruz-Jarmar Moon (Unfuwain (USA))
J Gallagher Mrs V W Jones

Placings:150/4P/0543PF620500/42332P14143-P133233   (1557)
2003/04: 16⁵G, 16¹GF, 16³GF, 17³G, 16²G, 16³GF, 20⁵GF,

	Starts	1st	2nd	3rd	Win & Pl
Chases	7	1	1	4	11352
Career Total	35	4	4	8	29697
115	5/03	NAbb	2m110y	D(0-115)HCh	G-F £5408
110	9/02	Plum	2m1f	E(0-105)HCh	GD £4095
102	8/02	NAbb	2m110y	D(0-125)HCh	G-F £4867
94	10/99	Weth	2m	H Hdl	G-F £3129

Total win prize-money £17499

Going:	Sf: 0-0 GS: 0-0 Gd: 0-3 GF: - Fm: 1-4
Distance:	**2m/2m3:** 1-6 2m4-2m7: 0-1 3m+: 0-0
Track:	**LH:** 1-7 RH: 0-0 **Tight:** 1-4 Gall: 0-0
Aids:	Bl: 0-0 Vi: 0-0 Tstrap: 0-0 Ckp: 0-0
Best Rating:	117 7/03 NAbb 2m110y good Ch

Fair chaser; won at Plumpton and Newton Abbot in 2002; pulled up after being kicked in running at Worcester May 2003; bounced back when winning 2m handicap at Newton Abbot next time; likes fast ground; yet to win when wearing blinkers.

Moon Mist

92   **66**

6-y-o gr m Accondy (IRE)-Lillie's Brig (New Brig)
N W Alexander Alexander Family

Placings:P005PP   (4909)
2003/04: 20⁹S, 16⁶S, 16⁹HY, 24⁵GS, 24⁹HY, 24⁹S,

	Starts	1st	2nd	3rd	Win & Pl
Hurdles	6	0	0	0	0
Career Total	6	0	0	0	0

Going:	Sf: 0-5 GS: 0-1 Gd: 0-0 GF: - Fm: 0-0
Distance:	2m/2m3: 0-2 2m4-2m7: 0-1 3m+: 0-3
Track:	LH: 0-4 RH: 0-2 Tight: 0-2 Gall: 0-0
Aids:	Bl: 0-0 Vi: 0-0 Tstrap: 0-0 Ckp: 0-0
Best Rating:	66 1/04 Kels 2m110y soft Hdl

Moon Spinner

106   **91**

7-y-o b m Elmaamul (USA)-Lunabelle (Idiots Delight)
J M Bradley J H Lee

Placings:5f224/0032023004020064-6134   (0625)
2003/04: 16⁶GF, 16¹G, 16³G, 16⁴GF,

	Starts	1st	2nd	3rd	Win & Pl
Hurdles	4	1	0	1	3630
Career Total	24	2	5	3	11521
91	5/03	Strf	2m110y	G Hdl	GD £2982
90	7/01	Worc	2m	H NHF	GD £1477

Total win prize-money £4459

Going:	Sf: 0-0 GS: 0-0 Gd: 1-2 GF: - Fm: 0-2
Distance:	**2m/2m3:** 1-4 2m4-2m7: 0-0 3m+: 0-0
Track:	**LH:** 1-4 RH: 0-0 **Tight:** 1-2 Gall: 0-0
Aids:	Bl: 0-0 Vi: 0-0 Tstrap: 0-0 **Ckp:** 1-3
Best Rating:	96 2/02 Hntg 2m110y soft Hdl

Plating-class hurdler; took advantage of a drop in grade when winning 2m mares only novices seller at Stratford May 2003; stays 2m 4f; seems to act on most types of ground.

Moonlake (IRE)

103   (108h)**100**

9-y-o b g Durgam (USA)-Joyful Prospect (Hello Gorgeous (USA))
Ferdy Murphy Mr And Mrs Neil Iveson

Placings:002601/230100/1P   (2307)
2003/04: 16¹F, 16⁵GF,

	Starts	1st	2nd	3rd	Win & Pl
Chases	2	1	0	0	2933
Career Total	14	3	2	1	11240
100	9/03	Hexm	2m110y	E Ch	FRM £2933
108	3/02	Ludl	2m	E(0-105)HHdl	SFT £4104
108	10/00	Aint	2m110y	E Hdl	GD £2470

Total win prize-money £9508

Going:	Sf: 0-0 GS: 0-0 Gd: 0-0 GF: - Fm: 1-2
Distance:	**2m/2m3:** 1-2 2m4-2m7: 0-0 3m+: 0-0
Track:	**LH:** 1-2 RH: 0-0 Tight: 0-1 Gall: 0-0
Aids:	Bl: 0-0 Vi: 0-0 Tstrap: 0-0 Ckp: 0-0
Best Rating:	108 3/02 Ludl 2m soft Hdl

Modest handicap hurdler/ novice chaser; effective at two miles; acts on soft ground.

Moonlight Dancer

92   **84**

6-y-o b g Polar Falcon (USA)-Guanhumara (Caerleon (USA))
Mrs S Gardner D V Gardner

Placings:0026600   (2034)
2003/04: 22²G, 17⁰GF, 16²GF, 17⁶G, 22⁶GF, 22⁰GF, 16⁶GF,

	Starts	1st	2nd	3rd	Win & Pl
Hurdles	7	0	1	0	1201
Career Total	7	0	1	0	1201

Going:	Sf: 0-0 GS: 0-0 Gd: 0-2 GF: - Fm: 0-5
Distance:	2m/2m3: 0-4 2m4-2m7: 0-3 3m+: 0-0
Track:	LH: 0-5 RH: 0-2 Tight: 0-3 Gall: 0-0
Aids:	Bl: 0-0 Vi: 0-0 Tstrap: 0-0 Ckp: 0-0
Best Rating:	85 6/03 NAbb 2m1f good Hdl

Plating-class hurdler; acts on fast ground.

Moonlight Gold

(64h)   (40h)

8-y-o b g Jupiter Island-Moonlight Bay (Palm Track)
J C Haynes J C Haynes

Placings:P50PP   (3336)
2003/04: 20⁰GS, 20⁵G, 17⁰HY, 25⁹GS, 19⁰GS,

	Starts	1st	2nd	3rd	Win & Pl
Hurdles	4	0	0	0	0

Chases	1	0	0	0
Career Total	5	0	0	0

Going: Sf: 0-1 GS: 0-3 Gd: 0-1 GF: - Fm: 0-0
Distance: 2m/2m3: 0-2 2m4-2m7: 0-2 3m+: 0-1
Track: LH: 0-3 RH: 0-2 Tight: 0-1 Gall: 0-1
Aids: Bl: 0-0 Vi: 0-0 Tstrap: 0-0 Ckp: 0-0
Best Rating: 40 11/03 Carl 2m1f heavy Hdl

Moonlighting

(80c)**63**

7-y-o b m Lugana Beach-White Flash (Sure Blade (USA))
Mrs N S Sharpe B Owen

Placings:6UP/P4043-PP (0612)
2003/04: 19PGF, 19PGF,

	Starts	1st	2nd	3rd	Win & Pl
Hurdles	2	0	0	0	
Career Total	10	0	0	1	334

Going: Sf: 0-0 GS: 0-0 Gd: 0-0 GF: - Fm: 0-2
Distance: 2m/2m3: 0-2 2m4-2m7: 0-2 3m+: 0-0
Track: LH: 0-0 RH: 0-2 Tight: 0-0 Gall: 0-0
Aids: Bl: 0-0 Vi: 0-0 Tstrap: 0-0 Ckp: 0-2
Best Rating: 70 4/02 Plum 2m1f gd-fm Ch

Plating-class hurdler; often wears cheekpieces.

Moonlit Harbour

99 109

5-y-o b g Bal Harbour-Nuit De Lune (FR) (Crystal Palace (FR))
M W Easterby Steve Hull

Placings:133-112101 (4727)
2003/04: 16¹G, 17⁴G, 20²S, 17¹GS, 20⁰S, 17¹G,

	Starts	1st	2nd	3rd	Win & Pl
NH Flat	1	1	0	0	1470
Hurdles	5	3	1	0	11987
Career Total	9	5	1	2	16506
109	4/04	Carl	2m1f	E Hdl	GD	£3705
112	2/04	Sedg	2m1f	E Hdl	G-S	£3445
93	10/03	Sedg	2m1f	E Hdl	GD	£3045
93	10/03	Hexm	2m110y	H NHF	G-F	£1470
88	3/03	Weth	2m	H NHF	GD	£2478

Total win prize-money £14143

Going: Sf: 0-2 GS: 1-1 Gd: 2-2 GF: - Fm: 1-1
Distance: 2m/2m3: 4-4 2m4-2m7: 0-2 3m+: 0-0
Track: LH: 3-4 RH: 1-2 Tight: 2-2 Gall: 0-0
Aids: Bl: 0-0 Vi: 0-0 Tstrap: 0-0 Ckp: 0-0
Best Rating: 112 2/04 Sedg 2m1f gd-sft Hdl

Fair novice hurdler; won two of his four outings in bumpers; successful in two out of three hurdle races to date; stays two and a half miles; acts on most types of ground; consistent.

Moonlite Magic (IRE)

76

10-y-o br g Phardante (FR)-Lucey Allen (Strong Gale)
Miss Z C Davison The Secret Circle

Placings:3500/F02251U04/U6046-0 (0332)
2003/04: 26PGF,

	Starts	1st	2nd	3rd	Win & Pl
Hurdles	1	0	0	0	
Career Total	19	1	2	2	3359
93	11/01	Sedg	3m3f110yG(0-90)HHdl	SFT	£1547

Total win prize-money £1547

Going: Sf: 0-0 GS: 0-0 Gd: 0-0 GF: - Fm: 0-1
Distance: 2m/2m3: 0-0 2m4-2m7: 0-0 3m+: 0-1
Track: LH: 0-1 RH: 0-0 Tight: 0-0 Gall: 0-0
Aids: Bl: 0-0 Vi: 0-0 Tstrap: 0-0 Ckp: 0-1
Best Rating: 97 10/00 Sthl 2m soft NHF

Moonstream

111f 102+f

4-y-o b g Terimon-Lunabelle (Idiots Delight)
N J Henderson The Queen

Placings:11 (3874)
2003/04: 17¹GS, 17¹GS,

	Starts	1st	2nd	3rd	Win & Pl
NH Flat	2	2	0	0	3787
Career Total	2	2	0	0	3787
102	2/04	Folk	2m1f110yH NHF	G-S	£1869
102	1/04	Extr	2m1f	H NHF	G-S	£1918

Total win prize-money £3787

Going: Sf: 0-0 GS: 2-2 Gd: 0-0 GF: - Fm: 0-0
Distance: 2m/2m3: 2-2 2m4-2m7: 0-0 3m+: 0-0
Track: LH: 0-0 RH: 2-2 Tight: 1-1 Gall: 0-0
Aids: Bl: 0-0 Vi: 0-0 Tstrap: 0-0 Ckp: 0-0
Best Rating: 102 2/04 Folk 2m1f110y gd-sft NHF

Related to plenty of winners in the winter game; has won both of his bumper starts to date; best on good to soft; promising type.

Moonzie Laird (IRE)

96 74+

6-y-o b/br g Good Thyne (USA)-Sweet Roselier (IRE) (Roselier (FR))
J N R Billinge Sceptre House Golf Society

Placings:10-5P (3280)
2003/04: 22⁵G, 24PHY,

	Starts	1st	2nd	3rd	Win & Pl
Hurdles	2	0	0	0	0
Career Total	4	1	0	0	2215
99	3/03	Ayr	2m	H NHF	SFT	£2214

Total win prize-money £2215

Going: Sf: 0-1 GS: 0-0 Gd: 0-1 GF: - Fm: 0-0
Distance: 2m/2m3: 0-0 2m4-2m7: 0-1 3m+: 0-1
Track: LH: 0-2 RH: 0-0 Tight: 0-0 Gall: 0-0
Aids: Bl: 0-0 Vi: 0-0 Tstrap: 0-0 Ckp: 0-0
Best Rating: 99 3/03 Ayr 2m soft NHF

Moor Hall Hopper

8-y-o gr g Rock Hopper-Forgiving (Jellaby)
M Sheppard Mrs Rosie Newman

Placings:0/00-FFP (3652)
2003/04: 16PGS, 19PGS, 17PS,

	Starts	1st	2nd	3rd	Win & Pl
Hurdles	1	0	0	0	0
Chases	2	0	0	0	0
Career Total	6	0	0	0	0

Going: Sf: 0-1 GS: 0-2 Gd: 0-0 GF: - Fm: 0-0
Distance: 2m/2m3: 0-3 2m4-2m7: 0-0 3m+: 0-0
Track: LH: 0-0 RH: 0-3 Tight: 0-1 Gall: 0-0
Aids: Bl: 0-0 Vi: 0-0 Tstrap: 0-0 Ckp: 0-0
Best Rating: 64 11/00 Ludl 2m good NHF

Moor Lane

102 131

12-y-o b g Primitive Rising (USA)-Navos (Tymavos)
A M Balding R P B Michaelson

Placings:2/311F/12/51120/4FP61U0-243 (2674)
2003/04: 24²GF, 27⁴G, 22³GF,

	Starts	1st	2nd	3rd	Win & Pl
Chases	3	0	1	1	8604
Career Total	22	6	4	2	92032
130	2/03	Kemp	3m	D(0-125)HCh	GD	£6955
138	1/02	Donc	3m	A(0-145)HCh	SFT	£39871
122	1/02	Newb	3m	C(0-135)HCh	GD	£8931
134	9/99	Extr	2m6f110yE(0-115)HCh	G-S	£4279
124	1/99	Donc	2m3f110yD Ch	GD	£4211
127	11/98	Newb	2m4f	C Ch	SFT	£7108

Total win prize-money £71356

Going: Sf: 0-0 GS: 0-0 Gd: 0-1 GF: - Fm: 0-2
Distance: 2m/2m3: 0-2 2m4-2m7: 0-1 3m+: 0-2
Track: LH: 0-2 RH: 0-1 Tight: 0-1 Gall: 0-1
Aids: Bl: 0-0 Vi: 0-0 Tstrap: 0-0 Ckp: 0-0
Best Rating: 138 3/02 Newb 3m gd-sft Ch

Useful handicap chaser; effective at three miles; acts on good ground and faster; usually jumps well.

Moor Spirit

94(86h) (47h)**70+**

7-y-o b g Nomadic Way (USA)-Navos (Tymavos)
R D E Woodhouse Mrs C M Clarke

Placings:4-0P00044U (4880)
2003/04: 17⁰G, 20⁵S, 25⁰GS, 25⁰G, 21⁰GS, 19⁴G, 25⁴GS, 20UGS,

	Starts	1st	2nd	3rd	Win & Pl
NH Flat	1	0	0	0	0
Hurdles	3	0	0	0	0
Chases	4	0	0	0	314
Career Total	9	0	0	0	314

Going: Sf: 0-1 GS: 0-4 Gd: 0-3 GF: - Fm: 0-0
Distance: 2m/2m3: 0-2 2m4-2m7: 0-3 3m+: 0-3
Track: LH: 0-7 RH: 0-0 Tight: 0-3 Gall: 0-0
Aids: Bl: 0-5 Vi: 0-0 Tstrap: 0-0 Ckp: 0-0
Best Rating: 85 3/03 Weth 2m good NHF

Mooramana

97f 94f

5-y-o ch g Alflora (IRE)-Petit Primitive (Primitive Rising (USA))
P Beaumont Mrs Karen Ratcliffe

Placings:644 (4571)
2003/04: 16⁶GS, 16⁴GS, 17⁴GS,

	Starts	1st	2nd	3rd	Win & Pl
NH Flat	3	0	0	0	0
Career Total	3	0	0	0	0

Going: Sf: 0-1 GS: 0-1 Gd: 0-1 GF: - Fm: 0-0
Distance: 2m/2m3: 0-3 2m4-2m7: 0-0 3m+: 0-0
Track: LH: 0-2 RH: 0-1 Tight: 0-2 Gall: 0-0
Aids: Bl: 0-0 Vi: 0-0 Tstrap: 0-0 Ckp: 0-0
Best Rating: 94 3/04 Bang 2m1f gd-sft NHF

Well backed when respectable fourth on second start in bumper at Newcastle in March.

Moorhall (IRE)

75 81

5-y-o b g Persian Bold-Never Told (IRE) (Classic Secret (USA))

J G Cosgrave F Thompson

Placings:004-00 (0467)
2003/04: 20⁰YS, 16⁰G,

	Starts	1st	2nd	3rd	Win & Pl
Hurdles	2	0	0	0	
Career Total	5	0	0	0	260

Going: Sf: 0-0 GS: 0-0 Gd: 0-1 GF: - Fm: 0-0
Distance: 2m/2m3: 0-1 2m4-2m7: 0-1 3m+: 0-0
Track: LH: 0-1 RH: 0-0 Tight: 0-0 Gall: 0-0
Aids: Bl: 0-0 Vi: 0-0 Tstrap: 0-0 Ckp: 0-0
Best Rating: 81 4/03 Tram 2m gd-fm Hdl

Moorland Monarch
93   80
6-y-o b g Morpeth-Moorland Nell (Neltino)
J D Frost Peninsula Racegoers

Placings:0-4005U6 (4733)
2003/04: 17⁰S, 17⁴GF, 19⁰S, 17⁰GS, 24⁵G, 22ᵁGS, 22⁶G,

	Starts	1st	2nd	3rd	Win & Pl
NH Flat	2	0	0	0	264
Hurdles	5	0	0	0	0
Career Total	7	0	0	0	264

Going: Sf: 0-2 GS: 0-2 Gd: 0-2 GF: - Fm: 0-1
Distance: 2m/2m3: 0-4 2m4-2m7: 0-2 3m+: 0-1
Track: LH: 0-3 RH: 0-4 Tight: 0-4 Gall: 0-0
Aids: Bl: 0-0 Vi: 0-0 Tstrap: 0-0 Ckp: 0-0
Best Rating: 90 8/03 NAbb 2m1f gd-fm NHF

Moorlands Return
96f   100f
5-y-o b g Bob's Return (IRE)-Sandford Springs (USA) (Robellino (USA))
C L Tizzard Mrs Lynda M Williams

Placings:15 (4454)
2003/04: 16¹GS, 16⁵GS,

	Starts	1st	2nd	3rd	Win & Pl
NH Flat	2	1	0	0	2478
Career Total	2	1	0	0	2478

100 2/04 Kemp 2m H NHF G-S £2478
Total win prize-money £2478

Going: Sf: 0-0 GS: 1-2 Gd: 0-0 GF: - Fm: 0-0
Distance: 2m/2m3: 1-2 2m4-2m7: 0-0 3m+: 0-0
Track: LH: 0-0 RH: 1-2 Tight: 0-0 Gall: 0-0
Aids: Bl: 0-0 Vi: 0-0 Tstrap: 0-0 Ckp: 0-0
Best Rating: 100 3/04 Asct 2m110y gd-sft NHF

Made a winning debut in a Kempton bumper and ran well under a penalty; acts on easy ground.

Moose Malloy
77   66
7-y-o ch g Formidable (USA)-Jolimo (Fortissimo)
M J Ryan M J Ryan

Placings:40/603P/0P0 (4781)
2003/04: 16⁰GS, 16⁸G, 16⁸G,

	Starts	1st	2nd	3rd	Win & Pl
Hurdles	3	0	0	0	
Career Total	9	0	0	1	438

Going: Sf: 0-0 GS: 0-1 Gd: 0-2 GF: - Fm: 0-0
Distance: 2m/2m3: 0-3 2m4-2m7: 0-0 3m+: 0-0
Track: LH: 0-1 RH: 0-2 Tight: 0-1 Gall: 0-2
Aids: Bl: 0-2 Vi: 0-0 Tstrap: 0-0 Ckp: 0-1
Best Rating: 86 9/00 Hntg 2m110y gd-fm Hdl

Moral Justice (IRE)
105   100
11-y-o b g Lafontaine (USA)-Proven Right (IRE) (Kemal (FR))
S J Gilmore Miss Jumbo Frost

Placings:0152122PP/32112PPP-512324P3 (1584)
2003/04: 21⁵GF, 21¹GF, 20²GF, 23³GF, 22²GF, 21⁴GF, 17⁶GF, 20³GF,

	Starts	1st	2nd	3rd	Win & Pl
Chases	8	1	2	2	9552
Career Total	25	5	7	3	37061

92 6/03 NAbb 2m5f110yF(0-100)HCh G-F £4924
103 6/02 Uttx 2m5f C Ch G-F £6968
102 6/02 NAbb 2m5f110yD Ch GD £4357
109 9/01 Fair 2m4f Hdl FRM £5564
105 8/01 Kbgn 2m NHF GD £3616
Total win prize-money £25432

Going: Sf: 0-0 GS: 0-0 Gd: 0-0 GF: - Fm: 1-8
Distance: 2m/2m3: 0-1 2m4-2m7: 1-6 3m+: 0-1
Track: LH: 1-5 RH: 0-2 Tight: 1-4 Gall: 0-1
Aids: Bl: 0-0 Vi: 0-0 Tstrap: 0-0 Ckp: 0-0
Best Rating: 122 10/01 Gowr 2m6f good Ch

Moderate chaser, took advantage of having dropped 15lb in the handicap when all out to win a handicap at Newton Abbot June 2003; best on fast ground; effective at up to an extended two miles five; suited by forcing tactics.

Moral Support (IRE)
101   110
12-y-o ch g Zaffaran (USA)-Marians Pride (Pry)
J S Moore Tom & Evelyn Yates

Placings:4010/42F/345150P6/1111236B/23PP/0P02P-P5552P (3425)
2003/04: 26PGF, 26⁵G, 32⁵GF, 26⁵GS, 29²S, 25PS,

	Starts	1st	2nd	3rd	Win & Pl
Chases	6	0	1	0	1997
Career Total	38	6	5	3	76643

143 12/00 Chep 3m A HCh HVY £21000
125 11/00 Hntg 3m6f110yC(0-130)HCh G-S £6955
129 11/00 Newb 3m D(0-110)HCh SFT £4368
125 11/00 Kemp 3m D(0-110)HCh SFT £4777
104 2/00 Thur 3m (0-95)HHdl HVY £3588
102 3/97 Tipp 2m4f Hdl G-Y £3391
Total win prize-money £44080

Going: Sf: 0-2 GS: 0-1 Gd: 0-1 GF: - Fm: 0-2
Distance: 2m/2m3: 0-0 2m4-2m7: 0-0 3m+: 0-6
Track: LH: 0-5 RH: 0-1 Tight: 0-5 Gall: 0-1
Aids: Bl: 0-0 Vi: 0-0 Tstrap: 0-0 Ckp: 0-0
Best Rating: 143 2/01 Hayd 3m heavy Ch

Fair chaser; stays marathon trips well; best on soft ground; reportedly retired.

Moratorium (USA)
103   126
9-y-o b g El Gran Senor (USA)-Substance (USA) (Diesis)
Noel Meade John P McManus

Placings:000560/20126101/06-000 (1393a)
2003/04: 16⁶GS, 17⁰F, 16⁹G,

	Starts	1st	2nd	3rd	Win & Pl
Hurdles	3	0	0	0	
Career Total	19	3	2	0	21198

121 4/02 Punc 2m (0-130)HHdl GD £8000
115 8/01 Naas 2m (0-116)HHdl G-Y £5008
104 6/01 Naas 2m (0-109)HHdl GD £4729
Total win prize-money £17738

Going: Sf: 0-0 GS: 0-1 Gd: 0-1 GF: - Fm: 0-1
Distance: 2m/2m3: 0-3 2m4-2m7: 0-0 3m+: 0-0
Track: LH: 0-3 RH: 0-0 Tight: 0-0 Gall: 0-0
Aids: Bl: 0-0 Vi: 0-0 Tstrap: 0-0 Ckp: 0-0
Best Rating: 126 8/02 Gway 2m yld-sft Hdl

Fair Irish handicap hurdler, acts on any ground. Has worn blinkers and a tongue tie.

Morchard Mill
89   (0c)60+
12-y-o b g Out Of Hand-Dorothy Jane (He Loves Me)
Jean-Rene Auvray R T Grant

Placings:00/0/4P34 (1331)
2003/04: 23⁴G, 26PG, 22³GF, 26⁴GF,

	Starts	1st	2nd	3rd	Win & Pl
Hurdles	2	0	0	1	513
Chases	2	0	0	0	296
Career Total	7	0	0	1	809

Going: Sf: 0-0 GS: 0-0 Gd: 0-2 GF: - Fm: 0-2
Distance: 2m/2m3: 0-0 2m4-2m7: 0-1 3m+: 0-3
Track: LH: 0-3 RH: 0-1 Tight: 0-1 Gall: 0-0
Aids: Bl: 0-2 Vi: 0-0 Tstrap: 0-0 Ckp: 0-1
Best Rating: 64 9/03 Hrld 3m2f gd-fm Hdl

More Rainbows (IRE)
94   112
4-y-o b g Rainbows For Life (CAN)-Musical Myth (USA) (Crafty Prospector (USA))
Noel Meade Neighbours Racing Club

Placings:1120F (4828a)
2003/04: 16¹F, 16¹F, 16²GF, 16⁹G, 16⁴Y,

	Starts	1st	2nd	3rd	Win & Pl
Hurdles	5	2	1	0	12623
Career Total	5	2	1	0	12623

112 8/03 Tral 2m Hdl FRM £5824
97 8/03 Tram 2m Hdl FRM £4928
Total win prize-money £10754

Going: Sf: 0-0 GS: 0-0 Gd: 0-1 GF: - Fm: 2-3
Distance: 2m/2m3: 2-5 2m4-2m7: 0-0 3m+: 0-0
Track: LH: 0-2 RH: 0-1 Tight: 0-1 Gall: 0-0
Aids: Bl: 0-0 Vi: 0-0 Tstrap: 0-0 Ckp: 0-0
Best Rating: 112 8/03 Tral 2m firm Hdl

Fair Irish-trained novice hurdler; effective at two miles and acts well on fast ground.

Moreluck (IRE)
103   121
8-y-o b g Roselier (FR)-Vulcan Belle (Royal Vulcan)
K C Bailey Graham And Alison Jelley

Placings:3P1P25 (4930)
2003/04: 16³GS, 20PGS, 24¹G, 25PGS, 24²G, 22⁵G,

	Starts	1st	2nd	3rd	Win & Pl
Chases	6	1	1	1	6730
Career Total	6	1	1	1	6730

111 2/04 Muss 3m E Ch GD £4085
Total win prize-money £4085

Going: Sf: 0-0 GS: 0-3 Gd: 1-3 GF: - Fm: 0-0
Distance: 2m/2m3: 0-1 2m4-2m7: 0-2 **3m+: 1-3**
Track: LH: 0-1 RH: **1-4 Tight: 1-4** Gall: 0-1
Aids: Bl: 0-0 Vi: 0-0 Tstrap: 0-0 Ckp: 0-1
Best Rating: 111 4/04 Ludl 3m   good   Ch

Fair novice chaser; unbeaten in two points in Ireland; suited by three miles and will stay further; acts on good.

Morless

5-y-o b m Morpeth-Bush Radio (Hot Grove)
Dr J R J Naylor P Tosh

Placings:P-0P   (3933)
2003/04: 17⁰GS, 24ᴾG,

	Starts	1st	2nd	3rd	Win & Pl
Hurdles	2	0	0	0	
Career Total	3	0	0	0	

Going: Sf: 0-0 GS: 0-1 Gd: 0-1 GF: - Fm: 0-0
Distance: 2m/2m3: 0-1 2m4-2m7: 0-0 3m+: 0-1
Track: LH: 0-0 RH: 0-2 Tight: 0-1 Gall: 0-0
Aids: Bl: 0-0 Vi: 0-0 Tstrap: 0-0 Ckp: 0-0

Morning Melody
71f   29f

6-y-o b m Afzal-Pacific Overture (Southern Music)
Mrs N S Sharpe Graham Richards

Placings:0-00   (1195)
2003/04: 16⁰G, 16⁰GF,

	Starts	1st	2nd	3rd	Win & Pl
NH Flat	2	0	0	0	
Career Total	3	0	0	0	

Going: Sf: 0-0 GS: 0-0 Gd: 0-1 GF: - Fm: 0-0
Distance: 2m/2m3: 0-2 2m4-2m7: 0-0 3m+: 0-0
Track: LH: 0-2 RH: 0-0 Tight: 0-0 Gall: 0-0
Aids: Bl: 0-0 Vi: 0-0 Tstrap: 0-0 Ckp: 0-0
Best Rating: 29 6/03 Worc 2m   good   NHF

Morris Dancing (USA)

5-y-o b g Rahy (USA)-Summer Dance (Sadler's Wells (USA))
B P J Baugh Messrs Chrimes, Winn & Wilson

Placings:P   (4874)
2003/04: 20ᴾGS,

	Starts	1st	2nd	3rd	Win & Pl
Hurdles	1	0	0	0	
Career Total	1	0	0	0	

Going: Sf: 0-0 GS: 0-1 Gd: 0-0 GF: - Fm: 0-0
Distance: 2m/2m3: 0-0 2m4-2m7: 0-0 3m+: 0-0
Track: LH: 0-1 RH: 0-0 Tight: 0-1 Gall: 0-0
Aids: Bl: 0-0 Vi: 0-0 Tstrap: 0-0 Ckp: 0-0

Morris Piper

11-y-o b g Long Leave-Miss Cone (Celtic Cone)
Mrs R Partridge Daren Partridge

Placings:3/P/0P0P/P   (4696)
2003/04: 19ᴾG,

	Starts	1st	2nd	3rd	Win & Pl
Chases	1	0	0	0	
Career Total	7	0	0	1	172

Going: Sf: 0-0 GS: 0-0 Gd: 0-0 GF: - Fm: 0-0
Distance: 2m/2m3: 0-0 2m4-2m7: 0-1 3m+: 0-0
Track: LH: 0-0 RH: 0-0 Tight: 0-0 Gall: 0-0
Aids: Bl: 0-0 Vi: 0-0 Tstrap: 0-0 Ckp: 0-0
Best Rating: 94 3/00 Winc 2m5f   gd-sft   Ch

Morvern (IRE)
52

4-y-o ch g Titus Livius (FR)-Scotia Rose (Tap On Wood)
J G Given Mrs D Given

Placings:0   (4368)
2003/04: 16⁰GF,

	Starts	1st	2nd	3rd	Win & Pl
Hurdles	1	0	0	0	
Career Total	1	0	0	0	

Going: Sf: 0-0 GS: 0-0 Gd: 0-0 GF: - Fm: 0-1
Distance: 2m/2m3: 0-1 2m4-2m7: 0-0 3m+: 0-0
Track: LH: 0-1 RH: 0-0 Tight: 0-1 Gall: 0-0
Aids: Bl: 0-0 Vi: 0-0 Tstrap: 0-0 Ckp: 0-0

Morwick Mill

10-y-o b g Milieu-Charons Daughter (Another River)
S Waugh Mrs A J Howie

Placings:P   (0430)
2003/04: 26ᴾG,

	Starts	1st	2nd	3rd	Win & Pl
Chases	1	0	0	0	
Career Total	1	0	0	0	

Going: Sf: 0-0 GS: 0-0 Gd: 0-1 GF: - Fm: 0-0
Distance: 2m/2m3: 0-0 2m4-2m7: 0-0 3m+: 0-1
Track: LH: 0-1 RH: 0-0 Tight: 0-1 Gall: 0-0
Aids: Bl: 0-1 Vi: 0-0 Tstrap: 0-0 Ckp: 0-0

Moscow (IRE)

5-y-o ch g Cadeaux Genereux-Madame Nureyev (USA) (Nureyev (USA))
P D Evans (J H M Gosden 20/6) D Healy

Placings:P   (1481)
2003/04: 19ᴾGF,

	Starts	1st	2nd	3rd	Win & Pl
Hurdles	1	0	0	0	
Career Total	1	0	0	0	

Going: Sf: 0-0 GS: 0-0 Gd: 0-0 GF: - Fm: 0-1
Distance: 2m/2m3: 0-0 2m4-2m7: 0-0 3m+: 0-0
Track: LH: 0-0 RH: 0-1 Tight: 0-0 Gall: 0-0
Aids: Bl: 0-0 Vi: 0-0 Tstrap: 0-0 Ckp: 0-0

Moscow Dancer (IRE)
108   109+

7-y-o ch g Moscow Society (USA)-Cromhill Lady (Miners Lamp)

P Monteith J Stephenson

Placings:000/PP-111   (2729)
2003/04: 18¹S, 18¹S, 16¹S,

	Starts	1st	2nd	3rd	Win & Pl
Hurdles	3	3	0	0	9662
Career Total	8	3	0	0	9662
109 12/03 Hayd 2m	E(0-110)HHdl		SFT		£3416
109 12/03 Kels 2m2f	F(0-90)HHdl		SFT		£2723
86 11/03 Kels 2m2f	E(0-110)HHdl		SFT		£3523
		Total win prize-money £9662			

Going: Sf: 2-2 GS: 0-0 Gd: 1-1 GF: - Fm: 0-0
Distance: 2m/2m3: 3-3 2m4-2m7: 0-0 3m+: 0-0
Track: LH: 3-3 RH: 0-0 **Tight: 2-2** Gall: 0-0
Aids: Bl: 0-0 Vi: 0-0 Tstrap: 0-0 Ckp: 0-0
Best Rating: 109 12/03 Hayd 2m   soft   Hdl

Moderate hurdler; much improved form in late 2003 for Peter Monteith following wind operations; effective at up to two miles-two; should stay further; acts on good ground or softer.

Moscow Fields (IRE)
101   84

6-y-o ch g Moscow Society (USA)-Cloverlady (Decent Fellow)
Miss H C Knight J D N Tillyard

Placings:2-40   (2673)
2003/04: 16⁴G, 19⁰GF,

	Starts	1st	2nd	3rd	Win & Pl
Hurdles	2	0	0	0	264
Career Total	3	0	1	0	1192

Going: Sf: 0-0 GS: 0-0 Gd: 0-0 GF: - Fm: 0-1
Distance: 2m/2m3: 0-2 2m4-2m7: 0-0 3m+: 0-0
Track: LH: 0-1 RH: 0-1 Tight: 0-0 Gall: 0-1
Aids: Bl: 0-0 Vi: 0-0 Tstrap: 0-0 Ckp: 0-0
Best Rating: 102 3/03 Newb 2m110y   soft   NHF

Novice hurdler; runner-up in a good Newbury bumper behind top-class prospect Bourbon Manhattan; had a wind operation after; fourth on hurdling debut; will be suited by chasing.

Moscow Flyer (IRE)
121   (170h) 176

10-y-o b g Moscow Society (USA)-Meelick Lady (IRE) (Duky)
Mrs John Harrington Brian Kearney

Placings:6343/1110/13121F21/**F111F11**/1U111U-111U1   (4639)
2003/04: 16⁴GY, 16¹GF, 16¹S, 17¹S, 16⁴G, 20¹G,

	Starts	1st	2nd	3rd	Win & Pl
Chases	6	4	0	0	189458
Career Total	34	20	2	3	714846
176 4/04 Aint 2m4f	A Ch		GD		£89250
166 12/03 Leop 2m1f	Ch		SFT		£21103
176 12/03 Sand 2m	A Ch		GD		£58000
152 11/03 Navn 2m	Ch		G-F		£21103
174 3/03 Chel 2m	A Ch		GD		£145000
163 2/03 Punc 2m	Ch		SH		£16883
162 12/02 Leop 2m1f	Ch		HVY		£17944
168 11/02 DRoy 2m2f	Ch		SFT		£21165
155 4/02 Punc 2m	Ch		GD		£32331
167 3/02 Chel 2m	A Ch		G-S		£72500
151 12/01 Leop 2m1f	Ch		YLD		£39314
151 11/01 Punc 2m	Ch		SFT		£13104
123 11/01 DRoy 2m	Ch		YLD		£7233
170 4/01 Leop 2m	Hdl		SH		£55645

165	12/00	Leop	2m	Hdl	HVY £15600
151	11/00	Punc	2m	Hdl	SFT £10400
150	5/00	Punc	2m	Hdl	YLD £24800
133	11/99	Fair	2m	Hdl	SFT £26116
121	11/99	DRoy	2m	Hdl	SFT £8705
117	10/99	Punc	2m	Hdl	YLD £3696
					Total win prize-money £699899

Going:	Sf: 1-1 GS: 0-0 Gd: 2-3 GF: - Fm: 1-1
Distance:	2m/2m3: 3-5 2m4-2m7: 1-1 3m+: 0-0
Track:	LH: 3-4 RH: 1-2 Tight: 1-1 Gall: 0-1
Aids:	Bl: 0-0 Vi: 0-0 Tstrap: 0-0 Ckp: 0-0
Best Rating:	176 4/04 Aint 2m4f good Ch

Top-class two-mile chaser; former high-class hurdler; winner of the 2002 Arkle Trophy at Cheltenham; followed up in Grade One at Punchestown; successful three times in 2002/2003 before winning the Queen Mother Champion Chase at the 2003 Festival; unseated on final start of that campaign; scored on seasonal debut at Navan before taking the Tingle Creek at Sandown and followed up at Leopardstown on next outing; unseated rider in 2004 Queen Mother, when warm favourite; ready winner of the Melling Chase at Aintree; stays two and a half miles well; acts on any ground; usually jumps well, but can sometimes puts in a bad one; unbeaten in completed starts over fences.

Moscow Gold (IRE)

(80h)   (59h)
7-y-o ch g Moscow Society (USA)-Vesper Time (The Parson)
A E Price   Mrs Carol Davis

Placings:00/0005-F   (4566)
2003/04: 17FGS,

	Starts	1st	2nd	3rd	Win & Pl
Chases	1	0	0	0	
Career Total	7	0	0	0	0

Going:	Sf: 0-0 GS: 0-1 Gd: 0-0 GF: - Fm: 0-0
Distance:	2m/2m3: 0-1 2m4-2m7: 0-0 3m+: 0-0
Track:	LH: 0-1 RH: 0-0 Tight: 0-1 Gall: 0-0
Aids:	Bl: 0-0 Vi: 0-0 Tstrap: 0-0 Ckp: 0-0
Best Rating:	77 4/02 Weth 2m gd-fm NHF

Moscow Leader (IRE)

105(104h)   (107h)119+
6-y-o ch g Moscow Society (USA)-Catrionas Castle (IRE) (Orchestra)
R C Guest   Miss P Overy

Placings:053-31223F112031F   (4590)
2003/04: 20³GF, 22¹G, 24²GF, 21²F, 24³GS, 25FG, 20¹S, 16²G, 19⁴GS, 26³G, 24¹HY, 24FG,

	Starts	1st	2nd	3rd	Win & Pl
Hurdles	7	3	2	2	12781
Chases	6	1	1	1	8906
Career Total	16	4	3	4	22004
119	3/04	Carl	3m	D(0-115)HCh	HVY £7182
107	12/03	Weth	2m4f110yE(0-105)HHdl	GD £3167
106	12/03	Kels	2m6f110yE(0-105)HHdl	SFT £2754
100	8/03	Ctml	2m6f	E Hdl	GD £4102
					Total win prize-money £17208

Going:	Sf: 2-2 GS: 0-2 Gd: 2-6 GF: - Fm: 0-3
Distance:	2m/2m3: 0-2 2m4-2m7: 3-5 3m+: 1-6
Track:	LH: 3-7 RH: 1-6 Tight: 2-3 Gall: 0-3
Aids:	Bl: 0-0 Vi: 0-0 Tstrap: 0-0 Ckp: 3-6
Best Rating:	119 3/04 Carl 3m heavy Ch

Moderate performer; stays three miles; acts on good.

Moscow Tradition (IRE)

(103h)   (99h)
6-y-o b g Moscow Society (USA)-Bucks Grove (IRE) (Buckskin (FR))
Jonjo O'Neill   Mr & Mrs John Poynton

Placings:0265-3U   (1418)
2003/04: 17³G, 20ᵁGF,

	Starts	1st	2nd	3rd	Win & Pl
Hurdles	1	0	0	1	540
Chases	1	0	0	0	0
Career Total	6	0	1	1	1374

Going:	Sf: 0-0 GS: 0-0 Gd: 0-1 GF: - Fm: 0-1
Distance:	2m/2m3: 0-1 2m4-2m7: 0-1 3m+: 0-0
Track:	LH: 0-1 RH: 0-0 Tight: 0-2 Gall: 0-0
Aids:	Bl: 0-0 Vi: 0-0 Tstrap: 0-0 Ckp: 0-0
Best Rating:	99 1/03 Kemp 2m5f gd-sft Hdl

Moderate ex-Irish hurdler; won his only point in Ireland as a four-year-old; disappointing including on return when only third in weak event at Bangor in September; acts on soft ground.

Moscow Whisper (IRE)

103   102
7-y-o b g Moscow Society (USA)-Native Woodfire (IRE) (Mister Majestic)
P J Hobbs   Yusof Sepiuddin

Placings:331-12   (0530)
2003/04: 22¹G, 20²GF,

	Starts	1st	2nd	3rd	Win & Pl
Hurdles	2	1	1	0	6850
Career Total	5	2	1	2	13652
92	5/03	Strf	2m6f110yD Hdl	GD £5850
102	4/03	Prth	2m4f110yD Hdl	GD £5824
			Total win prize-money £11674	

Going:	Sf: 0-0 GS: 0-0 Gd: 1-1 GF: - Fm: 0-1
Distance:	2m/2m3: 0-0 2m4-2m7: 1-2 3m+: 0-0
Track:	LH: 1-2 RH: 0-0 Tight: 1-1 Gall: 0-0
Aids:	Bl: 0-0 Vi: 0-0 Tstrap: 0-0 Ckp: 0-0
Best Rating:	102 6/03 Worc 2m4f gd-fm Hdl

Got off the mark over hurdles when winning over 2m 4f at Perth in April 2003; followed up over 2m 6f at Stratford in May but he is better going right-handed; stays well; likes decent ground.

Moslob (IRE)

91   93
7-y-o b g Black Monday-Musical Millie (IRE) (Orchestra)
Miss J S Davis   Miss J Davis

Placings:PP4   (4713)
2003/04: 26ᴾG, 21ᴾS, 24⁴G,

	Starts	1st	2nd	3rd	Win & Pl
Hurdles	2	0	0	0	0
Chases	1	0	0	0	514
Career Total	3	0	0	0	514

Going:	Sf: 0-1 GS: 0-0 Gd: 0-2 GF: - Fm: 0-0
Distance:	2m/2m3: 0-0 2m4-2m7: 0-3 3m+: 0-0
Track:	LH: 0-1 RH: 0-2 Tight: 0-1 Gall: 0-0
Aids:	Bl: 0-0 Vi: 0-0 Tstrap: 0-0 Ckp: 0-0
Best Rating:	93 4/04 Ludl 3m good Ch

Moss Campian

6-y-o ch g Le Moss-Rose Rambler (Scallywag)
L Wells   W A Scott

Placings:00P   (4931)
2003/04: 18ᵒS, 17ᵒGS, 22ᴾG,

	Starts	1st	2nd	3rd	Win & Pl
NH Flat	2	0	0	0	0
Hurdles	1	0	0	0	0
Career Total	3	0	0	0	

Going:	Sf: 0-1 GS: 0-1 Gd: 0-1 GF: - Fm: 0-0
Distance:	2m/2m3: 0-2 2m4-2m7: 0-1 3m+: 0-0
Track:	LH: 0-2 RH: 0-1 Tight: 0-1 Gall: 0-0
Aids:	Bl: 0-0 Vi: 0-0 Tstrap: 0-0 Ckp: 0-0
Best Rating:	61 12/03 Plum 2m2f soft NHF

Moss Harvey

106(105h)   (136h)128
9-y-o ch g Le Moss-Wings Ground (Murrayfield)
J M Jefferson   J R Salter

Placings:53/1111226P/11534P-4P1   (4912)
2003/04: 24⁴S, 20ᴾG, 20¹S,

	Starts	1st	2nd	3rd	Win & Pl
Chases	3	1	0	0	13872
Career Total	19	7	2	2	53797
128	4/04	Prth	2m4f110yD(0-125)HCh	SFT £13193
128	11/02	Kels	3m1f	D Ch	SFT £6734
128	10/02	Fknm	2m5f110yC Ch	G-S £8073
140	12/01	Bang	3m	C(0-135)HHdl	G-S £6929
131	12/01	Newc	3m	D Hdl	G-S £3454
108	11/01	Kels	2m6f110yE Hdl	GD £3136
104	10/01	Kels	2m6f110yE Hdl	G-S £2544
				Total win prize-money £44066	

Going:	Sf: 1-2 GS: 0-0 Gd: 0-1 GF: - Fm: 0-0
Distance:	2m/2m3: 0-0 2m4-2m7: 1-2 3m+: 0-0
Track:	LH: 0-1 RH: 1-2 Tight: 0-0 Gall: 0-1
Aids:	Bl: 0-0 Vi: 0-0 Tstrap: 0-0 Ckp: 0-0
Best Rating:	140 2/02 Hayd 2m7f110y heavy Hdl

Fair chaser/ formerly smart novice hurdler; lost his way until winning at Perth in April 2004; stays three miles and handles soft ground.

Moss Run (IRE)

101   83
10-y-o b g Commanche Run-Glenreigh Moss (Le Moss)
A E Jessop   Mrs Gloria Jessop

Placings:0/50P/000U/P2/0421622060-5634666 (4750)
2003/04: 21⁵G, 22⁶GS, 22³G, 20⁴G, 24⁶S, 23⁶GS, 21⁶G,

	Starts	1st	2nd	3rd	Win & Pl
Hurdles	7	0	0	1	819
Career Total	27	1	4	7	10593
79	7/02	Klny	2m6f	(60-88)HHdl	GD £4233
				Total win prize-money £4233	

Going:	Sf: 0-1 GS: 0-2 Gd: 0-4 GF: - Fm: 0-0
Distance:	2m/2m3: 0-0 2m4-2m7: 0-6 3m+: 0-1
Track:	LH: 0-6 RH: 0-0 Tight: 0-5 Gall: 0-1
Aids:	Bl: 0-0 Vi: 0-0 Tstrap: 0-0 Ckp: 0-0
Best Rating:	85 2/00 Wwck 2m soft NHF

Plating-class hurdler; stays two miles six.

Mosscow Reality

68   **28**

11-y-o ch m Le Moss-La Verite (Vitiges (FR))
M D McMillan M D McMillan

Placings:0260/4/0   (4873)
2003/04: 20⁹GS,

	Starts	1st	2nd	3rd	Win & Pl
Hurdles	1	0	0	0	
Career Total	6	0	1	0	1135

Going: Sf: 0-0 GS: 0-1 Gd: 0-0 GF: - Fm: 0-0
Distance: 2m/2m3: 0-0 2m4-2m7: 0-1 3m+: 0-0
Track: LH: 0-1 RH: 0-0 Tight: 0-1 Gall: 0-0
Aids: Bl: 0-0 Vi: 0-0 Tstrap: 0-0 Ckp: 0-0
Best Rating: 88 12/00 Ludl 2m5f   soft   Hdl

Mosspat

86   **62**

5-y-o b g Reprimand-Queen And Country (Town And Country)
W G M Turner Mossie O'Connell

Placings:P60-000   (1059)
2003/04: 17⁰GS, 16⁹G, 20⁰GF,

	Starts	1st	2nd	3rd	Win & Pl
Hurdles	3	0	0	0	
Career Total	6	0	0	0	0

Going: Sf: 0-0 GS: 0-1 Gd: 0-1 GF: - Fm: 0-1
Distance: 2m/2m3: 0-2 2m4-2m7: 0-1 3m+: 0-0
Track: LH: 0-3 RH: 0-0 Tight: 0-2 Gall: 0-0
Aids: Bl: 0-0 Vi: 0-0 Tstrap: 0-0 Ckp: 0-1
Best Rating: 62 11/02 Leic 2m   heavy Hdl

Mossy Bay

91   **88**

9-y-o b g Phardante (FR)-Mossy Fern (Le Moss)
O Sherwood R Waters

Placings:10/12102/6   (0602)
2003/04: 22⁶G,

	Starts	1st	2nd	3rd	Win & Pl
Hurdles	1	0	0	0	
Career Total	8	3	2	0	7748
103	10/00	Towc	3m	D Hdl	GD	£2947
103	5/00	Folk	2m1f110yH NHF		GD	£1746
103	11/99	Ludl	2m	H NHF	GD	£1646
				Total win prize-money £6341		

Going: Sf: 0-0 GS: 0-0 Gd: 0-1 GF: - Fm: 0-0
Distance: 2m/2m3: 0-0 2m4-2m7: 0-1 3m+: 0-0
Track: LH: 0-1 RH: 0-0 Tight: 0-1 Gall: 0-0
Aids: Bl: 0-0 Vi: 0-0 Tstrap: 0-0 Ckp: 0-0
Best Rating: 103 4/01 Hrfd 3m2f   good   Hdl

Modest hurdler; has shaped well since returning to the action; stays two and a half miles; effective on a sound surface.

Mossy Green (IRE)

117(106h)   (146h)**155**

10-y-o b g Moscow Society (USA)-Green Ajo (Green Shoon)
W P Mullins Greenstar Syndicate

Placings:2321/2120-1142FF   (4827a)
2003/04: 16¹GY, 16¹YS, 17⁴YS, 21²YS, 24⁶G, 20⁰FY,

	Starts	1st	2nd	3rd	Win & Pl
Chases	6	2	1	0	32915

Career Total		14	4	5	1	53306
140	12/03	Cork	2m	Ch	Y-S	£8441
131	11/03	Naas	2m	Ch	G-Y	£8064
137	1/03	Naas	2m3f	Hdl	SFT	£6720
127	4/01	Baln	2m	NHF	SFT	£4173
				Total win prize-money £27401		

Going: Sf: 0-0 GS: 0-0 Gd: 0-1 GF: - Fm: 0-0
Distance: 2m/2m3: 2-3 2m4-2m7: 0-2 3m+: 0-1
Track: LH: 1-4 RH: 0-1 Tight: 0-1 Gall: 0-0
Aids: Bl: 0-0 Vi: 0-0 Tstrap: 0-0 Ckp: 0-0
Best Rating: 155 3/04 Chel 3m110y   good   Ch

Very useful Irish-trained hurdler; useful novice chaser; stays 2m 4f; suited by cut in the ground; front runner; progressive despite his age.

Mostakbel (USA)

92f   **85f**

5-y-o b/br g Saint Ballado (CAN)-Shamlegh (USA) (Flying Paster (USA))
M D I Usher Midweek Racing

Placings:2   (0837)
2003/04: 16²GF,

	Starts	1st	2nd	3rd	Win & Pl
NH Flat	1	0	1	0	545
Career Total	1	0	1	0	545

Going: Sf: 0-0 GS: 0-0 Gd: 0-0 GF: - Fm: 0-1
Distance: 2m/2m3: 0-1 2m4-2m7: 0-0 3m+: 0-0
Track: LH: 0-1 RH: 0-0 Tight: 0-0 Gall: 0-0
Aids: Bl: 0-0 Vi: 0-0 Tstrap: 0-0 Ckp: 0-0
Best Rating: 85 7/03 Worc 2m   gd-fm NHF

Caught close home when 33/1 chance on debut in Worcester bumper July 2003.

Motcomb Jam (IRE)

106(100h)   (114 h)**122+**

7-y-o b g Frimaire-Flying Flo Jo (USA) (Aloma's Ruler (USA))
C J Mann Bix Racers

Placings:40/B0134-32122   (4841)
2003/04: 20³GF, 19²GF, 21¹G, 18²G, 21²G,

	Starts	1st	2nd	3rd	Win & Pl
Chases	5	1	3	1	14531
Career Total	12	2	3	2	18655
98	11/03	Fknm	2m5f110yD Ch		GD	£5356
114	1/03	Donc	2m110y E Hdl		G-S	£3552
				Total win prize-money £8908		

Going: Sf: 0-0 GS: 0-0 Gd: 1-3 GF: - Fm: 0-2
Distance: 2m/2m3: 0-1 2m4-2m7: 1-4 3m+: 0-0
Track: LH: 1-4 RH: 0-1 Tight: 1-2 Gall: 0-2
Aids: Bl: 0-0 Vi: 0-0 Tstrap: 0-0 Ckp: 0-0
Best Rating: 122 4/04 Chel 2m5f   good   Ch

Modest novice chaser/fair hurdler; showed ability in bumper company; stays two and a half miles and acts on most types of ground.

Motcombe (IRE)

98   **93+**

6-y-o ch m Carroll House-Cooks Lawn (The Parson)
R H Alner Lady Cobham

Placings:03455220   (4733)
2003/04: 16⁸GS, 17³GF, 21⁴G, 21⁵GS, 16⁵S, 20²HY, 22²GS, 22⁰G,

	Starts	1st	2nd	3rd	Win & Pl
NH Flat	1	0	0	0	0

Hurdles	7	0	2	1	3100
Career Total	8	0	2	1	3100

Going: Sf: 0-2 GS: 0-3 Gd: 0-2 GF: - Fm: 0-1
Distance: 2m/2m3: 0-3 2m4-2m7: 0-5 3m+: 0-0
Track: LH: 0-7 RH: 0-1 Tight: 0-2 Gall: 0-1
Aids: Bl: 0-0 Vi: 0-0 Tstrap: 0-0 Ckp: 0-0
Best Rating: 99 3/04 Extr 2m6f110y gd-sft Hdl

Consistent efforts in novice hurdles; stays 2m 4f; acts on any ground.

Motown Melody (IRE)

75   **29**

6-y-o b m Detroit Sam (FR)-Hester Ann (Proverb)
C L Tizzard R G Tizzard

Placings:2320   (1813)
2003/04: 16²GF, 17³GF, 17²GF, 20⁴G,

	Starts	1st	2nd	3rd	Win & Pl
NH Flat	3	0	2	1	1365
Hurdles	1	0	0	0	0
Career Total	4	0	2	1	1365

Going: Sf: 0-0 GS: 0-0 Gd: 0-1 GF: - Fm: 0-3
Distance: 2m/2m3: 0-3 2m4-2m7: 0-1 3m+: 0-0
Track: LH: 0-4 RH: 0-0 Tight: 0-3 Gall: 0-0
Aids: Bl: 0-0 Vi: 0-0 Tstrap: 0-0 Ckp: 0-0
Best Rating: 85 8/03 NAbb 2m1f   gd-fm NHF

Very moderate bumper performer; well beaten on debut over hurdles.

Moulin Riche (FR)

107   **124**

4-y-o b g Video Rock (FR)-Gintonique (FR) (Royal Charter (FR))
F Doumen J C Seroul

Placings:2O02   (4422)
2003/04: 15²HO, 16⁰S, 17⁰G, 18²HO,

	Starts	1st	2nd	3rd	Win & Pl
Hurdles	4	0	2	0	14527
Career Total	4	0	2	0	14527

Going: Sf: 0-1 GS: 0-0 Gd: 0-1 GF: - Fm: 0-0
Distance: 2m/2m3: 0-3 2m4-2m7: 0-0 3m+: 0-0
Track: LH: 0-1 RH: 0-1 Tight: 0-0 Gall: 0-1
Aids: Bl: 0-1 Vi: 0-0 Tstrap: 0-0 Ckp: 0-0
Best Rating: 124 3/04 Chel 2m1f   good   Hdl

Promising French-trained juvenile hurdler; going well on British debut when running into a rail; ran in snatches when well fancied for the 2004 Triumph Hurdle; acts on most ground, but best with cut; suited by two miles.

Mounsey Castle

114(108h)   (110h)**123**

7-y-o ch g Carlingford Castle-Gay Ticket (New Member)
P J Hobbs Alan Peterson

Placings:46/12211-3123415   (4648)
2003/04: 22³G, 23¹GF, 24²GF, 24³G, 24⁴G, 20¹G, 20⁵G,

	Starts	1st	2nd	3rd	Win & Pl
Hurdles	1	0	0	1	768
Chases	6	2	1	1	14586
Career Total	14	5	3	2	29178
122	3/04	Sand	2m4f110yD(0-120)HCh	GD	£8092

117	9/03	Worc	2m7f110yE Ch		G-F	£3042
104	4/03	Strf	2m6f110yE Hdl		G-F	£4260
102	4/03	Hrfd	2m3f110yE Hdl		G-F	£3692
100	5/02	Chep	2m110y H NHF		G-F	£1967

Total win prize-money £21055

Going:	Sf: 0-0 GS: 0-0 Gd: 1-5 GF: - Fm: 1-2
Distance:	2m/2m3: 0-0 2m4-2m7: 1-3 3m+: 1-4
Track:	LH: 1-3 RH: 1-4 Tight: 0-1 Gall: 0-0
Aids:	Bl: 0-0 Vi: 0-0 Tstrap: 0-0 Ckp: 0-0
Best Rating:	**124** 12/03 Sand 3m110y good Ch

Fair chaser; stays three miles, but effective at shorter; best on a sound surface; looks the type to do well summer jumping.

Mount Clerigo (IRE)
114f   **129f**

6-y-o b g Supreme Leader-Fair Ava (IRE) (Strong Gale)
V R A Dartnall Stewart Andrew

Placings:*112*   **(3832)**
2003/04: 17¹G, 16¹HY, 16²G,

	Starts	1st	2nd	3rd	Win & Pl
NH Flat	3	2	1	0	13747
Career Total	**3**	**2**	**1**	**0**	**13747**
117	1/04	Uttx	2m	H NHF	HVY	£2198
117	11/03	Aint	2m1f	H NHF	GD	£6948

Total win prize-money £9147

Going:	Sf: 1-1 GS: 0-0 Gd: 1-2 GF: - Fm: 0-0
Distance:	**2m/2m3: 2-3** 2m4-2m7: 0-0 3m+: 0-0
Track:	**LH: 1-2** RH: 0-0 Tight: 0-0 Gall: 0-1
Aids:	Bl: 0-0 Vi: 0-0 Tstrap: 0-0 Ckp: 0-0
Best Rating:	**132** 2/04 Newb 2m110y good NHF

Won Aintree bumper on racecourse debut in November; narrowly defied a penalty at Uttoxeter in January before good effort at Newbury; handles good to heavy ground.

Mount Cook (FR)
99   **83+**

4-y-o b g Gold And Steel (FR)-Debandade (FR) (Le Pontet (FR))
Mrs H Dalton (G Cherel 24/11) Miss L Hales

Placings:*4*   **(3511)**
2003/04: 18⁴G,

	Starts	1st	2nd	3rd	Win & Pl
Hurdles	1	0	0	0	258
Career Total	**1**	**0**	**0**	**0**	**258**

Going:	Sf: 0-0 GS: 0-0 Gd: 0-1 GF: - Fm: 0-0
Distance:	2m/2m3: 0-1 2m4-2m7: 0-0 3m+: 0-0
Track:	LH: 0-1 RH: 0-0 Tight: 0-1 Gall: 0-0
Aids:	Bl: 0-0 Vi: 0-0 Tstrap: 0-0 Ckp: 0-0
Best Rating:	**93** 1/04 Font 2m2f110y good Hdl

Middle-distance winner in testing ground on the Flat in France; some promise on hurdling debut.

Mount Karinga
110   **128**

6-y-o b g Karinga Bay-Candarela (Damister (USA))
P F Nicholls Derek Millard

Placings:*1-412202*   **(4852)**
2003/04: 19⁴G, 20¹G, 16²G, 22²G, 20⁵S, 20²GS,

	Starts	1st	2nd	3rd	Win & Pl
Hurdles	6	1	3	0	16389
Career Total	**7**	**2**	**3**	**0**	**18377**
111	11/03	Chep	2m4f	E Hdl	GD	£2681

Mount Prague (IRE)
101   **124**

10-y-o br g Lord Americo-Celtic Duchess (Ya Zaman (USA))
K C Bailey W J Ives

Placings:*4/1305461/0F31F23/13453P/135P5-6F223105P*   **(4784)**
2003/04: 24⁶G, 20^FGF, 21²GS, 20²GS, 18³GF, 20¹GF, 20⁰G, 20⁵G, 24^PG,

	Starts	1st	2nd	3rd	Win & Pl
Chases	9	1	2	1	11511
Career Total	**35**	**6**	**3**	**7**	**39393**
124	12/03	Leic	2m4f110yD(0-125)HCh	G-F	£7609
124	11/02	Hntg	2m4f110yD(0-115)HCh	G-S	£5473
128	1/02	Ludl	2m4f	D(0-115)HCh	GD	£4537
123	12/00	Hntg	2m110y	F(0-105)HCh	HVY	£2699
112	3/00	DRoy	2m	Hdl	G-Y	£2760
111	10/99	Gway	2m	NHF	SFT	£4004

Total win prize-money £27083

Going:	Sf: 0-0 GS: 0-2 Gd: 0-4 GF: - Fm: 1-3
Distance:	2m/2m3: 0-1 **2m4-2m7: 1-6** 3m+: 0-2
Track:	LH: 0-2 **RH: 1-7** Tight: 0-1 Gall: 0-4
Aids:	Bl: 0-0 Vi: 0-0 Tstrap: 0-0 **Ckp: 1-8**
Best Rating:	**128** 1/02 Ludl 2m4f good Ch

Moderate chaser; suited by two and a half miles and soft ground; all his wins have been on right-handed tracks; goes well fresh.

Mount Vernon (IRE)
79   **68**

8-y-o b g Darshaan-Chellita (Habitat)
P Wegmann P Wegmann

Placings:*6P/0/5/P56-00*   **(0487)**
2003/04: 16⁰GS, 22⁰GF,

	Starts	1st	2nd	3rd	Win & Pl
Hurdles	2	0	0	0	0
Career Total	**9**	**0**	**0**	**0**	**0**

Going:	Sf: 0-0 GS: 0-0 Gd: 0-0 GF: - Fm: 0-1
Distance:	2m/2m3: 0-1 2m4-2m7: 0-0 3m+: 0-0
Track:	LH: 0-2 RH: 0-0 Tight: 0-1 Gall: 0-0
Aids:	Bl: 0-0 Vi: 0-0 Tstrap: 0-0 Ckp: 0-0
Best Rating:	**72** 5/01 Bang 2m1f gd-sft Hdl

Mountain Man (FR)
91   **94**

6-y-o b g Cadoudal (FR)-Montagne Bleue (Legend Of France (USA))
S E H Sherwood The Hon Mrs S Sherwood

Placings:*0/54-45*   **(4441)**
2003/04: 20⁴G, 21⁵S,

	Starts	1st	2nd	3rd	Win & Pl
Hurdles	2	0	0	0	0
Career Total	**5**	**0**	**0**	**0**	**0**

103	3/03	Chep	2m110y H NHF		GD	£1988

Total win prize-money £4669

Going:	Sf: 0-1 GS: 0-1 Gd: 1-4 GF: - Fm: 0-0
Distance:	2m/2m3: 0-2 **2m4-2m7: 1-4** 3m+: 0-0
Track:	**LH: 1-3** RH: 0-3 Tight: 0-0 Gall: 0-0
Aids:	Bl: 0-0 Vi: 0-0 Tstrap: 0-0 Ckp: 0-0
Best Rating:	**130** 12/03 Chel 2m110y good Hdl

Useful novice hurdler; stays two miles six; only raced on good ground; consistent and lightly raced.

Going:	Sf: 0-1 GS: 0-0 Gd: 0-1 GF: - Fm: 0-0
Distance:	2m/2m3: 0-0 2m4-2m7: 0-2 3m+: 0-0
Track:	LH: 0-2 RH: 0-0 Tight: 0-0 Gall: 0-0
Aids:	Bl: 0-0 Vi: 0-0 Tstrap: 0-0 Ckp: 0-0
Best Rating:	**90** 12/02 Donc 2m110y soft Hdl

Mountain Mayhem (IRE)

6-y-o br g Be My Native (USA)-Arctic Lucy (Lucifer (USA))
Jonjo O'Neill Terry Warner

Placings:0   **(2328)**
2003/04: 16⁰GS,

	Starts	1st	2nd	3rd	Win & Pl
Hurdles	1	0	0	0	
Career Total	**1**	**0**	**0**	**0**	

Going:	Sf: 0-0 GS: 0-1 Gd: 0-0 GF: - Fm: 0-0
Distance:	2m/2m3: 0-0 2m4-2m7: 0-0 3m+: 0-0
Track:	LH: 0-1 RH: 0-0 Tight: 0-1 Gall: 0-0
Aids:	Bl: 0-0 Vi: 0-0 Tstrap: 0-0 Ckp: 0-0

Mounthooley
85   **84**

8-y-o ch g Karinga Bay-Gladys Emmanuel (Idiots Delight)
B Mactaggart Ashleybank Investments Limited

Placings:*0042/3*   **(2402)**
2003/04: 17³HY,

	Starts	1st	2nd	3rd	Win & Pl
Hurdles	1	0	0	1	394
Career Total	**5**	**0**	**1**	**1**	**2108**

Going:	Sf: 0-1 GS: 0-0 Gd: 0-0 GF: - Fm: 0-0
Distance:	2m/2m3: 0-1 2m4-2m7: 0-0 3m+: 0-0
Track:	LH: 0-0 RH: 0-1 Tight: 0-0 Gall: 0-0
Aids:	Bl: 0-0 Vi: 0-0 Tstrap: 0-0 Ckp: 0-0
Best Rating:	**103** 4/02 Ayr 2m4f good Hdl

Moderate hurdler; lightly raced; acts on good ground or softer.

Mountrath Rock
90   **83**

7-y-o b m Rock Hopper-Point Of Law (Law Society (USA))
Miss B Sanders Mark L Champion

Placings:*4/3/4001-33*   **(1209)**
2003/04: 22³G, 20³GF,

	Starts	1st	2nd	3rd	Win & Pl
Hurdles	2	1	0	2	918
Career Total	**8**	**1**	**0**	**3**	**3821**
83	4/03	Plum	2m5f	G(0-90)HHdl	G-F	£2450

Total win prize-money £2450

Going:	Sf: 0-0 GS: 0-0 Gd: 0-1 GF: - Fm: 0-1
Distance:	2m/2m3: 0-0 2m4-2m7: 0-2 3m+: 0-1
Track:	LH: 0-1 RH: 0-0 Tight: 0-2 Gall: 0-0
Aids:	Bl: 0-2 Vi: 0-0 Tstrap: 0-2 Ckp: 0-0
Best Rating:	**83** 4/03 Plum 2m5f gd-fm Hdl

Plating-class hurdler; appreciated the drop in class when winning a Plumpton seller in April 2003; suited by fast ground; stays two miles five; wears tongue tie; has worn blinkers.

Mounts Bay

81   **54**

5-y-o ch m Karinga Bay-Sweet On Willie (USA) (Master Willie)
R J Hodges D F P Racing

Placings: 46050   (4736)
2003/04: 17⁴GF, 17⁶GF, 16⁹GF, 17⁵G, 17⁹G,

	Starts	1st	2nd	3rd	Win & Pl
NH Flat	4	0	0	0	0
Hurdles	1	0	0	0	0
Career Total	5	0	0	0	0

Going:	Sf: 0-0 GS: 0-0 Gd: 0-2 GF: - Fm: 0-3
Distance:	2m/2m3: 0-5 2m4-2m7: 0-0 3m+: 0-0
Track:	LH: 0-3 RH: 0-1 Tight: 0-2 Gall: 0-0
Aids:	Bl: 0-0 Vi: 0-0 Tstrap: 0-0 Ckp: 0-0
Best Rating:	79 11/03 Wwck 2m gd-fm NHF

Mountsorrel (IRE)

67   **30**

5-y-o b g Charnwood Forest (IRE)-Play The Queen (IRE) (King Of Clubs)
T Wall D Pugh

Placings: 00-0   (0761)
2003/04: 16⁹G,

	Starts	1st	2nd	3rd	Win & Pl
Hurdles	1	0	0	0	0
Career Total	3	0	0	0	

Going:	Sf: 0-0 GS: 0-0 Gd: 0-1 GF: - Fm: 0-0
Distance:	2m/2m3: 0-1 2m4-2m7: 0-0 3m+: 0-0
Track:	LH: 0-1 RH: 0-0 Tight: 0-0 Gall: 0-0
Aids:	Bl: 0-0 Vi: 0-0 Tstrap: 0-0 Ckp: 0-0
Best Rating:	31 9/02 Bang 2m1f good Hdl

Mouseski

10-y-o b g Petoski-Worth Matravers (National Trust)
R Barber M H Dare

Placings: 020/5/4P3F613/1   (4696)
2003/04: 19¹G,

	Starts	1st	2nd	3rd	Win & Pl
Chases	1	1	0	0	3679
Career Total	12	2	1	2	8086
107	4/04	Extr	2m3f110yH Ch		GD	£3679
100	3/02	Extr	2m1f	E(0-100)HHdl	GD	£2884
				Total win prize-money £6563	

Going:	Sf: 0-0 GS: 0-0 Gd: 1-1 GF: - Fm: 0-0
Distance:	2m/2m3: 0-0 **2m4-2m7: 1-1** 3m+: 0-0
Track:	LH: 0-0 **RH: 1-1** Tight: 0-0 Gall: 0-0
Aids:	Bl: 0-0 Vi: 0-0 Tstrap: 0-0 Ckp: 0-0
Best Rating:	107 4/04 Extr 2m3f110y good Ch

Modest hunter chaser; stays 2m 4f; acts on good ground.

Moving Earth (IRE)

109(108h)   (117h)**130**

11-y-o b g Brush Aside (USA)-Park Breeze (IRE) (Strong Gale)
A W Carroll Pursuit Media

Placings: 2/F/F1/31L6351/PR11P-2551P   (2186)
2003/04: 20²G, 20⁵GF, 24⁵GF, 20¹GF, 20⁹G,

	Starts	1st	2nd	3rd	Win & Pl
Hurdles	1	1	0	0	3556

Chases	4	0	1	0	4014
Career Total	21	6	2	2	41857
113	10/03	Chep	2m4f	D(0-120)HHdl	G-F	£3555
108	2/03	Donc	2m3f110yF	Hdl	G-S	£2702
104	11/02	Font	2m2f110yF	Hdl	G-S	£2712
126	4/02	Sand	2m4f110yB(0-145)HCh		GD	£17400
128	1/02	Winc	2m5f	D(0-120)HCh	GD	£5027
115	3/01	Font	2m2f	F Ch	SFT	£2873
				Total win prize-money £34272	

Going:	Sf: 0-0 GS: 0-0 Gd: 0-2 GF: - Fm: 1-3
Distance:	2m/2m3: 0-0 **2m4-2m7: 1-4** 3m+: 0-1
Track:	**LH: 1-4** RH: 0-1 Tight: 0-1 Gall: 0-1
Aids:	Bl: 0-0 Vi: 0-0 Tstrap: 0-0 Ckp: 0-0
Best Rating:	130 5/03 Weth 2m4f110y good Ch

Useful chaser/modest hurdler; point-to-point winner in the past; stays three miles and effective on good and soft ground; has refused to race on several occasions but has given no problems since joining Tony Carroll; has won his last three starts over hurdles.

Mr Albert (IRE)

96f   **89f**

5-y-o ch g Flemensfirth (USA)-Parkroe Lady (IRE) (Deep Run)
T D Easterby Mrs Jean P Connew

Placings: 0   (4962)
2003/04: 17⁰G,

	Starts	1st	2nd	3rd	Win & Pl
NH Flat	1	0	0	0	0
Career Total	1	0	0	0	0

Going:	Sf: 0-0 GS: 0-0 Gd: 0-0 GF: - Fm: 0-0
Distance:	2m/2m3: 0-1 2m4-2m7: 0-0 3m+: 0-0
Track:	LH: 0-0 RH: 0-1 Tight: 0-1 Gall: 0-0
Aids:	Bl: 0-0 Vi: 0-0 Tstrap: 0-0 Ckp: 0-0
Best Rating:	89 4/04 MRas 2m1f110y good NHF

Mr Auchterlonie (IRE)

96   **83**

7-y-o b g Mister Lord (USA)-Cahernane Girl (Bargello)
L Lungo Ashleybank Investments Limited

Placings: 5500   (4595)
2003/04: 16⁵G, 18⁵S, 24⁰GS, 22⁰G,

	Starts	1st	2nd	3rd	Win & Pl
NH Flat	1	0	0	0	0
Hurdles	3	0	0	0	0
Career Total	4	0	0	0	0

Going:	Sf: 0-1 GS: 0-1 Gd: 0-2 GF: - Fm: 0-0
Distance:	2m/2m3: 0-2 2m4-2m7: 0-1 3m+: 0-1
Track:	LH: 0-4 RH: 0-0 Tight: 0-2 Gall: 0-0
Aids:	Bl: 0-0 Vi: 0-0 Tstrap: 0-0 Ckp: 0-0
Best Rating:	93 11/03 Ayr 2m good NHF

Mr Banker

9-y-o b g Cashwyn-Flaming Fox (Healaugh Fox)
J C Tuck Mrs Carol Clift

Placings: PR   (4534)
2003/04: 24²GF, 22^PGS,

	Starts	1st	2nd	3rd	Win & Pl
Chases	2	0	0	0	

Career Total	2	0	0	0	

Going:	Sf: 0-0 GS: 0-1 Gd: 0-0 GF: - Fm: 0-1
Distance:	2m/2m3: 0-0 2m4-2m7: 0-1 3m+: 0-1
Track:	LH: 0-1 RH: 0-0 Tight: 0-0 Gall: 0-0
Aids:	Bl: 0-0 Vi: 0-0 Tstrap: 0-0 Ckp: 0-0

Mr Baxter Basics

108   **138**

13-y-o b g Lighter-Phyll-Tarquin (Tarqogan)
Miss Venetia Williams P Ryan

Placings: 0/661242/F512F21U/111/P041431/U0364/253P/6 22U2F2-1P52P   (2292)
2003/04: 20¹G, 20⁰G, 21⁵GS, 20²GF, 21^PGS,

	Starts	1st	2nd	3rd	Win & Pl
Chases	5	1	1	0	13125
Career Total	46	9	10	3	94094
136	5/03	Worc	2m4f110y	C(0-135)HCh	GD	£8307
141	4/00	Fair	2m100y	HCh	G-Y	£10400
137	1/00	Fair	2m100y	Ch	SFT	£6624
136	7/98	Klny	2m4f	Ch	G-Y	£8445
120	5/98	Cork	2m5f	Ch	GD	£0
136	5/98	Navn	2m2f	HCh	Y-S	£5956
130	3/98	Leop	2m2f	(0-130)HCh	G-Y	£2978
	12/97	Cork	2m	Ch	HVY	£3391
				Total win prize-money £46103	

Going:	Sf: 0-0 GS: 0-1 Gd: 1-3 GF: - Fm: 0-0
Distance:	2m/2m3: 0-0 **2m4-2m7: 1-5** 3m+: 0-0
Track:	**LH: 1-5** RH: 0-0 Tight: 0-2 Gall: 0-1
Aids:	Bl: 0-0 Vi: 0-0 Tstrap: 0-0 Ckp: 0-0
Best Rating:	141 4/00 Fair 2m100y gd-yld Ch

Useful handicap chaser; formerly trained in Ireland; now a veteran; best at around two and a half miles; effective on soft ground; can make mistakes.

Mr Ben Gunn

(90h)   (99h)**99**

12-y-o ch g Newski (USA)-Long John Silvia (Celtic Cone)
J D Frost P A Tylor

Placings: 64/5003F0/PP01333P-6   (1077)
2003/04: 20⁶GF,

	Starts	1st	2nd	3rd	Win & Pl
Hurdles	1	0	0	0	0
Career Total	17	1	0	4	7562
99	8/02	MRas	2m4f	D Ch	G-S	£5172
				Total win prize-money £5172	

Going:	Sf: 0-0 GS: 0-0 Gd: 0-0 GF: - Fm: 0-1
Distance:	2m/2m3: 0-0 2m4-2m7: 0-1 3m+: 0-0
Track:	LH: 0-1 RH: 0-0 Tight: 0-0 Gall: 0-0
Aids:	Bl: 0-0 Vi: 0-0 Tstrap: 0-0 Ckp: 0-0
Best Rating:	99 10/02 Hntg 2m4f110y gd-fm Ch

Mr Boo (IRE)

5-y-o b g Needle Gun (IRE)-Dasi (Bonne Noel)
D B Feek The Hon Mrs C Cameron

Placings: 00   (4793)
2003/04: 16⁰GS, 16⁹G,

	Starts	1st	2nd	3rd	Win & Pl
NH Flat	1	0	0	0	0
Hurdles	1	0	0	0	0
Career Total	2	0	0	0	0

Going:	Sf: 0-0 GS: 0-1 Gd: 0-1 GF: - Fm: 0-0				
Distance:	2m/2m3: 0-2 2m4-2m7: 0-0 3m+: 0-0				
Track:	LH: 0-1 RH: 0-1 Tight: 0-1 Gall: 0-0				
Aids:	Bl: 0-0 Vi: 0-0 Tstrap: 0-0 Ckp: 0-0				
Best Rating:	56	2/04	Kemp	2m	gd-sft NHF

Mr Bossman (IRE)

111   **129**

11-y-o b g Jolly Jake (NZ)-Imperial Greeting (Be My Guest (USA))
R C Guest T N Siviter

Placings:0/0/0000/1**PP5/52211133/P56602144-16P** (4640)
2003/04: 22¹G, 22⁶GS, 21⁷G,

	Starts	1st	2nd	3rd	Win & Pl
Chases	3	1	0	0	8171
Career Total	30	6	3	2	45938
129	5/03	Kels	2m6f110yC(0-130)HCh	GD	£8170
129	Fknm	2m5f110yD(0-120)HCh	GD	£6682
121	3/02	Fknm	2m5f110yD(0-120)HCh	GD	£4347
115	2/02	Muss	2m	D(0-110)HCh	SFT	£7150
121	1/02	Muss	2m4f	G-0(0-110)HCh	GD	£3640
103	2/01	Sedg	2m5f	H Ch	G-S	£1543
			Total win prize-money		£31534

Going:	Sf: 0-0 GS: 0-1 Gd: 1-2 GF: - Fm: 0-0				
Distance:	2m/2m3: 0-0 **2m4-2m7: 1-3** 3m+: 0-0				
Track:	**LH: 1-3** RH: 0-0 **Tight: 1-3** Gall: 0-0				
Aids:	Bl: 0-0 Vi: 0-0 Tstrap: 0-0 **Ckp: 1-3**				
Best Rating:	129	5/03	Kels	2m6f110y	good Ch

Fair chaser; stays two miles six; effective on good and soft ground; seems best on a sharp track; wears tongue tie and cheekpieces.

Mr Busby

11-y-o b g La Grange Music-Top-Anna (IRE) (Ela-Mana-Mou)
Michael Smith Michael Smith

Placings:100/21242130/4F/60P666P/023633403/0-3**PP** (4872)
2003/04: 21³GF, 25⁸PG, 24⁴S,

	Starts	1st	2nd	3rd	Win & Pl
Chases	3	0	0	1	277
Career Total	33	3	4	6	13467
110	2/99	Hayd	2m	C HHdl	SFT	£4485
97	11/98	MRas	2m1f110yE Hdl	HVY	£2477
111	1/98	Newc	2m	H NHF	G-S	£1392
			Total win prize-money		£8356

Going:	Sf: 0-1 GS: 0-0 Gd: 0-1 GF: - Fm: 0-1				
Distance:	2m/2m3: 0-0 2m4-2m7: 0-1 3m+: 0-2				
Track:	LH: 0-3 RH: 0-0 Tight: 0-2 Gall: 0-0				
Aids:	Bl: 0-0 Vi: 0-0 Tstrap: 0-0 Ckp: 0-0				
Best Rating:	113	3/99	Ayr	2m	soft Hdl

Moderate handicap hurdler; has not won a race for almost three years; best at two miles on soft ground.

Mr Cavallo (IRE)

99   (93c)**86**

12-y-o b g The Bart (USA)-Mrs Guru (Le Bavard (FR))
Miss Lucinda V Russell Peter J S Russell

Placings:000S/22230/P1211416140364450/033313204023
540/00324125006/023**P**S2140/00264254200-26P240 (1369)
2003/04: 27²S, 26⁶G, 24²G, 24²G, 27⁴GF, 20⁹F,

	Starts	1st	2nd	3rd	Win & Pl
Hurdles	6	0	2	0	2627

Career Total	78	8	15	9	41041
100	8/01	Sedg	3m3f110yF(0-110)HHdl	G-F	£2674
105	8/00	Prth	2m4f110yE(0-115)HHdl	GD	£3351
102	7/99	Wolv	2m4f110yE(0-110)HHdl	G-S	£2686
107	10/98	Carl	2m4f110yF(0-100)HHdl	GD	£2388
105	8/98	Ctml	2m6f	E(0-100)HHdl	GD	£2215
94	4/98	Bang	2m4f110yS(0-100)HCh	GD	£3631
99	7/98	Sedg	2m5f110yG(0-110)HHdl	G-S	£2250
86	7/98	Sedg	2m5f110yF Hdl	G-F	£1954
			Total win prize-money		£21149

Going:	Sf: 0-1 GS: 0-0 Gd: 0-3 GF: - Fm: 0-2				
Distance:	2m/2m3: 0-0 2m4-2m7: 0-1 3m+: 0-5				
Track:	LH: 0-4 RH: 0-2 Tight: 0-3 Gall: 0-0				
Aids:	Bl: 0-0 Vi: 0-0 Tstrap: 0-0 Ckp: 0-1				
Best Rating:	107	10/98	Carl	2m4f110y	good Hdl

Moderate hurdler/chaser; stays well; acts on most ground.

Mr Christie

91   **91d**

12-y-o b g Doulab (USA)-Hi There (High Top)
Miss L C Siddall Lynn Siddall Racing

Placings:000/3P0455325146502/124060501005/4**P506PU**
00305424/3020023354/026051131000/6361001062/056200
00-0400P040 (4956)
2003/04: 24⁰S, 26⁴GS, 24⁹HY, 26⁹GS, 27⁹G, 24⁹G, 26⁴G, 22⁰G,

	Starts	1st	2nd	3rd	Win & Pl
Hurdles	8	0	0	0	0
Career Total	93	8	9	8	31502
92	1/02	Newc	3m	F(0-100)HHdl	SFT	£2212
92	12/01	Hayd	2m7f110yF(0-110)HHdl	HVY	£3705
92	12/00	Hrfd	3m2f	F(0-100)HHdl	HVY	£3227
88	10/00	Sedg	3m3f110yF(0-100)HHdl	G-S	£2289
82	10/00	Hexm	3m	F(0-100)HHdl	HVY	£2107
103	3/98	Hntg	3m2f	E(0-110)HHdl	SFT	£2495
105	5/97	Uttx	3m110y	E Hdl	G-S	£2410
95	2/97	Muss	3m	E(0-100)HHdl	SFT	£2807
			Total win prize-money		£21253

Going:	Sf: 0-2 GS: 0-2 Gd: 0-4 GF: - Fm: 0-0				
Distance:	2m/2m3: 0-0 2m4-2m7: 0-1 3m+: 0-7				
Track:	LH: 0-4 RH: 0-3 Tight: 0-1 Gall: 0-3				
Aids:	Bl: 0-0 Vi: 0-0 Tstrap: 0-0 Ckp: 0-0				
Best Rating:	105	5/97	Uttx	3m110y	gd-sft Hdl

Plating-class staying hurdler; well suited by soft ground; usually tongue tied; often gets well behind and is far from reliable.

Mr Cool

116   (148c)**151**

10-y-o b g Jupiter Island-Laurel Diver (Celtic Cone)
M C Pipe N G Mills

Placings:10/111111/121023/**120114**/22562000-012P0 (3958)
2003/04: 25⁰VS, 20¹G, 25²G, 21⁸PG, 20⁰G,

	Starts	1st	2nd	3rd	Win & Pl
Hurdles	5	1	1	0	37100
Career Total	33	13	7	1	142148
151	11/03	Asct	2m4f	A Hdl	GD	£21700
136	4/02	Chep	2m110y	E Ch	G-F	£4204
133	4/02	Tntn	2m3f	D Ch	G-S	£4702
138	11/01	NAbb	2m110y	D Ch	SFT	£3812
156	12/00	Newb	2m110y	B Hdl	SFT	£7020
155	11/00	Newb	2m3f	C(0-135)HHdl	SFT	£5954
136	3/00	Uttx	2m	D Hdl	GD	£3688
119	2/00	Sand	2m110y	D Hdl	SFT	£3770
127	2/00	Folk	2m1f110yF Hdl	G-S	£2068
136	12/99	Chep	2m110y	A NHF	HVY	£7450
126	11/99	Aint	2m110y	H NHF	GD	£2008
119	11/99	Winc	2m	H NHF	GD	£1621

104	6/98	Sthl	2m	H NHF	GD	£1208
			Total win prize-money		£69209

Going:	Sf: 0-0 GS: 0-0 Gd: 1-4 GF: - Fm: 0-0				
Distance:	2m/2m3: 0-0 **2m4-2m7: 1-3** 3m+: 0-2				
Track:	LH: 0-2 **RH: 1-2** Tight: 0-1 Gall: 0-1				
Aids:	Bl: 0-0 Vi: 0-0 Tstrap: 0-0 Ckp: 0-0				
Best Rating:	160	11/00	Newb	2m110y	heavy Hdl

Smart hurdler/chaser; capable at the top level, but not consistent; won a Grade Two at Ascot in November 2003; runner-up in a Grade One next time before being pulled up at Cheltenham; effective at up to trips of three miles, suited by front-running tactics.

Mr Cooney (IRE)

10-y-o b g Van Der Linden (FR)-Green Orchid (Green Shoon)
J Parkes Derrick Mossop

Placings:P (3723)
2003/04: 25⁰PS,

	Starts	1st	2nd	3rd	Win & Pl
Chases	1	0	0	0	
Career Total	1	0	0	0	

Going:	Sf: 0-1 GS: 0-0 Gd: 0-0 GF: - Fm: 0-0				
Distance:	2m/2m3: 0-0 2m4-2m7: 0-0 3m+: 0-1				
Track:	LH: 0-1 RH: 0-0 Tight: 0-0 Gall: 0-0				
Aids:	Bl: 0-0 Vi: 0-0 Tstrap: 0-0 Ckp: 0-0				

Mr Cospector

114   (124h)**136+**

7-y-o b g Cosmonaut-L'Ancressaan (Dalsaan)
D L Williams The Eight Prospectors Syndicate

Placings:653F22143/O41F-P01126 (4572)
2003/04: 21⁸PG, 25⁰G, 20¹S, 24¹S, 19²GS, 24⁶G,

	Starts	1st	2nd	3rd	Win & Pl
Hurdles	1	0	0	0	0
Chases	5	2	1	0	17859
Career Total	19	4	3	2	35888
133	2/04	Hayd	3m	D(0-140)HCh	SFT	£11700
127	12/03	Plum	2m4f	D(0-125)HCh	SFT	£4062
122	12/02	Wwck	3m2f	D Ch	G-S	£4842
124	2/02	Hayd	2m4f	B HHdl	HVY	£8885
			Total win prize-money		£29492

Going:	Sf: 2-2 GS: 0-1 Gd: 0-3 GF: - Fm: 0-0				
Distance:	2m/2m3: 0-0 2m4-2m7: 1-3 3m+: 1-3				
Track:	**LH: 2-4** RH: 0-1 **Tight: 1-1** Gall: 0-1				
Aids:	Bl: 0-0 Vi: 0-0 Tstrap: 0-0 Ckp: 0-0				
Best Rating:	134	2/04	Towc	2m3f110y	gd-sft Ch

Useful chaser; stays at least three miles two, but effective at shorter; acts on soft ground.

Mr Custard

12-y-o b g Newski (USA)-May Owen (Master Owen)
Miss L J C Sweeting Miss L J C Sweeting

Placings:332P/50003/4-P (0018)
2003/04: 21⁸PS,

	Starts	1st	2nd	3rd	Win & Pl
Chases	1	0	0	0	
Career Total	11	0	1	3	2167

Going:	Sf: 0-1 GS: 0-0 Gd: 0-0 GF: - Fm: 0-0				

Distance: 2m/2m3: 0-0 2m4-2m7: 0-1 3m+: 0-0
Track: LH: 0-1 RH: 0-0 Tight: 0-1 Gall: 0-0
Aids: Bl: 0-0 Vi: 0-0 Tstrap: 0-0 Ckp: 0-0
Best Rating: 98 5/00 Strf 3m gd-fm Ch

Mr Don (IRE)

75   **61**

5-y-o b g Mister Lord (USA)-Paradiso (IRE) (Phardante (FR))
Mrs A M Thorpe Don Jones

Placings:00PP0   (4165)
2003/04: 17⁰G, 17⁰GS, 24PS, 19PS, 19⁰G,

	Starts	1st	2nd	3rd	Win & Pl
NH Flat	2	0	0	0	0
Hurdles	3	0	0	0	0
Career Total	5	0	0	0	

Going: Sf: 0-2 GS: 0-1 Gd: 0-2 GF: - Fm: 0-0
Distance: 2m/2m3: 0-3 2m4-2m7: 0-1 3m+: 0-1
Track: LH: 0-3 RH: 0-2 Tight: 0-1 Gall: 0-0
Aids: Bl: 0-0 Vi: 0-0 Tstrap: 0-0 Ckp: 0-0
Best Rating: 61 3/04 Donc 2m3f110y good Hdl

Mr Dow Jones (IRE)

105(73h)   (120+h)**120+**

12-y-o b g The Bart (USA)-Roseowen (Derring Rose)
W K Goldsworthy Mrs L A Goldsworthy

Placings:0F1/2P30/331U310/330011431/P53205-1134216202   (4932)
2003/04: 21⁵S, 25¹G, 23¹HY, 28³G, 26⁴G, 26²HY, 26¹G, 24⁸G, 29²GS, 26⁰GF, 27²G,

	Starts	1st	2nd	3rd	Win & Pl
Hurdles	1	0	1	0	1260
Chases	10	3	2	1	19733
Career Total	39	9	5	9	45164
120	2/04	Font	3m2f110yE(0-110)HCh	GD	£6773
116	5/03	Uttx	2m7f	H Ch	HVY	£3017
106	5/03	Hrfd	3m1f110yH Ch	GD	£1568
120	4/02	Chel	3m2f110yH Ch	GD	£5798
120	3/02	Hrfd	3m1f110yH Ch	GD	£1928
111	2/02	Hrfd	3m1f110yH Ch	HVY	£1865
104	4/01	Hrfd	2m3f	H Ch	GD	£2719
104	2/01	Ludl	3m	H Ch	G-S	£2628
108	4/99	Chep	3m	H Ch	HVY	£3598

Total win prize-money £29899

Going: Sf: 1-3 GS: 1-0 Gd: 2-6 GF: - Fm: 0-1
Distance: 2m/2m3: 0-0 2m4-2m7: 0-1 3m+: 2-9
Track: LH: 1-8 RH: 1-1 Tight: 1-4 Gall: 0-2
Aids: Bl: 0-0 Vi: 0-0 Tstrap: 0-0 Ckp: 0-0
Best Rating: 120 4/04 Font 3m3f good Hdl

Modest chaser; formerly useful hunter chaser; pays his way each season; scored back-to-back victories at Hereford and Uttoxeter spring 2003; possibly just failed to stay 3m 4f when third in 'Horse and Hound Cup'; back to winning ways in February 2004 at Fontwell; likes cut in the ground.

Mr Ed (IRE)

100   **129+**

6-y-o ch g In The Wings-Center Moriches (IRE) (Magical Wonder (USA))
P Bowen Gwilym J Morris

Placings:424-2112   (2183)
2003/04: 19²F, 20¹G, 20¹G, 21²G,

	Starts	1st	2nd	3rd	Win & Pl
Hurdles	4	2	2	0	14816

Career Total 7   2   3   0   **17328**
119 10/03 Aint 2m4f D Hdl GD £3848
115 10/03 Hntg 2m4f110yD Hdl G-F £3809
Total win prize-money £7657

Going: Sf: 0-0 GS: 0-0 Gd: 1-2 GF: - Fm: 1-2
Distance: 2m/2m3: 0-1 **2m4-2m7: 2-3** 3m+: 0-0
Track: LH: 1-2 RH: 1-2 Tight: 1-1 Gall: 1-2
Aids: Bl: 0-0 Vi: 0-0 Tstrap: 0-0 **Ckp: 2-3**
Best Rating: 129 11/03 Chel 2m5f good Hdl

Fair hurdler; effective at around two and a half miles; acts on fast ground; wears cheekpieces.

Mr Eye Popper (IRE)

77   **67**

5-y-o b g Sadler's Wells (USA)-Tipperary Tartan (Rarity)
B D Leavy J T S (International) Ltd

Placings:00   (4783)
2003/04: 16⁰G, 21⁹G,

	Starts	1st	2nd	3rd	Win & Pl
NH Flat	1	0	0	0	0
Hurdles	1	0	0	0	0
Career Total	2	0	0	0	

Going: Sf: 0-0 GS: 0-0 Gd: 0-2 GF: - Fm: 0-0
Distance: 2m/2m3: 0-1 2m4-2m7: 0-1 3m+: 0-0
Track: LH: 0-0 RH: 0-2 Tight: 0-0 Gall: 0-2
Aids: Bl: 0-0 Vi: 0-0 Tstrap: 0-0 Ckp: 0-0
Best Rating: 74 3/04 Hntg 2m110y good NHF

Mr Fisher (IRE)

55   **48**

7-y-o ch g Toulon-Parthian Opera (Dalsaan)
Miss E Hill (Edward U Hales 2/5) R G Langley

Placings:0-5PF   (4612)
2003/04: 19⁹G, 25PS, 21FG,

	Starts	1st	2nd	3rd	Win & Pl
Hurdles	3	0	0	0	0
Career Total	4	0	0	0	0

Going: Sf: 0-1 GS: 0-0 Gd: 0-1 GF: - Fm: 0-1
Distance: 2m/2m3: 0-0 2m4-2m7: 0-2 3m+: 0-1
Track: LH: 0-2 RH: 0-1 Tight: 0-1 Gall: 0-0
Aids: Bl: 0-0 Vi: 0-0 Tstrap: 0-0 Ckp: 0-0
Best Rating: 75 4/03 Fair 2m good NHF

Mr Fluffy

102   **130+**

7-y-o br g Charmer-Hinton Baim (Balinger)
P J Hobbs The Cockpit Crew

Placings:25/3504/F2111-U2F0   (4836)
2003/04: 24UG, 21²GF, 20FG, 21⁹GF,

	Starts	1st	2nd	3rd	Win & Pl
Hurdles	4	0	1	0	1466
Career Total	15	3	3	1	14515
129	9/02	NAbb	2m6f	E Hdl	GD	£3267
120	8/02	Worc	2m4f	E Hdl	GD	£3451
111	6/02	Uttx	2m4f110yD Hdl	GD	£3610

Total win prize-money £10331

Going: Sf: 0-0 GS: 0-0 Gd: 0-2 GF: - Fm: 0-2
Distance: 2m/2m3: 0-0 2m4-2m7: 0-3 3m+: 0-1
Track: LH: 0-3 RH: 0-1 Tight: 0-0 Gall: 0-2
Aids: Bl: 0-0 Vi: 0-0 Tstrap: 0-0 Ckp: 0-0
Best Rating: 130 5/03 Hntg 2m5f110y gd-fm Hdl

Useful hurdler; won three times in 2002; struggled in 2004; best at two and a half miles plus; likes a sound surface.

Mr George

82f   **52f**

5-y-o b g Whittingham (IRE)-Mossalier (Mazilier (USA))
B J Llewellyn T G B Racing Club

Placings:0   (0705)
2003/04: 17⁰GF,

	Starts	1st	2nd	3rd	Win & Pl
NH Flat	1	0	0	0	0
Career Total	1	0	0	0	

Going: Sf: 0-0 GS: 0-0 Gd: 0-0 GF: - Fm: 0-1
Distance: 2m/2m3: 0-1 2m4-2m7: 0-0 3m+: 0-0
Track: LH: 0-0 RH: 0-1 Tight: 0-1 Gall: 0-0
Aids: Bl: 0-0 Vi: 0-0 Tstrap: 0-0 Ckp: 0-0
Best Rating: 52 6/03 MRas 2m1f110y gd-fm NHF

Mr Gisby (USA)

94   **103**

6-y-o b g Chief's Crown (USA)-Double Lock (Home Guard (USA))
Mrs L Wadham Nightmare Partnership

Placings:3P55/5-160303   (4776)
2003/04: 20¹G, 19⁶G, 18⁰GS, 19³G, 19⁰GS, 20³G,

	Starts	1st	2nd	3rd	Win & Pl
Hurdles	6	1	0	2	4509
Career Total	11	1	0	3	5061
94	10/03	Fknm	2m4f	E Hdl	GD	£3318

Total win prize-money £3318

Going: Sf: 0-0 GS: 0-2 Gd: 1-4 GF: - Fm: 0-0
Distance: 2m/2m3: 0-3 **2m4-2m7: 1-3** 3m+: 0-0
Track: **LH: 1-6** RH: 0-0 Tight: 1-3 Gall: 0-2
Aids: Bl: 0-0 Vi: 0-0 Tstrap: 0-0 Ckp: 0-0
Best Rating: 103 12/01 Kemp 2m good Hdl

Moderate hurdler, he had shown ability over hurdles before getting off the mark at Fakenham in October 2003; seems best with cut in the ground.

Mr Hickman (IRE)

99(95h)   (87h)**94+**

7-y-o b g Montelimar (USA)-Cabin Glory (The Parson)
G Prodromou Alan Macalister

Placings:4426   (3431)
2003/04: 26⁴G, 21⁴G, 23²GF, 24⁶GS,

	Starts	1st	2nd	3rd	Win & Pl
Hurdles	1	0	0	0	0
Chases	3	0	1	0	1626
Career Total	4	0	1	0	1626

Going: Sf: 0-0 GS: 0-1 Gd: 0-2 GF: - Fm: 0-1
Distance: 2m/2m3: 0-0 2m4-2m7: 0-1 3m+: 0-3
Track: LH: 0-3 RH: 0-1 Tight: 0-2 Gall: 0-0
Aids: Bl: 0-0 Vi: 0-0 Tstrap: 0-0 Ckp: 0-0
Best Rating: 99 12/03 Leic 2m7f110y gd-fm Ch

Winning pointer; stays three miles; acts on fast ground.

Mr Hornblower (IRE)

74   **71**

10-y-o ch g Orchestra-Garland (Night Star)

L Lungo Ashleybank Investments Limited

Placings: 00/312/PFP0P   (4882)
2003/04: 16PHY, 25FHY, 21PGS, 20QG, 26PGS,

	Starts	1st	2nd	3rd	Win & Pl
Chases	5	0	0	0	
Career Total	10	1	0	1	4113
104	11/00 Newc	2m4f	D Hdl		G-S £2986

Total win prize-money £2987

Going:	Sf: 0-2 GS: 0-2 Gd: 0-1 GF: - Fm: 0-0
Distance:	2m/2m3: 0-0 2m4-2m7: 0-2 3m+: 0-2
Track:	LH: 0-3 RH: 0-2 Tight: 0-2 Gall: 0-1
Aids:	Bl: 0-0 Vi: 0-0 Tstrap: 0-0 Ckp: 0-0
Best Rating:	108 12/00 Weth 2m4f110y soft Hdl

Mr Jake

11-y-o b g Safawan-Miss Tealeaf (USA) (Lear Fan (USA))
H E Haynes Mrs H E Haynes

Placings: 200/0/06612/00314/PP   (4652)
2003/04: 21PGS, 25PG,

	Starts	1st	2nd	3rd	Win & Pl
Chases	2	0	0	0	
Career Total	16	2	2	1	8507
88	8/01 Strf	3m	E(0-105)HCh		G-F £3510
78	7/99 Strf	2m3f	E(0-105)HHdl		GD £2840

Total win prize-money £6350

Going:	Sf: 0-0 GS: 0-1 Gd: 0-1 GF: - Fm: 0-0
Distance:	2m/2m3: 0-0 2m4-2m7: 0-1 3m+: 0-1
Track:	LH: 0-1 RH: 0-1 Tight: 0-1 Gall: 0-0
Aids:	Bl: 0-0 Vi: 0-0 Tstrap: 0-0 Ckp: 0-0
Best Rating:	99 10/97 MRas 1m5f110y good NHF

Mr Kermit

13-y-o b g Rolfe (USA)-Sea Dart (Air Trooper)
Miss J Froggatt D G Blagden

Placings: 64023F414/60/0P03/P   (0073)
2003/04: 24PS,

	Starts	1st	2nd	3rd	Win & Pl
Chases	1	0	0	0	
Career Total	16	1	1	2	7253
117	3/96 Uttx	3m110y D Hdl		GD £3039

Total win prize-money £3039

Going:	Sf: 0-1 GS: 0-0 Gd: 0-0 GF: - Fm: 0-0
Distance:	2m/2m3: 0-0 2m4-2m7: 0-0 3m+: 0-1
Track:	LH: 0-1 RH: 0-0 Tight: 0-1 Gall: 0-0
Aids:	Bl: 0-0 Vi: 0-0 Tstrap: 0-0 Ckp: 0-0
Best Rating:	127 3/96 Aint 3m110y good Hdl

Mr Laggan
101(69h)   (74h)84

9-y-o b g Tina's Pet-Galway Gal (Proverb)
Miss Kate Milligan Mrs J M L Milligan

Placings: 56P4/30600P/240PPP5-03244414215   (3236)
2003/04: 25QG, 20QG, 22QG, 25FGF, 24FG, 21FGF, 20¹F, 20FGF, 22QGF, 20¹GF, 20PGF,

	Starts	1st	2nd	3rd	Win & Pl
Chases	11	2	2	1	9123
Career Total	28	2	3	2	10679
84	12/03 Muss	2m4f	F(0-95)HCh	G-F £2926
84	9/03 Hexm	2m4f110yF(0-95)HCh	FRM £2562

Total win prize-money £5488

Mr Lear (USA)
103   111+

5-y-o b g Lear Fan (USA)-Majestic Mae (USA) (Crow (FR))
R A Fahey (T D Barron 9/9) Christine Townley & Ms Laura Townley

Placings: 00115   (4513)
2003/04: 16QG, 17QGS, 16¹HY, 17¹GS, 16SGS,

	Starts	1st	2nd	3rd	Win & Pl
Hurdles	5	2	0	0	7300
Career Total	5	2	0	0	7300
111	2/04 Sedg	2m1f	E(0-110)HHdl	G-S £3464
102	2/04 Kels	2m110y E Hdl		HVY £3835

Total win prize-money £7300

Going:	Sf: 1-1 GS: 1-3 Gd: 0-1 GF: - Fm: 0-0
Distance:	2m/2m3: 2-5 2m4-2m7: 0-0 3m+: 0-0
Track:	LH: 2-5 RH: 0-0 Tight: 2-3 Gall: 0-0
Aids:	Bl: 0-0 Vi: 0-0 Tstrap: 0-0 Ckp: 0-0
Best Rating:	111 3/04 Weth 2m gd-sft Hdl

Improving novice hurdler; off the mark at Kelso in February; followed up under top-weight in handicap company at Sedgefield the following month; suited by soft ground.

Mr Lehman
92   73

7-y-o ch g Presidium-Lehmans Lot (Oats)
Mrs M Reveley D C Renton

Placings: 430-65F   (4654)
2003/04: 16GGF, 16SGF, 17FG,

	Starts	1st	2nd	3rd	Win & Pl
NH Flat	1	0	0	0	0
Hurdles	2	0	0	0	0
Career Total	6	0	0	1	286

Going:	Sf: 0-0 GS: 0-0 Gd: 0-0 GF: - Fm: 0-2
Distance:	2m/2m3: 0-3 2m4-2m7: 0-0 3m+: 0-0
Track:	LH: 0-1 RH: 0-2 Tight: 0-2 Gall: 0-0
Aids:	Bl: 0-0 Vi: 0-0 Tstrap: 0-0 Ckp: 0-0
Best Rating:	92 1/03 Muss 2m good NHF

Modest form in bumpers.

Mr Magget (IRE)
88   38

12-y-o gr g Salluceva-Linda Dudley (Owen Dudley)
D P Keane Richard Hawker

Placings: 0/0002054/04652/P00/F/3F0/5P   (0887)
2003/04: 23SGF, 23PG,

	Starts	1st	2nd	3rd	Win & Pl
Chases	2	0	0	0	0
Career Total	22	0	2	1	1326

Going:	Sf: 0-0 GS: 0-0 Gd: 0-0 GF: - Fm: 0-1
Distance:	2m/2m3: 0-0 2m4-2m7: 0-0 3m+: 0-1
Track:	LH: 0-2 RH: 0-0 Tight: 0-0 Gall: 0-0
Aids:	Bl: 0-1 Vi: 0-0 Tstrap: 0-0 Ckp: 0-1
Best Rating:	99 1/98 Tram 2m4f heavy Ch

Mr Magnetic (IRE)

13-y-o b g Point North-Miss Ironside (General Ironside)
Dominic Harvey Dominic Harvey

Placings: 505/041235F1/3FP340/0/1/5P-0   (0521)
2003/04: 24QG,

	Starts	1st	2nd	3rd	Win & Pl
Chases	1	0	0	0	
Career Total	22	3	1	3	11050
103	4/02 Tntn	3m	H Ch	GD £2664
114	4/98 Hrfd	3m1f110yE Ch	G-S £3130
104	6/97 Gowr	2m4f	NHF	G-Y £2712

Total win prize-money £8507

Going:	Sf: 0-0 GS: 0-0 Gd: 0-1 GF: - Fm: 0-0
Distance:	2m/2m3: 0-0 2m4-2m7: 0-0 3m+: 0-1
Track:	LH: 0-1 RH: 0-0 Tight: 0-1 Gall: 0-0
Aids:	Bl: 0-0 Vi: 0-0 Tstrap: 0-0 Ckp: 0-0
Best Rating:	114 4/98 Hrfd 3m1f110y gd-sft Ch

Mr Mahdlo

10-y-o b g Rakaposhi King-Fedelm (Celtic Cone)
R D E Woodhouse R D E Woodhouse

Placings: 000/335F25212PP/42P21PPP/P4P22PP/PPP/31PP13P3P-P3P   (4626)
2003/04: 25PS, 24³HY, 21PG,

	Starts	1st	2nd	3rd	Win & Pl
Chases	3	0	0	1	272
Career Total	44	4	7	6	25224
100	11/02 Sedg	3m3f	F(0-100)HCh	SFT £3406
103	6/02 Uttx	3m	D(0-120)HCh	SFT £4095
117	1/00 Weth	3m1f	D(0-125)HCh	SFT £3825
96	1/99 Ayr	3m110y	F(0-110)HHdl	HVY £2851

Total win prize-money £14177

Going:	Sf: 0-2 GS: 0-0 Gd: 0-1 GF: - Fm: 0-0
Distance:	2m/2m3: 0-0 2m4-2m7: 0-1 3m+: 0-3
Track:	LH: 0-3 RH: 0-0 Tight: 0-1 Gall: 0-1
Aids:	Bl: 0-0 Vi: 0-0 Tstrap: 0-0 Ckp: 0-0
Best Rating:	117 1/00 Weth 3m1f soft Ch

Modest staying chaser who is frequently pulled up; won a couple of points in February and March of 2004 before finishing a fair third in a hunter chase at Newcastle; well suited by soft ground; has worn sheepskin cheekpieces of late.

Mr Markham (IRE)
(93h)   (112h)129

12-y-o b g Naheez (USA)-Brighter Gail (Bustineto)
N J Gifford Felix Rosenstiel's Widow & Son

Placings: 115/221303/13441P210/400F/305015500/4U15F0-060   (3102)
2003/04: 23QGS, 24FS, 28QG,

	Starts	1st	2nd	3rd	Win & Pl
Hurdles	2	0	0	0	0
Chases	1	0	0	0	0
Career Total	40	8	3	4	73437
129	11/02 Plum	3m5f	C(0-130)HCh	SFT £15428
145	1/02 Kemp	2m5f	C(0-130)HHdl	G-S £7442
124	3/00 Font	2m4f	D Ch	G-S £3753
130	1/00 Plum	2m1f	E Ch	SFT £3006
140	10/99 Asct	2m110y	B(0-150)HHdl	GD £6097
143	12/97 Asct	2m110y B Hdl	G-S £8091
119	2/97 Newb	2m110y H NHF	GD £7006
107	11/96 Sand	2m110y H NHF	GD £1997

Total win prize-money £52824

Going:	Sf: 0-1 GS: 0-1 Gd: 0-1 GF: - Fm: 0-0

Distance:	2m/2m3: 0-0 2m4-2m7: 0-0 3m+: 0-3
Track:	LH: 0-1 RH: 0-1 Tight: 0-0 Gall: 0-0
Aids:	BI: 0-2 VI: 0-0 Tstrap: 0-0 Ckp: 0-0
Best Rating:	145 1/02 Kemp 2m5f gd-sft Hdl

Fair chaser/hurdler; now at the veteran stage; stays extreme distances and suited by cut in the ground; sometimes wears headgear.

Mr Max (IRE)

11-y-o b g Parliament-Aria (Saintly Song)
Miss S Caton N D Edden

Placings:0/0/P/45					(4761)
2003/04: 34⁴HY, 25⁵S,					
	Starts	1st	2nd	3rd	Win & Pl
Chases	2	0	0	0	259
Career Total	5	0	0	0	259

Going:	Sf: 0-2 GS: 0-0 Gd: 0-0 GF: - Fm: 0-0
Distance:	2m/2m3: 0-0 2m4-2m7: 0-0 3m+: 0-2
Track:	LH: 0-1 RH: 0-1 Tight: 0-0 Gall: 0-0
Aids:	BI: 0-0 VI: 0-0 Tstrap: 0-0 Ckp: 0-0
Best Rating:	61 4/04 Towc 3m1f soft Ch

Mr McAuley (IRE)
112f   **132f**

6-y-o b g Denel (FR)-Dusty Lane (IRE) (Electric)
M Halford Mrs Eugena Porter

Placings:215					(4400)
2003/04: 16²Y, 16¹Y, 16⁵G,					
	Starts	1st	2nd	3rd	Win & Pl
NH Flat	3	1	1	0	6189
Career Total	3	1	1	0	6189
115 2/04 DRoy 2m		NHF		YLD	£3892
			Total win prize-money £3893		

Going:	Sf: 0-0 GS: 0-0 Gd: 0-0 GF: - Fm: 0-0
Distance:	2m/2m3: 1-3 2m4-2m7: 0-0 3m+: 0-0
Track:	LH: 0-1 RH: 0-0 Tight: 0-0 Gall: 0-0
Aids:	BI: 0-0 VI: 0-0 Tstrap: 0-0 Ckp: 0-0
Best Rating:	132 3/04 Chel 2m110y good NHF

Second at Leopardstown in decent bumper in January; improved to win comfortably on next start in Down Royal in February; both outings have been on yielding ground, before running fifth in the Festival bumper; potentially useful.

Mr McDuck (IRE)

12-y-o ch g Denel (FR)-Coldwater Morning (Laurence O)
Ms S Duell J A V Duell

Placings:0F0/0/PP/0046/4-31					(0416)
2003/04: 21³S, 22¹G,					
	Starts	1st	2nd	3rd	Win & Pl
Chases	2	1	0	1	1818
Career Total	13	1	0	1	1818
102 5/03 MRas 2m6f110yH Ch				GD	£1603
			Total win prize-money £1603		

Going:	Sf: 0-1 GS: 0-0 Gd: 1-1 GF: - Fm: 0-0
Distance:	2m/2m3: 0-0 2m4-2m7: 1-2 3m+: 0-0
Track:	LH: 0-0 RH: 1-1 Tight: 1-2 Gall: 0-0
Aids:	BI: 0-0 VI: 0-0 Tstrap: 0-0 Ckp: 0-0
Best Rating:	102 5/03 MRas 2m6f110y good Ch

Mr McDuff (IRE)
81(97c)   (81c)**65**

8-y-o b g Mandalus-Le Glen (Le Bevard (FR))
M J Gingell The Duffers X

Placings:5/P55U36/25431450000-333F043U					(1758)
2003/04: 16⁹GF, 16⁹GF, 17³GF, 17⁵G, 16⁹GF, 17⁴GF, 19⁹F, 16⁰G,					
	Starts	1st	2nd	3rd	Win & Pl
Hurdles	3	0	0	1	263
Chases	5	0	0	3	2024
Career Total	26	1	1	6	8115
90 9/02 Worc 2m		E Hdl		GD	£2989
			Total win prize-money £2989		

Going:	Sf: 0-0 GS: 0-0 Gd: 0-2 GF: - Fm: 0-6
Distance:	2m/2m3: 0-7 2m4-2m7: 0-1 3m+: 0-0
Track:	LH: 0-7 RH: 0-0 Tight: 0-5 Gall: 0-0
Aids:	BI: 0-0 VI: 0-1 Tstrap: 0-0 Ckp: 0-0
Best Rating:	90 9/02 Worc 2m good Hdl

Plating-class chaser; seems best at around 2m; suited by a sound surface.

Mr Midaz
98   **84**

5-y-o ch g Danzig Connection (USA)-Marmy (Midyan (USA))
D W Whillans S C Carter

Placings:6450410-04000					(4688)
2003/04: 17⁰GS, 17⁴GF, 19⁹GS, 18⁹HY, 16⁹G,					
	Starts	1st	2nd	3rd	Win & Pl
Hurdles	5	0	0	0	4052
Career Total	12	1	0	0	4052
84 3/03 Sedg 2m1f		E(o-105)HHdl		GD	£3465
			Total win prize-money £3465		

Going:	Sf: 0-1 GS: 0-2 Gd: 0-1 GF: - Fm: 0-1
Distance:	2m/2m3: 0-5 2m4-2m7: 0-0 3m+: 0-0
Track:	LH: 0-4 RH: 0-1 Tight: 0-4 Gall: 0-0
Aids:	BI: 0-0 VI: 0-0 Tstrap: 0-0 Ckp: 0-0
Best Rating:	84 11/03 Carl 2m1f gd-sft Hdl

Plating-class hurdler, successful at Sedgefield in March; suited by two miles.

Mr Mighty (IRE)

8-y-o br g Montelimar (USA)-Laurie Belle (Boreen (FR))
N J Pewter N J Pewter

Placings:000/O-00					(0483)
2003/04: 20⁰GF, 24⁰GF,					
	Starts	1st	2nd	3rd	Win & Pl
Chases	2	0	0	0	
Career Total	6	0	0	0	

Going:	Sf: 0-0 GS: 0-0 Gd: 0-0 GF: - Fm: 0-2
Distance:	2m/2m3: 0-0 2m4-2m7: 0-0 3m+: 0-1
Track:	LH: 0-0 RH: 0-2 Tight: 0-0 Gall: 0-2
Aids:	BI: 0-0 VI: 0-0 Tstrap: 0-1 Ckp: 0-0
Best Rating:	73 4/02 Fair 2m yield NHF

Mr Miller (IRE)
63

12-y-o b g The Bart (USA)-Celtic Connection (Martinmas)
O Sherwood Pat & Peter Flaherty

Placings:P243/PPB434P64/P/644UFP-P					(0329)
2003/04: 26²GF,					
	Starts	1st	2nd	3rd	Win & Pl
Chases	1	0	0	0	

Career Total	21	0	1	2	2732

Going:	Sf: 0-0 GS: 0-0 Gd: 0-0 GF: - Fm: 0-1
Distance:	2m/2m3: 0-0 2m4-2m7: 0-0 3m+: 0-1
Track:	LH: 0-0 RH: 0-0 Tight: 0-0 Gall: 0-0
Aids:	BI: 0-1 VI: 0-0 Tstrap: 0-0 Ckp: 0-0
Best Rating:	86 2/99 Plum 3m1f110y soft Ch

Mr Morrissey

7-y-o ch g Karinga Bay-Barford Lass Vii (Damsire Unregistered)
K Bishop K Bishop

Placings:P					(4561)
2003/04: 24PGS,					
	Starts	1st	2nd	3rd	Win & Pl
Hurdles	1	0	0	0	
Career Total	1	0	0	0	

Going:	Sf: 0-0 GS: 0-1 Gd: 0-0 GF: - Fm: 0-0
Distance:	2m/2m3: 0-0 2m4-2m7: 0-0 3m+: 0-1
Track:	LH: 0-1 RH: 0-0 Tight: 0-0 Gall: 0-1
Aids:	BI: 0-0 VI: 0-0 Tstrap: 0-0 Ckp: 0-0

Mr Music Man (IRE)
65(91h)   (49h)**23**

11-y-o b g Accordion-A New Rose (IRE) (Saher)
Mrs G Harvey Brig C K Price

Placings:1300/P/2P0P/P/0P5004P-60					(4369)
2003/04: 18⁸G, 20⁰G,					
	Starts	1st	2nd	3rd	Win & Pl
Chases	2	0	0	0	0
Career Total	19	1	1	1	3383
115 1/98 Kemp 2m		H NHF		G-S	£1507
			Total win prize-money £1508		

Going:	Sf: 0-0 GS: 0-0 Gd: 0-2 GF: - Fm: 0-0
Distance:	2m/2m3: 0-1 2m4-2m7: 0-1 3m+: 0-0
Track:	LH: 0-1 RH: 0-0 Tight: 0-2 Gall: 0-0
Aids:	BI: 0-0 VI: 0-0 Tstrap: 0-1 Ckp: 0-0
Best Rating:	115 2/98 Newb 2m110y good NHF

Mr Nemo (IRE)
96   **96**

8-y-o b g Doubletour (USA)-Snowdrifter (Strong Gale)
Evan Williams Mike Dawson

Placings:0/3OP2432PF					(4672)
2003/04: 27³GF, 20⁰GF, 22PGF, 20²GF, 19⁴GF, 24³GF, 24²GF, 26PG, 25FG,					
	Starts	1st	2nd	3rd	Win & Pl
Chases	9	0	2	2	4476
Career Total	10	0	2	2	4476

Going:	Sf: 0-0 GS: 0-0 Gd: 0-2 GF: - Fm: 0-7
Distance:	2m/2m3: 0-0 2m4-2m7: 0-0 3m+: 0-5
Track:	LH: 0-6 RH: 0-2 Tight: 0-6 Gall: 0-0
Aids:	BI: 0-0 VI: 0-0 Tstrap: 0-0 Ckp: 0-1
Best Rating:	96 10/03 Chep 3m gd-fm Ch

Modest novice chaser; winning pointer; likes to front run; has shown ability, but also worrying temperament; stays well; acts on fast ground.

Mr No Man

(75h)   (47h)
8-y-o b g Cosmonaut-Christmas Show (Petorius)
T J Fitzgerald   J G Fitzgerald

Placings:5233/4/1/PP0-PP   (4221)
2003/04: 20PS, 22PGS,

	Starts	1st	2nd	3rd	Win & Pl
Chases	2	0	0	0	
Career Total	11	1	1	2	3787
91	5/01	Weth	2m	E Hdl	GD	£2856

Total win prize-money £2856

Going:	Sf: 0-1 GS: 0-1 Gd: 0-0 GF: - Fm: 0-0
Distance:	2m/2m3: 0-2 2m4-2m7: 0-2 3m+: 0-0
Track:	LH: 0-2 RH: 0-2 Tight: 0-1 Gall: 0-1
Aids:	Bl: 0-0 Vi: 0-0 Tstrap: 0-2 Ckp: 0-0
Best Rating:	97 3/01 MRas 2m1f110y gd-sft Hdl

Mr Norm

10-y-o ch g Nomadic Way (USA)-Miss Puck (Tepukei)
I A Brown   W Brown

Placings:P   (0387)
2003/04: 20PG,

	Starts	1st	2nd	3rd	Win & Pl
Hurdles	1	0	0	0	
Career Total	1	0	0	0	

Going:	Sf: 0-0 GS: 0-0 Gd: 0-1 GF: - Fm: 0-0
Distance:	2m/2m3: 0-0 2m4-2m7: 0-1 3m+: 0-0
Track:	LH: 0-1 RH: 0-0 Tight: 0-0 Gall: 0-0
Aids:	Bl: 0-0 Vi: 0-0 Tstrap: 0-0 Ckp: 0-0

Mr Perry (IRE)

81   (0c)89
8-y-o br g Perugino (USA)-Elegant Tune (USA) (Alysheba (USA))
Mrs P Ford   R A Champken

Placings:F33/P4F00/PP3343201/00P-3PP0   (4266)
2003/04: 16³GF, 16PGF, 16PG, 16PGF,

	Starts	1st	2nd	3rd	Win & Pl
Hurdles	4	0	0	1	275
Career Total	24	1	1	6	4600
89	10/01	Uttx	2m	G Hdl	G-S	£1750

Total win prize-money £1750

Going:	Sf: 0-0 GS: 0-0 Gd: 0-1 GF: - Fm: 0-3
Distance:	2m/2m3: 0-4 2m4-2m7: 0-0 3m+: 0-0
Track:	LH: 0-2 RH: 0-2 Tight: 0-0 Gall: 0-0
Aids:	Bl: 0-0 Vi: 0-0 Tstrap: 0-0 Ckp: 0-0
Best Rating:	91 1/01 Catt 2m gd-sft Hdl

Plating-class hurdler.

Mr Phipps

93   80
8-y-o b g Shareef Dancer (USA)-Frost In Summer (Busted)
R T Phillips   Bill Naylor

Placings:F060-60   (4519)
2003/04: 22⁶G, 22⁰GS,

	Starts	1st	2nd	3rd	Win & Pl
Hurdles	2	0	0	0	0
Career Total	6	0	0	0	0

Going:	Sf: 0-0 GS: 0-1 Gd: 0-1 GF: - Fm: 0-0
Distance:	2m/2m3: 0-0 2m4-2m7: 0-0 3m+: 0-0
Track:	LH: 0-0 RH: 0-1 Tight: 0-0 Gall: 0-0
Aids:	Bl: 0-0 Vi: 0-0 Tstrap: 0-0 Ckp: 0-0
Best Rating:	80 3/04 MRas 2m6f good Hdl

Mr President (GER)

92   97+
5-y-o br g Surako (GER)-Mostly Sure (IRE) (Sure Blade (USA))
Miss Venetia Williams   J M Boodle, A H M White, P M Shawyer

Placings:3   (4524)
2003/04: 16³GS,

	Starts	1st	2nd	3rd	Win & Pl
Hurdles	1	0	0	1	548
Career Total	1	0	0	1	548

Going:	Sf: 0-0 GS: 0-1 Gd: 0-0 GF: - Fm: 0-0
Distance:	2m/2m3: 0-1 2m4-2m7: 0-0 3m+: 0-0
Track:	LH: 0-1 RH: 0-0 Tight: 0-0 Gall: 0-0
Aids:	Bl: 0-0 Vi: 0-0 Tstrap: 0-0 Ckp: 0-0
Best Rating:	97 3/04 Chep 2m110y gd-sft Hdl

Three times a winner over middle-distances in Germany; made highly satisfactory debut in Chepstow 2m novice hurdle March 2004; acts on soft ground.

Mr Rhubarb (IRE)

94   79+
6-y-o ch g Shardari-Gale Griffin (IRE) (Strong Gale)
R T Phillips   Mr & Mrs C Schwick

Placings:0-405   (4098)
2003/04: 17⁰S, 16⁴GF, 21⁰GS, 21⁵G,

	Starts	1st	2nd	3rd	Win & Pl
NH Flat	2	0	0	0	0
Hurdles	2	0	0	0	0
Career Total	4	0	0	0	0

Going:	Sf: 0-1 GS: 0-1 Gd: 0-1 GF: - Fm: 0-1
Distance:	2m/2m3: 0-2 2m4-2m7: 0-2 3m+: 0-0
Track:	LH: 0-2 RH: 0-2 Tight: 0-2 Gall: 0-1
Aids:	Bl: 0-0 Vi: 0-0 Tstrap: 0-0 Ckp: 0-0
Best Rating:	95 5/03 Hntg 2m110y gd-fm NHF

Mr Scones

79   85
7-y-o b g North Col-Thetford Chase (Relkino)
Michael Hourigan   Mrs Laura O'Mara

Placings:000000-0   (0380)
2003/04: 16⁰G,

	Starts	1st	2nd	3rd	Win & Pl
Hurdles	1	0	0	0	
Career Total	8	0	0	0	

Going:	Sf: 0-0 GS: 0-0 Gd: 0-1 GF: - Fm: 0-0
Distance:	2m/2m3: 0-1 2m4-2m7: 0-0 3m+: 0-0
Track:	LH: 0-1 RH: 0-0 Tight: 0-1 Gall: 0-0
Aids:	Bl: 0-0 Vi: 0-0 Tstrap: 0-0 Ckp: 0-0
Best Rating:	100 10/02 Thur 2m yld-sft NHF

Mr Smudge

12-y-o ch g Fearless Action (USA)-Amerian County (Amerian (USA))
Mrs F J Marriott   C Marriott

Placings:3PPP/P1/25PP-P46   (4308)
2003/04: 25PG, 26⁴HY, 24⁶G,

	Starts	1st	2nd	3rd	Win & Pl
Chases	3	0	0	0	514
Career Total	13	1	1	1	6059
92	5/01	Chel	3m1f110yH Ch	GD	£3688

Total win prize-money £3689

Going:	Sf: 0-1 GS: 0-0 Gd: 0-2 GF: - Fm: 0-0
Distance:	2m/2m3: 0-0 2m4-2m7: 0-0 3m+: 0-3
Track:	LH: 0-2 RH: 0-1 Tight: 0-0 Gall: 0-1
Aids:	Bl: 0-0 Vi: 0-0 Tstrap: 0-0 Ckp: 0-0
Best Rating:	92 5/01 Chel 3m1f110y good Ch

Mr Sneaky Boo (IRE)

99(110h)   (115+h)126
8-y-o b g Little Wolf-Florabalda (Kambalda)
Michael Hourigan   Sneaky Boo Syndicate

Placings:000601P000P/56234103223/123351000015-32P0F   (1150a)
2003/04: 17³Y, 17²G, 24PF, 21⁰Y, 22PF,

	Starts	1st	2nd	3rd	Win & Pl
Hurdles	1	0	0	0	0
Chases	4	0	1	1	3049
Career Total	39	5	5	6	53399
93	4/03	Thur	Ch	G-F	£5824
122	1/03	Cork	2m4f	(74-116)HHdl	SFT	£10551
109	5/02	Limk	2m	(74-109)HHdl	G-Y	£5503
100	11/01	Clon	2m	(0-116)HHdl	SFT	£6120
99	1/01	Leop	2m	(0-102)HHdl	SFT	£9435

Total win prize-money £37436

Going:	Sf: 0-0 GS: 0-0 Gd: 0-1 GF: - Fm: 0-2
Distance:	2m/2m3: 0-2 2m4-2m7: 0-2 3m+: 0-1
Track:	LH: 0-1 RH: 0-1 Tight: 0-1 Gall: 0-0
Aids:	Bl: 0-0 Vi: 0-0 Tstrap: 0-0 Ckp: 0-0
Best Rating:	126 5/03 Tipp 2m1f yield Ch

Irish hurdler; beaten at odds on in a chase at Kelso in May; effective at around two miles on soft ground.

Mr Splodge

10-y-o b g Gildoran-Ethels Course (Crash Course)
Mrs T J Hill   Alan Hill

Placings:040/235P/0/44   (4302)
2003/04: 21⁴G, 20⁴G,

	Starts	1st	2nd	3rd	Win & Pl
Chases	2	0	0	0	285
Career Total	10	0	1	1	1413

Going:	Sf: 0-0 GS: 0-0 Gd: 0-2 GF: - Fm: 0-0
Distance:	2m/2m3: 0-0 2m4-2m7: 0-2 3m+: 0-0
Track:	LH: 0-0 RH: 0-2 Tight: 0-1 Gall: 0-0
Aids:	Bl: 0-0 Vi: 0-0 Tstrap: 0-0 Ckp: 0-0
Best Rating:	90 11/00 Plum 2m5f heavy Hdl

Mr Stitch

(75h)   (13h)
7-y-o br g Lancastrian-Hovian (Hotfoot)

Mrs L B Normile The Heatheryfour

Placings: 0PUP-PPP6   (2140)
2003/04: 24^{P}G, 24^{P}G, 20^{P}G, 20^{P}G,

	Starts	1st	2nd	3rd	Win & Pl
Hurdles	2	0	0	0	0
Chases	2	0	0	0	0
Career Total	8	0	0	0	0

Going: Sf: 0-0 GS: 0-0 Gd: 0-4 GF: - Fm: 0-0
Distance: 2m/2m3: 0-0 2m4-2m7: 0-2 3m+: 0-2
Track: LH: 0-1 RH: 0-3 Tight: 0-0 Gall: 0-1
Aids: Bl: 0-1 Vi: 0-0 Tstrap: 0-0 Ckp: 0-0
Best Rating: 17 11/02 Aint 2m1f   good NHF

Mr Tim (IRE)

88f   88f
6-y-o br g Naheez (USA)-Ari's Fashion (Aristocracy)
L Lungo Ashleybank Investments Limited

Placings: 004   (4663)
2003/04: 16^{H}Y, 17°G, 16^{I}S,

	Starts	1st	2nd	3rd	Win & Pl
NH Flat	3	0	0	0	0
Career Total	3	0	0	0	0

Going: Sf: 0-2 GS: 0-0 Gd: 0-1 GF: - Fm: 0-0
Distance: 2m/2m3: 0-3 2m4-2m7: 0-0 3m+: 0-0
Track: LH: 0-2 RH: 0-1 Tight: 0-0 Gall: 0-0
Aids: Bl: 0-1 Vi: 0-0 Tstrap: 0-0 Ckp: 0-0
Best Rating: 88 3/04 Carl 2m1f   good NHF

Mr Whizz

101   96+
7-y-o ch g Manhal-Panienka (POL) (Dom Racine (FR))
A P Jones (J S King 26/5) The Milk Sheiks

Placings: 6F061   (4781)
2003/04: 16^{G}GF, 20^{F}G, 17^{G}GS, 17^{F}G, 16^{I}G,

	Starts	1st	2nd	3rd	Win & Pl
Hurdles	5	1	0	0	2408
Career Total	5	1	0	0	2408

96 4/04 Hntg 2m110y G(0-90)HHdl   GD £2408
Total win prize-money £2408

Going: Sf: 0-0 GS: 0-1 Gd: 1-3 GF: - Fm: 0-1
Distance: 2m/2m3: 1-4 2m4-2m7: 0-1 3m+: 0-0
Track: LH: 0-1 RH: 1-2 Tight: 0-2 Gall: 1-1
Aids: Bl: 0-0 Vi: 0-0 Tstrap: 0-0 Ckp: 1-1
Best Rating: 96 4/04 Hntg 2m110y   good Hdl

First worthwhile form when easy winner of selling handicap hurdle at Huntingdon in April; suited by two miles.

Mr Woodentop (IRE)

107(105h)   (133h) 133+
8-y-o b g Roselier (FR)-Una's Polly (Pollerton)
L Lungo Ashleybank Investments Limited

Placings: 4/211S1/11P-21PFPP   (4861)
2003/04: 24^{R}G, 24^{I}S, 29^{P}S, 22^{F}HY, 32^{P}G, 33^{P}GS,

	Starts	1st	2nd	3rd	Win & Pl
Chases	6	1	1	0	10890
Career Total	15	6	2	0	34238

133 11/03 Carl 3m   C(0-135)HCh   SFT £8814
122 1/03 Ayr   3m11y   E Ch   SFT £4725
122 11/02 Ayr   3m110y D(0-125)HHdl   SFT £4728
122 4/02 Ayr   3m110y B HHdl   GD   £7250
127 12/01 Ayr   2m4f   E Hdl   SFT £2492
114 12/01 Hayd 2m4f   D Hdl   SFT £3640
Total win prize-money £31652

Going: Sf: 1-3 GS: 0-1 Gd: 0-2 GF: - Fm: 0-0
Distance: 2m/2m3: 0-0 2m4-2m7: 0-1 3m+: 1-5
Track: LH: 0-4 RH: 1-2 Tight: 0-2 Gall: 0-0
Aids: Bl: 0-0 Vi: 0-0 Tstrap: 0-0 Ckp: 0-0
Best Rating: 133 11/03 Carl 3m   soft Ch

Fair chaser; stays three miles plus; suited by soft ground.

Mr Woodland

99   (116h) 116
10-y-o br g Landyap (USA)-Wood Corner (Sit In The Corner (USA))
J D Frost P A Tylor

Placings: 4322150F3/12110-P5U   (1936)
2003/04: 21^{P}GF, 21^{S}GF, 23^{U}G,

	Starts	1st	2nd	3rd	Win & Pl
Chases	3	0	0	0	-
Career Total	17	4	3	2	23920

111 10/02 Hntg 3m   D Ch   G-F £4563
116 9/02 Worc 2m7f110yD Ch   GD   £4836
112 7/02 NAbb 2m5f110yD Ch   G-F £4754
116 1/02 Winc 2m6f   E Hdl   GD   £2859
Total win prize-money £17014

Going: Sf: 0-0 GS: 0-0 Gd: 0-1 GF: - Fm: 0-2
Distance: 2m/2m3: 0-0 2m4-2m7: 0-2 3m+: 0-1
Track: LH: 0-2 RH: 0-1 Tight: 0-2 Gall: 0-0
Aids: Bl: 0-0 Vi: 0-0 Tstrap: 0-0 Ckp: 0-0
Best Rating: 116 10/03 Strf 2m5f110y gd-fm Ch

Fair chaser; suited by two and a half to three miles and fast ground.

Mrs Be (IRE)

8-y-o ch m Be My Native (USA)-Kilbrack (Perspex)
Mrs O Bush J H Burbidge

Placings: 4/2   (3778)
2003/04: 24^{Q}G,

	Starts	1st	2nd	3rd	Win & Pl
Chases	1	0	1	0	978
Career Total	2	0	1	0	978

Going: Sf: 0-0 GS: 0-0 Gd: 0-0 GF: - Fm: 0-0
Distance: 2m/2m3: 0-0 2m4-2m7: 0-0 3m+: 0-1
Track: LH: 0-0 RH: 0-1 Tight: 0-1 Gall: 0-0
Aids: Bl: 0-0 Vi: 0-0 Tstrap: 0-0 Ckp: 0-0
Best Rating: 97 5/01 Font 2m2f110y gd-fm NHF

Multiple winning pointer; stays well.

Mrs Philip

91   86+
5-y-o b m Puissance-Lightning Legacy (USA) (Super Concorde (USA))
P J Hobbs Jack Joseph & Mrs Philip Hobbs

Placings: 22-41204   (4237)
2003/04: 17^{Q}GF, 19^{I}GF, 19^{Z}GF, 16°G, 18^{Q}GF,

	Starts	1st	2nd	3rd	Win & Pl
Hurdles	5	1	1	0	5451
Career Total	7	1	3	0	7208

86 10/03 Extr 2m3f   E Hdl   G-F £3419
Total win prize-money £3419

Going: Sf: 0-0 GS: 0-0 Gd: 0-1 GF: - Fm: 1-4
Distance: 2m/2m3: 1-4 2m4-2m7: 0-1 3m+: 0-0
Track: LH: 0-1 RH: 1-4 Tight: 0-2 Gall: 0-0
Aids: Bl: 0-0 Vi: 0-0 Tstrap: 0-0 Ckp: 0-0
Best Rating: 86 11/03 Tntn 2m3f110y gd-fm Hdl

Moderate hurdler; half-sister to the useful jumper Cabochon; runner-up in bumper on her debut; disqualified after narrow victory at Exeter next time; disappointing fourth on hurdling debut at the same course May 2003 but won there in the autumn; acts on fast ground.

Mrs Ritchie

100   90
7-y-o b m Teenoso (USA)-Material Girl (Busted)
M Pitman Just Good Fun Club

Placings: 53/4   (4375)
2003/04: 19^{Q}G,

	Starts	1st	2nd	3rd	Win & Pl
Hurdles	1	0	0	0	333
Career Total	3	0	0	1	581

Going: Sf: 0-0 GS: 0-0 Gd: 0-1 GF: - Fm: 0-0
Distance: 2m/2m3: 0-0 2m4-2m7: 0-1 3m+: 0-0
Track: LH: 0-0 RH: 0-1 Tight: 0-1 Gall: 0-0
Aids: Bl: 0-0 Vi: 0-0 Tstrap: 0-0 Ckp: 0-0
Best Rating: 90 3/04 Tntn 2m3f110y good Hdl

Ms Trude (IRE)

105(85h)   (61h)85
7-y-o b m Montelimar (USA)-Pencil (Crash Course)
A W Carroll Gary J Roberts

Placings: 200/R66PP-P6331U40F   (4112)
2003/04: 24^{P}G, 25^{R}G, 20^{Z}S, 21^{Z}GF, 24^{I}G, 23^{U}GF, 26^{A}GF, 17^{Q}GS, 20^{F}GF,

	Starts	1st	2nd	3rd	Win & Pl
Hurdles	1	0	0	0	0
Chases	8	1	0	2	6407
Career Total	17	1	4	2	7230

85 7/03 Strf 3m   E(0-105)HCh   GD £4745
Total win prize-money £4745

Going: Sf: 0-1 GS: 0-1 Gd: 1-3 GF: - Fm: 0-4
Distance: 2m/2m3: 0-1 2m4-2m7: 0-3 3m+: 1-5
Track: LH: 1-5 RH: 0-3 Tight: 1-5 Gall: 0-0
Aids: Bl: 0-2 Vi: 1-4 Tstrap: 0-0 Ckp: 0-0
Best Rating: 101 4/02 Chel 2m1f   good NHF

Plating-class chaser; improved for the fitting of a visor; stays three miles acts on a sound surface; suited by making the running.

Muallaf (IRE)

12-y-o b g Unfuwain (USA)-Honourable Sheba (USA) (Roberto (USA))
Mrs A M Woodrow Mrs Ann Woodrow

Placings: 002/0P0P0/PS/PP-P04R   (0614)
2003/04: 16^{P}GF, 17^{Q}GF, 16^{A}GF, 16^{P}GF,

	Starts	1st	2nd	3rd	Win & Pl
Hurdles	2	0	0	0	0
Chases	2	0	0	0	311
Career Total	16	0	1	0	782

Going: Sf: 0-0 GS: 0-0 Gd: 0-0 GF: - Fm: 0-4
Distance: 2m/2m3: 0-0 2m4-2m7: 0-0 3m+: 0-1
Track: LH: 0-0 RH: 0-4 Tight: 0-0 Gall: 0-1
Aids: Bl: 0-0 Vi: 0-0 Tstrap: 0-0 Ckp: 0-0
Best Rating: 79 4/97 Chep 2m110y   firm NHF

Muck Savage

109(107h)   (118h)**126+**
7-y-o b g Homo Sapien-Rare Luck (Rare One)
C J Mann Granville J Harper

Placings:3015600/06032U2P2-14P   (3143)
2003/04: 23¹G, 24⁴S, 25PS,

	Starts	1st	2nd	3rd	Win & Pl
Chases	3	1	0	0	7113
Career Total	19	2	3	2	21066
136 11/03 Extr	2m7f110yD Ch			GD	£5863
106 11/01 Tram	2m Hdl			YLD	£4173
			Total win prize-money £10036

Going:	Sf: 0-2 GS: 0-0 Gd: 1-1 GF: - Fm: 0-0
Distance:	2m/2m3: 0-0 2m4-2m7: 0-0 3m+: 1-3
Track:	LH: 0-4 RH: 1-2 Tight: 0-1 Gall: 0-0
Aids:	Bl: 0-0 Vi: 0-0 Tstrap: 0-0 Ckp: 0-0
Best Rating:	136 11/03 Extr 2m7f110y good Ch

Useful novice chaser; fair hurdler; surprise winner of a race that has worked out well on his chase debut; every chance when all but fell next time; stays three miles; acts on a soft surface.

Muckle Flugga (IRE)

96   **65**
5-y-o ch m Karinga Bay-Dancing Dove (IRE) (Denel (FR))
N G Richards Dr Kenneth S Fraser

Placings:5000   (4685)
2003/04: 16⁵GS, 21⁰GS, 17⁰GS, 16⁰G,

	Starts	1st	2nd	3rd	Win & Pl
NH Flat	1	0	0	0	0
Hurdles	3	0	0	0	0
Career Total	4	0	0	0	0

Going:	Sf: 0-0 GS: 0-3 Gd: 0-1 GF: - Fm: 0-0
Distance:	2m/2m3: 0-3 2m4-2m7: 0-1 3m+: 0-0
Track:	LH: 0-4 RH: 0-0 Tight: 0-3 Gall: 0-0
Aids:	Bl: 0-0 Vi: 0-0 Tstrap: 0-0 Ckp: 0-0
Best Rating:	74 11/03 Weth 2m gd-sft NHF

Mucky Mabel (IRE)

77f   **66f**
5-y-o b m Grand Plaisir (IRE)-Bolaney Girl (IRE) (Amazing Bust)
P D Niven Steve Hammond

Placings:0   (4886)
2003/04: 17⁰GS,

	Starts	1st	2nd	3rd	Win & Pl
NH Flat	1	0	0	0	0
Career Total	1	0	0	0	0

Going:	Sf: 0-0 GS: 0-1 Gd: 0-0 GF: - Fm: 0-0
Distance:	2m/2m3: 0-1 2m4-2m7: 0-0 3m+: 0-0
Track:	LH: 0-0 RH: 0-1 Tight: 0-0 Gall: 0-0
Aids:	Bl: 0-0 Vi: 0-0 Tstrap: 0-0 Ckp: 0-0
Best Rating:	65 4/04 Carl 2m1f gd-sft NHF

Muggy Moss

90   **58**
6-y-o b m Sovereign Water (FR)-Sudberry Lady (IRE) (Commanche Run)
Mrs J C McGregor The Don Raiders

Placings:005U0P   (3598)

2003/04: 16⁶G, 20⁹G, 22⁵F, 24ᵁGS, 24⁰S, 24PHY,

	Starts	1st	2nd	3rd	Win & Pl
NH Flat	1	0	0	0	0
Hurdles	5	0	0	0	0
Career Total	6	0	0	0	0

Going:	Sf: 0-2 GS: 0-1 Gd: 0-2 GF: - Fm: 0-1
Distance:	2m/2m3: 0-1 2m4-2m7: 0-2 3m+: 0-3
Track:	LH: 0-4 RH: 0-2 Tight: 0-1 Gall: 0-0
Aids:	Bl: 0-0 Vi: 0-0 Tstrap: 0-0 Ckp: 0-0
Best Rating:	58 12/03 Hexm 3m soft Hdl

Mughas (IRE)

122   **147**
5-y-o b g Sadler's Wells (USA)-Quest Of Passion (FR) (Saumarez)
A King B Winfield, C Fenton & A Longman

Placings:11256-0113440   (4643)
2003/04: 20⁰S, 20¹GS, 20¹GS, 21³S, 16⁴G, 21⁴G, 24⁰G,

	Starts	1st	2nd	3rd	Win & Pl
Hurdles	7	2	0	1	36727
Career Total	12	4	1	1	54749
144 12/03 Chep	2m4f	B(0-140)HHdl	G-S	£12278
143 11/03 Aint	2m4f	C(0-130)HHdl	G-S	£12870
114 2/03 Plum	E Hdl	HVY	£3562
110 1/03 Wwck	2m	E Hdl	HVY	£3710
		Total win prize-money £32421

Going:	Sf: 0-2 GS: 2-2 Gd: 0-3 GF: - Fm: 0-0
Distance:	2m/2m3: 0-1 2m4-2m7: 2-5 3m+: 0-1
Track:	LH: 2-7 RH: 0-0 Tight: 1-2 Gall: 0-2
Aids:	Bl: 0-0 Vi: 0-0 Tstrap: 0-0 Ckp: 0-0
Best Rating:	147 3/04 Chel 2m5f good Hdl

Smart hurdler; made successful reappearance in competitive 2m 4f handicap at Aintree November 2003; defied a 9lb hike in the ratings when winning a slowly-run similar event at Chepstow the following month; excuses when beaten at Warwick before running excellent race over an inadequate two miles in the Tote Gold Trophy; fair fourth in the Coral Cup at Cheltenham, slightly unlucky not to get closer; stays 2m 4f; enjoys some cut in the ground; improving.

Muharib Lady (IRE)

102(102h)   (90h)**90**
9-y-o b m Muharib (USA)-Brickhill Lady (Le Bavard (FR))
P G Murphy P G Murphy

Placings:0/0030/30342303556/3321300621-0053   (1153)
2003/04: 27⁰G, 24⁰GF, 24⁵GF, 26⁹GF,

	Starts	1st	2nd	3rd	Win & Pl
Hurdles	2	0	0	0	0
Chases	2	0	0	1	761
Career Total	30	2	3	9	18298
90 4/03 Font	3m3f	E(0-110)HHdl	G-F	£6864
90 10/02 Plum	3m2f	E(0-110)HCh	G-F	£4326
		Total win prize-money £11190

Going:	Sf: 0-0 GS: 0-0 Gd: 0-1 GF: - Fm: 0-0
Distance:	2m/2m3: 0-0 2m4-2m7: 0-0 3m+: 0-4
Track:	LH: 0-3 RH: 0-0 Tight: 0-2 Gall: 0-0
Aids:	Bl: 0-0 Vi: 0-0 Tstrap: 0-0 Ckp: 0-0
Best Rating:	90 4/03 Font 3m3f gd-fm Hdl

Plating-class hurdler; stays 3m 3f; suited by a sound surface.

Muhtadi (IRE)

97   **70**
11-y-o br g Marju (IRE)-Moon Parade (Welsh Pageant)

S B Clark S B Clark

Placings:0156/001/0000350/00/10P0/100/0000-34   (4614)
2003/04: 16⁸GF, 16²G, 174G,

	Starts	1st	2nd	3rd	Win & Pl
Hurdles	3	0	0	1	382
Career Total	29	4	0	2	9080
83 3/02 Sedg	2m1f	G(0-90)HHdl	SFT	£1946
79 1/01 Catt	2m	G(0-90)HHdl	G-S	£1666
85 3/98 Plum	2m	E Ch	SFT	£2956
92 3/97 Winc	2m	F Hdl	GD	£1900
		Total win prize-money £8468

Going:	Sf: 0-0 GS: 0-0 Gd: 0-2 GF: - Fm: 0-1
Distance:	2m/2m3: 0-3 2m4-2m7: 0-0 3m+: 0-1
Track:	LH: 0-3 RH: 0-0 Tight: 0-0 Gall: 0-1
Aids:	Bl: 0-3 Vi: 0-0 Tstrap: 0-0 Ckp: 0-0
Best Rating:	92 3/97 Bang 2m1f good Hdl

Plating-class hurdler/chaser; suited by give; best over two miles.

Muhtenbar

78f   **74f**
4-y-o b g Muhtarram (USA)-Ardenbar (Ardross)
J W Payne T J Wyatt

Placings:0   (4407)
2003/04: 16⁹G,

	Starts	1st	2nd	3rd	Win & Pl
NH Flat	1	0	0	0	0
Career Total	1	0	0	0	0

Going:	Sf: 0-0 GS: 0-0 Gd: 0-1 GF: - Fm: 0-0
Distance:	2m/2m3: 0-1 2m4-2m7: 0-0 3m+: 0-0
Track:	LH: 0-0 RH: 0-1 Tight: 0-0 Gall: 0-1
Aids:	Bl: 0-0 Vi: 0-0 Tstrap: 0-0 Ckp: 0-0
Best Rating:	74 3/04 Hntg 2m110y good NHF

Mulabee (USA)

93   **77+**
5-y-o br g Gulch (USA)-Shir Dar (FR) (Lead On Time (USA))
R T Phillips (R Brotherton 12/5) Richard Phillips

Placings:05   (1921)
2003/04: 16⁹GF, 16⁵G,

	Starts	1st	2nd	3rd	Win & Pl
Hurdles	2	0	0	0	0
Career Total	2	0	0	0	0

Going:	Sf: 0-0 GS: 0-0 Gd: 0-1 GF: - Fm: 0-1
Distance:	2m/2m3: 0-2 2m4-2m7: 0-0 3m+: 0-0
Track:	LH: 0-2 RH: 0-0 Tight: 0-2 Gall: 0-0
Aids:	Bl: 0-0 Vi: 0-0 Tstrap: 0-0 Ckp: 0-0
Best Rating:	77 11/03 Plum 2m good Hdl

Mulan Princess (IRE)

80   **54**
4-y-o b f Mukaddamah (USA)-Notley Park (Wolfhound (USA))
S C Burrough (T J Naughton 3/6) Mr & Mrs Charles Hill and Ray Moody

Placings:5O   (3902)
2003/04: 16⁵GF, 17⁰GS,

	Starts	1st	2nd	3rd	Win & Pl
Hurdles	2	0	0	0	0

Career Total	2	0	0	0	0

Going:	Sf: 0-0 GS: 0-1 Gd: 0-0 GF: - Fm: 0-1
Distance:	2m/2m3: 0-2 2m4-2m7: 0-0 3m+: 0-0
Track:	LH: 0-0 RH: 0-2 Tight: 0-1 Gall: 0-0
Aids:	Bl: 0-0 Vi: 0-0 Tstrap: 0-0 Ckp: 0-0
Best Rating:	54 11/03 Asct 2m110y gd-fm Hdl

Mulga Bill (NZ)
74   56

6-y-o br g Carolingian (AUS)-Replica (NZ) (Creag-An-Sgor)
R C Guest Miss C Metcalfe

Placings:0					(0380)
2003/04: 16⁵G,					

	Starts	1st	2nd	3rd	Win & Pl
Hurdles	1	0	0	0	
Career Total	1	0	0	0	

Going:	Sf: 0-0 GS: 0-0 Gd: 0-1 GF: - Fm: 0-0
Distance:	2m/2m3: 0-1 2m4-2m7: 0-0 3m+: 0-0
Track:	LH: 0-1 RH: 0-0 Tight: 0-1 Gall: 0-0
Aids:	Bl: 0-0 Vi: 0-0 Tstrap: 0-0 Ckp: 0-0
Best Rating:	56 5/03 Kels 2m110y good Hdl

New Zealand import; well beaten on hurdles debut.

Mulkev Prince (IRE)
104   (73h)121

13-y-o b g Lancastrian-Waltzing Shoon (Green Shoon)
David Pearson David Pearson

Placings:6/30O1O2/33OFP24P/6122102/625304/5					
411U3F/05F126/004P21U20110-24P46540					(4730)
2003/04: 20²G, 20⁴F, 16⁸HY, 20⁴G, 21⁵G, 20⁴HY, 20⁹G,					

	Starts	1st	2nd	3rd	Win & Pl
Chases	8	0	1	0	2204
Career Total	67	9	11	5	66853
121	3/03	Ludl	2m4f	D(0-115)HCh	G-F	£7224
115	3/03	Leic	2m4f110yE(0-110)HCh	G-S	£4069
115	11/02	Leic	2m4f110yH(0-100)HCh	G-F	£3464
110	3/02	Leic	2m4f110yH Ch	SFT	£2219
131	10/00	Carl	2m	D(0-125)HCh	GD	£4095
131	9/00	Prth	2m	E(0-115)HCh	HVY	£5408
139	2/98	Fair	2m	Ch	Y-S	£11217
115	11/97	Thur	2m	Ch	Y-S	£2204
112	2/96	Fair	2m2f	Hdl	G-Y	£3177
				Total win prize-money £43079		

Going:	Sf: 0-2 GS: 0-0 Gd: 0-4 GF: - Fm: 0-2
Distance:	2m/2m3: 0-2 2m4-2m7: 0-6 3m+: 0-0
Track:	LH: 0-3 RH: 0-5 Tight: 0-3 Gall: 0-0
Aids:	Bl: 0-0 Vi: 0-0 Tstrap: 0-0 Ckp: 0-0
Best Rating:	139 2/98 Fair 2m yld-sft Ch

Modest front-running handicap chaser at around two and a half miles; jumps well; acts on any ground, possibly best on fast though.

Mullensgrove

10-y-o b g Derrylin-Wedding Song (True Song)
D Lowe D Lowe

Placings:00/PP/2/1P62F0-2534101F51					(4872)
2003/04: 22²G, 28⁵G, 24³G, 26⁴G, 25¹G, 26⁰G, 20¹GS, 21⁶G,					
24⁵G, 24¹S,					

	Starts	1st	2nd	3rd	Win & Pl
Chases	10	3	1	1	9789
Career Total	21	4	3	1	12095

118	4/04	Bang	3m110y H Ch	SFT	£2404
118	3/04	Ludl	2m4f H Ch	G-S	£3125
102	3/04	Ludl	3m1f110yH Ch	GD	£2999
97	5/02	Bang	3m110y H Ch	GD	£1501
			Total win prize-money £10033		

Going:	Sf: 1-1 GS: 1-1 Gd: 1-8 GF: - Fm: 0-0
Distance:	2m/2m3: 0-0 2m4-2m7: 1-3 3m+: 2-7
Track:	LH: 1-4 RH: 1-4 Tight: 2-8 Gall: 0-1
Aids:	Bl: 0-0 Vi: 0-0 Tstrap: 0-0 Ckp: 0-0
Best Rating:	118 4/04 Bang 3m110y soft Ch

Useful hunter chaser; stays three miles plus; well suited by a sound surface.

Mulligans Fool (IRE)
96   95

7-y-o ch m Torus-Miss Mulligan (Whistling Deer)
A M Hales (A J Martin 11/7) William Rowley

Placings:00/P230U-420034					(4253)
2003/04: 16⁴F, 16²GF, 17⁹HY, 20⁹GS, 16³G, 17⁴G,					

	Starts	1st	2nd	3rd	Win & Pl
Hurdles	6	0	1	1	2135
Career Total	13	0	2	2	3776

Going:	Sf: 0-1 GS: 0-1 Gd: 0-2 GF: - Fm: 0-2
Distance:	2m/2m3: 0-5 2m4-2m7: 0-1 3m+: 0-0
Track:	LH: 0-2 RH: 0-3 Tight: 0-3 Gall: 0-0
Aids:	Bl: 0-0 Vi: 0-0 Tstrap: 0-1 Ckp: 0-1
Best Rating:	100 11/02 Clon 2m4f yld-sft NHF

Moderate hurdler; effective over two miles; acts on fast ground.

Mulligatawny (IRE)
109(105h)   (113 h)121+

10-y-o b g Abednego-Mullangale (Strong Gale)
N J Gifford Pell-Mell Partners

Placings:2F32/4/0134-31					(3782)
2003/04: 21³S, 24¹S,					

	Starts	1st	2nd	3rd	Win & Pl
Chases	2	1	0	1	9264
Career Total	11	2	2	3	20028
121	2/04	Hntg	3m	C(0-125)HCh	SFT	£8433
109	12/02	Asct	2m4f	D(0-115)HHdl	SFT	£7036
			Total win prize-money £15470		

Going:	Sf: 1-2 GS: 0-0 Gd: 0-0 GF: - Fm: 0-0
Distance:	2m/2m3: 0-0 2m4-2m7: 0-1 3m+: 1-1
Track:	LH: 0-0 RH: 1-2 Tight: 0-0 Gall: 1-1
Aids:	Bl: 0-0 Vi: 0-0 Tstrap: 0-0 Ckp: 0-0
Best Rating:	121 2/04 Hntg 3m soft Ch

Fair novice chaser/hurdler; lightly raced; stays three miles; acts well on soft ground; inconsistent.

Mulsanne

6-y-o b g Clantime-Prim Lass (Reprimand)
P A Pritchard P A Pritchard

Placings:00P/P-PP					(0879)
2003/04: 16⁶G, 16⁸GF,					

	Starts	1st	2nd	3rd	Win & Pl
Hurdles	1	0	0	0	0
Chases	1	0	0	0	0
Career Total	6	0	0	0	0

Going:	Sf: 0-0 GS: 0-0 Gd: 0-1 GF: - Fm: 0-1

Distance:	2m/2m3: 0-2 2m4-2m7: 0-0 3m+: 0-0
Track:	LH: 0-2 RH: 0-0 Tight: 0-0 Gall: 0-0
Aids:	Bl: 0-0 Vi: 0-0 Tstrap: 0-0 Ckp: 0-0

Multeen River (IRE)
109(99h)   (115+h)122+

8-y-o b g Supreme Leader-Blackwater Mist (IRE) (King's Ride)
Jonjo O'Neill John P McManus

Placings:03124/21-114F040					(4398)
2003/04: 17¹GF, 16¹GF, 19⁴G, 16⁸HY, 16⁶S, 18⁴G, 32⁰G,					

	Starts	1st	2nd	3rd	Win & Pl
Chases	7	2	0	0	8824
Career Total	14	4	2	1	19651
119	11/03	Hntg	2m110y	D Ch	G-F	£4390
111	10/03	Sthl	2m1f	E Ch	G-F	£2723
115	12/02	Bang	2m1f	E Hdl	G-S	£3374
109	3/02	Thur	2m	NHF	SFT	£3386
			Total win prize-money £13876		

Going:	Sf: 0-2 GS: 0-0 Gd: 0-3 GF: - Fm: 2-2
Distance:	2m/2m3: 2-5 2m4-2m7: 0-1 3m+: 0-1
Track:	LH: 1-5 RH: 1-2 Tight: 0-0 Gall: 1-4
Aids:	Bl: 0-0 Vi: 0-0 Tstrap: 0-0 Ckp: 0-0
Best Rating:	124 12/03 Asct 2m3f110y good Ch

Fair novice chaser/hurdler; effective on soft and fast ground; best at around two miles; has shown temperament in the past.

Multi Talented (IRE)
108   121+

8-y-o b g Montelimar (USA)-Boro Glen (Furry Glen)
L Wells David Cox

Placings:321P-425P215300					(4965)
2003/04: 24⁴G, 24²GF, 24⁵G, 26⁴GS, 26²HY, 24¹S, 30⁵G, 24³GS,					
26⁶GF, 29⁰GF,					

	Starts	1st	2nd	3rd	Win & Pl
Chases	10	1	2	1	10814
Career Total	14	2	3	2	18364
121	1/04	Asct	3m110y	E(0-110)HCh	SFT	£5330
114	3/03	Folk	3m1f	E Ch	GD	£4424
			Total win prize-money £9754		

Going:	Sf: 1-2 GS: 0-2 Gd: 0-3 GF: - Fm: 0-3
Distance:	2m/2m3: 0-0 2m4-2m7: 0-0 3m+: 1-10
Track:	LH: 0-3 RH: 1-6 Tight: 0-3 Gall: 0-1
Aids:	Bl: 1-5 Vi: 0-0 Tstrap: 0-0 Ckp: 0-0
Best Rating:	121 1/04 Asct 3m110y soft Ch

Modest chaser; stays three and a quarter miles; acts on both good and soft ground; successful in blinkers.

Multigirl
82   34

7-y-o br m Ballet Royal (USA)-Last Colours (Afzal)
H J Manners H J Manners

Placings:00U/PP/0P					(0593)
2003/04: 19⁰GF, 20⁸GF,					

	Starts	1st	2nd	3rd	Win & Pl
Hurdles	2	0	0	0	
Career Total	7	0	0	0	

Going:	Sf: 0-0 GS: 0-0 Gd: 0-0 GF: 0-0 Fm: 0-2
Distance:	2m/2m3: 0-0 2m4-2m7: 0-2 3m+: 0-0
Track:	LH: 0-1 RH: 0-1 Tight: 0-0 Gall: 0-0
Aids:	Bl: 0-0 Vi: 0-0 Tstrap: 0-0 Ckp: 0-0
Best Rating:	41 10/00 Winc 2m gd-sft Hdl

Mumaris (USA)

104   (126h)**112**

10-y-o b/br g Capote (USA)-Barakat (Bustino)
Miss Lucinda V Russell (Mark Campion 26/5) De Montfort Management Limited

Placings:31613/04043400/44405F5202231/2P51152P-3242364246   (4458)
2003/04: 16³GS, 16²GF, 16⁴G, 16²S, 16³G, 20⁶GF, 16⁴HY, 20²G, 19⁴G, 16⁶HY,

	Starts	1st	2nd	3rd	Win & Pl
Chases	10	0	3	2	7397
Career Total	44	5	8	6	34989
115 8/02	Sedg	2m110y E Ch		GD	£3731
109 8/02	Sedg	2m110y E Ch		GD	£3662
92 4/02	Newc	2m110y E Ch		GD	£2957
107 8/98	Cork	2m Hdl		FRM	£3586
119 7/98	Bell	2m1f Hdl		G-F	£2391
				Total win prize-money £16330

Going: Sf: 0-3 GS: 0-1 Gd: 0-4 GF: - Fm: 0-2
Distance: 2m/2m3: 0-8 2m4-2m7: 0-2 3m+: 0-0
Track: LH: 0-7 RH: 0-3 Tight: 0-2 Gall: 0-3
Aids: Bl: 0-0 Vi: 0-0 Tstrap: 0-0 Ckp: 0-5
Best Rating: 126 10/01 Gway 2m   sft-hvy   Hdl

Moderate chaser; ex-Irish; best when making the running; suited by two miles and good ground, but handles cut; has worn cheekpieces.

Mumbling (IRE)

101   **105+**

6-y-o ch g Dr Devious (IRE)-Valley Lights (IRE) (Dance Of Life (USA))
B G Powell (M H Tompkins 24/10) Robert Gunn

Placings:164   (2449)
2003/04: 16¹GF, 17⁶G, 16⁴GS,

	Starts	1st	2nd	3rd	Win & Pl
Hurdles	3	1	0	0	4841
Career Total	3	1	0	0	4841
101 11/03	Leic	2m	D Hdl	G-F	£4270
				Total win prize-money £4271

Going: Sf: 0-0 GS: 0-1 Gd: 0-1 GF: - Fm: 1-1
Distance: 2m/2m3: 1-3 2m4-2m7: 0-0 3m+: 0-0
Track: LH: 0-1 RH: 1-2 Tight: 0-0 Gall: 0-1
Aids: Bl: 0-0 Vi: 0-0 Tstrap: 0-0 Ckp: 0-0
Best Rating: 105 11/03 Newb 2m110y   gd-sft   Hdl

Former fair Flat performer; won well on hurdle debut in November 2003 and has not been disgraced since in better company; acts on most ground; suited by trips around two miles.

Mumuqa (IRE)

81   **61**

12-y-o ch g Noalto-Princess Isabella (Divine Gift)
B S Rothwell J T Brown

Placings:42/11/F/03245P34P604/3P-5P   (1093)
2003/04: 17⁵G, 17⁷G,

	Starts	1st	2nd	3rd	Win & Pl
Chases	2	0	0	0	
Career Total	21	2	2	3	10744
113 9/99	Sedg	2m110y E Ch		G-F	£3650
106 9/99	NAbb	2m110y E Ch		G-F	£2766
				Total win prize-money £6418

Going: Sf: 0-0 GS: 0-0 Gd: 0-2 GF: - Fm: 0-0
Distance: 2m/2m3: 0-2 2m4-2m7: 0-0 3m+: 0-0
Track: LH: 0-2 RH: 0-0 Tight: 0-0 Gall: 0-0
Aids: Bl: 0-0 Vi: 0-0 Tstrap: 0-0 Ckp: 0-0

Best Rating: 113 7/01 Wolv 2m   gd-sft   Ch

Munny Hill

79f   **59f**

4-y-o b g Golden Heights-More Laughter (Oats)
M Appleby Eamon Spain

Placings:00   (3948)
2003/04: 16⁹GS, 16⁹G,

	Starts	1st	2nd	3rd	Win & Pl
NH Flat	2	0	0	0	
Career Total	2	0	0	0	

Going: Sf: 0-0 GS: 0-1 Gd: 0-1 GF: - Fm: 0-0
Distance: 2m/2m3: 0-2 2m4-2m7: 0-0 3m+: 0-0
Track: LH: 0-0 RH: 0-2 Tight: 0-0 Gall: 0-0
Aids: Bl: 0-0 Vi: 0-0 Tstrap: 0-0 Ckp: 0-0
Best Rating: 59 2/04 Winc 2m   good   NHF

Muntasir

102   **77**

4-y-o b g Rainbow Quest (USA)-Licorne (Sadler's Wells (USA))
P G Murphy J Cooper

Placings:60464   (4573)
2003/04: 13⁶GS, 16⁰S, 17⁴GS, 20⁶GF, 19⁴G,

	Starts	1st	2nd	3rd	Win & Pl
NH Flat	1	0	0	0	0
Hurdles	4	0	0	0	648
Career Total	5	0	0	0	648

Going: Sf: 0-1 GS: 0-2 Gd: 0-1 GF: - Fm: 0-1
Distance: 2m/2m3: 0-3 2m4-2m7: 0-1 3m+: 0-0
Track: LH: 0-2 RH: 0-2 Tight: 0-1 Gall: 0-1
Aids: Bl: 0-0 Vi: 0-0 Tstrap: 0-0 Ckp: 0-0
Best Rating: 79 1/04 Hrfd 2m1f   gd-sft   Hdl

Well held in a bumper on debut.

Muqarrar (IRE)

89f   **82f**

5-y-o ch h Alhaarth (IRE)-Narjis (USA) (Blushing Groom (FR))
T J Fitzgerald N H T Wrigley

Placings:0-0   (0422)
2003/04: 17⁰GF,

	Starts	1st	2nd	3rd	Win & Pl
NH Flat	1	0	0	0	
Career Total	2	0	0	0	

Going: Sf: 0-0 GS: 0-0 Gd: 0-0 GF: - Fm: 0-1
Distance: 2m/2m3: 0-1 2m4-2m7: 0-0 3m+: 0-0
Track: LH: 0-0 RH: 0-1 Tight: 0-1 Gall: 0-0
Aids: Bl: 0-0 Vi: 0-0 Tstrap: 0-0 Ckp: 0-0
Best Rating: 82 5/03 MRas 2m1f110y   gd-fm   NHF

Muqtadi (IRE)

90   **69+**

6-y-o b g Marju (IRE)-Kadwah (USA) (Mr Prospector (USA))
M Quinn (C R Dore 18/10) Mrs S G Davies

Placings:5   (1698)
2003/04: 16⁵GF,

	Starts	1st	2nd	3rd	Win & Pl
Hurdles	1	0	0	0	0
Career Total	1	0	0	0	0

Going: Sf: 0-0 GS: 0-0 Gd: 0-0 GF: - Fm: 0-1
Distance: 2m/2m3: 0-1 2m4-2m7: 0-0 3m+: 0-0
Track: LH: 0-1 RH: 0-0 Tight: 0-1 Gall: 0-0
Aids: Bl: 0-0 Vi: 0-0 Tstrap: 0-0 Ckp: 0-0
Best Rating: 69 10/03 Strf 2m110y   gd-fm   Hdl

Pulled too hard when supported in the market on hurdling debut in Stratford seller; doubtful stayer.

Murat (FR)

107   **96**

4-y-o b g Useful (FR)-La Marianne (FR) (Don Roberto (USA))
M C Pipe P A Deal

Placings:233   (3901)
2003/04: 17²GS, 17³G, 17³GS,

	Starts	1st	2nd	3rd	Win & Pl
Hurdles	3	0	1	2	2525
Career Total	3	0	1	2	2525

Going: Sf: 0-0 GS: 0-2 Gd: 0-1 GF: - Fm: 0-0
Distance: 2m/2m3: 0-3 2m4-2m7: 0-0 3m+: 0-0
Track: LH: 0-0 RH: 0-3 Tight: 0-2 Gall: 0-0
Aids: Bl: 0-0 Vi: 0-0 Tstrap: 0-0 Ckp: 0-0
Best Rating: 97 2/04 Tntn 2m1f   gd-sft   Hdl

Placed in modest novice hurdles, but looks quirky.

Murdinga

91   **99**

5-y-o br g Emperor Jones (USA)-Tintinara (Selkirk (USA))
A M Hales (Lady Herries 30/6) The Cornish 'Crac' Partnership

Placings:3PP5   (4899)
2003/04: 16³G, 17⁶GS, 17⁰G, 16⁵G,

	Starts	1st	2nd	3rd	Win & Pl
Hurdles	4	0	0	1	659
Career Total	4	0	0	1	659

Going: Sf: 0-0 GS: 0-1 Gd: 0-3 GF: - Fm: 0-0
Distance: 2m/2m3: 0-4 2m4-2m7: 0-0 3m+: 0-0
Track: LH: 0-0 RH: 0-4 Tight: 0-2 Gall: 0-0
Aids: Bl: 0-0 Vi: 0-0 Tstrap: 0-0 Ckp: 0-0
Best Rating: 99 12/03 Leic 2m   good   Hdl

Murhill's Pride (IRE)

94f   **74+f**

6-y-o b g Great Marquess-Penny's Wishing (Clantime)
W M Brisbourne Mike Murray

Placings:052   (1594)
2003/04: 16⁰GF, 17⁵GF, 16²GF,

	Starts	1st	2nd	3rd	Win & Pl
NH Flat	3	0	1	0	520
Career Total	3	0	1	0	520

Going: Sf: 0-0 GS: 0-0 Gd: 0-0 GF: - Fm: 0-3
Distance: 2m/2m3: 0-3 2m4-2m7: 0-0 3m+: 0-0
Track: LH: 0-1 RH: 0-2 Tight: 0-0 Gall: 0-0
Aids: Bl: 0-0 Vi: 0-0 Tstrap: 0-0 Ckp: 0-1
Best Rating: 74 10/03 Ludl 2m   gd-fm   NHF

Headstrong sort; has shown a little ability in bumpers.

Murphy's Cardinal (IRE)

107(103h)   (140+h)**129+**
8-y-o b g Shemazar-Lady Swinford (Ardross)
Noel T Chance T Conway & Mrs Conway

Placings:f111-1   (2532)
2003/04: 20¹S,

	Starts	1st	2nd	3rd	Win & Pl
Chases	1	1	0	0	3588
Career Total	5	5	0	0	16461
127 12/03 Plum	2m4f	E Ch		SFT	£3588
140 2/03 Asct	3m	D Hdl		SFT	£5187
140 1/03 Folk	2m6f110yE Hdl			HVY	£3472
117 12/02 Folk	2m6f110yF Hdl			HVY	£2275
99 11/02 Folk	2m1f110yH NHF			SFT	£1939
			Total win prize-money £16461		

Going:	Sf: 1-1 GS: 0-0 Gd: 0-0 GF: - Fm: 0-0
Distance:	2m/2m3: 0-0 **2m4-2m7: 1-1** 3m+: 0-0
Track:	**LH: 1-1** RH: 0-0 Tight: 1-1 Gall: 0-0
Aids:	Bl: 0-0 Vi: 0-0 Tstrap: 0-0 Ckp: 0-0
Best Rating:	140 2/03 Asct 3m soft Hdl

Novice chaser/useful hurdler; won his only bumper; unbeaten in three starts over hurdles; won on his chasing debut despite jumping right; acts in testing ground; stays three miles; promising.

Murphy's Nails (IRE)

92   **109+**
7-y-o b g Bob's Return (IRE)-Southern Run (Deep Run)
C R Egerton R K Carvill

Placings:0-42   (0449)
2003/04: 16⁶G, 20²GF,

	Starts	1st	2nd	3rd	Win & Pl
Hurdles	2	0	1	0	1016
Career Total	3	0	1	0	1016

Going:	Sf: 0-0 GS: 0-0 Gd: 0-1 GF: - Fm: 0-1
Distance:	2m/2m3: 0-1 2m4-2m7: 0-1 3m+: 0-0
Track:	LH: 0-1 RH: 0-1 Tight: 0-0 Gall: 0-1
Aids:	Bl: 0-0 Vi: 0-0 Tstrap: 0-0 Ckp: 0-0
Best Rating:	113 5/03 Hntg 2m4f110y gd-fm Hdl

Modest novice hurdler; showed promise on hurdles debut; may do better when handicapped.

Murray River (FR)

106(95c)   (76c)**126**
8-y-o b g Esprit Du Nord (USA)-Mulika (FR) (Procida (USA))
M C Pipe D A Johnson

Placings:22/5310/202-06531422   (1554)
2003/04: 23⁰GS, 20⁶GF, 21⁵GF, 17³GF, 22¹GF, 17⁴GF, 22²GF, 19²GF,

	Starts	1st	2nd	3rd	Win & Pl
Hurdles	7	1	2	1	6327
Chases	1	0	0	0	
Career Total	17	2	6	2	22259
110 8/03 Strf	2m6f110yF Hdl		G-F	£4168
130 11/00 Tntn	2m1f	D(0-125)HHdl	G-S	£4800
		Total win prize-money £8968		

Going:	Sf: 0-0 GS: 0-1 Gd: 0-0 GF: - Fm: 1-7
Distance:	2m/2m3: 0-3 **2m4-2m7: 1-4** 3m+: 0-1
Track:	**LH: 1-8** RH: 0-0 Tight: 1-6 Gall: 0-0
Aids:	Bl: 0-1 Vi: 1-7 Tstrap: 1-8 Ckp: 0-0
Best Rating:	130 11/00 Tntn 2m1f gd-sft Hdl

Fair hurdler; good efforts in the spring of 2003; disappointed on chase debut; beaten odds-on favourite when dropped into a claimer over hurdles but won again when stepped up to two miles six; effective at up to two miles six and acts on any ground; wears a visor; has become a bit of an enigma.

Murt's Man (IRE)

95(86h)   (52h)**129**
10-y-o b g Be My Native (USA)-Autumn Queen (Menelek)
Ms Bridget Nicholls (P F Nicholls 29/4) Derek Millard

Placings:3F1B/2F21PU/262P21PP/6500-4300   (3705)
2003/04: 27⁰S, 28⁴S, 31³G, 28⁰G, 26⁰HY,

	Starts	1st	2nd	3rd	Win & Pl
Hurdles	1	0	0	0	0
Chases	4	0	0	1	2593
Career Total	26	3	5	2	42286
145 3/02 Chep	3m2f110yB(0-145)HCh		G-S	£10773
135 1/01 Winc	3m11f110yC(0-135)HCh		SFT	£8307
111 3/00 Donc	3m	E Ch	G-S	£3006
		Total win prize-money £22086		

Going:	Sf: 0-3 GS: 0-0 Gd: 0-2 GF: - Fm: 0-0
Distance:	2m/2m3: 0-0 2m4-2m7: 0-0 3m+: 0-5
Track:	LH: 0-3 RH: 0-0 Tight: 0-1 Gall: 0-0
Aids:	Bl: 0-0 Vi: 0-0 Tstrap: 0-0 Ckp: 0-2
Best Rating:	145 3/02 Chep 3m2f110y gd-sft Ch

Fair handicap chaser; not the most fluent of jumpers; stays 3m 7f; acts on most types of ground; has worn blinkers/cheekpieces.

Murtakez

55
4-y-o b g Alhaarth (IRE)-Raaqiyya (USA) (Blushing Groom (FR))
S C Burrough (S Dow 13/8) Martin Smith (frome)

Placings:P000FP   (4899)
2003/04: 16⁵PS, 17⁰GS, 16⁰HY, 16⁰G, 16⁰FG, 16⁰PG,

	Starts	1st	2nd	3rd	Win & Pl
Hurdles	6	0	0	0	
Career Total	6	0	0	0	

Going:	Sf: 0-2 GS: 0-1 Gd: 0-3 GF: - Fm: 0-0
Distance:	2m/2m3: 0-6 2m4-2m7: 0-0 3m+: 0-0
Track:	LH: 0-3 RH: 0-3 Tight: 0-2 Gall: 0-0
Aids:	Bl: 0-0 Vi: 0-0 Tstrap: 0-0 Ckp: 0-0

Murzim

91   **84**
5-y-o b g Salse (USA)-Guilty Secret (IRE) (Kris)
J Gallagher C R Marks (banbury)

Placings:6   (1866)
2003/04: 16⁶GF,

	Starts	1st	2nd	3rd	Win & Pl
Hurdles	1	0	0	0	0
Career Total	1	0	0	0	0

Going:	Sf: 0-0 GS: 0-0 Gd: 0-0 GF: - Fm: 0-1
Distance:	2m/2m3: 0-1 2m4-2m7: 0-0 3m+: 0-0
Track:	LH: 0-0 RH: 0-1 Tight: 0-0 Gall: 0-0
Aids:	Bl: 0-0 Vi: 0-0 Tstrap: 0-0 Ckp: 0-0
Best Rating:	84 11/03 Asct 2m110y gd-fm Hdl

Musally

109(102c)   (82c)**100**
7-y-o ch g Muhtarram (USA)-Flourishing (IRE) (Trojan Fen)
W Jenks The Glazeley Partnership

Placings:P0/06F0/36353-214142UP43420   (4343)
2003/04: 21²G, 21¹GF, 26⁴GF, 21¹GF, 24⁴GF, 20²G, 20⁴G, 20⁰GF, 20⁴G, 24³GF, 20⁴G, 21²G, 21⁰GS,

	Starts	1st	2nd	3rd	Win & Pl
Hurdles	10	2	2	1	11321
Chases	3	0	1	0	1266
Career Total	24	2	4	3	14353
94 6/03 Sthl	2m5f110yE Hdl		G-F	£3479
83 5/03 Ludl	2m5f	F(0-95)HHdl	G-F	£4260
		Total win prize-money £7740		

Going:	Sf: 0-0 GS: 0-1 Gd: 0-6 GF: - Fm: 2-6
Distance:	2m/2m3: 0-0 **2m4-2m7: 2-10** 3m+: 0-3
Track:	LH: 1-8 RH: 1-5 Tight: 0-2 Gall: 0-1
Aids:	Bl: 0-0 Vi: 0-0 Tstrap: 0-0 Ckp: 0-0
Best Rating:	97 7/03 Worc 3m gd-fm Hdl

Modest hurdler/chaser; raised a total of 17lb after hurdle wins at Ludlow and Southwell in May and June 2003; yet to shine over fences; suited by fast ground; stays two miles five.

Muscadin

85   **70**
6-y-o br g Shaamit (IRE)-As Mustard (Keen)
M J Gingell (A C Whillans 14/5) The Real Tadzio Partnership

Placings:P/2P-660F   (1291)
2003/04: 16⁶G, 20⁰G, 24⁰GF, 22⁶GF,

	Starts	1st	2nd	3rd	Win & Pl
Hurdles	4	0	0	0	0
Career Total	7	0	1	0	580

Going:	Sf: 0-0 GS: 0-0 Gd: 0-0 GF: - Fm: 0-2
Distance:	2m/2m3: 0-1 2m4-2m7: 0-2 3m+: 0-1
Track:	LH: 0-3 RH: 0-1 Tight: 0-2 Gall: 0-0
Aids:	Bl: 0-0 Vi: 0-0 Tstrap: 0-0 Ckp: 0-0
Best Rating:	89 10/02 MRas 2m1f110y gd-fm NHF

Muscatelli

7-y-o b m Perpendicular-Small Money (Altosa Palace)
R D Wylie Giles Bracewell

Placings:0   (0373)
2003/04: 16⁰G,

	Starts	1st	2nd	3rd	Win & Pl
NH Flat	1	0	0	0	
Career Total	1	0	0	0	

Going:	Sf: 0-0 GS: 0-0 Gd: 0-1 GF: - Fm: 0-0
Distance:	2m/2m3: 0-1 2m4-2m7: 0-0 3m+: 0-0
Track:	LH: 0-1 RH: 0-0 Tight: 0-0 Gall: 0-0
Aids:	Bl: 0-0 Vi: 0-0 Tstrap: 0-0 Ckp: 0-0

Music To My Ears (IRE)

(99h)   (96+h)
6-y-o ch g Phardante (FR)-Evas Charm (Carlburg)
Jonjo O'Neill John P McManus

Placings: *12*-114P   (1831)
2003/04: 20¹GF, 19¹GF, 21⁴G, 20⁸GF,

	Starts	1st	2nd	3rd	Win & Pl
Hurdles	3	2	0	0	5547
Chases	1	0	0	0	0
Career Total	6	3	1	0	8142
96	10/03 MRas	2m3f110yE Hdl		G-F	£2959
96	9/03 Worc	2m4f	E Hdl	G-F	£2587
100	1/03 Sthl	2m	H NHF	GD	£2023

Total win prize-money £7570

Going:	Sf: 0-0 GS: 0-0 Gd: 0-1 GF: - Fm: 2-3
Distance:	2m/2m3: 0-0 2m4-2m7: 2-4 3m+: 0-0
Track:	LH: 1-3 RH: 1-1 Tight: 1-2 Gall: 0-1
Aids:	Bl: 0-0 Vi: 0-0 Tstrap: 0-0 Ckp: 0-0
Best Rating:	107 3/03 Donc 2m110y gd-sft NHF

Modest hurdler; well-backed when winning 2m 4f novices' hurdle at Worcester in September and followed up at Market Rasen; looks a promising long-term chasing prospect; acts on fast.

Musical Stage (USA)

104   114+

5-y-o b g Theatrical-Changed Tune (USA) (Tunerup (USA))
P R Webber N Ruddell & D Heath

Placings: FP13   (4847)
2003/04: 16²G, 17ᴾGS, 16¹G, 16³GS,

	Starts	1st	2nd	3rd	Win & Pl
Hurdles	4	1	0	1	4666
Career Total	4	1	0	1	4666
110	3/04 Hntg	2m110y E Hdl		GD	£3536

Total win prize-money £3536

Going:	Sf: 0-0 GS: 0-2 Gd: 1-2 GF: - Fm: 0-0
Distance:	2m/2m3: 1-4 2m4-2m7: 0-0 3m+: 0-0
Track:	LH: 0-1 RH: 1-3 Tight: 0-1 Gall: 1-1
Aids:	Bl: 0-0 Vi: 0-0 Tstrap: 1-2 Ckp: 0-0
Best Rating:	114 4/04 Ayr 2m gd-sft Hdl

Fair hurdler; acts on good and easy ground.

Musimaro (FR)

96   97+

6-y-o b g Solid Illusion (USA)-Musimara (FR) (Margouillat (FR))
O Sherwood O M C Sherwood

Placings: *3*103-550P4510   (4785)
2003/04: 20⁵GF, 21⁵GF, 20⁴GS, 25⁵S, 22⁴GS, 20⁵G, 19¹GS, 21⁰G,

	Starts	1st	2nd	3rd	Win & Pl
Hurdles	8	1	0	0	2317
Career Total	12	2	0	2	5714
97	3/04 Hrfd	2m3f110yG Hdl		G-S	£2317
101	11/02 Ludl	2m	H NHF	GD	£2499

Total win prize-money £4816

Going:	Sf: 0-1 GS: 1-3 Gd: 0-2 GF: - Fm: 0-2
Distance:	2m/2m3: 0-0 2m4-2m7: 1-7 3m+: 0-1
Track:	LH: 0-4 RH: 1-4 Tight: 0-1 Gall: 0-3
Aids:	Bl: 0-1 Vi: 0-0 Tstrap: 0-0 Ckp: 1-4
Best Rating:	101 11/02 Ludl 2m good NHF

Moderate hurdler; does not appear to stay 2m 4f over hurdles; acts on good and easy ground.

Muskatsturm (GER)

82   77

5-y-o b g Lecroix (GER)-Myrthe (GER) (Konigsstuhl (GER))
B J Curley Mrs B J Curley

Placings: 264-P3PP   (4343)
2003/04: 19⁹G, 20³GS, 20⁸S, 21ᴾGS,

	Starts	1st	2nd	3rd	Win & Pl
Hurdles	4	0	0	1	548
Career Total	7	0	1	1	1898

Going:	Sf: 0-1 GS: 0-2 Gd: 0-1 GF: - Fm: 0-0
Distance:	2m/2m3: 0-1 2m4-2m7: 0-3 3m+: 0-0
Track:	LH: 0-3 RH: 0-1 Tight: 0-0 Gall: 0-0
Aids:	Bl: 0-0 Vi: 0-0 Tstrap: 0-0 Ckp: 0-0
Best Rating:	78 3/03 Hntg 2m4f110y good Hdl

Moderate hurdler; stays 2m 4f; seems best on good ground.

Must Bite

98   119+

8-y-o b g Bustino-Once Bitten (Brave Invader (USA))
Jonjo O'Neill John P McManus

Placings: UU000/030/3-0126   (4693)
2003/04: 22⁰G, 22¹G, 22²G, 22⁶G,

	Starts	1st	2nd	3rd	Win & Pl
Hurdles	4	1	1	0	5144
Career Total	13	1	1	2	6228
105	3/04 Folk	2m6f110yE(0-110)HHdl		GD	£3591

Total win prize-money £3591

Going:	Sf: 0-0 GS: 0-0 Gd: 1-4 GF: - Fm: 0-0
Distance:	2m/2m3: 0-0 2m4-2m7: 1-4 3m+: 0-0
Track:	LH: 0-0 RH: 1-2 Tight: 1-1 Gall: 0-0
Aids:	Bl: 0-0 Vi: 0-0 Tstrap: 0-0 Ckp: 0-0
Best Rating:	119 3/04 MRas 2m6f good Hdl

Fair hurdler; stays two miles-six; acts on good.

Mustang Molly

12-y-o br m Soldier Rose-Little 'N' Game (Convolvulus)
Andrew J Martin Andrew J Martin

Placings: P5/2P0P/P442234P-PPP   (4439)
2003/04: 16²G, 21ᴾG, 21ᴾGS,

	Starts	1st	2nd	3rd	Win & Pl
Chases	3	0	0	0	
Career Total	17	0	3	1	4651

Going:	Sf: 0-0 GS: 0-1 Gd: 0-2 GF: - Fm: 0-0
Distance:	2m/2m3: 0-1 2m4-2m7: 0-2 3m+: 0-1
Track:	LH: 0-3 RH: 0-0 Tight: 0-1 Gall: 0-1
Aids:	Bl: 0-0 Vi: 0-0 Tstrap: 0-0 Ckp: 0-0
Best Rating:	90 5/01 Chel 2m110y good Ch

Mutabari (USA)

82   70

10-y-o ch g Seeking The Gold (USA)-Cagey Exuberance (USA) (Exuberant (USA))
J L Spearing J Spearing

Placings: 040/4-00   (0676)
2003/04: 17⁰GS, 16⁰GF,

	Starts	1st	2nd	3rd	Win & Pl
Hurdles	2	0	0	0	
Career Total	6	0	0	0	0

Going:	Sf: 0-0 GS: 0-1 Gd: 0-0 GF: - Fm: 0-1
Distance:	2m/2m3: 0-2 2m4-2m7: 0-0 3m+: 0-0
Track:	LH: 0-1 RH: 0-1 Tight: 0-0 Gall: 0-0
Aids:	Bl: 0-0 Vi: 0-0 Tstrap: 0-0 Ckp: 0-1

Best Rating: 70 10/02 Ludl 2m firm Hdl

Mutadarra (IRE)

88(106h)   (93h)80

11-y-o ch g Mujtahid (USA)-Silver Echo (Caerleon (USA))
J W Mullins M S Green

Placings: 014/634/310454300P/2250051140-50052054F420U0   (2702)
2003/04: 16⁵GF, 20⁴GF, 16⁸G, 20⁵G, 19²G, 18⁹GF, 17⁵GF, 22⁴F, 19⁴GF, 16⁴GF, 16²F, 17⁹G, 19¹⁰GF, 19⁹GF,

	Starts	1st	2nd	3rd	Win & Pl
Hurdles	12	0	2	0	2035
Chases	2	0	0	0	0
Career Total	40	4	4	3	16533
93	10/02 Strf	2m110y F(0-100)HHdl		GD	£3010
93	10/02 Winc	2m	E(0-105)HHdl	FRM	£3445
86	8/01 Worc	2m	G Hdl	G-F	£1591
97	3/00 Hntg	2m110y E Hdl		G-F	£2870

Total win prize-money £10917

Going:	Sf: 0-0 GS: 0-0 Gd: 0-4 GF: - Fm: 0-10
Distance:	2m/2m3: 0-10 2m4-2m7: 0-4 3m+: 0-0
Track:	LH: 0-7 RH: 0-6 Tight: 0-6 Gall: 0-0
Aids:	Bl: 0-0 Vi: 0-0 Tstrap: 0-0 Ckp: 0-1
Best Rating:	97 10/00 Hrfd 2m3f110y good Hdl

Plating-class handicap hurdler; acts on a sound surface; yet to prove he can be effective beyond 2m.

Mutared (IRE)

59   20

6-y-o b g Marju (IRE)-Shahaada (USA) (Private Account (USA))
N P Littmoden Mrs Emma Littmoden

Placings: P0   (1457)
2003/04: 17ᴾG, 16⁰GF,

	Starts	1st	2nd	3rd	Win & Pl
Hurdles	2	0	0	0	
Career Total	2	0	0	0	

Going:	Sf: 0-0 GS: 0-0 Gd: 0-1 GF: - Fm: 0-1
Distance:	2m/2m3: 0-2 2m4-2m7: 0-0 3m+: 0-0
Track:	LH: 0-2 RH: 0-0 Tight: 0-2 Gall: 0-0
Aids:	Bl: 0-0 Vi: 0-0 Tstrap: 0-0 Ckp: 0-0
Best Rating:	20 9/03 Plum 2m gd-fm Hdl

Mutineer (IRE)

115   132

5-y-o gr g Highest Honor (FR)-Miss Amy R (USA) (Deputy Minister (CAN))
D T Hughes Seven To Eleven Syndicate

Placings: 33331110-500601360   (4806a)
2003/04: 16⁵GY, 20⁰GY, 20⁰YS, 20⁶S, 24⁰S, 19¹S, 24³S, 25⁶G, 22⁰Y,

	Starts	1st	2nd	3rd	Win & Pl
Hurdles	9	1	0	1	14036
Career Total	17	4	0	5	58769
129	1/04 Naas	2m3f	(81-123)HHdl	SFT	£8503
136	2/03 Leop	2m	Hdl	SFT	£21103
129	1/03 Punc	2m	Hdl	Y-S	£13506
123	12/02 Leop	2m	Hdl	HVY	£7975

Total win prize-money £51089

Going:	Sf: 1-4 GS: 0-0 Gd: 0-1 GF: - Fm: 0-0
Distance:	2m/2m3: 1-2 2m4-2m7: 0-4 3m+: 0-3
Track:	LH: 1-5 RH: 0-2 Tight: 0-0 Gall: 0-1
Aids:	Bl: 0-4 Vi: 0-0 Tstrap: 1-7 Ckp: 0-0

Best Rating: 136 2/03 Leop 2m   soft   Hdl

Useful hurdler; likes to race up with the pace; best at around two and a half miles; suited by soft ground; has worn blinkers and a tongue tie.

Mvezo

98f   **87f**

6-y-o ch g Karinga Bay-Queen Of The Celts (Celtic Cone)
Evan Williams Celtic Racing

Placings:*0*   (4447)
2003/04: 16⁰S,

	Starts	1st	2nd	3rd	Win & Pl
NH Flat	1	0	0	0	
Career Total	1	0	0	0	

Going:	Sf: 0-1 GS: 0-0 Gd: 0-0 GF: - Fm: 0-0
Distance:	2m/2m3: 0-1 2m4-2m7: 0-0 3m+: 0-0
Track:	LH: 0-0 RH: 0-1 Tight: 0-0 Gall: 0-0
Aids:	Bl: 0-0 Vi: 0-0 Tstrap: 0-0 Ckp: 0-0
Best Rating:	87 3/04 Wwck 2m soft NHF

My Ace

104   **92**

6-y-o b m Definite Article-Miss Springtime (Bluebird (USA))
James Moffatt (Mrs H Dalton 22/11) R Naylor

Placings:*3/24204-0043132*   (4297)
2003/04: 16⁰G, 17⁰GF, 17⁴GF, 16³GF, 16¹GF, 16³GF, 16²GF,

	Starts	1st	2nd	3rd	Win & Pl
Hurdles	7	1	1	2	6474
Career Total	13	1	3	3	7893
92 11/03 Ludl	2m	D Hdl		G-F	£4007
			Total win prize-money £4007		

Going:	Sf: 0-0 GS: 0-0 Gd: 0-0 GF: - Fm: 1-6
Distance:	2m/2m3: 1-7 2m4-2m7: 0-0 3m+: 0-0
Track:	LH: 0-4 RH: 1-3 Tight: 0-3 Gall: 0-0
Aids:	Bl: 1-2 Vi: 0-1 Tstrap: 1-5 Ckp: 0-0
Best Rating:	93 10/02 Tntn 2m1f firm NHF

Plating-class hurdler; best in blinkers and on fast ground.

My Big Sister

64f   **32f**

5-y-o gr m Thethingaboutitis (USA)-My Concordia (Belfort (FR))
A W Carroll John Halsey

Placings:*0*   (4608)
2003/04: 17⁰G,

	Starts	1st	2nd	3rd	Win & Pl
NH Flat	1	0	0	0	
Career Total	1	0	0	0	

Going:	Sf: 0-0 GS: 0-0 Gd: 0-1 GF: - Fm: 0-0
Distance:	2m/2m3: 0-1 2m4-2m7: 0-0 3m+: 0-0
Track:	LH: 0-0 RH: 0-1 Tight: 0-1 Gall: 0-0
Aids:	Bl: 0-0 Vi: 0-0 Tstrap: 0-0 Ckp: 0-0
Best Rating:	34 3/04 MRas 2m1f110y good NHF

My Bold Boyo

100(80c)   (71c)**103**

9-y-o b g Never So Bold-My Rosie (Forzando)
K Bishop E T Roberts

Placings:*3006P511/00110600F2-0*   (0035)
2003/04: 22⁶G,

	Starts	1st	2nd	3rd	Win & Pl
Hurdles	1	0	0	0	
Career Total	19	4	1	1	15785
103 10/02 Extr	2m1f	E(0-110)HHdl	FRM	£4017
103 10/02 Extr	2m1f	D(0-120)HHdl	FRM	£4069
94 4/02 Extr	2m1f	D(0-105)HHdl	FRM	£2954
82 4/02 Extr	2m1f	F(0-100)HHdl	FRM	£2870
		Total win prize-money £13910		

Going:	Sf: 0-0 GS: 0-0 Gd: 0-0 GF: - Fm: 0-0
Distance:	2m/2m3: 0-0 2m4-2m7: 0-1 3m+: 0-0
Track:	LH: 0-0 RH: 0-1 Tight: 0-0 Gall: 0-0
Aids:	Bl: 0-0 Vi: 0-0 Tstrap: 0-0 Ckp: 0-0
Best Rating:	103 4/03 Extr 2m3f gd-fm Hdl

Modest handicap hurdler; four times a winner over 17 furlongs at Exeter in 2002; suited by a stiff track; acts on fast ground.

My Caraidd

89   **66**

8-y-o b m Rakaposhi King-Tochenka (Fine Blue)
D G Bridgwater Anita & Relton Minton

Placings:*0*   (1970)
2003/04: 16⁰G,

	Starts	1st	2nd	3rd	Win & Pl
Hurdles	1	0	0	0	
Career Total	1	0	0	0	

Going:	Sf: 0-0 GS: 0-0 Gd: 0-1 GF: - Fm: 0-0
Distance:	2m/2m3: 0-1 2m4-2m7: 0-0 3m+: 0-0
Track:	LH: 0-0 RH: 0-1 Tight: 0-0 Gall: 0-0
Aids:	Bl: 0-0 Vi: 0-0 Tstrap: 0-0 Ckp: 0-0
Best Rating:	66 11/03 Towc 2m good Hdl

My Galliano (IRE)

104(100c)   (103+c)**103+**

8-y-o b g Muharib (USA)-Hogan Stand (Buckskin (FR))
B G Powell L Gilbert

Placings:*00/0452125/U60FP31425/454235-301440* (4210)
2003/04: 16³G, 16⁹G, 16¹GS, 16⁴S, 16⁴GS, 16⁹G,

	Starts	1st	2nd	3rd	Win & Pl
Hurdles	4	0	0	1	1171
Chases	2	1	0	0	3708
Career Total	31	3	4	3	17606
103 12/03 Hntg	2m110y	E(0-105)HCh	G-S	£3396
99 11/01 Winc	2m	E(0-115)HHdl	G-F	£3523
94 11/00 Kemp	2m	F(0-100)HHdl	SFT	£2756
		Total win prize-money £9675		

Going:	Sf: 0-1 GS: 1-2 Gd: 0-3 GF: - Fm: 0-0
Distance:	2m/2m3: 1-6 2m4-2m7: 0-0 3m+: 0-0
Track:	LH: 0-0 RH: 1-6 Tight: 0-1 Gall: 1-1
Aids:	Bl: 0-0 Vi: 0-0 Tstrap: 0-0 Ckp: 0-0
Best Rating:	103 12/03 Hntg 2m110y gd-sft Ch

Moderate hurdler/winning chaser; suited by two miles; effective on any ground, but may not want it too soft.

My Good Son (NZ)

100(95c)   (100c)**98+**

9-y-o b g The Son (NZ)-Meadow Hall (NZ) (Pikehall (USA))
Ian Williams Men Behaving Sadly Partnership

Placings:*4003210/010P/U0P650P1F1/FPPP31223U-3* (0858)
2003/04: 22³GF,

	Starts	1st	2nd	3rd	Win & Pl
Hurdles	1	0	0	1	556
Career Total	32	5	3	4	22925
91 7/02 Worc	3m	D(0-125)HHdl	G-F	£4095
100 4/02 Sedg	2m5f	D(0-120)HCh	G-F	£4075
100 4/02 Plum	3m2f	F(0-90)HCh	G-F	£2828
103 2/01 Hayd	2m4f	D(0-120)HHdl	HVY	£3552
99 3/00 Ludl	2m5f	E Hdl	GD	£2899
		Total win prize-money £17451		

Going:	Sf: 0-0 GS: 0-0 Gd: 0-0 GF: - Fm: 0-1
Distance:	2m/2m3: 0-0 2m4-2m7: 0-1 3m+: 0-0
Track:	LH: 0-1 RH: 0-0 Tight: 0-1 Gall: 0-0
Aids:	Bl: 0-0 Vi: 0-0 Tstrap: 0-0 Ckp: 0-0
Best Rating:	103 2/01 Hayd 2m4f heavy Hdl

Moderate hurdler/chaser; handles heavy ground but prefers faster; stays three miles.

My Lady Link (FR)

84   **92**

5-y-o bl m Sleeping Car (FR)-Cadoudaline (FR) (Cadoudal (FR))
Miss Venetia Williams (T Trapenard 26/11) Six Diamonds Partnership

Placings:*20-2030003410U*   (4162)
2003/04: 18²VS, 18⁶S, 18³VS, 17⁰VS, 18⁰HO, 19⁰VS, 18³VS, 17⁴HO, 17¹HO, 20⁰GS, 24⁴Ug,

	Starts	1st	2nd	3rd	Win & Pl
Hurdles	6	0	1	1	6546
Chases	5	1	0	1	11045
Career Total	13	1	2	2	23201
11/03 Autl	2m1f110y Ch		HLD	£6545
		Total win prize-money £6545		

Going:	Sf: 0-1 GS: 0-1 Gd: 0-1 GF: - Fm: 0-0
Distance:	2m/2m3: 1-8 2m4-2m7: 0-2 3m+: 0-1
Track:	LH: 0-3 RH: 0-0 Tight: 0-1 Gall: 0-1
Aids:	Bl: 0-0 Vi: 0-0 Tstrap: 0-0 Ckp: 0-0
Best Rating:	92 3/04 Donc 3m good Ch

Winner over fences in France at four; very modest form so far here.

My Last Bean (IRE)

107   **113**

7-y-o gr g Soviet Lad (USA)-Meanz Beanz (High Top)
B Smart The Coopyline Racing Club Ltd

Placings:*4410P*   (4638)
2003/04: 16⁴S, 16⁴S, 16¹GF, 16⁰GS, 16²G,

	Starts	1st	2nd	3rd	Win & Pl
Hurdles	5	1	0	0	7152
Career Total	5	1	0	0	7152
110 1/04 Muss	2m	C Hdl	G-F	£6864
		Total win prize-money £6864		

Going:	Sf: 0-2 GS: 0-1 Gd: 0-1 GF: - Fm: 1-1
Distance:	2m/2m3: 1-5 2m4-2m7: 0-0 3m+: 0-0
Track:	LH: 0-4 RH: 1-1 Tight: 1-2 Gall: 0-1
Aids:	Bl: 0-0 Vi: 0-0 Tstrap: 0-0 Ckp: 0-0
Best Rating:	113 2/04 Newc 2m gd-sft Hdl

Fair novice hurdler; suited by two miles and fast ground.

My Legal Eagle (IRE)

109   **103**

10-y-o b g Law Society (USA)-Majestic Nurse (On Your Mark)
R J Price E G Bevan

Placings:420/6/5P06/4122-1   (1296)
2003/04: 16¹GF,

	Starts	1st	2nd	3rd	Win & Pl
Hurdles	1	1	0	0	4706
Career Total	13	2	3	0	10518
103 9/03 Strf	2m110y	D(0-105)HHdl	G-F		£4706
103 5/02 Worc	2m	E(0-105)HHdl	G-F		£2625
				Total win prize-money £7331	

Going:	Sf: 0-0 GS: 0-0 Gd: 0-0 GF: - Fm: 1-1
Distance:	2m/2m3: 1-1 2m4-2m7: 0-0 3m+: 0-0
Track:	LH: 1-1 RH: 0-0 Tight: 1-1 Gall: 0-0
Aids:	Bl: 0-0 Vi: 0-0 Tstrap: 0-0 Ckp: 0-0
Best Rating:	103 9/03 Strf 2m110y gd-fm Hdl

Modest handicap hurdler; effective at around 2m; acts on most types of ground.

My Line
109   125+
7-y-o b g Perpendicular-My Desire (Grey Desire)
Mrs M Reveley   Mrs M Hoey

Placings:0/30F6-2142632311   (4838)
2003/04: 17²GF, 17¹G, 17⁴GS, 17²HY, 16⁶GS, 23³GS, 22²G, 20³GS, 24¹GF, 24¹GF,

	Starts	1st	2nd	3rd	Win & Pl
Hurdles	10	3	3	2	33618
Career Total	15	3	3	3	34050
125 4/04 Chel	3m	D(0-120)HHdl	G-F		£10440
115 3/04 Ayr	3m110y	D(0-115)HHdl	G-F		£5005
107 10/03 Carl	2m1f	D(0-125)HHdl	GD		£14007
				Total win prize-money £29453	

Going:	Sf: 0-1 GS: 0-4 Gd: 1-2 GF: - Fm: 2-3
Distance:	2m/2m3: 1-5 2m4-2m7: 0-2 3m+: 2-3
Track:	LH: 2-5 RH: 1-5 Tight: 0-0 Gall: 1-2
Aids:	Bl: 1-3 Vi: 0-0 Tstrap: 0-0 Ckp: 0-0
Best Rating:	125 4/04 Chel 3m gd-fm Hdl

Modest hurdler; stays three miles and acts on most types of ground; disappointed in blinkers.

My Maite (IRE)

5-y-o b g Komaite (USA)-Mena (Blakeney)
R Ingram   The Stargazers 2nd Xi

Placings:0   (2778)
2003/04: 17⁰GS,

	Starts	1st	2nd	3rd	Win & Pl
Hurdles	1	0	0	0	
Career Total	1	0	0	0	

Going:	Sf: 0-0 GS: 0-1 Gd: 0-0 GF: - Fm: 0-0
Distance:	2m/2m3: 0-1 2m4-2m7: 0-0 3m+: 0-0
Track:	LH: 0-0 RH: 0-1 Tight: 0-1 Gall: 0-0
Aids:	Bl: 0-0 Vi: 0-0 Tstrap: 0-1 Ckp: 0-0

My Mate Whitey (IRE)
11
5-y-o ch g Millkom-Imagery (Vision (USA))
M A Allen   Brendan Laverty

Placings:P0-0   (0449)
2003/04: 20⁰GF,

	Starts	1st	2nd	3rd	Win & Pl
Hurdles	1	0	0	0	

Career Total   3   0   0   0

Going:	Sf: 0-0 GS: 0-0 Gd: 0-0 GF: - Fm: 0-1
Distance:	2m/2m3: 0-0 2m4-2m7: 0-1 3m+: 0-0
Track:	LH: 0-0 RH: 0-1 Tight: 0-0 Gall: 0-1
Aids:	Bl: 0-0 Vi: 0-0 Tstrap: 0-0 Ckp: 0-0
Best Rating:	11 12/02 Font 2m2f110y good Hdl

My Native Cork (IRE)
82   64
9-y-o b m Be My Native (USA)-Autumn Glen (Furry Glen)
A J Martin   Daniel O'Shea

Placings:00000/0P   (0574)
2003/04: 16⁰Y, 16⁵G,

	Starts	1st	2nd	3rd	Win & Pl
Hurdles	2	0	0	0	
Career Total	7	0	0	0	

Going:	Sf: 0-0 GS: 0-0 Gd: 0-1 GF: - Fm: 0-0
Distance:	2m/2m3: 0-2 2m4-2m7: 0-0 3m+: 0-0
Track:	LH: 0-0 RH: 0-2 Tight: 0-0 Gall: 0-0
Aids:	Bl: 0-0 Vi: 0-0 Tstrap: 0-0 Ckp: 0-0
Best Rating:	67 11/01 Clon 2m4f yield Hdl

My Pal Val (IRE)
53f
4-y-o br g Classic Cliche (IRE)-Lessons Lass (IRE) (Doyoun)
Miss H C Knight   Harold Winton

Placings:0   (4509)
2003/04: 14⁰GS,

	Starts	1st	2nd	3rd	Win & Pl
NH Flat	1	0	0	0	
Career Total	1	0	0	0	

Going:	Sf: 0-0 GS: 0-1 Gd: 0-0 GF: - Fm: 0-0
Distance:	2m/2m3: 0-0 2m4-2m7: 0-0 3m+: 0-0
Track:	LH: 0-0 RH: 0-0 Tight: 0-0 Gall: 0-0
Aids:	Bl: 0-0 Vi: 0-0 Tstrap: 0-0 Ckp: 0-0
Best Rating:	53 3/04 Hrfd 1m6f gd-sft NHF

My Retreat (USA)
100   91
7-y-o b g Hermitage (USA)-My Jessica Ann (USA) (Native Rythm)
R Fielder (G L Moore 9/9) R Fielder

Placings:02500   (4103)
2003/04: 17⁰GS, 16²HY, 16⁵S, 17⁰GS, 16⁰G,

	Starts	1st	2nd	3rd	Win & Pl
Hurdles	5	0	1	0	1278
Career Total	5	0	1	0	1278

Going:	Sf: 0-2 GS: 0-2 Gd: 0-1 GF: - Fm: 0-0
Distance:	2m/2m3: 0-5 2m4-2m7: 0-0 3m+: 0-0
Track:	LH: 0-2 RH: 0-3 Tight: 0-4 Gall: 0-0
Aids:	Bl: 0-0 Vi: 0-0 Tstrap: 0-0 Ckp: 0-0
Best Rating:	91 1/04 Plum 2m soft Hdl

Modest hurdler; formerly a plater on the Flat; suited by two miles and soft ground.

My Sharp Grey
106   101+
5-y-o gr m Tragic Role (USA)-Sharp Anne (Belfort (FR))
J Gallagher (M C Pipe 3/11) Bob Bevan

Placings:R312U11604   (4210)
2003/04: 17ᴿGF, 16²GF, 16¹G, 16²G, 16ᵁGF, 16¹GF, 16¹G, 16⁶GF, 16⁶G, 16⁴G,

	Starts	1st	2nd	3rd	Win & Pl
Hurdles	10	3	1	1	12631
Career Total	10	3	1	1	12631
101 12/03 Ludl	2m	E(0-110)HHdl	GD		£6760
92 11/03 Ludl	2m	G Hdl	G-F		£2320
84 10/03 Strf	2m110y	G Hdl	G-F		£2247
				Total win prize-money £11328	

Going:	Sf: 0-0 GS: 0-0 Gd: 2-5 GF: - Fm: 1-5
Distance:	2m/2m3: 3-10 2m4-2m7: 0-0 3m+: 0-0
Track:	LH: 1-3 RH: 2-7 Tight: 1-3 Gall: 0-0
Aids:	Bl: 0-0 Vi: 0-1 Tstrap: 0-0 Ckp: 0-0
Best Rating:	101 12/03 Ludl 2m good Hdl

Moderate hurdler; twice a winner at Ludlow; suited by an easy 2m; and a sound surface.

My True Love (IRE)
83f   85f
5-y-o b g Beneficial-Elfi (IRE) (Le Moss)
R J Baker   Surerak Ins Cons (Racing)/Mrs S Rowe

Placings:5-50   (2850)
2003/04: 17⁵GF, 16⁰S,

	Starts	1st	2nd	3rd	Win & Pl
NH Flat	2	0	0	0	
Career Total	3	0	0	0	

Going:	Sf: 0-1 GS: 0-0 Gd: 0-0 GF: - Fm: 0-1
Distance:	2m/2m3: 0-2 2m4-2m7: 0-0 3m+: 0-0
Track:	LH: 0-0 RH: 0-2 Tight: 0-0 Gall: 0-0
Aids:	Bl: 0-0 Vi: 0-0 Tstrap: 0-0 Ckp: 0-0
Best Rating:	84 4/03 NAbb 2m1f gd-fm NHF

My Whisper (IRE)
81f   62f
5-y-o b m Zaffaran (USA)-Floreamus (Quayside)
A King   Mrs M C Sweeney

Placings:0-0   (0216)
2003/04: 16⁰G,

	Starts	1st	2nd	3rd	Win & Pl
NH Flat	1	0	0	0	
Career Total	2	0	0	0	

Going:	Sf: 0-0 GS: 0-0 Gd: 0-1 GF: - Fm: 0-0
Distance:	2m/2m3: 0-1 2m4-2m7: 0-0 3m+: 0-0
Track:	LH: 0-1 RH: 0-0 Tight: 0-0 Gall: 0-0
Aids:	Bl: 0-0 Vi: 0-0 Tstrap: 0-0 Ckp: 0-0
Best Rating:	62 4/03 MRas 2m1f110y good NHF

Well beaten on first ever outing in bumper at Market Rasen in April.

My Will (FR)
110   130
4-y-o b g Saint Preuil (FR)-Gleep Will (FR) (Laniste)
P F Nicholls (G Macaire 23/11) Mrs J Stewart

Placings:1123   (4625)
2003/04: 16¹S, 16¹VS, 16²S, 16³G,

	Starts	1st	2nd	3rd	Win & Pl
Hurdles	4	2	1	1	31148
Career Total	4	2	1	1	31148
98 11/03 Engh 2m110y Hdl				VS	£11221
10/03 Fntb 2m Hdl				SFT	£4675
				Total win prize-money	£15896

Going: Sf: 1-2 GS: 0-0 Gd: 0-1 GF: - Fm: 0-0
Distance: 2m/2m3: 2-4 2m4-2m7: 0-0 3m+: 0-0
Track: LH: 1-3 RH: 0-0 Tight: 0-1 Gall: 0-0
Aids: Bl: 0-0 Vi: 0-0 Tstrap: 0-0 Ckp: 0-0
Best Rating: 130 4/04 Aint 2m110y good Hdl

Useful juvenile hurdler; dual winner over hurdles in France; blundered two out when just missing out on British debut in a fair event at Haydock in February; third in Grade 2 at Aintree; fully effective at two miles but will be suited by further; handles testing ground.

Mydante (IRE)

9-y-o b m Phardante (FR)-Carminda (Proverb)
S Flook S Flook

Placings:340/310366433/505142/1260243354310/12-46   (4542)
2003/04: 25^{4}G, 20^{6}GS,

	Starts	1st	2nd	3rd	Win & Pl
Chases	2	0	0	0	84
Career Total	35	5	4	8	44764
111 5/02 Towc 3m				G-S	£6191
116 4/02 Uttx 3m110y D(0-125)HHdl				G-F	£4329
111 5/01 Extr 3m110y D(0-135)HHdl				GD	£5664
99 4/01 Newb 3m110y F(0-100)HHdl				SFT	£3461
91 10/99 Navn 2m2f Hdl				Y-S	£13258
				Total win prize-money	£32905

Going: Sf: 0-0 GS: 0-1 Gd: 0-0 GF: - Fm: 0-1
Distance: 2m/2m3: 0-0 2m4-2m7: 0-0 3m+: 0-1
Track: LH: 0-1 RH: 0-1 Tight: 0-2 Gall: 0-0
Aids: Bl: 0-0 Vi: 0-0 Tstrap: 0-0 Ckp: 0-0
Best Rating: 116 4/02 Uttx 3m110y gd-fm Hdl

Mylo

103   **96d**

6-y-o gr g Faustus (USA)-Bellifontaine (FR) (Bellypha)
Jonjo O'Neill John P McManus

Placings:2/2224065-3245   (4873)
2003/04: 16^{3}G, 19^{2}G, 17^{4}GF, 20^{5}GS,

	Starts	1st	2nd	3rd	Win & Pl
Hurdles	4	0	1	1	3048
Career Total	12	0	5	1	5743

Going: Sf: 0-0 GS: 0-1 Gd: 0-2 GF: - Fm: 0-1
Distance: 2m/2m3: 0-2 2m4-2m7: 0-2 3m+: 0-1
Track: LH: 0-2 RH: 0-2 Tight: 0-3 Gall: 0-0
Aids: Bl: 0-1 Vi: 0-0 Tstrap: 0-0 Ckp: 0-0
Best Rating: 101 5/02 Worc 2m good NHF

Modest frustrating novice hurdler; stays two and a half miles; seems best on good ground; no improvement when tried in blinkers.

Mylo (GER)

5-y-o b h Second Set (IRE)-Meerdunung (GDR) (Tauchsport (GER))
C Von Der Recke Gestut Rangau Stall Fairy Tale

Placings:343P   (3645)

2003/04: 18^{3}G, 18^{4}S, 16^{3}G, 24^{5}PGS,

	Starts	1st	2nd	3rd	Win & Pl
Chases	4	0	0	2	3463
Career Total	4	0	0	2	3463

Going: Sf: 0-1 GS: 0-1 Gd: 0-2 GF: - Fm: 0-0
Distance: 2m/2m3: 0-3 2m4-2m7: 0-0 3m+: 0-1
Track: LH: 0-0 RH: 0-2 Tight: 0-0 Gall: 0-0
Aids: Bl: 0-0 Vi: 0-0 Tstrap: 0-0 Ckp: 0-0
Best Rating: 0 2/04 Kemp 3m gd-sft Ch

German-trained novice chaser; has a tendency to jump left.

Myson (IRE)

103   (85h)**91**

5-y-o ch g Accordion-Ah Suzie (IRE) (King's Ride)
D B Feek (D M Grissell 5/5) R Winchester & Son

Placings:4F-0P45   (3171)
2003/04: 18^{9}G, 21^{5}PS, 16^{4}G, 16^{5}GS,

	Starts	1st	2nd	3rd	Win & Pl
Hurdles	2	0	0	0	0
Chases	2	0	0	0	215
Career Total	6	0	0	0	215

Going: Sf: 0-1 GS: 0-1 Gd: 0-2 GF: - Fm: 0-0
Distance: 2m/2m3: 0-3 2m4-2m7: 0-1 3m+: 0-0
Track: LH: 0-2 RH: 0-2 Tight: 0-4 Gall: 0-0
Aids: Bl: 0-0 Vi: 0-0 Tstrap: 0-0 Ckp: 0-0
Best Rating: 90 1/04 Folk 2m gd-sft Ch

Mysteri Dancer

108   **96**

6-y-o b g Rudimentary (USA)-Mystery Ship (Decoy Boy)
P J Hobbs Jack Joseph

Placings:244-F1   (1095)
2003/04: 16^{6}G, 16^{1}GF,

	Starts	1st	2nd	3rd	Win & Pl
Hurdles	2	1	0	0	3445
Career Total	5	1	0	0	4703
100 8/03 Strf 2m110y E(0-105)HHdl				G-F	£3445
				Total win prize-money	£3445

Going: Sf: 0-0 GS: 0-0 Gd: 0-1 GF: - Fm: 1-1
Distance: 2m/2m3: 1-2 2m4-2m7: 0-0 3m+: 0-0
Track: LH: 1-2 RH: 0-0 Tight: 1-2 Gall: 0-0
Aids: Bl: 0-0 Vi: 0-0 Tstrap: 0-0 Ckp: 0-0
Best Rating: 100 8/03 Strf 2m110y gd-fm Hdl

Plating-class hurdler; tends to take a keen hold; settled better when getting off the mark at Stratford in august 2003; best at around two miles; acts on a sound surface.

Mystery (GER)

85   **87**

6-y-o br g Java Gold (USA)-My Secret (USA) (Sabona (USA))
T R George P J Kennedy

Placings:6PP   (3328)
2003/04: 16^{6}G, 16^{6}PS, 19^{5}PS,

	Starts	1st	2nd	3rd	Win & Pl
Hurdles	3	0	0	0	0
Career Total	3	0	0	0	0

Going: Sf: 0-1 GS: 0-1 Gd: 0-1 GF: - Fm: 0-0
Distance: 2m/2m3: 0-3 2m4-2m7: 0-0 3m+: 0-0
Track: LH: 0-1 RH: 0-2 Tight: 0-0 Gall: 0-1

Aids: Bl: 0-0 Vi: 0-0 Tstrap: 0-1 Ckp: 0-0
Best Rating: 87 12/03 Leic 2m good Hdl

Mystic Forest

107   **87**

5-y-o b g Charnwood Forest (IRE)-Mystic Beauty (IRE) (Alzao (USA))
C J Mann (B J Meehan 17/5) Lee Bolingbroke & Partners II

Placings:F31   (0990)
2003/04: 20^{6}G, 19^{3}G, 22^{1}G,

	Starts	1st	2nd	3rd	Win & Pl
Hurdles	3	1	0	1	5594
Career Total	3	1	0	1	5594
87 7/03 NAbb 2m6f D Hdl				GD	£4784
				Total win prize-money	£4784

Going: Sf: 0-0 GS: 0-0 Gd: 1-3 GF: - Fm: 0-0
Distance: 2m/2m3: 0-0 2m4-2m7: 1-3 3m+: 0-0
Track: LH: 1-1 RH: 0-2 Tight: 1-2 Gall: 0-0
Aids: Bl: 0-0 Vi: 0-0 Tstrap: 0-0 Ckp: 0-0
Best Rating: 87 7/03 NAbb 2m6f good Hdl

Modest staying handicapper on the Flat; appreciated the longer trip when winning an uncompetitive 2m 6f maiden hurdle at Newton Abbot July 2003.

Mystic Glen

89   **69**

5-y-o b m Vettori (IRE)-Mystic Memory (Ela-Mana-Mou)
P D Niven Mrs J A Niven

Placings:0-40060   (4685)
2003/04: 16^{4}GF, 16^{9}GS, 16^{0}GF, 17^{6}G, 16^{0}G,

	Starts	1st	2nd	3rd	Win & Pl
NH Flat	2	0	0	0	0
Hurdles	3	0	0	0	0
Career Total	6	0	0	0	0

Going: Sf: 0-0 GS: 0-1 Gd: 0-2 GF: - Fm: 0-2
Distance: 2m/2m3: 0-5 2m4-2m7: 0-0 3m+: 0-0
Track: LH: 0-3 RH: 0-2 Tight: 0-3 Gall: 0-0
Aids: Bl: 0-0 Vi: 0-0 Tstrap: 0-0 Ckp: 0-0
Best Rating: 73 3/04 MRas 2m1f110y good Hdl

Better effort when modest fourth in weak bumper at Hexham in November on second start.

Mystic Hill

98   **73**

13-y-o b g Shirley Heights-Nuryana (Nureyev (USA))
J Joseph Jack Joseph

Placings:044121/4363031/212240/6/0/P06000/15003-2   (0479)
2003/04: 21^{2}GF,

	Starts	1st	2nd	3rd	Win & Pl
Hurdles	1	0	1	0	714
Career Total	33	5	5	4	17683
77 9/02 Strf 2m6f110yG(0-95)HHdl				G-F	£2338
114 6/98 NAbb 2m6f D(0-120)HHdl				GD	£2775
94 3/98 NAbb 2m1f F(0-100)HHdl				SFT	£1827
96 4/97 Extr 2m3f110yG(0-110)HHdl				G-F	£2528
79 4/97 Tntn 2m1f F Hdl				FRM	£2039
				Total win prize-money	£11509

Going: Sf: 0-0 GS: 0-0 Gd: 0-0 GF: - Fm: 0-1
Distance: 2m/2m3: 0-0 2m4-2m7: 0-1 3m+: 0-0
Track: LH: 0-0 RH: 0-1 Tight: 0-0 Gall: 0-1
Aids: Bl: 0-0 Vi: 0-0 Tstrap: 0-0 Ckp: 0-0
Best Rating: 114 6/98 NAbb 2m6f good Hdl

Plating-class hurdler; stays two and three-quarter miles; suited by fast ground.

Mystic Mayhem

5-y-o b m Danzig Connection (USA)-Mrs Meyrick (Owen Dudley)
R Bastiman Czech Mates

Placings:0   (0940)
2003/04: 17⁰GF,

	Starts	1st	2nd	3rd	Win & Pl
NH Flat	1	0	0	0	
Career Total	1	0	0	0	

Going:	Sf: 0-0 GS: 0-0 Gd: 0-0 GF: - Fm: 0-1
Distance:	2m2m3: 0-1 2m4-2m7: 0-0 3m+: 0-1
Track:	LH: 0-1 RH: 0-0 Tight: 0-1 Gall: 0-0
Aids:	Bl: 0-0 Vi: 0-0 Tstrap: 0-0 Ckp: 0-0

Mystic Native (IRE)
66

11-y-o ch g Be My Native (USA)-Mystic River (IRE) (Over The River (FR))
David Pearson David Pearson

Placings:00/0-33PP0   (4612)
2003/04: 24³GF, 24³GS, 20ᴾGY, 20ᴾG, 21⁰G,

	Starts	1st	2nd	3rd	Win & Pl
Hurdles	1	0	0	0	
Chases	4	0	0	2	1044
Career Total	8	0	0	2	1044

Going:	Sf: 0-1 GS: 0-1 Gd: 0-2 GF: - Fm: 0-1
Distance:	2m/2m3: 0-0 2m4-2m7: 0-3 3m+: 0-2
Track:	LH: 0-4 RH: 0-0 Tight: 0-2 Gall: 0-0
Aids:	Bl: 0-0 Vi: 0-0 Tstrap: 0-0 Ckp: 0-1
Best Rating:	66 11/03 Uttx 3m gd-fm Ch

Mystic Ridge
92(83h)   (71 h)79

10-y-o ch g Mystiko (USA)-Vallauris (Faustus (USA))
R Lee Osborne House Limited

Placings:P000/0/63/004-F3   (0303)
2003/04: 17ᶠS, 17³G,

	Starts	1st	2nd	3rd	Win & Pl
Chases	2	0	0	1	643
Career Total	12	0	0	2	1574

Going:	Sf: 0-1 GS: 0-0 Gd: 0-1 GF: - Fm: 0-0
Distance:	2m/2m3: 0-2 2m4-2m7: 0-0 3m+: 0-0
Track:	LH: 0-2 RH: 0-0 Tight: 0-2 Gall: 0-0
Aids:	Bl: 0-0 Vi: 0-0 Tstrap: 0-0 Ckp: 0-0
Best Rating:	85 5/01 Bang 2m1f110y good Ch

Plating-class maiden chaser; (DEAD)

Mythical King (IRE)
103   125

7-y-o b g Fairy King (USA)-Whatcombe (USA) (Alleged (USA))
R Lee Richard Edwards

Placings:312510-5056150   (4628)
2003/04: 16⁵G, 20⁰GS, 20⁵G, 16⁶GS, 20¹HY, 20⁵G, 20⁰G,

	Starts	1st	2nd	3rd	Win & Pl
Hurdles	7	1	0	0	26774
Career Total	**13**	**3**	**1**	**1**	**40312**
125	1/04	Asct	2m4f	B(0-140)HHdl	HVY £26100
125	3/03	Strf	2m110y	D(0-125)HHdl	G-S £8443
114	12/02	Uttx	2m	E Hdl	SFT £3395
				Total win prize-money £37939

Going:	Sf: 1-1 GS: 0-2 Gd: 0-4 GF: - Fm: 0-0
Distance:	2m/2m3: 0-2 **2m4-2m7: 1-5** 3m+: 0-0
Track:	LH: 0-4 RH: 1-3 Tight: 0-4 Gall: 0-0
Aids:	Bl: 0-0 Vi: 0-0 Tstrap: 0-0 Ckp: 0-0
Best Rating:	125 1/04 Asct 2m4f heavy Hdl

Fair hurdler; stays two and a half miles; acts on soft ground.

Mytimie (IRE)

9-y-o b g Be My Native (USA)-Snoqualmie (Warpath)
David Parker (J M Jefferson 27/10) Mr & Mrs Raymond Anderson Green

Placings:134/260/P13222P/21332-P34   (4949)
2003/04: 20ᴾG, 25³G, 26⁴GS,

	Starts	1st	2nd	3rd	Win & Pl
Hurdles	1	0	0	0	0
Chases	2	0	0	1	661
Career Total	**21**	**3**	**6**	**5**	**23486**
113	11/02	Carl	2m	D Ch	HVY £5206
104	10/01	Kels	2m110y	E Hdl	G-S £2439
114	11/99	Carl	2m1f	H NHF	SFT £1658
				Total win prize-money £9305

Going:	Sf: 0-0 GS: 0-1 Gd: 0-2 GF: - Fm: 0-0
Distance:	2m/2m3: 0-0 2m4-2m7: 0-1 3m+: 0-2
Track:	LH: 0-2 RH: 0-0 Tight: 0-2 Gall: 0-0
Aids:	Bl: 0-0 Vi: 0-0 Tstrap: 0-0 Ckp: 0-0
Best Rating:	114 11/99 Carl 2m1f soft NHF

Moderate chaser; appreciates cut in the ground; stays three miles.

Mytton's Quest (IRE)
92   66

4-y-o ch g Grand Lodge (USA)-Fleeting Quest (Rainbow Quest (USA))
Mrs L Williamson (A Bailey 30/6) Bangor-On-Dee Racing Club

Placings:606556   (1926)
2003/04: 17⁶G, 16³GF, 17⁵G, 16⁵GF, 17⁵G, 16⁶GF,

	Starts	1st	2nd	3rd	Win & Pl
Hurdles	6	0	0	0	0
Career Total	6	0	0	0	0

Going:	Sf: 0-0 GS: 0-0 Gd: 0-3 GF: - Fm: 0-3
Distance:	2m/2m3: 0-6 2m4-2m7: 0-0 3m+: 0-0
Track:	LH: 0-5 RH: 0-1 Tight: 0-3 Gall: 0-0
Aids:	Bl: 0-0 Vi: 0-0 Tstrap: 0-5 Ckp: 0-0
Best Rating:	66 11/03 Wwck 2m gd-fm Hdl

Nadderwater

12-y-o br g Arctic Lord-Flying Cherub (Osiris)
Mrs J G Retter Mrs J G Retter

Placings:P/PP/PP   (0941)
2003/04: 23ᴾGF, 20ᴾG,

	Starts	1st	2nd	3rd	Win & Pl
Hurdles	1	0	0	0	0

Chases	1 0 0 0 0
Career Total	**5 0 0 0**

Going:	Sf: 0-0 GS: 0-0 Gd: 0-1 GF: - Fm: 0-1
Distance:	2m/2m3: 0-0 2m4-2m7: 0-1 3m+: 0-1
Track:	LH: 0-2 RH: 0-0 Tight: 0-0 Gall: 0-0
Aids:	Bl: 0-0 Vi: 0-0 Tstrap: 0-0 Ckp: 0-0

Nadeema (FR)

6-y-o gr m Linamix (FR)-Nabagha (FR) (Fabulous Dancer (USA))
B N Pollock S G B Morrison

Placings:P/0P-P   (3877)
2003/04: 16ᴾS,

	Starts	1st	2nd	3rd	Win & Pl
Hurdles	1	0	0	0	
Career Total	4	0	0	0	

Going:	Sf: 0-1 GS: 0-0 Gd: 0-0 GF: - Fm: 0-0
Distance:	2m/2m3: 0-1 2m4-2m7: 0-0 3m+: 0-0
Track:	LH: 0-0 RH: 0-1 Tight: 0-0 Gall: 0-0
Aids:	Bl: 0-0 Vi: 0-0 Tstrap: 0-0 Ckp: 0-0

Nafsika (USA)
88   74

4-y-o b f Sky Classic (CAN)-Exotic Beauty (USA) (Java Gold (USA))
R C Harper (N J Henderson 2/11) R C Harper

Placings:2PPP0P   (4159)
2003/04: 16²GF, 16ᴾGF, 16ᴾHY, 16ᴾG, 19⁰GS, 19ᴾG,

	Starts	1st	2nd	3rd	Win & Pl
Hurdles	6	0	1	0	839
Career Total	6	0	1	0	839

Going:	Sf: 0-1 GS: 0-1 Gd: 0-2 GF: - Fm: 0-2
Distance:	2m/2m3: 0-4 2m4-2m7: 0-2 3m+: 0-0
Track:	LH: 0-1 RH: 0-5 Tight: 0-0 Gall: 0-1
Aids:	Bl: 0-0 Vi: 0-0 Tstrap: 0-0 Ckp: 0-0
Best Rating:	74 10/03 Ludl 2m gd-fm Hdl

Nagano (FR)
93   85+

6-y-o b g Hero's Honor (USA)-Sadinskaya (FR) (Niniski (USA))
Ian Williams Allan Stennett & Terry Warner

Placings:3F206-6   (2289)
2003/04: 20⁶G,

	Starts	1st	2nd	3rd	Win & Pl
Hurdles	1	0	0	0	0
Career Total	6	0	1	1	8737

Going:	Sf: 0-0 GS: 0-0 Gd: 0-1 GF: - Fm: 0-0
Distance:	2m/2m3: 0-0 2m4-2m7: 0-1 3m+: 0-0
Track:	LH: 0-1 RH: 0-0 Tight: 0-1 Gall: 0-0
Aids:	Bl: 0-0 Vi: 0-0 Tstrap: 0-0 Ckp: 0-0
Best Rating:	85 11/03 Aint 2m4f good Hdl

Nahthen Lad (IRE)

15-y-o b g Good Thyne (USA)-Current Call (Electrify)
J A Danahar J A Danahar

Placings:4/1P311606/121121/6P2P0/33P6F4/52P30P/13/P
320/P0-F   (4344)
2003/04: 26FGS,

	Starts	1st	2nd	3rd	Win & Pl
Chases	1	0	0	0	
Career Total	41	8	5	6	122505
139	10/99 Asct	3m110y B HCh		GD	£8486
157	3/96 Chel	3m110y A Ch		G-S	£54672
139	1/96 Hayd	2m4f D Ch		SFT	£3779
127	1/96 Wwck	2m4f110yD Ch		G-S	£4074
124	11/95 Chel	2m5f C(0-130)HHdl		GD	£2827
113	2/95 Hntg	2m5f110yC Hdl		G-S	£7230
113	1/95 Hayd	2m4f E Hdl		HVY	£2472
103	10/94 Towc	2m Hdl		GD	£2075

Total win prize-money £85617

Going: Sf: 0-0 GS: 0-1 Gd: 0-0 GF: - Fm: 0-0
Distance: 2m/2m3: 0-0 2m4-2m7: 0-0 3m+: 0-1
Track: LH: 0-1 RH: 0-0 Tight: 0-0 Gall: 0-0
Aids: Bl: 0-0 Vi: 0-1 Tstrap: 0-0 Ckp: 0-0
Best Rating: 157 3/96 Chel 3m110y gd-sft Ch

Nailbiter
84

5-y-o b g Night Shift (USA)-Scylla (Rock City)
Mrs A Duffield Middleham Park Racing Xvi

Placings:503F5325-P   (0445)
2003/04: 16PG,

	Starts	1st	2nd	3rd	Win & Pl
Hurdles	1	0	0	0	
Career Total	9	0	1	2	1813

Going: Sf: 0-0 GS: 0-0 Gd: 0-1 GF: - Fm: 0-0
Distance: 2m/2m3: 0-1 2m4-2m7: 0-0 3m+: 0-0
Track: LH: 0-0 RH: 0-1 Tight: 0-0 Gall: 0-1
Aids: Bl: 0-0 Vi: 0-0 Tstrap: 0-1 Ckp: 0-0
Best Rating: 84 3/03 Weth 2m gd-fm Hdl

Naked Flame
54f   17f

5-y-o b g Blushing Flame (USA)-Final Attraction (Jalmood (USA))
A G Blackmore A G Blackmore

Placings:00   (4934)
2003/04: 16FGS, 18FG,

	Starts	1st	2nd	3rd	Win & Pl
NH Flat	2	0	0	0	
Career Total	2	0	0	0	

Going: Sf: 0-0 GS: 0-1 Gd: 0-1 GF: - Fm: 0-0
Distance: 2m/2m3: 0-2 2m4-2m7: 0-0 3m+: 0-0
Track: LH: 0-1 RH: 0-1 Tight: 0-1 Gall: 0-0
Aids: Bl: 0-0 Vi: 0-0 Tstrap: 0-0 Ckp: 0-0
Best Rating: 17 3/04 Asct 2m110y gd-sft NHF

Naked Oat
101   81

9-y-o b g Imp Society (USA)-Bajina (Dancing Brave (USA))
Mrs L Wadham The Dyball Partnership

Placings:0/0533   (4774)
2003/04: 16QG, 16SGS, 17QG, 16QG,

	Starts	1st	2nd	3rd	Win & Pl
Hurdles	4	0	0	2	740
Career Total	5	0	0	2	740

Going: Sf: 0-0 GS: 0-1 Gd: 0-3 GF: - Fm: 0-0
Distance: 2m/2m3: 0-4 2m4-2m7: 0-0 3m+: 0-0
Track: LH: 0-3 RH: 0-1 Tight: 0-4 Gall: 0-0
Aids: Bl: 0-0 Vi: 0-0 Tstrap: 0-0 Ckp: 0-0
Best Rating: 81 4/04 Fknm 2m good Hdl

Nameless Wonder (IRE)
100   96

8-y-o b g Supreme Leader-Miss Kylogue (IRE) (Lancastrian)
J Howard Johnson (N J Henderson 15/5) Group Captain J A Prideaux

Placings:600/0043-03   (3326)
2003/04: 21QGF, 21SGS,

	Starts	1st	2nd	3rd	Win & Pl
Hurdles	2	0	0	1	650
Career Total	9	0	0	2	1036

Going: Sf: 0-0 GS: 1-0 Gd: 0-0 GF: - Fm: 0-1
Distance: 2m/2m3: 0-0 2m4-2m7: 0-2 3m+: 0-1
Track: LH: 0-1 RH: 0-1 Tight: 0-1 Gall: 0-0
Aids: Bl: 0-0 Vi: 0-1 Tstrap: 0-0 Ckp: 0-0
Best Rating: 102 3/02 Newb 2m5f soft Hdl

Fair novice hurdler; suited by distances of around two and a half miles; has worn blinkers.

Nandoo
98   95+

5-y-o b m Forzando-Ascend (IRE) (Glint Of Gold)
A G Juckes (M D Hammond 15/10) Mrs K C Price

Placings:121P   (1844)
2003/04: 21¹GF, 21²G, 20¹F, 16PG,

	Starts	1st	2nd	3rd	Win & Pl
Hurdles	4	2	1	0	7499
Career Total	4	2	1	0	7499
95	10/03 Weth	2m4f110yD Hdl		FRM	£4257
89	9/03 Sedg	2m5f110yE Hdl		G-F	£2541

Total win prize-money £6799

Going: Sf: 0-0 GS: 0-0 Gd: 0-2 GF: - Fm: 2-2
Distance: 2m/2m3: 0-1 2m4-2m7: 2-3 3m+: 0-0
Track: LH: 2-4 RH: 0-0 Tight: 1-3 Gall: 0-0
Aids: Bl: 0-0 Vi: 0-0 Tstrap: 0-0 Ckp: 2-4
Best Rating: 95 10/03 Weth 2m4f110y firm Hdl

Plating-class maiden on the Flat; winner of two modest events over hurdles; stays two miles five; acts on fast ground; wears cheekpieces.

Narwhal (IRE)
105   127

6-y-o b/br g Naheez (USA)-Well Why (IRE) (The Parson)
N J Gifford Mrs S N J Embiricos

Placings:2/3-1312P   (4449)
2003/04: 20¹G, 18³HY, 20¹S, 21²G, 20PGS,

	Starts	1st	2nd	3rd	Win & Pl
Hurdles	5	2	1	1	15518
Career Total	7	2	2	2	16914
117	2/04 Sand	2m4f110yD(0-120)HHdl		SFT	£5759
113	12/03 Font	2m4f E Hdl		GD	£2611

Total win prize-money £8370

Going: Sf: 1-2 GS: 0-1 Gd: 1-2 GF: - Fm: 0-0
Distance: 2m/2m3: 0-1 2m4-2m7: 2-4 3m+: 0-0
Track: LH: 0-1 RH: 1-3 Tight: 1-2 Gall: 0-0
Aids: Bl: 0-0 Vi: 0-0 Tstrap: 0-0 Ckp: 0-0
Best Rating: 127 2/04 Kemp 2m5f good Hdl

Fair handicap hurdler; stays 2m4f; best on good to soft.

Nas Na Riogh (IRE)
98(111c)   (114+c) 131

5-y-o b m King's Theatre (IRE)-Abstraite (Groom Dancer (USA))
N J Henderson Brian Twojohns Partnership

Placings:212211F-033   (3722)
2003/04: 16QGY, 17QG, 16QS,

	Starts	1st	2nd	3rd	Win & Pl
Hurdles	2	0	0	1	1052
Chases	1	0	0	1	1650
Career Total	10	3	3	3	35142
112	3/03 Font	2m2f110yE Hdl		SFT	£3367
131	12/02 Chep	2m110y A Hdl		HVY	£21420
115	11/02 Sand	2m110y D Hdl		SFT	£4251

Total win prize-money £29038

Going: Sf: 0-1 GS: 0-0 Gd: 0-1 GF: - Fm: 0-0
Distance: 2m/2m3: 0-3 2m4-2m7: 0-0 3m+: 0-0
Track: LH: 0-1 RH: 0-2 Tight: 0-0 Gall: 0-0
Aids: Bl: 0-0 Vi: 0-0 Tstrap: 0-0 Ckp: 0-0
Best Rating: 131 12/02 Chep 2m110y heavy Hdl

Useful hurdler; won three times as a juvenile; showed promise on only start over fences at Exeter; disappointing back over hurdles next time; suited by forcing tactics and effective in testing ground; has shown her best form at around two miles.

Nashville Star (USA)

13-y-o ch g Star De Naskra (USA)-Mary Davies (Tyrnavos)
Miss C Herrington Robin Mathew

Placings:211340P10/6P5/4054010660/34331424363/5023045/P00/0P6/650/PP-02 (4487)
2003/04: 20QG, 20²G,

	Starts	1st	2nd	3rd	Win & Pl
Chases	2	0	1	0	426
Career Total	53	5	4	7	29011
95	12/97 Wind	2m D(0-125)HCh		GD	£4232
102	2/97 Bang	2m1f E(0-110)HHdl		GD	£3517
104	3/95 Newb	2m110y B HHdl		GD	£5994
91	10/94 Newc	2m110y Hdl		FRM	£2232
90	10/94 Carl	2m1f Hdl		GD	£1927

Total win prize-money £17905

Going: Sf: 0-0 GS: 0-0 Gd: 0-0 GF: - Fm: 0-0
Distance: 2m/2m3: 0-0 2m4-2m7: 0-2 3m+: 0-0
Track: LH: 0-0 RH: 0-1 Tight: 0-1 Gall: 0-0
Aids: Bl: 0-0 Vi: 0-2 Tstrap: 0-0 Ckp: 0-0
Best Rating: 122 3/98 Chel 2m110y good Ch

Nat Gold
98   95

8-y-o b g Push On-April Airs (Grey Mirage)
Mrs D A Hamer E L Harries

Placings:4P-1   (0563)

2003/04: 24¹GF,

	Starts	1st	2nd	3rd	Win & Pl
Hurdles	1	1	0	0	3017
Career Total	3	1	0	0	3017
95	6/03	Uttx	3m110y	F Hdl		G-F £3017

Total win prize-money £3017

Going:	Sf: 0-0 GS: 0-0 Gd: 0-0 GF: - Fm: 1-1
Distance:	2m/2m3: 0-0 2m4-2m7: 0-0 3m+: 1-1
Track:	LH: 1-1 RH: 0-0 Tight: 0-0 Gall: 0-0
Aids:	Bl: 0-0 Vi: 0-0 Tstrap: 0-0 Ckp: 0-0
Best Rating:	95 6/03 Uttx 3m110y gd-fm Hdl

Runner-up in two points; wide margin winner of a poor novices' hurdle at Uttoxeter in June 2003 but looked to finish lame; stays well; acts on fast ground.

Nathos (GER)
106　　　　　　121

7-y-o b g Zaizoom (USA)-Nathania (GER) (Athenagoras (GER))
C J Mann John Davies & John Trickett

Placings: 211242410　　　　　　　　(4628)
2003/04: 20²GF, 16¹GS, 16¹GS, 19²G, 16⁴S, 16²G, 21⁴G, 16¹GS, 20⁰G,

	Starts	1st	2nd	3rd	Win & Pl
Hurdles	9	3	3	0	17894
Career Total	9	3	3	0	17894
119	3/04	Plum	2m	D Hdl		G-S £5018
121	12/03	Sand	2m110y	D(0-110)HHdl		G-S £4888
121	11/03	Uttx	2m	E Hdl		G-S £2674

Total win prize-money £12580

Going:	Sf: 0-1 GS: 3-3 Gd: 0-4 GF: - Fm: 0-1
Distance:	2m/2m3: 3-6 2m4-2m7: 0-3 3m+: 0-0
Track:	LH: 2-3 RH: 1-5 Tight: 1-3 Gall: 0-0
Aids:	Bl: 0-0 Vi: 0-0 Tstrap: 0-0 Ckp: 0-0
Best Rating:	121 2/04 Kemp 2m5f good Hdl

Fair novice hurdler; ex-German Flat winner; effective over two miles; acts on easy ground; tough.

Natiain

5-y-o ch g Danzig Connection (USA)-Fen Princess (IRE) (Trojan Fen)
W S Coltherd Mrs June Brown

Placings: P　　　　　　　　　　　(4731)
2003/04: 20⁰G,

	Starts	1st	2nd	3rd	Win & Pl
Hurdles	1	0	0	0	
Career Total	1	0	0	0	

Going:	Sf: 0-0 GS: 0-0 Gd: 0-1 GF: - Fm: 0-0
Distance:	2m/2m3: 0-0 2m4-2m7: 0-1 3m+: 0-0
Track:	LH: 0-0 RH: 0-1 Tight: 0-0 Gall: 0-0
Aids:	Bl: 0-0 Vi: 0-0 Tstrap: 0-0 Ckp: 0-0

Native Alibi (IRE)

7-y-o b g Be My Native (USA)-Perfect Excuse (Certingo)
Mrs S H Shirley-Beavan Mrs S H Shirley-Beavan

Placings: 5U5-3　　　　　　　　　(4687)
2003/04: 25³G,

	Starts	1st	2nd	3rd	Win & Pl
Chases	1	0	0	1	323
Career Total	4	0	0	1	323

Going:	Sf: 0-0 GS: 0-0 Gd: 0-1 GF: - Fm: 0-0
Distance:	2m/2m3: 0-0 2m4-2m7: 0-1 3m+: 0-0
Track:	LH: 0-0 RH: 0-1 Tight: 0-1 Gall: 0-0
Aids:	Bl: 0-0 Vi: 0-0 Tstrap: 0-0 Ckp: 0-0
Best Rating:	82 2/03 Sedg 3m3f heavy Ch

Consistent pointer; form in hunter chases at around three miles.

Native Beat (IRE)
109　　　　　　(113h)114

9-y-o b g Be My Native (USA)-Deeprunonthepound (IRE) (Deep Run)
J R H Fowler Miss Daisy Duggan

Placings: 06/00231640/640044610/055466031-303310U
　　　　　　　　　　　　　　　　　(4640)
2003/04: 24¹GY, 19³GY, 18⁰GY, 20³S, 25³S, 22¹S, 21⁰G, 21ᵁG,

	Starts	1st	2nd	3rd	Win & Pl
Chases	8	2	0	3	18502
Career Total	35	4	1	5	38460
116	2/04	Punc	2m6f	(0-123)HCh	SFT	£9002
113	4/03	Punc	3m	Ch	G-Y	£7168
113	3/02	Fair	2m4f	Ch	G-Y	£9312
109	2/01	Gowr	2m	Hdl	HVY	£5564

Total win prize-money £31049

Going:	Sf: 1-3 GS: 0-0 Gd: 0-2 GF: - Fm: 0-0
Distance:	2m/2m3: 0-2 2m4-2m7: 1-4 3m+: 1-2
Track:	LH: 0-4 RH: 1-3 Tight: 0-1 Gall: 0-0
Aids:	Bl: 0-0 Vi: 0-0 Tstrap: 0-0 Ckp: 0-0
Best Rating:	117 12/02 Punc 2m4f sft-hvy Ch

Modest Irish chaser; stays three miles; likes soft ground.

Native Buck (IRE)
(92h)　　　　　　(78h)123

11-y-o ch g Be My Native (USA)-Buckskins Chat (Buckskin (FR))
M F Harris (T R George 7/2) Mrs D J Brown

Placings: 00/063212/22P/1411P/2P16-PP50　(4870)
2003/04: 26³PG, 28³PG, 23⁵S, 24⁰GS,

	Starts	1st	2nd	3rd	Win & Pl
Hurdles	2	0	0	0	0
Chases	2	0	0	0	0
Career Total	24	5	5	1	41817
123	2/03	Catt	3m6f	C(0-130)HCh	GD	£10276
123	2/02	Uttx	3m2f	B HCh	HVY	£10976
116	12/01	Hayd	3m	D(0-110)HCh	HVY	£4114
109	11/01	Uttx	2m5f	F(0-110)HCh	SFT	£3532
91	12/98	Uttx	3m110y	E(0-100)HHdl	SFT	£2431

Total win prize-money £31333

Going:	Sf: 0-1 GS: 0-1 Gd: 0-2 GF: - Fm: 0-0
Distance:	2m/2m3: 0-0 2m4-2m7: 0-1 3m+: 0-3
Track:	LH: 0-3 RH: 0-0 Tight: 0-1 Gall: 0-1
Aids:	Bl: 0-1 Vi: 0-0 Tstrap: 0-0 Ckp: 0-0
Best Rating:	123 2/03 Catt 3m6f good Ch

Fair staying chaser, gets three and a quarter miles and is especially well suited to testing conditions; has worn blinkers.

Native Cove (IRE)

12-y-o b g Be My Native (USA)-Down All The Coves (Athenius)
E Haddock Miss H M Newell

Placings: P/2/F0PP/P3025/P2-P　　　(0029)
2003/04: 26⁰PG,

	Starts	1st	2nd	3rd	Win & Pl
Chases	1	0	0	0	
Career Total	14	0	3	1	2952

Going:	Sf: 0-0 GS: 0-0 Gd: 0-1 GF: - Fm: 0-0
Distance:	2m/2m3: 0-0 2m4-2m7: 0-0 3m+: 0-1
Track:	LH: 0-1 RH: 0-0 Tight: 0-0 Gall: 0-1
Aids:	Bl: 0-0 Vi: 0-0 Tstrap: 0-0 Ckp: 0-0
Best Rating:	101 4/00 Ludl 3m good Ch

Modest hunter chaser, stays well.

Native Cunning
104　　　　　　76

6-y-o b g Be My Native (USA)-Icy Miss (Random Shot)
R H Buckler Nick Elliott

Placings: 000-45004165　　　　　(4749)
2003/04: 16⁴GF, 24⁵G, 22⁰GS, 21⁰G, 22⁴GS, 25¹GS, 26⁶G, 25⁵G,

	Starts	1st	2nd	3rd	Win & Pl
NH Flat	1	0	0	0	
Hurdles	7	1	0	0	2639
Career Total	11	1	0	0	2639
76	3/04	Plum	3m1f110yF(0-95)HHdl		G-S	£2639

Total win prize-money £2639

Going:	Sf: 0-0 GS: 1-3 Gd: 0-4 GF: - Fm: 0-1
Distance:	2m/2m3: 0-1 2m4-2m7: 0-0 3m+: 1-4
Track:	LH: 0-1 RH: 0-5 Tight: 0-2 Gall: 0-0
Aids:	Bl: 0-0 Vi: 0-0 Tstrap: 0-0 Ckp: 0-0
Best Rating:	87 11/03 Winc 2m gd-fm NHF

Native Daisy (IRE)
89　　　　　　56

9-y-o b m Be My Native (USA)-Castleblagh (General Ironside)
K J Burke K Burke

Placings: 00/0/0U-45000064　　　(4538)
2003/04: 25⁴G, 24⁵G, 24⁰F, 23⁰F, 25⁰F, 28⁰YS, 24⁶G, 24⁴GS,

	Starts	1st	2nd	3rd	Win & Pl
Chases	8	0	0	0	846
Career Total	12	0	0	0	846

Going:	Sf: 0-0 GS: 0-1 Gd: 0-3 GF: - Fm: 0-3
Distance:	2m/2m3: 0-0 2m4-2m7: 0-1 3m+: 0-7
Track:	LH: 0-0 RH: 0-3 Tight: 0-1 Gall: 0-0
Aids:	Bl: 0-0 Vi: 0-0 Tstrap: 0-0 Ckp: 0-1
Best Rating:	98 4/00 Asct 2m110y soft NHF

Native Eire (IRE)
102　　　　　　88+

10-y-o b g Be My Native (USA)-Ballyline Dancer (Giolla Mear)
N Wilson Mrs N C Wilson

Placings: 0/065B/0F5051/0B3-6P11P　(4730)
2003/04: 20⁶G, 20⁰G, 20¹G, 21¹GS, 20⁰G,

	Starts	1st	2nd	3rd	Win & Pl
Hurdles	1	0	0	0	0
Chases	4	2	0	0	6071
Career Total	19	3	0	1	9470
92	1/04	Sedg	2m5f	F(0-95)HCh	G-S	£3432
74	11/03	Weth	2m4f110yG(0-90)HCh	GD	£2639
98	3/02	Sedg	2m5f110yE Hdl	SFT	£2569

Total win prize-money £8640

Going:	Sf: 0-0 GS: 1-1 Gd: 1-4 GF: - Fm: 0-0
Distance:	2m/2m3: 0-0 2m4-2m7: 2-5 3m+: 0-0

Track: LH: 2-3 RH: 0-2 Tight: 1-1 Gall: 0-0
Aids: Bl: 0-0 Vi: 0-0 Tstrap: 0-0 Ckp: 0-0
Best Rating: 98 3/02 Sedg 2m5f110y soft Hdl

Plating-class chaser; took a selling handicap chase at Wetherby in November; successful again in better company at Sedgefield in January; stays two and a half miles plus; handles soft.

Native Emperor

116(112h)   (158h)147+
8-y-o br g Be My Native (USA)-Fiona's Blue (Crash Course)
Jonjo O'Neill J C, J R And S R Hitchins

Placings: 55/13145P/012114/123P-22121P   (4861)
2003/04: 24²GS, 24²S, 24¹GS, 25²S, 32¹G, 33³GS

	Starts	1st	2nd	3rd	Win & Pl
Chases	6	2	3	0	55164
Career Total	24	8	5	2	132849
147	3/04	Chel	4m	B Ch		GD	£29000
118	12/03	Strf	3m	D Ch		G-S	£5264
143	11/02	Chel	3m1f110yA HHdl			G-S	£31175
139	2/02	Uttx	2m6f110yC(0-135)HHdl		HVY	£10504
132	1/02	Wwck	3m1f	D(0-125)HHdl		HVY	£3688
114	12/01	NAbb	3m1f	D(0-125)HHdl		HVY	£5382
123	11/00	Asct	2m4f	C Hdl		SFT	£4862
100	10/00	Strf	2m6f110yD Hdl			HVY	£2219
				Total win prize-money £93165			

Going: Sf: 0-2 GS: 1-3 Gd: 1-1 GF: - Fm: 0-0
Distance: 2m/2m3: 0-0 2m4-2m7: 0-0 **3m+: 2-6**
Track: LH: 2-6 RH: 0-0 Tight: 1-2 Gall: 1-2
Aids: Bl: 0-0 Vi: 0-0 Tstrap: 0-0 Ckp: 0-0
Best Rating: 157 11/02 Newb 3m110y soft Hdl

Smart staying hurdler; promising novice chaser; lucky winner of 3m novice chase at Stratford in December 2003, but no fluke about his victory in the 4m National Hunt Chase at the 2004 Festival; looks a stayer and prefers testing conditions.

Native Glen (IRE)

10-y-o b g Be My Native (USA)-The Gargle Monster (Furry Glen)
S Lloyd J Huckle

Placings: 000550/0140P/000P/00PP/U-F   (0224)
2003/04: 16⁶FG,

	Starts	1st	2nd	3rd	Win & Pl
Chases	1	0	0	0	
Career Total	21	1	0	0	3295
90	9/99	Gowr	2m	Hdl		Y-S	£3080
				Total win prize-money £3080			

Going: Sf: 0-0 GS: 0-0 Gd: 0-1 GF: - Fm: 0-0
Distance: 2m/2m3: 0-1 2m4-2m7: 0-0 3m+: 0-0
Track: LH: 0-1 RH: 0-0 Tight: 0-0 Gall: 0-0
Aids: Bl: 0-0 Vi: 0-0 Tstrap: 0-0 Ckp: 0-0
Best Rating: 90 9/99 Gowr 2m yld-sft Hdl

Native Ivy (IRE)

103   112+
6-y-o b g Be My Native (USA)-Outdoor Ivy (Deep Run)
C Tinkler (A J Lidderdale 3/5) George Ward

Placings: 1331   (4445)
2003/04: 16¹S, 20³GS, 20³GS, 25¹S,

	Starts	1st	2nd	3rd	Win & Pl
NH Flat	1	1	0	0	2219
Hurdles	3	1	0	2	4800
Career Total	4	2	0	2	7019

---

112 3/04 Wwck 3m1f E Hdl SFT £3808
112 5/03 Uttx 2m H NHF SFT £2219
Total win prize-money £6027

Going: Sf: 2-2 GS: 0-2 Gd: 0-0 GF: - Fm: 0-0
Distance: 2m/2m3: 1-1 2m4-2m7: 0-2 3m+: 1-1
Track: LH: 2-3 RH: 0-1 Tight: 0-1 Gall: 0-0
Aids: Bl: 0-0 Vi: 0-0 Tstrap: 0-0 Ckp: 0-0
Best Rating: 112 3/04 Wwck 3m1f soft Hdl

Modest hurdler; successful in bumper on debut at Uttoxeter in April 2003; built on some promising efforts to win 3m 1f novices hurdle at Warwick March 2004; looks a staying chasing in the making; acts on soft ground.

Native Legend (IRE)

(104h)   (108+h)
9-y-o b g Be My Native (USA)-Tickhill (General Assembly (USA))
Ferdy Murphy J D Gordon

Placings: 0/35041/4/F21-F43   (4728)
2003/04: 24⁵S, 20⁴HY, 24³G,

	Starts	1st	2nd	3rd	Win & Pl
Chases	3	0	0	1	1426
Career Total	13	2	1	2	9368
108	1/03	Ayr	3m110y	F(0-100)HHdl		HVY	£2996
93	2/00	Muss	2m4f	D Hdl		GD	£2925
				Total win prize-money £5921			

Going: Sf: 0-2 GS: 0-0 Gd: 0-1 GF: - Fm: 0-0
Distance: 2m/2m3: 0-0 2m4-2m7: 0-1 3m+: 0-2
Track: LH: 0-1 RH: 0-0 Tight: 0-0 Gall: 0-2
Aids: Bl: 0-1 Vi: 0-0 Tstrap: 0-0 Ckp: 0-0
Best Rating: 108 1/03 Ayr 3m110y heavy Hdl

Lightly-raced hurdler; stays three miles plus, acts on a soft surface.

Native New Yorker (IRE)

134+
9-y-o b g Be My Native (USA)-Sunbath (Krayyan)
R Rowe Ann & John Symes

Placings: 1200/1/F1F01P-0   (4963)
2003/04: 20⁰G,

	Starts	1st	2nd	3rd	Win & Pl
Hurdles	1	0	0	0	
Career Total	12	4	1	0	23511
136	1/03	Chel	2m1f	B(0-145)HHdl		G-S	£13108
128	10/02	Strf	2m3f	C(0-135)HHdl		GD	£7020
112	10/01	Font	2m2f110yE Hdl		SFT	£2460
				Total win prize-money £22589			

Going: Sf: 0-0 GS: 0-0 Gd: 0-1 GF: - Fm: 0-0
Distance: 2m/2m3: 0-0 2m4-2m7: 0-1 3m+: 0-0
Track: LH: 0-0 RH: 0-1 Tight: 0-0 Gall: 0-0
Aids: Bl: 0-0 Vi: 0-0 Tstrap: 0-0 Ckp: 0-0
Best Rating: 136 1/03 Chel 2m1f gd-sft Hdl

Useful handicap hurdler; lightly raced; stays two miles three; acts on most types of ground.

Native Peach (IRE)

80   (117h)74
9-y-o ch g Be My Native (USA)-Larry's Peach (Laurence O)
J A B Old W E Sturt

Placings: 0/1366/5-6   (3270)
2003/04: 24⁶GS,

	Starts	1st	2nd	3rd	Win & Pl
Chases	1	0	0	0	0
Career Total	7	1	0	1	3920
96	5/01	Wwck	3m1f	E Hdl		GD	£2824
				Total win prize-money £2825			

Going: Sf: 0-0 GS: 0-1 Gd: 0-0 GF: - Fm: 0-0
Distance: 2m/2m3: 0-0 2m4-2m7: 0-0 3m+: 0-1
Track: LH: 0-0 RH: 0-1 Tight: 0-0 Gall: 0-0
Aids: Bl: 0-0 Vi: 0-0 Tstrap: 0-0 Ckp: 0-0
Best Rating: 117 10/01 Chel 3m1f110y good Hdl

Plating-class hurdler/chaser; stays three miles; effective on good ground.

Native Performance (IRE)

105   (109h)123
9-y-o b g Be My Native (USA)-Noon Performance (Strong Gale)
Michael Hourigan Donal O'Connor

Placings: 305/0000.30P65/6P142F2452P1/560632364-2000362110200P   (4805a)
2003/04: 25⁴GY, 24²G, 24⁵GY, 25⁰F, 23⁰G, 24³G, 16⁶GF, 24²F, 20¹F, 24¹G, 24⁰GF, 20²GF, 26⁹GS, 22⁹S, 29⁰FY,

	Starts	1st	2nd	3rd	Win & Pl
Hurdles	5	1	1	1	10045
Chases	10	1	2	0	66516
Career Total	47	4	7	5	112141
123	9/03	List	3m	HCh		GD	£58685
106	9/03	Punc	2m4f	(88-130)HHdl		FRM	£7840
110	4/02	Cork	2m4f	(0-116)HCh		Y-S	£9969
97	6/01	Dpat	2m6f	Ch		FRM	£4451
				Total win prize-money £80947			

Going: Sf: 0-1 GS: 0-1 Gd: 1-4 GF: - Fm: 1-6
Distance: 2m/2m3: 0-1 2m4-2m7: 1-4 3m+: 1-10
Track: LH: 1-2 RH: 1-5 Tight: 0-0 Gall: 0-1
Aids: Bl: 0-0 Vi: 0-0 Tstrap: 0-0 Ckp: 0-0
Best Rating: 123 9/03 List 3m good Ch

Modest handicap hurdler/chaser; successful between two and a half miles and two miles six, but stays three miles; best on a sound surface.

Native Scout (IRE)

119   (146h)156
8-y-o b g Be My Native (USA)-Carmels Castle (Deep Run)
Donal Hassett N F Glynn

Placings: 32002/1301121264/1FP120-2124124   (4769a)
2003/04: 17²Y, 17¹S, 17²S, 16⁴GS, 16¹HY, 16²Y, 17⁴Y,

	Starts	1st	2nd	3rd	Win & Pl
Chases	7	2	3	0	52091
Career Total	28	8	8	2	118571
156	2/04	Punc	2m	Ch		HVY	£18309
146	11/03	Fair	2m1f	(0-135)HCh		SFT	£8441
141	12/02	Uttx	2m	D Ch		SFT	£5408
132	10/02	Wxfd	2m	Ch		Y-S	£4868
130	12/01	Limk	2m	Hdl		SFT	£8346
120	11/01	Clon	2m	Hdl		YLD	£6120
120	10/01	Gway	2m	Hdl		SH	£5286
113	5/01	Klny	2m1f	NHF		GD	£4173
				Total win prize-money £60955			

Going: Sf: 2-3 GS: 0-1 Gd: 0-0 GF: - Fm: 0-0
Distance: **2m/2m3: 2-7** 2m4-2m7: 0-0 3m+: 0-0
Track: LH: 0-2 RH: 2-4 Tight: 0-0 Gall: 0-0
Aids: Bl: 0-0 Vi: 0-0 **Tstrap: 2-7** Ckp: 0-0
Best Rating: 156 2/04 Punc 2m heavy Ch

Smart Irish-trained chaser; best at two miles; acts well in soft ground; wears a tongue tie.

Native Speaker (IRE)

124

11-y-o ch g Be My Native (USA)-My Wonder (Deep Run)
P R Webber J Dougall

Placings: *13*/35/**13P53/1PP/3-P** (4606)
2003/04: 20PGS,

	Starts	1st	2nd	3rd	Win & Pl
Chases	1	0	0	0	
Career Total	14	3	0	5	16218
124	2/02	Winc	2m5f	D(0-120)HCh	G-S	£7215
126	11/99	MRas	2m4f	D Ch	G-S	£4221
109	3/98	Newb	2m110y	H NHF	G-S	£1411
				Total win prize-money		£12847

Going:	Sf: 0-0 GS: 0-1 Gd: 0-0 GF: - Fm: 0-0
Distance:	2m/2m3: 0-0 2m4-2m7: 0-1 3m+: 0-0
Track:	LH: 0-0 RH: 0-1 Tight: 0-1 Gall: 0-0
Aids:	Bl: 0-0 Vi: 0-0 Tstrap: 0-0 Ckp: 0-0
Best Rating:	126 12/99 Sand 2m4f110y good Ch

Native Star (IRE)

6-y-o b g Be My Native (USA)-Star Chamber (FR) (Tower Walk)
P J Hobbs M J Tuckey

Placings: *461*-P (2264)
2003/04: 22PGF,

	Starts	1st	2nd	3rd	Win & Pl
Hurdles	1	0	0	0	
Career Total	4	1	0	0	3575
96	4/03	Ayr	2m	H NHF	GD	£3575
				Total win prize-money		£3575

Going:	Sf: 0-0 GS: 0-0 Gd: 0-0 GF: - Fm: 0-1
Distance:	2m/2m3: 0-0 2m4-2m7: 0-0 3m+: 0-0
Track:	LH: 0-0 RH: 0-1 Tight: 0-0 Gall: 0-0
Aids:	Bl: 0-0 Vi: 0-0 Tstrap: 0-0 Ckp: 0-0
Best Rating:	96 4/03 Ayr 2m good NHF

Bumper performer; got his head in front on his third start in an ordinary event at Ayr; effective on good ground.

Native Thunder (IRE)

9-y-o b g Be My Native (USA)-Huntstown Gale (IRE) (Strong Gale)
Geoffrey Deacon Mrs Sandra A Roe

Placings: *5*/645/P (0073)
2003/04: 24PS,

	Starts	1st	2nd	3rd	Win & Pl
Chases	1	0	0	0	
Career Total	5	0	0	0	348

Going:	Sf: 0-1 GS: 0-0 Gd: 0-0 GF: - Fm: 0-0
Distance:	2m/2m3: 0-0 2m4-2m7: 0-0 3m+: 0-0
Track:	LH: 0-1 RH: 0-0 Tight: 0-1 Gall: 0-0
Aids:	Bl: 0-0 Vi: 0-0 Tstrap: 0-0 Ckp: 0-0
Best Rating:	119 2/00 Kemp 2m soft NHF

Native Upmanship (IRE)

115 **170**

11-y-o ch g Be My Native (USA)-Hi' Upham (Deep Run)

A L T Moore Mrs John Magnier

Placings: *31*/4012221/11141/114P4/2221212/215121-35133 (4639)
2003/04: 25³G, 20⁵Y, 20¹S, 16³Y, 20³G,

	Starts	1st	2nd	3rd	Win & Pl
Chases	5	1	0	3	52903
Career Total	37	15	10	4	636297
152	2/04	Thur	2m4f	Ch	SFT	£22887
167	4/03	Aint	2m4f	A Ch	GD	£87000
152	1/03	Thur	2m4f	Ch	SFT	£21103
166	12/02	Punc	2m4f	Ch	SH	£35889
164	4/02	Aint	2m4f	A Ch	GD	£69600
167	1/02	Thur	2m4f	Ch	HVY	£19938
166	12/00	Punc	2m4f	Ch	SH	£26000
150	11/00	Navn	2m	Ch	HVY	£10880
160	4/00	Fair	2m4f	Ch	SFT	£31880
142	2/00	Leop	2m5f	Ch	YLD	£26000
150	12/99	Leop	2m1f	Ch	SH	£29017
127	11/99	Navn	2m4f	Ch	YLD	£4312
138	4/99	Punc	2m4f	Hdl	YLD	£27678
114	12/98	Leop	2m2f	Hdl	SFT	£4184
114	4/98	Punc	2m	NHF	HVY	£5956
				Total win prize-money		£422332

Going:	Sf: 1-1 GS: 0-0 Gd: 0-2 GF: - Fm: 0-0
Distance:	2m/2m3: 0-1 2m4-2m7: 1-3 3m+: 0-1
Track:	LH: 0-2 RH: 1-3 Tight: 0-1 Gall: 0-0
Aids:	Bl: 0-0 Vi: 0-0 Tstrap: 0-0 Ckp: 0-0
Best Rating:	167 4/03 Aint 2m4f good Ch

High-class chaser; seems best at 2m 4f these days and landed both the 2002 and 2003 Martell Chases at Aintree; finished runner-up in the Queen Mother Champion Chase in both 2002 and 2003; appeared not to stay when tried over 3m; suited by soft ground.

Nativetrial (IRE)

95 (42h) **115**

9-y-o ch g Be My Native (USA)-Protrial (Proverb)
C J Mann Mrs P Dodd, Mr & Mrs Mark Hunter

Placings: *00241P0*/4033350/0/42112P-2PB44P (3938)
2003/04: 26²G, 30PGS, 26⁸HY, 25⁴S, 25⁴S, 33PG,

	Starts	1st	2nd	3rd	Win & Pl
Chases	6	0	1	0	2151
Career Total	27	3	4	3	27024
115	1/03	Font	3m2f110yE(0-110)HCh	HVY	£4007
110	12/02	MRas	4m1f	D(0-120)HCh	SFT	£10800
100	2/00	Clon	2m4f	Hdl	SH	£3036
				Total win prize-money		£17843

Going:	Sf: 0-3 GS: 0-1 Gd: 0-2 GF: - Fm: 0-0
Distance:	2m/2m3: 0-0 2m4-2m7: 0-0 3m+: 0-6
Track:	LH: 0-3 RH: 0-1 Tight: 0-0 Gall: 0-1
Aids:	Bl: 0-1 Vi: 0-0 Tstrap: 0-2 Ckp: 0-1
Best Rating:	115 1/03 Font 3m2f110y heavy Ch

Moderate ex-Irish chaser, stays very well and handles testing ground.

Natterjack (IRE)

91f **90f**

6-y-o b g Roselier (FR)-Hansel's Lady (IRE) (The Parson)
A King Elite Racing Club

Placings: *650* (4529)
2003/04: 16⁶GS, 16⁵G, 16⁰GS,

	Starts	1st	2nd	3rd	Win & Pl
NH Flat	3	0	0	0	
Career Total	3	0	0	0	0

Going:	Sf: 0-0 GS: 0-2 Gd: 0-1 GF: - Fm: 0-0

Distance:	2m/2m3: 0-3 2m4-2m7: 0-0 3m+: 0-0
Track:	LH: 0-1 RH: 0-2 Tight: 0-0 Gall: 0-0
Aids:	Bl: 0-0 Vi: 0-0 Tstrap: 0-0 Ckp: 0-0
Best Rating:	90 2/04 Kemp 2m good NHF

Natural (IRE)

108(105h) (99dh)**88**

7-y-o b g Bigstone (IRE)-You Make Me Real (USA) (Give Me Strength (USA))
F P Murtagh G & P Barker Ltd/globe Engineering

Placings: *450P2P*/21F2000P-0060325U5R (4684)
2003/04: 20⁴G, 18⁰S, 16⁶GS, 16⁰GS, 16³HY, 16²HY, 20⁵G, 16⁴GF, 20⁵HY, 25⁵RG,

	Starts	1st	2nd	3rd	Win & Pl
Hurdles	4	0	0	0	
Chases	6	0	1	1	2038
Career Total	24	1	1	1	8142
98	10/02	Bang	2m1f	E(0-105)HHdl	SFT	£3445
				Total win prize-money		£3445

Going:	Sf: 0-4 GS: 0-2 Gd: 0-3 GF: - Fm: 0-1
Distance:	2m/2m3: 0-6 2m4-2m7: 0-3 3m+: 0-1
Track:	LH: 0-7 RH: 0-3 Tight: 0-2 Gall: 0-2
Aids:	Bl: 0-1 Vi: 0-0 Tstrap: 0-0 Ckp: 0-0
Best Rating:	99 11/02 Carl 2m1f heavy Hdl

Modest hurdler, best around two miles; suited by soft ground.

Naughtynelly's Pet

56f **4f**

5-y-o b g Balnibarbi-Naughty Nessie (Celtic Cone)
D A Nolan William Prentice

Placings: *00* (2790)
2003/04: 16⁰G, 16⁰GF,

	Starts	1st	2nd	3rd	Win & Pl
NH Flat	2	0	0	0	
Career Total	2	0	0	0	

Going:	Sf: 0-0 GS: 0-0 Gd: 0-0 GF: 0-1 Fm: 0-1
Distance:	2m/2m3: 0-2 2m4-2m7: 0-0 3m+: 0-0
Track:	LH: 0-0 RH: 0-2 Tight: 0-1 Gall: 0-0
Aids:	Bl: 0-0 Vi: 0-0 Tstrap: 0-0 Ckp: 0-0
Best Rating:	4 12/03 Muss 2m gd-fm NHF

Naunton Brook

102 **112+**

5-y-o b g Alderbrook-Give Me An Answer (True Song)
N A Twiston-Davies David Langdon

Placings: *40132* (4959)
2003/04: 17⁴G, 17⁰GS, 25¹G, 24³S, 19²G,

	Starts	1st	2nd	3rd	Win & Pl
NH Flat	2	0	0	0	0
Hurdles	3	1	1	1	5868
Career Total	5	1	1	1	5868
112	3/04	Wwck	3m1f	E Hdl	GD	£3794
				Total win prize-money		£3794

Going:	Sf: 0-1 GS: 0-1 Gd: 1-3 GF: - Fm: 0-0
Distance:	2m/2m3: 0-2 2m4-2m7: 0-1 3m+: 1-2
Track:	LH: 1-4 RH: 0-1 Tight: 0-3 Gall: 0-0
Aids:	Bl: 0-0 Vi: 0-0 Tstrap: 0-0 Ckp: 0-0
Best Rating:	112 3/04 Wwck 3m1f good Hdl

Confirmed promise of bumper debut when winning on hurdles debut over three miles and one furlong in March; not disgraced at Hexham last time; may do better in handicap company in due course.

Nautical

88

6-y-o gr g Lion Cavern (USA)-Russian Royal (USA) (Nureyev (USA))
A W Carroll (M C Pipe 30/7) Gary J Roberts

Placings:P03-PP   (4285)
2003/04: 17PGF, 16PG,

	Starts	1st	2nd	3rd	Win & Pl
Hurdles	2	0	0	0	
Career Total	5	0	0	1	546

Going:	Sf: 0-0 GS: 0-0 Gd: 0-1 GF: - Fm: 0-1
Distance:	2m/2m3: 0-2 2m4-2m7: 0-0 3m+: 0-0
Track:	LH: 0-0 RH: 0-2 Tight: 0-1 Gall: 0-0
Aids:	Bl: 0-0 Vi: 0-0 Tstrap: 0-1 Ckp: 0-0
Best Rating:	88 4/03 Chep 2m110y gd-fm Hdl

Nautical Star

97   **79**

9-y-o b g Slip Anchor-Comic Talent (Pharly (FR))
A C Whillans Mrs Helen Greggan

Placings:005P41/00P-23050   (3476)
2003/04: 17²G, 20³GF, 18⁰S, 17⁵GS, 16⁰G,

	Starts	1st	2nd	3rd	Win & Pl
Hurdles	5	0	1	1	847
Career Total	14	1	1	1	4539
86	4/02 Prth 2m110y G(0-90)HHdl		GD		£3692
				Total win prize-money £3692	

Going:	Sf: 0-1 GS: 0-1 Gd: 0-2 GF: - Fm: 0-1
Distance:	2m/2m3: 0-4 2m4-2m7: 0-1 3m+: 0-0
Track:	LH: 0-5 RH: 0-0 Tight: 0-4 Gall: 0-0
Aids:	Bl: 0-0 Vi: 0-0 Tstrap: 0-0 Ckp: 0-1
Best Rating:	86 4/02 Prth 2m110y good Hdl

Poor selling hurdler; stays two and a half miles.

Navado (USA)

107   **110+**

5-y-o b g Rainbow Quest (USA)-Miznah (IRE) (Sadler's Wells (USA))
Jonjo O'Neill (Sir Michael Stoute 11/10) John P McManus

Placings:001   (4214)
2003/04: 20⁴G, 20⁰S, 17¹G,

	Starts	1st	2nd	3rd	Win & Pl
Hurdles	3	1	0	0	3618
Career Total	3	1	0	0	3618
110	3/04 MRas 2m1f110yE Hdl		GD		£3617
				Total win prize-money £3618	

Going:	Sf: 0-1 GS: 0-0 Gd: 1-2 GF: - Fm: 0-0
Distance:	2m/2m3: 1-1 2m4-2m7: 0-2 3m+: 0-0
Track:	LH: 0-2 RH: 1-1 Tight: 1-1 Gall: 0-0
Aids:	Bl: 0-0 Vi: 0-0 Tstrap: 0-0 Ckp: 0-0
Best Rating:	110 3/04 MRas 2m1f110y good Hdl

Very useful handicapper on the Flat; much improved effort on third start when easy winner of novices' hurdle at Market Rasen in March; probably unsuited by testing ground.

Navarone

104   **127**

10-y-o b g Gunner B-Anamasi (Idiots Delight)
Ian Williams A J Cresser

Placings:554/4224315/33PP110/4221P11-U400P2 (4371)
2003/04: 25ᵁG, 24⁴G, 24⁰GF, 24⁰G, 24⁴G, 24²G,

	Starts	1st	2nd	3rd	Win & Pl
Chases	6	0	1	0	4807
Career Total	30	6	5	3	63202
127	4/03 Prth 3m B HCh	GD	£18677
117	4/03 Bang 3m110y C(0-135)HCh	G-F	£10660
116	12/02 Newb 2m6f110yC(0-130)HCh	GD	£8547
115	4/02 Uttx 2m4f E(0-100)HCh	G-F	£3373
109	4/02 Wwck 2m4f110yF(0-90)HCh	G-F	£3220
104	3/00 Ling 2m7f D Hdl	GD	£3373
		Total win prize-money £47853	

Going:	Sf: 0-0 GS: 0-0 Gd: 0-5 GF: - Fm: 0-1
Distance:	2m/2m3: 0-0 2m4-2m7: 0-0 3m+: 0-6
Track:	LH: 0-4 RH: 0-2 Tight: 0-2 Gall: 0-0
Aids:	Bl: 0-0 Vi: 0-0 Tstrap: 0-0 Ckp: 0-0
Best Rating:	127 4/03 Prth 3m good Ch

Fair chaser; stays three miles; suited by positive tactics and a sound surface; has worn a tongue tie.

Nawamees (IRE)

109   **122+**

6-y-o b h Darshaan-Truly Generous (IRE) (Generous (IRE))
G L Moore Paul Stamp

Placings:543-16243   (4698)
2003/04: 16¹GF, 16⁶GS, 16²G, 16⁴G, 18³G,

	Starts	1st	2nd	3rd	Win & Pl
Hurdles	5	1	1	1	8216
Career Total	8	1	1	2	9597
122	11/03 Asct 2m110y D Hdl	G-F	£4576
		Total win prize-money £4576	

Going:	Sf: 0-0 GS: 0-1 Gd: 0-3 GF: - Fm: 1-1
Distance:	2m/2m3: 1-5 2m4-2m7: 0-0 3m+: 0-0
Track:	LH: 0-2 RH: 1-3 Tight: 0-1 Gall: 0-1
Aids:	Bl: 0-0 Vi: 0-0 Tstrap: 0-0 Ckp: 0-0
Best Rating:	122 12/03 Kemp 2m good Hdl

Fair hurdler; ex-French; useful on the Flat; acts on good ground and effective at around two miles; likes to race prominently.

Nawow

96   **94+**

4-y-o b g Blushing Flame (USA)-Fair Test (Fair Season)
P D Cundell Ian M Brown

Placings:105   (4368)
2003/04: 16¹GS, 16⁹GS, 16⁵GF,

	Starts	1st	2nd	3rd	Win & Pl
Hurdles	3	1	0	0	3416
Career Total	3	1	0	0	3416
94	12/03 Sand 2m110y D Hdl	G-S	£3415
		Total win prize-money £3416	

Going:	Sf: 0-0 GS: 1-2 Gd: 0-0 GF: - Fm: 0-1
Distance:	2m/2m3: 1-3 2m4-2m7: 0-0 3m+: 0-0
Track:	LH: 0-1 RH: 1-2 Tight: 0-1 Gall: 0-0
Aids:	Bl: 0-0 Vi: 0-0 Tstrap: 0-0 Ckp: 0-0
Best Rating:	94 12/03 Sand 2m110y gd-sft Hdl

Moderate novice hurdler; winner at Sandown on his debut; effective over two miles; acts well with cut in the ground.

Ndr's Cash For Fun

79   **26**

11-y-o b g Ballacashtal (CAN)-Basic Fun (Teenoso (USA))
A W Carroll Group 1 Racing (1994) Ltd

Placings:00/0P/0P1P1430/000F0-063   (0315)
2003/04: 20⁰S, 27⁶S, 18³F,

	Starts	1st	2nd	3rd	Win & Pl
Hurdles	3	0	0	1	315
Career Total	20	2	0	4	4254
73	2/02 Tntn 2m3f110yG(0-95)HHdl	SFT	£1750
73	1/02 Leic 2m G(0-90)HHdl	SFT	£1939
		Total win prize-money £3689	

Going:	Sf: 0-2 GS: 0-0 Gd: 0-0 GF: - Fm: 0-1
Distance:	2m/2m3: 0-1 2m4-2m7: 0-1 3m+: 0-0
Track:	LH: 0-0 RH: 0-0 Tight: 0-1 Gall: 0-0
Aids:	Bl: 0-1 Vi: 0-0 Tstrap: 0-0 Ckp: 0-0
Best Rating:	82 4/98 Asct 2m110y good NHF

Lightly raced selling-class hurdler, needs humouring.

Needwood Bucolic (IRE)

6-y-o br g Charnwood Forest (IRE)-Greek Icon (Thatching)
R Shiels R Shiels

Placings:PF   (4937)
2003/04: 20PGS, 16PGS,

	Starts	1st	2nd	3rd	Win & Pl
Hurdles	2	0	0	0	
Career Total	2	0	0	0	

Going:	Sf: 0-0 GS: 0-2 Gd: 0-0 GF: - Fm: 0-0
Distance:	2m/2m3: 0-1 2m4-2m7: 0-1 3m+: 0-0
Track:	LH: 0-0 RH: 0-2 Tight: 0-0 Gall: 0-0
Aids:	Bl: 0-0 Vi: 0-0 Tstrap: 0-0 Ckp: 0-0

Needwood Lion

96   (107h)**125**

11-y-o b g Rolfe (USA)-Arctic Lion (Arctic Slave)
Miss Venetia Williams Tweenhills Racing (Gadbury Syndicate)

Placings:26/606511/021FF46/305352/641213403-5 (2870)
2003/04: 20⁵G,

	Starts	1st	2nd	3rd	Win & Pl
Chases	1	0	0	0	0
Career Total	31	5	4	4	35700
125	12/02 Kemp 2m4f110yD(0-120)HCh	SFT	£10653
120	12/02 Hrfd 2m3f D(0-115)HCh	GD	£5031
130	1/01 Uttx 2m D Ch	HVY	£4143
104	4/00 Hrfd 2m3f110yE(0-105)HHdl	SFT	£2970
96	3/00 Tntn 2m1f F(0-105)HHdl	SFT	£2524
		Total win prize-money £25323	

Going:	Sf: 0-0 GS: 0-0 Gd: 0-1 GF: - Fm: 0-0
Distance:	2m/2m3: 0-0 2m4-2m7: 0-1 3m+: 0-0
Track:	LH: 0-1 RH: 0-0 Tight: 0-0 Gall: 0-0
Aids:	Bl: 0-0 Vi: 0-0 Tstrap: 0-0 Ckp: 0-0
Best Rating:	130 1/01 Winc 2m5f soft Ch

Fair handicap chaser; headstrong individual, likes to have his own way out in front; stays two and a half miles; effective on good ground or softer.

Needwood Merlin

8-y-o b g Sizzling Melody-Enchanting Kate (Enchantment)
K W Hogg K W Hogg

Placings:PP-P   (0194)
2003/04: 20PG,

	Starts	1st	2nd	3rd	Win & Pl
Hurdles	1	0	0	0	
Career Total	3	0	0	0	

Going:	Sf: 0-0 GS: 0-0 Gd: 0-1 GF: - Fm: 0-0
Distance:	2m/2m3: 0-0 2m4-2m7: 0-1 3m+: 0-0
Track:	LH: 0-1 RH: 0-0 Tight: 0-0 Gall: 0-0
Aids:	Bl: 0-0 Vi: 0-0 Tstrap: 0-0 Ckp: 0-0

Needwood Spirit

105   **109**

9-y-o b g Rolfe (USA)-Needwood Nymph (Bold Owl)
Mrs A M Naughton Famous Five Racing

Placings:45/00P01/5611146/4620-6044060   (3326)
2003/04: 20⁶G, 20⁰G, 17⁴GS, 17⁴HY, 16⁹S, 16⁶S, 21⁰GS,

	Starts	1st	2nd	3rd	Win & Pl
Hurdles	7	0	0	0	608
Career Total	**25**	**4**	**1**	**0**	**16159**
95 12/01 Hexm	2m	D(0-125)HHdl		SFT	£7020
110 11/01 Carl	2m4f	F(0-105)HHdl		HVY	£2299
110 11/01 Carl	2m1f	F(0-110)HHdl		SFT	£2664
87 4/01 Fknm	2m	G(0-90)HHdl		G-S	£1926
			Total win prize-money £13910		

Going:	Sf: 0-3 GS: 0-2 Gd: 0-2 GF: - Fm: 0-0
Distance:	2m/2m3: 0-4 2m4-2m7: 0-3 3m+: 0-0
Track:	LH: 0-4 RH: 0-3 Tight: 0-1 Gall: 0-0
Aids:	Bl: 0-0 Vi: 0-0 Tstrap: 0-0 Ckp: 0-0
Best Rating:	110 11/01 Carl 2m4f heavy Hdl

Modest front-running handicap hurdler; ideally suited by a stiff track and testing ground; stays two and a half miles.

Negresko (FR)

99   (0c)**118**

5-y-o gr g Great Palm (USA)-Negra (FR) (Tropular)
J Bertran De Balanda (M C Pipe 22/5) J Bertran De Balanda

Placings:00/0P3111113553-5   (0382)
2003/04: 18⁵G,

	Starts	1st	2nd	3rd	Win & Pl
Hurdles	1	0	0	0	390
Career Total	**15**	**5**	**0**	**3**	**26773**
10/02 Pari	2m1f	Hdl		SFT	£5890
10/02 MARS	2m1f110y	Hdl		SFT	£4417
9/02 Lyrh	1m7f110y	Hdl		HLD	£4712
8/02 Divo	2m	Hdl		G-S	£2945
7/02 Divo	2m	Hdl		GD	£2650
			Total win prize-money £20614		

Going:	Sf: 0-0 GS: 0-0 Gd: 0-0 GF: - Fm: 0-0
Distance:	2m/2m3: 0-1 2m4-2m7: 0-0 3m+: 0-0
Track:	LH: 0-1 RH: 0-0 Tight: 0-1 Gall: 0-0
Aids:	Bl: 0-0 Vi: 0-0 Tstrap: 0-0 Ckp: 0-0
Best Rating:	118 4/03 Chel 2m1f good Hdl

Fair hurdler; won five times over hurdles in France in 2002; third on chase debut; has looked reluctant; handles soft ground; often blinkered.

Neidpath Castle

37f   **95f**

5-y-o b g Alflora (IRE)-Pennant Cottage (IRE) (Denel (FR))
A C Whillans B McKie, G Harrow, K Creighton, W Scott

Placings:1   (4482)
2003/04: 17¹HY,

	Starts	1st	2nd	3rd	Win & Pl
NH Flat	1	1	0	0	1918
Career Total	**1**	**1**	**0**	**0**	**1918**
95 3/04 Carl	2m1f	H NHF		HVY	£1918
			Total win prize-money £1918		

Going:	Sf: 1-1 GS: 0-0 Gd: 0-0 GF: - Fm: 0-0
Distance:	2m/2m3: 1-1 2m4-2m7: 0-0 3m+: 0-0
Track:	LH: 0-0 RH: 1-1 Tight: 0-0 Gall: 0-0
Aids:	Bl: 0-0 Vi: 0-0 Tstrap: 0-0 Ckp: 0-0
Best Rating:	95 3/04 Carl 2m1f heavy NHF

Won moderate bumper on debut in April 2004; acts on heavy.

Nelly Moser

91   **74**

7-y-o gr m Neltino-Boreen's Glory (Boreen (FR))
Mrs A J Hamilton-Fairley Mrs A Hamilton-Fairley

Placings:0/40-25   (0485)
2003/04: 19²GS, 22⁵GF,

	Starts	1st	2nd	3rd	Win & Pl
Hurdles	2	0	1	0	1202
Career Total	**5**	**0**	**1**	**0**	**1202**

Going:	Sf: 0-0 GS: 0-1 Gd: 0-0 GF: - Fm: 0-1
Distance:	2m/2m3: 0-0 2m4-2m7: 0-2 3m+: 0-0
Track:	LH: 0-1 RH: 0-1 Tight: 0-1 Gall: 0-0
Aids:	Bl: 0-0 Vi: 0-0 Tstrap: 0-0 Ckp: 0-0
Best Rating:	89 5/02 Font 2m2f110y gd-fm NHF

Modest form in bumpers and hurdles.

Nelsons Nell (IRE)

(79h)   (82h)

8-y-o b m Supreme Leader-Lough Neagh Lady (Furry Glen)
Miss Lucinda V Russell (George Young 3/3) Mrs Kay Owens

Placings:053600   (4947)
2003/04: 17⁰G, 22⁵GY, 20³S, 18⁶GY, 20⁰S, 20⁰GS,

	Starts	1st	2nd	3rd	Win & Pl
NH Flat	1	0	0	0	0
Hurdles	4	0	0	1	641
Chases	1	0	0	0	0
Career Total	**6**	**0**	**0**	**1**	**641**

Going:	Sf: 0-2 GS: 0-1 Gd: 0-1 GF: - Fm: 0-0
Distance:	2m/2m3: 0-2 2m4-2m7: 0-4 3m+: 0-0
Track:	LH: 0-1 RH: 0-1 Tight: 0-0 Gall: 0-0
Aids:	Bl: 0-0 Vi: 0-0 Tstrap: 0-0 Ckp: 0-0
Best Rating:	82 1/04 DRoy 2m4f soft Hdl

Nemisto

100   (119c)**101**

10-y-o gr g Mystiko (USA)-Nemesia (Mill Reef (USA))
R Lee R L C Hartley

Placings:62P/5330201/51252201/0056F/33355PP/42230P 46-31   (0487)
2003/04: 21³GF, 22¹GF,

	Starts	1st	2nd	3rd	Win & Pl
Hurdles	2	1	0	1	3636
Career Total	**40**	**4**	**7**	**7**	**27137**
99 5/03 NAbb	2m6f	G(0-95)HHdl		G-F	£3066
128 3/00 Chep	2m110y	D Hdl		GD	£3256
124 12/99 Hrfd	2m1f	E(0-115)HHdl		SFT	£2762
114 5/99 Hrfd	2m1f	D(0-110)HHdl		GD	£2560
			Total win prize-money £11645		

Going:	Sf: 0-0 GS: 0-0 Gd: 0-0 GF: - Fm: 1-2
Distance:	2m/2m3: 0-0 2m4-2m7: 1-2 3m+: 0-0
Track:	LH: 1-2 RH: 0-0 Tight: 1-1 Gall: 0-0
Aids:	Bl: 0-0 Vi: 0-0 Tstrap: 0-0 Ckp: 0-0

Best Rating:	128 3/00 Chep 2m110y good Hdl

Modest hurdler/chaser; had not won since March 2000 until defying top weight in competitive 2m 6f selling handicap at Newton Abbot May 2003; acts on soft, but handles a sound surface; stays 2m 4f.

Neophyte (IRE)

90f   **84+f**

5-y-o gr g Broken Hearted-Dunmahon Lady (General Ironside)
B De Haan The Neophyte Four

Placings:5   (0606)
2003/04: 17⁵G,

	Starts	1st	2nd	3rd	Win & Pl
NH Flat	1	0	0	0	0
Career Total	**1**	**0**	**0**	**0**	**0**

Going:	Sf: 0-0 GS: 0-0 Gd: 0-0 GF: - Fm: 0-0
Distance:	2m/2m3: 0-1 2m4-2m7: 0-0 3m+: 0-0
Track:	LH: 0-1 RH: 0-0 Tight: 0-1 Gall: 0-0
Aids:	Bl: 0-0 Vi: 0-0 Tstrap: 0-0 Ckp: 0-0
Best Rating:	86 6/03 NAbb 2m1f good NHF

Stoutly bred; ran well on bumper debut; effective at two miles, will want further in time; acts on good ground.

Nephite (NZ)

103(95h)   (75h)**105**

10-y-o b g Star Way-Te Akau Charmer (NZ) (Sir Tristram)
Miss Venetia Williams (R C Guest 4/8) Mrs H Spencer

Placings:56633233005/441365131231P/064P4352161-6005205041034P   (1377)
2003/04: 16⁶G, 16⁹G, 17⁹GS, 17⁵GF, 17²G, 17⁰G, 17⁵GF, 19⁰G, 16⁴G, 16¹GF, 17⁰G, 17³G, 17⁴GF, 16⁸GF,

	Starts	1st	2nd	3rd	Win & Pl
Hurdles	5	0	0	0	0
Chases	9	1	1	6	9135
Career Total	**49**	**7**	**4**	**9**	**39905**
105 8/03 NAbb	2m110y	E(0-105)HCh		G-F	£5343
105 3/03 MRas	2m1f110yE(0-105)HCh		GD	£4075
100 3/03 Newc	2m1f110y	E(0-105)HCh		G-S	£4332
98 4/02 MRas	2m1f110yG(0-105)HCh		GD	£3570
98 1/02 Newc	2m110y	E(0-105)HCh		SFT	£3032
87 1/02 Fknm	2m110y	F(0-100)HCh		SFT	£4342
82 10/01 Carl	2m	F(0-100)HCh		SFT	£2938
			Total win prize-money £27633		

Going:	Sf: 0-0 GS: 0-1 Gd: 0-8 GF: - Fm: 1-5
Distance:	2m/2m3: 1-14 2m4-2m7: 0-0 3m+: 0-0
Track:	LH: 1-11 RH: 0-3 Tight: 1-8 Gall: 0-0
Aids:	Bl: 1-5 Vi: 0-0 Tstrap: 1-3 Ckp: 0-9
Best Rating:	105 8/03 Ctml 2m1f110y good Ch

Moderate chaser; fitted from first-time blinkers instead of his regular cheekpieces when landing extended 2m handicap chase at Newton Abbot August 2003; suited by 2m on both soft and good ground, best when allowed to front-run; usually wears tongue tie.

Neptune

80

8-y-o b g Dolphin Street (FR)-Seal Indigo (IRE) (Glenstal (USA))
J C Fox S J V Construction

Placings:00041-P   (3642)
2003/04: 19⁰S,

	Starts	1st	2nd	3rd	Win & Pl
Hurdles	1	0	0	0	

Career Total	6	1	0	0	3724
80	3/03	Extr	2m1f	G Hdl	GD £3388

Total win prize-money £3388

Going:	Sf: 0-1 GS: 0-0 Gd: 0-0 GF: - Fm: 0-0
Distance:	2m/2m3: 0-1 2m4-2m7: 0-0 3m+: 0-0
Track:	LH: 0-0 RH: 0-1 Tight: 0-0 Gall: 0-0
Aids:	Bl: 0-0 Vi: 0-0 Tstrap: 0-0 Ckp: 0-0
Best Rating:	80 3/03 Extr 2m1f good Hdl

Plating-class hurdler; appreciated the combination of a drop in class and better ground when winning extended two mile selling hurdle at Exeter March 2003.

Neutron (IRE)

95   **128+**

7-y-o g Nucleon (USA)-Balistic Princess (Lomond (USA))
M C Pipe Matt Archer & Miss Jean Broadhurst

Placings:2212200/4600/1412F-0   (3590)
2003/04: 20⁰HY,

	Starts	1st	2nd	3rd	Win & Pl
Hurdles	1	0	0	0	
Career Total	17	3	5	0	20125
123	12/02	Winc	2m	D(0-120)HHdl	G-S £5398
115	10/02	Winc	2m	E(0-110)HHdl	GD £3542
110	9/00	Cork		Hdl	GD £3864

Total win prize-money £12805

Going:	Sf: 0-1 GS: 0-0 Gd: 0-0 GF: - Fm: 0-0
Distance:	2m/2m3: 0-0 2m4-2m7: 0-1 3m+: 0-0
Track:	LH: 0-0 RH: 0-1 Tight: 0-0 Gall: 0-0
Aids:	Bl: 0-0 Vi: 0-0 Tstrap: 0-0 Ckp: 0-0
Best Rating:	128 12/02 Kemp 2m5f soft Hdl

Useful handicap hurdler; ex-Irish; has never won beyond two miles, but does stay two mile five; acts on most ground; wears a visor; has shown a questionable attitude.

Nev Brown (IRE)

99(74h)   (49h)**106+**

8-y-o b/br g Executive Perk-Brandy Hill Girl (Green Shoon)
N A Twiston-Davies Geoffrey & Donna Keeys

Placings:032P   (4645)
2003/04: 21⁰G, 16³HY, 17²G, 16⁶G,

	Starts	1st	2nd	3rd	Win & Pl
Hurdles	1	0	0	0	0
Chases	3	0	1	1	2339
Career Total	4	0	1	1	2339

Going:	Sf: 0-1 GS: 0-0 Gd: 0-3 GF: - Fm: 0-0
Distance:	2m/2m3: 0-3 2m4-2m7: 0-1 3m+: 0-0
Track:	LH: 0-2 RH: 0-2 Tight: 0-2 Gall: 0-0
Aids:	Bl: 0-0 Vi: 0-0 Tstrap: 0-0 Ckp: 0-0
Best Rating:	106 2/04 Hrfd 2m heavy Ch

Useful novice chaser; still a maiden; effective over two miles; acts on good ground.

Neven

54   **61**

5-y-o b g Casteddu-Rose Burton (Lucky Wednesday)
Miss Lucinda V Russell (T D Barron 25/11) White Horse Racing Club

Placings:00   (4937)
2003/04: 17⁰G, 16⁰GS,

	Starts	1st	2nd	3rd	Win & Pl
Hurdles	2	0	0	0	
Career Total	2	0	0	0	

Going:	Sf: 0-0 GS: 0-1 Gd: 0-1 GF: - Fm: 0-0
Distance:	2m/2m3: 0-2 2m4-2m7: 0-0 3m+: 0-0
Track:	LH: 0-0 RH: 0-2 Tight: 0-0 Gall: 0-0
Aids:	Bl: 0-0 Vi: 0-0 Tstrap: 0-1 Ckp: 0-0
Best Rating:	61 4/04 Carl 2m1f good Hdl

Never (FR)

109   **148d**

7-y-o b g Vettori (IRE)-Neraida (USA) (Giboulee (CAN))
Jonjo O'Neill (F Doumen 6/12) Sir Peter O'Sullevan

Placings:411000/15001-0006   (4559)
2003/04: 16⁰GS, 16⁰G, 16⁰S, 16⁶GS,

	Starts	1st	2nd	3rd	Win & Pl
Hurdles	4	0	0	0	322
Career Total	15	4	0	0	50097
	4/03	Engh	2m3f	Hdl	VS £10601
148	11/02	Newb	2m110y	A(0-145)Hdl	SFT £14500
140	12/01	Asct	2m110y	A Hdl	GD £13100
	11/01	Engh	2m1f110y	Hdl	HVY £9699

Total win prize-money £47900

Going:	Sf: 0-1 GS: 0-2 Gd: 0-1 GF: - Fm: 0-0
Distance:	2m/2m3: 0-4 2m4-2m7: 0-0 3m+: 0-0
Track:	LH: 0-2 RH: 0-2 Tight: 0-0 Gall: 0-2
Aids:	Bl: 0-0 Vi: 0-0 Tstrap: 0-0 Ckp: 0-0
Best Rating:	150 12/02 Chel 2m1f good Hdl

Very useful hurdler; ex-French; best at two miles, does stay further; suited by soft ground.

Never Can Tell

100   **90**

8-y-o ch g Emarati (USA)-Farmer's Pet (Sharrood (USA))
B D Leavy Mrs Renee Farrington-Kirkham

Placings:P22050024F0/0020514/402644403/5P62-1   (0139)
2003/04: 16¹G,

	Starts	1st	2nd	3rd	Win & Pl
Hurdles	1	1	0	0	4914
Career Total	32	2	6	1	12818
92	5/03	Ludl	2m	E(0-105)HHdl	GD £4914
92	1/01	Winc	2m	F Hdl	G-S £1949

Total win prize-money £6864

Going:	Sf: 0-0 GS: 0-0 Gd: 1-1 GF: - Fm: 0-0
Distance:	2m/2m3: 1-1 2m4-2m7: 0-0 3m+: 0-0
Track:	LH: 0-0 RH: 1-1 Tight: 0-0 Gall: 0-0
Aids:	Bl: 0-0 Vi: 0-0 Tstrap: 0-0 Ckp: 0-0
Best Rating:	94 2/00 MRas 2m1f110y gd-sft Hdl

Modest handicap hurdler; acts on good or softer.

Never Compromise (IRE)

99(80h)   (94h)**135**

9-y-o br g Glacial Storm (USA)-Banderole (IRE) (Roselier (FR))
T M Walsh D F Desmond

Placings:00/003B052F6/53245320-1112F   (4805a)
2003/04: 22¹GY, 24¹Y, 24¹YS, 26²G, 29²FY,

	Starts	1st	2nd	3rd	Win & Pl
Chases	5	3	1	0	24241
Career Total	24	3	4	3	31778
116	2/04	Leop	3m	Ch	Y-S £8272
107	12/03	DRoy	3m	Ch	YLD £3584
116	12/03	Dpat	2m6f	Ch	G-Y £3584

Total win prize-money £15441

Never (FR) [see right column — Never In Debt]

Going:	Sf: 0-0 GS: 0-0 Gd: 0-1 GF: - Fm: 0-0
Distance:	2m/2m3: 0-0 2m4-2m7: 1-1 3m+: 2-4
Track:	LH: 1-2 RH: 0-1 Tight: 0-0 Gall: 0-1
Aids:	Bl: 0-0 Vi: 0-0 Tstrap: 0-0 Ckp: 0-0
Best Rating:	135 3/04 Chel 3m2f110y good Ch

Useful hunter chaser; former maiden chaser/hurdler under rules; had won six races in a row, combination of point and hunter chases, before meeting defeat when second in the Cheltenham Foxhunters'; stays three miles; best on soft ground.

Never In Debt

89   **64**

12-y-o ch g Nicholas Bill-Deep In Debt (Deep Run)
E R Clough E R Clough

Placings:120/341104/2P/P524F425/4P/FPP/0P-60 (1015)
2003/04: 20⁶G, 20⁹GF,

	Starts	1st	2nd	3rd	Win & Pl
Hurdles	2	0	0	0	
Career Total	28	3	4	1	13020
110	2/98	Tntn	2m3f110yD(0-120)HHdl	G-F £2814
108	1/98	Tntn	2m3f110yD Hdl	SFT £2913
101	9/96	Worc	2m	H NHF	G-F £1385

Total win prize-money £7112

Going:	Sf: 0-0 GS: 0-0 Gd: 0-1 GF: - Fm: 0-1
Distance:	2m/2m3: 0-0 2m4-2m7: 0-2 3m+: 0-0
Track:	LH: 0-2 RH: 0-0 Tight: 0-0 Gall: 0-0
Aids:	Bl: 0-0 Vi: 0-0 Tstrap: 0-0 Ckp: 0-1
Best Rating:	115 11/98 Chel 2m5f gd-sft Hdl

Never Promise (FR)

    60

6-y-o b m Cadeaux Genereux-Yazeanhaa (USA) (Zilzal (USA))
Daniel Mark Loughnane (C Roberts 20/8) Mrs Theresa O'Toole

Placings:00/P0   (1972a)
2003/04: 17²GF, 16⁰GF,

	Starts	1st	2nd	3rd	Win & Pl
Hurdles	2	0	0	0	
Career Total	4	0	0	0	

Going:	Sf: 0-0 GS: 0-1 Gd: 0-0 GF: - Fm: 0-1
Distance:	2m/2m3: 0-2 2m4-2m7: 0-0 3m+: 0-0
Track:	LH: 0-1 RH: 0-1 Tight: 0-0 Gall: 0-0
Aids:	Bl: 0-0 Vi: 0-1 Tstrap: 0-0 Ckp: 0-0
Best Rating:	60 11/03 Thur 2m gd-fm Hdl

Neverbitethehand (IRE)

73f   **46f**

6-y-o b g Aragon-We're Joken (Statoblest)
R J Baker Miss S A Ryder

Placings:00   (0947)
2003/04: 17⁰GF, 16⁰G,

	Starts	1st	2nd	3rd	Win & Pl
NH Flat	2	0	0	0	
Career Total	2	0	0	0	

Going:	Sf: 0-0 GS: 0-0 Gd: 0-1 GF: - Fm: 0-1
Distance:	2m/2m3: 0-2 2m4-2m7: 0-0 3m+: 0-0
Track:	LH: 0-1 RH: 0-1 Tight: 0-0 Gall: 0-0
Aids:	Bl: 0-0 Vi: 0-0 Tstrap: 0-0 Ckp: 0-0

Best Rating: 53   6/03   Hrfd   2m1f   gd-fm NHF

New Bird (GER)
108   125+

9-y-o b g Bluebird (USA)-Nouvelle Amour (GER) (Esclavo (FR))
Mrs H Dalton David M Hughes

Placings:3124012/3060/31/216F302/P356-22113P2 (4843)
2003/04: 16²GS, 16²GF, 16¹G, 16¹GF, 17³GF, 16PGF, 16²G,

	Starts	1st	2nd	3rd	Win & Pl
Chases	7	2	3	1	22243
Career Total	31	6	7	6	51512
121	8/03	NAbb	2m110y	D(0-120)HCh	G-F	£9008
117	7/03	NAbb	2m110y	D(0-125)HCh	GD	£5328
125	5/01	Aint	2m	D(0-125)HCh	GD	£5502
117	4/01	Weth	2m	E Ch	G-S	£3233
122	4/99	Hrfd	2m1f	D Hdl	G-F	£3009
117	12/98	Kemp	2m	C Hdl	SFT	£5083

Total win prize-money £31167

Going:	Sf: 0-0 GS: 0-1 Gd: 1-2 GF: - Fm: 1-4
Distance:	2m/2m3: 2-7 2m4-2m7: 0-0 3m+: 0-0
Track:	LH: 2-7 RH: 0-0 Tight: 2-5 Gall: 0-1
Aids:	Bl: 0-0 Vi: 0-0 Tstrap: 0-0 Ckp: 0-0
Best Rating:	130 3/00 Chel 2m1f gd-fm Hdl

Fair handicap chaser, best at 2m and likes to make the running; does not want the ground too soft.

New Diamond

5-y-o ch g Bijou D'Inde-Nannie Annie (Persian Bold)
Mrs P Ford (J M P Eustace 28/6) R S Herbert

Placings:PP   (4762)
2003/04: 19PG, 19PS,

	Starts	1st	2nd	3rd	Win & Pl
Hurdles	2	0	0	0	
Career Total	2	0	0	0	

Going:	Sf: 0-1 GS: 0-0 Gd: 0-1 GF: - Fm: 0-0
Distance:	2m/2m3: 0-0 2m4-2m7: 0-0 3m+: 0-0
Track:	LH: 0-0 RH: 0-1 Tight: 0-0 Gall: 0-0
Aids:	Bl: 0-0 Vi: 0-0 Tstrap: 0-0 Ckp: 0-0

New Era (IRE)
97   89

10-y-o b g Distinctly North (USA)-Vaguely Deesse (USA) (Vaguely Noble)
B De Haan Sidtenga Syndicate

Placings:363/21201/6-55   (4667)
2003/04: 23⁵S, 24⁵S,

	Starts	1st	2nd	3rd	Win & Pl
Chases	2	0	0	0	
Career Total	11	2	2	2	11558
113	4/01	Kemp	3m	D Ch	GD	£5265
113	1/01	Wwck	2m4f110yF(0-90)HCh	HVY	£2695

Total win prize-money £7960

Going:	Sf: 0-2 GS: 0-0 Gd: 0-0 GF: - Fm: 0-0
Distance:	2m/2m3: 0-0 2m4-2m7: 0-0 3m+: 0-2
Track:	LH: 0-1 RH: 0-1 Tight: 0-1 Gall: 0-0
Aids:	Bl: 0-0 Vi: 0-0 Tstrap: 0-0 Ckp: 0-0
Best Rating:	118 2/01 Sand 2m4f110y soft Ch

New Leader (IRE)
85(107h)   (88 h)35

7-y-o b g Supreme Leader-Two Spots (Deep Run)
Mrs L Richards M E Thompsett

Placings:00020-060PPFU0   (4209)
2003/04: 26³GS, 22³GF, 21⁰G, 24PGF, 22PGS, 20FGS, 24⁰G,

	Starts	1st	2nd	3rd	Win & Pl
Hurdles	2	0	0	0	159
Chases	6	0	0	0	0
Career Total	13	0	1	0	1258

Going:	Sf: 0-0 GS: 0-4 Gd: 0-2 GF: - Fm: 0-2
Distance:	2m/2m3: 0-2 2m4-2m7: 0-4 3m+: 0-4
Track:	LH: 0-3 RH: 0-5 Tight: 0-4 Gall: 0-1
Aids:	Bl: 0-0 Vi: 0-0 Tstrap: 0-3 Ckp: 0-0
Best Rating:	88 3/03 Wwck 3m1f gd-fm Hdl

New Mischief (IRE)
102   90+

6-y-o b g Accordion-Alone Party (IRE) (Phardante (FR))
Noel T Chance R W And J R Fidler

Placings:4-1302   (4893)
2003/04: 16¹GF, 16³G, 16⁰GS, 16²G,

	Starts	1st	2nd	3rd	Win & Pl
NH Flat	2	1	0	1	5529
Hurdles	2	0	1	0	1018
Career Total	5	1	1	1	6547
112	10/03	Chel	2m110y	H NHF	G-F	£3672

Total win prize-money £3673

Going:	Sf: 0-0 GS: 0-1 Gd: 0-2 GF: - Fm: 1-1
Distance:	2m/2m3: 1-4 2m4-2m7: 0-0 3m+: 0-0
Track:	LH: 1-3 RH: 0-1 Tight: 0-0 Gall: 0-1
Aids:	Bl: 0-0 Vi: 0-0 Tstrap: 0-0 Ckp: 0-0
Best Rating:	112 10/03 Chel 2m110y gd-fm NHF

Moderate bumper horse; likely to need a test of stamina over hurdles.

New Perk (IRE)
96(96c)   (80c)90

6-y-o b g Executive Perk-New Cello (IRE) (Orchestra)
M J Gingell A White

Placings:55026-300334PB560   (4588)
2003/04: 21³GF, 19⁰G, 19⁰GF, 16³GF, 20³G, 20⁴G, 21PS, 22BG, 20⁵S, 22BGS, 21⁰G,

	Starts	1st	2nd	3rd	Win & Pl
Hurdles	9	0	0	3	1353
Chases	2	0	0	0	0
Career Total	16	0	1	3	2461

Going:	Sf: 0-2 GS: 0-1 Gd: 0-5 GF: - Fm: 0-3
Distance:	2m/2m3: 0-2 2m4-2m7: 0-9 3m+: 0-0
Track:	LH: 0-4 RH: 0-7 Tight: 0-6 Gall: 0-3
Aids:	Bl: 0-0 Vi: 0-1 Tstrap: 0-0 Ckp: 0-0
Best Rating:	90 10/03 Fknm 2m4f good Hdl

Plating-class hurdler; stays two and a half miles; suited by soft ground, but effective on faster.

New Rising
101

12-y-o b g Primitive Rising (USA)-Saucy (Muhtarram (USA))
R T Phillips Bill Naylor

Placings:5F43/0F/433254454/42412/FPP04P/P342FP-P   (2225)
2003/04: 25PGS,

	Starts	1st	2nd	3rd	Win & Pl
Chases	1	0	0	0	
Career Total	33	1	4	4	20978
116	1/01	Fknm	3m5f110yC(0-130)HCh	SFT	£6630

Total win prize-money £6630

Going:	Sf: 0-0 GS: 0-1 Gd: 0-0 GF: - Fm: 0-0
Distance:	2m/2m3: 0-0 2m4-2m7: 0-0 3m+: 0-1
Track:	LH: 0-0 RH: 0-1 Tight: 0-0 Gall: 0-0
Aids:	Bl: 0-0 Vi: 0-0 Tstrap: 0-0 Ckp: 0-0
Best Rating:	116 3/01 Ling 3m4f110y heavy Ch

Moderate handicap chaser; rather slow, he requires a real test of stamina; suited by heavy ground; usually visored.

New Ross (IRE)

12-y-o gr g Roselier (FR)-Miss Lucille (Fine Blade (USA))
M J Bloom A W K Merriam

Placings:0/50/6U3U/P-P   (0349)
2003/04: 26PGF,

	Starts	1st	2nd	3rd	Win & Pl
Chases	1	0	0	0	
Career Total	9	0	0	1	270

Going:	Sf: 0-0 GS: 0-0 Gd: 0-0 GF: - Fm: 0-1
Distance:	2m/2m3: 0-0 2m4-2m7: 0-0 3m+: 0-1
Track:	LH: 0-0 RH: 0-1 Tight: 0-1 Gall: 0-0
Aids:	Bl: 0-1 Vi: 0-0 Tstrap: 0-0 Ckp: 0-0
Best Rating:	71 5/97 Ludl 2m gd-fm Hdl

New Time (IRE)
94f   88f

5-y-o b g Topanoora-Fast Time (IRE) (Be My Native (USA))
Jonjo O'Neill John P McManus

Placings:0   (4920)
2003/04: 16⁰GS,

	Starts	1st	2nd	3rd	Win & Pl
NH Flat	1	0	0	0	
Career Total	1	0	0	0	

Going:	Sf: 0-0 GS: 0-1 Gd: 0-0 GF: - Fm: 0-0
Distance:	2m/2m3: 0-1 2m4-2m7: 0-0 3m+: 0-0
Track:	LH: 0-1 RH: 0-0 Tight: 0-0 Gall: 0-0
Aids:	Bl: 0-0 Vi: 0-0 Tstrap: 0-0 Ckp: 0-0
Best Rating:	88 4/04 Worc 2m gd-sft NHF

New Venture
54f   33f

5-y-o b m Alflora (IRE)-Purple Silk (Belfalas)
W Storey F W W Chapman

Placings:0   (1985)
2003/04: 16⁰GF,

	Starts	1st	2nd	3rd	Win & Pl
NH Flat	1	0	0	0	
Career Total	1	0	0	0	

Going:	Sf: 0-0 GS: 0-0 Gd: 0-0 GF: - Fm: 0-1
Distance:	2m/2m3: 0-1 2m4-2m7: 0-0 3m+: 0-0
Track:	LH: 0-1 RH: 0-0 Tight: 0-0 Gall: 0-0
Aids:	Bl: 0-0 Vi: 0-0 Tstrap: 0-0 Ckp: 0-0
Best Rating:	33 11/03 Hexm 2m110y gd-fm NHF

Newgate Times

50f   **25f**

5-y-o b g Timeless Times (USA)-Newgate Bubbles (Hubbly Bubbly (USA))
N Wilson W P S Johnson

Placings:*0*   (4517)
2003/04: 16⁰GS,

	Starts	1st	2nd	3rd	Win & Pl
NH Flat	1	0	0	0	
Career Total	1	0	0	0	

Going:	Sf: 0-0 GS: 0-1 Gd: 0-0 GF: - Fm: 0-0
Distance:	2m/2m3: 0-1 2m4-2m7: 0-0 3m+: 0-0
Track:	LH: 0-1 RH: 0-0 Tight: 0-0 Gall: 0-0
Aids:	Bl: 0-0 Vi: 0-0 Tstrap: 0-0 Ckp: 0-0
Best Rating:	19 3/04 Weth 2m gd-sft NHF

Newhall (IRE)

109   **134**

6-y-o b m Shernazar-Graffogue (IRE) (Red Sunset)
F Flood T McParland

Placings:3121232/06F4260-4240   (4428)
2003/04: 20⁴S, 16²S, 16⁴S, 17⁰G,

	Starts	1st	2nd	3rd	Win & Pl
Hurdles	4	0	1	0	5350
Career Total	18	2	5	2	102916
135	2/02	Leop	2m		Hdl	HVY	£16748
117	12/01	Leop			Hdl	YLD	£20967
				Total win prize-money £37716			

Going:	Sf: 0-3 GS: 0-0 Gd: 0-1 GF: - Fm: 0-0
Distance:	2m/2m3: 0-3 2m4-2m7: 0-1 3m+: 0-0
Track:	LH: 0-4 RH: 0-0 Tight: 0-0 Gall: 0-1
Aids:	Bl: 0-0 Vi: 0-0 Tstrap: 0-0 Ckp: 0-0
Best Rating:	135 2/02 Leop 2m heavy Hdl

Useful Irish-trained hurdler; runner-up in the 2002 Triumph Hurdle, but has not won since; acts on ground ranging from fast to heavy; effective over two miles.

Newick Park

108   **107**

9-y-o gr g Chilibang-Quilpee Mai (Pee Mai)
R Dickin Newick Park Partnership

Placings:151P/1616P/534PP-1122F   (4211)
2003/04: 16¹GF, 18¹S, 16²G, 21²G, 20⁰F,

	Starts	1st	2nd	3rd	Win & Pl
Chases	5	2	2	0	14593
Career Total	19	6	2	1	30631
110	1/04	Newb	2m2f110y(0-120)HCh	SFT	£5538
100	11/03	Wwck	2m110y E(0-105)HCh	G-F	£3370
110	12/01	Sand	2m4f110y(0-115)HCh	G-S	£5694
95	10/01	Folk	2m	E Ch	GD	£3406
100	11/00	Folk	2m1f110yE Hdl	HVY	£2390
105	6/00	Folk	2m1f110yF Hdl	GD	£1948
			Total win prize-money £22349		

Going:	Sf: 1-1 GS: 0-0 Gd: 0-3 GF: - Fm: 1-1
Distance:	**2m/2m3: 2-3** 2m4-2m7: 0-2 3m+: 0-0
Track:	**LH: 2-2** RH: 0-3 Tight: 0-0 **Gall: 1-1**
Aids:	Bl: 0-0 Vi: 0-0 Tstrap: 0-0 Ckp: 0-0
Best Rating:	110 1/04 Newb 2m2f110y soft Ch

Plating-class chaser; effective at 2m 4f; acts on most types of ground.

Newkidontheblock (IRE)

99   **82+**

9-y-o b g Be My Native (USA)-Jenny's Child (Crash Course)
J R Jenkins The Beaver Group

Placings:*106*/65/5/2-00236   (4892)
2003/04: 16⁸G, 16⁶S, 16²G, 20³G, 16⁶GF,

	Starts	1st	2nd	3rd	Win & Pl
Hurdles	5	0	1	1	1126
Career Total	12	1	2	1	3592
99	3/00	Hntg	2m110y H NHF	G-F	£1694
			Total win prize-money £1694		

Going:	Sf: 0-1 GS: 0-0 Gd: 0-3 GF: - Fm: 0-1
Distance:	2m/2m3: 0-4 2m4-2m7: 0-1 3m+: 0-0
Track:	LH: 0-2 RH: 0-3 Tight: 0-2 Gall: 0-1
Aids:	Bl: 0-0 Vi: 0-0 Tstrap: 0-0 Ckp: 0-0
Best Rating:	107 4/00 Font 2m2f110y good NHF

Plating-class hurdler; effective over two miles; acts on good ground.

News Flash (IRE)

12-y-o b g Strong Gale-Gale Flash (News Item)
Lady Susan Brooke (E R Clough 23/7) Lady Susan Brooke

Placings:0/0F6/P/455FU-0C2   (4891)
2003/04: 20⁰G, 24ᶜG, 24²GF,

	Starts	1st	2nd	3rd	Win & Pl
Hurdles	1	0	0	0	0
Chases	2	0	1	0	836
Career Total	13	0	1	0	836

Going:	Sf: 0-0 GS: 0-0 Gd: 0-2 GF: - Fm: 0-1
Distance:	2m/2m3: 0-0 2m4-2m7: 0-1 3m+: 0-2
Track:	LH: 0-2 RH: 0-1 Tight: 0-2 Gall: 0-0
Aids:	Bl: 0-0 Vi: 0-0 Tstrap: 0-0 Ckp: 0-0
Best Rating:	86 11/97 Newb 2m110y good Hdl

News Maker (IRE)

95(107h)   **129**

8-y-o b g Good Thyne (USA)-Announcement (Laurence O)
Mrs H Dalton Mrs Caroline Shaw

Placings:301334/2121P-4   (1828)
2003/04: 24⁴GF,

	Starts	1st	2nd	3rd	Win & Pl
Chases	1	0	0	0	535
Career Total	12	3	2	3	21573
129	3/03	Weth	2m7f110yD Ch	GD	£6624
126	12/02	Hayd	3m	D(0-110)HCh	SFT	£5018
100	12/01	Uttx	2m4f110yE Hdl	SFT	£2681
			Total win prize-money £14323		

Going:	Sf: 0-0 GS: 0-0 Gd: 0-0 GF: - Fm: 0-1
Distance:	2m/2m3: 0-0 2m4-2m7: 0-0 3m+: 0-1
Track:	LH: 0-1 RH: 0-0 Tight: 0-0 Gall: 0-1
Aids:	Bl: 0-0 Vi: 0-0 Tstrap: 0-0 Ckp: 0-0
Best Rating:	129 3/03 Weth 2m7f110y good Ch

Modest hurdler/fair chaser; acts on soft ground; stays three miles.

Newsplayer (IRE)

104(100h)   (91h)**119**

8-y-o br g Alphabatim (USA)-Another Tycoon (IRE)

(Phardante (FR))
R T Phillips Bradley, Dale, Deal, Hirschfeld

Placings:*0/30*/5003-0211   (1658)
2003/04: 20⁰G, 17²GF, 16¹GS, 16¹G,

	Starts	1st	2nd	3rd	Win & Pl
Hurdles	1	0	0	0	0
Chases	3	2	1	0	8755
Career Total	11	2	1	2	9428
119	10/03	Sedg	2m110y	E(0-105)HCh	GD	£3692
105	7/03	NAbb	2m110y	E Ch	G-S	£4026
			Total win prize-money £7719		

Going:	Sf: 0-0 GS: 1-1 Gd: 1-2 GF: - Fm: 0-1
Distance:	**2m/2m3: 2-3** 2m4-2m7: 0-1 3m+: 0-0
Track:	**LH: 2-3** RH: 0-1 **Tight: 2-2** Gall: 0-0
Aids:	Bl: 0-0 Vi: 0-0 **Tstrap:** 0-2 Ckp: 0-0
Best Rating:	119 10/03 Sedg 2m110y good Ch

Fair chaser; jumped right on chasing debut July 2003; won next two races; acts on good and easy ground; does not appear to stay 2m4f.

Newtown

5-y-o b g Darshaan-Calypso Run (Lycius (USA))
M F Harris Warwick Racecourse Owners Club

Placings:PP   (3983)
2003/04: 20⁰GS, 17⁰GS,

	Starts	1st	2nd	3rd	Win & Pl
Hurdles	2	0	0	0	
Career Total	2	0	0	0	

Going:	Sf: 0-0 GS: 0-2 Gd: 0-0 GF: - Fm: 0-0
Distance:	2m/2m3: 0-1 2m4-2m7: 0-1 3m+: 0-0
Track:	LH: 0-1 RH: 0-1 Tight: 0-2 Gall: 0-0
Aids:	Bl: 0-0 Vi: 0-0 Tstrap: 0-0 Ckp: 0-0

Next To Nothing (IRE)

95(100h)   (104+h)**114+**

7-y-o b g Bob's Return (IRE)-Shuil Abhaile (Quayside)
N G Richards Ashleybank Investments Limited

Placings:5P-2P11P   (4726)
2003/04: 24²GS, 25⁴GS, 24¹G, 24¹HY, 24⁰G,

	Starts	1st	2nd	3rd	Win & Pl
Hurdles	2	0	1	0	863
Chases	3	2	0	0	11295
Career Total	7	2	1	0	12158
114	3/04	Newc	3m	E(0-110)HCh	HVY	£5021
104	2/04	Carl	3m	D Ch	GD	£6274
			Total win prize-money £11295		

Going:	Sf: 1-1 GS: 0-2 Gd: 1-2 GF: - Fm: 0-0
Distance:	2m/2m3: 0-0 2m4-2m7: 0-0 **3m+: 2-5**
Track:	LH: 1-3 RH: 1-2 Tight: 0-0 **Gall: 1-1**
Aids:	Bl: 0-0 Vi: 0-0 Tstrap: 0-0 Ckp: 0-0
Best Rating:	114 3/04 Newc 3m heavy Ch

Modest novice hurdler/chaser; front runner; ran his best race when stepped up to three miles; acts on easy ground; type to improve again over fences.

Niagara (IRE)

100(106h)   (104h)**105**

7-y-o b g Rainbows For Life (CAN)-Highbrook (USA) (Alphabatim (USA))
M H Tompkins Pollards Stables

Placings:2/2P40-323211 (1574)
2003/04: 16³GF, 20²GF, 19³G, 17²GF, 20¹GF, 16¹F,

	Starts	1st	2nd	3rd	Win & Pl
Hurdles	4	0	2	2	4284
Chases	2	2	0	0	8730
Career Total	11	2	4	2	15252
105 10/03 Towc	2m110y	D Ch			FRM £4686
101 9/03 Plum	2m4f	D Ch			G-F £4043
			Total win prize-money £8730		

Going:	Sf: 0-0 GS: 0-0 Gd: 0-1 GF: - Fm: 2-5
Distance:	2m/2m3: 1-4 2m4-2m7: 1-2 3m+: 0-0
Track:	LH: 1-4 RH: 1-2 Tight: 1-3 Gall: 0-0
Aids:	Bl: 0-1 Vi: 0-0 Tstrap: 0-0 Ckp: 0-0
Best Rating:	105 10/03 Towc 2m110y firm Ch

Moderate hurdler; winner of his first two novice chases; acts on fast ground; best at two miles but appears to get farther; front runner; has worn blinkers.

Nice Guy Eddie
55f
5-y-o g Thowra (FR)-Mrs Guyb Vii (Damsire Unregistered)
N J Hawke   N J Hawke

Placings:0 (0871)
2003/04: 17⁰GF,

	Starts	1st	2nd	3rd	Win & Pl
NH Flat	1	0	0	0	
Career Total	1	0	0	0	

Going:	Sf: 0-0 GS: 0-0 Gd: 0-0 GF: - Fm: 0-1
Distance:	2m/2m3: 0-1 2m4-2m7: 0-0 3m+: 0-0
Track:	LH: 0-1 RH: 0-0 Tight: 0-1 Gall: 0-0
Aids:	Bl: 0-0 Vi: 0-0 Tstrap: 0-0 Ckp: 0-0

Nice N Spicey

7-y-o br m Sure Blade (USA)-Dusty Chimes (Foggy Bell)
J White   H J H Reynolds

Placings:00P (1679)
2003/04: 16⁰G, 17⁰GF, 16²F,

	Starts	1st	2nd	3rd	Win & Pl
NH Flat	3	0	0	0	
Career Total	3	0	0	0	

Going:	Sf: 0-0 GS: 0-0 Gd: 0-1 GF: - Fm: 0-2
Distance:	2m/2m3: 0-3 2m4-2m7: 0-0 3m+: 0-0
Track:	LH: 0-1 RH: 0-2 Tight: 0-0 Gall: 0-0
Aids:	Bl: 0-0 Vi: 0-0 Tstrap: 0-0 Ckp: 0-0

Nice One Ted (IRE)

8-y-o b g Posen (USA)-Arburie (Exbury)
Mrs Pippa Bickerton   Mrs Pippa Bickerton

Placings:400P-P0P (3226)
2003/04: 24⁰GS, 19⁰GS, 26⁰GS,

	Starts	1st	2nd	3rd	Win & Pl
Hurdles	3	0	0	0	
Career Total	7	0	0	0	0

Going:	Sf: 0-0 GS: 0-2 Gd: 0-1 GF: - Fm: 0-0
Distance:	2m/2m3: 0-0 2m4-2m7: 0-1 3m+: 0-2
Track:	LH: 0-0 RH: 0-3 Tight: 0-1 Gall: 0-0
Aids:	Bl: 0-0 Vi: 0-0 Tstrap: 0-1 Ckp: 0-0

Best Rating: 77 10/02 Hrfd 2m1f gd-fm NHF

Nicely Presented (IRE)
103   102
7-y-o b g Executive Perk-Minimum Choice (IRE) (Miners Lamp)
Jonjo O'Neill   John P McManus

Placings:433-PP034 (4946)
2003/04: 17⁵S, 20⁰GS, 21⁰G, 16³G, 16⁴GS,

	Starts	1st	2nd	3rd	Win & Pl
Hurdles	5	0	0	1	980
Career Total	8	0	0	3	1623

Going:	Sf: 0-1 GS: 0-2 Gd: 0-2 GF: - Fm: 0-0
Distance:	2m/2m3: 0-3 2m4-2m7: 0-2 3m+: 0-0
Track:	LH: 0-1 RH: 0-4 Tight: 0-2 Gall: 0-2
Aids:	Bl: 0-0 Vi: 0-0 Tstrap: 0-0 Ckp: 0-0
Best Rating:	102 3/04 Hntg 2m110y good Hdl

Moderate hurdler; acts on good ground or softer.

Nicho-Line
63f   46f
7-y-o b g Homo Sapien-Littoral (Crash Course)
Mrs J A Saunders   John Nicholls (banbury) Ltd

Placings:000 (1378)
2003/04: 16⁰GF, 16⁰GF, 16⁰GF,

	Starts	1st	2nd	3rd	Win & Pl
NH Flat	3	0	0	0	
Career Total	3	0	0	0	

Going:	Sf: 0-0 GS: 0-0 Gd: 0-0 GF: - Fm: 0-3
Distance:	2m/2m3: 0-3 2m4-2m7: 0-0 3m+: 0-0
Track:	LH: 0-2 RH: 0-1 Tight: 0-0 Gall: 0-1
Aids:	Bl: 0-0 Vi: 0-0 Tstrap: 0-0 Ckp: 0-0
Best Rating:	49 9/03 Worc 2m gd-fm NHF

Nichol Fifty
78   90
10-y-o b g Old Vic-Jawaher (IRE) (Dancing Brave (USA))
N Wilson   E J Govan

Placings:41P/00/P/305-0 (1184)
2003/04: 22⁰G,

	Starts	1st	2nd	3rd	Win & Pl
Hurdles	1	0	0	0	
Career Total	10	1	0	1	3758
114 3/98 MRas	2m1f110yD Hdl			G-S	£2979
			Total win prize-money £2980		

Going:	Sf: 0-0 GS: 0-0 Gd: 0-1 GF: - Fm: 0-0
Distance:	2m/2m3: 0-0 2m4-2m7: 0-1 3m+: 0-0
Track:	LH: 0-1 RH: 0-0 Tight: 0-1 Gall: 0-0
Aids:	Bl: 0-0 Vi: 0-0 Tstrap: 0-0 Ckp: 0-0
Best Rating:	114 3/98 MRas 2m1f110y gd-sft Hdl

Selling hurdler, largely out of form.

Nicholls Cross (IRE)

12-y-o b g Mandalus-Milan Pride (Northern Guest (USA))
D McCain Jnr   D A Malam

Placings:4/40224/F31F21/3633F611U33F3/0533F526424/030004300/B651506-F (4002)

2003/04: 20⁵G,

	Starts	1st	2nd	3rd	Win & Pl
Chases	1	0	0	0	
Career Total	53	5	5	11	54153
110 8/02 Kbgn	3m1f	(0-109)HCh	Y-S	£5503
128 10/99 Gowr	2m	(0-116)HCh	G-Y	£6776
135 9/99 List	2m3f	(0-123)HCh	HVY	£5544
119 9/98 Baln	2m1f	Ch	G-Y	£5978
112 7/98 Klny	2m1f	(0-109)HHdl	G-F	£2690
		Total win prize-money £26493		

Going:	Sf: 0-0 GS: 0-0 Gd: 0-1 GF: - Fm: 0-0
Distance:	2m/2m3: 0-2 2m4-2m7: 0-1 3m+: 0-0
Track:	LH: 0-0 RH: 0-1 Tight: 0-1 Gall: 0-0
Aids:	Bl: 0-0 Vi: 0-0 Tstrap: 0-0 Ckp: 0-0
Best Rating:	135 9/99 List 2m3f heavy Ch

Niciara (IRE)
102   93
7-y-o b g Soviet Lad (USA)-Verusa (IRE) (Petorius)
M C Chapman   Alan Mann

Placings:11/45/054 (4605)
2003/04: 16⁰GS, 19⁵G, 22⁴G,

	Starts	1st	2nd	3rd	Win & Pl
Hurdles	3	0	0	0	388
Career Total	7	2	0	0	5509
111 9/00 Sedg	2m1f	E Hdl	GD	£2408
102 8/00 Ctml	2m1f110yE Hdl		G-S	£2712
		Total win prize-money £5121		

Going:	Sf: 0-0 GS: 0-1 Gd: 0-2 GF: - Fm: 0-0
Distance:	2m/2m3: 0-2 2m4-2m7: 0-1 3m+: 0-0
Track:	LH: 0-2 RH: 0-0 Tight: 0-0 Gall: 0-0
Aids:	Bl: 0-0 Vi: 0-0 Tstrap: 0-0 Ckp: 0-0
Best Rating:	111 9/00 Sedg 2m1f good Hdl

Moderate hurdler; best at two miles; acts on good and goes to soft ground.

Nick The Jewel
106   (36h)122
9-y-o b g Nicholas Bill-Bijou Georgie (Rhodomantade)
J S King   Marlborough Racing Partnership

Placings:0F004/P111FP03-11332 (2954)
2003/04: 17¹GF, 16¹GF, 16³GF, 16³GF, 16²G,

	Starts	1st	2nd	3rd	Win & Pl
Chases	5	2	1	2	11577
Career Total	18	5	1	3	25091
122 10/03 Uttx	2m	E(0-110)HCh	G-F	£3563
113 10/03 Strf	2m1f110yE(0-105)HCh		G-F	£3406
108 12/02 Hntg	2m110y	E(0-105)HCh	G-S	£3545
115 11/02 Hrfd	2m	E(0-105)HCh	SFT	£4446
112 11/02 Ludl	2m	E(0-105)HCh	GD	£4433
		Total win prize-money £19394		

Going:	Sf: 0-0 GS: 0-0 Gd: 0-1 GF: - Fm: 2-4
Distance:	2m/2m3: 2-5 2m4-2m7: 0-0 3m+: 0-0
Track:	LH: 2-3 RH: 0-2 Tight: 1-2 Gall: 0-0
Aids:	Bl: 0-0 Vi: 0-0 Tstrap: 0-0 Ckp: 0-0
Best Rating:	122 10/03 Uttx 2m gd-fm Ch

Modest chaser; raised 13lb after back-to-back wins in October 2003; stays 2m; acts on good and soft ground; front-runner; neat jumper.

Nick's Choice
103   112+
8-y-o b g Sula Bula-Clare's Choice (Pragmatic)
D Burchell   Don Gould

Placings:343005263/P0134/421P00611F/50601-5163

(3050)

2003/04: 16⁶GF, 16¹S, 16⁶G, 17³G,

		Starts	1st	2nd	3rd	Win & Pl
Hurdles		4	1	0	1	4592
Career Total		33	6	2	5	23087
112	11/03	Plum	2m	E(0-110)HHdl	SFT	£3474
102	3/03	Ludl	2m5f	E(0-105)HHdl	GD	£3552
110	3/02	Hrfd	2m3f110yF(0-100)HHdl	SFT	£3653
94	2/02	Tntn	2m1f	E(0-105)HHdl	SFT	£2782
101	5/01	Bang	2m4f	E(0-100)HHdl	GD	£2530
92	3/01	Extr	2m1f	F(0-100)HHdl	HVY	£2506
				Total win prize-money £18499		

Going:	Sf: 1-1 GS: 0-0 Gd: 0-2 GF: - Fm: 0-1
Distance:	2m/2m3: 1-4 2m4-2m7: 0-0 3m+: 0-0
Track:	LH: 1-3 RH: 0-1 Tight: 1-2 Gall: 0-0
Aids:	Bl: 0-0 Vi: 0-0 Tstrap: 0-0 Ckp: 0-0
Best Rating:	115 3/02 NAbb 2m1f good Hdl

Moderate hurdler; stays two and a half miles and acts on good and heavy ground.

Nickel Plate

7-y-o b g Perpendicular-Tinstone (Nishapour (FR))
J G M O'Shea Ms N McGrail

Placings:6P

(3256)

2003/04: 16⁶G, 21⁶GS,

		Starts	1st	2nd	3rd	Win & Pl
NH Flat		1	0	0	0	0
Hurdles		1	0	0	0	0
Career Total		2	0	0	0	0

Going:	Sf: 0-0 GS: 0-1 Gd: 0-0 GF: - Fm: 0-1
Distance:	2m/2m3: 0-0 2m4-2m7: 0-1 3m+: 0-0
Track:	LH: 0-0 RH: 0-0 Tight: 0-0 Gall: 0-0
Aids:	Bl: 0-0 Vi: 0-0 Tstrap: 0-0 Ckp: 0-0
Best Rating:	75 12/03 Ludl 2m gd-fm NHF

Nickel Sun (IRE)

105   124

8-y-o b g Phardante (FR)-Deep Green (Deep Run)
Mrs S J Smith Keith Nicholson

Placings:22153512/11010433-3F

(0384)

2003/04: 20³S, 22⁶G,

		Starts	1st	2nd	3rd	Win & Pl
Hurdles		2	0	0	1	1772
Career Total		18	5	3	4	40777
120	12/02	Hayd	2m4f	B HHdl	GD	£16835
120	5/02	Uttx	2m4f110yB(0-140)HHdl	GD	£6854
111	5/02	Weth	2m4f110yD Hdl	G-F	£3605
103	4/02	Carl	2m1f	E Hdl	GD	£2975
96	9/01	MRas	2m1f110yH NHF	SFT	£1596
				Total win prize-money £31865		

Going:	Sf: 0-1 GS: 0-0 Gd: 0-1 GF: 0-0 Fm: 0-0
Distance:	2m/2m3: 0-0 2m4-2m7: 0-5 3m+: 0-0
Track:	LH: 0-2 RH: 0-0 Tight: 0-1 Gall: 0-0
Aids:	Bl: 0-0 Vi: 0-0 Tstrap: 0-0 Ckp: 0-0
Best Rating:	124 5/03 Uttx 2m4f110y soft Hdl

Fair hurdler; stays two miles four; acts on most types of ground.

Nickel Suntoo (IRE)

98   82+

7-y-o b g Convinced-The Scarlet Dragon (Oats)
Mrs S J Smith Keith Nicholson

Placings:200-6205

(1190)

2003/04: 17⁶GF, 17²G, 20⁰GF, 20⁵GF,

		Starts	1st	2nd	3rd	Win & Pl
NH Flat		1	0	0	0	0
Hurdles		3	0	1	0	1150
Career Total		7	0	2	0	1831

Going:	Sf: 0-0 GS: 0-0 Gd: 0-1 GF: - Fm: 0-3
Distance:	2m/2m3: 0-2 2m4-2m7: 0-2 3m+: 0-0
Track:	LH: 0-3 RH: 0-1 Tight: 0-1 Gall: 0-1
Aids:	Bl: 0-0 Vi: 0-0 Tstrap: 0-0 Ckp: 0-0
Best Rating:	97 11/02 Sthl 2m gd-sft NHF

Modest form in bumpers; runner-up to very easy winner in weak novices hurdle at Market Rasen in June 2003; has failed to progress since.

Niembro

106   91

4-y-o b g Victory Note (USA)-Diabaig (Precocious)
Mrs T J McInnes Skinner (Mrs Lydia Pearce 17/11) Mrs T J McInnes Skinner

Placings:443210P05

(4959)

2003/04: 16⁶GF, 16⁴GF, 16³GF, 16²GF, 16¹G, 16⁰S, 16⁶G, 16⁹G, 19⁵G,

		Starts	1st	2nd	3rd	Win & Pl
Hurdles		9	1	1	1	5468
Career Total		9	1	1	1	5468
91	12/03	Leic	2m	D Hdl	GD	£4241
				Total win prize-money £4241		

Going:	Sf: 0-1 GS: 0-0 Gd: 1-4 GF: - Fm: 0-4
Distance:	2m/2m3: 1-8 2m4-2m7: 0-1 3m+: 0-0
Track:	LH: 0-2 RH: 1-7 Tight: 0-1 Gall: 0-5
Aids:	Bl: 0-0 Vi: 0-0 Tstrap: 0-0 Ckp: 0-0
Best Rating:	91 12/03 Leic 2m good Hdl

Modest hurdler; got off the mark at Leicester last time; stays two miles; acts on good ground; has been tried in blinkers and cheekpieces on the Flat.

Nigello

85(89h)   (67h)84+

12-y-o b g El Conquistador-Saffron Poser (Sagaro)
Miss V A Stephens D G Stephens

Placings:505P/21312P3/2P1P4/2F3F0400/440U0

(4814)

2003/04: 21⁴G, 21⁴GS, 19⁰G, 21⁰G, 19⁰G,

		Starts	1st	2nd	3rd	Win & Pl
Hurdles		1	0	0	0	0
Chases		4	0	0	0	581
Career Total		29	3	4	3	19929
115	11/00	Ludl	3m	E(0-115)HCh	G-F	£4114
108	12/99	Ludl	2m4f	D(0-115)HCh	GD	£4357
111	10/99	Hrfd	2m3f	E(0-105)HCh	G-F	£3615
				Total win prize-money £12088		

Going:	Sf: 0-0 GS: 0-1 Gd: 0-4 GF: - Fm: 0-0
Distance:	2m/2m3: 0-0 2m4-2m7: 0-5 3m+: 0-0
Track:	LH: 0-3 RH: 0-2 Tight: 0-3 Gall: 0-0
Aids:	Bl: 0-0 Vi: 0-0 Tstrap: 0-0 Ckp: 0-0
Best Rating:	115 11/01 Ludl 3m gd-fm Ch

Night Driver (IRE)

94   96

5-y-o b g Night Shift (USA)-Highshaan (Pistolet Bleu (IRE))
P J Hobbs Colin Brown Racing li

Placings:44-0F352U0P

(4304)

2003/04: 16⁰GS, 17⁶GF, 17³GF, 17⁵GF, 17²G, 16¹S, 16⁹G, 16⁶G,

		Starts	1st	2nd	3rd	Win & Pl
Hurdles		8	0	1	1	1907
Career Total		10	0	1	1	2621

Going:	Sf: 0-1 GS: 0-1 Gd: 0-3 GF: - Fm: 0-3
Distance:	2m/2m3: 0-8 2m4-2m7: 0-0 3m+: 0-0
Track:	LH: 0-4 RH: 0-4 Tight: 0-4 Gall: 0-0
Aids:	Bl: 0-1 Vi: 0-0 Tstrap: 0-0 Ckp: 0-0
Best Rating:	100 12/03 Tntn 2m1f good Hdl

Moderate hurdler; best around two miles; acts on a sound surface.

Night Fighter (GER)

105(104h)   (114+h)114

9-y-o b g Dashing Blade-Nouvelle (GER) (Nandino (GER))
R C Guest N B Mason

Placings:060/2240056/P/121F44305/301P222314F0U-51P

(0920)

2003/04: 17⁵G, 17¹G, 17⁸GF,

		Starts	1st	2nd	3rd	Win & Pl
Chases		3	1	0	0	4108
Career Total		36	5	6	3	26629
114	7/03	MRas	2m1f110yE(0-110)HCh	GD	£4108
114	2/03	Donc	2m110y D(0-110)HCh	GD	£5443
114	8/02	Ctml	2m1f110yD(0-120)HHdl	GD	£4533
106	10/01	Towc	2m	F(0-100)HHdl	GD	£2723
98	9/01	Worc	2m	G(0-90)HHdl	G-F	£1671
				Total win prize-money £18481		

Going:	Sf: 0-0 GS: 0-0 Gd: 1-2 GF: - Fm: 0-1
Distance:	2m/2m3: 1-3 2m4-2m7: 0-0 3m+: 0-0
Track:	LH: 0-1 RH: 1-2 Tight: 1-2 Gall: 0-0
Aids:	Bl: 0-0 Vi: 0-0 Tstrap: 0-1 Ckp: 1-2
Best Rating:	114 7/03 MRas 2m1f110y good Ch

Modest chaser; suited by trips of around two miles and good ground; usually tongue tied and wears cheekpieces; pulled up lame July 2003.

Night Mail

82   78

4-y-o b g Shaamit (IRE)-Penlanfeigan (Abutammam)
M W Easterby Night Mail Partnership

Placings:06

(2528)

2003/04: 16⁰G, 16⁶GS,

		Starts	1st	2nd	3rd	Win & Pl
Hurdles		2	0	0	0	0
Career Total		2	0	0	0	0

Going:	Sf: 0-0 GS: 0-1 Gd: 0-1 GF: - Fm: 0-0
Distance:	2m/2m3: 0-2 2m4-2m7: 0-0 3m+: 0-0
Track:	LH: 0-2 RH: 0-0 Tight: 0-1 Gall: 0-1
Aids:	Bl: 0-0 Vi: 0-0 Tstrap: 0-0 Ckp: 0-0
Best Rating:	78 12/03 Catt 2m gd-sft Hdl

Night Music

74

7-y-o b/br m Piccolo-Oribi (Top Ville)
G F Edwards G F Edwards

Placings:00F4/F3P0-F

(0034)

2003/04: 22⁵G,

		Starts	1st	2nd	3rd	Win & Pl
Hurdles		1	0	0	0	
Career Total		9	0	0	1	360

Going: Sf: 0-0 GS: 0-0 Gd: 0-1 GF: - Fm: 0-0
Distance: 2m/2m3: 0-0 2m4-2m7: 0-1 3m+: 0-0
Track: LH: 0-0 RH: 0-1 Tight: 0-0 Gall: 0-0
Aids: Bl: 0-0 Vi: 0-0 Tstrap: 0-0 Ckp: 0-1
Best Rating: 79   4/03   Extr   2m6f110y   good   Hdl

Nijway

101(84h)   (45h)**76**
14-y-o b g Nijin (USA)-Runaway Girl (FR) (Homeric)
M A Barnes M Barnes

Placings:00P40/P2R044241/33F06U4FU31U12P1/312405
2/P13P/PUP44/1400P/S00P6060/PP0-P0U3FP   (1492)
2003/04: 24⁰GF, 16ᴾG, 22⁰G, 21ᵁG, 27³GF, 24ᶠG, 25ᴾGF,

	Starts	1st	2nd	3rd	Win & Pl
Hurdles	1	0	0	0	0
Chases	6	0	0	1	514
Career Total	68	7	5	6	33023
100	5/00	Sedg	3m3f	F(0-110)HCh	G-F	£3955
104	3/99	Ayr	2m4f	D(0-120)HCh	SFT	£3736
95	5/97	Hexm	3m1f	E(0-115)HCh	G-F	£2406
98	4/97	Kels	3m1f	D(0-120)HCh	G-F	£3986
90	3/97	Carl	3m	F(0-105)HCh	GD	£3355
90	3/97	Sedg	2m5f	E Ch	GD	£3023
86	4/96	Prth	2m110y	D(0-110)HHdl	SFT	£3941

Total win prize-money £24405

Going: Sf: 0-0 GS: 0-0 Gd: 0-4 GF: - Fm: 0-3
Distance: 2m/2m3: 0-1 2m4-2m7: 0-2 3m+: 0-4
Track: LH: 0-5 RH: 0-2 Tight: 0-3 Gall: 0-1
Aids: Bl: 0-5 Vi: 0-0 Tstrap: 0-7 Ckp: 0-1
Best Rating: 104   3/99   Newc   3m   soft   Ch

Plating-class chaser; stays forever, but one-paced with it.

Nimbus Stratus

87   **48**
11-y-o br g Welsh Captain-Touching Clouds (Touching Wood (USA))
J D Frost Miss M McCarthy

Placings:53436P/06/0/60-P5   (1077)
2003/04: 22ᴾG, 20⁵GF,

	Starts	1st	2nd	3rd	Win & Pl
Hurdles	2	0	0	0	0
Career Total	13	0	0	2	821

Going: Sf: 0-0 GS: 0-0 Gd: 0-1 GF: - Fm: 0-1
Distance: 2m/2m3: 0-0 2m4-2m7: 0-2 3m+: 0-0
Track: LH: 0-2 RH: 0-0 Tight: 0-0 Gall: 0-0
Aids: Bl: 0-0 Vi: 0-0 Tstrap: 0-0 Ckp: 0-2
Best Rating: 86   10/99   Chep   2m110y   soft   Hdl

Nine O Three (IRE)

93   **88**
15-y-o b g Supreme Leader-Grenache (Menelek)
Mrs S D Williams Bideford Tool Ltd

Placings:0/630000 /33040/3F2005343/350001/61226/1006/
405/03F1114/2000/6143F/4322-60F   (0754)
2003/04: 24⁶G, 27⁰GF, 27ᶠGF,

	Starts	1st	2nd	3rd	Win & Pl
Hurdles	3	0	0	0	0
Career Total	63	8	6	10	45693
122	6/01	NAbb	3m3f	C(0-130)HHdl	G-F	£4867
117	10/99	Worc	2m4f	C(0-130)HHdl	GD	£6840
110	9/99	NAbb	3m3f	D(0-120)HHdl	G-F	£2859
99	7/99	Worc	3m	C(0-135)HHdl	G-F	£4796
115	12/97	Tntn	2m1f	D(0-125)HHdl	G-F	£2794
106	6/96	Worc	2m4f	D(0-130)HHdl	G-F	£3965

107	2/96	Tntn	2m1f	F(0-105)HHdl	G-S	£2284
	2/94	Thur	2m	NHF	SFT	£2628

Total win prize-money £31036

Going: Sf: 0-0 GS: 0-0 Gd: 0-1 GF: - Fm: 0-2
Distance: 2m/2m3: 0-0 2m4-2m7: 0-3 3m+: 0-3
Track: LH: 0-3 RH: 0-0 Tight: 0-2 Gall: 0-0
Aids: Bl: 0-0 Vi: 0-0 Tstrap: 0-0 Ckp: 0-0
Best Rating: 124   9/00   MRas   3m   gd-fm   Hdl

Nip On

91(102h)   (95h)**57**
10-y-o b g Dunbeath (USA)-Popping On (Sonnen Gold)
J R Turner Robin Ellerbeck

Placings:0001/053P53F10/0/20/P3234-P0P24   (1837)
2003/04: 25ᴾG, 25⁰G, 25ᴾG, 20²F, 27⁴G,

	Starts	1st	2nd	3rd	Win & Pl
Hurdles	2	0	1	0	2056
Chases	3	0	0	0	0
Career Total	26	2	3	4	11143
102	3/00	Sedg	3m3f110y	D(0-120)HHdl	G-F	£2938
95	4/99	Hexm	2m4f110y	E Hdl	GD	£2196

Total win prize-money £5134

Going: Sf: 0-0 GS: 0-0 Gd: 0-4 GF: - Fm: 0-0
Distance: 2m/2m3: 0-0 2m4-2m7: 0-1 3m+: 0-4
Track: LH: 0-5 RH: 0-0 Tight: 0-1 Gall: 0-0
Aids: Bl: 0-0 Vi: 0-0 Tstrap: 0-1 Ckp: 0-1
Best Rating: 102   3/00   Sedg   3m3f110y   gd-fm   Hdl

Moderate hurdler; stays three miles plus but effective over much shorter; often wears cheekpieces.

Nisbet

10-y-o b g Lithgie-Brig-Drummond Lass (Peacock (FR))
Miss M Bremner (Miss Lucinda V Russell 3/7) Mrs Ann Rutherford

Placings:4455P33P4526-P30312   (4949)
2003/04: 25ᴾG, 24³GF, 25⁹GF, 24³G, 25¹G, 26²GS,

	Starts	1st	2nd	3rd	Win & Pl
Chases	6	1	1	2	5145
Career Total	18	1	2	4	9388
93	4/04	Kels	3m1f	H Ch	GD	£2096

Total win prize-money £2096

Going: Sf: 0-0 GS: 0-0 Gd: 1-3 GF: - Fm: 0-2
Distance: 2m/2m3: 0-0 2m4-2m7: 0-0 3m+: 1-6
Track: LH: 1-3 RH: 0-2 Tight: 1-1 Gall: 0-0
Aids: Bl: 0-0 Vi: 0-0 Tstrap: 0-0 Ckp: 0-0
Best Rating: 93   4/04   Kels   3m1f   good   Ch

Plating-class chaser; winning pointer, opened account under Rules at Kelso in maiden hunter chase in April; stays three miles; acts on any ground.

Nite Fox (IRE)

95f   **84f**
5-y-o ch m Anshan-New Talent (The Parson)
Mrs H Dalton Mrs A Beard Miss M Knapper & J Dalton

Placings:65   (4920)
2003/04: 16⁶G, 16⁵GS,

	Starts	1st	2nd	3rd	Win & Pl
NH Flat	2	0	0	0	0
Career Total	2	0	0	0	0

Going: Sf: 0-0 GS: 0-1 Gd: 0-1 GF: - Fm: 0-0
Distance: 2m/2m3: 0-2 2m4-2m7: 0-0 3m+: 0-0

Track: LH: 0-1 RH: 0-1 Tight: 0-0 Gall: 0-1
Aids: Bl: 0-0 Vi: 0-0 Tstrap: 0-0 Ckp: 0-0
Best Rating: 84   4/04   Worc   2m   gd-sft   NHF

No Argument

5-y-o b g Young Em-As Sharp As (Handsome Sailor)
C C Bealby (D W Chapman 16/6) Michael Hill

Placings:PP   (2421)
2003/04: 17ᴾGF, 20ᴾGS,

	Starts	1st	2nd	3rd	Win & Pl
Hurdles	2	0	0	0	0
Career Total	2	0	0	0	0

Going: Sf: 0-0 GS: 0-1 Gd: 0-0 GF: - Fm: 0-1
Distance: 2m/2m3: 0-1 2m4-2m7: 0-1 3m+: 0-0
Track: LH: 0-1 RH: 0-1 Tight: 0-1 Gall: 0-0
Aids: Bl: 0-0 Vi: 0-0 Tstrap: 0-0 Ckp: 0-0

No Fear (IRE)

8-y-o b g Warcraft (USA)-Mandalaw (IRE) (Mandalus)
Mrs S J Smith Mrs S Smith

Placings:2/P   (0495)
2003/04: 20ᴾG,

	Starts	1st	2nd	3rd	Win & Pl
Hurdles	1	0	0	0	0
Career Total	2	0	1	0	714

Going: Sf: 0-0 GS: 0-0 Gd: 0-1 GF: - Fm: 0-0
Distance: 2m/2m3: 0-0 2m4-2m7: 0-0 3m+: 0-0
Track: LH: 0-1 RH: 0-0 Tight: 0-0 Gall: 0-0
Aids: Bl: 0-0 Vi: 0-0 Tstrap: 0-0 Ckp: 0-0
Best Rating: 98   4/02   Carl   2m1f   good   NHF

No Finer Man (IRE)

13-y-o b g Lord Americo-Ballaroe Bar (Bargello)
Miss Angela Stephenson Andy Hogan

Placings:055/425/54P2/PP/0   (0430)
2003/04: 26⁶G,

	Starts	1st	2nd	3rd	Win & Pl
Chases	1	0	0	0	0
Career Total	13	0	2	0	2066

Going: Sf: 0-0 GS: 0-0 Gd: 0-1 GF: - Fm: 0-0
Distance: 2m/2m3: 0-0 2m4-2m7: 0-0 3m+: 0-1
Track: LH: 0-1 RH: 0-0 Tight: 0-0 Gall: 0-0
Aids: Bl: 0-0 Vi: 0-0 Tstrap: 0-0 Ckp: 0-0
Best Rating: 106   2/01   Carl   2m4f110y   soft   Ch

No Forecast (IRE)

101   **115**
10-y-o b g Executive Perk-Guess Twice (Deep Run)
A M Hales Coach House Racing

Placings:5120/0F6/4/1/3-2PP   (4255)
2003/04: 24²G, 24ᴾGS, 24ᴾG,

	Starts	1st	2nd	3rd	Win & Pl
Hurdles	1	0	0	0	0
Chases	2	0	1	0	1725

Career Total	13	2	2	1		12629
121	12/01	Newb	2m6f110yD(0-110)HCh	GD	£5996
108	12/98	Folk	2m1f110yH NHF	SFT	£1234
			Total win prize-money £7231		

Going:	Sf: 0-0 GS: 0-1 Gd: 0-2 GF: - Fm: 0-0
Distance:	2m/2m3: 0-0 2m4-2m7: 0-0 3m+: 0-3
Track:	LH: 0-2 RH: 0-1 Tight: 0-1 Gall: 0-1
Aids:	Bl: 0-0 Vi: 0-0 Tstrap: 0-0 Ckp: 0-0
Best Rating:	123 2/99 Newb 2m110y good NHF

Fair chaser; lightly raced; stays two miles six but may not quite stay three miles; handles cut in the ground.

No Gloating (IRE)

5-y-o b g King's Ride-Arctic Gale (IRE) (Strong Gale)
P D Niven IBT Racing

Placings:0 (4867)
2003/04: 16⁰S,

	Starts	1st	2nd	3rd	Win & Pl
NH Flat	1	0	0	0	
Career Total	1	0	0	0	

Going:	Sf: 0-1 GS: 0-0 Gd: 0-0 GF: - Fm: 0-0
Distance:	2m/2m3: 0-1 2m4-2m7: 0-0 3m+: 0-0
Track:	LH: 0-1 RH: 0-0 Tight: 0-0 Gall: 0-0
Aids:	Bl: 0-0 Vi: 0-0 Tstrap: 0-0 Ckp: 0-0

No Kidding

99 (98h)108

10-y-o b g Teenoso (USA)-Vaigly Fine (Vaigly Great)
J I A Charlton Miss J Palmer

Placings:0200P/214F5020/42561F403452/PPP1P610-
0050312305 (2911)
2003/04: 16⁰GF, 20⁰G, 16⁵GF, 26⁰F, 20³F, 16¹GF, 20²GF, 17³G,
16⁰GS, 16⁵GS,

	Starts	1st	2nd	3rd	Win & Pl
Chases	10	1	1	2	3910
Career Total	43	5	6	3	24554
103	10/03	Hexm	2m110y F(0-100)HCh	G-F	£2268
108	4/03	Hexm	2m4f110yF(0-95)HCh	GD	£3454
104	12/02	Muss	2m F(0-95)HCh	G-F	£4017
98	11/01	Catt	2m D Ch	G-F	£4153
84	5/00	Kels	2m2f D Hdl	G-F	£3035
			Total win prize-money £16930		

Going:	Sf: 0-0 GS: 0-2 Gd: 0-2 GF: - Fm: 1-6
Distance:	2m/2m3: 1-6 2m4-2m7: 0-3 3m+: 0-1
Track:	LH: 1-9 RH: 0-1 Tight: 0-3 Gall: 0-1
Aids:	Bl: 0-0 Vi: 0-0 Tstrap: 0-0 Ckp: 0-0
Best Rating:	108 4/03 Hexm 2m4f110y good Ch

Modest chaser; effective from two to two and a half miles on fast ground; not totally reliable.

No Mercy

96 83

8-y-o ch g Faustus (USA)-Nashville Blues (IRE) (Try My Best (USA))
B A Pearce Patrick Barter

Placings:6550/P0P/200-00205566 (2329)
2003/04: 16⁰HY, 16⁰GF, 20²GF, 19⁰G, 24⁵GF, 20⁵GF, 21⁶G, 20⁶G,

	Starts	1st	2nd	3rd	Win & Pl
Hurdles	8	0	1	0	1028
Career Total	18	0	2	0	1900

Going:	Sf: 0-1 GS: 0-0 Gd: 0-3 GF: - Fm: 0-4
Distance:	2m/2m3: 0-3 2m4-2m7: 0-4 3m+: 0-1
Track:	LH: 0-6 RH: 0-1 Tight: 0-5 Gall: 0-0
Aids:	Bl: 0-1 Vi: 0-0 Tstrap: 0-0 Ckp: 0-4
Best Rating:	86 9/00 Worc 2m gd-fm Hdl

Poor novice hurdler.

No More Money

97 84

6-y-o b m Alflora (IRE)-Cover Your Money (Precipice Wood)
Miss H C Knight David Jenks

Placings:24443 (4239)
2003/04: 17²G, 16⁴GS, 17⁴GS, 19⁴GS, 19³G,

	Starts	1st	2nd	3rd	Win & Pl
NH Flat	3	0	1	0	580
Hurdles	2	0	0	1	1224
Career Total	5	0	1	1	1804

Going:	Sf: 0-0 GS: 0-3 Gd: 0-2 GF: - Fm: 0-0
Distance:	2m/2m3: 0-4 2m4-2m7: 0-1 3m+: 0-0
Track:	LH: 0-1 RH: 0-3 Tight: 0-1 Gall: 0-1
Aids:	Bl: 0-0 Vi: 0-0 Tstrap: 0-1 Ckp: 0-0
Best Rating:	96 1/04 Tntn 2m1f gd-sft NHF

Half-sister to high-class chasers Red Marauder and Red Striker; placed in bumpers.

No Muckin' About

(0c)

9-y-o br g Muqadar (USA)-Planet Suite (Space King)
V Y Gethin V Y Gethin

Placings:P6P (0367)
2003/04: 19³GS, 16⁶GF, 16⁸G,

	Starts	1st	2nd	3rd	Win & Pl
Hurdles	1	0	0	0	0
Chases	2	0	0	0	0
Career Total	3	0	0	0	0

Going:	Sf: 0-0 GS: 0-1 Gd: 0-1 GF: - Fm: 0-1
Distance:	2m/2m3: 0-3 2m4-2m7: 0-0 3m+: 0-0
Track:	LH: 0-2 RH: 0-1 Tight: 0-0 Gall: 0-0
Aids:	Bl: 0-0 Vi: 0-0 Tstrap: 0-0 Ckp: 0-2

No Nay Never (IRE)

(90h) (70h)

9-y-o b g Tremblant-Monread (Le Tricolore)
J W Mullins Ian M McGready

Placings:034/6/60B0/4-04 (0274)
2003/04: 20⁰GF, 16⁴GF,

	Starts	1st	2nd	3rd	Win & Pl
Hurdles	1	0	0	0	0
Chases	1	0	0	0	309
Career Total	11	0	0	1	541

Going:	Sf: 0-0 GS: 0-0 Gd: 0-0 GF: - Fm: 0-2
Distance:	2m/2m3: 0-1 2m4-2m7: 0-1 3m+: 0-0
Track:	LH: 0-1 RH: 0-1 Tight: 0-0 Gall: 0-0
Aids:	Bl: 0-0 Vi: 0-0 Tstrap: 0-0 Ckp: 0-0
Best Rating:	83 3/00 Ludl 2m good NHF

No Picnic (IRE)

107 113

6-y-o ch g Be My Native (USA)-Emmagreen (Green Shoon)

Mrs S C Bradburne Broad and Cochrane

Placings:50230-3643243212 (4939)
2003/04: 22³F, 20⁶G, 22⁴G, 24³GF, 20²S, 21⁴GS, 24³GF, 24²GF,
24¹S, 24²GS,

	Starts	1st	2nd	3rd	Win & Pl
Hurdles	10	1	3	3	11240
Career Total	15	1	4	4	12950
110	4/04	Hexm	3m	E Hdl	SFT	£3668
			Total win prize-money £3668		

Going:	Sf: 1-2 GS: 0-2 Gd: 0-2 GF: - Fm: 0-4
Distance:	2m/2m3: 0-0 2m4-2m7: 0-5 3m+: 1-5
Track:	LH: 1-8 RH: 0-1 Tight: 0-3 Gall: 0-1
Aids:	Bl: 0-0 Vi: 0-0 Tstrap: 0-0 Ckp: 0-0
Best Rating:	113 4/04 Prth 3m110y gd-sft Hdl

Moderate hurdler; has shown some promise; stays three miles; acts on fast and soft ground.

No Retreat (NZ)

100 103+

11-y-o b g Exattic (USA)-Lerwick (NZ) (Thoreau (FR))
R T Phillips M W & A N Harris

Placings:3/11322/1/5PPPP/5503400P/3P (4615)
2003/04: 24³G, 28⁶G,

	Starts	1st	2nd	3rd	Win & Pl
Chases	2	0	0	1	850
Career Total	22	3	2	4	55110
139	10/99	Winc	2m5f	A HCh	G-F	£19350
135	11/98	Hayd	2m4f	B Ch	HVY	£11160
126	11/96	Newb	2m4f	D(0-120)Ch	G-S	£4286
			Total win prize-money £34796		

Going:	Sf: 0-0 GS: 0-0 Gd: 0-2 GF: - Fm: 0-0
Distance:	2m/2m3: 0-0 2m4-2m7: 0-0 3m+: 0-2
Track:	LH: 0-2 RH: 0-0 Tight: 0-2 Gall: 0-0
Aids:	Bl: 0-0 Vi: 0-0 Tstrap: 0-0 Ckp: 0-0
Best Rating:	143 2/99 Kemp 2m4f110y soft Ch

Modest chaser; acts on most types of ground; best at three miles plus.

No Sam No

104(103c) (81c)81

6-y-o b m Reprimand-Samjamalifran (Blakeney)
S C Burrough (Mrs K Walton 3/7) G Regan

Placings:40006/34P240P204-51FP0P50P655 (4290)
2003/04: 25⁵GF, 24¹G, 26⁵G, 26⁶GF, 25⁰G, 25⁶GS, 21⁵S, 19⁰GS,
24²HY, 24⁶GS, 17⁵G, 22⁵G,

	Starts	1st	2nd	3rd	Win & Pl
Hurdles	3	0	0	0	0
Chases	9	1	0	0	4633
Career Total	27	1	2	1	7077
81	7/03	Prth	3m	E Ch	GD	£4633
			Total win prize-money £4633		

Going:	Sf: 0-2 GS: 0-3 Gd: 1-5 GF: - Fm: 0-2
Distance:	2m/2m3: 0-2 2m4-2m7: 0-2 3m+: 1-8
Track:	LH: 0-5 RH: 1-7 Tight: 0-3 Gall: 0-1
Aids:	Bl: 0-6 Vi: 0-0 Tstrap: 0-0 Ckp: 0-0
Best Rating:	81 7/03 Prth 3m good Ch

Selling-class hurdler; stays well; acts on good ground.

No Shenanigans (IRE)

88 120

7-y-o b g King's Ride-Melarka (Dara Monarch)
N J Henderson Mrs Christopher Hanbury

Placings: *14/320* (4645)
2003/04: 16³S, 16²GS, 16⁶G,

	Starts	1st	2nd	3rd	Win & Pl
Chases	3	0	1	1	3136
Career Total	5	1	1	1	7338
116 3/02 Sand 2m110y H NHF			G-S		£2551

Total win prize-money £2552

Going:	Sf: 0-1 GS: 0-1 Gd: 0-1 GF: - Fm: 0-0
Distance:	2m/2m3: 0-3 2m4-2m7: 0-0 3m+: 0-0
Track:	LH: 0-1 RH: 0-0 Tight: 0-2 Gall: 0-0
Aids:	Bl: 0-0 Vi: 0-0 Tstrap: 0-0 Ckp: 0-0
Best Rating:	134 4/02 Aint 2m1f good NHF

Fair novice chaser; off the track 22 months prior to finishing third on chase debut in February 2004; effective at two miles; suited by cut in the ground.

No Visibility (IRE)

112(92h) (104h)137
9-y-o b g Glacial Storm (USA)-Duhallow Lady (IRE) (Torus)
R H Alner David O Moon

Placings: *60/43000P/0005U/0311F-3U3444* (4426)
2003/04: 16²G, 16⁴US, 20³G, 20⁴G, 20⁴G, 16⁴G,

	Starts	1st	2nd	3rd	Win & Pl
Chases	6	0	0	2	9126
Career Total	24	2	0	4	21586
137 3/03 Tntn 2m110y D Ch			HVY		£4322
117 1/03 Tntn 2m110y E Ch			SFT		£4732

Total win prize-money £10955

Going:	Sf: 0-0 GS: 0-1 Gd: 0-5 GF: - Fm: 0-0
Distance:	2m/2m3: 0-3 2m4-2m7: 0-3 3m+: 0-0
Track:	LH: 0-2 RH: 0-4 Tight: 0-0 Gall: 0-2
Aids:	Bl: 0-0 Vi: 0-0 Tstrap: 0-0 Ckp: 0-0
Best Rating:	137 11/03 Asct 2m good Ch

Useful ex-Irish hurdler/chaser; best at around two miles; acts on soft ground.

No Way Home (IRE)

6-y-o b g Arctic Lord-Soldeu Creek (IRE) (Buckskin (FR))
J K Magee J K Magee

Placings: *00* (0774a)
2003/04: 16⁰GF, 16⁶F,

	Starts	1st	2nd	3rd	Win & Pl
NH Flat	2	0	0	0	
Career Total	2	0	0	0	

Going:	Sf: 0-0 GS: 0-0 Gd: 0-0 GF: - Fm: 0-2
Distance:	2m/2m3: 0-2 2m4-2m7: 0-0 3m+: 0-0
Track:	LH: 0-1 RH: 0-1 Tight: 0-0 Gall: 0-0
Aids:	Bl: 0-0 Vi: 0-0 Tstrap: 0-0 Ckp: 0-0

Noaff (IRE)

10-y-o b g Mandalus-Good Sailing (Scorpio (FR))
John Moore Iwan Thomas

Placings: *000500/0/0P2-3* (4815)
2003/04: 24³G,

	Starts	1st	2nd	3rd	Win & Pl
Chases	1	0	0	1	518
Career Total	11	0	1	1	1566

Going:	Sf: 0-0 GS: 0-0 Gd: 0-1 GF: - Fm: 0-0

Distance:	2m/2m3: 0-0 2m4-2m7: 0-0 3m+: 0-1
Track:	LH: 0-1 RH: 0-0 Tight: 0-0 Gall: 0-0
Aids:	Bl: 0-0 Vi: 0-0 Tstrap: 0-1 Ckp: 0-0
Best Rating:	85 4/03 Chep 3m gd-fm Ch

Three times a winner between the flags; placed in point-to-point final at Chepstow in both 2003 and 2004.

Noble Affair

9-y-o b m Lancastrian-Abinovian (Ra Nova)
Mrs L Pomfret J R Noble

Placings: *4* (4439)
2003/04: 21⁴GS,

	Starts	1st	2nd	3rd	Win & Pl
Chases	1	0	0	0	188
Career Total	1	0	0	0	188

Going:	Sf: 0-0 GS: 0-1 Gd: 0-0 GF: - Fm: 0-0
Distance:	2m/2m3: 0-0 2m4-2m7: 0-1 3m+: 0-0
Track:	LH: 0-1 RH: 0-0 Tight: 0-1 Gall: 0-0
Aids:	Bl: 0-0 Vi: 0-0 Tstrap: 0-0 Ckp: 0-0
Best Rating:	57 3/04 Fknm 2m5f110y gd-sft Ch

Noble Baron

103 120
8-y-o gr g Karinga Bay-Grey Baroness (Baron Blakeney)
C G Cox T Y Bissett

Placings: *01//003-PU1411* (4693)
2003/04: 21²G, 24⁰GS, 22¹S, 24⁴S, 22¹GS, 22¹G,

	Starts	1st	2nd	3rd	Win & Pl
Hurdles	4	3	0	0	13062
Chases	2	0	0	0	
Career Total	11	4	0	1	15849
120 4/04 Extr 2m6f110yD(0-125)HHdl			GD		£5086
116 3/04 Extr 2m6f110yE(-105)HHdl			G-S		£4238
101 1/04 Extr 2m6f110yE(0-100)HHdl			SFT		£3738
104 1/02 Kemp 2m H NHF			SFT		£2012

Total win prize-money £15075

Going:	Sf: 1-2 GS: 1-2 Gd: 1-2 GF: - Fm: 0-0
Distance:	2m/2m3: 0-0 2m4-2m7: 3-4 3m+: 0-2
Track:	LH: 0-2 RH: 3-4 Tight: 0-0 Gall: 0-1
Aids:	Bl: 0-0 Vi: 0-0 Tstrap: 0-0 Ckp: 0-0
Best Rating:	120 4/04 Extr 2m6f110y good Hdl

Fair novice hurdler; failed to take to chasing; acts on soft ground; stays two miles six.

Noble Caesar (IRE)

6-y-o b/br g Montelimar (USA)-Timely Run (IRE) (Deep Run)
M Todhunter (J R Adam 7/5) J W Hazeldean

Placings: *PP-P0* (2804)
2003/04: 20²PS, 16⁰S,

	Starts	1st	2nd	3rd	Win & Pl
Hurdles	1	0	0	0	
Chases	1	0	0	0	
Career Total	4	0	0	0	

Going:	Sf: 0-2 GS: 0-0 Gd: 0-0 GF: - Fm: 0-0
Distance:	2m/2m3: 0-1 2m4-2m7: 0-1 3m+: 0-0
Track:	LH: 0-1 RH: 0-1 Tight: 0-0 Gall: 0-0
Aids:	Bl: 0-0 Vi: 0-0 Tstrap: 0-0 Ckp: 0-0

Noble Calling (FR)

100 98
7-y-o b h Caller I.D. (USA)-Specificity (USA) (Alleged (USA))
R J Hodges Nineways

Placings: *0/63050143* (4898)
2003/04: 16⁶G, 17³G, 16⁰S, 17⁵GS, 17⁰G, 17¹GS, 17⁴GF, 16³G,

	Starts	1st	2nd	3rd	Win & Pl
Hurdles	8	1	0	2	4429
Career Total	9	1	0	2	4429
97 3/04 Extr 2m1f G Hdl			G-S		£3052

Total win prize-money £3052

Going:	Sf: 0-1 GS: 1-2 Gd: 0-4 GF: - Fm: 0-1
Distance:	2m/2m3: 1-8 2m4-2m7: 0-0 3m+: 0-0
Track:	LH: 0-1 RH: 1-7 Tight: 0-3 Gall: 0-0
Aids:	Bl: 0-0 Vi: 0-0 Tstrap: 0-0 Ckp: 0-0
Best Rating:	98 4/04 Winc 2m good Hdl

Noble Colours

11-y-o b g Distinctly North (USA)-Kentucky Tears (USA)
(Cougar (CHI))
Mrs P J Ikin Mrs P J Ikin

Placings: *B00331F/03FF13214424/5536F4/15244365/50/P5P* (4775)
2003/04: 16²G, 21⁵SS, 21²G,

	Starts	1st	2nd	3rd	Win & Pl
Chases	3	0	0	0	0
Career Total	38	4	3	6	23429
121 6/99 Hrfd 2m1f D(0-125)HHdl			GD		£5251
110 11/97 Chep 2m110y E(0-115)HHdl			GD		£3030
113 10/97 Chep 2m4f110yD(0-125)HHdl			G-F		£3783
111 3/97 Hrfd 2m1f E Hdl			G-F		£2402

Total win prize-money £14467

Going:	Sf: 0-0 GS: 0-1 Gd: 0-2 GF: - Fm: 0-0
Distance:	2m/2m3: 0-1 2m4-2m7: 0-2 3m+: 0-0
Track:	LH: 0-2 RH: 0-1 Tight: 0-2 Gall: 0-0
Aids:	Bl: 0-0 Vi: 0-0 Tstrap: 0-2 Ckp: 0-0
Best Rating:	121 9/99 Strf 2m110y gd-fm Hdl

Noble Comic

103 103
13-y-o b g Silly Prices-Barony (Ribston)
C L Tizzard R E Dimond

Placings: *0P/6FP/413152P5/0211504/2321352614-06P2P20443P* (2552)
2003/04: 16⁰G, 16⁶G, 21⁵GF, 16²GF, 21⁵GF, 16²GF, 17⁰GF, 21⁴F, 21⁴GF, 16³GF, 21⁵G,

	Starts	1st	2nd	3rd	Win & Pl
Chases	11	0	2	1	7839
Career Total	41	6	7	4	41353
103 10/02 Winc 2m5f E(0-110)HCh			FRM		£5964
109 3/02 NAbb 2m110y E(0-105)HCh			GD		£3360
101 8/01 NAbb 2m110y F(0-110)HCh			GD		£4315
104 7/01 NAbb 2m5f110yD(0-120)HCh			GD		£3776
109 6/00 NAbb 2m110y D Ch			G-F		£3711
105 6/00 NAbb 2m5f110yD Ch			GD		£3779

Total win prize-money £24909

Going:	Sf: 0-0 GS: 0-0 Gd: 0-3 GF: - Fm: 0-8
Distance:	2m/2m3: 0-6 2m4-2m7: 0-5 3m+: 0-0
Track:	LH: 0-7 RH: 0-4 Tight: 0-6 Gall: 0-0
Aids:	Bl: 0-0 Vi: 0-0 Tstrap: 0-0 Ckp: 0-0
Best Rating:	109 8/02 NAbb 2m110y gd-fm Ch

Fair handicap chaser; successful five times at Newton Abbot; likes good/fast ground; effective at up to 21 furlongs;

well suited to making the running; very disappointing when tried in cheekpieces.

Noble Deed (IRE)
76

7-y-o b g Lord Americo-Legal Statement (IRE) (Strong Statement (USA))
Miss H C Knight Winter Madness

Placings:0/P40-P   (3899)
2003/04: 20PGS,

	Starts	1st	2nd	3rd	Win & Pl
Hurdles	1	0	0	0	
Career Total	5	0	0	0	0

Going:	Sf: 0-0 GS: 0-1 Gd: 0-0 GF: - Fm: 0-0
Distance:	2m2m3: 0-0 2m4-2m7: 0-1 3m+: 0-0
Track:	LH: 0-0 RH: 0-1 Tight: 0-0 Gall: 0-0
Aids:	Bl: 0-0 Vi: 0-0 Tstrap: 0-0 Ckp: 0-0
Best Rating:	74 3/02 Newb 2m110y gd-sft NHF

Noble House
102   86

7-y-o ch g Gildoran-Trust To Luck (Mandamus)
Mrs A Duffield R Renny

Placings:562   (2139)
2003/04: 17⁵G, 24⁶GF, 20²G,

	Starts	1st	2nd	3rd	Win & Pl
Hurdles	3	0	1	0	746
Career Total	3	0	1	0	746

Going:	Sf: 0-0 GS: 0-0 Gd: 0-2 GF: - Fm: 0-1
Distance:	2m2m3: 0-1 2m4-2m7: 0-1 3m+: 0-1
Track:	LH: 0-2 RH: 0-1 Tight: 0-1 Gall: 0-1
Aids:	Bl: 0-0 Vi: 0-0 Tstrap: 0-0 Ckp: 0-0
Best Rating:	86 11/03 Newc 2m4f good Hdl

Novice hurdler; stays 2m 4f; has jumped left.

Noble Hymn

11-y-o br g Arctic Lord-Soraway (Choral Society)
Mrs C M Mulhall Mrs C M Mulhall

Placings:3000/5P/F/624-325   (4392)
2003/04: 20⁴GS, 25⁵G, 20²G, 27⁵G,

	Starts	1st	2nd	3rd	Win & Pl
Chases	4	0	1	1	936
Career Total	13	0	2	2	1537

Going:	Sf: 0-0 GS: 0-0 Gd: 0-3 GF: - Fm: 0-1
Distance:	2m2m3: 0-0 2m4-2m7: 0-2 3m+: 0-2
Track:	LH: 0-4 RH: 0-0 Tight: 0-1 Gall: 0-1
Aids:	Bl: 0-0 Vi: 0-0 Tstrap: 0-0 Ckp: 0-0
Best Rating:	87 5/03 Hexm 2m4f110y good Ch

Hunter chaser; stays three miles; acts well with cut in the ground.

Noble Justice (IRE)
88   115

8-y-o b g Jurado (USA)-Furry Hope (Furry Glen)
R J Hodges Fieldspring Racing

Placings:03212/PP-P1   (2018)
2003/04: 20PG, 21¹GF,

	Starts	1st	2nd	3rd	Win & Pl
Chases	2	1	0	0	5356
Career Total	9	2	2	1	13415
115 11/03	Winc	2m5f	D(0-115)HCh	G-F	£5356
106 11/01	Winc	2m5f	D Ch	G-F	£4290

Total win prize-money £9646

Going:	Sf: 0-0 GS: 0-0 Gd: 0-1 GF: - Fm: 1-1
Distance:	2m/2m3: 0-0 2m4-2m7: 1-2 3m+: 0-0
Track:	LH: 0-1 RH: 1-1 Tight: 0-0 Gall: 0-0
Aids:	Bl: 0-0 Vi: 0-0 Tstrap: 0-0 Ckp: 0-0
Best Rating:	115 11/03 Winc 2m5f gd-fm Ch

Lightly-raced chaser; stays two miles five furlongs; suited by a sound surface.

Noble Philosopher

4-y-o ch g Faustus (USA)-Princess Lucy (Local Suitor (USA))
R M Beckett Trajan Partners

Placings:PP   (3465)
2003/04: 16PG, 16PS,

	Starts	1st	2nd	3rd	Win & Pl
Hurdles	2	0	0	0	
Career Total	2	0	0	0	

Going:	Sf: 0-1 GS: 0-0 Gd: 0-1 GF: - Fm: 0-0
Distance:	2m/2m3: 0-2 2m4-2m7: 0-0 3m+: 0-0
Track:	LH: 0-1 RH: 0-1 Tight: 0-0 Gall: 0-0
Aids:	Bl: 0-1 Vi: 0-0 Tstrap: 0-0 Ckp: 0-0

Noble Pursuit (FR)

6-y-o b g Pursuit Of Love-Pipitina (Bustino)
I R Brown I R Brown

Placings:PP   (3774)
2003/04: 20PG, 24PG,

	Starts	1st	2nd	3rd	Win & Pl
Chases	2	0	0	0	
Career Total	2	0	0	0	

Going:	Sf: 0-0 GS: 0-0 Gd: 0-2 GF: - Fm: 0-0
Distance:	2m/2m3: 0-0 2m4-2m7: 0-1 3m+: 0-1
Track:	LH: 0-0 RH: 0-2 Tight: 0-0 Gall: 0-0
Aids:	Bl: 0-0 Vi: 0-0 Tstrap: 0-1 Ckp: 0-0

Noble Spy (IRE)
95   (0c)81

10-y-o b g Lord Americo-Flashey Blond (Buckskin (FR))
Mrs D A Hamer Hanford's Chemist Ltd

Placings:405/F00/1334F232/0P0-005   (2036)
2003/04: 21⁹GF, 20⁰GF, 24⁵GF,

	Starts	1st	2nd	3rd	Win & Pl
Hurdles	3	0	0	0	0
Career Total	20	1	2	3	6386
84 8/01	Worc	2m4f	F Hdl	G-F	£1981

Total win prize-money £1981

Going:	Sf: 0-0 GS: 0-0 Gd: 0-0 GF: - Fm: 0-3
Distance:	2m/2m3: 0-0 2m4-2m7: 0-2 3m+: 0-1
Track:	LH: 0-3 RH: 0-0 Tight: 0-0 Gall: 0-0
Aids:	Bl: 0-0 Vi: 0-1 Tstrap: 0-0 Ckp: 0-0
Best Rating:	105 2/02 Wwck 3m1f soft Hdl

Noble Teviot
85   84+

6-y-o b g Lithgie-Brig-Polly Peril (Politico (USA))
Miss S E Forster R J Kyle

Placings:040050   (4273)
2003/04: 17⁹G, 17⁴HY, 16⁰S, 16⁰S, 16⁵HY, 24⁴G,

	Starts	1st	2nd	3rd	Win & Pl
NH Flat	1	0	0	0	0
Hurdles	5	0	0	0	0
Career Total	6	0	0	0	0

Going:	Sf: 0-4 GS: 0-0 Gd: 0-2 GF: - Fm: 0-0
Distance:	2m/2m3: 0-2 2m4-2m7: 0-0 3m+: 0-1
Track:	LH: 0-4 RH: 0-2 Tight: 0-2 Gall: 0-1
Aids:	Bl: 0-0 Vi: 0-0 Tstrap: 0-0 Ckp: 0-0
Best Rating:	84 11/03 Carl 2m1f heavy Hdl

Ex-pointer; has shown moderate ability under Rules so far.

Noblefir (IRE)
92   91

6-y-o b g Shernazar-Chrisali (IRE) (Strong Gale)
L Lungo P Gaffney & J N Stevenson

Placings:023-26P   (3209)
2003/04: 17²HY, 20⁶S, 25PGS,

	Starts	1st	2nd	3rd	Win & Pl
Hurdles	3	0	1	0	788
Career Total	6	0	2	1	2191

Going:	Sf: 0-2 GS: 0-1 Gd: 0-0 GF: - Fm: 0-0
Distance:	2m/2m3: 0-1 2m4-2m7: 0-0 3m+: 0-1
Track:	LH: 0-2 RH: 0-1 Tight: 0-0 Gall: 0-0
Aids:	Bl: 0-0 Vi: 0-0 Tstrap: 0-0 Ckp: 0-0
Best Rating:	98 4/03 Carl 2m1f gd-fm NHF

Fair hurdler/bumper performer; Irish point winner; has shown promise under Rules; acts on good ground or softer.

Nobody's Fool

9-y-o ch g St Ninian-Majestic Form (IRE) (Double Schwartz)
Mrs Dianne Sayer Greengate Lease Syndicate

Placings:0/P   (0557)
2003/04: 16PGF,

	Starts	1st	2nd	3rd	Win & Pl
Hurdles	1	0	0	0	
Career Total	2	0	0	0	

Going:	Sf: 0-0 GS: 0-0 Gd: 0-0 GF: - Fm: 0-1
Distance:	2m/2m3: 0-1 2m4-2m7: 0-0 3m+: 0-0
Track:	LH: 0-0 RH: 0-0 Tight: 0-0 Gall: 0-0
Aids:	Bl: 0-0 Vi: 0-0 Tstrap: 0-0 Ckp: 0-0
Best Rating:	52 6/99 MRas 1m5f110y gd-fm NHF

Nocksky (IRE)
82   104+

11-y-o b g Niniski (USA)-Olivana (GER) (Sparkler)
M C Pipe Terry Neill

Placings:211F0P/P103/111/PP0/P1   (4737)
2003/04: 25PGS, 21¹G,

	Starts	1st	2nd	3rd	Win & Pl
Chases	2	1	0	0	2968
Career Total	18	7	1	1	27317
104 4/04	NAbb	2m5f110yG(0-95)HCh	GD	£2968

125	7/99	Worc	2m7f110yE Ch	G-F	£3195
121	7/99	Wolv	2m4f110yE Ch	G-F	£3329
116	7/99	NAbb	3m2f110yE Ch	G-S	£3176
131	2/99	Hayd	2m4f	D(0-120)HHdl	SFT	£2840
132	12/97	Leop	3m	Hdl	HVY	£6782
82	9/97	Dund	3m	Hdl	Y-S	£2204

Total win prize-money £24496

Going:	Sf: 0-0 GS: 0-1 Gd: 1-1 GF: - Fm: 0-1
Distance:	2m/2m3: 0-0 **2m4-2m7: 1-1** 3m+: 0-1
Track:	**LH: 1-1** RH: 0-1 **Tight: 1-1** Gall: 0-0
Aids:	Bl: 0-0 Vi: 0-0 Tstrap: 0-0 Ckp: 0-0
Best Rating:	**132** 4/99 Aint 3m110y gd-sft Hdl

Moderate chaser these days; lightly raced; acts on a sound surface; stays three miles.

Nod 'N' A Wink
68f   27f

6-y-o b g Factual (USA)-Singing Reply (USA) (The Minstrel (CAN))
C A Dwyer Mrs C M Goode

Placings:0   (2690)
2003/04: 16⁰GS,

	Starts	1st	2nd	3rd	Win & Pl
NH Flat	1	0	0	0	
Career Total	**1**	**0**	**0**	**0**	

Going:	Sf: 0-0 GS: 0-1 Gd: 0-0 GF: - Fm: 0-0
Distance:	2m/2m3: 0-1 2m4-2m7: 0-0 3m+: 0-0
Track:	LH: 0-0 RH: 0-1 Tight: 0-0 Gall: 0-1
Aids:	Bl: 0-0 Vi: 0-0 Tstrap: 0-0 Ckp: 0-0
Best Rating:	27 12/03 Hntg 2m110y gd-sft NHF

Nod Ya Head
89   66

8-y-o ch m Minster Son-Little Mittens (Little Buskins)
R E Barr R E Barr

Placings:0-004034   (4388)
2003/04: 17⁰GS, 16⁰Gd, 20⁴GF, 20⁵GS, 27³F, 21⁴G,

	Starts	1st	2nd	3rd	Win & Pl
Hurdles	6	0	0	1	675
Career Total	**7**	**0**	**0**	**1**	**675**

Going:	Sf: 0-0 GS: 0-2 Gd: 0-1 GF: - Fm: 0-3
Distance:	2m/2m3: 0-0 2m4-2m7: 0-3 3m+: 0-1
Track:	LH: 0-5 RH: 0-1 Tight: 0-3 Gall: 0-0
Aids:	Bl: 0-0 Vi: 0-0 Tstrap: 0-0 Ckp: 0-0
Best Rating:	70 3/04 Sedg 2m5f110y good Hdl

Noisetine (FR)
109(104h)   (107h)115+

6-y-o ch m Mansonnien (FR)-Notabilite (FR) (No Pass No Sale)
Miss Venetia Williams Mrs Jean F P Yeomans

Placings:303/1511/063062-2241222   (4699)
2003/04: 25²GF, 19²S, 22⁴S, 19¹G, 21²GS, 20²G, 18²G,

	Starts	1st	2nd	3rd	Win & Pl
Chases	7	1	5	0	11603
Career Total	**20**	**4**	**6**	**3**	**28769**
117	2/04	Catt	2m3f E Ch	GD	£3861
99	4/02	Uttx	2m4f110yE Hdl	GD	£3045
105	3/02	Winc	2m6f E Hdl	SFT	£2744
5/01	Fntb	1m7f	Hdl	GD	£3880

Total win prize-money £13530

Nolife (IRE)
97   (0c)70

8-y-o b g Religiously (USA)-Garnerstown Lady (Pitpan)
Miss Lucinda V Russell Fair City Flyers

Placings:04-FP654   (0791)
2003/04: 16⁶G, 20⁰P, 20⁹G, 20⁵G, 24⁴G,

	Starts	1st	2nd	3rd	Win & Pl
Hurdles	4	0	0	0	309
Chases	1	0	0	0	0
Career Total	**7**	**0**	**0**	**0**	**309**

Going:	Sf: 0-0 GS: 0-0 Gd: 0-5 GF: - Fm: 0-0
Distance:	2m/2m3: 0-1 2m4-2m7: 0-3 3m+: 0-0
Track:	LH: 0-2 RH: 0-3 Tight: 0-1 Gall: 0-0
Aids:	Bl: 0-0 Vi: 0-0 Tstrap: 0-0 Ckp: 0-0
Best Rating:	70 7/03 Prth 3m110y good Hdl

Nomadic Ice

7-y-o b g Nomadic Way (USA)-Icelolly (Idiots Delight)
Mrs G Harvey Blowing Stone Quartet

Placings:PP00   (4888)
2003/04: 25³S, 22⁰G, 19⁰GS, 24⁰GF,

	Starts	1st	2nd	3rd	Win & Pl
Hurdles	3	0	0	0	0
Chases	1	0	0	0	0
Career Total	**4**	**0**	**0**	**0**	**0**

Going:	Sf: 0-0 GS: 0-1 Gd: 0-1 GF: - Fm: 0-1
Distance:	2m/2m3: 0-0 2m4-2m7: 0-2 3m+: 0-2
Track:	LH: 0-4 RH: 0-0 Tight: 0-3 Gall: 0-0
Aids:	Bl: 0-0 Vi: 0-0 Tstrap: 0-0 Ckp: 0-0

Nomadic Star

9-y-o br g Nomadic Way (USA)-Dreamago (Sir Mago)
Mrs F J Browne (D G Atkinson 3/5) Mark Lilly and Adrian Vivier

Placings:5-56   (4522)
2003/04: 25⁵GS, 25⁶GS,

	Starts	1st	2nd	3rd	Win & Pl
Chases	2	0	0	0	0
Career Total	**3**	**0**	**0**	**0**	0

Going:	Sf: 0-0 GS: 0-1 Gd: 0-1 GF: - Fm: 0-0
Distance:	2m/2m3: 0-0 2m4-2m7: 0-0 3m+: 0-2
Track:	LH: 0-1 RH: 0-1 Tight: 0-0 Gall: 0-0
Aids:	Bl: 0-0 Vi: 0-0 Tstrap: 0-1 Ckp: 0-0
Best Rating:	66 3/03 Kels 3m1f gd-sft Ch

Nominate (GER)

4-y-o b g Desert King (IRE)-Northern Goddess (Night Shift (USA))

Going: Sf: 0-2 GS: 0-1 Gd: 1-3 GF: - Fm: 0-1
Distance: **2m/2m3: 1-2** 2m4-2m7: 0-4 3m+: 0-1
Track: **LH: 1-4** RH: 0-2 **Tight: 1-5** Gall: 0-1
Aids: Bl: 0-0 Vi: 0-0 Tstrap: 0-0 Ckp: 0-0
Best Rating: 117 2/04 Sedg 2m5f gd-sft Ch

Fair novice chaser; stays two and a half miles plus; and acts on most types of ground; has sometimes not looked a straightforward ride.

S T Lewis (P F I Cole 23/7) Simon T Lewis

Placings:P   (1451)
2003/04: 16⁰GF,

	Starts	1st	2nd	3rd	Win & Pl
Hurdles	1	0	0	0	
Career Total	**1**	**0**	**0**	**0**	

Going:	Sf: 0-0 GS: 0-0 Gd: 0-0 GF: - Fm: 0-1
Distance:	2m/2m3: 0-1 2m4-2m7: 0-0 3m+: 0-0
Track:	LH: 0-1 RH: 0-0 Tight: 0-1 Gall: 0-0
Aids:	Bl: 0-0 Vi: 0-0 Tstrap: 0-0 Ckp: 0-0
Best Rating:	0 9/03 Plum 2m gd-fm Hdl

Juvenile hurdler; disappointing maiden on the Flat.

Non So (FR)
109(117h)   (146h)138+

6-y-o b g Definite Article-Irish Woman (FR) (Assert)
N J Henderson Roa Dawn Run Partnership

Placings:0211P/511240-112   (3269)
2003/04: 17¹GS, 17¹S, 16²GS,

	Starts	1st	2nd	3rd	Win & Pl
Chases	3	2	1	0	18740
Career Total	**14**	**6**	**3**	**0**	**90621**
133	1/04	Plum	2m1f	D Ch	SFT	£6841
123	12/03	Plum	2m1f	D Ch	G-S	£4199
139	1/03	Kemp	2m	B(0-145)HHdl	GD	£29000
131	12/02	Kemp	2m	D(0-125)HHdl	SFT	£6728
107	1/02	Font	2m2f110yE Hdl	SFT	£2653
115	1/02	Folk	2m1f110yE Hdl	SFT	£2632

Total win prize-money £52053

Going:	Sf: 1-1 GS: 1-2 Gd: 0-0 GF: - Fm: 0-0
Distance:	**2m/2m3: 2-3** 2m4-2m7: 0-0 3m+: 0-0
Track:	**LH: 2-2** RH: 0-1 **Tight: 2-2** Gall: 0-0
Aids:	Bl: 0-0 Vi: 0-0 Tstrap: 0-0 Ckp: 0-0
Best Rating:	**146** 3/03 Chel 2m1f good Hdl

Very useful novice chaser; very useful handicap hurdler in 2002/3; won the Lanzarote at Kempton in January 2003 and runner-up in the Tote Gold Trophy next time; impressive winner of first two novice chases at Plumpton; second of three in a better race at Ascot; suited by good ground or softer; stays two and a quarter miles.

Non Stop Aims
54f   24f

6-y-o ch m Gunner B-Prevada (Soldier Rose)
J L Spearing Bryan Mathieson

Placings:0   (4407)
2003/04: 16⁰G,

	Starts	1st	2nd	3rd	Win & Pl
NH Flat	1	0	0	0	
Career Total	**1**	**0**	**0**	**0**	

Going:	Sf: 0-0 GS: 0-0 Gd: 0-1 GF: - Fm: 0-0
Distance:	2m/2m3: 0-1 2m4-2m7: 0-0 3m+: 0-0
Track:	LH: 0-0 RH: 0-1 Tight: 0-0 Gall: 0-1
Aids:	Bl: 0-0 Vi: 0-0 Tstrap: 0-0 Ckp: 0-0
Best Rating:	24 3/04 Hntg 2m110y good NHF

Non Vintage (IRE)
79(102h)   (68h)55

13-y-o ch g Shy Groom (USA)-Great Alexandra (Runnett)
M C Chapman Mrs J E Seston

Placings:34231/21300364356/024144FO6650010/4533040

5243P2003/34635432133436230405/55053065/65400/041/
66P4044-0PP0   (0428)
2003/04: 21⁰GF, 21PGF, 30PG, 17⁰G,

		Starts	1st	2nd	3rd	Win & Pl
Hurdles		1	0	0	0	0
Chases		3	0	0	0	0
Career Total		94	6	7	17	66347
76	7/01	Uttx	3m2f	F(0-90)HCh	G-F	£3575
107	8/98	Ctml	2m1f110yD(0-120)HCh	G-S	£3418
130	2/97	MRas	2m1f110yD(0-120)HHdl	GD	£2796
132	10/96	MRas	2m1f110yC(0-135)HHdl	GD	£3355
123	11/95	Asct	2m110y B(0-145)HHdl	GD	£6691
94	3/95	Ludl	2m	E Hdl	G-S	£2528
			Total win prize-money £22364

Going:	Sf: 0-0 GS: 0-0 Gd: 0-2 GF: - Fm: 0-2
Distance:	2m/2m3: 0-1 2m4-2m7: 0-2 3m+: 0-1
Track:	LH: 0-3 RH: 0-0 Tight: 0-3 Gall: 0-0
Aids:	Bl: 0-0 Vi: 0-0 Tstrap: 0-0 Ckp: 0-0
Best Rating:	137 11/95 Newc 2m good Hdl

Nonantais (FR)
109(112h)   (120+h)120+
7-y-o b g Nikos-Sanhia (FR) (Sanhedrin (USA))
M Bradstock The Frankly Intolerable

Placings:363112-23   (4208)
2003/04: 21²GS, 20³G,

		Starts	1st	2nd	3rd	Win & Pl
Chases		2	0	1	1	2332
Career Total		8	2	2	3	25026
120	2/03	Tntn	2m3f110yD Hdl	G-S	£5369
108	2/03	Tntn	2m1f	D Hdl	SFT	£5232
			Total win prize-money £10602

Going:	Sf: 0-0 GS: 0-1 Gd: 0-1 GF: - Fm: 0-0
Distance:	2m/2m3: 0-0 2m4-2m7: 0-2 3m+: 0-0
Track:	LH: 0-0 RH: 0-2 Tight: 0-1 Gall: 0-0
Aids:	Bl: 0-0 Vi: 0-0 Tstrap: 0-0 Ckp: 0-0
Best Rating:	120 2/04 Folk 2m5f gd-sft Ch

Fair novice hurdler; effective over two miles, but probably better over further; acts well on soft ground; progressive.

Nopekan (IRE)
109   128+
4-y-o b g Sri Pekan (USA)-Giadamar (IRE) (Be My Guest (USA))
P Mullins Mrs Helen Mullins

Placings:4252154   (4802a)
2003/04: 164S, 162GY, 165S, 162S, 161G, 165G, 164Y,

		Starts	1st	2nd	3rd	Win & Pl
Hurdles		7	1	2	0	20976
Career Total		7	1	2	0	20976
102	2/04	Leop	Hdl	GD	£7785
			Total win prize-money £7786

Going:	Sf: 0-3 GS: 0-0 Gd: 1-2 GF: - Fm: 0-0
Distance:	2m/2m3: 1-7 2m4-2m7: 0-0 3m+: 0-0
Track:	LH: 1-4 RH: 0-2 Tight: 0-1 Gall: 0-0
Aids:	Bl: 0-0 Vi: 0-0 Tstrap: 0-0 Ckp: 0-0
Best Rating:	128 4/04 Aint 2m110y good Hdl

Useful Irish juvenile hurdler; effective over two miles; acts on soft ground and good ground.

Noplanofaction (IRE)
85   111+
7-y-o ch g Be My Native (USA)-Creative Music (Creative

Plan (USA))
Jonjo O'Neill Byrne Bros (Formwork) Limited

Placings:12   (3331)
2003/04: 161S, 192S,

		Starts	1st	2nd	3rd	Win & Pl
NH Flat		1	1	0	0	8700
Hurdles		1	0	1	0	1120
Career Total		2	1	1	0	9820
122	12/03	Chep	2m110y	A NHF	SFT	£8700
			Total win prize-money £8700

Going:	Sf: 1-2 GS: 0-0 Gd: 0-0 GF: - Fm: 0-0
Distance:	2m/2m3: 1-2 2m4-2m7: 0-0 3m+: 0-0
Track:	LH: 1-2 RH: 0-0 Tight: 0-0 Gall: 0-1
Aids:	Bl: 0-0 Vi: 0-0 Tstrap: 0-0 Ckp: 0-0
Best Rating:	122 12/03 Chep 2m110y soft NHF

Son of top sire Be My Native who won a Grade 2 bumper on his debut at Chepstow in December 2003 over two miles on soft ground; runner-up on hurdles debutunt finished lame; effective in soft ground.

Noras Legacy (IRE)
95   68
6-y-o b m Old Vic-Balda Girl (IRE) (Mandalus)
Miss Lucinda V Russell Harry Gettings

Placings:00U40   (4685)
2003/04: 16⁰G, 16⁰GF, 21UGS, 20⁴HY, 16⁰G,

		Starts	1st	2nd	3rd	Win & Pl
NH Flat		2	0	0	0	0
Hurdles		3	0	0	0	0
Career Total		5	0	0	0	

Going:	Sf: 0-1 GS: 0-1 Gd: 0-2 GF: - Fm: 0-1
Distance:	2m/2m3: 0-3 2m4-2m7: 0-2 3m+: 0-0
Track:	LH: 0-2 RH: 0-2 Tight: 0-3 Gall: 0-0
Aids:	Bl: 0-0 Vi: 0-0 Tstrap: 0-0 Ckp: 0-0
Best Rating:	80 5/03 Kels 2m110y good NHF

Norbert (IRE)
69   24
6-y-o ch g Imperial Frontier (USA)-Glowing Reeds (Kalaglow)
M F Harris M Harris

Placings:00-0   (0156)
2003/04: 16⁰GF,

		Starts	1st	2nd	3rd	Win & Pl
Hurdles		1	0	0	0	
Career Total		3	0	0	0	

Going:	Sf: 0-0 GS: 0-0 Gd: 0-0 GF: - Fm: 0-1
Distance:	2m/2m3: 0-1 2m4-2m7: 0-0 3m+: 0-0
Track:	LH: 0-1 RH: 0-0 Tight: 0-1 Gall: 0-0
Aids:	Bl: 0-0 Vi: 0-0 Tstrap: 0-0 Ckp: 0-0
Best Rating:	66 4/03 Ludl 2m good NHF

Nordance Prince (IRE)
144
13-y-o b g Nordance (USA)-Shirleys Princess (Sandhurst Prince)
Miss Venetia Williams D C Pierce

Placings:3/335534/112211001/11/1211FFF4/053/3F-PF   (4211)

2003/04: 19PS, 20FG,

		Starts	1st	2nd	3rd	Win & Pl
Chases		2	0	0	0	
Career Total		33	10	3	6	134283
151	1/00	Asct	2m	A HCh	G-S	£30000
151	12/99	Weth	2m	A HCh	G-S	£19300
151	11/99	Asct	2m3f110yA HCh	GD	£29775
140	10/98	Chel	2m	C Ch	GD	£4719
131	10/98	Towc	2m110y	E(0-120)Ch	GD	£2815
128	4/98	Prth	2m110y	D Hdl	GD	£3499
128	2/98	Donc	2m110y	B(0-140)HHdl	G-F	£5234
130	2/98	Sand	2m110y	E(0-115)HHdl	GD	£2840
101	5/97	Hntg	2m110y	E Hdl	G-F	£2355
115	5/97	NAbb	2m1f	E Hdl	G-F	£2505
			Total win prize-money £103045

Going:	Sf: 0-1 GS: 0-0 Gd: 0-1 GF: - Fm: 0-0
Distance:	2m/2m3: 0-0 2m4-2m7: 0-2 3m+: 0-0
Track:	LH: 0-1 RH: 0-1 Tight: 0-0 Gall: 0-0
Aids:	Bl: 0-0 Vi: 0-0 Tstrap: 0-0 Ckp: 0-0
Best Rating:	151 1/00 Asct 2m gd-sft Ch

Formerly a high-class handicap chaser; lightly raced nowadays; best at two to two and a half miles; likes decent ground.

Nordic Crest (IRE)
10-y-o b g Danehill (USA)-Feather Glen (Glenstal (USA))
Mrs C A Coward T D Rose & Miss K P Barron

Placings:04251/3/14P3/P22/4-0   (0475)
2003/04: 26⁰GS,

		Starts	1st	2nd	3rd	Win & Pl
Chases		1	0	0	0	
Career Total		15	2	3	2	17673
102	10/00	Towc	2m110y	E Ch	G-F	£3504
102	4/98	Ayr	2m	C HHdl	GD	£3817
			Total win prize-money £7322

Going:	Sf: 0-0 GS: 0-1 Gd: 0-0 GF: - Fm: 0-0
Distance:	2m/2m3: 0-0 2m4-2m7: 0-0 3m+: 0-1
Track:	LH: 0-1 RH: 0-0 Tight: 0-1 Gall: 0-0
Aids:	Bl: 0-0 Vi: 0-0 Tstrap: 0-1 Ckp: 0-0
Best Rating:	118 6/01 Strf 3m gd-fm Ch

Nordic Prince (IRE)
95(113c)   (118c)114
13-y-o b g Nordance (USA)-Royal Desire (Royal Match)
J G M O'Shea Blue Shirts

Placings:11/03/133123P/1P/R3440/423231111231PP230/4
6264/32B141P3P-16   (4567)
2003/04: 20¹HY, 24⁶GS,

		Starts	1st	2nd	3rd	Win & Pl
Hurdles		2	1	0	0	2499
Career Total		51	4	7	11	64650
102	1/04	Uttx	2m4f110yG Hdl	HVY	£2499
99	2/03	Hntg	2m4f110yG Hdl	GD	£2548
118	1/03	Sthl	3m110y D(0-125)HCh	G-S	£5499
118	11/00	Wwck	3m2f	D(0-120)HCh	HVY	£4020
115	10/00	Strf	3m	D(0-125)HCh	G-S	£3757
108	10/00	Bang	3m110y	D(0-120)HCh	SFT	£6857
82	8/00	Sthl	3m110y	E Ch	GD	£2815
92	8/00	Sthl	3m110y	G Hdl	G-F	£1501
126	10/98	Worc	2m4f	C(0-130)HHdl	G-F	£3769
108	2/98	Font	2m6f110yE Hdl	GD	£2553
101	8/97	Uttx	2m4f110yD Hdl	GD	£2773
	11/95	Hexm	2m	H NHF	G-F	£1371
	11/95	Worc	2m	H NHF	G-F	£2052
			Total win prize-money £42017

| Going: | Sf: 1-1 GS: 0-1 Gd: 0-0 GF: - Fm: 0-0 |

Distance: 2m/2m3: 0-0 **2m4-2m7: 1-1** 3m+: 0-1
Track: LH: **1-2** RH: 0-0 Tight: 0-1 Gall: 0-0
Aids: Bl: 0-0 Vi: 0-0 Tstrap: 0-0 Ckp: 0-0
Best Rating: 126 10/98 Worc 2m4f   good   Hdl

Fair hurdler/chaser; now at the veteran stage; 11th career win when reappearing in a selling hurdle at Uttoxeter in January; stays beyond three miles, but effective at shorter; handles any ground.

Norlandic (NZ)

12-y-o ch g First Norman (USA)-April Snow (NZ) (Icelandic)
L Jefford (P J Hobbs 14/5) Mrs S M Trump

Placings:06/3/5521511/2122/154UP3/33/3FP3-01P (4522)
2003/04: 23⁰G, 25¹GF, 25PGS,

	Starts	1st	2nd	3rd	Win & Pl
Chases	3	1	0	0	7228
Career Total	29	6	4	6	41106
103 5/03	Extr	3m1f110yD(0-115)HCh		G-F	7228
129 10/00	Extr	2m7f110yD(0-125)HCh		SFT	£5096
129 12/99	Winc	3m1f110yD(0-120)HCh		GD	£4143
124 4/99	Extr	2m7f110yE(0-105)HCh		G-S	£4079
115 3/99	Extr	3m110y E(0-105)HCh		GD	£5054
103 2/99	Tntn	3m110y F(0-110)HHdl		G-S	£2246

Total win prize-money £27847

Going: Sf: 0-0 GS: 0-1 Gd: 0-1 GF: - Fm: 1-1
Distance: 2m/2m3: 0-0 2m4-2m7: 0-0 **3m+: 1-3**
Track: LH: 0-0 **RH: 1-3** Tight: 0-0 Gall: 0-0
Aids: Bl: 0-0 Vi: 0-0 Tstrap: 0-0 Ckp: 0-0
Best Rating: 129 10/00 Extr 2m7f110y soft   Ch

Modest staying chaser on good ground or softer; has won all his races on right-handed courses and goes well at Exeter; has been hindered by a tendency to make mistakes.

Normand De Fer (FR)

90   73

7-y-o b g Genereux Genie-Xav Wood (FR) (Le Pontet (FR))
John Allen   John Allen

Placings:50 (4561)
2003/04: 19⁵G, 24⁹GS,

	Starts	1st	2nd	3rd	Win & Pl
Hurdles	2	0	0	0	0
Career Total	2	0	0	0	0

Going: Sf: 0-0 GS: 0-1 Gd: 0-1 GF: - Fm: 0-0
Distance: 2m/2m3: 0-0 2m4-2m7: 0-1 3m+: 0-1
Track: LH: 0-2 RH: 0-0 Tight: 0-0 Gall: 0-0
Aids: Bl: 0-0 Vi: 0-0 Tstrap: 0-0 Ckp: 0-0
Best Rating: 69 3/04 Donc 2m3f110y   good   Hdl

Normandy Sands (IRE)

101   89

6-y-o b/br g Namaqualand (USA)-Buzz Along (Prince Bee)
Mrs J Candlish   N M Wynne

Placings:0665-235326002 (4656)
2003/04: 24²GF, 24³GF, 26⁵GS, 26³GS, 24²HY, 26⁶GS, 27⁰GS, 24⁹HY, 26²G,

	Starts	1st	2nd	3rd	Win & Pl
Hurdles	9	0	3	2	3817
Career Total	13	0	3	2	3817

Going: Sf: 0-2 GS: 0-4 Gd: 0-1 GF: - Fm: 0-2
Distance: 2m/2m3: 0-0 2m4-2m7: 0-0 3m+: 0-9
Track: LH: 0-4 RH: 0-5 Tight: 0-1 Gall: 0-2
Aids: Bl: 0-0 Vi: 0-0 Tstrap: 0-0 Ckp: 0-1
Best Rating: 89 4/04 Hrfd 3m2f   good   Hdl

Moderate hurdler; placed in weak novice hurdles in June; stays well; has worn a visor on good.

Normania (NZ)

12-y-o b g First Norman (USA)-Brigania (NZ) (Brigand (USA))
Miss Sarah West   C D J West

Placings:20/0430214/3P3F/FP3/FF/5/42F-54P (4775)
2003/04: 24⁵G, 22⁴G, 21PG,

	Starts	1st	2nd	3rd	Win & Pl
Chases	3	0	0	0	0
Career Total	25	1	3	4	7932
9	2/98	Hntg	2m4f110y		E(0-105)HHdl
GD	£2897				

Total win prize-money £2898

Going: Sf: 0-0 GS: 0-0 Gd: 0-3 GF: - Fm: 0-0
Distance: 2m/2m3: 0-0 2m4-2m7: 0-2 3m+: 0-1
Track: LH: 0-3 RH: 0-0 Tight: 0-2 Gall: 0-1
Aids: Bl: 0-0 Vi: 0-0 Tstrap: 0-0 Ckp: 0-0
Best Rating: 97 3/97 Winc 2m   gd-fm NHF

North (IRE)

35

6-y-o br g Mukaddamah (USA)-Flamenco (USA) (Dance Spell (USA))
A C Wilson   Cooper Wilson

Placings:0P-P (4868)
2003/04: 20PGS,

	Starts	1st	2nd	3rd	Win & Pl
Hurdles	1	0	0	0	
Career Total	3	0	0	0	

Going: Sf: 0-0 GS: 0-1 Gd: 0-0 GF: - Fm: 0-0
Distance: 2m/2m3: 0-0 2m4-2m7: 0-1 3m+: 0-0
Track: LH: 0-1 RH: 0-0 Tight: 0-1 Gall: 0-0
Aids: Bl: 0-0 Vi: 0-0 Tstrap: 0-0 Ckp: 0-0
Best Rating: 35 1/03 Muss 2m   good   Hdl

North Croft

8-y-o b g North Street-Sock Jinks (New Member)
C J Gray   Mrs T Frampton

Placings:00/54P-PP44 (1725)
2003/04: 16PGF, 22PGF, 17⁴GF, 17⁴GF,

	Starts	1st	2nd	3rd	Win & Pl
Hurdles	4	0	0	0	324
Career Total	9	0	0	0	613

Going: Sf: 0-0 GS: 0-0 Gd: 0-0 GF: - Fm: 0-4
Distance: 2m/2m3: 0-3 2m4-2m7: 0-1 3m+: 0-0
Track: LH: 0-2 RH: 0-2 Tight: 0-1 Gall: 0-0
Aids: Bl: 0-0 Vi: 0-0 Tstrap: 0-0 Ckp: 0-1
Best Rating: 51 9/01 Hrfd 2m1f   gd-fm NHF

Very modest form in novice hurdles.

North Face

89(76c)   (49c)65

7-y-o ch g Factual (USA)-Northgate Dancer (Ile De Bourbon (USA))
Miss Lucinda V Russell   Mrs L R Joughin

Placings:060/41F2P/0-0 (0576)
2003/04: 16⁰G,

	Starts	1st	2nd	3rd	Win & Pl
Hurdles	1	0	0	0	
Career Total	10	1	1	0	3960
80 6/01	Prth	2m110y E Hdl		G-F	£3003

Total win prize-money £3003

Going: Sf: 0-0 GS: 0-0 Gd: 0-1 GF: - Fm: 0-0
Distance: 2m/2m3: 0-1 2m4-2m7: 0-0 3m+: 0-0
Track: LH: 0-0 RH: 0-1 Tight: 0-0 Gall: 0-0
Aids: Bl: 0-0 Vi: 0-0 Tstrap: 0-0 Ckp: 0-0
Best Rating: 80 12/01 Donc 2m110y   good   Hdl

North Of Kala (IRE)

100   107

11-y-o b g Distinctly North (USA)-Hi Kala (Kampala)
G L Moore   B Lennard

Placings:00/00S440/200U0F/24410/2113/3P122/24P (0866)

2003/04: 18²GF, 16⁴G, 16PGF,

	Starts	1st	2nd	3rd	Win & Pl
Chases	3	0	1	0	1034
Career Total	31	4	6	2	17094
105 6/01	Fknm	2m110y E Ch		G-F	£2902
114 8/00	Font	2m2f110yE(0-115)HHdl		G-F	£2576
112 5/00	Font	2m2f110yF(0-105)HHdl		GD	£2369
114 11/99	Winc	2m	F(0-100)HHdl	GD	£2374

Total win prize-money £10222

Going: Sf: 0-0 GS: 0-0 Gd: 0-1 GF: - Fm: 0-2
Distance: 2m/2m3: 0-3 2m4-2m7: 0-0 3m+: 0-0
Track: LH: 0-2 RH: 0-0 Tight: 0-3 Gall: 0-0
Aids: Bl: 0-0 Vi: 0-0 Tstrap: 0-0 Ckp: 0-0
Best Rating: 114 5/01 Wwck 2m   gd-fm Hdl

North Point (IRE)

85   115

6-y-o b g Definite Article-Friendly Song (Song)
R Curtis   Heart Of The South Racing

Placings:1041-5P0 (4859)
2003/04: 16⁵GF, 18PG, 19⁹GF,

	Starts	1st	2nd	3rd	Win & Pl
Hurdles	3	0	0	0	0
Career Total	7	2	0	0	8110
108 4/03	Plum	2m	E Hdl	G-F	£3376
116 2/03	Ludl	2m	E Hdl	GD	£4358

Total win prize-money £7735

Going: Sf: 0-0 GS: 0-0 Gd: 0-1 GF: - Fm: 0-0
Distance: 2m/2m3: 0-2 2m4-2m7: 0-1 3m+: 0-0
Track: LH: 0-2 RH: 0-1 Tight: 0-2 Gall: 0-0
Aids: Bl: 0-0 Vi: 0-0 Tstrap: 0-0 Ckp: 0-0
Best Rating: 116 2/03 Ludl 2m   good   Hdl

Fair hurdler; suited by fast ground; effective at two miles.

Northaw Lad (IRE)

104   100+

6-y-o ch g Executive Perk-Black Tulip (Pals Passage)
C Tinkler (A J Lidderdale 3/11) J Fishpool

Placings:5-3314 (3775)
2003/04: 18^3G, 16^3G, 16^1GS, 16^6G,

	Starts	1st	2nd	3rd	Win & Pl
NH Flat	3	1	0	2	2539
Hurdles	1	0	0	0	310
Career Total	5	1	0	2	2849
103 12/03 Uttx	2m	H NHF		G-S	£1904

Total win prize-money £1904

Going:	Sf: 0-0 GS: 1-1 Gd: 0-3 GF: - Fm: 0-0
Distance:	2m/2m3: 1-4 2m4-2m7: 0-0 3m+: 0-0
Track:	LH: 1-3 RH: 0-1 Tight: 0-0 Gall: 0-0
Aids:	Bl: 0-0 Vi: 0-0 Tstrap: 0-0 Ckp: 0-0
Best Rating:	103 12/03 Uttx 2m gd-sft NHF

Consistent form in bumpers and novice hurdles on good ground; did not mind the soft when easy winner at Uttoxeter Boxing Day 2003; slow maturing type.

Northern Echo
100   74
7-y-o b g Pursuit Of Love-Stop Press (USA) (Sharpen Up)
Keith Thomas Keith Thomas

Placings:643FP2P0R/60P036004P0-6405066655 (1838)
2003/04: 16^6G, 16^4GF, 17^0GF, 16^5GF, 17^0G, 17^6GF, 16^6F, 17^6G, 20^5GF, 17^5G,

	Starts	1st	2nd	3rd	Win & Pl
Hurdles	10	0	0	0	0
Career Total	30	0	1	2	1033

Going:	Sf: 0-0 GS: 0-0 Gd: 0-4 GF: - Fm: 0-6
Distance:	2m/2m3: 0-9 2m4-2m7: 0-1 3m+: 0-0
Track:	LH: 0-9 RH: 0-1 Tight: 0-5 Gall: 0-0
Aids:	Bl: 0-0 Vi: 0-0 Tstrap: 0-0 Ckp: 0-9
Best Rating:	79 9/01 Hrfd 2m1f gd-fm Hdl

Northern Edition (IRE)
105   114+
7-y-o br g Good Thyne (USA)-Early Pace (Black Minstrel)
P F Nicholls You Boyz Is Lost

Placings:1P (4398)
2003/04: 26^1GS, 32^5G,

	Starts	1st	2nd	3rd	Win & Pl
Chases	2	1	0	0	6711
Career Total	2	1	0	0	6711
114 2/04 Plum	3m2f	D Ch		G-S	£6711

Total win prize-money £6711

Going:	Sf: 0-0 GS: 1-1 Gd: 0-1 GF: - Fm: 0-0
Distance:	2m/2m3: 0-0 2m4-2m7: 0-0 3m+: 1-2
Track:	LH: 1-2 RH: 0-0 Tight: 1-1 Gall: 0-1
Aids:	Bl: 0-0 Vi: 0-0 Tstrap: 0-0 Ckp: 0-0
Best Rating:	114 2/04 Plum 3m2f gd-sft Ch

Former maiden point-to-point winner; opened account on debut under Rules at Plumpton in February; stays three miles plus; acts on soft ground.

Northern Flash
101(67h)   (12h)77
10-y-o b g Rambo Dancer (CAN)-Spinster (Grundy)
J C Haynes J C Haynes

Placings:5064P0P00/603006000PP/0344P44404365/6232/ PP604-406044305PP (4880)
2003/04: 16^4GF, 22^0GS, 24^6G, 27^0G, 16^4GS, 20^4HY, 20^3HY, 21^9GS, 16^5G, 17^6G, 20^0GS,

	Starts	1st	2nd	3rd	Win & Pl
Chases	11	0	0	1	1445
Career Total	53	0	2	5	7839

Going:	Sf: 0-2 GS: 0-4 Gd: 0-4 GF: - Fm: 0-1
Distance:	2m/2m3: 0-4 2m4-2m7: 0-5 3m+: 0-2
Track:	LH: 0-10 RH: 0-1 Tight: 0-5 Gall: 0-3
Aids:	Bl: 0-0 Vi: 0-3 Tstrap: 0-0 Ckp: 0-8
Best Rating:	95 5/00 Ctml 2m1f110y good Ch

Plating-class chaser; still a maiden; acts on good or easier; has worn various headgear.

Northern Minster
100   79
5-y-o b g Minster Son-Hand On Heart (IRE) (Taufan (USA))
F P Murtagh L Irving & T Littleton

Placings:500-00416P1005 (4688)
2003/04: 16^9G, 22^0F, 20^4GS, 16^1GF, 16^6S, 20^0GF, 16^1HY, 17^0GS, 17^0G, 16^5G,

	Starts	1st	2nd	3rd	Win & Pl
Hurdles	10	2	0	0	6622
Career Total	13	2	0	0	6622
84 2/04 Newc	2m	E(0-100)HHdl	HVY	£3367
75 11/03 Catt	2m	E(0-100)HHdl	G-F	£3255

Total win prize-money £6622

Going:	Sf: 1-2 GS: 0-2 Gd: 0-3 GF: - Fm: 1-3
Distance:	2m/2m3: 2-7 2m4-2m7: 0-3 3m+: 0-0
Track:	LH: 2-8 RH: 0-2 Tight: 1-7 Gall: 1-1
Aids:	Bl: 0-0 Vi: 0-0 Tstrap: 0-0 Ckp: 0-0
Best Rating:	84 2/04 Newc 2m heavy Hdl

Plating-class hurdler; took weak event at Catterick in November; best over two miles.

Northern Motto
11-y-o b g Mtoto-Soulful (FR) (Zino)
T Jewitt T Jewitt

Placings:U/025U3/2543/30/55343/00P4F0/50-U (0521)
2003/04: 24^UG,

	Starts	1st	2nd	3rd	Win & Pl
Chases	1	0	0	0	
Career Total	26	0	2	5	4282

Going:	Sf: 0-0 GS: 0-0 Gd: 0-1 GF: - Fm: 0-0
Distance:	2m/2m3: 0-0 2m4-2m7: 0-0 3m+: 0-1
Track:	LH: 0-1 RH: 0-0 Tight: 0-1 Gall: 0-0
Aids:	Bl: 0-0 Vi: 0-0 Tstrap: 0-0 Ckp: 0-0
Best Rating:	104 10/99 Weth 3m1f gd-fm Hdl

Northern Raider (IRE)
(85c)   (66c)57
6-y-o b g College Chapel-Pepper And Salt (IRE) (Double Schwartz)
Miss T Jackson H L Thompson

Placings:0100P/5-P (4433)
2003/04: 24^PG,

	Starts	1st	2nd	3rd	Win & Pl
Hurdles	1	0	0	0	
Career Total	7	1	0	0	1897
57 12/01 Uttx	2m	G Hdl	SFT	£1897

Total win prize-money £1897

Going:	Sf: 0-0 GS: 0-0 Gd: 0-1 GF: - Fm: 0-0
Distance:	2m/2m3: 0-0 2m4-2m7: 0-0 3m+: 0-1
Track:	LH: 0-1 RH: 0-0 Tight: 0-0 Gall: 0-0
Aids:	Bl: 0-0 Vi: 0-0 Tstrap: 0-0 Ckp: 0-0
Best Rating:	66 3/03 Catt 3m1f110y soft Ch

Northern Rambler (IRE)
92(100h)   (81h)64
7-y-o gr g Roselier (FR)-Ramble Bramble (Random Shot)
Mrs M Reveley W J Smith And M D Dudley

Placings:05060-P33053 (4259)
2003/04: 24^5PS, 23^9GF, 22^3G, 23^9GS, 22^5S, 25^3GF,

	Starts	1st	2nd	3rd	Win & Pl
Hurdles	5	0	0	2	854
Chases	1	0	0	1	615
Career Total	11	0	0	3	1469

Going:	Sf: 0-2 GS: 0-1 Gd: 0-1 GF: - Fm: 0-2
Distance:	2m/2m3: 0-0 2m4-2m7: 0-4 3m+: 0-0
Track:	LH: 0-6 RH: 0-0 Tight: 0-3 Gall: 0-0
Aids:	Bl: 0-0 Vi: 0-0 Tstrap: 0-0 Ckp: 0-0
Best Rating:	88 1/03 Ayr 2m heavy NHF

Only very moderate form so far in bumpers, over hurdles and novice chases; will stay well; acts on fast.

Northern Shadows
96f   97f
5-y-o b m Rock Hopper-Shadows Of Silver (Carwhite)
Mrs M Reveley M J Hutton, Mrs M Laing, Mrs G Waters

Placings:30 (4787)
2003/04: 16^9GS, 16^0G,

	Starts	1st	2nd	3rd	Win & Pl
NH Flat	2	0	0	1	285
Career Total	2	0	0	1	285

Going:	Sf: 0-0 GS: 0-1 Gd: 0-1 GF: - Fm: 0-0
Distance:	2m/2m3: 0-2 2m4-2m7: 0-0 3m+: 0-0
Track:	LH: 0-1 RH: 0-1 Tight: 0-0 Gall: 0-0
Aids:	Bl: 0-0 Vi: 0-0 Tstrap: 0-0 Ckp: 0-0
Best Rating:	97 3/04 Wwck 2m gd-sft NHF

Northern Svengali (IRE)
83   54
8-y-o b g Distinctly North (USA)-Trilby's Dream (IRE) (Mansooj)
D A Nolan Miss McFadyen-Murray

Placings:6 (2784)
2003/04: 16^6GF,

	Starts	1st	2nd	3rd	Win & Pl
Hurdles	1	0	0	0	0
Career Total	1	0	0	0	0

Going:	Sf: 0-0 GS: 0-0 Gd: 0-0 GF: - Fm: 0-1
Distance:	2m/2m3: 0-1 2m4-2m7: 0-0 3m+: 0-0
Track:	LH: 0-0 RH: 0-1 Tight: 0-1 Gall: 0-0
Aids:	Bl: 0-0 Vi: 0-0 Tstrap: 0-1 Ckp: 0-0
Best Rating:	54 12/03 Muss 2m gd-fm Hdl

Norton Sapphire

90   **66+**

5-y-o ch m Karinga Bay-Sea Of Pearls (IRE) (King's Ride)
M J Gingell Gentlemen Don't Work On Mondays

Placings:00P0502   (4750)
2003/04: 16⁶G, 17⁰G, 21⁶S, 19⁰GF, 16⁵S, 21⁰G, 21²G,

	Starts	1st	2nd	3rd	Win & Pl
NH Flat	1	0	0	0	0
Hurdles	6	0	1	0	721
Career Total	7	0	1	0	721

Going:	Sf: 0-2 GS: 0-1 Gd: 0-4 GF: - Fm: 0-1
Distance:	2m/2m3: 0-3 2m4-2m7: 0-4 3m+: 0-0
Track:	LH: 0-7 RH: 0-0 Tight: 0-5 Gall: 0-0
Aids:	Bl: 0-0 Vi: 0-0 Tstrap: 0-0 Ckp: 0-0
Best Rating:	70 4/04 Plum 2m5f good Hdl

Nosam

105(99h)   (93h)**119**

14-y-o b g Idiots Delight-Socher (Anax)
R C Guest N B Mason

Placings:0/6/1120/406U5113313423P3/23343114112200/0
6254622F1/3120352105/FP52463300-35F0660212320463   (4313)
2003/04: 20³S, 20⁵G, 20⁵GF, 24⁰GS, 22⁵GF, 21⁶GF, 24⁰GF, 24²G,
21¹G, 25²F, 25³GF, 24²G, 21⁰G, 20⁴G, 19⁶G, 25³GF,

	Starts	1st	2nd	3rd	Win & Pl
Hurdles	3	0	0	0	0
Chases	13	1	3	3	14417
Career Total	82	13	14	15	108840

114	9/03	Sedg	2m5f	E(0-110)HCh	GD	£3423
119	3/02	Donc	2m3f110yE(0-110)HCh	SFT	£3514
122	9/01	List	2m3f	(0-123)HCh	G-F	£7862
115	4/01	Prth	2m4f110yD(0-125)HCh	HVY	£7962
125	1/00	Donc	2m3f110yD(0-120)HCh	GD	£7020
124	1/00	Leic	2m4f110yD(0-120)HCh	GD	£5785
118	11/99	Catt	2m3f	E(0-115)HCh	G-F	£5572
114	11/99	Ayr	2m4f	D(0-120)HCh	GD	£3821
111	1/99	Donc	2m3f110yC(0-130)HCh	G-S	£5930
101	11/98	Sedg	E Ch		G-S	£2940
97	10/98	Sedg	2m5f	E Ch	G-S	£3065
103	8/97	Ctml	2m6f	E Hdl	G-F	£2250
105	5/97	Ctml	2m6f	E Hdl	G-F	£2447
				Total win prize-money £61597		

Going:	Sf: 0-1 GS: 0-1 Gd: 1-7 GF: - Fm: 0-7
Distance:	2m/2m3: 0-1 2m4-2m7: 1-8 3m+: 0-7
Track:	LH: 1-13 RH: 0-3 Tight: 1-8 Gall: 0-0
Aids:	Bl: 0-0 Vi: 0-0 Tstrap: 0-5 Ckp: 1-10
Best Rating:	125 9/00 Uttx 2m5f gd-sft Ch

Moderate chaser; as tough as old boots; effective on any ground; best around two and a half miles; usually races with his tongue tied; often wears cheekpieces.

Noshinannikin

107(106h)   (117 h)**129d**

10-y-o ch g Anshan-Preziosa (Homing)
Mrs S J Smith (M W Easterby 28/4) M C V Racing

Placings:202/41045/14F1UR2/PP3P/P4412241P0C/40000
60642115-2230   (4426)
2003/04: 16⁵G, 16²G, 19²G, 19³G, 16⁰G,

	Starts	1st	2nd	3rd	Win & Pl
Hurdles	2	0	1	0	2056
Chases	3	0	1	1	3624
Career Total	47	7	8	2	40537

117	4/03	Weth	2m	F(0-100)HHdl	G-F	£2688
104	4/03	Hexm	2m110y	E(0-110)HHdl	GD	£3647

129	2/02	Hntg	2m110y	D(0-120)HCh	G-S	£3864
128	12/01	Newc	2m	E(0-115)HHdl	G-S	£3396
129	1/00	Weth	2m	E Ch	SFT	£3003
98	11/99	Hexm	2m110y	E Ch	GD	£3152
107	11/98	Newc	2m4f	E Hdl	G-S	£2410
				Total win prize-money £22161		

Going:	Sf: 0-0 GS: 0-0 Gd: 0-5 GF: - Fm: 0-0
Distance:	2m/2m3: 0-4 2m4-2m7: 0-1 3m+: 0-0
Track:	LH: 0-4 RH: 0-1 Tight: 0-0 Gall: 0-2
Aids:	Bl: 0-0 Vi: 0-0 Tstrap: 0-1 Ckp: 0-0
Best Rating:	133 4/00 Aint 2m4f good Ch

Fair hurdler/chaser; looked rejuvenated when winning over hurdles at Hexham and Wetherby in April 2003; effective over two miles; usually wears tongue strap; has worn blinkers.

Nostradamus (USA)

74   **90**

5-y-o b h Gone West (USA)-Madam North (CAN) (Halo (USA))
K J Burke Joseph A Kelly

Placings:F600   (4493)
2003/04: 17⁵GS, 16⁶HY, 16⁰YS, 16⁰G,

	Starts	1st	2nd	3rd	Win & Pl
Hurdles	4	0	0	0	
Career Total	4	0	0	0	

Going:	Sf: 0-1 GS: 0-1 Gd: 0-1 GF: - Fm: 0-0
Distance:	2m/2m3: 0-4 2m4-2m7: 0-0 3m+: 0-0
Track:	LH: 0-2 RH: 0-1 Tight: 0-2 Gall: 0-0
Aids:	Bl: 0-0 Vi: 0-0 Tstrap: 0-0 Ckp: 0-0
Best Rating:	90 2/04 Punc 2m heavy Hdl

Not Now George

61   **36**

5-y-o b g Sovereign Water (FR)-Threads (Bedford (USA))
T H Caldwell Mrs S J Wall and T H Caldwell

Placings:00-00F   (3825)
2003/04: 16⁰HY, 17⁰HY, 20⁵S,

	Starts	1st	2nd	3rd	Win & Pl
NH Flat	1	0	0	0	0
Hurdles	2	0	0	0	0
Career Total	5	0	0	0	0

Going:	Sf: 0-3 GS: 0-0 Gd: 0-0 GF: - Fm: 0-0
Distance:	2m/2m3: 0-2 2m4-2m7: 0-1 3m+: 0-0
Track:	LH: 0-2 RH: 0-1 Tight: 0-0 Gall: 0-0
Aids:	Bl: 0-0 Vi: 0-0 Tstrap: 0-0 Ckp: 0-0
Best Rating:	71 11/02 Wwck 1m6f gd-sft NHF

Not To Be Missed

96   **85**

6-y-o gr m Missed Flight-Petinata (Petong)
R Dickin Only Horses And Fools

Placings:0005-F0260   (1587)
2003/04: 16⁵GS, 16⁰G, 16²GF, 17⁵GF, 16⁰GF,

	Starts	1st	2nd	3rd	Win & Pl
Hurdles	5	0	1	0	1233
Career Total	9	0	1	0	1233

Going:	Sf: 0-0 GS: 0-1 Gd: 0-1 GF: - Fm: 0-3
Distance:	2m/2m3: 0-5 2m4-2m7: 0-0 3m+: 0-0
Track:	LH: 0-3 RH: 0-2 Tight: 0-2 Gall: 0-1

Aids:	Bl: 0-0 Vi: 0-0 Tstrap: 0-0 Ckp: 0-0
Best Rating:	85 4/03 Uttx 2m good Hdl

Poor novice hurdler; can pull hard.

Notanotherdonkey (IRE)

82f

4-y-o b g Zaffaran (USA)-Sporting Talent (IRE) (Seymour Hicks (FR))
M Scudamore Nick Ponting

Placings:003   (4374)
2003/04: 13⁰GS, 12⁰G, 16³GF,

	Starts	1st	2nd	3rd	Win & Pl
NH Flat	3	0	0	1	587
Career Total	3	0	0	1	587

Going:	Sf: 0-0 GS: 0-1 Gd: 0-1 GF: - Fm: 0-0
Distance:	2m/2m3: 0-0 2m4-2m7: 0-3 3m+: 0-0
Track:	LH: 0-0 RH: 0-1 Tight: 0-0 Gall: 0-0
Aids:	Bl: 0-0 Vi: 0-0 Tstrap: 0-0 Ckp: 0-0
Best Rating:	86 1/04 Chel 1m4f good NHF

Notsotiny

78   **47**

8-y-o b g Southern Music-Goodbye Roscoe (Roscoe Blake)
Evan Williams Mrs J M Hegarty

Placings:0F60   (1024)
2003/04: 16⁰G, 20⁰GF, 16⁶GF, 17⁰GF,

	Starts	1st	2nd	3rd	Win & Pl
Hurdles	4	0	0	0	0
Career Total	4	0	0	0	0

Going:	Sf: 0-0 GS: 0-0 Gd: 0-1 GF: - Fm: 0-3
Distance:	2m/2m3: 0-3 2m4-2m7: 0-0 3m+: 0-0
Track:	LH: 0-3 RH: 0-1 Tight: 0-1 Gall: 0-0
Aids:	Bl: 0-0 Vi: 0-1 Tstrap: 0-0 Ckp: 0-0
Best Rating:	47 6/03 Worc 2m good Hdl

Notwhatshewanted (IRE)

94   **84**

7-y-o b g Supreme Leader-Wise Nellie (IRE) (Brush Aside (USA))
J W Mullins Mrs M M Rayner

Placings:000P-4P005   (4819)
2003/04: 22⁴GF, 21⁰S, 21⁰G, 22⁰G, 22⁵GF,

	Starts	1st	2nd	3rd	Win & Pl
Hurdles	5	0	0	0	0
Career Total	9	0	0	0	0

Going:	Sf: 0-0 GS: 0-1 Gd: 0-2 GF: - Fm: 0-2
Distance:	2m/2m3: 0-0 2m4-2m7: 0-5 3m+: 0-0
Track:	LH: 0-2 RH: 0-3 Tight: 0-2 Gall: 0-0
Aids:	Bl: 0-0 Vi: 0-0 Tstrap: 0-0 Ckp: 0-0
Best Rating:	84 4/04 Extr 2m6f110y gd-fm Hdl

Nought To Ninety

6-y-o b g Mazaad-Bonnyhill Lass (Royal Fountain)
C Grant Chris Grant

Placings:0/0					(0162)
2003/04: 22⁶G,					

	Starts	1st	2nd	3rd	Win & Pl
Hurdles	1	0	0	0	0
Career Total	2	0	0	0	0

Going:	Sf: 0-0 GS: 0-0 Gd: 0-1 GF: - Fm: 0-0
Distance:	2m/2m3: 0-0 2m4-2m7: 0-1 3m+: 0-0
Track:	LH: 0-1 RH: 0-0 Tight: 0-1 Gall: 0-0
Aids:	Bl: 0-0 Vi: 0-0 Tstrap: 0-0 Ckp: 0-0
Best Rating:	31 4/02 Hexm 2m110y good NHF

Nousayri (IRE)

9-y-o b g Slip Anchor-Noufiyla (Top Ville)
N B King A R Humphrey

Placings:6/132/232666/320/405525F-5					(0198)
2003/04: 20⁵GF,					

	Starts	1st	2nd	3rd	Win & Pl
Chases	1	0	0	0	0
Career Total	21	1	5	3	7314
103 5/99 Prth 2m110y H NHF HVY £1987					
				Total win prize-money £1987	

Going:	Sf: 0-0 GS: 0-0 Gd: 0-0 GF: - Fm: 0-1
Distance:	2m/2m3: 0-0 2m4-2m7: 0-1 3m+: 0-0
Track:	LH: 0-0 RH: 0-1 Tight: 0-0 Gall: 0-1
Aids:	Bl: 0-0 Vi: 0-0 Tstrap: 0-0 Ckp: 0-0
Best Rating:	122 12/99 Hntg 2m110y good NHF

Nousyr
79   **36**

5-y-o b m Syrtos-Noushy (Ahonoora)
D McCain Mrs D McCain

Placings:00P					(0852)
2003/04: 17⁰G, 16⁰GF, 16⁶GF,					

	Starts	1st	2nd	3rd	Win & Pl
NH Flat	1	0	0	0	0
Hurdles	2	0	0	0	0
Career Total	3	0	0	0	0

Going:	Sf: 0-0 GS: 0-0 Gd: 0-1 GF: - Fm: 0-2
Distance:	2m/2m3: 0-3 2m4-2m7: 0-0 3m+: 0-0
Track:	LH: 0-3 RH: 0-0 Tight: 0-2 Gall: 0-0
Aids:	Bl: 0-0 Vi: 0-0 Tstrap: 0-0 Ckp: 0-0
Best Rating:	36 6/03 Uttx 2m gd-fm Hdl

Nova Beacon
68   **42**

12-y-o b g Ra Nova-Ditchling Beacon (High Line)
S J Gilmore Steve Mouring

Placings:0/0					(4783)
2003/04: 21⁰G,					

	Starts	1st	2nd	3rd	Win & Pl
Hurdles	1	0	0	0	0
Career Total	2	0	0	0	0

Going:	Sf: 0-0 GS: 0-0 Gd: 0-1 GF: - Fm: 0-0
Distance:	2m/2m3: 0-0 2m4-2m7: 0-1 3m+: 0-0
Track:	LH: 0-0 RH: 0-1 Tight: 0-0 Gall: 0-1
Aids:	Bl: 0-0 Vi: 0-0 Tstrap: 0-0 Ckp: 0-0
Best Rating:	56 11/99 Bang 2m1f soft Hdl

Novatara
92(105h)   (88h)**76+**

12-y-o ch g Ra Nova-Asphaltara (Scallywag)
B G Powell (P G Murphy 7/1) A Ayers

Placings:32/0/P11/5P22333					(4792)
2003/04: 25⁵GS, 25⁵S, 26²GS, 26²GS, 26³GS, 26³G, 26³G,					

	Starts	1st	2nd	3rd	Win & Pl
Hurdles	4	0	2	2	3047
Chases	3	0	0	1	486
Career Total	13	2	3	4	9620
88 3/02 Sand 3m110y H Ch GD £2912					
88 5/01 Folk 2m5f H Ch GD £2184					
				Total win prize-money £5096	

Going:	Sf: 0-1 GS: 0-4 Gd: 0-2 GF: - Fm: 0-0
Distance:	2m/2m3: 0-0 2m4-2m7: 0-0 3m+: 0-7
Track:	LH: 0-1 RH: 0-6 Tight: 0-1 Gall: 0-2
Aids:	Bl: 0-5 Vi: 0-2 Tstrap: 0-0 Ckp: 0-0
Best Rating:	88 3/04 Hntg 3m2f good Hdl

Plating-class chaser/hurdler; has broke blood vessels over fences; acts on ground good and softer; usually wears blinkers or a visor.

Novel Idea (IRE)
73   **70**

6-y-o ch g Phardante (FR)-Novelist (Quayside)
Mrs H Dalton Mrs Caroline Shaw

Placings:60F40					(4512)
2003/04: 16⁶G, 16⁰GS, 25⁶GS, 25⁴G, 20⁰GS,					

	Starts	1st	2nd	3rd	Win & Pl
NH Flat	2	0	0	0	0
Hurdles	3	0	0	0	0
Career Total	5	0	0	0	0

Going:	Sf: 0-0 GS: 0-3 Gd: 0-2 GF: - Fm: 0-0
Distance:	2m/2m3: 0-2 2m4-2m7: 0-1 3m+: 0-2
Track:	LH: 0-4 RH: 0-1 Tight: 0-0 Gall: 0-1
Aids:	Bl: 0-0 Vi: 0-0 Tstrap: 0-0 Ckp: 0-0
Best Rating:	92 11/03 Weth 2m good NHF

Novi Sad (IRE)
93   **97+**

6-y-o b g Norwich-Shuil Na Gale (Strong Gale)
L Wells Mrs Carrie Zetter-Wells

Placings:02/510P53134-5002					(2239)
2003/04: 17⁵S, 16⁰G, 16⁰G, 25²G,					

	Starts	1st	2nd	3rd	Win & Pl
Hurdles	4	0	1	0	1245
Career Total	15	2	2	5	11493
96 3/03 Asct 2m110y D(0-110)HHdl GD £5603					
97 11/02 Plum 2m2f H NHF SFT £2404					
				Total win prize-money £8008	

Going:	Sf: 0-1 GS: 0-0 Gd: 0-3 GF: - Fm: 0-0
Distance:	2m/2m3: 0-3 2m4-2m7: 0-0 3m+: 0-1
Track:	LH: 0-2 RH: 0-2 Tight: 0-1 Gall: 0-0
Aids:	Bl: 0-1 Vi: 0-0 Tstrap: 0-0 Ckp: 0-1
Best Rating:	97 3/03 Font 2m2f110y good Hdl

Modest hurdler; collared the reluctant favourite to land first hurdles success in March 2003; acts on soft and good ground; suited by further than two miles.

Now And Again
92   **75**

5-y-o b g Shaamit (IRE)-Sweet Allegiance (Alleging (USA))

M W Easterby Mrs M E Curtis

Placings:00600					(4431)
2003/04: 17⁰GF, 16⁰G, 19⁶G, 17⁰G, 24⁰G,					

	Starts	1st	2nd	3rd	Win & Pl
NH Flat	2	0	0	0	0
Hurdles	3	0	0	0	0
Career Total	5	0	0	0	0

Going:	Sf: 0-0 GS: 0-0 Gd: 0-4 GF: - Fm: 0-1
Distance:	2m/2m3: 0-3 2m4-2m7: 0-1 3m+: 0-1
Track:	LH: 0-4 RH: 0-3 Tight: 0-3 Gall: 0-0
Aids:	Bl: 0-0 Vi: 0-0 Tstrap: 0-0 Ckp: 0-0
Best Rating:	85 9/03 MRas 2m1f110y gd-fm NHF

Now Then Sid
101   **92+**

5-y-o ch g Presidium-Callace (Royal Palace)
Mrs S A Watt Mrs S A Watt

Placings:4056-201340					(3233)
2003/04: 20²F, 20⁰G, 20¹GF, 20³G, 20⁴G, 20⁰GF,					

	Starts	1st	2nd	3rd	Win & Pl
Hurdles	6	1	1	1	3572
Career Total	10	1	1	1	3572
92 11/03 Hexm 2m4f110yE Hdl G-F £2226					
				Total win prize-money £2226	

Going:	Sf: 0-0 GS: 0-0 Gd: 0-3 GF: - Fm: 1-3
Distance:	2m/2m3: 0-0 **2m4-2m7: 1-6** 3m+: 0-0
Track:	**LH: 1-5** RH: 0-1 Tight: 0-2 Gall: 0-0
Aids:	Bl: 0-0 Vi: 0-0 Tstrap: 0-0 Ckp: 0-0
Best Rating:	92 12/03 Weth 2m4f110y good Hdl

Moderate novice hurdler; wide margin winner of poor event at Hexham in November; stays 2m 4f.

Nowator (POL)
109   **107+**

7-y-o ch g Jape (USA)-Naradka (POL) (Dakota)
T R George Mrs Sharon C Nelson

Placings:040-1304P20					(3050)
2003/04: 17¹GS, 16³G, 16⁰G, 16⁴GS, 16⁶G, 16²GF, 17⁰G,					

	Starts	1st	2nd	3rd	Win & Pl
Hurdles	7	1	1	1	5981
Career Total	10	1	1	1	5981
105 5/03 Hrfd 2m1f E(0-105)HHdl G-S £3477					
				Total win prize-money £3478	

Going:	Sf: 0-0 GS: 1-2 Gd: 0-4 GF: - Fm: 0-1
Distance:	**2m/2m3: 1-7** 2m4-2m7: 0-0 3m+: 0-0
Track:	LH: 0-2 **RH: 1-5** Tight: 0-1 Gall: 0-0
Aids:	Bl: 0-0 Vi: 0-0 Tstrap: 0-0 Ckp: 0-0
Best Rating:	107 5/03 Weth 2m good Hdl

Moderate hurdler; decent on the Flat in Poland; off the mark in novice handicap hurdle at Hereford in May 2003; seems suited by good ground or softer.

Nowbytheway (IRE)
58   **50**

7-y-o b g Wakashan-Gilded Empress (Menelek)
J R Jenkins Jack McGrath

Placings:00F					(4588)
2003/04: 16⁰GS, 23⁹GS, 21⁶GF,					

	Starts	1st	2nd	3rd	Win & Pl
Hurdles	2	0	0	0	0
Chases	1	0	0	0	0
Career Total	3	0	0	0	0

Going:	Sf: 0-0 GS: 0-2 Gd: 0-1 GF: - Fm: 0-0
Distance:	2m/2m3: 0-1 2m4-2m7: 0-1 3m+: 0-1
Track:	LH: 0-1 RH: 0-2 Tight: 0-2 Gall: 0-1
Aids:	Bl: 0-0 Vi: 0-0 Tstrap: 0-0 Ckp: 0-0
Best Rating:	50 1/04 Fknm 2m7f110y gd-sft Hdl

Nowell House

111   131

8-y-o ch g Polar Falcon (USA)-Langtry Lady (Pas De Seul)
M W Easterby   John Walsh

Placings:214/406/2515-110   (4644)
2003/04: 17¹G, 16¹GS, 16⁶G,

	Starts	1st	2nd	3rd	Win & Pl
Hurdles	3	2	0		10023
Career Total	13	4	2	0	18158
131	3/04	Weth	2m		D(0-125)HHdl	G-S	£4972
121	2/04	Carl	2m1f		D(0-120)HHdl	GD	£5050
110	1/03	Newc	2m		E(0-105)HHdl	HVY	£3479
101	2/01	Sedg	2m1f		E Hdl	G-S	£2044

Total win prize-money £15547

Going:	Sf: 0-0 GS: 1-1 Gd: 1-2 GF: 0-0
Distance:	2m/2m3: 2-3 2m4-2m7: 0-0 3m+: 0-0
Track:	LH: 1-2 RH: 1-1 Tight: 0-1 Gall: 0-0
Aids:	Bl: 0-0 Vi: 0-0 Tstrap: 0-0 Ckp: 0-0
Best Rating:	131 3/04 Weth 2m gd-sft Hdl

Fair hurdler; better known as a Flat performer; scored at Carlisle in February and followed up narrowly at Wetherby thhe following month; best over two miles; suited by cut in the ground.

Nowt

92   67

7-y-o b m Derrylin-Jolejester (Relkino)
D McCain   Champ Chicken Co Ltd

Placings:P5-5PP   (1073)
2003/04: 20⁵G, 16⁶G, 17⁵GS, 17⁶GF,

	Starts	1st	2nd	3rd	Win & Pl
Hurdles	4	0	0	0	0
Career Total	5	0	0	0	0

Going:	Sf: 0-0 GS: 0-1 Gd: 0-2 GF: - Fm: 0-1
Distance:	2m/2m3: 0-3 2m4-2m7: 0-1 3m+: 0-0
Track:	LH: 0-4 RH: 0-0 Tight: 0-2 Gall: 0-0
Aids:	Bl: 0-0 Vi: 0-0 Tstrap: 0-0 Ckp: 0-0
Best Rating:	67 5/03 Uttx 2m good Hdl

Nuclear Prospect (IRE)

81   78

4-y-o ch g Nucleon (USA)-Carraigbyrne (IRE) (Over The River (FR))
G M Moore   Mrs Mary And Miss Susan Hatfield

Placings:0P54P   (4657)
2003/04: 16⁶GS, 16ᴾGS, 16⁵G, 16⁴G, 16ᴾS,

	Starts	1st	2nd	3rd	Win & Pl
Hurdles	5	0	0	0	322
Career Total	5	0	0	0	322

Going:	Sf: 0-1 GS: 0-2 Gd: 0-2 GF: - Fm: 0-0
Distance:	2m/2m3: 0-5 2m4-2m7: 0-0 3m+: 0-0
Track:	LH: 0-5 RH: 0-0 Tight: 0-3 Gall: 0-0
Aids:	Bl: 0-0 Vi: 0-0 Tstrap: 0-0 Ckp: 0-0

Best Rating: 78   2/04   Catt   2m   good   Hdl

Numitas (GER)

105   119

4-y-o b c Lomitas-Narola (GER) (Nebos (GER))
P J Hobbs (Sir Mark Prescott 18/10)   Mrs David Thompson

Placings:R16   (4629)
2003/04: 16ᴿS, 16¹G, 20⁶G,

	Starts	1st	2nd	3rd	Win & Pl
Hurdles	3	1	0	0	4676
Career Total	3	1	0	0	4676
112	3/04	Newb	2m110y	E Hdl		GD	£3926

Total win prize-money £3926

Going:	Sf: 0-1 GS: 0-0 Gd: 1-2 GF: - Fm: 0-0
Distance:	2m/2m3: 1-2 2m4-2m7: 0-1 3m+: 0-0
Track:	LH: 0-1 RH: 1-0 Tight: 0-1 Gall: 1-1
Aids:	Bl: 1-2 Vi: 0-0 Tstrap: 0-0 Ckp: 0-0
Best Rating:	119 4/04 Aint 2m4f good Hdl

Fair novice hurdler; winner at Newbury in February; wore blinkers and looked ungenuine at Aintree; stays two and a half miles; best on a sound surface.

Nurseryman (IRE)

77   32

7-y-o b g Mandalus-The Mighty Midge (Hardgreen (USA))
P Winkworth   P Winkworth

Placings:0-00   (2838)
2003/04: 20⁰G, 20⁰GS,

	Starts	1st	2nd	3rd	Win & Pl
Hurdles	2	0	0	0	
Career Total	3	0	0	0	

Going:	Sf: 0-0 GS: 0-1 Gd: 0-1 GF: - Fm: 0-0
Distance:	2m/2m3: 0-0 2m4-2m7: 0-1 3m+: 0-0
Track:	LH: 0-2 RH: 0-0 Tight: 0-0 Gall: 0-0
Aids:	Bl: 0-0 Vi: 0-0 Tstrap: 0-0 Ckp: 0-0
Best Rating:	48 4/03 Asct 2m110y good NHF

Nurzyk (POL)

103   81+

7-y-o ch g Freedom's Choice (USA)-Numeria (POL) (Dakota)
T R George   C Davies,S Nelson,A Stennett,T Warner

Placings:P00-12   (0366)
2003/04: 27¹S, 24²S,

	Starts	1st	2nd	3rd	Win & Pl
Hurdles	2	1	1	0	4451
Career Total	5	1	1	0	4451
75	5/03	Sedg	3m3f110yE(0-100)HHdl	SFT	£3451

Total win prize-money £3451

Going:	Sf: 1-2 GS: 0-0 Gd: 0-0 GF: - Fm: 0-0
Distance:	2m/2m3: 0-0 2m4-2m7: 0-0 3m+: 1-2
Track:	LH: 1-2 RH: 0-0 Tight: 1-1 Gall: 0-0
Aids:	Bl: 0-0 Vi: 0-0 Tstrap: 0-0 Ckp: 0-0
Best Rating:	81 5/03 Uttx 3m110y soft Hdl

Flat winner in Poland; winner over an extreme distance at Sedgefield in May 2003; acts well in soft ground.

Nutcracker Lad (IRE)

99   73+

6-y-o ch g Duky-Allercashin Moon (IRE) (Callernish)

M J Gingell   C N & Mrs A V Roberts

Placings:0-0PPP001P   (4592)
2003/04: 20⁰GF, 20ᴾGF, 21ᴾS, 17ᴾGS, 16⁰S, 17⁰G, 21¹G, 26ᴾG,

	Starts	1st	2nd	3rd	Win & Pl
Hurdles	8	1	0	0	2443
Career Total	9	1	0	0	2443
73	3/04	Hntg	2m5f110y		G(0-90)HHdl	
GD	£2443					

Total win prize-money £2443

Going:	Sf: 0-2 GS: 0-1 Gd: 1-3 GF: - Fm: 0-2
Distance:	2m/2m3: 0-3 2m4-2m7: 1-4 3m+: 0-1
Track:	LH: 0-4 RH: 1-6 Tight: 0-3 Gall: 1-3
Aids:	Bl: 0-0 Vi: 1-5 Tstrap: 0-0 Ckp: 0-0
Best Rating:	73 3/04 Hntg 2m5f110y good Hdl

Selling hudle winner; stays 21f; acts on good ground.

Nutty (IRE)

4-y-o b f Sri Pekan (USA)-Mitra (IRE) (Archway (IRE))
Mrs S Gardner (Mrs P N Dutfield 28/5)   Graham Brown

Placings:P   (3997)
2003/04: 21ᴾG,

	Starts	1st	2nd	3rd	Win & Pl
Hurdles	1	0	0	0	
Career Total	1	0	0	0	

Going:	Sf: 0-0 GS: 0-0 Gd: 0-1 GF: - Fm: 0-0
Distance:	2m/2m3: 0-0 2m4-2m7: 0-1 3m+: 0-0
Track:	LH: 0-0 RH: 0-1 Tight: 0-0 Gall: 0-0
Aids:	Bl: 0-0 Vi: 0-0 Tstrap: 0-0 Ckp: 0-0

Nuzum Road Makers (IRE)

75(105h)   (119h)114

13-y-o b g Lafontaine (USA)-Dark Gold (Raise You Ten)
W G Young   W G Young

Placings:00/6f0010/B011410610/06/02P406/000046023/10200-00   (3359)
2003/04: 20⁰GF, 25⁰S,

	Starts	1st	2nd	3rd	Win & Pl
Chases	2	0	0	0	
Career Total	42	7	3	1	69116
114	5/02	DRoy	3m		(0-123)HCh	G-F	£15950
122	4/99	Fair	2m6f		HHdl	YLD	£8671
129	11/98	Fair	3m1f		HCh	Y-S	£11260
122	10/98	Rosc	2m		Ch	Y-S	£7472
93	9/98	Gway	2m6f		Ch	Y-S	£3885
120	4/98	Fair	2m6f		Hdl	G-Y	£5956
113	2/98	Navn	2m		NHF	HVY	£2680

Total win prize-money £55880

Going:	Sf: 0-1 GS: 0-0 Gd: 0-0 GF: - Fm: 0-1
Distance:	2m/2m3: 0-0 2m4-2m7: 0-1 3m+: 0-1
Track:	LH: 0-1 RH: 0-1 Tight: 0-2 Gall: 0-0
Aids:	Bl: 0-0 Vi: 0-0 Tstrap: 0-0 Ckp: 0-0
Best Rating:	129 11/98 Fair 3m1f yld-sft Ch

Fair chaser; ex-Irish veteran; stays three miles; acts on easy ground.

Nyrche (FR)

97   100+

4-y-o b g Medaaly-Thoiry (USA) (Sagace (FR))
A King (A Lamotte D'Argy 7/1)   Tony Fisher & Mrs Jeni Fisher

Placings:0322   (4309)
2003/04: 15⁰HO, 15³VS, 16²VS, 16²G,

	Starts	1st	2nd	3rd	Win & Pl
Hurdles	4	0	2	1	8873
Career Total	4	0	2	1	8873

Going:	Sf: 0-0 GS: 0-0 Gd: 0-1 GF: - Fm: 0-0
Distance:	2m/2m3: 0-2 2m4-2m7: 0-0 3m+: 0-0
Track:	LH: 0-1 RH: 0-1 Tight: 0-0 Gall: 0-0
Aids:	Bl: 0-0 Vi: 0-0 Tstrap: 0-0 Ckp: 0-0
Best Rating:	100 3/04 Sand 2m110y good Hdl

Novice hurdler; French import; chased home useful prospect Back To Ben Alder on his British debut; likely to be campaigned as a novice in 2004/05; nice prospect.

O Cinza (IRE)

6-y-o gr g Norwich-Queenlier (IRE) (Roselier (FR))
Miss H C Knight Martin Broughton

Placings:0P   (3447)
2003/04: 16⁰GS, 19ᴾGS,

	Starts	1st	2nd	3rd	Win & Pl
NH Flat	1	0	0	0	0
Hurdles	1	0	0	0	0
Career Total	2	0	0	0	

Going:	Sf: 0-0 GS: 0-2 Gd: 0-0 GF: - Fm: 0-0
Distance:	2m/2m3: 0-1 2m4-2m7: 0-1 3m+: 0-0
Track:	LH: 0-1 RH: 0-1 Tight: 0-1 Gall: 0-1
Aids:	Bl: 0-0 Vi: 0-0 Tstrap: 0-0 Ckp: 0-0
Best Rating:	81 12/03 Newb 2m110y gd-sft NHF

O So Bossy

14-y-o ch g Sousa-Bubbling Spirit (Hubble Bubble)
A W Congdon A W Congdon

Placings:F/4/U/3-5F   (4150)
2003/04: 19⁵GF, 24ᶠG,

	Starts	1st	2nd	3rd	Win & Pl
Chases	2	0	0	0	0
Career Total	6	0	0	1	513

Going:	Sf: 0-0 GS: 0-0 Gd: 0-0 GF: 0-1 Fm: 0-1
Distance:	2m/2m3: 0-0 2m4-2m7: 0-0 3m+: 0-1
Track:	LH: 0-0 RH: 0-2 Tight: 0-1 Gall: 0-0
Aids:	Bl: 0-0 Vi: 0-0 Tstrap: 0-0 Ckp: 0-0
Best Rating:	87 5/02 NAbb 3m2f110y soft Ch

O'Flaherty'S (IRE)

12-y-o ch g Balinger-Deise Lady (Le Bavard (FR))
G D Blagbrough G D Blagbrough

Placings:0/30U-50F   (4302)
2003/04: 20⁵GS, 21⁰G, 20ᶠG,

	Starts	1st	2nd	3rd	Win & Pl
Chases	3	0	0	0	0
Career Total	7	0	0	1	315

Going:	Sf: 0-0 GS: 0-1 Gd: 0-2 GF: - Fm: 0-0
Distance:	2m/2m3: 0-0 2m4-2m7: 0-3 3m+: 0-0
Track:	LH: 0-1 RH: 0-2 Tight: 0-0 Gall: 0-0
Aids:	Bl: 0-1 Vi: 0-0 Tstrap: 0-0 Ckp: 0-0

Best Rating: 68 5/02 Strf 2m4f gd-fm Ch

O'Toole (IRE)

98f   **102f**

5-y-o b g Toulon-Legs Burke (IRE) (Buckskin (FR))
P J Hobbs Mrs L R Lovell

Placings:233   (4816)
2003/04: 16²G, 16³GS, 16³G,

	Starts	1st	2nd	3rd	Win & Pl
NH Flat	3	0	1	2	1278
Career Total	3	0	1	2	1278

Going:	Sf: 0-0 GS: 0-1 Gd: 0-2 GF: - Fm: 0-0
Distance:	2m/2m3: 0-3 2m4-2m7: 0-0 3m+: 0-0
Track:	LH: 0-2 RH: 0-1 Tight: 0-0 Gall: 0-0
Aids:	Bl: 0-0 Vi: 0-0 Tstrap: 0-0 Ckp: 0-0
Best Rating:	102 4/04 Chep 2m110y good NHF

Plenty of stamina in breeding; good second on debut in Wincanton bumper February 2004; subsequently slightly disappointing on softer ground at Chepstow; no excuses at the same venue next time.

Oakley Gold

93f   **88f**

6-y-o ch m Afzal-Romany Gold (Pauper)
S E H Sherwood Mrs J Tarran

Placings:0   (3453)
2003/04: 17⁰GS,

	Starts	1st	2nd	3rd	Win & Pl
NH Flat	1	0	0	0	
Career Total	1	0	0	0	

Going:	Sf: 0-0 GS: 0-1 Gd: 0-0 GF: - Fm: 0-0
Distance:	2m/2m3: 0-1 2m4-2m7: 0-0 3m+: 0-0
Track:	LH: 0-0 RH: 0-0 Tight: 0-0 Gall: 0-0
Aids:	Bl: 0-0 Vi: 0-0 Tstrap: 0-0 Ckp: 0-0
Best Rating:	88 1/04 Tntn 2m1f gd-sft NHF

Oaksy

4-y-o b/br g Turtle Island (IRE)-Safe Secret (Seclude (USA))
I A Brown I A Brown

Placings:PP   (2528)
2003/04: 16⁵GS, 16ᴾGS,

	Starts	1st	2nd	3rd	Win & Pl
Hurdles	2	0	0	0	
Career Total	2	0	0	0	

Going:	Sf: 0-0 GS: 0-2 Gd: 0-0 GF: - Fm: 0-0
Distance:	2m/2m3: 0-2 2m4-2m7: 0-0 3m+: 0-0
Track:	LH: 0-2 RH: 0-0 Tight: 0-1 Gall: 0-0
Aids:	Bl: 0-0 Vi: 0-0 Tstrap: 0-0 Ckp: 0-0

Oatis Brook

6-y-o b g Alderbrook-Lagrimass (Oats)
Ian Williams Mcmahon (contractors services) Ltd

Placings:00P   (4145)
2003/04: 16⁰G, 21⁰GS, 19ᴾG,

	Starts	1st	2nd	3rd	Win & Pl
NH Flat	1	0	0	0	

Hurdles	2	0	0	0	0
Career Total	3	0	0	0	

Going:	Sf: 0-0 GS: 0-1 Gd: 0-2 GF: - Fm: 0-0
Distance:	2m/2m3: 0-1 2m4-2m7: 0-2 3m+: 0-0
Track:	LH: 0-1 RH: 0-2 Tight: 0-1 Gall: 0-0
Aids:	Bl: 0-0 Vi: 0-0 Tstrap: 0-0 Ckp: 0-0
Best Rating:	80 12/03 Wwck 2m good NHF

Oboedire (IRE)

99   **83**

11-y-o br g Royal Fountain-Another Pride (Golden Love)
Sir John Barlow Bt T D B Barlow

Placings:21P3P/P4-4P   (0493)
2003/04: 25⁴GS, 25ᴾG,

	Starts	1st	2nd	3rd	Win & Pl
Chases	2	0	0	0	430
Career Total	9	1	1	1	14331
101 11/01 Hayd 3m	B Ch		SFT	£9597
		Total win prize-money £9598

Going:	Sf: 0-0 GS: 0-1 Gd: 0-1 GF: - Fm: 0-0
Distance:	2m/2m3: 0-0 2m4-2m7: 0-0 3m+: 0-2
Track:	LH: 0-2 RH: 0-0 Tight: 0-1 Gall: 0-0
Aids:	Bl: 0-0 Vi: 0-0 Tstrap: 0-0 Ckp: 0-0
Best Rating:	101 11/01 Hayd 3m soft Ch

Modest chaser; winning point-to-pointer; likes soft ground; stays three miles plus.

Occam (IRE)

80(105h)   (80 h)**89**

10-y-o ch g Sharp Victor (USA)-Monterana (Sallust)
A Bailey Mrs J Bailey

Placings:00/0/0/304130304440P023-44F   (2121)
2003/04: 17⁴G, 17⁴G, 16ᶠF,

	Starts	1st	2nd	3rd	Win & Pl
Chases	3	0	0	0	695
Career Total	23	1	1	4	8208
94 8/02 Bang 2m1f	E(0-105)HHdl		G-F	£3770
		Total win prize-money £3770

Going:	Sf: 0-0 GS: 0-0 Gd: 0-2 GF: - Fm: 0-1
Distance:	2m/2m3: 0-3 2m4-2m7: 0-0 3m+: 0-0
Track:	LH: 0-2 RH: 0-0 Tight: 0-3 Gall: 0-0
Aids:	Bl: 0-0 Vi: 0-0 Tstrap: 0-0 Ckp: 0-3
Best Rating:	94 8/02 Bang 2m1f gd-fm Hdl

Winning hurdler; plating-class chaser; best at around two miles (DEAD).

Ocean Dancer

96(101h)   (101h)**103**

7-y-o b g Primitive Rising (USA)-Bally Small (Sunyboy)
P Beaumont Mrs S Sunter

Placings:60062-2F142   (4161)
2003/04: 16²G, 17ᶠGS, 16¹G, 17⁴G, 16²G,

	Starts	1st	2nd	3rd	Win & Pl
Hurdles	1	0	1	0	1156
Chases	4	1	1	0	4887
Career Total	10	1	3	0	7145
98 12/03 Donc 2m110y E Ch			GD	£3367
		Total win prize-money £3367

Going:	Sf: 0-0 GS: 0-1 Gd: 1-4 GF: - Fm: 0-0
Distance:	2m/2m3: 1-5 2m4-2m7: 0-0 3m+: 0-0
Track:	LH: 1-4 RH: 0-1 Tight: 0-3 Gall: 1-2
Aids:	Bl: 0-0 Vi: 0-0 Tstrap: 0-0 Ckp: 0-0

Best Rating: 103 3/04 Donc 2m110y good Ch

Maiden hurdler; took weak novices' chase on second start over fences at Doncaster in December; runner-up in better company there in March; best suited by two miles.

Ocki

11-y-o gr g Octogenarian-Royalty Miss (Royalty)
Mrs M R Eagleton R S Eagleton

Placings:P/0/F   (0353)
2003/04: 21FGF,

	Starts	1st	2nd	3rd	Win & Pl
Chases	1	0	0	0	
Career Total	3	0	0	0	

Going:	Sf: 0-0 GS: 0-0 Gd: 0-0 GF: - Fm: 0-1
Distance:	2m/2m3: 0-0 2m4-2m7: 0-1 3m+: 0-0
Track:	LH: 0-0 RH: 0-1 Tight: 0-0 Gall: 0-0
Aids:	Bl: 0-0 Vi: 0-0 Tstrap: 0-0 Ckp: 0-0

Ockley Flyer

83   74

5-y-o b g Sir Harry Lewis (USA)-Bewails (IRE) (Caerleon (USA))
Miss Z C Davison Alan Walder

Placings:06300-060P   (4290)
2003/04: 19QS, 18RG, 22QG, 22FG,

	Starts	1st	2nd	3rd	Win & Pl
Hurdles	4	0	0	0	0
Career Total	9	0	0	1	548

Going:	Sf: 0-1 GS: 0-0 Gd: 0-3 GF: - Fm: 0-0
Distance:	2m/2m3: 0-1 2m4-2m7: 0-3 3m+: 0-0
Track:	LH: 0-3 RH: 0-1 Tight: 0-3 Gall: 0-0
Aids:	Bl: 0-0 Vi: 0-0 Tstrap: 0-0 Ckp: 0-0
Best Rating:	74 3/03 Winc 2m gd-fm Hdl

October Magic

54f

5-y-o b m Hatim (USA)-Wand Of Youth (Mandamus)
A R Dicken Jim & Wendy Beaumont

Placings:0   (2790)
2003/04: 16QGF,

	Starts	1st	2nd	3rd	Win & Pl
NH Flat	1	0	0	0	
Career Total	1	0	0	0	

Going:	Sf: 0-0 GS: 0-0 Gd: 0-0 GF: - Fm: 0-1
Distance:	2m/2m3: 0-1 2m4-2m7: 0-0 3m+: 0-0
Track:	LH: 0-0 RH: 0-1 Tight: 0-1 Gall: 0-0
Aids:	Bl: 0-0 Vi: 0-0 Tstrap: 0-0 Ckp: 0-0

October Mist (IRE)

100(113h)   (140h)144

10-y-o gr g Roselier (FR)-Bonny Joe (Derring Rose)
Mrs M Reveley Mrs E A Murray

Placings:2/3311116/1163/121FP5/44204-2265046F6   (4853)

2003/04: 23QGS, 20QG, 24RG, 20RG, 20PS, 194G, 20QG, 22FGS, 22RGS,

	Starts	1st	2nd	3rd	Win & Pl
Hurdles	5	0	2	0	9909
Chases	4	0	0	0	420
Career Total	32	8	5	3	64441
123	12/01 Weth	2m4f110yD Ch		SFT	£4576
134	11/01 Weth	2m E Ch		GD	£3857
159	11/00 Hayd	2m6f B(0-140)HHdl		HVY	£6683
150	11/00 Ayr	2m4f C(0-130)HHdl		SFT	£5018
148	2/00 Hayd	2m C HHdl		HVY	£4914
122	1/00 Kels	2m E Hdl		GD	£2394
119	12/99 Weth	2m4f110yD(0-110)HHdl		G-S	£3577
96	12/99 MRas	2m1f110yD Hdl		G-S	£3051
			Total win prize-money		£34073

Going:	Sf: 0-1 GS: 0-3 Gd: 0-5 GF: - Fm: 0-0
Distance:	2m/2m3: 0-1 2m4-2m7: 0-6 3m+: 0-2
Track:	LH: 0-9 RH: 0-0 Tight: 0-3 Gall: 0-1
Aids:	Bl: 0-0 Vi: 0-0 Tstrap: 0-0 Ckp: 0-3
Best Rating:	159 11/00 Hayd 2m6f heavy Hdl

Very useful hurdler/fair chaser; not a good jumper of fences; suited by a flat, left-handed track; best on easy ground; stays two miles four; has worn cheekpieces.

Odagh Odyssey (IRE)

100(102c)   (128c)111

10-y-o ch g Ikdam-Riverside Willow (Callernish)
Miss E C Lavelle R J Lavelle

Placings:40004/F111/3P11/5F-26U0P22   (4785)
2003/04: 22QGS, 20RG, 19UGS, 20QG, 20PG, 192G, 21ZG,

	Starts	1st	2nd	3rd	Win & Pl
Hurdles	4	0	3	0	3056
Chases	3	0	1	0	
Career Total	22	5	3	1	37551
137	12/01 Asct	2m3f110yB(0-145)HCh		GD	£17342
134	12/01 Leic	2m4f110yE(0-115)HCh		GD	£4403
134	4/01 Hntg	2m4f110yE Ch		SFT	£3777
120	1/01 Tntn	2m3f D(0-110)HCh		SFT	£4407
116	12/00 Tntn	2m3f F(0-95)HCh		SFT	£3224
			Total win prize-money		£33155

Going:	Sf: 0-0 GS: 0-2 Gd: 0-5 GF: - Fm: 0-0
Distance:	2m/2m3: 0-0 2m4-2m7: 0-7 3m+: 0-0
Track:	LH: 0-0 RH: 0-7 Tight: 0-2 Gall: 0-1
Aids:	Bl: 0-0 Vi: 0-0 Tstrap: 0-0 Ckp: 0-0
Best Rating:	137 12/01 Asct 2m3f110y good Ch

Useful chaser; not as good over hurdles; just denied in modest handicap hurdle at Haydock in April; suited by two miles six; suited by good ground or softer; needs to race right-handed.

Odd Job (IRE)

81f   87f

6-y-o b/br g Jolly Jake (NZ)-Kristellita (FR) (Crystal Palace (FR))
Jonjo O'Neill Mr & Mrs Peter S Thompson/Mrs J O'Neill

Placings:04-0   (0251)
2003/04: 17QGF,

	Starts	1st	2nd	3rd	Win & Pl
NH Flat	1	0	0	0	
Career Total	3	0	0	0	0

Going:	Sf: 0-0 GS: 0-0 Gd: 0-0 GF: - Fm: 0-0
Distance:	2m/2m3: 0-1 2m4-2m7: 0-0 3m+: 0-0
Track:	LH: 0-0 RH: 0-1 Tight: 0-0 Gall: 0-0
Aids:	Bl: 0-0 Vi: 0-0 Tstrap: 0-0 Ckp: 0-0
Best Rating:	84 4/03 MRas 2m1f110y good NHF

Well beaten fourth on first run here in modest bumper at Market Rasen in April 2003.

Oddlydodd (IRE)

(0c)101

8-y-o b g Tremblant-Poor Times (IRE) (Roselier (FR))
T Keddy Mrs H Keddy

Placings:00PP410/P6PP03603-0   (0671)
2003/04: 26QGF,

	Starts	1st	2nd	3rd	Win & Pl
Hurdles	1	0	0	0	
Career Total	17	1	0	2	4440
101	3/02 Wwck	2m5f D(0-115)HHdl		G-S	£3570
			Total win prize-money		£3570

Going:	Sf: 0-0 GS: 0-0 Gd: 0-0 GF: - Fm: 0-1
Distance:	2m/2m3: 0-0 2m4-2m7: 0-0 3m+: 0-1
Track:	LH: 0-1 RH: 0-0 Tight: 0-0 Gall: 0-0
Aids:	Bl: 0-0 Vi: 0-0 Tstrap: 0-0 Ckp: 0-0
Best Rating:	101 2/03 Hntg 2m4f110y good Hdl

Modest hurdler; acts on a soft surface; stays two miles five.

Odyn Dancer

57   24

7-y-o b m Minshaanshu Amad (USA)-Themeda (Sure Blade (USA))
M D I Usher G A Summers

Placings:0   (0149)
2003/04: 20QGF,

	Starts	1st	2nd	3rd	Win & Pl
Hurdles	1	0	0	0	
Career Total	1	0	0	0	

Going:	Sf: 0-0 GS: 0-0 Gd: 0-0 GF: - Fm: 0-1
Distance:	2m/2m3: 0-0 2m4-2m7: 0-1 3m+: 0-0
Track:	LH: 0-1 RH: 0-0 Tight: 0-0 Gall: 0-0
Aids:	Bl: 0-0 Vi: 0-0 Tstrap: 0-0 Ckp: 0-0
Best Rating:	24 5/03 Chep 2m4f gd-fm Hdl

Off Broadway (IRE)

98   92

6-y-o b g Presenting-Mona Curra Gale (IRE) (Strong Gale)
A King The Presenters

Placings:2-64P0   (4819)
2003/04: 20QGS, 214G, 25PG, 22QG,

	Starts	1st	2nd	3rd	Win & Pl
Hurdles	4	0	0	0	288
Career Total	5	0	1	0	858

Going:	Sf: 0-0 GS: 0-1 Gd: 0-2 GF: - Fm: 0-1
Distance:	2m/2m3: 0-0 2m4-2m7: 0-3 3m+: 0-1
Track:	LH: 0-2 RH: 0-2 Tight: 0-0 Gall: 0-0
Aids:	Bl: 0-0 Vi: 0-0 Tstrap: 0-0 Ckp: 0-0
Best Rating:	106 3/03 Winc 2m soft NHF

Placed in a bumper; well beaten over hurdles.

Off The Seal (NZ)

91   48+

8-y-o b g Imperial Seal-Grand Countess (NZ) (St Puckle)
B G Powell Miss Sasha Harrison

Placings:6   (0832)
2003/04: 20QGF,

	Starts	1st	2nd	3rd	Win & Pl
Hurdles	1	0	0	0	0
Career Total	1	0	0	0	0

Going: Sf: 0-0 GS: 0-0 Gd: 0-0 GF: - Fm: 0-1
Distance: 2m/2m3: 0-0 2m4-2m7: 0-1 3m+: 0-0
Track: LH: 0-1 RH: 0-0 Tight: 0-0 Gall: 0-0
Aids: Bl: 0-0 Vi: 0-0 Tstrap: 0-0 Ckp: 0-0
Best Rating: 53 7/03 Worc 2m4f   gd-fm   Hdl

Offshore (IRE)

11-y-o b g Over The River (FR)-Parsons Princess (The Parson)
S A Saltmarsh Puttenden Partnership

Placings: 344/P/P2PP-PP   (4283)
2003/04: 25PGS, 25PG,

	Starts	1st	2nd	3rd	Win & Pl
Chases	2	0	0	0	
Career Total	10	0	1	1	1441

Going: Sf: 0-0 GS: 0-1 Gd: 0-0 GF: - Fm: 0-0
Distance: 2m/2m3: 0-0 2m4-2m7: 0-0 3m+: 0-2
Track: LH: 0-0 RH: 0-2 Tight: 0-1 Gall: 0-0
Aids: Bl: 0-0 Vi: 0-0 Tstrap: 0-0 Ckp: 0-0
Best Rating: 103 4/98 Chel 2m1f   heavy   NHF

Oh Lordie Be (IRE)

73f   52f

6-y-o gr m Arctic Lord-Beagan Rose (IRE) (Roselier (FR))
T P Walshe Mrs Penny Walshe

Placings: 000   (4345)
2003/04: 16OS, 16OGS, 16OGS,

	Starts	1st	2nd	3rd	Win & Pl
NH Flat	3	0	0	0	
Career Total	3	0	0	0	

Going: Sf: 0-1 GS: 0-2 Gd: 0-0 GF: - Fm: 0-0
Distance: 2m/2m3: 0-3 2m4-2m7: 0-0 3m+: 0-0
Track: LH: 0-1 RH: 0-2 Tight: 0-0 Gall: 0-0
Aids: Bl: 0-0 Vi: 0-0 Tstrap: 0-0 Ckp: 0-0
Best Rating: 54 1/04 Ludl 2m   gd-sft   NHF

Oh So Brave

94   72+

7-y-o gr g Arzanni-Goodbye Roscoe (Roscoe Blake)
Evan Williams Mrs J M Hegarty

Placings: 564   (4856)
2003/04: 17SG, 16OG, 19AGF,

	Starts	1st	2nd	3rd	Win & Pl
Hurdles	3	0	0	0	371
Career Total	3	0	0	0	371

Going: Sf: 0-0 GS: 0-0 Gd: 0-2 GF: - Fm: 0-1
Distance: 2m/2m3: 0-2 2m4-2m7: 0-1 3m+: 0-0
Track: LH: 0-1 RH: 0-2 Tight: 0-1 Gall: 0-0
Aids: Bl: 0-0 Vi: 0-0 Tstrap: 0-0 Ckp: 0-0
Best Rating: 72 4/04 Tntn 2m3f110y   gd-fm   Hdl

Winning pointer; modest efforts over hurdles.

Oh So Posh

5-y-o b m Overbury (IRE)-Sally Ho (Gildoran)
B Llewellyn (Mrs A M Thorpe 26/10) Mrs M Llewellyn

Placings: 000-4PP   (4915)
2003/04: 174GF, 16PGF, 16PGS,

	Starts	1st	2nd	3rd	Win & Pl
NH Flat	1	0	0	0	0
Hurdles	2	0	0	0	0
Career Total	6	0	0	0	0

Going: Sf: 0-0 GS: 0-1 Gd: 0-0 GF: - Fm: 0-2
Distance: 2m/2m3: 0-3 2m4-2m7: 0-0 3m+: 0-0
Track: LH: 0-2 RH: 0-1 Tight: 0-0 Gall: 0-0
Aids: Bl: 0-0 Vi: 0-0 Tstrap: 0-0 Ckp: 0-0
Best Rating: 69 10/03 Hrfd 2m1f   gd-fm   NHF

Oh So Rosie (IRE)

94   54

4-y-o b f Danehill Dancer (IRE)-Shinkoh Rose (FR) (Warning)
J S Moore Ada's Racing Boys

Placings: 3   (2331)
2003/04: 16³G,

	Starts	1st	2nd	3rd	Win & Pl
Hurdles	1	0	0	1	688
Career Total	1	0	0	1	688

Going: Sf: 0-0 GS: 0-0 Gd: 0-1 GF: - Fm: 0-0
Distance: 2m/2m3: 0-1 2m4-2m7: 0-0 3m+: 0-0
Track: LH: 0-1 RH: 0-0 Tight: 0-1 Gall: 0-0
Aids: Bl: 0-0 Vi: 0-0 Tstrap: 0-0 Ckp: 0-0
Best Rating: 54 11/03 Fknm 2m   good   Hdl

Fair two-year-old on the Flat, but a little bit disappointing at three; acts on fast ground; has worn cheekpieces.

Oh So Wisley

103(101c)   (105c)109

9-y-o g g Teenoso (USA)-Easy Horse (FR) (Carmarthen (FR))
N A Twiston-Davies Gavin Macechern

Placings: 0006/3213164/1/P230-140P   (3827)
2003/04: 24¹G, 21⁴G, 22OGS, 24PG,

	Starts	1st	2nd	3rd	Win & Pl
Hurdles	4	1	0	0	4362
Career Total	20	4	2	3	16304
111 11/03 Extr	3m110y E(0-110)HHdl			GD	£3432
103 9/01 Worc	3m F(0-100)HHdl			G-F	£2838
105 1/01 Tntn	3m110y F(0-110)HHdl			HVY	£2271
98 11/00 Wwck	2m5f D(0-110)HHdl			HVY	£2850
	Total win prize-money £11393				

Going: Sf: 0-0 GS: 0-1 Gd: 1-3 GF: - Fm: 0-0
Distance: 2m/2m3: 0-0 2m4-2m7: 0-2 3m+: 1-2
Track: LH: 0-2 RH: 1-2 Tight: 0-0 Gall: 0-2
Aids: Bl: 0-0 Vi: 0-0 Tstrap: 0-0 Ckp: 0-0
Best Rating: 111 11/03 Extr 3m110y   good   Hdl

Modest hurdler; has been placed over fences; acts in most types of ground.

Oh Vlo (FR)

90   (0c)86

5-y-o b/br g Sassanian (USA)-Lady Christine (FR) (Vayrann)
M C Pipe (J Bertran De Balanda 24/10) Mrs Judith E Wilson

Placings: 00-046043053P   (4859)
2003/04: 17OVS, 174VS, 19⁶VS, 17OG, 18⁴VS, 18³HO, 16⁶S, 20⁵S, 19³GF, 19PGF,

---

	Starts	1st	2nd	3rd	Win & Pl
Hurdles	9	0	0	2	5305
Chases	1	0	0	0	0
Career Total	12	0	0	2	5305

Going: Sf: 0-2 GS: 0-0 Gd: 0-1 GF: - Fm: 0-2
Distance: 2m/2m3: 0-6 2m4-2m7: 0-4 3m+: 0-0
Track: LH: 0-1 RH: 0-4 Tight: 0-1 Gall: 0-0
Aids: Bl: 0-0 Vi: 0-0 Tstrap: 0-0 Ckp: 0-0
Best Rating: 100 10/03 Autl 2m2f   holding   Hdl

Ojays Alibi (IRE)

99   102+

8-y-o b g Witness Box (USA)-Tinkers Lady (Sheer Grit)
J D Frost Mrs C Irish

Placings: 63-F34331   (4242)
2003/04: 17⁵G, 19³G, 19⁴S, 16³S, 17³HY, 24¹G,

	Starts	1st	2nd	3rd	Win & Pl
Hurdles	6	1	0	3	5859
Career Total	8	1	0	4	6664
102 3/04 Extr	3m110y E Hdl			GD	£3926
	Total win prize-money £3926				

Going: Sf: 0-3 GS: 0-0 Gd: 1-3 GF: - Fm: 0-0
Distance: 2m/2m3: 0-5 2m4-2m7: 0-0 3m+: 1-1
Track: LH: 0-1 RH: 1-5 Tight: 0-1 Gall: 0-0
Aids: Bl: 0-0 Vi: 0-0 Tstrap: 0-0 Ckp: 0-0
Best Rating: 102 3/04 Extr 3m110y   good   Hdl

Modest novice hurdler; acts on soft and good ground; improved when stepped up to three miles.

Old Barns (IRE)

64f   51f

4-y-o b g Nucleon (USA)-Surfer Katie (IRE) (Be My Native (USA))
G A Swinbank M Sawers

Placings: 0   (4050)
2003/04: 16OG,

	Starts	1st	2nd	3rd	Win & Pl
NH Flat	1	0	0	0	
Career Total	1	0	0	0	

Going: Sf: 0-0 GS: 0-0 Gd: 0-1 GF: - Fm: 0-0
Distance: 2m/2m3: 0-1 2m4-2m7: 0-0 3m+: 0-0
Track: LH: 0-1 RH: 0-0 Tight: 0-0 Gall: 0-0
Aids: Bl: 0-0 Vi: 0-0 Tstrap: 0-0 Ckp: 0-0
Best Rating: 50 2/04 Hayd 2m   good   NHF

Old Bean (IRE)

102   100+

8-y-o b g Eurobus-Princess Petara (IRE) (Petorius)
N J Henderson Wrestlers Racing

Placings: 151/0-01PP   (4790)
2003/04: 16OG, 21¹S, 22PG, 21PG,

	Starts	1st	2nd	3rd	Win & Pl
Hurdles	4	1	0	0	3504
Career Total	3	0	0	0	7760
100 1/04 Plum	2m5f E Hdl			SFT	£3503
104 3/02 Ludl	2m H NHF			SFT	£2044
114 1/02 Ludl	2m H NHF			GD	£2212
	Total win prize-money £7760				

Going: Sf: 1-1 GS: 0-1 Gd: 0-2 GF: - Fm: 0-0
Distance: 2m/2m3: 0-1 2m4-2m7: 1-3 3m+: 0-0
Track: LH: 1-2 RH: 0-2 Tight: 1-2 Gall: 0-0

Aids: Bl: 0-0 Vi: 0-0 Tstrap: 0-0 Ckp: 0-0
Best Rating: 114 1/02 Ludl 2m   good NHF

Moderate hurdler; stays two miles-five; acts on good and soft ground.

Old Flame (IRE)

99   **118**

5-y-o b g Oscar (IRE)-Flameing Run (Deep Run)
C F Swan Banagher Glen Syndicate

Placings:33351512130   (4628)
2003/04: 16³F, 16²S, 16⁵Y, 16⁵GY, 17¹GY, 18⁵S, 16¹S, 16²S, 18¹YS, 20³GY, 20⁹G,

	Starts	1st	2nd	3rd	Win & Pl
NH Flat	5	1	0	3	5084
Hurdles	6	2	1	1	19040
Career Total	11	3	1	4	24125
121 2/04	Limk	2m2f		Hdl	Y-S £8272
114 1/04	Navn	2m		Hdl	SFT £5345
105 12/03	Dpat	2m1f172y	NHF		G-Y £3584

Total win prize-money £17202

Going: Sf: 1-4 GS: 0-0 Gd: 0-1 GF: - Fm: 0-1
Distance: 2m/2m3: 3-9 2m4-2m7: 0-2 3m+: 0-0
Track: LH: 1-3 RH: 0-2 Tight: 0-1 Gall: 0-0
Aids: Bl: 0-0 Vi: 0-0 Tstrap: 0-0 Ckp: 0-0
Best Rating: 121 2/04 Limk 2m2f   yld-sft Hdl

Irish-trained novice hurdler; suited by give and trips around two miles.

Old Golden Grey

7-y-o gr g Thethingaboutitis (USA)-Modina April (New Member)
M Wellings Stephen Williams

Placings:00PP   (3277)
2003/04: 17⁰G, 16⁰GF, 20⁴S, 20⁶G,

	Starts	1st	2nd	3rd	Win & Pl
NH Flat	2	0	0	0	0
Hurdles	2	0	0	0	0
Career Total	4	0	0	0	

Going: Sf: 0-1 GS: 0-0 Gd: 0-2 GF: - Fm: 0-1
Distance: 2m/2m3: 0-2 2m4-2m7: 0-2 3m+: 0-0
Track: LH: 0-4 RH: 0-0 Tight: 0-1 Gall: 0-0
Aids: Bl: 0-1 Vi: 0-1 Tstrap: 0-0 Ckp: 0-0

Old Hush Wing (IRE)

97(91h)   (100h)**105**

11-y-o b g Tirol-Saneena (Kris)
Mrs S J Smith Mrs B Ramsden

Placings:4/1O521/5223136/13334/11005/6U454B6/4-41P

    (0759)
2003/04: 25⁴G, 21¹S, 23ᴾG,

	Starts	1st	2nd	3rd	Win & Pl
Chases	3	1	0	0	4698
Career Total	34	7	3	5	33912
105 5/03	Sedg	2m5f	E(0-110)HCh		SFT £4400
112 12/00	Hntg	2m5f110yF Hdl			SFT £1789
122 11/00	Hayd	2m4f	F Hdl		HVY £2019
128 11/99	Sedg	2m5f110yB HHdl			GD £6273
125 11/98	Sedg	2m5f110yB HHdl			G-S £6677
106 5/98	Sedg	2m5f110yE Hdl			GD £2425
115 11/97	Sedg	2m5f110yE Hdl			GD £2705

Total win prize-money £26291

Going: Sf: 1-1 GS: 0-0 Gd: 0-2 GF: - Fm: 0-0

Distance: 2m/2m3: 0-0 2m4-2m7: 1-1 3m+: 0-2
Track: LH: 1-3 RH: 0-0 Tight: 1-1 Gall: 0-0
Aids: Bl: 0-0 Vi: 0-0 Tstrap: 0-0 Ckp: 0-0
Best Rating: 130 1/00 Wwck 2m4f110y soft Hdl

Moderate chaser/hurdler; he has done all his winning over hurdles at Sedgefield, although is tough and consistent and capable of a good show anywhere over two and a half miles; opened his account over fences on third start at favourite track in May; acts on soft/heavy ground but is getting a bit long in the tooth now.

Old King Coal

91   **97+**

8-y-o b g Miners Lamp-Mill Shine (Milan)
R Ford G B Barlow

Placings:6-F335P   (3435)
2003/04: 20⁶G, 16³GF, 16³G, 16⁵GF, 20ᴾHY,

	Starts	1st	2nd	3rd	Win & Pl
Hurdles	1	0	0	0	0
Chases	4	0	0	2	916
Career Total	6	0	0	2	916

Going: Sf: 0-1 GS: 0-0 Gd: 0-2 GF: - Fm: 0-2
Distance: 2m/2m3: 0-3 2m4-2m7: 0-2 3m+: 0-0
Track: LH: 0-3 RH: 0-2 Tight: 0-1 Gall: 0-1
Aids: Bl: 0-0 Vi: 0-0 Tstrap: 0-0 Ckp: 0-0
Best Rating: 96 11/03 Towc 2m110y good Ch

Little worthwhile form shown to date; suited by a sound surface.

Old Marsh (IRE)

107(113h)   (126 h)**126+**

8-y-o b g Grand Lodge (USA)-Lolly Dolly (Alleged (USA))
Miss Venetia Williams Seasons And Paradise

Placings:4/4020/131125CF04-422260   (4627)
2003/04: 19⁴GS, 20²G, 16²HY, 16⁴G, 16⁶G, 16⁰G,

	Starts	1st	2nd	3rd	Win & Pl
Chases	6	0	3	0	9160
Career Total	21	3	5	1	26179
110 7/02	Worc	2m	D Hdl		G-F £3601
120 7/02	Uttx	2m	E Hdl		G-F £3464
119 5/02	Aint	2m110y	D Hdl		GD £3523

Total win prize-money £10589

Going: Sf: 0-1 GS: 0-1 Gd: 0-4 GF: - Fm: 0-0
Distance: 2m/2m3: 0-5 2m4-2m7: 0-3 3m+: 0-0
Track: LH: 0-2 RH: 0-4 Tight: 0-1 Gall: 0-1
Aids: Bl: 0-0 Vi: 0-0 Tstrap: 0-2 Ckp: 0-0
Best Rating: 126 2/04 Sand 2m good Ch

Useful novice chaser; effective at around two miles; suited by fast ground; has worn a tongue tie and blinkers; front-runner.

Old Nosey (IRE)

104   **89**

8-y-o b g Muharib (USA)-Regent Star (Prince Regent (FR))
B Mactaggart The Potassium Partnership

Placings:400/0566365F6002-233213656   (4879)
2003/04: 22²G, 20³G, 24³G, 22²GF, 24¹GF, 22³GF, 24⁶GF, 22⁵F, 20⁶GS,

	Starts	1st	2nd	3rd	Win & Pl
Hurdles	9	1	2	3	9104
Career Total	25	1	3	4	10830
89 8/03	Prth	3m110y	E(0-100)HHdl		G-F £4657

Total win prize-money £4657

Going: Sf: 1-5 GS: 0-1 Gd: 0-3 GF: - Fm: 1-5
Distance: 2m/2m3: 0-0 2m4-2m7: 0-6 3m+: 1-3
Track: LH: 0-4 RH: 1-3 Tight: 0-2 Gall: 0-0
Aids: Bl: 0-0 Vi: 0-0 Tstrap: 0-0 Ckp: 0-0
Best Rating: 89 8/03 MRas 2m6f gd-fm Hdl

Plating-class hurdler; ex-Irish; hardly winning out of turn when breaking his duck in handicap at Perth in August 2003; stays 3m; suited by a sound surface.

Old Rolla (IRE)

91(101h)   (97h)**77**

6-y-o b g Old Vic-Criswood (IRE) (Chromite (USA))
C Grant A Dawson

Placings:0033006-P4F635P   (4880)
2003/04: 25⁵GF, 27⁴G, 25⁵S, 25⁶HY, 25³GF, 24⁵GS, 20ᴾGS,

	Starts	1st	2nd	3rd	Win & Pl
Hurdles	1	0	0	0	0
Chases	6	0	0	1	757
Career Total	14	0	0	3	2036

Going: Sf: 0-2 GS: 0-2 Gd: 0-1 GF: - Fm: 0-2
Distance: 2m/2m3: 0-0 2m4-2m7: 0-1 3m+: 0-6
Track: LH: 0-6 RH: 0-1 Tight: 0-3 Gall: 0-0
Aids: Bl: 0-0 Vi: 0-0 Tstrap: 0-0 Ckp: 0-0
Best Rating: 91 2/03 Ayr 3m110y soft Hdl

Modest staying novice hurdler/chaser; acts on testing ground.

Ole Gunnar (IRE)

82   **73**

12-y-o b g Le Bavard (FR)-Rareitess (Rarity)
M S Wilesmith M S Wilesmith

Placings:P/3-4   (4918)
2003/04: 20⁴GS,

	Starts	1st	2nd	3rd	Win & Pl
Hurdles	1	0	0	0	0
Career Total	3	0	0	1	386

Going: Sf: 0-0 GS: 0-1 Gd: 0-0 GF: - Fm: 0-0
Distance: 2m/2m3: 0-0 2m4-2m7: 0-1 3m+: 0-0
Track: LH: 0-1 RH: 0-0 Tight: 0-0 Gall: 0-0
Aids: Bl: 0-0 Vi: 0-0 Tstrap: 0-0 Ckp: 0-1
Best Rating: 66 6/02 Worc 2m4f good Hdl

Maiden pointer/novice hurdler.

Olimp (POL)

84   **54**

8-y-o ch g Saphir (GER)-Olgierda (POL) (Sentyment (POL))
Miss A M Newton-Smith Mrs Sharon C Nelson

Placings:U6U0   (3424)
2003/04: 20ᵁGS, 19⁶S, 20ᵁG, 22ᴾHY,

	Starts	1st	2nd	3rd	Win & Pl
Hurdles	4	0	0	0	0
Career Total	4	0	0	0	0

Going: Sf: 0-2 GS: 0-1 Gd: 0-1 GF: - Fm: 0-0
Distance: 2m/2m3: 0-0 2m4-2m7: 0-4 3m+: 0-0
Track: LH: 0-1 RH: 0-2 Tight: 0-4 Gall: 0-0
Aids: Bl: 0-2 Vi: 0-0 Tstrap: 0-0 Ckp: 0-0
Best Rating: 55 12/03 Ling 2m3f110y soft Hdl

Olitheaga

82   85

9-y-o ch g Safawan-Lyaaric (Privy Seal)
N E Berry (C J Mann 26/5) Box 40 Racing

Placings: 12/P0-316   (1554)
2003/04: 22³GF, 22¹G, 19⁶GF,

	Starts	1st	2nd	3rd	Win & Pl
Hurdles	3	1	0	1	6285
Career Total	7	2	1	1	8910
62 5/03 Ctml	2m6f	E Hdl		GD	£5780
96 5/01 Hntg	2m110y	H NHF		G-F	£1729
				Total win prize-money £7509

Going:	Sf: 0-0 GS: 0-0 Gd: 1-1 GF: - Fm: 0-2
Distance:	2m/2m3: 0-1 2m4-2m7: 1-2 3m+: 0-0
Track:	LH: 1-2 RH: 0-1 Tight: 1-2 Gall: 0-0
Aids:	Bl: 1-1 Vi: 0-0 Tstrap: 0-0 Ckp: 0-1
Best Rating:	96 10/01 Bang 2m1f good Hdl

Plating-class hurdler; struggled to land the odds in a very weak novices' hurdle at Cartmel in May in first time blinkers; acts on a sound surface.

Oliver Cromwell (IRE)

99(102h)   (131h)122

9-y-o br g Mandalus-Gemini Gale (Strong Gale)
P R Hedger Howard Spooner

Placings: 556U513/221P1/P223301/06305302-5U4P (4448)
2003/04: 19⁵S, 25ᵁG, 24⁴G, 24ᴾGS,

	Starts	1st	2nd	3rd	Win & Pl
Chases	4	0	0	0	325
Career Total	31	4	5	5	46044
131 4/02 Chel	3m	B(0-145)HHdl		GD	£10871
122 2/01 Kemp	2m5f	C(0-130)HHdl		G-S	£14072
129 1/01 Extr	2m3f	E(0-115)HHdl		HVY	£3136
98 3/00 Towc	2m	E(0-105)HHdl		GD	£2562
				Total win prize-money £30642

Going:	Sf: 0-1 GS: 0-2 Gd: 0-1 GF: - Fm: 0-0
Distance:	2m/2m3: 0-1 2m4-2m7: 0-0 3m+: 0-3
Track:	LH: 0-0 RH: 0-4 Tight: 0-2 Gall: 0-0
Aids:	Bl: 0-1 Vi: 0-0 Tstrap: 0-0 Ckp: 0-3
Best Rating:	131 4/02 Chel 3m good Hdl

Fair novice chaser; stays three miles and should be suited by further; acts on ground good or softer; has worn blinkers and cheekpieces.

Olivier (USA)

99   103+

6-y-o ch g Theatrical-Izara (USA) (Blushing John (USA))
Miss Venetia Williams You Can Be Sure

Placings: 2/63-U65   (4343)
2003/04: 20ᵁS, 17⁶GS, 21⁵GS,

	Starts	1st	2nd	3rd	Win & Pl
Hurdles	3	0	0	0	0
Career Total	6	0	1	1	1561

Going:	Sf: 0-1 GS: 0-2 Gd: 0-0 GF: - Fm: 0-0
Distance:	2m/2m3: 0-1 2m4-2m7: 0-0 3m+: 0-0
Track:	LH: 0-1 RH: 0-0 Tight: 0-1 Gall: 0-0
Aids:	Bl: 0-0 Vi: 0-0 Tstrap: 0-0 Ckp: 0-0
Best Rating:	110 4/02 Prth 2m110y good NHF

Ollie Magern

112   128

6-y-o b g Alderbrook-Outfield (Monksfield)
N A Twiston-Davies Roger Nicholls

Placings: 0002-421121110564   (4939)
2003/04: 26⁶GS, 27⁶G, 22¹G, 26¹GF, 22²GF, 22¹G, 26¹GF, 25¹GF, 21⁰G, 24⁵G, 21⁶GF, 24⁴GS,

	Starts	1st	2nd	3rd	Win & Pl
Hurdles	12	5	2	0	28934
Career Total	16	5	3	0	30245
120 10/03 Chel	3m1f110yC Hdl			G-F	£6247
110 10/03 Hntg	3m2f	E Hdl		G-F	£2870
120 7/03 Strf	2m6f110yD Hdl			GD	£5356
116 6/03 Hrfd	3m2f	E Hdl		G-F	£3493
105 5/03 Strf	2m6f110yD Hdl			GD	£5538
				Total win prize-money £23505

Going:	Sf: 0-0 GS: 0-2 Gd: 2-5 GF: - Fm: 3-5
Distance:	2m/2m3: 0-0 2m4-2m7: 2-5 3m+: 3-7
Track:	LH: 3-8 RH: 2-4 Tight: 2-5 Gall: 2-4
Aids:	Bl: 0-0 Vi: 0-0 Tstrap: 0-0 Ckp: 0-0
Best Rating:	127 4/04 Chel 2m5f110y gd-fm Hdl

Fair novice hurdler; consistent form over staying distances winning five times in 2003; stays three miles well; considered best with cut in the ground but handles good to firm; tends to hit flat spots in his races, but stays on strongly; improving.

Olney Lad

103   118+

5-y-o b g Democratic (USA)-Alipampa (IRE) (Glenstal (USA))
Mrs P Robeson The Tyringham Partnership

Placings: 55-61310   (3942)
2003/04: 16⁶GF, 20¹GS, 20³GS, 20¹GS, 22⁰G,

	Starts	1st	2nd	3rd	Win & Pl
Hurdles	5	2	0	1	6625
Career Total	7	2	0	1	6625
121 12/03 Leic	2m4f110yD Hdl			G-S	£3562
108 11/03 Uttx	2m4f110yE(0-105)HHdl			G-S	£2667
				Total win prize-money £6229

Going:	Sf: 0-0 GS: 2-3 Gd: 0-1 GF: - Fm: 0-1
Distance:	2m/2m3: 0-1 2m4-2m7: 2-4 3m+: 0-0
Track:	LH: 1-3 RH: 1-2 Tight: 0-1 Gall: 0-0
Aids:	Bl: 0-0 Vi: 0-0 Tstrap: 0-0 Ckp: 0-0
Best Rating:	121 12/03 Leic 2m4f110y gd-sft Hdl

Fair hurdler; acts on easy ground; stays two and a half miles.

Olympic Storm (IRE)

74f   53f

6-y-o b g Glacial Storm (USA)-Philly Athletic (Sit In The Corner (USA))
N W Alexander Jamie Alexander

Placings: 00   (4952)
2003/04: 16⁰S, 16⁰GS,

	Starts	1st	2nd	3rd	Win & Pl
NH Flat	2	0	0	0	
Career Total	2	0	0	0	

Going:	Sf: 0-0 GS: 0-1 Gd: 0-0 GF: - Fm: 0-0
Distance:	2m/2m3: 0-2 2m4-2m7: 0-0 3m+: 0-0
Track:	LH: 0-1 RH: 0-1 Tight: 0-0 Gall: 0-0
Aids:	Bl: 0-0 Vi: 0-0 Tstrap: 0-0 Ckp: 0-0

Best Rating: 53 4/04 Prth 2m110y gd-sft NHF

Omni Cosmo Touch (USA)

8-y-o b g Trempolino (USA)-Wooden Pudden (USA) (Top Ville)
Joss Saville Alan Potts

Placings: 221122/51412RR/6R6R-1U2   (4872)
2003/04: 21¹GS, 26ᵁG, 24²S,

	Starts	1st	2nd	3rd	Win & Pl
Chases	3	1	1	0	2202
Career Total	20	5	6	0	24570
109 2/04 Sedg	2m5f	H Ch		G-S	£1514
120 6/01 Worc	2m4f	C(0-135)HHdl		GD	£5525
120 5/01 Ling	2m3f110yD(0-125)HHdl			G-F	£7250
111 5/00 Tntn	2m1f	E Hdl		GD	£2891
98 9/00 Worc	2m	E Hdl		G-F	£1904
				Total win prize-money £19086

Going:	Sf: 0-1 GS: 1-1 Gd: 0-1 GF: - Fm: 0-0
Distance:	2m/2m3: 0-0 2m4-2m7: 1-1 3m+: 0-2
Track:	LH: 1-3 RH: 0-0 Tight: 1-2 Gall: 0-1
Aids:	Bl: 0-0 Vi: 0-0 Tstrap: 0-0 Ckp: 0-0
Best Rating:	120 6/01 Worc 2m4f good Hdl

Modest hurdler/chaser; effective on a sound surface; stays three miles.

On A Deal

89   90

6-y-o b g Teenoso (USA)-Gale Spring (IRE) (Strong Gale)
R J Hodges Unity Farm Holiday Centre Ltd

Placings: 04O5-B2   (0184)
2003/04: 22⁸G, 22²GF,

	Starts	1st	2nd	3rd	Win & Pl
Hurdles	2	0	1	0	1036
Career Total	6	0	1	0	1036

Going:	Sf: 0-0 GS: 0-0 Gd: 0-1 GF: - Fm: 0-1
Distance:	2m/2m3: 0-0 2m4-2m7: 0-2 3m+: 0-0
Track:	LH: 0-0 RH: 0-2 Tight: 0-0 Gall: 0-0
Aids:	Bl: 0-0 Vi: 0-0 Tstrap: 0-0 Ckp: 0-0
Best Rating:	99 1/03 Tntn 2m1f soft NHF

Novice hurdler; inclined to run freely in his bumpers; some promise over hurdles; stays two miles six and should stay further; appears to act on most ground.

On A Full Wager

7-y-o b g Homo Sapien-Ntombi (Trasi's Son)
Mrs K Lawther R Owen

Placings: 40000P-P   (4302)
2003/04: 20ᴾG,

	Starts	1st	2nd	3rd	Win & Pl
Chases	1	0	0	0	0
Career Total	7	0	0	0	0

Going:	Sf: 0-0 GS: 0-0 Gd: 0-1 GF: - Fm: 0-0
Distance:	2m/2m3: 0-0 2m4-2m7: 0-1 3m+: 0-0
Track:	LH: 0-0 RH: 0-1 Tight: 0-0 Gall: 0-0
Aids:	Bl: 0-0 Vi: 0-0 Tstrap: 0-0 Ckp: 0-0
Best Rating:	85 6/02 Hrfd 2m1f gd-fm NHF

On Les Aura (IRE)

98   **105+**

5-y-o b g Germany (USA)-Another Thurn (IRE) (Trimmingham)
R H Alner David Constant

Placings:000362   (4819)
2003/04: 17⁰G, 19⁰G, 22⁰HY, 19³S, 22⁶G, 22²GF,

	Starts	1st	2nd	3rd	Win & Pl
NH Flat	1	0	0	0	0
Hurdles	5	0	1	1	1848
Career Total	6	0	1	1	1848

Going: Sf: 0-2 GS: 0-0 Gd: 0-3 GF: - Fm: 0-1
Distance: 2m/2m3: 0-3 2m4-2m7: 0-3 3m+: 0-0
Track: LH: 0-3 RH: 0-3 Tight: 0-3 Gall: 0-0
Aids: Bl: 0-0 Vi: 0-0 Tstrap: 0-0 Ckp: 0-0
Best Rating: 105 4/04 Extr 2m6f110y gd-fm Hdl

On The Bone

12-y-o b m Lyphento (USA)-Lydia Languish (Hotfoot)
C N Kellett K And A K Smith

Placings:6S/P-6F5F46   (4757)
2003/04: 20⁶HY, 20⁶G, 25⁵GS, 25⁵GF, 22⁴GS, 25⁶S,

	Starts	1st	2nd	3rd	Win & Pl
Hurdles	1	0	0	0	0
Chases	5	0	0	0	304
Career Total	9	0	0	0	304

Going: Sf: 0-2 GS: 0-2 Gd: 0-1 GF: - Fm: 0-1
Distance: 2m/2m3: 0-0 2m4-2m7: 0-3 3m+: 0-3
Track: LH: 0-1 RH: 0-5 Tight: 0-1 Gall: 0-0
Aids: Bl: 0-0 Vi: 0-0 Tstrap: 0-0 Ckp: 0-0

On The Luce

98   **95+**

7-y-o b g Karinga Bay-Lirchur (Lir)
Miss P Robson (W T Reed 28/4) Mrs P R Crawfurd

Placings:60/P0-341P41   (4514)
2003/04: 20⁰GF, 21³GF, 20⁴S, 24¹HY, 25⁰HY, 20⁴S, 25¹GS,

	Starts	1st	2nd	3rd	Win & Pl
Chases	7	2	0	1	8606
Career Total	10	2	0	1	8606
95 3/04 Weth 3m1f		E(0-105)HCh		G-S	£4078
95 1/04 Newc 3m		F(0-100)HCh		HVY	£3367
				Total win prize-money	£7446

Going: Sf: 1-4 GS: 1-1 Gd: 0-0 GF: - Fm: 0-2
Distance: 2m/2m3: 0-0 2m4-2m7: 0-4 3m+: 2-3
Track: LH: 2-7 RH: 0-0 Tight: 0-2 Gall: 1-3
Aids: Bl: 0-0 Vi: 0-0 Tstrap: 0-0 Ckp: 0-0
Best Rating: 95 3/04 Weth 3m1f gd-sft Ch

Point winner; took a modest handicap at Newcastle in January; back to winning form at Wetherby two months later; suited by give; stays well.

On The Mend (IRE)

11-y-o b g Broken Hearted-Mugs Away (Mugatpura)
Miss S Balshaw (M J P O'Brien 29/7) Mrs J M Newitt

Placings:666/00034/423/3511/60U23321UP/3P12F160U-056P   (4542)
2003/04: 20⁰GF, 22⁵S, 20⁶G, 20⁶GS,

	Starts	1st	2nd	3rd	Win & Pl
Hurdles	1	0	0	0	0
Chases	3	0	0	0	0
Career Total	38	5	4	6	50189
127 2/03 Clon 2m2f		Ch		SFT	£8441
112 12/02 Cork 2m4f		(74-109)HHdl		SFT	£5503
119 3/02 Dpat 2m2f		Ch		SFT	£4021
114 4/01 Fair 2m4f		(0-130)HHdl		SFT	£15725
101 11/00 DRoy 2m6f		Hdl		Y-S	£5520
				Total win prize-money	£39212

Going: Sf: 0-1 GS: 0-1 Gd: 0-1 GF: - Fm: 0-1
Distance: 2m/2m3: 0-2 2m4-2m7: 0-4 3m+: 0-0
Track: LH: 0-4 RH: 0-4 Tight: 0-1 Gall: 0-0
Aids: Bl: 0-0 Vi: 0-0 Tstrap: 0-0 Ckp: 0-0
Best Rating: 127 2/03 Clon 2m2f soft Ch

Hunter/chaser; ex-Irish; effective on soft ground at around two and a half miles.

On The Outside (IRE)

88f   **87f**

5-y-o ch m Anshan-Kate Fisher (IRE) (Over The River (FR))
S E H Sherwood (P F Cashman 9/11) Geoffrey Vos

Placings:55   (4345)
2003/04: 16⁵GF, 16⁵GS,

	Starts	1st	2nd	3rd	Win & Pl
NH Flat	2	0	0	0	0
Career Total	2	0	0	0	0

Going: Sf: 0-0 GS: 0-1 Gd: 0-0 GF: - Fm: 0-1
Distance: 2m/2m3: 0-2 2m4-2m7: 0-0 3m+: 0-0
Track: LH: 0-1 RH: 0-0 Tight: 0-0 Gall: 0-0
Aids: Bl: 0-0 Vi: 0-0 Tstrap: 0-0 Ckp: 0-0
Best Rating: 87 11/03 Cork 2m gd-fm NHF

On The Run (IRE)

(102h)   **(90h)**

10-y-o ch m Don't Forget Me-Chepstow House (USA) (Northern Baby (CAN))
D J Wintle D A Thorpe

Placings:00/206/632000/023F20/34061000/223424UP-0   (1154)
2003/04: 18⁰GF,

	Starts	1st	2nd	3rd	Win & Pl
Hurdles	1	0	0	0	0
Career Total	34	1	7	4	8933
85 8/01 Sthl 2m		G Hdl		G-F	£1570
				Total win prize-money	£1571

Going: Sf: 0-0 GS: 0-0 Gd: 0-0 GF: - Fm: 0-1
Distance: 2m/2m3: 0-1 2m4-2m7: 0-0 3m+: 0-0
Track: LH: 0-1 RH: 0-0 Tight: 0-0 Gall: 0-0
Aids: Bl: 0-0 Vi: 0-0 Tstrap: 0-0 Ckp: 0-0
Best Rating: 97 7/00 Worc 2m gd-fm Hdl

On The Verge (IRE)

94   **83**

6-y-o ch g Alphabatim (USA)-Come On Lis (Domynsky)
J R Jenkins James Roche

Placings:21O400   (4181)
2003/04: 16²G, 16¹G, 16⁰HY, 16⁴S, 21⁰GS, 16⁰G,

	Starts	1st	2nd	3rd	Win & Pl
NH Flat	2	1	1	0	1889
Hurdles	4	0	0	0	376
Career Total	6	1	1	0	2265
101 11/03 Fknm 2m		H NHF		GD	£1470
				Total win prize-money	£1470

Going: Sf: 0-2 GS: 0-1 Gd: 1-3 GF: - Fm: 0-0
Distance: 2m/2m3: 1-5 2m4-2m7: 0-1 3m+: 0-0
Track: LH: 1-2 RH: 0-4 Tight: 1-2 Gall: 0-2
Aids: Bl: 0-0 Vi: 0-0 Tstrap: 0-0 Ckp: 0-0
Best Rating: 101 11/03 Fknm 2m good NHF

Very moderate bumper performer; has shown little over hurdles.

On Y Va (FR)

85   **72**

6-y-o b g Goldneyev (USA)-Shakna (FR) (Le Nain Jaune (FR))
R T Phillips (T Trapenard 10/11) ROA Red Alligator Partnership

Placings:05P20424234623-062550   (4097)
2003/04: 18⁰VS, 19⁶VS, 19⁴VS, 18⁵VS, 20⁵HY, 16⁰G,

	Starts	1st	2nd	3rd	Win & Pl
Hurdles	6	0	1	0	17425
Career Total	20	0	5	2	54790

Going: Sf: 0-1 GS: 0-0 Gd: 0-1 GF: - Fm: 0-0
Distance: 2m/2m3: 0-4 2m4-2m7: 0-2 3m+: 0-0
Track: LH: 0-3 RH: 0-0 Tight: 0-1 Gall: 0-0
Aids: Bl: 0-0 Vi: 0-0 Tstrap: 0-0 Ckp: 0-0
Best Rating: 79 1/04 Hayd 2m4f heavy Hdl

Placed on the Flat and over hurdles in France; yet to show much here.

Onassis

79 (100h)   (88h) **63**

7-y-o b g Roselier (FR)-Jack's The Girl (IRE) (Supreme Leader)
O Sherwood P Joe Davis & Peter McNeil

Placings:352PP3-266P   (2217)
2003/04: 24²S, 26⁶GF, 21⁶G, 26⁶G,

	Starts	1st	2nd	3rd	Win & Pl
Hurdles	2	0	1	0	1148
Chases	2	0	0	0	0
Career Total	10	0	2	2	3441

Going: Sf: 0-1 GS: 0-0 Gd: 0-2 GF: - Fm: 0-1
Distance: 2m/2m3: 0-0 2m4-2m7: 0-1 3m+: 0-3
Track: LH: 0-4 RH: 0-0 Tight: 0-3 Gall: 0-0
Aids: Bl: 0-4 Vi: 0-0 Tstrap: 0-0 Ckp: 0-0
Best Rating: 88 5/03 Bang 3m soft Hdl

Some ability over hurdles and fences, but looks short of pace.

Once Seen

103   **93+**

4-y-o b g Celtic Swing-Brief Glimpse (IRE) (Taufan (USA))
O Sherwood (R M Beckett 28/10) R Fallon & Associates

Placings:1060   (4915)
2003/04: 16¹S, 16⁰G, 16⁶G, 16⁰GS,

	Starts	1st	2nd	3rd	Win & Pl
Hurdles	4	1	0	0	4163
Career Total	4	1	0	0	4163
98 2/04 Plum		E Hdl		SFT	£4163
				Total win prize-money	£4163

Going: Sf: 1-1 GS: 0-1 Gd: 0-2 GF: - Fm: 0-0

Distance: 2m/2m3: 1-4 2m4-2m7: 0-0 3m+: 0-0
Track: LH: 1-4 RH: 0-0 **Tight:** 1-2 Gall: 0-1
Aids: Bl: 0-1 Vi: 0-1 Tstrap: 0-0 Ckp: 0-0
Best Rating: 98 2/04 Plum 2m   soft   Hdl

Made a winning debut over hurdles at Plumpton; held subsequently; Flat winner; wore a visor on the level; handles soft ground.

Oncourse (IRE)
43

8-y-o b g Toulon-Slaney Jazz (Orchestra)
R D Tudor R D Tudor

Placings:1/P0-PP   (0367)
2003/04: 16PGF, 16PG,

	Starts	1st	2nd	3rd	Win & Pl
Hurdles	2	0	0	0	
Career Total	5	1	0	0	3339
102	7/01	Dund	2m135y	NHF	FRM £3338

Total win prize-money £3339

Going: Sf: 0-0 GS: 0-0 Gd: 0-1 GF: 0-0 Fm: 0-1
Distance: 2m/2m3: 0-2 2m4-2m7: 0-0 3m+: 0-0
Track: LH: 0-1 RH: 0-1 Tight: 0-0 Gall: 0-0
Aids: Bl: 0-0 Vi: 0-0 Tstrap: 0-0 Ckp: 0-0
Best Rating: 102 7/01 Dund 2m135y   firm   NHF

One A Dackie
68f

5-y-o b m Lord Americo-Oriel Dream (Oats)
Ferdy Murphy Jack Iddon

Placings:60-   (0007)
2003/04: 16PG,

	Starts	1st	2nd	3rd	Win & Pl
NH Flat	1	0	0	0	
Career Total	2	0	0	0	0

Going: Sf: 0-0 GS: 0-0 Gd: 0-1 GF: 0-0 Fm: 0-0
Distance: 2m/2m3: 0-1 2m4-2m7: 0-0 3m+: 0-0
Track: LH: 0-1 RH: 0-0 Tight: 0-0 Gall: 0-0
Aids: Bl: 0-0 Vi: 0-0 Tstrap: 0-0 Ckp: 0-0
Best Rating: 68 3/03 Hayd 2m   gd-fm   NHF

One Cornetto (IRE)
92f   83f

5-y-o b g Eurobus-Costenetta (IRE) (Runnett)
L Wells Mrs Carrie Zetter-Wells

Placings:05   (4936)
2003/04: 16PHY, 18PG,

	Starts	1st	2nd	3rd	Win & Pl
NH Flat	2	0	0	0	0
Career Total	2	0	0	0	0

Going: Sf: 0-1 GS: 0-0 Gd: 0 GF: 0-0
Distance: 2m/2m3: 0-2 2m4-2m7: 0-0 3m+: 0-0
Track: LH: 0-1 RH: 0-1 Tight: 0-1 Gall: 0-0
Aids: Bl: 0-0 Vi: 0-0 Tstrap: 0-0 Ckp: 0-0
Best Rating: 83 4/04 Font 2m2f110y   good   NHF

One Day (NZ)
100   102+

6-y-o ch g Stark South (USA)-Dragon Pearl (USA)
(Ahonoora)

R C Guest Paul Beck

Placings:13P00   (4455)
2003/04: 201GS, 243GS, 20PGS, 20PG, 24PHY,

	Starts	1st	2nd	3rd	Win & Pl
Hurdles	5	1	0	1	3308
Career Total	5	1	0	1	3308
102	11/03	Carl	2m4f	E Hdl	G-S £2747

Total win prize-money £2748

Going: Sf: 0-1 GS: 1-3 Gd: 0-1 GF: 0-0 Fm: 0-0
Distance: 2m/2m3: 0-0 2m4-2m7: 1-3 3m+: 0-2
Track: LH: 0-4 RH: 1-1 Tight: 0-0 Gall: 0-2
Aids: Bl: 0-0 Vi: 0-0 Tstrap: 0-0 Ckp: 0-0
Best Rating: 102 11/03 Carl 2m4f   gd-sft   Hdl

Modest novice hurdler; created a favourable impression on hurdles debut when beating subsequent dual winner over two and a half miles at Carlisle in November 2003; failed to build on that promising run since; probably stays 3m; acts on good to soft.

One Five Eight
88   75+

5-y-o b g Alflora (IRE)-Dark Nightingale (Strong Gale)
M W Easterby J W P Curtis

Placings:0-31130   (2549)
2003/04: 173GF, 171GF, 203GF, 70PGS,

	Starts	1st	2nd	3rd	Win & Pl
NH Flat	3	2	0	1	3711
Hurdles	2	0	0	1	318
Career Total	6	2	0	2	4029
96	10/03	Sedg	2m1f	H NHF	GD £1519
86	10/03	MRas	2m1f110yH	NHF	G-F £1918

Total win prize-money £3437

Going: Sf: 0-0 GS: 0-1 Gd: 1-1 GF: 0-0 Fm: 1-3
Distance: 2m/2m3: 2-4 2m4-2m7: 0-1 3m+: 0-0
Track: LH: 1-2 RH: 1-3 Tight: 2-4 Gall: 0-0
Aids: Bl: 0-0 Vi: 0-0 Tstrap: 0-0 Ckp: 0-0
Best Rating: 96 10/03 Sedg 2m1f   good   NHF

Won bumper on third attempt at Market Rasen in October; followed up next time under a penalty at Sedgefield in good style; held over hurdles; acts on a sound surface.

One For Me
102   107+

6-y-o br m Tragic Role (USA)-Chantallee's Pride (Mansooj)
Jean-Rene Auvray M J Lewin

Placings:1P-6U1311100   (2990)
2003/04: 176GF, 16UG, 181GF, 193GF, 221G, 191GF, 221GF, 16PG, 24PG,

	Starts	1st	2nd	3rd	Win & Pl
Hurdles	9	4	0	1	29500
Career Total	11	5	0	1	33933
106	11/03	Winc	2m6f	B HHdl	G-F £18052
109	10/03	Extr	2m3f	D(0-115)HHdl	G-F £4147
97	10/03	Font	2m6f110yE(0-110)HHdl	GD	£3290
89	8/03	Font	2m2f110yE(0-105)HHdl	G-F	£3721
92	10/02	Strf	2m110y	D Hdl	G-F £4433

Total win prize-money £33643

Going: Sf: 0-0 GS: 0-0 Gd: 1-4 GF: 0-0 Fm: 3-5
Distance: 2m/2m3: 2-5 2m4-2m7: 2-3 3m+: 0-1
Track: LH: 2-3 RH: 2-6 Tight: 2-3 Gall: 0-0
Aids: Bl: 0-0 Vi: 0-0 Tstrap: 0-0 Ckp: 0-0
Best Rating: 109 10/03 Extr 2m3f   gd-fm   Hdl

Modest hurdler; in good form autumn 2003 winning four times; stays two miles six and needs fast ground; seems to go well for Marcus Foley.

One Knight (IRE)
(134h)159+

8-y-o ch g Roselier (FR)-Midnights Daughter (IRE) (Long Pond)
P J Hobbs R Gibbs

Placings:131/1136/13111-F   (2453)
2003/04: 26FGS,

	Starts	1st	2nd	3rd	Win & Pl
Chases	1	0	0	0	
Career Total	13	8	0	3	133782
159	3/03	Chel	3m110y	A Ch	GD £81200
138	1/03	Extr	2m7f110yE Ch	G-S	£4849
119	12/02	Extr	2m7f110yD Ch	G-S	£5518
151	11/02	Chep	2m3f110yA Ch	SFT	£17980
134	11/01	Chep	2m4f	A Hdl	G-S £10500
119	10/01	Chep	2m4f	E Hdl	SFT £2569
119	3/01	Newb	2m110y	H NHF	HVY £2660
116	11/00	Winc	2m	H NHF	G-S £1645

Total win prize-money £126922

Going: Sf: 0-0 GS: 0-1 Gd: 0-0 GF: - Fm: 0-0
Distance: 2m/2m3: 0-2 2m4-2m7: 0-0 3m+: 0-0
Track: LH: 0-1 RH: 0-0 Tight: 0-0 Gall: 0-1
Aids: Bl: 0-0 Vi: 0-0 Tstrap: 0-0 Ckp: 0-0
Best Rating: 159 3/03 Chel 3m110y   good   Ch

Very smart novice chaser in 2002/3, winning four times including making all in the 2003 Royal & SunAlliance Chase; fell at the first in the Hennessy on seasonal reappearance, and reportedly sustained an injury; effective at 3m; suited by forcing tactics; acts on any ground; prone to mistakes.

One More Native (IRE)
78

7-y-o ch g Be My Native (USA)-Romany Fortune (Sunyboy)
J L Needham Miss Joanna Needham

Placings:34-0F   (4003)
2003/04: 170GS, 16FG,

	Starts	1st	2nd	3rd	Win & Pl
NH Flat	1	0	0	0	0
Hurdles	1	0	0	0	0
Career Total	4	0	0	1	341

Going: Sf: 0-0 GS: 0-1 Gd: 0 GF: - Fm: 0-0
Distance: 2m/2m3: 0-2 2m4-2m7: 0-0 3m+: 0-0
Track: LH: 0-0 RH: 0-2 Tight: 0-0 Gall: 0-0
Aids: Bl: 0-0 Vi: 0-0 Tstrap: 0-0 Ckp: 0-0
Best Rating: 94 11/02 Sthl 2m   gd-sft NHF

One More Stride
101   77+

8-y-o gr g Beveled (USA)-Gem Of Gold (Jellaby)
Miss Victoria Roberts C F Stratford

Placings:00/P600-2   (1593)
2003/04: 212GF,

	Starts	1st	2nd	3rd	Win & Pl
Hurdles	1	0	1	0	830
Career Total	7	0	1	0	830

Going: Sf: 0-0 GS: 0-0 Gd: 0-0 GF: - Fm: 0-1
Distance: 2m/2m3: 0-0 2m4-2m7: 0-1 3m+: 0-0
Track: LH: 0-0 RH: 0-1 Tight: 0-0 Gall: 0-0
Aids: Bl: 0-0 Vi: 0-0 Tstrap: 0-0 Ckp: 0-0
Best Rating: 77 10/03 Ludl 2m5f   gd-fm   Hdl

Showed tremendous improvement on first outing for new yard when second at 80/1 in 2m 5f classified hurdle at Ludlow October 2003; acts on fast.

One Nation (IRE)

107(94h) (114h)**131+**

9-y-o br g Be My Native (USA)-Diklers Run (Deep Run)
Miss H C Knight The Earl Cadogan

Placings:3/24F211/144134/23/P300-15313P (4642)
2003/04: 19¹G, 17⁵G, 19³S, 21¹GS, 20³S, 25⁶G,

	Starts	1st	2nd	3rd	Win & Pl
Chases	6	2	0	2	21606
Career Total	25	6	3	6	47120
131	1/04	Winc	2m5f	D Ch	G-S	£5443
120	11/03	Extr	2m3f110yD Ch		GD	£6812
129	1/01	Winc	2m	D(0-125)HHdl	SFT	£5187
121	10/00	Hrfd	2m1f	D(0-120)HHdl	GD	£2977
115	4/00	Winc	2m	E Hdl	G-S	£2604
112	3/00	Hntg	2m110y	E Hdl	SFT	£2440

Total win prize-money £25464

Going:	Sf: 0-2 GS: 1-1 Gd: 1-3 GF: - Fm: 0-0
Distance:	2m/2m3: 0-1 2m4-2m7: 2-4 3m+: 0-1
Track:	LH: 0-1 RH: 2-5 Tight: 0-1 Gall: 0-0
Aids:	Bl: 0-0 Vi: 0-0 Tstrap: 0-0 Ckp: 0-0
Best Rating:	131 2/04 Sand 2m4f110y soft Ch

Useful hurdler/novice chaser; stays beyond two and a half miles and acts on most types of ground; best going right-handed; has had back problems in the past.

One Of The Natives (IRE)

10-y-o b g Be My Native (USA)-Take Me Home (Amoristic (USA))
Miss J H Jenner Miss J H Jenner

Placings:50/P/P34F/0P-0 (4563)
2003/04: 22⁰G,

	Starts	1st	2nd	3rd	Win & Pl
Chases	1	0	0	0	
Career Total	10	0	0	1	976

Going:	Sf: 0-0 GS: 0-0 Gd: 0-1 GF: - Fm: 0-0
Distance:	2m/2m3: 0-0 2m4-2m7: 0-1 3m+: 0-0
Track:	LH: 0-1 RH: 0-0 Tight: 0-0 Gall: 0-1
Aids:	Bl: 0-0 Vi: 0-1 Tstrap: 0-0 Ckp: 0-0
Best Rating:	95 2/02 Tntn 3m soft Ch

One Of Them

87 **80**

5-y-o ch g Pharly (FR)-Hicklam Millie (Absalom)
J S Moore Cistm Racing Club Ltd

Placings:6000 (4818)
2003/04: 17⁶GS, 17⁰S, 22²⁰G, 17⁰GF,

	Starts	1st	2nd	3rd	Win & Pl
Hurdles	4	0	0	0	0
Career Total	4	0	0	0	0

Going:	Sf: 0-1 GS: 0-1 Gd: 0-1 GF: - Fm: 0-1
Distance:	2m/2m3: 0-3 2m4-2m7: 0-1 3m+: 0-0
Track:	LH: 0-1 RH: 0-3 Tight: 0-3 Gall: 0-0
Aids:	Bl: 0-0 Vi: 0-0 Tstrap: 0-0 Ckp: 0-0
Best Rating:	80 2/04 Tntn 2m1f soft Hdl

One Up (IRE)

57

6-y-o b m Bob Back (USA)-Strong Desire (IRE) (Strong Gale)
M Todhunter Steve Baron

Placings:005-0 (0197)
2003/04: 24⁰G,

	Starts	1st	2nd	3rd	Win & Pl
Hurdles	1	0	0	0	
Career Total	4	0	0	0	0

Going:	Sf: 0-0 GS: 0-0 Gd: 0-1 GF: - Fm: 0-0
Distance:	2m/2m3: 0-0 2m4-2m7: 0-0 3m+: 0-1
Track:	LH: 0-1 RH: 0-0 Tight: 0-0 Gall: 0-0
Aids:	Bl: 0-0 Vi: 0-0 Tstrap: 0-0 Ckp: 0-0
Best Rating:	57 4/03 Carl 2m1f gd-fm Hdl

Oneforbertandhenry (IRE)

92 **67**

5-y-o b g Rashar (USA)-Roi Vision (Roi Guillaume (FR))
G M Moore J B Partnership

Placings:004 (3481)
2003/04: 16⁰G, 16⁰GS, 25⁴G,

	Starts	1st	2nd	3rd	Win & Pl
NH Flat	2	0	0	0	0
Hurdles	1	0	0	0	274
Career Total	3	0	0	0	274

Going:	Sf: 0-0 GS: 0-1 Gd: 0-2 GF: - Fm: 0-0
Distance:	2m/2m3: 0-2 2m4-2m7: 0-1 3m+: 0-0
Track:	LH: 0-3 RH: 0-0 Tight: 0-1 Gall: 0-0
Aids:	Bl: 0-0 Vi: 0-0 Tstrap: 0-0 Ckp: 0-0
Best Rating:	86 11/03 Ayr 2m good NHF

Onefourseven

102 **104+**

11-y-o b g Jumbo Hirt (USA)-Dominance (Dominion)
P C Haslam J Roundtree

Placings:2224500/0-4211 (1076)
2003/04: 20⁴GF, 26²G, 21¹GF, 21¹GF,

	Starts	1st	2nd	3rd	Win & Pl
Hurdles	4	2	1	0	7900
Career Total	12	2	4	0	10488
105	8/03	Sedg	2m5f110yE(0-110)HHdl	G-F	£3451
102	7/03	Sedg	2m5f110yE Hdl	G-F	£3479

Total win prize-money £6930

Going:	Sf: 0-0 GS: 0-0 Gd: 0-1 GF: - Fm: 2-3
Distance:	2m/2m3: 0-0 2m4-2m7: 2-3 3m+: 0-1
Track:	LH: 2-4 RH: 0-0 Tight: 2-2 Gall: 0-0
Aids:	Bl: 0-0 Vi: 0-0 Tstrap: 2-2 Ckp: 0-0
Best Rating:	105 8/03 Sedg 2m5f110y gd-fm Hdl

Moderate novice hurdler; winner at Sedgefield in July and again there the following month; tongue tied both times; stays 3m; effective on fast ground.

Oneminutetofive

7-y-o b g Neltino-Island Beat (Jupiter Island)
D Pipe B A Kilpatrick

Placings:4 (4425)

2003/04: 26⁴G,

	Starts	1st	2nd	3rd	Win & Pl
Chases	1	0	0	0	2000
Career Total	1	0	0	0	2000

Going:	Sf: 0-0 GS: 0-0 Gd: 0-1 GF: - Fm: 0-0
Distance:	2m/2m3: 0-0 2m4-2m7: 0-0 3m+: 0-1
Track:	LH: 0-1 RH: 0-0 Tight: 0-0 Gall: 0-1
Aids:	Bl: 0-0 Vi: 0-0 Tstrap: 0-0 Ckp: 0-0
Best Rating:	117 3/04 Chel 3m2f110y good Ch

Useful pointer; fourth in Cheltenham Foxhunters' on debut under Rules; bright prospect.

Oneofthemongoes (IRE)

89 **70**

8-y-o b g Ikdam-Miss Hganavak (Abednego)
Mrs L C Jewell Mrs A Greengrow

Placings:005 (4664)
2003/04: 16⁰G, 18⁰G, 19⁵GS,

	Starts	1st	2nd	3rd	Win & Pl
Hurdles	3	0	0	0	0
Career Total	3	0	0	0	0

Going:	Sf: 0-0 GS: 0-1 Gd: 0-2 GF: - Fm: 0-0
Distance:	2m/2m3: 0-2 2m4-2m7: 0-1 3m+: 0-0
Track:	LH: 0-3 RH: 0-0 Tight: 0-3 Gall: 0-0
Aids:	Bl: 0-0 Vi: 0-0 Tstrap: 0-0 Ckp: 0-0
Best Rating:	73 3/04 Plum 2m good Hdl

Oneway (IRE)

90(101h) (103 h)**110+**

7-y-o b g Bob's Return (IRE)-Rendezvous (Lorenzaccio)
M G Rimell Mrs Charlotte Oram

Placings:05245-315P (4527)
2003/04: 16³S, 20¹S, 22²⁵G, 19⁰GS,

	Starts	1st	2nd	3rd	Win & Pl
Chases	4	1	0	1	4653
Career Total	9	1	1	1	6349
114	12/03	Ling	2m4f110yE(0-110)HCh	SFT	£4026

Total win prize-money £4027

Going:	Sf: 1-2 GS: 0-1 Gd: 0-1 GF: - Fm: 0-0
Distance:	2m/2m3: 0-1 2m4-2m7: 1-3 3m+: 0-0
Track:	LH: 1-3 RH: 0-0 Tight: 1-1 Gall: 0-0
Aids:	Bl: 0-0 Vi: 0-0 Tstrap: 0-0 Ckp: 0-0
Best Rating:	114 12/03 Ling 2m4f110y soft Ch

Moderate chaser; stays 2m 4f; acts on soft.

Only For Gold

64 **33**

9-y-o b g Presidium-Calvanne Miss (Martinmas)
Dr P Pritchard (A Berry 8/8) Juro Antiques

Placings:6P0 (3355)
2003/04: 21⁶G, 16⁰G, 16⁰S,

	Starts	1st	2nd	3rd	Win & Pl
Hurdles	3	0	0	0	332
Career Total	3	0	0	0	332

Going:	Sf: 0-1 GS: 0-1 Gd: 0-1 GF: - Fm: 0-0
Distance:	2m/2m3: 0-2 2m4-2m7: 0-1 3m+: 0-0
Track:	LH: 0-3 RH: 0-0 Tight: 0-1 Gall: 0-1
Aids:	Bl: 0-0 Vi: 0-0 Tstrap: 0-0 Ckp: 0-0

Best Rating: **33** 1/04 Kels 2m110y soft Hdl

Only Once

(98h)   (101+h) **118**

9-y-o b g King's Ride-Rambling Gold (Little Buskins)
L Lungo Ashleybank Investments Limited

Placings:11-2P   (3938)
2003/04: 20²GS, 33³PG,

	Starts	1st	2nd	3rd	Win & Pl
Hurdles	1	0	1	0	1116
Chases	1	0	0	0	0
Career Total	4	2	1	0	10900
118 3/03	Kels	3m1f	D Ch	GD	£5838
97 1/03	Sedg	3m3f	E Ch	HVY	£3945
			Total win prize-money £9784		

Going:	Sf: 0-0 GS: 0-1 Gd: 0-1 GF: - Fm: 0-0
Distance:	2m2m3: 0-0 2m4-2m7: 0-1 3m+: 0-1
Track:	LH: 0-2 RH: 0-0 Tight: 0-0 Gall: 0-1
Aids:	Bl: 0-0 Vi: 0-0 Tstrap: 0-0 Ckp: 0-0
Best Rating:	118 3/03 Kels 3m1f good Ch

Useful chaser; winning Irish pointer; winner of his first two starts over fences in this country, but finished lame on the second occasion; shaped well over two and a half miles on hurdles debut in February 2004; pulled up in the Eider Chase; stays three miles three and acts on good and heavy ground; type to win more races.

Only One Matty (IRE)

104   112+

7-y-o b g Satco (FR)-Poundworld (IRE) (Orchestra)
Mrs K Walton The White Liners

Placings:040000/33400-0412103   (4601)
2003/04: 20⁰GS, 16⁴GS, 24¹GF, 20²G, 24¹G, 24⁰G, 22³GS,

	Starts	1st	2nd	3rd	Win & Pl
Hurdles	7	2	1	1	9575
Career Total	18	2	1	3	11230
112 2/04	Muss	3m110y	D(0-110)HHdl	GD	£4706
101 1/04	Muss	3m110y	E(0-105)HHdl	G-F	£3445
			Total win prize-money £8151		

Going:	Sf: 0-0 GS: 0-3 Gd: 1-3 GF: - Fm: 1-1
Distance:	2m2m3: 0-1 2m4-2m7: 0-0 3m+: 2-3
Track:	LH: 0-3 RH: 0-2 Tight: 0-4 Gall: 0-1
Aids:	Bl: 0-0 Vi: 0-0 Tstrap: 0-0 Ckp: 0-0
Best Rating:	112 2/04 Muss 3m110y good Hdl

Moderate ex-Irish hurdler; won twice at Musselburgh in early 2004; stays three miles but highly effective over shorter; hurdles well; acts on a sound surface; has worn a tongue tie.

Only Vintage (USA)

111f   124+f

4-y-o b g Diesis-Wild Vintage (USA) (Alysheba (USA))
Michael Hourigan Lady Bamford

Placings:6410   (4400)
2003/04: 16⁶HY, 16⁴GY, 16¹G, 16⁰G,

	Starts	1st	2nd	3rd	Win & Pl
NH Flat	4	1	0	0	6557
Career Total	4	1	0	0	6557
110 2/04	Leop	2m	NHF	GD	£6326
			Total win prize-money £6326		

Going:	Sf: 0-1 GS: 0-0 Gd: 1-2 GF: - Fm: 0-0
Distance:	2m2m3: 1-4 2m4-2m7: 0-0 3m+: 0-0
Track:	LH: 0-1 RH: 0-1 Tight: 0-0 Gall: 0-0

Aids: Bl: 0-0 Vi: 0-0 Tstrap: 0-0 Ckp: 0-0
Best Rating: **124** 3/04 Chel 2m110y good NHF

Off the mark on third outing in a bumper at Leopardstown in February before running well at Cheltenham; acts on soft, but seems best on good ground.

Only Wallis (IRE)

88   65

7-y-o b g Supreme Leader-Laurdella Lady (Golden Love)
C L Tizzard D J Hinks

Placings:366   (4445)
2003/04: 16³S, 24⁶GS, 25⁶S,

	Starts	1st	2nd	3rd	Win & Pl
NH Flat	1	0	0	1	1113
Hurdles	2	0	0	0	0
Career Total	3	0	0	1	1113

Going:	Sf: 0-2 GS: 0-1 Gd: 0-0 GF: - Fm: 0-0
Distance:	2m2m3: 0-1 2m4-2m7: 0-0 3m+: 0-2
Track:	LH: 0-1 RH: 0-2 Tight: 0-0 Gall: 0-0
Aids:	Bl: 0-0 Vi: 0-0 Tstrap: 0-0 Ckp: 0-0
Best Rating:	103 12/03 Asct 2m110y soft NHF

Good bumper run on debut disappointing over hurdles over three miles.

Only Words (USA)

105   96

7-y-o ch g Shuailaan (USA)-Conversation Piece (USA) (Seeking The Gold (USA))
A J Lockwood Mrs Lynne Lumley

Placings:500356/202001252402P0-6123304   (4262)
2003/04: 17⁶G, 16¹GS, 16²S, 16⁹HY, 17³GS, 19⁴GF,

	Starts	1st	2nd	3rd	Win & Pl
Hurdles	7	1	1	2	5944
Career Total	27	2	6	3	12204
92 1/04	Weth	2m	F(0-100)HHdl	G-S	£3620
82 10/02	Sedg	2m1f	G(0-90)HHdl	GD	£2289
			Total win prize-money £5910		

Going:	Sf: 0-2 GS: 1-3 Gd: 0-1 GF: - Fm: 0-1
Distance:	2m2m3: 1-7 2m4-2m7: 0-0 3m+: 0-0
Track:	LH: 1-7 RH: 0-0 Tight: 0-4 Gall: 0-1
Aids:	Bl: 0-0 Vi: 0-0 Tstrap: 0-0 Ckp: 0-0
Best Rating:	96 2/04 Sedg 2m1f gd-sft Hdl

Plating-class hurdler; 25/1 winner at Wetherby in January; best over two miles; acts on soft.

Only You

96   76

8-y-o b g Gildoran-Outfield (Monksfield)
N A Twiston-Davies Roger Nicholls

Placings:0FP/5U00554PU4326/33-064   (3642)
2003/04: 16⁶GS, 19⁶HY, 19⁴S,

	Starts	1st	2nd	3rd	Win & Pl
Hurdles	3	0	0	0	0
Career Total	21	0	1	3	1485

Going:	Sf: 0-2 GS: 0-0 Gd: 0-0 GF: - Fm: 0-0
Distance:	2m2m3: 0-2 2m4-2m7: 0-1 3m+: 0-0
Track:	LH: 0-0 RH: 0-2 Tight: 0-0 Gall: 0-0
Aids:	Bl: 0-0 Vi: 0-0 Tstrap: 0-0 Ckp: 0-0
Best Rating:	76 5/02 Worc 2m4f good Hdl

Modest maiden including selling company; suited by two and a half miles and fast ground.

Onmywayhome (IRE)

9-y-o br m Alphabatim (USA)-Mammy's Friend (Miners Lamp)
Mrs Susan Smith Mrs Susan Smith

Placings:0/P   (0151)
2003/04: 24⁰GF,

	Starts	1st	2nd	3rd	Win & Pl
Chases	1	0	0	0	
Career Total	2	0	0	0	

Going:	Sf: 0-0 GS: 0-0 Gd: 0-0 GF: - Fm: 0-1
Distance:	2m2m3: 0-0 2m4-2m7: 0-0 3m+: 0-1
Track:	LH: 0-1 RH: 0-0 Tight: 0-0 Gall: 0-0
Aids:	Bl: 0-0 Vi: 0-0 Tstrap: 0-0 Ckp: 0-0

Ontos (GER)

102   120+

8-y-o b g Super Abound (USA)-Onestep (GER) (Konigsstuhl (GER))
Miss V Scott (N M L Ewart 16/1) Miss Victoria Scott Jnr

Placings:P/0002344/F4F5511145140433434-5P5   (3360)
2003/04: 16⁵G, 16⁶S, 16⁶S,

	Starts	1st	2nd	3rd	Win & Pl
Hurdles	3	0	0	0	1125
Career Total	30	4	1	4	26750
122 11/02	Kels	2m110y	D(0-125)HHdl	SFT	£4043
110 9/02	Prth	2m110y	D Hdl	G-F	£4303
108 9/02	Sedg	2m1f	E Hdl	G-F	£2968
102 8/02	Hntg	2m110y	F Hdl	G-F	£2223
			Total win prize-money £13537		

Going:	Sf: 0-2 GS: 0-0 Gd: 0-1 GF: - Fm: 0-0
Distance:	2m2m3: 0-3 2m4-2m7: 0-0 3m+: 0-0
Track:	LH: 0-3 RH: 0-0 Tight: 0-1 Gall: 0-1
Aids:	Bl: 0-0 Vi: 0-0 Tstrap: 0-0 Ckp: 0-0
Best Rating:	122 4/03 Aint 2m110y good Hdl

Fair hurdler; ex-Irish; in good form in the autumn of 2002 and consistent efforts since without winning; best at two miles; effective on most types of ground.

Onwardsandupwards (IRE)

108   118+

5-y-o b/br g Un Desperado (FR)-Kalifornia Katie (IRE) (Sharp Charter)
P F Nicholls Paul K Barber & Barry Marshall

Placings:1-26220P   (4853)
2003/04: 17²G, 16⁶GS, 22²GS, 24²S, 20⁰S, 22⁰PGS,

	Starts	1st	2nd	3rd	Win & Pl
Hurdles	6	0	3	0	3768
Career Total	7	1	3	0	6330
90 1/03	Tntn	2m1f	H NHF	SFT	£2562
			Total win prize-money £2562		

Going:	Sf: 0-2 GS: 0-3 Gd: 0-1 GF: - Fm: 0-0
Distance:	2m2m3: 0-2 2m4-2m7: 0-3 3m+: 0-1
Track:	LH: 0-2 RH: 0-4 Tight: 0-1 Gall: 0-1
Aids:	Bl: 0-0 Vi: 0-0 Tstrap: 0-0 Ckp: 0-0
Best Rating:	118 2/04 Tntn 3m110y soft Hdl

Justified favouritism when narrow winner of soft ground bumper at Taunton on his racecourse debut January 2003; has shown ability over hurdles, but likely to be best over fences; should stay a real trip.

Onyourheadbeit (IRE)

92   **83**

6-y-o b g Glacial Storm (USA)-Family Birthday (Sandalay)
K C Bailey Mr and Mrs Giles Wilson

Placings: f0   (4560)
2003/04: 17¹GS, 21⁰GS,

	Starts	1st	2nd	3rd	Win & Pl
NH Flat	1	1	0	0	1953
Hurdles	1	0	0	0	
Career Total	2	1	0	0	1953
97 2/04 Sedg 2m1f H NHF				G-S	£1953
				Total win prize-money £1953

Going: Sf: 0-0 GS: 1-2 Gd: 0-0 GF: - Fm: 0-0
Distance: 2m/2m3: 1-1 2m4-2m7: 0-0 3m+: 0-0
Track: LH: 1-2 RH: 0-0 Tight: 1-1 Gall: 0-1
Aids: Bl: 0-0 Vi: 0-0 Tstrap: 0-0 Ckp: 0-0
Best Rating: 97 2/04 Sedg 2m1f gd-sft NHF

Well-backed winner of a Sedgefield bumper on his debut; beaten on hurdles debut; acts on easy ground; will stay three miles in time.

Oos And Ahs

71   **60**

4-y-o b f Silver Wizard (USA)-Hot Feet (Marching On)
C W Fairhurst C W Fairhurst

Placings: P0   (2528)
2003/04: 16⁰GF, 16⁰GS,

	Starts	1st	2nd	3rd	Win & Pl
Hurdles	2	0	0	0	
Career Total	2	0	0	0	

Going: Sf: 0-0 GS: 0-1 Gd: 0-0 GF: - Fm: 0-1
Distance: 2m/2m3: 0-2 2m4-2m7: 0-0 3m+: 0-0
Track: LH: 0-2 RH: 0-0 Tight: 0-0 Gall: 0-0
Aids: Bl: 0-0 Vi: 0-0 Tstrap: 0-0 Ckp: 0-0
Best Rating: 60 12/03 Catt 2m gd-sft Hdl

Opal Ridge

99   **95+**

7-y-o ch g Jupiter Island-The Beginning (Goldhill)
P R Webber D l Bare

Placings: 4-5   (4146)
2003/04: 24⁵G,

	Starts	1st	2nd	3rd	Win & Pl
Chases	1	0	0	0	0
Career Total	2	0	0	0	0

Going: Sf: 0-0 GS: 0-0 Gd: 0-1 GF: - Fm: 0-0
Distance: 2m/2m3: 0-0 2m4-2m7: 0-0 3m+: 0-1
Track: LH: 0-0 RH: 0-1 Tight: 0-1 Gall: 0-0
Aids: Bl: 0-0 Vi: 0-0 Tstrap: 0-0 Ckp: 0-0
Best Rating: 95 3/04 Tntn 3m good Ch

Opal'Lou (FR)

105

8-y-o b m Garde Royale-Calligraphie (FR) (Rb Chesne)
P F Nicholls Formpave Ltd

Placings: 5060/250040F/32363636/25332-P   (0183)
2003/04: 21⁵PGF,

	Starts	1st	2nd	3rd	Win & Pl
Chases	1	0	0	0	

| Career Total | 25 | 0 | 4 | 6 | 11992 |

Going: Sf: 0-0 GS: 0-0 Gd: 0-0 GF: - Fm: 0-1
Distance: 2m/2m3: 0-0 2m4-2m7: 0-1 3m+: 0-0
Track: LH: 0-0 RH: 0-1 Tight: 0-0 Gall: 0-0
Aids: Bl: 0-0 Vi: 0-0 Tstrap: 0-0 Ckp: 0-0
Best Rating: 105 12/02 Extr 2m3f110y gd-sft Ch

Modest chaser; effective at around two and a half miles; has become disappointing.

Opera Hall

94f   **83+f**

4-y-o b f Saddlers' Hall (IRE)-Opera Hat (IRE) (Strong Gale)
H D Daly Ladywood Farm

Placings: 36   (4594)
2003/04: 16³G, 16⁶G,

	Starts	1st	2nd	3rd	Win & Pl
NH Flat	2	0	0	1	369
Career Total	2	0	0	1	369

Going: Sf: 0-0 GS: 0-0 Gd: 0-2 GF: - Fm: 0-0
Distance: 2m/2m3: 0-2 2m4-2m7: 0-0 3m+: 0-0
Track: LH: 0-1 RH: 0-1 Tight: 0-1 Gall: 0-1
Aids: Bl: 0-0 Vi: 0-0 Tstrap: 0-0 Ckp: 0-0
Best Rating: 87 2/04 Fknm 2m good NHF

Promising third at Fakenham on debut; should get further over hurdles; acts on good ground.

Operashaan (IRE)

54   **23**

4-y-o b g Darshaan-Comic Opera (IRE) (Royal Academy (USA))
G L Moore (T T Clement 18/5) Brighthelm Racing

Placings: 0   (3364)
2003/04: 16⁰G,

	Starts	1st	2nd	3rd	Win & Pl
Hurdles	1	0	0	0	
Career Total	1	0	0	0	

Going: Sf: 0-0 GS: 0-0 Gd: 0-1 GF: - Fm: 0-0
Distance: 2m/2m3: 0-1 2m4-2m7: 0-0 3m+: 0-0
Track: LH: 0-0 RH: 0-1 Tight: 0-0 Gall: 0-0
Aids: Bl: 0-0 Vi: 0-0 Tstrap: 0-0 Ckp: 0-0
Best Rating: 23 1/04 Kemp 2m good Hdl

Optimaite

103   **111+**

7-y-o b g Komaite (USA)-Leprechaun Lady (Royal Blend)
B R Millman Always Hopeful Partnership

Placings: 2416   (3315)
2003/04: 16²GF, 16⁴GF, 16¹G, 16⁶S,

	Starts	1st	2nd	3rd	Win & Pl
Hurdles	4	1	1	0	7188
Career Total	4	1	1	0	7188
107 12/03 Leic 2m D Hdl				GD	£4280
				Total win prize-money £4280

Going: Sf: 0-1 GS: 0-0 Gd: 1-1 GF: - Fm: 0-2
Distance: 2m/2m3: 1-4 2m4-2m7: 0-0 3m+: 0-0
Track: LH: 0-1 RH: 1-3 Tight: 0-0 Gall: 0-0
Aids: Bl: 0-0 Vi: 0-0 Tstrap: 1-4 Ckp: 0-0
Best Rating: 111 11/03 Chel 2m110y gd-fm Hdl

Modest novice hurdler; effective over two miles; acts on good ground.

Optimistic Harry

73

5-y-o b g Sir Harry Lewis (USA)-Miss Optimist (Relkino)
P A Blockley bellhouseracing.com

Placings: 0UP   (4756)
2003/04: 24⁰G, 21ᵁG, 19ᴾS,

	Starts	1st	2nd	3rd	Win & Pl
Hurdles	3	0	0	0	
Career Total	3	0	0	0	

Going: Sf: 0-1 GS: 0-0 Gd: 0-2 GF: - Fm: 0-0
Distance: 2m/2m3: 0-0 2m4-2m7: 0-2 3m+: 0-1
Track: LH: 0-1 RH: 0-1 Tight: 0-1 Gall: 0-0
Aids: Bl: 0-0 Vi: 0-0 Tstrap: 0-0 Ckp: 0-0

Optimistic Thinker

10-y-o ch g Beveled (USA)-Racemosa (Town Crier)
Miss T McCurrich (T R George 2/5) 47th Regiment Royal Artillery

Placings: 102P61P/2223/412P1UP6/P234014P/4PPPP-50
                                                          (3896)
2003/04: 16⁵GS, 24⁰G,

	Starts	1st	2nd	3rd	Win & Pl
Chases	2	0	0	0	0
Career Total	34	5	6	2	21409
115 1/02 Hntg 2m110y D(0-115)HCh G-S £3893					
118 11/00 Uttx 2m D Ch HVY £3944					
113 10/00 Hntg 2m110y E(0-105)HCh G-F £3052					
103 3/99 NAbb 2m1f F(0-100)HHdl SFT £1760					
109 10/98 MRas 1m5f110yH NHF HVY £1234					
				Total win prize-money £13886

Going: Sf: 0-0 GS: 0-1 Gd: 0-1 GF: - Fm: 0-0
Distance: 2m/2m3: 0-1 2m4-2m7: 0-0 3m+: 0-1
Track: LH: 0-1 RH: 0-1 Tight: 0-0 Gall: 0-0
Aids: Bl: 0-0 Vi: 0-0 Tstrap: 0-0 Ckp: 0-2
Best Rating: 118 11/00 Uttx 2m heavy Ch

Oracle Des Mottes (FR)

112   **115+**

5-y-o b g Signe Divin (USA)-Daisy Des Mottes (FR) (Abdonski (FR))
P F Nicholls Mark Tincknell

Placings: 23O3-5213   (2815)
2003/04: 16⁶GF, 16²GF, 16¹GS, 17³G,

	Starts	1st	2nd	3rd	Win & Pl
Hurdles	4	1	1	1	10816
Career Total	8	1	2	3	13001
108 12/03 Chep 2m110y D Hdl				G-S	£3406
				Total win prize-money £3406

Going: Sf: 0-0 GS: 1-1 Gd: 0-1 GF: - Fm: 0-2
Distance: 2m/2m3: 1-4 2m4-2m7: 0-0 3m+: 0-0
Track: LH: 1-3 RH: 0-1 Tight: 0-0 Gall: 0-0
Aids: Bl: 0-0 Vi: 0-0 Tstrap: 0-0 Ckp: 0-0
Best Rating: 115 12/03 Extr 2m1f good Hdl

Modest hurdler; French import; ran better than finishing position suggests when close fifth in Free Handicap Hurdle at Chepstow October 2003; respectable second at Cheltenham next time; won maiden back at Chepstow in December; stays an extended 2m and should get further; acts on soft ground.

Orake Prince

84   **54**

5-y-o b g Bluegrass Prince (IRE)-Kiri Te (Liboi (USA))
W G M Turner D A Drake

Placings: PP-600   **(2514)**
2003/04: 16⁵GS, 16⁰GF, 17⁰GS,

	Starts	1st	2nd	3rd	Win & Pl
Hurdles	3	0	0	0	0
Career Total	5	0	0	0	0

Going:	Sf: 0-0 GS: 0-2 Gd: 0-0 GF: - Fm: 0-1
Distance:	2m/2m3: 0-3 2m4-2m7: 0-0 3m+: 0-0
Track:	LH: 0-0 RH: 0-3 Tight: 0-0 Gall: 0-0
Aids:	Bl: 0-0 Vi: 0-0 Tstrap: 0-0 Ckp: 0-0
Best Rating:	59 12/03 Hrfd 2m1f gd-sft Hdl

Orange Order (IRE)

101(101c)   **(73c)86**

11-y-o ch g Generous (IRE)-Fleur D'Oranger (Northfields (USA))
G M Moore Mrs A Roddis

Placings: 6P/62106504/013502060L00/11615062/11354331
50/4214123F3/P5P336P33P0-65   **(0671)**
2003/04: 22⁶GS, 26⁵GF,

	Starts	1st	2nd	3rd	Win & Pl
Hurdles	2	0	0	0	0
Career Total	62	10	5	10	37602
101	7/01	Wolv	2m4f110yE Ch	G-F	£3376
115	6/01	MRas	2m4f	E Ch	G-F	£3851
119	9/00	Sedg	2m5f110yD(0-120)HHdl	G-F	£3575
114	5/00	Weth	2m	E(0-115)HHdl	G-S	£2485
101	5/00	Sedg	2m1f	F(0-100)HHdl	G-F	£2492
102	9/99	Sedg	2m1f	G(0-95)HHdl	G-F	£2066
102	7/99	Sedg	2m1f	G(0-95)HHdl	G-F	£1884
100	7/99	Sedg	2m1f	F(0-100)HHdl	G-F	£2010
109	6/98	Tral	2m	(0-102)Hdl	GD	£2382
102	9/97	Clon	2m	Hdl	Y-S	£2543
				Total win prize-money £26666

Going:	Sf: 0-0 GS: 0-1 Gd: 0-0 GF: - Fm: 0-1
Distance:	2m/2m3: 0-0 2m4-2m7: 0-1 3m+: 0-1
Track:	LH: 0-2 RH: 0-0 Tight: 0-1 Gall: 0-0
Aids:	Bl: 0-0 Vi: 0-0 Tstrap: 0-0 Ckp: 0-0
Best Rating:	119 9/00 Sedg 2m5f110y good Hdl

Plating-class hurdler; Sedgefield specialist over hurdles, ordinary handicap chaser, best at distances short of three miles.

Orange Tree Lad

77

6-y-o b g Tragic Role (USA)-Adorable Cherub (USA) (Halo (USA))
D W Thompson Growing on Trees Partnership

Placings: P033343506U-P   **(1204)**
2003/04: 17⁵G,

	Starts	1st	2nd	3rd	Win & Pl
Hurdles	1	0	0	0	0
Career Total	12	0	0	4	1329

Going:	Sf: 0-0 GS: 0-0 Gd: 0-0 GF: - Fm: 0-0
Distance:	2m/2m3: 0-1 2m4-2m7: 0-0 3m+: 0-0
Track:	LH: 0-1 RH: 0-0 Tight: 0-0 Gall: 0-0
Aids:	Bl: 0-0 Vi: 0-0 Tstrap: 0-0 Ckp: 0-0
Best Rating:	77 1/03 Ludl 2m soft Hdl

Orangerie (IRE)

(106h)   **(112 h)**

6-y-o b g Darshaan-Fleur D'Oranger (Northfields (USA))
P J Hobbs Richard Green (fine Paintings)

Placings: 4/1204U2365-U   **(0131)**
2003/04: 20ᵁGF,

	Starts	1st	2nd	3rd	Win & Pl
Chases	1	0	0	0	
Career Total	11	1	2	1	12422
119	10/02	Chel	2m110y D Hdl	G-F	£7586
				Total win prize-money £7586

Going:	Sf: 0-0 GS: 0-0 Gd: 0-0 GF: - Fm: 0-1
Distance:	2m/2m3: 0-0 2m4-2m7: 0-1 3m+: 0-0
Track:	LH: 0-0 RH: 0-1 Tight: 0-0 Gall: 0-1
Aids:	Bl: 0-1 Vi: 0-0 Tstrap: 0-0 Ckp: 0-0
Best Rating:	119 11/02 Winc 2m6f gd-sft Hdl

Modest hurdler; effective at up to two miles six furlongs; acts on a sound surface, but is also effective with cut; often wears blinkers; is probably not a straightforward ride.

Orapa

31

5-y-o b g Spectrum (IRE)-African Dance (USA) (El Gran Senor (USA))
T D McCarthy The Jump For Joy Partnership

Placings: 0-P   **(4664)**
2003/04: 19⁰GS,

	Starts	1st	2nd	3rd	Win & Pl
Hurdles	1	0	0	0	
Career Total	2	0	0	0	

Going:	Sf: 0-0 GS: 0-1 Gd: 0-0 GF: - Fm: 0-0
Distance:	2m/2m3: 0-0 2m4-2m7: 0-1 3m+: 0-0
Track:	LH: 0-1 RH: 0-0 Tight: 0-1 Gall: 0-0
Aids:	Bl: 0-0 Vi: 0-0 Tstrap: 0-0 Ckp: 0-0
Best Rating:	31 2/03 Weth 2m good Hdl

Orbicularis (IRE)

102   **91+**

8-y-o b g Supreme Leader-Liffey Travel (Le Bavard (FR))
Mrs A M Thorpe (R F Fisher 17/5) Don Jones

Placings: 000/000-5100   **(3272)**
2003/04: 17⁵S, 22¹G, 24⁰GS, 22⁰G,

	Starts	1st	2nd	3rd	Win & Pl
Hurdles	4	1	0	0	2611
Career Total	10	1	0	0	2611
91	12/03	Extr	2m6f110yF(0-100)HHdl	GD	£2611
				Total win prize-money £2611

Going:	Sf: 0-1 GS: 0-1 Gd: 1-2 GF: - Fm: 0-0
Distance:	2m/2m3: 0-1 2m4-2m7: 1-2 3m+: 0-1
Track:	LH: 0-3 RH: 1-1 Tight: 0-1 Gall: 0-0
Aids:	Bl: 0-0 Vi: 0-0 Tstrap: 0-0 Ckp: 0-0
Best Rating:	91 12/03 Extr 2m6f110y good Hdl

Plating-class hurder; improved form on first start for new trainer when winning 2m 6f amateur riders' handicap hurdle at Exeter December 2003; appeared to be unsuited by soft ground at Uttoxeter next time; needs a sound surface.

Orient Bay (IRE)

102(106c)   **(67c)78**

9-y-o b g Commanche Run-East Link (IRE) (Over The River (FR))
M Sheppard R W Guilding

Placings: 4/U/PR44P33U-0P2440032   **(4716)**
2003/04: 25⁹GF, 25⁵GF, 20²GF, 20⁴GF, 26⁴GS, 26⁹GS, 21⁰S, 26³GF, 21²G,

	Starts	1st	2nd	3rd	Win & Pl
Hurdles	5	0	1	1	2157
Chases	4	0	1	0	1142
Career Total	19	0	2	3	5787

Going:	Sf: 0-1 GS: 0-2 Gd: 0-1 GF: - Fm: 0-5
Distance:	2m/2m3: 0-0 2m4-2m7: 0-4 3m+: 0-5
Track:	LH: 0-1 RH: 0-8 Tight: 0-1 Gall: 0-1
Aids:	Bl: 0-2 Vi: 0-0 Tstrap: 0-2 Ckp: 0-7
Best Rating:	92 5/00 Prth 2m110y gd-sft NHF

Point-to-point winner in 2002 but only moderate form in chases and hurdles; has shown a tendency to jump left handed.

Oriental Mist (IRE)

54

6-y-o gr g Balla Cove-Donna Katrina (King's Lake (USA))
P Monteith Oriental Mist Partnership

Placings: 50P/P   **(0713)**
2003/04: 16⁶G,

	Starts	1st	2nd	3rd	Win & Pl
Hurdles	1	0	0	0	
Career Total	4	0	0	0	0

Going:	Sf: 0-0 GS: 0-0 Gd: 0-1 GF: - Fm: 0-0
Distance:	2m/2m3: 0-0 2m4-2m7: 0-0 3m+: 0-0
Track:	LH: 0-0 RH: 0-1 Tight: 0-0 Gall: 0-0
Aids:	Bl: 0-1 Vi: 0-0 Tstrap: 0-0 Ckp: 0-0
Best Rating:	55 12/01 Muss 2m good Hdl

Oriental Moon (IRE)

87   **54**

5-y-o ch m Spectrum (IRE)-La Grande Cascade (USA) (Beaudelaire (USA))
M J Gingell (G C H Chung 22/12) M J Gingell

Placings: P0540   **(4774)**
2003/04: 16⁵PHY, 16⁰S, 17⁵GS, 16⁴GS, 16⁰G,

	Starts	1st	2nd	3rd	Win & Pl
Hurdles	5	0	0	0	0
Career Total	5	0	0	0	0

Going:	Sf: 0-2 GS: 0-1 Gd: 0-2 GF: - Fm: 0-0
Distance:	2m/2m3: 0-5 2m4-2m7: 0-0 3m+: 0-0
Track:	LH: 0-4 RH: 0-1 Tight: 0-4 Gall: 0-0
Aids:	Bl: 0-0 Vi: 0-0 Tstrap: 0-0 Ckp: 0-0
Best Rating:	54 2/04 Plum 2m soft Hdl

Orinocovsky (IRE)

85   **74**

5-y-o ch g Grand Lodge (USA)-Brillantina (FR) (Crystal Glitters (USA))
N P Littmoden (C R Egerton 15/1) Nigel Shields

Placings: 56P   **(3245)**
2003/04: 16⁵GS, 19⁰GS, 16⁶GS,

	Starts	1st	2nd	3rd	Win & Pl
Hurdles	3	0	0	0	0
Career Total	3	0	0	0	0

Going:	Sf: 0-0 GS: 0-3 Gd: 0-0 GF: - Fm: 0-0

Distance: 2m/2m3: 0-2 2m4-2m7: 0-1 3m+: 0-0
Track: LH: 0-2 RH: 0-1 Tight: 0-0 Gall: 0-0
Aids: Bl: 0-1 Vi: 0-1 Tstrap: 0-0 Ckp: 0-0
Best Rating: 74 11/03 Uttx   2m   gd-sft Hdl

Orlando Sunrise (IRE)

84(96h)   (93h)80
7-y-o ch m Dolphin Street (FR)-Miss Belgravia (USA)
(Smarten (USA))
R Dickin   Charles Eden

Placings:3060/00-4F1PRUF   (1730)
2003/04: 17⁴GF, 17⁵F, 20¹GF, 20PGF, 16RF, 20UGF, 19FGF,

	Starts	1st	2nd	3rd	Win & Pl
Chases	7	1	0	0	4365
Career Total	13	1	0	1	4835
78 8/03 Worc 2m4f110yE Ch				G-F	£4105

Total win prize-money £4106

Going: Sf: 0-0 GS: 0-0 Gd: 0-1 GF: - Fm: 1-6
Distance: 2m/2m3: 0-3 2m4-2m7: 1-4 3m+: 0-0
Track: LH: 1-5 RH: 0-2 Tight: 0-0 Gall: 0-1
Aids: Bl: 0-1 Vi: 0-1 Tstrap: 0-0 Ckp: 0-0
Best Rating: 93 10/01 Strf 2m110y   gd-sft Hdl

Plating-class hurdler; stays two and a half miles; acts on fast ground.

Orleans (IRE)

9-y-o b g Scenic-Guest House (What A Guest)
S J Robinson   S J Robinson

Placings:03/5/2OO/F-40   (3987)
2003/04: 21⁴S, 21⁰GS,

	Starts	1st	2nd	3rd	Win & Pl
Chases	2	0	0	0	0
Career Total	9	0	1	1	910

Going: Sf: 0-1 GS: 0-1 Gd: 0-0 GF: - Fm: 0-0
Distance: 2m/2m3: 0-1 2m4-2m7: 0-2 3m+: 0-0
Track: LH: 0-2 RH: 0-0 Tight: 0-2 Gall: 0-0
Aids: Bl: 0-2 Vi: 0-0 Tstrap: 0-0 Ckp: 0-0
Best Rating: 92 6/01 Worc   2m   gd-fm Hdl

Oro Street (IRE)

98   88
8-y-o b g Dolphin Street (FR)-Love Unlimited (Dominion)
G F Bridgwater   Mrs Gail Bridgwater

Placings:124/0520/30060/00542263P00   (4339)
2003/04: 16⁸GF, 16⁰G, 16⁴GF, 16⁴GF, 17²GS, 16²G, 16⁵S, 16³GS, 25PGS, 16⁰G, 16⁰G,

	Starts	1st	2nd	3rd	Win & Pl
Hurdles	11	0	2	1	1516
Career Total	23	1	4	2	8512
120 2/00 Wwck 2m			E Hdl	GD	£2913

Total win prize-money £2913

Going: Sf: 0-1 GS: 0-3 Gd: 0-4 GF: - Fm: 0-3
Distance: 2m/2m3: 0-10 2m4-2m7: 0-0 3m+: 0-0
Track: LH: 0-2 RH: 0-9 Tight: 0-0 Gall: 0-0
Aids: Bl: 0-0 Vi: 0-0 Tstrap: 0-0 Ckp: 0-0
Best Rating: 120 2/00 Wwck   2m   good   Hdl

Plating-class hurdler; effective at up to two and a half miles; acts on ground good and softer.

Orswell Crest

111   120+
10-y-o b g Crested Lark-Slave's Bangle (Prince Rheingold)
P J Hobbs   The Mane Chance Partnership

Placings:0/063/0245U/1133314-43163U3   (4547)
2003/04: 24⁴G, 25⁵G, 24¹GF, 24⁸GF, 25³G, 25UG, 25³GS,

	Starts	1st	2nd	3rd	Win & Pl
Chases	7	1	0	3	8447
Career Total	23	4	1	7	61613
120 11/03 Sand 3m110y C(0-130)HCh				G-F	£5138
116 4/03 Ayr 3m1f B HCh				GD	£21255
115 11/02 Aint 3m1f D(0-115)HCh				GD	£14218
108 11/02 Winc 3m1f110yD(0-110)HCh				GD	£10188

Total win prize-money £50801

Going: Sf: 0-0 GS: 0-1 Gd: 0-4 GF: - Fm: 1-2
Distance: 2m/2m3: 0-0 2m4-2m7: 0-0 3m+: 1-7
Track: LH: 0-2 RH: 1-5 Tight: 0-1 Gall: 0-1
Aids: Bl: 0-0 Vi: 0-0 Tstrap: 0-0 Ckp: 0-0
Best Rating: 120 3/04 Winc 3m1f110y gd-sft Ch

Modest handicap chaser; stays beyond three miles and suited by ground good or faster; likes flat tracks; prefers to race prominently.

Orthodox

5-y-o gr g Baryshnikov (AUS)-Sancta (So Blessed)
G L Moore   Mrs Elizabeth Kiernan

Placings:P   (2449)
2003/04: 16PGS,

	Starts	1st	2nd	3rd	Win & Pl
Hurdles	1	0	0	0	0
Career Total	1	0	0	0	0

Going: Sf: 0-0 GS: 0-1 Gd: 0-0 GF: - Fm: 0-0
Distance: 2m/2m3: 0-1 2m4-2m7: 0-0 3m+: 0-0
Track: LH: 0-1 RH: 0-0 Tight: 0-0 Gall: 0-1
Aids: Bl: 0-1 Vi: 0-0 Tstrap: 0-0 Ckp: 0-0

Oscar Bill (IRE)

91f   84f
5-y-o b g Oscar (IRE)-Forecast Rain (IRE) (Phardante (FR))
M J Coombe   Chris Pugsley

Placings:05   (4738)
2003/04: 16⁰GS, 17⁵G,

	Starts	1st	2nd	3rd	Win & Pl
NH Flat	2	0	0	0	0
Career Total	2	0	0	0	0

Going: Sf: 0-0 GS: 0-1 Gd: 0-1 GF: - Fm: 0-0
Distance: 2m/2m3: 0-2 2m4-2m7: 0-0 3m+: 0-0
Track: LH: 0-1 RH: 0-1 Tight: 0-1 Gall: 0-0
Aids: Bl: 0-0 Vi: 0-0 Tstrap: 0-0 Ckp: 0-0
Best Rating: 84 4/04 NAbb 2m1f   good   NHF

Oscar The Boxer (IRE)

97f   87f
5-y-o b g Oscar (IRE)-Here She Comes (Deep Run)
J M Jefferson   The New Phoenix Racing Club

Placings:2300   (4962)
2003/04: 17²GF, 16³G, 16⁰GS, 17⁰G,

	Starts	1st	2nd	3rd	Win & Pl
NH Flat	4	0	1	1	758
Career Total	4	0	1	1	758

Going: Sf: 0-0 GS: 0-1 Gd: 0-2 GF: - Fm: 0-1
Distance: 2m/2m3: 0-2 2m4-2m7: 0-0 3m+: 0-0
Track: LH: 0-1 RH: 0-3 Tight: 0-3 Gall: 0-1
Aids: Bl: 0-0 Vi: 0-0 Tstrap: 0-0 Ckp: 0-0
Best Rating: 87 4/04 MRas 2m1f110y good NHF

Has shown form in modest bumpers on a sound surface.

Oscar Wilde

12-y-o b g Arctic Lord-Topsy Bee (Be Friendly)
Mrs S Alner   R Alner

Placings:50/422/F014F/0P2/0-0   (4172)
2003/04: 24⁰G,

	Starts	1st	2nd	3rd	Win & Pl
Chases	1	0	0	0	
Career Total	15	1	3	0	10540
108 11/99 Winc 2m5f E(0-105)HCh				GD	£5381

Total win prize-money £5381

Going: Sf: 0-0 GS: 0-0 Gd: 0-1 GF: - Fm: 0-0
Distance: 2m/2m3: 0-0 2m4-2m7: 0-0 3m+: 0-1
Track: LH: 0-1 RH: 0-0 Tight: 0-0 Gall: 0-1
Aids: Bl: 0-0 Vi: 0-0 Tstrap: 0-0 Ckp: 0-0
Best Rating: 108 11/99 Winc 2m5f   good   Ch

Oscars Vision (IRE)

71   37
4-y-o ch f Oscar Schindler (IRE)-Eyelet (IRE) (Satco (FR))
B W Duke   Brendan W Duke Racing

Placings:10   (2987)
2003/04: 12¹GF, 16⁰G,

	Starts	1st	2nd	3rd	Win & Pl
NH Flat	1	1	0	0	2681
Hurdles	1	0	0	0	0
Career Total	2	1	0	0	2681
88 12/03 Newb 1m4f110yH NHF				G-F	£2681

Total win prize-money £2681

Going: Sf: 0-0 GS: 0-0 Gd: 0-0 GF: - Fm: 1-1
Distance: 2m/2m3: 0-1 2m4-2m7: 0-0 3m+: 0-0
Track: LH: 1-1 RH: 0-1 Tight: 0-0 Gall: 0-0
Aids: Bl: 0-0 Vi: 0-0 Tstrap: 0-0 Ckp: 0-0
Best Rating: 88 12/03 Newb 1m4f110y gd-fm NHF

Won on debut at Newbury in a Junior bumper over 12 furlongs at odds of 100/1 in December 2003; well beaten on hurdling debut; acts on good to firm.

Oso Magic

94   84
6-y-o b g Teenoso (USA)-Scottish Clover (Scottish Reel)
Mrs S J Smith   Michael Thompson

Placings:66   (4732)
2003/04: 16⁰G, 17⁵G,

	Starts	1st	2nd	3rd	Win & Pl
Hurdles	2	0	0	0	0
Career Total	2	0	0	0	0

Going: Sf: 0-0 GS: 0-0 Gd: 0-2 GF: - Fm: 0-0
Distance: 2m/2m3: 0-2 2m4-2m7: 0-0 3m+: 0-0
Track: LH: 0-1 RH: 0-1 Tight: 0-0 Gall: 0-0
Aids: Bl: 0-0 Vi: 0-0 Tstrap: 0-0 Ckp: 0-0

Best Rating: 84   12/03 Weth 2m   good   Hdl

Big type, will make a chaser in time; showed a little ability on debut over hurdles at Wetherby in December.

Osoglad

92f   81f

6-y-o b m Teenoso (USA)-Gladys Emmanuel (Idiots Delight)
Jane Southcombe P L Southcombe

Placings: 35P   (1334)
2003/04: 17³GF, 17⁵GF, 17ᵖGF,

	Starts	1st	2nd	3rd	Win & Pl
NH Flat	3	0	0	1	285
Career Total	3	0	0	1	285

Going: Sf: 0-0 GS: 0-0 Gd: 0-0 GF: - Fm: 0-3
Distance: 2m/2m3: 0-3 2m4-2m7: 0-0 3m+: 0-0
Track: LH: 0-1 RH: 0-2 Tight: 0-1 Gall: 0-0
Aids: Bl: 0-0 Vi: 0-0 Tstrap: 0-0 Ckp: 0-0
Best Rating: 88   6/03 Hrfd 2m1f   gd-fm NHF

Out of a mare who won a couple of 2m chases; springer in the market when close third on debut in Hereford bumper June 2003; easy to back when disappointing at Newton Abbot next time; pulled up lame third run.

Ososhot

102   106

11-y-o b g Teenoso (USA)-Duckdown (Blast)
A J Wilson Favourites Racing

Placings: 1/U/52564F5/060113/0F2003-206354   (4343)
2003/04: 17²GS, 22⁴GS, 23⁶GS, 22³S, 24⁵GS, 21⁴GS,

	Starts	1st	2nd	3rd	Win & Pl
Hurdles	6	0	1	1	1908
Career Total	27	3	3	3	14309
114	1/02	Winc	2m6f	D(0-115)HHdl	G-S	£3556
104	12/01	Winc	2m6f	F(0-100)HHdl	GD	£2709
116	3/99	Ludl	2m	H NHF	SFT	£1493

Total win prize-money £7759

Going: Sf: 0-1 GS: 0-4 Gd: 0-1 GF: - Fm: 0-0
Distance: 2m/2m3: 0-1 2m4-2m7: 0-3 3m+: 0-2
Track: LH: 0-3 RH: 0-3 Tight: 0-1 Gall: 0-0
Aids: Bl: 0-0 Vi: 0-0 Tstrap: 0-0 Ckp: 0-0
Best Rating: 116   11/00 MRas 2m1f110y gd-sft Hdl

Moderate staying hurdler; goes well at Wincanton; acts on good and soft ground.

Ossmoses (IRE)

97(99h)   (71h)104+

7-y-o gr g Roselier (FR)-Sugarstown (Sassafras (FR))
D M Forster D M Forster

Placings: 4315   (3721)
2003/04: 23⁴G, 25³G, 25¹S, 25⁵S,

	Starts	1st	2nd	3rd	Win & Pl
Hurdles	1	0	0	0	366
Chases	3	1	0	1	7141
Career Total	4	1	0	1	7507
104	1/04	Weth	3m1f	E Ch	SFT	£5400

Total win prize-money £5400

Going: Sf: 1-2 GS: 0-0 Gd: 0-2 GF: - Fm: 0-0
Distance: 2m/2m3: 0-0 2m4-2m7: 0-0 3m+: 1-3
Track: LH: 1-4 RH: 0-0 Tight: 0-0 Gall: 0-0
Aids: Bl: 0-0 Vi: 0-0 Tstrap: 0-0 Ckp: 0-0
Best Rating: 104   1/04 Weth 3m1f   soft   Ch

Chasing-type; not disgraced on hurdling bow at Wetherby in

May; took weak novices' chase at Wetherby in January; will stay beyond three miles; acts on soft.

Ottoman (AUS)

(101h)   (98h)

8-y-o br g Grand Lodge (USA)-Cushti (AUS) (Gypsy Kingdom (AUS))
R C Guest Leslie John Garrett

Placings: 301000U   (3981)
2003/04: 16³G, 16⁶S, 19¹G, 16⁸GS, 19⁰G, 18⁰HY, 20⁰G,

	Starts	1st	2nd	3rd	Win & Pl
Hurdles	6	1	0	1	2850
Chases	1	0	0	0	0
Career Total	7	1	0	1	2850
98	12/03	MRas	2m3f110yF Hdl		GD	£2290

Total win prize-money £2290

Going: Sf: 0-2 GS: 0-1 Gd: 1-4 GF: - Fm: 0-0
Distance: 2m/2m3: 1-4 2m4-2m7: 0-0 3m+: 0-0
Track: LH: 0-5 RH: 1-2 Tight: 1-3 Gall: 0-0
Aids: Bl: 0-0 Vi: 0-0 Tstrap: 0-0 Ckp: 0-0
Best Rating: 98   12/03 MRas 2m3f110y   good   Hdl

Moderate novice hurdler; ex-Australian middle-distance Flat winner; showed promise before winning a maiden hurdle at Market Rasen; stays two miles three.

Oubus Hill (IRE)

81(82h)   (43h)59

8-y-o b g Zaffaran (USA)-Gamerstown Queen (Push On)
R F Fisher Great Head House Estates Limited

Placings: 60PP0FO0   (4390)
2003/04: 22⁶G, 24⁰GS, 20⁰S, 21ᵖG, 19⁰GS, 25ᴴHY, 20⁰HY, 27⁰G,

	Starts	1st	2nd	3rd	Win & Pl
Hurdles	4	0	0	0	0
Chases	4	0	0	0	0
Career Total	8	0	0	0	0

Going: Sf: 0-3 GS: 0-2 Gd: 0-3 GF: - Fm: 0-0
Distance: 2m/2m3: 0-1 2m4-2m7: 0-4 3m+: 0-3
Track: LH: 0-6 RH: 0-2 Tight: 0-5 Gall: 0-0
Aids: Bl: 0-0 Vi: 0-0 Tstrap: 0-0 Ckp: 0-0
Best Rating: 59   1/04 Catt 2m3f   gd-sft   Ch

Oudalmuteena (IRE)

96(72c)   (38c)94

9-y-o b g Lahib (USA)-Roxy Music (IRE) (Song)
C J Gray Riverdance Consortium

Placings: 040/060123P400P/4P04400/0-0005020600   (4632)
2003/04: 21⁰G, 22⁰GS, 22⁶G, 24⁵G, 26⁰GS, 22²HY, 22⁰G, 16⁶GS, 19⁰G, 24⁰G,

	Starts	1st	2nd	3rd	Win & Pl
Hurdles	10	0	1	0	734
Career Total	32	1	2	1	4877
88	12/00	Extr	2m3f	F(0-100)HHdl	HVY	£2548

Total win prize-money £2548

Going: Sf: 0-1 GS: 0-3 Gd: 0-6 GF: - Fm: 0-0
Distance: 2m/2m3: 0-6 2m4-2m7: 0-6 3m+: 0-3
Track: LH: 0-2 RH: 0-8 Tight: 0-6 Gall: 0-0
Aids: Bl: 0-0 Vi: 0-1 Tstrap: 0-0 Ckp: 0-3
Best Rating: 94   2/02 Winc 2m   soft   Hdl

Plating-class hurdler; stays three miles; best suited by soft ground.

Oulton Broad

107   115+

8-y-o b g Midyan (USA)-Lady Quachita (USA) (Sovereign Dancer (USA))
F Jordan (R Ford 19/3) Marcus Reeder

Placings: 55F31111P/000PP/003060P4P/641412U631-011 (4537)
2003/04: 24⁹G, 21¹S, 16¹GS,

	Starts	1st	2nd	3rd	Win & Pl
Hurdles	3	2	0	0	5838
Career Total	36	9	1	3	36857
115	3/04	Ludl	2m	F Hdl	G-S	£2968
110	3/04	Wwck	2m5f	F Hdl	SFT	£2870
104	10/02	Hayd	2m7f110yD(0-115)HHdl	GD	£4257
105	6/02	Uttx	2m4f110yD(0-120)HHdl	G-F	£5330
104	6/02	Prth	2m4f110yD(0-115)HHdl	GS	£3396
122	4/00	Asct	2m4f	C(0-130)HHdl	GD	£6402
102	3/00	Hrfd	2m4f110yD Hdl	SFT	£3497
115	2/00	Folk	2m1f110yF(0-95)HHdl	SFT	£2366
106	2/00	Hrfd	2m3f110yF Hdl	GD	£2534

Total win prize-money £33622

Going: Sf: 1-1 GS: 1-1 Gd: 0-1 GF: - Fm: 0-0
Distance: 2m/2m3: 1-1 2m4-2m7: 1-1 3m+: 0-1
Track: LH: 1-2 RH: 1-1 Tight: 0-0 Gall: 0-1
Aids: Bl: 0-0 Vi: 0-0 Tstrap: 0-0 Ckp: 2-3
Best Rating: 122   4/00 Asct 2m4f   soft   Hdl

Modest hurdler; stays three miles, but effective at much shorter; acts on soft, but handles good ground.

Our Armageddon (NZ)

119(114h)   (131+h)153+

7-y-o b g Sky Chase (NZ)-Monte D'Oro (NZ) (Cache Of Gold (USA))
R C Guest Leslie John Garrett

Placings: 21301-2111121P14   (4648)
2003/04: 21²G, 17¹G, 20¹G, 19¹S, 20¹G, 16²S, 20¹G, 16ᵖG, 21¹G, 20⁴G,

	Starts	1st	2nd	3rd	Win & Pl
Chases	10	6	2	0	99203
Career Total	15	8	3	1	111883
153	3/04	Chel	2m5f	A Ch	GD	£46400
150	1/04	Hayd	2m4f	B Ch	GD	£20124
140	12/03	Weth	2m4f110yC Ch	GD	£9341
144	11/03	Asct	2m3f110yD Ch	SFT	£7171
131	11/03	Ayr	2m4f	D Ch	GD	£5557
122	11/03	Kels	2m1f	E Ch	GD	£3808
131	3/03	MRas	2m1f110yC Hdl	GD	£3555
111	12/02	Newc	2m	E Hdl	SFT	£3555

Total win prize-money £102996

Going: Sf: 1-2 GS: 0-0 Gd: 5-8 GF: - Fm: 0-0
Distance: 2m/2m3: 1-3 2m4-2m7: 5-7 3m+: 0-0
Track: LH: 5-9 RH: 1-1 Tight: 1-3 Gall: 1-2
Aids: Bl: 0-0 Vi: 0-0 Tstrap: 0-0 Ckp: 0-0
Best Rating: 153   3/04 Chel 2m5f   good   Ch

Smart novice chaser; won three uncompetitive events over fences in November; quite impressive when following up at Wetherby the following month; beaten by Caracciola at Haydock, but returned there to win his fifth race over fences in January; pulled up after a bad mistake in the Arkle, but came out again two days later to win the Cathcart, making all and jumping brilliantly for a game success; disappointing just two weeks later at Aintree; stays two and a half miles and acts ground good or softer; could still be anything.

Our Ben

101f   **109+f**

5-y-o ch g Presenting-Forest Pride (IRE) (Be My Native (USA))
W P Mullins   Trevor Hemmings

Placings: 10   **(4400)**
2003/04: 16¹YS, 16⁹G,

	Starts	1st	2nd	3rd	Win & Pl
NH Flat	2	1	0	0	4866
Career Total	2	1	0	0	4866
106 2/04 Limk 2m	NHF			Y-S	£4866
			Total win prize-money £4866

Going:	Sf: 0-0 GS: 0-0 Gd: 0-1 GF: - Fm: 0-0
Distance:	2m/2m3: 1-2 2m4-2m7: 0-0 3m+: 0-0
Track:	LH: 0-1 RH: 0-0 Tight: 0-0 Gall: 0-0
Aids:	Bl: 0-0 Vi: 0-0 Tstrap: 0-0 Ckp: 0-0
Best Rating:	109 3/04 Chel 2m110y good NHF

Well-backed winner of soft ground bumper at Limerick in February; looks to have a bright future.

Our Dream (IRE)

105   **101+**

5-y-o b m Bob Back (USA)-Baybush (Boreen (FR))
Mrs M Reveley   Scart Stud

Placings: 5-3221   **(3704)**
2003/04: 16³GS, 21²GS, 22²HY, 20¹HY,

	Starts	1st	2nd	3rd	Win & Pl
NH Flat	1	0	0	1	338
Hurdles	3	1	2	0	6534
Career Total	5	1	2	1	6872
101 2/04 Chep 2m4f	E Hdl			HVY	£3770
			Total win prize-money £3770

Going:	Sf: 1-2 GS: 0-2 Gd: 0-0 GF: - Fm: 0-0
Distance:	2m/2m3: 0-1 2m4-2m7: 1-3 3m+: 0-0
Track:	LH: 1-4 RH: 0-0 Tight: 0-0 Gall: 0-1
Aids:	Bl: 0-0 Vi: 0-0 Tstrap: 0-0 Ckp: 0-0
Best Rating:	101 2/04 Chep 2m4f heavy Hdl

Modest form in bumpers; very easy winner of modest 2m 4f mares' only novices hurdle at Chepstow February 2004; handles soft ground; improving.

Our Ethel

85   **71**

6-y-o ch m Be My Chief (USA)-Annes Gift (Ballymoss)
Mrs M Reveley   Minster Commercials

Placings: 10/00-3   **(0170)**
2003/04: 20³GF,

	Starts	1st	2nd	3rd	Win & Pl
Hurdles	1	0	0	1	775
Career Total	5	1	0	1	3096
86 2/02 Muss 2m	H NHF			SFT	£2320
			Total win prize-money £2321

Going:	Sf: 0-0 GS: 0-0 Gd: 0-0 GF: - Fm: 0-1
Distance:	2m/2m3: 0-0 2m4-2m7: 0-1 3m+: 0-0
Track:	LH: 0-1 RH: 0-0 Tight: 0-0 Gall: 0-0
Aids:	Bl: 0-0 Vi: 0-0 Tstrap: 0-0 Ckp: 0-0
Best Rating:	86 2/03 Ludl 2m good NHF

From a good family, she made a winning debut on soft ground in a Musselburgh bumper, February 2002; showed little on hurdling bow at Wetherby in May.

Our House (IRE)

89   **89+**

5-y-o ch g Carroll House-Farinella (IRE) (Salmon Leap (USA))
M C Pipe   D A Johnson

Placings: 4P0   **(3775)**
2003/04: 19⁴G, 19⁹S, 16⁹G,

	Starts	1st	2nd	3rd	Win & Pl
Hurdles	3	0	0	0	0
Career Total	3	0	0	0	0

Going:	Sf: 0-1 GS: 0-0 Gd: 0-2 GF: - Fm: 0-0
Distance:	2m/2m3: 0-2 2m4-2m7: 0-1 3m+: 0-0
Track:	LH: 0-0 RH: 0-3 Tight: 0-1 Gall: 0-0
Aids:	Bl: 0-0 Vi: 0-0 Tstrap: 0-0 Ckp: 0-0
Best Rating:	90 12/03 Tntn 2m3f110y good Hdl

Half-brother to high-class chaser Beef Or Slamon; pulled too hard on debut; held since.

Our Imperial Bay (USA)

89   **62**

5-y-o b g Smart Strike (CAN)-Heat Lightning (USA) (Summer Squall (USA))
R M Stronge   Mrs Bernice Stronge

Placings: 65-6P655   **(1373)**
2003/04: 16⁶G, 20⁰G, 20⁶G, 17⁵GF, 24⁵GF,

	Starts	1st	2nd	3rd	Win & Pl
Hurdles	5	0	0	0	0
Career Total	7	0	0	0	0

Going:	Sf: 0-0 GS: 0-0 Gd: 0-3 GF: - Fm: 0-2
Distance:	2m/2m3: 0-2 2m4-2m7: 0-3 3m+: 0-1
Track:	LH: 0-5 RH: 0-0 Tight: 0-1 Gall: 0-0
Aids:	Bl: 0-2 Vi: 0-1 Tstrap: 0-0 Ckp: 0-0
Best Rating:	95 12/02 Newb 2m110y good Hdl

Our Jolly Swagman

110   **126+**

9-y-o b g Thowra (FR)-Queens Dowry (Dominion)
J W Mullins   F G Matthews

Placings: 50P6/U0P121/54131PU26/PPP3012P1-11P01P
                       (3138)
2003/04: 24¹GF, 28¹GS, 32²GF, 20⁰G, 24¹S, 33⁰G,

	Starts	1st	2nd	3rd	Win & Pl
Chases	6	3	0	0	18395
Career Total	34	9	6	2	46556
126 12/03 Ling	3m	D(0-125)HCh	SFT	£5590
121 5/03 Strf	3m4f	D(0-120)HCh	G-S	£6948
115 5/03 Chep	3m	D(0-125)HCh	G-F	£5856
119 4/03 NAbb	3m2f110yD(0-115)HCh		SFT	£6403
87 2/03 Folk	3m1f	F(0-90)HCh	SFT	£3523
103 1/02 Plum	2m4f	D(0-125)HCh	HVY	£3916
93 12/01 Plum	3m2f	F(0-110)HCh	GD	£3916
87 4/01 Plum	3m2f	F(0-90)HCh	SFT	£3038
77 1/01 Plum	3m2f	F(0-90)HCh	G-S	£3094
			Total win prize-money £42286

Going:	Sf: 1-1 GS: 1-1 Gd: 0-2 GF: - Fm: 1-2
Distance:	2m/2m3: 0-0 2m4-2m7: 0-1 3m+: 3-5
Track:	LH: 3-5 RH: 0-0 Tight: 2-2 Gall: 0-2
Aids:	Bl: 0-0 Vi: 3-5 Tstrap: 0-0 Ckp: 0-0
Best Rating:	126 12/03 Ling 3m soft Ch

Fair staying chaser; improved form when swapping usual cheekpieces for a visor when winning at Newton Abbot in April 2003; went on to complete hat-trick; acts on all types of ground and showed improved form again when winning at Lingfield in December; stays three and a quarter miles; acts on any ground.

Our Kev (IRE)

100   (96h)**96**

8-y-o b g Be My Native (USA)-Sunbath (Krayyan)
B G Powell   Mrs Jean R Bishop

Placings: 06P0/P-2561P   **(4209)**
2003/04: 24²GS, 21⁵GS, 25⁶S, 24¹G, 24³PG,

	Starts	1st	2nd	3rd	Win & Pl
Chases	5	1	1	0	4763
Career Total	10	1	1	0	4763
96 2/04 Muss 3m	F(0-95)HCh		GD	£3399
			Total win prize-money £3400

Going:	Sf: 0-1 GS: 0-2 Gd: 1-2 GF: - Fm: 0-0
Distance:	2m/2m3: 0-0 2m4-2m7: 0-1 3m+: 1-4
Track:	LH: 0-0 RH: 1-5 Tight: 1-2 Gall: 0-1
Aids:	Bl: 0-0 Vi: 0-0 Tstrap: 0-0 Ckp: 0-0
Best Rating:	96 2/04 Muss 3m good Ch

Moderate chaser; stays three miles; acts on good ground.

Our Lawman

63   **30**

5-y-o b g Shareef Dancer (USA)-Motoqua (Mtoto)
Mrs S J Smith   Trevor Hemmings

Placings: 050   **(4881)**
2003/04: 16⁰G, 17⁵HY, 17⁰GS,

	Starts	1st	2nd	3rd	Win & Pl
NH Flat	2	0	0	0	0
Hurdles	1	0	0	0	0
Career Total	3	0	0	0	0

Going:	Sf: 0-1 GS: 0-1 Gd: 0-1 GF: - Fm: 0-0
Distance:	2m/2m3: 0-3 2m4-2m7: 0-0 3m+: 0-0
Track:	LH: 0-1 RH: 0-2 Tight: 0-0 Gall: 0-1
Aids:	Bl: 0-0 Vi: 0-0 Tstrap: 0-0 Ckp: 0-0
Best Rating:	85 3/04 Carl 2m1f heavy NHF

Our Man Dennis

95   **85**

10-y-o b g Arzanni-Pendocks Polly (Grey Steel)
Mrs P Ford   Mrs S J Williams

Placings: 50/00/43450/PP/P0056P   **(4916)**
2003/04: 16⁶G, 24⁴G, 20⁰G, 16⁵GS, 19⁶G, 23⁰GS,

	Starts	1st	2nd	3rd	Win & Pl
Hurdles	1	0	0	0	0
Chases	5	0	0	0	0
Career Total	17	0	0	1	736

Going:	Sf: 0-0 GS: 0-3 Gd: 0-3 GF: - Fm: 0-0
Distance:	2m/2m3: 0-3 2m4-2m7: 0-1 3m+: 0-2
Track:	LH: 0-3 RH: 0-3 Tight: 0-2 Gall: 0-0
Aids:	Bl: 0-0 Vi: 0-0 Tstrap: 0-0 Ckp: 0-0
Best Rating:	85 4/04 Hrfd 2m3f good Ch

Our Men

79f   **73f**

5-y-o b g Classic Cliche (IRE)-Praise The Lord (Lord Gayle (USA))
C R Egerton   Nicholas Alexander

Placings:0   (0109)
2003/04: 16⁰S,

	Starts	1st	2nd	3rd	Win & Pl
NH Flat	1	0	0	0	
Career Total	1	0	0	0	

Going:	Sf: 0-1 GS: 0-0 Gd: 0-0 GF: - Fm: 0-0
Distance:	2m/2m3: 0-1 2m4-2m7: 0-0 3m+: 0-0
Track:	LH: 0-1 RH: 0-0 Tight: 0-0 Gall: 0-0
Aids:	Bl: 0-0 Vi: 0-0 Tstrap: 0-0 Ckp: 0-0
Best Rating:	73 5/03 Uttx 2m soft NHF

Our Paddy (IRE)

5-y-o b g Ali-Royal (IRE)-Lilting Air (IRE) (Glenstal (USA))
Mrs L C Jewell (W A Murphy 13/10) Ms Ann Cully

Placings:P   (1844)
2003/04: 16⁰G,

	Starts	1st	2nd	3rd	Win & Pl
Hurdles	1	0	0	0	
Career Total	1	0	0	0	

Going:	Sf: 0-0 GS: 0-0 Gd: 0-0 GF: - Fm: 0-0
Distance:	2m/2m3: 0-1 2m4-2m7: 0-0 3m+: 0-0
Track:	LH: 0-1 RH: 0-0 Tight: 0-1 Gall: 0-0
Aids:	Bl: 0-0 Vi: 0-0 Tstrap: 0-0 Ckp: 0-0

Our Prima Donna (IRE)

102   98

6-y-o ch m Be My Native (USA)-Stage Debut (Decent
Fellow)
Miss H C Knight GPS Racing

Placings:02340   (4574)
2003/04: 20⁹GS, 21²GS, 21³G, 22⁴G, 21⁰G,

	Starts	1st	2nd	3rd	Win & Pl
Hurdles	5	0	1	1	2048
Career Total	5	0	1	1	2048

Going:	Sf: 0-0 GS: 0-2 Gd: 0-3 GF: - Fm: 0-0
Distance:	2m/2m3: 0-0 2m4-2m7: 0-5 3m+: 0-0
Track:	LH: 0-1 RH: 0-4 Tight: 0-0 Gall: 0-2
Aids:	Bl: 0-0 Vi: 0-0 Tstrap: 0-0 Ckp: 0-0
Best Rating:	100 2/04 Winc 2m6f good Hdl

Placed in novice hurdles; should stay three miles.

Our Tommy

95   92

11-y-o ch g Ardross-Ina's Farewell (Random Shot)
A E Price Mrs H L Price

Placings:F/P501/6223PP-5605P   (4919)
2003/04: 21⁵GS, 20⁶S, 20⁰S, 19⁵G, 20⁰GS,

	Starts	1st	2nd	3rd	Win & Pl
Chases	5	0	0	0	0
Career Total	16	1	2	1	7200
92 3/02 Wwck 2m4f110yE(0-105)HCh GD £4046					
		Total win prize-money £4046			

Going:	Sf: 0-2 GS: 0-2 Gd: 0-1 GF: - Fm: 0-0
Distance:	2m/2m3: 0-0 2m4-2m7: 0-5 3m+: 0-0
Track:	LH: 0-3 RH: 0-2 Tight: 0-2 Gall: 0-1
Aids:	Bl: 0-0 Vi: 0-0 Tstrap: 0-0 Ckp: 0-0

Best Rating: 92   3/03   Leic   2m4f110y   gd-sft   Ch

Moderate chaser; winning pointer; best at two and a half
miles; likes good or soft ground.

Our Vic (IRE)

116(116h)   (147h)158+

6-y-o b g Old Vic-Shabra Princess (Buckskin (FR))
M C Pipe D A Johnson

Placings:111-2113   (4395)
2003/04: 16²GS, 19¹S, 24¹G, 24³G,

	Starts	1st	2nd	3rd	Win & Pl
Hurdles	1	0	1	0	11000
Chases	3	2	0	1	40515
Career Total	7	5	1	1	65684
151 2/04 Asct 3m110y A Ch GD £20825					
133 2/04 Extr 2m3f110yE Ch SFT £4290					
147 2/03 Winc 2m D(0-125)HHdl G-S £5073					
135 1/03 Tntn 2m3f110yD Hdl SFT £5427					
118 12/02 Extr 2m1f E Hdl SFT £3668					
		Total win prize-money £39284			

Going:	Sf: 1-1 GS: 0-1 Gd: 1-2 GF: - Fm: 0-0
Distance:	2m/2m3: 0-1 2m4-2m7: 1-1 3m+: 1-2
Track:	LH: 0-1 RH: 2-3 Tight: 0-0 Gall: 0-1
Aids:	Bl: 0-0 Vi: 0-0 Tstrap: 0-0 Ckp: 0-0
Best Rating:	158 3/04 Chel 3m110y good Ch

Smart novice chaser; won his first three hurdle races easily
from the front, before finishing second in the William Hill
Handicap Hurdle; facile victory on chase debut at Exeter in
testing ground; most impressive winner of Grade 2
Reynoldstown Chase at Ascot in February; third in the Royal
& SunAlliance Chase at Cheltenham; possibly best suited
going left-handed; effective over two and a half miles but
stays three; acts on soft ground; potentially very smart.

Ourman (IRE)

8-y-o b g Good Thyne (USA)-Magic Minstrel (Pitpan)
Mrs A Bell Mrs A Bell

Placings:0633/12C/U3U-12   (0364)
2003/04: 25¹G, 26²HY,

	Starts	1st	2nd	3rd	Win & Pl
Chases	2	1	1	0	4289
Career Total	12	2	2	3	9585
97 5/03 Hexm 3m1f H Ch GD £2233					
102 1/02 Sedg 3m3f E Ch HVY £3045					
		Total win prize-money £5278			

Going:	Sf: 0-1 GS: 0-0 Gd: 1-1 GF: - Fm: 0-0
Distance:	2m/2m3: 0-0 2m4-2m7: 0-0 3m+: 1-2
Track:	LH: 1-2 RH: 0-0 Tight: 0-0 Gall: 0-0
Aids:	Bl: 0-0 Vi: 0-0 Tstrap: 0-0 Ckp: 0-0
Best Rating:	102 5/03 Uttx 3m2f heavy Ch

Moderate hunter chaser; stays three and a half miles; acts
on soft ground.

Out Of The Shadows

91   113

8-y-o gr m Rock Hopper-Shadows Of Silver (Carwhite)
Mrs M Reveley Ms Linda Redmond

Placings:0/03/F1416/3053134P424-5   (0173)
2003/04: 16⁵GF,

	Starts	1st	2nd	3rd	Win & Pl
Hurdles	1	0	0	0	0
Career Total	20	3	1	4	17692

112   11/02   Hayd   2m   D(0-120)HHdl   GD   £3737
112   1/02   Donc   2m110y   E Hdl   GD   £3290
107   11/01   Hayd   2m   D Hdl   GD   £3535
Total win prize-money £10563

Going:	Sf: 0-0 GS: 0-0 Gd: 0-0 GF: - Fm: 0-1
Distance:	2m/2m3: 0-1 2m4-2m7: 0-0 3m+: 0-0
Track:	LH: 0-1 RH: 0-0 Tight: 0-0 Gall: 0-0
Aids:	Bl: 0-0 Vi: 0-0 Tstrap: 0-0 Ckp: 0-1
Best Rating:	113 3/03 Weth 2m gd-fm Hdl

Fair handicap hurdler; acts on good ground and is effective
at around two miles.

Out Of Westwood

6-y-o ch m Out Of Hand-Brandy Season (High Season)
Mrs S Gardner J Sluggett

Placings:P   (1226)
2003/04: 17⁰GF,

	Starts	1st	2nd	3rd	Win & Pl
NH Flat	1	0	0	0	
Career Total	1	0	0	0	

Going:	Sf: 0-0 GS: 0-0 Gd: 0-0 GF: - Fm: 0-1
Distance:	2m/2m3: 0-1 2m4-2m7: 0-0 3m+: 0-0
Track:	LH: 0-1 RH: 0-0 Tight: 0-1 Gall: 0-0
Aids:	Bl: 0-0 Vi: 0-0 Tstrap: 0-0 Ckp: 0-0

Outlaw Express (IRE)

100   (92h)73

8-y-o b g Un Desperado (FR)-Surprise Packet (Torus)
P R Webber Economic Security 2

Placings:35006000P/3002P   (4753)
2003/04: 21³GF, 19⁰G, 23⁰G, 24²G, 26⁰G,

	Starts	1st	2nd	3rd	Win & Pl
Chases	5	0	1	1	1414
Career Total	14	0	1	2	1686

Going:	Sf: 0-0 GS: 0-0 Gd: 0-4 GF: - Fm: 0-1
Distance:	2m/2m3: 0-1 2m4-2m7: 0-1 3m+: 0-3
Track:	LH: 0-1 RH: 0-4 Tight: 0-3 Gall: 0-1
Aids:	Bl: 0-0 Vi: 0-1 Tstrap: 0-0 Ckp: 0-1
Best Rating:	106 5/01 Folk 2m1f110y gd-sft NHF

Moderate performer over fences.

Outside Investor (IRE)

100   85+

4-y-o b/br g Cadeaux Genereux-Desert Ease (IRE) (Green
Desert (USA))
Ferdy Murphy (D K Weld 16/10) Anthony O'Gorman

Placings:510   (3472)
2003/04: 16⁵GS, 16¹GF, 16⁰GF,

	Starts	1st	2nd	3rd	Win & Pl
Hurdles	3	1	0	0	3387
Career Total	3	1	0	0	3387
85 1/04 Muss 2m E Hdl G-F £3386					
		Total win prize-money £3387			

Going:	Sf: 0-0 GS: 0-1 Gd: 0-0 GF: - Fm: 1-2
Distance:	2m/2m3: 1-3 2m4-2m7: 0-0 3m+: 0-0
Track:	LH: 0-1 RH: 1-2 Tight: 1-3 Gall: 0-0
Aids:	Bl: 1-2 Vi: 0-0 Tstrap: 0-0 Ckp: 0-0

Best Rating: 85 1/04 Muss 2m   gd-fm Hdl

Modest maiden on the Flat; blinkered when narrow winner of poor event at Musselburgh in January; acts on fast.

Outside The Door (IRE)

(98h)   (84h)
8-y-o b g Husyan (USA)-Twilight Sunset (Deep Run)
Mrs J R Buckley (A L T Moore 20/7) Mrs J R Buckley

Placings:0/0000-45P463F   (2922)
2003/04: 20⁴Y, 20⁵GF, 24⁸PGY, 20⁴Y, 19⁶G, 19³GS, 17⁷FG,

	Starts	1st	2nd	3rd	Win & Pl
NH Flat	2	0	0	0	208
Hurdles	4	0	0	1	757
Chases	1	0	0	0	0
Career Total	**12**	**0**	**0**	**1**	**965**

Going:	Sf: 0-0 GS: 0-1 Gd: 0-2 GF: - Fm: 0-1
Distance:	2m/2m3: 0-2 2m4-2m7: 0-4 3m+: 0-1
Track:	LH: 0-1 RH: 0-2 Tight: 0-3 Gall: 0-0
Aids:	Bl: 0-0 Vi: 0-0 Tstrap: 0-0 Ckp: 0-0
Best Rating: 91	6/03 Wxfd 2m4f gd-fm NHF

Plating-class hurdler; ex-Irish; stays two and a half miles; does not want the ground too soft.

Over Bridge

101   87
6-y-o b g Overbury (IRE)-Celtic Bridge (Celtic Cone)
Mrs S M Johnson I K Johnson

Placings:00500PR00-15B020   (4716)
2003/04: 19¹GS, 19⁵GS, 22⁸G, 19⁴G, 19²GS, 21⁰G,

	Starts	1st	2nd	3rd	Win & Pl
Hurdles	6	1	1	0	4214
Career Total	**15**	**1**	**1**	**0**	**4214**
86	11/03 Hrfd	2m3f110yE(0-100)HHdl		G-F	£3122

Total win prize-money £3122

Going:	Sf: 0-0 GS: 0-2 Gd: 0-3 GF: - Fm: 1-1
Distance:	2m/2m3: 0-2 2m4-2m7: 1-4 3m+: 0-0
Track:	LH: 0-4 RH: 1-2 Tight: 0-0 Gall: 0-1
Aids:	Bl: 0-0 Vi: 0-0 Tstrap: 0-0 Ckp: 0-0
Best Rating: 87	3/04 Newb 2m3f gd-sft Hdl

Plating-class hurdler; better run when scoring at Hereford in November; stays 2m 3f; effective on fast ground.

Over The Creek

93   100+
5-y-o br g Over The River (FR)-Solo Girl (IRE) (Le Bavard (FR))
M C Pipe D A Johnson

Placings:5B2   (3376)
2003/04: 19⁵G, 18⁸HY, 16²S,

	Starts	1st	2nd	3rd	Win & Pl
Hurdles	3	0	1	0	1009
Career Total	**3**	**0**	**1**	**0**	**1009**

Going:	Sf: 0-2 GS: 0-0 Gd: 0-1 GF: - Fm: 0-0
Distance:	2m/2m3: 0-2 2m4-2m7: 0-1 3m+: 0-0
Track:	LH: 0-1 RH: 0-2 Tight: 0-0 Gall: 0-0
Aids:	Bl: 0-0 Vi: 0-0 Tstrap: 0-0 Ckp: 0-0
Best Rating: 100	1/04 Winc 2m soft Hdl

Has shown ability in novice hurdles; probably stays 2m 4f; acts on soft.

Over The First (IRE)

111(111h)   (130h)134
9-y-o b/br g Orchestra-Ruby Lodge (Peacock (FR))
C F Swan Trotters Ind Trading Syndicate

Placings:0030/135015016/031610PU5310/0U21141F40-30FP051615   (4580a)
2003/04: 20³YS, 19⁰GY, 18⁵GY, 16⁸S, 19⁹S, 17⁵S, 20¹S, 21⁸G, 16¹S, 20⁵Y,

	Starts	1st	2nd	3rd	Win & Pl
Hurdles	1	0	0	0	0
Chases	9	2	0	1	26991
Career Total	**45**	**11**	**1**	**5**	**97448**
131	3/04 Punc	2m HCh	SFT	£13753
134	2/04 Navn	2m4f (0-130)HCh	SFT	£10315
130	1/03 Navn	2m4f HHdl	SFT	£12662
119	11/02 Fair	2m HHdl	SFT	£15153
115	11/02 Clon	2m (67-109)HHdl	HVY	£3809
119	3/02 Navn	2m1f (0-127)HCh	SH	£7975
126	11/01 Cork	2m (0-109)HCh	Y-S	£6677
104	10/01 Tipp	2m Ch	HVY	£5842
120	1/01 Thur	2m Hdl	HVY	£6677
116	11/00 Thur	2m Hdl	SFT	£2760
104	8/00 Tral	2m1f NHF	SFT	£3588

Total win prize-money £89214

Going:	Sf: 2-5 GS: 0-0 Gd: 0-1 GF: - Fm: 0-0
Distance:	2m/2m3: 1-6 2m4-2m7: 1-4 3m+: 0-0
Track:	LH: 1-6 RH: 1-4 Tight: 0-0 Gall: 0-0
Aids:	Bl: 0-0 Vi: 0-0 Tstrap: 0-0 Ckp: 0-0
Best Rating: 134	2/04 Navn 2m4f soft Ch

Fair Irish handicap hurdler/chaser; effective at around two miles; goes well on a soft surface.

Over The Hill (IRE)

89(106h)   (90h)88
12-y-o b g Over The River (FR)-Joint Equity (Callernish)
J A Pickering (S J Magnier 2/5) A Hartgrove

Placings:P/12PUP/3F0R/526113023-3P23P   (0818)
2003/04: 27³S, 30⁸PG, 25²GF, 26³GF, 24⁴FG,

	Starts	1st	2nd	3rd	Win & Pl
Hurdles	2	0	0	1	507
Chases	3	0	1	1	1427
Career Total	**24**	**3**	**4**	**5**	**12788**
90	10/02 Sedg	3m3f110yF(0-100)HHdl	GD	£2618
78	10/02 Sedg	2m5f110yG(0-90)HHdl	GD	£2170
87	5/99 Ctml	3m2f H Ch	GD	£1943

Total win prize-money £6731

Going:	Sf: 0-1 GS: 0-0 Gd: 0-2 GF: - Fm: 0-2
Distance:	2m/2m3: 0-0 2m4-2m7: 0-0 3m+: 0-5
Track:	LH: 0-2 RH: 0-2 Tight: 0-2 Gall: 0-0
Aids:	Bl: 0-3 Vi: 0-2 Tstrap: 0-0 Ckp: 0-0
Best Rating: 93	4/00 Ayr 3m3f110y good Ch

Plating-class hurdler/chaser; won twice at Sedgefield in October 2002; stays 3m 3f but effective at shorter; acts on a sound surface; has worn blinkers.

Over The Kohls (IRE)

6-y-o ch g Over The River (FR)-Forever Second (IRE) (Parliament)
John R Upson T L Brooks

Placings:P   (2844)
2003/04: 16⁸PGS,

	Starts	1st	2nd	3rd	Win & Pl
NH Flat	1	0	0	0	

Career Total   1   0   0   0

Going:	Sf: 0-0 GS: 0-1 Gd: 0-0 GF: - Fm: 0-0
Distance:	2m/2m3: 0-1 2m4-2m7: 0-0 3m+: 0-0
Track:	LH: 0-1 RH: 0-0 Tight: 0-0 Gall: 0-0
Aids:	Bl: 0-0 Vi: 0-0 Tstrap: 0-0 Ckp: 0-0

Over The Storm (IRE)

112   138+
7-y-o b g Over The River (FR)-Naas (Ballymore)
Miss H C Knight Hogarth Racing

Placings:1230-321   (3186)
2003/04: 24³GS, 25²G, 24¹G,

	Starts	1st	2nd	3rd	Win & Pl
Chases	3	1	1	1	18542
Career Total	**7**	**2**	**2**	**2**	**26588**
140	1/04 Sand	3m110y C(0-135)HCh	GD	£15109
112	12/02 Donc	3m D Ch	GD	£4904

Total win prize-money £20014

Going:	Sf: 0-0 GS: 0-1 Gd: 1-2 GF: - Fm: 0-0
Distance:	2m/2m3: 0-0 2m4-2m7: 0-0 3m+: 1-3
Track:	LH: 0-1 RH: 1-2 Tight: 0-1 Gall: 0-0
Aids:	Bl: 0-0 Vi: 0-0 Tstrap: 0-0 Ckp: 0-0
Best Rating: 140	1/04 Sand 3m110y good Ch

Useful chaser; winning Irish pointer; stays three miles and looks the sort to get much farther; acts on good and easy ground.

Over To You Bert

88   59
5-y-o b g Overbury (IRE)-Silvers Era (Balidar)
R J Hodges (Mrs P N Dutfield 21/6) Unity Farm Holiday Centre Ltd

Placings:0-5   (0709)
2003/04: 17⁵GF,

	Starts	1st	2nd	3rd	Win & Pl
Hurdles	1	0	0	0	0
Career Total	**2**	**0**	**0**	**0**	**0**

Going:	Sf: 0-0 GS: 0-0 Gd: 0-0 GF: - Fm: 0-1
Distance:	2m/2m3: 0-1 2m4-2m7: 0-0 3m+: 0-0
Track:	LH: 0-1 RH: 0-0 Tight: 0-1 Gall: 0-0
Aids:	Bl: 0-0 Vi: 0-0 Tstrap: 0-0 Ckp: 0-0
Best Rating: 59	6/03 NAbb 2m1f gd-fm Hdl

Over Zealous (IRE)

108   (59h)107
12-y-o ch g Over The River (FR)-Chatty Di (Le Bavard (FR))
John R Upson Middleham Park Racing X

Placings:0000/245/U11112/22P4RP/05361PPP/322411-61U65U   (4757)
2003/04: 30⁶GS, 29¹G, 27⁰GS, 26⁶G, 25⁵G, 25⁰S,

	Starts	1st	2nd	3rd	Win & Pl
Chases	6	1	0	0	4498
Career Total	**39**	**8**	**6**	**2**	**36317**
103	12/03 Wwck	3m5f	D(0-120)HCh	GD	£4497
106	3/03 Wwck	3m5f	E(0-110)HCh	GD	£4030
106	2/03 Chep	3m2f110yF(0-90)HCh	G-S	£3688
97	1/02 Wwck	3m2f	F(0-95)HCh	SFT	£2705
98	1/00 Newc	3m6f	D(0-125)HCh	SFT	£3753
93	12/99 Sedg	3m3f	F(0-110)HCh	G-S	£3579
95	11/99 Newc	3m	F(0-90)HCh	G-S	£2866

93   11/99 Sedg   3m3f   F(0-100)HCh   GD   £2670
                                    Total win prize-money £27792

Going:	Sf: 0-1 GS: 0-2 Gd: 1-3 GF: - Fm: 0-0
Distance:	2m/2m3: 0-0 2m4-2m7: 0-0 3m+: 1-6
Track:	LH: 1-2 RH: 0-3 Tight: 0-2 Gall: 0-1
Aids:	Bl: 0-4 Vi: 1-2 Tstrap: 0-0 Ckp: 0-0
Best Rating:	106 3/03 Wwck 3m5f good Ch

Moderate handicap chaser; genuine and stays very well; best on ground good and softer.

Overlord (IRE)

87   70

7-y-o b g Lord Americo-Straddler's Hill (IRE) (Torus)
B De Haan The Longhedge Partnership

Placings:000-3   (0289)
2003/04: 20³GS,

	Starts	1st	2nd	3rd	Win & Pl
Hurdles	1	0	0	1	760
Career Total	4	0	0	1	760

Going:	Sf: 0-0 GS: 0-1 Gd: 0-0 GF: - Fm: 0-0
Distance:	2m/2m3: 0-0 2m4-2m7: 0-1 3m+: 0-0
Track:	LH: 0-1 RH: 0-0 Tight: 0-1 Gall: 0-0
Aids:	Bl: 0-0 Vi: 0-0 Tstrap: 0-0 Ckp: 0-0
Best Rating:	85 11/02 Winc 2m good NHF

Overserved

87   63

5-y-o b/br g Supreme Leader-Divine Comedy (IRE) (Phardante (FR))
A Parker Mr & Mrs Raymond Anderson Green

Placings:0   (3356)
2003/04: 18⁰S,

	Starts	1st	2nd	3rd	Win & Pl
Hurdles	1	0	0	0	
Career Total	1	0	0	0	

Going:	Sf: 0-1 GS: 0-0 Gd: 0-0 GF: - Fm: 0-0
Distance:	2m/2m3: 0-1 2m4-2m7: 0-0 3m+: 0-0
Track:	LH: 0-1 RH: 0-0 Tight: 0-1 Gall: 0-0
Aids:	Bl: 0-0 Vi: 0-0 Tstrap: 0-0 Ckp: 0-0
Best Rating:	63 1/04 Kels 2m2f soft Hdl

Overstrand (IRE)

119   135+

5-y-o b g In The Wings-Vaison La Romaine (Arctic Tern (USA))
Mrs M Reveley F F Racing Services Partnership IV

Placings:360-11110240   (4326)
2003/04: 20¹G, 17¹G, 17¹HY, 16¹GS, 16⁶S, 21²G, 21⁴GS, 16⁶S,

	Starts	1st	2nd	3rd	Win & Pl
Hurdles	8	4	1	0	40978
Career Total	11	4	1	1	42089

135 12/03 Sand   2m110y A(0-140)HHdl   G-S £29000
116 11/03 Carl   2m1f   E Hdl   HVY £2759
114 11/03 MRas   2m1f110yE Hdl   GD   £3017
99   5/03 Prth   2m4f110yE Hdl   GD   £4260
                                    Total win prize-money £39037

Going:	Sf: 1-3 GS: 1-2 Gd: 2-3 GF: - Fm: 0-0
Distance:	2m/2m3: 3-5 2m4-2m7: 1-3 3m+: 0-0
Track:	LH: 0-4 RH: 4-8 Tight: 1-1 Gall: 0-0
Aids:	Bl: 0-0 Vi: 0-0 Tstrap: 0-0 Ckp: 0-0
Best Rating:	135 12/03 Sand 2m110y gd-sft Hdl

Useful hurdler; won the 2003 William Hill Handicap Hurdle at Sandown; beaten back in novice company since; effective from two to two and a half miles; acts on good and soft ground.

Overton Rose

7-y-o b m Cut The Mustard (IRE)-Palmy (USA) (Buckfinder (USA))
J R Bewley R Bewley

Placings:00   (3358)
2003/04: 17⁰GF, 16⁰S,

	Starts	1st	2nd	3rd	Win & Pl
NH Flat	1	0	0	0	0
Hurdles	1	0	0	0	0
Career Total	2	0	0	0	

Going:	Sf: 0-1 GS: 0-0 Gd: 0-0 GF: - Fm: 0-1
Distance:	2m/2m3: 0-2 2m4-2m7: 0-0 3m+: 0-0
Track:	LH: 0-1 RH: 0-1 Tight: 0-1 Gall: 0-0
Aids:	Bl: 0-0 Vi: 0-0 Tstrap: 0-0 Ckp: 0-0

Owen's Pet (IRE)

10-y-o b g Alphabatim (USA)-Ballinlovane (Le Moss)
Miss S A Loggin Miss N A McKim

Placings:63/P023/6-P3   (4703)
2003/04: 25⁸GS, 26³G,

	Starts	1st	2nd	3rd	Win & Pl
Chases	2	0	0	1	218
Career Total	9	0	1	3	2597

Going:	Sf: 0-0 GS: 0-1 Gd: 0-0 GF: - Fm: 0-0
Distance:	2m/2m3: 0-0 2m4-2m7: 0-0 3m+: 0-0
Track:	LH: 0-0 RH: 0-1 Tight: 0-2 Gall: 0-0
Aids:	Bl: 0-0 Vi: 0-0 Tstrap: 0-0 Ckp: 0-0
Best Rating:	99 4/02 Carl 3m2f gd-sft Ch

Owenweld

(94c)   (46c)

11-y-o ch g Weld-Owen Belle (Master Owen)
D R Gandolfo Edward M Kirtland

Placings:4/PP4P/5P/50P   (0833)
2003/04: 24⁵GF, 25⁰GF, 24⁴GF,

	Starts	1st	2nd	3rd	Win & Pl
Hurdles	1	0	0	0	0
Chases	2	0	0	0	0
Career Total	10	0	0	0	250

Going:	Sf: 0-0 GS: 0-0 Gd: 0-0 GF: - Fm: 0-3
Distance:	2m/2m3: 0-0 2m4-2m7: 0-0 3m+: 0-3
Track:	LH: 0-1 RH: 0-2 Tight: 0-0 Gall: 0-0
Aids:	Bl: 0-0 Vi: 0-0 Tstrap: 0-0 Ckp: 0-0
Best Rating:	84 9/98 Carl 2m4f110y good Hdl

Oxidor (IRE)

86   87

9-y-o br g Be My Native (USA)-Euroblend (IRE) (The Parson)
C P Morlock D And Mrs H Woodhall

Placings:6/000015/6360015/30530-P0P0   (4405)

2003/04: 24⁸S, 26⁶GS, 24⁸GS, 26⁸G,

	Starts	1st	2nd	3rd	Win & Pl
Hurdles	4	0	0	0	
Career Total	23	2	0	3	6890

90   3/02 Hntg   3m2f   E(0-110)HHdl   G-F   £2492
96   2/01 Uttx   2m6f110yF(0-105)HHdl   SFT   £3041
                                    Total win prize-money £5534

Going:	Sf: 0-1 GS: 0-2 Gd: 0-1 GF: - Fm: 0-0
Distance:	2m/2m3: 0-0 2m4-2m7: 0-0 3m+: 0-4
Track:	LH: 0-1 RH: 0-3 Tight: 0-0 Gall: 0-3
Aids:	Bl: 0-4 Vi: 0-0 Tstrap: 0-4 Ckp: 0-0
Best Rating:	100 11/99 Weth 2m good NHF

Oyster Shell (IRE)

97   92+

7-y-o b g Be My Native (USA)-Judys View (King's Ride)
N J Henderson The Oyster Shell Partnership

Placings:6-3   (1946)
2003/04: 21³G,

	Starts	1st	2nd	3rd	Win & Pl
Hurdles	1	0	0	1	543
Career Total	2	0	0	1	543

Going:	Sf: 0-0 GS: 0-0 Gd: 0-1 GF: - Fm: 0-0
Distance:	2m/2m3: 0-0 2m4-2m7: 0-1 3m+: 0-0
Track:	LH: 0-0 RH: 0-1 Tight: 0-0 Gall: 0-0
Aids:	Bl: 0-0 Vi: 0-0 Tstrap: 0-0 Ckp: 0-0
Best Rating:	92 11/03 Kemp 2m5f good Hdl

Novice hurdler; Irish points winner; promise in first two hurdles starts; lovely big type, who will come into his own when sent chasing.

Oysterhaven (IRE)

                                                    104

6-y-o b g Mister Lord (USA)-Haven's Glory (IRE) (Supreme Leader)
D P Keane Avon Thoroughbreds Ltd

Placings:01P   (4561)
2003/04: 16⁰G, 20¹G, 24⁰GS,

	Starts	1st	2nd	3rd	Win & Pl
NH Flat	1	0	0	0	0
Hurdles	2	1	0	0	2618
Career Total	3	1	0	0	2618

108 12/03 Font   2m4f   E Hdl   GD   £2618
                                    Total win prize-money £2618

Going:	Sf: 0-0 GS: 0-1 Gd: 1-2 GF: - Fm: 0-0
Distance:	2m/2m3: 0-1 2m4-2m7: 1-1 3m+: 0-1
Track:	LH: 0-2 RH: 0-0 Tight: 1-1 Gall: 0-1
Aids:	Bl: 0-0 Vi: 0-0 Tstrap: 0-0 Ckp: 0-0
Best Rating:	108 12/03 Font 2m4f good Hdl

Moderate hurdler; stays two miles four; acts on good ground.

Paarl Rock

72   109

9-y-o ch g Common Grounds-Markievicz (IRE) (Doyoun)
S T Lewis J C Bradbury

Placings:3/5   (4630)
2003/04: 17⁵G,

	Starts	1st	2nd	3rd	Win & Pl
Hurdles	1	0	0	0	0
Career Total	2	0	0	1	592

Going: Sf: 0-0 GS: 0-0 Gd: 0-1 GF: - Fm: 0-0
Distance: 2m/2m3: 0-1 2m4-2m7: 0-0 3m+: 0-0
Track: LH: 0-0 RH: 0-1 Tight: 0-1 Gall: 0-0
Aids: Bl: 0-1 Vi: 0-0 Tstrap: 0-0 Ckp: 0-0
Best Rating: 109 6/01 Strf 2m110y gd-fm Hdl

Pachinco

90   60

6-y-o ch g Bluebird (USA)-Lady Philippa (IRE) (Taufan (USA))
J G M O'Shea K A Ayres

Placings:P6PP-P02605P   (2188)
2003/04: 20⁰G, 16⁰G, 22²G, 22⁶G, 22⁰GF, 20⁵G, 16⁹GS,

	Starts	1st	2nd	3rd	Win & Pl
Hurdles	7	0	1	0	1080
Career Total	11	0	1	0	1080

Going: Sf: 0-0 GS: 0-1 Gd: 0-5 GF: - Fm: 0-1
Distance: 2m/2m3: 0-2 2m4-2m7: 0-5 3m+: 0-0
Track: LH: 0-7 RH: 0-0 Tight: 0-4 Gall: 0-0
Aids: Bl: 0-0 Vi: 0-0 Tstrap: 0-0 Ckp: 0-0
Best Rating: 60 5/03 Ctml 2m6f good Hdl

Runner-up in a very weak three-runner novices' hurdle at Cartmel in May; well beaten in selling company previously.

Pacific Alliance (IRE)

98   84

8-y-o b g Fayruz-La Gravotte (FR) (Habitat)
Michael Butler (R M Stronge 21/7) Crack Of Dawn Syndicate

Placings:53515-P5512   (2106a)
2003/04: 16⁶G, 17⁵G, 17⁵GF, 16¹G, 16²GY,

	Starts	1st	2nd	3rd	Win & Pl
Hurdles	5	1	1	0	7088
Career Total	10	2	1	1	9640
82	10/03	Wxfd	2m	(74-102)HHdl	GD	£6048
86	10/02	MRas	2m1f110yG(0-95)HHdl	GD	£2268

Total win prize-money £8317

Going: Sf: 0-0 GS: 0-0 Gd: 1-3 GF: - Fm: 0-1
Distance: 2m/2m3: 1-5 2m4-2m7: 0-0 3m+: 0-0
Track: LH: 0-1 RH: 0-3 Tight: 0-2 Gall: 0-1
Aids: Bl: 0-0 Vi: 0-0 Tstrap: 0-0 Ckp: 0-0
Best Rating: 86 10/02 MRas 2m1f110y good Hdl

Sellin-class hurdler, acts on good ground and is effective at around two miles.

Pacific Highway (IRE)

86f   59f

5-y-o b g Sadler's Wells (USA)-Obeah (Cure The Blues (USA))
Mrs L B Normile Red Rock Racing

Placings:000   (4323)
2003/04: 16⁰HY, 16⁰HY, 16⁰S,

	Starts	1st	2nd	3rd	Win & Pl
NH Flat	3	0	0	0	
Career Total	3	0	0	0	

Going: Sf: 0-3 GS: 0-0 Gd: 0-0 GF: - Fm: 0-0
Distance: 2m/2m3: 0-3 2m4-2m7: 0-0 3m+: 0-0
Track: LH: 0-3 RH: 0-0 Tight: 0-0 Gall: 0-0
Aids: Bl: 0-0 Vi: 0-0 Tstrap: 0-0 Ckp: 0-0

Best Rating: 59 1/04 Uttx 2m heavy NHF

Pacifyc (IRE)

88   91

9-y-o b g Brief Truce (USA)-Ocean Blue (IRE) (Bluebird (USA))
John A Harris Mrs A E Harris

Placings:1P00/240206-0   (0420)
2003/04: 17⁰GF,

	Starts	1st	2nd	3rd	Win & Pl
Hurdles	1	0	0	0	
Career Total	11	1	2	0	3143
98	9/01	MRas	2m1f110yG Hdl	G-F	£1673

Total win prize-money £1673

Going: Sf: 0-0 GS: 0-0 Gd: 0-0 GF: - Fm: 0-1
Distance: 2m/2m3: 0-1 2m4-2m7: 0-0 3m+: 0-0
Track: LH: 0-0 RH: 0-1 Tight: 0-1 Gall: 0-0
Aids: Bl: 0-0 Vi: 0-0 Tstrap: 0-0 Ckp: 0-0
Best Rating: 98 9/01 MRas 2m1f110y gd-fm Hdl

Pack Leader (IRE)

(97h)   (91 h)

8-y-o b g Muharib (USA)-Royal Broderick (IRE) (Lancastrian)
Jonjo O'Neill John Connor

Placings:0P050-PP   (1304)
2003/04: 20⁰G, 20⁰GF,

	Starts	1st	2nd	3rd	Win & Pl
Chases	2	0	0	0	
Career Total	7	0	0	0	

Going: Sf: 0-0 GS: 0-0 Gd: 0-1 GF: - Fm: 0-1
Distance: 2m/2m3: 0-0 2m4-2m7: 0-2 3m+: 0-0
Track: LH: 0-2 RH: 0-0 Tight: 0-1 Gall: 0-0
Aids: Bl: 0-0 Vi: 0-0 Tstrap: 0-0 Ckp: 0-0
Best Rating: 91 11/02 Hayd 2m4f soft Hdl

Paco Venture (IRE)

100(108h)   (119 h)100

9-y-o b g Supreme Leader-Ethelsdaughter (Deep Run)
Miss Venetia Williams Ashleybank Investments Limited

Placings:4/00/26/035511212150-F2   (1610)
2003/04: 24⁴GF, 24²GF,

	Starts	1st	2nd	3rd	Win & Pl
Chases	2	0	1	0	1336
Career Total	19	4	4	1	26397
119	12/02	Bang	3m	C(0-135)HHdl	G-S	£7527
109	10/02	Tntn	3m110y	D Hdl	G-F	£4396
106	10/02	Uttx	2m6f110yD Hdl	G-F	£5600
104	9/02	Worc	3m	F Hdl	GF	£2233

Total win prize-money £19756

Going: Sf: 0-0 GS: 0-0 Gd: 0-0 GF: - Fm: 0-2
Distance: 2m/2m3: 0-0 2m4-2m7: 0-0 3m+: 0-2
Track: LH: 0-1 RH: 0-1 Tight: 0-1 Gall: 0-1
Aids: Bl: 0-0 Vi: 0-0 Tstrap: 0-0 Ckp: 0-0
Best Rating: 119 12/02 Bang 3m gd-sft Hdl

Moderate chaser/fair hurdler; in fine form in 2002/3; stays three miles; does not want the ground too soft.

Paddington Green

97   92

6-y-o b g Primitive Rising (USA)-Mayfair Minx (St Columbus)

H Morrison R Sweet,Mrs M Wilson,F Flynn,R Madden

Placings:04P0022   (4777)
2003/04: 17⁰GS, 19⁴GS, 22⁵GS, 17⁰GS, 19⁰GS, 22²G, 23⁶G,

	Starts	1st	2nd	3rd	Win & Pl
NH Flat	1	0	0	0	0
Hurdles	6	0	2	0	3241
Career Total	7	0	2	0	3241

Going: Sf: 0-0 GS: 0-5 Gd: 0-2 GF: - Fm: 0-0
Distance: 2m/2m3: 0-2 2m4-2m7: 0-4 3m+: 0-1
Track: LH: 0-1 RH: 0-5 Tight: 0-2 Gall: 0-0
Aids: Bl: 0-0 Vi: 0-0 Tstrap: 0-0 Ckp: 0-0
Best Rating: 92 4/04 Winc 2m6f good Hdl

Plating-class hurdler; half-brother to Marble Arch and Tom Paddington; stays two miles seven furlongs; acts on good.

Paddy For Paddy (IRE)

10-y-o b g Mandalus-Lady Rerico (Pamroy)
G L Landau Mrs Jane Thornton

Placings:12P-P   (4522)
2003/04: 25⁵GS,

	Starts	1st	2nd	3rd	Win & Pl
Chases	1	0	0	0	
Career Total	4	1	1	0	2646
100	2/03	Folk	3m1f	H Ch	SFT	£1554

Total win prize-money £1554

Going: Sf: 0-0 GS: 0-1 Gd: 0-0 GF: - Fm: 0-0
Distance: 2m/2m3: 0-0 2m4-2m7: 0-0 3m+: 0-1
Track: LH: 0-0 RH: 0-1 Tight: 0-0 Gall: 0-0
Aids: Bl: 0-0 Vi: 0-0 Tstrap: 0-0 Ckp: 0-0
Best Rating: 100 3/03 Extr 3m1f110y good Ch

Moderate hunter; acts on ground good and softer; seems sure to win more hunter chases.

Paddy Mul

77   64

7-y-o ch h Democratic (USA)-My Pretty Niece (Great Nephew)
W Storey Gremlin Racing

Placings:0P/0   (2508)
2003/04: 16⁰S,

	Starts	1st	2nd	3rd	Win & Pl
Hurdles	1	0	0	0	
Career Total	3	0	0	0	

Going: Sf: 0-1 GS: 0-0 Gd: 0-0 GF: - Fm: 0-0
Distance: 2m/2m3: 0-1 2m4-2m7: 0-0 3m+: 0-0
Track: LH: 0-1 RH: 0-0 Tight: 0-1 Gall: 0-0
Aids: Bl: 0-0 Vi: 0-0 Tstrap: 0-0 Ckp: 0-0
Best Rating: 75 12/03 Kels 2m110y soft Hdl

Paddy The Driver (IRE)

84   54

8-y-o b g Grand Plaisir (IRE)-Jude's Hollow (IRE) (Hollow Hand)
P J Hobbs Torquay Boyz Racing Syndicate

Placings:40/64306P/6-0P   (2564)
2003/04: 16⁰G, 19⁷GS,

	Starts	1st	2nd	3rd	Win & Pl
Hurdles	2	0	0	0	

| Career Total | 11 | 0 | 0 | 1 | 866 |

Going:	Sf: 0-0 GS: 0-1 Gd: 0-0 GF: - Fm: 0-0
Distance:	2m/2m3: 0-2 2m4-2m7: 0-0 3m+: 0-0
Track:	LH: 0-0 RH: 0-2 Tight: 0-0 Gall: 0-0
Aids:	Bl: 0-0 Vi: 0-0 Tstrap: 0-0 Ckp: 0-0
Best Rating:	90 7/01 NAbb 2m1f gd-fm Hdl

Paddy The Optimist (IRE)

104(92h)   (86h)**94**

8-y-o b g Leading Counsel (USA)-Erne Duchess (IRE) (Duky)
D Burchell (T R George 13/4) Don Gould, Mervyn Phillips

Placings:6/66-43PP3P13   (4947)
2003/04: 16⁴GS, 20³S, 26⁵S, 24⁴HY, 25³G, 20⁶S, 19¹G, 20³GS,

	Starts	1st	2nd	3rd	Win & Pl
Hurdles	1	0	0	0	262
Chases	7	1	0	3	5400
Career Total	11	1	0	3	5661
78	4/04	Chep	2m3f110yG(0-90)HCh	GD	£2688

Total win prize-money £2688

Going:	Sf: 0-4 GS: 0-2 Gd: 1-2 GF: - Fm: 0-0
Distance:	2m/2m3: 0-1 **2m4-2m7: 1-4** 3m+: 0-3
Track:	LH: 1-5 RH: 0-2 Tight: 0-2 Gall: 0-0
Aids:	Bl: 1-4 Vi: 0-0 Tstrap: 0-0 Ckp: 0-0
Best Rating:	94 4/04 Prth 2m4f110y gd-sft Ch

Appreciated a drop in grade when breaking his duck with a wide margin win in 2m 4f selling handicap chase at Chepstow April 2004; subsequently changed hands for 7,500 gns; acts on good ground.

Paddy The Piper (IRE)

112   **136+**

7-y-o b g Witness Box (USA)-Divine Dibs (Raise You Ten)
L Lungo Mr & Mrs Raymond Anderson Green

Placings:3/211-1111   (4599)
2003/04: 16¹S, 20¹GS, 18¹GS, 18¹G,

	Starts	1st	2nd	3rd	Win & Pl
Hurdles	4	4	0	0	32942
Career Total	8	6	1	1	38091
136	3/04	Kels	2m2f	C(0-135)HHdl	GD	£8248
134	3/04	Kels	2m2f	A Hdl	G-S	£17400
116	2/04	Ayr	2m4f	E Hdl	G-S	£3627
114	1/04	Kels	2m110y	E Hdl	SFT	£3666
110	3/03	Weth	2m	H NHF	G-F	£2037
100	2/03	Catt	2m	H NHF	GD	£2058

Total win prize-money £37037

Going:	Sf: 1-1 GS: 2-2 Gd: 1-1 GF: - Fm: 0-0
Distance:	**2m/2m3: 3-3** 2m4-2m7: 1-1 3m+: 0-0
Track:	LH: 4-4 RH: 0-0 **Tight: 3-3** Gall: 0-0
Aids:	Bl: 0-0 Vi: 0-0 Tstrap: 0-0 Ckp: 0-0
Best Rating:	136 3/04 Kels 2m2f good Hdl

Very useful novice hurdler; showed ability in bumpers winning at Catterick and Wetherby; unbeaten in four starts over hurdles including a grade two event at Kelso; stays two miles four; very game; will make a smart chaser in time.

Paddy's Profiles (IRE)

72   **16**

10-y-o b g Euphemism-Dame Niamh (IRE) (Buckskin (FR))

Miss K M George Stableline

Placings:0/004/65/0005-0   (0152)
2003/04: 20⁶GF,

	Starts	1st	2nd	3rd	Win & Pl
Hurdles	1	0	0	0	
Career Total	11	0	0	0	0

Going:	Sf: 0-0 GS: 0-0 Gd: 0-0 GF: - Fm: 0-1
Distance:	2m/2m3: 0-0 2m4-2m7: 0-1 3m+: 0-0
Track:	LH: 0-1 RH: 0-0 Tight: 0-0 Gall: 0-0
Aids:	Bl: 0-0 Vi: 0-1 Tstrap: 0-0 Ckp: 0-0
Best Rating:	79 1/01 Tntn 2m3f110y soft Hdl

Paddy's Thyme (IRE)

(97h)   (71h)

8-y-o gr g Good Thyne (USA)-Nanny Kehoe (IRE) (Sexton Blake)
B G Powell Paddy O'Donnell

Placings:055/0FU2-P   (2204)
2003/04: 25⁶GF,

	Starts	1st	2nd	3rd	Win & Pl
Chases	1	0	0	0	
Career Total	8	0	1	0	766

Going:	Sf: 0-0 GS: 0-0 Gd: 0-0 GF: - Fm: 0-1
Distance:	2m/2m3: 0-0 2m4-2m7: 0-0 3m+: 0-0
Track:	LH: 0-0 RH: 0-1 Tight: 0-1 Gall: 0-0
Aids:	Bl: 0-0 Vi: 0-0 Tstrap: 0-0 Ckp: 0-0
Best Rating:	89 11/00 Chel 2m110y gd-sft NHF

Pagan Dance (IRE)

88   **115+**

5-y-o b g Revoque (IRE)-Ballade D'Ainhoa (FR) (Al Nasr (FR))
Mrs A J Perrett The Gap Partnership

Placings:30   (3042)
2003/04: 16³GS, 16⁰GS,

	Starts	1st	2nd	3rd	Win & Pl
Hurdles	2	0	0	1	1254
Career Total	2	0	0	1	1254

Going:	Sf: 0-0 GS: 0-2 Gd: 0-0 GF: - Fm: 0-0
Distance:	2m/2m3: 0-2 2m4-2m7: 0-0 3m+: 0-0
Track:	LH: 0-0 RH: 0-0 Tight: 0-0 Gall: 0-2
Aids:	Bl: 0-0 Vi: 0-0 Tstrap: 0-0 Ckp: 0-0
Best Rating:	115 11/03 Newb 2m110y gd-sft Hdl

Very useful Flat performer; pleasing hurdle debut at Newbury in November 2003 when third, but failed to get anywhere near that form on next outing back over course-and-distance; acts over two miles, but should stay further; effective on most ground.

Pagermar (IRE)

10-y-o b/br g Camden Town-Another Coup (Le Patron)
Mrs W D Sykes Mrs Richard Cambray

Placings:F/P0/P   (0073)
2003/04: 24³PS,

	Starts	1st	2nd	3rd	Win & Pl
Chases	1	0	0	0	
Career Total	4	0	0	0	

Going:	Sf: 0-1 GS: 0-0 Gd: 0-0 GF: - 0-0
Distance:	2m/2m3: 0-0 2m4-2m7: 0-0 3m+: 0-1
Track:	LH: 0-1 RH: 0-0 Tight: 0-1 Gall: 0-0
Aids:	Bl: 0-0 Vi: 0-0 Tstrap: 0-0 Ckp: 0-0
Best Rating:	51 6/01 Clon 2m4f gd-fm Ch

Pailitas (GER)

107   **86**

7-y-o b g Lomitas-Pradera (GER) (Abary (GER))
G A Swinbank (Ian Williams 1/10) C N Barnes

Placings:0P0P/120O60-0534134   (1838)
2003/04: 17⁰G, 17⁵GF, 16³GF, 16⁴GF, 16¹GF, 17³GF, 17⁴G,

	Starts	1st	2nd	3rd	Win & Pl
Hurdles	7	1	0	2	4007
Career Total	17	2	1	2	6786
86	8/03	Hntg	2m110y	E(0-110)HHdl	G-F	£3402
77	6/02	Hntg	2m110y	G(0-95)HHdl	G-F	£1661

Total win prize-money £5064

Going:	Sf: 0-0 GS: 0-0 Gd: 0-2 GF: - Fm: 1-5
Distance:	**2m/2m3: 1-7** 2m4-2m7: 0-0 3m+: 0-0
Track:	LH: 0-5 RH: 1-2 Tight: 0-3 **Gall: 1-1**
Aids:	Bl: 0-0 Vi: 0-0 Tstrap: 0-0 Ckp: 0-0
Best Rating:	86 9/03 Sedg 2m1f gd-fm Hdl

Winner on the Flat in Germany; selling-class hurdler; best at 2m; acts on fast ground; does not always find that much off the bridle.

Palace (FR)

8-y-o b g Rahotep (FR)-La Musardiere (FR) (Cadoudal (FR))
P F Nicholls B L Blinman

Placings:0/06P/P   (0943)
2003/04: 23³⁶G, 19⁵GS,

	Starts	1st	2nd	3rd	Win & Pl
Chases	1	0	0	0	
Career Total	5	0	0	0	0

Going:	Sf: 0-0 GS: 0-0 Gd: 0-0 GF: - Fm: 0-0
Distance:	2m/2m3: 0-0 2m4-2m7: 0-0 3m+: 0-1
Track:	LH: 0-1 RH: 0-0 Tight: 0-0 Gall: 0-0
Aids:	Bl: 0-0 Vi: 0-0 Tstrap: 0-0 Ckp: 0-0
Best Rating:	83 11/01 Winc 2m good NHF

Palais (IRE)

80   **81**

9-y-o b g Darshaan-Dance Festival (Nureyev (USA))
John A Harris J South

Placings:46000/300/P6P/1020-P600   (2544)
2003/04: 26⁶GF, 24⁸G, 22⁰G, 19⁰GS,

	Starts	1st	2nd	3rd	Win & Pl
Hurdles	4	0	0	0	0
Career Total	19	1	1	1	5197
73	8/02	MRas	3m	D Hdl	G-S	£3851

Total win prize-money £3851

Going:	Sf: 0-0 GS: 0-1 Gd: 0-2 GF: - Fm: 0-1
Distance:	2m/2m3: 0-0 2m4-2m7: 0-2 3m+: 0-2
Track:	LH: 0-1 RH: 0-2 Tight: 0-1 Gall: 0-0
Aids:	Bl: 0-0 Vi: 0-0 Tstrap: 0-0 Ckp: 0-0
Best Rating:	93 10/99 Strf 2m110y gd-fm Hdl

Palarshan (FR)

106 (133h)**151**

6-y-o b/br g Darshaan-Palavera (FR) (Bikala)
H D Daly Mrs A L Wood

Placings:131/22311-020 (4426)
2003/04: 16⁶GS, 16²S, 16⁶G,

	Starts	1st	2nd	3rd	Win & Pl
Chases	3	0	1	0	4561
Career Total	11	4	3	2	70939

144	3/03	Chel	2m110y	A HCh	GD	£43500
131	2/03	Leic	2m	E Ch	G-S	£4745
140	4/02	Chel	2m1f	B Hdl	G-F	£8541
	8/01	Pard	1m6f	Hdl	GD	£542
					Total win prize-money	£57328

Going: Sf: 0-1 GS: 0-1 Gd: 0-1 GF: - Fm: 0-0
Distance: 2m/2m3: 0-3 2m4-2m7: 0-0 3m+: 0-0
Track: LH: 0-1 RH: 0-2 Tight: 0-0 Gall: 0-1
Aids: Bl: 0-0 Vi: 0-0 Tstrap: 0-0 Ckp: 0-0
Best Rating: 151 2/04 Sand 2m soft Ch

Very useful chaser; won the Grand Annual at the Cheltenham Festival in 2003; lightly raced since; probably best at two miles; suited by good ground.

Palma (IRE)

90f **86f**

6-y-o b/br g Rashar (USA)-Quaybreeze (IRE) (Quayside)
P R Webber J Dougall

Placings:5 (2537)
2003/04: 18⁵S,

	Starts	1st	2nd	3rd	Win & Pl
NH Flat	1	0	0	0	0
Career Total	1	0	0	0	0

Going: Sf: 0-1 GS: 0-0 Gd: 0-0 GF: - Fm: 0-0
Distance: 2m/2m3: 0-1 2m4-2m7: 0-0 3m+: 0-0
Track: LH: 0-1 RH: 0-0 Tight: 0-0 Gall: 0-0
Aids: Bl: 0-0 Vi: 0-0 Tstrap: 0-0 Ckp: 0-0
Best Rating: 86 12/03 Plum 2m2f soft NHF

Palmac's Pride

4-y-o ch g Atraf-Nashwanah (Nashwan (USA))
M F Harris The Virtual Partnership

Placings:0P (3420)
2003/04: 12⁰G, 17ᴾGS,

	Starts	1st	2nd	3rd	Win & Pl
NH Flat	2	0	0	0	0
Career Total	2	0	0	0	0

Going: Sf: 0-0 GS: 0-1 Gd: 0-1 GF: - Fm: 0-0
Distance: 2m/2m3: 0-1 2m4-2m7: 0-0 3m+: 0-0
Track: LH: 0-0 RH: 0-1 Tight: 0-0 Gall: 0-0
Aids: Bl: 0-0 Vi: 0-0 Tstrap: 0-0 Ckp: 0-0

Palouse (IRE)

92(98h) (116h)**102**

8-y-o gr g Toulon-Hop Picker (USA) (Plugged Nickle (USA))
R H Buckler (P J Rothwell 17/9) Woodland Flowers

Placings:60/020411244/3031134F0/0-PP603063P5 (4896)
2003/04: 20ᴾHY, 16ᴾF, 16⁶F, 20ᴾF, 18³F, 20⁴GF, 19⁵GS, 18³G, 22ᴾG, 16⁵G,

	Starts	1st	2nd	3rd	Win & Pl
Hurdles	3	0	0	1	1723

Chases		7	0	0	1	795
Career Total		31	4	2	5	35372
120	9/01	Tral	2m4f	Ch	GD	£7233
105	8/01	Baln	2m1f	Ch	GD	£7790
139	9/00	Kbgn	2m	Hdl	G-Y	£3312
122	8/00	Rosc	2m	Hdl	FRM	£2760
					Total win prize-money	£21096

Going: Sf: 0-1 GS: 0-1 Gd: 0-3 GF: - Fm: 0-5
Distance: 2m/2m3: 0-6 2m4-2m7: 0-4 3m+: 0-0
Track: LH: 0-1 RH: 0-5 Tight: 0-1 Gall: 0-0
Aids: Bl: 0-5 Vi: 0-0 Tstrap: 0-0 Ckp: 0-0
Best Rating: 139 5/01 Fair 2m good Hdl

Fair hurdler; ex-Irish; disappointing so far over fences; has worn blinkers; stays 2m 4f; effective on fast ground.

Palua

107(106h) (139+h)**139+**

7-y-o b g Sri Pekan (USA)-Reticent Bride (IRE) (Shy Groom (USA))
Miss E C Lavelle Mark Barrett And Partners

Placings:4/2120-1561P6 (4645)
2003/04: 20¹GF, 25⁵GS, 20⁶GS, 16¹G, 16ᴾG, 16⁶G,

	Starts	1st	2nd	3rd	Win & Pl
Chases	6	2	0	0	14953
Career Total	11	3	2	0	29814

139	1/04	Kemp	2m	C Ch	GD	£8073
127	11/03	Hntg	2m4f110yD Ch		G-F	£5380
111	2/03	Folk	2m4f110yE Hdl		HVY	£3689
					Total win prize-money	£17142

Going: Sf: 0-0 GS: 0-2 Gd: 1-3 GF: - Fm: 1-1
Distance: 2m/2m3: 1-3 2m4-2m7: 1-2 3m+: 0-1
Track: LH: 0-3 RH: 2-3 Tight: 0-2 Gall: 1-2
Aids: Bl: 0-0 Vi: 0-0 Tstrap: 0-0 Ckp: 0-0
Best Rating: 139 4/04 Aint 2m good Ch

Very useful novice chaser; lightly-raced over hurdles; indifferent form over fences until winning at his first try at two miles; enigmatic character who travels well but finds little off the bit; stays two miles four, but effective at two miles; acts on most ground.

Pamela Anshan

102(93h) (66 h)**96**

7-y-o b m Anshan-Have Form (Haveroid)
S C Burrough Mrs Christine Priest

Placings:5555/606P42-051P (4146)
2003/04: 16⁸G, 19⁵GS, 24¹GS, 24ᴾG,

	Starts	1st	2nd	3rd	Win & Pl
Chases	4	1	0	0	5571
Career Total	14	1	1	0	7158

98	2/04	Tntn	3m	D Ch	G-S	£5570
					Total win prize-money	£5571

Going: Sf: 0-0 GS: 1-2 Gd: 0-2 GF: - Fm: 0-0
Distance: 2m/2m3: 0-2 2m4-2m7: 0-0 3m+: 1-2
Track: LH: 0-0 RH: 1-4 Tight: 1-3 Gall: 0-0
Aids: Bl: 0-0 Vi: 0-0 Tstrap: 0-0 Ckp: 0-0
Best Rating: 98 2/04 Tntn 3m gd-sft Ch

Plating-class chaser; stays three miles; acts on easy ground; almost certainly flattered by her victory at Taunton in February 2004.

Panama (IRE)

4-y-o b c Peintre Celebre (USA)-Bay Queen (Damister (USA))
D R Wellicome (M L W Bell 16/7) D R Wellicome

Placings:P (4166)
2003/04: 16ᴾG,

	Starts	1st	2nd	3rd	Win & Pl
Hurdles	1	0	0	0	0
Career Total	1	0	0	0	0

Going: Sf: 0-0 GS: 0-0 Gd: 0-1 GF: - Fm: 0-0
Distance: 2m/2m3: 0-1 2m4-2m7: 0-0 3m+: 0-0
Track: LH: 0-1 RH: 0-0 Tight: 0-0 Gall: 0-1
Aids: Bl: 0-0 Vi: 0-0 Tstrap: 0-0 Ckp: 0-0

Pangeran (USA)

105 **82**

12-y-o ch g Forty Niner (USA)-Smart Heiress (USA) (Vaguely Noble)
N B King R Oliver Smith

Placings:42622505/423U/3622/143UU/31P3/32460/53-36644322234 (2382)
2003/04: 24³GF, 24⁶GF, 23⁶GF, 20⁴GF, 24⁴GF, 24³GF, 24²G, 26²GF, 24²G, 24³G, 26⁴GF,

	Starts	1st	2nd	3rd	Win & Pl
Chases	11	0	3	3	4650
Career Total	43	2	10	14	14407

106	5/00	Uttx	2m5f	H Ch	GD	£1742
92	5/99	Folk	2m5f	H Ch	G-F	£1472
					Total win prize-money	£3214

Going: Sf: 0-0 GS: 0-0 Gd: 0-3 GF: - Fm: 0-8
Distance: 2m/2m3: 0-0 2m4-2m7: 0-1 3m+: 0-10
Track: LH: 0-6 RH: 0-4 Tight: 0-4 Gall: 0-4
Aids: Bl: 0-0 Vi: 0-0 Tstrap: 0-0 Ckp: 0-0
Best Rating: 106 5/00 Uttx 2m5f good Ch

Plating-class chaser; multiple winner between the flags; best at three miles, but effective at shorter; best on a sound surface.

Panmure (IRE)

108(98h) (88h)**103**

8-y-o b g Alphabatim (USA)-Serjitak (Saher)
P D Niven The Poppet Partnership

Placings:304/040P0U-5115 (1898)
2003/04: 16⁵GF, 16¹GF, 16¹G, 16⁵GF,

	Starts	1st	2nd	3rd	Win & Pl
Chases	4	2	0	0	6064
Career Total	13	2	0	1	6672

103	10/03	Carl	2m	E(0-100)HCh	GD	£3477
96	10/03	Hexm	2m110y	F(0-90)Ch	G-F	£2586
					Total win prize-money	£6065

Going: Sf: 0-0 GS: 0-0 Gd: 1-1 GF: - Fm: 1-3
Distance: 2m/2m3: 2-4 2m4-2m7: 0-0 3m+: 0-0
Track: LH: 1-2 RH: 1-2 Tight: 0-0 Gall: 0-0
Aids: Bl: 0-0 Vi: 0-0 Tstrap: 0-1 Ckp: 0-0
Best Rating: 104 10/01 Chel 2m110y good NHF

Moderate chaser/plating-class hurdler; stays 2m; acts on fast ground; has been tried in blinkers and a tongue tie.

Panooras Lord (IRE)

10-y-o b g Topanoora-Ladyship (Windjammer (USA))
Martyn Hill (J S Wainwright 29/10) Ms Julie French

Placings:6320/5P0200010/U0/1PP046/0005/F50-4F (4218)
2003/04: 21⁴G, 25ᶠGS,

	Starts	1st	2nd	3rd	Win & Pl
Chases	2	0	0	0	238

Career Total	30	2	2	1	5356
98	6/00	Fknm	2m	G(0-90)HHdl	GD	£1876
87	4/99	Hntg	2m110y	G(0-100)HHdl	G-F	£1926

Total win prize-money £3802

Going:	Sf: 0-0 GS: 0-0 Gd: 0-1 GF: - Fm: 0-0
Distance:	2m/2m3: 0-0 2m4-2m7: 0-1 3m+: 0-1
Track:	LH: 0-1 RH: 0-0 Tight: 0-0 Gall: 0-0
Aids:	Bl: 0-0 Vi: 0-0 Tstrap: 0-0 Ckp: 0-0
Best Rating:	98 6/00 Fknm 2m good Hdl

Paperound

36f

6-y-o ch m Primitive Rising (USA)-Eye Bee Aitch (Move Off)
N G Richards The Jockeys Whips

Placings:0-   (0007)
2003/04: 16[G],

	Starts	1st	2nd	3rd	Win & Pl
NH Flat	1	0	0	0	
Career Total	1	0	0	0	

Going:	Sf: 0-0 GS: 0-0 Gd: 0-0 GF: - Fm: 0-0
Distance:	2m/2m3: 0-1 2m4-2m7: 0-0 3m+: 0-0
Track:	LH: 0-1 RH: 0-0 Tight: 0-0 Gall: 0-0
Aids:	Bl: 0-0 Vi: 0-0 Tstrap: 0-0 Ckp: 0-0
Best Rating:	36 4/03 Hexm 2m110y good NHF

Paperprophet

107   **130**

6-y-o b g Glory Of Dancer-Living Legend (ITY) (Archway (IRE))
N G Richards The Jockeys Whips

Placings:3112-112   (4449)
2003/04: 16[1]S, 20[1]G, 20[2]GS,

	Starts	1st	2nd	3rd	Win & Pl
Hurdles	3	2	1	0	31503
Career Total	7	4	2	1	43938
125	2/04	Hayd	2m4f	B HHdl	GD	£15631
121	12/03	Ayr	2m	C(0-135)HHdl	SFT	£7072
110	11/02	Ayr	2m4f	D(0-110)HHdl	SFT	£4420
97	10/02	Bang	2m1f	E Hdl	G-S	£3038

Total win prize-money £30161

Going:	Sf: 1-1 GS: 0-1 Gd: 1-1 GF: - Fm: 0-0
Distance:	2m/2m3: 1-1 2m4-2m7: 1-2 3m+: 0-0
Track:	LH: 2-2 RH: 0-0 Tight: 0-0 Gall: 0-0
Aids:	Bl: 0-0 Vi: 0-0 Tstrap: 0-0 Ckp: 0-0
Best Rating:	135 3/04 Asct 2m4f gd-sft Hdl

Useful hurdler; has won four of his seven outings to date, latest competitive handicap at Haydock in February; stays 2m 4f and should get further; acts on fast ground but is best with cut; progressive.

Paphian Bay

92   **96**

6-y-o b g Karinga Bay-Bichette (Lidhame)
Ferdy Murphy S Hubbard Rodwell

Placings:0-512P   (2907)
2003/04: 17[5]GS, 20[1]G, 20[2]G, 26[P]GS,

	Starts	1st	2nd	3rd	Win & Pl
NH Flat	1	0	0	0	0
Hurdles	3	1	1	0	4465
Career Total	5	1	1	0	4465
91	11/03	Weth	2m4f110yE Hdl		GD	£3559

Total win prize-money £3560

Going: Sf: 0-0 GS: 0-1 Gd: 1-3 GF: - Fm: 0-0
Distance: 2m/2m3: 0-1 2m4-2m7: 1-2 3m+: 0-1
Track: LH: 1-3 RH: 0-1 Tight: 0-1 Gall: 0-1
Aids: Bl: 0-0 Vi: 0-0 Tstrap: 0-0 Ckp: 0-0
Best Rating: 96 12/03 Weth 2m4f110y good Hdl

Took a weak novices' hurdle on first try over timber at Wetherby in November; narrowly beaten on a return there the following month; stays 2m 4f; acts on good.

Papillon De Iena (FR)

108   **118+**

4-y-o ch g Varese (FR)-Belle du Chesne (FR) (Rb Chesne)
M C Pipe Joe Moran

Placings:310   (4863)
2003/04: 17[3]GS, 18[1]G, 16[0]S,

	Starts	1st	2nd	3rd	Win & Pl
Hurdles	3	1	0	1	3928
Career Total	3	1	0	1	3928
118	3/04	Font	2m2f110yE Hdl		GD	£3490

Total win prize-money £3491

Going:	Sf: 0-1 GS: 0-1 Gd: 1-1 GF: - Fm: 0-0
Distance:	2m/2m3: 1-3 2m4-2m7: 0-0 3m+: 0-0
Track:	LH: 1-2 RH: 0-1 Tight: 1-2 Gall: 0-0
Aids:	Bl: 0-0 Vi: 0-0 Tstrap: 0-0 Ckp: 0-0
Best Rating:	118 3/04 Font 2m2f110y good Hdl

Fair hurdler; stays 2m 2f; acts on good.

Papua

110   **116**

10-y-o ch g Green Dancer (USA)-Fairy Tern (Mill Reef (USA))
J White Nick Quesnel

Placings:61P/242042/260613533/32P1413   (1692)
2003/04: 18[3]G, 21[2]GF, 21[P]GS, 16[1]GF, 20[4]GF, 16[1]GF, 17[3]GF,

	Starts	1st	2nd	3rd	Win & Pl
Chases	7	2	1	2	12045
Career Total	25	4	5	5	40302
116	10/03	Uttx	2m	E Ch	G-F	£3701
112	7/03	Uttx	2m	E Ch	G-F	£5040
127	8/01	Ctml	2m1f110yD(0-125)HHdl	G-S	£3464
126	2/98	Wind	2m	B Hdl	G-F	£7351

Total win prize-money £19559

Going:	Sf: 0-0 GS: 0-1 Gd: 0-1 GF: - Fm: 2-5
Distance:	2m/2m3: 2-4 2m4-2m7: 0-3 3m+: 0-0
Track:	LH: 2-4 RH: 0-1 Tight: 0-4 Gall: 0-0
Aids:	Bl: 2-5 Vi: 0-0 Tstrap: 1-2 Ckp: 0-0
Best Rating:	134 6/01 Strf 2m110y gd-fm Hdl

Fair novice chaser; finally off the mark at Uttoxeter in July; tongue tied when scoring again there in October; best around two miles; needs fast ground; moody.

Parade Racer

13-y-o b g Derring Rose-Dusky Damsel (Sahib (USA))
Tim Butt Tim Butt

Placings:56/PP42F153/F/PP43444P/3/3203/11P-1PR0P   (4949)
2003/04: 25[1]G, 25[P]G, 24[R]HY, 25[P]G, 26[P]GS,

	Starts	1st	2nd	3rd	Win & Pl
Chases	5	1	0	0	3038
Career Total	32	4	2	5	15804
104	5/03	Kels	3m1f	H Ch	GD	£3038
99	5/02	Prth	2m4f110yH Ch	G-F	£2743

| 104 | 5/02 | Kels | 3m1f | H Ch | G-S | £1876 |
| 82 | 1/97 | Towc | 2m5f | G(0-95)HHdl | G-S | £2232 |

Total win prize-money £9890

Going:	Sf: 0-1 GS: 0-1 Gd: 1-3 GF: - Fm: 0-0
Distance:	2m/2m3: 0-2 2m4-2m7: 0-0 3m+: 1-5
Track:	LH: 1-4 RH: 0-0 Tight: 1-3 Gall: 0-1
Aids:	Bl: 0-0 Vi: 0-0 Tstrap: 0-0 Ckp: 0-0
Best Rating:	104 5/03 Kels 3m1f good Ch

Moderate pointer/hunter chaser; stays three miles; acts on any ground.

Parahandy (IRE)

14-y-o b g Lancastrian-Dishcloth (Fury Royal)
Giles Smyly G E Dowty

Placings:2246/UF11/4P345/1/224224/53/025-P3   (3723)
2003/04: 33[P]G, 25[3]S,

	Starts	1st	2nd	3rd	Win & Pl
Chases	2	0	0	1	238
Career Total	27	3	7	3	30348
125	11/99	NAbb	3m2f110yD(0-140)HCh	G-S	£8439
127	4/98	Winc	3m1f110yE Ch	G-S	£3226
133	4/98	Font	3m2f110yE(0-115)HCh	G-S	£3377

Total win prize-money £15043

Going:	Sf: 0-1 GS: 0-0 Gd: 0-1 GF: - Fm: 0-0
Distance:	2m/2m3: 0-0 2m4-2m7: 0-0 3m+: 0-2
Track:	LH: 0-2 RH: 0-0 Tight: 0-0 Gall: 0-1
Aids:	Bl: 0-0 Vi: 0-0 Tstrap: 0-0 Ckp: 0-0
Best Rating:	133 4/98 Font 3m2f110y gd-sft Ch

Veteran hunter chaser; a thorough stayer; suited by plenty of give.

Pardini (USA)

97   **94**

5-y-o b g Quest For Fame-Noblissima (IRE) (Sadler's Wells (USA))
M F Harris M Harris

Placings:4-F06PP4P23   (4890)
2003/04: 22[F]S, 20[0]G, 22[6]G, 23[P]G, 25[P]S, 21[4]S, 24[P]S, 22[2]G, 19[3]GF,

	Starts	1st	2nd	3rd	Win & Pl
Hurdles	9	0	1	1	2221
Career Total	10	0	1	1	2650

Going:	Sf: 0-4 GS: 0-0 Gd: 0-4 GF: - Fm: 0-1
Distance:	2m/2m3: 0-1 2m4-2m7: 0-5 3m+: 0-3
Track:	LH: 0-5 RH: 0-3 Tight: 0-5 Gall: 0-1
Aids:	Bl: 0-2 Vi: 0-0 Tstrap: 0-0 Ckp: 0-0
Best Rating:	94 5/03 Uttx 2m6f110y soft Hdl

Plating-class hurdler; has only raced on good or softer.

Pardishar (IRE)

113   **112**

6-y-o b g Kahyasi-Parapa (IRE) (Akarad (FR))
G L Moore D R Hunnisett

Placings:0/5-P122242   (4704)
2003/04: 16[P]S, 18[1]G, 17[2]GS, 16[2]GS, 16[2]G, 18[4]G, 18[2]G,

	Starts	1st	2nd	3rd	Win & Pl
Hurdles	7	1	4	0	12390
Career Total	9	1	4	0	12390
98	12/03	Font	2m2f110yD(0-115)HHdl	GD	£3633

Total win prize-money £3634

Going:	Sf: 0-1 GS: 0-2 Gd: 1-4 GF: - Fm: 0-0
Distance:	2m/2m3: 1-7 2m4-2m7: 0-0 3m+: 0-0

Track:	LH: 1-6 RH: 0-1 Tight: 1-5 Gall: 0-1
Aids:	Bl: 0-0 Vi: 0-0 Tstrap: 0-0 Ckp: 0-0
Best Rating:	112 4/04 Font 2m2f110y good Hdl

Progressive novice hurdler; stays 2m 2f; acts on yielding ground.

Pardon What

101(100c)   (96c)**90d**

8-y-o b g Theatrical Charmer-Tree Poppy (Rolfe (USA))
B G Powell   Mrs A Ellis

Placings:*31*UP54014P-0FP400224   (4488)
2003/04: 20UG, 26FG, 25PGS, 224G, 16PGS, 19UG, 222GF, 252GS, 224G,

	Starts	1st	2nd	3rd	Win & Pl
Hurdles	7	0	2	0	1454
Chases	2	0	0	0	0
Career Total	19	2	2	1	8492
96	3/03	Bang	2m4f110yE(0-105)HCh		SFT £4858
108	6/02	Worc	2m	H NHF	SFT £1519
				Total win prize-money £6378	

Going:	Sf: 0-0 GS: 0-3 Gd: 0-5 GF: - Fm: 0-1
Distance:	2m/2m3: 0-1 2m4-2m7: 0-5 3m+: 0-3
Track:	LH: 0-8 RH: 0-0 Tight: 0-0 Gall: 0-0
Aids:	Bl: 0-3 Vi: 0-2 Tstrap: 0-0 Ckp: 0-2
Best Rating:	108 6/02 Worc 2m soft NHF

Moderate chaser, winner at Bangor on debut; effective at two and a half miles; acts on soft ground.

Paris Latino (FR)

90   **68**

5-y-o b g Nikos-Tarbelissima (FR) (Tarbes (FR))
C L Tizzard   R G Tizzard

Placings:*00-04*P0006   (4899)
2003/04: 17UGF, 164GF, 16PS, 17UG, 16UG, 22UG, 16PG,

	Starts	1st	2nd	3rd	Win & Pl
NH Flat	1	0	0	0	0
Hurdles	6	0	0	0	0
Career Total	9	0	0	0	0

Going:	Sf: 0-1 GS: 0-0 Gd: 0-4 GF: - Fm: 0-2
Distance:	2m/2m3: 0-6 2m4-2m7: 0-1 3m+: 0-0
Track:	LH: 0-2 RH: 0-5 Tight: 0-3 Gall: 0-0
Aids:	Bl: 0-0 Vi: 0-0 Tstrap: 0-0 Ckp: 0-0
Best Rating:	72 11/02 Newb 1m4f110y gd-sft NHF

Parisian Storm (IRE)

80   **112**

8-y-o b g Glacial Storm (USA)-Lost In Paris (Deep Run)
Evan Williams   Mark Glastonbury Grant Lewis

Placings:*0*-U2PP4   (4811)
2003/04: 22US, 252S, 23PS, 24PGS, 244G,

	Starts	1st	2nd	3rd	Win & Pl
Chases	5	0	1	0	1665
Career Total	6	0	1	0	1665

Going:	Sf: 0-3 GS: 0-1 Gd: 0-1 GF: - Fm: 0-0
Distance:	2m/2m3: 0-0 2m4-2m7: 0-1 3m+: 0-4
Track:	LH: 0-2 RH: 0-3 Tight: 0-1 Gall: 0-0
Aids:	Bl: 0-0 Vi: 0-0 Tstrap: 0-0 Ckp: 0-0
Best Rating:	112 1/04 Extr 3m1f110y soft Ch

Modest novice chaser; winner of two point-to-points; stays three miles; effective in soft ground.

Parisienne Gale (IRE)

5-y-o b m Lapierre-Elegant Gale (IRE) (Strong Gale)
D McCain   Ray Pattison

Placings:*50*U   (4253)
2003/04: 16SG, 17UGS, 17UG,

	Starts	1st	2nd	3rd	Win & Pl
NH Flat	2	0	0	0	0
Hurdles	1	0	0	0	0
Career Total	3	0	0	0	0

Going:	Sf: 0-0 GS: 0-1 Gd: 0-2 GF: - Fm: 0-0
Distance:	2m/2m3: 0-3 2m4-2m7: 0-0 3m+: 0-0
Track:	LH: 0-3 RH: 0-0 Tight: 0-2 Gall: 0-0
Aids:	Bl: 0-0 Vi: 0-0 Tstrap: 0-0 Ckp: 0-0
Best Rating:	78 11/03 Newc 2m good NHF

Park City

104   **94**

5-y-o b g Slip Anchor-Cryptal (Persian Bold)
J Joseph (P J Hobbs 2/5)   Jack Joseph

Placings:B3021P503-3000   (4917)
2003/04: 163GS, 16UG, 18UG, 20PGS,

	Starts	1st	2nd	3rd	Win & Pl
Hurdles	4	0	0	1	559
Career Total	13	1	1	3	5538
85	12/02	Wwck	2m	F(0-100)HHdl	SFT £2541
				Total win prize-money £2541	

Going:	Sf: 0-0 GS: 0-2 Gd: 0-2 GF: - Fm: 0-0
Distance:	2m/2m3: 0-3 2m4-2m7: 0-1 3m+: 0-0
Track:	LH: 0-3 RH: 0-1 Tight: 0-1 Gall: 0-0
Aids:	Bl: 0-0 Vi: 0-0 Tstrap: 0-0 Ckp: 0-0
Best Rating:	94 5/03 Worc 2m gd-sft Hdl

Modest handicap hurdler; effective at around two miles and on good and soft ground.

Park Lane Billie

72f   **67f**

4-y-o b f Double Eclipse (IRE)-Kathy's Role (Rolfe (USA))
J Mackie   Mrs Nigel Batho

Placings:*00*   (4186)
2003/04: 16UG, 16UG,

	Starts	1st	2nd	3rd	Win & Pl
NH Flat	2	0	0	0	0
Career Total	2	0	0	0	0

Going:	Sf: 0-0 GS: 0-0 Gd: 0-2 GF: - Fm: 0-0
Distance:	2m/2m3: 0-2 2m4-2m7: 0-0 3m+: 0-0
Track:	LH: 0-1 RH: 0-1 Tight: 0-0 Gall: 0-1
Aids:	Bl: 0-0 Vi: 0-0 Tstrap: 0-0 Ckp: 0-0
Best Rating:	67 3/04 Hntg 2m110y good NHF

Park Lane Freddie

91   **88**

6-y-o b g Nalchik (USA)-Kathy's Role (Rolfe (USA))
J Mackie   Mrs Nigel Batho

Placings:*00*600-46   (0522)
2003/04: 17UG, 16PG,

	Starts	1st	2nd	3rd	Win & Pl
Hurdles	2	0	0	0	293

Career Total	7	0	0	0	293

Going:	Sf: 0-0 GS: 0-0 Gd: 0-2 GF: - Fm: 0-0
Distance:	2m/2m3: 0-2 2m4-2m7: 0-0 3m+: 0-0
Track:	LH: 0-2 RH: 0-0 Tight: 0-2 Gall: 0-0
Aids:	Bl: 0-0 Vi: 0-0 Tstrap: 0-0 Ckp: 0-0
Best Rating:	88 5/03 Strf 2m110y good Hdl

Well held in bumpers and novice hurdles.

Park Place (IRE)

(77c)   (60c)**90**

9-y-o gr g Husyan (USA)-Iron Mermaid (General Ironside)
J I A Charlton   W F Trueman

Placings:*105/*665/0434-P   (0170)
2003/04: 20PGF,

	Starts	1st	2nd	3rd	Win & Pl
Hurdles	1	0	0	0	0
Career Total	11	1	0	1	2902
112	5/00	Prth	2m110y	H NHF	G-S £1918
				Total win prize-money £1918	

Going:	Sf: 0-0 GS: 0-0 Gd: 0-0 GF: - Fm: 0-1
Distance:	2m/2m3: 0-0 2m4-2m7: 0-1 3m+: 0-0
Track:	LH: 0-1 RH: 0-0 Tight: 0-0 Gall: 0-0
Aids:	Bl: 0-0 Vi: 0-0 Tstrap: 0-0 Ckp: 0-0
Best Rating:	112 5/00 Prth 2m110y gd-sft NHF

Moderate novice hurdler; stayed three miles; acted on a sound surface; (DEAD)

Parknasilla

102   **117**

4-y-o b g Marju (IRE)-Top Berry (High Top)
M W Easterby   Lady Bland

Placings:1222   (4863)
2003/04: 16TS, 16PG, 16PS, 16PS,

	Starts	1st	2nd	3rd	Win & Pl
Hurdles	4	1	3	0	9932
Career Total	4	1	3	0	9932
104	1/04	Leic	2m	D Hdl	SFT £5109
				Total win prize-money £5109	

Going:	Sf: 1-3 GS: 0-0 Gd: 0-1 GF: - Fm: 0-0
Distance:	2m/2m3: 1-4 2m4-2m7: 0-0 3m+: 0-0
Track:	LH: 0-2 RH: 1-2 Tight: 0-1 Gall: 0-0
Aids:	Bl: 0-0 Vi: 0-0 Tstrap: 0-0 Ckp: 0-0
Best Rating:	117 4/04 Ayr 2m soft Hdl

Fair novice hurdler; suited by two miles; acts on good and soft ground; type to win more races.

Parlour Game

111   (112h)**110**

8-y-o br m Petoski-Henry's True Love (Random Shot)
H D Daly   G A Greaves

Placings:*31*F0/63P55/F4U32P2-14125P   (3705)
2003/04: 201HY, 244G, 251G, 25PGS, 245GS, 26PHY,

	Starts	1st	2nd	3rd	Win & Pl
Chases	6	2	1	0	9087
Career Total	22	3	3	3	16419
110	10/03	Towc	3m1f	E(0-105)HCh	GD £3297
110	5/03	Uttx	2m4f	E(0-105)HCh	HVY £4429
117	1/01	Sthl	2m	E Hdl	HVY £2590
				Total win prize-money £10317	

Going:	Sf: 1-2 GS: 0-2 Gd: 1-2 GF: - Fm: 0-0
Distance:	2m/2m3: 0-0 2m4-2m7: 1-1 3m+: 1-5
Track:	LH: 1-2 RH: 1-4 Tight: 0-1 Gall: 0-0

Career Total	7	0	0	0	293

Going:	Sf: 0-0 GS: 0-0 Gd: 0-2 GF: - Fm: 0-0
Distance:	2m/2m3: 0-2 2m4-2m7: 0-0 3m+: 0-0
Track:	LH: 0-2 RH: 0-0 Tight: 0-2 Gall: 0-0
Aids:	Bl: 0-0 Vi: 0-0 Tstrap: 0-0 Ckp: 0-0
Best Rating:	88 5/03 Strf 2m110y good Hdl

Aids: Bl: 0-0 Vi: 0-0 Tstrap: 0-0 Ckp: 0-0
Best Rating: 117 1/01 Sthl 2m   heavy Hdl

Modest chaser; appreciated step up to 3m1f when winning Towcester handicap October 2003; acts on any going between good and heavy.

Parole Officer

5-y-o b g Priolo (USA)-Twosixtythreewest (FR) (Kris)
J Wade John Wade

Placings:0   (4481)
2003/04: 17⁰HY,

	Starts	1st	2nd	3rd	Win & Pl
NH Flat	1	0	0	0	
Career Total	1	0	0	0	

Going: Sf: 0-1 GS: 0-0 Gd: 0-0 GF: - Fm: 0-0
Distance: 2m/2m3: 0-1 2m4-2m7: 0-0 3m+: 0-0
Track: LH: 0-0 RH: 0-1 Tight: 0-0 Gall: 0-0
Aids: Bl: 0-0 Vi: 0-0 Tstrap: 0-0 Ckp: 0-0

Parsifal
109   91+

5-y-o b g Sadler's Wells (USA)-Moss (USA) (Woodman (USA))
J Howard Johnson M McKernan

Placings:00P6-32   (1480)
2003/04: 17³S, 17²G,

	Starts	1st	2nd	3rd	Win & Pl
Hurdles	2	0	1	1	1317
Career Total	6	0	1	1	1317

Going: Sf: 0-1 GS: 0-0 Gd: 0-1 GF: - Fm: 0-0
Distance: 2m/2m3: 0-2 2m4-2m7: 0-0 3m+: 0-0
Track: LH: 0-2 RH: 0-0 Tight: 0-2 Gall: 0-0
Aids: Bl: 0-0 Vi: 0-0 Tstrap: 0-0 Ckp: 0-0
Best Rating: 91 9/03 Sedg 2m1f   good Hdl

Moderate novice hurdler; ran best race on latest start when close third in handicap company at Sedgefield in May and went one place better when just caught in novice race at same venue in September; acts on good and easy ground; improving type.

Parson Jack

7-y-o b g Bedford (USA)-Scobitora (Thesauros)
R Dickin R T S Matthews

Placings:P   (3262)
2003/04: 16⁰HY,

	Starts	1st	2nd	3rd	Win & Pl
Hurdles	1	0	0	0	
Career Total	1	0	0	0	

Going: Sf: 0-1 GS: 0-0 Gd: 0-0 GF: - Fm: 0-0
Distance: 2m/2m3: 0-1 2m4-2m7: 0-0 3m+: 0-0
Track: LH: 0-0 RH: 0-1 Tight: 0-0 Gall: 0-0
Aids: Bl: 0-0 Vi: 0-0 Tstrap: 0-0 Ckp: 0-0

Parson Ploughman
96   81

9-y-o br g Riverwise (USA)-Pretty Pantoes (Lepanto (GER))

P F Nicholls Andrew Wadsworth

Placings:0/0040   (4676)
2003/04: 19⁰S, 24⁰GS, 19⁴S, 22⁰G,

	Starts	1st	2nd	3rd	Win & Pl
Hurdles	4	0	0	0	284
Career Total	5	0	0	0	284

Going: Sf: 0-2 GS: 0-1 Gd: 0-1 GF: - Fm: 0-0
Distance: 2m/2m3: 0-2 2m4-2m7: 0-1 3m+: 0-1
Track: LH: 0-0 RH: 0-4 Tight: 0-0 Gall: 0-0
Aids: Bl: 0-0 Vi: 0-0 Tstrap: 0-0 Ckp: 0-0
Best Rating: 81 2/04 Extr 2m3f   soft Hdl

Parsons Legacy (IRE)
111   126+

6-y-o b g Leading Counsel (USA)-The Parson's Girl (IRE) (The Parson)
P J Hobbs R A S Offer

Placings:040332-1P104P2   (4838)
2003/04: 19¹GF, 21⁵S, 20¹GS, 20⁰S, 22⁴G, 24⁰GS, 24²GF,

	Starts	1st	2nd	3rd	Win & Pl
Hurdles	7	2	1	0	14173
Career Total	13	2	2	2	17382
110 12/03 Leic	2m4f110yD Hdl			G-S	£3552
122 11/03 Newb	2m3f	D Hdl		G-F	£5021
			Total win prize-money £8573		

Going: Sf: 0-2 GS: 1-2 Gd: 0-1 GF: - Fm: 1-2
Distance: 2m/2m3: 1-1 2m4-2m7: 1-4 3m+: 0-2
Track: LH: 1-2 RH: 1-5 Tight: 0-0 Gall: 1-2
Aids: Bl: 0-0 Vi: 0-0 Tstrap: 0-0 Ckp: 0-0
Best Rating: 122 4/04 Chel 3m   gd-fm Hdl

Fair hurdler; stays 2m 4f; effective on a fast surface and with give underfoot, but has won on fast ground.

Parsons Pride (IRE)
103   90

8-y-o b g Persian Mews-First Prize (IRE) (The Parson)
J W Tudor Mrs Jeffrey Bird

Placings:30PP-015325   (1824)
2003/04: 17⁰GS, 24¹GF, 24⁴GF, 22³F, 26²GF, 25⁵GF,

	Starts	1st	2nd	3rd	Win & Pl
Hurdles	6	1	1	1	3939
Career Total	10	1	1	2	4223
90 9/03 Worc	3m	E Hdl		G-F	£2611
			Total win prize-money £2611		

Going: Sf: 0-0 GS: 0-1 Gd: 0-0 GF: - Fm: 1-5
Distance: 2m/2m3: 0-1 2m4-2m7: 0-1 3m+: 1-4
Track: LH: 1-5 RH: 0-1 Tight: 0-1 Gall: 0-1
Aids: Bl: 0-0 Vi: 0-0 Tstrap: 0-0 Ckp: 0-0
Best Rating: 91 9/02 Worc 2m   good NHF

First signs of form when winning 3m novices' hurdle at Worcester in September 2003; beaten favourite when effectively carrying 5lb more than his long handicap mark over the same course and distance next time; acts on fast ground.

Parte Prima

8-y-o b g Perpendicular-Pendle's Secret (Le Johnstan)
Alan Walter Mrs Jane Walter

Placings:0U/U136   (4655)

2003/04: 21⁰GS, 21¹G, 16³G, 16⁶G,

	Starts	1st	2nd	3rd	Win & Pl
Chases	4	1	0	1	1789
Career Total	6	1	0	1	1789
95 3/04 Folk	2m5f	H Ch		GD	£1469
			Total win prize-money £1469		

Going: Sf: 0-0 GS: 0-1 Gd: 1-3 GF: - Fm: 0-0
Distance: 2m/2m3: 0-2 2m4-2m7: 1-2 3m+: 0-1
Track: LH: 0-1 RH: 1-3 Tight: 1-2 Gall: 0-0
Aids: Bl: 0-0 Vi: 0-0 Tstrap: 0-0 Ckp: 0-0
Best Rating: 95 3/04 Folk 2m5f   good Ch

Hunter chaser; stays 2m5f; acts on good.

Party Animal (IRE)
104   97

12-y-o b g Buckskin (FR)-More Chat (Torenaga)
K C Bailey Racing Club Kcb

Placings:453/23/1U/3/P-3   (0056)
2003/04: 25³GS,

	Starts	1st	2nd	3rd	Win & Pl
Chases	1	0	0	1	760
Career Total	10	1	1	4	5915
110 11/00 Hrfd	3m1f110yF(0-90)HCh			G-S	£2710
			Total win prize-money £2711		

Going: Sf: 0-0 GS: 0-1 Gd: 0-0 GF: - Fm: 0-0
Distance: 2m/2m3: 0-2 2m4-2m7: 0-0 3m+: 0-1
Track: LH: 0-0 RH: 0-1 Tight: 0-0 Gall: 0-0
Aids: Bl: 0-0 Vi: 0-0 Tstrap: 0-0 Ckp: 0-0
Best Rating: 110 11/01 Wwck 3m2f   good Ch

Lightly raced chaser; broke blood vessel when pulled up at Chepstow February 2003; has obviously been difficult to train.

Party Games (IRE)
102   100

7-y-o b g King's Ride-Shady Miss (Mandamus)
D B Feek Gregory Barker

Placings:4/5-2353P32   (4793)
2003/04: 17²GS, 17³GS, 18⁵G, 16³S, 20⁰GS, 21³GS, 16²G,

	Starts	1st	2nd	3rd	Win & Pl
Hurdles	6	0	2	3	3526
Chases	1	0	0	0	
Career Total	9	0	2	3	3526

Going: Sf: 0-1 GS: 0-4 Gd: 0-2 GF: - Fm: 0-0
Distance: 2m/2m3: 0-5 2m4-2m7: 0-2 3m+: 0-0
Track: LH: 0-4 RH: 0-3 Tight: 0-6 Gall: 0-0
Aids: Bl: 0-0 Vi: 0-0 Tstrap: 0-0 Ckp: 0-0
Best Rating: 100 12/03 Folk 2m1f110y gd-sft Hdl

Moderate novice hurdler; stays two miles-five; acts on good and easy ground.

Pas De Surprise

6-y-o b g Dancing Spree (USA)-Supreme Rose (Frimley Park)
P D Evans (J G Portman 3/6) D Healy

Placings:P   (1702)
2003/04: 16⁰GF,

	Starts	1st	2nd	3rd	Win & Pl
Hurdles	1	0	0	0	
Career Total	1	0	0	0	

Going: Sf: 0-0 GS: 0-0 Gd: 0-0 GF: - Fm: 0-1

Distance: 2m/2m3: 0-1 2m4-2m7: 0-0 3m+: 0-0
Track: LH: 0-1 RH: 0-0 Tight: 0-1 Gall: 0-0
Aids: Bl: 0-0 Vi: 0-0 Tstrap: 0-0 Ckp: 0-0

Pasha

8-y-o b m Ardkinglass-Infanta Maria (King Of Spain)
R J Baker Churchgoers Anonymous

Placings: P   (0182)
2003/04: 16PGF,

	Starts	1st	2nd	3rd	Win & Pl
Hurdles	1	0	0	0	
Career Total	1	0	0	0	

Going: Sf: 0-0 GS: 0-0 Gd: 0-0 GF: 0-1
Distance: 2m/2m3: 0-1 2m4-2m7: 0-0 3m+: 0-1
Track: LH: 0-0 RH: 0-1 Tight: 0-0 Gall: 0-0
Aids: Bl: 0-0 Vi: 0-0 Tstrap: 0-0 Ckp: 0-0

Pass Me By
106   126+

5-y-o b g Balnibarbi-Errol Emerald (Dom Racine (FR))
T D Walford Mrs M Cooper

Placings: 104-2101000   (4729)
2003/04: 20²GS, 21¹GS, 20⁹S, 20¹S, 20⁹G, 24⁰HY, 20⁴G,

	Starts	1st	2nd	3rd	Win & Pl
Hurdles	7	2	1	0	9674
Career Total	10	3	1	0	12649
126	2/04	Hayd	2m4f		D Hdl	SFT	£5248
113	11/03	Hayd	2m4f		D Hdl	G-S	£3640
93	1/03	Muss	2m		H NHF	GD	£2975
						Total win prize-money £11864

Going: Sf: 1-3 GS: 1-2 Gd: 0-2 GF: - Fm: 0-0
Distance: 2m/2m3: 0-0 2m4-2m7: 2-6 3m+: 0-1
Track: LH: 2-5 RH: 0-2 Tight: 0-0 Gall: 0-0
Aids: Bl: 0-0 Vi: 0-0 Tstrap: 0-0 Ckp: 0-0
Best Rating: 126 2/04 Hayd 2m4f   soft   Hdl

Fair hurdler; bumper winner; has won twice over Haydock's 'fixed brush' hurdles, latest in February 2004; suited by two and a half miles; handles testing conditions.

Passed Out (IRE)

6-y-o b g Shahanndeh-Ah Suzie (IRE) (King's Ride)
B N Pollock Mrs Nicola Pollock

Placings: P   (2193)
2003/04: 20PGS,

	Starts	1st	2nd	3rd	Win & Pl
Hurdles	1	0	0	0	
Career Total	1	0	0	0	

Going: Sf: 0-0 GS: 0-1 Gd: 0-0 GF: - Fm: 0-0
Distance: 2m/2m3: 0-0 2m4-2m7: 0-1 3m+: 0-0
Track: LH: 0-1 RH: 0-0 Tight: 0-0 Gall: 0-0
Aids: Bl: 0-0 Vi: 0-0 Tstrap: 0-0 Ckp: 0-0

Passenger Omar (IRE)
96   81

6-y-o b g Safety Catch (USA)-Princess Douglas (Bishop Of Orange)

Noel T Chance Mrs V Griffiths

Placings: R0-044   (4887)
2003/04: 20⁹GF, 25⁴S, 22⁴GF,

	Starts	1st	2nd	3rd	Win & Pl
Hurdles	3	0	0	0	471
Career Total	5	0	0	0	471

Going: Sf: 0-1 GS: 0-0 Gd: 0-0 GF: - Fm: 0-2
Distance: 2m/2m3: 0-0 2m4-2m7: 0-2 3m+: 0-1
Track: LH: 0-3 RH: 0-0 Tight: 0-1 Gall: 0-0
Aids: Bl: 0-0 Vi: 0-0 Tstrap: 0-3 Ckp: 0-0
Best Rating: 81 4/04 Strf 2m6f110y gd-fm Hdl

Passing Wind (NZ)
105   (96h)96

10-y-o br g Beau Zephyr (AUS)-Miss Row (NZ) (Long Row)
R C Guest George and Doris Racing

Placings: 33F03FFP/1F22060P/31F   (3253)
2003/04: 24³G, 21¹G, 20⁵G,

	Starts	1st	2nd	3rd	Win & Pl
Chases	3	1	0	1	3541
Career Total	19	2	2	4	9450
96	11/03	Fknm	2m5f110yE(0-105)HCh	GD	£2905
93	8/01	Bang	2m1f	E(0-105)HHdl	G-S	£3122
				Total win prize-money £6027

Going: Sf: 0-0 GS: 0-0 Gd: 1-3 GF: - Fm: 0-0
Distance: 2m/2m3: 0-0 2m4-2m7: 1-2 3m+: 1-1
Track: LH: 1-2 RH: 0-1 Tight: 1-3 Gall: 0-0
Aids: Bl: 0-0 Vi: 0-0 Tstrap: 0-0 Ckp: 0-0
Best Rating: 99 9/03 Bang 3m110y   good   Ch

New Zealand import; has shown ability over hurdles, but had problems completing; promising third on debut over fences at Bangor in September and was gifted race next time; best at distances short of three miles; appreciates a little cut in the ground.

Pat N Dec
82f   90f

5-y-o b g Overbury (IRE)-Princess Semele (Imperial Fling (USA))
Ian Williams Dsm Demolition Limited

Placings: 66   (4787)
2003/04: 16⁶G, 16⁶G,

	Starts	1st	2nd	3rd	Win & Pl
NH Flat	2	0	0	0	0
Career Total	2	0	0	0	0

Going: Sf: 0-0 GS: 0-0 Gd: 0-2 GF: - Fm: 0-0
Distance: 2m/2m3: 0-2 2m4-2m7: 0-0 3m+: 0-0
Track: LH: 0-0 RH: 0-2 Tight: 0-0 Gall: 0-2
Aids: Bl: 0-0 Vi: 0-0 Tstrap: 0-0 Ckp: 0-0
Best Rating: 90 3/04 Hntg 2m110y   good   NHF

Patches (IRE)
96   111

5-y-o b/br g Presenting-Ballykilleen (The Parson)
P F Nicholls Mrs Marianne G Barber

Placings: 265   (3789)
2003/04: 16²GS, 16⁶GS, 22⁵G,

	Starts	1st	2nd	3rd	Win & Pl
Hurdles	3	0	1	0	1646
Career Total	3	0	1	0	1646

Going: Sf: 0-0 GS: 0-2 Gd: 0-1 GF: - Fm: 0-0
Distance: 2m/2m3: 0-2 2m4-2m7: 0-0 3m+: 0-0
Track: LH: 0-0 RH: 0-0 Tight: 0-0 Gall: 0-0
Aids: Bl: 0-0 Vi: 0-0 Tstrap: 0-0 Ckp: 0-0
Best Rating: 111 12/03 Chep 2m110y gd-sft Hdl

Impressive winner of Irish point in heavy ground March 2003; promising debut over inadequate 2m when narrowly beaten at Chepstow maiden hurdle December 2003.

Patriarch (IRE)
101   98

8-y-o b g Alphabatim (USA)-Strong Language (Formidable (USA))
M Pitman Malcolm C Denmark

Placings: 13/502132/P-3   (3870)
2003/04: 21³GS,

	Starts	1st	2nd	3rd	Win & Pl
Chases	1	0	0	1	644
Career Total	10	2	2	3	22351
135	2/01	Wwck	2m5f		B Hdl	SFT	£9217
117	2/00	Newb	2m110y	B NHF	G-S	£7670
				Total win prize-money £16887

Going: Sf: 0-0 GS: 0-1 Gd: 0-0 GF: - Fm: 0-0
Distance: 2m/2m3: 0-0 2m4-2m7: 0-1 3m+: 0-0
Track: LH: 0-0 RH: 0-1 Tight: 0-1 Gall: 0-0
Aids: Bl: 0-0 Vi: 0-0 Tstrap: 0-0 Ckp: 0-0
Best Rating: 135 2/01 Wwck 2m5f   soft   Hdl

Modest chaser/former decent novice hurdler; suited by forcing the pace; stays two miles five; acts on a soft surface.

Patriarch Express
107   127

7-y-o b g Noble Patriarch-Jaydeeglen (Bay Express)
G A Harker A P Muir

Placings: 2/11100-1162635   (4641)
2003/04: 20¹G, 20¹S, 21⁶GS, 18²S, 19⁶S, 18³GS, 24⁵G,

	Starts	1st	2nd	3rd	Win & Pl
Hurdles	7	2	1	1	13147
Career Total	12	4	2	1	20763
123	11/03	Hayd	2m4f		D Hdl	SFT	£3770
101	11/03	Newc	2m4f		E Hdl	GD	£2611
111	10/02	Chel	2m110y	H NHF	GD	£4127
107	9/02	Prth	2m110y	H NHF	G-F	£3003
				Total win prize-money £13512

Going: Sf: 1-3 GS: 0-2 Gd: 1-2 GF: - Fm: 0-0
Distance: 2m/2m3: 2-4 2m4-2m7: 2-4 3m+: 0-1
Track: LH: 2-7 RH: 0-0 Tight: 0-3 Gall: 1-2
Aids: Bl: 0-0 Vi: 0-0 Tstrap: 0-0 Ckp: 0-0
Best Rating: 127 4/04 Aint 3m110y   good   Hdl

Useful hurdler; decent bumper horse in 2002/3; won well on hurdles debut at Newcastle in November; followed up in easy fashion at Haydock but limitations exposed after; stays 2m 4f; acts on good and soft.

Patricksnineteenth (IRE)
112   148+

7-y-o b g Mister Lord (USA)-Many Miracles (Le Moss)
P R Webber The Large G & T Partnership

Placings: 310-2214   (4395)
2003/04: 20²GS, 20²G, 20¹S, 24⁴G,

	Starts	1st	2nd	3rd	Win & Pl
Chases	4	1	2	0	44859
Career Total	7	2	2	1	47818

148 2/04 Sand 2m4f110y   A Ch SFT
£32725
111 2/03 Sand 2m110y H NHF   HVY £2656
Total win prize-money £35382

Going: Sf: 1-1 GS: 0-1 Gd: 0-2 GF: - Fm: 0-0
Distance: 2m/2m3: 0-0 **2m4-2m7: 1-3** 3m+: 0-1
Track: LH: 0-2 **RH: 1-2** Tight: 0-1 Gall: 0-1
Aids: Bl: 0-0 Vi: 0-0 Tstrap: 0-0 Ckp: 0-0
Best Rating: 148 2/04 Sand 2m4f110y   soft   Ch

Smart novice chaser; bumper winner; got off the mark over fences in the Grade One Scilly Isles Novices' Chase at Sandown in February; stays two and a half miles and appeared to not stay when upped to three; acts on most ground; open to more improvement.

Pats Future
85   **64**
5-y-o ch m King's Signet (USA)-Bedelia (Mr Fluorocarbon)
P R Rodford P R Rodford

Placings:00-3000   (2818)
2003/04: 17³GS, 16⁶GF, 17⁰GS, 19⁰G,

	Starts	1st	2nd	3rd	Win & Pl
NH Flat	2	0	0	1	339
Hurdles	2	0	0	0	0
Career Total	6	0	0	1	339

Going: Sf: 0-0 GS: 0-1 Gd: 0-1 GF: - Fm: 0-2
Distance: 2m/2m3: 0-4 2m4-2m7: 0-0 3m+: 0-0
Track: LH: 0-1 RH: 0-3 Tight: 0-0 Gall: 0-0
Aids: Bl: 0-0 Vi: 0-0 Tstrap: 0-0 Ckp: 0-0
Best Rating: 77 10/03 Extr 2m1f   gd-fm NHF

Patsy Veale (IRE)
111   **130**
9-y-o b g Accordion-Bermuda Castle (Carlingford Castle)
John Queally M A Ryan

Placings:20/2 f213/13403006/102-20   (1239a)
2003/04: 16²GS, 17⁰F,

	Starts	1st	2nd	3rd	Win & Pl
Hurdles	2	0	1	0	15400
Career Total	20	4	5	3	57468
125 5/02	Klny	2m1f	HHdl	G-Y	£19938
120 5/01	Dund	2m4f153y (0-123)HHdl	FRM	£6677
107 9/00	Gway	2m	Hdl	YLD	£4416
107 6/00	Dund	2m135y	NHF	FRM	£2760

Total win prize-money £33792

Going: Sf: 0-0 GS: 0-1 Gd: 0-0 GF: - Fm: 0-1
Distance: 2m/2m3: 0-2 2m4-2m7: 0-0 3m+: 0-0
Track: LH: 0-2 RH: 0-0 Tight: 0-0 Gall: 0-0
Aids: Bl: 0-0 Vi: 0-0 Tstrap: 0-0 Ckp: 0-0
Best Rating: 130 5/03 Hayd 2m   gd-sft Hdl

Irish-trained; winner of a bumper and has been successful over hurdles; acts on a sound surface and is effective from two to two and a half miles.

Pattella Wood (IRE)
6-y-o ch m Denel (FR)-West Cove (Quayside)
R A Curran Mrs Mary Curran

Placings:PP   (3056a)
2003/04: 19⁰GF, 20⁰Y,

	Starts	1st	2nd	3rd	Win & Pl
Hurdles	2	0	0	0	
Career Total	2	0	0	0	

Paula
75f   **50f**
4-y-o b f Compton Place-Be My Bird (Be My Chief (USA))
M Dods D Vic Roper

Placings:0   (4608)
2003/04: 17⁰G,

	Starts	1st	2nd	3rd	Win & Pl
NH Flat	1	0	0	0	
Career Total	1	0	0	0	

Going: Sf: 0-0 GS: 0-0 Gd: 0-1 GF: - Fm: 0-0
Distance: 2m/2m3: 0-1 2m4-2m7: 0-0 3m+: 0-0
Track: LH: 0-0 RH: 0-1 Tight: 0-1 Gall: 0-0
Aids: Bl: 0-0 Vi: 0-0 Tstrap: 0-0 Ckp: 0-0
Best Rating: 52 3/04 MRas 2m1f110y good NHF

Paula Lane
72   **38**
4-y-o b f Factual (USA)-Colfax Classic (Jareer (USA))
R Curtis Mrs R A Smith

Placings:0   (2871)
2003/04: 16⁰S,

	Starts	1st	2nd	3rd	Win & Pl
Hurdles	1	0	0	0	
Career Total	1	0	0	0	

Going: Sf: 0-1 GS: 0-0 Gd: 0-0 GF: - Fm: 0-0
Distance: 2m/2m3: 0-1 2m4-2m7: 0-0 3m+: 0-0
Track: LH: 0-1 RH: 0-0 Tight: 0-0 Gall: 0-0
Aids: Bl: 0-0 Vi: 0-0 Tstrap: 0-0 Ckp: 0-0
Best Rating: 38 12/03 Wwck 2m   soft   Hdl

Pauluke
84   **70+**
5-y-o b m Bishop Of Cashel-Beacon Blaze (Rudimentary (USA))
N J Hawke Mrs S Robinson

Placings:005   (2589)
2003/04: 16⁰G, 16⁰GS, 16⁵GS,

	Starts	1st	2nd	3rd	Win & Pl
Hurdles	3	0	0	0	
Career Total	3	0	0	0	

Going: Sf: 0-0 GS: 0-2 Gd: 0-1 GF: - Fm: 0-0
Distance: 2m/2m3: 0-3 2m4-2m7: 0-0 3m+: 0-0
Track: LH: 0-3 RH: 0-0 Tight: 0-1 Gall: 0-0
Aids: Bl: 0-0 Vi: 0-0 Tstrap: 0-0 Ckp: 0-1
Best Rating: 70 12/03 Chep 2m110y gd-sft Hdl

Pavey Ark (IRE)
91   **61**
6-y-o b g King's Ride-Splendid Run (Deep Run)
James Moffatt Mr & Mrs A G Milligan

Placings:052-06P6P   (4273)

2003/04: 16⁰G, 20⁶GS, 17⁶G, 19⁶G, 24⁶G,

	Starts	1st	2nd	3rd	Win & Pl
NH Flat	1	0	0	0	0
Hurdles	4	0	0	0	0
Career Total	8	0	1	0	544

Going: Sf: 0-0 GS: 0-1 Gd: 0-4 GF: - Fm: 0-0
Distance: 2m/2m3: 0-3 2m4-2m7: 0-1 3m+: 0-0
Track: LH: 0-2 RH: 0-3 Tight: 0-2 Gall: 0-0
Aids: Bl: 0-0 Vi: 0-0 Tstrap: 0-0 Ckp: 0-0
Best Rating: 96 4/03 Hexm 2m110y good NHF

Pavone Quest
7-y-o ch g Jumbo Hirt (USA)-Gilsan Grey (Grey Ghost)
G M Moore Inter Enterprise Ies Ltd

Placings:OP   (3371)
2003/04: 16⁰GS, 20⁰S,

	Starts	1st	2nd	3rd	Win & Pl
NH Flat	1	0	0	0	0
Hurdles	1	0	0	0	0
Career Total	2	0	0	0	

Going: Sf: 0-1 GS: 0-1 Gd: 0-0 GF: - Fm: 0-0
Distance: 2m/2m3: 0-1 2m4-2m7: 0-1 3m+: 0-0
Track: LH: 0-2 RH: 0-0 Tight: 0-0 Gall: 0-0
Aids: Bl: 0-0 Vi: 0-0 Tstrap: 0-0 Ckp: 0-0
Best Rating: 63 12/03 Newc 2m   gd-sft NHF

Pawn Broker
109   **116**
7-y-o ch g Selkirk (USA)-Dime Bag (High Line)
D R C Elsworth Raymond Tooth

Placings:6-43   (2914)
2003/04: 16⁴S, 16³G,

	Starts	1st	2nd	3rd	Win & Pl
Hurdles	2	0	0	1	2246
Career Total	3	0	0	1	2246

Going: Sf: 0-1 GS: 0-0 Gd: 0-1 GF: - Fm: 0-0
Distance: 2m/2m3: 0-2 2m4-2m7: 0-0 3m+: 0-0
Track: LH: 0-0 RH: 0-2 Tight: 0-0 Gall: 0-0
Aids: Bl: 0-0 Vi: 0-0 Tstrap: 0-0 Ckp: 0-0
Best Rating: 116 12/03 Kemp 2m   good Hdl

Smart performer on the Flat; best run over hurdles so far when third at Kempton on Boxing Day 2003; only just gets the two miles.

Paxford Lady
98   **81**
7-y-o b m Alflora (IRE)-Rakajack (Rakaposhi King)
M F Harris M Harris

Placings:500PP/P-2PF5FPP   (3439)
2003/04: 20²HY, 21²HY, 20⁶G, 16⁵GS, 16⁶GS, 20⁶S, 20⁶HY,

	Starts	1st	2nd	3rd	Win & Pl
Chases	7	0	1	0	1363
Career Total	13	0	1	0	1363

Going: Sf: 0-4 GS: 0-2 Gd: 0-1 GF: - Fm: 0-0
Distance: 2m/2m3: 0-2 2m4-2m7: 0-5 3m+: 0-0
Track: LH: 0-5 RH: 0-2 Tight: 0-0 Gall: 0-2
Aids: Bl: 0-1 Vi: 0-0 Tstrap: 0-0 Ckp: 0-0
Best Rating: 81 12/03 Hntg 2m110y gd-sft Ch

First worthwhile form over fences when well beaten runner-up in weak mares' only 2m 4f handicap in soft ground at Uttoxeter April 2003.

Paxford Trooper

66 **13**

10-y-o b g Gunner B-Say Shanaz (Tickled Pink)
M F Harris M Harris

Placings: 5/P0/P-F0 (2909)
2003/04: 24FG, 21OGS,

	Starts	1st	2nd	Win & Pl
Hurdles	1	0	0	0
Chases	1	0	0	0
Career Total	6	0	0	0

Going:	Sf: 0-0 GS: 0-1 Gd: 0-1 GF: - Fm: 0-0
Distance:	2m/2m3: 0-0 2m4-2m7: 0-1 3m+: 0-1
Track:	LH: 0-0 RH: 0-0 Tight: 0-0 Gall: 0-0
Aids:	Bl: 0-0 Vi: 0-0 Tstrap: 0-0 Ckp: 0-0
Best Rating:	87 5/98 Worc 2m gd-fm NHF

Poor hurdler; winning pointer.

Pay It Forward

104(111h) (139 h)**123**

6-y-o b g Anshan-Kellsboro Kate (Paddy's Stream)
Mrs John Harrington Paid Thru The Nose Syndicate

Placings: 405123241-3250F20 (3742a)
2003/04: 20³YS, 20²S, 25⁶G, 20⁰S, 18FS, 20²S, 21⁰YS,

	Starts	1st	2nd	3rd	Win & Pl
Hurdles	4	0	1	1	10328
Chases	3	0	0	0	1870
Career Total	16	2	4	2	37177
119	4/03	Fair	2m4f		G-F £14772
110	12/02	Fair	2m2f	Hdl	SH £6561

Total win prize-money £21334

Going:	Sf: 0-4 GS: 0-0 Gd: 0-1 GF: - Fm: 0-0
Distance:	2m/2m3: 0-1 2m4-2m7: 0-5 3m+: 0-2
Track:	LH: 0-4 RH: 0-2 Tight: 0-0 Gall: 0-0
Aids:	Bl: 0-0 Vi: 0-0 Tstrap: 0-0 Ckp: 0-0
Best Rating:	139 11/03 Weth 3m1f good Hdl

Useful hurdler in Ireland; consistent; stays two and a half miles; acts on fast and soft ground.

Payford Bridge

54

11-y-o br g Lighter-Saucy Laura (Crozier)
M Sheppard Mrs Rosie Newman

Placings: P/P/0/PP6/P (4874)
2003/04: 20⁰GS,

	Starts	1st	2nd	3rd	Win & Pl
Hurdles	1	0	0	0	0
Career Total	7	0	0	0	0

Going:	Sf: 0-0 GS: 0-1 Gd: 0-0 GF: - Fm: 0-0
Distance:	2m/2m3: 0-0 2m4-2m7: 0-1 3m+: 0-0
Track:	LH: 0-1 RH: 0-0 Tight: 0-1 Gall: 0-0
Aids:	Bl: 0-0 Vi: 0-0 Tstrap: 0-0 Ckp: 0-0
Best Rating:	54 4/02 Uttx 2m4f110y gd-fm Hdl

Paynestown Lad (IRE)

88 **86**

8-y-o b g Bravefoot-Athy Lady (Welsh Captain)

Miss C J E Caroe   Miss C J E Caroe

Placings: 006P6U1-604 (1025)
2003/04: 21⁶GF, 22⁰GF, 24⁴GF,

	Starts	1st	2nd	3rd	Win & Pl
Hurdles	3	0	0	0	363
Career Total	10	1	0	0	3847
86	4/03	Plum	2m5f	E Hdl	G-F £3484

Total win prize-money £3484

Going:	Sf: 0-0 GS: 0-0 Gd: 0-0 GF: - Fm: 0-3
Distance:	2m/2m3: 0-0 2m4-2m7: 0-2 3m+: 0-1
Track:	LH: 0-2 RH: 0-1 Tight: 0-2 Gall: 0-0
Aids:	Bl: 0-0 Vi: 0-0 Tstrap: 0-0 Ckp: 0-0
Best Rating:	86 4/03 Plum 2m5f gd-fm Hdl

Plating-class hurdler; first worthwhile form when slightly fortunate winner of a novice hurdle at Plumpton in April 2003; stays two miles five; effective on good to firm.

PC's Eurocruiser (IRE)

91 **73**

8-y-o b g Fayruz-Kuwait Night (Morston (FR))
Mrs Dianne Sayer Mrs M A Kendall

Placings: 0OP/055261/P00033/430-50F (0428)
2003/04: 16⁰G, 16⁶G, 16⁹G, 17⁷G,

	Starts	1st	2nd	3rd	Win & Pl
Hurdles	4	0	0	0	0
Career Total	21	1	1	3	4006
82	9/00	MRas	2m1f110yF(0-100)HHdl	G-F	£2747

Total win prize-money £2748

Going:	Sf: 0-0 GS: 0-0 Gd: 0-0 GF: - Fm: 0-1
Distance:	2m/2m3: 0-4 2m4-2m7: 0-0 3m+: 0-0
Track:	LH: 0-4 RH: 0-0 Tight: 0-1 Gall: 0-1
Aids:	Bl: 0-0 Vi: 0-0 Tstrap: 0-0 Ckp: 0-0
Best Rating:	86 2/02 Fknm 2m gd-sft Hdl

Peacemaker (IRE)

105 **80**

12-y-o br g Strong Gale-Gamonda (Gala Performance (USA))
J R Cornwall J R Cornwall

Placings: 0OP3/404/040P/P22035/121222F5F4/005P3-2631260 (3526)
2003/04: 21²GF, 25⁶G, 23³GF, 25¹F, 21²G, 24⁶GS, 23⁰G,

	Starts	1st	2nd	3rd	Win & Pl
Chases	7	1	2	1	5583
Career Total	39	3	8	4	24336
80	10/03	Towc	3m1f	F(0-90)HCh	FRM £2936
86	7/01	Strf	2m5f110yE(0-105)HCh	GD	£3328
86	6/01	Fknm	2m5f110yF(0-100)HCh	G-F	£3562

Total win prize-money £9828

Going:	Sf: 0-0 GS: 0-1 Gd: 0-3 GF: - Fm: 1-3
Distance:	2m/2m3: 0-0 2m4-2m7: 0-2 3m+: 1-5
Track:	LH: 0-5 RH: 1-2 Tight: 0-2 Gall: 0-0
Aids:	Bl: 0-0 Vi: 0-0 Tstrap: 0-0 Ckp: 0-0
Best Rating:	98 7/01 Sthl 2m4f110y gd-fm Ch

Plating-class chaser; stays three miles; acts on fast ground.

Peachy (IRE)

9-y-o b g Un Desperado (FR)-Little Peach (Ragapan)
R T Phillips Colin Pocock

Placings: 1/F/3F/P (2727)

2003/04: 19⁶G,

	Starts	1st	2nd	Win & Pl
Hurdles	1	0	0	0
Career Total	5	1	0	1	2099
104	3/00	Folk	2m1f110yH	NHF	G-F £1715

Total win prize-money £1715

Going:	Sf: 0-0 GS: 0-0 Gd: 0-1 GF: - Fm: 0-0
Distance:	2m/2m3: 0-0 2m4-2m7: 0-1 3m+: 0-0
Track:	LH: 0-1 RH: 0-0 Tight: 0-0 Gall: 0-0
Aids:	Bl: 0-0 Vi: 0-0 Tstrap: 0-0 Ckp: 0-0
Best Rating:	104 3/02 Hrfd 2m3f110y good Hdl

Peafield (IRE)

15-y-o b g Torus-La'Bavette (Le Bavard (FR))
P York A R Parrish

Placings: 65203504P/20F4/00405/220/3 (0349)
2003/04: 26³GF,

	Starts	1st	2nd	3rd	Win & Pl
Chases	1	0	0	1	217
Career Total	22	0	4	2	3710

Going:	Sf: 0-0 GS: 0-0 Gd: 0-0 GF: - Fm: 0-1
Distance:	2m/2m3: 0-0 2m4-2m7: 0-0 3m+: 0-1
Track:	LH: 0-0 RH: 0-1 Tight: 0-1 Gall: 0-0
Aids:	Bl: 0-0 Vi: 0-0 Tstrap: 0-0 Ckp: 0-0
Best Rating:	97 5/01 Folk 3m2f good Ch

Pearliwhirl

92 **81+**

5-y-o b m Alflora (IRE)-Pearlossa (Teenoso (USA))
N J Henderson P J Hughes Developments Ltd

Placings: 0-406 (4253)
2003/04: 17⁴GF, 21⁰GS, 17⁶G,

	Starts	1st	2nd	3rd	Win & Pl
NH Flat	1	0	0	0	0
Hurdles	2	0	0	0	0
Career Total	4	0	0	0	0

Going:	Sf: 0-0 GS: 0-1 Gd: 0-1 GF: - Fm: 0-1
Distance:	2m/2m3: 0-2 2m4-2m7: 0-0 3m+: 0-1
Track:	LH: 0-2 RH: 0-1 Tight: 0-1 Gall: 0-1
Aids:	Bl: 0-0 Vi: 0-0 Tstrap: 0-0 Ckp: 0-0
Best Rating:	93 11/03 Hrfd 2m1f gd-fm NHF

Pearly Bay

102f **99+f**

6-y-o b m Karinga Bay-Marina Bird (Julio Mariner)
M G Rimell Mark Rimell

Placings: 1 (4571)
2003/04: 17¹GS,

	Starts	1st	2nd	3rd	Win & Pl
NH Flat	1	1	0	0	2093
Career Total	1	1	0	0	2093
99	3/04	Bang	2m1f	H NHF	G-S £2093

Total win prize-money £2093

Going:	Sf: 0-0 GS: 1-1 Gd: 0-0 GF: - Fm: 0-0
Distance:	2m/2m3: 1-1 2m4-2m7: 0-0 3m+: 0-0
Track:	LH: 1-1 RH: 0-0 Tight: 1-1 Gall: 0-0
Aids:	Bl: 0-0 Vi: 0-0 Tstrap: 0-0 Ckp: 0-0
Best Rating:	99 3/04 Bang 2m1f gd-sft NHF

Bumper winner on easy ground.

Pease Blossom (IRE)

101   **93**

5-y-o b m Revoque (IRE)-Saneena (Kris)
T G McCourt John J Hughes

Placings:0552-256430P0   (4332a)
2003/04: 16²GY, 16⁵G, 16⁶Y, 17⁴GY, 16³S, 16²G, 16⁰YS,

	Starts	1st	2nd	3rd	Win & Pl
Hurdles	8	0	1	0	2161
Career Total	12	0	2	1	3304

Going:	Sf: 0-2 GS: 0-0 Gd: 0-2 GF: - Fm: 0-0
Distance:	2m/2m3: 0-8 2m4-2m7: 0-0 3m+: 0-0
Track:	LH: 0-0 RH: 0-6 Tight: 0-1 Gall: 0-0
Aids:	Bl: 0-0 Vi: 0-1 Tstrap: 0-0 Ckp: 0-6
Best Rating:	101 2/03 Naas 2m soft Hdl

Pebble Bay

83   **78**

9-y-o br g Perpendicular-Milly L'Attaque (Military)
G A Harker M F Spence

Placings:2PF05   (2530)
2003/04: 16²GF, 21PGF, 17FGF, 19⁰G, 19⁵GS,

	Starts	1st	2nd	3rd	Win & Pl
Hurdles	5	0	1	0	972
Career Total	5	0	1	0	972

Going:	Sf: 0-0 GS: 0-1 Gd: 0-1 GF: - Fm: 0-3
Distance:	2m/2m3: 0-3 2m4-2m7: 0-2 3m+: 0-0
Track:	LH: 0-4 RH: 0-1 Tight: 0-4 Gall: 0-0
Aids:	Bl: 0-3 Vi: 0-0 Tstrap: 0-0 Ckp: 0-0
Best Rating:	78 12/03 Catt 2m3f gd-sft Hdl

Remote second behind effortless winner on his first ever outing in a novices' hurdle at Hexham in June; well beaten since.

Peccadillo (IRE)

110   **138**

10-y-o br g Un Desperado (FR)-First Mistake (Posse (USA))
R H Alner Dwight Makins

Placings:60/63212/315/2133143F/11430P15-2235U0   (4057)

2003/04: 20²GF, 24²GF, 24³GF, 20⁵GF, 24UG, 20⁰G,

	Starts	1st	2nd	3rd	Win & Pl
Chases	6	0	2	1	8502
Career Total	32	7	5	7	60446
137	4/03	Asct	2m3f110yD(0-125)HCh	GD	£10341
137	9/02	Hntg	2m4f110yC(0-135)HCh	G-F	£7995
133	9/02	Uttx	2m5f	D(0-125)HCh	GD	£5411
137	12/01	Winc	2m	E(0-115)HCh	GD	£4075
120	10/01	Winc	2m5f	F(0-110)HCh	G-S	£4173
115	12/00	Winc	2m	E(0-115)HCh	G-S	£4290
99	3/00	Folk	2m	F(0-100)HCh	G-F	£2422
			Total win prize-money £38710		

Going:	Sf: 0-0 GS: 0-0 Gd: 0-2 GF: - Fm: 0-4
Distance:	2m/2m3: 0-0 2m4-2m7: 0-3 3m+: 0-3
Track:	LH: 0-0 RH: 0-6 Tight: 0-0 Gall: 0-1
Aids:	Bl: 0-0 Vi: 0-0 Tstrap: 0-0 Ckp: 0-0
Best Rating:	138 10/03 Kemp 3m gd-fm Ch

Useful handicap chaser; at his best when able to establish an uncontested lead; jumps well, acts on fast ground and goes particularly well at Wincanton; stays 3m, effective at shorter.

Peddars Way

90f   **79f**

5-y-o b g Nomadic Way (USA)-Deep Selection (IRE) (Deep Run)
A King Mrs Peter Mason

Placings:0   (4594)
2003/04: 16⁰G,

	Starts	1st	2nd	3rd	Win & Pl
NH Flat	1	0	0	0	
Career Total	1	0	0	0	

Going:	Sf: 0-0 GS: 0-0 Gd: 0-1 GF: - Fm: 0-0
Distance:	2m/2m3: 0-1 2m4-2m7: 0-0 3m+: 0-0
Track:	LH: 0-0 RH: 0-0 Tight: 0-0 Gall: 0-1
Aids:	Bl: 0-0 Vi: 0-0 Tstrap: 0-0 Ckp: 0-0
Best Rating:	79 3/04 Hntg 2m110y good NHF

Pedler's Profiles

84   **42**

4-y-o br g Topanoora-La Vie En Primrose (Henbit (USA))
Miss K M George Exterior Profiles Ltd

Placings:0   (4854)
2003/04: 17⁰GF,

	Starts	1st	2nd	3rd	Win & Pl
Hurdles	1	0	0	0	
Career Total	1	0	0	0	

Going:	Sf: 0-0 GS: 0-0 Gd: 0-0 GF: - Fm: 0-1
Distance:	2m/2m3: 0-0 2m4-2m7: 0-0 3m+: 0-0
Track:	LH: 0-0 RH: 0-0 Tight: 0-1 Gall: 0-0
Aids:	Bl: 0-0 Vi: 0-0 Tstrap: 0-0 Ckp: 0-0
Best Rating:	42 4/04 Tntn 2m1f gd-fm Hdl

Peeyoutwo

100   **89**

9-y-o b g Golden Heights-Nyika (Town And Country)
Mrs D A Hamer Power Units (1953) Ltd

Placings:100P/0-361243   (2034)
2003/04: 20³GF, 16⁸G, 16¹GF, 17²G, 16⁴G, 16³GF,

	Starts	1st	2nd	3rd	Win & Pl
Hurdles	6	1	1	2	6289
Career Total	11	2	1	2	8459
89	9/03	Strf	2m110y D Hdl	G-F	£4007
91	8/01	NAbb	2m1f	H NHF	G-F	£2170
			Total win prize-money £6177		

Going:	Sf: 0-0 GS: 0-0 Gd: 0-3 GF: - Fm: 1-3
Distance:	2m/2m3: 1-5 2m4-2m7: 0-0 3m+: 0-0
Track:	LH: 1-6 RH: 0-0 Tight: 1-3 Gall: 0-0
Aids:	Bl: 0-0 Vi: 0-0 Tstrap: 0-0 Ckp: 0-0
Best Rating:	97 10/01 Chel 2m110y good NHF

Free-running sort; lightly-raced; acts on fast; won poor 2m novice hurdle at Stratford September 2003; has given the impression he fails to stay 2m 4f.

Peggy Lou

84   **73**

4-y-o b f Washington State (USA)-Rosemary Nalden (Great Commotion (USA))
B J Llewellyn T G B Racing Club

Placings:530   (1958)
2003/04: 16⁵GF, 16³F, 16⁰GF,

	Starts	1st	2nd	3rd	Win & Pl
Hurdles	3	0	0	1	376
Career Total	3	0	0	1	376

Going:	Sf: 0-0 GS: 0-0 Gd: 0-0 GF: - Fm: 0-3
Distance:	2m/2m3: 0-3 2m4-2m7: 0-0 3m+: 0-0
Track:	LH: 0-2 RH: 0-1 Tight: 0-0 Gall: 0-0
Aids:	Bl: 0-0 Vi: 0-0 Tstrap: 0-0 Ckp: 0-1
Best Rating:	73 10/03 Towc 2m firm Hdl

Juvenile hurdler; disappointing third in weak Towcester claimer second start.

Peggy Sioux (IRE)

93   **75**

7-y-o b m Little Bighorn-Gayable (Gay Fandango (USA))
J I A Charlton John Hogg

Placings:300/25-P0P20   (4429)
2003/04: 20PGS, 21⁰GS, 16PHY, 20²F, 16⁰G,

	Starts	1st	2nd	3rd	Win & Pl
Hurdles	5	0	1	0	1708
Career Total	10	0	2	1	2542

Going:	Sf: 0-1 GS: 0-2 Gd: 0-1 GF: - Fm: 0-1
Distance:	2m/2m3: 0-2 2m4-2m7: 0-3 3m+: 0-0
Track:	LH: 0-4 RH: 0-1 Tight: 0-2 Gall: 0-1
Aids:	Bl: 0-0 Vi: 0-0 Tstrap: 0-0 Ckp: 0-0
Best Rating:	93 11/02 Hexm 2m110y heavy NHF

Peggy's Prince

91f   **88f**

6-y-o b g Morpeth-Prudent Peggy (Kambalda)
J D Frost Mrs J McCormack

Placings:3-26   (4738)
2003/04: 16²G, 17⁶G,

	Starts	1st	2nd	3rd	Win & Pl
NH Flat	2	0	1	0	536
Career Total	3	0	1	1	1002

Going:	Sf: 0-0 GS: 0-0 Gd: 0-2 GF: - Fm: 0-0
Distance:	2m/2m3: 0-2 2m4-2m7: 0-0 3m+: 0-0
Track:	LH: 0-1 RH: 0-0 Tight: 0-1 Gall: 0-0
Aids:	Bl: 0-0 Vi: 0-0 Tstrap: 0-0 Ckp: 0-0
Best Rating:	88 3/04 Strf 2m110y good NHF

Out of a mare who won over three miles over fences; modest form in bumpers on good.

Pembroke Square (IRE)

9-y-o b g Tenby-The Poachers Lady (IRE) (Salmon Leap (USA))
Miss E C Lavelle Fraser Miller Racing

Placings:05325/13142/0P/6432/S   (2076)
2003/04: 24⁵G,

	Starts	1st	2nd	3rd	Win & Pl
Chases	1	0	0	0	
Career Total	17	2	3	3	14876
130	11/99	Asct	3m	C Hdl	GD	£4856
111	5/99	Towc	3m	D Hdl	G-F	£3406
			Total win prize-money £8263		

Going:	Sf: 0-0 GS: 0-0 Gd: 0-1 GF: - Fm: 0-0
Distance:	2m/2m3: 0-0 2m4-2m7: 0-0 3m+: 0-1

Track: LH: 0-1 RH: 0-0 Tight: 0-1 Gall: 0-0
Aids: Bl: 0-0 Vi: 0-1 Tstrap: 0-1 Ckp: 0-0
Best Rating: 137 2/00 Asct 3m   soft   Hdl

Penalta

97   83

8-y-o ch g Cosmonaut-Targuette (Targowice (USA))
W M Brisbourne John Smallman

Placings:46   (2838)
2003/04: 21⁴GF, 20⁶GS,

	Starts	1st	2nd	3rd	Win & Pl
Hurdles	2	0	0	0	260
Career Total	2	0	0	0	260

Going: Sf: 0-0 GS: 0-1 Gd: 0-0 GF: - Fm: 0-1
Distance: 2m/2m3: 0-0 2m4-2m7: 0-2 3m+: 0-0
Track: LH: 0-1 RH: 0-1 Tight: 0-0 Gall: 0-0
Aids: Bl: 0-1 Vi: 0-0 Tstrap: 0-0 Ckp: 0-0
Best Rating: 91 12/03 Uttx   2m4f110y   gd-sft   Hdl

Penalty Clause (IRE)

96   79

4-y-o b g Namaqualand (USA)-Lady Be Lucky (IRE) (Taufan (USA))
K A Morgan (G Prodromou 27/9) Hall Farm Racing

Placings:30320F100   (3780)
2003/04: 17³GF, 16⁶G, 16³GF, 17²GF, 16⁹G, 16⁶GF, 16¹GS, 21⁹G, 16⁸GS,

	Starts	1st	2nd	3rd	Win & Pl
Hurdles	9	1	1	2	4516
Career Total	9	1	1	2	4516
79 12/03 Donc 2m110y G Hdl				G-S	£2282

Total win prize-money £2282

Going: Sf: 0-0 GS: 1-2 Gd: 0-3 GF: - Fm: 0-4
Distance: 2m/2m3: 1-8 2m4-2m7: 0-1 3m+: 0-0
Track: LH: 1-6 RH: 0-3 Tight: 0-7 Gall: 1-2
Aids: Bl: 0-0 Vi: 0-2 Tstrap: 0-1 Ckp: 1-5
Best Rating: 79 2/04 Hntg   2m110y   gd-sft   Hdl

Plating-class form in juvenile hurdles; narrow winner at Doncaster in December; best on fast ground; has worn cheekpieces.

Pendant

72   17

9-y-o b g Warning-Emerald (USA) (El Gran Senor (USA))
Mrs J Candlish Friends R Four

Placings:3P104/00/6PP/P3-60   (0613)
2003/04: 17⁶G, 25⁰GF,

	Starts	1st	2nd	3rd	Win & Pl
Chases	2	0	0	0	0
Career Total	14	1	0	2	3355
96 1/00 Catt 2m3f E Hdl				GD	£2362

Total win prize-money £2363

Going: Sf: 0-0 GS: 0-0 Gd: 0-1 GF: - Fm: 0-1
Distance: 2m/2m3: 0-1 2m4-2m7: 0-0 3m+: 0-1
Track: LH: 0-1 RH: 0-1 Tight: 0-1 Gall: 0-1
Aids: Bl: 0-0 Vi: 0-1 Tstrap: 0-0 Ckp: 0-0
Best Rating: 96 4/00 MRas   2m5f110y   gd-fm   Hdl

Pendil's Princess

88f   77f

5-y-o b m Afzal-Pendil's Delight (Scorpio (FR))
S E H Sherwood N F Williams

Placings:6   (4144)
2003/04: 16⁶G,

	Starts	1st	2nd	3rd	Win & Pl
NH Flat	1	0	0	0	0
Career Total	1	0	0	0	0

Going: Sf: 0-0 GS: 0-0 Gd: 0-1 GF: - Fm: 0-0
Distance: 2m/2m3: 0-0 2m4-2m7: 0-0 3m+: 0-0
Track: LH: 0-0 RH: 0-1 Tight: 0-0 Gall: 0-0
Aids: Bl: 0-0 Vi: 0-0 Tstrap: 0-0 Ckp: 0-0
Best Rating: 77 3/04 Ludl   2m   good   NHF

Pendle Forest (IRE)

102f   90+f

4-y-o gr f Charnwood Forest (IRE)-Pride Of Pendle (Grey Desire)
R A Fahey Mrs Linda Miller

Placings:10   (3818)
2003/04: 16¹HY, 16⁹GS,

	Starts	1st	2nd	3rd	Win & Pl
NH Flat	2	1	0	0	1974
Career Total	2	1	0	0	1974
90 1/04 Newc 2m	H NHF			HVY	£1974

Total win prize-money £1974

Going: Sf: 1-1 GS: 0-1 Gd: 0-0 GF: - Fm: 0-0
Distance: 2m/2m3: 1-2 2m4-2m7: 0-0 3m+: 0-0
Track: LH: 1-2 RH: 0-0 Tight: 0-0 Gall: 0-0
Aids: Bl: 0-0 Vi: 0-0 Tstrap: 0-0 Ckp: 0-0
Best Rating: 90 1/04 Newc   2m   heavy   NHF

Made a winning debut in a Newcastle bumper but long way below that level on less testing ground at Ayr in February 2004; handles heavy ground.

Pendle Hill

9-y-o gr g Roscoe Blake-Pendle Princess (Broxted)
Mrs S J Hickman Mrs Kate Digweed

Placings:4003/665002610/5224640-5   (3785)
2003/04: 24⁴S,

	Starts	1st	2nd	3rd	Win & Pl
Chases	1	0	0	0	0
Career Total	21	1	3	1	8013
98 2/01 Newc 2m4f E Hdl				HVY	£2555

Total win prize-money £2555

Going: Sf: 0-1 GS: 0-0 Gd: 0-0 GF: - Fm: 0-0
Distance: 2m/2m3: 0-0 2m4-2m7: 0-0 3m+: 0-1
Track: LH: 0-0 RH: 0-1 Tight: 0-0 Gall: 0-1
Aids: Bl: 0-0 Vi: 0-0 Tstrap: 0-0 Ckp: 0-0
Best Rating: 112 11/02 Carl   2m4f   heavy   Ch

Modest hurdler chaser; successful over hurdles over two and a half miles; has shown ability over fences at around the same distance; goes well in the mud.

Pendragon

12-y-o b g Bold Fox-Celtic Royale (Celtic Cone)
Mrs Sarah Faulks Mrs Sarah Faulks

Placings:26/F-P   (4522)

2003/04: 25⁸GS,

	Starts	1st	2nd	3rd	Win & Pl
Chases	1	0	0	0	
Career Total	4	0	1	0	621

Going: Sf: 0-0 GS: 0-1 Gd: 0-0 GF: - Fm: 0-0
Distance: 2m/2m3: 0-0 2m4-2m7: 0-0 3m+: 0-1
Track: LH: 0-0 RH: 0-1 Tight: 0-0 Gall: 0-0
Aids: Bl: 0-0 Vi: 0-0 Tstrap: 0-0 Ckp: 0-0
Best Rating: 86 3/02 Towc   3m1f   soft   Ch

Penguin Bay

(77c)   (55c)84

8-y-o b g Rock Hopper-Corn Lily (Aragon)
N Wilson Mrs Susan McDonald

Placings:330/3030/506042004-P   (0466)
2003/04: 16⁴GF, 16⁸G,

	Starts	1st	2nd	3rd	Win & Pl
Hurdles	1	0	0	0	0
Chases	1	0	0	0	306
Career Total	17	0	1	4	2406

Going: Sf: 0-0 GS: 0-0 Gd: 0-1 GF: - Fm: 0-1
Distance: 2m/2m3: 0-2 2m4-2m7: 0-0 3m+: 0-0
Track: LH: 0-2 RH: 0-0 Tight: 0-0 Gall: 0-1
Aids: Bl: 0-1 Vi: 0-0 Tstrap: 0-0 Ckp: 0-0
Best Rating: 107 5/00 Hntg   2m110y   gd-sft   NHF

Pennant Castle

23f

6-y-o b g Alflora (IRE)-Pennant Cottage (IRE) (Denel (FR))
Mrs H Dalton P J Woolley

Placings:0   (0334)
2003/04: 17⁰GF,

	Starts	1st	2nd	3rd	Win & Pl
NH Flat	1	0	0	0	
Career Total	1	0	0	0	

Going: Sf: 0-0 GS: 0-0 Gd: 0-0 GF: - Fm: 0-1
Distance: 2m/2m3: 0-1 2m4-2m7: 0-0 3m+: 0-0
Track: LH: 0-1 RH: 0-0 Tight: 0-0 Gall: 0-0
Aids: Bl: 0-0 Vi: 0-0 Tstrap: 0-0 Ckp: 0-0
Best Rating: 23 5/03 Sthl   2m1f   gd-fm   NHF

Penneless Dancer

69   36

5-y-o b g Pennekamp (USA)-Villella (Sadler's Wells (USA))
M E Sowersby M E Sowersby

Placings:00-0   (0432)
2003/04: 17⁰G,

	Starts	1st	2nd	3rd	Win & Pl
Hurdles	1	0	0	0	
Career Total	3	0	0	0	

Going: Sf: 0-0 GS: 0-0 Gd: 0-0 GF: - Fm: 0-0
Distance: 2m/2m3: 0-1 2m4-2m7: 0-0 3m+: 0-0
Track: LH: 0-1 RH: 0-0 Tight: 0-1 Gall: 0-0
Aids: Bl: 0-0 Vi: 0-0 Tstrap: 0-0 Ckp: 0-0
Best Rating: 36 11/02 Catt   2m   good   Hdl

Penneyrose Bay

92f   **90f**

5-y-o ch m Karinga Bay-Pennethorne Place (Deep Run)
G B Balding Sir Christopher Wates

Placings:06   (3709)
2003/04: 16⁰GS, 16⁶HY,

	Starts	1st	2nd	3rd	Win & Pl
NH Flat	2	0	0	0	0
Career Total	2	0	0	0	0

Going:	Sf: 0-1 GS: 0-1 Gd: 0-0 GF: - Fm: 0-0
Distance:	2m/2m3: 0-2 2m4-2m7: 0-0 3m+: 0-0
Track:	LH: 0-2 RH: 0-0 Tight: 0-0 Gall: 0-1
Aids:	Bl: 0-0 Vi: 0-0 Tstrap: 0-0 Ckp: 0-0
Best Rating:	90 12/03 Newb 2m110y gd-sft NHF

Half-sister to stable's Latimer's Place; showed ability on debut in hot bumper at Newbury in December.

Pennillion

4-y-o b g Pennekamp (USA)-Brave Princess (Dancing Brave (USA)
D P Keane Avon Thoroughbreds Ltd

Placings:PP   (2764)
2003/04: 16⁶GS, 16⁶GS,

	Starts	1st	2nd	3rd	Win & Pl
Hurdles	2	0	0	0	0
Career Total	2	0	0	0	0

Going:	Sf: 0-0 GS: 0-2 Gd: 0-0 GF: - Fm: 0-0
Distance:	2m/2m3: 0-2 2m4-2m7: 0-0 3m+: 0-0
Track:	LH: 0-1 RH: 0-1 Tight: 0-1 Gall: 0-0
Aids:	Bl: 0-0 Vi: 0-0 Tstrap: 0-0 Ckp: 0-0

Penny Native (IRE)

12-y-o ch g Be My Native (USA)-Penny Maes (Welsh Saint)
Miss J M Furness (W F Kerr 29/2) W F Kerr

Placings:0/2121/P000042/4/502/352221402/026-220   (4689)

2003/04: 24²F, 21²GF, 25⁰G,

	Starts	1st	2nd	3rd	Win & Pl
Chases	3	0	2	0	1194
Career Total	31	3	11	1	35399
115	10/01	Wxfd	2m	Ch		Y-S	£7233
117	3/98	Gowr	2m	Hdl		Y-S	£2382
111	12/97	Leop	2m	Hdl		HVY	£4069
			Total win prize-money £13686				

Going:	Sf: 0-0 GS: 0-0 Gd: 0-1 GF: - Fm: 0-2
Distance:	2m/2m3: 0-0 2m4-2m7: 0-1 3m+: 0-2
Track:	LH: 0-2 RH: 0-1 Tight: 0-2 Gall: 0-0
Aids:	Bl: 0-0 Vi: 0-0 Tstrap: 0-0 Ckp: 0-0
Best Rating:	120 7/99 Gway 2m gd-fm Hdl

Penny Pictures (IRE)

100   **110**

5-y-o b h Theatrical-Copper Creek (Habitat)
M C Pipe Terry Neill

Placings:311-60603   (4859)
2003/04: 16⁶G, 16⁰G, 16⁶GS, 20⁰G, 19³GF,

	Starts	1st	2nd	3rd	Win & Pl
Hurdles	5	0	0	1	880
Career Total	8	2	0	2	9329
106	4/03	Ludl	2m	E Hdl		GD	£4186
127	3/03	Bang	2m1f	E Hdl		SFT	£3493
			Total win prize-money £7680				

Going:	Sf: 0-0 GS: 0-1 Gd: 0-3 GF: - Fm: 0-1
Distance:	2m/2m3: 0-3 2m4-2m7: 0-2 3m+: 0-0
Track:	LH: 0-1 RH: 0-4 Tight: 0-2 Gall: 0-0
Aids:	Bl: 0-0 Vi: 0-0 Tstrap: 0-0 Ckp: 0-0
Best Rating:	127 3/03 Bang 2m1f soft Hdl

Fair handicapper on the Flat; ran well on hurdles debut and easy winner of next two starts; keen sort; effective over two miles; prefers decent ground, although effective on soft; will need to learn to settle if he is going to reach his full potential over hurdles; held this season.

Penny Rich (IRE)

10-y-o br g Little Bighorn-Musical Puss (Orchestra)
R Ford (Michael Hourigan 20/7) David Bostock

Placings:232/210065161013202030335/PF3PP/0F-0P   (4613)
2003/04: 16⁰S, 16⁶G,

	Starts	1st	2nd	3rd	Win & Pl
Hurdles	1	0	0	0	0
Chases	1	0	0	0	0
Career Total	31	4	5	5	59602
126	9/00	List	2m	HHdl		HVY	£13480
131	8/00	Tral	2m	Hdl		SFT	£6424
118	8/00	Tram	2m	(0-130)HHdl		G-F	£6560
101	5/00	Kiny	2m1f	NHF		GD	£3588
			Total win prize-money £30052				

Going:	Sf: 0-1 GS: 0-0 Gd: 0-1 GF: - Fm: 0-0
Distance:	2m/2m3: 0-2 2m4-2m7: 0-0 3m+: 0-0
Track:	LH: 0-1 RH: 0-0 Tight: 0-1 Gall: 0-0
Aids:	Bl: 0-0 Vi: 0-0 Tstrap: 0-0 Ckp: 0-0
Best Rating:	159 1/01 Leop 2m soft Hdl

Penny's Crown

74   **28**

5-y-o b m Reprimand-Two And Sixpence (USA) (Chief's Crown (USA))
G A Ham (H M Kavanagh 22/1) Sally & Tom Dalley

Placings:425000   (4544)
2003/04: 17⁴GF, 16²GF, 16⁵GF, 17⁰GS, 19⁰G, 22⁰GS,

	Starts	1st	2nd	3rd	Win & Pl
NH Flat	4	0	1	0	436
Hurdles	2	0	0	0	0
Career Total	6	0	1	0	436

Going:	Sf: 0-0 GS: 0-2 Gd: 0-1 GF: - Fm: 0-3
Distance:	2m/2m3: 0-4 2m4-2m7: 0-2 3m+: 0-0
Track:	LH: 0-2 RH: 0-3 Tight: 0-1 Gall: 0-0
Aids:	Bl: 0-0 Vi: 0-0 Tstrap: 0-0 Ckp: 0-0
Best Rating:	87 10/03 Chel 2m110y gd-fm NHF

Fair fourth on bumper debut; better effort when runner-up at Chepstow next time; held since.

Penny's Loss

57

6-y-o b m Primitive Rising (USA)-Lingham Bride (Deep Run)
Evan Williams W Ralph Thomas

Placings:00   (0869)
2003/04: 20⁰GF, 22⁰GF,

	Starts	1st	2nd	3rd	Win & Pl
Hurdles	2	0	0	0	0
Career Total	2	0	0	0	0

Going:	Sf: 0-0 GS: 0-0 Gd: 0-0 GF: - Fm: 0-2
Distance:	2m/2m3: 0-0 2m4-2m7: 0-2 3m+: 0-0
Track:	LH: 0-2 RH: 0-0 Tight: 0-1 Gall: 0-0
Aids:	Bl: 0-0 Vi: 0-0 Tstrap: 0-0 Ckp: 0-0

Pennyahei

13-y-o b m Malaspina-Pennyazena (Pamroy)
S A Brookshaw Miss H Brookshaw

Placings:P/UO6P065P4/2203220530/5P0F2041U/4466026
0P/5-2P   (0519)
2003/04: 24²G, 28⁶G,

	Starts	1st	2nd	3rd	Win & Pl
Chases	2	0	1	0	1296
Career Total	41	1	7	2	11603
92	3/00	Uttx	3m2f	F(0-110)HCh		GD	£3835
			Total win prize-money £3835				

Going:	Sf: 0-0 GS: 0-0 Gd: 0-2 GF: - Fm: 0-2
Distance:	2m/2m3: 0-0 2m4-2m7: 0-0 3m+: 0-2
Track:	LH: 0-2 RH: 0-0 Tight: 0-2 Gall: 0-0
Aids:	Bl: 0-0 Vi: 0-0 Tstrap: 0-0 Ckp: 0-0
Best Rating:	92 5/03 Bang 3m110y good Ch

Winning chaser/decent pointer.

Pennys From Heaven

85   **89**

10-y-o gr g Generous (IRE)-Heavenly Cause (USA) (Grey Dawn Ii)
Miss T M Ide Miss Tracey Ide

Placings:05/040/023/53430326-0U03   (4899)
2003/04: 19⁰GS, 16⁰U, 16⁰G, 16³G,

	Starts	1st	2nd	3rd	Win & Pl
Hurdles	4	0	0	1	508
Career Total	20	0	2	5	4130

Going:	Sf: 0-0 GS: 0-0 Gd: 0-3 GF: - Fm: 0-0
Distance:	2m/2m3: 0-3 2m4-2m7: 0-1 3m+: 0-0
Track:	LH: 0-1 RH: 0-3 Tight: 0-1 Gall: 0-1
Aids:	Bl: 0-0 Vi: 0-0 Tstrap: 0-0 Ckp: 0-0
Best Rating:	95 3/98 Kels 2m110y good Hdl

Plating-class hurdler; acts on most ground.

Penric

100   **87**

4-y-o b g Marju (IRE)-Nafhaat (USA) (Roberto (USA))
C G Cox P G Horrocks

Placings:454P00   (4818)
2003/04: 16⁴GS, 16⁰G, 16⁴S, 16⁶S, 19⁰G, 17⁰GF,

	Starts	1st	2nd	3rd	Win & Pl
Hurdles	6	0	0	0	1038
Career Total	6	0	0	0	1038

Going:	Sf: 0-2 GS: 0-1 Gd: 0-2 GF: - Fm: 0-1
Distance:	2m/2m3: 0-6 2m4-2m7: 0-0 3m+: 0-0
Track:	LH: 0-4 RH: 0-2 Tight: 0-0 Gall: 0-3
Aids:	Bl: 0-1 Vi: 0-0 Tstrap: 0-0 Ckp: 0-0
Best Rating:	87 4/04 Extr 2m1f gd-fm Hdl

Penthouse Minstrel

106   **109+**

10-y-o b/br g Seven Hearts-Pentameron (Heres)
R J Hodges (Miss N Stephens 30/5) Bob Andrews

Placings:542P/PP-343P41142P44011   (4841)
2003/04: 25³G, 19⁴GF, 20³GS, 28⁸GS, 20⁴GF, 25¹F, 20¹GF,
25⁴GF, 19²G, 18⁸GS, 21⁴G, 21⁴G, 21⁰G, 21¹GS, 21¹G,

	Starts	1st	2nd	3rd	Win & Pl
Chases	15	4	1	2	36620
Career Total	**21**	**4**	**2**	**2**	**37311**
109	4/04	Chel	2m5f	D(0-115)HCh	GD	£11764
104	3/04	Winc	2m5f	E(0-110)HCh	G-S	£3900
95	10/03	Chel	2m4f110yD(0-110)HCh	G-F	£9526
	10/03	Winc	3m1f110yD Ch	FRM	£6135

Total win prize-money £31326

Going:	Sf: 0-0 GS: 1-4 Gd: 1-6 GF: - Fm: 2-5
Distance:	2m/2m3: 0-1 **2m4-2m7: 3-10** 3m+: 1-4
Track:	LH: 2-8 RH: 2-7 Tight: 0-0 **Gall: 2-5**
Aids:	Bl: 0-0 **Vi: 3-14** Tstrap: 0-0 Ckp: 0-0
Best Rating:	109 4/04 Chel 2m5f good Ch

Modest chaser; won maiden open point April 2003; improved over fences when upped to three miles, but has also won over 2m4f; seems best on good/good to firm; usually wears a visor.

Pepe Galvez (SWE)

106   **124**

7-y-o br g Mango Express-Mango Sampaquita (SWE) (Colombian Friend (USA))
Mrs L C Taylor Mrs D Barnett

Placings:213215-2   (2097)
2003/04: 19²GF,

	Starts	1st	2nd	3rd	Win & Pl
Hurdles	1	0	1	0	2180
Career Total	**7**	**2**	**3**	**1**	**17673**
124	3/03	Newb	2m110y	D Hdl	GD	£5291
100	11/02	Tntn	2m1f	E Hdl	G-S	£3540

Total win prize-money £8832

Going:	Sf: 0-0 GS: 0-0 Gd: 0-0 GF: - Fm: 0-1
Distance:	2m/2m3: 0-1 2m4-2m7: 0-0 3m+: 0-0
Track:	LH: 0-1 RH: 0-0 Tight: 0-0 Gall: 0-1
Aids:	Bl: 0-0 Vi: 0-0 Tstrap: 0-0 Ckp: 0-0
Best Rating:	124 11/03 Newb 2m3f gd-fm Hdl

Fair performer; suited by around two to two and a half miles; acts on decent ground.

Pepeta

97   (54h)**84**

7-y-o b m Presidium-Mighty Flash (Rolfe (USA))
D L Williams Miss L Horner

Placings:0P00/P2UP34   (2816)
2003/04: 26⁸GF, 24²GF, 20⁴G, 21⁷GF, 16³G, 19⁴G,

	Starts	1st	2nd	3rd	Win & Pl
Chases	6	0	1	1	2128
Career Total	**10**	**0**	**1**	**1**	**2128**

Going:	Sf: 0-0 GS: 0-0 Gd: 0-3 GF: - Fm: 0-3
Distance:	2m/2m3: 0-1 2m4-2m7: 0-3 3m+: 0-2
Track:	LH: 0-2 RH: 0-4 Tight: 0-2 Gall: 0-0
Aids:	Bl: 0-0 Vi: 0-0 Tstrap: 0-2 Ckp: 0-0
Best Rating:	79 12/03 Ludl 2m good Ch

Peppershot

99   **92**

4-y-o b g Vettori (IRE)-No Chili (Glint Of Gold)
G P Enright (A M Balding 14/8) R Gurney

Placings:33550   (4452)
2003/04: 16³S, 17³HY, 16⁵S, 16⁵GS, 16⁹GS,

	Starts	1st	2nd	3rd	Win & Pl
Hurdles	5	0	0	2	1330
Career Total	**5**	**0**	**0**	**2**	**1330**

Going:	Sf: 0-3 GS: 0-2 Gd: 0-0 GF: - Fm: 0-0
Distance:	2m/2m3: 0-5 2m4-2m7: 0-0 3m+: 0-0
Track:	LH: 0-1 RH: 0-4 Tight: 0-2 Gall: 0-0
Aids:	Bl: 0-0 Vi: 0-0 Tstrap: 0-0 Ckp: 0-0
Best Rating:	92 2/04 Sand 2m110y soft Hdl

Pequenita

99   **108**

4-y-o b f Rudimentary (USA)-Sierra Madrona (USA) (Woodman (USA))
G L Moore (J G Given 13/10) N J Jones

Placings:122P   (3432)
2003/04: 17¹G, 16²GS, 16²GS, 16⁹GS,

	Starts	1st	2nd	3rd	Win & Pl
Hurdles	4	1	2	0	5931
Career Total	**4**	**1**	**2**	**0**	**5931**
108	11/03	Folk	2m1f110yE Hdl	GD	£2947

Total win prize-money £2947

Going:	Sf: 0-0 GS: 0-3 Gd: 1-1 GF: - Fm: 0-0
Distance:	**2m/2m3: 1-4** 2m4-2m7: 0-0 3m+: 0-0
Track:	LH: 0-3 RH: 1-1 Tight: 1-3 Gall: 0-1
Aids:	Bl: 0-0 Vi: 0-0 Tstrap: 0-0 Ckp: 0-0
Best Rating:	108 11/03 Folk 2m1f110y good Hdl

Made a winning hurdles debut at Folkestone in November; runner-up in better races; may stay 2m 4f; has worn blinkers.

Per Amore (IRE)

106(106h)   (121h)**126**

6-y-o ch g General Monash (USA)-Danny's Miracle (Superlative)
P J Hobbs Mrs J F Deithrick

Placings:323311/221003-2114312P   (1825)
2003/04: 17²G, 20¹GF, 21¹GF, 21⁴GF, 21³G, 17¹GF, 17²F, 16⁶GF,

	Starts	1st	2nd	3rd	Win & Pl
Hurdles	1	0	1	0	1206
Chases	7	3	1	2	20355
Career Total	**20**	**6**	**5**	**5**	**37917**
126	9/03	Strf	2m1f110yD(0-120)HCh	G-F	£4706
115	6/03	NAbb	2m5f110yC Ch	G-F	£9052
123	5/03	Hntg	2m4f110yE Ch	G-F	£3829
121	11/02	Winc	2m	E(0-115)HHdl	G-S	£3428
103	4/02	Ludl	2m	E Hdl	G-F	£3020
116	4/02	Ludl	2m	D Hdl	G-F	£3900

Total win prize-money £27939

Going:	Sf: 0-0 GS: 0-0 Gd: 0-2 GF: - Fm: 3-6
Distance:	2m/2m3: 1-4 **2m4-2m7: 2-4** 3m+: 0-0
Track:	**LH: 2-5** RH: 1-3 Tight: 2-4 Gall: 1-2
Aids:	Bl: 3-8 Vi: 0-0 Tstrap: 0-0 Ckp: 0-0
Best Rating:	126 9/03 Strf 2m1f110y gd-fm Ch

Useful handicap hurdler/fair chaser; acts on all ground except extremes; regularly blinkered; won back-to-back novice chases at Huntingdon and Newton Abbot May/June 2003; bounced back after a couple of disappointing efforts to

make successful handicap debut at Stratford in September; stays 21 furlongs but is possible more effective over shorter.

Perange (FR)

108   **135+**

8-y-o ch g Perrault-La Mesange (FR) (Olmeto)
P F Nicholls Mrs Kathy Stuart

Placings:0060541/313321/54F1-PP16FP   (4850)
2003/04: 17²G, 20⁸GF, 19¹S, 19⁶G, 21²GF, 20⁸GS,

	Starts	1st	2nd	3rd	Win & Pl
Chases	6	5	1	0	5907
Career Total	**23**	**5**	**1**	**3**	**42054**
135	2/04	Tntn	2m3f	D(0-125)HCh	SFT	£5642
119	4/03	NAbb	2m5f110yD(0-125)HCh	GD	£5460
131	2/02	Font	2m4f	C Ch	SFT	£6230
112	10/01	Uttx	2m	D Ch	G-S	£4875
	3/01	Autl	2m3f110y HHdl	HVY	£9699

Total win prize-money £31906

Going:	Sf: 1-1 GS: 0-1 Gd: 0-2 GF: - Fm: 0-2
Distance:	**2m/2m3: 1-2** 2m4-2m7: 0-3 3m+: 0-0
Track:	LH: 0-3 **RH: 1-3** Tight: 1-2 Gall: 0-0
Aids:	Bl: 0-0 Vi: 0-0 Tstrap: 0-0 Ckp: 0-0
Best Rating:	135 3/04 Winc 2m5f gd-fm Ch

Useful handicap chaser; suited by soft ground; has won on faster but jumped right when doing so; effective at two and a half miles.

Perchancer (IRE)

102(95h)   (118h)**96**

8-y-o ch g Perugino (USA)-Irish Hope (Nishapour (FR))
P C Haslam N P Green

Placings:3/1F24/5-2F   (1186)
2003/04: 16²GF, 21⁷G,

	Starts	1st	2nd	3rd	Win & Pl
Chases	2	0	1	0	1199
Career Total	**8**	**1**	**2**	**1**	**5631**
116	11/01	Weth	2m4f110yE Hdl	GD	£2744

Total win prize-money £2744

Going:	Sf: 0-0 GS: 0-0 Gd: 0-0 GF: - Fm: 0-1
Distance:	2m/2m3: 0-1 2m4-2m7: 0-1 3m+: 0-0
Track:	LH: 0-2 RH: 0-0 Tight: 0-2 Gall: 0-0
Aids:	Bl: 0-0 Vi: 0-0 Tstrap: 0-0 Ckp: 0-0
Best Rating:	118 4/02 Strf 2m110y good Hdl

Modest hurdler; runner-up on chasing debut at Sedgefield in August; best around two and a half miles; best on a sound surface.

Perchcourt Steel (IRE)

8-y-o b g Grand Lodge (USA)-Scaravie (IRE) (Drumalis)
A M Hales J Smith

Placings:PP   (3403)
2003/04: 22⁸G, 19⁷G,

	Starts	1st	2nd	3rd	Win & Pl
Hurdles	2	0	0	0	
Career Total	**2**	**0**	**0**	**0**	

Going:	Sf: 0-0 GS: 0-1 Gd: 0-1 GF: - Fm: 0-0
Distance:	2m/2m3: 0-0 2m4-2m7: 0-2 3m+: 0-0
Track:	LH: 0-1 RH: 0-1 Tight: 0-1 Gall: 0-0
Aids:	Bl: 0-0 Vi: 0-0 Tstrap: 0-1 Ckp: 0-0

Perching (IRE)

73

10-y-o b g Strong Gale-Fiona's Blue (Crash Course)
P Butler John Plackett

Placings:50/UF0412/P5/02-P   (0437)
2003/04: 22PGF,

	Starts	1st	2nd	3rd	Win & Pl
Chases	1	0	0	0	
Career Total	13	1	2	0	7548
108	3/00	Ling	3m	D Ch	GD £4186

Total win prize-money £4186

Going:	Sf: 0-0 GS: 0-0 Gd: 0-0 GF: - Fm: 0-1
Distance:	2m/2m3: 0-0 2m4-2m7: 0-1 3m+: 0-0
Track:	LH: 0-0 RH: 0-1 Tight: 0-1 Gall: 0-0
Aids:	Bl: 0-0 Vi: 0-0 Tstrap: 0-0 Ckp: 0-1
Best Rating:	113 4/00 Font 2m6f good Ch

Plating-class chaser; lightly raced in recent seasons; has shown only moderate form; best on a sound surface; stays three miles; has worn cheekpieces.

Percipient

102   91+

6-y-o b g Pennekamp (USA)-Annie Albright (USA) (Verbatim (USA))
D R Gandolfo Nigel Stafford

Placings:5-06020   (4198)
2003/04: 17PG, 17PGS, 16PGS, 16PGS, 16PG,

	Starts	1st	2nd	3rd	Win & Pl
Hurdles	5	0	1	0	984
Career Total	6	0	1	0	984

Going:	Sf: 0-0 GS: 0-3 Gd: 0-2 GF: - Fm: 0-0
Distance:	2m/2m3: 0-5 2m4-2m7: 0-0 3m+: 0-0
Track:	LH: 0-4 RH: 0-1 Tight: 0-3 Gall: 0-1
Aids:	Bl: 0-0 Vi: 0-0 Tstrap: 0-0 Ckp: 0-0
Best Rating:	91 1/04 Fknm 2m gd-sft Hdl

Plating-class hurdler; acts on easy ground.

Percy Basil

5-y-o b g Petoski-Madam-M (Tina's Pet)
Ian Williams C B Compton

Placings:0-00   (2328)
2003/04: 17PG, 16PGS,

	Starts	1st	2nd	3rd	Win & Pl
NH Flat	1	0	0	0	0
Hurdles	1	0	0	0	0
Career Total	3	0	0	0	

Going:	Sf: 0-0 GS: 0-1 Gd: 0-1 GF: 0-0 Fm: 0-0
Distance:	2m/2m3: 0-2 2m4-2m7: 0-0 3m+: 0-0
Track:	LH: 0-2 RH: 0-0 Tight: 0-2 Gall: 0-0
Aids:	Bl: 0-0 Vi: 0-0 Tstrap: 0-0 Ckp: 0-0
Best Rating:	30 10/03 Bang 2m1f good NHF

Percy Braithwaite (IRE)

12-y-o b g Kahyasi-Nasseem (FR) (Zeddaan)
Mrs P Ford W E Donohue, K Marritt, K R Ford

Placings:41001U/22362530/3P234/464411/23F46P/04445
200/606-P   (0259)

2003/04: 21PGF,

	Starts	1st	2nd	3rd	Win & Pl
Hurdles	1	0	0	0	
Career Total	43	4	6	5	22153
101	4/00	Hntg	2m110y	D(0-115)HCh	GD £4048
86	2/00	Ludl	2m	F(0-100)HCh	GD £2873
107	4/97	Ludl	2m	E Hdl	FRM £2248
102	1/97	Ludl	2m	E Hdl	G-F £2682

Total win prize-money £11852

Going:	Sf: 0-0 GS: 0-0 Gd: 0-0 GF: - Fm: 0-1
Distance:	2m/2m3: 0-0 2m4-2m7: 0-1 3m+: 0-0
Track:	LH: 0-0 RH: 0-1 Tight: 0-0 Gall: 0-0
Aids:	Bl: 0-0 Vi: 0-0 Tstrap: 0-0 Ckp: 0-0
Best Rating:	112 5/97 Ludl 2m gd-fm Hdl

Percy Parkeeper

105   122

11-y-o b g Teenoso (USA)-True Clown (True Song)
N A Twiston-Davies Mr & Mrs Peter Orton

Placings:1224/F40213F/3454/0113450PP/124333-25
                              (0532)
2003/04: 24²GS, 23PGF,

	Starts	1st	2nd	3rd	Win & Pl
Chases	2	0	1	0	2526
Career Total	32	5	5	6	38225
121	9/02	Strf	2m1f110yD(0-120)HCh	G-F £5473
123	10/01	Hrfd	2m	E(0-115)HCh	GD £3376
119	9/01	Prth	2m	E(0-115)HCh	GD £5369
124	2/99	Kemp	2m5f	D Hdl	GD £3009
107	1/98	Hntg	2m110y	H NHF	G-S £1402

Total win prize-money £18631

Going:	Sf: 0-0 GS: 0-1 Gd: 0-0 GF: - Fm: 0-1
Distance:	2m/2m3: 0-0 2m4-2m7: 0-0 3m+: 0-2
Track:	LH: 0-2 RH: 0-0 Tight: 0-1 Gall: 0-0
Aids:	Bl: 0-0 Vi: 0-0 Tstrap: 0-0 Ckp: 0-0
Best Rating:	124 2/99 Kemp 2m5f good Hdl

Fair handicap chaser; yet to win beyond an extended 2m but does stay much further; best on good ground; likes to dominate; has worn blinkers.

Percy-Verance (IRE)

74   83

6-y-o ch g Dolphin Street (FR)-Sinology (Rainbow Quest (USA))
J J Quinn J H Hewitt

Placings:00/5   (3989)
2003/04: 17PGS,

	Starts	1st	2nd	3rd	Win & Pl
Hurdles	1	0	0	0	
Career Total	3	0	0	0	

Going:	Sf: 0-0 GS: 0-1 Gd: 0-0 GF: - Fm: 0-0
Distance:	2m/2m3: 0-1 2m4-2m7: 0-0 3m+: 0-0
Track:	LH: 0-1 RH: 0-0 Tight: 0-1 Gall: 0-0
Aids:	Bl: 0-0 Vi: 0-0 Tstrap: 0-0 Ckp: 0-0
Best Rating:	83 2/04 Sedg 2m1f gd-sft Hdl

Perfect Fellow

112   133

10-y-o b g Teamster-G W Supermare (Rymer)
Miss H C Knight The Unlucky For Some Partnership

Placings:10/11/0/31/41/1F-PP1P   (4871)
2003/04: 20PYS, 24PGS, 24¹GS, 24PS,

	Starts	1st	2nd	3rd	Win & Pl
Chases	4	1	0	0	8249

Career Total	15	7	0	1	42662
133	3/04	Sand	3m110y C(0-135)HCh	G-S £8248
133	10/02	Chel	2m4f110yC(0-135)HCh	GD £12852
133	12/01	Kemp	2m4f110yD(0-120)HCh	GD £10676
116	12/00	Folk	2m5f D Ch	SFT £3848
126	1/99	Folk	2m6f110yE Hdl	HVY £2427
108	12/98	Strf	2m6f110yE Hdl	SFT £2250
90	3/98	NAbb	2m1f H NHF	SFT £1236

Total win prize-money £41538

Going:	Sf: 0-1 GS: 1-1 Gd: 0-1 GF: - Fm: 0-0
Distance:	2m/2m3: 0-0 2m4-2m7: 0-1 3m+: 1-3
Track:	LH: 0-1 RH: 1-3 Tight: 0-1 Gall: 0-0
Aids:	Bl: 0-0 Vi: 0-0 Tstrap: 0-0 Ckp: 0-0
Best Rating:	133 3/04 Sand 3m110y gd-sft Ch

Useful chaser; stays 3m, effective at 2m 4f; acts on most types of ground; has had his problems and does not stand much racing.

Perfect Finisher

13-y-o b g Captain Maverick (USA)-Miss Eutopia (Dunphy)
Mrs Jackie Hunt Miss T Habgood

Placings:0/P   (4302)
2003/04: 20PG,

	Starts	1st	2nd	3rd	Win & Pl
Chases	1	0	0	0	
Career Total	2	0	0	0	

Going:	Sf: 0-0 GS: 0-0 Gd: 0-1 GF: - Fm: 0-0
Distance:	2m/2m3: 0-0 2m4-2m7: 0-1 3m+: 0-0
Track:	LH: 0-0 RH: 0-1 Tight: 0-0 Gall: 0-0
Aids:	Bl: 0-0 Vi: 0-0 Tstrap: 0-0 Ckp: 0-0

Perfect Liaison

103   109

7-y-o b g Alflora (IRE)-Connie's Pet (National Trust)
R H Alner Neil & Susie Dalgren

Placings:06-13   (4324)
2003/04: 19¹S, 20³S,

	Starts	1st	2nd	3rd	Win & Pl
Hurdles	2	1	0	1	4468
Career Total	4	1	0	1	4468
97	2/04	Extr	2m3f E Hdl	SFT £3692

Total win prize-money £3692

Going:	Sf: 1-2 GS: 0-0 Gd: 0-0 GF: - Fm: 0-0
Distance:	2m/2m3: 1-1 2m4-2m7: 0-1 3m+: 0-0
Track:	LH: 0-0 RH: 1-2 Tight: 0-0 Gall: 0-0
Aids:	Bl: 0-0 Vi: 0-0 Tstrap: 0-0 Ckp: 0-0
Best Rating:	109 3/04 Sand 2m4f110y soft Hdl

Modest novice hurdler; showed promise in bumpers; won his hurdling debut at Exeter and ran well in a fair race at Sandown after; acts best on soft ground.

Perfect Venue (IRE)

54   56

11-y-o b g Danehill (USA)-Welsh Fantasy (Welsh Pageant)
A J Wilson Mrs M J Wilson

Placings:53/21132000/66006/4000F/0   (2418)
2003/04: 16PGS,

	Starts	1st	2nd	3rd	Win & Pl
Hurdles	1	0	0	0	
Career Total	21	2	2	2	11018
128	1/99	Tntn	2m1f E Hdl	SFT £2421
118	12/98	Tntn	2m1f C Hdl	GD £4197

Total win prize-money £6618

Going:	Sf: 0-0 GS: 0-1 Gd: 0-0 GF: - Fm: 0-0
Distance:	2m/2m3: 0-1 2m4-2m7: 0-0 3m+: 0-0
Track:	LH: 0-1 RH: 0-0 Tight: 0-0 Gall: 0-0
Aids:	Bl: 0-0 Vi: 0-0 Tstrap: 0-0 Ckp: 0-0
Best Rating:	131 11/00 Newb 2m110y gd-sft Hdl

Perhaps This Time (IRE)

92f   **85f**

5-y-o b g Flemensfirth (USA)-Royal Chapeau (IRE) (Royal Fountain)
D P Keane Mrs L J Robins

Placings:*64*   (4738)
2003/04: 16^{P}GS, 17^{4}G,

	Starts	1st	2nd	3rd	Win & Pl
NH Flat	2	0	0	0	0
Career Total	2	0	0	0	0

Going:	Sf: 0-0 GS: 0-1 Gd: 0-1 GF: - Fm: 0-0
Distance:	2m/2m3: 0-2 2m4-2m7: 0-0 3m+: 0-0
Track:	LH: 0-2 RH: 0-0 Tight: 0-1 Gall: 0-0
Aids:	Bl: 0-0 Vi: 0-0 Tstrap: 0-Ckp: 0-0
Best Rating:	85 4/04 NAbb 2m1f good NHF

Periwinkle Lad (IRE)

112(83c)   (94c)**107**

7-y-o b g Perugino (USA)-Bold Kate (Bold Lad (IRE))
Miss Victoria Roberts (C A Dwyer 10/11) D C Roberts

Placings:*S/000000/026U0030301321660***2013-0325522**   (3759)
2003/04: 24^{D}YS, 20^{3}GF, 22^{2}G, 21^{5}GF, 25^{5}G, 22^{2}GF, 22^{2}G,

	Starts	1st	2nd	3rd	Win & Pl
Hurdles	5	0	2	0	2010
Chases	2	0	1	1	1448
Career Total	35	3	6	5	28933
102 4/03 List 3m		(81-123)HHdl		G-F	£9918
95 12/02 Tram 2m4f		(60-88)HHdl		HVY	£3809
85 11/02 Thur 2m6f110y		(60-88)HHdl		SFT	£3809
				Total win prize-money	£17539

Going:	Sf: 0-0 GS: 0-0 Gd: 0-3 GF: - Fm: 0-3
Distance:	2m/2m3: 0-0 2m4-2m7: 0-5 3m+: 0-2
Track:	LH: 0-2 RH: 0-3 Tight: 0-3 Gall: 0-0
Aids:	Bl: 0-0 Vi: 0-0 Tstrap: 0-Ckp: 0-1
Best Rating:	109 2/04 MRas 2m6f good Hdl

Moderate ex-Irish hurdler; appears to act on most types of ground; stays three miles.

Perk Alert (IRE)

103   **82**

10-y-o b g Executive Perk-Clondo Blue (IRE) (Miners Lamp)
A King Mrs Dawn Perrett

Placings:*210/3033F/4/***P061-2PP**   (0446)
2003/04: 24^{2}GF, 25^{5}GF, 24^{6}G,

	Starts	1st	2nd	3rd	Win & Pl
Chases	3	0	1	0	1162
Career Total	16	2	2	3	8231
76 3/03 Hrfd 3m1f110yF(0-90)HCh				G-F	£3445
106 12/98 Wwck 2m H NHF				SFT	£1444
				Total win prize-money	£4890

Going:	Sf: 0-0 GS: 0-0 Gd: 0-1 GF: - Fm: 0-2

Distance:	2m/2m3: 0-0 2m4-2m7: 0-0 3m+: 0-3
Track:	LH: 0-0 RH: 0-3 Tight: 0-0 Gall: 0-2
Aids:	Bl: 0-0 Vi: 0-0 Tstrap: 0-0 Ckp: 0-0
Best Rating:	118 11/98 Wwck 2m soft NHF

Plating-class staying chaser; suited by fast ground.

Perkys Pride (IRE)

102

8-y-o b g Executive Perk-Josie Mac (Pitpan)
M C Pipe D A Johnson

Placings:*3/2/231311035/500***P064-P**   (0756)
2003/04: 22^{P}GF,

	Starts	1st	2nd	3rd	Win & Pl
Hurdles	1	0	0	0	
Career Total	19	3	2	4	24260
124 1/02 Navn 2m6f		Hdl		Y-S	£7196
121 12/01 Navn 2m2f		Hdl		Y-S	£5842
108 11/01 DRoy 2m		NHF		YLD	£5008
				Total win prize-money	£18047

Going:	Sf: 0-0 GS: 0-0 Gd: 0-0 GF: - Fm: 0-1
Distance:	2m/2m3: 0-0 2m4-2m7: 0-1 3m+: 0-0
Track:	LH: 0-1 RH: 0-0 Tight: 0-1 Gall: 0-0
Aids:	Bl: 0-0 Vi: 0-1 Tstrap: 0-0 Ckp: 0-0
Best Rating:	125 4/02 Fair 2m4f gd-yld Hdl

Fair hurdler; ex-Irish; acts on a soft surface, stays two miles six.

Perle De Puce (FR)

111   **143+**

5-y-o b m Snurge-Ma Puce (FR) (Tip Moss (FR))
N J Henderson (A Hosselet 16/11) Robert Waley-Cohen

Placings:*21P03011***FP0**   (4629)
2003/04: 17^{2}VS, 18^{1}HY, 18^{8}S, 18^{0}VS, 18^{3}VS, 19^{0}VS, 18^{1}HO, 16^{1}G, 16^{6}GS, 16^{6}G, 20^{0}G,

	Starts	1st	2nd	3rd	Win & Pl
Hurdles	11	3	1	1	54357
Career Total	11	3	1	1	54357
143 12/03 Asct 2m110y A Hdl				GD	£14500
11/03 Autl 2m2f HHdl				HLD	£14961
5/03 Autl 2m2f Hdl				HVY	£12468
				Total win prize-money	£41929

Going:	Sf: 1-2 GS: 0-1 Gd: 1-3 GF: - Fm: 0-0
Distance:	2m/2m3: 3-9 2m4-2m7: 0-2 3m+: 0-0
Track:	LH: 0-3 RH: 1-2 Tight: 0-1 Gall: 0-0
Aids:	Bl: 0-0 Vi: 0-0 Tstrap: 0-0 Ckp: 0-1
Best Rating:	143 12/03 Asct 2m110y good Hdl

Useful ex-French hurdler; good winner in Grade Two on British debut and fell when still in contention in a Grade One next time; disappointing at the spring festivals; stays 2m 2f; acts on testing ground and good ground; promises to do better still.

Pernickety King

87f   **62f**

5-y-o b g Rakaposhi King-Fussy Lady (Idiots Delight)
P J Hobbs The Hedonists

Placings:*00*   (0871)
2003/04: 16^{0}G, 17^{0}GF,

	Starts	1st	2nd	3rd	Win & Pl
NH Flat	2	0	0	0	
Career Total	2	0	0	0	

Going:	Sf: 0-0 GS: 0-0 Gd: 0-1 GF: - Fm: 0-1
Distance:	2m/2m3: 0-2 2m4-2m7: 0-0 3m+: 0-0

Track:	LH: 0-2 RH: 0-0 Tight: 0-1 Gall: 0-0
Aids:	Bl: 0-0 Vi: 0-0 Tstrap: 0-0 Ckp: 0-0
Best Rating:	62 6/03 Worc 2m good NHF

Perouse

115   **149**

6-y-o ch g Alderbrook-Track Angel (Ardoon)
P F Nicholls J Dickson & S McVie

Placings:*221/0211-062111220P*   (4862)
2003/04: 16^{8}GF, 16^{6}GF, 16^{2}GS, 16^{1}G, 18^{1}G, 16^{1}G, 17^{2}G, 16^{2}G, 16^{9}G, 16^{8}GS,

	Starts	1st	2nd	3rd	Win & Pl
Hurdles	10	3	3	0	50426
Career Total	17	6	6	0	62111
136 12/03 Chel 2m110y C(0-135)HHdl				GD	£16457
135 12/03 Font 2m2f110yC(0-130)HHdl				GD	£9317
131 12/03 Winc 2m D(0-120)HHdl				GD	£5122
105 4/03 Winc 2m E Hdl				FRM	£3521
86 4/03 Tntn 2m1f E Hdl				FRM	£3906
93 4/02 Hexm 2m110y H NHF				GD	£1701
				Total win prize-money	£40025

Going:	Sf: 0-0 GS: 0-2 Gd: 3-6 GF: - Fm: 0-2
Distance:	2m/2m3: 3-10 2m4-2m7: 0-0 3m+: 0-0
Track:	LH: 2-5 RH: 1-5 Tight: 1-1 Gall: 0-2
Aids:	Bl: 0-0 Vi: 0-0 Tstrap: 3-8 Ckp: 0-0
Best Rating:	149 1/04 Kemp 2m good Hdl

Smart hurdler; progressive; completed a treble in decent handicap company in December 2003; later runner-up in two very competitive handicaps; suited by two miles and good ground; usually tongue tied.

Persian Brook

4-y-o b g Atraf-Persian Role (Tragic Role (USA))
M W Easterby M Sutton

Placings:*P*   (1448)
2003/04: 17^{P}GF,

	Starts	1st	2nd	3rd	Win & Pl
Hurdles	1	0	0	0	
Career Total	1	0	0	0	

Going:	Sf: 0-0 GS: 0-0 Gd: 0-0 GF: - Fm: 0-1
Distance:	2m/2m3: 0-1 2m4-2m7: 0-0 3m+: 0-0
Track:	LH: 0-0 RH: 0-1 Tight: 0-1 Gall: 0-0
Aids:	Bl: 0-0 Vi: 0-0 Tstrap: 0-0 Ckp: 0-0

Persian King (IRE)

104(108h)   (121h)**119**

7-y-o ch g Persian Bold-Queen's Share (Main Reef)
J A B Old W E Sturt

Placings:*5/66/23110-3341F*   (1363)
2003/04: 16^{3}G, 16^{3}G, 16^{6}GF, 16^{1}GF, 16^{6}GF,

	Starts	1st	2nd	3rd	Win & Pl
Hurdles	2	0	0	2	4195
Chases	3	1	0	0	3619
Career Total	13	3	1	3	16241
119 9/03 Worc 2m E Ch				G-F	£3360
115 10/02 Chep 2m110y D Hdl				G-F	£4143
90 9/02 Worc 2m E Hdl				GD	£2982
				Total win prize-money	£10486

Going:	Sf: 0-0 GS: 0-0 Gd: 0-2 GF: - Fm: 1-3
Distance:	2m/2m3: 1-5 2m4-2m7: 0-0 3m+: 0-0
Track:	LH: 1-5 RH: 0-0 Tight: 0-2 Gall: 0-0
Aids:	Bl: 0-0 Vi: 0-0 Tstrap: 0-0 Ckp: 0-0

Best Rating: 121 5/03 Strf 2m110y good Hdl

Useful hurdler; bit of a flop when even money favourite on chasing debut at Newton Abbot September 2003, but won at Worcester four days later; effective at two miles; acts on a sound surface.

Persian Waters (IRE)

110   137+

8-y-o b g Persian Bold-Emerald Waters (King's Lake (USA))
J R Fanshawe Paul Green

Placings:1224/200/230-1   (0095)
2003/04: 23¹GS,

	Starts	1st	2nd	3rd	Win & Pl
Hurdles	1	1	0	0	15008
Career Total	11	2	4	1	35144
139 5/03	Hayd	2m7f110yB HHdl		G-S	£15008
115 11/99	Hntg	2m110y C Hdl		G-F	£5327
		Total win prize-money £20335			

Going: Sf: 0-0 GS: 1-1 Gd: 0-0 GF: - Fm: 0-0
Distance: 2m/2m3: 0-0 2m4-2m7: 0-0 3m+: 1-1
Track: LH: 1-1 RH: 0-0 Tight: 0-0 Gall: 0-0
Aids: Bl: 0-0 Vi: 0-0 Tstrap: 0-0 Ckp: 0-0
Best Rating: 139 5/03 Hayd 2m7f110y gd-sft Hdl

Useful handicap hurdler; lightly raced; stays two miles seven; suited by a sound surface, but does handle softer ground

Persona Pride

10-y-o gr g St Enodoc-Le Jour Fortune (Twilight Alley)
Mrs B Brown Percy Priday

Placings:P64P/PP-P   (3778)
2003/04: 24²G,

	Starts	1st	2nd	3rd	Win & Pl
Chases	1	0	0	0	0
Career Total	7	0	0	0	0

Going: Sf: 0-0 GS: 0-0 Gd: 0-1 GF: - Fm: 0-0
Distance: 2m/2m3: 0-0 2m4-2m7: 0-0 3m+: 0-1
Track: LH: 0-0 RH: 0-1 Tight: 0-0 Gall: 0-0
Aids: Bl: 0-0 Vi: 0-0 Tstrap: 0-0 Ckp: 0-0
Best Rating: 80 3/02 Hrfd 3m1f110y good Ch

Personal Assurance

108   125+

7-y-o b/br g Un Desperado (FR)-Steel Typhoon (General Ironside)
Jonjo O'Neill Christopher W T Johnston

Placings:3233154-122400P   (4643)
2003/04: 21¹GF, 20²G, 22²GS, 21⁴S, 23⁹S, 25⁰G, 24⁴G,

	Starts	1st	2nd	3rd	Win & Pl
Hurdles	7	1	2	0	10061
Career Total	14	2	3	3	18647
125 10/03	Sthl	2m5f110yC(0-130)HHdl		G-F	£5408
112 2/03	Sand	2m110y D Hdl		HVY	£5414
		Total win prize-money £10823			

Going: Sf: 0-2 GS: 0-1 Gd: 0-3 GF: - Fm: 1-1
Distance: 2m/2m3: 0-0 2m4-2m7: 1-4 3m+: 0-3
Track: LH: 1-6 RH: 0-1 Tight: 0-0 Gall: 0-1
Aids: Bl: 0-0 Vi: 0-0 Tstrap: 0-0 Ckp: 0-0
Best Rating: 127 11/03 Weth 2m4f110y good Hdl

Fair hurdler; stays two and a half miles plus; acts on any ground but best on a sound surface.

Persuets (IRE)

77   50

6-y-o b m Gildoran-Furry Queen (Furry Glen)
Ronald Thompson (J I A Charlton 17/5) Ronald Thompson

Placings:4-40   (0976)
2003/04: 17⁴G, 17⁰GF,

	Starts	1st	2nd	3rd	Win & Pl
NH Flat	1	0	0	0	0
Hurdles	1	0	0	0	0
Career Total	3	0	0	0	0

Going: Sf: 0-0 GS: 0-0 Gd: 0-1 GF: - Fm: 0-1
Distance: 2m/2m3: 0-2 2m4-2m7: 0-0 3m+: 0-0
Track: LH: 0-2 RH: 0-0 Tight: 0-0 Gall: 0-0
Aids: Bl: 0-0 Vi: 0-0 Tstrap: 0-0 Ckp: 0-0
Best Rating: 92 4/03 Carl 2m1f gd-fm NHF

Pertemps Cindrella

(93c)   (91c) 81

9-y-o ch m Almoojid-Cinderella Derek (Hittite Glory)
B D Leavy J A Provan

Placings:33060/P030/0F522250/5F012200P4/204361-P6
                         (0366)
2003/04: 20²HY, 24⁶S,

	Starts	1st	2nd	3rd	Win & Pl
Hurdles	1	0	0	0	0
Chases	1	0	0	0	0
Career Total	35	2	6	4	10965
91 3/03	MRas	2m6f110yE(0-105)HCh		SFT	£4315
82 11/01	Uttx	2m	G(0-90)HHdl	HVY	£1897
		Total win prize-money £6213			

Going: Sf: 0-2 GS: 0-0 Gd: 0-0 GF: - Fm: 0-0
Distance: 2m/2m3: 0-0 2m4-2m7: 0-1 3m+: 0-1
Track: LH: 0-2 RH: 0-0 Tight: 0-0 Gall: 0-0
Aids: Bl: 0-0 Vi: 0-0 Tstrap: 0-0 Ckp: 0-0
Best Rating: 91 3/03 MRas 2m6f110y soft Ch

Plating-class hurdler; suited by testing conditions, had luck on her side when making a winning debut over fences at Market Rasen in March; stays two miles-six.

Pertemps Machine

79   60

5-y-o b g Danzig Connection (USA)-Shamrock Dancer (IRE) (Dance Of Life (USA))
A D Smith Duckhaven Stud

Placings:P-00F   (3049)
2003/04: 16⁶GS, 19⁰G, 24²G,

	Starts	1st	2nd	3rd	Win & Pl
Hurdles	3	0	0	0	0
Career Total	4	0	0	0	0

Going: Sf: 0-0 GS: 0-1 Gd: 0-2 GF: - Fm: 0-0
Distance: 2m/2m3: 0-1 2m4-2m7: 0-1 3m+: 0-1
Track: LH: 0-1 RH: 0-2 Tight: 0-0 Gall: 0-0
Aids: Bl: 0-0 Vi: 0-0 Tstrap: 0-0 Ckp: 0-0
Best Rating: 64 11/03 Chep 2m110y gd-sft Hdl

Pertemps Profile

83   (103h)69

8-y-o b g Petoski-Peristyle (Tolomeo)
Ian Williams Pertemps Group Limited

Placings:165/UP4/16P35020/P05P   (4341)
2003/04: 20⁰GS, 23⁰G, 25⁵HY, 20⁰GS,

	Starts	1st	2nd	3rd	Win & Pl
Chases	4	0	0	0	0
Career Total	18	2	1	1	6550
100 5/01	Bang	2m4f	D(0-110)HHdl	G-S	£3612
96 2/00	Towc	2m	H NHF	HVY	£1820
		Total win prize-money £5432			

Going: Sf: 0-1 GS: 0-2 Gd: 0-1 GF: - Fm: 0-0
Distance: 2m/2m3: 0-0 2m4-2m7: 0-2 3m+: 0-2
Track: LH: 0-1 RH: 0-3 Tight: 0-0 Gall: 0-1
Aids: Bl: 0-3 Vi: 0-0 Tstrap: 0-0 Ckp: 0-0
Best Rating: 103 2/02 Hntg 3m2f soft Hdl

Pertemps Silenus

6-y-o b g Silca Blanka (IRE)-Silvie (Kind Of Hush)
A D Smith Pertemps Group Limited

Placings:00/0PP-F   (0631)
2003/04: 17⁵GF,

	Starts	1st	2nd	3rd	Win & Pl
Hurdles	1	0	0	0	0
Career Total	6	0	0	0	0

Going: Sf: 0-0 GS: 0-0 Gd: 0-0 GF: - Fm: 0-1
Distance: 2m/2m3: 0-1 2m4-2m7: 0-0 3m+: 0-0
Track: LH: 0-1 RH: 0-0 Tight: 0-1 Gall: 0-0
Aids: Bl: 0-0 Vi: 0-0 Tstrap: 0-0 Ckp: 0-0
Best Rating: 68 2/02 Sand 2m110y soft NHF

Pertemps Susie

93   92

8-y-o b m Gildoran-Brilliant Future (Welsh Saint)
Ian Williams Martin Green

Placings:006/ 164/05325-5   (0207)
2003/04: 16⁵GF,

	Starts	1st	2nd	3rd	Win & Pl
Hurdles	1	0	0	0	0
Career Total	12	1	1	1	3985
95 5/01	Extr	2m1f	H NHF	FRM	£2187
		Total win prize-money £2188			

Going: Sf: 0-0 GS: 0-0 Gd: 0-0 GF: - Fm: 0-1
Distance: 2m/2m3: 0-1 2m4-2m7: 0-0 3m+: 0-0
Track: LH: 0-1 RH: 0-0 Tight: 0-0 Gall: 0-0
Aids: Bl: 0-0 Vi: 0-0 Tstrap: 0-0 Ckp: 0-0
Best Rating: 95 5/01 Extr 2m1f firm NHF

Moderate hurdler; best at distances short of two and a half miles; acts on fast ground.

Pertemps Wizard

4-y-o br g Silver Wizard (USA)-Peristyle (Tolomeo)
A D Smith Pertemps Group Limited

Placings:P   (3708)
2003/04: 16⁰HY,

	Starts	1st	2nd	3rd	Win & Pl
Hurdles	1	0	0	0	0
Career Total	1	0	0	0	0

Going: Sf: 0-1 GS: 0-0 Gd: 0-0 GF: - Fm: 0-0
Distance: 2m/2m3: 0-1 2m4-2m7: 0-0 3m+: 0-0
Track: LH: 0-1 RH: 0-0 Tight: 0-0 Gall: 0-0
Aids: Bl: 0-0 Vi: 0-0 Tstrap: 0-0 Ckp: 0-0

Pertino

104(108h)   (113h)**117**
8-y-o b g Terimon-Persian Fountain (IRE) (Persian Heights)
J M Jefferson W Fouracres, T Pryke & D Willis

Placings:5412153/P0056P/P0F12205212/5412120-5466140605   (4686)
2003/04: 17^5GF, 16^4GF, 16^6G, 21^6G, 16^1S, 16^4G, 16^0HY, 19^6G, 16^0G, 17^5G,

	Starts	1st	2nd	3rd	Win & Pl
Hurdles	2	0	0	0	0
Chases	8	1	0	0	6051
Career Total	41	7	7	1	35545
117 11/03 Ayr	2m	D(0-115)HCh		SFT	£5408
117 10/02 Sthl	2m1f	E Ch		GD	£4315
106 9/02 Hexm	2m110y	E Ch		G-F	£3357
112 4/02 Carl	2m1f	D(0-120)HHdl		GD	£3486
106 10/01 Kels	2m110y	E(0-115)HHdl		GD	£2821
120 2/00 Muss	2m	D Hdl		G-S	£3087
104 1/00 Newc	2m	E Hdl		SFT	£2558
				Total win prize-money	£25035

Going: Sf: 1-2 GS: 0-0 Gd: 0-6 GF: - Fm: 0-2
Distance: 2m/2m3: 1-9 2m4-2m7: 0-1 3m+: 0-0
Track: LH: 1-8 RH: 0-2 Tight: 0-5 Gall: 0-1
Aids: Bl: 0-2 Vi: 0-0 Tstrap: 0-0 **Ckp: 1-5**
Best Rating: 120 2/00 Muss 2m   gd-sft Hdl

Modest hurdler/chaser; suited by a sound surface but handles softer; effective at around two miles; has worn sheepskin cheekpieces.

Peruvia (IRE)

80   **49**
4-y-o b f Perugino (USA)-Dane's Lane (IRE) (Danehill (USA))
Mrs A J Hamilton-Fairley (H Morrison 13/10) Quenby Racing

Placings:00P   (4452)
2003/04: 17^0S, 16^0G, 16^0GS,

	Starts	1st	2nd	3rd	Win & Pl
Hurdles	3	0	0	0	0
Career Total	3	0	0	0	0

Going: Sf: 0-1 GS: 0-1 Gd: 0-1 GF: - Fm: 0-0
Distance: 2m/2m3: 0-2 2m4-2m7: 0-0 3m+: 0-0
Track: LH: 0-1 RH: 0-0 Tight: 0-1 Gall: 0-1
Aids: Bl: 0-0 Vi: 0-0 Tstrap: 0-0 Ckp: 0-0
Best Rating: 49 3/04 Newb 2m110y good Hdl

Modest hurdler; winner over nine furlongs on the Flat; suited by cut in the ground.

Peruvian Princess

5-y-o gr m Missed Flight-Misty View (Absalom)
W M Brisbourne Ms Rosario Cornejo S C

Placings:0   (4846)
2003/04: 17^0G,

	Starts	1st	2nd	3rd	Win & Pl
NH Flat	1	0	0	0	0
Career Total	1	0	0	0	0

Going: Sf: 0-0 GS: 0-0 Gd: 0-1 GF: - Fm: 0-0
Distance: 2m/2m3: 0-1 2m4-2m7: 0-0 3m+: 0-0
Track: LH: 0-1 RH: 0-0 Tight: 0-0 Gall: 0-1
Aids: Bl: 0-0 Vi: 0-0 Tstrap: 0-0 Ckp: 0-0

Pessimistic Dick

105   **121**
11-y-o b g Derrylin-Tycoon Moon (Tycoon Ii)
H Morrison Frank Flynn And Richard Madden

Placings:5505/262P4533/P1036F30F52/PP0P/P534/14511115P5-54P5215U5   (2578)
2003/04: 24^5GF, 30^4G, 32^8GF, 24^5G, 26^2GF, 26^1GF, 24^5GF, 27^0G, 24^5GF,

	Starts	1st	2nd	3rd	Win & Pl
Chases	9	1	1	0	5412
Career Total	50	7	4	5	43995
106 10/03 Plum	3m2f	E(0-110)HCh		G-F	£3213
121 10/02 Chel	3m110y	E(0-125)HCh		G-F	£7829
113 10/02 Carl	3m2f	D(0-115)HCh		G-F	£6678
103 9/02 Sedg	3m3f	D(0-115)HCh		GD	£4680
98 8/02 Ctml	3m2f	D(0-120)HCh		G-F	£5200
90 6/02 Worc	2m7f110y	E(0-110)HCh		G-F	£3757
75 10/01 Carl	2m4f110y	E Ch		G-F	£3096
				Total win prize-money	£34453

Going: Sf: 0-0 GS: 0-0 Gd: 0-3 GF: - Fm: 1-6
Distance: 2m/2m3: 0-0 2m4-2m7: 0-0 3m+: 1-9
Track: LH: 1-7 RH: 0-0 Tight: 1-4 Gall: 0-1
Aids: Bl: 0-1 Vi: 0-0 Tstrap: 0-0 Ckp: 0-0
Best Rating: 121 10/02 Chel 3m110y gd-fm Ch

Moderate staying chaser; not always the most consistent; suited by three miles plus and ground good or faster.

Petanque (IRE)

110   **123**
8-y-o b g King's Ride-Phargara (IRE) (Phardante (FR))
N J Henderson P J D Pottinger

Placings:1/5146-4434   (3607)
2003/04: 16^4GS, 17^4G, 16^5S, 16^4S,

	Starts	1st	2nd	3rd	Win & Pl
Hurdles	4	0	0	1	4739
Career Total	9	1	0	1	12768
117 1/03 Donc	2m3f110y	D Hdl		G-S	£5863
105 12/01 Hntg	2m110y	H NHF		G-S	£1750
				Total win prize-money	£7613

Going: Sf: 0-0 GS: 0-1 Gd: 0-1 GF: - Fm: 0-0
Distance: 2m/2m3: 0-4 2m4-2m7: 0-0 3m+: 0-0
Track: LH: 0-3 RH: 0-1 Tight: 0-0 Gall: 0-3
Aids: Bl: 0-0 Vi: 0-0 Tstrap: 0-0 Ckp: 0-0
Best Rating: 123 1/04 Winc 2m soft Hdl

Fair hurdler; bumper winner; effective over trips of around two and half miles; handles cut in the ground, but disappointed when tried on heavy

Petara (IRE)

68   **32**
9-y-o ch g Petardia-Romangoddess (IRE) (Rhoman Rule (USA))
J S Wainwright J S Wainwright

Placings:0/0P-0   (0417)
2003/04: 17^0G,

	Starts	1st	2nd	3rd	Win & Pl
Hurdles	1	0	0	0	
Career Total	4	0	0	0	

Going: Sf: 0-0 GS: 0-0 Gd: 0-1 GF: - Fm: 0-0
Distance: 2m/2m3: 0-1 2m4-2m7: 0-0 3m+: 0-0
Track: LH: 0-0 RH: 0-1 Tight: 0-1 Gall: 0-0
Aids: Bl: 0-0 Vi: 0-0 Tstrap: 0-0 Ckp: 0-0
Best Rating: 58 7/99 Sedg 2m1f   gd-fm Hdl

Peter's Imp (IRE)

100   **79**
9-y-o b g Imp Society (USA)-Catherine Clare (Sallust)
A Berry Ian A Bolland

Placings:060/050021006   (1765)
2003/04: 17^0GF, 17^5G, 17^0G, 17^0GF, 22^2G, 17^1G, 16^0F, 20^0G, 20^6GF,

	Starts	1st	2nd	3rd	Win & Pl
Hurdles	9	1	1	0	3932
Career Total	12	1	1	0	3932
79 8/03 Ctml	2m1f110y	G(0-90)HHdl		GD	£3062
				Total win prize-money	£3063

Going: Sf: 0-0 GS: 0-0 Gd: 1-5 GF: - Fm: 0-4
Distance: 2m/2m3: 1-6 2m4-2m7: 0-3 3m+: 0-0
Track: LH: 1-8 RH: 0-1 Tight: 1-6 Gall: 0-0
Aids: Bl: 0-0 Vi: 0-0 Tstrap: 0-0 Ckp: 0-0
Best Rating: 79 8/03 Ctml 2m1f110y good Hdl

Poor hurdler; runner-up in a seller at Cartmel in August; took similar event at the track two days later; effective over two miles but stays two mile six.

Peter's Two Fun (FR)

80(104h)   (97 h)**85+**
7-y-o b g Funambule (USA)-Spinner's Mate (FR) (Miller's Mate)
A S T Holdsworth (J L Flint 9/1) N J Holdsworth

Placings:F30P/25S543/231202034520P-5P53   (4737)
2003/04: 16^5GS, 19^6G, 16^5GS, 21^3G,

	Starts	1st	2nd	3rd	Win & Pl
Hurdles	3	0	0	0	0
Chases	1	0	0	1	424
Career Total	27	1	5	5	13152
99 6/02 Worc	2m4f	E Hdl		GD	£2702
				Total win prize-money	£2702

Going: Sf: 0-0 GS: 0-2 Gd: 0-2 GF: - Fm: 0-0
Distance: 2m/2m3: 0-2 2m4-2m7: 0-2 3m+: 0-0
Track: LH: 0-2 RH: 0-1 Tight: 0-2 Gall: 0-0
Aids: Bl: 0-1 Vi: 0-0 Tstrap: 0-0 Ckp: 0-0
Best Rating: 99 6/02 NAbb 2m6f   gd-fm Hdl

Peterhouse

5-y-o b g Persian Bold-Run With Pride (Mandrake Major)
R Johnson A Slack

Placings:6P0   (4727)
2003/04: 16^6HY, 17^6GS, 17^0G,

	Starts	1st	2nd	3rd	Win & Pl
NH Flat	1	0	0	0	0
Hurdles	2	0	0	0	0
Career Total	3	0	0	0	0

Going: Sf: 0-1 GS: 0-1 Gd: 0-1 GF: - Fm: 0-0
Distance: 2m/2m3: 0-3 2m4-2m7: 0-3 3m+: 0-0
Track: LH: 0-2 RH: 0-1 Tight: 0-1 Gall: 0-0
Aids: Bl: 0-0 Vi: 0-0 Tstrap: 0-0 Ckp: 0-0
Best Rating: 71 2/04 Newc 2m heavy NHF

Peterson's Cay (IRE)

95   **96**

6-y-o b g Grand Lodge (USA)-Columbian Sand (IRE) (Salmon Leap (USA))
Mrs M Reveley A Frame

Placings:42/435P4-301   (3841)
2003/04: 20³GF, 16⁶G, 19¹GS,

	Starts	1st	2nd	3rd	Win & Pl
Hurdles	3	1	0	1	3462
Career Total	10	1	1	2	4881
96 2/04 Hrfd	2m3f110yF Hdl			G-S	£3024
				Total win prize-money £3024

Going:	Sf: 0-0 GS: 1-1 Gd: 0-1 GF: - Fm: 0-1
Distance:	2m/2m3: 0-1 **2m4-2m7: 1-2** 3m+: 0-0
Track:	LH: 0-1 **RH: 1-2** Tight: 0-1 Gall: 0-1
Aids:	Bl: 0-0 Vi: 0-0 Tstrap: 0-0 Ckp: 0-0
Best Rating:	**96** 2/04 Hrfd 2m3f110y gd-sft Hdl

Moderate hurdler; claimed out of Mary Reveley's yard after winning at Hereford in February; stays 2m 4f.

Petite Margot

111   **128+**

5-y-o b m Alderbrook-Outfield (Monksfield)
N A Twiston-Davies (D J Caro 26/5) Roger Nicholls

Placings:043111142341   (4909)
2003/04: 16⁸GF, 16⁴G, 17³GF, 16¹GF, 24¹GF, 25¹G, 21¹G, 24⁴GS, 24²G, 24³G, 21⁴G, 24¹S,

	Starts	1st	2nd	3rd	Win & Pl
NH Flat	4	1	0	1	2045
Hurdles	8	4	1	1	19463
Career Total	12	5	1	2	21508
128 4/04 Prth	3m110y D Hdl		SFT	£5564
110 12/03 Ludl	2m5f	E(0-105)HHdl	GD	£3750
101 11/03 Wwck	3m1f	E Hdl	G-F	£3073
88 10/03 Towc	3m	E Hdl	G-F	£2597
95 10/03 Ludl	2m	H NHF	G-F	£1820
				Total win prize-money £16805

Going:	Sf: 1-1 GS: 0-1 Gd: 1-5 GF: - Fm: 3-5
Distance:	2m/2m3: 1-4 2m4-2m7: 1-2 **3m+: 3-6**
Track:	LH: 1-5 **RH: 4-7** Tight: 0-0 Gall: 0-3
Aids:	Bl: 0-0 Vi: 0-0 Tstrap: 0-0 Ckp: 0-0
Best Rating:	**128** 4/04 Prth 3m110y soft Hdl

Fair hurdler; had shown ability in modest bumpers prior to winning poor 4-runner affair at Ludlow October 2003; won first three races over hurdles and scored again in the spring; stays 3m; acts on any ground; needs plenty of driving.

Petolinski

102(109h)   (100h)**83**

6-y-o b g Petoski-Olnistar (FR) (Balsamo (FR))
J S King R B Denny

Placings:60/00130P-54PP4P   (4695)
2003/04: 20⁵G, 25⁴S, 26⁶S, 24⁵PHY, 23⁴GS, 23⁹G,

	Starts	1st	2nd	3rd	Win & Pl
Chases	6	0	0	0	783
Career Total	14	1	0	1	4501
100 12/02 Chep	2m4f	E Hdl	SFT	£2912
				Total win prize-money £2912

Going:	Sf: 0-4 GS: 0-1 Gd: 0-1 GF: - Fm: 0-0
Distance:	2m/2m3: 0-0 2m4-2m7: 0-1 3m+: 0-5
Track:	LH: 0-3 RH: 0-3 Tight: 0-1 Gall: 0-2
Aids:	Bl: 0-0 Vi: 0-0 Tstrap: 0-0 Ckp: 0-2
Best Rating:	**100** 12/02 Leic 2m4f110y heavy Hdl

Petrea

102(91c)   (33c)**87+**

9-y-o b/br m St Ninian-Polypodium (Politico (USA))
T D Walford (W M Burnell 3/5) Mrs E C York

Placings:50/00PP/3-01P16   (4433)
2003/04: 25⁰G, 23¹GS, 25⁸GS, 24¹HY, 24⁶G,

	Starts	1st	2nd	3rd	Win & Pl
Hurdles	4	2	0	0	4970
Chases	1	0	0	0	0
Career Total	12	2	0	1	5405
87 2/04 Newc	3m	F(0-100)HHdl	HVY	£2709
75 11/03 Weth	2m7f	F(0-100)HHdl	G-S	£2261
				Total win prize-money £4970

Going:	Sf: 1-1 GS: 1-2 Gd: 0-2 GF: - Fm: 0-0
Distance:	2m/2m3: 0-0 2m4-2m7: 1-1 3m+: 1-4
Track:	LH: 2-5 RH: 0-0 Tight: 0-0 **Gall: 1-1**
Aids:	Bl: 0-0 Vi: 0-0 Tstrap: 0-0 Ckp: 0-0
Best Rating:	**88** 5/02 Strf 3m good Ch

Plating-class hurdler; showed promise in points and has now won twice from three outings since returning under rules; stays three miles; acts on any ground.

Petrouge

110   (4302)

8-y-o b g Petoski-Red Spider (Red God))
Mrs C J Robinson Jeremy Beasley

Placings:500305P/P   (4302)
2003/04: 20²G,

	Starts	1st	2nd	3rd	Win & Pl
Chases	1	0	0	0	
Career Total	8	0	0	1	407

Going:	Sf: 0-0 GS: 0-0 Gd: 0-1 GF: - Fm: 0-0
Distance:	2m/2m3: 0-0 2m4-2m7: 0-1 3m+: 0-0
Track:	LH: 0-0 RH: 0-1 Tight: 0-0 Gall: 0-0
Aids:	Bl: 0-0 Vi: 0-0 Tstrap: 0-0 Ckp: 0-0
Best Rating:	**86** 1/02 Hrfd 2m3f110y soft Hdl

Petrula

110   **127+**

5-y-o ch g Tagula (IRE)-Bouffant (High Top)
K A Ryan Mr & Mrs Peter Foden

Placings:2F2145B2   (4513)
2003/04: 17²G, 16⁶F, 16²S, 20¹G, 20⁴S, 16⁵G, 17⁶G, 16²GS,

	Starts	1st	2nd	3rd	Win & Pl
Hurdles	8	1	3	0	8636
Career Total	8	1	3	0	8636
117 12/03 Weth	2m4f110yD(0-110)HHdl	GD	£4517
			Total win prize-money £4518

Going:	Sf: 0-2 GS: 0-1 Gd: 1-5 GF: - Fm: 0-0
Distance:	2m/2m3: 0-6 **2m4-2m7: 1-2** 3m+: 0-0
Track:	**LH: 1-6** RH: 0-2 Tight: 0-3 Gall: 1-4
Aids:	Bl: 0-0 Vi: 0-0 Tstrap: 0-0 **Ckp: 1-4**
Best Rating:	**127** 3/04 Weth 2m gd-sft Hdl

Fair handicapper on the Flat; winning novice hurdler; stays two and a half miles; acts on most ground; sometimes wears cheekpieces; has been tried in blinkers.

Pettree (IRE)

109   **108**

10-y-o ch g King Persian-Whackers World (Whistling Deer)

N A Twiston-Davies Pettifer Group Limited

Placings:U02/6623FP/1UU/64052-2P154FP   (1617)
2003/04: 24²GF, 28⁸GS, 26¹GF, 32⁵GF, 26⁴GF, 26⁶GF, 24⁶G,

	Starts	1st	2nd	3rd	Win & Pl
Chases	7	1	1	0	7989
Career Total	24	2	4	1	15979
108 6/03 Sthl	3m2f	E(0-110)HCh	G-F	£4065
108 11/01 Wwck	2m4f110yD(0-125)HCh	GD	£4153
			Total win prize-money £8220

Going:	Sf: 0-0 GS: 0-1 Gd: 0-1 GF: - Fm: 1-5
Distance:	2m/2m3: 0-0 2m4-2m7: 0-0 **3m+: 1-7**
Track:	**LH: 1-6** RH: 0-0 Tight: 0-3 Gall: 0-0
Aids:	Bl: 0-0 Vi: 0-0 Tstrap: 0-0 Ckp: 0-0
Best Rating:	**114** 2/00 Newb 3m110y gd-sft Hdl

Moderate chaser; inclined to be let down by his jumping; often loses his place during his races; stays acts on good ground; stays marathon trips.

Peveril Pride

107   **103**

6-y-o b g Past Glories-Peveril Princess (Town And Country)
M J Weeden Mrs E A Haycock

Placings:5P0R03   (4147)
2003/04: 16⁵GF, 19⁸S, 16⁶G, 22⁸G, 16⁹G, 24³G,

	Starts	1st	2nd	3rd	Win & Pl
NH Flat	1	0	0	0	0
Hurdles	5	0	0	1	745
Career Total	6	0	0	1	745

Going:	Sf: 0-2 GS: 0-0 Gd: 0-3 GF: - Fm: 0-1
Distance:	2m/2m3: 0-4 2m4-2m7: 0-1 3m+: 0-1
Track:	LH: 0-1 RH: 0-5 Tight: 0-1 Gall: 0-1
Aids:	Bl: 0-0 Vi: 0-0 Tstrap: 0-0 Ckp: 0-0
Best Rating:	**103** 3/04 Tntn 3m110y good Hdl

Pewter Light (IRE)

96(82h)   (58h)**79+**

7-y-o g g g Roselier (FR)-Luminous Light (Cardinal Flower)
B J M Ryall I & Mrs K G Fawcett

Placings:PP0-63PP23   (4672)
2003/04: 25⁶GS, 23⁹G, 25⁷S, 26⁶GF, 25²G, 25³G,

	Starts	1st	2nd	3rd	Win & Pl
Chases	6	0	1	2	2743
Career Total	9	0	1	2	2743

Going:	Sf: 0-1 GS: 0-1 Gd: 0-3 GF: - Fm: 0-1
Distance:	2m/2m3: 0-0 2m4-2m7: 0-0 3m+: 0-6
Track:	LH: 0-1 RH: 0-5 Tight: 0-0 Gall: 0-1
Aids:	Bl: 0-0 Vi: 0-0 Tstrap: 0-0 Ckp: 0-1
Best Rating:	**79** 3/04 Hrfd 3m1f110y good Ch

Phantom Haze

11-y-o g r g Absalom-Caroline Lamb (Hotfoot)
J Parkes Derrick Mossop

Placings:334/02/50/P6/P   (4794)
2003/04: 21¹G,

	Starts	1st	2nd	3rd	Win & Pl
Chases	1	0	0	0	
Career Total	10	0	1	2	1519

| Going: | Sf: 0-0 GS: 0-0 Gd: 0-1 GF: - Fm: 0-0 |

Distance: 2m/2m3: 0-0 2m4-2m7: 0-1 3m+: 0-0
Track: LH: 0-1 RH: 0-0 Tight: 0-1 Gall: 0-0
Aids: Bl: 0-0 Vi: 0-0 Tstrap: 0-0 Ckp: 0-0
Best Rating: 89   12/97   Muss   2m4f   good   Hdl

Phar City (IRE)

100(103h)   (90h)102

7-y-o b g Phardante (FR)-Aunty Dawn (IRE) (Strong Gale)
R H Buckler   Mrs Timothy Lewis

Placings:6/503P5021F-3F   (4734)
2003/04: 25FGY, 233GF, 26FG,

	Starts	1st	2nd	3rd	Win & Pl
Chases	3	0	0	1	742
Career Total	12	1	1	2	5546

102	4/03	Plum	2m4f	F Ch	G-F	£3318

Total win prize-money £3318

Going: Sf: 0-0 GS: 0-0 Gd: 0-1 GF: - Fm: 0-1
Distance: 2m/2m3: 0-0 2m4-2m7: 0-0 3m+: 0-3
Track: LH: 0-0 RH: 0-2 Tight: 0-1 Gall: 0-0
Aids: Bl: 0-0 Vi: 0-0 Tstrap: 0-0 Ckp: 0-0
Best Rating: 102   4/03   Plum   2m4f   gd-fm   Ch

Moderate hurdler/chaser; got off the mark on his chase debut; suited by fast ground; stays two miles five.

Phar Far Away

80   43

6-y-o b m Phardante (FR)-Shannon Juliette (Julio Mariner)
D R Gandolfo   Stephen Freud & Friends

Placings:2UP0P   (4929)
2003/04: 16²GS, 20UG, 21PGS, 22QGS, 18PG,

	Starts	1st	2nd	3rd	Win & Pl
NH Flat	1	0	1	0	612
Hurdles	4	0	0	0	0
Career Total	5	0	1	0	612

Going: Sf: 0-0 GS: 0-3 Gd: 0-2 GF: - Fm: 0-0
Distance: 2m/2m3: 0-2 2m4-2m7: 0-3 3m+: 0-0
Track: LH: 0-2 RH: 0-2 Tight: 0-2 Gall: 0-0
Aids: Bl: 0-0 Vi: 0-0 Tstrap: 0-0 Ckp: 0-0
Best Rating: 96   12/03   Uttx   2m   gd-sft   NHF

Dam staying hurdler; runner-up on debut in bumper at Uttoxeter in December; held over hurdles.

Phar From A Fiddle (IRE)

104(106h)   (107h)120

8-y-o b/br g Phardante (FR)-Lucycello (Monksfield)
P F Nicholls   Mrs J Stewart

Placings:0U2/22114444/45-512PP   (2363)
2003/04: 235GF, 221G, 22²GF, 24PGF, 24PGF,

	Starts	1st	2nd	3rd	Win & Pl
Hurdles	1	0	1	0	860
Chases	4	1	0	0	5382
Career Total	18	3	4	0	36059

120	10/03	Font	2m6f	D(0-120)HCh	GD	£5382
130	11/01	Winc	3m1f110yD(0-110)HCh		GD	£6955
130	10/01	Chel	2m4f110yD(0-110)HCh		GD	£8697

Total win prize-money £21034

Going: Sf: 0-0 GS: 0-0 Gd: 1-1 GF: - Fm: 0-4
Distance: 2m/2m3: 0-0 2m4-2m7: 1-2 3m+: 0-3
Track: LH: 0-1 RH: 0-3 Tight: 1-2 Gall: 0-0
Aids: Bl: 0-0 Vi: 0-0 Tstrap: 1-5 Ckp: 0-0
Best Rating: 130   7/02   MRas   2m4f   gd-sft   Ch

Phar From Frosty (IRE)

114   128+

7-y-o br g Phardante (FR)-Cold Evening (IRE) (Strong Gale)
C R Egerton   Mrs Sandra A Roe

Placings:014F-43113112   (2722)
2003/04: 204GF, 273GF, 241GF, 231GF, 263G, 261GS, 271GF, 252GS,

	Starts	1st	2nd	3rd	Win & Pl
Hurdles	8	4	1	2	19012
Career Total	12	5	1	2	21364

122	11/03	Sedg	3m3f110yE Hdl		G-F	£2478
128	11/03	Hntg	3m2f	E(0-110)HHdl	G-S	£2702
107	10/03	Weth	2m7f	E(0-105)HHdl	G-F	£2212
102	10/03	MRas	3m	D Hdl	G-F	£3454
90	11/02	Ludl	2m	H NHF	G-S	£2352

Total win prize-money £13199

Going: Sf: 0-0 GS: 1-2 Gd: 0-1 GF: - Fm: 3-5
Distance: 2m/2m3: 0-0 2m4-2m7: 1-2 3m+: 3-6
Track: LH: 2-6 RH: 2-2 Tight: 2-3 Gall: 1-2
Aids: Bl: 0-0 Vi: 0-0 Tstrap: 0-0 Ckp: 0-0
Best Rating: 132   12/03   Chel   3m1f110y   gd-sft   Hdl

Fair hurdler; rattled up a sequence in weak staying hurdles in the autumn of 2003; stays well beyond three miles and acts on most types of ground; should make a chaser.

Phar Jeffen (IRE)

99   130

9-y-o ch g Phardante (FR)-Clever Milly (Precipice Wood)
R J Hodges   Fieldspring Racing

Placings:6056420/2113/64F213211/152FPF   (3378)
2003/04: 161GF, 165G, 162G, 16FG, 16PG, 21FS,

	Starts	1st	2nd	3rd	Win & Pl
Chases	6	1	1	0	11076
Career Total	26	6	5	2	41937

130	10/03	Kemp	2m	B(0-140)HCh	G-F	£9816
130	3/02	Towc	2m110y	C Ch	G-S	£6126
128	3/02	Sand	2m	C Ch	GD	£6760
112	12/01	Ludl	2m	E(0-115)HCh	GD	£5782
97	6/00	Baln	2m	Hdl	G-Y	£3036
	5/00	DRoy	2m	NHF	GD	£2760

Total win prize-money £34280

Going: Sf: 0-1 GS: 0-0 Gd: 0-4 GF: - Fm: 1-1
Distance: 2m/2m3: 1-5 2m4-2m7: 0-1 3m+: 0-0
Track: LH: 0-1 RH: 1-5 Tight: 0-0 Gall: 0-0
Aids: Bl: 0-1 Vi: 0-0 Tstrap: 0-0 Ckp: 0-0
Best Rating: 130   10/03   Kemp   2m   gd-fm   Ch

Fair chaser; returned from lengthy absence to win two-horse race at Kempton in October 2003; has run well without winning since; effective at two miles, but seems best on fast.

Phar Out Phavorite (IRE)

94f   102+f

5-y-o b g Beneficial-Phar From Men (IRE) (Phardante (FR))
Miss E C Lavelle   Favourites Racing

Placings:420   (4578)
2003/04: 164GS, 182S, 169G,

	Starts	1st	2nd	3rd	Win & Pl
NH Flat	3	0	1	0	654
Career Total	3	0	1	0	654

Going: Sf: 0-1 GS: 0-1 Gd: 0-1 GF: - Fm: 0-0
Distance: 2m/2m3: 0-3 2m4-2m7: 0-0 3m+: 0-0
Track: LH: 0-2 RH: 0-1 Tight: 0-0 Gall: 0-1
Aids: Bl: 0-0 Vi: 0-0 Tstrap: 0-0 Ckp: 0-0
Best Rating: 102   2/04   Plum   2m2f   soft   NHF

Promising form shown in bumper runs to date; stays 2m 2f; acts on good to soft; promising.

Pharagon (IRE)

(41h)

6-y-o b g Phardante (FR)-Hogan (IRE) (Black Minstrel)
Mrs C J Kerr   Mrs C J Kerr

Placings:000-PPP0P   (4940)
2003/04: 20PG, 24PGS, 24PG, 21UG, 16PGS,

	Starts	1st	2nd	3rd	Win & Pl
Hurdles	3	0	0	0	0
Chases	2	0	0	0	0
Career Total	8	0	0	0	0

Going: Sf: 0-0 GS: 0-2 Gd: 0-3 GF: - Fm: 0-0
Distance: 2m/2m3: 0-1 2m4-2m7: 0-2 3m+: 0-2
Track: LH: 0-4 RH: 0-1 Tight: 0-1 Gall: 0-0
Aids: Bl: 0-0 Vi: 0-0 Tstrap: 0-0 Ckp: 0-0
Best Rating: 26   12/02   Ayr   1m6f   gd-sft   NHF

Pharaway Citizen (IRE)

106(62h)   (100h)128

9-y-o ch g Phardante (FR)-Boreen Citizen (Boreen (FR))
T R George   Pharaway Partnership

Placings:P32/3PP1P53-P6R1412133   (4834)
2003/04: 27PGS, 205GS, 25PGF, 241G, 264HY, 251HY, 242GS, 241G, 243G, 263GF,

	Starts	1st	2nd	3rd	Win & Pl
Chases	10	3	1	2	19330
Career Total	20	4	2	5	30787

119	3/04	Bang	3m110y	D(0-120)HCh	GD	£5525
127	2/04	Hrfd	3m1f110yE(0-105)HCh		HVY	£4901
107	12/03	Tntn	3m	E(0-105)HCh	GD	£3598
115	2/03	Newb	2m6f110yD(0-120)HCh		SFT	£8736

Total win prize-money £22760

Going: Sf: 1-3 GS: 0-2 Gd: 2-3 GF: - Fm: 0-2
Distance: 2m/2m3: 0-0 2m4-2m7: 0-1 3m+: 3-9
Track: LH: 1-3 RH: 2-6 Tight: 2-7 Gall: 0-0
Aids: Bl: 0-0 Vi: 0-0 Tstrap: 0-0 Ckp: 0-0
Best Rating: 128   4/04   Chel   3m2f110y   gd-fm   Ch

Fair chaser; successful between the flags in Ireland; stays 3m 2f; acts on soft and good to firm ground.

Pharbeit (IRE)

95   78

7-y-o b g King's Ride-Phargara (IRE) (Phardante (FR))
E L James   Lady Thompson

Placings:060-020UP   (0990)
2003/04: 16QGS, 162GF, 16QG, 20UGF, 22PG,

	Starts	1st	2nd	3rd	Win & Pl
Hurdles	5	0	1	0	984
Career Total	8	0	1	0	984

Fair chaser; has shown ability over hurdles but was always going to come into his own when tackling fences; thought not to want the ground too soft; stays three miles plus.

Going: Sf: 0-0 GS: 0-1 Gd: 0-2 GF: - Fm: 0-2
Distance: 2m/2m3: 0-3 2m4-2m7: 0-2 3m+: 0-0
Track: LH: 0-4 RH: 0-1 Tight: 0-2 Gall: 0-1
Aids: Bl: 0-4 Vi: 0-0 Tstrap: 0-0 Ckp: 0-0
Best Rating: 84 12/02 Uttx   2m   soft   NHF

PLating-class novice hurdler; yet to prove he stays further than two miles; wears blinkers.

Pharbeitfrome (IRE)
106   95

10-y-o b g Phardante (FR)-Asigh Glen (Furry Glen)
N Wilson   Steven Downes

Placings: 0/00F310F/P04P/0UPF43/31PP3F1U05-325F12U232P253   (2947)
2003/04: 16³G, 16²G, 20⁵G, 16⁶G, 17¹GF, 16²GF, 17⁴UG, 16²GF, 16³GF, 16²GF, 17⁶G, 16²GF, 16⁵GS, 16³G,

	Starts	1st	2nd	3rd	Win & Pl
Chases	14	1	5	3	14755
Career Total	42	4	5	7	26497
95	7/03	Sthl	2m1f	F(0-100)HCh	G-F	£3367
83	1/03	Sedg	2m110y	F(0-90)HCh	HVY	£3297
83	6/02	MRas	2m1f110yF(0-100)HCh	G-F	£3388
99	3/00	Dpat	2m2f	Ch	SFT	£2345

Total win prize-money £12398

Going: Sf: 0-0 GS: 0-1 Gd: 0-7 GF: - Fm: 1-6
Distance: 2m/2m3: 1-13 2m4-2m7: 0-1 3m+: 0-0
Track: LH: 1-13 RH: 0-1 Tight: 0-5 Gall: 0-0
Aids: Bl: 0-0 Vi: 0-0 Tstrap: 1-14 Ckp: 0-0
Best Rating: 99 3/00 Dpat 2m2f   soft   Ch

Moderate chaser; not the best of jumpers; best at around two miles and acts on all types of ground; wears a tongue tie.

Pharchancier
66   43

8-y-o gr g Pharly (FR)-Lots Of Luck (Neltino)
O Brennan   Mrs Pat Brennan

Placings: 0   (0168)
2003/04: 16⁰GF,

	Starts	1st	2nd	3rd	Win & Pl
Hurdles	1	0	0	0	
Career Total	1	0	0	0	

Going: Sf: 0-0 GS: 0-0 Gd: 0-0 GF: - Fm: 0-1
Distance: 2m/2m3: 0-1 2m4-2m7: 0-0 3m+: 0-0
Track: LH: 0-1 RH: 0-0 Tight: 0-0 Gall: 0-0
Aids: Bl: 0-0 Vi: 0-0 Tstrap: 0-0 Ckp: 0-0
Best Rating: 43 5/03 Weth 2m   gd-fm Hdl

Phardante Flyer (IRE)
80(89h)   64

10-y-o ch g Phardante (FR)-Shannon Lek (Menelek)
P J Hobbs   Mrs Karola Vann

Placings: 2/1141141/24/2P/04-5   (0303)
2003/04: 17⁵G,

	Starts	1st	2nd	3rd	Win & Pl
Chases	1	0	0	0	
Career Total	15	5	3	0	38900
144	4/00	Aint	2m110y	A Hdl	GD	£21000
123	2/00	Ludl	2m	E Hdl	GD	£2352
120	1/00	Winc	2m	E Hdl	G-S	£2205
114	11/99	Wwck	2m	H NHF	GD	£1856
113	11/99	Sand	2m110y	H NHF	GD	£1658

Total win prize-money £29071

Going: Sf: 0-0 GS: 0-0 Gd: 0-1 GF: - Fm: 0-0
Distance: 2m/2m3: 0-1 2m4-2m7: 0-0 3m+: 0-0
Track: LH: 0-1 RH: 0-0 Tight: 0-1 Gall: 0-0
Aids: Bl: 0-0 Vi: 0-0 Tstrap: 0-0 Ckp: 0-0
Best Rating: 144 4/00 Aint 2m110y good Hdl

Fair hurdler; goes well on good ground, but effective with cut; best over two miles; formerly useful but lightly raced in recent seasons; finished lame in novice chase in May 2003.

Pharly Reef
97   102

12-y-o b g Pharly (FR)-Hay Reef (Mill Reef (USA))
D Burchell   Mrs Ruth Burchell

Placings: 6020/00612/4U26621/1154/S35065/6102-000P5   (4673)
2003/04: 16⁰S, 17⁹GS, 16⁰G, 16⁶G, 16⁵G,

	Starts	1st	2nd	3rd	Win & Pl
Hurdles	5	0	0	0	
Career Total	35	5	5	1	24217
102	6/02	Uttx	2m	D(0-115)HHdl	SFT	£3276
113	11/99	Chep	2m110y	D(0-125)HHdl	SFT	£2845
109	7/99	Strf	2m110y	C(0-130)HHdl	GD	£4926
98	4/99	Bang	2m1f	F(0-100)HHdl	GD	£3858
82	12/96	Fknm	2m	G(0-95)HHdl	GD	£2733

Total win prize-money £17640

Going: Sf: 0-1 GS: 0-1 Gd: 0-3 GF: - Fm: 0-0
Distance: 2m/2m3: 0-5 2m4-2m7: 0-0 3m+: 0-0
Track: LH: 0-2 RH: 0-3 Tight: 0-2 Gall: 0-0
Aids: Bl: 0-0 Vi: 0-0 Tstrap: 0-0 Ckp: 0-0
Best Rating: 113 11/99 Chep 2m110y soft Hdl

Moderate hurdler these days; goes well in soft ground; best at around 2m.

Pharly Star

10-y-o ch g Pharly (FR)-Norapa (Ahonoora)
Mrs F M Midwood   W H Midwood

Placings: 2   (0199)
2003/04: 24²GF,

	Starts	1st	2nd	3rd	Win & Pl
Chases	1	0	1	0	430
Career Total	1	0	1	0	430

Going: Sf: 0-0 GS: 0-0 Gd: 0-0 GF: - Fm: 0-1
Distance: 2m/2m3: 0-0 2m4-2m7: 0-0 3m+: 0-1
Track: LH: 0-0 RH: 0-1 Tight: 0-0 Gall: 0-1
Aids: Bl: 0-0 Vi: 0-0 Tstrap: 0-0 Ckp: 0-0
Best Rating: 76 5/03 Hntg 3m   gd-fm Ch

Hunter chaser; dual winning pointing; stays three miles; acts on fast ground.

Pharmistice (IRE)

13-y-o b g Phardante (FR)-Lucylet (Kinglet)
Miss N Stirling   Mrs P C Stirling

Placings: 006/10/2140/0/4/13-UP   (4689)
2003/04: 25⁰G, 25⁵G,

	Starts	1st	2nd	3rd	Win & Pl
Chases	2	0	0	0	
Career Total	15	3	1	1	9370
102	5/02	Kels	3m1f	H Ch	G-F	£2999
83	11/97	Kels	2m6f110yD(0-125)HHdl	G-F	£2738
82	12/96	Kels	2m6f110yE Hdl	GD	£2346

Going: Sf: 0-0 GS: 0-0 Gd: 0-2 GF: - Fm: 0-0
Distance: 2m/2m3: 0-0 2m4-2m7: 0-0 3m+: 0-2
Track: LH: 0-2 RH: 0-0 Tight: 0-2 Gall: 0-0
Aids: Bl: 0-0 Vi: 0-0 Tstrap: 0-0 Ckp: 0-0
Best Rating: 102 4/03 Kels 3m1f   good Ch

Pharpost (IRE)
107   (103+h)126

9-y-o b g Phardante (FR)-Branston Lady (Deep Run)
Miss Venetia Williams   Direct Sales UK Ltd

Placings: 136/41/2F3F424-12322132303U6   (4841)
2003/04: 20¹GF, 20²GF, 26⁵GF, 20²G, 20²G, 20¹GF, 24³GF, 24²GF, 24³GF, 22⁰G, 24³G, 20⁰G, 21⁶G,

	Starts	1st	2nd	3rd	Win & Pl
Hurdles	1	0	0	0	
Chases	12	2	4	4	26685
Career Total	25	4	6	6	39972
120	10/03	Carl	2m4f	D Ch	G-F	£7595
119	6/03	Uttx	2m4f	C(0-135)HCh	G-F	£8984
120	11/01	Strf	2m6f110yE Hdl	SFT	£2618
114	11/00	Ludl	2m	H NHF	GD	£1652

Total win prize-money £20850

Going: Sf: 0-0 GS: 0-0 Gd: 0-6 GF: - Fm: 2-7
Distance: 2m/2m3: 0-0 2m4-2m7: 2-8 3m+: 0-5
Track: LH: 1-7 RH: 1-4 Tight: 0-7 Gall: 0-2
Aids: Bl: 0-0 Vi: 0-0 Tstrap: 0-0 Ckp: 0-0
Best Rating: 126 11/02 Winc 3m1f110y good Ch

Modest chaser; won 2m 4f handicap at Uttoxeter June 2003 and uncompetitive novice event at Carlisle in October; stays 3m; suited by the ground good or softer; can front run or be held up but often finds little under pressure.

Phartodante (IRE)
86   41

7-y-o b m Phardante (FR)-Hennywood (IRE) (Henbit (USA))
Mrs L C Jewell   R B Morton

Placings: 0P-000PP0   (4929)
2003/04: 20⁶G, 20⁰GF, 21⁰G, 22⁹G, 23ᴾGS, 18⁰G,

	Starts	1st	2nd	3rd	Win & Pl
Hurdles	6	0	0	0	
Career Total	8	0	0	0	

Going: Sf: 0-0 GS: 0-1 Gd: 0-4 GF: - Fm: 0-1
Distance: 2m/2m3: 0-1 2m4-2m7: 0-5 3m+: 0-0
Track: LH: 0-5 RH: 0-0 Tight: 0-6 Gall: 0-0
Aids: Bl: 0-0 Vi: 0-0 Tstrap: 0-0 Ckp: 0-1
Best Rating: 58 3/03 Hntg 2m110y gd-fm NHF

Phase Eight Girl
78

8-y-o b m Warrshan (USA)-Bugsy's Sister (Aragon)
J Hetherton   Peter Urquhart

Placings: 363P0046/4124544/313-PP0P4   (4956)
2003/04: 21ᴾGS, 21ᴾG, 22⁰G, 26ᴾG, 22⁴G,

	Starts	1st	2nd	3rd	Win & Pl
Hurdles	5	0	0	0	
Career Total	23	2	1	4	6417
78	8/02	Hntg	3m2f	F(0-95)HHdl	G-F	£2262
77	5/01	Hntg	2m110y	G(0-95)HHdl	G-F	£1736

Total win prize-money £3998

Going: Sf: 0-0 GS: 0-1 Gd: 0-4 GF: - Fm: 0-0
Distance: 2m/2m3: 0-0 2m4-2m7: 0-4 3m+: 0-1

Track: LH: 0-1 RH: 0-2 Tight: 0-1 Gall: 0-1
Aids: Bl: 0-0 Vi: 0-0 Tstrap: 0-0 Ckp: 0-0
Best Rating: 78 8/02 Hntg 3m2f   gd-fm Hdl

Small mare; winning hurdler who needs good ground; stays well.

Phazar

89f   77f

4-y-o b g Zamindar (USA)-Ypha (USA) (Lyphard (USA))
N J Hawke   Set To Stun Partnership

Placings:0   (3649)
2003/04: 16⁰GS,

	Starts	1st	2nd	3rd	Win & Pl
NH Flat	1	0	0	0	
Career Total	1	0	0	0	

Going: Sf: 0-0 GS: 0-1 Gd: 0-0 GF: - Fm: 0-0
Distance: 2m/2m3: 0-1 2m4-2m7: 0-0 3m+: 0-0
Track: LH: 0-0 RH: 0-1 Tight: 0-0 Gall: 0-0
Aids: Bl: 0-0 Vi: 0-0 Tstrap: 0-0 Ckp: 0-0
Best Rating: 77 2/04 Kemp 2m   gd-sft NHF

Phenomenon

89   68

6-y-o b m Unfuwain (USA)-Pure (Slip Anchor)
M C Pipe W J Gredley

Placings:0   (2663)
2003/04: 16⁰G,

	Starts	1st	2nd	3rd	Win & Pl
Hurdles	1	0	0	0	
Career Total	1	0	0	0	

Going: Sf: 0-0 GS: 0-0 Gd: 0-1 GF: - Fm: 0-0
Distance: 2m/2m3: 0-1 2m4-2m7: 0-0 3m+: 0-0
Track: LH: 0-0 RH: 0-0 Tight: 0-0 Gall: 0-0
Aids: Bl: 0-0 Vi: 0-0 Tstrap: 0-0 Ckp: 0-0
Best Rating: 68 12/03 Leic 2m   good Hdl

Phil The Fencer

80   85

8-y-o gr g Neltino-Who's Free (Sit In The Corner (USA))
John Allen   Gray, Jameson and Trio Partnership

Placings:5/50FP2/0   (4492)
2003/04: 22⁰G,

	Starts	1st	2nd	3rd	Win & Pl
Hurdles	1	0	0	0	
Career Total	7	0	1	0	955

Going: Sf: 0-0 GS: 0-0 Gd: 0-1 GF: - Fm: 0-0
Distance: 2m/2m3: 0-0 2m4-2m7: 0-1 3m+: 0-0
Track: LH: 0-1 RH: 0-0 Tight: 0-1 Gall: 0-0
Aids: Bl: 0-0 Vi: 0-0 Tstrap: 0-0 Ckp: 0-0
Best Rating: 85 2/02 Fknm 2m4f   gd-sft Chs

Phildari (IRE)

109(97h)   (108h)115

8-y-o b g Shardari-Philosophical (Welsh Chanter)
P R Webber Michael Coghlan

Placings:00/022423/34P5242-213PF325   (4841)
2003/04: 24²G, 21¹GF, 24³GF, 20PGF, 20FGF, 25³GF, 21²GF,

21⁵G,

	Starts	1st	2nd	3rd	Win & Pl
Chases	8	1	2	2	9723
Career Total	23	1	7	4	17620
115 9/03 Sthl	2m5f110yE Ch			G-F	£3276

Total win prize-money £3276

Going: Sf: 0-0 GS: 0-0 Gd: 0-0 GF: - Fm: 1-6
Distance: 2m/2m3: 0-0 2m4-2m7: 1-5 3m+: 0-3
Track: LH: 1-3 RH: 0-5 Tight: 0-2 Gall: 0-4
Aids: Bl: 0-0 Vi: 0-0 Tstrap: 1-7 Ckp: 0-1
Best Rating: 115 11/03 Folk 2m5f   gd-fm Ch

Moderate chaser; improved over hurdles for the fitting of a tongue tie; consistent efforts before winning at Southwell in September 2003; acts on good and soft ground; stays three miles; has worn cheekpieces.

Philippa Yeates (IRE)

84   70

5-y-o b m Hushang (IRE)-Miss Bobby Bennett (King's Lake (USA))
M C Pipe   B A Kilpatrick

Placings:000   (4003)
2003/04: 16⁰G, 17⁰GS, 16⁰G,

	Starts	1st	2nd	3rd	Win & Pl
Hurdles	3	0	0	0	
Career Total	3	0	0	0	

Going: Sf: 0-0 GS: 0-1 Gd: 0-2 GF: - Fm: 0-0
Distance: 2m/2m3: 0-3 2m4-2m7: 0-0 3m+: 0-0
Track: LH: 0-0 RH: 0-3 Tight: 0-1 Gall: 0-0
Aids: Bl: 0-0 Vi: 0-0 Tstrap: 0-0 Ckp: 0-0
Best Rating: 70 2/04 Ludl 2m   good Hdl

Philomena

75f   50f

5-y-o b m Bedford (USA)-Mandalay Miss (Mandalus)
V R A Dartnall   Dorset Racing

Placings:0   (4816)
2003/04: 16⁰G,

	Starts	1st	2nd	3rd	Win & Pl
NH Flat	1	0	0	0	
Career Total	1	0	0	0	

Going: Sf: 0-0 GS: 0-0 Gd: 0-1 GF: - Fm: 0-0
Distance: 2m/2m3: 0-0 2m4-2m7: 0-0 3m+: 0-0
Track: LH: 0-1 RH: 0-0 Tight: 0-0 Gall: 0-0
Aids: Bl: 0-0 Vi: 0-0 Tstrap: 0-0 Ckp: 0-0
Best Rating: 50 4/04 Chep 2m110y   good NHF

Philson Run (IRE)

8-y-o b g Un Desperado (FR)-Isis (Deep Run)
Nick Williams   Gale Force One

Placings:1   (3792)
2003/04: 25¹G,

	Starts	1st	2nd	3rd	Win & Pl
Chases	1	1	0	0	1561
Career Total	1	1	0	0	1561
121 2/04 Winc	3m1f110yH Ch			GD	£1561

Total win prize-money £1561

Going: Sf: 0-0 GS: 0-0 Gd: 1-1 GF: - Fm: 0-0

Distance: 2m/2m3: 0-0 2m4-2m7: 0-0 3m+: 1-1
Track: LH: 0-0 RH: 1-1 Tight: 0-0 Gall: 0-0
Aids: Bl: 0-0 Vi: 0-0 Tstrap: 0-0 Ckp: 0-0
Best Rating: 121 2/04 Winc 3m1f110y   good Ch

Fair hunter chaser; stays 3m1f plus; acts on good ground.

Philtre (IRE)

10-y-o b g Phardante (FR)-Forest Gale (Strong Gale)
Mrs H L Needham   J D Callow

Placings:2P3U/1311046/P-P5   (0759)
2003/04: 28PG, 23⁵G,

	Starts	1st	2nd	3rd	Win & Pl
Chases	2	0	0	0	0
Career Total	14	3	1	2	16372
110 6/01 Worc	2m7f110yE Ch			G-F	£3190
110 6/01 Strf	3m4f			G-F	£8287
110 5/01 Hntg	3m	E Ch		GD	£3731

Total win prize-money £15209

Going: Sf: 0-0 GS: 0-0 Gd: 0-2 GF: - Fm: 0-0
Distance: 2m/2m3: 0-0 2m4-2m7: 0-0 3m+: 0-2
Track: LH: 0-2 RH: 0-0 Tight: 0-1 Gall: 0-0
Aids: Bl: 0-0 Vi: 0-0 Tstrap: 0-0 Ckp: 0-0
Best Rating: 110 6/01 Worc 2m7f110y   gd-fm Ch

Useful hunter chaser; needs a sound surface; stays three and a half miles.

Phinda Forest (IRE)

80   40

5-y-o br m Charnwood Forest (IRE)-Shatalia (USA) (Shahrastani (USA))
W Storey   Gremlin Racing

Placings:00P-06   (0472)
2003/04: 16⁰G, 17⁶GS,

	Starts	1st	2nd	3rd	Win & Pl
Hurdles	2	0	0	0	0
Career Total	5	0	0	0	0

Going: Sf: 0-0 GS: 0-1 Gd: 0-1 GF: - Fm: 0-0
Distance: 2m/2m3: 0-2 2m4-2m7: 0-0 3m+: 0-0
Track: LH: 0-1 RH: 0-1 Tight: 0-1 Gall: 0-0
Aids: Bl: 0-0 Vi: 0-0 Tstrap: 0-0 Ckp: 0-2
Best Rating: 45 2/03 Muss 2m   good Hdl

Phoenix Phlyer

10-y-o b g Ardross-Brown Coast (Oats)
D Pipe   Miss Charlotte C Stucley

Placings:500/005023/020P34312/00/0-51U25   (4696)
2003/04: 20⁵GF, 20¹GL, 24⁴UG, 20²GS, 19⁶G,

	Starts	1st	2nd	3rd	Win & Pl
Chases	5	1	1	0	3637
Career Total	26	2	4	3	12223
105 2/04 Ludl	2m4f	H Ch		GD	£2744
108 4/01 Extr	2m3f110yF(0-95)HCh			G-S	£3447

Total win prize-money £6192

Going: Sf: 0-0 GS: 0-1 Gd: 1-3 GF: - Fm: 0-1
Distance: 2m/2m3: 0-0 2m4-2m7: 1-4 3m+: 1-4
Track: LH: 0-0 RH: 1-5 Tight: 1-4 Gall: 0-0
Aids: Bl: 0-0 Vi: 0-0 Tstrap: 0-0 Ckp: 1-4
Best Rating: 108 4/01 Extr 2m3f110y   gd-sft Ch

Hunter chaser; showed promise in points before running away with a fair contest at Ludlow; acts on fast ground; effective at 2m4f; has worn cheekpieces.

Phone Back (IRE)

71f   **25f**

5-y-o b g Bob Back (USA)-Will Phone (Buckskin (FR))
G L Moore Mrs Patricia Gilmore

Placings:0   (4578)
2003/04: 16⁰G,

	Starts	1st	2nd	3rd	Win & Pl
NH Flat	1	0	0	0	
Career Total	1	0	0	0	

Going:	Sf: 0-0 GS: 0-0 Gd: 0-1 GF: - Fm: 0-0
Distance:	2m/2m3: 0-1 2m4-2m7: 0-0 3m+: 0-0
Track:	LH: 0-1 RH: 0-0 Tight: 0-0 Gall: 0-1
Aids:	Bl: 0-0 Vi: 0-0 Tstrap: 0-0 Ckp: 0-0
Best Rating:	25 3/04 Newb 2m110y good NHF

Photographer (USA)

97   **101**

6-y-o b/br g Mountain Cat (USA)-Clickety Click (USA)
(Sovereign Dancer (USA))
Mrs N Smith Tony Hayward, Barry Fulton, Jamie Bruce

Placings:404/5-04   (2952)
2003/04: 16⁵GS, 16⁴G,

	Starts	1st	2nd	3rd	Win & Pl
Hurdles	2	0	0	0	0
Career Total	6	0	0	0	

Going:	Sf: 0-0 GS: 0-1 Gd: 0-1 GF: 0-0 Fm: 0-0
Distance:	2m/2m3: 0-2 2m4-2m7: 0-0 3m+: 0-0
Track:	LH: 0-0 RH: 0-2 Tight: 0-0 Gall: 0-0
Aids:	Bl: 0-0 Vi: 0-0 Tstrap: 0-0 Ckp: 0-0
Best Rating:	101 2/02 Kemp 2m good Hdl

Phred

80   **59**

4-y-o ch g Safawan-Phlirty (Pharly (FR))
R F Johnson Houghton Mrs R F Johnson Houghton

Placings:00   (3806)
2003/04: 17⁰GS, 16⁰G,

	Starts	1st	2nd	3rd	Win & Pl
Hurdles	2	0	0	0	
Career Total	2	0	0	0	

Going:	Sf: 0-0 GS: 0-1 Gd: 0-1 GF: 0-0 Fm: 0-0
Distance:	2m/2m3: 0-2 2m4-2m7: 0-0 3m+: 0-0
Track:	LH: 0-0 RH: 0-2 Tight: 0-1 Gall: 0-0
Aids:	Bl: 0-0 Vi: 0-0 Tstrap: 0-0 Ckp: 0-0
Best Rating:	59 2/04 Kemp 2m good Hdl

Physical Graffiti (USA)

95   **95**

7-y-o b g Mister Baileys-Gleaming Water (USA) (Pago Pago)
J A B Old Old Fools Partnership

Placings:04/40/F14-5PC00   (4760)
2003/04: 16⁵GS, 16⁸HY, 16⁶S, 20⁹GS, 16⁶S,

	Starts	1st	2nd	3rd	Win & Pl
Hurdles	5	0	0	0	0
Career Total	12	1	0	0	5616
95 2/03 Leic 2m E(0-105)HHdl HVY £4914

Total win prize-money £4914

Going:	Sf: 0-3 GS: 0-2 Gd: 0-0 GF: - Fm: 0-0
Distance:	2m/2m3: 0-4 2m4-2m7: 0-1 3m+: 0-0
Track:	LH: 0-1 RH: 0-4 Tight: 0-0 Gall: 0-0
Aids:	Bl: 0-0 Vi: 0-0 Tstrap: 0-0 Ckp: 0-0
Best Rating:	95 2/03 Leic 2m heavy Hdl

Moderate hurdler; acts on very soft ground; should stay further than two miles.

Picquet Officer (IRE)

93   **76**

6-y-o b g Safety Catch (USA)-Pitea (Corvaro (USA))
Miss S E Forster Peter Innes

Placings:0S   (1684)
2003/04: 17⁰G, 16⁵GF,

	Starts	1st	2nd	3rd	Win & Pl
Hurdles	2	0	0	0	
Career Total	2	0	0	0	

Going:	Sf: 0-0 GS: 0-0 Gd: 0-1 GF: - Fm: 0-1
Distance:	2m/2m3: 0-2 2m4-2m7: 0-0 3m+: 0-0
Track:	LH: 0-1 RH: 0-0 Tight: 0-1 Gall: 0-0
Aids:	Bl: 0-0 Vi: 0-0 Tstrap: 0-0 Ckp: 0-0
Best Rating:	80 10/03 Sedg 2m1f good Hdl

Picture Palace

90   **109+**

6-y-o ch g Salse (USA)-Moviegoer (Pharly (FR))
T R George Mrs V Beeching,Alan Waller,James Layton

Placings:22220343/P5431-10   (4785)
2003/04: 26¹GF, 21⁹G,

	Starts	1st	2nd	3rd	Win & Pl
Hurdles	2	1	0	0	5122
Career Total	15	2	4	3	18437
109 5/03 Sthl 3m2f D(0-125)HHdl G-F £5122
102 3/03 Hrfd 3m2f E(0-110)HHdl G-F £3528
Total win prize-money £8650

Going:	Sf: 0-0 GS: 0-0 Gd: 0-1 GF: - Fm: 1-1
Distance:	2m/2m3: 0-0 2m4-2m7: 0-1 3m+: 1-1
Track:	LH: 1-1 RH: 0-1 Tight: 0-0 Gall: 0-1
Aids:	Bl: 1-1 Vi: 0-0 Tstrap: 0-0 Ckp: 0-0
Best Rating:	109 5/03 Sthl 3m2f gd-fm Hdl

Modest hurdler; stays really well; winner at Hereford in March and Southwell two months later.

Pierpoint (IRE)

80   **70**

9-y-o g Archway (IRE)-Lavinia (Habitat)
Mrs A M Thorpe (J M Bradley 27/9) Mrs A M Thorpe

Placings:0P50   (1852)
2003/04: 16⁸GF, 16⁷GF, 16⁵F, 16⁹G,

	Starts	1st	2nd	3rd	Win & Pl
Hurdles	4	0	0	0	0
Career Total	4	0	0	0	0

Going:	Sf: 0-0 GS: 0-0 Gd: 0-1 GF: - Fm: 0-3
Distance:	2m/2m3: 0-4 2m4-2m7: 0-0 3m+: 0-0
Track:	LH: 0-2 RH: 0-2 Tight: 0-1 Gall: 0-0
Aids:	Bl: 0-0 Vi: 0-0 Tstrap: 0-0 Ckp: 0-0
Best Rating:	70 10/03 Towc 2m firm Hdl

Pierre Du Forez (FR)

6-y-o ch g Sicyos (USA)-Pierre Du Luizet (FR) (Fulgus (FR))
M C Pipe M C Pipe

Placings:PP0RPP   (4518)
2003/04: 16⁸GS, 19⁸HY, 16⁰GS, 17⁷GS, 18⁵GF, 17⁸GS,

	Starts	1st	2nd	3rd	Win & Pl
Hurdles	6	0	0	0	
Career Total	6	0	0	0	

Going:	Sf: 0-1 GS: 0-4 Gd: 0-0 GF: - Fm: 0-1
Distance:	2m/2m3: 0-5 2m4-2m7: 0-1 3m+: 0-0
Track:	LH: 0-1 RH: 0-5 Tight: 0-2 Gall: 0-1
Aids:	Bl: 0-0 Vi: 0-5 Tstrap: 0-0 Ckp: 0-0

Pierre Precieuse

78f

5-y-o ch m Bijou D'Inde-Time Or Never (FR) (Dowsing (USA))
J S Goldie J S Morrison

Placings:066-0   (0270)
2003/04: 16⁰G,

	Starts	1st	2nd	3rd	Win & Pl
NH Flat	1	0	0	0	
Career Total	4	0	0	0	0

Going:	Sf: 0-0 GS: 0-0 Gd: 0-1 GF: - Fm: 0-0
Distance:	2m/2m3: 0-1 2m4-2m7: 0-0 3m+: 0-0
Track:	LH: 0-0 RH: 0-1 Tight: 0-0 Gall: 0-0
Aids:	Bl: 0-0 Vi: 0-0 Tstrap: 0-0 Ckp: 0-0
Best Rating:	78 4/03 Prth 2m110y good NHF

Pietro Bembo (IRE)

106   **102**

10-y-o b g Midyan (USA)-Cut No Ice (Great Nephew)
P R Chamings Fraser Miller Racing

Placings:0/42613125/F4100/0P5401/43/60-2P42254   (1335)
2003/04: 17²GS, 17⁰G, 16⁴GF, 20²GF, 24⁴GF, 24⁵GS, 19⁴GF,

	Starts	1st	2nd	3rd	Win & Pl
Chases	7	0	3	0	6236
Career Total	31	4	5	2	34710
133 3/01 Asct 2m110y B(0-140)HHdl HVY £7254
133 2/00 Kemp 2m C(0-135)HHdl SFT £10481
130 3/99 Folk 2m1f110yE Hdl G-S £2488
133 12/98 Winc 2m E(0-100)HHdl SFT £2528
Total win prize-money £22751

Going:	Sf: 0-0 GS: 0-2 Gd: 0-1 GF: - Fm: 0-4
Distance:	2m/2m3: 0-4 2m4-2m7: 0-1 3m+: 0-2
Track:	LH: 0-2 RH: 0-1 Tight: 0-5 Gall: 0-0
Aids:	Bl: 0-0 Vi: 0-0 Tstrap: 0-0 Ckp: 0-0
Best Rating:	133 3/01 Asct 2m110y heavy Hdl

Useful hurdler/moderate chaser; likes to force the pace; best on soft ground, but acts on faster; yet to prove he stays three miles.

Pikestaff (USA)

94   **93d**

6-y-o ch g Diesis-Navarene (USA) (Known Fact (USA))
M A Barnes J M Carlyle

Placings:0002-10P00500   (3767)
2003/04: 16¹G, 16⁰G, 16⁶F, 20⁵GS, 16⁹GS, 17⁵G, 16⁹HY, 17⁰HY,

	Starts	1st	2nd	3rd	Win & Pl
Hurdles	8	1	0	0	3653
Career Total	12	1	1	0	4737

88 4/03 Kels 2m110y E Hdl   GD £3653
Total win prize-money £3653

Going: Sf: 0-2 GS: 0-2 Gd: 1-3 GF: - Fm: 0-1
Distance: 2m/2m3: 1-7 2m4-2m7: 0-1 3m+: 0-0
Track: LH: 1-6 RH: 0-2 Tight: 1-3 Gall: 0-2
Aids: Bl: 0-0 Vi: 0-0 Tstrap: 0-5 Ckp: 0-0
Best Rating: 88 4/03 Kels 2m110y good Hdl

Plating-class hurdler; suited by fast ground.

Pilca (FR)
98   94

4-y-o ch g Pistolet Bleu (IRE)-Caricoe (Baillamont (USA))
M C Pipe (J-P Bernhardt 5/9) Eminence Grise Partnership

Placings:03-F4311514P6033   (4363)
2003/04: 15FHY, 174VS, 163S, 171S, 171S, 185GS, 151S, 164GF, 16PGS, 176G, 190GS, 173G, 163GS,

	Starts	1st	2nd	3rd	Win & Pl
Hurdles	13	3	0	3	19140
Career Total	15	3	0	4	21049

9/03 Autl 1m7f Hdl   SFT £6545
8/03 Claf 2m1f Hdl   SFT £4675
7/03 Diep 2m1f Hdl   SFT £3117
Total win prize-money £14337

Going: Sf: 3-5 GS: 0-4 Gd: 0-2 GF: - Fm: 0-1
Distance: 2m/2m3: 2-10 2m4-2m7: 0-1 3m+: 0-0
Track: LH: 0-4 RH: 1-4 Tight: 0-3 Gall: 0-1
Aids: Bl: 0-0 Vi: 0-0 Tstrap: 0-0 Ckp: 0-0
Best Rating: 99 3/04 Tntn 2m1f good Hdl

Ex-French hurdler; now with Martin Pipe; acts in soft ground; stays two miles one.

Pilgrims Progress (IRE)
98   108

4-y-o b g Entrepreneur-Rose Bonbon (FR) (High Top)
P J Hobbs (T Stack 28/6) P A Newey

Placings:235410   (4573)
2003/04: 172G, 163GS, 165S, 164S, 171G, 190G,

	Starts	1st	2nd	3rd	Win & Pl
Hurdles	6	1	1	1	7327
Career Total	6	1	1	1	7327

107 3/04 Bang 2m1f F Hdl   GD £3164
Total win prize-money £3164

Going: Sf: 0-2 GS: 0-1 Gd: 1-3 GF: - Fm: 0-0
Distance: 2m/2m3: 1-6 2m4-2m7: 0-0 3m+: 0-0
Track: LH: 1-4 RH: 0-2 Tight: 1-2 Gall: 0-1
Aids: Bl: 0-0 Vi: 0-0 Tstrap: 0-0 Ckp: 0-0
Best Rating: 108 12/03 Chel 2m110y gd-sft Hdl

Modest novice hurdler; Flat winner in heavy ground; effective over two miles; acts on softish ground, but may be best on good; has been tried in headgear, but seems better without.

Pillaging Pict
98   126

9-y-o ch g Primitive Rising (USA)-Carat Stick (Gold Rod)
J B Walton Messrs F T Walton

Placings:F63415F311/31351P-UP6   (3281)
2003/04: 25UG, 25PS, 16RHY,

	Starts	1st	2nd	3rd	Win & Pl
Chases	3	0	0	0	309
Career Total	19	5	0	4	36387

126 3/03 Kels 2m6f110yC(0-130)HCh G-S £11482
126 11/02 Kels 2m1f D(0-115)HCh SFT £4823
114 4/02 Prth 2m4f110yD(0-115)HCh GD £5863
105 4/02 Carl 2m4f E(0-100)HCh G-S £3867
101 1/02 Catt 2m E(0-105)HCh G-S £6071
Total win prize-money £32107

Going: Sf: 0-2 GS: 0-0 Gd: 0-1 GF: - Fm: 0-0
Distance: 2m/2m3: 0-1 2m4-2m7: 0-0 3m+: 0-2
Track: LH: 0-3 RH: 0-0 Tight: 0-2 Gall: 0-0
Aids: Bl: 0-0 Vi: 0-0 Tstrap: 0-0 Ckp: 0-0
Best Rating: 126 3/03 Kels 2m6f110y gd-sft Ch

Fair chaser; stays two and three-quarter miles; appreciates cut, but does not want it too soft.

Pillar Of Fire (IRE)
88 (103h)   (101h) 103

10-y-o gr g Roselier (FR)-Cousin Flo (True Song)
Ian Williams Paul Robson

Placings:633/40101/02P4PF04P/O0100-4422U3   (4341)
2003/04: 244GF, 214GF, 20²GF, 20²G, 24UG, 203GS,

	Starts	1st	2nd	3rd	Win & Pl
Hurdles	2	0	0	0	829
Chases	4	0	2	1	3427
Career Total	28	3	3	3	19752

101 10/02 MRas 2m5f110yD(0-125)HHdl GD £6344
103 4/01 MRas 2m3f110yD(0-120)HHdl G-S £3932
100 12/00 MRas 2m3f110yF Hdl G-S £2562
Total win prize-money £12839

Going: Sf: 0-0 GS: 0-1 Gd: 0-2 GF: - Fm: 0-3
Distance: 2m/2m3: 0-0 2m4-2m7: 0-4 3m+: 0-2
Track: LH: 0-1 RH: 0-5 Tight: 0-4 Gall: 0-0
Aids: Bl: 0-0 Vi: 0-0 Tstrap: 0-0 Ckp: 0-0
Best Rating: 103 4/01 MRas 2m3f110y gd-sft Hdl

Modest hurdler/plating-class chaser; likes Market Rasen; effective at around two miles five.

Pillar To Post
91f   74f

5-y-o b g Bluegrass Prince (IRE)-Parisana (FR) (Gift Card (FR))
Ian Williams T J & Mrs H Parrott

Placings:00   (4447)
2003/04: 16°GS, 16PS,

	Starts	1st	2nd	3rd	Win & Pl
NH Flat	2	0	0	0	
Career Total	2	0	0	0	

Going: Sf: 0-1 GS: 0-1 Gd: 0-0 GF: - Fm: 0-0
Distance: 2m/2m3: 0-2 2m4-2m7: 0-0 3m+: 0-0
Track: LH: 0-2 RH: 0-0 Tight: 0-0 Gall: 0-0
Aids: Bl: 0-0 Vi: 0-0 Tstrap: 0-0 Ckp: 0-0
Best Rating: 74 3/04 Wwck 2m soft NHF

Pilot's Harbour
87 (92h)   (91h) 56

8-y-o b g Distant Relative-Lillemor (Connaught)
F P Murtagh F P Murtagh

Placings:312342P0666/251P/4FP054P   (1842)
2003/04: 214G, 26PGF, 27PGF, 22PG, 245GF, 214G, 27PG,

	Starts	1st	2nd	3rd	Win & Pl
Hurdles	4	0	0	0	0

	Chases	3	0	0	0	464
	Career Total	22	2	3	2	9416

92 5/01 Hexm 3m F(0-100)HHdl FRM £2485
95 5/00 Ctrl 2m1f110yD Hdl GD £3152
Total win prize-money £5638

Going: Sf: 0-2 GS: 0-0 Gd: 0-4 GF: - Fm: 0-3
Distance: 2m/2m3: 0-0 2m4-2m7: 0-3 3m+: 0-4
Track: LH: 0-7 RH: 0-0 Tight: 0-6 Gall: 0-0
Aids: Bl: 0-0 Vi: 0-0 Tstrap: 0-0 Ckp: 0-0
Best Rating: 95 8/00 Ctrl 2m6f good Hdl

Pimlico (IRE)

6-y-o ch g Imp Society (USA)-Willow Gale (Strong Gale)
B G Powell John Plackett

Placings:50-P0   (2673)
2003/04: 16PGS, 19PGS,

	Starts	1st	2nd	3rd	Win & Pl
Hurdles	2	0	0	0	
Career Total	4	0	0	0	0

Going: Sf: 0-0 GS: 0-1 Gd: 0-0 GF: - Fm: 0-1
Distance: 2m/2m3: 0-2 2m4-2m7: 0-0 3m+: 0-0
Track: LH: 0-2 RH: 0-0 Tight: 0-0 Gall: 0-2
Aids: Bl: 0-0 Vi: 0-0 Tstrap: 0-0 Ckp: 0-0
Best Rating: 96 11/02 Chel 2m110y gd-sft NHF

Well held first time out in a Folkestone bumper.

Pin High (IRE)
97   100

5-y-o b g Needle Gun (IRE)-Eva's Fancy (Distinctly (USA))
Miss H C Knight M B J Kimmins & & Mrs D Anderson

Placings:50020   (4819)
2003/04: 16°G, 17PGS, 16RGS, 16²G, 22PGF,

	Starts	1st	2nd	3rd	Win & Pl
NH Flat	2	0	0	0	0
Hurdles	3	0	1	0	1093
Career Total	5	0	1	0	1093

Going: Sf: 0-0 GS: 0-2 Gd: 0-2 GF: - Fm: 0-1
Distance: 2m/2m3: 0-4 2m4-2m7: 0-1 3m+: 0-0
Track: LH: 0-2 RH: 0-3 Tight: 0-0 Gall: 0-0
Aids: Bl: 0-0 Vi: 0-0 Tstrap: 0-0 Ckp: 0-0
Best Rating: 100 2/04 Ludl 2m good Hdl

Moderate novice hurdler; has shown some promise.

Pink Eclipse
87f   49f

4-y-o b f Double Eclipse (IRE)-Caspian Mist (Remainder Man)
C Roberts J Milton

Placings:P00   (3832)
2003/04: 13PS, 16PHY, 16PG,

	Starts	1st	2nd	3rd	Win & Pl
NH Flat	3	0	0	0	
Career Total	3	0	0	0	

Going: Sf: 0-2 GS: 0-0 Gd: 0-1 GF: - Fm: 0-0
Distance: 2m/2m3: 0-3 2m4-2m7: 0-0 3m+: 0-0
Track: LH: 0-2 RH: 0-0 Tight: 0-0 Gall: 0-1
Aids: Bl: 0-0 Vi: 0-0 Tstrap: 0-0 Ckp: 0-0
Best Rating: 52 2/04 Newb 2m110y good NHF

Pink Harbour

95   **54**

6-y-o b m Rakaposhi King-Let Me Finish (Chantro)
D McCain D McCain

Placings:5004UUU05   (4390)
2003/04: 20⁵GF, 17⁰G, 20⁰GS, 17⁴GS, 16ᵁGS, 17ᵁGS, 19ᵁHY, 21¹⁰G, 27⁵G,

	Starts	1st	2nd	3rd	Win & Pl
Hurdles	9	0	0	0	0
Career Total	9	0	0	0	0

Going:	Sf: 0-1 GS: 0-4 Gd: 0-3 GF: - Fm: 0-0
Distance:	2m/2m3: 0-4 2m4-2m7: 0-0 3m+: 0-1
Track:	LH: 0-5 RH: 0-4 Tight: 0-2 Gall: 0-0
Aids:	Bl: 0-0 Vi: 0-0 Tstrap: 0-0 Ckp: 0-0
Best Rating:	54 2/04 Ludl 2m5f good Hdl

Pinot Noir

76   **38**

6-y-o b g Saddlers' Hall (IRE)-Go For Red (IRE) (Thatching)
G J Smith Mrs Joanne Woods

Placings:0P   (0852)
2003/04: 17⁰G, 16ᴾGF,

	Starts	1st	2nd	3rd	Win & Pl
Hurdles	2	0	0	0	
Career Total	2	0	0	0	

Going:	Sf: 0-0 GS: 0-0 Gd: 0-1 GF: - Fm: 0-1
Distance:	2m/2m3: 0-2 2m4-2m7: 0-0 3m+: 0-0
Track:	LH: 0-1 RH: 0-1 Tight: 0-2 Gall: 0-0
Aids:	Bl: 0-0 Vi: 0-0 Tstrap: 0-0 Ckp: 0-1
Best Rating:	38 6/03 MRas 2m1f110y good Hdl

Pip Moss

(103h)   **(85h)**

9-y-o ch g Le Moss-My Aisling (John De Coombe)
J A B Old Mrs Jim Old

Placings:0/5F/0063-P   (3710)
2003/04: 24ᴾHY,

	Starts	1st	2nd	3rd	Win & Pl
Chases	1	0	0	0	
Career Total	8	0	0	1	837

Going:	Sf: 0-1 GS: 0-0 Gd: 0-0 GF: - Fm: 0-0
Distance:	2m/2m3: 0-0 2m4-2m7: 0-0 3m+: 0-1
Track:	LH: 0-1 RH: 0-0 Tight: 0-0 Gall: 0-0
Aids:	Bl: 0-0 Vi: 0-0 Tstrap: 0-0 Ckp: 0-0
Best Rating:	95 12/01 NAbb 2m1f heavy NHF

Piper's Rock (IRE)

13-y-o ch g Zaffaran (USA)-Misclaire (Steeple Aston)
Miss M A Neill Miss V A Russell

Placings:000P55413/2/21F2P0/3/1214P141F40/04P5PP/6   (4600)
2003/04: 25⁶G,

	Starts	1st	2nd	3rd	Win & Pl
Chases	1	0	0	0	0
Career Total	35	6	4	2	30578
112 10/00 Towc 2m	F(0-100)HHdl		G-F	£2289	
114 8/00 NAbb 2m110y	D(0-125)HCh		G-S	£4007	
114 6/00 NAbb 2m110y	E(0-115)HCh		GD	£3415	
105 5/00 Bang 2m4f110y	D(0-120)HCh		G-S	£5577	
1G8 10/98 Plum 2m5f	E(0-105)HCh		GD	£4901	
90 4/97 Ludl 2m5f110y	E(0-100)HHdl		G-F	£2528	
				Total win prize-money £22719	

Going:	Sf: 0-0 GS: 0-0 Gd: 0-1 GF: - Fm: 0-0
Distance:	2m/2m3: 0-0 2m4-2m7: 0-0 3m+: 0-1
Track:	LH: 0-1 RH: 0-0 Tight: 0-1 Gall: 0-0
Aids:	Bl: 0-0 Vi: 0-0 Tstrap: 0-0 Ckp: 0-0
Best Rating:	114 5/01 NAbb 2m110y gd-fm Ch

Pipersland

75   **51**

7-y-o b g Lir-Celtic Mist (Celtic Cone)
Ms Sue Willcock Ms Sue Willcock

Placings:0P   (3643)
2003/04: 19⁰G, 19ᴾS,

	Starts	1st	2nd	3rd	Win & Pl
Hurdles	2	0	0	0	
Career Total	2	0	0	0	

Going:	Sf: 0-1 GS: 0-0 Gd: 0-1 GF: - Fm: 0-0
Distance:	2m/2m3: 0-1 2m4-2m7: 0-1 3m+: 0-0
Track:	LH: 0-0 RH: 0-2 Tight: 0-1 Gall: 0-0
Aids:	Bl: 0-0 Vi: 0-0 Tstrap: 0-0 Ckp: 0-0
Best Rating:	52 12/03 Tntn 2m3f110y good Hdl

Pipssalio (SPA)

100   **113+**

7-y-o b g Pips Pride-Tesalia (SPA) (Finissimo (SPA))
Jamie Poulton Chris Steward

Placings:03/3401   (4664)
2003/04: 16⁹GS, 20⁴S, 20⁰GS, 19¹GS,

	Starts	1st	2nd	3rd	Win & Pl
Hurdles	4	1	0	1	4931
Career Total	6	1	0	2	5503
113 4/04 Ling 2m3f110yE Hdl			G-S	£3766	
				Total win prize-money £3767	

Going:	Sf: 0-1 GS: 1-3 Gd: 0-0 GF: - Fm: 0-0
Distance:	2m/2m3: 0-1 2m4-2m7: 1-3 3m+: 0-0
Track:	LH: 1-1 RH: 0-3 Tight: 1-1 Gall: 0-0
Aids:	Bl: 0-0 Vi: 0-0 Tstrap: 1-4 Ckp: 0-0
Best Rating:	113 4/04 Ling 2m3f110y gd-sft Hdl

Modest novice hurdler; plating-class on the Flat; stays two miles four; wears a tongue tie; acts on soft ground.

Pirandello (IRE)

113   **128**

6-y-o ch g Shalford (IRE)-Scenic Villa (Top Ville)
K C Bailey Quicksilver Racing Partnership

Placings:611-6231200F   (3367)
2003/04: 16⁶G, 16²G, 16³G, 16¹GS, 16²GS, 16⁵S, 17⁰G, 16⁶G,

	Starts	1st	2nd	3rd	Win & Pl
Hurdles	8	1	2	1	14350
Career Total	11	3	2	1	23899
124 11/03 Hntg 2m110y	D(0-120)HHdl		G-S	£7371	
110 4/03 Strf 2m110y	D(0-110)HHdl		G-F	£5850	
90 3/03 Hntg 2m110y	E Hdl		G-F	£3698	
				Total win prize-money £16920	

Going:	Sf: 0-1 GS: 1-2 Gd: 0-5 GF: - Fm: 0-0
Distance:	2m/2m3: 1-8 2m4-2m7: 0-0 3m+: 0-0
Track:	LH: 0-1 RH: 1-7 Tight: 0-0 Gall: 1-3
Aids:	Bl: 0-0 Vi: 0-0 Tstrap: 0-0 Ckp: 0-0
Best Rating:	128 12/03 Hntg 2m110y gd-sft Hdl

Fair hurdler; suited by two miles; goes well on fast ground, but also effective with cut.

Pirandello Due

84(69h)   **(8h)67**

10-y-o b g Teenoso (USA)-Bay Girl (Persian Bold)
D P Keane Carol & Richard Stainer

Placings:P0/4P/004FP   (4185)
2003/04: 21⁰S, 22⁰G, 19⁴HY, 20ᶠS, 24ᴾG,

	Starts	1st	2nd	3rd	Win & Pl
Hurdles	2	0	0	0	0
Chases	3	0	0	0	348
Career Total	9	0	0	0	348

Going:	Sf: 0-3 GS: 0-0 Gd: 0-2 GF: - Fm: 0-0
Distance:	2m/2m3: 0-1 2m4-2m7: 0-3 3m+: 0-1
Track:	LH: 0-4 RH: 0-4 Tight: 0-1 Gall: 0-3
Aids:	Bl: 0-0 Vi: 0-0 Tstrap: 0-0 Ckp: 0-0
Best Rating:	74 4/01 Font 2m6f110y good Hdl

Piste Bleu (FR)

81   **59**

4-y-o b f Pistolet Bleu (IRE)-Thamissia (FR) (Riverman (USA))
R Ford (R M Beckett 26/7) M Dunlevy & N Morgan

Placings:6   (1590)
2003/04: 16⁶GF,

	Starts	1st	2nd	3rd	Win & Pl
Hurdles	1	0	0	0	0
Career Total	1	0	0	0	0

Going:	Sf: 0-0 GS: 0-0 Gd: 0-0 GF: - Fm: 0-1
Distance:	2m/2m3: 0-1 2m4-2m7: 0-0 3m+: 0-0
Track:	LH: 0-0 RH: 0-1 Tight: 0-0 Gall: 0-0
Aids:	Bl: 0-0 Vi: 0-0 Tstrap: 0-0 Ckp: 0-0
Best Rating:	59 10/03 Ludl 2m gd-fm Hdl

Pistol Knight

10-y-o b g Jupiter Island-Porchester Run (Deep Run)
Mrs S Bowman N J Bowman

Placings:3   (4122)
2003/04: 21³G,

	Starts	1st	2nd	3rd	Win & Pl
Chases	1	0	0	1	226
Career Total	1	0	0	1	226

Going:	Sf: 0-0 GS: 0-0 Gd: 0-1 GF: - Fm: 0-0
Distance:	2m/2m3: 0-0 2m4-2m7: 0-1 3m+: 0-0
Track:	LH: 0-0 RH: 0-1 Tight: 0-1 Gall: 0-0
Aids:	Bl: 0-0 Vi: 0-0 Tstrap: 0-0 Ckp: 0-0
Best Rating:	75 3/04 Folk 2m5f good Ch

Pitminster

93   **93+**

6-y-o b g Karinga Bay-Eleanora Muse (Idiots Delight)
P F Nicholls R H Dunn

Placings:026   (3900)
2003/04: 17⁰G, 17²GS, 17⁶GS,

	Starts	1st	2nd	3rd	Win & Pl
NH Flat	1	0	0	0	0

Hurdles	2	0	1	0	1304
Career Total	3	0	1	0	1304

Going:	Sf: 0-0 GS: 0-2 Gd: 0-1 GF: - Fm: 0-0
Distance:	2m/2m3: 0-3 2m4-2m7: 0-0 3m+: 0-0
Track:	LH: 0-1 RH: 0-2 Tight: 0-3 Gall: 0-0
Aids:	Bl: 0-0 Vi: 0-0 Tstrap: 0-0 Ckp: 0-0
Best Rating:	95 2/04 Tntn 2m1f gd-sft Hdl

Pittsburgh Phil (IRE)

73   125+

7-y-o b g Sadler's Wells (USA)-Broadway Joan (USA) (Bold Arian (USA))
Jonjo O'Neill   John P McManus

Placings:210/2F446/U4U   (4726)
2003/04: 17^UGS, 17⁴GS, 24^UG,

	Starts	1st	2nd	3rd	Win & Pl
Chases	3	0	0	0	323
Career Total	11	1	2	0	17699
140 12/00 Leop 2m		Hdl		SH	£13000

Total win prize-money £13000

Going:	Sf: 0-0 GS: 0-2 Gd: 0-1 GF: - Fm: 0-0
Distance:	2m/2m3: 0-2 2m4-2m7: 0-0 3m+: 0-1
Track:	LH: 0-1 RH: 0-2 Tight: 0-2 Gall: 0-0
Aids:	Bl: 0-0 Vi: 0-0 Tstrap: 0-0 Ckp: 0-0
Best Rating:	140 12/00 Leop 2m sft-hvy Hdl

Former smart juvenile hurdler; in the process of running a creditable first race over fences when departing at halfway at Market Rasen in December; suited by two miles; best on soft ground.

Pixley

63f   76f

4-y-o ch g Saxon Farm-Lady Renton (Rolfe (USA))
Mrs Pippa Bickerton   Mrs Pippa Bickerton

Placings:0   (4824)
2003/04: 17⁰GF,

	Starts	1st	2nd	3rd	Win & Pl
NH Flat	1	0	0	0	
Career Total	1	0	0	0	

Going:	Sf: 0-0 GS: 0-0 Gd: 0-0 GF: - Fm: 0-1
Distance:	2m/2m3: 0-1 2m4-2m7: 0-0 3m+: 0-0
Track:	LH: 0-0 RH: 0-1 Tight: 0-0 Gall: 0-0
Aids:	Bl: 0-0 Vi: 0-0 Tstrap: 0-0 Ckp: 0-0
Best Rating:	76 4/04 Extr 2m1f gd-fm NHF

Pizarro (IRE)

117(113h)   (147h)155

7-y-o b g Broken Hearted-Our Swan Lady (Swan's Rock)
E J O'Grady   Edward Wallace

Placings:1/11/1312F-41P11B   (4395)
2003/04: 20⁴YS, 17¹G, 20^PS, 24¹YS, 21¹YS, 24^BG,

	Starts	1st	2nd	3rd	Win & Pl
Hurdles	1	0	0	0	1753
Chases	5	3	0	0	88729
Career Total	14	8	1	1	164097
150 2/04 Leop	2m5f	Ch		Y-S	£50352
147 12/03 Leop	3m	Ch		Y-S	£31655
128 11/03 Clon	2m1f	Ch		GD	£6720
132 2/03 DRoy	2m4f	Hdl		SFT	£5376
147 11/02 Navn	2m4f	Hdl		SFT	£14355
152 3/02 Chel	2m110y	A NHF		G-S	£18000

---

127 2/02 Naas	2m		NHF		HVY	£4444
126 4/01 Fair	2m		NHF		SFT	£6677

Total win prize-money £137584

Going:	Sf: 0-1 GS: 0-0 Gd: 1-2 GF: - Fm: 0-0
Distance:	2m/2m3: 1-1 2m4-2m7: 1-3 3m+: 1-2
Track:	LH: 2-3 RH: 0-2 Tight: 0-0 Gall: 0-1
Aids:	Bl: 0-0 Vi: 0-0 Tstrap: 0-0 Ckp: 0-0
Best Rating:	155 3/04 Chel 3m110y good Ch

Winner of the 2002 Champion Bumper at Cheltenham; progressed into high-class novice hurdler and finished second after being promoted a place in the Royal & SunAlliance Novices' Hurdle at the 2003 Festival; early casualty on last outing over hurdles; has developed into smart novice chaser this season, and was still going well when brought down in the Royal & Sun Alliance Chase; still has room for improvement; stays three miles; suited by soft ground.

Place Above (IRE)

8-y-o b g Alphabatim (USA)-Lucky Pit (Pitpan)
E A Elliott   Eric A Elliott

Placings:05-00UR   (4460)
2003/04: 24⁰G, 24⁰G, 24^UG, 24^RHY,

	Starts	1st	2nd	3rd	Win & Pl
Hurdles	2	0	0	0	0
Chases	2	0	0	0	0
Career Total	6	0	0	0	0

Going:	Sf: 0-1 GS: 0-0 Gd: 0-3 GF: - Fm: 0-0
Distance:	2m/2m3: 0-0 2m4-2m7: 0-0 3m+: 0-4
Track:	LH: 0-4 RH: 0-0 Tight: 0-1 Gall: 0-1
Aids:	Bl: 0-0 Vi: 0-0 Tstrap: 0-0 Ckp: 0-0
Best Rating:	50 2/03 Ayr 2m4f gd-sft Hdl

Placid Man (IRE)

10-y-o br g Un Desperado (FR)-Sparkling Gale (Strong Gale)
Ms A E Embiricos   Tim Jones and Partners

Placings:2/3/P1-1   (4487)
2003/04: 20¹G,

	Starts	1st	2nd	3rd	Win & Pl
Chases	1	1	0	0	1491
Career Total	5	2	1	1	6917
122 3/04 Font	2m4f	H Ch		GD	£1491
130 1/03 Font	2m4f	E Ch		HVY	£4085

Total win prize-money £5576

Going:	Sf: 0-0 GS: 0-0 Gd: 1-1 GF: - Fm: 0-0
Distance:	2m/2m3: 0-0 2m4-2m7: 1-1 3m+: 0-0
Track:	LH: 0-0 RH: 0-0 Tight: 1-1 Gall: 0-0
Aids:	Bl: 0-0 Vi: 0-0 Tstrap: 0-0 Ckp: 0-0
Best Rating:	130 1/03 Font 2m4f heavy Ch

Fair chaser; stays two miles four furlongs; acts on good and heavy ground.

Plaisance (GER)

80

5-y-o b m Monsun (GER)-Pariana (USA) (Bering)
A M Hales   Jack McGrath

Placings:F23P-P   (4488)
2003/04: 22^PG,

	Starts	1st	2nd	3rd	Win & Pl
Hurdles	1	0	0	0	

Career Total	5	0	1	1	1477

Going:	Sf: 0-0 GS: 0-0 Gd: 0-1 GF: - Fm: 0-0
Distance:	2m/2m3: 0-0 2m4-2m7: 0-1 3m+: 0-0
Track:	LH: 0-1 RH: 0-0 Tight: 0-1 Gall: 0-0
Aids:	Bl: 0-0 Vi: 0-0 Tstrap: 0-0 Ckp: 0-0
Best Rating:	80 3/03 Folk 2m1f110y good Hdl

Plantaganet (FR)

99   91

6-y-o br g Cadoudal (FR)-Ever Young (FR) (Royal Charter (FR))
Ian Williams   Sir Robert Ogden

Placings:00-05   (4145)
2003/04: 16⁰G, 19⁵G,

	Starts	1st	2nd	3rd	Win & Pl
Hurdles	2	0	0	0	0
Career Total	4	0	0	0	0

Going:	Sf: 0-0 GS: 0-0 Gd: 0-2 GF: - Fm: 0-0
Distance:	2m/2m3: 0-1 2m4-2m7: 0-1 3m+: 0-0
Track:	LH: 0-0 RH: 0-2 Tight: 0-1 Gall: 0-0
Aids:	Bl: 0-0 Vi: 0-0 Tstrap: 0-0 Ckp: 0-0
Best Rating:	93 2/03 Kemp 2m good NHF

Plantagenet Prince

73f   38f

5-y-o b g Lancastrian-Yuan Princess (Tender King)
M Scudamore   N F Williams

Placings:0   (4934)
2003/04: 18⁰G,

	Starts	1st	2nd	3rd	Win & Pl
NH Flat	1	0	0	0	
Career Total	1	0	0	0	

Going:	Sf: 0-0 GS: 0-0 Gd: 0-1 GF: - Fm: 0-0
Distance:	2m/2m3: 0-1 2m4-2m7: 0-0 3m+: 0-0
Track:	LH: 0-1 RH: 0-0 Tight: 0-1 Gall: 0-0
Aids:	Bl: 0-0 Vi: 0-0 Tstrap: 0-0 Ckp: 0-0
Best Rating:	38 4/04 Font 2m2f110y good NHF

Plastic Paddy (IRE)

97   103

7-y-o b g Beau Sher-Vultang Lady (Le Bavard (FR))
D P Keane   Mrs S Clifford

Placings:12-U30   (2939)
2003/04: 20^UGS, 16³GS, 20⁰GS,

	Starts	1st	2nd	3rd	Win & Pl
Hurdles	3	0	0	1	524
Career Total	5	1	1	1	3236
110 12/02 Uttx	2m	H NHF		SFT	£1953

Total win prize-money £1953

Going:	Sf: 0-0 GS: 0-3 Gd: 0-0 GF: - Fm: 0-0
Distance:	2m/2m3: 0-1 2m4-2m7: 0-0 3m+: 0-0
Track:	LH: 0-3 RH: 0-0 Tight: 0-0 Gall: 0-0
Aids:	Bl: 0-0 Vi: 0-0 Tstrap: 0-0 Ckp: 0-0
Best Rating:	115 2/03 Sand 2m110y heavy NHF

Chasing-bred; finished first and second in his two bumpers; good effort when third in 2m maiden hurdle at Chepstow December 2003; can get off the mark over further; acts very well on testing ground.

Plenty

64f   **21f**

5-y-o b m Terimon-Mrs Moneypenny (Relkino)
N A Gaselee P T Fenwick

Placings:0   (3312)
2003/04: 18⁰HY,

	Starts	1st	2nd	3rd	Win & Pl
NH Flat	1	0	0	0	
Career Total	1	0	0	0	

Going:	Sf: 0-1 GS: 0-0 Gd: 0-0 GF: - Fm: 0-0
Distance:	2m/2m3: 0-1 2m4-2m7: 0-0 3m+: 0-0
Track:	LH: 0-1 RH: 0-0 Tight: 0-1 Gall: 0-0
Aids:	Bl: 0-0 Vi: 0-0 Tstrap: 0-0 Ckp: 0-0
Best Rating:	21 1/04 Font 2m2f110y heavy NHF

Plenty Courage

105(108c)   (77c)**92**

10-y-o ch g Gildoran-Fastlass (Celtic Cone)
F S Storey F S Storey

Placings:035111F/406P31/605F0/0255212510P34/246000
525-3443346P   (2929)
2003/04: 22³G, 224G, 24⁴G, 22³F, 22³GF, 21⁴G, 20⁶HY, 21⁶G,

	Starts	1st	2nd	3rd	Win & Pl
Hurdles	8	0	0	3	2383
Career Total	48	6	5	6	27181
107	11/01	Ayr	2m4f	C(0-130)HHdl	G-S	£5148
107	10/01	Sedg	2m5f110yD(0-125)HHdl	GD	£3265
114	4/00	Carl	2m4f110yD(0-125)HHdl	SFT	£3388
100	3/99	Hexm	2m	E Hdl	G-S	£2427
106	3/99	Ayr	F Hdl	SFT	£2145
102	2/99	Muss	2m	H NHF	G-F	£1702
				Total win prize-money £18076

Going:	Sf: 0-1 GS: 0-0 Gd: 0-5 GF: - Fm: 0-2
Distance:	2m/2m3: 0-0 2m4-2m7: 0-7 3m+: 0-1
Track:	LH: 0-6 RH: 0-2 Tight: 0-6 Gall: 0-0
Aids:	Bl: 0-0 Vi: 0-0 Tstrap: 0-0 Ckp: 0-2
Best Rating:	114 4/00 Carl 2m4f110y soft Hdl

Moderate handicap hurdler; best when ridden with forcing tactics; stays two miles six; suited by good or softer; looked only modest over fences in the spring of 2002; has worn cheekpieces.

Plenty Inn Hand

(96h)   (87dh)

8-y-o b g Alflora (IRE)-Shean Deas (Le Moss)
M F Harris M Harris

Placings:303P0-FUPP   (0906)
2003/04: 24⁶G, 21⁴UG, 21⁴GF, 26⁴GF,

	Starts	1st	2nd	3rd	Win & Pl
Chases	4	0	0	0	
Career Total	9	0	0	2	1343

Going:	Sf: 0-0 GS: 0-0 Gd: 0-2 GF: - Fm: 0-2
Distance:	2m/2m3: 0-0 2m4-2m7: 0-2 3m+: 0-2
Track:	LH: 0-4 RH: 0-0 Tight: 0-2 Gall: 0-0
Aids:	Bl: 0-0 Vi: 0-0 Tstrap: 0-0 Ckp: 0-0
Best Rating:	87 11/02 Uttx 2m4f110y soft Hdl

Plumier (FR)

103   **110+**

6-y-o b g Beyssac (FR)-Plume Rose (FR) (Rose Laurel)
Ms Bridget Nicholls Sir Robert Ogden

Placings:5P-P21P   (4894)
2003/04: 23⁶PS, 19²G, 24¹S, 25⁶PG,

	Starts	1st	2nd	3rd	Win & Pl
Chases	4	1	1	0	5444
Career Total	6	1	1	0	5444
110	4/04	Ling	3m	E Ch	SFT	£4124
				Total win prize-money £4124

Going:	Sf: 1-2 GS: 0-0 Gd: 0-2 GF: - Fm: 0-0
Distance:	2m/2m3: 0-0 2m4-2m7: 0-1 3m+: 1-3
Track:	LH: 1-1 RH: 0-3 Tight: 1-1 Gall: 0-0
Aids:	Bl: 0-0 Vi: 0-0 Tstrap: 1-3 Ckp: 0-0
Best Rating:	110 4/04 Ling 3m soft Ch

Late maturing type; well beat on debut in Ascot bumper in 2003; going the right way in 2004 and won latest at Lingfield over fences on only fifth career outing; best on soft ground, but handles good; stays well.

Pluralist (IRE)

67   **23**

8-y-o b g Mujadil (USA)-Encore Une Fois (IRE) (Shirley Heights)
A P Jones (J S Moore 9/8) G Last

Placings:00/10332P/P0   (3320)
2003/04: 17⁵PGS, 16⁰S,

	Starts	1st	2nd	3rd	Win & Pl
Hurdles	2	0	0	0	
Career Total	10	1	1	2	4194
87	5/01	Bang	2m1f	E Hdl	G-S	£2870
				Total win prize-money £2870

Going:	Sf: 0-1 GS: 0-1 Gd: 0-0 GF: - Fm: 0-0
Distance:	2m/2m3: 0-2 2m4-2m7: 0-0 3m+: 0-0
Track:	LH: 0-0 RH: 0-2 Tight: 0-0 Gall: 0-0
Aids:	Bl: 0-0 Vi: 0-0 Tstrap: 0-2 Ckp: 0-0
Best Rating:	87 8/01 Sedg 2m5f110y gd-fm Hdl

Plutocrat

99   **128**

8-y-o b g Polar Falcon (USA)-Choire Mhor (Dominion)
L Lungo A W Jack

Placings:00P111/0P0P/6612P3/2002152-540   (3360)
2003/04: 21⁵PGS, 24⁴GS, 16⁰S,

	Starts	1st	2nd	3rd	Win & Pl
Hurdles	3	0	0	0	424
Career Total	26	5	4	1	32273
128	12/02	Muss	2m4f	C(0-135)HHdl	G-S	£12267
122	11/01	Newc	2m	E(0-115)HHdl	G-S	£2541
106	2/00	Sand	2m110y	E(0-115)HHdl	SFT	£3575
94	1/00	Muss	2m	G(0-95)HHdl	GD	£2338
72	1/00	Muss	2m	G Hdl	SFT	£2324
				Total win prize-money £23045

Going:	Sf: 0-1 GS: 0-1 Gd: 0-0 GF: - Fm: 0-1
Distance:	2m/2m3: 0-1 2m4-2m7: 0-1 3m+: 0-1
Track:	LH: 0-3 RH: 0-0 Tight: 0-2 Gall: 0-1
Aids:	Bl: 0-0 Vi: 0-0 Tstrap: 0-0 Ckp: 0-0
Best Rating:	128 12/02 Muss 2m4f gd-sft Hdl

Fair hurdler; effective from two to three miles; suited by hold-up tactics off a strong pace; acts on most types of ground.

Poacher's Paddy (IRE)

9-y-o b m Jurado (USA)-Ross Maid (Random Shot)

N Poacher N Poacher

Placings:1P   (0509)
2003/04: 19¹GF, 28⁶PGS,

	Starts	1st	2nd	3rd	Win & Pl
Chases	2	1	0	0	2860
Career Total	2	1	0	0	2860
91	5/03	Extr	2m3f110yH Ch	G-F	£2860
				Total win prize-money £2860

Going:	Sf: 0-0 GS: 0-1 Gd: 0-0 GF: - Fm: 1-1
Distance:	2m/2m3: 0-0 2m4-2m7: 1-1 3m+: 0-0
Track:	LH: 0-1 RH: 1-1 Tight: 0-1 Gall: 0-0
Aids:	Bl: 0-0 Vi: 0-0 Tstrap: 0-0 Ckp: 0-0
Best Rating:	91 5/03 Extr 2m3f110y gd-fm Ch

The winner of two points; had plenty of use made of her when winning 2m 3f novice hunter at Exeter May 2003; acts on fast ground.

Poachers Run (IRE)

97   (79c)**91**

9-y-o b m Executive Perk-Rugged Run (Deep Run)
G M Moore D J Bushell

Placings:115110/2250P40/5F045P/3P1U50-P4   (1076)
2003/04: 21⁵PGF, 21⁴GF,

	Starts	1st	2nd	3rd	Win & Pl
Hurdles	2	0	0	0	0
Career Total	27	5	2	1	14945
91	10/02	Sedg	2m5f110yD(0-125)HHdl	G-F	£3682
106	1/00	Sedg	2m5f110yE Hdl	SFT	£2537
97	1/00	Sedg	2m5f110yE Hdl	SFT	£2502
106	11/99	Hexm	2m	H NHF	GD	£1618
105	10/99	Carl	2m1f	H NHF	GD	£1710
				Total win prize-money £12052

Going:	Sf: 0-0 GS: 0-0 Gd: 0-0 GF: - Fm: 0-2
Distance:	2m/2m3: 0-0 2m4-2m7: 0-2 3m+: 0-0
Track:	LH: 0-2 RH: 0-0 Tight: 0-2 Gall: 0-0
Aids:	Bl: 0-0 Vi: 0-0 Tstrap: 0-0 Ckp: 0-0
Best Rating:	112 11/00 Hayd 2m7f110y soft Hdl

Plating-class hurdler; has won at up to two miles five; acts on good and soft ground.

Poaching (IRE)

55f

6-y-o b g Gone Fishin-Riveress (Dunphy)
Miss S E Forster Should Be Fun Racing

Placings:00-6   (0940)
2003/04: 17⁶GF,

	Starts	1st	2nd	3rd	Win & Pl
NH Flat	1	0	0	0	0
Career Total	3	0	0	0	

Going:	Sf: 0-0 GS: 0-0 Gd: 0-0 GF: - Fm: 0-1
Distance:	2m/2m3: 0-1 2m4-2m7: 0-0 3m+: 0-0
Track:	LH: 0-1 RH: 0-0 Tight: 0-1 Gall: 0-0
Aids:	Bl: 0-0 Vi: 0-0 Tstrap: 0-0 Ckp: 0-0
Best Rating:	55 10/02 Sedg 2m1f good NHF

Poetry And Jazz

72f   **54f**

5-y-o b g Nomadic Way (USA)-Indian Crown (Welsh Captain)
Dr P Pritchard Miss T R Johnson

Placings:PP00   (3948)
2003/04: 16⁶PGS, 17⁶GS, 16⁶HY, 16⁶G,

	Starts	1st	2nd	3rd	Win & Pl
NH Flat	4	0	0	0	
Career Total	4	0	0	0	

Going:	Sf: 0-1 GS: 0-2 Gd: 0-1 GF: - Fm: 0-0
Distance:	2m/2m3: 0-4 2m4-2m7: 0-0 3m+: 0-0
Track:	LH: 0-3 RH: 0-3 Tight: 0-0 Gall: 0-1
Aids:	Bl: 0-0 Vi: 0-0 Tstrap: 0-0 Ckp: 0-0
Best Rating:	54 2/04 Winc 2m good NHF

Pulled-up on both bumper outings to date.

Poggenip

85f   91f

5-y-o b m Petoski-Princess Tria (Space King)
B G Powell The Poggen Partners

Placings:3   (4407)
2003/04: 16³G,

	Starts	1st	2nd	3rd	Win & Pl
NH Flat	1	0	0	1	272
Career Total	1	0	0	1	272

Going:	Sf: 0-0 GS: 0-0 Gd: 0-1 GF: - Fm: 0-0
Distance:	2m/2m3: 0-1 2m4-2m7: 0-0 3m+: 0-0
Track:	LH: 0-0 RH: 0-1 Tight: 0-0 Gall: 0-1
Aids:	Bl: 0-0 Vi: 0-0 Tstrap: 0-0 Ckp: 0-0
Best Rating:	91 3/04 Hntg 2m110y good NHF

Poilu

86   67

6-y-o ch g Fearless Action (USA)-Marielou (FR) (Carwhite)
J M Jefferson Richard Collins

Placings:4000   (3941)
2003/04: 16⁴GS, 20⁰G, 20⁰HY, 20⁰GS,

	Starts	1st	2nd	3rd	Win & Pl
NH Flat	1	0	0	0	0
Hurdles	3	0	0	0	0
Career Total	4	0	0	0	0

Going:	Sf: 0-1 GS: 0-2 Gd: 0-1 GF: - Fm: 0-0
Distance:	2m/2m3: 0-1 2m4-2m7: 0-3 3m+: 0-0
Track:	LH: 0-4 RH: 0-0 Tight: 0-0 Gall: 0-1
Aids:	Bl: 0-0 Vi: 0-0 Tstrap: 0-0 Ckp: 0-0
Best Rating:	77 12/03 Newc 2m gd-sft NHF

Point Of Origin (IRE)

101(72h)   (35h)97+

7-y-o b g Caerleon (USA)-Aptostar (USA) (Fappiano (USA))
C C Bealby Get Em Off

Placings:4/45PP-1PPP   (4961)
2003/04: 20¹S, 20⁰S, 19⁰PG, 20⁰GS,

	Starts	1st	2nd	3rd	Win & Pl
Chases	4	1	0	0	3465
Career Total	9	1	0	0	3465
98 1/04 Hntg 2m4f110yF(0-100)HCh SFT £3464					
				Total win prize-money £3465

Going:	Sf: 1-2 GS: 0-1 Gd: 0-1 GF: - Fm: 0-0
Distance:	2m/2m3: 0-1 2m4-2m7: 1-3 3m+: 0-0
Track:	LH: 0-1 RH: 1-3 Tight: 0-0 Gall: 1-2
Aids:	Bl: 0-0 Vi: 0-0 Tstrap: 0-2 Ckp: 0-0
Best Rating:	98 1/04 Hntg 2m4f110y soft Ch

Moderate chaser; stays two miles four; acts on soft.

Pointalism (IRE)

84   68

5-y-o br g Roselier (FR)-Ballinahowna Dream (IRE) (Treasure Kay)
Miss H C Knight The Hon Mrs Peter Tower

Placings:P5   (4539)
2003/04: 19⁵S, 21⁵GS,

	Starts	1st	2nd	3rd	Win & Pl
Hurdles	2	0	0	0	0
Career Total	2	0	0	0	0

Going:	Sf: 0-1 GS: 0-1 Gd: 0-0 GF: - Fm: 0-0
Distance:	2m/2m3: 0-1 2m4-2m7: 0-1 3m+: 0-0
Track:	LH: 0-1 RH: 0-1 Tight: 0-0 Gall: 0-1
Aids:	Bl: 0-0 Vi: 0-0 Tstrap: 0-0 Ckp: 0-0
Best Rating:	68 3/04 Ludl 2m5f gd-sft Hdl

Irish point winner; pulled up on hurdling debut.

Poitiers (FR)

109(103h)   (115h)121+

5-y-o b g Bering-Prusse (USA) (Ogygian (USA))
M C Pipe (J Bertran De Balanda 24/10) David Manning Associates

Placings:4000F-5F411330322   (4869)
2003/04: 17⁵G, 18⁵VS, 17⁴HO, 18¹HO, 16¹GF, 21³S, 16³G, 17⁰G, 19³GS, 16²GS, 17²S,

	Starts	1st	2nd	3rd	Win & Pl
Hurdles	10	2	1	3	15091
Chases	1	0	1	0	1714
Career Total	16	2	2	3	17679
109 11/03 Winc 2m D Hdl G-F £2940					
105 10/03 Autl 2m2f Hdl HLD £6545					
				Total win prize-money £9485

Going:	Sf: 0-2 GS: 0-2 Gd: 0-3 GF: - Fm: 1-1
Distance:	2m/2m3: 2-9 2m4-2m7: 0-2 3m+: 0-0
Track:	LH: 0-4 RH: 1-3 Tight: 0-3 Gall: 0-1
Aids:	Bl: 1-1 Vi: 1-7 Tstrap: 0-0 Ckp: 0-0
Best Rating:	121 4/04 Bang 2m1f110y soft Ch

Modest novice hurdler; runner-up on chase debut; stays two and a half miles; acts on most ground; has worn blinkers, but normally visored; likes to force the pace.

Polar Champ

11-y-o b g Polar Falcon (USA)-Ceramic (USA) (Raja Baba (USA))
D Pipe (M C Pipe 28/6) Mrs Angie Malde

Placings:441200/54000/1111111430P/4101/31112142PU3-P00   (4425)
2003/04: 27⁶G, 27⁰GF, 26⁶G,

	Starts	1st	2nd	3rd	Win & Pl
Hurdles	2	0	0	0	0
Chases	1	0	0	0	0
Career Total	40	14	3	3	62948
134 10/02 Extr 2m7f110yD Ch GD £4959					
107 7/02 NAbb 3m2f110yE Ch G-F £4026					
117 6/02 Strf 3m E Ch G-F £3575					
127 6/02 NAbb 3m2f110yD Ch GD £4017					
116 3/02 NAbb 3m3f F Hdl GD £2374					
130 1/02 Leic 2m4f110yF Hdl SFT £3125					
155 10/00 Towc 3m C(0-135)HHdl G-S £4745					
141 8/00 Worc 3m C(0-135)HHdl G-F £6710					
154 7/00 NAbb 3m3f C(0-130)HHdl G-F £4654					
135 6/00 NAbb 2m6f D(0-120)HHdl G-F £2887					
134 6/00 Strf 3m3f D(0-125)HHdl GD £3185					
129 5/00 Uttx 3m110y F(0-105)HHdl G-F £2051					

113 5/00 Uttx 2m4f110y G(0-100)HHdl GD £1715					
115 12/98 Bang 2m1f E Hdl G-S £2358					
				Total win prize-money £50264

Going:	Sf: 0-0 GS: 0-0 Gd: 0-2 GF: - Fm: 0-1
Distance:	2m/2m3: 0-0 2m4-2m7: 0-0 3m+: 0-3
Track:	LH: 0-3 RH: 0-0 Tight: 0-2 Gall: 0-1
Aids:	Bl: 0-0 Vi: 0-3 Tstrap: 0-0 Ckp: 0-0
Best Rating:	155 10/00 Towc 3m gd-sft Hdl

Useful hurdler/chaser; decent pointer these days; acts well on good ground, but goes on a soft surface; often fitted with a visor.

Polar Gunner

84   37

7-y-o b g Gunner B-Polar Belle (Arctic Lord)
J M Jefferson Mrs M E Dixon

Placings:4/000-4   (1283)
2003/04: 21⁴GF,

	Starts	1st	2nd	3rd	Win & Pl
Hurdles	1	0	0	0	0
Career Total	5	0	0	0	0

Going:	Sf: 0-0 GS: 0-0 Gd: 0-0 GF: - Fm: 0-1
Distance:	2m/2m3: 0-0 2m4-2m7: 0-1 3m+: 0-0
Track:	LH: 0-1 RH: 0-0 Tight: 0-1 Gall: 0-0
Aids:	Bl: 0-0 Vi: 0-0 Tstrap: 0-0 Ckp: 0-0
Best Rating:	83 4/02 Hexm 2m110y good NHF

Polar Prospect

11-y-o b g Polar Falcon (USA)-Littlemisstrouble (USA) (My Gallant (USA))
Miss Sarah George (Mrs M J McGuinness 30/4) M Woodman and D Nibblett

Placings:1413021/222531252020/F530/3212336312/PP0   (4542)
2003/04: 21⁰PG, 24⁰PG, 20⁰GS,

	Starts	1st	2nd	3rd	Win & Pl
Chases	3	0	0	0	
Career Total	36	6	10	7	78076
135 3/02 Extr 2m3f110yD Ch GD £4013					
111 10/01 Towc 2m110y D Ch SFT £6129					
141 12/98 Sand 2m110y B(0-150)HHdl GD £34562					
125 4/98 Chep 2m110y E Hdl HVY £2374					
119 1/98 Tntn 2m1f E Hdl SFT £2351					
110 12/97 Uttx 2m E Hdl G-S £2557					
				Total win prize-money £51989

Going:	Sf: 0-0 GS: 0-1 Gd: 0-2 GF: - Fm: 0-0
Distance:	2m/2m3: 0-0 2m4-2m7: 0-2 3m+: 0-1
Track:	LH: 0-1 RH: 0-2 Tight: 0-2 Gall: 0-1
Aids:	Bl: 0-1 Vi: 0-0 Tstrap: 0-0 Ckp: 0-0
Best Rating:	150 2/99 Asct 2m4f gd-sft Hdl

Polar Red

113(115h)   (150h)142

7-y-o ch g Polar Falcon (USA)-Sharp Top (Sharpo)
M C Pipe Lady Clarke

Placings:222110/P000-211U631   (4821)
2003/04: 16⁶GS, 19¹S, 16¹HY, 17⁴GS, 20⁶G, 20³G, 19¹GF,

	Starts	1st	2nd	3rd	Win & Pl
Chases	7	3	1	1	18975
Career Total	17	5	4	1	60399
142 4/04 Extr 2m3f110yE Ch G-F £4387					

127	2/04	Chep	2m110y E Ch	HVY	£4410
137	12/03	Chep	2m3f110y	D Ch SFT	
£4221					
154	3/02	Sand	2m110y B(0-150)HHdl	G-S	£26100
153	1/02	Chel	2m1f D(0-120)HHdl	HVY	£9360
			Total win prize-money £48480		

Going: Sf: 2-2 GS: 0-2 Gd: 0-2 GF: - Fm: 1-1
Distance: 2m/2m3: 1-3 **2m4-2m7: 2-4** 3m+: 0-0
Track: LH: **2-6** RH: 1-1 Tight: 0-2 Gall: 0-1
Aids: Bl: 0-0 Vi: 0-0 Tstrap: 0-0 Ckp: 0-0
Best Rating: 154 3/02 Sand 2m110y gd-sft Hdl

Former smart hurdler; very useful novice chaser; effective up to 2m 4f; suited by cut in the ground; usually wore a visor over hurdles.

Polar Scout (IRE)
96(98h)   (98h)107+
7-y-o b g Arctic Lord-Baden (IRE) (Furry Glen)
C J Mann Mrs L G Turner

Placings:0/00000004420-531U21   (4733)
2003/04: 21^5G, 24^3GS, 22^1G, 22^2G, 22^1G,

	Starts	1st	2nd	3rd	Win & Pl
Hurdles	1	1	0	0	3588
Chases	5	1	1	1	7494
Career Total	18	2	2	1	12952
98	4/04	NAbb 2m6f E(0-105)HHdl	GD	£3588	
107	2/04	MRas 2m6f110yE(0-105)HCh	GD	£4149	
		Total win prize-money £7738			

Going: Sf: 0-0 GS: 0-2 Gd: 2-4 GF: - Fm: 0-0
Distance: 2m/2m3: 0-0 **2m4-2m7: 2-4** 3m+: 0-2
Track: LH: 1-3 RH: 1-3 **Tight: 2-4** Gall: 0-2
Aids: Bl: 0-0 Vi: 0-0 **Tstrap: 2-5** Ckp: 0-0
Best Rating: 107 2/04 MRas 2m6f110y good Ch

Modest chaser; will stay three miles; sometimes tongue tied.

Polar Summit (IRE)
(84h)
8-y-o br g Top Of The World-Blackrath Beauty (Le Tricolore)
N A Twiston-Davies The Summit Partnership

Placings:50P/40/FF   (3228)
2003/04: 24^6GS, 25^6GS,

	Starts	1st	2nd	3rd	Win & Pl
Chases	2	0	0	0	0
Career Total	7	0	0	0	0

Going: Sf: 0-0 GS: 0-2 Gd: 0-0 GF: - Fm: 0-0
Distance: 2m/2m3: 0-0 2m4-2m7: 0-0 3m+: 0-2
Track: LH: 0-0 RH: 0-2 Tight: 0-0 Gall: 0-1
Aids: Bl: 0-0 Vi: 0-0 Tstrap: 0-0 Ckp: 0-0
Best Rating: 99 11/00 Chel 2m110y gd-sft NHF

Poliantas (FR)
111   158
7-y-o b g Rasi Brasak-Popie D'Ecorcei (FR) (Balsamo (FR))
P F Nicholls Mark Tincknell

Placings:212P331/112121/212651-2   (2151)
2003/04: 20^2G,

	Starts	1st	2nd	3rd	Win & Pl
Chases	1	0	1	0	24200
Career Total	20	8	7	2	157525
158	4/03	Chel 2m5f A HCh	GD	£29000	
149	12/02	Winc 2m5f B HCh	G-S	£17922	
135	4/02	Sand 3m110y B Ch	GD	£16337	
101	3/02	Tntn 2m3f D Ch	SFT	£4777	

126	2/02	Sand	2m4f110yD Ch	SFT	£4845
	6/01	Pari	2m1f Hdl	G-S	£10669
	4/01	Nanc	2m1f Hdl	HLD	£3880
	10/00	Pari	2m1f Hdl	HVY	£4365
			Total win prize-money £91797		

Going: Sf: 0-0 GS: 0-0 Gd: 0-1 GF: - Fm: 0-0
Distance: 2m/2m3: 0-0 2m4-2m7: 0-1 3m+: 0-0
Track: LH: 0-1 RH: 0-0 Tight: 0-0 Gall: 0-1
Aids: Bl: 0-0 Vi: 0-0 Tstrap: 0-0 Ckp: 0-0
Best Rating: 158 11/03 Chel 2m4f110y good Ch

Smart chaser; runner-up in the Thomas Pink in November 2002, and won a good race at Wincanton next time; returned to form winning a valuable prize at Cheltenham in April; runner-up in the Paddy Power Gold Cup on seasonal debut, but sadly collapsed and died after the race; stayed three miles, but best at around two and a half; was effective on good and soft ground.(DEAD)

Policastro
6-y-o b g Anabaa (USA)-Belle Arrivee (Bustino)
Miss K M George R M Page

Placings:P-P   (0135)
2003/04: 16^2G,

	Starts	1st	2nd	3rd	Win & Pl
Hurdles	1	0	0	0	
Career Total	2	0	0	0	

Going: Sf: 0-0 GS: 0-0 Gd: 0-1 GF: - Fm: 0-0
Distance: 2m/2m3: 0-0 2m4-2m7: 0-0 3m+: 0-0
Track: LH: 0-0 RH: 0-0 Tight: 0-0 Gall: 0-0
Aids: Bl: 0-0 Vi: 0-0 Tstrap: 0-0 Ckp: 0-0

Polish Baron (IRE)
96(92h)   (92h)99
7-y-o b g Barathea (IRE)-Polish Mission (Polish Precedent (USA))
J R Cornwall (J White 8/1) J R Cornwall

Placings:1156/121F41P0/3-0304613   (4910)
2003/04: 16^6G, 16^3GS, 17^0GS, 20^4G, 17^6GS, 16^1S, 24^3S,

	Starts	1st	2nd	3rd	Win & Pl
Hurdles	3	1	0	1	514
Chases	4	1	0	1	7959
Career Total	20	6	1	3	27571
99	4/04	Towc 2m110y D Ch	SFT	£5936	
103	2/02	Hntg 2m110y F Hdl	SFT	£1895	
113	12/01	Font 2m2f110yG Hdl	GD	£3094	
110	5/01	NAbb 2m1f D(0-125)HHdl	G-F	£4134	
107	1/01	Plum 2m E Hdl	SFT	£1918	
107	11/00	Hntg 2m110y B Hdl	G-S	£6857	
		Total win prize-money £23836			

Going: Sf: 1-3 GS: 0-2 Gd: 0-2 GF: - Fm: 0-0
Distance: **2m/2m3: 1-5** 2m4-2m7: 0-1 3m+: 0-1
Track: LH: 0-1 **RH: 1-6** Tight: 0-1 Gall: 0-1
Aids: Bl: 0-0 Vi: 0-0 Tstrap: 0-0 Ckp: 0-0
Best Rating: 113 12/01 Font 2m2f110y good Hdl

Moderate handicap hurdler/chaser; best at two to two and a quarter miles; acts on fast ground, but is suited by softer.

Polish Cloud (FR)
104   112+
7-y-o gr g Bering-Batchelor's Button (FR) (Kenmare (FR))
T R George Mrs Grace Frankel & Partners

Placings:10243-23226041   (4942)

2003/04: 16^2G, 16^3GS, 17^2HY, 22^2S, 24^5GS, 21^9G, 19^4G, 20^1GS,

	Starts	1st	2nd	3rd	Win & Pl
Hurdles	8	1	3	1	13363
Career Total	13	2	4	2	19001
109	4/04	Prth 2m4f110yE(0-130)HHdl	G-S	£8645	
95	12/02	Donc 2m110y E Hdl	SFT	£3102	
		Total win prize-money £11747			

Going: Sf: 0-2 GS: 1-3 Gd: 0-3 GF: - Fm: 0-0
Distance: 2m/2m3: 0-3 **2m4-2m7: 1-4** 3m+: 0-1
Track: LH: 0-2 **RH: 1-6** Tight: 0-3 Gall: 0-1
Aids: Bl: 0-0 Vi: 0-0 Tstrap: 0-0 Ckp: 0-0
Best Rating: 110 3/03 Newb 2m110y soft Hdl

Modest hurdler; Polish import; best over two miles, although stays further; acts on good and soft ground.

Polish Legend
95   87
5-y-o b g Polish Precedent (USA)-Chita Rivera (Chief Singer)
B R Millman (R J Baker 29/4) M A Swift, A J Chapman And T Warden

Placings:0444-PF023   (4714)
2003/04: 17^4S, 16^6G, 17^7G, 17^9G, 17^2G, 16^3G,

	Starts	1st	2nd	3rd	Win & Pl
Hurdles	6	0	1	1	1512
Career Total	9	0	1	1	2143

Going: Sf: 0-1 GS: 0-0 Gd: 0-5 GF: - Fm: 0-0
Distance: 2m/2m3: 0-6 2m4-2m7: 0-0 3m+: 0-0
Track: LH: 0-3 RH: 0-3 Tight: 0-5 Gall: 0-0
Aids: Bl: 0-1 Vi: 0-0 Tstrap: 0-4 Ckp: 0-0
Best Rating: 87 4/04 Ludl 2m good Hdl

Moderate hurdler; acts on good.

Polish Paddy (IRE)
88+
6-y-o b g Priolo (USA)-Polish Widow (Polish Precedent (USA))
A G Hobbs Furnish With Abbey

Placings:050006014/1-0PPP   (3227)
2003/04: 20^0S, 22^2G, 24^4G, 26^2GS,

	Starts	1st	2nd	3rd	Win & Pl
Hurdles	4	0	0	0	
Career Total	14	2	0	0	3471
88	5/02	Hntg 2m5f110yG(0-95)HHdl	GD	£1720	
80	4/02	Tntn 3m110y G(0-95)HHdl	GD	£1750	
		Total win prize-money £3471			

Going: Sf: 0-1 GS: 0-1 Gd: 0-2 GF: - Fm: 0-0
Distance: 2m/2m3: 0-0 2m4-2m7: 0-2 3m+: 0-2
Track: LH: 0-2 RH: 0-2 Tight: 0-2 Gall: 0-0
Aids: Bl: 0-2 Vi: 0-2 Tstrap: 0-0 Ckp: 0-0
Best Rating: 88 5/02 Hntg 2m5f110y good Hdl

Polish Pilot (IRE)
106   (76h)85
9-y-o b g Polish Patriot (USA)-Va Toujours (Alzao (USA))
J R Cornwall J R Cornwall

Placings:3321602/43P0040/4P0P531543P4/2P4P0304553 4454-331024330443   (4957)
2003/04: 20^3GS, 17^3GS, 17^1GF, 17^0GF, 16^2F, 17^4GF, 16^3GF, 16^3GS, 16^0GS, 16^4G, 16^4GS, 17^3GS,

	Starts	1st	2nd	3rd	Win & Pl
Chases	12	1	1	5	10650
Career Total	53	3	4	12	22658

80	5/03	MRas	2m1f110yF(0-100)HCh	G-F	£3445	
76	1/02	Sthl	2m F(0-95)HHdl	G-S	£2352	
105	11/99	Worc	2m E(0-105)HHdl	GD	£2267	
			Total win prize-money		£8065	

Going:	Sf: 0-0 GS: 0-3 Gd: 0-2 GF: - Fm: 1-7
Distance:	**2m/2m3: 1-11** 2m4-2m7: 0-1 3m+: 0-0
Track:	LH: 0-4 **RH: 1-8 Tight: 1-4** Gall: 0-5
Aids:	Bl: 0-0 Vi: 0-0 Tstrap: 0-0 Ckp: 0-0
Best Rating:	105 11/99 Worc 2m good Hdl

Very moderate hurdler/chaser; best at around two miles; acts on fast and easy ground.

Polished

109(106h) (85h)**96**
5-y-o ch g Danzig Connection (USA)-Glitter (FR) (Reliance li)
R C Guest The Cherry Blossom Partnership

Placings:5-P0211U (4164)
2003/04: 17PS, 17OGF, 17²GS, 16¹HY, 16¹GS, 19UG,

	Starts	1st	2nd	3rd	Win & Pl
Hurdles	3	0	1	0	684
Chases	3	2	0	0	8408
Career Total	**7**	**2**	**1**	**0**	**9092**
96	2/04	Sedg	2m110y E(0-110)HCh	G-S	£4322
96	2/04	Newc	2m110y E(0-105)HCh	HVY	£4085
			Total win prize-money		£8408

Going:	Sf: 1-2 GS: 1-2 Gd: 0-1 GF: - Fm: 0-1
Distance:	**2m/2m3: 2-6** 2m4-2m7: 0-0 3m+: 0-0
Track:	**LH: 2-6** RH: 0-0 Tight: 1-4 Gall: 1-1
Aids:	Bl: 0-0 Vi: 0-0 Tstrap: 0-0 Ckp: 0-0
Best Rating:	96 2/04 Sedg 2m110y gd-sft Ch

Plating-class hurdler, but has looked a much better novice chaser; successful at Newcastle and Sedgefield; best at two miles; handles testing conditions, but should act on good ground.

Politburo

9-y-o b g Presidium-Kitty Come Home (Monsanto (FR))
N J Gifford Mrs J F Hall

Placings:0/0/005FP501/4PP-PP (0749)
2003/04: 17PGF, 16PG,

	Starts	1st	2nd	3rd	Win & Pl
Hurdles	1	0	0	0	0
Chases	1	0	0	0	0
Career Total	**15**	**1**	**0**	**0**	**3416**
97	4/02	Plum	2m1f E Ch	G-F	£3415
			Total win prize-money		£3416

Going:	Sf: 0-0 GS: 0-0 Gd: 0-1 GF: - Fm: 0-1
Distance:	2m/2m3: 0-2 2m4-2m7: 0-0 3m+: 0-0
Track:	LH: 0-2 RH: 0-0 Tight: 0-1 Gall: 0-0
Aids:	Bl: 0-0 Vi: 0-0 Tstrap: 0-0 Ckp: 0-0
Best Rating:	97 4/02 Plum 2m1f gd-fm Ch

Political Cruise

86 **51**
6-y-o b g Royal Fountain-Political Mill (Politico (USA))
R Nixon G R S Nixon

Placings:040-000 (4595)
2003/04: 20PG, 20³S, 22PG,

	Starts	1st	2nd	3rd	Win & Pl
Hurdles	3	0	0	0	0
Career Total	**6**	**0**	**0**	**0**	**0**

Going:	Sf: 0-1 GS: 0-0 Gd: 0-2 GF: - Fm: 0-0
Distance:	2m/2m3: 0-0 2m4-2m7: 0-3 3m+: 0-0
Track:	LH: 0-2 RH: 0-1 Tight: 0-1 Gall: 0-0
Aids:	Bl: 0-0 Vi: 0-0 Tstrap: 0-0 Ckp: 0-0
Best Rating:	70 1/03 Ayr 2m heavy NHF

Political Sox

110(100c) (0c)**98**
10-y-o br g Mirror Boy-Political Mill (Politico (USA))
R Nixon G R S Nixon

Placings:640/466000425P340/605100/0500523032 23404/6 43P01120044364-33214624500 5004552 (4942)
2003/04: 24³G, 22³G, 22²GS, 24¹G, 24⁴G, 17⁶G, 22²G, 24⁴G, 20⁵HY, 24⁰GS, 16⁰S, 20⁵S, 25⁹G, 22⁰GS, 22⁴GF, 24⁵HY, 17⁵GS, 20²GS,

	Starts	1st	2nd	3rd	Win & Pl
Hurdles	18	1	3	2	12301
Career Total	**70**	**4**	**8**	**8**	**31790**
97	6/03	Prth	3m110y E(0-110)HHdl	GD	£4110
98	12/02	Newc	2m4f F Hdl	SFT	£2926
95	12/02	Kels	2m2f F(0-90)HHdl	HVY	£3458
84	2/01	Kels	2m110y F(0-100)HHdl	SFT	£2772
			Total win prize-money		£13267

Going:	Sf: 0-4 GS: 0-5 Gd: 1-8 GF: - Fm: 0-1
Distance:	2m/2m3: 0-3 2m4-2m7: 0-8 **3m+: 1-7**
Track:	LH: 0-11 **RH: 1-7** Tight: 0-6 Gall: 0-2
Aids:	Bl: 0-0 Vi: 0-0 Tstrap: 0-0 Ckp: 0-0
Best Rating:	98 4/04 Prth 2m4f110y gd-sft Hdl

Moderate hurdler; best around two and a half miles but stays three; suited by soft ground, but acts on faster.

Pollensa Bay

98 **88**
5-y-o b g Overbury (IRE)-Cloncoose (IRE) (Remainder Man)
S A Brookshaw Ken Edwards

Placings:462304P6PP (4874)
2003/04: 16⁴G, 16⁶GF, 17²GF, 16³GF, 17⁰G, 21⁴GS, 20⁷G, 21⁶G, 24PG, 20PGS,

	Starts	1st	2nd	3rd	Win & Pl
NH Flat	3	0	1	0	434
Hurdles	7	0	0	1	844
Career Total	**10**	**0**	**1**	**1**	**1278**

Going:	Sf: 0-0 GS: 0-2 Gd: 0-5 GF: - Fm: 0-3
Distance:	2m/2m3: 0-5 2m4-2m7: 0-4 3m+: 0-1
Track:	LH: 0-5 RH: 0-5 Tight: 0-2 Gall: 0-0
Aids:	Bl: 0-0 Vi: 0-1 Tstrap: 0-0 Ckp: 0-0
Best Rating:	96 5/03 Ludl 2m good NHF

Modest form in bumpers and novice hurdle company.

Polligana

110(99h) (90h)**100**
8-y-o b g Lugana Beach-Pollibrig (Politico (USA))
V R A Dartnall W Westacott

Placings:00023/P0F5-325 (4734)
2003/04: 22³GF, 26²GF, 26⁵G,

	Starts	1st	2nd	3rd	Win & Pl
Hurdles	1	0	0	1	458
Chases	2	0	1	0	1030
Career Total	**12**	**0**	**2**	**2**	**2822**

Going:	Sf: 0-0 GS: 0-0 Gd: 0-1 GF: - Fm: 0-2
Distance:	2m/2m3: 0-0 2m4-2m7: 0-1 3m+: 0-2
Track:	LH: 0-2 RH: 0-1 Tight: 0-2 Gall: 0-0
Aids:	Bl: 0-0 Vi: 0-0 Tstrap: 0-0 Ckp: 0-0
Best Rating:	103 4/02 Winc 2m6f good Hdl

Modest novice hurdler; supported in the ring when second after being given a lot to do on chasing debut in 3m 2f handicap at Newton Abbot September 2003; acts on good ground; stays 3m 2f.

Polly's Pride

5-y-o b m Syrtos-Polly Minor (Sunley Builds)
C L Popham L A Heard

Placings:P (2844)
2003/04: 16PGS,

	Starts	1st	2nd	3rd	Win & Pl
NH Flat	1	0	0	0	
Career Total	**1**	**0**	**0**	**0**	

Going:	Sf: 0-0 GS: 0-1 Gd: 0-0 GF: - Fm: 0-0
Distance:	2m/2m3: 0-1 2m4-2m7: 0-0 3m+: 0-0
Track:	LH: 0-1 RH: 0-0 Tight: 0-0 Gall: 0-0
Aids:	Bl: 0-0 Vi: 0-0 Tstrap: 0-0 Ckp: 0-0

Polo Pony (IRE)

12-y-o b g The Noble Player (USA)-Mangan Lane (Le Moss)
Mrs K D Horan Miss T Habgood

Placings:0/002001P/4100UUF40234/133P56/0PP0/U (4283)
2003/04: 25UG,

	Starts	1st	2nd	3rd	Win & Pl
Chases	1	0	0	0	
Career Total	**31**	**3**	**2**	**3**	**9675**
79	10/98	Sedg	3m3f F(0-100)HCh	GD	£2901
76	11/97	Sedg	3m3f110yG(0-95)HHdl	GD	£1884
74	4/97	Uttx	2m4f110yG(0-95)HHdl	G-F	£1857
			Total win prize-money		£6644

Going:	Sf: 0-0 GS: 0-0 Gd: 0-1 GF: - Fm: 0-0
Distance:	2m/2m3: 0-0 2m4-2m7: 0-0 3m+: 0-1
Track:	LH: 0-0 RH: 0-1 Tight: 0-0 Gall: 0-0
Best Rating:	79 10/98 Sedg 3m3f good Ch

Poly Amanshaa (IRE)

109 (100h)**118+**
12-y-o b/br g Nashamaa-Mombones (Lord Gayle (USA))
M C Banks M C Banks

Placings:005143/22/3532/312/0515414P/02U/24/142P-P5411 (2072)
2003/04: 20PG, 20⁵GF, 21⁴GF, 20¹GF, 20¹GF,

	Starts	1st	2nd	3rd	Win & Pl
Chases	5	2	0	0	13818
Career Total	**37**	**7**	**7**	**4**	**44667**
118	11/03	Hntg	2m4f110yC(0-130)HCh	G-F	£6682
116	11/03	Hntg	2m4f110yD(0-115)HCh	G-F	£6877
110	12/02	Donc	2m110y D(0-115)HCh	G-S	£4754
113	1/00	Donc	2m3f110yD Ch	GD	£4134
111	12/99	Fknm	2m5f110yD Ch	GD	£3635
97	5/98	Towc	2m D(0-125)HHdl	G-F	£2805
91	4/96	Fknm	2m E(0-100)HHdl	GD	£2885
			Total win prize-money		£31773

Going:	Sf: 0-0 GS: 0-0 Gd: 0-1 GF: - Fm: 2-4
Distance:	2m/2m3: 0-0 **2m4-2m7: 2-5** 3m+: 0-0

Track: LH: 0-2 **RH: 2-3** Tight: 0-0 **Gall: 2-3**
Aids: Bl: 0-0 Vi: 0-0 Tstrap: 0-0 Ckp: 0-0
Best Rating: 118 11/03 Hntg 2m4f110y gd-fm   Ch

Modest chaser; effective at 2m 4f; acts well on all goings bar extremes.

Polyanthus Jones

100f   99f

5-y-o b m Sovereign Water (FR)-Cindie Girl (Orchestra)
H D Daly Patrick Burling Developments Ltd

Placings: 02   (4144)
2003/04: 16⁰G, 16²G,

	Starts	1st	2nd	3rd	Win & Pl
NH Flat	2	0	1	0	766
Career Total	2	0	1	0	766

Going: Sf: 0-0 GS: 0-0 Gd: 0-2 GF: - Fm: 0-0
Distance: 2m/2m3: 0-2 2m4-2m7: 0-0 3m+: 0-0
Track: LH: 0-1 RH: 0-1 Tight: 0-0 Gall: 0-0
Aids: Bl: 0-0 Vi: 0-0 Tstrap: 0-0 Ckp: 0-0
Best Rating: 99 3/04 Ludl 2m   good NHF

Fair bumper efforts on good ground.

Polyphon (FR)

107(96h)   (80h)94+

6-y-o b g Murmure (FR)-Petite Folie (Salmon Leap (USA))
P Monteith (Miss P Robson 15/5) Mr & Mrs Raymond Anderson Green

Placings: 00/2P630   (4686)
2003/04: 20²G, 21⁸S, 20⁶HY, 16³GF, 17⁰G,

	Starts	1st	2nd	3rd	Win & Pl
Hurdles	1	0	0	0	0
Chases	4	0	1	1	1683
Career Total	7	0	1	1	1683

Going: Sf: 0-2 GS: 0-0 Gd: 0-2 GF: - Fm: 0-1
Distance: 2m/2m3: 0-2 2m4-2m7: 0-3 3m+: 0-0
Track: LH: 0-4 RH: 0-1 Tight: 0-1 Gall: 0-1
Aids: Bl: 0-0 Vi: 0-0 Tstrap: 0-0 Ckp: 0-0
Best Rating: 94 3/04 Ayr 2m   gd-fm   Ch

Ordinary chaser who failed to justify market support when dropped in trip to two miles at Ayr in March 2004; once again not finding as much off the bridle as seemed likely and tending to make mistakes under pressure; best around two miles; acts on a sound surface.

Polyphony (USA)

96   75

10-y-o b g Cox's Ridge (USA)-Populi (USA) (Star Envoy (USA))
D C O'Brien Mrs V O'Brien

Placings: 5/32400/66/36F6P/PP65/26-50PP   (3173)
2003/04: 20⁵G, 17⁰GF, 17⁷GS, 22⁸HY,

	Starts	1st	2nd	3rd	Win & Pl
Hurdles	4	0	0	0	0
Career Total	23	0	2	2	2149

Going: Sf: 0-1 GS: 0-1 Gd: 0-1 GF: - Fm: 0-1
Distance: 2m/2m3: 0-2 2m4-2m7: 0-2 3m+: 0-0
Track: LH: 0-2 RH: 0-1 Tight: 0-3 Gall: 0-0
Aids: Bl: 0-0 Vi: 0-0 Tstrap: 0-0 Ckp: 0-0
Best Rating: 90 1/99 Folk 2m6f110y heavy Hdl

Plating-class hurdler/chaser; runner-up in a seller at Fontwell in March 2003; has worn headgear.

Pompeii (IRE)

104   93

7-y-o b g Salse (USA)-Before Dawn (USA) (Raise A Cup (USA))
A J Lockwood (Ronald Thompson 4/6) J B Slatcher

Placings: 233002/41206022P00   (4513)
2003/04: 17⁴G, 17¹GF, 17²GF, 16⁰G, 17⁶GF, 17⁰G, 16²GS, 19²GS, 17⁸GS, 16⁰G, 16⁰GS,

	Starts	1st	2nd	3rd	Win & Pl
Hurdles	11	1	3	0	6329
Career Total	17	1	5	2	9414
83 9/03 MRas 2m1f110yE(0-100)HHdl G-F £3102
			Total win prize-money £3102

Going: Sf: 0-0 GS: 0-4 Gd: 0-4 GF: - Fm: 1-3
Distance: 2m/2m3: 1-11 2m4-2m7: 0-0 3m+: 0-0
Track: LH: 0-8 RH: 1-3 Tight: 1-7 Gall: 0-1
Aids: Bl: 0-0 Vi: 0-0 Tstrap: 0-0 Ckp: 0-0
Best Rating: 107 4/01 Ayr 2m4f   gd-fm   Hdl

Plating-class hurdler; suited by two and a half miles; best on fast ground though handles cut.

Pontius

106(96h)   (107h)111

7-y-o b g Terimon-Coole Pilate (Celtic Cone)
N A Twiston-Davies H R Mould

Placings: 033/53FF3BP31-1U   (0505)
2003/04: 22¹G, 21⁰G,

	Starts	1st	2nd	3rd	Win & Pl
Chases	2	1	0	0	6929
Career Total	14	2	0	5	16661
108 5/03 Kels 2m6f110yF(0-90)HCh   GD £6929
107 4/03 Prth 3m3f   D(0-125)HHdl GD £6942
			Total win prize-money £13871

Going: Sf: 0-0 GS: 0-1 Gd: 1-1 GF: - Fm: 0-0
Distance: 2m/2m3: 0-0 2m4-2m7: 1-2 3m+: 0-0
Track: LH: 1-2 RH: 0-0 Tight: 1-2 Gall: 0-0
Aids: Bl: 0-0 Vi: 0-0 Tstrap: 0-0 Ckp: 0-0
Best Rating: 111 5/03 Strf 2m5f110y gd-sft   Ch

Modest chaser/hurdler; has had problems getting round; stays three miles plus; seems to appreciate good ground.

Poony Haw

5-y-o b m Minster Son-Miss Brook (Meadowbrook)
W S Coltherd S Coltherd

Placings: 0PPPP   (3468)
2003/04: 16⁰GF, 16²S, 24⁵S, 18⁸S, 20⁰GF,

	Starts	1st	2nd	3rd	Win & Pl
NH Flat	1	0	0	0	0
Hurdles	4	0	0	0	0
Career Total	5	0	0	0	0

Going: Sf: 0-3 GS: 0-0 Gd: 0-0 GF: - Fm: 0-2
Distance: 2m/2m3: 0-3 2m4-2m7: 0-1 3m+: 0-0
Track: LH: 0-4 RH: 0-1 Tight: 0-3 Gall: 0-0
Aids: Bl: 0-0 Vi: 0-1 Tstrap: 0-0 Ckp: 0-1

Pop Gun

95   82

5-y-o ch g Pharly (FR)-Angel Fire (Nashwan (USA))
Miss K Marks (B W Hills 16/6) Nick Shutts

Placings: 03P   (2120)

2003/04: 16⁰GF, 20³GF, 21⁸GF,

	Starts	1st	2nd	3rd	Win & Pl
Hurdles	3	0	0	1	401
Career Total	3	0	0	1	401

Going: Sf: 0-0 GS: 0-0 Gd: 0-0 GF: - Fm: 0-3
Distance: 2m/2m3: 0-1 2m4-2m7: 0-2 3m+: 0-0
Track: LH: 0-2 RH: 0-1 Tight: 0-1 Gall: 0-0
Aids: Bl: 0-0 Vi: 0-0 Tstrap: 0-0 Ckp: 0-0
Best Rating: 82 10/03 Strf 2m110y gd-fm   Hdl

Poppy's Progress

75f   67f

7-y-o ch m Carlton (GER)-Countess Blakeney (Baron Blakeney)
T D McCarthy Philip Sheehan

Placings: 06-0   (0451)
2003/04: 16⁰GF,

	Starts	1st	2nd	3rd	Win & Pl
NH Flat	1	0	0	0	
Career Total	3	0	0	0	0

Going: Sf: 0-0 GS: 0-0 Gd: 0-0 GF: - Fm: 0-1
Distance: 2m/2m3: 0-1 2m4-2m7: 0-0 3m+: 0-0
Track: LH: 0-0 RH: 0-1 Tight: 0-0 Gall: 0-1
Aids: Bl: 0-0 Vi: 0-0 Tstrap: 0-0 Ckp: 0-0
Best Rating: 67 5/03 Hntg 2m110y gd-fm   NHF

Porak (IRE)

99   123

7-y-o ch g Perugino (USA)-Gayla Orchestra (Lord Gayle (USA))
G L Moore Allen, Manley, Prichard, Russell

Placings: 242/120-0   (0515)
2003/04: 16⁰G,

	Starts	1st	2nd	3rd	Win & Pl
Hurdles	1	0	0	0	
Career Total	7	1	3	0	9669
123 11/02 Asct 2m110y D Hdl   G-S £5213
			Total win prize-money £5213

Going: Sf: 0-0 GS: 0-0 Gd: 0-1 GF: - Fm: 0-0
Distance: 2m/2m3: 0-1 2m4-2m7: 0-0 3m+: 0-0
Track: LH: 0-1 RH: 0-0 Tight: 0-1 Gall: 0-0
Aids: Bl: 0-0 Vi: 0-0 Tstrap: 0-0 Ckp: 0-0
Best Rating: 123 11/02 Asct 2m110y gd-sft   Hdl

Fair hurdler; won very nicely at Ascot in November 2002; effective over two miles with cut in the ground; lightly raced since.

Pornic (FR)

103(104h)   (96h)90+

10-y-o b g Shining Steel-Marie De Geneve (FR) (Nishapour (FR))
A Crook John Sinclair (haulage) Ltd

Placings: 11436233/P5F053324223/110326431/50064033P PP/14332-0542600241   (4961)
2003/04: 17⁰GS, 16⁵G, 19⁴GS, 20²GF, 17⁶S, 19⁰G, 20⁰G, 21²G, 21⁴G, 20¹GS,

	Starts	1st	2nd	3rd	Win & Pl
Hurdles	3	0	0	0	0
Chases	7	1	2	0	6197
Career Total	55	7	8	12	47688
90 4/04 MRas 2m4f   E(0-105)HCh   G-S £3892
98 11/02 Carl 2m1f E(0-110)HHdl G-S £2870

98	4/01	MRas	2m1f110yE(0-115)HCh	G-S	£4078
108	6/00	Prth	2m	E(0-115)HCh	SFT	£4095
110	5/00	MRas	2m1f110yD(0-120)HCh	G-F	£4192
	5/98	Autl	2m2f	Ch	SFT	£10101

Total win prize-money £29230

Going: Sf: 0-1 GS: 1-3 Gd: 0-5 GF: - Fm: 0-1
Distance: 2m/2m3: 0-5 2m4-2m7: 1-5 3m+: 0-0
Track: LH: 0-7 RH: 1-3 Tight: 1-6 Gall: 0-1
Aids: Bl: 0-0 Vi: 0-0 Tstrap: 0-0 Ckp: 0-0
Best Rating: 114 3/99 Newc 2m110y soft Ch

Moderate handicap hurdler/chaser; effective over two miles; handles heavy.

Port Du Salut (FR)
54   23
4-y-o br g Garde Royale-Landevennec (FR) (Gairloch)
A Ennis A T A Wates

Placings:00   (3364)
2003/04: 14⁰G, 16⁰G,

	Starts	1st	2nd	3rd	Win & Pl
NH Flat	1	0	0	0	0
Hurdles	1	0	0	0	0
Career Total	2	0	0	0	

Going: Sf: 0-0 GS: 0-0 Gd: 0-2 GF: 0-0 Fm: 0-0
Distance: 2m/2m3: 0-1 2m4-2m7: 0-0 3m+: 0-0
Track: LH: 0-1 RH: 0-1 Tight: 0-0 Gall: 0-0
Aids: Bl: 0-0 Vi: 0-0 Tstrap: 0-0 Ckp: 0-0
Best Rating: 71 11/03 Wwck 1m6f good NHF

Port Moreno (IRE)
102   85+
4-y-o b g Turtle Island (IRE)-Infra Blue (IRE) (Bluebird (USA))
J G M O'Shea C B Beck

Placings:02   (4654)
2003/04: 17⁰GF, 17²G,

	Starts	1st	2nd	3rd	Win & Pl
Hurdles	2	0	1	0	714
Career Total	2	0	1	0	714

Going: Sf: 0-0 GS: 0-0 Gd: 0-1 GF: 0-0 Fm: 0-1
Distance: 2m/2m3: 0-2 2m4-2m7: 0-0 3m+: 0-0
Track: LH: 0-0 RH: 0-2 Tight: 0-0 Gall: 0-0
Aids: Bl: 0-1 Vi: 0-0 Tstrap: 0-0 Ckp: 0-0
Best Rating: 85 4/04 Hrfd 2m1f good Hdl

Portant Fella
105   116
5-y-o b g Greensmith-Jubilata (USA) (The Minstrel (CAN))
Ms Joanna Morgan Portant Fellas Syndicate

Placings:050-41112060B0   (4828a)
2003/04: 16⁴HY, 16¹F, 16¹GF, 16¹F, 16²F, 16⁹G, 16⁶GF, 16⁹GF, 16⁸G, 16⁰Y,

	Starts	1st	2nd	3rd	Win & Pl
Hurdles	10	3	1	0	22805
Career Total	13	3	1	0	22805
111	8/03	Cork	2m	(88-130)HHdl	FRM	£8288
105	7/03	Navn	2m	(74-116)HHdl	G-F	£5600
103	6/03	Slig	2m	(67-95)HHdl	FRM	£4928

Total win prize-money £18819

Going: Sf: 0-1 GS: 0-0 Gd: 0-2 GF: - Fm: 3-6
Distance: 2m/2m3: 3-10 2m4-2m7: 0-0 3m+: 0-0

Track: LH: 1-3 RH: 0-1 Tight: 0-1 Gall: 0-0
Aids: Bl: 0-0 Vi: 0-0 Tstrap: 0-0 Ckp: 0-0
Best Rating: 116 10/03 Gowr 2m gd-fm Hdl

Fair Irish-trained hurdler; effective at around two miles; suited by fast ground; has worn cheekpieces.

Portichol Princess
56
4-y-o b f Bluegrass Prince (IRE)-Barbrallen (Rambo Dancer (CAN))
R M Stronge Peter J Allen

Placings:P000   (4378)
2003/04: 16⁸GS, 16⁰GS, 16⁰S, 17⁰G,

	Starts	1st	2nd	3rd	Win & Pl
Hurdles	4	0	0	0	
Career Total	4	0	0	0	

Going: Sf: 0-1 GS: 0-2 Gd: 0-1 GF: - Fm: 0-0
Distance: 2m/2m3: 0-4 2m4-2m7: 0-0 3m+: 0-0
Track: LH: 0-1 RH: 0-3 Tight: 0-2 Gall: 0-0
Aids: Bl: 0-0 Vi: 0-0 Tstrap: 0-2 Ckp: 0-0

Posh Pearl
107   96
9-y-o b/br m Rakaposhi King-Rim Of Pearl (Rymer)
Miss Venetia Williams David Jenks

Placings:11125/F3-2   (0376)
2003/04: 20²S,

	Starts	1st	2nd	3rd	Win & Pl
Hurdles	1	0	1	0	1112
Career Total	8	3	2	1	14067
120	3/01	Wwck	2m	H NHF	HVY	£1967
111	12/00	Tntn	2m1f	H NHF	SFT	£1694
116	11/00	Extr	2m1f	H NHF	G-S	£1652

Total win prize-money £5313

Going: Sf: 0-1 GS: 0-0 Gd: 0-0 GF: - Fm: 0-0
Distance: 2m/2m3: 0-0 2m4-2m7: 0-1 3m+: 0-0
Track: LH: 0-1 RH: 0-0 Tight: 0-1 Gall: 0-0
Aids: Bl: 0-0 Vi: 0-0 Tstrap: 0-0 Ckp: 0-0
Best Rating: 120 4/01 Kemp 2m good NHF

Moderate hurdler; useful bumper performer 2000/1; refused to settle when falling on hurdling debut at Taunton March 2003; better efforts since; stays two and a half miles.

Posh Stick
96   71
7-y-o b m Rakaposhi King-Carat Stick (Gold Rod)
J B Walton Messrs F T Walton

Placings:0000/PP0250-4555   (0781)
2003/04: 16⁴G, 16⁵G, 20⁵GF, 20⁵G,

	Starts	1st	2nd	3rd	Win & Pl
Hurdles	4	0	0	0	315
Career Total	14	0	1	0	1071

Going: Sf: 0-0 GS: 0-0 Gd: 0-3 GF: - Fm: 0-1
Distance: 2m/2m3: 0-2 2m4-2m7: 0-2 3m+: 0-0
Track: LH: 0-2 RH: 0-2 Tight: 0-0 Gall: 0-0
Aids: Bl: 0-0 Vi: 0-0 Tstrap: 0-0 Ckp: 0-0
Best Rating: 86 3/02 Ayr 2m heavy NHF

Positive Profile (IRE)
114   126+
6-y-o b g Definite Article-Leyete Gulf (IRE) (Slip Anchor)
P C Haslam Chelgate Public Relations Ltd

Placings:30-113   (2708)
2003/04: 16¹G, 19¹GF, 25³G,

	Starts	1st	2nd	3rd	Win & Pl
Hurdles	3	2	0	1	12622
Career Total	5	2	0	2	13235
126	11/03	Donc	2m3f110yC(0-135)HHdl	G-F	£6792
110	11/03	Kels	2m110y E Hdl	GD	£3640

Total win prize-money £10433

Going: Sf: 0-0 GS: 0-0 Gd: 1-2 GF: - Fm: 1-1
Distance: 2m/2m3: 1-1 2m4-2m7: 1-1 3m+: 0-1
Track: LH: 2-3 RH: 0-0 Tight: 1-1 Gall: 0-1
Aids: Bl: 0-0 Vi: 0-0 Tstrap: 0-0 Ckp: 0-0
Best Rating: 126 12/03 Chel 3m1f110y good Hdl

Fair hurdler; stays two miles four, did not get home over three miles one at Cheltenham in December; acts on good ground.

Possible Pardon (NZ)
93   128
10-y-o b g Iades (FR)-Wonderful Excuse (NZ) (Alibhai (NZ))
P J Hobbs B Pike

Placings:245/1144/216F10-64P   (2574)
2003/04: 26⁶G, 26⁴G, 24⁹G,

	Starts	1st	2nd	3rd	Win & Pl
Chases	3	0	0	0	283
Career Total	16	4	2	0	23508
128	1/03	Chep	3m	D(0-125)HCh	HVY	£5902
122	11/02	Tntn	3m3f	D(0-115)HCh	G-S	£6890
113	1/02	Font	3m2f110yE(0-110)HCh	GD	£3304
105	11/01	Plum	3m2f	D(0-110)HCh	G-S	£3818

Total win prize-money £19915

Going: Sf: 0-0 GS: 0-0 Gd: 0-3 GF: - Fm: 0-0
Distance: 2m/2m3: 0-0 2m4-2m7: 0-0 3m+: 0-3
Track: LH: 0-2 RH: 0-1 Tight: 0-2 Gall: 0-0
Aids: Bl: 0-3 Vi: 0-0 Tstrap: 0-0 Ckp: 0-0
Best Rating: 128 1/03 Chep 3m heavy Ch

Fair staying handicap chaser, he stays further than three miles and acts on ground good or softer.

Potts Of Magic
71f
5-y-o b g Classic Cliche (IRE)-Potter's Gale (IRE) (Strong Gale)
R Lee J E Potter

Placings:0   (4495)
2003/04: 16⁹G,

	Starts	1st	2nd	3rd	Win & Pl
NH Flat	1	0	0	0	
Career Total	1	0	0	0	

Going: Sf: 0-0 GS: 0-0 Gd: 0-1 GF: - Fm: 0-0
Distance: 2m/2m3: 0-1 2m4-2m7: 0-0 3m+: 0-0
Track: LH: 0-0 RH: 0-0 Tight: 0-0 Gall: 0-0
Aids: Bl: 0-0 Vi: 0-0 Tstrap: 0-0 Ckp: 0-0
Best Rating: 71 3/04 Strf 2m110y good NHF

Pottsy's Joy

93   **100**

7-y-o b g Syrtos-Orange Spice (Orange Bay)
Mrs S J Smith Mrs A Potts

Placings:050F5   (4511)
2003/04: 17⁰G, 16⁵GS, 16⁰G, 19⁰FG, 20⁵GS,

	Starts	1st	2nd	3rd	Win & Pl
NH Flat	1	0	0	0	0
Hurdles	4	0	0	0	0
Career Total	5	0	0	0	0

Going:	Sf: 0-0 GS: 0-2 Gd: 0-3 GF: - Fm: 0-0
Distance:	2m2/m3: 0-3 2m4-2m7: 0-2 3m+: 0-0
Track:	LH: 0-4 RH: 0-0 Tight: 0-0 Gall: 0-1
Aids:	Bl: 0-0 Vi: 0-0 Tstrap: 0-0 Ckp: 0-0
Best Rating:	100 3/04 Donc 2m3f110y good Hdl

Moderate hurdler; booked for modest third spot when falling at the last in novices' hurdle at Doncaster in March; suited by two and a half miles.

Pougatcheva (FR)

105   **99+**

5-y-o ch m Epervier Bleu-Notabilite (FR) (No Pass No Sale)
Miss Venetia Williams Direct Sales UK Ltd

Placings:63-31455036140   (4100)
2003/04: 20³GS, 16¹HY, 17⁴GF, 20⁵G, 22⁵GF, 17⁰G, 19⁶GS, 19¹HY, 21⁴G, 21⁰G,

	Starts	1st	2nd	3rd	Win & Pl
Hurdles	11	2	0	2	8476
Career Total	13	2	0	3	10280
99	2/04	Hrfd	2m3f110yF(0-100)HHdl		HVY	£2975
91	5/03	Uttx	2m	E Hdl		HVY	£3507
					Total win prize-money £6482

Going:	Sf: 2-3 GS: 0-2 Gd: 0-4 GF: - Fm: 0-2
Distance:	2m2/m3: 1-4 2m4-2m7: 1-7 3m+: 0-0
Track:	LH: 1-8 RH: 1-3 Tight: 0-5 Gall: 0-0
Aids:	Bl: 0-0 Vi: 0-0 Tstrap: 0-0 Ckp: 0-0
Best Rating:	99 2/04 Kemp 2m5f good Hdl

Moderate hurdler; stays 2m 4f; needs testing ground.

Pounsley Mill (IRE)

100   **101**

11-y-o b g Asir-Clonroche Abendego (Pauper)
N J Gifford Mrs John Shipley

Placings:404505/2232050/52140/132   (3083)
2003/04: 20¹G, 19³GS, 21²GS,

	Starts	1st	2nd	3rd	Win & Pl
Chases	3	1	1	1	6673
Career Total	21	2	5	2	13949
101	5/03	Font	2m4f	E(0-110)HCh	GD	£4754
111	1/01	Folk	2m	E Ch	SFT	£3648
					Total win prize-money £8403

Going:	Sf: 0-0 GS: 0-1 Gd: 1-1 GF: - Fm: 0-1
Distance:	2m2/m3: 0-1 2m4-2m7: 1-2 3m+: 0-0
Track:	LH: 0-1 RH: 0-1 Tight: 1-2 Gall: 0-0
Aids:	Bl: 0-0 Vi: 0-0 Tstrap: 0-0 Ckp: 0-0
Best Rating:	111 1/01 Folk 2m soft Ch

Moderate chaser; returned from two year absence to land 2m 4f handicap at Fontwell May 2003; acts on good ground or softer.

Powder Creek (IRE)

104   **102**

7-y-o b g Little Bighorn-Our Dorcet (Condorcet (FR))

Mrs M Reveley T M McKain

Placings:230/1-360213   (4685)
2003/04: 20³G, 16⁶S, 16⁰G, 16²GS, 20¹GS, 16³G,

	Starts	1st	2nd	3rd	Win & Pl
Hurdles	6	1	1	2	7148
Career Total	10	2	2	3	9447
97	3/04	Weth	2m4f110yF Hdl		G-S	£2744
108	5/02	Worc	2m	H NHF	GD	£1594
					Total win prize-money £4339

Going:	Sf: 0-1 GS: 1-2 Gd: 0-3 GF: - Fm: 0-0
Distance:	2m2/m3: 0-4 2m4-2m7: 1-2 3m+: 0-0
Track:	LH: 1-6 RH: 0-0 Tight: 0-1 Gall: 0-3
Aids:	Bl: 0-0 Vi: 0-0 Tstrap: 0-0 Ckp: 0-0
Best Rating:	108 5/02 Worc 2m good NHF

Moderate hurdler; bumper winner; eventually broke duck over hurdles at Wetherby in March; suited by two and a half miles; should make a chaser.

Power Factor (IRE)

     66

8-y-o ch g Fayruz-Shragraddy Lass (IRE) (Jareer (USA))
P Butler (T J Nagle Jr 20/6) Mrs E Lucey-Butler

Placings:000060-0005050   (1415)
2003/04: 17⁰S, 16⁰Y, 16⁰GF, 16⁵GY, 16⁰Y, 18⁵GF, 18⁰GF,

	Starts	1st	2nd	3rd	Win & Pl
Hurdles	7	0	0	0	0
Career Total	13	0	0	0	0

Going:	Sf: 0-1 GS: 0-0 Gd: 0-0 GF: - Fm: 0-0
Distance:	2m2/m3: 0-7 2m4-2m7: 0-0 3m+: 0-0
Track:	LH: 0-2 RH: 0-0 Tight: 0-2 Gall: 0-0
Aids:	Bl: 0-2 Vi: 0-0 Tstrap: 0-5 Ckp: 0-2
Best Rating:	75 4/03 Cork 2m firm NHF

Power Hit (USA)

     51

8-y-o b g Leo Castelli (USA)-Rajana (USA) (Rajab (USA))
K Bishop G A Doble

Placings:220/23PP/PP0-P   (0706)
2003/04: 22PGF,

	Starts	1st	2nd	3rd	Win & Pl
Hurdles	1	0	0	0	0
Career Total	10	0	3	1	3234

Going:	Sf: 0-0 GS: 0-0 Gd: 0-0 GF: - Fm: 0-1
Distance:	2m2/m3: 0-0 2m4-2m7: 0-1 3m+: 0-0
Track:	LH: 0-1 RH: 0-0 Tight: 0-1 Gall: 0-0
Aids:	Bl: 0-1 Vi: 0-0 Tstrap: 0-0 Ckp: 0-0
Best Rating:	102 9/99 Extr 2m1f gd-sft Hdl

Power Unit

94(98h)   (109+h)**115+**

9-y-o ch g Risk Me (FR)-Hazel Bee (Starch Reduced)
Mrs D A Hamer Power Units (1953) Ltd

Placings:2204/351440-1UP3P1   (4892)
2003/04: 16¹G, 16⁰GF, 20PGF, 19³GF, 17PS, 16¹GF,

	Starts	1st	2nd	3rd	Win & Pl
Hurdles	1	1	0	0	5915
Chases	5	1	0	1	4617
Career Total	16	3	2	2	18993
109	4/04	Strf	2m110y D(0-110)HHdl		G-F	£5915
115	5/03	Worc	2m	E(0-110)HCh	GD	£4026
105	1/03	Tntn	2m3f	D(0-110)HCh	SFT	£5703

Total win prize-money £15646

Going:	Sf: 0-1 GS: 0-0 Gd: 1-1 GF: - Fm: 1-4
Distance:	2m2/m3: 2-5 2m4-2m7: 0-1 3m+: 0-0
Track:	LH: 2-4 RH: 0-0 Tight: 1-3 Gall: 0-0
Aids:	Bl: 0-0 Vi: 0-1 Tstrap: 0-0 Ckp: 1-4
Best Rating:	115 12/03 Tntn 2m3f gd-fm Ch

Modest chaser/hurdler; stays two miles-three; seems to handle any ground.

Poynder Park (IRE)

13-y-o b g Mandalus-So Deep (Deep Run)
Mrs J Williamson Len Stevenson

Placings:PP/2-5   (0044)
2003/04: 25⁵G,

	Starts	1st	2nd	3rd	Win & Pl
Chases	1	0	0	0	0
Career Total	4	0	1	0	444

Going:	Sf: 0-0 GS: 0-0 Gd: 0-1 GF: - Fm: 0-0
Distance:	2m2/m3: 0-0 2m4-2m7: 0-0 3m+: 0-1
Track:	LH: 0-1 RH: 0-0 Tight: 0-1 Gall: 0-0
Aids:	Bl: 0-0 Vi: 0-0 Tstrap: 0-0 Ckp: 0-1
Best Rating:	84 4/03 Carl 3m gd-fm Ch

Moderate hunter/pointer; stays three miles; suited by fast ground; wears cheekpieces.

Poynton Henry (IRE)

86   (91h)**62**

8-y-o b g Supreme Leader-Short Memories (Quisling)
R H Buckler The Desirables

Placings:00P/1P/0P4F0P   (4737)
2003/04: 19⁰S, 22PS, 26⁴GS, 26FG, 23⁰GS, 21PG,

	Starts	1st	2nd	3rd	Win & Pl
Chases	6	0	0	0	317
Career Total	11	1	0	0	2781
91	10/01	Extr	2m6f110yE Hdl		G-F	£2464
					Total win prize-money £2464

Going:	Sf: 0-2 GS: 0-2 Gd: 0-2 GF: - Fm: 0-0
Distance:	2m2/m3: 0-0 2m4-2m7: 0-3 3m+: 0-3
Track:	LH: 0-3 RH: 0-2 Tight: 0-3 Gall: 0-1
Aids:	Bl: 0-3 Vi: 0-0 Tstrap: 0-0 Ckp: 0-0
Best Rating:	91 10/01 Extr 2m6f110y gd-fm Hdl

Praetorian Gold

89   (88h)**89**

9-y-o ch g Presidium-Chinese Princess (Sunny Way)
N F Glynn N F Glynn

Placings:00013/30155/005045F/0000-F4400UP0P00   (2750a)
2003/04: 20FYS, 21⁴GF, 21⁴GF, 22⁰Y, 24⁰V, 16⁴F, 25PGF, 24⁰G, 24PG, 16⁰YS, 20⁰Y,

	Starts	1st	2nd	3rd	Win & Pl
Hurdles	3	0	0	0	0
Chases	8	0	0	0	911
Career Total	32	2	0	2	9327
120	6/00	Tral	2m	(0-116)HHdl	Y-S	£3588
103	3/00	Thur	2m	Hdl	GD	£3312
					Total win prize-money £6900

Going:	Sf: 0-0 GS: 0-0 Gd: 0-2 GF: - Fm: 0-4
Distance:	2m2/m3: 0-2 2m4-2m7: 0-5 3m+: 0-4
Track:	LH: 0-4 RH: 0-0 Tight: 0-1 Gall: 0-0
Aids:	Bl: 0-5 Vi: 0-0 Tstrap: 0-0 Ckp: 0-1

Best Rating: 120 6/00 Tral 2m yld-sft Hdl

Prairie Minstrel (USA)

101   106

10-y-o b g Regal Intention (CAN)-Prairie Sky (USA) (Gone West (USA))
R Dickin E R C Beech & B Wilkinson

Placings:2223125P152/0025025622/21F111P/3/0021P60-F131235P (4889)
2003/04: 20FG, 201GF, 243G, 201F, 202GF, 173G, 205GF, 20PGF,

	Starts	1st	2nd	3rd	Win & Pl
Chases	8	2	1	2	12280
Career Total	44	9	12	4	45727

102	12/03	Leic	2m4f110yD(0-115)HCh	FRM	£4202
97	11/03	Worc	2m4f110yD(0-120)HCh	G-F	£4221
100	12/02	Leic	2m4f110yD(0-115)HCh	GD	£4758
106	8/99	Sthl	2m4f110yE(0-105)HCh	G-F	£3125
97	8/99	MRas	2m4f D Ch	G-F	£4413
104	7/99	MRas	2m4f D Ch	G-F	£3795
109	5/99	Hntg	2m4f110yE Ch	G-F	£2860
88	3/98	Wwck	2m F(0-100)HHdl	SFT	£2244
92	11/97	Wind	2m E Hdl	GD	£2407

Total win prize-money £33028

Going: Sf: 0-0 GS: 0-0 Gd: 0-3 GF: - Fm: 2-5
Distance: 2m/2m3: 0-1 2m4-2m7: 2-6 3m+: 0-1
Track: LH: 1-3 RH: 1-5 Tight: 0-2 Gall: 0-0
Aids: Bl: 0-0 Vi: 0-0 Tstrap: 0-0 Ckp: 2-7
Best Rating: 109 5/99 Hntg 2m4f110y gd-fm Ch

Moderate chaser; best at two and a half miles; acts on decent ground.

Prancing Blade

110   113

11-y-o b g Broadsword (USA)-Sparkling Cinders (Netherkelly)
N A Twiston-Davies Gavin Macechern

Placings:60/C4P0F6/222112F06/31115U4F/PP/2434214F PP00P-01P610 (4141)
2003/04: 240G, 261GF, 31PG, 206G, 241G, 240G,

	Starts	1st	2nd	3rd	Win & Pl
Chases	6	2	0	0	7833
Career Total	46	8	6	2	51198

113	2/04	Ludl	3m E(0-105)HCh	GD	£4823
101	11/03	Wwck	3m2f F(0-95)HCh	G-F	£3010
125	9/02	Prth	3m D(0-115)HCh	G-F	£8862
131	10/00	MRas	2m1f110yC Ch	GD	£7215
128	9/00	Chep	2m3f110yC Ch	GD	£6743
116	5/00	Bang	2m1f110yE Ch	G-F	£3510
116	10/99	Worc	2m2f E Hdl	G-F	£2402
104	10/99	Hexm	2m E Hdl	GD	£2364

Total win prize-money £38930

Going: Sf: 0-0 GS: 0-0 Gd: 1-5 GF: - Fm: 1-1
Distance: 2m/2m3: 0-4 2m4-2m7: 0-1 3m+: 2-5
Track: LH: 1-2 RH: 1-3 Tight: 1-4 Gall: 0-0
Aids: Bl: 0-0 Vi: 0-0 Tstrap: 0-0 Ckp: 0-0
Best Rating: 131 10/00 MRas 2m1f110y good Ch

Moderate handicap chaser; stays three miles two; best on a sound surface; likes to force the pace.

Prate Box (IRE)

14-y-o b g Ela-Mana-Mou-Prattle On (Ballymore)
F A Hutsby Mrs Peter Corbett

Placings:U/06033110/2602/0006441311F0/21F2/PPP/F/P-24 (4250)
2003/04: 242G, 254GF,

	Starts	1st	2nd	3rd	Win & Pl
Chases	2	0	1	0	1024
Career Total	36	6	5	3	31434

129	11/97	Chep	2m3f110yC(0-135)HCh	G-S	£6905
123	3/97	Fair	2m4f (0-109)HCh	GD	£4747
123	3/97	Naas	2m40y (0-109)HCh	Y-S	£3051
113	1/97	Punc	2m (0-109)HCh	Y-S	£3730
127	2/95	Clon	2m Hdl	HVY	£3051
110	11/94	Clon	2m Hdl	Y-S	£2446

Total win prize-money £23933

Going: Sf: 0-0 GS: 0-0 Gd: 0-1 GF: - Fm: 0-1
Distance: 2m/2m3: 0-0 2m4-2m7: 0-0 3m+: 0-2
Track: LH: 0-1 RH: 0-1 Tight: 0-0 Gall: 0-0
Aids: Bl: 0-0 Vi: 0-0 Tstrap: 0-0 Ckp: 0-0
Best Rating: 131 1/98 Kemp 2m4f110y gd-sft Ch

Prayerful

97   69+

5-y-o b m Syrtos-Pure Formality (Forzando)
B N Doran P N Exton

Placings:0U0-P664303032 (4756)
2003/04: 26PGF, 16BGF, 17BGF, 214GF, 203G, 220G, 193HY, 160GS, 193GF, 192S,

	Starts	1st	2nd	3rd	Win & Pl
Hurdles	10	0	1	3	2348
Career Total	13	0	1	3	2348

Going: Sf: 0-2 GS: 0-1 Gd: 0-2 GF: - Fm: 0-5
Distance: 2m/2m3: 0-4 2m4-2m7: 0-5 3m+: 0-1
Track: LH: 0-1 RH: 0-7 Tight: 0-1 Gall: 0-1
Aids: Bl: 0-0 Vi: 0-0 Tstrap: 0-0 Ckp: 0-5
Best Rating: 69 4/04 Towc 2m3f110y soft Hdl

Plating-class hurdler; stays two and a half miles; acts on good ground.

Precious Lucy (FR)

83   59

5-y-o gr m Kadrou (FR)-Teardrops Fall (FR) (Law Society (USA))
C J Down G Doel

Placings:00 (4736)
2003/04: 22BGS, 17BG,

	Starts	1st	2nd	3rd	Win & Pl
Hurdles	2	0	0	0	
Career Total	2	0	0	0	

Going: Sf: 0-0 GS: 0-0 Gd: 0-1 GF: - Fm: 0-0
Distance: 2m/2m3: 0-1 2m4-2m7: 0-1 3m+: 0-0
Track: LH: 0-1 RH: 0-1 Tight: 0-1 Gall: 0-0
Aids: Bl: 0-0 Vi: 0-0 Tstrap: 0-0 Ckp: 0-0
Best Rating: 64 4/04 NAbb 2m1f good Hdl

Precious Mystery (IRE)

108   101

4-y-o ch f Titus Livius (FR)-Ascoli (Skyliner)
A King (J Nicol 4/10) The Dunnkirk Partnership

Placings:01466 (4931)
2003/04: 16BS, 161GS, 16KG, 199G, 226G,

	Starts	1st	2nd	3rd	Win & Pl
Hurdles	5	1	0	0	5296
Career Total	5	1	0	0	5296

101	1/04	Fknm	2m D Hdl	G-S	£4959

Total win prize-money £4960

Going: Sf: 0-1 GS: 1-1 Gd: 0-3 GF: - Fm: 0-0
Distance: 2m/2m3: 1-4 2m4-2m7: 0-1 3m+: 0-0
Track: LH: 1-4 RH: 0-1 Tight: 1-2 Gall: 0-2
Aids: Bl: 0-0 Vi: 0-0 Tstrap: 0-0 Ckp: 0-0
Best Rating: 101 1/04 Fknm 2m gd-sft Hdl

Fair novice hurdler; suited by two miles and cut in the ground, but handled fast ground on the Flat.

Predestine (FR)

108   103

4-y-o ch g Signe Divin (USA)-Smyrna (FR) (Lightning (FR))
K C Bailey Dream Makers Partnership

Placings:24-312P (3825)
2003/04: 163S, 171GS, 202HY, 20PS,

	Starts	1st	2nd	3rd	Win & Pl
Hurdles	4	1	1	1	5357
Career Total	6	1	2	1	8838

98	1/04	Hrfd	2m1f E Hdl	G-S	£3347

Total win prize-money £3348

Going: Sf: 0-3 GS: 1-1 Gd: 0-0 GF: - Fm: 0-0
Distance: 2m/2m3: 1-2 2m4-2m7: 0-2 3m+: 0-0
Track: LH: 0-3 RH: 1-1 Tight: 0-0 Gall: 0-0
Aids: Bl: 0-0 Vi: 0-0 Tstrap: 0-0 Ckp: 0-0
Best Rating: 103 1/04 Hayd 2m4f heavy Hdl

Moderate ex-French hurdler; won at Hereford in January; stays 2m4f; best in soft ground; ran badly and pulled out latest.

Premier Cheval (USA)

5-y-o ch g Irish River (FR)-Restikarada (FR) (Akarad (FR))
R Rowe R C Stillwell

Placings:PPP (3871)
2003/04: 16PGS, 21PGS, 17PGS,

	Starts	1st	2nd	3rd	Win & Pl
Hurdles	3	0	0	0	
Career Total	3	0	0	0	

Going: Sf: 0-0 GS: 0-3 Gd: 0-0 GF: - Fm: 0-0
Distance: 2m/2m3: 0-2 2m4-2m7: 0-1 3m+: 0-0
Track: LH: 0-0 RH: 0-3 Tight: 0-1 Gall: 0-0
Aids: Bl: 0-0 Vi: 0-0 Tstrap: 0-0 Ckp: 0-0

Premier Drive (IRE)

103(112c)   (117c)121

11-y-o ch g Black Minstrel-Ballyanihan (Le Moss)
G M Moore A W Sergeant

Placings:U6665/600315/21153P1/322F32111P/F533F6-FF006PU60 (4662)
2003/04: 20FGF, 20FGF, 20PG, 160GS, 196GS, 20PS, 22UG, 206HY, 20PS,

	Starts	1st	2nd	3rd	Win & Pl
Hurdles	6	0	0	0	0
Chases	3	0	0	0	0
Career Total	43	7	4	6	33323

117	3/02	Hexm	2m110y E Ch	HVY	£3107
108	2/02	Leic	2m4f110yE Ch	SFT	£3094
122	1/02	Leic	2m4f110yD Ch	GD	£4403
121	4/01	Weth	2m4f110yD Hdl	G-S	£3395

121	12/00	Weth	2m4f110yE(0-105)HHdl	SFT	£2702
115	11/00	Weth	2m4f110yD Hdl	HVY	£3250
99	1/00	Tram	2m NHF	Y-S	£2760
				Total win prize-money	£22712

Going:	Sf: 0-3 GS: 0-2 Gd: 0-3 GF: 0-1 Fm: 0-1
Distance:	2m/2m3: 0-2 2m4-2m7: 0-7 3m+: 0-0
Track:	LH: 0-5 RH: 0-4 Tight: 0-2 Gall: 0-0
Aids:	Bl: 0-0 Vi: 0-0 Tstrap: 0-0 Ckp: 0-0
Best Rating:	122 1/02 Leic 2m4f110y good Ch

Fair chaser/hurdler; effective from two to two and a half miles; acts on ground good or softer; suited by forcing tactics.

Premier Estate (IRE)

105   108+

7-y-o b g Satco (FR)-Kettleby (IRE) (Tale Quale)
R Rowe Mrs Jacky Field

Placings:6/05334U-1101   (3310)
2003/04: 22¹GF, 22¹GS, 20⁶G, 20¹HY,

	Starts	1st	2nd	3rd	Win & Pl
Hurdles	4	3	0	0	12495
Career Total	11	3	0	2	13494
108 1/04 Font 2m4f			D(0-125)HHdl	HVY	£5304
99 12/03 Extr 2m6f110yD(0-115)HHdl				G-S	£4663
90 11/03 Font 2m6f110yE(0-110)HHdl				G-F	£2527
				Total win prize-money	£12495

Going:	Sf: 1-1 GS: 1-1 Gd: 0-1 GF: - Fm: 1-1
Distance:	2m/2m3: 0-0 2m4-2m7: 3-4 3m+: 0-0
Track:	LH: 1-1 RH: 1-2 Tight: 2-2 Gall: 0-0
Aids:	Bl: 0-0 Vi: 0-0 Tstrap: 0-0 Ckp: 0-0
Best Rating:	108 1/04 Font 2m4f heavy Hdl

Progressive hurdler; stays two miles six and handles most types of ground.

Premier Generation (IRE)

93(90h)   (80h)89

11-y-o b g Cadeaux Genereux-Bristle (Thatch (USA))
Dr P Pritchard Ray Edwards

Placings:00/23/1211020/402/05001303/00550045/4P4-
PP66065   (4249)
2003/04: 17⁵G, 20⁵S, 17⁶G, 16⁶S, 16⁹S, 16⁶GS, 16⁵GF,

	Starts	1st	2nd	3rd	Win & Pl
Hurdles	3	0	0	0	0
Chases	4	0	0	0	0
Career Total	40	4	4	3	31681
120 12/00 Ludl 2m		E Ch		SFT	£3493
141 2/99 Kemp 2m		A Hdl		SFT	£9465
124 12/98 Wwck 2m		A Hdl		SFT	£3036
112 11/98 Chel 2m110y		D(0-110)HHdl		G-S	£7457
				Total win prize-money	£23453

Going:	Sf: 0-3 GS: 0-1 Gd: 0-2 GF: - Fm: 0-1
Distance:	2m/2m3: 0-6 2m4-2m7: 0-1 3m+: 0-0
Track:	LH: 0-3 RH: 0-4 Tight: 0-3 Gall: 0-0
Aids:	Bl: 0-0 Vi: 0-0 Tstrap: 0-0 Ckp: 0-5
Best Rating:	141 2/99 Kemp 2m soft Hdl

Plating-class chaser; best at 2m; acted on most ground (DEAD).

Premium First (IRE)

95   94

5-y-o ch g Naheez (USA)-Regular Rose (IRE) (Regular Guy)
Mrs H Dalton Hill Fuels Limited

Placings:3156   (4783)
2003/04: 16³G, 16¹GS, 20⁵GS, 21⁶G,

	Starts	1st	2nd	3rd	Win & Pl
NH Flat	2	1	0	1	2335
Hurdles	2	0	0	0	0
Career Total	4	1	0	1	2335
100 1/04 Weth 2m		H NHF		G-S	£2051
				Total win prize-money	£2051

Going:	Sf: 0-0 GS: 1-2 Gd: 0-2 GF: - Fm: 0-0
Distance:	2m/2m3: 1-2 2m4-2m7: 0-2 3m+: 0-0
Track:	LH: 1-2 RH: 0-2 Tight: 0-1 Gall: 0-1
Aids:	Bl: 0-0 Vi: 0-0 Tstrap: 0-0 Ckp: 0-0
Best Rating:	100 1/04 Weth 2m gd-sft NHF

Plating-class hurdler; Irish point winner; acts on easy ground.

Presence Of Mind (IRE)

91   97

6-y-o ch g Presenting-Blue Rose (IRE) (Good Thyne (USA))
Miss E C Lavelle J M Layton

Placings:0P24   (4819)
2003/04: 17⁰GS, 19⁰GS, 24²G, 22⁴GF,

	Starts	1st	2nd	3rd	Win & Pl
NH Flat	1	0	0	0	0
Hurdles	3	0	1	0	1528
Career Total	4	0	1	0	1528

Going:	Sf: 0-0 GS: 0-2 Gd: 0-1 GF: - Fm: 0-1
Distance:	2m/2m3: 0-1 2m4-2m7: 0-2 3m+: 0-1
Track:	LH: 0-0 RH: 0-1 Tight: 0-1 Gall: 0-0
Aids:	Bl: 0-0 Vi: 0-0 Tstrap: 0-0 Ckp: 0-0
Best Rating:	97 4/04 Extr 2m6f110y gd-fm Hdl

Present Glory (IRE)

69f   94f

5-y-o br g Presenting-Prudent Rose (IRE) (Strong Gale)
C Tinkler George Ward

Placings:0   (4824)
2003/04: 17⁰GF,

	Starts	1st	2nd	3rd	Win & Pl
NH Flat	1	0	0	0	
Career Total	1	0	0	0	

Going:	Sf: 0-0 GS: 0-0 Gd: 0-0 GF: - Fm: 0-1
Distance:	2m/2m3: 0-1 2m4-2m7: 0-0 3m+: 0-0
Track:	LH: 0-0 RH: 0-1 Tight: 0-0 Gall: 0-0
Aids:	Bl: 0-0 Vi: 0-0 Tstrap: 0-0 Ckp: 0-0
Best Rating:	94 4/04 Extr 2m1f gd-fm NHF

Presenting Roxy (IRE)

67f   13f

6-y-o br m Presenting-Two Hills Folly (IRE) (Pollerton)
G A Harker David Adair

Placings:0   (2401)
2003/04: 16⁰GS,

	Starts	1st	2nd	3rd	Win & Pl
NH Flat	1	0	0	0	
Career Total	1	0	0	0	

Presentingthecase (IRE)

(82h)   (48h)

6-y-o b g Presenting-Let The Hare Run (IRE) (Tale Quale)
Jonjo O'Neill Mrs Jonjo O'Neill

Placings:000U   (4786)
2003/04: 17⁰HY, 22²⁰G, 21⁰G, 16⁰G,

	Starts	1st	2nd	3rd	Win & Pl
Hurdles	3	0	0	0	0
Chases	1	0	0	0	0
Career Total	4	0	0	0	

Going:	Sf: 0-1 GS: 0-0 Gd: 0-3 GF: - Fm: 0-0
Distance:	2m/2m3: 0-2 2m4-2m7: 0-2 3m+: 0-0
Track:	LH: 0-1 RH: 0-3 Tight: 0-1 Gall: 0-2
Aids:	Bl: 0-0 Vi: 0-0 Tstrap: 0-0 Ckp: 0-0
Best Rating:	48 3/04 Hntg 2m5f110y good Hdl

Presidio (GER)

81(93h)   (61h)61

9-y-o b g Konigsstuhl (GER)-Pradera (GER) (Abary (GER))
N J Hawke The Fairway Boys

Placings:F0/0P063/0P06P   (4737)
2003/04: 16⁰GF, 19⁰S, 16⁶G, 20⁶G, 21⁰G,

	Starts	1st	2nd	3rd	Win & Pl
Hurdles	2	0	0	0	0
Chases	3	0	0	0	0
Career Total	12	0	0	1	287

Going:	Sf: 0-1 GS: 0-0 Gd: 0-3 GF: - Fm: 0-0
Distance:	2m/2m3: 0-3 2m4-2m7: 0-2 3m+: 0-0
Track:	LH: 0-2 RH: 0-3 Tight: 0-2 Gall: 0-0
Aids:	Bl: 0-0 Vi: 0-0 Tstrap: 0-0 Ckp: 0-0
Best Rating:	81 2/01 Ludl 2m gd-sft Hdl

Preston Brook

100(77c)   (80+c)103

7-y-o b g Perpendicular-Tommys Dream (Le Bavard (FR))
M W Easterby Lord Daresbury

Placings:20/2322251P/F546   (4956)
2003/04: 24⁴S, 25⁴GS, 16⁴S, 22⁶G,

	Starts	1st	2nd	3rd	Win & Pl
Hurdles	2	0	0	0	389
Chases	2	0	0	0	0
Career Total	14	1	5	1	6733
103 3/02 Sthl 2m4f110yE Hdl				HVY	£2667
				Total win prize-money	£2667

Going:	Sf: 0-2 GS: 0-1 Gd: 0-1 GF: - Fm: 0-0
Distance:	2m/2m3: 0-1 2m4-2m7: 0-1 3m+: 0-2
Track:	LH: 0-1 RH: 0-2 Tight: 0-1 Gall: 0-1
Aids:	Bl: 0-0 Vi: 0-0 Tstrap: 0-0 Ckp: 0-0
Best Rating:	106 11/01 Newc 2m4f gd-sft Hdl

Presumptuous

94   106+

4-y-o ch g Double Trigger (IRE)-T O O Mamma'S (IRE)
(Classic Secret (USA))

Mrs S J Smith C Bradford-Nutter

Placings:215   (4863)
2003/04: 17²G, 16¹G, 16⁶S,

	Starts	1st	2nd	3rd	Win & Pl
Hurdles	3	1	1	0	5090
Career Total	3	1	1	0	5090
106 3/04 Kels	2m110y E Hdl			GD	£4186
			Total win prize-money £4186		

Going:	Sf: 0-1 GS: 0-0 Gd: 1-2 GF: - Fm: 0-0
Distance:	2m/2m3: 1-3 2m4-2m7: 0-0 3m+: 0-0
Track:	LH: 1-3 RH: 0-0 Tight: 1-2 Gall: 0-0
Aids:	Bl: 0-0 Vi: 0-0 Tstrap: 0-0 Ckp: 0-0
Best Rating:	106 3/04 Kels 2m110y good Hdl

Juvenile hurdler; much improved effort when upsetting hot-pot at Kelso in March despite some indifferent jumping; acts on good.

Pretty Boy Blue

(64h)   (2h)
9-y-o gr g Portogon-Nicola Lisa (Dumbarnie)
W Davies Bill Davies

Placings:PP/P0P0B   (4531)
2003/04: 24ᴾHY, 17ᴾHY, 16ᴾGS, 17ᴾGF, 16ᴮGS,

	Starts	1st	2nd	3rd	Win & Pl
Hurdles	4	0	0	0	0
Chases	1	0	0	0	
Career Total	7	0	0	0	

Going:	Sf: 0-2 GS: 0-2 Gd: 0-0 GF: - Fm: 0-1
Distance:	2m/2m3: 0-4 2m4-2m7: 0-0 3m+: 0-1
Track:	LH: 0-0 RH: 0-5 Tight: 0-0 Gall: 0-0
Aids:	Bl: 0-0 Vi: 0-0 Tstrap: 0-0 Ckp: 0-0
Best Rating:	2 3/04 Hrfd 2m1f gd-fm Hdl

Priaisy (IRE)

99f   75f
5-y-o b g Priolo (USA)-Daisy Dobson (Gorytus (USA))
J Wade John Wade

Placings:30   (1195)
2003/04: 17³GF, 16⁰GF,

	Starts	1st	2nd	3rd	Win & Pl
NH Flat	2	0	0	1	260
Career Total	2	0	0	1	260

Going:	Sf: 0-0 GS: 0-0 Gd: 0-0 GF: - Fm: 0-2
Distance:	2m/2m3: 0-2 2m4-2m7: 0-0 3m+: 0-0
Track:	LH: 0-2 RH: 0-0 Tight: 0-1 Gall: 0-0
Aids:	Bl: 0-0 Vi: 0-0 Tstrap: 0-0 Ckp: 0-0
Best Rating:	89 7/03 Sedg 2m1f gd-fm NHF

Third in a poor bumper on his debut.

Pride Of Finewood (IRE)

79f   88f
6-y-o ch g Old Vic-Macamore Rose (Torus)
Noel T Chance Finewood Joinery Products

Placings:0   (4179)
2003/04: 16⁰G,

	Starts	1st	2nd	3rd	Win & Pl
NH Flat	1	0	0	0	
Career Total	1	0	0	0	

Going:	Sf: 0-0 GS: 0-0 Gd: 0-1 GF: - Fm: 0-0
Distance:	2m/2m3: 0-1 2m4-2m7: 0-0 3m+: 0-0
Track:	LH: 0-1 RH: 0-0 Tight: 0-0 Gall: 0-1
Aids:	Bl: 0-0 Vi: 0-0 Tstrap: 0-0 Ckp: 0-0
Best Rating:	88 3/04 Donc 2m110y good NHF

Pride Of Penlee

4-y-o b g Pontevecchio Notte-Kindly Lady (Kind Of Hush)
J D Frost D C & Mrs T M Fisher

Placings:0   (3752)
2003/04: 18⁰GS,

	Starts	1st	2nd	3rd	Win & Pl
NH Flat	1	0	0	0	
Career Total	1	0	0	0	

Going:	Sf: 0-0 GS: 0-1 Gd: 0-0 GF: - Fm: 0-0
Distance:	2m/2m3: 0-1 2m4-2m7: 0-0 3m+: 0-0
Track:	LH: 0-1 RH: 0-0 Tight: 0-1 Gall: 0-0
Aids:	Bl: 0-0 Vi: 0-0 Tstrap: 0-0 Ckp: 0-0

Pride Of Pennker (IRE)

89   66
11-y-o b m Glacial Storm (USA)-Quitrentina (Green Shoon)
G A Ham C F Caple

Placings:0P0P/4P12400/640/FP3UP/P3454P-F04P3P4P
                       (1483)
2003/04: 16ᶠGF, 20⁰GF, 25⁴GF, 22ᴾGF, 16³GF, 20ᴾG, 20⁴GF, 19ᴾGF,

	Starts	1st	2nd	3rd	Win & Pl
Hurdles	1	0	0	0	0
Chases	7	0	0	1	1083
Career Total	33	1	1	3	6610
75 10/98 Tntn	2m3f110yE Hdl			FRM	£2669
			Total win prize-money £2669		

Going:	Sf: 0-0 GS: 0-0 Gd: 0-1 GF: - Fm: 0-7
Distance:	2m/2m3: 0-3 2m4-2m7: 0-4 3m+: 0-1
Track:	LH: 0-5 RH: 0-2 Tight: 0-4 Gall: 0-0
Aids:	Bl: 0-0 Vi: 0-0 Tstrap: 0-0 Ckp: 0-0
Best Rating:	86 10/98 Ludl 2m5f110y gd-fm Hdl

Plating-class chaser; best at distances short of 3m.

Pride Of The Oaks

4-y-o b f Faustus (USA)-Annabel's Baby (IRE) (Alzao (USA))
G G Margarson Oaks Racing

Placings:0   (4608)
2003/04: 17⁰G,

	Starts	1st	2nd	3rd	Win & Pl
NH Flat	1	0	0	0	
Career Total	1	0	0	0	

Going:	Sf: 0-0 GS: 0-0 Gd: 0-1 GF: - Fm: 0-0
Distance:	2m/2m3: 0-1 2m4-2m7: 0-0 3m+: 0-0
Track:	LH: 0-0 RH: 0-1 Tight: 0-1 Gall: 0-0
Aids:	Bl: 0-0 Vi: 0-0 Tstrap: 0-0 Ckp: 0-0

Pridewood Dove

5-y-o b m Alderbrook-Flighty Dove (Cruise Missile)

R J Price Mrs B Morris

Placings:0   (1195)
2003/04: 16⁰GF,

	Starts	1st	2nd	3rd	Win & Pl
NH Flat	1	0	0	0	
Career Total	1	0	0	0	

Going:	Sf: 0-0 GS: 0-0 Gd: 0-0 GF: - Fm: 0-1
Distance:	2m/2m3: 0-1 2m4-2m7: 0-0 3m+: 0-0
Track:	LH: 0-1 RH: 0-0 Tight: 0-0 Gall: 0-0
Aids:	Bl: 0-0 Vi: 0-0 Tstrap: 0-0 Ckp: 0-0

Priests Bridge (IRE)

108   129
8-y-o ch m Mr Ditton-Paddys Gale (Strong Gale)
N A Twiston-Davies Geoffrey & Donna Keeys

Placings:12213012B-4   (1358)
2003/04: 17⁴G,

	Starts	1st	2nd	3rd	Win & Pl
Hurdles	1	0	0	0	1038
Career Total	10	3	3	1	26689
122 2/03 Kemp	3m110y D Hdl			G-S	£5255
122 11/02 Uttx	2m4f110yE Hdl			SFT	£3489
125 10/02 Bang	2m1f H NHF			G-S	£1873
			Total win prize-money £10618		

Going:	Sf: 0-0 GS: 0-0 Gd: 0-1 GF: - Fm: 0-0
Distance:	2m/2m3: 0-1 2m4-2m7: 0-0 3m+: 0-0
Track:	LH: 0-1 RH: 0-0 Tight: 0-1 Gall: 0-0
Aids:	Bl: 0-0 Vi: 0-0 Tstrap: 0-0 Ckp: 0-0
Best Rating:	129 3/03 Hayd 2m7f110y good Hdl

Irish point winner; useful novice hurdler; stays 3m; effective in soft ground; front runner; tough.

Prima Casa

72f   58f
4-y-o ch f First Trump-Welcome Home (Most Welcome)
P T Dalton Mrs Joanne Woods

Placings:00   (4186)
2003/04: 16⁰G, 16⁰G,

	Starts	1st	2nd	3rd	Win & Pl
NH Flat	2	0	0	0	
Career Total	2	0	0	0	

Going:	Sf: 0-0 GS: 0-0 Gd: 0-2 GF: - Fm: 0-0
Distance:	2m/2m3: 0-2 2m4-2m7: 0-0 3m+: 0-0
Track:	LH: 0-1 RH: 0-1 Tight: 0-0 Gall: 0-1
Aids:	Bl: 0-0 Vi: 0-0 Tstrap: 0-0 Ckp: 0-0
Best Rating:	58 3/04 Hntg 2m10y good NHF

Primaticcio (IRE)

9-y-o b g Priolo (USA)-Martinova (Martinmas)
Ian Williams Ian Williams

Placings:04/2/1111-P   (4143)
2003/04: 25ᴾG,

	Starts	1st	2nd	3rd	Win & Pl
Chases	1	0	0	0	
Career Total	8	4	1	0	27096
126 6/02 Strf	3m4f	B Ch		G-F	£17680
125 5/02 Folk	2m5f	H Ch		GD	£1976
110 5/02 Winc	2m5f	H Ch		G-F	£3575
104 5/02 Chel	2m5f	H Ch		G-F	£2821
			Total win prize-money £26053		

Going:	Sf: 0-0 GS: 0-0 Gd: 0-1 GF: - Fm: 0-0
Distance:	2m/2m3: 0-0 2m4-2m7: 0-0 3m+: 0-0
Track:	LH: 0-0 RH: 0-0 Tight: 0-0 Gall: 0-0
Aids:	Bl: 0-1 Vi: 0-0 Tstrap: 0-0 Ckp: 0-0
Best Rating:	126 6/02 Strf 3m4f gd-fm Ch

Progressive hunter chaser back in 2002; completed a four-timer when winning the Justitia Champion Hunters Chase at Stratford June 2002; pulled up on first outing since at Ludlow in March; stays 3m4f; likes fast ground, wears headgear.

Prime Attraction
85+

7-y-o gr m Primitive Rising (USA)-My Friend Melody (Sizzling Melody)
W M Brisbourne Positive Partners

Placings:*100/12*U-F   (1608)
2003/04: 20FGF,

	Starts	1st	2nd	3rd	Win & Pl
Hurdles	1	0	0	0	
Career Total	7	2	1	0	3856
103	6/02 Hexm 2m110y H NHF			GD	£1547
83	7/01 Uttx 2m H NHF			G-F	£1470
			Total win prize-money £3017		

Going:	Sf: 0-0 GS: 0-0 Gd: 0-0 GF: - Fm: 0-1
Distance:	2m/2m3: 0-0 2m4-2m7: 0-0 3m+: 0-0
Track:	LH: 0-0 RH: 0-1 Tight: 0-0 Gall: 0-1
Aids:	Bl: 0-0 Vi: 0-0 Tstrap: 0-0 Ckp: 0-0
Best Rating:	103 6/02 Hexm 2m110y good NHF

Prime Minister
102   85

10-y-o ch g Be My Chief (USA)-Classic Design (Busted)
G E Jones G Elwyn Jones

Placings:P/6045/33P04-545   (0517)
2003/04: 17PGS, 174GF, 195G,

	Starts	1st	2nd	3rd	Win & Pl
Hurdles	3	0	0	0	264
Career Total	13	0	0	2	988

Going:	Sf: 0-0 GS: 0-1 Gd: 0-1 GF: - Fm: 0-0
Distance:	2m/2m3: 0-3 2m4-2m7: 0-0 3m+: 0-0
Track:	LH: 0-1 RH: 0-2 Tight: 0-1 Gall: 0-0
Aids:	Bl: 0-0 Vi: 0-0 Tstrap: 0-0 Ckp: 0-0
Best Rating:	82 5/03 Strf 2m3f good Hdl

Plating-class hurdler, acts on fast ground; does not truly stay 2m.

Primitive Jean

5-y-o b m Primitive Rising (USA)-Gemma Jean (Derek H)
C W Fairhurst David Bartlett

Placings:0P   (3034)
2003/04: 16QG, 16PGS,

	Starts	1st	2nd	3rd	Win & Pl
NH Flat	1	0	0	0	0
Hurdles	1	0	0	0	0
Career Total	2	0	0	0	

Going:	Sf: 0-0 GS: 0-1 Gd: 0-1 GF: - Fm: 0-0
Distance:	2m/2m3: 0-2 2m4-2m7: 0-0 3m+: 0-0
Track:	LH: 0-2 RH: 0-0 Tight: 0-0 Gall: 0-0
Aids:	Bl: 0-0 Vi: 0-0 Tstrap: 0-0 Ckp: 0-0

Best Rating:	61	11/03 Hexm 2m110y	good	NHF

Primitive Rites

7-y-o b g Primitive Rising (USA)-Sun Goddess (FR) (Deep Roots)
M J Brown M J Brown

Placings:P   (3723)
2003/04: 25PS,

	Starts	1st	2nd	3rd	Win & Pl
Chases	1	0	0	0	
Career Total	1	0	0	0	

Going:	Sf: 0-1 GS: 0-0 Gd: 0-0 GF: - Fm: 0-0
Distance:	2m/2m3: 0-0 2m4-2m7: 0-0 3m+: 0-0
Track:	LH: 0-1 RH: 0-0 Tight: 0-0 Gall: 0-0
Aids:	Bl: 0-1 Vi: 0-0 Tstrap: 0-0 Ckp: 0-0

Primitive Satin

9-y-o ch g Primitive Rising (USA)-Satinanda (Leander)
Mrs R Tate R Tate

Placings:PU41/25-F   (4607)
2003/04: 25FGS,

	Starts	1st	2nd	3rd	Win & Pl
Chases	1	0	0	0	
Career Total	7	1	1	0	2227
80	4/02 Hexm 3m1f	H Ch		GD	£1566
			Total win prize-money £1567		

Going:	Sf: 0-0 GS: 0-1 Gd: 0-0 GF: - Fm: 0-0
Distance:	2m/2m3: 0-0 2m4-2m7: 0-0 3m+: 0-1
Track:	LH: 0-0 RH: 0-1 Tight: 0-0 Gall: 0-0
Aids:	Bl: 0-1 Vi: 0-0 Tstrap: 0-0 Ckp: 0-0
Best Rating:	80 5/02 Hexm 3m1f gd-sft Ch

Primitive Way

12-y-o b g Primitive Rising (USA)-Potterway (Velvet Prince)
Miss S E Forster (C Storey 20/3) The Hon Gerald Maitland-Carew

Placings:6213353P04P2/440-5512P3256   (4851)
2003/04: 255G, 255G, 251GF, 272G, 27PG, 243F, 242HY, 255G, 275GS,

	Starts	1st	2nd	3rd	Win & Pl
Chases	9	1	2	1	4171
Career Total	24	2	4	4	14667
87	10/03 Hexm 3m1f	F(0-100)HCh		G-F	£2586
90	10/01 Kels 3m1f	E Ch		G-F	£3201
			Total win prize-money £5788		

Going:	Sf: 0-1 GS: 0-1 Gd: 0-5 GF: - Fm: 1-2
Distance:	2m/2m3: 0-0 2m4-2m7: 0-0 **3m+: 1-9**
Track:	**LH: 1-8** RH: 0-1 Tight: 0-5 Gall: 0-1
Aids:	Bl: 0-2 Vi: 0-0 Tstrap: 0-0 **Ckp: 1-7**
Best Rating:	104 4/02 Hexm 3m1f good Ch

Modest hunter chaser; acts on fast ground; stays three miles plus.

Primrose Hill
14

11-y-o b m Lord David S (USA)-Country Carnival (Town And Country)

Ms A E Embiricos
D Wilsher

Placings:0/PPOP/0   (0672)
2003/04: 21QGF,

	Starts	1st	2nd	3rd	Win & Pl
Hurdles	1	0	0	0	
Career Total	6	0	0	0	

Going:	Sf: 0-0 GS: 0-0 Gd: 0-0 GF: - Fm: 0-1
Distance:	2m/2m3: 0-0 2m4-2m7: 0-1 3m+: 0-0
Track:	LH: 0-1 RH: 0-0 Tight: 0-0 Gall: 0-0
Aids:	Bl: 0-0 Vi: 0-0 Tstrap: 0-0 Ckp: 0-0
Best Rating:	36 5/98 Sedg 2m5f110y good Hdl

Prince Adjal (IRE)
84   89+

4-y-o b g Desert Prince (IRE)-Adjalisa (IRE) (Darshaan)
G M Moore J & M Leisure / Unos Restaurant

Placings:1002   (2839)
2003/04: 161F, 16QG, 16QGF, 162GS,

	Starts	1st	2nd	3rd	Win & Pl
Hurdles	4	1	1	0	3558
Career Total	4	1	1	0	3558
89	10/03 Kels 2m	D Hdl		FRM	£2996
			Total win prize-money £2996		

Going:	Sf: 0-0 GS: 0-1 Gd: 0-1 GF: - Fm: 1-2
Distance:	**2m/2m3: 1-4** 2m4-2m7: 0-0 3m+: 0-0
Track:	LH: 0-3 RH: 0-0 Tight: 0-1 Gall: 0-0
Aids:	Bl: 0-0 Vi: 0-0 Tstrap: 0-0 Ckp: 0-0
Best Rating:	89 12/03 Uttx 2m gd-sft Hdl

Sprinter on the Flat; made all to win unchallenged on hurdling debut at Kelso in October; runner-up in poor seller at Uttoxeter in December; acts on any ground.

Prince Among Men
108   116+

7-y-o b g Robellino (USA)-Forelino (USA) (Trempolino (USA))
N G Richards Jim Ennis

Placings:1212/330/12341-31105   (4911)
2003/04: 163G, 161GF, 161G, 179GF, 165S,

	Starts	1st	2nd	3rd	Win & Pl
Hurdles	5	2	0	1	18734
Career Total	17	6	3	4	35018
116	7/03 Prth	2m110y C(0-130)HHdl		GD	£12017
110	6/03 Uttx	2m E(0-110)HHdl		G-F	£6148
111	4/03 MRas	2m1f110y G Hdl		G-F	£2517
104	11/02 Hrfd	2m1f G Hdl		GD	£2261
106	10/00 Ludl	2m E Hdl		G-F	£2807
106	8/00 Worc	2m E Hdl		G-F	£2775
			Total win prize-money £28527		

Going:	Sf: 0-1 GS: 0-0 Gd: 1-2 GF: - Fm: 1-2
Distance:	**2m/2m3: 2-5** 2m4-2m7: 0-0 3m+: 0-0
Track:	LH: 1-2 RH: 1-3 Tight: 0-1 Gall: 0-0
Aids:	Bl: 0-1 Vi: 0-0 Tstrap: 0-0 Ckp: 0-0
Best Rating:	116 7/03 Prth 2m110y good Hdl

Fair hurdler; suited by trips of around two miles and handles cut in the ground, but looks better on a sound surface; consistent.

Prince Aurum

9-y-o ch g Mystiko (USA)-Jarin Rose (IRE) (Jareer (USA))
B G Powell Miss Sheila Smith

Placings:00   (3448)
2003/04: 18⁰HY, 17⁰GS,

	Starts	1st	2nd	3rd	Win & Pl
Hurdles	2	0	0	0	
Career Total	**2**	**0**	**0**	**0**	

Going: Sf: 0-1 GS: 0-1 Gd: 0-0 GF: - Fm: 0-0
Distance: 2m/2m3: 0-2 2m4-2m7: 0-0 3m+: 0-0
Track: LH: 0-1 RH: 0-1 Tight: 0-2 Gall: 0-0
Aids: Bl: 0-0 Vi: 0-0 Tstrap: 0-0 Ckp: 0-0

Prince Darkhan (IRE)

8-y-o br g Doyoun-Sovereign Dona (Sovereign Path)
G A Harker Malcolm Smith

Placings:F/P   (0802)
2003/04: 17ᴾG,

	Starts	1st	2nd	3rd	Win & Pl
Hurdles	1	0	0	0	
Career Total	**2**	**0**	**0**	**0**	

Going: Sf: 0-0 GS: 0-0 Gd: 0-1 GF: - Fm: 0-0
Distance: 2m/2m3: 0-1 2m4-2m7: 0-0 3m+: 0-0
Track: LH: 0-1 RH: 0-0 Tight: 0-0 Gall: 0-0
Aids: Bl: 0-0 Vi: 0-0 Tstrap: 0-0 Ckp: 0-0

Prince De Galles

93   84

11-y-o b g Prince Des Coeurs (USA)-Royal Brush (King Of Spain)
P Bowen Homebred Racing

Placings:0/2600221U30P/FFF04506/501P44P-4304PP   (1474)
2003/04: 24⁴S, 24³GF, 26⁹GF, 24⁴GF, 24ᴾGF, 22ᴾF,

	Starts	1st	2nd	3rd	Win & Pl
Hurdles	6	0	0	1	744
Career Total	**33**	**2**	**3**	**2**	**10552**
93	6/02 Uttx	3m110y	E(0-105)HHdl	SFT	£2660
97	11/00 Ludl	3m	F(0-105)HHdl	GD	£3493

Total win prize-money £6154

Going: Sf: 0-1 GS: 0-0 Gd: 0-0 GF: - Fm: 0-5
Distance: 2m/2m3: 0-0 2m4-2m7: 0-1 3m+: 0-5
Track: LH: 0-5 RH: 0-1 Tight: 0-0 Gall: 0-0
Aids: Bl: 0-5 Vi: 0-0 Tstrap: 0-0 Ckp: 0-0
Best Rating: 99 6/00 Uttx 2m4f110y good Hdl

Moderate handicap hurdler; best in soft ground; stays well; needs blinkers.

Prince Dimitri

80   106d

5-y-o ch g Desert King (IRE)-Pinta (IRE) (Ahonoora)
M C Pipe Lucayan Stud

Placings:1F024-P0506   (3251)
2003/04: 16ᴾGF, 16ᴾGF, 20⁵GF, 16⁹G, 16ᴾGS,

	Starts	1st	2nd	3rd	Win & Pl
Hurdles	5	0	0	0	
Career Total	**10**	**1**	**1**	**0**	**5308**
110	12/02 Wwck	2m	E Hdl	SFT	£3213

Total win prize-money £3213

Going: Sf: 0-0 GS: 0-1 Gd: 0-1 GF: - Fm: 0-3
Distance: 2m/2m3: 0-4 2m4-2m7: 0-1 3m+: 0-0

Track: LH: 0-3 RH: 0-2 Tight: 0-0 Gall: 0-0
Aids: Bl: 0-0 Vi: 0-1 Tstrap: 0-2 Ckp: 0-2
Best Rating: 110 1/03 Wwck 2m heavy Hdl

Moderate hurdler hurdler; effective on soft ground; has worn a visor.

Prince Du Soleil (FR)

74   85

8-y-o b g Cardoun (FR)-Revelry (FR) (Blakeney)
J R Jenkins Mrs Wendy Jenkins

Placings:6/5   (2113)
2003/04: 16⁵G,

	Starts	1st	2nd	3rd	Win & Pl
Hurdles	1	0	0	0	0
Career Total	**2**	**0**	**0**	**0**	**0**

Going: Sf: 0-0 GS: 0-0 Gd: 0-1 GF: - Fm: 0-0
Distance: 2m/2m3: 0-1 2m4-2m7: 0-0 3m+: 0-0
Track: LH: 0-1 RH: 0-0 Tight: 0-1 Gall: 0-0
Aids: Bl: 0-0 Vi: 0-0 Tstrap: 0-0 Ckp: 0-0
Best Rating: 84 11/03 Fknm 2m good Hdl

Prince Holing

4-y-o ch g Halling (USA)-Ella Mon Amour (Ela-Mana-Mou)
Miss Venetia Williams (J H M Gosden 24/8) FF Racing Services Partnership X

Placings:P   (3711)
2003/04: 16ᴾS,

	Starts	1st	2nd	3rd	Win & Pl
Hurdles	1	0	0	0	
Career Total	**1**	**0**	**0**	**0**	

Going: Sf: 0-1 GS: 0-0 Gd: 0-0 GF: - Fm: 0-0
Distance: 2m/2m3: 0-1 2m4-2m7: 0-0 3m+: 0-0
Track: LH: 0-0 RH: 0-1 Tight: 0-0 Gall: 0-0
Aids: Bl: 0-0 Vi: 0-0 Tstrap: 0-0 Ckp: 0-0

Prince Ivor

4-y-o b g Polar Falcon (USA)-Mistook (USA) (Phone Trick (USA))
J C Fox (R Hannon 8/9) Mitchell Block

Placings:P   (4368)
2003/04: 16ᴾGF,

	Starts	1st	2nd	3rd	Win & Pl
Hurdles	1	0	0	0	
Career Total	**1**	**0**	**0**	**0**	

Going: Sf: 0-0 GS: 0-0 Gd: 0-0 GF: - Fm: 0-1
Distance: 2m/2m3: 0-1 2m4-2m7: 0-0 3m+: 0-0
Track: LH: 0-1 RH: 0-0 Tight: 0-1 Gall: 0-0
Aids: Bl: 0-0 Vi: 0-0 Tstrap: 0-0 Ckp: 0-0

Prince Millennium

6-y-o b g First Trump-Petit Point (IRE) (Petorius)
R A Fahey G Morrill

Placings:0   (1208)

2003/04: 17⁰G,

	Starts	1st	2nd	3rd	Win & Pl
Hurdles	1	0	0	0	
Career Total	**1**	**0**	**0**	**0**	

Going: Sf: 0-0 GS: 0-0 Gd: 0-1 GF: - Fm: 0-0
Distance: 2m/2m3: 0-1 2m4-2m7: 0-0 3m+: 0-0
Track: LH: 0-1 RH: 0-0 Tight: 0-1 Gall: 0-0
Aids: Bl: 0-0 Vi: 0-0 Tstrap: 0-0 Ckp: 0-0

Prince Nasseem (GER)

7-y-o b h Neshad (USA)-Penola (GER) (Acatenango (GER))
A G Juckes Whispering Winds

Placings:5   (2512)
2003/04: 19⁰GS,

	Starts	1st	2nd	3rd	Win & Pl
Hurdles	1	0	0	0	0
Career Total	**1**	**0**	**0**	**0**	**0**

Going: Sf: 0-0 GS: 0-1 Gd: 0-0 GF: - Fm: 0-0
Distance: 2m/2m3: 0-0 2m4-2m7: 0-0 3m+: 0-0
Track: LH: 0-0 RH: 0-1 Tight: 0-0 Gall: 0-0
Aids: Bl: 0-0 Vi: 0-0 Tstrap: 0-0 Ckp: 0-0

Prince Of Perils

105   88+

10-y-o b g Lord Bud-Kumari Peril (Rebel Prince)
J S Haldane John & Mary Stenhouse

Placings:0/F061   (4390)
2003/04: 25ᶠG, 20⁰HY, 17⁶HY, 27¹G,

	Starts	1st	2nd	3rd	Win & Pl
Hurdles	3	1	0	0	2359
Chases	1	0	0	0	0
Career Total	**88**	**1**	**0**	**0**	**2359**
88	3/04 Sedg	3m3f110yG(0-90)HHdl		GD	£2359

Total win prize-money £2359

Going: Sf: 0-2 GS: 0-0 Gd: 1-2 GF: - Fm: 0-0
Distance: 2m/2m3: 0-1 2m4-2m7: 0-1 **3m+: 1-2**
Track: **LH: 1-3** RH: 0-1 **Tight: 1-1** Gall: 0-1
Aids: Bl: 0-0 Vi: 0-0 Tstrap: 0-0 Ckp: 0-0
Best Rating: 88 3/04 Sedg 3m3f110y good Hdl

Point winner in the past; wide margin winner of selling handicap at Sedgefield in March; stays really well; suited by soft ground.

Prince Of Persia

95   96+

4-y-o b g Turtle Island (IRE)-Sianiski (Niniski (USA))
R S Brookhouse (R C Guest 8/4) R S Brookhouse

Placings:F64415   (4915)
2003/04: 16ᶠG, 16⁶GS, 16⁴GS, 16⁴GS, 16¹G, 16⁵GS,

	Starts	1st	2nd	3rd	Win & Pl
Hurdles	6	1	0	0	3748
Career Total	**6**	**1**	**0**	**0**	**3748**
87	4/04 Ludl	2m	G Hdl	GD	£3454

Total win prize-money £3455

Going: Sf: 0-0 GS: 0-4 Gd: 1-2 GF: - Fm: 0-0
Distance: **2m/2m3: 1-6** 2m4-2m7: 0-0 3m+: 0-0
Track: LH: 0-4 **RH: 1-2** Tight: 0-3 Gall: 0-1
Aids: Bl: 0-0 Vi: 0-0 Tstrap: 0-0 **Ckp: 1-2**

Best Rating: 96 4/04 Worc 2m gd-sft Hdl

Moderate performer at up to a mile on the Flat; moderate hurdler; effective over two miles; successful in cheekpieces; acts on good.

Prince Of Saints (IRE)

13-y-o ch g Boyne Valley-Sandy's Daughter (Raise You Ten)
Miss L Ingram Miss L Ingram

Placings:0/6005/F112P311/6FP01P/3/PP/5   (0389)
2003/04: 25[5]G,

	Starts	1st	2nd	3rd	Win & Pl
Chases	1	0	0	0	0
Career Total	23	5	1	2	16096
108	3/99	Catt	2m	E(0-115)HCh	SFT	£2726
112	4/98	Weth	2m	E(0-115)HCh	GD	£3119
112	3/98	Catt	2m	E(0-115)HCh	G-S	£2765
107	12/97	Catt	2m	F(0-105)HCh	G-S	£2556
103	11/97	Catt	2m	E(0-100)HCh	SFT	£2950

Total win prize-money £14116

Going: Sf: 0-0 GS: 0-0 Gd: 0-1 GF: - Fm: 0-0
Distance: 2m/2m3: 0-0 2m4-2m7: 0-0 3m+: 0-1
Track: LH: 0-1 RH: 0-0 Tight: 0-0 Gall: 0-0
Aids: Bl: 0-1 Vi: 0-0 Tstrap: 0-0 Ckp: 0-0
Best Rating: 115 2/98 Newc 2m110y good Ch

Prince Of Slane
98f   100f

5-y-o b g Prince Daniel (USA)-Singing Slane (Cree Song)
G A Swinbank (C Grant 14/6) J H Richardson

Placings:2-534   (4962)
2003/04: 17[5]GF, 16[3]GF, 17[4]G,

	Starts	1st	2nd	3rd	Win & Pl
NH Flat	3	0	0	1	266
Career Total	4	0	1	1	846

Going: Sf: 0-0 GS: 0-0 Gd: 0-1 GF: - Fm: 0-0
Distance: 2m/2m3: 0-3 2m4-2m7: 0-0 3m+: 0-0
Track: LH: 0-1 RH: 0-2 Tight: 0-0 Gall: 0-0
Aids: Bl: 0-0 Vi: 0-0 Tstrap: 0-0 Ckp: 0-0
Best Rating: 100 4/03 MRas 2m1f110y good NHF

Moderate bumper performer; acts on a sound surface.

Prince Of The Wood (IRE)
99   87

4-y-o ch g Woodborough (USA)-Ard Dauphine (IRE) (Forest Wind (USA))
A Bailey (D J S Cosgrove 2/8) The Four Of Us

Placings:356   (2871)
2003/04: 16[3]G, 16[5]GS, 16[6]S,

	Starts	1st	2nd	3rd	Win & Pl
Hurdles	3	0	0	1	529
Career Total	3	0	0	1	529

Going: Sf: 0-1 GS: 0-0 Gd: 0-1 GF: - Fm: 0-0
Distance: 2m/2m3: 0-3 2m4-2m7: 0-0 3m+: 0-0
Track: LH: 0-2 RH: 0-1 Tight: 0-0 Gall: 0-1
Aids: Bl: 0-0 Vi: 0-0 Tstrap: 0-0 Ckp: 0-0
Best Rating: 87 11/03 Hntg 2m110y gd-sft Hdl

Plating-class on the level; just fair form so far over hurdles; seems best on good ground.

Prince Sandrovitch (IRE)
93   59

10-y-o b g Camden Town-Devon Royale (Le Prince)
Mrs Jane Galpin Mrs C D Farmer

Placings:5/264135/P-P6P6   (4933)
2003/04: 26[8]GS, 22[6]HY, 25[5]G, 26[6]G,

	Starts	1st	2nd	3rd	Win & Pl
Chases	4	0	0	0	0
Career Total	12	1	1	1	3836
96	2/00	Chep	2m110y	E Hdl	SFT	£2824

Total win prize-money £2825

Going: Sf: 0-1 GS: 0-1 Gd: 0-2 GF: - Fm: 0-0
Distance: 2m/2m3: 0-0 2m4-2m7: 0-0 3m+: 0-3
Track: LH: 0-1 RH: 0-0 Tight: 0-3 Gall: 0-0
Aids: Bl: 0-0 Vi: 0-0 Tstrap: 0-0 Ckp: 0-1
Best Rating: 102 3/00 Chep 2m110y gd-sft Hdl

Prince Shaamaal
97   90

6-y-o b g Shaamit (IRE)-Princess Alaska (Northern State (USA))
K Bell The Upshire Racing Partnership

Placings:U05-0   (0135)
2003/04: 16[5]G,

	Starts	1st	2nd	3rd	Win & Pl
Hurdles	1	0	0	0	0
Career Total	4	0	0	0	0

Going: Sf: 0-0 GS: 0-0 Gd: 0-1 GF: - Fm: 0-0
Distance: 2m/2m3: 0-1 2m4-2m7: 0-0 3m+: 0-0
Track: LH: 0-0 RH: 0-1 Tight: 0-0 Gall: 0-0
Aids: Bl: 0-0 Vi: 0-0 Tstrap: 0-0 Ckp: 0-0
Best Rating: 90 5/03 Ludl 2m good Hdl

Prince Slayer
99   91

8-y-o b g Batshoof-Top Sovereign (High Top)
T P McGovern Ahmed Abdel-Khaleq

Placings:2P3/6/63-046004   (4752)
2003/04: 16[9]GF, 16[4]GF, 16[6]GS, 16[9]GS, 16[9]S, 16[4]G,

	Starts	1st	2nd	3rd	Win & Pl
Hurdles	6	0	0	0	0
Career Total	12	0	1	2	1644

Going: Sf: 0-1 GS: 0-2 Gd: 0-1 GF: - Fm: 0-2
Distance: 2m/2m3: 0-6 2m4-2m7: 0-0 3m+: 0-0
Track: LH: 0-6 RH: 0-0 Tight: 0-4 Gall: 0-0
Aids: Bl: 0-0 Vi: 0-0 Tstrap: 0-0 Ckp: 0-0
Best Rating: 103 2/01 Plum 2m soft Hdl

Plating-class novice hurdler; still a maiden; has been tried in cheekpieces.

Prince Sorinieres (FR)
102   125

9-y-o br g Valanjou (FR)-Somewhat Better (Rheingold)
M C Pipe The Arthur White Partnership

Placings:11/111F422F30/P/P/5P1-2346P   (0868)
2003/04: 23[2]G, 25[3]GF, 23[4]GF, 24[6]G, 26[6]GF,

	Starts	1st	2nd	3rd	Win & Pl
Chases	5	0	1	1	4682
Career Total	22	6	3	2	51192
125	4/03	Tntn	3m	D(0-120)HCh	FRM	£7020
	8/99	Mesl	2m1f110y	Ch	SFT	£4306
	6/99	Toul	2m1f110y	Ch	GD	£4844
	5/99	Mesl	2m1f110y	Ch	SFT	£3767
	3/99	Toul	2m1f110y	Hdl	VS	£11841
	3/99	Chol	2m1f	Hdl	VS	£3229

Total win prize-money £35007

Going: Sf: 0-0 GS: 0-0 Gd: 0-2 GF: - Fm: 0-3
Distance: 2m/2m3: 0-0 2m4-2m7: 0-0 3m+: 0-5
Track: LH: 0-3 RH: 0-1 Tight: 0-2 Gall: 0-0
Aids: Bl: 0-0 Vi: 0-1 Tstrap: 0-0 Ckp: 0-0
Best Rating: 138 11/99 Towc 2m110y good Ch

Prince Zar (IRE)
78   68

4-y-o b g Inzar (USA)-Salonniere (FR) (Bikala)
A M Hales (C G Cox 6/6) J Smith

Placings:56   (1583)
2003/04: 16[5]GF, 16[6]GF,

	Starts	1st	2nd	3rd	Win & Pl
Hurdles	2	0	0	0	0
Career Total	2	0	0	0	0

Going: Sf: 0-0 GS: 0-0 Gd: 0-0 GF: - Fm: 0-2
Distance: 2m/2m3: 0-2 2m4-2m7: 0-0 3m+: 0-0
Track: LH: 0-0 RH: 0-2 Tight: 0-0 Gall: 0-2
Aids: Bl: 0-1 Vi: 0-0 Tstrap: 0-2 Ckp: 0-0
Best Rating: 68 10/03 Hntg 2m110y gd-fm Hdl

Princess Aimee

4-y-o b f Wizard King-Off The Air (IRE) (Taufan (USA))
P Bowen Eamonn O'Malley

Placings:PP   (3512)
2003/04: 16[6]G, 18[6]G,

	Starts	1st	2nd	3rd	Win & Pl
Hurdles	2	0	0	0	0
Career Total	2	0	0	0	0

Going: Sf: 0-0 GS: 0-0 Gd: 0-2 GF: - Fm: 0-0
Distance: 2m/2m3: 0-2 2m4-2m7: 0-0 3m+: 0-0
Track: LH: 0-2 RH: 0-0 Tight: 0-2 Gall: 0-0
Aids: Bl: 0-0 Vi: 0-0 Tstrap: 0-0 Ckp: 0-0

Princess Claudia (IRE)
97   75

6-y-o b m Kahyasi-Shamarra (FR) (Zayyani)
M F Harris M Harris

Placings:244-20P434043   (1291)
2003/04: 21[5]S, 20[9]GF, 20[6]G, 22[4]GF, 22[3]GF, 22[4]GF, 17[9]GF, 27[4]GF, 22[3]GF,

	Starts	1st	2nd	3rd	Win & Pl
Hurdles	9	0	1	2	2310
Career Total	12	0	2	2	3785

Going:	Sf: 0-1 GS: 0-0 Gd: 0-2 GF: - Fm: 0-6
Distance:	2m/2m3: 0-1 2m4-2m7: 0-7 3m+: 0-1
Track:	LH: 0-7 RH: 0-1 Tight: 0-7 Gall: 0-0
Aids:	Bl: 0-0 Vi: 0-0 Tstrap: 0-0 Ckp: 0-0
Best Rating:	89 3/03 Plum 2m gd-fm Hdl

Maiden hurdler; beaten in sellers at up to 3m 3f.

Princess Faith

61   **8**

4-y-o b f Polar Prince (IRE)-Crissem (IRE) (Thatching)
A J Chamberlain   Mrs S L Routley

Placings:4F   (2226)
2003/04: 17⁴GF, 16ᶠGS,

	Starts	1st	2nd	3rd	Win & Pl
Hurdles	2	0	0	0	0
Career Total	2	0	0	0	0

Going:	Sf: 0-0 GS: 0-0 Gd: 0-0 GF: - Fm: 0-0
Distance:	2m/2m3: 0-2 2m4-2m7: 0-0 3m+: 0-0
Track:	LH: 0-0 RH: 0-2 Tight: 0-0 Gall: 0-0
Aids:	Bl: 0-0 Vi: 0-0 Tstrap: 0-0 Ckp: 0-0

Princess Gillie

59f   **77f**

5-y-o br m Prince Daniel (USA)-Gilmanscleuch (IRE) (Mandalus)
Mrs J K M Oliver   Miss J S Peat

Placings:00   (4316)
2003/04: 17⁰G, 16⁰GF,

	Starts	1st	2nd	3rd	Win & Pl
NH Flat	2	0	0	0	
Career Total	2	0	0	0	

Going:	Sf: 0-0 GS: 0-0 Gd: 0-0 GF: 0-1 Fm: 0-1
Distance:	2m/2m3: 0-2 2m4-2m7: 0-0 3m+: 0-0
Track:	LH: 0-1 RH: 0-1 Tight: 0-0 Gall: 0-0
Aids:	Bl: 0-0 Vi: 0-0 Tstrap: 0-0 Ckp: 0-0
Best Rating:	77 3/04 Ayr 2m gd-fm NHF

Princess Magdalena

84   **38**

4-y-o ch f Pennekamp (USA)-Reason To Dance (Damister (USA))
L G Cottrell   Eric Gadsden

Placings:0P0   (4854)
2003/04: 16⁰G, 16ᴾGS, 17⁰GS,

	Starts	1st	2nd	3rd	Win & Pl
Hurdles	3	0	0	0	
Career Total	3	0	0	0	

Going:	Sf: 0-0 GS: 0-1 Gd: 0-1 GF: - Fm: 0-1
Distance:	2m/2m3: 0-3 2m4-2m7: 0-0 3m+: 0-0
Track:	LH: 0-1 RH: 0-2 Tight: 0-1 Gall: 0-0
Aids:	Bl: 0-0 Vi: 0-0 Tstrap: 0-0 Ckp: 0-0
Best Rating:	46 12/03 Wwck 2m good Hdl

Middle-distance plater on the Flat; did not jump that well on hurdles debut; suited by a sound surface.

Princess Stephanie

73   **55**

6-y-o b m Shaab-Waterloo Princess (IRE) (Le Moss)

M J Gingell   Dave (Ben) Heath

Placings:0-00030   (2114)
2003/04: 16⁰G, 17⁰GF, 16⁹GF, 19³GF, 16⁰G,

	Starts	1st	2nd	3rd	Win & Pl
NH Flat	1	0	0	0	
Hurdles	4	0	0	1	423
Career Total	6	0	0	1	423

Going:	Sf: 0-0 GS: 0-0 Gd: 0-0 GF: - Fm: 0-3
Distance:	2m/2m3: 0-4 2m4-2m7: 0-1 3m+: 0-0
Track:	LH: 0-3 RH: 0-2 Tight: 0-3 Gall: 0-0
Aids:	Bl: 0-0 Vi: 0-1 Tstrap: 0-0 Ckp: 0-0
Best Rating:	58 7/03 Worc 2m good NHF

Princess Tessa

                   66+

8-y-o b m King's Ride-Kathy Cook (Glenstal (USA))
N A Twiston-Davies   M P Wareing

Placings:240/3   (2823)
2003/04: 21³GF,

	Starts	1st	2nd	3rd	Win & Pl
Hurdles	1	0	0	1	632
Career Total	4	0	1	1	1137

Going:	Sf: 0-0 GS: 0-0 Gd: 0-0 GF: - Fm: 0-1
Distance:	2m/2m3: 0-0 2m4-2m7: 0-1 3m+: 0-0
Track:	LH: 0-0 RH: 0-1 Tight: 0-0 Gall: 0-0
Aids:	Bl: 0-0 Vi: 0-0 Tstrap: 0-0 Ckp: 0-0
Best Rating:	93 12/01 Towc 2m heavy NHF

Off the track for two years prior to finishing third in a novices' hurdle in December 2003.

Princesse Grec (FR)

96(102h)   (78h)**72**

6-y-o ch m Grand Tresor (FR)-Perimele (FR) (Mon Fils)
Dr P Pritchard   The Honfleur Syndicate

Placings:00P0P00/4256200PPU56-24332P403F   (2944)
2003/04: 20²G, 16⁴GF, 21³GF, 16³GS, 21²GF, 23ᶠGF, 18⁴GF, 22⁰G, 17³F, 20ᶠS,

	Starts	1st	2nd	3rd	Win & Pl
Chases	10	0	2	3	6031
Career Total	29	0	4	3	7679

Going:	Sf: 0-1 GS: 0-1 Gd: 0-2 GF: - Fm: 0-6
Distance:	2m/2m3: 0-4 2m4-2m7: 0-5 3m+: 0-1
Track:	LH: 0-6 RH: 0-2 Tight: 0-5 Gall: 0-0
Aids:	Bl: 0-0 Vi: 0-0 Tstrap: 0-0 Ckp: 0-0
Best Rating:	78 8/02 Strf 2m110y gd-sft Hdl

Plating-class chaser; outclassed when picking up place money in small races in the summer of 2003; stays two miles five.

Priory Wood

83   (41h)**77**

8-y-o ch m Gunner B-Penlea Lady (Leading Man)
M Sheppard   Mrs S G Addinsell

Placings:100/P-P4P   (3223)
2003/04: 21ᴾGS, 16⁴GS, 19ᴾGS,

	Starts	1st	2nd	3rd	Win & Pl
Hurdles	1	0	0	0	
Chases	2	0	0	0	199
Career Total	7	1	0	0	1795
	87	12/01	Hrfd	2m1f	H NHF	SFT	£1596

Total win prize-money £1596

Going:	Sf: 0-0 GS: 0-3 Gd: 0-0 GF: - Fm: 0-0
Distance:	2m/2m3: 0-2 2m4-2m7: 0-1 3m+: 0-0
Track:	LH: 0-0 RH: 0-3 Tight: 0-0 Gall: 0-0
Aids:	Bl: 0-0 Vi: 0-0 Tstrap: 0-0 Ckp: 0-0
Best Rating:	87 12/01 Hrfd 2m1f soft NHF

Pristeen Spy

92   **72**

7-y-o b g Teenoso (USA)-Sikera Spy (Harvest Spirit)
R Ford   D W Heys

Placings:P40   (0473)
2003/04: 24ᴾS, 20⁴GS, 17⁰GS,

	Starts	1st	2nd	3rd	Win & Pl
Hurdles	3	0	0	0	380
Career Total	3	0	0	0	380

Going:	Sf: 0-1 GS: 0-2 Gd: 0-0 GF: - Fm: 0-0
Distance:	2m/2m3: 0-1 2m4-2m7: 0-1 3m+: 0-1
Track:	LH: 0-3 RH: 0-0 Tight: 0-3 Gall: 0-0
Aids:	Bl: 0-0 Vi: 0-1 Tstrap: 0-0 Ckp: 0-0
Best Rating:	72 5/03 Ctml 2m1f110y gd-sft Hdl

Private Benjamin

89   **99**

4-y-o gr g Ridgewood Ben-Jilly Woo (Environment Friend)
Jamie Poulton   Mrs J Wotherspoon

Placings:10   (1827)
2003/04: 16¹GF, 16⁰GF,

	Starts	1st	2nd	3rd	Win & Pl
Hurdles	2	1	0	0	3445
Career Total	2	1	0	0	3445
	99	9/03	Plum	2m	D Hdl	G-F	£3445

Total win prize-money £3445

Going:	Sf: 0-0 GS: 0-0 Gd: 0-0 GF: - Fm: 1-2
Distance:	2m/2m3: 1-2 2m4-2m7: 0-0 3m+: 0-0
Track:	LH: 1-2 RH: 0-0 Tight: 1-1 Gall: 0-0
Aids:	Bl: 0-0 Vi: 0-0 Tstrap: 0-0 Ckp: 0-0
Best Rating:	99 9/03 Plum 2m gd-fm Hdl

Winning juvenile hurdler; acts on fast ground.

Private Pete

11-y-o ch g Gunner B-Vedra (IRE) (Carlingford Castle)
Lady Connell   Sir Michael Connell

Placings:P/1/30-3   (0364)
2003/04: 26³HY,

	Starts	1st	2nd	3rd	Win & Pl
Chases	1	0	0	1	1028
Career Total	5	1	0	2	3389
	91	3/02	Leic	2m7f110yH Ch	SFT	£2138

Total win prize-money £2139

Going:	Sf: 0-1 GS: 0-0 Gd: 0-0 GF: - Fm: 0-0
Distance:	2m/2m3: 0-0 2m4-2m7: 0-0 3m+: 0-1
Track:	LH: 0-1 RH: 0-0 Tight: 0-0 Gall: 0-0
Aids:	Bl: 0-0 Vi: 0-0 Tstrap: 0-0 Ckp: 0-0
Best Rating:	91 2/03 Folk 3m1f soft Ch

Hunter chaser/ pointer; acts on soft ground.

Prize Ring

104   **97**

5-y-o ch g Bering-Spot Prize (USA) (Seattle Dancer (USA))
G M Moore (Mrs J R Ramsden 15/8) Gordon Brown/bert
Watson

Placings:161064   (4799)
2003/04: 17¹GF, 16⁶G, 17¹G, 17⁹G, 16⁶G, 17⁴G,

	Starts	1st	2nd	3rd	Win & Pl
Hurdles	6	2	0	0	6026
Career Total	6	2	0	0	6026
97	9/03	Sedg	2m1f	E Hdl	GD	2527
82	9/03	Sedg	2m1f	E Hdl	G-F	3104
				Total win prize-money	£5631

Going:	Sf: 0-0 GS: 0-0 Gd: 1-5 GF: - Fm: 1-1
Distance:	2m/2m3: 2-6 2m4-2m7: 0-0 3m+: 0-0
Track:	LH: 2-5 RH: 0-1 Tight: 2-5 Gall: 0-0
Aids:	Bl: 0-0 Vi: 0-0 Tstrap: 0-0 Ckp: 0-0
Best Rating:	97 10/03 Sedg 2m1f good Hdl

Plating-class on the level; has won two novice races over
hurdles to date, both at Sedgefield in September; stays two
miles one; acts on fast ground.

Pro Bono (IRE)

14-y-o ch g Tale Quale-Quality Suite (Prince Hansel)
M G Hazell W F Caudwell

Placings:00030100/4F3P2521/F3PU321/31U4P/34315U/P
654/02F2P36/14/PPP-P   (0032)
2003/04: 25ᴾG,

	Starts	1st	2nd	3rd	Win & Pl
Chases	1	0	0	0	
Career Total	51	6	5	8	20775
96	5/01	Strf	3m	H Ch	G-F	£3374
104	2/99	Fknm	2m5f110yH Ch		G-S	£2168
100	2/98	Fknm	2m5f110yH Ch		GD	£2158
100	4/97	Chel	2m110y H Ch		G-F	£2190
98	3/96	Fknm	2m5f110yH Ch		G-F	£2440
107	4/95	Thur	2m	Hdl	GD	£2204
				Total win prize-money	£14536

Going:	Sf: 0-0 GS: 0-0 Gd: 0-1 GF: - Fm: 0-0
Distance:	2m/2m3: 0-0 2m4-2m7: 0-0 3m+: 0-1
Track:	LH: 0-1 RH: 0-0 Tight: 0-0 Gall: 0-1
Aids:	Bl: 0-0 Vi: 0-0 Tstrap: 0-0 Ckp: 0-0
Best Rating:	110 5/98 Sthl 2m4f110y good Ch

Probus Lady

85   **65**

7-y-o ch m Good Times (ITY)-Decoyanne (Decoy Boy)
C J Down E G M Beard

Placings:P-04   (0970)
2003/04: 22¹⁰GF, 17⁴GS,

	Starts	1st	2nd	3rd	Win & Pl
Hurdles	2	0	0	0	317
Career Total	3	0	0	0	317

Going:	Sf: 0-0 GS: 0-1 Gd: 0-0 GF: - Fm: 0-1
Distance:	2m/2m3: 0-1 2m4-2m7: 0-1 3m+: 0-0
Track:	LH: 0-2 RH: 0-0 Tight: 0-2 Gall: 0-0
Aids:	Bl: 0-0 Vi: 0-0 Tstrap: 0-0 Ckp: 0-0
Best Rating:	65 7/03 NAbb 2m1f gd-sft Hdl

Probus Lord

102   **104**

9-y-o b g Rough Stones-Decoyanne (Decoy Boy)

C J Down E G M Beard

Placings:05/P/0P2-F2   (0611)
2003/04: 27²S, 24⁴GF, 26²GF,

	Starts	1st	2nd	3rd	Win & Pl
Hurdles	3	0	2	0	2086
Career Total	8	0	2	0	2086

Going:	Sf: 0-1 GS: 0-0 Gd: 0-0 GF: - Fm: 0-2
Distance:	2m/2m3: 0-0 2m4-2m7: 0-0 3m+: 0-3
Track:	LH: 0-2 RH: 0-0 Tight: 0-1 Gall: 0-0
Aids:	Bl: 0-0 Vi: 0-0 Tstrap: 0-0 Ckp: 0-0
Best Rating:	104 6/03 Hrfd 3m2f gd-fm Hdl

Moderate chaser; runner-up in stamina test run in soft
ground at Newton Abbot in April 2003 and again over 3m 2f
on fast ground at Hereford in June.

Procedure (USA)

(88c)   (89c)

8-y-o b/br g Strolling Along (USA)-Bold Courtesan (USA)
(Bold Bidder)
J A B Old W E Sturt

Placings:60206/3P-P   (0150)
2003/04: 21ᴾS, 16ᴾGF,

	Starts	1st	2nd	3rd	Win & Pl
Hurdles	1	0	0	0	0
Chases	1	0	0	0	0
Career Total	8	0	1	1	1485

Going:	Sf: 0-1 GS: 0-0 Gd: 0-0 GF: - Fm: 0-1
Distance:	2m/2m3: 0-1 2m4-2m7: 0-1 3m+: 0-0
Track:	LH: 0-2 RH: 0-0 Tight: 0-1 Gall: 0-0
Aids:	Bl: 0-0 Vi: 0-0 Tstrap: 0-0 Ckp: 0-0
Best Rating:	109 1/02 Tntn 2m1f soft Hdl

Profiler (USA)

(71h)   (24h) **75**

9-y-o b g Capote (USA)-Magnificent Star (USA) (Silver
Hawk (USA))
Ferdy Murphy Miss J V Morgan

Placings:55/2046444/0U1F1/PPPP3U/6PU3BP0-00 (2511)
2003/04: 24⁹GF, 18⁰S,

	Starts	1st	2nd	3rd	Win & Pl
Hurdles	1	0	0	0	0
Chases	1	0	0	0	0
Career Total	29	2	1	2	7248
96	1/01	Donc	2m4f	E Hdl	GD	£2254
111	10/00	Folk	2m	E Ch	G-F	£2808
				Total win prize-money	£5062

Going:	Sf: 0-1 GS: 0-0 Gd: 0-0 GF: - Fm: 0-1
Distance:	2m/2m3: 0-1 2m4-2m7: 0-0 3m+: 0-1
Track:	LH: 0-1 RH: 0-1 Tight: 0-1 Gall: 0-1
Aids:	Bl: 0-0 Vi: 0-0 Tstrap: 0-0 Ckp: 0-2
Best Rating:	111 10/00 Folk 2m gd-fm Ch

Profowens (IRE)

103f   **93f**

6-y-o b g Welsh Term-Cutty Sark (Strong Gale)
P Beaumont Trevor Hemmings

Placings:020   (4050)
2003/04: 16⁹S, 16²HY, 16⁹G,

	Starts	1st	2nd	3rd	Win & Pl
NH Flat	3	0	1	0	576
Career Total	3	0	1	0	576

Progressive (IRE)

111f   **113+f**

6-y-o ch g Be My Native (USA)-Move Forward (Deep Run)
Jonjo O'Neill John P McManus

Placings:1   (2912)
2003/04: 16¹GS,

	Starts	1st	2nd	3rd	Win & Pl
NH Flat	1	1	0	0	1645
Career Total	1	1	0	0	1645
113	12/03	Hntg	2m110y	H NHF	G-S	£1645
				Total win prize-money	£1645

Going:	Sf: 0-0 GS: 1-1 Gd: 0-0 GF: - Fm: 0-0
Distance:	2m/2m3: 1-1 2m4-2m7: 0-0 3m+: 0-0
Track:	LH: 0-0 RH: 1-1 Tight: 0-0 Gall: 1-1
Aids:	Bl: 0-0 Vi: 0-0 Tstrap: 0-0 Ckp: 0-0
Best Rating:	113 12/03 Hntg 2m110y gd-sft NHF

Fair bumper performer; acts on easy ground.

Prokofiev (USA)

102(112h)   (125+h)**123**

8-y-o br g Nureyev (USA)-Aviara (USA) (Cox's Ridge (USA))
Jonjo O'Neill Mrs Sylvia Darlington

Placings:14/5520010/52350344/616305P1-11PP51P0
                                                     (4871)
2003/04: 20¹G, 20¹G, 22ᴾGS, 24ᴾGF, 23⁵G, 22¹G, 24ᴾGS, 24⁰S,

	Starts	1st	2nd	3rd	Win & Pl
Chases	8	3	0	0	20639
Career Total	33	7	2	3	56452
123	3/04	Newb	2m6f110yC(0-125)HCh		GD	£9048
123	10/03	Bang	2m4f110yD(0-125)HCh		GD	£5570
114	10/03	Bang	2m4f110yD Ch		GD	£6020
125	4/03	Bang	3m	D(0-120)HHdl	G-F	£5619
125	12/02	Band	2m6f	C(0-120)HHdl	SFT	£7442
134	2/01	Newc	2m4f	B(0-140)HHdl	HVY	£6366
109	12/99	Wwck	2m	C Hdl	SFT	£5912
				Total win prize-money	£45980

Going:	Sf: 0-1 GS: 0-2 Gd: 3-4 GF: - Fm: 0-1
Distance:	2m/2m3: 0-0 2m4-2m7: 3-4 3m+: 0-4
Track:	LH: 3-5 RH: 0-3 Tight: 2-4 Gall: 1-2
Aids:	Bl: 3-8 Vi: 0-0 Tstrap: 0-0 Ckp: 0-0
Best Rating:	134 2/01 Newc 2m4f heavy Hdl

Fair hurdler/novice chaser; won three of his six outings over
fences; enigmatic and not a straightforward ride; needs at
least two miles four; acts on most types of ground; has worn
a tongue tie and usually wears blinkers.

Prominent Profile (IRE)

110   **123**

11-y-o ch g Mazaad-Nakuru (IRE) (Mandalus)
N A Twiston-Davies The Son Partnership

Placings:1011303⁴/13FU4/050U50/U1P4-2U1B221052
                                                     (4951)
2003/04: 17²G, 22ᵁGS, 20¹G, 16⁸GS, 20²G, 18²S, 24¹G, 24⁰G, 24⁵G, 24²GS,

	Starts	1st	2nd	3rd	Win & Pl
Chases	10	2	4	0	31214

Career Total	33	7	4	3		62578
123 2/04 Sand	3m110y B(0-140)HCh				GD	£12046
114 11/03 Aint	2m4f D(0-125)HCh				GD	£6162
104 12/02 Newb	2m2f110yD(0-120)HCh				GD	£6162
135 10/99 Chep	2m3f110yD Ch				SFT	£4182
146 1/99 Weth	2m4f110yD Hdl				SFT	£3038
132 12/98 Chep	2m110y A NHF				HVY	£6280
115 10/98 Chel	2m110y H NHF				G-S	£1940
			Total win prize-money £39811			

Going: Sf: 0-1 GS: 0-3 Gd: 2-6 GF: - Fm: 0-0
Distance: 2m2/m3: 0-3 2m4-2m7: 1-3 3m+: 1-4
Track: LH: 1-8 RH: 1-2 **Tight: 1-2** Gall: 0-4
Aids: Bl: 0-0 Vi: 0-0 Tstrap: 0-0 Ckp: 0-0
Best Rating: 146 1/99 Weth 2m4f110y soft   Hdl

Fair chaser, former very useful novice hurdler; effective at up to two and a half miles; acts on soft ground; has worn blinkers; likes to dominate.

Promises

71f   68f

4-y-o b/br f Nashwan (USA)-Balliasta (USA) (Lyphard (USA))
D Shaw Mrs Jackie Cornwell

Placings:050   (3426)
2003/04: 12⁰GF, 13⁵GF, 17⁹HY,

	Starts	1st	2nd	3rd	Win & Pl
NH Flat	3	0	0	0	0
Career Total	3	0	0	0	0

Going: Sf: 0-1 GS: 0-0 Gd: 0-0 GF: - Fm: 0-2
Distance: 2m2/m3: 0-1 2m4-2m7: 0-0 3m+: 0-0
Track: LH: 0-1 RH: 0-1 Tight: 0-1 Gall: 0-0
Aids: Bl: 0-0 Vi: 0-0 Tstrap: 0-0 Ckp: 0-0
Best Rating: 71 11/03 Donc 1m5f   gd-fm NHF

Promising (FR)

101   75

6-y-o ch m Ashkalani (IRE)-Sea Thunder (Salse (USA))
M C Chapman Mrs S M Richards

Placings:4620F0-3504   (1001)
2003/04: 16³GF, 17⁵GF, 17⁰GF, 19⁴G,

	Starts	1st	2nd	3rd	Win & Pl
Hurdles	4	0	0	1	835
Career Total	10	0	1	1	1515

Going: Sf: 0-0 GS: 0-0 Gd: 0-1 GF: - Fm: 0-3
Distance: 2m2/m3: 0-4 2m4-2m7: 0-0 3m+: 0-0
Track: LH: 0-3 RH: 0-1 Tight: 0-3 Gall: 0-0
Aids: Bl: 0-0 Vi: 0-0 Tstrap: 0-4 Ckp: 0-0
Best Rating: 75 6/03 MRas 2m1f110y gd-fm Hdl

Plating-class hurdler; effective over two miles on good ground.

Proper Posh

6-y-o b m Rakaposhi King-Rim Of Pearl (Rymer)
Mrs H Dalton W D Hockenhull

Placings:00PP   (4511)
2003/04: 17⁰GS, 16⁰HY, 21⁶GS, 20⁶GS,

	Starts	1st	2nd	3rd	Win & Pl
NH Flat	2	0	0	0	0
Hurdles	2	0	0	0	0
Career Total	4	0	0	0	

Going: Sf: 0-0 GS: 0-1 Gd: 0-3 GF: - Fm: 0-0

Going: Sf: 0-1 GS: 0-3 Gd: 0-0 GF: - Fm: 0-0
Distance: 2m2/m3: 0-2 2m4-2m7: 0-2 3m+: 0-0
Track: LH: 0-2 RH: 0-1 Tight: 0-0 Gall: 0-0
Aids: Bl: 0-0 Vi: 0-0 Tstrap: 0-0 Ckp: 0-0
Best Rating: 81 1/04 Tntn 2m1f   gd-sft NHF

Proper Squire (USA)

105(107h)   (122 h)122

7-y-o b g Bien Bien (USA)-La Cumbre (Sadler's Wells (USA))
C J Mann The Icy Fire Partnership

Placings:214P/1313400-132F333F   (4861)
2003/04: 24¹GF, 25³G, 26²GF, 26⁶GF, 24³GF, 32³GF, 30³G, 33⁶GS,

	Starts	1st	2nd	3rd	Win & Pl
Chases	8	1	1	4	14556
Career Total	19	4	2	6	30857
106 5/03 Fknm	3m110y E Ch			G-F	£5007
121 11/02 Kemp	3m110y D(0-120)HHdl			GD	£5330
112 5/02 Font	2m6f110yE(0-110)HHdl			G-F	£2562
110 12/01 Strf	2m6f110yE Hdl			SFT	£3125
		Total win prize-money £16026			

Going: Sf: 0-0 GS: 0-1 Gd: 0-2 GF: - Fm: 1-5
Distance: 2m2/m3: 0-0 2m4-2m7: 0-0 **3m+: 1-8**
Track: **LH: 1-6** RH: 0-0 Tight: 1-3 Gall: 0-1
Aids: Bl: 0-0 Vi: 0-0 Tstrap: 0-0 Ckp: 0-1
Best Rating: 122 3/04 Extr 3m6f110y good   Ch

Fair novice chaser; formerly a useful handicap hurdler; has performed creditably since being switched to fences; probably stays four miles; best on fast ground, but acts on softer; has been tried in blinkers and cheekpieces.

Property Zone

(0c)102

6-y-o b g Cool Jazz-Prime Property (IRE) (Tirol)
C Grant Mrs A Meller

Placings:60554/06F332141-P   (0286)
2003/04: 16⁶GS,

	Starts	1st	2nd	3rd	Win & Pl
Hurdles	1	0	0	0	
Career Total	15	2	1	2	13300
102 4/03 Prth	2m110y D(0-120)HHdl			GD	£7104
99 3/03 Donc	2m110y E(0-105)HHdl			G-S	£3552
		Total win prize-money £10657			

Going: Sf: 0-0 GS: 0-1 Gd: 0-0 GF: - Fm: 0-0
Distance: 2m2/m3: 0-1 2m4-2m7: 0-0 3m+: 0-0
Track: LH: 0-1 RH: 0-0 Tight: 0-1 Gall: 0-0
Aids: Bl: 0-0 Vi: 0-0 Tstrap: 0-0 Ckp: 0-0
Best Rating: 102 4/03 Prth 2m110y good   Hdl

Plating-class hurdler; acts on good to soft ground; effective over two miles.

Protection Money

97   82

4-y-o ch g Hector Protector (USA)-Three Piece (Jaazeiro (USA))
Mrs M Reveley P D Savill

Placings:0U52   (4401)
2003/04: 16⁰GS, 16⁴U, 16⁵G, 21²G,

	Starts	1st	2nd	3rd	Win & Pl
Hurdles	4	0	1	0	698
Career Total	4	0	1	0	698

Going: Sf: 0-0 GS: 0-1 Gd: 0-3 GF: - Fm: 0-0

Showed first signs of ability in poor seller; stays 21f; acts on good.

Protector

60   10

7-y-o b g Be My Chief (USA)-Clicquot (Bold Lad (IRE))
C J Price Dextra Lighting Systems

Placings:3125/4025205/0   (0081)
2003/04: 16⁰GS,

	Starts	1st	2nd	3rd	Win & Pl
Hurdles	1	0	0	0	
Career Total	12	1	3	1	5503
102 9/00 Font	2m2f110yE Hdl			GD	£2275
		Total win prize-money £2275			

Going: Sf: 0-0 GS: 0-1 Gd: 0-0 GF: - Fm: 0-0
Distance: 2m2/m3: 0-1 2m4-2m7: 0-0 3m+: 0-0
Track: LH: 0-1 RH: 0-0 Tight: 0-0 Gall: 0-0
Aids: Bl: 0-0 Vi: 0-0 Tstrap: 0-0 Ckp: 0-0
Best Rating: 109 9/00 Chep 2m110y good   Hdl

Protocol (IRE)

100   95

10-y-o b g Taufan (USA)-Ukraine's Affair (USA) (The Minstrel (CAN))
Mrs S Lamyman P Lamyman

Placings:43/2450422/006/246015500-05003014   (4603)
2003/04: 17⁰GF, 17⁵GF, 16⁶GF, 22⁶G, 17³G, 22⁰G, 16¹GS, 17⁴G,

	Starts	1st	2nd	3rd	Win & Pl
Hurdles	8	1	0	1	2982
Career Total	29	2	4	2	11071
93 3/04 Fknm	2m G(0-90)HHdl			G-S	£2716
99 12/02 MRas	2m1f110yG(0-95)HHdl			G-S	£2425
		Total win prize-money £5142			

Going: Sf: 0-0 GS: 1-1 Gd: 0-4 GF: - Fm: 0-3
Distance: **2m2/m3: 1-6** 2m4-2m7: 0-2 3m+: 0-0
Track: **LH: 1-2** RH: 0-4 **Tight: 1-5** Gall: 0-0
Aids: Bl: 0-0 Vi: 0-0 **Tstrap: 1-7** Ckp: 0-1
Best Rating: 109 3/00 Donc 2m110y good   Hdl

Moderate hurdler; won a selling handicap hurdle at Market Rasen in December; acts on easy ground.

Proud Peer (IRE)

54f   88f

6-y-o ch g Mister Lord (USA)-Raffeen Pride (Shackleton)
M Pitman G C Stevens

Placings:55-0   (0087)
2003/04: 16⁰GS,

	Starts	1st	2nd	3rd	Win & Pl
NH Flat	1	0	0	0	
Career Total	3	0	0	0	0

Going: Sf: 0-0 GS: 0-1 Gd: 0-0 GF: - Fm: 0-0
Distance: 2m2/m3: 0-1 2m4-2m7: 0-0 3m+: 0-0
Track: LH: 0-1 RH: 0-0 Tight: 0-0 Gall: 0-0
Aids: Bl: 0-0 Vi: 0-0 Tstrap: 0-0 Ckp: 0-0
Best Rating: 88 1/03 Kemp 2m   gd-sft NHF

Provence Dreamer

94   76

7-y-o b g Alflora (IRE)-Kilbragh Dreamer (IRE) (Decent Fellow)
Jonjo O'Neill Mrs Jonjo O'Neill

Placings:22P53-P0P   (1012)
2003/04: 20PG, 19QG, 24PG,

	Starts	1st	2nd	3rd	Win & Pl
Hurdles	3	0	0	0	
Career Total	8	0	2	1	1655

Going:	Sf: 0-0 GS: 0-0 Gd: 0-3 GF: - Fm: 0-0
Distance:	2m/2m3: 0-1 2m4-2m7: 0-1 3m+: 0-1
Track:	LH: 0-3 RH: 0-0 Tight: 0-2 Gall: 0-0
Aids:	Bl: 0-0 Vi: 0-0 Tstrap: 0-0 Ckp: 0-0
Best Rating:	104 10/02 MRas 2m1f110y good NHF

Proverbial Gray

95   73

7-y-o ro m Norton Challenger-Clove Bud (Beau Charmeur (FR))
D R Gandolfo D R Gandolfo Ltd

Placings:500/506403S-2   (0082)
2003/04: 16²GS,

	Starts	1st	2nd	3rd	Win & Pl
Hurdles	1	0	1	0	756
Career Total	11	0	1	1	1109

Going:	Sf: 0-0 GS: 0-0 Gd: 0-0 GF: - Fm: 0-0
Distance:	2m/2m3: 0-1 2m4-2m7: 0-0 3m+: 0-0
Track:	LH: 0-1 RH: 0-0 Tight: 0-0 Gall: 0-0
Aids:	Bl: 0-0 Vi: 0-0 Tstrap: 0-0 Ckp: 0-0
Best Rating:	75 10/02 Bang 2m1f gd-sft Hdl

Plating-class hurdler; tends to pull hard; appreciates cut.

Provocative (FR)

108   129+

6-y-o b/br g Useful (FR)-All Blue (FR) (Noir Et Or)
M Todhunter Sir Robert Ogden

Placings:23-10130   (4595)
2003/04: 20¹GS, 20⁹GS, 20¹S, 24³S, 22⁰G,

	Starts	1st	2nd	3rd	Win & Pl
Hurdles	5	2	0	1	9559
Career Total	7	2	1	2	10440
125 12/03 Ayr	2m4f	E Hdl		SFT	£3523
116 11/03 Carl	2m4f	E Hdl		G-S	£2735
				Total win prize-money £6259	

Going:	Sf: 1-2 GS: 1-2 Gd: 0-1 GF: - Fm: 0-0
Distance:	2m/2m3: 0-0 2m4-2m7: 2-3 3m+: 0-0
Track:	LH: 1-4 RH: 1-1 Tight: 0-1 Gall: 0-1
Aids:	Bl: 0-0 Vi: 0-0 Tstrap: 0-0 Ckp: 0-0
Best Rating:	125 12/03 Ayr 2m4f soft Hdl

Fair hurdler; showed ability in bumpers and has shown fair form over hurdles with victories over two and a half miles at Carlisle in November 2003 and at Ayr the following month; headstrong and disappointing since; suited by soft.

Prudish Lass

7-y-o b m Warcraft (USA)-Bella Delite (Uncle Pokey)
A J Lidderdale Goforbroke

Placings:0-P   (0058)

2003/04: 19PGS,

	Starts	1st	2nd	3rd	Win & Pl
Hurdles	1	0	0	0	
Career Total	2	0	0	0	

Going:	Sf: 0-0 GS: 0-1 Gd: 0-0 GF: - Fm: 0-0
Distance:	2m/2m3: 0-0 2m4-2m7: 0-1 3m+: 0-0
Track:	LH: 0-0 RH: 0-1 Tight: 0-0 Gall: 0-0
Aids:	Bl: 0-0 Vi: 0-0 Tstrap: 0-0 Ckp: 0-0

Puck Out (IRE)

110   139+

6-y-o ch g Topanoora-Prosaic Star (IRE) (Common Grounds)
C Roche John P McManus

Placings:714-102201   (4644)
2003/04: 16¹YS, 16⁰Y, 16²GF, 16²S, 16⁰S, 16¹G,

	Starts	1st	2nd	3rd	Win & Pl
Hurdles	6	2	2	0	38275
Career Total	9	4	2	0	47671
139 4/04 Aint	2m110y	A HHdl		GD	£26100
119 6/03 Rosc	2m	Hdl		Y-S	£5824
121 7/02 Gway	2m	Hdl		YLD	£5503
104 6/02 Baln	2m	NHF		SH	£3598
			Total win prize-money £41026		

Going:	Sf: 0-2 GS: 0-0 Gd: 1-1 GF: - Fm: 0-1
Distance:	2m/2m3: 2-6 2m4-2m7: 0-0 3m+: 0-0
Track:	LH: 1-1 RH: 0-3 Tight: 1-1 Gall: 0-0
Aids:	Bl: 0-0 Vi: 0-0 Tstrap: 0-0 Ckp: 0-0
Best Rating:	139 4/04 Aint 2m110y good Hdl

Useful Irish-trained hurdler; landed the Cordon Bleu Handicap Hurdle at Aintree; effective over two miles; effective with some give in the ground.

Pucks Court

71   43

7-y-o b g Nomadic Way (USA)-Miss Puck (Tepukei)
I A Brown W Brown

Placings:P00-6PP6   (4618)
2003/04: 17⁶G, 20⁰G, 22⁸PG, 21⁶G,

	Starts	1st	2nd	3rd	Win & Pl
Hurdles	4	0	0	0	0
Career Total	7	0	0	0	0

Going:	Sf: 0-0 GS: 0-0 Gd: 0-4 GF: - Fm: 0-0
Distance:	2m/2m3: 0-1 2m4-2m7: 0-3 3m+: 0-0
Track:	LH: 0-3 RH: 0-0 Tight: 0-2 Gall: 0-0
Aids:	Bl: 0-0 Vi: 0-0 Tstrap: 0-0 Ckp: 0-0
Best Rating:	43 10/03 Sedg 2m1f good Hdl

Pucks Way

74   41

5-y-o b g Nomadic Way (USA)-Adventurous Lady (Roman Warrior)
D G Bridgwater Miss E E Hill

Placings:5-5   (1987)
2003/04: 16⁰GF,

	Starts	1st	2nd	3rd	Win & Pl
Hurdles	1	0	0	0	0
Career Total	2	0	0	0	0

Going:	Sf: 0-0 GS: 0-0 Gd: 0-0 GF: - Fm: 0-0
Distance:	2m/2m3: 0-1 2m4-2m7: 0-0 3m+: 0-0

Pudlicott Mill (IRE)

53

5-y-o b g Definite Article-Mimining (Tower Walk)
M F Harris M Harris

Placings:P-F0P   (0507)
2003/04: 23⁶GF, 20⁰GF, 16⁶G,

	Starts	1st	2nd	3rd	Win & Pl
Hurdles	3	0	0	0	
Career Total	4	0	0	0	

Going:	Sf: 0-0 GS: 0-0 Gd: 0-1 GF: - Fm: 0-2
Distance:	2m/2m3: 0-1 2m4-2m7: 0-1 3m+: 0-1
Track:	LH: 0-3 RH: 0-0 Tight: 0-3 Gall: 0-0
Aids:	Bl: 0-0 Vi: 0-0 Tstrap: 0-0 Ckp: 0-0

Pulham Downe

9-y-o ch g Baron Blakeney-Dame Nellie (Dominion)
Mrs A L Tory Stan The Man's Gang

Placings:P   (4696)
2003/04: 19PG,

	Starts	1st	2nd	3rd	Win & Pl
Chases	1	0	0	0	
Career Total	1	0	0	0	

Going:	Sf: 0-0 GS: 0-0 Gd: 0-1 GF: - Fm: 0-0
Distance:	2m/2m3: 0-0 2m4-2m7: 0-1 3m+: 0-0
Track:	LH: 0-0 RH: 0-1 Tight: 0-0 Gall: 0-0
Aids:	Bl: 0-0 Vi: 0-0 Tstrap: 0-0 Ckp: 0-0

Punchy (IRE)

112(105h)   (115+h)112

8-y-o b/br g Freddie's Star-Baltimore Fox (IRE) (Arapahos (FR))
M C Pipe G-Force Partnership

Placings:1/20/12212256/P11P51125666   (3905)
2003/04: 22PG, 20¹S, 22¹GF, 20PG, 24⁵GF, 26¹GF, 23¹F, 24²GF, 20⁵F, 25⁶G, 19⁸GS, 24⁶GS,

	Starts	1st	2nd	3rd	Win & Pl
Hurdles	5	2	0	0	10474
Chases	7	2	1	0	12779
Career Total	23	7	6	0	36528
109 10/03 Extr	2m7f110yD	Ch		FRM	£5395
109 10/03 Uttx	3m2f	E Ch		G-F	£3577
115 5/03 Font	2m6f110yD(0-115)HHdl			G-F	£5070
115 5/03 Bang	2m4f	D(0-115)HHdl		SFT	£5404
108 10/01 Nabb	2m6f	E Hdl		G-F	£2912
107 5/01 Wwck	2m5f	E Hdl		G-F	£2950
112 4/00 Font	2m2f110yH	NHF		GD	£1998
			Total win prize-money £27308		

Going:	Sf: 1-1 GS: 0-2 Gd: 0-3 GF: - Fm: 3-6
Distance:	2m/2m3: 0-1 2m4-2m7: 2-5 3m+: 2-6
Track:	LH: 3-6 RH: 1-6 Tight: 2-5 Gall: 0-0
Aids:	Bl: 0-0 Vi: 0-0 Tstrap: 0-0 Ckp: 0-0
Best Rating:	115 10/03 Chel 3m110y gd-fm Ch

Modest novice chaser/fair hurdler; won twice over hurdles since joining Martin Pipe; won his first two races over fences; disappointing since; stays three miles; seems to require a sound surface, although is does act on soft ground; inconsistent.

Puntal (FR)

109(114h)   (146 h)149

8-y-o b g Bering-Saveur (Ardross)
M C Pipe   Terry Neill

Placings:32P2224/05600/1111F122010P-1211415UU1
     (4965)
2003/04: 16¹GF, 19²G, 20¹G, 20¹GS, 16⁴G, 16¹S, 20⁵S, 16⁴UG,
36⁰UG, 29¹GF,

	Starts	1st	2nd	3rd	Win & Pl
Chases	10	5	1	0	149171
Career Total	34	11	7	1	253099
148 4/04 Sand	3m5f110yA HCh			G-F	£87000
149 1/04 Asct	2m	C Ch		SFT	£8092
149 11/03 Newb	2m4f	A Ch		G-S	£16286
149 11/03 Chel	2m4f110yB Ch			GD	£16614
149 10/03 Chel	2m	C Ch		G-F	£10602
148 2/03 Kemp	2m	A Hdl		GD	£17400
149 7/02 MRas	2m1f110yB(0-140)HHdl			G-S	£23200
140 5/02 Strf	2m110y	D Hdl		G-F	£4322
134 5/02 Worc	2m	E Hdl		GD	£2709
124 5/02 Hrfd	2m1f	E Hdl		GD	£3188
122 5/02 Sthl	2m	D Hdl		GD	£3469
				Total win prize-money £192886	

Going:	Sf: 1-2 GS: 1-1 Gd: 1-4 GF: - Fm: 2-3
Distance:	2m/2m3: 2-4 2m4-2m7: 2-4 3m+: 1-2
Track:	LH: 3-6 RH: 2-4 Tight: 0-1 Gall: 3-4
Aids:	Bl: 0-0 Vi: 0-1 Tstrap: 1-4 Ckp: 0-0
Best Rating:	149 1/04 Asct 2m soft Ch

Smart novice chaser on his day; formerly useful hurdler; unseated his rider in the Arkle at Cheltenham; ran well until unseating in the Grand National; won the BetFred Gold Cup over 3m5f at Sandown; needs things his own way up front and can sulk; effective at 2m, but seemingly stays 3m5f; acts on most types of ground; has worn a visor and tongue tie.

Puppet King

64   65

5-y-o b g Mistertopogigo (IRE)-Bold Gift (Persian Bold)
A C Whillans   Jethart Justice

Placings:P0   (2145)
2003/04: 16⁶G, 16⁰G,

	Starts	1st	2nd	3rd	Win & Pl
Hurdles	2	0	0	0	
Career Total	2	0	0	0	

Going:	Sf: 0-0 GS: 0-0 Gd: 0-2 GF: - Fm: 0-0
Distance:	2m/2m3: 0-2 2m4-2m7: 0-0 3m+: 0-0
Track:	LH: 0-1 RH: 0-1 Tight: 0-0 Gall: 0-0
Aids:	Bl: 0-0 Vi: 0-0 Tstrap: 0-0 Ckp: 0-0
Best Rating:	66 11/03 Ayr 2m good Hdl

Pure Brief (IRE)

86(99h)   (82h)74

7-y-o b g Brief Truce (USA)-Epure (Bellypha)
Mrs J Candlish   Mrs V D Gandola-Gray

Placings:U000/1P5535-6U6P   (1216)
2003/04: 20⁶GF, 21ᵁGF, 21⁶GF, 16⁶GF,

	Starts	1st	2nd	3rd	Win & Pl
Hurdles	1	0	0	0	0
Chases	3	0	0	0	0
Career Total	14	1	0	1	4267
82 7/02 Uttx	2m	E(0-110)HHdl	G-F	£3770
			Total win prize-money £3770	

Going:	Sf: 0-0 GS: 0-0 Gd: 0-0 GF: - Fm: 0-4

Pure Fast Bellevue (FR)

7-y-o ch m Start Fast (FR)-Si Pure (FR) (Pure Flight (USA))
Jean-Rene Auvray   Lambourn Racing

Placings:FPP   (4483)
2003/04: 20⁰G, 19ᴾGS, 18ᴾG,

	Starts	1st	2nd	3rd	Win & Pl
Hurdles	3	0	0	0	
Career Total	3	0	0	0	

Going:	Sf: 0-0 GS: 0-1 Gd: 0-2 GF: - Fm: 0-0
Distance:	2m/2m3: 0-1 2m4-2m7: 0-2 3m+: 0-0
Track:	LH: 0-1 RH: 0-1 Tight: 0-2 Gall: 0-0
Aids:	Bl: 0-0 Vi: 0-0 Tstrap: 0-1 Ckp: 0-0

Pure Fun (IRE)

93(104h)   (109+h)66

7-y-o b g Lord Americo-Rath Caola (Neltino)
P J Hobbs   Miss I D Du Pre

Placings:F0055244/04140421-21653   (1014)
2003/04: 24²GF, 27¹G, 27⁶GF, 24⁵G, 23⁰G,

	Starts	1st	2nd	3rd	Win & Pl
Hurdles	4	1	1	0	7589
Chases	1	0	0	1	593
Career Total	21	4	3	1	22092
109 5/03 Strf	3m3f	D(0-125)HHdl	GD	£5382
105 4/03 Winc	2m6f	E(0-105)HHdl	FRM	£3542
109 10/02 Ludl	3m	D(0-115)HHdl	FRM	£5348
95 8/01 Worc	2m	H NHF	G-F	£1449
			Total win prize-money £15721	

Going:	Sf: 0-0 GS: 0-0 Gd: 1-3 GF: - Fm: 0-2
Distance:	2m/2m3: 0-0 2m4-2m7: 0-0 3m+: 1-5
Track:	LH: 1-4 RH: 0-1 Tight: 1-2 Gall: 0-0
Aids:	Bl: 0-0 Vi: 0-0 Tstrap: 0-0 Ckp: 0-0
Best Rating:	109 5/03 Strf 3m3f good Hdl

Fast ground bumper winner; appreciated step up to three miles when winning a three-runner race at Ludlow October 2002; good efforts in the summer of 2003; reported by his rider to have hung right-handed when well beaten third on chasing debut at Worcester August 2003.

Pure Mischief (IRE)

105   93

5-y-o b g Alhaarth (IRE)-Bellissi (IRE) (Bluebird (USA))
W M Brisbourne (M Todhunter 3/7) The Cartmel Syndicate

Placings:3U610-30U   (0792)
2003/04: 16³GF, 22⁰GS, 20ᵁG,

	Starts	1st	2nd	3rd	Win & Pl
Hurdles	3	0	0	1	370
Career Total	8	1	0	2	3413
90 3/03 Plum	2m	F Hdl	HVY	£2548
			Total win prize-money £2548	

Going:	Sf: 0-0 GS: 0-1 Gd: 0-1 GF: - Fm: 0-1
Distance:	2m/2m3: 0-1 2m4-2m7: 0-2 3m+: 0-0
Track:	LH: 0-2 RH: 1-1 Tight: 0-2 Gall: 0-0
Aids:	Bl: 0-0 Vi: 0-0 Tstrap: 0-0 Ckp: 0-0
Best Rating:	90 7/03 Prth 2m4f110y good Hdl

Distance: 2m/2m3: 0-1 2m4-2m7: 0-3 3m+: 0-0
Track: LH: 0-3 RH: 0-1 Tight: 0-1 Gall: 0-1
Aids: Bl: 0-0 Vi: 0-1 Tstrap: 0-1 Ckp: 0-1
Best Rating: 82   9/02   MRas   2m1f110y   gd-fm   Hdl

Winning claiming hurdler; suited by a tight track; acts on any ground.

Pure Platinum (IRE)

90   69

6-y-o gr g Roselier (FR)-Waterloo Ball (IRE) (Where To Dance (USA))
Jonjo O'Neill   Home Run Syndicate Ltd

Placings:3P00   (4167)
2003/04: 16³GS, 25ᴾGS, 19⁰G, 21⁰G,

	Starts	1st	2nd	3rd	Win & Pl
NH Flat	1	0	0	1	306
Hurdles	3	0	0	0	0
Career Total	4	0	0	1	306

Going:	Sf: 0-0 GS: 0-2 Gd: 0-2 GF: - Fm: 0-0
Distance:	2m/2m3: 0-3 2m4-2m7: 0-3 3m+: 0-1
Track:	LH: 0-3 RH: 0-1 Tight: 0-1 Gall: 0-1
Aids:	Bl: 0-0 Vi: 0-0 Tstrap: 0-0 Ckp: 0-0
Best Rating:	96 12/03 Uttx 2m gd-sft NHF

Well beaten third on debut at Uttoxeter in December; should stay well; held since.

Purple Patch

95f   95f

6-y-o b m Afzal-My Purple Prose (Rymer)
C L Popham   Mrs C C Scott

Placings:042   (4636)
2003/04: 16⁰G, 16⁴GS, 17²G,

	Starts	1st	2nd	3rd	Win & Pl
NH Flat	3	0	1	0	542
Career Total	3	0	1	0	542

Going:	Sf: 0-0 GS: 0-1 Gd: 0-2 GF: - Fm: 0-0
Distance:	2m/2m3: 0-3 2m4-2m7: 0-3 3m+: 0-0
Track:	LH: 0-1 RH: 0-1 Tight: 0-0 Gall: 0-0
Aids:	Bl: 0-0 Vi: 0-0 Tstrap: 0-0 Ckp: 0-0
Best Rating:	95 3/04 Wwck 2m gd-sft NHF

Moderate form in bumpers on good ground.

Purrfect Prince (IRE)

6-y-o b g Commanche Run-Castle Leney (Mandalus)
Jonjo O'Neill   Home Run Syndicate Ltd

Placings:06FPP   (4445)
2003/04: 16⁰GS, 16⁶HY, 20ᶠHY, 22ᴾG, 25ᴾS,

	Starts	1st	2nd	3rd	Win & Pl
NH Flat	2	0	0	0	0
Hurdles	3	0	0	0	0
Career Total	5	0	0	0	0

Going:	Sf: 0-3 GS: 0-1 Gd: 0-1 GF: - Fm: 0-0
Distance:	2m/2m3: 0-3 2m4-2m7: 0-2 3m+: 0-1
Track:	LH: 0-5 RH: 0-0 Tight: 0-1 Gall: 0-0
Aids:	Bl: 0-0 Vi: 0-0 Tstrap: 0-0 Ckp: 0-0
Best Rating:	79 1/04 Uttx 2m heavy NHF

Pyrrhic

79   60

5-y-o b g Salse (USA)-Bint Lariaaf (USA) (Diesis)

R M Flower M Lickert

Placings:55 (1457)
2003/04: 17⁵GF, 16⁵GF,

	Starts	1st	2nd	3rd	Win & Pl
Hurdles	2	0	0	0	0
Career Total	2	0	0	0	0

Going:	Sf: 0-0 GS: 0-0 Gd: 0-0 GF: - Fm: 0-2
Distance:	2m/2m3: 0-2 2m4-2m7: 0-0 3m+: 0-0
Track:	LH: 0-2 RH: 0-0 Tight: 0-1 Gall: 0-0
Aids:	Bl: 0-0 Vi: 0-0 Tstrap: 0-0 Ckp: 0-1
Best Rating:	60 9/03 Plum 2m gd-fm Hdl

Pythagoras

86(98h)   (81h)**74**
7-y-o ch g Kris-Tricorne (Green Desert (USA))
M Sheppard Mike Drake, Tim Doxsey, Ray Hitchin

Placings:2306/64-00400P (0885)
2003/04: 17⁰GS, 16⁵GF, 16⁴GF, 16⁶GF, 16⁰G, 16⁵G,

	Starts	1st	2nd	3rd	Win & Pl
Hurdles	3	0	0	0	0
Chases	3	0	0	0	313
Career Total	12	0	1	1	1222

Going:	Sf: 0-0 GS: 1-0 Gd: 0-2 GF: - Fm: 0-3
Distance:	2m/2m3: 0-6 2m4-2m7: 0-0 3m+: 0-0
Track:	LH: 0-4 RH: 0-2 Tight: 0-1 Gall: 0-0
Aids:	Bl: 0-0 Vi: 0-0 Tstrap: 0-0 Ckp: 0-2
Best Rating:	81 4/03 Uttx 2m good Hdl

Plating-class hurdler; acts on a sound surface.

Qabas (USA)

86   **73**
4-y-o b g Swain (IRE)-Classical Dance (CAN) (Regal Classic (CAN))
P R Webber (A C Stewart 25/10) Mrs Christine Painting

Placings:060 (4788)
2003/04: 16⁵GS, 16⁶GF, 16⁰G,

	Starts	1st	2nd	3rd	Win & Pl
Hurdles	3	0	0	0	0
Career Total	3	0	0	0	0

Going:	Sf: 0-0 GS: 0-1 Gd: 0-1 GF: - Fm: 0-1
Distance:	2m/2m3: 0-3 2m4-2m7: 0-0 3m+: 0-0
Track:	LH: 0-2 RH: 0-1 Tight: 0-2 Gall: 0-0
Aids:	Bl: 0-0 Vi: 0-0 Tstrap: 0-0 Ckp: 0-0
Best Rating:	72 3/04 Strf 2m110y gd-fm Hdl

Poor form in novice hurdles on varying ground.

Quabmatic

102   **104**
11-y-o b g Pragmatic-Good Skills (Bustino)
K Bishop Eric's Friends Racing Partnership

Placings:4/543533/540/426101/0/16P/PP03311B-0305630
(3906)
2003/04: 22⁸S, 20⁰S, 19³G, 22²GS, 19⁵S, 17⁵GS, 19⁸S, 19⁰GS,

	Starts	1st	2nd	3rd	Win & Pl
Hurdles	8	0	0	2	1161
Career Total	35	5	1	7	21445
104	3/03	Extr	2m1f	D(0-115)HHdl	GD	£4823
104	2/03	Tntn	2m3f110yE(0-110)HHdl	SFT	£4046
98	11/01	Uttx	2m4f110yE(0-115)HHdl	SFT	£2618
104	4/00	Extr	2m1f110yE(0-105)HHdl	HVY	£2928

---

104 3/00 Tntn 2m3f110yE(0-115)HHdl GD £3209
Total win prize-money £17625

Going:	Sf: 0-4 GS: 0-3 Gd: 0-1 GF: - Fm: 0-0
Distance:	2m/2m3: 0-4 2m4-2m7: 0-4 3m+: 0-0
Track:	LH: 0-2 RH: 0-6 Tight: 0-3 Gall: 0-0
Aids:	Bl: 0-0 Vi: 0-0 Tstrap: 0-0 Ckp: 0-0
Best Rating:	104 3/03 Extr 2m1f good Hdl

Moderate hurdler; stays two and a half miles; acts on ground good and softer.

Quainton Hills

106(89h)   (79h)**104+**
10-y-o b g Gildoran-Spin Again (Royalty)
D R Stoddart D R Stoddart

Placings:203/42F12U/4234/PP0-P31U022 (4113)
2003/04: 20⁰GF, 20³GS, 22¹S, 25⁰S, 23⁰S, 20²G, 23⁰GF,

	Starts	1st	2nd	3rd	Win & Pl
Hurdles	1	0	0	0	0
Chases	6	1	2	1	7004
Career Total	23	2	6	3	16674
100	11/03	Towc	2m6f	D(0-130)HCh	SFT	£3290
112	1/01	Leic	2m7f110yF	Ch	SFT	£2824

Total win prize-money £6114

Going:	Sf: 1-3 GS: 0-1 Gd: 0-1 GF: - Fm: 0-2
Distance:	2m/2m3: 0-0 **2m4-2m7: 1-5** 3m+: 0-2
Track:	LH: 0-1 **RH: 1-6** Tight: 0-0 Gall: 0-2
Aids:	Bl: 0-0 Vi: 0-0 Tstrap: 0-0 Ckp: 0-0
Best Rating:	112 1/01 Leic 2m7f110y soft Ch

Moderate chaser; stays three miles; acts on any ground; can be a sketchy jumper.

Qualicum (IRE)

5-y-o br g Son Of Sharp Shot (IRE)-Rugged Perk (IRE) (Executive Perk)
G Brown (J S Moore 15/12) Mrs Amanda Killick

Placings:0060P0 (3424)
2003/04: 16⁰G, 16⁸GF, 17⁵GF, 16⁶GS, 21⁵GS, 22⁰HY,

	Starts	1st	2nd	3rd	Win & Pl
NH Flat	3	0	0	0	0
Hurdles	3	0	0	0	0
Career Total	6	0	0	0	0

Going:	Sf: 0-1 GS: 0-2 Gd: 0-1 GF: - Fm: 0-2
Distance:	2m/2m3: 0-4 2m4-2m7: 0-2 3m+: 0-0
Track:	LH: 0-5 RH: 0-1 Tight: 0-3 Gall: 0-1
Aids:	Bl: 0-1 Vi: 0-0 Tstrap: 0-0 Ckp: 0-0
Best Rating:	66 7/03 Worc 2m good NHF

Qualitair Pleasure

82f   **84f**
4-y-o b f Slip Anchor-Qualitair Ridge (Indian Ridge)
J Hetherton Qualitair Holdings Limited

Placings:01 (4316)
2003/04: 16⁰G, 16¹GF,

	Starts	1st	2nd	3rd	Win & Pl
NH Flat	2	1	0	0	2086
Career Total	2	1	0	0	2086
84	3/04	Ayr	2m	H NHF	G-F	£2086

Total win prize-money £2086

Going:	Sf: 0-0 GS: 0-0 Gd: 0-0 GF: - Fm: 1-1
Distance:	**2m/2m3: 1-2** 2m4-2m7: 0-0 3m+: 0-0
Track:	**LH: 1-1** RH: 0-1 Tight: 0-1 Gall: 0-1

Aids:	Bl: 0-0 Vi: 0-0 Tstrap: 0-0 Ckp: 0-0
Best Rating:	84 3/04 Ayr 2m gd-fm NHF

Half-sister to Flat winners Cyber Santa and Indian Welcome; bettered debut effort by some way when winning Ayr bumper in March 2004; will be suited by further than two miles when sent over hurdles.

Quality First (IRE)

103(82h)   (111h)**133**
11-y-o b g Un Desperado (FR)-Vipsania (General Ironside)
Mrs H Dalton A N Dalton

Placings:5/R0L00/0001001513130F2F4/P4313204/4B2F01
042163-603 (4889)
2003/04: 20⁶G, 20⁰HY, 20³GF,

	Starts	1st	2nd	3rd	Win & Pl
Hurdles	1	0	0	0	0
Chases	2	0	1	0	2201
Career Total	46	7	4	6	73740
133	3/03	Bang	2m4f110yC(0-135)HCh	GD	£10595
127	1/03	Chel	2m5f	C(0-130)HCh	HVY	£11424
104	2/02	Navn	2m	(0-120)HHdl	SFT	£6349
125	11/00	Naas	2m	(0-130)HCh	Y-S	£4416
110	9/00	List	2m3f	Ch	HVY	£4968
116	8/00	Tral	2m4f	Ch	Y-S	£3864
75	6/00	Navn	2m	(0-102)HHdl	GD	£3312

Total win prize-money £44929

Going:	Sf: 0-1 GS: 0-0 Gd: 0-1 GF: - Fm: 0-1
Distance:	2m/2m3: 0-0 2m4-2m7: 0-3 3m+: 0-0
Track:	LH: 0-3 RH: 0-0 Tight: 0-2 Gall: 0-0
Aids:	Bl: 0-0 Vi: 0-0 Tstrap: 0-0 Ckp: 0-1
Best Rating:	133 4/03 Aint 2m5f110y good Ch

Fair chaser; ex-Irish; best over trips of around two and a half miles; suited by good ground or softer.

Quango

12-y-o b g Charmer-Quaranta (Hotfoot)
Miss J E Foster Miss J E Foster

Placings:105/3202412P3014/52P4332403P/000/5 (0416)
2003/04: 22⁵G,

	Starts	1st	2nd	3rd	Win & Pl
Chases	1	0	0	0	0
Career Total	30	3	5	5	16461
112	4/98	Sedg	2m110y	D Ch	G-S	£4081
114	12/97	Sedg	2m1f	E(0-110)HHdl	SFT	£2582
97	1/97	Carl	2m1f	E Hdl	GD	£2108

Total win prize-money £8772

Going:	Sf: 0-0 GS: 0-0 Gd: 0-1 GF: - Fm: 0-0
Distance:	2m/2m3: 0-0 2m4-2m7: 0-1 3m+: 0-0
Track:	LH: 0-0 RH: 0-1 Tight: 0-1 Gall: 0-0
Aids:	Bl: 0-0 Vi: 0-0 Tstrap: 0-0 Ckp: 0-1
Best Rating:	114 1/98 Donc 2m110y good Hdl

Quarter Masters (IRE)

91(105h)   (93h)**90**
5-y-o b g Mujadil (USA)-Kentucky Wildcat (Be My Guest (USA))
G M Moore The Dowdstown Boy'S

Placings:P601300P-P26F022U6 (4616)
2003/04: 21⁵G, 17²GF, 16⁶S, 19⁶GS, 16⁰G, 21²GS, 20²S, 20⁰HY, 21⁸G,

	Starts	1st	2nd	3rd	Win & Pl
Hurdles	2	0	1	0	546

Chases	7	0	2	0		3220
Career Total	**17**	**1**	**3**	**1**		**7209**
93 11/02 Ayr	2m	E Hdl		SFT	£2989
				Total win prize-money £2989

Going:	Sf: 0-3 GS: 0-2 Gd: 0-3 GF: - Fm: 0-1
Distance:	2m/2m3: 0-4 2m4-2m7: 0-5 3m+: 0-0
Track:	LH: 0-9 RH: 0-0 Tight: 0-5 Gall: 0-2
Aids:	Bl: 0-0 Vi: 0-0 Tstrap: 0-0 Ckp: 0-1
Best Rating:	93 11/03 Sedg 2m1f gd-fm Hdl

Plating-class hurdler/chaser; stays two miles five; acts on soft and fast ground.

Quarterstaff
107   121+
10-y-o b g Charmer-Quaranta (Hotfoot)
C R Wilson Mrs J Wilson (durham)

Placings:36P/2C33P2/23U21-15F2   (4726)
2003/04: 25¹G, 24⁵G, 24⁶G, 24²G,

	Starts	1st	2nd	3rd	Win & Pl
Chases	4	1	1	0	12600
Career Total	**18**	**2**	**5**	**4**	**28365**
116 4/03 Kels	3m1f	C(0-130)HCh	GD	£8190
106 3/03 Carl	3m	D(0-115)HCh	GD	£8612
		Total win prize-money £16803

Going:	Sf: 0-0 GS: 0-0 Gd: 1-4 GF: - Fm: 0-0
Distance:	2m/2m3: 0-0 2m4-2m7: 0-0 **3m+:** 1-4
Track:	**LH:** 1-1 RH: 0-3 Tight: 1-1 Gall: 0-0
Aids:	Bl: 0-0 Vi: 0-0 Tstrap: 0-0 Ckp: 0-0
Best Rating:	121 4/04 Carl 3m good Ch

Moderate chaser; stays three miles one; acts on good ground; not the most reliable jumper.

Quatrain (IRE)
96f   80f
4-y-o ch g Anshan-Gray's Ellergy (Oats)
D R Gandolfo Starlight Racing

Placings:400   (4199)
2003/04: 12⁴S, 16⁸S, 16⁹G,

	Starts	1st	2nd	3rd	Win & Pl
NH Flat	3	0	0	0	0
Career Total	**3**	**0**	**0**	**0**	**0**

Going:	Sf: 0-2 GS: 0-0 Gd: 0-1 GF: - Fm: 0-0
Distance:	2m/2m3: 0-0 2m4-2m7: 0-0 3m+: 0-0
Track:	LH: 0-1 RH: 0-1 Tight: 0-0 Gall: 0-2
Aids:	Bl: 0-0 Vi: 0-0 Tstrap: 0-0 Ckp: 0-0
Best Rating:	80 3/04 Newb 2m110y good NHF

Some ability in bumpers.

Quazar (IRE)
122   157
6-y-o b g Inzar (USA)-Evictress (IRE) (Sharp Victor (USA))
Jonjo O'Neill C D Carr

Placings:1111P12011/32010104-12245400   (4646)
2003/04: 16¹YS, 16²GF, 20²G, 16⁴S, 16⁵G, 20⁴G, 21⁰G, 20⁰G,

	Starts	1st	2nd	3rd	Win & Pl
Hurdles	8	1	2	0	73825
Career Total	**26**	**10**	**4**	**1**	**260500**
157 5/03 Punc	2m	Hdl	Y-S	£52597
152 3/03 Hayd	2m4f	B HHdl	GD	£15065
146 1/03 Hayd	2m4f	B HHdl	G-S	£10933
137 4/02 Punc	2m	Hdl	GD	£41901
137 4/02 Aint	2m110y	A Hdl	GD	£58000
132 1/02 Wwck	2m	B Hdl	SFT	£8736

---

117 11/01 Weth	2m	A Hdl	GD	£10627
116 10/01 Chel	2m110y	B Hdl	GD	£6857
108 9/01 Bang	2m1f	D Hdl	GD	£3402
89 8/01 Bang	2m1f	E Hdl	GD	£3052
			Total win prize-money £211173

Going:	Sf: 0-1 GS: 0-0 Gd: 0-5 GF: - Fm: 0-1
Distance:	**2m/2m3:** 1-4 2m4-2m7: 0-4 3m+: 0-0
Track:	LH: 0-3 **RH:** 1-4 Tight: 0-2 Gall: 0-2
Aids:	Bl: 0-0 Vi: 0-0 **Tstrap:** 1-7 Ckp: 0-1
Best Rating:	157 2/04 Newb 2m110y good Hdl

Smart hurdler, career-best effort when winning Grade One Champion Hurdle at the 2003 Punchestown Festival; disappointing in 2003/2004 prior to good fifth in the Tote Gold Trophy; best suited to a strongly run two miles; acts on ground good or softer; usually wears a tongue-tie; tough.

Quedex
80   100
8-y-o b g Deploy-Alwal (Pharly (FR))
R J Price Fox And Cub Partnership

Placings:225431-P   (0261)
2003/04: 24⁷GF,

	Starts	1st	2nd	3rd	Win & Pl
Hurdles	1	0	0	0	
Career Total	**7**	**1**	**2**	**1**	**6041**
100 4/03 Strf	2m3f	F Hdl	G-F	£3010
		Total win prize-money £3010

Going:	Sf: 0-0 GS: 0-0 Gd: 0-0 GF: - Fm: 0-1
Distance:	2m/2m3: 0-0 2m4-2m7: 0-0 3m+: 0-1
Track:	LH: 0-0 RH: 0-1 Tight: 0-0 Gall: 0-0
Aids:	Bl: 0-0 Vi: 0-0 Tstrap: 0-0 Ckp: 0-1
Best Rating:	101 1/03 Tntn 2m1f soft Hdl

Fair stayer on the Flat; finally got off the mark over hurdles when winning modest maiden at Stratford April 2003; acts on a sound surface; should be suited by two and a half miles plus.

Queen Of Jazz
87   66
7-y-o b m Sovereign Water (FR)-When The Saints (Bay Express)
V Y Gethin V Y Gethin

Placings:00-4P5P   (4874)
2003/04: 16⁸G, 25⁸G, 19⁵G, 20⁹G,

	Starts	1st	2nd	3rd	Win & Pl
Hurdles	4	0	0	0	367
Career Total	**6**	**0**	**0**	**0**	**367**

Going:	Sf: 0-0 GS: 0-1 Gd: 0-3 GF: - Fm: 0-0
Distance:	2m/2m3: 0-1 2m4-2m7: 0-2 3m+: 0-1
Track:	LH: 0-2 RH: 0-2 Tight: 0-1 Gall: 0-0
Aids:	Bl: 0-0 Vi: 0-0 Tstrap: 0-0 Ckp: 0-0
Best Rating:	66 2/04 Asct 2m110y good Hdl

Poor form in bumpers and novice hurdles.

Queen Of Light (IRE)
50   60
4-y-o b/br f Ali-Royal (IRE)-Blaze Of Light (Blakeney)
J K Magee (J G Burns 6/10) T Foy

Placings:00   (2460)
2003/04: 16⁹GF, 16⁰G,

	Starts	1st	2nd	3rd	Win & Pl
Hurdles	2	0	0	0	

Career Total	2 0 0 0

Going:	Sf: 0-0 GS: 0-0 Gd: 0-1 GF: - Fm: 0-1
Distance:	2m/2m3: 0-2 2m4-2m7: 0-0 3m+: 0-0
Track:	LH: 0-1 RH: 0-0 Tight: 0-0 Gall: 0-1
Aids:	Bl: 0-0 Vi: 0-0 Tstrap: 0-0 Ckp: 0-0
Best Rating:	60 11/03 DRoy 2m gd-fm Hdl

Queen Of The South
79   82
7-y-o b m Cut The Mustard (IRE)-Kawarau Queen (Taufan (USA))
L Lungo G G Fraser

Placings:3PPP   (4940)
2003/04: 16³G, 17⁰GS, 17⁰GS, 16³GS,

	Starts	1st	2nd	3rd	Win & Pl
Chases	4	0	0	1	677
Career Total	**4**	**0**	**0**	**1**	**677**

Going:	Sf: 0-0 GS: 0-3 Gd: 0-1 GF: - Fm: 0-0
Distance:	2m/2m3: 0-4 2m4-2m7: 0-0 3m+: 0-0
Track:	LH: 0-3 RH: 0-1 Tight: 0-2 Gall: 0-1
Aids:	Bl: 0-0 Vi: 0-0 Tstrap: 0-0 Ckp: 0-0
Best Rating:	82 2/04 Newc 2m110y good Ch

Modest form in points in 2002 and only modest form (had the run of the race) on debut over regulation fences in February 2004.

Queen Soraya
103f   100f
6-y-o b m Persian Bold-Fairlead (Slip Anchor)
Miss H C Knight Mrs Oliver Fox-Pitt

Placings:1106   (4649)
2003/04: 16¹GF, 16¹G, 16⁰S, 17⁶G,

	Starts	1st	2nd	3rd	Win & Pl
NH Flat	4	2	0	0	5770
Career Total	**4**	**2**	**0**	**0**	**5770**
100 12/03 Ludl	2m	H NHF	GD	£3486
87 11/03 Ludl	2m	H NHF	G-F	£1834
		Total win prize-money £5320

Going:	Sf: 0-1 GS: 0-0 Gd: 1-2 GF: - Fm: 1-1
Distance:	2m/2m3: 2-4 2m4-2m7: 0-0 3m+: 0-0
Track:	LH: 0-0 **RH:** 2-3 Tight: 0-0 Gall: 0-0
Aids:	Bl: 0-0 Vi: 0-0 Tstrap: 0-0 Ckp: 0-0
Best Rating:	100 4/04 Aint 2m1f good NHF

Moderate bumper performer; should stay further than two miles over hurdles; best form to date on a sound surface.

Queen's Banquet
7-y-o b m Glacial Storm (USA)-Culinary (Tower Walk)
P R Webber The Alchemists 2

Placings:300O-P   (1813)
2003/04: 20⁰G,

	Starts	1st	2nd	3rd	Win & Pl
Hurdles	1	0	0	0	
Career Total	**5**	**0**	**0**	**1**	**401**

Going:	Sf: 0-0 GS: 0-0 Gd: 0-1 GF: - Fm: 0-0
Distance:	2m/2m3: 0-0 2m4-2m7: 0-1 3m+: 0-0
Track:	LH: 0-1 RH: 0-0 Tight: 0-1 Gall: 0-0
Aids:	Bl: 0-0 Vi: 0-0 Tstrap: 0-0 Ckp: 0-0
Best Rating:	96 4/03 Chel 2m1f good NHF

Queen's Pageant

102	(0c)106

10-y-o ch m Risk Me (FR)-Mistral's Dancer (Shareef Dancer (USA))
J L Spearing Mrs Robert Heathcote

Placings:0431/5510020-4   (1016)
2003/04: 24⁴GF,

	Starts	1st	2nd	3rd	Win & Pl
Hurdles	1	0	0	0	519
Career Total	12	2	1	1	10113
104	11/02	Tntn		2m3f110yD(0-120)HHdl	G-S	£4550
95	4/02	Hrfd		2m3f110yE Hdl	G-S	£3080
				Total win prize-money £7630

Going:	Sf: 0-0 GS: 0-0 Gd: 0-0 GF: - Fm: 0-1
Distance:	2m/2m3: 0-0 2m4-2m7: 0-0 3m+: 0-1
Track:	LH: 0-1 RH: 0-0 Tight: 0-0 Gall: 0-0
Aids:	Bl: 0-0 Vi: 0-0 Tstrap: 0-0 Ckp: 0-1
Best Rating:	106 2/03 Sand 2m4f110y heavy Hdl

Fair hurdler; best at around two and a half miles; acts on both fast and heavy ground; has gone well in cheekpieces.

Queens Brigade

104	87

12-y-o b g K-Battery-Queen Of Dara (Dara Monarch)
Miss V A Stephens D G Stephens

Placings:00/566234/12U353B414P/1U00244U4/4U244F31
305/0500/122   (3642)
2003/04: 24¹G, 16²G, 19²S,

	Starts	1st	2nd	3rd	Win & Pl
Hurdles	3	1	2	0	3670
Career Total	46	5	6	5	26177
77	12/03	Tntn	3m110y	G(0-90)HHdl	GD	£1876
96	11/00	Catt	2m	F(0-105)HCh	G-S	£3802
99	5/99	Hexm	2m110y	E Ch	G-F	£2212
107	3/99	Hexm	2m110y	E Ch	G-S	£2946
92	5/98	Hexm	2m4f110yF Hdl		G-S	£2390
				Total win prize-money £13229

Going:	Sf: 0-1 GS: 0-0 Gd: 1-2 GF: - Fm: 0-0
Distance:	2m/2m3: 0-2 2m4-2m7: 0-0 3m+: 1-1
Track:	LH: 0-0 RH: 1-3 Tight: 1-1 Gall: 0-0
Aids:	Bl: 0-0 Vi: 0-0 Tstrap: 0-0 Ckp: 0-0
Best Rating:	107 3/99 Hexm 2m110y gd-sft Ch

Plating-class chaser/hurdler; returned from two years off to win selling hurdle at Taunton in December 2003; stays three miles but effective at shorter; acts on easy ground.

Queens Wood

5-y-o br m Abzu-Fleur De Tal (Primitive Rising (USA))
N M Babbage John Cantrill

Placings:0   (1622)
2003/04: 17⁰G,

	Starts	1st	2nd	3rd	Win & Pl
NH Flat	1	0	0	0	
Career Total	1	0	0	0	

Going:	Sf: 0-0 GS: 0-0 Gd: 0-0 GF: - Fm: 0-0
Distance:	2m/2m3: 0-0 2m4-2m7: 0-0 3m+: 0-0
Track:	LH: 0-1 RH: 0-0 Tight: 0-1 Gall: 0-0
Aids:	Bl: 0-0 Vi: 0-0 Tstrap: 0-0 Ckp: 0-0

Queensberry

93	91

5-y-o b g Up And At 'Em-Princess Poquito (Hard Fought)

Miss L J Sheen (J O'Reilly 16/12) Mrs P J Sheen

Placings:6400   (4564)
2003/04: 16⁵S, 17⁴GS, 21⁰G, 19⁰GS,

	Starts	1st	2nd	3rd	Win & Pl
Hurdles	4	0	0	0	0
Career Total	4	0	0	0	0

Going:	Sf: 0-1 GS: 0-2 Gd: 0-1 GF: - Fm: 0-0
Distance:	2m/2m3: 0-3 2m4-2m7: 0-1 3m+: 0-0
Track:	LH: 0-2 RH: 0-2 Tight: 0-2 Gall: 0-1
Aids:	Bl: 0-0 Vi: 0-0 Tstrap: 0-0 Ckp: 0-0
Best Rating:	91 2/04 Folk 2m1f110y gd-sft Hdl

Queensland Bay

93f	63f

5-y-o ch m Primitive Rising (USA)-Hysteria (Prince Bee)
T D Easterby C H Stevens

Placings:06-6   (1696)
2003/04: 17⁵GF,

	Starts	1st	2nd	3rd	Win & Pl
NH Flat	1	0	0	0	0
Career Total	3	0	0	0	0

Going:	Sf: 0-0 GS: 0-0 Gd: 0-0 GF: - Fm: 0-1
Distance:	2m/2m3: 0-1 2m4-2m7: 0-0 3m+: 0-0
Track:	LH: 0-0 RH: 0-1 Tight: 0-1 Gall: 0-0
Aids:	Bl: 0-0 Vi: 0-0 Tstrap: 0-0 Ckp: 0-0
Best Rating:	63 10/03 MRas 2m1f110y gd-fm NHF

Queensway (IRE)

96	74

12-y-o b g Pennine Walk-Polaregina (FR) (Rex Magna (FR))
R M Carson Mrs P Carson

Placings:12013/3445P21/1422/4FU100/561F35600/P52P-363F   (1044)
2003/04: 16³GF, 16⁶GF, 16³GF, 16⁶GF,

	Starts	1st	2nd	3rd	Win & Pl
Chases	4	0	0	2	1391
Career Total	39	6	5	5	25997
103	8/01	Strf	2m1f110yF(0-105)HCh	G-F	£4160
101	10/00	Ludl	2m	G(0-95)HCh	G-F	£2730
107	8/99	Prth	2m	F(0-100)HCh	G-F	£4182
87	4/99	Kels	2m1f	E Ch	G-F	£3582
100	4/98	Sedg	2m1f	E Hdl	SFT	£2582
111	5/97	Prth	2m110y	H NHF	G-S	£1020
				Total win prize-money £18258

Going:	Sf: 0-0 GS: 0-0 Gd: 0-0 GF: - Fm: 0-4
Distance:	2m/2m3: 0-4 2m4-2m7: 0-0 3m+: 0-0
Track:	LH: 0-4 RH: 0-0 Tight: 0-3 Gall: 0-0
Aids:	Bl: 0-0 Vi: 0-0 Tstrap: 0-0 Ckp: 0-0
Best Rating:	111 5/97 Prth 2m110y gd-sft NHF

Poor chaser, best on fast ground at around two miles.

Quel Bon Choix (FR)

6-y-o b g Tel Quel (FR)-Special Marianna (FR) (Kaldoun (FR))
M C Pipe B A Kilpatrick

Placings:3232634212/PP   (0957)
2003/04: 19⁰PG, 22⁰PG,

	Starts	1st	2nd	3rd	Win & Pl
Hurdles	2	0	0	0	0
Career Total	12	1	4	3	13365

110 4/02 Uttx 2m4f110yD Hdl G-F £4000
Total win prize-money £4001

Going:	Sf: 0-0 GS: 0-0 Gd: 0-2 GF: - Fm: 0-0
Distance:	2m/2m3: 0-0 2m4-2m7: 0-2 3m+: 0-0
Track:	LH: 0-1 RH: 0-1 Tight: 0-2 Gall: 0-0
Aids:	Bl: 0-0 Vi: 0-0 Tstrap: 0-0 Ckp: 0-0
Best Rating:	110 4/02 Strf 2m6f110y good Hdl

Quel Regal (FR)

6-y-o b g Comte Du Bourg (FR)-Rigala (FR) (Roi Dagobert)
A R Dicken Mr & Mrs Raymond Anderson Green

Placings:0030/P-P   (0196)
2003/04: 20⁰PG, 16⁰G,

	Starts	1st	2nd	3rd	Win & Pl
Hurdles	2	0	0	0	
Career Total	6	0	0	1	380

Going:	Sf: 0-0 GS: 0-0 Gd: 0-2 GF: - Fm: 0-0
Distance:	2m/2m3: 0-1 2m4-2m7: 0-1 3m+: 0-0
Track:	LH: 0-2 RH: 0-0 Tight: 0-0 Gall: 0-0
Aids:	Bl: 0-0 Vi: 0-0 Tstrap: 0-0 Ckp: 0-0
Best Rating:	65 2/02 Muss 2m soft Hdl

Quest For Rome

8-y-o ch g Question Of Pride-Unbeknown (Most Secret)
M Appleby Clovers

Placings:P   (3195)
2003/04: 21⁰PS,

	Starts	1st	2nd	3rd	Win & Pl
Hurdles	1	0	0	0	
Career Total	1	0	0	0	

Going:	Sf: 0-1 GS: 0-0 Gd: 0-0 GF: - Fm: 0-0
Distance:	2m/2m3: 0-0 2m4-2m7: 0-1 3m+: 0-0
Track:	LH: 0-1 RH: 0-0 Tight: 0-1 Gall: 0-0
Aids:	Bl: 0-0 Vi: 0-0 Tstrap: 0-0 Ckp: 0-0

Quetal (IRE)

11-y-o ch g Buckskin (FR)-Cantafleur (Cantab)
Mrs Laura J Young Miss K J Kitching

Placings:2F44/F6P/11/10-6PPF   (4761)
2003/04: 33⁶G, 25⁶PG, 26⁶PG, 25⁶S,

	Starts	1st	2nd	3rd	Win & Pl
Chases	4	0	0	0	0
Career Total	15	3	1	0	15255
129	2/03	Newb	3m	H Ch	SFT	£1974
115	4/02	Aint	3m1f	B Ch	GD	£10822
104	3/02	Wwck	3m2f	H Ch	GD	£1176
				Total win prize-money £13973

Going:	Sf: 0-1 GS: 0-0 Gd: 0-3 GF: - Fm: 0-0
Distance:	2m/2m3: 0-0 2m4-2m7: 0-0 3m+: 0-4
Track:	LH: 0-2 RH: 0-2 Tight: 0-2 Gall: 0-2
Aids:	Bl: 0-0 Vi: 0-0 Tstrap: 0-0 Ckp: 0-2
Best Rating:	129 2/03 Newb 3m soft Ch

Winning pointer and hunter chaser; loves soft ground.

Quick

111   **127+**

4-y-o b g Kahyasi-Prompt (Old Vic)
M C Pipe (R M H Cowell 19/6) Kinsford Champagne Partnership

Placings:1111014030   (4963)
2003/04: 17¹GF, 22¹GF, 24¹GF, 25¹S, 24⁰G, 22¹G, 24⁴GS, 24⁰G, 24³G, 20⁰G,

	Starts	1st	2nd	3rd	Win & Pl
Hurdles	10	5	0	1	23120
Career Total	10	5	0	1	23120
123	3/04	Sand	2m6f	D(0-120)HHdl	GD £8443
106	12/03	Plum	3m1f110yE(0-105)HHdl	SFT £2565
100	11/03	Tntn	3m110y D(0-110)HHdl	G-F £5026
85	10/03	Extr	2m1f110yE(0-100)HHdl	G-F £2555
96	9/03	MRas	2m1f110yG Hdl	G-F £1862

Total win prize-money £20453

Going:	Sf: 1-1 GS: 0-1 Gd: 1-5 GF: - Fm: 3-3
Distance:	2m/2m3: 1-1 2m4-2m7: 2-3 3m+: 2-6
Track:	LH: 0-3 RH: 4-6 Tight: 2-3 Gall: 0-2
Aids:	Bl: 0-0 Vi: 5-10 Tstrap: 0-0 Ckp: 0-0
Best Rating:	127 4/04 Chel 3m good Hdl

Useful four-year-old hurdler; winner of five hurdles at up to an extended three miles one; acts on any ground; wears a visor; fairly progressive.

Quick To Move (IRE)

56   **32**

4-y-o b g Night Shift (USA)-Corynida (USA) (Alleged (USA))
C N Kellett J E Titley

Placings:0P   (1007)
2003/04: 17⁰GF, 17⁰G,

	Starts	1st	2nd	3rd	Win & Pl
Hurdles	2	0	0	0	
Career Total	2	0	0	0	

Going:	Sf: 0-0 GS: 0-0 Gd: 0-1 GF: 0-1 Fm: 0-1
Distance:	2m/2m3: 0-2 2m4-2m7: 0-0 3m+: 0-0
Track:	LH: 0-1 RH: 0-1 Tight: 0-2 Gall: 0-0
Aids:	Bl: 0-0 Vi: 0-0 Tstrap: 0-0 Ckp: 0-0
Best Rating:	32 7/03 MRas 2m1f110y gd-fm Hdl

Quid Pro Quo (FR)

110f   **109+f**

5-y-o b g Cadoudal (FR)-Luzenia (FR) (Armos)
P F Nicholls Sir Robert Ogden

Placings:4212   (4550)
2003/04: 17⁴G, 17²GS, 17¹S, 16²GS,

	Starts	1st	2nd	3rd	Win & Pl
NH Flat	4	1	2	0	4369
Career Total	4	1	2	0	4369
109	2/04	Tntn	2m1f	H NHF	SFT £2604

Total win prize-money £2604

Going:	Sf: 1-1 GS: 0-2 Gd: 0-1 GF: - Fm: 0-0
Distance:	2m/2m3: 1-4 2m4-2m7: 0-0 3m+: 0-0
Track:	LH: 0-0 RH: 0-2 Tight: 0-0 Gall: 0-0
Aids:	Bl: 0-0 Vi: 0-0 Tstrap: 0-0 Ckp: 0-0
Best Rating:	109 2/04 Tntn 2m1f soft NHF

Brother to Luzcadou; good efforts in decent bumpers so far.

Quidditch

4-y-o b f Wizard King-Celtic Chimes (Celtic Cone)
P Bowen Homebred Racing

Placings:P   (2764)
2003/04: 16⁰GS,

	Starts	1st	2nd	3rd	Win & Pl
Hurdles	1	0	0	0	
Career Total	1	0	0	0	

Going:	Sf: 0-0 GS: 0-1 Gd: 0-0 GF: - Fm: 0-0
Distance:	2m/2m3: 0-1 2m4-2m7: 0-0 3m+: 0-0
Track:	LH: 0-1 RH: 0-0 Tight: 0-1 Gall: 0-0
Aids:	Bl: 0-0 Vi: 0-0 Tstrap: 0-0 Ckp: 0-0

Quiet Desperation

69   **35**

8-y-o b g Supreme Leader-Wing On (Quayside)
J D Frost (K J Burke 5/5) Arthur Watling

Placings:P0P0   (2812)
2003/04: 22⁰G, 17⁰G, 16⁰GS, 19⁰G,

	Starts	1st	2nd	3rd	Win & Pl
Hurdles	4	0	0	0	
Career Total	4	0	0	0	

Going:	Sf: 0-0 GS: 0-1 Gd: 0-3 GF: - Fm: 0-0
Distance:	2m/2m3: 0-3 2m4-2m7: 0-1 3m+: 0-0
Track:	LH: 0-1 RH: 0-2 Tight: 0-0 Gall: 0-0
Aids:	Bl: 0-0 Vi: 0-0 Tstrap: 0-0 Ckp: 0-0
Best Rating:	35 12/03 Extr 2m3f good Hdl

Quiet Water (IRE)

91(109h)   (112 h) **112**

8-y-o br g Lord Americo-Sirana (Al Sirat)
P J Hobbs Network Training 4

Placings:040/450/103110-0141   (0870)
2003/04: 18⁰G, 19¹G, 20⁴G, 21¹GF,

	Starts	1st	2nd	3rd	Win & Pl
Hurdles	3	1	0	0	4048
Chases	1	1	0	0	5382
Career Total	16	5	0	1	22122
112	7/03	NAbb	2m5f110yD Ch	G-F £5382
109	5/03	Strf	2m3f	E(0-110)HHdl	GD £3523
109	3/03	Newb	2m3f	E(0-110)HHdl	GD £3682
100	2/03	Ludl	2m5f	D(0-120)HHdl	GD £5642
89	5/02	Hntg	2m5f110yE(0-110)HHdl	G-F £2415

Total win prize-money £20644

Going:	Sf: 0-0 GS: 0-0 Gd: 1-3 GF: - Fm: 1-1
Distance:	2m/2m3: 1-2 2m4-2m7: 1-2 3m+: 0-0
Track:	LH: 2-3 RH: 0-0 Tight: 2-2 Gall: 0-0
Aids:	Bl: 0-0 Vi: 0-0 Tstrap: 0-0 Ckp: 0-0
Best Rating:	112 7/03 NAbb 2m5f110y gd-fm Ch

Improving handicap hurdler; made winning chasing debut when beating Miss Cool in 2m 5f novice chase at Newton Abbot July 2003; stays 2m 5f; suited by a sound surface.

Quincy's Perk (IRE)

99   **99**

11-y-o ch g Executive Perk-Quincy Bay (Buckskin (FR))
C T Pogson C T Pogson

Placings:432P21PPPP   (4782)
2003/04: 21⁶G, 25³G, 24²GF, 24⁰GS, 24²G, 21¹GS, 24⁰G, 21⁰G, 24⁰GS, 24⁰G,

Quidditch (cont.)

	Starts	1st	2nd	3rd	Win & Pl
Chases	10	1	2	1	7510
Career Total	10	1	2	1	7510
96	2/04	Sedg	2m5f	E Ch	G-S £4706

Total win prize-money £4706

Going:	Sf: 0-0 GS: 1-3 Gd: 0-6 GF: - Fm: 0-1
Distance:	2m/2m3: 0-0 2m4-2m7: 1-3 3m+: 0-7
Track:	LH: 1-7 RH: 0-3 Tight: 1-5 Gall: 0-3
Aids:	Bl: 0-1 Vi: 0-0 Tstrap: 0-0 Ckp: 0-0
Best Rating:	96 2/04 Sedg 2m5f gd-sft Ch

Poor pointer; little impact under Rules until winning a very weak race at Sedgefield in February.

Quintrell Downs

95

9-y-o b g Efisio-Nineteenth Of May (Homing)
T R George Mr & Mrs D A Gamble

Placings:000/13/3-PP   (0517)
2003/04: 17⁰G, 19⁰G,

	Starts	1st	2nd	3rd	Win & Pl
Hurdles	2	0	0	0	
Career Total	8	1	0	2	3707
94	7/99	Wolv	2m	E(0-105)HHdl	G-F £2692

Total win prize-money £2693

Going:	Sf: 0-0 GS: 0-0 Gd: 0-2 GF: - Fm: 0-0
Distance:	2m/2m3: 0-2 2m4-2m7: 0-0 3m+: 0-0
Track:	LH: 0-2 RH: 0-0 Tight: 0-2 Gall: 0-0
Aids:	Bl: 0-0 Vi: 0-0 Tstrap: 0-0 Ckp: 0-0
Best Rating:	95 10/02 Hrfd 2m1f good Hdl

Quite Remarkable

89   **80**

5-y-o b g Danzig Connection (USA)-Kathy Fair (IRE) (Nicholas Bill)
Ian Williams J Tredwell

Placings:000   (4524)
2003/04: 17⁰GS, 17⁰G, 16⁰GS,

	Starts	1st	2nd	3rd	Win & Pl
Hurdles	3	0	0	0	
Career Total	3	0	0	0	

Going:	Sf: 0-0 GS: 0-2 Gd: 0-1 GF: - Fm: 0-0
Distance:	2m/2m3: 0-3 2m4-2m7: 0-0 3m+: 0-0
Track:	LH: 0-1 RH: 0-2 Tight: 0-2 Gall: 0-0
Aids:	Bl: 0-0 Vi: 0-0 Tstrap: 0-0 Ckp: 0-0
Best Rating:	80 2/04 Folk 2m1f110y gd-sft Hdl

Quizzical

70(104h)   (87h)**76**

6-y-o ch g Indian Ridge-Mount Row (Alzao (USA))
John G Carr James Hepburn

Placings:FP/06320000P-4F23230600FP   (4473a)
2003/04: 24⁰GY, 20⁴GY, 22⁰G, 17²G, 24³G, 24²GF, 24³GF, 21⁰G, 20⁶Y, 17⁰S, 17⁰S, 20⁴FYS, 20⁰G,

	Starts	1st	2nd	3rd	Win & Pl
Hurdles	7	0	2	2	2601
Chases	6	0	0	0	0
Career Total	23	0	3	3	4182

Going:	Sf: 0-3 GS: 0-0 Gd: 0-4 GF: - Fm: 0-2
Distance:	2m/2m3: 0-3 2m4-2m7: 0-6 3m+: 0-4
Track:	LH: 0-7 RH: 0-3 Tight: 0-2 Gall: 0-1
Aids:	Bl: 0-0 Vi: 0-0 Tstrap: 0-0 Ckp: 0-1

Best Rating: 98 3/02 Wxfd 2m   soft   Hdl

Selling-class maiden hurdler; acts on a sound surface.

Quizzling (IRE)
98   77
6-y-o b g Jurado (USA)-Monksville (Monksfield)
B J M Ryall I & Mrs K G Fawcett

Placings: 6660   (4147)
2003/04: 16⁶GS, 19⁹S, 22⁶G, 24⁰G,

	Starts	1st	2nd	3rd	Win & Pl
NH Flat	1	0	0	0	0
Hurdles	3	0	0	0	0
Career Total	**4**	**0**	**0**	**0**	

Going: Sf: 0-1 GS: 0-1 Gd: 0-2 GF: - Fm: 0-0
Distance: 2m/2m3: 0-2 2m4-2m7: 0-1 3m+: 0-1
Track: LH: 0-2 RH: 0-2 Tight: 0-2 Gall: 0-0
Aids: Bl: 0-0 Vi: 0-0 Tstrap: 0-0 Ckp: 0-0
Best Rating: 87 5/03 Worc 2m   gd-sft NHF

Racing Demon (IRE)
103f   98f
4-y-o b g Old Vic-All Set (IRE) (Electric)
Miss H C Knight Mrs T P Radford

Placings: 1   (4594)
2003/04: 16¹G,

	Starts	1st	2nd	3rd	Win & Pl
NH Flat	1	1	0	0	1876
Career Total	**1**	**1**	**0**	**0**	**1876**
98	3/04	Hntg	2m110y	H NHF	GD	£1876
				Total win prize-money £1876

Going: Sf: 0-0 GS: 0-0 Gd: 1-1 GF: - Fm: 0-0
Distance: 2m/2m3: 1-1 2m4-2m7: 0-0 3m+: 0-0
Track: LH: 0-0 RH: 1-1 Tight: 0-0 Gall: 1-1
Aids: Bl: 0-0 Vi: 0-0 Tstrap: 0-0 Ckp: 0-0
Best Rating: 98 3/04 Hntg 2m110y   good   NHF

Racing Surveyor

9-y-o b m Mazilier (USA)-Ruthenia (IRE) (Taufan (USA))
H Alexander Alastair Baillie

Placings: P   (1625)
2003/04: 16ᴾGF,

	Starts	1st	2nd	3rd	Win & Pl
Hurdles	1	0	0	0	
Career Total	**1**	**0**	**0**	**0**	

Going: Sf: 0-0 GS: 0-0 Gd: 0-0 GF: - Fm: 0-1
Distance: 2m/2m3: 0-1 2m4-2m7: 0-0 3m+: 0-0
Track: LH: 0-1 RH: 0-0 Tight: 0-0 Gall: 0-0
Aids: Bl: 0-0 Vi: 0-0 Tstrap: 0-0 Ckp: 0-0

Raconteur (IRE)

10-y-o b g Top Of The World-Blackrath Gem (Bargello)
G D Hanmer W Puddifer

Placings: 04504400000465032/33100F000/P (0073)
2003/04: 24ᴾS,

	Starts	1st	2nd	3rd	Win & Pl
Chases	1	0	0	0	

Career Total 27 1 1 3 5797
100 6/00 Tral 2m1f   Hdl   SH   £2760
Total win prize-money £2760

Going: Sf: 0-1 GS: 0-0 Gd: 0-0 GF: - Fm: 0-0
Distance: 2m/2m3: 0-0 2m4-2m7: 0-0 3m+: 0-1
Track: LH: 0-1 RH: 0-0 Tight: 0-0 Gall: 0-0
Aids: Bl: 0-0 Vi: 0-0 Tstrap: 0-0 Ckp: 0-0
Best Rating: 100 6/00 Tral 2m1f   sft-hvy Hdl

Radar (IRE)
105(113c)   (118c)106
9-y-o b g Petardia-Soignee (Night Shift (USA))
Miss S E Forster C Storey

Placings: 345/321/0112F4/53541-23224   (4314)
2003/04: 17⁴GS, 17³HY, 16²S, 17²GS, 20⁴GF,

	Starts	1st	2nd	3rd	Win & Pl
Hurdles	5	0	3	1	6323
Career Total	**22**	**4**	**5**	**4**	**27350**
118	2/03	Sedg	2m110y	E(0-110)HCh	HVY	£4046
103	3/02	Sedg	2m110y	D Ch	SFT	£3844
118	3/02	Sedg	2m110y	C Ch	SFT	£6077
107	8/00	Worc	2m	E Hdl	G-F	£2756
				Total win prize-money £16725

Going: Sf: 0-2 GS: 0-2 Gd: 0-0 GF: - Fm: 0-1
Distance: 2m/2m3: 0-4 2m4-2m7: 0-1 3m+: 0-0
Track: LH: 0-3 RH: 0-2 Tight: 0-2 Gall: 0-0
Aids: Bl: 0-0 Vi: 0-0 Tstrap: 0-0 Ckp: 0-0
Best Rating: 118 2/03 Sedg 2m110y   heavy   Ch

Modest hurdler/chaser, a winner on the Flat; been successful over hurdles and fences; effective over two miles; acts on most types of ground.

Radcliffe (IRE)
107(95h)   (96h)113
7-y-o b g Supreme Leader-Marys Course (Crash Course)
Miss Venetia Williams M L Shone

Placings: 6106-6233251F456P2   (4364)
2003/04: 26⁶GS, 16²GS, 20⁵GF, 21³GF, 18²GF, 22⁵G, 26¹G, 26⁴GF, 28⁴G, 24⁵GS, 24⁶S, 22²G, 26²G,

	Starts	1st	2nd	3rd	Win & Pl
Hurdles	3	0	1	1	1976
Chases	10	1	2	1	8273
Career Total	**17**	**2**	**3**	**2**	**12258**
110	11/03	Plum	3m2f	D(0-110)HCh	GD	£4707
108	12/02	Fknm	2m	H NHF	G-S	£2009
				Total win prize-money £6717

Going: Sf: 0-1 GS: 0-3 Gd: 1-5 GF: - Fm: 0-4
Distance: 2m/2m3: 0-2 2m4-2m7: 0-4 3m+: 1-7
Track: LH: 1-6 RH: 0-3 Tight: 1-6 Gall: 0-1
Aids: Bl: 0-0 Vi: 0-0 Tstrap: 0-0 Ckp: 0-0
Best Rating: 110 11/03 Plum 3m2f   good   Ch

Moderate hurdler/chaser, stays 3m 2f; acts on a sound surface.

Radical Jack
(47h)
7-y-o b g Presidium-Luckifosome (Smackover)
C W Fairhurst Mrs B J Boocock

Placings: 00/PPU-PP   (4161)
2003/04: 16⁶S, 16ᴾG,

	Starts	1st	2nd	3rd	Win & Pl
Chases	2	0	0	0	
Career Total	**7**	**0**	**0**	**0**	

Going: Sf: 0-1 GS: 0-0 Gd: 0-1 GF: - Fm: 0-0
Distance: 2m/2m3: 0-2 2m4-2m7: 0-0 3m+: 0-0
Track: LH: 0-2 RH: 0-0 Tight: 0-0 Gall: 0-1
Aids: Bl: 0-0 Vi: 0-0 Tstrap: 0-0 Ckp: 0-0
Best Rating: 47 9/01 Sedg 2m1f   gd-fm Hdl

Radmore Spirit

4-y-o b f Whittingham (IRE)-Ruda (FR) (Free Round (USA))
G A Ham J R Salter

Placings: 00   (3657)
2003/04: 17⁰GS, 17⁰S,

	Starts	1st	2nd	3rd	Win & Pl
NH Flat	2	0	0	0	
Career Total	**2**	**0**	**0**	**0**	

Going: Sf: 0-1 GS: 0-1 Gd: 0-0 GF: - Fm: 0-0
Distance: 2m/2m3: 0-2 2m4-2m7: 0-0 3m+: 0-0
Track: LH: 0-0 RH: 0-0 Tight: 0-0 Gall: 0-0
Aids: Bl: 0-0 Vi: 0-0 Tstrap: 0-0 Ckp: 0-0

Raffles Rooster

12-y-o ch g Galetto (FR)-Singapore Girl (FR) (Lyphard (USA))
Miss L Revell Mark A Leatham

Placings: 35/232/142U1/251/51F01326/31524/5222-P5U   (4607)
2003/04: 25ᴾS, 24⁵GS, 25ᵁGS,

	Starts	1st	2nd	3rd	Win & Pl
Chases	3	0	0	0	
Career Total	**33**	**6**	**9**	**4**	**52638**
126	12/01	Sand	3m110y	D(0-130)HCh	G-S	£7150
125	2/01	Towc	3m1f	C(0-130)HCh	HVY	£5941
125	11/00	NAbb	3m2f110yC(0-130)HCh	HVY	£7315
119	3/00	Tntn	3m	F(0-105)HCh	GD	£4777
108	2/99	Tntn	3m	C(0-115)HCh	G-F	£3875
115	11/98	Font	3m3f	E Ch	SFT	£2786
				Total win prize-money £31845

Going: Sf: 0-1 GS: 0-1 Gd: 0-1 GF: - Fm: 0-0
Distance: 2m/2m3: 0-2 2m4-2m7: 0-0 3m+: 0-3
Track: LH: 0-1 RH: 0-2 Tight: 0-1 Gall: 0-0
Aids: Bl: 0-0 Vi: 0-0 Tstrap: 0-0 Ckp: 0-0
Best Rating: 129 12/02 Hayd 3m   soft   Ch

Once a useful Flat handicapper, he is a capable chaser. Suited to hold-up tactics and a test of stamina, although he does not find a great deal off the bit. Acts on any ground softer than good.

Ragdale Hall (USA)
108(107c)   (107c)124+
7-y-o b g Bien Bien (USA)-Gift Of Dance (USA) (Trempolino (USA))
J Joseph (P J Hobbs 8/10) Jack Joseph

Placings: 2/2132422141-616151344   (4963)
2003/04: 16⁶G, 16¹G, 17⁵GF, 16¹GF, 17⁵GF, 16³F, 16⁴G, 20⁴G,

	Starts	1st	2nd	3rd	Win & Pl
Hurdles	6	1	0	0	8489
Chases	3	2	1	0	11648
Career Total	**20**	**6**	**5**	**2**	**38431**
110	9/03	Prth	2m4f110yD Ch	GD	£5622
92	8/03	NAbb	2m110y D Ch	G-F	£5356
124	6/03	Strf	2m110y D(0-120)HHdl	GD	£5564
121	4/03	Strf	2m110y D(0-125)HHdl	G-F	£4849

105	9/02	Hrfd	2m3f110yE Hdl		G-F	£3195
96	6/02	Uttx	2m	E Hdl	GD	£2639
				Total win prize-money £27227		

Going:	Sf: 0-0 GS: 0-0 Gd: 2-5 GF: - Fm: 1-4
Distance:	2m/2m3: 2-7 2m4-2m7: 1-2 3m+: 0-0
Track:	LH: 2-5 RH: 1-4 Tight: 2-5 Gall: 0-0
Aids:	Bl: 0-0 Vi: 0-0 Tstrap: 0-0 Ckp: 0-0
Best Rating:	124 6/03 Strf 2m110y good Hdl

Fair hurdler; won his first two novice chases, but did not look a natural; effective from two to two and a half miles and suited by a sound surface.

Raging Torrent

9-y-o b g Meadowbrook-Charons Daughter (Another River)
S Waugh S Waugh

Placings:40					(3987)
2003/04: 26⁴G, 21⁰G,					

	Starts	1st	2nd	3rd	Win & Pl
Chases	2	0	0	0	168
Career Total	2	0	0	0	168

Going:	Sf: 0-0 GS: 0-1 Gd: 0-1 GF: - Fm: 0-0
Distance:	2m/2m3: 0-0 2m4-2m7: 0-1 3m+: 0-1
Track:	LH: 0-2 RH: 0-0 Tight: 0-2 Gall: 0-0
Aids:	Bl: 0-0 Vi: 0-0 Tstrap: 0-0 Ckp: 0-0
Best Rating:	71 5/03 Ctml 3m2f good Ch

Ragstone Lad

5-y-o b g Zamindar (USA)-Thahabyah (USA) (Sheikh Albadou)
M A Barnes T A Barnes

Placings:0PP					(3358)
2003/04: 16⁰GF, 16⁵S, 16⁰S,					

	Starts	1st	2nd	3rd	Win & Pl
NH Flat	1	0	0	0	0
Hurdles	2	0	0	0	0
Career Total	3	0	0	0	

Going:	Sf: 0-2 GS: 0-0 Gd: 0-0 GF: - Fm: 0-1
Distance:	2m/2m3: 0-3 2m4-2m7: 0-0 3m+: 0-0
Track:	LH: 0-3 RH: 0-0 Tight: 0-1 Gall: 0-0
Aids:	Bl: 0-0 Vi: 0-0 Tstrap: 0-0 Ckp: 0-0

Ragu

95   94+

6-y-o b m Contract Law (USA)-Mamworth (Funny Man)
M J Gingell (Ferdy Murphy 23/1) W Stanger, P Whittall and G Plastow

Placings:0323/5432004-215F00P					(4776)
2003/04: 20²GF, 20¹GF, 21⁵G, 21²GF, 16⁹HY, 24⁰GF, 20⁰G,					

	Starts	1st	2nd	3rd	Win & Pl
Hurdles	7	1	1	0	3030
Career Total	18	1	3	3	6362
94	10/03	Hayd	2m4f	E Hdl	G-F	£2394
				Total win prize-money £2394		

Going:	Sf: 0-1 GS: 0-0 Gd: 0-2 GF: - Fm: 1-4
Distance:	2m/2m3: 0-1 2m4-2m7: 1-5 3m+: 0-1
Track:	LH: 1-6 RH: 0-0 Tight: 0-3 Gall: 0-0
Aids:	Bl: 0-0 Vi: 0-0 Tstrap: 0-0 Ckp: 0-1
Best Rating:	94 11/03 Sedg 2m5f110y gd-fm Hdl

Modest novice hurdler; stays two miles five; acts on most types of ground.

Raheel (IRE)

4-y-o ch g Barathea (IRE)-Tajawuz (Kris)
P Mitchell Mrs S and Mr S L Sheldon

Placings:P					(2205)
2003/04: 17⁶G,					

	Starts	1st	2nd	3rd	Win & Pl
Hurdles	1	0	0	0	
Career Total	1	0	0	0	

Going:	Sf: 0-0 GS: 0-0 Gd: 0-1 GF: - Fm: 0-0
Distance:	2m/2m3: 0-1 2m4-2m7: 0-0 3m+: 0-0
Track:	LH: 0-0 RH: 0-1 Tight: 0-1 Gall: 0-0
Aids:	Bl: 0-0 Vi: 0-0 Tstrap: 0-0 Ckp: 0-0

Rahwaan (IRE)

110   110+

5-y-o b g Darshaan-Fawaakeh (USA) (Lyphard (USA))
C W Fairhurst Six Iron Partnership

Placings:1					(4260)
2003/04: 16¹GF,					

	Starts	1st	2nd	3rd	Win & Pl
Hurdles	1	1	0	0	3658
Career Total	1	1	0	0	3658
110	3/04	Catt	2m	E Hdl	G-F	£3657
				Total win prize-money £3658		

Going:	Sf: 0-0 GS: 0-0 Gd: 0-0 GF: - Fm: 1-1
Distance:	2m/2m3: 1-1 2m4-2m7: 0-0 3m+: 0-0
Track:	LH: 1-1 RH: 0-0 Tight: 1-1 Gall: 0-0
Aids:	Bl: 0-0 Vi: 0-0 Tstrap: 0-0 Ckp: 0-0
Best Rating:	110 3/04 Catt 2m gd-fm Hdl

Useful staying handicapper on the Flat; made virtually all on hurdling bow at Catterick in March, jumping well; handles a fast surface but may be even more effective in the mud.

Raikkonen (IRE)

106   121

4-y-o b g Lake Coniston (IRE)-Jour Ferie (IRE) (Taufan (USA))
W P Mullins (Augustine Leahy 30/8) Austin Fanning

Placings:2344100					(4802a)
2003/04: 16²GF, 16³GF, 16⁴S, 16⁴S, 16¹YS, 17⁰G, 16⁰Y,					

	Starts	1st	2nd	3rd	Win & Pl
Hurdles	7	1	1	1	9426
Career Total	7	1	1	1	9426
105	2/04	Gowr	2m	Hdl	Y-S	£6082
				Total win prize-money £6083		

Going:	Sf: 0-2 GS: 0-0 Gd: 0-1 GF: - Fm: 0-2
Distance:	2m/2m3: 1-7 2m4-2m7: 0-0 3m+: 0-0
Track:	LH: 0-2 RH: 0-3 Tight: 0-0 Gall: 0-1
Aids:	Bl: 0-0 Vi: 0-0 Tstrap: 0-0 Ckp: 0-0
Best Rating:	121 3/04 Chel 2m1f good Hdl

Fair Irish juvenile hurdler; effective at two miles; acts on fast and soft ground.

Rainbow Dance (IRE)

107(109h)   (124+h)107

8-y-o ch g Rainbows For Life (CAN)-Nishila (USA) (Green Dancer (USA))
Jonjo O'Neill Mrs G Smith

Placings:053254/00 126562/1212335-24F422P		(1658)

2003/04: 20²G, 20⁴GF, 20⁵FGF, 23⁴GF, 16²GF, 20²GF, 16⁶G,					

	Starts	1st	2nd	3rd	Win & Pl
Hurdles	1	0	1	0	550
Chases	6	0	2	0	5301
Career Total	28	3	8	3	25804
120	6/02	Worc	2m4f	C(0-135)HHdl	GD	£5109
124	5/02	Ludl	2m5f	E(0-105)HHdl	G-F	£3150
104	7/01	Tipp	2m	NHF	GD	£3895
				Total win prize-money £12154		

Going:	Sf: 0-0 GS: 0-0 Gd: 0-2 GF: - Fm: 0-5
Distance:	2m/2m3: 0-2 2m4-2m7: 0-4 3m+: 0-1
Track:	LH: 0-4 RH: 0-3 Tight: 0-4 Gall: 0-0
Aids:	Bl: 0-7 Vi: 0-0 Tstrap: 0-4 Ckp: 0-0
Best Rating:	124 5/02 Ludl 2m5f gd-fm Hdl

Modest novice chaser/selling-class hurdler; tends to find one to beat him and does not look reliable; has yet to prove he stays 3m over fences; effective on fast ground; jumped left when well beaten second at Ludlow October 2003.

Rainbow River (IRE)

97   110

6-y-o ch g Rainbows For Life (CAN)-Shrewd Girl (USA) (Sagace (FR))
M C Chapman Patrick Darcy

Placings:2114-0					(0404)
2003/04: 17⁰G,					

	Starts	1st	2nd	3rd	Win & Pl
Hurdles	1	0	0	0	
Career Total	5	2	1	0	8865
98	3/03	Ludl	2m5f	E Hdl	G-F	£3799
110	3/03	Fknm	2m	E Hdl	GD	£3528
				Total win prize-money £7327		

Going:	Sf: 0-0 GS: 0-0 Gd: 0-1 GF: - Fm: 0-0
Distance:	2m/2m3: 0-1 2m4-2m7: 0-0 3m+: 0-0
Track:	LH: 0-1 RH: 0-0 Tight: 0-1 Gall: 0-0
Aids:	Bl: 0-0 Vi: 0-0 Tstrap: 0-0 Ckp: 0-0
Best Rating:	110 3/03 Fknm 2m good Hdl

Fair hurdler; acts on decent ground; effective at up to two miles five.

Rainbow Star (FR)

10-y-o b/br g Saumarez-In The Star (FR) (In Fijar (USA))
Mrs Myfanwy Miles P B Miles

Placings:221P/214P5/4P11F/1P/P000P/R03P-R		(4002)

2003/04: 20⁰RG,					

	Starts	1st	2nd	3rd	Win & Pl
Chases	2	0	0	0	
Career Total	26	5	3	1	13486
106	5/00	Hrfd	2m3f110yG Hdl	GD	£1974
105	1/00	Plum	2m5f	G Hdl	SFT	£2292
99	1/00	Tntn	2m3f110yG Hdl	SFT	£1519
116	5/98	NAbb	2m1f	D Hdl	G-F	£2832
99	3/98	NAbb	2m1f	F Hdl	SFT	£1962
				Total win prize-money £10580		

Going:	Sf: 0-0 GS: 0-0 Gd: 0-1 GF: - Fm: 0-0
Distance:	2m/2m3: 0-0 2m4-2m7: 0-1 3m+: 0-0
Track:	LH: 0-0 RH: 0-0 Tight: 0-1 Gall: 0-0
Aids:	Bl: 0-1 Vi: 0-0 Tstrap: 0-0 Ckp: 0-0
Best Rating:	116 5/98 NAbb 2m1f gd-fm Hdl

Rainbow Sun

(88h)   (72+h)

8-y-o ch g Minster Son-Rilin (Ribston)
N M Babbage B Babbage

Placings:	40/00P0-P				(0235)

2003/04: 19⁰GF,

	Starts	1st	2nd	3rd	Win & Pl
Chases	1	0	0	0	
Career Total	7	0	0	0	0

Going: Sf: 0-0 GS: 0-0 Gd: 0-0 GF: - Fm: 0-1
Distance: 2m/2m3: 0-1 2m4-2m7: 0-0 3m+: 0-0
Track: LH: 0-0 RH: 0-1 Tight: 0-0 Gall: 0-0
Aids: Bl: 0-0 Vi: 0-0 Tstrap: 0-0 Ckp: 0-1
Best Rating: 91 4/02 Wwck 2m gd-fm NHF

Rainbows Aglitter

102(110h)　　　　　(119 h)120+
7-y-o ch g Rainbows For Life (CAN)-Chalet Waldegg (Monsanto (FR))
D R Gandolfo　Nigel Stafford

Placings:	1/12324P/233020-23122P				(2692)

2003/04: 17²G, 17³G, 16¹GF, 20²GF, 19²S, 20⁰PG,

	Starts	1st	2nd	3rd	Win & Pl
Hurdles	2	0	1	1	5028
Chases	4	1	2	0	6786
Career Total	19	3	7	4	30524
109	10/03	Towc	2m110y	E Ch		G-F	£2681
114	10/01	Sthl	2m	E Hdl		GD	£2247
105	1/01	Kemp	2m	H NHF		SFT	£1683

Total win prize-money £6612

Going: Sf: 0-1 GS: 0-0 Gd: 0-3 GF: - Fm: 1-2
Distance: 2m/2m3: 1-3 2m4-2m7: 0-3 3m+: 0-0
Track: LH: 0-2 RH: 1-5 Tight: 0-3 Gall: 0-1
Aids: Bl: 0-0 Vi: 0-0 Tstrap: 0-0 Ckp: 0-0
Best Rating: 120 11/03 Asct 2m3f110y soft Ch

Modest hurdler/chaser; effective at up to two miles five; acts on good and soft ground; likes to be held up.

Raise A McGregor

100(82h)　　　　　(74h)95
8-y-o br g Perpendicular-Gregory's Lady (Meldrum)
Mrs S J Smith　Keith Nicholson

Placings:	3O0/04/P00-P05413				(1304)

2003/04: 20PG, 20³G, 16⁵G, 16⁴GF, 20¹G, 20³GF,

	Starts	1st	2nd	3rd	Win & Pl
Hurdles	1	0	0	0	0
Chases	5	1	0	1	5054
Career Total	14	1	0	2	5267
95	8/03	Bang	2m4f110yE(0-100)HCh		GD	£4241

Total win prize-money £4241

Going: Sf: 0-0 GS: 0-0 Gd: 1-3 GF: - Fm: 0-3
Distance: 2m/2m3: 0-2 2m4-2m7: 1-4 3m+: 0-0
Track: LH: 1-6 RH: 0-0 Tight: 1-1 Gall: 0-0
Aids: Bl: 0-0 Vi: 0-0 Tstrap: 0-0 Ckp: 0-0
Best Rating: 95 8/03 Bang 2m4f110y good Ch

Plating-class; pulled up on chasing debut May 2003; won handicap over two and a half miles in August; acts on sound surface.

Raise Your Glass (IRE)

108　　　　　100+
5-y-o b/br g Namaqualand (USA)-Toast And Honey (IRE) (Glow (USA))
Miss V Scott (N M L Ewart 23/1)　Miss Victoria Scott Jnr

Placings:	060-F050311005				(3978)

2003/04: 16FGF, 17⁰GF, 17⁵GF, 16⁸GF, 16³GF, 21¹G, 20¹GF, 20⁶G, 24⁰GF, 20⁵G,

	Starts	1st	2nd	3rd	Win & Pl
Hurdles	10	2	0	1	5351
Career Total	13	2	0	1	5351
100	10/03	Carl	2m4f	E(0-105)HHdl		G-F	£3276
86	10/03	Sedg	2m5f110yG(0-90)HHdl		GD	£1813

Total win prize-money £5089

Going: Sf: 0-0 GS: 0-0 Gd: 1-3 GF: - Fm: 1-7
Distance: 2m/2m3: 0-5 2m4-2m7: 2-4 3m+: 0-1
Track: LH: 1-6 RH: 1-3 Tight: 1-4 Gall: 0-0
Aids: Bl: 2-7 Vi: 0-0 Tstrap: 0-0 Ckp: 0-0
Best Rating: 100 2/04 Carl 2m4f good Hdl

Moderate over hurdles; found his form in October 2003 with a win at Sedgefield over 2m5f but turned in much improved effort when successful at Carlisle later that month; acts on firm and good ground.

Rajam

103　　　　　104
6-y-o b g Sadler's Wells (USA)-Rafff (USA) (Riverman (USA))
D Nicholls (R C Guest 17/3)　A A Bloodstock Ltd

Placings:	33				(4402)

2003/04: 16³S, 16³G,

	Starts	1st	2nd	3rd	Win & Pl
Hurdles	2	0	0	2	1088
Career Total	2	0	0	2	1088

Going: Sf: 0-1 GS: 0-0 Gd: 0-1 GF: - Fm: 0-0
Distance: 2m/2m3: 0-2 2m4-2m7: 0-0 3m+: 0-0
Track: LH: 0-1 RH: 0-1 Tight: 0-1 Gall: 0-1
Aids: Bl: 0-0 Vi: 0-0 Tstrap: 0-0 Ckp: 0-0
Best Rating: 104 1/04 Kels 2m110y soft Hdl

Promise in low grade novice hurdles; acts on soft ground;

Raka King

11-y-o b g Rakaposhi King-Spartan Native (Native Bazaar)
J A T De Giles　J A T De Giles

Placings:	6664/2FFF/6/P				(0613)

2003/04: 25PGF,

	Starts	1st	2nd	3rd	Win & Pl
Chases	1	0	0	0	0
Career Total	10	0	1	0	672

Going: Sf: 0-0 GS: 0-0 Gd: 0-0 GF: - Fm: 0-1
Distance: 2m/2m3: 0-0 2m4-2m7: 0-0 3m+: 0-1
Track: LH: 0-0 RH: 0-1 Tight: 0-0 Gall: 0-1
Aids: Bl: 0-0 Vi: 0-0 Tstrap: 0-0 Ckp: 0-0
Best Rating: 95 12/99 Towc 2m good NHF

Rakalackey

105　　　　　121
6-y-o br g Rakaposhi King-Celtic Slave (Celtic Cone)
H D Daly　B G Hellyer

Placings:	55-1610P				(4887)

2003/04: 19¹G, 22⁶GS, 21¹G, 20⁰G, 22PGF,

	Starts	1st	2nd	3rd	Win & Pl
Hurdles	5	2	0	0	7270
Career Total	7	2	0	0	7270
117	2/04	Ludl	2m5f	E Hdl		GD	£3747
121	11/03	MRas	2m3f110yE Hdl		GD	£3523

Total win prize-money £7270

Going: Sf: 0-0 GS: 0-1 Gd: 2-3 GF: - Fm: 0-1
Distance: 2m/2m3: 0-0 2m4-2m7: 2-5 3m+: 0-0
Track: LH: 0-2 RH: 2-3 Tight: 1-3 Gall: 0-0
Aids: Bl: 0-0 Vi: 0-0 Tstrap: 0-0 Ckp: 0-0
Best Rating: 121 4/04 Aint 2m4f good Hdl

Fair hurdler; half-brother to Young Spartacus; suited by sharp right-hand tracks; stays two and a half miles; best on decent ground.

Rakassa

106　　　　　107
6-y-o ch m Ballet Royal (USA)-Shafayif (Ela-Mana-Mou)
H J Manners　H J Manners

Placings:	00530-44F3231424				(4544)

2003/04: 16⁴GF, 20⁴G, 21²G, 19³GS, 21²G, 24³S, 21¹G, 22⁴G, 22²G, 22⁴GS,

	Starts	1st	2nd	3rd	Win & Pl
Hurdles	10	1	2	2	10418
Career Total	15	1	2	3	10701
107	2/04	Kemp	2m5f	D(0-115)HHdl		GD	£6090

Total win prize-money £6090

Going: Sf: 0-1 GS: 0-2 Gd: 1-6 GF: - Fm: 0-1
Distance: 2m/2m3: 0-1 2m4-2m7: 1-8 3m+: 0-0
Track: LH: 0-3 RH: 1-7 Tight: 0-3 Gall: 0-0
Aids: Bl: 0-0 Vi: 0-0 Tstrap: 0-0 Ckp: 0-0
Best Rating: 107 3/04 Winc 2m6f gd-sft Hdl

Ramblees Holly

98　　　　　94
6-y-o ch g Alfie Dickins-Lucky Holly (General David)
R S Wood　R S Wood

Placings:	30/0630P650-153350120355000				(4605)

2003/04: 21¹S, 20²G, 24³G, 17³GF, 16⁵GF, 17⁰G, 21¹GF, 21²GF, 19³GF, 20³F, 20⁵GF, 21⁵G, 17⁰GS, 20⁰HY, 22⁶G,

	Starts	1st	2nd	3rd	Win & Pl
Hurdles	15	2	1	3	9523
Career Total	25	2	1	5	10457
94	7/03	Sedg	2m5f110yE(0-110)HHdl		G-F	£3701
94	5/03	Sedg	2m5f110yE Hdl		SFT	£3451

Total win prize-money £7153

Going: Sf: 1-2 GS: 0-1 Gd: 0-5 GF: - Fm: 1-7
Distance: 2m/2m3: 0-4 2m4-2m7: 2-10 3m+: 0-1
Track: LH: 2-9 RH: 0-5 Tight: 2-9 Gall: 0-2
Aids: Bl: 0-0 Vi: 0-0 Tstrap: 0-0 Ckp: 0-0
Best Rating: 94 9/03 Hntg 2m4f110y gd-fm Hdl

Moderate hurdler; stays three miles; acts on a sound surface; goes well at Sedgefield.

Rambling Minster

106　　　　　109+
6-y-o b g Minster Son-Howcleuch (Buckskin (FR))
Mrs M Reveley　The Lingdale Optimists

Placings:	231526				(4577)

2003/04: 17²GF, 17³G, 16¹G, 16⁵S, 19²G, 16⁶G,

	Starts	1st	2nd	3rd	Win & Pl
NH Flat	4	1	1	1	2678
Hurdles	2	0	1	0	1738
Career Total	6	1	2	1	4416
104	11/03	Hexm	2m110y	H NHF		GD	£1904

Total win prize-money £1904

Going: Sf: 0-1 GS: 0-0 Gd: 1-4 GF: - Fm: 0-1
Distance: 2m/2m3: 1-5 2m4-2m7: 0-1 3m+: 0-0

Track: LH: 1-3 RH: 0-3 Tight: 0-3 Gall: 0-1
Aids: Bl: 0-0 Vi: 0-0 Tstrap: 0-0 Ckp: 0-0
Best Rating: 108 2/04 MRas 2m3f110y good Hdl

National Hunt-bred; won bumper at the third attempt at Hexham in November; promising runner-up on hurdling debut at Market Rasen in February; will be suited by three miles; acts on good.

Ramon Allones (IRE)

6-y-o br g Good Thyne (USA)-Cuban Vacation (Ovac (ITY))
Mrs R L Elliot D Davidson

Placings:0 　　　　　　　　　　　　(1769)
2003/04: 17⁰G,

	Starts	1st	2nd	3rd	Win & Pl
NH Flat	1	0	0	0	
Career Total	1	0	0	0	

Going: Sf: 0-0 GS: 0-0 Gd: 0-1 GF: - Fm: 0-0
Distance: 2m/2m3: 0-1 2m4-2m7: 0-0 3m+: 0-0
Track: LH: 0-0 RH: 0-1 Tight: 0-0 Gall: 0-0
Aids: Bl: 0-0 Vi: 0-0 Tstrap: 0-0 Ckp: 0-0

Rampant (IRE)

6-y-o b g Pursuit Of Love-Flourishing (IRE) (Trojan Fen)
C J Teague Reg Richardson

Placings:P 　　　　　　　　　　　　(2941)
2003/04: 16ᴾGS,

	Starts	1st	2nd	3rd	Win & Pl
Hurdles	1	0	0	0	
Career Total	1	0	0	0	

Going: Sf: 0-0 GS: 0-1 Gd: 0-0 GF: - Fm: 0-0
Distance: 2m/2m3: 0-1 2m4-2m7: 0-0 3m+: 0-0
Track: LH: 0-1 RH: 0-0 Tight: 0-0 Gall: 0-0
Aids: Bl: 0-0 Vi: 0-0 Tstrap: 0-0 Ckp: 0-0

Randolph O'Brien (IRE)

95 　　　　　　　　　　　　**87**

4-y-o b g Zaffaran (USA)-Gala's Pride (Gala Performance (ZIM))
N A Twiston-Davies Geoffrey & Donna Keeys

Placings:5024 　　　　　　　　　　(4251)
2003/04: 12⁵S, 13⁰S, 17²S, 17⁴G,

	Starts	1st	2nd	3rd	Win & Pl
NH Flat	2	0	0	0	0
Hurdles	2	0	1	0	1048
Career Total	4	0	1	0	1048

Going: Sf: 0-3 GS: 0-0 Gd: 0-1 GF: - Fm: 0-0
Distance: 2m/2m3: 0-2 2m4-2m7: 0-0 3m+: 0-0
Track: LH: 0-1 RH: 0-1 Tight: 0-1 Gall: 0-0
Aids: Bl: 0-0 Vi: 0-0 Tstrap: 0-0 Ckp: 0-0
Best Rating: 87 3/04 Bang 2m1f good Hdl

Random Harvest (IRE)

102(101h) 　　　　　(105+h)**124**

15-y-o br g Strong Gale-Bavello (Le Bavard (FR))
Mrs M Reveley C C Buckley

Placings:5/426/24120PU/B5324/U14121130/1/PP1245PP/
F321600F/0P23P461351-050456 　　(4615)
2003/04: 24⁰GF, 23⁵GF, 25⁰G, 25⁴G, 24⁵G, 28⁶G,

	Starts	1st	2nd	3rd	Win & Pl
Hurdles	2	0	0	0	0
Chases	4	0	0	0	446
Career Total	59	10	8	5	99992
117 4/03 Sedg	3m4f	D(0-125)HCh	G-F	£12110
116 3/03 Weth	2m7f110yD(0-125)HCh	G-F	£6792
138 12/01 Weth	3m1f	C(0-130)HCh	SFT	£7560
136 11/00 Weth	3m1f	C(0-125)HCh	SFT	£3828
129 12/99 Weth	2m7f	D Hdl	G-S	£3207
150 12/98 Weth	3m1f	B HCh	SFT	£14732
150 12/98 Weth	3m1f	B(0-145)HCh	GD	£7100
137 10/98 MRas	3m1f	C(0-130)HCh	G-S	£6905
122 5/98 Weth	3m1f	C(0-135)HCh	G-F	£4719
118 1/97 Carl	2m4f110yD(0-120)HCh	GD	£3566
		Total win prize-money £70523		

Going: Sf: 0-0 GS: 0-0 Gd: 0-4 GF: - Fm: 0-2
Distance: 2m/2m3: 0-0 2m4-2m7: 0-0 3m+: 0-6
Track: LH: 0-5 RH: 0-1 Tight: 0-1 Gall: 0-1
Aids: Bl: 0-0 Vi: 0-0 Tstrap: 0-0 Ckp: 0-0
Best Rating: 153 1/99 Hayd 3m soft Ch

Fair handicap chaser; useful in his prime, but well into the veteran stage now; goes well at Wetherby and recorded his seventh win there in March 2003; best at around three miles on soft ground, although does handle a faster surface.

Random Precision (IRE)

93 　　　　　　　　　　　　**80**

5-y-o ch g Presenting-Rendezvous (Lorenzaccio)
B G Powell John Studd

Placings:20P05 　　　　　　　　　(4671)
2003/04: 18²HY, 16⁰HY, 21ᴾG, 18⁰G, 16⁵G,

	Starts	1st	2nd	3rd	Win & Pl
NH Flat	2	0	1	0	578
Hurdles	3	0	0	0	0
Career Total	5	0	1	0	578

Going: Sf: 0-2 GS: 0-0 Gd: 0-3 GF: - Fm: 0-0
Distance: 2m/2m3: 0-4 2m4-2m7: 0-1 3m+: 0-0
Track: LH: 0-3 RH: 0-2 Tight: 0-2 Gall: 0-1
Aids: Bl: 0-0 Vi: 0-0 Tstrap: 0-0 Ckp: 0-0
Best Rating: 88 1/04 Font 2m2f110y heavy NHF

Made promising debut on heavy ground in a 2m2f bumper at Fontwell in January, despite running keenly; held over hurdles.

Randy (GER)

105 　　　　　　　　　　　　**77**

6-y-o gr g Neshad (USA)-Regal Beauty (GER) (Windwurf (GER))
M C Pipe M C Pipe

Placings:P0PP-40 　　　　　　　　(0676)
2003/04: 17⁴GF, 16⁰GF,

	Starts	1st	2nd	3rd	Win & Pl
Hurdles	2	0	0	0	0
Career Total	6	0	0	0	0

Going: Sf: 0-0 GS: 0-0 Gd: 0-0 GF: - Fm: 0-2
Distance: 2m/2m3: 0-2 2m4-2m7: 0-0 3m+: 0-0
Track: LH: 0-2 RH: 0-0 Tight: 0-1 Gall: 0-0
Aids: Bl: 0-0 Vi: 0-0 Tstrap: 0-0 Ckp: 0-0
Best Rating: 77 12/02 Tntn 2m3f110y gd-sft Hdl

Selling hurdler; seemed to appreciate first run on a sound surface when fourth at Newton Abbot June 2003.

Raneen Nashwan

78 　　　　　　　　　　　　**94**

8-y-o b g Nashwan (USA)-Raneen Alwatar (Sadler's Wells (USA))
R J Baker M Channon

Placings:F0020/4063-60 　　　　　(1268)
2003/04: 19⁶G, 17⁰GF,

	Starts	1st	2nd	3rd	Win & Pl
Hurdles	2	0	0	0	0
Career Total	11	0	1	1	1326

Going: Sf: 0-0 GS: 0-0 Gd: 0-1 GF: - Fm: 0-1
Distance: 2m/2m3: 0-2 2m4-2m7: 0-0 3m+: 0-0
Track: LH: 0-1 RH: 0-0 Tight: 0-1 Gall: 0-0
Aids: Bl: 0-0 Vi: 0-0 Tstrap: 0-0 Ckp: 0-0
Best Rating: 94 5/02 Winc 2m gd-fm Hdl

Moderate hurdler; suited by cut in the ground; has a tendency to hinder himself by racing too keenly.

Ranelagh Gray (IRE)

104 　　　　　　　　　　　　**109+**

7-y-o gr g Roselier (FR)-Bea Marie (IRE) (King's Ride)
Miss Venetia Williams Christopher Drury

Placings:05P50-01201 　　　　　　(4760)
2003/04: 21⁰G, 17¹HY, 16²S, 16⁰G, 16¹S,

	Starts	1st	2nd	3rd	Win & Pl
Hurdles	5	2	1	0	11933
Career Total	10	2	1	0	11933
109 4/04 Towc	2m	E(0-105)HHdl	SFT	£5057
104 1/04 Folk	2m1f110yE(0-105)HHdl	HVY	£3437
		Total win prize-money £8494		

Going: Sf: 2-3 GS: 0-0 Gd: 0-2 GF: - Fm: 0-0
Distance: 2m/2m3: 2-4 2m4-2m7: 0-1 3m+: 0-0
Track: LH: 0-2 RH: 2-3 Tight: 1-1 Gall: 0-2
Aids: Bl: 0-0 Vi: 0-0 Tstrap: 0-0 Ckp: 0-0
Best Rating: 109 4/04 Towc 2m soft Hdl

Moderate hurdler; suited by two miles and cut in the ground.

Raoul Dufy (USA)

4-y-o gr g El Prado (IRE)-Parrish Empress (USA) (His Majesty (USA))
P J Hobbs (P F I Cole 26/7) Richard Green (fine Paintings)

Placings:0 　　　　　　　　　　　(3187)
2003/04: 16⁰GS,

	Starts	1st	2nd	3rd	Win & Pl
Hurdles	1	0	0	0	0
Career Total	1	0	0	0	0

Going: Sf: 0-0 GS: 0-1 Gd: 0-0 GF: - Fm: 0-0
Distance: 2m/2m3: 0-1 2m4-2m7: 0-0 3m+: 0-0
Track: LH: 0-0 RH: 0-1 Tight: 0-0 Gall: 0-0
Aids: Bl: 0-0 Vi: 0-0 Tstrap: 0-0 Ckp: 0-0

Rapid Liner

81   (81c)**66**

11-y-o b g Skyliner-Stellaris (Star Appeal)
B G Powell Mrs G Elliott And G Jarvie

Placings:00P6035/5P5/00006/P00P0/00PP/602-0   (0768)
2003/04: 22⁰GF,

	Starts	1st	2nd	3rd	Win & Pl
Hurdles	1	0	0	0	
Career Total	28	0	1	1	997

Going:	Sf: 0-0 GS: 0-0 Gd: 0-0 GF: 0-0 Fm: 0-1
Distance:	2m2m3: 0-0 2m4-2m7: 0-1 3m+: 0-0
Track:	LH: 0-1 RH: 0-0 Tight: 0-0 Gall: 0-0
Aids:	Bl: 0-0 Vi: 0-0 Tstrap: 0-0 Ckp: 0-0
Best Rating:	71 4/01 Font 2m2f good Ch

Poor hurdler/chaser; only worthwhile form when runner-up in Plumpton seller in April 2003.

Rapt (IRE)

101   **93+**

6-y-o b g Septieme Ciel (USA)-Dream Play (USA) (Blushing Groom (FR))
M A Barnes Thirdtimelucky

Placings:0P00-65150P   (4915)
2003/04: 17⁶G, 17⁵G, 16¹GF, 16⁵GF, 17⁰G, 16PGS,

	Starts	1st	2nd	3rd	Win & Pl
Hurdles	6	1	0	0	2303
Career Total	10	1	0	0	2303
93 10/03 Strf 2m110y G Hdl				G-F	2303
				Total win prize-money	£2303

Going:	Sf: 0-0 GS: 0-1 Gd: 0-2 GF: 0-0 Fm: 1-3
Distance:	2m2m3: 1-6 2m4-2m7: 0-0 3m+: 0-0
Track:	LH: 1-5 RH: 0-1 Tight: 1-4 Gall: 0-0
Aids:	Bl: 0-0 Vi: 0-0 Tstrap: 1-5 Ckp: 0-0
Best Rating:	93 10/03 Strf 2m110y gd-fm Hdl

Plating-class hurdler; took advantage of a drop in class when convincing winner of 2m Stratford seller October 2003.

Rarchnamara (IRE)

92   **80+**

9-y-o b g Commanche Run-Knollwood Court (Le Jean)
Ferdy Murphy John Duddy

Placings:400/42122322/4U-F5   (4432)
2003/04: 25FGS, 32⁵G,

	Starts	1st	2nd	3rd	Win & Pl
Chases	2	0	0	0	0
Career Total	15	1	5	1	7087
103 6/01 Hexm 2m4f110yE(0-105)HHdl				G-S	£2626
				Total win prize-money	£2626

Going:	Sf: 0-0 GS: 0-1 Gd: 0-1 GF: 0-0 Fm: 0-0
Distance:	2m2m3: 0-0 2m4-2m7: 0-0 3m+: 0-2
Track:	LH: 0-1 RH: 0-1 Tight: 0-0 Gall: 0-0
Aids:	Bl: 0-0 Vi: 0-0 Tstrap: 0-0 Ckp: 0-0
Best Rating:	109 12/01 Hexm 3m soft Hdl

He has been stepped up in trip since his Hexham win over an extended mile and a half in June 2001 and has bot disgraced himself, with near misses in his three races since then. He has worn blinkers, although not as a permanent fixture and is suited by cut in the ground.

Rare Presence (IRE)

94   **80+**

5-y-o b g Sadler's Wells (USA)-Celebrity Style (USA) (Seeking The Gold (USA))

C P Morlock The Shouting Men

Placings:004-6PP030   (4488)
2003/04: 18⁶G, 24PGS, 22PGS, 20⁰GS, 22³G, 22⁰G,

	Starts	1st	2nd	3rd	Win & Pl
Hurdles	6	0	0	1	513
Career Total	9	0	0	1	513

Going:	Sf: 0-0 GS: 0-3 Gd: 0-3 GF: 0-0 Fm: 0-0
Distance:	2m2m3: 0-1 2m4-2m7: 0-4 3m+: 0-1
Track:	LH: 0-2 RH: 0-4 Tight: 0-4 Gall: 0-1
Aids:	Bl: 0-4 Vi: 0-1 Tstrap: 0-3 Ckp: 0-0
Best Rating:	80 3/04 Folk 2m6f110y good Hdl

Moderate hurdler; limited potential; has worn blinkers.

Rare Quality

93   **76**

6-y-o b m Chaddleworth (IRE)-Pink Mex (Tickled Pink)
N J Henderson Magno-Pulse Ltd

Placings:400PP   (4377)
2003/04: 16⁴G, 10⁰HY, 21⁰G, 21PG, 17PG,

	Starts	1st	2nd	3rd	Win & Pl
Hurdles	5	0	0	0	284
Career Total	5	0	0	0	284

Going:	Sf: 0-1 GS: 0-0 Gd: 0-4 GF: 0-0 Fm: 0-0
Distance:	2m2m3: 0-3 2m4-2m7: 0-2 3m+: 0-0
Track:	LH: 0-2 RH: 0-3 Tight: 0-2 Gall: 0-0
Aids:	Bl: 0-0 Vi: 0-0 Tstrap: 0-0 Ckp: 0-0
Best Rating:	76 12/03 Leic 2m good Hdl

Moderate maiden on the Flat; fourth on hurdling debut over two miles.

Rare Vintage (IRE)

(85h)   (64h)

6-y-o b m Germany (USA)-Tatlock (Paico)
Miss H C Knight Trevor Hemmings

Placings:PP04   (4702)
2003/04: 20PG, 21PG, 17⁰G, 20⁴G,

	Starts	1st	2nd	3rd	Win & Pl
Hurdles	4	0	0	0	0
Career Total	4	0	0	0	0

Going:	Sf: 0-0 GS: 0-0 Gd: 0-4 GF: 0-0 Fm: 0-0
Distance:	2m2m3: 0-1 2m4-2m7: 0-3 3m+: 0-0
Track:	LH: 0-3 RH: 0-0 Tight: 0-3 Gall: 0-0
Aids:	Bl: 0-0 Vi: 0-0 Tstrap: 0-0 Ckp: 0-0
Best Rating:	64 3/04 Bang 2m1f good Hdl

Rascella

101   **90**

9-y-o gr m Scallywag-Blue Gift (Hasty Word)
Mrs S J Smith J Townson & A A Thomason

Placings:20/264342   (2233)
2003/04: 16²G, 17⁶GS, 16⁴GF, 20³G, 20⁴G, 20²G,

	Starts	1st	2nd	3rd	Win & Pl
Hurdles	6	0	2	1	3252
Career Total	8	0	3	1	3692

Going:	Sf: 0-0 GS: 0-1 Gd: 0-4 GF: 0-0 Fm: 0-1
Distance:	2m2m3: 0-3 2m4-2m7: 0-3 3m+: 0-0
Track:	LH: 0-6 RH: 0-0 Tight: 0-3 Gall: 0-0
Aids:	Bl: 0-0 Vi: 0-0 Tstrap: 0-0 Ckp: 0-0
Best Rating:	90 11/03 Hexm 2m4f110y good Hdl

Lightly-raced novice hurdler; stays 2m4f; acts on good.

Rathbawn Prince (IRE)

12-y-o ch g All Haste (USA)-Ellis Town (Camden Town)
Miss H C Knight (D T Hughes 2/5) Miss S L Samworth

Placings:141/55100/133200/0P2P3214U/21115U55P/2056 F0/0F43P0-P22   (4172)
2003/04: 20PYS, 25²G, 24²G,

	Starts	1st	2nd	3rd		Win & Pl
Chases	3	0	2	0		1016
Career Total	47	8	7	4		84680
145	11/00	DRoy	2m2f	Ch	G-Y	£10400
122	10/00	Thur	2m6f	Ch	Y-S	£4416
121	10/00	Fair	2m2f	Hdl	G-Y	£3864
130	2/00	Fair	2m2f	Ch	HVY	£4692
105	10/98	Fair	2m	Hdl	YLD	£2989
120	3/98	Navn	2m	NHF	Y-S	£2680
119	4/97	Punc	2m	NHF	GD	£6782
107	10/96	Punc	2m	NHF	GD	£3177
					Total win prize-money	£39001

Going:	Sf: 0-0 GS: 0-0 Gd: 0-2 GF: 0-0 Fm: 0-0
Distance:	2m2m3: 0-0 2m4-2m7: 0-1 3m+: 0-2
Track:	LH: 0-1 RH: 0-2 Tight: 0-0 Gall: 0-1
Aids:	Bl: 0-0 Vi: 0-0 Tstrap: 0-0 Ckp: 0-1
Best Rating:	157 5/01 Fair 3m5f good Ch

Smart Irish staying chaser; runner-up in the 2001 Irish National, been lightly raced since; has won on a sound surface but effective on heavy; has worn blinkers on one single occasion.

Rathgar Beau (IRE)

118(97h)   (133h)**149**

8-y-o b/br g Beau Sher-Salerina (Orchestra)
E Sheehy One-O-Eight Racing Club

Placings:165/F212312523/2B43213211F-3322F320015   (4769a)
2003/04: 16³GY, 16³GF, 16²GY, 16²YS, 17FS, 17³S, 16²HY, 20⁰YS, 12⁰G, 20¹Y, 17⁵Y,

	Starts	1st	2nd	3rd		Win & Pl
Hurdles	1	0	0	0		
Chases	10	1	3	3		40057
Career Total	35	7	10	7		101730
145	3/04	Navn	2m4f	Ch	YLD	£14670
144	3/03	Naas	2m	Ch	HVY	£8441
139	2/03	Thur	2m	Ch	YLD	£6272
105	12/02	Limk	2m1f	Ch	HVY	£7196
126	1/02	Thur	2m	Hdl	Y-S	£5079
122	11/01	Thur	2m	Hdl	Y-S	£5008
122	12/00	Fair	2m	NHF	SFT	£3312
					Total win prize-money	£49981

Going:	Sf: 0-3 GS: 0-0 Gd: 0-1 GF: 0-0 Fm: 0-1
Distance:	2m2m3: 0-9 2m4-2m7: 1-2 3m+: 0-0
Track:	LH: 1-5 RH: 0-5 Tight: 0-0 Gall: 0-1
Aids:	Bl: 0-2 Vi: 0-0 Tstrap: 0-0 Ckp: 0-0
Best Rating:	149 4/04 Fair 2m1f yield Ch

Smart Irish chaser; suited by two miles, but stays 2m 4f; loves the mud; often held-up.

Rathowen (IRE)

57f

5-y-o b g Good Thyne (USA)-Owenageera (IRE) (Riot Helmet)

J I A Charlton J I A Charlton

Placings:0 (4649)
2003/04: 17[P]G,

	Starts	1st	2nd	3rd	Win & Pl
NH Flat	1	0	0	0	
Career Total	1	0	0	0	

Going:	Sf: 0-0 GS: 0-0 Gd: 0-1 GF: - Fm: 0-0
Distance:	2m2m3: 0-1 2m4-2m7: 0-0 3m+: 0-0
Track:	LH: 0-0 RH: 0-0 Tight: 0-0 Gall: 0-0
Aids:	Bl: 0-0 Vi: 0-0 Tstrap: 0-0 Ckp: 0-0
Best Rating:	57 4/04 Aint 2m1f good NHF

Ratling

8-y-o gr g Pittacus (USA)-Sedgewell Orchid (John De Coombe)
J F Panvert J F Panvert

Placings:4 (1549)
2003/04: 21[4]GF,

	Starts	1st	2nd	3rd	Win & Pl
Hurdles	1	0	0	0	0
Career Total	1	0	0	0	0

Going:	Sf: 0-0 GS: 0-0 Gd: 0-0 GF: - Fm: 0-1
Distance:	2m/2m3: 0-0 2m4-2m7: 0-1 3m+: 0-0
Track:	LH: 0-1 RH: 0-0 Tight: 0-1 Gall: 0-0
Aids:	Bl: 0-0 Vi: 0-0 Tstrap: 0-0 Ckp: 0-0

Ratty's Band

77 (67h)82+

10-y-o ch g Gunner B-Arctic Ander (Leander)
Mrs L B Normile Perth Racers

Placings:0PP/50/P2P (4940)
2003/04: 16[P]HY, 16[2]GS, 16[P]GS,

	Starts	1st	2nd	3rd	Win & Pl
Chases	3	0	1	0	1685
Career Total	8	0	1	0	1685

Going:	Sf: 0-1 GS: 0-1 Gd: 0-0 GF: - Fm: 0-1
Distance:	2m/2m3: 0-3 2m4-2m7: 0-0 3m+: 0-0
Track:	LH: 0-2 RH: 0-1 Tight: 0-1 Gall: 0-0
Aids:	Bl: 0-0 Vi: 0-0 Tstrap: 0-0 Ckp: 0-0
Best Rating:	82 3/04 Catt 2m gd-fm Ch

Plating-class novice chaser; narrowly beaten in very weak event at Catterick in March.

Raven's Last

106f 101f

5-y-o b g Sea Raven (IRE)-Lavenham's Last (Rymer)
R T Phillips Mrs Stewart Catherwood

Placings:12 (4323)
2003/04: 16[1]HY, 16[2]S,

	Starts	1st	2nd	3rd	Win & Pl
NH Flat	2	1	1	0	2628
Career Total	2	1	1	0	2628
107	2/04 Newc 2m		H NHF	HVY	£2016
				Total win prize-money	£2016

Going:	Sf: 1-2 GS: 0-0 Gd: 0-0 GF: - Fm: 0-0
Distance:	2m/2m3: 1-2 2m4-2m7: 0-0 3m+: 0-0
Track:	LH: 1-2 RH: 0-0 Tight: 0-0 Gall: 0-0
Aids:	Bl: 0-0 Vi: 0-0 Tstrap: 0-0 Ckp: 0-0

Best Rating: 107 2/04 Newc 2m heavy NHF

Irish point winner; impressive winner of bumper at Newcastle in February; only runner-up there the following month.

Raving Lord (IRE)

79 50

7-y-o b g Lord Americo-Miss Kertina (IRE) (Orchestra)
J P Dodds Tom Batey

Placings:65540P-0U (4297)
2003/04: 16[0]G, 16[U]GF,

	Starts	1st	2nd	3rd	Win & Pl
Hurdles	2	0	0	0	
Career Total	8	0	0	0	0

Going:	Sf: 0-0 GS: 0-0 Gd: 0-1 GF: - Fm: 0-1
Distance:	2m/2m3: 0-2 2m4-2m7: 0-0 3m+: 0-0
Track:	LH: 0-1 RH: 0-1 Tight: 0-0 Gall: 0-0
Aids:	Bl: 0-0 Vi: 0-0 Tstrap: 0-0 Ckp: 0-0
Best Rating:	93 11/02 Ayr 2m soft NHF

Raw Silk

111 117

6-y-o b g Rudimentary (USA)-Misty Silks (Scottish Reel)
M Todhunter The Cartmel Syndicate

Placings:04200201113/440232-210P6 (1185)
2003/04: 16[2]GF, 17[1]G, 17[0]GF, 16[P]G, 17[6]G,

	Starts	1st	2nd	3rd	Win & Pl
Hurdles	5	1	1	0	5040
Career Total	22	4	5	2	17095
117	5/03 Ctml	2m1f110yE(0-110)HHdl	GD	£4004
97	4/02 Newc 2m	F Hdl	FRM	£2079
94	4/02 Fknm 2m	D(0-110)HHdl	GD	£3410
93	3/02 Fknm 2m	G(0-90)HHdl	GD	£1857
			Total win prize-money	£11351

Going:	Sf: 0-0 GS: 0-0 Gd: 1-3 GF: - Fm: 0-2
Distance:	2m/2m3: 1-5 2m4-2m7: 0-0 3m+: 0-0
Track:	LH: 1-4 RH: 0-1 Tight: 1-4 Gall: 0-0
Aids:	Bl: 0-1 Vi: 0-0 Tstrap: 0-0 Ckp: 0-0
Best Rating:	117 5/03 Ctml 2m1f110y good Hdl

Modest hurdler; recorded fourth career win at Cartmel in May; best on decent ground; best at around two miles.

Ray Source (IRE)

105(89h) (99h)106+

9-y-o b g Lashkari-Salote (USA) (Forli (ARG))
Ian Williams C J Leech

Placings:42/006252/230/144/P123151 (2278)
2003/04: 22[P]GF, 26[1]GF, 24[2]G, 25[3]GF, 24[1]GF, 25[5]GF, 24[1]G,

	Starts	1st	2nd	3rd	Win & Pl
Hurdles	2	1	0	0	2597
Chases	5	2	1	1	13214
Career Total	21	4	5	2	23498
106	11/03 Asct	3m110y D(0-115)HCh	GD	£6037
99	10/03 Chep	3m D Ch	G-F	£4968
99	8/03 Hntg	3m2f F(0-95)HHdl	G-F	£2597
97	10/01 Sthl	3m110y E Hdl	GD	£2982
			Total win prize-money	£16585

Going:	Sf: 0-0 GS: 0-0 Gd: 1-2 GF: - Fm: 2-5
Distance:	2m/2m3: 0-0 2m4-2m7: 0-1 3m+: 3-6
Track:	LH: 1-3 RH: 2-4 Tight: 0-2 Gall: 1-1
Aids:	Bl: 1-1 Vi: 0-0 Tstrap: 0-0 Ckp: 0-0
Best Rating:	106 11/03 Asct 3m110y good Ch

Moderate hurdler/chaser; stays three miles and acts on fast ground.

Raybaan (IRE)

73 52

5-y-o b g Flying Spur (AUS)-Genetta (Green Desert (USA))
Miss J S Davis (S Dow 23/10) Miss J Davis

Placings:0-65 (4537)
2003/04: 17[6]G, 16[5]GS,

	Starts	1st	2nd	3rd	Win & Pl
Hurdles	2	0	0	0	0
Career Total	3	0	0	0	0

Going:	Sf: 0-0 GS: 0-0 Gd: 0-1 GF: - Fm: 0-0
Distance:	2m/2m3: 0-2 2m4-2m7: 0-0 3m+: 0-0
Track:	LH: 0-0 RH: 0-2 Tight: 0-1 Gall: 0-0
Aids:	Bl: 0-0 Vi: 0-0 Tstrap: 0-0 Ckp: 0-0
Best Rating:	62 4/03 Chel 2m1f good Hdl

Raygale

82 83

7-y-o b g Superpower-Little Missile (Ile De Bourbon (USA))
K C Bailey Simon Cordingley

Placings:6/6420/602UPP (4756)
2003/04: 16[6]S, 20[P]GS, 16[2]HY, 19[U]GS, 26[P]G, 19[P]S,

	Starts	1st	2nd	3rd	Win & Pl
Hurdles	6	0	1	0	1278
Career Total	11	0	2	0	1726

Going:	Sf: 0-3 GS: 0-2 Gd: 0-1 GF: - Fm: 0-0
Distance:	2m/2m3: 0-2 2m4-2m7: 0-3 3m+: 0-1
Track:	LH: 0-1 RH: 0-3 Tight: 0-0 Gall: 0-1
Aids:	Bl: 0-0 Vi: 0-0 Tstrap: 0-0 Ckp: 0-0
Best Rating:	97 1/02 Newc 2m soft NHF

Placed in bumpers and modest novice hurdles.

Rayshan (IRE)

99 111

4-y-o b g Darshaan-Rayseka (IRE) (Dancing Brave (USA))
J Howard Johnson (John M Oxx 13/9) Andrea & Graham Wylie

Placings:12 (4597)
2003/04: 16[1]G, 16[2]G,

	Starts	1st	2nd	3rd	Win & Pl
Hurdles	2	1	1	0	6072
Career Total	2	1	1	0	6072
104	2/04 Muss 2m	D Hdl	GD	£4784
			Total win prize-money	£4784

Going:	Sf: 0-0 GS: 0-0 Gd: 1-2 GF: - Fm: 0-0
Distance:	2m/2m3: 1-2 2m4-2m7: 0-0 3m+: 0-0
Track:	LH: 0-1 RH: 1-1 Tight: 1-2 Gall: 0-0
Aids:	Bl: 0-0 Vi: 0-0 Tstrap: 0-0 Ckp: 0-0
Best Rating:	111 3/04 Kels 2m110y good Hdl

Modest juvenile hurdler; smart middle-distance performer on the Flat; showed impressive turn of foot to win on his hurdles debut at Musselburgh, outstaying runner-up; most disappointing next time when runner-up in weak company at Kelso in March; effective at two miles, but will want further; acts on good ground.

Rayware Boy (IRE)
103   **92**

8-y-o b g Scenic-Amata (USA) (Nodouble (USA))
D Shaw Rayton Racing

Placings:0256F0/05/1051U3/06230R0-0345205R4RR
(4776)
2003/04: 17⁹GF, 20³HY, 16⁴G, 16⁵GS, 20²G, 19⁰GS, 16⁵S, 16⁶G, 19⁴G, 17⁸G, 20⁸G,

	Starts	1st	2nd	3rd	Win & Pl
Hurdles	11	0	1	1	2260
Career Total	32	2	3	3	9927
92	1/02	Donc	2m110y	F(0-100)HHdl	SFT £2754
82	12/01	Bang	2m1f	F(0-100)HHdl	G-S £2086
				Total win prize-money £4841	

Going:	Sf: 0-2 GS: 0-2 Gd: 0-6 GF: - Fm: 0-1
Distance:	2m/2m3: 0-6 2m4-2m7: 0-5 3m+: 0-0
Track:	LH: 0-6 RH: 0-5 Tight: 0-6 Gall: 0-0
Aids:	Bl: 0-0 Vi: 0-11 Tstrap: 0-0 Ckp: 0-0
Best Rating:	92 3/04 Donc 2m3f110y good Hdl

Plating-class hurdler, acts on soft ground and wears a visor; has refused to race in the past.

Razzmatazz (IRE)
       57

10-y-o br g Camden Town-Sallys Wish (Proverb)
J Howard Johnson George Thursby

Placings:00/00000.5500/0-4
(1491)
2003/04: 16⁴GF,

	Starts	1st	2nd	3rd	Win & Pl
Hurdles	1	0	0	0	0
Career Total	12	0	0	0	0

Going:	Sf: 0-0 GS: 0-0 Gd: 0-0 GF: - Fm: 0-1
Distance:	2m/2m3: 0-1 2m4-2m7: 0-0 3m+: 0-0
Track:	LH: 0-1 RH: 0-0 Tight: 0-0 Gall: 0-0
Aids:	Bl: 0-0 Vi: 0-0 Tstrap: 0-0 Ckp: 0-0
Best Rating:	92 12/00 Navn 2m heavy NHF

Poor plater nowadays.

Reach The Clouds (IRE)
102(87h)   (95h)**102**

12-y-o b g Lord Americo-Dusky Stream (Paddy's Stream)
John R Upson The Three Horseshoes Sporting Club

Placings:0P0F63/1302325230/1325152/1323241/4F64432 20/522432F035/F42232-26132PF625
(4752)
2003/04: 16²GS, 16⁶G, 17¹G, 16³GF, 16²GF, 17⁸GS, 17⁵S, 16⁶GS, 16²GS, 16⁸G,

	Starts	1st	2nd	3rd	Win & Pl
Hurdles	1	0	0	0	0
Chases	9	1	3	1	6789
Career Total	65	6	18	12	59109
102	11/03	Plum	2m1f	E(0-110)HCh	GD £3244
118	4/00	Chel	2m110y	C(0-135)HCh	SFT £10244
115	10/99	Bang	2m1f110y	F(0-110)HCh	G-S £4045
109	4/99	Plum	2m2f	F(0-110)HCh	G-S £2932
107	11/98	Folk	2m	E(0-100)HCh	G-S £3436
82	10/97	Plum	2m1f	E(0-100)HHdl	GD £2511
				Total win prize-money £26415	

Going:	Sf: 0-1 GS: 0-3 Gd: 1-4 GF: - Fm: 0-2
Distance:	2m/2m3: 1-10 2m4-2m7: 0-0 3m+: 0-0
Track:	LH: 1-10 RH: 0-0 Tight: 1-6 Gall: 0-0
Aids:	Bl: 0-0 Vi: 0-0 Tstrap: 0-0 Ckp: 0-0
Best Rating:	118 5/01 Sthl 2m gd-fm Ch

Reachforthestars

8-y-o b m Royal Fountain-China's Way (USA) (Native Uproar (USA))
J Mackie Fools Who Dream

Placings:00/0P-PPPP
(3338)
2003/04: 20⁵S, 21⁸GS, 21⁸GS, 16⁸GS,

	Starts	1st	2nd	3rd	Win & Pl
Hurdles	3	0	0	0	0
Chases	1	0	0	0	0
Career Total	7	0	0	0	

Going:	Sf: 0-1 GS: 0-3 Gd: 0-0 GF: - Fm: 0-0
Distance:	2m/2m3: 0-1 2m4-2m7: 0-3 3m+: 0-0
Track:	LH: 0-2 RH: 0-2 Tight: 0-2 Gall: 0-1
Aids:	Bl: 0-0 Vi: 0-0 Tstrap: 0-0 Ckp: 0-0
Best Rating:	40 4/01 MRas 2m1f110y heavy NHF

Ready To Rumble (IRE)
99   **114**

9-y-o ch g Phardante (FR)-My Only Hope (Brave Invader (USA))
Noel T Chance Let's Get Ready To Rumble Partnership

Placings:203/221P/64P
(4169)
2003/04: 19⁶GS, 20⁴G, 22⁸G,

	Starts	1st	2nd	3rd	Win & Pl
Chases	3	0	0	0	431
Career Total	10	1	3	1	13453
121	2/01	Wwck	2m5f	D Hdl	£4042
				Total win prize-money £4043	

Going:	Sf: 0-0 GS: 0-1 Gd: 0-2 GF: - Fm: 0-0
Distance:	2m/2m3: 0-0 2m4-2m7: 0-3 3m+: 0-0
Track:	LH: 0-2 RH: 0-1 Tight: 0-0 Gall: 0-1
Aids:	Bl: 0-0 Vi: 0-0 Tstrap: 0-0 Ckp: 0-0
Best Rating:	127 3/00 Chel 2m110y good NHF

Modest novice chaser, formerly useful in bumpers and hurdles; off for three years prior to comeback at Chepstow in December 2003; stays three miles; best with cut; fragile sort.

Real Cracker (IRE)
       94

5-y-o b g Lahib (USA)-Loreo (IRE) (Lord Chancellor (USA))
Miss Venetia Williams Peter Diamond

Placings:1PF
(4003)
2003/04: 17¹GF, 19⁸G, 16⁸FG,

	Starts	1st	2nd	3rd	Win & Pl
NH Flat	1	1	0	0	2078
Hurdles	2	0	0	0	0
Career Total	3	1	0	0	2078
98	5/03	MRas	2m1f110y	H NHF	G-F £2077
				Total win prize-money £2078	

Going:	Sf: 0-0 GS: 0-0 Gd: 0-2 GF: - Fm: 1-1
Distance:	2m/2m3: 1-2 2m4-2m7: 0-1 3m+: 0-0
Track:	LH: 0-0 RH: 1-3 Tight: 1-2 Gall: 0-1
Aids:	Bl: 0-0 Vi: 0-0 Tstrap: 0-0 Ckp: 0-0
Best Rating:	98 5/03 MRas 2m1f110y gd-fm NHF

Real Definition
103f   **96+f**

5-y-o gr g Highest Honor (FR)-Segovia (Groom Dancer (USA))
D J Wintle Lady Blyth

Placings:401
(4447)
2003/04: 16⁴S, 16⁰GS, 16¹S,

	Starts	1st	2nd	3rd	Win & Pl
NH Flat	3	1	0	0	2303
Career Total	3	1	0	0	2303
96	3/04	Wwck	2m	H NHF	SFT £2303
				Total win prize-money £2303	

Going:	Sf: 1-2 GS: 0-1 Gd: 0-0 GF: - Fm: 0-0
Distance:	2m/2m3: 1-3 2m4-2m7: 0-0 3m+: 0-0
Track:	LH: 1-1 RH: 0-1 Tight: 0-0 Gall: 0-1
Aids:	Bl: 0-0 Vi: 0-0 Tstrap: 0-0 Ckp: 0-0
Best Rating:	96 3/04 Wwck 2m soft NHF

Half-brother to useful Irish bumper and hurdle winner Govamix; showed promise on his debut and won Warwick bumper third start; should be interesting over hurdles.

Real Fire (IRE)
97(99c)   (75c)**73**

10-y-o b g Astronef-Golden Arum (Home Guard (USA))
R Johnson Jack Thornton

Placings:331202P/4PPP040245P602400/0/0P/040510/0P3 0404043042044-4345
(1468)
2003/04: 16⁴G, 16⁴G, 22³GF, 22⁴G, 26⁵GF,

	Starts	1st	2nd	3rd	Win & Pl
Hurdles	3	0	0	1	385
Chases	2	0	0	0	824
Career Total	53	2	5	5	11345
73	10/01	Sedg	2m5f110yG(0-95)HHdl	GD £1862
77	9/97	Prth	2m110y	E Hdl	G-F £2558
				Total win prize-money £4420	

Going:	Sf: 0-0 GS: 0-0 Gd: 0-3 GF: - Fm: 0-2
Distance:	2m/2m3: 0-2 2m4-2m7: 0-2 3m+: 0-1
Track:	LH: 0-3 RH: 0-2 Tight: 0-2 Gall: 0-1
Aids:	Bl: 0-1 Vi: 0-0 Tstrap: 0-1 Ckp: 0-3
Best Rating:	82 10/97 Carl 2m1f gd-fm Hdl

Poor hurdler/chaser; stays two mile six.

Real Shady
108   **108+**

7-y-o b g Bob's Return (IRE)-Madam Margeaux (IRE) (Ardross)
M W Easterby Lord Daresbury

Placings:1/400/PP2-12263
(3320)
2003/04: 16¹GF, 16²G, 20⁴HY, 23⁸G, 16³S,

	Starts	1st	2nd	3rd	Win & Pl
Hurdles	5	1	2	1	4547
Career Total	12	2	3	1	7181
104	11/03	Hexm	2m110y	F(0-100)HHdl	G-F £2240
90	1/01	Newc	2m	H NHF	SFT £1589
				Total win prize-money £3829	

Going:	Sf: 0-2 GS: 0-0 Gd: 0-2 GF: - Fm: 1-1
Distance:	2m/2m3: 1-3 2m4-2m7: 0-2 3m+: 0-0
Track:	LH: 1-3 RH: 0-2 Tight: 0-0 Gall: 0-0
Aids:	Bl: 0-0 Vi: 0-0 Tstrap: 0-0 Ckp: 0-0
Best Rating:	108 11/03 Carl 2m4f heavy Hdl

Modest hurdler; off the mark over hurdles at Hexham in November; acts on fast and soft ground; best over two miles.

Real Sharp (IRE)

84   39

6-y-o br g Son Of Sharp Shot (IRE)-Lady By Chance (IRE) (Never Got A Chance)
S E H Sherwood The Perseverance Mob

Placings:6040-00   (3786)
2003/04: 21⁰G, 20⁰GS,

	Starts	1st	2nd	3rd	Win & Pl
Hurdles	2	0	0	0	
Career Total	6	0	0	0	269

Going:	Sf: 0-0 GS: 0-1 Gd: 0-1 GF: - Fm: 0-0
Distance:	2m/2m3: 0-0 2m4-2m7: 0-2 3m+: 0-0
Track:	LH: 0-0 RH: 0-2 Tight: 0-0 Gall: 0-1
Aids:	Bl: 0-1 Vi: 0-0 Tstrap: 0-0 Ckp: 0-0
Best Rating:	66 11/02 Ludl 2m gd-sft NHF

Real Value (IRE)

13-y-o b g Matching Pair-Silent Verb (Proverb)
Mrs D M Grissell Cockerell Cowing Racing

Placings:12F2/P05513/F20P/021F-3PP   (3873)
2003/04: 24³G, 28ᴾG, 25ᴾGS,

	Starts	1st	2nd	3rd	Win & Pl
Chases	3	0	0	1	512
Career Total	21	3	4	2	29505
108	3/03	Leic	2m7f110yH Ch		G-S	£5486
131	2/01	Sand	3m110y	B(0-140)HCh	SFT	£9948
121	3/00	Newb	3m	H Ch	SFT	£1557
			Total win prize-money £16992

Going:	Sf: 0-0 GS: 0-0 Gd: 0-2 GF: - Fm: 0-0
Distance:	2m/2m3: 0-0 2m4-2m7: 0-0 3m+: 0-3
Track:	LH: 0-2 RH: 0-1 Tight: 0-2 Gall: 0-0
Aids:	Bl: 0-0 Vi: 0-0 Tstrap: 0-0 Ckp: 0-0
Best Rating:	136 3/00 Chel 3m2f110y gd-fm Ch

Fair hunter chaser; thorough stayer; seems to handle any ground; can make mistakes.

Reasonable Reserve (IRE)

(107h)   (109h)90

7-y-o ch g Fourstars Allstar (USA)-Alice O'Malley (The Parson)
B G Powell (C F Swan 1/6) Seamus Mannion

Placings:0006/40³-0611132OUU   (1732)
2003/04: 24⁰S, 24⁶GF, 24¹G, 24¹GF, 24¹G, 24³GF, 24²GF, 24⁰GF, 26ᵁGF, 24ᵁGF,

	Starts	1st	2nd	3rd	Win & Pl
Hurdles	7	3	0	1	13090
Chases	3	0	1	0	868
Career Total	17	3	1	2	14776
101	7/03	Worc	3m	D(0-125)HHdl	GD	£5031
109	7/03	Worc	3m	E(0-100)HHdl	G-F	£3451
96	6/03	Worc	3m	E Hdl	GD	£3570
			Total win prize-money £12052

Going:	Sf: 0-1 GS: 0-0 Gd: 2-2 GF: - Fm: 1-7
Distance:	2m/2m3: 0-0 2m4-2m7: 0-0 3m+: 3-10
Track:	LH: 3-7 RH: 0-2 Tight: 0-0 Gall: 0-1
Aids:	Bl: 0-0 Vi: 0-0 Tstrap: 0-0 Ckp: 0-2
Best Rating:	109 8/03 Worc 3m gd-fm Hdl

Modest hurdler/novice chaser; ex-Irish; completed a hat-trick over hurdles in the summer of 2003; did not jump well on chase debut; ran over hurdles next start; likes fast ground; stays well; has been tried in cheekpieces.

Rebel Raider (IRE)

100   93

5-y-o b g Mujadil (USA)-Emily's Pride (Shirley Heights)
B N Pollock S G B Morrison

Placings:C-222   (0889)
2003/04: 16²G, 17²G, 16²G,

	Starts	1st	2nd	3rd	Win & Pl
Hurdles	3	0	3	0	3207
Career Total	4	0	3	0	3207

Going:	Sf: 0-0 GS: 0-0 Gd: 0-3 GF: - Fm: 0-0
Distance:	2m/2m3: 0-3 2m4-2m7: 0-0 3m+: 0-0
Track:	LH: 0-2 RH: 0-1 Tight: 0-0 Gall: 0-0
Aids:	Bl: 0-0 Vi: 0-0 Tstrap: 0-0 Ckp: 0-0
Best Rating:	93 7/03 Worc 2m good Hdl

Modrate hurdler; clearly second best on all three outings since being carried out on his British debut; acts on good.

Rebel Rhythm

98f   126+f

5-y-o b g Robellino (USA)-Celt Song (IRE) (Unfuwain (USA))
Mrs S J Smith The Fees R Us Syndicate

Placings:133   (4866)
2003/04: 16¹GS, 17³G, 16⁹S,

	Starts	1st	2nd	3rd	Win & Pl
NH Flat	3	1	0	2	5883
Career Total	3	1	0	2	5883
120	3/04	Weth	2m	H NHF	G-S	£2037
			Total win prize-money £2037

Going:	Sf: 0-1 GS: 1-1 Gd: 0-1 GF: - Fm: 0-0
Distance:	2m/2m3: 1-3 2m4-2m7: 0-0 3m+: 0-0
Track:	LH: 1-2 RH: 0-0 Tight: 0-0 Gall: 0-0
Aids:	Bl: 0-0 Vi: 0-0 Tstrap: 0-0 Ckp: 0-0
Best Rating:	120 3/04 Weth 2m gd-sft NHF

Flat-bred; wide margin winner on debut in bumper at Wetherby in March; third in the Aintree Champion Bumper and anything but disgraced at Ayr in April 2004; bags of physical scope and looks sure to win more races when sent over obstacles.

Rebel's Gift

        56

11-y-o b g Genuine Gift (CAN)-Princess Veronica (Rebel Prince)
F P Murtagh S R Bainbridge & Mrs G Bainbridge

Placings:0P5/4FPP00104/6010F60/3303PP/0PP5-P (0197)
2003/04: 24ᴾG,

	Starts	1st	2nd	3rd	Win & Pl
Hurdles	1	0	0	0	
Career Total	30	2	0	3	5294
78	10/00	Kels	2m6f110yF(0-105)HHdl	GD	£2786
78	2/00	Catt	2m3f	G(0-90)HHdl	GD	£1617
			Total win prize-money £4403

Going:	Sf: 0-0 GS: 0-0 Gd: 0-1 GF: - Fm: 0-0
Distance:	2m/2m3: 0-0 2m4-2m7: 0-0 3m+: 0-1
Track:	LH: 0-1 RH: 0-0 Tight: 0-0 Gall: 0-0
Aids:	Bl: 0-0 Vi: 0-0 Tstrap: 0-0 Ckp: 0-0
Best Rating:	78 9/01 Sedg 2m5f110y good Hdl

Rebelle

5-y-o b/br g Reprimand-Blushing Belle (Local Suitor (USA))

P Bowen P Bowen

Placings:P   (3084)
2003/04: 22ᴾGS,

	Starts	1st	2nd	3rd	Win & Pl
Hurdles	1	0	0	0	
Career Total	1	0	0	0	

Going:	Sf: 0-0 GS: 0-1 Gd: 0-0 GF: - Fm: 0-0
Distance:	2m/2m3: 0-0 2m4-2m7: 0-1 3m+: 0-0
Track:	LH: 0-1 RH: 0-0 Tight: 0-1 Gall: 0-0
Aids:	Bl: 0-0 Vi: 0-0 Tstrap: 0-0 Ckp: 0-0

Recoleta

7-y-o b m Ezzoud (IRE)-Hug Me (Shareef Dancer (USA))
F Jordan Mrs J E Crisell

Placings:03000PP/PP   (2465)
2003/04: 16ᴾGF, 16ᴾS,

	Starts	1st	2nd	3rd	Win & Pl
Hurdles	2	0	0	0	
Career Total	9	0	0	1	323

Going:	Sf: 0-1 GS: 0-0 Gd: 0-0 GF: - Fm: 0-1
Distance:	2m/2m3: 0-2 2m4-2m7: 0-0 3m+: 0-0
Track:	LH: 0-0 RH: 0-2 Tight: 0-0 Gall: 0-0
Aids:	Bl: 0-0 Vi: 0-0 Tstrap: 0-0 Ckp: 0-0
Best Rating:	46 11/00 Wwck 2m heavy Hdl

Rectory (IRE)

87f   84f

5-y-o b g Presenting-Billys Pet (Le Moss)
Mrs S J Smith J Henderson (co Durham)

Placings:00   (3482)
2003/04: 16⁰GS, 16⁰G,

	Starts	1st	2nd	3rd	Win & Pl
NH Flat	2	0	0	0	
Career Total	2	0	0	0	

Going:	Sf: 0-0 GS: 0-1 Gd: 0-1 GF: - Fm: 0-0
Distance:	2m/2m3: 0-2 2m4-2m7: 0-0 3m+: 0-0
Track:	LH: 0-2 RH: 0-0 Tight: 0-1 Gall: 0-0
Aids:	Bl: 0-0 Vi: 0-0 Tstrap: 0-0 Ckp: 0-0
Best Rating:	84 1/04 Catt 2m good NHF

Red Addick (IRE)

5-y-o gr g Grand Lodge (USA)-Glad's Night (IRE) (Sexton Blake)
Miss Suzy Smith Miss Z Anthony

Placings:0P   (0619)
2003/04: 16⁰GF, 24ᴾG,

	Starts	1st	2nd	3rd	Win & Pl
Hurdles	2	0	0	0	
Career Total	2	0	0	0	

Going:	Sf: 0-0 GS: 0-0 Gd: 0-1 GF: - Fm: 0-1
Distance:	2m/2m3: 0-1 2m4-2m7: 0-0 3m+: 0-1
Track:	LH: 0-0 RH: 0-2 Tight: 0-1 Gall: 0-1
Aids:	Bl: 0-1 Vi: 0-0 Tstrap: 0-0 Ckp: 0-0

Red Afgem

88   **49**

7-y-o ch m Afzal-Preacher's Gem (The Parson)
Mrs S M Johnson Mrs P A Wallis

Placings:030-P0   (4712)
2003/04: 21PGS, 240G,

	Starts	1st	2nd	3rd	Win & Pl
Hurdles	2	0	0	0	
Career Total	5	0	0	1	240

Going:	Sf: 0-0 GS: 0-1 Gd: 0-1 GF: - Fm: 0-0
Distance:	2m/2m3: 0-0 2m4-2m7: 0-1 3m+: 0-0
Track:	LH: 0-1 RH: 0-1 Tight: 0-0 Gall: 0-1
Aids:	Bl: 0-0 Vi: 0-0 Tstrap: 0-0 Ckp: 0-0
Best Rating:	63 6/02 Hrfd 2m1f gd-fm NHF

Red Alert Man (IRE)

90   **(77h)76**

8-y-o ch g Sharp Charter-Tukurua (Noalto)
Mrs L Williamson Halewood International Ltd

Placings:006/F0F0P/44PP563U1-3423P   (4914)
2003/04: 17PS, 204S, 242GF, 213GF, 24PGS,

	Starts	1st	2nd	3rd	Win & Pl
Hurdles	1	0	0	0	0
Chases	4	0	1	2	3022
Career Total	22	1	1	3	8525
76 4/03 Uttx			2m5f		E Ch GD £4389
				Total win prize-money £4389	

Going:	Sf: 0-2 GS: 0-1 Gd: 0-0 GF: - Fm: 0-2
Distance:	2m/2m3: 0-1 2m4-2m7: 0-2 3m+: 0-1
Track:	LH: 0-5 RH: 0-0 Tight: 0-2 Gall: 0-0
Aids:	Bl: 0-4 Vi: 0-0 Tstrap: 0-0 Ckp: 0-0
Best Rating:	79 3/01 Hayd 2m heavy NHF

Selling-class chaser; stays two and a half miles; acts well on good ground.

Red Blazer (NZ)

97   **(101h)94**

11-y-o ch g Omnicorp (NZ)-Gay Reef (Reform)
A W Carroll K Marshall

Placings:1235P/P6132P0/5/P6620   (3781)
2003/04: 16PGS, 22PGS, 23RG, 202GS, 20PS,

	Starts	1st	2nd	3rd	Win & Pl
Hurdles	1	0	0	0	0
Chases	4	0	1	0	1668
Career Total	18	2	3	2	8291
109 12/00 Fknm		2m4f		F(0-100)HHdl	G-S £1771
8/99 Foxt		1m6f		Hdl	SFT £2063
				Total win prize-money £3834	

Going:	Sf: 0-1 GS: 0-3 Gd: 0-1 GF: - Fm: 0-0
Distance:	2m/2m3: 0-1 2m4-2m7: 0-3 3m+: 0-1
Track:	LH: 0-2 RH: 0-3 Tight: 0-0 Gall: 0-0
Aids:	Bl: 0-0 Vi: 0-0 Tstrap: 0-0 Ckp: 0-0
Best Rating:	109 3/01 Hntg 2m5f110y soft Hdl

Moderate chaser; effective at around two and a half miles; acts on soft.

Red Blooded (IRE)

(94c)   **(78c)10**

7-y-o b g River Falls-Volkova (Green Desert (USA))
Mrs L C Jewell Mrs A Greengrow

Placings:0P5-P5PP0   (1543)

2003/04: 20PG, 175GS, 18PGF, 21PGF, 16QGF,

	Starts	1st	2nd	3rd	Win & Pl
Hurdles	3	0	0	0	0
Chases	2	0	0	0	0
Career Total	8	0	0	0	0

Going:	Sf: 0-0 GS: 0-1 Gd: 0-1 GF: - Fm: 0-3
Distance:	2m/2m3: 0-3 2m4-2m7: 0-2 3m+: 0-0
Track:	LH: 0-4 RH: 0-0 Tight: 0-4 Gall: 0-0
Aids:	Bl: 0-0 Vi: 0-1 Tstrap: 0-4 Ckp: 0-0
Best Rating:	78 3/03 Hntg 2m110y good Ch

Red Boy (GER)

5-y-o ch h Royal Abjar (USA)-Royal Wind (GER) (Windwurf (GER))
Mario Hofer Stall Lucky Owner

Placings:P   (3871)
2003/04: 17PGS,

	Starts	1st	2nd	3rd	Win & Pl
Hurdles	1	0	0	0	0
Career Total	1	0	0	0	0

Going:	Sf: 0-0 GS: 0-0 Gd: 0-0 GF: - Fm: 0-0
Distance:	2m/2m3: 0-1 2m4-2m7: 0-0 3m+: 0-0
Track:	LH: 0-0 RH: 0-1 Tight: 0-1 Gall: 0-0
Aids:	Bl: 0-0 Vi: 0-0 Tstrap: 0-0 Ckp: 0-0

Red Brae

96(86h)   **(67h)75+**

7-y-o b g Rakaposhi King-Sayshar (Sayfar)
P D Niven C D Carr

Placings:5/04/P-00053B015P   (4880)
2003/04: 20PHY, 179GS, 16QGS, 16PGF, 16QGS, 25PHY, 24QG, 16IGS, 16QG, 20PGS,

	Starts	1st	2nd	3rd	Win & Pl
Hurdles	3	0	0	0	0
Chases	7	1	0	1	3712
Career Total	14	1	0	1	3712
75 3/04 Towc		2m110y		F(0-95)HCh	G-S £3120
				Total win prize-money £3120	

Going:	Sf: 0-2 GS: 1-5 Gd: 0-2 GF: - Fm: 0-1
Distance:	2m/2m3: 1-6 2m4-2m7: 0-2 3m+: 0-2
Track:	LH: 0-3 RH: 1-7 Tight: 0-4 Gall: 0-3
Aids:	Bl: 0-0 Vi: 0-2 Tstrap: 0-0 Ckp: 1-1
Best Rating:	100 3/02 Chep 2m110y soft NHF

Plating-class hurdler/chaser; has worn blinkers; effective over two miles.

Red Brook Lad

9-y-o ch g Nomadic Way (USA)-Silently Yours (USA) (Silent Screen (USA))
C St V Fox C St V Fox

Placings:P053060/UF2-111P0   (4696)
2003/04: 21IG, 25IGF, 20IG, 26PG, 19QG,

	Starts	1st	2nd	3rd	Win & Pl
Chases	5	3	0	0	8896
Career Total	15	3	1	1	10342
118 2/04 Sand		2m4f110yH Ch			GD £2331
99 5/03 Winc		3m1f110yH Ch			G-F £3406
100 4/03 Chel		2m5f		H Ch	GD £3159
				Total win prize-money £8896	

Going:	Sf: 0-0 GS: 0-0 Gd: 2-4 GF: - Fm: 1-1
Distance:	2m/2m3: 0-0 2m4-2m7: 2-3 3m+: 1-2
Track:	LH: 1-2 RH: 2-3 Tight: 0-0 Gall: 1-2
Aids:	Bl: 0-0 Vi: 0-0 Tstrap: 0-0 Ckp: 0-0
Best Rating:	118 2/04 Sand 2m4f110y good Ch

Fair hunter chaser; prolific winning pointer; stays three miles one; unlikely to stay further; suited by a sound surface.

Red Canyon (IRE)

108   **98**

7-y-o ch g Zieten (USA)-Bayazida (Bustino)
A G Hobbs Miss Jayne Brace & Gwyn Brace

Placings:0/04000435P/001114425-435642236F4   (1733)
2003/04: 204GF, 203GF, 20PG, 24PG, 24AGF, 212GS, 202GF, 203GF, 226GF, 22PGF, 20PGF,

	Starts	1st	2nd	3rd	Win & Pl
Hurdles	11	0	2	2	4266
Career Total	30	3	3	3	14969
98 8/02 NAbb		2m6f		E(0-110)HHdl	G-F £2884
95 7/02 Strf		2m6f110yE(0-110)HHdl			G-F £3209
79 6/02 Worc		2m4f		E(0-105)HHdl	G-F £2653
				Total win prize-money £8747	

Going:	Sf: 0-0 GS: 0-1 Gd: 0-2 GF: - Fm: 0-8
Distance:	2m/2m3: 0-0 2m4-2m7: 0-10 3m+: 0-1
Track:	LH: 0-11 RH: 0-0 Tight: 0-3 Gall: 0-0
Aids:	Bl: 0-0 Vi: 0-4 Tstrap: 0-0 Ckp: 0-0
Best Rating:	98 8/03 Worc 2m4f gd-fm Hdl

Moderate hurdler; in top form when completing a hat-trick in the summer of 2002; stays 2m 6f; acts on fast ground; signs of a return to form since being fitted with a visor in August 2003.

Red Chief (IRE)

90   **85+**

4-y-o b g Lahib (USA)-Karayb (IRE) (Last Tycoon)
R Lee (M L W Bell 6/10) Gareth Samuel

Placings:5   (4251)
2003/04: 17PG,

	Starts	1st	2nd	3rd	Win & Pl
Hurdles	1	0	0	0	0
Career Total	1	0	0	0	0

Going:	Sf: 0-0 GS: 0-0 Gd: 0-1 GF: - Fm: 0-0
Distance:	2m/2m3: 0-1 2m4-2m7: 0-0 3m+: 0-0
Track:	LH: 0-1 RH: 0-0 Tight: 0-1 Gall: 0-0
Aids:	Bl: 0-0 Vi: 0-0 Tstrap: 0-0 Ckp: 0-0
Best Rating:	85 3/04 Bang 2m1f good Hdl

Red Crystal

6-y-o b m Presidium-Crystallography (Primitive Rising (USA))
C R Wilson Mrs V C Sugden

Placings:PPPP   (3481)
2003/04: 19PG, 21PGF, 17PG, 25PG,

	Starts	1st	2nd	3rd	Win & Pl
Hurdles	4	0	0	0	
Career Total	4	0	0	0	

Going:	Sf: 0-0 GS: 0-0 Gd: 0-3 GF: - Fm: 0-1
Distance:	2m/2m3: 0-1 2m4-2m7: 0-2 3m+: 0-1
Track:	LH: 0-3 RH: 0-1 Tight: 0-4 Gall: 0-0
Aids:	Bl: 0-0 Vi: 0-0 Tstrap: 0-0 Ckp: 0-1

Red Dahlia

89   **67**

7-y-o b m Afflora (IRE)-Redgrave Devil (Tug Of War)
M Pitman The Barrossa Syndicate

Placings:00P-4F6P   (4123)
2003/04: 21⁴GF, 21²G, 16⁶S, 17⁶G,

	Starts	1st	2nd	3rd	Win & Pl
Hurdles	4	0	0	0	316
Career Total	7	0	0	0	316

Going:	Sf: 0-1 GS: 0-0 Gd: 0-2 GF: - Fm: 0-1
Distance:	2m/2m3: 0-2 2m4-2m7: 0-2 3m+: 0-0
Track:	LH: 0-2 RH: 0-3 Tight: 0-2 Gall: 0-0
Aids:	Bl: 0-0 Vi: 0-0 Tstrap: 0-0 Ckp: 0-0
Best Rating:	81 5/02 Naas 2m good NHF

Red Devil Robert (IRE)

106   **113**

6-y-o ch g Carroll House-Well Over (Over The River (FR))
P F Nicholls Barry Marshall & Paul K Barber

Placings:2322   (4895)
2003/04: 20²GS, 24³S, 21²GS, 22²G,

	Starts	1st	2nd	3rd	Win & Pl
Hurdles	4	0	3	1	5675
Career Total	4	0	3	1	5675

Going:	Sf: 0-1 GS: 0-2 Gd: 0-1 GF: - Fm: 0-0
Distance:	2m/2m3: 0-0 2m4-2m7: 0-3 3m+: 0-1
Track:	LH: 0-2 RH: 0-2 Tight: 0-0 Gall: 0-1
Aids:	Bl: 0-0 Vi: 0-0 Tstrap: 0-0 Ckp: 0-0
Best Rating:	113 4/04 Winc 2m6f good Hdl

Fair hurdler; yet to win but often placed; yet to prove he truly stays beyond two and a half miles.

Red Emperor

80(81h)   (49h)**97**

10-y-o b g Emperor Fountain-Golden Curd (FR) (Nice Havrais (USA))
Dr P Pritchard Mrs T Pritchard

Placings:3043535652611523/0060U1436U05/512632P156 /3531P50-3430000600   (4777)
2003/04: 20³G, 24⁴G, 24³GF, 17⁹GS, 25⁹GS, 22⁰S, 22⁰GS, 25⁶G, 24⁰G, 23⁰G,

	Starts	1st	2nd	3rd	Win & Pl
Hurdles	4	0	0	0	0
Chases	6	0	0	2	2572
Career Total	55	6	4	10	28149
97	11/02	Newc	3m	F(0-90)HCh	G-S	£3292
98	3/02	Newc	3m	F(0-100)HCh	HVY	£2989
99	11/01	Newc	3m	F(0-90)HCh	G-S	£2597
94	11/00	Newc	3m	F(0-90)HCh	G-S	£2457
93	2/00	Carl	2m4f110y	F(0-110)HCh	HVY	£3526
81	1/00	Sthl	3m110y	F(0-90)HCh	G-S	£2643
				Total win prize-money		£17505

Going:	Sf: 0-1 GS: 0-3 Gd: 0-5 GF: - Fm: 0-1
Distance:	2m/2m3: 0-1 2m4-2m7: 0-3 3m+: 0-6
Track:	LH: 0-4 RH: 0-5 Tight: 0-5 Gall: 0-1
Aids:	Bl: 0-0 Vi: 0-0 Tstrap: 0-0 Ckp: 0-5
Best Rating:	99 2/02 Sedg 3m3f soft Ch

Plating-class hurdler/chaser; stays three miles plus; effective on soft ground; likes Newcastle; usually wears blinkers and a tongue tie.

Red Ensign

95   **54**

7-y-o ch g Lancastrian-Medway Queen (Pitpan)
Mrs L C Jewell Mrs S Stanier, P Oppenheimer, R Young

Placings:00-00655   (4367)
2003/04: 21⁰S, 22⁰GS, 22⁶HY, 22⁵GS, 25⁵GS,

	Starts	1st	2nd	3rd	Win & Pl
Hurdles	5	0	0	0	0
Career Total	7	0	0	0	0

Going:	Sf: 0-2 GS: 0-3 Gd: 0-0 GF: - Fm: 0-0
Distance:	2m/2m3: 0-0 2m4-2m7: 0-3 3m+: 0-1
Track:	LH: 0-2 RH: 0-2 Tight: 0-4 Gall: 0-0
Aids:	Bl: 0-0 Vi: 0-0 Tstrap: 0-0 Ckp: 0-0
Best Rating:	73 3/03 Plum 2m2f gd-fm NHF

Red Flyer (IRE)

104   **98**

5-y-o br g Catrail (USA)-Marostica (ITY) (Stone)
P C Haslam Mrs C Barclay

Placings:122FP-6254   (1879)
2003/04: 20⁶G, 16²GF, 16⁵G, 18⁴G,

	Starts	1st	2nd	3rd	Win & Pl
Hurdles	4	0	1	0	821
Career Total	9	1	3	0	7684
96	11/02	Newc	2m	D Hdl	G-S	£4173
				Total win prize-money £4173

Going:	Sf: 0-0 GS: 0-0 Gd: 0-3 GF: - Fm: 0-1
Distance:	2m/2m3: 0-3 2m4-2m7: 0-1 3m+: 0-0
Track:	LH: 0-4 RH: 0-0 Tight: 0-3 Gall: 0-0
Aids:	Bl: 0-0 Vi: 0-0 Tstrap: 0-0 Ckp: 0-0
Best Rating:	100 11/03 Kels 2m2f good Hdl

Moderate novice hurdler; beaten in selling company; best over two miles; acts on any ground

Red Forest (IRE)

5-y-o b g Charnwood Forest (IRE)-High Atlas (Shirley Heights)
J Mackie P Riley

Placings:PP-P   (2154)
2003/04: 16⁶GS,

	Starts	1st	2nd	3rd	Win & Pl
Hurdles	1	0	0	0	
Career Total	3	0	0	0	

Going:	Sf: 0-0 GS: 0-1 Gd: 0-0 GF: - Fm: 0-0
Distance:	2m/2m3: 0-1 2m4-2m7: 0-0 3m+: 0-0
Track:	LH: 0-1 RH: 0-0 Tight: 0-0 Gall: 0-0
Aids:	Bl: 0-0 Vi: 0-0 Tstrap: 0-1 Ckp: 0-0

Red Fred

4-y-o ch g Case Law-Mississipi Maid (All Systems Go)
P D Evans T Jarvis

Placings:P   (0958)
2003/04: 16⁰G,

	Starts	1st	2nd	3rd	Win & Pl
Hurdles	1	0	0	0	
Career Total	1	0	0	0	

Going:	Sf: 0-0 GS: 0-0 Gd: 0-1 GF: - Fm: 0-0
Distance:	2m/2m3: 0-1 2m4-2m7: 0-0 3m+: 0-0
Track:	LH: 0-1 RH: 0-0 Tight: 0-1 Gall: 0-0
Aids:	Bl: 0-0 Vi: 0-0 Tstrap: 0-0 Ckp: 0-0

Red Genie

95   **75**

6-y-o ch g Primitive Rising (USA)-Marsden Rock (Tina's Pet)
C J Gray (R C Guest 5/5) The Hilltop Seven Partnership

Placings:34043-56F0   (1362)
2003/04: 20³G, 16⁵GF, 17⁶GF, 16⁶GF, 16⁹GF,

	Starts	1st	2nd	3rd	Win & Pl
Hurdles	5	0	0	1	366
Career Total	9	0	0	2	627

Going:	Sf: 0-0 GS: 0-0 Gd: 0-1 GF: - Fm: 0-4
Distance:	2m/2m3: 0-4 2m4-2m7: 0-1 3m+: 0-0
Track:	LH: 0-4 RH: 0-1 Tight: 0-2 Gall: 0-1
Aids:	Bl: 0-0 Vi: 0-0 Tstrap: 0-0 Ckp: 0-0
Best Rating:	85 3/03 Hexm 2m110y good NHF

Moderate form in bumpers; only plating-class over hurdles.

Red Gold

109   **85+**

10-y-o ch g Sula Bula-Ruby Celebration (New Member)
Andrew Turnell Mrs C C Williams

Placings:0563PF/0F4/P-2P2UP3UP   (4916)
2003/04: 24²GS, 24ᴾGS, 25²GS, 24⁰HY, 24ᴾG, 24³G, 25⁰S, 23ᴾGS,

	Starts	1st	2nd	3rd	Win & Pl
Chases	8	0	2	1	2574
Career Total	18	0	2	2	3247

Going:	Sf: 0-2 GS: 0-4 Gd: 0-2 GF: - Fm: 0-0
Distance:	2m/2m3: 0-0 2m4-2m7: 0-0 3m+: 0-8
Track:	LH: 0-5 RH: 0-3 Tight: 0-1 Gall: 0-2
Aids:	Bl: 0-0 Vi: 0-0 Tstrap: 0-5 Ckp: 0-0
Best Rating:	104 1/01 Leic 2m4f110y soft Ch

Moderate form over fences; acts on soft; can make mistakes.

Red Guard

103(96h)   (107+h)**124**

10-y-o ch g Soviet Star (USA)-Zinzara (USA) (Stagedoor Johnny)
N J Gifford The Marvellous Partnership

Placings:4552/062140/11/0410P/622234F1/2F5P331F2- 54P2   (4701)
2003/04: 25⁵G, 20⁴GF, 24ᴾG, 22²G,

	Starts	1st	2nd	3rd	Win & Pl
Chases	4	0	1	0	2665
Career Total	38	6	8	3	54696
121	1/03	Hntg	3m	D(0-120)HCh	SFT	£5950
109	4/02	Font	2m6f	C Ch	G-F	£7345
138	1/01	Asct	2m110y	B HHdl	SFT	£10185
133	10/99	Weth	2m	C(0-135)HHdl	G-F	£5018
120	10/99	Font	2m2f110y C(0-135)HHdl	GD	£4719
124	12/98	Sand	2m110y	D(0-115)HHdl	GD	£4924
				Total win prize-money	£38145

Going:	Sf: 0-0 GS: 0-0 Gd: 0-3 GF: - Fm: 0-1
Distance:	2m/2m3: 0-0 2m4-2m7: 0-2 3m+: 0-2
Track:	LH: 0-3 RH: 0-0 Tight: 0-0 Gall: 0-0
Aids:	Bl: 0-3 Vi: 0-0 Tstrap: 0-0 Ckp: 0-0
Best Rating:	138 1/01 Asct 2m110y soft Hdl

Fair chaser; acts on most types of ground; effective at up to three miles; has not always convinced in a finish and needs to come late; has worn sheepskin cheekpieces and blinkers.

Red Halo

(104h)   (110 h)
5-y-o b g Be My Guest (USA)-Pray (IRE) (Priolo (USA))
S Kirk Terry Neill

Placings:111P0-F   (2385)
2003/04: 16FGF,

	Starts	1st	2nd	3rd	Win & Pl
Chases	1	0	0	0	
Career Total	6	3	0	0	11876
110	8/02	Bang	2m1f	E Hdl	G-F	£3672
95	8/02	Strf	2m110y	D Hdl	G-S	£5053
110	8/02	Bang	2m1f	E Hdl	SFT	£3150

Total win prize-money £11877

Going: Sf: 0-0 GS: 0-0 Gd: 0-0 GF: - Fm: 0-1
Distance: 2m2/m3: 0-1 2m4-2m7: 0-0 3m+: 0-0
Track: LH: 0-1 RH: 0-0 Tight: 0-0 Gall: 0-0
Aids: Bl: 0-0 Vi: 0-0 Tstrap: 0-0 Ckp: 0-0
Best Rating: 110 8/02 Bang 2m1f   gd-fm   Hdl

Fair enough hurdler; took a fatal fall on chasing debut; was best at around two miles; went on soft and fast ground (DEAD).

Red Hare (NZ)

103
10-y-o ch g Famous Star-Mutual Belle (NZ) (Western Bay (NZ))
Miss K Marks Nick Shutts

Placings:420/01PF6146/F3261PP2-PP   (0613)
2003/04: 21PG, 25PGF,

	Starts	1st	2nd	3rd	Win & Pl
Chases	2	0	0	0	
Career Total	21	3	3	1	16908
103	10/02	Tntn	3m	E(0-105)HCh	G-F	£4712
96	11/01	Kemp	3m110y	D(0-120)HHdl	GD	£5352
95	6/01	Fknm	2m4f	E Hdl	G-F	£2891

Total win prize-money £12957

Going: Sf: 0-0 GS: 0-0 Gd: 0-1 GF: - Fm: 0-1
Distance: 2m2/m3: 0-0 2m4-2m7: 0-1 3m+: 0-1
Track: LH: 0-1 RH: 0-1 Tight: 0-0 Gall: 0-0
Aids: Bl: 0-0 Vi: 0-0 Tstrap: 0-0 Ckp: 0-1
Best Rating: 105 11/00 Wwck 2m   soft   Hdl

Plating-class chaser; stays three miles; acts on decent ground.

Red Heather

61
7-y-o b m Mistertopogigo (IRE)-That's Rich (Hot Spark)
D W Whillans Mrs H M Whillans

Placings:0/P   (2508)
2003/04: 16PS,

	Starts	1st	2nd	3rd	Win & Pl
Hurdles	1	0	0	0	
Career Total	2	0	0	0	

Going: Sf: 0-1 GS: 0-0 Gd: 0-0 GF: - Fm: 0-0
Distance: 2m2/m3: 0-1 2m4-2m7: 0-0 3m+: 0-0
Track: LH: 0-1 RH: 0-0 Tight: 0-0 Gall: 0-0
Aids: Bl: 0-0 Vi: 0-0 Tstrap: 0-0 Ckp: 0-0
Best Rating: 63 3/02 Kels 2m110y   soft   Hdl

Red Hot Robbie

81
11-y-o ch g Gildoran-Quarry Machine (Laurence O)
Mrs N S Sharpe Mrs M Gittings-Watts

Placings:0/P63P-P   (1090)
2003/04: 22PGF,

	Starts	1st	2nd	3rd	Win & Pl
Hurdles	1	0	0	0	
Career Total	6	0	0	1	636

Going: Sf: 0-0 GS: 0-0 Gd: 0-0 GF: - Fm: 0-1
Distance: 2m2/m3: 0-0 2m4-2m7: 0-1 3m+: 0-0
Track: LH: 0-1 RH: 0-0 Tight: 0-1 Gall: 0-0
Aids: Bl: 0-0 Vi: 0-0 Tstrap: 0-0 Ckp: 0-0
Best Rating: 81 10/02 Strf   2m6f110y   good   Hdl

Plating-class hurdler; difficult to train; best effort so far when third in a modest 22 furlong maiden hurdle at Stratford October 2002; ran well until pulled up lame over the same track the following summer.

Red Hustler (IRE)

97   (47h)88
8-y-o ch g Husyan (USA)-Isoldes Tower (Balliol)
C Grant W Raw

Placings:/056/5F231-4F0620P0   (4797)
2003/04: 164S, 17FS, 199G, 166HY, 222GS, 20PGS, 20PG, 219G,

	Starts	1st	2nd	3rd	Win & Pl
Chases	8	0	1	0	1670
Career Total	16	1	2	1	8311
88	4/03	Weth	2m	E Ch	G-F	£4354

Total win prize-money £4354

Going: Sf: 0-3 GS: 0-2 Gd: 0-3 GF: - Fm: 0-0
Distance: 2m2/m3: 0-2 2m4-2m7: 0-4 3m+: 0-0
Track: LH: 0-4 RH: 0-4 Tight: 0-5 Gall: 0-0
Aids: Bl: 0-0 Vi: 0-1 Tstrap: 0-0 Ckp: 0-0
Best Rating: 88 3/04 MRas 2m6f110y gd-sft   Ch

Moderate chaser; off the mark in weak four-runner event at Wetherby in April 2003; just held at Market Rasen in March; stays two miles six; acts on any ground.

Red Lady

46
8-y-o b g Toulon-Winter Music (Young Emperor)
Peter McCreery (Mrs A M Naughton 4/7) Citrus Racing Syndicate

Placings:60   (3116a)
2003/04: 17SG, 16OS,

	Starts	1st	2nd	3rd	Win & Pl
Hurdles	1	0	0	0	0
Chases	1	0	0	0	0
Career Total	2	0	0	0	0

Going: Sf: 0-1 GS: 0-0 Gd: 0-1 GF: - Fm: 0-0
Distance: 2m2/m3: 0-2 2m4-2m7: 0-0 3m+: 0-0
Track: LH: 0-1 RH: 0-1 Tight: 0-0 Gall: 0-0
Aids: Bl: 0-0 Vi: 0-0 Tstrap: 0-0 Ckp: 0-0
Best Rating: 43 12/03 Punc 2m   soft   Ch

Red Lion (FR)

92   95d
7-y-o ch g Lion Cavern (USA)-Mahogany River (Irish River (FR))
N J Henderson W H Ponsonby

Placings:30340-00   (2590)
2003/04: 16OG, 16OGS,

	Starts	1st	2nd	3rd	Win & Pl
Hurdles	2	0	0	0	
Career Total	7	0	0	2	1684

Going: Sf: 0-0 GS: 0-1 Gd: 0-1 GF: - Fm: 0-0
Distance: 2m2/m3: 0-2 2m4-2m7: 0-1 3m+: 0-0
Track: LH: 0-1 RH: 0-1 Tight: 0-1 Gall: 0-0
Aids: Bl: 0-0 Vi: 0-0 Tstrap: 0-0 Ckp: 0-0
Best Rating: 99 2/03 Winc 2m   gd-sft   Hdl

Modest middle-distance/stayer on the Flat; made a decent hurdling debut at Wincanton in February 2003, but has not gone on from that; acts on a sound surface.

Red Mail (USA)

104(84h)   (59h)90
6-y-o b g Red Ransom (USA)-Seattle Byline (USA) (Slew City Slew (USA))
M A Barnes T A Barnes

Placings:0/5P0053-24P   (0410)
2003/04: 172G, 174G, 20PG,

	Starts	1st	2nd	3rd	Win & Pl
Chases	3	0	1	0	1976
Career Total	10	0	1	1	2666

Going: Sf: 0-0 GS: 0-0 Gd: 0-3 GF: - Fm: 0-0
Distance: 2m2/m3: 0-2 2m4-2m7: 0-1 3m+: 0-0
Track: LH: 0-3 RH: 0-0 Tight: 0-2 Gall: 0-0
Aids: Bl: 0-0 Vi: 0-0 Tstrap: 0-0 Ckp: 0-0
Best Rating: 90 5/03 Kels 2m1f   good   Ch

Poor hurdler/chaser; limited promise over fences; stays two miles five, but shapes as if further will suit.

Red Man (IRE)

106   100+
7-y-o ch g Toulon-Jamie's Lady (Ashmore (FR))
Mrs E Slack A Slack

Placings:500-21   (1527)
2003/04: 20PG, 22LF,

	Starts	1st	2nd	3rd	Win & Pl
Hurdles	2	1	1	0	3496
Career Total	5	1	1	0	3496
105	10/03	Kels	2m6f110yE Hdl	FRM	£2576

Total win prize-money £2576

Going: Sf: 0-0 GS: 0-0 Gd: 0-1 GF: - Fm: 1-1
Distance: 2m2/m3: 0-0 2m4-2m7: 1-2 3m+: 0-0
Track: LH: 1-1 RH: 0-1 Tight: 1-1 Gall: 0-0
Aids: Bl: 0-0 Vi: 0-0 Tstrap: 0-0 Ckp: 0-0
Best Rating: 105 10/03 Kels 2m6f110y   firm   Hdl

Moderate hurdler; stays two miles-six and may to get further; acts on a sound surface.

Red Marsala

(76h)   (38h)
6-y-o b/br g Tragic Role (USA)-Southend Scallywag (Tina's Pet)
R C Guest N B Mason

Placings:0-PFPF6UP4   (4593)
2003/04: 20PGS, 19FGS, 25PGS, 20FS, 166HY, 20UGS, 20PG, 164G,

	Starts	1st	2nd	3rd	Win & Pl
Hurdles	6	0	0	0	0

Chases	2	0	0	0	312
Career Total	9	0	0	0	312

Going:	Sf: 0-2 GS: 0-4 Gd: 0-2 GF: - Fm: 0-0
Distance:	2m/2m3: 0-3 2m4-2m7: 0-4 3m+: 0-1
Track:	LH: 0-5 RH: 0-3 Tight: 0-1 Gall: 0-2
Aids:	Bl: 0-1 Vi: 0-0 Tstrap: 0-0 Ckp: 0-3
Best Rating:	64 3/03 Weth 2m good NHF

Half-brother to two winners for the stable; showed ability though well beaten in the end in bumper at Wetherby in March on debut.

Red Minster

59   (17h)**94**

7-y-o b g Minster Son-Minty Muncher (Idiots Delight)
R C Guest N B Mason

Placings:000/0031P33-P0   (4730)
2003/04: 24PG, 20QG,

	Starts	1st	2nd	3rd	Win & Pl
Chases	2	0	0	0	
Career Total	12	1	0	3	5849
94	1/03	Newc	2m110y	E(0-105)HCh	HVY £3958
			Total win prize-money £3959		

Going:	Sf: 0-0 GS: 0-0 Gd: 0-2 GF: - Fm: 0-0
Distance:	2m/2m3: 0-0 2m4-2m7: 0-1 3m+: 0-1
Track:	LH: 0-0 RH: 0-2 Tight: 0-0 Gall: 0-1
Aids:	Bl: 0-0 Vi: 0-0 Tstrap: 0-0 Ckp: 0-1
Best Rating:	94 1/03 Newc 2m110y heavy Ch

Moderate chaser; acts well on a soft surface; has won over two miles, but gets further; goes well in cheekpieces.

Red Native (IRE)

8-y-o b g Be My Native (USA)-Larry's Peach (Laurence O)
R Barber P Maltby

Placings:00/F   (4675)
2003/04: 25FG,

	Starts	1st	2nd	3rd	Win & Pl
Chases	1	0	0	0	
Career Total	3	0	0	0	

Going:	Sf: 0-0 GS: 0-0 Gd: 0-1 GF: - Fm: 0-0
Distance:	2m/2m3: 0-0 2m4-2m7: 0-0 3m+: 0-1
Track:	LH: 0-0 RH: 0-2 Tight: 0-0 Gall: 0-0
Aids:	Bl: 0-1 Vi: 0-0 Tstrap: 0-0 Ckp: 0-0
Best Rating:	67 5/00 Worc 2m gd-fm NHF

Red Nose Lady

95   **97**

7-y-o b m Teenoso (USA)-Red Rambler (Rymer)
J M Jefferson Mrs M E Dixon

Placings:225P/546P-50P5PP40   (4914)
2003/04: 20SG, 20QG, 25PS, 16SHY, 16PHY, 22PHY, 24AHY, 24QGS,

	Starts	1st	2nd	3rd	Win & Pl
Hurdles	7	0	0	0	0
Chases	1	0	0	0	0
Career Total	16	0	2	0	1018

Going:	Sf: 0-5 GS: 0-1 Gd: 0-2 GF: - Fm: 0-0
Distance:	2m/2m3: 0-2 2m4-2m7: 0-3 3m+: 0-3
Track:	LH: 0-8 RH: 0-4 Tight: 0-1 Gall: 0-2
Aids:	Bl: 0-0 Vi: 0-1 Tstrap: 0-0 Ckp: 0-2
Best Rating:	97 11/02 Hexm 2m4f110y heavy Hdl

Red Oassis

97   (13h)**83**

13-y-o ch g Rymer-Heron's Mirage (Grey Mirage)
M J M Evans Mrs J Z Munday

Placings:00F/4U10/P022/54U1-46546   (4814)
2003/04: 16AGF, 20SGS, 20SG, 16AGS, 19SG,

	Starts	1st	2nd	3rd	Win & Pl
Chases	5	0	0	0	259
Career Total	20	2	2	2	8385
83	3/03	Chep	2m110y	F(0-100)HCh	GD £3416
76	3/01	Wwck	2m110y	F(0-90)HCh	HVY £2538
			Total win prize-money £5954		

Going:	Sf: 0-0 GS: 0-2 Gd: 0-2 GF: - Fm: 0-1
Distance:	2m/2m3: 0-2 2m4-2m7: 0-3 3m+: 0-0
Track:	LH: 0-4 RH: 0-1 Tight: 0-0 Gall: 0-0
Aids:	Bl: 0-0 Vi: 0-0 Tstrap: 0-0 Ckp: 0-0
Best Rating:	86 3/02 Uttx 2m heavy Ch

Plating-class chaser; gets three miles, effective over shorter.

Red Perk (IRE)

100(90h)   (78+h)**93**

7-y-o b g Executive Perk-Supreme View (Supreme Leader)
R C Guest N B Mason

Placings:0/52-P6P422   (4882)
2003/04: 25PGS, 20PS, 25PHY, 24AGS, 32QG, 26QGS,

	Starts	1st	2nd	3rd	Win & Pl
Hurdles	3	0	0	0	0
Chases	3	0	2	0	2588
Career Total	9	0	3	0	3414

Going:	Sf: 0-2 GS: 0-3 Gd: 0-1 GF: - Fm: 0-0
Distance:	2m/2m3: 0-0 2m4-2m7: 0-1 3m+: 0-5
Track:	LH: 0-5 RH: 0-1 Tight: 0-1 Gall: 0-1
Aids:	Bl: 0-0 Vi: 0-0 Tstrap: 0-0 Ckp: 0-2
Best Rating:	93 4/04 Carl 3m2f gd-sft Ch

Modest performer but has not had much racing and has hinted at ability over hurdles and fences; type to improve, especially if he can brush up his jumping in both departments; acts on good and easy ground.

Red Raja

92(72c)   (66c)**60**

11-y-o b/br g Persian Heights-Jenny Splendid (John Splendid)
Miss Victoria Roberts (C R Cox 12/5) C R Cox

Placings:01251510/223/64465/0653/6/P30-FP06   (4180)
2003/04: 16FG, 16PG, 16QGS, 20QG,

	Starts	1st	2nd	3rd	Win & Pl
Hurdles	2	0	0	0	
Chases	2	0	0	0	
Career Total	28	3	3	3	46245
133	3/97	Newb	2m110y	D(0-125)HHdl	GD £3317
127	2/97	Wind	2m	B Hdl	GD £7546
112	12/96	Folk	2m1f110yE	Hdl	G-S £2427
			Total win prize-money £13291		

Going:	Sf: 0-0 GS: 0-1 Gd: 0-3 GF: - Fm: 0-0
Distance:	2m/2m3: 0-3 2m4-2m7: 0-1 3m+: 0-0
Track:	LH: 0-2 RH: 0-2 Tight: 0-0 Gall: 0-2
Aids:	Bl: 0-0 Vi: 0-0 Tstrap: 0-0 Ckp: 0-1
Best Rating:	133 12/97 Chel 2m4f110y good Hdl

Red Ramona

74   **66**

9-y-o b g Rudimentary (USA)-Apply (King's Lake (USA))
R M Stronge Mrs Bernice Stronge

Placings:54FR/R0   (0701)
2003/04: 24RGF, 17QGF,

	Starts	1st	2nd	3rd	Win & Pl
Hurdles	2	0	0	0	
Career Total	6	0	0	0	0

Going:	Sf: 0-0 GS: 0-0 Gd: 0-0 GF: - Fm: 0-0
Distance:	2m/2m3: 0-1 2m4-2m7: 0-0 3m+: 0-1
Track:	LH: 0-1 RH: 0-1 Tight: 0-1 Gall: 0-0
Aids:	Bl: 0-0 Vi: 0-0 Tstrap: 0-0 Ckp: 0-0
Best Rating:	101 12/01 Extr 2m3f good Hdl

Moderate hurdler; stays well; suited by a sound surface; has become reluctant to start and is one to be wary of.

Red Rampage

104   (87h)**113+**

9-y-o b g King's Ride-Mighty Fly (Comedy Star (USA))
H P Hogarth (R C Guest 22/5) Hogarth Racing

Placings:U40042464/5042031420P/5O3F1PC31P-44P222132   (4941)
2003/04: 24AG, 24AS, 25PG, 27QGS, 24AHY, 27QGS, 26QG, 24QG, 31QGS,

	Starts	1st	2nd	3rd	Win & Pl
Chases	9	1	4	1	17214
Career Total	39	4	7	4	35373
113	3/04	Carl	3m2f	E(0-110)HCh	GD £4504
105	3/03	Carl	3m2f	E(0-110)HCh	SFT £4582
107	12/02	Newc	3m	E(0-115)HCh	SFT £4305
110	3/02	Catt	3m1f110yE(0-100)HCh	G-S	£3113
			Total win prize-money £16507		

Going:	Sf: 0-2 GS: 0-3 Gd: 1-4 GF: - Fm: 0-0
Distance:	2m/2m3: 0-2 2m4-2m7: 0-0 3m+: 1-9
Track:	LH: 0-5 RH: 1-3 Tight: 0-4 Gall: 0-1
Aids:	Bl: 1-8 Vi: 0-0 Tstrap: 1-7 Ckp: 0-0
Best Rating:	113 4/04 Prth 3m7f gd-sft Ch

Moderate handicap chaser; stays very well; acts on good and soft ground; usually wears a tongue tie and blinkers.

Red Return (IRE)

92   **82**

7-y-o ch g Bob's Return (IRE)-Kerrie's Pearl (Proverb)
L A Dace Mrs Yvonne Davess

Placings:50-4P00   (3145)
2003/04: 24AG, 24PGF, 20QG, 22QS,

	Starts	1st	2nd	3rd	Win & Pl
Hurdles	4	0	0	0	0
Career Total	6	0	0	0	0

Going:	Sf: 0-1 GS: 0-0 Gd: 0-2 GF: - Fm: 0-1
Distance:	2m/2m3: 0-0 2m4-2m7: 0-2 3m+: 0-2
Track:	LH: 0-1 RH: 0-2 Tight: 0-2 Gall: 0-0
Aids:	Bl: 0-0 Vi: 0-0 Tstrap: 0-0 Ckp: 0-0
Best Rating:	87 6/03 Worc 3m good Hdl

Red Rover

106   **76+**

7-y-o ch m Infantry-M I Babe (Celtic Cone)
Mrs M Reveley J F Mernagh

Placings:PU00P/51P60 (4476)
2003/04: 22^5G, 24^1GS, 20^PG, 24^6S, 24^0HY,

	Starts	1st	2nd	3rd	Win & Pl
Hurdles	5	1	0	0	2569
Career Total	10	1	0	0	2569
80	11/03 Carl	3m110y E(0-100)HHdl		G-S	£2569
			Total win prize-money		£2569

Going: Sf: 0-2 GS: 1-1 Gd: 0-2 GF: - Fm: 0-0
Distance: 2m/2m3: 0-0 2m4-2m7: 0-2 3m+: 1-3
Track: LH: 0-3 RH: 1-2 Tight: 0-1 Gall: 0-1
Aids: Bl: 0-1 Vi: 0-0 Tstrap: 0-0 Ckp: 0-0
Best Rating: 80 11/03 Carl 3m110y gd-sft Hdl

Plating-class hurdler, stays three miles; acts on easy ground.

Red Ruffles (IRE)
105   110
5-y-o b g Anshan-Rosie Ruffles (IRE) (Homo Sapien)
Noel T Chance T F C Partnership

Placings:14212 (4887)
2003/04: 16^1GS, 16^4HY, 16^2HY, 19^1G, 22^2GF,

	Starts	1st	2nd	3rd	Win & Pl
NH Flat	1	1	0	0	7605
Hurdles	4	1	2	0	7248
Career Total	5	2	2	0	14853
110	3/04 Donc	2m3f110yE Hdl		GD	£3600
112	11/03 Newb	2m110y H NHF		G-S	£7605
			Total win prize-money		£11206

Going: Sf: 0-2 GS: 1-1 Gd: 1-1 GF: - Fm: 0-1
Distance: 2m/2m3: 1-3 2m4-2m7: 1-2 3m+: 0-0
Track: LH: 2-4 RH: 0-1 Tight: 0-1 Gall: 1-1
Aids: Bl: 0-0 Vi: 0-0 Tstrap: 0-0 Ckp: 0-0
Best Rating: 112 11/03 Newb 2m110y gd-sft NHF

Modest hurdler; made winning debut in competitive bumper at Newbury November 2003; off the mark over hurdles with runaway success at Doncaster in March; suited by two and a half miles.

Red Socialite (IRE)
(102h)   (108+h)91
7-y-o ch g Moscow Society (USA)-Dees Darling (IRE) (King Persian)
D R Gandolfo Starlight Racing

Placings:05/401-4 (1935)
2003/04: 19^4G,

	Starts	1st	2nd	3rd	Win & Pl
Chases	1	0	0	0	524
Career Total	6	1	0	0	7647
108	3/03 Newb	2m5f D Hdl		GD	£6815
			Total win prize-money		£6815

Going: Sf: 0-0 GS: 0-0 Gd: 0-1 GF: - Fm: 0-0
Distance: 2m/2m3: 0-0 2m4-2m7: 0-1 3m+: 0-0
Track: LH: 0-0 RH: 0-1 Tight: 0-0 Gall: 0-0
Aids: Bl: 0-0 Vi: 0-0 Tstrap: 0-0 Ckp: 0-0
Best Rating: 108 3/03 Newb 2m5f good Hdl

Fair novice hurdler; caused a 40/1 surprise at Newbury in March 2003; held on chase debut; stays 2m 5f and handles any ground.

Red Society (IRE)
106(110h)   (82h)104+
6-y-o ch g Moscow Society (USA)-Allendara (IRE) (Phardante (FR))
Ferdy Murphy Eamonn J Kelly

Placings:000500-43232055301 (4389)
2003/04: 20^4F, 21^3G, 20^2GF, 21^3G, 23^2GF, 24^0GF, 16^5S, 21^5GS, 21^3GS, 16^6G, 21^1G,

	Starts	1st	2nd	3rd	Win & Pl
Hurdles	6	0	2	2	2159
Chases	5	1	0	1	5095
Career Total	17	1	2	3	7254
104	3/04 Sedg	2m5f E Ch		GD	£4371
			Total win prize-money		£4371

Going: Sf: 0-1 GS: 0-2 Gd: 1-4 GF: - Fm: 0-4
Distance: 2m/2m3: 0-2 2m4-2m7: 1-8 3m+: 0-1
Track: LH: 1-9 RH: 0-2 Tight: 1-6 Gall: 0-1
Aids: Bl: 0-0 Vi: 0-0 Tstrap: 0-0 Ckp: 1-4
Best Rating: 104 3/04 Sedg 2m5f good Ch

Plating-class; ex-Irish; showed some ability in bumpers in Ireland before joining current yard; won novice chase on 17th outing over fences at Sedgefield in March; stays 2m7f; handles soft.

Red Square Dawn
82   77
8-y-o b m Derrylin-Raise The Dawn (Rymer)
Mrs L Williamson Halewood International Ltd

Placings:020/P0P6420/0202053-000 (0629)
2003/04: 20^0G, 22^0G, 24^0GF,

	Starts	1st	2nd	3rd	Win & Pl
Hurdles	3	0	0	0	
Career Total	20	0	4	1	3558

Going: Sf: 0-0 GS: 0-0 Gd: 0-2 GF: - Fm: 0-1
Distance: 2m/2m3: 0-0 2m4-2m7: 0-2 3m+: 0-1
Track: LH: 0-3 RH: 0-0 Tight: 0-1 Gall: 0-0
Aids: Bl: 0-1 Vi: 0-0 Tstrap: 0-0 Ckp: 0-0
Best Rating: 77 4/03 Uttx 2m4f110y good Hdl

Plating-class; modest form in novice hurdles; possibly best at around two miles; acts on decent ground.

Red Square King
75(87h)   (69dh)17
6-y-o ch g Sure Blade (USA)-Patscilla (Squill (USA))
Mrs L Williamson Halewood International Ltd

Placings:050/505P-P5P (0614)
2003/04: 16^2G, 17^5G, 16^6GF,

	Starts	1st	2nd	3rd	Win & Pl
Hurdles	1	0	0	0	0
Chases	2	0	0	0	0
Career Total	10	0	0	0	0

Going: Sf: 0-0 GS: 0-0 Gd: 0-2 GF: - Fm: 0-0
Distance: 2m/2m3: 0-3 2m4-2m7: 0-0 3m+: 0-0
Track: LH: 0-2 RH: 0-1 Tight: 0-1 Gall: 0-0
Aids: Bl: 0-0 Vi: 0-0 Tstrap: 0-0 Ckp: 0-0
Best Rating: 71 6/02 Uttx 2m good Hdl

Poor novice hurdler/chaser.

Red Square Lad (IRE)
76   26
8-y-o ch g Toulon-Tempestuous Girl (Tumble Wind (USA))
Mrs L Williamson Halewood International Ltd

Placings:0 (1874)
2003/04: 22^0G,

	Starts	1st	2nd	3rd	Win & Pl
Hurdles	1	0	0	0	
Career Total	1	0	0	0	

Going: Sf: 0-0 GS: 0-1 Gd: 0-1 GF: - Fm: 0-0
Distance: 2m/2m3: 0-0 2m4-2m7: 0-0 3m+: 0-0
Track: LH: 0-1 RH: 0-0 Tight: 0-1 Gall: 0-0
Aids: Bl: 0-0 Vi: 0-0 Tstrap: 0-0 Ckp: 0-0
Best Rating: 36 11/03 Kels 2m6f110y good Hdl

Red Square Man (IRE)
94(69c)   (31c)66
9-y-o b g Rashar (USA)-November Tide (Laurence O)
Mrs L Williamson Halewood International Ltd

Placings:05/4P663P-00UU6P (1281)
2003/04: 17^0GF, 16^0G, 17^UGF, 17^UGS, 17^6G, 21^PGF,

	Starts	1st	2nd	3rd	Win & Pl
Hurdles	4	0	0	0	0
Chases	2	0	0	0	0
Career Total	14	0	0	1	714

Going: Sf: 0-0 GS: 0-1 Gd: 0-2 GF: - Fm: 0-3
Distance: 2m/2m3: 0-5 2m4-2m7: 0-1 3m+: 0-0
Track: LH: 0-5 RH: 0-1 Tight: 0-4 Gall: 0-0
Aids: Bl: 0-0 Vi: 0-0 Tstrap: 0-0 Ckp: 0-3
Best Rating: 91 10/02 Hayd 2m good Hdl

Red Square Prince (IRE)
8-y-o b g Alphabatim (USA)-Dawn Rising (Le Moss)
Mrs Alison Hickman Mrs Alison Hickman

Placings:06/P (0349)
2003/04: 26^PGF,

	Starts	1st	2nd	3rd	Win & Pl
Chases	1	0	0	0	
Career Total	3	0	0	0	0

Going: Sf: 0-0 GS: 0-0 Gd: 0-0 GF: - Fm: 0-1
Distance: 2m/2m3: 0-0 2m4-2m7: 0-0 3m+: 0-1
Track: LH: 0-0 RH: 0-0 Tight: 0-1 Gall: 0-0
Aids: Bl: 0-0 Vi: 0-0 Tstrap: 0-0 Ckp: 0-0
Best Rating: 53 1/01 Catt 2m gd-sft NHF

Red Storm
5-y-o ch m Dancing Spree (USA)-Dam Certain (IRE) (Damister (USA))
J R Boyle Brian McAtavey

Placings:PP (4490)
2003/04: 17^PGS, 16^PG,

	Starts	1st	2nd	3rd	Win & Pl
Hurdles	2	0	0	0	
Career Total	2	0	0	0	

Going: Sf: 0-0 GS: 0-1 Gd: 0-1 GF: - Fm: 0-0
Distance: 2m/2m3: 0-0 2m4-2m7: 0-0 3m+: 0-0
Track: LH: 0-1 RH: 0-1 Tight: 0-2 Gall: 0-0
Aids: Bl: 0-0 Vi: 0-1 Tstrap: 0-0 Ckp: 0-0

Red Sun

107   **130+**

7-y-o b g Foxhound (USA)-Superetta (Superlative)
J Mackie Bulls Head Racing Club

Placings:F6P/32FP662/216231043-1211005F   (4644)
2003/04: 19¹G, 19²G, 17¹GF, 16¹GF, 16⁹GF, 16⁹G, 16⁴G, 16⁶G,

	Starts	1st	2nd	3rd	Win & Pl
Hurdles	8	3	1	0	15442
Career Total	27	5	5	3	29919

130	10/03	Uttx	2m	D(0-120)HHdl	G-F	£4739
125	1/03	MRas	2m1f110yD(0-120)HHdl		G-F	£3396
112	5/03	Hrfd	2m3f110yD(0-120)HHdl		GD	£4946
112	12/02	Donc	2m3f110yD(0-115)HHdl		SFT	£3857
100	6/02	MRas	2m1f110yE Hdl		G-F	£2702

Total win prize-money £19642

Going:	Sf: 0-0 GS: 0-0 Gd: 1-5 GF: - Fm: 2-3
Distance:	2m/2m3: 2-6 2m4-2m7: 1-2 3m+: 0-0
Track:	LH: 1-3 RH: 2-5 Tight: 1-3 Gall: 0-1
Aids:	Bl: 0-0 Vi: 0-0 Tstrap: 0-1 Ckp: 0-0
Best Rating:	130 10/03 Uttx 2m gd-fm Hdl

Useful hurdler; stays two miles three; best on a sound surface; likes to race prominently.

Red Tyrant

100   **88**

6-y-o b g Minster Son-By The Lake (Tyrant (USA))
R C Guest Mason Jobe

Placings:50060343-6O4   (0468)
2003/04: 20³GF, 20⁶G, 22⁰G, 20⁴G,

	Starts	1st	2nd	3rd	Win & Pl
Hurdles	4	0	0	1	526
Career Total	11	0	0	2	1049

Going:	Sf: 0-0 GS: 0-0 Gd: 0-3 GF: - Fm: 0-1
Distance:	2m/2m3: 0-2 2m4-2m7: 0-4 3m+: 0-0
Track:	LH: 0-4 RH: 0-0 Tight: 0-2 Gall: 0-1
Aids:	Bl: 0-0 Vi: 0-0 Tstrap: 0-0 Ckp: 0-2
Best Rating:	92 3/03 Catt 2m soft NHF

Red Will Danagher (IRE)

96   **89**

7-y-o b g Glacial Storm (USA)-Clodas Pet (IRE) (Andretti)
John Allen John Allen

Placings:P020-0420   (0588)
2003/04: 26⁰GF, 22⁴G, 22⁶G, 24⁹GF,

	Starts	1st	2nd	3rd	Win & Pl
Hurdles	4	0	1	0	1362
Career Total	8	0	2	0	3050

Going:	Sf: 0-0 GS: 0-0 Gd: 0-1 GF: 0-2 Fm: 0-1
Distance:	2m/2m3: 0-0 2m4-2m7: 0-2 3m+: 0-2
Track:	LH: 0-3 RH: 0-1 Tight: 0-2 Gall: 0-0
Aids:	Bl: 0-0 Vi: 0-0 Tstrap: 0-0 Ckp: 0-0
Best Rating:	89 5/03 Ctrnl 2m6f good Hdl

Moderate novice hurdler; stays 2m 6f; acts on good.

Red Willie

71   **25**

5-y-o b g Master Willie-Ormania (FR) (Synefos (USA))
M C Pipe Terry Neill

Placings:00PP6   (4518)
2003/04: 16⁸GF, 16⁰GS, 19⁵HY, 19⁹G, 17⁶GS,

	Starts	1st	2nd	3rd	Win & Pl
NH Flat	2	0	0	0	0
Hurdles	3	0	0	0	0
Career Total	5	0	0	0	0

Going:	Sf: 0-1 GS: 0-2 Gd: 0-1 GF: - Fm: 0-1
Distance:	2m/2m3: 0-3 2m4-2m7: 0-2 3m+: 0-0
Track:	LH: 0-2 RH: 0-3 Tight: 0-1 Gall: 0-1
Aids:	Bl: 0-0 Vi: 0-1 Tstrap: 0-0 Ckp: 0-0
Best Rating:	78 8/03 Worc 2m gd-fm NHF

Red Wizard

95   **94**

4-y-o b g Wizard King-Drudwen (Sayf El Arab (USA))
Jonjo O'Neill (W A O'Gorman 26/8) T Mohan

Placings:1230   (3286)
2003/04: 16¹GF, 16²F, 16³GF, 16⁹GS,

	Starts	1st	2nd	3rd	Win & Pl
Hurdles	4	1	1	1	4920
Career Total	4	1	1	1	4920

81	10/03	Ludl	2m	E Hdl	G-F	£2936

Total win prize-money £2937

Going:	Sf: 0-0 GS: 0-1 Gd: 0-0 GF: - Fm: 1-3
Distance:	2m/2m3: 1-4 2m4-2m7: 0-0 3m+: 0-0
Track:	LH: 0-2 RH: 1-2 Tight: 0-0 Gall: 0-0
Aids:	Bl: 0-0 Vi: 0-0 Tstrap: 0-0 Ckp: 0-0
Best Rating:	94 11/03 Asct 2m110y gd-fm Hdl

Moderate hurdler; made winning debut in modest fast-ground juvenile event at Ludlow October 2003; placed under penalty; acts on fast ground.

Redberry Holly (IRE)

94(88h)   (59h)**52+**

6-y-o g m Roselier (FR)-Solvia (IRE) (Persian Mews)
R H Buckler R H Buckler

Placings:00P0F43   (4753)
2003/04: 21⁹GS, 21⁰S, 25⁹GS, 26⁸GF, 22⁴GS, 26⁸G,

	Starts	1st	2nd	3rd	Win & Pl
Hurdles	3	0	0	0	0
Chases	4	0	0	1	492
Career Total	7	0	0	1	492

Going:	Sf: 0-2 GS: 0-3 Gd: 0-1 GF: - Fm: 0-1
Distance:	2m/2m3: 0-0 2m4-2m7: 0-4 3m+: 0-3
Track:	LH: 0-5 RH: 0-1 Tight: 0-5 Gall: 0-0
Aids:	Bl: 0-0 Vi: 0-0 Tstrap: 0-0 Ckp: 0-0
Best Rating:	59 1/04 Plum 2m5f soft Hdl

Redde (IRE)

103(87h)   (119h)**110**

9-y-o ch g Classic Memory-Stoney Broke (Pauper)
R J Smith D Jackson,M Stock,R W Hibberd,C Harrison

Placings:2110/F51P21/P-P1P4063   (4695)
2003/04: 23⁸GS, 23¹HY, 26⁸S, 20⁴S, 21⁹G, 24⁶GS, 23⁵G,

	Starts	1st	2nd	3rd	Win & Pl
Hurdles	2	0	0	0	0
Chases	5	1	0	1	6666
Career Total	18	5	2	1	27939

110	5/03	Uttx	2m7f	E Ch	HVY	£5064
119	3/02	Chep	2m4f	C(0-135)HHdl	G-S	£5018

116	1/02	Carl	2m1f	D Hdl	HVY	£3526
123	2/01	Newb	2m110y	B NHF	SFT	£8190
110	11/00	Chep	2m110y	H NHF	HVY	£1505

Total win prize-money £23303

Going:	Sf: 1-3 GS: 2-0 Gd: 0-2 GF: - Fm: 0-0
Distance:	2m/2m3: 0-0 2m4-2m7: 1-3 3m+: 0-4
Track:	LH: 1-5 RH: 0-2 Tight: 0-2 Gall: 0-1
Aids:	Bl: 1-2 Vi: 0-0 Tstrap: 0-0 Ckp: 0-0
Best Rating:	123 2/01 Newb 2m110y soft NHF

Fair hurdler/modest chaser; won very poor 2m 7f novice chase in bad ground at Uttoxeter May 2003; disappointing since; goes well in soft/heavy ground; has worn blinkers; inconsistent.

Redemption

114(114c)   (157c)**142+**

9-y-o b g Sanglamore (USA)-Ypha (USA) (Lyphard (USA))
N A Twiston-Davies John Duggan & Michael Purtill

Placings:60460/31150F/2FF116/12136P/3F5F4-UP1F1U5003   (4628)
2003/04: 20⁰GF, 20⁰G, 20¹GS, 20⁴GS, 21¹G, 16⁰GS, 20⁵GS, 21⁹G, 24⁹G, 20³G,

	Starts	1st	2nd	3rd	Win & Pl
Hurdles	5	1	0	1	20831
Chases	5	1	0	0	23200
Career Total	38	8	2	4	93324

141	1/04	Chel	2m5f110yB HHdl	GD	£15181
157	11/03	Newb	2m4f	B(0-145)HCh	G-S	£23200
145	11/01	Asct	2m	B HCh	GF	£13380
149	10/01	Weth	2m4f110yB(0-145)HCh	GD	£9064
135	1/01	Weth	2m	E Ch	HVY	£3003
133	1/01	Plum	2m4f	E Ch	GS	£2964
121	2/00	Ludl	2m	E Hdl	GD	£2352
118	12/99	Weth	2m	D Hdl	G-S	£3460

Total win prize-money £72605

Going:	Sf: 0-0 GS: 1-4 Gd: 1-5 GF: - Fm: 0-1
Distance:	2m/2m3: 0-1 2m4-2m7: 2-8 3m+: 0-1
Track:	LH: 2-9 RH: 0-1 Tight: 0-1 Gall: 2-8
Aids:	Bl: 0-0 Vi: 0-0 Tstrap: 0-0 Ckp: 0-0
Best Rating:	157 11/03 Newb 2m4f gd-sft Ch

Very useful chaser/hurdler; stays 2m 5f and acts on any ground, although arguably best on good or slightly softer; not the safest of jumpers over fences; has worn blinkers.

Redgrave Wolf

77   **75**

11-y-o ch m Little Wolf-Redgrave Rose (Tug Of War)
K Bishop K Bishop

Placings:3/000600/20255/12/P0/0/244P-60   (1969)
2003/04: 25⁶G, 22⁰G,

	Starts	1st	2nd	3rd	Win & Pl
Chases	2	0	0	0	0
Career Total	23	1	4	1	5716

85	5/99	Towc	3m	F(0-100)HHdl	G-F	£1807

Total win prize-money £1807

Going:	Sf: 0-0 GS: 0-0 Gd: 0-2 GF: - Fm: 0-0
Distance:	2m/2m3: 0-0 2m4-2m7: 0-1 3m+: 0-1
Track:	LH: 0-0 RH: 0-2 Tight: 0-0 Gall: 0-0
Aids:	Bl: 0-1 Vi: 0-0 Tstrap: 0-0 Ckp: 0-0
Best Rating:	85 5/99 Extr 2m6f gd-fm Hdl

Redouble

99   **81**

8-y-o b g First Trump-Sunflower Seed (Mummy's Pet)
E L James E James

| Placings:0/0060202/254004444550-45555 | | | | (1792) |
| 2003/04: 20⁴GF, 20⁵G, 22²F, 22⁵GF, 16⁵GF, | | | | |

	Starts	1st	2nd	3rd	Win & Pl
Hurdles	5	0	0	0	0
Career Total	25	0	3	0	2249

Going:	Sf: 0-0 GS: 0-0 Gd: 0-1 GF: - Fm: 0-4
Distance:	2m/2m3: 0-1 2m4-2m7: 0-4 3m+: 0-0
Track:	LH: 0-2 RH: 0-3 Tight: 0-1 Gall: 0-0
Aids:	Bl: 0-1 Vi: 0-2 Tstrap: 0-0 Ckp: 0-2
Best Rating:	90 10/02 Extr 2m3f firm Hdl

Modest maiden hurdler, stays two and a half miles and acts on soft ground.

Redskin Raider (IRE)

106   (105h)**105+**

8-y-o b g Commanche Run-Sheltered (IRE) (Strong Gale)
T R George Mrs Christine Davies

| Placings:00/0033P20/P-U4FP2 | | | | (4672) |
| 2003/04: 22ᵁGS, 16⁴GS, 24⁴FG, 24⁴PG, 25²G, | | | | |

	Starts	1st	2nd	3rd	Win & Pl
Chases	5	0	1	0	1974
Career Total	15	0	2	2	3930

Going:	Sf: 0-0 GS: 0-2 Gd: 0-3 GF: - Fm: 0-0
Distance:	2m/2m3: 0-2 2m4-2m7: 0-1 3m+: 0-3
Track:	LH: 0-2 RH: 0-3 Tight: 0-1 Gall: 0-1
Aids:	Bl: 0-0 Vi: 0-0 Tstrap: 0-0 Ckp: 0-0
Best Rating:	105 4/04 Winc 3m1f110y good Ch

Fair novice hurdler, finds it hard to complete over fences; acts on an easy surface; stays two miles six.

Redspin (IRE)

93   **93**

4-y-o ch g Spectrum (IRE)-Trendy Indian (IRE) (Indian Ridge)
J S Moore (J W Hills 1/10) Mrs Fitri Hay

| Placings:25205 | | | | (2740) |
| 2003/04: 16²GS, 16⁵G, 16²GF, 16⁶S, 16⁵S, | | | | |

	Starts	1st	2nd	3rd	Win & Pl
Hurdles	5	0	2	0	5548
Career Total	5	0	2	0	5548

Going:	Sf: 0-2 GS: 0-0 Gd: 0-1 GF: - Fm: 0-2
Distance:	2m/2m3: 0-5 2m4-2m7: 0-0 3m+: 0-0
Track:	LH: 0-3 RH: 0-2 Tight: 0-1 Gall: 0-1
Aids:	Bl: 0-0 Vi: 0-0 Tstrap: 0-0 Ckp: 0-0
Best Rating:	93 11/03 Newb 2m110y gd-fm Hdl

Moderate maiden hurdler; acts on fast ground..

Redstar Attraction

81f   **66f**

6-y-o ch g Nalchik (USA)-Star Gal (Starch Reduced)
W M Brisbourne Magnate Racing

| Placings:0 | | | | (3446) |
| 2003/04: 16⁶G, | | | | |

	Starts	1st	2nd	3rd	Win & Pl
NH Flat	1	0	0	0	
Career Total	1	0	0	0	

Going:	Sf: 0-0 GS: 0-0 Gd: 0-1 GF: - Fm: 0-0
Distance:	2m/2m3: 0-0 2m4-2m7: 0-0 3m+: 0-0
Track:	LH: 0-0 RH: 0-0 Tight: 0-0 Gall: 0-0
Aids:	Bl: 0-0 Vi: 0-0 Tstrap: 0-0 Ckp: 0-0
Best Rating:	70 1/04 Ludl 2m good NHF

Redvic

4-y-o b g Alhaatmi-Sweet Fortune (Dubassoff) (USA))
G J Smith (Mrs N Macauley 1/5) K G Kitchen

| Placings:P | | | | (4756) |
| 2003/04: 19⁽P⁾S, | | | | |

	Starts	1st	2nd	3rd	Win & Pl
Hurdles	1	0	0	0	
Career Total	1	0	0	0	

Going:	Sf: 0-1 GS: 0-0 Gd: 0-0 GF: - Fm: 0-0
Distance:	2m/2m3: 0-0 2m4-2m7: 0-1 3m+: 0-0
Track:	LH: 0-0 RH: 0-0 Tight: 0-0 Gall: 0-0
Aids:	Bl: 0-0 Vi: 0-0 Tstrap: 0-0 Ckp: 0-0

Reefa's Mill (IRE)

12-y-o b g Astronef-Pharly's Myth (Pharly (FR))
B P J Baugh G W Briscoe

| Placings:002/656003P/614PUF3360/P | | | | (1204) |
| 2003/04: 17²G, | | | | |

	Starts	1st	2nd	3rd	Win & Pl
Hurdles	1	0	0	0	
Career Total	21	1	1	3	3613
				73 6/98 Sthl 2m4f110yG(0-90)HHdl GD £1586

Total win prize-money £1586

Going:	Sf: 0-0 GS: 0-0 Gd: 0-1 GF: - Fm: 0-0
Distance:	2m/2m3: 0-1 2m4-2m7: 0-0 3m+: 0-0
Track:	LH: 0-1 RH: 0-0 Tight: 0-0 Gall: 0-0
Aids:	Bl: 0-0 Vi: 0-0 Tstrap: 0-0 Ckp: 0-0
Best Rating:	77 8/96 NAbb 2m1f good Hdl

Reel Dancer

100(86h)   (73h)**117**

7-y-o g g Minshaanshu Amad (USA)-Sister Rosarii (USA) (Properantes (USA))
B De Haan The Play 4 Partnership

| Placings:632/26-2P | | | | (2985) |
| 2003/04: 19²GS, 19⁶S, | | | | |

	Starts	1st	2nd	3rd	Win & Pl
Chases	2	0	1	0	1269
Career Total	7	0	3	1	2709

Going:	Sf: 0-1 GS: 0-1 Gd: 0-0 GF: - Fm: 0-0
Distance:	2m/2m3: 0-0 2m4-2m7: 0-2 3m+: 0-0
Track:	LH: 0-2 RH: 0-0 Tight: 0-0 Gall: 0-0
Aids:	Bl: 0-0 Vi: 0-0 Tstrap: 0-0 Ckp: 0-0
Best Rating:	117 12/03 Chep 2m3f110y gd-sft Ch

Fair chaser/hurdler; fragile sort; acts on soft ground.

Reel Handsome

                                                  86

12-y-o ch g Handsome Sailor-Reel Chance (Proverb)
C T Pogson C T Pogson

| Placings:PPB360/3SP452/P4PU35F266400/3004324PU-464 | | | | (0456) |
| 2003/04: 20⁴GF, 17⁶GF, 21⁴HY, | | | | |

	Starts	1st	2nd	3rd	Win & Pl
Chases	3	0	0	0	423
Career Total	37	0	3	5	9683

Going:	Sf: 0-1 GS: 0-0 Gd: 0-0 GF: - Fm: 0-2
Distance:	2m/2m3: 0-1 2m4-2m7: 0-2 3m+: 0-0
Track:	LH: 0-2 RH: 0-1 Tight: 0-0 Gall: 0-1
Aids:	Bl: 0-0 Vi: 0-0 Tstrap: 0-3 Ckp: 0-0
Best Rating:	86 10/02 Sthl 2m1f good Ch

Reel Missile

101f   **108f**

5-y-o b g Weld-Landsker Missile (Cruise Missile)
C T Pogson C T Pogson

| Placings:12 | | | | (4594) |
| 2003/04: 16¹G, 16²G, | | | | |

	Starts	1st	2nd	3rd	Win & Pl
NH Flat	2	1	1	0	2643
Career Total	2	1	1	0	2643
				108 3/04 Donc 2m110y H NHF GD £2107

Total win prize-money £2107

Going:	Sf: 0-0 GS: 0-0 Gd: 0-1-2 GF: - Fm: 0-0
Distance:	2m/2m3: 1-2 2m4-2m7: 0-0 3m+: 0-0
Track:	LH: 1-1 RH: 0-1 Tight: 0-0 Gall: 1-2
Aids:	Bl: 0-0 Vi: 0-0 Tstrap: 0-0 Ckp: 0-0
Best Rating:	108 3/04 Hntg 2m110y good NHF

100/1 all-the-way winner of a Doncaster bumper on his debut; beaten under a penalty; acts on good.

Refinement (IRE)

115f   **133+f**

5-y-o b m Oscar (IRE)-Maneree (Mandalus)
Jonjo O'Neill M Tabor

| Placings:112 | | | | (4400) |
| 2003/04: 17¹G, 16¹S, 16²G, | | | | |

	Starts	1st	2nd	3rd	Win & Pl
NH Flat	3	2	1	0	17704
Career Total	3	2	1	0	17704
				122 12/03 Asct 2m110y H NHF SFT £7231
				106 10/03 Bang 2m1f H NHF GD £1673

Total win prize-money £8904

Going:	Sf: 1-1 GS: 0-0 Gd: 1-2 GF: - Fm: 0-0
Distance:	2m/2m3: 2-3 2m4-2m7: 0-0 3m+: 0-0
Track:	LH: 1-2 RH: 1-1 Tight: 1-1 Gall: 0-0
Aids:	Bl: 0-0 Vi: 0-0 Tstrap: 0-0 Ckp: 0-0
Best Rating:	133 3/04 Chel 2m110y good NHF

Useful bumper performer; well backed favourite when quickening to make successful debut in Bangor bumper October 2003 and followed up at Ascot before Christmas; good runner-up in the Festival bumper; decent hurdles prospect; acts on good or softer.

Reflective Way

100   **86+**

11-y-o ch m Mirror Boy-Craigie Way (Palm Track)
A C Whillans Robert Robinson

| Placings:P0234/11P-P52P3F226 | | | | (3986) |
| 2003/04: 24⁶GS, 25⁵G, 20²G, 25⁵GS, 20³S, 25⁵HY, 25²HY, 20²HY, 27⁶GS, | | | | |

	Starts	1st	2nd	3rd	Win & Pl
Chases	9	0	3	1	3374

Career Total		17	2	4	2	14578
92	6/02 Prth	3m	D Ch		G-S	£5124
92	5/02 Hexm	3m1f	E(0-105)HCh		GD	£3672
			Total win prize-money £8797			

Going:	Sf: 0-4 GS: 0-2 Gd: 0-3 GF: - Fm: 0-0
Distance:	2m/2m3: 0-0 2m4-2m7: 0-3 3m+: 0-6
Track:	LH: 0-6 RH: 0-3 Tight: 0-3 Gall: 0-0
Aids:	Bl: 0-0 Vi: 0-0 Tstrap: 0-0 Ckp: 0-0
Best Rating:	92 6/02 Prth 3m gd-sft Ch

Plating-class chaser; suited by trips of around three miles; acts on fast ground.

Reflex Blue

97   91+

7-y-o b g Ezzoud (IRE)-Briggsmaid (Elegant Air)
R J Price Fox And Cub Partnership

Placings:460006/23344-441510						(3964)
2003/04: 16⁴GF, 17⁴GF, 16¹GS, 16⁵GS, 16¹G, 16⁰GS,						

	Starts	1st	2nd	3rd	Win & Pl
Hurdles	6	2	0	0	4655
Career Total	17	2	1	2	6536
94	1/04 Ludl	2m	G(0-95)HHdl	GD	£2723
86	11/03 Uttx	2m	G(0-90)HHdl	G-S	£1932
			Total win prize-money £4655		

Going:	Sf: 0-0 GS: 1-3 Gd: 1-1 GF: - Fm: 0-2
Distance:	2m/2m3: 2-6 2m4-2m7: 0-0 3m+: 0-0
Track:	LH: 1-3 RH: 1-3 Tight: 0-1 Gall: 0-0
Aids:	Bl: 0-0 Vi: 1-5 Tstrap: 0-0 Ckp: 0-0
Best Rating:	94 1/04 Ludl 2m good Hdl

Plating-class hurdler; had visor removed when bought in for 3,200gns after winning at Uttoxeter November 2003;scored again at Ludlow in January; acts on fast and yielding ground; not an easy ride.

Reflex Courier (IRE)

96   99

12-y-o b g Over The River (FR)-Thornpark Lady (Mandalus)
John R Upson The Nap Hand Partnership

Placings:425PBPF0/11PP23/314254/14PU36/P41350-						
61554						(4221)
2003/04: 22⁶GS, 21¹¹GS, 24⁵HY, 22⁵GS, 22⁴GS,						

	Starts	1st	2nd	3rd	Win & Pl
Chases	5	1	0	0	4409
Career Total	37	6	3	4	30126
92	12/03 Strf	2m5f110yE(0-105)HCh	G-S	£4095
97	11/02 Hayd	3m	D(0-115)HCh	SFT	£5075
96	11/01 Hayd	2m6f	F(0-110)HCh	GD	£3601
104	11/00 Leic	2m7f110yF(0-110)HCh	G-S	£2678
104	11/99 MRas	3m1f	F(0-105)HCh	G-S	£3018
93	10/99 Bang	3m110y	F(0-105)HCh	SFT	£3875
			Total win prize-money £22343		

Going:	Sf: 0-1 GS: 1-4 Gd: 0-0 GF: - Fm: 0-0
Distance:	2m/2m3: 0-0 2m4-2m7: 1-4 3m+: 0-1
Track:	LH: 1-3 RH: 0-1 Tight: 1-3 Gall: 0-0
Aids:	Bl: 0-0 Vi: 0-0 Tstrap: 0-0 Ckp: 0-0
Best Rating:	104 11/00 Leic 2m7f110y gd-sft Ch

Moderate chaser; a lucky winner of 2m 5f handicap chase at Stratford December 2003; stays 3m; acts on good ground or softer; seems best held up for a late run.

Regal Act (IRE)

(102h)   (109h)91

8-y-o ch g Montelimar (USA)-Portal Lady (Pals Passage)
C J Mann M Rowland, B Beacham

Placings:5/10/043260-PB3						(2834)
2003/04: 20²GS, 20⁸S, 16³G,						

	Starts	1st	2nd	3rd	Win & Pl
Chases	3	0	0	1	1030
Career Total	12	1	1	2	7549
112	5/01 Wxfd	2m	NHF	Y-S	£4451
			Total win prize-money £4452		

Going:	Sf: 0-1 GS: 0-1 Gd: 0-1 GF: - Fm: 0-0
Distance:	2m/2m3: 0-1 2m4-2m7: 0-2 3m+: 0-0
Track:	LH: 0-1 RH: 0-2 Tight: 0-1 Gall: 0-1
Aids:	Bl: 0-0 Vi: 0-0 Tstrap: 0-0 Ckp: 0-0
Best Rating:	112 5/01 Wxfd 2m yld-sft NHF

Regal Ali (IRE)

13

5-y-o ch g Ali-Royal (IRE)-Depeche (FR) (King's Lake (USA))
G A Ham (Mrs A Malzard 25/8) N G Ahier

Placings:0P0-42110						(4673)
2003/04: 16⁴G, 16²G, 16¹G, 16¹GF, 16⁰G,						

	Starts	1st	2nd	3rd	Win & Pl
Hurdles	5	2	1	0	3045
Career Total	8	2	1	0	3045
8/03	LesL	2m	HHdl	G-F	£1260
7/03	LesL	2m	Hdl	GD	£1260
			Total win prize-money £2520		

Going:	Sf: 0-0 GS: 0-0 Gd: 1-4 GF: - Fm: 1-1
Distance:	2m/2m3: 2-5 2m4-2m7: 0-0 3m+: 0-0
Track:	LH: 2-4 RH: 0-1 Tight: 0-0 Gall: 0-0
Aids:	Bl: 0-0 Vi: 0-0 Tstrap: 0-0 Ckp: 0-0
Best Rating:	24 4/03 Tntn 2m1f firm Hdl

Dual hurdles winner in Jersey; acts on a sound surface.

Regal Applause

83   72

5-y-o b m Royal Applause-Panchellita (USA) (Pancho Villa (USA))
Mrs J A Ewer Mrs J A Ewer

Placings:00-06P						(4898)
2003/04: 16⁵S, 16⁶G, 16⁶G,						

	Starts	1st	2nd	3rd	Win & Pl
Hurdles	3	0	0	0	0
Career Total	5	0	0	0	0

Going:	Sf: 0-1 GS: 0-0 Gd: 0-2 GF: - Fm: 0-0
Distance:	2m/2m3: 0-3 2m4-2m7: 0-0 3m+: 0-0
Track:	LH: 0-1 RH: 0-2 Tight: 0-1 Gall: 0-0
Aids:	Bl: 0-0 Vi: 0-0 Tstrap: 0-0 Ckp: 0-0
Best Rating:	75 3/04 Winc 2m good Hdl

Regal Bandit (IRE)

91   95

6-y-o b g Un Desperado (FR)-Rainbow Alliance (IRE) (Golden Love)
Miss H C Knight The Bandits

Placings:5306P						(4167)
2003/04: 17⁵G, 16³GF, 22⁰GS, 22⁵G, 21⁹G,						

	Starts	1st	2nd	3rd	Win & Pl
NH Flat	2	0	0	1	389
Hurdles	3	0	0	1	167
Career Total	5	0	0	1	556

Going:	Sf: 0-0 GS: 0-1 Gd: 0-3 GF: - Fm: 0-1

Distance:	2m/2m3: 0-2 2m4-2m7: 0-3 3m+: 0-0
Track:	LH: 0-2 RH: 0-3 Tight: 0-1 Gall: 0-1
Aids:	Bl: 0-0 Vi: 0-0 Tstrap: 0-0 Ckp: 0-0
Best Rating:	95 2/04 Winc 2m6f good Hdl

Regal Chance

91   94

11-y-o b g Cisto (FR)-Regal Flutter (Henry The Seventh)
A King Mrs A A Shutes

Placings:0/0/FP2001-3P4						(4857)
2003/04: 20³GS, 20⁰G, 19⁴GF,						

	Starts	1st	2nd	3rd	Win & Pl
Chases	3	0	0	1	968
Career Total	11	1	1	1	5848
94	3/03 Hntg	2m4f110yF(0-90)HCh	GD	£3412
			Total win prize-money £3413		

Going:	Sf: 0-0 GS: 0-1 Gd: 0-1 GF: - Fm: 0-1
Distance:	2m/2m3: 0-1 2m4-2m7: 0-2 3m+: 0-0
Track:	LH: 0-1 RH: 0-2 Tight: 0-3 Gall: 0-0
Aids:	Bl: 0-0 Vi: 0-0 Tstrap: 0-0 Ckp: 0-0
Best Rating:	94 3/03 Hntg 2m4f110y good Ch

Lightly-raced chaser, moderate form until finishing runner-up at Leicester in January 2003.

Regal Custom

87f   84+f

6-y-o ch g Royal Vulcan-Rural Custom (Country Retreat)
N B King Mrs Jane Cotton

Placings:05						(3861)
2003/04: 18⁰GS, 18⁵S,						

	Starts	1st	2nd	3rd	Win & Pl
NH Flat	2	0	0	0	0
Career Total	2	0	0	0	0

Going:	Sf: 0-1 GS: 0-1 Gd: 0-0 GF: - Fm: 0-0
Distance:	2m/2m3: 0-2 2m4-2m7: 0-0 3m+: 0-0
Track:	LH: 0-2 RH: 0-0 Tight: 0-1 Gall: 0-0
Aids:	Bl: 0-0 Vi: 0-0 Tstrap: 0-0 Ckp: 0-0
Best Rating:	84 2/04 Plum 2m2f soft NHF

Modest ability shown in two bumpers to date.

Regal Empress

6-y-o b m Regal Embers (IRE)-Mis-E-Fishant (Sunyboy)
C J Price (G H Jones 13/5) H E Turberfield

Placings:600P						(3775)
2003/04: 17⁵G, 17⁰GF, 16⁸GF, 16⁸G,						

	Starts	1st	2nd	3rd	Win & Pl
NH Flat	3	0	0	0	0
Hurdles	1	0	0	0	0
Career Total	4	0	0	0	0

Going:	Sf: 0-0 GS: 0-0 Gd: 0-2 GF: - Fm: 0-2
Distance:	2m/2m3: 0-4 2m4-2m7: 0-0 3m+: 0-0
Track:	LH: 0-1 RH: 0-3 Tight: 0-0 Gall: 0-0
Aids:	Bl: 0-1 Vi: 0-0 Tstrap: 0-0 Ckp: 0-0

Regal Exit (FR)

109(110c)   (127c)135+

8-y-o ch g Exit To Nowhere (USA)-Regalante (Gairloch)
N J Henderson Brian Buckley

Placings:1312/6/000/12010P-0103F0 (4428)
2003/04: 17⁰GS, 16¹G, 16⁶S, 20³G, 19²G, 17⁰G,

	Starts	1st	2nd	3rd	Win & Pl
Hurdles	3	1	0	0	6683
Chases	3	0	0	1	2283
Career Total	20	5	2	2	47891
135 12/03 Donc	2m110y	B(0-140)HHdl		GD	£6683
126 3/03 Donc	2m3f	E Ch		GD	£4043
118 12/02 Ludl	2m	E Ch		GD	£4095
134 3/00 Newb	2m110y	D Hdl		SFT	£3835
130 1/00 Chel	2m1f	B Hdl		SFT	£7020
			Total win prize-money		£25676

Going:	Sf: 0-1 GS: 0-1 Gd: 1-4 GF: - Fm: 0-0
Distance:	2m/2m3: 1-4 2m4-2m7: 0-2 3m+: 0-0
Track:	LH: 1-3 RH: 0-3 Tight: 0-0 Gall: 1-3
Aids:	Bl: 0-0 Vi: 0-0 Tstrap: 0-0 Ckp: 0-0
Best Rating:	140 3/00 Chel 2m1f gd-fm Hdl

Useful chaser/hurdler; runner-up in the 2000 Triumph Hurdle, but has had training setbacks; took quite well to fences in 2002/2003 and fair effort to win back over hurdles at Doncaster in December; stays 2m 4f; most effective on a sound surface.

Regal Holly
(102h) (118h)121
9-y-o b m Gildoran-Pusey Street (Native Bazaar)
C J Mann Dr David Harris & Peter Simpson

Placings:1123/11135/034F00F5/212221-P40 (3655)
2003/04: 24⁴PS, 24⁴G, 24⁰S,

	Starts	1st	2nd	3rd	Win & Pl
Hurdles	2	0	0	0	1045
Chases	1	0	0	0	0
Career Total	27	8	5	3	73871
121 3/03 Uttx	2m5f	A HCh		SFT	£18600
121 12/02 Folk	3m1f	E Ch		SFT	£3487
130 2/01 Asct	2m4f	B(0-150)HHdl		HVY	£20923
123 1/01 Font	2m2f110yD(0-125)HHdl			SFT	£4231
120 12/00 MRas	2m3f110yD(0-125)HHdl			G-S	£7410
98 11/00 Catt	2m3f	F Hdl		GD	£1438
106 7/99 Worc	2m	H NHF		G-F	£1563
106 6/99 Worc	2m	H NHF		G-S	£1378
			Total win prize-money		£59034

Going:	Sf: 0-2 GS: 0-0 Gd: 0-1 GF: - Fm: 0-0
Distance:	2m/2m3: 0-0 2m4-2m7: 0-0 3m+: 0-3
Track:	LH: 0-1 RH: 0-2 Tight: 0-2 Gall: 0-0
Aids:	Bl: 0-3 Vi: 0-0 Tstrap: 0-0 Ckp: 0-0
Best Rating:	130 2/01 Asct 2m4f heavy Hdl

Modest chaser; suited by ease in the ground; stays three miles; likes to front run; usually wears blinkers.

Regal Jones (IRE)
4-y-o b f Sovereign Water (FR)-Juleit Jones (IRE) (Phardante (FR))
P Butler Mrs E Lucey-Butler

Placings:0 (3961)
2003/04: 18⁰G,

	Starts	1st	2nd	3rd	Win & Pl
NH Flat	1	0	0	0	
Career Total	1	0	0	0	

Going:	Sf: 0-0 GS: 0-0 Gd: 0-1 GF: - Fm: 0-0
Distance:	2m/2m3: 0-1 2m4-2m7: 0-0 3m+: 0-0
Track:	LH: 0-1 RH: 0-0 Tight: 0-1 Gall: 0-0
Aids:	Bl: 0-0 Vi: 0-0 Tstrap: 0-0 Ckp: 0-0

Regal Light
(69h) (69h)
9-y-o gr g Gran Alba (USA)-Light Of Zion (Pieces Of Eight)
J C Tuck J W Storkey

Placings:0PP6-P (0056)
2003/04: 25⁵GS,

	Starts	1st	2nd	3rd	Win & Pl
Chases	1	0	0	0	
Career Total	5	0	0	0	0

Going:	Sf: 0-0 GS: 0-1 Gd: 0-0 GF: - Fm: 0-0
Distance:	2m/2m3: 0-0 2m4-2m7: 0-0 3m+: 0-1
Track:	LH: 0-0 RH: 0-1 Tight: 0-0 Gall: 0-0
Aids:	Bl: 0-0 Vi: 0-0 Tstrap: 0-0 Ckp: 0-0
Best Rating:	66 4/03 Bang 2m4f gd-fm Hdl

Regal River (IRE)
(83h)103
7-y-o b g Over The River (FR)-My Friend Fashion (Laurence O)
John R Upson Middleham Park Racing Xix

Placings:005P10/F231P-UUPP (3986)
2003/04: 25¹US, 25⁵US, 29⁵S, 27⁰GS,

	Starts	1st	2nd	3rd	Win & Pl
Chases	4	0	0	0	
Career Total	15	2	1	1	7702
103 1/03 Leic	2m7f110yF(0-90)HCh			SFT	£3435
82 3/02 Towc	3m	F(0-100)HHdl		SFT	£2670
			Total win prize-money		£6106

Going:	Sf: 0-3 GS: 0-1 Gd: 0-0 GF: - Fm: 0-0
Distance:	2m/2m3: 0-0 2m4-2m7: 0-0 3m+: 0-4
Track:	LH: 0-2 RH: 0-2 Tight: 0-2 Gall: 0-0
Aids:	Bl: 0-0 Vi: 0-0 Tstrap: 0-0 Ckp: 0-0
Best Rating:	103 1/03 Leic 2m7f110y soft Ch

Moderate handicap hurdler/chaser; acts on a soft surface; well suited by three miles.

Regal Statesman (NZ)
(83h) (49h)66
11-y-o br g Vice Regal (NZ)-Hykit (NZ) (Swinging Junior)
O Brennan Lady Anne Bentinck

Placings:0/2PP/412PPP64/4405-0P (4605)
2003/04: 21⁹GF, 22⁷G,

	Starts	1st	2nd	3rd	Win & Pl
Hurdles	2	0	0	0	
Career Total	18	1	2	0	5709
89 5/01 Weth	2m7f	D Hdl		FRM	£3549
			Total win prize-money		£3549

Going:	Sf: 0-0 GS: 0-0 Gd: 0-1 GF: - Fm: 0-1
Distance:	2m/2m3: 0-0 2m4-2m7: 0-2 3m+: 0-1
Track:	LH: 0-0 RH: 0-1 Tight: 0-0 Gall: 0-1
Aids:	Bl: 0-0 Vi: 0-0 Tstrap: 0-0 Ckp: 0-0
Best Rating:	98 5/00 MRas 2m1f110y gd-fm Hdl

Regal Vintage (USA)
90 65
4-y-o ch g Kingmambo (USA)-Grapevine (IRE) (Sadler's Wells (USA))
C Grant J C Garbutt

Placings:P040P (4319)
2003/04: 16⁷PF, 16⁶G, 16⁴GF, 19⁰G, 20⁵PS,

	Starts	1st	2nd	3rd	Win & Pl
Hurdles	5	0	0	0	0
Career Total	5	0	0	0	0

Going:	Sf: 0-1 GS: 0-0 Gd: 0-2 GF: - Fm: 0-2
Distance:	2m/2m3: 0-3 2m4-2m7: 0-2 3m+: 0-0
Track:	LH: 0-5 RH: 0-0 Tight: 0-1 Gall: 0-2
Aids:	Bl: 0-0 Vi: 0-4 Tstrap: 0-3 Ckp: 0-0
Best Rating:	65 11/03 Catt 2m gd-fm Hdl

Regal Vision (IRE)
99(99h) (101h)101
7-y-o b g Emperor Jones (USA)-Shining Eyes (USA) (Mr Prospector (USA))
C J Mann (C G Cox 29/10) The Whitcoombe Partnership

Placings:0/U124P34030/54640-U15U0P2600024R3 (4857)
2003/04: 21¹UGF, 21¹GF, 21⁵GF, 21¹⁰GF, 23⁹GF, 24²GF, 20⁵GF, 20⁰G, 24⁰S, 24⁰G, 20²GF, 20⁴G, 21⁸G, 19³GF,

	Starts	1st	2nd	3rd	Win & Pl
Hurdles	2	0	0	0	
Chases	13	1	2	1	10771
Career Total	31	2	3	3	15258
98 6/03 NAbb	2m5f110yD Ch			G-F	£6541
105 8/01 Bang	2m4f	F Hdl		GD	£2268
			Total win prize-money		£8810

Going:	Sf: 0-1 GS: 0-0 Gd: 0-4 GF: - Fm: 1-0
Distance:	2m/2m3: 0-1 2m4-2m7: 1-10 3m+: 0-4
Track:	LH: 1-10 RH: 0-5 Tight: 1-7 Gall: 0-2
Aids:	Bl: 0-7 Vi: 0-0 Tstrap: 0-0 Ckp: 0-0
Best Rating:	105 4/02 Hntg 2m5f110y gd-fm Hdl

Moderate chaser; stays 2m 6f; acts on a sound surface.

Regar (IRE)
98 84
12-y-o b g Buckskin (FR)-Pass Thurn (Trimmingham)
M A Barnes (Mrs E Jestin 3/5) Brian McNichol

Placings:000/0P60/F/U2-P052430 (1072)
2003/04: 25⁸G, 16⁸S, 20⁶GF, 16²G, 17⁴GF, 16³GF, 16⁰GF,

	Starts	1st	2nd	3rd	Win & Pl
Chases	7	0	1	1	2706
Career Total	17	0	2	1	3156

Going:	Sf: 0-1 GS: 0-0 Gd: 0-2 GF: - Fm: 0-4
Distance:	2m/2m3: 0-5 2m4-2m7: 0-1 3m+: 0-0
Track:	LH: 0-6 RH: 0-1 Tight: 0-4 Gall: 0-0
Aids:	Bl: 0-0 Vi: 0-0 Tstrap: 0-1 Ckp: 0-0
Best Rating:	84 7/03 Prth 2m good Ch

Poor chaser; stays 2m 4f.

Regardez-Moi
89 64
7-y-o b m Distinctly North (USA)-Tomard (Thatching)
Miss M Bragg Friends Of Rock Park

Placings:6B56665-56 (0487)
2003/04: 16⁵GS, 22⁶GF,

	Starts	1st	2nd	3rd	Win & Pl
Hurdles	2	0	0	0	0
Career Total	9	0	0	0	0

Going:	Sf: 0-0 GS: 0-1 Gd: 0-0 GF: - Fm: 0-1

Distance: 2m/2m3: 0-1 2m4-2m7: 0-1 3m+: 0-0
Track: LH: 0-2 RH: 0-0 Tight: 0-1 Gall: 0-0
Aids: Bl: 0-0 Vi: 0-0 Tstrap: 0-1 Ckp: 0-0
Best Rating: 64 5/03 Worc 2m gd-sft Hdl

Poor hurdler; does not appear to stay 2m 6f.

Regents Walk (IRE)
83   91

6-y-o b g Phardante (FR)-Raw Courage (IRE) (The Parson)
B De Haan Mrs D Vaughan

Placings:3-6   (3947)
2003/04: 16⁶G,

	Starts	1st	2nd	3rd	Win & Pl
Hurdles	1	0	0	0	0
Career Total	2	0	0	1	281

Going: Sf: 0-0 GS: 0-0 Gd: 0-1 GF: - Fm: 0-0
Distance: 2m/2m3: 0-1 2m4-2m7: 0-0 3m+: 0-0
Track: LH: 0-0 RH: 0-1 Tight: 0-0 Gall: 0-0
Aids: Bl: 0-0 Vi: 0-0 Tstrap: 0-0 Ckp: 0-0
Best Rating: 103 3/03 Sthl 2m gd-fm NHF

Reggae Rhythm (IRE)
82(102c)   (90c)81

10-y-o b g Be My Native (USA)-Invery Lady (Sharpen Up)
R N Bevis Peter J Doyle

Placings:0005313363/0020PF00/66231B465/025/050P2P-02P0   (4785)
2003/04: 16⁰GS, 16²GS, 16⁶GS, 21⁰G,

	Starts	1st	2nd	3rd	Win & Pl
Hurdles	2	0	0	0	0
Chases	2	0	1	0	1332
Career Total	40	4	2	5	13705
105 1/01 Tram 2m		Hdl		HVY	£4451
102 11/98 Clon 2m		NHF		SFT	£1942
				Total win prize-money £6395

Going: Sf: 0-0 GS: 0-2 Gd: 0-2 GF: - Fm: 0-0
Distance: 2m/2m3: 0-3 2m4-2m7: 0-0 3m+: 0-0
Track: LH: 0-0 RH: 0-4 Tight: 0-0 Gall: 0-1
Aids: Bl: 0-0 Vi: 0-0 Tstrap: 0-0 Ckp: 0-3
Best Rating: 113 11/01 Tram 2m yield Hdl

Plating-class hurdler; best around 2m; acts on soft/heavy ground.

Reggie Buck (USA)
104   96

10-y-o b/br g Alleged (USA)-Hello Memphis (USA) (Super Concorde (USA))
J Mackie Fools Who Dream

Placings:P0/25146/05121225/203UP2300/16U1215355/066560031-32   (0497)
2003/04: 16¹G, 16³GF, 16²G,

	Starts	1st	2nd	3rd	Win & Pl
Hurdles	3	1	1	1	4704
Career Total	45	7	8	5	37894
96 4/03 Hexm 2m110y		E(0-105)HHdl	GD	£3425
114 11/01 Weth 2m		D(0-125)HHdl	GD	£3445
114 10/01 Sthl 2m		E(0-115)HHdl	GD	£2912
113 5/01 Hntg 2m110y		F(0-105)HHdl	GD	£2922
113 1/00 Catt 2m		D(0-120)HHdl	GD	£5547
100 12/99 Leic 2m		F(0-110)HHdl	GD	£2332
99 1/99 Donc 2m110y		F(0-110)HHdl	GD	£2066
			Total win prize-money £22652

Going: Sf: 0-0 GS: 0-0 Gd: 1-2 GF: - Fm: 0-1
Distance: 2m/2m3: 1-3 2m4-2m7: 0-0 3m+: 0-0
Track: LH: 1-3 RH: 0-0 Tight: 0-0 Gall: 0-0
Aids: Bl: 0-0 Vi: 0-0 Tstrap: 0-0 Ckp: 0-0
Best Rating: 114 12/01 Hntg 2m110y gd-sft Hdl

Moderate hurdler; acts well on good ground; effective at around two miles; has been tried in blinkers.

Regimental Dance

4-y-o b f Groom Dancer (USA)-Enlisted (IRE) (Sadler's Wells (USA))
C Grant (D Nicholls 29/7) Ian W Glenton

Placings:F   (1448)
2003/04: 17⁵GF,

	Starts	1st	2nd	3rd	Win & Pl
Hurdles	1	0	0	0	
Career Total	1	0	0	0	

Going: Sf: 0-0 GS: 0-0 Gd: 0-0 GF: - Fm: 0-1
Distance: 2m/2m3: 0-1 2m4-2m7: 0-0 3m+: 0-0
Track: LH: 0-0 RH: 0-1 Tight: 0-1 Gall: 0-0
Aids: Bl: 0-0 Vi: 0-0 Tstrap: 0-0 Ckp: 0-0

Reivers Moon
103   92

5-y-o b/br m Midnight Legend-Here Comes Tibby (Royal Fountain)
W Amos J W McNeill

Placings:016-203332320   (3734)
2003/04: 21²S, 20⁰G, 22³GF, 22³G, 16³S, 20²GF, 21³GS, 20²GF, 20⁴G,

	Starts	1st	2nd	3rd	Win & Pl
Hurdles	9	0	3	4	4705
Career Total	12	1	3	4	6925
89 3/03 Carl 2m1f		H NHF		GD	£2220
			Total win prize-money £2220

Going: Sf: 0-2 GS: 0-1 Gd: 0-3 GF: - Fm: 0-3
Distance: 2m/2m3: 0-1 2m4-2m7: 0-8 3m+: 0-0
Track: LH: 0-5 RH: 0-4 Tight: 0-8 Gall: 0-0
Aids: Bl: 0-0 Vi: 0-0 Tstrap: 0-0 Ckp: 0-0
Best Rating: 92 1/04 Muss 2m4f gd-fm Hdl

Moderate stays 2m6f; acts on a sound surface.

Reiziger (FR)
111(109h)   (121+h)133

8-y-o gr g Balleroy (USA)-Dany Ohio (FR) (Script Ohio (USA))
P J Hobbs D Jones & B Thomas

Placings:121131133P/304141/400252413   (4426)
2003/04: 16⁴G, 16⁶S, 17⁰G, 19²S, 20⁵G, 20²G, 20⁴G, 16¹GS, 16³G,

	Starts	1st	2nd	3rd	Win & Pl
Hurdles	3	0	0	0	423
Chases	6	1	2	1	21917
Career Total	25	8	3	5	66635
125 3/04 Sand 2m		D(0-125)HCh	G-S	£6727
133 3/02 Newb 2m2f110yC Ch			GD	£6890
107 12/01 Ludl 2m		E Ch		GD	£3120
135 11/00 Chel 2m110y		A Hdl		G-S	£12000
128 10/00 Extr 2m1f		E Hdl		GD	£2710
115 6/00 NAbb 2m1f		E Hdl		GD	£2492
115 5/00 Worc 2m		E Hdl		GD	£2429
114 5/00 Ludl 2m		E Hdl		GD	£2600
			Total win prize-money £38969

Going: Sf: 0-2 GS: 1-1 Gd: 0-6 GF: - Fm: 0-0
Distance: 2m/2m3: 1-6 2m4-2m7: 0-3 3m+: 0-0
Track: LH: 0-2 RH: 1-7 Tight: 0-2 Gall: 0-2
Aids: Bl: 0-0 Vi: 0-0 Tstrap: 0-0 Ckp: 0-0
Best Rating: 138 5/01 Hayd 2m good Hdl

Fair hurdler/winning chaser; not the best of jumpers; acts well on good ground, but handles softer; effective over two miles to two miles two.

Relative Hero (IRE)
79   42

4-y-o ch g Entrepreneur-Aunty (FR) (Riverman (USA))
Miss S J Wilton (H Morrison 17/10) John Pointon And Sons

Placings:0   (2436)
2003/04: 17⁰G,

	Starts	1st	2nd	3rd	Win & Pl
Hurdles	1	0	0	0	
Career Total	1	0	0	0	

Going: Sf: 0-0 GS: 0-0 Gd: 0-1 GF: - Fm: 0-0
Distance: 2m/2m3: 0-1 2m4-2m7: 0-0 3m+: 0-0
Track: LH: 0-1 RH: 0-0 Tight: 0-1 Gall: 0-0
Aids: Bl: 0-0 Vi: 0-0 Tstrap: 0-0 Ckp: 0-0
Best Rating: 42 11/03 Bang 2m1f good Hdl

Relix (FR)
69   53

4-y-o gr g Linamix (FR)-Resleona (Caerleon (USA))
Ferdy Murphy (G Henrot 18/11) Stuart Taylor, David Hardy, Lee Seaton

Placings:0P0   (4795)
2003/04: 17⁰GS, 17⁵G, 17⁰G,

	Starts	1st	2nd	3rd	Win & Pl
Hurdles	3	0	0	0	
Career Total	3	0	0	0	

Going: Sf: 0-0 GS: 0-1 Gd: 0-2 GF: - Fm: 0-0
Distance: 2m/2m3: 0-3 2m4-2m7: 0-0 3m+: 0-0
Track: LH: 0-2 RH: 0-1 Tight: 0-3 Gall: 0-0
Aids: Bl: 0-0 Vi: 0-0 Tstrap: 0-0 Ckp: 0-0
Best Rating: 64 2/04 Sedg 2m1f gd-sft Hdl

Remembrance
92   69+

4-y-o b g Sabrehill (USA)-Perfect Poppy (Shareef Dancer (USA))
M J Gingell (J M P Eustace 30/12) W Stanger, P Whittall and G Plastow

Placings:00F   (4440)
2003/04: 16⁶G, 17⁰G, 16⁵GS,

	Starts	1st	2nd	3rd	Win & Pl
Hurdles	3	0	0	0	
Career Total	3	0	0	0	

Going: Sf: 0-0 GS: 0-1 Gd: 0-2 GF: - Fm: 0-0
Distance: 2m/2m3: 0-3 2m4-2m7: 0-0 3m+: 0-0
Track: LH: 0-1 RH: 0-2 Tight: 0-2 Gall: 0-0
Aids: Bl: 0-0 Vi: 0-0 Tstrap: 0-3 Ckp: 0-0
Best Rating: 69 3/04 MRas 2m1f110y good Hdl

Reminiscent (IRE)
101   **97**
5-y-o b g Kahyasi-Eliza Orzeszkowa (IRE) (Polish Patriot (USA))
R F Johnson Houghton R F Johnson Houghton

Placings:25   (4232)
2003/04: 17²GS, 20⁵GF,

	Starts	1st	2nd	3rd	Win & Pl
Hurdles	2	0	1	0	1568
Career Total	2	0	1	0	1568

Going: Sf: 0-0 GS: 0-1 Gd: 0-0 GF: - Fm: 0-1
Distance: 2m/2m3: 0-1 2m4-2m7: 0-1 3m+: 0-0
Track: LH: 0-0 RH: 0-1 Tight: 0-2 Gall: 0-0
Aids: Bl: 0-0 Vi: 0-0 Tstrap: 0-0 Ckp: 0-0
Best Rating: 99   3/04   Font   2m4f   gd-fm   Hdl

Stayer on the Flat; ran well on his hurdling debut; will probably need beyond two miles; handles cut.

Ren's Magic
93   **89+**
6-y-o gr g Petong-Bath (Runnett)
J R Jenkins H Thomas

Placings:52P   (1702)
2003/04: 16⁵GS, 16²GF, 16⁶PG,

	Starts	1st	2nd	3rd	Win & Pl
Hurdles	3	0	1	0	884
Career Total	3	0	1	0	884

Going: Sf: 0-0 GS: 0-0 Gd: 0-0 GF: - Fm: 0-3
Distance: 2m/2m3: 0-3 2m4-2m7: 0-0 3m+: 0-0
Track: LH: 0-3 RH: 0-0 Tight: 0-2 Gall: 0-0
Aids: Bl: 0-0 Vi: 0-1 Tstrap: 0-0 Ckp: 0-0
Best Rating: 89   9/03   Plum   2m   gd-fm   Hdl

Runner-up in novice hurdle in September on fast ground.

Renaloo (IRE)
(90h)   (41h)**91**
9-y-o gr g Tremblant-Rare Flower (Decent Fellow)
R Rowe Tim Clowes

Placings:50046/006/056/F521F331P-P6PP   (4119)
2003/04: 17²G, 23⁶G, 22⁶G, 16⁶PG,

	Starts	1st	2nd	3rd	Win & Pl
Hurdles	1	0	0	0	0
Chases	3	0	0	0	0
Career Total	24	2	1	2	10480
91 3/03 Folk 2m   E(0-110)HCh   GD £4095
91 1/03 Folk 2m   E(0-105)HCh   SFT £4075
Total win prize-money £8171

Going: Sf: 0-0 GS: 0-0 Gd: 0-4 GF: - Fm: 0-0
Distance: 2m/2m3: 0-2 2m4-2m7: 0-2 3m+: 0-0
Track: LH: 0-2 RH: 0-1 Tight: 0-4 Gall: 0-0
Aids: Bl: 0-0 Vi: 0-0 Tstrap: 0-0 Ckp: 0-0
Best Rating: 99   11/99   Wwck   2m   good   NHF

Modest chaser, effective at 2m and acts on any ground; suited by positive tactics.

Rendari (IRE)
96   **98+**
9-y-o b g Shardari-Reneagh (Prince Regent (FR))
R Ford D C Fillingham

Placings:52f6-0P031P   (4777)

2003/04: 20⁰GS, 16⁶HY, 17⁹GS, 24³GF, 26¹G, 23⁶PG,

	Starts	1st	2nd	3rd	Win & Pl
Hurdles	6	1	0	1	3544
Career Total	10	2	1	1	8139
98 3/04 Hntg 3m2f   F(0-100)HHdl   GD £2996
97 7/02 Bell 2m1f   NHF   GD £3809
Total win prize-money £6806

Going: Sf: 0-1 GS: 0-2 Gd: 1-2 GF: - Fm: 0-1
Distance: 2m/2m3: 0-2 2m4-2m7: 0-1 3m+: 1-3
Track: LH: 0-4 RH: 1-2 Tight: 0-2 Gall: 1-1
Aids: Bl: 0-0 Vi: 0-0 Tstrap: 0-0 Ckp: 0-0
Best Rating: 98   3/04   Hntg   3m2f   good   Hdl

Moderate hurdler; stays three miles two furlongs; acts on good.

Rendova
101f   **95f**
5-y-o b g Darshaan-Mary Astor (FR) (Groom Dancer (USA))
A M Balding J C, J R And S R Hitchins

Placings:00   (4649)
2003/04: 16⁵G, 17⁹G,

	Starts	1st	2nd	3rd	Win & Pl
NH Flat	2	0	0	0	
Career Total	2	0	0	0	

Going: Sf: 0-0 GS: 0-0 Gd: 0-2 GF: - Fm: 0-0
Distance: 2m/2m3: 0-2 2m4-2m7: 0-0 3m+: 0-0
Track: LH: 0-1 RH: 0-0 Tight: 0-0 Gall: 0-1
Aids: Bl: 0-0 Vi: 0-0 Tstrap: 0-0 Ckp: 0-0
Best Rating: 98   2/04   Newb   2m110y   good   NHF

Reno
101   **87**
4-y-o ch f Efisio-Los Alamos (Keen)
C W Thornton The Reno Partnership

Placings:22324F003   (4795)
2003/04: 16²G, 16²GF, 16⁹GS, 16²GS, 16⁴S, 17⁶GS, 16⁹G, 20⁰HY, 17⁹G,

	Starts	1st	2nd	3rd	Win & Pl
Hurdles	9	0	3	2	3321
Career Total	9	0	3	2	3321

Going: Sf: 0-2 GS: 0-3 Gd: 0-3 GF: - Fm: 0-1
Distance: 2m/2m3: 0-8 2m4-2m7: 0-1 3m+: 0-0
Track: LH: 0-9 RH: 0-0 Tight: 0-0 Gall: 0-3
Aids: Bl: 0-0 Vi: 0-0 Tstrap: 0-2 Ckp: 0-0
Best Rating: 87   12/03   Catt   2m   gd-sft   Hdl

Plating-class hurdler; acts on fast and easy ground.

Renvyle (IRE)
103(98h)   (98+h)**118**
6-y-o b/br g Satco (FR)-Kara's Dream (IRE) (Bulldozer)
Jonjo O'Neill (Henry De Bromhead 24/6) The Four Exiles

Placings:01244041   (4256)
2003/04: 16⁶F, 17¹GF, 16²GF, 17⁴G, 24⁴GS, 21⁰GS, 16⁴GS, 20¹G,

	Starts	1st	2nd	3rd	Win & Pl
NH Flat	4	1	1	0	3370
Hurdles	3	0	0	0	388
Chases	1	1	0	0	4323
Career Total	8	2	1	0	8081
118 3/04 Bang 2m4f110yE(0-105)HCh G-F £4322
104 9/03 NAbb 2m1f   H NHF   G-F £2933
Total win prize-money £7256

Renzo (IRE)
65   **114**
11-y-o b g Alzao (USA)-Watership (USA) (Foolish Pleasure (USA))
John A Harris Cleartherm Ltd

Placings:1F2240/23220/U/60F24/41040-50   (3320)
2003/04: 16⁵GS, 16⁶S,

	Starts	1st	2nd	3rd	Win & Pl
Hurdles	2	0	0	0	0
Career Total	24	2	6	1	24890
114 6/02 MRas 2m3f110y C(0-130)HHdl G-F £5512
139 11/98 Asct 2m110y C Hdl G-S £3940
Total win prize-money £9452

Going: Sf: 0-1 GS: 0-1 Gd: 0-0 GF: - Fm: 0-0
Distance: 2m/2m3: 0-2 2m4-2m7: 0-0 3m+: 0-0
Track: LH: 0-1 RH: 0-1 Tight: 0-0 Gall: 0-0
Aids: Bl: 0-0 Vi: 0-0 Tstrap: 0-0 Ckp: 0-0
Best Rating: 139   2/99   Asct   2m110y   gd-sft   Hdl

Modest hurdler, lightly raced of late; acts on any ground; stays two and a half miles.

Repunzel
101   (95h)**95**
9-y-o b m Carlingford Castle-Hi-Rise Lady (Sunyboy)
N A Gaselee Michael Watt

Placings:20/0641/F05/64UP0P13/F0152-P230B3   (4535)
2003/04: 16²G, 16²GS, 20³GS, 16⁹GS, 17⁹G, 19³GS,

	Starts	1st	2nd	3rd	Win & Pl
Chases	6	0	1	2	1817
Career Total	28	3	3	3	13490
95 1/03 Plum 2m1f   F(0-90)HCh   HVY £3081
95 1/02 Plum 2m   D(0-115)HHdl HVY £3304
98 4/00 Plum 2m   D Hdl   G-S £2811
Total win prize-money £9196

Going: Sf: 0-0 GS: 0-4 Gd: 0-2 GF: - Fm: 0-0
Distance: 2m/2m3: 0-4 2m4-2m7: 0-2 3m+: 0-0
Track: LH: 0-3 RH: 0-2 Tight: 0-2 Gall: 0-0
Aids: Bl: 0-0 Vi: 0-0 Tstrap: 0-0 Ckp: 0-0
Best Rating: 98   4/00   Plum   2m   gd-sft   Hdl

Modest handicap hurdler/chaser, suited by soft ground over two miles.

Requestor
98   **95+**
9-y-o br g Distinctly North (USA)-Bebe Altesse (GER) (Alpenkonig (GER))
T J Fitzgerald Marquesa De Moratalla

Placings:00461-2   (0130)
2003/04: 16²GF,

	Starts	1st	2nd	3rd	Win & Pl
Hurdles	1	0	1	0	768
Career Total	6	1	1	0	3295
95 4/03 Newc 2m4f   G(0-95)HHdl   GD £2527
Total win prize-money £2527

Going: Sf: 0-0 GS: 0-0 Gd: 0-0 GF: - Fm: 0-1

Distance: 2m/2m3: 0-1 2m4-2m7: 0-0 3m+: 0-0
Track: LH: 0-0 RH: 0-1 Tight: 0-1 Gall: 0-1
Aids: Bl: 0-0 Vi: 0-0 Tstrap: 0-1 Ckp: 0-0
Best Rating: 95 4/03 Newc 2m4f good Hdl

Rescator (FR)
99   88

8-y-o gr g Saint Estephe (FR)-La Narquoise (FR) (Al Nasr (FR))
Mrs S J Smith Mrs S Smith

Placings:1/420P/6643-1600   (4873)
2003/04: 16¹G, 16⁸G, 20⁹HY, 20⁹GS,

	Starts	1st	2nd	3rd	Win & Pl
Hurdles	4	1	0	0	2443
Career Total	13	2	1	1	5965
88	5/03	Hexm	2m110y	G Hdl	GD £2443
109	1/00	Font	2m2f110yH NHF		G-S £1792

Total win prize-money £4235

Going: Sf: 0-1 GS: 0-1 Gd: 1-2 GF: - Fm: 0-0
Distance: 2m/2m3: 1-2 2m4-2m7: 0-2 3m+: 0-0
Track: LH: 1-3 RH: 0-1 Tight: 0-1 Gall: 0-0
Aids: Bl: 0-0 Vi: 0-0 Tstrap: 0-0 Ckp: 0-0
Best Rating: 119 1/01 Plum 2m5f soft Hdl

Plating-class hurdler; stays 2m 2f; acts on good and easy ground.

Rescind (IRE)
98   81

4-y-o b f Revoque (IRE)-Sunlit Ride (Ahonoora)
Jedd O'Keeffe Wetherby Racing Bureau 58

Placings:34   (2331)
2003/04: 16³GF, 16⁴G,

	Starts	1st	2nd	3rd	Win & Pl
Hurdles	2	0	0	1	737
Career Total	2	0	0	1	737

Going: Sf: 0-0 GS: 0-0 Gd: 0-1 GF: - Fm: 0-1
Distance: 2m/2m3: 0-2 2m4-2m7: 0-0 3m+: 0-0
Track: LH: 0-1 RH: 0-1 Tight: 0-1 Gall: 0-i
Aids: Bl: 0-0 Vi: 0-0 Tstrap: 0-0 Ckp: 0-0
Best Rating: 81 11/03 Hntg 2m110y gd-fm Hdl

Showed promise over hurdles on a sound surface.

Rescindo (IRE)
103   108

5-y-o b g Revoque (IRE)-Mystic Dispute (IRE) (Magical Strike (USA))
M C Pipe Joy And Valentine Feerick

Placings:224-434242   (1001)
2003/04: 16⁴GF, 18³GF, 17⁴GF, 17²GF, 17⁴GF, 19²G,

	Starts	1st	2nd	3rd	Win & Pl
Hurdles	6	0	2	1	4064
Career Total	9	0	4	1	7155

Going: Sf: 0-0 GS: 0-0 Gd: 0-1 GF: 0-5
Distance: 2m/2m3: 0-6 2m4-2m7: 0-0 3m+: 0-0
Track: LH: 0-5 RH: 0-1 Tight: 0-4 Gall: 0-0
Aids: Bl: 0-0 Vi: 0-5 Tstrap: 0-0 Ckp: 0-0
Best Rating: 108 7/03 Strf 2m3f good Hdl

Moderate hurdler; still a maiden; shown form at around 2m but stays further; acts on decent ground; wears a visor.

Researcher
109   112+

5-y-o ch m Cosmonaut-Rest (Dance In Time (CAN))
Miss Venetia Williams Mrs Kathy Stuart

Placings:6226-146131000   (4842)
2003/04: 17¹G, 17⁴G, 16⁶GS, 19¹GF, 24³G, 17¹GS, 21⁰G, 22⁰G, 21⁰G,

	Starts	1st	2nd	3rd	Win & Pl
Hurdles	9	3	0	1	15598
Career Total	13	3	2	1	18077
112	1/04	Extr	2m1f	D(0-120)HHdl	G-S £4657
105	11/03	Donc	2m3f110yD Hdl	G-F	£4875
88	4/03	Extr	2m1f	E Hdl	GD £3458

Total win prize-money £12990

Going: Sf: 0-0 GS: 1-2 Gd: 1-6 GF: - Fm: 0-0
Distance: 2m/2m3: 2-4 2m4-2m7: 1-4 3m+: 0-1
Track: LH: 1-4 RH: 2-5 Tight: 0-2 Gall: 0-1
Aids: Bl: 0-0 Vi: 0-0 Tstrap: 0-0 Ckp: 0-1
Best Rating: 112 1/04 Extr 2m1f gd-sft Hdl

Modest novice hurdler; stays 2m 4f; acts on fast and yielding ground.

Reseda (GER)
72f   96f

5-y-o b m Lavirco (GER)-Reklame (GER) (Immer (HUN))
Ian Williams R J Turton

Placings:4   (4824)
2003/04: 17⁴GF,

	Starts	1st	2nd	3rd	Win & Pl
NH Flat	1	0	0	0	0
Career Total	1	0	0	0	0

Going: Sf: 0-0 GS: 0-0 Gd: 0-0 GF: - Fm: 0-1
Distance: 2m/2m3: 0-1 2m4-2m7: 0-0 3m+: 0-1
Track: LH: 0-0 RH: 0-1 Tight: 0-0 Gall: 0-0
Aids: Bl: 0-0 Vi: 0-0 Tstrap: 0-0 Ckp: 0-1
Best Rating: 96 4/04 Extr 2m1f gd-fm NHF

Resilience

4-y-o b f Most Welcome-Abstone Queen (Presidium)
B Mactaggart Harlequin Racing

Placings:5   (1525)
2003/04: 16⁵F,

	Starts	1st	2nd	3rd	Win & Pl
Hurdles	1	0	0	0	0
Career Total	1	0	0	0	0

Going: Sf: 0-0 GS: 0-0 Gd: 0-0 GF: - Fm: 0-1
Distance: 2m/2m3: 0-1 2m4-2m7: 0-0 3m+: 0-1
Track: LH: 0-0 RH: 0-0 Tight: 0-0 Gall: 0-0
Aids: Bl: 0-0 Vi: 0-0 Tstrap: 0-0 Ckp: 0-0

Resistance (IRE)
89

7-y-o br g Phardante (FR)-Shean Hill (IRE) (Bar Dexter (USA))
G A Ham Sally and Tom Dalley and Dave Durbin

Placings:3/160/4F6-P   (3317)
2003/04: 16⁵PS,

	Starts	1st	2nd	3rd	Win & Pl
Hurdles	1	0	0	0	

Career Total 8 1 0 1 2478
99 5/01 Extr 2m1f H NHF GD £1785

Total win prize-money £1785

Going: Sf: 0-1 GS: 0-0 Gd: 0-0 GF: - Fm: 0-0
Distance: 2m/2m3: 0-1 2m4-2m7: 0-0 3m+: 0-0
Track: LH: 0-0 RH: 0-1 Tight: 0-0 Gall: 0-0
Aids: Bl: 0-0 Vi: 0-0 Tstrap: 0-0 Ckp: 0-0
Best Rating: 99 5/01 Extr 2m1f good NHF

Ressource (FR)
101   90

5-y-o b g Broadway Flyer (USA)-Rayonne (Sadler's Wells (USA))
G L Moore Miss S M Eastes

Placings:05424306-62F2433   (4752)
2003/04: 16⁶G, 18²GF, 17⁶GS, 17²GS, 17⁴HY, 17³GS, 16³G,

	Starts	1st	2nd	3rd	Win & Pl
Hurdles	7	0	2	2	1914
Career Total	15	0	3	3	3184

Going: Sf: 0-1 GS: 0-3 Gd: 0-2 GF: - Fm: 0-1
Distance: 2m/2m3: 0-7 2m4-2m7: 0-0 3m+: 0-0
Track: LH: 0-3 RH: 0-4 Tight: 0-6 Gall: 0-0
Aids: Bl: 0-7 Vi: 0-0 Tstrap: 0-0 Ckp: 0-0
Best Rating: 90 11/03 Font 2m2f110y gd-fm Hdl

Plating-class hurdler; yet to win a race; acts on fast and easy ground; may need further than two miles.

Restless Wind (IRE)
106   113

12-y-o b g Celio Rufo-Trulos (Three Dons)
G B Balding The Kingfisher Partnership

Placings:3UP/F5/340123/413521-P3P0612   (4633)
2003/04: 23⁹PS, 19³GS, 24⁵PS, 24⁰G, 24⁶G, 24¹G, 24²G,

	Starts	1st	2nd	3rd	Win & Pl
Chases	7	1	1	1	6275
Career Total	24	4	3	5	29312
100	3/04	Tntn	3m	F(0-90)Ch	GD £3430
111	4/03	Hntg	3m	D(0-120)HCh	G-F £5460
111	11/02	Kemp	3m	D(0-120)HCh	GD £6922
96	3/02	Tntn	3m	F(0-90)Ch	SFT £3150

Total win prize-money £18963

Going: Sf: 0-2 GS: 0-1 Gd: 1-4 GF: - Fm: 0-0
Distance: 2m/2m3: 0-0 2m4-2m7: 0-0 3m+: 1-6
Track: LH: 0-0 RH: 1-7 Tight: 1-2 Gall: 0-0
Aids: Bl: 0-0 Vi: 0-0 Tstrap: 0-0 Ckp: 0-0
Best Rating: 111 4/03 Hntg 3m gd-fm Ch

Modest handicap chaser; stays three miles and acts on most types of ground.

Retail Therapy (IRE)
97   84+

4-y-o b f Bahhare (USA)-Elect (USA) (Vaguely Noble)
M A Buckley C C Buckley

Placings:1P00   (4166)
2003/04: 16¹GF, 16⁶PS, 16⁹GS, 16⁹G,

	Starts	1st	2nd	3rd	Win & Pl
Hurdles	4	1	0	0	2751
Career Total	4	1	0	0	2751
84	11/03	Hntg	2m110y	E Hdl	G-F £2751

Total win prize-money £2751

Going: Sf: 0-1 GS: 0-1 Gd: 0-1 GF: - Fm: 1-1
Distance: 2m/2m3: 1-4 2m4-2m7: 0-0 3m+: 0-0

Track: LH: 0-1 **RH: 1-3** Tight: 0-0 **Gall: 1-3**
Aids: Bl: 0-0 Vi: 0-0 Tstrap: 0-0 Ckp: 0-0
Best Rating: 84   11/03   Hntg   2m110y   gd-fm   Hdl

Made winning hurdles debut at Huntingdon in November; held since; effective at around two miles; acts on fast ground; has been tried in a visor and eyeshield.

Return Ticket

92f   84f

5-y-o br g Bob's Return (IRE)-Mrs Jennifer (River Knight (FR))
R T Phillips   Mr & Mrs F C Welch

Placings:4   (4934)
2003/04: 18⁴G,

	Starts	1st	2nd	3rd	Win & Pl
NH Flat	1	0	0	0	0
Career Total	1	0	0	0	0

Going: Sf: 0-0 GS: 0-0 Gd: 0-1 GF: - Fm: 0-0
Distance: 2m/2m3: 0-1 2m4-2m7: 0-0 3m+: 0-0
Track: LH: 0-1 RH: 0-0 Tight: 0-1 Gall: 0-0
Aids: Bl: 0-0 Vi: 0-0 Tstrap: 0-0 Ckp: 0-0
Best Rating: 84   4/04   Font   2m2f110y   good   NHF

Returned Un Paid (IRE)

98   (76h)81

7-y-o b g Actinium (FR)-Claregalway Lass (Ardross)
Mrs S J Smith (P A Blockley 4/10)   Mrs M Ashby

Placings:P443P1FP330   (3768)
2003/04: 20⁰GF, 26⁴GF, 23⁴GF, 26⁵GS, 27⁰GF, 26¹GF, 26⁶GF, 26⁶GF, 25³S, 27³GS, 20⁰HY,

	Starts	1st	2nd	3rd	Win & Pl
Hurdles	3	0	0	1	361
Chases	8	1	0	2	5791
Career Total	11	1	0	3	6152
76 8/03 Sthl	3m2f	E Ch		G-F	£3978

Total win prize-money £3978

Going: Sf: 0-2 GS: 0-2 Gd: 0-0 GF: - Fm: 1-7
Distance: 2m/2m3: 0-0 2m4-2m7: 0-0 **3m+: 1-8**
Track: **LH: 1-9** RH: 0-1 Tight: 0-0 Gall: 0-0
Aids: **Bl: 1-3** Vi: 0-0 Tstrap: 0-0 Ckp: 0-0
Best Rating: 81   12/03   Hexm   3m1f   soft   Ch

Plating-class chaser; off the mark at Southwell in August when blinkered for the first time; stays 3m 2f; acts on good to firm ground.

Revelino (IRE)

99   75+

5-y-o b g Revoque (IRE)-Forelino (USA) (Trempolino (USA))
Miss S J Wilton   John Pointon And Sons

Placings:004-03405   (4404)
2003/04: 16⁰GS, 17³G, 19⁴GS, 16⁰GS, 16⁵G,

	Starts	1st	2nd	3rd	Win & Pl
Hurdles	5	0	0	1	430
Career Total	8	0	0	1	690

Going: Sf: 0-0 GS: 0-3 Gd: 0-0 GF: - Fm: 0-0
Distance: 2m/2m3: 0-4 2m4-2m7: 0-1 3m+: 0-0
Track: LH: 0-4 RH: 0-1 Tight: 0-1 Gall: 0-0
Aids: Bl: 0-0 Vi: 0-0 Tstrap: 0-0 Ckp: 0-0
Best Rating: 75   11/03   Bang   2m1f   good   Hdl

Plating-class hurdler; fair handicapper at around ten furlongs on the Flat; yet to prove he stays two miles; best on good ground.

Reverse Pace (IRE)

99f

7-y-o b g Leading Counsel (USA)-Drumscap (IRE) (Remainder Man)
Mrs H Dalton   Terry O'Connor & Mark Ball

Placings:06/0   (2294)
2003/04: 17⁰G,

	Starts	1st	2nd	3rd	Win & Pl
NH Flat	1	0	0	0	0
Career Total	3	0	0	0	0

Going: Sf: 0-0 GS: 0-0 Gd: 0-0 GF: - Fm: 0-0
Distance: 2m/2m3: 0-1 2m4-2m7: 0-0 3m+: 0-0
Track: LH: 0-0 RH: 0-0 Tight: 0-0 Gall: 0-0
Aids: Bl: 0-0 Vi: 0-0 Tstrap: 0-0 Ckp: 0-0
Best Rating: 99   3/02   Sand   2m110y   gd-sft   NHF

Reverse Swing

83   80d

7-y-o b m Charmer-Milly Kelly (Murrayfield)
Mrs H Dalton   The Herons Partnership

Placings:060/5051F006-0   (0082)
2003/04: 16⁰GS,

	Starts	1st	2nd	3rd	Win & Pl
Hurdles	1	0	0	0	0
Career Total	12	1	0	0	3494
80 11/02 Winc	2m	E(0-100)HHdl		G-S	£3493

Total win prize-money £3494

Going: Sf: 0-0 GS: 0-1 Gd: 0-0 GF: - Fm: 0-0
Distance: 2m/2m3: 0-1 2m4-2m7: 0-0 3m+: 0-0
Track: LH: 0-1 RH: 0-0 Tight: 0-0 Gall: 0-0
Aids: Bl: 0-0 Vi: 0-0 Tstrap: 0-0 Ckp: 0-0
Best Rating: 80   12/02   Ludl   2m   good   Hdl

Reverso (FR)

4-y-o b g Kaldounevees (FR)-Sweet Racine (FR) (Dom Racine (FR))
N J Hawke   R J & Mrs J A Peake

Placings:0P   (4560)
2003/04: 19⁰S, 21ᴾGS,

	Starts	1st	2nd	3rd	Win & Pl
Hurdles	2	0	0	0	0
Career Total	2	0	0	0	0

Going: Sf: 0-1 GS: 0-1 Gd: 0-0 GF: - Fm: 0-0
Distance: 2m/2m3: 0-1 2m4-2m7: 0-0 3m+: 0-0
Track: LH: 0-1 RH: 0-1 Tight: 0-0 Gall: 0-1
Aids: Bl: 0-0 Vi: 0-0 Tstrap: 0-0 Ckp: 0-0
Best Rating: 0   3/04   Newb   2m5f   gd-sft   Hdl

Has shown promise on both starts; will do better in time.

Reviewer (IRE)

108   128

6-y-o b g Sadler's Wells (USA)-Clandestina (USA) (Secretariat (USA))
M Meade   Ladyswood Stud

Placings:21P/0320-0300   (4567)
2003/04: 22⁰G, 22³G, 21⁰G, 24⁰GS,

	Starts	1st	2nd	3rd	Win & Pl
Hurdles	4	0	0	1	1299
Career Total	11	1	2	2	11130
128 2/02 MRas	2m1f110yD Hdl			G-S	£3612

Total win prize-money £3612

Going: Sf: 0-0 GS: 0-1 Gd: 0-3 GF: - Fm: 0-0
Distance: 2m/2m3: 0-0 2m4-2m7: 0-3 3m+: 0-1
Track: LH: 0-2 RH: 0-2 Tight: 0-1 Gall: 0-1
Aids: Bl: 0-0 Vi: 0-0 Tstrap: 0-0 Ckp: 0-0
Best Rating: 128   3/03   Newb   2m110y   soft   Hdl

Fair dual-purpose performer; suited by two miles and good or easy ground; keen sort; has not won since 2002.

Rhapsody In Blue (IRE)

(96h)   (90 h)73

9-y-o b g Magical Strike (USA)-Palace Blue (IRE) (Dara Monarch)
R Ford   Bricks, Bills & Beer

Placings:6300/00036/P/P30F121420/F120-PP   (0398)
2003/04: 20ᴾS, 24ᴾGS,

	Starts	1st	2nd	3rd	Win & Pl
Hurdles	1	0	0	0	0
Chases	1	0	0	0	0
Career Total	26	3	3	3	7555
90 1/03 Newc	2m4f	G(0-95)HHdl		HVY	£2310
83 12/01 Tntn	3m110y	G(0-90)HHdl		G-S	£1722

Total win prize-money £4032

Going: Sf: 0-1 GS: 0-1 Gd: 0-0 GF: - Fm: 0-0
Distance: 2m/2m3: 0-0 2m4-2m7: 0-1 3m+: 0-1
Track: LH: 0-1 RH: 0-1 Tight: 0-0 Gall: 0-1
Aids: Bl: 0-0 Vi: 0-0 Tstrap: 0-2 Ckp: 0-0
Best Rating: 99   3/99   Newb   2m110y   gd-fm   Hdl

Poor chaser; plating-class hurdler; effective from two and a half to three miles; handles good ground, but better on softer.

Rhetoric (IRE)

83   66

5-y-o b g Desert King (IRE)-Squaw Talk (USA) (Gulch (USA))
D G Bridgwater   Alan A Wright

Placings:60P6P40-00   (0479)
2003/04: 16⁰G, 21⁰GF,

	Starts	1st	2nd	3rd	Win & Pl
Hurdles	2	0	0	0	0
Career Total	9	0	0	0	177

Going: Sf: 0-0 GS: 0-0 Gd: 0-1 GF: - Fm: 0-1
Distance: 2m/2m3: 0-1 2m4-2m7: 0-1 3m+: 0-0
Track: LH: 0-1 RH: 0-1 Tight: 0-0 Gall: 0-1
Aids: Bl: 0-0 Vi: 0-0 Tstrap: 0-0 Ckp: 0-0
Best Rating: 66   4/03   Tntn   3m110y   firm   Hdl

Rhinestone Cowboy (IRE)

119   170+

8-y-o b g Be My Native (USA)-Monumental Gesture (Head For Heights)
Jonjo O'Neill   Mrs John Magnier

Placings:12/111113-16131   (4646)

2003/04: 20¹S, 16⁶Y, 16¹S, 21³G, 20¹G,

	Starts	1st	2nd	3rd	Win & Pl
Hurdles	5	3	0	1	130903
Career Total	13	6	1	2	245480
160	4/04 Aint	2m4f	A Hdl		GD £87000
161	2/04 Sand	2m110y A Hdl		SFT £15499
170	12/03 Hayd	2m4f	B HHdl		SFT £20153
162	2/03 Winc	2m	A Hdl		G-S £29750
142	2/03 Weth	2m	A Hdl		G-S £17400
117	12/02 Chel	2m1f	B Hdl		GD £10230
131	11/02 Newb	2m110y D Hdl		SFT £4277
131	11/02 Chel	2m110y A NHF		G-S £10570
131	2/02 Asct	2m110y H NHF		SFT £2450
				Total win prize-money £197330

Going:	Sf: 2-2 GS: 0-0 Gd: 1-2 GF: - Fm: 0-0
Distance:	2m/2m3: 1-2 2m4-2m7: 2-3 3m+: 0-0
Track:	LH: 2-4 RH: 1-1 Tight: 1-1 Gall: 0-1
Aids:	Bl: 0-0 Vi: 0-0 Tstrap: 0-0 Ckp: 0-0
Best Rating:	170 12/03 Hayd 2m4f　　soft　　Hdl

High-class hurdler; runner-up in the 2002 Cheltenham Festival bumper; had a successful 2002/3 season, winning novice hurdles at Newbury, Cheltenham and the Kingwell Hurdle at Wincanton, before finishing a well-beaten third in the Champion Hurdle; made a winning return in a Haydock handicap in 2003/4, but ran below form in a Grade One at Leopardstown; bounced back to form in the Agfa at Sandown, before running a respectable third in the Coral Cup; narrowly defeated Rooster Booster in Aintree Hurdle; amateur ridden these days; stays two and a half miles and will be suited by three; acts on good and soft ground; usually held up.

Rhossili (IRE)

62 　　　　　　　　　　　　　45

4-y-o b g Perugino (USA)-Velinowski (Malinowski (USA))
John Allen Dingley Dell Racing Ltd

Placings:0 　　　　　　　　　　　　(0919)
2003/04: 17⁰GF,

	Starts	1st	2nd	3rd	Win & Pl
Hurdles	1	0	0	0	
Career Total	1	0	0	0	

Going:	Sf: 0-0 GS: 0-0 Gd: 0-0 GF: - Fm: 0-1
Distance:	2m/2m3: 0-1 2m4-2m7: 0-0 3m+: 0-0
Track:	LH: 0-0 RH: 0-0 Tight: 0-1 Gall: 0-0
Aids:	Bl: 0-0 Vi: 0-0 Tstrap: 0-0 Ckp: 0-0
Best Rating:	45 7/03 MRas 2m1f110y gd-fm Hdl

Rhythm King

　　　　　　　　　　　　　(86h)93

9-y-o b g Rakaposhi King-Minim (Rymer)
J A B Old Mrs J A Fowler/the Kentish Men

Placings:00/600/U0FU0-F 　　　　　　(0038)
2003/04: 19⁰G,

	Starts	1st	2nd	3rd	Win & Pl
Chases	1	0	0	0	
Career Total	11	0	0	0	0

Going:	Sf: 0-0 GS: 0-0 Gd: 0-0 GF: - Fm: 0-0
Distance:	2m/2m3: 0-0 2m4-2m7: 0-0 3m+: 0-0
Track:	LH: 0-0 RH: 0-1 Tight: 0-0 Gall: 0-0
Aids:	Bl: 0-0 Vi: 0-0 Tstrap: 0-0 Ckp: 0-0
Best Rating:	93 3/03 Wwck 2m4f110y gd-sft Ch

Rhythmicall (IRE)

68 　　　　　　　　　　　　　43

7-y-o b g In The Wings-Rhoman Ruby (IRE) (Rhoman Rule (USA))
B S Rothwell Ron Macdonald

Placings:0/0 　　　　　　　　　　(2399)
2003/04: 16⁰GS,

	Starts	1st	2nd	3rd	Win & Pl
Hurdles	1	0	0	0	
Career Total	2	0	0	0	

Going:	Sf: 0-0 GS: 0-1 Gd: 0-0 GF: - Fm: 0-0
Distance:	2m/2m3: 0-1 2m4-2m7: 0-0 3m+: 0-0
Track:	LH: 0-1 RH: 0-0 Tight: 0-0 Gall: 0-0
Aids:	Bl: 0-0 Vi: 0-0 Tstrap: 0-0 Ckp: 0-0
Best Rating:	43 11/03 Weth 2m　　gd-sft　　Hdl

Riccarton

93(100h) 　　　　　　　(83 h)88

11-y-o b g Nomination-Legendary Dancer (Shareef Dancer (USA))
D C Turner Mrs M E Turner

Placings:560/12603/06455P/4322535-524 　　(0866)
2003/04: 16⁵GF, 16²GF, 16⁴GF,

	Starts	1st	2nd	3rd	Win & Pl
Chases	3	0	1	0	1944
Career Total	24	1	4	3	9912
89	9/99 Tntn	2m3f110yD Hdl		G-F £2626
				Total win prize-money £2626

Going:	Sf: 0-0 GS: 0-0 Gd: 0-0 GF: - Fm: 0-3
Distance:	2m/2m3: 0-3 2m4-2m7: 0-0 3m+: 0-0
Track:	LH: 0-3 RH: 0-0 Tight: 0-3 Gall: 0-0
Aids:	Bl: 0-0 Vi: 0-0 Tstrap: 0-0 Ckp: 0-0
Best Rating:	99 11/99 Chel 2m110y good Hdl

Low-grade chaser, in the frame in the summer of 2002; acts on fast.

Richie's Delight (IRE)

104(99c) 　　　　　　　(100c)100

11-y-o br g Phardante (FR)-Johnstown Love (IRE) (Golden Love)
J A Supple Geoff Hubbard Racing

Placings:S/405452P/351S42312F1/44P43364/4P022/U434 232242P0-46352F133F6430 　　(2909)
2003/04: 22⁴G, 20⁶G, 22³G, 23⁵G, 20²GF, 20⁴GF, 22¹GF, 19³GF, 19³GF, 21⁵G, 20⁵G, 20⁴G, 19³GS, 21⁵G,

	Starts	1st	2nd	3rd	Win & Pl
Hurdles	9	1	1	3	4103
Chases	5	0	1	0	985
Career Total	58	4	10	10	30082
91	9/03 Strf	2m6f110yOg(0-95)HHdl	G-F £2254
99	4/00 Hntg	2m4f110yE Ch	GD £3180
119	11/99 Hntg	2m4f110yD Ch	G-F £4177
96	8/99 Hntg	2m4f110yE Hdl	G-F £2835
			Total win prize-money £12446

Going:	Sf: 0-0 GS: 0-2 Gd: 0-7 GF: - Fm: 1-5
Distance:	2m/2m3: 0-1 2m4-2m7: 1-12 3m+: 0-1
Track:	LH: 1-7 RH: 0-7 Tight: 1-9 Gall: 0-2
Aids:	Bl: 0-0 Vi: 0-0 Tstrap: 0-0 Ckp: 1-13
Best Rating:	119 12/99 Leic 2m4f110y gd-fm Ch

Moderate hurdler/chaser; acts on any ground; particularly suited by two miles four at Huntingdon; usually wears cheekpieces; has been tried in blinkers.

Rickham Glory

6-y-o b g Past Glories-Rickham Bay (Snow Warning)
H E Haynes Miss Alison Joy

Placings:000-0U 　　　　　　　　(3700)
2003/04: 16⁵G, 19⁰HY,

	Starts	1st	2nd	3rd	Win & Pl
NH Flat	1	0	0	0	0
Hurdles	1	0	0	0	0
Career Total	5	0	0	0	0

Going:	Sf: 0-1 GS: 0-0 Gd: 0-1 GF: - Fm: 0-0
Distance:	2m/2m3: 0-1 2m4-2m7: 0-1 3m+: 0-0
Track:	LH: 0-1 RH: 0-1 Tight: 0-0 Gall: 0-0
Aids:	Bl: 0-1 Vi: 0-0 Tstrap: 0-0 Ckp: 0-0

Ricko (NZ)

　　　　　　　　　　　　104

10-y-o b g Defensive Play (USA)-Native Hawk (NZ) (War Hawk)
B G Powell D & J Newell

Placings:42212F/0/364F211F5-P 　　(0215)
2003/04: 20⁰G,

	Starts	1st	2nd	3rd	Win & Pl
Chases	1	0	0	0	
Career Total	17	3	4	1	25007
100	9/02 Strf	2m5f110yD Ch	G-F £5375
107	8/02 NAbb	2m5f110yB HCh	G-F £12722
	6/00 Trap	1m4f110y Hdl	HVY £1393
			Total win prize-money £19492

Going:	Sf: 0-0 GS: 0-0 Gd: 0-1 GF: - Fm: 0-0
Distance:	2m/2m3: 0-0 2m4-2m7: 0-1 3m+: 0-0
Track:	LH: 0-1 RH: 0-0 Tight: 0-0 Gall: 0-0
Aids:	Bl: 0-0 Vi: 0-0 Tstrap: 0-0 Ckp: 0-0
Best Rating:	110 1/01 Plum 2m　　soft　　Hdl

Moderate chaser; stays 2m5f; acts on any ground.

Rico Hombre (FR)

98f 　　　　　　　　　　106+f

5-y-o b g Cadoudal (FR)-Lady Carolina (FR) (Noir Et Or)
N J Henderson Sir Robert Ogden

Placings:1 　　　　　　　　　　(3752)
2003/04: 18¹GS,

	Starts	1st	2nd	3rd	Win & Pl
NH Flat	1	1	0	0	1974
Career Total	1	1	0	0	1974
106	2/04 Font	2m2f110yH NHF	G-S £1974
			Total win prize-money £1974

Going:	Sf: 0-0 GS: 1-1 Gd: 0-0 GF: - Fm: 0-0
Distance:	2m/2m3: 1-1 2m4-2m7: 0-0 3m+: 0-0
Track:	LH: 1-1 RH: 0-0 Tight: 1-1 Gall: 0-0
Aids:	Bl: 0-0 Vi: 0-0 Tstrap: 0-0 Ckp: 0-0
Best Rating:	106 2/04 Font 2m2f110y gd-sft NHF

Won debut bumper at Fontwell in February on good to soft despite running green.

Ridapour (IRE)

101 　　　　　　　　　　　90

5-y-o b g Kahyasi-Ridiyara (IRE) (Persian Bold)
D J Wintle Frinton Bloodstock

Placings:3-0554035315P 　　　　　(3963)
2003/04: 16⁹GS, 16⁵G, 20⁵GF, 17⁴GF, 20⁰GF, 16²GF, 16⁵G, 19³GS, 19¹HY, 22⁵G, 24⁵PG,

	Starts	1st	2nd	3rd	Win & Pl
Hurdles	11	1	0	2	3834
Career Total	12	1	0	3	4406

89 1/04 Towc 2m3f110yF(0-90)HHdl   HVY £3010

Total win prize-money £3010

Going:	Sf: 1-1 GS: 0-3 Gd: 0-3 GF: - Fm: 0-4
Distance:	2m/2m3: 0-6 2m4-2m7: 1-4 3m+: 0-1
Track:	LH: 0-5 RH: 0-5 Tight: 0-2 Gall: 0-1
Aids:	Bl: 0-0 Vi: 0-0 Tstrap: 0-0 Ckp: 0-1
Best Rating:	89 1/04 Towc 2m3f110y heavy Hdl

Plating-class hurdler; suited by two and a half miles and very soft ground.

Rideaway Rose (IRE)

(91h)   (76h)

8-y-o b m King's Ride-Miss Rockaway (Le Moss)
C J Down G Waterman

Placings: 04/P350P   (3638)
2003/04: 21PGS, 19³GF, 24⁴S, 26⁹GS, 19⁹S,

	Starts	1st	2nd	3rd	Win & Pl
Hurdles	4	0	0	1	863
Chases	1	0	0	0	0
Career Total	7	0	0	1	863

Going:	Sf: 0-2 GS: 0-2 Gd: 0-0 GF: - Fm: 0-1
Distance:	2m/2m3: 0-0 2m4-2m7: 0-3 3m+: 0-2
Track:	LH: 0-0 RH: 0-5 Tight: 0-1 Gall: 0-0
Aids:	Bl: 0-0 Vi: 0-0 Tstrap: 0-0 Ckp: 0-0
Best Rating:	90 10/01 Chep 2m110y soft NHF

Riders Revenge (IRE)

100   91

6-y-o b g Norwich-Paico Ana (Paico)
Miss Venetia Williams Dr Moira Hamlin

Placings: 300-23   (3637)
2003/04: 16²HY, 19³S,

	Starts	1st	2nd	3rd	Win & Pl
NH Flat	1	0	1	0	672
Hurdles	1	0	0	1	568
Career Total	5	0	1	2	1584

Going:	Sf: 0-2 GS: 0-0 Gd: 0-0 GF: - Fm: 0-0
Distance:	2m/2m3: 0-2 2m4-2m7: 0-0 3m+: 0-0
Track:	LH: 0-0 RH: 0-2 Tight: 0-0 Gall: 0-0
Aids:	Bl: 0-0 Vi: 0-0 Tstrap: 0-0 Ckp: 0-0
Best Rating:	104 10/02 Thur 2m yld-sft NHF

Moderate bumper performer/hurdler; acts on soft.

Ridgeway (IRE)

9-y-o b g Indian Ridge-Regal Promise (Pitskelly)
Miss J E Foster (M W Easterby 14/6) Stuart Hardy

Placings: 32/55/4412F-223   (4143)
2003/04: 20⁶GF, 25²G, 25⁴G, 25³G,

	Starts	1st	2nd	3rd	Win & Pl
Chases	4	0	2	1	2003
Career Total	12	1	4	2	5815

102 3/03 Catt 3m1f110yH Ch   SFT £1423

Total win prize-money £1424

Going:	Sf: 0-0 GS: 0-0 Gd: 0-3 GF: - Fm: 0-1

Distance:	2m/2m3: 0-0 2m4-2m7: 0-1 3m+: 0-3
Track:	LH: 0-2 RH: 0-1 Tight: 0-1 Gall: 0-1
Aids:	Bl: 0-0 Vi: 0-0 Tstrap: 0-0 Ckp: 0-3
Best Rating:	104 12/00 Donc 2m110y gd-sft Hdl

Modest hunter chaser; best over trips of three miles plus and acts on any ground; tends to make mistakes.

Rift Valley (IRE)

109(104h)   (117 h)127

9-y-o b g Good Thyne (USA)-Necochea (Julio Mariner)
P J Hobbs Mrs Kathy Stuart

Placings: 4210/6446020/11111/00U016-112   (0677)
2003/04: 23¹GF, 23¹GF, 23⁹GF,

	Starts	1st	2nd	3rd	Win & Pl
Chases	3	2	1	0	9901
Career Total	25	9	3	0	40340

127	6/03	Worc	2m7f110yE Ch	G-F	£3890
127	5/03	Extr	2m7f110yE Ch	G-F	£4823
117	3/03	Extr	2m6f110yD(0-125)HHdl	FRM	£5395
117	8/01	Worc	2m4f D(0-120)HHdl	G-F	£4238
115	8/01	Worc	3m C(0-135)HHdl	G-F	£5363
110	7/01	Wolv	2m4f110yD(0-135)HHdl	G-F	£6727
117	7/01	MRas	2m1f110yE(0-105)HHdl	GD	£3206
108	6/01	Worc	2m4f E(0-135)HHdl	GD	£2534
98	12/99	Ludl	2m H NHF	G-S	£1763

Total win prize-money £37941

Going:	Sf: 0-0 GS: 0-0 Gd: 0-0 GF: - Fm: 2-3
Distance:	2m/2m3: 0-0 2m4-2m7: 0-0 3m+: 2-3
Track:	LH: 1-2 RH: 1-1 Tight: 0-0 Gall: 0-0
Aids:	Bl: 0-0 Vi: 2-3 Tstrap: 0-0 Ckp: 0-0
Best Rating:	127 6/03 Worc 2m7f110y gd-fm Ch

Fair chaser; won twice over fences in the summer of 2003; stays 3m; acts on fast ground; jumps badly to his right; best in a visor.

Right On Target (IRE)

6-y-o b m Presenting-Owenageera (IRE) (Riot Helmet)
J Howard Johnson Dr B Mayoh

Placings: PP   (3762)
2003/04: 16PGS, 21PGS,

	Starts	1st	2nd	3rd	Win & Pl
Hurdles	2	0	0	0	
Career Total	2	0	0	0	

Going:	Sf: 0-0 GS: 0-2 Gd: 0-0 GF: - Fm: 0-0
Distance:	2m/2m3: 0-1 2m4-2m7: 0-1 3m+: 0-0
Track:	LH: 0-2 RH: 0-0 Tight: 0-0 Gall: 0-0
Aids:	Bl: 0-0 Vi: 0-0 Tstrap: 0-0 Ckp: 0-0

Right To Reply (IRE)

10-y-o b/br g Executive Perk-Sesheta (Tumble Wind (USA))
J R Scott Mrs Marilyn Cook

Placings: 2410/12/1/13P   (4696)
2003/04: 24¹G, 25⁵GS, 19⁹G,

	Starts	1st	2nd	3rd	Win & Pl
Chases	3	1	0	1	2555
Career Total	10	4	2	1	15170

125	3/04	Newb	3m H Ch	GD	£1995
117	11/01	Wwck	2m4f110yD Ch	GD	£4030
141	3/01	Asct	2m4f D Ch	HVY	£5148
111	3/00	Folk	2m1f110yH NHF	GD	£1683

Total win prize-money £12857

Going:	Sf: 0-0 GS: 0-1 Gd: 1-2 GF: - Fm: 0-0
Distance:	2m/2m3: 0-0 2m4-2m7: 0-1 3m+: 1-2
Track:	LH: 1-1 RH: 0-2 Tight: 0-0 Gall: 1-1
Aids:	Bl: 0-0 Vi: 0-0 Tstrap: 0-0 Ckp: 0-0
Best Rating:	141 3/01 Asct 2m4f heavy Hdl

Smart hunter; stays three miles and acts on a sound surface.

Rigmarole

114(100c)   (101c)157+

6-y-o b g Fairy King (USA)-Cattermole (USA) (Roberto (USA))
P F Nicholls Mr & Mrs Mark Woodhouse

Placings: 1463011/302002-24FF1121411102   (4954)
2003/04: 18²G, 16⁴G, 17⁵GF, 17⁵GF, 17¹GF, 17¹G, 16²F, 16¹GF, 16⁴GF, 16¹G, 16¹GS, 16¹G, 16⁹G, 16²G,

	Starts	1st	2nd	3rd	Win & Pl
Hurdles	13	6	2	0	164756
Chases	1	0	1	0	1266
Career Total	27	9	5	2	182580

137	2/04	Winc	2m A Hdl	GD	£34800
157	12/03	Chel	2m110y A Hdl	G-S	£43500
154	11/03	Chel	2m110y A HHdl	GD	£29000
131	10/03	Kemp	2m B Hdl	GF	£9495
142	9/03	Bang	2m1f C(0-135)HHdl	GF	£13494
134	8/03	NAbb	2m1f C(0-135)HHdl	G-F	£12316
126	4/02	Sedg	2m1f E Hdl	G-F	£2576
104	4/02	Weth	2m E Hdl	G-F	£3220
109	12/01	Weth	2m D Hdl	G-S	£3759

Total win prize-money £152161

Going:	Sf: 0-0 GS: 1-1 Gd: 3-7 GF: - Fm: 2-6
Distance:	2m/2m3: 6-14 2m4-2m7: 0-0 3m+: 0-0
Track:	LH: 4-7 RH: 2-6 Tight: 2-6 Gall: 0-0
Aids:	Bl: 0-0 Vi: 0-0 Tstrap: 6-14 Ckp: 0-0
Best Rating:	157 12/03 Chel 2m110y gd-sft Hdl

High-class hurdler; most progressive in 2003/4, landing a valuable handicap and the Bula at Cheltenham, together with an impressive win in the Kingwell Hurdle at Wincanton; disappointing eighth in the Champion Hurdle; suited by two miles and fast ground; wears a tongue tie.

Rimosa

92   91

9-y-o b m Miners Lamp-Crosa (Crozier)
A P Jones A P Jones

Placings: 00/PF035U/55P4-425   (2933)
2003/04: 18⁴G, 17²GS, 16⁵S,

	Starts	1st	2nd	3rd	Win & Pl
Hurdles	3	0	1	0	570
Career Total	15	0	1	1	963

Going:	Sf: 0-1 GS: 0-1 Gd: 0-1 GF: - Fm: 0-0
Distance:	2m/2m3: 0-3 2m4-2m7: 0-0 3m+: 0-0
Track:	LH: 0-1 RH: 0-2 Tight: 0-1 Gall: 0-0
Aids:	Bl: 0-0 Vi: 0-0 Tstrap: 0-0 Ckp: 0-0
Best Rating:	91 5/02 Extr 2m1f good Hdl

Plating-class maiden; acts on good ground; best around 2m1f.

Rimpton Boy

9-y-o gr g Interrex (CAN)-Ardelle Grey (Ardross)
R Barber Mrs Elaine Hutchinson

Placings:0/4/1 (0225)
2003/04: 21³G,

	Starts	1st	2nd	3rd	Win & Pl
Chases	1	1	0	0	2730
Career Total	3	1	0	0	2730
98 5/03 Uttx	2m5f			GD	£2730

Total win prize-money £2730

Going:	Sf: 0-0 GS: 0-0 Gd: 1-1 GF: - Fm: 0-0
Distance:	2m/2m3: 0-0 2m4-2m7: 1-1 3m+: 0-0
Track:	LH: 1-1 RH: 0-0 Tight: 0-0 Gall: 0-0
Aids:	Bl: 0-0 Vi: 0-0 Tstrap: 0-0 Ckp: 0-0
Best Rating:	98 5/03 Uttx 2m5f good Ch

Rince Ri (IRE)
119 (130h) 164
11-y-o ch g Orchestra-Mildred's Ball (Blue Refrain)
T M Walsh F M Moriarty

Placings:1114/11121/3213U/1/444213/2663411-23F223
(3744a)
2003/04: 25²G, 20³Y, 24⁴YS, 17²S, 25²GS, 24³YS,

	Starts	1st	2nd	3rd	Win & Pl
Chases	6	0	3	2	57093
Career Total	34	12	7	6	358442
159 3/03 Navn	2m4f	Ch		G-Y	£12662
159 2/03 Fair	3m1f	Ch		Y-S	£14772
164 1/02 Chel	3m1f110y A Ch			HVY	£45000
157 12/00 Leop	3m	Ch		HVY	£52240
160 12/99 Leop	3m	Ch		SFT	£43750
151 4/99 Fair	2m4f	Ch		G-Y	£29017
125 2/99 Naas	2m4f	Ch		SH	£11562
107 1/99 Naas	3m	Ch		HVY	£8671
132 11/98 Navn	2m4f	Ch		SFT	£4184
141 2/98 Navn	3m	Hdl		SFT	£8413
130 1/98 Navn	2m6f	Hdl		HVY	£3573
122 12/97 Navn	2m	Hdl		SFT	£3051

Total win prize-money £236902

Going:	Sf: 0-1 GS: 0-1 Gd: 0-1 GF: - Fm: 0-0
Distance:	2m/2m3: 0-1 2m4-2m7: 0-1 3m+: 0-4
Track:	LH: 0-3 RH: 0-3 Tight: 0-0 Gall: 0-1
Aids:	Bl: 0-0 Vi: 0-0 Tstrap: 0-0 Ckp: 0-0
Best Rating:	166 3/00 Chel 3m2f110y gd-fm Ch

High-class Irish chaser; twice a winner of the Ericsson Chase at Leopardstown; won the Pillar Property Chase at Cheltenham in January 2002 and runner-up to Jair du Cochet in same event in 2004; stays 3m 2f; effective in soft and heavy ground; has worn headgear; very tough.

Rincoola (IRE)
76f 61f
5-y-o br m Warcraft (USA)-Very Tense (IRE) (Orchestra)
J S Wainwright Andrew Nicholls

Placings:0 (4608)
2003/04: 17⁰G,

	Starts	1st	2nd	3rd	Win & Pl
NH Flat	1	0	0	0	
Career Total	1	0	0	0	

Going:	Sf: 0-0 GS: 0-0 Gd: 0-0 GF: - Fm: 0-0
Distance:	2m/2m3: 0-0 2m4-2m7: 0-0 3m+: 0-0
Track:	LH: 0-0 RH: 0-1 Tight: 0-0 Gall: 0-0
Aids:	Bl: 0-0 Vi: 0-0 Tstrap: 0-0 Ckp: 0-0
Best Rating:	63 3/04 MRas 2m1f110y good NHF

Ring Of Roses
74f 51f
5-y-o b m Efisio-True Ring (High Top)

M W Easterby Guy Reed

Placings:00 (4277)
2003/04: 16⁰G, 17⁰G,

	Starts	1st	2nd	3rd	Win & Pl
NH Flat	2	0	0	0	
Career Total	2	0	0	0	

Going:	Sf: 0-0 GS: 0-0 Gd: 0-2 GF: - Fm: 0-0
Distance:	2m/2m3: 0-2 2m4-2m7: 0-0 3m+: 0-0
Track:	LH: 0-1 RH: 0-1 Tight: 0-1 Gall: 0-0
Aids:	Bl: 0-0 Vi: 0-0 Tstrap: 0-1 Ckp: 0-0
Best Rating:	51 1/04 Catt 2m good NHF

Ringagold
5-y-o ch m Karinga Bay-Miss Marigold (Norwick (USA))
R J Hodges John & Greer Norman

Placings:PP (4636)
2003/04: 16⁶GS, 17⁶G,

	Starts	1st	2nd	3rd	Win & Pl
NH Flat	2	0	0	0	
Career Total	2	0	0	0	

Going:	Sf: 0-0 GS: 0-1 Gd: 0-1 GF: - Fm: 0-0
Distance:	2m/2m3: 0-2 2m4-2m7: 0-0 3m+: 0-0
Track:	LH: 0-0 RH: 0-1 Tight: 0-0 Gall: 0-0
Aids:	Bl: 0-0 Vi: 0-0 Tstrap: 0-0 Ckp: 0-0

Ringside Jack
101 94
8-y-o b g Batshoof-Celestine (Skyliner)
C W Fairhurst M J G Partnership

Placings:44 (4461)
2003/04: 17⁴G, 16⁴HY,

	Starts	1st	2nd	3rd	Win & Pl
Hurdles	2	0	0	0	272
Career Total	2	0	0	0	272

Going:	Sf: 0-1 GS: 0-0 Gd: 0-1 GF: - Fm: 0-0
Distance:	2m/2m3: 0-2 2m4-2m7: 0-0 3m+: 0-0
Track:	LH: 0-1 RH: 0-1 Tight: 0-0 Gall: 0-1
Aids:	Bl: 0-0 Vi: 0-0 Tstrap: 0-0 Ckp: 0-0
Best Rating:	94 3/04 MRas 2m1f110y good Hdl

Plating-class hurdler; acts on good or softer.

Rio Real (IRE)
91 96
8-y-o b g Case Law-Fine Flame (Le Prince)
J Mackie Mrs Sue Adams

Placings:33321/2/1634-6054 (2665)
2003/04: 20⁶G, 16⁰GS, 17⁵GS, 16⁴G,

	Starts	1st	2nd	3rd	Win & Pl
Hurdles	4	0	0	0	
Career Total	14	2	2	4	6381
93 5/02 Towc	2m	G Hdl		GD	£1862
94 12/99 Uttx	2m	G Hdl		SFT	£1679

Total win prize-money £3541

Going:	Sf: 0-0 GS: 0-2 Gd: 0-2 GF: - Fm: 0-0
Distance:	2m/2m3: 0-2 2m4-2m7: 0-1 3m+: 0-0
Track:	LH: 0-2 RH: 0-2 Tight: 0-1 Gall: 0-0
Aids:	Bl: 0-2 Vi: 0-2 Tstrap: 0-0 Ckp: 0-0
Best Rating:	104 11/00 Leic 2m heavy Hdl

Riothamus (IRE)
103 113+
6-y-o b g Supreme Leader-Kemchee (Kemal (FR))
Ferdy Murphy RP Racing

Placings:1-12324 (4838)
2003/04: 24¹GS, 20²HY, 20³S, 24²GS, 24⁴GF,

	Starts	1st	2nd	3rd	Win & Pl
Hurdles	5	1	2	1	6361
Career Total	6	2	2	1	8370
113 11/03 Carl	3m110y E Hdl			G-S	£2771
108 3/03 Carl	2m1f	H NHF		G-S	£2009

Total win prize-money £4780

Going:	Sf: 0-2 GS: 1-2 Gd: 0-0 GF: - Fm: 0-1
Distance:	2m/2m3: 0-0 2m4-2m7: 0-2 3m+: 1-3
Track:	LH: 0-3 RH: 1-2 Tight: 0-0 Gall: 0-1
Aids:	Bl: 0-0 Vi: 0-0 Tstrap: 0-0 Ckp: 0-0
Best Rating:	113 11/03 Carl 3m110y gd-sft Hdl

Modest hurdler; stays 3m; acts on yielding ground; type to do well over fences.

Ripcord (IRE)
97 73+
6-y-o b g Diesis-Native Twine (Be My Native (USA))
Lady Herries Lady Herries

Placings:0 (2069)
2003/04: 16⁰GF,

	Starts	1st	2nd	3rd	Win & Pl
Hurdles	1	0	0	0	
Career Total	1	0	0	0	

Going:	Sf: 0-0 GS: 0-0 Gd: 0-0 GF: - Fm: 0-1
Distance:	2m/2m3: 0-1 2m4-2m7: 0-0 3m+: 0-0
Track:	LH: 0-0 RH: 0-0 Tight: 0-0 Gall: 0-0
Aids:	Bl: 0-0 Vi: 0-0 Tstrap: 0-0 Ckp: 0-0
Best Rating:	76 11/03 Hntg 2m110y gd-fm Hdl

Rising Generation (FR)
105 114
7-y-o ch g Risen Star (USA)-Queen's Victory (FR) (Carmarthen (FR))
N G Richards Greystoke Stables Ltd

Placings:43/2112F5/1131143P/54P52-25F0500 (4883)
2003/04: 16²GS, 16⁵G, 21⁵GF, 16⁶S, 17⁵GS, 16⁹G, 17⁰GS,

	Starts	1st	2nd	3rd	Win & Pl
Hurdles	7	0	1	0	1708
Career Total	28	6	4	3	37148
131 1/02 Hrfd	2m3f	E Ch		SFT	£3302
10/01 Nanc	2m3f	Hdl		VS	£4364
9/01 Crao	2m2f110y Ch			SFT	£5819

Total win prize-money £23151

Going:	Sf: 0-1 GS: 0-2 Gd: 0-3 GF: - Fm: 0-1
Distance:	2m/2m3: 0-6 2m4-2m7: 0-1 3m+: 0-0
Track:	LH: 0-3 RH: 0-4 Tight: 0-2 Gall: 0-0
Aids:	Bl: 0-0 Vi: 0-0 Tstrap: 0-0 Ckp: 0-0
Best Rating:	131 1/02 Hrfd 2m3f soft Ch

Moderate hurdler; winning chaser; stays 2m 5f; acts on fast ground; not the most consistent.

Rising Talisker
11-y-o ch m Primitive Rising (USA)-Dialect (Connaught)

O R Dukes Miss D Hill

Placings:0036/5FU50/P/P/P   (4607)
2003/04: 25PGS,

	Starts	1st	2nd	3rd	Win & Pl
Chases	1	0	0	0	
Career Total	12	0	0	1	460

Going:	Sf: 0-0 GS: 0-1 Gd: 0-0 GF: - Fm: 0-0
Distance:	2m/2m3: 0-0 2m4-2m7: 0-0 3m+: 0-1
Track:	LH: 0-0 RH: 0-1 Tight: 0-1 Gall: 0-0
Aids:	Bl: 0-1 Vi: 0-0 Tstrap: 0-0 Ckp: 0-0
Best Rating:	85 1/00 Sthl 2m4f110y gd-sft Hdl

Risk Accessor (IRE)
117   (148h)148+
9-y-o b g Commanche Run-Bellatollah (Bellman (FR))
C Roche John P McManus

Placings:22/21251323/11F2331F2/40223-161F20U4
                                            (4835)
2003/04: 16¹S, 22⁶Y, 18¹GF, 20⁴G, 20²GS, 20⁶G, 36⁵U, 21⁴GF,

	Starts	1st	2nd	3rd	Win & Pl
Hurdles	1	0	0	0	25325
Chases	7	1	1	0	37516
Career Total	32	7	10	5	183709
134	10/03	Thur	2m2f			Ch	G-F	£11798
130	7/03	Tipp	2m			Hdl	SFT	£25324
128	2/02	Thur	2m			Ch	HVY	£6349
130	10/01	Thur	2m6f			Ch	YLD	£7790
146	5/01	Fair	2m4f			Hdl	G-Y	£14677
130	1/01	Naas	2m4f			Hdl	SFT	£18346
135	10/00	Fair	2m4f			Hdl	G-Y	£4416
						Total win prize-money £88704

Going:	Sf: 1-1 GS: 0-1 Gd: 0-3 GF: - Fm: 1-2
Distance:	2m/2m3: 2-2 2m4-2m7: 0-5 3m+: 0-1
Track:	LH: 0-5 RH: 1-2 Tight: 0-1 Gall: 0-4
Aids:	Bl: 0-0 Vi: 0-0 Tstrap: 0-1 Ckp: 0-0
Best Rating:	148 12/03 Chel 2m4f110y gd-sft Ch

Smart Irish-trained handicap chaser; still in with a chance when falling two out in the Paddy Power Gold Cup in November 2003; runner-up in the Tripleprint Gold Cup at the same track next time; can be a tricky ride; stays two miles six, but effective at shorter, looks best on a soft surface; has worn a tongue tie.

Risk And Reward (IRE)
81   91
6-y-o b m Topanoora-Khaiylasha (IRE) (Kahyasi)
Jonjo O'Neill John P McManus

Placings:P656-0P   (1907)
2003/04: 20⁴G, 16⁶GF,

	Starts	1st	2nd	3rd	Win & Pl
Hurdles	2	0	0	0	
Career Total	6	0	0	0	

Going:	Sf: 0-0 GS: 0-0 Gd: 0-1 GF: - Fm: 0-1
Distance:	2m/2m3: 0-1 2m4-2m7: 0-1 3m+: 0-1
Track:	LH: 0-1 RH: 0-1 Tight: 0-0 Gall: 0-1
Aids:	Bl: 0-1 Vi: 0-0 Tstrap: 0-0 Ckp: 0-0
Best Rating:	91 2/03 Gowr 2m yield Hdl

Risker (USA)
89   66
5-y-o b g Gone West (USA)-Trampoli (USA) (Trempolino (USA))

J Joseph Jack Joseph

Placings:F056-P0PP00P   (4401)
2003/04: 16PGF, 20⁰GF, 19PG, 16PS, 16⁰S, 19⁰G, 21PG,

	Starts	1st	2nd	3rd	Win & Pl
Hurdles	7	0	0	0	
Career Total	11	0	0	0	314

Going:	Sf: 0-2 GS: 0-0 Gd: 0-3 GF: - Fm: 0-2
Distance:	2m/2m3: 0-4 2m4-2m7: 0-3 3m+: 0-0
Track:	LH: 0-3 RH: 0-4 Tight: 0-1 Gall: 0-2
Aids:	Bl: 0-0 Vi: 0-0 Tstrap: 0-0 Ckp: 0-0
Best Rating:	80 9/02 NAbb 2m1f good Hdl

Risky Reef
113   147
7-y-o ch g Risk Me (FR)-Pas De Reef (Pas De Seul)
Andrew Lee Ergon Syndicate

Placings:14/3211-440   (3829)
2003/04: 16⁴YS, 16⁴GY, 16⁰G,

	Starts	1st	2nd	3rd	Win & Pl
Hurdles	3	0	0	0	3545
Career Total	9	3	1	1	45973
137	4/03	Aint	2m110y	A	HHdl	GD	£23200
133	1/03	Thur	2m		Hdl	SFT	£6272
121	12/01	Limk	2m		Hdl	SFT	£7862
					Total win prize-money £37336

Going:	Sf: 0-0 GS: 0-0 Gd: 0-1 GF: - Fm: 0-0
Distance:	2m/2m3: 0-3 2m4-2m7: 0-0 3m+: 0-0
Track:	LH: 0-1 RH: 0-2 Tight: 0-0 Gall: 0-1
Aids:	Bl: 0-0 Vi: 0-0 Tstrap: 0-0 Ckp: 0-0
Best Rating:	147 11/03 Punc 2m gd-yld Hdl

Smart Irish-trained hurdler; followed up a Thurles success in January 2003 with victory in a valuable handicap at Aintree; suited by two miles and decent ground; consistent.

Risky Way
99(96h)   (87+h)97
8-y-o b g Risk Me (FR)-Hot Sunday Sport (Star Appeal)
B S Rothwell Mike Gosse

Placings:104300/2/32U42P/U212-5P4604160000 (4164)
2003/04: 16⁵GF, 17PG, 21⁴GF, 17⁶G, 19⁰GF, 17⁴GF, 19¹GF, 17⁶G, 16⁸GF, 20⁰G, 19⁰G, 19⁰G,

	Starts	1st	2nd	3rd	Win & Pl
Hurdles	7	1	0	0	3659
Chases	5	0	0	0	308
Career Total	31	3	5	2	18018
87	9/03	MRas	2m3f110yE(0-110)HHdl	G-F	£3398
97	2/03	Catt	2m	D(0-115)HCh	G-F	£5343
85	9/99	MRas	2m1f110yG Hdl	G-F	£1688
			Total win prize-money £10429

Going:	Sf: 0-0 GS: 0-0 Gd: 0-6 GF: - Fm: 1-6
Distance:	2m/2m3: 0-8 2m4-2m7: 1-4 3m+: 0-0
Track:	LH: 0-10 RH: 1-2 Tight: 1-8 Gall: 0-0
Aids:	Bl: 0-0 Vi: 0-1 Tstrap: 0-0 Ckp: 1-7
Best Rating:	99 8/01 Worc 2m4f110y gd-fm Ch

Plating-class hurdler/ chaser; stays two and a half miles; not a fluent jumper of fences; wears cheekpieces.

Rival (IRE)
5-y-o b g Desert Style (IRE)-Arab Scimetar (IRE) (Sure Blade (USA))
S T Lewis Simon T Lewis

Placings:0   (3773)
2003/04: 16⁰G,

	Starts	1st	2nd	3rd	Win & Pl
Hurdles	1	0	0	0	
Career Total	1	0	0	0	

Going:	Sf: 0-0 GS: 0-0 Gd: 0-1 GF: - Fm: 0-0
Distance:	2m/2m3: 0-1 2m4-2m7: 0-0 3m+: 0-0
Track:	LH: 0-0 RH: 0-1 Tight: 0-0 Gall: 0-0
Aids:	Bl: 0-0 Vi: 0-0 Tstrap: 0-0 Ckp: 0-0

Rival Bidder
104   103
7-y-o ch g Arzanni-Beltalong (Belfort (FR))
Mrs S J Smith Keith Nicholson

Placings:0/0/1210U   (3369)
2003/04: 16¹GF, 16²GF, 16¹GF, 16⁰GS, 16⁰S,

	Starts	1st	2nd	3rd	Win & Pl
Hurdles	5	2	1	0	7037
Career Total	7	2	1	0	7037
100	10/03	Hayd	2m	D Hdl	G-F	£3934
103	9/03	Worc	2m	F Hdl	G-F	£2373
			Total win prize-money £6307

Going:	Sf: 0-1 GS: 0-1 Gd: 0-0 GF: - Fm: 2-3
Distance:	2m/2m3: 2-5 2m4-2m7: 0-0 3m+: 0-0
Track:	LH: 2-5 RH: 0-0 Tight: 0-0 Gall: 0-0
Aids:	Bl: 0-0 Vi: 0-0 Tstrap: 0-0 Ckp: 0-0
Best Rating:	103 10/03 Hexm 2m110y gd-fm Hdl

Moderate hurdler; easy 33/1 winner of maiden hurdle at Worcester in September after more than two years off the course; runner-up under a penalty at Hexham next time and won a three-runner affair over brush hurdles at Haydock subsequently; acts on fast ground.

Rivelli (IRE)
5-y-o b m Lure (USA)-Kama Tashoof (Mtoto)
B R Foster (P R Webber 11/9) Michael Brownrigg

Placings:P   (4565)
2003/04: 17PGS,

	Starts	1st	2nd	3rd	Win & Pl
Hurdles	1	0	0	0	
Career Total	1	0	0	0	

Going:	Sf: 0-0 GS: 0-1 Gd: 0-0 GF: - Fm: 0-0
Distance:	2m/2m3: 0-1 2m4-2m7: 0-0 3m+: 0-0
Track:	LH: 0-1 RH: 0-0 Tight: 0-1 Gall: 0-0
Aids:	Bl: 0-0 Vi: 0-0 Tstrap: 0-0 Ckp: 0-0

Rivendell
8-y-o b m Saddlers' Hall (IRE)-Fairy Kingdom (Prince Sabo)
M Wigham Maurice Kirby

Placings:P   (0291)
2003/04: 16PG,

	Starts	1st	2nd	3rd	Win & Pl
Hurdles	1	0	0	0	
Career Total	1	0	0	0	

Going:	Sf: 0-0 GS: 0-0 Gd: 0-1 GF: - Fm: 0-0
Distance:	2m/2m3: 0-1 2m4-2m7: 0-0 3m+: 0-0
Track:	LH: 0-1 RH: 0-0 Tight: 0-1 Gall: 0-0
Aids:	Bl: 0-0 Vi: 0-0 Tstrap: 0-1 Ckp: 0-0

River Alder

112   **104+**

6-y-o b m Alderbrook-River Pearl (Oats)
Miss S E Forster J M Dun

Placings:1   (4731)
2003/04: 20¹G,

	Starts	1st	2nd	3rd	Win & Pl
Hurdles	1	1	0	0	4014
Career Total	1	1	0	0	4014
104 4/04 Carl 2m4f		E Hdl		GD	£4013
				Total win prize-money £4014	

Going: Sf: 0-0 GS: 0-0 Gd: 1-1 GF: - Fm: 0-0
Distance: 2m/2m3: 0-0 **2m4-2m7: 1-1** 3m+: 0-0
Track: LH: 0-0 **RH: 1-1** Tight: 0-0 Gall: 0-0
Aids: Bl: 0-0 Vi: 0-0 Tstrap: 0-0 Ckp: 0-0
Best Rating: **104** 4/04 Carl 2m4f   good   Hdl

Moderate hurdler; stays 2m 4f: acts on good.

River Amora (IRE)

105   (86h)**76**

9-y-o b g Willie Joe (IRE)-That's Amora (Paddy's Stream)
P Butler Mrs P A Wood

Placings:055200034U660134/30563535P536-325 (4961)
2003/04: 17³G, 20²S, 20⁵GS,

	Starts	1st	2nd	3rd	Win & Pl
Chases	3	0	1	1	1600
Career Total	31	1	2	7	8895
88 4/02 Plum 2m4f		F Ch		G-F	£2557
				Total win prize-money £2558	

Going: Sf: 0-1 GS: 0-1 Gd: 0-1 GF: - Fm: 0-0
Distance: 2m/2m3: 0-1 2m4-2m7: 0-2 3m+: 0-0
Track: LH: 0-2 RH: 0-1 Tight: 0-3 Gall: 0-0
Aids: Bl: 0-0 Vi: 0-0 Tstrap: 0-0 Ckp: 0-0
Best Rating: **88** 9/02 Plum 2m4f   good   Ch

Moderate, lightly-raced hurdler/chaser; suited by good/fast ground; usually amateur ridden.

River Bailiff (IRE)

8-y-o ch g Over The River (FR)-Rath Caola (Neltino)
R Gurney S Garrott

Placings:464655-0   (3898)
2003/04: 20⁰G,

	Starts	1st	2nd	3rd	Win & Pl
Chases	1	0	0	0	
Career Total	7	0	0	0	410

Going: Sf: 0-0 GS: 0-0 Gd: 0-1 GF: - Fm: 0-0
Distance: 2m/2m3: 0-0 2m4-2m7: 0-1 3m+: 0-0
Track: LH: 0-0 RH: 0-1 Tight: 0-0 Gall: 0-0
Aids: Bl: 0-0 Vi: 0-0 Tstrap: 0-0 Ckp: 0-0
Best Rating: 79 2/03 Weth 2m   good   Ch

River Bann (USA)

105   **110+**

7-y-o ch g Irish River (FR)-Spiritual Star (USA) (Soviet Star (USA))
Mrs Jane Galpin Mrs C D Farmer

Placings:46423-350531   (3700)
2003/04: 16³GF, 16⁵GS, 22⁰G, 20⁵HY, 16³G, 19¹HY,

	Starts	1st	2nd	3rd	Win & Pl
Hurdles	6	1	0	2	3259

Career Total   11   1   1   3   5870
97 2/04 Hrfd 2m3f110yG Hdl   HVY £2527
Total win prize-money £2527

Going: Sf: 1-2 GS: 0-1 Gd: 0-2 GF: - Fm: 0-1
Distance: 2m/2m3: 0-3 **2m4-2m7: 1-3** 3m+: 0-0
Track: LH: 0-1 **RH: 1-4** Tight: 0-2 Gall: 0-0
Aids: Bl: 0-0 Vi: 0-0 Tstrap: 0-0 Ckp: 0-0
Best Rating: **100** 1/04 Ludl 2m   good   Hdl

Moderate hurdler; best over trips beyond two miles.

River Bug (IRE)

90   **127**

10-y-o ch g Over The River (FR)-Fiona's Wish (Wishing Star)
Jamie Poulton Ormonde Racing

Placings:050/1P1/320P114-556U0   (4342)
2003/04: 29⁵S, 29⁵G, 28⁶G, 33ᵁG, 29⁰GS,

	Starts	1st	2nd	3rd	Win & Pl
Chases	5	0	0	0	1926
Career Total	18	4	1	1	44925
123 2/03 Plum 3m2f		E(0-115)Ch		G-S	£5382
105 1/03 Folk 3m2f		F(0-100)HCh		HVY	£3367
106 3/02 Font 3m4f		D(0-125)HCh		SFT	£17615
86 3/02 Towc 3m1f		F(0-100)HCh		SFT	£4504
				Total win prize-money £30869	

Going: Sf: 0-1 GS: 0-1 Gd: 0-3 GF: - Fm: 0-0
Distance: 2m/2m3: 0-0 2m4-2m7: 0-0 3m+: 0-5
Track: LH: 0-3 RH: 0-1 Tight: 0-1 Gall: 0-1
Aids: Bl: 0-5 Vi: 0-0 Tstrap: 0-0 Ckp: 0-0
Best Rating: **123** 2/03 Plum 3m2f   gd-sft   Ch

Moderate chaser; ex-Irish; stays near to four miles; suited by soft ground; has worn blinkers.

River City (IRE)

109   **131+**

7-y-o b g Norwich-Shuil Na Lee (IRE) (Phardante (FR))
Noel T Chance Mrs S Rowley-Williams & Partners

Placings:01/2511P4-1   (4813)
2003/04: 16¹G,

	Starts	1st	2nd	3rd	Win & Pl
Hurdles	1	1	0	0	5639
Career Total	9	4	1	0	18039
131 4/04 Chep 2m110y		D(0-125)HHdl		GD	£5638
106 1/03 Donc 2m110y		E Hdl		G-S	£3581
110 11/02 NAbb 2m1f		E Hdl		SFT	£3613
100 4/02 Asct 2m110y		H NHF		G-F	£2709
				Total win prize-money £15543	

Going: Sf: 0-0 GS: 0-0 Gd: 0-0 GF: - Fm: 0-0
Distance: **2m/2m3: 1-1** 2m4-2m7: 0-0 3m+: 0-0
Track: **LH: 1-1** RH: 0-0 Tight: 0-0 Gall: 0-0
Aids: Bl: 0-0 Vi: 0-0 Tstrap: 0-0 Ckp: 0-0
Best Rating: **131** 4/04 Chep 2m110y   good   Hdl

Fair hurdler; returned after a year's absence to record fast time when easy winner of competitive Class D 2m handicap at Chepstow April 2004; suited by 2m, but may stay further; acts on any ground.

River Cottage

11-y-o b g Henbit (USA)-Tamorina (Quayside)
S T Lewis Simon T Lewis

Placings:PP   (4888)
2003/04: 24ᴾG, 24ᴾGF,

	Starts	1st	2nd	3rd	Win & Pl
Hurdles	1	0	0	0	0
Chases	1	0	0	0	0
Career Total	2	0	0	0	

Going: Sf: 0-0 GS: 0-0 Gd: 0-1 GF: - Fm: 0-1
Distance: 2m/2m3: 0-0 2m4-2m7: 0-0 3m+: 0-2
Track: LH: 0-1 RH: 0-1 Tight: 0-1 Gall: 0-0
Aids: Bl: 0-0 Vi: 0-0 Tstrap: 0-0 Ckp: 0-0

River Dante (IRE)

7-y-o ch g Phardante (FR)-Astral River (Over The River (FR))
Miss L Blackford 18 Red Lions Partnership

Placings:F   (4302)
2003/04: 20ᶠG,

	Starts	1st	2nd	3rd	Win & Pl
Chases	1	0	0	0	
Career Total	1	0	0	0	

Going: Sf: 0-0 GS: 0-0 Gd: 0-1 GF: - Fm: 0-0
Distance: 2m/2m3: 0-0 2m4-2m7: 0-1 3m+: 0-0
Track: LH: 0-0 RH: 0-1 Tight: 0-0 Gall: 0-0
Aids: Bl: 0-0 Vi: 0-0 Tstrap: 0-0 Ckp: 0-0

River Joy (IRE)

    76f

6-y-o b g Norwich-Vanessa's Palace (Quayside)
Noel T Chance C Green & J Dennis

Placings:000-0   (0251)
2003/04: 17⁰GF,

	Starts	1st	2nd	3rd	Win & Pl
NH Flat	1	0	0	0	
Career Total	4	0	0	0	

Going: Sf: 0-0 GS: 0-0 Gd: 0-0 GF: - Fm: 0-1
Distance: 2m/2m3: 0-0 2m4-2m7: 0-0 3m+: 0-0
Track: LH: 0-0 RH: 0-1 Tight: 0-0 Gall: 0-0
Aids: Bl: 0-0 Vi: 0-0 Tstrap: 0-0 Ckp: 0-0
Best Rating: 76 2/03 Folk 2m1f110y heavy NHF

River Marshal (IRE)

89   **97+**

6-y-o b g Synefos (USA)-Marshallstown (Callernish)
S Gollings R L Houlton

Placings:623-303P   (4589)
2003/04: 16³HY, 16⁰GS, 19³G, 16ᴾG,

	Starts	1st	2nd	3rd	Win & Pl
NH Flat	1	0	0	1	314
Hurdles	3	0	0	1	513
Career Total	7	0	1	3	1763

Going: Sf: 0-1 GS: 0-1 Gd: 0-2 GF: - Fm: 0-0
Distance: 2m/2m3: 0-3 2m4-2m7: 0-1 3m+: 0-0
Track: LH: 0-2 RH: 0-2 Tight: 0-0 Gall: 0-1
Aids: Bl: 0-0 Vi: 0-0 Tstrap: 0-0 Ckp: 0-0
Best Rating: **97** 3/04 Donc 2m3f110y good   Hdl

Moderate hurdler; suited by two and a half miles; acts on good or softer.

River Mere

100   **90**

10-y-o b g River God (USA)-Rupert's Daughter (Rupert Bear)
Mrs L Williamson Mrs J E Webster

Placings:502/PP4P/054-04205316   (1192)
2003/04: 16⁶G, 16⁴GF, 17²G, 17⁹GF, 17⁵GF, 16³GF, 17¹G, 16⁶GF,

	Starts	1st	2nd	3rd	Win & Pl
Hurdles	8	1	1	1	5311
Career Total	18	1	2	1	6160
84	8/03	Bang	2m1f	E(0-105)HHdl	GD	£3526

Total win prize-money £3526

Going:	Sf: 0-0 GS: 0-0 Gd: 1-3 GF: - Fm: 0-5
Distance:	2m/2m3: 1-8 2m4-2m7: 0-0 3m+: 0-0
Track:	LH: 1-7 RH: 0-1 Tight: 1-3 Gall: 0-0
Aids:	Bl: 0-0 Vi: 0-0 Tstrap: 0-0 Ckp: 0-0
Best Rating:	91 10/00 Ludl 2m gd-fm NHF

Plating-class novice hurdler; acts on fast ground; off the mark in novices' handicap at Bangor in August 2003; free running sort.

River Mist (IRE)

108   **92+**

5-y-o ch m Over The River (FR)-Minature Miss (Move Off)
D Eddy Mrs H Scotto

Placings:2-05O33   (4731)
2003/04: 16⁶GF, 16⁵G, 17⁰G, 21³G, 20³G,

	Starts	1st	2nd	3rd	Win & Pl
NH Flat	3	0	0	0	0
Hurdles	2	0	0	2	1131
Career Total	6	0	1	2	1765

Going:	Sf: 0-0 GS: 0-0 Gd: 0-4 GF: - Fm: 0-1
Distance:	2m/2m3: 0-3 2m4-2m7: 0-0 3m+: 0-0
Track:	LH: 0-1 RH: 0-4 Tight: 0-3 Gall: 0-0
Aids:	Bl: 0-0 Vi: 0-0 Tstrap: 0-0 Ckp: 0-0
Best Rating:	92 4/04 Carl 2m4f good Hdl

Very modest form in bumpers and novice hurdle.

River Ness

85(79c)   (56c)**110**

8-y-o br m Buckskin (FR)-Stubbin Moor (Kinglet)
N G Richards Dr Kenneth S Fraser

Placings:P/022011/22524P5-0   (0411)
2003/04: 16⁰G,

	Starts	1st	2nd	3rd	Win & Pl
Hurdles	1	0	0	0	0
Career Total	15	2	5	0	12058
100	4/02	Prth	3m110y	D Hdl	GD	£3731
100	3/02	Sedg	2m5f110yE Hdl	SFT	£2618

Total win prize-money £6349

Going:	Sf: 0-0 GS: 0-0 Gd: 0-1 GF: - Fm: 0-0
Distance:	2m/2m3: 0-1 2m4-2m7: 0-0 3m+: 0-0
Track:	LH: 0-1 RH: 0-0 Tight: 0-0 Gall: 0-0
Aids:	Bl: 0-0 Vi: 0-0 Tstrap: 0-0 Ckp: 0-0
Best Rating:	110 1/03 Ayr 2m heavy Hdl

Fair hurdler; disappointed on chae debut; stays three miles; handles good ground or softer.

River Paradise (IRE)

     (93h)

8-y-o ch g John French-Barbara Brook (Over The River (FR))

R H Alner Jobs Racing

Placings:F02/3UP   (3466)
2003/04: 20³S, 25ᵁGS, 26ᴾS,

	Starts	1st	2nd	3rd	Win & Pl
Chases	3	0	0	1	536
Career Total	6	0	0	1	1434

Going:	Sf: 0-2 GS: 0-1 Gd: 0-0 GF: - Fm: 0-0
Distance:	2m/2m3: 0-0 2m4-2m7: 0-1 3m+: 0-2
Track:	LH: 0-2 RH: 0-1 Tight: 0-1 Gall: 0-0
Aids:	Bl: 0-0 Vi: 0-0 Tstrap: 0-3 Ckp: 0-0
Best Rating:	104 4/02 Weth 2m4f110y good Hdl

River Phantom (IRE)

102f   **101f**

5-y-o b g Over The River (FR)-Cathilda (IRE) (Cataldi)
Ian Williams Graham Ketley

Placings:04   (4920)
2003/04: 16⁹G, 16⁴GS,

	Starts	1st	2nd	3rd	Win & Pl
NH Flat	2	0	0	0	0
Career Total	2	0	0	0	0

Going:	Sf: 0-0 GS: 0-1 Gd: 0-1 GF: - Fm: 0-0
Distance:	2m/2m3: 0-2 2m4-2m7: 0-0 3m+: 0-0
Track:	LH: 0-2 RH: 0-0 Tight: 0-0 Gall: 0-1
Aids:	Bl: 0-0 Vi: 0-0 Tstrap: 0-0 Ckp: 0-0
Best Rating:	101 3/04 Newb 2m110y good NHF

River Pilot

     114

10-y-o b g Unfuwain (USA)-Cut Ahead (Kalaglow)
C J Mann Terry Grove

Placings:1231/02222/5/P1233/F0544-PFP   (3463)
2003/04: 20ᴾGS, 24ᶠGS, 24ᴾS,

	Starts	1st	2nd	3rd	Win & Pl
Chases	3	0	0	0	
Career Total	23	3	6	3	26562
123	8/01	Gway	2m1f	Ch	Y-S	£6955
129	4/99	Punc	2m	Hdl	YLD	£6752
114	5/98	Navn	2m	Hdl	Y-S	£3573

Total win prize-money £17282

Going:	Sf: 0-1 GS: 0-2 Gd: 0-0 GF: - Fm: 0-0
Distance:	2m/2m3: 0-0 2m4-2m7: 0-1 3m+: 0-2
Track:	LH: 0-2 RH: 0-1 Tight: 0-1 Gall: 0-0
Aids:	Bl: 0-0 Vi: 0-0 Tstrap: 0-2 Ckp: 0-0
Best Rating:	129 4/99 Punc 2m yield Hdl

Fair ex-Irish chaser, best at around two miles; suited by soft ground.

River Pirate (IRE)

107   **114**

7-y-o b g Un Desperado (FR)-Kigali (IRE) (Torus)
N J Henderson Riverwood Racing II

Placings:3335-115024   (4704)
2003/04: 16¹G, 17¹GF, 17⁵G, 21⁹G, 16²G, 18⁴G,

	Starts	1st	2nd	3rd	Win & Pl
Hurdles	6	2	1	0	9933
Career Total	10	2	1	3	11480
111	5/03	Hrfd	2m1f	E Hdl	G-F	£3425
110	5/03	Ludl	2m	D Hdl	GD	£4225

Total win prize-money £7651

Going:	Sf: 0-0 GS: 0-0 Gd: 1-5 GF: - Fm: 1-1
Distance:	2m/2m3: 2-5 2m4-2m7: 0-1 3m+: 0-0
Track:	LH: 0-2 RH: 2-4 Tight: 0-1 Gall: 0-1
Aids:	Bl: 0-0 Vi: 0-0 Tstrap: 0-0 Ckp: 0-0
Best Rating:	114 2/04 Asct 2m110y good Hdl

Fair hurdler; won two novice hurdles in May; acts on most types of ground; should stay beyond 2m 1f.

River Quoile

103(99h)   (92h)**105**

8-y-o b g Terimon-Carrikins (Buckskin (FR)) R Alner
R H Alner (Michael Cunningham 19/11) R Alner

Placings:00/0-4200053F03F3F44   (4364)
2003/04: 22⁴G, 22²Y, 24⁴G, 22⁴GF, 22⁰S, 20⁵GF, 25³F, 24²G, 24⁹F, 24³GF, 20ᶠG, 24³G, 24ᶠG, 24⁴G, 26⁴G,

	Starts	1st	2nd	3rd	Win & Pl
Hurdles	5	0	1	0	1403
Chases	10	0	0	3	2489
Career Total	18	0	1	3	3892

Going:	Sf: 0-1 GS: 0-0 Gd: 0-8 GF: - Fm: 0-5
Distance:	2m/2m3: 0-0 2m4-2m7: 0-5 3m+: 0-10
Track:	LH: 0-3 RH: 0-3 Tight: 0-1 Gall: 0-0
Aids:	Bl: 0-1 Vi: 0-0 Tstrap: 0-0 Ckp: 0-0
Best Rating:	105 3/04 Kemp 3m good Ch

River Rambler

5-y-o ch m River Falls-Horsepower (Superpower)
J R Norton J Norton

Placings:0-0PP   (4214)
2003/04: 16⁰G, 16ᴾHY, 17ᴾG,

	Starts	1st	2nd	3rd	Win & Pl
NH Flat	1	0	0	0	0
Hurdles	2	0	0	0	0
Career Total	4	0	0	0	

Going:	Sf: 0-1 GS: 0-1 Gd: 0-1 GF: - Fm: 0-0
Distance:	2m/2m3: 0-3 2m4-2m7: 0-0 3m+: 0-0
Track:	LH: 0-2 RH: 0-0 Tight: 0-1 Gall: 0-1
Aids:	Bl: 0-0 Vi: 0-0 Tstrap: 0-0 Ckp: 0-0
Best Rating:	63 3/03 Weth 2m gd-fm NHF

River Reine (IRE)

97   **91**

5-y-o br m Lahib (USA)-Talahari (IRE) (Roi Danzig (USA))
R H Buckler L G Kimber

Placings:0-023564   (4929)
2003/04: 20⁰GF, 19²GF, 22³G, 23⁵G, 23⁶GS, 18⁴G,

	Starts	1st	2nd	3rd	Win & Pl
Hurdles	6	0	1	1	1972
Career Total	7	0	1	1	1972

Going:	Sf: 0-0 GS: 0-1 Gd: 0-3 GF: - Fm: 0-2
Distance:	2m/2m3: 0-0 2m4-2m7: 0-4 3m+: 0-0
Track:	LH: 0-5 RH: 0-1 Tight: 0-4 Gall: 0-0
Aids:	Bl: 0-0 Vi: 0-0 Tstrap: 0-0 Ckp: 0-0
Best Rating:	91 4/04 Font 2m2f110y good Hdl

Plating-class hurdler; acts on a sound surface.

River Ride (IRE)

86(82h)   (44h)**62**

10-y-o b g King's Ride-Over The Village (IRE) (Over The River (FR))

C J Teague B Batey

Placings:P/P0P46   (0977)
2003/04: 16⁶G, 17⁰S, 21⁸GF, 21⁴GF, 21⁶GF,

	Starts	1st	2nd	3rd	Win & Pl
Hurdles	4	0	0	0	0
Chases	1	0	0	0	0
Career Total	6	0	0	0	0

Going:	Sf: 0-1 GS: 0-0 Gd: 0-1 GF: - Fm: 0-3
Distance:	2m/2m3: 0-2 2m4-2m7: 0-3 3m+: 0-0
Track:	LH: 0-5 RH: 0-0 Tight: 0-3 Gall: 0-0
Aids:	Bl: 0-0 Vi: 0-0 Tstrap: 0-0 Ckp: 0-0
Best Rating:	62 7/03 Sedg 2m5f gd-fm Ch

River Rising

100(61h)   (85dh)**82**
10-y-o b g Primitive Rising (USA)-Dragons Daughter (Mandrake Major)
C R Wilson W R Wilson

Placings:P/430/0-46PFP6P   (3327)
2003/04: 16⁴G, 16⁶G, 20⁰G, 16⁶GF, 16⁶GF, 16⁶GS, 21⁸GS,

	Starts	1st	2nd	3rd	Win & Pl
Chases	7	0	0	0	307
Career Total	12	0	0	1	731

Going:	Sf: 0-0 GS: 0-2 Gd: 0-3 GF: - Fm: 0-2
Distance:	2m/2m3: 0-5 2m4-2m7: 0-2 3m+: 0-0
Track:	LH: 0-7 RH: 0-0 Tight: 0-3 Gall: 0-0
Aids:	Bl: 0-1 Vi: 0-0 Tstrap: 0-0 Ckp: 0-1
Best Rating:	85 5/01 Sedg 2m5f110y gd-fm Hdl

River Slave (IRE)

93
10-y-o b/br g Over The River (FR)-Sally Slave (Paddy's Stream)
T R George Mrs P Miller

Placings:10/P24P/3323P-FPP   (3313)
2003/04: 20⁶S, 20⁶GS, 22⁸HY,

	Starts	1st	2nd	3rd	Win & Pl
Chases	3	0	0	0	
Career Total	14	1	2	3	5859
113	2/00	Carl	2m1f	H NHF	HVY	£1694

Total win prize-money £1694

Going:	Sf: 0-2 GS: 0-1 Gd: 0-0 GF: - Fm: 0-0
Distance:	2m/2m3: 0-0 2m4-2m7: 0-3 3m+: 0-0
Track:	LH: 0-2 RH: 0-0 Tight: 0-3 Gall: 0-0
Aids:	Bl: 0-0 Vi: 0-0 Tstrap: 0-0 Ckp: 0-0
Best Rating:	113 2/00 Carl 2m1f heavy NHF

Moderate chaser; stays well; acts in soft ground.

River Styx (IRE)

106(88h)   (85h)**87**
9-y-o ch g Over The River (FR)-Money For Honey (New Brig)
D McCain The Bankhouse Confederacy

Placings:000/2600/00442330/P332124-P345   (1930)
2003/04: 16⁸GF, 16³GF, 19⁴GF, 26⁵GF,

	Starts	1st	2nd	3rd	Win & Pl
Chases	4	0	0	1	509
Career Total	26	1	4	5	15810
87	2/03	Muss	2m	D(0-110)HCh	GD	£6643

Total win prize-money £6643

River Wye (IRE)

93   **75**
12-y-o b g Jareer (USA)-Sun Gift (Guillaume Tell (USA))
G H Yardley Woodsfield Wanderers

Placings:64325/01P/241/224612U1F/32112/303/6064/P-0P44   (4535)
2003/04: 20⁰G, 24⁷G, 19⁴GF, 19⁴GS,

	Starts	1st	2nd	3rd	Win & Pl
Chases	4	0	0	0	600
Career Total	37	6	7	4	42931
133	3/00	Bang	2m4f110yC(0-135)HCh	GD	£7247
133	2/00	Kemp	2m4f110yC(0-130)HCh	SFT	£10481
135	2/99	Bang	2m1f110yD(0-110)HCh	G-S	£3696
119	12/98	Ludl	2m	E Ch	G-S	£2775
117	5/98	Bang	2m1f	E(0-110)HHdl	GD	£2879
105	2/97	Strf	2m3f	(0-105)Hdl	GD	£2368

Total win prize-money £29448

Going:	Sf: 0-0 GS: 0-1 Gd: 0-2 GF: - Fm: 0-1
Distance:	2m/2m3: 0-0 2m4-2m7: 0-3 3m+: 0-1
Track:	LH: 0-1 RH: 0-0 Tight: 0-2 Gall: 0-0
Aids:	Bl: 0-1 Vi: 0-0 Tstrap: 0-1 Ckp: 0-0
Best Rating:	135 2/99 Bang 2m1f110y gd-sft Ch

Ro Eridani

64   **15**
4-y-o b f Binary Star (USA)-Hat Hill (Roan Rocket)
Miss S E Forster (T J Etherington 16/2) C Storey

Placings:0   (4795)
2003/04: 17⁰G,

	Starts	1st	2nd	3rd	Win & Pl
Hurdles	1	0	0	0	
Career Total	1	0	0	0	

Going:	Sf: 0-0 GS: 0-0 Gd: 0-1 GF: - Fm: 0-0
Distance:	2m/2m3: 0-1 2m4-2m7: 0-0 3m+: 0-0
Track:	LH: 0-1 RH: 0-0 Tight: 0-1 Gall: 0-0
Aids:	Bl: 0-0 Vi: 0-0 Tstrap: 0-0 Ckp: 0-0
Best Rating:	15 4/04 Sedg 2m1f good Hdl

Ro Gema Ri

87f   **70f**
6-y-o b g Perpendicular-Pretty Soon (Tina's Pet)
T D Walford G W Singleton

Placings:0   (4962)
2003/04: 17⁰G,

	Starts	1st	2nd	3rd	Win & Pl
NH Flat	1	0	0	0	
Career Total	1	0	0	0	

Going:	Sf: 0-0 GS: 0-0 Gd: 0-1 GF: - Fm: 0-0
Distance:	2m/2m3: 0-1 2m4-2m7: 0-0 3m+: 0-0
Track:	LH: 0-0 RH: 0-1 Tight: 0-1 Gall: 0-0
Aids:	Bl: 0-0 Vi: 0-0 Tstrap: 0-0 Ckp: 0-0
Best Rating:	70 4/04 MRas 2m1f110y good NHF

Modest chaser; found the combination of a tongue strap and blinkers together for the first time doing the trick when winning 2m handicap chase at Musselburgh February 2003; suited to 2m and good ground.

River Surprise (IRE)

11-y-o b g Over The River (FR)-Reelin Surprise (Royal Match)
Mike Lurcock City Racing Club

Placings:P-P6P   (0483)
2003/04: 16⁸G, 24⁸GF, 24⁸GF,

	Starts	1st	2nd	3rd	Win & Pl
Chases	3	0	0	0	0
Career Total	4	0	0	0	0

Going:	Sf: 0-0 GS: 0-0 Gd: 0-1 GF: - Fm: 0-2
Distance:	2m/2m3: 0-1 2m4-2m7: 0-0 3m+: 0-2
Track:	LH: 0-2 RH: 0-1 Tight: 0-1 Gall: 0-2
Aids:	Bl: 0-0 Vi: 0-0 Tstrap: 0-0 Ckp: 0-0

River Trapper (IRE)

111f   **109f**
5-y-o b g Over The River (FR)-Mousa (Callernish)
Miss H C Knight Mrs C A Waters

Placings:31   (4578)
2003/04: 16³G, 16¹G,

	Starts	1st	2nd	3rd	Win & Pl
NH Flat	2	1	0	1	3713
Career Total	2	1	0	1	3713
109	3/04	Newb	2m110y	H NHF	GD	£3318

Total win prize-money £3318

Going:	Sf: 0-0 GS: 0-0 Gd: 1-2 GF: - Fm: 0-0
Distance:	2m/2m3: 1-2 2m4-2m7: 0-0 3m+: 0-0
Track:	LH: 1-1 RH: 0-1 Tight: 0-0 Gall: 1-1
Aids:	Bl: 0-0 Vi: 0-0 Tstrap: 0-0 Ckp: 0-0
Best Rating:	109 3/04 Newb 2m110y good NHF

River Trix (IRE)

109(83h)   (100h)**99**
10-y-o b g Riverhead (USA)-Game Trix (Buckskin (FR))
M Scudamore (M C Pipe 13/7) The Viva Vialli Partnership

Placings:0/0P2/UPP20/0503-313F51   (4754)
2003/04: 25³GF, 20¹G, 26⁵GF, 21⁶GF, 24⁵GS, 20¹G,

	Starts	1st	2nd	3rd	Win & Pl
Chases	6	2	0	2	7515
Career Total	19	2	2	3	9521
97	4/04	Plum	2m4f	F(0-100)HCh	GD	£3370
99	5/03	Hexm	2m4f110yF Ch	GD	£3081

Total win prize-money £6452

Going:	Sf: 0-0 GS: 0-1 Gd: 2-2 GF: - Fm: 0-3
Distance:	2m/2m3: 0-0 2m4-2m7: 2-3 3m+: 0-3
Track:	LH: 2-5 RH: 0-1 Tight: 1-3 Gall: 1-0
Aids:	Bl: 0-0 Vi: 0-0 Tstrap: 0-0 Ckp: 0-0
Best Rating:	100 4/01 Winc 2m6f soft Hdl

Moderate front-running chaser; won 2m 4f maiden chase at Hexham May 2003; stays 3m 2f; acts on good and soft ground.

Roadworthy (IRE)

73   **58**
7-y-o b m Lord Americo-Henry Woman (IRE) (Mandalus)
J K Magee Paul C Kelly

Placings:000-000   (0646)
2003/04: 16⁶S, 16⁵HY, 16⁰GF,

	Starts	1st	2nd	3rd	Win & Pl
NH Flat	1	0	0	0	0

Hurdles	2	0	0	0 0
Career Total	6	0	0	0

Going:	Sf: 0-2 GS: 0-0 Gd: 0-0 GF: - Fm: 0-1
Distance:	2m/2m3: 0-3 2m4-2m7: 0-0 3m+: 0-1
Track:	LH: 0-1 RH: 0-0 Tight: 0-0 Gall: 0-0
Aids:	Bl: 0-0 Vi: 0-0 Tstrap: 0-0 Ckp: 0-0
Best Rating:	62 8/02 Slig 2m4f heavy NHF

Roar Blizzard (IRE)
89   **53**

6-y-o b h Roar (USA)-Ragtime Rumble (USA) (Dixieland Band (USA))
T H Hansen (Frau A Bodenhagen 8/11) Stall Onextwo DE

Placings:060   (1300)
2003/04: 17⁰GS, 19⁶GS, 16⁰GF,

	Starts	1st	2nd	3rd	Win & Pl
Hurdles	3	0	0	0	
Career Total	3	0	0	0	

Going:	Sf: 0-1 GS: 0-1 Gd: 0-0 GF: - Fm: 0-0
Distance:	2m/2m3: 0-2 2m4-2m7: 0-1 3m+: 0-0
Track:	LH: 0-1 RH: 0-0 Tight: 0-0 Gall: 0-0
Aids:	Bl: 0-0 Vi: 0-0 Tstrap: 0-1 Ckp: 0-0
Best Rating:	63 9/03 Uttx 2m gd-fm Hdl

Roar With Me
82f   **63f**

6-y-o gr m Arzanni-Courtesy Call (Northfields (USA))
M A Buckley The Roaring Partnership

Placings:0   (1611)
2003/04: 16⁰GF,

	Starts	1st	2nd	3rd	Win & Pl
NH Flat	1	0	0	0	
Career Total	1	0	0	0	

Going:	Sf: 0-0 GS: 0-0 Gd: 0-0 GF: 0-0 Fm: 0-0
Distance:	2m/2m3: 0-1 2m4-2m7: 0-0 3m+: 0-0
Track:	LH: 0-0 RH: 0-0 Tight: 0-0 Gall: 0-1
Aids:	Bl: 0-0 Vi: 0-0 Tstrap: 0-0 Ckp: 0-0
Best Rating:	63 10/03 Hntg 2m110y gd-fm NHF

Robber (IRE)
98(98h)   **(87h)87+**

7-y-o ch g Un Desperado (FR)-Christy's Girl (IRE) (Buckskin (FR))
P J Hobbs The Hedonists

Placings:04/5030F0-063034   (4916)
2003/04: 22⁰G, 24⁶G, 25³S, 29³GS, 23⁴GS,

	Starts	1st	2nd	3rd	Win & Pl
Hurdles	1	0	0	0	0
Chases	5	0	0	2	1794
Career Total	14	0	0	3	2336

Going:	Sf: 0-1 GS: 0-2 Gd: 0-3 GF: - Fm: 0-0
Distance:	2m/2m3: 0-0 2m4-2m7: 0-1 3m+: 0-5
Track:	LH: 0-2 RH: 0-4 Tight: 0-1 Gall: 0-0
Aids:	Bl: 0-0 Vi: 0-0 Tstrap: 0-0 Ckp: 0-0
Best Rating:	92 3/02 Wwck 2m gd-sft NHF

Still a maiden over hurdles and fences at up to 3m 5f; does not find too much off the bridle; acts on soft.

Robbie Can Can
111   **105**

5-y-o b g Robellino (USA)-Can Can Lady (Anshan)
A W Carroll K F Coleman

Placings:5410-2023   (4304)
2003/04: 16²GF, 20⁴G, 16²S, 16³G,

	Starts	1st	2nd	3rd	Win & Pl
Hurdles	4	0	2	1	4431
Career Total	8	1	2	1	7414
91	1/03 Chep 2m110y F Hdl			HVY	£2688

Total win prize-money £2688

Going:	Sf: 0-1 GS: 0-0 Gd: 0-2 GF: - Fm: 0-1
Distance:	2m/2m3: 0-3 2m4-2m7: 0-1 3m+: 0-0
Track:	LH: 0-0 RH: 0-4 Tight: 0-0 Gall: 0-0
Aids:	Bl: 0-0 Vi: 0-0 Tstrap: 0-0 Ckp: 0-0
Best Rating:	105 11/03 Leic 2m gd-fm Hdl

Moderate hurdler; effective at two miles; acts on most ground.

Robbie On Tour (IRE)
85   **69**

5-y-o b g Oscar (IRE)-Mystery Woman (Tula Rocket)
M C Pipe D A Johnson

Placings:000   (3447)
2003/04: 17⁰GS, 19⁰G, 19⁰GS,

	Starts	1st	2nd	3rd	Win & Pl
Hurdles	3	0	0	0	
Career Total	3	0	0	0	

Going:	Sf: 0-0 GS: 0-2 Gd: 0-1 GF: - Fm: 0-0
Distance:	2m/2m3: 0-1 2m4-2m7: 0-2 3m+: 0-0
Track:	LH: 0-0 RH: 0-3 Tight: 0-2 Gall: 0-0
Aids:	Bl: 0-0 Vi: 0-0 Tstrap: 0-0 Ckp: 0-0
Best Rating:	75 12/03 Extr 2m1f gd-sft Hdl

Robbie Williams
84f   **55f**

6-y-o b g Missed Flight-Michelle's Ella (IRE) (Ela-Mana-Mou)
P M Rich Robert J Williams

Placings:0   (1817)
2003/04: 17⁰G,

	Starts	1st	2nd	3rd	Win & Pl
NH Flat	1	0	0	0	
Career Total	1	0	0	0	

Going:	Sf: 0-0 GS: 0-0 Gd: 0-1 GF: - Fm: 0-0
Distance:	2m/2m3: 0-1 2m4-2m7: 0-0 3m+: 0-0
Track:	LH: 0-1 RH: 0-0 Tight: 0-1 Gall: 0-0
Aids:	Bl: 0-0 Vi: 0-0 Tstrap: 0-0 Ckp: 0-0
Best Rating:	56 10/03 Bang 2m1f good NHF

Robbie's Adventure

10-y-o ch g Le Coq D'Or-Mendick Adventure (Mandrake Major)
Miss Emma Wettern (D L Williams 5/5) The Adventure partnership

Placings:04/0P045103/P3F134P/325/P4F3PP003P4-P5   (4703)

2003/04: 26⁰G, 26⁵G,

	Starts	1st	2nd	3rd	Win & Pl
Chases	2	0	0	0	0
Career Total	33	2	1	6	8948
86	1/01 Tntn 3m F(0-95)HCh			HVY	£3139
86	2/00 Folk 2m1f110yG(0-90)HCh			SFT	£1547

Total win prize-money £4687

Going:	Sf: 0-0 GS: 0-0 Gd: 0-2 GF: - Fm: 0-0
Distance:	2m/2m3: 0-0 2m4-2m7: 0-0 3m+: 0-2
Track:	LH: 0-0 RH: 0-0 Tight: 0-2 Gall: 0-0
Aids:	Bl: 0-0 Vi: 0-0 Tstrap: 0-0 Ckp: 0-0
Best Rating:	86 1/01 Tntn 3m heavy Ch

Robbo
108(104h)   **(117h)136**

10-y-o b g Robellino (USA)-Basha (USA) (Chief's Crown (USA))
Mrs M Reveley The Scarth Racing Partnership

Placings:1120/332221106/U21123115/0124363/042P006/0
1331054PU-43C20343524213   (4951)
2003/04: 24⁴GS, 26⁵G, 27⁰G, 25²S, 29⁰G, 24³GS, 24⁴G, 20³HY, 24⁴S, 33²G, 24⁴S, 32²G, 24¹G, 24³GS,

	Starts	1st	2nd	3rd	Win & Pl
Hurdles	2	0	0	1	1366
Chases	12	1	3	9	51539
Career Total	60	12	11	11	171153
136	4/04 Carl 3m D(0-125)HCh			GD	£14332
137	1/03 Donc 3m C(0-130)HCh			GD	£8141
127	11/02 Newc 2m4f D(0-125)HHdl			G-S	£5031
149	11/00 Kels 3m1f B(0-140)HCh			SFT	£8990
147	3/00 Carl 2m4f110yC Ch			HVY	£7560
142	2/00 Newc 2m4f B(0-140)Ch			HVY	£10432
108	11/99 Kels 2m6f110yE Ch			GD	£3355
113	11/99 Ayr 2m4f D Ch			GD	£3951
133	2/99 Newc 2m4f B(0-140)HHdl			SFT	£6937
134	2/99 Ayr 2m4f C(0-130)HHdl			SFT	£5790
118	1/98 Newc 2m E Hdl			G-S	£2248
116	1/98 Ayr 2m E Hdl			SFT	£2248

Total win prize-money £79140

Going:	Sf: 0-4 GS: 0-2 Gd: 1-8 GF: - Fm: 0-0
Distance:	2m/2m3: 0-0 2m4-2m7: 0-0 3m+: 1-13
Track:	LH: 0-10 RH: 1-4 Tight: 0-4 Gall: 0-4
Aids:	Bl: 0-2 Vi: 0-3 Tstrap: 0-0 Ckp: 1-5
Best Rating:	149 12/00 Chel 2m5f soft Ch

Fair chaser/hurdler; can appear a little quirky; tends to be best when coming from off the pace and needs plenty of driving; stays four miles and one furlong; acts on good and soft ground; has been tried in blinkers, visor and cheekpieces.

Robergerie (IRE)
90   **(65h)76**

8-y-o b g Robellino (USA)-Daisy Grey (Nordance (USA))
C A McBratney Cathal M McGovern

Placings:5460600/530450/0P/5506   (0937)
2003/04: 22⁵G, 16⁶G, 25⁰F, 27⁶GF,

	Starts	1st	2nd	3rd	Win & Pl
Chases	4	0	0	0	0
Career Total	19	0	0	1	619

Going:	Sf: 0-0 GS: 0-0 Gd: 0-2 GF: - Fm: 0-2
Distance:	2m/2m3: 0-1 2m4-2m7: 0-1 3m+: 0-0
Track:	LH: 0-2 RH: 0-0 Tight: 0-0 Gall: 0-0
Aids:	Bl: 0-2 Vi: 0-0 Tstrap: 0-0 Ckp: 0-0
Best Rating:	91 11/99 Navn 2m yld-sft Hdl

Robert The Rascal

11-y-o ch g Scottish Reel-Midnight Mary (Celtic Cone)
Mrs C M James Ceri James

Placings:0/6P4P   (4257)
2003/04: 24⁶S, 21ᴾG, 23⁴HY, 24ᴾG,

	Starts	1st	2nd	3rd	Win & Pl
Chases	4	0	0	0	0
Career Total	5	0	0	0	0

Going:	Sf: 0-2 GS: 0-0 Gd: 0-2 GF: - Fm: 0-0
Distance:	2m/2m3: 0-0 2m4-2m7: 0-2 3m+: 0-2
Track:	LH: 0-4 RH: 0-0 Tight: 0-2 Gall: 0-0
Aids:	Bl: 0-0 Vi: 0-0 Tstrap: 0-0 Ckp: 0-0
Best Rating:	63 5/03 Uttx 2m7f heavy Ch

Roberty Bob (IRE)

109(68h)   (96 h)**133**

9-y-o ch g Bob Back (USA)-Inesdela (Wolver Hollow)
H D Daly P J H Wills

Placings:43222/311/1423533-21   (0454)
2003/04: 24²HY, 26¹HY,

	Starts	1st	2nd	3rd	Win & Pl
Chases	2	1	1	0	10485
Career Total	17	4	5	5	50456
120	5/03	Uttx	3m2f	D(0-120)HCh	HVY £5928
133	5/02	Uttx	3m2f	D Ch	GD £4368
133	3/02	Uttx	3m2f	B HCh	HVY £19110
125	3/02	Towc	2m6f	D Ch	SFT £5538

Total win prize-money £34944

Going:	Sf: 1-2 GS: 0-0 Gd: 0-0 GF: - Fm: 0-0
Distance:	2m/2m3: 0-0 2m4-2m7: 0-0 3m+: 1-2
Track:	LH: 1-2 RH: 0-0 Tight: 0-0 Gall: 0-0
Aids:	Bl: 0-0 Vi: 0-0 Tstrap: 0-0 Ckp: 0-0
Best Rating:	133 11/02 Bang 3m110y heavy Ch

Fair consistent chaser; goes well at Uttoxeter; stays 3m 5f; suited by soft ground.

Robins Meg

8-y-o b m Skyliner-Home Dove (Homeboy)
M E Sowersby Mrs Jean W Robinson

Placings:30/00U-P   (0310)
2003/04: 21ᴾS,

	Starts	1st	2nd	3rd	Win & Pl
Hurdles	1	0	0	0	0
Career Total	6	0	0	1	228

Going:	Sf: 0-1 GS: 0-0 Gd: 0-0 GF: - Fm: 0-0
Distance:	2m/2m3: 0-0 2m4-2m7: 0-1 3m+: 0-0
Track:	LH: 0-1 RH: 0-0 Tight: 0-1 Gall: 0-0
Aids:	Bl: 0-0 Vi: 0-0 Tstrap: 0-0 Ckp: 0-0
Best Rating:	82 9/01 MRas 2m1f110y soft NHF

Robins Pride (IRE)

14-y-o b g Treasure Hunter-Barney's Sister (Abednego)
C L Popham Mrs Sue Popham

Placings:30/P0054/22F1521201/**P22P3U2/P3312353F/PU**
44142204F/053640624P1/655641U6U/00043/550P4342-3P
    (4002)
2003/04: 21³HY, 20ᴾG,

	Starts	1st	2nd	3rd	Win & Pl
Chases	2	0	0	1	503
Career Total	79	7	12	10	41519
89	1/01	Tntn	3m	F(0-110)HCh	HVY £3493
99	4/00	Winc	2m	E(0-115)HCh	G-S £4270
105	12/98	Winc	2m	D(0-125)HCh	SFT £3512
102	12/97	Winc	2m	D(0-125)HCh	G-S £3626
110	3/96	NAbb	2m1f	F(0-100)HHdl	SFT £2589
100	1/96	Winc	2m	F Hdl	G-S £2617
84	5/95	Ctml	2m1f110yE Hdl		GD £2416

Total win prize-money £22528

Going:	Sf: 0-1 GS: 0-0 Gd: 0-1 GF: - Fm: 0-0
Distance:	2m/2m3: 0-0 2m4-2m7: 0-2 3m+: 0-0
Track:	LH: 0-1 RH: 0-1 Tight: 0-1 Gall: 0-0
Aids:	Bl: 0-2 Vi: 0-0 Tstrap: 0-0 Ckp: 0-0
Best Rating:	114 1/98 Asct 2m gd-sft Ch

Plating-class chaser; fair sort in his prime, but into the veteran stage now and on the decline; won at Taunton in January 2001; runner-up in selling chase Chepstow April 2003; stays three miles; loves the mud.

Robshaw

4-y-o b g Robellino (USA)-Panorama (Shirley Heights)
T P Tate T P Tate

Placings:P   (3002)
2003/04: 16ᴾGS,

	Starts	1st	2nd	3rd	Win & Pl
Hurdles	1	0	0	0	0
Career Total	1	0	0	0	0

Going:	Sf: 0-0 GS: 0-1 Gd: 0-0 GF: - Fm: 0-0
Distance:	2m/2m3: 0-1 2m4-2m7: 0-0 3m+: 0-0
Track:	LH: 0-1 RH: 0-0 Tight: 0-0 Gall: 0-0
Aids:	Bl: 0-0 Vi: 0-0 Tstrap: 0-0 Ckp: 0-0

Robyn Alexander (IRE)

96(106h)   (124 h)**107+**

6-y-o ch m Sharifabad (IRE)-Flagship Ahoy (IRE) (Accordion)
P F Nicholls Jeffrey Hordle

Placings:0/5252310F31-2221   (2265)
2003/04: 16²GF, 16⁹G, 16²G, 21¹GF,

	Starts	1st	2nd	3rd	Win & Pl
Hurdles	2	0	2	0	2712
Chases	2	1	0	0	5274
Career Total	15	3	5	2	21429
107	11/03	Winc	2m5f	D Ch	G-F £4354
112	3/03	Tntn	2m3f110yD(0-115)HHdl	FRM	£5118
105	12/02	Font	2m2f110yD Hdl	SFT	£5122

Total win prize-money £14595

Going:	Sf: 0-0 GS: 0-0 Gd: 0-2 GF: - Fm: 1-2
Distance:	2m/2m3: 0-3 2m4-2m7: 1-1 3m+: 0-0
Track:	LH: 0-3 RH: 1-1 Tight: 0-2 Gall: 0-0
Aids:	Bl: 0-0 Vi: 0-0 Tstrap: 0-0 Ckp: 0-0
Best Rating:	124 5/03 Wwck 2m gd-fm Hdl

Modest hurdler/chaser; ex-Irish; handles soft ground but suited by fast.

Robyn's Delight

5-y-o b m Perpendicular-Woodram Delight (Idiots Delight)
M A Barnes R B Johnston

Robyns Chance

5-y-o b m Overbury (IRE)-Caithness Dawn (Deep Run)
Mrs A M Thorpe J H Lee

Placings:00P   (3700)
2003/04: 16⁰G, 17⁰HY, 19ᴾHY,

	Starts	1st	2nd	3rd	Win & Pl
NH Flat	2	0	0	0	0
Hurdles	1	0	0	0	0
Career Total	3	0	0	0	0

Going:	Sf: 0-1 GS: 0-1 Gd: 0-1 GF: - Fm: 0-0
Distance:	2m/2m3: 0-2 2m4-2m7: 0-1 3m+: 0-0
Track:	LH: 0-0 RH: 0-3 Tight: 0-0 Gall: 0-0
Aids:	Bl: 0-0 Vi: 0-0 Tstrap: 0-0 Ckp: 0-0
Best Rating:	18 12/03 Ludl 2m good NHF

Rocabee (IRE)

(77h)   (88h)

10-y-o b g Phardante (FR)-Auling (Tarqogan)
N B King (A J Chamberlain 22/2) St Gatien Racing Club

Placings:223F/24/P2P0PP   (4099)
2003/04: 21ᴾS, 21²S, 23ᴾGS, 22⁰GS, 25ᴾGS, 20ᴾG,

	Starts	1st	2nd	3rd	Win & Pl
Hurdles	3	0	1	0	1078
Chases	3	0	4	1	
Career Total	12	0	4	1	3146

Going:	Sf: 0-2 GS: 0-3 Gd: 0-1 GF: - Fm: 0-0
Distance:	2m/2m3: 0-2 2m4-2m7: 0-4 3m+: 0-0
Track:	LH: 0-3 RH: 0-3 Tight: 0-3 Gall: 0-0
Aids:	Bl: 0-1 Vi: 0-0 Tstrap: 0-0 Ckp: 0-0
Best Rating:	109 5/99 Towc 2m soft Hdl

Roches Fleuries (IRE)

78   **56**

4-y-o b f Barathea (IRE)-Princess Caraboo (IRE) (Alzao (USA)
Andrew Turnell Paradime Ltd

Placings:0   (1926)
2003/04: 16⁰GF,

	Starts	1st	2nd	3rd	Win & Pl
Hurdles	1	0	0	0	
Career Total	1	0	0	0	

Going:	Sf: 0-0 GS: 0-0 Gd: 0-0 GF: - Fm: 0-1
Distance:	2m/2m3: 0-1 2m4-2m7: 0-0 3m+: 0-0

Track:	LH: 0-1 RH: 0-0 Tight: 0-0 Gall: 0-0
Aids:	Bl: 0-0 Vi: 0-0 Tstrap: 0-0 Ckp: 0-0
Best Rating:	54 11/03 Wwck 2m gd-fm Hdl

Rock Concert

6-y-o b m Bishop Of Cashel-Summer Pageant (Chief's Crown (USA))
I W McInnes (P T Midgley 2/9) Ivy House Racing

Placings:U   (1029)
2003/04: 17^{U}GF,

	Starts	1st	2nd	3rd	Win & Pl
Hurdles	1	0	0	0	
Career Total	1	0	0	0	

Going:	Sf: 0-0 GS: 0-0 Gd: 0-0 GF: - Fm: 0-1
Distance:	2m/2m3: 0-1 2m4-2m7: 0-0 3m+: 0-0
Track:	LH: 0-0 RH: 0-1 Tight: 0-1 Gall: 0-0
Aids:	Bl: 0-0 Vi: 0-0 Tstrap: 0-0 Ckp: 0-0

Rock Garden (IRE)
107   110+

5-y-o br m Bigstone (IRE)-Woodland Garden (Godswalk (USA))
R F Johnson Houghton R F Johnson Houghton

Placings:1340-33155   (4574)
2003/04: 16^{3}GS, 20^{3}GS, 21^{1}G, 21^{5}G, 21^{5}G,

	Starts	1st	2nd	3rd	Win & Pl
Hurdles	5	1	0	2	7082
Career Total	9	2	0	3	10238
113	1/04	Ludl	2m5f	E Hdl	GD	£3562
88	11/02	Wwck	1m6f	H NHF	G-S	£2765
				Total win prize-money £6327

Going:	Sf: 0-0 GS: 0-2 Gd: 1-3 GF: - Fm: 0-0
Distance:	2m/2m3: 0-1 2m4-2m7: 1-4 3m+: 0-0
Track:	LH: 0-2 RH: 1-3 Tight: 0-0 Gall: 0-3
Aids:	Bl: 0-1 Vi: 0-0 Tstrap: 0-0 Ckp: 0-0
Best Rating:	113 1/04 Ludl 2m5f good Hdl

Modest bumper performer; winning hurdler; stays 2m 5f; acts on easy ground.

Rock Rose

11-y-o b m Arctic Lord-Ovington Court (Prefairy)
G L Davis Mrs Angela Davis

Placings:5U5/P602O3/3BU214P/46545-6U   (4150)
2003/04: 20^{6}G, 24^{U}G,

	Starts	1st	2nd	3rd	Win & Pl
Chases	2	0	0	0	0
Career Total	23	1	2	2	9076
100	2/02	Tntn	3m	D Ch	SFT	£5284
				Total win prize-money £5285

Going:	Sf: 0-0 GS: 0-0 Gd: 0-2 GF: - Fm: 0-0
Distance:	2m/2m3: 0-0 2m4-2m7: 0-1 3m+: 0-1
Track:	LH: 0-0 RH: 0-2 Tight: 0-1 Gall: 0-0
Aids:	Bl: 0-0 Vi: 0-0 Tstrap: 0-0 Ckp: 0-0
Best Rating:	100 2/02 Tntn 3m soft Ch

Rock'n Cold (IRE)
97(102h)   (107h)100

6-y-o b g Bigstone (IRE)-Unalaska (IRE) (High Estate)

J G Given A Clarke

Placings:5213/PP131-35   (0821)
2003/04: 19^{3}G, 20^{5}G,

	Starts	1st	2nd	3rd	Win & Pl
Hurdles	1	0	0	1	1180
Chases	1	0	0	0	0
Career Total	11	3	1	3	11242
100	4/03	Hrfd	2m1f	G Hdl	G-F	£2338
100	3/03	Catt	2m	G Hdl	SFT	£2436
109	3/02	MRas	2m1f110yE Hdl	G-S	£2765
				Total win prize-money £7539

Going:	Sf: 0-0 GS: 0-0 Gd: 0-2 GF: - Fm: 0-0
Distance:	2m/2m3: 0-0 2m4-2m7: 0-2 3m+: 0-0
Track:	LH: 0-0 RH: 0-2 Tight: 0-2 Gall: 0-0
Aids:	Bl: 0-0 Vi: 0-0 Tstrap: 0-0 Ckp: 0-1
Best Rating:	109 3/02 Chep 2m110y soft Hdl

Fair hurdler; won selling races either side of good third in handicap company at Market Rasen in March; acts on soft and fast ground; effective over two miles; wears cheek-pieces.

Rockcliffe Gossip
86   114

12-y-o ch g Phardante (FR)-Clonmello (Le Bavard (FR))
N A Twiston-Davies Mrs Caroline Beresford-Wylie

Placings:322/222501//22152U335/U33P4/0322335P2/4165
601-0605P   (4342)
2003/04: 24^{0}G, 24^{6}GF, 27^{0}GS, 26^{5}G, 29^{P}GS,

	Starts	1st	2nd	3rd	Win & Pl
Chases	5	0	0	0	0
Career Total	44	4	11	8	49199
108	4/03	Prth	3m7f	E(0-110)HCh	GD	£15515
114	10/02	Bang	3m110y	D(0-120)HCh	G-S	£10773
94	10/99	Towc	2m6f	E Ch	GD	£2739
118	4/99	Uttx	2m4f110yE(0-115)HHdl	G-S	£3225
				Total win prize-money £32253

Going:	Sf: 0-0 GS: 0-2 Gd: 0-2 GF: - Fm: 0-1
Distance:	2m/2m3: 0-0 2m4-2m7: 0-0 3m+: 0-5
Track:	LH: 0-3 RH: 0-1 Tight: 0-3 Gall: 0-1
Aids:	Bl: 0-0 Vi: 0-0 Tstrap: 0-0 Ckp: 0-0
Best Rating:	118 4/99 Uttx 2m4f110y gd-sft Hdl

Modest chaser; out-and-out stayer who is often tapped for speed; stays extreme distances; suited by a little ease in the ground; has worn blinkers.

Rockerfella Lad (IRE)
85   77

4-y-o b g Danetime (IRE)-Soucaro (Rusticaro (FR))
M Todhunter (K A Ryan 27/9) Mrs Kate Hall

Placings:000   (3355)
2003/04: 16^{0}G, 16^{0}GS, 16^{0}S,

	Starts	1st	2nd	3rd	Win & Pl
Hurdles	3	0	0	0	
Career Total	3	0	0	0	

Going:	Sf: 0-1 GS: 0-1 Gd: 0-1 GF: - Fm: 0-0
Distance:	2m/2m3: 0-3 2m4-2m7: 0-0 3m+: 0-0
Track:	LH: 0-3 RH: 0-0 Tight: 0-1 Gall: 0-0
Aids:	Bl: 0-0 Vi: 0-1 Tstrap: 0-0 Ckp: 0-0
Best Rating:	64 11/03 Newc 2m good Hdl

Rocket Bleu (FR)
96   86+

4-y-o ch g Epervier Bleu-Egeria (FR) (Baly Rockette)
N G Richards Jimmy Dudgeon

Placings:1514   (4657)
2003/04: 17^{1}GF, 17^{5}GS, 16^{1}S, 16^{4}S,

	Starts	1st	2nd	3rd	Win & Pl
Hurdles	4	2	0	0	5834
Career Total	4	2	0	0	5834
90	3/04	Newc	2m	E Hdl	SFT	£3318
90	10/03	Carl	2m1f	F Hdl	G-F	£2226
				Total win prize-money £5544

Going:	Sf: 1-2 GS: 0-1 Gd: 0-0 GF: - Fm: 1-1
Distance:	2m/2m3: 2-4 2m4-2m7: 0-0 3m+: 0-0
Track:	LH: 1-2 RH: 1-2 Tight: 0-0 Gall: 1-1
Aids:	Bl: 0-0 Vi: 0-0 Tstrap: 0-0 Ckp: 0-0
Best Rating:	90 3/04 Newc 2m soft Hdl

Plating-class hurdler; made a winning debut over hurdles at Carlisle; scored again in weak event at Newcastle in March; best at around two miles; acts on fast and soft ground.

Rocket Radar

13-y-o b g Vouchsafe-Courtney Pennant (Angus)
Mrs J Hughes Mrs J Hughes

Placings:4/1/34/4P6/421/153-32   (0483)
2003/04: 25^{3}G, 24^{2}GF,

	Starts	1st	2nd	3rd	Win & Pl
Chases	2	0	1	1	673
Career Total	15	3	2	3	8257
105	5/02	Hrfd	3m1f110yH Ch	GD	£2320
96	4/02	Ludl	3m	H Ch	GD	£2800
100	4/99	Worc	2m7f110yH Ch	G-S	£1193
				Total win prize-money £6314

Going:	Sf: 0-0 GS: 0-0 Gd: 0-1 GF: - Fm: 0-1
Distance:	2m/2m3: 0-0 2m4-2m7: 0-0 3m+: 0-2
Track:	LH: 0-0 RH: 0-2 Tight: 0-0 Gall: 0-1
Aids:	Bl: 0-0 Vi: 0-0 Tstrap: 0-0 Ckp: 0-0
Best Rating:	105 5/02 Hrfd 3m1f110y good Ch

Fair hunter chaser; stays three miles; likes yielding ground, but has also won on good to firm.

Rockfield Lane (IRE)
(96h)   (91h)

8-y-o b/br g Sharifabad (IRE)-Suir Surprise (Rusticaro (FR))
G F Bridgwater Michael Appleby

Placings:0/045504P000-063   (0853)
2003/04: 17^{0}GF, 17^{6}GF, 24^{3}GF,

	Starts	1st	2nd	3rd	Win & Pl
Hurdles	2	0	0	0	0
Chases	1	0	0	1	836
Career Total	14	0	0	1	1057

Going:	Sf: 0-0 GS: 0-0 Gd: 0-0 GF: - Fm: 0-3
Distance:	2m/2m3: 0-2 2m4-2m7: 0-0 3m+: 0-1
Track:	LH: 0-3 RH: 0-0 Tight: 0-2 Gall: 0-0
Aids:	Bl: 0-0 Vi: 0-1 Tstrap: 0-0 Ckp: 0-0
Best Rating:	93 7/02 Gway 2m soft NHF

Plating-class hurdler; tailed-off on chase debut; no worthwhile form since arriving from Ireland in 2002; has worn visor.

Rockley Beach (IRE)

5-y-o b g Tidaro (USA)-Green Fairy (Green Shoon)
V R A Dartnall Double P Partnership

Placings:60P   (4887)
2003/04: 16⁶G, 16⁰GS, 22ᴾGF,

	Starts	1st	2nd	3rd	Win & Pl
NH Flat	2	0	0	0	0
Hurdles	1	0	0	0	0
Career Total	3	0	0	0	0

Going: Sf: 0-0 GS: 0-1 Gd: 0-1 GF: - Fm: 0-1
Distance: 2m/2m3: 0-2 2m4-2m7: 0-1 3m+: 0-0
Track: LH: 0-1 RH: 0-2 Tight: 0-1 Gall: 0-0
Aids: Bl: 0-0 Vi: 0-0 Tstrap: 0-0 Ckp: 0-0
Best Rating: 105 2/04 Asct 2m110y good NHF

Rockwelda

9-y-o b m Weld-Hill's Rocket (Hills Forecast)
M P Muggeridge R W Vincent

Placings:0500/00U/B64/P   (1155)
2003/04: 22ᴾGF,

	Starts	1st	2nd	3rd	Win & Pl
Chases	1	0	0	0	
Career Total	11	0	0	0	0

Going: Sf: 0-0 GS: 0-0 Gd: 0-0 GF: - Fm: 0-0
Distance: 2m/2m3: 0-0 2m4-2m7: 0-1 3m+: 0-0
Track: LH: 0-0 RH: 0-0 Tight: 0-1 Gall: 0-0
Aids: Bl: 0-0 Vi: 0-0 Tstrap: 0-0 Ckp: 0-0
Best Rating: 71 5/01 Hntg 3m gd-fm Ch

Rodalko (FR)

109(108h)   (106h)140+
6-y-o b g Kadalko (FR)-Darling Rose (FR) (Rose Laurel)
O Sherwood J Palmer-Brown

Placings:02F14P0P-1F1114P   (4861)
2003/04: 23¹GF, 24²GF, 24¹GF, 24¹GF, 24¹G, 24⁴G, 33ᴾGS,

	Starts	1st	2nd	3rd	Win & Pl
Chases	7	4	0	0	35605
Career Total	15	5	1	0	40040
142 3/04	Ludl	3m	D(0-125)HCh	GD	£13702
135 12/03	Ludl	3m	D(0-125)HCh	GF	£10120
110 11/03	Ludl	3m	D Ch	G-F	£5726
125 11/03	Worc	2m7f110yD Ch		G-F	£4704
100 11/02	Ludl	2m5f	E Hdl	GD	£3562
			Total win prize-money £37815

Going: Sf: 0-0 GS: 0-0 Gd: 1-2 GF: 3-4
Distance: 2m/2m3: 0-0 2m4-2m7: 0-0 3m+: 4-7
Track: LH: 1-3 RH: 3-4 Tight: 3-3 Gall: 0-1
Aids: Bl: 0-0 Vi: 0-0 Tstrap: 0-0 Ckp: 0-0
Best Rating: 142 3/04 Ludl 3m good Ch

Useful novice chaser; winning hurdler; stays three miles; appreciates decent ground; front runner; on the upgrade.

Rodber (USA)

108(96h)   (94+h)117
8-y-o ch g Rodrigo De Triano (USA)-Berceau (USA) (Alleged (USA))
Mrs L B Normile K J Fehilly And A K Collins

Placings:43/3P4P-46622211U3   (4848)
2003/04: 20⁴S, 24⁶HY, 24⁶HY, 20²GS, 17²GS, 16²S, 17¹GS, 17¹GS, 20ᵁG, 16³GGS,

	Starts	1st	2nd	3rd	Win & Pl
Hurdles	3	0	0	0	271
Chases	7	2	3	1	19542
Career Total	16	2	3	3	21126
110 3/04	MRas	2m1f110yD Ch		G-S	£6721
98 3/04	Bang	2m1f110yD Ch		G-S	£5411
		Total win prize-money £12132

Going: Sf: 0-4 GS: 2-5 Gd: 0-1 GF: - Fm: 0-0
Distance: 2m/2m3: 2-5 2m4-2m7: 0-3 3m+: 0-2
Track: LH: 1-9 RH: 1-1 Tight: 2-4 Gall: 0-1
Aids: Bl: 0-0 Vi: 0-0 Tstrap: 0-0 Ckp: 0-0
Best Rating: 117 4/04 Ayr 2m gd-sft Ch

Modest form over hurdles at up to 2m4f; decent novice chaser; stays 2m 4f; effective on soft ground; has broken blood vessels.

Roddy The Vet (IRE)

103(91h)   (92 h)101
6-y-o ch g Be My Native (USA)-Caronia (IRE) (Cardinal Flower)
A Ennis Lady Wates

Placings:0/f6040-3332P   (3926)
2003/04: 21³F, 20³G, 22³GS, 23²G, 24ᴾG,

	Starts	1st	2nd	3rd	Win & Pl
Hurdles	1	0	0	1	573
Chases	4	0	1	2	3151
Career Total	11	1	1	3	8913
102 10/02	Gowr	2m	NHF	GD	£4868
			Total win prize-money £4868

Going: Sf: 0-0 GS: 0-1 Gd: 0-3 GF: - Fm: 0-1
Distance: 2m/2m3: 0-0 2m4-2m7: 0-3 3m+: 0-2
Track: LH: 0-1 RH: 0-4 Tight: 0-0 Gall: 0-1
Aids: Bl: 0-0 Vi: 0-0 Tstrap: 0-0 Ckp: 0-1
Best Rating: 103 1/04 Leic 2m7f110y good Ch

Plating-class hurdler/chaser; ex-Irish; effective at up to two and a half miles; acts on good ground.

Rodiak

88   74
5-y-o b g Distant Relative-Misty Silks (Scottish Reel)
P R Hedger P Iron Ltd

Placings:3224-0P00   (3200)
2003/04: 16⁰G, 16ᴾGS, 18⁰G, 16⁰S,

	Starts	1st	2nd	3rd	Win & Pl
Hurdles	4	0	0	0	
Career Total	8	0	2	1	2942

Going: Sf: 0-1 GS: 0-1 Gd: 0-2 GF: - Fm: 0-0
Distance: 2m/2m3: 0-4 2m4-2m7: 0-0 3m+: 0-0
Track: LH: 0-3 RH: 0-1 Tight: 0-3 Gall: 0-0
Aids: Bl: 0-1 Vi: 0-1 Tstrap: 0-0 Ckp: 0-2
Best Rating: 74 9/02 Strf 2m110y gd-fm Hdl

Maiden hurdler; effective at around two miles; sometimes wears headgear.

Rodolfo

100   102+
6-y-o b g Tragic Role (USA)-Be Discreet (Junius (USA))
O Sherwood P Joe Davis

Placings:1/063-216   (3053)

2003/04: 19²GF, 20¹GF, 19⁶G,

	Starts	1st	2nd	3rd	Win & Pl
Hurdles	3	1	1	0	3487
Career Total	7	2	1	1	5576
102 11/03	Uttx	2m4f110yE Hdl		G-F	£2807
104 4/02	MRas	2m1f110yH NHF		GD	£1799
			Total win prize-money £4606

Going: Sf: 0-0 GS: 0-0 Gd: 0-1 GF: - Fm: 1-2
Distance: 2m/2m3: 0-0 2m4-2m7: 1-3 3m+: 0-0
Track: LH: 1-1 RH: 0-2 Tight: 0-1 Gall: 0-0
Aids: Bl: 0-0 Vi: 0-0 Tstrap: 0-0 Ckp: 0-0
Best Rating: 104 4/03 MRas 2m1f110y good NHF

Moderate hurdler; won second outing over hurdles at Uttoxeter in November 2003; stays 2m4f; acts on good/good to soft.

Rody (IRE)

84   57
7-y-o b/br g Foxhound (USA)-Capable Kate (IRE) (Alzao (USA))
I R Brown I R Brown

Placings:FPP/605PP0P-0P0   (0680)
2003/04: 16⁰G, 19ᴾGF, 16⁶GF,

	Starts	1st	2nd	3rd	Win & Pl
Hurdles	3	0	0	0	
Career Total	13	0	0	0	0

Going: Sf: 0-0 GS: 0-0 Gd: 0-1 GF: - Fm: 0-2
Distance: 2m/2m3: 0-2 2m4-2m7: 0-1 3m+: 0-0
Track: LH: 0-2 RH: 0-1 Tight: 0-0 Gall: 0-0
Aids: Bl: 0-0 Vi: 0-1 Tstrap: 0-0 Ckp: 0-0
Best Rating: 57 5/03 Uttx 2m good Hdl

Rogero

83   55
5-y-o b g Presidium-Richesse (FR) (Far Away Son (USA))
R E Barr R E Barr

Placings:005P40   (4595)
2003/04: 16⁰G, 16⁶GF, 17⁵GF, 19ᴾG, 20⁴F, 22⁰G,

	Starts	1st	2nd	3rd	Win & Pl
NH Flat	3	0	0	0	0
Hurdles	3	0	0	0	427
Career Total	6	0	0	0	427

Going: Sf: 0-0 GS: 0-0 Gd: 0-3 GF: - Fm: 0-3
Distance: 2m/2m3: 0-4 2m4-2m7: 0-2 3m+: 0-0
Track: LH: 0-4 RH: 0-1 Tight: 0-4 Gall: 0-0
Aids: Bl: 0-0 Vi: 0-0 Tstrap: 0-0 Ckp: 0-0
Best Rating: 72 5/03 Kels 2m110y good NHF

Rohan

99   92
8-y-o gr g Norton Challenger-Acushla Macree (Mansingh (USA))
R F Johnson Houghton Mrs R F Johnson Houghton

Placings:06/5/02-404620   (4634)
2003/04: 19⁴G, 22⁰S, 20⁴GS, 19⁶G, 19²G, 19⁰G,

	Starts	1st	2nd	3rd	Win & Pl
Hurdles	6	0	1	0	1240
Career Total	11	0	2	0	2328

Going: Sf: 0-1 GS: 0-1 Gd: 0-4 GF: - Fm: 0-0
Distance: 2m/2m3: 0-1 2m4-2m7: 0-5 3m+: 0-0

Track: LH: 0-1 RH: 0-5 Tight: 0-3 Gall: 0-2
Aids: Bl: 0-1 Vi: 0-0 Tstrap: 0-0 Ckp: 0-0
Best Rating: 104 10/00 Extr 2m1f   good   NHF

Lightly-raced maiden hurdler; has shown only moderate form so far; stays two and a half miles; acts on decent ground.

Rojabaa

| 83 | | | | | | 70 |

5-y-o b g Anabaa (USA)-Slava (USA) (Diesis)
W G M Turner Rojabaa Partnership

| Placings:00056 | | | | | | (2516) |
2003/04: 16⁶G, 17⁰GF, 22⁰G, 17⁵GF, 17⁶GS,

	Starts	1st	2nd	3rd	Win & Pl
Hurdles	5	0	0	0	0
Career Total	5	0	0	0	0

Going: Sf: 0-0 GS: 0-1 Gd: 0-2 GF: - Fm: 0-2
Distance: 2m/2m3: 0-4 2m4-2m7: 0-1 3m+: 0-0
Track: LH: 0-2 RH: 0-3 Tight: 0-3 Gall: 0-0
Aids: Bl: 0-1 Vi: 0-0 Tstrap: 0-1 Ckp: 0-0
Best Rating: 70 5/03 Ludl 2m   good   Hdl

Roky Star (FR)

| 100 | | | | | | 93+ |

7-y-o b g Start Fast (FR)-Rosydolie (FR) (Dhausli (FR))
M R Bosley N Turner, D Kelly, D Merricks, R Jones

| Placings:33/0130/6344-664 | | | | | | (2598) |
2003/04: 17⁶GS, 20⁵S, 21⁴G,

	Starts	1st	2nd	3rd	Win & Pl
Hurdles	3	0	0	0	0
Career Total	13	1	0	4	3511
106	11/01	Folk	2m1f110yH NHF		SFT £1641

Total win prize-money £1642

Going: Sf: 0-1 GS: 0-1 Gd: 0-1 GF: - Fm: 0-0
Distance: 2m/2m3: 0-1 2m4-2m7: 0-2 3m+: 0-0
Track: LH: 0-2 RH: 0-1 Tight: 0-0 Gall: 0-0
Aids: Bl: 0-0 Vi: 0-0 Tstrap: 0-0 Ckp: 0-0
Best Rating: 106 11/01 Folk 2m1f110y   soft   NHF

Bumper winner, moderate hurdler at around two and a half miles.

Rolex Free (ARG)

| 92 | | | | | | 69+ |

6-y-o ch g Friul (ARG)-Karolera (ARG) (Kaljerry (ARG))
Mrs L C Taylor Mrs L C Taylor

| Placings:6-000PP | | | | | | (4915) |
2003/04: 16⁵GS, 20⁰G, 16⁰GF, 17⁷G, 16⁵GS,

	Starts	1st	2nd	3rd	Win & Pl
Hurdles	4	0	0	0	0
Chases	1	0	0	0	0
Career Total	6	0	0	0	450

Going: Sf: 0-1 GS: 0-1 Gd: 0-2 GF: - Fm: 0-1
Distance: 2m/2m3: 0-4 2m4-2m7: 0-1 3m+: 0-0
Track: LH: 0-4 RH: 0-0 Tight: 0-3 Gall: 0-0
Aids: Bl: 0-1 Vi: 0-0 Tstrap: 0-1 Ckp: 0-3
Best Rating: 69 3/04 Chep 2m110y   gd-fm   Hdl

Rolfes Delight

| 90(95h) | | | | | | (56h)90 |

12-y-o b g Rolfe (USA)-Idiot's Run (Idiots Delight)

A E Jones Miss Sophie Parmentier

Total win prize-money £3312

| Placings:5/16/PP/1F0515PP-1P | | | | | | (1058) |
2003/04: 25¹GF, 24PGF,

	Starts	1st	2nd	3rd	Win & Pl
Chases	2	1	0	0	2611
Career Total	15	4	0	0	12017
90	6/03	Hrfd	3m1f110yG(0-90)HCh	G-F	£2611
90	10/02	Winc	3m1f110yF(0-95)HCh	FRM	£3692
89	5/02	Winc	2m5f	E(0-100)HCh	G-F	£4251
100	5/00	Bang	3m110y	H Ch	G-S	£1462

Total win prize-money £12018

Going: Sf: 0-0 GS: 0-0 Gd: 0-0 GF: - Fm: 1-2
Distance: 2m/2m3: 0-0 2m4-2m7: 0-0 3m+: 1-2
Track: LH: 0-1 RH: 1-1 Tight: 0-0 Gall: 0-0
Aids: Bl: 0-1 Vi: 0-0 Tstrap: 0-0 Ckp: 0-0
Best Rating: 100 5/00 Bang 3m110y   gd-sft   Ch

Moderate chaser; returned from three month absence to land 3m 1f selling handicap chase at Hereford June 2003; stays three miles plus; acts on fast ground.

Roll With It (IRE)

11-y-o b g Royal Fountain-Deirdre Elizabeth (Salluceva)
I Anderson Ian Anderson

| Placings:05/6263/000300660/20/33-P | | | | | | (0073) |
2003/04: 24PS,

	Starts	1st	2nd	3rd	Win & Pl
Chases	1	0	0	0	0
Career Total	20	0	2	4	2140

Going: Sf: 0-1 GS: 0-0 Gd: 0-0 GF: - Fm: 0-0
Distance: 2m/2m3: 0-0 2m4-2m7: 0-0 3m+: 0-1
Track: LH: 0-1 RH: 0-0 Tight: 0-1 Gall: 0-0
Aids: Bl: 0-0 Vi: 0-0 Tstrap: 0-0 Ckp: 0-0
Best Rating: 94 7/98 Klny 2m1f   gd-yld   NHF

Roller

| 94 | | | | | | 73 |

8-y-o b g Bluebird (USA)-Tight Spin (High Top)
J M Bradley J M Bradley

| Placings:46PP | | | | | | (0889) |
2003/04: 16⁴GF, 16⁶GF, 17PG, 16PG,

	Starts	1st	2nd	3rd	Win & Pl
Hurdles	4	0	0	0	0
Career Total	4	0	0	0	0

Going: Sf: 0-0 GS: 0-0 Gd: 0-2 GF: - Fm: 0-2
Distance: 2m/2m3: 0-4 2m4-2m7: 0-0 3m+: 0-0
Track: LH: 0-4 RH: 0-0 Tight: 0-0 Gall: 0-0
Aids: Bl: 0-3 Vi: 0-0 Tstrap: 0-0 Ckp: 0-0
Best Rating: 73 6/03 Uttx 2m   gd-fm   Hdl

Rolling Maul (IRE)

| | | | | | | 58 |

9-y-o b g Simply Great (FR)-Soyez Sage (FR) (Grundy)
Miss C J E Caroe Miss C J E Caroe

| Placings:30/04025/05410F00030/200050364P/50P343-3 | | | | | | (0159) |
2003/04: 24³GF,

	Starts	1st	2nd	3rd	Win & Pl
Chases	1	0	0	1	715
Career Total	36	1	2	6	10698
82	7/00	Baln	2m4f	(0-95)HHdl	G-F	£3312

Total win prize-money £3312

Going: Sf: 0-0 GS: 0-0 Gd: 0-0 GF: - Fm: 0-1
Distance: 2m/2m3: 0-0 2m4-2m7: 0-0 3m+: 0-1
Track: LH: 0-1 RH: 0-0 Tight: 0-1 Gall: 0-0
Aids: Bl: 0-0 Vi: 0-0 Tstrap: 0-0 Ckp: 0-0
Best Rating: 97 11/00 Navn 2m4f   soft   Ch

Poor maiden chaser; tends to run in snatches.

Rolling Tide (IRE)

| 101 | | | | | | 107 |

8-y-o b g Alphabatim (USA)-St.Cristoph (The Parson)
Evan Williams (N J Henderson 16/7) R W J Willcox

| Placings:2/1/0P-1 | | | | | | (1209) |
2003/04: 20¹GF,

	Starts	1st	2nd	3rd	Win & Pl
Hurdles	1	1	0	0	2639
Career Total	5	2	1	0	5864
93	8/03	Font	2m4f	F Hdl	G-F	£2639
107	2/02	Ludl	2m	E Hdl	G-S	£2677

Total win prize-money £5317

Going: Sf: 0-0 GS: 0-0 Gd: 0-0 GF: - Fm: 1-1
Distance: 2m/2m3: 0-0 2m4-2m7: 1-1 3m+: 0-0
Track: LH: 0-1 RH: 1-1 Tight: 0-0 Gall: 0-0
Aids: Bl: 0-0 Vi: 0-0 Tstrap: 0-0 Ckp: 0-0
Best Rating: 107 2/02 Ludl 2m   gd-sft   Hdl

Modest hurdler; won a weak Fontwell claimer on first start for Evan Williams; stays two and a half miles.

Rollo (IRE)

| 92f | | | | | | 113f |

6-y-o gr g Roselier (FR)-Comeragh Queen (The Parson)
M G Rimell Mark Rimell

| Placings:305 | | | | | | (4529) |
2003/04: 16³HY, 16⁰GS, 16⁵GS,

	Starts	1st	2nd	3rd	Win & Pl
NH Flat	3	0	0	1	359
Career Total	3	0	0	1	359

Going: Sf: 0-1 GS: 0-2 Gd: 0-0 GF: - Fm: 0-0
Distance: 2m/2m3: 0-3 2m4-2m7: 0-0 3m+: 0-0
Track: LH: 0-1 RH: 0-2 Tight: 0-0 Gall: 0-0
Aids: Bl: 0-0 Vi: 0-0 Tstrap: 0-0 Ckp: 0-0
Best Rating: 108 1/04 Asct 2m110y   heavy   NHF

Rollswood (USA)

| 90f | | | | | | 83f |

4-y-o ch g Diesis-Spit Curl (USA) (Northern Dancer)
P R Hedger Howard Spooner

| Placings:00 | | | | | | (3657) |
2003/04: 12⁰G, 17⁰S,

	Starts	1st	2nd	3rd	Win & Pl
NH Flat	2	0	0	0	0
Career Total	2	0	0	0	0

Going: Sf: 0-1 GS: 0-0 Gd: 0-1 GF: - Fm: 0-0
Distance: 2m/2m3: 0-1 2m4-2m7: 0-0 3m+: 0-0
Track: LH: 0-0 RH: 0-0 Tight: 0-0 Gall: 0-0
Aids: Bl: 0-0 Vi: 0-0 Tstrap: 0-0 Ckp: 0-0
Best Rating: 87 1/04 Chel 1m4f   good   NHF

Roma Road

85   **68**

8-y-o b g Syrtos-Fair Cruise (Cruise Missile)
R J Smith Oliver Ryan & Mrs Gill Ryan

Placings:250-065   (0516)
2003/04: 16OGS, 17RGF, 225G,

	Starts	1st	2nd	3rd	Win & Pl
Hurdles	3	0	0	0	0
Career Total	6	0	1	0	562

Going: Sf: 0-0 GS: 0-1 Gd: 0-1 GF: - Fm: 0-1
Distance: 2m2m3: 0-2 2m4-2m7: 0-1 3m+: 0-0
Track: LH: 0-2 RH: 0-1 Tight: 0-1 Gall: 0-0
Aids: Bl: 0-0 Vi: 0-0 Tstrap: 0-0 Ckp: 0-0
Best Rating: **102** 5/02 Chep 2m110y   gd-fm NHF

Roman Ark

111   **101+**

6-y-o gr g Terimon-Larksmore (Royal Fountain)
J M Jefferson Richard Collins

Placings:1/32   (4319)
2003/04: 23RG, 20PS,

	Starts	1st	2nd	3rd	Win & Pl
Hurdles	2	0	1	1	1763
Career Total	3	1	1	1	3579
105	3/02	Newc	2m	H NHF	HVY £1816

Total win prize-money £1817

Going: Sf: 0-1 GS: 0-0 Gd: 0-1 GF: - Fm: 0-0
Distance: 2m2m3: 0-0 2m4-2m7: 0-2 3m+: 0-0
Track: LH: 0-2 RH: 0-0 Tight: 0-0 Gall: 0-1
Aids: Bl: 0-0 Vi: 0-0 Tstrap: 0-0 Ckp: 0-0
Best Rating: **105** 3/02 Newc 2m   heavy NHF

Made a winning debut in a Newcastle bumper in March 2002; absent until promising third over hurdles at Wetherby in December; runner-up to useful prospect next time at Newcastle in March; stays three miles; acts on soft.

Roman Candle (IRE)

99   **82**

8-y-o b g Sabrehill (USA)-Penny Banger (IRE) (Pennine Walk)
Mrs Lucinda Featherstone Largesse Racing

Placings:00F/6U05220F5-036464   (1062)
2003/04: 16OG, 16QG, 17RGF, 16RGF, 20RG, 16RGF,

	Starts	1st	2nd	3rd	Win & Pl
Hurdles	6	0	0	1	993
Career Total	18	0	2	1	2741

Going: Sf: 0-0 GS: 0-0 Gd: 0-3 GF: - Fm: 0-3
Distance: 2m2m3: 0-5 2m4-2m7: 0-1 3m+: 0-0
Track: LH: 0-5 RH: 0-1 Tight: 0-1 Gall: 0-0
Aids: Bl: 0-0 Vi: 0-0 Tstrap: 0-0 Ckp: 0-0
Best Rating: **84** 8/02 Worc 2m   gd-fm Hdl

Moderate maiden hurdler.

Roman Consul (IRE)

6-y-o ch g Alphabatim (USA)-Stella Romana (Roman Warrior)
Jonjo O'Neill John P McManus

Placings:P   (2448)
2003/04: 20PS,

	Starts	1st	2nd	3rd	Win & Pl
Hurdles	1	0	0	0	0
Career Total	1	0	0	0	0

Going: Sf: 0-1 GS: 0-0 Gd: 0-0 GF: - Fm: 0-0
Distance: 2m2m3: 0-0 2m4-2m7: 0-1 3m+: 0-0
Track: LH: 0-1 RH: 0-0 Tight: 0-0 Gall: 0-0
Aids: Bl: 0-0 Vi: 0-0 Tstrap: 0-0 Ckp: 0-0

Roman Court (IRE)

108   **88**

6-y-o b g Witness Box (USA)-Small Iron (General Ironside)
R H Alner Club Ten

Placings:62-033632633   (4749)
2003/04: 26QGS, 22RGF, 22RGF, 20RGF, 22RGF, 24PGF, 24RG, 24RG, 25RG,

	Starts	1st	2nd	3rd	Win & Pl
Hurdles	9	0	1	5	4051
Career Total	11	0	2	5	4923

Going: Sf: 0-0 GS: 0-1 Gd: 0-3 GF: - Fm: 0-5
Distance: 2m2m3: 0-0 2m4-2m7: 0-4 3m+: 0-5
Track: LH: 0-1 RH: 0-7 Tight: 0-2 Gall: 0-0
Aids: Bl: 0-0 Vi: 0-0 Tstrap: 0-0 Ckp: 0-0
Best Rating: **89** 3/03 Chep 2m110y   good NHF

Very modest novice hurdler; stays well; handles fast ground.

Roman Hideaway (IRE)

92   **57**

6-y-o b g Hernando (FR)-Vaison La Romaine (Arctic Tern (USA))
J A B Old W E Sturt

Placings:0   (3265)
2003/04: 16OS,

	Starts	1st	2nd	3rd	Win & Pl
Hurdles	1	0	0	0	0
Career Total	1	0	0	0	0

Going: Sf: 0-1 GS: 0-0 Gd: 0-0 GF: - Fm: 0-0
Distance: 2m2m3: 0-1 2m4-2m7: 0-0 3m+: 0-0
Track: LH: 0-0 RH: 0-1 Tight: 0-0 Gall: 0-0
Aids: Bl: 0-0 Vi: 0-0 Tstrap: 0-0 Ckp: 0-0
Best Rating: **57** 1/04 Asct 2m110y   soft Hdl

Roman Outlaw

70(89h)   (53h)**106**

12-y-o g g Alias Smith (USA)-Roman Moor (Owen Anthony)
Mrs K Walton Mrs K Walton

Placings:344/200441/4/0/623P/4211PU55P/P1650UP1PP-P600P   (3522)
2003/04: 25PG, 24PS, 28RGS, 24RS, 24QHY, 25PS,

	Starts	1st	2nd	3rd	Win & Pl
Hurdles	1	0	0	0	0
Chases	5	0	0	0	0
Career Total	39	5	3	2	22679
103	4/03	Newc	3m	D(0-120)HCh	GD £5733
106	1/03	Newc	3m	F(0-100)HCh	HVY £3339
105	1/02	Newc	3m6f	D(0-125)HCh	SFT £4104
106	12/01	Newc	3m6f	F(0-110)HCh	G-S £3386
102	4/98	Hexm	2m4f110yE	Hdl	HVY £2789

Total win prize-money £19354

Going: Sf: 0-4 GS: 0-1 Gd: 0-1 GF: - Fm: 0-0
Distance: 2m2m3: 0-0 2m4-2m7: 0-0 3m+: 0-6
Track: LH: 0-5 RH: 0-1 Tight: 0-1 Gall: 0-1
Aids: Bl: 0-3 Vi: 0-0 Tstrap: 0-0 Ckp: 0-2
Best Rating: **109** 11/97 Weth 2m   good NHF

Modest staying chaser, best at Newcastle; acts on testing ground; unreliable though.

Roman Rampage

66   **112**

9-y-o b g Perpendicular-Roman Moor (Owen Anthony)
Miss Z C Davison Barry Ward

Placings:221/34/1/P004   (4932)
2003/04: 24PG, 24QGS, 22QG, 27RG,

	Starts	1st	2nd	3rd	Win & Pl
Hurdles	4	0	0	0	315
Career Total	10	2	2	1	7021
112	10/01	Aint	2m4f	E Hdl	GD £3402
112	1/00	Ayr	2m	H NHF	SFT £1662

Total win prize-money £5065

Going: Sf: 0-0 GS: 0-1 Gd: 0-3 GF: - Fm: 0-0
Distance: 2m2m3: 0-0 2m4-2m7: 0-1 3m+: 0-3
Track: LH: 0-1 RH: 0-2 Tight: 0-1 Gall: 0-1
Aids: Bl: 0-0 Vi: 0-0 Tstrap: 0-0 Ckp: 0-0
Best Rating: **112** 10/01 Aint 2m4f   good Hdl

Moderate hurdler; won a novice hurdle in October 2001 when trained by Tim Easterby, but off the track for a long time afterwards; stays 2m 4f, should stay 3m; acts on soft ground.

Roman Rebel

93f   **88f**

5-y-o ch g Primitive Rising (USA)-Roman Moor (Owen Anthony)
Mrs K Walton Paul Lawson

Placings:0406   (4323)
2003/04: 16RG, 16RS, 17OG, 16RS,

	Starts	1st	2nd	3rd	Win & Pl
NH Flat	4	0	0	0	0
Career Total	4	0	0	0	0

Going: Sf: 0-2 GS: 0-0 Gd: 0-2 GF: - Fm: 0-0
Distance: 2m2m3: 0-4 2m4-2m7: 0-0 3m+: 0-0
Track: LH: 0-3 RH: 0-1 Tight: 0-0 Gall: 0-0
Aids: Bl: 0-0 Vi: 0-0 Tstrap: 0-0 Ckp: 0-0
Best Rating: **91** 3/04 Newc 2m   soft NHF

Modest form in bumpers; should stay well.

Roman Rodney

83   **61**

7-y-o b g Feelings (FR)-Pohet (Pongee)
G M Moore W J Laws

Placings:00   (3941)
2003/04: 20OHY, 20QGS,

	Starts	1st	2nd	3rd	Win & Pl
Hurdles	2	0	0	0	0
Career Total	2	0	0	0	0

Going: Sf: 0-1 GS: 0-1 Gd: 0-0 GF: - Fm: 0-0
Distance: 2m2m3: 0-0 2m4-2m7: 0-2 3m+: 0-0
Track: LH: 0-2 RH: 0-0 Tight: 0-0 Gall: 0-2
Aids: Bl: 0-0 Vi: 0-0 Tstrap: 0-0 Ckp: 0-0
Best Rating: **61** 2/04 Newc 2m4f   gd-sft Hdl

Romantic Affair (IRE)

99   **99+**

7-y-o ch g Persian Bold-Broken Romance (IRE) (Ela-Mana-Mou)
Miss H C Knight The Earl Cadogan

Placings:665   (4589)
2003/04: 16⁶GS, 16⁶GS, 16⁵G,

	Starts	1st	2nd	3rd	Win & Pl
Hurdles	3	0	0	0	0
Career Total	3	0	0	0	0

Going:	Sf: 0-0 GS: 0-2 Gd: 0-1 GF: - Fm: 0-0
Distance:	2m/2m3: 0-3 2m4-2m7: 0-0 3m+: 0-0
Track:	LH: 0-0 RH: 0-3 Tight: 0-0 Gall: 0-1
Aids:	Bl: 0-0 Vi: 0-0 Tstrap: 0-0 Ckp: 0-0
Best Rating:	99 3/04 Hntg 2m110y good Hdl

Modest form over hurdles; Listed-class stayer on the level; acts on any ground; should improve for further.

Romantic Hero (IRE)

(78h)**116**

8-y-o b g Supreme Leader-Right Love (Golden Love)
N A Gaselee Miss F M Fletcher

Placings:43/F41/FPP21-U   (2420)
2003/04: 24ᵁGS,

	Starts	1st	2nd	3rd	Win & Pl
Chases	1	0	0	0	
Career Total	11	2	1	1	11476
116 3/03	Chep	3m	F(0-100)HCh	GD	£3584
107 3/02	Newb	2m2f110yD(0-110)HCh	G-S	£5616
			Total win prize-money £9200		

Going:	Sf: 0-0 GS: 0-1 Gd: 0-0 GF: - Fm: 0-0
Distance:	2m/2m3: 0-0 2m4-2m7: 0-0 3m+: 0-1
Track:	LH: 0-0 RH: 0-0 Tight: 0-0 Gall: 0-0
Aids:	Bl: 0-1 Vi: 0-0 Tstrap: 0-Ckp: 0-0
Best Rating:	116 3/03 Chep 3m good Ch

Lightly-raced chaser; stays 3m; suited by soft ground.

Romany Chat

12-y-o b g Backchat (USA)-Ranee's Song (True Song)
Mrs Rosemary Gasson Mrs Rosemary Gasson

Placings:PP/0143P/64P-64P   (0519)
2003/04: 21⁶G, 25⁴G, 28ᴾG,

	Starts	1st	2nd	3rd	Win & Pl
Chases	3	0	1	0	0
Career Total	13	1	0	1	3870
101 5/01	Chel	2m5f	H Ch	GD	£2535
			Total win prize-money £2535		

Going:	Sf: 0-0 GS: 0-0 Gd: 0-3 GF: - Fm: 0-0
Distance:	2m/2m3: 0-0 2m4-2m7: 0-1 3m+: 0-2
Track:	LH: 0-2 RH: 0-1 Tight: 0-1 Gall: 0-1
Aids:	Bl: 0-0 Vi: 0-0 Tstrap: 0-0 Ckp: 0-0
Best Rating:	101 2/02 Hntg 3m gd-sft Ch

Romany Dream

90(65c)   (44c)**57**

6-y-o b m Nomadic Way (USA)-Half Asleep (Quiet Fling (USA))
R Dickin The Snoozy Partnership

Placings:70-40P000   (4833)
2003/04: 21⁴G, 21⁰G, 24⁵S, 17⁹GS, 16⁶GS, 21⁰GF,

	Starts	1st	2nd	3rd	Win & Pl
Hurdles	5	0	0	0	0
Chases	1	0	0	0	0
Career Total	8	1	0	0	2037
82 3/03	Wwck	2m	H NHF	G-F	£2037
			Total win prize-money £2037		

Going:	Sf: 0-1 GS: 0-2 Gd: 0-1 GF: - Fm: 0-2
Distance:	2m/2m3: 0-3 2m4-2m7: 0-3 3m+: 0-1
Track:	LH: 0-5 RH: 0-1 Tight: 0-1 Gall: 0-2
Aids:	Bl: 0-4 Vi: 0-0 Tstrap: 0-0 Ckp: 0-0
Best Rating:	82 3/03 Wwck 2m gd-fm NHF

Romany Move

10-y-o b g Silly Prices-Go Gipsy (Move Off)
Miss Maria D Myco Miss Maria D Myco

Placings:50/00054P/F   (0079)
2003/04: 21ᶠS,

	Starts	1st	2nd	3rd	Win & Pl
Chases	1	0	0	0	0
Career Total	9	0	0	0	238

Going:	Sf: 0-1 GS: 0-0 Gd: 0-0 GF: - Fm: 0-0
Distance:	2m/2m3: 0-0 2m4-2m7: 0-1 3m+: 0-0
Track:	LH: 0-1 RH: 0-0 Tight: 0-1 Gall: 0-0
Aids:	Bl: 0-0 Vi: 0-0 Tstrap: 0-0 Ckp: 0-1
Best Rating:	70 12/01 MRas 2m1f110y soft Ch

Romeo Jones

35f

5-y-o bl g Roselier (FR)-Juleit Jones (IRE) (Phardante (FR))
P Butler Mrs Jean Plackett

Placings:0   (3649)
2003/04: 16⁰GS,

	Starts	1st	2nd	3rd	Win & Pl
NH Flat	1	0	0	0	
Career Total	1	0	0	0	

Going:	Sf: 0-0 GS: 0-1 Gd: 0-0 GF: - Fm: 0-0
Distance:	2m/2m3: 0-1 2m4-2m7: 0-0 3m+: 0-0
Track:	LH: 0-0 RH: 0-1 Tight: 0-0 Gall: 0-0
Aids:	Bl: 0-0 Vi: 0-0 Tstrap: 0-0 Ckp: 0-0

Romero

106(105c)   (93c)**96**

8-y-o b g Robellino (USA)-Casamurrae (Be My Guest (USA))
P R Chamings Fraser Miller Racing

Placings:1126201/234004/2124000042/446351U440-04556   (4704)
2003/04: 16⁰GF, 23⁴G, 22⁵GS, 22⁵G, 18⁶G,

	Starts	1st	2nd	3rd	Win & Pl
Hurdles	5	0	0	0	523
Career Total	38	5	6	2	52746
118 11/02	Newb	2m6f110yD(0-120)HCh	SFT	£6500
131 11/01	Asct	2m110y	B(0-150)HHdl	GD	£7121
123 4/00	Asct	2m110y	C HHdl	GD	£4914
119 11/99	Asct	2m110y	B Hdl	GD	£6742
109 10/99	Asct	2m110y	C Hdl	GD	£4788
			Total win prize-money £30066		

Going:	Sf: 0-0 GS: 0-1 Gd: 0-3 GF: - Fm: 0-1
Distance:	2m/2m3: 0-2 2m4-2m7: 0-3 3m+: 0-0
Track:	LH: 0-2 RH: 0-3 Tight: 0-3 Gall: 0-0
Aids:	Bl: 0-0 Vi: 0-1 Tstrap: 0-0 Ckp: 0-0
Best Rating:	131 11/01 Sand 2m110y gd-sft Hdl

Modest chaser/hurdler; won his first race over fences in a handicap at Newbury in November 2002; goes really well on good ground but handles soft; had a good record at Ascot over hurdles; effective at up to two miles six; has worn a tongue tie and a visor.

Romil Star (GER)

96(107h)   (109h)**83+**

7-y-o b g Chief's Crown (USA)-Romelia (USA) (Woodman (USA))
K R Burke (G M Moore 30/3) M R Johnson

Placings:004/10-U02015034P0   (4613)
2003/04: 17⁵S, 16⁰G, 21²G, 24⁰G, 21¹GF, 25⁵GF, 20⁰G, 21³G, 21⁴GS, 19ᴾG, 16⁸G,

	Starts	1st	2nd	3rd	Win & Pl
Hurdles	8	1	1	1	5261
Chases	3	0	0	0	362
Career Total	16	2	1	1	9068
106 11/03	Sedg	2m5f110yD(0-125)HHdl	G-F	£4046
94 5/02	Prth	2m110y E(0-105)HHdl	G-F	£3445
			Total win prize-money £7491		

Going:	Sf: 0-1 GS: 0-1 Gd: 0-6 GF: - Fm: 1-3
Distance:	2m/2m3: 0-4 2m4-2m7: 1-5 3m+: 0-2
Track:	LH: 1-10 RH: 0-1 Tight: 1-9 Gall: 0-0
Aids:	Bl: 0-0 Vi: 0-0 Tstrap: 0-0 Ckp: 1-7
Best Rating:	112 12/03 Sedg 2m5f110y good Hdl

Poor chaser/modest hurdler; handles any ground but possibly best on a sound surface; effective at up to two miles five; has won in cheekpieces.

Romney

86   **24**

7-y-o ch g Timeless Times (USA)-Ewe Lamb (Free State)
Mrs P Sly Mrs P M Sly

Placings:54232/215200/0   (4183)
2003/04: 26⁰G,

	Starts	1st	2nd	3rd	Win & Pl
Hurdles	1	0	0	0	0
Career Total	12	1	3	2	6280
106 11/01	Folk	2m6f110yE Hdl	SFT	£3003
			Total win prize-money £3003		

Going:	Sf: 0-0 GS: 0-0 Gd: 0-1 GF: - Fm: 0-0
Distance:	2m/2m3: 0-0 2m4-2m7: 0-0 3m+: 0-1
Track:	LH: 0-0 RH: 0-0 Tight: 0-0 Gall: 0-0
Aids:	Bl: 0-0 Vi: 0-0 Tstrap: 0-0 Ckp: 0-0
Best Rating:	108 1/01 Folk 2m1f110y heavy Hdl

Ronald

83f   **63f**

5-y-o ch g Karinga Bay-Hy Wilma (Jalmood (USA))
N J Hawke Mrs C J Cole

Placings:0   (1226)
2003/04: 17⁰GF,

	Starts	1st	2nd	3rd	Win & Pl
NH Flat	1	0	0	0	
Career Total	1	0	0	0	

Going:	Sf: 0-0 GS: 0-0 Gd: 0-0 GF: - Fm: 0-1
Distance:	2m/2m3: 0-1 2m4-2m7: 0-0 3m+: 0-0

Track: LH: 0-1 RH: 0-0 Tight: 0-1 Gall: 0-0
Aids: Bl: 0-0 Vi: 0-0 Tstrap: 0-0 Ckp: 0-0
Best Rating: 63 8/03 NAbb 2m1f   gd-fm NHF

Ronans Choice (IRE)

11-y-o b g Yashgan-Petite Port (IRE) (Decent Fellow)
Miss Emma Oliver R O Oliver

Placings:602PP/61/PPP-2S   (4858)
2003/04: 26²G, 24SGF,

	Starts	1st	2nd	3rd	Win & Pl
Chases	2	0	1	0	436
Career Total	12	1	2	0	4134
87 4/02 Font	3m2f110yF(0-100)HCh		G-F		£2786

Total win prize-money £2786

Going: Sf: 0-0 GS: 0-0 Gd: 0-1 GF: - Fm: 0-1
Distance: 2m/2m3: 0-0 2m4-2m7: 0-0 3m+: 0-2
Track: LH: 0-0 RH: 0-1 Tight: 0-2 Gall: 0-0
Aids: Bl: 0-2 Vi: 0-0 Tstrap: 0-0 Ckp: 0-0
Best Rating: 112 4/04 Font 3m2f110y good   Ch

Fair hunter/pointer; ex-Irish; stays beyond three miles and seems to handle any ground.

Ronans Song (IRE)

9-y-o b g Insan (USA)-Start Singing (IRE) (Orchestra)
Mrs C J Kerr Mrs C J Kerr

Placings:50P0/P   (0252)
2003/04: 20PG,

	Starts	1st	2nd	3rd	Win & Pl
Hurdles	1	0	0	0	
Career Total	5	0	0	0	0

Going: Sf: 0-0 GS: 0-0 Gd: 0-1 GF: - Fm: 0-0
Distance: 2m/2m3: 0-0 2m4-2m7: 0-0 3m+: 0-0
Track: LH: 0-0 RH: 0-1 Tight: 0-0 Gall: 0-0
Aids: Bl: 0-0 Vi: 0-0 Tstrap: 0-1 Ckp: 0-0
Best Rating: 70 11/99 Ayr 2m   good NHF

Ronquista D'Or

10-y-o b g Ron's Victory (USA)-Gild The Lily (Ile De Bourbon (USA))
G A Ham D M Drury

Placings:PP   (0612)
2003/04: 17PGF, 19PGF,

	Starts	1st	2nd	3rd	Win & Pl
Hurdles	2	0	0	0	
Career Total	2	0	0	0	

Going: Sf: 0-0 GS: 0-0 Gd: 0-0 GF: - Fm: 0-2
Distance: 2m/2m3: 0-0 2m4-2m7: 0-0 3m+: 0-0
Track: LH: 0-0 RH: 0-2 Tight: 0-0 Gall: 0-0
Aids: Bl: 0-0 Vi: 0-0 Tstrap: 0-0 Ckp: 0-0

Roobihoo (IRE)
108   93

5-y-o b g Norwich-Griffinstown Lady (Over The River (FR))
C Grant Mrs H E Aitkin

Placings:55-66053U441   (4879)
2003/04: 17⁶G, 20⁶HY, 20⁹S, 20⁵GS, 20³HY, 22ᴜGS, 20⁴HY, 20⁴S, 20¹GS,

	Starts	1st	2nd	3rd	Win & Pl
NH Flat	1	0	0	0	0
Hurdles	8	1	0	1	4742
Career Total	11	1	0	1	4742
93 4/04 Carl	2m4f	E(0-105)HHdl	G-S		£3883

Total win prize-money £3884

Going: Sf: 0-5 GS: 1-3 Gd: 0-0 GF: - Fm: 0-1
Distance: 2m/2m3: 0-1 2m4-2m7: 1-8 3m+: 0-0
Track: LH: 0-6 RH: 1-3 Tight: 0-2 Gall: 0-1
Aids: Bl: 0-0 Vi: 0-0 Tstrap: 0-0 Ckp: 0-0
Best Rating: 93 4/04 Carl 2m4f   gd-sft Hdl

Moderate novice hurdler; much improved effort when off the mark at Carlisle in April; suited by two and a half miles; acts on soft ground.

Roofing Spirit (IRE)
104   99

6-y-o b g Beneficial-Vulcash (IRE) (Callernish)
D P Keane Clifford/Matthews

Placings:260402   (4339)
2003/04: 17²G, 16⁶S, 16⁹GS, 16⁴S, 20⁹GS, 16²G,

	Starts	1st	2nd	3rd	Win & Pl
NH Flat	1	0	1	0	854
Hurdles	5	0	1	0	883
Career Total	6	0	2	0	1737

Going: Sf: 0-2 GS: 0-2 Gd: 0-2 GF: - Fm: 0-0
Distance: 2m/2m3: 0-5 2m4-2m7: 0-1 3m+: 0-0
Track: LH: 0-4 RH: 0-2 Tight: 0-1 Gall: 0-2
Aids: Bl: 0-0 Vi: 0-0 Tstrap: 0-0 Ckp: 0-0
Best Rating: 103 11/03 NAbb 2m1f   good NHF

Moderate hudler; acts on good.

Rookery Lad
103   96+

6-y-o b g Makbul-Wayzgoose (USA) (Diesis)
C N Kellett S Kitching

Placings:00600402-122324P01   (4776)
2003/04: 16¹GF, 16²G, 17²GF, 17³G, 22²G, 20⁴GF, 24²G, 21⁹GS, 20¹G,

	Starts	1st	2nd	3rd	Win & Pl
Hurdles	9	2	3	1	12001
Career Total	17	2	4	1	12691
96 4/04 Fknm	2m4f	E(0-105)HHdl	GD		£4087
84 5/03 Hntg	2m110y	Hdl	G-F		£2688

Total win prize-money £6775

Going: Sf: 0-0 GS: 0-1 Gd: 1-5 GF: - Fm: 1-3
Distance: 2m/2m3: 1-4 2m4-2m7: 1-4 3m+: 0-1
Track: LH: 1-4 RH: 1-4 Tight: 1-7 Gall: 1-1
Aids: Bl: 0-0 Vi: 0-0 Tstrap: 0-0 Ckp: 0-0
Best Rating: 96 4/04 Fknm 2m4f   good Hdl

Moderate handicap hurdler; suited by trips of around two and a half miles; acts on a sound surface.

Rookwith (IRE)
92   99

4-y-o b g Revoque (IRE)-Resume (IRE) (Lahib (USA))
T G McCourt (J D Bethell 6/10) P Jordan

Placings:334   (3732)
2003/04: 16³S, 16³GY, 16⁴G,

	Starts	1st	2nd	3rd	Win & Pl
Hurdles	3	0	0	2	1524

Career Total   3   0   0   2   1524

Going: Sf: 0-1 GS: 0-0 Gd: 0-1 GF: - Fm: 0-0
Distance: 2m/2m3: 0-3 2m4-2m7: 0-0 3m+: 0-0
Track: LH: 0-0 RH: 0-2 Tight: 0-1 Gall: 0-0
Aids: Bl: 0-0 Vi: 0-1 Tstrap: 0-0 Ckp: 0-0
Best Rating: 99 1/04 Thur 2m   gd-yld Hdl

Modest winner on the Flat; placed over hurdles in Ireland; acts on soft.

Rooster

9-y-o b g Roi Danzig (USA)-Jussoli (Don)
Mrs Julie Read Mrs P King

Placings:35/4125/F/P43-2F6   (4775)
2003/04: 20²GF, 21FGS, 21⁶G,

	Starts	1st	2nd	3rd	Win & Pl
Chases	3	0	1	0	421
Career Total	13	1	2	2	7909
113 3/00 Donc	2m110y	E(0-105)HHdl	GD		£5551

Total win prize-money £5551

Going: Sf: 0-0 GS: 0-1 Gd: 0-1 GF: - Fm: 0-1
Distance: 2m/2m3: 0-0 2m4-2m7: 0-3 3m+: 0-0
Track: LH: 0-2 RH: 0-1 Tight: 0-2 Gall: 0-1
Aids: Bl: 0-0 Vi: 0-0 Tstrap: 0-0 Ckp: 0-0
Best Rating: 113 3/00 Newc 2m   good Hdl

Poor hunter chaser; best on a sound surface; stays two miles five.

Rooster Booster
122   178

10-y-o gr g Riverwise (USA)-Came Cottage (Nearly A Hand)
P J Hobbs Terry Warner

Placings:0/23F1332/3PF2323P/5542214/111112-521222   (4646)
2003/04: 16⁵GS, 16²G, 16¹G, 16²G, 16²G, 20²G,

	Starts	1st	2nd	3rd	Win & Pl
Hurdles	6	1	4	0	169175
Career Total	35	8	11	6	585231
163 1/04 Hayd	2m	A Hdl		GD	£23200
173 3/03 Chel	2m110y	A Hdl		GD	£174000
161 2/03 Sand	2m110y	B Hdl		HVY	£12180
160 12/02 Chel	2m1f	A Hdl		GD	£43500
170 11/02 Chel	2m110y	A HHdl		G-S	£29000
166 10/02 Kemp	2m	B Hdl		GD	£8151
155 3/02 Chel	2m1f	A Hdl		GD	£33000
120 1/00 Tntn	2m1f	D Hdl		SFT	£4284

Total win prize-money £327316

Going: Sf: 0-0 GS: 0-1 Gd: 1-5 GF: - Fm: 0-0
Distance: 2m/2m3: 1-5 2m4-2m7: 0-1 3m+: 0-0
Track: LH: 1-5 RH: 0-1 Tight: 0-1 Gall: 0-1
Aids: Bl: 0-0 Vi: 0-0 Tstrap: 0-0 Ckp: 0-0
Best Rating: 173 2/04 Newb 2m110y   good Hdl

Top-class hurdler, winner of the 2003 Champion Hurdle after making a great deal of improvement through the season; below his best in 2003/4 until winning at Haydock, but did not have his races run to suit; narrow second to Geos in Tote Gold Trophy at Newbury, an excellent effort at the weights; went down fighting in second to Hardy Eustace in attempt to regain his title in the Champion; just missed out in Aintree Hurdle; stays two and a half miles but best served by a strongly-run two miles; effective on good or soft ground, not at his best on heavy; consistent and goes well at Cheltenham.

Rooster's Reunion (IRE)

102   **109+**

5-y-o gr g Presenting-Court Town (Camden Town)
D R Gandolfo   Terry Warner

Placings: 02-201   (4181)
2003/04: 16²GS, 16⁰GS, 16¹G,

	Starts	1st	2nd	3rd	Win & Pl
Hurdles	3	1	1	0	4408
Career Total	5	1	2	0	4976
109 3/04	Hntg	2m110y	E Hdl		GD 3626

Total win prize-money £3626

Going:	Sf: 0-0 GS: 0-2 Gd: 1-1 GF: - Fm: 0-0
Distance:	2m/2m3: 1-3 2m4-2m7: 0-0 3m+: 0-0
Track:	LH: 0-2 RH: 1-1 Tight: 0-0 Gall: 1-2
Aids:	Bl: 0-0 Vi: 0-0 Tstrap: 0-0 Ckp: 0-0
Best Rating:	109 3/04 Hntg 2m110y good Hdl

Modest winning hurdler; acts on good/good to soft.

Roppongi Dancer

100   **83**

5-y-o b m Mtoto-Ice Chocolate (USA) (Icecapade (USA))
Mrs N Macauley (Mrs M Reveley 10/6)   Andy Peake

Placings: 5600-3223PP5PP   (4958)
2003/04: 17³GS, 17²GF, 20²GF, 19³GF, 16⁰G, 16⁰GF, 19⁵GF, 22⁵G, 17⁸G,

	Starts	1st	2nd	3rd	Win & Pl
Hurdles	9	0	2	2	2335
Career Total	13	0	2	2	2335

Going:	Sf: 0-0 GS: 0-1 Gd: 0-3 GF: - Fm: 0-5
Distance:	2m/2m3: 0-6 2m4-2m7: 0-3 3m+: 0-0
Track:	LH: 0-3 RH: 0-5 Tight: 0-6 Gall: 0-1
Aids:	Bl: 0-0 Vi: 0-1 Tstrap: 0-6 Ckp: 0-2
Best Rating:	82 9/03 MRas 2m1f110y gd-fm Hdl

Plating-class hurdler; suited by two and a half miles; acts on fast ground.

Rosaker (USA)

115   **150**

7-y-o b g Pleasant Tap (USA)-Rose Crescent (USA) (Nijinsky (CAN))
Noel Meade   High Street Ceathar Syndicate

Placings: 5110-012110   (4397)
2003/04: 20⁰YS, 20¹GF, 20²S, 24¹S, 24¹S, 21⁰G,

	Starts	1st	2nd	3rd	Win & Pl
Hurdles	6	3	1	0	67271
Career Total	10	5	1	0	92190
150 2/04	Navn	3m	Hdl		SFT £22922
144 1/04	Gowr	3m	Hdl		SFT £18309
144 11/03	Navn	2m4f	Hdl		G-F £21103
148 2/03	Naas	2m4f	Hdl		YLD £19415
114 12/02	Fair	2m	Hdl		SFT £5503

Total win prize-money £87256

Going:	Sf: 2-3 GS: 0-0 Gd: 0-1 GF: - Fm: 1-1
Distance:	2m/2m3: 0-0 2m4-2m7: 0-0 3m+: 2-2
Track:	LH: 2-4 RH: 0-1 Tight: 0-0 Gall: 0-1
Aids:	Bl: 0-0 Vi: 0-0 Tstrap: 0-0 Ckp: 0-0
Best Rating:	150 2/04 Navn 3m soft Hdl

Smart Irish-trained hurdler; winner on the Flat in Dubai; has won three times this season; stays three miles; effective with cut in the ground, but has won on good to firm.

Rosalee Royale

12-y-o ch m Out Of Hand-Miss Ark Royal (Broadsword (USA))
Mrs S Kittow   Mrs S Kittow

Placings: 00/0/6/6-P   (0249)
2003/04: 19⁹GF,

	Starts	1st	2nd	3rd	Win & Pl
Chases	1	0	0	0	
Career Total	6	0	0	0	0

Going:	Sf: 0-0 GS: 0-0 Gd: 0-0 GF: - Fm: 0-1
Distance:	2m/2m3: 0-0 2m4-2m7: 0-1 3m+: 0-0
Track:	LH: 0-0 RH: 0-1 Tight: 0-0 Gall: 0-0
Aids:	Bl: 0-0 Vi: 0-0 Tstrap: 0-0 Ckp: 0-0
Best Rating:	55 3/96 Wwck 2m good NHF

Rosalyons (IRE)

104(107c)   (82c)**96**

10-y-o gr g Roselier (FR)-Coffee Shop (Bargello)
Mrs H O Graham   Mrs H O Graham

Placings: 5/06000/011U330PP4F/050353614P-0625U4U00P0   (4662)
2003/04: 22⁹G, 20⁶G, 30²G, 25⁵S, 25ᵁS, 16⁴HY, 24ᵁHY, 27⁰GS, 22⁰GS, 32ᴾG, 20⁰S,

	Starts	1st	2nd	3rd	Win & Pl
Hurdles	5	0	0	0	0
Chases	6	0	1	0	1703
Career Total	38	3	1	4	15043
96 3/03	Kels	2m6f110yD(0-115)	HHdl		G-S £4797
102 10/01	Carl	2m4f	E(0-105)	HHdl		SFT £2609
85 10/01	Kels	2m6f110yF(0-110)	HHdl		G-S £2716

Total win prize-money £10123

Going:	Sf: 0-5 GS: 0-2 Gd: 0-4 GF: - Fm: 0-0
Distance:	2m/2m3: 0-1 2m4-2m7: 0-4 3m+: 0-6
Track:	LH: 0-11 RH: 0-0 Tight: 0-0 Gall: 0-3
Aids:	Bl: 0-1 Vi: 0-0 Tstrap: 0-0 Ckp: 0-0
Best Rating:	102 12/01 Kels 2m6f110y gd-sft Hdl

Moderate hurdler/chaser; stays three miles and six furlongs; has won on soft and good to soft.

Rosarian (IRE)

111   **124+**

7-y-o b g Fourstars Allstar (USA)-Only A Rose (Glint Of Gold)
V R A Dartnall   A Hordle

Placings: 4213/4431311F-1   (2001)
2003/04: 24¹GF,

	Starts	1st	2nd	3rd	Win & Pl
Hurdles	1	1	0	0	9114
Career Total	13	5	3	3	28046
124 11/03	Chep	3m	B(0-150)	HHdl		G-F £9114
122 3/03	Newb	3m110y	D Hdl		GD £5193
114 3/03	Font	3m3f	E Hdl		SFT £3451
123 1/03	Winc	2m6f	D(0-115)	HHdl		G-S £5460
115 1/02	Font	2m2f110yH	NHF		GD £1680

Total win prize-money £24899

Going:	Sf: 0-0 GS: 0-0 Gd: 0-0 GF: - Fm: 1-1
Distance:	2m/2m3: 0-0 2m4-2m7: 0-0 3m+: 1-1
Track:	LH: 1-1 RH: 0-0 Tight: 0-0 Gall: 0-0
Aids:	Bl: 0-0 Vi: 0-0 Tstrap: 0-0 Ckp: 1-1
Best Rating:	124 11/03 Chep 3m gd-fm Hdl

Progressive staying novice hurdler; finished lame after winning Pertemps Qualifier on reappearance at Chepstow.

November 2003; stays 3m plus; acts in soft ground, but better on a good surface.

Roschal (IRE)

89   **86+**

6-y-o gr g Roselier (FR)-Sunday World (USA) (Solford (USA))
P J Hobbs   Brian Walsh

Placings: 35660   (4290)
2003/04: 16³G, 20⁵GS, 19⁶G, 19⁶S, 22⁰G,

	Starts	1st	2nd	3rd	Win & Pl
NH Flat	1	0	0	1	229
Hurdles	4	0	0	0	0
Career Total	5	0	0	1	229

Going:	Sf: 0-1 GS: 0-1 Gd: 0-3 GF: - Fm: 0-0
Distance:	2m/2m3: 0-3 2m4-2m7: 0-2 3m+: 0-0
Track:	LH: 0-1 RH: 0-4 Tight: 0-0 Gall: 0-0
Aids:	Bl: 0-1 Vi: 0-0 Tstrap: 0-0 Ckp: 0-0
Best Rating:	102 11/03 Sand 2m110y good NHF

Roscoe Burn

12-y-o ch g Meadowbrook-Rosecko (White Speck)
Mrs K Massie   Mrs E Johnstone

Placings: P   (4884)
2003/04: 24ᴾGS,

	Starts	1st	2nd	3rd	Win & Pl
Chases	1	0	0	0	
Career Total	1	0	0	0	

Going:	Sf: 0-0 GS: 0-1 Gd: 0-0 GF: - Fm: 0-0
Distance:	2m/2m3: 0-0 2m4-2m7: 0-0 3m+: 0-0
Track:	LH: 0-0 RH: 0-1 Tight: 0-0 Gall: 0-0
Aids:	Bl: 0-0 Vi: 0-0 Tstrap: 0-0 Ckp: 0-0

Rosdari (IRE)

85(84c)   (27c)**63**

7-y-o b g Shardari-Tullahought (Jaazeiro (USA))
M C Pipe   P J Finn

Placings: 550406   (1012)
2003/04: 20⁵GF, 20⁵GF, 22⁰GF, 26⁴GF, 19⁰GF, 24⁶G,

	Starts	1st	2nd	3rd	Win & Pl
Hurdles	4	0	0	0	0
Chases	2	0	0	0	314
Career Total	6	0	0	0	314

Going:	Sf: 0-0 GS: 0-0 Gd: 0-1 GF: - Fm: 0-5
Distance:	2m/2m3: 0-1 2m4-2m7: 0-3 3m+: 0-2
Track:	LH: 0-6 RH: 0-0 Tight: 0-4 Gall: 0-0
Aids:	Bl: 0-0 Vi: 0-1 Tstrap: 0-2 Ckp: 0-0
Best Rating:	67 6/03 Uttx 2m4f110y gd-fm Hdl

Rose Bowl Boy (IRE)

80   **53**

6-y-o ch g Lahib (USA)-Danita (IRE) (Roi Danzig (USA))
B N Pollock   The All Blues

Placings: 000-00P   (4588)
2003/04: 16⁰G, 16⁰G, 21ᴾG,

	Starts	1st	2nd	3rd	Win & Pl
Hurdles	3	0	0	0	

Career Total   6   0   0   0

Going:	Sf: 0-0 GS: 0-0 Gd: 0-3 GF: - Fm: 0-0
Distance:	2m/2m3: 0-2 2m4-2m7: 0-1 3m+: 0-0
Track:	LH: 0-0 RH: 0-3 Tight: 0-0 Gall: 0-2
Aids:	Bl: 0-0 Vi: 0-0 Tstrap: 0-2 Ckp: 0-0
Best Rating:	53 3/04 Hntg 2m110y good Hdl

Rose D'April (FR)

76(107h)   (115dh)102

7-y-o gr g April Night (FR)-Rose De Hoc (FR) (Rose Laurel)
L Lungo Ashleybank Investments Limited

Placings:0/120/151P0-65U   (2928)
2003/04: 16⁰G, 20⁵GS, 21ᵁG,

	Starts	1st	2nd	3rd	Win & Pl
Chases	3	0	0	0	0
Career Total	12	3	1	0	8457
115 1/03	Muss	2m4f		E(0-100)HHdl	GD £3347
104 11/02	Carl	2m1f		E Hdl	HVY £3024
102 12/01	Catt	2m		H NHF	GD £1631
			Total win prize-money £8003		

Going:	Sf: 0-0 GS: 0-0 Gd: 0-2 GF: - Fm: 0-0
Distance:	2m/2m3: 0-0 2m4-2m7: 0-2 3m+: 0-0
Track:	LH: 0-2 RH: 0-1 Tight: 0-1 Gall: 0-0
Aids:	Bl: 0-0 Vi: 0-0 Tstrap: 0-0 Ckp: 0-0
Best Rating:	115 1/03 Muss 2m4f good Hdl

Winning hurdler; well beaten on chase debut; stays 2m 4f; acts on soft ground.

Rose Of York (IRE)

82   54

4-y-o b f Emarati (USA)-True Ring (High Top)
J G Portman Col E C York

Placings:00UOP   (3997)
2003/04: 16⁰GF, 17⁰G, 18ᵁG, 16⁰GS, 21ᵖG,

	Starts	1st	2nd	3rd	Win & Pl
Hurdles	5	0	0	0	
Career Total	5	0	0	0	

Going:	Sf: 0-0 GS: 0-1 Gd: 0-3 GF: - Fm: 0-1
Distance:	2m/2m3: 0-4 2m4-2m7: 0-1 3m+: 0-0
Track:	LH: 0-3 RH: 0-2 Tight: 0-2 Gall: 0-0
Aids:	Bl: 0-0 Vi: 0-0 Tstrap: 0-0 Ckp: 0-0
Best Rating:	54 11/03 Hayd 2m gd-fm Hdl

Very moderate form over hurdles so far.

Rose Palma (FR)

79   67

6-y-o gr/ro m Great Palm (USA)-Rose Angevine (FR)
(Master Thatch)
S J Gilmore S N Wilshire

Placings:F50/544R146344360-P0F   (4101)
2003/04: 20ᴾS, 17⁰G, 26ᶠG,

	Starts	1st	2nd	3rd	Win & Pl
Chases	3	0	0	0	
Career Total	19	1	0	2	12349
11/02	Maur	2m3f		Ch	VS £2945
			Total win prize-money £2945		

Going:	Sf: 0-1 GS: 0-0 Gd: 0-2 GF: - Fm: 0-0
Distance:	2m/2m3: 0-1 2m4-2m7: 0-1 3m+: 0-1
Track:	LH: 0-1 RH: 0-2 Tight: 0-2 Gall: 0-1
Aids:	Bl: 0-0 Vi: 0-0 Tstrap: 0-2 Ckp: 0-0
Best Rating:	67 2/04 MRas 2m1f110y good Ch

Rose Tea (IRE)

87   95+

5-y-o ro m Alhaarth (IRE)-Shakamiyn (Nishapour (FR))
N A Graham Paul G Jacobs

Placings:1120   (4842)
2003/04: 21¹GF, 20¹GF, 23²G, 21⁰G,

	Starts	1st	2nd	3rd	Win & Pl
Hurdles	4	2	1	0	6541
Career Total	4	2	1	0	6541
76 10/03	Hexm	2m4f110yE Hdl			G-F £2257
95 9/03	Sthl	2m5f110yE Hdl			G-F £3444
			Total win prize-money £5702		

Going:	Sf: 0-0 GS: 0-0 Gd: 0-2 GF: - Fm: 2-2
Distance:	2m/2m3: 0-0 2m4-2m7: 2-4 3m+: 0-0
Track:	LH: 2-4 RH: 0-0 Tight: 0-0 Gall: 0-1
Aids:	Bl: 0-0 Vi: 0-0 Tstrap: 0-0 Ckp: 0-0
Best Rating:	95 9/03 Sthl 2m5f110y gd-fm Hdl

Moderate ex-Flat racer; made a winning debut over hurdles at Southwell in September; followed up in a weak event at Hexham the following month; should stay three miles; best on a sound surface.

Rose Tina

101(101h)   (86+h)109

7-y-o b m Tina's Pet-Rosevear (IRE) (Contract Law (USA))
B G Powell Church Racing Partnership

Placings:U66/40450/0036224-3FO21211F3   (2006)
2003/04: 19³GF, 20ᶠGF, 19⁰GF, 21²GF, 18¹GF, 22²G, 19¹F,
19¹GF, 20ᶠGF, 20³G,

	Starts	1st	2nd	3rd	Win & Pl
Hurdles	1	0	0	1	422
Chases	9	3	2	1	13572
Career Total	25	3	4	3	18714
109 10/03	Towc	2m3f110yD(0-120)HCh			G-F £2695
109 10/03	Towc	2m3f110yD Ch			FRM £5440
109 9/03	Font	2m2f		F Ch	G-F £2320
			Total win prize-money £10456		

Going:	Sf: 0-0 GS: 0-0 Gd: 0-2 GF: - Fm: 3-8
Distance:	2m/2m3: 1-3 2m4-2m7: 2-7 3m+: 0-0
Track:	LH: 0-4 RH: 0-5 Tight: 1-2 Gall: 0-2
Aids:	Bl: 0-0 Vi: 0-0 Tstrap: 0-0 Ckp: 0-0
Best Rating:	109 10/03 Towc 2m3f110y gd-fm Ch

Modest novice chaser; stays trips of around two and a half miles and acts on a sound surface; suited by forcing tactics; keen sort.

Rose Tinted

89   70

5-y-o b m Spectrum (IRE)-Marie La Rose (FR) (Night Shift (USA))
M E Sowersby (M L W Bell 15/6) The Southwold Set

Placings:05   (2305)
2003/04: 16⁰GS, 19⁵GF,

	Starts	1st	2nd	3rd	Win & Pl
Hurdles	2	0	0	0	0
Career Total	2	0	0	0	0

Going:	Sf: 0-0 GS: 0-1 Gd: 0-0 GF: - Fm: 0-1
Distance:	2m/2m3: 0-2 2m4-2m7: 0-0 3m+: 0-0
Track:	LH: 0-2 RH: 0-0 Tight: 0-0 Gall: 0-0
Aids:	Bl: 0-0 Vi: 0-0 Tstrap: 0-0 Ckp: 0-0
Best Rating:	70 11/03 Hayd 2m gd-sft Hdl

Roseberry Rose

66f   60f

5-y-o ch m Keen-Scotch Imp (Imperial Fling (USA))
M E Sowersby James Ritchie

Placings:000   (4264)
2003/04: 16⁰GF, 16⁰G, 16⁰GF,

	Starts	1st	2nd	3rd	Win & Pl
NH Flat	3	0	0	0	
Career Total	3	0	0	0	

Going:	Sf: 0-0 GS: 0-0 Gd: 0-1 GF: - Fm: 0-2
Distance:	2m/2m3: 0-3 2m4-2m7: 0-0 3m+: 0-0
Track:	LH: 0-3 RH: 0-0 Tight: 0-1 Gall: 0-0
Aids:	Bl: 0-0 Vi: 0-0 Tstrap: 0-0 Ckp: 0-0
Best Rating:	60 11/03 Hexm 2m110y gd-fm NHF

Rosegrove Rooster

7-y-o b g Henbit (USA)-Cornbelt (Oats)
D J Caro Joe Roper

Placings:00/P-P   (0084)
2003/04: 16ᵖGS,

	Starts	1st	2nd	3rd	Win & Pl
Hurdles	1	0	0	0	
Career Total	4	0	0	0	

Going:	Sf: 0-0 GS: 0-1 Gd: 0-0 GF: - Fm: 0-0
Distance:	2m/2m3: 0-1 2m4-2m7: 0-0 3m+: 0-0
Track:	LH: 0-1 RH: 0-0 Tight: 0-0 Gall: 0-0
Aids:	Bl: 0-0 Vi: 0-0 Tstrap: 0-0 Ckp: 0-0
Best Rating:	72 3/02 Ludl 2m soft NHF

Rosemead Tye

87(81h)   (52h)50

8-y-o b m Kasakov-Nouvelle Cuisine (Yawa)
D W Thompson (J A Moore 2/5) Mrs J M Moore

Placings:0P0P0-003506   (1187)
2003/04: 16⁰GS, 16⁰GF, 17³GF, 17⁵GF, 17⁰GF, 17⁶G,

	Starts	1st	2nd	3rd	Win & Pl
Hurdles	3	0	0	0	0
Chases	3	0	0	1	954
Career Total	11	0	0	1	954

Going:	Sf: 0-0 GS: 0-1 Gd: 0-1 GF: - Fm: 0-4
Distance:	2m/2m3: 0-6 2m4-2m7: 0-0 3m+: 0-0
Track:	LH: 0-5 RH: 0-1 Tight: 0-4 Gall: 0-0
Aids:	Bl: 0-0 Vi: 0-0 Tstrap: 0-0 Ckp: 0-0
Best Rating:	56 6/03 Hexm 2m110y gd-fm Hdl

Plating-class hurdler/chaser; yet to show any worthwhile form.

Roses Are Wild (IRE)

77   68

6-y-o gr m Roselier (FR)-Wild Bramble (IRE) (Deep Run)
Mrs B K Thomson Mrs B K Thomson

Placings:003F   (4239)
2003/04: 16⁰G, 16⁰HY, 20³HY, 19⁰G,

	Starts	1st	2nd	3rd	Win & Pl
NH Flat	2	0	0	0	0
Hurdles	2	0	0	1	746

Career Total	4	0	0	1	746

Going:	Sf: 0-2 GS: 0-0 Gd: 0-2 GF: - Fm: 0-0
Distance:	2m/2m3: 0-3 2m4-2m7: 0-1 3m+: 0-0
Track:	LH: 0-2 RH: 0-2 Tight: 0-0 Gall: 0-0
Aids:	Bl: 0-0 Vi: 0-0 Tstrap: 0-0 Ckp: 0-0
Best Rating:	68 2/04 Carl 2m4f heavy Hdl

Roseta Pearl (IRE)
59
8-y-o gr m Roselier (FR)-Brown Pearl (Tap On Wood)
Mrs S Wall Mrs S Wall

Placings:3F5-PP					(3169)
2003/04: 26PS, 25PGS,					
	Starts	1st	2nd	3rd	Win & Pl
Chases	2	0	0	0	
Career Total	5	0	0	1	624

Going:	Sf: 0-1 GS: 0-1 Gd: 0-0 GF: - Fm: 0-0
Distance:	2m/2m3: 0-0 2m4-2m7: 0-0 3m+: 0-2
Track:	LH: 0-1 RH: 0-1 Tight: 0-2 Gall: 0-0
Aids:	Bl: 0-0 Vi: 0-0 Tstrap: 0-1 Ckp: 0-0
Best Rating:	59 3/03 Font 2m6f good Ch

Rosetown (IRE)
69   47
6-y-o gr g Roselier (FR)-Railstown Cheeky (IRE) (Strong Gale)
T R George Timothy N Chick

Placings:00P0					(3309)
2003/04: 17PG, 20PGS, 20PGS, 22PHY,					
	Starts	1st	2nd	3rd	Win & Pl
NH Flat	1	0	0	0	0
Hurdles	3	0	0	0	0
Career Total	4	0	0	0	

Going:	Sf: 0-1 GS: 0-2 Gd: 0-1 GF: - Fm: 0-0
Distance:	2m/2m3: 0-1 2m4-2m7: 0-3 3m+: 0-0
Track:	LH: 0-3 RH: 0-0 Tight: 0-1 Gall: 0-0
Aids:	Bl: 0-0 Vi: 0-0 Tstrap: 0-1 Ckp: 0-0
Best Rating:	58 11/03 Aint 2m1f good NHF

Rosie Redman (IRE)
105(101h)   (97+h)113+
7-y-o gr m Roselier (FR)-Carbia's Last (Palm Track)
J R Turner Miss S J Turner

Placings:3/54454-3C1111					(4865)
2003/04: 25³G, 24CGS, 25¹S, 22¹S, 20¹S, 25¹S,					
	Starts	1st	2nd	3rd	Win & Pl
Hurdles	1	1	0	0	3784
Chases	5	3	0	1	29681
Career Total	12	4	0	2	34150
113 4/04	Ayr	3m1f	B HCh		SFT £21255
100 4/04	Hexm	2m4f110yE(0-105)HHdl		SFT £3783
109 1/04	Kels	2m6f110yE Ch		SFT £4706
100 12/03	MRas	3m1f	E(0-105)HCh		GD £3360
			Total win prize-money £33105		

Going:	Sf: 3-3 GS: 0-1 Gd: 1-2 GF: - Fm: 0-0
Distance:	2m/2m3: 0-0 2m4-2m7: 2-2 3m+: 2-4
Track:	LH: 3-5 RH: 1-1 Tight: 2-2 Gall: 0-1
Aids:	Bl: 0-0 Vi: 0-0 Tstrap: 0-0 Ckp: 0-0
Best Rating:	113 4/04 Ayr 3m1f soft Ch

Moderate but progressive chaser/hurdler; jumping-bred; stays 3m 1f over fences and scored from lower mark over hurdles at Hexham in April 2004; effective on soft ground and best effort in ideal conditions at Ayr in April; may still be capable of better.

Ross Gee (IRE)
90   76
8-y-o gr g Roselier (FR)-Miss Leader (Taufan (USA))
Mrs S J Smith Mrs S Smith

Placings:0/00P6					(3693)
2003/04: 17PGS, 20PGS, 21PGS, 19PG,					
	Starts	1st	2nd	3rd	Win & Pl
Hurdles	2	0	0	0	0
Chases	2	0	0	0	0
Career Total	5	0	0	0	

Going:	Sf: 0-0 GS: 0-3 Gd: 0-1 GF: - Fm: 0-0
Distance:	2m/2m3: 0-2 2m4-2m7: 0-2 3m+: 0-0
Track:	LH: 0-3 RH: 0-1 Tight: 0-3 Gall: 0-0
Aids:	Bl: 0-0 Vi: 0-0 Tstrap: 0-0 Ckp: 0-0
Best Rating:	78 2/04 Catt 2m3f good Ch

Ross Leader (IRE)
92   85
7-y-o b g Supreme Leader-Emmagreen (Green Shoon)
Mrs Susan Nock Gerard Nock

Placings:P5P2					(4570)
2003/04: 24PGS, 24SGS, 23PGS, 24²GS,					
	Starts	1st	2nd	3rd	Win & Pl
Chases	4	0	1	0	1705
Career Total	4	0	1	0	1705

Going:	Sf: 0-0 GS: 0-4 Gd: 0-0 GF: - Fm: 0-0
Distance:	2m/2m3: 0-0 2m4-2m7: 0-3 3m+: 0-1
Track:	LH: 0-3 RH: 0-1 Tight: 0-2 Gall: 0-0
Aids:	Bl: 0-0 Vi: 0-0 Tstrap: 0-0 Ckp: 0-0
Best Rating:	85 3/04 Bang 3m110y gd-sft Ch

Plating-class chaser; stays three miles; acts on easy ground.

Ross Minster (IRE)
103   124+
10-y-o ro g Roselier (FR)-Face To Face (The Parson)
P J Hobbs The Country Side

Placings:62/150121/53P1352/1235501/P-2P4					(4342)
2003/04: 25²S, 26²HY, 29⁴GS,					
	Starts	1st	2nd	3rd	Win & Pl
Chases	3	0	1	0	2164
Career Total	26	6	5	3	35652
128 4/02	Chep	3m2f110yD(0-120)	G-S	£4124
124 11/01	NAbb	3m2f110yD(0-120)HCh	SFT	£3767
121 1/01	Chep	3m2f110yE(0-115)HCh	G-S	£3104
121 4/00	Uttx	3m2f	E Ch	HVY	£5540
120 2/00	Winc	3m1f110yD Ch	G-S	£4348
115 11/99	Towc	3m	D Hdl	GD	£3051
			Total win prize-money £23936		

Going:	Sf: 0-2 GS: 0-1 Gd: 0-0 GF: - Fm: 0-0
Distance:	2m/2m3: 0-0 2m4-2m7: 0-0 3m+: 0-3
Track:	LH: 0-2 RH: 0-1 Tight: 0-0 Gall: 0-0
Aids:	Bl: 0-0 Vi: 0-0 Tstrap: 0-0 Ckp: 0-0
Best Rating:	128 4/02 Chep 3m2f110y gd-sft Ch

Fair handicap chaser; stays extreme distances; acts on soft ground; tough; has been tried blinkered, inconsistent.

Ross Park (IRE)
80
8-y-o b g Roselier (FR)-La Christyana (IRE) (The Parson)
J Howard Johnson Gordon Brown/bert Watson

Placings:4/06F-0					(3691)
2003/04: 19PG,					
	Starts	1st	2nd	3rd	Win & Pl
Hurdles	1	0	0	0	
Career Total	5	0	0	0	

Going:	Sf: 0-0 GS: 0-0 Gd: 0-1 GF: - Fm: 0-0
Distance:	2m/2m3: 0-1 2m4-2m7: 0-0 3m+: 0-0
Track:	LH: 0-1 RH: 0-0 Tight: 0-1 Gall: 0-0
Aids:	Bl: 0-0 Vi: 0-0 Tstrap: 0-0 Ckp: 0-0
Best Rating:	80 3/02 Hexm 3m heavy Hdl

Ross River
108   127+
8-y-o gr g Over The River (FR)-Solo Rose (Roselier (FR))
P J Hobbs Seamus Ross

Placings:15/105					(4868)
2003/04: 20¹GS, 21⁰G, 20⁵GS,					
	Starts	1st	2nd	3rd	Win & Pl
Hurdles	3	1	0	0	2772
Career Total	5	2	0	0	9968
127 12/03	Chep	2m4f	E Hdl	G-S	£2772
116 4/02	Fair	2m2f	NHF	G-Y	£7196
			Total win prize-money £9968		

Going:	Sf: 0-0 GS: 1-2 Gd: 0-1 GF: - Fm: 0-0
Distance:	2m/2m3: 0-0 2m4-2m7: 1-3 3m+: 0-0
Track:	LH: 1-3 RH: 0-0 Tight: 0-1 Gall: 0-1
Aids:	Bl: 0-0 Vi: 0-0 Tstrap: 0-0 Ckp: 0-0
Best Rating:	127 12/03 Chep 2m4f gd-sft Hdl

Ex-Irish; has had his problems since winning a bumper at Fairyhouse in April 2002; very easy winner on hurdling debut over 2m 4f at Chepstow December 2003; well beaten next time at Cheltenham Festival and very disappointing at Bangor; effective over two and a half miles; operates well on soft ground.

Rosscarbery Grey (IRE)
6-y-o gr g Gothland (FR)-Millroad (Buckskin (FR))
S T Lewis Simon T Lewis

Placings:00-PP					(3524)
2003/04: 22PG, 20PS,					
	Starts	1st	2nd	3rd	Win & Pl
Hurdles	2	0	0	0	
Career Total	4	0	0	0	

Going:	Sf: 0-1 GS: 0-0 Gd: 0-1 GF: - Fm: 0-0
Distance:	2m/2m3: 0-0 2m4-2m7: 0-2 3m+: 0-0
Track:	LH: 0-1 RH: 0-1 Tight: 0-1 Gall: 0-0
Aids:	Bl: 0-0 Vi: 0-0 Tstrap: 0-0 Ckp: 0-0

Rosslea (IRE)
111(112h)   (125+h)136
6-y-o b g Roselier (FR)-Burren Gale (IRE) (Strong Gale)
Miss H C Knight Jim Lewis

Placings:P230-12212	(3931)

2003/04: 24¹GS, 25²G, 24²YS, 24¹GS, 24²G,

	Starts	1st	2nd	3rd	Win & Pl
Chases	5	2	3	0	33105
Career Total	**9**	**2**	**4**	**1**	**35990**
136 2/04	Kemp	3m	D Ch		G-S	£6873
136 11/03	Bang	3m110y	D Ch		G-S	£4504

Total win prize-money £11379

Going:	Sf: 0-0 GS: 2-2 Gd: 0-2 GF: - Fm: 0-0
Distance:	2m/2m3: 0-0 2m4-2m7: 0-0 3m+: 2-5
Track:	LH: 1-3 RH: 1-2 Tight: 1-1 Gall: 0-1
Aids:	Bl: 0-0 Vi: 0-0 Tstrap: 0-0 Ckp: 0-0
Best Rating:	136 2/04 Asct 3m110y good Ch

Former Irish point winner; in the frame in novice hurdles; made an impressive chase debut when winning at Bangor in November 2003, and ran well to chase home Therealbandit next time; back to winning ways at Kempton; stayed three miles plus; acted with give in the ground. (DEAD)

Rossmay (IRE)

7-y-o b g Kasmayo-Ross Rag (Ragapan)
G F Bridgwater Mrs Gail Bridgwater

Placings:PP03P					(3225)

2003/04: 16³GF, 20PGF, 16ºGF, 16³GF, 19PGS,

	Starts	1st	2nd	3rd	Win & Pl
Hurdles	3	0	0	0	0
Chases	2	0	0	1	383
Career Total	**5**	**0**	**0**	**1**	**383**

Going:	Sf: 0-0 GS: 0-1 Gd: 0-0 GF: - Fm: 0-4
Distance:	2m/2m3: 0-4 2m4-2m7: 0-1 3m+: 0-0
Track:	LH: 0-3 RH: 0-2 Tight: 0-0 Gall: 0-0
Aids:	Bl: 0-0 Vi: 0-0 Tstrap: 0-0 Ckp: 0-0

Rostropovich (IRE)

117　　　　　　　　　　　140

7-y-o gr g Sadler's Wells (USA)-Infamy (Shirley Heights)
M F Morris M A Kilduff

Placings:13316/14005/452424021-33030600					(4643)

2003/04: 24³GY, 25³G, 16ºGY, 24³YS, 24ºHY, 23ºS, 25ºG, 24ºG,

	Starts	1st	2nd	3rd	Win & Pl
Hurdles	8	0	0	3	12066
Career Total	**27**	**4**	**3**		**90989**
152 4/03	Sand	3m	B Hdl		G-F	£29000
137 5/01	Fair	2m	Hdl		GD	£10483
124 4/01	Cork	2m	Hdl		Y-S	£6120
109 1/01	Naas	2m	Hdl		SFT	£5564

Total win prize-money £51170

Going:	Sf: 0-2 GS: 0-0 Gd: 0-3 GF: - Fm: 0-0
Distance:	2m/2m3: 0-1 2m4-2m7: 0-0 3m+: 0-7
Track:	LH: 0-5 RH: 0-3 Tight: 0-1 Gall: 0-1
Aids:	Bl: 0-0 Vi: 0-0 Tstrap: 0-2 Ckp: 0-6
Best Rating:	152 4/03 Sand 3m gd-fm Hdl

High-class hurdler; won valuable event at Sandown April 2003; suited by 3m; acts on firm and good and soft ground; usually wears a tongue strap and cheekpieces.

Rothko (IRE)

81　　　　　　　　　　　74

6-y-o b g Naheez (USA)-Dizzy Lady (IRE) (Sarab)
P D Niven R A Bartlett

Placings:0PP					(4731)

2003/04: 19ºGS, 22PGS, 20PG,

	Starts	1st	2nd	3rd	Win & Pl
Hurdles	3	0	0	0	
Career Total	**3**	**0**	**0**	**0**	

Going:	Sf: 0-0 GS: 0-2 Gd: 0-1 GF: - Fm: 0-0
Distance:	2m/2m3: 0-1 2m4-2m7: 0-2 3m+: 0-0
Track:	LH: 0-2 RH: 0-1 Tight: 0-2 Gall: 0-0
Aids:	Bl: 0-0 Vi: 0-0 Tstrap: 0-0 Ckp: 0-0
Best Rating:	74 12/03 Catt 2m3f gd-sft Hdl

Rouge Blanc (USA)

81　　　　　　　　　　　61

4-y-o b f King Of Kings (IRE)-Style N' Elegance (USA) (Alysheba (USA))
G A Harker (P J McBride 20/10) John J Maguire

Placings:005					(4387)

2003/04: 16ºGS, 16ºGS, 21⁵G,

	Starts	1st	2nd	3rd	Win & Pl
Hurdles	3	0	0	0	0
Career Total	**3**	**0**	**0**	**0**	**0**

Going:	Sf: 0-0 GS: 0-2 Gd: 0-1 GF: - Fm: 0-0
Distance:	2m/2m3: 0-2 2m4-2m7: 0-1 3m+: 0-0
Track:	LH: 0-3 RH: 0-0 Tight: 0-2 Gall: 0-0
Aids:	Bl: 0-0 Vi: 0-0 Tstrap: 0-0 Ckp: 0-0
Best Rating:	58 11/03 Weth 2m gd-sft Hdl

Rouge Et Noir

105f　　　　　　　　　105+f

6-y-o b g Hernando (FR)-Bayrouge (IRE) (Gorytus (USA))
Mrs M Reveley The Mary Reveley Racing Club

Placings:20					(2435)

2003/04: 16²G, 16ºS,

	Starts	1st	2nd	3rd	Win & Pl
NH Flat	2	0	1	0	568
Career Total	**2**	**0**	**1**	**0**	**568**

Going:	Sf: 0-1 GS: 0-0 Gd: 0-1 GF: - Fm: 0-0
Distance:	2m/2m3: 0-2 2m4-2m7: 0-0 3m+: 0-0
Track:	LH: 0-2 RH: 0-0 Tight: 0-0 Gall: 0-0
Aids:	Bl: 0-0 Vi: 0-0 Tstrap: 0-0 Ckp: 0-0
Best Rating:	105 11/03 Weth 2m good NHF

Runner-up in bumper at Wetherby in November on racecourse debut but disappointed next time.

Rough Tiger (IRE)

11-y-o ch g Glacial Storm (USA)-Mourne Trix (Golden Love)
F A Hutsby Mrs Ian McKie

Placings:F-43					(0415)

2003/04: 33⁴G, 20³G,

	Starts	1st	2nd	3rd	Win & Pl
Chases	2	0	0	1	717
Career Total	**3**	**0**	**0**	**1**	**717**

Going:	Sf: 0-0 GS: 0-0 Gd: 0-2 GF: - Fm: 0-0
Distance:	2m/2m3: 0-0 2m4-2m7: 0-1 3m+: 0-1
Track:	LH: 0-2 RH: 0-0 Tight: 0-0 Gall: 0-1
Aids:	Bl: 0-0 Vi: 0-0 Tstrap: 0-0 Ckp: 0-0
Best Rating:	98 3/03 Leic 2m7f110y gd-sft Ch

Round The Bend

12-y-o b g Revolutionary (USA)-No Love (Bustiki)
Miss Louise Allan F Allan

Placings:25-P					(4439)

2003/04: 21PGS,

	Starts	1st	2nd	3rd	Win & Pl
Chases	1	0	0	0	
Career Total	**3**	**0**	**1**	**0**	**416**

Going:	Sf: 0-0 GS: 0-1 Gd: 0-0 GF: - Fm: 0-0
Distance:	2m/2m3: 0-0 2m4-2m7: 0-1 3m+: 0-0
Track:	LH: 0-1 RH: 0-0 Tight: 0-1 Gall: 0-0
Aids:	Bl: 0-0 Vi: 0-0 Tstrap: 0-0 Ckp: 0-0
Best Rating:	81 6/02 MRas 2m6f110y gd-fm Ch

Modest pointer/hunter chaser; handles fast ground.

Rousing Thunder

97　　　　　　　　　　　79

7-y-o b g Theatrical-Moss (USA) (Woodman (USA))
W Storey John J Maguire

Placings:53543					(2083)

2003/04: 16⁵G, 16³GF, 16⁵G, 16⁴G, 21³GF,

	Starts	1st	2nd	3rd	Win & Pl
Hurdles	5	0	0	2	788
Career Total	**5**	**0**	**0**	**2**	**788**

Going:	Sf: 0-0 GS: 0-0 Gd: 0-3 GF: - Fm: 0-2
Distance:	2m/2m3: 0-4 2m4-2m7: 0-1 3m+: 0-0
Track:	LH: 0-3 RH: 0-2 Tight: 0-3 Gall: 0-0
Aids:	Bl: 0-0 Vi: 0-0 Tstrap: 0-0 Ckp: 0-4
Best Rating:	82 8/03 Prth 2m110y gd-fm Hdl

Route One (IRE)

11-y-o b g Welsh Term-Skylin (Skyliner)
D Frankland D Frankland

Placings:1/2241/1F466/0/023221-31014					(4542)

2003/04: 16³G, 20¹GF, 20ºG, 16¹G, 20⁴GS,

	Starts	1st	2nd	3rd	Win & Pl
Chases	5	2	0	1	4151
Career Total	**22**	**6**	**5**	**2**	**18476**
99 3/04	Leic	2m	H Ch		GD	£2240
97 5/03	Hntg	2m4f110yH Ch		G-F	£1368
97 4/03	Asct	2m3f110yH Ch		GD	£2954
105 5/99	Towc	2m	E Hdl		G-F	£2985
106 4/99	Hrfd	2m1f	E Hdl		G-F	£2578
106 4/97	MRas	1m5f110yH NHF		GD	£1402

Total win prize-money £13529

Going:	Sf: 0-0 GS: 0-1 Gd: 1-3 GF: - Fm: 1-1
Distance:	2m/2m3: 1-2 2m4-2m7: 1-3 3m+: 0-0
Track:	LH: 0-1 RH: 2-4 Tight: 0-1 Gall: 1-2
Aids:	Bl: 0-0 Vi: 0-0 Tstrap: 0-0 Ckp: 0-0
Best Rating:	106 4/99 Hrfd 2m1f gd-fm Hdl

Modest hunter chaser; consistent sort; best form at around two and a half miles; likes fast ground.

Route Sixty Six (IRE)

103(98c)　　　　　　(85c)97

8-y-o b m Brief Truce (USA)-Lyphards Goddess (IRE) (Lyphard's Special (USA))

Jedd O'Keeffe WRB Racing 47 (wrbracing.com)

Placings:0F12/322PP/U10PP-65044P56   (4849)
2003/04: 16⁶GS, 16⁵GS, 16⁹S, 16⁴G, 16⁴G, 16⁶G, 17⁵G, 16⁶GS,

	Starts	1st	2nd	3rd	Win & Pl
Hurdles	8	0	0	0	2025
Career Total	22	2	3	1	17751
85	11/02 Ayr	2m	D Ch	SFT	£5872
90	1/01 Muss	2m	E Hdl	GD	£2362

Total win prize-money £8235

Going:	Sf: 0-1 GS: 0-2 Gd: 0-4 GF: - Fm: 0-1
Distance:	2m/2m3: 0-8 2m4-2m7: 0-0 3m+: 0-0
Track:	LH: 0-5 RH: 0-3 Tight: 0-2 Gall: 0-1
Aids:	Bl: 0-0 Vi: 0-0 Tstrap: 0-0 Ckp: 0-4
Best Rating:	110 12/01 Kemp 2m	good	Hdl

Plating-class hurdler; suited by good ground; best at two miles; has worn cheekpieces.

Rovestar
62

13-y-o b g Le Solaret (FR)-Gilberts Choice (My Swanee)
C L Popham The Rovestar Partnership

Placings:04/453000/61003/360R451412/4231310052/2332
05315336/11422P0FPU/0310413415/0P0600-P   (0038)
2003/04: 19⁸G,

	Starts	1st	2nd	3rd	Win & Pl
Chases	1	0	0	0	
Career Total	72	11	7	12	57532
109	4/02 Tntn	3m	D(0-120)HCh	GD	£7020
105	1/02 Tntn	3m	E(0-110)HCh	SFT	£3640
100	11/01 Chep	2m110y	E(0-115)HCh	G-S	£3307
109	5/00 Towc	2m110y	D(0-125)HCh	SFT	£3848
109	5/00 Towc	2m110y	E(0-115)HCh	SFT	£3198
109	2/00 Towc	2m110y	D(0-120)HCh	SFT	£3861
113	2/99 Towc	2m110y	D(0-120)HCh	SFT	£3658
108	11/98 Wwck	2m	D(0-125)HCh	SFT	£3415
112	4/98 Winc	2m	E(0-115)HCh	G-S	£3550
112	3/98 NAbb	2m110y	F(0-100)HCh	SFT	£2448
94	11/96 Wwck	2m	E(0-100)HHdl	GD	£2692

Total win prize-money £40640

Going:	Sf: 0-0 GS: 0-0 Gd: 0 GF: - Fm: 0-0
Distance:	2m/2m3: 0-0 2m4-2m7: 0-1 3m+: 0-0
Track:	LH: 0-0 RH: 0-1 Tight: 0-0 Gall: 0-0
Aids:	Bl: 0-1 Vi: 0-0 Tstrap: 0-0 Ckp: 0-0
Best Rating:	113 2/99 Towc 2m110y	soft	Ch

Rowley Hill
92   **77**

6-y-o b g Karinga Bay-Scarlet Dymond (Rymer)
A King J E Brown & Mrs S Faccenda

Placings:4650   (4197)
2003/04: 17⁴GS, 20⁶G, 25⁵GS, 24⁰G,

	Starts	1st	2nd	3rd	Win & Pl
NH Flat	1	0	0	0	0
Hurdles	3	0	0	0	0
Career Total	4	0	0	0	0

Going:	Sf: 0-0 GS: 0-2 Gd: 0-2 GF: - Fm: 0-0
Distance:	2m/2m3: 0-2 2m4-2m7: 0-1 3m+: 0-2
Track:	LH: 0-2 RH: 0-2 Tight: 0-0 Gall: 0-1
Aids:	Bl: 0-0 Vi: 0-0 Tstrap: 0-0 Ckp: 0-1
Best Rating:	96 12/03 Hrfd 2m1f	gd-sft	NHF

Satisfactory debut when fourth in Hereford bumper in December; has shown ability in novice hurdles; stays well.

Royal Allegiance
82   (35h)**57**

9-y-o ch g Kris-Wilayif (USA) (Danzig (USA))
P Wegmann R Koniger

Placings:P00003006/4013005000/00P0/P53-54640   (2513)
2003/04: 16⁵GS, 21⁴GF, 16⁶GF, 17⁴GF, 16⁹GS,

	Starts	1st	2nd	3rd	Win & Pl
Chases	5	0	0	0	724
Career Total	31	1	0	3	5765
85	10/00 Strf	2m110y F(0-100)HHdl	G-S	£2828

Total win prize-money £2828

Going:	Sf: 0-0 GS: 0-2 Gd: 0-0 GF: - Fm: 0-3
Distance:	2m/2m3: 0-2 2m4-2m7: 0-1 3m+: 0-0
Track:	LH: 0-4 RH: 0-1 Tight: 0-4 Gall: 0-0
Aids:	Bl: 0-1 Vi: 0-1 Tstrap: 0-0 Ckp: 0-1
Best Rating:	85 10/00 Strf 2m110y	gd-sft	Hdl

Royal Amaretto (IRE)
100   **113**

10-y-o b g Fairy King (USA)-Melbourne Miss (Chaparral (USA))
Mrs S J Smith M Keightley

Placings:1/P/24   (1017)
2003/04: 17²GF, 16⁴GF,

	Starts	1st	2nd	3rd	Win & Pl
Hurdles	2	0	1	0	1942
Career Total	4	1	1	0	3741
108	12/00 Muss	2m	E Hdl	GD	£1799

Total win prize-money £1799

Going:	Sf: 0-0 GS: 0-0 Gd: 0-0 GF: - Fm: 0-2
Distance:	2m/2m3: 0-2 2m4-2m7: 0-0 3m+: 0-0
Track:	LH: 0-2 RH: 0-0 Tight: 0-0 Gall: 0-0
Aids:	Bl: 0-1 Vi: 0-0 Tstrap: 0-0 Ckp: 0-0
Best Rating:	115 8/03 Worc 2m	gd-fm	Ch

Fair hurdler; lightly raced in recent seasons; good second when trying to concede a lot of weight in an in-form rival on first start for 21 months at Southwell July 2003; not beaten far when fourth after hanging right in a more competitive event at Worcester next time: use to be tongue-tied; acts on fast ground.

Royal Atalza (FR)
(91h)

7-y-o gr g Saint Preuil (FR)-Crystalza (FR) (Crystal Palace (FR))
C N Allen (B Barbier 16/11) T P Ramsden

Placings:1/002F005/40433010/0F4100606-0601PP (4647)
2003/04: 21⁰VS, 20⁶S, 24⁰VS, 21¹HO, 19⁵S, 36⁰G,

	Starts	1st	2nd	3rd	Win & Pl
Hurdles	2	0	0	0	0
Chases	4	1	0	0	23377
Career Total	31	4	1	2	117741
	11/03 Autl	2m5f110y HCh	HLD	£23377
	10/02 Autl	2m4f110y Ch	HLD	£19141
	3/02 Autl	2m3f110y HHdl	HVY	£26227
	4/00 Autl	1m7f	Hdl	HLD	£11527

Total win prize-money £80272

Going:	Sf: 0-2 GS: 0-0 Gd: 0-1 GF: - Fm: 0-0
Distance:	2m/2m3: 0-0 2m4-2m7: 1-4 3m+: 0-2
Track:	LH: 0-2 RH: 0-1 Tight: 0-1 Gall: 0-1
Aids:	Bl: 1-2 Vi: 0-0 Tstrap: 0-0 Ckp: 0-1

Very useful ex-French chaser/hurdler; pulled up on British debut at Ascot and in the Grand National; won on Fibresand in February; stays three miles; acts well in soft ground; has worn blinkers.

Royal Auclair (FR)
112   (96h)**146**

7-y-o ch g Garde Royale-Carmonera (FR) (Carmont (FR))
P F Nicholls Clive D Smith

Placings:531115/F111/440-4F04422302   (4965)
2003/04: 20⁴GS, 21²GF, 19⁹GS, 20⁴S, 24⁴G, 25²G, 24²G, 24³G, 25⁰G, 29²GF,

	Starts	1st	2nd	3rd	Win & Pl
Chases	10	0	3	1	67748
Career Total	23	6	3	2	165948
152	3/02 Chel	2m5f	A Ch	GD	£42000
139	1/02 Chel	2m5f	B HCh	HVY	£12720
132	12/01 Extr	2m1f110yC Ch	G-S	£8515
143	2/01 Sand	2m110y D Hdl	HVY	£4270
	12/00 Engh	2m1f110y Hdl	HVY	£10567
	11/00 Engh	2m1f110y Hdl	HVY	£9606

Total win prize-money £87680

Going:	Sf: 0-1 GS: 0-2 Gd: 0-6 GF: - Fm: 0-1
Distance:	2m/2m3: 0-0 2m4-2m7: 0-4 3m+: 0-6
Track:	LH: 0-7 RH: 0-3 Tight: 0-1 Gall: 0-5
Aids:	Bl: 0-1 Vi: 0-0 Tstrap: 0-10 Ckp: 0-0
Best Rating:	155 2/03 Newb 3m	good	Ch

Smart chaser; a leading novice in 2001/2 when trained by M. Pipe, making all in the Cathcart at the Festival; disappointing in 2002/3; in better form since joining Paul Nicholls without getting his head in front, including when runner-up in the BetFred Gold Cup at Sandown; stays 3m5f, effective at 2m 5f; acts on good and soft ground; has worn blinkers and a tongue tie.

Royal Barge

14-y-o b g Nearly A Hand-April Airs (Grey Mirage)
G Barber A D Quinn

Placings:3263/2311113321P/U20/P/4143-0   (4626)
2003/04: 21⁰G,

	Starts	1st	2nd	3rd	Win & Pl
Chases	1	0	0	0	
Career Total	24	6	4	6	29824
109	8/02 MRas	3m1f	E(0-110)HCh	G-F	£4439
120	12/98 Extr	3m2f	D(0-125)HCh	SFT	£5034
109	7/98 Sedg	3m3f	D Ch	GD	£3533
114	7/98 Worc	2m7f110yF(0-105)HCh	GD	£2798
117	6/98 Sthl	3m110y E(0-110)HHdl	GD	£2305
93	5/98 Ctml	2m5f	D Hdl	G-F	£2992

Total win prize-money £21106

Going:	Sf: 0-0 GS: 0-0 Gd: 0-1 GF: - Fm: 0-0
Distance:	2m/2m3: 0-0 2m4-2m7: 0-1 3m+: 0-0
Track:	LH: 0-1 RH: 0-0 Tight: 0-1 Gall: 0-0
Aids:	Bl: 0-0 Vi: 0-0 Tstrap: 0-0 Ckp: 0-0
Best Rating:	120 12/98 Extr 3m2f	soft	Ch

Fair chaser; performed creditably in a point latest; stays over three miles; acts on most ground, but possibly best on a sound surface.

Royal Beluga (USA)
104(100h)   (78h)**127**

7-y-o b g Rahy (USA)-Navratilovna (USA) (Nureyev (USA))
T R George M R C Opperman

Placings:24/5236/320011532152-54P1244P   (4385)
2003/04: 20⁵GF, 20⁴G, 21⁵PS, 19¹G, 20²GS, 20⁴G, 24⁴G, 24⁰GF,

		Starts	1st	2nd	3rd	Win & Pl
Hurdles		1	0	0	0	0
Chases		7	1	1	0	13106
Career Total		26	4	6	3	40990
127	12/03 Donc	2m3f	C(0-135)HCh	GD		£8288
124	3/03 Newb	2m2f110yD(0-110)HCh		GD		£5720
106	1/03 Ludl	2m4f	E(0-105)HCh	G-S		£5291
99	11/02 Bang	2m1f110yE(0-105)HCh		HVY		£4231
			Total win prize-money			£23531

Going:	Sf: 0-0 GS: 0-2 Gd: 1-5 GF: - Fm: 0-1
Distance:	2m/2m3: 1-1 2m4-2m7: 0-5 3m+: 0-2
Track:	LH: 1-6 RH: 0-2 Tight: 0-3 Gall: 0-3
Aids:	Bl: 0-0 Vi: 0-0 Tstrap: 0-0 Ckp: 0-0
Best Rating:	127 12/03 Donc 2m3f good Ch

Fair handicap chaser; possibly best on soft ground; stays two and a half miles; has worn a visor.

Royal Blazer (IRE)
97   75+
4-y-o b g Barathea (IRE)-Royale (IRE) (Royal Academy (USA))
C Grant Club 4 Racing

Placings:4000   (3988)
2003/04: 16⁴G, 16⁹G, 16⁹GF, 17⁰GS,

	Starts	1st	2nd	3rd	Win & Pl
Hurdles	4	0	0	0	
Career Total	4	0	0	0	

Going:	Sf: 0-0 GS: 0-1 Gd: 0-2 GF: - Fm: 0-1
Distance:	2m/2m3: 0-4 2m4-2m7: 0-0 3m+: 0-0
Track:	LH: 0-3 RH: 0-1 Tight: 0-2 Gall: 0-2
Aids:	Bl: 0-0 Vi: 0-0 Tstrap: 0-0 Ckp: 0-0
Best Rating:	75 11/03 Newc 2m good Hdl

Royal Bubbel (IRE)
95   84
6-y-o ch m Hubbly Bubbly (USA)-Last Royal (Kambalda)
D R Gandolfo Starlight Racing

Placings:3   (4736)
2003/04: 17³G,

	Starts	1st	2nd	3rd	Win & Pl
Hurdles	1	0	0	1	530
Career Total	1	0	0	1	530

Going:	Sf: 0-0 GS: 0-0 Gd: 0-1 GF: - Fm: 0-0
Distance:	2m/2m3: 0-1 2m4-2m7: 0-0 3m+: 0-0
Track:	LH: 0-1 RH: 0-0 Tight: 0-1 Gall: 0-0
Aids:	Bl: 0-0 Vi: 0-0 Tstrap: 0-0 Ckp: 0-0
Best Rating:	89 4/04 NAbb 2m1f good Hdl

Royal Castle (IRE)
95(105c)   (113c)126
10-y-o b g Caerleon (USA)-Sun Princess (English Prince)
Mrs K Walton Stan Clough and Dudley Bendall

Placings:223/11500/1/P/010P-11402FP05U0   (3694)
2003/04: 21¹S, 21¹G, 24⁴G, 21⁹G, 21²GF, 22⁴G, 26⁶P, 22⁰S, 24⁴GS, 30⁴UG, 25⁰G,

		Starts	1st	2nd	3rd	Win & Pl
Hurdles		3	0	0	0	
Chases		8	2	1	0	11920
Career Total		25	6	3	1	27723
113	5/03 Cctml	2m5f110yD Ch	GD			£6032
90	5/03 Sedg	2m5f E Ch	SFT			£4336
117	10/02 Sedg	2m5f110yD(0-125)HHdl	GD			£4030

		Starts	1st	2nd	3rd	Win & Pl
126	7/00 Strf	2m6f110yE(0-115)HHdl	G-F			£3542
114	12/99 Donc	2m4f E Hdl	G-F			£3113
109	11/99 Towc	2m5f E Hdl	GD			£2775
			Total win prize-money			£23830

Going:	Sf: 1-2 GS: 0-1 Gd: 1-7 GF: - Fm: 0-1
Distance:	2m/2m3: 0-2 2m4-2m7: 2-6 3m+: 0-1
Track:	LH: 2-10 RH: 0-1 Tight: 2-6 Gall: 0-1
Aids:	Bl: 0-0 Vi: 0-0 Tstrap: 0-0 Ckp: 0-0
Best Rating:	137 3/00 Chel 2m5f good Hdl

Fair hurdler at around two and a half miles; moderate chaser; acts on a sound surface; stays two miles six.

Royal Charlie
7-y-o br g Royal Fountain-Cool View (Kinglet)
Mrs R L Elliot D G Pryde

Placings:0-P0   (3358)
2003/04: 20⁵S, 16⁰S,

	Starts	1st	2nd	3rd	Win & Pl
Hurdles	2	0	0	0	
Career Total	3	0	0	0	

Going:	Sf: 0-2 GS: 0-0 Gd: 0-0 GF: - Fm: 0-0
Distance:	2m/2m3: 0-1 2m4-2m7: 0-3 3m+: 0-0
Track:	LH: 0-2 RH: 0-0 Tight: 0-1 Gall: 0-0
Aids:	Bl: 0-0 Vi: 0-0 Tstrap: 0-0 Ckp: 0-0
Best Rating:	69 1/03 Hayd 2m gd-sft NHF

Royal China (IRE)
98(95h)   (84h)90+
6-y-o b g Aristocracy-Luan Causca (Pampapaul)
Miss H C Knight David Zeffman

Placings:0405-4423FP0   (4785)
2003/04: 17⁴G, 20⁴GF, 21²G, 20³GS, 19⁶G, 20⁰GS, 21⁰G,

	Starts	1st	2nd	3rd	Win & Pl
Hurdles	1	0	0	0	
Chases	6	0	1	1	2593
Career Total	11	0	1	1	2926

Going:	Sf: 0-0 GS: 0-4 Gd: 0-2 GF: - Fm: 0-0
Distance:	2m/2m3: 0-2 2m4-2m7: 0-5 3m+: 0-1
Track:	LH: 0-0 RH: 0-5 Tight: 0-2 Gall: 0-1
Aids:	Bl: 0-0 Vi: 0-0 Tstrap: 0-0 Ckp: 0-0
Best Rating:	90 1/04 Fknm 2m5f110y gd-sft Ch

Modest novice chaser; stays 2m 4f; acts on fast and easy ground.

Royal County Buck (IRE)
101   (101h)111+
9-y-o b g Good Thyne (USA)-Little Quince (Laurence O)
A J Martin Dunsany Racing Syndicate

Placings:0000/4 1233/6005046-1401332   (2132)
2003/04: 25¹F, 23⁴G, 24⁰Y, 25¹GF, 24³GF, 24³GF, 32²GF,

		Starts	1st	2nd	3rd	Win & Pl
Hurdles		1	0	0	0	
Chases		6	2	1	2	27164
Career Total		23	3	2	4	33444
108	9/03 Kbgn	3m1f (0-116)HCh	G-F			£9707
105	6/03 Kbgn	3m1f (0-123)HCh	FRM			£7840
103	6/01 Dpat	2m4f110y NHF	FRM			£3338
			Total win prize-money			£20888

Going:	Sf: 0-0 GS: 0-0 Gd: 0-1 GF: - Fm: 2-5
Distance:	2m/2m3: 0-0 2m4-2m7: 0-1 3m+: 2-6
Track:	LH: 0-1 RH: 0-3 Tight: 0-0 Gall: 0-1
Aids:	Bl: 0-0 Vi: 0-0 Tstrap: 2-7 Ckp: 0-0
Best Rating:	111 11/03 Chel 4m gd-fm Ch

Fair hurdler/chaser; Irish trained; acts on fast ground; stays three mile plus; usually has tongue tied.

Royal Crimson
13-y-o b g Danehill (USA)-Fine Honey (USA) (Drone (USA))
Miss A Armitage (Mrs F E Needham 7/5) Major R R Alers-Hankey

Placings:0/3501/52P/5FP114/040/130P14/P320/3P-44   (4308)
2003/04: 25⁴G, 24⁴G,

		Starts	1st	2nd	3rd	Win & Pl
Chases		2	0	0	0	420
Career Total		31	5	2	4	20584
107	2/00 Muss	2m4f E(0-115)HCh	GD			£4550
101	10/99 Hexm	2m110y F(0-100)HCh	GD			£2862
100	3/98 Hexm	2m110y E Ch	GD			£3284
107	3/98 Catt	2m3f E Ch	G-S			£2979
106	2/96 Muss	2m E Hdl	G-F			£2154
			Total win prize-money			£15831

Going:	Sf: 0-0 GS: 0-0 Gd: 0-1 GF: - Fm: 0-1
Distance:	2m/2m3: 0-0 2m4-2m7: 0-0 3m+: 0-1
Track:	LH: 0-1 RH: 0-1 Tight: 0-0 Gall: 0-0
Aids:	Bl: 0-0 Vi: 0-0 Tstrap: 0-0 Ckp: 0-0
Best Rating:	107 2/00 Muss 2m4f good Ch

Royal Emperor (IRE)
120(116h)   (156h)163+
8-y-o gr g Roselier (FR)-Boreen Bro (Boreen (FR))
Mrs S J Smith Widdop Wanderers

Placings:30/03P/6F243/1121122-21F12F   (4642)
2003/04: 25²G, 22¹S, 24⁴GS, 25¹S, 24²G, 25⁴G,

		Starts	1st	2nd	3rd	Win & Pl
Hurdles		1	0	1	0	6600
Chases		5	2	1	0	55161
Career Total		23	6	6	3	123002
163	2/04 Weth	3m1f A Ch	SFT			£20825
128	12/03 Kels	2m6f110yE Ch	SFT			£3536
147	2/03 Hayd	2m7f110yB HHdl	G-S			£12651
143	12/02 Weth	2m7f C(0-130)HHdl	HVY			£6812
125	11/02 Carl	3m110y E Hdl	G-S			£3591
115	10/02 Carl	3m110y E Hdl	SFT			£3262
			Total win prize-money			£50678

Going:	Sf: 2-2 GS: 0-1 Gd: 0-3 GF: - Fm: 0-1
Distance:	2m/2m3: 0-0 2m4-2m7: 1-1 3m+: 1-5
Track:	LH: 2-6 RH: 0-0 Tight: 1-2 Gall: 0-1
Aids:	Bl: 0-0 Vi: 0-0 Tstrap: 0-0 Ckp: 0-0
Best Rating:	163 3/04 Chel 3m110y good Ch

Smart chaser; smart staying novice hurdler; narrow runner-up in Pertemps Handicap Final at Cheltenham in 2003; beaten by top-class novice when runner-up in a Grade One at Aintree; winner at Kelso and Wetherby (Grade 2) over fences before finishing second in the SunAlliance; fell at Aintree; handles fast ground but is best suited by soft ground; stays three miles; tough and genuine.

Royal Feelings
(70h)
10-y-o b g Feelings (FR)-Wedderburn (Royalty)
Mrs J C McGregor Capt Ben Coutts

Placings:0600/5404/00/4224F-4   (0253)
2003/04: 24⁴G,

	Starts	1st	2nd	3rd	Win & Pl
Chases	1	0	0	0	519
Career Total	16	0	2	0	3917

Going:	Sf: 0-0 GS: 0-0 Gd: 0-1 GF: - Fm: 0-0
Distance:	2m/2m3: 0-0 2m4-2m7: 0-0 3m+: 0-1
Track:	LH: 0-0 RH: 0-1 Tight: 0-0 Gall: 0-0
Aids:	Bl: 0-0 Vi: 0-0 Tstrap: 0-0 Ckp: 0-0
Best Rating:	85 10/99 Kels 2m110y good Hdl

Maiden hurdler/ chaser.

Royal Fontenailles (FR)

68   41

5-y-o ch g Tel Quel (FR)-Sissi Fontenailles (FR) (Pampabird)
R H Buckler The Ever Smiling Partnership

Placings:6   (1361)
2003/04: 16⁵GF,

	Starts	1st	2nd	3rd	Win & Pl
Hurdles	1	0	0	0	0
Career Total	1	0	0	0	0

Going:	Sf: 0-0 GS: 0-0 Gd: 0-0 GF: - Fm: 0-1
Distance:	2m/2m3: 0-1 2m4-2m7: 0-0 3m+: 0-0
Track:	LH: 0-1 RH: 0-0 Tight: 0-0 Gall: 0-0
Aids:	Bl: 0-0 Vi: 0-0 Tstrap: 0-0 Ckp: 0-0
Best Rating:	41 9/03 Worc 2m gd-fm Hdl

Royal Gillie

77   24

7-y-o br m Royal Fountain-Gilmanscleuch (IRE) (Mandalus)
Mrs J K M Oliver Miss J S Peat

Placings:0-00   (4685)
2003/04: 16⁹G, 16⁶G,

	Starts	1st	2nd	3rd	Win & Pl
NH Flat	1	0	0	0	0
Hurdles	1	0	0	0	0
Career Total	3	0	0	0	0

Going:	Sf: 0-0 GS: 0-0 Gd: 0-1 GF: - Fm: 0-1
Distance:	2m/2m3: 0-2 2m4-2m7: 0-0 3m+: 0-0
Track:	LH: 0-2 RH: 0-0 Tight: 0-1 Gall: 0-0
Aids:	Bl: 0-0 Vi: 0-0 Tstrap: 0-0 Ckp: 0-0
Best Rating:	71 4/03 Hexm 2m110y good NHF

Royal Hector (GER)

101   100

5-y-o b g Hector Protector (USA)-Rudolfina (CAN) (Pleasant Colony (USA))
A G Hobbs Three Counties Racing 2

Placings:25500-0044555400   (4917)
2003/04: 20⁹G, 16⁹G, 16⁴G, 17⁴GS, 16⁵GS, 20⁵GS, 19⁵G, 19⁴G, 21⁹G, 20⁴GS,

	Starts	1st	2nd	3rd	Win & Pl
Hurdles	10	0	0	0	704
Career Total	15	0	1	0	2096

Going:	Sf: 0-0 GS: 0-4 Gd: 0-6 GF: - Fm: 0-0
Distance:	2m/2m3: 0-5 2m4-2m7: 0-5 3m+: 0-0

Track:	LH: 0-6 RH: 0-4 Tight: 0-3 Gall: 0-3
Aids:	Bl: 0-0 Vi: 0-0 Tstrap: 0-0 Ckp: 0-0
Best Rating:	100 12/03 Winc 2m good Hdl

Moderate hurdler; second on jumps debut in Britain, but regressive form since; yet to prove he stays beyond two miles.

Royal Indulgence

66   26

4-y-o b g Royal Applause-Silent Indulgence (USA) (Woodman (USA))
M Dods Payne Riddell and Monk

Placings:0   (1355)
2003/04: 17⁰G,

	Starts	1st	2nd	3rd	Win & Pl
Hurdles	1	0	0	0	
Career Total	1	0	0	0	

Going:	Sf: 0-0 GS: 0-0 Gd: 0-1 GF: - Fm: 0-0
Distance:	2m/2m3: 0-1 2m4-2m7: 0-0 3m+: 0-0
Track:	LH: 0-1 RH: 0-0 Tight: 0-1 Gall: 0-0
Aids:	Bl: 0-0 Vi: 0-0 Tstrap: 0-0 Ckp: 0-0
Best Rating:	33 9/03 Bang 2m1f good Hdl

Royal Katidoki (FR)

108   111

4-y-o b g Rochesson (FR)-Miss Coco (FR) (Bay Comeau (FR))
N J Henderson (B Barbier 17/9) Anthony Speelman

Placings:22   (3894)
2003/04: 18⁴VS, 16²GS,

	Starts	1st	2nd	3rd	Win & Pl
Hurdles	2	0	2	0	9588
Career Total	2	0	2	0	9588

Going:	Sf: 0-0 GS: 0-1 Gd: 0-0 GF: - Fm: 0-0
Distance:	2m/2m3: 0-2 2m4-2m7: 0-0 3m+: 0-0
Track:	LH: 0-0 RH: 0-1 Tight: 0-0 Gall: 0-0
Aids:	Bl: 0-0 Vi: 0-0 Tstrap: 0-0 Ckp: 0-0
Best Rating:	118 2/04 Sand 2m110y gd-sft Hdl

Modest hurdler; ex-French; placed over 13 furlongs on the level and second on only start over hurdles in France in Listed event in September on soft ground over 2m2f; runner-up at Sandown on British debut; acts on soft.

Royal Maid (FR)

96   94+

6-y-o b g Bakharoff (USA)-Swimming Maid (FR) (Esprit Du Nord (USA))
J G M O'Shea (O Sherwood 6/2) Arthur Watling

Placings:302300   (4246)
2003/04: 16³GS, 16⁰GF, 16²GS, 19³HY, 19⁰GS, 17⁰GF,

	Starts	1st	2nd	3rd	Win & Pl
NH Flat	2	0	0	1	272
Hurdles	4	0	1	1	1021
Career Total	6	0	1	2	1293

Going:	Sf: 0-1 GS: 0-2 Gd: 0-0 GF: - Fm: 0-3
Distance:	2m/2m3: 0-4 2m4-2m7: 0-2 3m+: 0-0
Track:	LH: 0-2 RH: 0-4 Tight: 0-0 Gall: 0-0
Aids:	Bl: 0-0 Vi: 0-0 Tstrap: 0-0 Ckp: 0-0
Best Rating:	94 2/04 Hrld 2m3f110y heavy Hdl

Plating-class hurdler; placed in bumpers; stays 2m 4f.

Royal Niece (IRE)

78   70

5-y-o b m Rakaposhi King-Sister Stephanie (IRE) (Phardante (FR))
D J Wintle M & J Gent, C White, Mrs M Turner

Placings:30   (4692)
2003/04: 16³GS, 17⁰G,

	Starts	1st	2nd	3rd	Win & Pl
NH Flat	1	0	0	1	279
Hurdles	1	0	0	0	0
Career Total	2	0	0	1	279

Going:	Sf: 0-0 GS: 0-1 Gd: 0-1 GF: - Fm: 0-0
Distance:	2m/2m3: 0-2 2m4-2m7: 0-0 3m+: 0-0
Track:	LH: 0-0 RH: 0-2 Tight: 0-0 Gall: 0-0
Aids:	Bl: 0-0 Vi: 0-0 Tstrap: 0-0 Ckp: 0-0
Best Rating:	70 4/04 Extr 2m1f good Hdl

Royal Paradise (FR)

113f   127f

4-y-o b g Cadoudal (FR)-Crystalza (FR) (Crystal Palace (FR))
F Doumen Marc De Chambure

Placings:14   (4400)
2003/04: 16¹GS, 16⁴G,

	Starts	1st	2nd	3rd	Win & Pl
NH Flat	2	1	0	0	4422
Career Total	2	1	0	0	4422
110 2/04 Sand 2m110y H NHF				G-S	£2422
Total win prize-money £2422					

Going:	Sf: 0-0 GS: 1-1 Gd: 0-1 GF: - Fm: 0-0
Distance:	2m/2m3: 1-2 2m4-2m7: 0-0 3m+: 0-0
Track:	LH: 0-1 RH: 1-1 Tight: 0-0 Gall: 0-0
Aids:	Bl: 0-0 Vi: 0-0 Tstrap: 0-0 Ckp: 0-0
Best Rating:	127 3/04 Chel 2m110y good NHF

French-trained bumper performer; winner at Sandown on debut before fourth in Festival bumper; acts on good and easy ground.

Royal Plum

8-y-o ch g Inchinor-Miss Plum (Ardross)
S J Robinson S J Robinson

Placings:6/210/0501245/0-R   (4392)
2003/04: 27⁰G,

	Starts	1st	2nd	3rd	Win & Pl
Chases	1	0	0	0	
Career Total	13	2	2	0	6357
98 1/02 Muss 3m		E(0-105)HHdl	GD		£3514
111 7/00 Worc 2m		H NHF	GD		£1456
Total win prize-money £4970					

Going:	Sf: 0-0 GS: 0-0 Gd: 0-1 GF: - Fm: 0-0
Distance:	2m/2m3: 0-0 2m4-2m7: 0-0 3m+: 0-1
Track:	LH: 0-1 RH: 0-0 Tight: 0-1 Gall: 0-0
Aids:	Bl: 0-1 Vi: 0-0 Tstrap: 0-0 Ckp: 0-0
Best Rating:	111 7/00 Worc 2m good NHF

Royal Predica (FR)

99   147

10-y-o ch g Tip Moss (FR)-Girl Vamp (FR) (Kaldoun (FR))
M C Pipe P A Deal, J S Dale & A Stennett

Placings:1/344F2131P/4211FF/2PPP/2122P500/10P-0P5F0   (4965)

2003/04: 26⁶GS, 24⁷S, 20⁵G, 24⁶G, 29⁹GF,

	Starts	1st	2nd	3rd	Win & Pl
Chases	5	0	0	0	519
Career Total	36	7	6	2	114035
146	3/03	Chel	3m110y	B(0-140)HCh	GD	£29000
142	6/01	NAbb	2m5f110yD(0-125)HCh	GD	£4085
147	2/00	Wwck	2m4f	B(0-140)HCh	SFT	£8784
129	1/00	Wwck	2m4f	C(0-135)HCh	SFT	£7117
136	4/99	Aint	2m4f	C HCh	G-S	£11235
98	1/99	Plum	2m	E Ch	HVY	£2915
	7/97	Diep	1m7f	Hdl	FRM	£3591

Total win prize-money £66728

Going:	Sf: 0-1 GS: 0-1 Gd: 0-2 GF: - Fm: 0-1
Distance:	2m/2m3: 0-0 2m4-2m7: 0-1 3m+: 0-4
Track:	LH: 0-2 RH: 0-3 Tight: 0-0 Gall: 0-2
Aids:	Bl: 0-0 Vi: 0-0 Tstrap: 0-5 Ckp: 0-0
Best Rating:	147 12/00 Asct 3m110y soft Ch

Useful chaser when on song; ran out a surprise winner of the Kim Muir at the 2003 Cheltenham Festival; failed to stay in the National next time, and well held in 2004; stays three miles well; suited by good or softer ground; wears a tongue strap.

Royal Prodigy (USA)
98   92

5-y-o ch g Royal Academy (USA)-Prospector's Queen (USA) (Mr Prospector (USA))
R J Hodges (M C Pipe 8/10) The Gardens Entertainments Ltd

Placings:33P10612PF   (4673)
2003/04: 16³G, 17³G, 17⁶G, 16¹G, 17⁰G, 16⁶GF, 17¹F, 19²GF, 22²GS, 16⁶G,

	Starts	1st	2nd	3rd	Win & Pl
Hurdles	10	2	1	2	6928
Career Total	10	2	1	2	6928
90	9/03	Extr	2m1f	G(0-95)HHdl	FRM	£2226
78	7/03	Strf	2m110y	G Hdl	GD	£2982

Total win prize-money £5208

Going:	Sf: 0-0 GS: 0-1 Gd: 1-6 GF: - Fm: 1-3
Distance:	2m/2m3: 2-9 2m4-2m7: 0-1 3m+: 0-0
Track:	LH: 1-5 RH: 1-5 Tight: 1-3 Gall: 0-0
Aids:	Bl: 0-0 Vi: 0-1 Tstrap: 0-0 Ckp: 0-0
Best Rating:	94 10/03 Extr 2m3f gd-fm Hdl

Plating-class hurdler; plater on the Flat; got off the mark when dropped to selling grade at Stratford in July 2003 and won again at Exeter; acts on a sound surface.

Royal Rackeen

7-y-o b m Rakaposhi King-Snippet (Ragstone)
D McCain D McCain

Placings:0-0   (0291)
2003/04: 16⁰G, 16⁶G,

	Starts	1st	2nd	3rd	Win & Pl
NH Flat	1	0	0	0	0
Hurdles	1	0	0	0	0
Career Total	2	0	0	0	

Going:	Sf: 0-0 GS: 0-0 Gd: 0-2 GF: - Fm: 0-0
Distance:	2m/2m3: 0-2 2m4-2m7: 0-0 3m+: 0-0
Track:	LH: 0-2 RH: 0-0 Tight: 0-0 Gall: 0-0
Aids:	Bl: 0-0 Vi: 0-0 Tstrap: 0-0 Ckp: 0-0
Best Rating:	34 4/03 Hexm 2m110y good NHF

Royal Reference
(77h)   (64h)

8-y-o br m Royal Fountain-Cross Reference (Oats)
J E Brockbank Mrs J E Brockbank

Placings:0PP   (3370)
2003/04: 17⁰HY, 24⁸PS, 25⁸PS,

	Starts	1st	2nd	3rd	Win & Pl
Hurdles	2	0	0	0	0
Chases	1	0	0	0	0
Career Total	3	0	0	0	

Going:	Sf: 0-3 GS: 0-0 Gd: 0-0 GF: - Fm: 0-0
Distance:	2m/2m3: 0-1 2m4-2m7: 0-0 3m+: 0-2
Track:	LH: 0-2 RH: 0-1 Tight: 0-0 Gall: 0-0
Aids:	Bl: 0-0 Vi: 0-0 Tstrap: 0-0 Ckp: 0-0
Best Rating:	64 11/03 Carl 2m1f heavy Hdl

Royal Rocket (IRE)
87   46

7-y-o b m King's Ride-Carol's Cracker (IRE) (Persian Mews)
Miss Venetia Williams Miss L M Rochford

Placings:5-P0P0   (4712)
2003/04: 21⁸PG, 19⁰GS, 21⁸GS, 24⁰G,

	Starts	1st	2nd	3rd	Win & Pl
Hurdles	4	0	0	0	0
Career Total	5	0	0	0	0

Going:	Sf: 0-0 GS: 0-2 Gd: 0-2 GF: - Fm: 0-0
Distance:	2m/2m3: 0-0 2m4-2m7: 0-3 3m+: 0-1
Track:	LH: 0-0 RH: 0-4 Tight: 0-0 Gall: 0-0
Aids:	Bl: 0-0 Vi: 0-0 Tstrap: 0-0 Ckp: 0-0
Best Rating:	75 3/03 Hayd 2m gd-fm NHF

Royal Rosa (FR)
111   157

5-y-o ch g Garde Royale-Crystalza (FR) (Crystal Palace (FR))
J Howard Johnson (N J Henderson 30/4) Andrea & Graham Wylie

Placings:161-112112   (4623)
2003/04: 16¹G, 24¹S, 23²G, 20¹HY, 23¹G, 24²G,

	Starts	1st	2nd	3rd	Win & Pl
NH Flat	1	1	0	0	12662
Hurdles	5	3	2	0	43556
Career Total	9	6	2	0	61408
145	2/04	Hayd	2m7f110yA Hdl	GD	£17850
127	1/04	Ayr	2m4f	E Hdl	HVY	£3562
110	12/03	Hexm	3m	E Hdl	SFT	£2343
123	4/03	Punc	2m	NHF	GD	£12662
123	3/03	Sand	2m110y	H NHF	HVY	£2383
98	12/02	Newb	1m4f110yH NHF	GD	£2807

Total win prize-money £41609

Going:	Sf: 2-2 GS: 0-0 Gd: 2-4 GF: - Fm: 0-0
Distance:	2m/2m3: 1-1 2m4-2m7: 1-1 3m+: 2-4
Track:	LH: 3-5 RH: 1-1 Tight: 0-1 Gall: 0-0
Aids:	Bl: 0-0 Vi: 0-0 Tstrap: 0-0 Ckp: 0-0
Best Rating:	157 4/04 Aint 3m110y good Hdl

Very useful novice hurdler; smart bumper performer; winner of the 2003 Punchestown bumper; sold for 340,000gns afterwards; acts on good ground or softer; beat a modest field with plenty in hand on hurdles debut over three miles at Hexham in December, and followed up with a cracking effort to chase home Sh Boom at Haydock; did not have to improve to win at Ayr in January; followed up returned to

novices' company at Haydock in February when beating Fundamentalist; only one to give Iris's Gift a race at Aintree; suited by three miles; may prove best on easy ground.

Royal Satin (IRE)

6-y-o b g Royal Academy (USA)-Satinette (Shirley Heights)
B Mactaggart B Mactaggart

Placings:FP   (2089)
2003/04: 16⁵G, 16⁶G,

	Starts	1st	2nd	3rd	Win & Pl
Hurdles	2	0	0	0	
Career Total	2	0	0	0	

Going:	Sf: 0-0 GS: 0-0 Gd: 0-2 GF: - Fm: 0-0
Distance:	2m/2m3: 0-2 2m4-2m7: 0-0 3m+: 0-0
Track:	LH: 0-2 RH: 0-0 Tight: 0-2 Gall: 0-0
Aids:	Bl: 0-0 Vi: 0-0 Tstrap: 0-0 Ckp: 0-0

Royal Shakespeare (FR)
114   145+

5-y-o b g King's Theatre (IRE)-Persian Walk (FR) (Persian Bold)
S Gollings J B Webb

Placings:111   (4638)
2003/04: 17¹GS, 19¹G, 16¹G,

	Starts	1st	2nd	3rd	Win & Pl
Hurdles	3	3	0	0	39439
Career Total	3	3	0	0	39439
145	4/04	Aint	2m110y	A Hdl	GD	£29000
119	3/04	Donc	2m3f110yC Hdl	GD	£6987
113	2/04	Sedg	2m1f	E Hdl	G-S	£3451

Total win prize-money £39440

Going:	Sf: 0-0 GS: 1-1 Gd: 2-2 GF: - Fm: 0-0
Distance:	2m/2m3: 2-2 2m4-2m7: 1-1 3m+: 0-0
Track:	LH: 3-3 RH: 0-0 Tight: 2-2 Gall: 0-0
Aids:	Bl: 0-0 Vi: 0-0 Tstrap: 0-0 Ckp: 0-0
Best Rating:	145 4/04 Aint 2m110y good Hdl

Promising novice hurdler; former winning handicapper on the Flat in Dubai; took two minor events prior to a narrow success in Grade Two at Aintree; stays two and a half miles; acts on most types of ground; progressive and will make a chaser.

Royal Twist (USA)
86   63

4-y-o ch g Royal Academy (USA)-Musical Twist (USA) (Woodman (USA))
J S Wainwright (T P Tate 9/9) J S Wainwright

Placings:6   (1904)
2003/04: 16⁶GF,

	Starts	1st	2nd	3rd	Win & Pl
Hurdles	1	0	0	0	0
Career Total	1	0	0	0	0

Going:	Sf: 0-0 GS: 0-0 Gd: 0-0 GF: - Fm: 0-1
Distance:	2m/2m3: 0-1 2m4-2m7: 0-0 3m+: 0-0
Track:	LH: 0-0 RH: 0-1 Tight: 0-0 Gall: 0-1
Aids:	Bl: 0-0 Vi: 0-0 Tstrap: 0-0 Ckp: 0-0
Best Rating:	63 11/03 Hntg 2m110y gd-fm Hdl

Royal Variety (IRE)

87+

6-y-o gr g Roselier (FR)-Private Dancer (Deep Run)
L Lungo Elite Racing Club

Placings:3   (3212)
2003/04: 20³GS,

	Starts	1st	2nd	3rd	Win & Pl
Hurdles	1	0	0	1	684
Career Total	1	0	0	1	684

Going:	Sf: 0-0 GS: 0-1 Gd: 0-0 GF: - Fm: 0-0
Distance:	2m/2m3: 0-0 2m4-2m7: 0-1 3m+: 0-0
Track:	LH: 0-1 RH: 0-0 Tight: 0-0 Gall: 0-0
Aids:	Bl: 0-0 Vi: 0-0 Tstrap: 0-0 Ckp: 0-0
Best Rating:	88 1/04 Weth 2m4f110y gd-sft Hdl

Novice hurdler; showed ability when distant third on belated debut at Wetherby in January; should stay well; can improve.

Royal Whisper

74f   **34f**

5-y-o b g Prince Of Birds (USA)-Hush It Up (Tina's Pet)
R Ford The Haydock Club

Placings:0   (4264)
2003/04: 16⁰GF,

	Starts	1st	2nd	3rd	Win & Pl
NH Flat	1	0	0	0	
Career Total	1	0	0	0	

Going:	Sf: 0-0 GS: 0-0 Gd: 0-0 GF: - Fm: 0-1
Distance:	2m/2m3: 0-1 2m4-2m7: 0-0 3m+: 0-0
Track:	LH: 0-1 RH: 0-0 Tight: 0-0 Gall: 0-0
Aids:	Bl: 0-0 Vi: 0-0 Tstrap: 0-0 Ckp: 0-0
Best Rating:	34 3/04 Catt 2m gd-fm NHF

Royale Acadou (FR)

89   **92+**

6-y-o b/br m Cadoudal (FR)-Girl Vamp (FR) (Kaldoun (FR))
Miss L J Sheen (B Barbier 29/2) Mrs P J Sheen

Placings:0F0643310/00242600220-0PP5603004   (4930)
2003/04: 18⁰VS, 21ᴾVS, 22ᴾVS, 18⁵HO, 18⁶HO, 18⁰S, 18³S, 16⁰S, 18⁰S, 22⁴G,

	Starts	1st	2nd	3rd	Win & Pl
Hurdles	5	0	0	1	3769
Chases	5	0	0	0	314
Career Total	30	1	4	3	45632
	3/02 Autl 2m1f110y Hdl		HVY £11779
		Total win prize-money £11779

Going:	Sf: 0-4 GS: 0-0 Gd: 0-1 GF: - Fm: 0-0
Distance:	2m/2m3: 0-7 2m4-2m7: 0-3 3m+: 0-0
Track:	LH: 0-2 RH: 0-0 Tight: 0-1 Gall: 0-0
Aids:	Bl: 0-5 Vi: 0-0 Tstrap: 0-0 Ckp: 0-0
Best Rating:	92 4/04 Font 2m6f good Ch

Royale Angela (FR)

12-y-o ch g Garde Royale-Santa Angela (FR) (Son Of Silver)
C Roberts S N Shinton

Placings:126F3/2111120/020/10015P4/**22P**03/PP-PP
                                                              (0549)
2003/04: 21ᴾGF, 27ᴾGF,

		Starts	1st	2nd	3rd	Win & Pl
Hurdles		2	0	0	0	
Career Total		31	7	6	2	35865
128	2/00 Newc 3m	D(0-125)HHdl		SFT	£2879
125	11/99 NAbb 2m6f	D(0-125)HHdl		SFT	£2983
127	2/98 Uttx	2m6f110yC(0-135)HHdl	SFT	£10942
118	1/98 Plum	D(0-125)HHdl	HVY	£2910
105	12/97 Plum 2m4f	F(0-105)HHdl	SFT	£1970
106	12/97 Worc 2m4f	D(0-125)HHdl	SFT	£2756
106	10/95 Bang 2m1f	D Hdl	G-S	£2920
		Total win prize-money £27363

Going:	Sf: 0-0 GS: 0-0 Gd: 0-0 GF: - Fm: 0-2
Distance:	2m/2m3: 0-0 2m4-2m7: 0-1 3m+: 0-1
Track:	LH: 0-2 RH: 0-0 Tight: 0-1 Gall: 0-0
Aids:	Bl: 0-0 Vi: 0-1 Tstrap: 0-0 Ckp: 0-0
Best Rating:	133 3/00 Chel 3m1f110y good Hdl

Royale Pearl

91   **94+**

4-y-o gr f Cloudings (IRE)-Ivy Edith (Blakeney)
R Ingram Glen Antill

Placings:34   (3432)
2003/04: 17³G, 16⁴GS,

	Starts	1st	2nd	3rd	Win & Pl
Hurdles	2	0	0	1	803
Career Total	2	0	0	1	803

Going:	Sf: 0-0 GS: 0-1 Gd: 0-1 GF: - Fm: 0-0
Distance:	2m/2m3: 0-2 2m4-2m7: 0-0 3m+: 0-0
Track:	LH: 0-1 RH: 0-1 Tight: 0-2 Gall: 0-0
Aids:	Bl: 0-0 Vi: 0-0 Tstrap: 0-0 Ckp: 0-0
Best Rating:	94 11/03 Folk 2m1f110y good Hdl

Plating-class hurdler; maiden on the Flat; third having made the running on hurdles debut on good ground.

Royaleety (FR)

                                                                  131

5-y-o b g Garde Royale-La Grive (FR) (Pharly (FR))
Ian Williams (T Civel 2/11) Mr & Mrs John Poynton

Placings:11/131312105P-011510FPU   (4848)
2003/04: 18⁰VS, 17¹VS, 17¹VS, 20⁵VS, 19¹VS, 22⁰VS, 20⁶GS, 16⁰G, 16ᵁGS,

	Starts	1st	2nd	3rd	Win & Pl
Hurdles	1	0	0	0	0
Chases	8	3	0	0	51571
Career Total	21	9	1	2	227717
	10/03 Engh 2m3f	Ch		VS	£18078
	9/03 Autl 2m1f110y	Ch		VS	£14338
	9/03 Autl 2m1f	Ch		VS	£15584
	11/02 Autl 2m	Hdl		HVY	£57975
	9/02 Autl 2m2f	Hdl		VS	£19141
	6/02 Autl 2m1f110y	Hdl		VS	£30920
	5/02 Autl 1m7f	Hdl		VS	£11779
	4/02 Autl 1m7f	Hdl		VS	£11779
	3/02 Autl 1m7f	Hdl		HLD	£13546
		Total win prize-money £193140

Going:	Sf: 0-0 GS: 0-2 Gd: 0-1 GF: - Fm: 0-0
Distance:	2m/2m3: 3-6 2m4-2m7: 0-3 3m+: 0-0
Track:	LH: 0-4 RH: 0-0 Tight: 0-0 Gall: 0-1
Aids:	Bl: 0-0 Vi: 0-0 Tstrap: 0-0 Ckp: 0-0
Best Rating:	131 4/04 Ayr 2m gd-sft Ch

Novice chaser; Grade 1 hurdle winner and Listed chase winner in France; in the process of running well when coming to grief on first start for Ian Williams at Ayr in February; handles testing ground; likely to win more races; has worn a tongue tie.

Royalentertainment (IRE)

83f   **97+f**

6-y-o b/br m King's Ride-Spring Fiddler (IRE) (Fidel)
J R Best D S Nevison

Placings:1   (3426)
2003/04: 17¹HY,

	Starts	1st	2nd	3rd	Win & Pl
NH Flat	1	1	0	0	1918
Career Total	1	1	0	0	1918
97	1/04 Folk 2m1f110yH NHF		HVY	£1918
	Total win prize-money £1918

Going:	Sf: 1-1 GS: 0-0 Gd: 0-0 GF: - Fm: 0-0
Distance:	2m/2m3: 1-1 2m4-2m7: 0-0 3m+: 0-0
Track:	LH: 0-0 **RH: 1-1 Tight: 1-1** Gall: 0-0
Aids:	Bl: 0-0 Vi: 0-0 Tstrap: 0-0 Ckp: 0-0
Best Rating:	97 1/04 Folk 2m1f110y heavy NHF

From decent jumping family; won mares-only bumper on debut; acts on soft ground.

Royaloutlook

                                                                  77

7-y-o br g Royal Fountain-Broad Outlook (Broadsword (USA))
G A Harker Malcolm Smith

Placings:404P-1   (1684)
2003/04: 16¹GF,

	Starts	1st	2nd	3rd	Win & Pl
Hurdles	1	1	0	0	3808
Career Total	5	1	0	0	3808
91	10/03 Kels 2m	E Hdl		G-F	£3808
	Total win prize-money £3808

Going:	Sf: 0-0 GS: 0-0 Gd: 0-0 GF: - Fm: 1-1
Distance:	2m/2m3: 1-1 2m4-2m7: 0-0 3m+: 0-0
Track:	LH: 0-0 RH: 0-0 Tight: 0-0 Gall: 0-0
Aids:	Bl: 0-0 Vi: 0-0 Tstrap: 0-0 **Ckp: 1-1**
Best Rating:	91 10/03 Kels 2m gd-fm Hdl

Modest form in bumpers and over hurdles; gifted hurdle race where only two finished at Kelso in October; acts on fast ground.

Royaltino (IRE)

12-y-o b g Neltino-Royal Well (Royal Vulcan)
Miss T McCurrich Miss T McCurrich

Placings:1/2F310/11/2136/022P/P2-P   (3824)
2003/04: 22ᴾS,

	Starts	1st	2nd	3rd	Win & Pl
Chases	1	0	0	0	
Career Total	19	5	5	2	64007
	10/98 Engh 2m3f	Ch		VS	£15152
	4/98 Engh 2m3f	Hdl		HVY	£10101
	3/98 Vire 2m3f	Hdl		HLD	£3030
117	2/97 Kemp 2m5f	D Hdl		GD	£2969
103	2/96 Wwck 2m	H NHF		GD	£1867
	Total win prize-money £33119

Going:	Sf: 0-1 GS: 0-0 Gd: 0-0 GF: - Fm: 0-0
Distance:	2m/2m3: 0-0 2m4-2m7: 0-1 3m+: 0-0
Track:	LH: 0-1 RH: 0-0 Tight: 0-0 Gall: 0-0
Aids:	Bl: 0-0 Vi: 0-0 Tstrap: 0-0 Ckp: 0-0
Best Rating:	119 3/97 Chel 2m5f gd-fm Hdl

Modest hunter chaser; acts in soft ground; former useful hurdler when trained in France.

Roymillon (GER)

(108h) (87 h)
10-y-o b g Milesius (USA)-Royal Slope (USA) (His Majesty (USA))
D J Wintle John W Egan/graham Brown

Placings:005/06551403/514-6 (4916)
2003/04: 23⁶GS,

	Starts	1st	2nd	3rd	Win & Pl
Chases	1	0	0	0	0
Career Total	15	2	0	1	4834
87 9/02 Hntg	3m2f	F(0-90)HHdl		G-F	2234
85 7/01 Worc	3m	F(0-100)HHdl		G-F	£1946
		Total win prize-money £4180			

Going:	Sf: 0-0 GS: 0-1 Gd: 0-0 GF: - Fm: 0-0
Distance:	2m/2m3: 0-0 2m4-2m7: 0-0 3m+: 0-1
Track:	LH: 0-1 RH: 0-0 Tight: 0-1 Gall: 0-0
Aids:	Bl: 0-0 Vi: 0-0 Tstrap: 0-0 Ckp: 0-0
Best Rating:	87 9/02 Hntg 3m2f gd-fm Hdl

Roznic (FR)

105f 98+f
6-y-o b g Nikos-Rozamie (FR) (Azimut (FR))
P Winkworth P Winkworth

Placings:343 (4571)
2003/04: 16³GS, 16⁴G, 17³GS,

	Starts	1st	2nd	3rd	Win & Pl
NH Flat	3	0	0	2	653
Career Total	3	0	0	2	653

Going:	Sf: 0-0 GS: 0-2 Gd: 0-1 GF: - Fm: 0-0
Distance:	2m/2m3: 0-3 2m4-2m7: 0-0 3m+: 0-0
Track:	LH: 0-1 RH: 0-2 Tight: 0-1 Gall: 0-0
Aids:	Bl: 0-0 Vi: 0-0 Tstrap: 0-0 Ckp: 0-0
Best Rating:	98 3/04 Bang 2m1f gd-sft NHF

Rubberdubber

98f 97+f
4-y-o b g Teenoso (USA)-True Clown (True Song)
C R Egerton Mr & Mrs Peter Orton

Placings:1 (4550)
2003/04: 16¹GS,

	Starts	1st	2nd	3rd	Win & Pl
NH Flat	1	1	0	0	2387
Career Total	1	1	0	0	2387
97 3/04 Winc	2m	H NHF		G-S	£2387
		Total win prize-money £2387			

Going:	Sf: 0-0 GS: 0-0 Gd: 1-1 GF: 0-0 GF: - Fm: 0-0
Distance:	2m/2m3: 1-1 2m4-2m7: 0-0 3m+: 0-0
Track:	LH: 0-0 RH: 1-1 Tight: 0-0 Gall: 0-0
Aids:	Bl: 0-0 Vi: 0-0 Tstrap: 0-0 Ckp: 0-0
Best Rating:	97 3/04 Winc 2m gd-sft NHF

Bumper winner on easy ground.

Ruby Dante (IRE)

95f 82f
6-y-o b m Ajraad (USA)-Phar Glen (IRE) (Phardante (FR))
P Bowen M G Jones

Placings:030 (0947)
2003/04: 17⁰GF, 17³GF, 16⁰GS,

	Starts	1st	2nd	3rd	Win & Pl
NH Flat	3	0	0	1	421
Career Total	3	0	0	1	421

Showed improvement on her debut despite hanging left in the home straight when third in Newton Abbot bumper July 2003.

Ruby Gale (IRE)

106(86h) (128h)133
8-y-o b g Lord Americo-Well Over (Over The River (FR))
P F Nicholls Mrs Angela Tincknell

Placings:0/1210212/F6-202233 (3903)
2003/04: 22²G, 20⁰GS, 21²GS, 21²S, 21³GS, 24³GS,

	Starts	1st	2nd	3rd	Win & Pl
Hurdles	2	0	1	0	1439
Chases	4	0	2	2	6568
Career Total	16	3	6	2	21829
120 3/02 Extr	2m3f	E Hdl		GD	£2828
116 12/01 Extr	2m3f	E Hdl		GD	£2922
102 11/01 NAbb	2m1f	H NHF		GD	£2289
		Total win prize-money £8040			

Going:	Sf: 0-1 GS: 0-4 Gd: 0-1 GF: - Fm: 0-0
Distance:	2m/2m3: 0-0 2m4-2m7: 0-5 3m+: 0-1
Track:	LH: 0-3 RH: 0-0 Tight: 0-2 Gall: 0-1
Aids:	Bl: 0-0 Vi: 0-0 Tstrap: 0-0 Ckp: 0-0
Best Rating:	133 10/02 Extr 2m1f110y good Ch

Useful novice chaser; stays two miles six; travels well, but his jumping can be cause for concern over fences; suited to good ground; has had breathing difficulties; has worn a tongue-tie.

Ruby Glen (IRE)

75 59
6-y-o b m Insan (USA)-Le Glen (Le Bavard (FR))
B G Powell John Studd

Placings:6000 (4929)
2003/04: 17⁶GS, 18⁰HY, 20⁰G, 18⁰G,

	Starts	1st	2nd	3rd	Win & Pl
NH Flat	1	0	0	0	0
Hurdles	3	0	0	0	0
Career Total	4	0	0	0	0

Going:	Sf: 0-1 GS: 0-1 Gd: 0-2 GF: - Fm: 0-0
Distance:	2m/2m3: 0-3 2m4-2m7: 0-1 3m+: 0-0
Track:	LH: 0-2 RH: 0-1 Tight: 0-4 Gall: 0-0
Aids:	Bl: 0-0 Vi: 0-0 Tstrap: 0-0 Ckp: 0-0
Best Rating:	62 11/03 Folk 2m1f110y gd-sft NHF

Ruby Rainne

70f 61f
5-y-o gr m Perugino (USA)-Lady Shikari (Kala Shikari)
A P Jones T G N Burrage

Placings:00 (4636)
2003/04: 16⁰GS, 17⁰G,

	Starts	1st	2nd	3rd	Win & Pl
NH Flat	2	0	0	0	0
Career Total	2	0	0	0	0

Going:	Sf: 0-0 GS: 0-1 Gd: 0-0 GF: - Fm: 0-0
Distance:	2m/2m3: 0-2 2m4-2m7: 0-0 3m+: 0-0
Track:	LH: 0-0 RH: 0-1 Tight: 0-0 Gall: 0-0
Aids:	Bl: 0-0 Vi: 0-0 Tstrap: 0-0 Ckp: 0-0
Best Rating:	61 4/04 Tntn 2m1f good NHF

Ruby Too

99f 90+f
5-y-o b m El Conquistador-Ruby Flame (Tudor Flame)
J W Mullins Dr R Jowett

Placings:3140 (4550)
2003/04: 16³GF, 16⁴HY, 16⁰GS,

	Starts	1st	2nd	3rd	Win & Pl
NH Flat	4	1	0	1	1797
Career Total	4	1	0	1	1797

Going:	Sf: 0-1 GS: 0-1 Gd: 0-0 GF: - Fm: 0-1
Distance:	2m/2m3: 1-4 2m4-2m7: 0-0 3m+: 0-0
Track:	LH: 1-2 RH: 0-2 Tight: 0-0 Gall: 0-0
Aids:	Bl: 0-0 Vi: 0-0 Tstrap: 0-0 Ckp: 0-0
Best Rating:	90+ 12/02 Ling 2m std NHF

Won maiden bumper on Polytrack at Lingfield December 2003; unsuited by heavy ground at Chepstow next time; should get further over hurdles; acts on most ground.

Rubyluv

84f 63f
5-y-o ch m Rock Hopper-Hunting Cottage (Pyjama Hunt)
Miss S E Forster Mrs J Cadzow

Placings:00 (3669)
2003/04: 16⁰HY, 16⁰HY,

	Starts	1st	2nd	3rd	Win & Pl
NH Flat	2	0	0	0	
Career Total	2	0	0	0	

Going:	Sf: 0-2 GS: 0-0 Gd: 0-0 GF: - Fm: 0-0
Distance:	2m/2m3: 0-2 2m4-2m7: 0-0 3m+: 0-0
Track:	LH: 0-2 RH: 0-0 Tight: 0-0 Gall: 0-0
Aids:	Bl: 0-0 Vi: 0-0 Tstrap: 0-0 Ckp: 0-0
Best Rating:	63 1/04 Newc 2m heavy NHF

Rudetski

103(98h) (92 h)110+
7-y-o b g Rudimentary (USA)-Butosky (Busted)
M Sheppard (M Dods 2/6) M J Jordan and J N Jordan

Placings:005-524F1 (3407)
2003/04: 17⁵G, 16²G, 16⁴GF, 16⁶G, 16¹G,

	Starts	1st	2nd	3rd	Win & Pl
Hurdles	1	0	0	0	0
Chases	4	1	1	0	5551
Career Total	8	1	1	0	5551
110 1/04 Donc	2m110y	E(0-105)HCh		GD	£3939
		Total win prize-money £3939			

Going:	Sf: 0-0 GS: 0-0 Gd: 1-4 GF: - Fm: 0-0
Distance:	2m/2m3: 1-5 2m4-2m7: 0-0 3m+: 0-0
Track:	LH: 1-1 RH: 0-4 Tight: 0-3 Gall: 1-1
Aids:	Bl: 0-0 Vi: 0-0 Tstrap: 1-2 Ckp: 0-0
Best Rating:	110 1/04 Donc 2m110y good Ch

Moderate hurdler/chaser; wide margin winner of handicap chase at Doncaster in January; best over two miles; does not want the ground too soft.

Rudge Hill

77 39
8-y-o b g Almushmmir-Time After Time (High Award)

S C Burrough Martin Smith (frome)

Placings:00/P-P00P   (0990)
2003/04: 17PGF, 20QGF, 17QGF, 22PG,

	Starts	1st	2nd	3rd	Win & Pl
Hurdles	4	0	0		
Career Total	7	0	0		

Going:	Sf: 0-0 GS: 0-0 Gd: 0-0 GF: - Fm: 0-3
Distance:	2m/2m3: 0-2 2m4-2m7: 0-2 3m+: 0-0
Track:	LH: 0-3 RH: 0-1 Tight: 0-2 Gall: 0-0
Aids:	Bl: 0-0 Vi: 0-0 Tstrap: 0-0 Ckp: 0-0
Best Rating:	42 6/03 Worc 2m4f gd-fm Hdl

Rudi Knight

111(101h)   (132h)**119**
9-y-o ch g Rudimentary (USA)-Fleeting Affair (Hotfoot)
Miss Venetia Williams Derek And Jean Clee

Placings:413512362/3302122/0054/5331-316   (4562)
2003/04: 21¹S, 20³GS, 20¹G, 22⁶G,

	Starts	1st	2nd	3rd	Win & Pl
Chases	4	2	0	1	10401
Career Total	27	5	5	7	43982
112	7/03	MRas	2m4f	E Ch	GD	£4134
119	4/03	NAbb	2m5f110yD Ch	SFT	£5434
130	2/01	Kemp	2m	C(0-135)HHdl	G-S	£10676
119	1/00	Font	2m2f110yC(0-135)HHdl	G-S	£6142
107	7/99	NAbb	2m1f	E Hdl	G-F	£2671
			Total win prize-money £29058

Going:	Sf: 1-1 GS: 0-1 Gd: 1-2 GF: - Fm: 0-0
Distance:	2m/2m3: 0-0 **2m4-2m7: 2-4** 3m+: 0-0
Track:	LH: 1-3 RH: 1-1 **Tight: 2-3** Gall: 0-1
Aids:	Bl: 0-0 Vi: 0-0 Tstrap: 0-0 Ckp: 0-0
Best Rating:	138 3/01 Newb 2m110y heavy Hdl

Decent hurdler, winning novice chaser, but does not look a natural; recorded second win over fences at Market Rasen in July; stays two and a half miles; seems to act on most types of ground; often held up in his races.

Rudi's Charm

86   **52**
7-y-o b g Rudimentary (USA)-Irene's Charter (Persian Bold)
D W Thompson J A Moore

Placings:50-00   (4887)
2003/04: 22⁰G, 22⁰GF,

	Starts	1st	2nd	3rd	Win & Pl
Hurdles	2	0	0		
Career Total	4	0	0		0

Going:	Sf: 0-0 GS: 0-0 Gd: 0-0 GF: - Fm: 0-1
Distance:	2m/2m3: 0-0 2m4-2m7: 0-2 3m+: 0-0
Track:	LH: 0-2 RH: 0-0 Tight: 0-2 Gall: 0-0
Aids:	Bl: 0-0 Vi: 0-0 Tstrap: 0-0 Ckp: 0-0
Best Rating:	90 12/02 Muss 2m gd-fm NHF

Rudolf Rassendyll (IRE)

91(100h)   (103 h)**123**
9-y-o b g Supreme Leader-Chantel Rouge (Boreen (FR))
Miss Venetia Williams C R Nugent

Placings:060/51412-P15   (4941)
2003/04: 25PGS, 20¹G, 31⁵GS,

	Starts	1st	2nd	3rd	Win & Pl
Chases	3	1	0	0	5133

Career Total	11	3	1	0	15999
122	4/04	Carl	2m4f	E(0-105)HCh	GD	£4582
112	2/03	Chep	2m3f110yD(0-120)HCh	G-S	£5635
103	1/03	Hntg	2m4f110yF(0-95)HHdl	SFT	£2702
			Total win prize-money £12921

Going:	Sf: 0-0 GS: 0-2 Gd: 1-1 GF: - Fm: 0-0
Distance:	2m/2m3: 0-0 **2m4-2m7: 1-1** 3m+: 0-2
Track:	LH: 0-1 **RH: 1-1** Tight: 0-1 Gall: 0-0
Aids:	Bl: 0-0 Vi: 0-0 Tstrap: 0-0 Ckp: 0-0
Best Rating:	122 4/04 Carl 2m4f good Ch

Moderate chaser; won a novice handicap hurdle at Huntingdon in January 2003, and a handicap chase at Chepstow the following month; absent after May that year; stays two and a half miles; acts on soft ground.

Rue Du Rivoli

91f   **88f**
6-y-o ch g Rudimentary (USA)-Lovers Tryst (Castle Keep)
Lady Herries Lady Herries

Placings:450   (4787)
2003/04: 18⁴S, 18⁵HY, 16⁶G,

	Starts	1st	2nd	3rd	Win & Pl
NH Flat	3	0	0	0	0
Career Total	3	0	0	0	0

Going:	Sf: 0-2 GS: 0-0 Gd: 0-1 GF: - Fm: 0-0
Distance:	2m/2m3: 0-3 2m4-2m7: 0-0 3m+: 0-0
Track:	LH: 0-2 RH: 0-1 Tight: 0-0 Gall: 0-1
Aids:	Bl: 0-0 Vi: 0-0 Tstrap: 0-0 Ckp: 0-0
Best Rating:	88 12/03 Plum 2m2f soft NHF

Rufius (IRE)

104   **104**
11-y-o b g Celio Rufo-In View Lass (Tepukei)
P Kelsall Peter Kelsall

Placings:4000/000P3/OP055F/55240/2124216P0-
P415U4P40   (3647)
2003/04: 25PGS, 23⁴GF, 20¹GF, 20⁵GF, 32UGF, 25⁴G,
24⁴GS, 24⁹GS,

	Starts	1st	2nd	3rd	Win & Pl
Chases	9	1	0	0	5979
Career Total	38	3	4	1	30769
98	10/03	Hntg	2m4f110yE(0-110)HCh	G-F	£4095
104	12/02	Chel	3m1f110yD(0-120)HCh	SFT	£11221
100	9/02	Hntg	3m	E Ch	G-F	£3526
			Total win prize-money £18843

Going:	Sf: 0-0 GS: 0-4 Gd: 0-1 GF: - Fm: 1-4
Distance:	2m/2m3: 0-3 **2m4-2m7:** 0-0 3m+: 0-0
Track:	LH: 0-3 **RH: 1-6** Tight: 0-0 Gall: 1-4
Aids:	Bl: 0-0 Vi: 0-0 Tstrap: 0-0 Ckp: 0-0
Best Rating:	104 12/02 Chel 3m1f110y soft Ch

Moderate chaser; best at trips around two and a half to three miles; acts on a sound surface, although is effective on soft.

Rugged Man (IRE)

95   **89**
6-y-o b h Topanoora-The Grey (GER) (Pentathlon)
J G Cosgrave F Thompson

Placings:0/35004301-P2052   (0862a)
2003/04: 20PYS, 16²G, 16⁰F, 16⁵H, 16²F,

	Starts	1st	2nd	3rd	Win & Pl
Hurdles	5	0	2	0	2328
Career Total	14	1	2	2	7770
89	4/03	Slig	2m	Hdl	GD	£4480

Total win prize-money £4481

Going:	Sf: 0-0 GS: 0-0 Gd: 0-1 GF: - Fm: 0-3
Distance:	2m/2m3: 0-4 2m4-2m7: 0-1 3m+: 0-0
Track:	LH: 0-1 RH: 0-0 Tight: 0-0 Gall: 0-0
Aids:	Bl: 0-5 Vi: 0-0 Tstrap: 0-0 Ckp: 0-0
Best Rating:	90 5/03 Hexm 2m110y good Hdl

Poor novice hurdler; acts on fast ground.

Rugged River (IRE)

99   **137**
9-y-o b g Over The River (FR)-Early Dalus (IRE) (Mandalus)
R H Alner Miss H J Flower

Placings:351P/13PP3-2   (2445)
2003/04: 28²S,

	Starts	1st	2nd	3rd	Win & Pl
Chases	1	0	1	0	2180
Career Total	10	2	1	3	24165
133	11/02	NAbb	3m2f110yC(0-130)HCh	HVY	£7368
130	12/00	Extr	3m1f110yC Ch	HVY	£7805
			Total win prize-money £15173

Going:	Sf: 0-1 GS: 0-0 Gd: 0-0 GF: - Fm: 0-0
Distance:	2m/2m3: 0-0 2m4-2m7: 0-0 3m+: 0-1
Track:	LH: 0-1 RH: 0-0 Tight: 0-0 Gall: 0-0
Aids:	Bl: 0-0 Vi: 0-0 Tstrap: 0-0 Ckp: 0-0
Best Rating:	137 12/02 Chep 3m2f110y soft Ch

Useful staying chaser; has had injury problems; stays three miles two; likes the mud.

Rule Supreme (IRE)

118   (130h)**161+**
8-y-o b g Supreme Leader-Book Of Rules (IRE) (Phardante (FR))
W P Mullins John J Fallon

Placings:3602122214/45-1F13321U5   (4965)
2003/04: 25¹G, 20FY, 24¹G, 24³G, 24³S, 28²HY, 24¹G, 25UG,
29⁵GF,

	Starts	1st	2nd	3rd	Win & Pl
Chases	9	3	1	2	144711
Career Total	21	5	5	3	167344
161	3/04	Chel	3m110y	A Ch	GD	£81200
135	12/03	Thur	3m	Ch	GD	£8441
142	4/03	Punc	3m1f	HCh	GD	£36233
129	4/02	Fair	2m4f	Hdl	YLD	£7407
123	12/01	Leop	2m4f	Hdl	YLD	£6677
			Total win prize-money £139961

Going:	Sf: 0-2 GS: 0-0 Gd: 3-5 GF: - Fm: 0-1
Distance:	2m/2m3: 0-0 2m4-2m7: 0-1 **3m+:** 3-8
Track:	LH: 1-2 **RH: 2-6** Tight: 0-1 **Gall: 1-1**
Aids:	Bl: 0-0 Vi: 0-0 Tstrap: 0-0 Ckp: 0-0
Best Rating:	161 3/04 Chel 3m110y good Ch

Smart Irish chaser; won a valuable novices' handicap at the Punchestown Festival in 2003, beating Hedgehunter; third in the Feltham at Kempton over Christmas and surprise winner of the Royal & Sun Alliance Chase; unseated his rider at Aintree; stays 3m 4f; acts well with cut in the ground.

Rum Pointer (IRE)

110(110h)   (134h)**132**
8-y-o b g Turtle Island (IRE)-Osmunda (Mill Reef (USA))
R H Buckler K C B Mackenzie

Placings:432112/P/42260F-F314114   (4572)
2003/04: 20FS, 24³S, 24¹S, 24⁴GS, 22¹S, 22¹G, 24⁴G,

	Starts	1st	2nd	3rd	Win & Pl
Chases	7	3	0	1	23345

Career Total	20	5	4	2	49900
130 3/04 Towc	2m6f	D Ch		GD	£6594
125 2/04 Hayd	2m6f	D Ch		SFT	£6870
130 12/03 Uttx	3m	E Ch		SFT	£4634
130 1/01 Donc	2m4f	A Hdl		GD	£9600
119 1/01 Wwck	2m5f	D Hdl		SFT	£3874

Total win prize-money £31574

Going:	Sf: 2-4 GS: 0-1 Gd: 1-2 GF: - Fm: 0-0
Distance:	2m/2m3: 0-0 2m4-2m7: 2-3 3m+: 1-4
Track:	LH: 2-6 RH: 1-1 Tight: 0-2 Gall: 0-1
Aids:	Bl: 0-0 Vi: 0-0 Tstrap: 0-0 Ckp: 0-0
Best Rating:	132 3/04 Newb 3m good Ch

Useful hurdler/novice chaser; has stamina in abundance; best on an easy surface.

Run Atim

84f   107f

6-y-o ch g Hatim (USA)-Run Pet Run (Deep Run)
K C Bailey Mrs J Way

Placings:50   (4323)
2003/04: 16⁵G, 16⁰S,

	Starts	1st	2nd	3rd	Win & Pl
NH Flat	2	0	0	0	0
Career Total	2	0	0	0	0

Going:	Sf: 0-1 GS: 0-0 Gd: 0-1 GF: - Fm: 0-0
Distance:	2m/2m3: 0-2 2m4-2m7: 0-0 3m+: 0-0
Track:	LH: 0-1 RH: 0-1 Tight: 0-0 Gall: 0-0
Aids:	Bl: 0-0 Vi: 0-0 Tstrap: 0-0 Ckp: 0-0
Best Rating:	107 2/04 Asct 2m110y good NHF

Showed promise when fifth on debut in bumper at Ascot in February; ran moderately at Newcastle the following month.

Run For Paddy

(122h)122

8-y-o b g Michelozzo (USA)-Deep Selection (IRE) (Deep Run)
T Hogan (Mrs H Dalton 29/6) B J Perkins

Placings:230/3111263/23411P1P/1PP-P04P   (4805a)
2003/04: 20ᴾGF, 21⁰G, 20⁴YS, 29ᴾY,

	Starts	1st	2nd	3rd	Win & Pl
Chases	4	0	0	0	534
Career Total	25	7	3	4	60034
147 10/02 Chep	3m	B(0-145)HCh	G-F	£13578
140 4/02 MRas	3m1f	D Ch	GD	£4907
140 3/02 Donc	2m3f110yD Ch	G-S	£4368
111 2/02 Fknm	3m110y D Ch	G-S	£3874
132 10/00 Chel	2m5f	B(0-145)HHdl	GD	£8414
118 9/00 Uttx	2m6f110yC Hdl	G-S	£4771
107 9/00 Font	2m2f110yE Hdl	G-S	£2782

Total win prize-money £42695

Going:	Sf: 0-0 GS: 0-0 Gd: 0-1 GF: - Fm: 0-1
Distance:	2m/2m3: 0-0 2m4-2m7: 0-3 3m+: 0-1
Track:	LH: 0-2 RH: 0-1 Tight: 0-0 Gall: 0-0
Aids:	Bl: 0-0 Vi: 0-0 Tstrap: 0-0 Ckp: 0-0
Best Rating:	156 12/00 Chel 2m5f110y soft Hdl

Fair chaser; ex-English; stays three miles; acts on both good to firm and soft ground.

Run Forrest (IRE)

66

7-y-o ch g Forest Wind (USA)-Katie's Delight (Relko)
Miss Sheena West Mrs Sue Flight

Placings:5/4P   (1457)

2003/04: 16⁴GF, 16ᴾGF,

	Starts	1st	2nd	3rd	Win & Pl
Hurdles	2	0	0	0	308
Career Total	3	0	0	0	308

Going:	Sf: 0-0 GS: 0-0 Gd: 0-0 GF: - Fm: 0-2
Distance:	2m/2m3: 0-2 2m4-2m7: 0-0 3m+: 0-0
Track:	LH: 0-2 RH: 0-0 Tight: 0-2 Gall: 0-0
Aids:	Bl: 0-0 Vi: 0-0 Tstrap: 0-0 Ckp: 0-0
Best Rating:	66 9/01 Plum 2m gd-sft Hdl

Run Of Kings (IRE)

97   111

6-y-o b g King's Ride-Arctic Tartan (Deep Run)
M C Pipe D A Johnson

Placings:F50   (4833)
2003/04: 24ᶠG, 22⁵G, 21⁰GF,

	Starts	1st	2nd	3rd	Win & Pl
Hurdles	2	0	0	0	0
Chases	1	0	0	0	0
Career Total	3	0	0	0	0

Going:	Sf: 0-0 GS: 0-0 Gd: 0-0 GF: 0-2 Fm: - Fm: 0-1
Distance:	2m/2m3: 0-0 2m4-2m7: 0-2 3m+: 0-1
Track:	LH: 0-2 RH: 0-1 Tight: 0-2 Gall: 0-1
Aids:	Bl: 0-0 Vi: 0-0 Tstrap: 0-0 Ckp: 0-0
Best Rating:	111 4/04 Chel 2m5f110y gd-fm Hdl

Fell on chase debut; showed ability over hurdles next time.

Run River Run

71   66

10-y-o b m River God (USA)-Run Lady Run (General Ironside)
M A Hill M A Hill

Placings:040/5/5/FP   (4344)
2003/04: 20ᶠG, 26ᴾGS,

	Starts	1st	2nd	3rd	Win & Pl
Chases	2	0	0	0	0
Career Total	7	0	0	0	0

Going:	Sf: 0-0 GS: 0-1 Gd: 0-1 GF: - Fm: 0-0
Distance:	2m/2m3: 0-0 2m4-2m7: 0-1 3m+: 0-1
Track:	LH: 0-1 RH: 0-1 Tight: 0-0 Gall: 0-0
Aids:	Bl: 0-2 Vi: 0-0 Tstrap: 0-0 Ckp: 0-0
Best Rating:	83 12/99 Hntg 2m110y good NHF

Runaway Bishop (USA)

103(107h)   (94h)104+

9-y-o b/br g Lear Fan (USA)-Valid Linda (USA) (Valid Appeal (USA))
J R Cornwall J R Cornwall

Placings:230/322342313/F/242/3423334-44F550111   (4757)
2003/04: 20⁴GS, 20⁴GS, 24ᶠGS, 19⁵HY, 23⁵S, 22⁰GS, 24¹G, 19¹GS, 25¹S,

	Starts	1st	2nd	3rd	Win & Pl
Hurdles	2	0	0	0	0
Chases	7	3	0	0	10896
Career Total	32	4	7	9	24976
104 4/04 Towc	3m1f	F(0-100)HCh	SFT	£3444
90 3/04 Towc	2m3f110yF(0-95)HCh	G-S	£3373
96 3/04 Hntg	3m	F(0-95)HCh	GD	£3409

Rundetto (IRE)

70f   42f

7-y-o b g Warcraft (USA)-Deep Link (Deep Run)
R Bastiman John Endersby

Placings:0P   (0649)
2003/04: 17⁰GF, 16ᴾGF,

	Starts	1st	2nd	3rd	Win & Pl
NH Flat	2	0	0	0	
Career Total	2	0	0	0	

Going:	Sf: 0-0 GS: 0-0 Gd: 0-0 GF: - Fm: 0-2
Distance:	2m/2m3: 0-2 2m4-2m7: 0-0 3m+: 0-0
Track:	LH: 0-1 RH: 0-1 Tight: 0-0 Gall: 0-0
Aids:	Bl: 0-0 Vi: 0-0 Tstrap: 0-0 Ckp: 0-0
Best Rating:	42 5/03 MRas 2m1f110y gd-fm NHF

Runner Bean

108   (84h)111+

10-y-o b/br g Henbit (USA)-Bean Alainn (Candy Cane)
R Lee H F P Foods Limited

Placings:511634P/403P/424P21-310332234F   (4715)
2003/04: 16³GF, 16¹GF, 17⁰G, 16³GS, 16³GS, 16²GF, 16²GS, 16³G, 16⁴GF, 20ᶠG,

	Starts	1st	2nd	3rd	Win & Pl
Chases	10	1	2	4	9649
Career Total	27	4	4	6	23697
102 5/03 Hntg	2m110y E(0-105)HCh	G-F	£3837
98 4/03 Hntg	2m110y D(0-115)HCh	G-F	£5852
114 11/99 Ludl	2m	H NHF	GD	£1542
105 5/99 Uttx	2m	H NHF	G-F	£1763

Total win prize-money £12996

Going:	Sf: 0-0 GS: 0-3 Gd: 0-3 GF: - Fm: 1-4
Distance:	2m/2m3: 1-9 2m4-2m7: 0-1 3m+: 0-0
Track:	LH: 0-0 RH: 1-10 Tight: 0-4 Gall: 1-4
Aids:	Bl: 0-0 Vi: 0-0 Tstrap: 0-0 Ckp: 0-0
Best Rating:	114 11/99 Ludl 2m good NHF

Moderate chaser; stays two and a half miles but best over shorter; acts on any ground; can make mistakes.

Running De Cerisy (FR)

69

10-y-o ch g Lightning (FR)-Niloq (FR) (Nikos)
P L Clinton (Miss S J Wilton 22/10) In The Clear Racing

Placings:1F1133P04/041/FPP/65112132432403/PP-PPP0   (4890)
2003/04: 19ᶠGF, 19ᴾGF, 16ᴾS, 19ᴾGF,

	Starts	1st	2nd	3rd	Win & Pl
Hurdles	2	0	0	0	0
Chases	2	0	0	0	0
Career Total	35	7	3	5	27009
110 8/01 NAbb	2m1f	F Hdl	G-F	£2296
102 7/01 MRas	2m1f110yF(0-105)HCh	G-S	£4251

| 96 3/00 Folk | 2m5f | D Ch | G-F | £4036 |

Total win prize-money £14264

Going:	Sf: 1-3 GS: 1-5 Gd: 1-1 GF: - Fm: 0-0
Distance:	2m/2m3: 0-0 2m4-2m7: 1-6 3m+: 2-3
Track:	LH: 0-2 RH: 2-5 Tight: 0-2 Gall: 1-3
Aids:	Bl: 0-1 Vi: 0-0 Tstrap: 0-0 Ckp: 0-0
Best Rating:	109 4/00 Font 2m6f good Ch

Moderate chaser; plating class hurdler; stays three miles one furlong; acts on any ground.

114	7/01	Wolv	2m	G Hdl	G-S	£1621
110	11/98	Hrfd	2m	E(0-100)HCh	GD	£3126
114	9/97	NAbb	2m1f	E Hdl	SFT	£2148
108	8/97	Worc	2m	E Hdl	G-F	£2250
	6/97	Autl	1m7f	Hdl	SFT	£7295

Total win prize-money £22987

Going: Sf: 0-1 GS: 0-0 Gd: 0-0 GF: - Fm: 0-3
Distance: 2m/2m3: 0-3 2m4-2m7: 0-1 3m+: 0-0
Track: LH: 0-2 RH: 0-2 Tight: 0-1 Gall: 0-0
Aids: Bl: 0-0 Vi: 0-0 Tstrap: 0-0 Ckp: 0-1
Best Rating: 114 8/01 NAbb 2m1f good Hdl

Running Free (IRE)

10-y-o b g Waajib-Selchis (Main Reef)
W S Cunningham C P M Racing

Placings:55P50/0/0P/PP (0693)
2003/04: 16PG, 25PGF,

	Starts	1st	2nd	3rd	Win & Pl
Chases	2	0	0	0	
Career Total	10	0	0	0	0

Going: Sf: 0-0 GS: 0-0 Gd: 0-1 GF: - Fm: 0-1
Distance: 2m/2m3: 0-1 2m4-2m7: 0-0 3m+: 0-1
Track: LH: 0-2 RH: 0-0 Tight: 0-0 Gall: 0-0
Aids: Bl: 0-0 Vi: 0-0 Tstrap: 0-0 Ckp: 0-0
Best Rating: 76 10/98 Ludl 2m5f110y gd-fm Hdl

Running Machine (IRE)

106(100h)   (96 h)108+
7-y-o b g Classic Memory-Foxborough Lady (Crash Course)
Miss Venetia Williams (A M Hales 21/5) Favourites Racing

Placings:03F3F336-P153542 (3926)
2003/04: 26^PHY, 21^1GF, 20^5G, 24^3GS, 25^5S, 24^4G, 24^2G,

	Starts	1st	2nd	3rd	Win & Pl
Chases	7	1	1	1	6713
Career Total	15	1	1	5	8959
108 12/03 Folk 2m5f F(0-95)HCh G-F £2795					

Total win prize-money £2795

Going: Sf: 0-2 GS: 0-1 Gd: 0-3 GF: - Fm: 1-1
Distance: 2m/2m3: 0-0 2m4-2m7: 1-2 3m+: 0-5
Track: LH: 0-1 RH: 1-6 Tight: 1-2 Gall: 0-0
Aids: Bl: 0-0 Vi: 0-0 Tstrap: 0-1 Ckp: 0-0
Best Rating: 108 2/04 Sand 3m110y good Ch

Moderate chaser; stays three miles and acts on most types of ground; wears a tongue tie.

Running Moss

113
12-y-o ch g Le Moss-Run'n Fly (Deep Run)
A H Mactaggart Mrs A H Mactaggart

Placings:P62/344412/P314/1321/3P4-U0P (3675)
2003/04: 25US, 25^PS, 22^PHY,

	Starts	1st	2nd	3rd	Win & Pl
Chases	3	0	0	0	
Career Total	23	4	3	4	44889
110 3/02 Kels 4m C(0-135)HCh HVY £24534					
103 11/01 Kels 2m6f110yD(0-120)HCh GD £5148					
103 11/00 Catt 3m1f110yF(0-110)HCh G-S £4192					
97 12/99 Sedg 3m3f E Ch SFT £3299					

Total win prize-money £37175

Going: Sf: 0-3 GS: 0-0 Gd: 0-0 GF: - Fm: 0-0
Distance: 2m/2m3: 0-0 2m4-2m7: 0-1 3m+: 0-2
Track: LH: 0-3 RH: 0-0 Tight: 0-2 Gall: 0-0
Aids: Bl: 0-0 Vi: 0-0 Tstrap: 0-0 Ckp: 0-0
Best Rating: 113 12/02 Kels 3m1f heavy Ch

Suited by a strongly-run race, he is a three-mile staying chaser who has been effective on a soft surface and good ground.

Running Mute

108   98
10-y-o b g Roscoe Blake-Rose Albertine (Record Token)
S H Shirley-Beavan J E M Vestey

Placings:1-212P (4295)
2003/04: 22^2G, 20^1G, 24^2G, 20^PGF,

	Starts	1st	2nd	3rd	Win & Pl
Chases	4	1	2	0	13420
Career Total	5	2	2	0	15721
98 6/03 Prth 2m4f110yD(0-115)HCh GD £9228					
79 6/02 Ctml 3m2f H Ch GD £2301					

Total win prize-money £11529

Going: Sf: 0-0 GS: 0-0 Gd: 1-3 GF: - Fm: 0-1
Distance: 2m/2m3: 0-0 2m4-2m7: 1-3 3m+: 0-1
Track: LH: 0-2 RH: 1-2 Tight: 0-1 Gall: 0-0
Aids: Bl: 0-0 Vi: 0-0 Tstrap: 0-0 Ckp: 0-0
Best Rating: 98 7/03 Prth 3m good Ch

Moderate performer; has won plenty of points; stays three miles; acts on a sound surface.

Running Times (USA)

82   (0c)68
7-y-o b g Brocco (USA)-Concert Peace (USA) (Hold Your Peace (USA))
H J Manners H J Manners

Placings:04/122401/1P-0P056 (1792)
2003/04: 16^QG, 22^PGF, 16^PGF, 22^5G, 16^6GF,

	Starts	1st	2nd	3rd	Win & Pl
Hurdles	5	0	0	0	0
Career Total	15	3	2	0	10243
121 5/02 Hrfd 2m3f110yG Hdl GD £2002					
116 3/02 Chep 2m4f F Hdl SFT £2016					
102 5/01 Sedg 2m5f110yE Hdl GD £2786					

Total win prize-money £6804

Going: Sf: 0-0 GS: 0-0 Gd: 0-2 GF: - Fm: 0-3
Distance: 2m/2m3: 0-3 2m4-2m7: 0-2 3m+: 0-0
Track: LH: 0-4 RH: 0-1 Tight: 0-3 Gall: 0-0
Aids: Bl: 0-0 Vi: 0-2 Tstrap: 0-0 Ckp: 0-0
Best Rating: 121 5/02 Hrfd 2m3f110y good Hdl

Runningwiththemoon

(79h)   (58h)
8-y-o b g Homo Sapien-Ardeal (Ardross)
C C Bealby Mrs S M V Bealby

Placings:6P-643P (1106)
2003/04: 20^6GF, 21^4GF, 26^3G, 26^PG,

	Starts	1st	2nd	3rd	Win & Pl
Hurdles	3	0	0	1	485
Chases	1	0	0	0	
Career Total	6	0	0	1	485

Going: Sf: 0-0 GS: 0-0 Gd: 0-2 GF: - Fm: 0-2
Distance: 2m/2m3: 0-0 2m4-2m7: 0-2 3m+: 0-2

Track: LH: 0-4 RH: 0-0 Tight: 0-0 Gall: 0-0
Aids: Bl: 0-0 Vi: 0-0 Tstrap: 0-0 Ckp: 0-0
Best Rating: 63 6/03 Sthl 2m5f110y gd-fm Hdl

Rush About (IRE)

5-y-o ch g Kris-Rachrush (IRE) (Sadler's Wells (USA))
P A Blockley (Miss K Marks 4/10) Bell House Racing Limited

Placings:P5PPP (2154)
2003/04: 17^PG, 19^5G, 16^PGF, 26^PG, 16^PGS,

	Starts	1st	2nd	3rd	Win & Pl
Hurdles	5	0	0	0	0
Career Total	5	0	0	0	0

Going: Sf: 0-0 GS: 0-1 Gd: 0-3 GF: - Fm: 0-1
Distance: 2m/2m3: 0-4 2m4-2m7: 0-0 3m+: 0-1
Track: LH: 0-5 RH: 0-0 Tight: 0-2 Gall: 0-0
Aids: Bl: 0-1 Vi: 0-0 Tstrap: 0-0 Ckp: 0-0

Rushen Raider

73
12-y-o br g Reprimand-Travel Storm (Lord Gayle (USA))
P Needham P Needham

Placings:SP00/12/615/U22260/3P021050/40246306F0O/3 0-PU (2929)
2003/04: 20^PS, 21^UG,

	Starts	1st	2nd	3rd	Win & Pl
Hurdles	2	0	0	0	
Career Total	38	3	6	3	14769
103 9/00 Sedg 2m5f110yD(0-125)HHdl SFT £2892					
112 9/98 Sedg 2m5f110yD(0-120)HHdl GD £2726					
104 5/97 MRas 2m1f110yE Hdl G-F £2547					

Total win prize-money £8167

Going: Sf: 0-1 GS: 0-0 Gd: 0-1 GF: - Fm: 0-0
Distance: 2m/2m3: 0-2 2m4-2m7: 0-2 3m+: 0-0
Track: LH: 0-2 RH: 0-0 Tight: 0-1 Gall: 0-0
Aids: Bl: 0-0 Vi: 0-0 Tstrap: 0-0 Ckp: 0-0
Best Rating: 115 9/99 Sedg 2m5f110y gd-fm Hdl

Rushing Again

74   90
9-y-o br g Rushmere-Saunders Grove (IRE) (Sunyboy)
Dr P Pritchard The Shooting Stars

Placings:20/P4234U4PP4P-P5P65P (1523)
2003/04: 20^PGF, 21^5GF, 24^PGF, 24^6GF, 18^5GF, 22^PG,

	Starts	1st	2nd	3rd	Win & Pl
Hurdles	2	0	0	0	
Chases	4	0	0	0	
Career Total	19	0	2	1	6613

Going: Sf: 0-0 GS: 0-0 Gd: 0-1 GF: - Fm: 0-5
Distance: 2m/2m3: 0-1 2m4-2m7: 0-3 3m+: 0-2
Track: LH: 0-4 RH: 0-0 Tight: 0-2 Gall: 0-0
Aids: Bl: 0-1 Vi: 0-0 Tstrap: 0-0 Ckp: 0-0
Best Rating: 100 3/02 Font 3m3f soft Hdl

Plating-class chaser; winning pointer; modest placed efforts over fences in 2002/3; stays well; acts on any ground.

Rusinga

90f   71f
6-y-o gr g Homo Sapien-Royal Blaze (Scallywag)

L Wells Mrs Carrie Zetter-Wells

Placings:000 (4447)
2003/04: 18⁰GS, 16⁰G, 16⁰S,

	Starts	1st	2nd	3rd	Win & Pl
NH Flat	3	0	0		
Career Total	3	0	0		

Going: Sf: 0-1 GS: 0-1 Gd: 0-1 GF: - Fm: 0-0
Distance: 2m/2m3: 0-3 2m4-2m7: 0-3 3m+: 0-0
Track: LH: 0-3 RH: 0-0 Tight: 0-1 Gall: 0-1
Aids: Bl: 0-0 Vi: 0-0 Tstrap: 0-0 Ckp: 0-0
Best Rating: 71 3/04 Wwck 2m soft NHF

Russian Comrade (IRE)

63   92

8-y-o b g Polish Patriot (USA)-Tikama (FR) (Targowice (USA))
J C Tuck (William J Fitzpatrick 13/6) James R Tuck

Placings:0P0PP/20P00 (4138)
2003/04: 16²YS, 16⁰G, 16⁶S, 16⁰G, 16⁰G,

	Starts	1st	2nd	3rd	Win & Pl
Hurdles	5	0	1	0	1818
Career Total	10	0	1	0	1818

Going: Sf: 0-1 GS: 0-0 Gd: 0-3 GF: - Fm: 0-0
Distance: 2m/2m3: 0-5 2m4-2m7: 0-0 3m+: 0-0
Track: LH: 0-1 RH: 0-4 Tight: 0-0 Gall: 0-0
Aids: Bl: 0-0 Vi: 0-0 Tstrap: 0-0 Ckp: 0-0
Best Rating: 92 5/03 Punc 2m yld-sft Hdl

Plating-class hurdler; ex-Irish; best at around two miles.

Russian Court

102   104

8-y-o b g Soviet Lad (USA)-Court Town (Camden Town)
S E H Sherwood Rosemary Viscountess Boyne

Placings:4/06/3616540/540131F-20314500 (3921)
2003/04: 16²G, 21⁰GF, 16³GF, 17¹G, 16⁴GF, 19⁵G, 17⁰GS, 16⁰GS,

	Starts	1st	2nd	3rd	Win & Pl
Hurdles	8	1	1	1	5475
Career Total	25	4	1	3	17222

100	11/03	Bang	2m1f	E(0-110)HHdl	GD	£3010
95	2/03	Tntn	2m1f	E(0-105)HHdl	G-S	£4046
89	1/03	Ludl	2m	G(0-95)HHdl	SFT	£3146
87	10/01	Plum	2m	F(0-100)HHdl	SFT	£2639

Total win prize-money £12842

Going: Sf: 0-0 GS: 0-2 Gd: 1-3 GF: - Fm: 0-3
Distance: 2m/2m3: 1-6 2m4-2m7: 0-3 3m+: 0-0
Track: LH: 1-3 RH: 0-5 Tight: 1-2 Gall: 0-0
Aids: Bl: 0-0 Vi: 0-0 Tstrap: 0-0 Ckp: 0-1
Best Rating: 104 12/03 Ludl 2m gd-fm Hdl

Moderate hurdler; suited by two miles and soft ground; needs to come late off a strong pace and do it all on the bridle.

Russian Gigolo (IRE)

108(104h) (103dh)128

7-y-o b g Toulon-Nanogan (Tarqogan)
N A Twiston-Davies Mrs Caroline Beresford-Wylie

Placings:4006/25230P4-31123 (3922)
2003/04: 20³G, 21¹GS, 20¹GS, 25²G, 20³G,

	Starts	1st	2nd	3rd	Win & Pl
Hurdles	1	0	0	1	548
Chases	4	2	1	1	15085
Career Total	16	2	3	3	19899

128	12/03	Bang	2m4f110y	E(0-110)HCh	G-S	£4225
126	11/03	Uttx	2m5f	E(0-110)HCh	G-S	£5486

Total win prize-money £9711

Going: Sf: 0-0 GS: 2-2 Gd: 0-3 GF: - Fm: 0-0
Distance: 2m/2m3: 0-0 2m4-2m7: 2-4 3m+: 0-1
Track: LH: 2-4 RH: 0-1 Tight: 1-2 Gall: 0-1
Aids: Bl: 0-0 Vi: 0-0 Tstrap: 0-0 Ckp: 0-0
Best Rating: 128 12/03 Chel 3m1f110y good Ch

Moderate maiden hurdler/fair novice chaser; won first two starts over fences; acts on a soft surface; stays three miles one.

Russian Lord (IRE)

86f   81f

5-y-o br g Topanoora-Russian Gale (IRE) (Strong Gale)
V R A Dartnall Plain Peeps

Placings:0 (3649)
2003/04: 16⁰GS,

	Starts	1st	2nd	3rd	Win & Pl
NH Flat	1	0	0	0	
Career Total	1	0	0	0	

Going: Sf: 0-0 GS: 0-1 Gd: 0-0 GF: - Fm: 0-0
Distance: 2m/2m3: 0-1 2m4-2m7: 0-0 3m+: 0-0
Track: LH: 0-0 RH: 0-1 Tight: 0-0 Gall: 0-0
Aids: Bl: 0-0 Vi: 0-0 Tstrap: 0-0 Ckp: 0-0
Best Rating: 81 2/04 Kemp 2m gd-sft NHF

Russian Sky

98   77

5-y-o gr g Endoli (USA)-Anzarna (Zambrano)
Mrs H O Graham Mrs H O Graham

Placings:0P0440 (4690)
2003/04: 22⁰G, 24²G, 16⁰GS, 17⁴G, 22⁴G, 22⁰G,

	Starts	1st	2nd	3rd	Win & Pl
Hurdles	6	0	0	0	532
Career Total	6	0	0	0	532

Going: Sf: 0-0 GS: 0-1 Gd: 0-5 GF: - Fm: 0-0
Distance: 2m/2m3: 0-2 2m4-2m7: 0-3 3m+: 0-1
Track: LH: 0-4 RH: 0-0 Tight: 0-3 Gall: 0-2
Aids: Bl: 0-0 Vi: 0-0 Tstrap: 0-0 Ckp: 0-0
Best Rating: 77 3/04 Kels 2m6f110y good Hdl

Soundly beaten in novice hurdles; will stay well.

Russian Steppes (IRE)

87   64

6-y-o gr g Moscow Society (USA)-Pryana (Pry)
H D Daly Mrs John Nesbitt

Placings:06 (3779)
2003/04: 22⁰GS, 21⁰G,

	Starts	1st	2nd	3rd	Win & Pl
Hurdles	2	0	0	0	0
Career Total	2	0	0	0	0

Going: Sf: 0-0 GS: 0-1 Gd: 0-1 GF: - Fm: 0-0
Distance: 2m/2m3: 0-0 2m4-2m7: 0-2 3m+: 0-0
Track: LH: 0-1 RH: 0-1 Tight: 0-1 Gall: 0-0
Aids: Bl: 0-0 Vi: 0-1 Tstrap: 0-0 Ckp: 0-0
Best Rating: 62 2/04 Ludl 2m5f good Hdl

Rust En Vrede

104   80

5-y-o b g Royal Applause-Souveniers (Relko)
D Carroll Alan Mann

Placings:3050-06 (0895)
2003/04: 17⁰G, 17⁶GF,

	Starts	1st	2nd	3rd	Win & Pl
Hurdles	2	0	0	0	
Career Total	6	0	0	1	850

Going: Sf: 0-0 GS: 0-0 Gd: 0-1 GF: - Fm: 0-1
Distance: 2m/2m3: 0-2 2m4-2m7: 0-0 3m+: 0-0
Track: LH: 0-1 RH: 0-1 Tight: 0-2 Gall: 0-0
Aids: Bl: 0-0 Vi: 0-1 Tstrap: 0-0 Ckp: 0-0
Best Rating: 86 7/03 Ctml 2m1f110y gd-fm Hdl

Moderate on the Flat; has shown just fair form over hurdles.

Rustic Charm (IRE)

95   90

4-y-o b f Charnwood Forest (IRE)-Kabayil (Dancing Brave (USA))
C R Egerton (C G Cox 6/11) Elite Racing Club

Placings:0P (4736)
2003/04: 16⁰GS, 17²G,

	Starts	1st	2nd	3rd	Win & Pl
Hurdles	2	0	0	0	
Career Total	2	0	0	0	

Going: Sf: 0-0 GS: 0-1 Gd: 0-1 GF: - Fm: 0-0
Distance: 2m/2m3: 0-2 2m4-2m7: 0-0 3m+: 0-0
Track: LH: 0-1 RH: 0-1 Tight: 0-1 Gall: 0-0
Aids: Bl: 0-1 Vi: 0-0 Tstrap: 0-0 Ckp: 0-0
Best Rating: 90 1/04 Sand 2m110y gd-sft Hdl

Rustic Revelry

11-y-o b g Afzal-Country Festival (Town And Country)
R H York R H York

Placings:00000/45/5F4/216/36O6005/B62536-213 (0354)
2003/04: 16²G, 24¹GF, 21³GF,

	Starts	1st	2nd	3rd	Win & Pl
Chases	3	1	1	1	4251
Career Total	29	2	3	3	8427

93	5/03	Hntg	3m	H Ch	G-F	£2891
89	5/00	Folk	2m5f	H Ch	GD	£1456

Total win prize-money £4347

Going: Sf: 0-0 GS: 0-0 Gd: 0-1 GF: - Fm: 1-2
Distance: 2m/2m3: 0-1 2m4-2m7: 0-1 3m+: 1-1
Track: LH: 0-1 RH: 1-2 Tight: 0-1 Gall: 1-2
Aids: Bl: 1-3 Vi: 0-0 Tstrap: 0-0 Ckp: 0-0
Best Rating: 100 5/00 Hntg 2m4f110y good Ch

Moderate hunter chaser; prolific winner between the flags; likes a sound surface, but acts with cut; stays three miles, but effective at shorter; wears blinkers.

Rutland Chantry (USA)

93   90+

10-y-o b g Dixieland Band (USA)-Christchurch (FR) (So Blessed))
S Gollings   Mrs Allison L Bottomley

Placings:1P0/3O   (2943)
2003/04: 17³GS, 16⁰GS,

	Starts	1st	2nd	3rd	Win & Pl	
Hurdles	2	0	0	1	388	
Career Total	5	1	0	1	2852	
104 11/00 Uttx	2m		E Hdl		HVY	£2464

Total win prize-money £2464

Going:	Sf: 0-0 GS: 0-2 Gd: 0-0 GF: - Fm: 0-0
Distance:	2m/2m3: 0-2 2m4-2m7: 0-0 3m+: 0-0
Track:	LH: 0-2 RH: 0-0 Tight: 0-1 Gall: 0-0
Aids:	Bl: 0-0 Vi: 0-0 Tstrap: 0-0 Ckp: 0-0
Best Rating:	104 11/00 Uttx 2m heavy Hdl

Moderate middle-distance performer on the Flat; won on his hurdling debut back in 2000, but was having his first start over timber for 1094 days when third at Bangor in December.

Rutledge Red (IRE)

(105h)   (109h)

8-y-o gr g Roselier (FR)-Katebeaujolais (Politico (USA))
J M Jefferson   Ashleybank Investments Limited

Placings:0P20/1112-FU   (1533)
2003/04: 21FGF, 22UGF,

	Starts	1st	2nd	3rd	Win & Pl	
Chases	2	0	0	0		
Career Total	10	3	2	0	13572	
111 10/02 Fknm	2m4f		D Hdl		G-S	£3708
114 10/02 MRas	2m3f110yD Hdl				G-F	£4407
100 8/02 MRas	2m3f110yE Hdl				G-F	£3195

Total win prize-money £11311

Going:	Sf: 0-0 GS: 0-0 Gd: 0-0 GF: - Fm: 0-2
Distance:	2m/2m3: 0-0 2m4-2m7: 0-2 3m+: 0-0
Track:	LH: 0-1 RH: 0-1 Tight: 0-2 Gall: 0-0
Aids:	Bl: 0-0 Vi: 0-0 Tstrap: 0-0 Ckp: 0-0
Best Rating:	114 10/02 MRas 2m3f110y gd-fm Hdl

Fair novice hurdler; completed a hat-trick in the autumn of 2002 with two wins at Market Rasen and one at Fakenham; has failed to complete over fences; suited by at least two and a half miles; has won on good to firm and soft ground.

Ryalux (IRE)

(106h)   (119h)154

11-y-o b g Riverhead (USA)-Kings De Lema (IRE) (King's Ride)
A Crook   William Lomas

Placings:221/12F111/3331P/22223F21/312231-65 (2733)
2003/04: 22⁶G, 24⁵S,

	Starts	1st	2nd	3rd	Win & Pl	
Hurdles	1	0	0	0	0	
Chases	1	0	0	0	1500	
Career Total	30	9	10	6	160126	
154 4/03 Ayr	4m1f	A HCh			GD	£63800
139 11/02 Ayr	3m1f	C(0-135)HCh			SFT	£10080
134 4/02 Prth	3m	B Hdl			GD	£12203
129 1/01 Weth	4m1f110yD(0-125)HCh				G-S	£4160
125 3/00 Carl	2m	D Ch			G-S	£4368
109 3/00 Newc	2m4f	E Ch			GD	£3152
129 2/00 Newc	2m4f	E Ch			SFT	£3087
104 5/99 Hexm	2m	E Hdl			SFT	£2526

Rye Brook

7-y-o b g Romany Rye-Nearly A Brook (Nearly A Hand)
P F Nicholls   Mrs S J Maltby

Placings:0P/12P   (3084)
2003/04: 16¹GF, 16²GF, 22PGS,

---

109 3/99 Newc 2m4f   E Hdl   GD   £2253
Total win prize-money £105630

Going:	Sf: 0-1 GS: 0-0 Gd: 0-1 GF: - Fm: 0-0
Distance:	2m/2m3: 0-0 2m4-2m7: 0-1 3m+: 0-1
Track:	LH: 0-2 RH: 0-0 Tight: 0-1 Gall: 0-0
Aids:	Bl: 0-0 Vi: 0-0 Tstrap: 0-0 Ckp: 0-0
Best Rating:	154 4/03 Ayr 4m1f good Ch

Smart chaser; consistent; just touched off in the Great Yorkshire Chase at Doncaster in January 2003 and ran well in the Racing Post Chase; posted a career-best effort when stepped up to four miles one to land the Scottish National; lightly raced in 2003/4; stays well; acts on most types of ground.

Ryders Storm (USA)

108(98h)   (115dh)116

5-y-o b/br g Dynaformer (USA)-Justicara (Rusticaro (FR))
T R George   Ryder Racing Ltd

Placings:1114P-222P   (2859)
2003/04: 17²GF, 16²GF, 16²G, 16PGS,

	Starts	1st	2nd	3rd	Win & Pl	
Chases	4	0	3	0	9678	
Career Total	9	3	3	0	20200	
93 9/02 Font	2m2f110yE Hdl				G-F	£2926
116 9/02 Bang	2m1f	D Hdl			G-F	£3997
95 8/02 Font	2m2f110yE Hdl				GD	£3010

Total win prize-money £9934

Going:	Sf: 0-0 GS: 0-1 Gd: 0-1 GF: - Fm: 0-2
Distance:	2m/2m3: 0-4 2m4-2m7: 0-0 3m+: 0-0
Track:	LH: 0-4 RH: 0-0 Tight: 0-0 Gall: 0-2
Aids:	Bl: 0-0 Vi: 0-0 Tstrap: 0-0 Ckp: 0-0
Best Rating:	116 11/03 Chel 2m good Ch

Fair novice chaser; runner-up in first three novice chases before pulling up on easy ground; sound jumper of fences; best at around two miles on a sound surface; has worn a visor.

Rydon Lane (IRE)

105   (0c)100+

8-y-o br g Toca Madera-Polocracy (IRE) (Aristocracy)
Mrs S D Williams   D C Coard

Placings:0/004446/4F51P-32F4341P   (4634)
2003/04: 24³G, 19²G, 22⁴G, 24³S, 19⁴GS, 19¹G, 19PG,

	Starts	1st	2nd	3rd	Win & Pl	
Hurdles	8	1	1	2	7840	
Career Total	20	2	1	2	11434	
100 3/04 Extr	2m3f	D(0-115)HHdl			GD	£5151
95 1/03 Extr	2m3f	F(0-100)HHdl			G-S	£2838

Total win prize-money £7990

Going:	Sf: 0-1 GS: 0-2 Gd: 1-5 GF: - Fm: 0-0
Distance:	2m/2m3: 1-2 2m4-2m7: 0-4 3m+: 0-2
Track:	LH: 0-0 RH: 1-8 Tight: 0-0 Gall: 0-0
Aids:	Bl: 0-0 Vi: 0-0 Tstrap: 0-0 Ckp: 0-0
Best Rating:	100 3/04 Extr 2m3f good Hdl

Moderate hurdler; both wins have come at Exeter; stays three miles; acts on good and soft ground.

	Starts	1st	2nd	3rd	Win & Pl	
NH Flat	2	1	1	0	2469	
Hurdles	1	0	0	0	0	
Career Total	5	1	1	0	2469	
90 10/03 Chep	2m110y	H NHF			G-F	£1953

Total win prize-money £1953

Going:	Sf: 0-0 GS: 0-1 Gd: 0-0 GF: - Fm: 1-2
Distance:	2m/2m3: 1-2 2m4-2m7: 0-1 3m+: 0-0
Track:	LH: 1-2 RH: 0-1 Tight: 0-1 Gall: 0-0
Aids:	Bl: 0-0 Vi: 0-0 Tstrap: 0-0 Ckp: 0-0
Best Rating:	90 10/03 Chep 2m110y NHF

Had shown in a couple of soft ground bumpers for Ron Hodges 2001/2; won weak bumper on good to firm at Chepstow October 2003 on first start for Paul Nicholls.

Rye Rum (IRE)

83   17

13-y-o br g Strong Gale-Eimers Pet (Paddy's Stream)
J W F Aynsley   J W F Aynsley

Placings:0PP/PPP/P/PPP/P2/6035/P0LPP/5PP-P0 (0693)
2003/04: 20PGF, 25⁰GF,

	Starts	1st	2nd	3rd	Win & Pl
Chases	2	0	0	0	
Career Total	26	0	1	1	1253

Going:	Sf: 0-0 GS: 0-0 Gd: 0-0 GF: - Fm: 0-2
Distance:	2m/2m3: 0-2 2m4-2m7: 0-1 3m+: 0-1
Track:	LH: 0-2 RH: 0-0 Tight: 0-1 Gall: 0-1
Aids:	Bl: 0-0 Vi: 0-0 Tstrap: 0-0 Ckp: 0-0
Best Rating:	57 6/99 Hexm 2m4f110y gd-fm Ch

Ryhall (IRE)

94f   84f

4-y-o b f Saddlers' Hall (IRE)-Loshian (IRE) (Montelimar (USA))
T D Easterby   Mr & Mrs W J Williams

Placings:04   (4517)
2003/04: 16⁰G, 16⁴GS,

	Starts	1st	2nd	3rd	Win & Pl
NH Flat	2	0	0	0	0
Career Total	2	0	0	0	0

Going:	Sf: 0-0 GS: 0-1 Gd: 0-0 GF: - Fm: 0-0
Distance:	2m/2m3: 0-2 2m4-2m7: 0-0 3m+: 0-0
Track:	LH: 0-2 RH: 0-0 Tight: 0-0 Gall: 0-0
Aids:	Bl: 0-0 Vi: 0-0 Tstrap: 0-0 Ckp: 0-0
Best Rating:	78 3/04 Weth 2m gd-sft NHF

Ryminster

88   66

5-y-o ch g Minster Son-Shultan (IRE) (Rymer)
J Wade   John Wade

Placings:000   (4260)
2003/04: 19⁰GS, 18⁰S, 16⁰GF,

	Starts	1st	2nd	3rd	Win & Pl
Hurdles	3	0	0	0	
Career Total	3	0	0	0	

Going:	Sf: 0-1 GS: 0-1 Gd: 0-0 GF: - Fm: 0-1
Distance:	2m/2m3: 0-3 2m4-2m7: 0-0 3m+: 0-0
Track:	LH: 0-3 RH: 0-0 Tight: 0-3 Gall: 0-0
Aids:	Bl: 0-0 Vi: 0-0 Tstrap: 0-0 Ckp: 0-0
Best Rating:	66 3/04 Catt 2m gd-fm Hdl

Rymon

93f   64f

4-y-o br g Terimon-Rythmic Rymer (Rymer)
J M Jefferson Mrs M Barker

Placings:00   (4264)
2003/04: 13⁰GF, 16⁰GF,

	Starts	1st	2nd	3rd	Win & Pl
NH Flat	2	0	0	0	
Career Total	2	0	0	0	

Going:	Sf: 0-0 GS: 0-0 Gd: 0-0 GF: - Fm: 0-2
Distance:	2m/2m3: 0-1 2m4-2m7: 0-0 3m+: 0-0
Track:	LH: 0-1 RH: 0-0 Tight: 0-1 Gall: 0-0
Aids:	Bl: 0-0 Vi: 0-0 Tstrap: 0-0 Ckp: 0-0
Best Rating:	64 3/04 Catt 2m gd-fm NHF

S B S By Jove

11-y-o ch g Jupiter Island-Mill Shine (Milan)
Miss L Blackford David Cocks

Placings:P   (4823)
2003/04: 23⁰GF,

	Starts	1st	2nd	3rd	Win & Pl
Chases	1	0	0	0	
Career Total	1	0	0	0	

Going:	Sf: 0-0 GS: 0-0 Gd: 0-0 GF: - Fm: 0-1
Distance:	2m/2m3: 0-0 2m4-2m7: 0-0 3m+: 0-1
Track:	LH: 0-0 RH: 0-1 Tight: 0-0 Gall: 0-0
Aids:	Bl: 0-0 Vi: 0-0 Tstrap: 0-0 Ckp: 0-0

Saafend Rocket (IRE)

102   113

6-y-o b g Distinctly North (USA)-Simple Annie (Simply Great (FR))
H D Daly (R Lee 26/5) Ludlow Racing Partnership

Placings:6F-2241116043   (4718)
2003/04: 16²G, 16²G, 16⁴G, 16¹GF, 17¹GS, 16¹GF, 16⁶GS, 17⁰GS, 16⁴GS, 16⁴GS, 16³GF,

	Starts	1st	2nd	3rd	Win & Pl
Hurdles	10	3	2	1	12853
Career Total	12	3	2	1	12853
110 12/03 Ludl	2m	E(0-105)HHdl	G-F	£5499
103 12/03 Hrfd	2m1f	F(0-95)HHdl	G-S	£1995
84 11/03 Ludl	2m	G Hdl	G-F	£2320
		Total win prize-money £9815		

Going:	Sf: 0-0 GS: 1-4 Gd: 0-4 GF: - Fm: 2-2
Distance:	2m/2m3: 3-10 2m4-2m7: 0-0 3m+: 0-0
Track:	LH: 0-2 RH: 3-8 Tight: 0-0 Gall: 0-1
Aids:	Bl: 0-0 Vi: 0-0 Tstrap: 0-0 Ckp: 0-0
Best Rating:	113 1/04 Wwck 2m gd-sft Hdl

Moderate hurdler; improved form since joining Henry Daly and completed hat-trick in November and December 2003; best at 2m; acts on most types of ground..

Sabi Sand

 (84h)   (81h)97

8-y-o b m Minster Son-Radical Lady (Radical)
J R Turner Yarm Racing Partnership

Placings:00006/2014411P-PPPP   (3768)

2003/04: 22⁰PS, 27⁰G, 24⁰PHY, 20⁰PHY,

	Starts	1st	2nd	3rd	Win & Pl
Chases	4	0	0	0	
Career Total	17	3	1	0	13920
97 3/03 Catt	3m1f110yE(0-100)HCh	SFT	£4069
94 2/03 Newc	3m	E(0-110)HCh	SFT	£4400
97 11/02 Uttx	3m2f	F(0-100)HCh	HVY	£3445
		Total win prize-money £11915		

Going:	Sf: 0-3 GS: 0-0 Gd: 0-1 GF: - Fm: 0-0
Distance:	2m/2m3: 0-0 2m4-2m7: 0-2 3m+: 0-2
Track:	LH: 0-2 RH: 0-2 Tight: 0-0 Gall: 0-1
Aids:	Bl: 0-0 Vi: 0-0 Tstrap: 0-3 Ckp: 0-0
Best Rating:	97 3/03 Catt 3m1f110y soft Ch

Moderate chaser; stays well; suited by soft ground; out of form in 2003/4.

Sabreflight

101f   98f

4-y-o ch f Sabrehill (USA)-Little Redwing (Be My Chief (USA))
R A Fahey D S Coates

Placings:33   (4328)
2003/04: 16³G, 16³S,

	Starts	1st	2nd	3rd	Win & Pl
NH Flat	2	0	0	2	3176
Career Total	2	0	0	2	3176

Going:	Sf: 0-1 GS: 0-0 Gd: 0-1 GF: - Fm: 0-0
Distance:	2m/2m3: 0-2 2m4-2m7: 0-0 3m+: 0-0
Track:	LH: 0-0 RH: 0-2 Tight: 0-1 Gall: 0-0
Aids:	Bl: 0-0 Vi: 0-0 Tstrap: 0-0 Ckp: 0-0
Best Rating:	98 3/04 Sand 2m110y soft NHF

Showed promise when third at Musselburgh on debut and in the big mares' bumper at Sandown; will get further over hurdles; acts on a sound surface.

Saby (FR)

100(95h)   (86 h)114

6-y-o b/br g Sassanian (USA)-Valy Flett (FR) (Pietru (FR))
P J Hobbs Setsquare Recruitment

Placings:424022/36002-F40040633P   (4857)
2003/04: 19²GF, 17⁴G, 19⁰S, 16⁰G, 16⁴S, 19⁰GS, 18⁶G, 16³G, 16³G, 19⁰GF,

	Starts	1st	2nd	3rd	Win & Pl
Hurdles	3	0	0	0	0
Chases	7	0	0	2	2219
Career Total	21	0	4	3	10468

Going:	Sf: 0-2 GS: 0-1 Gd: 0-5 GF: - Fm: 0-2
Distance:	2m/2m3: 0-9 2m4-2m7: 0-1 3m+: 0-0
Track:	LH: 0-2 RH: 0-8 Tight: 0-5 Gall: 0-1
Aids:	Bl: 0-0 Vi: 0-0 Tstrap: 0-0 Ckp: 0-0
Best Rating:	114 4/03 NAbb 2m110y good Ch

Plating-class hurdler/modest chaser; goes well at around two miles; acts on decent ground.

Sachsenwalzer (GER)

96   86

6-y-o ch g Top Waltz (FR)-Stairway To Heaven (GER) (Nebos (GER))
C Grant Mrs A Meller

Placings:05054   (4438)

2003/04: 16⁰GF, 16⁵GS, 16⁹S, 16⁵G, 16⁴GS,

	Starts	1st	2nd	3rd	Win & Pl
Hurdles	5	0	0	0	512
Career Total	5	0	0	0	512

Going:	Sf: 0-1 GS: 0-2 Gd: 0-1 GF: - Fm: 0-1
Distance:	2m/2m3: 0-5 2m4-2m7: 0-0 3m+: 0-0
Track:	LH: 0-4 RH: 0-1 Tight: 0-3 Gall: 0-1
Aids:	Bl: 0-0 Vi: 0-0 Tstrap: 0-0 Ckp: 0-0
Best Rating:	85 3/04 Donc 2m110y good Hdl

Winner four times on the Flat in Germany; very moderate over hurdles here but ought to be capable of better.

Sacrebleu (FR)

89   89

5-y-o b g Epervier Bleu-Sa Majeste (FR) (Garde Royale)
M Todhunter Sir Robert Ogden

Placings:4PP   (3767)
2003/04: 16⁴S, 20⁰GS, 17⁰HY,

	Starts	1st	2nd	3rd	Win & Pl
Hurdles	3	0	0	0	303
Career Total	3	0	0	0	303

Going:	Sf: 0-2 GS: 0-1 Gd: 0-0 GF: - Fm: 0-0
Distance:	2m/2m3: 0-2 2m4-2m7: 0-1 3m+: 0-0
Track:	LH: 0-2 RH: 0-1 Tight: 0-0 Gall: 0-0
Aids:	Bl: 0-0 Vi: 0-0 Tstrap: 0-0 Ckp: 0-0
Best Rating:	89 12/03 Hayd 2m soft Hdl

Sacrifice

92   100

9-y-o b g Arctic Lord-Kellyann (Jellaby)
K Bishop (T Long 15/5) Mike Cornish

Placings:501/324313-44UP6634   (2157)
2003/04: 16⁴G, 20⁴GF, 21ᵁGF, 20⁰GF, 19⁶GF, 16⁶GF, 21³GF, 21⁴GS,

	Starts	1st	2nd	3rd	Win & Pl
Chases	8	0	0	1	1517
Career Total	17	2	1	4	6932
100 4/03 Hrfd	2m	H Ch	G-F	£1540
85 4/02 Hrfd	2m3f	H Ch	GD	£2299
		Total win prize-money £3840		

Going:	Sf: 0-0 GS: 0-1 Gd: 0-1 GF: - Fm: 0-6
Distance:	2m/2m3: 0-3 2m4-2m7: 0-5 3m+: 0-0
Track:	LH: 0-5 RH: 0-3 Tight: 0-2 Gall: 0-1
Aids:	Bl: 0-0 Vi: 0-0 Tstrap: 0-0 Ckp: 0-0
Best Rating:	100 4/03 Hrfd 2m gd-fm Ch

Moderate hunter chaser at two to two and a half miles.

Sacsayhuaman

87   47

5-y-o b m Halling (USA)-La Dolce Vita (Mazilier (USA))
D W Thompson (R M Beckett 10/6) Mrs Ann Davis

Placings:F000   (4774)
2003/04: 16⁶G, 16⁰HY, 16⁰HY, 16⁰G,

	Starts	1st	2nd	3rd	Win & Pl
Hurdles	4	0	0	0	
Career Total	4	0	0	0	

Going:	Sf: 0-2 GS: 0-0 Gd: 0-2 GF: - Fm: 0-0
Distance:	2m/2m3: 0-4 2m4-2m7: 0-0 3m+: 0-0
Track:	LH: 0-4 RH: 0-0 Tight: 0-0 Gall: 0-1
Aids:	Bl: 0-0 Vi: 0-0 Tstrap: 0-0 Ckp: 0-0
Best Rating:	47 4/04 Fknm 2m good Hdl

Sad Mad Bad (USA)

10-y-o b g Sunny's Halo (CAN)-Quite Attractive (USA) (Well Decorated (USA))
G Tuer (Mrs M Reveley 12/6) G Tuer

Placings:11410/13111060/312P25/40062U32/311FP/4140
00PP5-P512   (4851)
2003/04: 25⁵G, 28⁸GS, 24⁵GF, 27¹G, 27⁹GS,

	Starts	1st	2nd	3rd	Win & Pl
Chases	5	1	1	0	2568
Career Total	45	12	5	4	94388

101	3/04	Sedg	3m3f	H Ch	GD	£1512
121	11/02	Weth	3m1f	D(0-125)HCh	G-S	£4615
121	11/01	Plum	3m5f	C(0-130)HCh	GD	£13340
101	10/01	Uttx	3m2f	E(0-115)HCh	G-S	£6500
128	1/00	Uttx	3m	B(0-140)HCh	SFT	£23200
112	3/99	Carl	2m4f110yC	Ch	SFT	£5472
124	2/99	MRas	2m4f	D Ch	SFT	£4027
131	12/98	Bang	2m4f110yD	Ch	G-S	£3582
104	11/98	MRas	2m4f	D Ch	G-S	£4608
125	2/98	Hayd	2m	C HHdl	GD	£5083
120	11/97	Newc	2m	D Ch	GD	£2841
117	11/97	MRas	2m1f110yD	Hdl	GD	£2999

Total win prize-money £77781

Going: Sf: 0-0 GS: 0-2 Gd: 1-2 GF: - Fm: 0-1
Distance: 2m2m3: 0-0 2m4-2m7: 0-0 **3m+: 1-5**
Track: **LH: 1-5** RH: 0-0 **Tight: 1-2** Gall: 0-0
Aids: Bl: 0-0 Vi: 0-0 Tstrap: 0-0 Ckp: 0-0
Best Rating: **131** 12/98 Bang 2m4f110y gd-sft Ch

Fair chaser at his best; not the easiest of rides; stays extreme distances; now hunter chasing and winner at Sedgefield in March; has worn a visor; acts on soft ground.

Saddler's Quest

89   77

7-y-o b g Saddlers' Hall (IRE)-Seren Quest (Rainbow Quest (USA))
J White (C P Morlock 9/6) Nick Quesnel

Placings:0-000   (1543)
2003/04: 22⁰S, 19⁹G, 16⁰GF,

	Starts	1st	2nd	3rd	Win & Pl
Hurdles	3	0	0	0	
Career Total	4	0	0	0	

Going: Sf: 0-1 GS: 0-0 Gd: 0-1 GF: - Fm: 0-1
Distance: 2m2m3: 0-1 2m4-2m7: 0-0 3m+: 0-0
Track: LH: 0-2 RH: 0-1 Tight: 0-1 Gall: 0-0
Aids: Bl: 0-0 Vi: 0-0 Tstrap: 0-0 Ckp: 0-0
Best Rating: 77 2/03 Ludl 2m good Hdl

Sadie Jane

4-y-o b f Zahran (IRE)-So We Know (Daring March)
J M Bradley D Smith (saul)

Placings:P   (2410)
2003/04: 17⁰GF,

	Starts	1st	2nd	3rd	Win & Pl
Hurdles	1	0	0	0	
Career Total	1	0	0	0	

Going: Sf: 0-0 GS: 0-0 Gd: 0-0 GF: - Fm: 0-1
Distance: 2m2m3: 0-1 2m4-2m7: 0-0 3m+: 0-0
Track: LH: 0-0 RH: 0-1 Tight: 0-1 Gall: 0-0
Aids: Bl: 0-0 Vi: 0-0 Tstrap: 0-0 Ckp: 0-0

Sadler's Cove (FR)

74

6-y-o g g King's Theatre (IRE)-Mine D'Or (FR) (Posse (ZIM))
Mrs L C Jewell (B G Powell 5/5) Gallagher Equine Ltd

Placings:000-PP   (0322)
2003/04: 22⁸G, 16⁰GF,

	Starts	1st	2nd	3rd	Win & Pl
Hurdles	2	0	0	0	
Career Total	5	0	0	0	

Going: Sf: 0-0 GS: 0-0 Gd: 0-1 GF: - Fm: 0-1
Distance: 2m/2m3: 0-1 2m4-2m7: 0-1 3m+: 0-0
Track: LH: 0-2 RH: 0-0 Tight: 0-2 Gall: 0-0
Aids: Bl: 0-0 Vi: 0-0 Tstrap: 0-1 Ckp: 0-0
Best Rating: 74 4/03 Hrfd 2m3f110y gd-fm Hdl

Sadler's Realm

11-y-o b g Sadler's Wells (USA)-Rensaler (USA) (Stop The Music (USA))
Ms S J Gordon (P J Hobbs 3/5) J F Tucker

Placings:02/2012111220/1403043/3321/P551/4PF-013   (4696)
2003/04: 20⁰S, 19¹GS, 19³G,

	Starts	1st	2nd	3rd	Win & Pl
Hurdles	1	0	0	0	0
Chases	2	1	0	1	2575
Career Total	33	8	6	5	58603

112	3/04	Hrfd	2m3f	H Ch	G-S	£2009
131	4/02	Chep	2m3f110yD(0-125)HCh	G-S	£4085
122	2/01	Sand	2m4f110yD Ch	SFT	£4982
141	12/98	Chep	2m4f110yB(0-140)HHdl	GD	£5319
111	1/98	Extr	2m3f110yD(0-125)HHdl	HVY	£3340
115	12/97	Chep	2m110y E(0-120)HHdl	HVY	£2320
108	12/97	Extr	2m2f	F(0-105)HHdl	SFT	£2176
114	11/97	Kemp	2m	F(0-100)HHdl	G-S	£1898

Total win prize-money £26129

Going: Sf: 0-1 GS: 1-1 Gd: 0-1 GF: - Fm: 0-0
Distance: **2m/2m3: 1-1** 2m4-2m7: 0-2 3m+: 0-0
Track: LH: 0-1 **RH: 1-2** Tight: 0-0 Gall: 0-0
Aids: Bl: 0-0 Vi: 0-0 Tstrap: 0-0 Ckp: 0-0
Best Rating: **141** 2/99 Newb 2m110y good Hdl

Fair two and a half mile chaser; acts on soft ground and a sound surface.

Sadler's Rock (IRE)

6-y-o b g Sadler's Wells (USA)-Triple Couronne (USA) (Riverman (USA))
G L Moore Regal Racing

Placings:40/P   (2488)
2003/04: 16⁰GS,

	Starts	1st	2nd	3rd	Win & Pl
Hurdles	1	0	0	0	
Career Total	3	0	0	0	0

Going: Sf: 0-0 GS: 0-1 Gd: 0-0 GF: - Fm: 0-0
Distance: 2m/2m3: 0-1 2m4-2m7: 0-0 3m+: 0-0
Track: LH: 0-1 RH: 0-0 Tight: 0-0 Gall: 0-1
Aids: Bl: 0-0 Vi: 0-0 Tstrap: 0-0 Ckp: 0-0
Best Rating: 106 4/02 Aint 2m1f good NHF

Sadler's Secret (IRE)

110   115

9-y-o b g Sadler's Wells (USA)-Athyka (USA) (Secretariat (USA))
G J Smith (A J Deakin 29/11) Slow Donkey Partnership

Placings:F42143350/013/4203330PP/0043P/30P21233204
-22013P1   (4917)
2003/04: 20²G, 23²GF, 21⁰G, 20¹S, 19³G, 20⁵S, 20¹GS,

	Starts	1st	2nd	3rd	Win & Pl
Hurdles	7	2	2	1	10975
Career Total	44	5	7	11	33261

115	4/04	Worc	2m4f	D(0-115)HHdl	G-S	£5304
107	11/03	Hayd	2m4f	F Hdl	SFT	£2310
110	11/02	Hayd	2m4f	E(0-110)HHdl	GD	£3575
118	4/00	Tntn	2m1f	F(0-110)HHdl	G-S	£2926
107	12/98	Plum	2m1f	E Hdl	SFT	£2512

Total win prize-money £16628

Going: Sf: 1-2 GS: 1-1 Gd: 0-3 GF: - Fm: 0-1
Distance: 2m/2m3: 0-0 **2m4-2m7: 2-6** 3m+: 0-1
Track: **LH: 2-6** RH: 0-1 Tight: 0-2 Gall: 0-1
Aids: Bl: 0-0 Vi: 0-0 Tstrap: 0-0 **Ckp: 2-4**
Best Rating: 124 12/00 Tntn 3m110y soft Hdl

Fair hurdler; goes well at Haydock and won a claimer there in November with plenty to spare; acts on any ground, though best suited by soft surface; effective at two and a half miles.

Sadler's Vic

60f   27f

6-y-o g g Old Vic-Lorna-Gail (Callernish)
A J Chamberlain F J Brennan

Placings:0   (4787)
2003/04: 16⁰G,

	Starts	1st	2nd	3rd	Win & Pl
NH Flat	1	0	0	0	
Career Total	1	0	0	0	

Going: Sf: 0-0 GS: 0-0 Gd: 0-1 GF: - Fm: 0-0
Distance: 2m/2m3: 0-1 2m4-2m7: 0-0 3m+: 0-0
Track: LH: 0-0 RH: 0-1 Tight: 0-0 Gall: 0-1
Aids: Bl: 0-0 Vi: 0-0 Tstrap: 0-0 Ckp: 0-0
Best Rating: 27 4/04 Hntg 2m110y good NHF

Sadlers Wings (IRE)

114   146

6-y-o b h In The Wings-Anna Comnena (IRE) (Shareef Dancer (USA))
W P Mullins John J Brennan

Placings:1161   (4768a)
2003/04: 20¹Y, 16¹S, 21⁶G, 20¹Y,

	Starts	1st	2nd	3rd	Win & Pl
Hurdles	4	3	0	0	37039
Career Total	4	3	0	0	37039

143	4/04	Fair	2m4f	Hdl	YLD	£222005
135	2/04	Navn	2m	Hdl	SFT	£6812
119	12/03	Punc	2m4f	Hdl	YLD	£6720

Total win prize-money £35540

Going: Sf: 1-1 GS: 0-0 Gd: 0-1 GF: - Fm: 0-0
Distance: 2m/2m3: 1-1 **2m4-2m7: 2-3** 3m+: 0-0
Track: LH: 1-2 **RH: 2-2** Tight: 0-0 Gall: 0-1
Aids: Bl: 0-0 Vi: 0-0 **Tstrap: 2-3** Ckp: 0-0
Best Rating: **146** 3/04 Chel 2m5f good Hdl

Smart, exciting novice hurdler; Listed winner on the Flat in Ireland; won three of four starts over hurdles to date in impressive fashion, only defeat coming at Cheltenham in the Royal & SunAlliance Hurdle; stays 2m 4f, but has speed for minimum trip; best on soft ground; sometimes tongue tied.

Safari Paradise (FR)

89 (63c)**79**

7-y-o ch g Red Paradise-Safari Liz (USA) (Hawaii)
M C Pipe P Deal, J Dale, T Neill

Placings:600555640/F442505FP/U00640300-035   (2531)
2003/04: 21⁰G, 24³GF, 21⁵S,

	Starts	1st	2nd	3rd	Win & Pl
Hurdles	2	0	0	0	0
Chases	1	0	0	1	818
Career Total	30	0	1	2	50540

Going:	Sf: 0-1 GS: 0-0 Gd: 0-1 GF: - Fm: 0-1
Distance:	2m/2m3: 0-0 2m4-2m7: 0-2 3m+: 0-1
Track:	LH: 0-2 RH: 0-1 Tight: 0-0 Gall: 0-1
Aids:	Bl: 0-0 Vi: 0-0 Tstrap: 0-0 Ckp: 0-1
Best Rating:	113 2/03 Kemp 2m5f good Hdl

Fair ex-French hurdler/chaser; has shown only modest form over hurdles since coming to Britain; seems best on soft ground.

Safe Enough (IRE)

95 **100+**

8-y-o ch g Safety Catch (USA)-Godfreys Cross (IRE) (Fine Blade (USA))
N J Gifford D S Norden & R S Norden

Placings:00/3/4/01-2   (4790)
2003/04: 21²G,

	Starts	1st	2nd	3rd	Win & Pl
Hurdles	1	0	1	0	1120
Career Total	7	1	1	1	5026
97	10/02	Plum	2m5f	E(0-110)HHdl	G-F	£3445
			Total win prize-money £3445

Going:	Sf: 0-0 GS: 0-0 Gd: 0-1 GF: - Fm: 0-0
Distance:	2m/2m3: 0-0 2m4-2m7: 0-1 3m+: 0-0
Track:	LH: 0-1 RH: 0-0 Tight: 0-1 Gall: 0-0
Aids:	Bl: 0-0 Vi: 0-0 Tstrap: 0-0 Ckp: 0-0
Best Rating:	101 10/00 Chep 2m110y gd-sft Hdl

Modest hurdler, returned from an 18-month absence in April 2004; stays two miles-five, acts on fast ground.

Safe Shot

90 **67**

5-y-o b g Salse (USA)-Optaria (Song)
Mrs J C McGregor The Boozers Brigade

Placings:000-053PP   (4908)
2003/04: 16³G, 16⁵G, 20³G, 20⁵S,

	Starts	1st	2nd	3rd	Win & Pl
Hurdles	5	0	0	1	744
Career Total	8	0	0	1	744

Going:	Sf: 0-1 GS: 0-0 Gd: 0-3 GF: - Fm: 0-1
Distance:	2m/2m3: 0-2 2m4-2m7: 0-3 3m+: 0-0
Track:	LH: 0-2 RH: 0-3 Tight: 0-2 Gall: 0-0
Aids:	Bl: 0-0 Vi: 0-0 Tstrap: 0-0 Ckp: 0-4
Best Rating:	69 11/03 Kels 2m110y good Hdl

Safe To Blush

93f **88f**

6-y-o gr m Blushing Flame (USA)-Safe Arrival (USA) (Shadeed (USA))
P A Pritchard D R Pritchard

Placings:66   (4816)
2003/04: 16⁶G, 16⁶G,

	Starts	1st	2nd	3rd	Win & Pl
NH Flat	2	0	0	0	0
Career Total	2	0	0	0	0

Going:	Sf: 0-0 GS: 0-0 Gd: 0-2 GF: - Fm: 0-0
Distance:	2m/2m3: 0-2 2m4-2m7: 0-0 3m+: 0-0
Track:	LH: 0-0 RH: 0-0 Tight: 0-0 Gall: 0-0
Aids:	Bl: 0-0 Vi: 0-0 Tstrap: 0-0 Ckp: 0-0
Best Rating:	88 4/04 Chep 2m110y good NHF

Saffron Sun

104 (106h)**113**

9-y-o b g Landyap (USA)-Saffron Bun (Sit In The Corner (USA))
J D Frost Mrs J F Bury

Placings:000/3F005/01432613/60P124F-243P31P4 (4715)
2003/04: 20²GF, 24⁴GF, 24³GF, 25⁶G, 23⁶S, 19¹GS, 19⁵S, 20⁴G,

	Starts	1st	2nd	3rd	Win & Pl
Chases	8	1	1	2	10448
Career Total	31	4	3	5	27505
113	1/04	Extr	2m3f110yD(0-125)HCh	G-S	£5740
113	3/03	Extr	2m7f110yD(0-110)HCh	GD	£5006
104	4/02	Extr	2m1f	E Hdl	FRM	£3066
92	6/01	NAbb	2m1f	F(0-100)HHdl	GD	£2667
			Total win prize-money £17427

Going:	Sf: 0-2 GS: 1-1 Gd: 0-2 GF: - Fm: 0-3
Distance:	2m/2m3: 0-1 2m4-2m7: 1-3 3m+: 0-4
Track:	LH: 0-0 RH: 1-8 Tight: 0-0 Gall: 0-0
Aids:	Bl: 0-0 Vi: 0-0 Tstrap: 0-0 Ckp: 0-0
Best Rating:	113 1/04 Extr 2m3f110y gd-sft Ch

Modest chaser; stays three miles but effective at shorter; suited by racing prominently; best on fast ground.

Safi

9-y-o b g Generous (IRE)-Jasarah (IRE) (Green Desert (USA))
D McCain Jnr D McCain Jnr

Placings:PP/335003104/0204524U6/0/60-5   (0475)
2003/04: 26⁵GS,

	Starts	1st	2nd	3rd	Win & Pl
Chases	1	0	0	0	0
Career Total	24	1	2	3	4720
92	12/99	Donc	2m110y	G Hdl	G-F	£1864
			Total win prize-money £1864

Going:	Sf: 0-0 GS: 0-1 Gd: 0-0 GF: - Fm: 0-0
Distance:	2m/2m3: 0-0 2m4-2m7: 0-0 3m+: 0-1
Track:	LH: 0-1 RH: 0-0 Tight: 0-1 Gall: 0-0
Aids:	Bl: 0-0 Vi: 0-0 Tstrap: 0-1 Ckp: 0-0
Best Rating:	92 5/00 Hrfd 2m3f110y good Hdl

Sagardian (FR)

85 **61**

5-y-o b g Mister Mat (FR)-Tipnik (FR) (Nikos)
L Lungo Mrs S J Matthews

Placings (Safari entry continues - Sahhar)

Placings:50P005   (3881)
2003/04: 16⁵G, 17⁰HY, 16⁸S, 16⁹GF, 16⁰HY, 24⁵G,

	Starts	1st	2nd	3rd	Win & Pl
NH Flat	1	0	0	0	0
Hurdles	5	0	0	0	0
Career Total	6	0	0	0	0

Going:	Sf: 0-3 GS: 0-0 Gd: 0-2 GF: - Fm: 0-1
Distance:	2m/2m3: 0-5 2m4-2m7: 0-0 3m+: 0-1
Track:	LH: 0-2 RH: 0-3 Tight: 0-2 Gall: 0-0
Aids:	Bl: 0-0 Vi: 0-0 Tstrap: 0-0 Ckp: 0-1
Best Rating:	80 5/03 Prth 2m110y good NHF

Sahhar

101 **87**

11-y-o ch g Sayf El Arab (USA)-Native Magic (Be My Native (USA))
B D Leavy Mrs Margaret Underwood

Placings:4/6F/0126340/6/510/03/260465-253   (0761)
2003/04: 19²GF, 16⁵GF, 16⁹G,

	Starts	1st	2nd	3rd	Win & Pl
Hurdles	3	0	1	1	1338
Career Total	25	2	3	3	7184
91	11/00	Ludl	2m	G Hdl	GD	£1981
88	8/98	Worc	2m	G(0-95)HHdl	G-F	£1744
			Total win prize-money £3725

Going:	Sf: 0-0 GS: 0-0 Gd: 0-1 GF: - Fm: 0-2
Distance:	2m/2m3: 0-2 2m4-2m7: 0-1 3m+: 0-0
Track:	LH: 0-2 RH: 0-1 Tight: 0-0 Gall: 0-0
Aids:	Bl: 0-0 Vi: 0-0 Tstrap: 0-0 Ckp: 0-0
Best Rating:	91 6/01 Worc 2m gd-fm Hdl

Selling plater over hurdles; acts on a sound surface.

Sailing Through

84 **82**

4-y-o b g Bahhare (USA)-Hopesay (Warning)
R Dickin (T G Mills 22/10) Red Star Racing

Placings:P005   (4839)
2003/04: 16⁸S, 16⁹G, 16⁹GF, 17⁵GF,

	Starts	1st	2nd	3rd	Win & Pl
Hurdles	4	0	0	0	411
Career Total	4	0	0	0	411

Going:	Sf: 0-1 GS: 0-0 Gd: 0-1 GF: - Fm: 0-2
Distance:	2m/2m3: 0-4 2m4-2m7: 0-0 3m+: 0-0
Track:	LH: 0-2 RH: 0-2 Tight: 0-1 Gall: 0-1
Aids:	Bl: 0-0 Vi: 0-0 Tstrap: 0-0 Ckp: 0-0
Best Rating:	82 4/04 Chel 2m1f gd-fm Hdl

Sailor A'Hoy

101 **90**

8-y-o b g Handsome Sailor-Eye Sight (Roscoe Blake)
M Mullineaux R Williamson

Placings:00/204/0P2   (4377)
2003/04: 17⁰GS, 16⁸S, 17²G,

	Starts	1st	2nd	3rd	Win & Pl
Hurdles	3	0	1	0	1350
Career Total	8	0	2	0	2115

Going:	Sf: 0-1 GS: 0-1 Gd: 0-1 GF: - Fm: 0-0
Distance:	2m/2m3: 0-3 2m4-2m7: 0-0 3m+: 0-0
Track:	LH: 0-1 RH: 0-2 Tight: 0-2 Gall: 0-1
Aids:	Bl: 0-0 Vi: 0-0 Tstrap: 0-0 Ckp: 0-0

Best Rating: 95 7/01 MRas 2m1f110y good   Hdl

Plating-class hurdler; best around two miles; acts on a sound surface.

Saint Albert

9-y-o ch g Keen-Thimbalina (Salmon Leap (USA))
C C Bealby Mrs D C Samworth

Placings: 0P/P   (3427)
2003/04: 23^{P}GS,

	Starts	1st	2nd	3rd	Win & Pl
Hurdles	1	0	0	0	
Career Total	3	0	0	0	

Going: Sf: 0-0 GS: 0-1 Gd: 0-0 GF: - Fm: 0-0
Distance: 2m/2m3: 0-2 2m4-2m7: 0-0 3m+: 0-1
Track: LH: 0-1 RH: 0-0 Tight: 0-1 Gall: 0-0
Aids: Bl: 0-0 Vi: 0-0 Tstrap: 0-0 Ckp: 0-0

Saint Esteben (FR)
98   121

5-y-o b g Poliglote-Highest Tulip (FR) (Highest Honor (FR))
P F Nicholls Formpave Ltd

Placings: 312156-2223   (4631)
2003/04: 16^{2}GF, 16^{2}S, 21^{2}GF, 19^{3}G,

	Starts	1st	2nd	3rd	Win & Pl
Chases	4	0	3	1	5819
Career Total	10	2	4	2	33672
11/02	Engh	2m110y	Hdl		HLD £11779
8/02	Claf	2m1f	Hdl		SFT £6773
				Total win prize-money £18552

Going: Sf: 0-1 GS: 0-0 Gd: 0-0 GF: - Fm: 0-2
Distance: 2m/2m3: 0-3 2m4-2m7: 0-0 3m+: 0-0
Track: LH: 0-1 RH: 0-0 Tight: 0-2 Gall: 0-0
Aids: Bl: 0-0 Vi: 0-0 Tstrap: 0-0 Ckp: 0-0
Best Rating: 121 2/04 Tntn 2m110y soft   Ch

Ex-French; runner-up on chase debut; acts on soft ground.

Saint Reverien (FR)
89   (0c)71

5-y-o b g Silver Rainbow-La Briganderie (FR) (Noir Et Or)
Ian Williams (J Bertran De Balanda 9/5) Hill Fuels Limited

Placings: 04F22302-3F060   (4691)
2003/04: 23^{3}VS, 16^{F}G, 19^{9}S, 20^{6}GS, 17^{0}G,

	Starts	1st	2nd	3rd	Win & Pl
Hurdles	3	0	0	0	0
Chases	2	0	0	1	4545
Career Total	13	0	3	2	32525

Going: Sf: 0-1 GS: 0-1 Gd: 0-2 GF: - Fm: 0-0
Distance: 2m/2m3: 0-3 2m4-2m7: 0-2 3m+: 0-0
Track: LH: 0-3 RH: 0-1 Tight: 0-0 Gall: 0-2
Aids: Bl: 0-0 Vi: 0-0 Tstrap: 0-0 Ckp: 0-0
Best Rating: 106 4/03 Autl 2m1f110y v soft   Ch

Placed over hurdles and fences in France; no form yet over here; stays two and a half miles; acts on soft ground.

Saint Romble (FR)
94   100

7-y-o b g Sassanian (USA)-Limatge (FR) (Trac)

P J Hobbs P J Hobbs

Placings: 1/0064/P2123P4-146332   (4549)
2003/04: 16^{1}GS, 19^{4}GS, 17^{6}GS, 18^{3}GS, 20^{3}G, 21^{2}GS,

	Starts	1st	2nd	3rd	Win & Pl
Chases	6	1	1	2	5846
Career Total	18	3	3	3	26610
100	5/03	Worc	2m	F(0-90)Ch	G-S £3402
100	12/02	Asct	2m	D(0-110)HCh	G-S £6776
	4/01	Engh	2m110y	Hdl	HVY £9699
				Total win prize-money £19877

Going: Sf: 0-0 GS: 1-5 Gd: 0-1 GF: - Fm: 0-0
Distance: 2m/2m3: 1-4 2m4-2m7: 0-2 3m+: 0-0
Track: LH: 1-2 RH: 0-3 Tight: 0-2 Gall: 0-0
Aids: Bl: 0-0 Vi: 0-0 Tstrap: 0-0 Ckp: 0-0
Best Rating: 100 5/03 Worc 2m gd-sft   Ch

Modest chaser; flattered by winning distance when scoring at Ascot in December 2002; probably a lucky winner of Class F classified chase at Worcester May 2003; acts on good and soft ground; probably best at 2m in testing ground.

Saint-Declan (IRE)

11-y-o b g Polykratis-Welsh Symphony (Welsh Saint)
Richard Mathias Mrs Hilary Bubb

Placings: S00/2/03/6FP24/0554655-5   (4655)
2003/04: 16^{5}G,

	Starts	1st	2nd	3rd	Win & Pl
Chases	1	0	0	0	0
Career Total	19	0	2	1	3461

Going: Sf: 0-0 GS: 0-0 Gd: 0-1 GF: - Fm: 0-0
Distance: 2m/2m3: 0-1 2m4-2m7: 0-0 3m+: 0-0
Track: LH: 0-0 RH: 0-1 Tight: 0-0 Gall: 0-0
Aids: Bl: 0-0 Vi: 0-0 Tstrap: 0-0 Ckp: 0-0
Best Rating: 84 8/02 Tral 2m good   Ch

Saintly Thoughts (USA)
67   33

9-y-o b/br g St Jovite (USA)-Free Thinker (USA) (Shadeed (USA))
R J Hodges (B J Llewellyn 28/10) Bob Andrews

Placings: 423/PPP/0   (0761)
2003/04: 16^{0}G,

	Starts	1st	2nd	3rd	Win & Pl
Hurdles	1	0	0	0	
Career Total	7	0	1	1	1130

Going: Sf: 0-0 GS: 0-0 Gd: 0-0 GF: - Fm: 0-0
Distance: 2m/2m3: 0-0 2m4-2m7: 0-0 3m+: 0-0
Track: LH: 0-1 RH: 0-0 Tight: 0-0 Gall: 0-0
Aids: Bl: 0-0 Vi: 0-0 Tstrap: 0-0 Ckp: 0-0
Best Rating: 83 7/99 Klny 2m1f gd-fm   Hdl

Saintsaire (FR)
121   144

5-y-o b g Apeldoorn (FR)-Pro Wonder (FR) (The Wonder (FR))
N J Henderson Anthony Speelman

Placings: 1350-33003   (4862)
2003/04: 16^{3}GS, 16^{3}S, 16^{0}G, 16^{0}S, 16^{3}GS,

	Starts	1st	2nd	3rd	Win & Pl
Hurdles	5	0	0	3	18150

Career Total   9   1   0   4   26295
120 12/02 Newb 2m110y D Hdl   GD £4095
Total win prize-money £4095

Going: Sf: 0-2 GS: 0-2 Gd: 0-1 GF: - Fm: 0-0
Distance: 2m/2m3: 0-5 2m4-2m7: 0-0 3m+: 0-0
Track: LH: 0-3 RH: 0-2 Tight: 0-0 Gall: 0-2
Aids: Bl: 0-0 Vi: 0-0 Tstrap: 0-0 Ckp: 0-0
Best Rating: 144 2/04 Newb 2m110y good   Hdl

Very useful hurdler; does not find as much as he promises to; effective at two miles; acts in good and soft ground.

Sajomi Rona (IRE)
(102h)   (77h)

7-y-o ch g Riberetto-Mauma Lady (IRE) (Le Moss)
A Crook Jay Dee Bloodstock Limited

Placings: 00050/P5FP603U   (4661)
2003/04: 26^{P}GF, 20^{5}GF, 21^{F}G, 16^{P}GS, 25^{6}HY, 21^{0}GS, 20^{3}HY, 25^{U}S,

	Starts	1st	2nd	3rd	Win & Pl
Hurdles	2	0	0	0	0
Chases	6	0	0	1	671
Career Total	13	0	0	1	671

Going: Sf: 0-3 GS: 0-2 Gd: 0-1 GF: - Fm: 0-2
Distance: 2m/2m3: 0-1 2m4-2m7: 0-0 3m+: 0-3
Track: LH: 0-5 RH: 0-3 Tight: 0-3 Gall: 0-2
Aids: Bl: 0-2 Vi: 0-1 Tstrap: 0-1 Ckp: 0-1
Best Rating: 77 3/02 Ayr 2m heavy   Hdl

Modest hurdler/hunter chaser; stays three miles; acts on a sound surface.

Saleen (IRE)
33f

4-y-o b f Kahyasi-Sabrata (IRE) (Zino)
P D Cundell P D Cundell

Placings: 0   (2101)
2003/04: 12^{0}GF,

	Starts	1st	2nd	3rd	Win & Pl
NH Flat	1	0	0	0	
Career Total	1	0	0	0	

Going: Sf: 0-0 GS: 0-0 Gd: 0-0 GF: - Fm: 0-1
Distance: 2m/2m3: 0-0 2m4-2m7: 0-0 3m+: 0-0
Track: LH: 0-1 RH: 0-0 Tight: 0-0 Gall: 0-0
Aids: Bl: 0-0 Vi: 0-0 Tstrap: 0-0 Ckp: 0-0
Best Rating: 33 11/03 Newb 1m4f110y gd-fm   NHF

Salford
102(93h)   (75+h)96

9-y-o ch g Salse (USA)-Bustellina (Busted)
N J Hawke C E Handford

Placings: PP/02/51F1P030/P1PP/U4P122-P633P511
(1798)
2003/04: 20^{P}G, 21^{6}G, 21^{3}G, 22^{3}GF, 20^{P}GF, 21^{5}GF, 24^{1}GF, 25^{1}F,

	Starts	1st	2nd	3rd	Win & Pl
Hurdles	1	0	0	0	0
Chases	7	2	0	2	8728
Career Total	30	6	3	3	26670
96	10/03	Winc	3m1f110y	E(0-110)HCh	FRM £4680
88	10/03	Hntg	3m	F(0-95)HCh	G-F £2919
92	3/03	Winc	2m5f	E(0-110)HCh	G-F £3900
94	5/01	Winc	2m5f	F(0-100)HCh	G-F £4160
99	12/00	Ludl	2m5f	E(0-105)HHdl	SFT £2891
83	10/00	Extr	2m3f	E(0-115)HHdl	GD £3198
				Total win prize-money £21748

Going:	Sf: 0-0 GS: 0-0 Gd: 0-3 GF: - Fm: 2-5
Distance:	2m/2m3: 0-0 2m4-2m7: 0-6 3m+: 2-2
Track:	LH: 0-4 RH: 2-2 Tight: 0-4 Gall: 1-1
Aids:	Bl: 0-0 Vi: 0-0 Tstrap: 0-0 Ckp: 0-0
Best Rating:	99 12/00 Ludl 2m5f soft Hdl

Moderate handicap chaser; stays three miles; suited by fast ground.

Salford Flyer

8-y-o b g Pharly (FR)-Edge Of Darkness (Vaigly Great)
Jane Southcombe P L Southcombe

| Placings:6432321/5/P0 | | | | | (3588) |
| 2003/04: 21PG, 16DHY, | | | | | |

	Starts	1st	2nd	3rd	Win & Pl
Hurdles	2	0	0	0	
Career Total	10	1	2	2	6267
110 3/00 Winc 2m		E Hdl		G-S	£2247

Total win prize-money £2247

Going:	Sf: 0-1 GS: 0-0 Gd: 0-1 GF: - Fm: 0-0
Distance:	2m/2m3: 0-1 2m4-2m7: 0-1 3m+: 0-0
Track:	LH: 0-0 RH: 0-2 Tight: 0-0 Gall: 0-0
Aids:	Bl: 0-0 Vi: 0-0 Tstrap: 0-0 Ckp: 0-0
Best Rating:	115 2/00 Kemp 2m good Hdl

Salgrado (NZ)

72

8-y-o ch g Prince Salieri (AUS)-Musing (Music Maestro)
Jonjo O'Neill Ray & Sue Dodd Partnership

| Placings:00-S | | | | | (0367) |
| 2003/04: 16SG, | | | | | |

	Starts	1st	2nd	3rd	Win & Pl
Hurdles	1	0	0	0	
Career Total	3	0	0	0	

Going:	Sf: 0-0 GS: 0-0 Gd: 0-1 GF: - Fm: 0-0
Distance:	2m/2m3: 0-1 2m4-2m7: 0-0 3m+: 0-0
Track:	LH: 0-1 RH: 0-0 Tight: 0-0 Gall: 0-0
Aids:	Bl: 0-0 Vi: 0-0 Tstrap: 0-0 Ckp: 0-0
Best Rating:	77 3/03 Newb 2m110y good Hdl

Salhood

105   125

5-y-o b g Capote (USA)-Princess Haifa (USA) (Mr Prospector (USA))
S Gollings J B Webb

| Placings:20-10211314 | | | | | (4194) |
| 2003/04: 161GF, 17DG, 162SG, 161S, 161G, 163S, 161GS, 164G, | | | | | |

	Starts	1st	2nd	3rd	Win & Pl
NH Flat	2	1	0	0	2009
Hurdles	6	3	1	1	23638
Career Total	10	4	2	1	26209
125 2/04 Newc 2m		B HHdl		G-S	£9135
113 1/04 Donc 2m110y		E Hdl		GD	£3701
119 1/04 Leic 2m		D Hdl		SFT	£5109
106 5/03 Chep 2m110y		H NHF		GF	£2009

Total win prize-money £19955

Going:	Sf: 1-2 GS: 1-2 Gd: 1-3 GF: - Fm: 1-1
Distance:	2m/2m3: 4-8 2m4-2m7: 0-0 3m+: 0-0
Track:	LH: 3-6 RH: 1-1 Tight: 0-1 Gall: 2-3
Aids:	Bl: 0-0 Vi: 0-0 Tstrap: 0-0 Ckp: 0-0
Best Rating:	125 2/04 Newc 2m gd-sft Hdl

Fair hurdler; bumper winner; progressive form over hurdles and turned in best effort back in handicap at Newcastle in February; big type who will make an even better chaser in time; acts on fast and soft ground; best at two miles but looks well worth a try over further.

Salim

85(90h)   (74+h)82+

7-y-o b g Salse (USA)-Moviegoer (Pharly (FR))
Miss J S Davis (G L Moore 30/5) Miss J Davis

| Placings:0P-5P003P305 | | | | | (4379) |
| 2003/04: 16SG, 16PG, 17DGF, 17DGS, 163G, 23PGF, 20DG, 16DG, 24SG, | | | | | |

	Starts	1st	2nd	3rd	Win & Pl
Hurdles	5	0	0	1	395
Chases	4	0	0	1	680
Career Total	11	0	0	2	1075

Going:	Sf: 0-0 GS: 0-1 Gd: 0-6 GF: - Fm: 0-2
Distance:	2m/2m3: 0-6 2m4-2m7: 0-1 3m+: 0-2
Track:	LH: 0-2 RH: 0-7 Tight: 0-4 Gall: 0-0
Aids:	Bl: 0-0 Vi: 0-0 Tstrap: 0-4 Ckp: 0-0
Best Rating:	82 1/04 Ludl 2m4f good Ch

Salinas (GER)

106   112

5-y-o b g Macanal (USA)-Santa Ana (GER) (Acatenango (GER))
M F Harris (C Von Der Recke 26/12) Prevention & Detection Holdings Ltd

| Placings:043030 | | | | | (4651) |
| 2003/04: 16DG, 164G, 173GS, 16DG, 163GS, 17DG, | | | | | |

	Starts	1st	2nd	3rd	Win & Pl
Hurdles	6	0	0	2	1901
Career Total	6	0	0	2	1901

Going:	Sf: 0-0 GS: 0-2 Gd: 0-4 GF: - Fm: 0-0
Distance:	2m/2m3: 0-6 2m4-2m7: 0-0 3m+: 0-0
Track:	LH: 0-3 RH: 0-3 Tight: 0-2 Gall: 0-1
Aids:	Bl: 0-0 Vi: 0-0 Tstrap: 0-0 Ckp: 0-0
Best Rating:	112 12/03 Kemp 2m good Hdl

Modest novice hurdler; winner on the Flat in Germany; suited by a flat track; acts on easy ground.

Salliemak

6-y-o b m Makbul-Glenbrook Fort (Fort Nayef)
A J Wilson Tim Leadbeater

| Placings:0-000 | | | | | (4147) |
| 2003/04: 17DG, 17DG, 24DG, | | | | | |

	Starts	1st	2nd	3rd	Win & Pl
NH Flat	1	0	0	0	
Hurdles	2	0	0	0	0
Career Total	4	0	0	0	

Going:	Sf: 0-0 GS: 0-0 Gd: 0-2 GF: - Fm: 0-1
Distance:	2m/2m3: 0-2 2m4-2m7: 0-0 3m+: 0-1
Track:	LH: 0-1 RH: 0-2 Tight: 0-2 Gall: 0-0
Aids:	Bl: 0-0 Vi: 0-0 Tstrap: 0-0 Ckp: 0-0
Best Rating:	54 6/03 Hrfd 2m1f gd-fm NHF

Sally Lightfoot

81   29

10-y-o ch m Derrylin-Vino Festa (Nebbiolo)
P T Dalton P T Dalton

| Placings:6/540/03/P3530P/P0 | | | | | (0479) |
| 2003/04: 20PS, 21PG, | | | | | |

	Starts	1st	2nd	3rd	Win & Pl
Hurdles	2	0	0	0	
Career Total	14	0	0	3	1213

Going:	Sf: 0-1 GS: 0-0 Gd: 0-0 GF: - Fm: 0-1
Distance:	2m/2m3: 0-0 2m4-2m7: 0-2 3m+: 0-0
Track:	LH: 0-1 RH: 0-0 Tight: 0-1 Gall: 0-1
Aids:	Bl: 0-0 Vi: 0-0 Tstrap: 0-0 Ckp: 0-0
Best Rating:	90 3/99 Uttx 2m heavy NHF

Sally Scally

12-y-o ch m Scallywag-Petite Cone (Celtic Cone)
Miss T Jackson H L Thompson

| Placings:3/40666620P/6460/PPP/6/2/3P4-0 | | | | | (0430) |
| 2003/04: 26DG, | | | | | |

	Starts	1st	2nd	3rd	Win & Pl
Chases	1	0	0	0	
Career Total	23	0	2	2	1873

Going:	Sf: 0-0 GS: 0-0 Gd: 0-1 GF: - Fm: 0-0
Distance:	2m/2m3: 0-0 2m4-2m7: 0-0 3m+: 0-1
Track:	LH: 0-1 RH: 0-0 Tight: 0-1 Gall: 0-0
Aids:	Bl: 0-0 Vi: 0-0 Tstrap: 0-0 Ckp: 0-0
Best Rating:	120 2/98 Winc 2m gd-fm Hdl

Sally's Pride

7-y-o gr m Norton Challenger-Another Scally (Scallywag)
W Clay Fools Who Dream

| Placings:6-UP | | | | | (3279) |
| 2003/04: 20UGS, 16PHY, | | | | | |

	Starts	1st	2nd	3rd	Win & Pl
Hurdles	2	0	0	0	
Career Total	3	0	0	0	0

Going:	Sf: 0-1 GS: 0-1 Gd: 0-0 GF: - Fm: 0-0
Distance:	2m/2m3: 0-1 2m4-2m7: 0-1 3m+: 0-0
Track:	LH: 0-2 RH: 0-0 Tight: 0-0 Gall: 0-0
Aids:	Bl: 0-0 Vi: 0-0 Tstrap: 0-0 Ckp: 0-0
Best Rating:	78 12/02 Fknm 2m gd-sft NHF

Salmon Ladder (USA)

112   100

12-y-o b h Bering-Ballerina Princess (USA) (Mr Prospector (USA))
A J Martin Nicholas Butterly

| Placings:0400/320/3502-026 | | | | | (0826a) |
| 2003/04: 24DYS, 20DG, 24SGF, | | | | | |

	Starts	1st	2nd	3rd	Win & Pl
Hurdles	3	0	1	0	1260
Career Total	14	0	3	2	5401

Going:	Sf: 0-0 GS: 0-0 Gd: 0-1 GF: - Fm: 0-1
Distance:	2m/2m3: 0-0 2m4-2m7: 0-1 3m+: 0-2
Track:	LH: 0-0 RH: 0-2 Tight: 0-0 Gall: 0-0
Aids:	Bl: 0-0 Vi: 0-0 Tstrap: 0-0 Ckp: 0-0
Best Rating:	110 6/01 Tral 2m1f gd-fm Hdl

Moderate hurdler; smart flat horse in England in his prime; now trained in Ireland; runner-up at Perth in April and June; acts on good ground; stays two and a half miles.

Saloup

87

6-y-o b m Wolfhound (USA)-Sarcita (Primo Dominie)
O Sherwood Raymond Tooth

Placings:642/0-F   **(3050)**
2003/04: 17^FG,

	Starts	1st	2nd	3rd	Win & Pl
Hurdles	1	0	0	0	0
Career Total	5	0	1	0	1163

Going:	Sf: 0-0 GS: 0-0 Gd: 0-1 GF: - Fm: 0-0
Distance:	2m/2m3: 0-1 2m4-2m7: 0-0 3m+: 0-0
Track:	LH: 0-0 RH: 0-1 Tight: 0-1 Gall: 0-0
Aids:	Bl: 0-0 Vi: 0-0 Tstrap: 0-0 Ckp: 0-0
Best Rating:	91 12/03 Tntn 2m1f good Hdl

Moderate hurdler; lightly-raced; acts on a sound surface.

Salt Cellar (IRE)

99f   **90f**

5-y-o b g Salse (USA)-Athene (IRE) (Rousillon (USA))
P R Webber Paul Webber

Placings:06   **(4447)**
2003/04: 16⁹GS, 16⁶S,

	Starts	1st	2nd	3rd	Win & Pl
NH Flat	2	0	0	0	0
Career Total	2	0	0	0	0

Going:	Sf: 0-1 GS: 0-1 Gd: 0-0 GF: - Fm: 0-0
Distance:	2m/2m3: 0-2 2m4-2m7: 0-0 3m+: 0-0
Track:	LH: 0-2 RH: 0-0 Tight: 0-0 Gall: 0-1
Aids:	Bl: 0-0 Vi: 0-0 Tstrap: 0-0 Ckp: 0-0
Best Rating:	90 3/04 Wwck 2m soft NHF

Half-brother to useful French mile and a half winner; stepped up on his debut in Warwick bumper second start.

Salvage

105(89h)   (100h)**100**

9-y-o b g Kahyasi-Storm Weaver (USA) (Storm Bird (CAN))
Mrs J C McGregor Mrs E R Sneddon

Placings:031/33/254P23B4/344P535/P3056425-
221523332   **(4940)**
2003/04: 16²G, 16²G, 17¹G, 21⁵G, 17²S, 17³S, 17³GS, 17³G,
16²GS,

	Starts	1st	2nd	3rd	Win & Pl
Chases	9	1	4	3	12923
Career Total	37	2	7	10	26054
90	11/03	Kels	2m1f	E(0-110)HCh	GD	£3510
93	4/99	Carl	2m1f	E Hdl	GD	£2612
				Total win prize-money £6122

Going:	Sf: 0-2 GS: 0-2 Gd: 1-5 GF: - Fm: 0-0
Distance:	2m/2m3: 1-8 2m4-2m7: 0-0 3m+: 0-0
Track:	LH: 1-6 RH: 0-3 Tight: 1-5 Gall: 0-0
Aids:	Bl: 0-0 Vi: 0-0 Tstrap: 0-0 Ckp: 0-0
Best Rating:	105 9/00 Prth 2m1l0y heavy Hdl

Plating-class hurdler/chaser, has a real liking for Kelso; suited by two miles on quick ground; consistent.

Salvo

(79h)   (75h)

13-y-o ch g K-Battery-Saleander (Leander)
Miss M Bragg W H Whitley

Placings:000/12352/U/F5/045613/0P5   **(1269)**
2003/04: 22^QGF, 20^PGF, 26⁵GF,

	Starts	1st	2nd	3rd	Win & Pl
Hurdles	2	0	0	0	0
Chases	1	0	0	0	0
Career Total	20	2	2	2	7516
98	12/01	Tntn	2m3f	F(0-110)HCh	G-S	£3444
10/95	Hexm	2m	E Hdl	G-F	£2127
				Total win prize-money £5572

Going:	Sf: 0-0 GS: 0-0 Gd: 0-0 GF: - Fm: 0-3
Distance:	2m/2m3: 0-0 2m4-2m7: 0-0 3m+: 0-1
Track:	LH: 0-3 RH: 0-0 Tight: 0-2 Gall: 0-0
Aids:	Bl: 0-0 Vi: 0-0 Tstrap: 0-0 Ckp: 0-0
Best Rating:	98 12/01 Tntn 2m3f gd-sft Ch

Plating-class hurdler/chaser; seems to act on any ground.

Sam Adamson

108(95h)   (63h)**103**

9-y-o br g Domitor (USA)-Sardine (Saritamer (USA))
J W Mullins M Jenkins

Placings:600/000P0/45-12316211P   **(1521)**
2003/04: 21¹GF, 16²GF, 20³GF, 21¹GF, 24⁶G, 20²GF, 20¹GF,
19¹GF, 22^PG,

	Starts	1st	2nd	3rd	Win & Pl
Chases	9	4	2	1	19755
Career Total	19	4	2	1	20050
103	10/03	Hrfd	2m3f	D(0-115)HCh	G-F	£5759
103	9/03	Worc	2m4f110yE(0-100)HCh	G-F	£2975
93	7/03	Strf	2m5f110yE(0-105)HCh	G-F	£4124
93	5/03	Winc	2m5f	E(0-100)HCh	G-F	£3978
				Total win prize-money £16836

Going:	Sf: 0-0 GS: 0-0 Gd: 0-2 GF: - Fm: 4-7
Distance:	2m/2m3: 1-2 2m4-2m7: 3-6 3m+: 0-1
Track:	LH: 2-4 RH: 2-4 Tight: 1-3 Gall: 0-1
Aids:	Bl: 0-0 Vi: 0-0 Tstrap: 4-9 Ckp: 0-0
Best Rating:	103 10/03 Hrfd 2m3f gd-fm Ch

Moderate chaser; has improved in the summer of 2003; acts on good to firm; best at around two and a half miles; genuine type.

Sam Rockett

(101h)   (92h)

11-y-o b g Petong-Art Deco (Artaius (USA))
P J Hobbs L G Kennard

Placings:600100/2114126/3P/F00040/6054552114/004012
4/4053-600P   **(1191)**
2003/04: 22⁶GF, 27⁰G, 22⁰GF, 23^PGF,

	Starts	1st	2nd	3rd	Win & Pl
Hurdles	3	0	0	0	0
Chases	1	0	0	0	0
Career Total	46	7	4	2	20755
92	8/01	NAbb	3m3f	F(0-105)HHdl	GD	£2961
91	9/00	Hrfd	3m2f	E(0-115)HHdl	G-F	£3090
90	8/00	Font	2m4f	F(0-100)HHdl	G-F	£2289
104	11/97	NAbb	2m1f	E(0-110)HHdl	G-F	£2253
91	9/97	NAbb	2m1f	G Hdl	GD	£1784
100	8/97	NAbb	2m1f	G(0-95)HHdl	G-F	£1860
82	1/97	Tntn	2m1f	G Hdl	G-F	£1857
				Total win prize-money £16098

Going:	Sf: 0-0 GS: 0-0 Gd: 0-1 GF: - Fm: 0-3
Distance:	2m/2m3: 0-0 2m4-2m7: 0-2 3m+: 0-2
Track:	LH: 0-4 RH: 0-0 Tight: 0-3 Gall: 0-0
Aids:	Bl: 0-3 Vi: 0-0 Tstrap: 0-0 Ckp: 0-0
Best Rating:	104 11/97 NAbb 2m1f gd-fm Hdl

Moderate handicap hurdler; needs marathon distances these days; acts on ground good or faster.

Samandara (FR)

4-y-o b f Kris-Samneeza (USA) (Storm Bird (CAN))
A King (A De Royer-Dupre 19/11) Miss J M Bodycote

Placings:P   **(3806)**
2003/04: 16^PG,

	Starts	1st	2nd	3rd	Win & Pl
Hurdles	1	0	0	0	0
Career Total	1	0	0	0	0

Going:	Sf: 0-0 GS: 0-0 Gd: 0-1 GF: - Fm: 0-0
Distance:	2m/2m3: 0-1 2m4-2m7: 0-0 3m+: 0-0
Track:	LH: 0-0 RH: 0-1 Tight: 0-0 Gall: 0-0
Aids:	Bl: 0-0 Vi: 0-0 Tstrap: 0-0 Ckp: 0-0

Dual winner on the Flat in France; very disappointing on British hurdling debut.

Samar Qand

5-y-o b m Selkirk (USA)-Sit Alkul (USA) (Mr Prospector (USA))
Julian Poulton Gryffindor (www.racingtours.co.uk)

Placings:P   **(4783)**
2003/04: 21^PG,

	Starts	1st	2nd	3rd	Win & Pl
Hurdles	1	0	0	0	0
Career Total	1	0	0	0	0

Going:	Sf: 0-0 GS: 0-0 Gd: 0-1 GF: - Fm: 0-0
Distance:	2m/2m3: 0-0 2m4-2m7: 0-1 3m+: 0-0
Track:	LH: 0-0 RH: 0-1 Tight: 0-0 Gall: 0-1
Aids:	Bl: 0-0 Vi: 0-0 Tstrap: 0-0 Ckp: 0-0

Samby

109   **120+**

6-y-o ch g Anshan-Mossy Fern (Le Moss)
O Sherwood R Waters

Placings:221-121P   **(3604)**
2003/04: 16¹G, 19²G, 19¹GS, 24^PS,

	Starts	1st	2nd	3rd	Win & Pl
Hurdles	4	2	1	0	7742
Career Total	7	3	3	0	11128
120	12/03	Donc	2m3f110yE Hdl	G-S	£3043
95	10/03	Towc	2m	D Hdl	GD	£3614
100	3/03	Folk	2m1f110yH NHF	GD	£1960
				Total win prize-money £8618

Going:	Sf: 0-1 GS: 1-1 Gd: 1-2 GF: - Fm: 0-0
Distance:	2m/2m3: 1-1 2m4-2m7: 1-2 3m+: 0-1
Track:	LH: 1-2 RH: 1-2 Tight: 0-1 Gall: 0-1
Aids:	Bl: 0-0 Vi: 0-0 Tstrap: 0-0 Ckp: 0-0
Best Rating:	120 12/03 Donc 2m3f110y gd-sft Hdl

Promising novice hurdler; bumper winner; suited by two and a half miles.

Sammagefromtenesse (IRE)

106 **82**

7-y-o b g Petardia-Canoora (Ahonoora)
N F Glynn N F Glynn

Placings:6000/000000/P360P0-10006P0P (3064a)
2003/04: 17¹GS, 16⁰YS, 16⁰GY, 16⁰YS, 16⁸GF, 16ᴾGF, 16⁰G, 18ᴾS,

	Starts	1st	2nd	3rd	Win & Pl
Hurdles	8	1	0	0	2492
Career Total	24	1	0	1	2928
82 5/03 Hrfd 2m1f G(0-95)HHdl G-S £2492					
Total win prize-money £2492					

Going:	Sf: 0-1 GS: 1-1 Gd: 0-1 GF: - Fm: 0-2
Distance:	**2m2/m3: 1-8** 2m4-2m7: 0-0 3m+: 0-0
Track:	LH: 0-3 RH: **1-2** Tight: 0-1 Gall: 0-0
Aids:	Bl: 0-1 Vi: 0-0 Tstrap: 0-0 Ckp: 0-1
Best Rating:	92 7/01 Slig 2m good Hdl

Plating-class irish hurdler; acts on a sound surface.

Samon (GER)

100(115h) (145h)**119**

7-y-o ch g Monsun (GER)-Savanna (GER) (Sassafras (FR))
M C Pipe The Macca & Growler Partnership

Placings:10/0325-111 (0626)
2003/04: 21¹GF, 20¹GF, 21¹GF,

	Starts	1st	2nd	3rd	Win & Pl
Chases	3	3	0	0	12811
Career Total	9	4	1	1	35418
117 6/03 Uttx 2m5f E Ch G-F £4728					
119 5/03 Font 2m4f E Ch G-F £4075					
114 5/03 Sthl 2m5f110yE Ch G-F £4007					
145 1/02 Tntn 2m1f E Hdl SFT £3033					
Total win prize-money £15845					

Going:	Sf: 0-0 GS: 0-0 Gd: 0-0 GF: - Fm: 3-3
Distance:	2m/2m3: 0-0 **2m4-2m7: 3-3** 3m+: 0-0
Track:	**LH: 2-2** RH: 0-0 Tight: **1-1** Gall: 0-0
Aids:	Bl: 0-0 Vi: 0-0 Tstrap: 0-0 Ckp: 0-0
Best Rating:	145 3/03 Chel 2m5f good Hdl

Fair chaser, ex-German; stays two miles five; acts on soft and good ground; runner-up in the Coral Cup at the Cheltenham Festival in 2003.

Samsaam (IRE)

108 **133**

7-y-o b g Sadler's Wells (USA)-Azyaa (Kris)
M C Pipe Matt Archer & Miss Jean Broadhurst

Placings:41P/052-1B (0918)
2003/04: 20¹GF, 17⁸GF,

	Starts	1st	2nd	3rd	Win & Pl
Hurdles	2	1	0	0	5070
Career Total	8	2	1	0	10048
127 6/03 Uttx 2m4f110yD(0-115)HHdl G-F £5070					
108 3/02 Winc 2m E Hdl GD £2758					
Total win prize-money £7828					

Going:	Sf: 0-0 GS: 0-0 Gd: 0-0 GF: - Fm: 1-2
Distance:	2m/2m3: 0-1 **2m4-2m7: 1-1** 3m+: 0-0
Track:	**LH: 1-1** RH: 0-1 Tight: 1-2 Gall: 0-0
Aids:	Bl: 0-0 Vi: **1-2** Tstrap: 1-2 Ckp: 0-0
Best Rating:	127 6/03 Uttx 2m4f110y gd-fm Hdl

Fair hurdler, Group Three winner on the Flat for John Dunlop; stays two and a half miles; has worn blinkers or a visor and been tongue tied.

Samson Des Galas (FR)

6-y-o b/br g Agent Bleu (FR)-Sarema (FR) (Primo Dominie)
R Ford J & G Sporting Partners

Placings:6-P (4812)
2003/04: 16ᴾG,

	Starts	1st	2nd	3rd	Win & Pl
Hurdles	1	0	0	0	
Career Total	2	0	0	0	0

Going:	Sf: 0-0 GS: 0-0 Gd: 0-1 GF: - Fm: 0-0
Distance:	2m/2m3: 0-1 2m4-2m7: 0-0 3m+: 0-0
Track:	LH: 0-1 RH: 0-0 Tight: 0-0 Gall: 0-0
Aids:	Bl: 0-0 Vi: 0-0 Tstrap: 0-0 Ckp: 0-0
Best Rating:	91 2/03 Weth 2m gd-sft NHF

Samuel Wilderspin

107 **137**

12-y-o b g Henbit (USA)-Littoral (Crash Course)
R Lee Steve Smith

Placings:106/321143/6122P1/130/24P130/1512FP/23540P -54504P (4834)
2003/04: 24⁵GF, 32⁴G, 33⁵G, 24⁰S, 26⁴G, 26ᴾGF,

	Starts	1st	2nd	3rd	Win & Pl
Chases	6	0	0	0	2283
Career Total	42	9	6	5	83293
142 2/02 Hayd 3m E(0-140)HCh HVY £9653					
140 11/01 Chel 3m110y E(0-135)HCh GD £8736					
136 2/01 Weth 3m1f C(0-135)HCh SFT £6780					
130 5/99 Towc 3m1f E Ch SFT £3156					
119 4/99 Wwck 3m2f D Ch SFT £4465					
116 1/99 Wwck 2m4f110yD Ch SFT £4695					
134 2/98 Wwck 2m4f110yB Hdl GD £6807					
111 1/98 Donc 2m4f D Hdl GD £4136					
118 2/97 Wwck 2m H NHF GD £1028					
Total win prize-money £49461					

Going:	Sf: 0-1 GS: 0-0 Gd: 0-3 GF: - Fm: 0-2
Distance:	2m/2m3: 0-0 2m4-2m7: 0-0 3m+: 0-6
Track:	LH: 0-5 RH: 0-1 Tight: 0-1 Gall: 0-3
Aids:	Bl: 0-0 Vi: 0-0 Tstrap: 0-4 Ckp: 0-0
Best Rating:	142 2/02 Hayd 3m heavy Ch

Modest chaser; best at around three miles; stays well; acts on soft ground; runs well fresh; often wears a tongue tie; has broken blood vessels in the past.

San Dimas (USA)

99 **96+**

7-y-o gr g Distant View (USA)-Chrystophard (USA) (Lypheor)
R Allan Mrs R P Aggio

Placings:4/4P4026033/0135P4-1F (1688)
2003/04: 22¹F, 22ᴾGF,

	Starts	1st	2nd	3rd	Win & Pl
Hurdles	2	1	0	0	2608
Career Total	18	2	1	3	7866
100 10/03 Kels 2m6f110y E(0-105)HHdl FRM £2607					
95 10/03 Kels 2m6f110yE Hdl G-F £3445					
Total win prize-money £6053					

Going:	Sf: 0-0 GS: 0-0 Gd: 0-0 GF: - Fm: 1-2
Distance:	2m/2m3: 0-0 **2m4-2m7: 1-2** 3m+: 0-0
Track:	**LH: 1-2** RH: 0-0 **Tight: 1-2** Gall: 0-0
Aids:	Bl: 0-0 Vi: **1-2** Tstrap: 0-0 Ckp: 0-0
Best Rating:	100 10/03 Kels 2m6f110y firm Hdl

Moderate hurdler; goes well at Kelso; stays two miles six; acts on a sound surface; usually wears a visor, but has worn cheekpieces.

San Francisco

94 **95**

10-y-o b g Aragon-Sirene Bleu Marine (USA) (Secreto (USA))
A C Whillans C Bird

Placings:32030/00213/25534/P04133U3052/3466110F3/5 P5P446325-03 (0395)
2003/04: 22⁰G, 20³GS,

	Starts	1st	2nd	3rd	Win & Pl
Chases	2	0	0	1	465
Career Total	47	4	5	11	27292
99 3/02 Ayr 2m F(0-95)HCh SFT £2936					
89 3/02 Ayr 2m F(0-95)HCh HVY £4273					
94 12/00 Newc 2m110y F(0-90)Ch SFT £2380					
99 3/99 Ayr 2m D(0-110)HHdl SFT £2882					
Total win prize-money £12473					

Going:	Sf: 0-0 GS: 0-1 Gd: 0-1 GF: - Fm: 0-0
Distance:	2m/2m3: 0-0 2m4-2m7: 0-2 3m+: 0-0
Track:	LH: 0-1 RH: 0-1 Tight: 0-1 Gall: 0-0
Aids:	Bl: 0-0 Vi: 0-0 Tstrap: 0-0 Ckp: 0-0
Best Rating:	103 2/01 Kels 2m1f soft Ch

Moderate handicap chaser; handles testing ground; best at around two miles.

San Marco (IRE)

95(93h) (88h)**93**

6-y-o b g Brief Truce (USA)-Nuit Des Temps (Sadler's Wells (USA))
Mrs P Sly R Brazier

Placings:P03/P-3403324F (3318)
2003/04: 20³GF, 20⁴G, 20⁰GF, 16³G, 20³G, 20²F, 23⁴GF, 23⁰G,

	Starts	1st	2nd	3rd	Win & Pl
Hurdles	5	0	0	3	862
Chases	3	0	1	0	1549
Career Total	12	0	1	4	2840

Going:	Sf: 0-0 GS: 0-0 Gd: 0-4 GF: - Fm: 0-4
Distance:	2m/2m3: 0-1 2m4-2m7: 0-5 3m+: 0-2
Track:	LH: 0-4 RH: 0-4 Tight: 0-3 Gall: 0-0
Aids:	Bl: 0-0 Vi: 0-0 Tstrap: 0-0 Ckp: 0-8
Best Rating:	99 1/02 Tram 2m sft-hvy Hdl

Plating-class hurdler; runner-up on chasing debut; stays 2m4f easily; wears cheekpieces; frustrating.

San Marino (IRE)

86

8-y-o b g Torus-Lousion (Lucifer (USA))
Miss Venetia Williams P Ryan

Placings:4/3FF-F (0060)
2003/04: 17⁵GS,

	Starts	1st	2nd	3rd	Win & Pl
Hurdles	1	0	0	0	
Career Total	5	0	0	1	652

Going:	Sf: 0-0 GS: 0-1 Gd: 0-0 GF: - Fm: 0-0
Distance:	2m/2m3: 0-1 2m4-2m7: 0-0 3m+: 0-0
Track:	LH: 0-0 RH: 0-1 Tight: 0-0 Gall: 0-0
Aids:	Bl: 0-0 Vi: 0-0 Tstrap: 0-0 Ckp: 0-0
Best Rating:	88 10/01 Fknm 2m soft NHF

San Peire (FR)

98(103c)   (115+c)**107+**

7-y-o b g Cyborg (FR)-Shakapoura (FR) (Shakapour)
J Howard Johnson Comtake-Welding Engineering Specialists

Placings:0605/3P021-124155   **(4617)**
2003/04: 27¹S, 21²G, 21⁴G, 27¹GS, 27⁵GS, 27⁵G,

	Starts	1st	2nd	3rd	Win & Pl
Hurdles	5	1	1	0	4627
Chases	1	1	0	0	4391
Career Total	15	3	2	1	12814
115	2/04	Sedg	3m3f	E Ch	G-S	£4390
107	5/03	Sedg	3m3f110yF(0-90)HHdl	SFT	£3437
101	3/03	Sedg	3m3f110yF Hdl	GD	£2681
			Total win prize-money £10509		

Going:	Sf: 1-1 GS: 1-2 Gd: 0-3 GF: - Fm: 0-0
Distance:	2m/2m3: 0-0 2m4-2m7: 0-2 **3m+: 2-4**
Track:	LH: **2-6** RH: 0-0 **Tight: 2-6** Gall: 0-0
Aids:	Bl: 0-0 Vi: 0-0 Tstrap: 0-0 Ckp: 0-0
Best Rating:	115 2/04 Sedg 3m3f gd-sft Ch

Modest hurdler/chaser; much improved since stepping up to extreme distances; stays three miles-three; acts on good ground or softer; has worn cheekpieces.

Sandabar

94   **83**

11-y-o b g Green Desert (USA)-Children's Corner (FR) (Top Ville)
G A Swinbank (N Waggott 29/5) Miss T Waggott

Placings:2600002/1223111/145/24/03362613000/F043   **(1838)**
2003/04: 16²G, 17⁰G, 16⁴G, 17³G,

	Starts	1st	2nd	3rd	Win & Pl
Hurdles	4	0	0	1	269
Career Total	34	6	6	5	21692
97	7/01	Sedg	2m1f	F(0-105)HHdl	G-F	£1928
126	5/99	Weth	2m	D(0-120)HHdl	GD	£2786
116	9/98	Prth	2m110y	D Hdl	GD	£2788
113	9/98	Sedg	2m1f	F(0-105)HHdl	GD	£1954
104	8/98	Prth	2m110y	D Hdl	G-F	£2762
109	5/98	Kels	2m110y	E(0-105)HHdl	G-F	£1738
			Total win prize-money £13958		

Going:	Sf: 0-0 GS: 0-0 Gd: 0-3 GF: - Fm: 0-1
Distance:	2m/2m3: 0-4 2m4-2m7: 0-0 3m+: 0-0
Track:	LH: 0-4 RH: 0-0 Tight: 0-2 Gall: 0-0
Aids:	Bl: 0-0 Vi: 0-0 Tstrap: 0-4 Ckp: 0-0
Best Rating:	126 5/99 Weth 2m good Hdl

Plating-class hurdler; lightly-raced of late; acts on fast.

Sandal Saphire

5-y-o b m Danzig Connection (USA)-Mudflap (Slip Anchor)
K A Ryan W J Dobson

Placings:P   **(0940)**
2003/04: 17⁰GF,

	Starts	1st	2nd	3rd	Win & Pl
NH Flat	1	0	0	0	
Career Total	1	0	0	0	

Going:	Sf: 0-0 GS: 0-0 Gd: 0-0 GF: - Fm: 0-1
Distance:	2m/2m3: 0-1 2m4-2m7: 0-0 3m+: 0-0
Track:	LH: 0-1 RH: 0-0 Tight: 0-1 Gall: 0-0
Aids:	Bl: 0-0 Vi: 0-0 Tstrap: 0-0 Ckp: 0-0

Sandrone (IRE)

4-y-o b f In Command (IRE)-Florinda (CAN) (Vice Regent (CAN))
P M Phelan Andrew L Cohen

Placings:P   **(2205)**
2003/04: 17⁵G,

	Starts	1st	2nd	3rd	Win & Pl
Hurdles	1	0	0	0	
Career Total	1	0	0	0	

Going:	Sf: 0-0 GS: 0-0 Gd: 0-1 GF: - Fm: 0-0
Distance:	2m/2m3: 0-1 2m4-2m7: 0-0 3m+: 0-0
Track:	LH: 0-0 RH: 0-1 Tight: 0-1 Gall: 0-0
Aids:	Bl: 0-0 Vi: 0-0 Tstrap: 0-0 Ckp: 0-0

Sands Of Thyne (IRE)

6-y-o ch g Good Thyne (USA)-Yesterdays Gorby (IRE) (Strong Gale)
Noel T Chance A D Weller

Placings:20   **(2381)**
2003/04: 17²GF, 16⁰G,

	Starts	1st	2nd	3rd	Win & Pl
NH Flat	1	0	1	0	594
Hurdles	1	0	0	0	0
Career Total	2	0	1	0	594

Going:	Sf: 0-0 GS: 0-0 Gd: 0-1 GF: - Fm: 0-1
Distance:	2m/2m3: 0-2 2m4-2m7: 0-0 3m+: 0-0
Track:	LH: 0-1 RH: 0-1 Tight: 0-1 Gall: 0-0
Aids:	Bl: 0-0 Vi: 0-0 Tstrap: 0-0 Ckp: 0-0
Best Rating:	101 5/03 MRas 2m1f110y gd-fm NHF

Sands Rising

99   **98+**

7-y-o b g Primitive Rising (USA)-Celtic Sands (Celtic Cone)
R Johnson T L A Robson

Placings:00/030434-2105030   **(4662)**
2003/04: 22²G, 20¹HY, 20⁵S, 20⁵S, 20³HY, 20⁰S,

	Starts	1st	2nd	3rd	Win & Pl
Hurdles	7	1	1	1	4954
Career Total	15	1	1	3	6569
100	11/03	Carl	2m4f	E Hdl	HVY	£3596
			Total win prize-money £3597		

Going:	Sf: 1-6 GS: 0-0 Gd: 0-1 GF: - Fm: 0-0
Distance:	2m/2m3: 0-0 **2m4-2m7:** 1-7 3m+: 0-0
Track:	LH: 0-5 **RH:** 1-2 Tight: 0-1 Gall: 0-1
Aids:	Bl: 0-0 Vi: 0-0 Tstrap: 0-0 Ckp: 0-0
Best Rating:	100 11/03 Carl 2m4f heavy Hdl

Modest hurdler, won at Carlisle in November; stays three miles; acts on good and heavy ground.

Sandy Bay (IRE)

5-y-o b g Spectrum (IRE)-Karinski (USA) (Palace Music (USA))
R Allan (M W Easterby 19/7) Gary Harrison

Placings:5   **(0921)**
2003/04: 17³GF,

	Starts	1st	2nd	3rd	Win & Pl
Hurdles	1	0	0	0	0
Career Total	1	0	0	0	0

Going:	Sf: 0-0 GS: 0-0 Gd: 0-0 GF: - Fm: 0-1
Distance:	2m/2m3: 0-1 2m4-2m7: 0-0 3m+: 0-0
Track:	LH: 0-0 RH: 0-1 Tight: 0-1 Gall: 0-0
Aids:	Bl: 0-0 Vi: 0-0 Tstrap: 0-0 Ckp: 0-0

Sandy Duff

83   **107**

10-y-o ch g Scottish Reel-Not Enough (Balinger)
J D Frost The Tuesday Syndicate

Placings:10/211P/2336P/113502/F5-6   **(0486)**
2003/04: 16⁶GF,

	Starts	1st	2nd	3rd	Win & Pl
Chases	1	0	0	0	0
Career Total	20	5	3	3	24320
127	10/01	Sthl	2m	E Ch	GD	£3357
111	5/01	Ling	2m	E Ch	G-F	£3549
121	1/00	Donc	2m110y	E Hdl	GD	£2814
121	12/99	Folk	2m1f110y	E Hdl	SFT	£2512
116	1/99	Ludl	2m	H NHF	SFT	£1546
			Total win prize-money £13779		

Going:	Sf: 0-0 GS: 0-0 Gd: 0-0 GF: - Fm: 0-1
Distance:	2m/2m3: 0-1 2m4-2m7: 0-0 3m+: 0-0
Track:	LH: 0-1 RH: 0-0 Tight: 0-1 Gall: 0-0
Aids:	Bl: 0-1 Vi: 0-0 Tstrap: 0-0 Ckp: 0-0
Best Rating:	133 12/00 Kemp 2m gd-sft Ch

Modest chaser; disappointing when well backed in first-time blinkers at Newton Abbot May 2003; suited by 2m and a sound surface.

Sandywell George

98   **88**

9-y-o ch g Zambrano-Farmcote Air (True Song)
L P Grassick David Lloyd & Mrs Carole Lloyd

Placings:0/004P/P603P/6U00PP5-3025223231000   **(4488)**
2003/04: 21³GF, 24⁴S, 20²GF, 24⁵GF, 20²G, 20²GF, 20³GF, 20²GF, 19¹GS, 22⁰S, 18⁰G, 22⁰G,

	Starts	1st	2nd	3rd	Win & Pl
Hurdles	13	1	4	4	7422
Career Total	29	1	4	4	7876
95	12/03	Wwck	2m3f	F(0-95)HHdl	G-S	£2457
			Total win prize-money £2457		

Going:	Sf: 0-2 GS: 1-1 Gd: 0-3 GF: - Fm: 0-7
Distance:	2m/2m3: 1-2 2m4-2m7: 0-9 3m+: 0-2
Track:	LH: 1-12 RH: 0-1 Tight: 0-2 Gall: 0-0
Aids:	Bl: 0-0 Vi: 0-0 **Tstrap:** 1-13 Ckp: 0-0
Best Rating:	95 12/03 Wwck 2m3f gd-sft Hdl

Plating-class hurdler; acts on a sound surface; does not appear to stay 3m.

Sangatte (IRE)

92   **92**

6-y-o b g Un Desperado (FR)-Mad House (Kabour)
N J Henderson Trevor Hemmings

Placings:5P0   **(3265)**
2003/04: 16⁵S, 16²GF, 16⁰S,

	Starts	1st	2nd	3rd	Win & Pl
NH Flat	1	0	0	0	0
Hurdles	2	0	0	0	0
Career Total	3	0	0	0	0

Going: Sf: 0-2 GS: 0-1 Gd: 0-0 GF: - Fm: 0-0
Distance: 2m/2m3: 0-3 2m4-2m7: 0-0 3m+: 0-0
Track: LH: 0-1 RH: 0-2 Tight: 0-0 Gall: 0-0
Aids: Bl: 0-0 Vi: 0-0 Tstrap: 0-0 Ckp: 0-0
Best Rating: 86 1/04 Asct 2m110y soft Hdl

Well beaten so far in bumpers and novice hurdles.

Santa Lucia
102(106h)   (100h)87
8-y-o b m Namaqualand (USA)-Villasanta (Corvaro (USA))
Miss Lucinda V Russell (M Dods 3/7) Kelso Members Lowflyers Club

Placings:F/60241/042335-60313335F3 (4849)
2003/04: 20⁶G, 24⁴G, 20³GF, 20¹G, 21³GF, 20³G, 25³GF, 21⁵GS, 21¹FG, 16³GS,

	Starts	1st	2nd	3rd	Win & Pl
Hurdles	5	1	0	2	7103
Chases	5	0	0	3	1799
Career Total	22	2	2	7	15345
100 7/03 Prth	2m4f110yF Hdl		GD		£3419
100 4/02 Prth	2m4f110yD Hdl		GD		£3718
			Total win prize-money		£7137

Going: Sf: 0-0 GS: 0-2 Gd: 1-5 GF: - Fm: 0-3
Distance: 2m/2m3: 0-1 2m4-2m7: 1-7 3m+: 0-2
Track: LH: 0-7 RH: 1-3 Tight: 0-0 Gall: 0-0
Aids: Bl: 0-0 Vi: 0-0 Tstrap: 0-0 Ckp: 0-3
Best Rating: 100 4/04 Ayr 2m gd-sft Hdl

Modest selling hurdler; well beaten over fences so far; suited by fast ground but handles softer, stays two and a half miles.

Santella Boy (USA)
54   (50h)80+
12-y-o b g Turkoman (USA)-Dream Creek (USA) (The Minstrel (CAN))
Miss C Dyson Miss C Dyson

Placings:36/351321142F4/112132/0PP4P254/P0/00423/04633/014-P3P3 (4549)
2003/04: 24⁵GF, 24³G, 24⁵G, 21³GS,

	Starts	1st	2nd	3rd	Win & Pl
Hurdles	1	0	0	0	0
Chases	3	0	0	2	1017
Career Total	46	7	6	9	31876
80 8/02 NAbb	3m2f110yF(0-90)HCh		G-F		£2933
117 7/97 Sthl	3m110y E Ch		G-F		£3593
117 6/97 Uttx	2m7f D Ch		G-F		£3420
113 5/97 Extr	2m7f110yD Ch		GD		£3550
97 9/96 Extr	2m6f E(0-110)HHdl		FRM		£2611
103 8/96 Hntg	2m4f110yE Hdl		G-F		£2192
94 6/96 MRas	3m D Hdl		G-F		£2974
			Total win prize-money		£21276

Going: Sf: 0-0 GS: 0-1 Gd: 0-2 GF: - Fm: 0-1
Distance: 2m/2m3: 0-0 2m4-2m7: 0-1 3m+: 0-3
Track: LH: 0-2 RH: 0-2 Tight: 0-1 Gall: 0-1
Aids: Bl: 0-0 Vi: 0-0 Tstrap: 0-0 Ckp: 0-0
Best Rating: 117 7/97 Sthl 3m110y gd-fm Ch

Very modest chaser, stays well.

Santenay (FR)
111(126h)   (160h)145
6-y-o b g Mister Mat (FR)-Guigone (FR) (Esprit Du Nord (USA))
P F Nicholls The Hon Mrs Townshend

Placings:522P14/11201-22111F1306 (4954)
2003/04: 16²GF, 19²GF, 16¹GF, 16¹GF, 16¹G, 16⁶GS, 16¹G, 20³G, 16⁵G, 16⁶G,

	Starts	1st	2nd	3rd	Win & Pl
Hurdles	1	0	0	0	1050
Chases	9	4	2	1	41578
Career Total	21	8	5	1	131730
145 12/03 Chel	2m110y B Ch		GD		£13268
134 11/03 Aint	2m C Ch		GD		£8645
134 11/03 Sand	2m D Ch		G-F		£4860
10/03 Kemp	2m D Ch		G-F		£7140
137 4/03 Sand	2m110y B Hdl		G-F		£34800
146 11/02 Winc	2m A HHdl		GD		£20300
142 10/02 Chep	2m110y B HHdl		G-F		£9958
116 3/02 Winc	2m E Hdl		GD		£2758
			Total win prize-money		£101729

Going: Sf: 0-0 GS: 0-1 Gd: 2-5 GF: - Fm: 2-4
Distance: 2m/2m3: 4-8 2m4-2m7: 0-2 3m+: 0-0
Track: LH: 2-6 RH: 2-4 Tight: 1-3 Gall: 1-3
Aids: Bl: 0-0 Vi: 0-0 Tstrap: 0-0 Ckp: 0-0
Best Rating: 156 12/02 Kemp 2m soft Hdl

Very useful novice chaser; former high-class hurdler; goes well at speed tracks; still has to prove he is as good over fences as he was over hurdles; best at two miles and handles any ground, although at his best on a sound surface.

Santi (FR)
6-y-o b g Brief Truce (USA)-Sun River (IRE) (Last Tycoon)
Mrs K J Gilmore S N Wilshire

Placings:03100551/20352P000-P (4510)
2003/04: 19⁵GS,

	Starts	1st	2nd	3rd	Win & Pl
Chases	1	0	0	0	
Career Total	18	2	2	2	23235
4/02 Comp	2m1f110y Ch		VS		£3828
11/01 Pari	2m1f Hdl		SFT		£4074
			Total win prize-money		£7902

Going: Sf: 0-0 GS: 0-1 Gd: 0-0 GF: - Fm: 0-0
Distance: 2m/2m3: 0-1 2m4-2m7: 0-0 3m+: 0-0
Track: LH: 0-0 RH: 0-1 Tight: 0-0 Gall: 0-0
Aids: Bl: 0-0 Vi: 0-0 Tstrap: 0-0 Ckp: 0-0

Santiburi Lad (IRE)
85   69
7-y-o b g Namaqualand (USA)-Suggia (Alzao (USA))
N Wilson (N Tinkler 3/9) Mrs Karan Ridley

Placings:34 (1668)
2003/04: 20³GF, 16⁴F,

	Starts	1st	2nd	3rd	Win & Pl
Hurdles	2	0	0	1	632
Career Total	2	0	0	1	632

Going: Sf: 0-0 GS: 0-0 Gd: 0-0 GF: - Fm: 0-2
Distance: 2m/2m3: 0-1 2m4-2m7: 0-1 3m+: 0-0
Track: LH: 0-2 RH: 0-0 Tight: 0-0 Gall: 0-0
Aids: Bl: 0-0 Vi: 0-0 Tstrap: 0-0 Ckp: 0-0
Best Rating: 69 10/03 Hexm 2m4f110y gd-fm Hdl

Modest winner at up to 10 furlongs on the Flat; held in novice hurdles on fast ground.

Saorsie
106   106
6-y-o b g Emperor Jones (USA)-Exclusive Lottery (Presidium)
J C Fox Lord Mutton Racing Partnership

Placings:0500/B10644-1431P5332220000UP (4523)
2003/04: 16¹GS, 16⁴G, 16³HY, 17¹G, 17⁵GF, 16⁵G, 17³GF, 16³G, 17²GF, 16²GF, 17²G, 16⁹GF, 16⁹G, 16⁹GS, 16⁹G, 16⁴GF, 17⁹GS,

	Starts	1st	2nd	3rd	Win & Pl
Hurdles	17	2	3	3	11748
Career Total	27	3	3	3	15205
105 6/03 NAbb	2m1f F(0-100)HHdl		GD		£2968
90 5/03 Worc	2m1f E(0-110)HHdl		G-S		£3630
88 7/02 NAbb	2m1f F(0-100)HHdl		G-F		£2926
			Total win prize-money		£9524

Going: Sf: 0-1 GS: 1-3 Gd: 1-7 GF: - Fm: 0-6
Distance: 2m/2m3: 2-17 2m4-2m7: 0-0 3m+: 0-0
Track: LH: 2-14 RH: 0-3 Tight: 1-2 Gall: 0-1
Aids: Bl: 0-0 Vi: 0-0 Tstrap: 0-0 Ckp: 0-0
Best Rating: 106 10/03 Bang 2m1f good Hdl

Moderate handicap hurdler; in good form in the summer of 2003 winning twice; best at around 2m; acts on good to firm and good to soft; does not find a lot off the bridle and needs things to go his way.

Saposcat (IRE)
4-y-o b g Groom Dancer (USA)-Dance Of Joy (Shareef Dancer (USA))
D P Keane The It's My Job Partnership

Placings:P (4893)
2003/04: 16⁶G,

	Starts	1st	2nd	3rd	Win & Pl
Hurdles	1	0	0	0	
Career Total	1	0	0	0	

Going: Sf: 0-0 GS: 0-0 Gd: 0-1 GF: - Fm: 0-0
Distance: 2m/2m3: 0-1 2m4-2m7: 0-0 3m+: 0-0
Track: LH: 0-0 RH: 0-1 Tight: 0-0 Gall: 0-0
Aids: Bl: 0-0 Vi: 0-0 Tstrap: 0-0 Ckp: 0-0

Sara Monica (IRE)
106   94
7-y-o ch m Moscow Society (USA)-Swift Trip (IRE) (Duky)
L Lungo R J Gilbert

Placings:4013 (4476)
2003/04: 16⁴GS, 16⁹GS, 21¹GS, 24³HY,

	Starts	1st	2nd	3rd	Win & Pl
NH Flat	1	0	0	0	0
Hurdles	3	1	0	1	3962
Career Total	4	1	0	1	3962
87 1/04 Sedg	2m5f110yE Hdl		G-S		£3367
			Total win prize-money		£3367

Going: Sf: 0-1 GS: 1-3 Gd: 0-0 GF: - Fm: 0-0
Distance: 2m/2m3: 0-2 2m4-2m7: 1-1 3m+: 0-1
Track: LH: 1-3 RH: 0-1 Tight: 1-1 Gall: 0-0
Aids: Bl: 0-0 Vi: 0-0 Tstrap: 0-0 Ckp: 0-0
Best Rating: 94 3/04 Carl 3m110y heavy Hdl

Improved on debut effort when taking a very modest mares' only novice hurdle going away at Sedgefield in January; suited by two miles six; handles heavy ground.

Saragann (IRE)
111(98h)   (134h)130
9-y-o b g Danehill (USA)-Sarliya (IRE) (Doyoun)
P J Hobbs Jay Dee Bloodstock Limited

Placings:235PPP6/4U44113/2131/02P12UF3450-65315P44 (4938)
2003/04: 20⁶GF, 20⁵GF, 16³G, 16¹S, 16⁵G, 16⁶G, 20⁴S, 16⁴GS,

	Starts	1st	2nd	3rd	Win & Pl
Chases	8	1	0	1	8545
Career Total	**37**	**6**	**4**	**5**	**81265**

120	1/04	Hntg	2m1f10y	D(0-115)HCh	SFT	£5369
124	8/02	Strf	2m1f110yD(0-125)HCh	SFT	£6838
134	8/01	Sthl	2m	C(0-130)HHdl	G-F	£4810
130	6/01	Worc	2m	D(0-140)HHdl	G-F	£14384
124	1/01	Kemp	2m4f110yE(0-115)HCh	SFT	£3737
115	11/00	Carl	2m	E Ch	SFT	£3146

Total win prize-money £38286

Going:	Sf: 1-2 GS: 0-1 Gd: 0-3 GF: - Fm: 0-2
Distance:	2m/2m3: 1-5 2m4-2m7: 0-3 3m+: 0-0
Track:	LH: 0-4 RH: 1-4 Tight: 0-0 Gall: 1-4
Aids:	Bl: 0-1 Vi: 0-0 Tstrap: 0-0 Ckp: 0-0
Best Rating:	134 6/02 Worc 2m4f gd-fm Hdl

Useful chaser; stays two and a half miles, but effective over shorter; acts on any ground.

Saras Delight

12-y-o b g Idiots Delight-Lady Bess (Straight Lad)
Major General C A Ramsay Major General C A Ramsay

Placings:06/03F3/3U1233/15/5/F/PP3-U   (0044)
2003/04: 25^UG,

	Starts	1st	2nd	3rd	Win & Pl
Chases	1	0	0	0	
Career Total	**20**	**2**	**1**	**6**	**9212**

100	4/00	Newc	3m	F(0-105)HCh	G-S	£2902
101	12/98	Hrfd	3m1f110yF Ch		G-S	£2125

Total win prize-money £5027

Going:	Sf: 0-0 GS: 0-0 Gd: 0-1 GF: - Fm: 0-0
Distance:	2m/2m3: 0-0 2m4-2m7: 0-0 3m+: 0-1
Track:	LH: 0-1 RH: 0-1 Tight: 0-0 Gall: 0-0
Aids:	Bl: 0-0 Vi: 0-0 Tstrap: 0-0 Ckp: 0-0
Best Rating:	101 1/99 Winc 3m1f110y soft Ch

Plating-class hunter chaser; stays three miles; suited by cut in the ground.

Sarasota (IRE)
97   78

9-y-o b g Lord Americo-Ceoltoir Dubh (Black Minstrel)
P Bowen F W & E P Ridge

Placings:060P/02P05/P-5   (0140)
2003/04: 21⁵G,

	Starts	1st	2nd	3rd	Win & Pl
Hurdles	1	0	0	0	0
Career Total	**11**	**0**	**1**	**0**	**793**

Going:	Sf: 0-0 GS: 0-0 Gd: 0-1 GF: - Fm: 0-0
Distance:	2m/2m3: 0-0 2m4-2m7: 0-1 3m+: 0-0
Track:	LH: 0-0 RH: 0-1 Tight: 0-0 Gall: 0-0
Aids:	Bl: 0-0 Vi: 0-0 Tstrap: 0-0 Ckp: 0-0
Best Rating:	84 5/01 NAbb 2m1f gd-fm Hdl

Saratov (GER)
76   110

5-y-o b g Acatenango (GER)-Sovereign Touch (IRE)
(Pennine Walk)
Jonjo O'Neill P Piller

Placings:F-0P   (3258)
2003/04: 17⁹GS, 16^PHY,

	Starts	1st	2nd	3rd	Win & Pl
Hurdles	2	0	0	0	
Career Total	**3**	**0**	**0**	**0**	

Sarena Pride (IRE)
86   88

7-y-o b m Persian Bold-Avidal Park (Horage)
J D Frost Sarena Mfg Ltd

Placings:465P/3   (0752)
2003/04: 17³GF,

	Starts	1st	2nd	3rd	Win & Pl
Hurdles	1	0	0	1	754
Career Total	**5**	**0**	**0**	**1**	**754**

Going:	Sf: 0-0 GS: 0-0 Gd: 0-0 GF: - Fm: 0-1
Distance:	2m/2m3: 0-1 2m4-2m7: 0-0 3m+: 0-0
Track:	LH: 0-1 RH: 0-0 Tight: 0-1 Gall: 0-0
Aids:	Bl: 0-0 Vi: 0-0 Tstrap: 0-0 Ckp: 0-0
Best Rating:	93 9/01 Plum 2m gd-fm Hdl

Caught the eye of the Stewards when third in novice hurdle in June 2003.

Sargasso Sea
(104h)   (104+h)

7-y-o gr g Greensmith-Sea Spice (Precipice Wood)
J A B Old Miss S Blumberg

Placings:341-430P   (4631)
2003/04: 16⁴GS, 20⁵S, 19^PG,

	Starts	1st	2nd	3rd	Win & Pl
Hurdles	3	0	0	1	788
Chases	1	0	0	0	0
Career Total	**7**	**1**	**0**	**2**	**3069**
109	3/03	Winc	2m	H NHF	SFT	£1995

Total win prize-money £1995

Going:	Sf: 0-1 GS: 0-1 Gd: 0-2 GF: - Fm: 0-0
Distance:	2m/2m3: 0-2 2m4-2m7: 0-2 3m+: 0-0
Track:	LH: 0-1 RH: 0-3 Tight: 0-1 Gall: 0-0
Aids:	Bl: 0-0 Vi: 0-0 Tstrap: 0-0 Ckp: 0-0
Best Rating:	109 3/03 Winc 2m soft NHF

Moderate novice hurdler; bumper winner; suited by soft ground; pulled up on chase debut.

Sariba

5-y-o b m Persian Bold-En Vacances (IRE) (Old Vic)
A Charlton Woodhaven Racing Syndicate

Placings:P   (3328)
2003/04: 19^PS,

	Starts	1st	2nd	3rd	Win & Pl
Hurdles	1	0	0	0	
Career Total	**1**	**0**	**0**	**0**	

Going:	Sf: 0-1 GS: 0-0 Gd: 0-0 GF: - Fm: 0-0
Distance:	2m/2m3: 0-1 2m4-2m7: 0-0 3m+: 0-0
Track:	LH: 0-1 RH: 0-0 Tight: 0-0 Gall: 0-1
Aids:	Bl: 0-0 Vi: 0-0 Tstrap: 0-0 Ckp: 0-0

Saspys Lad
108   116

7-y-o b g Faustus (USA)-Legendary Lady (Reprimand)
W M Brisbourne K J Oulton

Placings:0003/05133/12F011-42410   (3282)
2003/04: 16⁴GF, 16²GF, 16⁴GF, 16¹G, 16⁹HY,

	Starts	1st	2nd	3rd	Win & Pl
Hurdles	5	1	1	0	14316
Career Total	**20**	**5**	**2**	**3**	**28963**

116	11/03	Weth	2m	C(0-130)HHdl	GD	£10237
113	9/02	Sthl	2m1f	D(0-115)HHdl	GD	£4065
102	8/02	Uttx	2m	D(0-125)HHdl	G-F	£4121
88	6/02	NAbb	2m1f	F(0-100)HHdl	GD	£2646
79	2/02	Fknm	2m	G(0-90)HHdl	G-S	£1892

Total win prize-money £22963

Going:	Sf: 0-1 GS: 0-0 Gd: 1-1 GF: - Fm: 0-3
Distance:	2m/2m3: 1-5 2m4-2m7: 0-0 3m+: 0-0
Track:	LH: 1-3 RH: 0-2 Tight: 0-0 Gall: 0-1
Aids:	Bl: 0-0 Vi: 0-0 Tstrap: 0-0 Ckp: 0-0
Best Rating:	116 11/03 Weth 2m good Hdl

Fair hurdler; recorded fifth career win at Wetherby in November 2003; best at two miles; acts well on fast ground.

Sassyrose

5-y-o b m Thowra (FR)-Atlantic Line (Capricorn Line)
B G Powell D & J Newell

Placings:00P   (0941)
2003/04: 17⁹G, 16⁸G, 20^PG,

	Starts	1st	2nd	3rd	Win & Pl
NH Flat	2	0	0	0	0
Hurdles	1	0	0	0	0
Career Total	**3**	**0**	**0**	**0**	

Going:	Sf: 0-0 GS: 0-0 Gd: 0-3 GF: - Fm: 0-0
Distance:	2m/2m3: 0-2 2m4-2m7: 0-1 3m+: 0-0
Track:	LH: 0-3 RH: 0-0 Tight: 0-1 Gall: 0-0
Aids:	Bl: 0-0 Vi: 0-0 Tstrap: 0-0 Ckp: 0-0
Best Rating:	67 6/03 Worc 2m good NHF

Satanas (FR)
67(79h)   (85h)7

6-y-o b g Dress Parade-Oiseau Noir (FR) (Rex Magna (FR))
O Sherwood M G St Quinton

Placings:00/P65P-5   (0070)
2003/04: 17⁵S,

	Starts	1st	2nd	3rd	Win & Pl
Chases	1	0	0	0	0
Career Total	**7**	**0**	**0**	**0**	**0**

Going:	Sf: 0-1 GS: 0-0 Gd: 0-0 GF: - Fm: 0-0
Distance:	2m/2m3: 0-1 2m4-2m7: 0-0 3m+: 0-0
Track:	LH: 0-1 RH: 0-0 Tight: 0-0 Gall: 0-0
Aids:	Bl: 0-0 Vi: 0-0 Tstrap: 0-0 Ckp: 0-0
Best Rating:	88 2/02 Kemp 2m good NHF

Satchmo (IRE)

12-y-o b g Satco (FR)-Taradale (Torus)
Mrs D M Grissell (E J O'Grady 12/5) G J D Wragg

Placings:21U/24F211FP/066/30-004   (4626)
2003/04: 20^DYS, 22^DS, 21⁴G,

	Starts	1st	2nd	Win & Pl
Chases	3	0	0	1675
Career Total	**19**	**3**	**3**	**35679**
147 3/01 Hntg	2m4f110yB HCh		SFT	£10328
147 2/01 Kemp	2m4f110yC(0-130)HCh		GD	£10871
136 3/00 Sand	2m4f110yH Ch		G-F	£2436
		Total win prize-money £23636

Going:	Sf: 0-1 GS: 0-0 Gd: 0-1 GF: - Fm: 0-0
Distance:	2m/2m3: 0-0 2m4-2m7: 0-3 3m+: 0-0
Track:	LH: 0-1 RH: 0-1 Tight: 0-1 Gall: 0-0
Aids:	Bl: 0-0 Vi: 0-0 Tstrap: 0-0 Ckp: 0-0
Best Rating:	147 3/01 Hntg 2m4f110y soft Ch

Useful chaser; formerly trained by Gardie Grissell; absent for 14 months before finishing third at Gowran in February 2003; won a point-to-point in February; well beaten fourth in Foxhunters' at Aintree; stays three miles; acts on good and soft ground.

Satco Express (IRE)
108(120h)   (139h)134
8-y-o b g Satco (FR)-Rosel Chris (Roselier (FR))
E Sheehy J B Ryan

Placings:5/1/214533*0/461511141-1144P10F   (4805a)
2003/04: 22¹G, 22¹GY, 20⁴S, 24⁴YS, 24⁵S, 24¹S, 32⁰G, 29⁰FY,

	Starts	1st	2nd	3rd	Win & Pl
Chases	8	3	0	0	46341
Career Total	**26**	**10**	**1**	**2**	**112329**
134 2/04 Navn	3m	Ch		SFT	£18338
133 11/03 Punc	2m6f	Ch		G-Y	£16250
122 11/03 Cork	2m6f	Ch		GD	£8831
140 1/03 Gowr	3m	Hdl		SH	£16883
132 12/02 Cork	3m	Hdl		SFT	£15950
123 11/02 Cork	3m	Hdl		SFT	£8374
129 11/02 Punc	2m6f	Hdl		SFT	£7975
112 10/02 Gowr	2m4f	Hdl		GD	£5503
120 11/01 Naas	2m	NHF		Y-S	£4451
120 10/00 Naas	2m	NHF		YLD	£3312
			Total win prize-money £105869

Going:	Sf: 1-3 GS: 0-0 Gd: 1-2 GF: - Fm: 0-0
Distance:	2m/2m3: 0-0 2m4-2m7: 2-3 3m+: 1-5
Track:	LH: 1-3 RH: 0-3 Tight: 0-4 Gall: 0-1
Aids:	Bl: 0-0 Vi: 0-0 Tstrap: 0-1 Ckp: 0-0
Best Rating:	140 1/03 Gowr 3m sft-hvy Hdl

Multiple winner in Ireland; has won a Grade 3 hurdle; stays three miles; acts well on soft ground.

Satineyeva (FR)
93f   70f
5-y-o b m Goldneyev (USA)-Sataga (FR) (Satingo)
R J Baker Miss J V May

Placings:0   (0763)
2003/04: 16⁰G,

	Starts	1st	2nd	3rd	Win & Pl
NH Flat	1	0	0	0	
Career Total	**1**	**0**	**0**	**0**	

Going:	Sf: 0-0 GS: 0-0 Gd: 0-1 GF: - Fm: 0-0
Distance:	2m/2m3: 0-1 2m4-2m7: 0-0 3m+: 0-0
Track:	LH: 0-1 RH: 0-0 Tight: 0-0 Gall: 0-0
Aids:	Bl: 0-0 Vi: 0-0 Tstrap: 0-0 Ckp: 0-0
Best Rating:	70 6/03 Worc 2m good NHF

Sativa Bay
91f   92f
5-y-o ch g Karinga Bay-Busy Mittens (Nearly A Hand)

J W Mullins D I Bare

Placings:0000   (4454)
2003/04: 16⁰G, 18⁰HY, 16⁰G, 16⁶GS,

	Starts	1st	2nd	3rd	Win & Pl
NH Flat	4	0	0	0	
Career Total	**4**	**0**	**0**	**0**	

Going:	Sf: 0-1 GS: 1-0 Gd: 0-2 GF: - Fm: 0-0
Distance:	2m/2m3: 0-4 2m4-2m7: 0-0 3m+: 0-0
Track:	LH: 0-2 RH: 0-2 Tight: 0-1 Gall: 0-0
Aids:	Bl: 0-0 Vi: 0-0 Tstrap: 0-0 Ckp: 0-0
Best Rating:	92 2/04 Winc 2m good NHF

Satshoon (IRE)
99(103h)   (116 h)133
11-y-o b g Satco (FR)-Tudor Lady (Green Shoon)
P F Nicholls Mick Coburn

Placings:221U11/P1/116040-11131F43133   (4306)
2003/04: 22¹G, 24¹GS, 26¹GS, 22³G, 24¹F, 24FGF, 25⁴GF, 25³GF, 31¹G, 24³G, 24³G,

	Starts	1st	2nd	3rd	Win & Pl
Hurdles	7	4	0	1	17406
Chases	4	1	1	0	17973
Career Total	**25**	**11**	**2**	**4**	**62612**
133 12/03 Ludl	3m7f	D(0-125)HCh	GD	£14336
116 9/03 Extr	3m110y	D(0-125)HHdl	FRM	£4396
113 5/03 Ctml	3m2f	E Hdl	G-S	£3796
113 5/03 Prth	3m110y	D Hdl	G-S	£4686
102 4/03 Extr	2m6f110yF Hdl		GD	£3150
133 11/02 Extr	2m7f110yD(0-125)HCh		GD	£6968
125 12/01 Winc	3m110yD(0-120)HCh		GD	£5187
129 4/01 Winc	3m1f110yD Ch		SFT	£4988
123 4/01 Winc	3m1f110yE Ch		SFT	£3757
119 1/01 Font	2m4f	E Ch		SFT	£3318
			Total win prize-money £54584

Going:	Sf: 0-0 GS: 2-2 Gd: 2-5 GF: - Fm: 1-4
Distance:	2m/2m3: 0-0 2m4-2m7: 1-2 3m+: 4-9
Track:	LH: 1-3 RH: 3-7 Tight: 1-2 Gall: 0-1
Aids:	Bl: 5-11 Vi: 0-0 Tstrap: 0-0 Ckp: 0-0
Best Rating:	133 12/03 Ludl 3m7f good Ch

Useful handicap chaser/fair hurdler; effective at around three miles and acts on any ground; suited by left-handed course and fast ground; usually wears blinkers.

Saucynorwich (IRE)
101   97
6-y-o b g Norwich-Kelly Gales (IRE) (Strong Gale)
J G Portman Mrs Richard Tice

Placings:0P05   (3756)
2003/04: 16⁰G, 20⁰G, 20⁰G, 19⁵G,

	Starts	1st	2nd	3rd	Win & Pl
NH Flat	1	0	0	0	
Hurdles	3	0	0	0	
Career Total	**4**	**0**	**0**	**0**	

Going:	Sf: 0-0 GS: 0-0 Gd: 0-4 GF: - Fm: 0-0
Distance:	2m/2m3: 0-1 2m4-2m7: 0-3 3m+: 0-0
Track:	LH: 0-1 RH: 0-3 Tight: 0-1 Gall: 0-0
Aids:	Bl: 0-0 Vi: 0-0 Tstrap: 0-0 Ckp: 0-0
Best Rating:	98 11/03 Sand 2m110y good NHF

Very modest form in bumpers and novice hurdles.

Savannah Mo (IRE)
95   92+
9-y-o ch m Husyan (USA)-Sweet Start (Candy Cane)

J N R Billinge Mrs M M Wilson & Fife Foxhounds Racing

Placings:00/012PP/0P02621-4PFF600   (4913)
2003/04: 20⁴G, 21⁵S, 22⁵S, 25⁵HY, 27⁵GS, 22⁰GF, 24⁰S,

	Starts	1st	2nd	3rd	Win & Pl
Hurdles	3	0	0	0	0
Chases	4	0	0	0	428
Career Total	**21**	**2**	**3**	**0**	**8786**
86 3/03 Ayr	2m6f	E(0-110)HHdl	SFT	£3484
83 11/00 Ayr	2m6f	E Hdl	SFT	£2548
			Total win prize-money £6032

Going:	Sf: 0-4 GS: 0-1 Gd: 0-1 GF: - Fm: 0-1
Distance:	2m/2m3: 0-0 2m4-2m7: 0-4 3m+: 0-3
Track:	LH: 0-6 RH: 0-1 Tight: 0-3 Gall: 0-0
Aids:	Bl: 0-0 Vi: 0-0 Tstrap: 0-0 Ckp: 0-0
Best Rating:	92 12/00 Ayr 2m4f soft Hdl

Plating-class hurdler; best at around two and a half miles; acts on soft ground.

Sawah
12f
4-y-o gr g Linamix (FR)-Tarhhib (Danzig (USA))
D Shaw Swann Racing Ltd

Placings:0   (2101)
2003/04: 12⁰GF,

	Starts	1st	2nd	3rd	Win & Pl
NH Flat	1	0	0	0	
Career Total	**1**	**0**	**0**	**0**	

Going:	Sf: 0-0 GS: 0-0 Gd: 0-0 GF: - Fm: 0-1
Distance:	2m/2m3: 0-0 2m4-2m7: 0-0 3m+: 0-1
Track:	LH: 0-1 RH: 0-0 Tight: 0-0 Gall: 0-0
Aids:	Bl: 0-0 Vi: 0-0 Tstrap: 0-0 Ckp: 0-0

Saxon Kingdom

5-y-o b g Petoski-Saxon Magic (Faustus (USA))
M Bradstock Miller Place Racing Club

Placings:00   (2797)
2003/04: 16⁰G, 17⁰GS,

	Starts	1st	2nd	3rd	Win & Pl
NH Flat	2	0	0	0	
Career Total	**2**	**0**	**0**	**0**	

Going:	Sf: 0-0 GS: 0-1 Gd: 0-1 GF: - Fm: 0-0
Distance:	2m/2m3: 0-2 2m4-2m7: 0-0 3m+: 0-0
Track:	LH: 0-1 RH: 0-1 Tight: 0-1 Gall: 0-0
Aids:	Bl: 0-0 Vi: 0-0 Tstrap: 0-0 Ckp: 0-0

Saxon Mill
72   101+
9-y-o ch g Saxon Farm-Djellaba (Decoy Boy)
Mrs Pippa Bickerton Mrs Pippa Bickerton

Placings:2602/403/0P24P/130-P0   (4219)
2003/04: 22PGS, 24⁰G,

	Starts	1st	2nd	3rd	Win & Pl
Hurdles	2	0	0	0	
Career Total	**17**	**1**	**3**	**2**	**7529**
101 12/02 MRas	2m1f110yD Hdl		SFT	£3900
			Total win prize-money £3900

Going:	Sf: 0-0 GS: 0-1 Gd: 0-1 GF: - Fm: 0-0
Distance:	2m/2m3: 0-0 2m4-2m7: 0-1 3m+: 0-1
Track:	LH: 0-1 RH: 0-1 Tight: 0-1 Gall: 0-0

Aids: Bl: 0-0 Vi: 0-0 Tstrap: 0-0 Ckp: 0-0
Best Rating: 101 12/02 MRas 2m3f110y gd-sft Hdl

Modest hurdler, feffective over two and a half miles in soft ground.

Saxon Mist

82f   97f

5-y-o b g Slip Anchor-Ruby Venture (Ballad Rock)
A King C W Lane

Placings:6   (4050)
2003/04: 16⁶G,

	Starts	1st	2nd	3rd	Win & Pl
NH Flat	1	0	0	0	0
Career Total	1	0	0	0	0

Going: Sf: 0-0 GS: 0-0 Gd: 0-1 GF: - Fm: 0-0
Distance: 2m2m3: 0-1 2m4-2m7: 0-0 3m+: 0-0
Track: LH: 0-1 RH: 0-0 Tight: 0-0 Gall: 0-0
Aids: Bl: 0-0 Vi: 0-0 Tstrap: 0-0 Ckp: 0-0
Best Rating: 96 2/04 Hayd 2m good NHF

Respectable first effort in bumper at Haydock in February.

Saxon Victory (USA)

9-y-o b g Nicholas (USA)-Saxon Shore (USA) (Halo (USA))
Tim Tarratt D E Jones

Placings:3222023/40323500030/F434502U600/6650046/5
P   (3785)
2003/04: 24⁵GF, 24ᴾS,

	Starts	1st	2nd	3rd	Win & Pl
Chases	2	0	0	0	0
Career Total	38	0	6	6	7280

Going: Sf: 0-0 GS: 0-0 Gd: 0-0 GF: - Fm: 0-1
Distance: 2m2m3: 0-0 2m4-2m7: 0-0 3m+: 0-2
Track: LH: 0-0 RH: 0-2 Tight: 0-0 Gall: 0-2
Aids: Bl: 0-0 Vi: 0-2 Tstrap: 0-0 Ckp: 0-0
Best Rating: 100 11/99 Hrfd 2m3f110y good Hdl

Fair hunter chaser; stays three miles; likes good to firm.

Sayeh (IRE)

94   90

12-y-o b g Fool's Holme (USA)-Piffle (Shirley Heights)
Mrs D Thomas Mrs D Thomas

Placings:14/11/1/01242PF6/53P   (2031)
2003/04: 17⁵GF, 16³G, 21ᴾG,

	Starts	1st	2nd	3rd	Win & Pl
Hurdles	3	0	0	1	489
Career Total	16	5	2	1	18350
125 6/01	Hrfd	2m1f	F(0-110)HHdl	FRM	£3542
128 8/99	Hrfd	2m1f110yD(0-125)HHdl	GD	£3532
105 5/98	Hrfd	2m1f	E Hdl	GD	£2431
113 5/98	Ludl	2m1f	E Hdl	G-F	£2425
105 2/98	Tntn	2m1f	E Hdl	G-F	£1990
			Total win prize-money		£13923

Going: Sf: 0-0 GS: 0-0 Gd: 0-1 GF: - Fm: 0-2
Distance: 2m2m3: 0-2 2m4-2m7: 0-1 3m+: 0-0
Track: LH: 0-2 RH: 0-1 Tight: 0-0 Gall: 0-0
Aids: Bl: 0-0 Vi: 0-0 Tstrap: 0-0 Ckp: 0-0
Best Rating: 128 8/99 Ctml 2m1f110y good Hdl

Veteran plating-class hurdler; acts on a sound surface.

Sayoun (IRE)

5-y-o gr g Primo Dominie-Sarafia (Dalsaan)
Mrs L B Normile Red Rock Racing

Placings:00P   (4685)
2003/04: 16⁶GS, 16⁹G, 16ᴾG,

	Starts	1st	2nd	3rd	Win & Pl
NH Flat	2	0	0	0	0
Hurdles	1	0	0	0	0
Career Total	3	0	0	0	0

Going: Sf: 0-0 GS: 0-1 Gd: 0-2 GF: - Fm: 0-0
Distance: 2m2m3: 0-3 2m4-2m7: 0-0 3m+: 0-0
Track: LH: 0-2 RH: 0-1 Tight: 0-3 Gall: 0-0
Aids: Bl: 0-0 Vi: 0-0 Tstrap: 0-0 Ckp: 0-0
Best Rating: 62 2/04 Muss 2m good NHF

Scalloway (IRE)

95   78

4-y-o b g Marju (IRE)-Zany (Junius (USA))
D J Wintle (J A Osborne 19/7) Lady Blyth

Placings:4   (1092)
2003/04: 16⁴GF,

	Starts	1st	2nd	3rd	Win & Pl
Hurdles	1	0	0	0	426
Career Total	1	0	0	0	426

Going: Sf: 0-0 GS: 0-0 Gd: 0-0 GF: - Fm: 0-1
Distance: 2m2m3: 0-1 2m4-2m7: 0-0 3m+: 0-0
Track: LH: 0-1 RH: 0-0 Tight: 0-1 Gall: 0-0
Aids: Bl: 0-0 Vi: 0-0 Tstrap: 0-0 Ckp: 0-0
Best Rating: 78 8/03 Strf 2m110y gd-fm Hdl

Ten-furlong winner on the Flat; ran well on hurdling debut despite being keen.

Scallybuck (IRE)

                                              (105h)89

12-y-o br g Scallywag-Miss McNight (Master Buck)
R H Buckler R H Buckler

Placings:0060F4554/0000/321440162P2/12243132665356
/55242U6632F6P/24450F065364P-55   (0670)
2003/04: 17⁵GF, 26⁵GF,

	Starts	1st	2nd	3rd	Win & Pl
Chases	2	0	0	0	0
Career Total	66	4	10	6	50409
115 7/00	Kbgn	2m7f	HCh	G-F	£10400
99 5/00	DRoy	3m	(0-123)HCh	YLD	£13000
92 9/99	List	2m3f	(0-102)HCh	Y-S	£4312
85 6/99	Kbgn	3m1f	(0-102)HCh	GD	£2915
			Total win prize-money		£30629

Going: Sf: 0-0 GS: 0-0 Gd: 0-0 GF: - Fm: 0-2
Distance: 2m2m3: 0-1 2m4-2m7: 0-0 3m+: 0-1
Track: LH: 0-2 RH: 0-0 Tight: 0-0 Gall: 0-0
Aids: Bl: 0-0 Vi: 0-0 Tstrap: 0-0 Ckp: 0-0
Best Rating: 116 8/00 Gway 2m6f good Ch

Scallywace

89   63

10-y-o br g Wace (USA)-Scally Jenks (Scallywag)
T Wall K C G Edwards

Placings:45F0PP   (4265)
2003/04: 24⁴GS, 23⁵GF, 24ᶠS, 23⁰G, 19ᴾGS, 26ᴾGF,

	Starts	1st	2nd	3rd	Win & Pl
Chases	6	0	0	0	347
Career Total	6	0	0	0	347

Going: Sf: 0-1 GS: 0-2 Gd: 0-1 GF: - Fm: 0-2
Distance: 2m2m3: 0-1 2m4-2m7: 0-0 3m+: 0-5
Track: LH: 0-2 RH: 0-4 Tight: 0-1 Gall: 0-1
Aids: Bl: 0-0 Vi: 0-0 Tstrap: 0-0 Ckp: 0-0
Best Rating: 69 12/03 Leic 2m7f110y gd-fm Ch

Scallywags Return

5-y-o b m Bob's Return (IRE)-Bee-A-Scally (Scallywag)
Miss Lucinda V Russell Roberts Racing

Placings:0   (4952)
2003/04: 16⁹GS,

	Starts	1st	2nd	3rd	Win & Pl
NH Flat	1	0	0	0	
Career Total	1	0	0	0	

Going: Sf: 0-0 GS: 0-1 Gd: 0-0 GF: - Fm: 0-0
Distance: 2m2m3: 0-1 2m4-2m7: 0-0 3m+: 0-0
Track: LH: 0-0 RH: 0-1 Tight: 0-0 Gall: 0-0
Aids: Bl: 0-0 Vi: 0-0 Tstrap: 0-0 Ckp: 0-0

Scamp

93f   91f

5-y-o b m Selkirk (USA)-Cut And Run (Slip Anchor)
S Gollings (H D Daly 15/5) J B Webb

Placings:201-20   (4649)
2003/04: 16²GF, 17⁰G,

	Starts	1st	2nd	3rd	Win & Pl
NH Flat	2	0	1	0	845
Career Total	5	1	2	0	4671
86 4/03	Extr	2m1f	H NHF	G-F	£3024
			Total win prize-money		£3024

Going: Sf: 0-0 GS: 0-0 Gd: 0-1 GF: - Fm: 0-0
Distance: 2m2m3: 0-2 2m4-2m7: 0-0 3m+: 0-0
Track: LH: 0-0 RH: 0-1 Tight: 0-0 Gall: 0-0
Aids: Bl: 0-0 Vi: 0-0 Tstrap: 0-0 Ckp: 0-0
Best Rating: 91 12/02 Newb 1m4f110y good NHF

Half-brother to the stayer Ski Run; awarded fast ground bumper after being short-headed at Exeter April 2003; runner-up next time.

Scaramouche

                                                       94f

4-y-o b c Busy Flight-Laura Lye (IRE) (Carlingford Castle)
B De Haan Flora Charlie Limited

Placings:16   (3139)
2003/04: 13¹S, 12⁶G,

	Starts	1st	2nd	3rd	Win & Pl
NH Flat	2	1	0	0	1988
Career Total	2	1	0	0	1988
94 12/03	Towc	1m5f110yH NHF	SFT	£1988
			Total win prize-money		£1988

Going: Sf: 1-1 GS: 0-0 Gd: 0-1 GF: - Fm: 0-0
Distance: 2m2m3: 0-0 2m4-2m7: 0-0 3m+: 0-0
Track: LH: 0-0 RH: 0-0 Tight: 0-0 Gall: 0-0
Aids: Bl: 0-0 Vi: 0-0 Tstrap: 0-0 Ckp: 0-0
Best Rating: 97 1/04 Chel 1m4f good NHF

Bumper winner on soft ground.

Scarborough Fair (IRE)

94(97h)   (105 h)**118+**

7-y-o b g Synefos (USA)-Hue 'N' Cry (IRE) (Denel (FR))
R C Guest (Jonjo O'Neill 26/10) Sir Robert Ogden

Placings:0/30P-P1PF   **(3214)**
2003/04: 25PG, 251S, 25PG, 25FGS,

	Starts	1st	2nd	3rd	Win & Pl
Chases	4	1	0	0	2805
Career Total	8	1	0	1	3183
118	12/03	Hexm	3m1f	E(0-105)HCh	SFT £2804

Total win prize-money £2805

Going: Sf: 1-1 GS: 0-1 Gd: 0-2 GF: - Fm: 0-0
Distance: 2m/2m3: 0-0 2m4-2m7: 0-0 3m+: 1-4
Track: LH: 1-3 RH: 0-1 Tight: 0-2 Gall: 0-0
Aids: Bl: 0-0 Vi: 0-0 Tstrap: 0-0 Ckp: 0-0
Best Rating: 118 12/03 Hexm 3m1f soft Ch

Fair chaser; placed over hurdles; won on first start for Richard Guest, but pulled up next time; stays three miles.

Scarface

103   **84**

7-y-o ch g Hernando (FR)-Scarlatine (IRE) (Alzao (USA))
A G Hobbs Three Counties Racing

Placings:0P600-2335   **(1357)**
2003/04: 20²G, 22³GF, 21³G, 20⁵G,

	Starts	1st	2nd	3rd	Win & Pl
Hurdles	4	0	1	2	3314
Career Total	9	0	1	2	3314

Going: Sf: 0-0 GS: 0-0 Gd: 0-3 GF: - Fm: 0-1
Distance: 2m/2m3: 0-0 2m4-2m7: 0-4 3m+: 0-0
Track: LH: 0-4 RH: 0-0 Tight: 0-3 Gall: 0-0
Aids: Bl: 0-0 Vi: 0-0 Tstrap: 0-0 Ckp: 0-0
Best Rating: 84 7/03 Sthl 2m5f110y good Hdl

Moderate hurdler; a winner on the Flat in Germany; shown limited promise over hurdles.

Scarlet Dawn (IRE)

76f   **69f**

6-y-o b m Supreme Leader-Dawn Appeal (Deep Run)
D A Rees D Rees

Placings:6   **(1378)**
2003/04: 16⁶GF,

	Starts	1st	2nd	3rd	Win & Pl
NH Flat	1	0	0	0	0
Career Total	1	0	0	0	0

Going: Sf: 0-0 GS: 0-0 Gd: 0-0 GF: - Fm: 0-1
Distance: 2m/2m3: 0-1 2m4-2m7: 0-0 3m+: 0-0
Track: LH: 0-1 RH: 0-0 Tight: 0-0 Gall: 0-0
Aids: Bl: 0-0 Vi: 0-0 Tstrap: 0-0 Ckp: 0-0
Best Rating: 72 9/03 Worc 2m gd-fm NHF

Scarlet Fantasy

97   **93+**

4-y-o b g Rudimentary (USA)-Katie Scarlett (Lochnager)
P A Pritchard (E A Wheeler 12/10) Thomas D Goodman

Placings:PPP14501   **(4758)**
2003/04: 16²G, 16PGF, 16PGF, 161S, 16⁴HY, 16⁵S, 17⁹G, 161S,

	Starts	1st	2nd	3rd	Win & Pl
Hurdles	8	2	0	0	7737

Career Total   8   2   0   0   7737
93   4/04   Towc   2m   D(0-110)HHdl   SFT £4764
85   1/04   Chep   2m110y   F Hdl   SFT £2611

Total win prize-money £7376

Going: Sf: 2-4 GS: 0-0 Gd: 0-2 GF: - Fm: 0-2
Distance: 2m/2m3: 2-8 2m4-2m7: 0-0 3m+: 0-0
Track: LH: 1-3 RH: 1-5 Tight: 0-0 Gall: 0-1
Aids: Bl: 0-0 Vi: 0-0 Tstrap: 0-0 Ckp: 0-0
Best Rating: 93 4/04 Towc 2m soft Hdl

Plating-class hurdler; pulled up on first three starts over hurdles prior to causing 66/1 shock when winning 2m claimer in soft ground at Chepstow January 2003; scored again at Towcester; acts on soft ground.

Scarletti (GER)

104   **117+**

7-y-o ch g Master Willie-Solidago (USA) (Decies)
I Semple (Jonjo O'Neill 19/7) Strathayr Publishing Ltd

Placings:2/2214122-4P   **(0918)**
2003/04: 16⁴G, 17PGF,

	Starts	1st	2nd	3rd	Win & Pl
Hurdles	2	0	0	0	1036
Career Total	10	2	5	0	20800
114	9/02	Worc	2m	D(0-115)HHdl	GD £4342
86	8/02	Prth	2m110y	D Hdl	G-S £4888

Total win prize-money £9230

Going: Sf: 0-0 GS: 0-0 Gd: 0-1 GF: - Fm: 0-1
Distance: 2m/2m3: 0-2 2m4-2m7: 0-0 3m+: 0-0
Track: LH: 0-0 RH: 0-2 Tight: 0-1 Gall: 0-0
Aids: Bl: 0-2 Vi: 0-0 Tstrap: 0-0 Ckp: 0-0
Best Rating: 114 10/02 Chel 2m110y good Hdl

Fair hurdler; stays two and a half miles; acts on ground either side of good; consistent.

Scenic Lady (IRE)

98   **72**

8-y-o b m Scenic-Tu Tu Maori (IRE) (King's Lake (USA))
L A Dace Mrs Yvonne Davess

Placings:4   **(1029)**
2003/04: 17⁴GF,

	Starts	1st	2nd	3rd	Win & Pl
Hurdles	1	0	0	0	371
Career Total	1	0	0	0	371

Going: Sf: 0-0 GS: 0-0 Gd: 0-0 GF: - Fm: 0-1
Distance: 2m/2m3: 0-1 2m4-2m7: 0-0 3m+: 0-0
Track: LH: 0-0 RH: 0-1 Tight: 0-1 Gall: 0-0
Aids: Bl: 0-0 Vi: 0-0 Tstrap: 0-0 Ckp: 0-0
Best Rating: 77 8/03 MRas 2m1f110y gd-fm Hdl

Moderate on the Flat; well beaten fourth on hurdling debut; suited by a sound surface.

Scented Air

103   **113**

7-y-o b m Lion Cavern (USA)-Jungle Rose (Shirley Heights)
J D Czerpak Stampede Racing

Placings:120104-15   **(0306)**
2003/04: 161GF, 17⁵G,

	Starts	1st	2nd	3rd	Win & Pl
Hurdles	2	1	0	0	3500
Career Total	8	3	1	0	13943
113	5/03	Wwck	2m	E(0-110)HHdl	G-F £3500
100	12/02	Ludl	2m	E(0-110)HHdl	GD £4056
87	10/02	Strf	2m110y	G Hdl	GD £2303

Total win prize-money £9859

Going: Sf: 0-0 GS: 0-0 Gd: 0-1 GF: - Fm: 1-1
Distance: 2m/2m3: 1-2 2m4-2m7: 0-0 3m+: 0-0
Track: LH: 1-2 RH: 0-0 Tight: 0-1 Gall: 0-0
Aids: Bl: 0-0 Vi: 0-0 Tstrap: 0-0 Ckp: 0-0
Best Rating: 113 5/03 Wwck 2m gd-fm Hdl

Modest hurdler; best at around two miles; acts on good ground; likes to race prominently.

Schoodic Point (IRE)

90   **80+**

9-y-o ch g Roselier (FR)-Madam Beau (Le Tricolore)
Mrs S J Smith Mrs M Ashby

Placings:0/P/3U2   **(1025)**
2003/04: 21³GF, 26⁵UG, 24²GF,

	Starts	1st	2nd	3rd	Win & Pl
Hurdles	3	0	1	1	1949
Career Total	5	0	1	1	1949

Going: Sf: 0-0 GS: 0-0 Gd: 0-1 GF: - Fm: 0-2
Distance: 2m/2m3: 0-0 2m4-2m7: 0-1 3m+: 0-2
Track: LH: 0-2 RH: 0-1 Tight: 0-1 Gall: 0-0
Aids: Bl: 0-0 Vi: 0-0 Tstrap: 0-0 Ckp: 0-0
Best Rating: 84 3/01 Hntg 2m110y soft NHF

Modest pointer; quirky; fair form in novice hurdles; probably best over short of three miles.

Schoolhouse Walk

95   **83+**

6-y-o b g Mistertopogigo (IRE)-Restandbejoyful (Takachiho)
M E Sowersby Lord Manton

Placings:4000-P531   **(4756)**
2003/04: 21PGF, 24⁵GF, 20³F, 191S,

	Starts	1st	2nd	3rd	Win & Pl
Hurdles	4	1	0	1	3749
Career Total	8	1	0	1	3749
83	4/04	Towc	2m3f110yF Hdl	SFT	£3094

Total win prize-money £3094

Going: Sf: 1-1 GS: 0-0 Gd: 0-0 GF: - Fm: 0-3
Distance: 2m/2m3: 0-0 2m4-2m7: 1-3 3m+: 0-1
Track: LH: 0-2 RH: 0-1 Tight: 0-2 Gall: 0-0
Aids: Bl: 0-0 Vi: 0-0 Tstrap: 0-0 Ckp: 0-0
Best Rating: 87 6/02 MRas 2m1f110y gd-fm NHF

Winning pointer over two and a half miles.

Schuh Shine (IRE)

105   **98**

7-y-o gr g Roselier (FR)-Naar Chamali (Salmon Leap (USA))
L Lungo Ashleybank Investments Limited

Placings:FP242   **(4660)**
2003/04: 23FG, 20PGS, 20³HY, 20⁴GS, 24²S,

	Starts	1st	2nd	3rd	Win & Pl
Hurdles	5	0	2	0	2418
Career Total	5	0	2	0	2418

Going: Sf: 0-2 GS: 0-2 Gd: 0-1 GF: - Fm: 0-0
Distance: 2m/2m3: 0-0 2m4-2m7: 0-4 3m+: 0-1
Track: LH: 0-5 RH: 0-0 Tight: 0-0 Gall: 0-1
Aids: Bl: 0-0 Vi: 0-0 Tstrap: 0-0 Ckp: 0-0
Best Rating: 105 4/04 Hexm 3m soft Hdl

Flattered by proximity but showed first worthwhile form when distant second to smart prospect Royal Rosa at Ayr in January and again shaped well at Newcastle following month; looks the type to do better when upped to three miles in modest handicaps.

Scippit

101   90

5-y-o ch g Unfuwain (USA)-Scierpan (USA) (Sharpen Up)
N Waggott (F Watson 12/5) Mrs J Waggott

Placings:0400354453542233460   (2730)
2003/04: 17⁰G, 17⁴G, 16⁰G, 17⁰G, 16³GF, 17⁵GF, 16⁴GF, 17⁴G, 16⁵GF, 16³F, 16⁵G, 16⁴GF, 16²F, 16²GF, 16³GF, 16³G, 16⁴G, 16⁰G, 16⁰S,

	Starts	1st	2nd	3rd	Win & Pl
Hurdles	19	0	2	4	4856
Career Total	19	0	2	4	4856

Going:	Sf: 0-1 GS: 0-0 Gd: 0-9 GF: - Fm: 0-9
Distance:	2m/2m3: 0-19 2m4-2m7: 0-0 3m+: 0-0
Track:	LH: 0-12 RH: 0-6 Tight: 0-7 Gall: 0-1
Aids:	Bl: 0-0 Vi: 0-0 Tstrap: 0-1 Ckp: 0-1
Best Rating:	90 10/03 Weth 2m firm Hdl

Poor maiden on the flat; plating-class over hurdles; acts on firm ground.

Scolt Head

95f   82f

5-y-o b g Bal Harbour-Curlew Calling (IRE) (Pennine Walk)
M W Easterby Lord Daresbury

Placings:2000   (3375)
2003/04: 16²GF, 17⁰GF, 16³GS, 16⁰S,

	Starts	1st	2nd	3rd	Win & Pl
NH Flat	4	0	1	0	420
Career Total	4	0	1	0	420

Going:	Sf: 0-1 GS: 0-1 Gd: 0-0 GF: - Fm: 0-2
Distance:	2m/2m3: 0-4 2m4-2m7: 0-0 3m+: 0-0
Track:	LH: 0-3 RH: 0-1 Tight: 0-1 Gall: 0-0
Aids:	Bl: 0-0 Vi: 0-0 Tstrap: 0-0 Ckp: 0-0
Best Rating:	82 10/03 Hexm 2m110y gd-fm NHF

Keen sort; runner-up in weak bumper on debut at Hexham in October; held subsequently.

Scoop Thirty Nine

98   84

6-y-o b m Petoski-Welsh Clover (Cruise Missile)
Mrs E Slack Mrs Evelyn Slack

Placings:P0/6P16-33   (4262)
2003/04: 17³GG, 19³GF,

	Starts	1st	2nd	3rd	Win & Pl
Hurdles	2	0	0	2	921
Career Total	8	1	0	2	3357
64 3/03 Sedg 2m1f G(0-90)HHdl			GD		£2436

Total win prize-money £2436

Going:	Sf: 0-0 GS: 0-1 Gd: 0-0 GF: - Fm: 0-1
Distance:	2m/2m3: 0-2 2m4-2m7: 0-0 3m+: 0-0
Track:	LH: 0-2 RH: 0-0 Tight: 0-2 Gall: 0-0
Aids:	Bl: 0-0 Vi: 0-0 Tstrap: 0-0 Ckp: 0-0
Best Rating:	84 3/04 Catt 2m3f gd-fm Hdl

Plating-class hurdler; seemed to show much improved form when good third on return at Sedgefield in February; ran well again next time; suited by two and a half miles.

Scorned (GER)

117   135+

9-y-o b g Selkirk (USA)-Spurned (USA) (Robellino (USA))
A M Balding Kingsclere Stud

Placings:2/6210   (4428)
2003/04: 16⁸HY, 16²G, 16¹S, 17⁰G,

	Starts	1st	2nd	3rd	Win & Pl
Hurdles	4	1	1	0	31320
Career Total	5	1	2	0	32260
135 3/04 Sand 2m110y B(0-150)HHdl			SFT		£29000

Total win prize-money £29000

Going:	Sf: 1-2 GS: 0-0 Gd: 0-2 GF: - Fm: 0-0
Distance:	2m/2m3: 1-4 2m4-2m7: 0-0 3m+: 0-0
Track:	LH: 0-2 RH: 1-2 Tight: 0-0 Gall: 0-2
Aids:	Bl: 0-0 Vi: 0-0 Tstrap: 0-1 Ckp: 0-0
Best Rating:	135 3/04 Sand 2m110y soft Hdl

Useful hurdler; Listed class on the Flat; chased home smart novice Albuhera at Newbury in February 2004; landed the Imperial Cup on testing ground the following month; suited by two miles; suited by soft ground.

Scotch Corner (IRE)

6-y-o b g Jurado (USA)-Quennie Mo Ghra (IRE) (Mandalus)
N A Twiston-Davies H R Mould

Placings:1PP   (2907)
2003/04: 16¹G, 20PGS, 26PGS,

	Starts	1st	2nd	3rd	Win & Pl
NH Flat	1	1	0	0	1988
Hurdles	2	0	0	0	
Career Total	3	1	0	0	1988
107 11/03 Weth 2m H NHF			GD		£1988

Total win prize-money £1988

Going:	Sf: 0-0 GS: 0-2 Gd: 1-1 GF: - Fm: 0-0
Distance:	2m/2m3: 1-1 2m4-2m7: 0-1 3m+: 0-1
Track:	LH: 1-2 RH: 0-1 Tight: 0-0 Gall: 0-1
Aids:	Bl: 0-0 Vi: 0-0 Tstrap: 0-0 Ckp: 0-0
Best Rating:	107 11/03 Weth 2m good NHF

Point winner; successful in a bumper at Wetherby in November 2003; weakening in third when making a mistake and losing his action when pulled-up on hurdling debut over 2m 4f at Chepstow next time; essentially a stayer.

Scotish Law (IRE)

102   101

6-y-o ch g Case Law-Scotia Rose (Tap On Wood)
P R Chamings Inhurst Farm Stables Partnership

Placings:023-332   (0960)
2003/04: 19³GF, 19³GF, 19²G,

	Starts	1st	2nd	3rd	Win & Pl
Hurdles	3	0	1	2	2301
Career Total	6	0	2	3	3960

Going:	Sf: 0-0 GS: 0-0 Gd: 0-1 GF: - Fm: 0-2
Distance:	2m/2m3: 0-2 2m4-2m7: 0-1 3m+: 0-0
Track:	LH: 0-1 RH: 0-2 Tight: 0-1 Gall: 0-0
Aids:	Bl: 0-0 Vi: 0-0 Tstrap: 0-3 Ckp: 0-0
Best Rating:	101 7/03 Strf 2m3f good Hdl

Moderate hurdler; keen sort; stays 2m 5f; acts on fast ground.

Scotmail Boy (IRE)

105   120

11-y-o b g Over The River (FR)-Princess Paula (Smoggy)
J Howard Johnson George Tobitt

Placings:05P/5000P/2P13212/61P3/02P06P/0443424-2113P   (4965)
2003/04: 24⁴GF, 21²GS, 24¹G, 20¹G, 21³G, 29PGF,

	Starts	1st	2nd	3rd	Win & Pl
Chases	6	2	1	1	28435
Career Total	37	5	6	4	56011
120 2/04 Carl 2m4f D(0-120)HCh			GD		£5616
117 12/03 Sand 3m110y D(0-120)HCh			GD		£5499
106 11/00 Carl 3m2f C(0-130)HCh			SFT		£6760
96 3/00 Sedg 2m5f E Ch			G-F		£3342
93 1/00 Sedg 3m3f E Ch			SFT		£2658

Total win prize-money £23877

Going:	Sf: 0-0 GS: 0-1 Gd: 2-3 GF: - Fm: 0-2
Distance:	2m/2m3: 0-2 2m4-2m7: 1-3 3m+: 1-3
Track:	LH: 0-3 RH: 2-3 Tight: 0-2 Gall: 0-1
Aids:	Bl: 0-0 Vi: 0-0 Tstrap: 0-0 Ckp: 0-1
Best Rating:	120 4/04 Aint 2m5f110y good Ch

Fair chaser; sound jumper; usually runs well over the Grand National fences at Aintree, and third in the Topham Trophy in 2004; acts on any ground and stays well; has worn cheekpieces.

Scotmail Lad (IRE)

107   117

10-y-o b g Ilium-Nicholas Ferry (Floriferous)
G M Moore Gordon Brown/bert Watson

Placings:041/3134115135/52406/222236322/P362245211PP/36324-41265550   (4797)
2003/04: 20⁴GF, 16¹GF, 17²G, 20PG, 20³GS, 16⁵S, 16⁵GS, 21⁰G,

	Starts	1st	2nd	3rd	Win & Pl
Chases	8	1	1	0	4910
Career Total	52	8	12	8	47231
117 11/03 Sedg 2m110y E(0-110)HCh			G-F		£3213
120 3/02 MRas 2m4f E Ch			SFT		£3419
114 2/02 Leic 2m4f110yE(0-105)HCh			SFT		£3627
122 3/99 Kels 2m6f110yE(0-120)HHdl			SFT		£2892
125 1/99 Weth 2m4f110yF(0-105)HHdl			HVY		£2066
123 12/98 Ayr 2m4f E Hdl			HVY		£2794
100 10/98 Carl 2m1f E Hdl			HVY		£2458
100 3/98 Hexm 2m H NHF			GF		£1455

Total win prize-money £21924

Going:	Sf: 0-1 GS: 0-2 Gd: 0-3 GF: - Fm: 1-2
Distance:	2m/2m3: 1-4 2m4-2m7: 0-4 3m+: 0-0
Track:	LH: 1-5 RH: 0-3 Tight: 1-4 Gall: 0-2
Aids:	Bl: 1-8 Vi: 0-0 Tstrap: 0-0 Ckp: 0-0
Best Rating:	127 3/99 Newc 3m soft Hdl

Fair chaser; best over two and a half miles; suited by soft ground; has worn a visor or blinkers; suited by forcing tactics.

Scotmail Park

5-y-o b g Presidium-Miss Tri Colour (Shavian)
G M Moore Gordon Brown/bert Watson

Placings:PP-F   (2087)
2003/04: 17FGF,

	Starts	1st	2nd	3rd	Win & Pl
Hurdles	1	0	0	0	
Career Total	3	0	0	0	

Going:	Sf: 0-0 GS: 0-0 Gd: 0-0 GF: - Fm: 0-1

Distance:	2m/2m3: 0-1 2m4-2m7: 0-0 3m+: 0-0
Track:	LH: 0-1 RH: 0-0 Tight: 0-1 Gall: 0-0
Aids:	Bl: 0-0 Vi: 0-0 Tstrap: 0-0 Ckp: 0-0

Scots Grey

104 (131h)**142**

9-y-o gr g Terimon-Misowni (Niniski (USA))
N J Henderson W H Ponsonby

Placings:2165/445110320/122133F-1F   (4640)
2003/04: 20¹G, 21⁶G,

	Starts	1st	2nd	3rd	Win & Pl
Chases	2	1	0	0	9446
Career Total	22	6	4	3	65375
142	12/03	Kemp	2m4f110yB(0-145)HCh	GD	£9445
133	2/03	Kemp	2m4f110yD Ch	G-S	£7150
132	11/02	Hntg	2m4f110yD Ch	G-S	£4732
125	12/01	Asct	2m4f	E(0-115)HHdl	GD	£6987
120	12/01	Ludl	2m	F(0-110)HHdl	GD	£3474
120	11/00	MRas	2m1f110yE Hdl	G-S	£2634
			Total win prize-money £34425

Going:	Sf: 0-0 GS: 0-0 Gd: 1-2 GF: - Fm: 0-0
Distance:	2m/2m3: 0-0 **2m4-2m7: 1-2** 3m+: 0-0
Track:	LH: 0-1 **RH: 1-1** Tight: 0-1 Gall: 0-0
Aids:	Bl: 0-0 Vi: 0-0 Tstrap: 0-0 Ckp: 0-0
Best Rating:	142 12/03 Kemp 2m4f110y good Ch

Very useful chaser; winning on chase debut at Huntingdon in November; ran well against potentially top-class opponents subsequently, and scored again at Kempton; all his wins have been on right-handed tracks; stays two and a half miles, handles good ground or softer; likes to make the running.

Scottie York

49

8-y-o b g Noble Patriarch-Devon Dancer (Shareef Dancer (USA))
A R Dicken D W Shaw

Placings:0/00/05-P   (3235)
2003/04: 24⁵GF,

	Starts	1st	2nd	3rd	Win & Pl
Hurdles	1	0	0	0	
Career Total	6	0	0	0	0

Going:	Sf: 0-0 GS: 0-0 Gd: 0-0 GF: - Fm: 0-1
Distance:	2m/2m3: 0-0 2m4-2m7: 0-0 3m+: 0-1
Track:	LH: 0-0 RH: 0-0 Tight: 0-0 Gall: 0-0
Aids:	Bl: 0-0 Vi: 0-0 Tstrap: 0-0 Ckp: 0-0
Best Rating:	68 10/99 Weth 2m gd-fm Hdl

Scottish Dance

98

7-y-o ch m Bustino-Highland Lyric (Rymer)
Mrs D A Hamer Stephen Owen

Placings:2122/0610-P   (2852)
2003/04: 19⁵GS,

	Starts	1st	2nd	3rd	Win & Pl
Hurdles	1	0	0	0	
Career Total	9	2	3	0	8313
98	2/03	Hrfd	2m3f110yD Hdl	GD	£5118
98	1/02	Hntg	2m110y H NHF	G-S	£1603
			Total win prize-money £6722

Going:	Sf: 0-0 GS: 0-1 Gd: 0-0 GF: - Fm: 0-0
Distance:	2m/2m3: 0-0 2m4-2m7: 0-0 3m+: 0-0
Track:	LH: 0-0 RH: 0-1 Tight: 0-0 Gall: 0-0

| Aids: | Bl: 0-0 Vi: 0-0 Tstrap: 0-1 Ckp: 0-0 |
| Best Rating: | 100 2/02 Ludl 2m good NHF |

Bumper winner; fair novice hurdler, stays two and a half miles; effective on good ground.

Scottish Roots

9-y-o b g Roscoe Blake-Lothian Queen (Scorpio (FR))
David M Easterby Mrs C N Weatherby

Placings:350/PP-3P   (4218)
2003/04: 21³GS, 25⁶GS,

	Starts	1st	2nd	3rd	Win & Pl
Chases	2	0	0	1	233
Career Total	7	0	0	2	441

Going:	Sf: 0-0 GS: 0-2 Gd: 0-0 GF: - Fm: 0-0
Distance:	2m/2m3: 0-0 2m4-2m7: 0-1 3m+: 0-1
Track:	LH: 0-1 RH: 0-1 Tight: 0-2 Gall: 0-0
Aids:	Bl: 0-0 Vi: 0-0 Tstrap: 0-0 Ckp: 0-0
Best Rating:	102 10/01 Chel 2m110y good NHF

Scottish Song

96 **80**

11-y-o b g Niniski (USA)-Miss Saint-Cloud (Nonoalco (USA))
Mrs M Reveley Mrs M Reveley

Placings:1/1/4/000/034-0P   (0619)
2003/04: 20⁴GF, 21⁰GF, 24⁶GS,

	Starts	1st	2nd	3rd	Win & Pl
Hurdles	3	0	0	0	263
Career Total	11	2	0	1	6784
117	5/98	Leop	2m	NHF	G-F	£2978
108	3/98	Leop	2m	NHF	G-Y	£2680
			Total win prize-money £5658

Going:	Sf: 0-0 GS: 0-0 Gd: 0-0 GF: - Fm: 0-2
Distance:	2m/2m3: 0-0 2m4-2m7: 0-2 3m+: 0-1
Track:	LH: 0-1 RH: 0-2 Tight: 0-1 Gall: 0-2
Aids:	Bl: 0-0 Vi: 0-0 Tstrap: 0-0 Ckp: 0-0
Best Rating:	117 5/98 Leop 2m gd-fm NHF

Plating-class hurdler; stayed two and a half miles. (DEAD)

Scoundrel

13-y-o gr g Scallywag-Nicholcone (Celtic Cone)
F L Matthews F L Matthews

Placings:23/111/PP/53/6U0/PPP   (4872)
2003/04: 26⁶GS, 20⁰GS, 24⁶S,

	Starts	1st	2nd	3rd	Win & Pl
Chases	3	0	0	0	
Career Total	15	3	1	2	6768
100	1/97	Wind	2m4f	E Hdl	G-F	£2757
112	10/96	Ludl	2m	H NHF	FRM	£1316
95	10/96	Hntg	2m110y	H NHF	G-F	£1763
			Total win prize-money £5838

Going:	Sf: 0-1 GS: 0-2 Gd: 0-0 GF: - Fm: 0-0
Distance:	2m/2m3: 0-0 2m4-2m7: 0-1 3m+: 0-2
Track:	LH: 0-2 RH: 0-1 Tight: 0-2 Gall: 0-0
Aids:	Bl: 0-0 Vi: 0-0 Tstrap: 0-0 Ckp: 0-0
Best Rating:	114 4/96 Ayr 2m soft NHF

Scowlin Brig

91 **69**

8-y-o ch g Minster Son-Gideonscleuch (Beverley Boy)

F P Murtagh D McLeod

Placings:05/P505/63P353-P4P   (0795)
2003/04: 25⁶G, 20⁴GF, 24⁶G,

	Starts	1st	2nd	3rd	Win & Pl
Chases	3	0	0	0	297
Career Total	15	0	0	3	2054

Going:	Sf: 0-0 GS: 0-0 Gd: 0-2 GF: - Fm: 0-0
Distance:	2m/2m3: 0-0 2m4-2m7: 0-1 3m+: 0-2
Track:	LH: 0-2 RH: 0-1 Tight: 0-0 Gall: 0-0
Aids:	Bl: 0-1 Vi: 0-0 Tstrap: 0-0 Ckp: 0-0
Best Rating:	76 2/01 Sedg 2m1f soft NHF

Has not shown much over fences.

Scramble (USA)

6-y-o ch g Gulch (USA)-Syzygy (ARG) (Big Play (USA))
B Ellison Keith Middleton

Placings:P/P   (1480)
2003/04: 17⁰G,

	Starts	1st	2nd	3rd	Win & Pl
Hurdles	1	0	0	0	
Career Total	2	0	0	0	

Going:	Sf: 0-0 GS: 0-0 Gd: 0-1 GF: - Fm: 0-0
Distance:	2m/2m3: 0-1 2m4-2m7: 0-0 3m+: 0-0
Track:	LH: 0-1 RH: 0-0 Tight: 0-1 Gall: 0-0
Aids:	Bl: 0-0 Vi: 0-0 Tstrap: 0-1 Ckp: 0-0

Scratch The Dove

108 **102**

7-y-o b m Henbit (USA)-Coney Dove (Celtic Cone)
C J Price Cecil J Price

Placings:400/2P1543-02200   (4842)
2003/04: 22⁰GS, 19²GS, 17²GS, 16⁰G, 21⁰G,

	Starts	1st	2nd	3rd	Win & Pl
Hurdles	5	0	2	0	2487
Career Total	14	1	3	1	8760
96	11/02	Leic	2m4f110yE(0-105)HHdl	HVY	£4104
			Total win prize-money £4105

Going:	Sf: 0-0 GS: 0-3 Gd: 0-2 GF: - Fm: 0-0
Distance:	2m/2m3: 0-2 2m4-2m7: 0-3 3m+: 0-0
Track:	LH: 0-1 RH: 0-4 Tight: 0-0 Gall: 0-1
Aids:	Bl: 0-0 Vi: 0-0 Tstrap: 0-0 Ckp: 0-0
Best Rating:	102 4/04 Chel 2m5f110y good Hdl

Moderate hurdler, stays two and a half miles but effective over shorter.

Scrumpy

82 **78**

5-y-o b g Sir Harry Lewis (USA)-Superfina (USA) (Fluorescent Light (USA))
S E H Sherwood Mrs
Strachan,Graham,Boyne,Lywood,Parkes

Placings:0-0060   (4783)
2003/04: 16⁰GS, 17⁰HY, 19⁶G, 21⁰G,

	Starts	1st	2nd	3rd	Win & Pl
NH Flat	1	0	0	0	0
Hurdles	3	0	0	0	0
Career Total	5	0	0	0	0

| Going: | Sf: 0-1 GS: 0-1 Gd: 0-2 GF: - Fm: 0-0 |

Distance:	2m/2m3: 0-2 2m4-2m7: 0-2 3m+: 0-0
Track:	LH: 0-1 RH: 0-3 Tight: 0-0 Gall: 0-2
Aids:	Bl: 0-0 Vi: 0-0 Tstrap: 0-1 Ckp: 0-0
Best Rating:	78 3/04 Donc 2m3f110y good Hdl

Sculptor

97   **96**

5-y-o b g Salse (USA)-Classic Colleen (IRE) (Sadler's Wells (USA))
C J Mann Magic Moments

Placings:0-2   (0182)
2003/04: 16²GF,

	Starts	1st	2nd	3rd	Win & Pl
Hurdles	1	0	1	0	1072
Career Total	2	0	1	0	1072

Going:	Sf: 0-0 GS: 0-0 Gd: 0-0 GF: - Fm: 0-1
Distance:	2m/2m3: 0-1 2m4-2m7: 0-0 3m+: 0-0
Track:	LH: 0-0 RH: 0-1 Tight: 0-0 Gall: 0-0
Aids:	Bl: 0-0 Vi: 0-0 Tstrap: 0-0 Ckp: 0-0
Best Rating:	96 5/03 Winc 2m gd-fm Hdl

Modest hurdler; stiff task on hurdles debut, but good second at Wincanton on second start;acts on fast.

Scurry Dancer (FR)

84   **60**

8-y-o b g Snurge-Fijar Dance (FR) (In Fijar (USA))
O Sherwood The St Joseph Partnership

Placings:1/31PP3/P0F4   (4789)
2003/04: 16⁶G, 20⁰G, 20⁶G, 17⁴G,

	Starts	1st	2nd	3rd	Win & Pl
Chases	4	0	0	0	0
Career Total	10	2	0	2	5789
88	11/01 NAbb	2m1f	D Hdl		GD £3259
103	12/00 Muss	2m	H NHF		GD £1575
				Total win prize-money £4834

Going:	Sf: 0-0 GS: 0-0 Gd: 0-4 GF: - Fm: 0-0
Distance:	2m/2m3: 0-2 2m4-2m7: 0-2 3m+: 0-0
Track:	LH: 0-3 RH: 0-1 Tight: 0-2 Gall: 0-1
Aids:	Bl: 0-0 Vi: 0-0 Tstrap: 0-0 Ckp: 0-1
Best Rating:	103 12/00 Muss 2m good NHF

Lightly-raced chaser/moderate hurdler; has had jumping problems; best on good ground.

Sea Cove

89   **72**

4-y-o b f Terimon-Regal Pursuit (IRE) (Roi Danzig (USA))
J M Jefferson W A Developments Ltd

Placings:4500   (3760)
2003/04: 16⁴GF, 16⁵G, 16⁹GS, 17⁹GS,

	Starts	1st	2nd	3rd	Win & Pl
Hurdles	4	0	0	0	266
Career Total	4	0	0	0	266

Going:	Sf: 0-0 GS: 0-2 Gd: 0-1 GF: - Fm: 0-1
Distance:	2m/2m3: 0-4 2m4-2m7: 0-0 3m+: 0-0
Track:	LH: 0-4 RH: 0-0 Tight: 0-1 Gall: 0-0
Aids:	Bl: 0-0 Vi: 0-0 Tstrap: 0-0 Ckp: 0-0
Best Rating:	72 11/03 Hayd 2m gd-fm Hdl

Sea Drifting

80(99h)   (123h)**128**

7-y-o b g Slip Anchor-Theme (IRE) (Sadler's Wells (USA))
K A Morgan Mr & Mrs S Giles & Mr & Mrs J Taqvi

Placings:110/114P32/F33134252-660   (3096)
2003/04: 20⁶G, 24⁶GS, 26⁰G,

	Starts	1st	2nd	3rd	Win & Pl
Hurdles	2	0	0	0	600
Chases	1	0	0	0	0
Career Total	21	5	3	4	48979
117	12/02 Muss	3m	D Ch	G-S	£6662
114	12/01 Ayr	2m	E Hdl	SFT	£2544
126	11/01 Newc	2m4f	D Hdl	G-S	£3328
112	2/01 Weth	2m	H NHF	SFT	£1701
108	1/01 Ludl	2m	H NHF	SFT	£2065
				Total win prize-money £16303

Going:	Sf: 0-0 GS: 0-1 Gd: 0-2 GF: - Fm: 0-0
Distance:	2m/2m3: 0-2 2m4-2m7: 0-1 3m+: 0-2
Track:	LH: 0-3 RH: 0-0 Tight: 0-0 Gall: 0-2
Aids:	Bl: 0-0 Vi: 0-0 Tstrap: 0-0 Ckp: 0-0
Best Rating:	128 3/03 Chel 3m110y good Ch

Useful chaser, previously decent bumper horse and novice hurdler; acts on soft ground although handles faster; stays three miles; has worn cheekpieces.

Sea Falcon (IRE)

84   **60**

5-y-o ch m Synefos (USA)-Kasterlee (FR) (Stay For Lunch (USA))
M J Ryan Extraman Ltd & Chambers Commodities Ltd

Placings:0   (3920)
2003/04: 16⁰G,

	Starts	1st	2nd	3rd	Win & Pl
NH Flat	1	0	0	0	
Career Total	1	0	0	0	

Going:	Sf: 0-0 GS: 0-0 Gd: 0-1 GF: - Fm: 0-0
Distance:	2m/2m3: 0-1 2m4-2m7: 0-0 3m+: 0-0
Track:	LH: 0-1 RH: 0-0 Tight: 0-1 Gall: 0-0
Aids:	Bl: 0-0 Vi: 0-0 Tstrap: 0-0 Ckp: 0-0

Sea Grass (IRE)

58f

6-y-o b g Jolly Jake (NZ)-Furry Dream (Furry Glen)
N A Twiston-Davies N A Twiston-Davies

Placings:0   (4495)
2003/04: 16⁰G,

	Starts	1st	2nd	3rd	Win & Pl
NH Flat	1	0	0	0	
Career Total	1	0	0	0	

Going:	Sf: 0-0 GS: 0-0 Gd: 0-1 GF: - Fm: 0-0
Distance:	2m/2m3: 0-1 2m4-2m7: 0-0 3m+: 0-0
Track:	LH: 0-0 RH: 0-0 Tight: 0-0 Gall: 0-0
Best Rating:	58 3/04 Strf 2m110y good NHF

Moderate form in bumpers so far; acts on good ground or softer.

Sea Haitch Em

9-y-o ch g Norton Challenger-One Way Circuit (Windjammer (USA))
V J Hughes V J Hughes

Placings:5000/045/2-1PPP   (4635)
2003/04: 21¹GF, 24²G, 20⁶GS, 24⁸G,

	Starts	1st	2nd	3rd	Win & Pl
Chases	4	1	0	0	2116
Career Total	12	1	1	0	2784
99	5/03 Folk	2m5f	H Ch	G-F	£2115
				Total win prize-money £2116

Going:	Sf: 0-0 GS: 0-1 Gd: 0-2 GF: - Fm: 1-1
Distance:	2m/2m3: 0-0 2m4-2m7: 1-2 3m+: 0-2
Track:	LH: 0-1 RH: 1-3 Tight: 1-3 Gall: 0-1
Aids:	Bl: 0-0 Vi: 0-0 Tstrap: 0-0 Ckp: 0-0
Best Rating:	99 5/03 Folk 2m5f gd-fm Ch

Sea Knight (IRE)

98   **78+**

7-y-o b g Beau Sher-Meaney (Delamain (USA))
J I A Charlton J I A Charlton

Placings:0/52603   (4273)
2003/04: 20⁵G, 24²GF, 24⁶G, 20⁰GS, 24³G,

	Starts	1st	2nd	3rd	Win & Pl
Hurdles	5	0	1	1	1844
Career Total	6	0	1	1	1844

Going:	Sf: 0-1 GS: 0-1 Gd: 0-3 GF: - Fm: 0-0
Distance:	2m/2m3: 0-0 2m4-2m7: 0-2 3m+: 0-3
Track:	LH: 0-4 RH: 0-1 Tight: 0-0 Gall: 0-1
Aids:	Bl: 0-0 Vi: 0-0 Tstrap: 0-0 Ckp: 0-0
Best Rating:	83 3/04 Carl 3m110y good Hdl

Very modest form in novices' hurdles; stays 3m.

Sea Laughter (IRE)

93f   **97f**

6-y-o gr m Presenting-Bruna Rosa (Roselier (FR))
J N R Billinge Mrs R Linzee Gordon & Mrs M M Wilson

Placings:024   (4482)
2003/04: 16⁶G, 16²S, 17⁴HY,

	Starts	1st	2nd	3rd	Win & Pl
NH Flat	3	0	1	0	672
Career Total	3	0	1	0	672

Going:	Sf: 0-2 GS: 0-0 Gd: 0-1 GF: - Fm: 0-0
Distance:	2m/2m3: 0-3 2m4-2m7: 0-0 3m+: 0-0
Track:	LH: 0-2 RH: 0-1 Tight: 0-0 Gall: 0-0
Aids:	Bl: 0-0 Vi: 0-0 Tstrap: 0-0 Ckp: 0-0
Best Rating:	97 11/03 Ayr 2m soft NHF

Moderate form in bumpers so far; acts on good ground or softer.

Sea Maize

80   **71**

6-y-o b m Sea Raven (IRE)-Dragons Daughter (Mandrake Major)
C R Wilson W R Wilson

Placings:00-600655   (4956)
2003/04: 16⁶GS, 21⁹GS, 22⁰G, 24⁶G, 22⁵GS, 22⁵G,

	Starts	1st	2nd	3rd	Win & Pl
NH Flat	1	0	0	0	0
Hurdles	5	0	0	0	0
Career Total	8	0	0	0	0

Going:	Sf: 0-0 GS: 0-3 Gd: 0-3 GF: - Fm: 0-0
Distance:	2m/2m3: 0-1 2m4-2m7: 0-4 3m+: 0-1
Track:	LH: 0-4 RH: 0-0 Tight: 0-2 Gall: 0-0

Aids: Bl: 0-0 Vi: 0-0 Tstrap: 0-0 Ckp: 0-2
Best Rating: 71 4/04 MRas 2m6f good Hdl

Sea Otter (IRE)

7-y-o b g King's Ride-Knockarctic (Quayside)
L Lungo Ashleybank Investments Limited

Placings:0 (0109)
2003/04: 16⁰S,

	Starts	1st	2nd	3rd	Win & Pl
NH Flat	1	0	0	0	
Career Total	1	0	0	0	

Going: Sf: 0-1 GS: 0-0 Gd: 0-0 GF: - Fm: 0-0
Distance: 2m/2m3: 0-1 2m4-2m7: 0-0 3m+: 0-0
Track: LH: 0-1 RH: 0-0 Tight: 0-0 Gall: 0-0
Aids: Bl: 0-0 Vi: 0-0 Tstrap: 0-0 Ckp: 0-0

Sea Swallow

5-y-o b m Sea Raven (IRE)-Denby Wood (Lord Bud)
J S Wainwright Tony Longbottom

Placings:0 (1372)
2003/04: 16⁰F,

	Starts	1st	2nd	3rd	Win & Pl
NH Flat	1	0	0	0	
Career Total	1	0	0	0	

Going: Sf: 0-0 GS: 0-0 Gd: 0-0 GF: - Fm: 0-1
Distance: 2m/2m3: 0-1 2m4-2m7: 0-0 3m+: 0-0
Track: LH: 0-1 RH: 0-0 Tight: 0-0 Gall: 0-0
Aids: Bl: 0-0 Vi: 0-0 Tstrap: 0-0 Ckp: 0-0

Sea Tern

4-y-o b f Emarati (USA)-Great Tern (Simply Great (FR))
N M Babbage Mrs P Cantrill

Placings:P (1092)
2003/04: 16⁰PGF,

	Starts	1st	2nd	3rd	Win & Pl
Hurdles	1	0	0	0	
Career Total	1	0	0	0	

Going: Sf: 0-0 GS: 0-0 Gd: 0-0 GF: - Fm: 0-1
Distance: 2m/2m3: 0-1 2m4-2m7: 0-0 3m+: 0-0
Track: LH: 0-1 RH: 0-0 Tight: 0-1 Gall: 0-0
Aids: Bl: 0-0 Vi: 0-0 Tstrap: 0-0 Ckp: 0-0

Sea Urchin

90 **69**

11-y-o b g Scallywag-Sailor's Shanty (Dubassoff (USA))
C J Gray (Mrs H J Wiegersma 29/5) J H Philips

Placings:P-03PP (1375)
2003/04: 19⁰GF, 26³GF, 20PGF, 23PGF,

	Starts	1st	2nd	3rd	Win & Pl
Chases	4	0	0	1	525
Career Total	5	0	0	1	525

Going: Sf: 0-0 GS: 0-0 Gd: 0-0 GF: - Fm: 0-4

Distance: 2m/2m3: 0-0 2m4-2m7: 0-2 3m+: 0-2
Track: LH: 0-3 RH: 0-1 Tight: 0-1 Gall: 0-0
Aids: Bl: 0-0 Vi: 0-0 Tstrap: 0-0 Ckp: 0-0
Best Rating: 69 5/03 Extr 2m3f110y gd-fm Ch

Seabrook Lad

13-y-o b g Derrylin-Moll (Rugantino)
Mrs F Kehoe A D Chorlton

Placings:005/4F0214/634/5U20115/23U2/PP/6P0/233-P (4344)
2003/04: 26PGS,

	Starts	1st	2nd	3rd	Win & Pl
Chases	1	0	0	0	
Career Total	32	3	5	4	18721
115	3/99	Ludl	3m	F(0-115)HCh	GD	£4758
114	2/99	Ludl	2m4f	F(0-100)HCh	GD	£2671
102	3/97	Hntg	2m5f110yE Hdl		G-F	£2867

Total win prize-money £10298

Going: Sf: 0-0 GS: 0-1 Gd: 0-0 GF: - Fm: 0-0
Distance: 2m/2m3: 0-0 2m4-2m7: 0-0 3m+: 1-0
Track: LH: 0-1 RH: 0-0 Tight: 0-0 Gall: 0-0
Aids: Bl: 0-0 Vi: 0-0 Tstrap: 0-0 Ckp: 0-1
Best Rating: 119 5/99 Ludl 3m gd-fm Ch

Fair pointer/hunter chaser, consistent sort; suited by a sound surface, although acts on softer; stays three miles.

Seaforde (IRE)

101 **114**

4-y-o ch g Titus Livius (FR)-Rosy Affair (IRE) (Red Sunset)
M F Morris (Kevin Prendergast 14/9) Sir Anthony O'Reilly

Placings:541100 (4422)
2003/04: 16⁵GY, 16⁴GY, 16¹Y, 16¹GY, 16⁰S, 17⁰G,

	Starts	1st	2nd	3rd	Win & Pl
Hurdles	6	2	0	0	12517
Career Total	6	2	0	0	12517
114	1/04	Thur	2m	Hdl	G-Y	£6802
111	12/03	Clon	2m	Hdl	YLD	£5376

Total win prize-money £12180

Going: Sf: 0-1 GS: 0-0 Gd: 0-1 GF: - Fm: 0-0
Distance: 2m/2m3: 2-6 2m4-2m7: 0-0 3m+: 0-0
Track: LH: 0-3 RH: 1-1 Tight: 0-0 Gall: 0-0
Aids: Bl: 0-0 Vi: 0-0 Tstrap: 0-0 Ckp: 0-0
Best Rating: 114 1/04 Thur 2m gd-yld Hdl

Decent Irish juvenile hurdler; effective on yielding ground; front runner.

Seahorse Girl

49

7-y-o b m Sea Raven (IRE)-Kakapo (Oats)
R J Smith R Smith

Placings:006 (4762)
2003/04: 16⁰Gd, 16⁰HY, 19⁶S,

	Starts	1st	2nd	3rd	Win & Pl
NH Flat	2	0	0	0	0
Hurdles	1	0	0	0	0
Career Total	3	0	0	0	0

Going: Sf: 0-2 GS: 0-0 Gd: 0-0 GF: - Fm: 0-1
Distance: 2m/2m3: 0-2 2m4-2m7: 0-1 3m+: 0-0
Track: LH: 0-2 RH: 0-0 Tight: 0-0 Gall: 0-0
Aids: Bl: 0-0 Vi: 0-0 Tstrap: 0-0 Ckp: 0-0
Best Rating: 71 6/03 Worc 2m gd-fm NHF

Sean At The Ivy (FR)

5-y-o b g Nikos-Matelica (FR) (Rb Chesne)
P F Nicholls Mrs J Stewart

Placings:P-43 (1794)
2003/04: 18⁴GF, 16³F,

	Starts	1st	2nd	3rd	Win & Pl
NH Flat	1	0	0	0	0
Hurdles	1	0	0	1	467
Career Total	3	0	0	1	467

Going: Sf: 0-0 GS: 0-0 Gd: 0-0 GF: - Fm: 0-2
Distance: 2m/2m3: 0-2 2m4-2m7: 0-0 3m+: 0-0
Track: LH: 0-1 RH: 0-1 Tight: 0-0 Gall: 0-0
Aids: Bl: 0-0 Vi: 0-0 Tstrap: 0-1 Ckp: 0-0

Disappointing in bumpers and showed little on hurdles debut at Wincanton in October 2003; acts on good ground; has suffered breating problems, very keen sort.

Sean's Minstrel (IRE)

11-y-o gr g Black Minstrel-Gala Star (Gail Star)
Miss Tina Hammond A S Nelson

Placings:FP/6-U (4392)
2003/04: 27UG,

	Starts	1st	2nd	3rd	Win & Pl
Chases	1	0	0	0	
Career Total	4	0	0	0	0

Going: Sf: 0-0 GS: 0-0 Gd: 0-1 GF: - Fm: 0-0
Distance: 2m/2m3: 0-0 2m4-2m7: 0-0 3m+: 0-1
Track: LH: 0-1 RH: 0-0 Tight: 0-1 Gall: 0-0
Aids: Bl: 0-0 Vi: 0-0 Tstrap: 0-0 Ckp: 0-0

Seaniethesmuggler (IRE)

101f **93f**

6-y-o b g Balla Cove-Sharp Shauna (Sayyaf)
S Gollings J B Webb

Placings:200 (3446)
2003/04: 16²G, 16⁰S, 16⁰G,

	Starts	1st	2nd	3rd	Win & Pl
NH Flat	3	0	1	0	598
Career Total	3	0	1	0	598

Going: Sf: 0-1 GS: 0-0 Gd: 0-2 GF: - Fm: 0-0
Distance: 2m/2m3: 0-3 2m4-2m7: 0-0 3m+: 0-0
Track: LH: 0-2 RH: 0-1 Tight: 0-0 Gall: 0-0
Aids: Bl: 0-0 Vi: 0-0 Tstrap: 0-0 Ckp: 0-0
Best Rating: 93 12/03 Wwck 2m good NHF

Winning Irish pointer; second on debut in 21-runner bumper at Warwick in December; acts on good.

Search And Destroy (USA)

111(105h) (107h)**120**

6-y-o b/br g Sky Classic (CAN)-Hunt The Thimble (USA) (Turn And Count (USA))

T R George　Mrs R E R Rumboll

Placings:246/10301-21126333　　(2189)
2003/04: 16¹GF, 16²G, 16¹GF, 20¹GF, 21²GF, 24⁶GF, 20³GF, 24³GF, 22³GS,

	Starts	1st	2nd	3rd	Win & Pl
Hurdles	1	0	1	0	833
Chases	8	3	1	3	23649
Career Total	16	4	3	4	29789
120	6/03	Prth	2m4f110yD(0-115)HCh		G-F £8108
112	5/03	Winc	2m	E(0-105)HCh	G-F £4017
91	4/03	Newc	2m110y	E Ch	G-F £3978
107	12/02	Donc	2m110y	F(0-100)HHdl	GD £3136

Total win prize-money £19240

Going:	Sf: 0-0 GS: 0-1 Gd: 0-1 GF: - Fm: 3-7
Distance:	2m/2m3: 2-3 2m4-2m7: 1-4 3m+: 0-2
Track:	LH: 1-6 RH: 2-3 Tight: 0-1 Gall: 1-3
Aids:	Bl: 0-3 Vi: 0-0 Tstrap: 0-0 Ckp: 0-0
Best Rating:	120　6/03　Prth　2m4f110y　gd-fm　Ch

Fair chaser/moderate hurdler; progressive form on fast ground; effective at up to two and a half miles; best on a sound surface.

Season Express

(89h)　　(70 h)
9-y-o ch g Vital Season-Coach Rd Express (Pony Express)
C L Tizzard　G F Gingell

Placings:464-P　　(0246)
2003/04: 23⁹GF,

	Starts	1st	2nd	3rd	Win & Pl
Chases	1	0	0	0	
Career Total	4	0	0	0	272

Going:	Sf: 0-0 GS: 0-0 Gd: 0-0 GF: - Fm: 0-1
Distance:	2m/2m3: 0-2 2m4-2m7: 0-0 3m+: 0-1
Track:	LH: 0-0 RH: 0-1 Tight: 0-0 Gall: 0-0
Aids:	Bl: 0-0 Vi: 0-0 Tstrap: 0-0 Ckp: 0-0
Best Rating:	70　4/03　Winc　2m6f　firm　Hdl

Seasquill (AUS)

102(97h)　　(86 h)102
9-y-o br g Squill (USA)-Sea Surge (AUS) (Rolfe)
Ferdy Murphy　G V Wilson Tom Murphy Ms J V Morgan

Placings:40660P-22434F　　(3232)
2003/04: 16²GF, 16²G, 16⁴GF, 20³F, 20⁴GF, 24²GF,

	Starts	1st	2nd	3rd	Win & Pl
Chases	6	0	2	1	3817
Career Total	12	0	2	1	4524

Going:	Sf: 0-0 GS: 0-0 Gd: 0-1 GF: - Fm: 0-5
Distance:	2m/2m3: 0-3 2m4-2m7: 0-2 3m+: 0-1
Track:	LH: 0-2 RH: 0-4 Tight: 0-2 Gall: 0-0
Aids:	Bl: 0-0 Vi: 0-0 Tstrap: 0-0 Ckp: 0-0
Best Rating:	102　11/03　Ayr　2m　good　Ch

Moderate chaser; acts on fast ground; stays two and a half miles.

Seattle Art (USA)

63　　(63h)90
10-y-o b g Seattle Slew (USA)-Artiste (Artaius (USA))
Dr P Pritchard　Lady Maria Coventry

Placings:0/0P/65553010F/63/52P00430FPP35U1/04140-0PPP0P　　(3965)
2003/04: 16⁰G, 24⁶GF, 20⁶G, 16⁶S, 22⁰GS, 19⁰GS,

Seattle Express

82　　54
4-y-o b g Salse (USA)-Seattle Ribbon (USA) (Seattle Dancer (USA))
M A Buckley (E A Elliott 23/8)　Eric A Elliott

Placings:0　　(1183)
2003/04: 17⁰G,

	Starts	1st	2nd	3rd	Win & Pl
Hurdles	1	0	0	0	
Career Total	1	0	0	0	

Going:	Sf: 0-0 GS: 0-0 Gd: 0-0 GF: - Fm: 0-0
Distance:	2m/2m3: 0-1 2m4-2m7: 0-0 3m+: 0-0
Track:	LH: 0-1 RH: 0-0 Tight: 0-0 Gall: 0-0
Aids:	Bl: 0-0 Vi: 0-0 Tstrap: 0-0 Ckp: 0-0
Best Rating:	54　8/03　Ctml　2m1f110y　good　Hdl

Dual winner on the Flat; showed temperament and did not jump well when well beaten on first try over hurdles at Cartmel in August.

Secam (POL)

76　　55
5-y-o gr g Alywar (USA)-Scytia (POL) (Euro Star)
Mrs P Townsley　Jamie Butler & Paul Townsley

Placings:63/24-1P560　　(4490)
2003/04: 15¹G, 17⁵G, 19⁵G, 18⁶G, 16⁰G,

	Starts	1st	2nd	3rd	Win & Pl
Hurdles	5	1	0	0	814
Career Total	9	1	1	1	1711
5/03	Sluz	1m7f		Hdl	GD £814

Total win prize-money £814

Going:	Sf: 0-0 GS: 0-0 Gd: 1-5 GF: - Fm: 0-0
Distance:	2m/2m3: 0-4 2m4-2m7: 0-0 3m+: 0-0
Track:	LH: 0-1 RH: 0-0 Tight: 0-1 Gall: 0-0
Aids:	Bl: 0-1 Vi: 0-0 Tstrap: 0-0 Ckp: 0-0
Best Rating:	55　3/04　Strf　2m110y　good　Hdl

Second Affair (IRE)

93　　78
7-y-o b m Pursuit of Love-Startino (Bustino)
Miss S E Hall　Miss S E Hall

Placings:P6　　(4073)
2003/04: 16⁶HY, 16⁶F,

	Starts	1st	2nd	3rd	Win & Pl
Hurdles	2	0	0	0	0
Career Total	2	0	0	0	0

Hurdles	2	0	0	0	0
Chases	4	0	0	0	0
Career Total	40	3	1	4	15309
89	7/02	MRas	2m6f110yE(0-105)HCh	GD	£4452
83	4/02	Hexm	2m4f110yF(0-95)HCh	GD	£3192
81	2/00	Muss	2m	E Ch	G-S £3071

Total win prize-money £10716

Going:	Sf: 0-1 GS: 0-2 Gd: 0-2 GF: - Fm: 0-1
Distance:	2m/2m3: 0-2 2m4-2m7: 0-3 3m+: 0-1
Track:	LH: 0-2 RH: 0-2 Tight: 0-2 Gall: 0-1
Aids:	Bl: 0-0 Vi: 0-0 Tstrap: 0-0 Ckp: 0-0
Best Rating:	89　8/02　Prth　3m　gd-sft　Ch

Plating-class chaser; stays two and a half miles and acts on good ground; suited by a right-handed track.

Second Paige (IRE)

111　　111
7-y-o b g Nicolotte-My First Paige (IRE) (Runnett)
N A Graham　Coronation Partnership

Placings:6/4311116　　(1833)
2003/04: 20⁴S, 20³GF, 17¹GF, 17¹GF, 19¹GF, 16¹G, 16⁶GF,

	Starts	1st	2nd	3rd	Win & Pl
Hurdles	7	4	0	1	13062
Career Total	8	4	0	1	13062
113	9/03	Prth	2m110y E Hdl		GD £3108
106	9/03	Hrfd	2m3f110yE Hdl		G-F £2541
106	8/03	Sedg	2m1f E Hdl		G-F £3458
106	7/03	Ctml	2m1f110yF(0-90)HHdl		G-F £3178

Total win prize-money £12285

Going:	Sf: 0-1 GS: 0-0 Gd: 1-1 GF: - Fm: 3-5
Distance:	2m/2m3: 3-4 2m4-2m7: 1-3 3m+: 0-0
Track:	LH: 2-5 RH: 2-2 Tight: 2-2 Gall: 0-1
Aids:	Bl: 0-0 Vi: 0-0 Tstrap: 0-0 Ckp: 0-0
Best Rating:	113　9/03　Prth　2m110y　good　Hdl

Modest novice hurdler; off the mark on handicap debut at Cartmel in July; took a novices' event under a penalty at Sedgefield the following month and completed hat-trick Hereford in September; best at around two miles; likes fast ground.

Second Pick (IRE)

66(78h)　　(22h)44
8-y-o b g Doubletour (USA)-Wurti (Wolver Hollow)
C J Gray　Bob Andrews

Placings:000P/PPPP-P50　　(1081)
2003/04: 21⁰GF, 16⁵GF, 16⁰GF,

	Starts	1st	2nd	3rd	Win & Pl
Hurdles	1	0	0	0	0
Chases	2	0	0	0	0
Career Total	11	0	0	0	0

Going:	Sf: 0-0 GS: 0-0 Gd: 0-0 GF: - Fm: 0-3
Distance:	2m/2m3: 0-2 2m4-2m7: 0-1 3m+: 0-0
Track:	LH: 0-3 RH: 0-0 Tight: 0-2 Gall: 0-0
Aids:	Bl: 0-0 Vi: 0-0 Tstrap: 0-0 Ckp: 0-0
Best Rating:	44　7/03　NAbb　2m110y　gd-fm　Ch

Secret Conquest

87　　82
7-y-o b m Secret Appeal-Mohibbah (USA) (Conquistador Cielo (USA))
A Crook (G M Moore 10/6)　Keith Nicholson

Placings:40P-P0　　(1633)
2003/04: 17²G, 17⁰GF,

	Starts	1st	2nd	3rd	Win & Pl
Hurdles	2	0	0	0	0
Career Total	5	0	0	0	0

Going:	Sf: 0-0 GS: 0-0 Gd: 0-0 GF: 0-1 Fm: 0-1
Distance:	2m/2m3: 0-2 2m4-2m7: 0-0 3m+: 0-0
Track:	LH: 0-2 RH: 0-0 Tight: 0-1 Gall: 0-0
Aids:	Bl: 0-0 Vi: 0-0 Tstrap: 0-1 Ckp: 0-0
Best Rating:	82　9/02　Sedg　2m1f　gd-fm　Hdl

Secret Drinker (IRE)

104 (78h)**90+**

8-y-o b g Husyan (USA)-Try Le Reste (IRE) (Le Moss)
O Sherwood S Channing-Williams

Placings:0/005221/55323P-U23 (3199)
2003/04: 25ᵁGS, 26²GS, 29³S,

	Starts	1st	2nd	3rd	Win & Pl
Chases	3	0	1	1	1964
Career Total	16	1	4	3	8525
78	3/02	Plum	3m1f110yF(0-95)HHdl		G-S £2278

Total win prize-money £2279

Going:	Sf: 0-1 GS: 0-2 Gd: 0-0 GF: - Fm: 0-0
Distance:	2m/2m3: 0-0 2m4-2m7: 0-0 3m+: 0-3
Track:	LH: 0-2 RH: 0-1 Tight: 0-2 Gall: 0-0
Aids:	Bl: 0-0 Vi: 0-0 Tstrap: 0-0 Ckp: 0-3
Best Rating:	85 1/04 Plum 3m5f soft Ch

Moderate chaser; stays three miles plus; acts on a soft surface; lacks a turn of foot.

Secret Native (IRE)

107 (112h)**112**

9-y-o b g Be My Native (USA)-Rivers Secret (Young Man (FR))
T J Taaffe Mrs Mary Ward

Placings:5/60000/10B020F112/30362100/1-140P (3819)
2003/04: 16¹Y, 244S, 19⁰YS, 23⁹S,

	Starts	1st	2nd	3rd	Win & Pl
Hurdles	1	0	0	0	0
Chases	3	1	0	0	10292
Career Total	29	6	3	2	54761
102	11/03	Gowr	2m	(0-109)HChv	YLD £6720
102	9/02	Klny	2m5f	(0-109)HCh	G-F £5291
134	1/02	Naas	2m3f	HHdl	SH £10966
126	1/01	Leop	2m6f	(0-140)HHdl	SFT £7862
122	12/00	Leop	2m2f	(0-120)HHdl	SH £6624
94	7/00	Slig	2m	Hdl	G-F £2760

Total win prize-money £40225

Going:	Sf: 0-2 GS: 0-0 Gd: 0-0 GF: - Fm: 0-0
Distance:	2m/2m3: 1-2 2m4-2m7: 0-0 3m+: 0-2
Track:	LH: 0-3 RH: 0-0 Tight: 0-0 Gall: 0-0
Aids:	Bl: 0-0 Vi: 0-0 Tstrap: 0-0 Ckp: 0-0
Best Rating:	134 1/02 Naas 2m3f sft-hvy Hdl

Fair hurdler/modest chaser; effective at two to two and a half miles; acts on fast and easy ground.

Secret Order

75 **51**

5-y-o ch m Chocolat De Meguro (USA)-Kilkenny Gorge (Deep Run)
W S Coltherd (M A Barnes 16/1) Tweedside Racing

Placings:0P6 (4387)
2003/04: 16⁰S, 20⁰GS, 21⁶G,

	Starts	1st	2nd	3rd	Win & Pl
Hurdles	3	0	0	0	0
Career Total	3	0	0	0	0

Going:	Sf: 0-1 GS: 0-1 Gd: 0-1 GF: - Fm: 0-0
Distance:	2m/2m3: 0-1 2m4-2m7: 0-0 3m+: 0-0
Track:	LH: 0-3 RH: 0-0 Tight: 0-2 Gall: 0-1
Aids:	Bl: 0-0 Vi: 0-0 Tstrap: 0-0 Ckp: 0-0
Best Rating:	51 1/04 Kels 2m110y soft Hdl

Secret Ploy

116f **127+f**

4-y-o b g Deploy-By Line (High Line)
H Morrison A M Carding

Placings:111 (3832)
2003/04: 12¹GF, 12¹G, 16¹G,

	Starts	1st	2nd	3rd	Win & Pl
NH Flat	3	3	0	0	22200
Career Total	3	3	0	0	22200
130	2/04	Newb	2m110y	A NHF	GD £12000
114	1/04	Chel	1m4f	NHF	GD £7345
102	11/03	Newb	1m4f110yH NHF		G-F £2854

Total win prize-money £22200

Going:	Sf: 0-0 GS: 0-0 Gd: 2-2 GF: - Fm: 1-1
Distance:	2m/2m3: 1-1 2m4-2m7: 0-0 3m+: 0-0
Track:	LH: 2-2 RH: 0-0 Tight: 0-0 Gall: 1-1
Aids:	Bl: 0-0 Vi: 0-0 Tstrap: 0-0 Ckp: 0-0
Best Rating:	130 2/04 Newb 2m110y good NHF

Useful winner of all three bumpers; effective on fast ground.

Secret Racine

5-y-o b m Secret Appeal-Miss Racine (Dom Racine (FR))
I A Brown Mrs Joanne Brown

Placings:0 (1372)
2003/04: 16⁰F,

	Starts	1st	2nd	3rd	Win & Pl
NH Flat	1	0	0	0	0
Career Total	1	0	0	0	0

Going:	Sf: 0-0 GS: 0-0 Gd: 0-0 GF: - Fm: 0-1
Distance:	2m/2m3: 0-1 2m4-2m7: 0-0 3m+: 0-0
Track:	LH: 0-1 RH: 0-0 Tight: 0-0 Gall: 0-0
Aids:	Bl: 0-0 Vi: 0-0 Tstrap: 0-0 Ckp: 0-0

Secret's Out

105 **88**

8-y-o b g Polish Precedent (USA)-Secret Obsession (USA) (Secretariat (USA))
W M Brisbourne (W Clay 2/10) F Lloyd

Placings:0033/235/060542223030/03425-335P23062 (2361)
2003/04: 17³G, 17³G, 16⁵GF, 17⁶GF, 17²GF, 16³GF, 17⁰G, 16⁶GS, 16²GF,

	Starts	1st	2nd	3rd	Win & Pl
Hurdles	9	0	2	3	3099
Career Total	33	0	7	9	9317

Going:	Sf: 0-0 GS: 0-1 Gd: 0-3 GF: - Fm: 0-5
Distance:	2m/2m3: 0-9 2m4-2m7: 0-0 3m+: 0-5
Track:	LH: 0-6 RH: 0-3 Tight: 0-5 Gall: 0-0
Aids:	Bl: 0-0 Vi: 0-4 Tstrap: 0-0 Ckp: 0-0
Best Rating:	96 9/00 Uttx 2m gd-sft Hdl

Plating-class hurdler; placed on a number of occasions without putting his head in front.

Securon Dancer

87 **54**

6-y-o b m Emperor Jones (USA)-Gena Ivor (USA) (Sir Ivor (USA))
R Rowe Mrs R A Proctor

Placings:0-P0 (2777)

(continued)

2003/04: 17ᴾG, 17⁰GS,

	Starts	1st	2nd	3rd	Win & Pl
Hurdles	2	0	0	0	
Career Total	3	0	0	0	

Going:	Sf: 0-0 GS: 0-1 Gd: 0-1 GF: - Fm: 0-0
Distance:	2m/2m3: 0-2 2m4-2m7: 0-0 3m+: 0-0
Track:	LH: 0-0 RH: 0-2 Tight: 0-2 Gall: 0-0
Aids:	Bl: 0-0 Vi: 0-1 Tstrap: 0-0 Ckp: 0-0
Best Rating:	54 12/03 Folk 2m1f110y gd-sft Hdl

Sedge (USA)

92f **76f**

4-y-o b g Lure (USA)-First Flyer (USA) (Riverman (USA))
P T Midgley Peter Mee

Placings:0 (4962)
2003/04: 17⁰G,

	Starts	1st	2nd	3rd	Win & Pl
NH Flat	1	0	0	0	0
Career Total	1	0	0	0	0

Going:	Sf: 0-0 GS: 0-0 Gd: 0-1 GF: - Fm: 0-0
Distance:	2m/2m3: 0-1 2m4-2m7: 0-0 3m+: 0-0
Track:	LH: 0-0 RH: 0-1 Tight: 0-1 Gall: 0-0
Aids:	Bl: 0-0 Vi: 0-0 Tstrap: 0-0 Ckp: 0-0
Best Rating:	76 4/04 MRas 2m1f110y good NHF

See Me There

84 **65**

4-y-o b g Busy Flight-See-A-Rose (Halyudh (USA))
J W Mullins J A G Meaden

Placings:504 (3416)
2003/04: 14⁵G, 16⁹GS, 17⁴GS,

	Starts	1st	2nd	3rd	Win & Pl
NH Flat	2	0	0	0	0
Hurdles	1	0	0	0	0
Career Total	3	0	0	0	0

Going:	Sf: 0-0 GS: 0-2 Gd: 0-1 GF: - Fm: 0-0
Distance:	2m/2m3: 0-2 2m4-2m7: 0-0 3m+: 0-0
Track:	LH: 0-1 RH: 0-2 Tight: 0-0 Gall: 0-0
Aids:	Bl: 0-0 Vi: 0-0 Tstrap: 0-0 Ckp: 0-0
Best Rating:	78 11/03 Wwck 1m6f good NHF

Modest form to date.

See More Business (IRE)

171

14-y-o b g Seymour Hicks (FR)-Miss Redlands (Dubassoff (USA))
P F Nicholls Sir Robert Ogden

Placings:111/122F/3111C/41P31/11141/1515/FP135/2110-4 (2586)
2003/04: 26⁴GS,

	Starts	1st	2nd	3rd	Win & Pl
Chases	1	0	0	0	2000
Career Total	36	18	3	3	701722
171	2/03	Winc	3m1f110yA Ch		G-S £23800
166	12/02	Chep	3m2f110yA HCh		SFT £23800
171	2/02	Winc	3m1f110yA Ch		G-S £16770
176	1/01	Chel	3m1f110yA Ch		SFT £49125
176	10/00	Weth	3m1f	A Ch	SFT £27000
176	4/00	Aint	3m1f	A Ch	GD £46900

170	2/00	Newb	3m	B Ch	G-S	£31000
176	12/99	Kemp	3m	A Ch	SFT	£65500
175	10/99	Weth	3m1f	A Ch	GD	£23800
172	3/99	Chel	3m2f110y	A Ch	G-S	£149600
172	12/98	Chep	3m	A HCh	GD	£20305
172	1/98	Chel	3m1f110y	B Ch	G-S	£16937
168	12/97	Kemp	3m	A Ch	SFT	£64374
158	12/97	Chep	3m	A HCh	SFT	£18606
133	11/96	Chep	3m3f110y	A Ch	G-S	£13786
148	12/95	Sand	2m6f	A Hdl	GD	£9555
130	11/95	Winc	2m6f	C Hdl		£3727
134	11/95	Chep	2m4f110y	D Hdl	G-S	£2845
					Total win prize-money	£607433

Going:	Sf: 0-0 GS: 0-1 Gd: 0-0 GF: - Fm: 0-0
Distance:	2m/2m3: 0-0 2m4-2m7: 0-0 3m+: 0-1
Track:	LH: 0-1 RH: 0-0 Tight: 0-0 Gall: 0-0
Aids:	Bl: 0-1 Vi: 0-0 Tstrap: 0-0 Ckp: 0-0
Best Rating:	176 1/01 Chel 3m1f110y soft Ch

Evergreen top-class chaser; winner of the Gold Cup in 1999 and 3rd in 2002; won the Rehearsal Chase at Chepstow for a third time in December 2002; scored again at Wincanton in February, but held in the Gold Cup; stays 3m 2f; acts on soft and good but does not want the ground too fast; usually wears blinkers. Reportedly retired.

See More Jock
99f   **103f**
6-y-o b g Seymour Hicks (FR)-Metafan (Last Fandango)
Dr J R J Naylor Mrs B Bishop

Placings:2000 (4787)
2003/04: 16[2]GS, 16[6]G, 16[6]G, 16[6]G,

	Starts	1st	2nd	3rd	Win & Pl
NH Flat	4	0	1	0	566
Career Total	4	0	1	0	566

Going:	Sf: 0-0 GS: 0-0 Gd: 0-3 GF: - Fm: 0-1
Distance:	2m/2m3: 0-4 2m4-2m7: 0-0 3m+: 0-0
Track:	LH: 0-3 RH: 0-1 Tight: 0-0 Gall: 0-1
Aids:	Bl: 0-0 Vi: 0-0 Tstrap: 0-0 Ckp: 0-0
Best Rating:	103 6/03 Worc 2m gd-fm NHF

Refused in both his points; no chance with the useful Alpine Fox despite staying on well when second on bumper debut at Worcester June 2003; held subsequently.

See More Snow
79(83c)   **(80+c)86**
7-y-o b g Seymour Hicks (FR)-Snow Child (Mandrake Major)
W G M Turner E Goody

Placings:64/6/435033-254 (2555)
2003/04: 20[2]F, 17[5]G, 22[4]G,

	Starts	1st	2nd	3rd	Win & Pl
Hurdles	1	0	0	0	0
Chases	2	0	1	0	1124
Career Total	12	0	1	3	2646

Going:	Sf: 0-0 GS: 0-0 Gd: 0-2 GF: - Fm: 0-1
Distance:	2m/2m3: 0-1 2m4-2m7: 0-2 3m+: 0-0
Track:	LH: 0-0 RH: 0-3 Tight: 0-1 Gall: 0-0
Aids:	Bl: 0-1 Vi: 0-0 Tstrap: 0-0 Ckp: 0-1
Best Rating:	89 3/03 Winc 2m gd-fm Hdl

Moderate hurdler; best at around two miles.

See My Girl
79   **78**
6-y-o gr m Terimon-Nessfield (Tumble Wind (USA))

K A Morgan J Duckworth

Placings:00-5 (3039)
2003/04: 20[5]GS,

	Starts	1st	2nd	3rd	Win & Pl
Hurdles	1	0	0	0	0
Career Total	3	0	0	0	0

Going:	Sf: 0-0 GS: 0-1 Gd: 0-0 GF: - Fm: 0-0
Distance:	2m/2m3: 0-0 2m4-2m7: 0-1 3m+: 0-0
Track:	LH: 0-1 RH: 0-0 Tight: 0-0 Gall: 0-0
Aids:	Bl: 0-1 Vi: 0-0 Tstrap: 0-0 Ckp: 0-0
Best Rating:	78 12/03 Hayd 2m4f gd-sft Hdl

See Red Billdan (IRE)
8-y-o br g Riverhead (USA)-Sweet Mayo (IRE) (Sexton Blake)
R J Lancaster R J Lancaster

Placings:P (4122)
2003/04: 21[5]G,

	Starts	1st	2nd	3rd	Win & Pl
Chases	1	0	0	0	0
Career Total	1	0	0	0	0

Going:	Sf: 0-0 GS: 0-0 Gd: 0-1 GF: - Fm: 0-0
Distance:	2m/2m3: 0-0 2m4-2m7: 0-1 3m+: 0-0
Track:	LH: 0-0 RH: 0-1 Tight: 0-1 Gall: 0-0
Aids:	Bl: 0-0 Vi: 0-0 Tstrap: 0-0 Ckp: 0-0

See You Around
102   **(94h)99**
9-y-o b g Sharp Deal-Seeborg (Lepanto (GER))
J W Mullins (C L Tizzard 9/5) The Infamous Five

Placings:0320P25P/4SP64U22P/25605324-P244P24 (4792)
2003/04: 21[4]S, 21[5]GF, 26[2]G, 24[4]GS, 24[5]HY, 26[8]GF, 24[2]GS, 26[4]G,

	Starts	1st	2nd	3rd	Win & Pl
Chases	8	0	2	0	2892
Career Total	32	0	8	2	9919

Going:	Sf: 0-2 GS: 0-2 Gd: 0-2 GF: - Fm: 0-2
Distance:	2m/2m3: 0-0 2m4-2m7: 0-2 3m+: 0-6
Track:	LH: 0-6 RH: 0-2 Tight: 0-3 Gall: 0-0
Aids:	Bl: 0-1 Vi: 0-0 Tstrap: 0-2 Ckp: 0-0
Best Rating:	109 12/00 Folk 2m1f110y heavy NHF

Moderate maiden hurdler/chaser; reported to have had a breathing problem when pulled up on fast ground at Chepstow March 2004; fitted with a tongue-tie when runner-up at the same venue on softer surface next time; suited to soft/heavy ground; stays three miles two.

See You Sometime
104(114h)   **(142h)133**
9-y-o b g Sharp Deal-Shepani (New Member)
J W Mullins J A G Meaden

Placings:43435/3111132/4101-23F6F (4642)
2003/04: 19[2]S, 19[3]S, 20[2]S, 20[6]G, 25[4]G,

	Starts	1st	2nd	3rd	Win & Pl
Chases	5	0	1	1	19183
Career Total	16	2	6	5	89563
142	4/03 Chel	2m5f110yB HHdl		GD	£11194
142	2/03 Winc	2m6f	C(0-135)HHdl	G-S	£16008

140	12/01	Newb	2m5f	B Hdl	G-S	£9993
132	11/01	Chel	2m5f	C(0-135)HHdl	GD	£18118
121	6/01	Strf	2m6f110y	D Hdl	G-F	£3796
118	5/01	Folk	2m4f110yF(0-100)HHdl		G-F	£2037
					Total win prize-money	£61148

Going:	Sf: 0-3 GS: 0-0 Gd: 0-2 GF: - Fm: 0-0
Distance:	2m/2m3: 0-0 2m4-2m7: 0-4 3m+: 0-1
Track:	LH: 0-2 RH: 0-3 Tight: 0-1 Gall: 0-1
Aids:	Bl: 0-0 Vi: 0-0 Tstrap: 0-0 Ckp: 0-0
Best Rating:	142 4/03 Chel 2m5f110y good Hdl

Very useful novice chaser; formerly useful hurdler; effective at up to two miles six furlongs and may stay further; acts on a sound surface, but handles cut; suited to forcing tactics.

Seeador
83   **85**
5-y-o b g El Conquistador-Shepani (New Member)
J W Mullins J A G Meaden

Placings:005 (4692)
2003/04: 16[0]GS, 16[0]GS, 17[5]G,

	Starts	1st	2nd	3rd	Win & Pl
NH Flat	2	0	0	0	0
Hurdles	1	0	0	0	0
Career Total	3	0	0	0	0

Going:	Sf: 0-0 GS: 0-2 Gd: 0-1 GF: - Fm: 0-0
Distance:	2m/2m3: 0-3 2m4-2m7: 0-0 3m+: 0-0
Track:	LH: 0-1 RH: 0-2 Tight: 0-0 Gall: 0-1
Aids:	Bl: 0-0 Vi: 0-0 Tstrap: 0-0 Ckp: 0-0
Best Rating:	85 4/04 Extr 2m1f good Hdl

Half-brother to yard's decent See You Sometime.

Seebald (GER)
118   **157**
9-y-o b g Mulberry (FR)-Spartina (USA) (Northern Baby (CAN))
M C Pipe The Macca & Growler Partnership

Placings:110/2630/111111122/222F21-46U03U510 (4964)
2003/04: 17[4]G, 16[6]G, 24[4]UG, 24[0]G, 20[3]G, 16[1]UG, 25[5]G, 21[1]GF, 16[8]GF,

	Starts	1st	2nd	3rd	Win & Pl
Chases	9	1	0	1	48357
Career Total	31	11	7	2	307220
157	4/04 Chel	2m5f	A HCh	G-F	£29000
162	4/03 Sand	2m	B Ch	GD	£59500
161	1/02 Wwck	2m4f110yC Ch		SFT	£8385
162	12/01 Asct	2m3f110yA Ch		GD	£16375
156	11/01 Chel	2m	A Ch	GD	£18000
131	10/01 Chel	2m	C Ch	GD	£10272
123	6/01 MRas	2m1f110yD Ch		G-F	£6045
117	6/01 Hrfd	2m	E Ch	FRM	£3159
117	5/01 Hrfd	2m	E Ch	GD	£3297
133	2/00 Newb	2m110y	C Hdl	G-S	£5226
123	1/00 Tntn	2m1f	E Hdl	G-S	£2513
				Total win prize-money	£161773

Going:	Sf: 0-0 GS: 0-0 Gd: 0-7 GF: - Fm: 1-2
Distance:	2m/2m3: 0-4 2m4-2m7: 1-2 3m+: 0-3
Track:	LH: 1-5 RH: 0-4 Tight: 0-1 Gall: 1-4
Aids:	Bl: 0-1 Vi: 0-0 Tstrap: 0-0 Ckp: 0-0
Best Rating:	163 3/03 Chel 2m good Ch

Smart chaser at his best; won his first seven races in the 2001/02 season before a good 2nd in the Arkle; going well when falling two out in the 2003 Champion Chase; jumped poorly when beaten in the 2003 Tingle Creek and has looked a non-stayer over three miles since; back to winning ways in valuable event over 2m 5f at Cheltenham; acts on good and soft ground; genuine sort.

Seef

95 (67h)**80**

10-y-o b g Slip Anchor-Compton Lady (USA) (Sovereign Dancer (USA))
J S King Mrs S Horton

Placings:20/60006/1435/35324/002352/1PP556U-55

(4933)

2003/04: 25⁵G, 26⁵G,

	Starts	1st	2nd	3rd	Win & Pl
Chases	2	0	0	0	0
Career Total	31	2	4	4	13027
80	5/02 Folk	3m2f	E Ch		GD	£3380
99	5/99 Extr	2m6f	E Hdl		G-F	£2915

Total win prize-money £6295

Going:	Sf: 0-0 GS: 0-0 Gd: 0-2 GF: - Fm: 0-0
Distance:	2m/2m3: 0-0 2m4-2m7: 0-0 3m+: 0-2
Track:	LH: 0-0 RH: 0-1 Tight: 0-1 Gall: 0-0
Aids:	Bl: 0-0 Vi: 0-0 Tstrap: 0-0 Ckp: 0-0
Best Rating:	99 10/99 Winc 2m6f gd-fm Hdl

Modest hurdler/fair chaser; best over staying distances; acts on a sound surface.

Seeking Shelter (IRE)

70f **48f**

5-y-o b m Glacial Storm (USA)-Seeking Gold (IRE) (Lancastrian)
N G Richards Kinneston Racing

Placings:0

(4866)

2003/04: 16⁰S,

	Starts	1st	2nd	3rd	Win & Pl
NH Flat	1	0	0	0	
Career Total	1	0	0	0	

Going:	Sf: 0-1 GS: 0-0 Gd: 0-0 GF: - Fm: 0-0
Distance:	2m/2m3: 0-1 2m4-2m7: 0-0 3m+: 0-0
Track:	LH: 0-1 RH: 0-0 Tight: 0-0 Gall: 0-0
Aids:	Bl: 0-0 Vi: 0-0 Tstrap: 0-0 Ckp: 0-0
Best Rating:	48 4/04 Ayr 2m soft NHF

Seemore Sunshine

94 **76**

7-y-o br g Seymour Hicks (FR)-Temporary Affair (Mandalus)
R Johnson Michael Smith

Placings:0P0

(4946)

2003/04: 22⁰GS, 24⁵PS, 16⁶GS,

	Starts	1st	2nd	3rd	Win & Pl
Hurdles	3	0	0	0	
Career Total	3	0	0	0	

Going:	Sf: 0-1 GS: 0-2 Gd: 0-0 GF: - Fm: 0-0
Distance:	2m/2m3: 0-1 2m4-2m7: 0-1 3m+: 0-1
Track:	LH: 0-2 RH: 0-1 Tight: 0-1 Gall: 0-0
Aids:	Bl: 0-0 Vi: 0-0 Tstrap: 0-0 Ckp: 0-0
Best Rating:	76 4/04 Prth 2m110y gd-sft Hdl

Seeyaaj

99 **88+**

4-y-o b g Darshaan-Subya (Night Shift (USA))
Jonjo O'Neill (A C Stewart 24/10) Wellers Racing Partnership

Placings:P0043

(4892)

2003/04: 16²S, 16⁹G, 20⁹S, 16⁴G, 16³GF,

	Starts	1st	2nd	3rd	Win & Pl
Hurdles	5	0	0	1	1428
Career Total	5	0	0	1	1428

Going:	Sf: 0-2 GS: 0-0 Gd: 0-2 GF: - Fm: 0-1
Distance:	2m/2m3: 0-4 2m4-2m7: 0-1 3m+: 0-0
Track:	LH: 0-3 RH: 0-2 Tight: 0-1 Gall: 0-3
Aids:	Bl: 0-0 Vi: 0-0 Tstrap: 0-0 Ckp: 0-0
Best Rating:	88 3/04 Hntg 2m110y good Hdl

Modest hurdler; useful middle-distance handicapper on the Flat; suited by good ground.

Sefton Blake

104 **79**

10-y-o b g Roscoe Blake-Rainbow Lady (Jaazeiro (USA))
R D Wylie M R Johnson

Placings:404P6/55243616/112P0/415P56/0P46/6-4P

(0431)

2003/04: 20⁴S, 26²G,

	Starts	1st	2nd	3rd	Win & Pl
Hurdles	2	0	0	0	0
Career Total	31	4	2	1	12549
93	8/00 Sthl	3m110y E Ch		G-F	£3133
93	11/99 Catt	3m1f110yE(0-115)HHdl		G-F	£2304
93	5/99 Ctml	2m6f F(0-95)HHdl		GD	£3100
84	4/99 Sedg	2m5f110yG(0-100)HHdl		FRM	£2164

Total win prize-money £10702

Going:	Sf: 0-1 GS: 0-0 Gd: 0-1 GF: - Fm: 0-1
Distance:	2m/2m3: 0-0 2m4-2m7: 0-1 3m+: 0-1
Track:	LH: 0-2 RH: 0-0 Tight: 0-2 Gall: 0-0
Aids:	Bl: 0-0 Vi: 0-0 Tstrap: 0-0 Ckp: 0-0
Best Rating:	96 11/99 Kels 2m6f110y good Hdl

Sefton Lodge

5-y-o b g Barathea (IRE)-Pine Needle (Kris)
M A Barnes (Andrew Reid 4/7) The Purple Patch Racing Club

Placings:P0-PPP

(2712)

2003/04: 16⁶GF, 17⁰GF, 16⁶GS,

	Starts	1st	2nd	3rd	Win & Pl
Hurdles	3	0	0	0	
Career Total	5	0	0	0	

Going:	Sf: 0-0 GS: 0-1 Gd: 0-0 GF: - Fm: 0-2
Distance:	2m/2m3: 0-3 2m4-2m7: 0-0 3m+: 0-0
Track:	LH: 0-3 RH: 0-0 Tight: 0-1 Gall: 0-1
Aids:	Bl: 0-0 Vi: 0-0 Tstrap: 0-2 Ckp: 0-0

Segsbury Belle

9-y-o b m Petoski-Rolling Dice (Balinger)
Mrs G Harvey R A Instone

Placings:0O/0/PP

(3947)

2003/04: 21⁶G, 16⁶G,

	Starts	1st	2nd	3rd	Win & Pl
Hurdles	2	0	0	0	
Career Total	5	0	0	0	

Going:	Sf: 0-0 GS: 0-0 Gd: 0-2 GF: - Fm: 0-0
Distance:	2m/2m3: 0-1 2m4-2m7: 0-1 3m+: 0-0

Track:	LH: 0-0 RH: 0-2 Tight: 0-0 Gall: 0-0
Aids:	Bl: 0-0 Vi: 0-0 Tstrap: 0-0 Ckp: 0-0
Best Rating:	56 11/01 Ludl 2m gd-fm NHF

Sekwana (POL)

66 **19**

5-y-o b m Duke Valentino-Surmia (POL) (Demon Club (POL))
Miss A M Newton-Smith Hugh Le Fanu

Placings:P-05P0P

(4931)

2003/04: 17⁰G, 18⁵GF, 16⁷GF, 16⁹S, 22⁹G,

	Starts	1st	2nd	3rd	Win & Pl
Hurdles	5	0	0	0	0
Career Total	6	0	0	0	0

Going:	Sf: 0-1 GS: 0-0 Gd: 0-2 GF: - Fm: 0-2
Distance:	2m/2m3: 0-4 2m4-2m7: 0-1 3m+: 0-0
Track:	LH: 0-3 RH: 0-2 Tight: 0-1 Gall: 0-0
Aids:	Bl: 0-0 Vi: 0-0 Tstrap: 0-1 Ckp: 0-4
Best Rating:	19 4/03 Extr 2m1f good Hdl

Selassie

5-y-o ch g Alflora (IRE)-Zanditu (Presidium)
M Scudamore Mrs V Stockdale

Placings:0F

(3697)

2003/04: 16⁰HY, 17⁰HY,

	Starts	1st	2nd	3rd	Win & Pl
NH Flat	1	0	0	0	0
Hurdles	1	0	0	0	0
Career Total	2	0	0	0	

Going:	Sf: 0-2 GS: 0-0 Gd: 0-0 GF: - Fm: 0-0
Distance:	2m/2m3: 0-2 2m4-2m7: 0-0 3m+: 0-0
Track:	LH: 0-0 RH: 0-2 Tight: 0-0 Gall: 0-0
Aids:	Bl: 0-0 Vi: 0-0 Tstrap: 0-0 Ckp: 0-0

Selberry

106 **115**

10-y-o b g Selkirk (USA)-Choke Cherry (Connaught)
E L James Mr & Mrs D W H Bell

Placings:66/5011142424/4260/3104114005/23525221/P22 33B05

(4935)

2003/04: 17⁹S, 16²G, 16²S, 17³GS, 21³S, 16⁸G, 18⁶G, 18⁵G,

	Starts	1st	2nd	3rd	Win & Pl
Hurdles	1	0	0	0	0
Chases	7	0	2	2	5927
Career Total	42	7	9	4	39257
113	2/02 Uttx	2m D(0-120)HCh		HVY	£5109
112	1/01 Chep	2m110y D(0-125)HHdl		G-S	£3160
112	1/01 Winc	2m F(0-110)HHdl		G-S	£2982
110	10/00 Wwck	2m D(0-125)HHdl		SFT	£2879
110	12/98 Hrfd	2m1f E(0-100)HHdl		SFT	£2920
95	12/98 MRas	2m1f110yD(0-100)HHdl		SFT	£2798
107	12/98 Extr	2m1f110yF(0-100)HHdl		GD	£1975

Total win prize-money £21825

Going:	Sf: 0-3 GS: 0-1 Gd: 0-4 GF: - Fm: 0-0
Distance:	2m/2m3: 0-7 2m4-2m7: 0-1 3m+: 0-0
Track:	LH: 0-4 RH: 0-3 Tight: 0-4 Gall: 0-2
Aids:	Bl: 0-8 Vi: 0-0 Tstrap: 0-0 Ckp: 0-0
Best Rating:	114 11/03 Ling 2m good Ch

Modest chaser; suited by cut in the ground; wears blinkers; best at around 2m.

Self Defense

118   160

7-y-o b h Warning-Dansara (Dancing Brave (USA))
Miss E C Lavelle Fraser Miller Racing

Placings:43324P-1240012   (4844)
2003/04: 16¹GF, 20²GS, 16⁴G, 16⁹G, 16⁹G, 16¹G, 17²G,

	Starts	1st	2nd	3rd	Win & Pl
Hurdles	7	2	2	0	33131
Career Total	**13**	**2**	**3**	**2**	**60489**
137 3/04 Newb	2m110y D Hdl			GD	£5252
132 11/03 Chel	2m110y A Hdl			G-F	£17400
			Total win prize-money £22652		

Going:	Sf: 0-0 GS: 0-1 Gd: 1-5 GF: - Fm: 1-1
Distance:	**2m/2m3:** 2-6 2m4-2m7: 0-1 3m+: 0-0
Track:	LH: **2-5** RH: 0-2 Tight: 0-0 **Gall: 1-3**
Aids:	Bl: 0-0 Vi: 0-0 Tstrap: 0-0 Ckp: 0-0
Best Rating:	155 3/03 Chel 2m110y good Hdl

Smart hurdler; ex-French; best efforts so far a narrow defeat by Rooster Booster in the 2003 Agfa Hurdle at Sandown and fourth in the Champion Hurdle; finally got off the mark with a narrow victory at Cheltenham on his reappearance, and won a little race at Newbury in March; exposed in better races, though; well suited by a stiff two miles in testing conditions.

Selvas (GER)

105   112+

4-y-o ch g Lomitas-Subia (GER) (Konigsstuhl (GER))
Jonjo O'Neill (P Schiergen 5/10) Getjar Limited

Placings:1   (4452)
2003/04: 16¹GS,

	Starts	1st	2nd	3rd	Win & Pl
Hurdles	1	1	0	0	4940
Career Total	**1**	**1**	**0**	**0**	**4940**
112 3/04 Asct	2m110y D Hdl			G-S	£4940
			Total win prize-money £4940		

Going:	Sf: 0-0 GS: 1-1 Gd: 0-0 GF: - Fm: 0-0
Distance:	**2m/2m3:** 1-1 2m4-2m7: 0-0 3m+: 0-0
Track:	LH: 0-0 **RH: 1-1** Tight: 0-0 Gall: 0-0
Aids:	Bl: 0-0 Vi: 0-0 Tstrap: 0-0 Ckp: 0-0
Best Rating:	112 3/04 Asct 2m110y gd-sft Hdl

Ex-German middle-distance handicapper, was able to outstay his rivals when making a successful hurdling debut at Ascot; handles cut in the ground.

Semi Precious (IRE)

105   86

6-y-o ch g Semillon-Precious Petra (Bing Ii)
D P Keane Richard & Carol Stainer

Placings:035013   (4523)
2003/04: 18⁶G, 21³S, 19⁵S, 20⁶S, 16¹S, 17³GS,

	Starts	1st	2nd	3rd	Win & Pl
NH Flat	1	0	0	0	0
Hurdles	5	1	0	2	4792
Career Total	**6**	**1**	**0**	**2**	**4792**
86 1/04 Hntg	2m110y E(0-100)HHdl			SFT	£3556
			Total win prize-money £3556		

Going:	Sf: 1-4 GS: 0-1 Gd: 0-1 GF: - Fm: 0-0
Distance:	**2m/2m3:** 1-3 2m4-2m7: 0-3 3m+: 0-0
Track:	LH: 0-4 **RH: 1-2** Tight: 0-2 **Gall: 1-1**
Aids:	Bl: 0-0 Vi: 0-0 Tstrap: 0-0 Ckp: 0-0
Best Rating:	88 3/04 Extr 2m1f gd-sft Hdl

Senna (IRE)

4166

4-y-o b g Petardia-Saborinie (Prince Sabo)
P D Cundell John Davies (stonehill)

Placings:P   (4166)
2003/04: 16²FG,

	Starts	1st	2nd	3rd	Win & Pl
Hurdles	1	0	0	0	
Career Total	**1**	**0**	**0**	**0**	

Going:	Sf: 0-0 GS: 0-0 Gd: 0-1 GF: - Fm: 0-0
Distance:	2m/2m3: 0-1 2m4-2m7: 0-0 3m+: 0-0
Track:	LH: 0-1 RH: 0-0 Tight: 0-0 Gall: 0-1
Aids:	Bl: 0-0 Vi: 0-0 Tstrap: 0-0 Ckp: 0-0

Senna Da Silva

101   71

4-y-o gr f Prince Of Birds (USA)-Impulsive Decision (IRE)
(Nomination)
J L Flint J L Flint

Placings:00644   (4266)
2003/04: 12⁹GF, 16⁹GS, 17⁶GS, 17⁴S, 16⁴GF,

	Starts	1st	2nd	3rd	Win & Pl
NH Flat	1	0	0	0	0
Hurdles	4	0	0	0	262
Career Total	**5**	**0**	**0**	**0**	**262**

Going:	Sf: 0-1 GS: 0-1 Gd: 0-1 GF: - Fm: 0-2
Distance:	2m/2m3: 0-4 2m4-2m7: 0-0 3m+: 0-0
Track:	LH: 0-2 RH: 0-3 Tight: 0-0 Gall: 0-0
Aids:	Bl: 0-0 Vi: 0-0 Tstrap: 0-0 Ckp: 0-0
Best Rating:	71 3/04 Chep 2m110y gd-fm Hdl

Senor Eduardo

88   79

7-y-o gr g Terimon-Jasmin Path (Warpath)
S Gollings R L Houlton

Placings:005/5-6P00   (4178)
2003/04: 16⁶GS, 16²G, 17⁹GS, 16⁹G,

	Starts	1st	2nd	3rd	Win & Pl
Hurdles	4	0	0	0	0
Career Total	**8**	**0**	**0**	**0**	**0**

Going:	Sf: 0-0 GS: 0-2 Gd: 0-2 GF: - Fm: 0-0
Distance:	2m/2m3: 0-4 2m4-2m7: 0-0 3m+: 0-0
Track:	LH: 0-3 RH: 0-1 Tight: 0-1 Gall: 0-1
Aids:	Bl: 0-0 Vi: 0-0 Tstrap: 0-0 Ckp: 0-0
Best Rating:	98 2/02 Wwck 2m soft NHF

Moderate ability in bumpers and over hurdles.

Senor Gigo

86   68

6-y-o b g Mistertopogigo (IRE)-Lady Carol (Lord Gayle (USA))
Miss V Scott (N M L Ewart 23/1) Mrs A Scott

Placings:00-F0   (4073)
2003/04: 16⁶F, 16⁹F,

	Starts	1st	2nd	3rd	Win & Pl
Hurdles	2	0	0	0	
Career Total	**4**	**0**	**0**	**0**	

Going:	Sf: 0-0 GS: 0-0 Gd: 0-0 GF: - Fm: 0-2
Distance:	2m/2m3: 0-2 2m4-2m7: 0-0 3m+: 0-0
Track:	LH: 0-0 RH: 0-0 Tight: 0-0 Gall: 0-0
Aids:	Bl: 0-0 Vi: 0-0 Tstrap: 0-0 Ckp: 0-0
Best Rating:	68 2/04 Muss 2m firm Hdl

Senor Hurst

97   71+

9-y-o b g Young Senor (USA)-Broadhurst (Workboy)
Mrs P Sly Thorney Racing Club

Placings:02P0/0/623F432/00-0563630P   (4774)
2003/04: 16⁹G, 17⁵G, 17⁶GS, 16²S, 16⁶GS, 16³G, 21⁰G, 16⁷G,

	Starts	1st	2nd	3rd	Win & Pl
Hurdles	7	0	0	2	762
Chases	1	0	0	0	
Career Total	**22**	**0**	**3**	**4**	**4120**

Going:	Sf: 0-1 GS: 0-2 Gd: 0-5 GF: - Fm: 0-0
Distance:	2m/2m3: 0-7 2m4-2m7: 0-1 3m+: 0-0
Track:	LH: 0-4 RH: 0-4 Tight: 0-6 Gall: 0-1
Aids:	Bl: 0-0 Vi: 0-0 Tstrap: 0-0 Ckp: 0-0
Best Rating:	87 7/00 MRas 2m1f110y good Hdl

Plating-class hurdler; still maiden.

Senor Sedona

93f   116f

5-y-o b g Royal Vulcan-Star Shell (Queens Hussar)
N J Gifford Felix Rosensteil's Widow & Son

Placings:22   (3934)
2003/04: 16²HY, 16²G,

	Starts	1st	2nd	3rd	Win & Pl
NH Flat	2	0	2	0	1413
Career Total	**2**	**0**	**2**	**0**	**1413**

Going:	Sf: 0-1 GS: 0-0 Gd: 0-1 GF: - Fm: 0-0
Distance:	2m/2m3: 0-2 2m4-2m7: 0-0 3m+: 0-0
Track:	LH: 0-0 RH: 0-2 Tight: 0-0 Gall: 0-0
Aids:	Bl: 0-0 Vi: 0-0 Tstrap: 0-0 Ckp: 0-0
Best Rating:	113 2/04 Asct 2m110y good NHF

Runner-up in bumpers at Ascot in January (somewhat unluckily) and again there the following month (no match for easy winner); deserves to go one better.

Senor Toran (USA)

4-y-o b g Barathea (IRE)-Applaud (USA) (Rahy (USA))
P Burgoyne (P F I Cole 1/5) Abacus Employment Services Ltd

Placings:U   (4368)
2003/04: 16ᵁGF,

	Starts	1st	2nd	3rd	Win & Pl
Hurdles	1	0	0	0	
Career Total	**1**	**0**	**0**	**0**	

Going:	Sf: 0-0 GS: 0-0 Gd: 0-0 GF: - Fm: 0-1
Distance:	2m/2m3: 0-1 2m4-2m7: 0-0 3m+: 0-0
Track:	LH: 0-1 RH: 0-0 Tight: 0-1 Gall: 0-0
Aids:	Bl: 0-0 Vi: 0-0 Tstrap: 0-0 Ckp: 0-0

Sento (IRE)

107   108+

6-y-o ch g Persian Bold-Esclava (USA) (Nureyev (USA))

A King Mrs M C Sweeney

Placings:1006041-443 (0957)
2003/04: 22⁴G, 21⁴GF, 22³G,

	Starts	1st	2nd	3rd	Win & Pl
Hurdles	3	0	0	1	1920
Career Total	10	2	0	1	10324
104 4/03 NAbb 2m6f		E(0-105)HHdl		G-F	£5928
108 8/02 NAbb 2m1f		H NHF		G-F	£2191
				Total win prize-money £8119	

Going:	Sf: 0-0 GS: 0-0 Gd: 0-2 GF: - Fm: 0-1
Distance:	2m/2m3: 0-0 2m4-2m7: 0-3 3m+: 0-0
Track:	LH: 0-1 RH: 0-0 Tight: 0-1 Gall: 0-1
Aids:	Bl: 0-0 Vi: 0-0 Tstrap: 0-0 Ckp: 0-0
Best Rating:	108 5/03 Hntg 2m5f110y gd-fm Hdl

Modest hurdler; has been held since raised 11b after showing improved form when stepped up to 2m 6f to win at Newton Abbot April 2003; suited by fast ground, but acts with cut.

Senza Scrupoli

97   69

4-y-o ch g Inchinor-Gravette (Kris)
M D Hammond (L M Cumani 7/7) WRB Racing 44 (wrbracing.com)

Placings:P0062 (4781)
2003/04: 18ᴾHY, 17⁰HY, 16⁴HY, 17⁶G, 16²G,

	Starts	1st	2nd	3rd	Win & Pl
Hurdles	5	0	1	0	688
Career Total	5	0	1	0	688

Going:	Sf: 0-2 GS: 0-0 Gd: 0-3 GF: - Fm: 0-0
Distance:	2m/2m3: 0-5 2m4-2m7: 0-0 3m+: 0-0
Track:	LH: 0-3 RH: 0-2 Tight: 0-3 Gall: 0-2
Aids:	Bl: 0-1 Vi: 0-0 Tstrap: 0-0 Ckp: 0-0
Best Rating:	69 4/04 Hntg 2m110y good Hdl

Selling hurdler; best effort when runner-up at Huntingdon in April when blinkered for the first time; best suited by two miles.

September Moon

85   95

6-y-o b m Bustino-Lunabelle (Idiots Delight)
Mrs A M Thorpe J H Lee

Placings:40001F-F0 (4842)
2003/04: 26⁵G, 21⁹G,

	Starts	1st	2nd	3rd	Win & Pl
Hurdles	2	0	0	0	
Career Total	8	1	0	0	4534
95 4/03 Extr	2m6f110yE Hdl			G-F	£4533
				Total win prize-money £4534	

Going:	Sf: 0-0 GS: 0-0 Gd: 0-2 GF: - Fm: 0-0
Distance:	2m/2m3: 0-0 2m4-2m7: 0-0 3m+: 0-1
Track:	LH: 0-1 RH: 0-1 Tight: 0-0 Gall: 0-1
Aids:	Bl: 0-0 Vi: 0-0 Tstrap: 0-0 Ckp: 0-1
Best Rating:	95 4/03 Extr 2m6f110y gd-fm Hdl

Moderate hurdler; stays two miles-six; acts on fast ground.

September Whisper

6-y-o b m Country Classic-Marjimel (Backchat (USA))
Miss L C Siddall Mrs M P Neatby

Placings:P (1019)
2003/04: 16ᴾGF,

	Starts	1st	2nd	3rd	Win & Pl
NH Flat	1	0	0	0	
Career Total	1	0	0	0	

Seraph

95   78+

4-y-o ch g Vettori (IRE)-Dahlawise (IRE) (Caerleon (USA))
John A Harris (I A Wood 10/6) M F Schofield

Placings:U000 (4602)
2003/04: 16ᵁGF, 16⁹GS, 16⁹GF, 17⁰G,

	Starts	1st	2nd	3rd	Win & Pl
Hurdles	4	0	0	0	
Career Total	4	0	0	0	

Going:	Sf: 0-0 GS: 0-1 Gd: 0-1 GF: - Fm: 0-2
Distance:	2m/2m3: 0-4 2m4-2m7: 0-0 3m+: 0-0
Track:	LH: 0-2 RH: 0-2 Tight: 0-2 Gall: 0-1
Aids:	Bl: 0-0 Vi: 0-0 Tstrap: 0-0 Ckp: 0-0
Best Rating:	78 12/03 Ludl 2m gd-fm Hdl

Modest form in juvenile hurdles; sometimes wears cheekpieces.

Seren Fach (IRE)

60f   1f

6-y-o b/br m Fourstars Allstar (USA)-Cauriedator (Laurence O)
Mrs D A Hamer Mike Thomas

Placings:0 (1487)
2003/04: 17⁰GF,

	Starts	1st	2nd	3rd	Win & Pl
NH Flat	1	0	0	0	
Career Total	1	0	0	0	

Going:	Sf: 0-0 GS: 0-0 Gd: 0-0 GF: - Fm: 0-1
Distance:	2m/2m3: 0-1 2m4-2m7: 0-0 3m+: 0-0
Track:	LH: 0-0 RH: 0-1 Tight: 0-0 Gall: 0-0
Aids:	Bl: 0-0 Vi: 0-0 Tstrap: 0-0 Ckp: 0-0
Best Rating:	1 10/03 Hrfd 2m1f gd-fm NHF

Serious Position (IRE)

(109h)   (91h)

9-y-o ch g Orchestra-Lady Temba (Callernish)
D R Stoddart D R Stoddart

Placings:5P6P4P/0PP336P/544-1P (1664)
2003/04: 22¹GF, 20ᴾGF,

	Starts	1st	2nd	3rd	Win & Pl
Hurdles	1	1	0	0	2905
Chases	1	0	0	0	0
Career Total	18	1	0	2	4867
91 10/03 Uttx	2m6f110yE Hdl			G-F	£2905
				Total win prize-money £2905	

Going:	Sf: 0-0 GS: 0-0 Gd: 0-0 GF: - Fm: 1-2
Distance:	2m/2m3: 0-0 2m4-2m7: 1-2 3m+: 0-0
Track:	LH: 1-2 RH: 0-0 Tight: 0-0 Gall: 0-0
Aids:	Bl: 0-0 Vi: 0-0 Tstrap: 0-0 Ckp: 0-0
Best Rating:	91 10/03 Uttx 2m6f110y gd-fm Hdl

Moderate novice hurdler/chaser; narrow winner of weak hurdle event at Uttoxeter in October 2003; stays well; acts on fast ground; went wrong on chase debut.

Serpentine Rock

85f   90f

4-y-o ch g Hernando (FR)-Serpentara (Kris)
Ferdy Murphy Burns Farm Racing

Placings:552 (4663)
2003/04: 12⁵GF, 17⁵G, 16²S,

	Starts	1st	2nd	3rd	Win & Pl
NH Flat	3	0	1	0	586
Career Total	3	0	1	0	586

Going:	Sf: 0-1 GS: 0-0 Gd: 0-1 GF: - Fm: 0-1
Distance:	2m/2m3: 0-2 2m4-2m7: 0-0 3m+: 0-0
Track:	LH: 0-2 RH: 0-1 Tight: 0-0 Gall: 0-0
Aids:	Bl: 0-0 Vi: 0-0 Tstrap: 0-0 Ckp: 0-0
Best Rating:	90 4/04 Hexm 2m110y soft NHF

Has hinted at ability in bumpers on a sound surface and on soft ground; should be suited by further than two miles over obstacles; sure to win a small race.

Setting Sun

93

11-y-o ch g Generous (IRE)-Suntrap (USA) (Roberto (USA))
N Waggott Mrs J Waggott

Placings:60322/0P/001/0P/44450-P (1027)
2003/04: 19ᴾGF,

	Starts	1st	2nd	3rd	Win & Pl
Hurdles	1	0	0	0	
Career Total	18	1	2	1	6114
100 2/00 Muss	3m	D(0-110)HHdl		G-S	£3250
				Total win prize-money £3250	

Going:	Sf: 0-0 GS: 0-0 Gd: 0-0 GF: - Fm: 0-1
Distance:	2m/2m3: 0-0 2m4-2m7: 0-1 3m+: 0-0
Track:	LH: 0-0 RH: 0-1 Tight: 0-1 Gall: 0-0
Aids:	Bl: 0-0 Vi: 0-0 Tstrap: 0-0 Ckp: 0-0
Best Rating:	105 3/98 Newc 2m gd-fm Hdl

Modest staying hurdler; handles a sound surface but suited by a little cut; stays three miles.

Seven Colours

79f   62f

4-y-o b g Spectrum (IRE)-Sinking Sun (Danehill (USA))
Miss V Scott G M Abercrombie

Placings:0 (4787)
2003/04: 16⁰G,

	Starts	1st	2nd	3rd	Win & Pl
NH Flat	1	0	0	0	
Career Total	1	0	0	0	

Going:	Sf: 0-0 GS: 0-0 Gd: 0-1 GF: - Fm: 0-0
Distance:	2m/2m3: 0-1 2m4-2m7: 0-0 3m+: 0-0
Track:	LH: 0-0 RH: 0-1 Tight: 0-0 Gall: 0-1
Aids:	Bl: 0-0 Vi: 0-0 Tstrap: 0-0 Ckp: 0-0
Best Rating:	62 4/04 Hntg 2m110y good NHF

Severn Air

101   97

6-y-o b m Alderbrook-Mariner's Air (Julio Mariner)
J L Spearing Mrs Peter Badger

Placings: *60-4420166* (4915)
2003/04: 16⁴GS, 17⁴G, 16²G, 19⁹GS, 17¹G, 18⁶G, 16⁶GS,

	Starts	1st	2nd	3rd	Win & Pl
NH Flat	1	0	0	0	0
Hurdles	6	1	1	0	4350
Career Total	9	1	1	0	4350
97	3/04	Bang	2m1f		E Hdl	GD	£3654

Total win prize-money £3654

Going:	Sf: 0-0 GS: 0-3 Gd: 1-4 GF: - Fm: 0-0
Distance:	2m/2m3: 1-6 2m4-2m7: 0-1 3m+: 0-0
Track:	LH: 1-5 RH: 0-2 Tight: 1-4 Gall: 0-0
Aids:	Bl: 0-0 Vi: 0-0 Tstrap: 0-0 Ckp: 0-0
Best Rating:	97	3/04	Bang	2m1f	good	Hdl

Moderate novice hurdler; effective over two miles; acts on good ground.

Severn Belle (IRE)
85   75

8-y-o ch m Executive Perk-Our Siveen (Deep Run)
Mrs S J Smith A P Russell

Placings: *30603/446* (2030)
2003/04: 17⁴G, 20⁴GF, 26⁶G,

	Starts	1st	2nd	3rd	Win & Pl
Hurdles	3	0	0	0	0
Career Total	8	0	0	2	665

Going:	Sf: 0-0 GS: 0-0 Gd: 0-2 GF: - Fm: 0-1
Distance:	2m/2m3: 0-1 2m4-2m7: 0-1 3m+: 0-1
Track:	LH: 0-3 RH: 0-0 Tight: 0-1 Gall: 0-0
Aids:	Bl: 0-0 Vi: 0-0 Tstrap: 0-0 Ckp: 0-0
Best Rating:	83	6/01	Hexm	2m	gd-sft	NHF

Severn Magic

11-y-o b m Buckley-La Margarite (Bonne Noel)
D Thomas R Packer

Placings: *P/5-U* (4150)
2003/04: 24ᵁG,

	Starts	1st	2nd	3rd	Win & Pl
Chases	1	0	0	0	0
Career Total	3	0	0	0	0

Going:	Sf: 0-0 GS: 0-0 Gd: 0-1 GF: - Fm: 0-0
Distance:	2m/2m3: 0-0 2m4-2m7: 0-0 3m+: 0-1
Track:	LH: 0-0 RH: 0-1 Tight: 0-1 Gall: 0-0
Aids:	Bl: 0-0 Vi: 0-0 Tstrap: 0-0 Ckp: 0-0
Best Rating:	60	5/02	Bang	3m110y	good	Ch

Sh Boom
114   148+

6-y-o b g Alderbrook-Muznah (Royal And Regal (USA))
Jonjo O'Neill T G K Construction Ltd

Placings: *61/11215P-2211F0* (4623)
2003/04: 24²G, 21²GS, 24¹G, 23¹G, 24²G, 24⁰G,

	Starts	1st	2nd	3rd	Win & Pl
Hurdles	6	2	2	0	44346
Career Total	14	6	3	0	63208
154	1/04	Hayd	2m7110yA	Hdl	GD	£23200
139	12/03	Chel	3m	B Hdl	GD	£12412
126	3/03	Hntg	2m4f110yE	Hdl	GD	£3766
133	12/02	Uttx	2m4f110yE	Hdl	SFT	£3669
100	11/02	Weth	2m	H NHF	HVY	£2478
98	4/02	Towc	2m	H NHF	GD	£1722

Total win prize-money £47248

Placings: Sf: 0-0 GS: 0-1 Gd: 2-5 GF: - Fm: 0-0

Going:	Sf: 0-0 GS: 0-1 Gd: 2-5 GF: - Fm: 0-0
Distance:	2m/2m3: 0-0 2m4-2m7: 0-1 3m+: 2-5
Track:	LH: 2-6 RH: 0-0 Tight: 0-2 Gall: 1-3
Aids:	Bl: 0-0 Vi: 0-0 Tstrap: 0-0 Ckp: 0-0
Best Rating:	154	1/04	Hayd	2m7f110y	good	Hdl

Smart hurdler; half-brother to Stayers' Hurdle winner Anzum; did well in bumpers, winning twice; useful novice hurdler in 2002/3; won valuable conditions hurdles at Cheltenham in December and Haydock in January; fell in the Stayers Hurdle and well beaten at Aintree; stays three miles; acts on good and soft ground.

Shaadiva
103   111+

6-y-o b m Shaamit (IRE)-Kristal Diva (Kris)
A King Cheltenham Racing Ltd

Placings: *0043-311P2P* (4574)
2003/04: 17³G, 16¹GF, 20¹GS, 21⁸G, 21²G, 21⁸G,

	Starts	1st	2nd	3rd	Win & Pl
Hurdles	6	2	1	1	10827
Career Total	10	2	1	2	11609
111	12/03	Hntg	2m4f110yD Hdl		G-S	£4891
100	11/03	Winc	2m	E(0-100)HHdl	G-F	£3376

Total win prize-money £8268

Going:	Sf: 0-0 GS: 1-1 Gd: 0-4 GF: - Fm: 1-1
Distance:	2m/2m3: 1-2 2m4-2m7: 1-4 3m+: 0-0
Track:	LH: 0-2 RH: 2-4 Tight: 0-1 Gall: 1-3
Aids:	Bl: 0-1 Vi: 0-0 Tstrap: 0-0 Ckp: 0-0
Best Rating:	111	3/04	Ludl	2m5f	good	Hdl

Modest novice hurdler; probably best over farther than two miles; acts on fast and easy ground.

Shaamit The Vaamit (IRE)
64f

4-y-o b g Shaamit (IRE)-Shocker (IRE) (Sabrehill (USA))
M Scudamore Mrs S Tainton

Placings: *5* (4509)
2003/04: 14⁵GS,

	Starts	1st	2nd	3rd	Win & Pl
NH Flat	1	0	0	0	0
Career Total	1	0	0	0	0

Going:	Sf: 0-0 GS: 0-1 Gd: 0-0 GF: - Fm: 0-0
Distance:	2m/2m3: 0-0 2m4-2m7: 0-0 3m+: 0-0
Track:	LH: 0-0 RH: 0-0 Tight: 0-0 Gall: 0-0
Aids:	Bl: 0-0 Vi: 0-0 Tstrap: 0-0 Ckp: 0-0
Best Rating:	64	3/04	Hrfd	1m6f	gd-sft	NHF

Shadbolt (NZ)
95f   87f

6-y-o gr g Heroicity (AUS)-Another Day (NZ) (Open Day)
L A Dace Michael H Watt

Placings: *00* (2690)
2003/04: 16⁰G, 16⁰GS,

	Starts	1st	2nd	3rd	Win & Pl
NH Flat	2	0	0	0	0
Career Total	2	0	0	0	0

Going:	Sf: 0-0 GS: 0-1 Gd: 0-1 GF: - Fm: 0-0
Distance:	2m/2m3: 0-2 2m4-2m7: 0-0 3m+: 0-0
Track:	LH: 0-0 RH: 0-2 Tight: 0-0 Gall: 0-1

Aids:	Bl: 0-0 Vi: 0-0 Tstrap: 0-0 Ckp: 0-0
Best Rating:	87	11/03	Sand	2m110y	good	NHF

Shade Lucky

8-y-o ch g Gildoran-Snowy Autumn (Deep Run)
B J M Ryall J F Tucker

Placings: *00/PP-P5F* (0591)
2003/04: 22⁸PG, 23⁵G, 23⁸GF,

	Starts	1st	2nd	3rd	Win & Pl
Hurdles	1	0	0	0	0
Chases	2	0	0	0	0
Career Total	7	0	0	0	0

Going:	Sf: 0-0 GS: 0-0 Gd: 0-2 GF: - Fm: 0-1
Distance:	2m/2m3: 0-0 2m4-2m7: 0-1 3m+: 0-2
Track:	LH: 0-2 RH: 0-1 Tight: 0-0 Gall: 0-0
Aids:	Bl: 0-1 Vi: 0-0 Tstrap: 0-0 Ckp: 0-0
Best Rating:	67	12/01	NAbb	2m1f	heavy	NHF

Shaded (IRE)
94(77c)   (47c)67

10-y-o b g Night Shift (USA)-Sarsaparilla (FR) (Shirley Heights)
D J Minty D J Minty

Placings: *06FP0/00P200P/00P0434534P/0/000301/FPP0-40006P* (4148)
2003/04: 22⁴GF, 17⁰G, 19⁰G, 17⁰GF, 19⁶GF, 19⁰PG,

	Starts	1st	2nd	3rd	Win & Pl
Hurdles	5	0	0	0	0
Chases	1	0	0	0	0
Career Total	40	1	1	3	3192
75	10/01	Tntn	2m3f110yG(0-90)HHdl	FRM	£1690

Total win prize-money £1691

Going:	Sf: 0-0 GS: 0-0 Gd: 0-3 GF: - Fm: 0-3
Distance:	2m/2m3: 0-4 2m4-2m7: 0-2 3m+: 0-0
Track:	LH: 0-2 RH: 0-3 Tight: 0-4 Gall: 0-0
Aids:	Bl: 0-0 Vi: 0-0 Tstrap: 0-0 Ckp: 0-0
Best Rating:	75	10/01	Tntn	2m3f110y	firm	Hdl

Shadow River (IRE)
97f   94f

6-y-o b g Over The River (FR)-Society Belle (Callernish)
P J Hobbs Ian David Ltd & Byrne Bros (FWK) Ltd

Placings: *02* (4936)
2003/04: 16⁰GS, 18²G,

	Starts	1st	2nd	3rd	Win & Pl
NH Flat	2	0	1	0	548
Career Total	2	0	1	0	548

Going:	Sf: 0-0 GS: 0-1 Gd: 0-1 GF: - Fm: 0-0
Distance:	2m/2m3: 0-2 2m4-2m7: 0-0 3m+: 0-0
Track:	LH: 0-2 RH: 0-0 Tight: 0-1 Gall: 0-1
Aids:	Bl: 0-0 Vi: 0-0 Tstrap: 0-0 Ckp: 0-0
Best Rating:	94	4/04	Font	2m2f110y	good	NHF

Half-brother to high-class hurdler Davenport Millenium; acts on good ground.

Shady Affair (IRE)
(0c)28

13-y-o b g Black Minstrel-Golden Ice (Golden Love)

R N Bevis Mrs S J Clutton

Placings: PP/25516UP/50P0-P **(0069)**
2003/04: 20PS,

	Starts	1st	2nd	3rd	Win & Pl
Hurdles	1	0	0	0	
Career Total	14	1	1	0	4528

82 11/01 Bang 2m1f110yE(0-105)HCh SFT £3607
Total win prize-money £3608

Going:	Sf: 0-1 GS: 0-0 Gd: 0-0 GF: - Fm: 0-0
Distance:	2m/2m3: 0-0 2m4-2m7: 0-1 3m+: 0-0
Track:	LH: 0-1 RH: 0-0 Tight: 0-1 Gall: 0-0
Aids:	Bl: 0-0 Vi: 0-0 Tstrap: 0-0 Ckp: 0-0
Best Rating:	82 11/01 Bang 2m1f110y soft Ch

Shady Anne

101   85

6-y-o ch m Derrylin-Juno Away (Strong Gale)
F Jordan D Pugh

Placings: 1/61050P-54P600 **(4873)**
2003/04: 24FS, 20AG, 16PS, 26RGS, 26PG, 20FGS,

	Starts	1st	2nd	3rd	Win & Pl
Hurdles	6	0	0	0	413
Career Total	13	2	0	0	4031

106 10/02 Bang 2m1f H NHF SFT £1881
93 4/02 Towc 2m H NHF G-S £1736
Total win prize-money £3618

Going:	Sf: 0-2 GS: 0-2 Gd: 0-2 GF: - Fm: 0-0
Distance:	2m/2m3: 0-1 2m4-2m7: 0-2 3m+: 0-3
Track:	LH: 0-3 RH: 0-3 Tight: 0-3 Gall: 0-2
Aids:	Bl: 0-0 Vi: 0-0 Tstrap: 0-0 Ckp: 0-2
Best Rating:	106 10/02 Bang 2m1f soft NHF

Shady Exchange (IRE)

89   61

9-y-o b g Le Bavard (FR)-Torus Light (Torus)
R Lee The Three Tees

Placings: PP5PP **(4713)**
2003/04: 22PS, 26PS, 24FS, 25PG, 24PG,

	Starts	1st	2nd	3rd	Win & Pl
Chases	5	0	0	0	0
Career Total	5	0	0	0	0

Going:	Sf: 0-2 GS: 0-3 Gd: 0-3 GF: - Fm: 0-0
Distance:	2m/2m3: 0-0 2m4-2m7: 0-1 3m+: 0-4
Track:	LH: 0-1 RH: 0-4 Tight: 0-3 Gall: 0-0
Aids:	Bl: 0-2 Vi: 0-0 Tstrap: 0-0 Ckp: 0-1
Best Rating:	60 2/04 Ludl 3m good Ch

Shady Grey

98   83

6-y-o gr m Minster Son-Yemaail (IRE) (Shaadi (USA))
Miss S E Forster A Dawson

Placings: 600-003254 **(4909)**
2003/04: 20HY, 16PGF, 16RH, 20PHY, 21FS, 24FS,

	Starts	1st	2nd	3rd	Win & Pl
Hurdles	6	0	1	1	2455
Career Total	9	0	1	1	2455

Going:	Sf: 0-4 GS: 0-0 Gd: 0-1 GF: - Fm: 0-1
Distance:	2m/2m3: 0-2 2m4-2m7: 0-3 3m+: 0-1

Track:	LH: 0-2 RH: 0-4 Tight: 0-2 Gall: 0-1
Aids:	Bl: 0-0 Vi: 0-0 Tstrap: 0-0 Ckp: 0-0
Best Rating:	83 2/04 Carl 2m4f heavy Hdl

Modest hurdler; suited by two and a half miles and soft ground.

Shady Man

89   96+

6-y-o b g Shaamit (IRE)-Miss Hardy (Formidable (USA))
Mrs S J Smith Trevor Hemmings

Placings: 0/P602-P1 **(4958)**
2003/04: 20PS, 17IG,

	Starts	1st	2nd	3rd	Win & Pl
Hurdles	2	1	0	0	2373
Career Total	7	1	1	0	3413

96 4/04 MRas 2m1f110yG(0-95)HHdl GD £2373
Total win prize-money £2373

Going:	Sf: 0-1 GS: 0-0 Gd: 1-1 GF: - Fm: 0-0
Distance:	2m/2m3: 1-1 2m4-2m7: 0-1 3m+: 0-0
Track:	LH: 0-1 RH: 1-1 Tight: 1-1 Gall: 0-0
Aids:	Bl: 0-0 Vi: 0-0 Tstrap: 0-0 Ckp: 0-0
Best Rating:	96 4/04 MRas 2m1f110y good Hdl

Plating-class hurdler; stays 2m 1f; acts on good.

Shaffishayes

105   95

12-y-o ch g Clantime-Mischievous Miss (Niniski (USA))
Mrs M Reveley P Davidson-Brown

Placings: F4/04333U2F-110623610 **(4159)**
2003/04: 16IG, 16IG, 16IIG, 16RGS, 17FG, 16RGS, 16RHY, 20IG, 19RG,

	Starts	1st	2nd	3rd	Win & Pl
Hurdles	9	3	1	1	13216
Career Total	19	3	2	4	15079

97 2/04 Muss 2m4f F(0-100)HHdl GD £3073
88 5/03 Kels 2m10y E(0-105)HHdl GD £5616
86 5/03 Prth 2m110y G(0-95)HHdl GD £3437
Total win prize-money £12126

Going:	Sf: 0-1 GS: 0-2 Gd: 3-6 GF: - Fm: 0-0
Distance:	2m/2m3: 2-7 2m4-2m7: 1-2 3m+: 0-0
Track:	LH: 1-6 RH: 2-3 Tight: 2-4 Gall: 0-1
Aids:	Bl: 0-0 Vi: 0-0 Tstrap: 0-0 Ckp: 0-0
Best Rating:	97 2/04 Muss 2m4f good Hdl

Plating-class veteran hurdler; recorded third career win at Musselburgh in February; best at two miles; suited by decent ground.

Shafts Chance (IRE)

(46h)60

7-y-o br m Over The River (FR)-Lunar Approach (IRE) (Mandalus)
C R Egerton (J A Flynn 11/7) Ian Jacombs & Partners

Placings: 50034FF **(1664)**
2003/04: 16FGY, 16PGF, 19FIF, 26RGF, 25FGF, 20FGF, 20FGF,

	Starts	1st	2nd	3rd	Win & Pl
NH Flat	2	0	0	0	0
Hurdles	1	0	0	0	0
Chases	4	0	0	1	819
Career Total	7	0	0	1	819

Going:	Sf: 0-0 GS: 0-0 Gd: 0-0 GF: - Fm: 0-6
Distance:	2m/2m3: 0-3 2m4-2m7: 0-2 3m+: 0-2
Track:	LH: 0-3 RH: 0-1 Tight: 0-1 Gall: 0-0
Aids:	Bl: 0-1 Vi: 0-0 Tstrap: 0-0 Ckp: 0-0

Best Rating:	78 6/03 Navn 2m	gd-fm NHF

Poor novice chaser; formerly fair bumper mare; yet to show much over fences.

Shah (IRE)

83   89+

11-y-o b g King Persian-Gay And Sharp (Fine Blade (USA))
P Kelsall Peter Kelsall

Placings: 00P0P/1/45/P1-P3PP **(3443)**
2003/04: 21PG, 16RGS, 16PS, 20PG,

	Starts	1st	2nd	3rd	Win & Pl
Chases	4	0	0	1	523
Career Total	14	2	0	1	7473

89 5/02 Worc 2m F(0-95)HCh GD £2978
78 10/00 Ludl 2m4f D(0-110)HCh G-F £3711
Total win prize-money £6691

Going:	Sf: 0-1 GS: 0-1 Gd: 0-2 GF: - Fm: 0-0
Distance:	2m/2m3: 0-2 2m4-2m7: 0-2 3m+: 0-0
Track:	LH: 0-0 RH: 0-4 Tight: 0-1 Gall: 0-2
Aids:	Bl: 0-1 Vi: 0-0 Tstrap: 0-0 Ckp: 0-0
Best Rating:	89 12/03 Hntg 2m10y gd-sft Ch

Plating-class hurdler; effective at up to two and a half miles; likes fast ground.

Shahboor (USA)

(123h)111

10-y-o b g Zilzal (USA)-Iva Reputation (USA) (Sir Ivor)
Mrs P Robeson Sir Evelyn De Rothschild

Placings: 0/24160/12104233/325F3435/21-F **(1584)**
2003/04: 20FGF,

	Starts	1st	2nd	3rd	Win & Pl
Chases	1	0	0	0	
Career Total	25	4	5	5	27536

111 4/03 Uttx 2m E Ch GD £4114
125 5/99 Uttx 2m C(0-135)HHdl GD £4440
125 5/99 Strf 2m110y D(0-120)HHdl G-S £3860
106 5/98 Uttx 2m E(0-100)HHdl GF £2547
Total win prize-money £14962

Going:	Sf: 0-0 GS: 0-0 Gd: 0-0 GF: - Fm: 0-1
Distance:	2m/2m3: 0-0 2m4-2m7: 0-1 3m+: 0-0
Track:	LH: 0-0 RH: 0-1 Tight: 0-0 Gall: 0-1
Aids:	Bl: 0-1 Vi: 0-0 Tstrap: 0-0 Ckp: 0-0
Best Rating:	125 5/99 Uttx 2m	good Hdl

Modest novice chaser; decent handicap hurdler in his time; finished runner-up at Market Rasen on his first outing for over two years and followed up with an impressive victory at Uttoxeter; acts on most types of ground; best at two miles; looks well handicapped over fences.

Shake Eddie Shake (IRE)

(87h)   (69h)

7-y-o b g Blues Traveller (IRE)-Fortune Teller (Troy)
H S Howe C I A Slocock

Placings: 05/PPP/P040-0P **(4376)**
2003/04: 16FIG, 16FG,

	Starts	1st	2nd	3rd	Win & Pl
Hurdles	1	0	0	0	0
Chases	1	0	0	0	0
Career Total	11	0	0	0	335

Going:	Sf: 0-0 GS: 0-0 Gd: 0-1 GF: - Fm: 0-1
Distance:	2m/2m3: 0-2 2m4-2m7: 0-0 3m+: 0-0

Track: LH: 0-0 RH: 0-2 Tight: 0-1 Gall: 0-0
Aids: Bl: 0-0 Vi: 0-0 Tstrap: 0-0 Ckp: 0-0
Best Rating: 69   5/03   Winc   2m   gd-fm   Hdl

Shakwaa

94   87

5-y-o ch m Lion Cavern (USA)-Shadha (USA) (Devil's Bag (USA))
E A Elliott Mrs Anne E Elliott

Placings:00-0003P   (4908)
2003/04: 17⁰G, 16⁹G, 21⁹G, 17⁹G, 20⁹S,

	Starts	1st	2nd	3rd	Win & Pl
Hurdles	5	0	0	1	570
Career Total	7	0	0	1	570

Going: Sf: 0-1 GS: 0-0 Gd: 0-4 GF: - Fm: 0-0
Distance: 2m/2m3: 0-3 2m4-2m7: 0-2 3m+: 0-0
Track: LH: 0-3 RH: 0-2 Tight: 0-2 Gall: 0-0
Aids: Bl: 0-0 Vi: 0-0 Tstrap: 0-0 Ckp: 0-0
Best Rating: 87   4/04   Carl   2m1f   good   Hdl

Shalako (USA)

114   130

6-y-o ch g Kingmambo (USA)-Sporades (USA) (Vaguely Noble)
P J Hobbs D J Jones

Placings:141-2542046600   (4813)
2003/04: 16²GF, 16⁵G, 20⁴GS, 16²G, 16⁹S, 21⁴G, 21⁶G, 16⁶S, 20⁰G, 16⁰G,

	Starts	1st	2nd	3rd	Win & Pl
Hurdles	10	0	2	0	19570
Career Total	13	2	2	0	29751
113	1/03	Tntn	2m1f	E Hdl	SFT £4615
118	11/02	Tntn	2m1f	D Hdl	G-S £4316
				Total win prize-money £8931	

Going: Sf: 0-2 GS: 0-1 Gd: 0-6 GF: - Fm: 0-1
Distance: 2m/2m3: 0-6 2m4-2m7: 0-4 3m+: 0-0
Track: LH: 0-6 RH: 0-4 Tight: 0-1 Gall: 0-1
Aids: Bl: 0-2 Vi: 0-1 Tstrap: 0-0 Ckp: 0-0
Best Rating: 128   12/03   Chel   2m110y   good   Hdl

Fair hurdler; effective at around two miles; acts on most types of ground, although prefers a sound surface; has worn blinkers.

Shalbeblue (IRE)

85(100h)   (110h)100

7-y-o b g Shalford (IRE)-Alberjas (IRE) (Sure Blade (USA))
B Ellison Four Clubs

Placings:3534P/16632116/63023233-63   (1476)
2003/04: 16⁶G, 17³G,

	Starts	1st	2nd	3rd	Win & Pl
Hurdles	1	0	0	1	283
Chases	3	0	0	0	0
Career Total	23	3	3	8	18758
108	3/02	Sedg	2m1f	E(0-110)HHdl	SFT £2548
110	2/02	Sedg	2m1f	E Hdl	SFT £2583
111	10/01	Sedg	2m1f	E Hdl	G-S £2576
				Total win prize-money £7707	

Going: Sf: 0-0 GS: 0-0 Gd: 0-2 GF: - Fm: 0-0
Distance: 2m/2m3: 0-2 2m4-2m7: 0-0 3m+: 0-0
Track: LH: 0-2 RH: 0-0 Tight: 0-1 Gall: 0-0
Aids: Bl: 0-2 Vi: 0-0 Tstrap: 0-0 Ckp: 0-0
Best Rating: 112   1/01   Donc   2m10y   good   Hdl

Sham Sharif

100   82

7-y-o b m Be My Chief (USA)-Syrian Queen (Slip Anchor)
C J Down Gordon James Cossey

Placings:606/PP202   (0970)
2003/04: 17⁵GF, 20²GF, 17²GF, 16⁰G, 17²GS,

	Starts	1st	2nd	3rd	Win & Pl
Hurdles	5	0	2	0	2994
Career Total	8	0	2	0	2994

Going: Sf: 0-0 GS: 0-1 Gd: 0-1 GF: - Fm: 0-3
Distance: 2m/2m3: 0-4 2m4-2m7: 0-1 3m+: 0-0
Track: LH: 0-4 RH: 0-1 Tight: 0-2 Gall: 0-0
Aids: Bl: 0-3 Vi: 0-0 Tstrap: 0-0 Ckp: 0-0
Best Rating: 82   7/03   NAbb   2m1f   gd-sft   Hdl

Plating-class hurdler; acts on fast and easy ground.

Shaman

104   103

7-y-o b g Fraam-Magic Maggie (Beveled (USA))
G L Moore Paul Chapman

Placings:P60-522621P   (4365)
2003/04: 17⁵G, 16²GF, 16²G, 16⁶G, 16²GS, 16¹S, 16⁶GS,

	Starts	1st	2nd	3rd	Win & Pl
Hurdles	7	1	3	0	6844
Career Total	10	1	3	0	6844
103	1/04	Plum	2m	E(0-110)HHdl	SFT £4163
				Total win prize-money £4163	

Going: Sf: 1-1 GS: 0-2 Gd: 0-3 GF: - Fm: 0-1
Distance: 2m/2m3: 1-7 2m4-2m7: 0-0 3m+: 0-0
Track: LH: 1-4 RH: 0-3 Tight: 1-5 Gall: 0-0
Aids: Bl: 0-0 Vi: 0-0 Tstrap: 0-0 Ckp: 0-0
Best Rating: 103   1/04   Plum   2m   soft   Hdl

Plating-class novice hurdler; acts on a sound surface; should stay further than two miles.

Shamawan (IRE)

(103h)   (100h)141

9-y-o b g Kris-Shamawna (IRE) (Darshaan)
Jonjo O'Neill John P McManus

Placings:050/020/3P632/2112/F132-5   (3717)
2003/04: 20⁵S,

	Starts	1st	2nd	3rd	Win & Pl
Hurdles	1	0	0	0	0
Career Total	20	3	5	3	41321
136	11/02	Asct	2m	B(0-145)HCh	HVY £10992
119	3/02	MRas	2m1f110yD Ch	G-S	£5936
126	3/02	Hntg	2m110y	D(0-115)HCh	SFT £3893
				Total win prize-money £20823	

Going: Sf: 0-1 GS: 0-0 Gd: 0-0 GF: - Fm: 0-0
Distance: 2m/2m3: 0-0 2m4-2m7: 0-1 3m+: 0-0
Track: LH: 0-0 RH: 0-0 Tight: 0-1 Gall: 0-0
Aids: Bl: 0-0 Vi: 0-0 Tstrap: 0-0 Ckp: 0-0
Best Rating: 141   1/03   Chel   2m5f   gd-sft   Ch

Very useful handicap chaser; acts on soft ground; effective at around two miles to two miles five; not the most fluent of jumpers; lightly raced of late.

Shamdian (IRE)

99   103

4-y-o b g Indian Ridge-Shamadara (IRE) (Kahyasi)
N J Henderson (A De Royer-Dupre 1/9) Thurloe Thoroughbreds XI

Placings:3P   (3364)
2003/04: 16³GS, 16⁶G,

	Starts	1st	2nd	3rd	Win & Pl
Hurdles	2	0	0	1	868
Career Total	2	0	0	1	868

Going: Sf: 0-0 GS: 0-1 Gd: 0-1 GF: - Fm: 0-0
Distance: 2m/2m3: 0-2 2m4-2m7: 0-0 3m+: 0-0
Track: LH: 0-0 RH: 0-2 Tight: 0-0 Gall: 0-0
Aids: Bl: 0-0 Vi: 0-0 Tstrap: 0-0 Ckp: 0-0
Best Rating: 103   1/04   Sand   2m110y   gd-sft   Hdl

Moderate juvenile hurdler; placed over a mile and ten furlongs on the Flat in France on easy ground.

Shamel

8-y-o b g Unfuwain (USA)-Narjis (USA) (Blushing Groom (FR))
S Flook (A E Price 3/5) Glyn Byard

Placings:P-0P   (4303)
2003/04: 22⁰S, 16²G,

	Starts	1st	2nd	3rd	Win & Pl
Hurdles	1	0	0	0	0
Chases	1	0	0	0	0
Career Total	3	0	0	0	0

Going: Sf: 0-1 GS: 0-0 Gd: 0-1 GF: - Fm: 0-0
Distance: 2m/2m3: 0-1 2m4-2m7: 0-1 3m+: 0-0
Track: LH: 0-1 RH: 0-1 Tight: 0-0 Gall: 0-0
Aids: Bl: 0-0 Vi: 0-0 Tstrap: 0-1 Ckp: 0-0
Best Rating: 32   5/03   Uttx   2m6f110y   soft   Hdl

Shameless

33

7-y-o ch g Prince Daniel (USA)-Level Edge (Beveled (USA))
H Alexander Mrs L Lever

Placings:4025/PPPP0P-P   (3324)
2003/04: 17⁷GS,

	Starts	1st	2nd	3rd	Win & Pl
Hurdles	1	0	0	0	0
Career Total	11	0	1	0	506

Going: Sf: 0-0 GS: 0-1 Gd: 0-0 GF: - Fm: 0-0
Distance: 2m/2m3: 0-1 2m4-2m7: 0-0 3m+: 0-0
Track: LH: 0-1 RH: 0-0 Tight: 0-1 Gall: 0-0
Aids: Bl: 0-0 Vi: 0-0 Tstrap: 0-0 Ckp: 0-0
Best Rating: 89   3/02   Sthl   2m   heavy   NHF

Shampooed (IRE)

113(97h)   (100h)116

10-y-o b m Law Society (USA)-White Cap'S (Shirley Heights)
R Dickin Warwick Members Racing Club

Placings:001/200/010511/114561300/4102553641/P16225 0-03241   (0855)
2003/04: 16⁶GF, 19³GF, 17²G, 17⁴G, 20¹GF,

	Starts	1st	2nd	3rd	Win & Pl
Hurdles	2	0	0	1	518

| Chases | 3 | 1 | 1 | 0 | 11139 |
| Career Total | 43 | 11 | 5 | 3 | 54599 |

116	7/03	Strf	2m4f	D(0-125)HCh	G-F	£8118
109	5/02	Worc	2m	E(0-110)HCh	G-F	£3368
99	4/02	Wwck	2m110y	E Ch	G-F	£3458
111	5/01	Strf	2m1f110yD Ch			£4403
113	2/01	Wwck	2m	C(0-130)HHdl	SFT	£5135
116	5/00	Hrfd	2m3f110yD(0-120)HHdl	G-S	£3071
116	5/00	Towc	2m	D(0-125)HHdl	SFT	£3211
109	4/00	Strf	2m110y	D(0-120)HHdl	GD	£3568
92	3/00	Wwck	2m	F(0-100)HHdl	SFT	£1960
98	12/99	Wwck	2m	F(0-110)HHdl	SFT	£1996
94	3/98	Clon		Hdl	YLD	£2382
				Total win prize-money £40674

Going:	Sf: 0-0 GS: 0-0 Gd: 0-2 GF: - Fm: 1-3
Distance:	2m/2m3: 0-2 2m4-2m7: 1-0 3m+: 0-0
Track:	LH: 1-4 RH: 0-1 Tight: 1-2 Gall: 0-0
Aids:	Bl: 0-0 Vi: 1-4 Tstrap: 0-0 Ckp: 0-0
Best Rating:	116 7/03 Strf 2m4f gd-fm Ch

Modest hurdler/chaser; multiple winner in her time; very game; effective on a sound surface but best when the mud is flying; stays 2m 4f; has worn a visor.

Shamrock

95f 93f

7-y-o ch m Sanglamore (USA)-Rockfest (USA) (Stagedoor Johnny)
Lady Herries Lady Herries

Placings: 2/03 (0422)
2003/04: 16⁰GS, 17³GF,

	Starts	1st	2nd	3rd	Win & Pl
NH Flat	2	0	1	1	297
Career Total	3	0	1		753

Going:	Sf: 0-0 GS: 0-1 Gd: 0-0 GF: - Fm: 0-1
Distance:	2m/2m3: 0-2 2m4-2m7: 0-0 3m+: 0-0
Track:	LH: 0-1 RH: 0-1 Tight: 0-1 Gall: 0-0
Aids:	Bl: 0-0 Vi: 0-0 Tstrap: 0-0 Ckp: 0-0
Best Rating:	93 5/03 MRas 2m1f110y gd-fm NHF

Shamsan (IRE)

106(106c) (100c)116

7-y-o ch g Night Shift (USA)-Awayil (USA) (Woodman (USA))
P J Hobbs (J Joseph 26/5) Jack Joseph

Placings: 03/1212116600/221222312246-640222 (1733)
2003/04: 21⁶GD, 16⁴GD, 20⁰GF, 20²GF, 16²GD, 20⁰GF,

	Starts	1st	2nd	3rd	Win & Pl
Hurdles	6	0	3	0	3305
Career Total	30	6	12	2	38938

96	9/02	Plum	2m4f	D Ch	GD	£5538
113	6/02	Hrfd	2m1f	E(0-110)HHdl	G-F	£3402
118	7/01	NAbb	2m1f	D Hdl	GD	£3376
106	7/01	Strf	2m110y	D Hdl	GD	£3472
110	6/01	Hrfd	2m1f	E Hdl	FRM	£2712
113	5/01	Sthl	2m	D Hdl	FRM	£3662
					Total win prize-money £22164

Going:	Sf: 0-0 GS: 0-0 Gd: 0-0 GF: - Fm: 0-6
Distance:	2m/2m3: 0-2 2m4-2m7: 0-4 3m+: 0-0
Track:	LH: 0-4 RH: 0-2 Tight: 0-2 Gall: 0-2
Aids:	Bl: 0-1 Vi: 0-0 Tstrap: 0-1 Ckp: 0-0
Best Rating:	121 6/01 Strf 2m110y gd-fm Hdl

Modest hurdler/chaser; multiple novice hurdle winner in his time; has shown ability over fences, winning a modest event at Plumpton; needs ground good or faster; stays two and a half miles; sometimes wears blinkers; held up.

Shanavoher (IRE)

69 42

12-y-o ch g Phardante (FR)-Lane Baloo (Lucky Brief)
B G Powell (David Phelan 21/5) Anthony Ward-Thomas

Placings: 650/2160006/5006046034P5/255F543F02/6P (0613)
2003/04: 21⁶GF, 25²GF,

	Starts	1st	2nd	3rd	Win & Pl
Chases	2	0	0	0	0
Career Total	34	1	3	2	5856
95	6/98	Rosc	2m	NHF	G-Y	£2233
					Total win prize-money £2234

Going:	Sf: 0-0 GS: 0-0 Gd: 0-0 GF: - Fm: 0-2
Distance:	2m/2m3: 0-0 2m4-2m7: 0-1 3m+: 0-1
Track:	LH: 0-0 RH: 0-2 Tight: 0-1 Gall: 0-0
Aids:	Bl: 0-0 Vi: 0-0 Tstrap: 0-0 Ckp: 0-0
Best Rating:	100 5/00 Klny 2m4f good Ch

Shankly

9-y-o g King's Ride-Brandy Run (Deep Run)
C J Barker A C Barker

Placings: P5/P6PP/U (0101)
2003/04: 25ᵁG,

	Starts	1st	2nd	3rd	Win & Pl
Chases	1	0	0	0	
Career Total	7	0	0	0	0

Going:	Sf: 0-0 GS: 0-0 Gd: 0-1 GF: - Fm: 0-0
Distance:	2m/2m3: 0-0 2m4-2m7: 0-0 3m+: 0-1
Track:	LH: 0-1 RH: 0-0 Tight: 0-0 Gall: 0-0
Aids:	Bl: 0-0 Vi: 0-0 Tstrap: 0-0 Ckp: 0-0
Best Rating:	43 1/01 Muss 2m good Ch

Shannon Light (IRE)

74 100

12-y-o b/br g Electric-Shannon Lass (Callernish)
N R Mitchell Mrs E Mitchell

Placings: 00202/30/0/P/2506410F/2P-6P (3748)
2003/04: 22⁶HY, 22⁰GS,

	Starts	1st	2nd	3rd	Win & Pl
Hurdles	2	0	0	0	0
Career Total	21	1	4	1	6876
101	3/02	Chep	3m	D(0-120)HHdl	SFT	£3575
					Total win prize-money £3575

Going:	Sf: 0-1 GS: 0-1 Gd: 0-0 GF: - Fm: 0-0
Distance:	2m/2m3: 0-0 2m4-2m7: 0-0 3m+: 0-1
Track:	LH: 0-1 RH: 0-1 Tight: 0-2 Gall: 0-0
Aids:	Bl: 0-0 Vi: 0-0 Tstrap: 0-0 Ckp: 0-1
Best Rating:	104 5/97 Tipp 2m4f yld-sft NHF

Shannon Quest (IRE)

104(107c) (90c)90

8-y-o b/br g Zaffaran (USA)-Carrick Shannon (Green Shoon)
O Sherwood Ledwidge Best Fforde

Placings: 0/030436F/2P5423F5P-2203 (0878)
2003/04: 22²GF, 20²GF, 24⁰GF, 20³GF,

	Starts	1st	2nd	3rd	Win & Pl
Hurdles	4	0	2	1	3083
Career Total	21	0	4	4	7585

Going:	Sf: 0-0 GS: 0-0 Gd: 0-0 GF: - Fm: 0-4
Distance:	2m/2m3: 0-0 2m4-2m7: 0-3 3m+: 0-1
Track:	LH: 0-3 RH: 0-1 Tight: 0-0 Gall: 0-0
Aids:	Bl: 0-4 Vi: 0-0 Tstrap: 0-0 Ckp: 0-0
Best Rating:	96 5/02 Folk 2m good Ch

Plating-class hurdler/chaser; sometimes wears blinkers; effective at around two miles, probably gets two miles six; not a straightforward ride.

Shannon Water's (IRE)

(100h) (95+h)61

8-y-o b m Moscow Society (USA)-Percy's Pet (Blakeney)
M C Pipe (Trevor Begley 19/6) T Begley

Placings: 00/00060/U-6P1F (4367)
2003/04: 20⁶Y, 20⁶F, 26¹GF, 25⁶GS,

	Starts	1st	2nd	3rd	Win & Pl
Hurdles	2	1	0	0	2835
Chases	2	0	0	0	
Career Total	12	1	0	0	2835
102	3/04	Hrfd	3m2f	F(0-95)HHdl	G-F	£2835
					Total win prize-money £2835

Going:	Sf: 0-0 GS: 0-1 Gd: 0-0 GF: - Fm: 1-2
Distance:	2m/2m3: 0-0 2m4-2m7: 0-2 3m+: 1-2
Track:	LH: 0-0 RH: 1-2 Tight: 0-0 Gall: 0-0
Aids:	Bl: 0-0 Vi: 0-0 Tstrap: 1-2 Ckp: 0-0
Best Rating:	102 3/04 Hrfd 3m2f gd-fm Hdl

Shannon's Pride (IRE)

(103h) (120+h)

8-y-o gr g Roselier (FR)-Spanish Flame (IRE) (Spanish Place (USA))
N G Richards J Hales

Placings: 3/113-PP (2902)
2003/04: 20⁶PG, 21³PS,

	Starts	1st	2nd	3rd	Win & Pl
Chases	2	0	0	0	
Career Total	6	2	0	2	7675
120	12/02	Ayr	2m4f	E Hdl	G-S	£3052
112	11/02	Ayr	2m6f	E Hdl	SFT	£3094
					Total win prize-money £6146

Going:	Sf: 0-1 GS: 0-0 Gd: 0-1 GF: - Fm: 0-0
Distance:	2m/2m3: 0-0 2m4-2m7: 0-2 3m+: 0-0
Track:	LH: 0-2 RH: 0-0 Tight: 0-0 Gall: 0-0
Aids:	Bl: 0-0 Vi: 0-0 Tstrap: 0-0 Ckp: 0-0
Best Rating:	120 12/02 Ayr 2m4f gd-sft Hdl

Fair hurdler; stays 2m 6f and should stay further; suited by cut in the ground; pulled up on both starts.

Sharabad (FR)

90 74+

6-y-o b g Ela-Mana-Mou-Sharbada (FR) (Kahyasi)
Mrs L B Normile A K Collins and D J Hindmarsh

Placings: 000300 (4685)
2003/04: 16⁶S, 16⁰HY, 16⁰G, 20³F, 18⁰GS, 16⁰G,

	Starts	1st	2nd	3rd	Win & Pl
NH Flat	3	0	0	0	0
Hurdles	3	0	0	1	854
Career Total	6	0	0	1	854

| **Going:** | Sf: 0-2 GS: 0-1 Gd: 0-2 GF: - Fm: 0-1 |

Distance:	2m/2m3: 0-5 2m4-2m7: 0-1 3m+: 0-0
Track:	LH: 0-4 RH: 0-2 Tight: 0-4 Gall: 0-0
Aids:	Bl: 0-0 Vi: 0-0 Tstrap: 0-0 Ckp: 0-0
Best Rating:	74 2/04 Muss 2m4f firm Hdl

Shardam (IRE)

119(99h)   (115h)151+

7-y-o b g Shardari-Knockea Hill (Buckskin (FR))
N A Twiston-Davies   Howard Parker

Placings:2526262/31U21512-U11P042U0   (4965)
2003/04: 25UG, 251G, 27IG, 26PGS, 24OG, 244G, 242G, 36UG, 29PGF,

	Starts	1st	2nd	3rd	Win & Pl
Chases	9	2	1	0	70684
Career Total	24	5	7	1	100529
149	11/03	Chel	3m3f110yA	HCh		GD	£29000
136	5/03	Kels	3m1f	B Ch		GD	£19083
125	2/03	Chep	3m	D Ch		G-S	£5713
129	12/02	Font	2m6f	D Ch		SFT	£6864
108	11/02	Chep	3m	F Hdl		SFT	£2646

Total win prize-money £63308

Going:	Sf: 0-0 GS: 0-1 Gd: 2-7 GF: - Fm: 0-1
Distance:	2m/2m3: 0-0 2m4-2m7: 0-0 3m+: 2-9
Track:	LH: 2-6 RH: 0-3 Tight: 1-2 Gall: 1-4
Aids:	Bl: 0-0 Vi: 0-0 Tstrap: 0-0 Ckp: 0-0
Best Rating:	151 3/04 Chel 3m110y good Ch

Smart chaser; made all to win very valuable chase at Cheltenham in November 2003; injured next time in the Hennessy, but ran much better to finish fourth in the 2004 Racing Post Chase and second at the Festival; acts on good and soft ground; stays three and a half miles; races prominently; a tough sort.

Shardante (IRE)

109   130+

11-y-o ch g Phardante (FR)-Shirabas (Karabas)
Mrs S J Smith   W A Bethell

Placings:0P/304524402P/152541/5/31531U0   (4174)
2003/04: 213GF, 251G, 255G, 263G, 251GS, 25UG, 24OG,

	Starts	1st	2nd	3rd	Win & Pl
Chases	7	2	0	2	12339
Career Total	26	4	3	3	24481
130	1/04	Weth	3m1f	D(0-120)HCh	G-S	£6968
122	10/03	Aint	3m1f	E(0-105)HCh	GD	£3601
117	2/01	Hntg	3m	D(0-120)HCh	G-S	£4426
110	9/00	Bang	2m4f110yD Ch		G-F	£4173

Total win prize-money £19169

Going:	Sf: 0-1 GS: 1-1 Gd: 1-4 GF: - Fm: 0-1
Distance:	2m/2m3: 0-0 2m4-2m7: 0-0 3m+: 2-6
Track:	LH: 2-7 RH: 0-0 Tight: 1-1 Gall: 0-2
Aids:	Bl: 0-0 Vi: 0-0 Tstrap: 0-0 Ckp: 0-0
Best Rating:	130 1/04 Weth 3m1f soft Ch

Fair chaser; in good form for new yard and wide margin winner at Wetherby in January 2004; stays beyond three miles and acts on most types of ground; has given problems before the start.

Shared Account (IRE)

109   112

10-y-o b g Supreme Leader-Ribble Rabble (Deep Run)
P A Blockley (F Flood 20/9) Carl Would

Placings:6200500/100103555/0146040/241542503005-100055025   (4275)

2003/04: 191YS, 190F, 20OY, 20OS, 24SG, 25SG, 270GS, 242G, 20SG,

	Starts	1st	2nd	3rd	Win & Pl
Hurdles	9	1	1	0	12099
Career Total	44	5	4	2	35108
112	5/03	Kbgn	2m3f	(81-123)HHdl	Y-S	£10551
97	6/02	Tral	2m4f	(67-109)HHdl	Y-S	£4233
102	10/01	Fair	2m4f	(0-109)HHdl	YLD	£5564
96	8/00	Tral	2m4f	(0-102)HHdl	SFT	£3864
96	6/00	Dund	2m135y	NHF		G-Y	£3312

Total win prize-money £27526

Going:	Sf: 0-1 GS: 0-1 Gd: 0-4 GF: - Fm: 0-0
Distance:	2m/2m3: 1-2 2m4-2m7: 0-3 3m+: 0-4
Track:	LH: 0-3 RH: 0-4 Tight: 0-3 Gall: 0-0
Aids:	Bl: 0-0 Vi: 0-0 Tstrap: 0-0 Ckp: 0-0
Best Rating:	116 11/02 Punc 2m4f soft Hdl

Fair hurdler; ex-Irish; stays three miles; best with cut.

Shared Expectation (IRE)

69   47

8-y-o ch g Husyan (USA)-Calmount (IRE) (Callernish)
J M Jefferson   R E Williams

Placings:0/0   (3358)
2003/04: 16PS,

	Starts	1st	2nd	3rd	Win & Pl
Hurdles	1	0	0	0	
Career Total	2	0	0	0	

Going:	Sf: 0-1 GS: 0-0 Gd: 0-0 GF: - Fm: 0-0
Distance:	2m/2m3: 0-1 2m4-2m7: 0-0 3m+: 0-0
Track:	LH: 0-1 RH: 0-0 Tight: 0-0 Gall: 0-0
Aids:	Bl: 0-0 Vi: 0-0 Tstrap: 0-0 Ckp: 0-0
Best Rating:	62 11/01 Carl 2m1f soft NHF

Shared-Interest

10-y-o ch m Interrex (CAN)-La Campagnola (Hubble Bubble)
K Bishop   David J Adams

Placings:0/P0/P-P   (0038)
2003/04: 19PG,

	Starts	1st	2nd	3rd	Win & Pl
Chases	1	0	0	0	
Career Total	5	0	0	0	

Going:	Sf: 0-0 GS: 0-0 Gd: 0-1 GF: - Fm: 0-0
Distance:	2m/2m3: 0-0 2m4-2m7: 0-1 3m+: 0-0
Track:	LH: 0-0 RH: 0-1 Tight: 0-0 Gall: 0-0
Aids:	Bl: 0-0 Vi: 0-0 Tstrap: 0-1 Ckp: 0-0
Best Rating:	32 2/99 Winc 2m gd-sft NHF

Shareef (FR)

87(94h)   (123h)132

7-y-o b g Port Lyautey (FR)-Saralik (Salse (USA))
A King   Tony Fisher & Mrs Jeni Fisher

Placings:1/5U12P44/P3U22-5   (2910)
2003/04: 20SG,

	Starts	1st	2nd	3rd	Win & Pl
Chases	1	0	0	0	0
Career Total	14	2	3	1	9636
114	10/01	Winc	2m6f	E Hdl	GD	£2275
91	4/01	Newb	2m110y	H NHF	SFT	£1750

Total win prize-money £4025

Going:	Sf: 0-0 GS: 0-1 Gd: 0-0 GF: - Fm: 0-0
Distance:	2m/2m3: 0-0 2m4-2m7: 0-1 3m+: 0-0
Track:	LH: 0-0 RH: 0-1 Tight: 0-0 Gall: 0-1
Aids:	Bl: 0-0 Vi: 0-0 Tstrap: 0-0 Ckp: 0-0
Best Rating:	130 11/02 Extr 2m3f110y good Ch

Modest hurdler/useful chaser; best on a soundish surface.

Shares (IRE)

98   92

4-y-o b g Turtle Island (IRE)-Glendora (Glenstal (USA))
P Monteith (G A Butler 16/7) The Dregs Of Humanity

Placings:551   (4187)
2003/04: 16SS, 18SHY, 16IGS,

	Starts	1st	2nd	3rd	Win & Pl
Hurdles	3	1	0	0	3710
Career Total	3	1	0	0	3710
92	3/04	Kels	2m110y	E Hdl		G-S	£3710

Total win prize-money £3710

Going:	Sf: 0-2 GS: 1-1 Gd: 0-0 GF: - Fm: 0-0
Distance:	2m/2m3: 1-3 2m4-2m7: 0-0 3m+: 0-0
Track:	LH: 1-3 RH: 0-0 Tight: 1-3 Gall: 0-0
Aids:	Bl: 0-0 Vi: 0-0 Tstrap: 0-0 Ckp: 0-0
Best Rating:	92 3/04 Kels 2m110y gd-sft Hdl

Plating-class hurdler; creditable efforts over hurdles and got off the mark in ordinary novice event at Kelso in March; travelled strongly for long way and may improve again in handicaps; should stay two and a half miles.

Sharmy (IRE)

106(105h)   (110h)124+

8-y-o b g Caerleon (USA)-Petticoat Lane (Ela-Mana-Mou)
Ian Williams   T J & Mrs H Parrott

Placings:525224/31F5-31313   (4896)
2003/04: 16SGS, 16IG, 16OG, 16IG, 16OG,

	Starts	1st	2nd	3rd	Win & Pl
Hurdles	1	0	0	1	1134
Chases	4	2	0	2	14850
Career Total	15	3	3	4	24516
122	3/04	Hntg	2m110y	D(0-120)HCh	GD	£8272
104	12/03	Ludl	2m	E Ch	GD	£4046
100	11/02	Hntg	2m110y	E Hdl	G-S	£2996

Total win prize-money £15314

Going:	Sf: 0-0 GS: 0-1 Gd: 2-4 GF: - Fm: 0-0
Distance:	2m/2m3: 2-5 2m4-2m7: 0-0 3m+: 0-0
Track:	LH: 0-0 RH: 2-5 Tight: 1-1 Gall: 1-2
Aids:	Bl: 0-0 Vi: 0-0 Tstrap: 0-0 Ckp: 0-0
Best Rating:	124 4/04 Winc 2m good Ch

Fair chaser/hurdler; very useful on the Flat on Polytrack; made a winning chasing debut at Ludlow in December 2003; beaten next time, but won again at Huntingdon in early March; effective over two miles; acts well with cut in the ground.

Sharp As Croesus

4-y-o b f Sesaro (USA)-Chushan Venture (Pursuit Of Love)
J R Best   Mrs L M Askew

Placings:P   (1451)
2003/04: 16PGF,

	Starts	1st	2nd	3rd	Win & Pl
Hurdles	1	0	0	0	
Career Total	1	0	0	0	

Going:	Sf: 0-0 GS: 0-0 Gd: 0-0 GF: - Fm: 0-1
Distance:	2m/2m3: 0-1 2m4-2m7: 0-0 3m+: 0-0
Track:	LH: 0-1 RH: 0-0 Tight: 0-1 Gall: 0-0
Aids:	Bl: 0-0 Vi: 0-0 Tstrap: 0-0 Ckp: 0-0

Sharp Belline (IRE)

91(109h)   (114h)97

7-y-o b g Robellino (USA)-Moon Watch (Night Shift (USA))
Mrs S J Smith (John A Harris 12/2) Townville C C Racing Club

Placings:01402/063304624/1240-465P60   (4617)
2003/04: 22⁴G, 19⁶GF, 24⁵GS, 24⁶S, 20⁶G, 27⁹G,

	Starts	1st	2nd	3rd	Win & Pl
Hurdles	3	0	0	0	724
Chases	3	0	0	0	0
Career Total	24	2	3	2	13626
114 5/02 Sthl	3m110y D(0-120)HHdl		G-S	£3523
117 2/01 Donc	2m4f			£2508
		Total win prize-money £6032

Going:	Sf: 0-1 GS: 0-1 Gd: 0-3 GF: - Fm: 0-0
Distance:	2m/2m3: 0-0 2m4-2m7: 0-3 3m+: 0-0
Track:	LH: 0-3 RH: 0-2 Tight: 0-2 Gall: 0-1
Aids:	Bl: 0-0 Vi: 0-0 Tstrap: 0-0 Ckp: 0-0
Best Rating:	117 2/01 Donc 2m4f good Hdl

Modest hurdler; stays 3m; acts on most ground; tough sort.

Sharp Exit (IRE)

79f   68f

5-y-o ch g Fourstars Allstar (USA)-Dipper's Gift (IRE) (Salluceva)
C Grant John Wade

Placings:0   (1450)
2003/04: 17⁰GF,

	Starts	1st	2nd	3rd	Win & Pl
NH Flat	1	0	0	0	
Career Total	1	0	0	0	

Going:	Sf: 0-0 GS: 0-0 Gd: 0-0 GF: - Fm: 0-0
Distance:	2m/2m3: 0-1 2m4-2m7: 0-0 3m+: 0-0
Track:	LH: 0-0 RH: 0-1 Tight: 0-1 Gall: 0-0
Aids:	Bl: 0-0 Vi: 0-0 Tstrap: 0-0 Ckp: 0-0
Best Rating:	68 9/03 MRas 2m1f110y gd-fm NHF

Sharp Hand

98   75

8-y-o ch g Handsome Sailor-Sharp Glance (IRE) (Deep Run)
J G M O'Shea N M Lowe

Placings:00P6535-0   (0057)
2003/04: 17⁰GS,

	Starts	1st	2nd	3rd	Win & Pl
Hurdles	1	0	0	0	
Career Total	8	0	0	1	500

Going:	Sf: 0-0 GS: 0-1 Gd: 0-0 GF: - Fm: 0-0
Distance:	2m/2m3: 0-1 2m4-2m7: 0-0 3m+: 0-0
Track:	LH: 0-0 RH: 0-1 Tight: 0-1 Gall: 0-0
Aids:	Bl: 0-0 Vi: 0-0 Tstrap: 0-0 Ckp: 0-0
Best Rating:	83 12/02 Bang 2m1f gd-sft NHF

Selling hurdler; seems best on ground good or faster.

Sharp Jack (IRE)

103   79

6-y-o b g Be My Native (USA)-Polly Sharp (Pollerton)
R T Phillips Mrs Claire Smith

Placings:05   (4319)
2003/04: 16⁵GS, 20⁵S,

	Starts	1st	2nd	3rd	Win & Pl
NH Flat	1	0	0	0	0
Hurdles	1	0	0	0	0
Career Total	2	0	0	0	0

Going:	Sf: 0-1 GS: 0-1 Gd: 0-0 GF: - Fm: 0-0
Distance:	2m/2m3: 0-1 2m4-2m7: 0-0 3m+: 0-0
Track:	LH: 0-1 RH: 0-1 Tight: 0-0 Gall: 0-2
Aids:	Bl: 0-0 Vi: 0-0 Tstrap: 0-0 Ckp: 0-0
Best Rating:	79 3/04 Newc 2m4f soft Hdl

Sharp Rigging (IRE)

105   115+

4-y-o b g Son Of Sharp Shot (IRE)-In The Rigging (USA) (Topsider (USA))
A M Hales (E A L Dunlop 29/9) Mrs S E Lindley

Placings:311   (4788)
2003/04: 16³GS, 17¹G, 16¹G,

	Starts	1st	2nd	3rd	Win & Pl
Hurdles	3	2	0	1	8711
Career Total	3	2	0	1	8711
115 4/04 Plum	2m	E Hdl	GD	£3668
111 3/04 Hrfd	2m1f	E Hdl	GD	£3471
		Total win prize-money £7139

Going:	Sf: 0-0 GS: 0-1 Gd: 2-2 GF: - Fm: 0-0
Distance:	2m/2m3: 2-3 2m4-2m7: 0-0 3m+: 0-0
Track:	LH: 1-1 RH: 1-2 Tight: 1-1 Gall: 0-1
Aids:	Bl: 0-0 Vi: 0-0 Tstrap: 0-0 Ckp: 0-0
Best Rating:	115 4/04 Plum 2m good Hdl

Fair juvenile hurdler; showed plenty of promise when third behind two useful sorts on his hurdling debut before winning two ordinary events comfortably; acts on good to soft ground.

Sharp Seal

99   91

10-y-o b g Broadsword (USA)-Little Beaver (Privy Seal)
M Madgwick M Madgwick

Placings:P/3U42FP5-33   (0435)
2003/04: 21³GF, 18³GF,

	Starts	1st	2nd	3rd	Win & Pl
Chases	2	0	0	2	974
Career Total	10	0	1	3	3567

Going:	Sf: 0-0 GS: 0-0 Gd: 0-0 GF: - Fm: 0-2
Distance:	2m/2m3: 0-1 2m4-2m7: 0-1 3m+: 0-0
Track:	LH: 0-0 RH: 0-1 Tight: 0-1 Gall: 0-0
Aids:	Bl: 0-0 Vi: 0-0 Tstrap: 0-0 Ckp: 0-0
Best Rating:	91 12/02 Font 2m4f soft Ch

Moderate novice chaser; stays three miles; acts on soft ground.

Sharp Single (IRE)

102(99h)   (84+h)95

8-y-o b m Supreme Leader-Pollyville (Pollerton)
P Beaumont W L Smith

Placings:PPPP-4354P53P   (4659)
2003/04: 20⁴S, 20³G, 20⁵G, 22⁴S, 20⁹G, 17⁵G, 16³G, 16⁹S,

	Starts	1st	2nd	3rd	Win & Pl
Hurdles	3	0	0	1	731
Chases	5	0	0	1	959
Career Total	12	0	0	2	1690

Going:	Sf: 0-3 GS: 0-0 Gd: 0-5 GF: - Fm: 0-0
Distance:	2m/2m3: 0-2 2m4-2m7: 0-5 3m+: 0-0
Track:	LH: 0-7 RH: 0-1 Tight: 0-4 Gall: 0-0
Aids:	Bl: 0-0 Vi: 0-0 Tstrap: 0-0 Ckp: 0-0
Best Rating:	95 3/04 Hexm 2m110y good Ch

Moderate chaser; much improved effort when good third in novices' handicap hurdle at Wetherby in December; stays two miles six.

Sharp Spice

94   69

8-y-o b m Lugana Beach-Ewar Empress (IRE) (Persian Bold)
D L Williams (D J Coakley 12/10) Symbol Of Success Racing

Placings:P5B4PP   (3671a)
2003/04: 16²G, 16⁵GF, 16⁹G, 16⁴GS, 17⁵HY, 17⁵PHO,

	Starts	1st	2nd	3rd	Win & Pl
Hurdles	6	0	0	0	0
Career Total	6	0	0	0	0

Going:	Sf: 0-1 GS: 0-1 Gd: 0-2 GF: - Fm: 0-1
Distance:	2m/2m3: 0-4 2m4-2m7: 0-1 3m+: 0-0
Track:	LH: 0-2 RH: 0-2 Tight: 0-2 Gall: 0-0
Aids:	Bl: 0-0 Vi: 0-0 Tstrap: 0-0 Ckp: 0-0
Best Rating:	71 12/03 Strf 2m110y gd-sft Hdl

Modest form in selling hurdles; looked a difficult ride when fourth at Stratford December 2003.

Sharp Steel

107(94h)   (84h)99

9-y-o ch g Beveled (USA)-Shift Over (USA) (Night Shift (USA))
Miss S J Wilton John Pointon And Sons

Placings:400/5P653-F31243PU2F   (2121)
2003/04: 16⁶GF, 16³GS, 16¹G, 17²G, 16⁴GF, 16³GF, 19⁹GF, 17⁴GF, 16²GF, 16⁶F,

	Starts	1st	2nd	3rd	Win & Pl
Chases	10	1	2	3	6961
Career Total	18	1	2	3	7788
95 7/03 Worc	2m	F(0-95)HCh	GD	£3425
		Total win prize-money £3426

Going:	Sf: 0-0 GS: 0-0 Gd: 1-3 GF: - Fm: 0-7
Distance:	2m/2m3: 1-10 2m4-2m7: 0-0 3m+: 0-0
Track:	LH: 1-6 RH: 0-4 Tight: 0-3 Gall: 0-2
Aids:	Bl: 0-0 Vi: 0-0 Tstrap: 0-0 Ckp: 0-0
Best Rating:	99 11/03 Ludl 2m firm Ch

Moderate novice chaser; best when held up; acted on good ground; probably best at 2m (DEAD).

Sharp's The Word

74f   57f

5-y-o b g Keen-Scally's Girl (Scallywag)
C Grant W Raw

Placings:00   (3482)
2003/04: 16⁰GS, 16⁰G,

	Starts	1st	2nd	3rd	Win & Pl
NH Flat	2	0	0	0	
Career Total	2	0	0	0	

Going:	Sf: 0-0 GS: 0-1 Gd: 0-1 GF: - Fm: 0-0
Distance:	2m/2m3: 0-2 2m4-2m7: 0-0 3m+: 0-0
Track:	LH: 0-2 RH: 0-0 Tight: 0-2 Gall: 0-0
Aids:	Bl: 0-0 Vi: 0-0 Tstrap: 0-0 Ckp: 0-0
Best Rating:	57 1/04 Catt 2m good NHF

Sharpastrizam (NZ)
104   (57h)112
9-y-o b g Try To Stop Me-Atristazam (NZ) (Zamazaan (FR))
P Beaumont Trevor Hemmings

Placings:2F060P/11P1211551/44044-64450133514 (4686)
2003/04: 16⁶GF, 16⁴GS, 16⁴G, 17⁵G, 20⁰G, 16¹GS, 16³S, 16³G, 17⁵G, 16¹GF, 17⁴G,

	Starts	1st	2nd	3rd	Win & Pl
Chases	11	2	0	2	10886
Career Total	32	8	2	2	38485
103 3/04	Leic	2m	F(0-95)Ch	G-F	£4017
103 12/03	Catt	2m	E(0-105)HCh	G-S	£3357
112 4/02	Prth	2m	C(0-130)HCh	GD	£7111
112 1/02	Donc	2m110y	E(0-105)HCh	GD	£3201
96 12/01	Catt	2m	F(0-105)HCh	GD	£3024
96 11/01	Weth	2m	D(0-110)HCh	GD	£4153
92 5/01	Bang	2m1f110yF(0-95)HCh	GD	£3486
91 5/01	Sthl	2m	F(0-100)HCh	FRM	£2775
			Total win prize-money £31126

Going:	Sf: 0-1 GS: 1-2 Gd: 0-6 GF: - Fm: 1-2
Distance:	2m/2m3: 2-10 2m4-2m7: 0-1 3m+: 0-0
Track:	LH: 1-8 RH: 1-3 Tight: 1-7 Gall: 0-0
Aids:	Bl: 0-0 Vi: 0-0 Tstrap: 0-0 Ckp: 0-0
Best Rating:	112 12/02 Donc 2m110y gd-sft Ch

Moderate chaser; suited by around two miles; handles cut, but best on a sound surface. (DEAD)

Sharpaten (IRE)
(110h)   (110h)
9-y-o b g Scenic-Sloane Ranger (Sharpen Up)
Ian Williams The Baron Rouge Partnership

Placings:233164/62632110/560400/162542F/030053240-0000041F (4330)
2003/04: 16⁰GS, 20⁰GS, 20⁰GS, 16⁹G, 16⁰HY, 16⁴GS, 16¹S, 16⁶GS,

	Starts	1st	2nd	3rd	Win & Pl
Hurdles	7	1	0	0	3582
Chases	1	0	0	0	
Career Total	44	5	6	5	55536
110 2/04	Leic	2m	F Hdl	SFT	£3581
115 5/01	Wxfd	2m		Y-S	£6677
140 4/00	Aint	2m110y	B HHdl	GD	£19500
128 3/00	Leop	2m	(0-144)HHdl	Y-S	£4968
111 3/99	Limk	2m1f		SH	£2700
			Total win prize-money £37428

Going:	Sf: 1-2 GS: 0-4 Gd: 0-1 GF: - Fm: 0-1
Distance:	2m/2m3: 1-6 2m4-2m7: 0-2 3m+: 0-0
Track:	LH: 0-3 RH: 1-5 Tight: 0-1 Gall: 0-1
Aids:	Bl: 0-0 Vi: 0-0 Tstrap: 0-0 Ckp: 0-0
Best Rating:	142 10/00 Gowr 2m soft Hdl

Fair handicap hurdler; ex-Irish; suited by two miles; acts on good and soft ground.

Sharvie
80   65
7-y-o b g Rock Hopper-Heresheis (Free State)

M R Bosley (C J Hemsley 20/12) Mrs Jill Hemsley

Placings:6000P4-P5205P (2854)
2003/04: 19⁵G, 19⁵GF, 26²G, 26⁹GF, 24⁵GF, 26⁶GS,

	Starts	1st	2nd	3rd	Win & Pl
Hurdles	6	0	1	0	968
Career Total	12	0	1	0	968

Going:	Sf: 0-0 GS: 0-1 Gd: 0-2 GF: - Fm: 0-3
Distance:	2m/2m3: 0-0 2m4-2m7: 0-2 3m+: 0-4
Track:	LH: 0-3 RH: 0-3 Tight: 0-0 Gall: 0-0
Aids:	Bl: 0-3 Vi: 0-0 Tstrap: 0-0 Ckp: 0-2
Best Rating:	65 7/03 Sthl 3m2f good Hdl

Poor novice hurdler; stays really well.

Shayadi (IRE)
112   115+
7-y-o b g Kahyasi-Shayrdia (IRE) (Storm Bird (CAN))
B Ellison (M Johnston 26/8) Ashley Carr

Placings:1100 (4644)
2003/04: 16¹G, 16¹GS, 16⁹S, 16⁹G,

	Starts	1st	2nd	3rd	Win & Pl
Hurdles	4	2	0	0	5299
Career Total	4	2	0	0	5299
115 12/03	Newc	2m	E Hdl	G-S	£3038
98 12/03	Leic	2m	G Hdl	GD	£2261
			Total win prize-money £5299

Going:	Sf: 0-1 GS: 1-1 Gd: 1-2 GF: - Fm: 0-0
Distance:	2m/2m3: 2-4 2m4-2m7: 0-0 3m+: 0-0
Track:	LH: 1-3 RH: 1-1 Tight: 0-2 Gall: 1-1
Aids:	Bl: 0-1 Vi: 0-0 Tstrap: 2-4 Ckp: 0-0
Best Rating:	115 12/03 Newc 2m gd-sft Hdl

Fair novice hurdler; winner of two modest events over hurdles before having limitations exposed in decent contest at Kelso; effective over two miles and acts on good ground; wears a tongue tie, has worn blinkers.

Shaydeylaydeh (IRE)
85   76
5-y-o b m Shaddad (USA)-Spirito Libro (USA) (Lear Fan (USA))
Miss J Feilden (C N Allen 21/6) Steven Rees

Placings:0-U563P50P (3904)
2003/04: 20⁰G, 16⁵GS, 17⁶GS, 21³GS, 19⁹HY, 23⁵GS, 19⁹HY, 24⁸GS,

	Starts	1st	2nd	3rd	Win & Pl
Hurdles	8	0	0	1	321
Career Total	9	0	0	1	321

Going:	Sf: 0-2 GS: 0-5 Gd: 0-1 GF: - Fm: 0-0
Distance:	2m/2m3: 0-2 2m4-2m7: 0-4 3m+: 0-2
Track:	LH: 0-1 RH: 0-5 Tight: 0-3 Gall: 0-1
Aids:	Bl: 0-0 Vi: 0-0 Tstrap: 0-0 Ckp: 0-0
Best Rating:	76 12/03 Hntg 2m5f110y gd-sft Hdl

Shays Lane (IRE)
101   (78h)92
10-y-o b g The Bart (USA)-Continuity Lass (Continuation)
Ferdy Murphy Mrs C McKeane

Placings:0000/54-311PP4P (4882)
2003/04: 25³G, 25¹G, 25¹GF, 25⁸S, 25⁶GS, 25⁴GF, 26⁶GS,

	Starts	1st	2nd	3rd	Win & Pl
Chases	7	2	0	1	8269

Career Total	13	2	0	1	8684
92 6/03	Hexm	3m1f	E(0-105)HCh	G-F	£3890
85 5/03	Hexm	3m1f	F(0-95)HCh	GD	£3475
			Total win prize-money £7366

Going:	Sf: 0-1 GS: 0-2 Gd: 1-2 GF: - Fm: 1-2
Distance:	2m/2m3: 0-0 2m4-2m7: 0-0 3m+: 2-7
Track:	LH: 2-6 RH: 0-1 Tight: 0-2 Gall: 0-0
Aids:	Bl: 0-0 Vi: 0-0 Tstrap: 0-0 Ckp: 0-0
Best Rating:	92 6/03 Hexm 3m1f gd-fm Ch

Moderate chaser; won twice at Hexham in the summer of 2003; stays very well; acts on fast ground.

Shazal
101   74
7-y-o b m Afzal-Isolationist (Welsh Pageant)
J N R Billinge Lordscairnie Racing

Placings:0/00F60-210P (2901)
2003/04: 16⁶G, 16²GS, 16¹G, 18⁰G, 16⁸S,

	Starts	1st	2nd	3rd	Win & Pl
Hurdles	5	1	1	0	5201
Career Total	10	1	1	0	5201
77 6/03	Prth	2m110y	F(0-90)HHdl	GD	£4143
			Total win prize-money £4144

Going:	Sf: 0-1 GS: 0-0 Gd: 1-4 GF: - Fm: 0-0
Distance:	2m/2m3: 1-5 2m4-2m7: 0-0 3m+: 0-0
Track:	LH: 0-3 RH: 1-2 Tight: 0-1 Gall: 0-0
Aids:	Bl: 0-0 Vi: 0-0 Tstrap: 0-0 Ckp: 0-0
Best Rating:	77 6/03 Prth 2m110y good Hdl

Plating-class hurdler; shock winner of a low-grade handicap at Perth in June 2003; acts on good ground.

She's Flash (IRE)
5-y-o b m Woodborough (USA)-Beechwood Quest (IRE) (River Falls)
J A Supple Geoff Hubbard Racing

Placings:0P (0291)
2003/04: 16⁸G, 16⁷G,

	Starts	1st	2nd	3rd	Win & Pl
Hurdles	2	0	0	0	
Career Total	2	0	0	0	

Going:	Sf: 0-0 GS: 0-0 Gd: 0-1 GF: - Fm: 0-1
Distance:	2m/2m3: 0-2 2m4-2m7: 0-0 3m+: 0-0
Track:	LH: 0-1 RH: 0-1 Tight: 0-1 Gall: 0-1
Aids:	Bl: 0-1 Vi: 0-0 Tstrap: 0-0 Ckp: 0-1

She's Our Native (IRE)
103   93+
6-y-o b m Be My Native (USA)-More Dash (IRE) (Strong Gale)
P J Hobbs Ian Brice

Placings:21-620U200 (4733)
2003/04: 16⁶GF, 16²GF, 16⁶G, 19⁰GS, 19³HY, 19⁰G, 22⁰G,

	Starts	1st	2nd	3rd	Win & Pl
Hurdles	7	1	2	0	2083
Career Total	9	1	3	0	4845
101 3/03	Ludl	2m	H NHF	GD	£1960
			Total win prize-money £1960

Going:	Sf: 0-1 GS: 0-1 Gd: 0-3 GF: - Fm: 0-2

Distance:	2m/2m3: 0-5 2m4-2m7: 0-2 3m+: 0-0
Track:	LH: 0-5 RH: 0-2 Tight: 0-1 Gall: 0-1
Aids:	Bl: 0-0 Vi: 0-0 Tstrap: 0-0 Ckp: 0-0
Best Rating:	101 3/03 Ludl 2m good NHF

Bumper winner; moderate hurdler; stays 2m 4f; acts on most types of ground.

She'ssomelady (IRE)

5-y-o b m Muroto-Designer (Celtic Cone)
R J Baker R J Baker

Placings:000					(2224)
2003/04: 17⁰GF, 17⁰G, 21⁰GS,					

	Starts	1st	2nd	3rd	Win & Pl
NH Flat	1	0	0	0	0
Hurdles	2	0	0	0	0
Career Total	3	0	0	0	

Going:	Sf: 0-0 GS: 0-1 Gd: 0-1 GF: - Fm: 0-1
Distance:	2m/2m3: 0-2 2m4-2m7: 0-1 3m+: 0-0
Track:	LH: 0-1 RH: 0-2 Tight: 0-1 Gall: 0-0
Aids:	Bl: 0-0 Vi: 0-0 Tstrap: 0-0 Ckp: 0-0
Best Rating:	56 8/03 NAbb 2m1f gd-fm NHF

Sheer Genius (IRE)
66   114

8-y-o b g Insan (USA)-Mulberry (IRE) (Denel (FR))
M Pitman Malcolm C Denmark

Placings:430/111332/30/2P					(3362)
2003/04: 16²GF, 24PG,					

	Starts	1st	2nd	3rd	Win & Pl
Chases	2	0	1	0	1215
Career Total	13	3	2	4	21094
129	11/00	Chel	2m5f	B Hdl		G-S	£7377
101	10/00	Towc	2m	D Hdl		GD	£2977
110	10/00	Font	2m2f110yE Hdl		GD	£1858
						Total win prize-money £12214

Going:	Sf: 0-0 GS: 0-0 Gd: 0-0 GF: - Fm: 0-1
Distance:	2m/2m3: 0-2 2m4-2m7: 0-0 3m+: 0-1
Track:	LH: 0-0 RH: 0-2 Tight: 0-0 Gall: 0-0
Aids:	Bl: 0-0 Vi: 0-0 Tstrap: 0-0 Ckp: 0-0
Best Rating:	131 4/01 Ayr 3m110y good Hdl

Modest chaser; stays 2m5f; acts on a sound surface.

Sheer Guts (IRE)
93   86

5-y-o b g Hamas (IRE)-Balakera (FR) (Lashkari)
John A Harris Cleartherm Ltd

Placings:1O10P000					(4603)
2003/04: 16¹G, 16⁰GF, 16¹S, 16⁰GS, 17⁰GS, 16⁰GS, 16⁰G, 17⁰G,					

	Starts	1st	2nd	3rd	Win & Pl
Hurdles	8	2	0	0	3808
Career Total	8	2	0	0	3808
86	12/03	Towc	2m	G(0-95)HHdl	SFT	£1904
76	11/03	Towc	2m	G Hdl	GD	£1904
					Total win prize-money £3808

Going:	Sf: 1-1 GS: 0-3 Gd: 1-3 GF: - Fm: 0-1
Distance:	2m/2m3: 2-8 2m4-2m7: 0-0 3m+: 0-0
Track:	LH: 0-3 RH: 2-5 Tight: 0-1 Gall: 0-1
Aids:	Bl: 1-4 Vi: 0-0 Tstrap: 0-1 Ckp: 0-1
Best Rating:	86 12/03 Towc 2m soft Hdl

Plating-class novice hurdler; acts on soft ground; often blinkered.

Sheila McKenzie

7-y-o b m Aragon-Lady Quachita (USA) (Sovereign Dancer (USA))
C O King C O King

Placings:P/P-U					(4655)
2003/04: 16ᵁG,					

	Starts	1st	2nd	3rd	Win & Pl
Chases	1	0	0	0	
Career Total	3	0	0	0	

Going:	Sf: 0-0 GS: 0-0 Gd: 0-1 GF: - Fm: 0-0
Distance:	2m/2m3: 0-4 2m4-2m7: 0-0 3m+: 0-0
Track:	LH: 0-0 RH: 0-1 Tight: 0-0 Gall: 0-0
Aids:	Bl: 0-0 Vi: 0-0 Tstrap: 0-0 Ckp: 0-0

Shellin Hill (IRE)
92   (87h)92

10-y-o ch g Sharp Victor (USA)-Queenspay (Sandhurst Prince)
R J Price My Left Foot Racing Syndicate

Placings:000/0532O0402P6/0423424F0P622/621FP3P043 F4P-P053645					(4919)
2003/04: 16PG, 20⁵S, 16⁵G, 16³GS, 16⁶GS, 19⁴G, 20⁵GS,					

	Starts	1st	2nd	3rd	Win & Pl
Chases	7	0	0	1	506
Career Total	47	1	7	5	14046
96	9/02	Sthl	2m1f	F(0-95)HCh	GD	£3049
					Total win prize-money £3050

Going:	Sf: 0-1 GS: 0-3 Gd: 0-3 GF: - Fm: 0-0
Distance:	2m/2m3: 0-4 2m4-2m7: 0-3 3m+: 0-0
Track:	LH: 0-4 RH: 0-3 Tight: 0-1 Gall: 0-1
Aids:	Bl: 0-0 Vi: 0-0 Tstrap: 0-0 Ckp: 0-2
Best Rating:	97 6/01 Worc 2m good Ch

Modest chaser, suited by two miles and fast ground.

Shelu
100(56h)   (94h)83+

6-y-o b g Good Thyne (USA)-Nearly Married (Nearly A Hand)
Ferdy Murphy Raj Patel

Placings:0/003P-1					(1980)
2003/04: 25¹GF,					

	Starts	1st	2nd	3rd	Win & Pl
Chases	1	1	0	0	2373
Career Total	6	1	0	1	2861
83	11/03	Hexm	3m1f	F Ch	G-F	£2372
					Total win prize-money £2373

Going:	Sf: 0-0 GS: 0-0 Gd: 0-0 GF: - Fm: 1-1
Distance:	2m/2m3: 0-0 2m4-2m7: 0-0 3m+: 1-1
Track:	LH: 1-1 RH: 0-0 Tight: 0-0 Gall: 0-0
Aids:	Bl: 0-0 Vi: 0-0 Tstrap: 0-0 Ckp: 0-0
Best Rating:	94 3/03 Hexm 3m soft Hdl

Poor maiden hurdler; took a very weak novices' chase on debut over fences at Hexham in November; acts on fast; stays well.

Shemdani (IRE)
87   133

7-y-o b g Unfuwain (USA)-Shemaka (IRE) (Nishapour (FR))

M C Pipe
Mr & Mrs M Bovingdon & C Langley

Placings:112/61-0					(2992)
2003/04: 16⁰G,					

	Starts	1st	2nd	3rd	Win & Pl
Hurdles	1	0	0	0	
Career Total	6	3	1	0	13115
124	2/03	Asct	2m110y	D(0-120)HHdl	SFT	£4979
128	3/02	MRas	2m1f110yE Hdl		G-S	£3304
102	1/02	Donc	2m110y	D Hdl	SFT	£3472
					Total win prize-money £11755

Going:	Sf: 0-0 GS: 0-0 Gd: 0-1 GF: - Fm: 0-0
Distance:	2m/2m3: 0-0 2m4-2m7: 0-0 3m+: 0-0
Track:	LH: 0-0 RH: 0-1 Tight: 0-0 Gall: 0-0
Aids:	Bl: 0-0 Vi: 0-0 Tstrap: 0-0 Ckp: 0-0
Best Rating:	128 3/02 MRas 2m1f110y gd-sft Hdl

Fair hurdler; lightly raced; acts on soft ground.

Shepherds Rest (IRE)
105   (57h)105

12-y-o b g Accordion-Mandy's Last (Krayyan)
C P Morlock The Odd Dozen

Placings:062640223/231U220/0322/P45P02/53322112215 P01/346P003PP0/PP02324133143411/F1252P5-23P					(1269)
2003/04: 26²GS, 24³G, 26PGF,					

	Starts	1st	2nd	3rd	Win & Pl
Chases	3	0	1	0	2295
Career Total	76	10	18	12	67534
110	6/02	Uttx	3m2f	D(0-120)HCh	GD	£4340
110	4/02	Uttx	3m2f	E(0-110)HCh	G-F	£3601
100	4/02	Wwck	3m110y	E(0-105)HCh	G-F	£4078
102	10/01	Folk	2m5f	F(0-95)HCh	GD	£3406
89	8/01	Ctml	2m5f110yF(0-110)HCh		GD	£4192
107	4/00	Uttx	2m4f110yE(0-115)HHdl		SFT	£2824
117	3/00	Newb	2m4f	D(0-125)HCh	SFT	£7091
119	1/00	Kemp	2m4f110yE(0-115)HHdl		SFT	£3477
116	1/00	Wwck	2m4f	E(0-115)HCh	SFT	£3198
106	12/96	Ling	2m110y	E(0-110)HHdl	G-S	£2364
					Total win prize-money £38575

Going:	Sf: 0-0 GS: 0-1 Gd: 0-1 GF: - Fm: 0-0
Distance:	2m/2m3: 0-0 2m4-2m7: 0-0 3m+: 0-3
Track:	LH: 0-3 RH: 0-0 Tight: 0-3 Gall: 0-0
Aids:	Bl: 0-0 Vi: 0-3 Tstrap: 0-0 Ckp: 0-0
Best Rating:	119 2/00 Wwck 2m4f soft Ch

Moderate handicap chaser; has developed stamina with age and now gets three and a quarter miles; likes to be held up, but finds little off the bridle; seems best on a sound surface these days although he handles cut.

Sherbet Fizz (IRE)
88   34

8-y-o b m Petardia-Skiddaw (USA) (Grey Dawn Ii)
C Roberts J Milton

Placings:P/0P					(1043)
2003/04: 20⁰GF, 22PGF,					

	Starts	1st	2nd	3rd	Win & Pl
Hurdles	2	0	0	0	
Career Total	3	0	0	0	

Going:	Sf: 0-0 GS: 0-0 Gd: 0-0 GF: - Fm: 0-2
Distance:	2m/2m3: 0-0 2m4-2m7: 0-2 3m+: 0-0
Track:	LH: 0-2 RH: 0-0 Tight: 0-1 Gall: 0-0
Aids:	Bl: 0-0 Vi: 0-0 Tstrap: 0-0 Ckp: 0-0
Best Rating:	39 7/03 Worc 2m4f gd-fm Hdl

Sherbet Lad (IRE)

112 **104**

8-y-o b g Cataldi-She's Foolish (IRE) (Callernish)
V R A Dartnall Lisa Mackenzie, M Foxon & J Darbishire

Placings:*02U3/01-0P* (0363)
2003/04: 24[0]YS, 20[P]S,

	Starts	1st	2nd	3rd	Win & Pl
Hurdles	8	0	0	0	
Career Total	8	1	1	1	5915

104 3/03 Sand 2m4f110yD Hdl HVY £5053
Total win prize-money £5054

Going:	Sf: 0-1 GS: 0-0 Gd: 0-0 GF: - Fm: 0-0
Distance:	2m/2m3: 0-0 2m4-2m7: 0-1 3m+: 0-1
Track:	LH: 0-1 RH: 0-0 Tight: 0-0 Gall: 0-0
Aids:	Bl: 0-0 Vi: 0-0 Tstrap: 0-0 Ckp: 0-0
Best Rating:	104 3/03 Sand 2m4f110y heavy Hdl

Showed promise in bumpers; winning novice hurdler; stays two and a half miles; effective in testing ground.

Sherfield Lass

71 **23**

6-y-o b m Tina's Pet-Mindyerownbusiness (IRE) (Roselier (FR))
Mrs H Dalton W D Edwards

Placings:*0-4* (0058)
2003/04: 19[4]GS,

	Starts	1st	2nd	3rd	Win & Pl
Hurdles	1	0	0	0	301
Career Total	2	0	0	0	301

Going:	Sf: 0-0 GS: 0-1 Gd: 0-0 GF: - Fm: 0-0
Distance:	2m/2m3: 0-0 2m4-2m7: 0-1 3m+: 0-0
Track:	LH: 0-0 RH: 0-1 Tight: 0-0 Gall: 0-0
Aids:	Bl: 0-0 Vi: 0-0 Tstrap: 0-0 Ckp: 0-0
Best Rating:	53 3/03 Hayd 2m gd-fm NHF

Sheriff's Friend (IRE)

9-y-o b/br g Supreme Leader-Arctic Scale (IRE) (Strong Gale)
Mrs Jenny Gordon S P Tindall

Placings:*P426P/1P* (4425)
2003/04: 28[1]GS, 26[P]G,

	Starts	1st	2nd	3rd	Win & Pl
Chases	2	1	0	0	12155
Career Total	7	1	1	0	13091

103 5/03 Strf 3m4f H Ch G-S £12155
Total win prize-money £12155

Going:	Sf: 0-0 GS: 1-1 Gd: 0-1 GF: - Fm: 0-0
Distance:	2m/2m3: 0-0 2m4-2m7: 0-0 3m+: 1-2
Track:	LH: 1-2 RH: 0-0 Tight: 1-1 Gall: 0-1
Aids:	Bl: 0-0 Vi: 0-0 Tstrap: 0-0 Ckp: 0-0
Best Rating:	103 5/03 Strf 3m4f gd-sft Ch

Sherkin Island (IRE)

96(83c) (116+c)**104+**

6-y-o b g Shemazar-Tullerolli (IRE) (Barbarolli (USA))
Jonjo O'Neill John P McManus

Placings:*4110* (4777)
2003/04: 26[4]GS, 24[1]HY, 18[1]G, 23[9]G,

	Starts	1st	2nd	3rd	Win & Pl
Hurdles	3	1	0	0	4713
Chases	1	1	0	0	4576
Career Total	4	2	0	0	9289

116 3/04 Newb 2m2f110yE(0-105)HCh GD £4576
104 1/04 Uttx 3m110y E Hdl   HVY £4712
Total win prize-money £9289

Going:	Sf: 1-1 GS: 0-1 Gd: 1-2 GF: - Fm: 0-0
Distance:	2m/2m3: 1-1 2m4-2m7: 0-0 3m+: 1-3
Track:	LH: 2-3 RH: 0-1 Tight: 0-1 Gall: 1-2
Aids:	Bl: 0-0 Vi: 0-0 Tstrap: 0-0 Ckp: 0-0
Best Rating:	116 3/04 Newb 2m2f110y good Ch

Maiden Irish pointer; took a modest novices' hurdle in testing conditions at Uttoxeter in January; won on chase debut at Newbury; stays exceptionally well; acts on soft.

Sherwood Rose (IRE)

85(96h) (70h)**64**

8-y-o gr m Mandalus-Cronlier (Roselier (FR))
K C Bailey Peter Granger

Placings:*0/0/0-P0P6P6PUP* (4716)
2003/04: 16[P]S, 16[9]G, 26[P]GS, 17[6]HY, 21[6]GS, 24[P]G, 22[5]UGS, 21[P]G,

	Starts	1st	2nd	3rd	Win & Pl
Hurdles	5	0	0	0	0
Chases	3	0	0	0	0
Career Total	11	0	0	0	0

Going:	Sf: 0-2 GS: 0-3 Gd: 0-3 GF: - Fm: 0-0
Distance:	2m/2m3: 0-3 2m4-2m7: 0-3 3m+: 0-2
Track:	LH: 0-1 RH: 0-7 Tight: 0-2 Gall: 0-1
Aids:	Bl: 0-0 Vi: 0-0 Tstrap: 0-0 Ckp: 0-0
Best Rating:	70 1/04 Folk 2m1f110y heavy Hdl

Plating-class hurdler; stays 2m 6f; suited by hold up tactics; has proved a flop over fences.

Sherzabad (IRE)

7-y-o b/br g Doyoun-Sheriya (USA) (Green Dancer (USA))
Miss I E Craig (H J Collingridge 4/10) Guy Luck

Placings:*P* (3652)
2003/04: 17[P]S,

	Starts	1st	2nd	3rd	Win & Pl
Hurdles	1	0	0	0	
Career Total	1	0	0	0	

Going:	Sf: 0-1 GS: 0-0 Gd: 0-0 GF: - Fm: 0-0
Distance:	2m/2m3: 0-1 2m4-2m7: 0-0 3m+: 0-0
Track:	LH: 0-0 RH: 0-1 Tight: 0-1 Gall: 0-0
Aids:	Bl: 0-0 Vi: 0-0 Tstrap: 0-0 Ckp: 0-0

Shes Elite (IRE)

77f **43f**

6-y-o b m Supreme Leader-Chic And Elite (Deep Run)
Jonjo O'Neill J R Weston

Placings:*00* (0705)
2003/04: 17[0]G, 17[0]GF,

	Starts	1st	2nd	3rd	Win & Pl
NH Flat	2	0	0	0	
Career Total	2	0	0	0	

Going:	Sf: 0-0 GS: 0-0 Gd: 0-1 GF: - Fm: 0-1
Distance:	2m/2m3: 0-2 2m4-2m7: 0-0 3m+: 0-0
Track:	LH: 0-1 RH: 0-1 Tight: 0-2 Gall: 0-0
Aids:	Bl: 0-0 Vi: 0-0 Tstrap: 0-0 Ckp: 0-0
Best Rating:	43 5/03 Bang 2m1f good NHF

Shifting Moon

103 (83c)**82**

12-y-o b g Night Shift (USA)-Moonscape (Ribero)
F Jordan Mrs K Roberts-Hindle

Placings:*2104500/0PP204031F/61211233P/0631/P001406 33634/00610534446/0P22050U3P/404125350U0-6210* (1012)
2003/04: 16[P]HY, 22[2]GF, 22[1]GF, 24[0]G,

	Starts	1st	2nd	3rd	Win & Pl
Hurdles	4	1	1	0	4491
Career Total	78	10	8	10	42991

79 7/03 Strf 2m6f110yE(0-105)HHdl G-F £3610
91 7/02 Strf 2m6f110yD(0-115)HHdl G-F £4186
100 9/00 Bang 2m4f F(0-110)HHdl   G-F £4251
95 11/99 NAbb 2m1f E(0-115)HHdl   G-S £2906
108 7/98 Strf 2m110y D(0-125)HHdl G-F £3496
91 8/97 Ctml 2m1f110yD(0-120)HHdl G-F £2784
89 8/97 NAbb 2m1f E(0-110)HHdl   G-F £2179
89 8/97 NAbb 2m1f E(0-110)HHdl   G-F £2116
77 4/97 Tntn 2m1f E(0-115)HHdl   FRM £2200
102 8/95 NAbb 2m1f D Hdl   G-F £2532
Total win prize-money £30265

Going:	Sf: 0-1 GS: 0-0 Gd: 0-1 GF: - Fm: 1-2
Distance:	2m/2m3: 0-2 2m4-2m7: 1-2 3m+: 0-1
Track:	LH: 1-4 RH: 0-0 Tight: 1-3 Gall: 0-0
Aids:	Bl: 0-0 Vi: 0-0 Tstrap: 1-4 Ckp: 0-0
Best Rating:	108 7/98 Strf 2m110y gd-fm Hdl

Plating-class hurdler; stays 2m 6f; suited by hold up tactics; has proved a flop over fences.

Shifty Shakomala (IRE)

7-y-o b g Lord Americo-I'Ll Say She Is (Ashmore (FR))
M J Ryan Andy Beard

Placings:*P* (0451)
2003/04: 16[P]GF,

	Starts	1st	2nd	3rd	Win & Pl
NH Flat	1	0	0	0	
Career Total	1	0	0	0	

Going:	Sf: 0-0 GS: 0-0 Gd: 0-0 GF: - Fm: 0-1
Distance:	2m/2m3: 0-1 2m4-2m7: 0-0 3m+: 0-0
Track:	LH: 0-0 RH: 0-1 Tight: 0-0 Gall: 0-1
Aids:	Bl: 0-0 Vi: 0-0 Tstrap: 0-0 Ckp: 0-0

Shillelah Law

(90h) (83h)

8-y-o ch g Weld-Compasita (Old Jocus)
M C Pipe P J Finn

Placings:*003P* (1091)
2003/04: 24[0]G, 20[0]G, 22[3]GF, 24[P]G,

	Starts	1st	2nd	3rd	Win & Pl
Hurdles	3	0	0	1	844
Chases	1	0	0	0	0
Career Total	4	0	0	1	844

Going:	Sf: 0-0 GS: 0-0 Gd: 0-2 GF: - Fm: 0-2
Distance:	2m/2m3: 0-0 2m4-2m7: 0-2 3m+: 0-2
Track:	LH: 0-4 RH: 0-0 Tight: 0-2 Gall: 0-0

Aids: Bl: 0-0 Vi: 0-0 Tstrap: 0-0 Ckp: 0-0
Best Rating: 85   7/03   Strf   2m6f110y   gd-fm   Hdl

Novice hurdler; first sign of ability when third behind two fair sorts at Stratford; should do better in handicaps.

Shilo (IRE)

99   **94**

10-y-o ch g Roselier (FR)-Cathedral Street (Boreen Beag)
Mrs Merrita Jones   Mrs D J Hughes

Placings:00/P-43F   (4757)
2003/04: 22⁴S, 26³S, 25⁵S,

	Starts	1st	2nd	3rd	Win & Pl
Chases	3	0	0	1	866
Career Total	6	0	0	1	866

Going: Sf: 0-3 GS: 0-0 Gd: 0-0 GF: - Fm: 0-0
Distance: 2m/2m3: 0-0 2m4-2m7: 0-1 3m+: 0-2
Track: LH: 0-1 RH: 0-2 Tight: 0-0 Gall: 0-0
Aids: Bl: 0-0 Vi: 0-0 Tstrap: 0-0 Ckp: 0-0
Best Rating: 94   12/03   Towc   2m6f   soft   Ch

Shining Strand

99f   **111f**

5-y-o ch g Karinga Bay-First Romance (Royalty)
N J Henderson   The Queen

Placings:2   (2489)
2003/04: 16²GS,

	Starts	1st	2nd	3rd	Win & Pl
NH Flat	1	0	1	0	2340
Career Total	1	0	1	0	2340

Going: Sf: 0-0 GS: 0-1 Gd: 0-0 GF: - Fm: 0-0
Distance: 2m/2m3: 0-1 2m4-2m7: 0-0 3m+: 0-0
Track: LH: 0-1 RH: 0-0 Tight: 0-0 Gall: 0-1
Aids: Bl: 0-0 Vi: 0-0 Tstrap: 0-0 Ckp: 0-0
Best Rating: 111   11/03   Newb   2m110y   gd-sft   NHF

Runner-up on debut; stays two miles; acts on good to soft ground.

Shining Tyne

95   **91**

10-y-o b g Primitive Rising (USA)-Shining Bann (Bargello)
R Johnson   David Blythe

Placings:0/00F/6RPP03/6423F/445652322-5432P   (3938)
2003/04: 24⁵G, 24⁴GS, 20³HY, 20²HY, 33⁶G,

	Starts	1st	2nd	3rd	Win & Pl
Chases	5	0	1	4	2155
Career Total	29	0	5	4	14802

Going: Sf: 0-2 GS: 0-1 Gd: 0-2 GF: - Fm: 0-0
Distance: 2m/2m3: 0-0 2m4-2m7: 0-2 3m+: 0-3
Track: LH: 0-5 RH: 0-0 Tight: 0-0 Gall: 0-5
Aids: Bl: 0-4 Vi: 0-0 Tstrap: 0-4 Ckp: 0-1
Best Rating: 91   4/03   Prth   3m   good   Ch

Moderate maiden chaser; stays three miles, acts on soft ground; has worn combinations of a tongue tie, cheekpieces and blinkers.

Shiny Bay (IRE)

11-y-o ch g Glacial Storm (USA)-Raby (Pongee)

Miss Jenny Garley   Mrs Donna Lowther

Placings:00/0005P50036/4310513123/0FF525031PF/3302
0/P   (4872)
2003/04: 24⁹S,

	Starts	1st	2nd	3rd	Win & Pl
Chases	1	0	0	0	
Career Total	41	4	3	7	32852
118	2/01	Gowr	2m2f	Ch	HVY	£7790
108	2/00	Punc	2m	(0-116)HHdl	Y-S	£4692
102	1/00	Naas	2m	(0-116)HHdl	SFT	£3864
98	12/99	Navn	2m4f	(0-109)HHdl	SFT	£4312

Total win prize-money £20659

Going: Sf: 0-1 GS: 0-0 Gd: 0-0 GF: - Fm: 0-0
Distance: 2m/2m3: 0-0 2m4-2m7: 0-0 3m+: 0-1
Track: LH: 0-1 RH: 0-0 Tight: 0-0 Gall: 0-0
Aids: Bl: 0-0 Vi: 0-0 Tstrap: 0-0 Ckp: 0-0
Best Rating: 127   4/00   Fair   2m   soft   Hdl

Shirazi

95   **103+**

6-y-o b g Mtoto-Al Shadeedah (USA) (Nureyev (USA))
D R Gandolfo   Starlight Racing

Placings:514000   (4651)
2003/04: 17⁵G, 17¹GF, 17⁴G, 16⁰G, 16⁰GS, 17⁰G,

	Starts	1st	2nd	3rd	Win & Pl
Hurdles	6	1	0	0	5543
Career Total	6	1	0	0	5543
103	6/03	NAbb	2m1f	D Hdl	G-F	£4901

Total win prize-money £4901

Going: Sf: 0-0 GS: 0-1 Gd: 0-4 GF: - Fm: 1-1
Distance: 2m/2m3: 1-6 2m4-2m7: 0-0 3m+: 0-0
Track: LH: 1-3 RH: 0-3 Tight: 1-3 Gall: 0-0
Aids: Bl: 0-0 Vi: 0-0 Tstrap: 0-0 Ckp: 0-0
Best Rating: 103   6/03   NAbb   2m1f   gd-fm   Hdl

Modest hurdler; won novice hurdle at Newton Abbot in June on second start; has since failed to build on his victory and looks exposed; acts on fast ground.

Shobrooke Mill

11-y-o ch g Shaab-Jubilee Leigh (Hubble Bubble)
Mrs S Prouse   Mrs S Prouse

Placings:U/U342/6U-F4   (4823)
2003/04: 21⁶GF, 23⁴GF,

	Starts	1st	2nd	3rd	Win & Pl
Chases	2	0	0	0	214
Career Total	9	0	1	1	1067

Going: Sf: 0-0 GS: 0-0 Gd: 0-1 GF: - Fm: 0-1
Distance: 2m/2m3: 0-0 2m4-2m7: 0-1 3m+: 0-1
Track: LH: 0-1 RH: 0-1 Tight: 0-0 Gall: 0-1
Aids: Bl: 0-0 Vi: 0-0 Tstrap: 0-0 Ckp: 0-0
Best Rating: 95   4/02   Extr   2m7f110y   firm   Ch

Shock's Pride (IRE)

12-y-o b g Glacial Storm (USA)-Ewood Park (Wishing Star)
Mrs S Clarke   C H Sclater

Placings:P/P-   (0020)
2003/04: 26³S,

	Starts	1st	2nd	3rd	Win & Pl
Chases	1	0	0	0	
Career Total	2	0	0	0	

Going: Sf: 0-1 GS: 0-0 Gd: 0-0 GF: - Fm: 0-0
Distance: 2m/2m3: 0-0 2m4-2m7: 0-0 3m+: 0-0
Track: LH: 0-1 RH: 0-0 Tight: 0-1 Gall: 0-0
Aids: Bl: 0-0 Vi: 0-0 Tstrap: 0-0 Ckp: 0-0

Shogoon (FR)

78   (43h)**75**

5-y-o b g Rangoon (FR)-Touranlad (FR) (Tourangeau (FR))
M D Hammond   The County Set

Placings:2-000F1F   (4880)
2003/04: 17⁰GS, 20⁰GS, 20⁰S, 24⁴FF, 16¹GF, 20⁴GS,

	Starts	1st	2nd	3rd	Win & Pl
Hurdles	3	0	0	0	0
Chases	3	1	0	0	6740
Career Total	7	1	1	0	7771
75	3/04	Catt	2m	D Ch	G-F	£6740

Total win prize-money £6740

Going: Sf: 0-1 GS: 0-3 Gd: 0-0 GF: - Fm: 1-2
Distance: 2m/2m3: 1-2 2m4-2m7: 0-3 3m+: 0-1
Track: LH: 1-3 RH: 0-3 Tight: 1-3 Gall: 0-0
Aids: Bl: 0-0 Vi: 0-0 Tstrap: 0-0 Ckp: 0-0
Best Rating: 75   3/04   Catt   2m   gd-fm   Ch

Runner-up over hurdles in France; reluctant winner of weak two-horse event at Catterick in March; best over two miles.

Sholay (IRE)

92   **90**

5-y-o b g Bluebird (USA)-Splicing (Sharpo)
P Mitchell (N A Twiston-Davies 3/2)   Mrs S Trikha

Placings:00   (3651)
2003/04: 16⁰S, 17⁰S,

	Starts	1st	2nd	3rd	Win & Pl
Hurdles	2	0	0	0	
Career Total	2	0	0	0	

Going: Sf: 0-2 GS: 0-0 Gd: 0-0 GF: - Fm: 0-0
Distance: 2m/2m3: 0-2 2m4-2m7: 0-0 3m+: 0-0
Track: LH: 0-0 RH: 0-2 Tight: 0-1 Gall: 0-0
Aids: Bl: 0-0 Vi: 0-0 Tstrap: 0-0 Ckp: 0-0
Best Rating: 90   2/04   Tntn   2m1f   soft   Hdl

Shooting Light (IRE)

108   (130h)**159**

11-y-o b g Shernazar-Church Light (Caerleon (USA))
M C Pipe   J M Brown & M J Blackburn

Placings:1213/24004/526/36B2365/3132350/111P/5P-1P   (4055)
2003/04: 24¹G, 24²G,

	Starts	1st	2nd	3rd	Win & Pl
Chases	2	1	0	0	40600
Career Total	34	7	5	6	215701
159	2/04	Newb	3m	A Ch	GD	£40600
169	12/01	Asct	3m110y	A HCh	GD	£32500
161	11/01	Chel	2m4f110yA HCh	GD	£58000
155	10/01	Chel	2m4f110yC(0-135)HCh	GD	£13013
132	11/00	Asct	2m3f110yB Ch	SFT	£9350
126	1/97	Chel	2m1f	A Hdl	G-F	£9779
114	11/96	Sand	2m110y	D Hdl	GD	£2801

Total win prize-money £166044

Going: Sf: 0-0 GS: 0-0 Gd: 1-2 GF: - Fm: 0-0
Distance: 2m/2m3: 0-0 2m4-2m7: 0-0 3m+: 1-2
Track: LH: 1-1 RH: 0-1 Tight: 0-0 Gall: 1-1
Aids: Bl: 0-0 Vi: 1-2 Tstrap: 0-0 Ckp: 0-0

Best Rating: 169 12/01 Asct 3m110y good Ch

High-class chaser; joined Martin Pipe at the start of 2001/02, when easy winner of the Thomas Pink Gold Cup and Tote Silver Cup; pulled up lame in the Gold Cup; only ran twice in 2002/3 season; bounced back to best when winning the AON Chase at Newbury on his return in February; stayed three miles, effective over shorter; won on good ground and soft; usually wore a visor.(DEAD)

Short Change (IRE)

103   **109+**

5-y-o b g Revoque (IRE)-Maafi Esm (Polish Precedent (USA))
A W Carroll Dennis Deacon

Placings:12B0-160   (2486)
2003/04: 16¹GF, 16⁶G, 16⁰GS,

	Starts	1st	2nd	3rd	Win & Pl
Hurdles	3	1	0	0	3308
Career Total	7	2	1	0	7899
109	11/03	Wwck	2m		E(0-110)HHdl	G-F	£3307
102	10/02	Hrfd	2m1f		E Hdl	GD	£3507
				Total win prize-money £6815

Going:	Sf: 0-0 GS: 0-1 Gd: 0-0 GF: - Fm: 1-1
Distance:	2m/2m3: 1-3 2m4-2m7: 0-0 3m+: 0-0
Track:	LH: 1-2 RH: 0-1 Tight: 0-0 Gall: 0-1
Aids:	Bl: 0-0 Vi: 0-0 Tstrap: 0-0 Ckp: 0-1
Best Rating:	109 11/03 Wwck 2m gd-fm Hdl

Moderate hurdler; best at around two miles; acts on fast ground.

Shosen (IRE)

88   **121**

8-y-o b g Persian Mews-Lugnagullagh (Pitpan)
A King Mrs M C Sweeney

Placings:341/0P   (3827)
2003/04: 20⁰S, 24ᴾG,

	Starts	1st	2nd	3rd	Win & Pl
Hurdles	2	0	0	0	
Career Total	5	1	0	1	7722
121	3/02	Newb	2m5f		D Hdl	SFT	£6318
				Total win prize-money £6318

Going:	Sf: 0-1 GS: 0-0 Gd: 0-1 GF: - Fm: 0-0
Distance:	2m/2m3: 0-0 2m4-2m7: 0-1 3m+: 0-1
Track:	LH: 0-2 RH: 0-0 Tight: 0-0 Gall: 0-1
Aids:	Bl: 0-0 Vi: 0-0 Tstrap: 0-0 Ckp: 0-1
Best Rating:	121 3/02 Newb 2m5f soft Hdl

Light-raced hurdler; easy winner of a novices' event Newbury in March 2002; started favourite but well beaten on return at Wetherby in January 2004 and again disappointing next time; best at around two and a half miles; suited by soft ground; chasing will eventually be his game.

Shotacross The Bow (IRE)

81

7-y-o b g Warning-Nordica (Northfields (USA))
Mrs H E Rees (M Blanshard 25/11) Mrs H E Rees

Placings:44/P   (4577)
2003/04: 16ᴾG,

	Starts	1st	2nd	3rd	Win & Pl
Hurdles	1	0	0	0	
Career Total	3	0	0	0	0

Going:	Sf: 0-0 GS: 0-0 Gd: 0-1 GF: - Fm: 0-0
Distance:	2m/2m3: 0-1 2m4-2m7: 0-0 3m+: 0-0
Track:	LH: 0-1 RH: 0-0 Tight: 0-0 Gall: 0-1
Aids:	Bl: 0-0 Vi: 0-0 Tstrap: 0-0 Ckp: 0-0
Best Rating:	81 8/01 Worc 2m gd-fm Hdl

Shotgun Annie

25f

4-y-o b f Double Trigger (IRE)-Coh Sho No (Old Vic)
S Dow Harold Nass

Placings:0   (2301)
2003/04: 12⁰S,

	Starts	1st	2nd	3rd	Win & Pl
NH Flat	1	0	0	0	
Career Total	1	0	0	0	

Going:	Sf: 0-1 GS: 0-0 Gd: 0-0 GF: - Fm: 0-0
Distance:	2m/2m3: 0-0 2m4-2m7: 0-0 3m+: 0-0
Track:	LH: 0-0 RH: 0-0 Tight: 0-0 Gall: 0-0
Aids:	Bl: 0-0 Vi: 0-0 Tstrap: 0-0 Ckp: 0-0
Best Rating:	25 11/03 Asct 1m4f soft NHF

Shoulton (IRE)

105(81h)   (35h)**94**

7-y-o br g Aristocracy-Jay Joy (Double U Jay)
G H Yardley Miss A J Yardley

Placings:05/000U-2CU2U4   (4570)
2003/04: 24²GS, 24ᶜGS, 24ᵁGS, 26²S, 24ᵁGS, 24⁴GS,

	Starts	1st	2nd	3rd	Win & Pl
Chases	6	0	2	0	2664
Career Total	12	0	2	0	2664

Going:	Sf: 0-1 GS: 0-5 Gd: 0-0 GF: - Fm: 0-0
Distance:	2m/2m3: 0-0 2m4-2m7: 0-0 3m+: 0-6
Track:	LH: 0-5 RH: 0-1 Tight: 0-1 Gall: 0-0
Aids:	Bl: 0-0 Vi: 0-0 Tstrap: 0-0 Ckp: 0-0
Best Rating:	102 1/04 Chep 3m2f110y soft Ch

Plating-class novice chaser; front runner; stays 3m; acts in soft ground; still a maiden.

Showpiece

112   **132**

6-y-o b g Selkirk (USA)-Hawayah (IRE) (Shareef Dancer (USA))
C J Mann C S G Limited

Placings:4-121120   (2131)
2003/04: 16¹GS, 18²G, 17¹GF, 17¹GF, 17²GF, 16⁰GF,

	Starts	1st	2nd	3rd	Win & Pl
Hurdles	6	3	2	0	37316
Career Total	7	3	2	0	37884
132	6/03	MRas	2m1f110yB(0-140)HHdl	G-F	£16757
97	6/03	NAbb	2m1f	E Hdl	G-F	£3503
97	5/03	Aint	2m110y	D Hdl	G-S	£4823
				Total win prize-money £25084

Going:	Sf: 0-0 GS: 1-1 Gd: 0-1 GF: - Fm: 2-4
Distance:	2m/2m3: 3-6 2m4-2m7: 0-0 3m+: 0-0
Track:	LH: 2-4 RH: 1-2 Tight: 3-5 Gall: 0-0
Aids:	Bl: 0-0 Vi: 0-0 Tstrap: 0-0 Ckp: 0-0
Best Rating:	134 7/03 MRas 2m1f110y gd-fm Hdl

Useful hurdler, in good form in the summer of 2003; suited by trips of around two miles and acts on most types of ground.

Shraden Edition

7-y-o b g Tina's Pet-Star Edition (Leading Man)
P A Jones Shraden Partnership

Placings:2P   (4872)
2003/04: 24²G, 24ᴾS,

	Starts	1st	2nd	3rd	Win & Pl
Chases	2	0	1	0	1102
Career Total	2	0	1	0	1102

Going:	Sf: 0-1 GS: 0-0 Gd: 0-1 GF: - Fm: 0-0
Distance:	2m/2m3: 0-0 2m4-2m7: 0-0 3m+: 0-2
Track:	LH: 0-2 RH: 0-0 Tight: 0-2 Gall: 0-0
Aids:	Bl: 0-0 Vi: 0-0 Tstrap: 0-0 Ckp: 0-0
Best Rating:	99 3/04 Strf 3m good Ch

Winning pointer; showed promise in first start over regulation fences at Stratford.

Shrilanka (IRE)

90(88h)   (66h)**55**

8-y-o b m Lashkari-Lady Nerak (Pitpan)
P J Hobbs Mr & Mrs A J Heywood

Placings:4/0555-0   (0236)
2003/04: 25⁰GF,

	Starts	1st	2nd	3rd	Win & Pl
Chases	1	0	0	0	
Career Total	6	0	0	0	323

Going:	Sf: 0-0 GS: 0-0 Gd: 0-0 GF: - Fm: 0-1
Distance:	2m/2m3: 0-0 2m4-2m7: 0-0 3m+: 0-1
Track:	LH: 0-0 RH: 0-0 Tight: 0-0 Gall: 0-0
Aids:	Bl: 0-0 Vi: 0-0 Tstrap: 0-0 Ckp: 0-0
Best Rating:	84 5/01 Tipp 2m2f heavy NHF

Shu Gaa (IRE)

11-y-o ch g Salse (USA)-River Reem (USA) (Irish River (FR))
C Goulding C Goulding

Placings:10411/3/4F3F4F0/545630/14P43/0P/P-10 (4563)
2003/04: 21¹GM, 22⁰G,

	Starts	1st	2nd	3rd	Win & Pl
Chases	2	0	0	4	24646
Career Total	29	5	0	4	24646
112	5/00	Bang	2m4f110yD(0-120)HCh	£7475
116	4/97	Ayr	2m	C HHdl	GD	£4402
106	3/97	Chep	2m110y	C HHdl	G-S	£3488
101	12/96	Hayd	2m	D Hdl	G-S	£2955
				Total win prize-money £18321

Going:	Sf: 0-0 GS: 0-0 Gd: 0-1 GF: - Fm: 1-1
Distance:	2m/2m3: 0-0 2m4-2m7: 1-2 3m+: 0-0
Track:	LH: 0-1 RH: 1-1 Tight: 1-1 Gall: 0-1
Aids:	Bl: 0-0 Vi: 0-0 Tstrap: 0-0 Ckp: 0-0
Best Rating:	116 5/97 Hayd 2m good Hdl

Modest hunter; stays 2m4f; acts on good or easy ground.

Shuhood (USA)

106   **118**

4-y-o b g Kingmambo (USA)-Nifty (USA) (Roberto (USA))
P R Webber (E A L Dunlop 27/6) Mr & Mrs M Dowd

Placings:30   (4625)
2003/04: 16³G, 16⁰G,

	Starts	1st	2nd	3rd	Win & Pl
Hurdles	2	0	0	1	3300
Career Total	2	0	0	1	3300

Going:	Sf: 0-0 GS: 0-0 Gd: 0-2 GF: - Fm: 0-0
Distance:	2m/2m3: 0-2 2m4-2m7: 0-0 3m+: 0-0
Track:	LH: 0-1 RH: 0-1 Tight: 0-0 Gall: 0-0
Aids:	Bl: 0-0 Vi: 0-0 Tstrap: 0-0 Ckp: 0-0
Best Rating:	118 4/04 Aint 2m110y good Hdl

Lightly-raced winner on the level; made a highly promising hurdling debut at Kempton when third in the Adonis; not disgraced at Aintree subsequently; stays two miles, may get further; acts well on a sound surface.

Shuil Back (IRE)
90   **51**

7-y-o b m Bob Back (USA)-Shuil Ar Aghaidh (The Parson)
A J Lidderdale   George Ward

Placings:3/P-0   (0107)
2003/04: 22⁰S,

	Starts	1st	2nd	3rd	Win & Pl
Hurdles	1	0	0	0	
Career Total	3	0	0	1	246

Going:	Sf: 0-1 GS: 0-0 Gd: 0-0 GF: - Fm: 0-0
Distance:	2m/2m3: 0-0 2m4-2m7: 0-1 3m+: 0-0
Track:	LH: 0-1 RH: 0-0 Tight: 0-0 Gall: 0-0
Aids:	Bl: 0-0 Vi: 0-0 Tstrap: 0-0 Ckp: 0-0
Best Rating:	82 4/02 Towc 2m good NHF

Daughter of a smart staying mare, likely to need a test of stamina in time.

Shuil Tsarina (IRE)
73   **57+**

6-y-o b m King's Ride-Shuil Realt (IRE) (Jolly Jake (NZ))
J M Jefferson   Mrs K S Gaffney & Mrs Alix Stevenson

Placings:0/3-00   (2688)
2003/04: 17⁰G, 20⁰GS,

	Starts	1st	2nd	3rd	Win & Pl
NH Flat	1	0	0	0	0
Hurdles	1	0	0	0	0
Career Total	4	0	0	1	251

Going:	Sf: 0-0 GS: 0-1 Gd: 0-1 GF: - Fm: 0-0
Distance:	2m/2m3: 0-1 2m4-2m7: 0-1 3m+: 0-0
Track:	LH: 0-1 RH: 0-1 Tight: 0-1 Gall: 0-1
Aids:	Bl: 0-0 Vi: 0-0 Tstrap: 0-0 Ckp: 0-0
Best Rating:	88 10/03 Bang 2m1f good NHF

Si Celia

9-y-o ch m Primitive Rising (USA)-Easterly Gael (Tudor Music)
Mrs J Williamson   J P R Deans & Co

Placings:6   (0101)
2003/04: 25⁰G,

	Starts	1st	2nd	3rd	Win & Pl
Chases	1	0	0	0	0
Career Total	1	0	0	0	0

Going:	Sf: 0-0 GS: 0-0 Gd: 0-1 GF: - Fm: 0-0
Distance:	2m/2m3: 0-0 2m4-2m7: 0-0 3m+: 0-1
Track:	LH: 0-1 RH: 0-0 Tight: 0-0 Gall: 0-0

Sidewinder (IRE)
108   (48h)**78**

9-y-o br g Jolly Jake (NZ)-Silk Empress (Young Emperor)
M C Pipe (L A Dace 30/7)   Mrs K Tobin

Placings:000F53/600P03PP/P0PP-00024   (1930)
2003/04: 18⁰YS, 26⁰GF, 19⁰G, 23²F, 26⁴GF,

	Starts	1st	2nd	3rd	Win & Pl
Hurdles	2	0	0	0	0
Chases	3	0	1	0	1660
Career Total	23	0	1	2	2845

Going:	Sf: 0-0 GS: 0-0 Gd: 0-1 GF: - Fm: 0-3
Distance:	2m/2m3: 0-2 2m4-2m7: 0-0 3m+: 0-3
Track:	LH: 0-2 RH: 0-2 Tight: 0-0 Gall: 0-0
Aids:	Bl: 0-1 Vi: 0-0 Tstrap: 0-0 Ckp: 0-1
Best Rating:	78 11/03 Wwck 3m2f gd-fm Ch

Maiden hurdler/chaser in Ireland; well backed when going off like a scalded cat on British debut in 3m2f handicap hurdle at Southwell July 2003; modest runner-up on chase bow in Britain.

Sienna Sunset (IRE)
85   **80**

5-y-o ch m Spectrum (IRE)-Wasabi (IRE) (Polar Falcon (USA))
Mrs H Dalton   Ray Bailey

Placings:005   (4365)
2003/04: 17⁰GS, 16⁰G, 16⁵GS,

	Starts	1st	2nd	3rd	Win & Pl
Hurdles	3	0	0	0	0
Career Total	3	0	0	0	0

Going:	Sf: 0-0 GS: 0-2 Gd: 0-1 GF: - Fm: 0-0
Distance:	2m/2m3: 0-3 2m4-2m7: 0-0 3m+: 0-0
Track:	LH: 0-1 RH: 0-2 Tight: 0-2 Gall: 0-0
Aids:	Bl: 0-0 Vi: 0-0 Tstrap: 0-0 Ckp: 0-0
Best Rating:	80 3/04 Ludl 2m good Hdl

Sigma Dotcomm (IRE)
115   (88h)**115**

8-y-o b g Safety Catch (USA)-Dream Academy (Town And Country)
James Joseph Mangan (Noel Meade 2/5)   J A Boyle

Placings:21/335105/01FF12P322F/03P30-U03PP0 (4640)
2003/04: 16⁰YS, 19⁰GY, 28³G, 29²S, 24⁴S, 21⁰G,

	Starts	1st	2nd	3rd	Win & Pl
Chases	6	0	0	1	2922
Career Total	30	4	4	6	38911
107 11/01	Dpat	2m6f		Ch		SFT	£6120
121 10/01	Gowr	2m6f		Ch		GD	£7790
110 2/01	Clon	2m4f		Hdl		HVY	£3895
101 2/00	Punc	2m		NHF		Y-S	£3864

Total win prize-money £21670

Going:	Sf: 0-2 GS: 0-0 Gd: 0-2 GF: - Fm: 0-0
Distance:	2m/2m3: 0-2 2m4-2m7: 0-1 3m+: 0-3
Track:	LH: 0-2 RH: 0-3 Tight: 0-1 Gall: 0-0
Aids:	Bl: 0-0 Vi: 0-0 Tstrap: 0-0 Ckp: 0-2
Best Rating:	125 12/01 Navn 2m4f yield Ch

Aids:	Bl: 0-0 Vi: 0-0 Tstrap: 0-0 Ckp: 0-0
Best Rating:	43 5/03 Hexm 3m1f good Ch

Fair Irish chaser; best on soft ground; stays three miles; has worn blinkers.

Sign Of Nike
63   **26**

6-y-o b h Mistertopogigo (IRE)-Infanta Maria (King Of Spain)
C Von Der Recke   C Von Der Recke

Placings:0   (1192)
2003/04: 16⁰GF,

	Starts	1st	2nd	3rd	Win & Pl
Hurdles	1	0	0	0	
Career Total	1	0	0	0	

Going:	Sf: 0-0 GS: 0-0 Gd: 0-0 GF: - Fm: 0-1
Distance:	2m/2m3: 0-1 2m4-2m7: 0-0 3m+: 0-0
Track:	LH: 0-1 RH: 0-0 Tight: 0-0 Gall: 0-0
Aids:	Bl: 0-0 Vi: 0-0 Tstrap: 0-0 Ckp: 0-0
Best Rating:	26 8/03 Worc 2m gd-fm Hdl

Signature Tune (IRE)

5-y-o b g Gothland (FR)-Divine Affair (IRE) (The Parson)
P Winkworth   Simon Martyn

Placings:00U   (4698)
2003/04: 16⁰GS, 18⁰HY, 18ᵁG,

	Starts	1st	2nd	3rd	Win & Pl
NH Flat	2	0	0	0	0
Hurdles	1	0	0	0	0
Career Total	3	0	0	0	

Going:	Sf: 0-1 GS: 0-1 Gd: 0-1 GF: - Fm: 0-0
Distance:	2m/2m3: 0-3 2m4-2m7: 0-0 3m+: 0-0
Track:	LH: 0-3 RH: 0-0 Tight: 0-2 Gall: 0-0
Aids:	Bl: 0-0 Vi: 0-0 Tstrap: 0-0 Ckp: 0-0
Best Rating:	66 12/03 Uttx 2m gd-sft NHF

Signed And Dated (USA)
97   **66**

5-y-o b g Red Ransom (USA)-Libeccio (NZ) (Danzatore (CAN))
Mrs E Slack   A Slack

Placings:P0F-6P0P   (1984)
2003/04: 16⁶G, 20ᴾGF, 20⁰GF, 16ᴾGF,

	Starts	1st	2nd	3rd	Win & Pl
Hurdles	4	0	0	0	0
Career Total	7	0	0	0	0

Going:	Sf: 0-0 GS: 0-0 Gd: 0-1 GF: - Fm: 0-3
Distance:	2m/2m3: 0-2 2m4-2m7: 0-2 3m+: 0-0
Track:	LH: 0-3 RH: 0-1 Tight: 0-1 Gall: 0-0
Aids:	Bl: 0-0 Vi: 0-0 Tstrap: 0-0 Ckp: 0-1
Best Rating:	66 5/03 Kels 2m110y good Hdl

Sigwells Club Boy
97   **82**

4-y-o b g Fayruz-Run With Pride (Mandrake Major)
J L Flint (W G M Turner 19/2)   J L Flint

Placings:5302432230   (4697)

2003/04: 17⁵GF, 17³GF, 16⁰GF, 16²GS, 16⁴S, 16³G, 17²GS, 18²GF, 16³S, 17⁰G,

	Starts	1st	2nd	3rd	Win & Pl
Hurdles	10	0	3	3	3605
Career Total	10	0	3	3	3605

Going:	Sf: 0-2 GS: 0-2 Gd: 0-2 GF: - Fm: 0-4
Distance:	2m/2m3: 0-10 2m4-2m7: 0-0 3m+: 0-0
Track:	LH: 0-4 RH: 0-6 Tight: 0-4 Gall: 0-0
Aids:	Bl: 0-0 Vi: 0-0 Tstrap: 0-0 Ckp: 0-2
Best Rating:	88 3/04 Wwck 2m soft Hdl

Plating-class hurdler; consistently placed in sellers; has worn cheekpieces.

Sijujama (IRE)

63   **61**

9-y-o b g Torus-Knights Bounty (IRE) (Henbit (USA))
Miss Lucinda V Russell Major R B H Young

Placings:00000/P0F/P3/2344PP-6PP2   (1526)
2003/04: 16⁶G, 16⁶G, 23⁶PG, 25²F,

	Starts	1st	2nd	3rd	Win & Pl
Chases	4	0	1	0	1028
Career Total	20	0	2	2	5180

Going:	Sf: 0-0 GS: 0-0 Gd: 0-2 GF: - Fm: 0-2
Distance:	2m/2m3: 0-2 2m4-2m7: 0-1 3m+: 0-1
Track:	LH: 0-2 RH: 0-0 Tight: 0-1 Gall: 0-0
Aids:	Bl: 0-0 Vi: 0-0 Tstrap: 0-1 Ckp: 0-0
Best Rating:	102 11/99 Naas 2m yld-sft Hdl

Modest form when placed over fences so far.

Sikander A Azam

11-y-o b g Arctic Lord-Shanlaragh (Gaberdine)
David M Easterby The Grand National Racing Club Limited

Placings:32140/F51106/61163/514/32003/12   (4626)
2003/04: 19¹GS, 21²G,

		Starts	1st	2nd	3rd	Win & Pl
Chases		2	1	1	0	9540
Career Total		26	7	3	4	35345
105	3/04	Asct	2m3f110y H Ch		G-S	£2170
133	5/00	Ctml	2m1f110y D(0-125) HCh		G-F	£3867
124	11/99	Ayr	2m D Ch		GD	£4055
133	10/99	MRas	2m1f110y D Ch		GD	£4435
115	12/98	Donc	2m110y E Hdl		GD	£2182
121	11/98	Aint	2m110y C Hdl		G-S	£3818
103	1/98	Muss	2m H NHF		G-S	£1175
			Total win prize-money £21704			

Going:	Sf: 0-0 GS: 1-1 Gd: 0-1 GF: - Fm: 0-0
Distance:	2m/2m3: 0-0 2m4-2m7: 1-2 3m+: 0-0
Track:	LH: 0-1 RH: 1-1 Tight: 1-1 Gall: 0-0
Aids:	Bl: 0-0 Vi: 0-0 Tstrap: 0-0 Ckp: 0-0
Best Rating:	133 5/00 Ctml 2m1f110y gd-fm Ch

One-time useful hurdler and chaser; winner of points at three miles but took a hunter chase at Ascot in 2004 over two and a half; excellent runner-up in the Foxhunters' at Aintree; stays three miles; best on a sound surface.

Silchester Dream

81   **63**

6-y-o ch m Karinga Bay-Raghill Hannah (Buckskin (FR))
C G Cox The Silchester Racing Club

Placings:004-00   (4819)

2003/04: 21⁰G, 22⁰GF,

	Starts	1st	2nd	3rd	Win & Pl
Hurdles	2	0	0	0	0
Career Total	5	0	0	0	266

Going:	Sf: 0-0 GS: 0-0 Gd: 0-1 GF: - Fm: 0-1
Distance:	2m/2m3: 0-0 2m4-2m7: 0-2 3m+: 0-0
Track:	LH: 0-1 RH: 0-1 Tight: 0-0 Gall: 0-0
Aids:	Bl: 0-0 Vi: 0-0 Tstrap: 0-0 Ckp: 0-0
Best Rating:	78 12/02 Newb 1m4f110y good NHF

Silence Reigns

10-y-o b g Saddlers' Hall (IRE)-Rensaler (USA) (Stop The Music (USA))
P F Nicholls The Madness Prevails Partnership

Placings:0/16310/0/1412P/FU6-U1B   (4626)
2003/04: 20ᵁG, 22¹G, 21⁸G,

		Starts	1st	2nd	3rd	Win & Pl
Chases		3	1	0	0	1935
Career Total		18	5	1	1	34609
118	3/04	Newb	2m6f110y H Ch		GD	£1934
126	12/01	Chep	2m3f110y D Ch		G-S	£4163
139	11/01	Chep	2m110y E Ch		SFT	£3415
127	3/00	Ludl	2m E Hdl		GD	£2880
127	11/99	Chel	2m110y A Hdl		GD	£9525
			Total win prize-money £21920			

Going:	Sf: 0-0 GS: 0-0 Gd: 1-3 GF: - Fm: 0-0
Distance:	2m/2m3: 0-0 **2m4-2m7: 1-3** 3m+: 0-0
Track:	**LH: 1-2** RH: 0-0 Tight: 0-2 **Gall: 1-1**
Aids:	**Bl: 1-2** Vi: 0-0 Tstrap: 0-0 Ckp: 0-0
Best Rating:	**143** 2/02 Sand 2m4f110y gd-sft Ch

Former smart hurdler; very useful novice chaser in 2001/2l; has since gone hunter chasing and would have made a successful debut but for unseating at the last; gained compensation in impressive fashion next time; stays two mile six; acts well on a sound surface.

Silent Action (USA)

98(89h)   **76**

12-y-o b/br g Greinton-Heather Bee (USA) (Drone (USA))
N A Smith (Miss E Grainger 21/5) V Hollier

Placings:25/00036/334/63P/03F53/0P5000060/5P5044-0554   (0677)
2003/04: 21⁰G, 21⁵GF, 25⁵GF, 23⁴GF,

	Starts	1st	2nd	3rd	Win & Pl
Chases	4	0	0	0	297
Career Total	37	0	1	6	3153

Going:	Sf: 0-0 GS: 0-0 Gd: 0-1 GF: - Fm: 0-3
Distance:	2m/2m3: 0-0 2m4-2m7: 0-2 3m+: 0-2
Track:	LH: 0-2 RH: 0-2 Tight: 0-1 Gall: 0-1
Aids:	Bl: 0-0 Vi: 0-0 Tstrap: 0-4 Ckp: 0-0
Best Rating:	96 2/96 Punc 2m soft NHF

Won two modest points spring 2003; well beaten in chases under Rules.

Silent Guest (IRE)

97   **64**

11-y-o b g Don't Forget Me-Guest House (What A Guest)
J D Frost R C Burridge

Placings:2164/53P/565/0200224/60/0-64   (4697)
2003/04: 17⁶G, 17⁴G,

	Starts	1st	2nd	3rd	Win & Pl
Hurdles	2	0	0	0	0

	Career Total	22	1	4	1	5770
87	11/96 Newc 2m	E Hdl		GF	£2274
			Total win prize-money £2274		

Going:	Sf: 0-0 GS: 0-0 Gd: 0-2 GF: - Fm: 0-0
Distance:	2m/2m3: 0-2 2m4-2m7: 0-0 3m+: 0-0
Track:	LH: 0-0 RH: 0-2 Tight: 0-0 Gall: 0-0
Aids:	Bl: 0-0 Vi: 0-0 Tstrap: 0-0 Ckp: 0-0
Best Rating:	87 11/96 Newc 2m gd-fm Hdl

Silent Gunner

6-y-o ch g Gunner B-Quiet Dawn (Lighter)
J S King T L Morshead

Placings:0-30PP   (4783)
2003/04: 17³GS, 18⁰HY, 25³PG, 21⁸PG,

	Starts	1st	2nd	3rd	Win & Pl
NH Flat	2	0	0	1	255
Hurdles	2	0	0	0	0
Career Total	5	0	0	1	255

Going:	Sf: 0-1 GS: 0-1 Gd: 0-2 GF: - Fm: 0-0
Distance:	2m/2m3: 0-2 2m4-2m7: 0-1 3m+: 0-0
Track:	LH: 0-2 RH: 0-2 Tight: 0-1 Gall: 0-0
Aids:	Bl: 0-0 Vi: 0-0 Tstrap: 0-0 Ckp: 0-0
Best Rating:	74 12/03 Hrfd 2m1f gd-sft NHF

No sign of ability in Chepstow bumper March 2003; better effort when 25/1 third at Hereford in December.

Silent Keys (SWE)

12-y-o br g Eighty Eight Keys (USA)-Habilage (Horage)
Mrs Alison Hickman (T Oscarsson 7/9) Capt T Oscarsson

Placings:1354046/4P543F421/2556321P/25433431/40341 3323/2121223P/36-0416P0P6   (4703)
2003/04: 21⁰VS, 17⁴G, 21¹GF, 18⁶S, 25⁷G, 20⁰G, 24⁵G, 26⁵G,

		Starts	1st	2nd	3rd	Win & Pl
Chases		8	1	0	0	10357
Career Total		59	8	9	12	72944
6/03	Stro	2m5f	Ch		G-F	£10014
8/01	Ovrl	2m3f	Ch		SFT	£3070
6/01	Stro	2m5f	Ch		GD	£10014
8/00	Taby	2m4f	Ch		GD	£3655
10/99	Taby	2m1f110y	Ch		SFT	£2224
10/98	Taby	2m6f110y	Ch		GD	£3060
10/97	Taby	2m1f110y	Ch		G-F	£2562
5/96	Taby	2m1f	Hdl		G-F	£1944
			Total win prize-money £36543			

Going:	Sf: 0-1 GS: 0-0 Gd: 0-5 GF: - Fm: 1-1
Distance:	2m/2m3: 0-2 **2m4-2m7: 1-3** 3m+: 0-0
Track:	LH: 0-0 **RH: 1-3** Tight: 0-3 Gall: 0-0
Aids:	Bl: 0-1 Vi: 0-0 Tstrap: 0-2 Ckp: 0-0
Best Rating:	0 4/04 Font 3m2f110y good Ch

He is a useful chaser in Norway; acts on any ground.

Silent Snipe

107(80h)   (51h)**82**

11-y-o ch g Jendali (USA)-Sasol (Bustino)
Miss L C Siddall Mrs D Ibbotson

Placings:P665P60P3010U/014P0130PP-03P023131223P10   (4615)
2003/04: 24⁶GF, 25⁰G, 25³GF, 26⁶GF, 24⁰GF, 27²GF, 25³GF, 27¹G, 25⁵G, 27¹GF, 23²F, 29²G, 27³G, 25⁵GS, 24¹GF, 26⁰G,

	Starts	1st	2nd	3rd	Win & Pl
Hurdles	1	0	0	0	0

Chases	15	3	3	4	13241		
Career Total	**38**	**6**	**3**	**6**	**23769**		
79	1/04	Muss	3m	F(0-100)HCh	G-F	£3295	
78	11/03	Sedg	3m3f	F(0-100)HCh	G-F	£2520	
80	10/03	Sedg	3m3f	F(0-100)HCh	GD	£2520	
82	10/02	Hexm	3m1f	F(0-100)HCh	G-F	£3150	
85	6/02	Hexm	3m1f	F(0-95)HCh	G-F	£2702	
80	4/02	Hexm	3m1f	E Ch	G-F	£3217	

Total win prize-money £17406

Going:	Sf: 0-0 GS: 0-1 Gd: 1-6 GF: - Fm: 2-9
Distance:	2m/2m3: 0-0 2m4-2m7: 0-0 **3m+: 3-16**
Track:	**LH: 2-10** RH: 1-5 **Tight: 3-6** Gall: 0-1
Aids:	Bl: 0-0 Vi: 0-0 Tstrap: 0-0 Ckp: 0-0
Best Rating:	85 6/02 Hexm 3m1f gd-fm Ch

Plating-class chaser; winning pointer; suited by three miles plus and fast ground; goes well at Hexham and Sedgefield.

Silent Sound (IRE)

96(104h)   (87h)95+

8-y-o b g Be My Guest (USA)-Whist Awhile (Caerleon (USA))
C L Tizzard Mrs P Tizzard

Placings:026-P0214624541PP   (3201)
2003/04: 18PG, 16PGF, 17PGS, 20¹GF, 22⁴GF, 18⁶GF, 17²GF, 22⁴GF, 16⁵GF, 16⁴GF, 19¹GF, 19⁰G, 17PS,

	Starts	1st	2nd	3rd	Win & Pl
Hurdles	8	1	2	0	4883
Chases	5	1	0	0	4173
Career Total	**16**	**2**	**3**	**0**	**9846**
95	12/03	Tntn	2m3f	E(0-110)HCh	G-F	£3835
87	8/03	Worc	2m4f	G Hdl	G-F	£2601

Total win prize-money £6436

Going:	Sf: 0-1 GS: 0-1 Gd: 0-2 GF: - Fm: 2-9
Distance:	2m/2m3: 1-10 2m4-2m7: 1-3 3m+: 0-0
Track:	LH: 1-8 RH: 1-4 **Tight: 1-9** Gall: 0-1
Aids:	Bl: 0-0 Vi: 0-1 Tstrap: 0-0 **Ckp: 1-8**
Best Rating:	95 12/03 Tntn 2m3f gd-fm Ch

Plating-class hurdler/chaser; seems to have benefitted since having cheekpieces fitted and took advantage of a drop in grade and step up in distance when landing 2m 4f seller at Worcester August 2003; acts on fast ground; yet to prove he stays 2m 6f.

Silenttouchoftime (IRE)

6-y-o b m Hymns On High-Ballinaboy Queen (IRE) (Black Minstrel)
C J Down J Selby

Placings:PP   (3841)
2003/04: 24PS, 19PGS,

	Starts	1st	2nd	3rd	Win & Pl
Hurdles	2	0	0	0	
Career Total	**2**	**0**	**0**	**0**	

Going:	Sf: 0-1 GS: 0-1 Gd: 0-0 GF: - Fm: 0-0
Distance:	2m/2m3: 0-0 2m4-2m7: 0-1 3m+: 0-1
Track:	LH: 0-0 RH: 0-2 Tight: 0-1 Gall: 0-0
Aids:	Bl: 0-0 Vi: 0-0 Tstrap: 0-0 Ckp: 0-0

Silistra

83   49

5-y-o gr g Sadler's Wells (USA)-Dundel (IRE) (Machiavellian (USA))

Mrs L C Jewell Mrs P S Donkin

Placings:0P   (4664)
2003/04: 20⁰GF, 19PGS,

	Starts	1st	2nd	3rd	Win & Pl
Hurdles	2	0	0	0	
Career Total	**2**	**0**	**0**	**0**	

Going:	Sf: 0-0 GS: 0-1 Gd: 0-0 GF: - Fm: 0-1
Distance:	2m/2m3: 0-0 2m4-2m7: 0-2 3m+: 0-0
Track:	LH: 0-1 RH: 0-1 Tight: 0-2 Gall: 0-0
Aids:	Bl: 0-0 Vi: 0-1 Tstrap: 0-0 Ckp: 0-1
Best Rating:	51 3/04 Font 2m4f gd-fm Hdl

Silk St John

10-y-o b g Damister (USA)-Silk St James (Pas De Seul)
W M Brisbourne C R S Partners

Placings:0/2/0-P   (0528)
2003/04: 16PGF,

	Starts	1st	2nd	3rd	Win & Pl
Hurdles	1	0	0	0	
Career Total	**4**	**0**	**1**	**0**	**694**

Going:	Sf: 0-0 GS: 0-0 Gd: 0-0 GF: - Fm: 0-1
Distance:	2m/2m3: 0-1 2m4-2m7: 0-0 3m+: 0-0
Track:	LH: 0-1 RH: 0-0 Tight: 0-0 Gall: 0-0
Aids:	Bl: 0-0 Vi: 0-0 Tstrap: 0-0 Ckp: 0-0
Best Rating:	91 11/01 Hntg 2m110y good Hdl

Silk Trader

110(105c)   (113+c)113

9-y-o b g Nomadic Way (USA)-Money Run (Deep Run)
J Mackie The Festival Dream Partnership

Placings:40/61U3/31400403163110/504414-60S12F3120
                                                   (4813)
2003/04: 16⁶G, 16⁰G, 16⁵GF, 19¹G, 19²G, 19FG, 16³GS, 16¹G, 18²G, 16⁶G,

	Starts	1st	2nd	3rd	Win & Pl
Hurdles	7	1	1	1	8544
Chases	3	1	1	0	5851
Career Total	**36**	**8**	**2**	**5**	**40145**
113	3/04	Sand	2m110y	E(0-115)HHdl	GD	£5356
	12/03	Donc	2m3f	E Ch	GD	£4156
113	3/03	Sand	2m110y	E(0-115)HHdl	HVY	£4732
113	3/03	Towc	2m	D(0-125)HHdl	G-S	£5174
104	3/02	Sand	2m110y	D(0-115)HHdl	G-S	£4231
108	12/01	Leic	2m	F(0-100)HHdl	SFT	£3146
113	5/01	Wwck	2m3f	E(0-115)HHdl	GD	£2660
100	2/01	Uttx	2m	D Hdl	SFT	£2849

Total win prize-money £32306

Going:	Sf: 0-0 GS: 0-1 Gd: 2-8 GF: - Fm: 0-1
Distance:	**2m/2m3: 2-10** 2m4-2m7: 0-0 3m+: 0-0
Track:	LH: 1-6 RH: 1-4 Tight: 0-3 Gall: 0-0
Aids:	Bl: 0-0 Vi: 0-0 Tstrap: 0-0 Ckp: 0-0
Best Rating:	113 3/04 Kels 2m2f good Hdl

Modest handicap hurdler; has won over two miles three, but is probably better over two miles; acts on good to soft ground; has won the amateur riders' hurdle on Grand Military Gold Cup day at Sandown three times; made mistakes over fences.

Silken Pearls

97+

8-y-o b m Leading Counsel (USA)-River Pearl (Oats)

L Lungo P E Truscott

Placings:4/110-P   (4478)
2003/04: 20PHY,

	Starts	1st	2nd	3rd	Win & Pl
Hurdles	1	0	0	0	
Career Total	**5**	**2**	**0**	**0**	**5784**
97	11/02	Kels	2m6f110yD Hdl		SFT	£4026
104	11/02	Hexm	2m110y	H NHF	HVY	£1757

Total win prize-money £5784

Going:	Sf: 0-1 GS: 0-0 Gd: 0-0 GF: - Fm: 0-0
Distance:	2m/2m3: 0-0 2m4-2m7: 0-1 3m+: 0-0
Track:	LH: 0-0 RH: 0-1 Tight: 0-0 Gall: 0-0
Aids:	Bl: 0-0 Vi: 0-0 Tstrap: 0-0 Ckp: 0-0
Best Rating:	104 11/02 Hexm 2m110y heavy NHF

Winner of a bumper and a novices' hurdle at Kelso at Kelso in November 2002, but has run poorly since.

Silken Thomas

73   39

9-y-o b g King's Ride-Padykin (Bustino)
N J Hawke N J Hawke

Placings:02/3030/435PU40/0F   (3083)
2003/04: 21⁰G, 21FGS,

	Starts	1st	2nd	3rd	Win & Pl
Chases	2	0	0	0	
Career Total	**15**	**0**	**1**	**3**	**1838**

Going:	Sf: 0-0 GS: 0-1 Gd: 0-1 GF: - Fm: 0-0
Distance:	2m/2m3: 0-0 2m4-2m7: 0-2 3m+: 0-0
Track:	LH: 0-1 RH: 0-1 Tight: 0-1 Gall: 0-0
Aids:	Bl: 0-0 Vi: 0-0 Tstrap: 0-0 Ckp: 0-0
Best Rating:	103 4/00 NAbb 2m1f heavy NHF

Silkie Pekin

73f   48f

5-y-o gr m Riverwise (USA)-Came Cottage (Nearly A Hand)
N R Mitchell Mrs E Mitchell

Placings:0   (4550)
2003/04: 16⁰GS,

	Starts	1st	2nd	3rd	Win & Pl
NH Flat	1	0	0	0	
Career Total	**1**	**0**	**0**	**0**	

Going:	Sf: 0-0 GS: 0-1 Gd: 0-0 GF: - Fm: 0-0
Distance:	2m/2m3: 0-1 2m4-2m7: 0-0 3m+: 0-0
Track:	LH: 0-0 RH: 0-1 Tight: 0-0 Gall: 0-0
Aids:	Bl: 0-0 Vi: 0-0 Tstrap: 0-0 Ckp: 0-0
Best Rating:	48 3/04 Winc 2m gd-sft NHF

Silkwood Top (IRE)

92f   87+f

5-y-o b g Norwich-Brave Mum (Brave Invader (USA))
V R A Dartnall O C R Wynne & Mrs S J Wynne

Placings:3   (4738)
2003/04: 17³G,

	Starts	1st	2nd	3rd	Win & Pl
NH Flat	1	0	0	1	425
Career Total	**1**	**0**	**0**	**1**	**425**

Going:	Sf: 0-0 GS: 0-0 Gd: 0-1 GF: - Fm: 0-0
Distance:	2m/2m3: 0-1 2m4-2m7: 0-0 3m+: 0-0
Track:	LH: 0-1 RH: 0-0 Tight: 0-1 Gall: 0-0

Aids: Bl: 0-0 Vi: 0-0 Tstrap: 0-0 Ckp: 0-0
Best Rating: 87 4/04 NAbb 2m1f   good NHF

Silly Boy

9-y-o ch g Crested Lark-Sutton Lass (Politico (USA))
R C Harper R C Harper

Placings:PF-P   (0059)
2003/04: 19PGS,

	Starts	1st	2nd	3rd	Win & Pl
Chases	1	0	0	0	
Career Total	3	0	0	0	

Going: Sf: 0-0 GS: 0-1 Gd: 0-0 GF: - Fm: 0-0
Distance: 2m/2m3: 0-1 2m4-2m7: 0-0 3m+: 0-0
Track: LH: 0-0 RH: 0-0 Tight: 0-0 Gall: 0-0
Aids: Bl: 0-0 Vi: 0-0 Tstrap: 0-0 Ckp: 0-0

Winning ex-pointer with a poor completion record, but no form under Rules.

Silly Sarah

27f

4-y-o b f Sovereign Water (FR)-Fortria's Delight (Idiots Delight)
Mrs A M Thorpe J H Lee

Placings:0   (2101)
2003/04: 12PGF,

	Starts	1st	2nd	3rd	Win & Pl
NH Flat	1	0	0	0	
Career Total	1	0	0	0	

Going: Sf: 0-0 GS: 0-0 Gd: 0-0 GF: - Fm: 0-1
Distance: 2m/2m3: 0-0 2m4-2m7: 0-0 3m+: 0-0
Track: LH: 0-1 RH: 0-0 Tight: 0-0 Gall: 0-0
Aids: Bl: 0-0 Vi: 0-0 Tstrap: 0-0 Ckp: 0-0

Silogue (IRE)

101   **74**

7-y-o b/br g Distinctly North (USA)-African Bloom (African Sky)
O Brennan O Brennan

Placings:5-0600034330   (1279)
2003/04: 16OGF, 17SG, 17OGF, 17OG, 20OG, 16³G, 17⁴GF, 17³GF, 17³GF, 17OGF,

	Starts	1st	2nd	3rd	Win & Pl
Hurdles	10	0	0	3	1145
Career Total	11	0	0	3	1145

Going: Sf: 0-0 GS: 0-0 Gd: 0-4 GF: 0-6
Distance: 2m/2m3: 0-9 2m4-2m7: 0-1 3m+: 0-0
Track: LH: 0-4 RH: 0-6 Tight: 0-7 Gall: 0-1
Aids: Bl: 0-0 Vi: 0-2 Tstrap: 0-0 Ckp: 0-0
Best Rating: 76 7/03 MRas 2m1f110y good Hdl

Plating-class hurdler; still a maiden; acts on a sound surface.

Silva Venture (IRE)

84   **73**

7-y-o b m Mandalus-Miss The Post (Bustino)
L Lungo Elite Racing Club

Placings:0/0004-00   (0644)
2003/04: 16⁴G, 16OG, 20OGF,

	Starts	1st	2nd	3rd	Win & Pl
Hurdles	3	0	0	0	259
Career Total	7	0	0	0	259

Going: Sf: 0-0 GS: 0-0 Gd: 0-2 GF: - Fm: 0-1
Distance: 2m/2m3: 0-2 2m4-2m7: 0-1 3m+: 0-0
Track: LH: 0-2 RH: 0-1 Tight: 0-0 Gall: 0-0
Aids: Bl: 0-0 Vi: 0-0 Tstrap: 0-0 Ckp: 0-0
Best Rating: 73 4/03 Hexm 2m110y good Hdl

Silver Birch (IRE)

115(106h)   (109 h)**132**

7-y-o b g Clearly Bust-All Gone (Giolla Mear)
P F Nicholls D J Nichols

Placings:4113-3124P   (4865)
2003/04: 25³S, 26¹S, 25²G, 32⁴G, 25PS,

	Starts	1st	2nd	3rd	Win & Pl
Chases	5	1	1	1	8779
Career Total	9	3	1	2	19146
107	1/04	Chep	3m2f110yF	Ch	SFT	£3906
100	1/03	Plum	3m1f110yD	Hdl	HVY	£5473
109	11/02	Chep	2m4f	D Hdl	SFT	£4231

Total win prize-money £13612

Going: Sf: 1-3 GS: 0-0 Gd: 0-2 GF: - Fm: 0-0
Distance: 2m/2m3: 0-0 2m4-2m7: 0-0 3m+: 1-5
Track: LH: 1-3 RH: 0-2 Tight: 0-0 Gall: 0-1
Aids: Bl: 0-0 Vi: 0-0 Tstrap: 0-0 Ckp: 0-0
Best Rating: 132 2/04 Winc 3m1f110y good Ch

Fair novice chaser; Irish point winner; suited by two and a half to three miles plus and a soft surface; old fashioned staying type who should progress.

Silver Buzzard (USA)

112   **108**

5-y-o b/br g Silver Hawk (USA)-Stellarina (USA) (Pleasant Colony (USA))
Jonjo O'Neill International Plywood Plc

Placings:521446-244   (1306)
2003/04: 17²GS, 16⁴GS, 20⁴GF,

	Starts	1st	2nd	3rd	Win & Pl
Hurdles	3	0	1	0	2662
Career Total	9	1	2	0	8978
91	11/02	Hayd	2m	D Hdl	GD	£4111

Total win prize-money £4111

Going: Sf: 0-1 GS: 0-1 Gd: 0-0 GF: - Fm: 0-1
Distance: 2m/2m3: 0-2 2m4-2m7: 0-1 3m+: 0-0
Track: LH: 0-3 RH: 0-0 Tight: 0-2 Gall: 0-0
Aids: Bl: 0-0 Vi: 0-0 Tstrap: 0-0 Ckp: 0-0
Best Rating: 108 5/03 Aint 2m110y gd-sft Hdl

Fair hurdler, suited by a soft surface and stays 2m 6f, although is effective over shorter.

Silver Charmer

108   **117+**

5-y-o b m Charmer-Sea Dart (Air Trooper)
H S Howe John Bull

Placings:F34041F0-0660U1   (4842)
2003/04: 16OGS, 19²GF, 16⁶GS, 22²G, 16UGF, 21¹G,

	Starts	1st	2nd	3rd	Win & Pl
Hurdles	6	1	0	0	14967

Career Total | 14 | 2 | 0 | 1 | 22934
117 | 4/04 | Chel | 2m5f110yA | HHdl | | GD | £14500
111 | 3/03 | Newb | 2m3f | | D(0-115) | HHdl | | GD | £4823

Total win prize-money £19323

Going: Sf: 0-0 GS: 0-1 Gd: 1-2 GF: - Fm: 0-3
Distance: 2m/2m3: 0-4 2m4-2m7: 1-2 3m+: 0-0
Track: LH: 1-3 RH: 0-3 Tight: 0-1 Gall: 1-2
Aids: Bl: 0-0 Vi: 0-0 Tstrap: 0-0 Ckp: 0-0
Best Rating: 117 4/04 Chel 2m5f110y good Hdl

Fair hurdler; stays two and a half miles.seemingly best on a sound surface.

Silver Charter (USA)

89(99h)   (87h)**49**

5-y-o b g Silver Hawk (USA)-Pride Of Darby (USA) (Danzig (USA))
H S Howe M J Moore

Placings:26040-00UF0   (4523)
2003/04: 20OGF, 19OGS, 17UGS, 20FG, 17OGS,

	Starts	1st	2nd	3rd	Win & Pl
Hurdles	2	0	0	0	0
Chases	3	0	0	0	0
Career Total	10	0	1	0	1661

Going: Sf: 0-0 GS: 0-3 Gd: 0-1 GF: - Fm: 0-1
Distance: 2m/2m3: 0-3 2m4-2m7: 0-1 3m+: 0-0
Track: LH: 0-1 RH: 0-4 Tight: 0-2 Gall: 0-0
Aids: Bl: 0-0 Vi: 0-0 Tstrap: 0-0 Ckp: 0-0
Best Rating: 89 3/03 Newb 2m3f   good Hdl

Moderate hurdler; effective on good to soft.

Silver Chevalier (IRE)

99   **80**

6-y-o gr g Petong-Princess Eurolink (Be My Guest (USA))
D Burchell Mrs Ruth Burchell

Placings:06P5/0PP0P-00   (0880)
2003/04: 17OGF, 16OGF,

	Starts	1st	2nd	3rd	Win & Pl
Hurdles	2	0	0	0	
Career Total	11	0	0	0	0

Going: Sf: 0-0 GS: 0-0 Gd: 0-0 GF: - Fm: 0-2
Distance: 2m/2m3: 0-2 2m4-2m7: 0-0 3m+: 0-0
Track: LH: 0-2 RH: 0-0 Tight: 0-1 Gall: 0-0
Aids: Bl: 0-0 Vi: 0-2 Tstrap: 0-0 Ckp: 0-0
Best Rating: 80 4/02 Ludl 2m   gd-fm Hdl

Silver Chieftan (IRE)

90   **86**

6-y-o gr g Be My Native (USA)-Mystery Rose (Roselier (FR))
P J Hobbs P A Newey

Placings:0-506F   (4950)
2003/04: 17⁵G, 20OS, 19⁶S, 20FGS,

	Starts	1st	2nd	3rd	Win & Pl
Hurdles	4	0	0	0	0
Career Total	5	0	0	0	0

Going: Sf: 0-2 GS: 0-1 Gd: 0-1 GF: - Fm: 0-0
Distance: 2m/2m3: 0-2 2m4-2m7: 0-2 3m+: 0-0
Track: LH: 0-1 RH: 0-3 Tight: 0-1 Gall: 0-0

Aids: Bl: 0-0 Vi: 0-0 Tstrap: 0-0 Ckp: 0-0
Best Rating: 86   12/03   Hayd   2m4f   soft   Hdl

Silver Coin (IRE)
105   105+
4-y-o gr g Night Shift (USA)-Eurythmic (Pharly (FR))
T D Easterby   C H Stevens

Placings:002013   (4310)
2003/04: 16⁰G, 16⁹GS, 16²GS, 20⁰G, 16¹F, 16³GF,

	Starts	1st	2nd	3rd	Win & Pl
Hurdles	6	1	1	1	4762
Career Total	6	1	1	1	4762
96	2/04	Muss	2m	F Hdl	FRM £3143
				Total win prize-money	£3143

Going: Sf: 0-0 GS: 0-2 Gd: 0-2 GF: - Fm: 1-2
Distance: 2m/2m3: 1-5 2m4-2m7: 0-1 3m+: 0-0
Track: LH: 0-5 RH: 1-1 Tight: 0-0 Gall: 0-0
Aids: Bl: 0-0 Vi: 0-0 Tstrap: 0-0 Ckp: 0-0
Best Rating: 105 3/04 Ayr 2m   gd-fm   Hdl

Fair novice hurdler who won over two miles at Musselburgh in February; probably best on fast ground.

Silver Dagger
82   90
6-y-o gr g Dr Devious (IRE)-La Belle Affair (USA) (Black Tie Affair)
Jonjo O'Neill (C Roche 3/5) John P McManus

Placings:005P60-0F00P   (4785)
2003/04: 16⁰Y, 20⁵S, 17⁰GF, 16⁹G, 21⁰G,

	Starts	1st	2nd	3rd	Win & Pl
Hurdles	5	0	0	0	
Career Total	11	0	0	0	

Going: Sf: 0-1 GS: 0-0 Gd: 0-2 GF: - Fm: 0-1
Distance: 2m/2m3: 0-3 2m4-2m7: 0-0 3m+: 0-0
Track: LH: 0-2 RH: 0-3 Tight: 0-2 Gall: 0-0
Aids: Bl: 0-0 Vi: 0-0 Tstrap: 0-2 Ckp: 0-0
Best Rating: 90 2/03 Naas 2m   yield   Hdl

Plating-class performer; one of stables lesser lights; best at two miles; effective on soft ground.

Silver Dancer (IRE)
71(79h)   (45h)56
8-y-o gr g Roselier (FR)-Fancy Step (Step Together (USA))
M G Rimell   Mark Rimell

Placings:050U-U6PU4   (4821)
2003/04: 16⁰U, 22⁶GS, 24⁰GS, 16⁰S, 19⁴GF,

	Starts	1st	2nd	3rd	Win & Pl
Chases	5	0	0	0	338
Career Total	9	0	0	0	338

Going: Sf: 0-2 GS: 0-2 Gd: 0-0 GF: - Fm: 0-1
Distance: 2m/2m3: 0-2 2m4-2m7: 0-2 3m+: 0-1
Track: LH: 0-2 RH: 0-2 Tight: 0-2 Gall: 0-0
Aids: Bl: 0-2 Vi: 0-0 Tstrap: 0-0 Ckp: 0-0
Best Rating: 57 2/04 Font 2m6f   gd-sft   Ch

Very moderate form so far.

Silver Ghost
92f   86f
5-y-o gr g Alderbrook-Belmore Cloud (Baron Blakeney)

M Bradstock The Silver Cloud Partnership

Placings:00   (4447)
2003/04: 16⁹GS, 16⁹S,

	Starts	1st	2nd	3rd	Win & Pl
NH Flat	2	0	0	0	
Career Total	2	0	0	0	

Going: Sf: 0-1 GS: 0-1 Gd: 0-0 GF: - Fm: 0-0
Distance: 2m/2m3: 0-2 2m4-2m7: 0-0 3m+: 0-0
Track: LH: 0-1 RH: 0-1 Tight: 0-0 Gall: 0-0
Aids: Bl: 0-0 Vi: 0-0 Tstrap: 0-0 Ckp: 0-0
Best Rating: 86 2/04 Sand 2m110y   gd-sft NHF

Silver Gift
101   (0c)97
7-y-o b m Rakaposhi King-Kellsboro Kate (Paddy's Stream)
G Fierro   G Fierro

Placings:0040/PP360P3/0FP52211U141PP04100-0U23644   (2309)
2003/04: 27⁰GF, 23ᵁGF, 26²GF, 24³F, 24⁶G, 24⁴GF, 26⁴GS,

	Starts	1st	2nd	3rd	Win & Pl
Hurdles	6	0	1	1	1248
Chases	1	0	0	0	
Career Total	37	5	3	3	18895
97	4/03	Hrfd	3m2f	E(0-105)HHdl	G-F £3568
97	10/02	Hntg	3m2f	E(0-110)HHdl	G-F £2884
94	9/02	Worc	3m	F(0-100)HHdl	GD £2828
84	8/02	Worc	3m	F(0-95)HHdl	GD £2653
81	8/02	Sedg	3m3f110yE(0-110)HHdl	GD £2891
				Total win prize-money	£14825

Going: Sf: 0-0 GS: 0-1 Gd: 0-1 GF: - Fm: 0-5
Distance: 2m/2m3: 0-0 2m4-2m7: 0-0 3m+: 0-7
Track: LH: 0-4 RH: 0-3 Tight: 0-2 Gall: 0-2
Aids: Bl: 0-0 Vi: 0-0 Tstrap: 0-0 Ckp: 0-0
Best Rating: 97 10/03 Hntg 3m2f   gd-fm   Hdl

Modest staying handicap hurdler; suited by extreme distances; acts on ground good and faster.

Silver Grey Annie
7-y-o gr m Arzanni-Celtic Berry (Celtic Cone)
F P Murtagh   Norman Furness

Placings:0/UP   (0781)
2003/04: 20ᵁGF, 20⁰G,

	Starts	1st	2nd	3rd	Win & Pl
Hurdles	2	0	0	0	
Career Total	3	0	0	0	

Going: Sf: 0-0 GS: 0-0 Gd: 0-1 GF: - Fm: 0-0
Distance: 2m/2m3: 0-0 2m4-2m7: 0-2 3m+: 0-0
Track: LH: 0-1 RH: 0-1 Tight: 0-0 Gall: 0-0
Aids: Bl: 0-0 Vi: 0-0 Tstrap: 0-0 Ckp: 0-0

Silver Inngot (IRE)
94   94
5-y-o gr g Gothland (FR)-Hotel Saltees (IRE) (Over The River (FR))
R H Alner   J Browne,Mrs C Robertson,Mrs E Woodhouse

Placings:5000   (4895)
2003/04: 19⁵G, 16⁰GS, 18⁰GS, 22⁰G,

	Starts	1st	2nd	3rd	Win & Pl
Hurdles	4	0	0	0	0
Career Total	4	0	0	0	0

Going: Sf: 0-0 GS: 0-1 Gd: 0-1 GF: - Fm: 0-0

Going: Sf: 0-0 GS: 0-2 Gd: 0-2 GF: - Fm: 0-0
Distance: 2m/2m3: 0-3 2m4-2m7: 0-1 3m+: 0-0
Track: LH: 0-1 RH: 0-3 Tight: 0-1 Gall: 0-0
Aids: Bl: 0-0 Vi: 0-0 Tstrap: 0-0 Ckp: 0-0
Best Rating: 93 12/03 Extr 2m3f   good   Hdl

Silver Jack (IRE)
96   80
6-y-o gr g Roselier (FR)-Consharon (IRE) (Strong Gale)
M Todhunter   B Batey

Placings:6-546   (3209)
2003/04: 20⁵HY, 24⁴S, 25⁶GS,

	Starts	1st	2nd	3rd	Win & Pl
Hurdles	3	0	0	0	0
Career Total	4	0	0	0	0

Going: Sf: 0-2 GS: 0-1 Gd: 0-0 GF: - Fm: 0-0
Distance: 2m/2m3: 0-0 2m4-2m7: 0-1 3m+: 0-0
Track: LH: 0-2 RH: 0-1 Tight: 0-0 Gall: 0-0
Aids: Bl: 0-0 Vi: 0-0 Tstrap: 0-0 Ckp: 0-0
Best Rating: 96 2/03 Ayr 2m   gd-sft NHF

Novice hurdler; stays well; will make a chaser in time.

Silver Knight
106(113h)   (119h)130+
6-y-o gr g Simply Great (FR)-Hysteria (Prince Bee)
T D Easterby   C H Stevens

Placings:16/0122163303-212133223   (4865)
2003/04: 24²GF, 25¹G, 20²G, 25¹G, 24³GS, 25³S, 25²GS, 25²G, 25³S,

	Starts	1st	2nd	3rd	Win & Pl
Chases	9	2	4	3	28171
Career Total	21	5	6	6	44848
130	12/03	Weth	3m1f	D Ch	GD £6062
130	11/03	Weth	3m1f	D Ch	GD £4882
112	1/03	Catt	3m1f110yE Hdl	GD £3590
107	11/02	Hexm	2m4f110yE Hdl	HVY £3003
109	3/02	Donc	2m110y H NHF	G-S £2186
				Total win prize-money	£19724

Going: Sf: 0-2 GS: 0-2 Gd: 2-4 GF: - Fm: 0-1
Distance: 2m/2m3: 0-0 2m4-2m7: 0-1 3m+: 2-8
Track: LH: 2-7 RH: 0-2 Tight: 0-2 Gall: 0-0
Aids: Bl: 0-0 Vi: 0-0 Tstrap: 0-0 Ckp: 0-0
Best Rating: 130 12/03 Weth 3m1f   good   Ch

Useful staying hurdler and novice chaser; twice successful in weak events over 3m 1f at Wetherby at the end of 2003; game; acts on good ground; may have stamina limitations on soft; has been tried in blinkers.

Silver Lake (IRE)
10-y-o gr g Roselier (FR)-Over The Pond (IRE) (Over The River (FR))
S Breen (F R Jackson 17/2) F R Jackson

Placings:113/PP   (4172)
2003/04: 25⁰GS, 24⁰G,

	Starts	1st	2nd	3rd	Win & Pl
Chases	2	0	0	0	
Career Total	5	2	0	1	5779
108	11/00	Plum	2m5f	E Hdl	HVY £2453
114	11/00	Winc	2m	E Hdl	G-S £2695
				Total win prize-money	£5149

Going: Sf: 0-0 GS: 0-1 Gd: 0-1 GF: - Fm: 0-0

Distance: 2m/2m3: 0-0 2m4-2m7: 0-0 3m+: 0-2
Track: LH: 0-1 RH: 0-1 Tight: 0-1 Gall: 0-1
Aids: Bl: 0-0 Vi: 0-0 Tstrap: 0-0 Ckp: 0-0
Best Rating: 114 11/00 Winc 2m   gd-sft Hdl

Silver Louie (IRE)
64   33

4-y-o gr f Titus Livius (FR)-Shakamiyn (Nishapour (FR))
G B Balding Mr & Mrs K Finch

Placings:0   (2253)
2003/04: 17⁰GF,

	Starts	1st	2nd	3rd	Win & Pl
Hurdles	1	0	0	0	
Career Total	1	0	0	0	

Going: Sf: 0-0 GS: 0-0 Gd: 0-0 GF: 0-0 Fm: 0-1
Distance: 2m/2m3: 0-1 2m4-2m7: 0-0 3m+: 0-0
Track: LH: 0-0 RH: 0-1 Tight: 0-0 Gall: 0-0
Aids: Bl: 0-0 Vi: 0-0 Tstrap: 0-0 Ckp: 0-0
Best Rating: 33 11/03 Hrfd 2m1f   gd-fm Hdl

Silver Man
82   46

10-y-o gr g Silver Owl-What An Experiance (Chance Meeting)
D C Turner Mrs M E Turner

Placings:P4-0P   (0712)
2003/04: 21⁰GF, 26ᴾGF,

	Starts	1st	2nd	3rd	Win & Pl
Chases	2	0	0	0	
Career Total	4	0	0	0	305

Going: Sf: 0-0 GS: 0-0 Gd: 0-0 GF: 0-0 Fm: 0-2
Distance: 2m/2m3: 0-0 2m4-2m7: 0-1 3m+: 0-1
Track: LH: 0-2 RH: 0-0 Tight: 0-2 Gall: 0-0
Aids: Bl: 0-0 Vi: 0-0 Tstrap: 0-0 Ckp: 0-2
Best Rating: 46 6/03 NAbb 2m5f110y   gd-fm Ch

Silver Prophet (IRE)
104   100

5-y-o gr g Idris (IRE)-Silver Heart (Yankee Gold)
M R Bosley Mrs Jean M O'Connor

Placings:0410   (4691)
2003/04: 16⁵GS, 17⁴GS, 16¹G, 17⁰G,

	Starts	1st	2nd	3rd	Win & Pl
Hurdles	4	1	0	0	3994
Career Total	4	1	0	0	3994
96	3/04 Hntg	2m110y E Hdl		GD	£3668
		Total win prize-money £3668			

Going: Sf: 0-1 GS: 0-1 Gd: 1-2 GF: - Fm: 0-0
Distance: 2m/2m3: 1-4 2m4-2m7: 0-0 3m+: 0-0
Track: LH: 0-0 RH: 1-4 Tight: 0-1 Gall: 1-1
Aids: Bl: 0-0 Vi: 0-0 Tstrap: 1-2 Ckp: 0-0
Best Rating: 100 1/04 Asct 2m110y   soft Hdl

Moderate hurdle winner; acts on good/soft;

Silver Samuel (NZ)

(91h)   (99+h)
7-y-o gr g Hula Town (NZ)-Offrande (NZ) (Decies)
S A Brookshaw Redcroft Racing

Placings:0/4P01450PP   (4713)
2003/04: 24⁴GF, 24ᴾGS, 20⁹GS, 20¹GS, 20⁴HY, 21⁵G, 20⁰G, 25ᴾS, 24ᴾG,

	Starts	1st	2nd	3rd	Win & Pl
Hurdles	5	1	0	0	4212
Chases	4	0	0	0	263
Career Total	10	1	0	0	4475
99	12/03 Hayd	2m4f	D Hdl	G-S	£3825
		Total win prize-money £3825			

Going: Sf: 0-2 GS: 1-3 Gd: 0-3 GF: - Fm: 0-1
Distance: 2m/2m3: 0-0 **2m4-2m7: 1-5** 3m+: 0-4
Track: **LH: 1-7** RH: 0-2 Tight: 0-0 Gall: 0-0
Aids: Bl: 0-0 Vi: 0-0 Tstrap: 0-0 Ckp: 0-1
Best Rating: 106 1/04 Hayd 2m4f   heavy Hdl

Winning pointer; won weak novices' hurdle in December; stays 2m 4f; suited by good ground.

Silver Sedge (IRE)
66

5-y-o br g Aristocracy-Pollyfaster (Polyfoto)
J Howard Johnson W M G Black

Placings:F   (4727)
2003/04: 17ᶠG,

	Starts	1st	2nd	3rd	Win & Pl
Hurdles	1	0	0	0	
Career Total	1	0	0	0	

Going: Sf: 0-0 GS: 0-0 Gd: 0 GF: - Fm: 0-0
Distance: 2m/2m3: 0-1 2m4-2m7: 0-0 3m+: 0-0
Track: LH: 0-0 RH: 0-1 Tight: 0-0 Gall: 0-0
Aids: Bl: 0-0 Vi: 0-0 Tstrap: 0-0 Ckp: 0-0
Best Rating: 66 4/04 Carl 2m1f   good Hdl

Silver Sleeve (IRE)
89(97h)   (65h)90

12-y-o b g Taufan (USA)-Sable Coated (Caerleon (USA))
Mrs H M Bridges Mrs H M Bridges

Placings:F0002035/4124430/P/0060/6UP40423040-P265045060P   (4919)
2003/04: 17⁰GS, 20²G, 21⁶GF, 17⁵GS, 19⁰HY, 16⁴S, 19⁵S, 17⁰G, 20⁶G, 19⁰G, 20ᴾGS,

	Starts	1st	2nd	3rd	Win & Pl
Hurdles	9	0	1	0	525
Chases	2	0	0	0	0
Career Total	42	1	4	3	5809
84	7/96 Strf	2m3f	E(0-100)HHdl	G-F	£2178
		Total win prize-money £2178			

Going: Sf: 0-3 GS: 0-3 Gd: 0-4 GF: - Fm: 0-1
Distance: 2m/2m3: 0-5 2m4-2m7: 0-6 3m+: 0-0
Track: LH: 0-5 RH: 0-4 Tight: 0-4 Gall: 0-0
Aids: Bl: 0-0 Vi: 0-0 Tstrap: 0-0 Ckp: 0-10
Best Rating: 90 3/02 Extr 2m3f110y   good Ch

Plating-class hurdler, a hard ride.

Silver Squirrel

4-y-o b f Silver Wizard (USA)-Farah (Lead On Time (USA))
J R Turner J R Turner

Placings:00P   (4388)
2003/04: 13⁰GS, 16⁰HY, 21ᴾG,

	Starts	1st	2nd	3rd	Win & Pl
NH Flat	2	0	0	0	0
Hurdles	1	0	0	0	0
Career Total	3	0	0	0	0

Silver Streak (IRE)
104   97

10-y-o gr g Roselier (FR)-Vulcash (IRE) (Callernish)
N J Gifford Mrs Timothy Pilkington

Placings:2/422013/33P5/52411P2/P-U50   (4834)
2003/04: 24ᵁGF, 24⁵S, 26⁰GF,

	Starts	1st	2nd	3rd	Win & Pl
Chases	3	0	0	0	
Career Total	22	3	5	3	32808
132	12/01 Chel	3m1f110yB Ch		GD	£12018
120	11/00 Weth	3m1f		GD	£4069
128	3/00 Sand	2m4f110yD Hdl		GD	£4426
		Total win prize-money £20515			

Going: Sf: 0-1 GS: 0-0 Gd: 0-0 GF: - Fm: 0-2
Distance: 2m/2m3: 0-0 2m4-2m7: 0-3 3m+: 0-3
Track: LH: 0-2 RH: 0-1 Tight: 0-0 Gall: 0-2
Aids: Bl: 0-0 Vi: 0-0 Tstrap: 0-0 Ckp: 0-0
Best Rating: 132 12/01 Chel 3m1f110y   good Ch

Fair chaser; lightly raced; stays three miles plus; best on good ground.

Silvertown
130

9-y-o b g Danehill (USA)-Docklands (USA) (Theatrical)
L Lungo R J Gilbert & Sw Transport (swindon) Ltd

Placings:5106P/030111-PP   (3373)
2003/04: 17⁰GF, 20ᴾS,

	Starts	1st	2nd	3rd	Win & Pl
Hurdles	2	0	0	0	
Career Total	13	4	0	1	19357
130	4/03 Carl	2m1f	D(0-120)HHdl	G-F	£4599
116	4/03 Hrfd	2m1f	D(0-115)HHdl	G-F	£7454
120	3/03 Carl	2m4f	D(0-110)HHdl	GD	£3864
105	5/01 Newc	2m	E Hdl	G-F	£2968
		Total win prize-money £18885			

Going: Sf: 0-1 GS: 0-0 Gd: 0-0 GF: - Fm: 0-0
Distance: 2m/2m3: 0-1 2m4-2m7: 0-1 3m+: 0-0
Track: LH: 0-1 RH: 0-0 Tight: 0-1 Gall: 0-0
Aids: Bl: 0-0 Vi: 0-0 Tstrap: 0-0 Ckp: 0-0
Best Rating: 130 4/03 Carl 2m1f   gd-fm Hdl

Useful hurdler; in fine form in the spring of 2003, completing a hat-trick in handicap hurdles and winning another two on the Flat; stays two and a half miles and suited by fast ground; likes to dominate from the front; has a good record at Carlisle.

Simber Hill (IRE)

10-y-o ch g Phardante (FR)-Princess Wager (Pollerton)
P J Hobbs C de P Berry, C Moore, P Rowe

Placings:105/25213/3F333545/31132215F3-3P24545   (4858)
2003/04: 24³GS, 24ᴾG, 24²GS, 23⁴GF, 24⁵G, 24⁴G, 24⁵GF,

	Starts	1st	2nd	3rd	Win & Pl
Chases	7	0	1	1	4256
Career Total	33	5	5	9	36421
122	10/02 Tntn	3m	D Ch	G-F	£5362
121	7/02 Uttx	3m	D(0-120)HCh	G-F	£6909

109	7/02	Strf	3m	E(0-110)HCh	GD	£4186
108	3/00	Newb	3m110y	D Hdl	G-F	£3770
108	12/98	Bang	2m1f	N HHF	G-S	£1266

Total win prize-money £21495

Going:	Sf: 0-0 GS: 0-2 Gd: 0-3 GF: - Fm: 0-2
Distance:	2m/2m3: 0-0 2m4-2m7: 0-0 3m+: 0-7
Track:	LH: 0-4 RH: 0-3 Tight: 0-5 Gall: 0-0
Aids:	Bl: 0-5 Vi: 0-0 Tstrap: 0-0 Ckp: 0-0
Best Rating:	122 10/02 Tntn 3m gd-fm Ch

Fair chaser; stays 3m; inclined to be let down by his jumping; best on a sound surface; wears blinkers.

Simiola

69   4

5-y-o b m Shaamit (IRE)-Brave Vanessa (USA) (Private Account (USA))
S T Lewis Simon T Lewis

Placings:PP6P   (2516)
2003/04: 16⁶GS, 16⁶GF, 19⁶GF, 17⁶GS,

	Starts	1st	2nd	3rd	Win & Pl
Hurdles	4	0	0	0	0
Career Total	4	0	0	0	0

Going:	Sf: 0-0 GS: 0-2 Gd: 0-0 GF: - Fm: 0-2
Distance:	2m/2m3: 0-3 2m4-2m7: 0-1 3m+: 0-0
Track:	LH: 0-2 RH: 0-2 Tight: 0-0 Gall: 0-0
Aids:	Bl: 0-0 Vi: 0-0 Tstrap: 0-0 Ckp: 0-0
Best Rating:	8 6/03 Hrfd 2m3f110y gd-fm Hdl

Simlet

104(109h)   (112h)108+

9-y-o b g Forzando-Besito (Wassl)
E W Tuer E Tuer

Placings:0P3603/62102F5442124/F1430/5131/3P133034   (4730)

2003/04: 24³G, 24²G, 20¹G, 20³GF, 19³G, 24⁰G, 21³G, 20⁴G,

	Starts	1st	2nd	3rd	Win & Pl
Hurdles	4	1	0	2	1512
Chases	4	0	0	2	1982
Career Total	36	6	4	8	26309
121	9/01	Prth	3m110y	D(0-125)HHdl	GD	£4036
112	8/01	Prth	2m4f110yE(0-115)HHdl	GD	£3386
111	5/00	Prth	2m4f110yF(0-110)HHdl	G-S	£3591
99	3/00	Muss	2m	D(0-120)HHdl	G-F	£3526
97	6/99	Sthl	2m	E Hdl	G-F	£2410

Total win prize-money £16952

Going:	Sf: 0-0 GS: 0-0 Gd: 1-7 GF: - Fm: 0-1
Distance:	2m/2m3: 0-1 **2m4-2m7: 1-4** 3m+: 0-3
Track:	**LH: 1-5** RH: 0-3 Tight: 0-5 **Gall: 1-1**
Aids:	Bl: 0-0 Vi: 0-0 Tstrap: 0-3 **Ckp: 1-3**
Best Rating:	121 9/01 Prth 3m110y good Hdl

Modest staying hurdler; acts on any ground; stays 3m; has worn a tongue tie; goes very well at Perth; not disgraced in novice chases in early 2004.

Simon The Poacher

5-y-o br g Chaddleworth (IRE)-Lady Crusty (Golden Dipper)
L P Grassick N Goodger & Postlip Racing

Placings:0   (4630)
2003/04: 17⁰G,

	Starts	1st	2nd	3rd	Win & Pl
Hurdles	1	0	0	0	
Career Total	1	0	0	0	

Going:	Sf: 0-0 GS: 0-0 Gd: 0-1 GF: - Fm: 0-0
Distance:	2m/2m3: 0-1 2m4-2m7: 0-0 3m+: 0-0
Track:	LH: 0-0 RH: 0-1 Tight: 0-1 Gall: 0-0
Aids:	Bl: 0-0 Vi: 0-0 Tstrap: 0-0 Ckp: 0-0

Simon's Seat (USA)

92   85

5-y-o ch g Woodman (USA)-Spire (USA) (Topsider (USA))
C Drew (J A R Toller 24/10) Mrs E Reid

Placings:06   (4051)
2003/04: 16⁰S, 21⁶G,

	Starts	1st	2nd	3rd	Win & Pl
Hurdles	2	0	0	0	161
Career Total	2	0	0	0	161

Going:	Sf: 0-1 GS: 0-0 Gd: 0-1 GF: - Fm: 0-0
Distance:	2m/2m3: 0-2 2m4-2m7: 0-0 3m+: 0-0
Track:	LH: 0-0 RH: 0-2 Tight: 0-0 Gall: 0-0
Aids:	Bl: 0-0 Vi: 0-0 Tstrap: 0-0 Ckp: 0-0
Best Rating:	85 1/04 Asct 2m110y soft Hdl

Simoski

101   (0c)81

7-y-o b g Petoski-Miss Simone (Ile De Bourbon (USA))
N A Twiston-Davies N A Twiston-Davies

Placings:0/0/03FU0-0235   (1469)
2003/04: 16⁰GF, 16²GF, 16³GF, 17⁵F,

	Starts	1st	2nd	3rd	Win & Pl
Hurdles	4	0	1	1	1021
Career Total	11	0	1	2	1453

Going:	Sf: 0-0 GS: 0-0 Gd: 0-0 GF: - Fm: 0-4
Distance:	2m/2m3: 0-4 2m4-2m7: 0-0 3m+: 0-0
Track:	LH: 0-3 RH: 0-1 Tight: 0-0 Gall: 0-0
Aids:	Bl: 0-0 Vi: 0-0 Tstrap: 0-0 Ckp: 0-0
Best Rating:	81 8/03 Worc 2m gd-fm Hdl

Selling hurdler; best efforts seemed to have come when front-running although he did not appear to last out the trip; ridden from behind when second at Worcester August 2003; raised 5lb finished third in similar event at the same venue next time.

Simoun (IRE)

102   130+

6-y-o b g Monsun (GER)-Suivez (FR) (Fioravanti (USA))
M C Pipe (P Schiergen 1/6) The Macca & Growler Partnership

Placings:512061   (4856)
2003/04: 16⁵GS, 17¹S, 16²GS, 16⁰G, 20⁶G, 19¹GF,

	Starts	1st	2nd	3rd	Win & Pl
Hurdles	6	2	1	0	11809
Career Total	6	2	1	0	11809
103	4/04	Tntn	2m3f110yE Hdl	G-F	£4816
123	2/04	Tntn	2m1f	E Hdl	SFT	£4303

Total win prize-money £9120

Going:	Sf: 1-1 GS: 0-2 Gd: 0-2 GF: - Fm: 1-1
Distance:	2m/2m3: 1-4 2m4-2m7: 0-0 3m+: 0-0
Track:	LH: 0-3 **RH: 2-3** Tight: 2-3 Gall: 0-1
Aids:	Bl: 0-0 Vi: 0-0 Tstrap: 2-5 Ckp: 0-0
Best Rating:	130 4/04 Aint 2m4f good Hdl

Useful hurdler; twice a Group Two winner on the Flat in Germany; stays 2m 4f; seems to act on most types of ground; wears a tongue tie.

Simply Gifted

116   141+

9-y-o b g Simply Great (FR)-Souveniers (Relko)
Jonjo O'Neill Steve Hammond

Placings:1F21104/331315333/P403/1U41   (4850)
2003/04: 16¹S, 16ᵁG, 16⁴G, 20¹GS,

	Starts	1st	2nd	3rd	Win & Pl
Chases	4	2	0	0	22677
Career Total	24	7	1	7	68836
133	4/04	Ayr	2m4f	B HCh	G-S	£13733
132	1/04	Chep	2m110y	D(0-125)HCh	SFT	£5694
137	1/01	Hayd	2m	C Ch	SFT	£7150
124	11/00	Leic	2m	E Ch	G-S	£3022
147	2/99	Hayd	2m	C HHdl	SFT	£5173
140	12/98	Weth	2m	D Hdl	SFT	£3008
118	10/98	Weth	2m	D Hdl	GD	£3037

Total win prize-money £40819

Going:	Sf: 1-1 GS: 1-1 Gd: 0-2 GF: - Fm: 0-0
Distance:	2m/2m3: 1-3 2m4-2m7: 1-1 3m+: 0-0
Track:	**LH: 2-4** RH: 0-0 Tight: 0-1 Gall: 0-1
Aids:	Bl: 0-0 Vi: 0-1 Tstrap: 0-0 Ckp: 0-0
Best Rating:	147 12/01 Newc 2m gd-sft Hdl

Very useful performer in his prime; placed in top Graded company; returned from over three years off to win at Chepstow in January and right up to best when winning at Ayr in April; effective from two to two and a half miles; acts on most ground and effective blinkered or without.

Simply Mystic

80f   86f

4-y-o ch f Simply Great (FR)-Mystic Memory (Ela-Mana-Mou)
P D Niven Mrs J A Niven

Placings:332   (4186)
2003/04: 13³GF, 16³G, 16²G,

	Starts	1st	2nd	3rd	Win & Pl
NH Flat	3	0	1	2	1405
Career Total	3	0	1	2	1405

Going:	Sf: 0-0 GS: 0-0 Gd: 0-2 GF: - Fm: 0-1
Distance:	2m/2m3: 0-2 2m4-2m7: 0-0 3m+: 0-0
Track:	LH: 0-0 RH: 0-2 Tight: 0-1 Gall: 0-1
Aids:	Bl: 0-0 Vi: 0-0 Tstrap: 0-0 Ckp: 0-0
Best Rating:	86 3/04 Hntg 2m110y good NHF

Modest form in bumpers on a sound surface.

Simply Silver Lady

9-y-o ch m Push On-Pentwd Mundy (Vital Season)
Mrs H O Graham R D Graham

Placings:0PP/P-   (0008)
2003/04: 20⁰GF,

	Starts	1st	2nd	3rd	Win & Pl
Chases	1	0	0	0	
Career Total	4	0	0	0	

Going:	Sf: 0-0 GS: 0-0 Gd: 0-0 GF: - Fm: 0-1
Distance:	2m/2m3: 0-0 2m4-2m7: 0-1 3m+: 0-0
Track:	LH: 0-1 RH: 0-0 Tight: 0-0 Gall: 0-1
Aids:	Bl: 0-0 Vi: 0-0 Tstrap: 0-1 Ckp: 0-0

Simply Stunning

5-y-o ch m Primitive Rising (USA)-Qurrat Al Ain (Wolver Hollow)
Jonjo O'Neill Steve Hammond

Placings:00P   (3490)
2003/04: 17⁰G, 17⁰GS, 22PHY,

	Starts	1st	2nd	3rd	Win & Pl
NH Flat	2	0	0	0	0
Hurdles	1	0	0	0	0
Career Total	**3**	**0**	**0**	**0**	

Going:	Sf: 0-1 GS: 0-1 Gd: 0-1 GF: - Fm: 0-0
Distance:	2m2m3: 0-2 2m4-2m7: 0-1 3m+: 0-0
Track:	LH: 0-3 RH: 0-0 Tight: 0-2 Gall: 0-0
Aids:	Bl: 0-0 Vi: 0-0 Tstrap: 0-0 Ckp: 0-0
Best Rating:	61 10/03 Bang 2m1f good NHF

Simply Supreme (IRE)

112(110h)   (133+h)156+
7-y-o b g Supreme Leader-Some Gift (Avocat)
Mrs S J Smith Trevor Hemmings

Placings:130/111244-22341F1F   (4861)
2003/04: 16²G, 20²S, 20³GS, 23⁴G, 23¹S, 25²FS, 25¹G, 33⁵GS,

	Starts	1st	2nd	3rd	Win & Pl
Hurdles	1	0	0	0	2000
Chases	7	2	2	1	60144
Career Total	**17**	**6**	**3**	**2**	**86016**
156	4/04	Aint	3m1f	A Ch	GD	£46500
145	1/04	Weth	2m7f110yE Ch		SFT	£4960
133	12/02	Hayd	2m4f	D Hdl	SFT	£4160
133	11/02	Hayd	2m4f	D Hdl	SFT	£3835
122	11/02	Kels	2m6f110yE Hdl		SFT	£3588
111	12/01	Bang	2m1f	H NHF	G-S	£1746
				Total win prize-money £64790

Going:	Sf: 1-3 GS: 0-2 Gd: 1-3 GF: - Fm: 0-0
Distance:	2m2m3: 0-1 2m4-2m7: 0-2 3m+: 2-5
Track:	LH: 1-5 RH: 0-2 Tight: 1-1 Gall: 0-1
Aids:	Bl: 0-0 Vi: 0-0 Tstrap: 0-0 Ckp: 0-0
Best Rating:	156 4/04 Aint 3m1f good Ch

Very useful performer; recorded a wide-margin success at Wetherby in January; took advantage of some indifferent jumping by his rivals when winning a Grade Two at Aintree easily; stays three miles; effective in soft ground; front-runner.

Sinalco (USA)

86   92+
6-y-o b g Quest For Fame-Sin Lucha (USA) (Northfields (USA))
Mrs L B Normile A K Collins and D J Hindmarsh

Placings:605-054P   (3595)
2003/04: 16⁰S, 16⁵S, 24⁴HY, 20⁵HY,

	Starts	1st	2nd	3rd	Win & Pl
NH Flat	1	0	0	0	0
Hurdles	3	0	0	0	363
Career Total	**7**	**0**	**0**	**0**	**363**

Going:	Sf: 0-4 GS: 0-0 Gd: 0-0 GF: - Fm: 0-0
Distance:	2m2m3: 0-2 2m4-2m7: 0-1 3m+: 0-1
Track:	LH: 0-4 RH: 0-0 Tight: 0-0 Gall: 0-0
Aids:	Bl: 0-0 Vi: 0-0 Tstrap: 0-0 Ckp: 0-0
Best Rating:	92 1/04 Uttx 3m110y heavy Hdl

Modest novice hurdler; stays well.

Sindapour (IRE)

109   122
6-y-o b g Priolo (USA)-Sinntara (IRE) (Lashkari)
M C Pipe Mrs Mary Burke

Placings:1033   (4887)
2003/04: 16¹G, 21⁹G, 17³G, 22³GF,

	Starts	1st	2nd	3rd	Win & Pl
Hurdles	4	1	0	2	4727
Career Total	**4**	**1**	**0**	**2**	**4727**
120	3/04	Plum	2m	F Hdl	GD	£3115
				Total win prize-money £3115

Going:	Sf: 0-0 GS: 0-0 Gd: 1-3 GF: - Fm: 0-1
Distance:	2m2m3: 1-2 2m4-2m7: 0-2 3m+: 0-0
Track:	LH: 1-3 RH: 0-1 Tight: 1-2 Gall: 0-1
Aids:	Bl: 0-0 Vi: 0-0 Tstrap: 0-0 Ckp: 0-0
Best Rating:	121 4/04 Extr 2m1f good Hdl

Fair novice hurdler; won at Plumpton on his hurdling debut; useful stayer on the Flat; won 2003 Ascot Stakes; acts on fast and soft ground.

Single Sourcing (IRE)

107   98
13-y-o b g Good Thyne (USA)-Lady Albron (Royal Match)
A C Whillans G L Harrow

Placings:142/P/P1PP3P/F304241/FPPP3/41146/32-P1P
                                            (0784)
2003/04: 25²G, 25⁵PGS, 30¹G, 24⁶PG,

	Starts	1st	2nd	3rd	Win & Pl
Chases	4	1	1	0	9955
Career Total	**32**	**6**	**3**	**4**	**39498**
98	5/03	Crtml	3m6f	D(0-125)HCh	GD	£8255
101	11/01	Kels	3m4f	F(0-110)HCh	G-S	£4212
98	10/01	Aint	3m1f	F(0-105)HCh	GD	£5232
102	1/99	Ayr	2m5f110yC HCh		HVY	£10480
94	5/97	Uttx	2m	E Hdl	G-S	£2389
103	5/95	Uttx	2m	H NHF	G-F	£1805
				Total win prize-money £32375

Going:	Sf: 0-0 GS: 0-1 Gd: 1-3 GF: - Fm: 0-0
Distance:	2m2m3: 0-0 2m4-2m7: 0-3 3m+: 1-4
Track:	LH: 0-2 RH: 0-1 Tight: 0-1 Gall: 0-0
Aids:	Bl: 0-0 Vi: 0-0 Tstrap: 0-0 Ckp: 0-0
Best Rating:	108 10/95 Newb 2m110y good NHF

Modest staying handicap chaser; took a veterans race at Cartmel in May; stays extremely well; acts on most types of ground; has broken blood vessels.

Singularity

4-y-o b g Rudimentary (USA)-Lyrical Bid (USA) (Lyphard (USA))
K F Clutterbuck (W R Muir 17/10) The T Class Partnership

Placings:P   (4664)
2003/04: 19PGS,

	Starts	1st	2nd	3rd	Win & Pl
Hurdles	1	0	0	0	
Career Total	**1**	**0**	**0**	**0**	

Going:	Sf: 0-0 GS: 0-1 Gd: 0-0 GF: - Fm: -
Distance:	2m2m3: 0-0 2m4-2m7: 0-1 3m+: 0-0
Track:	LH: 0-1 RH: 0-0 Tight: 0-1 Gall: 0-0
Aids:	Bl: 0-0 Vi: 0-0 Tstrap: 0-0 Ckp: 0-0

Sink Or Swim (IRE)

65
6-y-o b m Big Sink Hope (USA)-Cragreagh VII (Damsire Unregistered)
J J Bridger (William Flavin 15/9) J J Bridger

Placings:000-42340P   (2238)
2003/04: 16⁴G, 16²GY, 16³F, 16⁴F, 16⁰GF, 16⁰G,

	Starts	1st	2nd	3rd	Win & Pl
NH Flat	4	0	1	1	1786
Hurdles	2	0	0	0	0
Career Total	**9**	**0**	**1**	**1**	**1786**

Going:	Sf: 0-0 GS: 0-0 Gd: 0-2 GF: - Fm: 0-3
Distance:	2m2m3: 0-6 2m4-2m7: 0-0 3m+: 0-0
Track:	LH: 0-1 RH: 0-1 Tight: 0-0 Gall: 0-0
Aids:	Bl: 0-0 Vi: 0-0 Tstrap: 0-0 Ckp: 0-0
Best Rating:	96 7/03 Cork 2m good NHF

Sintos

94f   95+f
6-y-o b/br g Syrtos-Sindur (Rolfe (USA))
Miss A M Newton-Smith Mrs John Grist

Placings:20   (2209)
2003/04: 17²G, 17⁰GS,

	Starts	1st	2nd	3rd	Win & Pl
NH Flat	2	0	1	0	432
Career Total	**2**	**0**	**1**	**0**	**432**

Going:	Sf: 0-0 GS: 0-1 Gd: 0-1 GF: - Fm: 0-0
Distance:	2m2m3: 0-2 2m4-2m7: 0-0 3m+: 0-0
Track:	LH: 0-0 RH: 0-2 Tight: 0-2 Gall: 0-0
Aids:	Bl: 0-0 Vi: 0-0 Tstrap: 0-0 Ckp: 0-0
Best Rating:	95 11/03 Folk 2m1f110y good NHF

Runner-up in a five-runner Folkestone bumper on his debut.

Sip Of Brandy (IRE)

11-y-o ch g Sharp Charter-Manhattan Brandy (Frankincense)
Miss J Hughes Miss J Hughes

Placings:P44PP/PP/1-U260   (4717)
2003/04: 25⁵UGS, 25²GF, 22⁶G, 24⁰G,

	Starts	1st	2nd	3rd	Win & Pl
Chases	4	0	1	0	446
Career Total	**12**	**1**	**1**	**0**	**3607**
95	4/03	Ludl	3m	H Ch	GD	£2968
				Total win prize-money £2968

Going:	Sf: 0-0 GS: 0-1 Gd: 0-2 GF: - Fm: 0-1
Distance:	2m2m3: 0-0 2m4-2m7: 0-1 3m+: 0-3
Track:	LH: 0-1 RH: 0-3 Tight: 0-1 Gall: 0-1
Aids:	Bl: 0-0 Vi: 0-0 Tstrap: 0-0 Ckp: 0-0
Best Rating:	95 3/04 Hrfd 3m1f110y gd-fm Ch

Hunter chaser; sprang 33/1 shock when landing modest three mile hunter chase at Ludlow April 2003.

Sir Alfred

96   95
5-y-o b g Royal Academy (USA)-Magnificent Star (USA) (Silver Hawk (USA))
A King W A Harrison-Allan & D Bellamy

Placings:P514-6   (1017)
2003/04: 16⁶GF,

	Starts	1st	2nd	3rd	Win & Pl
Hurdles	1	0	0	0	
Career Total	5	1	0	0	5497

96 3/03 Hayd 2m   D Hdl   G-F £4927
Total win prize-money £4927

Going:	Sf: 0-0 GS: 0-0 Gd: 0-0 GF: - Fm: 0-1
Distance:	2m/2m3: 0-1 2m4-2m7: 0-0 3m+: 0-0
Track:	LH: 0-1 RH: 0-0 Tight: 0-0 Gall: 0-0
Aids:	Bl: 0-0 Vi: 0-0 Tstrap: 0-0 Ckp: 0-0
Best Rating:	96 8/03 Worc 2m gd-fm Hdl

Modest juvenile hurdler; fair middle-distance handicapper on the Flat; won a novice event on fast ground at Haydock in March 2003.

Sir Bob (IRE)

97   **119**

12-y-o br g Aristocracy-Wilden (Will Somers)
Mrs H Dalton   Mrs Lucia Farmer

Placings:02/4200/313112/F342/2U5/124P4/P23-030 **(4817)**
2003/04: 23⁰G, 25³S, 24⁰G,

	Starts	1st	2nd	3rd	Win & Pl
Chases	3	0	0	1	365
Career Total	30	4	7	5	25716

128	11/01	Towc	2m6f	D Ch		SFT	£5304
128	3/99	Carl	3m110y	E Hdl		SFT	£2318
128	2/99	Carl	3m110y	E Hdl		HVY	£2472
108	11/98	Newc	3m	E Hdl		G-S	£2379

Total win prize-money £12473

Going:	Sf: 0-1 GS: 0-0 Gd: 0-2 GF: - Fm: 0-0
Distance:	2m/2m3: 0-0 2m4-2m7: 0-1 3m+: 0-3
Track:	LH: 0-1 RH: 0-2 Tight: 0-0 Gall: 0-0
Aids:	Bl: 0-0 Vi: 0-0 Tstrap: 0-0 Ckp: 0-0
Best Rating:	128 11/01 Towc 2m6f soft Ch

Modest chaser; stays well; goes well in soft ground; has worn blinkers.

Sir Brastias

103   **93**

5-y-o b g Shaamit (IRE)-Premier Night (Old Vic)
K C Bailey (S Dow 25/6)   D G Churston

Placings:2   **(4402)**
2003/04: 16²G,

	Starts	1st	2nd	3rd	Win & Pl
Hurdles	1	0	1	0	1048
Career Total	1	0	1	0	1048

Going:	Sf: 0-0 GS: 0-0 Gd: 0-1 GF: - Fm: 0-0
Distance:	2m/2m3: 0-1 2m4-2m7: 0-0 3m+: 0-0
Track:	LH: 0-0 RH: 0-1 Tight: 0-0 Gall: 0-1
Aids:	Bl: 0-0 Vi: 0-0 Tstrap: 0-0 Ckp: 0-0
Best Rating:	95 3/04 Hntg 2m110y good Hdl

Promise in maiden hurdle on debut.

Sir Cumference

     100

8-y-o b g Sir Harry Lewis (USA)-Puki Puki (Roselier (FR))
Miss H C Knight   Mrs Nicola Moores

Placings:6P511-PF   **(2160)**
2003/04: 24⁵G, 24ᶠGS,

	Starts	1st	2nd	3rd	Win & Pl
Chases	2	0	0		
Career Total	7	2	0	0	8974

100	4/03	Strf	3m	F(0-100)HCh	GD	£3514
92	4/03	Ludl	3m	D(0-110)HCh	GD	£5460

Total win prize-money £8974

Going:	Sf: 0-0 GS: 0-1 Gd: 0-1 GF: - Fm: 0-0
Distance:	2m/2m3: 0-0 2m4-2m7: 0-0 3m+: 0-0
Track:	LH: 0-2 RH: 0-0 Tight: 0-1 Gall: 0-0
Aids:	Bl: 0-0 Vi: 0-0 Tstrap: 0-0 Ckp: 0-0
Best Rating:	100 4/03 Strf 3m good Ch

Moderate chaser; dual point-to-point winner; considered best suited to left-handed tracks; likes good ground; has suffered breathing problems in the past.

Sir D'Orton (FR)

98   **118**

8-y-o ch g Beyssac (FR)-Prime Target (FR) (Ti King (FR))
P F Nicholls   Mrs J Stewart

Placings:332/23P4233/2112232/P4P   **(0604)**
2003/04: 24ᴾHY, 20⁴G, 26ᴾG,

	Starts	1st	2nd	3rd	Win & Pl
Chases	3	0	0		546
Career Total	20	2	7	6	22965

119	11/01	Plum	2m4f	D(0-120)HCh	G-S	£5392
120	10/01	Plum	2m4f	D(0-120)HCh	SFT	£4111

Total win prize-money £9503

Going:	Sf: 0-1 GS: 0-0 Gd: 0-2 GF: - Fm: 0-0
Distance:	2m/2m3: 0-0 2m4-2m7: 0-1 3m+: 0-2
Track:	LH: 0-3 RH: 0-0 Tight: 0-2 Gall: 0-0
Aids:	Bl: 0-0 Vi: 0-0 Tstrap: 0-0 Ckp: 0-0
Best Rating:	123 2/02 Font 3m2f110y soft Ch

Modest hurdler/fair chaser; handles soft ground; stays more than three miles.

Sir Edward Burrow (IRE)

101   **93**

6-y-o b g Distinctly North (USA)-Alalja (IRE) (Entitled)
W Storey   W Storey

Placings:450/P6F-33   **(0266)**
2003/04: 16³G, 20³G,

	Starts	1st	2nd	3rd	Win & Pl
Hurdles	2	0	0	2	1370
Career Total	8	0	0	2	1678

Going:	Sf: 0-0 GS: 0-0 Gd: 0-2 GF: - Fm: 0-0
Distance:	2m/2m3: 0-1 2m4-2m7: 0-1 3m+: 0-0
Track:	LH: 0-1 RH: 0-1 Tight: 0-1 Gall: 0-0
Aids:	Bl: 0-0 Vi: 0-0 Tstrap: 0-0 Ckp: 0-0
Best Rating:	93 5/03 Prth 2m4f110y good Hdl

Sir Frosty

105   **131**

11-y-o b g Arctic Lord-Snowy Autumn (Deep Run)
B J M Ryall   J F Tucker

Placings:1341/11U-P06P   **(4861)**
2003/04: 29ᴾS, 30⁰G, 25ᴿG, 33ᴾGS,

	Starts	1st	2nd	3rd	Win & Pl
Chases	4	0	0		600
Career Total	11	4	0	1	34522

125	1/03	Chel	4m1f	B(0-145)HCh	SFT	£12620
131	12/02	Extr	4m	D(0-125)HCh	G-S	£10302
122	1/02	Tntn	3m8f	C(0-130)HCh	SFT	£7020
127	10/01	Hrfd	3m1f110yE Ch		SFT	£2941

Total win prize-money £32885

Going:	Sf: 0-1 GS: 0-1 Gd: 0-2 GF: - Fm: 0-0
Distance:	2m/2m3: 0-0 2m4-2m7: 0-0 3m+: 0-0

Track:	LH: 0-3 RH: 0-1 Tight: 0-2 Gall: 0-0
Aids:	Bl: 0-0 Vi: 0-0 Tstrap: 0-1 Ckp: 0-0
Best Rating:	131 12/02 Extr 4m gd-sft Ch

Useful handicap chaser; stays 4m 1f; effective on soft ground; often wears a tongue tie; goes well fresh.

Sir Gordon

6-y-o ch g Hatim (USA)-Sweet Colleen (Connaught)
C N Kellett   S Kitching

Placings:P   **(3966)**
2003/04: 16ᴾGS,

	Starts	1st	2nd	3rd	Win & Pl
Hurdles	1	0	0	0	
Career Total	1	0	0	0	

Going:	Sf: 0-0 GS: 0-0 Gd: 0-0 GF: - Fm: 0-0
Distance:	2m/2m3: 0-1 2m4-2m7: 0-0 3m+: 0-0
Track:	LH: 0-0 RH: 0-1 Tight: 0-0 Gall: 0-0
Aids:	Bl: 0-0 Vi: 0-0 Tstrap: 0-0 Ckp: 0-0

Sir Harvy (IRE)

5-y-o gr g Gothland (FR)-Promised Path (Hello Gorgeous (USA))
M Todhunter   Black Stripe Racing

Placings:P   **(1840)**
2003/04: 17ᴾG,

	Starts	1st	2nd	3rd	Win & Pl
Hurdles	1	0	0	0	
Career Total	1	0	0	0	

Going:	Sf: 0-0 GS: 0-0 Gd: 0-0 GF: - Fm: 0-0
Distance:	2m/2m3: 0-1 2m4-2m7: 0-0 3m+: 0-0
Track:	LH: 0-1 RH: 0-0 Tight: 0-1 Gall: 0-0
Aids:	Bl: 0-0 Vi: 0-0 Tstrap: 0-0 Ckp: 0-0

Sir Homo (IRE)

100   **84**

10-y-o b g Homo Sapien-Deise Lady (Le Bavard (FR))
E W Tuer   E Tuer

Placings:00660P/F0P/P0-022205030   **(4614)**
2003/04: 17⁰GF, 17²GF, 16²GF, 16²GF, 20⁰G, 19⁵GS, 17⁰GS, 20⁵S, 17⁰G,

	Starts	1st	2nd	3rd	Win & Pl
Hurdles	9	0	3	1	2743
Career Total	20	0	3	1	2743

Going:	Sf: 0-1 GS: 0-2 Gd: 0-2 GF: - Fm: 0-4
Distance:	2m/2m3: 0-7 2m4-2m7: 0-2 3m+: 0-0
Track:	LH: 0-8 RH: 0-1 Tight: 0-5 Gall: 0-1
Aids:	Bl: 0-0 Vi: 0-0 Tstrap: 0-0 Ckp: 0-0
Best Rating:	98 6/00 Naas 2m3f yield NHF

Plating-class hurdler; narrowly beaten at Wetherby in November; best over two miles; suited by fast ground.

Sir Mouse

96   **95**

8-y-o gr g Phardante (FR)-Place Stephanie (IRE) (Hatim (USA))
M F Harris   John J Murray

Placings:2/3P-10P20   (3694)
2003/04: 23¹G, 26⁰GS, 25⁵PS, 19²G, 25⁰G,

	Starts	1st	2nd	3rd	Win & Pl
Hurdles	5	1	1	0	3249
Career Total	8	1	2	1	4445
87 11/03 Fknm	2m7f110yE Hdl		GD		£2191

Total win prize-money £2191

Going:	Sf: 0-1 GS: 0-1 Gd: 1-3 GF: - Fm: 0-0
Distance:	2m/2m3: 0-2 2m4-2m7: 0-0 3m+: 1-4
Track:	LH: 1-3 RH: 0-1 Tight: 1-2 Gall: 0-1
Aids:	Bl: 0-0 Vi: 0-0 Tstrap: 0-0 Ckp: 0-0
Best Rating:	102 11/01 Font 2m4f gd-sft Hdl

Moderate novice hurdler; took a weak novices' hurdle at Fakenham in November; suited to three miles.

Sir Murphy

11-y-o ch g Brando-Bemas (Levanter)
Mrs B E Matthews R V Harraway

Placings:00/0F   (2005)
2003/04: 16⁰GF, 24ᶠGF,

	Starts	1st	2nd	3rd	Win & Pl
Hurdles	2	0	0	0	
Career Total	4	0	0	0	

Going:	Sf: 0-0 GS: 0-0 Gd: 0-0 GF: - Fm: 0-2
Distance:	2m/2m3: 0-1 2m4-2m7: 0-0 3m+: 0-1
Track:	LH: 0-2 RH: 0-0 Tight: 0-0 Gall: 0-0
Aids:	Bl: 0-0 Vi: 0-1 Tstrap: 0-0 Ckp: 0-0
Best Rating:	41 3/99 MRas 1m5f110y gd-sft NHF

Sir Night (IRE)

97   88

4-y-o b g Night Shift (USA)-Highly Respected (IRE) (High Estate)
Jedd O'Keeffe (J D Bethell 22/10) Highbeck Racing

Placings:0451   (4795)
2003/04: 16⁰GF, 16⁴G, 16⁵GS, 17¹G,

	Starts	1st	2nd	3rd	Win & Pl
Hurdles	4	1	0	0	3406
Career Total	4	1	0	0	3406
88 4/04 Sedg	2m1f	E Hdl		GD	£3406

Total win prize-money £3406

Going:	Sf: 0-0 GS: 0-1 Gd: 1-2 GF: - Fm: 0-1
Distance:	2m/2m3: 1-4 2m4-2m7: 0-0 3m+: 0-0
Track:	LH: 1-3 RH: 0-1 Tight: 1-4 Gall: 0-0
Aids:	Bl: 0-0 Vi: 0-0 Tstrap: 0-0 Ckp: 0-0
Best Rating:	88 4/04 Sedg 2m1f good Hdl

Modesthurdler; acts on good ground.

Sir Norman

109   (78h)108

9-y-o b g Arctic Lord-Moy Ran Lady (Black Minstrel)
R D E Woodhouse M A Sawyer

Placings:0/000P6PP/5512232-2105PP53P0   (4730)
2003/04: 16²GF, 17¹G, 20⁰G, 17⁵GF, 16⁰P, 20⁰GS, 17⁵S, 20³GF, 19⁰G, 20⁰G,

	Starts	1st	2nd	3rd	Win & Pl
Chases	10	1	1	1	14667
Career Total	25	2	4	2	24621
104 5/03 Kels	2m1f	D(0-125)HCh	GD	£12203
96 11/02 Ayr	2m5f110yD(0-110)HCh	SFT	£5057

Total win prize-money £17260

Sir Pelinore

62

9-y-o b g Caerleon (USA)-Soemba (General Assembly (USA))
Mrs A M Woodrow Mrs Ann Woodrow

Placings:0/PB0-PP05PP   (4762)
2003/04: 21⁵PS, 22⁵PGS, 16⁵GS, 19⁵GS, 26⁵PGS, 19⁵PS,

	Starts	1st	2nd	3rd	Win & Pl
Hurdles	6	0	0	0	0
Career Total	10	0	0	0	0

Going:	Sf: 0-2 GS: 0-4 Gd: 0-0 GF: - Fm: 0-0
Distance:	2m/2m3: 0-1 2m4-2m7: 0-0 3m+: 0-1
Track:	LH: 0-0 RH: 0-4 Tight: 0-1 Gall: 0-1
Aids:	Bl: 0-0 Vi: 0-0 Tstrap: 0-0 Ckp: 0-0
Best Rating:	62 3/04 Towc 2m3f110y gd-sft Hdl

Sir Rembrandt (IRE)

119   (113h)172

8-y-o b g Mandalus-Sue's A Lady (Le Moss)
R H Alner A Hordle

Placings:32021/11-F12P62   (4424)
2003/04: 26⁶GS, 26¹GS, 29²S, 25⁵PGS, 24⁶G, 26²G,

	Starts	1st	2nd	3rd	Win & Pl
Chases	6	1	2	0	119450
Career Total	13	4	4	1	146647
168 12/03 Chep	3m2f110yA HCh	G-S	£23800
155 12/02 Chel	3m1f110yA Ch	GD	£14500
130 11/02 Newb	2m6f110yD Ch	G-S	£5720
113 3/02 Newb	3m110y D Hdl	SFT	£4563

Total win prize-money £48583

Going:	Sf: 0-1 GS: 1-3 Gd: 0-2 GF: - Fm: 0-0
Distance:	2m/2m3: 0-0 2m4-2m7: 0-0 3m+: 1-6
Track:	LH: 1-6 RH: 0-0 Tight: 0-0 Gall: 0-4
Aids:	Bl: 0-0 Vi: 0-0 Tstrap: 0-0 Ckp: 0-0
Best Rating:	172 3/04 Chel 3m2f110y good Ch

High-class chaser; unbeaten in two starts as a novice including a Grade Two race at Cheltenham; made amends for an early fall in the Hennessy when running out an impressive winner of the Rehearsal Chase at Chepstow a week later; runner-up in the Welsh National; below form next two runs but ran a blinder when half-length second to Best Mate in the Cheltenham Gold Cup; stays well; effective in soft ground; has suffered muscular problems this term.

Sir Robbo (IRE)

95   76

10-y-o b g Glacial Storm (USA)-Polly's Slipper (Pollerton)
N A Twiston-Davies Melton Pets Direct Ltd

Placings:U03/01P1005546/1/525FP/1P-54P4   (3998)
2003/04: 25⁵GS, 24⁴GS, 25⁵PGS, 24⁴G,

	Starts	1st	2nd	3rd	Win & Pl
Chases	4	0	0	1	371
Career Total	25	4	1	1	14868
99 5/02 Hrfd	3m1f110yE(0-105)HCh	G-F	£3900
99 5/00 Hrfd	2m3f	D Ch	GD	£3900
96 10/99 Hrfd	2m1f	D Hdl	G-F	£2892

| 96 6/99 Hrfd | 2m1f | D Hdl | GD | £2801 |

Total win prize-money £13493

Going:	Sf: 0-0 GS: 0-2 Gd: 0-1 GF: - Fm: 0-1
Distance:	2m/2m3: 0-0 2m4-2m7: 0-0 3m+: 0-4
Track:	LH: 0-1 RH: 0-3 Tight: 0-1 Gall: 0-0
Aids:	Bl: 0-0 Vi: 0-0 Tstrap: 0-0 Ckp: 0-0
Best Rating:	101 4/99 Towc 2m good NHF

All his wins over hurdles and fences have come at Hereford; stays three miles plus; likes fast ground.

Sir Rowland Hill (IRE)

100   82+

5-y-o b g Kahyasi-Zaila (IRE) (Darshaan)
Ferdy Murphy A G Chappell

Placings:21-3403P   (3881)
2003/04: 16³G, 20⁴G, 20⁰GS, 20³S, 24ᵖG,

	Starts	1st	2nd	3rd	Win & Pl
NH Flat	1	0	0	1	530
Hurdles	4	0	0	1	896
Career Total	7	1	1	2	3882
92 4/03 Hexm	2m110y H NHF	GD	£1904

Total win prize-money £1904

Going:	Sf: 0-1 GS: 0-1 Gd: 0-3 GF: - Fm: 0-0
Distance:	2m/2m3: 0-1 2m4-2m7: 0-3 3m+: 0-0
Track:	LH: 0-3 RH: 0-0 Tight: 0-0 Gall: 0-0
Aids:	Bl: 0-0 Vi: 0-0 Tstrap: 0-0 Ckp: 0-0
Best Rating:	97 5/03 Kels 2m110y good NHF

Useful bumper performer; fourth on hurdles debut; stays 2m 4f.

Sir Storm (IRE)

114   (114h)138

8-y-o b g Ore-Yonder Bay (IRE) (Trimmingham)
G M Moore J R F (management Consultants) Ltd

Placings:301P2P/2123235-1042115011   (4938)
2003/04: 16¹G, 20⁰G, 16⁴GF, 16²G, 16¹G, 16¹S, 16⁵HY, 16⁰G, 16¹GS, 16¹GS,

	Starts	1st	2nd	3rd	Win & Pl
Chases	10	5	1	0	40840
Career Total	28	7	5	3	60069
138 4/04 Prth	2m	D(0-125)HCh	G-S	£8255
128 3/04 Weth	2m	D(0-120)HCh	G-S	£5434
128 12/03 Hayd	2m	D(0-125)HCh	SFT	£10182
122 11/03 Weth	2m	C(0-130)HCh	GD	£6734
118 9/03 Prth	2m	D(0-115)HCh	GD	£6851
109 11/02 Weth	2m	D(0-110)HCh	HVY	£5092
114 11/01 Bang	2m1f	E Hdl	G-S	£2828

Total win prize-money £45377

Going:	Sf: 1-2 GS: 2-2 Gd: 2-5 GF: - Fm: 0-1
Distance:	2m/2m3: 5-9 2m4-2m7: 0-1 3m+: 0-0
Track:	LH: 3-8 RH: 2-2 Tight: 0-1 Gall: 0-0
Aids:	Bl: 0-0 Vi: 0-0 Tstrap: 0-0 Ckp: 3-5
Best Rating:	138 4/04 Prth 2m gd-sft Ch

Useful chaser; best over two miles; acts on good ground or softer; seems most effective on a flat track; likes to race prominently; has worn cheekpieces; game.

Sir Talbot

110(98h)   (145h)123

10-y-o b g Ardross-Bermuda Lily (Dunbeath (USA))
J A B Old W E Sturt

Placings:12/15215/4F2/45FF5/3P621242   (4521)

2003/04: 20³G, 24PGS, 21⁶G, 16²G, 20¹G, 20²G, 20⁴G, 19²GS,

	Starts	1st	2nd	3rd	Win & Pl
Hurdles	3	0	0	1	4243
Chases	5	1	3	0	12465
Career Total	**23**	**4**	**6**	**1**	**63760**
117 1/04 Leic	2m4f110yD Ch			GD	£5603
152 3/99 Chel	2m1f A HHdl			G-S	£29750
142 10/98 Chep	2m110y C Hdl			G-S	£3740
109 1/98 Hntg	2m110y E Hdl			G-S	£2080
			Total win prize-money £41173

Going:	Sf: 0-0 GS: 0-2 Gd: 1-6 GF: - Fm: 0-0
Distance:	2m/2m3: 0-1 **2m4-2m7: 1-6** 3m+: 0-0
Track:	LH: 0-2 **RH: 1-6** Tight: 0-0 Gall: 0-2
Aids:	Bl: 0-0 Vi: 0-0 Tstrap: 0-0 Ckp: 0-0
Best Rating:	**159** 11/99 Chel 2m110y good Hdl

Formerly very useful hurdler, but off the track for two years after December 1999; won first race for a long time in a novice chase at Leicester in January; seems best at around two and a half miles; acts well on decent ground.

Sir Toby (IRE)

109 (86h) **122**

11-y-o bl g Strong Gale-Petite Deb (Cure The Blues (USA))
R Rowe Capt A Pratt

Placings:0430/530/3F2/1114-5621 (4778)
2003/04: 20⁵GF, 20⁶GF, 20²G, 21¹G,

	Starts	1st	2nd	3rd	Win & Pl
Chases	4	1	1	0	8592
Career Total	**18**	**4**	**2**	**3**	**29544**
112 4/04 Fknm	2m5f110yE(0-110)HCh			GD	£6084
122 11/02 Leic	2m4f110yC(0-130)HCh			GD	£8073
122 11/02 Kemp	2m4f110yD Ch			GD	£5316
107 10/02 Hntg	2m4f110yE(0-105)HCh			G-F	£3536
			Total win prize-money £23010

Going:	Sf: 0-0 GS: 0-0 Gd: 1-2 GF: - Fm: 0-2
Distance:	2m/2m3: 0-0 **2m4-2m7: 1-4** 3m+: 0-0
Track:	**LH: 1-2** RH: 0-2 **Tight: 1-1** Gall: 0-2
Aids:	Bl: 0-0 Vi: 0-0 Tstrap: 0-0 Ckp: 0-0
Best Rating:	**122** 11/02 Leic 2m4f110y good Ch

Modest chaser; suited by two and a half miles and acts on any ground; may be best on a tight track.

Sir Walter (IRE)

106 (108c) (78c) **78**

11-y-o b g The Bart (USA)-Glenbalda (Kambalda)
A G Hobbs Jason Parfitt

Placings:0000/0/044346F023/0304/PFF0200U6412361344 6134/**6240**-430565P006644 (4781)
2003/04: 16⁴GS, 17³G, 20⁴GF, 20⁵GF, 16⁶G, 17⁵G, 16⁴GS, 16⁰GS, 16⁸S, 16⁶G, 19⁶G, 21⁴G, 16⁴G,

	Starts	1st	2nd	3rd	Win & Pl
Hurdles	13	0	0	1	1057
Career Total	**58**	**3**	**4**	**7**	**13359**
105 3/02 Wwck	2m F(0-100)HHdl			G-S	£2159
97 12/01 Ludl	2m F Hdl			GD	£2383
91 10/01 MRas	2m1f110yG(0-95)HHdl			GD	£1680
			Total win prize-money £6224

Going:	Sf: 0-1 GS: 0-3 Gd: 0-7 GF: - Fm: 0-2
Distance:	2m/2m3: 0-9 2m4-2m7: 0-4 3m+: 0-0
Track:	LH: 0-8 RH: 0-5 Tight: 0-4 Gall: 0-2
Aids:	Bl: 0-0 Vi: 0-0 Tstrap: 0-0 Ckp: 0-0
Best Rating:	**105** 3/02 Wwck 2m gd-sft Hdl

Modest hurdler; suited by two miles and a sound surface, travels well in his races.

Sir Williamwallace (IRE)

11-y-o br g Strong Gale-Kemchee (Kernal (FR))
D L Claydon D L Claydon

Placings:0/0560000/F133F0/14626633/4P0PPP/P0630452 P26P-P (0201)
2003/04: 24PGF,

	Starts	1st	2nd	3rd	Win & Pl
Chases	1	0	0	0	
Career Total	**41**	**2**	**3**	**5**	12975
77 5/00 Dpat	2m2f (0-95)HCh			GD	£3174
75 7/99 Wxfd	2m (0-95)HCh			FRM	£3683
			Total win prize-money £6857

Going:	Sf: 0-0 GS: 0-0 Gd: 0-0 GF: - Fm: 0-1
Distance:	2m/2m3: 0-0 2m4-2m7: 0-0 3m+: 0-1
Track:	LH: 0-0 RH: 0-1 Tight: 0-0 Gall: 0-1
Aids:	Bl: 0-0 Vi: 0-0 Tstrap: 0-0 Ckp: 0-0
Best Rating:	**84** 9/00 Dpat 2m2f good Ch

Sireric (IRE)

106 (108h) (106h) **103**

14-y-o b g Asir-Twice Regal (Royal Prerogative)
R Johnson C H P Bell

Placings:0321/000/03/316213/F4U0P0/4221P2/33243/205 4112412203-03P (2458)
2003/04: 25³G, 24⁰G, 30³G, 30PG,

	Starts	1st	2nd	3rd	Win & Pl
Hurdles	1	0	0	0	0
Chases	3	0	0	2	2120
Career Total	**48**	**7**	**10**	**9**	**47065**
103 1/03 Newc	3m E(0-110)HCh			HVY	£5040
100 12/02 Sedg	3m3f F(0-95)HCh			SFT	£3386
98 12/02 Sedg	3m3f110yD(0-115)HHdl			SFT	£4459
97 1/01 Newc	3m E(0-115)HCh			HVY	£3391
108 3/98 Hexm	3m D(0-120)HCh			SFT	£4272
108 12/97 Sedg	3m3f E(0-110)HCh			SFT	£3738
109 4/95 Hexm	3m E Hdl			HVY	£2578
			Total win prize-money £26869

Going:	Sf: 0-0 GS: 0-0 Gd: 0-4 GF: - Fm: 0-0
Distance:	2m/2m3: 0-0 2m4-2m7: 0-0 3m+: 0-4
Track:	LH: 0-3 RH: 0-0 Tight: 0-0 Gall: 0-1
Aids:	Bl: 0-0 Vi: 0-0 Tstrap: 0-0 Ckp: 0-0
Best Rating:	**109** 4/95 Hexm 3m heavy Hdl

Modest hurdler/chaser; stays marathon trips; acts on a soft surface; suited by forcing tactics.

Sirinndi (IRE)

68

10-y-o b g Shahrastani (USA)-Sinntara (IRE) (Lashkari)
Miss K Marks Nick Shutts

Placings:0/630/0/54100654/00/P36-F (0069)
2003/04: 20FS,

	Starts	1st	2nd	3rd	Win & Pl
Hurdles	1	0	0	0	
Career Total	**19**	**1**	**0**	**2**	2261
90 12/00 Chep	2m4f G Hdl			HVY	£1526
			Total win prize-money £1526

Going:	Sf: 0-1 GS: 0-0 Gd: 0-0 GF: - Fm: 0-0
Distance:	2m/2m3: 0-0 2m4-2m7: 0-1 3m+: 0-0
Track:	LH: 0-1 RH: 0-0 Tight: 0-1 Gall: 0-0
Aids:	Bl: 0-0 Vi: 0-0 Tstrap: 0-0 Ckp: 0-0
Best Rating:	**90** 12/00 Chep 2m4f heavy Hdl

Sirius Lady

4-y-o b f Sir Harry Lewis (USA)-Intrepida (Fair Season)
E L James (A M Balding 2/6) Exors of the late Mrs D Hardy

Placings:P (1092)
2003/04: 16PGF,

	Starts	1st	2nd	3rd	Win & Pl
Hurdles	1	0	0	0	
Career Total	**1**	**0**	**0**	**0**	

Going:	Sf: 0-0 GS: 0-0 Gd: 0-0 GF: - Fm: 0-0
Distance:	2m/2m3: 0-1 2m4-2m7: 0-0 3m+: 0-0
Track:	LH: 0-1 RH: 0-0 Tight: 0-1 Gall: 0-0
Aids:	Bl: 0-0 Vi: 0-0 Tstrap: 0-1 Ckp: 0-0

Sissinghurst Storm (IRE)

99 (91h) (78h) **83+**

6-y-o b/br m Good Thyne (USA)-Mrs Hill (Strong Gale)
R Dickin Brian Clifford

Placings:03-0534123 (4841)
2003/04: 16⁰G, 21⁵GS, 26³GS, 20⁴GS, 25¹GF, 22²GS, 21³G,

	Starts	1st	2nd	3rd	Win & Pl
Hurdles	3	0	0	1	275
Chases	4	1	1	1	7585
Career Total	**9**	**1**	**1**	**3**	**8516**
83 3/04 Hrfd	3m1f110yE Ch			G-F	£4017
			Total win prize-money £4017

Going:	Sf: 0-0 GS: 0-4 Gd: 0-2 GF: - Fm: 1-1
Distance:	2m/2m3: 0-1 2m4-2m7: 0-4 **3m+: 1-2**
Track:	LH: 0-1 **RH: 1-6** Tight: 0-0 Gall: 0-1
Aids:	Bl: 0-0 Vi: 0-0 Tstrap: 0-0 Ckp: 0-0
Best Rating:	**83** 4/04 Chel 2m5f good Ch

Plating-class novice hurdler; blessed with stamina rather than speed; may do better over fences.

Sister Amy

7-y-o gr m Gods Solution-Amys Sister (Silly Prices)
J R Turner J Edward Boynton

Placings:00P- (0002)
2003/04: 20PG,

	Starts	1st	2nd	3rd	Win & Pl
Hurdles	1	0	0	0	
Career Total	**3**	**0**	**0**	**0**	

Going:	Sf: 0-0 GS: 0-0 Gd: 0-1 GF: - Fm: 0-0
Distance:	2m/2m3: 0-0 2m4-2m7: 0-1 3m+: 0-0
Track:	LH: 0-1 RH: 0-0 Tight: 0-0 Gall: 0-0
Aids:	Bl: 0-0 Vi: 0-0 Tstrap: 0-0 Ckp: 0-0
Best Rating:	**72** 3/03 Weth 2m gd-fm NHF

Sister Anna

99 **96**

6-y-o br m Gildoran-Take The Veil (Monksfield)
T D Walford Anthony Preston

Placings:206-F5261 (4956)
2003/04: 20FG, 16⁶GS, 23²S, 21⁶GS, 22¹G,

	Starts	1st	2nd	3rd	Win & Pl
Hurdles	5	1	1	0	3784
Career Total	**8**	**1**	**2**	**0**	**4492**

96   4/04   MRas 2m6f   F(0-100)HHdl   GD   £2772
Total win prize-money £2772

Going:	Sf: 0-1 GS: 0-2 Gd: 1-2 GF: - Fm: 0-0
Distance:	2m/2m3: 0-1 **2m4-2m7: 1-4** 3m+: 0-0
Track:	LH: 0-4 RH: 0-0 Tight: 0-0 Gall: 0-0
Aids:	Bl: 0-0 Vi: 0-0 Tstrap: 0-0 Ckp: 0-0
Best Rating:	96 4/04 MRas 2m6f good Hdl

Moderate novice hurdler;stays 2m6f; acts on good or softer.

Sister Cinnamon
97f   102f
6-y-o ch m Karinga Bay-Cinnamon Run (Deep Run)
S Gollings Mrs M A Hall

Placings:*2410*   **(4328)**
2003/04: 16²G, 17⁴GS, 16¹GS, 16⁰S,

	Starts	1st	2nd	3rd	Win & Pl
NH Flat	4	1	1	0	2541
Career Total	4	1	1	0	2541
102	2/04	Towc	2m	H NHF	G-S £1953

Total win prize-money £1953

Going:	Sf: 0-1 GS: 1-2 Gd: 0-1 GF: - Fm: 0-0
Distance:	**2m/2m3: 1-4** 2m4-2m7: 0-0 3m+: 0-0
Track:	LH: 0-2 **RH: 1-2** Tight: 0-1 Gall: 0-0
Aids:	Bl: 0-0 Vi: 0-0 Tstrap: 0-0 Ckp: 0-0
Best Rating:	102 2/04 Towc 2m gd-sft NHF

Moderate bumper performer; acts on good or easy ground;
should stay further over hurdles; acts on most ground.

Sister Superior (IRE)
(103h)   (101h)**77**
9-y-o b m Supreme Leader-Nicat (Wolver Hollow)
S Gollings The High Five Partnership

Placings:02263500516/35P/22503**P5**-0   **(0161)**
2003/04: 20⁰GF,

	Starts	1st	2nd	3rd	Win & Pl
Hurdles	1	0	0	0	
Career Total	22	1	4	3	23960
109	3/01	Newb	2m5f	HHdl	HVY £17400

Total win prize-money £17400

Going:	Sf: 0-0 GS: 0-0 Gd: 0-0 GF: - Fm: 0-1
Distance:	2m/2m3: 0-0 2m4-2m7: 0-1 3m+: 0-0
Track:	LH: 0-1 RH: 0-0 Tight: 0-1 Gall: 0-0
Aids:	Bl: 0-0 Vi: 0-0 Tstrap: 0-0 Ckp: 0-0
Best Rating:	111 6/00 Uttx 2m good NHF

Modest hurdler; distant third on chasing debut; stays 2m 6f;
acts on good ground and softer.

Six Bells

8-y-o b m Gildoran-Strikealightlady (Lighter)
J D Frost Fun In The Sun Partnership

Placings:*00/300*/P   **(1222)**
2003/04: 17PGF,

	Starts	1st	2nd	3rd	Win & Pl
Hurdles	1	0	0	0	
Career Total	6	0	0	1	215

Going:	Sf: 0-0 GS: 0-0 Gd: 0-0 GF: - Fm: 0-1
Distance:	2m/2m3: 0-1 2m4-2m7: 0-0 3m+: 0-0
Track:	LH: 0-1 RH: 0-0 Tight: 0-1 Gall: 0-0
Aids:	Bl: 0-0 Vi: 0-0 Tstrap: 0-0 Ckp: 0-0

Six Clerks (IRE)

11-y-o b g Shadeed (USA)-Skidmore Girl (USA) (Vaguely Noble)
Mrs S M Odell W J Odell

Placings:0421330/52325**263**/6P5P46/30**F3FP**/05530535/2
0PPF-0F   **(4373)**
2003/04: 21FS, 24⁰G, 24FG,

	Starts	1st	2nd	3rd	Win & Pl
Chases	3	0	0	0	
Career Total	42	1	5	8	9150
89	2/97	Catt	2m	F Hdl	GD £2029

Total win prize-money £2029

Going:	Sf: 0-1 GS: 0-0 Gd: 0-0 GF: - Fm: 0-0
Distance:	2m/2m3: 0-0 2m4-2m7: 0-1 3m+: 0-2
Track:	LH: 0-0 RH: 0-0 Tight: 0-0 Gall: 0-0
Aids:	Bl: 0-0 Vi: 0-0 Tstrap: 0-0 Ckp: 0-2
Best Rating:	99 3/97 MRas 2m1f110y good Hdl

Modest hunter chaser on a long losing run.

Six Of One
112   100
6-y-o b g Kahyasi-Ten To Six (Night Shift (USA))
R Rowe Mrs R A Proctor

Placings:6660-32623042   **(4856)**
2003/04: 16³GS, 17²G, 20⁶G, 18²G, 20³S, 21⁰G, 20⁴GS, 19²GF,

	Starts	1st	2nd	3rd	Win & Pl
Hurdles	8	0	3	2	9384
Career Total	12	0	3	2	9561

Going:	Sf: 0-1 GS: 0-2 Gd: 0-4 GF: - Fm: 0-1
Distance:	2m/2m3: 0-3 2m4-2m7: 0-5 3m+: 0-0
Track:	LH: 0-2 RH: 0-5 Tight: 0-3 Gall: 0-0
Aids:	Bl: 0-0 Vi: 0-0 Tstrap: 0-0 Ckp: 0-0
Best Rating:	103 2/04 Sand 2m4f110y soft Hdl

Moderate hurdler; has run some good races in defeat in
2003/4; remains a maiden over obstacles though; effective
up to two and a half miles; acts on good ground; has worn
blinkers.

Six Pack (IRE)
101(91h)   (86+h)**96**
6-y-o ch g Royal Abjar (USA)-Regal Entrance (Be My Guest (USA))
Andrew Turnell J J Canny

Placings:50-30321   **(2994)**
2003/04: 16³F, 16⁰G, 17³GF, 16²F, 16¹GF,

	Starts	1st	2nd	3rd	Win & Pl
Hurdles	3	0	0	2	960
Chases	2	1	1	0	6004
Career Total	7	1	1	2	6964
97	12/03	Leic	2m	D(0-110)HCh	G-F £4771

Total win prize-money £4771

Going:	Sf: 0-0 GS: 0-0 Gd: 0-1 GF: - Fm: 1-4
Distance:	**2m/2m3: 1-4** 2m4-2m7: 0-0 3m+: 0-0
Track:	LH: 0-2 **RH: 1-3** Tight: 0-2 Gall: 0-0
Aids:	Bl: 0-0 Vi: 0-0 Tstrap: 0-0 Ckp: 0-0
Best Rating:	97 12/03 Leic 2m gd-fm Ch

Plating-class hurdler; winning chaser; handles fast ground.

Six Star
90   76
4-y-o b f Desert Story (IRE)-Adriya (Vayrann)
B G Powell (B W Duke 4/1) Mrs Rachel A Powell

Placings:2460   **(3440)**
2003/04: 16²GF, 17⁴G, 16⁶S, 16⁰G,

	Starts	1st	2nd	3rd	Win & Pl
Hurdles	4	0	1	0	1166
Career Total	4	0	1	0	1166

Going:	Sf: 0-1 GS: 0-0 Gd: 0-2 GF: - Fm: 0-1
Distance:	2m/2m3: 0-4 2m4-2m7: 0-0 3m+: 0-0
Track:	LH: 0-2 RH: 0-2 Tight: 0-2 Gall: 0-1
Aids:	Bl: 0-0 Vi: 0-0 Tstrap: 0-0 Ckp: 0-0
Best Rating:	76 11/03 Hntg 2m110y gd-fm Hdl

Plating-class hurdler; acts on a sound surface.

Sixo (IRE)
112   125
7-y-o gr g Roselier (FR)-Miss Mangaroo (Oats)
M C Pipe Matt Archer & Miss Jean Broadhurst

Placings:*113*-14306   **(4641)**
2003/04: 16¹GS, 20⁴S, 21³G, 20⁰S, 24⁶G,

	Starts	1st	2nd	3rd	Win & Pl
Hurdles	5	1	0	1	6161
Career Total	8	3	0	2	13226
120	12/03	Sand	2m110y	D Hdl	G-S £3620
125	12/02	Newb	2m110y	H NHF	HVY £2646
109	11/02	NAbb	2m1f	H NHF	HVY £2219

Total win prize-money £8486

Going:	Sf: 0-2 GS: 1-1 Gd: 0-2 GF: - Fm: 0-0
Distance:	**2m/2m3: 1-1** 2m4-2m7: 0-3 3m+: 0-1
Track:	LH: 0-2 **RH: 1-3** Tight: 0-2 Gall: 0-0
Aids:	Bl: 0-0 Vi: 0-0 Tstrap: 0-0 Ckp: 0-0
Best Rating:	130 2/03 Newb 2m110y good NHF

Fair novice hurdler; bumper winner; won hurdle debut at
Sandown in December 2003; effective over two miles and
acts well on soft ground; suited by forcing tactics; has not
lived up to expectations this season.

Skenfrith
102   94+
5-y-o b g Atraf-Hobbs Choice (Superpower)
Miss S E Forster J M & Miss H M Crichton, Miss S Forster

Placings:00302-252533200146   **(4312)**
2003/04: 16²G, 24⁶G, 16⁶G, 20⁵G, 20³GF, 20³GS, 27²GF, 16⁵S,
19⁰GS, 20¹HY, 22⁴GS, 24⁶GF,

	Starts	1st	2nd	3rd	Win & Pl
Hurdles	12	1	3	2	7785
Career Total	17	1	4	3	9343
94	2/04	Newc	2m4f	E Hdl	HVY £3484

Total win prize-money £3484

Going:	Sf: 1-2 GS: 0-3 Gd: 0-4 GF: - Fm: 0-3
Distance:	2m/2m3: 0-4 **2m4-2m7: 1-5** 3m+: 0-0
Track:	**LH: 1-10** RH: 0-2 Tight: 0-5 **Gall: 1-1**
Aids:	Bl: 0-0 Vi: 0-0 Tstrap: 0-0 Ckp: 0-0
Best Rating:	94 3/04 Kels 2m6f110y gd-sft Hdl

Plating-class hurdler; stays two and a half miles; acts on fast
and easy ground.

Ski Seal

10-y-o b g Petoski-Roving Seal (Privy Seal)

Miss V A Stephens (B J M Ryall 17/2) I N Jones

Placings:0/FP/0P/PP0 (4930)
2003/04: 23⁵GS, 21⁵GS, 22⁹G,

	Starts	1st	2nd	3rd	Win & Pl
Chases	3	0	0	0	
Career Total	8	0	0	0	

Going: Sf: 0-0 GS: 0-2 Gd: 0-1 GF: - Fm: 0-0
Distance: 2m/2m3: 0-0 2m4-2m7: 0-2 3m+: 0-1
Track: LH: 0-0 RH: 0-2 Tight: 0-0 Gall: 0-0
Aids: Bl: 0-0 Vi: 0-0 Tstrap: 0-0 Ckp: 0-0
Best Rating: 86 2/00 Hrfd 2m3f110y good Hdl

Skiddaw Rose (IRE)

86(100h) (76h)76

8-y-o gr m Terimon-Whimbrel (Dara Monarch)
M A Barnes John Wills

Placings:06/00PP/44030300-6653044562U (1864)
2003/04: 16⁶G, 16⁶G, 16⁵GF, 20³G, 17⁰GF, 17⁴GF, 17⁴GF, 17⁵GF, 16⁸F, 16²GF, 16⁰GF,

	Starts	1st	2nd	3rd	Win & Pl
Hurdles	8	0	0	1	518
Chases	3	0	1	0	1440
Career Total	25	0	1	3	3024

Going: Sf: 0-0 GS: 0-0 Gd: 0-3 GF: - Fm: 0-8
Distance: 2m/2m3: 0-10 2m4-2m7: 0-1 3m+: 0-0
Track: LH: 0-8 RH: 0-2 Tight: 0-4 Gall: 0-0
Aids: Bl: 0-0 Vi: 0-0 Tstrap: 0-0 Ckp: 0-0
Best Rating: 76 10/03 Kels 2m110y gd-fm Ch

Poor novice hurdler/chaser; often a front runner.

Skillwise

92 104

12-y-o b g Buckley-Calametta (Oats)
T D Easterby M H Easterby

Placings:0/012252U51/3/02142P5/412264U16/432P34100U/PP565-45P6 (2932)
2003/04: 20⁴GF, 23⁵G, 25⁰G, 27⁶G,

	Starts	1st	2nd	3rd	Win & Pl
Chases	4	0	0	0	258
Career Total	46	6	8	3	59746
126 3/02	Donc	3m2f	B(0-145)HCh	G-S	£20640
123 4/01	Hayd	2m6f	B(0-140)HCh	SFT	£10093
114 11/00	Newc	3m	D(0-125)HCh	SFT	£3809
120 11/99	Weth	3m1f	D Ch	GD	£3925
114 4/98	Ayr	2m4f	C HHdl	GD	£4289
107 10/97	Sedg	2m1f	H NHF	GD	£1035

Total win prize-money £43792

Going: Sf: 0-0 GS: 0-0 Gd: 0-3 GF: - Fm: 0-1
Distance: 2m/2m3: 0-0 2m4-2m7: 0-1 3m+: 0-3
Track: LH: 0-3 RH: 0-0 Tight: 0-1 Gall: 0-0
Aids: Bl: 0-1 Vi: 0-0 Tstrap: 0-0 Ckp: 0-0
Best Rating: 126 3/02 Donc 3m2f gd-sft Ch

Veteran chaser; stays beyond three miles; acts on good or softer ground.

Skinsey Finnegan (IRE)

93 109

10-y-o b g Fresh Breeze (USA)-Rose Of Solway (Derring Rose)
C A Dwyer Casino Racing Partnership

Placings:23³3431225423-344 (1521)
2003/04: 20³GF, 26⁴GF, 22⁴G,

	Starts	1st	2nd	3rd	Win & Pl
Chases	3	0	0	1	1317
Career Total	15	1	4	5	11930
109 12/02	Folk	2m	F(0-90)HCh	SFT	£3425

Total win prize-money £3426

Going: Sf: 0-0 GS: 0-0 Gd: 0-1 GF: - Fm: 0-2
Distance: 2m/2m3: 0-0 2m4-2m7: 0-2 3m+: 0-1
Track: LH: 0-1 RH: 0-0 Tight: 0-3 Gall: 0-0
Aids: Bl: 0-0 Vi: 0-0 Tstrap: 0-0 Ckp: 0-3
Best Rating: 109 4/03 Plum 2m1f gd-fm Ch

Moderate chaser; winning pointer; effective at two miles, but stays further; usually wears a tongue tie; has been tried in cheekpieces.

Skiora

78 70

7-y-o br m Petoski-Coral Delight (Idiots Delight)
A J Wilson The Up And Running Partnership

Placings:0/3U04P-P0P05P (4544)
2003/04: 16⁰GF, 16⁰G, 19⁵GS, 17⁰GS, 26⁵GF, 22⁰GS,

	Starts	1st	2nd	3rd	Win & Pl
Hurdles	6	0	0	0	0
Career Total	12	0	0	1	240

Going: Sf: 0-0 GS: 0-3 Gd: 0-1 GF: - Fm: 0-2
Distance: 2m/2m3: 0-3 2m4-2m7: 0-2 3m+: 0-1
Track: LH: 0-1 RH: 0-5 Tight: 0-0 Gall: 0-0
Aids: Bl: 0-0 Vi: 0-0 Tstrap: 0-0 Ckp: 0-4
Best Rating: 82 5/02 Worc 2m gd-fm NHF

Skippers Cleuch (IRE)

116 146+

10-y-o b g Be My Native (USA)-Cloughoola Lady (Black Minstrel)
L Lungo Ashleybank Investments Limited

Placings:111/1111P/11U0-P12P (3597)
2003/04: 25⁵G, 25¹G, 25²GS, 20⁰HY,

	Starts	1st	2nd	3rd	Win & Pl
Chases	4	1	1	0	12398
Career Total	16	10	1	0	44264
146 12/03	Weth	3m1f	C(0-130)HCh	GD	£5798
122 12/02	Weth	2m4f110yD Ch		G-S	£5152
118 11/02	Kels	2m6f110yD Ch		HVY	£5057
151 1/01	Newc	2m4f	B Hdl	SFT	£6873
132 12/00	Newc	2m4f	E Hdl	SFT	£2723
138 12/00	Ayr	2m	E Hdl	SFT	£2380
120 11/00	Ayr	2m	E Hdl	SFT	£1974
138 4/00	Carl	2m1f	H NHF	G-S	£1652
126 3/00	Carl	2m1f	H NHF	G-S	£4465
124 3/00	Ayr	2m	H NHF	HVY	£1589

Total win prize-money £37665

Going: Sf: 0-1 GS: 0-1 Gd: 1-2 GF: - Fm: 0-0
Distance: 2m/2m3: 0-0 2m4-2m7: 0-1 3m+: 1-3
Track: LH: 1-4 RH: 0-0 Tight: 0-1 Gall: 0-0
Aids: Bl: 0-0 Vi: 0-0 Tstrap: 0-0 Ckp: 0-0
Best Rating: 151 1/01 Newc 2m4f soft Hdl

Smart chaser; formerly high-class novice hurdler; stays three miles plus; best on soft ground.

Skram

74(97h) (76h)57

11-y-o b g Rambo Dancer (CAN)-Skarberg (FR) (Noir Et Or)
R Dickin W P Evans & Mrs D L Weaver

Placings:F14552P20/122236224412/16010P/P2003425224
5/11U21113245/250F51204/5P-4000 (1295)
2003/04: 20⁴GF, 16⁶G, 21⁰GF, 17⁹GF,

	Starts	1st	2nd	3rd	Win & Pl
Hurdles	2	0	0	0	390
Chases	2	0	0	0	0
Career Total	65	11	16	3	63803
113 7/01	Strf	2m4f	D(0-125)HCh	GD	£7280
115 9/00	Strf	2m4f	D(0-120)HCh	GD	£4017
115 8/00	Worc	2m4f110yD Ch	G-F	£4147
117 7/00	Strf	2m1f110yE Ch	G-F	£3103
112 6/00	Worc	2m4f110yD(0-110)HCh	G-F	£4069
105 5/00	Wwck	2m	E Ch	G-F	£2948
101 2/99	Font	2m2f110yE(0-115)HHdl	SFT	£7327
107 5/98	Hntg	2m5f110yD(0-125)HHdl	G-F	£2931
107 4/98	Font	2m2f110yD(0-110)HHdl	G-S	£2427
97 9/97	Font	2m2f110yF(0-105)HHdl	G-F	£2048
77 8/96	Font	2m2f110yE Hdl	G-F	£2175

Total win prize-money £42475

Going: Sf: 0-0 GS: 0-0 Gd: 0-1 GF: - Fm: 0-3
Distance: 2m/2m3: 0-2 2m4-2m7: 0-2 3m+: 0-0
Track: LH: 0-4 RH: 0-0 Tight: 0-2 Gall: 0-0
Aids: Bl: 0-0 Vi: 0-0 Tstrap: 0-0 Ckp: 0-0
Best Rating: 117 9/00 MRas 2m6f110y gd-fm Ch

Sky Warrior (FR)

105(99h) (111h)125

6-y-o b g Warrshan (USA)-Sky Bibi (FR) (Sky Lawyer (FR))
Evan Williams Mr and Mrs Glynne Clay

Placings:541321/3060F21F121-604020 (4568)
2003/04: 20⁶GF, 19⁰S, 16⁴S, 24⁰S, 21³GF, 20⁰GS,

	Starts	1st	2nd	3rd	Win & Pl
Hurdles	2	0	0	0	0
Chases	4	0	1	0	2929
Career Total	23	5	4	2	31812
4/03	LE L	2m4f	Ch	G-S	£4052
3/03	Pchu	2m1f	Ch	GD	£3117
12/02	Agtn	2m4f	Ch	HLD	£2650
3/02	Sabl	2m1f	Hdl	G-S	£3828
11/01	Sbri	1m7f	Hdl	HVY	£2716

Total win prize-money £16363

Going: Sf: 0-3 GS: 0-1 Gd: 0-0 GF: - Fm: 0-0
Distance: 2m/2m3: 0-2 2m4-2m7: 0-3 3m+: 0-1
Track: LH: 0-3 RH: 0-3 Tight: 0-2 Gall: 0-0
Aids: Bl: 0-0 Vi: 0-0 Tstrap: 0-0 Ckp: 0-0
Best Rating: 125 3/04 Winc 2m5f gd-fm Ch

A winner over both hurdles and fences in France, but has yet to show much since coming to Britain; acts on good and soft ground; best at 2m 4f.

Skycab (IRE)

103 136

12-y-o b g Montelimar (USA)-Sams Money (Pry)
N J Gifford P H Betts (holdings) Ltd

Placings:4/522411/4225/2162140115/P0P4P/51/331P311-30U05U0 (4889)
2003/04: 25⁵G, 20⁰GS, 24¹G, 25⁰S, 24⁵G, 36¹G, 20⁰GF,

	Starts	1st	2nd	3rd	Win & Pl
Chases	7	0	0	1	4492
Career Total	42	10	6	4	96785
136 4/03	Sand	2m4f110yB(0-145)HCh	GD	£17400
133 4/03	Strf	2m4f	C(0-130)HCh	GD	£8287

136	12/02	Fknm	3m110y	D(0-125)HCh	G-S	£6630
132	10/01	Sthl	2m4f110yD(0-120)HCh		GD	£6841
135	4/00	Strf	2m4f	C(0-130)HCh	G	£6500
135	4/00	Asct	2m3f110yC(0-130)HCh		SFT	£13812
129	12/99	Hntg	2m4f110yE Ch		G-S	£3613
127	11/99	Sand	2m	D Ch	GD	£4401
127	4/98	MRas	2m3f110yD Hd		SFT	£3315
127	4/98	Fknm	2m	E(0-100)HHdl	G-S	£3001
				Total win prize-money £73803		

Going:	Sf:-0-1 GS: 0-1 Gd: 0-4 GF: - Fm: 0-1
Distance:	2m/2m3: 0-0 2m4-2m7: 0-2 3m+: 0-5
Track:	LH: 0-4 RH: 0-3 Tight: 0-3 Gall: 0-5
Aids:	Bl: 0-0 Vi: 0-0 Tstrap: 0-0 Ckp: 0-0
Best Rating:	136 5/03 Kels 3m1f good Ch

Fair chaser; stays three miles, but more effective at shorter; acts on most types of ground.

Skye Blue (IRE)

76   **58**

7-y-o b g Blues Traveller (IRE)-Hitopah (Bustino)
B J Llewellyn Maenllwyd Racing Club

Placings:231/P450/4   **(4526)**
2003/04: 16⁴GS,

	Starts	1st	2nd	3rd	Win & Pl
Hurdles	1	0	0	0	
Career Total	8	1	1		4042
113	4/01	Plum	2m	F Hdl	SFT	£2646
				Total win prize-money £2646		

Going:	Sf: 0-0 GS: 0-1 Gd: 0-0 GF: - Fm: 0-0
Distance:	2m/2m3: 0-1 2m4-2m7: 0-0 3m+: 0-0
Track:	LH: 0-1 RH: 0-0 Tight: 0-0 Gall: 0-0
Aids:	Bl: 0-0 Vi: 0-0 Tstrap: 0-0 Ckp: 0-0
Best Rating:	113 4/01 Plum 2m soft Hdl

Skylander

(85h)   **(74h)**

8-y-o b g Thethingaboutitis (USA)-Mesembryanthemum (Warpath)
Mrs Merrita Jones G I Isaac

Placings:06/5-64P   **(3223)**
2003/04: 16⁶GS, 20⁴GF, 19ᴾGS,

	Starts	1st	2nd	3rd	Win & Pl
Hurdles	2	0	0	0	0
Chases	1	0	0	0	0
Career Total	6	0	0	0	0

Going:	Sf: 0-0 GS: 0-2 Gd: 0-0 GF: - Fm: 0-1
Distance:	2m/2m3: 0-2 2m4-2m7: 0-1 3m+: 0-0
Track:	LH: 0-2 RH: 0-1 Tight: 0-0 Gall: 0-0
Aids:	Bl: 0-0 Vi: 0-0 Tstrap: 0-0 Ckp: 0-0
Best Rating:	85 4/02 Plum 2m2f good NHF

Skylarker (USA)

75

6-y-o b g Sky Classic (CAN)-O My Darling (USA) (Mr Prospector (USA))
W S Kittow Midd Shire Racing

Placings:55-P   **(4285)**
2003/04: 16ᵖG,

	Starts	1st	2nd	3rd	Win & Pl
Hurdles	1	0	0	0	0
Career Total	3	0	0	0	0

Going:	Sf: 0-0 GS: 0-0 Gd: 0-1 GF: - Fm: 0-0
Distance:	2m/2m3: 0-1 2m4-2m7: 0-0 3m+: 0-0
Track:	LH: 0-0 RH: 0-1 Tight: 0-0 Gall: 0-0
Aids:	Bl: 0-0 Vi: 0-0 Tstrap: 0-0 Ckp: 0-0
Best Rating:	75 12/02 Tntn 2m1f soft Hdl

Sledmere (IRE)

9-y-o ch g Shalford (IRE)-Jazirah (Main Reef)
George R Moscrop George R Moscrop

Placings:005PP/F/UU-P   **(4218)**
2003/04: 25ᴾGS,

	Starts	1st	2nd	3rd	Win & Pl
Chases	1	0	0	0	0
Career Total	9	0	0	0	0

Going:	Sf: 0-0 GS: 0-1 Gd: 0-0 GF: - Fm: 0-0
Distance:	2m/2m3: 0-0 2m4-2m7: 0-0 3m+: 0-1
Track:	LH: 0-0 RH: 0-1 Tight: 0-0 Gall: 0-0
Aids:	Bl: 0-0 Vi: 0-0 Tstrap: 0-0 Ckp: 0-0
Best Rating:	72 7/00 Uttx 2m4f110y gd-fm Hdl

Sleep Bal (FR)

101   **142**

5-y-o b g Sleeping Car (FR)-Balle Six (FR) (Balsamo (FR))
N J Henderson Mrs M O Bryant

Placings:1-600   **(4954)**
2003/04: 20⁶G, 20⁰G, 16⁰G,

	Starts	1st	2nd	3rd	Win & Pl
Hurdles	3	0	0	0	750
Career Total	4	1	0	0	11971
	3/03	Engh	2m110y	Hdl	VS	£11221
				Total win prize-money £11221		

Going:	Sf: 0-0 GS: 0-0 Gd: 0-3 GF: - Fm: 0-0
Distance:	2m/2m3: 0-1 2m4-2m7: 0-0 3m+: 0-0
Track:	LH: 0-1 RH: 0-0 Tight: 0-2 Gall: 0-0
Aids:	Bl: 0-0 Vi: 0-0 Tstrap: 0-0 Ckp: 0-0
Best Rating:	142 4/04 Sand 2m110y good Hdl

Has been highly-tried over hurdles; acts on very soft ground; effective over two miles.

Sleeping Night (FR)

(108h)   **(132h)**

8-y-o b g Sleeping Car (FR)-Doll Night (FR) (Karkour (FR))
P F Nicholls D J & F A Jackson

Placings:613141/3121213/2424/5   **(2452)**
2003/04: 24⁵GS,

	Starts	1st	2nd	3rd	Win & Pl
Hurdles	1	0	0	0	1000
Career Total	18	6	4	3	197294
	11/00	Autl	2m4f110y	Ch	HVY	£28818
150	10/00	Autl	2m4f110y	Ch	VS	£28818
	6/00	Autl	2m4f110y	Ch	VS	£28818
	4/00	Autl	2m1f110y	Ch	HVY	£11527
	2/00	Autl	2m1f110y	Hdl	VS	£10567
	12/99	Pau	2m110y	Hdl	HVY	£6459
				Total win prize-money £115007		

Going:	Sf: 0-0 GS: 0-1 Gd: 0-0 GF: - Fm: 0-0
Distance:	2m/2m3: 0-0 2m4-2m7: 0-0 3m+: 0-1
Track:	LH: 0-1 RH: 0-0 Tight: 0-0 Gall: 0-1
Aids:	Bl: 0-0 Vi: 0-0 Tstrap: 0-0 Ckp: 0-0
Best Rating:	163 11/01 Weth 3m1f good Ch

High-class chaser/smart hurdler; ex-French; showed good

---

form for Mary Reveley in 2001/2, but missed the following season; good run over hurdles on return in November 2003 for new yard; best at around 3m; suited by soft ground.

Sleepy River (IRE)

96   **73**

13-y-o ch g Over The River (FR)-Shreelane (Laurence O)
Miss Kate Milligan The Aunts

Placings:0103/005010/0050/1F14/36P3606/11/15P343/FP
P0-043F   **(3677)**
2003/04: 24⁰GS, 27⁰S, 27⁴G, 24³HY, 25³HY,

	Starts	1st	2nd	3rd	Win & Pl
Hurdles	1	0	0	0	0
Chases	4	0	0	1	518
Career Total	41	7	6		25330
104	11/01	Newc	3m	D(0-125)HCh	GD	£4075
96	11/00	Wwck	3m110y	E(0-105)HCh	HVY	£2886
96	10/00	Wwck	3m2f	F(0-105)HCh	SFT	£2467
109	11/98	Kels	2m6f110yD(0-125)HHdl		HVY	£2749
114	10/98	Kels	2m6f110yD(0-125)HHdl		SFT	£2871
113	3/97	Tipp	2m4f	(0-123)HHdl	G-Y	£4069
108	1/96	Tram	2m	Hdl	SFT	£2295
				Total win prize-money £21414		

Going:	Sf: 0-3 GS: 0-0 Gd: 0-1 GF: - Fm: 0-1
Distance:	2m/2m3: 0-0 2m4-2m7: 0-0 3m+: 0-5
Track:	LH: 0-5 RH: 0-0 Tight: 0-3 Gall: 0-0
Aids:	Bl: 0-0 Vi: 0-0 Tstrap: 0-0 Ckp: 0-2
Best Rating:	115 4/96 Punc 2m2f soft Hdl

Moderate staying chaser; lightly raced in recent seasons; likes soft ground.

Sleight

90   **69**

5-y-o ch m Bob's Return (IRE)-Jolejester (Relkino)
W Jenks The Wadeley Partnership

Placings:44-00   **(3445)**
2003/04: 17⁰G, 21⁰G,

	Starts	1st	2nd	3rd	Win & Pl
Hurdles	2	0	0	0	0
Career Total	4	0	0	0	0

Going:	Sf: 0-0 GS: 0-0 Gd: 0-2 GF: - Fm: 0-0
Distance:	2m/2m3: 0-2 2m4-2m7: 0-1 3m+: 0-0
Track:	LH: 0-1 RH: 0-1 Tight: 0-1 Gall: 0-0
Aids:	Bl: 0-0 Vi: 0-0 Tstrap: 0-0 Ckp: 0-0
Best Rating:	83 3/03 Wwck 2m soft NHF

Slinky Malinky

74f   **40f**

6-y-o b m Alderbrook-Winnie The Witch (Leading Man)
D G Bridgwater The Cats Whiskers

Placings:00   **(1273)**
2003/04: 16ᵖGF, 17⁰GF,

	Starts	1st	2nd	3rd	Win & Pl
NH Flat	2	0	0	0	0
Career Total	2	0	0	0	0

Going:	Sf: 0-0 GS: 0-0 Gd: 0-0 GF: - Fm: 0-2
Distance:	2m/2m3: 0-2 2m4-2m7: 0-0 3m+: 0-0
Track:	LH: 0-2 RH: 0-0 Tight: 0-1 Gall: 0-0
Aids:	Bl: 0-0 Vi: 0-0 Tstrap: 0-0 Ckp: 0-0
Best Rating:	40 9/03 NAbb 2m1f gd-fm NHF

Slip The Ring

10-y-o ch g Belmez (USA)-Sixslip (USA) (Diesis)
P Senter (Miss K Marks 3/5) P Senter

Placings:S52250/565/FP-54 (4344)
2003/04: 20⁵S, 26⁴GS,

	Starts	1st	2nd	3rd	Win & Pl
Hurdles	1	0	0	0	0
Chases	1	0	0	0	0
Career Total	**13**	**0**	**2**	**0**	**1532**

Going: Sf: 0-1 GS: 0-1 Gd: 0-0 GF: - Fm: 0-0
Distance: 2m/2m3: 0-0 2m4-2m7: 0-1 3m+: 0-1
Track: LH: 0-2 RH: 0-0 Tight: 0-0 Gall: 0-0
Aids: Bl: 0-0 Vi: 0-0 Tstrap: 0-0 Ckp: 0-1
Best Rating: 108 10/00 MRas 2m3f110y good Hdl

Slippy Hitherao

77 **45**

4-y-o f First Trump-Child Star (FR) (Bellypha)
Miss L J Sheen (B R Johnson 17/11) Mrs P J Sheen

Placings:0P0 (4788)
2003/04: 17⁰G, 16⁸S, 16⁹G,

	Starts	1st	2nd	3rd	Win & Pl
Hurdles	3	0	0	0	
Career Total	**3**	**0**	**0**	**0**	

Going: Sf: 0-1 GS: 0-0 Gd: 0-2 GF: - Fm: 0-0
Distance: 2m/2m3: 0-3 2m4-2m7: 0-0 3m+: 0-0
Track: LH: 0-2 RH: 0-1 Tight: 0-0 Gall: 0-1
Aids: Bl: 0-0 Vi: 0-0 Tstrap: 0-0 Ckp: 0-0
Best Rating: 45 4/04 Plum 2m good Hdl

Sloane Street (FR)

105 **100+**

5-y-o b g Sadler's Wells (USA)-Shy Danceuse (FR) (Groom
Dancer (USA))
M Scudamore (D J Caro 27/5) The Yes - No - Wait
Sorries

Placings:FP005320-522215P (3036)
2003/04: 16⁵G, 16²GF, 21²G, 24²GF, 24¹GF, 24⁵G, 23⁹GS,

	Starts	1st	2nd	3rd	Win & Pl
Hurdles	7	1	3	0	6808
Career Total	**15**	**1**	**4**	**1**	**8979**

100 11/03 Donc 3m110y E(0-100)HHdl G-F £4212
Total win prize-money £4212

Going: Sf: 0-0 GS: 0-1 Gd: 0-3 GF: - Fm: 1-3
Distance: 2m/2m3: 0-2 2m4-2m7: 0-1 3m+: 1-4
Track: LH: 1-4 RH: 0-3 Tight: 0-2 Gall: 1-2
Aids: Bl: 0-0 Vi: 0-0 Tstrap: 0-0 Ckp: 0-0
Best Rating: 100 11/03 Donc 3m110y gd-fm Hdl

Moderate hurdler; stays three miles; effective on fast
ground.

Sly Celebrity (IRE)

7-y-o ch g Fourstars Allstar (USA)-Over Slyguff (IRE) (Over
The River (FR))
J A B Old W E Sturt

Placings:0 (0109)
2003/04: 16⁰S,

	Starts	1st	2nd	3rd	Win & Pl
NH Flat	1	0	0	0	

Career Total 1 0 0 0

Going: Sf: 0-1 GS: 0-0 Gd: 0-0 GF: - Fm: 0-0
Distance: 2m/2m3: 0-1 2m4-2m7: 0-0 3m+: 0-0
Track: LH: 0-1 RH: 0-0 Tight: 0-0 Gall: 0-0
Aids: Bl: 0-0 Vi: 0-0 Tstrap: 0-0 Ckp: 0-0

Slyboots (GER)

100 **91**

5-y-o gr g Neshad (USA)-Shanice (USA) (Highland Park
(USA))
C J Mann J E Brown

Placings:5-01215 (1548)
2003/04: 24⁰G, 20¹GF, 20²G, 22¹GF, 21⁵GF,

	Starts	1st	2nd	3rd	Win & Pl
Hurdles	5	2	1	0	10279
Career Total	**6**	**2**	**1**	**0**	**10432**

91 8/03 Strf 2m6f110yD Hdl G-F £5782
70 7/03 Worc 2m4f E Hdl G-F £3493
Total win prize-money £9275

Going: Sf: 0-0 GS: 0-0 Gd: 0-2 GF: - Fm: 2-3
Distance: 2m/2m3: 0-0 2m4-2m7: 2-4 3m+: 0-1
Track: LH: 2-5 RH: 0-0 Tight: 1-2 Gall: 0-0
Aids: Bl: 0-0 Vi: 0-0 Tstrap: 0-0 Ckp: 0-0
Best Rating: 91 8/03 Strf 2m6f110y gd-fm Hdl

Moderate hurdler; winner on the Flat in Germany; stepped
up considerably on his debut when winning 2m 4f novices
hurdle at Worcester July 2003; scored again at Stratford in
August; stays two miles six; acts on fast ground; may stay
further.

Small Amount

49f

4-y-o ch f Sir Harry Lewis (USA)-Pretty Scarce (Handsome
Sailor)
W Jenks P Russell

Placings:00 (2675)
2003/04: 14⁰G, 12⁰GF,

	Starts	1st	2nd	3rd	Win & Pl
NH Flat	2	0	0	0	
Career Total	**2**	**0**	**0**	**0**	

Going: Sf: 0-0 GS: 0-0 Gd: 0-1 GF: - Fm: 0-1
Distance: 2m/2m3: 0-0 2m4-2m7: 0-0 3m+: 0-0
Track: LH: 0-2 RH: 0-0 Tight: 0-0 Gall: 0-0
Aids: Bl: 0-0 Vi: 0-0 Tstrap: 0-0 Ckp: 0-0
Best Rating: 49 12/03 Newb 1m4f110y gd-fm NHF

Smart Guy

98 **87+**

12-y-o ch g Gildoran-Talahache Bridge (New Brig)
Mrs L C Jewell Mrs P S Donkin

Placings:0/0P0F/0P0003U6U02U0/5U65P/3P3432633/U21
0P5P/PP5F061P2P30P2-0100056 (4935)
2003/04: 20⁰G, 22¹G, 22⁰HY, 22²GS, 20⁹GF, 22⁵G, 18⁶G,

	Starts	1st	2nd	3rd	Win & Pl
Chases	7	1	0	0	2933
Career Total	**60**	**3**	**5**	**7**	**19635**

87 12/03 Font 2m6f F(0-90)HCh GD £2933
81 12/02 Font 2m4f F(0-100)HCh SFT £4832
79 12/01 Font 2m4f F(0-100)HCh GD £3055
Total win prize-money £10821

Going: Sf: 0-1 GS: 0-1 Gd: 1-4 GF: - Fm: 0-1

Smart Lord

70(95h) **(74h)64**

13-y-o br g Arctic Lord-Lady Catcher (Free Boy)
M R Bosley The Blowingstone Partnership

Placings:5050/303545P/20FP/0/43/3/36223/0554-0306
(2820)
2003/04: 17⁰GS, 17⁹GF, 16⁹G, 20⁶GF,

	Starts	1st	2nd	3rd	Win & Pl
Hurdles	3	0	0	1	272
Chases	1	0	0	0	0
Career Total	**32**	**0**	**3**	**7**	**6268**

Going: Sf: 0-0 GS: 0-1 Gd: 0-1 GF: - Fm: 0-2
Distance: 2m/2m3: 0-3 2m4-2m7: 0-0 3m+: 0-0
Track: LH: 0-0 RH: 0-4 Tight: 0-1 Gall: 0-0
Aids: Bl: 0-0 Vi: 0-4 Tstrap: 0-0 Ckp: 0-0
Best Rating: 91 3/96 Folk 2m1f110y gd-fm NHF

Selling hurdler; long-standing maiden.

Smart Savannah

104 **130+**

8-y-o b g Primo Dominie-High Savannah (Rousillon (USA))
C Tinkler George Ward

Placings:4/2122220/20111 (4718)
2003/04: 17²GS, 17⁹GS, 16¹GS, 16¹GS, 16¹G,

	Starts	1st	2nd	3rd	Win & Pl
Hurdles	5	3	1	0	17292
Career Total	**13**	**4**	**6**	**0**	**25419**

130 4/04 Ludl 2m D(0-125)HHdl GD £6825
128 3/04 Ludl 2m D(0-115)HHdl G-S £5512
126 3/04 Strf 2m110y E(0-110)HHdl GD £3445
97 8/01 Worc 2m E Hdl G-F £3230
Total win prize-money £19013

Going: Sf: 0-0 GS: 1-3 Gd: 2-2 GF: - Fm: 0-0
Distance: 2m/2m3: 3-5 2m4-2m7: 0-0 3m+: 0-0
Track: LH: 1-1 RH: 2-4 Tight: 1-2 Gall: 0-0
Aids: Bl: 0-0 Vi: 0-0 Tstrap: 0-0 Ckp: 0-0
Best Rating: 130 4/04 Ludl 2m good Hdl

Fair hurdler; best over two miles, but does stay further; acts
on any ground; has worn a tongue-tie.

Smart Scot

90 **77**

5-y-o ch g Selkirk (USA)-Amazing Bay (Mazilier (USA))
B P J Baugh S Day

Placings:000P (3081)
2003/04: 16⁰G, 16⁰GS, 16⁰S, 16⁰GS,

	Starts	1st	2nd	3rd	Win & Pl
Hurdles	4	0	0	0	
Career Total	**4**	**0**	**0**	**0**	

Going: Sf: 0-1 GS: 0-2 Gd: 0-1 GF: - Fm: 0-0
Distance: 2m/2m3: 0-4 2m4-2m7: 0-0 3m+: 0-0
Track: LH: 0-4 RH: 0-0 Tight: 0-2 Gall: 0-0
Aids: Bl: 0-0 Vi: 0-0 Tstrap: 0-0 Ckp: 0-0
Best Rating: 77 11/03 Hayd 2m gd-sft Hdl

Smarty (IRE)

104 (102h)**111**

11-y-o b/br g Royal Fountain-Cahernane Girl (Bargello)
M Pitman Mrs T Brown

Placings: 0036P/45F11P11/132P2/12035PP/05-4065

(4861)

2003/04: 24⁴G, 24⁰G, 36⁶G, 33⁵GS,

	Starts	1st	2nd	3rd	Win & Pl
Chases	4	0	0		12000
Career Total	31	6	3	3	181594
91	11/01	Plum	2m5f	E Hdl	G-S	£2387
133	12/00	Leic	2m7f110yD(0-125)HCh	G-S	£4192
140	3/99	Uttx	3m2f	C HCh	G-S	£18643
135	2/99	Hntg	3m	D(0-120)HCh	G-S	£5836
123	1/99	Leic	2m7f110yF(0-110)HCh	SFT	£3262
118	12/98	Wwck	3m2f	E Ch	G-S	£2846

Total win prize-money £37168

Going:	Sf: 0-0 GS: 0-1 Gd: 0-3 GF: - Fm: 0-0
Distance:	2m2m3: 0-0 2m4-2m7: 0-0 3m+: 0-4
Track:	LH: 0-4 RH: 0-0 Tight: 0-1 Gall: 0-2
Aids:	Bl: 0-0 Vi: 0 Tstrap: 0-0 Ckp: 0-1
Best Rating:	140 3/99 Uttx 3m2f gd-sft Ch

Useful staying chaser on his day; runner-up in 2001 Grand National; generally well held since; fourth in the 2004 National; suited by good to soft ground; often wears head-gear.

Smarty Boots (IRE)

92f **81+f**

5-y-o b m Arctic Lord-Solmus (IRE) (Sexton Blake)
A M Crow Bartley Nolan

Placings: 6065

(3887)

2003/04: 16⁸GF, 16⁰GS, 16⁶HY, 16⁵G,

	Starts	1st	2nd	3rd	Win & Pl
NH Flat	4	0	0	0	0
Career Total	4	0	0	0	0

Going:	Sf: 0-1 GS: 0-1 Gd: 0-1 GF: - Fm: 0-1
Distance:	2m2m3: 0-4 2m4-2m7: 0-0 3m+: 0-0
Track:	LH: 0-3 RH: 0-1 Tight: 0-0 Gall: 0-0
Aids:	Bl: 0-0 Vi: 0-0 Tstrap: 0-0 Ckp: 0-0
Best Rating:	85 2/04 Muss 2m good NHF

Smashing Time (USA)

94 **68**

6-y-o b m Smart Strike (CAN)-Broken Peace (USA) (Devil's Bag (USA))
M C Chapman Eric Knowles

Placings: P0-300

(2544)

2003/04: 17³GF, 24⁰GF, 19⁰GS,

	Starts	1st	2nd	3rd	Win & Pl
Hurdles	3	0	0	1	535
Career Total	5	0	0	1	535

Going:	Sf: 0-0 GS: 0-1 Gd: 0-0 GF: - Fm: 0-2
Distance:	2m2m3: 0-1 2m4-2m7: 0-1 3m+: 0-1
Track:	LH: 0-0 RH: 0-3 Tight: 0-3 Gall: 0-0
Aids:	Bl: 0-0 Vi: 0-0 Tstrap: 0-0 Ckp: 0-0
Best Rating:	68 8/03 MRas 2m1f110y gd-fm Hdl

Poor maiden on the Flat; easily best effort over hurdles when well beaten third in weak mares' only novices' hurdle at Market Rasen in August; acts on fast.

Smeathe's Ridge

92f **75f**

6-y-o b g Rakaposhi King-Mrs Barty (IRE) (King's Ride)
J A B Old Peter Guntrip

Placings: 00

(4447)

2003/04: 16⁶G, 16⁰S,

	Starts	1st	2nd	3rd	Win & Pl
NH Flat	2	0	0	0	0
Career Total	2	0	0	0	0

Going:	Sf: 0-1 GS: 0-0 Gd: 0-1 GF: - Fm: 0-0
Distance:	2m2m3: 0-2 2m4-2m7: 0-0 3m+: 0-0
Track:	LH: 0-2 RH: 0-0 Tight: 0-0 Gall: 0-1
Aids:	Bl: 0-0 Vi: 0-0 Tstrap: 0-0 Ckp: 0-0
Best Rating:	77 2/04 Newb 2m110y good NHF

Smetherds Tom

95 **64**

10-y-o b g Dortino-Nellie's Joy Vii (Damsire Unregistered)
N R Mitchell Mrs J C Duffy

Placings: 6UPP30-0F450PU4F

(1169)

2003/04: 19⁰G, 21⁶GF, 18⁴GF, 21⁵GF, 21⁰GF, 21⁶GF, 16⁰G, 22⁴GF, 18⁷GF,

	Starts	1st	2nd	3rd	Win & Pl
Chases	9	0	0	0	308
Career Total	15	0	0	1	1164

Going:	Sf: 0-0 GS: 0-0 Gd: 0-2 GF: - Fm: 0-7
Distance:	2m2m3: 0-3 2m4-2m7: 0-6 3m+: 0-0
Track:	LH: 0-4 RH: 0-2 Tight: 0-0 Gall: 0-0
Aids:	Bl: 0-0 Vi: 0-0 Tstrap: 0-0 Ckp: 0-9
Best Rating:	70 5/03 Font 2m2f gd-fm Ch

Smile Pleeze (IRE)

12-y-o b g Naheez (USA)-Harkin Park (Pollerton)
M R Daniell Miss S Troughton

Placings: 66F/50/5/40P/4-5P

(0509)

2003/04: 25⁵G, 28⁷GS,

	Starts	1st	2nd	3rd	Win & Pl
Chases	2	0	0	0	0
Career Total	12	0	0	0	302

Going:	Sf: 0-0 GS: 0-1 Gd: 0-1 GF: - Fm: 0-0
Distance:	2m2m3: 0-0 2m4-2m7: 0-0 3m+: 0-2
Track:	LH: 0-2 RH: 0-0 Tight: 0-1 Gall: 0-1
Aids:	Bl: 0-0 Vi: 0-0 Tstrap: 0-0 Ckp: 0-0
Best Rating:	95 3/02 Chel 3m2f110y good Ch

Winning pointer, best on a sound surface although has won on good to soft.

Smiling Applause

80 **48**

5-y-o b g Royal Applause-Smilingatstrangers (Macmillion)
Mrs Barbara Waring Eddys 'A Team

Placings: 400

(2598)

2003/04: 19⁴GF, 22⁰G, 21⁰G,

	Starts	1st	2nd	3rd	Win & Pl
Hurdles	3	0	0	0	0
Career Total	3	0	0	0	0

Going:	Sf: 0-0 GS: 0-0 Gd: 0-2 GF: - Fm: 0-1
Distance:	2m2m3: 0-0 2m4-2m7: 0-3 3m+: 0-0

Track:	LH: 0-2 RH: 0-1 Tight: 0-1 Gall: 0-0
Aids:	Bl: 0-0 Vi: 0-0 Tstrap: 0-0 Ckp: 0-0
Best Rating:	48 10/03 Hrfd 2m3f110y gd-fm Hdl

Smith's Perk (IRE)

11-y-o b g Executive Perk-Sister Of Slane (The Parson)
Mrs L C Jewell R B Morton

Placings: 106/2/PP/0/5PP6-0

(0127)

2003/04: 18⁰G,

	Starts	1st	2nd	3rd	Win & Pl
Chases	1	0	0	0	
Career Total	12	1	1	0	2329
101	12/97	Hntg	2m110y	H NHF	GD	£1413

Total win prize-money £1413

Going:	Sf: 0-0 GS: 0-0 Gd: 0-1 GF: - Fm: 0-0
Distance:	2m2m3: 0-0 2m4-2m7: 0-0 3m+: 0-0
Track:	LH: 0-0 RH: 0-0 Tight: 0-1 Gall: 0-0
Aids:	Bl: 0-0 Vi: 0-0 Tstrap: 0-1 Ckp: 0-0
Best Rating:	107 2/98 Newb 2m110y good NHF

Smithlyn

100 **99+**

7-y-o b g Greensmith-Sunylyn (Sunyboy)
K C Bailey Mrs K C Bailey and Mrs F Wills

Placings: 1324

(4908)

2003/04: 16¹G, 16³GS, 21²G, 20⁴S,

	Starts	1st	2nd	3rd	Win & Pl
NH Flat	2	1	0	1	3238
Hurdles	2	0	1	0	1537
Career Total	4	1	1	1	4775
104	5/03	Prth	2m110y	H NHF	GD	£3010

Total win prize-money £3010

Going:	Sf: 0-1 GS: 0-0 Gd: 1-2 GF: - Fm: 0-0
Distance:	**2m2m3: 1-2** 2m4-2m7: 0-2 3m+: 0-0
Track:	LH: 0-1 **RH: 1-3** Tight: 0-0 Gall: 0-1
Aids:	Bl: 0-0 Vi: 0-0 Tstrap: 0-0 Ckp: 0-0
Best Rating:	104 11/03 Uttx 2m gd-sft NHF

Smiths Landing

113 **125**

7-y-o b g Primitive Rising (USA)-Landing Power (Hills Forecast)
Mrs S J Smith Billy McCullough

Placings: 6464512-1P1

(4662)

2003/04: 20¹G, 20⁰G, 20¹S,

	Starts	1st	2nd	3rd	Win & Pl
Hurdles	3	2	0	0	11973
Career Total	10	3	1	0	17116
124	4/04	Hexm	2m4f110yD(0-125)HHdl	SFT	£5109
120	5/04	Weth	2m4f110yD(0-120)HHdl	GD	£6864
111	3/03	Hexm	2m4f110yE(0-105)HHdl	GD	£3794

Total win prize-money £15767

Going:	Sf: 1-1 GS: 0-0 Gd: 1-2 GF: - Fm: 0-0
Distance:	2m2m3: 0-0 **2m4-2m7: 2-3** 3m+: 0-0
Track:	**LH: 2-3** RH: 0-0 Tight: 0-0 Gall: 0-0
Aids:	Bl: 0-0 Vi: 0-0 Tstrap: 0-0 Ckp: 0-0
Best Rating:	124 4/04 Hexm 2m4f110y soft Hdl

Fair novice hurdler; jumped much better than previously when getting off the mark at Hexham in March; progressive since and recorded another victory in handicap company at same course following April; stays two and a half miles and should get further; handles fast and soft ground.

Smokestack (IRE)

78   **91**

8-y-o b g Lord Americo-Chiminee Fly (Proverb)
J A B Old M Lovatt/c Jenkins

Placings:054/30-0P   (4733)
2003/04: 16⁰GS, 22⁰G,

	Starts	1st	2nd	3rd	Win & Pl
Hurdles	2	0	0	0	.
Career Total	7	0	0	1	1224

Going:	Sf: 0-0 GS: 0-1 Gd: 0-1 GF: - Fm: 0-0
Distance:	2m/2m3: 0-1 2m4-2m7: 0-1 3m+: 0-0
Track:	LH: 0-1 RH: 0-1 Tight: 0-1 Gall: 0-0
Aids:	Bl: 0-0 Vi: 0-0 Tstrap: 0-0 Ckp: 0-0
Best Rating:	91 12/02 Sand 2m110y soft Hdl

Smokey Robot (IRE)

46

11-y-o b g Riberetto-Smokey Queen (Proverb)
D S Dennis Peter G Fowler

Placings:00/3463/PU/253/0/0   (3896)
2003/04: 24⁰G,

	Starts	1st	2nd	3rd	Win & Pl
Chases	1	0	0	0	
Career Total	13	0	1	3	2120

Going:	Sf: 0-0 GS: 0-0 Gd: 0-1 GF: - Fm: 0-0
Distance:	2m/2m3: 0-0 2m4-2m7: 0-0 3m+: 0-1
Track:	LH: 0-0 RH: 0-1 Tight: 0-0 Gall: 0-0
Aids:	Bl: 0-0 Vi: 0-0 Tstrap: 0-0 Ckp: 0-0
Best Rating:	95 11/00 Font 2m6f heavy Ch

Smokin Grey

85f

4-y-o gr f Terimon-Wollow Maid (Wollow)
M J Gingell (G G Margarson 10/12) Gingells Disciples

Placings:44RP   (4328)
2003/04: 14⁴G, 12⁴GF, 16⁶G, 16⁰PS,

	Starts	1st	2nd	3rd	Win & Pl
NH Flat	4	0	0	0	0
Career Total	4	0	0	0	0

Going:	Sf: 0-1 GS: 0-0 Gd: 0-2 GF: - Fm: 0-1
Distance:	2m/2m3: 0-2 2m4-2m7: 0-0 3m+: 0-0
Track:	LH: 0-3 RH: 0-1 Tight: 0-0 Gall: 0-0
Aids:	Bl: 0-0 Vi: 0-0 Tstrap: 0-0 Ckp: 0-0
Best Rating:	85 12/03 Newb 1m4f110y gd-fm NHF

Plating-class hurdler; ended up taking no part; will get further than two miles over hurdles; acts on a sound surface.

Smooth Passage

34

5-y-o b g Suave Dancer (USA)-Flagship (Rainbow Quest (USA))
J Gallagher Colin Rashbrook

Placings:0-5   (0852)
2003/04: 16⁵GF,

	Starts	1st	2nd	3rd	Win & Pl
Hurdles	1	0	0	0	0
Career Total	2	0	0	0	0

Going:	Sf: 0-0 GS: 0-0 Gd: 0-0 GF: - Fm: 0-1
Distance:	2m/2m3: 0-1 2m4-2m7: 0-0 3m+: 0-0
Track:	LH: 0-1 RH: 0-0 Tight: 0-1 Gall: 0-0
Aids:	Bl: 0-1 Vi: 0-0 Tstrap: 0-0 Ckp: 0-0
Best Rating:	40 3/03 Strf 2m110y gd-sft Hdl

Smoothie (IRE)

84   **73+**

6-y-o gr g Definite Article-Limpopo (Green Desert (USA))
Ian Williams (P F I Cole 26/5) Miss S Howell

Placings:000   (4490)
2003/04: 16⁰GS, 17⁰G, 16⁰G,

	Starts	1st	2nd	3rd	Win & Pl
Hurdles	3	0	0	0	
Career Total	3	0	0	0	

Going:	Sf: 0-0 GS: 0-1 Gd: 0-2 GF: - Fm: 0-0
Distance:	2m/2m3: 0-3 2m4-2m7: 0-0 3m+: 0-0
Track:	LH: 0-1 RH: 0-2 Tight: 0-2 Gall: 0-0
Aids:	Bl: 0-0 Vi: 0-0 Tstrap: 0-0 Ckp: 0-0
Best Rating:	73 1/04 Winc 2m gd-sft Hdl

Smudge (IRE)

(96h)   (98h)

7-y-o br g Be My Native (USA)-Crash Call (Crash Course)
R Ford Mrs Brenda Siddall

Placings:0/P06-53F   (4880)
2003/04: 20⁵G, 20³GS, 20⁰GS,

	Starts	1st	2nd	3rd	Win & Pl
Hurdles	2	0	0	1	394
Chases	1	0	0	0	0
Career Total	7	0	0	1	394

Going:	Sf: 0-0 GS: 0-2 Gd: 0-1 GF: - Fm: 0-0
Distance:	2m/2m3: 0-0 2m4-2m7: 0-0 3m+: 0-0
Track:	LH: 0-2 RH: 0-1 Tight: 0-0 Gall: 0-0
Aids:	Bl: 0-0 Vi: 0-0 Tstrap: 0-1 Ckp: 0-0
Best Rating:	98 3/04 Weth 2m4f110y gd-sft Hdl

Modest novice hurdler; suited by two and a half miles.

Smudger Smith

77(94h)   (105h)**33**

7-y-o ch g Deploy-Parfait Amour (Clantime)
B S Rothwell S P Hudson

Placings:1140/001P/6000   (3325)
2003/04: 16⁶S, 16⁰GS, 23⁰GS, 21⁰GS,

	Starts	1st	2nd	3rd	Win & Pl
Hurdles	3	0	0	0	0
Chases	1	0	0	0	0
Career Total	12	3	0	0	10471
105	1/02	Leic	2m	E(0-110)HHdl	SFT	£2744
110	11/00	Newc	2m	D Hdl	SFT	£3090
89	11/00	Hayd	2m	D Hdl	HVY	£3136
				Total win prize-money £8971

Going:	Sf: 0-1 GS: 0-3 Gd: 0-0 GF: - Fm: 0-0
Distance:	2m/2m3: 0-2 2m4-2m7: 0-1 3m+: 0-1
Track:	LH: 0-4 RH: 0-0 Tight: 0-1 Gall: 0-0
Aids:	Bl: 0-0 Vi: 0-0 Tstrap: 0-0 Ckp: 0-0
Best Rating:	110 11/00 Newc 2m soft Hdl

Smyslov

93   **72**

6-y-o b g Rainbow Quest (USA)-Vlaanderen (IRE) (In The Wings)
P R Webber Trevor Sharman

Placings:553/0-0   (0628)
2003/04: 16⁰GF,

	Starts	1st	2nd	3rd	Win & Pl
Hurdles	1	0	0	0	
Career Total	5	0	0	1	432

Going:	Sf: 0-0 GS: 0-0 Gd: 0-0 GF: - Fm: 0-1
Distance:	2m/2m3: 0-1 2m4-2m7: 0-0 3m+: 0-0
Track:	LH: 0-1 RH: 0-0 Tight: 0-0 Gall: 0-0
Aids:	Bl: 0-0 Vi: 0-0 Tstrap: 0-0 Ckp: 0-0
Best Rating:	90 4/02 Ludl 2m gd-fm Hdl

Snails Castle (IRE)

91

5-y-o b g Danehill (USA)-Bean Island (USA) (Afleet (CAN))
E W Tuer Shore Property

Placings:03-6   (1370)
2003/04: 20⁶F,

	Starts	1st	2nd	3rd	Win & Pl
Hurdles	1	0	0	0	0
Career Total	3	0	0	1	596

Going:	Sf: 0-0 GS: 0-0 Gd: 0-0 GF: - Fm: 0-1
Distance:	2m/2m3: 0-0 2m4-2m7: 0-1 3m+: 0-0
Track:	LH: 0-1 RH: 0-0 Tight: 0-0 Gall: 0-0
Aids:	Bl: 0-0 Vi: 0-0 Tstrap: 0-0 Ckp: 0-0
Best Rating:	86 10/02 Kels 2m110y gd-fm Hdl

Poor form when placed in juvenile hurdle at Kelso in October.

Snipe

98   **95**

6-y-o ch g Anshan-Flexwing (Electric)
Ian Williams C J Tipton

Placings:04-054045   (4564)
2003/04: 20⁰GS, 17⁵G, 16⁴GS, 16⁰GS, 17⁴GS, 19⁵GS,

	Starts	1st	2nd	3rd	Win & Pl
Hurdles	6	0	0	0	297
Career Total	8	0	0	0	297

Going:	Sf: 0-0 GS: 0-5 Gd: 0-1 GF: - Fm: 0-0
Distance:	2m/2m3: 0-5 2m4-2m7: 0-1 3m+: 0-0
Track:	LH: 0-5 RH: 0-1 Tight: 0-1 Gall: 0-1
Aids:	Bl: 0-0 Vi: 0-0 Tstrap: 0-0 Ckp: 0-0
Best Rating:	95 12/03 Hayd 2m gd-sft Hdl

Moderate novice hurdler; stays 2m 4f; acts on easy ground.

Snitton West

8-y-o b g Derrylin-Snitton (Rymer)
G C Evans Capt J M G Lumsden

Placings:P   (0262)
2003/04: 20⁰PGF,

	Starts	1st	2nd	3rd	Win & Pl
Chases	1	0	0	0	
Career Total	1	0	0	0	

Going:	Sf: 0-0 GS: 0-0 Gd: 0-0 GF: - Fm: 0-1
Distance:	2m/2m3: 0-0 2m4-2m7: 0-1 3m+: 0-0
Track:	LH: 0-0 RH: 0-1 Tight: 0-1 Gall: 0-0
Aids:	Bl: 0-1 Vi: 0-0 Tstrap: 0-0 Ckp: 0-0

Snoopy Loopy (IRE)
101f　　　　　　　　　　**113f**
6-y-o ch g Old Vic-Lovely Snoopy (IRE) (Phardante (FR))
Miss V Scott Miss Victoria Scott Jnr

Placings: 1					(4787)
2003/04: 16¹G,					

	Starts	1st	2nd	3rd	Win & Pl
NH Flat	1	1	0	0	1985
Career Total	1	1	0	0	1985
113 4/04 Hntg	2m110y	H NHF		GD	£1984
				Total win prize-money £1985	

Going:	Sf: 0-0 GS: 0-0 Gd: 1-1 GF: - Fm: 0-0
Distance:	2m/2m3: 1-1 2m4-2m7: 0-0 3m+: 0-0
Track:	LH: 0-0 RH: 1-1 Tight: 0-0 Gall: 1-1
Aids:	Bl: 0-0 Vi: 0-0 Tstrap: 0-0 Ckp: 0-0
Best Rating:	113 4/04 Hntg 2m110y good NHF

Game winner of ordinary bumper on debut at Huntingdon in April on good.

Snooty Eskimo (IRE)

12-y-o ch g Aristocracy-Over The Arctic (Over The River (FR))
W T Reed T R P S Norton

Placings: 0050/PP2060/P05P00/6P0P/P43/P006P/0-6					(4191)
2003/04: 20⁹GF, 25⁶GS,					

	Starts	1st	2nd	3rd	Win & Pl
Chases	2	0	0	0	0
Career Total	30	0	1	1	1014

Going:	Sf: 0-0 GS: 0-1 Gd: 0-0 GF: - Fm: 0-1
Distance:	2m/2m3: 0-0 2m4-2m7: 0-1 3m+: 0-1
Track:	LH: 0-2 RH: 0-0 Tight: 0-0 Gall: 0-1
Aids:	Bl: 0-0 Vi: 0-0 Tstrap: 0-0 Ckp: 0-0
Best Rating:	80 2/01 Kels 3m1f soft Ch

Snowmore
114
8-y-o ch m Glacial Storm (USA)-Royal Typhoon (Royal Fountain)
Mrs S J Smith Paul J Dixon

Placings: 4622412P0/2110442P-1					(0333)
2003/04: 21¹GF,					

	Starts	1st	2nd	3rd	Win & Pl
Hurdles	1	1	0	0	3591
Career Total	18	4	5	0	21207
114 5/03 Sthl	2m5f110yE(0-105)HHdl	G-F	£3591
105 10/02 Sthl	2m5f110yC(0-130)HHdl	GD	£6890
99 8/02 Sthl	2m5f110yE(0-110)HHdl	G-F	£3410
83 11/01 Catt	2m3f F Hdl	G-F	£1907
	Total win prize-money £15799	

Going:	Sf: 0-0 GS: 0-0 Gd: 0-0 GF: - Fm: 1-1
Distance:	2m/2m3: 0-0 2m4-2m7: 1-1 3m+: 0-0
Track:	LH: 1-1 RH: 0-0 Tight: 0-0 Gall: 0-0
Aids:	Bl: 0-0 Vi: 0-0 Tstrap: 0-0 Ckp: 0-0
Best Rating:	114 5/03 Sthl 2m5f110y gd-fm Hdl

Modest hurdler, stays two miles-five, suited by a sound surface and positive tactics; recorded third win over Southwell's mini-fences in May 2003 but finished lame.

Snowy (IRE)
105　　　　　　　　　　**100+**
6-y-o gr g Pierre-Snowy Gunner (Gunner B)
J I A Charlton Mr & Mrs Raymond Anderson Green

Placings: 03013					(4879)
2003/04: 16⁵G, 17⁹HY, 20⁹G, 22¹G, 20³GS,					

	Starts	1st	2nd	3rd	Win & Pl
NH Flat	1	0	0	0	0
Hurdles	4	1	0	2	4955
Career Total	5	1	0	2	4955
100 3/04 Kels	2m6f110yE Hdl	GD	£3549
	Total win prize-money £3549	

Going:	Sf: 0-1 GS: 0-1 Gd: 1-3 GF: - Fm: 0-0
Distance:	2m/2m3: 0-2 2m4-2m7: 1-3 3m+: 0-0
Track:	LH: 1-2 RH: 0-3 Tight: 1-1 Gall: 0-0
Aids:	Bl: 0-0 Vi: 0-0 Tstrap: 0-0 Ckp: 0-0
Best Rating:	100 4/04 Carl 2m4f gd-sft Hdl

Much improved effort when wide margin winner of moderate novices' hurdle at Kelso in March; stays well; acts on good or softer.

So Daisy

6-y-o b m Teenoso (USA)-La Margarite (Bonne Noel)
C J Price W J Butler

Placings: 0					(4816)
2003/04: 16⁹G,					

	Starts	1st	2nd	3rd	Win & Pl
NH Flat	1	0	0	0	
Career Total	1	0	0	0	

Going:	Sf: 0-0 GS: 0-0 Gd: 0-1 GF: - Fm: 0-0
Distance:	2m/2m3: 0-1 2m4-2m7: 0-0 3m+: 0-0
Track:	LH: 0-1 RH: 0-0 Tight: 0-0 Gall: 0-0
Aids:	Bl: 0-0 Vi: 0-0 Tstrap: 0-0 Ckp: 0-0

So Sure (IRE)
104　　　　　　　　　　**94**
4-y-o b g Definite Article-Zorilla (Belmez (USA))
J G M O'Shea (P C Haslam 16/10) Premier-Racing.Net (2)

Placings: P15224046F6					(4898)
2003/04: 17⁵GF, 16¹F, 16⁵GF, 16²GF, 16²G, 16⁴GF, 16⁹S, 17⁴GS, 17⁶G, 17⁶GF, 16⁶G,					

	Starts	1st	2nd	3rd	Win & Pl
Hurdles	11	1	2	0	6310
Career Total	11	1	2	0	6310
85 10/03 Towc	2m F Hdl	FRM	£2628
	Total win prize-money £2629	

Going:	Sf: 0-1 GS: 0-1 Gd: 0-3 GF: - Fm: 1-6
Distance:	2m/2m3: 1-11 2m4-2m7: 0-0 3m+: 0-0
Track:	LH: 0-4 RH: 1-7 Tight: 0-3 Gall: 0-1
Aids:	Bl: 0-0 Vi: 0-0 Tstrap: 0-0 Ckp: 0-0
Best Rating:	94 2/04 Hrfd 2m1f gd-sft Hdl

Moderate hurdler, stays two miles; acts on good ground.

So Tempted

5-y-o br m So Factual (USA)-Bystrouska (Gorytus (USA))

N Wilson J Watson

Placings: SF-P					(1625)
2003/04: 16⁶GF,					

	Starts	1st	2nd	3rd	Win & Pl
Hurdles	1	0	0	0	
Career Total	3	0	0	0	

Going:	Sf: 0-0 GS: 0-0 Gd: 0-0 GF: - Fm: 0-1
Distance:	2m/2m3: 0-1 2m4-2m7: 0-0 3m+: 0-0
Track:	LH: 0-1 RH: 0-0 Tight: 0-0 Gall: 0-0
Aids:	Bl: 0-0 Vi: 0-0 Tstrap: 0-0 Ckp: 0-0

Sobraon (IRE)
93f　　　　　　　　　　**114+f**
5-y-o b g Topanoora-Anniepepp (IRE) (Montelimar (USA))
N G Richards Mrs Julia Young & Mrs Sarah Walsh

Placings: 31					(4277)
2003/04: 17³G, 17¹G,					

	Starts	1st	2nd	3rd	Win & Pl
NH Flat	2	1	0	1	3078
Career Total	2	1	0	1	3078
109 3/04 Carl	2m1f H NHF	GD	£2009
	Total win prize-money £2009	

Going:	Sf: 0-0 GS: 0-0 Gd: 1-2 GF: - Fm: 0-0
Distance:	2m/2m3: 1-2 2m4-2m7: 0-0 3m+: 0-0
Track:	LH: 0-0 RH: 1-1 Tight: 0-0 Gall: 0-0
Aids:	Bl: 0-0 Vi: 0-0 Tstrap: 0-0 Ckp: 0-0
Best Rating:	114 11/03 Aint 2m1f good NHF

Fair bumper performer; acts on good.

Society Affair
108　　　　　　　　　　**103+**
5-y-o b g Moscow Society (USA)-Society News (Law Society (USA))
Jonjo O'Neill John Power

Placings: 324P0510					(4948)
2003/04: 16³GD, 17²GF, 19⁴G, 20⁵GS, 21⁰GS, 20⁵GS, 26¹G, 27⁶GS,					

	Starts	1st	2nd	3rd	Win & Pl
NH Flat	2	0	1	1	752
Hurdles	6	1	0	0	7307
Career Total	8	1	1	1	8059
103 3/04 Hntg	3m2f	D(0-115)HHdl	GD	£7007
	Total win prize-money £7007	

Going:	Sf: 0-0 GS: 0-4 Gd: 1-2 GF: - Fm: 0-2
Distance:	2m/2m3: 0-3 2m4-2m7: 0-3 3m+: 1-2
Track:	LH: 0-1 RH: 1-6 Tight: 0-1 Gall: 1-2
Aids:	Bl: 0-0 Vi: 0-0 Tstrap: 0-0 Ckp: 0-0
Best Rating:	103 3/04 Hntg 3m2f good Hdl

Winning hurdler; stays three miles; acts on a sound surface.

Society Buck (IRE)
104　　　　　　　　　　**102**
7-y-o b g Moscow Society (USA)-Bucks Grove (IRE) (Buckskin (FR))
John Allen John Allen

Placings: 0/1040-3021					(4887)
2003/04: 17³GS, 22⁰G, 22²G, 22¹GF,					

	Starts	1st	2nd	3rd	Win & Pl
Hurdles	4	1	1	1	8773
Career Total	9	2	1	1	10927
102 4/04 Strf	2m6f110yD Hdl	G-F	£6123
89 7/02 Sedg	2m1f H NHF	G-F	£1848
	Total win prize-money £7971	

Going: Sf: 0-0 GS: 0-1 Gd: 0-2 GF: - Fm: 1-1
Distance: 2m/2m3: 0-1 **2m4-2m7: 1-3** 3m+: 0-0
Track: LH: 1-3 RH: 0-1 Tight: 1-3 Gall: 0-0
Aids: Bl: 0-0 Vi: 0-0 Tstrap: 0-0 Ckp: 0-0
Best Rating: 102 4/04 Strf 2m6f110y gd-fm Hdl

Moderate hurdler; stays two miles six furlongs; acts on fast.

Sohapara

9-y-o ch m Arapahos (FR)-Mistress Boreen (Boreen (FR))
Miss J E Mathias Mrs S E Mathias

Placings:05/2 (4815)
2003/04: 242G,

	Starts	1st	2nd	3rd	Win & Pl
Chases	1	0	1	0	1036
Career Total	3	0	1	0	1036

Going: Sf: 0-0 GS: 0-0 Gd: 0-1 GF: 0-0 Fm: 0-0
Distance: 2m/2m3: 0-0 2m4-2m7: 0-0 3m+: 0-1
Track: LH: 0-1 RH: 0-0 Tight: 0-0 Gall: 0-0
Aids: Bl: 0-0 Vi: 0-0 Tstrap: 0-0 Ckp: 0-0
Best Rating: 91 4/04 Chep 3m good Ch

Prolific winner between the flags; eventually well beaten second behind Cherry Gold in hunter chase at Chepstow April 2004.

Soho Fields (IRE)
100   103
7-y-o b g Good Thyne (USA)-Rosie Owen (IRE) (Roselier (FR))
Miss H C Knight The Earl Cadogan

Placings:1054-3 (0135)
2003/04: 163G,

	Starts	1st	2nd	3rd	Win & Pl
Hurdles	1	0	0	1	650
Career Total	5	1	0	1	6189
103 11/02 Ludl 2m D Hdl				G-S	£4706

Total win prize-money £4706

Going: Sf: 0-0 GS: 0-0 Gd: 0-1 GF: 0-0 Fm: 0-0
Distance: 2m/2m3: 0-0 2m4-2m7: 0-0 3m+: 0-0
Track: LH: 0-0 RH: 0-1 Tight: 0-0 Gall: 0-0
Aids: Bl: 0-0 Vi: 0-0 Tstrap: 0-0 Ckp: 0-0
Best Rating: 103 5/03 Ludl 2m good Hdl

Modest hurdler; won on his debut at Ludlow; has the scope to develop into a chaser in time; acts on good or softer.

Sol Chance
87   83
5-y-o ch g Jupiter Island-Super Sol (Rolfe (USA))
R S Brookhouse R S Brookhouse

Placings:6-40P00 (4959)
2003/04: 164GF, 169GF, 19PG, 240G, 190G,

	Starts	1st	2nd	3rd	Win & Pl
NH Flat	2	0	0	0	0
Hurdles	3	0	0	0	0
Career Total	6	0	0	0	0

Going: Sf: 0-0 GS: 0-1 Gd: 0-3 GF: - Fm: 0-1
Distance: 2m/2m3: 0-2 2m4-2m7: 0-2 3m+: 0-1
Track: LH: 0-3 RH: 0-2 Tight: 0-1 Gall: 0-0
Aids: Bl: 0-0 Vi: 0-0 Tstrap: 0-0 Ckp: 0-0
Best Rating: 93 2/03 Winc 2m gd-sft NHF

Sol Music

12-y-o ch g Southern Music-Tyqueen (Tycoon Ii)
Mrs V M Graham The G & P Partnership

Placings:0/55/245212/03551120/5P55600/131/01112-1434 (4696)
2003/04: 212S, 161G, 204G, 203G, 194G,

	Starts	1st	2nd	3rd	Win & Pl
Chases	5	1	1	1	8770
Career Total	36	9	5	3	36848

105	5/03	Uttx	2m H Ch		GD	£3373
107	3/03	Extr	2m3f110yH Ch		FRM	£3692
114	3/03	Leic	2m4f110yH Ch		G-S	£2660
107	5/02	Towc	2m110y H Ch		GD	£3010
107	3/02	Extr	2m3f110yH Ch		GD	£2156
110	5/01	NAbb	2m110y E(0-115)HCh		G-F	£3410
126	3/99	Hrfd	2m E Ch		G-S	£3160
118	3/99	Tntn	2m110y E(0-100)HCh		SFT	£3241
113	4/98	Hrfd	2m1f E Hdl		SFT	£2641

Total win prize-money £27346

Going: Sf: 0-1 GS: 0-0 Gd: 1-4 GF: - Fm: 0-0
Distance: **2m/2m3: 1-1** 2m4-2m7: 0-4 3m+: 0-0
Track: LH: 1-2 RH: 0-3 Tight: 0-2 Gall: 0-0
Aids: Bl: 0-0 Vi: 0-0 Tstrap: 0-0 Ckp: 0-0
Best Rating: 126 3/99 Hrfd 2m gd-sft Ch

A front-running hunter chaser, seems best in the spring on a right-handed track; suited by two miles and handles any ground.

Solar Dove
(91h)
8-y-o b g Jupiter Island-Celtic Dove (Celtic Cone)
C J Price M J Low

Placings:00F41/0PPU0/PF (3774)
2003/04: 20PG, 24FG,

	Starts	1st	2nd	3rd	Win & Pl
Chases	2	0	0	0	
Career Total	12	1	0	0	2304
91 4/01 Extr 2m6f110yE Hdl				SFT	£2304

Total win prize-money £2304

Going: Sf: 0-0 GS: 0-0 Gd: 0-2 GF: - Fm: 0-0
Distance: 2m/2m3: 0-0 2m4-2m7: 0-1 3m+: 0-1
Track: LH: 0-0 RH: 0-2 Tight: 0-2 Gall: 0-0
Aids: Bl: 0-1 Vi: 0-0 Tstrap: 0-0 Ckp: 0-0
Best Rating: 91 4/01 Extr 2m6f110y soft Hdl

Soldershire
57   91
7-y-o b g Weld-Dishcloth (Fury Royal)
S Dow P McCarthy

Placings:0/3P-5 (4755)
2003/04: 215G,

	Starts	1st	2nd	3rd	Win & Pl
Hurdles	1	0	0	0	0
Career Total	4	0	0	1	444

Going: Sf: 0-0 GS: 0-0 Gd: 0-1 GF: - Fm: 0-0
Distance: 2m/2m3: 0-0 2m4-2m7: 0-1 3m+: 0-0
Track: LH: 0-1 RH: 0-0 Tight: 0-1 Gall: 0-0
Aids: Bl: 0-0 Vi: 0-0 Tstrap: 0-0 Ckp: 0-0
Best Rating: 91 10/02 Font 2m2f110y good Hdl

Solerina (IRE)
115   154
7-y-o b m Toulon-Deep Peace (Deep Run)
James Bowe John P Bowe

Placings:2431/512111111-311414 (4423)
2003/04: 163GY, 201S, 201S, 164Y, 191S, 244G,

	Starts	1st	2nd	3rd	Win & Pl
Hurdles	6	3	0	1	68999
Career Total	19	11	2	2	187058

150	1/04	Naas	2m3f	Hdl	SFT	£9154
154	12/03	Navn	2m4f	Hdl	SFT	£16883
151	11/03	Fair	2m4f	Hdl	SFT	£31655
146	2/03	Leop	2m2f	Hdl	SFT	£31655
151	1/03	Leop	2m4f	Hdl	Y-S	£14350
151	12/02	Leop	2m	Hdl	HVY	£23620
151	12/02	Navn	2m4f	Hdl	Y-S	£19938
131	12/02	Punc	2m	Hdl	SH	£8972
151	11/02	Thur	2m6f110y	Hdl	SFT	£6138
111	11/02	Thur	2m	Hdl	G-Y	£3809
109	3/02	Naas	2m	NHF	HVY	£3809

Total win prize-money £169990

Going: Sf: 3-3 GS: 0-0 Gd: 0-1 GF: - Fm: 0-0
Distance: 2m/2m3: 1-3 **2m4-2m7: 2-2** 3m+: 0-1
Track: **LH: 2-4** RH: 1-2 Tight: 0-0 Gall: 0-1
Aids: Bl: 0-0 Vi: 0-0 Tstrap: 0-0 Ckp: 0-0
Best Rating: 154 12/03 Navn 2m4f soft Hdl

Smart front-running Irish hurdler from the stable of Limestone Lad; successful ten times over hurdles; stays 2m 4f, should get farther; suited by give in the ground; very tough.

Solmorin
50f
6-y-o b m Fraam-Reclusive (Sunley Builds)
R J Baker M Channon

Placings:0 (1273)
2003/04: 170GF,

	Starts	1st	2nd	3rd	Win & Pl
NH Flat	1	0	0	0	
Career Total	1	0	0	0	

Going: Sf: 0-0 GS: 0-0 Gd: 0-0 GF: - Fm: 0-1
Distance: 2m/2m3: 0-1 2m4-2m7: 0-0 3m+: 0-0
Track: LH: 0-1 RH: 0-0 Tight: 0-1 Gall: 0-0
Aids: Bl: 0-0 Vi: 0-0 Tstrap: 0-0 Ckp: 0-0

Solo Dancer
102   86+
6-y-o ch m Sayaarr (USA)-Oiseval (National Trust)
Mrs H M Bridges Mrs H M Bridges

Placings:0F630P/6PFFP3-65553103P (4897)
2003/04: 176G, 195GF, 195GF, 195GS, 163S, 211G, 220GS, 213G, 22PG,

	Starts	1st	2nd	3rd	Win & Pl
Hurdles	9	1	0	4	4608
Career Total	21	1	0	4	5510
86 3/04 Plum 2m5f E(0-105)HHdl				GD	£3513

Total win prize-money £3513

Going: Sf: 0-1 GS: 0-2 Gd: 1-4 GF: - Fm: 0-2
Distance: 2m/2m3: 0-4 **2m4-2m7: 1-5** 3m+: 0-0
Track: **LH: 1-3** RH: 0-6 Tight: 1-3 Gall: 0-0
Aids: Bl: 0-0 Vi: 0-0 Tstrap: 0-0 **Ckp: 1-9**
Best Rating: 86 4/04 Plum 2m5f good Hdl

Plating-class hurdler; modest form over hurdles so far; has worn cheekpieces.

Soloman (IRE)

11-y-o br g Mandalus-Solo Player (Blue Refrain)
Mrs Jane Galpin H T Pelham

Placings:32132/34433/123521/5/0P402/P   (3792)
2003/04: 25PG,

	Starts	1st	2nd	3rd	Win & Pl
Chases	1	0	0	0	
Career Total	23	3	5	6	28546
116 4/00 Plum	3m2f	E Ch		G-S	£3168
122 10/99 Chel	2m4f110yD(0-110)HCh		GD	£5550
123 2/98 Towc	2m	E Hdl		GD	£2652

Total win prize-money £11372

Going:	Sf: 0-0 GS: 0-0 Gd: 0-1 GF: - Fm: 0-0
Distance:	2m/2m3: 0-0 2m4-2m7: 0-0 3m+: 0-1
Track:	LH: 0-0 RH: 0-1 Tight: 0-0 Gall: 0-1
Aids:	Bl: 0-0 Vi: 0-0 Tstrap: 0-0 Ckp: 0-0
Best Rating:	130 12/97 Asct 2m110y gd-sft Hdl

Solvang (IRE)

12-y-o b g Carlingford Castle-Bramble Bird (Pitpan)
Mrs J Marles Mrs N A Hedges

Placings:10/1132FP3PP/10201613/232125/45F6/05/PP5P-
4PP   (4696)
2003/04: 204G, 20PGS, 19PG,

	Starts	1st	2nd	3rd	Win & Pl
Chases	3	0	0	0	0
Career Total	38	7	5	4	46451
130 11/99 Aint	2m4f	C(0-130)HCh	GD	£7067
110 10/98 Winc	2m6f	E Hdl	G-F	£2206
126 8/98 Tral	2m4f	HCh	GD	£11260
121 6/98 Rosc	3m100y	Ch	G-Y	£2382
125 7/97 Klny	2m4f	Ch	Y-S	£3391
113 6/97 Clon	2m2f	Ch	GD	£2712
109 4/97 Fair	2m2f	NHF	G-F	£6287

Total win prize-money £35309

Going:	Sf: 0-0 GS: 0-1 Gd: 0-2 GF: - Fm: 0-0
Distance:	2m/2m3: 0-0 2m4-2m7: 0-3 3m+: 0-0
Track:	LH: 0-0 RH: 0-3 Tight: 0-1 Gall: 0-0
Aids:	Bl: 0-0 Vi: 0-0 Tstrap: 0-0 Ckp: 0-0
Best Rating:	130 12/99 Leic 2m4f110y good Ch

Solve It Sober (IRE)

94(77h)   (49h)**67+**
10-y-o b g Carefree Dancer (USA)-Haunted Lady
(Trimmingham)
S G Griffiths (S Slevin 9/5) S G Griffiths

Placings:UPP002   (4814)
2003/04: 24UGF, 20PS, 19PGS, 19UHY, 19UG, 19²G,

	Starts	1st	2nd	3rd	Win & Pl
Hurdles	3	0	0	0	
Chases	3	0	1	0	768
Career Total	6	0	1	0	768

Going:	Sf: 0-2 GS: 0-1 Gd: 0-2 GF: - Fm: 0-1
Distance:	2m/2m3: 0-1 2m4-2m7: 0-4 3m+: 0-1
Track:	LH: 0-2 RH: 0-4 Tight: 0-0 Gall: 0-0
Aids:	Bl: 0-1 Vi: 0-0 Tstrap: 0-4 Ckp: 0-0
Best Rating:	67 4/04 Chep 2m3f110y good Ch

Finally showed signs of ability when well beaten second in
first-time blinkers in 2m 4f selling handicap chase at
Chepstow April 2004.

Solway Breeze (IRE)

99   **76**
11-y-o b m King's Ride-Spicey Cut (Cut Above)
Ms Liz Harrison David Alan Harrison

Placings:225/331P10/F4UP/3312/UPP0-U43UP   (4882)
2003/04: 25PG, 27UGS, 24PHY, 20PHY, 25US, 26PGS,

	Starts	1st	2nd	3rd	Win & Pl
Chases	6	0	0	1	1049
Career Total	26	3	3	5	16738
98 3/02 Ayr	3m1f	D Ch	SFT	£4367
116 1/00 Hayd	2m6f	D Hdl	SFT	£3666
97 12/99 Hexm	3m	E Hdl	HVY	£2658

Total win prize-money £10691

Going:	Sf: 0-3 GS: 0-2 Gd: 0-1 GF: - Fm: 0-0
Distance:	2m/2m3: 0-2 2m4-2m7: 0-1 3m+: 0-5
Track:	LH: 0-3 RH: 0-3 Tight: 0-1 Gall: 0-1
Aids:	Bl: 0-0 Vi: 0-0 Tstrap: 0-0 Ckp: 0-0
Best Rating:	116 1/00 Hayd 2m6f soft Hdl

Moderate chaser; stays three miles plus; suited by testing
ground.

Solway Dawn

98   **71**
9-y-o ch m Minster Son-Oh Dear (Paico)
Ms Liz Harrison David Alan Harrison

Placings:5110/53P/0/P40035P   (2431)
2003/04: 20PG, 164G, 16PGF, 20PG, 24³GF, 20⁵GS, 24PGS,

	Starts	1st	2nd	3rd	Win & Pl
Hurdles	7	0	0	1	638
Career Total	15	2	0	2	4451
102 3/00 Ludl	2m	H NHF	GD	£1683
100 3/00 Catt	2m	H NHF	G-F	£1652

Total win prize-money £3336

Going:	Sf: 0-0 GS: 0-2 Gd: 0-3 GF: - Fm: 0-2
Distance:	2m/2m3: 0-2 2m4-2m7: 0-3 3m+: 0-2
Track:	LH: 0-4 RH: 0-3 Tight: 0-0 Gall: 0-0
Aids:	Bl: 0-0 Vi: 0-0 Tstrap: 0-0 Ckp: 0-0
Best Rating:	102 3/00 Ludl 2m good NHF

Plating-class hurdler; dual bumper winner; yet to find a trip;
effective on a sound surface.

Solway Donal (IRE)

98   **80**
11-y-o b m Celio Rufo-Knockaville (Crozier)
Ms Liz Harrison David Alan Harrison

Placings:0FP/55/06P40PU316P/UPP635P-3   (0470)
2003/04: 24PGF, 20³G,

	Starts	1st	2nd	3rd	Win & Pl
Chases	2	0	0	1	606
Career Total	24	1	0	3	4276
72 1/02 Sedg	2m110y	F(0-90)HCh	HVY	£2499

Total win prize-money £2499

Going:	Sf: 0-0 GS: 0-0 Gd: 0-1 GF: - Fm: 0-1
Distance:	2m/2m3: 0-0 2m4-2m7: 0-1 3m+: 0-1
Track:	LH: 0-2 RH: 0-0 Tight: 0-0 Gall: 0-1
Aids:	Bl: 0-0 Vi: 0-0 Tstrap: 0-0 Ckp: 0-1
Best Rating:	80 5/03 Hexm 2m4f110y good Ch

Plating-class chaser; poor form in 2002/2003; handles
heavy ground, but has won on good.

Solway Gale (IRE)

89(96h)   (77+h)**83+**
7-y-o b m Husyan (USA)-Some Gale (Strong Gale)
Ms Liz Harrison David Alan Harrison

Placings:60/063056-154P53F   (3357)
2003/04: 20¹GF, 20⁵GF, 21⁴GF, 25PGS, 20⁵GF, 24³GF, 22FS,

	Starts	1st	2nd	3rd	Win & Pl
Hurdles	3	1	0	0	2184
Chases	4	0	0	1	627
Career Total	15	1	0	2	3341
77 10/03 Carl	2m4f	F Hdl	G-F	£2184

Total win prize-money £2184

Going:	Sf: 0-1 GS: 0-1 Gd: 0-0 GF: - Fm: 1-5
Distance:	2m/2m3: 0-2 2m4-2m7: 1-5 3m+: 0-2
Track:	LH: 0-3 RH: 1-4 Tight: 0-4 Gall: 0-0
Aids:	Bl: 0-0 Vi: 0-0 Tstrap: 0-0 Ckp: 0-0
Best Rating:	83 1/04 Muss 3m gd-fm Ch

Very modest novice hurdler; took a weak event at Carlisle
in October; erratic over fences so far.

Solway Gorge

8-y-o ch g Jumbo Hirt (USA)-Kilkenny Gorge (Deep Run)
Ms Liz Harrison David Alan Harrison

Placings:00P-PPP   (4273)
2003/04: 21PGS, 25PHY, 24FG,

	Starts	1st	2nd	3rd	Win & Pl
Hurdles	1	0	0	0	0
Chases	2	0	0	0	0
Career Total	6	0	0	0	

Going:	Sf: 0-1 GS: 0-1 Gd: 0-1 GF: - Fm: 0-0
Distance:	2m/2m3: 0-0 2m4-2m7: 0-1 3m+: 0-2
Track:	LH: 0-2 RH: 0-1 Tight: 0-2 Gall: 0-0
Aids:	Bl: 0-1 Vi: 0-0 Tstrap: 0-0 Ckp: 0-0
Best Rating:	31 9/02 Prth 2m110y gd-fm NHF

Solway Larkin (IRE)

78f   **57f**
6-y-o b m Supreme Leader-In Any Case (IRE) (Torus)
Ms Liz Harrison David Alan Harrison

Placings:6   (4952)
2003/04: 16²GS,

	Starts	1st	2nd	3rd	Win & Pl
NH Flat	1	0	0	0	0
Career Total	1	0	0	0	0

Going:	Sf: 0-0 GS: 0-1 Gd: 0-0 GF: - Fm: 0-0
Distance:	2m/2m3: 0-1 2m4-2m7: 0-0 3m+: 0-0
Track:	LH: 0-0 RH: 0-1 Tight: 0-0 Gall: 0-0
Aids:	Bl: 0-0 Vi: 0-0 Tstrap: 0-0 Ckp: 0-0
Best Rating:	57 4/04 Prth 2m110y gd-sft NHF

Solway Minstrel

104   **101+**
7-y-o ch g Jumbo Hirt (USA)-Spicey Cut (Cut Above)
Ms Liz Harrison David Alan Harrison

Placings:0-33243541   (4948)
2003/04: 24³GF, 22³G, 24²G, 24⁴GF, 22³GS, 24⁵HY, 24⁴S, 27¹GS,

	Starts	1st	2nd	3rd	Win & Pl
Hurdles	8	1	1	3	10428
Career Total	9	1	1	3	10428

101 4/04 Prth 3m3f D(0-125)HHdl G-S £6994
Total win prize-money £6994

Going:	Sf: 0-2 GS: 1-2 Gd: 0-2 GF: - Fm: 0-2
Distance:	2m/2m3: 0-2 2m4-2m7: 0-2 3m+: 1-6
Track:	LH: 0-2 RH: 0-5 Tight: 0-0 Gall: 0-0
Aids:	Bl: 0-0 Vi: 0-0 Tstrap: 0-0 Ckp: 0-0
Best Rating:	101 4/04 Prth 3m3f gd-sft Hdl

Moderate novice hurdler; stays three miles and three furlongs; acts on a sound surface.

Solway Plain
97 (76h)96
10-y-o b g King's Ride-Oh Dear (Paico)
Ms Liz Harrison David Alan Harrison

Placings:5635400/5PPP-P2F (0648)
2003/04: 25PG, 20²G, 20FGF,

	Starts	1st	2nd	3rd	Win & Pl
Chases	3	0	1	0	948
Career Total	14	0	1	1	1388

Going:	Sf: 0-0 GS: 0-0 Gd: 0-2 GF: - Fm: 0-1
Distance:	2m/2m3: 0-0 2m4-2m7: 0-2 3m+: 0-1
Track:	LH: 0-0 RH: 0-0 Tight: 0-0 Gall: 0-0
Aids:	Bl: 0-0 Vi: 0-0 Tstrap: 0-0 Ckp: 0-2
Best Rating:	96 5/03 Hexm 2m4f110y good Ch

Plating-class chaser; acts opn a sound surface.

Solway Quest
6-y-o ch m Jumbo Hirt (USA)-Kilkenny Gorge (Deep Run)
Ms Liz Harrison David Alan Harrison

Placings:0PPP (4909)
2003/04: 17DG, 21PG, 20PG, 24PS,

	Starts	1st	2nd	3rd	Win & Pl
NH Flat	1	0	0	0	0
Hurdles	3	0	0	0	0
Career Total	4	0	0	0	

Going:	Sf: 0-1 GS: 0-0 Gd: 0-3 GF: - Fm: 0-0
Distance:	2m/2m3: 0-1 2m4-2m7: 0-2 3m+: 0-1
Track:	LH: 0-1 RH: 0-3 Tight: 0-1 Gall: 0-0
Aids:	Bl: 0-0 Vi: 0-0 Tstrap: 0-0 Ckp: 0-0

Solway Raider
60f 37f
6-y-o ch g Jumbo Hirt (USA)-Lady Mag (Silver Season)
Ms Liz Harrison David Alan Harrison

Placings:00 (4886)
2003/04: 17⁰G, 17⁰GS,

	Starts	1st	2nd	3rd	Win & Pl
NH Flat	2	0	0	0	
Career Total	2	0	0	0	

Going:	Sf: 0-0 GS: 0-1 Gd: 0-1 GF: - Fm: 0-0
Distance:	2m/2m3: 0-2 2m4-2m7: 0-0 3m+: 0-0
Track:	LH: 0-0 RH: 0-2 Tight: 0-0 Gall: 0-0
Aids:	Bl: 0-0 Vi: 0-0 Tstrap: 0-0 Ckp: 0-0
Best Rating:	37 3/04 Carl 2m1f good NHF

Solway Rose
101 105
10-y-o ch m Minster Son-Lady Mag (Silver Season)

Ms Liz Harrison David Alan Harrison

Placings:346/31P/3F301/PUP1U4/P244U-30234 (4272)
2003/04: 25³G, 25⁰GS, 24²HY, 25³HY, 26⁴G,

	Starts	1st	2nd	3rd	Win & Pl
Chases	5	0	1	2	2766
Career Total	27	3	2	6	18962
105	3/02 Ayr	3m1f	D(0-125)HCh	HVY	£4745
105	10/00 Carl	3m2f	D(0-120)HCh	G-S	£3786
100	6/99 Prth	3m110y	E Hdl	G-S	£2724

Total win prize-money £11255

Going:	Sf: 0-2 GS: 0-1 Gd: 0-2 GF: - Fm: 0-0
Distance:	2m/2m3: 0-0 2m4-2m7: 0-0 3m+: 0-0
Track:	LH: 0-4 RH: 0-1 Tight: 0-2 Gall: 0-1
Aids:	Bl: 0-0 Vi: 0-0 Tstrap: 0-0 Ckp: 0-0
Best Rating:	105 11/02 Newc 3m soft Ch

Somayda (IRE)
87 65
9-y-o b g Last Tycoon-Flame Of Tara (Artaius (USA))
Miss Jacqueline S Doyle The Somayda Partnership

Placings:0P/0P-0 (1702)
2003/04: 16⁰GF,

	Starts	1st	2nd	3rd	Win & Pl
Hurdles	1	0	0	0	
Career Total	5	0	0	0	

Going:	Sf: 0-0 GS: 0-0 Gd: 0-0 GF: - Fm: 0-1
Distance:	2m/2m3: 0-1 2m4-2m7: 0-0 3m+: 0-0
Track:	LH: 0-1 RH: 0-0 Tight: 0-0 Gall: 0-0
Aids:	Bl: 0-0 Vi: 0-0 Tstrap: 0-0 Ckp: 0-0
Best Rating:	65 10/03 Strf 2m110y gd-fm Hdl

Some Judge
93 92+
7-y-o ch g Rakaposhi King-Si-Gaoith (Strong Gale)
Jonjo O'Neill John Power

Placings:25/606606 (4913)
2003/04: 17⁶G, 17⁰GS, 16⁸GS, 24⁶S, 20⁶S, 24⁶S,

	Starts	1st	2nd	3rd	Win & Pl
NH Flat	2	0	0	0	0
Hurdles	4	0	0	0	0
Career Total	8	0	1	0	1032

Going:	Sf: 0-3 GS: 0-2 Gd: 0-1 GF: - Fm: 0-0
Distance:	2m/2m3: 0-3 2m4-2m7: 0-1 3m+: 0-2
Track:	LH: 0-3 RH: 0-2 Tight: 0-2 Gall: 0-0
Aids:	Bl: 0-0 Vi: 0-0 Tstrap: 0-0 Ckp: 0-0
Best Rating:	106 2/02 Gowr 2m1f soft NHF

Some Operator (IRE)
99 91
10-y-o b g Lord Americo-Rathvilly Flier (Peacock (FR))
T Wall Michael Doocey

Placings:50/UU434U0/00300/02-0P1P (0749)
2003/04: 21⁰G, 20⁰G, 16¹G, 16⁶G,

	Starts	1st	2nd	3rd	Win & Pl
Hurdles	4	1	0	0	4212
Career Total	20	1	1	2	6476
91	5/03 Strf	2m110y	E(0-105)HHdl	GD	£4212

Total win prize-money £4212

Going:	Sf: 0-0 GS: 0-0 Gd: 1-3 GF: - Fm: 0-1
Distance:	2m/2m3: 1-2 2m4-2m7: 0-2 3m+: 0-0
Track:	LH: 1-3 RH: 0-1 Tight: 1-2 Gall: 0-0
Aids:	Bl: 0-0 Vi: 0-0 Tstrap: 0-0 Ckp: 0-0
Best Rating:	99 10/99 Chep 2m110y soft Hdl

Showed ability in 1999; relatively lightly-raced since; settled much better when springing 25/1 shock in low grade novices handicap hurdle at Stratford May 2003; acts on a sound surface.

Some Trainer (IRE)
99(98h) (82h)82
8-y-o b g Leading Counsel (USA)-Miss Polymer (Doulab (USA))
J G Cromwell M & G K Syndicate

Placings:00/640050/006642PP2/304P006003-2435202532140 (3730a)
2003/04: 17²G, 17⁴G, 20³GY, 17⁵G, 21²G, 20⁰F, 20²G, 16⁵GF, 20³GF, 16²G, 20¹Y, 20⁴HY, 20⁵S,

	Starts	1st	2nd	3rd	Win & Pl
Hurdles	2	0	1	1	1505
Chases	11	1	3	1	10781
Career Total	40	1	6	4	16575
82	12/03 DRoy	2m4f	(0-95)HCh	YLD	£5152

Total win prize-money £5153

Going:	Sf: 0-2 GS: 0-0 Gd: 0-4 GF: - Fm: 0-3
Distance:	2m/2m3: 0-5 2m4-2m7: 1-8 3m+: 0-0
Track:	LH: 0-4 RH: 0-2 Tight: 0-2 Gall: 0-0
Aids:	Bl: 0-0 Vi: 0-0 Tstrap: 0-9 Ckp: 1-4
Best Rating:	117 5/00 Punc 2m yield NHF

Selling-class chaser; stays two and a half miles; no battler.

Somemanforoneman (IRE)
85(97h) (93h)90
10-y-o b g Asir-Wintry Shower (Strong Gale)
R S Brookhouse R S Brookhouse

Placings:4500/352430/63301F646263/011232F/055P420/P4F6P-0P4UPP0 (3784)
2003/04: 22⁰G, 27⁸G, 24⁴GS, 30⁴GS, 25⁸G, 25⁸GS, 26⁰GS,

	Starts	1st	2nd	3rd	Win & Pl
Hurdles	3	0	0	0	0
Chases	4	0	0	0	573
Career Total	48	3	5	6	33517
145	11/00 Asct	3m110y	C(0-130)HCh	G-S	£6646
130	10/00 Wwck	2m4f110y D	Ch	SFT	£4030
105	12/99 Clon	2m6f	(0-95)Hdl	SH	£3388

Total win prize-money £14064

Going:	Sf: 0-0 GS: 0-4 Gd: 0-3 GF: - Fm: 0-0
Distance:	2m/2m3: 0-0 2m4-2m7: 0-1 3m+: 0-6
Track:	LH: 0-3 RH: 0-4 Tight: 0-3 Gall: 0-1
Aids:	Bl: 0-2 Vi: 0-0 Tstrap: 0-0 Ckp: 0-0
Best Rating:	145 11/00 Asct 3m110y gd-sft Ch

Moderate ex-Irish handicap chaser, very useful early on in Britain, but on the decline now; suited by cut in the ground; stays three miles, effective at two and a half, has worn blinkers and cheekpieces.

Something Dandy (IRE)
107(110h) (121h)101
11-y-o b g Brush Aside (USA)-Hawthorn Dandy (Deep Run)
J A B Old Blomeley/lovatt Partnership

Placings:00/F0U/2240/520/5641342112-5402233U (4820)

2003/04: 20^5GF, 23^4G, 20^0GF, 19^2GF, 19^2GS, 21^3G, 23^3G, 25^UGF,

	Starts	1st	2nd	3rd	Win & Pl
Hurdles	1	0	0	0	0
Chases	7	0	2	2	3949
Career Total	30	3	7	3	25156
101	11/02 Tntn 3m		E(0-105)HCh	G-S	£3640
101	11/02 Kemp 3m		D(0-110)HCh	GD	£5908
98	7/02 Worc 3m		E(0-100)HHdl	GD	£2905

Total win prize-money £12453

Going:	Sf: 0-0 GS: 0-1 Gd: 0-3 GF: - Fm: 0-4
Distance:	2m/2m3: 0-0 2m4-2m7: 0-5 3m+: 0-3
Track:	LH: 0-4 RH: 0-3 Tight: 0-0 Gall: 0-0
Aids:	Bl: 0-0 Vi: 0-0 Tstrap: 0-0 Ckp: 0-0
Best Rating:	121 4/03 Chel 2m1f good Hdl

Plating-class hurdler/chaser at around two and a half to three miles; acts on good or faster ground.

Something Gold (FR)
97f   101f
4-y-o gr g Baby Turk-Exiled (USA) (Iron Ruler (USA))
M Bradstock J Macleod

Placings:1   (4454)
2003/04: 16^1GS,

	Starts	1st	2nd	3rd	Win & Pl
NH Flat	1	1	0	0	2513
Career Total	1	1	0	0	2513
101	3/04 Asct 2m110y H NHF			G-S	£2513

Total win prize-money £2513

Going:	Sf: 0-0 GS: 1-1 Gd: 0-0 GF: - Fm: 0-0
Distance:	2m/2m3: 1-1 2m4-2m7: 0-0 3m+: 0-0
Track:	LH: 0-0 RH: 1-1 Tight: 0-0 Gall: 0-0
Aids:	Bl: 0-0 Vi: 0-0 Tstrap: 0-0 Ckp: 0-0
Best Rating:	101 3/04 Asct 2m110y gd-sft NHF

French-bred bumper performer; showed courage to win an Ascot bumper on racecourse debut; acts on easy ground.

Something Small
72f   95f
4-y-o br g Supreme Leader-Rachel C (IRE) (Phardante (FR))
R Waley-Cohen Robert Waley-Cohen

Placings:3   (4824)
2003/04: 17^3GF,

	Starts	1st	2nd	3rd	Win & Pl
NH Flat	1	0	0	1	396
Career Total	1	0	0	1	396

Going:	Sf: 0-0 GS: 0-0 Gd: 0-0 GF: - Fm: 0-1
Distance:	2m/2m3: 0-1 2m4-2m7: 0-0 3m+: 0-0
Track:	LH: 0-0 RH: 0-1 Tight: 0-0 Gall: 0-0
Aids:	Bl: 0-0 Vi: 0-0 Tstrap: 0-0 Ckp: 0-0
Best Rating:	95 4/04 Extr 2m1f gd-fm NHF

Somewin (IRE)
104f   82f
4-y-o b f Goldmark (USA)-Janet Oliphant (Red Sunset)
R A Fahey R A Fahey

Placings:21   (3737)
2003/04: 16^2G, 16^1G,

	Starts	1st	2nd	3rd	Win & Pl
NH Flat	2	1	1	0	844
Career Total	2	1	1	0	844

Going:	Sf: 0-0 GS: 0-0 Gd: 1-1 GF: - Fm: 0-1
Distance:	2m/2m3: 1-2 2m4-2m7: 0-0 3m+: 0-0
Track:	LH: 0-0 RH: 1-2 Tight: 1-2 Gall: 0-0
Aids:	Bl: 0-0 Vi: 0-0 Tstrap: 0-0 Ckp: 0-0
Best Rating:	82 2/04 Muss 2m good NHF

Son Of A Gun
105(100h)   (88h)91
10-y-o b g Gunner B-Sola Mia (Tolomeo)
M J Polglase Ron Spore & Michael Crompton

Placings:312223/330/360P4100-65052434PF   (2162)
2003/04: 16^6GF, 26^5GS, 21^0GF, 16^5GF, 16^2GF, 20^4GF, 17^3GF, 16^4GF, 16^7GF, 20^6G,

	Starts	1st	2nd	3rd	Win & Pl
Hurdles	3	0	0	0	0
Chases	7	0	1	1	2534
Career Total	27	2	4	6	12175
88	3/03 Fknm 2m		G(0-90)HHdl	GD	£2382
101	9/99 MRas 1m5f110yH NHF			G-F	£1595

Total win prize-money £3977

Going:	Sf: 0-0 GS: 0-1 Gd: 0-1 GF: - Fm: 0-8
Distance:	2m/2m3: 0-6 2m4-2m7: 0-3 3m+: 0-1
Track:	LH: 0-10 RH: 0-0 Tight: 0-2 Gall: 0-0
Aids:	Bl: 0-0 Vi: 0-0 Tstrap: 0-0 Ckp: 0-0
Best Rating:	126 12/99 Chep 2m110y heavy NHF

Plating-class hurdler/chaser; reported to have had breathing problems on chasing debut at Worcester September 2003; slightly unlucky when promoted to second at the same course a week later; best on a sound surface; rather inconsistent.

Son Of Anshan

11-y-o b g Anshan-Anhaar (Ela-Mana-Mou)
G Tuer G Tuer

Placings:0321F11/33P/314P3223/4450/P4/5213/311U-261   (4798)
2003/04: 24^2G, 25^6G, 27^1G,

	Starts	1st	2nd	3rd	Win & Pl
Chases	3	1	1	0	2083
Career Total	35	8	5	8	31509
108	4/04 Sedg 3m3f	H Ch		GD	£1463
104	3/03 Sedg 3m3f	H Ch		GD	£1540
113	3/03 Sedg 3m3f	H Ch		SFT	£1533
85	3/02 Sedg 3m3f	H Ch		SFT	£1498
113	11/98 Uttx 3m	D Ch		GD	£4370
133	3/97 Kels 2m	D Hdl		GD	£2815
121	3/97 Ayr 2m	E Hdl		SFT	£2134
109	12/96 Newc 2m	E Hdl		GD	£2337

Total win prize-money £17692

Going:	Sf: 0-0 GS: 0-0 Gd: 1-3 GF: - Fm: 0-0
Distance:	2m/2m3: 0-0 2m4-2m7: 0-0 3m+: 1-3
Track:	LH: 1-2 RH: 0-1 Tight: 1-3 Gall: 0-0
Aids:	Bl: 0-0 Vi: 0-0 Tstrap: 1-3 Ckp: 0-0
Best Rating:	133 3/97 Kels 2m2f good Hdl

Fair hunter chaser; one-time decent novice over fences; won his second Sedgefield hunter chaser in March 2003; stays well; usually tongue tied.

Son Of Flighty
88   81
6-y-o b g Then Again-Record Flight (Record Token)
R J Hodges Frank E Crumpler

Placings:4P0P30   (4818)

2003/04: 17^4GF, 26^6GS, 17^0S, 16^7G, 17^3G, 17^0GF,

	Starts	1st	2nd	3rd	Win & Pl
Hurdles	5	0	0	1	799
Chases	1	0	0	0	0
Career Total	6	0	0	1	799

Going:	Sf: 0-1 GS: 0-1 Gd: 0-2 GF: - Fm: 0-2
Distance:	2m/2m3: 0-5 2m4-2m7: 0-0 3m+: 0-1
Track:	LH: 0-0 RH: 0-6 Tight: 0-3 Gall: 0-0
Aids:	Bl: 0-0 Vi: 0-0 Tstrap: 0-0 Ckp: 0-0
Best Rating:	81 2/04 Tntn 2m1f soft Hdl

Son Of Ross
102(84c)   (22c)65
10-y-o b g Minster Son-Nancy Ardross (Ardross)
R W Thomson R W Thomson

Placings:0/00/4005/41PP00/U560-PP000U300202   (4390)
2003/04: 25^5G, 24^5GF, 25^0GF, 24^9G, 22^0GF, 21^UGF, 22^3G, 20^6G, 22^0F, 21^2G, 24^0HY, 27^2G,

	Starts	1st	2nd	3rd	Win & Pl
Hurdles	9	0	2	1	1627
Chases	3	0	0	0	0
Career Total	29	1	2	1	4525
70	6/01 Prth 3m110y E Hdl			G-F	£2898

Total win prize-money £2898

Going:	Sf: 0-1 GS: 0-0 Gd: 0-6 GF: - Fm: 0-5
Distance:	2m/2m3: 0-0 2m4-2m7: 0-6 3m+: 0-6
Track:	LH: 0-9 RH: 0-3 Tight: 0-7 Gall: 0-1
Aids:	Bl: 0-0 Vi: 0-0 Tstrap: 0-0 Ckp: 0-9
Best Rating:	71 10/03 Sedg 2m5f110y good Hdl

Poor hurdler; stays three miles plus; has worn cheekpieces.

Son Of Snurge (FR)
109   81
8-y-o b g Snurge-Swift Spring (FR) (Bluebird (USA))
W G Young W G Young

Placings:PP/F4662400P5540003355-303502333345524556P   (2233)
2003/04: 20^5GF, 24^3G, 24^0G, 26^3GS, 24^5GF, 20^0GF, 20^3G, 24^3G, 22^3GF, 21^3GF, 24^4GF, 20^5F, 24^5G, 24^2GF, 20^4GF, 24^5GF, 27^5G, 22^6G, 20^0G,

	Starts	1st	2nd	3rd	Win & Pl
Hurdles	20	0	2	6	5558
Career Total	40	0	3	8	7470

Going:	Sf: 0-0 GS: 0-1 Gd: 0-8 GF: - Fm: 0-11
Distance:	2m/2m3: 0-0 2m4-2m7: 0-10 3m+: 0-10
Track:	LH: 0-13 RH: 0-7 Tight: 0-5 Gall: 0-1
Aids:	Bl: 0-1 Vi: 0-0 Tstrap: 0-0 Ckp: 0-15
Best Rating:	81 7/03 Sedg 2m5f110y gd-fm Hdl

Plating-class hurdler; placed many times; stays 3m; acts on fast ground.

Sonevafushi (FR)
112   129
6-y-o b g Ganges (USA)-For Kicks (FR) (Top Ville)
Miss Venetia Williams B C Dice

Placings:130/1220460-320034P20400   (4836)
2003/04: 16^3GS, 16^2G, 16^9G, 16^9GF, 25^3G, 24^4S, 21^5S, 20^2S, 22^0S, 20^4G, 20^0GS, 21^0GF,

	Starts	1st	2nd	3rd	Win & Pl
Hurdles	12	0	2	2	16308
Career Total	22	2	4	3	36876
105	5/02 Sthl 2m4f110yE Hdl			GD	£2667

115 1/02 Newb 2m110y D Hdl   G-S   £4179
Total win prize-money £6847

Going:	Sf: 0-4 GS: 0-2 Gd: 0-4 GF: - Fm: 0-2	
Distance:	2m2/3: 0-4 2m4-2m7: 0-6 3m+: 0-2	
Track:	LH: 0-7 RH: 0-5 Tight: 0-2 Gall: 0-2	
Aids:	Bl: 0-11 Vi: 0-0 Tstrap: 0-0 Ckp: 0-0	
Best Rating:	129 2/04 Hayd 2m4f	good Hdl

Very useful handicap hurdler; does not find much off the bridle; effective from two to three miles; acts on most ground; usually wears blinkers; fairly consistent, but hard to win with.

Songino (IRE)

86   69

8-y-o ch g Perugino (USA)-Sonbere (Electric)
J Clements (J Parkes 2/9) James Clements

Placings:0000/0/0030000/600   (0773a)
2003/04: 16⁶G, 17⁰G, 20⁰F,

	Starts	1st	2nd	3rd	Win & Pl
Hurdles	3	0	0	0	0
Career Total	15	0	0	1	353

Going:	Sf: 0-0 GS: 0-0 Gd: 0-2 GF: - Fm: 0-1	
Distance:	2m2/3: 0-2 2m4-2m7: 0-1 3m+: 0-0	
Track:	LH: 0-1 RH: 0-1 Tight: 0-1 Gall: 0-0	
Aids:	Bl: 0-1 Vi: 0-0 Tstrap: 0-0 Ckp: 0-0	
Best Rating:	85 10/01 Dpat 2m1f172y gd-yld Hdl	

Sonic Sound

60f   27f

5-y-o b g Cosmonaut-Sophiesue (Balidar)
Miss C J E Caroe Skeltools Ltd

Placings:0   (4787)
2003/04: 16⁰G,

	Starts	1st	2nd	3rd	Win & Pl
NH Flat	1	0	0	0	
Career Total	1	0	0	0	

Going:	Sf: 0-0 GS: 0-0 Gd: 0-1 GF: - Fm: 0-0	
Distance:	2m2/3: 0-1 2m4-2m7: 0-0 3m+: 0-0	
Track:	LH: 0-0 RH: 0-1 Tight: 0-0 Gall: 0-1	
Aids:	Bl: 0-0 Vi: 0-0 Tstrap: 0-0 Ckp: 0-0	
Best Rating:	27 4/04 Hntg 2m110y good NHF	

Sonny Jim

109   84

6-y-o b g Timeless Times (USA)-Allesca (Alleging (USA))
N G Ayliffe (M D I Usher 16/7) Derek Walker

Placings:0F622010440/532323046-01U60040 (3049)
2003/04: 21⁰GF, 20¹GF, 20ᵁGF, 21⁶G, 20⁰G, 19⁰G, 19⁴GS, 24⁰G,

	Starts	1st	2nd	3rd	Win & Pl
Hurdles	8	1	0	0	3241
Career Total	28	2	4	3	12799
84	6/03 Worc 2m4f	F(0-100)HHdl	G-F	£3241
89	2/02 Plum 2m	F Hdl	HVY	£2247
			Total win prize-money £5488

Going:	Sf: 0-0 GS: 0-1 Gd: 0-4 GF: - Fm: 0-1	
Distance:	2m2/3: 0-1 2m4-2m7: 1-6 3m+: 0-1	
Track:	LH: 1-5 RH: 0-3 Tight: 0-1 Gall: 0-0	
Aids:	Bl: 0-0 Vi: 0-0 Tstrap: 0-0 Ckp: 0-0	
Best Rating:	91 2/03 Font 2m2f110y soft Hdl	

Plating-class handicap hurdler; unsuited by fast ground; stays 2m 4f; has worn headgear in the past.

Sono

103   103+

7-y-o b g Robellino (USA)-Sweet Holland (USA) (Alydar (USA))
P D Niven Kinloch Arms (Carnoustie) Ltd

Placings:5335046P5   (4950)
2003/04: 16⁵G, 16³S, 16³G, 16⁵S, 16⁰G, 20⁴S, 17⁶HY, 16ᴾGS, 20⁵GS,

	Starts	1st	2nd	3rd	Win & Pl
Hurdles	9	0	0	2	1563
Career Total	9	0	0	2	1563

Going:	Sf: 0-4 GS: 0-2 Gd: 0-3 GF: - Fm: 0-0	
Distance:	2m2/3: 0-7 2m4-2m7: 0-2 3m+: 0-0	
Track:	LH: 0-6 RH: 0-3 Tight: 0-2 Gall: 0-0	
Aids:	Bl: 0-0 Vi: 0-0 Tstrap: 0-0 Ckp: 0-2	
Best Rating:	103 1/04 Weth 2m4f110y soft Hdl	

Moderate but improving novice hurdler; effective at two miles; best effort when good third at Wetherby in December.

Sootsir

8-y-o b g Baron Blakeney-Furry Bear (Rymer)
Richard Hawker Richard Hawker

Placings:P   (4522)
2003/04: 25ᴾGS,

	Starts	1st	2nd	3rd	Win & Pl
Chases	1	0	0	0	
Career Total	1	0	0	0	

Going:	Sf: 0-0 GS: 0-1 Gd: 0-0 GF: - Fm: 0-0
Distance:	2m2/3: 0-0 2m4-2m7: 0-0 3m+: 0-1
Track:	LH: 0-0 RH: 0-1 Tight: 0-0 Gall: 0-0
Aids:	Bl: 0-0 Vi: 0-0 Tstrap: 0-0 Ckp: 0-0

Sophomore

83   68+

10-y-o b g Sanglamore (USA)-Livry (USA) (Lyphard (USA))
John A Harris D Wilcox

Placings:0P0P/04/020   (2842)
2003/04: 17⁰G, 16²GS, 16⁶GS,

	Starts	1st	2nd	3rd	Win & Pl
Hurdles	3	0	1	0	552
Career Total	9	0	1	0	552

Going:	Sf: 0-0 GS: 0-0 Gd: 0-1 GF: - Fm: 0-0	
Distance:	2m2/3: 0-3 2m4-2m7: 0-0 3m+: 0-0	
Track:	LH: 0-2 RH: 0-1 Tight: 0-0 Gall: 0-0	
Aids:	Bl: 0-0 Vi: 0-0 Tstrap: 0-0 Ckp: 0-0	
Best Rating:	74 2/00 Fknm 2m good Hdl	

Soprano Lass (IRE)

96   88

7-y-o ch m Black Monday-Kam Country (IRE) (Kambalda)
J G Portman Anthony Boswood

Placings:0P2UP3   (4855)
2003/04: 17⁰GS, 21ᴾGS, 23²GF, 25ᵁGF, 25ᴾG, 24³GF,

	Starts	1st	2nd	3rd	Win & Pl
NH Flat	1	0	0	0	0
Hurdles	1	0	0	0	0
Chases	4	0	1	1	2306
Career Total	6	0	1	1	2306

Going:	Sf: 0-0 GS: 0-2 Gd: 0-1 GF: - Fm: 0-3	
Distance:	2m2/3: 0-1 2m4-2m7: 0-1 3m+: 0-4	
Track:	LH: 0-1 RH: 0-5 Tight: 0-2 Gall: 0-1	
Aids:	Bl: 0-0 Vi: 0-0 Tstrap: 0-0 Ckp: 0-0	
Best Rating:	80 3/04 Leic 2m7f110y gd-fm Ch	

Plating-class chaser; has achieved little when finishing second and third in three mile novice chases; acts on fast ground.

Sorely Missed (IRE)

(86h)

9-y-o br g Yashgan-Well Honey (Al Sirat)
R Dickin Mrs M Payne

Placings:60P/0P613334/4PPP-P   (1664)
2003/04: 20ᴾGF,

	Starts	1st	2nd	3rd	Win & Pl
Chases	1	0	0	0	
Career Total	16	1	0	3	5134
78	11/01 Wwck 2m3f	F(0-100)HHdl	GD	£2059
			Total win prize-money £2059

Going:	Sf: 0-0 GS: 0-0 Gd: 0-0 GF: - Fm: 0-1	
Distance:	2m2/3: 0-0 2m4-2m7: 0-1 3m+: 0-0	
Track:	LH: 0-1 RH: 0-0 Tight: 0-0 Gall: 0-0	
Aids:	Bl: 0-0 Vi: 0-0 Tstrap: 0-0 Ckp: 0-0	
Best Rating:	87 10/00 Chep 2m110y gd-sft NHF	

Sorrento King

(99h)108

7-y-o ch g First Trump-Star Face (African Sky)
C N Kellett Trevor Farrow

Placings:4203U3102/33411F-P   (4873)
2003/04: 20ᴾGS,

	Starts	1st	2nd	3rd	Win & Pl
Hurdles	1	0	0	0	
Career Total	16	3	2	4	14828
108	10/02 Sedg 2m5f	E Ch	G-F	£3711
87	9/02 Sedg 2m5f	E Ch	GD	£3701
99	12/01 Kels 2m110y	E Hdl	G-S	£3346
			Total win prize-money £10760

Going:	Sf: 0-0 GS: 0-1 Gd: 0-0 GF: - Fm: 0-0	
Distance:	2m2/3: 0-0 2m4-2m7: 0-0 3m+: 0-0	
Track:	LH: 0-1 RH: 0-0 Tight: 0-0 Gall: 0-0	
Aids:	Bl: 0-0 Vi: 0-0 Tstrap: 0-0 Ckp: 0-0	
Best Rating:	108 10/02 Sedg 2m5f gd-fm Ch	

Modest chaser; effective at around two miles five; acts on fast ground.

Sossus Vlei

106(102h)   (114dh)118

8-y-o b g Inchinor-Sassalya (Sassafras (FR))
P Winkworth P Winkworth

Placings:300/20225-223U522U   (4699)
2003/04: 17²GS, 16²GS, 17³S, 24ᵁS, 21⁵GS, 20²G, 20²G, 18ᵁG,

	Starts	1st	2nd	3rd	Win & Pl
Chases	8	0	4	1	6920
Career Total	16	0	7	2	12131

Going:	Sf: 0-2 GS: 0-3 Gd: 0-3 GF: - Fm: 0-0	
Distance:	2m2/3: 0-4 2m4-2m7: 0-3 3m+: 0-1	
Track:	LH: 0-3 RH: 0-4 Tight: 0-6 Gall: 0-2	
Aids:	Bl: 0-0 Vi: 0-0 Tstrap: 0-0 Ckp: 0-0	
Best Rating:	134 2/02 Newb 2m110y soft Hdl	

A one-time decent performer on the Flat; fair novice hurdler;

has run into some decent prospects over fences; acts in soft ground; rather frustrating.

Sou'Wester

82   **49**

4-y-o b g Fleetwood (IRE)-Mayfair (Green Desert (USA))
B J Llewellyn E R Griffiths

Placings:60   **(3700)**
2003/04: 17⁶G, 19⁰HY,

	Starts	1st	2nd	3rd	Win & Pl
Hurdles	2	0	0	0	0
Career Total	2	0	0	0	0

Going:	Sf: 0-1 GS: 0-1 Gd: 0-1 GF: - Fm: 0-0
Distance:	2m/2m3: 0-2 2m4-2m7: 0-1 3m+: 0-0
Track:	LH: 0-1 RH: 0-1 Tight: 0-1 Gall: 0-0
Aids:	Bl: 0-0 Vi: 0-0 Tstrap: 0-0 Ckp: 0-0
Best Rating:	49 11/03 Bang 2m1f good Hdl

Soul (IRE)

103(97h)   (90h)**88+**

7-y-o b g Jurado (USA)-Pachamama (Glen Quaich)
C J Mann Charlie Mann

Placings:0U/0000301P30U6-0P2   **(3351)**
2003/04: 17⁰G, 17⁵GS, 16⁶S,

	Starts	1st	2nd	3rd	Win & Pl
Hurdles	2	0	0	0	0
Chases	1	0	1	0	1652
Career Total	17	1	1	2	7038
85	2/03 Thur 2m	(67-95)HHdl	SH	£4480

Total win prize-money £4481

Going:	Sf: 0-1 GS: 0-1 Gd: 0-1 GF: - Fm: 0-0
Distance:	2m/2m3: 0-3 2m4-2m7: 0-0 3m+: 0-0
Track:	LH: 0-2 RH: 0-1 Tight: 0-2 Gall: 0-1
Aids:	Bl: 0-0 Vi: 0-0 Tstrap: 0-0 Ckp: 0-0
Best Rating:	101 12/02 Cork 2m soft NHF

Soul King (IRE)

9-y-o b g King's Ride-Soul Lucy (Lucifer (USA))
Michael Blake Staverton Owners Group

Placings:40005/0FP/3P4   **(4761)**
2003/04: 25³G, 25⁵GS, 24⁵S,

	Starts	1st	2nd	3rd	Win & Pl
Chases	3	0	0	1	307
Career Total	11	0	0	1	307

Going:	Sf: 0-1 GS: 0-1 Gd: 0-1 GF: - Fm: 0-0
Distance:	2m/2m3: 0-0 2m4-2m7: 0-0 3m+: 0-3
Track:	LH: 0-0 RH: 0-2 Tight: 0-0 Gall: 0-0
Aids:	Bl: 0-0 Vi: 0-0 Tstrap: 0-0 Ckp: 0-0
Best Rating:	96 3/04 Towc 3m1f good Ch

Sound Of Cheers

112(89h)   (109h)**117+**

7-y-o b g Zilzal (USA)-Martha Stevens (USA) (Super Concorde (USA))
F Kirby Fred Kirby

Placings:061023/44P542620-32U4614011   **(4686)**
2003/04: 17³G, 16²S, 17⁰UG, 21⁴G, 19⁶GS, 16¹G, 16⁴GS, 16⁶G, 16¹HY, 17¹G,

---

	Starts	1st	2nd	3rd	Win & Pl
Chases	10	3	1	1	18278
Career Total	25	4	4	2	25517
117	4/04 Kels 2m1f	E(0-110)HCh	GD	£6909
109	3/04 Newc 2m110y	E(0-105)HCh	HVY	£4754
99	1/04 Catt 2m	E(0-105)HCh	GD	£4108
105	1/02 Newc 2m4f	E Hdl	SFT	£2667

Total win prize-money £18440

Going:	Sf: 1-2 GS: 0-2 Gd: 2-6 GF: - Fm: 0-0
Distance:	2m/2m3: 3-9 2m4-2m7: 0-1 3m+: 0-0
Track:	LH: 3-10 RH: 0-0 Tight: 2-8 Gall: 1-2
Aids:	Bl: 0-0 Vi: 0-0 Tstrap: 3-10 Ckp: 0-0
Best Rating:	117 4/04 Kels 2m1f good Ch

Modest chaser; finally off the mark at Catterick in January; then scored at Newcastle in March and comfortably followed up at Kelso in April; effective over two miles, but stays two and a half miles; acts on most ground; wears a tongue tie.

Sound Sense

6-y-o br g So Factual (USA)-Sight'n Sound (Chief Singer)
Mrs Laura J Young L W Wickett

Placings:P   **(4150)**
2003/04: 24⁰G,

	Starts	1st	2nd	3rd	Win & Pl
Chases	1	0	0	0	0
Career Total	1	0	0	0	0

Going:	Sf: 0-0 GS: 0-0 Gd: 0-0 GF: - Fm: 0-0
Distance:	2m/2m3: 0-0 2m4-2m7: 0-0 3m+: 0-1
Track:	LH: 0-0 RH: 0-1 Tight: 0-1 Gall: 0-0
Aids:	Bl: 0-0 Vi: 0-0 Tstrap: 0-0 Ckp: 0-0

Sounds Cool

102(98h)   (84h)**84**

8-y-o b g Savahra Sound-Lucky Candy (Lucky Wednesday)
Mrs A M Thorpe (Mrs S J Smith 11/10) Formula One Racing

Placings:0/00500F/U126P33/44P6-40303F61   **(4789)**
2003/04: 16⁶G, 16⁴S, 17⁰GF, 17³G, 16⁰G, 17³GS, 17⁴GF, 17⁶GF, 17¹G,

	Starts	1st	2nd	3rd	Win & Pl
Hurdles	3	0	0	1	377
Chases	6	1	0	1	3539
Career Total	26	2	1	4	7154
77	4/04 Plum 2m1f	G(0-90)HCh	GD	£2639
74	6/01 MRas 2m11y	10yG(0-90)HHdl	G-F	£1645

Total win prize-money £4284

Going:	Sf: 0-1 GS: 0-1 Gd: 1-4 GF: - Fm: 0-3
Distance:	2m/2m3: 1-9 2m4-2m7: 0-0 3m+: 0-0
Track:	LH: 1-8 RH: 0-1 Tight: 1-3 Gall: 0-0
Aids:	Bl: 0-0 Vi: 0-0 Tstrap: 0-0 Ckp: 0-0
Best Rating:	84 5/03 Sedg 2m110y soft Ch

Plating class hurdler; best over two miles; suited by fast ground.

Soundtrack (IRE)

100   **109**

11-y-o b g Orchestra-Misty Boosh (Tarboosh (USA))
Miss Venetia Williams (G D Hanmer 12/3) J M Kinnear

Placings:22111125/34111F/P0P/6-454   **(0819)**
2003/04: 25⁴GF, 24⁵G, 22⁴G,

	Starts	1st	2nd	3rd	Win & Pl
Chases	3	0	0	0	884

Career Total		21	7	3	1	28768
121	3/01 Plum 3m2f	E Ch	HVY	£3055
130	2/01 Tntn 3m	D Ch	HVY	£5715
140	1/01 Plum 3m2f	E Ch	HVY	£3318
123	10/99 Strf	2m6f110yD Hdl	G-F	£3717
120	10/99 Bang 2m4f	E Hdl	G-S	£2295
119	9/99 Hrfd	2m3f110yE Hdl	GD	£2472
98	9/99 Carl 2m1f	H NHF	G-F	£1647

Total win prize-money £22221

Going:	Sf: 0-0 GS: 0-0 Gd: 0-2 GF: - Fm: 0-1
Distance:	2m/2m3: 0-0 2m4-2m7: 0-1 3m+: 0-2
Track:	LH: 0-0 RH: 0-3 Tight: 0-0 Gall: 0-0
Aids:	Bl: 0-0 Vi: 0-0 Tstrap: 0-0 Ckp: 0-0
Best Rating:	140 1/01 Plum 3m2f heavy Ch

Decent chaser; an out-and-out stayer; did well in novice chases at the beginning of 2001, winning three times on heavy ground; lightly raced since and has dropped significantly in the handicap.

South West Won

6-y-o b g Bedford (USA)-Wood Heath (Heres)
Miss Sheena West B Cockerill

Placings:6-6PPP   **(3956)**
2003/04: 18⁶S, 21⁰PS, 19⁰PS, 22⁰PG,

	Starts	1st	2nd	3rd	Win & Pl
NH Flat	1	0	0	0	0
Hurdles	3	0	0	0	0
Career Total	5	0	0	0	0

Going:	Sf: 0-3 GS: 0-0 Gd: 0-1 GF: - Fm: 0-0
Distance:	2m/2m3: 0-2 2m4-2m7: 0-2 3m+: 0-0
Track:	LH: 0-4 RH: 0-0 Tight: 0-2 Gall: 0-1
Aids:	Bl: 0-0 Vi: 0-0 Tstrap: 0-0 Ckp: 0-2
Best Rating:	63 12/03 Plum 2m2f soft NHF

Southampton Joe (USA)

83   **47**

4-y-o ch g Just A Cat (USA)-Maple Hill Jill (USA) (Executive Pride)
J G M O'Shea (A M Balding 4/10) Arthur Watling

Placings:U6   **(4893)**
2003/04: 16⁰UG, 16⁶G,

	Starts	1st	2nd	3rd	Win & Pl
Hurdles	2	0	0	0	0
Career Total	2	0	0	0	0

Going:	Sf: 0-0 GS: 0-0 Gd: 0-2 GF: - Fm: 0-0
Distance:	2m/2m3: 0-2 2m4-2m7: 0-0 3m+: 0-0
Track:	LH: 0-0 RH: 0-2 Tight: 0-0 Gall: 0-0
Aids:	Bl: 0-0 Vi: 0-0 Tstrap: 0-0 Ckp: 0-0
Best Rating:	47 4/04 Winc 2m good Hdl

Southbay (IRE)

104   (91h)**101+**

10-y-o b g Montelimar (USA)-Herbal Lady (Good Thyne (USA))
A J Martin Lyreen Syndicate

Placings:06402464/21202554/635456351005/62PF-3F   **(4772a)**
2003/04: 24³G, 25⁵Y,

	Starts	1st	2nd	3rd	Win & Pl
Chases	2	0	0	1	1616

Career Total	34	2	5	3	18159
96 8/01 Dpat 3m	Ch			G-F	£4451
101 5/00 Navn 2m	NHF			G-Y	£4692
			Total win prize-money £9144		

Going:	Sf: 0-0 GS: 0-0 Gd: 0-1 GF: - Fm: 0-0
Distance:	2m/2m3: 0-0 2m4-2m7: 0-0 3m+: 0-2
Track:	LH: 0-1 RH: 0-1 Tight: 0-1 Gall: 0-0
Aids:	Bl: 0-0 Vi: 0-0 Tstrap: 0-0 Ckp: 0-0
Best Rating:	101 3/04 Strf 3m good Ch

Winning Irish chaser; stays three miles; acts on good to firm.

Southbound (IRE)
64f   49f
5-y-o ch g Zaffaran (USA)-Soxess (IRE) (Carlingford Castle)
J Howard Johnson R J Crake

Placings:0   (4885)
2003/04: 17³GS,

	Starts	1st	2nd	3rd	Win & Pl
NH Flat	1	0	0	0	
Career Total	1	0	0	0	

Going:	Sf: 0-0 GS: 0-1 Gd: 0-0 GF: - Fm: 0-0
Distance:	2m/2m3: 0-1 2m4-2m7: 0-0 3m+: 0-0
Track:	LH: 0-0 RH: 0-1 Tight: 0-0 Gall: 0-0
Aids:	Bl: 0-0 Vi: 0-0 Tstrap: 0-0 Ckp: 0-0
Best Rating:	49 4/04 Carl 2m1f gd-sft NHF

Southern Belize

10-y-o ch m Southern Music-Belize (Tom Noddy)
Miss M Ree Miss M Ree

Placings:P   (0249)
2003/04: 19ᴾGF,

	Starts	1st	2nd	3rd	Win & Pl
Chases	1	0	0	0	
Career Total	1	0	0	0	

Going:	Sf: 0-0 GS: 0-0 Gd: 0-0 GF: - Fm: 0-0
Distance:	2m/2m3: 0-0 2m4-2m7: 0-1 3m+: 0-0
Track:	LH: 0-0 RH: 0-1 Tight: 0-0 Gall: 0-0
Aids:	Bl: 0-0 Vi: 0-0 Tstrap: 0-0 Ckp: 0-0

Southern Star (IRE)
111   (128h)145
9-y-o ch g Montelimar (USA)-Flying Pegus (Beau Chapeau)
Miss H C Knight Trevor Hemmings

Placings:13/23113/11U34P2/202000-431P   (4647)
2003/04: 27⁴G, 33³G, 29¹GS, 36ᴾG,

	Starts	1st	2nd	3rd	Win & Pl
Chases	4	1	0	1	68683
Career Total	24	6	4	5	139533
150 1/04 Wwck 3m5f	A HCh			G-S	£63800
144 10/01 Chel	3m110y C Ch			GD	£8346
114 10/01 Bang	2m4f110yD Ch			GD	£4309
132 2/01 Hntg	2m4f110yB Hdl			G-S	£8970
133 1/01 Winc	2m E Hdl			G-S	£2047
123 10/99 Hntg	2m110y H NHF			G-F	£1842
		Total win prize-money £89316			

Going:	Sf: 0-0 GS: 1-1 Gd: 0-3 GF: - Fm: 0-0
Distance:	2m/2m3: 0-0 2m4-2m7: 0-0 3m+: 1-4
Track:	LH: 1-4 RH: 0-0 Tight: 0-1 Gall: 0-2
Aids:	Bl: 0-0 Vi: 0-0 Tstrap: 0-0 Ckp: 0-0
Best Rating:	150 1/04 Wwck 3m5f gd-sft Ch

Smart chaser; has run well in very decent staying handicaps; registered his first victory in handicap company when winning Tote Classic Chase at Warwick January 2004; acts on most types of ground and stays marathon trips.

Southern Star (GER)
94   76
4-y-o gr g Sternkoenig (IRE)-Sun Mate (IRE) (Miller's Mate)
R C Guest Mrs Monica Caine

Placings:620   (4260)
2003/04: 18⁶HY, 16²G, 16⁰GF,

	Starts	1st	2nd	3rd	Win & Pl
Hurdles	3	0	1	0	1064
Career Total	3	0	1	0	1064

Going:	Sf: 0-1 GS: 0-0 Gd: 0-1 GF: - Fm: 0-1
Distance:	2m/2m3: 0-3 2m4-2m7: 0-0 3m+: 0-0
Track:	LH: 0-2 RH: 0-1 Tight: 0-3 Gall: 0-0
Aids:	Bl: 0-0 Vi: 0-0 Tstrap: 0-0 Ckp: 0-0
Best Rating:	81 2/04 Muss 2m good Hdl

Fair novice hurdler, ex-German, maiden on the Flat; runner-up to wide margin winner on second start over hurdles.

Southerncrosspatch
100   88
13-y-o ch g Ra Nova-Southern Bird (Shiny Tenth)
Mrs Barbara Waring E S Chivers

Placings:0/040/0125F3P/111P/3PP204P4/03422P/133424 4022/P60P42-5663016P03   (4632)
2003/04: 24⁵GF, 21⁵GF, 22⁶GF, 26³GS, 24⁰GS, 26¹GS, 24⁶G, 23ᴾG, 26⁰G, 24³G,

	Starts	1st	2nd	3rd	Win & Pl
Hurdles	10	1	0	2	3447
Career Total	55	6	8	7	32151
85 1/04 Hrfd	3m2f	F(0-90)Hdl		G-S	£2716
101 6/01 NAbb	3m3f	E(0-115)HHdl		GD	£3038
101 6/98 Font	2m1f	E(0-115)HCh		G-S	£2921
86 6/98 Sthl	3m110y	F(0-105)HCh		G-F	£3777
107 6/98 Worc	2m4f110y	E(0-100)HCh		G-F	£3315
87 8/97 Sthl	3m110y	E Hdl		G-F	£2322
		Total win prize-money £18091			

Going:	Sf: 0-0 GS: 1-3 Gd: 0-4 GF: - Fm: 0-3
Distance:	2m/2m3: 0-0 2m4-2m7: 0-2 3m+: 1-8
Track:	LH: 0-5 RH: 1-5 Tight: 0-2 Gall: 0-2
Aids:	Bl: 0-0 Vi: 0-0 Tstrap: 0-0 Ckp: 0-0
Best Rating:	107 6/98 Worc 2m4f110y gd-fm Ch

Moderate handicap hurdler these days; has won three times over fences in the past; acts on fast and easy ground.

Southerndown (IRE)
100(95h)   (88h)98
11-y-o ch g Montelimar (USA)-Country Melody (IRE) (Orchestra)
R Lee Mrs Bill Neale And John Jackson

Placings:05/62265504/P5261055/040/4002260553033/2F5 24111440-0P4P1426525424   (4505)
2003/04: 25⁰GF, 25ᴾGF, 26⁴GF, 23ᴾGF, 26¹GS, 23⁴GF, 26²GF, 24⁶GF, 30⁵GS, 26²GS, 26⁶S, 24⁴GS, 26²GF, 25⁴G,

	Starts	1st	2nd	3rd	Win & Pl
Hurdles	4	1	1	0	3589
Chases	10	0	2	0	2516
Career Total	59	5	10	3	28980
87 8/03 Sthl	3m2f	G Hdl		G-S	£2527
98 10/02 Sthl	3m2f	F(0-100)HCh		GD	£3334
90 9/02 Bang	3m110y	E(0-100)HCh		GD	£5027
98 8/02 Sthl	3m2f	E Ch		G-F	£3672

80 9/99 Hntg	3m2f	F(0-90)HHdl		GD	£1955
		Total win prize-money £16519			

Going:	Sf: 0-1 GS: 1-4 Gd: 0-1 GF: - Fm: 0-8
Distance:	2m/2m3: 0-0 2m4-2m7: 0-0 3m+: 1-14
Track:	LH: 1-9 RH: 0-5 Tight: 0-2 Gall: 0-0
Aids:	Bl: 0-0 Vi: 0-0 Tstrap: 0-0 Ckp: 0-0
Best Rating:	98 10/02 Sthl 3m2f good Ch

Plating-class staying hurdler and chaser; suited by good ground or faster; stays extreme distances.

Sovereign
108   103
10-y-o b m Interrex (CAN)-Shiny Penny (Glint Of Gold)
J F Panvert J F Panvert

Placings:5524342/6220604060P5/60P6P66550500023303/610015/0/41003246632-44343311323   (1568)
2003/04: 20⁴GF, 19⁴GF, 22³GF, 22⁴GF, 22³GF, 22³GF, 22¹GF, 24¹GF, 20⁴GF, 24²F, 24³GF,

	Starts	1st	2nd	3rd	Win & Pl
Hurdles	11	2	1	5	14327
Career Total	67	5	8	11	31310
103 8/03 MRas	3m	C(0-130)HHdl		G-F	£6075
98 8/03 Font	2m6f110yF(0-100)HHdl			G-F	£2758
93 6/02 Hrfd	2m3f110yE(0-110)HHdl			GD	£3465
92 9/00 Hrfd	2m3f110yE Hdl			G-F	£2992
90 5/00 Fknm	2m7f110yE Hdl			FRM	£2229
		Total win prize-money £17520			

Going:	Sf: 0-0 GS: 0-0 Gd: 0-0 GF: - Fm: 2-11
Distance:	2m/2m3: 0-0 2m4-2m7: 1-8 3m+: 1-3
Track:	LH: 1-6 RH: 1-4 Tight: 2-7 Gall: 0-0
Aids:	Bl: 0-0 Vi: 0-0 Tstrap: 0-0 Ckp: 0-0
Best Rating:	103 10/03 Extr 3m110y gd-fm Hdl

Moderate hurdler; in good form in the summer of 2003, scoring second win in eight days at Market Rasen in August; likes the ground good or faster; stays three miles well; game and consistent.

Sovereign Gold
93   68
7-y-o b g Rakaposhi King-Page Of Gold (Goldhill)
D R Gandolfo K W Bell & Son Ltd

Placings:0/0-0P0   (4519)
2003/04: 20⁰S, 21ᴾGS, 22⁰GS,

	Starts	1st	2nd	3rd	Win & Pl
Hurdles	2	0	0	0	0
Chases	1	0	0	0	0
Career Total	5	0	0	0	

Going:	Sf: 0-1 GS: 0-2 Gd: 0-0 GF: - Fm: 0-0
Distance:	2m/2m3: 0-0 2m4-2m7: 0-3 3m+: 0-0
Track:	LH: 0-0 RH: 0-3 Tight: 0-1 Gall: 0-0
Aids:	Bl: 0-0 Vi: 0-0 Tstrap: 0-0 Ckp: 0-0
Best Rating:	88 11/01 Sand 2m110y gd-sft NHF

Sovereign State (IRE)
109   98
7-y-o b g Soviet Lad (USA)-Portree (Slip Anchor)
D W Thompson (J A Moore 5/6) J Greenbank

Placings:4P0635-132131103004   (4892)
2003/04: 16⁵GS, 16¹GF, 17³G, 16²GF, 16¹GF, 17³GF, 17¹G, 16¹GF, 16⁰GF, 16³GF, 16⁶GS, 16⁶G, 16⁴GF,

	Starts	1st	2nd	3rd	Win & Pl
Hurdles	13	4	1	3	14581

Career Total		18	4	1	4	15295
97	9/03 Worc 2m E(0-110)HHdl				G-F	£2623
98	8/03 Ctml 2m1f110yE(0-100)HHdl				GD	£3835
92	7/03 Strf 2m110y G Hdl				G-F	£2982
86	5/03 Fknm 2m G(0-90)HHdl				G-F	£2592

Total win prize-money £12033

Going:	Sf: 0-0 GS: 0-1 Gd: 1-3 GF: - Fm: 3-9
Distance:	2m/2m3: 4-13 2m4-2m7: 0-0 3m+: 0-0
Track:	LH: 4-12 RH: 0-1 Tight: 3-9 Gall: 0-2
Aids:	Bl: 0-0 Vi: 1-7 Tstrap: 0-0 Ckp: 2-3
Best Rating:	98 9/03 Plum 2m gd-fm Hdl

Moderate hurdler; keen sort; in good form in the summer of 2003 winning four times; seems best on a sound surface; goes well on a sharp track; has worn a visor and cheek-pieces; consistent and progressive.

Sovereign's Gift
99   95+
8-y-o ch m Elegant Monarch-Cadeau D'Aragon (Aragon)
Mrs S D Williams B W Gillbard

Placings:000/05030/4252P2-213   (0707)
2003/04: 17^2G, 17^1GF, 22^3GF,

	Starts	1st	2nd	3rd	Win & Pl
Hurdles	3	1	1	1	5950
Career Total	17	1	4	2	9687
95	6/03 NAbb 2m1f E Hdl		G-F		£4134

Total win prize-money £4134

Going:	Sf: 0-0 GS: 0-0 Gd: 0-1 GF: - Fm: 1-2
Distance:	2m/2m3: 1-2 2m4-2m7: 0-0 3m+: 0-0
Track:	LH: 1-2 RH: 0-1 Tight: 1-2 Gall: 0-0
Aids:	Bl: 0-0 Vi: 0-0 Tstrap: 0-0 Ckp: 0-0
Best Rating:	95 6/03 NAbb 2m1f gd-fm Hdl

Plating-class hurdler; put stamina to good use when winning 2m 1f mares only novice hurdle at Newton Abbot June 2003; stays 2m 6f; acts on a sound surface.

Soviet Society (IRE)
89f   80f
6-y-o b g Moscow Society (USA)-Catchmenot (IRE) (Bluebird (USA))
Noel T Chance Mrs Rose Boyd

Placings:00   (3650)
2003/04: 17^9GS, 16^9GS,

	Starts	1st	2nd	3rd	Win & Pl
NH Flat	2	0	0	0	
Career Total	2	0	0	0	

Going:	Sf: 0-0 GS: 0-2 Gd: 0-0 GF: - Fm: 0-0
Distance:	2m/2m3: 0-2 2m4-2m7: 0-0 3m+: 0-0
Track:	LH: 0-0 RH: 0-2 Tight: 0-1 Gall: 0-0
Aids:	Bl: 0-0 Vi: 0-0 Tstrap: 0-0 Ckp: 0-0
Best Rating:	84 2/04 Kemp 2m gd-sft NHF

Better than postion indicates on debut in bumper at Folkestone in November.

Space Cadet
8-y-o b g Teenoso (USA)-Spaced Out (Space King)
J Rudge David J Lee

Placings:P   (4782)
2003/04: 24^9G,

	Starts	1st	2nd	3rd	Win & Pl
Chases	1	0	0	0	
Career Total	1	0	0	0	

Going:	Sf: 0-0 GS: 0-0 Gd: 0-1 GF: - Fm: 0-0
Distance:	2m/2m3: 0-0 2m4-2m7: 0-0 3m+: 0-0
Track:	LH: 0-0 RH: 0-1 Tight: 0-0 Gall: 0-1
Aids:	Bl: 0-0 Vi: 0-0 Tstrap: 0-0 Ckp: 0-0

Modest hurdler; lightly-raced since his winning debut in 2002; stays two miles three; acts best on soft ground.

Space Cowboy (IRE)
100   100
4-y-o b c Anabaa (USA)-Lady Moranbon (USA) (Trempolino (USA))
G L Moore (Mrs A J Perrett 25/9) Platt Sanderson Partnership

Placings:F2533   (4097)
2003/04: 16^2S, 16^2GF, 16^5G, 16^3G, 16^9G,

	Starts	1st	2nd	3rd	Win & Pl
Hurdles	5	0	1	2	2775
Career Total	5	0	1	2	2775

Going:	Sf: 0-0 GS: 0-1 Gd: 0-3 GF: - Fm: 0-1
Distance:	2m/2m3: 0-5 2m4-2m7: 0-0 3m+: 0-0
Track:	LH: 0-2 RH: 0-3 Tight: 0-1 Gall: 0-2
Aids:	Bl: 0-2 Vi: 0-0 Tstrap: 0-0 Ckp: 0-0
Best Rating:	97 3/04 Plum 2m good Hdl

Fair hurdler; has shown ability in juvenile novice events; winner on the Flat; acts on fast ground.

Space Star
102   80+
4-y-o b g Cosmonaut-Sophiesue (Balidar)
P R Webber (J G Given 9/6) Skeltools Ltd

Placings:002   (4854)
2003/04: 16^5S, 16^9G, 17^2GF,

	Starts	1st	2nd	3rd	Win & Pl
Hurdles	3	0	1	0	1416
Career Total	3	0	1	0	1416

Going:	Sf: 0-1 GS: 0-0 Gd: 0-1 GF: - Fm: 0-1
Distance:	2m/2m3: 0-3 2m4-2m7: 0-0 3m+: 0-0
Track:	LH: 0-1 RH: 0-2 Tight: 0-1 Gall: 0-1
Aids:	Bl: 0-0 Vi: 0-0 Tstrap: 0-0 Ckp: 0-0
Best Rating:	80 4/04 Tntn 2m1f gd-fm Hdl

Modest novice hurdler; improved form when runner-up under tender handling third start; may do better in handicaps.

Spaghetti Junction
93   103
6-y-o ch m Sir Harry Lewis (USA)-Up The Junction (IRE) (Treasure Kay)
R H Alner Paul Murphy

Placings:1P340-0063   (4790)
2003/04: 22^9GS, 22^9G, 20^9GS, 21^3G,

	Starts	1st	2nd	3rd	Win & Pl
Hurdles	4	0	0	1	560
Career Total	9	1	0	2	7637
106	11/02 Hayd 2m D Hdl			SFT	£3770

Total win prize-money £3770

Going:	Sf: 0-0 GS: 0-2 Gd: 0-2 GF: - Fm: 0-0
Distance:	2m/2m3: 0-0 2m4-2m7: 0-4 3m+: 0-0
Track:	LH: 0-2 RH: 0-0 Tight: 0-2 Gall: 0-0
Aids:	Bl: 0-0 Vi: 0-0 Tstrap: 0-0 Ckp: 0-0
Best Rating:	106 3/03 Newb 2m5f good Hdl

Modest hurdler; lightly-raced since his winning debut in 2002; stays two miles three; acts best on soft ground.

Spainkris
97   105
5-y-o b g Kris-Pennycairn (Last Tycoon)
A Crook M Wainright

Placings:05U16-0040460   (4262)
2003/04: 19^0GF, 17^4S, 19^0GS, 23^4S, 17^6GS, 19^0GF,

	Starts	1st	2nd	3rd	Win & Pl
Hurdles	7	0	0	0	381
Career Total	12	1	0	0	5967
105	3/03 MRas 2m1f110yD Hdl			GD	£4836

Total win prize-money £4836

Going:	Sf: 0-2 GS: 0-2 Gd: 0-1 GF: - Fm: 0-2
Distance:	2m/2m3: 0-5 2m4-2m7: 0-2 3m+: 0-0
Track:	LH: 0-7 RH: 0-0 Tight: 0-0 Gall: 0-0
Aids:	Bl: 0-1 Vi: 0-0 Tstrap: 0-0 Ckp: 0-0
Best Rating:	105 3/03 MRas 2m1f110y good Hdl

Modest hurdler; keen sort and best suited by two miles; acts on good and heavy ground.

Spanchil Hill
100   69
4-y-o b g Sabrehill (USA)-War Shanty (Warrshan (USA))
J Howard Johnson (Cathal McCarthy 29/11) J Howard Johnson

Placings:0066   (4393)
2003/04: 16^9GY, 16^0S, 16^6G, 17^6G,

	Starts	1st	2nd	3rd	Win & Pl
Hurdles	4	0	0	0	0
Career Total	4	0	0	0	0

Going:	Sf: 0-0 GS: 0-0 Gd: 0-2 GF: - Fm: 0-0
Distance:	2m/2m3: 0-4 2m4-2m7: 0-0 3m+: 0-0
Track:	LH: 0-1 RH: 0-3 Tight: 0-2 Gall: 0-0
Aids:	Bl: 0-0 Vi: 0-0 Tstrap: 0-0 Ckp: 0-0
Best Rating:	69 2/04 Muss 2m good Hdl

Well beaten in two juvenile hurdles when trained in Ireland.

Spandau (NZ)
107   89+
10-y-o br g Fiesta Star (AUS)-Koru (NZ) (Diplomatic Agent (USA))
J C Tuck J C Tuck

Placings:00P/2600/1/P/P0530-015223   (1662)
2003/04: 16^9G, 17^1GF, 18^5GF, 20^2G, 19^2GF, 16^3GF,

	Starts	1st	2nd	3rd	Win & Pl
Hurdles	6	1	2	1	6495
Career Total	20	2	3	2	10324
87	8/03 NAbb 2m1f E(0-110)HHdl			G-F	£4063
95	5/00 Hrfd 2m1f D(0-110)HHdl			GD	£2762

Total win prize-money £6827

Going:	Sf: 0-0 GS: 0-0 Gd: 0-2 GF: - Fm: 1-4
Distance:	2m/2m3: 1-4 2m4-2m7: 0-2 3m+: 0-0
Track:	LH: 1-5 RH: 0-1 Tight: 1-4 Gall: 0-0
Aids:	Bl: 0-0 Vi: 0-1 Tstrap: 0-0 Ckp: 1-2
Best Rating:	95 5/00 Hrfd 2m1f good Hdl

Plating-class hurdler; lightly raced in recent seasons; controversial winner at Newton Abbot in August 2003; does not impress in a finish; has worn cheekpieces.

Spanish Archer (IRE)

84(100c)   **44**

9-y-o b g Spanish Place (USA)-Bow Gello (Bargello)
L Waring Mrs J Waring

Placings:6f0000/02213/P/P13P5043403P05-6P   (0487)
2003/04: 19⁰GF, 22ᴾGF,

	Starts	1st	2nd	3rd	Win & Pl
Hurdles	2	0	0	0	0
Career Total	28	3	2	4	10825
70	6/02	Uttx	2m5f	F(0-90)HCh	SFT	£2674
87	10/00	Folk	2m5f	F(0-95)HCh	G-F	£2387
99	11/99	Tntn	2m1f	H NHF	GD	£1680

Total win prize-money £6742

Going:	Sf: 0-0 GS: 0-0 Gd: 0-0 GF: - Fm: 0-2
Distance:	2m/2m3: 0-1 2m4-2m7: 0-1 3m+: 0-0
Track:	LH: 0-1 RH: 0-1 Tight: 0-1 Gall: 0-0
Aids:	Bl: 0-0 Vi: 0-0 Tstrap: 0-0 Ckp: 0-0
Best Rating:	99 11/99 Tntn 2m1f good NHF

Spanish Point (IRE)

101(73h)   (93h)**107**

7-y-o br g Un Desperado (FR)-Molly Murphy (IRE) (Phardante (FR))
D B Feek Mrs R M Hepburn

Placings:3355   (3926)
2003/04: 22³G, 25³G, 22⁵G, 24⁵G,

	Starts	1st	2nd	3rd	Win & Pl
Hurdles	1	0	0	1	370
Chases	3	0	0	1	480
Career Total	4	0	0	2	850

Going:	Sf: 0-0 GS: 0-0 Gd: 0-4 GF: - Fm: 0-0
Distance:	2m/2m3: 0-0 2m4-2m7: 0-2 3m+: 0-2
Track:	LH: 0-0 RH: 0-3 Tight: 0-3 Gall: 0-0
Aids:	Bl: 0-0 Vi: 0-0 Tstrap: 0-0 Ckp: 0-0
Best Rating:	107 1/04 Font 2m6f good Ch

Modest novice chaser; stays well; acts on good.

Sparkling Cascade (IRE)

101   **75**

12-y-o b m Royal Fountain-Yukon Law (Goldhill)
A G Newcombe Adam Fitzgerald

Placings:320/P62/2P52-4P5   (0987)
2003/04: 19⁴G, 20ᴾGF, 21⁵G,

	Starts	1st	2nd	3rd	Win & Pl
Chases	3	0	0	0	264
Career Total	13	0	4	1	4827

Going:	Sf: 0-0 GS: 0-0 Gd: 0-2 GF: - Fm: 0-1
Distance:	2m/2m3: 0-0 2m4-2m7: 0-3 3m+: 0-0
Track:	LH: 0-2 RH: 0-1 Tight: 0-1 Gall: 0-0
Aids:	Bl: 0-0 Vi: 0-0 Tstrap: 0-0 Ckp: 0-0
Best Rating:	92 8/00 NAbb 2m110y good Ch

Moderate chaser; placed in low-grade chases; stays three miles; probably best suited by a sound surface.

Sparkling Jess

5-y-o b m Alderbrook-Tasmin Gayle (IRE) (Strong Gale)
M J Roberts Mike Roberts

Placings:00-00   (3956)
2003/04: 20⁰G, 22⁰G,

	Starts	1st	2nd	3rd	Win & Pl
Hurdles	2	0	0	0	
Career Total	4	0	0	0	

Going:	Sf: 0-0 GS: 0-0 Gd: 0-2 GF: - Fm: 0-0
Distance:	2m/2m3: 0-0 2m4-2m7: 0-2 3m+: 0-0
Track:	LH: 0-1 RH: 0-0 Tight: 0-0 Gall: 0-0
Aids:	Bl: 0-0 Vi: 0-0 Tstrap: 0-0 Ckp: 0-0
Best Rating:	38 3/03 Hntg 2m110y good NHF

Sparkling Lass

86   (0c)**50**

10-y-o gr m Nicholas Bill-Sparkling Time (USA) (Olden Times)
N G Ayliffe Mrs M A Barrett

Placings:050P/06F52/00450544/04P004/000-U5356P0   (3637)
2003/04: 21ᵁGF, 22⁵G, 19³GF, 19⁵GF, 22⁶G, 22ᴾG, 19⁰S,

	Starts	1st	2nd	3rd	Win & Pl
Hurdles	6	0	0	1	523
Chases	1	0	0	0	
Career Total	33	0	1	1	1448

Going:	Sf: 0-1 GS: 0-0 Gd: 0-3 GF: - Fm: 0-3
Distance:	2m/2m3: 0-3 2m4-2m7: 0-4 3m+: 0-0
Track:	LH: 0-2 RH: 0-4 Tight: 0-2 Gall: 0-0
Aids:	Bl: 0-3 Vi: 0-0 Tstrap: 0-0 Ckp: 0-0
Best Rating:	88 4/01 Winc 2m6f soft Hdl

Moderate hurdler/chaser; acts on a sound surface.

Sparkling Sabrina

82f   **56f**

4-y-o b f Classic Cliche (IRE)-Sparkling Yasmin (Derring Rose)
B R Millman Victor G Palmer

Placings:000   (3927)
2003/04: 12⁰GF, 16⁰HY, 16⁹GS,

	Starts	1st	2nd	3rd	Win & Pl
NH Flat	3	0	0	0	
Career Total	3	0	0	0	

Going:	Sf: 0-1 GS: 0-1 Gd: 0-0 GF: - Fm: 0-1
Distance:	2m/2m3: 0-2 2m4-2m7: 0-0 3m+: 0-0
Track:	LH: 0-2 RH: 0-1 Tight: 0-0 Gall: 0-0
Aids:	Bl: 0-0 Vi: 0-0 Tstrap: 0-0 Ckp: 0-0
Best Rating:	56 2/04 Sand 2m110y gd-sft NHF

Sparkling Spring (IRE)

97   **91+**

13-y-o b g Strong Gale-Cherry Jubilee (Le Bavard (FR))
Evan Williams R Mason

Placings:12216/F25/13/21/3U/P/1   (4749)
2003/04: 25¹G,

	Starts	1st	2nd	3rd	Win & Pl
Hurdles	1	1	0	0	2786
Career Total	16	5	4	2	20378
91	4/04	Plum	3m1f110yF(0-100)HHdl	GD	£2786
123	10/99	Strf	3m4f	D(0-120)HCh	G-S	£3977
111	7/98	NAbb	3m2f110yE Ch	G-F	£2818

108	3/97	Plum	2m4f	E Hdl	G-F	£2826
98	11/96	Wind	2m4f	D Hdl	GD	£2581

Total win prize-money £14989

Going:	Sf: 0-0 GS: 0-0 Gd: 1-1 GF: - Fm: 0-0
Distance:	2m/2m3: 0-0 2m4-2m7: 0-0 3m+: 1-1
Track:	LH: 0-0 RH: 0-0 Tight: 0-0 Gall: 0-0
Aids:	Bl: 0-0 Vi: 0-0 Tstrap: 0-0 Ckp: 0-0
Best Rating:	123 10/99 Strf 3m4f gd-sft Ch

Former fair hurdler/chaser; prolific point-to-point winner; beaten just once in 13 starts in 2002/3; won over hurdles on his first attempt for six years in April 2004; stays beyond three miles and acts well on a sound surface.

Sparkling Water (USA)

106   **91**

5-y-o b h Woodman (USA)-Shirley Valentine (Shirley Heights)
D L Williams Mrs Jeffrey Robinson

Placings:354236   (1520)
2003/04: 16³GF, 16⁵GF, 17⁴GF, 22²GF, 21³GF, 18⁶G,

	Starts	1st	2nd	3rd	Win & Pl
Hurdles	6	0	1	2	2304
Career Total	6	0	1	2	2304

Going:	Sf: 0-0 GS: 0-0 Gd: 0-1 GF: - Fm: 0-5
Distance:	2m/2m3: 0-4 2m4-2m7: 0-2 3m+: 0-0
Track:	LH: 0-3 RH: 0-3 Tight: 0-4 Gall: 0-2
Aids:	Bl: 0-1 Vi: 0-0 Tstrap: 0-0 Ckp: 0-0
Best Rating:	91 7/03 MRas 2m1f110y gd-fm Hdl

Moderate hurdler; just about gets two miles five; acts on ground.

Special Agenda (IRE)

100(93h)   (90h)**117**

10-y-o b g Torus-Easter Blade (IRE) (Fine Blade (USA))
C J Mann The Safest Syndicate

Placings:445/P1132O3F2/222PU202P6/14UP56-242P4P460   (3847)
2003/04: 16²GF, 16⁴GF, 16²G, 20⁶G, 16⁴GF, 17ᴾGS, 16⁴HY, 16⁶S, 16⁹GS,

	Starts	1st	2nd	3rd	Win & Pl
Hurdles	1	0	1	0	1000
Chases	8	0	1	0	3195
Career Total	37	3	9	2	26983
124	5/02	NAbb	2m110y	D(0-115)HCh	G-S	£3922
122	11/00	Hrfd	2m	E(0-105)HCh	SFT	£2804
119	11/00	Plum	2m1f	E Ch	SFT	£3346

Total win prize-money £10074

Going:	Sf: 0-2 GS: 0-2 Gd: 0-2 GF: - Fm: 0-3
Distance:	2m/2m3: 0-8 2m4-2m7: 0-1 3m+: 0-0
Track:	LH: 0-6 RH: 0-3 Tight: 0-5 Gall: 0-0
Aids:	Bl: 0-1 Vi: 0-0 Tstrap: 0-1 Ckp: 0-3
Best Rating:	124 5/02 NAbb 2m110y gd-sft Ch

Modest chaser/hurdler; has shown good form with cut in the ground; effective at around two miles.

Special Branch

96   **85+**

4-y-o ch g Woodborough (USA)-Sixslip (USA) (Diesis)
Jedd O'Keeffe Wetherby Racing Bureau 56

Placings:35644   (4478)

2003/04: 17³GF, 16⁵GS, 16⁶G, 24⁴G, 20⁴HY,

	Starts	1st	2nd	3rd	Win & Pl
Hurdles	5	0	0	1	973
Career Total	5	0	0	1	973

Going:	Sf: 0-1 GS: 0-1 Gd: 0-2 GF: - Fm: 0-1
Distance:	2m/2m3: 0-2 2m4-2m7: 0-1 3m+: 0-1
Track:	LH: 0-2 RH: 0-2 Tight: 0-1 Gall: 0-0
Aids:	Bl: 0-0 Vi: 0-0 Tstrap: 0-0 Ckp: 0-0
Best Rating:	87 12/03 Weth 2m gd-sft Hdl

PLating-class hurdler; effective at around two miles; acts on fast ground.

Special Conquest
104   **117**

6-y-o b g El Conquistador-Kellys Special (Netherkelly)
J W Mullins F G Matthews

Placings:*1-0323*   (4561)
2003/04: 16⁰S, 20³HY, 20²S, 24³GS,

	Starts	1st	2nd	3rd	Win & Pl
NH Flat	1	0	0	0	0
Hurdles	3	0	1	2	3100
Career Total	5	1	1	2	6306
103	4/03	NAbb	2m1f	H NHF	G-F	£3206

Total win prize-money £3206

Going:	Sf: 0-3 GS: 0-1 Gd: 0-0 GF: - Fm: 0-0
Distance:	2m/2m3: 0-1 2m4-2m7: 0-2 3m+: 0-1
Track:	LH: 0-3 RH: 0-0 Tight: 0-0 Gall: 0-1
Aids:	Bl: 0-0 Vi: 0-0 Tstrap: 0-0 Ckp: 0-0
Best Rating:	117 2/04 Hayd 2m4f soft Hdl

Bumper winner; progressive over hurdles and runner-up at Haydock in February; suited by two and a half miles; handles testing conditions.

Special Constable
74(79h)   (56h)**51**

6-y-o b/br g Derrylin-Lavenham's Last (Rymer)
B I Case Case Racing Partnership

Placings:*0P-P0P35*   (4666)
2003/04: 20⁰S, 17⁰G, 24⁴GS, 20³GS, 20⁵S,

	Starts	1st	2nd	3rd	Win & Pl
Hurdles	2	0	0	0	0
Chases	3	0	0	1	648
Career Total	7	0	0	1	648

Going:	Sf: 0-1 GS: 0-2 Gd: 0-2 GF: - Fm: 0-0
Distance:	2m/2m3: 0-1 2m4-2m7: 0-3 3m+: 0-1
Track:	LH: 0-4 RH: 0-1 Tight: 0-4 Gall: 0-0
Aids:	Bl: 0-0 Vi: 0-0 Tstrap: 0-4 Ckp: 0-0
Best Rating:	62 11/02 Wwck 1m6f gd-sft NHF

Special Promise (IRE)
82   **99**

7-y-o ch g Anjiz (USA)-Woodenitbenice (USA) (Nasty And Bold (USA))
P Monteith Mrs D Santonocito

Placings:*11/0*   (4729)
2003/04: 20⁰G,

	Starts	1st	2nd	3rd	Win & Pl
Hurdles	1	0	0	0	
Career Total	3	2	0	0	2366
99	7/01	Sedg	2m5f110yE Hdl	G-F	£2366

Total win prize-money £2366

Going:	Sf: 0-0 GS: 0-0 Gd: 0-1 GF: - Fm: 0-0
Distance:	2m/2m3: 0-0 2m4-2m7: 0-1 3m+: 0-0
Track:	LH: 0-0 RH: 0-1 Tight: 0-0 Gall: 0-0
Aids:	Bl: 0-0 Vi: 0-0 Tstrap: 0-0 Ckp: 0-0
Best Rating:	99 7/01 Sedg 2m5f110y gd-fm Hdl

Lightly raced hurdler; stays 2m5f; acts on fast.

Special Rate (IRE)
109   **128**

7-y-o br g Grand Plaisir (IRE)-Clerical Artist (IRE) (The Parson)
A King (John E Kiely 9/11) J Brown,Mrs Bunter,M Deeley&Mrs Faccenda

Placings:*212113*   (4045)
2003/04: 16²GF, 16¹GF, 20²GS, 20¹S, 22¹G, 23³G,

	Starts	1st	2nd	3rd	Win & Pl
NH Flat	2	1	1	0	5519
Hurdles	4	2	1	1	16195
Career Total	6	3	2	1	21714
118	2/04	Winc	2m6f	C Hdl	GD	£6443
121	1/04	Leic	2m4f110yD Hdl	SFT	£5083
112	11/03	Navn	2m	NHF	G-F	£4480

Total win prize-money £16008

Going:	Sf: 1-1 GS: 0-1 Gd: 1-2 GF: - Fm: 1-2
Distance:	2m/2m3: 1-2 2m4-2m7: 2-3 3m+: 0-1
Track:	LH: 0-2 RH: 2-3 Tight: 0-0 Gall: 0-0
Aids:	Bl: 0-0 Vi: 0-0 Tstrap: 0-0 Ckp: 0-0
Best Rating:	136 2/04 Hayd 2m7f110y good Hdl

Ex-Irish bumper winner; promising novice hurdler; winner at up to two miles six; acts on soft ground.

Specialism
93   **49**

6-y-o ch g Spectrum (IRE)-Waft (USA) (Topsider (USA))
M J Gingell Miss K D Francis

Placings:*0-00066P*   (1756)
2003/04: 20⁰GF, 16⁰GF, 17⁰GF, 20⁵GF, 16⁶GF, 16⁶PG,

	Starts	1st	2nd	3rd	Win & Pl
Hurdles	6	0	0	0	0
Career Total	7	0	0	0	0

Going:	Sf: 0-0 GS: 0-0 Gd: 0-1 GF: - Fm: 0-5
Distance:	2m/2m3: 0-4 2m4-2m7: 0-2 3m+: 0-0
Track:	LH: 0-4 RH: 0-1 Tight: 0-5 Gall: 0-0
Aids:	Bl: 0-0 Vi: 0-0 Tstrap: 0-0 Ckp: 0-0
Best Rating:	54 10/03 Plum 2m gd-fm Hdl

Spectacular (IRE)
98   **92**

5-y-o b g Spectrum (IRE)-Azra (IRE) (Danehill (USA))
F P Murtagh (J S Bolger 9/10) Spectacular Partnership

Placings:*50055*   (4937)
2003/04: 16⁵GF, 16⁰S, 16⁵HY, 16⁵GF, 16⁵GS,

	Starts	1st	2nd	3rd	Win & Pl
Hurdles	5	0	0	0	0
Career Total	5	0	0	0	0

Going:	Sf: 0-2 GS: 0-1 Gd: 0-0 GF: - Fm: 0-2
Distance:	2m/2m3: 0-5 2m4-2m7: 0-0 3m+: 0-0
Track:	LH: 0-3 RH: 0-2 Tight: 0-3 Gall: 0-0
Aids:	Bl: 0-0 Vi: 0-0 Tstrap: 0-0 Ckp: 0-0
Best Rating:	92 1/04 Muss 2m gd-fm Hdl

Modest miler on the Flat; showed some ability on hurdling debut in very modest company at Musselburgh in January.

Spectacular Hope

4-y-o b f Marju (IRE)-Distant Music (Darshaan)
J W Mullins (R M Beckett 27/10) Woodford Valley Racing

Placings:UP   (3512)
2003/04: 16ᵁG, 18ᴾG,

	Starts	1st	2nd	3rd	Win & Pl
Hurdles	2	0	0	0	
Career Total	2	0	0	0	

Going:	Sf: 0-0 GS: 0-0 Gd: 0-2 GF: - Fm: 0-0
Distance:	2m/2m3: 0-2 2m4-2m7: 0-0 3m+: 0-0
Track:	LH: 0-1 RH: 0-1 Tight: 0-1 Gall: 0-0
Aids:	Bl: 0-0 Vi: 0-0 Tstrap: 0-0 Ckp: 0-0

Spectrometer
99   **149**

7-y-o ch g Rainbow Quest (USA)-Selection Board (Welsh Pageant)
R C Guest (M Johnston 12/9) Concertina Racing

Placings:21124/25222135-04   (4853)
2003/04: 20⁰G, 22⁴GS,

	Starts	1st	2nd	3rd	Win & Pl
Hurdles	2	0	0	0	795
Career Total	15	3	6	1	49289
140	12/02	Chel	2m1f	C(0-135)HHdl	GD	£16892
117	7/01	Worc	2m	D Hdl	GD	£3307
104	7/01	Strf	2m3f	E Hdl	GD	£2415

Total win prize-money £22615

Going:	Sf: 0-0 GS: 0-1 Gd: 0-1 GF: - Fm: 0-0
Distance:	2m/2m3: 0-0 2m4-2m7: 0-2 3m+: 0-0
Track:	LH: 0-2 RH: 0-0 Tight: 0-1 Gall: 0-0
Aids:	Bl: 0-0 Vi: 0-0 Tstrap: 0-0 Ckp: 0-0
Best Rating:	149 4/03 Aint 3m110y good Hdl

Very useful handicap hurdler; stays three miles; likes good/fast ground but also handles softer.

Spectroscope (IRE)
119   **137**

5-y-o b g Spectrum (IRE)-Paloma Bay (IRE) (Alzao (USA))
Jonjo O'Neill Mrs G Smith

Placings:1B4112-20P0P   (4449)
2003/04: 16²GY, 16⁹GS, 20ᴾHY, 20⁰G, 20ᴾGS,

	Starts	1st	2nd	3rd	Win & Pl
Hurdles	5	0	1	0	13571
Career Total	11	3	2	0	105529
137	3/03	Chel	2m1f	A Hdl	GD	£58000
121	2/03	Kemp	2m	D Hdl	G-S	£5005
112	10/02	Kemp	2m	D Hdl	GD	£4348

Total win prize-money £67354

Going:	Sf: 0-1 GS: 0-2 Gd: 0-1 GF: - Fm: 0-0
Distance:	2m/2m3: 0-2 2m4-2m7: 0-3 3m+: 0-0
Track:	LH: 0-2 RH: 0-3 Tight: 0-0 Gall: 0-1
Aids:	Bl: 0-0 Vi: 0-0 Tstrap: 0-0 Ckp: 0-0
Best Rating:	137 5/03 Punc 2m gd-yld Hdl

Useful hurdler; game winner of the Triumph Hurdle at the 2003 Cheltenham Festival and fine runner-up under a penalty at Aintree; well beaten so far in 2003/4; suited by good and yielding ground; tough sort; should stay two and a half miles.

Spectrum Star

77   **42**

4-y-o b g Spectrum (IRE)-Persia (IRE) (Persian Bold)
F P Murtagh (D K Ivory 1/5) D O'Connor

Placings:0P   (1298)
2003/04: 17DG, 16PGF,

	Starts	1st	2nd	3rd	Win & Pl
Hurdles	2	0	0	0	
Career Total	2	0	0	0	

Going: Sf: 0-0 GS: 0-0 Gd: 0-1 GF: - Fm: 0-1
Distance: 2m/2m3: 0-2 2m4-2m7: 0-0 3m+: 0-0
Track: LH: 0-2 RH: 0-0 Tight: 0-1 Gall: 0-0
Aids: Bl: 0-0 Vi: 0-0 Tstrap: 0-0 Ckp: 0-0
Best Rating: 42   8/03   Ctrnl   2m1f110y good   Hdl

Specular (AUS)

111   **147+**

8-y-o b g Danehill (USA)-Spyglass (NZ) (Sir Sian (NZ))
Jonjo O'Neill   John P McManus

Placings:1211111-11230U   (4862)
2003/04: 17IS, 17IG, 202GS, 163G, 169G, 16UGS,

	Starts	1st	2nd	3rd	Win & Pl
Hurdles	6	2	1		43291
Career Total	13	8	2	1	103696
6/03	Flem	2m1f	Hdl		GD	£13979
5/03	Flem	2m1f77y	Hdl		SFT	£12588
4/03	Flem	2m22y	Hdl		SFT	£11444
3/03	Sann	1m7f110y	Hdl		GD	£9155
9/02	Moon	2m	Hdl		G-S	£13908
8/02	Caul	1m7f	Hdl		G-S	£11796
7/02	Flem	1m6f99y	Hdl		GD	£5211
6/02	Caul	1m7f	Hdl		HVY	£5722

Total win prize-money £83803

Going: Sf: 1-1 GS: 0-2 Gd: 1-3 GF: - Fm: 0-0
Distance: 2m/2m3: 2-5 2m4-2m7: 0-1 3m+: 0-0
Track: LH: 0-3 RH: 0-0 Tight: 0-0 Gall: 0-0
Aids: Bl: 0-0 Vi: 0-0 Tstrap: 0-0 Ckp: 0-0
Best Rating: 147   1/04   Hayd   2m   good   Hdl

Smart ex-Australian trained hurdler; won eight of ten outings down under; has joined top connections and ran a promising race on ground too soft at Haydock on his first run in Britain; little show in the Champion Hurdle; stays 2m 4f; acts on soft ground; still open to improvement.

Speculative

10-y-o b g Suave Dancer (USA)-Gull Nook (Mill Reef (USA))
J W Mullins   K A Hicks

Placings:00P/P   (3642)
2003/04: 19PS,

	Starts	1st	2nd	3rd	Win & Pl
Hurdles	1	0	0	0	
Career Total	4	0	0	0	

Going: Sf: 0-1 GS: 0-0 Gd: 0-0 GF: - Fm: 0-0
Distance: 2m/2m3: 0-1 2m4-2m7: 0-0 3m+: 0-0
Track: LH: 0-0 RH: 0-1 Tight: 0-0 Gall: 0-0
Aids: Bl: 0-0 Vi: 0-0 Tstrap: 0-0 Ckp: 0-0
Best Rating: 61   11/97   Newc   2m   gd-fm   Hdl

Speed Board (IRE)

12-y-o b g Waajib-Pitty Pal (USA) (Caracolero (USA))
Dennis Pugh   Dennis Pugh

Placings:04002O536/P000/00215025P/10010050/0105P55
04P1P/0F31P10/0PP055P36/0333U-P   (3845)
2003/04: 25PGS,

	Starts	1st	2nd	3rd	Win & Pl
Chases	1	0	0	0	
Career Total	66	7	3	6	35084
107	2/01	Naas	2m4f	(0-116)HCh	SH	£6677
96	12/00	Navn	2m4f	(0-123)HCh	HVY	£5880
101	3/00	Wxfd	3m	(0-109)HCh	YLD	£3864
106	5/99	Gowr	3m1f	(0-116)HHdl	GD	£4910
108	1/99	Fair	2m6f	(0-116)HHdl	HVY	£3069
101	5/98	Fair	3m	(0-109)HHdl	Y-S	£2680
96	1/98	DRoy	2m4f	(0-109)HHdl	SFT	£1489

Total win prize-money £28570

Going: Sf: 0-0 GS: 0-1 Gd: 0-0 GF: - Fm: 0-0
Distance: 2m/2m3: 0-0 2m4-2m7: 0-0 3m+: 0-1
Track: LH: 0-0 RH: 0-1 Tight: 0-0 Gall: 0-0
Aids: Bl: 0-1 Vi: 0-0 Tstrap: 0-0 Ckp: 0-0
Best Rating: 108   1/99   Fair   2m6f   heavy   Hdl

Speed Kris (FR)

101   **102**

5-y-o b g Belmez (USA)-Pandia (USA) (Affirmed (USA))
Mrs S C Bradburne   Lord Cochrane And Partners

Placings:35P25-51403002   (4911)
2003/04: 17SGS, 17IG, 16AS, 16PGF, 203GS, 22UGS, 20VS, 162S,

	Starts	1st	2nd	3rd	Win & Pl
Hurdles	7	1	1		4884
Chases	1	0	0	0	468
Career Total	13	1	2	2	10855
10/03	Mtbn	2m1f110y	Hdl		GD	£1870

Total win prize-money £1870

Going: Sf: 0-3 GS: 0-3 Gd: 1-1 GF: - Fm: 0-1
Distance: 2m/2m3: 1-5 2m4-2m7: 0-3 3m+: 0-0
Track: LH: 0-4 RH: 0-2 Tight: 0-3 Gall: 0-0
Aids: Bl: 0-1 Vi: 0-4 Tstrap: 0-0 Ckp: 0-0
Best Rating: 102   4/04   Prth   2m110y   soft   Hdl

Claiming hurdle winner in France and signs of ability on an easy surface at up to two and a half miles for Sue Bradburne, including when tried in a visor at Ayr in February; may be capable of better in handicaps.

Speed Venture

105   **101**

7-y-o b g Owington-Jade Venture (Never So Bold)
J Mackie   Wall Racing Partners

Placings:13345/0005410-144000P1   (4873)
2003/04: 17IS, 17AG, 17AG, 19VG, 17PGS, 16AG, 17PG, 20IGS,

	Starts	1st	2nd	3rd	Win & Pl
Hurdles	8	2	0	0	10165
Career Total	20	4	0	2	18997
101	4/04	Bang	2m4f	F(0-100)HHdl	G-S	£4680
101	5/03	Bang	2m1f	D(0-115)HHdl	SFT	£5096
101	3/03	Hrfd	2m3f110yD(0-120)HHdl	SFT	£5297
99	11/01	Uttx	2m	E Hdl	SFT	£2758

Total win prize-money £17832

Going: Sf: 1-1 GS: 1-2 Gd: 0-5 GF: - Fm: 0-0
Distance: 2m/2m3: 1-6 2m4-2m7: 1-2 3m+: 0-0
Track: LH: 2-5 RH: 0-3 Tight: 2-6 Gall: 0-0
Aids: Bl: 0-0 Vi: 1-7 Tstrap: 2-8 Ckp: 0-0
Best Rating: 101   4/04   Bang   2m4f   gd-sft   Hdl

Moderate hurdler; stays 2m 3f; acts on soft ground; has worn a tongue tie and a visor.

Speedy Richard (IRE)

97f   **72f**

4-y-o ch g Zaffaran (USA)-Chadandy (USA) (Fast Enough (USA))
M Scudamore   Stephen W Molloy

Placings:00   (4213)
2003/04: 16DG, 16DG,

	Starts	1st	2nd	3rd	Win & Pl
NH Flat	2	0	0	0	
Career Total	2	0	0	0	

Going: Sf: 0-0 GS: 0-0 Gd: 0-2 GF: - Fm: 0-0
Distance: 2m/2m3: 0-2 2m4-2m7: 0-0 3m+: 0-0
Track: LH: 0-0 RH: 0-2 Tight: 0-0 Gall: 0-0
Aids: Bl: 0-0 Vi: 0-0 Tstrap: 0-0 Ckp: 0-0
Best Rating: 72   3/04   Kemp   2m   good   NHF

Speedy Taurub (USA)

4-y-o b g El Prado (IRE)-Off To Glory (USA) (Miswaki (USA))
N J Hawke   C E Handford

Placings:0   (4738)
2003/04: 17DG,

	Starts	1st	2nd	3rd	Win & Pl
NH Flat	1	0	0	0	
Career Total	1	0	0	0	

Going: Sf: 0-0 GS: 0-0 Gd: 0-1 GF: - Fm: 0-0
Distance: 2m/2m3: 0-1 2m4-2m7: 0-0 3m+: 0-0
Track: LH: 0-1 RH: 0-0 Tight: 0-0 Gall: 0-0
Aids: Bl: 0-0 Vi: 0-0 Tstrap: 0-0 Ckp: 0-0

Spendent

93   **75**

8-y-o ch h Generous (IRE)-Cattermole (USA) (Roberto (USA))
J J Sheehan   Mrs H J Cobb

Placings:00   (4698)
2003/04: 21DGS, 18DG,

	Starts	1st	2nd	3rd	Win & Pl
Hurdles	2	0	0	0	
Career Total	2	0	0	0	

Going: Sf: 0-0 GS: 0-1 Gd: 0-1 GF: - Fm: 0-0
Distance: 2m/2m3: 0-1 2m4-2m7: 0-1 3m+: 0-0
Track: LH: 0-2 RH: 0-0 Tight: 0-1 Gall: 0-1
Aids: Bl: 0-0 Vi: 0-0 Tstrap: 0-0 Ckp: 0-0
Best Rating: 76   3/04   Newb   2m5f   gd-sft   Hdl

Spendid (IRE)

111(101h)   (152dh)**145**

12-y-o b g Tidaro (USA)-Spendapromise (Goldhill)
A King   Mrs Stewart Catherwood

Placings:*201*311/11642321/**11122P1**/F225154/0P/2322461
6/30130-62   **(2728)**
2003/04: 25⁶G, 26²G,

	Starts	1st	2nd	3rd	Win & Pl
Hurdles	1	0	0	0	450
Chases	1	0	1	0	2504
Career Total	**45**	**13**	**11**	**5**	**206870**
143 12/02 Donc	3m2f	B(0-140)HCh	G-S	£12259
152 4/02 Asct	3m	A Hdl	G-F	£17400
157 3/02 Winc	3m1f110yB Ch		GD	£17306
161 4/99 Aint	3m1f	A Ch	GD	£26775
144 12/98 Chel	3m1f110yC Ch		GD	£7230
134 11/98 Chel	3m110y	B Ch	G-S	£9530
124 10/98 Weth	3m1f	C Ch	GD	£4770
144 4/98 Chel	2m5f110yB HHdl		HVY	£6208
132 11/97 Chel	2m5f	E(0-130)HHdl	GD	£2788
130 11/97 Towc	2m5f	D(0-125)HHdl	GD	£2912
119 2/97 Towc	2m	E Hdl	SFT	£1976
116 1/97 MRas	2m3f110yE Hdl		GD	£2700
111 9/96 List	2m	NHF		£3884
		Total win prize-money £115741

Going: Sf: 0-0 GS: 0-0 Gd: 0-2 GF: - Fm: 0-0
Distance: 2m/2m3: 0-0 2m4-2m7: 0-0 3m+: 0-2
Track: LH: 0-2 RH: 0-0 Tight: 0-0 Gall: 0-1
Aids: Bl: 0-0 Vi: 0-0 Tstrap: 0-0 Ckp: 0-0
Best Rating: 161 4/99 Aint 3m1f good Ch

Useful chaser/smart hurdler; third in the 2003 Scottish National and had shown high-class form over hurdles in the previous couple of seasons; stays four miles and acts on most types of ground.

Spider Boy

89   64

7-y-o b g Jupiter Island-Great Dilemma (Vaigly Great)
Miss Z C Davison   Derek Ash

Placings:*00*/03-P0334   **(1929)**
2003/04: 22⁵G, 20⁹GF, 21³GF, 16³GF, 25⁴GF,

	Starts	1st	2nd	3rd	Win & Pl
Hurdles	5	0	0	2	792
Career Total	**9**	**0**	**0**	**3**	**1083**

Going: Sf: 0-0 GS: 0-0 Gd: 0-1 GF: - Fm: 0-4
Distance: 2m/2m3: 0-1 2m4-2m7: 0-3 3m+: 0-1
Track: LH: 0-3 RH: 0-2 Tight: 0-2 Gall: 0-1
Aids: Bl: 0-0 Vi: 0-0 Tstrap: 0-0 Ckp: 0-2
Best Rating: 84 3/03 Wwck 2m gd-fm NHF

Spider McCoy (USA)

4-y-o ch g Irish River (FR)-Indy's Princess (USA) (A.P. Indy (USA))
Miss B Sanders (N Tinkler 9/8)   J M Quinn

Placings:P   **(1092)**
2003/04: 16⁵GF,

	Starts	1st	2nd	3rd	Win & Pl
Hurdles	1	0	0	0	
Career Total	**1**	**0**	**0**	**0**	

Going: Sf: 0-0 GS: 0-0 Gd: 0-0 GF: - Fm: 0-1
Distance: 2m/2m3: 0-1 2m4-2m7: 0-0 3m+: 0-0
Track: LH: 0-1 RH: 0-0 Tight: 0-1 Gall: 0-0
Aids: Bl: 0-0 Vi: 0-0 Tstrap: 0-0 Ckp: 0-0

Spider Music

97   88

8-y-o ch g Orchestra-Muffet's Spider (Rymer)

N G Richards   Mrs F D McInnes Skinner

Placings:*03*/3O36-0PP   **(4393)**
2003/04: 22⁰HY, 16²HY, 17²G,

	Starts	1st	2nd	3rd	Win & Pl
Hurdles	3	0	0	0	
Career Total	**9**	**0**	**0**	**3**	1623

Going: Sf: 0-1 GS: 0-0 Gd: 0-2 GF: - Fm: 0-0
Distance: 2m/2m3: 0-2 2m4-2m7: 0-1 3m+: 0-0
Track: LH: 0-3 RH: 0-0 Tight: 0-1 Gall: 0-1
Aids: Bl: 0-0 Vi: 0-0 Tstrap: 0-0 Ckp: 0-1
Best Rating: 102 2/02 Kemp 2m good NHF

Spike And Divel (IRE)

(99h)   (96h)

6-y-o b g Zaffaran (USA)-Lady Go Marching (USA) (Go Marching (USA))
Jonjo O'Neill (Ms Margaret Mullins 19/9)   John P McManus

Placings:24002   **(4490)**
2003/04: 16²S, 16⁴GS, 17⁰GS, 16⁶G, 16²G,

	Starts	1st	2nd	3rd	Win & Pl
NH Flat	2	0	1	0	1351
Hurdles	3	0	1	0	1068
Career Total	**5**	**0**	**2**	**0**	2419

Going: Sf: 0-1 GS: 0-2 Gd: 0-2 GF: - Fm: 0-0
Distance: 2m/2m3: 0-5 2m4-2m7: 0-0 3m+: 0-0
Track: LH: 0-1 RH: 0-3 Tight: 0-2 Gall: 0-2
Aids: Bl: 0-0 Vi: 0-0 Tstrap: 0-0 Ckp: 0-0
Best Rating: 97 9/03 List 2m soft NHF

Showed promise in bumpers; acts on good and soft.

Spike Jones (NZ)

96   96

6-y-o b g Colonel Collins (USA)-Gloss (NZ) (Kaapstad (NZ))
Jonjo O'Neill   Mrs Sarah Granger

Placings:*4*16B035   **(4718)**
2003/04: 16⁴GF, 16¹GF, 17⁶G, 16⁶G, 16⁹G, 16³G, 16⁵G,

	Starts	1st	2nd	3rd	Win & Pl
NH Flat	2	1	0	0	2089
Hurdles	5	0	0	1	530
Career Total	**7**	**1**	**0**	**1**	2619
108 11/03 Ludl	2m	H NHF	G-F	£1806
		Total win prize-money £1806

Going: Sf: 0-0 GS: 0-0 Gd: 0-5 GF: - Fm: 1-2
Distance: 2m/2m3: 1-7 2m4-2m7: 0-0 3m+: 0-0
Track: LH: 0-3 RH: 1-4 Tight: 0-2 Gall: 0-0
Aids: Bl: 0-0 Vi: 0-0 Tstrap: 0-0 Ckp: 0-0
Best Rating: 108 11/03 Ludl 2m gd-fm NHF

Spilaw (FR)

8-y-o b g Sky Lawyer (FR)-Spinage (FR) (Village Star (FR))
John Allen   John Allen

Placings:1/045/2614200400F0/00040U0130/53326446-
PFP   **(4344)**
2003/04: 25⁵GS, 24²G, 26⁶G,

	Starts	1st	2nd	3rd	Win & Pl
Chases	3	0	0	0	
Career Total	**37**	**3**	**3**	**3**	26134

---

95 11/01 Folk	2m	F(0-95)HCh	GD	£2541
11/00 Engh	2m2f	Ch	HLD	£6244
4/99 Toul	1m7f	Hdl	VS	£3229
		Total win prize-money £12014

Going: Sf: 0-0 GS: 0-2 Gd: 0-1 GF: - Fm: 0-0
Distance: 2m/2m3: 0-0 2m4-2m7: 0-0 3m+: 0-3
Track: LH: 0-1 RH: 0-2 Tight: 0-1 Gall: 0-0
Aids: Bl: 0-0 Vi: 0-0 Tstrap: 0-0 Ckp: 0-0
Best Rating: 95 11/01 Folk 2m good Ch

Spinaround

102   92

6-y-o br g Terimon-Re-Spin (Gildoran)
N A Gaselee   D R Stoddart

Placings:00-605264   **(4756)**
2003/04: 17⁶G, 17⁰G, 21⁵S, 17²GS, 16⁶G, 19⁴S,

	Starts	1st	2nd	3rd	Win & Pl
Hurdles	6	0	1	0	956
Career Total	**8**	**0**	**1**	**0**	956

Going: Sf: 0-2 GS: 0-1 Gd: 0-3 GF: - Fm: 0-0
Distance: 2m/2m3: 0-4 2m4-2m7: 0-2 3m+: 0-0
Track: LH: 0-2 RH: 0-3 Tight: 0-1 Gall: 0-1
Aids: Bl: 0-0 Vi: 0-0 Tstrap: 0-0 Ckp: 0-0
Best Rating: 92 2/04 Hrfd 2m1f gd-sft Hdl

Moderate novice hurdler; ran best race so far over 2m 4f but should stay farther.

Spinosa

6-y-o br m Afzal-Rosewater (Waterfall)
Mrs P Sly   T M Fowler

Placings:5-4   **(0619)**
2003/04: 24⁴G,

	Starts	1st	2nd	3rd	Win & Pl
Hurdles	1	0	0	0	271
Career Total	**2**	**0**	**0**	**0**	271

Going: Sf: 0-0 GS: 0-0 Gd: 0-1 GF: - Fm: 0-0
Distance: 2m/2m3: 0-0 2m4-2m7: 0-0 3m+: 0-1
Track: LH: 0-0 RH: 0-1 Tight: 0-1 Gall: 0-0
Aids: Bl: 0-0 Vi: 0-0 Tstrap: 0-0 Ckp: 0-0
Best Rating: 63 4/03 Fknm 2m good NHF

Spirit Leader (IRE)

115   154

8-y-o b/br m Supreme Leader-That's The Spirit (Mandalus)
Mrs John Harrington   D Thompson

Placings:*44*13/22222212/231511-624   **(3507a)**
2003/04: 16⁶GS, 16²Y, 16⁴Y,

	Starts	1st	2nd	3rd	Win & Pl
Hurdles	3	0	1	0	13847
Career Total	**21**	**5**	**9**	**2**	200766
154 3/03 Chel	2m1f	A HHdl	GD	£37700
144 2/03 Newb	2m110y	A HHdl	GD	£69600
136 12/02 Asct	3m 2m110y	A(0-150)HHdl	SFT	£40600
125 3/02 Punc	2m	Hdl	SFT	£6138
125 4/01 Gowr	2m	NHF	Y-S	£4173
		Total win prize-money £158211

Going: Sf: 0-0 GS: 0-1 Gd: 0-0 GF: - Fm: 0-0
Distance: 2m/2m3: 0-3 2m4-2m7: 0-0 3m+: 0-1
Track: LH: 0-3 RH: 0-0 Tight: 0-0 Gall: 0-0
Aids: Bl: 0-0 Vi: 0-0 Tstrap: 0-0 Ckp: 0-0

Best Rating: 154 12/03 Leop 2m   yield   Hdl

Smart Irish-trained hurdler; landed the valuable William Hill Handicap Hurdle at Sandown in December 2002 and the Tote Gold Trophy and County Hurdle in 2003; decent efforts in conditions races this term; effective at around two miles; acts on fast but well suited by soft ground; tough.

Spirit Of Destiny

7-y-o ch m Riverwise (USA)-Tearful Sarah (Rugantino)
C W Mitchell C W Mitchell

Placings:*00*/P-P					(4544)
2003/04: 22PGS,					
	Starts	1st	2nd	3rd	Win & Pl
Hurdles	1	0	0	0	
Career Total	4	0	0	0	

Going: Sf: 0-0 GS: 0-1 Gd: 0-0 GF: - Fm: 0-0
Distance: 2m/2m3: 0-0 2m4-2m7: 0-0 3m+: 0-0
Track: LH: 0-0 RH: 0-1 Tight: 0-0 Gall: 0-0
Aids: Bl: 0-0 Vi: 0-0 Tstrap: 0-0 Ckp: 0-0
Best Rating: 63 3/02 Winc 2m   soft   NHF

Spirit Of New York (IRE)

107f   **112f**

5-y-o b g Topanoora-Fiona's Blue (Crash Course)
Jonjo O'Neill John P McManus

Placings:*1*					(4199)
2003/04: 16¹G,					
	Starts	1st	2nd	3rd	Win & Pl
NH Flat	1	1	0	0	2667
Career Total	1	1	0	0	2667
112 3/04 Newb 2m110y H NHF				GD	£2667
Total win prize-money £2667					

Going: Sf: 0-0 GS: 0-0 Gd: 1-1 GF: - Fm: 0-0
Distance: 2m/2m3: 1-1 2m4-2m7: 0-0 3m+: 0-0
Track: LH: 1-1 RH: 0-0 Tight: 0-0 Gall: 1-1
Aids: Bl: 0-0 Vi: 0-0 Tstrap: 0-0 Ckp: 0-0
Best Rating: 112 3/04 Newb 2m110y good NHF

Well-backed when making a winning debut in a Newbury bumper.

Spirit Ofthe Green (IRE)

92   **74**

6-y-o br g Detroit Sam (FR)-Golden Hearted (Corvaro (USA))
L Wells Jazz Knight Partnership

Placings:*5*-35P					(3748)
2003/04: 21³S, 21⁵S, 22PGS,					
	Starts	1st	2nd	3rd	Win & Pl
Hurdles	3	0	0	1	263
Career Total	4	0	0	1	263

Going: Sf: 0-0 GS: 0-1 Gd: 0-0 GF: - Fm: 0-0
Distance: 2m/2m3: 0-0 2m4-2m7: 0-0 3m+: 0-0
Track: LH: 0-3 RH: 0-0 Tight: 0-0 Gall: 0-0
Aids: Bl: 0-1 Vi: 0-0 Tstrap: 0-0 Ckp: 0-0
Best Rating: 82 3/03 Folk 2m1f110y good NHF

Plating-class hurdler; limited promise in bumpers; third in weak race on hurdles debut; stays two miles five.

Spiritual Dancer (IRE)

99   **102+**

9-y-o b g King's Ride-Arctic Tartan (Deep Run)
L Wells D W Cox & Paul Zetter

Placings:2F2P/3/3					(2536)
2003/04: 25³S,					
	Starts	1st	2nd	3rd	Win & Pl
Hurdles	1	0	0	1	367
Career Total	6	0	2	2	2382

Going: Sf: 0-1 GS: 0-0 Gd: 0-0 GF: - Fm: 0-0
Distance: 2m/2m3: 0-0 2m4-2m7: 0-0 3m+: 0-0
Track: LH: 0-0 RH: 0-0 Tight: 0-0 Gall: 0-0
Aids: Bl: 0-0 Vi: 0-0 Tstrap: 0-0 Ckp: 0-0
Best Rating: 102 12/03 Plum 3m1f110y soft Hdl

Moderate staying hurdler; keen sort; has stamina in abundance; well suited by testing ground.

Splash And Dash (IRE)

9-y-o ch g Arcane (USA)-Quilty Rose (Buckskin (FR))
Mrs S J Hickman Maurice Smith

Placings:1-6F					(4703)
2003/04: 26⁶G, 26FG,					
	Starts	1st	2nd	3rd	Win & Pl
Chases	2	0	0	0	0
Career Total	3	1	0	0	3543
97 3/03 Strf 3m H Ch				G-S	£3542
Total win prize-money £3543					

Going: Sf: 0-0 GS: 0-0 Gd: 0-2 GF: - Fm: 0-0
Distance: 2m/2m3: 0-0 2m4-2m7: 0-0 3m+: 0-2
Track: LH: 0-0 RH: 0-0 Tight: 0-2 Gall: 0-0
Aids: Bl: 0-0 Vi: 0-0 Tstrap: 0-0 Ckp: 0-0
Best Rating: 97 3/03 Strf 3m gd-sft Ch

Hunter chaser; made winning start under Rules at Stratford in March 2003; won three from five in points; acts on good and good to soft.

Splash Out Again

89   **107+**

6-y-o b g River Falls-Kajetana (FR) (Caro)
H Morrison M T Bevan

Placings:010					(4838)
2003/04: 17OGS, 22¹GF, 24OGF,					
	Starts	1st	2nd	3rd	Win & Pl
Hurdles	3	1	0	0	3626
Career Total	3	1	0	0	3626
107 3/04 Font 2m6f110yE Hdl				G-F	£3626
Total win prize-money £3626					

Going: Sf: 0-0 GS: 0-1 Gd: 0-0 GF: - Fm: 1-2
Distance: 2m/2m3: 0-0 2m4-2m7: 1-1 3m+: 0-1
Track: LH: 1-2 RH: 0-0 Tight: 1-2 Gall: 0-1
Aids: Bl: 0-0 Vi: 0-0 Tstrap: 0-0 Ckp: 0-0
Best Rating: 107 3/04 Font 2m6f110y gd-fm Hdl

Splendid Touch

86   **47**

4-y-o b f Distinctly North (USA)-Soft Touch (GER) (Horst-Herbert)

J R Jenkins Kingsland Bloodstock

Placings:60					(2538)
2003/04: 16⁶G, 16⁹G,					
	Starts	1st	2nd	3rd	Win & Pl
Hurdles	2	0	0	0	232
Career Total	2	0	0	0	232

Going: Sf: 0-0 GS: 0-0 Gd: 0-2 GF: - Fm: 0-0
Distance: 2m/2m3: 0-2 2m4-2m7: 0-0 3m+: 0-0
Track: LH: 0-0 RH: 0-2 Tight: 0-0 Gall: 0-0
Aids: Bl: 0-0 Vi: 0-0 Tstrap: 0-1 Ckp: 0-0
Best Rating: 47 12/03 Leic 2m good Hdl

Spokesman

102   (132h)**111+**

10-y-o b g Rudimentary (USA)-Ravaro (Raga Navarro (ITY))
Jonjo O'Neill John P McManus

Placings:*141*/3P02/1330/0/332F0600/0F240-3UP0					(3755)
2003/04: 16³G, 20UG, 20PGS, 17OG,					
	Starts	1st	2nd	3rd	Win & Pl
Chases	4	0	0	1	828
Career Total	29	3	3	6	32115
141 12/99 Leop 2m HHdl				SFT	£7392
114 3/98 Leop 2m NHF				SFT	£2680
105 1/98 Leop 2m NHF				YLD	£3573
Total win prize-money £13647					

Going: Sf: 0-0 GS: 0-1 Gd: 0-3 GF: - Fm: 0-0
Distance: 2m/2m3: 0-2 2m4-2m7: 0-2 3m+: 0-0
Track: LH: 0-3 RH: 0-1 Tight: 0-3 Gall: 0-0
Aids: Bl: 0-0 Vi: 0-0 Tstrap: 0-0 Ckp: 0-0
Best Rating: 141 12/99 Leop 2m soft Hdl

Modest chaser; ex-Irish; best at around two miles on testing ground; does not find much off the bridle.

Sporazene (IRE)

120   **155+**

5-y-o gr g Cozzene (USA)-Sporades (USA) (Vaguely Noble)
P F Nicholls Ged Mason & David Jackson

Placings:331-123010					(4646)
2003/04: 16¹GY, 16²GS, 16³G, 16⁶G, 17¹G, 20⁰G,					
	Starts	1st	2nd	3rd	Win & Pl
Hurdles	6	2	1	1	96286
Career Total	9	3	1	3	105877
155 3/04 Chel 2m1f A HHdl				GD	£37700
139 5/03 Punc 2m Hdl				G-Y	£44285
117 4/03 Ayr 2m C Hdl				GD	£7403
Total win prize-money £89390					

Going: Sf: 0-0 GS: 0-1 Gd: 1-4 GF: - Fm: 0-0
Distance: 2m/2m3: 2-5 2m4-2m7: 0-1 3m+: 0-0
Track: LH: 1-4 RH: 1-2 Tight: 0-1 Gall: 1-3
Aids: Bl: 0-0 Vi: 0-0 Tstrap: 0-0 Ckp: 0-0
Best Rating: 155 3/04 Chel 2m1f good Hdl

Smart hurdler; middle-distance winner on the Flat in France; off the mark in weak event at Ayr in April 2003, but massive improvement when winning the Grade One four-year-old hurdle at the Punchestown Festival the following month; narrow defeat at Newbury on return and creditable third in Christmas Hurdle this term prior to finishing eighth in the Tote Gold Trophy; bounced right back to his best to win the County Hurdle; best at two miles; likes to get his toe in.

Sporting Chance

12-y-o ch g Ikdam-Tumbling Ego (Abednego)

Ms J Channon H S Channon

Placings:5000P/P/3004-P6P4   (4858)
2003/04: 21PG, 24&G, 19PG, 24&GF,

	Starts	1st	2nd	3rd	Win & Pl
Chases	4	0	0	0	0
Career Total	14	0	0	1	574

Going: Sf: 0-0 GS: 0-0 Gd: 0-3 GF: - Fm: 0-1
Distance: 2m/2m3: 0-0 2m4-2m7: 0-2 3m+: 0-2
Track: LH: 0-1 RH: 0-3 Tight: 0-2 Gall: 0-1
Aids: Bl: 0-0 Vi: 0-0 Tstrap: 0-0 Ckp: 0-0
Best Rating: 77 7/02 Strf   2m5f110y gd-fm   Ch

Sporting Hero
88   70
4-y-o b g Safawan-Cryptic Gold (Glint Of Gold)
M W Easterby Steve Hull

Placings:/030   (4795)
2003/04: 17&G, 16&G, 17&G,

	Starts	1st	2nd	3rd	Win & Pl
NH Flat	1	0	0	0	0
Hurdles	2	0	0	1	511
Career Total	3	0	0	1	511

Going: Sf: 0-1 GS: 0-0 Gd: 0-2 GF: - Fm: 0-0
Distance: 2m/2m3: 0-3 2m4-2m7: 0-0 3m+: 0-0
Track: LH: 0-2 RH: 0-1 Tight: 0-1 Gall: 0-1
Aids: Bl: 0-0 Vi: 0-0 Tstrap: 0-0 Ckp: 0-0
Best Rating: 70 4/04 Sedg   2m1f   good   Hdl

Poor form in bumpers and juvenile hurdles.

Sports Express
104   90
6-y-o ch m Then Again-Lady St Lawrence (USA) (Bering)
Miss Lucinda V Russell (G A Swinbank 7/10)
Powrie,Valentine,Hawkins & McManus

Placings:2222/4P4554   (4950)
2003/04: 19&GF, 22PG, 20&GS, 24&GF, 20&GS, 20&GS,

	Starts	1st	2nd	3rd	Win & Pl
Hurdles	6	0	0	0	1196
Career Total	10	0	4	0	4504

Going: Sf: 0-0 GS: 0-3 Gd: 0-1 GF: - Fm: 0-2
Distance: 2m/2m3: 0-0 2m4-2m7: 0-5 3m+: 0-2
Track: LH: 0-4 RH: 0-2 Tight: 0-0 Gall: 0-0
Aids: Bl: 0-0 Vi: 0-0 Tstrap: 0-0 Ckp: 0-0
Best Rating: 97 2/02 Donc   2m4f   soft   Hdl

Moderate hurdler; finished second on her first four starts in the 2002 season, missed the following campaign; effective over two and a half miles.

Sportsman (IRE)
87   99
5-y-o b g Sri Pekan (USA)-Ardent Range (IRE) (Archway (IRE))
M W Easterby The Shooting Syndicate

Placings:6253-50U   (4956)
2003/04: 16&S, 23&S, 22&G,

	Starts	1st	2nd	3rd	Win & Pl
Hurdles	3	0	0	0	0
Career Total	7	0	1	1	1852

Going: Sf: 0-2 GS: 0-0 Gd: 0-1 GF: - Fm: 0-0
Distance: 2m/2m3: 0-1 2m4-2m7: 0-2 3m+: 0-0
Track: LH: 0-2 RH: 0-0 Tight: 0-0 Gall: 0-0
Aids: Bl: 0-3 Vi: 0-0 Tstrap: 0-0 Ckp: 0-0
Best Rating: 99 10/02 Weth   2m   gd-fm   Hdl

Spot In Time
80f   77f
4-y-o b f Mtoto-Kelimutu (Top Ville)
J Pearce (Mrs Lydia Pearce 20/1) Jim Furlong

Placings:35   (3920)
2003/04: 17&HY, 16&G,

	Starts	1st	2nd	3rd	Win & Pl
NH Flat	2	0	0	1	274
Career Total	2	0	0	1	274

Going: Sf: 0-1 GS: 0-0 Gd: 0-1 GF: - Fm: 0-0
Distance: 2m/2m3: 0-2 2m4-2m7: 0-0 3m+: 0-0
Track: LH: 0-1 RH: 0-1 Tight: 0-2 Gall: 0-0
Aids: Bl: 0-0 Vi: 0-0 Tstrap: 0-0 Ckp: 0-0
Best Rating: 77 1/04 Folk   2m1f110y   heavy   NHF

Spot Thedifference (IRE)
105   (87h) 135
11-y-o b g Lafontaine (USA)-Spotted Choice (IRE) (Callernish)
E Bolger John P McManus

Placings:P13F/220/4142/311126UP/6U0-U042255 (4647)
2003/04: 33&UG, 16&YS, 20&Y, 32&GF, 24&YS, 26&G, 36&G,

	Starts	1st	2nd	3rd	Win & Pl
Hurdles	2	0	0	0	416
Chases	5	0	2	0	31127
Career Total	29	5	6	2	74645
130	6/01	Kbgn	3m1f	(0-123)HCh	GD £10483
119	6/01	Rosc	3m100y	(0-116)HCh	GD £5564
110	5/01	Kbgn	3m1f		Ch	GD £3895
108	2/01	Thur	3m		Ch	SFT £4729
100	2/99	Clon	3m		Ch	SFT £2455
				Total win prize-money £27129

Going: Sf: 0-0 GS: 0-0 Gd: 0-3 GF: - Fm: 0-1
Distance: 2m/2m3: 0-1 2m4-2m7: 0-1 3m+: 0-5
Track: LH: 0-3 RH: 0-2 Tight: 0-0 Gall: 0-0
Aids: Bl: 0-0 Vi: 0-0 Tstrap: 0-0 Ckp: 0-0
Best Rating: 141 6/03 Uttx   4m110y   gd-fm   Ch

Useful hunter/handicap chaser at best; fifth in the 2004 Cheltenham Foxhunters' and filled the same position in the Grand National; stays well; acts on most ground.

Spread The Dream
87   79
6-y-o ch g Alflora (IRE)-Cauchemar (Hot Brandy)
N J Henderson Mrs G M Tregaskes

Placings:2-6   (3350)
2003/04: 16&S,

	Starts	1st	2nd	3rd	Win & Pl
Hurdles	1	0	0	0	0
Career Total	2	0	1	0	666

Going: Sf: 0-1 GS: 0-0 Gd: 0-0 GF: - Fm: 0-0
Distance: 2m/2m3: 0-1 2m4-2m7: 0-0 3m+: 0-0
Track: LH: 0-0 RH: 0-1 Tight: 0-0 Gall: 0-1
Aids: Bl: 0-0 Vi: 0-0 Tstrap: 0-0 Ckp: 0-0
Best Rating: 94 3/03 Winc   2m   gd-fm   NHF

Spread The Word
110   104
12-y-o b m Deploy-Apply (King's Lake (USA))
J G Cann Mrs Pam Pengelly

Placings:55/P-2123   (2119)
2003/04: 25&GF, 25&F, 25&G, 24&F,

	Starts	1st	2nd	3rd	Win & Pl
Chases	4	1	2	1	7089
Career Total	7	1	2	1	7089
98	10/03	Towc	3m1f	D(0-120)HCh	FRM £4501
				Total win prize-money £4501

Going: Sf: 0-0 GS: 0-0 Gd: 0-1 GF: - Fm: 1-0
Distance: 2m/2m3: 0-0 2m4-2m7: 0-0 3m+: 1-4
Track: LH: 0-0 RH: 1-4 Tight: 0-1 Gall: 0-0
Aids: Bl: 0-0 Vi: 0-0 Tstrap: 0-0 Ckp: 0-0
Best Rating: 104 10/03 Towc   3m1f   good   Ch

Modest chaser; winning pointer; stays beyond three miles and best on fast ground; suited by stiff track.

Spree Vision
103   91
8-y-o b g Suave Dancer (USA)-Regent's Folly (IRE) (Touching Wood (USA))
P Monteith I Bell

Placings:6/30620/653/22163P040-5506030   (4688)
2003/04: 18&G, 16&G, 17&HY, 17&G, 20&GF, 17&G, 16&G,

	Starts	1st	2nd	3rd	Win & Pl
Hurdles	7	0	0	1	348
Career Total	25	1	3	4	9548
105	11/02	Newc	2m	D Hdl	G-S £3945
				Total win prize-money £3946

Going: Sf: 0-1 GS: 0-0 Gd: 0-5 GF: - Fm: 0-1
Distance: 2m/2m3: 0-6 2m4-2m7: 0-1 3m+: 0-0
Track: LH: 0-5 RH: 0-2 Tight: 0-4 Gall: 0-0
Aids: Bl: 0-0 Vi: 0-0 Tstrap: 0-0 Ckp: 0-0
Best Rating: 105 11/02 Newc   2m   gd-sft   Hdl

Modest hurdler, on the downgrade; seems best on good to soft ground.

Spreewald (GER)
96   81
5-y-o b g Dulcero (USA)-Spartina (USA) (Northern Baby (CAN))
J C Tuck Seven Star Racing Club

Placings:020000   (4523)
2003/04: 16&G, 16&GF, 17&G, 16&G, 17&GS, 17&GS,

	Starts	1st	2nd	3rd	Win & Pl
Hurdles	6	0	1	0	1314
Career Total	6	0	1	0	1314

Going: Sf: 0-0 GS: 0-2 Gd: 0-2 GF: - Fm: 0-2
Distance: 2m/2m3: 0-6 2m4-2m7: 0-0 3m+: 0-0
Track: LH: 0-2 RH: 0-4 Tight: 0-1 Gall: 0-1
Aids: Bl: 0-0 Vi: 0-0 Tstrap: 0-0 Ckp: 0-0
Best Rating: 81 12/03 Tntn   2m1f   good   Hdl

PLating-class novice hurdler; yet to race at beyond two miles; acts on fast ground.

Spring Bee
76   22
4-y-o b f Parthian Springs-First Bee (Gunner B)

T Wall D Pugh

Placings:00 (3224)
2003/04: 13⁴S, 17⁰GS,

	Starts	1st	2nd	3rd	Win & Pl
NH Flat	1	0	0	0	0
Hurdles	1	0	0	0	0
Career Total	2	0	0		0

Going:	Sf: 0-1 GS: 0-1 Gd: 0-0 GF: - Fm: 0-0
Distance:	2m/2m3: 0-1 2m4-2m7: 0-0 3m+: 0-0
Track:	LH: 0-0 RH: 0-1 Tight: 0-0 Gall: 0-0
Aids:	Bl: 0-0 Vi: 0-0 Tstrap: 0-0 Ckp: 0-0
Best Rating:	27 1/04 Hrfd 2m1f gd-sft Hdl

Spring Dawn

98(105h) (102h)**102**
9-y-o gr g Arzanni-Another Spring (Town Crier)
N J Henderson W H Ponsonby

Placings:34/45/3230-FP6P633 (4786)
2003/04: 16⁶G, 19⁵GS, 23⁶GS, 24⁴G, 20⁶GF, 16³GS, 16³G,

	Starts	1st	2nd	3rd	Win & Pl
Hurdles	1	0	0	0	0
Chases	6	0	0	2	1330
Career Total	15	0	1	5	3829

Going:	Sf: 0-0 GS: 0-3 Gd: 0-3 GF: - Fm: 0-1
Distance:	2m/2m3: 0-4 2m4-2m7: 0-1 3m+: 0-2
Track:	LH: 0-1 RH: 0-6 Tight: 0-2 Gall: 0-1
Aids:	Bl: 0-0 Vi: 0-0 Tstrap: 0-0 Ckp: 0-1
Best Rating:	113 11/02 Tntn 2m1f gd-sft Hdl

Moderate hurdler/novice chaser; best at around two miles; acts on good ground.

Spring Double (IRE)

96 (0c)**87**
13-y-o br g Seclude (USA)-Solar Jet (Mandalus)
N A Twiston-Davies Mrs Lorna Berryman

Placings:06/1340511P2/4333/22P313/63432PP43/1000P/6
-360 (0944)
2003/04: 27³G, 26⁶GF, 24⁰G,

	Starts	1st	2nd	3rd	Win & Pl
Hurdles	2	0	0	1	828
Chases	1	0	0	0	0
Career Total	39	5	4	10	29726
104	11/01	Kemp	3m110y D(0-120)HHdl	GD	£4446
110	4/99	Uttx	3m C(0-125)HCh	G-S	£4416
126	3/97	Newb	2m5f D Hdl	G-S	£3467
105	2/97	Hrfd	2m3f110yE(0-105)HHdl	SFT	£2337
110	5/96	Uttx	3m N HHF	GF	£1763
			Total win prize-money £16429

Going:	Sf: 0-0 GS: 0-0 Gd: 0-2 GF: - Fm: 0-1
Distance:	2m/2m3: 0-0 2m4-2m7: 0-0 3m+: 0-3
Track:	LH: 0-3 RH: 0-0 Tight: 0-2 Gall: 0-0
Aids:	Bl: 0-0 Vi: 0-0 Tstrap: 0-0 Ckp: 0-0
Best Rating:	126 3/97 Newb 2m5f gd-sft Hdl

Fair staying hurdler/chaser; stays three miles and is effective on good ground or softer.

Spring Gale (IRE)

13-y-o b g Strong Gale-Orospring (Tesoro Mio)
J M Turner J M Turner

Placings:3/012151P/2121243/22523P32/62/124/21/R3-3 (0351)

2003/04: 25³GF,

	Starts	1st	2nd	3rd	Win & Pl
Chases	1	0	0	1	274
Career Total	33	7	11	6	39139
115	5/01	Folk	3m1f H Ch	GD	£1934
105	5/00	Fknm	3m110y H Ch	FRM	£1473
127	12/97	Strf	2m5f110yD Ch	SFT	£4770
132	11/97	Uttx	2m4f D(0-125)HCh	G-S	£3468
115	3/97	Donc	2m4f E Hdl	G-F	£2679
111	1/97	Tntn	2m3f110yD Hdl	G-F	£3137
110	10/96	Font	2m6f110yE Hdl	GD	£2595
			Total win prize-money £20059

Going:	Sf: 0-0 GS: 0-0 Gd: 0-0 GF: - Fm: 0-1
Distance:	2m/2m3: 0-0 2m4-2m7: 0-0 3m+: 0-1
Track:	LH: 0-0 RH: 0-1 Tight: 0-0 Gall: 0-0
Aids:	Bl: 0-0 Vi: 0-0 Tstrap: 0-0 Ckp: 0-0
Best Rating:	132 1/98 Chel 2m5f gd-sft Ch

Decent pointer/hunter chaser, but is sometimes reluctant to start.

Spring Gamble (IRE)

107 **99**
5-y-o b g Norwich-Aurora Run (IRE) (Cyrano De Bergerac)
G M Moore J B Wallwin

Placings:34332346 (4658)
2003/04: 16³F, 17⁴G, 17³G, 16³GS, 19²G, 17³GS, 16⁴GF, 20⁶S,

	Starts	1st	2nd	3rd	Win & Pl
NH Flat	4	0	0	3	747
Hurdles	4	0	1	1	1758
Career Total	8	0	1	4	2505

Going:	Sf: 0-1 GS: 0-2 Gd: 0-3 GF: - Fm: 0-2
Distance:	2m/2m3: 0-7 2m4-2m7: 0-1 3m+: 0-0
Track:	LH: 0-8 RH: 0-0 Tight: 0-5 Gall: 0-0
Aids:	Bl: 0-0 Vi: 0-0 Tstrap: 0-0 Ckp: 0-0
Best Rating:	99 2/04 Sedg 2m1f gd-sft Hdl

Placed in bumpers; showed plenty of promise on his hurdling debut; should stay beyond two and a half miles.

Spring Gift

81 **42**
7-y-o b m Slip Anchor-Belmez Melody (Belmez (USA))
D W Thompson (P S McEntee 18/6) J Greenbank

Placings:F/P000 (3324)
2003/04: 16⁶GF, 16⁹GS, 16⁶GS, 17⁰GS,

	Starts	1st	2nd	3rd	Win & Pl
Hurdles	4	0	0	0	0
Career Total	5	0	0	0	0

Going:	Sf: 0-0 GS: 0-3 Gd: 0-0 GF: - Fm: 0-1
Distance:	2m/2m3: 0-4 2m4-2m7: 0-0 3m+: 0-0
Track:	LH: 0-4 RH: 0-0 Tight: 0-2 Gall: 0-0
Aids:	Bl: 0-0 Vi: 0-0 Tstrap: 0-0 Ckp: 0-0
Best Rating:	42 11/03 Hayd 2m gd-sft Hdl

Spring Grove (IRE)

117(105h) (112h)**135**
9-y-o b g Mandalus-Lucy Lorraine (IRE) (Buckskin (FR))
R H Alner H V Perry

Placings:1/52153/123313/FUPP34/P46-51412034 (4889)
2003/04: 22⁵G, 16¹G, 17⁴GS, 20¹G, 21²G, 20⁶G, 24³G, 20⁴GF,

	Starts	1st	2nd	3rd	Win & Pl
Hurdles	1	0	0	0	0
Chases	7	2	1	1	27075

Career Total | **29** | **6** | **3** | **6** | 48330
135	12/03	Wwck	2m4f110yC(0-130)HCh	GD	£6812
130	11/03	Ling	2m C(0-130)HCh	GD	£6734
132	2/01	Leic	2m E Ch	SFT	£3413
124	10/00	Kemp	2m D Ch	G-S	£4959
125	2/00	Font	2m2f110yE Hdl	SFT	£2537
108	3/99	Chep	2m110y H NHF	G-F	£1856
			Total win prize-money £26314

Going:	Sf: 0-0 GS: 0-1 Gd: 2-6 GF: - Fm: 0-1
Distance:	2m/2m3: 1-2 2m4-2m7: 1-5 3m+: 0-1
Track:	LH: 2-7 RH: 0-1 Tight: 1-2 Gall: 0-4
Aids:	Bl: 0-0 Vi: 0-0 Tstrap: 0-0 Ckp: 0-0
Best Rating:	135 3/04 Newb 3m good Ch

Useful chaser; effective at around two to two and a half miles; acts well on soft, but has won on good ground.

Spring Lover (FR)

98(97h) (95h)**87**
5-y-o b g Fijar Tango (FR)-Kailasa (FR) (Rb Chesne)
Miss Venetia Williams Malcolm Edwards

Placings:3F/523313-020034F5 (4757)
2003/04: 16⁹G, 22²G, 20⁰GS, 16⁹GF, 16³GS, 23⁴GF, 25⁶GS, 25⁶S,

	Starts	1st	2nd	3rd	Win & Pl
Hurdles	5	0	1	1	1329
Chases	3	0	0	0	433
Career Total	16	1	2	5	18935
12/02	Pau	2m1f	Ch	SFT	£7656
			Total win prize-money £7656

Going:	Sf: 0-1 GS: 0-3 Gd: 0-2 GF: - Fm: 0-2
Distance:	2m/2m3: 0-3 2m4-2m7: 0-2 3m+: 0-3
Track:	LH: 0-1 RH: 0-7 Tight: 0-1 Gall: 0-0
Aids:	Bl: 0-0 Vi: 0-0 Tstrap: 0-0 Ckp: 0-0
Best Rating:	95 1/04 Ludl 2m gd-sft Hdl

Plating-class hurdler/chaser; winner over fences in France; effective over two miles; acts on soft ground.

Spring Pursuit

112 **115**
8-y-o b g Rudimentary (USA)-Pursuit Of Truth (USA) (Irish River (FR))
E G Bevan (R J Price 21/2) E G Bevan

Placings:560-2553144455063 (4917)
2003/04: 16²GS, 16⁵GS, 16⁵GS, 16³G, 16¹GS, 17⁴GS, 20⁴S, 16⁴GS, 16⁵GS, 16⁵GS, 16⁹GS, 17⁶G, 20³GS,

	Starts	1st	2nd	3rd	Win & Pl
Hurdles	13	1	1	2	13178
Career Total	16	1	1	2	13178
114	1/04	Wwck	2m D(0-110)HHdl	G-S	£7514
			Total win prize-money £7514

Going:	Sf: 0-1 GS: 1-8 Gd: 0-4 GF: - Fm: 0-0
Distance:	2m/2m3: 1-11 2m4-2m7: 0-2 3m+: 0-0
Track:	LH: 1-8 RH: 0-5 Tight: 0-0 Gall: 0-4
Aids:	Bl: 0-0 Vi: 0-0 Tstrap: 0-0 Ckp: 0-0
Best Rating:	115 1/04 Chel 2m1f gd-sft Hdl

Modest hurdler; stays two and a half miles; acts on good and easy going.

Spring Rock

55f
7-y-o b g Rock Hopper-Shaft Of Sunlight (Sparkler)
R M Whitaker R M Whitaker

Placings:00-0 (0649)
2003/04: 16⁰GF,

	Starts	1st	2nd	3rd	Win & Pl
NH Flat	1	0	0	0	
Career Total	3	0	0	0	

Going:	Sf: 0-0 GS: 0-0 Gd: 0-0 GF: - Fm: 0-1
Distance:	2m/2m3: 0-1 2m4-2m7: 0-0 3m+: 0-0
Track:	LH: 0-1 RH: 0-0 Tight: 0-0 Gall: 0-0
Aids:	Bl: 0-0 Vi: 0-1 Tstrap: 0-0 Ckp: 0-0
Best Rating:	59 9/02 Hexm 2m110y gd-fm NHF

Springaway
95f   72f

5-y-o ch g Minster Son-Galway Gal (Proverb)
Miss Kate Milligan Mrs J M L Milligan

Placings: 60   (3474)
2003/04: 16⁶GF, 16⁹GF,

	Starts	1st	2nd	3rd	Win & Pl
NH Flat	2	0	0	0	0
Career Total	2	0	0	0	0

Going:	Sf: 0-0 GS: 0-0 Gd: 0-0 GF: - Fm: 0-2
Distance:	2m/2m3: 0-2 2m4-2m7: 0-0 3m+: 0-0
Track:	LH: 0-1 RH: 0-1 Tight: 0-1 Gall: 0-0
Aids:	Bl: 0-0 Vi: 0-0 Tstrap: 0-0 Ckp: 0-0
Best Rating:	72 1/04 Muss 2m gd-fm NHF

Springbok Attitude
70

7-y-o b g Pharly (FR)-Tugra (FR) (Baby Turk)
B Llewellyn Mrs M Llewellyn

Placings: 000/00042P0P/PPP00023-PPP   (3440)
2003/04: 16⁵G, 16⁸GF, 16⁶G,

	Starts	1st	2nd	3rd	Win & Pl
Hurdles	3	0	0	0	
Career Total	22	0	2	1	1950

Going:	Sf: 0-0 GS: 0-0 Gd: 0-2 GF: - Fm: 0-1
Distance:	2m/2m3: 0-3 2m4-2m7: 0-0 3m+: 0-0
Track:	LH: 0-1 RH: 0-2 Tight: 0-1 Gall: 0-0
Aids:	Bl: 0-0 Vi: 0-0 Tstrap: 0-0 Ckp: 0-1
Best Rating:	84 9/01 Strf 2m110y gd-fm Hdl

Springbrook Girl
93   75

6-y-o br m Alderbrook-Springaleak (Lafontaine (USA))
A G Hobbs Hill Fuels Limited

Placings: 30P0663   (4856)
2003/04: 16⁵GF, 16⁹GS, 20⁹GS, 19⁹G, 19⁶GS, 22⁶G, 19⁸GF,

	Starts	1st	2nd	3rd	Win & Pl
NH Flat	2	0	0	1	234
Hurdles	5	0	0	1	741
Career Total	7	0	0	2	975

Going:	Sf: 0-0 GS: 0-3 Gd: 0-2 GF: - Fm: 0-2
Distance:	2m/2m3: 0-2 2m4-2m7: 0-5 3m+: 0-0
Track:	LH: 0-2 RH: 0-5 Tight: 0-2 Gall: 0-1
Aids:	Bl: 0-0 Vi: 0-0 Tstrap: 0-0 Ckp: 0-0
Best Rating:	77 10/03 Uttx 2m gd-fm NHF

Out of prolific winner Springaleak; third on her debut in a weak Uttoxeter bumper; disappointing over hurdles so far.

Springer The Lad
93(81c)   (43c)90

7-y-o ch g Carlton (GER)-Also Kirsty (Twilight Alley)
Miss M P Bryant (D B Feek 3/12) Miss M Bryant

Placings: 04P6/34P-F31P06   (4120)
2003/04: 24⁵GF, 22³G, 21¹S, 21⁶GS, 22⁹HY, 17⁶G,

	Starts	1st	2nd	3rd	Win & Pl
Hurdles	5	1	0	1	2154
Chases	1	0	0	0	0
Career Total	13	1	0	2	2895
86 12/03 Plum 2m5f   F Hdl SFT £1841
Total win prize-money £1841

Going:	Sf: 1-2 GS: 0-1 Gd: 0-2 GF: - Fm: 0-1
Distance:	2m/2m3: 0-1 2m4-2m7: 1-4 3m+: 0-1
Track:	LH: 1-1 RH: 0-5 Tight: 1-4 Gall: 0-2
Aids:	Bl: 1-3 Vi: 0-0 Tstrap: 0-0 Ckp: 0-0
Best Rating:	90 1/02 Plum 2m5f soft Hdl

Plating-class hurdler; won a poor claiming hurdle in first-time blinkers at Plumpton in December; suited by soft ground; stays two miles five.

Springfield Gilda (IRE)
88   68

6-y-o b m Gildoran-Ledee (Le Bavard (FR))
S Gollings Mrs M A Hall

Placings: 052/2P-403   (2933)
2003/04: 17⁴G, 16⁹G, 16³S,

	Starts	1st	2nd	3rd	Win & Pl
Hurdles	3	0	0	1	700
Career Total	8	0	2	1	1786

Going:	Sf: 0-1 GS: 0-0 Gd: 0-2 GF: - Fm: 0-0
Distance:	2m/2m3: 0-3 2m4-2m7: 0-0 3m+: 0-0
Track:	LH: 0-1 RH: 0-2 Tight: 0-0 Gall: 0-0
Aids:	Bl: 0-0 Vi: 0-0 Tstrap: 0-0 Ckp: 0-0
Best Rating:	87 9/02 NAbb 2m1f good NHF

Springfield Scally
109   138

11-y-o ch g Scallywag-Ledee (Le Bavard (FR))
S Gollings Mrs M A Hall

Placings: 21114113246/222U33616/5324541220/F00/1403
5100-44306335   (4567)
2003/04: 24⁴GF, 24⁴G, 24³GS, 25⁰G, 25⁶G, 23⁹HY, 24³G, 24⁵GS,

	Starts	1st	2nd	3rd	Win & Pl
Hurdles	8	0	0	3	11674
Career Total	49	9	8	8	102167
138	3/03 Donc	3m110y B(0-140)HHdl	G-S £13639
138	11/02 Chep	3m B(0-150)HHdl	SFT £10145
145	2/01 Uttx	2m6f110yC(0-135)HHdl	HVY £10426
132	3/00 Uttx	2m6f110yB(0-140)HHdl	GD £10692
112	1/99 MRas	3m E Hdl	SFT £2337
96	12/98 MRas	2m3f110yF Hdl	SFT £2304
108	10/98 Fknm	2m H NHF	SFT £1143
103	9/98 MRas	1m5f110yH NHF	GD £1255
103	9/98 Worc	2m H NHF	G-F £1716
Total win prize-money £53661

Going:	Sf: 0-1 GS: 0-2 Gd: 0-4 GF: - Fm: 0-1
Distance:	2m/2m3: 0-0 2m4-2m7: 0-0 3m+: 0-8
Track:	LH: 0-2 RH: 0-5 Tight: 0-0 Gall: 0-3
Aids:	Bl: 0-0 Vi: 0-0 Tstrap: 0-0 Ckp: 0-0
Best Rating:	145 2/01 Uttx 2m6f110y heavy Hdl

Useful handicap hurdler; stays three miles; acts on soft/heavy ground; tremendously genuine; likes to front-run; stayed on into third in Grade Two at Newbury in November 2003.

Springford (IRE)

12-y-o b g King's Ride-Tickenor Wood (Le Bavard (FR))
Mrs Caroline Keevil M J O'Connor

Placings: 00P/224521P/3006/5-2   (4635)
2003/04: 24²G,

	Starts	1st	2nd	3rd	Win & Pl
Chases	1	0	1	0	687
Career Total	16	1	4	1	8691
92 3/00 Towc 2m6f   D Ch GD £4143
Total win prize-money £4144

Going:	Sf: 0-0 GS: 0-0 Gd: 0-1 GF: - Fm: 0-0
Distance:	2m/2m3: 0-0 2m4-2m7: 0-0 3m+: 0-1
Track:	LH: 0-0 RH: 0-1 Tight: 0-1 Gall: 0-0
Aids:	Bl: 0-0 Vi: 0-0 Tstrap: 0-0 Ckp: 0-0
Best Rating:	106 11/99 Hrfd 3m1f110y good Ch

Decent pointer; has run well in hunter chases; suited by three miles and a sound surface.

Springhill
94   111

9-y-o b g Relief Pitcher-Early Call (Kind Of Hush)
Mrs Mary Hambro Richard Hambro

Placings: 2132/25/335/0   (4915)
2003/04: 16⁰GS,

	Starts	1st	2nd	3rd	Win & Pl
Hurdles	1	0	0	0	0
Career Total	10	1	3	3	7736
113 10/99 Sedg 2m1f   H NHF G-F £1605
Total win prize-money £1606

Going:	Sf: 0-0 GS: 0-1 Gd: 0-0 GF: - Fm: 0-0
Distance:	2m/2m3: 0-1 2m4-2m7: 0-0 3m+: 0-0
Track:	LH: 0-1 RH: 0-0 Tight: 0-0 Gall: 0-0
Aids:	Bl: 0-0 Vi: 0-0 Tstrap: 0-0 Ckp: 0-0
Best Rating:	113 11/99 Winc 2m good NHF

Modest novice hurdler; promising return to action in April 2004 after well over two years' absence; should make a chaser.

Springwood White
100   72

10-y-o gr g Sharkskin Suit (USA)-Kale Brig (New Brig)
J L Gledson J L Gledson

Placings: P/U0035-03   (0693)
2003/04: 20⁵GF, 20⁰G, 25³GF,

	Starts	1st	2nd	3rd	Win & Pl
Chases	3	0	0	1	599
Career Total	8	0	0	2	823

Going:	Sf: 0-0 GS: 0-0 Gd: 0-0 GF: - Fm: 0-1
Distance:	2m/2m3: 0-0 2m4-2m7: 0-2 3m+: 0-1
Track:	LH: 0-3 RH: 0-0 Tight: 0-0 Gall: 0-1
Aids:	Bl: 0-0 Vi: 0-0 Tstrap: 0-0 Ckp: 0-3
Best Rating:	72 6/03 Hexm 3m1f gd-fm Ch

Winning pointer; tried to make all when third in modest novices' handicap chase at Hexham in June; stays three miles; acts on fast ground.

Spud's Fancy

5-y-o ch m You My Chief-Adelbaran (FR) (No Pass No Sale)
B J Llewellyn F H Williams

Placings:*0* (1622)
2003/04: 17ᴼG,

	Starts	1st	2nd	3rd	Win & Pl
NH Flat	1	0	0	0	
Career Total	1	0	0	0	

Going:	Sf: 0-0 GS: 0-0 Gd: 0-1 GF: - Fm: 0-0
Distance:	2m/2m3: 0-1 2m4-2m7: 0-0 3m+: 0-0
Track:	LH: 0-1 RH: 0-0 Tight: 0-1 Gall: 0-0
Aids:	Bl: 0-0 Vi: 0-0 Tstrap: 0-0 Ckp: 0-0

Spy Boy (IRE)

8-y-o b g Balla Cove-Spy Girl (Tanfirion)
Arun Green Arun Green

Placings:*3/F04440/53301U005U/P000O634P04000PP-3P* (4703)
2003/04: 20³G, 26ᴾG,

	Starts	1st	2nd	3rd	Win & Pl
Chases	2	0	0	1	213
Career Total	35	1	0	5	5318
80	10/01 Font	2m4f		F Hdl	G-S £2373
				Total win prize-money £2373	

Going:	Sf: 0-0 GS: 0-0 Gd: 0-2 GF: - Fm: 0-0
Distance:	2m/2m3: 0-0 2m4-2m7: 0-1 3m+: 0-1
Track:	LH: 0-0 RH: 0-0 Tight: 0-2 Gall: 0-0
Aids:	Bl: 0-0 Vi: 0-1 Tstrap: 0-0 Ckp: 0-0
Best Rating:	88 7/00 Worc 2m gd-fm NHF

Plating-class hurdler, all out to win a claiming hurdle at Fontwell in October but well held since.

Squandamania
93 **71**

11-y-o b g Ela-Mana-Mou-Garden Pink (FR) (Bellypha)
J R Norton Jaffa Racing Syndicate

Placings:*3005/3522/5644213/F261311/P00P060/R55055-2662* (4321)
2003/04: 20²HY, 24⁸HY, 24⁶GS, 20²S,

	Starts	1st	2nd	3rd	Win & Pl
Hurdles	4	0	2	0	1360
Career Total	39	4	6	4	18823
108	2/01 Sedg	2m1f	F(0-110)HHdl	G-S	£3038
101	2/01 Sedg	2m1f	D(0-120)HHdl	SFT	£5193
104	12/00 Sedg	2m1f	F(0-110)HHdl	SFT	£2383
101	2/00 Sedg	2m1f	F(0-110)HHdl	G-S	£2775
			Total win prize-money £13332		

Going:	Sf: 0-3 GS: 0-1 Gd: 0-0 GF: - Fm: 0-0
Distance:	2m/2m3: 0-0 2m4-2m7: 0-2 3m+: 0-2
Track:	LH: 0-4 RH: 0-0 Tight: 0-0 Gall: 0-4
Aids:	Bl: 0-0 Vi: 0-0 Tstrap: 0-0 Ckp: 0-0
Best Rating:	108 2/01 Sedg 2m1f gd-sft Hdl

Plating-class hurdler; best at two miles; on a long losing run.

Squeeze (IRE)
83f

6-y-o b g Old Vic-Petaluma Pet (Callernish)
B N Pollock Mrs Jenny Dale & J B Dale

Placings:*6-P* (0705)
2003/04: 17ᴾGF,

	Starts	1st	2nd	3rd	Win & Pl
NH Flat	1	0	0	0	
Career Total	2	0	0	0	0

Going:	Sf: 0-0 GS: 0-0 Gd: 0-0 GF: - Fm: 0-1
Distance:	2m/2m3: 0-1 2m4-2m7: 0-0 3m+: 0-0
Track:	LH: 0-0 RH: 0-1 Tight: 0-0 Gall: 0-0
Aids:	Bl: 0-0 Vi: 0-0 Tstrap: 0-0 Ckp: 0-0
Best Rating:	83 4/03 Hntg 2m110y gd-fm NHF

Squeeze Box (IRE)
93 **72+**

5-y-o b m Accordion-Spread Your Wings (IRE) (Decent Fellow)
J Howard Johnson Hoggy, Hammy, Hendy and Howy

Placings:*206-0504* (4387)
2003/04: 16⁹GS, 20⁵GF, 20⁹GS, 21⁴G,

	Starts	1st	2nd	3rd	Win & Pl
Hurdles	4	0	0	0	257
Career Total	7	0	1	0	1107

Going:	Sf: 0-0 GS: 0-2 Gd: 0-1 GF: - Fm: 0-0
Distance:	2m/2m3: 0-1 2m4-2m7: 0-3 3m+: 0-0
Track:	LH: 0-3 RH: 0-1 Tight: 0-0 Gall: 0-0
Aids:	Bl: 0-0 Vi: 0-0 Tstrap: 0-0 Ckp: 0-1
Best Rating:	86 2/03 Muss 2m good NHF

Moderate form in bumpers on good ground.

Squirtle Turtle
73 **36**

4-y-o ch g Peintre Celebre (USA)-Hatton Gardens (Auction Ring (USA))
P F I Cole Mrs P F I Cole

Placings:*0* (3422)
2003/04: 17ᴼHY,

	Starts	1st	2nd	3rd	Win & Pl
Hurdles	1	0	0	0	
Career Total	1	0	0	0	

Going:	Sf: 0-1 GS: 0-0 Gd: 0-0 GF: - Fm: 0-0
Distance:	2m/2m3: 0-1 2m4-2m7: 0-0 3m+: 0-0
Track:	LH: 0-0 RH: 0-1 Tight: 0-1 Gall: 0-0
Aids:	Bl: 0-0 Vi: 0-0 Tstrap: 0-0 Ckp: 0-0
Best Rating:	36 1/04 Folk 2m1f110y heavy Hdl

St Bee

9-y-o br g St Ninian-Regal Bee (Royal Fountain)
W G Reed W G Reed

Placings:*0P/U06FPPF45-PU400* (4078)
2003/04: 25ᴾG, 25ᵁG, 23⁴G, 25ᴼG, 24ᴼF,

	Starts	1st	2nd	3rd	Win & Pl
Chases	5	0	0	0	302
Career Total	16	0	0	0	302

Going:	Sf: 0-0 GS: 0-0 Gd: 0-4 GF: - Fm: 0-1
Distance:	2m/2m3: 0-0 2m4-2m7: 0-0 3m+: 0-5
Track:	LH: 0-3 RH: 0-1 Tight: 0-1 Gall: 0-0
Aids:	Bl: 0-0 Vi: 0-0 Tstrap: 0-0 Ckp: 0-4
Best Rating:	66 4/03 Hexm 3m1f good Ch

St Cassien (IRE)

4-y-o b g Goldmark (USA)-Moonlight Partner (IRE) (Red Sunset)
T M Jones Richard L Page

Placings:*F* (1901)
2003/04: 16ᶠGF,

	Starts	1st	2nd	3rd	Win & Pl
Hurdles	1	0	0	0	
Career Total	1	0	0	0	

Going:	Sf: 0-0 GS: 0-0 Gd: 0-0 GF: - Fm: 0-1
Distance:	2m/2m3: 0-1 2m4-2m7: 0-0 3m+: 0-0
Track:	LH: 0-0 RH: 0-1 Tight: 0-0 Gall: 0-1
Aids:	Bl: 0-0 Vi: 0-0 Tstrap: 0-0 Ckp: 0-0

St Kilda
(88h) (65h)**55**

7-y-o b m Past Glories-Oiseval (National Trust)
Mrs H M Bridges Mrs H M Bridges

Placings:*03663-F0304* (4485)
2003/04: 21ᶠS, 22⁹GS, 16³S, 19⁴HY, 22⁴G,

	Starts	1st	2nd	3rd	Win & Pl
Hurdles	4	0	0	0	406
Chases	1	0	0	0	308
Career Total	10	0	0	3	1518

Going:	Sf: 0-3 GS: 0-1 Gd: 0-1 GF: - Fm: 0-0
Distance:	2m/2m3: 0-1 2m4-2m7: 0-4 3m+: 0-0
Track:	LH: 0-2 RH: 0-2 Tight: 0-2 Gall: 0-0
Aids:	Bl: 0-0 Vi: 0-0 Tstrap: 0-0 Ckp: 0-0
Best Rating:	82 2/03 Ludl 2m good NHF

St Martins (IRE)

6-y-o b g Old Vic-Mardior (Martinmas)
Miss C J E Caroe Miss C J E Caroe

Placings:*P* (2913)
2003/04: 16ᴾGS,

	Starts	1st	2nd	3rd	Win & Pl
NH Flat	1	0	0	0	
Career Total	1	0	0	0	

Going:	Sf: 0-0 GS: 0-1 Gd: 0-0 GF: - Fm: 0-0
Distance:	2m/2m3: 0-1 2m4-2m7: 0-0 3m+: 0-0
Track:	LH: 0-0 RH: 0-1 Tight: 0-0 Gall: 0-1
Aids:	Bl: 0-0 Vi: 0-0 Tstrap: 0-0 Ckp: 0-0

St Palais
84 **55**

5-y-o b m Timeless Times (USA)-Crambella (IRE) (Red Sunset)
D L Williams Gumbrills Racing Partnership

Placings:*026PO04006-50* (0130)
2003/04: 19⁵GS, 16ᴼGF,

	Starts	1st	2nd	3rd	Win & Pl
Hurdles	2	0	0	0	0
Career Total	12	0	1	0	1262

Going:	Sf: 0-0 GS: 0-1 Gd: 0-0 GF: - Fm: 0-1
Distance:	2m/2m3: 0-1 2m4-2m7: 0-1 3m+: 0-0

Track: LH: 0-0 RH: 0-2 Tight: 0-0 Gall: 0-1
Aids: Bl: 0-0 Vi: 0-0 Tstrap: 0-0 Ckp: 0-1
Best Rating: 63   11/02   Newb   2m110y   gd-sft   Hdl

St Pirran (IRE)
116   (119h)150
9-y-o b/br g Be My Native (USA)-Guess Twice (Deep Run)
P F Nicholls   C G Roach

Placings:3211214/1U23264/61F130   (4964)
2003/04: 20⁶G, 16¹G, 16ᶠS, 16¹G, 16³G, 16⁰GF,

	Starts	1st	2nd	3rd	Win & Pl
Chases	6	2	0	1	60817
Career Total	20	6	4	3	106719
145	3/04	Chel	2m110y A HCh		GD £43500
139	1/04	Sand	2m	B(0-145)HCh	GD £10167
117	10/01	Extr	2m1f110yD Ch		GD £4329
136	2/01	Kemp	2m	A Hdl	G-S £12000
137	12/00	Chel	2m1f	B Hdl	SFT £7280
120	11/00	Extr	2m1f	E Hdl	G-S £3080

Total win prize-money £80356

Going: Sf: 0-1 GS: 0-0 Gd: 2-4 GF: - Fm: 0-1
Distance: 2m/2m3: 2-5 2m4-2m7: 0-1 3m+: 0-0
Track: LH: 1-3 RH: 1-3 Tight: 0-2 Gall: 1-1
Aids: Bl: 0-0 Vi: 0-0 Tstrap: 0-0 Ckp: 0-0
Best Rating: 150   4/04   Aint   2m   good   Ch

Smart chaser; returned from 18 months off in late 2003, scoring at Sandown in early 2004; fell next time, but won Grand Annual Chase impressively at the Festival; ideally needs a strongly-run race in yielding ground; effective at two miles, stays two and a half; acts well on good ground.

Stafford King (IRE)
75   96
7-y-o b h Nicolotte-Opening Day (Day Is Done)
J G M O'Shea   N G H Ayliffe

Placings:P/23222320-P0   (2866)
2003/04: 16²G, 16⁰GS,

	Starts	1st	2nd	3rd	Win & Pl
Hurdles	2	0	0	0	
Career Total	11	0	5	2	4900

Going: Sf: 0-0 GS: 0-1 Gd: 0-1 GF: - Fm: 0-0
Distance: 2m/2m3: 0-2 2m4-2m7: 0-0 3m+: 0-0
Track: LH: 0-2 RH: 0-0 Tight: 0-0 Gall: 0-0
Aids: Bl: 0-0 Vi: 0-0 Tstrap: 0-0 Ckp: 0-0
Best Rating: 96   7/02   Worc   2m4f   good   Hdl

Stage Friendly (IRE)
101f   82f
5-y-o ch g Old Vic-Just Affable (IRE) (Phardante (FR))
N A Twiston-Davies   I Guest

Placings:50   (2913)
2003/04: 16⁵GS, 16⁰GS,

	Starts	1st	2nd	3rd	Win & Pl
NH Flat	2	0	0	0	0
Career Total	2	0	0	0	0

Going: Sf: 0-0 GS: 0-2 Gd: 0-0 GF: - Fm: 0-0
Distance: 2m/2m3: 0-2 2m4-2m7: 0-0 3m+: 0-0
Track: LH: 0-1 RH: 0-1 Tight: 0-0 Gall: 0-1
Aids: Bl: 0-0 Vi: 0-0 Tstrap: 0-0 Ckp: 0-0
Best Rating: 82   11/03   Chep   2m110y   gd-sft   NHF

Stagecoachsapphire
88f   106f
6-y-o b g Teenoso (USA)-Zajira (IRE) (Ela-Mana-Mou)
Mrs S J Smith   Mrs Jacqueline Conroy

Placings:10   (4400)
2003/04: 17¹G, 16⁰G,

	Starts	1st	2nd	3rd	Win & Pl
NH Flat	2	1	0	0	1995
Career Total	2	1	0	0	1995
106	2/04	Carl	2m1f	H NHF	GD £1995

Total win prize-money £1995

Going: Sf: 0-0 GS: 0-0 Gd: 1-2 GF: - Fm: 0-0
Distance: 2m/2m3: 1-2 2m4-2m7: 0-0 3m+: 0-0
Track: LH: 0-1 RH: 1-1 Tight: 0-0 Gall: 0-0
Aids: Bl: 0-0 Vi: 0-0 Tstrap: 0-0 Ckp: 0-0
Best Rating: 106   2/04   Carl   2m1f   good   NHF

Won on debut, despite running green, at Carlisle in soft ground bumper.

Stakeholder (IRE)
84   58
6-y-o ch g Priolo (USA)-Island Goddess (Godswalk (USA))
M Sheppard   M J Drake

Placings:035/000-0P   (3226)
2003/04: 22⁰G, 26ᴾGS,

	Starts	1st	2nd	3rd	Win & Pl
Hurdles	2	0	0	0	
Career Total	8	0	0	1	256

Going: Sf: 0-0 GS: 0-1 Gd: 0-1 GF: - Fm: 0-0
Distance: 2m/2m3: 0-0 2m4-2m7: 0-1 3m+: 0-0
Track: LH: 0-1 RH: 0-1 Tight: 0-0 Gall: 0-0
Aids: Bl: 0-0 Vi: 0-0 Tstrap: 0-1 Ckp: 0-0
Best Rating: 95   4/02   Carl   2m1f   good   NHF

Stalky Dove
7-y-o b m Homo Sapien-Sally's Dove (Celtic Cone)
W M Brisbourne   Mrs J M Russell

Placings:4602-P   (0291)
2003/04: 16²G, 16ᴾG,

	Starts	1st	2nd	3rd	Win & Pl
NH Flat	1	0	1	0	536
Hurdles	1	0	0	0	
Career Total	5	0	1	0	536

Going: Sf: 0-0 GS: 0-0 Gd: 0-2 GF: - Fm: 0-0
Distance: 2m/2m3: 0-2 2m4-2m7: 0-0 3m+: 0-0
Track: LH: 0-2 RH: 0-0 Tight: 0-1 Gall: 0-0
Aids: Bl: 0-0 Vi: 0-0 Tstrap: 0-0 Ckp: 0-0
Best Rating: 85   4/03   Hexm   2m110y   good   NHF

Runner-up behind a useful sort in bumper at Hexham in April on fourth start (poached long lead).

Stallone
86
7-y-o ch g Brief Truce (USA)-Bering Honneur (USA) (Bering)
N Wilson   Mrs Karan Ridley

Placings:635F5-P   (1765)
2003/04: 20ᴾGF,

	Starts	1st	2nd	3rd	Win & Pl
Hurdles	1	0	0	0	

Stamparland Hill
112(95h)   (112h)140
9-y-o b g Gildoran-Woodland Flower (Furry Glen)
J M Jefferson   Ashleybank Investments Limited

Placings:355/1321FP3P/04P-5022   (4938)
2003/04: 17⁵HY, 24⁰GS, 16²GS, 16²GS,

	Starts	1st	2nd	3rd	Win & Pl
Hurdles	2	0	0	0	
Chases	2	0	2	0	4212
Career Total	18	2	3	3	13129
130	1/02	Weth	2m	E Ch	G-S £3342
93	9/01	Sedg	2m1f	E Hdl	GD £2380

Total win prize-money £5723

Going: Sf: 0-1 GS: 0-3 Gd: 0-0 GF: - Fm: 0-0
Distance: 2m/2m3: 0-3 2m4-2m7: 0-0 3m+: 0-1
Track: LH: 0-2 RH: 0-2 Tight: 0-1 Gall: 0-0
Aids: Bl: 0-0 Vi: 0-0 Tstrap: 0-0 Ckp: 0-0
Best Rating: 130   1/02   Weth   2m   gd-sft   Ch

Mixes hurdling and chasing; is a fair sort over hurdles and quite decent over fences; acts on good and soft ground; has never won beyond two miles one.

Stance
106   104
5-y-o b g Salse (USA)-De Stael (USA) (Nijinsky (CAN))
P R Hedger (C Von Der Recke 14/1)   N J Jones

Placings:0441   (4704)
2003/04: 19⁰S, 17⁴GS, 20⁴GF, 18¹G,

	Starts	1st	2nd	3rd	Win & Pl
Hurdles	4	1	0	0	5469
Career Total	4	1	0	0	5469
104	4/04	Font	2m2f110y	D(0-125)HHdl	GD £5079

Total win prize-money £5080

Going: Sf: 0-1 GS: 0-1 Gd: 1-1 GF: - Fm: 0-1
Distance: 2m/2m3: 1-3 2m4-2m7: 0-1 3m+: 0-0
Track: LH: 1-2 RH: 0-1 Tight: 1-3 Gall: 0-1
Aids: Bl: 0-0 Vi: 0-0 Tstrap: 0-0 Ckp: 0-0
Best Rating: 104   4/04   Font   2m2f110y   good   Hdl

Moderate hurdler; suited by trips just beyond two miles and acts on good ground.

Stand Easy (IRE)
103(91h)   (77h)109
11-y-o b g Buckskin (FR)-Geeaway (Gala Performance (ZIM))
J R Cornwall   J R Cornwall

Placings:1/3355222/25303/FP0433-11P6   (2324)
2003/04: 26¹HY, 26¹HY, 24ᴾGF, 25⁶G,

	Starts	1st	2nd	3rd	Win & Pl
Chases	4	2	0	0	9854
Career Total	23	3	4	6	21751
109	5/03	Uttx	3m2f	E Ch	HVY £4095
109	5/03	Uttx	3m2f	E Ch	HVY £5452
98	4/99	NAbb	2m1f	H NHF	SFT £1397

Total win prize-money £10944

Going:	Sf: 2-2 GS: 0-0 Gd: 0-1 GF: - Fm: 0-1
Distance:	2m/2m3: 0-0 2m4-2m7: 0-0 **3m+: 2-4**
Track:	LH: **2-4** RH: 0-0 Tight: 0-1 Gall: 0-1
Aids:	Bl: 0-0 Vi: 0-0 Tstrap: 0-0 Ckp: 0-0
Best Rating:	113 11/99 Chep 2m110y gd-sft NHF

Modest staying chaser; won twice over three miles two at Uttoxeter in heavy ground in May 2003; stays well; has worn cheekpieces.

Standing Applause (USA)

97   86

6-y-o b/br g Theatrical-Pent (USA) (Mr Prospector (USA))
Mrs A J Hamilton-Fairley Hamilton-Fairley Racing

Placings:P05-03P   (4897)
2003/04: 22QGS, 223G, 22PG,

	Starts	1st	2nd	3rd	Win & Pl
Hurdles	3	0	0	1	552
Career Total	6	0	0	1	552

Going:	Sf: 0-0 GS: 0-1 Gd: 0-2 GF: - Fm: 0-0
Distance:	2m/2m3: 0-0 2m4-2m7: 0-3 3m+: 0-0
Track:	LH: 0-1 RH: 0-2 Tight: 0-1 Gall: 0-0
Aids:	Bl: 0-0 Vi: 0-0 Tstrap: 0-3 Ckp: 0-0
Best Rating:	86 4/04 NAbb 2m6f good Hdl

Plating-class hurdler; stays 2m6f; acts on any ground.

Standing Bloom

101 (105h)   (99 h) 99+

8-y-o ch m Presidium-Rosie Cone (Celtic Cone)
Mrs P Sly The Stablemates

Placings:4536/065P/032140-P0014   (3757)
2003/04: 20QGS, 20QG, 23QGS, 241S, 20QG,

	Starts	1st	2nd	3rd	Win & Pl
Hurdles	3	0	0	0	0
Chases	2	1	0	0	4731
Career Total	19	2	1	2	9891
99	1/04 Hntg 3m			E Ch	SFT £4241
99	1/03 Wwck 2m5f			F(0-90)Hdl	HVY £2828
			Total win prize-money £7069		

Going:	Sf: 1-1 GS: 0-2 Gd: 0-2 GF: - Fm: 0-0
Distance:	2m/2m3: 0-0 2m4-2m7: 0-3 **3m+: 1-2**
Track:	LH: 0-1 **RH: 1-4** Tight: 0-0 Gall: 1-1
Aids:	Bl: 0-0 Vi: 0-0 Tstrap: 0-0 Ckp: 0-0
Best Rating:	102 4/01 Kemp 2m good NHF

Modest hurdler/novice chaser; stays two miles five; effective in heavy ground.

Stanley Park

95   74

6-y-o ch g Bold Arrangement-Queen Buzzard (Buzzard's Bay)
J R Weymes Neil Palamountain

Placings:00P-342   (1535)
2003/04: 17QS, 164G, 192GF,

	Starts	1st	2nd	3rd	Win & Pl
Hurdles	3	0	1	1	1349
Career Total	6	0	1	1	1349

Going:	Sf: 0-1 GS: 0-0 Gd: 0-1 GF: - Fm: 0-1
Distance:	2m/2m3: 0-2 2m4-2m7: 0-1 3m+: 0-0
Track:	LH: 0-2 RH: 0-1 Tight: 0-2 Gall: 0-0

| Aids: | Bl: 0-0 Vi: 0-0 Tstrap: 0-0 Ckp: 0-0 |
| Best Rating: | 74 10/03 MRas 2m3f110y gd-fm Hdl |

First form when well beaten third in modest novices' hurdle at Sedgefield in May.

Stanmore (IRE)

103   103

12-y-o b g Aristocracy-Lady Go Marching (USA) (Go Marching (USA))
Mrs J A Saunders Mr & Mrs Simon E Bown

Placings:500/3U21P51F0/313PF2P1/423/6153/1P4010/P4 321143144-P6613663   (2214)
2003/04: 24PGF, 22PG, 24PG, 211GF, 243GF, 24PGF, 22PG, 29PF,

	Starts	1st	2nd	3rd	Win & Pl
Chases	8	1	0	2	5362
Career Total	52	11	4	9	54487
103	8/03 Sthl	2m5f110yF(0-100)HCh	G-F	£3357
103	10/02 Fknm	3m110y E(0-110)HCh	G-S	£5148
99	9/02 Strf	3m D(0-125)HCh	G-F	£8138
99	8/02 Sthl	2m5f110yE(0-105)HCh	G-F	£3770
99	11/01 Leic	2m4f110yF(0-100)HCh	G-F	£3125
88	5/01 Hntg	3m H Ch	G-F	£1820
99	5/00 MRas	2m6f110yH Ch	G-S	£1976
106	5/99 Hrfd	2m3f110yE Hdl	GD	£2560
130	5/98 Strf	2m5f110yC(0-135)HCh	G-F	£5182
112	12/97 Wwck	2m4f110yD(0-120)HCh	G-S	£3551
103	10/97 Chel	2m4f110yD(0-110)HCh	GD	£3876
		Total win prize-money £42508		

Going:	Sf: 0-0 GS: 0-0 Gd: 0-3 GF: - Fm: 1-5
Distance:	2m/2m3: 0-0 **2m4-2m7: 1-3** 3m+: 0-5
Track:	LH: **1-4** RH: 0-4 Tight: 0-4 Gall: 0-0
Aids:	Bl: 0-0 Vi: 0-0 Tstrap: 0-0 Ckp: 0-1
Best Rating:	130 5/98 Strf 2m5f110y gd-fm Ch

Moderate handicap chaser; suited by forcing tactics; appreciated a drop in grade when winning Class F handicap at Southwell August 2003; stays 3m and handles cut in the ground, but is best suited by fast.

Stans Man Can

6-y-o gr g Arzanni-Tais Toi (Vitiges (FR))
S C Burrough Cliff Gaylard & Sara Ellis

Placings:6PP   (4811)
2003/04: 196S, 25PG, 24PG,

	Starts	1st	2nd	3rd	Win & Pl
Hurdles	2	0	0	0	0
Chases	1	0	0	0	0
Career Total	3	0	0	0	0

Going:	Sf: 0-1 GS: 0-0 Gd: 0-2 GF: - Fm: 0-0
Distance:	2m/2m3: 0-1 2m4-2m7: 0-0 3m+: 0-2
Track:	LH: 0-2 RH: 0-1 Tight: 0-0 Gall: 0-0
Aids:	Bl: 0-0 Vi: 0-0 Tstrap: 0-0 Ckp: 0-0

Stantons Church

7-y-o b g Homo Sapien-Valkyrie Reef (Miramar Reef)
Mark Doyle (H D Daly 13/5) M W Jones

Placings:545P-00P   (4302)
2003/04: 17QG, 19QG, 20PG,

	Starts	1st	2nd	3rd	Win & Pl
Hurdles	2	0	0	0	0
Chases	1	0	0	0	0
Career Total	7	0	0	0	0

Going:	Sf: 0-0 GS: 0-1 Gd: 0-2 GF: - Fm: 0-0
Distance:	2m/2m3: 0-1 2m4-2m7: 0-2 3m+: 0-0
Track:	LH: 0-0 RH: 0-3 Tight: 0-0 Gall: 0-0
Aids:	Bl: 0-0 Vi: 0-0 Tstrap: 0-0 Ckp: 0-1
Best Rating:	84 12/02 Ludl 2m good Hdl

Stanway

95   94

5-y-o b g Presenting-Nicklup (Netherkelly)
Mrs Mary Hambro Richard Hambro

Placings:2430F06   (4887)
2003/04: 172G, 164G, 163GS, 16QGS, 20FG, 17QG, 22BGF,

	Starts	1st	2nd	3rd	Win & Pl
NH Flat	3	0	1	1	1084
Hurdles	4	0	0	0	0
Career Total	7	0	1	1	1084

Going:	Sf: 0-0 GS: 0-2 Gd: 0-4 GF: - Fm: 0-1
Distance:	2m/2m3: 0-5 2m4-2m7: 0-2 3m+: 0-0
Track:	LH: 0-6 RH: 0-1 Tight: 0-3 Gall: 0-0
Aids:	Bl: 0-0 Vi: 0-0 Tstrap: 0-0 Ckp: 0-0
Best Rating:	94 11/03 Chep 2m110y gd-sft NHF

Moderate performer in bumpers.

Staple Sound

78   50

7-y-o b g Afflora (IRE)-Loch Scavaig (IRE) (The Parson)
James Moffatt Mrs G A Turnbull

Placings:00/000P-P0   (0896)
2003/04: 27PS, 22PGF,

	Starts	1st	2nd	3rd	Win & Pl
Hurdles	2	0	0	0	0
Career Total	8	0	0	0	0

Going:	Sf: 0-1 GS: 0-0 Gd: 0-0 GF: - Fm: 0-1
Distance:	2m/2m3: 0-0 2m4-2m7: 0-1 3m+: 0-1
Track:	LH: 0-2 RH: 0-0 Tight: 0-2 Gall: 0-0
Aids:	Bl: 0-0 Vi: 0-2 Tstrap: 0-0 Ckp: 0-0
Best Rating:	83 10/02 Carl 2m1f soft NHF

Star Buster (IRE)

47f   10f

6-y-o b g Eurobus-Lucciola (FR) (Auction Ring (USA))
H M Kavanagh Mrs S Kavanagh

Placings:0   (2518)
2003/04: 17QGS,

	Starts	1st	2nd	3rd	Win & Pl
NH Flat	1	0	0	0	0
Career Total	1	0	0	0	0

Going:	Sf: 0-0 GS: 0-1 Gd: 0-0 GF: - Fm: 0-0
Distance:	2m/2m3: 0-1 2m4-2m7: 0-0 3m+: 0-0
Track:	LH: 0-0 RH: 0-1 Tight: 0-0 Gall: 0-0
Aids:	Bl: 0-0 Vi: 0-0 Tstrap: 0-0 Ckp: 0-0
Best Rating:	10 12/03 Hrfd 2m1f gd-sft NHF

Star Catcher (IRE)

8-y-o b g Toulon-Paper Merchant (Hays)
B G Powell L J Brotherton

Placings: 00/PP/P0-P   (1078)
2003/04: 20PGF,

	Starts	1st	2nd	3rd	Win & Pl
Hurdles	1	0	0	0	
Career Total	7	0	0	0	

Going:	Sf: 0-0 GS: 0-0 Gd: 0-0 GF: - Fm: 0-1
Distance:	2m/2m3: 0-0 2m4-2m7: 0-1 3m+: 0-0
Track:	LH: 0-1 RH: 0-0 Tight: 0-0 Gall: 0-0
Aids:	Bl: 0-0 Vi: 0-0 Tstrap: 0-0 Ckp: 0-0
Best Rating:	54 10/00 Fknm 2m good NHF

Star Changes

11-y-o b g Derrylin-Sweet Linda (Saucy Kit)
A Hollingsworth   A Hollingsworth

Placings: 0/6/00/0   (0521)
2003/04: 24PG,

	Starts	1st	2nd	3rd	Win & Pl
Chases	1	0	0	0	
Career Total	5	0	0	0	

Going:	Sf: 0-0 GS: 0-0 Gd: 0-1 GF: - Fm: 0-0
Distance:	2m/2m3: 0-0 2m4-2m7: 0-0 3m+: 0-1
Track:	LH: 0-1 RH: 0-0 Tight: 0-0 Gall: 0-0
Aids:	Bl: 0-0 Vi: 0-0 Tstrap: 0-0 Ckp: 0-0
Best Rating:	80 6/01 Strf 3m gd-fm Ch

Star Councel (IRE)

110(92c)   (72c)98+

8-y-o b m Leading Counsel (USA)-Black Avenue (IRE)
(Strong Gale)
B S Rothwell   Mrs Liz Hunt

Placings: 00/455 f314436P00440P/5C0P524201-
5354000013600   (3694)
2003/04: 21SGF, 26PG, 17SGF, 26PGF, 23PGF, 20PHY, 20PG, 24PS,
231GS, 24PGF, 23PG, 16PG, 25PG,

	Starts	1st	2nd	3rd	Win & Pl
Hurdles	11	1	0	2	5268
Chases	2	0	0	0	0
Career Total	42	4	2	4	23119
98	12/03	Hayd	2m7f110yE(0-110)HHdl		G-S	£3262
95	3/03	Sthl	3m110y F(0-100)HHdl		G-F	£3584
100	9/01	List	2m4f	Hdl	G-F	£6004
98	8/01	Slig	2m4f	NHF	SH	£3338
			Total win prize-money £16189			

Going:	Sf: 0-2 GS: 1-1 Gd: 0-5 GF: - Fm: 0-5
Distance:	2m/2m3: 0-2 2m4-2m7: 0-3 **3m+: 1-8**
Track:	**LH: 1-10** RH: 0-2 Tight: 0-3 Gall: 0-0
Aids:	Bl: 0-0 Vi: 0-0 Tstrap: 0-0 **Ckp: 1-5**
Best Rating:	100 9/01 List 2m4f gd-fm Hdl

Moderate hurdler; stays three miles, acts on any ground;
successful in cheekpieces.

Star Jack (FR)

130

9-y-o b g Epervier Bleu-Little Point (FR) (Le Nain Jaune
(FR))
T J Fitzgerald   Mr & Mrs Raymond Anderson Green

Placings: 1115/3213/PF/PP1P/P022311PP-0   (0384)
2003/04: 22PG,

	Starts	1st	2nd	3rd	Win & Pl
Hurdles	1	0	0	0	
Career Total	24	7	3	3	84265

130	11/02	Weth	2m	B(0-150)HCh	G-S	£10916
129	11/02	Ayr	2m	C(0-130)HCh	SFT	£7975
124	4/02	Ayr	2m4f	B HCh	GD	£10397
	1/00	Pau	2m110y	Hdl	GD	£6244
	2/99	Pau	2m2f110y	Ch	HVY	£15070
	1/99	Pau	2m1f	Ch	GD	£6459
	10/98	Toul	2m1f110y	Hdl	HVY	£4041
			Total win prize-money £61104			

Going:	Sf: 0-0 GS: 0-0 Gd: 0-1 GF: - Fm: 0-0
Distance:	2m/2m3: 0-0 2m4-2m7: 0-1 3m+: 0-0
Track:	LH: 0-1 RH: 0-0 Tight: 0-1 Gall: 0-0
Aids:	Bl: 0-0 Vi: 0-0 Tstrap: 0-0 Ckp: 0-1
Best Rating:	130 11/02 Weth 2m gd-sft Ch

Useful handicap chaser; tends to have two ways of running;
often wears tongue-strap and sheepskin cheekpieces; best
over two/two and a half miles; effective on most types of
ground.

Star Of Germany (IRE)

93   67

4-y-o b g Germany (USA)-Twinkle Bright (USA) (Star De
Naskra (USA))
Ferdy Murphy   Brendan J O'Rourke

Placings: 000404   (4321)
2003/04: 17PGF, 16PG, 16PS, 16AG, 16PG, 20PS,

	Starts	1st	2nd	3rd	Win & Pl
Hurdles	6	0	0	0	0
Career Total	6	0	0	0	0

Going:	Sf: 0-2 GS: 0-1 Gd: 0-2 GF: - Fm: 0-1
Distance:	2m/2m3: 0-1 2m4-2m7: 0-1 3m+: 0-0
Track:	LH: 0-5 RH: 0-1 Tight: 0-2 Gall: 0-2
Aids:	Bl: 0-0 Vi: 0-0 Tstrap: 0-0 Ckp: 0-0
Best Rating:	67 3/04 Newc 2m4f soft Hdl

Star Of Raven

7-y-o b m Sea Raven (IRE)-Lucy At The Minute (Silly
Prices)
Joss Saville   Joss Saville

Placings: 000/F-12   (4301)
2003/04: 251S, 232G,

	Starts	1st	2nd	3rd	Win & Pl
Chases	2	1	1	0	3778
Career Total	6	1	1	0	3778
103	2/04	Weth	3m1f	H Ch	SFT	£1666
			Total win prize-money £1666			

Going:	Sf: 1-1 GS: 0-0 Gd: 0-1 GF: - Fm: 0-0
Distance:	2m/2m3: 0-0 2m4-2m7: 0-0 **3m+: 1-2**
Track:	**LH: 1-1** RH: 0-1 Tight: 0-0 Gall: 0-0
Aids:	Bl: 0-0 Vi: 0-3 Tstrap: 0-0 Ckp: 0-0
Best Rating:	103 3/04 Leic 2m7f110y good Ch

Surprise winner of a hunter chase at Wetherby in February;
stays three miles well; handles testing conditions.

Star Prize (IRE)

92   100+

7-y-o b g Fourstars Allstar (USA)-Dipper's Gift (IRE)
(Salluceva)
N J Henderson   N J Henderson

Placings: 24   (3897)
2003/04: 16PGF, 164GS,

	Starts	1st	2nd	3rd	Win & Pl
NH Flat	1	0	1	0	534
Hurdles	1	0	0	0	393
Career Total	2	0	1	0	927

Going:	Sf: 0-0 GS: 0-1 Gd: 0-0 GF: - Fm: 0-1
Distance:	2m/2m3: 0-2 2m4-2m7: 0-0 3m+: 0-0
Track:	LH: 0-1 RH: 0-1 Tight: 0-0 Gall: 0-0
Aids:	Bl: 0-0 Vi: 0-0 Tstrap: 0-0 Ckp: 0-0
Best Rating:	100 2/04 Sand 2m110y gd-sft Hdl

Bought for 30,000 gns at Doncaster Sales in 2001; hung
right on home turn when runner-up in weak Worcester
bumper on debut August 2003.

Star Seventeen

72   58

6-y-o ch m Rock City-Westminster Waltz (Dance In Time
(CAN))
Mrs N S Sharpe   Islwyn Thomas

Placings: 6000P-0   (3902)
2003/04: 17PGS,

	Starts	1st	2nd	3rd	Win & Pl
Hurdles	1	0	0	0	0
Career Total	6	0	0	0	0

Going:	Sf: 0-0 GS: 0-1 Gd: 0-0 GF: - Fm: 0-0
Distance:	2m/2m3: 0-1 2m4-2m7: 0-0 3m+: 0-0
Track:	LH: 0-0 RH: 0-1 Tight: 0-0 Gall: 0-0
Aids:	Bl: 0-0 Vi: 0-0 Tstrap: 0-0 Ckp: 0-0
Best Rating:	59 8/02 Hntg 2m110y gd-fm Hdl

Star Time (IRE)

98   72

5-y-o b g Fourstars Allstar (USA)-Punctual (Lead On Time
(USA))
M Scudamore   successracing.com

Placings: 0P-003PP   (4519)
2003/04: 16PGS, 16PS, 22PGS, 26PGF, 22PGS,

	Starts	1st	2nd	3rd	Win & Pl
Hurdles	5	0	0	1	428
Career Total	7	0	0	1	428

Going:	Sf: 0-1 GS: 0-3 Gd: 0-0 GF: - Fm: 0-1
Distance:	2m/2m3: 0-2 2m4-2m7: 0-1 3m+: 0-1
Track:	LH: 0-1 RH: 0-4 Tight: 0-1 Gall: 0-0
Aids:	Bl: 0-0 Vi: 0-3 Tstrap: 0-0 Ckp: 0-0
Best Rating:	74 2/04 Folk 2m6f110y gd-sft Hdl

Star Trooper (IRE)

104(109h)   (98 h)85

8-y-o b/br g Brief Truce (USA)-Star Cream (Star Appeal)
Miss S E Forster   Should Be Fun Racing

Placings: 0040/000023500/0000220630/041210002-
003251300050036   (4797)
2003/04: 16PG, 18PG, 16PG, 162F, 16PGF, 201HY, 18PS, 24PS,
16PHY, 20PG, 20PGS, 17PGS, 20PG, 16PG, 21PG,

	Starts	1st	2nd	3rd	Win & Pl
Hurdles	13	1	1	2	5549
Chases	2	0	0	0	680
Career Total	47	3	6	5	18518
92	11/03	Carl	2m4f	E(0-105)HHdl	HVY	£2759
101	12/02	Sedg	2m1f	E(0-110)HHdl	SFT	£3346
84	11/02	Sedg	2m1f	G(0-95)HHdl	SFT	£2100
			Total win prize-money £8205			

Going:	Sf: 1-4 GS: 0-2 Gd: 0-7 GF: - Fm: 0-2
Distance:	2m/2m3: 0-9 **2m4-2m7: 1-5** 3m+: 0-1
Track:	LH: 0-8 **RH: 1-5** Tight: 0-6 Gall: 0-1
Aids:	Bl: 0-0 Vi: 0-0 Tstrap: 0-0 **Ckp: 1-10**
Best Rating:	**107** 8/00 Tral 2m1f soft Hdl

Moderate hurdler, ex-Irish; best around two miles; suited by soft ground; also handles faster going; has worn cheek-pieces.

Star Wonder

53

4-y-o b f Syrtos-Galava (CAN) (Graustark)
B N Doran R P & M Berrow

| Placings:UPP0 | | | | | (3529) |
| 2003/04: 17UGF, 16PG, 16PHY, 16PS, | | | | | |

	Starts	1st	2nd	3rd	Win & Pl
Hurdles	4	0	0	0	
Career Total	**4**	**0**	**0**	**0**	

Going:	Sf: 0-2 GS: 0-0 Gd: 0-1 GF: - Fm: 0-1
Distance:	2m/2m3: 0-4 2m4-2m7: 0-0 3m+: 0-1
Track:	LH: 0-0 RH: 0-4 Tight: 0-0 Gall: 0-0
Aids:	Bl: 0-1 Vi: 0-0 Tstrap: 0-0 Ckp: 0-0

Starbuck

10-y-o b g Brush Aside (USA)-Clonmello (Le Bavard (FR))
Miss J Fisher Miss J Fisher

| Placings:0/2604/4P/6 | | | | | (4078) |
| 2003/04: 24FF, | | | | | |

	Starts	1st	2nd	3rd	Win & Pl
Chases	1	0	0	0	0
Career Total	**8**	**0**	**1**	**0**	**730**

Going:	Sf: 0-0 GS: 0-0 Gd: 0-0 GF: 0-0 Fm: 0-1
Distance:	2m/2m3: 0-0 2m4-2m7: 0-0 3m+: 0-1
Track:	LH: 0-0 RH: 0-1 Tight: 0-1 Gall: 0-0
Aids:	Bl: 0-0 Vi: 0-0 Tstrap: 0-0 Ckp: 0-0
Best Rating:	**90** 10/99 Carl 2m1f good NHF

Starello

87f **81f**

5-y-o b m Supreme Leader-Oubava (FR) (Groom Dancer (USA))
N J Henderson R A Ballin

| Placings:60 | | | | | (4594) |
| 2003/04: 18GG, 16PG, | | | | | |

	Starts	1st	2nd	3rd	Win & Pl
NH Flat	2	0	0	0	0
Career Total	**2**	**0**	**0**	**0**	**0**

Going:	Sf: 0-0 GS: 0-0 Gd: 0-2 GF: - Fm: 0-0
Distance:	2m/2m3: 0-2 2m4-2m7: 0-0 3m+: 0-0
Track:	LH: 0-1 RH: 0-1 Tight: 0-1 Gall: 0-0
Aids:	Bl: 0-0 Vi: 0-0 Tstrap: 0-0 Ckp: 0-0
Best Rating:	**81** 2/04 Font 2m2f110y good NHF

Starlight Express (FR)

97 **76**

4-y-o b f Air Express (IRE)-Muramixa (FR) (Linamix (FR))

Miss E C Lavelle D M Bell

| Placings:40024 | | | | | (4668) |
| 2003/04: 124GF, 130GS, 170HY, 192G, 234GS, | | | | | |

	Starts	1st	2nd	3rd	Win & Pl
NH Flat	2	0	0	0	0
Hurdles	3	0	1	0	1855
Career Total	**5**	**0**	**1**	**0**	**1855**

Going:	Sf: 0-1 GS: 0-2 Gd: 0-1 GF: - Fm: 0-1
Distance:	2m/2m3: 0-2 2m4-2m7: 0-1 3m+: 0-0
Track:	LH: 0-2 RH: 0-3 Tight: 0-1 Gall: 0-0
Aids:	Bl: 0-0 Vi: 0-0 Tstrap: 0-0 Ckp: 0-0
Best Rating:	**80** 11/03 Newb 1m4f110y gd-fm NHF

Scopey filly; stayed on nicely on bumper debut.

Staroski

84f **83f**

7-y-o b m Petoski-Olnistar (FR) (Balsamo (FR))
Simon Earle E Wilmott

| Placings:503/5 | | | | | (2504) |
| 2003/04: 175GS, | | | | | |

	Starts	1st	2nd	3rd	Win & Pl
NH Flat	1	0	0	0	0
Career Total	**4**	**0**	**0**	**1**	**221**

Going:	Sf: 0-0 GS: 0-1 Gd: 0-0 GF: - Fm: 0-0
Distance:	2m/2m3: 0-1 2m4-2m7: 0-0 3m+: 0-0
Track:	LH: 0-0 RH: 0-1 Tight: 0-1 Gall: 0-0
Aids:	Bl: 0-0 Vi: 0-0 Tstrap: 0-0 Ckp: 0-0
Best Rating:	**83** 2/02 Fknm 2m gd-sft NHF

Starpath (NZ)

12-y-o ch g Starjo (NZ)-Centa Belle (NZ) (Centurius)
J J Boulter J J Boulter

| Placings:F1/2/P | | | | | (0030) |
| 2003/04: 33PG, | | | | | |

	Starts	1st	2nd	3rd	Win & Pl
Chases	1	0	0	0	0
Career Total	**4**	**1**	**1**	**0**	**5005**
103 4/01 Prth 3m7f H Ch				HVY	£3304
			Total win prize-money		£3304

Going:	Sf: 0-0 GS: 0-0 Gd: 0-1 GF: - Fm: 0-0
Distance:	2m/2m3: 0-0 2m4-2m7: 0-0 3m+: 0-0
Track:	LH: 0-1 RH: 0-0 Tight: 0-0 Gall: 0-1
Aids:	Bl: 0-0 Vi: 0-0 Tstrap: 0-0 Ckp: 0-1
Best Rating:	**107** 5/01 Chel 4m1f good Ch

Stars Delight (IRE)

101 **113**

7-y-o ch g Fourstars Allstar (USA)-Celtic Cygnet (Celtic Cone)
G L Moore Leon Best

| Placings:050/40311-23 | | | | | (0517) |
| 2003/04: 212GF, 193G, | | | | | |

	Starts	1st	2nd	3rd	Win & Pl
Hurdles	2	0	1	1	1542
Career Total	**10**	**2**	**1**	**2**	**10290**
100 3/03 Tntn 2m3f110yE Hdl				FRM	£4348
109 3/03 Font 2m4f E Hdl				SFT	£3598
			Total win prize-money		£7947

| Going: | Sf: 0-0 GS: 0-0 Gd: 0-1 GF: - Fm: 0-1 |

Distance:	2m/2m3: 0-1 2m4-2m7: 0-1 3m+: 0-0
Track:	LH: 0-1 RH: 0-1 Tight: 0-1 Gall: 0-1
Aids:	Bl: 0-0 Vi: 0-0 Tstrap: 0-0 Ckp: 0-0
Best Rating:	**113** 5/03 Hntg 2m5f110y gd-fm Hdl

Modest hurdler; won two modest 2m 4f novice hurdles on contrasting ground in March 2003; acts on soft and firm going.

Stars Out Tonight (IRE)

100 (137h)**137**

7-y-o b g Insan (USA)-Go And Tell (Kemal (FR))
Miss H C Knight Jim Lewis

| Placings:0//11004/131P-2P | | | | | (2989) |
| 2003/04: 222GS, 24PG, | | | | | |

	Starts	1st	2nd	3rd	Win & Pl
Chases	2	0	1	0	3647
Career Total	**12**	**4**	**1**	**1**	**25886**
125 2/03 Winc 3m1f110yD Ch				G-S	£5642
137 10/02 Extr 2m1f110yD Ch				GD	£5243
115 11/01 Kemp 2m D Hdl				GD	£3412
108 10/01 Chel 2m110y H NHF				GD	£3948
			Total win prize-money		£18247

Going:	Sf: 0-0 GS: 0-1 Gd: 0-1 GF: - Fm: 0-0
Distance:	2m/2m3: 0-0 2m4-2m7: 0-1 3m+: 0-1
Track:	LH: 0-1 RH: 0-1 Tight: 0-0 Gall: 0-1
Aids:	Bl: 0-0 Vi: 0-0 Tstrap: 0-0 Ckp: 0-0
Best Rating:	**137** 11/03 Newb 2m6f110y gd-sft Ch

Useful novice chaser in 2002/3; stays three miles plus; suited by good ground or a bit softer; jumps well; likes to race prominently.

Stars'N'Stripes (IRE)

78f **58f**

6-y-o b g Lord Americo-Drumdeels Star (IRE) (Le Bavard (FR))
W W Dennis W W Dennis

| Placings:0 | | | | | (0606) |
| 2003/04: 170G, | | | | | |

	Starts	1st	2nd	3rd	Win & Pl
NH Flat	1	0	0	0	0
Career Total	**1**	**0**	**0**	**0**	

Going:	Sf: 0-0 GS: 0-0 Gd: 0-1 GF: - Fm: 0-0
Distance:	2m/2m3: 0-1 2m4-2m7: 0-0 3m+: 0-0
Track:	LH: 0-1 RH: 0-0 Tight: 0-1 Gall: 0-0
Aids:	Bl: 0-0 Vi: 0-0 Tstrap: 0-0 Ckp: 0-0
Best Rating:	**60** 6/03 NAbb 2m1f good NHF

Starshipenterprise

88 **70**

6-y-o b g The Star Of Orion Vii-Lequest (Lepanto (GER))
L Wells L Wells

| Placings:665U | | | | | (4791) |
| 2003/04: 216S, 190G, 245S, 20UG, | | | | | |

	Starts	1st	2nd	3rd	Win & Pl
Hurdles	1	0	0	0	0
Chases	3	0	0	0	0
Career Total	**4**	**0**	**0**	**0**	**0**

| Going: | Sf: 0-2 GS: 0-0 Gd: 0-2 GF: - Fm: 0-0 |
| Distance: | 2m/2m3: 0-0 2m4-2m7: 0-3 3m+: 0-1 |

Track: LH: 0-3 RH: 0-1 Tight: 0-3 Gall: 0-0
Aids: Bl: 0-0 Vi: 0-0 Tstrap: 0-0 Ckp: 0-0
Best Rating: 77   3/04   Extr   2m3f110y   good   Ch

Starting Again

101   **112**

10-y-o b g Petoski-Lynemore (Nearly A Hand)
H D Daly   Mr & Mrs M P Wiggin

Placings:1/32/21PF2313/5-PF60   (4141)
2003/04: 19P GS, 20F G, 20G G, 24G G,

	Starts	1st	2nd	3rd	Win & Pl
Chases	4	0	0	0	
Career Total	16	3	3	3	16809
120 4/02	Ludl	2m4f	D(0-115)HCh	GD	£6500
106 10/01	Ludl	2m4f	E Ch	G-F	£3386
105 12/98	Ludl	2m	H NHF	G-S	£1318
			Total win prize-money £11206

Going: Sf: 0-0 GS: 0-1 Gd: 0-3 GF: 0-0 Fm: 0-0
Distance: 2m/2m3: 0-0 2m4-2m7: 0-3 3m+: 0-1
Track: LH: 0-1 RH: 0-3 Tight: 0-3 Gall: 0-0
Aids: Bl: 0-0 Vi: 0-0 Tstrap: 0-0 Ckp: 0-0
Best Rating: 120   4/02   Ludl   2m4f   good   Ch

Fair chaser, stays two and a half miles; acts on most types of ground.

Starzaan (IRE)

116   **155+**

5-y-o b g Darshaan-Stellina (IRE) (Caerleon (USA))
H Morrison   Ben Arbib

Placings:4104-424331054   (4954)
2003/04: 16A GY, 22G G, 16K GS, 21G GS, 25G GS, 20G G, 21G G, 20G G, 16G G,

	Starts	1st	2nd	3rd	Win & Pl
Hurdles	9	1	1	2	48728
Career Total	13	2	1	2	58050
155 2/04	Font	2m4f	A Hdl	GD	£29000
116 1/03	Folk	2m1f110yE Hdl	HVY	£3507
		Total win prize-money £32507

Going: Sf: 0-0 GS: 0-3 Gd: 1-5 GF: - Fm: 0-0
Distance: 2m/2m3: 0-3 2m4-2m7: 1-5 3m+: 0-1
Track: LH: 0-4 RH: 0-3 Tight: 1-2 Gall: 0-2
Aids: Bl: 0-0 Vi: 0-0 Tstrap: 0-0 Ckp: 0-0
Best Rating: 155   4/04   Sand   2m110y   good   Hdl

Smart hurdler; progressing well and won first race of the season in the National Spirit Hurdle at Fontwell; excellent fifth in the Aintree Hurdle; best at two and a half miles; acts in soft ground, but effective on faster.

State Express

13-y-o b m State Diplomacy (USA)-Roman Bonnet (Roman Warrior)
Mrs H E Oxendale   Mrs H E Oxendale

Placings:U   (0199)
2003/04: 24U GF,

	Starts	1st	2nd	3rd	Win & Pl
Chases	1	0	0	0	
Career Total	1	0	0	0	

Going: Sf: 0-0 GS: 0-0 Gd: 0-0 GF: - Fm: 0-0
Distance: 2m/2m3: 0-0 2m4-2m7: 0-0 3m+: 0-1
Track: LH: 0-0 RH: 0-1 Tight: 0-0 Gall: 0-1
Aids: Bl: 0-0 Vi: 0-0 Tstrap: 0-0 Ckp: 0-0

State Of Play

102f   **94+f**

4-y-o b g Hernando (FR)-Kaprice (GER) (Windwurf (GER))
P R Webber   Mrs C A Waters

Placings:01   (4543)
2003/04: 16G G, 16T GS,

	Starts	1st	2nd	3rd	Win & Pl
NH Flat	2	1	0	0	2562
Career Total	2	1	0	0	2562
94 3/04	Ludl	2m	H NHF	G-S	£2562
		Total win prize-money £2562

Going: Sf: 0-0 GS: 1-1 Gd: 0-1 GF: - Fm: 0-0
Distance: 2m/2m3: 1-2 2m4-2m7: 0-0 3m+: 0-0
Track: LH: 0-1 RH: 1-1 Tight: 0-0 Gall: 0-0
Aids: Bl: 0-0 Vi: 0-0 Tstrap: 0-0 Ckp: 0-0
Best Rating: 94   3/04   Ludl   2m   gd-sft   NHF

Bumper winner on second start; previously midfield in a Grade Two at Newbury.

State Power (IRE)

104   **93**

6-y-o b g Sadler's Wells (USA)-Lady Liberty (NZ) (Noble Bijou (USA))
A J Martin   State Power Syndicate

Placings:0/000041-3   (0561)
2003/04: 20G GF,

	Starts	1st	2nd	3rd	Win & Pl
Hurdles	1	0	0	1	846
Career Total	8	1	0	1	5651
90 4/03	Slig	2m	(67-88)HHdl	GD	£4480
		Total win prize-money £4481

Going: Sf: 0-0 GS: 0-0 Gd: 0-0 GF: - Fm: 0-0
Distance: 2m/2m3: 0-0 2m4-2m7: 0-1 3m+: 0-0
Track: LH: 0-0 RH: 0-1 Tight: 0-0 Gall: 0-0
Aids: Bl: 0-0 Vi: 0-0 Tstrap: 0-0 Ckp: 0-0
Best Rating: 93   6/03   Prth   2m4f110y   gd-fm   Hdl

Plating-class hurdler; trained in Ireland; third in ordinary event at Perth on British debut; stays two and a half miles; effective on a sound surface.

Stateley Lord (IRE)

65

8-y-o b/br g Good Thyne (USA)-Sixfoursix (Balinger)
Miss E C Lavelle   Mrs Betty Hobbs

Placings:UP0P/P-P   (2555)
2003/04: 22P G,

	Starts	1st	2nd	3rd	Win & Pl
Hurdles	1	0	0	0	
Career Total	6	0	0	0	

Going: Sf: 0-0 GS: 0-0 Gd: 0-1 GF: - Fm: 0-0
Distance: 2m/2m3: 0-0 2m4-2m7: 0-1 3m+: 0-0
Track: LH: 0-0 RH: 0-0 Tight: 0-1 Gall: 0-0
Aids: Bl: 0-0 Vi: 0-0 Tstrap: 0-0 Ckp: 0-0
Best Rating: 65   3/02   Newb   2m3f   soft   Hdl

Station Island (IRE)

106   **115+**

7-y-o ch g Roselier (FR)-Sweet Tulip (Beau Chapeau)
J Mackie   J S Harlow

Placings:5-22P5F43116   (4838)
2003/04: 23G G, 21L GS, 25P GS, 22G GS, 25F G, 24G G, 26G G, 26T GS, 27T G, 24G G,

	Starts	1st	2nd	3rd	Win & Pl
Hurdles	10	2	2	1	10390
Career Total	11	2	2	1	10390
106 3/04	Sedg	3m3f110yE(0-110)HHdl	GD	£3464
115 3/04	Hrfd	3m2f	E(0-110)HHdl	G-S	£3445
		Total win prize-money £6910

Going: Sf: 0-2 GS: 1-1 Gd: 1-6 GF: - Fm: 0-1
Distance: 2m/2m3: 0-0 2m4-2m7: 0-3 3m+: 2-7
Track: LH: 1-6 RH: 1-4 Tight: 1-3 Gall: 0-2
Aids: Bl: 0-0 Vi: 0-0 Tstrap: 2-6 Ckp: 0-0
Best Rating: 115   3/04   Hrfd   3m2f   gd-sft   Hdl

Moderate staying hurdler; Irish point winner; half-brother to Truckers Tavern; dual winner in the spring of 2004; stays well; acts on good and easy ground.

Statley Raj (IND)

5-y-o b g Mtoto-Donna Star (Stately Don (USA))
R Rowe   The Colonial Partnership

Placings:00P   (4671)
2003/04: 16G S, 16G GS, 16P G,

	Starts	1st	2nd	3rd	Win & Pl
NH Flat	2	0	0	0	0
Hurdles	1	0	0	0	0
Career Total	3	0	0	0	

Going: Sf: 0-1 GS: 0-1 Gd: 0-1 GF: - Fm: 0-0
Distance: 2m/2m3: 0-3 2m4-2m7: 0-0 3m+: 0-0
Track: LH: 0-0 RH: 0-3 Tight: 0-0 Gall: 0-1
Aids: Bl: 0-0 Vi: 0-0 Tstrap: 0-0 Ckp: 0-0
Best Rating: 83   1/04   Hntg   2m110y   soft   NHF

Stavordale Lad (IRE)

100   **118**

6-y-o b g Mister Lord (USA)-Ath Trasna (Amoristic (USA))
P F Nicholls   T G A Chappell & Paul K Barber

Placings:42F   (3419)
2003/04: 23G G, 25G GS, 23F GS,

	Starts	1st	2nd	3rd	Win & Pl
Chases	3	0	1	0	1767
Career Total	3	0	1	0	1767

Going: Sf: 0-0 GS: 0-2 Gd: 0-1 GF: - Fm: 0-0
Distance: 2m/2m3: 0-0 2m4-2m7: 0-0 3m+: 0-3
Track: LH: 0-0 RH: 0-3 Tight: 0-1 Gall: 0-0
Aids: Bl: 0-0 Vi: 0-0 Tstrap: 0-0 Ckp: 0-0
Best Rating: 117   1/04   Folk   3m1f   gd-sft   Ch

Winning pointer, modest form so far under Rules; looks to need good ground.

Steel Edge (IRE)

(97h)

10-y-o ch g Torus-Lasting Impression (Proverb)
Miss Venetia Williams   Worcester Racing Club

Placings:215/P54335/UF-0PP   (0589)
2003/04: 22G G, 24P S, 20P GF,

	Starts	1st	2nd	3rd	Win & Pl
Hurdles	2	0	0	0	0
Chases	1	0	0	0	0
Career Total	14	1	1	2	3571
109 2/00	Folk	2m1f110yH NHF	SFT	£1599
		Total win prize-money £1600

Going:	Sf: 0-1 GS: 0-0 Gd: 0-1 GF: - Fm: 0-1
Distance:	2m/2m3: 0-0 2m4-2m7: 0-2 3m+: 0-1
Track:	LH: 0-2 RH: 0-1 Tight: 0-0 Gall: 0-0
Aids:	Bl: 0-0 Vi: 0-0 Tstrap: 0-0 Ckp: 0-0
Best Rating:	109 4/00 Font 2m2f110y good NHF

Steel Mill (IRE)

102(103h)   (82+h)83+

9-y-o gr g Roselier (FR)-Chatmando (IRE) (Mandalus)
D J Caro   Mrs J F Billington

Placings: 000/PP63P/325-25F1U   (4757)
2003/04: 22²GS, 24⁵G, 24⁶FG, 25¹GS, 25ᵁS,

	Starts	1st	2nd	3rd	Win & Pl
Chases	5	1	1	0	5113
Career Total	16	1	2	2	6772
83	3/04	Towc	3m1f	E(0-110)HCh	G-S	£4137

Total win prize-money £4137

Going:	Sf: 0-1 GS: 1-2 Gd: 0-2 GF: - Fm: 0-0
Distance:	2m/2m3: 0-0 2m4-2m7: 0-1 3m+: 1-4
Track:	LH: 0-0 RH: 1-4 Tight: 0-1 Gall: 0-2
Aids:	Bl: 0-0 Vi: 0-0 Tstrap: 0-0 Ckp: 0-0
Best Rating:	86 3/01 Wwck 2m heavy NHF

Maiden over hurdles and fences; stays three miles; acts on soft ground.

Steel Warrior

87f   63f

7-y-o ch g Michelozzo (USA)-Iskra Bay (IRE) (Un Desperado (FR))
J S Smith   Donald Smith

Placings: 6   (2159)
2003/04: 16⁶GS,

	Starts	1st	2nd	3rd	Win & Pl
NH Flat	1	0	0	0	0
Career Total	1	0	0	0	0

Going:	Sf: 0-0 GS: 0-1 Gd: 0-0 GF: - Fm: 0-0
Distance:	2m/2m3: 0-1 2m4-2m7: 0-0 3m+: 0-0
Track:	LH: 0-1 RH: 0-0 Tight: 0-0 Gall: 0-0
Aids:	Bl: 0-0 Vi: 0-0 Tstrap: 0-0 Ckp: 0-0
Best Rating:	63 11/03 Uttx 2m gd-sft NHF

Step On Eyre (IRE)

14-y-o b g Step Together (USA)-Jane Eyre (Master Buck)
S Wynne   J E Stockton

Placings: 00/115/151/222P331/22111P/042435/6P16/641P 2/4P4-3P   (4257)
2003/04: 34³HY, 24PG,

	Starts	1st	2nd	3rd	Win & Pl
Chases	2	0	0	1	518
Career Total	41	10	7	4	72079
130	12/01	Bang	4m1f	D(0-120)HCh	SFT	£4494
134	2/01	Bang	3m6f	D(0-120)HCh	HVY	£5209
154	2/99	Hayd	3m	B(0-145)HCh	SFT	£12518
148	1/99	Weth	3m1f	B HCh	HVY	£8130
127	12/98	Bang	2m4f110yD(0-120)HCh	G-S	£4299
117	4/98	Towc	2m6f	E Ch	G-S	£2921
123	4/97	Punc	2m	Hdl	GD	£4747
111	11/96	Tipp	2m	Hdl	SFT	£2824
121	6/95	Tipp	2m	NHF	Y-S	£2712
112	5/95	Tipp	2m4f	NHF	GD	£2712

Total win prize-money £50571

Going:	Sf: 0-1 GS: 0-0 Gd: 0-1 GF: - Fm: 0-0
Distance:	2m/2m3: 0-0 2m4-2m7: 0-0 3m+: 0-2
Track:	LH: 0-2 RH: 0-0 Tight: 0-0 Gall: 0-0
Aids:	Bl: 0-0 Vi: 0-0 Tstrap: 0-0 Ckp: 0-0
Best Rating:	154 2/99 Hayd 3m soft Ch

One time useful handicap chaser; winning pointer; goes well under testing conditions but is inconsistent; stays four miles plus.

Step Quick (IRE)

100   94+

10-y-o ch g All Haste (USA)-Little Steps (Step Together (USA))
P Bowen   (W Bryan 17/5) David A Smith

Placings: 60/222P-6431223   (2362)
2003/04: 21PS, 24⁶G, 21⁴GF, 22³G, 22¹GF, 25²F, 20²GF, 20³GF,

	Starts	1st	2nd	3rd	Win & Pl
Chases	8	1	2	2	6852
Career Total	13	1	5	2	9096
92	10/03	MRas	2m6f110yE(0-105)HCh	G-F	£3022

Total win prize-money £3023

Going:	Sf: 0-1 GS: 0-0 Gd: 0-2 GF: - Fm: 1-5
Distance:	2m/2m3: 0-0 2m4-2m7: 1-6 3m+: 0-1
Track:	LH: 0-4 RH: 1-3 Tight: 1-5 Gall: 0-0
Aids:	Bl: 0-0 Vi: 0-0 Tstrap: 0-0 Ckp: 0-1
Best Rating:	94 11/03 Worc 2m4f110y gd-fm Ch

Former hunter chaser; stays three miles; acts on fast ground.

Stepastray

55   16

7-y-o gr g Alhijaz-Wandering Stranger (Petong)
R E Barr   D Thomson

Placings: P-0   (2399)
2003/04: 16⁰GS,

	Starts	1st	2nd	3rd	Win & Pl
Hurdles	1	0	0	0	0
Career Total	2	0	0	0	

Going:	Sf: 0-0 GS: 0-1 Gd: 0-0 GF: - Fm: 0-0
Distance:	2m/2m3: 0-1 2m4-2m7: 0-0 3m+: 0-0
Track:	LH: 0-1 RH: 0-0 Tight: 0-0 Gall: 0-0
Aids:	Bl: 0-0 Vi: 0-0 Tstrap: 0-0 Ckp: 0-0
Best Rating:	16 11/03 Weth 2m gd-sft Hdl

Steppes

(92h)89

9-y-o b g Jendali (USA)-Asoness (Laxton)
M J Gingell   T Alexander And G S Plastow

Placings: 001PPP-UPP   (4778)
2003/04: 24ᵁGF, 21PGS, 21PG,

	Starts	1st	2nd	3rd	Win & Pl
Chases	3	0	0	0	
Career Total	9	1	0	0	2226
78	9/02	Worc	3m	F Hdl	GD	£2226

Total win prize-money £2226

Going:	Sf: 0-0 GS: 0-1 Gd: 0-1 GF: - Fm: 0-1
Distance:	2m/2m3: 0-0 2m4-2m7: 0-2 3m+: 0-1
Track:	LH: 0-3 RH: 0-0 Tight: 0-3 Gall: 0-0
Aids:	Bl: 0-0 Vi: 0-0 Tstrap: 0-0 Ckp: 0-0
Best Rating:	89 5/03 Fknm 3m110y gd-fm Ch

Steppes Of Gold (IRE)

111   136+

7-y-o b g Moscow Society (USA)-Trysting Place (He Loves Me)
N G Richards   Independent Twine Manufacturing Co Ltd

Placings: 1-1125   (4638)
2003/04: 16¹S, 18¹S, 18²GS, 16⁶G,

	Starts	1st	2nd	3rd	Win & Pl
Hurdles	4	2	1	0	15533
Career Total	5	3	1	0	17598
106	1/04	Kels	2m2f	E Hdl	SFT	£3744
105	12/03	Hayd	2m	D Hdl	SFT	£3939
111	4/03	Newc	2m	H NHF	GD	£2065

Total win prize-money £9748

Going:	Sf: 2-2 GS: 0-1 Gd: 0-1 GF: - Fm: 0-0
Distance:	2m/2m3: 2-4 2m4-2m7: 0-0 3m+: 0-0
Track:	LH: 2-4 RH: 0-0 Tight: 1-3 Gall: 0-0
Aids:	Bl: 0-0 Vi: 0-0 Tstrap: 0-0 Ckp: 0-0
Best Rating:	136 4/04 Aint 2m110y good Hdl

Useful novice hurdler; bumper winner; won first two starts over hurdles before finishing second in a grade two at Kelso; good fifth in Grade Two at Aintree; effective on a sound surface and on soft; should make a decent chaser in time.

Sterling Dot Com (IRE)

99   (116h)104+

8-y-o b g Roselier (FR)-Daddy's Folly (Le Moss)
P J Hobbs   Sterling Racing Syndicate

Placings: 3¹134/F540P-3243455   (4820)
2003/04: 24³GF, 23⁶G, 22⁴GS, 25³HY, 24⁴G, 29⁵GS, 25⁵GF,

	Starts	1st	2nd	3rd	Win & Pl
Chases	7	0	1	2	3728
Career Total	16	1	1	4	8174
116	12/01	Wwck	2m5f	E Hdl	SFT	£2844

Total win prize-money £2845

Going:	Sf: 0-1 GS: 0-2 Gd: 0-2 GF: - Fm: 0-2
Distance:	2m/2m3: 0-2 2m4-2m7: 0-1 3m+: 0-6
Track:	LH: 0-3 RH: 0-4 Tight: 0-0 Gall: 0-2
Aids:	Bl: 0-0 Vi: 0-0 Tstrap: 0-0 Ckp: 0-0
Best Rating:	116 12/01 Wwck 2m5f soft Hdl

Moderate chaser; appears to stay 3m 5f; likes soft ground; has been let down by his jumping.

Stern Leader (IRE)

83   62

5-y-o b g Supreme Leader-Strong Stern (IRE) (Lancastrian)
D J Wintle   D Bishop,J Bull,T Hickman & Friends

Placings: 440P   (4098)
2003/04: 16⁴S, 16⁴HY, 17⁰GS, 21⁰G,

	Starts	1st	2nd	3rd	Win & Pl
NH Flat	2	0	0	0	0
Hurdles	2	0	0	0	0
Career Total	4	0	0	0	0

Going:	Sf: 0-2 GS: 0-1 Gd: 0-1 GF: - Fm: 0-0
Distance:	2m/2m3: 0-3 2m4-2m7: 0-1 3m+: 0-0
Track:	LH: 0-1 RH: 0-3 Tight: 0-2 Gall: 0-0
Aids:	Bl: 0-0 Vi: 0-0 Tstrap: 0-0 Ckp: 0-0
Best Rating:	87 12/03 Towc 2m soft NHF

Steve Ford

15-y-o gr g Another Realm-Sky Miss (Skymaster)
Mrs S S Harbour Miss E Harbour

Placings:60/P/30F0V3/5140450/U632/15223/1123/U5P/P0 P/F-F   (4891)
2003/04: 24^FGF,

	Starts	1st	2nd	3rd	Win & Pl
Chases	1	0	0		
Career Total	37	4	4	5	19259
110 5/98	Worc	2m4f110yD(0-125)HCh		G-F	£4235
105 5/98	Winc	2m5f		E(0-100)HCh	GD	£3480
99 5/97	Uttx	2m4f110yD(0-125)HHdl		GD	£2913
97 5/95	Worc	2m		E(0-110)HHdl	GD	£2547
		Total win prize-money £13176			

Going:	Sf: 0-0 GS: 0-0 Gd: 0-0 GF: - Fm: 0-1
Distance:	2m/2m3: 0-0 2m4-2m7: 0-0 3m+: 0-1
Track:	LH: 0-1 RH: 0-0 Tight: 0-1 Gall: 0-0
Aids:	Bl: 0-0 Vi: 0-0 Tstrap: 0-0 Ckp: 0-0
Best Rating:	110 5/98 Worc 2m4f110y gd-fm Ch

Steve The Fish (IRE)

(105h)   (104h)**89**
8-y-o ch g Dry Dock-Country Clothing (Salluceva)
J A B Old The Old Boys Partnership

Placings:06/05FF2/P5U0-10RP   (4525)
2003/04: 22^PS, 24¹S, 24^PS, 25^PG, 24^PGFS,

	Starts	1st	2nd	3rd	Win & Pl
Hurdles	3	1	0	0	2261
Chases	2	0	0	0	0
Career Total	15	1	1	0	2819
104 11/03	Towc	3m	D(0-115)HHdl	SFT	£2261
		Total win prize-money £2261			

Going:	Sf: 1-3 GS: 0-1 Gd: 0-1 GF: - Fm: 0-0
Distance:	2m/2m3: 0-0 2m4-2m7: 0-1 3m+: 1-4
Track:	LH: 0-3 RH: 1-2 Tight: 0-1 Gall: 0-0
Aids:	Bl: 0-0 Vi: 0-0 Tstrap: 0-0 Ckp: 0-0
Best Rating:	104 11/03 Towc 3m soft Hdl

Moderate novice hurdler/chaser; stays two miles five; acts on easy ground.

Stevie Dee

10-y-o ch g Emperor Fountain-Babe In The Wood (Athens Wood)
R A Maletroit Dr Carla Mahmoud

Placings:00050/003345020/0P03PP/P   (4218)
2003/04: 25^PGS,

	Starts	1st	2nd	3rd	Win & Pl
Chases	1	0	0	0	
Career Total	21	0	1	3	1849

Going:	Sf: 0-0 GS: 0-1 Gd: 0-0 GF: - Fm: 0-0
Distance:	2m/2m3: 0-0 2m4-2m7: 0-0 3m+: 0-0
Track:	LH: 0-0 RH: 0-1 Tight: 0-1 Gall: 0-0
Aids:	Bl: 0-0 Vi: 0-0 Tstrap: 0-1 Ckp: 0-0
Best Rating:	93 11/99 Clon 2m4f yld-sft NHF

Stewart's Lad
89   97
7-y-o b g Well Beloved-Moneyacre (Veloski)

B D Leavy S H Riley

Placings:0453F/0-54   (3697)
2003/04: 20⁵GS, 17⁴HY,

	Starts	1st	2nd	3rd	Win & Pl
Hurdles	2	0	0	0	268
Career Total	8	0	0	1	654

Going:	Sf: 0-1 GS: 0-1 Gd: 0-0 GF: - Fm: 0-0
Distance:	2m/2m3: 0-1 2m4-2m7: 0-1 3m+: 0-0
Track:	LH: 0-1 RH: 0-1 Tight: 0-0 Gall: 0-0
Aids:	Bl: 0-0 Vi: 0-0 Tstrap: 0-0 Ckp: 0-0
Best Rating:	97 4/02 Uttx 2m good Hdl

Has shown ability in novice hurdles.

Still Going On
96   96+
7-y-o b g Prince Sabo-Floppie (FR) (Law Society (USA))
Eoin Doyle J J P Murphy

Placings:0000453-02204P   (3154a)
2003/04: 16⁰GY, 16²G, 16⁰G, 16⁴GY, 16^PSH,

	Starts	1st	2nd	3rd	Win & Pl
Hurdles	6	0	2	0	2805
Career Total	13	0	2	1	3466

Going:	Sf: 0-0 GS: 0-0 Gd: 0-3 GF: - Fm: 0-0
Distance:	2m/2m3: 0-6 2m4-2m7: 0-0 3m+: 0-0
Track:	LH: 0-1 RH: 0-1 Tight: 0-0 Gall: 0-0
Aids:	Bl: 0-0 Vi: 0-0 Tstrap: 0-3 Ckp: 0-2
Best Rating:	93 11/03 Chel 2m110y good Hdl

Plating-class Irish-trained hurdler; still a maiden; suited by a sound surface; yet to race over further than two miles; has worn a tongue tie.

Still Speedy (IRE)
77   79+
7-y-o b g Toulon-Gorge (Mount Hagen (FR))
Noel T Chance The Cardinal Syndicate

Placings:004-3F3   (4812)
2003/04: 16³GF, 16^FGS, 16³G,

	Starts	1st	2nd	3rd	Win & Pl
NH Flat	1	0	0	1	423
Hurdles	2	0	0	1	554
Career Total	6	0	0	2	977

Going:	Sf: 0-0 GS: 0-1 Gd: 0-1 GF: - Fm: 0-1
Distance:	2m/2m3: 0-3 2m4-2m7: 0-0 3m+: 0-0
Track:	LH: 0-2 RH: 0-1 Tight: 0-1 Gall: 0-0
Aids:	Bl: 0-0 Vi: 0-0 Tstrap: 0-0 Ckp: 0-0
Best Rating:	95 11/02 Winc 2m good NHF

Has shown ability in bumpers and over hurdles but carries his head high and is not a straightforward ride.

Stillmore Business

13-y-o ch g Don Enrico (USA)-Mill Miss (Typhoon)
Mrs F J Walker Mrs F J Walker

Placings:0/04/P   (0249)
2003/04: 19^PGF,

	Starts	1st	2nd	3rd	Win & Pl
Chases	1	0	0	0	
Career Total	4	0	0	0	389

Sting Like A Bee (IRE)
100   85
5-y-o b g Ali-Royal (IRE)-Hidden Agenda (FR) (Machiavellian (USA))
J S Goldie Mrs C Brown

Placings:005356-1FFP00   (3233)
2003/04: 20¹GF, 20^FG, 16^FG, 16^PS, 16⁰GS, 20⁰GF,

	Starts	1st	2nd	3rd	Win & Pl
Hurdles	6	1	0	0	2163
Career Total	12	1	0	1	2516
85 11/03	Hexm	2m4f110yG(0-90)HHdl	G-F	£2163
		Total win prize-money £2163			

Going:	Sf: 0-1 GS: 0-1 Gd: 0-0 GF: - Fm: 1-2
Distance:	2m/2m3: 0-3 2m4-2m7: 1-3 3m+: 0-0
Track:	LH: 1-5 RH: 0-1 Tight: 0-1 Gall: 0-2
Aids:	Bl: 0-0 Vi: 0-0 Tstrap: 0-0 Ckp: 0-0
Best Rating:	85 11/03 Ayr 2m4f good Hdl

Plating-class hurdler; finally broke his duck with narrow success at Hexham in November 2003 and bang in contention when falling at Ayr later in month; held since; stays two and a half miles; acts best on a sound surface.

Stirred Not Shaken (IRE)

5-y-o b g Revoque (IRE)-Shakey (IRE) (Caerleon (USA))
Miss J S Davis Miss J Davis

Placings:P   (3900)
2003/04: 17^PGS,

	Starts	1st	2nd	3rd	Win & Pl
Hurdles	1	0	0	0	
Career Total	1	0	0	0	

Going:	Sf: 0-0 GS: 0-1 Gd: 0-0 GF: - Fm: 0-0
Distance:	2m/2m3: 0-1 2m4-2m7: 0-0 3m+: 0-0
Track:	LH: 0-0 RH: 0-1 Tight: 0-1 Gall: 0-0
Aids:	Bl: 0-0 Vi: 0-0 Tstrap: 0-0 Ckp: 0-0

Stittenham
71+f
5-y-o b g Blushing Flame (USA)-Coronati (IRE) (Bluebird (USA))
M W Easterby Mrs M E Curtis

Placings:5   (1372)
2003/04: 16⁵F,

	Starts	1st	2nd	3rd	Win & Pl
NH Flat	1	0	0	0	0
Career Total	1	0	0	0	0

Going:	Sf: 0-0 GS: 0-0 Gd: 0-0 GF: - Fm: 0-1
Distance:	2m/2m3: 0-1 2m4-2m7: 0-0 3m+: 0-0
Track:	LH: 0-1 RH: 0-0 Tight: 0-0 Gall: 0-0
Aids:	Bl: 0-0 Vi: 0-0 Tstrap: 0-0 Ckp: 0-0
Best Rating:	71 9/03 Hexm 2m110y firm NHF

Stock Dove

75   **63**

6-y-o ch m Deploy-Lady Stock (Crofter (USA))
Mrs P Robeson   Mrs P Robeson

Placings:*200*   (3213)
2003/04: 16²GS, 17⁹GS, 16⁹GS,

	Starts	1st	2nd	3rd	Win & Pl
NH Flat	2	0	1	0	456
Hurdles	1	0	0	0	0
Career Total	3	0	1	0	456

Going:	Sf: 0-0 GS: 0-3 Gd: 0-0 GF: - Fm: 0-0
Distance:	2m/2m3: 0-3 2m4-2m7: 0-0 3m+: 0-0
Track:	LH: 0-2 RH: 0-1 Tight: 0-1 Gall: 0-0
Aids:	Bl: 0-0 Vi: 0-0 Tstrap: 0-0 Ckp: 0-0
Best Rating:	94 11/03 Uttx 2m gd-sft NHF

Stockers Pride

77   (0c)**106**

9-y-o b g Sula Bula-Fille De Soleil (Sunyboy)
P R Hedger   J D Sells

Placings:*062313/PFP-PP0*   (4183)
2003/04: 24⁵GS, 22⁸GS, 26⁶G,

	Starts	1st	2nd	3rd	Win & Pl
Hurdles	3	0	0	0	
Career Total	12	1	1	2	3968
106 1/02 Plum	3m1f110yE Hdl			HVY	£2572
			Total win prize-money £2573		

Going:	Sf: 0-0 GS: 0-2 Gd: 0-1 GF: - Fm: 0-0
Distance:	2m/2m3: 0-0 2m4-2m7: 0-1 3m+: 0-2
Track:	LH: 0-0 RH: 0-3 Tight: 0-1 Gall: 0-1
Aids:	Bl: 0-1 Vi: 0-0 Tstrap: 0-0 Ckp: 0-0
Best Rating:	106 1/02 Plum 3m1f110y heavy Hdl

Modest novice hurdler, stays well and acts in the mud.

Stocks 'n Shares

105(98h)   (85h)**112+**

8-y-o b m Jupiter Island-Norstock (Norwich (USA))
J White   The Norstock Partnership

Placings:*0/0500-61312231U44*   (4305)
2003/04: 19⁶G, 16¹GF, 16³GF, 16¹GS, 20²GS, 16²GF, 17³HY, 19¹GS, 20⁴G, 20⁴G,

	Starts	1st	2nd	3rd	Win & Pl
Hurdles	3	0	1	0	490
Chases	8	3	2	1	17165
Career Total	16	3	2	2	17655
112 1/04 Tntn	2m3f	D(0-110)HCh		G-S	£5622
112 12/03 Hrfd	2m	F(0-95)HCh		G-S	£2405
82 11/03 Folk	2m	E Ch		G-F	£4120
			Total win prize-money £12148		

Going:	Sf: 0-1 GS: 2-4 Gd: 0-3 GF: - Fm: 1-3
Distance:	2m/2m3: 3-7 2m4-2m7: 0-4 3m+: 0-0
Track:	LH: 0-0 RH: 3-10 Tight: 2-4 Gall: 0-0
Aids:	Bl: 0-0 Vi: 0-0 Tstrap: 3-11 Ckp: 0-0
Best Rating:	112 3/04 Sand 2m4f110y good Ch

Modest novice chaser; plating-class hurdler; best at 2m; acts on soft ground; wears a tongue tie.

Stokesies Boy

96   **78**

4-y-o gr c Key Of Luck (USA)-Lesley's Fashion (Dominion)
J L Spearing   Byron J Stokes

Placings:*405*   (4854)
2003/04: 16⁴GF, 17⁰G, 17⁵GF,

	Starts	1st	2nd	3rd	Win & Pl
Hurdles	3	0	0	0	292
Career Total	3	0	0	0	292

Going:	Sf: 0-0 GS: 0-0 Gd: 0-1 GF: - Fm: 0-2
Distance:	2m/2m3: 0-3 2m4-2m7: 0-0 3m+: 0-0
Track:	LH: 0-0 RH: 0-3 Tight: 0-2 Gall: 0-1
Aids:	Bl: 0-0 Vi: 0-0 Tstrap: 0-0 Ckp: 0-0
Best Rating:	78 11/03 Hntg 2m10y gd-fm Hdl

Modest maiden at up to a mile on the Flat; pulls hard and has yet to show he can get the trip over hurdles.

Stolen Hours (USA)

98   **96**

4-y-o b/br c Silver Deputy (CAN)-Fasta (USA) (Seattle Song (USA))
J Akehurst (E A L Dunlop 22/10)   A D Spence

Placings:*4650*   (3899)
2003/04: 16⁴GS, 16⁶G, 16⁵S, 20⁰GS,

	Starts	1st	2nd	3rd	Win & Pl
Hurdles	4	0	0	0	167
Career Total	4	0	0	0	167

Going:	Sf: 0-1 GS: 0-2 Gd: 0-1 GF: - Fm: 0-0
Distance:	2m/2m3: 0-3 2m4-2m7: 0-1 3m+: 0-0
Track:	LH: 0-2 RH: 0-2 Tight: 0-1 Gall: 0-1
Aids:	Bl: 0-0 Vi: 0-0 Tstrap: 0-0 Ckp: 0-0
Best Rating:	92 12/03 Kemp 2m good Hdl

Staying maiden on the Flat; bits of ability over hurdles to date on good to soft ground over two miles.

Stolen Song

103   **95+**

4-y-o b g Sheikh Albadou-Sparky's Song (Electric)
M J Ryan   The Aldora Partnership

Placings:*52P051*   (4591)
2003/04: 16⁵GF, 16²G, 16⁸P, 16⁹GS, 16⁵S, 16¹G,

	Starts	1st	2nd	3rd	Win & Pl
Hurdles	6	1	1	0	9908
Career Total	6	1	1	0	9908
91 3/04 Hntg	2m110y	D(0-120)HHdl		GD	£6727
			Total win prize-money £6728		

Going:	Sf: 0-1 GS: 0-1 Gd: 1-3 GF: - Fm: 0-1
Distance:	2m/2m3: 1-6 2m4-2m7: 0-0 3m+: 0-0
Track:	LH: 0-2 RH: 1-4 Tight: 0-0 Gall: 1-3
Aids:	Bl: 0-4 Vi: 0-0 Tstrap: 0-0 Ckp: 0-0
Best Rating:	103 12/03 Wwck 2m good Hdl

Moderate hurdler; acts on a sound surface; has worn blinkers.

Stone Cold

103   (97h)**107**

7-y-o ch g Inchinor-Vaula (Henbit (USA))
T D Easterby   Six Diamonds Partnership

Placings:*45551040/0525P021F51/643462212-2P612352P*   (3340)
2003/04: 25²G, 25⁵GS, 24⁶G, 20¹G, 19²GF, 20³G, 20⁵GS, 20²GF, 25⁵GS,

	Starts	1st	2nd	3rd	Win & Pl
Chases	9	1	3	1	10851
Career Total	37	5	8	2	35673
101 11/03 Carl	2m4f	D(0-115)HCh		GD	£4556

---

104 2/03 Weth	2m4f110yD(0-125)HCh		GD	£5629
97 4/02 MRas	2m1f110yE(0-105)HCh		G-F	£3786
97 3/02 Donc	2m110y D(0-110)HCh		SFT	£4160
97 2/01 Sedg	2m1f	F(0-95)HHdl	SFT	£2009
			Total win prize-money £20141	

Going:	Sf: 0-0 GS: 0-3 Gd: 1-4 GF: - Fm: 0-2
Distance:	2m/2m3: 0-1 **2m4-2m7: 1-4** 3m+: 0-4
Track:	LH: 0-7 **RH: 1-2** Tight: 0-7 Gall: 0-1
Aids:	**Bl: 1-6** Vi: 0-0 Tstrap: 0-0 Ckp: 0-1
Best Rating:	107 3/03 Weth 2m7f110y gd-fm Ch

Moderate chaser/hurdler; stays three miles, but is effective over shorter; has worn blinkers; acts on any ground; consistent.

Stone Craic

6-y-o b/br g Safawan-Stone Madness (Yukon Eric (CAN))
Miss Z C Davison   Miss Z C Davison

Placings:*0*   (4529)
2003/04: 16⁹GS,

	Starts	1st	2nd	3rd	Win & Pl
NH Flat	1	0	0	0	
Career Total	1	0	0	0	

Going:	Sf: 0-0 GS: 0-1 Gd: 0-0 GF: - Fm: 0-0
Distance:	2m/2m3: 0-1 2m4-2m7: 0-0 3m+: 0-0
Track:	LH: 0-1 RH: 0-0 Tight: 0-0 Gall: 0-0
Aids:	Bl: 0-0 Vi: 0-0 Tstrap: 0-0 Ckp: 0-0

Stoned (IRE)

82   **55**

4-y-o b g Bigstone (IRE)-Lady Celina (FR) (Crystal Palace (FR))
L Wells   L Wells

Placings:*00P*   (4895)
2003/04: 14⁰G, 17⁰GS, 22⁸G,

	Starts	1st	2nd	3rd	Win & Pl
NH Flat	1	0	0	0	0
Hurdles	2	0	0	0	0
Career Total	3	0	0	0	

Going:	Sf: 0-0 GS: 0-1 Gd: 0-2 GF: - Fm: 0-0
Distance:	2m/2m3: 0-1 2m4-2m7: 0-1 3m+: 0-0
Track:	LH: 0-1 RH: 0-2 Tight: 0-1 Gall: 0-0
Aids:	Bl: 0-0 Vi: 0-0 Tstrap: 0-0 Ckp: 0-1
Best Rating:	71 11/03 Wwck 1m6f good NHF

Stonehenge (IRE)

(89c)   (77c)**91d**

7-y-o b g Caerleon (USA)-Sharata (IRE) (Darshaan)
D Burchell   Three Acres Racing

Placings:*5P0/512535PP05/06PP0-P*   (4750)
2003/04: 21⁸G,

	Starts	1st	2nd	3rd	Win & Pl
Hurdles	1	0	0	0	
Career Total	19	1	1	1	4155
95 6/01 NAbb	2m6f	F(0-105)HHdl	GD	£2793
			Total win prize-money £2793	

Going:	Sf: 0-0 GS: 0-0 Gd: 0-1 GF: - Fm: 0-0
Distance:	2m/2m3: 0-0 2m4-2m7: 0-1 3m+: 0-0
Track:	LH: 0-1 RH: 0-0 Tight: 0-1 Gall: 0-0
Aids:	Bl: 0-0 Vi: 0-0 Tstrap: 0-0 Ckp: 0-0
Best Rating:	95 6/01 NAbb 2m6f gd-fm Hdl

Stoneravinmad

80 (0c)**34**

6-y-o ch g Never So Bold-Premier Princess (Hard Fought)
Mrs E Slack Mrs Evelyn Slack

Placings:0U00-U35   (3000)
2003/04: 22^UG, 25^3F, 25^5GS,

	Starts	1st	2nd	3rd	Win & Pl
Hurdles	2	0	0	0	0
Chases	1	0	0	1	514
Career Total	7	0	0	1	514

Going:	Sf: 0-0 GS: 0-1 Gd: 0-1 GF: - Fm: 0-1
Distance:	2m/2m3: 0-0 2m4-2m7: 0-0 3m+: 0-2
Track:	LH: 0-3 RH: 0-0 Tight: 0-2 Gall: 0-0
Aids:	Bl: 0-0 Vi: 0-0 Tstrap: 0-0 Ckp: 0-0
Best Rating:	44 11/02 Newc 2m4f soft Hdl

Stoneyford Ben (IRE)

91f **103f**

5-y-o b g Beneficial-Rosie Rock (Swan's Rock)
S Gollings J B Webb

Placings:336   (4517)
2003/04: 17^3GS, 16^3G, 16^6GS,

	Starts	1st	2nd	3rd	Win & Pl
NH Flat	3	0	0	2	568
Career Total	3	0	0	2	568

Going:	Sf: 0-0 GS: 0-2 Gd: 0-1 GF: - Fm: 0-0
Distance:	2m/2m3: 0-3 2m4-2m7: 0-0 3m+: 0-0
Track:	LH: 0-2 RH: 0-1 Tight: 0-1 Gall: 0-1
Aids:	Bl: 0-0 Vi: 0-0 Tstrap: 0-0 Ckp: 0-0
Best Rating:	103 2/04 Folk 2m1f110y gd-sft NHF

Stopwatch (IRE)

95(95h) (63h)**90**

9-y-o b g Lead On Time (USA)-Rose Bonbon (FR) (High Top)
Mrs L C Jewell The Stopwatch Partnership

Placings:03015/5P40/3542500/64360016/3F022UFF0-U544060   (4237)
2003/04: 19^UG, 18^5G, 21^4GF, 20^4GF, 20^9G, 18^6G, 18^9GF,

	Starts	1st	2nd	3rd	Win & Pl
Hurdles	1	0	0	0	0
Chases	6	0	0	0	650
Career Total	40	2	3	4	11511
82	3/02	Hntg	2m110y F(0-100)HHdl		G-F £1848
104	4/99	Plum	2m1f E(0-105)HHdl		GD £2302
			Total win prize-money £4151

Going:	Sf: 0-0 GS: 0-0 Gd: 0-4 GF: - Fm: 0-3
Distance:	2m/2m3: 0-3 2m4-2m7: 0-4 3m+: 0-0
Track:	LH: 0-3 RH: 0-2 Tight: 0-5 Gall: 0-0
Aids:	Bl: 0-0 Vi: 0-0 Tstrap: 0-0 Ckp: 0-5
Best Rating:	104 4/99 Chel 2m1f good Hdl

Moderate chaser; effective at two and a half miles; not the best of jumpers.

Storm A Brewing

92 **72**

8-y-o ch g Glacial Storm (USA)-Southern Squaw (Buckskin (FR))
R M Stronge Mrs Bernice Stronge

Placings:20/004-2   (0295)
2003/04: 22^2G,

	Starts	1st	2nd	3rd	Win & Pl
Hurdles	1	0	1	0	1800
Career Total	6	0	2	0	2707

Going:	Sf: 0-0 GS: 0-0 Gd: 0-1 GF: - Fm: 0-0
Distance:	2m/2m3: 0-0 2m4-2m7: 0-1 3m+: 0-0
Track:	LH: 0-1 RH: 0-1 Tight: 0-1 Gall: 0-0
Aids:	Bl: 0-0 Vi: 0-0 Tstrap: 0-0 Ckp: 0-0
Best Rating:	98 1/02 Ludl 2m good NHF

Out of half-sister to Docklands Express; runner-up in bumper on debut; gradually improving in staying novice hurdles; may do better in handicaps.

Storm Ahead (IRE)

86(83h) (64h)**63**

10-y-o b g Glacial Storm (USA)-Little Slip (Super Slip)
A Parker It's A Bargain Syndicate

Placings:04320/0000/F425P/06P0P-44U   (0693)
2003/04: 21^4S, 20^4G, 25^UGF,

	Starts	1st	2nd	3rd	Win & Pl
Hurdles	1	0	0	0	0
Chases	2	0	0	0	237
Career Total	22	0	2	1	2167

Going:	Sf: 0-1 GS: 0-0 Gd: 0-1 GF: - Fm: 0-1
Distance:	2m/2m3: 0-0 2m4-2m7: 0-2 3m+: 0-1
Track:	LH: 0-3 RH: 0-0 Tight: 0-1 Gall: 0-0
Aids:	Bl: 0-0 Vi: 0-0 Tstrap: 0-0 Ckp: 0-1
Best Rating:	101 11/99 Dpat 2m1f87y yield NHF

Storm Clear (IRE)

100 **89**

5-y-o b h Mujadil (USA)-Escape Path (Wolver Hollow)
D J Wintle (R Hannon 20/10) D Boocock

Placings:P0000   (4339)
2003/04: 16^PGS, 17^0GS, 16^6S, 16^0GS, 16^6G,

	Starts	1st	2nd	3rd	Win & Pl
Hurdles	5	0	0	0	0
Career Total	5	0	0	0	0

Going:	Sf: 0-1 GS: 0-3 Gd: 0-1 GF: - Fm: 0-0
Distance:	2m/2m3: 0-5 2m4-2m7: 0-0 3m+: 0-0
Track:	LH: 0-3 RH: 0-2 Tight: 0-2 Gall: 0-0
Aids:	Bl: 0-0 Vi: 0-0 Tstrap: 0-1 Ckp: 0-0
Best Rating:	89 1/04 Plum 2m soft Hdl

Storm Damage (IRE)

131

12-y-o b g Waajib-Connaught Lace (Connaught)
P F Nicholls T Curry,C Lewis,Penny Mitchell & J Olds

Placings:65113/00/F21245/33112334/3132305/3422150/20 64B10/22351-P   (0105)
2003/04: 24^PHY,

	Starts	1st	2nd	3rd	Win & Pl
Chases	1	0	0	0	
Career Total	48	9	9	10	117804
126	2/03	Sand	3m110y E Ch		SFT £6942
135	3/02	Sand	3m110y C(0-135)HCh		GD £6987
135	2/01	Sand	3m110y B(0-145)HCh		HVY £20825

135	11/99	Chep	2m3f110yC(0-130)HCh		GD £6006
139	1/99	Kemp	2m4f110yB(0-145)HCh		SFT £10386
139	12/98	Chep	2m3f110yC(0-130)HCh		HVY £4955
116	1/98	Wind	2m E Ch		GD £2921
119	2/96	Clon	2m Hdl		SFT £2295
117	2/96	Gowr	2m Hdl		Y-S £3177
			Total win prize-money £64498

Going:	Sf: 0-1 GS: 0-0 Gd: 0-0 GF: - Fm: 0-0
Distance:	2m/2m3: 0-0 2m4-2m7: 0-0 3m+: 0-1
Track:	LH: 0-1 RH: 0-0 Tight: 0-0 Gall: 0-0
Aids:	Bl: 0-0 Vi: 0-0 Tstrap: 0-0 Ckp: 0-0
Best Rating:	139 1/99 Kemp 2m4f110y soft Ch

Decent staying chaser; had conditions in his favour when winning a sub-standard renewal of the Agfa Chase at Sandown in February 2001; shade disappointing after that success, but won back at Sandown in March 2002 and when winning the Royal Artillery Gold Cup in February 2003; stays three miles plus; acts on soft ground; sometimes blinkered.

Storm Of Gold (IRE)

11-y-o b g Glacial Storm (USA)-Tipperary Tartan (Rarity)
D L Williams Reliance Car Hire Services Ltd

Placings:235/11320/21F/0020/61PP/26P4P66-3   (0030)
2003/04: 33^3G,

	Starts	1st	2nd	3rd	Win & Pl
Chases	1	0	0	1	995
Career Total	27	4	5	3	25439
101	2/02	Ludl	3m7f H Ch		G-S £2618
124	12/99	MRas	3m1f E Ch		G-S £3070
124	12/98	Uttx	2m4f110yE Hdl		G-S £1966
121	11/98	Hayd	2m4f D Hdl		G-S £2885
			Total win prize-money £10540

Going:	Sf: 0-0 GS: 0-0 Gd: 0-1 GF: - Fm: 0-0
Distance:	2m/2m3: 0-0 2m4-2m7: 0-0 3m+: 0-0
Track:	LH: 0-1 RH: 0-0 Tight: 0-0 Gall: 0-1
Aids:	Bl: 0-0 Vi: 0-0 Tstrap: 0-0 Ckp: 0-1
Best Rating:	134 3/99 Sand 2m4f110y soft Hdl

Moderate hunter chaser; stays very well but may not be the most hearty.

Storm Prince (IRE)

107 **103+**

7-y-o ch g Prince Of Birds (USA)-Petersford Girl (IRE) (Taufan (USA))
J L Spearing D J Oseman

Placings:2113P0/0506-360551130   (4693)
2003/04: 17^3GS, 16^6S, 19^4G, 24^5S, 22^6G, 22^1G, 21^1GS, 22^3G, 22^6G,

	Starts	1st	2nd	3rd	Win & Pl
Hurdles	9	2	0	2	8438
Career Total	19	4	1	3	15530
103	3/04	Wwck	2m5f E(0-110)HHdl		G-S £3874
103	3/04	Winc	2m6f F(0-100)HHdl		GD £3003
118	11/00	Hrfd	2m1f E Hdl		G-S £2723
116	10/00	Wwck	2m D Hdl		SFT £3048
			Total win prize-money £12649

Going:	Sf: 0-3 GS: 1-1 Gd: 1-5 GF: - Fm: 0-0
Distance:	2m/2m3: 2-5 2m4-2m7: 2-6 3m+: 0-0
Track:	LH: 1-4 RH: 1-3 Tight: 0-3 Gall: 0-0
Aids:	Bl: 2-5 Vi: 0-1 Tstrap: 0-1 Ckp: 0-0
Best Rating:	118 12/00 Newb 2m110y soft Hdl

Modest hurdler; stays two miles six; best with cut in the ground.

Storm Valley (IRE)

12-y-o b g Strong Gale-Windy Run (Deep Run)
T Wall R Wilding

Placings:0P0/56/650UP5P4/133/P1PP/F5U-P   (0613)
2003/04: 25PGF,

	Starts	1st	2nd	3rd	Win & Pl
Chases	1	0	0	0	
Career Total	24	2	0	2	7877
95	10/01	Sthl	3m10y	F(0-100)HCh	GD	£2940
86	9/00	Plum	2m4f	D(0-110)HCh	G-F	£3770

Total win prize-money £6710

Going:	Sf: 0-0 GS: 0-0 Gd: 0-0 GF: - Fm: 0-1
Distance:	2m/2m3: 0-0 2m4-2m7: 0-0 3m+: 0-1
Track:	LH: 0-0 RH: 0-1 Tight: 0-0 Gall: 0-0
Aids:	Bl: 0-0 Vi: 0-0 Tstrap: 0-0 Ckp: 0-0
Best Rating:	95 10/01 Sthl 3m10y good Ch

Stormdancer (IRE)

7-y-o ch g Bluebird (USA)-Unspoiled (Tina's Pet)
Mrs Lucinda Featherstone Largesse Racing

Placings:PPP-0   (0158)
2003/04: 23QGF,

	Starts	1st	2nd	3rd	Win & Pl
Hurdles	1	0	0	0	
Career Total	4	0	0	0	

Going:	Sf: 0-0 GS: 0-0 Gd: 0-0 GF: - Fm: 0-1
Distance:	2m/2m3: 0-0 2m4-2m7: 0-0 3m+: 0-1
Track:	LH: 0-1 RH: 0-0 Tight: 0-1 Gall: 0-0
Aids:	Bl: 0-0 Vi: 0-0 Tstrap: 0-0 Ckp: 0-0

Stormez (FR)

109(115h)   (141 h)158
7-y-o b g Ezzoud (IRE)-Stormy Scene (USA) (Storm Bird (CAN))
M C Pipe D A Johnson

Placings:02163011541033/112110111222-23306U (4965)
2003/04: 27²G, 26³GS, 23³S, 25QG, 33QGS, 29UGF,

	Starts	1st	2nd	3rd	Win & Pl
Hurdles	2	0	0	1	1980
Chases	4	0	1	1	17200
Career Total	32	11	6	5	288551
143	2/03	Kemp	3m	C Ch	GD	£12753
145	2/03	Newb	3m	C Ch	GD	£8287
139	1/03	Kemp	3m	C Ch	GD	£8346
150	11/02	Chel	3m3f110yA HCh		G-S	£34800
141	6/02	Uttx	4m110y	B(0-140)HCh	G-F	£32500
111	5/02	Worc	2m7f110yE Ch		GD	£3190
122	5/02	Worc	2m7f110yD Ch		G-F	£5362
134	2/02	Asct	3m	C Hdl	SFT	£5005
140	11/01	Engh	2m3f	Hdl	HVY	£31038
	11/01	Engh	2m2f	Hdl	HVY	£17459
	7/01	Autl	2m3f110y Hdl		G-S	£19399

Total win prize-money £178141

Going:	Sf: 0-1 GS: 0-2 Gd: 0-2 GF: - Fm: 0-1
Distance:	2m/2m3: 0-0 2m4-2m7: 0-0 3m+: 0-6
Track:	LH: 0-5 RH: 0-1 Tight: 0-0 Gall: 0-2
Aids:	Bl: 0-0 Vi: 0-1 Tstrap: 0-6 Ckp: 0-1
Best Rating:	158 4/03 Ayr 4m1f good Ch

Smart chaser/very useful hurdler; successful seven times in 2002/3 and runner-up in National Hunt Challenge Cup at Cheltenham, Scottish National and Attheraces Gold Cup;

good return at Cheltenham; well beaten third in Rehearsal Chase at Chepstow the following month; reverted to hurdles with a sound effort when third at Haydock in February; well beaten sixth in Scottish National; stays 4m; only small, but usually jumps soundly; at his best on decent ground; has won on a soft surface; usually wears a tongue tie; very tough.

Stormhill Stag

101(96h)   (92h)119
12-y-o b g Buckley-Sweet Sirenia (Al Sirat)
R Lee R Taylor

Placings:2112/426431F/534P0/2230F/1220113/5P422- (4919)
461U6436P
2003/04: 23⁴G, 19⁶GS, 25¹S, 19UGS, 23⁶G, 21⁴G, 20³GS, 23⁶G, 20PGS,

	Starts	1st	2nd	3rd	Win & Pl
Chases	9	1	0	1	4217
Career Total	42	7	9	5	41638
73	12/03	Towc	3m1f	E(0-115)HCh	SFT	£2555
118	3/02	Newb	2m4f	D(0-125)HCh	G-S	£9512
120	1/02	Towc	2m110y	D(0-120)HCh	HVY	£5083
106	5/01	Extr	2m3f110yF(0-95)HCh		G-S	£3248
110	1/99	Font	2m6f110yF(0-110)HHdl		SFT	£2845
113	6/97	Sthl	2m	N NHF		G-S	£1203
115	5/97	Uttx	2m	H NHF		G-F	£1287

Total win prize-money £25733

Going:	Sf: 1-1 GS: 0-4 Gd: 0-4 GF: - Fm: 0-0
Distance:	2m/2m3: 0-0 2m4-2m7: 0-5 3m+: 1-4
Track:	LH: 0-3 RH: 1-6 Tight: 0-2 Gall: 0-0
Aids:	Bl: 0-3 Vi: 0-0 Tstrap: 0-0 Ckp: 0-0
Best Rating:	120 3/02 Chep 2m3f110y gd-sft Ch

Modest chaser; very fortunate winner of a farcical race at Towcester in December when the majority of the runners took the wrong course; effective at up to 3m; best with give in the ground.

Storming Back

95f   86f
5-y-o b g Bob Back (USA)-Prussian Storm (IRE) (Strong Gale)
R Waley-Cohen Robert Waley-Cohen

Placings:50   (4199)
2003/04: 16⁵S, 16⁰G,

	Starts	1st	2nd	3rd	Win & Pl
NH Flat	2	0	0	0	
Career Total	2	0	0	0	0

Going:	Sf: 0-1 GS: 0-0 Gd: 0-0 GF: - Fm: 0-0
Distance:	2m/2m3: 0-2 2m4-2m7: 0-0 3m+: 0-0
Track:	LH: 0-2 RH: 0-0 Tight: 0-0 Gall: 0-1
Aids:	Bl: 0-0 Vi: 0-0 Tstrap: 0-0 Ckp: 0-0
Best Rating:	86 2/04 Weth 2m soft NHF

Rangy type; showed some ability on debut in soft ground bumper at Wetherby in February.

Stormy Beech

109(107h)   (93 h)95
8-y-o b g Glacial Storm (USA)-Cheeny's Brig (New Brig)
R Johnson Peter & Paul Kelly

Placings:0/P00/P00526131020-16320000150P (4947)
2003/04: 16⁶G, 17¹S, 17⁶G, 21³G, 21²GF, 17⁰GF, 16⁹GS, 19⁴GS, 16⁹HY, 16¹HY, 16⁵G, 20⁴HY, 20PGS,

	Starts	1st	2nd	3rd	Win & Pl
Hurdles	9	1	1	1	4606
Chases	4	1	0	0	4232

	Career Total	28	4	3	2	16155
95	2/04	Carl	2m	E(0-105)HCh	HVY	£4231
90	5/03	Sedg	2m1f	F(0-100)HHdl	SFT	£2933
95	2/03	Sedg	2m1f	F(0-95)HHdl	HVY	£2730
84	1/03	Catt	2m	G(0-90)HHdl	GD	£2471

Total win prize-money £12366

Going:	Sf: 2-4 GS: 0-3 Gd: 0-4 GF: - Fm: 0-2
Distance:	2m/2m3: 2-9 2m4-2m7: 0-4 3m+: 0-0
Track:	LH: 1-9 RH: 1-4 Tight: 1-6 Gall: 0-0
Aids:	Bl: 1-9 Vi: 0-0 Tstrap: 0-1 Ckp: 0-0
Best Rating:	95 2/04 Carl 2m heavy Ch

Moderate hurdler; made a winning chasing debut in February 2004; acts on soft and good; usually wears blinkers.

Stormy Session

(22h)
14-y-o b g Celestial Storm (USA)-No Jazz (Jaazeiro (USA))
M F Harris M Harris

Placings:60/P/40P6/25420/2PPF/312306/UR0F/S00/P (0613)
2003/04: 25PGF,

	Starts	1st	2nd	3rd	Win & Pl
Chases	1	0	0	0	
Career Total	30	1	4	2	10502
103	5/99	Strf	2m5f110yD(0-110)HCh	GD	£4315

Total win prize-money £4315

Going:	Sf: 0-0 GS: 0-0 Gd: 0-0 GF: - Fm: 0-1
Distance:	2m/2m3: 0-0 2m4-2m7: 0-0 3m+: 0-1
Track:	LH: 0-0 RH: 0-1 Tight: 0-0 Gall: 0-0
Aids:	Bl: 0-0 Vi: 0-0 Tstrap: 0-0 Ckp: 0-0
Best Rating:	103 5/99 Uttx 3m2f gd-fm Ch

Stormy Skye (IRE)

96   (122h)116
8-y-o b g Bluebird (USA)-Canna (Caerleon (USA))
G L Moore Jayne Moore, T Pollock, J Driscoll

Placings:435122/102P/36300536/234F33F3-U1 (2076)
2003/04: 24UGF, 24¹G,

	Starts	1st	2nd	3rd	Win & Pl
Chases	2	1	0	0	3696
Career Total	28	3	4	8	29648
113	11/03	Ling	3m	E Ch	GD	£3696
122	11/00	Asct	2m110y	C(0-135)HHdl	SFT	£8365
108	2/00	Plum	2m	E Hdl	SFT	£2534

Total win prize-money £14596

Going:	Sf: 0-0 GS: 0-0 Gd: 1-1 GF: - Fm: 0-0
Distance:	2m/2m3: 0-0 2m4-2m7: 0-0 3m+: 1-2
Track:	LH: 1-1 RH: 0-1 Tight: 1-1 Gall: 0-0
Aids:	Bl: 1-2 Vi: 0-0 Tstrap: 0-0 Ckp: 0-0
Best Rating:	125 2/01 Kemp 2m5f gd-sft Hdl

Fair chaser; stays three miles; acts on soft ground; has worn blinkers.

Stormy Sunrise (IRE)

8-y-o b g Glacial Storm (USA)-Commanche Maid (Commanche Run)
Miss A Armitage (E Bolger 24/6) Major R R Alers-Hankey

Placings:00060P/000000-S000   (4303)
2003/04: 24⁰GY, 33⁵G, 21⁰G, 20⁰F, 16⁰G,

	Starts	1st	2nd	3rd	Win & Pl
Chases	5	0	0	0	
Career Total	16	0	0	0	

Going:	Sf: 0-0 GS: 0-0 Gd: 0-3 GF: - Fm: 0-1
Distance:	2m/2m3: 0-1 2m4-2m7: 0-2 3m+: 0-2
Track:	LH: 0-0 RH: 0-3 Tight: 0-0 Gall: 0-0
Aids:	Bl: 0-0 Vi: 0-0 Tstrap: 0-0 Ckp: 0-0
Best Rating:	70 8/01 Slig 2m sft-hvy Hdl

Stormyfairweather (IRE)

82   79

12-y-o b g Strong Gale-Game Sunset (Menelek)
N J Henderson   Mrs Christopher Hanbury

Placings:62011/110P/2133112/P1/5/P-P0UP   (3647)
2003/04: 25PGY, 19QG, 24UG, 24PGS,

	Starts	1st	2nd	3rd	Win & Pl		
Chases	4	0	0	0			
Career Total	24	8	3	2	111058		
163	3/00	Chel	2m5f	A Ch		G-F	£36000
150	3/99	Chel	2m5f	A Ch		G-S	£32700
120	2/99	Donc	3m	E Ch		G-F	£2999
133	11/98	Chel	2m4f110yB Ch			GD	£9394
129	11/97	Newb	2m110y B(0-140)HHdl			SFT	£5492
120	5/97	Towc	2m	D Hdl		SFT	£2966
114	4/97	Chel	2m5f110yE(0-105)HHdl			G-F	£2996
101	3/97	Towc	2m5f	E Hdl		G-F	£2722

Total win prize-money £95271

Going:	Sf: 0-0 GS: 0-1 Gd: 0-2 GF: - Fm: 0-0
Distance:	2m/2m3: 0-0 2m4-2m7: 0-1 3m+: 0-3
Track:	LH: 0-0 RH: 0-4 Tight: 0-0 Gall: 0-0
Aids:	Bl: 0-0 Vi: 0-0 Tstrap: 0-0 Ckp: 0-0
Best Rating:	163 3/00 Chel 2m5f gd-fm Ch

Formerly very useful performer; dual winner of the Cathcart at Cheltenham; reportedly retired.

Straight Eight

5-y-o b g Octagonal (NZ)-Kalymnia (GER) (Mondrian (GER))
T D Easterby   Giles W Pritchard-Gordon

Placings:B   (2087)
2003/04: 17BGF,

	Starts	1st	2nd	3rd	Win & Pl
Hurdles	1	0	0	0	
Career Total	1	0	0	0	

Going:	Sf: 0-0 GS: 0-0 Gd: 0-0 GF: - Fm: 0-1
Distance:	2m/2m3: 0-1 2m4-2m7: 0-0 3m+: 0-0
Track:	LH: 0-1 RH: 0-0 Tight: 0-1 Gall: 0-0
Aids:	Bl: 0-0 Vi: 0-0 Tstrap: 0-0 Ckp: 0-0

Strain The Rein

92

9-y-o b g Petoski-Valls D'Andorra (Free State)
M C Pipe   Mrs Belinda Harvey

Placings:061/20/00/0   (1503)
2003/04: 16QGF,

	Starts	1st	2nd	3rd	Win & Pl		
Hurdles	1	0	0	0			
Career Total	8	1	1	0	2500		
107	4/00	Hexm	2m	H NHF		GD	£1883

Total win prize-money £1883

Going:	Sf: 0-0 GS: 0-0 Gd: 0-0 GF: - Fm: 0-1
Distance:	2m/2m3: 0-1 2m4-2m7: 0-0 3m+: 0-1
Track:	LH: 0-1 RH: 0-0 Tight: 0-0 Gall: 0-0
Aids:	Bl: 0-0 Vi: 0-0 Tstrap: 0-0 Ckp: 0-0
Best Rating:	114 2/01 Hayd 2m soft NHF

Strait Talking (FR)

74   (0c)86

6-y-o b g Bering-Servia (Le Marmot (FR))
Jedd O'Keeffe   E Rider

Placings:040/06302F021-0   (0647)
2003/04: 16QGF,

	Starts	1st	2nd	3rd	Win & Pl
Hurdles	1	0	0	0	
Career Total	13	1	2	1	4337
88	4/03	Fknm	2m	G(0-90)HHdl	GD	£2367

Total win prize-money £2367

Going:	Sf: 0-0 GS: 0-0 Gd: 0-0 GF: - Fm: 0-1
Distance:	2m/2m3: 0-1 2m4-2m7: 0-0 3m+: 0-0
Track:	LH: 0-1 RH: 0-0 Tight: 0-0 Gall: 0-0
Aids:	Bl: 0-0 Vi: 0-0 Tstrap: 0-0 Ckp: 0-0
Best Rating:	88 4/03 Fknm 2m good Hdl

Selling-class hurdler; runner-up at Catterick and Uttoxeter in 2003 before scoring at Fakenham; fell on only chase start; acts on good ground; stays two miles;likes a sharp track; front-runner.

Strath Fillan

85   61

6-y-o b m Dolphin Street (FR)-Adarama (IRE) (Persian Bold)
H J Collingridge   L M Power

Placings:0/6600-0   (0438)
2003/04: 18QGY,

	Starts	1st	2nd	3rd	Win & Pl
Hurdles	1	0	0	0	
Career Total	6	0	0	0	0

Going:	Sf: 0-0 GS: 0-0 Gd: 0-0 GF: - Fm: 0-1
Distance:	2m/2m3: 0-1 2m4-2m7: 0-0 3m+: 0-0
Track:	LH: 0-1 RH: 0-0 Tight: 0-1 Gall: 0-0
Aids:	Bl: 0-0 Vi: 0-0 Tstrap: 0-0 Ckp: 0-0
Best Rating:	73 3/02 Hntg 2m110y gd-fm Hdl

Strawberry Hill (IRE)

(103h)   (88h)

10-y-o b g Lancastrian-Tudor Lady (Green Shoon)
B Mactaggart (Miss V Scott 1/11)   W A Chisholm

Placings:546P/5P526-50PP   (3232)
2003/04: 17PS, 24QGF, 17PG, 24PGF,

	Starts	1st	2nd	3rd	Win & Pl
Hurdles	2	0	0	0	0
Chases	2	0	0	0	0
Career Total	13	0	1	0	1509

Going:	Sf: 0-1 GS: 0-0 Gd: 0-1 GF: - Fm: 0-2
Distance:	2m/2m3: 0-2 2m4-2m7: 0-0 3m+: 0-2
Track:	LH: 0-2 RH: 0-2 Tight: 0-3 Gall: 0-0
Aids:	Bl: 0-0 Vi: 0-0 Tstrap: 0-0 Ckp: 0-0
Best Rating:	88 4/03 Sedg 2m1f good Hdl

Moderate hurdler; showed little worthwhile form before fin-

ishing second at Sedgefield in April 2003; connections appear to be struggling to find his trip.

Strawman

108   (79h)92

7-y-o b g Ela-Mana-Mou-Oatfield (Great Nephew)
C N Kellett   J E Titley

Placings:44P4P/60660/4FP6U312P-PP0U1424   (4933)
2003/04: 21PGS, 25PGS, 23QG, 24UG, 16PG, 17QG, 21QG, 26QG,

	Starts	1st	2nd	3rd	Win & Pl		
Chases	8	1	1	0	5578		
Career Total	27	2	2	1	11729		
80	3/04	Folk	2m	F(0-90)HCh		GD	£3445
92	8/02	Font	2m2f	E Ch		GD	£4007

Total win prize-money £7453

Going:	Sf: 0-0 GS: 0-2 Gd: 1-6 GF: - Fm: 0-0
Distance:	2m/2m3: 1-2 2m4-2m7: 0-2 3m+: 0-4
Track:	LH: 0-4 RH: 1-3 Tight: 1-6 Gall: 0-0
Aids:	Bl: 0-0 Vi: 1-4 Tstrap: 0-0 Ckp: 0-1
Best Rating:	92 9/02 Sedg 2m5f good Ch

Plating-class chaser; in and out performer; best form is at around two miles, but he stays father; seems best on good ground.

Stray Raven

73f   48f

5-y-o b g Sea Raven (IRE)-Gone Astray (The Parson)
J B Walton   Messrs F T Walton

Placings:00   (4663)
2003/04: 16QS, 16PS,

	Starts	1st	2nd	3rd	Win & Pl
NH Flat	2	0	0	0	
Career Total	2	0	0	0	

Going:	Sf: 0-2 GS: 0-0 Gd: 0-0 GF: - Fm: 0-0
Distance:	2m/2m3: 0-2 2m4-2m7: 0-0 3m+: 0-0
Track:	LH: 0-2 RH: 0-0 Tight: 0-0 Gall: 0-0
Aids:	Bl: 0-0 Vi: 0-0 Tstrap: 0-0 Ckp: 0-0
Best Rating:	51 3/04 Newc 2m soft NHF

Streamsforth Lad (IRE)

(100h)   (88h)

7-y-o b g Be My Native (USA)-Protrial (Proverb)
S A Brookshaw   T G K Construction Ltd

Placings:00/263P50P44-P   (0138)
2003/04: 24PG,

	Starts	1st	2nd	3rd	Win & Pl
Chases	1	0	0	0	
Career Total	12	0	1	1	2030

Going:	Sf: 0-0 GS: 0-0 Gd: 0-1 GF: - Fm: 0-0
Distance:	2m/2m3: 0-0 2m4-2m7: 0-0 3m+: 0-1
Track:	LH: 0-0 RH: 0-1 Tight: 0-1 Gall: 0-0
Aids:	Bl: 0-0 Vi: 0-0 Tstrap: 0-0 Ckp: 0-0
Best Rating:	92 10/02 Chel 2m110y good NHF

Streamstown (IRE)

104

10-y-o br g Rashar (USA)-Lady Torsil (Torus)
Ferdy Murphy   Haydock Park National Hunt Partnership

Placings:3104100/540551212/4F21115/56P1P0/0-P (2733)
2003/04: 24PS,

	Starts	1st	2nd	3rd	Win & Pl
Chases	1	0	0	0	
Career Total	**31**	**8**	**3**	**1**	**87969**

149	2/02	Uttx	3m4f	A HCh	HVY	£40600
144	1/01	Weth	3m1f	B HCh	G-S	£10056
143	11/00	Hayd	3m	E(0-115)HCh	HVY	£3510
128	11/00	Aint	2m4f	D(0-125)HCh	G-S	£7280
102	3/00	Clon	2m6f	Ch	G-Y	£4416
98	2/00	Punc	2m4f	(0-116)HCh	SFT	£4968
110	3/99	Gowr	2m4f	Hdl	YLD	£2700
104	1/99	Naas	2m	NHF	HVY	£2762
				Total win prize-money		£76294

Going: Sf: 0-1 GS: 0-0 Gd: 0-0 GF: - Fm: 0-0
Distance: 2m/2m3: 0-0 2m4-2m7: 0-0 3m+: 0-1
Track: LH: 0-1 RH: 0-0 Tight: 0-0 Gall: 0-0
Aids: Bl: 0-0 Vi: 0-0 Tstrap: 0-0 Ckp: 0-0
Best Rating: 149 2/02 Uttx 3m4f heavy Ch

Very useful ex-Irish chaser; testing conditions saw him win the National Trial at Uttoxeter in February 2002; lightly raced and held since; stays three miles plus; acts on soft ground.

Strenue (USA)

72   54

4-y-o ch g Crafty Prospector (USA)-Shawgatny (USA) (Danzig Connection (USA))
M C Pipe Mrs Belinda Harvey

Placings:0PP0 (4138)
2003/04: 16GGF, 17PGF, 18PGF, 16GG,

	Starts	1st	2nd	3rd	Win & Pl
Hurdles	4	0	0	0	
Career Total	**4**	**0**	**0**	**0**	

Going: Sf: 0-0 GS: 0-0 Gd: 0-1 GF: - Fm: 0-3
Distance: 2m/2m3: 0-4 2m4-2m7: 0-0 3m+: 0-0
Track: LH: 0-3 RH: 0-1 Tight: 0-3 Gall: 0-0
Aids: Bl: 0-0 Vi: 0-0 Tstrap: 0-0 Ckp: 0-0
Best Rating: 54 3/04 Ludl 2m good Hdl

Strewth

10-y-o b g Cruise Missile-Storm Foot (Import)
Mrs L Pomfret A Witcomb

Placings:00P/0/P6-5 (0073)
2003/04: 24PS,

	Starts	1st	2nd	3rd	Win & Pl
Chases	1	0	0	0	0
Career Total	**7**	**0**	**0**	**0**	**0**

Going: Sf: 0-1 GS: 0-0 Gd: 0-0 GF: - Fm: 0-0
Distance: 2m/2m3: 0-0 2m4-2m7: 0-0 3m+: 0-1
Track: LH: 0-1 RH: 0-0 Tight: 0-1 Gall: 0-0
Aids: Bl: 0-0 Vi: 0-0 Tstrap: 0-0 Ckp: 0-0
Best Rating: 76 5/00 Chel 2m5f good Ch

Strictly Speaking (IRE)

102   84

7-y-o b g Sri Pekan (USA)-Gaijin (Caerleon (USA))
R Brotherton (P F I Cole 31/7) Roy Brotherton

Placings:0340/6P-425 (1506)
2003/04: 16RG, 20PG, 16PGF,

	Starts	1st	2nd	3rd	Win & Pl
Hurdles	3	0	1	0	1095
Career Total	**9**	**0**	**1**	**1**	**1777**

Going: Sf: 0-0 GS: 0-0 Gd: 0-2 GF: - Fm: 0-1
Distance: 2m/2m3: 0-2 2m4-2m7: 0-1 3m+: 0-0
Track: LH: 0-3 RH: 0-0 Tight: 0-2 Gall: 0-0
Aids: Bl: 0-0 Vi: 0-0 Tstrap: 0-0 Ckp: 0-0
Best Rating: 112 1/02 Newb 2m3f gd-sft Hdl

Plating-class hurdler; winner on the Flat; stays two miles three furlongs over hurdles; acts on good to soft ground.

Strike Back (IRE)

106   140

6-y-o b g Bob Back (USA)-First Strike (IRE) (Magical Strike (USA))
Mrs John Harrington Commonstown Racing Syndicate

Placings:0-12113625 (4629)
2003/04: 16RG, 16QG, 16RGY, 19RGY, 16RS, 20RS, 20QGY, 20QG,

	Starts	1st	2nd	3rd	Win & Pl
NH Flat	2	1	1	0	5143
Hurdles	6	2	1	1	27230
Career Total	**9**	**3**	**2**	**1**	**32372**

115	11/03	Naas	2m3f	Hdl	G-Y	£8441
108	10/03	Rosc	2m	Hdl	GD	£5376
105	5/03	DRoy	2m	NHF	GD	£3584
				Total win prize-money		£17403

Going: Sf: 0-2 GS: 0-0 Gd: 2-4 GF: - Fm: 0-0
Distance: 2m/2m3: 3-5 2m4-2m7: 0-3 3m+: 0-0
Track: LH: 1-2 RH: 0-1 Tight: 0-1 Gall: 0-0
Aids: Bl: 0-0 Vi: 0-0 Tstrap: 0-0 Ckp: 0-0
Best Rating: 140 4/04 Aint 2m4f good Hdl

Useful hurdler; bumper winner; took two novice hurdles in Ireland before finishing creditable fifth in Grade 2 at Aintree; suited by two and a half miles.

Strolling

88f   86f

7-y-o br g Alflora (IRE)-Emmabella (True Song)
A Hollingsworth A Hollingsworth

Placings:0 (0533)
2003/04: 16GGF,

	Starts	1st	2nd	3rd	Win & Pl
NH Flat	1	0	0	0	
Career Total	**1**	**0**	**0**	**0**	

Going: Sf: 0-0 GS: 0-0 Gd: 0-0 GF: - Fm: 0-1
Distance: 2m/2m3: 0-1 2m4-2m7: 0-0 3m+: 0-0
Track: LH: 0-1 RH: 0-0 Tight: 0-0 Gall: 0-0
Aids: Bl: 0-0 Vi: 0-0 Tstrap: 0-0 Ckp: 0-0
Best Rating: 86 6/03 Worc 2m gd-fm NHF

Stromness (USA)

105(108c)   (130c)139

7-y-o ch g Trempolino (USA)-Caithness (USA) (Roberto (USA))
A King Lady Harris

Placings:5225/25112241/613633-221441F640 (4386)
2003/04: 23QGF, 23PGF, 23RG, 25RG, 25RG, 24RG, 23FGF, 25RGS, 24RG, 20QGS,

	Starts	1st	2nd	3rd	Win & Pl
Hurdles	5	0	0	0	4568
Chases	5	2	2	0	11090
Career Total	**28**	**6**	**7**	**3**	**104006**

130	12/03	Donc	3m	E Ch	GD	£4180
118	7/03	Worc	2m7f110yE Ch		GD	£4105
145	12/02	Chel	3m	N Hdl	SFT	£12435
151	4/02	Aint	3m110y	A Hdl	GD	£34800
130	1/02	Kemp	2m5f	D Hdl	G-S	£5073
121	1/02	Font	2m6f110yE Hdl		GD	£2730
				Total win prize-money		£63325

Going: Sf: 0-0 GS: 0-2 Gd: 2-6 GF: - Fm: 0-2
Distance: 2m/2m3: 0-0 2m4-2m7: 1-3 3m+: 2-10
Track: LH: 2-8 RH: 0-2 Tight: 0-0 Gall: 1-4
Aids: Bl: 0-0 Vi: 0-0 Tstrap: 2-7 Ckp: 0-0
Best Rating: 151 4/02 Aint 3m110y good Hdl

Very useful staying hurdler, but only a fair chaser; only small; has persistently suffered from wind problems; returned after third soft palate operation to win weakly contested four-runner novice chase at Worcester July 2003 and scored at Doncaster in December; suited by 3m; acts on good and soft ground, although better on the former; usually wears a tongue tie.

Strong Flow (IRE)

120(110h)   (130+h)169

7-y-o br g Over The River (FR)-Stormy Skies (Strong Gale)
P F Nicholls B C Marshall

Placings:21-11F111 (2915)
2003/04: 23RGS, 25RG, 25FGS, 21RG, 26RGS, 24RG,

	Starts	1st	2nd	3rd	Win & Pl
Chases	6	5	0	0	130703
Career Total	**8**	**6**	**1**	**0**	**136011**

159	12/03	Kemp	3m	A Ch	GD	£36850
169	11/03	Newb	3m2f110yA HCh		G-S	£63800
140	11/03	NAbb	2m5f110yD Ch		GD	£4813
147	5/03	Kels	3m1f	B(0-150)HCh	GD	£20949
137	5/03	Worc	2m7f110yE Ch		G-S	£4290
130	2/03	Tntn	3m110y	E Hdl	G-S	£4452
				Total win prize-money		£135156

Going: Sf: 0-0 GS: 2-2 Gd: 3-4 GF: - Fm: 0-0
Distance: 2m/2m3: 0-0 2m4-2m7: 1-1 3m+: 4-5
Track: LH: 4-5 RH: 1-1 Tight: 2-3 Gall: 1-1
Aids: Bl: 0-0 Vi: 0-0 Tstrap: 0-0 Ckp: 0-0
Best Rating: 169 11/03 Newb 3m2f110y gd-sft Ch

Very useful novice chaser; Irish point winner; won five of his first six starts over fences, including a hugely impressive win in the Hennessy Cognac Gold Cup at Newbury; won the Feltham subsequently despite two serious jumping errors which saw him sustain a season-ending injury; stays three miles plus; acts on good and soft ground; most progressive and an outstanding prospect.

Strong Magic (IRE)

108   101

12-y-o br g Strong Gale-Baybush (Boreen (FR))
J R Cornwall J R Cornwall

Placings:00/5/503040/4536F542/30/B3FB1123220/504222 4405-PU5332542321515 (4639)
2003/04: 24PGF, 20PGF, 25RF, 24RG, 20RGF, 24RGF, 20RGS, 24RGF, 20PGS, 21RGS, 20RS, 24RG, 24RGS, 19RGS, 20RS,

	Starts	1st	2nd	3rd	Win & Pl
Chases	15	2	3	3	19137
Career Total	**55**	**4**	**10**	**8**	**54169**

101	3/04	Towc	2m3f110yF(0-95)Ch		G-S	£3262
100	2/04	Asct	3m110y	E(0-110)HCh	GD	£5161
100	11/01	Aint	3m1f	D(0-115)HCh	G-S	£10627
107	11/01	Hntg	3m	F(0-105)HCh	GD	£2625
				Total win prize-money		£21676

Going: Sf: 0-1 GS: 1-4 Gd: 1-4 GF: - Fm: 0-6
Distance: 2m/2m3: 0-0 2m4-2m7: 1-8 3m+: 1-7

Track:	LH: 0-7 **RH: 1-7** Tight: 0-6 Gall: 0-5
Aids:	Bl: 0-0 Vi: 0-0 Tstrap: 0-0 Ckp: 0-0
Best Rating:	107 11/01 Hntg 3m good Ch

Moderate chaser; ended a long losing sequence at Ascot in February; scored again at Towcester; stays three miles; best on a sound surface but handles cut; jumps well generally.

Strong Paladin (IRE)
94   **120**

13-y-o b g Strong Gale-Kalanshoe (Random Shot)
N A Gaselee Mrs Angela Brodie

Placings:50/6011/F53332/3F233/32334/312/1224/33614-4
                                              (0437)
2003/04: 22⁴GF,

	Starts	1st	2nd	3rd	Win & Pl
Chases	1	0	0	0	345
Career Total	35	5	6	12	60446
114	3/03	Font	3m2f110y		D(0-125)HCh
G-F	£5993				
127	10/01	Font	2m6f	D(0-120)HCh	G-S £6922
109	10/00	Folk	3m1f	F(0-100)HCh	G-F £2656
110	3/97	Font	2m2f110yE	Hdl	G-F £2385
97	2/97	Tntn	2m3f110yD	Hdl	G-S £2567

Total win prize-money £20524

Going:	Sf: 0-0 GS: 0-0 Gd: 0-0 GF: - Fm: 0-1
Distance:	2m/2m3: 0-0 2m4-2m7: 0-1 3m+: 0-0
Track:	LH: 0-0 RH: 0-0 Tight: 0-1 Gall: 0-0
Aids:	Bl: 0-0 Vi: 0-0 Tstrap: 0-0 Ckp: 0-0
Best Rating:	127 12/01 Kemp 3m good Ch

Fair chaser; a little one-paced; stays 3m 2f; acts on both fast and easy surfaces.

Strong Project (IRE)
110   **(94c)130**

8-y-o ch g Project Manager-Hurricane Girl (IRE) (Strong Gale)
C F Swan J J Buckley

Placings:024/12313/655/F331F20F06-3136230   **(4806a)**
2003/04: 20³GF, 22¹G, 20³YS, 24⁸YS, 24²Y, 24³G, 20²Y,

	Starts	1st	2nd	3rd	Win & Pl
Hurdles	7	1	1	3	15957
Career Total	30	4	4	7	37700
127	12/03	Thur	2m6f110y	Hdl	GD £5376
105	7/02	Wxfd	2m4f	Hdl	G-F £5079
95	8/00	Naas	2m4f	Hdl	FRM £3312
95	6/00	Kbgn	2m3f	NHF	G-F £2760

Total win prize-money £16529

Going:	Sf: 0-0 GS: 0-0 Gd: 1-2 GF: - Fm: 0-1
Distance:	2m/2m3: 0-0 2m4-2m7: 1-4 3m+: 0-3
Track:	LH: 0-4 RH: 0-1 Tight: 0-1 Gall: 0-0
Aids:	Bl: 0-0 Vi: 0-0 Tstrap: 0-0 Ckp: 0-0
Best Rating:	130 4/04 Aint 3m110y good Hdl

Useful hurdler; stays well; acts on good and easy ground.

Strong Resolve (IRE)
104(105h)   **(93h)125**

8-y-o gr g Roselier (FR)-Farmerette (Teofane)
Miss Lucinda V Russell Fair City Flyers

Placings:62F3UP50/P333545P541P-321P22112   **(4865)**
2003/04: 20³G, 25²GS, 251S, 20²G, 25²HY, 25²GS, 251GF, 251G, 25²S,

	Starts	1st	2nd	3rd	Win & Pl
Chases	9	3	4	1	26250

Career Total		29	4	5	5	32384
125	3/04	Kels	3m1f	D Ch	GD £5512
104	3/04	Ayr	3m1f	E Ch	G-F £4920
120	12/03	Ayr	3m1f	E(0-110)HCh	SFT £3978
93	3/03	Ayr	2m	F Hdl	SFT £2670

Total win prize-money £17082

Going:	Sf: 1-3 GS: 0-2 Gd: 1-3 GF: - Fm: 1-1
Distance:	2m/2m3: 0-0 2m4-2m7: 0-2 3m+: 3-7
Track:	LH: 3-9 RH: 0-0 Tight: 1-2 Gall: 0-0
Aids:	Bl: 0-0 Vi: 0-0 Tstrap: 0-0 Ckp: 0-0
Best Rating:	125 4/04 Ayr 3m1f soft Ch

Moderate hurdler/improving chaser; won on handicap debut over fences at Ayr in December, mainly creditable efforts since (did not have to improve to win again back at Ayr); career best when successful in useful event at Kelso in March; stays three miles one furlong; acts on soft ground; sound jumper who likes to dominate.

Strong Run (IRE)
104   **(114h)149**

11-y-o b g Strong Gale-Arctic Run (Deep Run)
Noel Meade M D McGrath

Placings:225/33411/11FF/0010/1F411/5152   **(4580a)**
2003/04: 16⁵HY, 16¹Y, 16⁵G, 20²Y,

	Starts	1st	2nd	3rd	Win & Pl
Chases	4	1	1	0	35979
Career Total	25	9	3	2	135323
142	2/04	Naas	2m	Ch	YLD £29799
140	4/02	Punc	2m	Ch	Y-S £38159
138	4/02	Fair	2m100y	HCh	G-Y £15950
129	1/02	Navn	2m	(0-123)HCh	Y-S £7407
137	2/01	Fair	2m4f	(0-140)HHdl	Y-S £6677
105	11/99	Naas	2m	Ch	Y-S £6589
123	10/99	Punc	2m	Ch	GD £4312
125	4/99	Punc	2m	(0-135)HHdl	YLD £8671
123	4/99	Fair		Hdl	YLD £6138

Total win prize-money £123707

Going:	Sf: 0-1 GS: 0-0 Gd: 0-1 GF: - Fm: 0-0
Distance:	2m/2m3: 1-3 2m4-2m7: 0-1 3m+: 0-0
Track:	LH: 1-3 RH: 0-1 Tight: 0-0 Gall: 0-1
Aids:	Bl: 0-0 Vi: 0-0 Tstrap: 1-4 Ckp: 0-0
Best Rating:	149 3/04 Navn 2m4f yield Ch

Smart Irish chaser; 4th in the 2002 Mildmay of Flete at Cheltenham before winning twice in April, including a weak Grade One at Punchestown; won at Navan this season; stays 2m 4f; suited by cut in the ground; wears a tongue tie.

Strong Tartan (IRE)

10-y-o br g Strong Gale-Kemchee (Kemal (FR))
A Parker Mr & Mrs Raymond Anderson Green

Placings:0/153F/132F/33FP-31143P4   **(4851)**
2003/04: 22³G, 201GF, 241G, 244GS, 243GF, 21²GF, 274GS,

	Starts	1st	2nd	3rd	Win & Pl
Hurdles	1	0	0	1	717
Chases	6	2	0	1	12649
Career Total	20	4	1	6	22822
108	7/03	Prth	3m	D(0-120)HCh	GD £6695
106	6/03	Hexm	2m4f110yE(0-110)HCh	G-F £4004
103	11/01	Ayr	2m5f110yD(0-110)HCh	GD £4251
100	1/00	Muss	2m	H NHF	SFT £1599

Total win prize-money £16550

Going:	Sf: 0-0 GS: 0-2 Gd: 1-2 GF: - Fm: 1-3
Distance:	2m/2m3: 0-0 2m4-2m7: 1-3 3m+: 1-4
Track:	LH: 1-5 RH: 1-2 Tight: 0-2 Gall: 0-0
Aids:	Bl: 0-0 Vi: 0-0 Tstrap: 0-0 Ckp: 2-6
Best Rating:	108 7/03 Strf 3m gd-sft Ch

Strong Tea (IRE)

13-y-o b g Electric-Cutty Sark (Strong Gale)
Miss S Waugh M R Lilley

Placings:2   **(4761)**
2003/04: 25²S,

	Starts	1st	2nd	3rd	Win & Pl
Chases	1	0	1	0	652
Career Total	1	0	1	0	652

Going:	Sf: 0-1 GS: 0-0 Gd: 0-0 GF: - Fm: 0-0
Distance:	2m/2m3: 0-0 2m4-2m7: 0-0 3m+: 0-1
Track:	LH: 0-0 RH: 0-1 Tight: 0-0 Gall: 0-0
Aids:	Bl: 0-0 Vi: 0-0 Tstrap: 0-0 Ckp: 0-0
Best Rating:	76 4/04 Towc 3m1f soft Ch

Strongtrooper (IRE)
109   **109**

9-y-o b g Doubletour (USA)-Moss Gale (Strong Gale)
O Sherwood Munro, Milne, Hoddell, Robertson

Placings:4/10/FPF341F/6-321U0F2P   **(2782)**
2003/04: 24³GF, 25²G, 22¹G, 22UG, 24⁹G, 24FG, 20²F, 21PG,

	Starts	1st	2nd	3rd	Win & Pl
Chases	8	1	2	1	7828
Career Total	19	3	2	2	16178
107	6/03	MRas	2m6f110yE(0-105)HCh	GD £4270
89	4/02	Uttx	2m5f	E Ch	G-S £4264
106	11/00	Ludl	2m5f	E Hdl	GD £2723

Total win prize-money £11258

Going:	Sf: 0-0 GS: 0-0 Gd: 1-6 GF: - Fm: 0-2
Distance:	2m/2m3: 0-0 2m4-2m7: 1-4 3m+: 0-4
Track:	LH: 0-4 RH: 1-4 Tight: 1-6 Gall: 0-0
Aids:	Bl: 0-0 Vi: 0-0 Tstrap: 0-0 Ckp: 0-0
Best Rating:	109 12/03 Leic 2m4f110y firm Ch

Moderate chaser; stays three miles; acts on good ground.

Struggles Glory (IRE)

13-y-o b g Kamehameha (USA)-Another Struggle (Cheval)
D C Robinson D C Robinson

Placings:11/2/2/41F/114/56100B/P   **(0519)**
2003/04: 28PG,

	Starts	1st	2nd	3rd	Win & Pl
Chases	1	0	0	0	
Career Total	17	6	2	0	43691
139	1/02	Winc	3m1f110yC(0-135)HCh	G-S £8580
139	1/01	Kemp	3m	D(0-125)HCh	SFT £7247
127	12/00	Kemp	2m4f110yD(0-120)HCh	G-S £14950
100	3/00	Plum	3m2f	H Ch	GD £1141
118	4/97	Hntg	3m1f	H Ch	GD £1141
110	4/97	Asct	3m110y	H Ch	G-F £2879

Total win prize-money £36346

Going:	Sf: 0-0 GS: 0-0 Gd: 0-1 GF: - Fm: 0-0
Distance:	2m/2m3: 0-0 2m4-2m7: 0-0 3m+: 0-0
Track:	LH: 0-1 RH: 0-0 Tight: 0-1 Gall: 0-0
Aids:	Bl: 0-0 Vi: 0-0 Tstrap: 0-0 Ckp: 0-0
Best Rating:	139 1/02 Winc 3m1f110y gd-sft Ch

Sturm Und Drang

99(95h)   (91 h)**91**

10-y-o ch g Selkirk (USA)-Historiette (Chief's Crown (USA))
C J Down B Reeder

Placings:*0006/02/652*-0P232123   (1303)
2003/04: 16⁶GF, 16⁶F, 17²GF, 16³G, 16²GS, 16¹GF, 16²GF, 16³GF,

	Starts	1st	2nd	3rd	Win & Pl
Hurdles	3	0	1	0	1508
Chases	5	1	2	2	8405
Career Total	17	1	5	2	11881
91	8/03 NAbb	2m110y E Ch		G-F	£5164
		Total win prize-money £5165			

Going:	Sf: 0-0 GS: 0-1 Gd: 0-1 GF: - Fm: 1-6
Distance:	2m/2m3: 1-8 2m4-2m7: 0-0 3m+: 0-0
Track:	LH: 1-8 RH: 0-0 Tight: 1-4 Gall: 0-0
Aids:	Bl: 0-1 Vi: 0-0 Tstrap: 0-0 Ckp: 0-0
Best Rating:	91 9/03 NAbb 2m110y gd-fm Ch

Modest, lightly-raced hurdler; let down by his jumping in a couple of outings over fences for Jimmy Frost summer 2002; jumped better on return to fences when well beaten third at Worcester in July 2003; benefitted from the fall of the favourite when lucky winner at Newton Abbot in August; runner-up in first-time blinkers at the same venue next time; suited by a sound surface; best at 2m.

Stutter

89   **99**

6-y-o ch h Polish Precedent (USA)-Bright Spells (Salse (USA))
John G Carr J Stanley

Placings:0/0050-450552121   (4679a)
2003/04: 16⁴GY, 17⁵G, 17⁰G, 16⁵G, 16⁵HY, 16²SH, 16¹GY, 16²S, 16¹YS,

	Starts	1st	2nd	3rd	Win & Pl
Hurdles	9	2	2	0	14386
Career Total	14	2	2	0	14386
99	4/04 Tram	2m	(81-109)HHdl	Y-S	£6569
88	2/04 Thur	2m	(70-95)HHdl	G-Y	£4866
		Total win prize-money £11435			

Going:	Sf: 0-2 GS: 0-0 Gd: 0-3 GF: - Fm: 0-0
Distance:	2m/2m3: 2-9 2m4-2m7: 0-0 3m+: 0-0
Track:	LH: 0-2 RH: 1-3 Tight: 0-2 Gall: 0-0
Aids:	Bl: 0-0 Vi: 0-0 Tstrap: 0-0 Ckp: 0-1
Best Rating:	99 4/04 Tram 2m yld-sft Hdl

Stylish Prince

4-y-o b g Polar Prince (IRE)-Simply Style (Bairn (USA))
J G M O'Shea Gary Roberts

Placings:P   (1007)
2003/04: 17⁰G,

	Starts	1st	2nd	3rd	Win & Pl
Hurdles	1	0	0	0	0
Career Total	1	0	0	0	0

Going:	Sf: 0-0 GS: 0-0 Gd: 0-1 GF: - Fm: 0-0
Distance:	2m/2m3: 0-1 2m4-2m7: 0-0 3m+: 0-0
Track:	LH: 0-1 RH: 0-0 Tight: 0-1 Gall: 0-0
Aids:	Bl: 0-0 Vi: 0-0 Tstrap: 0-0 Ckp: 0-0

Suaverof (IRE)

87   (110h)**73**

9-y-o ch g Suave Dancer (USA)-Mild Intrigue (USA) (Sir Ivor)
J Rudge Tom Hayes

Placings:4/3P31122P/P0P   (4570)
2003/04: 24⁵GF, 25⁰G, 24⁵GS,

	Starts	1st	2nd	3rd	Win & Pl
Chases	3	0	0	0	
Career Total	12	2	2	2	7724
110	6/01 Worc	3m	E Hdl	GD	£2562
110	6/01 Worc	2m4f	E Hdl	G-F	£2597
		Total win prize-money £5159			

Going:	Sf: 0-0 GS: 0-1 Gd: 0-1 GF: - Fm: 0-1
Distance:	2m/2m3: 0-0 2m4-2m7: 0-0 3m+: 0-3
Track:	LH: 0-1 RH: 0-2 Tight: 0-2 Gall: 0-1
Aids:	Bl: 0-0 Vi: 0-0 Tstrap: 0-3 Ckp: 0-0
Best Rating:	110 8/01 Sthl 2m4f110y gd-fm Hdl

Sud Bleu (FR)

119   **140**

6-y-o b g Pistolet Bleu (IRE)-Sudaka (FR) (Garde Royale)
P F Nicholls Barry Marshall & Terry Warner

Placings:043200/13204355-2200000   (4643)
2003/04: 16²GS, 16²S, 17⁰GS, 16⁹G, 16⁰S, 21⁰G, 24⁰G,

	Starts	1st	2nd	3rd	Win & Pl
Hurdles	7	0	2	0	26873
Career Total	21	1	4	3	48071
121	10/02 Extr	2m1f	D Hdl	GD	£4329
		Total win prize-money £4329			

Going:	Sf: 0-2 GS: 0-2 Gd: 0-3 GF: - Fm: 0-0
Distance:	2m/2m3: 0-5 2m4-2m7: 0-1 3m+: 0-1
Track:	LH: 0-5 RH: 0-2 Tight: 0-1 Gall: 0-4
Aids:	Bl: 0-0 Vi: 0-0 Tstrap: 0-0 Ckp: 0-0
Best Rating:	140 12/03 Asct 2m110y soft Hdl

Useful hurdler; ex-French; always travels well but does not see his race out; has had an operation to work on his breathing; just about stays two miles and acts on soft ground, but looks best on good; very hard to win with.

Sudden Shock (GER)

(106h)   (150h)**139**

9-y-o br g Motley (USA)-Santalina (Relko)
Jonjo O'Neill Darren C Mercer

Placings:11/312212/122216126/06PP12/FF34210-0P   (2595)
2003/04: 25⁰G, 29⁰G,

	Starts	1st	2nd	3rd	Win & Pl
Hurdles	1	0	0	0	0
Chases	1	0	0	0	0
Career Total	32	9	9	2	184885
139	3/03 Chel	4m	B Ch	GD	£26100
134	4/02 Aint	3m110y	A HHdl	GD	£23200
11/00	Siro	2m4f	Hdl	HVY	£16266
9/00	Maia	2m4f110y	Hdl	GD	£35785
5/00	Badn	2m4f165y	Hdl	HVY	£9677
11/99	Turi	2m2f	Hdl	SFT	£10935
8/99	Gels	2m1f	Hdl	SFT	£2708
4/99	Gels	2m	Hdl	HVY	£2166
3/99	Gels	2m	Hdl	HVY	£2166
		Total win prize-money £129003			

Going:	Sf: 0-0 GS: 0-0 Gd: 0-2 GF: - Fm: 0-0
Distance:	2m/2m3: 0-0 2m4-2m7: 0-0 3m+: 0-2

Track / Best Rating (Sudden Shock top-right)

Track:	LH: 0-1 RH: 0-1 Tight: 0-0 Gall: 0-0
Aids:	Bl: 0-0 Vi: 0-0 Tstrap: 0-0 Ckp: 0-0
Best Rating:	148 4/02 Sand 3m good Hdl

Very useful chaser; former smart hurdler; successful for the first time over fences in National Hunt Challenge Cup at Cheltenham in 2003; held in the Scottish National next time; stays four miles; acts on good ground and softer.

Suggest

110   **91**

9-y-o b g Midyan (USA)-Awham (USA) (Lear Fan (USA))
W Storey Mrs M Tindale

Placings:066/03110025/01110PP/35/P20401P0   (4617)
2003/04: 24⁵G, 25²GF, 24⁰GF, 25⁴G, 27⁰GS, 27¹F, 24⁵HY, 27⁰G,

	Starts	1st	2nd	3rd	Win & Pl
Hurdles	8	1	1	0	4746
Career Total	28	4	2	1	19991
87	2/04 Muss	3m3f	F(0-100)HHdl	FRM	£2926
112	5/00 Ctml	3m2f	D(0-125)HHdl	GD	£4170
106	5/00 Hexm	2m4f110yE(0-115)HHdl	GD	£2039
87	5/00 Hexm	2m4f110yD(0-125)HHdl	G-F	£3230
107	2/00 Newc	3m	F(0-110)HHdl	SFT	£2023
93	1/00 Sedg	2m5f110yE(0-115)HHdl	SFT	£2380
		Total win prize-money £16770			

Going:	Sf: 0-1 GS: 0-1 Gd: 0-3 GF: - Fm: 1-3
Distance:	2m/2m3: 0-0 2m4-2m7: 0-0 3m+: 1-8
Track:	LH: 0-6 RH: 1-1 Tight: 0-4 Gall: 0-1
Aids:	Bl: 0-0 Vi: 0-0 Tstrap: 0-0 Ckp: 0-0
Best Rating:	112 5/00 Ctml 3m2f good Hdl

Modest staying hurdler; lightly-raced of late; stays really well; suited by a sound surface.

Sulagh Run

10-y-o b g Sula Bula-Brackagh Run (Deep Run)
R Nixon G R S Nixon

Placings:P6   (2786)
2003/04: 17⁵HY, 20⁶GF,

	Starts	1st	2nd	3rd	Win & Pl
Hurdles	2	0	0	0	0
Career Total	2	0	0	0	0

Going:	Sf: 0-1 GS: 0-0 Gd: 0-0 GF: - Fm: 0-1
Distance:	2m/2m3: 0-1 2m4-2m7: 0-1 3m+: 0-0
Track:	LH: 0-0 RH: 0-2 Tight: 0-1 Gall: 0-0
Aids:	Bl: 0-0 Vi: 0-0 Tstrap: 0-0 Ckp: 0-0

Sullane Storm (IRE)

             96

9-y-o b g Glacial Storm (USA)-Heather Point (Pollerton)
M C Pipe Sean Lucey

Placings:0U5433P/PPU011-PPP   (2420)
2003/04: 25⁵GF, 26⁵HY, 24⁵GS,

	Starts	1st	2nd	3rd	Win & Pl
Chases	3	0	0	0	
Career Total	16	2	0	2	9922
96	4/03 Chep	3m	E(0-110)HCh	G-F	£4221
96	3/03 Tntn	3m	F(0-90)Ch	HVY	£3430
		Total win prize-money £7652			

Going:	Sf: 0-1 GS: 0-1 Gd: 0-0 GF: - Fm: 0-1
Distance:	2m/2m3: 0-0 2m4-2m7: 0-0 3m+: 0-3
Track:	LH: 0-2 RH: 0-1 Tight: 0-0 Gall: 0-0
Aids:	Bl: 0-0 Vi: 0-0 Tstrap: 0-0 Ckp: 0-0
Best Rating:	106 12/01 Limk 2m6f heavy Ch

Moderate chaser; ex-irish; won a weakly contested contest at Taunton March 2003; all out to follow up at Chepstow on fast ground the following month; inclined to make mistakes; acts on soft ground.

Sully Shuffles (IRE)

114   (0c)**105**

9-y-o b g Broken Hearted-Green Legend (IRE) (Montekin)
M Todhunter (M A Barnes 13/1) Murphy's Law Partnership

Placings: 5/000000211/00/0022000BFP/100540001050P-F0404   (3937)
2003/04: 24FS, 17OGS, 23⁴GS, 21⁰GS, 20⁴GS,

	Starts	1st	2nd	3rd	Win & Pl
Hurdles	4	0	0	0	528
Chases	1	0	0	0	0
Career Total	40	4	3	0	21722
99	12/02	Navn	2m6f		(74-109)HHdl	SFT	£5503
95	5/02	Naas	2m4f		(0-123)HHdl	GD	£5926
88	4/00	DRoy	2m4f		(0-102)HHdl	G-F	£3091
79	3/00	DRoy	2m		(0-95)HHdl	G-Y	£2760
				Total win prize-money £17280

Going:	Sf: 0-1 GS: 0-4 Gd: 0-0 GF: - Fm: 0-0
Distance:	2m/2m3: 0-1 2m4-2m7: 0-2 3m+: 0-2
Track:	LH: 0-3 RH: 0-2 Tight: 0-1 Gall: 0-1
Aids:	Bl: 0-0 Vi: 0-0 Tstrap: 0-0 Ckp: 0-0
Best Rating:	105 2/04 Newc 2m4f gd-sft Hdl

Ex-Irish hurdler; stays 3m; acts in soft ground.

Sulphur Springs (IRE)

97   **105+**

12-y-o ch g Don't Forget Me-Short Wave (FR) (Trepan (FR))
M C Pipe P A D Scouller

Placings: 0/056P25/22F3P22/45533/066/1/PS1111161/30P-PP0   (4889)
2003/04: 28PG, 24PG, 20⁰GF,

	Starts	1st	2nd	3rd	Win & Pl
Chases	3	0	0	0	
Career Total	38	7	5	4	113669
145	4/02	Strf	2m4f		C(0-130)HCh	GD	£7124
140	9/01	MRas	2m6f110yC Ch			SFT	£7665
130	9/01	NAbb	3m2f110yD(0-120)HCh			G-F	£3997
130	7/01	Strf	3m		E(0-115)HCh	GD	£4920
135	6/01	MRas	2m6f110yE(0-105)HCh			G-F	£4160
121	6/01	Strf	3m		F(0-111)HCh	G-F	£1337
100	4/01	MRas	2m6f110yH Ch			G-S	£1266
				Total win prize-money £30471

Going:	Sf: 0-0 GS: 0-0 Gd: 0-2 GF: - Fm: 0-1
Distance:	2m/2m3: 0-0 2m4-2m7: 0-1 3m+: 0-2
Track:	LH: 0-2 RH: 0-1 Tight: 0-2 Gall: 0-1
Aids:	Bl: 0-0 Vi: 0-0 Tstrap: 0-3 Ckp: 0-1
Best Rating:	145 4/02 Strf 2m4f good Ch

Fair chaser; lightly raced nowadays; acts on most types of ground; stays three miles; usually tongue tied.

Summer Bounty

98   **95+**

8-y-o b g Lugana Beach-Tender Moment (IRE) (Caerleon (USA))
F Jordan Tim Powell

Placings: 55P/24/000/40F-13240   (2821)
2003/04: 16¹F, 16³GF, 19²GF, 16⁴G, 16⁰GF,

	Starts	1st	2nd	3rd	Win & Pl
Hurdles	5	1	1	1	5202

Career Total   16   1   2   1   6248
93   10/03   Towc   2m   F(0-100)HHdl   FRM   £4046
Total win prize-money £4046

Going:	Sf: 0-0 GS: 0-0 Gd: 0-1 GF: - Fm: 1-4
Distance:	2m/2m3: 1-4 2m4-2m7: 0-1 3m+: 0-0
Track:	LH: 0-0 RH: 1-5 Tight: 0-0 Gall: 0-0
Aids:	Bl: 0-0 Vi: 0-0 Tstrap: 0-0 Ckp: 0-0
Best Rating:	94 11/03 Hrfd 2m3f110y gd-fm Hdl

Summer In The Sun (IRE)

10-y-o ch g Shardari-Sacajawea (Tanfirion)
Mrs Edward Crow George Wilson

Placings: P/P   (0073)
2003/04: 24PS,

	Starts	1st	2nd	3rd	Win & Pl
Chases	1	0	0	0	
Career Total	2	0	0	0	

Going:	Sf: 0-1 GS: 0-0 Gd: 0-0 GF: - Fm: 0-0
Distance:	2m/2m3: 0-0 2m4-2m7: 0-0 3m+: 0-1
Track:	LH: 0-1 RH: 0-0 Tight: 0-1 Gall: 0-0
Aids:	Bl: 0-0 Vi: 0-0 Tstrap: 0-1 Ckp: 0-0

Summer Stock (USA)

96   **92+**

6-y-o b g Theatrical-Lake Placid (IRE) (Royal Academy (USA))
J A Supple Peter Botham

Placings: 36333   (2710)
2003/04: 16³G, 16⁶G, 16³G, 16³G, 16³GS,

	Starts	1st	2nd	3rd	Win & Pl
Hurdles	5	0	0	4	1375
Career Total	5	0	0	4	1375

Going:	Sf: 0-0 GS: 0-1 Gd: 0-3 GF: - Fm: 0-1
Distance:	2m/2m3: 0-5 2m4-2m7: 0-0 3m+: 0-0
Track:	LH: 0-4 RH: 0-1 Tight: 0-3 Gall: 0-2
Aids:	Bl: 0-0 Vi: 0-0 Tstrap: 0-5 Ckp: 0-0
Best Rating:	92 11/03 Fknm 2m good Hdl

Moderate novice hurdler; acts on any ground.

Summerwood Lilley

4-y-o b f Tragic Role (USA)-Celtic Lilley (Celtic Cone)
M R Hoad Mrs J E Taylor

Placings: P   (3752)
2003/04: 18PGS,

	Starts	1st	2nd	3rd	Win & Pl
NH Flat	1	0	0	0	
Career Total	1	0	0	0	

Going:	Sf: 0-0 GS: 0-1 Gd: 0-0 GF: - Fm: 0-0
Distance:	2m/2m3: 0-1 2m4-2m7: 0-0 3m+: 0-0
Track:	LH: 0-1 RH: 0-0 Tight: 0-1 Gall: 0-0
Aids:	Bl: 0-0 Vi: 0-0 Tstrap: 0-0 Ckp: 0-0

Sumthyne Special (IRE)

93   **74**

12-y-o b g Good Thyne (USA)-Condonstown Rose (Giolla Mear)
L Lungo J M Crichton

Placings: 2312/P6/4F2/2112FP1/PPP4   (4275)
2003/04: 20PG, 24FGS, 20PHY, 20⁴G,

	Starts	1st	2nd	3rd	Win & Pl
Hurdles	4	0	0	0	0
Career Total	20	4	5	1	13798
119	3/02	Kels	2m6f110yE Hdl			HVY	£3178
116	11/01	Carl	3m110y E Hdl			SFT	£2765
114	10/01	Carl	3m110y E Hdl			SFT	£2564
97	3/98	Carl	2m1f		H NHF		HVY	£1245
				Total win prize-money £9753

Going:	Sf: 0-1 GS: 0-1 Gd: 0-2 GF: - Fm: 0-0
Distance:	2m/2m3: 0-0 2m4-2m7: 0-3 3m+: 0-1
Track:	LH: 0-3 RH: 0-1 Tight: 0-0 Gall: 0-0
Aids:	Bl: 0-0 Vi: 0-0 Tstrap: 0-0 Ckp: 0-0
Best Rating:	119 3/02 Kels 2m6f110y heavy Hdl

Fair hurdler; lightly raced in recent seasons; stays three miles; acts on soft ground.

Sumut

91   **65+**

5-y-o b g Hamas (IRE)-Simaat (USA) (Mr Prospector (USA))
G A Swinbank Elsa Crankshaw & G Allan Ii

Placings: 0-6   (1480)
2003/04: 17⁶G,

	Starts	1st	2nd	3rd	Win & Pl
Hurdles	1	0	0	0	0
Career Total	2	0	0	0	0

Going:	Sf: 0-0 GS: 0-0 Gd: 0-1 GF: - Fm: 0-0
Distance:	2m/2m3: 0-1 2m4-2m7: 0-0 3m+: 0-0
Track:	LH: 0-1 RH: 0-0 Tight: 0-1 Gall: 0-0
Aids:	Bl: 0-0 Vi: 0-0 Tstrap: 0-0 Ckp: 0-0
Best Rating:	82 2/03 Ayr 2m gd-sft NHF

Sun Bird (IRE)

108   **113**

6-y-o ch g Prince Of Birds (USA)-Summer Fashion (Moorestyle)
R Allan Mrs R P Aggio

Placings: 2-23   (0382)
2003/04: 16²G, 18³G,

	Starts	1st	2nd	3rd	Win & Pl
Hurdles	2	0	1	1	4624
Career Total	3	0	2	1	5756

Going:	Sf: 0-0 GS: 0-0 Gd: 0-2 GF: - Fm: 0-0
Distance:	2m/2m3: 0-2 2m4-2m7: 0-0 3m+: 0-0
Track:	LH: 0-2 RH: 0-0 Tight: 0-2 Gall: 0-0
Aids:	Bl: 0-0 Vi: 0-0 Tstrap: 0-0 Ckp: 0-0
Best Rating:	113 5/03 Kels 2m2f good Hdl

Useful novice hurdler; good debut performance when runner-up at Kelso in November and has twice run well there since; effective at two miles; acts on fast ground.

Sun Cat (IRE)

101   **112+**

4-y-o br g Catrail (USA)-Susie Sunshine (IRE) (Waajib)

Mrs S J Smith (M J Polglase 1/5) Paul J Dixon

Placings:245210 (4625)
2003/04: 16²GF, 16⁴GS, 19⁵G, 16²S, 16¹GF, 16⁶G,

	Starts	1st	2nd	3rd	Win & Pl
Hurdles	6	1	2	0	7720
Career Total	6	1	2	0	**7720**
112 3/04 Ayr	2m	E Hdl		G-F	£3458
				Total win prize-money £3458	

Going:	Sf: 0-1 GS: 0-1 Gd: 0-2 GF: - Fm: 1-2
Distance:	**2m/2m3: 1-5** 2m4-2m7: 0-1 3m+: 0-0
Track:	**LH: 1-6** RH: 0-0 Tight: 0-1 Gall: 0-1
Aids:	Bl: 0-0 Vi: 0-0 Tstrap: 0-0 Ckp: 0-0
Best Rating:	112 3/04 Ayr 2m gd-fm Hdl

Modest juvenile hurdler; won uncompetitive novices' event at Ayr in March; should stay two and a half miles; acts well on a sound surface.

Sun Hill

4-y-o b g Robellino (USA)-Manhattan Sunset (USA) (El Gran Senor (USA))
M Blanshard Stanley Hinton

Placings:P (3329)
2003/04: 16⁰S,

	Starts	1st	2nd	3rd	Win & Pl
Hurdles	1	0	0	0	
Career Total	1	0	0	0	

Going:	Sf: 0-1 GS: 0-0 Gd: 0-0 GF: - Fm: 0-0
Distance:	2m/2m3: 0-1 2m4-2m7: 0-0 3m+: 0-0
Track:	LH: 0-1 RH: 0-0 Tight: 0-0 Gall: 0-1
Aids:	Bl: 0-0 Vi: 0-0 Tstrap: 0-0 Ckp: 0-0

Sun King

110 107

7-y-o ch g Zilzal (USA)-Opus One (Slip Anchor)
Mrs M Reveley The Mary Reveley Racing Club

Placings:4/21²S015/11232P0-3233406000 (4478)
2003/04: 16³GF, 16²GF, 16³G, 16³GS, 19⁴G, 16⁶G, 16⁶G, 24⁰G, 16⁶G, 20⁰HY,

	Starts	1st	2nd	3rd	Win & Pl
Hurdles	10	0	1	3	4369
Career Total	24	4	4	4	20306
86 5/02 Towc	2m	D Hdl		GD	£3150
107 5/02 Weth	2m	E Hdl		G-F	£2562
96 4/02 MRas	2m3f110yD Hdl			G-F	£3780
94 6/01 Worc	2m	H NHF		G-F	£1536
				Total win prize-money £11029	

Going:	Sf: 0-1 GS: 0-1 Gd: 0-6 GF: - Fm: 0-2
Distance:	2m/2m3: 0-7 2m4-2m7: 0-2 3m+: 0-1
Track:	LH: 0-3 RH: 0-7 Tight: 0-4 Gall: 0-3
Aids:	Bl: 0-0 Vi: 0-0 Tstrap: 0-0 Ckp: 0-0
Best Rating:	107 8/02 MRas 2m1f110y gd-sft Hdl

Moderate hurdler, effective on fast ground; stays two and a half miles, but effective at shorter.

Sun Lark

10-y-o b g Crested Lark-Sunylyn (Sunboy)
A D Old Mrs C Wilson

Placings:P (0350)
2003/04: 21⁰GF,

	Starts	1st	2nd	3rd	Win & Pl
Chases	1	0	0	0	
Career Total	1	0	0	0	

Sunburnt

10-y-o b g Henbit (USA)-Sunshine Gal (Alto Volante)
Miss J Houldey G Salter

Placings:45/05PP03/0P12/P34400P5/3 (0521)
2003/04: 24³G,

	Starts	1st	2nd	3rd	Win & Pl
Chases	1	0	0	1	563
Career Total	21	1	1	3	4873
86 8/00 Sthl	2m	F(0-100)HCh	G-F	£2707
			Total win prize-money £2707	

Going:	Sf: 0-0 GS: 0-0 Gd: 0-1 GF: - Fm: 0-0
Distance:	2m/2m3: 0-0 2m4-2m7: 0-0 3m+: 0-1
Track:	LH: 0-1 RH: 0-0 Tight: 0-1 Gall: 0-0
Aids:	Bl: 0-0 Vi: 0-0 Tstrap: 0-0 Ckp: 0-0
Best Rating:	102 2/99 Winc 2m gd-sft NHF

Hunter chaser; won back-to-back points spring 2003; springer in the market when third in 3m ladies hunter chase at Stratford; best on fast ground.

Sunczech (IRE)

14-y-o b m Sunyboy-Miss Prague (Mon Capitaine)
Mrs S S Harbour S C Clark

Placings:3/P/654-P4 (4298)
2003/04: 21⁶G, 23⁴G,

	Starts	1st	2nd	3rd	Win & Pl
Chases	2	0	0	0	170
Career Total	7	0	0	1	318

Going:	Sf: 0-0 GS: 0-0 Gd: 0-2 GF: - Fm: 0-0
Distance:	2m/2m3: 0-2 2m4-2m7: 0-1 3m+: 0-1
Track:	LH: 0-1 RH: 0-1 Tight: 0-0 Gall: 0-1
Aids:	Bl: 0-0 Vi: 0-0 Tstrap: 0-0 Ckp: 0-0
Best Rating:	85 2/99 Folk 2m5f gd-sft Ch

Sundance Sid (IRE)

(0c)65

8-y-o b g Phardante (FR)-The Kid's Sister (Black Minstrel)
V Y Gethin V Y Gethin

Placings:0PF0060/0-PP (0676)
2003/04: 16⁰GF, 16⁰GF,

	Starts	1st	2nd	3rd	Win & Pl
Hurdles	1	0	0	0	0
Chases	1	0	0	0	0
Career Total	10	0	0	0	0

Going:	Sf: 0-0 GS: 0-0 Gd: 0-0 GF: - Fm: 0-2
Distance:	2m/2m3: 0-2 2m4-2m7: 0-0 3m+: 0-1
Track:	LH: 0-2 RH: 0-0 Tight: 0-0 Gall: 0-1
Aids:	Bl: 0-0 Vi: 0-0 Tstrap: 0-1 Ckp: 0-0
Best Rating:	65 4/02 Extr 2m1f firm Hdl

Chases	1	0	0	0
Career Total	1	0	0	0

Sundawn Lady

95 86

6-y-o b m Faustus (USA)-Game Domino (Derring Rose)
C P Morlock Michael Padfield & Philip Dean

Placings:00225-63P (2288)
2003/04: 22⁶GF, 20³G, 22⁰G,

	Starts	1st	2nd	3rd	Win & Pl
Hurdles	3	0	0	1	380
Career Total	8	0	2	1	2781

Going:	Sf: 0-0 GS: 0-0 Gd: 0-2 GF: - Fm: 0-1
Distance:	2m/2m3: 0-0 2m4-2m7: 0-3 3m+: 0-0
Track:	LH: 0-1 RH: 0-2 Tight: 0-0 Gall: 0-0
Aids:	Bl: 0-0 Vi: 0-0 Tstrap: 0-0 Ckp: 0-0
Best Rating:	86 4/03 Strf 2m6f110y Hdl

Plating-class hurdler; appears suited by a sound surface; effective at around two miles six.

Sunday Habits (IRE)

102 88

10-y-o ch g Montelimar (USA)-Robertina (USA) (Roberto (USA))
D P Keane The It's My Job Partnership

Placings:400/0P05/1U-2222BP (0997)
2003/04: 26²GF, 25²GF, 24²GF, 26²GF, 26⁶GF, 24⁶G,

	Starts	1st	2nd	3rd	Win & Pl
Chases	6	0	4	0	5288
Career Total	15	1	4	0	8639
81 4/03 Plum	3m2f	F(0-95)HCh	G-F	£3159
			Total win prize-money £3159	

Going:	Sf: 0-0 GS: 0-0 Gd: 0-1 GF: - Fm: 0-5
Distance:	2m/2m3: 0-0 2m4-2m7: 0-0 3m+: 0-6
Track:	LH: 0-5 RH: 0-1 Tight: 0-2 Gall: 0-0
Aids:	Bl: 0-0 Vi: 0-1 Tstrap: 0-0 Ckp: 0-1
Best Rating:	88 6/03 Sthl 3m2f gd-fm Ch

Plating-class chaser; won weak Plumpton event on British debut in April 2003 after showing limited ability in Ireland; stays three miles two.

Sunday Rain (USA)

106(110h) (102h)117

7-y-o b g Summer Squall (USA)-Oxava (FR) (Antheus (USA))
Miss Lucinda V Russell Peter K Dale Ltd

Placings:233P0/3524001/331230305-43311422F (4686)
2003/04: 18⁴G, 17³G, 16³G, 16¹G, 20¹G, 20⁴GF, 20²G, 17²G, 17²FG,

	Starts	1st	2nd	3rd	Win & Pl
Hurdles	1	0	0	0	518
Chases	8	2	2	2	16158
Career Total	30	4	5	9	34493
117 8/03 Bang	2m4f110yD Ch	GD	£5518
97 7/03 Prth	2m	D Ch	GD	£5343
97 6/02 Hexm	2m110y D Hdl	G-F	£3472
98 4/02 Hexm	2m110y E Hdl	G-F	£2604
			Total win prize-money £16938	

Going:	Sf: 0-0 GS: 0-0 Gd: 2-8 GF: - Fm: 0-1
Distance:	2m/2m3: 1-6 2m4-2m7: 1-3 3m+: 0-0
Track:	LH: 1-5 RH: 1-4 **Tight: 1-5** Gall: 0-0
Aids:	Bl: 0-0 Vi: 0-0 Tstrap: 0-0 Ckp: 0-0
Best Rating:	117 11/03 Kels 2m1f good Ch

Modest novice chaser/fair handicap hurdler; won back to back chases in the summer of 2003; best at around two miles; best on ground good or faster.

Sundays Sarah

6-y-o b m Sea Raven (IRE)-Sundays Off (Dubassoff (USA))
M A Barnes S C Brown

Placings:0   (0897)
2003/04: 17⁰GF,

	Starts	1st	2nd	3rd	Win & Pl
Hurdles	1	0	0	0	
Career Total	1	0	0	0	

Going:	Sf: 0-0 GS: 0-0 Gd: 0-0 GF: - Fm: 0-1
Distance:	2m/2m3: 0-1 2m4-2m7: 0-0 3m+: 0-0
Track:	LH: 0-1 RH: 0-0 Tight: 0-1 Gall: 0-0
Aids:	Bl: 0-0 Vi: 0-0 Tstrap: 0-0 Ckp: 0-0

Sundial

5-y-o ch m Cadeaux Genereux-Ruby Setting (Gorytus (USA))
A E Jones Gregory Molen

Placings:P   (1361)
2003/04: 16⁷GF,

	Starts	1st	2nd	3rd	Win & Pl
Hurdles	1	0	0	0	
Career Total	1	0	0	0	

Going:	Sf: 0-0 GS: 0-0 Gd: 0-0 GF: - Fm: 0-1
Distance:	2m/2m3: 0-1 2m4-2m7: 0-0 3m+: 0-0
Track:	LH: 0-1 RH: 0-0 Tight: 0-0 Gall: 0-0
Aids:	Bl: 0-0 Vi: 0-0 Tstrap: 0-0 Ckp: 0-0

Sungates (IRE)

103   **114+**

8-y-o ch g Glacial Storm (USA)-Live It Up (Le Coq D'Or)
C Tinkler Team George Ii

Placings:2/65-6101   (4656)
2003/04: 21⁶GS, 22¹HY, 26⁹GS, 26¹G,

	Starts	1st	2nd	3rd	Win & Pl
Hurdles	4	2	0	0	7739
Career Total	7	2	1	0	8298
114 4/04 Hrfd		3m2f	E(0-105)HHdl	GD	£4182
95 1/04 Folk		2m6f110yE Hdl		HVY	£3556

Total win prize-money £7739

Going:	Sf: 1-1 GS: 0-2 Gd: 1-1 GF: - Fm: 0-0
Distance:	2m/2m3: 0-0 2m4-2m7: 1-2 3m+: 1-2
Track:	LH: 0-1 RH: 2-3 Tight: 1-2 Gall: 0-1
Aids:	Bl: 0-0 Vi: 0-0 Tstrap: 0-0 Ckp: 0-0
Best Rating:	114 4/04 Hrfd 3m2f good Hdl

Fair hurdler; caused a shock when winning a modest novice event at Folkestone in January 2004; stays two miles six; acts on heavy ground.

Sunley Future (IRE)

94f   **88+f**

5-y-o b g Broken Hearted-The Wicked Chicken (IRE) (Saher)
N J Henderson A K Collins

Placings:006   (4866)
2003/04: 16⁸GS, 16⁰S, 16⁵S,

	Starts	1st	2nd	3rd	Win & Pl
NH Flat	3	0	0	0	0
Career Total	3	0	0	0	0

Going:	Sf: 0-2 GS: 0-1 Gd: 0-0 GF: - Fm: 0-0
Distance:	2m/2m3: 0-3 2m4-2m7: 0-0 3m+: 0-0
Track:	LH: 0-2 RH: 0-1 Tight: 0-0 Gall: 0-0
Aids:	Bl: 0-0 Vi: 0-0 Tstrap: 0-0 Ckp: 0-0
Best Rating:	88 2/04 Kemp 2m gd-sft NHF

Sunlit Boy

72

12-y-o ch g Ardross-Sunlit River (Roi Soleil)
J J Bridger J J Bridger

Placings:5PP/P3P0/0P-06P   (3313)
2003/04: 16⁰G, 26⁶G, 22ᴾHY,

	Starts	1st	2nd	3rd	Win & Pl
Chases	3	0	0	0	0
Career Total	12	0	0	1	650

Going:	Sf: 0-1 GS: 0-0 Gd: 0-0 GF: - Fm: 0-0
Distance:	2m/2m3: 0-1 2m4-2m7: 0-1 3m+: 0-1
Track:	LH: 0-0 RH: 0-1 Tight: 0-3 Gall: 0-0
Aids:	Bl: 0-1 Vi: 0-0 Tstrap: 0-0 Ckp: 0-0
Best Rating:	92 12/98 Wwck 2m soft NHF

Sunne Lord (IRE)

97   **89**

7-y-o b g Mister Lord (USA)-Happy Party (Invited (USA))
A King Mrs S Warren

Placings:000-4564P   (4343)
2003/04: 19⁴S, 22⁵GS, 21⁶GS, 20⁴GS, 21ᴾGS,

	Starts	1st	2nd	3rd	Win & Pl
Hurdles	5	0	0	0	392
Career Total	8	0	0	0	392

Going:	Sf: 0-1 GS: 0-4 Gd: 0-0 GF: - Fm: 0-0
Distance:	2m/2m3: 0-0 2m4-2m7: 0-5 3m+: 0-0
Track:	LH: 0-3 RH: 0-2 Tight: 0-2 Gall: 0-0
Aids:	Bl: 0-0 Vi: 0-0 Tstrap: 0-0 Ckp: 0-0
Best Rating:	94 2/04 Kemp 2m5f gd-sft Hdl

Sunny Native (IRE)

101   **88+**

7-y-o ch m Be My Native (USA)-My Sunny South (Strong Gale)
Mrs H Dalton (W J Burke 25/9) Thomas O'Mahony

Placings:ʃ606/04P-242015   (2480)
2003/04: 20²F, 20⁴G, 20²GF, 22⁰G, 21¹GF, 19⁵GF,

	Starts	1st	2nd	3rd	Win & Pl
Hurdles	6	1	2	0	5819
Career Total	13	2	2	0	9755
78 11/03 Ludl		2m5f	E Hdl	G-F	£3376
106 6/01 Baln		2m	NHF	GD	£3616

Total win prize-money £6994

Going:	Sf: 0-0 GS: 0-0 Gd: 0-2 GF: - Fm: 1-4
Distance:	2m/2m3: 0-3 2m4-2m7: 1-6 3m+: 0-0
Track:	LH: 0-2 RH: 1-3 Tight: 0-1 Gall: 0-0
Aids:	Bl: 0-0 Vi: 0-0 Tstrap: 1-2 Ckp: 0-1
Best Rating:	106 6/01 Baln 2m good NHF

Bumper winner in Ireland who has shown ability at up to two and a half miles over hurdles, including on first start in Britain in October 2003; acts on fast and good ground.

Sunnyarjun

80   **65**

6-y-o ch g Afzal-Hush Tina (Tina's Pet)
J C Tuck The Japica Partnership

Placings:000-00   (0992)
2003/04: 16⁰GF, 19⁶G,

	Starts	1st	2nd	3rd	Win & Pl
Hurdles	2	0	0	0	
Career Total	5	0	0	0	

Going:	Sf: 0-0 GS: 0-0 Gd: 0-0 GF: - Fm: 0-1
Distance:	2m/2m3: 0-2 2m4-2m7: 0-0 3m+: 0-0
Track:	LH: 0-0 RH: 0-1 Tight: 0-0 Gall: 0-0
Aids:	Bl: 0-0 Vi: 0-0 Tstrap: 0-0 Ckp: 0-0
Best Rating:	73 1/03 Kemp 2m gd-sft NHF

Sunnycliff

101   **90**

11-y-o b g Dancing High-Nicolini (Nicholas Bill)
Miss R Brewis R Brewis

Placings:1/3/PP4U66P   (3882)
2003/04: 22ᴾG, 20ᴾG, 16⁴GF, 20ᵁGF, 25⁶GS, 20⁶GF, 24ᴾG,

	Starts	1st	2nd	3rd	Win & Pl
Chases	7	0	0	0	0
Career Total	9	1	0	1	2718
102 5/00 Prth		2m4f110yH Ch		G-S	£2060

Total win prize-money £2061

Going:	Sf: 0-0 GS: 0-1 Gd: 0-3 GF: - Fm: 0-3
Distance:	2m/2m3: 0-1 2m4-2m7: 0-4 3m+: 0-2
Track:	LH: 0-5 RH: 0-2 Tight: 0-4 Gall: 0-0
Aids:	Bl: 0-0 Vi: 0-0 Tstrap: 0-7 Ckp: 0-0
Best Rating:	102 5/00 Prth 2m4f110y gd-sft Ch

Plating-class chaser; suited by two and a half miles; wears a tongue tie.

Sunnyland

96   **80**

5-y-o b m Sovereign Water (FR)-Quadrapol (Pollerton)
P J Hobbs C D Harrison

Placings:40550   (4712)
2003/04: 16⁴G, 16⁰GS, 19⁵G, 22⁵GS, 24⁰G,

	Starts	1st	2nd	3rd	Win & Pl
NH Flat	2	0	0	0	0
Hurdles	3	0	0	0	0
Career Total	5	0	0	0	0

Going:	Sf: 0-0 GS: 0-2 Gd: 0-3 GF: - Fm: 0-0
Distance:	2m/2m3: 0-3 2m4-2m7: 0-1 3m+: 0-1
Track:	LH: 0-1 RH: 0-4 Tight: 0-0 Gall: 0-0
Aids:	Bl: 0-0 Vi: 0-0 Tstrap: 0-0 Ckp: 0-0
Best Rating:	83 1/04 Hayd 2m good NHF

Sunnyside Royale (IRE)

105   **90+**

5-y-o b g Ali-Royal (IRE)-Kuwah (IRE) (Be My Guest (USA))
R Bastiman (M W Easterby 21/6) S Durkin, P Earnshaw & J Greenan

Placings:00-P0PF153   (4178)
2003/04: 16ᴾGS, 20⁰G, 25ᴾGS, 20ᶠGF, 17¹GS, 17⁵GS, 16³G,

	Starts	1st	2nd	3rd	Win & Pl
Hurdles	7	1	0	1	3297

Career Total	9	1	0	1	3297

89 2/04 Sedg 2m1f F(0-95)HHdl G-S £2730
Total win prize-money £2730

Track:	LH: 0-0 RH: 1-6 Tight: 1-3 Gall: 0-0
Aids:	Bl: 0-0 Vi: 0-0 Tstrap: 0-1 Ckp: 0-0
Best Rating:	85 4/04 Tntn 3m gd-fm Ch

Winning pointer; relished the step up to three miles when winning weak novices' handicap chase at Taunton April 2004; acts on a sound surface.

Sunshine Boy

81(107h)   (94h)62

8-y-o b g Cadeaux Genereux-Sahara Baladee (USA) (Shadeed (USA))
Miss E C Lavelle David Cliff And Philippa Clunes

Placings:P0/51122/26/P3P-30   (0589)
2003/04: 21³GF, 20⁶GF,

	Starts	1st	2nd	3rd	Win & Pl
Hurdles	1	0	0	1	656
Chases	1	0	0	0	0
Career Total	14	2	3	2	9720

100 6/00 Fknm 2m7f110yF(0-100)HHdl GD £2671
93 5/00 Worc 2m4f F(0-100)HHdl GD £2065
Total win prize-money £4737

Going:	Sf: 0-0 GS: 0-0 Gd: 0-0 GF: - Fm: 0-2
Distance:	2m/2m3: 0-2 2m4-2m7: 0-2 3m+: 0-0
Track:	LH: 0-1 RH: 0-1 Tight: 0-0 Gall: 0-0
Aids:	Bl: 0-0 Vi: 0-0 Tstrap: 0-0 Ckp: 0-0
Best Rating:	100 7/01 Worc 3m good Hdl

Moderate hurdler; stays 3m; suited by a decent surface.

Super Blue (IRE)

85   62

7-y-o b m Supreme Leader-Tip Marie (IRE) (Celio Rufo)
Mrs S D Williams Mrs Angela Tincknell

Placings:06P-05   (4812)
2003/04: 19⁰G, 16⁵G,

	Starts	1st	2nd	3rd	Win & Pl
Hurdles	2	0	0	0	0
Career Total	5	0	0	0	0

Going:	Sf: 0-0 GS: 0-0 Gd: 0-2 GF: - Fm: 0-0
Distance:	2m/2m3: 0-2 2m4-2m7: 0-0 3m+: 0-0
Track:	LH: 0-1 RH: 0-1 Tight: 0-0 Gall: 0-0
Aids:	Bl: 0-0 Vi: 0-0 Tstrap: 0-0 Ckp: 0-0
Best Rating:	75 10/02 Extr 2m1f good NHF

Super Boston

58f   3f

4-y-o b g Saddlers' Hall (IRE)-Nasowas (IRE) (Cardinal Flower)
R D E Woodhouse M K Oldham

Placings:00   (3766)
2003/04: 16⁹S, 17⁰GS,

	Starts	1st	2nd	3rd	Win & Pl
NH Flat	2	0	0	0	
Career Total	2	0	0	0	

Going:	Sf: 0-1 GS: 0-1 Gd: 0-0 GF: - Fm: 0-0
Distance:	2m/2m3: 0-2 2m4-2m7: 0-0 3m+: 0-0
Track:	LH: 0-2 RH: 0-0 Tight: 0-1 Gall: 0-0
Aids:	Bl: 0-1 Vi: 0-0 Tstrap: 0-0 Ckp: 0-0
Best Rating:	3 2/04 Weth 2m soft NHF

| Career Total | 9 | 1 | 0 | 1 | 3297 |

Going:	Sf: 0-0 GS: 1-4 Gd: 0-2 GF: - Fm: 0-1
Distance:	2m/2m3: 1-4 2m4-2m7: 0-2 3m+: 0-1
Track:	LH: 1-6 RH: 0-1 Tight: 1-3 Gall: 0-1
Aids:	Bl: 0-0 Vi: 0-0 Tstrap: 1-7 Ckp: 0-0
Best Rating:	89 3/04 Donc 2m110y good Hdl

Plating-class hurdler; reportedly suffers from a breathing problem; winner at Sedgefield in February; effective over two miles but suited by farther.

Sunray

100   127

4-y-o b g Spectrum (IRE)-Sharkashka (IRE) (Shardari)
Evan Williams Mr Rose Mr Hague Mr Spierling Mr Powell

Placings:44342P160   (3711)
2003/04: 16⁴G, 17⁴G, 17³GF, 16⁴GF, 16²GF, 16⁶GF, 16¹S, 17⁶GS, 16⁶S,

	Starts	1st	2nd	3rd	Win & Pl
Hurdles	9	1	1	1	21875
Career Total	9	1	1	1	21875

127 12/03 Chep 2m110y A Hdl SFT £19140
Total win prize-money £19140

Going:	Sf: 1-2 GS: 0-1 Gd: 0-2 GF: - Fm: 0-4
Distance:	2m/2m3: 1-9 2m4-2m7: 0-0 3m+: 0-0
Track:	LH: 1-8 RH: 0-1 Tight: 0-3 Gall: 0-1
Aids:	Bl: 0-0 Vi: 0-2 Tstrap: 0-0 Ckp: 0-0
Best Rating:	127 12/03 Chep 2m110y soft Hdl

Useful juvenile hurdler; ran best race to date over hurdles when scoring at 40/1 in a Grade One at Chepstow; effective over two miles; acts on soft ground; has worn a visor.

Sunset King (USA)

78   67

4-y-o b c King Of Kings (IRE)-Sunset River (USA) (Northern Flagship (USA))
J C Fox (S Kirk 3/9) B J Weddle

Placings:000   (4489)
2003/04: 16⁰G, 16⁰GF, 16⁰G,

	Starts	1st	2nd	3rd	Win & Pl
Hurdles	3	0	0	0	
Career Total	3	0	0	0	

Going:	Sf: 0-0 GS: 0-0 Gd: 0-2 GF: - Fm: 0-1
Distance:	2m/2m3: 0-3 2m4-2m7: 0-0 3m+: 0-0
Track:	LH: 0-2 RH: 0-1 Tight: 0-2 Gall: 0-0
Aids:	Bl: 0-0 Vi: 0-0 Tstrap: 0-0 Ckp: 0-0
Best Rating:	67 3/04 Kemp 2m good Hdl

Sunshan

103   85+

8-y-o b g Anshan-Kyrenia Sunset (CYP) (Lucky Look (CYP))
R J Hodges (T Long 14/5) Unity Farm Holiday Centre Ltd

Placings:60/6565-P34641   (4855)
2003/04: 19⁵GF, 16³G, 16⁴G, 16⁶GS, 16⁴G, 24¹GF,

	Starts	1st	2nd	3rd	Win & Pl
Chases	6	1	0	1	5419
Career Total	12	1	0	1	5419

85 4/04 Tntn 3m F(0-90)HCh £3835
Total win prize-money £3835

Going:	Sf: 0-0 GS: 0-1 Gd: 0-3 GF: - Fm: 1-2
Distance:	2m/2m3: 0-4 2m4-2m7: 0-1 3m+: 1-1

Super Fellow (IRE)

105   (114h)119

10-y-o b g Shy Groom (USA)-Killough (Lord Gayle (USA))
Denis P Murphy R & P Syndicate

Placings:0504323/12643354/211F/02006/53012154-00203004   (4834)
2003/04: 24⁰HY, 20⁰GF, 19²GY, 24⁰GY, 24³S, 24⁰S, 24⁰G, 26⁴GF,

	Starts	1st	2nd	3rd	Win & Pl
Chases	8	0	1	1	3993
Career Total	40	5	6	6	44249

112 11/02 Chel 3m110y B Ch GD £13764
118 8/02 NAbb 3m2f110yD Ch G-F £4678
120 6/99 Navn 2m4f HHdl G-F £4603
122 5/99 Cotml 2m1f110yD Hdl GD £3160
103 5/98 Dund 2m135y Hdl G-Y £1935
Total win prize-money £28143

Going:	Sf: 0-3 GS: 0-0 Gd: 0-1 GF: - Fm: 0-2
Distance:	2m/2m3: 0-1 2m4-2m7: 0-1 3m+: 0-6
Track:	LH: 0-7 RH: 0-0 Tight: 0-0 Gall: 0-2
Aids:	Bl: 0-2 Vi: 0-0 Tstrap: 0-3 Ckp: 0-3
Best Rating:	131 11/00 Naas 2m sft-hvy Hdl

Modest Irish-trained chaser; stays an extended three and a quarter miles; prefers a sound surface; sometimes wears a tongue tie; sometimes blinkered.

Super Lucky (IRE)

100   (0c)103

8-y-o b m Moscow Society (USA)-Ballela Maid (Boreen (FR))
J J Lambe J P Kearney

Placings:00²6P00/P33000⁰P0-123P   (1142)
2003/04: 20¹G, 17²GF, 21³GF, 24⁶GF,

	Starts	1st	2nd	3rd	Win & Pl
Hurdles	4	1	1	1	4848
Career Total	19	1	2	3	9468

86 7/03 Prth 2m4f110yE Hdl GD £3367
Total win prize-money £3367

Going:	Sf: 0-0 GS: 0-0 Gd: 1-1 GF: - Fm: 0-3
Distance:	2m/2m3: 0-1 2m4-2m7: 1-2 3m+: 0-0
Track:	LH: 0-2 RH: 1-2 Tight: 0-2 Gall: 0-0
Aids:	Bl: 0-0 Vi: 0-0 Tstrap: 0-0 Ckp: 0-0
Best Rating:	103 11/01 Navn 2m2f yield Hdl

Irish-trained novice hurdler; won at Perth in July 2003; acts on good and fast.

Super Nomad

110(103h)   (112h)122

9-y-o b g Nomadic Way (USA)-Super Sue (Lochnager)
M W Easterby Brian Hutchinson & David & Steven Dudley

Placings:245/05315136123/214P/1F452123/5FP2422-3323022R0   (4843)
2003/04: 16³G, 20³G, 16²S, 20³G, 16⁶S, 19²GS, 16²GS, 21⁸G, 16⁶G,

	Starts	1st	2nd	3rd	Win & Pl
Chases	9	0	3	3	10121
Career Total	42	6	11	7	54013

122 2/02 Newc 2m110y E Ch SFT £3055
106 11/01 Kels 2m1f E Ch GD £3445
128 11/00 Aint 2m4f C(0-135)HHdl G-S £10871
121 3/00 Newc 2m4f D(0-110)HHdl SFT £3256
112 1/00 Donc 2m110y F(0-100)HHdl G-F £2138
107 12/99 Newc 2m4f E Hdl SFT £2690
Total win prize-money £25458

Going:	Sf: 0-2 GS: 0-1 Gd: 0-6 GF: - Fm: 0-0
Distance:	2m/2m3: 0-6 2m4-2m7: 0-3 3m+: 0-0

Track: LH: 0-8 RH: 0-1 Tight: 0-1 Gall: 0-2
Aids: Bl: 0-1 Vi: 0-0 Tstrap: 0-0 Ckp: 0-0
Best Rating: 128 11/00 Aint 2m4f   gd-sft Hdl

Fair handicap chaser; effective at two to two and a half miles and seems to act on any ground; has worn a tongue tie and blinkers.

Super Road Train

69   86

5-y-o b g Petoski-Foehn Gale (IRE) (Strong Gale)
L Wells   David Knox

Placings: 1-40F2   (4755)
2003/04: 21⁴S, 25⁰S, 20ᶠG, 21²G,

	Starts	1st	2nd	3rd	Win & Pl
Hurdles	4	0	1	0	1543
Career Total	5	1	1	0	5105
102	3/03	Plum	2m2f	H NHF	G-F £3562

Total win prize-money £3562

Going: Sf: 0-2 GS: 0-0 Gd: 0-2 GF: - Fm: 0-0
Distance: 2m/2m3: 0-0 2m4-2m7: 0-3 3m+: 0-1
Track: LH: 0-3 RH: 0-0 Tight: 0-3 Gall: 0-0
Aids: Bl: 0-1 Vi: 0-0 Tstrap: 0-0 Ckp: 0-2
Best Rating: 102 3/03 Plum 2m2f   gd-fm NHF

Plating-class hurdler; acts on fast ground.

Super Sammy

108(106h)   (93h)106

8-y-o br m Mesleh-Super Sue (Lochnager)
M W Easterby   Whitestonecliffe Racing Partnership

Placings: 0/311642/022316026-42U3F56P   (4957)
2003/04: 16⁴G, 17²GS, 21¹UG, 19³GS, 20ᶠG, 20⁵HY, 20ᵖS, 17ᵖGS,

	Starts	1st	2nd	3rd	Win & Pl
Hurdles	1	0	0	0	0
Chases	7	0	1	1	2125
Career Total	24	3	5	3	14531
92	1/03	Newc	2m	E Hdl	HVY £3438
105	1/02	Newc	2m	H NHF	SFT £1988
96	12/01	Donc	2m110y	H NHF	GD £2562

Total win prize-money £7989

Going: Sf: 0-2 GS: 0-3 Gd: 0-3 GF: - Fm: 0-0
Distance: 2m/2m3: 0-4 2m4-2m7: 0-4 3m+: 0-0
Track: LH: 0-3 RH: 0-5 Tight: 0-4 Gall: 0-0
Aids: Bl: 0-0 Vi: 0-0 Tstrap: 0-0 Ckp: 0-0
Best Rating: 109 12/03 MRas 2m1f110y gd-sft Ch

Modest hurdler; stays two and a half miles; effective on ground from good to heavy; runner-up on second start over fences at Market Rasen in December.

Super Satco (IRE)

6-y-o b g Satco (FR)-Brae (IRE) (Runnett)
J J Lambe   W Hitchen

Placings: 50-055   (0935)
2003/04: 16⁰G, 16⁵F, 21⁵GF,

	Starts	1st	2nd	3rd	Win & Pl
NH Flat	2	0	0	0	0
Hurdles	1	0	0	0	0
Career Total	5	0	0	0	0

Going: Sf: 0-0 GS: 0-0 Gd: 0-2 GF: - Fm: 0-0
Distance: 2m/2m3: 0-2 2m4-2m7: 0-1 3m+: 0-0
Track: LH: 0-1 RH: 0-1 Tight: 0-1 Gall: 0-0
Aids: Bl: 0-0 Vi: 0-0 Tstrap: 0-0 Ckp: 0-0
Best Rating: 87 9/02 Hexm 2m110y   gd-fm NHF

Super Tip (IRE)

91   83

6-y-o b g Supreme Leader-Tip Marie (IRE) (Celio Rufo)
P Winkworth   P Winkworth

Placings: 500600P   (4669)
2003/04: 16⁵G, 17⁰G, 16⁰GS, 16ᵖS, 18⁰GS, 17⁰G, 23ᵖGS,

	Starts	1st	2nd	3rd	Win & Pl
NH Flat	2	0	0	0	0
Hurdles	5	0	0	0	0
Career Total	7	0	0	0	0

Going: Sf: 0-1 GS: 0-3 Gd: 0-3 GF: - Fm: 0-0
Distance: 2m/2m3: 0-6 2m4-2m7: 0-1 3m+: 0-0
Track: LH: 0-3 RH: 0-3 Tight: 0-3 Gall: 0-1
Aids: Bl: 0-1 Vi: 0-0 Tstrap: 0-0 Ckp: 0-0
Best Rating: 101 11/03 Sand 2m110y   good NHF

Superb Leader (IRE)

100(100h)   (103h)107+

10-y-o b g Supreme Leader-Emmagreen (Green Shoon)
Miss Venetia Williams   The Geisha Girls

Placings: 2/P4P/43241-43PF2445   (4715)
2003/04: 20⁴G, 24³S, 20ᵖGF, 20ᶠGF, 20²GS, 17⁴GS, 20⁴GF, 20⁵G,

	Starts	1st	2nd	3rd	Win & Pl
Chases	8	0	1	1	3475
Career Total	17	1	3	2	12023
107	3/03	Bang	2m1f110yD Ch	GD	£5378

Total win prize-money £5379

Going: Sf: 0-1 GS: 0-2 Gd: 0-2 GF: - Fm: 0-3
Distance: 2m/2m3: 0-1 2m4-2m7: 0-6 3m+: 0-1
Track: LH: 0-4 RH: 0-3 Tight: 0-5 Gall: 0-0
Aids: Bl: 0-0 Vi: 0-0 Tstrap: 0-0 Ckp: 0-0
Best Rating: 107 12/03 Bang 2m4f110y   gd-sft Ch

Won extended 2m 1f maiden chase at Bangor March 2003; confirmed his liking for that venue when second over 2m 4f in December; acts on good and good to soft.

Supercharmer

10-y-o ch g Charmer-Surpassing (Superlative)
M A Humphreys   M A Humphreys

Placings: 00/6/F/U00   (4302)
2003/04: 20⁰GF, 22⁰G, 20⁰G,

	Starts	1st	2nd	3rd	Win & Pl
Chases	3	0	0	0	0
Career Total	7	0	0	0	0

Going: Sf: 0-0 GS: 0-0 Gd: 0-2 GF: - Fm: 0-1
Distance: 2m/2m3: 0-0 2m4-2m7: 0-3 3m+: 0-0
Track: LH: 0-0 RH: 0-3 Tight: 0-1 Gall: 0-1
Aids: Bl: 0-0 Vi: 0-0 Tstrap: 0-0 Ckp: 0-0
Best Rating: 70 5/00 MRas 2m6f110y gd-sft Ch

Superior Weapon (IRE)

111   88+

10-y-o b g Riverhead (USA)-Ballytrustan Maid (IRE) (Orchestra)
Mrs A Hamilton   Ian Hamilton

Placings: P/6353100/2PP-5120   (4686)
2003/04: 20⁵HY, 16¹GF, 16²HY, 17⁰G,

	Starts	1st	2nd	3rd	Win & Pl
Chases	4	1	1	0	5704
Career Total	15	2	2	2	12090
83	3/04	Ayr	2m	F(0-95)HCh	G-F £4241
98	3/02	Kels	2m1f	E Ch	SFT £3796

Total win prize-money £8037

Going: Sf: 0-2 GS: 0-0 Gd: 0-1 GF: - Fm: 1-1
Distance: 2m/2m3: 1-3 2m4-2m7: 0-1 3m+: 0-0
Track: LH: 1-3 RH: 0-1 Tight: 0-1 Gall: 0-1
Aids: Bl: 0-0 Vi: 0-0 Tstrap: 1-4 Ckp: 0-0
Best Rating: 98 5/02 Prth 3m   gd-fm Ch

Plating-class chaser; off for 14 months after November 2002 but showed he retains plenty of ability and showed the right attitude when winning at Ayr in March 2004; acts on any ground.

Supraluna

88   84

5-y-o ch m Classic Cliche (IRE)-Spring Flyer (IRE) (Waajib)
M C Pipe   Codan Trust Company Limited

Placings: 00-2U6P   (1078)
2003/04: 17²GF, 16⁰UG, 17⁶GS, 20ᵖGF,

	Starts	1st	2nd	3rd	Win & Pl
Hurdles	4	0	1	0	1272
Career Total	6	0	1	0	1272

Going: Sf: 0-0 GS: 0-1 Gd: 0-1 GF: - Fm: 0-2
Distance: 2m/2m3: 0-3 2m4-2m7: 0-1 3m+: 0-0
Track: LH: 0-4 RH: 0-0 Tight: 0-3 Gall: 0-0
Aids: Bl: 0-0 Vi: 0-0 Tstrap: 0-0 Ckp: 0-0
Best Rating: 84 6/03 NAbb 2m1f   gd-fm Hdl

Half-sister to winning hurdlers Miss Tango and Roveretto; showed nothing in two bumpers for Mary Reveley; fitted with an eyeshield when runner-up in modest Newton Abbot novice hurdle June 2003 on first run for Martin Pipe.

Supreme Arrow (IRE)

107(108h)   (116+h)122+

9-y-o b m Supreme Leader-Clover Run (IRE) (Deep Run)
Miss E C Lavelle   Mrs Jillian Twomey

Placings: 423/1231/6F3P-121245   (4362)
2003/04: 22¹GF, 21²GF, 24¹GF, 24²GS, 21⁴G, 20⁵G,

	Starts	1st	2nd	3rd	Win & Pl
Hurdles	3	1	1	0	5134
Chases	3	1	1	0	4193
Career Total	17	4	4	3	21549
122	11/03	Hntg	3m	E(0-105)HCh	G-F £3073
107	10/03	Strf	2m6f110yE(0-105)HHdl	G-F £3493
107	10/01	Thur	3m	Ch	GD £5008
107	6/01	Baln	3m	NHF	G-F £3616

Total win prize-money £15192

Going: Sf: 0-0 GS: 0-1 Gd: 0-2 GF: - Fm: 2-3
Distance: 2m/2m3: 0-0 2m4-2m7: 1-4 3m+: 1-2
Track: LH: 1-2 RH: 1-4 Tight: 1-2 Gall: 1-2
Aids: Bl: 0-0 Vi: 0-0 Tstrap: 0-0 Ckp: 0-0
Best Rating: 122 11/03 Hntg 3m   gd-fm Ch

Modest hurdler/chaser; ex-Irish; made a winning British debut for new yard in October 2003 at Stratford over hurdles; ran well in defeat next time; stays three miles; acts on most ground; improving front-runner.

Supreme Breeze (IRE)

106 **99**

9-y-o b g Supreme Leader-Merry Breeze (Strong Gale)
Mrs S J Smith (Ferdy Murphy 11/12) The Supreme Three

Placings:0/21530/PF252F2/U456233-34UP346   (4880)
2003/04: 26³G, 27⁴GF, 25ᵁGS, 24ᴾGS, 20³G, 28⁴G, 20⁶GS,

	Starts	1st	2nd	3rd	Win & Pl
Chases	7	0	0	2	2231
Career Total	27	1	5	5	15206
95 11/00 Newc 2m4f E Hdl				SFT	£2478
			Total win prize-money £2478		

Going:	Sf: 0-0 GS: 0-3 Gd: 0-3 GF: - Fm: 0-0	
Distance:	2m/2m3: 0-0 2m4-2m7: 0-2 3m+: 0-5	
Track:	LH: 0-4 RH: 0-3 Tight: 0-4 Gall: 0-1	
Aids:	Bl: 0-3 Vi: 0-0 Tstrap: 0-0 Ckp: 0-1	
Best Rating:	99 3/04 Sedg 3m4f	good Ch

Plating-class staying chaser; stays three miles seven; acts on any ground.

Supreme Catch (IRE)

109 (121h)**135**

7-y-o b g Supreme Leader-Lucky Trout (Beau Charmeur (FR))
Miss H C Knight Bucknall Street Partnership

Placings:12/512-1426   (4953)
2003/04: 19¹GS, 24⁴S, 19²G, 20⁶G,

	Starts	1st	2nd	3rd	Win & Pl
Chases	4	1	1	0	23577
Career Total	9	3	3	0	43890
133 1/04 Asct 2m3f110yB(0-150)HCh	G-S	£16783			
128 11/02 Hntg 2m4f110yD Ch	G-S	£5642			
128 3/02 Font 2m4f E Hdl	SFT	£2530			
		Total win prize-money £24956			

Going:	Sf: 0-1 GS: 1-1 Gd: 0-2 GF: - Fm: 0-0	
Distance:	2m/2m3: 0-0 2m4-2m7: 1-3 3m+: 0-1	
Track:	LH: 0-0 RH: 1-4 Tight: 0-0 Gall: 0-0	
Aids:	Bl: 0-0 Vi: 0-0 Tstrap: 0-0 Ckp: 0-0	
Best Rating:	135 2/04 Asct 2m3f110y	good Ch

Useful chaser; ex-Irish pointer, stays 2m 4f; acts on good but suited by soft ground.

Supreme Dawn (IRE)

104 **104+**

7-y-o b g Supreme Leader-Tudor Dawn (Deep Run)
C Tinkler (A J Lidderdale 29/4) George Ward

Placings:4/430-23F   (3408)
2003/04: 17⁰S, 16²G, 21³G, 16ᶠG,

	Starts	1st	2nd	3rd	Win & Pl
NH Flat	1	0	0	0	
Hurdles	3	0	1	1	1473
Career Total	7	0	1	2	1752

Going:	Sf: 0-1 GS: 0-0 Gd: 0-3 GF: - Fm: 0-0	
Distance:	2m/2m3: 0-3 2m4-2m7: 0-1 3m+: 0-0	
Track:	LH: 0-4 RH: 0-0 Tight: 0-1 Gall: 0-1	
Aids:	Bl: 0-0 Vi: 0-0 Tstrap: 0-0 Ckp: 0-0	
Best Rating:	104 11/03 Wwck 2m	good Hdl

Moderate novice hurdler; half-brother to smart hurdler Dawn Leader amongst others; effective over two miles; beaten when falling heavily at Doncaster in January.

Supreme Destiny (IRE)

87f **89f**

6-y-o b g Supreme Leader-Shuil Le Gaoth (IRE) (Strong Gale)
Miss V Scott A Butler

Placings:0   (2435)
2003/04: 16⁰S,

	Starts	1st	2nd	3rd	Win & Pl
NH Flat	1	0	0	0	
Career Total	1	0	0	0	

Going:	Sf: 0-1 GS: 0-0 Gd: 0-0 GF: - Fm: 0-0	
Distance:	2m/2m3: 0-1 2m4-2m7: 0-0 3m+: 0-0	
Track:	LH: 0-1 RH: 0-0 Tight: 0-0 Gall: 0-0	
Aids:	Bl: 0-0 Vi: 0-0 Tstrap: 0-0 Ckp: 0-0	
Best Rating:	89 11/03 Ayr 2m	soft NHF

Supreme Fortune (IRE)

(101h) **102**

10-y-o b g Supreme Leader-Lucylet (Kinglet)
Mrs M Reveley The Supreme Partnership

Placings:2034/133515113555/02U14P/003352066/036222
241-5P   (2442)
2003/04: 17⁵G, 20ᴾS,

	Starts	1st	2nd	3rd	Win & Pl
Hurdles	1	0	0	0	0
Chases	1	0	0	0	0
Career Total	42	6	7	7	41392
99 4/03 Newc 2m110y E Ch	GD	£4075			
124 1/01 Hayd 2m B(0-140)HHdl	SFT	£8392			
117 2/00 Catt 2m3f D Hdl	GD	£3198			
121 1/00 Newc 2m B Hdl	SFT	£6857			
124 12/99 Newc 2m F(0-105)HHdl	SFT	£2305			
110 5/99 Aint 2m110y D Hdl	G-S	£2905			
		Total win prize-money £27736			

Going:	Sf: 0-1 GS: 0-0 Gd: 0-1 GF: - Fm: 0-0	
Distance:	2m/2m3: 0-1 2m4-2m7: 0-1 3m+: 0-0	
Track:	LH: 0-2 RH: 0-0 Tight: 0-1 Gall: 0-0	
Aids:	Bl: 0-0 Vi: 0-0 Tstrap: 0-0 Ckp: 0-0	
Best Rating:	127 12/01 Hayd 2m4f	soft Hdl

Fair hurdler/chaser; if not as good as he was, he showed ability on his chasing debut and got off the mark over fences at Newcastle in early April; ran badly on return to hurdling at Haydock in November.

Supreme Hill (IRE)

99 **121+**

7-y-o br g Supreme Leader-Regents Prancer (Prince Regent (FR))
C J Mann J E Brown

Placings:1522/324-FF5   (3170)
2003/04: 24ᶠGS, 24ᶠG, 22⁵HY,

	Starts	1st	2nd	3rd	Win & Pl
Hurdles	1	0	0	0	0
Chases	2	0	0	0	0
Career Total	10	1	3	1	8136
121 12/01 Wwck 2m H NHF	SFT	£1708			
		Total win prize-money £1708			

Going:	Sf: 0-1 GS: 0-1 Gd: 0-1 GF: - Fm: 0-0	
Distance:	2m/2m3: 0-0 2m4-2m7: 0-1 3m+: 0-2	
Track:	LH: 0-2 RH: 0-1 Tight: 0-2 Gall: 0-0	
Aids:	Bl: 0-0 Vi: 0-0 Tstrap: 0-0 Ckp: 0-0	

Best Rating:	121 12/01 Wwck 2m	soft NHF

Decent bumper performer and had shown promise over hurdles; fell in first two chases and reverted to hurdles; stays two and a half miles; acts on soft ground.

Supreme Hope (USA)

92f **82f**

5-y-o b g Supreme Leader-Flaming Hope (IRE) (Callernish)
H D Daly Mrs Geoffrey Churton

Placings:2   (2367)
2003/04: 16²GF,

	Starts	1st	2nd	3rd	Win & Pl
NH Flat	1	0	1	0	524
Career Total	1	0	1	0	524

Going:	Sf: 0-0 GS: 0-0 Gd: 0-0 GF: - Fm: 0-1	
Distance:	2m/2m3: 0-1 2m4-2m7: 0-0 3m+: 0-0	
Track:	LH: 0-0 RH: 0-1 Tight: 0-0 Gall: 0-0	
Aids:	Bl: 0-0 Vi: 0-0 Tstrap: 0-0 Ckp: 0-0	
Best Rating:	89 11/03 Ludl 2m	gd-fm NHF

Supreme Lass (IRE)

97 **83**

8-y-o b m Supreme Leader-Falas Lass (Belfalas)
G M Moore A J Racehorses

Placings:2401/0P0-03242P   (3769)
2003/04: 16⁸F, 17³G, 19²GF, 19⁴GS, 21²GS, 20ᴾHY,

	Starts	1st	2nd	3rd	Win & Pl
Hurdles	6	0	2	1	2202
Career Total	13	1	3	1	4331
99 3/02 Donc 2m110y H NHF	SFT	£1666			
		Total win prize-money £1666			

Going:	Sf: 0-1 GS: 0-2 Gd: 0-1 GF: - Fm: 0-0	
Distance:	2m/2m3: 0-4 2m4-2m7: 0-2 3m+: 0-0	
Track:	LH: 0-5 RH: 0-1 Tight: 0-3 Gall: 0-0	
Aids:	Bl: 0-0 Vi: 0-0 Tstrap: 0-0 Ckp: 0-0	
Best Rating:	99 3/02 Donc 2m110y	soft NHF

Plating-class mare; stays two and a half miles.

Supreme Leisure (IRE)

99f **110+f**

7-y-o b g Supreme Leader-Maid Of Leisure (Le Moss)
Noel T Chance Mrs J M Porter

Placings:21   (3510a)
2003/04: 16²GS, 16¹Y,

	Starts	1st	2nd	3rd	Win & Pl
NH Flat	2	1	1	0	6344
Career Total	2	1	1	0	6344
110 1/04 Leop 2m NHF	YLD	£5588			
		Total win prize-money £5588			

Going:	Sf: 0-0 GS: 0-1 Gd: 0-0 GF: - Fm: 0-0	
Distance:	2m/2m3: 1-2 2m4-2m7: 0-0 3m+: 0-0	
Track:	LH: 0-1 RH: 0-0 Tight: 0-0 Gall: 0-1	
Aids:	Bl: 0-0 Vi: 0-0 Tstrap: 0-0 Ckp: 0-0	
Best Rating:	110 1/04 Leop 2m	yield NHF

Well-regarded half-brother to Native Leisure; highly promising second on debut at Newbury in a bumper on good to soft; should stay a trip; promising.

Supreme Optimist (IRE)

88   **103**

7-y-o b g Supreme Leader-Armagale (IRE) (Strong Gale)
N G Richards   H R C Catherwood

Placings:50/033-00   (3326)
2003/04: 16⁹S, 21⁹GS,

	Starts	1st	2nd	3rd	Win & Pl
Hurdles	2	0	0	0	
Career Total	7	0	0	2	1006

Going:	Sf: 0-1 GS: 0-1 Gd: 0-0 GF: - Fm: 0-0
Distance:	2m/2m3: 0-1 2m4-2m7: 0-1 3m+: 0-0
Track:	LH: 0-2 RH: 0-0 Tight: 0-1 Gall: 0-0
Aids:	Bl: 0-0 Vi: 0-0 Tstrap: 0-0 Ckp: 0-0
Best Rating:	108 11/02 Kels 2m110y soft Hdl

Has only shown moderate form in novice hurdles to date.

Supreme Piper (IRE)

102   **124+**

6-y-o b g Supreme Leader-Whistling Doe (Whistling Deer)
P J Hobbs   Mrs Karola Vann

Placings:34226-F1   (4702)
2003/04: 19⁶G, 20¹G,

	Starts	1st	2nd	3rd	Win & Pl
Hurdles	2	1	0	0	3591
Career Total	7	1	2	1	8292
120	4/04	Font	2m4f	E Hdl	GD	£3591
			Total win prize-money £3591			

Going:	Sf: 0-0 GS: 0-0 Gd: 1-2 GF: - Fm: 0-0
Distance:	2m/2m3: 0-1 2m4-2m7: 1-1 3m+: 0-0
Track:	LH: 0-0 RH: 0-0 Tight: 1-1 Gall: 0-0
Aids:	Bl: 0-0 Vi: 0-0 Tstrap: 0-0 Ckp: 0-0
Best Rating:	124 11/03 Extr 2m3f good Hdl

Fair novice hurdler; stays two and a half miles and suited by good ground.

Supreme Prince (IRE)

108(109h)   (146+h)**141+**

7-y-o b g Supreme Leader-Strong Serenade (IRE) (Strong Gale)
P J Hobbs   Mrs Karola Vann

Placings:1//11103-211P2   (4695)
2003/04: 23²G, 19¹GS, 19¹S, 24²G, 23²G,

	Starts	1st	2nd	3rd	Win & Pl
Chases	5	2	2	0	28172
Career Total	11	6	2	1	65354
141	12/03	Asct	2m3f110yA Ch	SFT	£20100
137	12/03	Chep	2m3f110yD Ch	G-S	£4124
132	2/03	Winc	2m6f	B Hdl	G-S	£9256
146	11/02	Chep	2m4f	A Hdl	SFT	£13685
132	10/02	Chep	2m4f	E Hdl	GD	£3630
117	10/01	Extr	2m1f	H NHF	G-S	£1809
			Total win prize-money £52606			

Going:	Sf: 1-1 GS: 1-1 Gd: 0-3 GF: - Fm: 0-0
Distance:	2m/2m3: 0-0 2m4-2m7: 2-2 3m+: 0-3
Track:	LH: 1-2 RH: 1-3 Tight: 0-0 Gall: 0-1
Aids:	Bl: 0-0 Vi: 0-0 Tstrap: 0-0 Ckp: 0-0
Best Rating:	146 4/03 Aint 3m110y good Hdl

Very useful novice chaser; good seventh in the Royal & SunAlliance Hurdle in 2003; was considered to have run too free when second on chasing debut over 3m at Exeter

November 2003; made amends over 2m 4f at Chepstow next time and won Grade A chase at Ascot latest in December; pulled up at Cheltenham and disappointed again next time; just gets three miles; acts on good or softer.

Supreme Priority (IRE)

112   **89**

6-y-o b g Supreme Leader-Kakemona (Kambalda)
C Roberts (Jonjo O'Neill 8/10)   A J Williams

Placings:03300-P1P004   (4656)
2003/04: 24⁸GF, 21¹F, 24⁸S, 19⁰G, 22⁰G, 26⁴G,

	Starts	1st	2nd	3rd	Win & Pl
Hurdles	6	1	0	2	2142
Career Total	11	1	0	2	3016
87	10/03	Towc	2m5f	G Hdl	FRM	£1820
			Total win prize-money £1820			

Going:	Sf: 0-1 GS: 0-0 Gd: 0-3 GF: - Fm: 1-2
Distance:	2m/2m3: 0-1 2m4-2m7: 1-2 3m+: 0-3
Track:	LH: 0-3 RH: 1-3 Tight: 0-2 Gall: 0-1
Aids:	Bl: 0-0 Vi: 0-0 Tstrap: 0-0 Ckp: 0-0
Best Rating:	101 12/02 Newb 2m110y heavy NHF

Moderate hurdler; acts on fast ground; stays two miles furlongs.

Supreme Return

97f   **104f**

5-y-o b g Bob's Return (IRE)-Supreme Wonder (IRE) (Supreme Leader)
A King   Lady Harris

Placings:50   (4213)
2003/04: 16⁵HY, 16⁹G,

	Starts	1st	2nd	3rd	Win & Pl
NH Flat	2	0	0	0	0
Career Total	2	0	0	0	0

Going:	Sf: 0-1 GS: 0-0 Gd: 0-1 GF: - Fm: 0-0
Distance:	2m/2m3: 0-2 2m4-2m7: 0-0 3m+: 0-0
Track:	LH: 0-0 RH: 0-0 Tight: 0-0 Gall: 0-0
Aids:	Bl: 0-0 Vi: 0-0 Tstrap: 0-0 Ckp: 0-0
Best Rating:	99 1/04 Asct 2m110y heavy NHF

Supreme Rullah (IRE)

73

7-y-o b m Supreme Leader-Trapper Jean (Orchestra)
I R Ferguson   Shanes Castle Racing Syndicate

Placings:00006P   (4913)
2003/04: 17⁰GY, 20⁰S, 20⁰Y, 18⁰GY, 20⁰Y, 24⁸S,

	Starts	1st	2nd	3rd	Win & Pl
NH Flat	1	0	0	0	0
Hurdles	5	0	0	0	0
Career Total	6	0	0	0	0

Going:	Sf: 0-2 GS: 0-0 Gd: 0-0 GF: - Fm: 0-0
Distance:	2m/2m3: 0-2 2m4-2m7: 0-3 3m+: 0-1
Track:	LH: 0-0 RH: 0-1 Tight: 0-0 Gall: 0-0
Aids:	Bl: 0-0 Vi: 0-0 Tstrap: 0-3 Ckp: 0-0
Best Rating:	73 4/04 DRoy 2m4f yield Hdl

Supreme Serenade (IRE)

108   **115+**

5-y-o b m Supreme Leader-Strong Serenade (IRE) (Strong Gale)
P J Hobbs   Mrs Karola Vann

Placings:1-21323   (4574)
2003/04: 17¹S, 17²G, 17¹GS, 19³S, 20²G, 21³G,

	Starts	1st	2nd	3rd	Win & Pl
NH Flat	1	1	0	0	3080
Hurdles	5	1	2	2	11430
Career Total	6	2	2	2	14510
105	12/03	Folk	2m1f110yE Hdl	G-S	£3052
112	4/03	NAbb	2m1f	H NHF	SFT	£3080
			Total win prize-money £6132			

Going:	Sf: 1-2 GS: 1-1 Gd: 0-3 GF: - Fm: 0-0
Distance:	2m/2m3: 2-4 2m4-2m7: 0-2 3m+: 0-0
Track:	LH: 1-2 RH: 1-3 Tight: 2-3 Gall: 0-1
Aids:	Bl: 0-0 Vi: 0-0 Tstrap: 0-0 Ckp: 0-0
Best Rating:	115 3/04 Newb 2m5f good Hdl

Promising novice hurdler; effective at around two miles; acts on easy ground.

Supreme Silence (IRE)

7-y-o b g Bluebird (USA)-Why So Silent (Mill Reef (USA))
Nick Kent (Jedd O'Keeffe 10/5)   Russel H Lee

Placings:P/5651PPP0/03P-PP2PP   (4607)
2003/04: 24⁶G, 25⁶S, 25²GS, 21⁸GS, 25⁸GS,

	Starts	1st	2nd	3rd	Win & Pl
Hurdles	1	0	0	0	0
Chases	4	0	1	0	383
Career Total	17	1	1	1	3554
88	6/01	Hexm	2m4f110yE Hdl	GD	£2397
			Total win prize-money £2398			

Going:	Sf: 0-1 GS: 0-3 Gd: 0-1 GF: - Fm: 0-0
Distance:	2m/2m3: 0-0 2m4-2m7: 0-1 3m+: 0-4
Track:	LH: 0-3 RH: 0-2 Tight: 0-3 Gall: 0-0
Aids:	Bl: 0-0 Vi: 0-1 Tstrap: 0-0 Ckp: 0-0
Best Rating:	88 6/01 Hexm 2m4f110y good Hdl

Flat and hurdle-race winner; took a point prior to finishing runner-up in weak hunters' chase at Market Rasen in March; stays three miles.

Supreme's Legacy (IRE)

115f

5-y-o b g Supreme Leader-Lucylet (Kinglet)
Mrs M Reveley   The Supreme Alliance

Placings:2   (2294)
2003/04: 17²G,

	Starts	1st	2nd	3rd	Win & Pl
NH Flat	1	0	1	0	2138
Career Total	1	0	1	0	2138

Going:	Sf: 0-0 GS: 0-0 Gd: 0-1 GF: - Fm: 0-0
Distance:	2m/2m3: 0-1 2m4-2m7: 0-0 3m+: 0-0
Track:	LH: 0-0 RH: 0-0 Tight: 0-0 Gall: 0-0
Aids:	Bl: 0-0 Vi: 0-0 Tstrap: 0-0 Ckp: 0-0
Best Rating:	115 11/03 Aint 2m1f good NHF

Promising effort on bumper debut.

Supremely Bright

7-y-o b m Supreme Leader-Oh So Bright (Celtic Cone)
M J Ryan P Picton-Warlow

Placings:00-P   (0156)
2003/04: 16PGF,

	Starts	1st	2nd	3rd	Win & Pl
Hurdles	1	0	0		
Career Total	3	0	0		

Going:	Sf: 0-0 GS: 0-0 Gd: 0-0 GF: - Fm: 0-1
Distance:	2m/2m3: 0-1 2m4-2m7: 0-0 3m+: 0-0
Track:	LH: 0-1 RH: 0-0 Tight: 0-1 Gall: 0-0
Aids:	Bl: 0-0 Vi: 0-0 Tstrap: 0-0 Ckp: 0-0

Supremely Red (IRE)

89

7-y-o b g Supreme Leader-Her Name Was Lola (Pitskelly)
D A Rees D A Rees & P Harris

Placings:4/3P100P-P   (2031)
2003/04: 21PG,

	Starts	1st	2nd	3rd	Win & Pl
Hurdles	1	0	0		
Career Total	8	1	0	1	2961
89	6/02	NAbb	2m6f		E Hdl	GD	£2961

Total win prize-money £2961

Going:	Sf: 0-0 GS: 0-0 Gd: 0-1 GF: - Fm: 0-0
Distance:	2m/2m3: 0-0 2m4-2m7: 0-1 3m+: 0-0
Track:	LH: 0-1 RH: 0-0 Tight: 0-0 Gall: 0-0
Aids:	Bl: 0-0 Vi: 0-0 Tstrap: 0-0 Ckp: 0-0
Best Rating:	89 6/02 NAbb 2m6f good Hdl

Sure Future

99(109h)   (120+h)**96**

8-y-o b g Kylian (USA)-Lady Ever-So-Sure (Malicious)
R M Stronge The Test Valley Partnership

Placings:34046/336/5450122/43121-2U6P06630 (4817)
2003/04: 24²GS, 22UGS, 25⁶G, 22PS, 19⁰G, 21⁶GS, 23⁶GS, 24³S, 24⁶G,

	Starts	1st	2nd	3rd	Win & Pl
Hurdles	3	0	1	0	1871
Chases	6	0	0	1	635
Career Total	29	3	4	5	22806
120	12/02	Kemp	3m110y	C(0-135)HHdl	SFT	£6380
117	12/02	Folk	2m6f110yE(0-105)HHdl	HVY	£4153
103	3/02	Newb	2m6f	E(0-105)HHdl	SFT	£3640

Total win prize-money £14174

Going:	Sf: 0-2 GS: 0-4 Gd: 0-3 GF: - Fm: 0-0
Distance:	2m/2m3: 0-1 2m4-2m7: 0-3 3m+: 0-5
Track:	LH: 0-6 RH: 0-3 Tight: 0-3 Gall: 0-2
Aids:	Bl: 0-0 Vi: 0-0 Tstrap: 0-0 Ckp: 0-0
Best Rating:	120 12/02 Kemp 3m110y soft Hdl

Fair hurdler/moderate chaser; stays three miles and loves soft ground; very consistent; has worn a tongue tie.

Surefast

108(99h)   (80h)**92+**

9-y-o ch g Nearly A Hand-Meldon Lady (Ballymoss)
K Bishop Brian Derrick

Placings:0/00/60F0U55/300636-PP512   (4916)

2003/04: 25PS, 24PG, 23⁵GS, 20¹S, 23²GS,

	Starts	1st	2nd	3rd	Win & Pl
Chases	5	1	1	0	5064
Career Total	21	1	1	2	6304
90	4/04	Ling	2m4f110yF(0-90)HCh	SFT	£3659

Total win prize-money £3660

Going:	Sf: 1-2 GS: 0-2 Gd: 0-1 GF: - Fm: 0-0
Distance:	2m/2m3: 0-0 2m4-2m7: 1-1 3m+: 0-4
Track:	LH: 1-2 RH: 0-3 Tight: 1-2 Gall: 0-0
Aids:	Bl: 0-0 Vi: 0-0 Tstrap: 0-0 Ckp: 0-0
Best Rating:	92 4/04 Worc 2m7f110y gd-sft Ch

Very modest novice hurdler/chaser; stays two and a half miles; unsuited by fast ground.

Surprise Gunner

69(96h)   (97h)**51**

14-y-o b g Gunner B-Heckley Loch (Lochnager)
A P Jones Mrs T Lewis

Placings:5/020001/1P/24P/465O0P   (4185)
2003/04: 19⁴G, 20⁶G, 22⁵G, 19⁰HY, 22⁰GS, 24PG,

	Starts	1st	2nd	3rd	Win & Pl
Hurdles	4	0	0	0	0
Chases	2	0	0	0	0
Career Total	18	2	2	0	6481
94	1/01	Leic	2m	F(0-110)HHdl	HVY	£2733
97	2/99	Folk	2m4f110yF(0-100)HHdl	SFT	£1953

Total win prize-money £4687

Going:	Sf: 0-1 GS: 0-1 Gd: 0-4 GF: - Fm: 0-0
Distance:	2m/2m3: 0-0 2m4-2m7: 0-5 3m+: 0-1
Track:	LH: 0-1 RH: 0-2 Tight: 0-2 Gall: 0-1
Aids:	Bl: 0-0 Vi: 0-0 Tstrap: 0-0 Ckp: 0-0
Best Rating:	97 6/01 Strf 2m3f gd-fm Hdl

Surprising

104(105h)   (113 h)**131**

9-y-o b g Primitive Rising (USA)-Ascot Lass (Touching Wood (USA))
O Sherwood M G St Quinton

Placings:4/212P/1133221/103420005-12   (2259)
2003/04: 24¹GF, 28²G,

	Starts	1st	2nd	3rd	Win & Pl
Chases	2	1	1	0	4650
Career Total	23	6	6	3	68818
120	11/03	Carl	3m	E Ch	G-F	£3526
137	5/02	Hayd	2m7f110yB HHdl	GD	£12247
135	4/02	Prth	3m110y	B Hdl	GD	£8978
121	11/01	Kemp	2m5f	D Hdl	GD	£3558
112	10/01	Plum	2m5f	E Hdl	SFT	£2481
118	10/00	Extr	2m1f	H NHF	GD	£1652

Total win prize-money £32444

Going:	Sf: 0-0 GS: 0-0 Gd: 0-1 GF: - Fm: 1-1
Distance:	2m/2m3: 0-0 2m4-2m7: 0-0 3m+: 1-2
Track:	LH: 0-0 RH: 1-2 Tight: 0-1 Gall: 0-0
Aids:	Bl: 0-0 Vi: 0-0 Tstrap: 0-0 Ckp: 0-0
Best Rating:	137 5/02 Hayd 2m7f110y good Hdl

Formerly very useful staying hurdler; fair chaser; did not take to chasing straight away, but was given a forceful ride to win at Carlisle in November 2003; stays three miles plus and acts on decent ground, but goes on soft; described as a stuffy sort, he idles in front; wears blinkers.

Sursum Corda

13-y-o b g Idiots Delight-Childhay (Roi Soleil)
John Wall M Ward-Thomas

Placings:4/2/342F3211/4252R14/2112330/030/P1P231/35
343F-U   (0224)
2003/04: 21FS, 16UG,

	Starts	1st	2nd	3rd	Win & Pl
Chases	2	0	0	0	
Career Total	40	7	8	9	42245
107	4/02	Asct	2m3f110yH Ch	G-F	£2947
90	5/01	Folk	2m5f	H Ch	GD	£1909
123	12/99	Hayd	2m	B(0-140)HCh	HVY	£10113
120	11/99	Wwck	2m	D(0-125)HCh	GD	£4042
112	3/99	Hntg	2m4f110yE Ch	SFT	£2997
94	4/98	Hntg	2m110y E Hdl	G-S	£2425
116	4/98	Extr	2m3f110yE Hdl	SFT	£2889

Total win prize-money £27324

Going:	Sf: 0-1 GS: 0-0 Gd: 0-1 GF: - Fm: 0-0
Distance:	2m/2m3: 0-1 2m4-2m7: 0-1 3m+: 0-0
Track:	LH: 0-2 RH: 0-0 Tight: 0-1 Gall: 0-0
Aids:	Bl: 0-0 Vi: 0-0 Tstrap: 0-1 Ckp: 0-0
Best Rating:	126 2/00 Sand 2m4f110y gd-sft Ch

Hunter chaser; formerly a decent hurdler/chaser; effective over two and two and a half miles; suited by a sound surafce; wears tongue tie.

Susie Bury

80f   **60f**

5-y-o b m Overbury (IRE)-Susie's Money (Seymour Hicks (FR))
S A Brookshaw The Highly Sociable Syndicate

Placings:00   (4144)
2003/04: 16⁶GS, 16⁰G,

	Starts	1st	2nd	3rd	Win & Pl
NH Flat	2	0	0	0	
Career Total	2	0	0	0	

Going:	Sf: 0-0 GS: 0-1 Gd: 0-1 GF: - Fm: 0-0
Distance:	2m/2m3: 0-2 2m4-2m7: 0-0 3m+: 0-0
Track:	LH: 0-1 RH: 0-1 Tight: 0-0 Gall: 0-0
Aids:	Bl: 0-0 Vi: 0-0 Tstrap: 0-0 Ckp: 0-0
Best Rating:	60 3/04 Ludl 2m good NHF

Suspendid (IRE)

108   **121**

11-y-o b g Yashgan-Spendapromise (Goldhill)
R Lee Stockton Heath Racing

Placings:f0/11P0/143/PP0211-05101P   (1835)
2003/04: 20⁶G, 21⁵GF, 20¹GF, 21⁰GF, 21¹GF, 20PGF,

	Starts	1st	2nd	3rd	Win & Pl
Chases	6	2	0	0	8827
Career Total	21	8	1	1	39909
119	10/03	Sthl	2m5f110yD(0-120)HCh	G-F	£3367
121	6/03	Worc	2m4f110yD(0-120)HCh	G-F	£5460
116	4/03	Ludl	2m4f	D(0-120)HCh	GD	£6727
109	4/03	Ludl	2m4f	D(0-115)HCh	GD	£7800
114	9/01	Prth	2m4f110yE Ch	GD	£4901
113	9/00	Hrfd	2m3f110yE Hdl	G-S	£2170
106	6/00	Strf	2m110y E Hdl	G-S	£2702
94	6/99	Rosc	2m	NHF	G-F	£2455

Total win prize-money £35583

Going:	Sf: 0-0 GS: 0-0 Gd: 0-1 GF: - Fm: 2-5
Distance:	2m/2m3: 0-0 2m4-2m7: 2-6 3m+: 0-0
Track:	LH: 2-6 RH: 0-0 Tight: 0-0 Gall: 0-1
Aids:	Bl: 0-0 Vi: 0-0 Tstrap: 0-0 Ckp: 0-0
Best Rating:	121 6/03 Worc 2m4f110y gd-fm Ch

Modest handicap chaser; has had blood-vessel problems; suited by 2m 4f; jumps well; acts on a sound surface.

Sussex Mist

62f   42f

5-y-o b m Phountzi (USA)-Dumerica (Yukon Eric (CAN))
J E Long   Amaroni Racing

Placings:*00*   (4816)
2003/04: 16⁰G, 16⁰G,

	Starts	1st	2nd	3rd	Win & Pl
NH Flat	2	0	0	0	
Career Total	2	0	0	0	

Going: Sf: 0-0 GS: 0-0 Gd: 0-0 GF: - Fm: 0-0
Distance: 2m/2m3: 0-2 2m4-2m7: 0-0 3m+: 0-0
Track: LH: 0-1 RH: 0-1 Tight: 0-0 Gall: 0-1
Aids: Bl: 0-0 Vi: 0-0 Tstrap: 0-0 Ckp: 0-0
Best Rating: 42   3/04   Hntg   2m110y   good   NHF

Susy Wells (IRE)

58   28

9-y-o b m Masad (IRE)-My Best Susy (IRE) (Try My Best (USA))
C W Moore   C W Moore

Placings:*0P0*   (4654)
2003/04: 16⁶G, 17⁵GS, 17⁰G,

	Starts	1st	2nd	3rd	Win & Pl
Hurdles	3	0	0	0	
Career Total	3	0	0	0	

Going: Sf: 0-0 GS: 0-1 Gd: 0-2 GF: 0-0 Fm: 0-0
Distance: 2m/2m3: 0-3 2m4-2m7: 0-0 3m+: 0-0
Track: LH: 0-1 RH: 0-2 Tight: 0-1 Gall: 0-0
Aids: Bl: 0-0 Vi: 0-0 Tstrap: 0-0 Ckp: 0-2
Best Rating: 28   3/04   Ludl   2m   good   Hdl

Sutton Ballad

10-y-o b m Emperor Fountain-Crescent Cottage (Cornuto)
P D Purdy   P D Purdy

Placings:*P*   (0135)
2003/04: 16⁸PG,

	Starts	1st	2nd	3rd	Win & Pl
Hurdles	1	0	0	0	
Career Total	1	0	0	0	

Going: Sf: 0-0 GS: 0-0 Gd: 0-1 GF: - Fm: 0-0
Distance: 2m/2m3: 0-1 2m4-2m7: 0-0 3m+: 0-0
Track: LH: 0-1 RH: 0-1 Tight: 0-0 Gall: 0-0
Aids: Bl: 0-0 Vi: 0-0 Tstrap: 0-0 Ckp: 0-0

Sutton Lion

12-y-o b g Lyphento (USA)-Crescent Cottage (Cornuto)
P D Purdy   P D Purdy

Placings:*R*   (2818)
2003/04: 19⁸RG,

	Starts	1st	2nd	3rd	Win & Pl
Hurdles	1	0	0	0	
Career Total	1	0	0	0	

Going: Sf: 0-0 GS: 0-0 Gd: 0-1 GF: - Fm: 0-0
Distance: 2m/2m3: 0-1 2m4-2m7: 0-0 3m+: 0-0
Track: LH: 0-0 RH: 0-1 Tight: 0-0 Gall: 0-0

Suzy Spitfire

6-y-o ch m Afzal-Oatis Rose (Oats)
B G Powell   J Howson

Placings:*00P*   (2075)
2003/04: 16⁸G, 17⁹G, 23⁸PG,

	Starts	1st	2nd	3rd	Win & Pl
NH Flat	2	0	0	0	0
Hurdles	1	0	0	0	0
Career Total	3	0	0	0	0

Going: Sf: 0-0 GS: 0-0 Gd: 0-3 GF: - Fm: 0-0
Distance: 2m/2m3: 0-2 2m4-2m7: 0-1 3m+: 0-0
Track: LH: 0-3 RH: 0-0 Tight: 0-2 Gall: 0-0
Aids: Bl: 0-0 Vi: 0-0 Tstrap: 0-0 Ckp: 0-0
Best Rating: 68   5/03   Worc   2m   good   NHF

Swan Knight (USA)

104(103h)   (123h)108+

8-y-o b/br g Sadler's Wells (USA)-Shannkara (IRE) (Akarad (FR))
R A Fahey   J J Staunton

Placings:*1P2/0/0526-5544F*   (3702)
2003/04: 17⁵GS, 16⁵HY, 16⁴G, 17⁴GS, 16⁶HY,

	Starts	1st	2nd	3rd	Win & Pl
Hurdles	3	0	0	0	3995
Chases	2	0	0	0	
Career Total	13	1	2	0	12716
127 2/01 Winc 2m	D Hdl			GD	£3969
		Total win prize-money £3969			

Going: Sf: 0-2 GS: 0-2 Gd: 0-1 GF: - Fm: 0-0
Distance: 2m/2m3: 0-5 2m4-2m7: 0-0 3m+: 0-0
Track: LH: 0-2 RH: 0-3 Tight: 0-1 Gall: 0-1
Aids: Bl: 0-0 Vi: 0-0 Tstrap: 0-0 Ckp: 0-0
Best Rating: 127   2/01   Winc   2m   good   Hdl

Modest hurdler/novice chaser; effective at two miles; best on good ground.

Swansea Bay

111   (89h)155+

8-y-o b g Jurado (USA)-Slave's Bangle (Prince Rheingold)
P Bowen   Peter Bowling

Placings:*26244/130/04211116116P-11110*   (2917)
2003/04: 23¹GF, 24¹GF, 25¹GF, 24¹GS, 24⁰G,

	Starts	1st	2nd	3rd	Win & Pl
Chases	5	4	0	0	79744
Career Total	25	11	3	1	138631
155 11/03 Hayd	3m	A HCh		G-S	£32750
154 11/03 Winc	3m1f110yA(0-150)HCh			G-F	£29750
147 10/03 Kemp	3m	B(0-145)HCh		G-F	£12232
137 9/03 Worc	2m7f110yD(0-125)HCh			G-F	£5011
135 11/02 Winc	3m1f110yA(0-150)HCh			GD	£29000
123 10/02 Winc	3m1f110yE(0-110)HCh			GD	£4936
122 9/02 Worc	2m7f110yC(0-135)HCh			GD	£7413
106 8/02 Worc	2m7f110yE(0-105)HCh			GD	£3555
105 8/02 Bang	3m110y D(0-115)HCh			SFT	£5964
111 7/02 Worc	2m7f110yF(0-100)HCh			G-F	£3059
89 9/01 Worc	3m	F Hdl		G-F	£1883
		Total win prize-money £135557			

Going: Sf: 0-0 GS: 1-1 Gd: 0-1 GF: - Fm: 3-3
Distance: 2m/2m3: 0-0 2m4-2m7: 0-0 3m+: 4-5
Track: LH: 2-2 RH: 2-3 Tight: 0-0 Gall: 0-0

Best Rating: 155   11/03   Hayd   3m   gd-sft   Ch

High-class chaser; most progressive; since winning his first chase rated 83, he has won nine races, including two Badger Ales Chases at Wincanton and a Grade Two at Haydock; has improved 71lb; found wanting in the King George at Kempton; stays three miles; acts on fast ground but has won on soft; suited by flat tracks; very solid jumper; has worn cheekpieces.

Swazi Prince

103f   101f

5-y-o b g Rakaposhi King-Swazi Princess (IRE) (Brush Aside (USA))
N A Gaselee   Mrs P T Orchart

Placings:*0-300*   (4739)
2003/04: 16³GS, 16⁰S, 17⁰G,

	Starts	1st	2nd	3rd	Win & Pl
NH Flat	3	0	0	1	226
Career Total	4	0	0	1	226

Going: Sf: 0-1 GS: 0-1 Gd: 0-1 GF: - Fm: 0-0
Distance: 2m/2m3: 0-3 2m4-2m7: 0-0 3m+: 0-0
Track: LH: 0-1 RH: 0-0 Tight: 0-1 Gall: 0-2
Aids: Bl: 0-0 Vi: 0-0 Tstrap: 0-0 Ckp: 0-0
Best Rating: 101   12/03   Hntg   2m110y   gd-sft   NHF

Sweet Auburn (IRE)

98(98h)   (85h)83

8-y-o b/br g Tidaro (USA)-Sweet View (King's Ride)
Mrs B K Thomson   Mrs B K Thomson

Placings:*5P0-5404434P4536*   (4950)
2003/04: 16⁵S, 16⁴GF, 16⁰S, 25⁴GS, 23⁴S, 20⁰HY, 24⁴GS, 17⁸G, 21⁴G, 25⁵GS, 25³G, 20⁶GS,

	Starts	1st	2nd	3rd	Win & Pl
Hurdles	9	0	0	1	816
Chases	3	0	0	1	1070
Career Total	15	0	0	2	1886

Going: Sf: 0-4 GS: 0-4 Gd: 0-3 GF: - Fm: 0-1
Distance: 2m/2m3: 0-4 2m4-2m7: 0-4 3m+: 0-4
Track: LH: 0-9 RH: 0-3 Tight: 0-4 Gall: 0-1
Aids: Bl: 0-1 Vi: 0-0 Tstrap: 0-0 Ckp: 0-1
Best Rating: 85   2/04   Ayr   3m110y   gd-sft   Hdl

Modest form in bumpers; well beaten so far over hurdles and fences; stays three miles.

Sweet Bird (FR)

95   96

7-y-o ch g Epervier Bleu-Sweet Virginia (FR) (Tapioca Ii)
P M Phelan   Andrew L Cohen

Placings:*3/40/56-40*   (4790)
2003/04: 24⁴G, 21⁰G,

	Starts	1st	2nd	3rd	Win & Pl
Hurdles	2	0	0	0	372
Career Total	7	0	0	0	582

Going: Sf: 0-0 GS: 0-0 Gd: 0-2 GF: - Fm: 0-0
Distance: 2m/2m3: 0-0 2m4-2m7: 0-1 3m+: 0-1
Track: LH: 0-0 RH: 0-1 Tight: 0-0 Gall: 0-0
Aids: Bl: 0-0 Vi: 0-0 Tstrap: 0-1 Ckp: 0-0
Best Rating: 99   1/02   Towc   2m   heavy   Hdl

Moderate hurdler; stays two miles; acts on a soft surface.

Sweet Champagne

5-y-o m Mazaad-Pink Sensation (Sagaro)
G A Harker   P I Harker

Placings:PP   (4258)
2003/04: 21[P]GS, 16[P]GF,

	Starts	1st	2nd	3rd	Win & Pl
Hurdles	2	0	0	0	
Career Total	2	0	0	0	

Going:	Sf: 0-0 GS: 0-1 Gd: 0-0 GF: - Fm: 0-1
Distance:	2m/2m3: 0-1 2m4-2m7: 0-1 3m+: 0-0
Track:	LH: 0-2 RH: 0-0 Tight: 0-2 Gall: 0-0
Aids:	Bl: 0-0 Vi: 0-0 Tstrap: 0-0 Ckp: 0-0

Sweet Chariot

79f   **83f**

5-y-o b g Hatim (USA)-Evening Dusk (IRE) (Phardante (FR))
B G Powell   R Barrs

Placings:00   (4824)
2003/04: 16[0]G, 17[0]GF,

	Starts	1st	2nd	3rd	Win & Pl
NH Flat	2	0	0	0	
Career Total	2	0	0	0	

Going:	Sf: 0-0 GS: 0-0 Gd: 0-1 GF: - Fm: 0-1
Distance:	2m/2m3: 0-2 2m4-2m7: 0-0 3m+: 0-0
Track:	LH: 0-0 RH: 0-2 Tight: 0-0 Gall: 0-1
Aids:	Bl: 0-0 Vi: 0-0 Tstrap: 0-0 Ckp: 0-0
Best Rating:	83 4/04 Extr 2m1f gd-fm NHF

Sweet Diversion (IRE)

109   **122**

5-y-o b g Carroll House-Serocco Wind (Roi Guillaume (FR))
P F Nicholls   Mr & Mrs Ian Marshall

Placings:22-332144   (4833)
2003/04: 16[3]GF, 16[3]GS, 19[2]GS, 20[1]G, 20[4]S, 21[4]GF,

	Starts	1st	2nd	3rd	Win & Pl
NH Flat	1	0	0	1	218
Hurdles	5	1	1	1	12985
Career Total	8	1	3	2	14335
118 2/04 Fknm 2m4f	D Hdl		GD	£5933	
			Total win prize-money £5933		

Going:	Sf: 0-1 GS: 0-2 Gd: 1-1 GF: - Fm: 0-2
Distance:	2m/2m3: 0-2 2m4-2m7: 1-4 3m+: 0-0
Track:	LH: 1-3 RH: 0-3 Tight: 1-2 Gall: 0-1
Aids:	Bl: 0-0 Vi: 0-0 Tstrap: 0-0 Ckp: 0-0
Best Rating:	122 4/04 Chel 2m5f110y gd-fm Hdl

Fair novice hurdler; placed in bumpers; may be best suited to soft ground, but acts on good; effective over two miles.

Sweet Milly

92   **81**

9-y-o b m Milieu-Another Joyful (Rubor)
J E Dixon   Mrs S F Dixon

Placings:0/FPP/4/630P4434-4PP   (2093)
2003/04: 16[4]G, 16[P]G, 22[P]G,

	Starts	1st	2nd	3rd	Win & Pl
Hurdles	3	0	0	0	281
Career Total	16	0	0	2	1516

Going:	Sf: 0-0 GS: 0-0 Gd: 0-3 GF: - Fm: 0-0
Distance:	2m/2m3: 0-2 2m4-2m7: 0-1 3m+: 0-0
Track:	LH: 0-2 RH: 0-1 Tight: 0-2 Gall: 0-0
Aids:	Bl: 0-0 Vi: 0-0 Tstrap: 0-0 Ckp: 0-0
Best Rating:	81 4/03 Kels 2m110y good Hdl

Plating-class novice hurdler; very limited ability to date; seems best with cut in the ground.

Sweet Minuet

93   **85**

7-y-o b m Minshaanshu Amad (USA)-Sweet N' Twenty (High Top)
M Madgwick   W E Baird

Placings:3006P/4306/441-4   (0436)
2003/04: 22[4]GF,

	Starts	1st	2nd	3rd	Win & Pl
Hurdles	1	0	0	0	390
Career Total	13	1	0	2	5446
85 4/03 Font 2m2f110yE Hdl			G-F	£3584	
			Total win prize-money £3584		

Going:	Sf: 0-0 GS: 0-0 Gd: 0-0 GF: - Fm: 0-1
Distance:	2m/2m3: 0-0 2m4-2m7: 0-1 3m+: 0-0
Track:	LH: 0-1 RH: 0-0 Tight: 0-1 Gall: 0-0
Aids:	Bl: 0-0 Vi: 0-0 Tstrap: 0-0 Ckp: 0-0
Best Rating:	85 5/03 Font 2m6f110y gd-fm Hdl

Modest novice hurdler; stays two miles-five; acts on any ground.

Sweet Roi (GER)

90   **64**

4-y-o b c Roi Danzig (USA)-Sweet Royale (GER) (Garde Royale)
Mario Hofer   Stall Lucky Owner

Placings:0   (3869)
2003/04: 20[0]GS,

	Starts	1st	2nd	3rd	Win & Pl
Hurdles	1	0	0	0	
Career Total	1	0	0	0	

Going:	Sf: 0-0 GS: 0-1 Gd: 0-0 GF: - Fm: 0-0
Distance:	2m/2m3: 0-0 2m4-2m7: 0-1 3m+: 0-0
Track:	LH: 0-0 RH: 0-1 Tight: 0-1 Gall: 0-0
Aids:	Bl: 0-0 Vi: 0-0 Tstrap: 0-0 Ckp: 0-0
Best Rating:	64 2/04 Folk 2m4f110y gd-sft Hdl

Sweet Sensation

73   **37**

9-y-o ch m Carlingford Castle-Pink Sensation (Sagaro)
C Grant   Mrs A Meller

Placings:0434/0P0U-P0   (0472)
2003/04: 21[P]S, 17[0]GS,

	Starts	1st	2nd	3rd	Win & Pl
Hurdles	2	0	0	0	
Career Total	10	0	0	1	227

Going:	Sf: 0-1 GS: 0-1 Gd: 0-0 GF: - Fm: 0-0
Distance:	2m/2m3: 0-1 2m4-2m7: 0-1 3m+: 0-0
Track:	LH: 0-2 RH: 0-0 Tight: 0-2 Gall: 0-0
Aids:	Bl: 0-2 Vi: 0-0 Tstrap: 0-0 Ckp: 0-0
Best Rating:	99 5/01 Newc 2m gd-fm NHF

Sweet Shooter

97f   **74f**

4-y-o ch f Double Trigger (IRE)-Sweet N' Twenty (High Top)
M Madgwick   W E Baird

Placings:550   (4578)
2003/04: 17[5]HY, 18[5]G, 16[0]G,

	Starts	1st	2nd	3rd	Win & Pl
NH Flat	3	0	0	0	0
Career Total	3	0	0	0	0

Going:	Sf: 0-1 GS: 0-0 Gd: 0-2 GF: - Fm: 0-0
Distance:	2m/2m3: 0-3 2m4-2m7: 0-0 3m+: 0-0
Track:	LH: 0-2 RH: 0-1 Tight: 0-2 Gall: 0-1
Aids:	Bl: 0-0 Vi: 0-0 Tstrap: 0-0 Ckp: 0-0
Best Rating:	74 2/04 Font 2m2f110y good NHF

Half-sister to Sweet Senorita; showed ability on bumper debut.

Swift Settlement

5-y-o br m King's Ride-Swift Conveyance (IRE) (Strong Gale)
J Rudge   Geoffrey Vos

Placings:0   (4780)
2003/04: 16[0]S,

	Starts	1st	2nd	3rd	Win & Pl
NH Flat	1	0	0	0	
Career Total	1	0	0	0	

Going:	Sf: 0-1 GS: 0-0 Gd: 0-0 GF: - Fm: 0-0
Distance:	2m/2m3: 0-1 2m4-2m7: 0-0 3m+: 0-0
Track:	LH: 0-1 RH: 0-0 Tight: 0-1 Gall: 0-0
Aids:	Bl: 0-0 Vi: 0-0 Tstrap: 0-0 Ckp: 0-0

Swift Swallow

87f   **100f**

6-y-o ch g Missed Flight-Alhargah (Be My Guest (USA))
O Brennan   Richard J Marshall

Placings:3-662   (4407)
2003/04: 16[6]GF, 16[6]G, 16[2]G,

	Starts	1st	2nd	3rd	Win & Pl
NH Flat	3	0	1	0	544
Career Total	4	0	1	1	820

Going:	Sf: 0-0 GS: 0-0 Gd: 0-2 GF: - Fm: 0-1
Distance:	2m/2m3: 0-3 2m4-2m7: 0-0 3m+: 0-0
Track:	LH: 0-1 RH: 0-2 Tight: 0-0 Gall: 0-3
Aids:	Bl: 0-0 Vi: 0-0 Tstrap: 0-0 Ckp: 0-0
Best Rating:	100 3/04 Hntg 2m110y good NHF

Moderate hurdler; acts on a sound surface.

Swiftway

10-y-o ch g Anshan-Solemn Occasion (USA) (Secreto (USA))
Mrs E Slack   A Slack

Placings:121/1P4/P503/PP   (0407)
2003/04: 22[P]G, 26[P]G,

	Starts	1st	2nd	3rd	Win & Pl
Chases	2	0	0	0	
Career Total	12	3	1	1	11538
126 9/99 MRas 3m		C(0-130)HHdl		G-F	£5151

111	4/99	Carl	2m4f110yE(0-105)HHdl	G-S	£2486
97	12/98	Muss	2m4f	E Hdl	G-F	£1996
			Total win prize-money £9634		

Going:	Sf: 0-0 GS: 0-0 Gd: 0-2 GF: - Fm: 0-0
Distance:	2m/2m3: 0-0 2m4-2m7: 0-1 3m+: 0-1
Track:	LH: 0-2 RH: 0-0 Tight: 0-0 Gall: 0-0
Aids:	Bl: 0-0 Vi: 0-0 Tstrap: 0-0 Ckp: 0-0
Best Rating:	126 9/99 MRas 3m gd-fm Hdl

Swincombe (IRE)

104   **115**

9-y-o b g Good Thyne (USA)-Gladtogetit (Green Shoon)
R H Alner T J Whitley

Placings:0121P-P042P0P   (4633)
2003/04: 24PG, 255S, 234S, 242S, 26PHY, 299GS, 24PG,

	Starts	1st	2nd	3rd	Win & Pl
Chases	7	0	1	0	2614
Career Total	12	2	2	0	12341
115	12/02	Winc	3m1f110yD(0-125)HCh	G-S	£7757
102	5/02	Chep	3m	H Ch	G-F	£1397
			Total win prize-money £9156		

Going:	Sf: 0-4 GS: 0-2 Gd: 0-1 GF: - Fm: 0-0
Distance:	2m/2m3: 0-0 2m4-2m7: 0-0 3m+: 0-7
Track:	LH: 0-4 RH: 0-3 Tight: 0-2 Gall: 0-0
Aids:	Bl: 0-0 Vi: 0-1 Tstrap: 0-0 Ckp: 0-0
Best Rating:	115 12/02 Winc 3m1f110y gd-sft Ch

Moderate chaser; former pointer; effective on fast and easy ground; stays three miles two.

Swing West (USA)

(95h)   **35**

10-y-o b g Gone West (USA)-Danlu (USA) (Danzig (USA))
A E Jones (N F Glynn 8/12) N F Glynn

Placings:212002/35U0006/5PF20U25/03U0F/0022450515
PP0PPP/300P0P-P50PPP   (4933)
2003/04: 24PY, 205YS, 229G, 24PY, 21PG, 26PG,

	Starts	1st	2nd	3rd	Win & Pl
Chases	6	0	0	0	
Career Total	54	2	7	3	16736
91	11/01	Tram	2m4f	(0-102)HCh	YLD	£5286
112	12/97	Ling	2m110y E Hdl	G-S	£2546
			Total win prize-money £7832		

Going:	Sf: 0-0 GS: 0-0 Gd: 0-3 GF: - Fm: 0-0
Distance:	2m/2m3: 0-0 2m4-2m7: 0-3 3m+: 0-3
Track:	LH: 0-1 RH: 0-3 Tight: 0-2 Gall: 0-0
Aids:	Bl: 0-3 Vi: 0-0 Tstrap: 0-0 Ckp: 0-1
Best Rating:	113 1/98 Newc 2m gd-sft Hdl

Swinging Sarah

86   **61**

5-y-o ch m Dr Devious (IRE)-Lupescu (Dixieland Band (USA))
N Wilson Mrs N C Wilson

Placings:0500P   (3322)
2003/04: 17PGF, 165G, 16PGS, 16PG, 21PGS,

	Starts	1st	2nd	3rd	Win & Pl
NH Flat	3	0	0	0	0
Hurdles	2	0	0	0	0
Career Total	5	0	0	0	0

Going:	Sf: 0-0 GS: 0-2 Gd: 0-2 GF: - Fm: 0-1
Distance:	2m/2m3: 0-4 2m4-2m7: 0-1 3m+: 0-0
Track:	LH: 0-3 RH: 0-2 Tight: 0-2 Gall: 0-0

| Aids: | Bl: 0-0 Vi: 0-0 Tstrap: 0-0 Ckp: 0-0 |
| Best Rating: | 73 7/03 Prth 2m110y good NHF |

Swinker

65   **29**

5-y-o b g Roscoe Blake-Fly-Girl (Clantime)
P G Atkinson D G Atkinson

Placings:00P   (3762)
2003/04: 16PG, 16PGS, 21PGS,

	Starts	1st	2nd	3rd	Win & Pl
NH Flat	1	0	0	0	0
Hurdles	2	0	0	0	0
Career Total	3	0	0	0	0

Going:	Sf: 0-0 GS: 0-2 Gd: 0-1 GF: - Fm: 0-0
Distance:	2m/2m3: 0-2 2m4-2m7: 0-1 3m+: 0-0
Track:	LH: 0-3 RH: 0-0 Tight: 0-2 Gall: 0-0
Aids:	Bl: 0-0 Vi: 0-0 Tstrap: 0-0 Ckp: 0-0
Best Rating:	29 1/04 Catt 2m gd-sft Hdl

Sword Lady

106   **101**

6-y-o b m Broadsword (USA)-Speckyfoureyes (Blue Cashmere)
Mrs S D Williams Berry Racing

Placings:6-123310   (4574)
2003/04: 16¹S, 16²S, 19³S, 22³HY, 21¹GS, 21⁰G,

	Starts	1st	2nd	3rd	Win & Pl
Hurdles	6	2	1	2	7775
Career Total	7	2	1	2	7775
100	3/04	Towc	2m5f	E Hdl	G-S	£3445
80	11/03	Towc	2m	E Hdl	SFT	£2352
			Total win prize-money £5797		

Going:	Sf: 1-4 GS: 1-1 Gd: 0-1 GF: - Fm: 0-0
Distance:	2m/2m3: 0-2 2m4-2m7: 1-3 3m+: 0-0
Track:	LH: 0-2 RH: 2-4 Tight: 0-0 Gall: 0-1
Aids:	Bl: 0-0 Vi: 0-0 Tstrap: 0-0 Ckp: 0-0
Best Rating:	101 1/04 Hayd 2m6f heavy Hdl

Moderate novice hurdler; stas two miles six; effective on soft ground.

Sylphide

101   (58h)**99**

9-y-o b m Ballet Royal (USA)-Shafayif (Ela-Mana-Mou)
H J Manners H J Manners

Placings:P033052/00/F0300/P55P4/41UPP53433021
                                                  (4701)
2003/04: 19⁴GF, 26¹G, 26UGF, 26PGF, 20PGF, 235GF, 243GF,
26⁴GF, 19³GF, 22³GS, 25⁰G, 21²GS, 22¹G,

	Starts	1st	2nd	3rd	Win & Pl
Chases	13	2	1	3	11307
Career Total	32	2	2	6	12501
93	4/04	Font	2m6f	E(0-110)HCh	GD	£4361
83	6/03	NAbb	3m2f110yE Ch	GD	£4026
			Total win prize-money £8389		

Going:	Sf: 0-0 GS: 0-2 Gd: 2-3 GF: - Fm: 0-8
Distance:	2m/2m3: 0-1 2m4-2m7: 1-5 3m+: 1-7
Track:	LH: 1-7 RH: 0-3 Tight: 2-8 Gall: 0-1
Aids:	Bl: 0-0 Vi: 0-0 Tstrap: 0-0 Ckp: 0-0
Best Rating:	99 6/03 NAbb 3m2f110y gd-fm Ch

Plating-class chaser; decent point-to-pointer; stays beyond three miles and acts on good ground.

Sylviajazz

5-y-o b m Alhijaz-Dispol Princess (IRE) (Cyrano De Bergerac)
Miss J Feilden J W Jenkins

Placings:0-0   (0291)
2003/04: 16⁰G,

	Starts	1st	2nd	3rd	Win & Pl
Hurdles	1	0	0	0	
Career Total	1	0	0	0	

Going:	Sf: 0-0 GS: 0-0 Gd: 0-1 GF: - Fm: 0-0
Distance:	2m/2m3: 0-1 2m4-2m7: 0-0 3m+: 0-0
Track:	LH: 0-1 RH: 0-0 Tight: 0-1 Gall: 0-0
Aids:	Bl: 0-0 Vi: 0-0 Tstrap: 0-0 Ckp: 0-1

Sylviesbuck (IRE)

103(89h)   (91h)**101+**

7-y-o b g Kasmayo-Sylvies Missiles (IRE) (Buckskin (FR))
G M Moore Mrs I I Plumb

Placings:2500-45U123U   (3986)
2003/04: 21⁴GF, 205S, 25US, 271GS, 232S, 273GS, 27UGS,

	Starts	1st	2nd	3rd	Win & Pl
Chases	7	1	1	1	6896
Career Total	11	1	2	1	7604
101	1/04	Sedg	3m3f	E(0-105)HCh	G-S	£4754
			Total win prize-money £4755		

Going:	Sf: 0-3 GS: 1-3 Gd: 0-0 GF: - Fm: 0-1
Distance:	2m/2m3: 0-2 2m4-2m7: 0-2 3m+: 1-5
Track:	LH: 1-5 RH: 0-1 Tight: 1-4 Gall: 0-0
Aids:	Bl: 0-1 Vi: 0-0 Tstrap: 0-1 Ckp: 0-0
Best Rating:	101 1/04 Sedg 3m3f gd-sft Ch

Irish point winner; ducked and dived when narrow winner of modest handicap chase at Sedgefield in January; stays really well; handles testing conditions.

Szeroki Bor (POL)

99   **106**

5-y-o b h In Camera (IRE)-Szuana (POL) (Five Star Camp (USA))
M Pitman G Pascoe, S Brewer, J Newton & I Mcewen

Placings:0022   (4103)
2003/04: 16⁰GS, 16⁰S, 172GS, 16²G,

	Starts	1st	2nd	3rd	Win & Pl
Hurdles	4	0	2	0	1914
Career Total	4	0	2	0	1914

Going:	Sf: 0-1 GS: 0-2 Gd: 0-1 GF: - Fm: 0-0
Distance:	2m/2m3: 0-4 2m4-2m7: 0-0 3m+: 0-0
Track:	LH: 0-2 RH: 0-2 Tight: 0-2 Gall: 0-1
Aids:	Bl: 0-0 Vi: 0-0 Tstrap: 0-0 Ckp: 0-0
Best Rating:	109 3/04 Plum 2m good Hdl

Modest hurdler; Flat winner in Poland; acts on good and easy ground.

T'Nightsthenight

10-y-o b g Scallywag-Misty Sky (Hot Brandy)
Miss Liz Slattery Larry Slattery

Placings:F   (4296)
2003/04: 21²GF,

| | Starts | 1st | 2nd | 3rd | Win & Pl |
| Chases | 1 | 0 | 0 | 0 | |

Career Total	1	0	0	0

Going: Sf: 0-0 GS: 0-0 Gd: 0-0 GF: - Fm: 0-1
Distance: 2m/2m3: 0-0 2m4-2m7: 0-1 3m+: 0-0
Track: LH: 0-1 RH: 0-0 Tight: 0-0 Gall: 0-0
Aids: Bl: 0-0 Vi: 0-0 Tstrap: 0-0 Ckp: 0-0

Ta Ta For Now

90(100c)   (90c)**101**
7-y-o b g Ezzoud (IRE)-Exit Laughing (Shaab)
Mrs S C Bradburne (P Beaumont 10/3) Mrs V M Stewart

Placings:05F0P1/4430034-5F00PP03   (4913)
2003/04: 20⁴G, 25⁵G, 22⁶G, 24⁰G, 24⁰GF, 25⁵S, 20⁰G, 19⁰GF, 24³S,

	Starts	1st	2nd	3rd	Win & Pl
Hurdles	3	0	0	1	874
Chases	6	0	0	0	416
Career Total	21	1	0	3	5148
101 4/02 Hexm	2m4f110yE Hdl			GD	£2520

Total win prize-money £2520

Going: Sf: 0-2 GS: 0-0 Gd: 0-5 GF: - Fm: 0-2
Distance: 2m/2m3: 0-1 2m4-2m7: 0-3 3m+: 0-5
Track: LH: 0-5 RH: 0-4 Tight: 0-0 Gall: 0-0
Aids: Bl: 0-3 Vi: 0-0 Tstrap: 0-0 Ckp: 0-0
Best Rating: 101 12/02 Ayr 2m4f soft Hdl

Moderate form in bumpers and over hurdles; stays 3m; acts on good or softer; but erratic over fences so far.

Taakid (USA)

84   **108**
9-y-o b g Diesis-Tanwi (Vision (USA))
Mrs S J Smith Daggers Drawn

Placings:660/360305/301P/55F/1255325313-10   (0470)
2003/04: 17¹GF, 20⁰G,

	Starts	1st	2nd	3rd	Win & Pl
Chases	2	1	0	0	4134
Career Total	28	4	2	6	21194
108 5/03 Sthl	2m1f	E(0-110)HCh	G-F	£4134
95 10/02 Sedg	2m5f	D(0-115)HCh	G-F	£4667
93 5/02 Hexm	2m110y	E(0-105)HCh	G-S	£3465
95 7/00 Wolv	2m4f110yE Ch		GD	£3386

Total win prize-money £15653

Going: Sf: 0-0 GS: 0-0 Gd: 0-1 GF: - Fm: 1-1
Distance: 2m/2m3: 1-1 2m4-2m7: 0-1 3m+: 0-0
Track: LH: 1-2 RH: 0-0 Tight: 0-0 Gall: 0-0
Aids: Bl: 0-0 Vi: 0-0 Tstrap: 0-0 Ckp: 0-0
Best Rating: 108 5/03 Sthl 2m1f gd-fm Ch

Modest handicap chaser; quite impressive on return at Southwell in May; stays two miles five and acts on any ground but is ideally suited by firm.

Table For Five

84   **78+**
10-y-o b g Sunley Builds-Prying Nell (Pry)
Miss Victoria Roberts C R Cox

Placings:F54/21224P1/PR0P/0   (3784)
2003/04: 26⁰GS,

	Starts	1st	2nd	3rd	Win & Pl
Hurdles	1	0	0	0	9801
Career Total	15	2	3	0	9801
109 4/01 Winc	2m6f	E Hdl	SFT	£2422
112 11/00 Newb	2m5f	D Hdl	SFT	£4316

Total win prize-money £6738

Going: Sf: 0-0 GS: 0-1 Gd: 0-0 GF: - Fm: 0-0
Distance: 2m/2m3: 0-0 2m4-2m7: 0-0 3m+: 0-1
Track: LH: 0-1 RH: 0-1 Tight: 0-0 Gall: 0-0
Aids: Bl: 0-0 Vi: 0-0 Tstrap: 0-0 Ckp: 0-1
Best Rating: 112 11/00 Newb 2m5f soft Hdl

Tacin (IRE)

(111h)   (119+h)
7-y-o b/br g Supreme Leader-Nicat (Wolver Hollow)
B G Powell Mrs Jean R Bishop

Placings:3F-1P   (2485)
2003/04: 24¹Y, 24⁰GS,

	Starts	1st	2nd	3rd	Win & Pl
Hurdles	1	1	0	0	5377
Chases	1	0	0	0	
Career Total	4	1	0	1	6248
119 5/03 Punc	3m	Hdl	YLD	£5376

Total win prize-money £5377

Going: Sf: 0-0 GS: 0-1 Gd: 0-0 GF: - Fm: 0-0
Distance: 2m/2m3: 0-0 2m4-2m7: 0-0 3m+: 1-2
Track: LH: 0-1 RH: 1-1 Tight: 0-0 Gall: 0-1
Aids: Bl: 0-0 Vi: 0-0 Tstrap: 0-0 Ckp: 0-0
Best Rating: 119 5/03 Punc 3m yield Hdl

Promising hurdler; former Irish Point winner who showed his talent when off the mark at the third attempt when winning useful maiden hurdle at Punchestown in May 2003; pulled up on chase debut; stays three miles; suited by cut.

Taco's Revenge

11-y-o b g Henbit (USA)-Taco (High Season)
M D McMillan M D McMillan

Placings:0/00P/P   (0159)
2003/04: 24⁵GF,

	Starts	1st	2nd	3rd	Win & Pl
Chases	1	0	0	0	
Career Total	5	0	0	0	

Going: Sf: 0-0 GS: 0-0 Gd: 0-0 GF: - Fm: 0-1
Distance: 2m/2m3: 0-0 2m4-2m7: 0-0 3m+: 0-1
Track: LH: 0-1 RH: 0-0 Tight: 0-1 Gall: 0-0
Aids: Bl: 0-0 Vi: 0-0 Tstrap: 0-0 Ckp: 0-0
Best Rating: 92 12/97 Uttx 2m gd-sft NHF

Tacolino (FR)

114   **127**
10-y-o ch g Royal Charter (FR)-Tamilda (FR) (Rose Laurel)
O Brennan John Sheridan

Placings:40/0035/30406/F1460F215/P3/00F51-06111
                                                 (1444)
2003/04: 16⁸G, 16⁶GF, 20¹GF, 20¹GF, 17¹GF,

	Starts	1st	2nd	3rd	Win & Pl
Chases	5	3	0	0	28017
Career Total	32	6	1	3	47215
127 9/03 MRas	2m1f110yD(0-125)HCh	G-F	£6857
120 6/03 MRas	2m4f	C(0-135)HCh	G-F	£13757
109 6/03 Worc	2m4f110yD(0-125)HCh	G-F	£7402
99 4/03 MRas	2m1f110yD(0-115)HCh	GD	£5856
109 12/00 Fair	2m100y (0-116)HCh	Y-S	£5520
89 5/00 Rosc	2m (0-123)HCh	FRM	£4416

Total win prize-money £43811

Going: Sf: 0-0 GS: 0-0 Gd: 0-0 GF: - Fm: 3-5
Distance: 2m/2m3: 1-3 2m4-2m7: 2-2 3m+: 0-0
Track: LH: 1-2 RH: 2-3 Tight: 2-2 Gall: 0-1

Aids: Bl: 0-0 Vi: 0-0 Tstrap: 0-0 Ckp: 0-0
Best Rating: 127 9/03 MRas 2m1f110y gd-fm Ch

Useful ex-Irish chaser; has done really well for present trainer recording fourth success here at Market Rasen in September; stays two miles four but highly effective over two miles; seems to act on most types of going but suited by fast ground.

Tactful Remark (USA)

98(113h)   (124+h)**104**
8-y-o ch g Lord At War (ARG)-Right Word (USA) (Verbatim (USA))
M C Pipe Professor D B A Silk & Mrs Heather Silk

Placings:113P3-51P14   (1505)
2003/04: 16⁵G, 17¹GF, 16⁰GF, 16¹GF, 16⁴GF,

	Starts	1st	2nd	3rd	Win & Pl
Hurdles	3	1	0	0	3367
Chases	2	1	0	0	3314
Career Total	10	4	0	2	14336
104 9/03 Worc	2m	E Ch	G-F	£3029
124 6/03 Sthl	2m1f	E Hdl	G-F	£3367
131 6/02 NAbb	2m1f	D Hdl	G-F	£3469
131 6/02 Worc	2m	E Hdl	SFT	£2765

Total win prize-money £12631

Going: Sf: 0-0 GS: 0-0 Gd: 0-1 GF: - Fm: 2-4
Distance: 2m/2m3: 2-5 2m4-2m7: 0-0 3m+: 0-0
Track: LH: 2-5 RH: 0-0 Tight: 0-2 Gall: 0-0
Aids: Bl: 0-0 Vi: 0-0 Tstrap: 0-0 Ckp: 0-0
Best Rating: 131 6/02 NAbb 2m1f gd-fm Hdl

Decent novice hurdler; found it more difficult to front-run in handicap company; apparently in command when left clear four out on chasing debut at Worcester September; looked ungenuine when well beaten next time; best at 2m; acts on any ground.

Tadzio

5-y-o bl g Mtoto-Fresher (Fabulous Dancer (USA))
M J Gingell (P R Webber 15/5) The Real Tadzio Partnership

Placings:0-50FUFP   (2113)
2003/04: 16⁵GF, 16⁰GF, 16⁶GF, 20⁰G, 16⁵G, 16⁸G,

	Starts	1st	2nd	3rd	Win & Pl
NH Flat	2	0	0	0	0
Hurdles	4	0	0	0	0
Career Total	7	0	0	0	0

Going: Sf: 0-0 GS: 0-0 Gd: 0-3 GF: - Fm: 0-3
Distance: 2m/2m3: 0-5 2m4-2m7: 0-1 3m+: 0-0
Track: LH: 0-5 RH: 0-1 Tight: 0-3 Gall: 0-0
Aids: Bl: 0-0 Vi: 0-0 Tstrap: 0-0 Ckp: 0-0
Best Rating: 77 5/03 Ludl 2m gd-fm NHF

Taffrail

85   **86**
6-y-o b g Slip Anchor-Tizona (Pharly (FR))
D Burchell (J L Dunlop 18/9) P S & Mrs N G Pritchard

Placings:0000   (4524)
2003/04: 16⁵G, 16⁰G, 16⁰G, 16⁰GS,

	Starts	1st	2nd	3rd	Win & Pl
Hurdles	4	0	0	0	
Career Total	4	0	0	0	

Going:	Sf: 0-1 GS: 0-1 Gd: 0-2 GF: - Fm: 0-0
Distance:	2m/2m3: 0-4 2m4-2m7: 0-0 3m+: 0-0
Track:	LH: 0-2 RH: 0-2 Tight: 0-0 Gall: 0-1
Aids:	Bl: 0-2 Vi: 0-0 Tstrap: 0-0 Ckp: 0-0
Best Rating:	91 2/04 Newb 2m110y good Hdl

Taffy Dancer

103   **108+**

6-y-o b g Emperor Jones (USA)-Ballerina Bay (Myjinski (USA))
H Morrison Rosemary Jenks & Partners

Placings:2520   (4232)
2003/04: 20²G, 24⁵G, 20²G, 20⁹GF,

	Starts	1st	2nd	3rd	Win & Pl
Hurdles	4	0	2	0	1820
Career Total	4	0	2	0	1820

Going:	Sf: 0-1 GS: 0-1 Gd: 0-1 GF: - Fm: 0-1
Distance:	2m/2m3: 0-0 2m4-2m7: 0-3 3m+: 0-1
Track:	LH: 0-1 RH: 0-1 Tight: 0-3 Gall: 0-0
Aids:	Bl: 0-0 Vi: 0-0 Tstrap: 0-0 Ckp: 0-0
Best Rating:	108 2/04 Folk 2m4f110y gd-sft Hdl

Moderate hurdler; stayer on the Flat; gets 2m4f; acts on good and easy ground.

Tagar (FR)

106(105h)   (95h)**108**

7-y-o b g Fijar Tango (FR)-Fight For Arfact (Salmon Leap (USA))
C Grant (N J Henderson 13/5) Lord Daresbury

Placings:3640/522/340-441   (1425)
2003/04: 16⁴GS, 19⁴GF, 16¹G,

	Starts	1st	2nd	3rd	Win & Pl
Hurdles	1	0	0	0	0
Chases	2	1	0	0	5771
Career Total	13	1	2	2	14668
108 9/03	Prth	2m		D Ch	GD £5508
				Total win prize-money £5509

Going:	Sf: 0-0 GS: 0-1 Gd: 1-1 GF: - Fm: 0-1
Distance:	2m/2m3: 1-3 2m4-2m7: 0-0 3m+: 0-0
Track:	LH: 0-1 RH: 1-2 Tight: 0-0 Gall: 0-0
Aids:	Bl: 0-0 Vi: 0-0 Tstrap: 0-0 Ckp: 0-0
Best Rating:	124 3/02 Newb 2m110y gd-sft Hdl

Moderate novice chaser/hurdler; disappointing for Nicky Henderson, now with Chris Grant; won first time out on the Flat; stays two and a half miles; suited by soft ground, but acts on good.

Tahrima

74f   **67f**

5-y-o b m Slip Anchor-Khandjar (Kris)
P Monteith I Bell

Placings:0-0   (2141)
2003/04: 16⁰G,

	Starts	1st	2nd	3rd	Win & Pl
NH Flat	1	0	0	0	
Career Total	2	0	0	0	

Going:	Sf: 0-0 GS: 0-0 Gd: 0-0 GF: - Fm: 0-0
Distance:	2m/2m3: 0-1 2m4-2m7: 0-0 3m+: 0-0
Track:	LH: 0-1 RH: 0-0 Tight: 0-0 Gall: 0-0
Aids:	Bl: 0-0 Vi: 0-0 Tstrap: 0-0 Ckp: 0-0
Best Rating:	67 2/03 Hntg 2m110y good NHF

Tai Lass

102   **100**

4-y-o b/br f Taipan (IRE)-Kerry's Oats (Derrylin)
P R Hedger J J Whelan

Placings:33622   (4591)
2003/04: 16²GF, 16³GS, 16⁶S, 16²G, 16²G,

	Starts	1st	2nd	3rd	Win & Pl
Hurdles	5	0	2	2	5358
Career Total	5	0	2	2	5358

Going:	Sf: 0-1 GS: 0-1 Gd: 0-2 GF: - Fm: 0-1
Distance:	2m/2m3: 0-5 2m4-2m7: 0-0 3m+: 0-0
Track:	LH: 0-4 RH: 0-1 Tight: 0-1 Gall: 0-4
Aids:	Bl: 0-0 Vi: 0-0 Tstrap: 0-0 Ckp: 0-0
Best Rating:	99 3/04 Hntg 2m110y good Hdl

Moderate hurdler; may need farther than two miles; acts on any ground.

Taillefer (FR)

81(105h)   (104h)**57**

8-y-o b g Cyborg (FR)-Tourka (FR) (Rose Laurel)
M E D Francis Mrs Merrick Francis Iii

Placings:0F503123126/0/PBPP6213-0   (0305)
2003/04: 20⁰G,

	Starts	1st	2nd	3rd	Win & Pl
Chases	1	0	0	0	
Career Total	21	3	3	3	21795
102 2/03	Sand	2m4f110yD(0-120)HHdl		HVY	£5027
122 3/01	Hntg	2m4f110yE Ch		SFT	£3276
9/00	Fntb	2m3f		Ch	GD £3362
				Total win prize-money £11666

Going:	Sf: 0-0 GS: 0-0 Gd: 0-1 GF: - Fm: 0-0
Distance:	2m/2m3: 0-0 2m4-2m7: 0-0 3m+: 0-0
Track:	LH: 0-1 RH: 0-0 Tight: 0-1 Gall: 0-0
Aids:	Bl: 0-0 Vi: 0-0 Tstrap: 0-0 Ckp: 0-0
Best Rating:	122 3/01 Hayd 2m6f heavy Ch

Modest handicap hurdler; has won over fences, but failed to progress over the larger obstacles; effective at around two and a half miles; acts on good and soft ground.

Tails I Win

97f   **84f**

5-y-o b g Petoski-Spinayab (King Of Spain)
J W Mullins J H Mead

Placings:0-25   (1944)
2003/04: 16²GF, 17⁵G,

	Starts	1st	2nd	3rd	Win & Pl
NH Flat	2	0	1	0	468
Career Total	3	0	1	0	468

Going:	Sf: 0-0 GS: 0-0 Gd: 0-1 GF: - Fm: 0-1
Distance:	2m/2m3: 0-2 2m4-2m7: 0-0 3m+: 0-0
Track:	LH: 0-1 RH: 0-1 Tight: 0-1 Gall: 0-0
Aids:	Bl: 0-0 Vi: 0-0 Tstrap: 0-0 Ckp: 0-0
Best Rating:	84 10/03 Uttx 2m gd-fm NHF

Some promise in bumpers.

Taipo Prince (IRE)

99   **83**

4-y-o b g Entrepreneur-Dedicated Lady (IRE) (Pennine Walk)
Miss Kate Milligan (A P Jarvis 11/7) E Whalley

Placings:03603   (4657)
2003/04: 17⁰G, 16³GF, 16⁶G, 19⁹GF, 16³S,

	Starts	1st	2nd	3rd	Win & Pl
Hurdles	5	0	0	2	1100
Career Total	5	0	0	2	1100

Going:	Sf: 0-1 GS: 0-0 Gd: 0-2 GF: - Fm: 0-2
Distance:	2m/2m3: 0-5 2m4-2m7: 0-0 3m+: 0-0
Track:	LH: 0-3 RH: 0-2 Tight: 0-4 Gall: 0-0
Aids:	Bl: 0-0 Vi: 0-0 Tstrap: 0-0 Ckp: 0-0
Best Rating:	83 1/04 Muss 2m gd-fm Hdl

Plating-class hurdler; best around 2m; acts on good ground.

Takagi (IRE)

105(105h)   (129h)**146**

9-y-o b g Husyan (USA)-Ballyclough Gale (Strong Gale)
E J O'Grady D Cox

Placings:0/2/3 1145/3U311F2152/1P2P230-435601U   (4647)
2003/04: 25⁴GY, 24³GY, 24⁴S, 24⁶S, 24⁰HY, 25¹Y, 36⁰G,

	Starts	1st	2nd	3rd	Win & Pl
Hurdles	2	0	0	0	0
Chases	5	1	0	1	21695
Career Total	31	7	5	5	131088
141 2/04	Fair	3m1f	Ch	YLD	£16045
150 11/02	Navn	3m	HCh	SFT	£25920
143 3/02	Navn	3m	HCh	SH	£15950
143 1/02	Naas	3m	Ch	SH	£17944
126 1/02	Naas	2m3f	Ch	YLD	£7831
123 1/01	Naas	2m3f	Hdl	SFT	£5564
135 12/00	Gowr	2m2f	NHF	HVY	£3588
				Total win prize-money £92846

Going:	Sf: 0-3 GS: 0-0 Gd: 0-3 GF: - Fm: 0-0
Distance:	2m/2m3: 0-1 2m4-2m7: 0-0 3m+: 1-7
Track:	LH: 0-3 RH: 1-4 Tight: 0-1 Gall: 0-0
Aids:	Bl: 1-1 Vi: 0-1 Tstrap: 0-0 Ckp: 0-0
Best Rating:	151 2/03 Fair 3m1f yld-sft Ch

Smart Irish chaser; stays beyond three miles; effective in soft ground; blinkered for the first time when winning at Fairyhouse in February 2004; unseated at the Chair in the National.

Take A Rain Check (IRE)

     33

7-y-o b m Rainbows For Life (CAN)-Just A Second (Jimsun)
C J Drewe The Coskett Partnership

Placings:PP/PP0-5P6P   (3513)
2003/04: 16⁵G, 21⁰GS, 20⁶G, 20⁰PG,

	Starts	1st	2nd	3rd	Win & Pl
Hurdles	4	0	0	0	0
Career Total	9	0	0	0	0

Going:	Sf: 0-0 GS: 0-1 Gd: 0-3 GF: - Fm: 0-0
Distance:	2m/2m3: 0-1 2m4-2m7: 0-3 3m+: 0-0
Track:	LH: 0-0 RH: 0-2 Tight: 0-2 Gall: 0-0
Aids:	Bl: 0-0 Vi: 0-0 Tstrap: 0-0 Ckp: 0-1
Best Rating:	33 4/03 Strf 2m6f110y gd-fm Hdl

Take Control (IRE)

115   **146**

10-y-o b g Roselier (FR)-Frosty Fairy (Paddy's Stream)
M C Pipe D A Johnson

Placings:050 1/113101/**11225130**/36P4P51/04F0P6-33PF
(3291)

2003/04: 32³GF, 26³GS, 29PS, 29FGS,

	Starts	1st	2nd	3rd	Win & Pl
Chases	4	0	0	2	18700
Career Total	35	9	2	5	173602
153	4/02	Ayr	4m1f	A HCh	GD	£60000
131	2/01	Wwck	3m2f	C Ch	SFT	£7046
138	11/00	NAbb	3m2f110yC Ch		HVY	£5768
143	10/00	Extr	2m3f110yD Ch		SFT	£5655
145	4/00	Chel	3m	B(0-145)HHdl	SFT	£10582
126	2/00	Plum	2m5f	D Hdl	SFT	£3797
117	12/99	Hayd	2m7f110yC(0-110)HHdl		SFT	£3257
112	12/99	Winc	2m6f	F(0-100)HHdl	GD	£2472
118	2/99	Naas	2m3f	NHF		SFT	£3069
				Total win prize-money £101649		

Going:	Sf: 0-1 GS: 0-2 Gd: 0-0 GF: - Fm: 0-1
Distance:	2m/2m3: 0-0 2m4-2m7: 0-0 3m+: 0-4
Track:	LH: 0-3 RH: 0-0 Tight: 0-1 Gall: 0-0
Aids:	Bl: 0-0 Vi: 0-4 Tstrap: 0-0 Ckp: 0-0
Best Rating:	153 4/02 Ayr 4m1f good Ch

Smart chaser; won the Scottish Grand National in 2002; relishes testing conditions, but also effective on a sound surface; stays four miles; inconsistent, but ran well in the Hennessy in November; off the track since January; has worn visor.

Take Heed
88   86

8-y-o b g Warning-Tunaria (USA) (Lyphard (USA))
K A Morgan   Roemex Ltd

Placings:U/0FP/05122606-4   (0077)
2003/04: 17⁴S,

	Starts	1st	2nd	3rd	Win & Pl
Hurdles	1	0	0	0	0
Career Total	13	1	2	0	5514
88	11/02	Kemp	2m	E(0-100)HHdl	GD	£3591
				Total win prize-money £3591		

Going:	Sf: 0-1 GS: 0-0 Gd: 0-0 GF: - Fm: 0-0
Distance:	2m/2m3: 0-1 2m4-2m7: 0-0 3m+: 0-0
Track:	LH: 0-1 RH: 0-0 Tight: 0-1 Gall: 0-0
Aids:	Bl: 0-0 Vi: 0-0 Tstrap: 0-1 Ckp: 0-0
Best Rating:	88 11/02 Fknm 2m gd-sft Hdl

Moderate novice hurdler, winner at Kempton in November 2002, suited by a sound surface.

Take The Odds (IRE)
55   (0c)73

8-y-o gr g Roselier (FR)-Skinana (Buckskin (FR))
G Prodromou   Alan Macalister

Placings:FP3   (2109)
2003/04: 24FGF, 22PGF, 23³G,

	Starts	1st	2nd	3rd	Win & Pl
Hurdles	1	0	0	1	313
Chases	2	0	0	0	0
Career Total	3	0	0	1	313

Going:	Sf: 0-0 GS: 0-0 Gd: 0-1 GF: - Fm: 0-2
Distance:	2m/2m3: 0-0 2m4-2m7: 0-1 3m+: 0-0
Track:	LH: 0-1 RH: 0-0 Tight: 0-2 Gall: 0-1
Aids:	Bl: 0-0 Vi: 0-0 Tstrap: 0-0 Ckp: 0-0
Best Rating:	72 11/03 Fknm 2m7f110y good Hdl

Take The Stand (IRE)
112   (97h)141+

8-y-o b g Witness Box (USA)-Denys Daughter (IRE) (Crash Course)
P Bowen   The Courters

Placings:00/64224135/P211-F121B14F   (3606)
2003/04: 32²GF, 26¹GF, 23²GF, 24¹GF, 26BGS, 25¹G, 29⁴S, 24FS,

	Starts	1st	2nd	3rd	Win & Pl
Chases	8	3	1	0	32048
Career Total	22	6	4	1	51647
145	12/03	Extr	3m1f110yC(0-135)HCh	GD	£7436
131	10/03	Chep	3m	B(0-145)HCh	G-F	£10478
129	7/03	NAbb	3m2f110yC(0-135)HCh	G-F	£8073
124	3/03	Plum	3m2f	D Ch	G-F	£6890
116	3/03	Fknm	3m110y	D Ch	G-F	£6440
92	9/01	Worc	3m	F Hdl	G-F	£1876
				Total win prize-money £41194		

Going:	Sf: 0-2 GS: 0-1 Gd: 1-1 GF: - Fm: 2-4
Distance:	2m/2m3: 0-0 2m4-2m7: 0-0 **3m+: 3-8**
Track:	**LH: 2-6** RH: 1-1 Tight: 1-1 Gall: 0-2
Aids:	Bl: 0-0 Vi: 0-0 Tstrap: 0-0 Ckp: 0-0
Best Rating:	145 12/03 Extr 3m1f110y good Ch

Useful chaser; vastly improved for new yard in 2003; effective from three to four miles and likes fast ground; suited by a left-handed track.

Takeachanceonhim
93f   78f

6-y-o b g Dilum (USA)-Smilingatstrangers (Macmillion)
Mrs Barbara Waring   A G Gibbs

Placings:06   (0947)
2003/04: 16⁰G, 16⁶G,

	Starts	1st	2nd	3rd	Win & Pl
NH Flat	2	0	0	0	0
Career Total	2	0	0	0	0

Going:	Sf: 0-0 GS: 0-0 Gd: 0-2 GF: - Fm: 0-0
Distance:	2m/2m3: 0-2 2m4-2m7: 0-0 3m+: 0-0
Track:	LH: 0-2 RH: 0-0 Tight: 0-0 Gall: 0-0
Aids:	Bl: 0-0 Vi: 0-0 Tstrap: 0-0 Ckp: 0-0
Best Rating:	78 6/03 Worc 2m good NHF

Taking (FR)

8-y-o gr g Take Risks (FR)-Sonning (FR) (Moulin)
C N Kellett   Sean A Taylor

Placings:P265033/565640364621/**P0F22/503621P3P**-PFPP   (3758)
2003/04: 16PS, 19FS, 20PS, 22PG,

	Starts	1st	2nd	3rd	Win & Pl
Chases	4	0	0	0	
Career Total	37	2	5	5	36583
92	7/02	Sthl	2m5f110yF(0-95)HCh	G-F	£3087
87	2/01	Folk	2m	F(0-90)HCh	SFT	£2926
				Total win prize-money £6013		

Going:	Sf: 0-3 GS: 0-0 Gd: 0-1 GF: - Fm: 0-0
Distance:	2m/2m3: 0-1 2m4-2m7: 0-3 3m+: 0-1
Track:	LH: 0-0 RH: 0-3 Tight: 0-1 Gall: 0-1
Aids:	Bl: 0-2 Vi: 0-0 Tstrap: 0-0 Ckp: 0-0
Best Rating:	92 7/02 Sthl 2m5f110y gd-fm Ch

Taksina
86(83h)   (43h)59

5-y-o b m Wace (USA)-Quago (New Member)
R H Buckler   Mrs Timothy Lewis

Placings:0056-035003F4   (4791)
2003/04: 17⁰GF, 17³S, 22⁵GF, 19⁴HY, 21⁰G, 25³GF, 22FGS, 20⁴G,

	Starts	1st	2nd	3rd	Win & Pl
Hurdles	5	0	0	1	544
Chases	3	0	0	1	863
Career Total	12	0	0	2	1407

Going:	Sf: 0-2 GS: 0-1 Gd: 0-2 GF: - Fm: 0-3
Distance:	2m/2m3: 0-2 2m4-2m7: 0-5 3m+: 0-1
Track:	LH: 0-3 RH: 0-5 Tight: 0-3 Gall: 0-0
Aids:	Bl: 0-0 Vi: 0-0 Tstrap: 0-0 Ckp: 0-0
Best Rating:	59 4/04 Plum 2m4f good Ch

Talama Lady (IRE)
104   99+

7-y-o b m Persian Bold-Talama (FR) (Shakapour)
G A Swinbank   Mrs B Watson

Placings:1/1/062P   (4881)
2003/04: 16⁰G, 16⁶G, 17²GS, 17PGS,

	Starts	1st	2nd	3rd	Win & Pl
NH Flat	2	1	0	0	0
Hurdles	2	0	1	0	1260
Career Total	6	2	1	0	4816
99	5/01	Hntg	2m110y	H NHF	G-F	£1687
97	4/01	MRas	1m5f110y	H NHF	G-S	£1869
				Total win prize-money £3556		

Going:	Sf: 0-0 GS: 0-3 Gd: 0-1 GF: - Fm: 0-0
Distance:	2m/2m3: 0-4 2m4-2m7: 0-0 3m+: 0-0
Track:	LH: 0-2 RH: 0-2 Tight: 0-2 Gall: 0-0
Aids:	Bl: 0-0 Vi: 0-0 Tstrap: 0-0 Ckp: 0-0
Best Rating:	99 3/04 Bang 2m1f gd-sft Hdl

Won both starts in bumpers back in 2001 before suffering an injury; struggled since returning.

Talarive (USA)
107   115

8-y-o ch g Riverman (USA)-Estala (Be My Guest (USA))
P D Niven   Ian G M Dalgleish

Placings:00000/4P00/425023/2112322P-36600P2000   (3722)

2003/04: 16³G, 16⁶GS, 16PG, 16⁰GS, 16PS, 16²HY, 20⁰S, 18⁰HY, 16⁰S,

	Starts	1st	2nd	3rd	Win & Pl
Hurdles	10	0	1	1	4885
Career Total	33	2	7	3	28414
115	1/03	Ayr	2m	D(0-125)HHdl	HVY	£4745
105	12/02	Leic	2m	F(0-100)HHdl	HVY	£3513
				Total win prize-money £8258		

Going:	Sf: 0-6 GS: 0-2 Gd: 0-2 GF: - Fm: 0-0
Distance:	2m/2m3: 0-9 2m4-2m7: 0-1 3m+: 0-0
Track:	LH: 0-9 RH: 0-1 Tight: 0-2 Gall: 0-1
Aids:	Bl: 0-0 Vi: 0-0 Tstrap: 0-0 Ckp: 0-3
Best Rating:	128 3/03 Kels 2m2f gd-sft Hdl

Modest hurdler; ex-Irish; stays two and a half miles, but effective over shorter; suited by testing ground; has worn cheekpieces.

Talbot Lad

109(99h)   (89h)**122+**

8-y-o b g Weld-Greenacres Girl (Tycoon li)
S A Brookshaw M J Talbot

Placings:**202255020/35P0423526-2121F1**   (4715)
2003/04: 19²GF, 20¹G, 16²G, 18¹G, 20²G, 20¹G,

	Starts	1st	2nd	3rd	Win & Pl
Chases	6	3	2	0	26756
Career Total	25	3	8	2	33527
122 4/04 Ludl	2m4f	D(0-115)HCh		GD	£10198
118 3/04 Newb	2m2f110yC(0-125)HCh			GD	£8417
106 1/04 Ludl	2m4f	E(0-105)HCh		GD	£4813

Total win prize-money £23430

Going:	Sf: 0-0 GS: 0-0 Gd: 3-5 GF: -: Fm: 0-1
Distance:	2m/2m3: 1-3 2m4-2m7: 2-3 3m+: 0-0
Track:	LH: 1-2 RH: 2-4 Tight: 2-4 Gall: 1-1
Aids:	Bl: 0-0 Vi: 0-0 Tstrap: 3-6 Ckp: 0-0
Best Rating:	122 4/04 Ludl 2m4f good Ch

Moderate chaser; placed in bumpers and over hurdles; stays 2m4f but effective at shorter; acts on fast ground; wears tongue tie.

Tale Bridge (IRE)

11-y-o b g Tale Quale-Loobagh Bridge (River Beauty)
Mrs O Bush J Grant Cann

Placings:**0600/P3P6-**   (0020)
2003/04: 26⁶S,

	Starts	1st	2nd	3rd	Win & Pl
Chases	1	0	0	0	0
Career Total	8	0	0	1	208

Going:	Sf: 0-1 GS: 0-0 Gd: 0-0 GF: -: Fm: 0-0
Distance:	2m/2m3: 0-0 2m4-2m7: 0-0 3m+: 0-1
Track:	LH: 0-1 RH: 0-0 Tight: 0-1 Gall: 0-0
Aids:	Bl: 0-0 Vi: 0-0 Tstrap: 0-0 Ckp: 0-0
Best Rating:	78 3/03 Winc 3m1f110y soft Ch

Taleban

9-y-o b g Alleged (USA)-Triode (USA) (Sharpen Up)
J Wade John Wade

Placings:**6/044320/000/25243**   (4263)
2003/04: 21²GF, 21⁵G, 21²GF, 16⁴F, 25³GF,

	Starts	1st	2nd	3rd	Win & Pl
Chases	5	0	2	1	2302
Career Total	15	0	3	2	3636

Going:	Sf: 0-0 GS: 0-0 Gd: 0-1 GF: -: Fm: 0-4
Distance:	2m/2m3: 0-1 2m4-2m7: 0-3 3m+: 0-1
Track:	LH: 0-5 RH: 0-0 Tight: 0-4 Gall: 0-0
Aids:	Bl: 0-0 Vi: 0-0 Tstrap: 0-0 Ckp: 0-2
Best Rating:	108 1/00 Ludl 2m gd-sft Hdl

Moderate novice hunter chaser, stays two miles five; acts on fast ground.

Tales Of Bounty (IRE)

9-y-o b g Ela-Mana-Mou-Tales Of Wisdom (Rousillon (USA)
P F Nicholls (R Barber 12/3) H B Geddes

Placings:**36532/100/31/2/1014-261P**   (4872)
2003/04: 24²G, 22⁶G, 24¹G, 24⁴S,

	Starts	1st	2nd	3rd	Win & Pl
Hurdles	2	0	1	0	2584
Chases	2	1	0	0	5460
Career Total	19	5	3	3	28886
109 3/04 Sand	3m110y H Ch		GD	£5460
121 12/02 Tntn	3m	D Ch	G-S	£4875
121 11/02 Extr	3m110y E(0-110)HHdl		G-S	£3444
123 4/01 Winc	2m6f	D(0-120)HHdl	SFT	£4225
116 11/99 Extr	2m1f	E Hdl	G-S	£3297

Total win prize-money £21301

Going:	Sf: 0-1 GS: 0-0 Gd: 1-3 GF: -: Fm: 0-0
Distance:	2m/2m3: 0-0 2m4-2m7: 0-1 3m+: 1-3
Track:	LH: 0-0 RH: 1-1 Tight: 0-2 Gall: 0-0
Aids:	Bl: 1-3 Vi: 0-0 Tstrap: 0-0 Ckp: 0-0
Best Rating:	123 5/03 Worc 3m good Hdl

Hunter chaser; formerly a useful chaser/hurdler for Paul Nicholls; stays three miles; acts on soft ground.

Talk On Corners (IRE)

84   **44**

9-y-o b m Alphabatim (USA)-Shannon Lass (Callernish)
N R Mitchell Mrs E Mitchell

Placings:**0F0000/00P/00PP-0P**   (0706)
2003/04: 19⁰GF, 22⁰GF,

	Starts	1st	2nd	3rd	Win & Pl
Hurdles	2	0	0	0	0
Career Total	15	0	0	0	0

Going:	Sf: 0-0 GS: 0-0 Gd: 0-0 GF: -: Fm: 0-2
Distance:	2m/2m3: 0-1 2m4-2m7: 0-1 3m+: 0-0
Track:	LH: 0-1 RH: 0-1 Tight: 0-1 Gall: 0-0
Aids:	Bl: 0-0 Vi: 0-0 Tstrap: 0-0 Ckp: 0-0
Best Rating:	64 1/02 Punc 2m yld-sft Hdl

Tall Tale (IRE)

97   **74**

12-y-o b g Tale Quale-Prudent Rose (IRE) (Strong Gale)
R Johnson The Jolly Boys Partnership

Placings:**52/34P/PP0425520/03UP4/345340F343/5354U40 P64P1-5**   (0898)
2003/04: 26⁵GF,

	Starts	1st	2nd	3rd	Win & Pl
Chases	1	0	0	0	0
Career Total	42	1	3	7	11607
74 3/03 Hexm	3m1f	G(0-90)HCh	GD	£2681

Total win prize-money £2681

Going:	Sf: 0-0 GS: 0-0 Gd: 0-0 GF: -: Fm: 0-1
Distance:	2m/2m3: 0-0 2m4-2m7: 0-0 3m+: 0-1
Track:	LH: 0-1 RH: 0-0 Tight: 0-1 Gall: 0-0
Aids:	Bl: 0-0 Vi: 0-0 Tstrap: 0-0 Ckp: 0-1
Best Rating:	98 10/01 Kels 3m1f good Ch

Poor staying chaser; finally broke his duck at Hexham in March 2003; stays 3m1f; suited by a sound surface.

Tallahassee (IRE)

80f   **72f**

6-y-o ch g Moscow Society (USA)-Kemperstrat (The Parson)
D R MacLeod Maurice W Chapman

Placings:**000**   (4517)
2003/04: 16⁰HY, 16⁰GS, 16⁰GS,

	Starts	1st	2nd	3rd	Win & Pl
NH Flat	3	0	0	0	
Career Total	3	0	0	0	

Going:	Sf: 0-1 GS: 0-2 Gd: 0-0 GF: -: Fm: 0-0
Distance:	2m/2m3: 0-3 2m4-2m7: 0-0 3m+: 0-0
Track:	LH: 0-3 RH: 0-0 Tight: 0-0 Gall: 0-0
Aids:	Bl: 0-0 Vi: 0-0 Tstrap: 0-0 Ckp: 0-0
Best Rating:	66 3/04 Weth 2m gd-sft NHF

Talldark'N'Andsome

99   **103+**

5-y-o b g Efisio-Fleur Du Val (Valiyar)
N P Littmoden Mrs Gillian Curley

Placings:**2**   (2534)
2003/04: 16²S,

	Starts	1st	2nd	3rd	Win & Pl
Hurdles	1	0	1	0	857
Career Total	1	0	1	0	857

Going:	Sf: 0-1 GS: 0-0 Gd: 0-0 GF: -: Fm: 0-0
Distance:	2m/2m3: 0-1 2m4-2m7: 0-0 3m+: 0-0
Track:	LH: 0-1 RH: 0-0 Tight: 0-1 Gall: 0-0
Aids:	Bl: 0-0 Vi: 0-0 Tstrap: 0-0 Ckp: 0-0
Best Rating:	103 12/03 Plum 2m soft Hdl

Novice hurdler; ran into a promising sort on his hurdles debut; acts in soft ground.

Tallow Bay (IRE)

98   **84+**

9-y-o b g Glacial Storm (USA)-Minimum Choice (IRE) (Miners Lamp)
Mrs S Wall Mrs S Wall

Placings:**000/5054600/243F25U2P/6116P5-05P566 (4666)**
2003/04: 20⁰G, 22⁵S, 25⁵S, 24⁵G, 19⁶GS, 20⁶S,

	Starts	1st	2nd	3rd	Win & Pl
Chases	6	0	0	0	0
Career Total	31	2	3	1	13142
106 1/03 Folk	2m5f	E Ch	HVY	£4238
104 1/03 Folk	2m5f	F(0-95)HCh	SFT	£3421

Total win prize-money £7660

Going:	Sf: 0-3 GS: 0-1 Gd: 0-2 GF: -: Fm: 0-0
Distance:	2m/2m3: 0-0 2m4-2m7: 0-4 3m+: 0-2
Track:	LH: 0-1 RH: 0-3 Tight: 0-3 Gall: 0-0
Aids:	Bl: 0-0 Vi: 0-0 Tstrap: 0-0 Ckp: 0-1
Best Rating:	109 4/00 Asct 2m110y soft NHF

Plating-class handicap chaser; acts on testing ground; stays three miles.

Tam O'Shanter

100   (97c)**97**

10-y-o gr g Persian Bold-No More Rosies (Warpath)
J G M O'Shea N M Lowe

Placings:F220/0/035112025635325/2F3**331143/5P3**152/54   (4632)
2003/04: 22⁵GF, 24⁴G,

	Starts	1st	2nd	3rd	Win & Pl
Hurdles	2	0	0	0	0
Career Total	37	5	7	8	25793
97 7/01 Sedg	3m3f110yF(0-110)HHdl		G-F	£2814
93 8/00 NAbb	3m2f110yE Ch		G-S	£3347
93 7/00 Sedg	3m3f	D Ch	G-F	£3757

103	7/99	Worc	2m4f	D Hdl		G-F	£3104
108	6/99	Uttx	2m4f110yG(0-95)HHdl		G-S	£2186
				Total win prize-money £15211			

Going:	Sf: 0-0 GS: 0-0 Gd: 0-1 GF: - Fm: 0-1
Distance:	2m/2m3: 0-0 2m4-2m7: 0-1 3m+: 0-1
Track:	LH: 0-1 RH: 0-1 Tight: 0-2 Gall: 0-0
Aids:	Bl: 0-0 Vi: 0-0 Tstrap: 0-0 Ckp: 0-0
Best Rating:	108 6/99 Uttx 2m4f110y gd-sft Hdl

Tamango (FR)

112(102h)   (117 h)**125**

7-y-o gr g Klimt (FR)-Timposa (FR) (Tip Moss (FR))
P J Hobbs The Brushmakers

Placings:32401/2223F3-1122F14   (1869)
2003/04: 18¹G, 16¹GF, 17²GS, 17²G, 16²G, 17¹GF, 16⁴GF,

	Starts	1st	2nd	3rd	Win & Pl
Chases	7	3	2	0	18581
Career Total	18	4	6	3	30803

125	10/03	Strf	2m1f110yD(0-120)HCh	G-F	£4719
109	5/03	Hrfd	2m	E Ch	G-F	£4036
117	5/03	Font	2m2f	E Ch	GD	£4114
103	4/02	Tntn	2m1f	E Hdl	G-S	£2800
				Total win prize-money £15671	

Going:	Sf: 0-0 GS: 0-1 Gd: 1-3 GF: - Fm: 2-3
Distance:	2m/2m3: 3-7 2m4-2m7: 0-0 3m+: 0-0
Track:	LH: 4-3 RH: 1-3 Tight: 2-4 Gall: 0-0
Aids:	Bl: 0-1 Vi: 0-0 Tstrap: 0-0 Ckp: 0-0
Best Rating:	125 11/03 Asct 2m gd-fm Ch

Fair novice chaser; successful twice in May 2003; subsequently threw away two Stratford chases when caught on the run-in; lit up and jumped badly when tried in blinkers at Perth; made amends with easy win back at Stratford next time; acts well on fast ground; stays two and a half miles; has room for improvement in his jumping; not one to trust.

Tamarinbleu (FR)

105   **130+**

4-y-o b g Epervier Bleu-Tamainia (FR) (Lashkari)
M C Pipe The Arthur White Partnership

Placings:12300   (4629)
2003/04: 16¹S, 16²GF, 17³S, 17⁰G, 20⁰G,

	Starts	1st	2nd	3rd	Win & Pl
Hurdles	5	1	1	1	9513
Career Total	5	1	1	1	9513

114	11/03	Asct	2m110y	D Hdl	SFT	£4784
				Total win prize-money £4784	

Going:	Sf: 1-2 GS: 0-1 Gd: 0-2 GF: - Fm: 0-0
Distance:	2m/2m3: 1-4 2m4-2m7: 0-1 3m+: 0-0
Track:	LH: 0-3 RH: 1-2 Tight: 0-1 Gall: 0-1
Aids:	Bl: 0-0 Vi: 0-0 Tstrap: 0-0 Ckp: 0-0
Best Rating:	130 12/03 Chel 2m110y gd-sft Hdl

Juvenile hurdler; bolted up on his Ascot debut, but held in fair events since; best at two miles; acts well in soft ground.

Tambo (IRE)

106   **116**

9-y-o b g Shardari-Carmen Lady (Torus)
M Bradstock Mark Tamburro

Placings:040221/40/3P/P2-1411   (4437)
2003/04: 22¹GF, 23⁴G, 21¹GF, 21¹GS,

	Starts	1st	2nd	3rd	Win & Pl
Chases	4	3	0	0	18047
Career Total	16	4	3	1	24610

116	3/04	Fknm	2m5f110yD(0-120)HCh	G-S	£7612

111	9/03	Uttx	2m5f	D(0-125)HCh	G-F	£5690
95	5/03	Font	2m6f	E(0-105)HCh	G-F	£4478
113	3/00	Plum	2m5f	E Hdl	GD	£2450
				Total win prize-money £20233		

Going:	Sf: 0-0 GS: 1-1 Gd: 0-1 GF: - Fm: 2-2
Distance:	2m/2m3: 0-0 2m4-2m7: 3-3 3m+: 0-1
Track:	LH: 2-3 RH: 0-0 Tight: 2-2 Gall: 0-0
Aids:	Bl: 0-0 Vi: 0-0 Tstrap: 0-0 Ckp: 0-0
Best Rating:	116 3/04 Fknm 2m5f110y gd-sft Ch

Modest handicap chaser; has run well since coming back; acts on fast ground; stays 2m5f; suited by racing prominently.

Tanager

9-y-o ch g Carlingford Castle-Tangara (Town Crier)
Mrs K Lawther R Owen & P Fullagar

Placings:0/3   (4298)
2003/04: 23³G,

	Starts	1st	2nd	3rd	Win & Pl
Chases	1	0	0	1	339
Career Total	2	0	0	1	339

Going:	Sf: 0-0 GS: 0-0 Gd: 0-1 GF: - Fm: 0-0
Distance:	2m/2m3: 0-0 2m4-2m7: 0-0 3m+: 0-1
Track:	LH: 0-0 RH: 0-1 Tight: 0-0 Gall: 0-0
Aids:	Bl: 0-1 Vi: 0-0 Tstrap: 0-0 Ckp: 0-0
Best Rating:	77 3/04 Leic 2m7f110y good Ch

Tanaji

5-y-o b m Marju (IRE)-Hamsaat (IRE) (Sadler's Wells (USA))
P R Webber The Dream On Partnership

Placings:P   (2465)
2003/04: 16⁰S,

	Starts	1st	2nd	3rd	Win & Pl
Hurdles	1	0	0	0	
Career Total	1	0	0	0	

Going:	Sf: 0-1 GS: 0-0 Gd: 0-0 GF: - Fm: 0-0
Distance:	2m/2m3: 0-1 2m4-2m7: 0-0 3m+: 0-0
Track:	LH: 0-0 RH: 0-1 Tight: 0-0 Gall: 0-0
Aids:	Bl: 0-0 Vi: 0-0 Tstrap: 0-0 Ckp: 0-0

Tandawizi

90f   **77f**

7-y-o b m Relief Pitcher-Arctic Ander (Leander)
Mrs L B Normile Perth Racers

Placings:6   (0270)
2003/04: 16⁶G,

	Starts	1st	2nd	3rd	Win & Pl
NH Flat	1	0	0	0	0
Career Total	1	0	0	0	0

Going:	Sf: 0-0 GS: 0-0 Gd: 0-1 GF: - Fm: 0-0
Distance:	2m/2m3: 0-1 2m4-2m7: 0-0 3m+: 0-0
Track:	LH: 0-0 RH: 0-1 Tight: 0-0 Gall: 0-0
Aids:	Bl: 0-0 Vi: 0-0 Tstrap: 0-0 Ckp: 0-0
Best Rating:	77 5/03 Prth 2m110y good NHF

Tanglin Blaze

10-y-o ch g Southern Music-Wessex Flyer (Pony Express)
A J Chamberlain Mrs A G Sims

Placings:P   (4524)
2003/04: 16⁰GS,

	Starts	1st	2nd	3rd	Win & Pl
Hurdles	1	0	0	0	
Career Total	1	0	0	0	

Going:	Sf: 0-0 GS: 0-1 Gd: 0-0 GF: - Fm: 0-0
Distance:	2m/2m3: 0-1 2m4-2m7: 0-0 3m+: 0-0
Track:	LH: 0-1 RH: 0-0 Tight: 0-0 Gall: 0-0
Aids:	Bl: 0-0 Vi: 0-0 Tstrap: 0-0 Ckp: 0-0

Tango Bojangles

6-y-o ch m Fraam-Hips'n Haws (IRE) (Thatching)
N Wilson Steven Downes

Placings:0P   (4388)
2003/04: 17⁰G, 21⁰G,

	Starts	1st	2nd	3rd	Win & Pl
NH Flat	1	0	0	0	0
Hurdles	1	0	0	0	0
Career Total	2	0	0	0	0

Going:	Sf: 0-0 GS: 0-0 Gd: 0-2 GF: - Fm: 0-0
Distance:	2m/2m3: 0-1 2m4-2m7: 0-1 3m+: 0-0
Track:	LH: 0-1 RH: 0-1 Tight: 0-0 Gall: 0-0
Aids:	Bl: 0-0 Vi: 0-0 Tstrap: 0-0 Ckp: 0-0
Best Rating:	65 2/04 Carl 2m1f good NHF

Tango Royal (FR)

114(110h)   (126+h)**146**

8-y-o gr g Royal Charter (FR)-Nazia (FR) (Zino)
M C Pipe B A Kilpatrick

Placings:01310112/03154F4/600/FF06635-14122420U1   (4843)
2003/04: 16¹G, 17⁴GF, 22¹GS, 22²G, 17²GS, 16⁴GS, 20²GS, 20⁰GS, 16⁰G, 16¹G,

	Starts	1st	2nd	3rd	Win & Pl
Hurdles	5	2	1	0	23689
Chases	5	1	2	0	18436
Career Total	35	8	4	3	158264

143	4/04	Chel	2m110y	C(0-135)HCh	GD	£11159
126	7/03	NAbb	2m6f	C(0-130)HHdl	G-S	£7700
120	5/03	Strf	2m110y	C(0-135)HHdl	GD	£13552
	9/00	Comp	2m1f110y	Hdl	G-S	£3362
	3/00	Autl	2m4f110y	Ch	VS	£28818
	3/00	Autl	2m1f110y	Ch	HVY	£28818
	11/99	Engh	2m1f	Ch	HLD	£10764
	10/99	Toul	2m1f110y	Ch	SFT	£4844
				Total win prize-money £109018		

Going:	Sf: 0-0 GS: 1-5 Gd: 2-4 GF: - Fm: 0-1
Distance:	2m/2m3: 2-6 2m4-2m7: 1-4 3m+: 0-0
Track:	LH: 3-9 RH: 0-1 Tight: 2-4 Gall: 1-5
Aids:	Bl: 0-0 Vi: 0-0 Tstrap: 3-10 Ckp: 0-0
Best Rating:	146 11/03 Newb 2m1f gd-sft Ch

Useful hurdler/smart chaser; ex-French; returned to fences in 2003; scored at Cheltenham in April; effective at up to 2m 6f and best on soft ground, although handles quicker conditions too; wears a tongue tie.

Tanikos (FR)

107(100h)   (101h)**116+**

5-y-o b g Nikos-Tamana (USA) (Northern Baby (CAN))
N J Henderson Studwell Two Partnership

Placings:130-021225   (4169)
2003/04: 16⁰G, 19²G, 19¹GS, 20²S, 20²G, 22⁵G,

	Starts	1st	2nd	3rd	Win & Pl
Hurdles	1	0	0	0	0
Chases	5	1	3	0	9989
Career Total	9	2	3	1	14991
113 1/04 Hrfd	2m3f	E Ch		G-S	£4754
11/02 Pari	2m1f	Hdl		HVY	£4418
			Total win prize-money		£9173

Going:	Sf: 0-1 GS: 1-1 Gd: 0-4 GF: - Fm: 0-0
Distance:	2m/2m3: 1-3 2m4-2m7: 0-3 3m+: 0-0
Track:	LH: 0-3 RH: 1-3 Tight: 0-1 Gall: 0-1
Aids:	Bl: 0-0 Vi: 0-0 Tstrap: 0-0 Ckp: 0-0
Best Rating:	116 2/04 Sand 2m4f110y good Ch

Fair novice chaser; stays 2m3f; acts on soft.

Tank Buster

66f   **37f**

4-y-o b g Executive Perk-Macfarly (IRE) (Phardante (FR))
Miss E Hill R G Langley

Placings:6   (4284)
2003/04: 16⁶GS,

	Starts	1st	2nd	3rd	Win & Pl
NH Flat	1	0	0	0	0
Career Total	1	0	0	0	0

Going:	Sf: 0-0 GS: 0-1 Gd: 0-0 GF: - Fm: 0-0
Distance:	2m/2m3: 0-1 2m4-2m7: 0-0 3m+: 0-0
Track:	LH: 0-0 RH: 0-0 Tight: 0-0 Gall: 0-0
Aids:	Bl: 0-0 Vi: 0-0 Tstrap: 0-0 Ckp: 0-0
Best Rating:	37 3/04 Towc 2m gd-sft NHF

Tanners Court

103   **111**

7-y-o b g Framlington Court-True Nell (Neltino)
Miss C Dyson Miss C Dyson

Placings:0030-045523   (4492)
2003/04: 20⁰S, 20⁴S, 20⁵G, 21⁵GS, 20²G, 22³G,

	Starts	1st	2nd	3rd	Win & Pl
Hurdles	6	0	1	1	5556
Career Total	10	0	1	2	5898

Going:	Sf: 0-2 GS: 0-1 Gd: 0-3 GF: - Fm: 0-0
Distance:	2m/2m3: 0-0 2m4-2m7: 0-6 3m+: 0-1
Track:	LH: 0-4 RH: 0-2 Tight: 0-1 Gall: 0-0
Aids:	Bl: 0-0 Vi: 0-0 Tstrap: 0-0 Ckp: 0-0
Best Rating:	111 3/04 Strf 2m6f110y good Hdl

Modest novice hurdler; improved effort on handicap bow when narrowly beaten at Haydock in February; stays 2m 5f; acts on good and soft ground.

Tanners Friend

84   **58**

7-y-o b m Environment Friend-Glenn's Slipper (Furry Glen)
Miss C Dyson Miss C Dyson

Placings:0000P-05   (2999)
2003/04: 16⁰G, 20⁵GS,

	Starts	1st	2nd	3rd	Win & Pl
Hurdles	2	0	0	0	0

Career Total   7   0   0   0   0

Going:	Sf: 0-0 GS: 0-1 Gd: 0-1 GF: - Fm: 0-0
Distance:	2m/2m3: 0-1 2m4-2m7: 0-0 3m+: 0-0
Track:	LH: 0-0 RH: 0-2 Tight: 0-0 Gall: 0-0
Aids:	Bl: 0-0 Vi: 0-0 Tstrap: 0-0 Ckp: 0-0
Best Rating:	79 2/03 Ludl 2m good NHF

Tanshan

(0c)**31**

9-y-o ch g Anshan-Nafla (FR) (Arctic Tern (USA))
R Rowe Richard Rowe

Placings:0/00/PP   (4401)
2003/04: 22⁵PHY, 21⁵PG,

	Starts	1st	2nd	3rd	Win & Pl
Hurdles	2	0	0	0	0
Career Total	5	0	0	0	0

Going:	Sf: 0-1 GS: 0-0 Gd: 0-1 GF: - Fm: 0-0
Distance:	2m/2m3: 0-0 2m4-2m7: 0-2 3m+: 0-0
Track:	LH: 0-0 RH: 0-2 Tight: 0-0 Gall: 0-1
Aids:	Bl: 0-0 Vi: 0-0 Tstrap: 0-0 Ckp: 0-0
Best Rating:	88 11/99 Hntg 2m10y good Hdl

Tanterari (IRE)

105   **96**

6-y-o b g Safety Catch (USA)-Cobblers Crest (IRE) (Step Together (USA))
M C Pipe (Denis Ahern 18/12) D A Johnson

Placings:0-1PF5   (4147)
2003/04: 16¹Y, 23⁵S, 26⁶GS, 24⁵G,

	Starts	1st	2nd	3rd	Win & Pl
NH Flat	1	1	0	0	4032
Hurdles	1	0	0	0	0
Chases	2	0	0	0	0
Career Total	5	1	0	0	4032
108 12/03 Gowr	2m	NHF		YLD	£4032
			Total win prize-money		£4032

Going:	Sf: 0-1 GS: 0-1 Gd: 0-1 GF: - Fm: 0-0
Distance:	2m/2m3: 1-1 2m4-2m7: 0-0 3m+: 0-3
Track:	LH: 0-1 RH: 0-2 Tight: 0-2 Gall: 0-0
Aids:	Bl: 0-0 Vi: 0-0 Tstrap: 0-0 Ckp: 0-0
Best Rating:	108 12/03 Gowr 2m yield NHF

Irish bumper winner; put straight over fences by current yard and has disappointed in both outings to date; staying type; acts on good to soft; probably capable of much better.

Tantico (IRE)

89   **72**

7-y-o b g Lord Americo-Tanti's Last (Ardoon)
D J Wintle (Anthony Mullins 5/7) The Lavender Hill Mob

Placings:22-450   (4565)
2003/04: 16⁴F, 16⁵GF, 17⁰GS,

	Starts	1st	2nd	3rd	Win & Pl
NH Flat	2	0	0	0	247
Hurdles	1	0	0	0	0
Career Total	5	0	2	0	2063

Going:	Sf: 0-0 GS: 0-1 Gd: 0-0 GF: - Fm: 0-2
Distance:	2m/2m3: 0-3 2m4-2m7: 0-0 3m+: 0-0
Track:	LH: 0-1 RH: 0-0 Tight: 0-1 Gall: 0-0
Aids:	Bl: 0-0 Vi: 0-0 Tstrap: 0-2 Ckp: 0-0
Best Rating:	100 7/03 Limk 2m gd-fm NHF

Tara's Flame

81   **56**

4-y-o ch g Blushing Flame (USA)-Lady Emm (Emarati (USA))
Mrs M Reveley (J G Given 19/6) R Wardlaw

Placings:0P   (3337)
2003/04: 16⁰GS, 16⁶GS,

	Starts	1st	2nd	3rd	Win & Pl
Hurdles	2	0	0	0	0
Career Total	2	0	0	0	0

Going:	Sf: 0-0 GS: 0-2 Gd: 0-0 GF: - Fm: 0-0
Distance:	2m/2m3: 0-2 2m4-2m7: 0-0 3m+: 0-0
Track:	LH: 0-0 RH: 0-0 Tight: 0-1 Gall: 0-0
Aids:	Bl: 0-0 Vi: 0-0 Tstrap: 0-0 Ckp: 0-0
Best Rating:	58 12/03 Weth 2m gd-sft Hdl

Tara-Brogan

102   **123**

11-y-o b g Jupiter Island-Princess Semele (Imperial Fling (USA))
Ian Williams Patrick Kelly

Placings:45/1153203/F232U/2/111/22   (1452)
2003/04: 26²GF, 26²GF,

	Starts	1st	2nd	3rd	Win & Pl
Chases	2	0	2	0	4034
Career Total	20	5	6	3	32410
120 9/01 Hntg	3m	E Ch		G-F	£3753
125 5/01 Weth	2m7f110yD Ch		FRM	£4108
123 5/01 Sthl	3m110y C Ch		G-F	£7296
118 6/98 MRas	2m3f110yD Hdl		GD	£3140
112 6/98 Worc	2m4f	E Hdl		G-F	£2005
			Total win prize-money		£20303

Going:	Sf: 0-0 GS: 0-0 Gd: 0-0 GF: - Fm: 0-2
Distance:	2m/2m3: 0-0 2m4-2m7: 0-0 3m+: 0-2
Track:	LH: 0-2 RH: 0-0 Tight: 0-2 Gall: 0-0
Aids:	Bl: 0-0 Vi: 0-0 Tstrap: 0-0 Ckp: 0-0
Best Rating:	125 5/01 Weth 2m7f110y firm Ch

Fair chaser; rattled up a hat-trick in 2001; lightly raced since; best on decent ground; stays well.

Tarashani (IRE)

88   **84**

6-y-o ch g Primo Dominie-Tarakana (USA) (Shahrastani (USA))
B Ellison R W L Bowden

Placings:006/444-0   (1279)
2003/04: 17⁰GF,

	Starts	1st	2nd	3rd	Win & Pl
Hurdles	1	0	0	0	0
Career Total	7	0	0	0	263

Going:	Sf: 0-0 GS: 0-0 Gd: 0-0 GF: - Fm: 0-1
Distance:	2m/2m3: 0-1 2m4-2m7: 0-0 3m+: 0-0
Track:	LH: 0-1 RH: 0-0 Tight: 0-1 Gall: 0-0
Aids:	Bl: 0-0 Vi: 0-0 Tstrap: 0-0 Ckp: 0-1
Best Rating:	84 11/02 Weth 2m heavy Hdl

Tarbolton Moss

104(96h)   (101h)**116+**

9-y-o b m Le Moss-Priceless Peril (Silly Prices)
M Todhunter Mrs David Marshall

Placings: 0505/40331212/42P13-10P6U   (4941)
2003/04: 25¹S, 25⁰GS, 32ᶠG, 20⁶G, 31ᵁGS,

	Starts	1st	2nd	3rd	Win & Pl
Hurdles	1	0	0	0	0
Chases	4	1	0	0	4251
Career Total	22	4	3	3	24769
116	1/04	Kels	3m1f	E(0-110)HCh	SFT	£4251
112	2/03	Ayr	3m1f	E Ch	G-S	£4036
101	3/02	Kels	3m3f	F(0-95)HHdl	SFT	£2999
93	2/02	Newc	3m	F(0-100)HHdl	SFT	£1904

Total win prize-money £13192

Going: Sf: 1-1 GS: 0-2 Gd: 0-2 GF: - Fm: 0-0
Distance: 2m/2m3: 0-0 2m4-2m7: 0-1 3m+: 1-4
Track: LH: 1-3 RH: 0-1 Tight: 1-2 Gall: 0-0
Aids: Bl: 0-0 Vi: 0-0 Tstrap: 0-0 Ckp: 0-0
Best Rating: 116 1/04 Kels 3m1f soft Ch

Modest hurdler/chaser; stays three miles plus; appreciates soft ground.

Tarboush
100   **100+**
7-y-o b g Polish Precedent (USA)-Barboukh (Night Shift (USA))
B G Powell Gallagher Equine Ltd

Placings: 6032-000041   (4899)
2003/04: 16⁰G, 16⁰S, 21⁰GS, 16⁰G, 16⁴G, 16¹G,

	Starts	1st	2nd	3rd	Win & Pl
Hurdles	6	1	0	0	3823
Career Total	10	1	1	1	5503
100	4/04	Winc	2m	E Hdl	GD	£3552

Total win prize-money £3553

Going: Sf: 0-0 GS: 0-1 Gd: 1-4 GF: - Fm: 0-0
Distance: 2m/2m3: 1-5 2m4-2m7: 0-1 3m+: 0-0
Track: LH: 0-0 RH: 1-6 Tight: 0-0 Gall: 0-0
Aids: Bl: 0-0 Vi: 0-0 Tstrap: 0-0 Ckp: 0-0
Best Rating: 100 4/04 Winc 2m good Hdl

Modest hurdler; acts on any ground; suited by waiting tactics

Tardar (NZ)
117   **145**
8-y-o br g Prince Ferdinand-La Magnifique (NZ) (Kampala)
Jonjo O'Neill Ray & Sue Dodd Partnership

Placings: 3110-01F   (4386)
2003/04: 20⁰GS, 23¹S, 25ᶠG,

	Starts	1st	2nd	3rd	Win & Pl
Hurdles	3	1	0	0	12870
Career Total	7	3	0	1	22407
145	2/04	Hayd	2m7f110yB HHdl	SFT	£12870
125	2/03	Chep	2m110y D Hdl	HVY	£5034
120	12/02	Chep	2m110y D Hdl	SFT	£3926

Total win prize-money £21830

Going: Sf: 1-1 GS: 0-1 Gd: 0-1 GF: - Fm: 0-0
Distance: 2m/2m3: 0-0 2m4-2m7: 0-1 3m+: 1-2
Track: LH: 1-3 RH: 0-0 Tight: 0-0 Gall: 0-1
Aids: Bl: 0-0 Vi: 0-0 Tstrap: 0-0 Ckp: 0-0
Best Rating: 145 2/04 Hayd 2m7f110y soft Hdl

Fair hurdler; formerly a winner on the Flat in Australia and New Zealand; recorded third career win from way out of the handicap at Haydock in February; stays three miles; suited by soft ground.

Tareno (GER)
6-y-o b g Saddlers' Hall (IRE)-Triclaria (GER) (Surumu (GER))

B J Curley P Byrne

Placings: F   (2069)
2003/04: 16ᶠGF,

	Starts	1st	2nd	3rd	Win & Pl
Hurdles	1	0	0	0	0
Career Total	1	0	0	0	0

Going: Sf: 0-0 GS: 0-0 Gd: 0-0 GF: - Fm: 0-1
Distance: 2m/2m3: 0-0 2m4-2m7: 0-0 3m+: 0-1
Track: LH: 0-0 RH: 0-0 Tight: 0-0 Gall: 0-1
Aids: Bl: 0-0 Vi: 0-0 Tstrap: 0-0 Ckp: 0-0

Tarn Beck (IRE)
5-y-o b m Alderbrook-Skiddaw Samba (Viking (USA))
T D Walford Mrs M Cooper

Placings: P   (3982)
2003/04: 17ᴾG,

	Starts	1st	2nd	3rd	Win & Pl
NH Flat	1	0	0	0	
Career Total	1	0	0	0	

Going: Sf: 0-0 GS: 0-0 Gd: 0-1 GF: - Fm: 0-0
Distance: 2m/2m3: 0-1 2m4-2m7: 0-0 3m+: 0-0
Track: LH: 0-0 RH: 0-0 Tight: 0-0 Gall: 0-0
Aids: Bl: 0-0 Vi: 0-0 Tstrap: 0-0 Ckp: 0-0

Tarongo (FR)
104   **87**
6-y-o b g Tel Quel (FR)-Rainbow Rainbow (Vision (USA))
Mrs L C Taylor Mrs L C Taylor

Placings: PP/PF2-531U2F   (4754)
2003/04: 17⁵G, 16³GF, 18¹GF, 17ᵁG, 16²GS, 20ᶠG,

	Starts	1st	2nd	3rd	Win & Pl
Chases	6	1	1	1	4597
Career Total	11	1	2	1	7075
87	5/03	Font	2m2f	G(0-90)HCh	G-F	£2534

Total win prize-money £2534

Going: Sf: 0-0 GS: 0-1 Gd: 0-3 GF: - Fm: 1-2
Distance: 2m/2m3: 1-5 2m4-2m7: 0-1 3m+: 0-0
Track: LH: 0-2 RH: 0-3 Tight: 1-3 Gall: 0-0
Aids: Bl: 0-0 Vi: 0-0 Tstrap: 1-5 Ckp: 0-0
Best Rating: 87 4/04 Plum 2m4f good Ch

Still a maiden over both hurdles and fences.

Tarpon Tale (IRE)
77   (82h)**46**
7-y-o b g Mujadil (USA)-Lady Of The Mist (IRE) (Digamist (USA))
M C Pipe M C Pipe

Placings: 00000/000066/PPP-5P4O4   (1724)
2003/04: 26ᴾGF, 26ᴾGF, 25⁴GF, 22⁰F, 23⁴F,

	Starts	1st	2nd	3rd	Win & Pl
Hurdles	2	0	0	0	0
Chases	3	0	0	0	631
Career Total	19	0	0	0	631

Going: Sf: 0-0 GS: 0-0 Gd: 0-0 GF: - Fm: 0-5
Distance: 2m/2m3: 0-0 2m4-2m7: 0-1 3m+: 0-4
Track: LH: 0-2 RH: 0-3 Tight: 0-1 Gall: 0-0
Aids: Bl: 0-0 Vi: 0-5 Tstrap: 0-0 Ckp: 0-0
Best Rating: 82 9/01 Clon 2m4f gd-fm Hdl

Poor chaser/hurdler; wore first-time visor when possibly failing to stay 3m2f at Southwell on British debut; no form over fences; best on a sound surface.

Tarque (IRE)
112   **128+**
4-y-o b g Revoque (IRE)-Tarquinia (IRE) (In The Wings)
Miss Venetia Williams (F Doumen 27/12) John Nicholls (banbury) Ltd

Placings: U2B21B4   (4625)
2003/04: 16ᵁHO, 18²VS, 18ᴮVS, 17²HO, 16¹G, 17ᴮG, 16⁴G,

	Starts	1st	2nd	3rd	Win & Pl
Hurdles	7	1	2	0	23187
Career Total	7	1	2	0	23187
124	12/03	Kemp	2m	C Hdl	GD	£6467

Total win prize-money £6467

Going: Sf: 0-0 GS: 0-0 Gd: 1-3 GF: - Fm: 0-0
Distance: 2m/2m3: 1-7 2m4-2m7: 0-0 3m+: 0-0
Track: LH: 0-3 RH: 1-1 Tight: 0-1 Gall: 0-1
Aids: Bl: 0-0 Vi: 0-0 Tstrap: 1-3 Ckp: 0-0
Best Rating: 128 4/04 Aint 2m110y good Hdl

Useful juvenile hurdler, ex-French; impressive on hurdling debut in this country at Kempton; brought down in the Triumph; well beaten fourth in GradeTwo at Aintree; effective over two miles; acts on good ground; has worn tongue tie.

Tarski
106   **102**
10-y-o ch g Polish Precedent (USA)-Illusory (King's Lake (USA))
W S Kittow Midd Shire Racing

Placings: 66/10102P-01P0246   (1727)
2003/04: 16⁰G, 20¹G, 20ᴾGF, 16ᴾGF, 22²F, 24⁴GF, 19ᴾGF,

	Starts	1st	2nd	3rd	Win & Pl
Hurdles	7	1	1	0	3528
Career Total	15	3	2	0	9548
102	7/03	Worc	2m4f	G(0-90)HHdl	GD	£2601
92	8/02	NAbb	2m1f	F Hdl	G-F	£2205
93	7/02	Worc	2m	E Hdl	G-F	£2940

Total win prize-money £7747

Going: Sf: 0-0 GS: 0-0 Gd: 1-2 GF: - Fm: 0-5
Distance: 2m/2m3: 0-3 2m4-2m7: 1-3 3m+: 1-0
Track: LH: 1-4 RH: 0-3 Tight: 0-0 Gall: 0-0
Aids: Bl: 1-6 Vi: 0-1 Tstrap: 0-0 Ckp: 0-0
Best Rating: 102 9/03 Extr 2m6f110y firm Hdl

Moderate hurdler; stays two miles six; acts on ground good and faster; usually wears blinkers and has worn visor.

Tarxien
116(110c)   (153c)**142**
10-y-o b g Kendor (FR)-Tanz (IRE) (Sadler's Wells (USA))
M C Pipe B A Kilpatrick

Placings: 4/443/54302/4111111B2/1121F2-3F4006   (4840)
2003/04: 19³S, 21ᶠG, 20⁴GS, 23⁹S, 24⁹G, 24⁶G,

	Starts	1st	2nd	3rd	Win & Pl
Hurdles	4	0	0	0	2811
Chases	2	0	0	1	6600
Career Total	30	9	4	3	143755
153	2/03	Sand	2m4f110yA Ch	HVY	£34100
153	12/02	Asct	2m3f110yA Ch	SFT	£18000
145	11/02	Chel	2m4f110yB Ch	G-S	£12354
134	12/01	Asct	3m	B Hdl	GD	£11340
140	11/01	Chel	2m5f	B Hdl	GD	£8736
136	9/01	Worc	2m4f	C(0-135)HHdl	G-F	£5554
126	8/01	NAbb	2m6f	E Hdl	G-F	£2954

130	8/01	MRas	2m3f110yC(0-130)HHdl	G-F	£6179
125	7/01	NAbb	2m6f C(0-130)HHdl	GD	£4867

Total win prize-money £104086

Going:	Sf: 0-2 GS: 0-1 Gd: 0-3 GF: - Fm: 0-0
Distance:	2m/2m3: 0-2 2m4-2m7: 0-3 3m+: 0-3
Track:	LH: 0-5 RH: 0-1 Tight: 0-0 Gall: 0-4
Aids:	Bl: 0-0 Vi: 0-0 Tstrap: 0-6 Ckp: 0-0
Best Rating:	153 2/03 Sand 2m4f110y heavy Ch

Smart chaser/very useful hurdler; high-class form in novice chases in 2002/3; not the most fluent jumper of fences; stays three miles, but effective at shorter; acts well on a soft surface, but is probably better on faster ground; wears a tongue tie; disappointing in 2004.

Taskmaster
(79h)   (104 h)
7-y-o b g Alflora (IRE)-Travail Girl (Forties Field (FR))
P J Hobbs   Andrew & Philippa Wyer

Placings:0/F-0400P (4530)
2003/04: 17⁰G, 19⁴S, 17⁰GS, 16⁰G, 16ᴾGS,

	Starts	1st	2nd	3rd	Win & Pl
Hurdles	4	0	0	0	280
Chases	1	0	0	0	0
Career Total	7	0	0	0	280

Going:	Sf: 0-1 GS: 0-2 Gd: 0-2 GF: - Fm: 0-0
Distance:	2m/2m3: 0-5 2m4-2m7: 0-0 3m+: 0-0
Track:	LH: 0-3 RH: 0-2 Tight: 0-0 Gall: 0-2
Aids:	Bl: 0-0 Vi: 0-0 Tstrap: 0-0 Ckp: 0-0
Best Rating:	104 10/02 Chep 2m110y good Hdl

Has shown ability in novice hurdles; stays 2m 4f.

Tasneef (USA)
85   73
5-y-o b g Gulch (USA)-Min Alhawa (USA) (Riverman (USA))
T D McCarthy   A D Spence

Placings:30 (3047)
2003/04: 17³GF, 17⁰G,

	Starts	1st	2nd	3rd	Win & Pl
Hurdles	2	0	0	1	686
Career Total	2	0	0	1	686

Going:	Sf: 0-0 GS: 0-0 Gd: 0-1 GF: - Fm: 0-1
Distance:	2m/2m3: 0-2 2m4-2m7: 0-0 3m+: 0-1
Track:	LH: 0-0 RH: 0-2 Tight: 0-2 Gall: 0-0
Aids:	Bl: 0-0 Vi: 0-0 Tstrap: 0-0 Ckp: 0-0
Best Rating:	79 12/03 Tntn 2m1f good Hdl

Tates Avenue (IRE)
78f   84f
6-y-o b g Zaffaran (USA)-Tate Divinity (IRE) (Tate Gallery (USA))
N A Twiston-Davies   S P Tindall

Placings:60 (4374)
2003/04: 16ᴾHY, 16⁰GF,

	Starts	1st	2nd	3rd	Win & Pl
NH Flat	2	0	0	0	0
Career Total	2	0	0	0	0

Going:	Sf: 0-1 GS: 0-0 Gd: 0-0 GF: - Fm: 0-1
Distance:	2m/2m3: 0-2 2m4-2m7: 0-0 3m+: 0-0
Track:	LH: 0-0 RH: 0-1 Tight: 0-0 Gall: 0-0
Aids:	Bl: 0-0

Best Rating: 79 1/04 Asct 2m110y heavy NHF

Taw Park
99   95
10-y-o b g Inca Chief (USA)-Parklands Belle (Stanford)
R J Baker   R P Maddock

Placings:5560/31 (1041)
2003/04: 17³GS, 17¹GF,

	Starts	1st	2nd	3rd	Win & Pl
Hurdles	2	1	0	1	3343
Career Total	6	1	0	1	3343

95	8/03	NAbb	2m1f	F Hdl	G-F	£2919

Total win prize-money £2919

Going:	Sf: 0-0 GS: 0-0 Gd: 0-0 GF: - Fm: 1-1
Distance:	2m/2m3: 1-2 2m4-2m7: 0-0 3m+: 0-0
Track:	LH: 1-2 RH: 0-0 Tight: 1-2 Gall: 0-0
Aids:	Bl: 0-0 Vi: 0-0 Tstrap: 0-0 Ckp: 0-0
Best Rating:	95 8/03 NAbb 2m1f gd-fm Hdl

Plating-class hurdler; lightly raced; not disgraced on come back when third in 2m 1f handicap at Newton Abbot July 2003; got up on line to win four-runner claimer over the same course and distance next time; appears to act on most types of ground.

Tea's Maid
92   78
4-y-o b f Wizard King-Come To Tea (IRE) (Be My Guest (USA))
M A Barnes (J G Given 29/10)   J G White

Placings:P340 (4310)
2003/04: 16ᴾHY, 16³G, 16⁴G, 16⁰GS,

	Starts	1st	2nd	3rd	Win & Pl
Hurdles	4	0	0	1	900
Career Total	4	0	0	1	900

Going:	Sf: 0-1 GS: 0-0 Gd: 0-2 GF: - Fm: 0-1
Distance:	2m/2m3: 0-4 2m4-2m7: 0-0 3m+: 0-0
Track:	LH: 0-2 RH: 0-2 Tight: 0-2 Gall: 0-1
Aids:	Bl: 0-0 Vi: 0-0 Tstrap: 0-0 Ckp: 0-0
Best Rating:	78 2/04 Muss 2m good Hdl

Poor maiden on the Flat; well beaten third over hurdles at Musselburgh in February; best on good.

Teaatral
103(105c)   (112c)119
10-y-o b g Saddlers' Hall (IRE)-La Cabrilla (Carwhite)
C R Egerton   Bernard Gover Bloodstock Trading Ltd

Placings:210112/013110/U3111/P412P56/5430PP/5-121RR536 (4052)
2003/04: 20¹GF, 20²GF, 20¹G, 24²G, 25ᴿGS, 25⁵G, 16³S, 24⁶G,

	Starts	1st	2nd	3rd	Win & Pl
Hurdles	3	0	0	1	5216
Chases	5	2	1	0	11514
Career Total	39	12	4	4	149374

93	6/03	MRas	2m4f	E Ch	GD	£4309
102	5/03	Hntg	2m4f110yD	Ch	G-F	£5499
164	2/01	Sand	2m110y	B Hdl	HVY	£13468
164	4/00	Asct	3m	A Hdl	GD	£18600
158	2/00	Kemp	3m110y	A HHdl	SFT	£13200
162	2/00	Asct	2m4f	B(0-150)HHdl	SFT	£20579
150	2/99	Sand	2m6f	A Hdl	G-S	£26800
148	1/99	Kemp	2m5f	C(0-135)HHdl	HVY	£5628
131	12/98	Leic	2m4f110yD(0-120)HHdl		SFT	£3002
105	4/98	Hrfd	2m1f	E Hdl	G-S	£2624
110	4/98	Tntn	2m1f	E(0-115)HHdl	GD	£2710

111 1/98 Folk 2m1f110yE Hdl G-S £1976
Total win prize-money £118397

Going:	Sf: 0-1 GS: 0-1 Gd: 1-4 GF: - Fm: 1-2
Distance:	2m/2m3: 2-6 2m4-2m7: 2-3 3m+: 0-4
Track:	LH: 0-1 RH: 2-7 Tight: 1-3 Gall: 1-1
Aids:	Bl: 2-5 Vi: 0-0 Tstrap: 0-0 Ckp: 0-0
Best Rating:	164 2/01 Kemp 3m110y gd-sft Hdl

Fair chaser; high-class staying hurdler in his time, but not so good these days; recent wins have been in weak novice chases; has only ever won on right-handed tracks; acts on most types of ground; usually wears blinkers.

Teach Altra (IRE)
7-y-o b g Warcraft (USA)-Miss Pushover (Push On)
M J Roberts (W J Burke 26/7)   Mike Roberts

Placings:0⁵ (3873)
2003/04: 17⁰SH, 25⁵GS,

	Starts	1st	2nd	3rd	Win & Pl
NH Flat	1	0	0	0	0
Chases	1	0	0	0	0
Career Total	2	0	0	0	0

Going:	Sf: 0-0 GS: 0-1 Gd: 0-0 GF: - Fm: 0-0
Distance:	2m/2m3: 0-1 2m4-2m7: 0-0 3m+: 0-0
Track:	LH: 0-0 RH: 0-1 Tight: 0-1 Gall: 0-0
Aids:	Bl: 0-0 Vi: 0-0 Tstrap: 0-0 Ckp: 0-1
Best Rating:	79 7/03 Klny 2m1f sft-hvy NHF

Tealby
103   109+
7-y-o b m Efisio-Al Raja (King's Lake (USA))
Mrs L Wadham   The Dyball Partnership

Placings:21214/122-5P1 (3430)
2003/04: 16⁵G, 16ᴾGS, 16¹GS,

	Starts	1st	2nd	3rd	Win & Pl
Hurdles	3	1	0	0	3712
Career Total	11	4	4	0	15193

107	1/04	Fknm	2m	E(0-105)HHdl	G-S	£3444
92	12/02	Sthl	2m	E Hdl	G-S	£2961
95	7/01	Worc	2m	H NHF	GD	£1494
109	6/01	MRas	2m1f110yH	HHdl	G-F	£1589

Total win prize-money £9489

Going:	Sf: 0-0 GS: 1-2 Gd: 0-1 GF: - Fm: 0-0
Distance:	2m/2m3: 1-3 2m4-2m7: 0-0 3m+: 0-0
Track:	LH: 1-1 RH: 0-2 Tight: 1-1 Gall: 0-0
Aids:	Bl: 0-0 Vi: 0-0 Tstrap: 0-0 Ckp: 0-0
Best Rating:	109 12/02 Chel 2m1f good Hdl

Modest hurdler; best around 2m; acts on fast and easy ground.

Team Captain
104   105+
10-y-o ch g Teamster-Silly Sausage (Silly Answer)
C J Down   P J Hickman

Placings:0/P/2PF2122/2U46-PP1 (4652)
2003/04: 25ᴾGS, 20ᴾG, 25¹G,

	Starts	1st	2nd	3rd	Win & Pl
Chases	3	1	0	0	7020
Career Total	16	2	5	0	12825

105	4/04	Hrfd	3m1f110yE(0-110)HCh	GD	£7020
100	3/02	Winc	3m1f110yH Ch	GD	£1684

Total win prize-money £8704

Going: Sf: 0-0 GS: 0-1 Gd: 1-2 GF: - Fm: 0-0
Distance: 2m/2m3: 0-0 2m4-2m7: 0-1 3m+: 1-2
Track: LH: 0-1 RH: 1-2 Tight: 0-0 Gall: 0-0
Aids: Bl: 0-0 Vi: 0-0 Tstrap: 0-0 Ckp: 0-0
Best Rating: 105 4/04 Hrfd 3m1f110y good Ch

Moderate hunter/pointer, he stays three miles and acts on fast ground.

Team Tassel (IRE)
107   117+
6-y-o b g Be My Native (USA)-Alcmena's Last (Pauper)
M C Pipe Matt Archer & Miss Jean Broadhurst

Placings:1   (3756)
2003/04: 19¹G,

	Starts	1st	2nd	3rd	Win & Pl
Hurdles	1	1	0	0	5647
Career Total	1	1	0	0	5647
117 2/04 MRas 2m3f110yD Hdl				£5647
			Total win prize-money £5647

Going: Sf: 0-0 GS: 0-0 Gd: 1-1 GF: - Fm: 0-0
Distance: 2m/2m3: 0-0 2m4-2m7: 1-1 3m+: 0-0
Track: LH: 0-0 RH: 1-1 Tight: 1-1 Gall: 0-0
Aids: Bl: 0-0 Vi: 0-0 Tstrap: 0-0 Ckp: 0-0
Best Rating: 117 2/04 MRas 2m3f110y good Hdl

Third in Irish point; successful on debut over hurdles at Market Rasen in February; suited by two and a half miles; acts on good.

Tee-Jay (IRE)
110(89c)   (94c)111
8-y-o ch g Un Desperado (FR)-N T Nad (Welsh Pageant)
M D Hammond T J Equestrian Ltd

Placings:03⁵5131PP/5P03032-110P04   (4729)
2003/04: 24¹G, 20¹GF, 20⁹S, 25⁸G, 24⁹G, 20⁴G,

	Starts	1st	2nd	3rd	Win & Pl
Hurdles	6	2	0	0	8975
Career Total	21	4	1	4	18430
111 12/03 Sthl 2m4f110yD(0-125)HHdl	G-F	£5655
108 5/03 Hexm 3m F(0-100)HHdl	GD	£2730
111 2/02 Muss 2m4f D Hdl	G-S	£3510
108 12/01 Catt 2m3f E Hdl	SFT	£2492
			Total win prize-money £14387

Going: Sf: 0-1 GS: 0-0 Gd: 1-4 GF: - Fm: 1-1
Distance: 2m/2m3: 0-0 2m4-2m7: 1-3 3m+: 1-3
Track: LH: 2-4 RH: 0-0 Tight: 1-3 Gall: 0-0
Aids: Bl: 0-0 Vi: 0-0 Tstrap: 0-0 Ckp: 0-0
Best Rating: 111 12/03 Sthl 2m4f110y gd-fm Hdl

Modest hurdler; stays three miles, acts on good ground; made little impact when tried over fences.

Teenager
89f   69+f
4-y-o b f Young Ern-Washita (Valiyar)
P Wegmann (Mrs K Walton 15/1) P Wegmann

Placings:50   (4571)
2003/04: 16⁵GS, 17⁹GS,

	Starts	1st	2nd	3rd	Win & Pl
NH Flat	2	0	0	0	0
Career Total	2	0	0	0	0

Going: Sf: 0-0 GS: 0-2 Gd: 0-0 GF: - Fm: 0-0
Distance: 2m/2m3: 0-2 2m4-2m7: 0-0 3m+: 0-0
Track: LH: 0-2 RH: 0-0 Tight: 0-2 Gall: 0-0
Aids: Bl: 0-0 Vi: 0-0 Tstrap: 0-3 Ckp: 0-0

Best Rating: 69 1/04 Catt 2m gd-sft NHF

Teeno Rossi (IRE)
65   26
6-y-o b m Teenoso (USA)-Mistress Ross (Impecunious)
J R Norton Miss A J Hurst

Placings:40000P   (4660)
2003/04: 16⁵F, 16⁹G, 17⁹GS, 16⁹GS, 21⁹G, 24⁸PS,

	Starts	1st	2nd	3rd	Win & Pl
NH Flat	4	0	0	0	0
Hurdles	2	0	0	0	0
Career Total	6	0	0	0	0

Going: Sf: 0-1 GS: 0-2 Gd: 0-2 GF: - Fm: 0-1
Distance: 2m/2m3: 0-4 2m4-2m7: 0-1 3m+: 0-1
Track: LH: 0-5 RH: 0-1 Tight: 0-2 Gall: 0-0
Aids: Bl: 0-0 Vi: 0-0 Tstrap: 0-0 Ckp: 0-0
Best Rating: 73 9/03 Hexm 2m110y firm NHF

Tees Components
104   152
9-y-o b g Risk Me (FR)-Lady Warninglid (Ela-Mana-Mou)
Mrs M Reveley Tees Components Ltd

Placings:211/11/1213-1   (0162)
2003/04: 22¹G,

	Starts	1st	2nd	3rd	Win & Pl
Hurdles	1	1	0	0	3484
Career Total	10	7	2	1	44685
142 5/03 Kels 2m6f110yE Hdl	GD	£3484
152 1/03 Donc 3m110y A Hdl	G-S	£17400
152 11/02 Newc 3m D Hdl	G-S	£4056
134 12/01 Chep 2m110y A NHF	G-S	£9000
123 11/01 Weth 2m H NHF	GD	£2359
120 2/00 Weth 2m H NHF	SFT	£1862
129 11/99 Weth 2m H NHF	GD	£1618
			Total win prize-money £39779

Going: Sf: 0-0 GS: 0-0 Gd: 1-1 GF: - Fm: 0-0
Distance: 2m/2m3: 0-0 2m4-2m7: 1-1 3m+: 0-0
Track: LH: 1-1 RH: 0-0 Tight: 1-1 Gall: 0-0
Aids: Bl: 0-0 Vi: 0-0 Tstrap: 0-0 Ckp: 0-0
Best Rating: 152 1/03 Donc 3m110y gd-sft Hdl

Very useful hurdler; talented bumper horse and stayer on the Flat; not seen since winning at Kelso in May 2003; best on soft; stays 3m.

Tefi
86   72
6-y-o ch g Efisio-Masuri Kabisa (USA) (Ascot Knight (CAN))
J Balding (S R Bowring 25/6) Watchman Racing

Placings:P-P00   (0623)
2003/04: 20⁸G, 17⁹G, 17⁹G,

	Starts	1st	2nd	3rd	Win & Pl
Hurdles	3	0	0	0	0
Career Total	4	0	0	0	0

Going: Sf: 0-0 GS: 0-0 Gd: 0-3 GF: - Fm: 0-0
Distance: 2m/2m3: 0-2 2m4-2m7: 0-1 3m+: 0-0
Track: LH: 0-1 RH: 0-2 Tight: 0-2 Gall: 0-0
Aids: Bl: 0-0 Vi: 0-0 Tstrap: 0-3 Ckp: 0-0
Best Rating: 70 5/03 MRas 2m1f110y good Hdl

Telemoss (IRE)
112   (154h)138
10-y-o b g Montelimar (USA)-Shan's Moss (Le Moss)
N G Richards Ashleybank Investments Limited

Placings:15/021/1121244/1114-3P   (3488)
2003/04: 20³GS, 21⁸PGS,

	Starts	1st	2nd	3rd	Win & Pl
Chases	2	0	0	1	11000
Career Total	18	8	3	1	72131
138 1/03 Newc 2m110y E Ch	HVY	£3997
125 12/02 Kels 2m6f110yE Ch	HVY	£4147
117 11/02 Ayr 2m4f D Ch	SFT	£5407
140 12/01 Hayd 2m4f B HHdl	SFT	£11921
130 10/01 Weth 2m C(0-135)HHdl	GD	£5430
127 5/01 Hexm 2m4f110yD(0-125)HHdl	SFT	£3570
124 2/01 Kels 2m2f E Hdl	SFT	£2912
105 11/99 Hayd 2m H NHF	GD	£1934
			Total win prize-money £39322

Going: Sf: 0-0 GS: 0-2 Gd: 0-0 GF: - Fm: 0-0
Distance: 2m/2m3: 0-0 2m4-2m7: 0-2 3m+: 0-0
Track: LH: 0-2 RH: 0-0 Tight: 0-0 Gall: 0-2
Aids: Bl: 0-0 Vi: 0-0 Tstrap: 0-0 Ckp: 0-0
Best Rating: 154 3/02 Chel 3m good Hdl

Very useful chaser; formerly high-class hurdler, best over trips of around two and a half miles; effective on good ground, but very much suited by soft; unbeaten over fences until breaking a blood-vessel and reportedly injuring a knee at Sandown in February 2003; lightly raced since.

Tell Her Off
90   65
4-y-o b f Reprimand-My Valentina (Royal Academy (USA))
Miss Victoria Roberts (Mrs C A Dunnett 13/10) Andy Middleton

Placings:00000   (4668)
2003/04: 16⁹G, 16⁹GS, 21⁹G, 19⁹G, 23⁹GS,

	Starts	1st	2nd	3rd	Win & Pl
Hurdles	5	0	0	0	
Career Total	5	0	0	0	

Going: Sf: 0-0 GS: 0-2 Gd: 0-3 GF: - Fm: 0-0
Distance: 2m/2m3: 0-2 2m4-2m7: 0-3 3m+: 0-0
Track: LH: 0-2 RH: 0-3 Tight: 0-3 Gall: 0-0
Aids: Bl: 0-0 Vi: 0-0 Tstrap: 0-0 Ckp: 0-3
Best Rating: 65 12/03 Winc 2m good Hdl

Tell Me Why (IRE)
90   (97h)116
8-y-o gr g Roselier (FR)-Clonarctic Slave (Sir Mordred)
P R Webber Mrs C A Waters

Placings:5/2-2   (3770)
2003/04: 24⁸HY,

	Starts	1st	2nd	3rd	Win & Pl
Chases	1	0	1	0	1736
Career Total	3	0	2	0	4116

Going: Sf: 0-1 GS: 0-0 Gd: 0-0 GF: - Fm: 0-0
Distance: 2m/2m3: 0-0 2m4-2m7: 0-0 3m+: 0-1
Track: LH: 0-0 RH: 0-1 Tight: 0-0 Gall: 0-0
Aids: Bl: 0-0 Vi: 0-0 Tstrap: 0-0 Ckp: 0-0
Best Rating: 116 12/02 Wwck 3m110y gd-sft Ch

Fair chaser; a full-brother to a winning staying hurdler; stays 3m; acts on soft.

Tell Tale (IRE)

12-y-o b g Tale Quale-Loobagh Bridge (River Beauty)
J G Cann (Mrs O Bush 30/5) Mrs Pam Pengelly

Placings:PP2622   (4823)
2003/04: 28^RGS, 23^RS, 24²G, 26^RGS, 25²G, 23²GF,

	Starts	1st	2nd	3rd	Win & Pl
Chases	6	0	3	0	2067
Career Total	6	0	3	0	2067

Going:	Sf: 0-1 GS: 0-2 Gd: 0-2 GF: - Fm: 0-1	
Distance:	2m/2m3: 0-0 2m4-2m7: 0-0 3m+: 0-6	
Track:	LH: 0-2 RH: 0-4 Tight: 0-2 Gall: 0-0	
Aids:	Bl: 0-0 Vi: 0-0 Tstrap: 0-0 Ckp: 0-0	
Best Rating:	102 4/04 Extr 2m7f110y gd-fm	Ch

Telmar Flyer

77   **52**

7-y-o gr m Neltino-Flying Mistress (Lear Jet)
P R Webber (J Cullinan 8/10) Dodson & Partners

Placings:00/F0PP-555BP   (3168)
2003/04: 16⁵GF, 16³F, 16⁵GF, 16^RG, 17^PHY,

	Starts	1st	2nd	3rd	Win & Pl
Hurdles	5	0	0	0	0
Career Total	11	0	0	0	0

Going:	Sf: 0-1 GS: 0-0 Gd: 0-1 GF: - Fm: 0-3	
Distance:	2m/2m3: 0-5 2m4-2m7: 0-0 3m+: 0-0	
Track:	LH: 0-1 RH: 0-4 Tight: 0-2 Gall: 0-0	
Aids:	Bl: 0-0 Vi: 0-0 Tstrap: 0-3 Ckp: 0-0	
Best Rating:	73 10/02 Chel 2m110y good	NHF

Teme Valley

106(108c)   (95+c)**113**

10-y-o br g Polish Precedent (USA)-Sudeley (Dancing Brave (USA))
J Howard Johnson Chris Heron

Placings:065U01/0F60132211/550150/00020016/4001001-
65003111   (4799)
2003/04: 18⁶G, 16⁵S, 16⁹GF, 16^RG, 20⁹GF, 17¹G, 16¹G, 17¹G,

	Starts	1st	2nd	3rd	Win & Pl
Hurdles	6	2	0	1	8878
Chases	2	1	0	0	4420
Career Total	45	11	3	2	41376
113	4/04	Sedg	2m1f	D(0-120)HHdl	GD	£5128
95	3/04	Sedg	2m110y	E Ch	GD	£4420
113	12/03	Sedg	2m1f	E(0-110)HHdl	GD	£2709
110	4/03	Sedg	2m1f	D(0-120)HHdl	GD	£4904
103	11/02	Sedg	2m1f	D(0-115)HHdl	SFT	£4036
110	4/02	Sedg	2m1f	D(0-115)HHdl	G-F	£3276
115	1/01	Catt	2m3f	F(0-110)HHdl	G-S	£2373
121	4/00	Sedg	2m1f	E(0-115)HHdl	GD	£2394
116	3/00	Sedg	2m1f	F(0-110)HHdl	G-F	£2677
110	12/99	Sedg	2m1f	F(0-110)HHdl	G-S	£2460
96	4/99	Sedg	2m1f	E Hdl	G-S	£2495
				Total win prize-money £36875		

Going:	Sf: 0-1 GS: 0-0 Gd: 3-5 GF: - Fm: 0-2	
Distance:	2m/2m3: 3-7 2m4-2m7: 0-0 3m+: 0-0	
Track:	LH: 3-7 RH: 0-1 Tight: 3-6 Gall: 0-1	
Aids:	Bl: 0-0 Vi: 0-0 Tstrap: 0-0 Ckp: 0-0	
Best Rating:	121 4/00 Sedg 2m1f good	Hdl

Modest hurdler; got off the mark over fences in March 2004; a multiple winner at his favoured Sedgefield; does not want the ground too soft; effective at around two miles.

Temper Lad (USA)

94   **82**

9-y-o b g Riverman (USA)-Dokki (USA) (Northern Dancer)
J Joseph Jack Joseph

Placings:P11331/6210P3404/00/5404/2-050   (4669)
2003/04: 24⁰S, 21⁵G, 23^RGS,

	Starts	1st	2nd	3rd	Win & Pl
Hurdles	3	0	0	0	0
Career Total	25	4	2	3	18872
129	10/99	Chep	2m110y	C Hdl	GD	£4658
116	4/99	Strf	2m110y	D(0-110)HHdl	GD	£2612
110	9/98	Hntg	2m110y	E Hdl	G-F	£2326
105	9/98	Strf	2m110y	E Hdl	GD	£2318
				Total win prize-money £11915		

Going:	Sf: 0-1 GS: 0-1 Gd: 0-1 GF: - Fm: - 0-1	
Distance:	2m/2m3: 0-0 2m4-2m7: 0-2 3m+: 0-1	
Track:	LH: 0-2 RH: 0-1 Tight: 0-1 Gall: 0-2	
Aids:	Bl: 0-0 Vi: 0-0 Tstrap: 0-3 Ckp: 0-0	
Best Rating:	130 1/00 Kemp 2m5f good	Hdl

One time useful hurdler, but poor form in recent years.

Temple Dog (IRE)

95(108h)   (122+h)**109+**

8-y-o ch g Un Desperado (FR)-Shower (King's Lake (USA))
T P Tate The Ivy Syndicate

Placings:4/103/111-31P60   (4455)
2003/04: 20³GS, 20¹HY, 23^PS, 20⁶G, 24⁰HY,

	Starts	1st	2nd	3rd	Win & Pl
Hurdles	2	0	0	0	0
Chases	3	1	0	1	6500
Career Total	12	5	0	2	19758
115	1/04	Uttx	2m4f	E Ch	HVY	£5245
125	3/03	Newc	2m	E Hdl	G-S	£3464
118	12/02	Hayd	2m	D Hdl	SFT	£4719
116	12/02	Ayr	2m	E Hdl	G-S	£3073
131	2/02	Ayr	2m	H NHF	HVY	£1739
				Total win prize-money £18243		

Going:	Sf: 1-3 GS: 0-1 Gd: 0-1 GF: - Fm: 0-0	
Distance:	2m/2m3: 0-0 2m4-2m7: 1-3 3m+: 0-2	
Track:	LH: 1-3 RH: 0-1 Tight: 0-0 Gall: 0-1	
Aids:	Bl: 0-2 Vi: 0-0 Tstrap: 0-0 Ckp: 0-0	
Best Rating:	131 2/02 Ayr 2m heavy	NHF

Formerly useful bumper horse/novice hurdler; disappointed on chase bow at Haydock in December; much better when wide-margin winner at Uttoxeter the following month; took no interest and pulled up next time; reverted to hurdles; stays 2m 4f; suited by soft ground.

Temple Of Artemis

5-y-o b h Spinning World (USA)-Casessa (USA) (Caro)
P A Blockley David Wright

Placings:0   (2030)
2003/04: 26⁰G,

	Starts	1st	2nd	3rd	Win & Pl
Hurdles	1	0	0	0	0
Career Total	1	0	0	0	0

Going:	Sf: 0-0 GS: 0-0 Gd: 0-1 GF: - Fm: 0-0	
Distance:	2m/2m3: 0-0 2m4-2m7: 0-0 3m+: 0-0	
Track:	LH: 0-1 RH: 0-0 Tight: 0-0 Gall: 0-0	
Aids:	Bl: 0-0 Vi: 0-0 Tstrap: 0-0 Ckp: 0-0	

Templebreedy (IRE)

10-y-o br g Torenaga-Points Review (Major Point)
Mrs Edward Crow R J French

Placings:P   (4542)
2003/04: 20^PGS,

	Starts	1st	2nd	3rd	Win & Pl
Chases	1	0	0	0	0
Career Total	1	0	0	0	0

Going:	Sf: 0-0 GS: 0-1 Gd: 0-0 GF: - Fm: 0-0	
Distance:	2m/2m3: 0-0 2m4-2m7: 0-1 3m+: 0-0	
Track:	LH: 0-0 RH: 0-1 Tight: 0-1 Gall: 0-0	
Aids:	Bl: 0-0 Vi: 0-0 Tstrap: 0-0 Ckp: 0-0	

Ten Past Six

12-y-o ch g Kris-Tashinsky (USA) (Niijinsky (CAN))
R C Guest (H A McWilliams 7/9) James S Kennerley And Miss Jenny Hall

Placings:60PP0/24040/0/06PP/P   (3435)
2003/04: 20^PHY,

	Starts	1st	2nd	3rd	Win & Pl
Hurdles	1	0	0	0	0
Career Total	16	0	1	0	885

Going:	Sf: 0-1 GS: 0-0 Gd: 0-0 GF: - Fm: 0-0	
Distance:	2m/2m3: 0-0 2m4-2m7: 0-1 3m+: 0-0	
Track:	LH: 0-1 RH: 0-0 Tight: 0-0 Gall: 0-1	
Aids:	Bl: 0-0 Vi: 0-0 Tstrap: 0-0 Ckp: 0-0	
Best Rating:	71 10/98 Carl 2m4f110y good	Hdl

Ten Pressed Men (FR)

106f   **93+f**

4-y-o b g Video Rock (FR)-Recolte D'Estruval (FR) (Kouban (FR))
Jonjo O'Neill Mrs Valda Burke

Placings:30   (4649)
2003/04: 16³G, 17⁹G,

	Starts	1st	2nd	3rd	Win & Pl
NH Flat	2	0	0	1	357
Career Total	2	0	0	1	357

Going:	Sf: 0-0 GS: 0-0 Gd: 0-2 GF: - Fm: 0-0	
Distance:	2m/2m3: 0-0 2m4-2m7: 0-0 3m+: 0-0	
Track:	LH: 0-0 RH: 0-1 Tight: 0-0 Gall: 0-0	
Aids:	Bl: 0-0 Vi: 0-0 Tstrap: 0-0 Ckp: 0-0	
Best Rating:	93 3/04 Kemp 2m good	NHF

Ran green on debut in March at Kempton in maiden bumper; acts on good ground.

Tender Touch (IRE)

98(97h)   (74h)**79**

9-y-o gr m Weldnaas (USA)-Moments Peace (Adonijah)
Miss Kate Milligan J D Gordon

Placings:23545/B00/6632322054/105464/5553032-
041U3246   (1344)
2003/04: 16²G, 16⁹G, 16⁴GF, 17¹GF, 20^UG, 17³GF, 21²G, 17⁴G, 17⁶GF,

	Starts	1st	2nd	3rd	Win & Pl
Chases	9	1	2	2	7382

Career Total	39	2	6	6	14825
79	6/03	Sthl	2m1f	E(0-100)HCh	G-F £3880
82	11/01	Kels	2m10y	G Hdl	GD £2702
				Total win prize-money £6583	

Going:	Sf: 0-0 GS: 0-0 Gd: 0-5 GF: - Fm: 1-4
Distance:	**2m/2m3: 1-7** 2m4-2m7: 0-2 3m+: 0-0
Track:	LH: 1-7 RH: 0-2 Tight: 0-0 Gall: 0-0
Aids:	Bl: 0-0 Vi: 0-0 Tstrap: 0-0 Ckp: 0-0
Best Rating:	84 4/02 Prth 2m110y good Hdl

Moderate chaser; did not achieve much when winning 2m1f handicap at Southwell June 2003; best at two miles and yet to convince she stays further; effective on decent ground.

Tennant Creek (IRE)

6-y-o b g Lord Americo-Coolstuff (Over The River (FR))
Miss E C Lavelle R J Lavelle

Placings:0-4P4					(1170)
2003/04: 17⁴GF, 22⁵G, 18⁴GF,					

	Starts	1st	2nd	3rd	Win & Pl
NH Flat	1	0	0	0	0
Hurdles	2	0	0	0	259
Career Total	4	0	0	0	259

Going:	Sf: 0-0 GS: 0-0 Gd: 0-1 GF: - Fm: 0-2
Distance:	2m/2m3: 0-2 2m4-2m7: 0-1 3m+: 0-0
Track:	LH: 0-2 RH: 0-1 Tight: 0-2 Gall: 0-0
Aids:	Bl: 0-0 Vi: 0-0 Tstrap: 0-0 Ckp: 0-0
Best Rating:	88 6/03 Hrfd 2m1f gd-fm NHF

Tenshookmen (IRE)
94   112

10-y-o ch g Cardinal Flower-April Rise (Prominer))
W F Codd W J Codd

Placings:620¹/P505/441140630/0P110465P-050060					
					(4640)
2003/04: 22⁰GY, 16⁵Y, 20⁰Y, 21⁰YS, 22⁵SH, 21⁰G,					

	Starts	1st	2nd	3rd	Win & Pl
Hurdles	1	0	0	0	0
Chases	5	0	0	0	0
Career Total	32	5	1	1	33521
109	11/02	Punc	2m2f	(0-116)HCh	SFT £6773
98	10/02	Thur	2m2f	(0-95)HCh	Y-S £4868
112	10/01	Punc	2m4f	(0-109)HCh	YLD £6677
106	9/01	List	2m3f	Ch	G-F £7790
105	4/00	List	3m	Ch	Y-S £4416
				Total win prize-money £30524	

Going:	Sf: 0-0 GS: 0-0 Gd: 0-1 GF: - Fm: 0-0
Distance:	2m/2m3: 0-1 2m4-2m7: 0-5 3m+: 0-0
Track:	LH: 0-1 RH: 0-1 Tight: 0-1 Gall: 0-0
Aids:	Bl: 0-1 Vi: 0-0 Tstrap: 0-0 Ckp: 0-0
Best Rating:	112 11/03 Gowr 2m yield Ch

Modest winning chaser in Ireland, effective at up to three miles, but effective at shorter, acts on a soft surface.

Tensile (IRE)
103(105c)   (121c)136

9-y-o b g Tenby-Bonnie Isle (Pitcairn)
P J Hobbs D Charlesworth

Placings:1/1211P/343P201/41F1331355-5					(0095)
2003/04: 23⁵GS,					

Starts		1st	2nd	3rd	Win & Pl
Hurdles	1	0	0	0	647
Career Total	24	8	2	5	66698
132	10/02	Uttx	2m4f110yC(0-130)HHdl	G-F	£7150
120	7/02	Strf	3m	D Ch	G-F	£5590
120	5/02	NAbb	2m5f110yD Ch	G-S	£4163
139	3/02	Hayd	2m6f	C(0-135)HHdl	GD	£6929
144	12/00	Hayd	2m4f	B HHdl	HVY £12174
144	12/00	Chep	2m4f	C(0-130)HHdl	HVY £8716
132	11/00	Tntn	2m3f110yF(0-110)HHdl	GD	£2564
110	11/99	Leic	2m	E Hdl	G-S	£2945
				Total win prize-money £50234	

Going:	Sf: 0-0 GS: 0-1 Gd: 0-0 GF: - Fm: 0-1
Distance:	2m/2m3: 0-0 2m4-2m7: 0-0 3m+: 0-1
Track:	LH: 0-1 RH: 0-0 Tight: 0-0 Gall: 0-0
Aids:	Bl: 0-0 Vi: 0-0 Tstrap: 0-0 Ckp: 0-0
Best Rating:	144 12/00 Hayd 2m4f heavy Hdl

Useful handicap hurdler; winner of novice chases in the summer of 2002 but not a natural jumper; stays three miles; acts on most types of ground.

Tentsmuir
95   75

8-y-o b m Arctic Lord-Deep Pier (Deep Run)
D W Whillans D McComb

Placings:10/P04-02FP0P5					(4079)
2003/04: 22⁰G, 24²GF, 20⁰GF, 22⁶S, 20⁰GF, 27⁵F,					

	Starts	1st	2nd	3rd	Win & Pl
Hurdles	7	0	1	0	1253
Career Total	12	1	1	0	3659
95	1/02	Newc	2m	H NHF	SFT £1932
				Total win prize-money £1932	

Going:	Sf: 0-0 GS: 0-0 Gd: 0-1 GF: - Fm: 0-5
Distance:	2m/2m3: 0-0 2m4-2m7: 0-4 3m+: 0-3
Track:	LH: 0-3 RH: 0-3 Tight: 0-3 Gall: 0-0
Aids:	Bl: 0-0 Vi: 0-0 Tstrap: 0-0 Ckp: 0-0
Best Rating:	95 1/02 Newc 2m soft NHF

Plating-class hurdler; bumper winner on racecourse debut; first sign of ability since when second in modest event at Perth; stays three miles; seems to act on most ground.

Teorban (POL)
103   90

5-y-o b g Don Corleone-Tabaka (POL) (Pyjama Hunt)
M Pitman Something In The City Partnership

Placings:6-430P3P66					(4183)
2003/04: 16⁴G, 21³GF, 20⁰GF, 20⁰GS, 21³GS, 24⁰HY, 20⁰GS, 26⁰G,					

	Starts	1st	2nd	3rd	Win & Pl
Hurdles	8	0	0	2	832
Career Total	9	0	0	2	832

Going:	Sf: 0-1 GS: 0-3 Gd: 0-2 GF: - Fm: 0-2
Distance:	2m/2m3: 0-1 2m4-2m7: 0-5 3m+: 0-2
Track:	LH: 0-2 RH: 0-6 Tight: 0-2 Gall: 0-3
Aids:	Bl: 0-0 Vi: 0-0 Tstrap: 0-0 Ckp: 0-0
Best Rating:	90 12/03 Hntg 2m5f110y gd-sft Hdl

Plating-class hurdler; stays 2m5f; acts on fast and easy ground.

Terdad (USA)
110(87c)   (0c)101

11-y-o ch g Lomond (USA)-Istiska (FR) (Irish River (FR))
J G Given (M C Chapman 17/7) Tremousser Partnership

Placings:1142/1040/332116336/052062203/0001551615/5					
0F004P06340-24223322P60					(3784)
2003/04: 26²G, 24⁴GF, 24²G, 22²GF, 26³GF, 26³GF, 24²F, 27²G, 24⁴PGS, 21⁶GS, 26⁹GS,					

	Starts	1st	2nd	3rd	Win & Pl
Hurdles	11	0	5	2	5274
Career Total	59	8	10	8	34151
115	12/01	Catt	2m3f	F(0-110)HHdl	SFT £1890
111	10/01	Sedg	2m1f	F Hdl	GD £1974
106	8/01	MRas	2m1f110yG(0-95)HHdl	G-F £1785
118	12/99	Hntg	2m110y	D(0-125)HHdl	GD £5204
111	11/99	Wwck	2m	G Hdl	GD £1637
109	5/98	Prth	2m110y	E(0-105)HHdl	G-F £2892
93	9/97	Prth	2m110y	E Hdl	G-F £2633
91	8/97	Sedg	2m1f	E Hdl	G-F £2304
				Total win prize-money £20320	

Going:	Sf: 0-0 GS: 0-3 Gd: 0-3 GF: - Fm: 0-5
Distance:	2m/2m3: 0-0 2m4-2m7: 0-2 3m+: 0-9
Track:	LH: 0-5 RH: 0-6 Tight: 0-5 Gall: 0-3
Aids:	Bl: 0-0 Vi: 0-0 Tstrap: 0-0 Ckp: 0-6
Best Rating:	118 12/99 Hntg 2m110y good Hdl

Moderate hurdler; stays three miles; acts on any going; has had usual blinkers replaced by cheekpieces recently.

Terek (GER)
101(109h)   (106+h)101+

8-y-o ch g Irish River (FR)-Turbaine (USA) (Trempolino (USA))
R T Phillips Ford Associated Racing Team Ii

Placings:2P/424-41264U1F					(4576)
2003/04: 17⁴S, 17¹GF, 17²G, 16⁶GS, 20⁴G, 16⁰G, 16¹G, 18²G,					

	Starts	1st	2nd	3rd	Win & Pl
Hurdles	4	1	1	0	4925
Chases	4	1	0	0	5933
Career Total	13	2	3	0	13128
106	3/04	Tntn	2m110y	D Ch	GD £5609
97	7/03	Ctml	2m1f110yE Hdl	G-F £3542
				Total win prize-money £9153	

Going:	Sf: 0-1 GS: 0-1 Gd: 1-5 GF: - Fm: 1-1
Distance:	**2m/2m3: 2-7** 2m4-2m7: 0-1 3m+: 0-0
Track:	LH: 1-5 RH: 1-3 Tight: 2-5 Gall: 0-1
Aids:	Bl: 0-0 Vi: 0-0 Tstrap: 0-0 Ckp: 0-0
Best Rating:	106 3/04 Tntn 2m110y good Ch

Modest hurdler/chaser; Group Three winner on the Flat in Germany, suited by cut in the ground; has a tendency to race keenly.

Teridove

7-y-o b g Terimon-Flakey Dove (Oats)
A E Price Mrs M Price

Placings:00-P					(0528)
2003/04: 16⁰GF,					

	Starts	1st	2nd	3rd	Win & Pl
Hurdles	1	0	0	0	
Career Total	3	0	0	0	

Going:	Sf: 0-0 GS: 0-0 Gd: 0-0 GF: - Fm: 0-0
Distance:	2m/2m3: 0-1 2m4-2m7: 0-0 3m+: 0-0
Track:	LH: 0-1 RH: 0-0 Tight: 0-0 Gall: 0-0
Aids:	Bl: 0-0 Vi: 0-0 Tstrap: 0-0 Ckp: 0-0
Best Rating:	58 11/02 Ludl 2m good NHF

Terimons Daughter
76f   33f

5-y-o b m Terimon-Fun While It Lasts (Idiots Delight)

E W Tuer E Tuer

Placings:0   (1605)
2003/04: 17^{9}GF,

	Starts	1st	2nd	3rd	Win & Pl
NH Flat	1	0	0	0	
Career Total	1	0	0	0	

Going:	Sf: 0-0 GS: 0-0 Gd: 0-0 GF: - Fm: 0-1
Distance:	2m/2m3: 0-1 2m4-2m7: 0-0 3m+: 0-0
Track:	LH: 0-0 RH: 0-1 Tight: 0-0 Gall: 0-0
Aids:	Bl: 0-0 Vi: 0-0 Tstrap: 0-0 Ckp: 0-0
Best Rating:	33 10/03 Carl 2m1f gd-fm NHF

Terino

59

8-y-o b g Terimon-Ashmo (Ashmore (FR))
A E Jessop A Jessop

Placings:500/500004-F0   (0449)
2003/04: 20^{6}G, 20^{9}GF,

	Starts	1st	2nd	3rd	Win & Pl
Hurdles	2	0	0	0	
Career Total	11	0	0	0	0

Going:	Sf: 0-0 GS: 0-0 Gd: 0-1 GF: - Fm: 0-1
Distance:	2m/2m3: 0-0 2m4-2m7: 0-2 3m+: 0-0
Track:	LH: 0-0 RH: 0-1 Tight: 0-0 Gall: 0-1
Aids:	Bl: 0-0 Vi: 0-0 Tstrap: 0-0 Ckp: 0-0
Best Rating:	91 12/01 Hntg 2m110y gd-sft NHF

Modest bumper form; only plating-class over hurdles.

Terivic

88f   82f

4-y-o br g Terimon-Ludoviciana (Oats)
J W Payne G W Paul

Placings:30   (4594)
2003/04: 16^{3}GS, 16^{9}G,

	Starts	1st	2nd	3rd	Win & Pl
NH Flat	2	0	0	1	296
Career Total	2	0	0	1	296

Going:	Sf: 0-0 GS: 0-1 Gd: 0-1 GF: - Fm: 0-0
Distance:	2m/2m3: 0-2 2m4-2m7: 0-0 3m+: 0-0
Track:	LH: 0-0 RH: 0-2 Tight: 0-0 Gall: 0-1
Aids:	Bl: 0-0 Vi: 0-0 Tstrap: 0-0 Ckp: 0-0
Best Rating:	82 3/04 Towc 2m gd-sft NHF

Terminology

101f   93f

6-y-o gr g Terimon-Rhyming Moppet (Rymer)
K C Bailey J Perriss

Placings:44   (4447)
2003/04: 16^{4}HY, 16^{4}S,

	Starts	1st	2nd	3rd	Win & Pl
NH Flat	2	0	0	0	0
Career Total	2	0	0	0	0

Going:	Sf: 0-2 GS: 0-0 Gd: 0-0 GF: - Fm: 0-0
Distance:	2m/2m3: 0-2 2m4-2m7: 0-0 3m+: 0-0
Track:	LH: 0-2 RH: 0-0 Tight: 0-0 Gall: 0-0
Aids:	Bl: 0-0 Vi: 0-0 Tstrap: 0-0 Ckp: 0-0
Best Rating:	93 3/04 Wwck 2m soft NHF

Big type; showed ability in first two starts over bumpers; likely to need a stamina test over hurdles; acts on soft.

Tern Intern (IRE)

57

5-y-o b/br g Dr Devious (IRE)-Arctic Bird (USA) (Storm Bird (CAN))
Miss J Feilden Miss F C Brown

Placings:00   (0680)
2003/04: 16^{9}GS, 16^{9}GF,

	Starts	1st	2nd	3rd	Win & Pl
Hurdles	2	0	0	0	
Career Total	2	0	0	0	

Going:	Sf: 0-0 GS: 0-0 Gd: 0-0 GF: - Fm: 0-2
Distance:	2m/2m3: 0-2 2m4-2m7: 0-0 3m+: 0-0
Track:	LH: 0-2 RH: 0-0 Tight: 0-0 Gall: 0-0
Aids:	Bl: 0-0 Vi: 0-0 Tstrap: 0-0 Ckp: 0-1

Terre De Java (FR)

100   106+

6-y-o b g Cadoudal (FR)-Terre D'Argent (FR) (Count Ivor (USA))
Mrs H Dalton Miss L Hales

Placings:322/2023   (4915)
2003/04: 20^{2}G, 20^{9}G, 20^{2}GS, 16^{9}GS,

	Starts	1st	2nd	3rd	Win & Pl
Hurdles	4	0	2	1	2535
Career Total	7	0	4	2	13358

Going:	Sf: 0-0 GS: 0-2 Gd: 0-2 GF: - Fm: 0-0
Distance:	2m/2m3: 0-1 2m4-2m7: 0-3 3m+: 0-0
Track:	LH: 0-4 RH: 0-0 Tight: 0-2 Gall: 0-0
Aids:	Bl: 0-0 Vi: 0-0 Tstrap: 0-0 Ckp: 0-0
Best Rating:	111 3/04 Weth 2m4f110y gd-sft Hdl

Ex-French, placed in novice hurdles; stays 2m 4f; acts on soft ground.

Terrible Tenant

(65h)   (9h)

5-y-o gr g Terimon-Rent Day (Town And Country)
J W Mullins D I Bare

Placings:0P   (3377)
2003/04: 20^{9}G, 16^{P}S,

	Starts	1st	2nd	3rd	Win & Pl
Hurdles	2	0	0	0	
Career Total	2	0	0	0	

Going:	Sf: 0-1 GS: 0-0 Gd: 0-1 GF: - Fm: 0-0
Distance:	2m/2m3: 0-1 2m4-2m7: 0-1 3m+: 0-0
Track:	LH: 0-0 RH: 0-2 Tight: 0-0 Gall: 0-0
Aids:	Bl: 0-0 Vi: 0-0 Tstrap: 0-0 Ckp: 0-0
Best Rating:	12 12/03 Asct 2m4f good Hdl

Test Of Faith

37f

5-y-o b g Weld-Gold Pigeon (IRE) (Goldhill)
J N R Billinge Hilton Racing Partnership

Placings:0   (4952)
2003/04: 16^{9}GS,

	Starts	1st	2nd	3rd	Win & Pl
NH Flat	1	0	0	0	

Career Total   1   0   0   0

Going:	Sf: 0-0 GS: 0-1 Gd: 0-0 GF: - Fm: 0-0
Distance:	2m/2m3: 0-1 2m4-2m7: 0-0 3m+: 0-0
Track:	LH: 0-0 RH: 0-1 Tight: 0-0 Gall: 0-0
Aids:	Bl: 0-0 Vi: 0-0 Tstrap: 0-0 Ckp: 0-0

Test Of Friendship

90   83+

7-y-o br g Roselier (FR)-Grease Pot (Gala Performance (ZIM))
Mrs H Dalton (Ian Williams 8/1) Miss L Hales

Placings:0P3   (4570)
2003/04: 16^{9}GS, 22^{P}GS, 24^{3}GS,

	Starts	1st	2nd	3rd	Win & Pl
NH Flat	1	0	0	0	0
Hurdles	1	0	0	0	0
Chases	1	0	0	1	853
Career Total	3	0	0	1	853

Going:	Sf: 0-0 GS: 0-3 Gd: 0-0 GF: - Fm: 0-0
Distance:	2m/2m3: 0-1 2m4-2m7: 0-1 3m+: 0-1
Track:	LH: 0-1 RH: 0-2 Tight: 0-1 Gall: 0-1
Aids:	Bl: 0-0 Vi: 0-0 Tstrap: 0-0 Ckp: 0-0
Best Rating:	83 3/04 Bang 3m110y gd-sft Ch

Test Of Loyalty

80   (71h)83

10-y-o b g Niniski (USA)-River Chimes (Forlorn River)
J N R Billinge Hilton Racing Partnership

Placings:0/P/0364P206/4116544-5P6P   (2379)
2003/04: 20^{5}GS, 16^{P}GF, 17^{6}G, 16^{P}GF,

	Starts	1st	2nd	3rd	Win & Pl
Chases	4	0	0	0	0
Career Total	21	2	1	1	12387
93 9/02	Sthl	2m1f	E(0-105)HCh	GD	£4036
85 6/02	Prth	2m	F(0-100)HCh	G-S	£5382
			Total win prize-money £9419		

Going:	Sf: 0-0 GS: 0-1 Gd: 0-1 GF: - Fm: 0-2
Distance:	2m/2m3: 0-3 2m4-2m7: 0-1 3m+: 0-0
Track:	LH: 0-2 RH: 0-2 Tight: 0-2 Gall: 0-0
Aids:	Bl: 0-0 Vi: 0-0 Tstrap: 0-0 Ckp: 0-0
Best Rating:	93 9/02 Sthl 2m1f good Ch

Moderate handicap chaser; best at around two miles; acts on most types of ground; suited by a flat track.

Test The Water (IRE)

83   51

10-y-o ch g Maelstrom Lake-Baliana (CAN) (Riverman (USA))
Dr J R J Naylor Mrs Kay Stone

Placings:65   (0530)
2003/04: 17^{6}G, 20^{5}GF,

	Starts	1st	2nd	3rd	Win & Pl
Hurdles	2	0	0	0	0
Career Total	2	0	0	0	0

Going:	Sf: 0-0 GS: 0-0 Gd: 0-1 GF: - Fm: 0-1
Distance:	2m/2m3: 0-1 2m4-2m7: 0-1 3m+: 0-0
Track:	LH: 0-2 RH: 0-0 Tight: 0-1 Gall: 0-0
Aids:	Bl: 0-0 Vi: 0-0 Tstrap: 0-1 Ckp: 0-0

Best Rating: 54 5/03 Bang 2m1f good Hdl

Tetragon (IRE)
87   **69+**

4-y-o b g Octagonal (NZ)-Viva Verdi (IRE) (Green Desert (USA))
Miss Lucinda V Russell (K R Burke 11/6) William A Powrie

Placings: 045460P				(3883)
2003/04: 16⁹G, 16⁴G, 17⁵G, 16⁴G, 16⁶G, 16⁰HY, 16⁸G,				

	Starts	1st	2nd	3rd	Win & Pl
Hurdles	7	0	0	0	864
Career Total	7	0	0	0	864

Going:	Sf: 0-1 GS: 0-0 Gd: 0-4 GF: - Fm: 0-2
Distance:	2m/2m3: 0-7 2m4-2m7: 0-0 3m+: 0-0
Track:	LH: 0-4 RH: 0-3 Tight: 0-3 Gall: 0-0
Aids:	Bl: 0-2 Vi: 0-0 Tstrap: 0-2 Ckp: 0-4
Best Rating:	78 10/03 Carl 2m1f gd-fm Hdl

Moderate novice hurdler; acts on sound surface.

Th'Moons A Balloon (IRE)

10-y-o b g Euphemism-Gerti's Quay (Quayside)
S J Partridge Miss E A Baverstock

Placings: 3P				(0490)
2003/04: 19³G, 26⁸GF,				

	Starts	1st	2nd	3rd	Win & Pl
Chases	2	0	0	1	440
Career Total	2	0	0	1	440

Going:	Sf: 0-0 GS: 0-0 Gd: 0-0 GF: - Fm: 0-2
Distance:	2m/2m3: 0-0 2m4-2m7: 0-1 3m+: 0-1
Track:	LH: 0-1 RH: 0-1 Tight: 0-1 Gall: 0-0
Aids:	Bl: 0-0 Vi: 0-0 Tstrap: 0-0 Ckp: 0-0
Best Rating:	86 5/03 Extr 2m3f110y gd-fm Ch

Winner of two points; found trip inadequate when third at around 2m 4f at Exeter May 2003 on debut under Rules.

Thai La

4-y-o gr/ro g Rashik-Bonyalua Mill (Chilibang)
Mrs J Candlish A J Cartlich

Placings: P5P				(2839)
2003/04: 17⁸G, 18⁵G, 16⁸GS,				

	Starts	1st	2nd	3rd	Win & Pl
Hurdles	3	0	0	0	0
Career Total	3	0	0	0	0

Going:	Sf: 0-0 GS: 0-1 Gd: 0-2 GF: - Fm: 0-0
Distance:	2m/2m3: 0-3 2m4-2m7: 0-0 3m+: 0-0
Track:	LH: 0-2 RH: 0-0 Tight: 0-2 Gall: 0-0
Aids:	Bl: 0-0 Vi: 0-0 Tstrap: 0-0 Ckp: 0-0

Thalys (GER)
103(95h)   (107+h)**105**

6-y-o bl g Gold And Ivory (USA)-Tachira (Faraway Times (USA))
N A Graham (Mrs H Dalton 27/9) Miss P Theobald

Placings: 0/23212-P62131				(3842)
2003/04: 16⁸G, 17⁵G, 16²GF, 17¹GF, 17³GF, 19¹GS,				

	Starts	1st	2nd	3rd	Win & Pl
Chases	6	2	1	1	10662
Career Total	12	3	4	2	17945

102	2/04	Hrfd	2m3f	E(0-100)HCh	G-S	£5226
105	9/03	Sthl	2m1f	F(0-95)HCh	G-F	£3432
107	7/02	MRas	2m3f110yD Hdl		G-F	£4143
				Total win prize-money £12802		

Going:	Sf: 0-0 GS: 1-1 Gd: 0-2 GF: - Fm: 1-3
Distance:	2m/2m3: 2-6 2m4-2m7: 0-0 3m+: 0-0
Track:	LH: 1-5 RH: 1-1 Tight: 0-1 Gall: 0-0
Aids:	Bl: 0-0 Vi: 0-0 Tstrap: 1-4 Ckp: 0-0
Best Rating:	107 7/02 MRas 2m3f110y gd-fm Hdl

Moderate chaser; winner on the Flat in native Germany; stays 2m 3f; best on a sound surface; has been let down by his jumping.

Thames (IRE)
106   **111**

6-y-o b g Over The River (FR)-Aon Dochas (IRE) (Strong Gale)
N J Henderson Trevor Hemmings

Placings: 34-3P				(4641)
2003/04: 20³G, 24⁷PG,				

	Starts	1st	2nd	3rd	Win & Pl
Hurdles	2	0	0	1	1081
Career Total	4	0	0	2	2876

Going:	Sf: 0-0 GS: 0-0 Gd: 0-2 GF: - Fm: 0-0
Distance:	2m/2m3: 0-0 2m4-2m7: 0-1 3m+: 0-1
Track:	LH: 0-2 RH: 0-0 Tight: 0-2 Gall: 0-0
Aids:	Bl: 0-0 Vi: 0-0 Tstrap: 0-0 Ckp: 0-0
Best Rating:	111 11/03 Aint 2m4f good Hdl

Has shown a fair level of ability in bumpers; third in good race on hurdles debut; acts on good.

Thatchers Longshot
93(73h)   (48h)**74**

7-y-o ch g Gunner B-Formidable Lady (Formidable (USA))
S A Brookshaw S A Brookshaw

Placings: 6-5404				(3774)
2003/04: 24⁵GS, 24⁴S, 20⁰HY, 24⁴G,				

	Starts	1st	2nd	3rd	Win & Pl
Hurdles	1	0	0	0	0
Chases	3	0	0	0	728
Career Total	5	0	0	0	728

Going:	Sf: 0-2 GS: 0-1 Gd: 0-1 GF: - Fm: 0-0
Distance:	2m/2m3: 0-0 2m4-2m7: 0-1 3m+: 0-3
Track:	LH: 0-3 RH: 0-1 Tight: 0-2 Gall: 0-0
Aids:	Bl: 0-0 Vi: 0-0 Tstrap: 0-0 Ckp: 0-0
Best Rating:	73 2/04 Ludl 3m good Ch

Thats All Jazz
84   **46**

6-y-o b m Prince Sabo-Gate Of Heaven (Starry Night (USA))
C R Dore A N Inglis

Placings: 0P				(3780)
2003/04: 16⁰GF, 16⁸GS,				

	Starts	1st	2nd	3rd	Win & Pl
Hurdles	2	0	0	0	0
Career Total	2	0	0	0	0

Going:	Sf: 0-0 GS: 0-1 Gd: 0-0 GF: - Fm: 0-1
Distance:	2m/2m3: 0-1 2m4-2m7: 0-0 3m+: 0-0
Track:	LH: 0-0 RH: 0-2 Tight: 0-0 Gall: 0-2
Aids:	Bl: 0-0 Vi: 0-0 Tstrap: 0-0 Ckp: 0-1
Best Rating:	46 5/03 Hntg 2m110y gd-fm Hdl

Thatsforeel

11-y-o b g Scottish Reel-That Space (Space King)
Miss Joanne Tremain C J Hitchings

Placings: 2/32PPP0/1-4				(0032)
2003/04: 25⁴G,				

	Starts	1st	2nd	3rd	Win & Pl
Chases	1	0	0	0	327
Career Total	9	1	2	1	4787

87	4/03	Uttx	3m	H Ch	GD	£1547
				Total win prize-money £1547		

Going:	Sf: 0-0 GS: 0-0 Gd: 0-1 GF: - Fm: 0-0
Distance:	2m/2m3: 0-0 2m4-2m7: 0-0 3m+: 0-1
Track:	LH: 0-1 RH: 0-0 Tight: 0-0 Gall: 0-1
Aids:	Bl: 0-0 Vi: 0-0 Tstrap: 0-0 Ckp: 0-0
Best Rating:	112 4/01 Winc 3m1f110y soft Ch

A winning pointer/hunter chaser; effective in soft ground.

The Alleycat (IRE)
109(86h)   (79h)**96+**

13-y-o b g Tidaro (USA)-Allitess (Mugatpura)
R Ford Tarporley Turf Club

Placings: 0F/61152150/0051-34P2056214644P				(4814)
2003/04: 16³GF, 17⁴G, 22⁸GF, 21²GF, 19⁰GF, 21⁵G, 16⁶GF, 19²GF, 18¹GF, 17⁴G, 16⁶G, 16⁴GF, 20⁴G, 19⁸G,				

	Starts	1st	2nd	3rd	Win & Pl
Hurdles	2	0	0	0	0
Chases	12	1	2	1	6357
Career Total	28	5	3	1	21392

96	11/03	Font	2m2f	F(0-100)HCh	G-F	£2534
96	4/03	Plum	2m1f	G(0-90)HCh	G-F	£2586
92	7/01	Sedg	2m110y	E(0-115)HCh	G-F	£3363
86	6/01	Prth	2m	F(0-100)HCh	G-F	£4823
80	5/01	Hntg	2m4f110yF(0-100)HCh		G-F	£2990
				Total win prize-money £16298		

Going:	Sf: 0-0 GS: 0-0 Gd: 0-6 GF: - Fm: 1-8
Distance:	2m/2m3: 1-8 2m4-2m7: 0-6 3m+: 0-0
Track:	LH: 0-6 RH: 0-6 Tight: 1-7 Gall: 0-0
Aids:	Bl: 0-0 Vi: 0-0 Tstrap: 0-0 Ckp: 0-1
Best Rating:	96 11/03 Font 2m2f gd-fm Ch

Plating-class chaser; multiple winning pointer in his time; likes fast ground; stays two and a half miles.

The Baillie (IRE)
97f   **93f**

5-y-o b g Castle Keep-Regular Dolan (IRE) (Regular Guy)
C R Egerton Mrs D E H Turner

Placings: 5				(4571)
2003/04: 17⁵GS,				

	Starts	1st	2nd	3rd	Win & Pl
NH Flat	1	0	0	0	0
Career Total	1	0	0	0	0

Going:	Sf: 0-0 GS: 0-1 Gd: 0-0 GF: - Fm: 0-0
Distance:	2m/2m3: 0-1 2m4-2m7: 0-0 3m+: 0-0
Track:	LH: 0-1 RH: 0-0 Tight: 0-1 Gall: 0-0
Aids:	Bl: 0-0 Vi: 0-0 Tstrap: 0-0 Ckp: 0-0
Best Rating:	93 3/04 Bang 2m1f gd-sft NHF

The Bajan Bandit (IRE)

110(108c)   (144c)140+

9-y-o b g Commanche Run-Sunrise Highway Vii (Damsire Unregistered)
L Lungo Ashleybank Investments Limited

Placings:1/1/111/11101/112PP-0P1P   (4386)
2003/04: 23⁰GS, 25ᴾGS, 20¹HY, 25ᴾG,

	Starts	1st	2nd	3rd	Win & Pl
Hurdles	4	1	0	0	9503
Career Total	18	11	1	0	67937
140	1/04	Ayr	2m4f	B(0-150)HHdl	HVY	£9503
144	12/02	Ayr	2m5fH10yE Ch		G-S	£3770
120	11/02	Carl	2m4f	D Ch	HVY	£5307
131	4/02	Ayr	2m4f	C Hdl	GD	£5570
134	2/02	Ayr	2m4f	E Hdl	HVY	£3108
126	11/01	Carl	2m1f	E Hdl	HVY	£2531
115	11/01	Ayr	2m	E Hdl	G-S	£2597
147	4/01	Aint	2m1f	A NHF	HVY	£18000
142	12/00	Chep	2m110y	A NHF	SFT	£9000
129	11/00	Ayr	2m	H NHF	SFT	£1767
108	4/00	Carl	2m1f	H NHF	G-S	£1662
				Total win prize-money £62818

Going: Sf: 1-1 GS: 0-2 Gd: 0-1 GF: - Fm: 0-0
Distance: 2m2/2m3: 0-0 **2m4-2m7: 1-1** 3m+: 0-3
Track: LH: **1-4** RH: 0-0 Tight: 0-0 Gall: 0-1
Aids: Bl: 0-0 Vi: 0-0 Tstrap: 0-0 Ckp: 0-0
Best Rating: 147 4/01 Aint 2m1f heavy NHF

Very useful chaser/hurdler; seemed to lose his way over fences after a promising start; stays at least 2m 6f; goes very well on heavy ground and had conditions to suit when returning to something like his best at Ayr in January 2004.

The Bandit (IRE)

112(102h)   (116+h)134+

7-y-o b g Un Desperado (FR)-Sweet Friendship (Alleging (USA))
Miss E C Lavelle R J Lavelle

Placings:0/0F62-01611P23   (4955)
2003/04: 22⁰G, 20¹GF, 20⁶G, 20¹GS, 20¹S, 20ᴾG, 20²G, 20³G,

	Starts	1st	2nd	3rd	Win & Pl
Hurdles	3	1	0	0	4472
Chases	5	2	1	1	22095
Career Total	13	3	2	1	27708
127	1/04	Plum	2m4f	D Ch	SFT	£6890
131	12/03	Hntg	2m4f110yD Ch		G-S	£4953
116	11/03	Asct	2m4f	E(0-105)HHdl	G-F	£4472
				Total win prize-money £16315

Going: Sf: 1-1 GS: 1-1 Gd: 0-5 GF: - Fm: 1-1
Distance: 2m2/2m3: 0-0 **2m4-2m7: 3-8** 3m+: 0-0
Track: LH: 1-2 RH: **2-6** Tight: 0-0 Gall: 1-1
Aids: Bl: 0-0 Vi: 0-0 Tstrap: 0-0 Ckp: 0-0
Best Rating: 134 4/04 Aint 2m4f good Ch

Fair hurdler, novice chaser; stays 2m 4f; acts on fast ground; progressing.

The Bar Maid

105   90

6-y-o b m Alderbrook-Corny Story (Oats)
Mrs G Harvey Brig C K Price

Placings:00602PP202   (4762)
2003/04: 17⁰GS, 17⁰GF, 16⁶GS, 16⁹G, 21²GS, 22ᴾGS, 21ᴾG,
21²GS, 23⁰GS, 19⁰S,

	Starts	1st	2nd	3rd	Win & Pl
NH Flat	3	0	0	0	0

The Barge (IRE)

66

11-y-o b g Un Desperado (FR)-Marble Owen (Master Owen)
J White Mrs P A White

Placings:3/B3100/0000/P5P/P6623/26-P   (0329)
2003/04: 26ᴾGF,

	Starts	1st	2nd	3rd	Win & Pl
Chases	1	0	0	0	
Career Total	21	1	2	3	5931
115	2/99	Thur	2m6f	Hdl	HVY	£2455
				Total win prize-money £2455

Going: Sf: 0-0 GS: 0-0 Gd: 0-0 GF: - Fm: 0-1
Distance: 2m2/2m3: 0-0 2m4-2m7: 0-0 3m+: 0-1
Track: LH: 0-1 RH: 0-0 Tight: 0-0 Gall: 0-0
Aids: Bl: 0-0 Vi: 0-0 Tstrap: 0-0 Ckp: 0-0
Best Rating: 115 2/99 Thur 2m6f heavy Hdl

Moderate chaser; acts on soft ground; stays two and a half miles; jumps well.

The Battlin Bishop

47f

5-y-o br g Bishop Of Cashel-Angel Drummer (Dance In Time (CAN))
Ian Williams T J & Mrs H Parrott

Placings:0   (4787)
2003/04: 16⁰G,

	Starts	1st	2nd	3rd	Win & Pl
NH Flat	1	0	0	0	
Career Total	1	0	0	0	

Going: Sf: 0-0 GS: 0-0 Gd: 0-0 GF: - Fm: 0-0
Distance: 2m2/2m3: 0-0 2m4-2m7: 0-0 3m+: 0-0
Track: LH: 0-0 RH: 0-1 Tight: 0-0 Gall: 0-0
Aids: Bl: 0-0 Vi: 0-0 Tstrap: 0-0 Ckp: 0-0

The Bay Bridge (IRE)

70f   51f

5-y-o b/br g Over The River (FR)-Alamo Bay (Torenaga)
Miss E C Lavelle Frisky Fillies 2

Placings:0   (4454)
2003/04: 16⁰GS,

	Starts	1st	2nd	3rd	Win & Pl
NH Flat	1	0	0	0	
Career Total	1	0	0	0	

Going: Sf: 0-0 GS: 0-1 Gd: 0-0 GF: - Fm: 0-0
Distance: 2m2/2m3: 0-1 2m4-2m7: 0-0 3m+: 0-0
Track: LH: 0-0 RH: 0-1 Tight: 0-0 Gall: 0-0

The Beanfield (IRE)

74f   54f

5-y-o b g Good Thyne (USA)-Carry Me (IRE) (Lafontaine (USA))
J W Mullins Miss S A Ryder

Placings:0   (3861)
2003/04: 18⁰S,

	Starts	1st	2nd	3rd	Win & Pl
NH Flat	1	0	0	0	
Career Total	1	0	0	0	

Going: Sf: 0-1 GS: 0-0 Gd: 0-0 GF: - Fm: 0-0
Distance: 2m2/2m3: 0-1 2m4-2m7: 0-0 3m+: 0-0
Track: LH: 0-1 RH: 0-0 Tight: 0-0 Gall: 0-0
Aids: Bl: 0-0 Vi: 0-0 Tstrap: 0-0 Ckp: 0-0
Best Rating: 54 2/04 Plum 2m2f soft NHF

The Big'Un

93   90

10-y-o b g Green-Fingered-Lismore (Relkino)
G L Moore The P G Partnership

Placings:P243/46/P63-0   (0133)
2003/04: 24⁰GF,

	Starts	1st	2nd	3rd	Win & Pl
Chases	1	0	0	0	
Career Total	10	0	1	2	2737

Going: Sf: 0-0 GS: 0-0 Gd: 0-0 GF: - Fm: 0-1
Distance: 2m2/2m3: 0-0 2m4-2m7: 0-0 3m+: 0-1
Track: LH: 0-0 RH: 0-1 Tight: 0-0 Gall: 0-1
Aids: Bl: 0-0 Vi: 0-0 Tstrap: 0-0 Ckp: 0-0
Best Rating: 103 3/00 Font 2m4f gd-sft Ch

The Biker (IRE)

93   111

7-y-o br g Arctic Lord-Glenraval (Lucifer (USA))
M C Pipe D A Johnson

Placings:13/11-0P04FP0   (4859)
2003/04: 21⁰G, 16ᴾGS, 16⁶G, 22⁴GS, 16ᶠS, 22ᴾG, 19⁰GF,

	Starts	1st	2nd	3rd	Win & Pl
Hurdles	7	0	0	0	694
Career Total	11	3	0	1	17588
127	11/02	NAbb	2m1f	D Hdl	HVY	£3997
126	11/02	Uttx	2m	E Hdl	SFT	£3620
115	4/02	Fair	2m	NHF	G-Y	£7619
				Total win prize-money £15239

Going: Sf: 0-1 GS: 0-1 Gd: 0-4 GF: - Fm: 0-0
Distance: 2m2/2m3: 0-3 2m4-2m7: 0-4 3m+: 0-0
Track: LH: 0-2 RH: 0-5 Tight: 0-1 Gall: 0-1
Aids: Bl: 0-0 Vi: 0-3 Tstrap: 0-0 Ckp: 0-0
Best Rating: 127 11/02 NAbb 2m1f heavy Hdl

Fair hurdler; bumper winner in Ireland, won both starts in novice hurdles November 2002; off for a year after and disappointing since return; form so far at two miles, but wants further; acts on soft ground; effective under forcing tactics; has been tried in a visor.

The Biscuit

96   71

10-y-o ch m Nomadic Way (USA)-Not To Worry (USA)

Hurdles   7   0   3   0   2536
Career Total 10   0   3   0   2536

Aids: Bl: 0-0 Vi: 0-0 Tstrap: 0-0 Ckp: 0-0
Best Rating: 51 3/04 Asct 2m110y gd-sft NHF

Going: Sf: 0-1 GS: 0-4 Gd: 0-2 GF: - Fm: 0-3
Distance: 2m2/2m3: 0-4 2m4-2m7: 0-6 3m+: 0-0
Track: LH: 0-3 RH: 0-6 Tight: 0-4 Gall: 0-0
Aids: Bl: 0-0 Vi: 0-0 Tstrap: 0-0 Ckp: 0-0
Best Rating: 90 3/04 Towc 2m5f gd-sft Hdl

Moderate hurdler; best effort to date when second to decent prospect at Towcester in November 2003; stays 2m5f, but should be better over further; acts on good to firm, but looks best suited by cut in the ground.

(Stevvard)
B Mactaggart K Bruce

Placings:	0/00/2-4006				(4601)

2003/04: 20⁴GF, 24⁹GF, 20⁹G, 22⁶GS,

	Starts	1st	2nd	3rd	Win & Pl
Hurdles	4	0	0	0	0
Career Total	8	0	1	0	1272

Going:	Sf: 0-0 GS: 0-1 Gd: 0-1 GF: - Fm: 0-2
Distance:	2m/2m3: 0-0 2m4-2m7: 0-3 3m+: 0-1
Track:	LH: 0-1 RH: 0-2 Tight: 0-3 Gall: 0-0
Aids:	Bl: 0-0 Vi: 0-0 Tstrap: 0-2 Ckp: 0-0
Best Rating:	71 12/03 Muss 2m4f gd-fm Hdl

Poor novice hurdler.

The Bo'Sun

74f   **82f**

7-y-o b g Charmer-Sailors Joy (Handsome Sailor)
A E Jessop Mrs Gloria Jessop

Placings:	00-00				(0451)

2003/04: 16⁹G, 16⁸GF,

	Starts	1st	2nd	3rd	Win & Pl
NH Flat	2	0	0	0	
Career Total	4	0	0	0	

Going:	Sf: 0-0 GS: 0-0 Gd: 0-1 GF: - Fm: 0-1
Distance:	2m/2m3: 0-0 2m4-2m7: 0-0 3m+: 0-0
Track:	LH: 0-1 RH: 0-1 Tight: 0-1 Gall: 0-0
Aids:	Bl: 0-0 Vi: 0-0 Tstrap: 0-2 Ckp: 0-0
Best Rating:	82 4/03 Hntg 2m110y gd-fm NHF

The Bombers Moon

11-y-o br g Lord Bud-Oakington (Henry The Seventh)
Mrs C H Covell Mrs C H Covell

Placings:	0/0/0PP/0				(0416)

2003/04: 22⁹G,

	Starts	1st	2nd	3rd	Win & Pl
Chases	1	0	0	0	
Career Total	5	0	0	0	

Going:	Sf: 0-0 GS: 0-0 Gd: 0-1 GF: - Fm: 0-0
Distance:	2m/2m3: 0-0 2m4-2m7: 0-1 3m+: 0-0
Track:	LH: 0-0 RH: 0-1 Tight: 0-1 Gall: 0-0
Aids:	Bl: 0-0 Vi: 0-0 Tstrap: 0-0 Ckp: 0-0
Best Rating:	56 5/03 MRas 2m6f110y good Ch

The Bongo Man (IRE)

96   **(89c)85**

11-y-o b g Be My Native (USA)-Fight For It (Strong Gale)
Lindsay Woods (D J Wintle 28/4) Hugh M Duffy

Placings:	1/3360/6123350/064412124F/016/2P0PF/P6310P				(4740a)
	05-050U00				

2003/04: 24⁵GF, 18⁰G, 20⁵YS, 20⁰S, 16ᵁHY, 20⁰Y, 16⁰Y,

	Starts	1st	2nd	3rd	Win & Pl
Hurdles	4	0	0	0	0
Chases	3	0	0	0	0
Career Total	46	6	4	5	40989
110	10/02	Tntn	3m110y	E(0-110)HHdl	FRM	£3402
118	9/00	Clon	2m4f	(0-109)HHdl	GD	£2760
117	11/99	Tram	2m	(0-109)HCh	YLD	£6160
109	6/99	Tram	2m	Ch	G-Y	£2926

118	9/98	Clon	2m	(0-102)HHdl	G-F	£2540
115	4/97	Punc	2m	NHF	GD	£6782
				Total win prize-money £24572		

Going:	Sf: 0-2 GS: 0-0 Gd: 0-1 GF: - Fm: 0-1
Distance:	2m/2m3: 0-3 2m4-2m7: 0-3 3m+: 0-1
Track:	LH: 0-2 RH: 0-1 Tight: 0-0 Gall: 0-1
Aids:	Bl: 0-0 Vi: 0-0 Tstrap: 0-0 Ckp: 0-1
Best Rating:	120 10/98 Gowr 2m yld-sft Hdl

Modest hurdler, now trained in Ireland; has been tried over fences; acts on most types of ground; effective at up to three miles; has worn a tongue tie.

The Bounder

14-y-o b g Uncle Pokey-Young Romance (Kings Troop)
A J Tizzard Mrs M J Tizzard

Placings:	10/03P30120/323/1/P/0PP21P/F				(0521)

2003/04: 24⁶G,

	Starts	1st	2nd	3rd	Win & Pl
Chases	1	0	0	0	
Career Total	22	4	3	4	15865
113	4/01	Winc	3m	E(0-115)HCh	SFT	£4251
137	2/98	Winc	3m1f110yH Ch	GD	£1150
116	3/96	Hntg	2m110y D(0-105)HHdl	GD	£3335
102	3/94	Donc	2m110y	NHF	G-F	£1814
				Total win prize-money £10551		

Going:	Sf: 0-0 GS: 0-0 Gd: 0-1 GF: - Fm: 0-0
Distance:	2m/2m3: 0-0 2m4-2m7: 0-0 3m+: 0-1
Track:	LH: 0-1 RH: 0-0 Tight: 0-1 Gall: 0-0
Aids:	Bl: 0-0 Vi: 0-0 Tstrap: 0-0 Ckp: 0-0
Best Rating:	137 2/98 Winc 3m1f110y good Ch

The Bunny Boiler (IRE)

94(110h)   **(137 h)122**

10-y-o b g Tremblant-Danny's Charm (IRE) (Arapahos (FR))
Noel Meade The Usual Suspects Syndicate

Placings:	2/15210/FU00U21/5312F11/21P00U0-0P00				(4647)

2003/04: 20⁰S, 24ᴾS, 21⁰G, 36⁰G,

	Starts	1st	2nd	3rd	Win & Pl
Hurdles	1	0	0	0	0
Chases	3	0	0	0	0
Career Total	31	7	5	1	175144
137	12/02	Navn	3m	HHdl	Y-S	£11963
145	4/02	Fair	3m5f	HCh	G-Y	£65693
145	3/02	Uttx	4m2f	A HCh	HVY	£49600
122	12/01	Thur	2m6f	Hdl	HVY	£5008
118	1/01	DRoy	3m	Ch	G-Y	£6677
113	3/00	Naas	3m	Hdl	Y-S	£3588
84	5/99	Dpat	2m4f110y	NHF	GD	£1994
				Total win prize-money £144524		

Going:	Sf: 0-2 GS: 0-0 Gd: 0-2 GF: - Fm: 0-0
Distance:	2m/2m3: 0-0 2m4-2m7: 0-2 3m+: 0-2
Track:	LH: 0-3 RH: 0-1 Tight: 0-1 Gall: 0-0
Aids:	Bl: 0-1 Vi: 0-0 Tstrap: 0-0 Ckp: 0-0
Best Rating:	145 4/02 Fair 3m5f gd-yld Ch

Very useful chaser; won the Midlands and Irish Grand Nationals in 2002, but largely disappointing since; stays extreme distances; acts on soft and heavy ground.

The Butterwick Kid

11-y-o ch g Interrex (CAN)-Ville Air (Town Crier)

T P Tate R T A Tate

Placings:	4/2134/4152PR/2631U2636/60113610/413103				(4872)

2003/04: 25⁴G, 25¹GF, 22³S, 24¹HY, 21⁰G, 24³S,

	Starts	1st	2nd	3rd	Win & Pl
Chases	6	2	0	2	5077
Career Total	34	8	4	6	37641
110	3/04	Newc	3m	H Ch	HVY	£1904
113	5/03	Weth	3m1f	H Ch	G-F	£1449
122	3/02	Carl	2m4f	E(0-110)HCh	G-S	£3688
122	1/02	Sthl	2m4f110yD(0-115)HCh	G-S	£4193
123	1/02	Carl	2m4f	D(0-120)HCh	SFT	£4503
110	12/00	Weth	3m1f	D Ch	SFT	£4043
127	12/98	Weth	2m	B(0-140)HHdl	SFT	£5052
120	12/97	Hexm	2m	E Hdl	SFT	£2106
				Total win prize-money £26941		

Going:	Sf: 1-3 GS: 0-0 Gd: 0-2 GF: - Fm: 1-1
Distance:	2m/2m3: 0-0 2m4-2m7: 0-2 3m+: 2-4
Track:	LH: 2-6 RH: 0-0 Tight: 0-2 Gall: 1-1
Aids:	Bl: 2-5 Vi: 0-0 Tstrap: 0-0 Ckp: 0-0
Best Rating:	127 12/98 Weth 2m7f soft Hdl

A winner in the past on the Flat, over hurdles and over fences; pointing and hunter chasing nowadays; effective between two miles and three miles one furlong over hurdles and fences; acts on most ground.

The Byedein (IRE)

99(89h)   **(72h)89+**

7-y-o b m Afflora (IRE)-Southern Squaw (Buckskin (FR))
A H Mactaggart A H Mactaggart

Placings:	00/505255-P3				(3357)

2003/04: 21ᴾS, 22³S,

	Starts	1st	2nd	3rd	Win & Pl
Chases	2	0	0	1	724
Career Total	10	0	1	1	1784

Going:	Sf: 0-2 GS: 0-0 Gd: 0-0 GF: - Fm: 0-0
Distance:	2m/2m3: 0-0 2m4-2m7: 0-2 3m+: 0-0
Track:	LH: 0-2 RH: 0-0 Tight: 0-1 Gall: 0-0
Aids:	Bl: 0-0 Vi: 0-0 Tstrap: 0-0 Ckp: 0-0
Best Rating:	93 1/04 Kels 2m6f110y soft Ch

Plating-class hurdler/chaser; has shown some ability; looks essentially a stayer.

The Chain Gang

11-y-o b g Baron Blakeney-Delvin Princess (Aglojo)
N Thomas N Thomas

Placings:	P				(0032)

2003/04: 25ᴾG,

	Starts	1st	2nd	3rd	Win & Pl
Chases	1	0	0	0	
Career Total	1	0	0	0	

Going:	Sf: 0-0 GS: 0-0 Gd: 0-1 GF: - Fm: 0-0
Distance:	2m/2m3: 0-0 2m4-2m7: 0-0 3m+: 0-1
Track:	LH: 0-1 RH: 0-0 Tight: 0-0 Gall: 0-1
Aids:	Bl: 0-0 Vi: 0-0 Tstrap: 0-0 Ckp: 0-0

The Cockney Kid (IRE)

77   **30**

9-y-o ch g Glacial Storm (USA)-Rainbow Days (Sunyboy)

N A Twiston-Davies N A Twiston-Davies

Placings:*560/03P/P0*   (4246)
2003/04: 19PHY, 17PGF,

	Starts	1st	2nd	3rd	Win & Pl
Hurdles	2	0	0	0	
Career Total	8	0	1		376

Going:	Sf: 0-1 GS: 0-0 Gd: 0-0 GF: - Fm: 0-1
Distance:	2m/2m3: 0-1 2m4-2m7: 0-1 3m+: 0-0
Track:	LH: 0-0 RH: 0-2 Tight: 0-0 Gall: 0-0
Aids:	Bl: 0-0 Vi: 0-0 Tstrap: 0-0 Ckp: 0-0
Best Rating:	90 9/00 Extr 2m6f110y good Hdl

The Collector (IRE)
86f   76f

5-y-o ch g Forest Wind (USA)-Glowing Reeds (Kalaglow)
N P McCormack (M C Pipe 22/10) Mrs D McCormack

Placings:*40*   (3669)
2003/04: 16AGF, 16PHY,

	Starts	1st	2nd	3rd	Win & Pl
NH Flat	2	0	0		0
Career Total	2	0	0	0	0

Going:	Sf: 0-1 GS: 0-0 Gd: 0-0 GF: - Fm: 0-1
Distance:	2m/2m3: 0-2 2m4-2m7: 0-0 3m+: 0-0
Track:	LH: 0-2 RH: 0-0 Tight: 0-0 Gall: 0-0
Aids:	Bl: 0-0 Vi: 0-0 Tstrap: 0-0 Ckp: 0-0
Best Rating:	76 10/03 Chep 2m110y gd-fm NHF

Beaten favourite on debut when only fourth in poor Chepstow bumper October 2003.

The Count (FR)
96   69

5-y-o b g Sillery (USA)-Dear Countess (FR) (Fabulous Dancer (USA))
F P Murtagh Jack The Lads

Placings:*300P-446R*   (1208)
2003/04: 17AG, 17AGF, 16AGF, 17PG,

	Starts	1st	2nd	3rd	Win & Pl
Hurdles	4	0	0		268
Career Total	8	0	1		591

Going:	Sf: 0-0 GS: 0-0 Gd: 0-2 GF: - Fm: 0-2
Distance:	2m/2m3: 0-4 2m4-2m7: 0-0 3m+: 0-0
Track:	LH: 0-3 RH: 0-1 Tight: 0-0 Gall: 0-0
Aids:	Bl: 0-0 Vi: 0-0 Tstrap: 0-0 Ckp: 0-0
Best Rating:	69 6/03 MRas 2m1f110y gd-fm Hdl

The Crooked Oak

12-y-o ch g Fearless Action (USA)-Life Goes On (Pharly (FR))
Keith Thomas Keith Thomas

Placings:*2/400P/0343/0U4/PU5/56/41410U040/F-PP*   (1142)

2003/04: 24PG, 24PGF,

	Starts	1st	2nd	3rd	Win & Pl
Hurdles	2	0	0		
Career Total	29	2	1	2	7544

96	6/01	Hexm	3m1f	E(0-105)HCh	GD £3204
75	5/01	Hexm	2m4f110yF Ch		G-F £2115
				Total win prize-money £5321	

Going:	Sf: 0-0 GS: 0-0 Gd: 0-1 GF: - Fm: 0-1
Distance:	2m/2m3: 0-0 2m4-2m7: 0-0 3m+: 0-2
Track:	LH: 0-1 RH: 0-1 Tight: 0-0 Gall: 0-0
Aids:	Bl: 0-0 Vi: 0-0 Tstrap: 0-0 Ckp: 0-0
Best Rating:	97 11/96 Carl 2m1f good NHF

The Croppy Boy
79   44

12-y-o b g Arctic Lord-Deep Cut (Deep Run)
Mrs N S Sharpe J V C Davenport

Placings:*5400/0/454P/F4P/P430-6P*   (1374)
2003/04: 24SGF, 24PGF,

	Starts	1st	2nd	3rd	Win & Pl
Hurdles	2	0	0	0	0
Career Total	18	0	0	1	741

Going:	Sf: 0-0 GS: 0-0 Gd: 0-0 GF: - Fm: 0-2
Distance:	2m/2m3: 0-0 2m4-2m7: 0-0 3m+: 0-2
Track:	LH: 0-2 RH: 0-0 Tight: 0-0 Gall: 0-0
Aids:	Bl: 0-0 Vi: 0-0 Tstrap: 0-0 Ckp: 0-0
Best Rating:	85 11/96 Wwck 2m good NHF

The Dark Flasher (IRE)
100(112h)   (124 h)117

7-y-o b h Lucky Guest-Perpignan (Rousillon (USA))
C F Swan N O'Flaherty

Placings:*1343204F/0632000F43-0652236B5*   (3062a)
2003/04: 16PGS, 16PY, 16SG, 16PG, 16PGF, 17PG, 16PGY, 17PYS, 17PSH,

	Starts	1st	2nd	3rd	Win & Pl
Hurdles	3	0	0		1380
Chases	6	0	2	1	3175
Career Total	27	1	4	5	22137

111	11/01	Naas	2m	Hdl	Y-S £4729
				Total win prize-money £4730	

Going:	Sf: 0-0 GS: 0-1 Gd: 0-3 GF: - Fm: 0-1
Distance:	2m/2m3: 0-9 2m4-2m7: 0-0 3m+: 0-0
Track:	LH: 0-3 RH: 0-1 Tight: 0-0 Gall: 0-0
Aids:	Bl: 0-0 Vi: 0-0 Tstrap: 0-0 Ckp: 0-0
Best Rating:	124 3/03 Winc 2m soft Hdl

Fair Irish-trained handicap hurdler; effective at two miles and acts on good ground, but handles heavy.

The Dark Lord (IRE)
105   117+

7-y-o b g Lord Americo-Khalkeys Shoon (Green Shoon)
Mrs L Wadham A E Pakenham

Placings:*42-1F143F*   (4325)
2003/04: 20¹GF, 21PGF, 20¹GS, 21⁴G, 19³G, 20PS,

	Starts	1st	2nd	3rd	Win & Pl
Hurdles	6	2	0	1	8497
Career Total	8	2	1	1	10007

116	11/03	Hayd	2m4f	D Hdl	G-S £3653
95	6/03	Worc	2m4f	E Hdl	G-F £3444
				Total win prize-money £7097	

Going:	Sf: 0-1 GS: 1-1 Gd: 0-2 GF: - Fm: 1-2
Distance:	2m/2m3: 0-0 2m4-2m7: 2-6 3m+: 0-0
Track:	LH: 2-2 RH: 0-4 Tight: 0-1 Gall: 0-1
Aids:	Bl: 0-0 Vi: 0-0 Tstrap: 0-0 Ckp: 0-0
Best Rating:	117 11/03 Hntg 2m5f110y gd-fm Hdl

Fair novice hurdler; dual winner and has given a good

---

account of himself since; effective at 2m4f; acts on any ground.

The Dream Lives On (IRE)
73

8-y-o ch g Phardante (FR)-Rare Dream (Pollerton)
T P McGovern B & M McHugh Ltd Civil Engineering

Placings:*05P/4P*   (2338)
2003/04: 22⁴G, 21PS,

	Starts	1st	2nd	3rd	Win & Pl
Hurdles	2	0	0	0	0
Career Total	5	0	0	0	0

Going:	Sf: 0-1 GS: 0-0 Gd: 0-1 GF: - Fm: 0-0
Distance:	2m/2m3: 0-2 2m4-2m7: 0-2 3m+: 0-0
Track:	LH: 0-1 RH: 0-1 Tight: 0-2 Gall: 0-0
Aids:	Bl: 0-0 Vi: 0-0 Tstrap: 0-0 Ckp: 0-0
Best Rating:	75 10/01 Hntg 2m110y good NHF

The Eens
95   (18h)85

12-y-o b g Rakaposhi King-Snippet (Ragstone)
D McCain Shaw Hill Golf Club (sage Cott Props Ltd

Placings:*5064/26P4P1/124231U0/4P440522143/4623P5P/03623541313/P44465-655PPP*   (4390)
2003/04: 24SG, 22SGS, 20²S, 19PHY, 24²G, 27PG,

	Starts	1st	2nd	3rd	Win & Pl
Hurdles	2	0	0		0
Chases	4	0	0		0
Career Total	59	6	7	7	35180

90	4/02	Uttx	3m4f	E(0-110)HCh	G-S £4221
85	3/02	MRas	3m1f	F(0-95)HCh	SFT £3031
101	3/00	Carl	2m1f	E(0-115)HHdl	HVY £2436
101	3/00	Uttx	3m2f	F(0-110)HHdl	HVY £3631
105	11/98	Hayd	2m	C(0-130)HCh	SFT £4697
94	3/98	Bang	2m4f110yD Ch		G-S £3598
				Total win prize-money £21616	

Going:	Sf: 0-2 GS: 0-1 Gd: 0-3 GF: - Fm: 0-0
Distance:	2m/2m3: 0-0 2m4-2m7: 0-3 3m+: 0-3
Track:	LH: 0-4 RH: 0-1 Tight: 0-3 Gall: 0-0
Aids:	Bl: 0-0 Vi: 0-0 Tstrap: 0-0 Ckp: 0-0
Best Rating:	105 11/98 Hayd 2m soft Ch

PLating-class chaser; normally a sound jumper; needs cut in the ground to be seen at his best; stays three miles two.

The Extra Man (IRE)
106   112+

10-y-o b g Sayaarr (USA)-Chez Georges (Welsh Saint)
M J Ryan Extraman Ltd

Placings:*610P/011520/12131/23P2/326F1*   (4406)
2003/04: 20³GS, 20²G, 24⁶G, 21PGS, 20¹G,

	Starts	1st	2nd	3rd	Win & Pl
Chases	5	1	1		6652
Career Total	24	7	5	3	78998

112	3/04	Hntg	2m4f110yE Ch		GD £3909
131	2/01	Sand	2m4f	A HHdl	HVY £29000
122	11/00	Chel	2m6f	C(0-135)HHdl	G-S £19337
116	10/00	MRas	2m5f110yD(0-125)HHdl		GD £7312
110	10/99	Asct	2m4f	E(0-105)HHdl	GD £3647
100	9/99	Hntg	2m5f110yE(0-105)HHdl		GD £2582
99	1/99	Kemp	2m	H NHF	SFT £1661
				Total win prize-money £67453	

Going:	Sf: 0-0 GS: 0-2 Gd: 1-3 GF: - Fm: 0-0

Distance: 2m/2m3: 0-0 2m4-2m7: 1-4 3m+: 0-1
Track: LH: 0-1 RH: 1-4 Tight: 0-0 Gall: 1-3
Aids: Bl: 1-5 Vi: 0-0 Tstrap: 0-0 Ckp: 0-0
Best Rating: 131 2/01 Sand 2m6f heavy Hdl

Modest chaser/fair hurdler; can go well fresh; stays three miles well; likes soft ground; usually wears blinkers.

The Fairy Flag (IRE)
95 **86**
6-y-o ch m Inchinor-Good Reference (IRE) (Reference Point)
A Bailey Mrs V Farrington

Placings:115/PP5-30P (4429)
2003/04: 16^3GF, 16^5S, 16^6G,

	Starts	1st	2nd	3rd	Win & Pl
Hurdles	3	0	0	1	326
Career Total	9	2	0	1	8143
97	11/01 Sand	2m110y	D Hdl	G-S	£4212
97	11/01 Hayd	2m	H Hdl	SFT	£3605
			Total win prize-money		£7817

Going: Sf: 0-1 GS: 0-0 Gd: 0-1 GF: - Fm: 0-1
Distance: 2m/2m3: 0-3 2m4-2m7: 0-0 3m+: 0-0
Track: LH: 0-3 RH: 0-0 Tight: 0-0 Gall: 0-0
Aids: Bl: 0-0 Vi: 0-0 Tstrap: 0-0 Ckp: 0-3
Best Rating: 97 11/01 Sand 2m110y gd-sft Hdl

Plating-class hurdler; dual winner as a juvenile in 2001; lightly-raced since; suited by two miles on soft ground.

The Fenman
96 **82d**
6-y-o b g Mazaad-Dalgorian (IRE) (Lancastrian)
R J Armson R J Armson

Placings:000/P200230000-60543 (4506)
2003/04: 20^6G, 26^0GS, 21^5G, 19^4GF, 19^3GS,

	Starts	1st	2nd	3rd	Win & Pl
Hurdles	5	0	0	1	331
Career Total	18	0	2	2	2179

Going: Sf: 0-0 GS: 0-2 Gd: 0-2 GF: - Fm: 0-1
Distance: 2m/2m3: 0-1 2m4-2m7: 0-3 3m+: 0-1
Track: LH: 0-1 RH: 0-4 Tight: 0-0 Gall: 0-0
Aids: Bl: 0-0 Vi: 0-0 Tstrap: 0-0 Ckp: 0-3
Best Rating: 82 2/03 Hrfd 2m3f110y good Hdl

Plating-class hurdler; stays two and a half miles.

The Flyer (IRE)
101 **118**
7-y-o b g Blues Traveller (IRE)-National Ballet (Shareef Dancer (USA))
Miss S J Wilton John Pointon And Sons

Placings:1314/0301201320/2142-00P0605 (4870)
2003/04: 20^0G, 20^0GS, 22^0GS, 24^0GS, 22^6S, 22^0G, 24^5GS,

	Starts	1st	2nd	3rd	Win & Pl
Hurdles	7	0	0	0	
Career Total	25	5	4	3	24964
118	11/02 Hrfd	2m3f110yD(0-125)HHdl	GD	£6987
101	2/02 Hrfd	2m1f D(0-115)HHdl	HVY	£3381
101	12/01 Hrfd	2m1f D(0-115)HHdl	GD	£2968
97	11/00 Uttx	2m E Hdl	HVY	£2303
97	9/00 MRas	2m1f110yG Hdl	G-F	£1561
		Total win prize-money		£17201

Going: Sf: 0-1 GS: 0-4 Gd: 0-2 GF: - Fm: 0-0
Distance: 2m/2m3: 0-0 2m4-2m7: 0-5 3m+: 0-2
Track: LH: 0-4 RH: 0-2 Tight: 0-3 Gall: 0-0
Aids: Bl: 0-0 Vi: 0-0 Tstrap: 0-0 Ckp: 0-0
Best Rating: 118 12/02 Wwck 2m5f soft Hdl

Fair handicap hurdler; stays two and a half miles; acts on all types of ground.

The French Furze (IRE)
121(100c) (124c)**150**
10-y-o ch g Be My Guest (USA)-Exciting (Mill Reef (USA))
N G Richards Jim Ennis

Placings:1261131PP/P2060/2110P/222065/2222304/0265 1F-011053004 (4862)
2003/04: 16^0GF, 20^1G, 16^1G, 16^9GS, 23^5G, 20^3GS, 21^0G, 20^0G, 16^4GS,

	Starts	1st	2nd	3rd	Win & Pl
Hurdles	9	2	0	1	48302
Career Total	47	9	11	3	168440
150	11/03 Newc	2m A Hdl	GD	£26100
136	11/03 Ayr	2m4f B(0-140)HHdl	GD	£13702
124	3/03 Sedg	2m5f E Ch	SFT	£3887
146	1/00 Chel	2m1f B(0-145)HHdl	G-S	£10140
141	1/00 Hayd	2m1 B(0-145)HHdl	SFT	£6652
134	2/98 Hntg	2m110y C Hdl	GD	£4202
137	11/97 Chel	2m110y B Hdl	GD	£5121
135	11/97 Plum	2m1f E Hdl	G-F	£2385
96	8/97 Tram	2m Hdl	GD	£2712
		Total win prize-money		£74903

Going: Sf: 0-0 GS: 0-3 Gd: 2-5 GF: - Fm: 0-1
Distance: 2m/2m3: 1-4 2m4-2m7: 1-4 3m+: 0-1
Track: LH: 2-9 RH: 0-1 Tight: 0-1 Gall: 1-3
Aids: Bl: 0-0 Vi: 0-0 Tstrap: 0-0 Ckp: 0-0
Best Rating: 153 1/02 Leop 2m heavy Hdl

Smart hurdler/chaser; deservedly won Fighting Fifth Hurdle at Newcastle in November 2003, having been runner-up in the previous three runnings; suited by two miles, but stays 2m 5f; acts on good or softer ground; usually a front runner.

The Fridge
97f **107f**
6-y-o ch g Karinga Bay-Sovereign Maiden (Nearly A Hand)
P R Webber J F Dean

Placings:22 (4454)
2003/04: 18^2GS, 16^2GS,

	Starts	1st	2nd	3rd	Win & Pl
NH Flat	2	0	2	0	1282
Career Total	2	0	2	0	1282

Going: Sf: 0-0 GS: 0-2 Gd: 0-0 GF: - Fm: 0-0
Distance: 2m/2m3: 0-2 2m4-2m7: 0-0 3m+: 0-0
Track: LH: 0-1 RH: 0-1 Tight: 0-1 Gall: 0-0
Aids: Bl: 0-0 Vi: 0-0 Tstrap: 0-0 Ckp: 0-0
Best Rating: 107 3/04 Asct 2m110y gd-sft NHF

Narrowly beaten in two bumpers on good to soft ground.

The Frosty Ferret (IRE)
92 **81**
6-y-o b g Zaffaran (USA)-Frostbite (Prince Tenderfoot (USA))
J M Jefferson Ashleybank Investments Limited

Placings:0003 (4881)
2003/04: 16^6G, 17^0G, 21^0G, 17^3GS,

	Starts	1st	2nd	3rd	Win & Pl
NH Flat	2	0	0	0	0
Hurdles	2	0	0	1	580
Career Total	4	0	0	1	580

Going: Sf: 0-0 GS: 0-1 Gd: 0-3 GF: - Fm: 0-0
Distance: 2m/2m3: 0-3 2m4-2m7: 0-1 3m+: 0-0
Track: LH: 0-1 RH: 0-0 Tight: 0-0 Gall: 0-1
Aids: Bl: 0-0 Vi: 0-0 Tstrap: 0-0 Ckp: 0-0
Best Rating: 86 3/04 Carl 2m1f good NHF

Very modest novice hurdler; looks basically slow.

The Gene Genie
103(95c) (97c)**104**
9-y-o b g Syrtos-Sally Maxwell (Roscoe Blake)
R J Hodges Mrs Carol Taylor

Placings:32506/13230/21232243P/5532-020514000 (3944)
2003/04: 17^0G, 16^2G, 16^9GF, 17^5G, 16^1S, 16^4S, 16^6HY, 16^0G, 16^9G,

	Starts	1st	2nd	3rd	Win & Pl
Hurdles	9	1	1	0	6326
Career Total	32	3	8	6	23597
103	1/04 Winc	2m E(0-110)HHdl	SFT	£3968
103	12/01 Winc	2m D(0-120)HHdl	GD	£5213
91	12/00 Hrfd	2m1f G Hdl	HVY	£2023
		Total win prize-money		£11204

Going: Sf: 1-3 GS: 0-0 Gd: 0-5 GF: - Fm: 0-1
Distance: 2m/2m3: 1-9 2m4-2m7: 0-0 3m+: 0-0
Track: LH: 0-1 RH: 1-8 Tight: 0-2 Gall: 0-0
Aids: Bl: 0-0 Vi: 0-0 Tstrap: 0-0 Ckp: 0-0
Best Rating: 113 1/01 Tntn 2m1f soft Hdl

Moderate hurdler; acts on good ground or softer; best at around two miles.

The Gerry Man (IRE)
75f **73f**
5-y-o b g Arctic Lord-Soldeu Creek (IRE) (Buckskin (FR))
D J Wintle G M McGuinness

Placings:0 (4407)
2003/04: 16^0G,

	Starts	1st	2nd	3rd	Win & Pl
NH Flat	1	0	0	0	
Career Total	1	0	0	0	

Going: Sf: 0-0 GS: 0-0 Gd: 0-1 GF: - Fm: 0-0
Distance: 2m/2m3: 0-1 2m4-2m7: 0-0 3m+: 0-0
Track: LH: 0-0 RH: 0-1 Tight: 0-0 Gall: 0-1
Aids: Bl: 0-0 Vi: 0-0 Tstrap: 0-0 Ckp: 0-0
Best Rating: 73 3/04 Hntg 2m110y good NHF

The Ginger Prince
66f **55f**
4-y-o ch g Alderbrook-Chapel Haven (IRE) (King Persian)
D McCain Ray Pattison

Placings:0 (4050)
2003/04: 16^0G,

	Starts	1st	2nd	3rd	Win & Pl
NH Flat	1	0	0	0	
Career Total	1	0	0	0	

Going: Sf: 0-0 GS: 0-0 Gd: 0-1 GF: - Fm: 0-0
Distance: 2m/2m3: 0-1 2m4-2m7: 0-0 3m+: 0-0
Track: LH: 0-1 RH: 0-0 Tight: 0-0 Gall: 0-1
Aids: Bl: 0-0 Vi: 0-0 Tstrap: 0-0 Ckp: 0-0
Best Rating: 54 2/04 Hayd 2m good NHF

The Glen

95   **89**

6-y-o gr g Mtoto-Silver Singer (Pharly (FR))
R Lee (M H Tompkins 13/10) W Roseff and Partners

Placings:04   (4490)
2003/04: 17⁰S, 16⁴G,

	Starts	1st	2nd	3rd	Win & Pl
Hurdles	2	0	0	0	267
Career Total	2	0	0	0	267

Going:	Sf: 0-1 GS: 0-0 Gd: 0-1 GF: - Fm: 0-0
Distance:	2m/2m3: 0-2 2m4-2m7: 0-0 3m+: 0-0
Track:	LH: 0-1 RH: 0-1 Tight: 0-2 Gall: 0-0
Aids:	Bl: 0-0 Vi: 0-0 Tstrap: 0-0 Ckp: 0-0
Best Rating:	89 3/04 Strf 2m110y good Hdl

The Granby (IRE)

10-y-o b g Insan (USA)-Elteetee (Paddy's Stream)
Miss H M Irving Miss H M Irving

Placings:4063/2F11111/3311U/6403-22U   (4891)
2003/04: 25²G, 25²GS, 24ᵁGF,

	Starts	1st	2nd	3rd	Win & Pl
Chases	3	0	2	0	1734
Career Total	23	7	3	4	33139
135	2/02	Donc	3m		E Ch	SFT	£3354
117	12/01	Muss	3m		D Ch	GD	£4231
135	4/00	Ayr	2m4f		C Hdl	GD	£5572
135	1/00	Donc	2m4f		D Hdl	G-F	£3493
124	1/00	Catt	2m		E Hdl	GD	£2835
127	12/99	Catt	2m3f		D Hdl	G-F	£1940
112	10/99	Sedg	2m1f		D Hdl	GD	£3168
					Total win prize-money £24595

Going:	Sf: 0-0 GS: 0-1 Gd: 0-1 GF: - Fm: 0-1
Distance:	2m/2m3: 0-0 2m4-2m7: 0-0 3m+: 0-3
Track:	LH: 0-1 RH: 0-2 Tight: 0-1 Gall: 0-0
Aids:	Bl: 0-0 Vi: 0-0 Tstrap: 0-0 Ckp: 0-0
Best Rating:	135 2/02 Donc 3m soft Ch

Useful chaser/hurdler; stays three miles; did most of his winning over hurdles on a sound surface but has won over fences on good to soft/soft ground.

The Grand Duke (IRE)

61f   **22f**

6-y-o ch g Moscow Society (USA)-In For It (IRE) (Tale Quale)
P R Webber The Patient Ones

Placings:0   (2602)
2003/04: 16⁰G,

	Starts	1st	2nd	3rd	Win & Pl
NH Flat	1	0	0	0	
Career Total	1	0	0	0	

Going:	Sf: 0-0 GS: 0-0 Gd: 0-1 GF: - Fm: 0-0
Distance:	2m/2m3: 0-1 2m4-2m7: 0-0 3m+: 0-0
Track:	LH: 0-1 RH: 0-0 Tight: 0-0 Gall: 0-0
Aids:	Bl: 0-0 Vi: 0-0 Tstrap: 0-0 Ckp: 0-0
Best Rating:	22 12/03 Wwck 2m good NHF

The Grey Butler (IRE)

105   **105**

7-y-o gr g Roselier (FR)-Georgic (Tumble Gold)
B De Haan Mrs D Vaughan

Placings:34-21000   (4836)
2003/04: 21²G, 22¹GS, 22⁰HV, 24⁰G, 21⁰GF,

	Starts	1st	2nd	3rd	Win & Pl
Hurdles	5	1	1	0	6057
Career Total	7	1	1	1	6406
105	12/03	Strf		2m6f110yD Hdl	G-S	£5161
				Total win prize-money £5161

Going:	Sf: 0-1 GS: 1-1 Gd: 0-2 GF: - Fm: 0-1
Distance:	2m/2m3: 0-0 2m4-2m7: 1-4 3m+: 0-1
Track:	LH: 1-4 RH: 0-1 Tight: 1-3 Gall: 0-1
Aids:	Bl: 0-0 Vi: 0-0 Tstrap: 0-0 Ckp: 0-0
Best Rating:	105 12/03 Strf 2m6f110y gd-sft Hdl

Moderate hurdler; showed ability in bumpers; built on the promise of his hurdling debut when landing 2m 6f maiden hurdle at Startford December 2003; acts on ground good and softer; progressive.

The Grey Dyer (IRE)

82   (120h)**123+**

10-y-o gr g Roselier (FR)-Tawny Kate (IRE) (Crash Course)
L Lungo Ashleybank Investments Limited

Placings:05/52/421/UF132/2F1PP2-O6   (3214)
2003/04: 24⁰S, 25⁶GS,

	Starts	1st	2nd	3rd	Win & Pl
Chases	2	0	0	0	0
Career Total	20	3	5	1	18387
125	12/02	Ayr		3m1f	D(0-125)HCh	G-S	£6792
109	11/01	Weth		2m4f110yF(0-110)HHdl	GD	£2478
105	4/01	Prth		2m4f110yD Hdl	HVY	£2828
				Total win prize-money £12099

Going:	Sf: 0-1 GS: 0-1 Gd: 0-0 GF: - Fm: 0-0
Distance:	2m/2m3: 0-0 2m4-2m7: 0-0 3m+: 0-2
Track:	LH: 0-2 RH: 0-0 Tight: 0-0 Gall: 0-0
Aids:	Bl: 0-0 Vi: 0-0 Tstrap: 0-0 Ckp: 0-0
Best Rating:	125 11/03 Hayd 3m soft Ch

Fair chaser, looked likely winner when missing out the final fence at Haydock in November; stays beyond three miles and suited by ground good or softer; not altogether reliable.

The Grey Gunner

7-y-o gr g Paris Of Troy-Aldington Annie (Baron Blakeney)
P R Johnson (B P J Baugh 10/9) Mrs L V Durnall

Placings:0P   (3283)
2003/04: 17⁰GF, 20PHY,

	Starts	1st	2nd	3rd	Win & Pl
NH Flat	1	0	0	0	0
Hurdles	1	0	0	0	0
Career Total	2	0	0	0	

Going:	Sf: 0-1 GS: 0-0 Gd: 0-0 GF: - Fm: 0-1
Distance:	2m/2m3: 0-1 2m4-2m7: 0-1 3m+: 0-0
Track:	LH: 0-1 RH: 0-1 Tight: 0-0 Gall: 0-0
Aids:	Bl: 0-0 Vi: 0-0 Tstrap: 0-0 Ckp: 0-0
Best Rating:	0 1/04 Uttx 2m4f110y heavy Hdl

The Guinea Stamp

81   **61**

5-y-o b g Overbury (IRE)-Gagajulu (Al Hareb (USA))
C Grant (A Berry 10/5) Dingley Dell Racing Ltd

Placings:00PP-0506056   (3435)
2003/04: 16⁰G, 21⁵GF, 22⁰G, 19⁶GS, 17⁰G, 20⁵HY, 20⁶HY,

	Starts	1st	2nd	3rd	Win & Pl
Hurdles	7	0	0	0	0
Career Total	11	0	0	0	0

Going:	Sf: 0-2 GS: 0-1 Gd: 0-3 GF: - Fm: 0-1
Distance:	2m/2m3: 0-2 2m4-2m7: 0-5 3m+: 0-0
Track:	LH: 0-4 RH: 0-2 Tight: 0-4 Gall: 0-1
Aids:	Bl: 0-0 Vi: 0-0 Tstrap: 0-2 Ckp: 0-0
Best Rating:	61 12/03 MRas 2m3f110y gd-sft Hdl

The Hairy Lemon

69   **60**

4-y-o b g Eagle Eyed (USA)-Angie's Darling (Milford)
M F Harris John J Murray

Placings:06PU0   (4489)
2003/04: 13⁰GF, 13⁶S, 17⁰GS, 16ᵁS, 16⁰G,

	Starts	1st	2nd	3rd	Win & Pl
NH Flat	2	0	0	0	0
Hurdles	3	0	0	0	0
Career Total	5	0	0	0	0

Going:	Sf: 0-2 GS: 0-1 Gd: 0-1 GF: - Fm: 0-1
Distance:	2m/2m3: 0-3 2m4-2m7: 0-0 3m+: 0-0
Track:	LH: 0-2 RH: 0-1 Tight: 0-1 Gall: 0-1
Aids:	Bl: 0-0 Vi: 0-0 Tstrap: 0-0 Ckp: 0-0
Best Rating:	64 3/04 Newc 2m soft Hdl

The Hearty Joker (IRE)

9-y-o b g Broken Hearted-Furryway (Furry Glen)
B G Powell Mrs Marygold O'Kelly

Placings:P0/P6P422/4323236-P521340F4430P30 (4696)
2003/04: 21PGF, 20⁵GF, 22²GF, 22¹G, 21³GF, 22⁴GF, 20⁰GF, 19FGF, 19⁴GF, 22⁴GF, 19³G, 20⁰G, 25PG, 19³GS, 19⁰G,

	Starts	1st	2nd	3rd	Win & Pl
Chases	15	1	1	3	8071
Career Total	30	1	5	6	15518
88	7/03	MRas		2m6f110yE(0-105)HCh	GD	£4264
				Total win prize-money £4264

Going:	Sf: 0-0 GS: 0-1 Gd: 1-5 GF: - Fm: 0-9
Distance:	2m/2m3: 0-3 2m4-2m7: 1-11 3m+: 0-1
Track:	LH: 0-3 RH: 1-10 Tight: 1-5 Gall: 0-0
Aids:	Bl: 0-1 Vi: 0-3 Tstrap: 0-0 Ckp: 0-0
Best Rating:	88 2/04 Sand 2m4f110y good Ch

Plating-class chaser; finally broke his duck when 10lb 'wrong' in modest 2m6f handicap at Market Rasen in July 2003; front runner; suited by a sound surface; has worn a visor.

The Higherho

81f   **78f**

4-y-o ch g Forzando-Own Free Will (Nicholas Bill)
M W Easterby Lord Daresbury

Placings:5   (4481)

2003/04: 17⁵HY,

	Starts	1st	2nd	3rd	Win & Pl
NH Flat	1	0	0	0	0
Career Total	1	0	0	0	0

Going:	Sf: 0-1 GS: 0-0 Gd: 0-0 GF: - Fm: 0-0
Distance:	2m/2m3: 0-1 2m4-2m7: 0-0 3m+: 0-0
Track:	LH: 0-0 RH: 0-1 Tight: 0-0 Gall: 0-0
Aids:	Bl: 0-0 Vi: 0-0 Tstrap: 0-0 Ckp: 0-0
Best Rating:	83 3/04 Carl 2m1f heavy NHF

The Indispensable (IRE)
104   114
8-y-o ch g College Chapel-Fanellan (Try My Best (USA))
Jonjo O'Neill John P McManus

Placings:00/246/4050/201   (2741)
2003/04: 21²GF, 17⁹HY, 16¹S,

	Starts	1st	2nd	3rd	Win & Pl
Hurdles	3	1	1	0	5714
Career Total	12	1	2	0	7992
110	12/03 Ling	2m110y D(0-120)HHdl		SFT	£4888
		Total win prize-money £4888			

Going:	Sf: 1-2 GS: 0-0 Gd: 0-0 GF: - Fm: 0-1
Distance:	2m/2m3: 1-2 2m4-2m7: 0-1 3m+: 0-0
Track:	LH: 1-1 RH: 0-2 Tight: 1-1 Gall: 0-1
Aids:	Bl: 0-0 Vi: 0-0 Tstrap: 0-0 Ckp: 0-0
Best Rating:	110 12/03 Ling 2m110y soft Hdl

Modest novice hurdler; stays 2m 5f; acts on any ground.

The Joker (IRE)
103   120+
6-y-o ch g Montelimar (USA)-How Doudo (Oats)
J K Magee J Killen

Placings:5¹¹4-1101   (2456)
2003/04: 16¹GY, 20¹F, 16⁰GF, 16¹G,

	Starts	1st	2nd	3rd	Win & Pl
Hurdles	4	3	0	0	10088
Career Total	8	5	0	0	15364
120	11/03 Newc	2m	E(0-110)HHdl	GD	£2933
96	9/03 Hexm	2m4f110yE Hdl		FRM	£2226
112	8/03 Slig	2m	Hdl	G-Y	£4928
112	1/03 Ayr	2m	H NHF	HVY	£1890
109	12/02 Dpat	2m1f172y NHF		Y-S	£3386
		Total win prize-money £15365			

Going:	Sf: 0-0 GS: 0-0 Gd: 1-1 GF: - Fm: 1-2
Distance:	2m/2m3: 2-3 2m4-2m7: 0-1 3m+: 0-0
Track:	LH: 2-3 RH: 0-0 Tight: 0-0 Gall: 1-1
Aids:	Bl: 0-0 Vi: 0-0 Tstrap: 0-0 Ckp: 0-0
Best Rating:	120 11/03 Newc 2m good Hdl

Progressive hurdler; Irish-trained; stays two and a half miles and acts on most ground.

The Jolly Beggar (IRE)
67f   46f
6-y-o gr g Jolly Jake (NZ)-Silk Empress (Young Emperor)
Noel T Chance Shearwater Bray Syndicate

Placings:0   (4454)
2003/04: 16⁰GS,

	Starts	1st	2nd	3rd	Win & Pl
NH Flat	1	0	0	0	
Career Total	1	0	0	0	

Going:	Sf: 0-0 GS: 0-1 Gd: 0-0 GF: - Fm: 0-0
Distance:	2m/2m3: 0-1 2m4-2m7: 0-0 3m+: 0-0
Track:	LH: 0-1 RH: 0-0 Tight: 0-0 Gall: 0-0
Aids:	Bl: 0-0 Vi: 0-0 Tstrap: 0-0 Ckp: 0-0
Best Rating:	46 3/04 Asct 2m110y gd-sft NHF

The Kelt (IRE)
100   93
7-y-o b g Leading Counsel (USA)-Casheral (Le Soleil)
Eoin Doyle J J P Murphy

Placings:0000/1   (4785)
2003/04: 21¹G,

	Starts	1st	2nd	3rd	Win & Pl
Hurdles	1	1	0	0	3612
Career Total	5	1	0	0	3612
93	4/04 Hntg	2m5f110yE(0-110)HHdl		GD	£3612
		Total win prize-money £3612			

Going:	Sf: 0-0 GS: 0-0 Gd: 0-1 GF: - Fm: 0-0
Distance:	2m/2m3: 0-0 2m4-2m7: 1-1 3m+: 0-0
Track:	LH: 0-0 RH: 1-1 Tight: 0-0 Gall: 1-1
Aids:	Bl: 0-0 Vi: 0-0 Tstrap: 1-1 Ckp: 0-0
Best Rating:	93 4/04 Hntg 2m5f110y good Hdl

Much improved effort after a lengthy absence when narrow winner of handicap hurdle at Huntingdon in April 2004; will stay three miles.

The Kew Tour (IRE)
102(105h)   (114h)125+
8-y-o ch g Un Desperado (FR)-Drivers Bureau (Proverb)
Mrs S J Smith Keith Nicholson

Placings:640/112-41F2312   (4728)
2003/04: 24⁴G, 25¹GF, 26⁶GF, 25²G, 22³S, 24¹G, 24²G,

	Starts	1st	2nd	3rd	Win & Pl
Hurdles	1	0	0	0	549
Chases	6	2	2	1	15001
Career Total	13	4	3	1	25305
119	3/04 Donc	3m	E Ch	GD	£4231
118	10/03 Weth	3m1f	D Ch	G-F	£5800
108	3/03 Weth	2m4f110yE Hdl		G-F	£3532
92	3/03 Weth	3m1f	F(0-100)HHdl	GD	£3041
		Total win prize-money £16607			

Going:	Sf: 0-1 GS: 0-0 Gd: 1-4 GF: - Fm: 1-2
Distance:	2m/2m3: 0-0 2m4-2m7: 0-0 3m+: 2-6
Track:	LH: 2-6 RH: 0-1 Tight: 0-0 Gall: 1-2
Aids:	Bl: 0-0 Vi: 0-0 Tstrap: 0-0 Ckp: 0-0
Best Rating:	123 2/04 Hayd 2m6f soft Ch

Moderate hurdler/fair novice chaser; winning pointer in Ireland; made a successful chasing bow at Wetherby in November; in front when blundering at the last at Haydock in February (finished good third); made amends with narrow success at Doncaster the following month; stays beyond three miles; handles the mud but probably better on a sound surface.

The King's Doctor (IRE)
(88h)
10-y-o gr g Glacial Storm (USA)-Grandpa's River (Over The River (FR))
J D Frost C Johnston

Placings:300/12024U203B4/060/P   (0083)
2003/04: 16⁶GS,

	Starts	1st	2nd	3rd	Win & Pl
Chases	1	0	0	0	

	Career Total	18	1	3	2	4260

Going:	Sf: 0-0 GS: 0-1 Gd: 0-0 GF: - Fm: 0-0
Distance:	2m/2m3: 0-1 2m4-2m7: 0-0 3m+: 0-0
Track:	LH: 0-1 RH: 0-0 Tight: 0-0 Gall: 0-0
Aids:	Bl: 0-0 Vi: 0-0 Tstrap: 0-0 Ckp: 0-0
Best Rating:	114 9/00 DRoy 2m4f good Hdl

The Kings Fling
8-y-o b g Rakaposhi King-Poetic Light (Ardross)
James Richardson Countess Goess-Saurau

Placings:4   (3873)
2003/04: 25⁴GS,

	Starts	1st	2nd	3rd	Win & Pl
Chases	1	0	0	0	0
Career Total	1	0	0	0	0

Going:	Sf: 0-0 GS: 0-1 Gd: 0-0 GF: - Fm: 0-0
Distance:	2m/2m3: 0-0 2m4-2m7: 0-0 3m+: 0-1
Track:	LH: 0-0 RH: 0-1 Tight: 0-1 Gall: 0-0
Aids:	Bl: 0-0 Vi: 0-0 Tstrap: 0-0 Ckp: 0-0
Best Rating:	68 2/04 Folk 3m1f gd-sft Ch

The Laird's Entry (IRE)
99(86h)   (111h)111
9-y-o b g King's Ride-Balancing Act (Balinger)
L Lungo Ashleybank Investments Limited

Placings:3315/6-24F1   (4293)
2003/04: 21²S, 21⁴GS, 16²HY, 20¹GF,

	Starts	1st	2nd	3rd	Win & Pl
Chases	4	1	1	0	6466
Career Total	9	2	1	2	10532
111	3/04 Ayr	2m4f	E Ch	G-F	£4840
111	1/02 Catt	2m3f	D Hdl	SFT	£3360
		Total win prize-money £8200			

Going:	Sf: 0-2 GS: 0-1 Gd: 0-0 GF: - Fm: 1-1
Distance:	2m/2m3: 0-1 2m4-2m7: 1-3 3m+: 0-0
Track:	LH: 1-4 RH: 0-0 Tight: 0-1 Gall: 0-0
Aids:	Bl: 0-0 Vi: 0-0 Tstrap: 0-0 Ckp: 0-0
Best Rating:	111 3/04 Ayr 2m4f gd-fm Ch

Modest hurdler/novice chaser; suited by trips of around two and a half miles and best with cut in the ground.

The Land Agent
98   108
13-y-o b g Town And Country-Notinhand (Nearly A Hand)
J W Mullins D I Bare

Placings:31/20/53424311/PP431224U5/U2441453/2U4P/5
6F004/43103P6431-365   (1335)
2003/04: 20³G, 21⁶GF, 19⁵GF,

	Starts	1st	2nd	3rd	Win & Pl
Chases	3	0	0	1	732
Career Total	53	7	6	9	103267
104	4/03 Hrfd	2m3f	E(0-110)HCh	G-F	£4468
109	6/02 Strf	2m4f	D(0-115)HCh	G-F	£4371
145	2/00 Winc	2m5f	B Ch	G-S	£10432
144	1/99 Winc	2m5f	B Ch	G-S	£10162
139	4/98 Sand	2m4f110yC HCh		G-S	£14975
139	4/98 Asct	2m3f110yC Ch		G-S	£5924
128	4/96 NAbb	2m1f	H NHF	SFT	£1509
		Total win prize-money £51844			

Going:	Sf: 0-0 GS: 0-0 Gd: 0-1 GF: - Fm: 0-2
Distance:	2m/2m3: 0-1 2m4-2m7: 0-2 3m+: 0-0
Track:	LH: 0-0 RH: 0-1 Tight: 0-2 Gall: 0-0
Aids:	Bl: 0-0 Vi: 0-0 Tstrap: 0-0 Ckp: 0-0
Best Rating:	**145** 2/00 Winc 2m5f gd-sft Ch

Modest chaser nowadays, formerly useful,; effective at around two and a half miles; acts on most types of ground.

The Last Cast

102   **125+**

5-y-o ch g Prince Of Birds (USA)-Atan's Gem (USA) (Sharpen Up)
H Morrison D P Barrie

Placings:53111-0610					(4449)
2003/04: 16^G, 17^GS, 21¹G, 20⁹GS,					

	Starts	1st	2nd	3rd	Win & Pl
Hurdles	4	1	0	0	5603
Career Total	9	4	0	1	22013
125	3/04	Newb	2m5f	D(0-125)HHdl	GD	£5271
123	1/03	Chel	2m1f	B Hdl	HVY	£9526
106	12/02	MRas	2m1f110yE Hdl	SFT	£3094
96	11/02	Bang	2m1f	E Hdl	SFT	£3136
			Total win prize-money £21028			

Going:	Sf: 0-0 GS: 0-2 Gd: 1-2 GF: - Fm: 0-0
Distance:	2m/2m3: 0-3 **2m4-2m7: 1-2** 3m+: 0-0
Track:	**LH: 1-2** RH: 0-2 Tight: 0-0 **Gall: 1-2**
Aids:	Bl: 0-0 Vi: 0-0 Tstrap: 0-0 Ckp: 0-0
Best Rating:	**125** 3/04 Asct 2m4f gd-sft Hdl

Fair hurdler; completed a hat-trick for Charlie Egerton in the winter of 2002/2003; returned to action after 11 months off and scored at Newbury in March 2004; suited by forcing tactics; effective in soft ground.

The Last Mohican

94   **99d**

5-y-o b g Common Grounds-Arndilly (Robellino (USA))
P Howling P Woodward

Placings:4352204-354460					(4278)
2003/04: 18³GF, 20⁵G, 20⁴S, 16⁴GS, 16⁶GS, 19⁹GS,					

	Starts	1st	2nd	3rd	Win & Pl
Hurdles	6	0	0	1	502
Career Total	13	0	2	2	2439

Going:	Sf: 0-1 GS: 0-3 Gd: 0-1 GF: - Fm: 0-1
Distance:	2m/2m3: 0-3 2m4-2m7: 0-3 3m+: 0-0
Track:	LH: 0-3 RH: 0-1 Tight: 0-2 Gall: 0-1
Aids:	Bl: 0-0 Vi: 0-0 Tstrap: 0-0 Ckp: 0-0
Best Rating:	**92** 2/03 Donc 2m3f110y gd-sft Hdl

Modest and disappointing novice hurdler; effective from two to two and a half miles; acts on good and soft ground.

The Leader

97   **105**

11-y-o b g Ardross-Leading Line (Leading Man)
P R Chamings Inhurst Farm Stables Partnership

Placings:546P/31U644/2541355/P2P441200/02010P-13060					(4817)
2003/04: 16¹S, 17³S, 16⁰GS, 16⁶GS, 24⁰G,					

	Starts	1st	2nd	3rd	Win & Pl
Chases	5	1	0	1	4154
Career Total	37	5	4	3	22067
100	12/03	Towc	2m110y	D(0-120)HCh	SFT	£3321
105	1/03	Folk	2m	F(0-100)HCh	HVY	£3374
105	1/02	Folk	2m	F(0-100)HCh	SFT	£3250

105	1/01	Folk	2m	F(0-100)HCh	HVY	£2478
102	1/00	Folk	2m	E Ch	SFT	£2866
			Total win prize-money £15293			

Going:	Sf: 1-2 GS: 0-2 Gd: 0-1 GF: - Fm: 0-0
Distance:	**2m/2m3: 1-4** 2m4-2m7: 0-3 3m+: 0-1
Track:	LH: 0-3 **RH: 1-2** Tight: 0-1 Gall: 0-0
Aids:	Bl: 0-0 Vi: 0-0 Tstrap: 0-0 Ckp: 0-0
Best Rating:	**105** 1/03 Folk 2m heavy Ch

Plating-class chaser; runs by far his best races at Folkestone; suited by two miles and soft ground.

The Leazes

86f   **61f**

5-y-o b g Shaamit (IRE)-Air Of Elegance (Elegant Air)
A Dickman The Maroon Stud

Placings:PP-00					(0797)
2003/04: 17⁹GF, 16⁰G,					

	Starts	1st	2nd	3rd	Win & Pl
NH Flat	2	0	0	0	
Career Total	4	0	0	0	

Going:	Sf: 0-0 GS: 0-0 Gd: 0-1 GF: - Fm: 0-1
Distance:	2m/2m3: 0-2 2m4-2m7: 0-0 3m+: 0-0
Track:	LH: 0-0 RH: 0-2 Tight: 0-1 Gall: 0-0
Aids:	Bl: 0-0 Vi: 0-0 Tstrap: 0-0 Ckp: 0-0
Best Rating:	**61** 6/03 MRas 2m1f110y gd-fm NHF

The Little Lad (IRE)

89   **88**

8-y-o ch g Phardante (FR)-Lady Bar (Crash Course)
T P McGovern T P McGovern

Placings:00000000/64P640/4-2					(1215)
2003/04: 20²GF,					

	Starts	1st	2nd	3rd	Win & Pl
Hurdles	1	0	1	0	684
Career Total	16	0	1	0	1486

Going:	Sf: 0-0 GS: 0-0 Gd: 0-0 GF: - Fm: 0-1
Distance:	2m/2m3: 0-0 2m4-2m7: 0-1 3m+: 0-0
Track:	LH: 0-0 RH: 0-1 Tight: 0-0 Gall: 0-1
Aids:	Bl: 0-0 Vi: 0-0 Tstrap: 0-0 Ckp: 0-0
Best Rating:	**108** 5/00 Punc 2m yield NHF

Former Irish-trained selling-class hurdler; stays two and a half miles; has worn blinkers.

The Local

104   **93**

4-y-o b g Selkirk (USA)-Finger Of Light (Green Desert (USA))
N A Gaselee (M Blanshard 21/10) Barry Marsden

Placings:60P16255					(4788)
2003/04: 16⁶GS, 16⁰GS, 18^PG, 16¹S, 17⁶G, 16²S, 16⁵G, 16⁶G,					

	Starts	1st	2nd	3rd	Win & Pl
Hurdles	8	1	1	0	4094
Career Total	8	1	1	0	4094
85	2/04	Plum	2m	F(0-90)HHdl	SFT	£2954
			Total win prize-money £2954			

Going:	Sf: 1-2 GS: 0-2 Gd: 0-4 GF: - Fm: 0-0
Distance:	2m/2m3: 1-8 2m4-2m7: 0-0 3m+: 0-0
Track:	**LH: 1-5** RH: 0-3 **Tight: 1-5** Gall: 0-1
Aids:	Bl: 0-0 Vi: 0-0 Tstrap: 0-0 Ckp: 0-0
Best Rating:	**93** 4/04 Plum 2m good Hdl

Moderate hurdler; front runner; won on handicap debut at Plumpton over two miles in February; should stay further; best on soft ground, but did win on good ground on the Flat.

The Lordof Mystery (IRE)

89   **68**

6-y-o b g Mister Lord (USA)-Cooline Mist (IRE) (Actinium (FR))
Mrs H Dalton A Ayers and B Belchem

Placings:3					(4918)
2003/04: 20³GS,					

	Starts	1st	2nd	3rd	Win & Pl
Hurdles	1	0	0	1	469
Career Total	1	0	0	1	469

Going:	Sf: 0-0 GS: 0-1 Gd: 0-0 GF: - Fm: 0-0
Distance:	2m/2m3: 0-0 2m4-2m7: 0-1 3m+: 0-0
Track:	LH: 0-1 RH: 0-0 Tight: 0-0 Gall: 0-0
Aids:	Bl: 0-0 Vi: 0-0 Tstrap: 0-0 Ckp: 0-0
Best Rating:	**68** 4/04 Worc 2m4f gd-sft Hdl

Maiden pointer; modest third on hurdles debut.

The Lyme Volunteer (IRE)

98(104h)   (115h)**106+**

7-y-o b m Zaffaran (USA)-Dooley O'Brien (The Parson)
O Sherwood The Chamberlain Addiscott Partnership

Placings:6/053321251-4232					(3701)
2003/04: 22⁴GF, 22²G, 23³GF, 25²HY,					

	Starts	1st	2nd	3rd	Win & Pl
Chases	4	0	2	1	3783
Career Total	14	2	4	3	17656
106	4/03	Hrfd	3m2f	E Hdl	G-F	£3438
115	11/02	Ludl	3m	E(0-105)HHdl	GD	£4550
			Total win prize-money £7989			

Going:	Sf: 0-1 GS: 0-0 Gd: 0-1 GF: - Fm: 0-2
Distance:	2m/2m3: 0-0 2m4-2m7: 0-2 3m+: 0-2
Track:	LH: 0-1 RH: 0-2 Tight: 0-1 Gall: 0-1
Aids:	Bl: 0-0 Vi: 0-0 Tstrap: 0-0 Ckp: 0-0
Best Rating:	**115** 2/04 Hrfd 3m1f110y heavy Ch

Modest novice hurdler; has not looked a natural over fences so far; stays 3m 2f; acts on fast and soft ground.

The Major (NZ)

97   **119**

11-y-o ch g Try To Stop Me-Equation (NZ) (Palatable (USA))
J R Cornwall J R Cornwall

Placings:232U1/444P11113/P35F-P53600					(4640)
2003/04: 20^PG, 20⁵G, 20³S, 17⁶G, 24⁰G, 21⁰G,					

	Starts	1st	2nd	3rd	Win & Pl
Chases	6	0	0	1	2115
Career Total	24	5	2	4	35436
133	12/01	Newc	2m4f	D(0-125)HCh	G-S	£4085
125	11/01	Ayr	2m4f	D(0-120)HCh	G-S	£4111
118	10/01	Bang	3m110y	D(0-120)HCh	GD	£6825
118	10/01	Uttx	2m5f	D(0-125)HCh	G-S	£4875
120	2/01	Uttx	2m	D(0-120)HCh	HVY	£5070
			Total win prize-money £24966			

Going:	Sf: 0-1 GS: 0-0 Gd: 0-0 GF: - Fm: 0-0
Distance:	2m/2m3: 0-1 2m4-2m7: 0-4 3m+: 0-1
Track:	LH: 0-6 RH: 0-0 Tight: 0-2 Gall: 0-3
Aids:	Bl: 0-0 Vi: 0-0 Tstrap: 0-0 Ckp: 0-0

Best Rating: 133 12/01 Newc 2m4f gd-sft Ch

Moderate chaser; stays three miles, but effective over shorter; acts on most types of ground.

The Masareti Kid (IRE)

101 (0c)90+

7-y-o b g Commanche Run-Little Crack (IRE) (Lancastrian)
G A Harker (Miss Venetia Williams 10/9) R Ward

Placings:501/15-333P1223P0P (4192)
2003/04: 22³GF, 17³G, 24³G, 25PGF, 22¹G, 23²GS, 22²S, 27³G, 24PHY, 20⁰G, 22PGS,

	Starts	1st	2nd	3rd	Win & Pl
Hurdles	10	1	2	4	6724
Chases	1	0	0	0	0
Career Total	16	3	2	4	10994
87	11/03 Kels	2m6f110yE(0-100)HHdl		GD	£3497
93	9/02 Hexm	2m110y H NHF		G-F	£1827
104	4/02 Hexm	2m110y H NHF		G-F	£2443

Total win prize-money £7767

Going: Sf: 0-2 GS: 2 Gd: 1-5 GF: - Fm: 0-2
Distance: 2m/2m3: 0-1 **2m4-2m7: 1-6** 3m+: 0-4
Track: LH: 1-9 RH: 0-2 Tight: 1-6 Gall: 0-1
Aids: Bl: 0-0 Vi: 0-0 Tstrap: 0-0 **Ckp: 1-2**
Best Rating: 104 4/02 Hexm 2m110y gd-fm Ch

Plating-class hurdler; stays two miles six furlongs; acts on a sound surface.

The Merry Mason (IRE)

100(93h) (80h)91+

8-y-o gr g Roselier (FR)-Busters Lodge (Antwerp City)
J M Jefferson Ashleybank Investments Limited

Placings:06P/11-P24P3P (3882)
2003/04: 25PG, 25²GF, 27⁴GF, 26PGF, 24³G, 24PG,

	Starts	1st	2nd	3rd	Win & Pl
Chases	6	0	1	1	2029
Career Total	11	2	1	1	7829
80	10/02 Weth	3m1f	F(0-90)HHdl	G-F	£2341
75	10/02 MRas	3m	F(0-100)HHdl	G-F	£3458

Total win prize-money £5800

Going: Sf: 0-0 GS: 0-0 Gd: 0-3 GF: - Fm: 0-3
Distance: 2m/2m3: 0-0 2m4-2m7: 0-0 3m+: 0-6
Track: LH: 0-4 RH: 0-2 Tight: 0-3 Gall: 0-0
Aids: Bl: 0-0 Vi: 0-0 Tstrap: 0-0 Ckp: 0-0
Best Rating: 91 2/04 Muss 3m good Ch

Staying hurdler/chaser; stays well; acts on fast ground; not totally reliable.

The Met Man (IRE)

8-y-o b g Executive Perk-Supplicate (Furry Glen)
Michael Smith Michael Smith

Placings:0-P (4949)
2003/04: 26PGS,

	Starts	1st	2nd	3rd	Win & Pl
Chases	1	0	0	0	
Career Total	2	0	0	0	

Going: Sf: 0-0 GS: 0-1 Gd: 0-0 GF: - Fm: 0-0
Distance: 2m/2m3: 0-0 2m4-2m7: 0-0 3m+: 0-1
Track: LH: 0-0 RH: 0-0 Tight: 0-0 Gall: 0-0
Aids: Bl: 0-0 Vi: 0-0 Tstrap: 0-0 Ckp: 0-0

The Mighty Flynn

60 11

5-y-o ch g Botanic (USA)-Owdbetts (IRE) (High Estate)
P Monteith J W D Campbell

Placings:0-00 (3230)
2003/04: 17⁰G, 16⁰GF,

	Starts	1st	2nd	3rd	Win & Pl
NH Flat	1	0	0	0	0
Hurdles	1	0	0	0	0
Career Total	3	0	0	0	

Going: Sf: 0-0 GS: 0-0 Gd: 0-1 GF: - Fm: 0-1
Distance: 2m/2m3: 0-2 2m4-2m7: 0-0 3m+: 0-0
Track: LH: 0-0 RH: 0-2 Tight: 0-1 Gall: 0-0
Aids: Bl: 0-0 Vi: 0-0 Tstrap: 0-0 Ckp: 0-0
Best Rating: 17 1/04 Muss 2m gd-fm Hdl

The Mighty Sparrow (IRE)

(104h) (90h)100

11-y-o b g Montelimar (USA)-Tamers Belle (Tamerlane)
N F Glynn N F Glynn

Placings:0/400F/23210040/2300P/0003-P14F400 (4005)
2003/04: 17PGS, 20¹GF, 17⁴Y, 21²F, 19⁴GF, 16⁰HY, 16⁰YS,

	Starts	1st	2nd	3rd	Win & Pl
Hurdles	4	1	0	0	4664
Chases	3	0	0	0	896
Career Total	29	2	3	3	13891
90	6/03 Uttx	2m4f110yE(0-110)HHdl	G-F	£4663
109	12/99 Punc	2m	NHF	SFT	£3080

Total win prize-money £7744

Going: Sf: 0-1 GS: 0-1 Gd: 0-0 GF: - Fm: 1-3
Distance: 2m/2m3: 0-5 **2m4-2m7: 1-2** 3m+: 0-0
Track: LH: 1-1 RH: 0-2 Tight: 0-0 Gall: 0-0
Aids: Bl: 0-0 Vi: 0-0 Tstrap: 0-0 Ckp: 0-0
Best Rating: 109 12/99 Punc 2m soft NHF

Moderate hurdler; suited by soft ground; stays 2m 4f.

The Miner

104 91

6-y-o ch g Hatim (USA)-Glen Morvern (Carlingford Castle)
Miss S E Forster C Storey

Placings:35-P003603 (4908)
2003/04: 22PG, 16⁰GS, 16⁰S, 18³HY, 22⁶GS, 20⁰HY, 20³S,

	Starts	1st	2nd	3rd	Win & Pl
Hurdles	7	0	0	2	1782
Career Total	9	0	0	3	2211

Going: Sf: 0-4 GS: 0-2 Gd: 0-1 GF: - Fm: 0-0
Distance: 2m/2m3: 0-3 2m4-2m7: 0-4 3m+: 0-0
Track: LH: 0-6 RH: 0-1 Tight: 0-3 Gall: 0-1
Aids: Bl: 0-0 Vi: 0-0 Tstrap: 0-0 Ckp: 0-1
Best Rating: 91 4/04 Prth 2m4f110y soft Hdl

Moderate form in bumpers on a sound surface; stays two miles and six furlongs.

The Mog

96 76

5-y-o b g Atraf-Safe Secret (Seclude (USA))

Miss M E Rowland (S R Bowring 18/7) Miss M E Rowland

Placings:02P-P002P40 (4781)
2003/04: 16PG, 17⁰GF, 19⁶G, 16²GF, 21PGF, 16⁴GS, 16⁰G,

	Starts	1st	2nd	3rd	Win & Pl
Hurdles	7	0	1	0	788
Career Total	10	0	2	0	1826

Going: Sf: 0-0 GS: 0-1 Gd: 0-3 GF: - Fm: 0-3
Distance: 2m/2m3: 0-5 2m4-2m7: 0-2 3m+: 0-0
Track: LH: 0-4 RH: 0-3 Tight: 0-3 Gall: 0-1
Aids: Bl: 0-0 Vi: 0-0 Tstrap: 0-4 Ckp: 0-3
Best Rating: 76 6/03 Worc 2m gd-fm Hdl

Poor performer on the Flat; plating-class hurdler; acts on decent ground.

The Muratti

98f 99f

6-y-o b g Alflora (IRE)-Grayrose Double (Celtic Cone)
D J Caro Mrs J F Billington

Placings:160 (4179)
2003/04: 16¹G, 18⁶GS, 16⁰G,

	Starts	1st	2nd	3rd	Win & Pl
NH Flat	3	1	0	0	2093
Career Total	3	1	0	0	2093
95	12/03 Wwck 2m	H NHF	GD	£2093

Total win prize-money £2093

Going: Sf: 0-0 GS: 0-1 Gd: 1-2 GF: - Fm: 0-0
Distance: 2m/2m3: **1-3** 2m4-2m7: 0-0 3m+: 0-0
Track: LH: 1-3 RH: 0-0 Tight: 0-1 Gall: 0-1
Aids: Bl: 0-0 Vi: 0-0 Tstrap: 0-0 Ckp: 0-0
Best Rating: 99 3/04 Donc 2m110y good NHF

Won a bumper at Warwick in December 2003 on good ground, but exposed next outing at Fontwell in February.

The Names Bond

88 99

6-y-o b g Tragic Role (USA)-Artistic Licence (High Top)
Andrew Turnell Mrs Claire Hollowood

Placings:25322/6342F-0 (0081)
2003/04: 16⁰GS,

	Starts	1st	2nd	3rd	Win & Pl
Hurdles	1	0	0	0	
Career Total	11	0	4	2	4369

Going: Sf: 0-0 GS: 0-1 Gd: 0-0 GF: - Fm: 0-0
Distance: 2m/2m3: 0-1 2m4-2m7: 0-0 3m+: 0-0
Track: LH: 0-1 RH: 0-0 Tight: 0-0 Gall: 0-0
Aids: Bl: 0-0 Vi: 0-0 Tstrap: 0-0 Ckp: 0-0
Best Rating: 99 1/03 Donc 2m110y gd-sft Hdl

Moderate performer, regularly in the frame in hurdle races but has yet to get his head in front.

The Negotiator

93 (98h)112

10-y-o ch g Nebos (GER)-Baie Des Anges (Pas De Seul)
M A Barnes T A Barnes

Placings:444P/04422/123/4401331330/5213442213236/52124PPF34-03U (4076)
2003/04: 17⁰S, 16³HY, 20ᵁF,

	Starts	1st	2nd	3rd	Win & Pl
Chases	3	0	0	1	836
Career Total	48	6	9	10	46196
119	5/02 Weth	2m4f110yD Ch	GD	£3932

110	11/01	Ayr	2m	C(0-130)HCh	GD	£6045
100	6/01	Prth	2m	D Ch	FRM	£4186
102	10/00	Kels	2m110y	E(0-115)HHdl	G-S	£2737
103	8/00	Prth	2m110y	G Hdl	GD	£2717
100	5/99	Bang	2m4f	D(0-110)HHdl	GD	£3243
					Total win prize-money	£22861

Going:	Sf: 0-2 GS: 0-0 Gd: 0-0 GF: - Fm: 0-1
Distance:	2m/2m3: 0-2 2m4-2m7: 0-1 3m+: 0-0
Track:	LH: 0-2 RH: 0-1 Tight: 0-2 Gall: 0-0
Aids:	Bl: 0-0 Vi: 0-0 Tstrap: 0-0 Ckp: 0-0
Best Rating:	119 6/02 Strf 2m1f110y gd-fm Ch

Moderate chaser; effective up to two and a half miles; handles most types of ground; sometimes takes a keen hold.

The Nelson Touch
(93h)   (73h)
7-y-o b g Past Glories-Kellys Special (Netherkelly)
J W Mullins F G Matthews

Placings:04P6/P0P-P3P   (0601)
2003/04: 21PG, 23³G, 26PG,

	Starts	1st	2nd	3rd	Win & Pl
Hurdles	1	0	0	0	0
Chases	2	0	0	1	609
Career Total	10	0	0	1	609

Going:	Sf: 0-0 GS: 0-0 Gd: 0-3 GF: - Fm: 0-0
Distance:	2m/2m3: 0-0 2m4-2m7: 0-1 3m+: 0-2
Track:	LH: 0-2 RH: 0-1 Tight: 0-1 Gall: 0-0
Aids:	Bl: 0-0 Vi: 0-0 Tstrap: 0-0 Ckp: 0-0
Best Rating:	86 4/02 Chep 2m4f gd-fm Hdl

The Newsman (IRE)
104(102h)   (112h)124
12-y-o b g Homo Sapien-Miller Fall'S (Stubbs Gazette)
G Wareham G Wareham

Placings:041/405006/201/4343/23161131-112140P   (4704)
2003/04: 18¹GF, 18¹GF, 18²G, 20¹G, 20⁴GF, 20⁶G, 18PG,

	Starts	1st	2nd	3rd	Win & Pl
Hurdles	4	2	1	0	9306
Chases	3	1	0	0	5041
Career Total	31	9	3	4	47263

124	11/03	Plum	2m4f	C(0-120)HCh	GD	£4420
109	8/03	Font	2m2f110yE(0-110)HHdl		G-F	£4696
101	5/03	Font	2m2f110yE(0-105)HHdl		G-F	£3445
115	4/03	Font	2m2f	E(0-110)HCh	G-F	£4036
108	3/03	Font	2m2f	E(0-105)HCh	SFT	£4114
106	12/02	Font	2m4f	E(0-100)HCh	GD	£4114
87	10/02	Plum	2m1f	E(0-100)HCh	G-F	£4404
	4/00	Fntb	2m4f	Hdl	SFT	£3074
107	3/98	Font	2m2f110yE Hdl		G-F	£2659
					Total win prize-money	£34566

Going:	Sf: 0-0 GS: 0-0 Gd: 1-4 GF: - Fm: 2-3
Distance:	2m/2m3: 2-4 2m4-2m7: 1-3 3m+: 0-0
Track:	LH: 3-6 RH: 0-1 Tight: 3-5 Gall: 0-1
Aids:	Bl: 0-0 Vi: 0-0 Tstrap: 0-0 Ckp: 0-0
Best Rating:	124 11/03 Plum 2m4f good Ch

Moderate hurdler/Fair chaser; Fontwell specialist; not the most fluent jumper of fences; stays two miles five; acts on fast ground and soft; has worn blinkers.

The Noble Moor (IRE)
57
8-y-o br g Euphemism-Who Says (IRE) (Amazing Bust)

T R George Mrs Sharon C Nelson

Placings:00/0P-P   (0075)
2003/04: 21PS,

	Starts	1st	2nd	3rd	Win & Pl
Hurdles	1	0	0	0	
Career Total	5	0	0	0	

Going:	Sf: 0-1 GS: 0-0 Gd: 0-0 GF: - Fm: 0-0
Distance:	2m/2m3: 0-0 2m4-2m7: 0-1 3m+: 0-0
Track:	LH: 0-1 RH: 0-0 Tight: 0-1 Gall: 0-0
Aids:	Bl: 0-0 Vi: 0-0 Tstrap: 0-0 Ckp: 0-0
Best Rating:	86 11/01 Sand 2m10y gd-sft NHF

The Nobleman (USA)
8-y-o b g Quiet American (USA)-Furajet (USA) (The Minstrel (CAN))
Mrs M Morris Mrs J E Todd

Placings:5/0650/0414P05/4   (0201)
2003/04: 24⁴GF,

	Starts	1st	2nd	3rd	Win & Pl
Chases	1	0	0	0	0
Career Total	13	1	0	0	2366
86	5/01	Hexm	2m4f110yE(0-105)HHdl	FRM	£2366
				Total win prize-money	£2366

Going:	Sf: 0-0 GS: 0-0 Gd: 0-0 GF: - Fm: 0-0
Distance:	2m/2m3: 0-0 2m4-2m7: 0-0 3m+: 0-1
Track:	LH: 0-0 RH: 0-1 Tight: 0-0 Gall: 0-1
Aids:	Bl: 0-0 Vi: 0-0 Tstrap: 0-0 Ckp: 0-0
Best Rating:	86 5/01 Hexm 2m4f110y firm Hdl

The Nomad
108(103h)   (110 h)121
8-y-o b g Nomadic Way (USA)-Bubbling (Tremblant) (CAN))
M W Easterby S Brewer,D Sugars & B Parker

Placings:35/2O55622/2111P1-32F45112   (4960)
2003/04: 20³G, 17²GS, 16⁶GS, 19⁴G, 25⁵GS, 16¹S, 20²GS,

	Starts	1st	2nd	3rd	Win & Pl
Chases	8	2	2	1	12880
Career Total	23	6	6	2	31188

118	4/04	Hexm	2m110y	E Ch	SFT	£4007
112	3/04	Hexm	2m110y	E Ch	GD	£3880
108	4/03	Newc	2m4f	E Hdl	GD	£3425
110	12/02	Weth	2m4f110yD(0-110)HHdl		HVY	£4306
108	11/02	MRas	2m1f110yE Hdl		G-S	£3486
98	10/02	Sedg	2m1f	D Hdl	GD	£4186
					Total win prize-money	£23292

Going:	Sf: 1-1 GS: 0-3 Gd: 1-4 GF: - Fm: 0-0
Distance:	2m/2m3: 2-5 2m4-2m7: 0-2 3m+: 0-1
Track:	LH: 2-5 RH: 0-3 Tight: 0-4 Gall: 0-0
Aids:	Bl: 0-0 Vi: 0-0 Tstrap: 0-0 Ckp: 0-0
Best Rating:	121 4/04 MRas 2m4f gd-sft Ch

Fair hurdler/chaser; has been let down by jumping but faced straightforward task when getting off the mark at Hexham in March and did not have to improve to follow up over same course and distance following month; effective up to 2m4f; acts on good or softer; front runner.

The October Man
79(88h)   (71h)80+
7-y-o ch g Afzal-Florence May (Grange Melody)
Jonjo O'Neill P Byrne

(3526)
2003/04: 20⁹GF, 20⁵GF, 23PG,

	Starts	1st	2nd	3rd	Win & Pl
Hurdles	1	0	0	0	0
Chases	2	0	0	0	0
Career Total	6	0	0	0	0

Going:	Sf: 0-0 GS: 0-0 Gd: 0-1 GF: - Fm: 0-2
Distance:	2m/2m3: 0-0 2m4-2m7: 0-2 3m+: 0-1
Track:	LH: 0-1 RH: 0-2 Tight: 0-2 Gall: 0-0
Aids:	Bl: 0-0 Vi: 0-0 Tstrap: 0-0 Ckp: 0-0
Best Rating:	80 11/03 Worc 2m4f110y gd-fm Ch

Lightly-raced chaser/hurdler; acts on a sound surface.

The Outlier (IRE)
86f   102f
6-y-o br g Roselier (FR)-Shuil A Cuig (Quayside)
Miss Venetia Williams P J Murphy

Placings:20   (4481)
2003/04: 17²G, 17⁰HY,

	Starts	1st	2nd	3rd	Win & Pl
NH Flat	2	0	1	0	570
Career Total	2	0	1	0	570

Going:	Sf: 0-1 GS: 0-0 Gd: 0-1 GF: - Fm: 0-0
Distance:	2m/2m3: 0-2 2m4-2m7: 0-0 3m+: 0-0
Track:	LH: 0-0 RH: 0-2 Tight: 0-0 Gall: 0-0
Aids:	Bl: 0-0 Vi: 0-0 Tstrap: 0-0 Ckp: 0-0
Best Rating:	102 2/04 Carl 2m1f good NHF

The Palletman
4-y-o ch g Lion Cavern (USA)-Aquarela (Shirley Heights)
M F Harris Mrs Ruth Nelmes

Placings:PP   (1583)
2003/04: 17PF, 16PGF,

	Starts	1st	2nd	3rd	Win & Pl
Hurdles	2	0	0	0	
Career Total	2	0	0	0	

Going:	Sf: 0-0 GS: 0-0 Gd: 0-0 GF: - Fm: 0-2
Distance:	2m/2m3: 0-2 2m4-2m7: 0-0 3m+: 0-0
Track:	LH: 0-0 RH: 0-2 Tight: 0-0 Gall: 0-1
Aids:	Bl: 0-0 Vi: 0-0 Tstrap: 0-0 Ckp: 0-0

The Parsons Dingle
81(90h)   (90h)106
9-y-o ch g Le Moss-Not Enough (Balinger)
T P Walshe Mrs Penny Walshe

Placings:41/66/2/0414P-5446506   (4919)
2003/04: 19⁵GF, 21⁴G, 19⁴GS, 17⁶GS, 21⁵G, 22⁰G, 20⁶GS,

	Starts	1st	2nd	3rd	Win & Pl
Hurdles	6	0	0	0	289
Chases	1	0	0	0	0
Career Total	17	2	1	0	8875
106	2/03	Bang	2m1f110yE(0-105)HCh	SFT	£5135
110	3/00	Bang	2m1f	H NHF	GD	£1904
				Total win prize-money	£7039

Going:	Sf: 0-0 GS: 0-3 Gd: 0-3 GF: - Fm: 0-1
Distance:	2m/2m3: 0-2 2m4-2m7: 0-5 3m+: 0-0
Track:	LH: 0-2 RH: 0-5 Tight: 0-0 Gall: 0-0
Aids:	Bl: 0-0 Vi: 0-0 Tstrap: 0-0 Ckp: 0-0

Best Rating: 110 3/00   Bang 2m1f   good   NHF

Bumper winner; moderate hurdler/chaser; best at two miles; acts on good or softer.

The Pecker Dunn (IRE)

93   **93**

10-y-o b g Be My Native (USA)-Riversdale Shadow (Kemal (FR))
Mrs N S Sharpe   The Illiney Group

Placings:0/300/3/5/4P1   (3963)
2003/04: 22⁴G, 24⁶S, 24¹GS,

	Starts	1st	2nd	3rd	Win & Pl
Hurdles	3	1	0	0	4130
Career Total	9	1	0	2	4780
93	2/04	Towc	3m		E(0-105)HHdl	G-S	£3718
				Total win prize-money £3718

Going:	Sf: 0-1 GS: 1-1 Gd: 0-1 GF: - Fm: 0-0
Distance:	2m/2m3: 0-0 2m4-2m7: 0-1 **3m+: 1-2**
Track:	LH: 0-1 **RH: 1-2** Tight: 0-0 Gall: 0-0
Aids:	Bl: 0-0 Vi: 0-0 Tstrap: 0-0 Ckp: 0-0
Best Rating:	93 2/04 Towc 3m gd-sft Hdl

Plating-class hurdler; stays 3m; handles easy ground.

The Pennys Dropped (IRE)

106(109h)   (107h)**108**

7-y-o ch g Bob's Return (IRE)-Shuil Alainn (Levanter)
Jonjo O'Neill   John P McManus

Placings:0/020F1-4F555PP   (4221)
2003/04: 16⁴G, 22⁵GS, 20⁵GS, 25⁵G, 24⁵S, 24⁵PS, 22⁵GS,

	Starts	1st	2nd	3rd	Win & Pl
Chases	7	0	0		1939
Career Total	13	1	1	0	6266
107	3/03	Carl	2m1f		E Hdl	G-S	£3640
				Total win prize-money £3640

Going:	Sf: 0-2 GS: 0-3 Gd: 0-2 GF: - Fm: 0-0
Distance:	2m/2m3: 0-1 2m4-2m7: 0-3 3m+: 0-3
Track:	LH: 0-2 RH: 0-5 Tight: 0-0 Gall: 0-3
Aids:	Bl: 0-0 Vi: 0-0 Tstrap: 0-1 Ckp: 0-0
Best Rating:	107 3/03 Carl 2m1f gd-sft Hdl

Modest chaser; has shown some fair form over hurdles; disappointing in chase starts to date; best at around two miles; acts on soft ground.

The Phair Crier (IRE)

103   **114**

9-y-o ch g Phardante (FR)-Maul-More (Deep Run)
L Lungo   Ashleybank Investments Limited

Placings:13/F14P/0P-35   (2446)
2003/04: 20³G, 22⁵S,

	Starts	1st	2nd	3rd	Win & Pl
Hurdles	2	0	0	1	752
Career Total	10	2	0	2	9672
133	1/02	Newc	3m		B Hdl	SFT	£6938
104	1/01	Ayr	2m		H NHF	G-S	£1673
				Total win prize-money £8612

Going:	Sf: 0-1 GS: 0-0 Gd: 0-1 GF: - Fm: 0-0
Distance:	2m/2m3: 0-0 2m4-2m7: 0-2 3m+: 0-0
Track:	LH: 0-2 RH: 0-0 Tight: 0-0 Gall: 0-0
Aids:	Bl: 0-0 Vi: 0-0 Tstrap: 0-0 Ckp: 0-0

Best Rating: 133 1/02   Newc 3m   soft   Hdl

Useful hurdler and bumper winner; well beaten on handicap debut after lengthy absence; stays three miles and acts on soft ground; has suffered breathing problems.

The Posh Nipper

85f   **61f**

5-y-o b g Rakaposhi King-Jindabyne (Good Times (ITY))
M Mullineaux   Mrs C S Wilson

Placings:00   (4447)
2003/04: 17⁰GS, 16⁹S,

	Starts	1st	2nd	3rd	Win & Pl
NH Flat	2	0	0	0	
Career Total	2	0	0	0	

Going:	Sf: 0-1 GS: 0-1 Gd: 0-0 GF: - Fm: 0-0
Distance:	2m/2m3: 0-2 2m4-2m7: 0-0 3m+: 0-0
Track:	LH: 0-2 RH: 0-0 Tight: 0-1 Gall: 0-0
Aids:	Bl: 0-0 Vi: 0-0 Tstrap: 0-0 Ckp: 0-0
Best Rating:	61 3/04 Wwck 2m soft NHF

The Posh Paddy (IRE)

104   **109**

7-y-o b/br g Be My Native (USA)-Dizzy Dot (Bargello)
Anthony Mullins (David Wachman 19/6)   Barry Connell

Placings:0-1115   (2746a)
2003/04: 16¹F, 16¹GF, 16¹G, 16⁵S,

	Starts	1st	2nd	3rd	Win & Pl
NH Flat	3	3	0		18300
Hurdles	1	0	0		
Career Total	5	3	0	0	18300
125	11/03	Chel	2m110y	A NHF	GD	£9787
115	8/03	Rosc	2m	NHF	G-F	£4928
108	6/03	Clon	2m	NHF	FRM	£3584
				Total win prize-money £18300

Going:	Sf: 0-1 GS: 0-0 Gd: 1-1 GF: - Fm: 2-2
Distance:	**2m/2m3: 3-4** 2m4-2m7: 0-0 3m+: 0-0
Track:	**LH: 1-1** RH: 0-1 Tight: 0-0 Gall: 0-0
Aids:	Bl: 0-0 Vi: 0-0 Tstrap: 0-0 Ckp: 0-0
Best Rating:	125 11/03 Chel 2m110y good NHF

Useful bumper performer; Irish trained; winner of the valuable bumper at the 2003 Cheltenham Open Meeting; suited by forcing tactics; sure to make up into a nice hurdler.

The Preacher Man (IRE)

95(67c)   (52c)**70**

9-y-o b g Be My Native (USA)-Frankford Run (Deep Run)
V Thompson   V Thompson

Placings:0200/40/U-06050   (4476)
2003/04: 20⁰HY, 27⁶GS, 21⁰GS, 24⁵G, 24⁰HY,

	Starts	1st	2nd	3rd	Win & Pl
Hurdles	3	0	0	0	0
Chases	2	0	0	0	0
Career Total	12	0	1	0	962

Going:	Sf: 0-2 GS: 0-2 Gd: 0-1 GF: - Fm: 0-0
Distance:	2m/2m3: 0-0 2m4-2m7: 0-2 3m+: 0-3
Track:	LH: 0-3 RH: 0-2 Tight: 0-2 Gall: 0-1
Aids:	Bl: 0-0 Vi: 0-0 Tstrap: 0-0 Ckp: 0-0
Best Rating:	100 8/00 Naas 2m3f firm NHF

The Premier Cat (IRE)

(92h)   (118h)**150**

8-y-o b g Glacial Storm (USA)-Carraigaloe (Little Buskins)
T Cahill   J C Whyte

Placings:2/0010310/6132112-04PF340   (4349a)
2003/04: 24⁰GF, 20⁴YS, 26⁰GS, 24⁴S, 22⁰SH, 24⁴Y, 24⁰S,

	Starts	1st	2nd	3rd	Win & Pl
Hurdles	2	0	0	0	437
Chases	5	0	0	1	2848
Career Total	22	5	3	3	61888
150	2/03	Navn	3m	Ch	Y-S	£16883
150	2/03	Clon	2m4f	Ch	SH	£8441
131	11/02	Clon	2m1f	Ch	SFT	£5926
131	3/02	Clon	3m	Hdl	HVY	£5079
116	11/01	Clon	3m	Hdl	SFT	£5008
				Total win prize-money £41339

Going:	Sf: 0-2 GS: 0-1 Gd: 0-0 GF: - Fm: 0-1
Distance:	2m/2m3: 0-0 2m4-2m7: 0-2 3m+: 0-5
Track:	LH: 0-4 RH: 0-2 Tight: 0-0 Gall: 0-1
Aids:	Bl: 0-0 Vi: 0-0 Tstrap: 0-0 Ckp: 0-0
Best Rating:	150 2/03 Navn 3m yld-sft Ch

Very useful Irish chaser; stays three miles; acts on soft ground; had gained all his wins at Clonmel before scoring at Navan in February 2003.

The Prince

110

10-y-o b g Machiavellian (USA)-Mohican Girl (Dancing Brave (USA))
Ian Williams   Patrick Kelly

Placings:16F13/00/P   (1454)
2003/04: 16⁰GF,

	Starts	1st	2nd	3rd	Win & Pl
Hurdles	1	0	0	0	
Career Total	8	2	0	1	6315
124	1/01	Catt	2m	E Hdl	G-S	£2891
120	7/00	NAbb	2m1f	D Hdl	G-F	£2957
				Total win prize-money £5849

Going:	Sf: 0-0 GS: 0-0 Gd: 0-0 GF: - Fm: 0-1
Distance:	2m/2m3: 0-1 2m4-2m7: 0-0 3m+: 0-0
Track:	LH: 0-1 RH: 0-0 Tight: 0-1 Gall: 0-0
Aids:	Bl: 0-0 Vi: 0-0 Tstrap: 0-1 Ckp: 0-0
Best Rating:	124 1/01 Catt 2m gd-sft Hdl

Fair hurdler; best at around two miles; seems to acts on most ground.

The Project

8-y-o b g Prince Of Darkness (IRE)-Kerry Calluna (Celtic Cone)
J C Fox   Shirley M & Peter G Palmer

Placings:0/00PP-P   (0184)
2003/04: 22⁰GF,

	Starts	1st	2nd	3rd	Win & Pl
Hurdles	1	0	0	0	
Career Total	6	0	0	0	

Going:	Sf: 0-0 GS: 0-0 Gd: 0-0 GF: - Fm: 0-1
Distance:	2m/2m3: 0-0 2m4-2m7: 0-0 3m+: 0-0
Track:	LH: 0-0 RH: 0-1 Tight: 0-0 Gall: 0-0
Aids:	Bl: 0-0 Vi: 0-0 Tstrap: 0-0 Ckp: 0-0
Best Rating:	81 10/02 Chep 2m110y good NHF

The Proof

101   87

7-y-o b g Rudimentary (USA)-Indubitable (Sharpo)
G B Balding Miss B Swire

Placings: 0/50-5F   (4523)
2003/04: 17^{S}G, 17^{F}GS,

	Starts	1st	2nd	3rd	Win & Pl
Hurdles	2	0	0	0	0
Career Total	5	0	0	0	0

Going:	Sf: 0-0 GS: 0-1 Gd: 0-1 GF: 0-0 Fm: 0-0
Distance:	2m/2m3: 0-2 2m4-2m7: 0-0 3m+: 0-0
Track:	LH: 0-0 RH: 0-2 Tight: 0-0 Gall: 0-0
Aids:	Bl: 0-0 Vi: 0-0 Tstrap: 0-0 Ckp: 0-0
Best Rating:	85 3/04 Folk 2m1f110y good Hdl

The Quads

(84h)   (47h)125

12-y-o b g Tinoco-Queen's Royale (Tobrouk (FR))
Ferdy Murphy John Duddy

Placings: 430064/531131/605302231300/050124264/P00/4
03240106/03104P40P/P21P5U-30   (1251)
2003/04: 33^{3}G, 24^{0}GF,

	Starts	1st	2nd	3rd	Win & Pl
Hurdles	1	0	0	0	0
Chases	1	0	0	1	1403
Career Total	62	8	6	9	105513
125	12/02	Chel	3m7f	C(0-135)HCh	G-S	£13940
125	10/01	Carl	3m2f	D(0-120)HCh	SFT	£4290
125	1/01	Navn	2m4f	HHdl	SFT	£13104
120	10/98	Gowr	3m	HHdl	SH	£14076
121	1/98	Leop	2m3f	HCh	Y-S	£7147
108	4/97	Punc	2m2f	HHdl	GD	£8138
105	3/97	Navn	3m	HHdl	SFT	£5425
99	1/97	Leop	2m6f	(0-130)HHdl	G-Y	£3051
				Total win prize-money £69177		

Going:	Sf: 0-0 GS: 0-0 Gd: 0 GF: - Fm: 0-1
Distance:	2m/2m3: 0-0 2m4-2m7: 0-0 3m+: 0-2
Track:	LH: 0-0 RH: 0-2 Tight: 0-1 Gall: 0-0
Aids:	Bl: 0-2 Vi: 0-0 Tstrap: 0-2 Ckp: 0-0
Best Rating:	128 1/99 Gowr 3m soft Ch

Fair chaser; stays 3m 7f; regularly tongue tied; wears blinkers.

The Rebel Lady (IRE)

97(97h)   (86h)110

7-y-o br m Mister Lord (USA)-Arborfield Brook (Over The
River (FR))
Miss H C Knight The Rebel Partnership

Placings: 60303-1PF51P   (4820)
2003/04: 24^{1}GF, 24^{P}GS, 24^{F}G, 24^{5}G, 25^{P}GF,

	Starts	1st	2nd	3rd	Win & Pl
Chases	6	2	0	0	7953
Career Total	11	2	0	2	9359
110	2/04	Ludl	3m	E Ch	GD	£4400
110	11/03	Hntg	3m	E(0-100)HCh	G-F	£3552
				Total win prize-money £7953		

Going:	Sf: 0-0 GS: 0-1 Gd: 1-3 GF: - Fm: 1-2
Distance:	2m/2m3: 0-0 2m4-2m7: 0-0 3m+: 2-6
Track:	LH: 0-0 RH: 2-6 Tight: 1-3 Gall: 1-2
Aids:	Bl: 0-0 Vi: 0-0 Tstrap: 0-0 Ckp: 0-0
Best Rating:	110 2/04 Ludl 3m good Ch

Moderate chaser; Irish point-to-point winner; showed ability over hurdles; has had breathing problems; reportedly likes fast ground and small fields; stays 3m.

The Recruiter

4-y-o gr g Danzig Connection (USA)-Tabeeba (Diesis)
J G M O'Shea premier-racing.net

Placings: P   (2871)
2003/04: 16^{P}S,

	Starts	1st	2nd	3rd	Win & Pl
Hurdles	1	0	0	0	
Career Total	1	0	0	0	

Going:	Sf: 0-1 GS: 0-0 Gd: 0-0 GF: - Fm: 0-0
Distance:	2m/2m3: 0-1 2m4-2m7: 0-0 3m+: 0-0
Track:	LH: 0-1 RH: 0-0 Tight: 0-0 Gall: 0-0
Aids:	Bl: 0-0 Vi: 0-0 Tstrap: 0-0 Ckp: 0-0

The Red Boy (IRE)

10-y-o ch g Boyne Valley-River Regent (Over The River
(FR))
C Sporborg Christopher Sporborg

Placings: 5   (4775)
2003/04: 21^{5}G,

	Starts	1st	2nd	3rd	Win & Pl
Chases	1	0	0	0	0
Career Total	1	0	0	0	0

Going:	Sf: 0-0 GS: 0-0 Gd: 0-1 GF: - Fm: 0-0
Distance:	2m/2m3: 0-0 2m4-2m7: 0-1 3m+: 0-0
Track:	LH: 0-1 RH: 0-0 Tight: 0-0 Gall: 0-0
Aids:	Bl: 0-0 Vi: 0-0 Tstrap: 0-0 Ckp: 0-0
Best Rating:	84 4/04 Fknm 2m5f110y good Ch

The Rile (IRE)

(108h)   (122+h)122

10-y-o ch g Alphabatim (USA)-Donna Chimene (Royal
Gunner (USA))
L Lungo Mr & Mrs Raymond Anderson Green

Placings: 0212/64010/0000100/551121-2PP   (4455)
2003/04: 16^{2}S, 25^{P}GS, 24^{P}HY,

	Starts	1st	2nd	3rd	Win & Pl
Hurdles	2	0	1	0	2176
Chases	1	0	0	0	0
Career Total	25	6	4	0	26244
121	3/03	Ayr	2m4f	E Ch	SFT	£4235
122	1/03	Ayr	2m5f110yD Ch		SFT	£5460
122	11/02	Weth	2m4f110yE(0-110)HHdl		G-S	£2919
117	1/02	Carl	2m4f	D(0-125)HHdl	SFT	£3526
112	2/01	Carl	2m4f110yE HHdl		SFT	£1964
111	3/00	Carl	2m1f	H NHF	HVY	£1704
				Total win prize-money £19809		

Going:	Sf: 0-2 GS: 0-1 Gd: 0-0 GF: - Fm: 0-0
Distance:	2m/2m3: 0-1 2m4-2m7: 0-0 3m+: 0-2
Track:	LH: 0-3 RH: 0-0 Tight: 0-0 Gall: 0-1
Aids:	Bl: 0-0 Vi: 0-0 Tstrap: 0-0 Ckp: 0-0
Best Rating:	122 1/03 Ayr 2m5f110y soft Ch

Modest hurdler/fair chaser; effective on soft ground; stays two and a half miles.

The Rising Moon (IRE)

5-y-o br g Anshan-I'm So Happy (IRE) (Miners Lamp)
Jonjo O'Neill John P McManus

Placings: 1P   (3290)
2003/04: 16^{1}GS, 21^{P}GS,

	Starts	1st	2nd	3rd	Win & Pl
NH Flat	1	1	0	0	2646
Hurdles	1	0	0	0	0
Career Total	2	1	0	0	2646
113	12/03	Newb	2m110y	H NHF	G-S	£2646
				Total win prize-money £2646		

Going:	Sf: 0-0 GS: 1-2 Gd: 0-0 GF: - Fm: 0-0
Distance:	2m/2m3: 1-1 2m4-2m7: 0-1 3m+: 0-0
Track:	LH: 1-2 RH: 0-0 Tight: 0-0 Gall: 1-1
Aids:	Bl: 0-0 Vi: 0-0 Tstrap: 0-0 Ckp: 0-0
Best Rating:	113 12/03 Newb 2m110y gd-sft NHF

Won an Irish point by 12 lengths in March 2003; scored on British debut in hot bumper at Newbury in December 2003; pulled up on hurdling debut after blundering in GradeTwo event at Warwick; should stay a trip; acts on good to soft; highly-promising sort.

The River Joker (IRE)

110(106h)   (91h)98+

8-y-o ch g Over The River (FR)-Augustaeliza (IRE)
(Callernish)
John R Upson Graeme P McPherson

Placings: 000/FB50P/126P0-2212P0   (4592)
2003/04: 24^{2}G, 24^{2}S, 25^{1}S, 25^{2}HY, 24^{P}HY, 26^{9}G,

	Starts	1st	2nd	3rd	Win & Pl
Hurdles	3	0	2	0	1278
Chases	3	1	1	0	4301
Career Total	19	2	4	0	8776
98	12/03	Towc	3m1f	F(0-90)Ch	SFT	£3241
89	11/02	Hntg	3m2f	F(0-100)HHdl	G-S	£2289
				Total win prize-money £5530		

Going:	Sf: 1-4 GS: 0-0 Gd: 0-2 GF: - Fm: 0-0
Distance:	2m/2m3: 0-0 2m4-2m7: 0-0 3m+: 1-6
Track:	LH: 0-1 RH: 1-5 Tight: 0-0 Gall: 0-2
Aids:	Bl: 0-0 Vi: 0-0 Tstrap: 0-0 Ckp: 0-0
Best Rating:	98 12/03 Towc 3m1f soft Ch

Moderate chaser/hurdler; stays three miles one; acts on soft ground.

The Sawdust Kid

100(93h)   (64h)102

10-y-o ch g River God (USA)-Susie's Money (Seymour
Hicks (FR))
R H Buckler Golden Cap

Placings: 3/1323P/1654P0/5P2511125P4P6-U202P (1040)
2003/04: 25^{U}GF, 25^{2}GF, 27^{0}GF, 26^{2}GF, 26^{P}GF,

	Starts	1st	2nd	3rd	Win & Pl
Hurdles	1	0	0	0	0
Chases	4	0	2	0	3478
Career Total	30	5	5	3	25681
102	9/02	Font	3m2f110yE(0-105)HCh	G-F	£4389
100	9/02	Sthl	3m2f	E(0-110)HCh	GD	£4326
98	8/02	Font	3m2f110yE(0-105)HCh	GD	£4600
104	10/01	Worc	2m6f	E Hdl	G-F	£2474
98	8/00	Worc	2m	H NHF	G-F	£1473
				Total win prize-money £17264		

Going:	Sf: 0-0 GS: 0-0 Gd: 0-0 GF: - Fm: 0-5
Distance:	2m/2m3: 0-0 2m4-2m7: 0-0 3m+: 0-5
Track:	LH: 0-3 RH: 0-2 Tight: 0-3 Gall: 0-0
Aids:	Bl: 0-0 Vi: 0-0 Tstrap: 0-0 Ckp: 0-0
Best Rating:	111 10/00 Chel 3m1f110y Hdl

Modest, strong-galloping chaser; completed a hat-trick in dire races in the autumn of 2002; good effort when runner up at Exeter May 2003; stays 3m 2f; acts on fast ground.

The Sawyer (BEL)
100f   108f

4-y-o ch g Fleetwood (IRE)-Green Land (BEL) (Hero's Honor (USA))
R H Buckler   D R Fear

Placings:12   (4816)
2003/04: 16¹GS, 16²G,

	Starts	1st	2nd	3rd	Win & Pl
NH Flat	2	1	1	0	2658
Career Total	2	1	1	0	2658
99	3/04	Towc	2m	H NHF	G-S £2072

Total win prize-money £2072

Going:	Sf: 0-0 GS: 1-1 Gd: 0-1 GF: - Fm: 0-0
Distance:	**2m/2m3: 1-2** 2m4-2m7: 0-0 3m+: 0-0
Track:	LH: 0-1 **RH: 1-1** Tight: 0-0 Gall: 0-0
Aids:	Bl: 0-0 Vi: 0-0 Tstrap: 0-0 Ckp: 0-0
Best Rating:	108 4/04 Chep 2m110y good NHF

Stayed on well when making winning debut in uncompetitive Towcester bumper March 2004; sound effort when runner-up in ordinary event at Chepstow next time; acts on good and easy ground.

The Sea Club (IRE)

9-y-o b g Be My Native (USA)-Furry Slipper (Furry Glen)
Andrew Nicholls   Andrew Nicholls

Placings:00/4P5P5/U   (4607)
2003/04: 25ᵁGS,

	Starts	1st	2nd	3rd	Win & Pl
Chases	1	0	0	0	
Career Total	8	0	0	0	0

Going:	Sf: 0-0 GS: 0-1 Gd: 0-0 GF: - Fm: 0-0
Distance:	2m/2m3: 0-0 2m4-2m7: 0-0 3m+: 0-1
Track:	LH: 0-0 RH: 0-1 Tight: 0-1 Gall: 0-0
Aids:	Bl: 0-0 Vi: 0-0 Tstrap: 0-0 Ckp: 0-0
Best Rating:	74 5/01 Prth 2m4f110y gd-sft Hdl

The Secretary (IRE)
93   65

7-y-o b m Shernazar-Exemplary Fashion (Master Owen)
E J O'Grady (Mrs H Dalton 1/5) Brian Kennedy

Placings:0/33P60P-00   (0815a)
2003/04: 17⁰GS, 20⁰GF,

	Starts	1st	2nd	3rd	Win & Pl
Hurdles	2	0	0	0	
Career Total	9	0	0	2	913

Going:	Sf: 0-0 GS: 0-1 Gd: 0-0 GF: - Fm: 0-1
Distance:	2m/2m3: 0-1 2m4-2m7: 0-1 3m+: 0-0
Track:	LH: 0-0 RH: 0-2 Tight: 0-0 Gall: 0-0
Aids:	Bl: 0-0 Vi: 0-0 Tstrap: 0-1 Ckp: 0-0
Best Rating:	86 7/02 Worc 2m good NHF

The Sister
102   96+

7-y-o b m Alflora (IRE)-Donna Farina (Little Buskins)
Jonjo O'Neill   Mrs R H Thompson

Placings:54-1233P4   (4870)
2003/04: 24¹GF, 24²GF, 20³G, 24³GF, 22⁴G, 24⁴GS,

	Starts	1st	2nd	3rd	Win & Pl
Hurdles	6	1	1	2	4548
Career Total	8	1	1	2	4816
93	9/03	Worc	3m	F Hdl	G-F £2017

Total win prize-money £2017

Going:	Sf: 0-0 GS: 0-1 Gd: 0-2 GF: - Fm: 1-3
Distance:	2m/2m3: 0-0 2m4-2m7: 0-2 **3m+: 1-4**
Track:	**LH: 1-5** RH: 0-1 Tight: 0-3 Gall: 0-0
Aids:	Bl: 0-0 Vi: 0-0 Tstrap: 0-0 Ckp: 0-0
Best Rating:	96 10/03 Bang 2m4f good Hdl

Moderate hurdler; suited by a sound surface.

The Sleeper
94(95h)   (78h)96

8-y-o ch g Perpendicular-Distant Cherry (General Ironside)
H P Hogarth   Hogarth Racing

Placings:00/0000-653   (1864)
2003/04: 16⁶GS, 20⁵G, 16³GF,

	Starts	1st	2nd	3rd	Win & Pl
Hurdles	1	0	0	0	0
Chases	2	0	0	1	570
Career Total	9	0	0	1	570

Going:	Sf: 0-0 GS: 0-0 Gd: 0-1 GF: - Fm: 0-2
Distance:	2m/2m3: 0-2 2m4-2m7: 0-1 3m+: 0-0
Track:	LH: 0-3 RH: 0-0 Tight: 0-0 Gall: 0-0
Aids:	Bl: 0-0 Vi: 0-0 Tstrap: 0-0 Ckp: 0-0
Best Rating:	96 10/03 Weth 2m gd-fm Ch

The Staggery Boy (IRE)
104   100

8-y-o b g Shalford (IRE)-Murroe Star (Glenstal (USA))
M R Hoad   Foray Racing

Placings:00/000/61056P443/425P44-2411   (0634)
2003/04: 16²GF, 20⁴GF, 16¹G, 16¹GF,

	Starts	1st	2nd	3rd	Win & Pl
Chases	4	2	1	0	9641
Career Total	24	3	2	1	17886
100	6/03	NAbb	2m110y	E(0-105)HCh	G-F £4124
96	6/03	NAbb	2m110y	D(0-110)HCh	G-F £4026
91	6/01	Navn	2m	(0-102)HHdl	GD £5564

Total win prize-money £13716

Going:	Sf: 0-0 GS: 0-0 Gd: 1-1 GF: - Fm: 1-3
Distance:	**2m/2m3: 2-3** 2m4-2m7: 0-1 3m+: 0-0
Track:	**LH: 2-3** RH: 0-0 **Tight: 2-4** Gall: 0-0
Aids:	Bl: 0-0 Vi: 0-0 Tstrap: 0-0 Ckp: 0-0
Best Rating:	104 11/01 Sedg 2m1f good Hdl

Moderate hurdler/modest novice chaser; won a couple of 2m handicap chases at Newton Abbot in the space of four days in June 2003; acts on good ground unsuited by soft; has worn tongue tie.

The Tall Guy (IRE)
104(100h)   (89h)112+

8-y-o b/br g Zaffaran (USA)-Mullangle (Strong Gale)

N A Twiston-Davies Mrs Jill Scott & Mrs Sarah Macechern

Placings:1/40P/5PF-21112P   (4341)
2003/04: 20²GF, 24¹GF, 20¹GF, 24¹G, 20²G, 20PGS,

	Starts	1st	2nd	3rd	Win & Pl
Chases	6	3	2	0	20332
Career Total	13	4	2	0	23946
112	1/04	Ludl	3m	E(0-105)HCh	GD £4764
102	12/03	Ludl	2m4f	F(0-95)HCh	G-F £4212
96	11/03	Newb	3m	D(0-110)HCh	G-F £5642
100	4/01	Ayr	2m	H NHF	G-F £3307

Total win prize-money £17927

Going:	Sf: 0-0 GS: 0-1 Gd: 1-2 GF: - Fm: 2-3
Distance:	2m/2m3: 0-0 2m4-2m7: 1-4 **3m+: 2-3**
Track:	LH: 1-3 **RH: 2-3 Tight: 2-3** Gall: 1-2
Aids:	Bl: 0-0 Vi: 0-0 Tstrap: 0-0 Ckp: 0-0
Best Rating:	112 1/04 Ludl 3m good Ch

Moderate chaser; completed a hat-trick in ther winter of 2003/4; effective from two miles four to three miles; acts very well on fast ground; has worn a tongue tie.

The Tallet
87(83h)   (55h)58+

6-y-o ch g Alflora (IRE)-Bustle'Em (IRE) (Burslem)
D McCain   D McCain

Placings:56-06P5   (3338)
2003/04: 16⁶G, 20⁰GS, 21⁶GF, 17PGS, 16⁵GS,

	Starts	1st	2nd	3rd	Win & Pl
Hurdles	2	0	0	0	0
Chases	3	0	0	0	0
Career Total	6	0	0	0	0

Going:	Sf: 0-0 GS: 0-3 Gd: 0-1 GF: - Fm: 0-1
Distance:	2m/2m3: 0-3 2m4-2m7: 0-2 3m+: 0-0
Track:	LH: 0-4 RH: 0-1 Tight: 0-3 Gall: 0-0
Aids:	Bl: 0-1 Vi: 0-0 Tstrap: 0-0 Ckp: 0-0
Best Rating:	58 1/04 Catt 2m gd-sft Ch

The Teuchter
97   82+

5-y-o b g First Trump-Barefoot Landing (USA) (Cozzene (USA))
N A Dunger   N A Dunger

Placings:006-622P03   (4367)
2003/04: 19⁰G, 16²GS, 21²S, 18PG, 16⁹GS, 25³GS,

	Starts	1st	2nd	3rd	Win & Pl
Hurdles	6	0	2	1	1443
Career Total	9	0	2	1	1443

Going:	Sf: 0-1 GS: 0-3 Gd: 0-2 GF: - Fm: 0-0
Distance:	2m/2m3: 0-3 2m4-2m7: 0-2 3m+: 0-1
Track:	LH: 0-2 RH: 0-2 Tight: 0-2 Gall: 0-0
Aids:	Bl: 0-1 Vi: 0-0 Tstrap: 0-0 Ckp: 0-3
Best Rating:	87 11/03 Towc 2m gd-sft Hdl

Plating-class hurdler; tends to make mistakes; not straight-forward; stays two miles five; acts on soft.

The Three Bandits (IRE)
83   57

4-y-o b g Accordion-Katie Baggage (IRE) (Brush Aside (USA))
M C Pipe   D A Johnson

Placings:0P0 (4097)
2003/04: 24⁶S, 16ᴾG, 16⁹G,

	Starts	1st	2nd	3rd	Win & Pl
Hurdles	3	0	0	0	
Career Total	3	0	0	0	

Going:	Sf: 0-1 GS: 0-0 Gd: 0-2 GF: - Fm: 0-0
Distance:	2m/2m3: 0-2 2m4-2m7: 0-0 3m+: 0-1
Track:	LH: 0-2 RH: 0-1 Tight: 0-1 Gall: 0-0
Aids:	Bl: 0-0 Vi: 0-0 Tstrap: 0-0 Ckp: 0-0
Best Rating:	57 3/04 Plum 2m good Hdl

The Thunderer

86f   122+f
5-y-o gr g Terimon-By Line (High Line)
N J Henderson Tom Wilson

Placings:010 (4400)
2003/04: 16⁹S, 16¹GF, 16⁹G,

	Starts	1st	2nd	3rd	Win & Pl
NH Flat	3	1	0	0	2436
Career Total	3	1	0	0	2436
122 2/04 Asct 2m110y H NHF				GD	£2436

Total win prize-money £2436

Going:	Sf: 0-1 GS: 0-0 Gd: 1-2 GF: - Fm: 0-0
Distance:	2m/2m3: 1-3 2m4-2m7: 0-0 3m+: 0-0
Track:	LH: 0-0 RH: 1-2 Tight: 0-0 Gall: 0-0
Aids:	Bl: 0-0 Vi: 0-0 Tstrap: 0-0 Ckp: 0-0
Best Rating:	122 2/04 Asct 2m110y good NHF

Half-brother to decent bumper horse Secret Ploy; readily improved on debut effort when facile winner of a bumper at Ascot in February; best on good ground; potentially very useful.

The Tile Baron (IRE)

97   80
7-y-o b g Little Bighorn-Elegant Miss (Prince Tenderfoot (USA))
L Lungo The Tile Barons

Placings:5/000-1 (0405)
2003/04: 22¹G,

	Starts	1st	2nd	3rd	Win & Pl
Hurdles	1	1	0	0	3192
Career Total	1	1	0	0	3192
80 5/03 Ctml 2m6f	F(0-95)HHdl			GD	£3192

Total win prize-money £3192

Going:	Sf: 0-0 GS: 0-0 Gd: 1-1 GF: - Fm: 0-0
Distance:	2m/2m3: 0-0 2m4-2m7: 1-1 3m+: 0-0
Track:	LH: 1-1 RH: 0-0 Tight: 1-1 Gall: 0-0
Aids:	Bl: 0-0 Vi: 0-0 Tstrap: 0-0 Ckp: 0-0
Best Rating:	82 3/02 Newc 2m heavy NHF

First worthwhile form when landing a modest novices' handicap hurdle at Cartmel in May; stays well and will be suited by three miles.

The Tinker

108   (45h)111
9-y-o b g Nomadic Way (USA)-Miss Tino (Relkino)
Mrs S C Bradburne Mrs S Irwin

Placings:00P/600²P2P6/FUF32F43-4U3F130133 (4938)
2003/04: 20³G, 16⁴G, 16ᵁG, 16³GF, 17⁷G, 16¹G, 16³GS, 20⁹GF, 20¹GF, 20³GF, 16³GS,

	Starts	1st	2nd	3rd	Win & Pl
Chases	11	2	0	5	15069
Career Total	28	2	2	6	19441

111 1/04 Muss	2m4f	E Ch	G-F	£4647
105 11/03 Ayr	2m	D Ch	GD	£5838

Total win prize-money £10486

Going:	Sf: 0-0 GS: 0-2 Gd: 1-5 GF: - Fm: 1-4
Distance:	2m/2m3: 1-7 2m4-2m7: 1-4 3m+: 0-0
Track:	LH: 1-6 RH: 1-4 Tight: 1-4 Gall: 0-0
Aids:	Bl: 0-0 Vi: 0-0 Tstrap: 0-0 Ckp: 0-0
Best Rating:	111 4/04 Prth 2m gd-sft Ch

Modest novice chaser; suited by two miles and ground good or faster; not the best of jumpers.

The Trojan Horse (IRE)

81f   60f
4-y-o b g Ilium-Miss Cynthia (Dawn Review)
Miss H C Knight The Trojan Horse Partnership

Placings:0 (3927)
2003/04: 16⁸GS,

	Starts	1st	2nd	3rd	Win & Pl
NH Flat	1	0	0	0	
Career Total	1	0	0	0	

Going:	Sf: 0-0 GS: 0-1 Gd: 0-0 GF: - Fm: 0-0
Distance:	2m/2m3: 0-1 2m4-2m7: 0-0 3m+: 0-0
Track:	LH: 0-0 RH: 0-1 Tight: 0-0 Gall: 0-0
Aids:	Bl: 0-0 Vi: 0-0 Tstrap: 0-0 Ckp: 0-0
Best Rating:	60 2/04 Sand 2m110y gd-sft NHF

The Villager (IRE)

107(104h)   (126+h)133
8-y-o br g Zaffaran (USA)-Kitty Wren (Warpath)
M Scudamore Mrs S Tainton

Placings:210¹131140/11321P-55 (3809)
2003/04: 21⁵GS, 20⁵G,

	Starts	1st	2nd	3rd	Win & Pl
Chases	2	0	0	0	1398
Career Total	17	7	2	2	34022
131 1/03 Extr	2m3f110yE Ch		G-S	£4979
128 11/02 Bang	3m110y D Ch		HVY	£4875
132 10/02 Chep	2m4f	D(0-120)HHdl	GD	£4104
121 12/01 Hayd	2m4f	D Hdl	SFT	£3770
115 11/01 Hayd	2m4f	D Hdl	GD	£3861
109 10/01 Hntg	2m110y H NHF		GD	£1452
109 1/01 Donc	2m110y H NHF		GD	£1771

Total win prize-money £24814

Going:	Sf: 0-0 GS: 0-1 Gd: 0-1 GF: - Fm: 0-0
Distance:	2m/2m3: 0-0 2m4-2m7: 0-2 3m+: 0-0
Track:	LH: 0-1 RH: 0-1 Tight: 0-0 Gall: 0-1
Aids:	Bl: 0-0 Vi: 0-0 Tstrap: 0-1 Ckp: 0-0
Best Rating:	135 12/02 Hayd 2m4f soft Ch

Useful handicap chaser; stays three miles well, effective at shorter; acts well on good to heavy ground.

The Vintage Dancer (IRE)

8-y-o b g Riberetto-Strong Swimmer (IRE) (Black Minstrel)
Mrs Nicola Pollock G R Kerr

Placings:33 (4775)
2003/04: 20³G, 21³G,

	Starts	1st	2nd	3rd	Win & Pl
Chases	2	0	0	2	869
Career Total	2	0	0	2	869

Going:	Sf: 0-0 GS: 0-0 Gd: 0-2 GF: - Fm: 0-0
Distance:	2m/2m3: 0-0 2m4-2m7: 0-2 3m+: 0-0
Track:	LH: 0-1 RH: 0-1 Tight: 0-1 Gall: 0-0
Aids:	Bl: 0-0 Vi: 0-0 Tstrap: 0-0 Ckp: 0-0
Best Rating:	87 4/04 Fknm 2m5f110y good Ch

The Weaver (FR)

105f   95f
5-y-o ch g Villez (USA)-Miss Planette (FR) (Tip Moss (FR))
L Lungo P Gaffney & J N Stevenson

Placings:013 (4885)
2003/04: 16⁹G, 16¹GF, 17³GS,

	Starts	1st	2nd	3rd	Win & Pl
NH Flat	3	1	0	1	2355
Career Total	3	1	0	1	2355
95 3/04 Catt	2m	H NHF	G-F	£2058

Total win prize-money £2058

Going:	Sf: 0-0 GS: 0-1 Gd: 0-1 GF: - Fm: 1-1
Distance:	2m/2m3: 1-3 2m4-2m7: 0-0 3m+: 0-0
Track:	LH: 1-1 RH: 0-2 Tight: 1-2 Gall: 0-0
Aids:	Bl: 0-0 Vi: 0-0 Tstrap: 0-0 Ckp: 0-0
Best Rating:	95 4/04 Carl 2m1f gd-sft NHF

Improved greatly on first effort when narrow winner of a bumper at Catterick in March despite saddle having slipped; well beaten under a penalty at Carlisle the following month.

The Welder

(70h)
10-y-o b g Buckley-Crystal Run Vii (Damsire Unregistered)
V Y Gethin V Y Gethin

Placings:503/P60F/P-5P (0369)
2003/04: 23⁵GS, 23ᴾG,

	Starts	1st	2nd	3rd	Win & Pl
Chases	2	0	0	0	0
Career Total	10	0	0	1	241

Going:	Sf: 0-0 GS: 0-1 Gd: 0-1 GF: - Fm: 0-0
Distance:	2m/2m3: 0-0 2m4-2m7: 0-0 3m+: 0-2
Track:	LH: 0-2 RH: 0-0 Tight: 0-0 Gall: 0-0
Aids:	Bl: 0-0 Vi: 0-0 Tstrap: 0-0 Ckp: 0-0
Best Rating:	91 3/00 Ludl 2m good NHF

The Who Shall (IRE)

86
6-y-o b/br g Warcraft (USA)-Pollerton Park (Pollerton)
Jonjo O'Neill John P McManus

Placings:000000-P (2419)
2003/04: 22ᴾGS,

	Starts	1st	2nd	3rd	Win & Pl
Hurdles	1	0	0	0	
Career Total	7	0	0	0	

Going:	Sf: 0-0 GS: 0-1 Gd: 0-0 GF: - Fm: 0-0
Distance:	2m/2m3: 0-0 2m4-2m7: 0-1 3m+: 0-0
Track:	LH: 0-1 RH: 0-0 Tight: 0-0 Gall: 0-0
Aids:	Bl: 0-0 Vi: 0-0 Tstrap: 0-0 Ckp: 0-0
Best Rating:	90 12/02 Gowr 2m yld-sft Hdl

The Wooden Spoon (IRE)

98f   103f
6-y-o b g Old Vic-Amy's Gale (IRE) (Strong Gale)

L Wells Hills, Smith And Wearne

Placings:3				(2537)
2003/04: 18³S,				

	Starts	1st	2nd	3rd	Win & Pl
NH Flat	1	0	0	1	335
Career Total	1	0	0	1	335

Going:	Sf: 0-1 GS: 0-0 Gd: 0-0 GF: - Fm: 0-0
Distance:	2m/2m3: 0-1 2m4-2m7: 0-0 3m+: 0-0
Track:	LH: 0-1 RH: 0-0 Tight: 0-0 Gall: 0-0
Aids:	Bl: 0-0 Vi: 0-0 Tstrap: 0-0 Ckp: 0-0
Best Rating:	103 12/03 Plum 2m2f soft NHF

Third in a Plumpton bumper on his racecourse debut; won his only completed start in Irish points.

The Writer (IRE)

11-y-o b g Royal Fountain-Novelist (Quayside)
The Hon Mrs S Sherwood Rosemary Viscountess Boyne

Placings:1355/P5/13/5				(4344)
2003/04: 26⁵GS,				

	Starts	1st	2nd	3rd	Win & Pl
Chases	1	0	0	0	0
Career Total	9	2	0	0	7816
104 11/00 Ludl	3m		F(0-110)HCh	GD	£3367
105 11/98 Tntn	3m110y		D Hdl	GD	£2788
			Total win prize-money £6155

Going:	Sf: 0-0 GS: 0-1 Gd: 0-0 GF: - Fm: 0-0
Distance:	2m/2m3: 0-0 2m4-2m7: 0-0 3m+: 0-1
Track:	LH: 0-1 RH: 0-0 Tight: 0-0 Gall: 0-0
Aids:	Bl: 0-0 Vi: 0-0 Tstrap: 0-0 Ckp: 0-0
Best Rating:	105 11/98 Tntn 3m110y good Hdl

Theatre Call (IRE)
84   84

6-y-o b g Old Vic-Jennycomequick (Furry Glen)
J A B Old W E Sturt

Placings:4-6P00P				(4733)
2003/04: 16⁶GS, 22⁵PGS, 16⁹G, 16⁰GS, 22⁶PG,				

	Starts	1st	2nd	3rd	Win & Pl
NH Flat	1	0	0	0	0
Hurdles	4	0	0	0	0
Career Total	6	0	0	0	0

Going:	Sf: 0-0 GS: 0-2 Gd: 0-3 GF: - Fm: 0-0
Distance:	2m/2m3: 0-3 2m4-2m7: 0-2 3m+: 0-0
Track:	LH: 0-3 RH: 0-2 Tight: 0-1 Gall: 0-1
Aids:	Bl: 0-0 Vi: 0-0 Tstrap: 0-0 Ckp: 0-0
Best Rating:	89 2/04 Newb 2m110y good Hdl

Theatre Groom (USA)
108f   104+f

5-y-o ch g Theatrical-Model Bride (USA) (Blushing Groom (FR))
Mrs G Harvey Mrs J Draper, C Jefferies, R Smith

Placings:21P				(1226)
2003/04: 16²G, 161GF, 17⁷GF,				

	Starts	1st	2nd	3rd	Win & Pl
NH Flat	3	1	1	0	2424
Career Total	3	1	1	0	2424
90 8/03 Worc	2m		H NHF	G-F	£1877

Total win prize-money £1877

Going:	Sf: 0-0 GS: 0-0 Gd: 0-1 GF: - Fm: 1-2
Distance:	2m/2m3: 1-3 2m4-2m7: 0-0 3m+: 0-0
Track:	LH: 1-3 RH: 0-0 Tight: 0-1 Gall: 0-0
Aids:	Bl: 0-0 Vi: 0-0 Tstrap: 0-0 Ckp: 0-0
Best Rating:	104 6/03 Worc 2m good NHF

Runner-up to the potentially useful Debatable on debut in Worcester bumper June 2003; went one better at the same course in August; pulled up lame when favourite next time; acts on fast ground.

Thebellinnbroadway
91f   77f

4-y-o b f El Conquistador-Ten Deep (Deep Run)
S C Burrough Greg and Jan Knight

Placings:4				(4739)
2003/04: 17⁴G,				

	Starts	1st	2nd	3rd	Win & Pl
NH Flat	1	0	0	0	0
Career Total	1	0	0	0	0

Going:	Sf: 0-0 GS: 0-0 Gd: 0-1 GF: - Fm: 0-0
Distance:	2m/2m3: 0-1 2m4-2m7: 0-0 3m+: 0-0
Track:	LH: 0-1 RH: 0-0 Tight: 0-0 Gall: 0-0
Aids:	Bl: 0-0 Vi: 0-0 Tstrap: 0-0 Ckp: 0-0
Best Rating:	77 4/04 NAbb 2m1f good NHF

Theicecreamman (IRE)
98   97d

7-y-o ch g Glacial Storm (USA)-Miss Cornetto (IRE) (Parliament)
G Prodromou Mrs L Middleton

Placings:63563013-P04F				(0768)
2003/04: 26⁶GF, 20⁰HY, 17⁴GF, 22⁸GF,				

	Starts	1st	2nd	3rd	Win & Pl
Hurdles	4	0	0	3	258
Career Total	12	1	0	3	6443
97 2/03 Clon	2m4f		Hdl	SH	£4480
			Total win prize-money £4481

Going:	Sf: 0-1 GS: 0-0 Gd: 0-0 GF: - Fm: 0-3
Distance:	2m/2m3: 0-1 2m4-2m7: 0-2 3m+: 0-1
Track:	LH: 0-2 RH: 0-2 Tight: 0-0 Gall: 0-1
Aids:	Bl: 0-0 Vi: 0-0 Tstrap: 0-2 Ckp: 0-0
Best Rating:	104 12/02 Limk 2m4f soft Hdl

Ex-Irish novice hurdler; winner of maiden hurdle at Clonmel in February 2003; acted in soft ground; stayed two miles four (DEAD).

Thelonius (IRE)
71   60+

9-y-o ch g Statoblest-Little Sega (FR) (Bellypha)
C J Down Michael C Morris

Placings:01120/53/P0				(4890)
2003/04: 16⁶PGS, 19⁰GF,				

	Starts	1st	2nd	3rd	Win & Pl
Hurdles	2	0	0	0	0
Career Total	9	2	1	1	9059
122 11/99 Winc	2m		D(0-125)HHdl	GD	£3454
96 10/99 Tntn	2m1f		E Hdl	G-F	£3151
			Total win prize-money £6605

Going:	Sf: 0-0 GS: 0-1 Gd: 0-0 GF: - Fm: 0-1

Distance: 2m/2m3: 0-2 2m4-2m7: 0-0 3m+: 0-0

Track:	LH: 0-1 RH: 0-1 Tight: 0-1 Gall: 0-0
Aids:	Bl: 0-0 Vi: 0-0 Tstrap: 0-0 Ckp: 0-0
Best Rating:	128 5/01 Hayd 2m good Hdl

Modest hurdler; off the track for nearly three years after June 2001; suited by two miles and a sound surface.

Themanfromcarlisle
108(100h)   (95h)100

8-y-o br g Jupiter Island-Country Mistress (Town And Country)
S H Shirley-Beavan (M Pitman 6/10) Mrs S H Shirley-Beavan

Placings:4/P0014-P4414				(2084)
2003/04: 21⁸GF, 18⁴GF, 22⁴GF, 20¹GF, 16⁴GF,				

	Starts	1st	2nd	3rd	Win & Pl
Hurdles	3	0	0	0	361
Chases	2	1	0	0	3266
Career Total	11	2	0	0	7586
100 10/03 Plum	2m4f		E Ch	G-F	£3265
95 3/03 Font	2m4f		E Hdl	G-F	£3536
			Total win prize-money £6802

Going:	Sf: 0-0 GS: 0-0 Gd: 0-0 GF: - Fm: 1-5
Distance:	2m/2m3: 0-2 2m4-2m7: 1-3 3m+: 0-0
Track:	LH: 1-5 RH: 0-0 Tight: 1-4 Gall: 0-0
Aids:	Bl: 0-0 Vi: 0-0 Tstrap: 0-0 Ckp: 0-0
Best Rating:	100 10/03 Plum 2m4f gd-fm Ch

Moderate novice chaser/hurdler; point winner; acts on decent ground; stays two and a half miles.

Theorist

4-y-o b g Machiavellian (USA)-Clerio (Soviet Star (USA))
J L Spearing (M Johnston 2/8) I Astle

Placings:PF				(3806)
2003/04: 16⁵G, 16²G,				

	Starts	1st	2nd	3rd	Win & Pl
Hurdles	2	0	0	0	0
Career Total	2	0	0	0	0

Going:	Sf: 0-1 GS: 0-0 Gd: 0-0 GF: - Fm: 0-0
Distance:	2m/2m3: 0-2 2m4-2m7: 0-0 3m+: 0-0
Track:	LH: 0-1 RH: 0-1 Tight: 0-0 Gall: 0-0
Aids:	Bl: 0-0 Vi: 0-0 Tstrap: 0-0 Ckp: 0-0

There Goes Wally

6-y-o b g Lyphento (USA)-Dutch Majesty (Homing)
A Ennis Mrs Frances Smith

Placings:00PP				(4931)
2003/04: 18⁸GS, 16⁰G, 19⁷PGS, 22⁶PG,				

	Starts	1st	2nd	3rd	Win & Pl
NH Flat	2	0	0	0	0
Hurdles	2	0	0	0	0
Career Total	4	0	0	0	0

Going:	Sf: 0-0 GS: 0-2 Gd: 0-2 GF: - Fm: 0-0
Distance:	2m/2m3: 0-2 2m4-2m7: 0-0 3m+: 0-0
Track:	LH: 0-3 RH: 0-1 Tight: 0-3 Gall: 0-0
Aids:	Bl: 0-0 Vi: 0-0 Tstrap: 0-0 Ckp: 0-1
Best Rating:	82 2/04 Asct 2m110y good NHF

Therealbandit (IRE)

114(109h)   (143+h)**146+**
7-y-o b g Torus-Sunrise Highway Vii (Damsire Unregistered)
M C Pipe D A Johnson

Placings:06312-111111F0   (4424)
2003/04: 22²S, 27¹G, 22¹GF, 22¹GF, 25¹G, 25¹G, 21¹G, 25FGS, 26³G,

	Starts	1st	2nd	3rd	Win & Pl
Hurdles	5	4	1	0	38600
Chases	4	2	0	0	27058
Career Total	**13**	**7**	**1**	**1**	**69841**
146	1/04	Chel	2m5f	B Ch	GD	£14472
146	12/03	Chel	3m1f110y	B Ch	GD	£12586
143	11/03	Chel	3m1f110yA	HHdl	GD	£23200
124	6/03	NAbb	2m6f	D Hdl	G-F	£4889
125	5/03	NAbb	2m6f	E Hdl	G-F	£3579
129	5/03	Strf	3m3f	D(0-115)HHdl	GD	£4966
114	4/03	NAbb	2m6f	E(0-105)HHdl	GD	£3630

Total win prize-money £67323

Going:	Sf: 0-1 GS: 0-1 Gd: 4-5 GF: - Fm: 2-2
Distance:	2m/2m3: 0-0 2m4-2m7: 7-1 3m+: 0-0
Track:	LH: 6-9 RH: 0-0 Tight: 3-4 Gall: 3-5
Aids:	Bl: 0-0 Vi: 0-0 Tstrap: 0-0 Ckp: 0-0
Best Rating:	146 1/04 Chel 2m5f good Ch

Smart novice chaser; formerly a useful hurdler; hugely progressive; won four times over hurdles early in the season and a handicap at Cheltenham in November; returned to Prestbury Park to score in impressive style on chasing debut and again next time out; fell when in still in contention when upped in class in the Pillar Property Chase; took his chance in the Gold Cup but was well beaten; acts on most ground; remains bright prospect.

Thesis (IRE)

120   **145+**
6-y-o ch g Definite Article-Chouette (Try My Best (USA))
Miss Venetia Williams The 1961 Partnership

Placings:2236-111331   (2848)
2003/04: 16¹GS, 16¹G, 16¹G, 16³GS, 16³G, 16¹S,

	Starts	1st	2nd	3rd	Win & Pl
Hurdles	6	4	0	2	77890
Career Total	**10**	**4**	**2**	**3**	**82476**
145	12/03	Asct	2m110y	A(0-150)HHdl	SFT	£58000
129	11/03	Weth	2m	C Hdl	GD	£7150
121	5/03	Worc	2m	E Hdl	GD	£3577
120	5/03	Worc	2m	E Hdl	G-S	£3605

Total win prize-money £72332

Going:	Sf: 1-1 GS: 1-2 Gd: 2-3 GF: - Fm: 0-0
Distance:	2m/2m3: 4-6 2m4-2m7: 0-0 3m+: 0-0
Track:	LH: 3-5 RH: 1-1 Tight: 0-0 Gall: 0-1
Aids:	Bl: 0-0 Vi: 0-0 Tstrap: 0-0 Ckp: 0-0
Best Rating:	145 12/03 Asct 2m110y soft Hdl

Very useful novice hurdler; suited by two miles; shock winner of the Ladbroke Hurdle in December 2003; acts on any ground; progressive.

Thieves'Glen

110   **110**
6-y-o b g Teenoso (USA)-Hollow Creek (Tarqogan)
H Morrison Panda Christie & Rory Sweet

Placings:4/534-5F   (3271)
2003/04: 25⁵GS, 20⁵S,

	Starts	1st	2nd	3rd	Win & Pl
Hurdles	2	0	0	0	750
Career Total	**6**	**0**	**0**	**1**	**1315**

Half-brother to Frenchman's Creek, some promise in bumpers and noice hurdles; injured when brought down at Ascot in January 2004.

This Thyne

(109h)   (103h)
8-y-o b m Good Thyne (USA)-Dalkey Sound (Crash Course)
Mrs M Reveley G S Brown

Placings:50P0/60061222F-0F   (2685)
2003/04: 20⁰S, 20FGS,

	Starts	1st	2nd	3rd	Win & Pl
Chases	5	0	0	0	
Career Total	**15**	**1**	**3**	**0**	**6148**
77	8/02	Prth	3m110y	E(0-100)HHdl	GD	£4046

Total win prize-money £4046

Going:	Sf: 0-1 GS: 0-1 Gd: 0-0 GF: - Fm: 0-0
Distance:	2m/2m3: 0-0 2m4-2m7: 0-2 3m+: 0-0
Track:	LH: 0-0 RH: 0-0 Tight: 0-0 Gall: 0-1
Aids:	Bl: 0-0 Vi: 0-0 Tstrap: 0-0 Ckp: 0-0
Best Rating:	103 11/02 Newc 2m4f soft Hdl

Modest hurdler; yet to show much over fences; stays 3m; acts on good or softer.

Thisisyourlife (IRE)

95   **99+**
6-y-o b g Lord Americo-Your Life (Le Bavard (FR))
H D Daly The Earl Cadogan

Placings:2F0   (4145)
2003/04: 17²GS, 16FGS, 19⁰G,

	Starts	1st	2nd	3rd	Win & Pl
NH Flat	1	0	1	0	484
Hurdles	2	0	0	0	
Career Total	**3**	**0**	**1**	**0**	**484**

Going:	Sf: 0-0 GS: 0-2 Gd: 0-1 GF: - Fm: 0-0
Distance:	2m/2m3: 0-2 2m4-2m7: 0-1 3m+: 0-0
Track:	LH: 0-0 RH: 0-2 Tight: 0-1 Gall: 0-0
Aids:	Bl: 0-0 Vi: 0-0 Tstrap: 0-0 Ckp: 0-0
Best Rating:	102 12/03 Hrfd 2m1f gd-sft NHF

Half-brother to Irish winning 3m hurdler and chaser Lifes A Flyer; shaped as though stamina is also going to be his forte when second at Hereford December 2003 and ran too keen when falling on hurdle debut.

Thisthatandtother (IRE)

117(115h)   (148 h)**154+**
8-y-o b g Bob Back (USA)-Baden (IRE) (Furry Glen)
P F Nicholls C G Roach

Placings:2145/1121252-11121F22   (4860)
2003/04: 17¹G, 16¹G, 16¹G, 16²G, 16¹G, 16FG, 16²G, 20²GS,

	Starts	1st	2nd	3rd	Win & Pl
Chases	8	4	3	0	86443
Career Total	**19**	**8**	**7**	**0**	**150236**
154	2/04	Winc	2m	C Ch	GD	£10846
151	12/03	Sand	2m	A Ch	GD	£17400
154	11/03	Chel	2m	A Ch	GD	£20825
135	10/03	Bang	2m1f110yD	Ch	GD	£4225
148	1/03	Winc	2m	A Hdl	G-S	£23800

117	11/02	Winc	2m	D Hdl	GD	£4891
100	10/02	Winc	2m	D Hdl	GD	£3916
118	2/02	Winc	2m	N HHF	SFT	£1736

Total win prize-money £87640

Going:	Sf: 0-0 GS: 0-1 Gd: 4-7 GF: - Fm: 0-0
Distance:	2m/2m3: 4-7 2m4-2m7: 0-1 3m+: 0-0
Track:	LH: 2-5 RH: 2-3 Tight: 1-2 Gall: 1-2
Aids:	Bl: 0-0 Vi: 0-0 Tstrap: 0-0 Ckp: 0-0
Best Rating:	154 2/04 Winc 2m good Ch

High-class novice chaser; winner of first three starts over fences, including two Grade 2s, before surprisingly beaten by Palua at Kempton; back to winning ways at Wincanton next time; bad blunder at the first in the Arkle, and came down at the second; runner-up to Well Chief in Grade 2 at Aintree, and could only manage second at Ayr over two and a half miles; suited by ground good or softer.

Thistle Do

90d

6-y-o b g College Chapel-Fishki (Niniski (USA))
M D Hammond S T Brankin

Placings:0/6P50PP0-P   (0468)
2003/04: 20PG,

	Starts	1st	2nd	3rd	Win & Pl
Hurdles	1	0	0	0	
Career Total	**9**	**0**	**0**	**0**	**0**

Going:	Sf: 0-0 GS: 0-0 Gd: 0-1 GF: - Fm: 0-0
Distance:	2m/2m3: 0-0 2m4-2m7: 0-1 3m+: 0-0
Track:	LH: 0-1 RH: 0-0 Tight: 0-0 Gall: 0-0
Aids:	Bl: 0-0 Vi: 0-0 Tstrap: 0-0 Ckp: 0-0
Best Rating:	90 12/02 Ayr 2m4f gd-sft Hdl

Thistlecraft (IRE)

82   **114+**
5-y-o b g Warcraft (USA)-Thistletopper (Le Bavard (FR))
C C Bealby The Wally Partnership

Placings:1P20   (4197)
2003/04: 16¹GS, 20PGS, 20²G, 24⁰G,

	Starts	1st	2nd	3rd	Win & Pl
NH Flat	1	1	0	0	1579
Hurdles	3	0	1	0	1826
Career Total	**4**	**1**	**1**	**0**	**3404**
113	12/03	Hntg	2m110y	H NHF	G-S	£1578

Total win prize-money £1579

Going:	Sf: 0-0 GS: 1-2 Gd: 0-2 GF: - Fm: 0-0
Distance:	2m/2m3: 1-1 2m4-2m7: 0-2 3m+: 0-1
Track:	LH: 0-3 RH: 1-1 Tight: 0-1 Gall: 1-2
Aids:	Bl: 0-0 Vi: 0-0 Tstrap: 0-0 Ckp: 0-0
Best Rating:	114 2/04 Fknm 2m4f good Hdl

Fair novice hurdler; acts on good ground; effective over two miles.

Thistlekicker (IRE)

96   **79**
12-y-o b g Mandalus-Miss Ranova (Giacometti)
Mrs J C McGregor Mrs Jean McGregor

Placings:00/04OP/P2P0/34F0034P2650/010343F050-5603440   (1841)
2003/04: 16⁵G, 16⁶GF, 16⁹GF, 17³GF, 16⁴GF, 16⁴GF, 21⁰G,

	Starts	1st	2nd	3rd	Win & Pl
Hurdles	7	0	0	1	871
Career Total	**39**	**1**	**2**	**5**	**7386**
81	5/02	Prth	2m110y	G(0-95)HHdl	G-F	£2954

Total win prize-money £2954

Going:	Sf: 0-0 GS: 0-0 Gd: 0-2 GF: - Fm: 0-5
Distance:	2m/2m3: 0-6 2m4-2m7: 0-1 3m+: 0-0
Track:	LH: 0-4 RH: 0-2 Tight: 0-2 Gall: 0-0
Aids:	Bl: 0-0 Vi: 0-0 Tstrap: 0-0 Ckp: 0-0
Best Rating:	81 7/02 MRas 2m1f110y gd-fm Hdl

Plating-class hurdler; suited by fast ground.

Thixendale

7-y-o b m Reprimand-Havenwood Lady (Fair Season)
Miss J E Foster (M W Easterby 29/10) Miss J E Foster

Placings:50P   (3987)
2003/04: 17⁵GF, 17⁰G, 21ᴾGS,

	Starts	1st	2nd	3rd	Win & Pl
NH Flat	2	0	0	0	0
Chases	1	0	0	0	0
Career Total	3	0	0	0	0

Going:	Sf: 0-0 GS: 0-1 Gd: 0-1 GF: - Fm: 0-1
Distance:	2m/2m3: 0-2 2m4-2m7: 0-1 3m+: 0-0
Track:	LH: 0-2 RH: 0-1 Tight: 0-3 Gall: 0-0
Aids:	Bl: 0-0 Vi: 0-0 Tstrap: 0-0 Ckp: 0-0
Best Rating:	64 10/03 MRas 2m1f110y gd-fm NHF

Thomo (IRE)
93f   70f

6-y-o b g Faustus (USA)-Dawn O'Er Kells (IRE) (Pitskelly)
P M Rich A J Cook

Placings:00   (2602)
2003/04: 16⁰GS, 16⁰G,

	Starts	1st	2nd	3rd	Win & Pl
NH Flat	2	0	0	0	0
Career Total	2	0	0	0	0

Going:	Sf: 0-0 GS: 0-1 Gd: 0-1 GF: - Fm: 0-0
Distance:	2m/2m3: 0-2 2m4-2m7: 0-0 3m+: 0-0
Track:	LH: 0-2 RH: 0-0 Tight: 0-0 Gall: 0-0
Aids:	Bl: 0-0 Vi: 0-0 Tstrap: 0-0 Ckp: 0-0
Best Rating:	70 12/03 Wwck 2m good NHF

Thor's Phantom

11-y-o ch g Weldnaas (USA)-La Carlotta (Ela-Mana-Mou)
Mrs F J Marriott Miss D J Day

Placings:0/4   (0294)
2003/04: 20⁴GS,

	Starts	1st	2nd	3rd	Win & Pl
Chases	1	0	0	0	215
Career Total	2	0	0	0	215

Going:	Sf: 0-0 GS: 0-1 Gd: 0-0 GF: - Fm: 0-0
Distance:	2m/2m3: 0-0 2m4-2m7: 0-1 3m+: 0-0
Track:	LH: 0-1 RH: 0-0 Tight: 0-1 Gall: 0-0
Aids:	Bl: 0-0 Vi: 0-0 Tstrap: 0-0 Ckp: 0-0
Best Rating:	68 5/03 Strf 2m4f gd-sft Ch

Thoralby
92   71

5-y-o b g Son Pardo-Polish Lady (IRE) (Posen (USA))

M Dods Harris Racing Partnership

Placings:42000   (3324)
2003/04: 20⁴F, 16²G, 17⁰HY, 16⁰GS, 17⁰GS,

	Starts	1st	2nd	3rd	Win & Pl
Hurdles	5	0	1	0	1088
Career Total	5	0	1	0	1088

Going:	Sf: 0-1 GS: 0-2 Gd: 0-1 GF: - Fm: 0-1
Distance:	2m/2m3: 0-4 2m4-2m7: 0-1 3m+: 0-0
Track:	LH: 0-4 RH: 0-1 Tight: 0-2 Gall: 0-1
Aids:	Bl: 0-0 Vi: 0-0 Tstrap: 0-0 Ckp: 0-1
Best Rating:	73 11/03 Kels 2m110y good Hdl

Thornbird Lass

8-y-o b m Alflora (IRE)-Burling Moss (Le Moss)
R Johnson Jack Thornton

Placings:P   (4595)
2003/04: 22ᴾG,

	Starts	1st	2nd	3rd	Win & Pl
Hurdles	1	0	0	0	0
Career Total	1	0	0	0	0

Going:	Sf: 0-0 GS: 0-0 Gd: 0-0 GF: - Fm: 0-0
Distance:	2m/2m3: 0-0 2m4-2m7: 0-1 3m+: 0-0
Track:	LH: 0-1 RH: 0-0 Tight: 0-1 Gall: 0-0
Aids:	Bl: 0-0 Vi: 0-0 Tstrap: 0-0 Ckp: 0-0

Thorntoun Holm
91   71

6-y-o ch g Dancing Spree (USA)-Furry Friend (USA) (Bold Bidder)
P F Nicholls Richard Barber

Placings:1254   (2699)
2003/04: 18¹GF, 16²F, 17⁵GF, 19⁴G,

	Starts	1st	2nd	3rd	Win & Pl
NH Flat	3	1	1	0	2278
Hurdles	1	0	0	0	0
Career Total	4	1	1	0	2278

85   8/03   Font   2m2f110yH NHF   G-F   £1848
Total win prize-money £1848

Going:	Sf: 0-0 GS: 0-0 Gd: 0-1 GF: - Fm: 1-3
Distance:	2m/2m3: 1-3 2m4-2m7: 0-1 3m+: 0-0
Track:	LH: 1-1 RH: 0-3 Tight: 1-2 Gall: 0-0
Aids:	Bl: 0-0 Vi: 0-0 Tstrap: 0-0 Ckp: 0-0
Best Rating:	85 10/03 Towc 2m firm NHF

Failed to achieve much when winning Fontwell bumper on debut August 2003; held subsequently; handles fast.

Thorpeness (IRE)
           88

5-y-o b g Barathea (IRE)-Brisighella (IRE) (Al Hareb (USA))
J White Mrs Elga Moran

Placings:03-PP   (3170)
2003/04: 20ᴾGS, 22ᴾHY,

	Starts	1st	2nd	3rd	Win & Pl
Hurdles	2	0	0	0	0
Career Total	4	0	0	1	497

Going:	Sf: 0-1 GS: 0-1 Gd: 0-0 GF: - Fm: 0-0
Distance:	2m/2m3: 0-0 2m4-2m7: 0-2 3m+: 0-0
Track:	LH: 0-0 RH: 0-2 Tight: 0-1 Gall: 0-0
Aids:	Bl: 0-0 Vi: 0-0 Tstrap: 0-0 Ckp: 0-0
Best Rating:	90 11/02 Hrfd 2m1f soft Hdl

Stayed on into third on his second run over hurdles.

Thosewerethedays
(96h)   (113+h)147

11-y-o b g Past Glories-Charlotte's Festival (Gala Performance (ZIM))
Miss P Robson Mrs J D Goodfellow

Placings:3131FP/13-1F   (3597)
2003/04: 19¹GS, 20ᶠHY,

	Starts	1st	2nd	3rd	Win & Pl
Hurdles	1	1	0	0	3497
Chases	3	0	0	0	0
Career Total	10	4	0	3	14245

113   12/03   Catt   2m3f   E Hdl   G-S   £3496
143   3/03   Ayr   2m5f110yH Ch   SFT   £1876
135   2/02   Kemp   2m4f110yD Ch   SFT   £5300
115   12/01   Hrfd   2m   F Ch   GD   £2431
Total win prize-money £13105

Going:	Sf: 0-1 GS: 1-1 Gd: 0-0 GF: - Fm: 0-0
Distance:	2m/2m3: 1-1 2m4-2m7: 0-1 3m+: 0-0
Track:	LH: 1-2 RH: 0-1 Tight: 1-1 Gall: 0-0
Aids:	Bl: 0-0 Vi: 0-0 Tstrap: 0-0 Ckp: 0-0
Best Rating:	147 1/04 Ayr 2m4f heavy Ch

Smart chaser/novice hurdler; best over two and a half miles, but stays further; suited by soft ground and in the process of running best race at Ayr in January 2004 despite falling (when clear at the last) in competitive handicap.

Thoutmosis (USA)
96   104+

5-y-o ch g Woodman (USA)-Toujours Elle (USA) (Lyphard (USA))
L Lungo The Border Reivers

Placings:13-63266   (4294)
2003/04: 16⁶G, 17³GS, 17²GF, 24⁶GF, 22⁶GF,

	Starts	1st	2nd	3rd	Win & Pl
Hurdles	5	0	1	1	1433
Career Total	7	1	1	2	6217

98   3/03   Kels   2m2f   E Hdl   GD   £4186
Total win prize-money £4186

Going:	Sf: 0-0 GS: 0-1 Gd: 0-1 GF: - Fm: 0-3
Distance:	2m/2m3: 0-3 2m4-2m7: 0-1 3m+: 0-1
Track:	LH: 0-2 RH: 0-2 Tight: 0-1 Gall: 0-0
Aids:	Bl: 0-0 Vi: 0-0 Tstrap: 0-0 Ckp: 0-0
Best Rating:	104 11/03 Sedg 2m1f gd-fm Hdl

Moderate ex-French novice hurdler; made a winning debut over hurdles at Kelso; stays 2m 2f and suited by good ground; should stay further.

Thrashing
104   (0c)97+

9-y-o b g Kahyasi-White-Wash (Final Straw)
A E Jones Graham Brown

Placings:06365300/022F32P5U/221/035PP01   (4632)
2003/04: 22⁰GF, 21³GF, 17⁵GS, 16⁸GF, 24²G, 24⁹G, 24¹G,

	Starts	1st	2nd	3rd	Win & Pl
Hurdles	5	1	0	0	2416
Chases	2	0	0	1	935
Career Total	27	2	5	4	10033

97   4/04   Tntn   3m110y   G(0-95)HHdl   GD   £2416
87   7/01   Wolv   3m1f   F Hdl   G-F   £1962
Total win prize-money £4379

Going:	Sf: 0-0 GS: 0-1 Gd: 1-3 GF: - Fm: 0-3
Distance:	2m/2m3: 0-2 2m4-2m7: 0-2 3m+: 1-3
Track:	LH: 0-3 RH: 1-4 Tight: 1-5 Gall: 0-0
Aids:	Bl: 0-3 Vi: 0-0 Tstrap: 0-5 Ckp: 1-2
Best Rating:	106 7/00 Sedg 2m5f110y gd-fm Hdl

Moderate hurdler; stays beyond three miles and acts very well on a sound surface; usually wears tongue tie.

Thread Of Honour (IRE)

99   97+

7-y-o gr g Roselier (FR)-Sharkezan (IRE) (Double Schwartz)
Miss H C Knight Sir Stephen Hastings And Partners

Placings:030-230   (3779)
2003/04: 17²GS, 19³GS, 21⁰G,

	Starts	1st	2nd	3rd	Win & Pl
Hurdles	3	0	1	1	1471
Career Total	6	0	1	2	1760

Going:	Sf: 0-0 GS: 0-2 Gd: 0-1 GF: - Fm: 0-0
Distance:	2m/2m3: 0-1 2m4-2m7: 0-2 3m+: 0-0
Track:	LH: 0-0 RH: 0-3 Tight: 0-1 Gall: 0-0
Aids:	Bl: 0-0 Vi: 0-0 Tstrap: 0-0 Ckp: 0-0
Best Rating:	97 12/03 MRas 2m1f110y gd-sft Hdl

Modest bumper form; runner-up to effortless winner in novices' hurdle at Market Rasen in December 2003; showed just how flattered he was by that effort when well beaten third over slightly further next time; should stay at least two and a half miles.

Three Days Reign (IRE)

113   (91h)99

10-y-o br g Camden Town-Little Treat (Miners Lamp)
P D Cundell Entre-Nous

Placings:2/500/30/3-212   (0759)
2003/04: 20²GS, 20¹G, 23²G,

	Starts	1st	2nd	3rd	Win & Pl
Chases	3	1	2	0	7021
Career Total	10	1	3	2	8774
99 5/03 Worc 2m4f110yE(0-110)HCh GD £4143					
				Total win prize-money	£4144

Going:	Sf: 0-0 GS: 0-1 Gd: 1-2 GF: - Fm: 0-0
Distance:	2m/2m3: 0-0 2m4-2m7: 1-2 3m+: 0-1
Track:	LH: 1-3 RH: 0-0 Tight: 0-1 Gall: 0-0
Aids:	Bl: 0-0 Vi: 0-0 Tstrap: 0-0 Ckp: 0-0
Best Rating:	107 5/99 Chep 2m110y good NHF

Lightly-raced in novice hurdles; has taken to fences; raised 11lb after winning 2m 4f handicap at Worcester May 2003; runner-up over 3m at the same course next time; acts on good and easy ground.

Three Eagles (USA)

115 (107h)   (117h)118

7-y-o ch g Eagle Eyed (USA)-Tertiary (USA) (Vaguely Noble)
M Scudamore (M C Pipe 16/7) Granite By Design Ltd

Placings:50/414026F504P435/13FF-022F11222P4U3
                                                    (2700)
2003/04: 20⁴GF, 16²GF, 16²GF, 23⁵G, 24¹G, 21¹GF, 23²GF, 21²G, 21²GF, 24⁶G, 25⁴G, 26⁵GF, 24³GF,

	Starts	1st	2nd	3rd	Win & Pl
Hurdles	5	1	1	0	5349
Chases	8	1	4	1	11958

Career Total	33	4	6	3	24979
117 8/03 Sthl 2m5f110yF(0-100)HHdl G-F £3374					
118 8/03 Bang 3m110y D(0-120)HCh GD £6825					
96 5/02 Wwck 2m5f E(0-110)HHdl FRM £2614					
101 8/01 Bang 2m4f F Hdl G-S £2268					
				Total win prize-money	£15082

Going:	Sf: 0-0 GS: 0-0 Gd: 1-6 GF: - Fm: 1-7
Distance:	2m/2m3: 0-0 2m4-2m7: 0-2 3m+: 1-7
Track:	LH: 2-11 RH: 0-2 Tight: 1-4 Gall: 0-1
Aids:	Bl: 0-0 Vi: 0-0 Tstrap: 0-0 Ckp: 0-0
Best Rating:	118 9/03 Sedg 2m5f good Ch

Modest hurdler/chaser; likes to front run; handles most ground; in good form in the summer of 2003, winning twice; stays three miles and acts well on fast ground; suited by forcing tactics.

Three Lions

98   107

7-y-o ch g Jupiter Island-Super Sol (Rolfe (USA))
R S Brookhouse R S Brookhouse

Placings:32F5/PP01-5P653003   (4873)
2003/04: 16⁵GF, 19⁰G, 16⁸G, 16⁵S, 18³G, 20⁰GS, 23⁰GS, 20³GS,

	Starts	1st	2nd	3rd	Win & Pl
Hurdles	8	0	0	2	1664
Career Total	16	1	1	3	7320
107 2/03 Hrfd 2m1f E(0-110)HHdl GD £3406					
				Total win prize-money	£3406

Going:	Sf: 0-1 GS: 0-3 Gd: 0-3 GF: - Fm: 0-1
Distance:	2m/2m3: 0-5 2m4-2m7: 0-3 3m+: 0-0
Track:	LH: 0-4 RH: 0-4 Tight: 0-3 Gall: 0-1
Aids:	Bl: 0-0 Vi: 0-0 Tstrap: 0-0 Ckp: 0-0
Best Rating:	118 2/02 Tntn 2m1f soft Hdl

Moderate hurdler; best at two miles; effective on good ground.

Three Times A Lady

4-y-o b f Syrtos-Pure Formality (Forzando)
D W Thompson I Fox

Placings:4   (4780)
2003/04: 16⁴S,

	Starts	1st	2nd	3rd	Win & Pl
NH Flat	1	0	0	0	0
Career Total	1	0	0	0	0

Going:	Sf: 0-0 GS: 0-0 Gd: 0-0 GF: - Fm: 0-0
Distance:	2m/2m3: 0-1 2m4-2m7: 0-0 3m+: 0-0
Track:	LH: 0-1 RH: 0-0 Tight: 0-0 Gall: 0-0
Aids:	Bl: 0-0 Vi: 0-0 Tstrap: 0-0 Ckp: 0-0

Threepenny Bit

65   21

6-y-o b m Safawan-Tuppence In Clover (Petoski)
Mrs S M Johnson J P and Mrs M A Skues

Placings:00P0   (4736)
2003/04: 17⁰GS, 17⁰GS, 20⁸G, 17⁰G,

	Starts	1st	2nd	3rd	Win & Pl
NH Flat	2	0	0	0	0
Hurdles	2	0	0	0	0
Career Total	4	0	0	0	0

| Going: | Sf: 0-0 GS: 0-1 Gd: 0-2 GF: - Fm: 0-1 |
| Distance: | 2m/2m3: 0-3 2m4-2m7: 0-1 3m+: 0-1 |

Track:	LH: 0-3 RH: 0-1 Tight: 0-2 Gall: 0-0
Aids:	Bl: 0-0 Vi: 0-0 Tstrap: 0-0 Ckp: 0-0
Best Rating:	75 11/03 Hrfd 2m1f gd-fm NHF

Threezedzz

95   96

6-y-o ch g Emarati (USA)-Exotic Forest (Dominion)
Mrs P N Dutfield Steve Evans

Placings:525-46   (4673)
2003/04: 16⁴GS, 16⁶G,

	Starts	1st	2nd	3rd	Win & Pl
Hurdles	2	0	0	0	386
Career Total	5	0	1	0	1306

Going:	Sf: 0-0 GS: 0-1 Gd: 0-1 GF: - Fm: 0-0
Distance:	2m/2m3: 0-2 2m4-2m7: 0-0 3m+: 0-0
Track:	LH: 0-1 RH: 0-1 Tight: 0-1 Gall: 0-0
Aids:	Bl: 0-0 Vi: 0-0 Tstrap: 0-0 Ckp: 0-0
Best Rating:	99 9/02 Plum 2m good Hdl

Moderate hurdler; best over sprint trips on the Flat but seemed to stay Plumpton's sharp two miles when runner-up over hurdles there in September; acts on good.

Thrilling Prospect (IRE)

97   94+

7-y-o b m King's Ride-Bail Out (Quayside)
R T Phillips H Fowler

Placings:0624   (4874)
2003/04: 17⁰G, 17⁶GF, 20²GS, 20⁴GS,

	Starts	1st	2nd	3rd	Win & Pl
NH Flat	2	0	0	0	0
Hurdles	2	0	1	0	1072
Career Total	4	0	1	0	1072

Going:	Sf: 0-0 GS: 0-2 Gd: 0-1 GF: - Fm: 0-1
Distance:	2m/2m3: 0-2 2m4-2m7: 0-2 3m+: 0-0
Track:	LH: 0-4 RH: 0-0 Tight: 0-2 Gall: 0-0
Aids:	Bl: 0-0 Vi: 0-0 Tstrap: 0-0 Ckp: 0-0
Best Rating:	94 4/04 Bang 2m4f gd-sft Hdl

Very modest form in two bumpers; runner-up on hurdling debut at Wetherby in March despite some sloppy jumping; suited by two and a half miles; acts on easy ground.

Through The Rye

108   142

8-y-o ch g Sabrehill (USA)-Baharlilys (Green Dancer (USA))
G A Swinbank Nice To See You Euro-Racing

Placings:116F/011141/62033P-F00100   (4428)
2003/04: 16⁶GF, 16⁶S, 16⁰HY, 16¹S, 16⁸G, 17⁰G,

	Starts	1st	2nd	3rd	Win & Pl
Hurdles	5	1	0	0	6838
Chases	1	0	0	0	0
Career Total	22	7	1	2	45511
138 2/04 Weth 2m C(0-135)HHdl SFT £6838					
133 2/04 Kels 2m2f C(0-135)HHdl HVY £8515					
124 3/02 Donc 2m110y D(0-120)HHdl SFT £3486					
136 2/02 Sedg 2m1f E(0-110)HHdl SFT £2947					
115 2/02 Muss 2m E(0-110)HHdl SFT £5746					
122 2/00 Folk 2m1f110yE Hdl G-S £2604					
122 1/00 Folk 2m1f110yE Hdl SFT £2422					
				Total win prize-money	£32558

| Going: | Sf: 1-3 GS: 0-0 Gd: 0-2 GF: - Fm: 0-1 |

Distance: 2m/2m3: 1-6 2m4-2m7: 0-0 3m+: 0-0
Track: LH: 1-6 RH: 0-0 Tight: 0-1 Gall: 0-2
Aids: Bl: 0-0 Vi: 0-0 Tstrap: 0-0 Ckp: 0-0
Best Rating: 142 3/03 Chel 2m1f   good   Hdl

Useful hurdler; suited by soft ground; effective at up to two and a quarter miles; excelled himself when third in the County Hurdle in 2003; back to winning ways with game success at Wetherby in February 2004; best at distances around two miles and suited by plenty of give.

Throwaline

114

8-y-o b g Thowra (FR)-Stockline (Capricorn Line)
P J Hobbs Yusof Sepiuddin

Placings: 1/2121-P   (1426)
2003/04: 24FG,

			Starts	1st	2nd	3rd	Win & Pl
Hurdles			1	0	0	0	
Career Total			6	3	2	0	12197
110	4/03	Font	2m6f110yE Hdl		G-F	£3570
107	3/03	Hrfd	2m3f110yE Hdl		SFT	£3490
104	2/02	Winc	2m	H NHF		G-S	£1708

Total win prize-money £8769

Going: Sf: 0-0 GS: 0-0 Gd: 0-1 GF: - Fm: 0-0
Distance: 2m/2m3: 0-0 2m4-2m7: 0-0 3m+: 0-1
Track: LH: 0-0 RH: 0-1 Tight: 0-0 Gall: 0-0
Aids: Bl: 0-0 Vi: 0-0 Tstrap: 0-0 Ckp: 0-0
Best Rating: 114 4/03 Ayr 2m4f   good   Hdl

Fair novice hurdler; stays two miles-six; acts on any ground.

Thumper (IRE)

102   **97**

6-y-o b g Grand Lodge (USA)-Parkeen Princess (He Loves Me)
Jonjo O'Neill Mrs Susan Granger

Placings: 2-13PP   (4917)
2003/04: 16¹GF, 16³G, 20²GF, 20²GS,

			Starts	1st	2nd	3rd	Win & Pl
Hurdles			4	1	0	1	4018
Career Total			5	1	1	1	5087
95	8/03	Worc	2m	E Hdl		G-F	£3573

Total win prize-money £3574

Going: Sf: 0-0 GS: 0-0 Gd: 0-1 GF: - Fm: 1-2
Distance: 2m/2m3: 1-2 2m4-2m7: 0-2 3m+: 0-0
Track: LH: 1-2 RH: 0-0 Tight: 0-0 Gall: 0-0
Aids: Bl: 0-2 Vi: 0-0 Tstrap: 0-0 Ckp: 0-0
Best Rating: 103 3/03 Hntg 2m110y good Hdl

Dual winner on the Flat; promising second on hurdling debut for John Mackie at Huntingdon March 2003; overcame mistake two out when winning on first run over hurdles for present stable at Worcester in August.

Thunder Canyon (USA)

95   **94**

5-y-o b/br g Gulch (USA)-Naazeq (Nashwan (USA))
Evan Williams (P A Blockley 15/6) A J Reid

Placings: 5223-044644   (4441)
2003/04: 16⁰G, 17⁴GS, 16⁴GS, 16⁶GS, 22⁴GF, 21⁴S,

			Starts	1st	2nd	3rd	Win & Pl
Hurdles			6	0	0	0	298
Career Total			10	0	2	1	3155

Going: Sf: 0-1 GS: 0-3 Gd: 0-1 GF: - Fm: 0-1
Distance: 2m/2m3: 0-4 2m4-2m7: 0-2 3m+: 0-0
Track: LH: 0-3 RH: 0-3 Tight: 0-2 Gall: 0-0
Aids: Bl: 0-0 Vi: 0-0 Tstrap: 0-0 Ckp: 0-1
Best Rating: 94 4/03 Fknm 2m4f   good   Hdl

Moderate hurdler; winning stayer on the Flat; fair efforts over hurdles; acts on any ground.

Thunderpoint (IRE)

12-y-o b g Glacial Storm (USA)-Urdite (FR) (Concertino (FR))
R J Price E J Whilding

Placings: 035/2155P25/1FF1300PP/RP00FP/04R022032F4 24P/0F6041344/2452656-1U212422140   (4299)
2003/04: 20¹GF, 20⁰G, 21²HY, 19¹GF, 21²GF, 20⁴G, 20²G, 17²G, 24¹G, 24⁴G, 20⁰G,

			Starts	1st	2nd	3rd	Win & Pl
Hurdles			2	1	1	0	3305
Chases			9	2	3	0	13690
Career Total			66	7	12	4	37812
105	8/03	Strf	3m	E(0-105)HCh	GD	£4836
87	6/03	Hrfd	2m3f	E(0-110)HCh	G-F	£4277
70	5/03	Chep	2m4f	G(0-90)HHdl	G-F	£2562
86	8/01	Bang	2m4f110yF(0-100)HCh	GD	£4348
107	8/98	MRas	2m1f110yF(0-105)HHdl	G-F	£1912
101	5/98	Hexm	2m	E Hdl		G-F	£2033
110	10/97	Sedg	2m1f	D Hdl		GD	£2847

Total win prize-money £22817

Going: Sf: 0-1 GS: 0-0 Gd: 1-7 GF: - Fm: 2-3
Distance: 2m/2m3: 1-2 2m4-2m7: 1-7 3m+: 1-2
Track: LH: 2-9 RH: 1-2 Tight: 1-5 Gall: 0-0
Aids: Bl: 3-10 Vi: 0-0 Tstrap: 0-0 Ckp: 0-0
Best Rating: 110 2/98 Sedg 2m1f   good   Hdl

Moderate chaser; plating-class handicap hurdler; returned from chasing to land 2m 4f selling handicap hurdle at Chepstow May 2003; showed his versatility by landing 2m 3f handicap chase at Hereford in June despite being 8lb 'wrong'; stays three miles; acts on ground good and faster; usually wears blinkers.

Thyne For Intersky (IRE)

107f   **114+f**

5-y-o ch g Good Thyne (USA)-One Last Chance (Le Bavard (FR))
Jonjo O'Neill interskyracing.com

Placings: 11   (1605)
2003/04: 17¹GF, 17¹GF,

			Starts	1st	2nd	3rd	Win & Pl
NH Flat			2	2	0	0	3864
Career Total			2	2	0	0	3864
114	10/03	Carl	2m1f	H NHF		G-F	£1946
108	9/03	MRas	2m1f110yH NHF		G-F	£1918

Total win prize-money £3864

Going: Sf: 0-0 GS: 0-0 Gd: 0-0 GF: - Fm: 2-2
Distance: 2m/2m3: 2-2 2m4-2m7: 0-0 3m+: 0-0
Track: LH: 0-0 RH: 2-2 Tight: 1-1 Gall: 0-0
Aids: Bl: 0-0 Vi: 0-0 Tstrap: 0-0 Ckp: 0-0
Best Rating: 114 10/03 Carl 2m1f   gd-fm   NHF

Modest bumper performer; won first two starts in bumpers; effective over two miles; will get further.

Thyne Will Tell (IRE)

(126h) **141**

9-y-o ch g Good Thyne (USA)-Deep Khaletta (Deep Run)
P J Hobbs Mrs J F Deithrick

Placings: 1/220/111221/11F4-F3   (0769)
2003/04: 20²GF, 20³GF,

			Starts	1st	2nd	3rd	Win & Pl
Chases			2	0	0	1	1284
Career Total			16	7	4	1	38182
141	10/02	Strf	2m5f110yC(0-135)HCh	GD	£10530
141	8/02	NAbb	2m5f110yD(0-120)HCh	G-F	£4585
118	9/01	Strf	2m5f110yD Ch		G-F	£4208
116	5/01	NAbb	2m6f	E Hdl		G-F	£3045
120	5/01	Winc	2m6f	E Hdl		G-F	£3283
118	5/01	Hrfd	2m3f110yE Hdl		GD	£2800
110	10/99	Gway	2m	NHF		SFT	£3234

Total win prize-money £31687

Going: Sf: 0-0 GS: 0-0 Gd: 0-0 GF: - Fm: 0-2
Distance: 2m/2m3: 0-0 2m4-2m7: 0-2 3m+: 0-0
Track: LH: 0-1 RH: 0-1 Tight: 0-0 Gall: 0-0
Aids: Bl: 0-0 Vi: 0-0 Tstrap: 0-0 Ckp: 0-0
Best Rating: 141 10/02 Strf 2m5f110y good Ch

Useful chaser; lightly raced in recent seasons; best at around 2m 5f; effective on a sound surface; his jumping has room for improvement.

Tianyi (IRE)

107   (0c) **85**

8-y-o b g Mujadil (USA)-Skinity (Rarity)
M Scudamore (D J Caro 27/9) Eddie Moss

Placings: P0PP/0050012104-40P34451233206   (4752)
2003/04: 16⁴G, 18⁰GF, 22²GF, 16³GF, 18⁴GF, 20⁴GF, 17⁵GF, 16¹GF, 19²GF, 16³GS, 16³G, 18²G, 17⁰GS, 16⁶G,

			Starts	1st	2nd	3rd	Win & Pl
Hurdles			13	1	2	3	6827
Chases			1	0	0	0	
Career Total			28	3	3	3	13576
85	10/03	Hntg	2m110y	E(0-105)HHdl	G-F	£2898
83	10/02	Tntn	2m1f	F(0-100)HHdl	G-F	£2859
71	10/02	Winc	2m	F(0-95)HHdl	FRM	£3038

Total win prize-money £8796

Going: Sf: 0-0 GS: 0-2 Gd: 0-4 GF: - Fm: 1-8
Distance: 2m/2m3: 1-12 2m4-2m7: 0-2 3m+: 0-0
Track: LH: 0-9 RH: 1-5 Tight: 0-6 Gall: 1-2
Aids: Bl: 1-3 Vi: 0-0 Tstrap: 0-0 Ckp: 0-0
Best Rating: 85 12/03 Font 2m2f110y good Hdl

Plating-class hurdler; suited by two miles and fast ground; often blinkered or visored.

Ticker

111

6-y-o b g Timeless Times (USA)-Lady Day (FR) (Lightning (FR))
P J Hobbs P R Bateman

Placings: 001-F   (0746)
2003/04: 16FG,

			Starts	1st	2nd	3rd	Win & Pl
Hurdles			1	0	0	0	
Career Total			4	1	0	0	4929
111	2/03	Naas	2m	Hdl		SFT	£4928

Total win prize-money £4929

Going: Sf: 0-0 GS: 0-0 Gd: 0-1 GF: - Fm: 0-0
Distance: 2m/2m3: 0-1 2m4-2m7: 0-0 3m+: 0-0

Track:	LH: 0-1 RH: 0-0 Tight: 0-1 Gall: 0-0
Aids:	Bl: 0-0 Vi: 0-0 Tstrap: 0-0 Ckp: 0-0
Best Rating:	111 2/03 Naas 2m soft Hdl

Tickton Flyer

107   **101+**

6-y-o b g Sovereign Water (FR)-Contradictory (Reprimand)
M W Easterby   T D Rose & J S Dale

Placings:2/2112532-10   (4220)
2003/04: 20²GS, 24¹G, 17⁰G,

	Starts	1st	2nd	3rd	Win & Pl
Hurdles	3	1	1	0	4608
Career Total	10	3	4	1	10924

101	5/03	Hexm	3m	E Hdl	GD £3556
101	9/02	MRas	2m1f110yH NHF		G-F £1988
101	6/02	MRas	2m1f110yH NHF		G-F £1687

Total win prize-money £7231

Going:	Sf: 0-0 GS: 0-0 Gd: 1-2 GF: - Fm: 0-1
Distance:	2m/2m3: 0-1 2m4-2m7: 0-0 3m+: 1-1
Track:	LH: 1-2 RH: 0-1 Tight: 0-1 Gall: 0-1
Aids:	Bl: 1-2 Vi: 0-0 Tstrap: 0-0 Ckp: 0-0
Best Rating:	105 4/03 Newc 2m4f gd-fm Hdl

Fair hurdler; bumper winner; stays two and a half miles and will get further; very much suited by fast ground.

Tidjani (IRE)

(107h)   (108h)

12-y-o b g Alleged (USA)-Tikarna (FR) (Targowice (USA))
Jonjo O'Neill   John P McManus

Placings:0000/1403005/002304230/01240005230/05035/043/313/P0-41P2P   (4494)
2003/04: 17⁴GS, 21¹GS, 20⁹HY, 20²HY, 24⁸GS,

	Starts	1st	2nd	3rd	Win & Pl
Hurdles	4	1	1	0	4192
Chases	1	0	0	0	0
Career Total	49	4	5	8	59788

102	12/03	Hntg	2m5f110yF(0-100)HHdl	G-S £2401
116	12/01	Fair	2m100y (0-130)HCh	YLD £7862
124	7/98	Tipp	2m2f (0-130)HHdl	SFT £3586
95	9/96	List	2m (0-109)HHdl	G-F £4237

Total win prize-money £18088

Going:	Sf: 0-2 GS: 1-3 Gd: 0-0 GF: - Fm: 0-0
Distance:	2m/2m3: 0-1 2m4-2m7: 1-3 3m+: 0-1
Track:	LH: 0-2 RH: 1-2 Tight: 0-3 Gall: 1-1
Aids:	Bl: 0-0 Vi: 0-0 Tstrap: 0-0 Ckp: 0-0
Best Rating:	126 7/98 Gway 2m yield Hdl

Moderate chaser; bounced back to form over hurdles when winning 2m5f handicap at Huntingdon on Boxing Day December 2003; effective over two miles but gets further; acts on easy ground.

Tidour (FR)

121   (113h)**156+**

8-y-o b g Rahotep (FR)-Softway (FR) (Tyrant (USA))
P R Webber   Mrs M Fisher

Placings:00263/1221F1   (4627)
2003/04: 16¹GS, 17²S, 16²HY, 17¹GS, 16¹G, 16¹G,

	Starts	1st	2nd	3rd	Win & Pl
Chases	6	3	2	0	53052
Career Total	11	3	3	1	59027

156	4/04	Aint	2m	A HCh	GD £37700
136	2/04	Plum	2m1f	D Ch	G-S £6743
126	12/03	Uttx	2m	E Ch	G-S £3425

Total win prize-money £47870

Going:	Sf: 0-2 GS: 2-2 Gd: 1-2 GF: - Fm: 0-0
Distance:	2m/2m3: 3-6 2m4-2m7: 0-0 3m+: 0-0
Track:	LH: 3-6 RH: 0-0 Tight: 2-3 Gall: 0-1
Aids:	Bl: 0-0 Vi: 0-0 Tstrap: 0-0 Ckp: 0-0
Best Rating:	156 4/04 Aint 2m good Ch

Smart novice chaser; returned after a lengthy break when impressive winner on chasing bow at Uttoxeter in December; has been decent runner-up twice since; back to winning ways at Plumpton; running an excellent race when falling two out in the Arkle; impressive winner of the Red Rum Handicap Chase at Aintree; best at two miles; suited by soft ground; can progress further.

Tidy (IRE)

4-y-o b c Mujadil (USA)-Neat Shilling (IRE) (Bob Back (USA))
M D Hammond (J A Osborne 3/7) P Davies and L Crowther

Placings:P   (3690)
2003/04: 16²PG,

	Starts	1st	2nd	3rd	Win & Pl
Hurdles	1	0	0	0	
Career Total	1	0	0	0	

Going:	Sf: 0-0 GS: 0-0 Gd: 0-0 GF: - Fm: 0-0
Distance:	2m/2m3: 0-1 2m4-2m7: 0-0 3m+: 0-0
Track:	LH: 0-1 RH: 0-0 Tight: 0-1 Gall: 0-0
Aids:	Bl: 0-0 Vi: 0-0 Tstrap: 0-0 Ckp: 0-0

Tierkely (IRE)

102   **105**

9-y-o br g Yashgan-Island Dream (Lucifer (USA))
J J Lambe   Brian W Dougan

Placings:211P60   (4500a)
2003/04: 24²G, 27¹GF, 21¹GF, 26⁸PG, 28⁶GY, 24⁰YS,

	Starts	1st	2nd	3rd	Win & Pl
Chases	6	2	1	0	9450
Career Total	6	2	1	0	9450

105	8/03	Sedg	2m5f	E(0-110)HCh	G-F £4007
92	7/03	Sedg	3m3f	E Ch	G-F £4017

Total win prize-money £8024

Going:	Sf: 0-0 GS: 0-0 Gd: 0-2 GF: - Fm: 2-2
Distance:	2m/2m3: 0-0 2m4-2m7: 1-1 3m+: 1-5
Track:	LH: 2-3 RH: 0-1 Tight: 2-3 Gall: 0-0
Aids:	Bl: 0-0 Vi: 0-0 Tstrap: 0-0 Ckp: 0-0
Best Rating:	105 8/03 Sedg 2m5f gd-fm Ch

Moderate novice chaser; won over three mile three at Sedgefield in July; returned to score again there the following month; stays really well; acts on a sound surface.

Tiger Frog (USA)

102(97c)   (78+c)**87**

5-y-o b g French Deputy (USA)-Woodyoubelieveit (USA) (Woodman (USA))
J Mackie (R C Guest 6/2) Fools Who Dream

Placings:6000-00050153022462   (4760)
2003/04: 16⁸GF, 16⁰G, 16⁹G, 22⁵G, 23⁹GS, 16¹GS, 16⁵GS, 20³GF, 21¹⁰GS, 16²GS, 19²G, 16⁴G, 16⁰G, 16²S,

	Starts	1st	2nd	3rd	Win & Pl
Hurdles	12	1	2	1	4958
Chases	2	0	1	0	1184
Career Total	18	1	3	1	6142

81	12/03	Catt	2m	G(0-95)HHdl	G-S £1904

Total win prize-money £1904

Going:	Sf: 0-1 GS: 1-5 Gd: 0-5 GF: - Fm: 0-3
Distance:	2m/2m3: 1-10 2m4-2m7: 0-4 3m+: 0-0
Track:	LH: 1-11 RH: 0-3 Tight: 1-7 Gall: 0-2
Aids:	Bl: 1-8 Vi: 0-0 Tstrap: 0-4 Ckp: 0-2
Best Rating:	87 4/04 Towc 2m soft Hdl

Plating-class hurdler/chaser; effective over two miles, but stays further; suited by cut in the ground; often tongue tied and has worn blinkers and cheekpieces.

Tiger Talk

103(91c)   (79c)**82**

8-y-o ch g Sabrehill (USA)-Tebre (USA) (Sir Ivor (USA))
M E Sowersby   The Southwold Set

Placings:U453604P0/2630300063/1351PP052P0645-20P304P   (0938)
2003/04: 17²S, 17⁰S, 16²PG, 19³G, 17⁰GF, 24⁴G, 21²PGF,

	Starts	1st	2nd	3rd	Win & Pl
Hurdles	7	0	1	1	1205
Career Total	40	2	3	6	12325

89	6/02	MRas	2m1f110yE(0-100)HHdl	G-F £2635
93	5/02	Sedg	2m1f	F(0-100)HHdl	G-F £2219

Total win prize-money £4855

Going:	Sf: 0-2 GS: 0-0 Gd: 0-3 GF: - Fm: 0-2
Distance:	2m/2m3: 0-4 2m4-2m7: 0-2 3m+: 0-1
Track:	LH: 0-4 RH: 0-3 Tight: 0-6 Gall: 0-0
Aids:	Bl: 0-0 Vi: 0-0 Tstrap: 0-0 Ckp: 0-1
Best Rating:	98 11/00 Newc 2m gd-sft Hdl

Plating-class hurdler/chaser, stays two and a half miles; suited by a sound surface; has worn blinkers.

Tiger Tips Lad (IRE)

105   **102+**

5-y-o b g Zaffaran (USA)-Halens Match (IRE) (Matching Pair)
N A Twiston-Davies   Gary Hopkins

Placings:00642   (4365)
2003/04: 16⁰G, 16⁰GS, 22⁶GS, 24⁴S, 16²GS,

	Starts	1st	2nd	3rd	Win & Pl
NH Flat	2	0	0	0	0
Hurdles	3	0	1	0	1544
Career Total	5	0	1	0	1544

Going:	Sf: 0-1 GS: 0-3 Gd: 0-1 GF: - Fm: 0-0
Distance:	2m/2m3: 0-3 2m4-2m7: 0-1 3m+: 0-1
Track:	LH: 0-4 RH: 0-1 Tight: 0-2 Gall: 0-1
Aids:	Bl: 0-0 Vi: 0-0 Tstrap: 0-0 Ckp: 0-0
Best Rating:	102 3/04 Plum 2m gd-sft Hdl

Moderate hurdler; off the mark at the sixth attempt over two miles at Towcester in April 2004; did not settle only try at three miles; acts on good and soft ground; future chaser.

Tiger Tops

5-y-o ch g Sabrehill (USA)-Rose Chime (IRE) (Tirol)
J A Supple (C F Wall 22/9) M Tilbrook

Placings:P   (4440)
2003/04: 16²GS,

	Starts	1st	2nd	3rd	Win & Pl
Hurdles	1	0	0	0	
Career Total	1	0	0	0	

Going:	Sf: 0-0 GS: 0-1 Gd: 0-0 GF: - Fm: 0-0
Distance:	2m/2m3: 0-1 2m4-2m7: 0-0 3m+: 0-0

Track: LH: 0-1 RH: 0-0 Tight: 0-1 Gall: 0-0
Aids: Bl: 0-0 Vi: 0-0 Tstrap: 0-0 Ckp: 0-0

Tiger Typhoon (IRE)
90(86h) (76+h)80
8-y-o b g Cataldi-Churchtown Breeze (Tarqogan)
R J Hodges   Mrs Anna L Sanders

Placings:0/3/03PU3-43O (0274)
2003/04: 17[4]G, 16[3]GS, 16[O]GF,

	Starts	1st	2nd	3rd	Win & Pl
Chases	3	0	0	1	853
Career Total	10	0	0	4	2142

Going: Sf: 0-0 GS: 0-1 Gd: 0-1 GF: - Fm: 0-1
Distance: 2m/2m3: 0-3 2m4-2m7: 0-0 3m+: 0-0
Track: LH: 0-1 RH: 0-2 Tight: 0-0 Gall: 0-0
Aids: Bl: 0-0 Vi: 0-0 Tstrap: 0-0 Ckp: 0-0
Best Rating: 80 4/03 Extr 2m1f110y good Ch

Tigers Lair (IRE)
93f   108f
5-y-o b/br g Accordion-Eadie (IRE) (Strong Gale)
Jonjo O'Neill   Mrs G Smith

Placings:424 (4649)
2003/04: 16[3]GS, 16[2]G, 17[4]G,

	Starts	1st	2nd	3rd	Win & Pl
NH Flat	3	0	1	0	2124
Career Total	3	0	1	0	2124

Going: Sf: 0-0 GS: 0-1 Gd: 0-2 GF: - Fm: 0-0
Distance: 2m/2m3: 0-3 2m4-2m7: 0-0 3m+: 0-0
Track: LH: 0-2 RH: 0-0 Tight: 0-0 Gall: 0-0
Aids: Bl: 0-0 Vi: 0-0 Tstrap: 0-0 Ckp: 0-0
Best Rating: 108 4/04 Aint 2m1f good NHF

Moderate hurdler; acts on good and easy ground.

Tighe Caster
89f   91f
5-y-o b g Makbul-Miss Fire (Gunner B)
P R Webber   D P Barrie & M J Rees

Placings:30 (4454)
2003/04: 18[3]HY, 16[O]GS,

	Starts	1st	2nd	3rd	Win & Pl
NH Flat	2	0	0	1	289
Career Total	2	0	0	1	289

Going: Sf: 0-1 GS: 0-1 Gd: 0-0 GF: - Fm: 0-0
Distance: 2m/2m3: 0-2 2m4-2m7: 0-0 3m+: 0-0
Track: LH: 0-1 RH: 0-1 Tight: 0-1 Gall: 0-0
Aids: Bl: 0-0 Vi: 0-0 Tstrap: 0-0 Ckp: 0-0
Best Rating: 91 3/04 Asct 2m110y gd-sft NHF

Fair debut in bumper at Fontwell in January on heavy ground; will improve for better ground.

Tighten Your Belt (IRE)
110   142
7-y-o b g Phardante (FR)-Hi' Upham (Deep Run)
Miss Venetia Williams   The MerseyClyde Partnership

Placings:13-110 (4394)

2003/04: 16[1]HY, 16[1]GS, 21[9]G,

	Starts	1st	2nd	3rd	Win & Pl
Hurdles	3	2	0	0	10696
Career Total	5	3	0	1	17519
105 2/04 Towc 2m C Hdl				G-S	£6542
111 1/04 Towc 2m E Hdl				HVY	£4153
111 3/03 Strf 2m110y H NHF				G-S	£3523

Total win prize-money £14219

Going: Sf: 1-1 GS: 1-1 Gd: 0-1 GF: - Fm: 0-0
Distance: 2m/2m3: 2-2 2m4-2m7: 0-1 3m+: 0-0
Track: LH: 0-1 RH: 2-2 Tight: 0-0 Gall: 0-1
Aids: Bl: 0-0 Vi: 0-0 Tstrap: 0-0 Ckp: 0-0
Best Rating: 142 3/04 Chel 2m5f good Hdl

Useful hurdler; previously winner of a bumper and an Irish point; half-brother to high-class chaser Native Upmanship; effective over two miles, but will stay much further; acts in soft ground; a smart prospect.

Tik-A-Tai (IRE)
108(101c) (124c)134+
9-y-o b g Alphabatim (USA)-Carrig Ross (Lord Ha Ha)
O Sherwood   The Chamberlain Addiscott Partnership

Placings:1PP/14221P/5313P-221 (3607)
2003/04: 20[2]GF, 21[2]S, 16[1]S,

	Starts	1st	2nd	3rd	Win & Pl
Hurdles	3	1	2	0	16607
Career Total	17	5	4	2	40773
134 1/04 Donc 2m110y C(0-130)HHdl				SFT	£6851
128 11/02 Font 2m6f110yE(0-110)HHdl				G-S	£3157
128 2/02 Ludl 2m4f D(0-125)HCh				G-S	£5369
118 10/01 Fknm 2m5f110yC Ch				SFT	£6776
123 10/00 Font 2m6f110yE Hdl				G-S	£2338

Total win prize-money £24491

Going: Sf: 1-2 GS: 0-0 Gd: 0-0 GF: - Fm: 0-1
Distance: 2m/2m3: 1-1 2m4-2m7: 0-2 3m+: 0-0
Track: LH: 1-3 RH: 0-0 Tight: 0-0 Gall: 1-1
Aids: Bl: 0-0 Vi: 0-0 Tstrap: 0-0 Ckp: 0-0
Best Rating: 134 1/04 Donc 2m110y soft Hdl

Fair hurdler/chaser; ran well on his first outing for the best part of a year when second in Tote Silver Trophy at Chepstow November 2003; solid effort in defeat next time before winning easily at Doncaster; stays up to three miles; acts on soft and fast ground; goes well fresh.

Tikram
117(114h) (139h)147
7-y-o ch g Lycius (USA)-Black Fighter (USA) (Secretariat (USA))
G L Moore   Mike Charlton And Rodger Sargent

Placings:2316/22360/42P4014360-32214112 (4835)
2003/04: 16[3]GF, 20[2]G, 16[2]G, 22[1]G, 20[4]S, 20[1]G, 20[1]G, 21[2]GF,

	Starts	1st	2nd	3rd	Win & Pl
Hurdles	1	0	0	1	4400
Chases	7	3	3	0	80962
Career Total	27	5	7	4	155385
144 2/04 Chel 2m4f110yA HCh				GD	£43500
134 2/04 Font 2m4f C Ch				GD	£9936
124 1/04 Font 2m6f E Ch				GD	£4381
137 12/02 Font 2m2f110yC(0-130)HHdl				GD	£12087
120 1/01 Donc 2m110y C Hdl				GD	£6305

Total win prize-money £76210

Going: Sf: 0-1 GS: 0-0 Gd: 3-5 GF: - Fm: 0-2
Distance: 2m/2m3: 0-2 2m4-2m7: 3-6 3m+: 0-2
Track: LH: 1-4 RH: 0-2 Tight: 2-2 Gall: 1-4
Aids: Bl: 0-0 Vi: 0-0 Tstrap: 0-0 Ckp: 0-0
Best Rating: 147 4/04 Chel 2m5f gd-fm Ch

Smart novice chaser; formerly useful hurdler; winner of the 2004 Mildmay Of Flete; suited by around two to two and a half miles, acts on soft ground, although is better on good; pulled too hard when tried in blinkers.

Tilley Lane (IRE)
7-y-o b g Blues Traveller (IRE)-Divine Apsara (Godswalk (USA))
R A Fahey   Mike Caulfield

Placings:P (4565)
2003/04: 17[P]GS,

	Starts	1st	2nd	3rd	Win & Pl
Hurdles	1	0	0	0	
Career Total	1	0	0	0	

Going: Sf: 0-0 GS: 0-1 Gd: 0-0 GF: - Fm: 0-0
Distance: 2m/2m3: 0-1 2m4-2m7: 0-0 3m+: 0-0
Track: LH: 0-1 RH: 0-0 Tight: 0-1 Gall: 0-0
Aids: Bl: 0-0 Vi: 0-0 Tstrap: 0-0 Ckp: 0-0

Tim's The Man (IRE)
99(99h) (93h)86
8-y-o gr g Roselier (FR)-Pindas (Bargello)
C J Mann   The Life Of Riley Partnership

Placings:3540/1042-0566 (3527)
2003/04: 26[0]G, 20[5]G, 19[6]S, 20[6]S,

	Starts	1st	2nd	3rd	Win & Pl
Hurdles	1	0	0	0	0
Chases	3	0	0	0	0
Career Total	12	1	1	1	5542
109 11/02 Leic 2m E Hdl				HVY	£3552

Total win prize-money £3552

Going: Sf: 0-2 GS: 0-0 Gd: 0-2 GF: - Fm: 0-0
Distance: 2m/2m3: 0-0 2m4-2m7: 0-3 3m+: 0-1
Track: LH: 0-1 RH: 0-3 Tight: 0-1 Gall: 0-0
Aids: Bl: 0-0 Vi: 0-0 Tstrap: 0-0 Ckp: 0-3
Best Rating: 109 11/02 Leic 2m heavy Hdl

Timberley
10-y-o ch g Dancing High-Kimberley Rose (Monksfield)
Miss R Brewis   Miss Rhona Brewis

Placings:P (1839)
2003/04: 21[P]G,

	Starts	1st	2nd	3rd	Win & Pl
Chases	1	0	0	0	
Career Total	1	0	0	0	

Going: Sf: 0-0 GS: 0-0 Gd: 0-0 GF: - Fm: 0-0
Distance: 2m/2m3: 0-0 2m4-2m7: 0-1 3m+: 0-0
Track: LH: 0-1 RH: 0-0 Tight: 0-0 Gall: 0-0
Aids: Bl: 0-0 Vi: 0-0 Tstrap: 0-1 Ckp: 0-0

Time For Action (IRE)
88   82+
12-y-o b g Alzao (USA)-Beyond Words (Ballad Rock)
H J Evans   Mrs Jane Evans

Placings:23/13260314355/36/60/400/P02P0 (4148)
2003/04: 21[P]GS, 17[0]G, 20[2]G, 17[P]GS, 19[0]G,

	Starts	1st	2nd	3rd	Win & Pl
Hurdles	5	0	1	0	664
Career Total	25	2	3	5	10703
116 12/98 Tntn	2m1f	E(0-115)HHdl		G-S	£2274
100 5/98 Bang	2m1f	E Hdl		GD	£2578

Total win prize-money £4853

Going:	Sf: 0-0 GS: 0-1 Gd: 0-3 GF: - Fm: 0-1
Distance:	2m2m3: 0-2 2m4-2m7: 0-3 3m+: 0-0
Track:	LH: 0-1 RH: 0-4 Tight: 0-3 Gall: 0-1
Aids:	Bl: 0-0 Vi: 0-0 Tstrap: 0-5 Ckp: 0-0
Best Rating:	116 2/99 Donc 2m110y gd-fm Hdl

Plating-class hurdler; stays two miles four; seems to acts on most ground; wears a tongue tie.

Time Marches On
82   89
6-y-o b g Timeless Times (USA)-Tees Gazette Girl (Kalaglow)
Mrs M Reveley Mrs M B Thwaites

Placings:610-0   (0004)
2003/04: 16⁰G,

	Starts	1st	2nd	3rd	Win & Pl
Hurdles	1	0	0	0	
Career Total	4	1	0	0	3471
89 11/02 Kels	2m110y	G Hdl		SFT	£3471

Total win prize-money £3471

Going:	Sf: 0-0 GS: 0-0 Gd: 0-1 GF: - Fm: 0-0
Distance:	2m2m3: 0-1 2m4-2m7: 0-0 3m+: 0-0
Track:	LH: 0-1 RH: 0-0 Tight: 0-0 Gall: 0-0
Aids:	Bl: 0-0 Vi: 0-0 Tstrap: 0-0 Ckp: 0-0
Best Rating:	89 11/02 Kels 2m110y soft Hdl

Time N Tide (IRE)
122d
8-y-o b g Namaqualand (USA)-Now Then (Sandford Lad)
Jonjo O'Neill Mccourt Fine Meats Ltd & D J Rushen

Placings:6512312/500/53/101P0-PP   (0332)
2003/04: 26⁹GF, 26⁶GF,

	Starts	1st	2nd	3rd	Win & Pl
Hurdles	2	0	0	0	
Career Total	19	4	2	2	25182
122 1/03 Donc	2m3f110yC(0-135)HHdl		G-S	£7143
121 11/02 Bang	2m1f	E(0-110)HHdl	SFT	£3412
104 4/00 Ludl	2m	D Hdl	GD	£2925
117 1/00 Donc	2m110y	C Hdl	GD	£5876

Total win prize-money £19358

Going:	Sf: 0-0 GS: 0-0 Gd: 0-0 GF: - Fm: 0-2
Distance:	2m2m3: 0-0 2m4-2m7: 0-0 3m+: 0-2
Track:	LH: 0-1 RH: 0-1 Tight: 0-0 Gall: 0-1
Aids:	Bl: 0-1 Vi: 0-0 Tstrap: 0-0 Ckp: 0-0
Best Rating:	122 1/03 Donc 2m3f110y gd-sft Hdl

Fair handicap hurdler; stays two and a half miles and acts on soft ground.

Time Of Flight (IRE)
106
11-y-o ch g Over The River (FR)-Icy Lou (Blue Rullah)
Mrs M Reveley Andy Peake

Placings:150/33UP41/215P4P/25112233F/034-PP   (3771)
2003/04: 20⁵PS, 16⁶PHY,

	Starts	1st	2nd	3rd	Win & Pl
Chases	2	0	0	0	
Career Total	29	5	4	5	33188
120 11/01 Weth	2m	C(0-135)HCh	GD	£7085

---

109 10/01 Carl	2m	D(0-125)HCh	G-S	£3900
127 10/00 Weth	2m4f110yC(0-130)HCh	HVY	£5882
110 3/00 Newc	2m	E Hdl	GD	£2684
111 12/98 Newc	2m	H NHF	SFT	£1318

Total win prize-money £20872

Going:	Sf: 0-2 GS: 0-0 Gd: 0-0 GF: - Fm: 0-0
Distance:	2m2m3: 0-1 2m4-2m7: 0-1 3m+: 0-0
Track:	LH: 0-1 RH: 0-1 Tight: 0-0 Gall: 0-0
Aids:	Bl: 0-0 Vi: 0-0 Tstrap: 0-0 Ckp: 0-0
Best Rating:	129 11/01 Weth 2m good Ch

Fair chaser; best over two miles, but does stay further; acts on ground good or softer; best when held up

Time Spin
98   94
4-y-o b g Robellino (USA)-Chiltern Court (USA) (Topsider (USA))
C Grant J C Garbutt B Woods Mrs L Swainston

Placings:6P2   (3672)
2003/04: 16⁶GS, 16⁶PGS, 18²HY,

	Starts	1st	2nd	3rd	Win & Pl
Hurdles	3	0	1	0	1080
Career Total	3	0	1	0	1080

Going:	Sf: 0-1 GS: 0-2 Gd: 0-0 GF: - Fm: 0-0
Distance:	2m2m3: 0-3 2m4-2m7: 0-0 3m+: 0-0
Track:	LH: 0-3 RH: 0-0 Tight: 0-1 Gall: 0-0
Aids:	Bl: 0-0 Vi: 0-0 Tstrap: 0-0 Ckp: 0-0
Best Rating:	94 2/04 Kels 2m2f heavy Hdl

Time To Parlez
78
13-y-o b g Amboise-Image Of War (Warpath)
C J Drewe Mrs J Strange

Placings:00/6/PPP44/P02250/B532P1PP/021UPP4P/6P0P136024-4P5   (2382)
2003/04: 25⁴G, 25⁵PGS, 26⁵PGS,

	Starts	1st	2nd	3rd	Win & Pl
Chases	3	0	0	0	
Career Total	43	3	5	2	18173
78 1/03 Plum	3m2f	F(0-90)HCh	SFT	£3276
86 12/01 Towc	3m1f	F(0-110)HCh	HVY	£4438
86 1/01 Font	3m2f110yF(0-100)HCh	SFT	£2847

Total win prize-money £10561

Going:	Sf: 0-0 GS: 0-1 Gd: 0-1 GF: - Fm: 0-1
Distance:	2m2m3: 0-0 2m4-2m7: 0-0 3m+: 0-3
Track:	LH: 0-1 RH: 0-2 Tight: 0-0 Gall: 0-0
Aids:	Bl: 0-0 Vi: 0-0 Tstrap: 0-0 Ckp: 0-0
Best Rating:	93 12/97 Chep 2m4f110y heavy Hdl

Plating-class chaser; stays well; suited by testing ground; likes to front run.

Time To Reflect (IRE)
107   103
5-y-o ch g Anshan-Castlemitchle (IRE) (Roselier (FR))
M C Pipe D A Johnson

Placings:/31200P00P   (4833)
2003/04: 18¹GF, 17⁹G, 24¹GF, 16²G, 20⁹GS, 22⁰G, 25⁹G, 22⁰G, 20⁸G, 21⁹GF,

	Starts	1st	2nd	3rd	Win & Pl
NH Flat	1	1	0	0	2247
Hurdles	8	1	1	1	3765

Chases	1	0	0	0		0
Career Total	10	2	1	1	6012
100 11/03 Chep	3m	F Hdl			G-F	£2037
88 10/03 Plum	2m2f	H NHF			G-F	£2247

Total win prize-money £4284

Going:	Sf: 0-1 GS: 0-1 Gd: 0-5 GF: - Fm: 2-3
Distance:	2m2m3: 1-3 2m4-2m7: 0-5 3m+: 1-2
Track:	LH: 2-6 RH: 0-4 Tight: 0-1 Gall: 0-2
Aids:	Bl: 0-0 Vi: 0-2 Tstrap: 0-0 Ckp: 0-0
Best Rating:	103 11/03 Extr 2m1f good Hdl

Moderate novice hurdler; bumper winner; promising third on hurdling debut at Exeter the following month; made hard work of winning novices' hurdle when stepped up to 3m at Chepstow four days later; has regressed since and pulled up on chase debut; raced mainly on good ground; has worn a visor.

Time To Regret
88   61+
4-y-o b g Presidium-Scoffera (Scottish Reel)
J J Quinn B Selective Partnership

Placings:0   (1071)
2003/04: 17⁰GF,

	Starts	1st	2nd	3rd	Win & Pl
Hurdles	1	0	0	0	
Career Total	1	0	0	0	

Going:	Sf: 0-0 GS: 0-0 Gd: 0-0 GF: - Fm: 0-1
Distance:	2m2m3: 0-1 2m4-2m7: 0-0 3m+: 0-0
Track:	LH: 0-1 RH: 0-0 Tight: 0-1 Gall: 0-0
Aids:	Bl: 0-0 Vi: 0-0 Tstrap: 0-0 Ckp: 0-0
Best Rating:	65 8/03 Sedg 2m1f gd-fm Hdl

Time To Shine
110   123+
5-y-o b m Pivotal-Sweet Jaffa (Never So Bold)
Miss L J Sheen (B R Johnson 7/5) Mrs P J Sheen

Placings:1142120   (4629)
2003/04: 16¹GY, 17¹HY, 19⁴S, 16²FY, 16¹G, 20²S, 20⁹G,

	Starts	1st	2nd	3rd	Win & Pl
Hurdles	7	3	2	0	13870
Career Total	7	3	2	0	13870
123 2/04 Asct	2m110y	D Hdl		GD	£4771
108 1/04 Folk	2m1f110yE(0-100)HHdl	HVY	£3430
80 5/03 Fknm	2m	G Hdl		G-F	£2352

Total win prize-money £10554

Going:	Sf: 1-4 GS: 0-0 Gd: 1-2 GF: - Fm: 1-1
Distance:	2m2m3: 3-5 2m4-2m7: 0-2 3m+: 0-0
Track:	LH: 1-3 RH: 2-4 Tight: 2-3 Gall: 0-1
Aids:	Bl: 0-0 Vi: 0-0 Tstrap: 0-0 Ckp: 0-0
Best Rating:	123 2/04 Asct 2m110y good Hdl

Useful hurdler, winner of her first two outings at a modest level; left clear at the final flight when recording third career win at Ascot in February; best at two miles; acts on fast and heavy ground.

Time To Tell
(83h)   (55h)
8-y-o b m Keen-Meet Again (Lomond (USA))
B G Powell D Coles, P Moore, J King, J Whittle

Placings:040P5-P   (0124)
2003/04: 26⁰PG,

	Starts	1st	2nd	3rd	Win & Pl
Chases	1	0	0	0	

Career Total	6	0	0	0	0

Going: Sf: 0-0 GS: 0-0 Gd: 0-1 GF: - Fm: 0-0
Distance: 2m/2m3: 0-0 2m4-2m7: 0-0 3m+: 0-1
Track: LH: 0-0 RH: 0-0 Tight: 0-1 Gall: 0-0
Aids: Bl: 0-0 Vi: 0-0 Tstrap: 0-0 Ckp: 0-0
Best Rating: 83 12/02 Fknm 2m   gd-sft NHF

Timeless Chick

102   **81**

7-y-o ch m Timeless Times (USA)-Be My Bird (Be My Chief (USA))
J L Spearing Be Luckies

Placings: 55343P0/5326-24   (1015)
2003/04: 21²GF, 20⁴GF,

	Starts	1st	2nd	3rd	Win & Pl
Hurdles	2	0	1	0	744
Career Total	13	0	2	3	2268

Going: Sf: 0-0 GS: 0-0 Gd: 0-0 GF: - Fm: 0-2
Distance: 2m/2m3: 0-0 2m4-2m7: 0-2 3m+: 0-0
Track: LH: 0-2 RH: 0-0 Tight: 0-0 Gall: 0-0
Aids: Bl: 0-0 Vi: 0-0 Tstrap: 0-0 Ckp: 0-0
Best Rating: 84 12/01 Hrfd 2m1f   good Hdl

Poor selling hurdler.

Times Past (IRE)

87(91c)   (67c)**78**

9-y-o b g Commanche Run-Orient Moonbeam (Deep Run)
J W Unett (P Jones 10/5) M W & A N Harris

Placings: 14/4-4540   (2865)
2003/04: 20⁴GF, 20⁵G, 24⁴GF, 19⁰GS,

	Starts	1st	2nd	3rd	Win & Pl
Hurdles	3	0	0	0	324
Chases	1	0	0	0	105
Career Total	7	1	0	0	4827
103	6/01 Navn 2m	NHF		YLD	£3895

Total win prize-money £3895

Going: Sf: 0-0 GS: 0-1 Gd: 0-1 GF: - Fm: 0-2
Distance: 2m/2m3: 0-1 2m4-2m7: 0-2 3m+: 0-1
Track: LH: 0-3 RH: 0-1 Tight: 0-1 Gall: 0-0
Aids: Bl: 0-0 Vi: 0-0 Tstrap: 0-0 Ckp: 0-0
Best Rating: 106 9/01 List 2m   gd-fm Hdl

Novice hunter chaser; Irish bumper winner and twice successful between the flags; acts on a sound surface; stays three miles.

Timidjar (IRE)

108   **78**

11-y-o b g Doyoun-Timissara (USA) (Shahrastani (USA))
Mrs D Thomas Mrs D Thomas

Placings: 603/236P/2006/26011/1440/0040000/00033-230P560   (1333)
2003/04: 17²GF, 17³GF, 16⁰GF, 17⁰PGS, 16⁵GF, 17⁶GF, 19⁰GS,

	Starts	1st	2nd	3rd	Win & Pl
Hurdles	7	0	1	0	1225
Career Total	39	3	4	5	10907
100	5/00 Hrfd	2m1f	G(0-95)HHdl	GD	£2100
99	4/00 Hrfd	2m1f	G Hdl	GD	£2159
95	3/00 NAbb	2m1f	F(0-100)HHdl	GD	£1862

Total win prize-money £6122

Going: Sf: 0-0 GS: 0-1 Gd: 0-0 GF: - Fm: 0-6
Distance: 2m/2m3: 0-6 2m4-2m7: 0-1 3m+: 0-0

Track: LH: 0-5 RH: 0-2 Tight: 0-4 Gall: 0-0
Aids: Bl: 0-0 Vi: 0-0 Tstrap: 0-0 Ckp: 0-0
Best Rating: 102 5/97 Chep 2m110y   good Hdl

Selling hurdler; signs of a return to form in the spring of 2003; acts on good ground and suited by soft.

Tin Symphony

99   **87**

6-y-o ch m Opera Ghost-Bronze Age (Celtic Cone)
B J M Ryall The Wessex Cornflower Partnership

Placings: U05-B526   (3698)
2003/04: 16⁸G, 17⁵G, 16²S, 17⁶HY,

	Starts	1st	2nd	3rd	Win & Pl
Hurdles	4	0	1	0	1009
Career Total	7	0	1	0	1009

Going: Sf: 0-2 GS: 0-0 Gd: 0-0 GF: - Fm: 0-0
Distance: 2m/2m3: 0-4 2m4-2m7: 0-0 3m+: 0-0
Track: LH: 0-0 RH: 0-4 Tight: 0-1 Gall: 0-0
Aids: Bl: 0-0 Vi: 0-0 Tstrap: 0-0 Ckp: 0-0
Best Rating: 88 3/03 Newb 2m110y   good NHF

Has shown some promise in bumpers and novice hurdles; acts on good or softer.

Tina Cooke

92(89h)   (62h)**73**

8-y-o gr m Tina's Pet-Up Cooke (Deep Run)
Miss Kate Milligan Mrs J M L Milligan

Placings: 50/P0404P-4PP50   (4659)
2003/04: 16⁴G, 17⁵GF, 21⁸GF, 21⁵GF, 16⁰S,

	Starts	1st	2nd	3rd	Win & Pl
Hurdles	1	0	0	0	0
Chases	4	0	0	0	299
Career Total	13	0	0	0	609

Going: Sf: 0-1 GS: 0-0 Gd: 0-1 GF: - Fm: 0-3
Distance: 2m/2m3: 0-3 2m4-2m7: 0-2 3m+: 0-0
Track: LH: 0-5 RH: 0-0 Tight: 0-1 Gall: 0-0
Aids: Bl: 0-0 Vi: 0-0 Tstrap: 0-0 Ckp: 0-0
Best Rating: 85 1/02 Muss 2m   good NHF

Tina Thyne (IRE)

(99h)   (89h)

10-y-o b m Good Thyne (USA)-Tiny Tina (Deep Run)
J G M O'Shea Gary Roberts

Placings: 12/0042326/5524146-P   (0136)
2003/04: 20⁰G,

	Starts	1st	2nd	3rd	Win & Pl
Chases	1	0	0	0	
Career Total	17	2	4	1	12790
89	3/03 Tntn	2m3f110y	E Hdl	HVY	£4322
107	3/00 Uttx	2m	H NHF	GD	£1610

Total win prize-money £5933

Going: Sf: 0-0 GS: 0-0 Gd: 0-1 GF: - Fm: 0-0
Distance: 2m/2m3: 0-0 2m4-2m7: 0-1 3m+: 0-0
Track: LH: 0-0 RH: 0-1 Tight: 0-1 Gall: 0-0
Aids: Bl: 0-0 Vi: 0-0 Tstrap: 0-0 Ckp: 0-0
Best Rating: 119 4/00 Chel 2m1f   soft NHF

Plating-class hurdler; winner of a bumper in 2000; had headgear left off when winning 19 furlong mares only maiden at Taunton March 2003; acts on ground good and softer.

Tinerana House (IRE)

5-y-o gr g Paris House-Tony Award (USA) (Kirtling)
Miss C J E Caroe Les McLaughlin

Placings: 0-0   (0837)
2003/04: 16⁸GF,

	Starts	1st	2nd	3rd	Win & Pl
NH Flat	1	0	0	0	
Career Total	2	0	0	0	

Going: Sf: 0-0 GS: 0-0 Gd: 0-0 GF: - Fm: 0-1
Distance: 2m/2m3: 0-0 2m4-2m7: 0-0 3m+: 0-0
Track: LH: 0-1 RH: 0-0 Tight: 0-0 Gall: 0-0
Aids: Bl: 0-0 Vi: 0-0 Tstrap: 0-0 Ckp: 0-0

Tino (IRE)

105   (72h)**87+**

8-y-o ch g Torus-Delphic Thunder (Viking (USA))
J S King Robert Skillen

Placings: 0/00P3536/P10032-PPP2211150   (3052)
2003/04: 26⁸GF, 23⁸G, 23⁰G, 26²GF, 23²F, 21¹GF, 24¹F, 23¹F, 22⁴G, 24⁰G,

	Starts	1st	2nd	3rd	Win & Pl
Chases	10	3	2	0	14615
Career Total	24	4	3	3	20409
85	11/03 Leic	2m7f110y		E(0-105)HCh	
FRM £4378					
87	11/03 Ludl	3m	D(0-115)HCh	FRM	£5330
85	11/03 Folk	2m5f	F(0-95)HCh	G-F	£2936
87	11/02 Folk	2m5f	F(0-95)HCh	G-F	£4104

Total win prize-money £16751

Going: Sf: 0-0 GS: 0-0 Gd: 0-0 GF: - Fm: 3-6
Distance: 2m/2m3: 0-0 2m4-2m7: 1-2 3m+: 2-8
Track: LH: 0-4 RH: 3-5 Tight: 2-4 Gall: 0-0
Aids: Bl: 0-2 Vi: 0-0 Tstrap: 0-0 Ckp: 0-0
Best Rating: 90 3/02 Hntg 2m4f110y   gd-fm Ch

Very moderate chaser; stays three miles and acts on fast ground; goes well at Folkestone.

Tinoveritas (FR)

112   **114**

6-y-o b g Saint Estephe (FR)-Tinorosa (FR) (Concertino (FR))
P F Nicholls C G Roach

Placings: 20-f31631   (4692)
2003/04: 16¹GS, 17³G, 19¹GF, 21⁶G, 16³G, 17¹G,

	Starts	1st	2nd	3rd	Win & Pl
NH Flat	1	1	0	0	2226
Hurdles	5	2	2	1	11443
Career Total	8	3	1	0	14450
114	4/04 Extr	2m1f	E Hdl	GD	£4338
112	12/03 Newb	2m3f	D Hdl	GF	£5596
107	5/03 Worc	2m	H NHF	G-S	£2226

Total win prize-money £12164

Going: Sf: 0-0 GS: 1-1 Gd: 1-4 GF: - Fm: 1-1
Distance: 2m/2m3: 3-5 2m4-2m7: 0-1 3m+: 0-0
Track: LH: 2-2 RH: 1-4 Tight: 0-0 Gall: 1-1
Aids: Bl: 0-0 Vi: 0-0 Tstrap: 0-0 Ckp: 0-0
Best Rating: 114 4/04 Extr 2m1f   good Hdl

Useful novice hurdler; stays trips of around two and a half miles and acts on most types of ground; looks a decent prospect.

Tinton Mill

5-y-o b m Shambo-Mill Thyme (Thowra (FR))
Jane Southcombe Mark Savill

Placings:0   (4824)
2003/04: 17⁰GF,

	Starts	1st	2nd	3rd	Win & Pl
NH Flat	1	0	0	0	
Career Total	1	0	0	0	

Going:	Sf: 0-0 GS: 0-0 Gd: 0-0 GF: - Fm: 0-1
Distance:	2m/2m3: 0-1 2m4-2m7: 0-0 3m+: 0-0
Track:	LH: 0-0 RH: 0-1 Tight: 0-0 Gall: 0-0
Aids:	Bl: 0-0 Vi: 0-0 Tstrap: 0-0 Ckp: 0-0

Tioga Gold (IRE)
79   **88**

5-y-o b g Goldmark (USA)-Coffee Bean (Doulab (USA))
L R James Nelson Unit Ltd

Placings:300   (4073)
2003/04: 16³G, 19⁰G, 16⁰F,

	Starts	1st	2nd	3rd	Win & Pl
Hurdles	3	0	0	1	1100
Career Total	3	0	0	1	1100

Going:	Sf: 0-0 GS: 0-0 Gd: 0-2 GF: - Fm: 0-1
Distance:	2m/2m3: 0-2 2m4-2m7: 0-1 3m+: 0-0
Track:	LH: 0-2 RH: 0-1 Tight: 0-1 Gall: 0-0
Aids:	Bl: 0-0 Vi: 0-0 Tstrap: 0-0 Ckp: 0-0
Best Rating:	88 11/03 Weth 2m good Hdl

Plater on the flat; well beaten third on hurdling bow at Wetherby in November; held subsequently.

Tioman (IRE)
80   **58**

5-y-o b/br g Dr Devious (IRE)-Tochar Ban (USA) (Assert)
Mary Meek (M A Jarvis 25/6) Mrs Mary Meek

Placings:060   (4577)
2003/04: 17⁰GS, 16⁶GS, 16⁰G,

	Starts	1st	2nd	3rd	Win & Pl
Hurdles	3	0	0	0	0
Career Total	3	0	0	0	0

Going:	Sf: 0-0 GS: 0-2 Gd: 0-1 GF: - Fm: 0-0
Distance:	2m/2m3: 0-3 2m4-2m7: 0-0 3m+: 0-0
Track:	LH: 0-2 RH: 0-1 Tight: 0-2 Gall: 0-1
Aids:	Bl: 0-0 Vi: 0-0 Tstrap: 0-0 Ckp: 0-0
Best Rating:	63 3/04 Newb 2m110y good Hdl

Tip Kash (FR)
78(103h)   (112 h)**52**

7-y-o ch g Kashtan (FR)-Tipas (FR) (Tip Moss (FR))
P M Phelan Andrew L Cohen

Placings:0/1443P-340PP030   (4841)
2003/04: 20³GF, 22⁴GS, 24⁰GS, 20⁰HY, 16⁰GS, 21⁰GS, 24³GS, 21⁰G,

	Starts	1st	2nd	3rd	Win & Pl
Hurdles	6	0	0	1	1399
Chases	2	0	0	1	718
Career Total	14	1	0	3	7688
112 11/02 MRas 2m3f110yE Hdl			SFT	£3654
Total win prize-money £3654				

Going:	Sf: 0-1 GS: 0-5 Gd: 0-1 GF: - Fm: 0-1
Distance:	2m/2m3: 0-1 2m4-2m7: 0-5 3m+: 0-2
Track:	LH: 0-5 RH: 0-1 Tight: 0-3 Gall: 0-1
Aids:	Bl: 0-0 Vi: 0-0 Tstrap: 0-4 Ckp: 0-0
Best Rating:	112 11/02 MRas 2m3f110y soft Hdl

Modest chaser/hurdler; acts on soft ground; stays two miles four; has suffered from breathing problems.

Tipp Top Lord (IRE)
107   **120+**

7-y-o gr g Mister Lord (USA)-Dark Fluff (Mandalus)
N A Twiston-Davies Mrs R Vaughan

Placings:6-P32110   (4398)
2003/04: 25⁰GS, 24³G, 26²S, 24¹HY, 25¹G, 32⁰G,

	Starts	1st	2nd	3rd	Win & Pl
Chases	6	2	1	1	9008
Career Total	7	2	1	1	9008
120 3/04 Towc 3m1f		F(0-100)HCh	GD	£3542
111 2/04 Chep 3m		F(0-95)HCh	HVY	£3445
Total win prize-money £6988				

Going:	Sf: 1-2 GS: 0-1 Gd: 1-3 GF: - Fm: 0-0
Distance:	2m/2m3: 0-0 2m4-2m7: 0-0 **3m+: 2-6**
Track:	LH: 1-4 RH: 1-2 Tight: 0-1 Gall: 0-1
Aids:	Bl: 0-0 Vi: 0-0 Tstrap: 0-0 Ckp: 0-0
Best Rating:	120 3/04 Towc 3m1f good Ch

Modest novice chaser; lightly-raced; relished the test of stamina when winning Class F 3m handicap in heavy ground at Chepstow February 2004; stays 3m 2f; suited by the mud; entitled to improve as he is a big horse.

Tipsy Mouse (IRE)
105(99h)   (102 h)**120**

8-y-o ch g Roselier (FR)-Darjoy (Darantus)
Mrs S J Smith Trevor Hemmings

Placings:P004242-12211F14   (4861)
2003/04: 20²G, 25¹G, 23²G, 24²S, 24¹GS, 24¹HY, 33⁰G, 32¹G, 33⁴GS,

	Starts	1st	2nd	3rd	Win & Pl
Chases	9	4	3	0	52926
Career Total	15	4	4	0	54467
129 3/04 Kels 4m		C(0-135)HCh	GD	£25114
117 1/04 Hayd 3m		C(0-135)HCh	HVY	£9343
125 12/03 Hayd 3m		D(0-110)HCh	G-S	£4338
113 5/03 Hexm 3m1f		E(0-105)HCh	GD	£3919
Total win prize-money £42717				

Going:	Sf: 1-2 GS: 1-2 Gd: 2-5 GF: - Fm: 0-0
Distance:	2m/2m3: 0-0 2m4-2m7: 0-1 **3m+: 4-8**
Track:	**LH: 4-8** RH: 0-0 **Tight: 1-1** Gall: 0-1
Aids:	Bl: 0-0 Vi: 0-0 Tstrap: 0-0 Ckp: 0-0
Best Rating:	129 3/04 Kels 4m good Ch

Fair novice chaser; winning Irish pointer; brother to Grand National winner Royal Athlete; recorded fourth career win in valuable event at Kelso in March 2004; stays really well; acts on soft ground.

Tiquet
91   **76**

5-y-o b g Bedford (USA)-Lady Kay-Lee (Cruise Missile)
N J Henderson The T K Partnership

Placings:00FP   (4560)
2003/04: 16⁰GS, 20⁰GS, 24⁰G, 21⁰GS,

	Starts	1st	2nd	3rd	Win & Pl
NH Flat	1	0	0	0	0
Hurdles	3	0	0	0	0

Career Total		4	0	0	0

Going:	Sf: 0-0 GS: 0-3 Gd: 0-1 GF: 0-0 Fm: 0-0
Distance:	2m/2m3: 0-1 2m4-2m7: 0-2 3m+: 0-1
Track:	LH: 0-2 RH: 0-2 Tight: 0-1 Gall: 0-3
Aids:	Bl: 0-0 Vi: 0-0 Tstrap: 0-0 Ckp: 0-0
Best Rating:	76 2/04 Folk 2m4f110y gd-sft Hdl

Has shown nothing to date; will do better once handicapped.

Tirailleur (IRE)
90   **58+**

4-y-o b f Eagle Eyed (USA)-Tiralle (IRE) (Tirol)
J White Nick Quesnel

Placings:4   (1472)
2003/04: 17⁴F,

	Starts	1st	2nd	3rd	Win & Pl
Hurdles	1	0	0	0	257
Career Total	1	0	0	0	257

Going:	Sf: 0-0 GS: 0-0 Gd: 0-0 GF: - Fm: 0-1
Distance:	2m/2m3: 0-1 2m4-2m7: 0-0 3m+: 0-0
Track:	LH: 0-0 RH: 0-1 Tight: 0-0 Gall: 0-0
Aids:	Bl: 0-0 Vi: 0-0 Tstrap: 0-0 Ckp: 0-0
Best Rating:	58 9/03 Extr 2m1f firm Hdl

Tiraldo (FR)

11-y-o b g Royal Charter (FR)-Tamilda (FR) (Rose Laurel)
S Flook (A G Juckes 26/5) Mrs S E Vaughan

Placings:4/5/22F1F1/23142P2F/40/PP444/5013P-600   (3845)
2003/04: 30⁶GF, 25⁰S, 25⁰GS,

	Starts	1st	2nd	3rd	Win & Pl
Chases	3	0	0	0	0
Career Total	31	4	5	2	41666
74 8/02 Strf 3m		E(0-105)HCh	SFT	£4095
122 11/99 Towc 3m1f		D(0-120)HCh	GD	£6905
121 2/99 Hntg 2m4f110yD Ch			G-S	£5160
112 12/98 Strf 2m5f110yD Ch			SFT	£4224
Total win prize-money £20384				

Going:	Sf: 0-1 GS: 0-1 Gd: 0-0 GF: - Fm: 0-1
Distance:	2m/2m3: 0-0 2m4-2m7: 0-0 3m+: 0-3
Track:	LH: 0-1 RH: 0-2 Tight: 0-0 Gall: 0-1
Aids:	Bl: 0-1 Vi: 0-0 Tstrap: 0-0 Ckp: 0-2
Best Rating:	126 5/99 Strf 2m5f110y gd-sft Ch

Formerly decent chaser, but very moderate nowadays; stays three miles; appreciates cut in the ground.

Tirikumba
106   **97**

8-y-o ch m Le Moss-Ntombi (Trasi's Son)
S G Griffiths S G Griffiths

Placings:166-2030   (4574)
2003/04: 22²G, 21⁰G, 19³GS, 21⁰G,

	Starts	1st	2nd	3rd	Win & Pl
Hurdles	4	0	1	1	2572
Career Total	7	1	1	1	5978
95 12/02 Ludl 2m		H NHF	GD	£3031
Total win prize-money £3031				

Going:	Sf: 0-0 GS: 0-1 Gd: 0-3 GF: - Fm: 0-0
Distance:	2m/2m3: 0-0 2m4-2m7: 0-4 3m+: 0-0
Track:	LH: 0-2 RH: 0-2 Tight: 0-1 Gall: 0-1
Aids:	Bl: 0-0 Vi: 0-0 Tstrap: 0-0 Ckp: 0-0

Best Rating: 97 3/04 Newb 2m5f good Hdl

Successful in a mares' bumper at Ludlow on her debut; subsequently highly tried; placed in novice hurdles; stays well.

Tirley Gale

90   83

12-y-o b g Strong Gale-Mascara VII (Damsire Unregistered)
J S Smith (Miss N Brookes 7/5) Donald Smith

Placings:000P/0FP35/153P5R6F/04P/04PR/3-40   (0414)
2003/04: 24⁴G, 25⁰G,

	Starts	1st	2nd	3rd	Win & Pl
Chases	2	0	0	0	0
Career Total	27	1	0	3	5086
98	5/99	Worc	2m7f110yHCh		good Ch
			Total win prize-money £3003

Going:	Sf: 0-0 GS: 0-0 Gd: 0-1 GF: - Fm: 0-1
Distance:	2m/2m3: 0-0 2m4-2m7: 0-0 3m+: 0-2
Track:	LH: 0-2 RH: 0-0 Tight: 0-1 Gall: 0-0
Aids:	Bl: 0-0 Vi: 0-0 Tstrap: 0-0 Ckp: 0-0
Best Rating:	104 3/99 Wwck 2m4f110y good Ch

Tirley Storm

100   (66h)88

9-y-o b g Tirley Gale-Random Select (Random Shot)
J S Smith Donald Smith

Placings:6/P0044P2P/PP460P00-120321236   (3048)
2003/04: 21¹G, 20²S, 21⁰GF, 21³G, 22²G, 21¹G, 20²GF, 21³G, 19⁶G,

	Starts	1st	2nd	3rd	Win & Pl
Chases	9	2	3	2	11591
Career Total	26	2	4	2	13631
88	10/03	Fknm	2m5f110yF(0-100)HCh		£2989
76	5/03	Fknm	2m5f110yF(0-90)HCh		G-F £3739
			Total win prize-money £6728

Going:	Sf: 0-1 GS: 0-0 Gd: 1-5 GF: - Fm: 1-3
Distance:	2m/2m3: 0-1 2m4-2m7: 2-6 3m+: 0-0
Track:	LH: 2-7 RH: 0-0 Tight: 2-8 Gall: 0-0
Aids:	Bl: 0-0 Vi: 0-0 Tstrap: 0-0 Ckp: 0-0
Best Rating:	88 11/03 Fknm 2m5f110y good Ch

Moderate form over hurdles and fences; goes well at Fakenham; best over two and a half miles.

Tis Gromit

89(70h)   (75h)83

10-y-o b m Bedford (USA)-Lac Royale (Lochnager)
Miss Sheena West Mucky Duck Partnership

Placings:0/6P/56323/P6402-UPP44   (3413)
2003/04: 26⁵U, 25⁵P, 24⁴GS, 29⁴S, 26⁴S,

	Starts	1st	2nd	3rd	Win & Pl
Chases	5	0	0	2	399
Career Total	18	0	2	2	2965

Going:	Sf: 0-4 GS: 0-1 Gd: 0-0 GF: - Fm: 0-0
Distance:	2m/2m3: 0-0 2m4-2m7: 0-0 3m+: 0-5
Track:	LH: 0-4 RH: 0-1 Tight: 0-3 Gall: 0-0
Aids:	Bl: 0-0 Vi: 0-0 Tstrap: 0-0 Ckp: 0-5
Best Rating:	90 4/00 Plum 2m5f gd-sft Hdl

Plating-class hurdler/chaser; effective in soft ground; stays three miles.

Tisho

104   116+

8-y-o ch m Sir Harry Lewis (USA)-Sister-In-Law (Legal Tender)
P R Webber Mrs P Scott-Dunn

Placings:134F-3111000   (4842)
2003/04: 16³G, 19¹GF, 16¹G, 21¹GS, 16⁰GS, 21⁰G, 21⁰G,

	Starts	1st	2nd	3rd	Win & Pl
Hurdles	7	3	0	1	13852
Career Total	11	4	0	2	15899
116	12/03	Newb	2m5f	D Hdl	G-S £4238
104	12/03	Leic	2m	E Hdl	GD £3688
90	11/03	Tntn	2m3f110yC Hdl		G-F £5609
108	5/02	Bang	2m1f	H NHF	SFT £1771
			Total win prize-money £15308

Going:	Sf: 0-0 GS: 1-2 Gd: 1-4 GF: - Fm: 1-1
Distance:	2m/2m3: 1-3 2m4-2m7: 2-4 3m+: 0-0
Track:	LH: 1-3 RH: 2-4 Tight: 1-1 Gall: 1-3
Aids:	Bl: 0-0 Vi: 0-0 Tstrap: 0-0 Ckp: 0-0
Best Rating:	116 1/04 Sand 2m110y gd-sft Hdl

Decent novice hurdler; stays two miles five, but effective at shorter; acts on any ground; keen sort.

Tisn't Easy (IRE)

97   93

6-y-o b m Mandalus-Gemini Gale (Strong Gale)
C F Swan Seamus Mannion

Placings:0-025062345310   (4764a)
2003/04: 16⁶R, 18²GF, 16⁵GY, 18⁰G, 20⁶S, 16²S, 20³GF, 16⁴HY, 20⁵YS, 18³GY, 22¹Y, 20⁰G,

	Starts	1st	2nd	3rd	Win & Pl
NH Flat	3	0	1	0	1247
Hurdles	9	1	1	2	7763
Career Total	13	1	2	2	9010
99	3/04	Thur	2m6f	Hdl	YLD £4866
			Total win prize-money £4866

Going:	Sf: 0-3 GS: 0-0 Gd: 0-2 GF: - Fm: 0-3
Distance:	2m/2m3: 0-7 2m4-2m7: 1-5 3m+: 0-0
Track:	LH: 0-0 RH: 1-6 Tight: 0-1 Gall: 0-0
Aids:	Bl: 0-0 Vi: 0-0 Tstrap: 0-0 Ckp: 0-0
Best Rating:	99 3/04 Thur 2m6f yield Hdl

Titian Flame (IRE)

99   91

4-y-o ch f Titus Livius (FR)-Golden Choice (Midyan (USA))
Mrs P N Dutfield P J Quinn

Placings:452U6   (4735)
2003/04: 17⁴G, 17⁵HY, 16²S, 16⁰G, 17⁶G,

	Starts	1st	2nd	3rd	Win & Pl
Hurdles	5	0	1	0	1069
Career Total	5	0	1	0	1069

Going:	Sf: 0-2 GS: 0-0 Gd: 0-3 GF: - Fm: 0-0
Distance:	2m/2m3: 0-5 2m4-2m7: 0-0 3m+: 0-0
Track:	LH: 0-2 RH: 0-3 Tight: 0-4 Gall: 0-0
Aids:	Bl: 0-0 Vi: 0-0 Tstrap: 0-0 Ckp: 0-0
Best Rating:	91 11/03 Folk 2m1f110y good Hdl

Not disgraced so far over hurdles; handles good ground or softer.

Tiutchev

116(107h)   (143h)171+

11-y-o b g Soviet Star (USA)-Cut Ahead (Kalaglow)

M C Pipe The Liars Poker Partnership

Placings:4FU/U2311/21F1662/111/1061U5/3154/21F0-422F31   (4624)
2003/04: 20⁴GF, 20²Y, 24²G, 19⁵S, 16³G, 25¹G,

	Starts	1st	2nd	3rd	Win & Pl
Hurdles	1	0	0	0	1500
Chases	5	1	2	1	160804
Career Total	38	12	6	3	444752
171	4/04	Aint	3m1f	A Ch	GD £87000
170	2/03	Asct	2m3f110yA Ch		G-S £59500
170	2/02	Sand	2m	B HCh	G-S £10179
170	2/01	Asct	2m3f110yA Ch		SFT £42575
162	5/00	Punc	2m	Ch	GD £24800
164	3/00	Chel	2m	A Ch	GD £66700
145	1/00	Sand	2m4f110yC Ch		SFT £7785
144	12/99	Extr	2m1f110yC Ch		G-S £7220
152	1/99	Kemp	2m	B(0-145)HHdl	HVY £21280
142	12/98	Chel	2m1f	C(0-135)HHdl	GD £4622
113	11/97	Chel	2m110y	D(0-110)HHdl	G-F £7490
117	10/97	Extr	2m110yE Hdl		GD £2326
			Total win prize-money £341479

Going:	Sf: 0-1 GS: 0-0 Gd: 1-3 GF: - Fm: 1-1
Distance:	2m/2m3: 0-1 2m4-2m7: 0-3 3m+: 1-2
Track:	LH: 1-3 RH: 0-0 Tight: 1-1 Gall: 0-1
Aids:	Bl: 0-0 Vi: 0-0 Tstrap: 0-0 Ckp: 0-0
Best Rating:	171 4/04 Aint 3m1f good Ch

High-class chaser; won the Arkle in 2000; inconsistent since, largely due to problems with colic; excelled himself this season when runner-up in the King George and third in the Queen Mother at Cheltenham; recorded fifth Grade One succss in the Martell Cup at Aintree; effective from 2m to 3m; acts on good and heavy ground.

Tiverton Tryer

77f   56f

6-y-o b g Gran Alba (USA)-Chester Belle (Ballacashtal (CAN))
N A Twiston-Davies C W Jenkins

Placings:0   (0617)
2003/04: 17⁰GF,

	Starts	1st	2nd	3rd	Win & Pl
NH Flat	1	0	0	0	
Career Total	1	0	0	0	

Going:	Sf: 0-0 GS: 0-0 Gd: 0-0 GF: - Fm: 0-1
Distance:	2m/2m3: 0-1 2m4-2m7: 0-0 3m+: 0-0
Track:	LH: 0-0 RH: 0-0 Tight: 0-0 Gall: 0-0
Aids:	Bl: 0-0 Vi: 0-0 Tstrap: 0-0 Ckp: 0-0
Best Rating:	63 6/03 Hrfd 2m1f gd-fm NHF

To The Future (IRE)

93   97

8-y-o ch g Bob Back (USA)-Lady Graduate (IRE) (Le Bavard (FR))
A Parker Mr & Mrs Raymond Anderson Green

Placings:4454/1/P21P-6   (0001)
2003/04: 25⁶G,

	Starts	1st	2nd	3rd	Win & Pl
Chases	1	0	0	0	0
Career Total	10	2	1	0	6406
97	1/03	Ayr	3m1f	E(0-105)HCh	SFT £3867
97	4/02	Carl	3m2f	H Ch	G-S £1430
			Total win prize-money £5298

Going:	Sf: 0-0 GS: 0-0 Gd: 0-1 GF: - Fm: 0-0
Distance:	2m/2m3: 0-0 2m4-2m7: 0-0 3m+: 0-1
Track:	LH: 0-1 RH: 0-0 Tight: 0-0 Gall: 0-0

Aids: Bl: 0-0 Vi: 0-0 Tstrap: 0-0 Ckp: 0-0
Best Rating: 97 1/03 Ayr 3m1f soft Ch

Ex-hunter chaser, won twice in points before completing the hat-trick in a Carlisle hunter chase in April 2002. Won a novices handicap at Ayr in Janury; stays well, acts on soft ground.

To-Day To-Day (IRE)

11-y-o b g Waajib-Balela (African Sky)
T P Tate T P Tate

Placings:263332/P4611P/635654054/U0/025311/0 (0416)
2003/04: 22⁶G,

	Starts	1st	2nd	3rd	Win & Pl
Chases	1	0	0	0	
Career Total	30	4	3	5	17276
104 3/02 Ayr	2m5f110yD(0-110)HCh		SFT	£4121	
97 3/02 Sedg	2m5f	F(0-95)HCh	SFT	£3318	
101 3/99 Newc	2m4f	D(0-110)HHdl	SFT	£2866	
94 3/99 Catt	3m1f110yF(0-100)HHdl		SFT	£2472	
				Total win prize-money	£12777

Going: Sf: 0-0 GS: 0-0 Gd: 0-1 GF: - Fm: 0-0
Distance: 2m/2m3: 0-0 2m4-2m7: 0-1 3m+: 0-0
Track: LH: 0-0 RH: 0-1 Tight: 0-1 Gall: 0-0
Aids: Bl: 0-0 Vi: 0-1 Tstrap: 0-0 Ckp: 0-0
Best Rating: 104 3/02 Ayr 2m5f110y soft Ch

Toad Hall

92   94

10-y-o b g Henbit (USA)-Candlebright (Lighter)
Mrs L B Normile John Findlay

Placings:60/21/P4-6P343U (1428)
2003/04: 16⁶S, 24²PGF, 20³GF, 20⁴GF, 16³GF, 24⁴UG,

	Starts	1st	2nd	3rd	Win & Pl
Chases	6	0	0	2	2468
Career Total	12	1	1	2	6716
87 8/00 Prth	2m4f110yE Hdl		GD	£2555	
				Total win prize-money	£2555

Going: Sf: 0-1 GS: 0-0 Gd: 0-1 GF: - Fm: 0-4
Distance: 2m/2m3: 0-2 2m4-2m7: 0-2 3m+: 0-2
Track: LH: 0-1 RH: 0-5 Tight: 0-3 Gall: 0-0
Aids: Bl: 0-0 Vi: 0-0 Tstrap: 0-0 Ckp: 0-0
Best Rating: 94 7/03 MRas 2m4f gd-fm Ch

Plating-class hurdler/chaser; has shown littlefor current connections; acts on fast.

Toberoe Commotion (IRE)

90   75

6-y-o b g Great Commotion (USA)-Fionn Varragh (IRE) (Tender King)
B J Llewellyn (W R Muir 27/9) Martin Brown

Placings:40600 (4781)
2003/04: 16⁴GF, 17⁰G, 17⁵GF, 17⁹G, 16⁹G,

	Starts	1st	2nd	3rd	Win & Pl
Hurdles	5	0	0	0	0
Career Total	5	0	0	0	0

Going: Sf: 0-0 GS: 0-0 Gd: 0-0 GF: - Fm: 0-2
Distance: 2m/2m3: 0-5 2m4-2m7: 0-0 3m+: 0-0
Track: LH: 0-1 RH: 0-4 Tight: 0-3 Gall: 0-1
Aids: Bl: 0-0 Vi: 0-0 Tstrap: 0-0 Ckp: 0-0
Best Rating: 75 9/03 Plum 2m gd-fm Hdl

Tobesure (IRE)

97(106c)   (109c)101

10-y-o b g Asir-Princess Citrus (IRE) (Auction Ring (USA))
J I A Charlton Richard Nixon

Placings:250352/64124460/4024P32F/50123603200-212P05236 (4948)
2003/04: 22²F, 25¹G, 25²S, 25⁵GS, 24⁹GS, 22⁵GS, 24²G, 22³G, 27⁶GS,

	Starts	1st	2nd	3rd	Win & Pl
Hurdles	6	0	2	1	2193
Chases	3	1	1	0	3203
Career Total	42	3	10	5	21302
101 11/03 Hexm	3m1f	E(0-105)HCh	GD	£2340	
93 10/02 Kels	2m6f110yE(0-105)HHdl		G-F	£3549	
96 10/00 Kels	2m6f110yE Hdl		GD	£2800	
				Total win prize-money	£8689

Going: Sf: 0-1 GS: 0-4 Gd: 1-3 GF: - Fm: 0-0
Distance: 2m/2m3: 0-0 2m4-2m7: 0-3 3m+: 1-6
Track: LH: 1-8 RH: 0-4 Tight: 0-4 Gall: 0-1
Aids: Bl: 0-0 Vi: 0-0 Tstrap: 0-0 Ckp: 0-0
Best Rating: 101 4/04 Kels 2m6f110y good Hdl

Modest hurdler; stays three miles; goes well at Kelso.

Tod's Brother

10-y-o b g Gildoran-Versina (Leander)
Mrs D M Grissell A W K Merriam

Placings:P (4373)
2003/04: 24⁰PG,

	Starts	1st	2nd	3rd	Win & Pl
Chases	1	0	0	0	
Career Total	1	0	0	0	

Going: Sf: 0-0 GS: 0-0 Gd: 0-0 GF: - Fm: 0-0
Distance: 2m/2m3: 0-0 2m4-2m7: 0-0 3m+: 0-1
Track: LH: 0-1 RH: 0-0 Tight: 0-0 Gall: 0-0
Aids: Bl: 0-0 Vi: 0-0 Tstrap: 0-0 Ckp: 0-0

Toejam

100   76

11-y-o ch g Move Off-Cheeky Pigeon (Brave Invader (USA))
R E Barr Mrs R E Barr

Placings:0/45-25606 (4258)
2003/04: 17²S, 17⁵GS, 16⁸GS, 20⁹G, 16⁶GF,

	Starts	1st	2nd	3rd	Win & Pl
Hurdles	5	0	1	0	1006
Career Total	8	0	1	0	1006

Going: Sf: 0-1 GS: 0-2 Gd: 0-1 GF: - Fm: 0-1
Distance: 2m/2m3: 0-4 2m4-2m7: 0-1 3m+: 0-0
Track: LH: 0-4 RH: 0-1 Tight: 0-4 Gall: 0-1
Aids: Bl: 0-0 Vi: 0-0 Tstrap: 0-0 Ckp: 0-0
Best Rating: 76 2/04 Muss 2m4f good Hdl

Plating-class hurdler; acts with cut in the ground..

Toemac

107f   116+f

5-y-o b g Slip Anchor-Bobanlyn (IRE) (Dance Of Life (USA))
M Bradstock J Macleod

Placings:0511 (4636)
2003/04: 16⁵S, 16⁵G, 16¹G, 17¹G,

	Starts	1st	2nd	3rd	Win & Pl
NH Flat	4	2	0	0	4396
Career Total	4	2	0	0	4396
116 4/04 Tntn	2m1f	H NHF	GD	£1897	
100 3/04 Kemp	2m	H NHF	GD	£2499	
				Total win prize-money £4396

Going: Sf: 0-1 GS: 0-0 Gd: 2-3 GF: - Fm: 0-0
Distance: 2m/2m3: 2-4 2m4-2m7: 0-0 3m+: 0-0
Track: LH: 0-0 RH: 1-3 Tight: 0-0 Gall: 0-1
Aids: Bl: 0-0 Vi: 0-0 Tstrap: 0-0 Ckp: 0-0
Best Rating: 116 4/04 Tntn 2m1f good NHF

Dual bumper winner; suited by good ground; should do well over hurdles.

Tohunga

9-y-o b/br g Rudimentary (USA)-Refinancing (USA) (Forli (ARG))
C Roberts F J Ayres

Placings:1/2022/0/P/P (0768)
2003/04: 22⁰GF,

	Starts	1st	2nd	3rd	Win & Pl
Hurdles	1	0	0	0	
Career Total	8	1	3	0	4019
99 4/99 MRas	1m5f110yH NHF		GD	£1567	
				Total win prize-money £1567

Going: Sf: 0-0 GS: 0-0 Gd: 0-0 GF: - Fm: 0-1
Distance: 2m/2m3: 0-0 2m4-2m7: 0-1 3m+: 0-0
Track: LH: 0-1 RH: 0-0 Tight: 0-0 Gall: 0-0
Aids: Bl: 0-0 Vi: 0-0 Tstrap: 0-1 Ckp: 0-0
Best Rating: 116 10/99 Chel 2m110y good NHF

Toi Express (IRE)

103(103h)   (113+h)124+

8-y-o ch g Phardante (FR)-Toi Figures (Deep Run)
P J Hobbs D F P Racing

Placings:5S/2563/F2311-12111F3 (2078)
2003/04: 19¹G, 19²GF, 19¹F, 17¹GF, 16¹F, 16²GF, 16³G,

	Starts	1st	2nd	3rd	Win & Pl
Hurdles	5	4	1	0	14916
Chases	2	0	0	1	1036
Career Total	18	6	3	3	27767
113 10/03 Winc	2m	E Hdl	FRM	£3269	
116 10/03 Extr	2m1f	D Hdl	G-F	£4208	
113 9/03 Extr	2m3f	E Hdl	G-F	£3206	
100 8/03 NAbb	2m3f	E Hdl	G-F	£3402	
103 9/02 Worc	2m	E Ch	GD	£4920	
95 9/02 NAbb	2m110y E Ch		GD	£3966	
				Total win prize-money £22274

Going: Sf: 0-0 GS: 0-0 Gd: 0-1 GF: - Fm: 4-6
Distance: 2m/2m3: 4-7 2m4-2m7: 0-0 3m+: 0-0
Track: LH: 0-2 RH: 3-3 Tight: 0-1 Gall: 0-0
Aids: Bl: 0-0 Vi: 0-0 Tstrap: 0-0 Ckp: 0-0
Best Rating: 124 11/03 Chep 2m110y gd-fm Ch

Fair chaser/hurdler; absent for a year before winning weakly contested 2m 3f novices' hurdle at Newton Abbot in August 2003; has since won twice at Exeter and at Wincanton; unlucky not to make winning return to fences when falling at the last at Chepstow in November; best at around 2m; acts on a sound surface.

Tojoneski

5-y-o b g Emperor Jones (USA)-Sampower Lady (Rock City)
I W McInnes (K A Morgan 27/12) M Shirley

Placings:UF   (2995)
2003/04: 17^UG, 16^FGS,

	Starts	1st	2nd	3rd	Win & Pl
Hurdles	2	0	0	0	
Career Total	2	0	0	0	

Going:	Sf: 0-0 GS: 0-1 Gd: 0-1 GF: - Fm: 0-0
Distance:	2m/2m3: 0-2 2m4-2m7: 0-0 3m+: 0-0
Track:	LH: 0-0 RH: 0-2 Tight: 0-1 Gall: 0-0
Aids:	Bl: 0-0 Vi: 0-0 Tstrap: 0-0 Ckp: 0-0

Tolcea (IRE)

76   **38**

5-y-o ch g Barathea (IRE)-Mosaique Bleue (Shirley Heights)
W Storey S Hogg

Placings:P-0600   (1895)
2003/04: 20⁰G, 17⁶G, 20⁰GF, 20⁰GS,

	Starts	1st	2nd	3rd	Win & Pl
Hurdles	4	0	0	0	0
Career Total	5	0	0	0	0

Going:	Sf: 0-0 GS: 0-1 Gd: 0-2 GF: - Fm: 0-1
Distance:	2m/2m3: 0-1 2m4-2m7: 0-3 3m+: 0-0
Track:	LH: 0-3 RH: 0-1 Tight: 0-1 Gall: 0-0
Aids:	Bl: 0-0 Vi: 0-0 Tstrap: 0-0 Ckp: 0-0
Best Rating:	51 5/03 Ctml good Hdl

Toledo Sun

98   **98**

4-y-o b g Zamindar (USA)-Shafir (IRE) (Shaadi (USA))
V Smith (H J Collingridge 17/2) Monkey A Month Racing

Placings:5P   (4504)
2003/04: 17⁵GS, 17^PG,

	Starts	1st	2nd	3rd	Win & Pl
Hurdles	2	0	0	0	0
Career Total	2	0	0	0	0

Going:	Sf: 0-0 GS: 0-1 Gd: 0-1 GF: - Fm: 0-0
Distance:	2m/2m3: 0-2 2m4-2m7: 0-0 3m+: 0-0
Track:	LH: 0-0 RH: 0-2 Tight: 0-1 Gall: 0-0
Aids:	Bl: 0-0 Vi: 0-0 Tstrap: 0-0 Ckp: 0-0
Best Rating:	80 2/04 Folk 2m1f110y gd-sft Hdl

Tollbrae (IRE)

104(107h)   (107h)**120+**

7-y-o gr g Supreme Leader-Miss Henrietta (IRE) (Step
Together (USA))
N J Henderson R A Bartlett

Placings:14/324-2421   (4791)
2003/04: 20²GS, 20⁴GS, 16²G, 20¹G,

	Starts	1st	2nd	3rd	Win & Pl
Hurdles	1	0	1	0	790
Chases	3	1	1	0	6954
Career Total	9	2	3	1	11300
120	4/04	Plum	2m4f	F Ch	GD	£3178
123	3/02	Hrfd	2m1f	H NHF	SFT	£1701
				Total win prize-money £4880

Going:	Sf: 0-0 GS: 0-2 Gd: 1-2 GF: - Fm: 0-0
Distance:	2m/2m3: 0-1 **2m4-2m7: 1-3** 3m+: 0-0
Track:	**LH: 1-3** RH: 0-0 **Tight: 1-1** Gall: 0-1
Aids:	Bl: 0-0 Vi: 0-0 Tstrap: 0-0 Ckp: 0-0
Best Rating:	123 3/02 Hrfd 2m1f soft NHF

Fair chaser/hurdler; stays two and a half miles; acts on good
ground, but looks better on soft.

Tom Barry (IRE)

8-y-o ch g Samhoi (USA)-Royal Custody (Reform)
K D Giles K D Giles

Placings:P   (0350)
2003/04: 21^PGF,

	Starts	1st	2nd	3rd	Win & Pl
Chases	1	0	0	0	
Career Total	1	0	0	0	

Going:	Sf: 0-0 GS: 0-0 Gd: 0-0 GF: - Fm: 0-1
Distance:	2m/2m3: 0-0 2m4-2m7: 0-1 3m+: 0-0
Track:	LH: 0-0 RH: 0-1 Tight: 0-1 Gall: 0-0
Aids:	Bl: 0-0 Vi: 0-0 Tstrap: 0-0 Ckp: 0-0

Tom Cobbler (IRE)

10-y-o ch g Zaffaran (USA)-Po Bo Pu (Pollerton)
Mrs C S Hall Christopher Hall

Placings:6213/133144/1U244505/005/3   (0352)
2003/04: 31³GF,

	Starts	1st	2nd	3rd	Win & Pl
Chases	1	0	0	1	536
Career Total	22	4	2	4	15810
114	9/00	Worc	2m7f110yD Ch		G-F	£4056
114	1/00	Folk	2m6f110yE Hdl		SFT	£2573
102	9/99	Worc	2m		E Hdl	SFT	£2455
110	4/99	NAbb	2m1f		H NHF	SFT	£1397
					Total win prize-money £10481

Going:	Sf: 0-0 GS: 0-0 Gd: 0-0 GF: - Fm: 0-1
Distance:	2m/2m3: 0-0 2m4-2m7: 0-0 3m+: 0-1
Track:	LH: 0-0 RH: 0-1 Tight: 0-1 Gall: 0-0
Aids:	Bl: 0-0 Vi: 0-0 Tstrap: 0-0 Ckp: 0-0
Best Rating:	114 9/00 Worc 2m7f110y gd-fm Ch

Tom Costalot (IRE)

105   (84h)**129**

9-y-o gr g Black Minstrel-Hop Picker (USA) (Plugged Nickle
(USA))
Mrs Susan Nock Gerard Nock

Placings:6055/B420/351112/311600-P326P   (4450)
2003/04: 20^PGS, 24³GS, 21²G, 20⁶G, 24^PGS,

	Starts	1st	2nd	3rd	Win & Pl
Chases	5	0	1	1	9369
Career Total	25	5	3	3	42705
129	12/02	Chel	2m5f	E(0-125)HCh	GD	£9352
129	11/02	Wwck	2m4f110yD(0-125)HCh	GD	£4563
127	2/02	Donc	2m3f110yE(0-105)HCh	SFT	£3302
109	12/01	Leic	2m4f110yD(0-125)HCh	GD	£7672
112	12/01	Winc	2m5f	F(0-105)HCh	GD	£3588
				Total win prize-money £28477

Going:	Sf: 0-0 GS: 0-1 Gd: 0-4 GF: - Fm: 0-0
Distance:	2m/2m3: 0-0 2m4-2m7: 0-3 3m+: 0-2
Track:	LH: 0-2 RH: 0-3 Tight: 0-0 Gall: 0-1
Aids:	Bl: 0-0 Vi: 0-0 Tstrap: 0-0 Ckp: 0-0
Best Rating:	129 1/04 Chel 2m5f good Ch

Fair handicap chaser; jumps well; suited by trips of around
two and a half miles; probably best on a sound surface, but
handles soft.

Tom Jelly

73f   **35f**

6-y-o b g Elmaamul (USA)-Primitive Gift (Primitive Rising
(USA))
A Crook M Wainright

Placings:0U   (3474)
2003/04: 16⁰GS, 16^UGF,

	Starts	1st	2nd	3rd	Win & Pl
NH Flat	2	0	0	0	
Career Total	2	0	0	0	

Going:	Sf: 0-0 GS: 0-1 Gd: 0-0 GF: - Fm: 0-1
Distance:	2m/2m3: 0-2 2m4-2m7: 0-0 3m+: 0-0
Track:	LH: 0-1 RH: 0-1 Tight: 0-1 Gall: 0-0
Aids:	Bl: 0-0 Vi: 0-0 Tstrap: 0-0 Ckp: 0-0
Best Rating:	35 1/04 Weth 2m gd-sft NHF

Tom Paddington

115   **142**

9-y-o b g Rock Hopper-Mayfair Minx (St Columbus)
H Morrison M S Wilson Mrs Wilson (camp Farm Racing)

Placings:112/1F0P   (4052)
2003/04: 16¹GS, 16^FS, 16⁰G, 24^PG,

	Starts	1st	2nd	3rd	Win & Pl
Hurdles	4	2	1	0	12847
Career Total	7	3	1	0	21072
142	11/03	Newb	2m110y	C(0-130)HHdl	G-S	£12847
142	12/98	Chel	2m1f	C Hdl	GD	£4576
126	12/98	Winc	2m	E Hdl	G-S	£2288
				Total win prize-money £19712

Going:	Sf: 0-1 GS: 1-1 Gd: 0-2 GF: - Fm: 0-0
Distance:	**2m/2m3: 1-3** 2m4-2m7: 0-0 3m+: 0-1
Track:	**LH: 1-2** RH: 0-2 Tight: 0-0 **Gall: 1-2**
Aids:	Bl: 0-0 Vi: 0-0 Tstrap: 0-0 Ckp: 0-0
Best Rating:	142 11/03 Newb 2m110y gd-sft Hdl

Useful hurdler; also useful stayer on the Flat; progressed
well over hurdles until breaking down in February 1999; winner on the Flat when returning in October 2002 and on first
run back over hurdles at Newbury in November 2003; effective at two miles, but may stay further; suited by softish
ground.

Tom Pinch (IRE)

15-y-o b g Mandalus-Spanish Royale (Royal Buck)
Mark Bennison Lord Yarborough

Placings:2/00/53FF3331U/P4/P23/P6P3/344UP-P   (0031)
2003/04: 21^PG,

	Starts	1st	2nd	3rd	Win & Pl
Chases	1	0	0	0	
Career Total	27	1	2	7	8104
95	4/99	Uttx	3m	G(0-90)HCh	G-S	£2207
				Total win prize-money £2208

Going:	Sf: 0-0 GS: 0-0 Gd: 0-1 GF: - Fm: 0-0
Distance:	2m/2m3: 0-0 2m4-2m7: 0-1 3m+: 0-0
Track:	LH: 0-1 RH: 0-0 Tight: 0-0 Gall: 0-1
Aids:	Bl: 0-1 Vi: 0-0 Tstrap: 0-0 Ckp: 0-0
Best Rating:	104 4/99 MRas 2m4f soft Ch

Tom's Man

10-y-o ch g Milieu-Lorna's Choice (Oats)
G F White F V White

Placings:*B*0P/0/P04/P3PPP/P　　(3886)
2003/04: 24PG,

	Starts	1st	2nd	3rd	Win & Pl
Chases	1	0	0		
Career Total	13	0	0	1	477

Going:	Sf: 0-0 GS: 0-0 Gd: 0-1 GF: - Fm: 0-0
Distance:	2m/2m3: 0-0 2m4-2m7: 0-0 3m+: 0-1
Track:	LH: 0-0 RH: 0-1 Tight: 0-1 Gall: 0-0
Aids:	Bl: 0-0 Vi: 0-0 Tstrap: 0-1 Ckp: 0-0
Best Rating:	77　4/01　Weth　2m　　gd-sft　Ch

Tom's Prize

108(111h)　　　　(130+h)130
9-y-o ch g Gunner B-Pandora's Prize (Royal Vulcan)
J L Spearing　Mrs P Joynes

Placings:0054/U/2514241/F22F110-P102412　　(4871)
2003/04: 24PGS, 261G, 26PGS, 252S, 24GGS, 241GS, 24PS,

	Starts	1st	2nd	3rd	Win & Pl
Hurdles	3	2	1	0	8506
Chases	4	0	1	0	3712
Career Total	26	6	6	0	59352
134	3/04	Newb	3m110y E Hdl		G-S	£4621
134	11/03	Sthl	3m2f	E Hdl	GD	£2982
125	3/03	Donc	3m	B(0-145)HCh		£22750
130	2/03	Leic	2m7f110yD(0-125)HCh		SFT	£8528
116	4/02	Strf	3m	D Ch		£4322
109	12/01	Towc	2m6f	D Ch		HVY	£5089

Total win prize-money £48295

Going:	Sf: 0-2 GS: 1-4 Gd: 1-1 GF: - Fm: 0-0
Distance:	2m/2m3: 0-0 2m4-2m7: 0-0 **3m+: 2-7**
Track:	**LH: 2-7** RH: 0-0 Tight: 0-2 **Gall: 1-2**
Aids:	Bl: 0-0 Vi: 0-0 Tstrap: 0-0 Ckp: 0-0
Best Rating:	**134**　3/04　Newb　3m110y　gd-sft　Hdl

Useful handicap chaser/hurdler; best when able to dominate; stays three miles; acts on any ground; tough.

Tom's River (IRE)

12-y-o ch g Over The River (FR)-Nesford (Walshford)
Chris Nenadich (R J Hodges 13/5) Chris Nenadich

Placings:120/200/U11P4/4213F/023UU/45415P/5364PPP4
3-36P　　(3845)
2003/04: 19GG, 25RGF, 25PS,

	Starts	1st	2nd	3rd	Win & Pl
Chases	3	0	0	1	528
Career Total	39	5	4	5	25335
104	1/02	Catt	3m1f110yF(0-100)HCh	G-S	£3514
122	11/00	Catt	3m1f110yF(0-110)HCh	GD	£5004
120	1/99	Catt	3m1f110yF(0-110)HCh	SFT	£3096
101	1/99	Catt	3m1f110y E Ch	GD	£2814
99	2/97	Carl	2m1f	H NHF	SFT	£1035

Total win prize-money £15464

Going:	Sf: 0-0 GS: 0-1 Gd: 0-1 GF: - Fm: 0-1
Distance:	2m/2m3: 0-0 2m4-2m7: 0-1 3m+: 0-2
Track:	LH: 0-0 RH: 0-3 Tight: 0-0 Gall: 0-0
Aids:	Bl: 0-0 Vi: 0-0 Tstrap: 0-0 Ckp: 0-0
Best Rating:	122　10/00　Kels　2m6f110y　soft　Ch

Moderate chaser; fair sort in his prime, but on the downgrade; goes well at Catterick; suited by easy ground.

Tomcappagh (IRE)

103　　94　　88
13-y-o br g Riberetto-Shuil Suas (Menelek)

Mrs S Wall　Mrs S Wall

Placings:F3P3P/4312/F55P/P0UP323P3/0045133U2CP3P/
PP64PP-P　　(0437)
2003/04: 22PGF,

	Starts	1st	2nd	3rd	Win & Pl
Chases	1	0	0	0	
Career Total	42	2	3	9	12787
86	12/01	Plum	3m2f	F(0-100)HCh	SFT	£4127
103	2/99	Folk	2m5f	H Ch	G-S	£1096

Total win prize-money £5224

Going:	Sf: 0-0 GS: 0-0 Gd: 0-0 GF: - Fm: 0-1
Distance:	2m/2m3: 0-0 2m4-2m7: 0-1 3m+: 0-0
Track:	LH: 0-0 RH: 0-0 Tight: 0-0 Gall: 0-0
Aids:	Bl: 0-0 Vi: 0-0 Tstrap: 0-0 Ckp: 0-0
Best Rating:	110　3/99　Strf　3m　　heavy　Ch

Moderate staying chaser, effective in soft ground, stays three miles-two.

Tomenoso

106　　　　115+
6-y-o b g Teenoso (USA)-Guarded Expression (Siberian Express (USA))
Mrs S J Smith　Keith Nicholson

Placings:44223/30111-2551　　(4729)
2003/04: 20²S, 17⁵G, 20⁵G, 20¹G,

	Starts	1st	2nd	3rd	Win & Pl
Hurdles	4	1	1	0	9786
Career Total	14	4	3	2	26721
115	4/04	Carl	2m4f	D(0-125)HHdl	GD	£7670
102	4/03	Carl	2m4f	D(0-125)HHdl	G-F	£7182
95	3/03	Sedg	2m5f110yE(0-110)HHdl	GD	£3507
101	3/03	Weth	2m	E(0-110)HHdl	GD	£3464

Total win prize-money £21825

Going:	Sf: 0-1 GS: 0-0 Gd: 1-3 GF: - Fm: 0-0
Distance:	2m/2m3: 0-1 **2m4-2m7: 1-3** 3m+: 0-0
Track:	LH: 0-2 **RH: 1-2** Tight: 0-0 Gall: 0-1
Aids:	Bl: 0-0 Vi: 0-0 Tstrap: 0-0 Ckp: 0-0
Best Rating:	115　4/04　Carl　2m4f　　good　Hdl

Modest hurdler; progressive form in 2003 completing a hat-trick at Wetherby, Sedgefield and Carlisle; best on a sound surface but handled the mud; effective at two miles five and should stay further.

Tomfoolary (IRE)

74
7-y-o ch g Erin's Isle-Liberty Bird (USA) (Danzatore (CAN))
J A B Old　Mrs C H Antrobus

Placings:3/0350/0-0PPP　　(4676)
2003/04: 16⁶G, 24PS, 19PGS, 22PG,

	Starts	1st	2nd	3rd	Win & Pl
Hurdles	3	0	0	0	0
Chases	1	0	0	0	0
Career Total	10	0	0	0	677

Going:	Sf: 0-1 GS: 0-1 Gd: 0-2 GF: - Fm: 0-0
Distance:	2m/2m3: 0-1 2m4-2m7: 0-2 3m+: 0-1
Track:	LH: 0-2 RH: 0-2 Tight: 0-0 Gall: 0-1
Aids:	Bl: 0-0 Vi: 0-0 Tstrap: 0-0 Ckp: 0-0
Best Rating:	94　4/01　Slig　2m　　heavy　NHF

Tommy Carson

103　　94
9-y-o b g Last Tycoon-Ivory Palm (USA) (Sir Ivor (USA))
Jamie Poulton　J Logan

Placings:035P/5424P3045/24/3013352P13440/41P (4667)
2003/04: 24⁴GS, 20¹G, 24PS,

	Starts	1st	2nd	3rd	Win & Pl
Chases	3	1	0	0	5155
Career Total	31	3	3	6	20408
94	3/04	Plum	2m4f	E(0-110)HCh	GD	£4719
98	1/02	Plum	2m4f	E(0-105)HCh	SFT	£3360
95	9/01	Plum	2m4f	D(0-115)HCh	G-F	£4075

Total win prize-money £12155

Going:	Sf: 0-1 GS: 0-1 Gd: 1-1 GF: - Fm: 0-0
Distance:	2m/2m3: 0-0 2m4-2m7: 1-1 3m+: 0-2
Track:	**LH: 1-2** RH: 0-1 **Tight: 1-3** Gall: 0-0
Aids:	Bl: 0-0 Vi: 0-0 Tstrap: 0-0 Ckp: 0-0
Best Rating:	**98**　1/02　Plum　2m4f　　soft　Ch

Plating-class chaser; stays two and a half miles and acts on soft ground; not the best of jumpers.

Tommy Nutter (IRE)

75　　　　40
4-y-o b g Desert Style (IRE)-Ahakista (IRE) (Persian Bold)
R Brotherton　W M Rollett

Placings:0　　(1007)
2003/04: 17⁰G,

	Starts	1st	2nd	3rd	Win & Pl
Hurdles	1	0	0	0	
Career Total	1	0	0	0	

Going:	Sf: 0-0 GS: 0-0 Gd: 0-0 GF: - Fm: 0-0
Distance:	2m/2m3: 0-0 2m4-2m7: 0-0 3m+: 0-0
Track:	LH: 0-1 RH: 0-0 Tight: 0-1 Gall: 0-0
Aids:	Bl: 0-0 Vi: 0-0 Tstrap: 0-0 Ckp: 0-0
Best Rating:	40　8/03　Bang　2m1f　　good　Hdl

Tommy Spar

70f　　34f
4-y-o b g Silver Owl-Lady Of Mine (Cruise Missile)
P Bowen　Ralph Morgans

Placings:0　　(3446)
2003/04: 16⁰G,

	Starts	1st	2nd	3rd	Win & Pl
NH Flat	1	0	0	0	
Career Total	1	0	0	0	

Going:	Sf: 0-0 GS: 0-0 Gd: 0-1 GF: - Fm: 0-0
Distance:	2m/2m3: 0-1 2m4-2m7: 0-0 3m+: 0-0
Track:	LH: 0-0 RH: 0-1 Tight: 0-0 Gall: 0-0
Aids:	Bl: 0-0 Vi: 0-0 Tstrap: 0-0 Ckp: 0-0
Best Rating:	38　1/04　Ludl　2m　　good　NHF

Tommy Trooper

(92c)　　(88c)102
9-y-o ch g Infantry-Steady Saunter Vii (Damsire Unregistered)
Miss K M George　Exterior Profiles Ltd

Placings:6316/14/0F062-0　　(0803)
2003/04: 21⁰G,

	Starts	1st	2nd	3rd	Win & Pl
Hurdles	1	0	0	0	
Career Total	12	2	1	1	5514
116	2/02	Font	2m2f110yE Hdl	HVY	£2614
120	2/00	Winc	2m	H NHF	GD	£1575

Total win prize-money £4190

Going: Sf: 0-0 GS: 0-0 Gd: 0-1 GF: - Fm: 0-0
Distance: 2m/2m3: 0-0 2m4-2m7: 0-1 3m+: 0-0
Track: LH: 0-1 RH: 0-0 Tight: 0-0 Gall: 0-0
Aids: Bl: 0-0 Vi: 0-0 Tstrap: 0-0 Ckp: 0-0
Best Rating: 120 4/00 Aint 2m110y good NHF

Moderate hurdler; stays two and a quarter miles; has won on good ground and heavy.

Tomorrows Treasure
35f

4-y-o ch f Bahamian Bounty-Yesterday's Song (Shirley Heights)
C W Fairhurst David Hawes

Placings:0   (2482)
2003/04: 13⁹GF,

	Starts	1st	2nd	3rd	Win & Pl
NH Flat	1	0	0	0	
Career Total	1	0	0	0	

Going: Sf: 0-0 GS: 0-0 Gd: 0-0 GF: - Fm: 0-1
Distance: 2m/2m3: 0-0 2m4-2m7: 0-0 3m+: 0-0
Track: LH: 0-0 RH: 0-0 Tight: 0-0 Gall: 0-0
Aids: Bl: 0-0 Vi: 0-0 Tstrap: 0-0 Ckp: 0-0
Best Rating: 38 11/03 Donc 1m5f gd-fm NHF

Toms Gone Grey (IRE)
102   **94**

5-y-o gr g Gothland (FR)-Cpv Lady (Le Moss)
R H Alner T H Chadney

Placings:04060335P   (4897)
2003/04: 16⁹G, 19⁴G, 20⁰G, 17⁶G, 19⁰S, 17³G, 19³GS, 22⁵G, 22⁶G,

	Starts	1st	2nd	3rd	Win & Pl
NH Flat	1	0	0	0	0
Hurdles	8	0	0	2	1320
Career Total	9	0	0	2	1320

Going: Sf: 0-1 GS: 0-0 Gd: 0-7 GF: - Fm: 0-0
Distance: 2m/2m3: 0-5 2m4-2m7: 0-4 3m+: 0-0
Track: LH: 0-3 RH: 0-5 Tight: 0-4 Gall: 0-1
Aids: Bl: 0-0 Vi: 0-0 Tstrap: 0-0 Ckp: 0-0
Best Rating: 92 3/04 Folk 2m1f110y good Hdl

Tomsk (IRE)

4-y-o b g Definite Article-Merry Twinkle (Martinmas)
A Berry Alan Berry

Placings:P   (2528)
2003/04: 16⁶GS,

	Starts	1st	2nd	3rd	Win & Pl
Hurdles	1	0	0	0	
Career Total	1	0	0	0	

Going: Sf: 0-0 GS: 0-1 Gd: 0-0 GF: - Fm: 0-0
Distance: 2m/2m3: 0-1 2m4-2m7: 0-0 3m+: 0-0
Track: LH: 0-1 RH: 0-0 Tight: 0-1 Gall: 0-0
Aids: Bl: 0-0 Vi: 0-0 Tstrap: 0-0 Ckp: 0-0

Tomsway

5-y-o b g Relief Pitcher-Thank Yourself (Le Bavard (FR))
Mrs P A Tetley Brian Tetley

Placings:PP6   (4755)
2003/04: 20⁵GS, 24⁵G, 21⁶G,

	Starts	1st	2nd	3rd	Win & Pl
Hurdles	3	0	0	0	0
Career Total	3	0	0	0	0

Going: Sf: 0-0 GS: 0-1 Gd: 0-2 GF: - Fm: 0-0
Distance: 2m/2m3: 0-0 2m4-2m7: 0-2 3m+: 0-1
Track: LH: 0-1 RH: 0-2 Tight: 0-2 Gall: 0-0
Aids: Bl: 0-0 Vi: 0-0 Tstrap: 0-0 Ckp: 0-0

Tomwontpayalot
101   **85+**

5-y-o gr g Overbury (IRE)-Alice Smith (Alias Smith (USA))
M C Pipe D A Johnson

Placings:22-2PFPP   (4749)
2003/04: 16²GF, 19⁵GS, 16⁶G, 17⁶G, 25⁵G,

	Starts	1st	2nd	3rd	Win & Pl
Hurdles	5	0	1	0	1074
Career Total	7	0	3	0	2375

Going: Sf: 0-0 GS: 0-1 Gd: 0-3 GF: - Fm: 0-1
Distance: 2m/2m3: 0-3 2m4-2m7: 0-1 3m+: 0-1
Track: LH: 0-3 RH: 0-1 Tight: 0-0 Gall: 0-1
Aids: Bl: 0-0 Vi: 0-0 Tstrap: 0-0 Ckp: 0-0
Best Rating: 99 4/03 Asct 2m110y good NHF

Plating-class hurdler; acts on a sound surface.

Toni's Pet

4-y-o b g Wizard King-Dannistar (Puissance)
B N Pollock P Andrew & M Brandwood

Placings:P   (1901)
2003/04: 16⁶GF,

	Starts	1st	2nd	3rd	Win & Pl
Hurdles	1	0	0	0	
Career Total	1	0	0	0	

Going: Sf: 0-0 GS: 0-0 Gd: 0-0 GF: - Fm: 0-1
Distance: 2m/2m3: 0-1 2m4-2m7: 0-0 3m+: 0-0
Track: LH: 0-0 RH: 0-1 Tight: 0-0 Gall: 0-1
Aids: Bl: 0-0 Vi: 0-0 Tstrap: 0-0 Ckp: 0-0

Tonoco
113   **128**

11-y-o b g Teenoso (USA)-Lady Shoco (Montekin)
Mrs S J Smith Trevor Hemmings

Placings:1/41116P/50211F2/PPP/F2132P01-62253 (3822)
2003/04: 21⁶GS, 25²G, 24²GS, 24⁴S, 24³S,

	Starts	1st	2nd	3rd	Win & Pl
Chases	5	0	2	1	8636
Career Total	30	8	6	2	69364
123	4/03	Weth	3m1f	B(0-150)HCh	G-F £11362
118	12/02	Hayd	3m	D(0-125)HCh	SFT £6223
132	3/01	MRas	2m1f110yD	Ch	G-S £5027
132	2/01	Carl	2m	D Ch	SFT £4536
138	2/99	Weth	2m	A Hdl	GD £9509
133	1/99	Hntg	2m110y	D Hdl	SFT £2762

132	12/98	Hayd	2m	D Hdl	SFT £2866
106	4/98	Ayr	2m	H NHF	GD £3598

Total win prize-money £45887

Going: Sf: 0-2 GS: 0-2 Gd: 0-1 GF: - Fm: 0-0
Distance: 2m/2m3: 0-0 2m4-2m7: 0-1 3m+: 0-4
Track: LH: 0-5 RH: 0-0 Tight: 0-1 Gall: 0-1
Aids: Bl: 0-0 Vi: 0-0 Tstrap: 0-0 Ckp: 0-0
Best Rating: 138 2/99 Weth 2m good Hdl

Fair chaser; stays three miles; seems to go on most ground; goes well at Haydock; has been tubed.

Tony's Time

10-y-o b g Tina's Pet-Time Warp (Town And Country)
Mrs Sarah Faulks Mrs Sarah Faulks

Placings:P/P/6   (0151)
2003/04: 24⁶GF,

	Starts	1st	2nd	3rd	Win & Pl
Chases	1	0	0	0	
Career Total	3	0	0	0	

Going: Sf: 0-0 GS: 0-0 Gd: 0-0 GF: - Fm: 0-1
Distance: 2m/2m3: 0-0 2m4-2m7: 0-0 3m+: 0-1
Track: LH: 0-1 RH: 0-0 Tight: 0-0 Gall: 0-0
Aids: Bl: 0-0 Vi: 0-0 Tstrap: 0-0 Ckp: 0-0
Best Rating: 61 5/03 Chep 3m gd-fm Ch

Too Phar To Touch

9-y-o br m Wace (USA)-Carew Mill (Hubble Bubble)
Miss F Goldsworthy Miss F Goldsworthy

Placings:P   (0294)
2003/04: 20⁶GS,

	Starts	1st	2nd	3rd	Win & Pl
Chases	1	0	0	0	
Career Total	1	0	0	0	

Going: Sf: 0-0 GS: 0-1 Gd: 0-0 GF: - Fm: 0-0
Distance: 2m/2m3: 0-0 2m4-2m7: 0-1 3m+: 0-0
Track: LH: 0-1 RH: 0-0 Tight: 0-1 Gall: 0-0
Aids: Bl: 0-0 Vi: 0-0 Tstrap: 0-0 Ckp: 0-0

Too Technical (IRE)
104   **95**

9-y-o b g Archway (IRE)-Another Side (Bold Lad (IRE))
J M Jefferson John Wade

Placings:1/30/005-11P   (1094)
2003/04: 20¹GF, 19¹G, 22⁶GF,

	Starts	1st	2nd	3rd	Win & Pl
Hurdles	3	2	0	0	7623
Career Total	9	3	0	1	9430
98	7/03	Strf	2m3f	E(0-105)HHdl	GD £4143
98	6/03	Hexm	2m4f110yE(0-105)HHdl		G-F £3479
101	4/00	MRas	1m5f110yH NHF		SFT £1533

Total win prize-money £9156

Going: Sf: 0-0 GS: 0-0 Gd: 1-1 GF: - Fm: 1-2
Distance: 2m/2m3: 1-1 2m4-2m7: 1-2 3m+: 0-0
Track: LH: 2-3 RH: 0-0 Tight: 1-2 Gall: 0-0
Aids: Bl: 0-0 Vi: 0-0 Tstrap: 0-0 Ckp: 0-0
Best Rating: 112 5/00 Prth 2m110y gd-sft NHF

Moderate hurdler; lightly raced; has improved over hurdles since being stepped up in distance with back-to-back wins

over 2m 4f at Hexham and 2m 3f at Stratford; pulled up lame next time; stays well; acts on all types of ground.

Toomebridge (IRE)
98   91

6-y-o b g Warcraft (USA)-The Foalicule (Imperial Fling (USA))
J S King Miss S Douglas-Pennant

Placings:2   (4650)
2003/04: 19³G,

	Starts	1st	2nd	3rd	Win & Pl
Hurdles	1	0	1	0	1323
Career Total	1	0	1	0	1323

Going:	Sf: 0-0 GS: 0-0 Gd: 0-1 GF: - Fm: 0-0
Distance:	2m/2m3: 0-0 2m4-2m7: 0-1 3m+: 0-0
Track:	LH: 0-1 RH: 0-0 Tight: 0-0 Gall: 0-0
Aids:	Bl: 0-1 Vi: 0-0 Tstrap: 0-0 Ckp: 0-0
Best Rating:	93 4/04 Hrfd 2m3f110y good Hdl

Former maiden Irish Pointer; pleasing hurdle debut at Hereford on good ground in April; will stay 2m 4f at least.

Toon Society (IRE)

6-y-o b g Moscow Society (USA)-Sweet Defeet (Deep Run)
Jonjo O'Neill Mike Browne

Placings:564   (1572)
2003/04: 17⁵GF, 16⁶G, 21⁴F,

	Starts	1st	2nd	3rd	Win & Pl
NH Flat	2	0	0	0	0
Hurdles	1	0	0	0	0
Career Total	3	0	0	0	0

Going:	Sf: 0-0 GS: 0-0 Gd: 0-1 GF: - Fm: 0-2
Distance:	2m/2m3: 0-2 2m4-2m7: 0-1 3m+: 0-0
Track:	LH: 0-1 RH: 0-2 Tight: 0-1 Gall: 0-0
Aids:	Bl: 0-2 Vi: 0-0 Tstrap: 0-0 Ckp: 0-0
Best Rating:	80 8/03 NAbb 2m1f gd-fm NHF

Plating-class from shown to date in two bumpers and one run over hurdles; has worn blinkers.

Toon Trooper (IRE)
103   107+

7-y-o ch g Bob Back (USA)-Salmoncita (Salmon Leap (USA))
Jonjo O'Neill Mike Browne

Placings:6-3014P   (3827)
2003/04: 20³HY, 23⁰G, 25¹S, 24⁴HY, 24ᴾG,

	Starts	1st	2nd	3rd	Win & Pl
Hurdles	5	1	0	1	3994
Career Total	6	1	0	1	3994
114	12/03	Wwck	3m1f	E Hdl	SFT	£3157
			Total win prize-money £3157			

Going:	Sf: 1-3 GS: 0-0 Gd: 0-2 GF: - Fm: 0-0
Distance:	2m/2m3: 0-0 2m4-2m7: 0-2 3m+: 1-3
Track:	LH: 1-3 RH: 0-2 Tight: 0-0 Gall: 0-1
Aids:	Bl: 0-0 Vi: 0-0 Tstrap: 0-0 Ckp: 0-0
Best Rating:	114 12/03 Wwck 3m1f soft Hdl

Fair hurdler; ex-Irish; stays beyond three miles and acts on soft ground.

Toorak (USA)
81   49

7-y-o b g Irish River (FR)-Just Juliet (USA) (What A Pleasure (USA))
Mrs T J McInnes Skinner Mrs T J McInnes Skinner

Placings:4300/0-00P   (0420)
2003/04: 16⁵GS, 16⁰G, 17ᴾGF,

	Starts	1st	2nd	3rd	Win & Pl
Hurdles	3	0	0	0	
Career Total	8	0	0	1	523

Going:	Sf: 0-0 GS: 0-1 Gd: 0-1 GF: - Fm: 0-1
Distance:	2m/2m3: 0-3 2m4-2m7: 0-0 3m+: 0-0
Track:	LH: 0-2 RH: 0-1 Tight: 0-1 Gall: 0-0
Aids:	Bl: 0-0 Vi: 0-0 Tstrap: 0-0 Ckp: 0-0
Best Rating:	98 12/01 Hayd 2m soft Hdl

Top Buck (IRE)
101   (118h) 132

10-y-o b/br g Top Of The World-Orlita (Master Buck)
K C Bailey A N Solomons

Placings:2F/235/1331430/11-35UF   (4912)
2003/04: 20³GF, 24⁵G, 20ᵁG, 20ᶠS,

	Starts	1st	2nd	3rd	Win & Pl
Chases	4	0	0	1	2028
Career Total	18	4	2	5	23515
132	2/03	Font	2m4f	D Ch	G-S	£5694
128	11/02	Asct	2m3f110y	D Ch	G-S	£4589
114	1/02	Winc	2m6f	E Hdl	GD	£2859
118	10/01	Extr	2m1f	D Hdl	GD	£4238
			Total win prize-money £17381			

Going:	Sf: 0-1 GS: 0-0 Gd: 0-2 GF: - Fm: 0-1
Distance:	2m/2m3: 0-0 2m4-2m7: 0-3 3m+: 0-1
Track:	LH: 0-0 RH: 0-4 Tight: 0-0 Gall: 0-1
Aids:	Bl: 0-0 Vi: 0-0 Tstrap: 0-0 Ckp: 0-1
Best Rating:	132 2/03 Font 2m4f gd-sft Ch

Useful chaser; lightly raced; stays two miles six; acts in yielding conditions but does not want the ground too soft.

Top Dog (IRE)
91f   82f

5-y-o b g Topanoora-Dun Oengus (IRE) (Strong Gale)
L Wells Mrs Carrie Zetter-Wells

Placings:5   (4934)
2003/04: 18⁵G,

	Starts	1st	2nd	3rd	Win & Pl
NH Flat	1	0	0	0	0
Career Total	1	0	0	0	0

Going:	Sf: 0-0 GS: 0-0 Gd: 0-1 GF: - Fm: 0-0
Distance:	2m/2m3: 0-1 2m4-2m7: 0-0 3m+: 0-0
Track:	LH: 0-1 RH: 0-0 Tight: 0-1 Gall: 0-0
Aids:	Bl: 0-0 Vi: 0-0 Tstrap: 0-0 Ckp: 0-0
Best Rating:	82 4/04 Font 2m2f110y good NHF

Top Gale (IRE)
94

5-y-o b m Topanoora-Amy's Gale (IRE) (Strong Gale)
R Dickin Pieces Of Eight

Placings:0   (0309)
2003/04: 17⁰G,

	Starts	1st	2nd	3rd	Win & Pl
NH Flat	1	0	0	0	

Career Total   1   0   0   0

Going:	Sf: 0-0 GS: 0-0 Gd: 0-1 GF: - Fm: 0-0
Distance:	2m/2m3: 0-1 2m4-2m7: 0-0 3m+: 0-0
Track:	LH: 0-1 RH: 0-0 Tight: 0-1 Gall: 0-0
Aids:	Bl: 0-0 Vi: 0-0 Tstrap: 0-0 Ckp: 0-0
Best Rating:	37 5/03 Bang 2m1f good NHF

Top Guard (IRE)

6-y-o b g Topanoora-Garter Royale (IRE) (Garde Royale)
Edward U Hales Mrs J Radbourne

Placings:00-04   (0492)
2003/04: 16⁰YS, 25⁴G,

	Starts	1st	2nd	3rd	Win & Pl
NH Flat	1	0	0	0	0
Hurdles	1	0	0	0	370
Career Total	4	0	0	0	370

Going:	Sf: 0-0 GS: 0-0 Gd: 0-1 GF: - Fm: 0-0
Distance:	2m/2m3: 0-1 2m4-2m7: 0-0 3m+: 0-1
Track:	LH: 0-1 RH: 0-1 Tight: 0-0 Gall: 0-0
Aids:	Bl: 0-0 Vi: 0-0 Tstrap: 0-0 Ckp: 0-0
Best Rating:	82 10/02 Gway 2m heavy NHF

No form in three starts in bumpers in Ireland and a novices' hurdle here (tailed off).

Top Notch
89   60

6-y-o br m Alderbrook-Gaygo Lady (Gay Fandango (USA))
K C Bailey Mrs Sharon C Nelson

Placings:60-05560   (3213)
2003/04: 16⁰G, 16⁵GF, 16⁵GS, 17⁵GS, 16⁰GS,

	Starts	1st	2nd	3rd	Win & Pl
NH Flat	2	0	0	0	0
Hurdles	3	0	0	0	0
Career Total	7	0	0	0	0

Going:	Sf: 0-0 GS: 0-3 Gd: 0-1 GF: - Fm: 0-1
Distance:	2m/2m3: 0-5 2m4-2m7: 0-0 3m+: 0-0
Track:	LH: 0-2 RH: 0-4 Tight: 0-1 Gall: 0-0
Aids:	Bl: 0-0 Vi: 0-0 Tstrap: 0-0 Ckp: 0-0
Best Rating:	87 5/03 Hntg 2m110y gd-fm NHF

Top Of The Agenda
100f   106f

5-y-o b g Michelozzo (USA)-Expensive Lark (Sir Lark)
M Pitman The Leaflet Company Ltd

Placings:2   (1611)
2003/04: 16²GF,

	Starts	1st	2nd	3rd	Win & Pl
NH Flat	1	0	1	0	423
Career Total	1	0	1	0	423

Going:	Sf: 0-0 GS: 0-0 Gd: 0-0 GF: - Fm: 0-1
Distance:	2m/2m3: 0-1 2m4-2m7: 0-0 3m+: 0-0
Track:	LH: 0-0 RH: 0-1 Tight: 0-0 Gall: 0-1
Aids:	Bl: 0-0 Vi: 0-0 Tstrap: 0-0 Ckp: 0-0
Best Rating:	106 10/03 Hntg 2m110y gd-fm NHF

Showed promise on bumper debut on fast ground.

Career Total   1   0   0   0

Top Of The Charts

8-y-o b g Salse (USA)-Celebrity (Troy)
Miss T McCurrich Miss T McCurrich

Placings:405045/032604PF0/P (0352)
2003/04: 31^{P}GF,

	Starts	1st	2nd	3rd	Win & Pl
Chases	1	0	0	0	
Career Total	16	0	1	1	1320

Going:	Sf: 0-0 GS: 0-0 Gd: 0-0 GF: 0-0 Fm: 0-1
Distance:	2m/2m3: 0-0 2m4-2m7: 0-0 3m+: 0-1
Track:	LH: 0-0 RH: 0-1 Tight: 0-1 Gall: 0-0
Aids:	Bl: 0-0 Vi: 0-0 Tstrap: 0-0 Ckp: 0-0
Best Rating:	80 11/00 Ludl 2m5f good Hdl

Plating-class staying hurdler. Seems to handle any ground.

Top Of The Dee
79 75

7-y-o ch m Rakaposhi King-Lavenham's Last (Rymer)
Mrs L Williamson Bangor-On-Dee Racing Club

Placings:600/650334236-3P0P (4868)
2003/04: 16^{3}HY, 20^{P}GF, 16^{9}GF, 20^{P}GS,

	Starts	1st	2nd	3rd	Win & Pl
Hurdles	4	0	0	1	501
Career Total	16	0	1	4	3754

Going:	Sf: 0-1 GS: 0-1 Gd: 0-0 GF: - Fm: 0-2
Distance:	2m/2m3: 0-2 2m4-2m7: 0-2 3m+: 0-0
Track:	LH: 0-4 RH: 0-0 Tight: 0-1 Gall: 0-0
Aids:	Bl: 0-0 Vi: 0-0 Tstrap: 0-0 Ckp: 0-0
Best Rating:	82 7/02 Uttx 2m4f110y gd-fm Hdl

Poor maiden hurdler.

Top Of The Left

(107h) (103+h)
9-y-o b/br g Nomination-Diva Madonna (Chief Singer)
Jonjo O'Neill John P McManus

Placings:35/0-22F (3333)
2003/04: 20^{2}G, 19^{2}S, 18^{F}S,

	Starts	1st	2nd	3rd	Win & Pl
Hurdles	2	0	2	0	2930
Chases	1	0	0	0	0
Career Total	6	0	2	1	3270

Going:	Sf: 0-2 GS: 0-0 Gd: 0-1 GF: - Fm: 0-0
Distance:	2m/2m3: 0-2 2m4-2m7: 0-1 3m+: 0-0
Track:	LH: 0-2 RH: 0-1 Tight: 0-0 Gall: 0-1
Aids:	Bl: 0-0 Vi: 0-0 Tstrap: 0-0 Ckp: 0-0
Best Rating:	105 12/03 Weth 2m4f110y good Hdl

Moderate hurdler; stays two and a half miles; not the strongest of finishers.

Top Stoppa
65f 50f

6-y-o gr g Environment Friend-Orchid Valley (IRE) (Cyrano De Bergerac)
Miss V Scott Exors of the late Andy Scott

Placings:0-0 (1436)
2003/04: 16^{0}G,

	Starts	1st	2nd	3rd	Win & Pl
NH Flat	1	0	0	0	

Career Total 2 0 0 0

Going:	Sf: 0-0 GS: 0-0 Gd: 0-1 GF: - Fm: 0-0
Distance:	2m/2m3: 0-1 2m4-2m7: 0-0 3m+: 0-0
Track:	LH: 0-0 RH: 0-1 Tight: 0-0 Gall: 0-0
Aids:	Bl: 0-0 Vi: 0-0 Tstrap: 0-0 Ckp: 0-0
Best Rating:	50 9/02 Hexm 2m110y gd-fm NHF

Top Strategy (IRE)
113 138

4-y-o b g Hernando (FR)-Sudden Stir (USA) (Woodman (USA))
T M Walsh (D K Weld 14/6) W J Kane

Placings:02124053 (4422)
2003/04: 16^{0}GY, 16^{2}S, 16^{1}S, 16^{2}HY, 16^{4}S, 16^{0}Y, 16^{5}Y, 17^{3}G,

	Starts	1st	2nd	3rd	Win & Pl
Hurdles	8	1	2	1	41904
Career Total	8	1	2	1	41904
127 12/03 Leop	2m		Hdl	SFT	£21103
		Total win prize-money £21104			

Going:	Sf: 1-4 GS: 0-0 Gd: 0-1 GF: - Fm: 0-0
Distance:	2m/2m3: 1-8 2m4-2m7: 0-0 3m+: 0-0
Track:	LH: 1-4 RH: 0-4 Tight: 0-0 Gall: 0-0
Aids:	Bl: 0-2 Vi: 0-0 Tstrap: 0-0 Ckp: 0-0
Best Rating:	138 3/04 Chel 2m1f good Hdl

Useful Irish-trained juvenile hurdler; third in the 2004 Triumph Hurdle; effective on soft ground; best at two miles.

Top Tenor (IRE)
76 44

4-y-o b g Sadler's Wells (USA)-Posta Vecchia (USA) (Rainbow Quest (USA))
V Thompson (B R Johnson 24/3) V Thompson

Placings:0 (4795)
2003/04: 17^{0}G,

	Starts	1st	2nd	3rd	Win & Pl
Hurdles	1	0	0	0	
Career Total	1	0	0	0	

Going:	Sf: 0-0 GS: 0-0 Gd: 0-0 GF: - Fm: 0-0
Distance:	2m/2m3: 0-1 2m4-2m7: 0-0 3m+: 0-0
Track:	LH: 0-1 RH: 0-0 Tight: 0-1 Gall: 0-0
Aids:	Bl: 0-0 Vi: 0-0 Tstrap: 0-0 Ckp: 0-0
Best Rating:	44 4/04 Sedg 2m1f good Hdl

Top The Bill (IRE)
85f 81f

4-y-o b g Topanoora-Rio Star (IRE) (Riot Helmet)
Mrs S A Watt Mrs S A Watt

Placings:004 (3737)
2003/04: 16^{0}GS, 16^{0}G, 16^{4}G,

	Starts	1st	2nd	3rd	Win & Pl
NH Flat	3	0	0	0	0
Career Total	3	0	0	0	0

Going:	Sf: 0-0 GS: 0-1 Gd: 0-2 GF: - Fm: 0-0
Distance:	2m/2m3: 0-3 2m4-2m7: 0-0 3m+: 0-0
Track:	LH: 0-2 RH: 0-1 Tight: 0-3 Gall: 0-0
Aids:	Bl: 0-0 Vi: 0-0 Tstrap: 0-0 Ckp: 0-0
Best Rating:	81 2/04 Muss 2m good NHF

Top Trees
105 87

6-y-o b g Charnwood Forest (IRE)-Low Line (High Line)
W S Kittow Mrs P E Hawkings

Placings:40-FR3435F (2411)
2003/04: 16^{6}G, 17^{R}GF, 17^{3}GF, 17^{4}F, 19^{3}GF, 16^{5}G, 19^{F}GF,

	Starts	1st	2nd	3rd	Win & Pl
Hurdles	7	0	0	2	1315
Career Total	9	0	0	2	1315

Going:	Sf: 0-0 GS: 0-0 Gd: 0-2 GF: - Fm: 0-5
Distance:	2m/2m3: 0-6 2m4-2m7: 0-1 3m+: 0-0
Track:	LH: 0-4 RH: 0-3 Tight: 0-4 Gall: 0-0
Aids:	Bl: 0-0 Vi: 0-0 Tstrap: 0-0 Ckp: 0-1
Best Rating:	87 9/03 Extr 2m1f firm Hdl

Plating-class hurdler; acts on fast ground; often wears cheekpieces.

Topanberry (IRE)
85f 81f

5-y-o ch m Topanoora-Mulberry (IRE) (Denel (FR))
N G Richards Mrs D McGawn

Placings:20 (4328)
2003/04: 16^{2}GF, 16^{0}S,

	Starts	1st	2nd	3rd	Win & Pl
NH Flat	2	0	1	0	756
Career Total	2	0	1	0	756

Going:	Sf: 0-1 GS: 0-0 Gd: 0-0 GF: - Fm: 0-1
Distance:	2m/2m3: 0-2 2m4-2m7: 0-0 3m+: 0-0
Track:	LH: 0-1 RH: 0-1 Tight: 0-0 Gall: 0-0
Aids:	Bl: 0-0 Vi: 0-0 Tstrap: 0-0 Ckp: 0-0
Best Rating:	81 11/03 Hexm 2m110y gd-fm NHF

Narrowly denied in modest mares' only bumper on debut at Hexham in November; will stay further over hurdles; acts on decent going.

Topol (IRE)
102(86h) (79h)101

6-y-o br g Topanoora-Kislev (IRE) (Be My Guest (USA))
Miss H C Knight Top Brass Partnership

Placings:0/000-2064P (4786)
2003/04: 16^{2}GS, 20^{0}GS, 16^{6}G, 18^{4}G, 16^{P}G,

	Starts	1st	2nd	3rd	Win & Pl
Chases	5	0	1	0	1092
Career Total	9	0	1	0	1092

Going:	Sf: 0-0 GS: 0-2 Gd: 0-3 GF: - Fm: 0-0
Distance:	2m/2m3: 0-4 2m4-2m7: 0-1 3m+: 0-0
Track:	LH: 0-3 RH: 0-2 Tight: 0-1 Gall: 0-3
Aids:	Bl: 0-0 Vi: 0-0 Tstrap: 0-0 Ckp: 0-0
Best Rating:	101 12/03 Hrfd 2m gd-sft Ch

Some signs of ability in bumper and over hurdles; improved form when runner-up in 2m novices' handicap chase at Hereford December 2003 despite hanging right.

Tor Head
103 102

8-y-o b g Then Again-Free Form (Glenstal (USA))
J Howard Johnson Group Captain J A Prideaux

Placings:2F2P (4794)
2003/04: 21^{2}GS, 25^{F}GS, 16^{2}G, 21^{P}G,

	Starts	1st	2nd	3rd	Win & Pl
Chases	4	0	2	0	1660
Career Total	**4**	**0**	**2**	**0**	**1660**

Going: Sf: 0-0 GS: 0-2 Gd: 0-2 GF: - Fm: 0-0
Distance: 2m/2m3: 0-1 2m4-2m7: 0-2 3m+: 0-1
Track: LH: 0-4 RH: 0-0 Tight: 0-3 Gall: 0-0
Aids: Bl: 0-1 Vi: 0-0 Tstrap: 0-0 Ckp: 0-0
Best Rating: 102 3/04 Hexm 2m110y good Ch

Hinted at ability in hunters chase over two miles and five furlongs and in beginners chase over two miles; will be suited by three miles; one to keep an eye out for in handicaps over that trip.

Torche (IRE)
100   **106+**
6-y-o b g Taos (IRE)-Orchette (IRE) (Orchestra)
M Scudamore (D J Caro 29/4) Mrs S Tainton

Placings:40-4R04143   (4340)
2003/04: 17⁰S, 20⁴GS, 20⁰S, 23⁰G, 25⁴S, 25¹GS, 24⁴S, 25³G,

	Starts	1st	2nd	3rd	Win & Pl
NH Flat	1	0	0	0	0
Hurdles	7	1	0	1	5059
Career Total	**9**	**1**	**0**	**1**	**5059**
106	1/04	Weth	3m1f	F Hdl	G-S £2737
				Total win prize-money £2737	

Going: Sf: 0-4 GS: 1-2 Gd: 0-2 GF: - Fm: 0-0
Distance: 2m/2m3: 0-1 2m4-2m7: 0-0 3m+: 1-4
Track: LH: 1-8 RH: 0-0 Tight: 0-1 Gall: 0-1
Aids: Bl: 0-0 Vi: 1-3 Tstrap: 0-0 Ckp: 0-0
Best Rating: 106 3/04 Wwck 3m1f good Hdl

Staying novice hurdler; wore first-time visor when decisive winner at Wetherby in January 2004; stays three miles well; suited by easy ground.

Torduff Express (IRE)
13-y-o b g Kambalda-Marhabtain (Touching Wood (USA))
P F Nicholls Two Plus Two

Placings:121321/12104/33F/1562P/2131/21U4-205 (4626)
2003/04: 22²S, 26⁹G, 21⁵G,

	Starts	1st	2nd	3rd	Win & Pl
Chases	3	0	1	0	3598
Career Total	**30**	**9**	**1**	**4**	**111060**
130	2/03	Font	3m2f110yH Ch	G-S	£3328
131	4/02	Aint	2m5f110yB Ch	GD	£21645
126	2/02	Font	3m2f110yH Ch	SFT	£6922
112	10/00	Extr	2m6f110yE Hdl	GD	£2540
144	12/98	Asct	3m110y B HCh	GS	£27230
128	10/98	Plum	3m1f110yC(0-130)HCh	GD	£5257
122	4/98	Sand	3m110y E Ch	GS	£4598
103	2/98	Font	3m2f110yE Ch	GD	£3116
103	12/97	Hrfd	3m1f110yE Ch	GD	£2697
				Total win prize-money £77335	

Going: Sf: 0-1 GS: 0-0 Gd: 0-2 GF: - Fm: 0-0
Distance: 2m/2m3: 0-0 2m4-2m7: 0-2 3m+: 0-1
Track: LH: 0-3 RH: 0-0 Tight: 0-1 Gall: 0-1
Aids: Bl: 0-3 Vi: 0-0 Tstrap: 0-0 Ckp: 0-0
Best Rating: 144 12/98 Asct 3m110y gd-sft Ch

Useful hunter chaser; won the Aintree Fox Hunters' in 2002 and landed a hunter chase at Fontwell in February 2003; stays three miles two; goes well in soft ground; effective in blinkers.

Toreo (FR)
85   **63**
10-y-o ch g Bakharoff (USA)-Becerrada (FR) (Tip Moss (FR))
M Todhunter (J R Adam 14/5) James R Adam

Placings:3642/00/6/PF-00   (2506)
2003/04: 16⁰G, 22⁰S,

	Starts	1st	2nd	3rd	Win & Pl
Hurdles	2	0	0	0	
Career Total	**11**	**0**	**1**	**1**	**721**

Going: Sf: 0-1 GS: 0-0 Gd: 0-1 GF: - Fm: 0-0
Distance: 2m/2m3: 0-1 2m4-2m7: 0-1 3m+: 0-0
Track: LH: 0-1 RH: 0-1 Tight: 0-1 Gall: 0-0
Aids: Bl: 0-0 Vi: 0-0 Tstrap: 0-1 Ckp: 0-0
Best Rating: 103 4/99 Hntg 2m110y gd-fm NHF

Toringa Rose
71f   **27f**
5-y-o ch m Karinga Bay-Topsy Turvy (IRE) (Roselier (FR))
R H York R H York

Placings:0   (0871)
2003/04: 17⁰GF,

	Starts	1st	2nd	3rd	Win & Pl
NH Flat	1	0	0	0	
Career Total	**1**	**0**	**0**	**0**	

Going: Sf: 0-0 GS: 0-0 Gd: 0-0 GF: - Fm: 0-1
Distance: 2m/2m3: 0-1 2m4-2m7: 0-0 3m+: 0-0
Track: LH: 0-1 RH: 0-0 Tight: 0-1 Gall: 0-0
Aids: Bl: 0-0 Vi: 0-0 Tstrap: 0-0 Ckp: 0-0
Best Rating: 27 7/03 NAbb 2m1f gd-fm NHF

Torosay (IRE)
93   **86**
6-y-o b g Presenting-Mazuma (IRE) (Mazaad)
N G Richards J Hales

Placings:5-555   (4431)
2003/04: 20⁵S, 20⁵HY, 24⁵G,

	Starts	1st	2nd	3rd	Win & Pl
Hurdles	3	0	0	0	0
Career Total	**4**	**0**	**0**	**0**	**0**

Going: Sf: 0-2 GS: 0-0 Gd: 0-1 GF: - Fm: 0-0
Distance: 2m/2m3: 0-0 2m4-2m7: 0-2 3m+: 0-1
Track: LH: 0-3 RH: 0-0 Tight: 0-0 Gall: 0-0
Aids: Bl: 0-0 Vi: 0-0 Tstrap: 0-0 Ckp: 0-0
Best Rating: 105 3/03 Carl 2m1f gd-sft NHF

Fourth in a point; showed ability in bumper and bit better than bare form suggests on hurdles debut; type to do better over fences in due course.

Torpica
   (77h)
8-y-o br g Be My Native (USA)-Irish Mint (Dusky Boy)
P Winkworth Miss Jessica Winkworth

Placings:0/03062P/PF   (4665)
2003/04: 20⁰GS, 24⁵S,

	Starts	1st	2nd	3rd	Win & Pl
Chases	2	0	0	0	
Career Total	**9**	**0**	**1**	**1**	**992**

Going: Sf: 0-1 GS: 0-1 Gd: 0-0 GF: - Fm: 0-0
Distance: 2m/2m3: 0-0 2m4-2m7: 0-1 3m+: 0-1
Track: LH: 0-2 RH: 0-0 Tight: 0-1 Gall: 0-0
Aids: Bl: 0-1 Vi: 0-0 Tstrap: 0-0 Ckp: 0-0
Best Rating: 77 3/02 Plum 3m1f110y gd-sft Hdl

Torrid Kentavr (USA)
110(110c)   (115c)**125**
7-y-o b g Trempolino (USA)-Torrid Tango (USA) (Green Dancer (USA))
B Ellison Graeme Redpath

Placings:226/11312   (1862)
2003/04: 16¹S, 16¹GF, 17³G, 16¹GF, 16²GF,

	Starts	1st	2nd	3rd	Win & Pl
Hurdles	3	1	1	1	16051
Chases	2	2	0	0	10933
Career Total	**8**	**3**	**3**	**1**	**28410**
115	9/03	Plum	2m	D(0-125)HHdl	G-F £12267
115	6/03	Prth	2m	F(0-100)HCh	G-F £6877
104	5/03	Sedg	2m110y	E Ch	SFT £4056
				Total win prize-money £23200	

Going: Sf: 1-1 GS: 0-0 Gd: 0-1 GF: - Fm: 2-3
Distance: 2m/2m3: 3-5 2m4-2m7: 0-0 3m+: 0-0
Track: LH: 2-4 RH: 1-1 Tight: 2-3 Gall: 0-0
Aids: Bl: 0-0 Vi: 0-0 Tstrap: 0-0 Ckp: 0-0
Best Rating: 123 10/03 Weth 2m gd-fm Hdl

Modest handicap hurdler/ novice chaser; won first two starts over fences, although lucky to collect in the latter; won valuable handicap hurdle at Plumpton in September; best at two miles; acts on soft and fast ground.

Tortuga Dream (IRE)
89   **56**
5-y-o b g Turtle Island (IRE)-Tycoon's Catch (IRE) (Thatching)
A Charlton P J Haycock

Placings:0600-0   (2543)
2003/04: 16⁰G,

	Starts	1st	2nd	3rd	Win & Pl
Hurdles	1	0	0	0	
Career Total	**5**	**0**	**0**	**0**	**0**

Going: Sf: 0-0 GS: 0-0 Gd: 0-1 GF: - Fm: 0-0
Distance: 2m/2m3: 0-1 2m4-2m7: 0-0 3m+: 0-0
Track: LH: 0-0 RH: 0-1 Tight: 0-0 Gall: 0-0
Aids: Bl: 0-0 Vi: 0-1 Tstrap: 0-0 Ckp: 0-0
Best Rating: 56 12/03 Leic 2m good Hdl

Tortugas (FR)
(75h)   (48h)**61**
7-y-o b g Subotica (FR)-Northern Whisper (FR) (Vacarme (USA))
Mrs H Dalton Miss Julia Oakey

Placings:01206/P3P50/044FFF-0   (0676)
2003/04: 16⁰GF,

	Starts	1st	2nd	3rd	Win & Pl
Hurdles	1	0	0	0	
Career Total	**17**	**1**	**1**	**1**	**2970**
97	11/00	Tntn	2m1f	G Hdl	G-S £1578
				Total win prize-money £1579	

Going: Sf: 0-0 GS: 0-0 Gd: 0-0 GF: - Fm: 0-1

Distance: 2m/2m3: 0-1 2m4-2m7: 0-0 3m+: 0-0
Track: LH: 0-1 RH: 0-0 Tight: 0-0 Gall: 0-0
Aids: Bl: 0-0 Vi: 0-0 Tstrap: 0-0 Ckp: 0-0
Best Rating: 97 11/00 Tntn 2m1f gd-sft Hdl

Tosawi (IRE)

106   **106**

8-y-o b g Commanche Run-Deep Satisfaction (Deep Run)
R J Hodges John & Greer Norman

Placings:5/030/04P1421PP/6040032-F0P61463   (4822)
2003/04: 16⁶G, 19⁰S, 22⁸S, 16⁶GS, 17⁷G, 16⁴G, 17⁹GS, 19³GF,

	Starts	1st	2nd	3rd	Win & Pl
Hurdles	7	1	0	1	3995
Chases	1	0	0	0	0
Career Total	28	3	2	3	13174
103 3/04 Extr	2m1f	F(0-100)HHdl		GD	£2817
109 1/02 Tntn	2m3f110yF(0-100)HHdl		SFT	£2714
97 12/01 Extr	2m1f	F(0-100)HHdl		GD	£2520

Total win prize-money £8053

Going: Sf: 0-2 GS: 0-2 Gd: 1-3 GF: - Fm: 0-1
Distance: **2m/2m3: 1-7** 2m4-2m7: 0-1 3m+: 0-0
Track: LH: 0-0 **RH: 1-8** Tight: 0-0 Gall: 0-0
Aids: Bl: 0-0 Vi: 0-0 Tstrap: 0-0 Ckp: 0-0
Best Rating: 109 1/02 Tntn 2m3f110y soft Hdl

Modest hurdler; acts well on a soft surface; stays two and a half miles.

Toscanini (GER)

99   **100**

8-y-o b g Goofalik (USA)-Tosca Stella (GER) (Surumu (GER))
D R Gandolfo Mrs John Lee

Placings:3404/5P16-3   (0379)
2003/04: 22⁶S, 20³S,

	Starts	1st	2nd	3rd	Win & Pl
Hurdles	2	0	0	1	772
Career Total	9	1	0	2	6445
100 3/03 Extr	2m3f	D(0-115)HHdl		SFT	£4858

Total win prize-money £4859

Going: Sf: 0-2 GS: 0-0 Gd: 0-0 GF: - Fm: 0-0
Distance: 2m/2m3: 0-0 2m4-2m7: 0-2 3m+: 0-0
Track: LH: 0-2 RH: 0-0 Tight: 0-0 Gall: 0-0
Aids: Bl: 0-0 Vi: 0-0 Tstrap: 0-0 Ckp: 0-0
Best Rating: 100 3/03 Extr 2m3f soft Hdl

Fair Flat form in Germany; described as a bit of a thinker by his trainer was suited by the small field when winning a falsely-run four-runner handicap at Exeter March 2003; acts on soft ground.

Tosheroon (IRE)

       110

8-y-o b g Good Thyne (USA)-Rare Currency (Rarity)
A M Hales Andrew L Cohen

Placings:13-P   (0132)
2003/04: 26⁷GF,

	Starts	1st	2nd	3rd	Win & Pl
Hurdles	1	0	0	0	
Career Total	3	1	0	1	3880
110 10/02 Plum	2m5f	E Hdl		GD	£3220

Total win prize-money £3220

Going: Sf: 0-0 GS: 0-0 Gd: 0-0 GF: - Fm: 0-1
Distance: 2m/2m3: 0-0 2m4-2m7: 0-0 3m+: 0-1
Track: LH: 0-0 RH: 0-1 Tight: 0-0 Gall: 0-1
Aids: Bl: 0-0 Vi: 0-0 Tstrap: 0-0 Ckp: 0-0

Best Rating: 110 11/02 Asct 2m4f gd-sft Hdl

Made a very impressive debut under Rules when winning a moderate novice hurdle at Plumpton in October 2002; lightly raced since; acts good.

Total Enjoyment (IRE)

117f   **135+f**

5-y-o b m Flemensfirth (USA)-Oak Court (IRE) (Bustineto)
Thomas Cooper It Will Never Last Syndicate

Placings:3111   (4400)
2003/04: 16³GY, 16¹S, 16¹Y, 16¹G,

	Starts	1st	2nd	3rd	Win & Pl
NH Flat	4	3	0	1	34681
Career Total	4	3	0	1	34681
135 3/04 Chel	2m110y	A NHF		GD	£23200
122 12/03 Leop	2m		NHF	YLD	£6272
119 12/03 Fair	2m		NHF	SFT	£4480

Total win prize-money £33954

Going: Sf: 1-1 GS: 0-0 Gd: 1-1 GF: - Fm: 0-0
Distance: **2m/2m3: 3-4** 2m4-2m7: 0-0 3m+: 0-0
Track: LH: 1-1 RH: 1-2 Tight: 0-0 Gall: 0-0
Aids: Bl: 0-0 Vi: 0-0 Tstrap: 0-0 Ckp: 0-0
Best Rating: 135 3/04 Chel 2m110y good NHF

Useful mare; third in decent bumper at Punchestown on debut in May 2003; improved to win next two outings in December and then took the Cheltenham Festival bumper; acts on good and soft ground; promising type for hurdling.

Totally Scottish

108   **117**

8-y-o b g Mtoto-Glenfinlass (Lomond (USA))
Mrs M Reveley The Phoenix Racing C O

Placings:0002/32451164464402/U21252-0343650025   (4599)
2003/04: 18⁶G, 20³G, 16⁴G, 19³GF, 16⁶G, 20⁵HY, 17⁹GS, 20⁰G, 20²G, 18⁵G,

	Starts	1st	2nd	3rd	Win & Pl
Hurdles	10	0	1	2	3685
Career Total	34	3	7	3	22241
114 11/02 Carl	2m1f	D(0-120)HHdl	HVY	£3623
103 11/01 Kels	2m110y	D(0-125)HHdl	G-S	£3325
99 10/01 Carl	2m4f	F(0-100)HHdl	G-S	£2108

Total win prize-money £9057

Going: Sf: 0-1 GS: 0-1 Gd: 0-7 GF: - Fm: 0-1
Distance: 2m/2m3: 0-5 2m4-2m7: 0-5 3m+: 0-1
Track: LH: 0-7 RH: 0-3 Tight: 0-3 Gall: 0-1
Aids: Bl: 0-0 Vi: 0-0 Tstrap: 0-0 Ckp: 0-0
Best Rating: 117 3/03 Kels 2m2f good Hdl

Fair hurdler; goes well on a stiff track and has a good record at Carlisle; stays two and a half miles, but probably best over shorter; suited by soft ground.

Totland Bay (IRE)

101   (0c)**107**

8-y-o br g Phardante (FR)-Seanaphobal Lady (Kambalda)
B D Leavy (J W Mullins 3/9) J A Provan

Placings:43040P2/401232232-4P2430   (1374)
2003/04: 22⁴G, 21⁵GF, 22²GF, 20⁴G, 22³GF, 24⁰GF,

	Starts	1st	2nd	3rd	Win & Pl
Hurdles	5	0	1	1	2417
Chases	1	0	0	0	0
Career Total	22	1	6	4	12037
91 7/02 NAbb	2m6f	D Hdl		G-F	£3581

Best Rating: 110 11/02 Asct 2m4f gd-sft Hdl   Total win prize-money £3582

Going: Sf: 0-0 GS: 0-1 Gd: 0-2 GF: - Fm: 0-3
Distance: 2m/2m3: 0-0 2m4-2m7: 0-5 3m+: 0-1
Track: LH: 0-6 RH: 0-0 Tight: 0-5 Gall: 0-0
Aids: Bl: 0-0 Vi: 0-0 Tstrap: 0-1 Ckp: 0-0
Best Rating: 105 10/02 Font 2m6f110y good Hdl

Modest hurdler; did not seem to take to fences; consistent sort; subsequently claimed for £6,000 after being fitted with a tongue strap for selling debut at Newton Abbot September 2003; best on a sound surface; effective at around two miles six furlongs.

Toto Taleca

91   **49**

7-y-o b m Mtoto-Miss Taleca (Pharly (FR))
M E Sowersby M E Sowersby

Placings:00/4/000P00UP-P00   (0703)
2003/04: 17⁸S, 17⁹G, 17⁹GF,

	Starts	1st	2nd	3rd	Win & Pl
Hurdles	3	0	0	0	
Career Total	14	0	0	0	0

Going: Sf: 0-1 GS: 0-0 Gd: 0-1 GF: - Fm: 0-1
Distance: 2m/2m3: 0-3 2m4-2m7: 0-0 3m+: 0-0
Track: LH: 0-2 RH: 0-1 Tight: 0-3 Gall: 0-0
Aids: Bl: 0-0 Vi: 0-1 Tstrap: 0-1 Ckp: 0-0
Best Rating: 75 11/01 Aint 2m1f gd-sft NHF

Toto Toscato (FR)

10-y-o br g Lesotho (USA)-Tosca De Bellouet (FR) (Olmeto)
M C Pipe Lady Clarke

Placings:1104/64113335/1221133/PP   (4637)
2003/04: 24⁹G, 25⁷G,

	Starts	1st	2nd	3rd	Win & Pl
Chases	2	0	0	0	
Career Total	21	7	2	5	117538
148 1/00 Hayd	2m6f	B Ch		SFT	£9938
148 12/99 Asct	2m3f110yA B Ch		G-S	£12500
101 11/99 Uttx	2m	D Ch		SFT	£3940
152 12/98 Asct	2m110y B Hdl		SFT	£8325
155 11/98 Chep	2m110y B Hdl		SFT	£6775
6/97 Autl	2m1f110y Hdl		VS	£33670
6/97 Autl	1m7f	Hdl		VS	£12346

Total win prize-money £87494

Going: Sf: 0-0 GS: 0-0 Gd: 0-2 GF: - Fm: 0-0
Distance: 2m/2m3: 0-0 2m4-2m7: 0-0 3m+: 0-2
Track: LH: 0-2 RH: 0-0 Tight: 0-1 Gall: 0-1
Aids: Bl: 0-0 Vi: 0-0 Tstrap: 0-1 Ckp: 0-0
Best Rating: 156 4/99 Aint 2m110y good Hdl

Formerly high-class novice chaser when trained by Alan King, but off the track after finishing third in the 2000 Royal & SunAlliance Chase; pulled up in the Kim Muir first start since then at the 2004 Festival; appeared to go wrong at Aintree; stays 3m; effective in soft, but has run some solid races on faster ground.

Touch Closer

104(91c)   (88c)**107+**

7-y-o b g Inchinor-Ryewater Dream (Touching Wood (USA))
Miss V Scott (G A Swinbank 28/3) Miss Victoria Scott Jnr

Placings:13/060P-05162513   (4942)
2003/04: 17⁹GF, 20⁵G, 21¹G, 20⁶GF, 16²S, 20⁵G, 22¹G, 20³GS,

	Starts	1st	2nd	3rd	Win & Pl
Hurdles	7	2	1	1	9695
Chases	1	0	0	0	0
Career Total	14	3	1	2	14818

110 4/04 Kels 2m6f110yE(0-110)HHdl GD £4342
98 12/03 Sedg 2m5f110yE(0-110)HHdl GD £2709
115 3/02 Ayr 2m H NHF SFT £1673
Total win prize-money £8724

Going:	Sf: 0-1 GS: 0-1 Gd: 2-4 GF: - Fm: 0-2
Distance:	2m/2m3: 0-2 2m4-2m7: 2-6 3m+: 0-0
Track:	LH: 2-3 RH: 0-5 Tight: 2-4 Gall: 0-1
Aids:	Bl: 0-0 Vi: 0-0 Tstrap: 0-0 Ckp: 0-0
Best Rating:	135 4/02 Aint 2m1f good NHF

Moderate hurdler; stays two miles six; acts on good ground or softer

Touch Of Spirit
93   **58**

5-y-o b m Dancing Spree (USA)-Soft Touch (GER) (Horst-Herbert)
J R Jenkins Kingsland Bloodstock

Placings:0F (2580)
2003/04: 16^{0}GF, 16^{F}GF,

	Starts	1st	2nd	3rd	Win & Pl
Hurdles	2	0	0	0	
Career Total	2	0	0	0	

Going:	Sf: 0-0 GS: 0-0 Gd: 0-0 GF: - Fm: 0-2
Distance:	2m/2m3: 0-2 2m4-2m7: 0-0 3m+: 0-0
Track:	LH: 0-1 RH: 0-1 Tight: 0-1 Gall: 0-1
Aids:	Bl: 0-0 Vi: 0-0 Tstrap: 0-0 Ckp: 0-0
Best Rating:	61 11/03 Hntg 2m110y gd-fm Hdl

Touch The Tambour (IRE)

7-y-o b g Insan (USA)-Queen River (Over The River (FR))
P R Webber A J Davies

Placings:P (2393)
2003/04: 16^{P}GS,

	Starts	1st	2nd	3rd	Win & Pl
NH Flat	1	0	0	0	
Career Total	1	0	0	0	

Going:	Sf: 0-0 GS: 0-0 Gd: 0-0 GF: 0-0 Fm: 0-0
Distance:	2m/2m3: 0-2 2m4-2m7: 0-0 3m+: 0-0
Track:	LH: 0-1 RH: 0-0 Tight: 0-0 Gall: 0-0
Aids:	Bl: 0-0 Vi: 0-0 Tstrap: 0-0 Ckp: 0-0

Toulon Crest (IRE)
94   **94**

7-y-o b g Toulon-Another Contact (Martin John)
G Prodromou Alan Macalister

Placings:000P3-F3023P (2994)
2003/04: 20^{6}GF, 16^{3}GF, 16^{6}G, 17^{2}GF, 17^{3}G, 16^{6}GF,

	Starts	1st	2nd	3rd	Win & Pl
Chases	6	0	1	2	3568
Career Total	11	0	1	3	4401

Going:	Sf: 0-0 GS: 0-0 Gd: 0-0 GF: - Fm: 0-4
Distance:	2m/2m3: 0-5 2m4-2m7: 0-1 3m+: 0-0
Track:	LH: 0-2 RH: 0-4 Tight: 0-1 Gall: 0-1
Aids:	Bl: 0-0 Vi: 0-0 Tstrap: 0-0 Ckp: 0-0
Best Rating:	94 7/03 MRas 2m1f110y gd-fm Ch

Plating-class chaser; still a maiden over hurdles and fences; yet to prove he stays further than two miles.

Toulouse (IRE)
97(107h)   (114h)**103**

7-y-o b g Toulon-Neasham (Nishapour (FR))
R H Alner Pell-Mell Partners

Placings:31500-FP43 (4193)
2003/04: 19^{5}GS, 20^{P}G, 21^{4}GS, 18^{3}G,

	Starts	1st	2nd	3rd	Win & Pl
Chases	4	0	0	1	1617
Career Total	9	1	0	2	9044

114 12/02 Tntn 2m1f C Hdl G-S £7085
Total win prize-money £7085

Going:	Sf: 0-0 GS: 0-2 Gd: 0-2 GF: - Fm: 0-0
Distance:	2m/2m3: 0-1 2m4-2m7: 0-3 3m+: 0-0
Track:	LH: 0-2 RH: 0-2 Tight: 0-1 Gall: 0-1
Aids:	Bl: 0-0 Vi: 0-0 Tstrap: 0-0 Ckp: 0-0
Best Rating:	114 1/03 Winc 2m gd-sft Hdl

Fair hurdler/novice chaser; seems best at around two miles; acts on good and soft ground; lightly raced.

Toulouse-Lautrec (IRE)
90   (87h)**123**

8-y-o ch g Toulon-Bucks Slave (Buckskin (FR))
T R George John French

Placings:6500/131-P2P (3705)
2003/04: 33^{P}G, 24^{2}S, 26^{P}HY,

	Starts	1st	2nd	3rd	Win & Pl
Chases	3	0	1	0	1800
Career Total	10	2	1	1	15282

123 12/02 Uttx 3m F(0-90)HCh SFT £3484
96 11/02 Uttx 2m4f E(0-105)HCh SFT £4498
Total win prize-money £7982

Going:	Sf: 0-2 GS: 0-0 Gd: 0-1 GF: - Fm: 0-0
Distance:	2m/2m3: 0-0 2m4-2m7: 0-0 3m+: 0-3
Track:	LH: 0-3 RH: 0-0 Tight: 0-0 Gall: 0-1
Aids:	Bl: 0-0 Vi: 0-0 Tstrap: 0-0 Ckp: 0-0
Best Rating:	123 12/02 Uttx 3m soft Ch

Progressive staying chaser at the end of 2002; stays 3m; effective in soft ground.

Tourniquet (IRE)
96(106h)   (108dh)**111+**

9-y-o b g Torus-Treidlia (Mandalus)
D J Caro D J Caro

Placings:230P-1U (3425)
2003/04: 27^{P}S, 22^{1}S, 25^{U}S,

	Starts	1st	2nd	3rd	Win & Pl
Hurdles	1	0	0	0	
Chases	2	1	0	0	4396
Career Total	6	1	1	1	5971

111 12/03 Towc 2m6f E Ch SFT £4396
Total win prize-money £4396

Going:	Sf: 1-3 GS: 0-0 Gd: 0-0 GF: - Fm: 0-0
Distance:	2m/2m3: 0-0 2m4-2m7: 1-1 3m+: 0-2
Track:	LH: 0-1 RH: 1-2 Tight: 0-2 Gall: 0-0
Aids:	Bl: 0-0 Vi: 0-0 Tstrap: 0-0 Ckp: 0-0
Best Rating:	111 12/03 Towc 2m6f soft Ch

Fair chaser; winning pointer in Ireland, made winning debut in Towcester novice chase on Boxing Day 2003; stays 3m; effective in soft ground.

Town Crier (IRE)
105   **105+**

9-y-o br g Beau Sher-Ballymacarett (Menelek)
Mrs S J Smith Trevor Hemmings

Placings:00/5F-1F1 (1060)
2003/04: 16^{1}GF, 17^{F}G, 16^{1}GF,

	Starts	1st	2nd	3rd	Win & Pl
Hurdles	3	2	0	0	6760
Career Total	7	2	0	0	6760

109 8/03 Uttx 2m E Hdl G-F £3393
91 7/03 Uttx 2m E Hdl G-F £3367
Total win prize-money £6760

Going:	Sf: 0-0 GS: 0-0 Gd: 0-1 GF: - Fm: 2-2
Distance:	2m/2m3: 2-3 2m4-2m7: 0-0 3m+: 0-0
Track:	LH: 2-3 RH: 0-0 Tight: 0-1 Gall: 0-0
Aids:	Bl: 0-0 Vi: 0-0 Tstrap: 0-0 Ckp: 0-0
Best Rating:	109 8/03 Uttx 2m gd-fm Hdl

Modest hurdler; grand, big type; facile winner of a novices' hurdle at Uttoxeter in July; acts on fast; should make a useful chaser.

Towns Ender (IRE)
107(102h)   (87h)**92**

6-y-o b g Zaffaran (USA)-Delway (Fidel)
M Scudamore Mrs S Tainton

Placings:005-30P35 (3842)
2003/04: 17^{3}G, 19^{0}GF, 22^{P}G, 16^{3}G, 19^{5}GS,

	Starts	1st	2nd	3rd	Win & Pl
Hurdles	3	0	0	1	498
Chases	2	0	0	1	530
Career Total	8	0	0	2	1028

Going:	Sf: 0-0 GS: 0-1 Gd: 0-3 GF: - Fm: 0-1
Distance:	2m/2m3: 0-4 2m4-2m7: 0-1 3m+: 0-0
Track:	LH: 0-3 RH: 0-2 Tight: 0-1 Gall: 0-1
Aids:	Bl: 0-0 Vi: 0-0 Tstrap: 0-5 Ckp: 0-0
Best Rating:	98 1/04 Leic 2m good Ch

Plating-class maiden hurdler; has shown a little ability over fences; stays 2m 6f; acts on good.

Toy Boy (IRE)
105   **93**

6-y-o b g Un Desperado (FR)-Too Sharp (True Song)
Miss H C Knight Sir Anthony Scott

Placings:0-5PP (4868)
2003/04: 19^{5}GF, 21^{P}G, 20^{P}GS,

	Starts	1st	2nd	3rd	Win & Pl
Hurdles	3	0	0	0	
Career Total	4	0	0	0	

Going:	Sf: 0-0 GS: 0-1 Gd: 0-1 GF: - Fm: 0-1
Distance:	2m/2m3: 0-1 2m4-2m7: 0-2 3m+: 0-0
Track:	LH: 0-2 RH: 0-1 Tight: 0-1 Gall: 0-1
Aids:	Bl: 0-0 Vi: 0-0 Tstrap: 0-0 Ckp: 0-0
Best Rating:	90 12/03 Newb 2m3f gd-fm Hdl

Has shown promise; will do better in handicaps.

Trabolgan (IRE)
108   **133+**

6-y-o b g King's Ride-Derrella (Derrylin)

N J Henderson Trevor Hemmings

Placings:222-F11P   (3756)
2003/04: 16^FGS, 20¹G, 19¹S, 19^PG,

	Starts	1st	2nd	3rd	Win & Pl
Hurdles	4	2	0		11115
Career Total	7	2	3	0	21678
133 1/04 Newb	2m3f		E Hdl	SFT	£3640
127 12/03 Asct	2m4f		D Hdl	GD	£7475
				Total win prize-money £11115

Going:	Sf: 1-1 GS: 0-1 Gd: 1-2 GF: - Fm: 0-0
Distance:	2m2m3: 1-2 2m4-2m7: 1-2 3m+: 0-0
Track:	LH: 1-2 RH: 1-2 Tight: 0-2 Gall: 1-1
Aids:	Bl: 0-0 Vi: 0-0 Tstrap: 0-0 Ckp: 0-0
Best Rating:	141 3/03 Chel 2m110y good NHF

Favourite when creditable runner-up in bumpers at Uttoxeter in December and Kempton in February; filled the same position behind Liberman at Cheltenham Festival; easy winner of novice hurdles at Ascot and Newbury; pulled up at an early stage at Market Rasen in February; stays 2m 4f; effective on soft ground; potentially very useful.

Track O' Profit (IRE)

12-y-o ch g Kambalda-Teazle (Quayside)
Miss S Young B R J Young

Placings:30/P44253632/42P/1U/13-P   (0490)
2003/04: 26^PGF,

	Starts	1st	2nd	3rd	Win & Pl
Chases	1	0	0	0	
Career Total	19	2	3	4	17032
105 2/03 Tntn	3m	H Ch		G-S	£2394
98 5/01 NAbb	2m5f110yB	HCh	G-F	£10290
				Total win prize-money £12685

Going:	Sf: 0-0 GS: 0-0 Gd: 0-0 GF: - Fm: 0-1
Distance:	2m2m3: 0-0 2m4-2m7: 0-0 3m+: 0-1
Track:	LH: 0-1 RH: 0-0 Tight: 0-1 Gall: 0-0
Aids:	Bl: 0-0 Vi: 0-0 Tstrap: 0-0 Ckp: 0-0
Best Rating:	105 2/03 Tntn 3m gd-sft Ch

Fair hunter chaser; stays three miles and best on soft ground.

Trade Off (IRE)

91(91h)   (92h)100+
6-y-o br g Roselier (FR)-Lady Owenette (IRE) (Salluceva)
M C Pipe D A Johnson

Placings:4003F52   (4753)
2003/04: 17⁴G, 16⁰GS, 16⁰G, 19³G, 24^FS, 24⁵G, 26⁶G,

	Starts	1st	2nd	3rd	Win & Pl
NH Flat	1	0	0	0	
Hurdles	3	0	0	1	394
Chases	3	0	1	0	984
Career Total	7	0	1	1	1378

Going:	Sf: 0-1 GS: 0-2 Gd: 0-4 GF: - Fm: 0-0
Distance:	2m2m3: 0-3 2m4-2m7: 0-1 3m+: 0-3
Track:	LH: 0-4 RH: 0-3 Tight: 0-3 Gall: 0-1
Aids:	Bl: 0-0 Vi: 0-0 Tstrap: 0-0 Ckp: 0-0
Best Rating:	100 4/04 Plum 3m2f good Ch

Modest form in novice hurdles and handicap chase; stays two and a half miles; acts on good ground.

Trading Trouble

98   (125h)113
7-y-o b g Petoski-Marielou (FR) (Carwhite)

J M Jefferson Richard Collins

Placings:261/22116/3F3-2U30   (0924)
2003/04: 16²G, 20^UG, 20³G, 22⁰GF,

	Starts	1st	2nd	3rd	Win & Pl
Hurdles	1	0	0	0	0
Chases	3	0	1	1	2708
Career Total	15	3	4	3	16013
116 3/02 Uttx	2m4f110yD Hdl		HVY	£3484
125 3/02 Uttx	2m4f110yD Hdl		HVY	£3993
98 3/01 Hntg	2m110y H NHF		SFT	£1960
				Total win prize-money £9438

Going:	Sf: 0-0 GS: 0-0 Gd: 0-3 GF: - Fm: 0-1
Distance:	2m2m3: 0-1 2m4-2m7: 0-3 3m+: 0-0
Track:	LH: 0-0 RH: 0-3 Tight: 0-1 Gall: 0-0
Aids:	Bl: 0-0 Vi: 0-0 Tstrap: 0-0 Ckp: 0-0
Best Rating:	125 3/02 Uttx 2m4f110y heavy Hdl

Modest novice chaser; bumper and hurdle winner; suited by two and a half miles; best on soft ground.

Traditional (IRE)

8-y-o ch g Erin's Isle-Noorajo (IRE) (Ahonoora)
Miss Chloe Newman (N J Hawke 26/5) Granville Taylor

Placings:6/4/00500211065406-P5PP4PP   (4858)
2003/04: 24^PG, 21⁵GF, 22^PGF, 23^PG, 19⁴GS, 19^PG, 24^PGF,

	Starts	1st	2nd	3rd	Win & Pl
Chases	7	0	0	0	
Career Total	23	2	1	0	8822
92 10/02 Dpat	2m6f	Hdl		G-F	£3809
92 9/02 Dpat	2m4f110y Hdl		GD	£3809
				Total win prize-money £7620

Going:	Sf: 0-0 GS: 0-1 Gd: 0-3 GF: - Fm: 0-3
Distance:	2m2m3: 0-1 2m4-2m7: 0-3 3m+: 0-3
Track:	LH: 0-0 RH: 0-6 Tight: 0-3 Gall: 0-0
Aids:	Bl: 0-2 Vi: 0-0 Tstrap: 0-0 Ckp: 0-3
Best Rating:	94 4/02 Fair 2m yield Hdl

Tragic Dancer

97   83+
8-y-o b g Tragic Role (USA)-Chantallee's Pride (Mansooj)
D J Wintle E Treadwell/miss M Butler

Placings:PP/0056P   (4750)
2003/04: 16⁰G, 16⁰S, 16⁵GS, 17⁶G, 21^PG,

	Starts	1st	2nd	3rd	Win & Pl
Hurdles	5	0	0	0	0
Career Total	7	0	0	0	0

Going:	Sf: 0-1 GS: 0-1 Gd: 0-3 GF: - Fm: 0-0
Distance:	2m2m3: 0-4 2m4-2m7: 0-1 3m+: 0-0
Track:	LH: 0-2 RH: 0-3 Tight: 0-2 Gall: 0-0
Aids:	Bl: 0-0 Vi: 0-0 Tstrap: 0-0 Ckp: 0-0
Best Rating:	83 3/04 Tntn 2m1f good Hdl

Tragic Ohio

104   125+
5-y-o b g Tragic Role (USA)-Kiniohio (FR) (Script Ohio (USA))
P F Nicholls Sandicroft Stud I

Placings:14-11P   (4190)
2003/04: 16¹S, 17¹HY, 18^PGS,

	Starts	1st	2nd	3rd	Win & Pl
Hurdles	3	2	0	0	7009
Career Total	5	3	0	0	9067

125 2/04 Hrfd	2m1f	E Hdl	HVY	£3477
100 1/04 Winc	2m	E Hdl	SFT	£3531
110 2/03 Extr	2m1f	H NHF	G-S	£2058
			Total win prize-money £9068

Going:	Sf: 2-2 GS: 0-1 Gd: 0-0 GF: - Fm: 0-0
Distance:	2m/2m3: 2-3 2m4-2m7: 0-0 3m+: 0-0
Track:	LH: 0-1 RH: 2-2 Tight: 0-1 Gall: 0-0
Aids:	Bl: 0-0 Vi: 0-0 Tstrap: 0-0 Ckp: 0-0
Best Rating:	125 2/04 Hrfd 2m1f heavy Hdl

Useful novice hurdler; bumper winner; won on hurdling debut at Wincanton and followed up at Hereford; should stay 2m 4f; acts well on soft ground.

Trained Bythe Best

112
6-y-o b m Alderbrook-Princess Moodyshoe (Jalmood (USA))
M C Pipe Mrs Alison C Farrant

Placings:13P3/03P-P   (2419)
2003/04: 22^PGS,

	Starts	1st	2nd	3rd	Win & Pl
Hurdles	1	0	0	0	
Career Total	8	1	0	3	3788
113 12/01 Font	2m2f110yE Hdl		GD	£2502
				Total win prize-money £2503

Going:	Sf: 0-0 GS: 0-1 Gd: 0-0 GF: - Fm: 0-0
Distance:	2m/2m3: 0-0 2m4-2m7: 0-1 3m+: 0-0
Track:	LH: 0-1 RH: 0-0 Tight: 0-0 Gall: 0-0
Aids:	Bl: 0-0 Vi: 0-1 Tstrap: 0-1 Ckp: 0-0
Best Rating:	113 11/02 Hayd 2m4f good Hdl

Modest hurdler; stays well; acts on a sound surface; lightly raced recently.

Tramantano

110   138+
5-y-o b g Muhtarram (USA)-Hatta Breeze (Night Shift (USA))
N A Twiston-Davies H R Mould

Placings:14440-521   (2455)
2003/04: 16⁵GS, 22²G, 16¹GS,

	Starts	1st	2nd	3rd	Win & Pl
Hurdles	3	1	1	0	20773
Career Total	8	2	1	0	29650
144 11/03 Newb	2m110y A(0-145)Hdl	G-S	£14500
111 11/02 Newb	2m110y C Hdl	SFT	£6708
			Total win prize-money £21208

Going:	Sf: 0-0 GS: 1-2 Gd: 0-1 GF: - Fm: 0-0
Distance:	2m/2m3: 1-2 2m4-2m7: 0-1 3m+: 0-0
Track:	LH: 1-3 RH: 0-0 Tight: 0-1 Gall: 1-1
Aids:	Bl: 0-0 Vi: 0-0 Tstrap: 0-2 Ckp: 0-0
Best Rating:	144 11/03 Newb 2m110y gd-sft Hdl

Very useful hurdler; suited by two miles, but stays two miles six; acts on good and soft ground; has worn a tongue tie; more to come.

Transatlantic (USA)

103   81
6-y-o gr g Dumaani (USA)-Viendra (USA) (Raise A Native)
H D Daly Mrs A Timpson

Placings:000P-62P   (2791)
2003/04: 20⁶GS, 16²G, 17^PGS,

	Starts	1st	2nd	3rd	Win & Pl
Hurdles	3	0	1	0	864
Career Total	7	0	1	0	864

Going: Sf: 0-0 GS: 0-1 Gd: 0-1 GF: - Fm: 0-1
Distance: 2m/2m3: 0-2 2m4-2m7: 0-1 3m+: 0-0
Track: LH: 0-2 RH: 0-1 Tight: 0-0 Gall: 0-0
Aids: Bl: 0-0 Vi: 0-0 Tstrap: 0-0 Ckp: 0-0
Best Rating: 81 12/03 Leic 2m   good   Hdl

Plating-class hurdler; headstrong sort; effective over two miles.

Transit

102(98h)   (97h)113+
5-y-o b g Lion Cavern (USA)-Black Fighter (USA)
(Secretariat (USA))
B Ellison Graeme Redpath

		Placings:552-0344U21P				(4391)

2003/04: 16⁰G, 21³S, 17⁴GF, 16⁴GS, 16ᵁGS, 16²G, 17¹GS, 21²FG,

	Starts	1st	2nd	3rd	Win & Pl
Hurdles	5	0	0	1	493
Chases	3	1	1	0	8909
Career Total	11	1	2	1	10598
113 3/04 MRas 2m1f110yD(0-120)HCh G-S £6825

Total win prize-money £6825

Going: Sf: 0-1 GS: 1-3 Gd: 0-3 GF: - Fm: 0-1
Distance: 2m/2m3: 1-6 2m4-2m7: 0-2 3m+: 0-0
Track: LH: 0-5 RH: 1-3 Tight: 1-5 Gall: 0-2
Aids: Bl: 0-1 Vi: 0-0 Tstrap: 0-0 Ckp: 1-7
Best Rating: 113 3/04 MRas 2m1f110y gd-sft   Ch

Plating-class hurdler; revelation on second start over fences landing a gamble from an in-form opponent at Market Rasen in March; best at two miles; acts on any ground; has worn cheekpieces.

Translucid (USA)

104(106h)   (119+h)128+
6-y-o b/br h Woodman (USA)-Gossamer (USA) (Seattle Slew (USA))
C Von Der Recke Bmk Racing

		Placings:2216-24620				(4193)

2003/04: 17²G, 16⁴GF, 16⁶G, 20²G, 18⁰G,

	Starts	1st	2nd	3rd	Win & Pl
Hurdles	2	0	1	0	3156
Chases	3	0	1	0	3858
Career Total	9	1	4	0	17937
117 11/02 Wwck 2m E Hdl G-S £3747

Total win prize-money £3747

Going: Sf: 0-0 GS: 0-0 Gd: 0-4 GF: - Fm: 0-1
Distance: 2m/2m3: 0-4 2m4-2m7: 0-1 3m+: 0-0
Track: LH: 0-2 RH: 0-2 Tight: 0-0 Gall: 0-1
Aids: Bl: 0-0 Vi: 0-0 Tstrap: 0-0 Ckp: 0-0
Best Rating: 128 12/03 Kemp 2m4f110y good   Ch

Fair hurdler/novice chaser; keen sort; best at two miles; acts with cut in the ground.

Travel (POL)

76   72
4-y-o gr g Freedom's Choice (USA)-Transylwania (POL) (Baby Bid (USA))
T R George Mrs Sharon C Nelson

		Placings:0P0				(3422)

2003/04: 17⁰G, 16ᴾS, 17⁰HY,

	Starts	1st	2nd	3rd	Win & Pl
Hurdles	3	0	0	0	
Career Total	3	0	0	0	

Going: Sf: 0-2 GS: 0-0 Gd: 0-1 GF: - Fm: 0-0

Distance: 2m/2m3: 0-3 2m4-2m7: 0-0 3m+: 0-0
Track: LH: 0-2 RH: 0-1 Tight: 0-1 Gall: 0-2
Aids: Bl: 0-0 Vi: 0-0 Tstrap: 0-0 Ckp: 0-0
Best Rating: 75 1/04 Chel 2m1f   good   Hdl

Decent on the level in Poland; acts with cut; well beaten over hurdles.

Traveller's Fayre (IRE)

5-y-o b g Fayruz-The Way She Moves (North Stoke)
Mrs Dianne Sayer (Mrs E Slack 3/12) A Slack

		Placings:000PPF				(3767)

2003/04: 17⁰GF, 17⁰G, 16⁰G, 19ᴾGS, 20ᴾHY, 17ᶠHY,

	Starts	1st	2nd	3rd	Win & Pl
NH Flat	3	0	0	0	0
Hurdles	3	0	0	0	0
Career Total	6	0	0	0	

Going: Sf: 0-2 GS: 0-1 Gd: 0-2 GF: - Fm: 0-1
Distance: 2m/2m3: 0-5 2m4-2m7: 0-1 3m+: 0-0
Track: LH: 0-4 RH: 0-2 Tight: 0-2 Gall: 0-1
Aids: Bl: 0-0 Vi: 0-0 Tstrap: 0-1 Ckp: 0-0
Best Rating: 38 10/03 Carl 2m1f   gd-fm   NHF

Travellers Heir (IRE)

107   113+
6-y-o ch g Montelimar (USA)-Allaracket (IRE) (The Parson)
H D Daly Mrs Strachan, Griffith, Lewis & Graham

		Placings:3/402-P11004				(4372)

2003/04: 20ᴾGF, 16¹GF, 17¹G, 17⁰G, 19⁰G, 16⁴GF,

	Starts	1st	2nd	3rd	Win & Pl
Hurdles	6	2	0	0	7198
Career Total	10	2	1	1	8643
114 11/03 Bang 2m1f E Hdl GD £3486
111 11/03 Worc 2m E(0-105)HHdl G-F £3059

Total win prize-money £6545

Going: Sf: 0-0 GS: 0-0 Gd: 1-3 GF: - Fm: 1-3
Distance: 2m/2m3: 2-4 2m4-2m7: 0-2 3m+: 0-0
Track: LH: 2-4 RH: 0-2 Tight: 1-3 Gall: 0-2
Aids: Bl: 0-0 Vi: 0-0 Tstrap: 0-0 Ckp: 0-0
Best Rating: 114 11/03 Bang 2m1f   good   Hdl

Modest novice hurdler; off the mark at Worcester in November 2003 over two miles; won easily under a penalty; stays 2m5f; acts on fast ground.

Travelling Band (IRE)

99   105+
6-y-o b g Blues Traveller (IRE)-Kind Of Cute (Prince Sabo)
A M Balding Park House Partnership

		Placings:125				(2914)

2003/04: 16¹S, 16²S, 16⁵G,

	Starts	1st	2nd	3rd	Win & Pl
Hurdles	3	1	1	0	5222
Career Total	3	1	1	0	5222
94 11/03 Hayd 2m D Hdl SFT £3744

Total win prize-money £3744

Going: Sf: 1-2 GS: 0-0 Gd: 0-1 GF: - Fm: 0-0
Distance: 2m/2m3: 1-3 2m4-2m7: 0-0 3m+: 0-0
Track: LH: 1-2 RH: 0-1 Tight: 0-0 Gall: 0-0

Aids: Bl: 0-0 Vi: 0 Tstrap: 0-0 Ckp: 0-0
Best Rating: 105 12/03 Kemp 2m   good   Hdl

Promising hurdler, successful on debut at Haydock in November but beaten by a potentially useful opponent next time; useful on the Flat; suited by two miles and soft ground; likely to progress further.

Travelling Warrior

94f   82f
5-y-o b g Emperor Fountain-Gipsy Princess (Prince Daniel (USA))
M F Harris The Golden Anorak Partnership

		Placings:5				(1019)

2003/04: 16⁵GF,

	Starts	1st	2nd	3rd	Win & Pl
NH Flat	1	0	0	0	0
Career Total	1	0	0	0	0

Going: Sf: 0-0 GS: 0-0 Gd: 0-0 GF: - Fm: 0-1
Distance: 2m/2m3: 0-1 2m4-2m7: 0-0 3m+: 0-0
Track: LH: 0-1 RH: 0-0 Tight: 0-0 Gall: 0-0
Aids: Bl: 0-0 Vi: 0-0 Tstrap: 0-0 Ckp: 0-0
Best Rating: 82 8/03 Worc 2m   gd-fm   NHF

Promising fifth when 50/1 on bumper debut at Worcester August 2003.

Travello (GER)

101   98+
4-y-o b c Bakharoff (USA)-Travista (GER) (Days At Sea (USA))
M F Harris (C Von Der Recke 26/11) M Harris

		Placings:F34P				(2740)

2003/04: 16ᶠG, 16³GS, 16⁴G, 16ᴾS,

	Starts	1st	2nd	3rd	Win & Pl
Hurdles	4	0	0	1	876
Career Total	4	0	0	1	876

Going: Sf: 0-1 GS: 0-1 Gd: 0-2 GF: - Fm: 0-0
Distance: 2m/2m3: 0-4 2m4-2m7: 0-0 3m+: 0-0
Track: LH: 0-2 RH: 0-1 Tight: 0-1 Gall: 0-0
Aids: Bl: 0-0 Vi: 0-0 Tstrap: 0-0 Ckp: 0-0
Best Rating: 95 11/03 Weth 2m   gd-sft   Hdl

Ex-German hurdler; only moderate form so far in Britain.

Treasure Trail

84   92
5-y-o b g Millkom-Forever Shineing (Glint Of Gold)
S Kirk T Neill & Mrs John Lee

		Placings:100				(2652)

2003/04: 16¹G, 16⁶GS, 20⁰G,

	Starts	1st	2nd	3rd	Win & Pl
Hurdles	3	1	0	0	2121
Career Total	3	1	0	0	2121
92 11/03 Fknm 2m F Hdl GD £2121

Total win prize-money £2121

Going: Sf: 0-0 GS: 0-1 Gd: 1-2 GF: - Fm: 0-0
Distance: 2m/2m3: 1-2 2m4-2m7: 0-1 3m+: 0-0
Track: LH: 1-2 RH: 0-0 Tight: 1-2 Gall: 0-1
Aids: Bl: 0-0 Vi: 0-0 Tstrap: 0-0 Ckp: 0-0
Best Rating: 92 11/03 Fknm 2m   good   Hdl

Fair Flat handicapper; made a winning hurdles debut but well beaten in a warm race next time.

Treasured Coin

96 **76**

6-y-o b g Overbury (IRE)-Slip A Coin (Slip Anchor)
P Bowen Eamonn O'Malley

Placings:004P0/2P-4 (0981)
2003/04: 21⁴GF,

	Starts	1st	2nd	3rd	Win & Pl
Hurdles	1	0	0	0	0
Career Total	8	0	1	0	884

Going:	Sf: 0-0 GS: 0-0 Gd: 0-0 GF: - Fm: 0-1
Distance:	2m/2m3: 0-0 2m4-2m7: 0-1 3m+: 0-0
Track:	LH: 0-1 RH: 0-0 Tight: 0-1 Gall: 0-0
Aids:	Bl: 0-0 Vi: 0-0 Tstrap: 0-0 Ckp: 0-0
Best Rating:	76 7/03 Sedg 2m5f110y gd-fm Hdl

Plating-class hurdler, stays two and a half miles.

Treble Vision (IRE)

10-y-o ch g Down The Hatch-General Vision (General Ironside)
W G Young W G Young

Placings:P (4660)
2003/04: 24⁵S,

	Starts	1st	2nd	3rd	Win & Pl
Hurdles	1	0	0	0	
Career Total	1	0	0	0	

Going:	Sf: 0-1 GS: 0-0 Gd: 0-0 GF: - Fm: 0-0
Distance:	2m/2m3: 0-0 2m4-2m7: 0-0 3m+: 0-1
Track:	LH: 0-1 RH: 0-0 Tight: 0-0 Gall: 0-0
Aids:	Bl: 0-0 Vi: 0-0 Tstrap: 0-0 Ckp: 0-0

Treen (IRE)

84 **60+**

5-y-o b m Charnwood Forest (IRE)-Legende D'Or (FR) (Diesis)
K J Burke Dr Paschal Carmody

Placings:04 (1588)
2003/04: 18⁰GF, 16⁴GF,

	Starts	1st	2nd	3rd	Win & Pl
Hurdles	2	0	0	0	
Career Total	2	0	0	0	

Going:	Sf: 0-0 GS: 0-0 Gd: 0-0 GF: - Fm: 0-2
Distance:	2m/2m3: 0-2 2m4-2m7: 0-0 3m+: 0-0
Track:	LH: 0-0 RH: 0-2 Tight: 0-0 Gall: 0-0
Aids:	Bl: 0-0 Vi: 0-0 Tstrap: 0-0 Ckp: 0-0
Best Rating:	60 10/03 Ludl 2m gd-fm Hdl

Showed nothing on the Flat in Ireland; tailed off on hurdling debut at Fairyhouse September 2003; dead-heated for fourth in poor seller at Ludlow the following month.

Tregastel (FR)

104

9-y-o b g Tel Quel (FR)-Myrtlewood (FR) (Home Guard (USA))
R Ford (E Chevalier Du Fau 23/6) D W Watson

Placings:P/2016/044F531/06P-32UB (2406)
2003/04: 22³VS, 21²VS, 22⁰UG, 24⁶S,

	Starts	1st	2nd	3rd	Win & Pl
Chases	4	0	1	1	7091

Career Total | 19 | 2 | 2 | 2 | 48691
4/02 Autl 2m5f110y Ch VS £13252
9/99 Autl 2m2f Hdl SFT £11840
Total win prize-money £25092

Going:	Sf: 0-1 GS: 0-0 Gd: 0-1 GF: - Fm: 0-0
Distance:	2m/2m3: 0-0 2m4-2m7: 0-3 3m+: 0-1
Track:	LH: 0-2 RH: 0-1 Tight: 0-1 Gall: 0-0
Aids:	Bl: 0-0 Vi: 0-0 Tstrap: 0-0 Ckp: 0-0

Fair novice chaser; ex-French; did not jump well and unseated his rider on his British debut; winner over two miles five on soft ground in his native country.

Tremallt (IRE)

113(89h) (102h)**130**

13-y-o b g Henbit (USA)-Secret Romance (Gala Performance (ZIM))
T R George Silkword Racing Partnership

Placings:2/226/U12FF1F11/16UP/5146FF/10616/0030-4F2PU22422 (4784)
2003/04: 22⁴G, 27⁶G, 24²S, 24⁹GF, 25⁰S, 25²S, 20²S, 24⁴G, 24²GS, 24²G,

	Starts	1st	2nd	3rd	Win & Pl
Hurdles	1	0	0	0	360
Chases	9	0	5	0	17860
Career Total	42	8	9	1	99166
144	12/01 Kemp 3m	C(0-135)HCh	GD	£29000
102	10/01 MRas 3m	E Hdl	G-S	£3374
144	10/00 Kemp 3m	B(0-145)HCh	G-S	£14794
144	10/99 Worc 2m7f110yC(0-130)HCh	GD	£6807
142	4/99 Uttx 2m4f	D(0-125)HCh	G-S	£4455
134	3/99 Uttx 2m4f	F(0-100)HCh	HVY	£3809
114	2/99 Uttx 2m5f	C HCh	HVY	£7002
107	11/98 Bang 2m4f110yE(0-105)HCh	SFT	£3598

Total win prize-money £72042

Going:	Sf: 0-4 GS: 0-1 Gd: 0-4 GF: - Fm: 0-1
Distance:	2m/2m3: 0-0 2m4-2m7: 0-2 3m+: 0-8
Track:	LH: 0-5 RH: 0-5 Tight: 0-4 Gall: 0-2
Aids:	Bl: 0-0 Vi: 0-0 Tstrap: 0-0 Ckp: 0-0
Best Rating:	144 12/01 Kemp 3m good Ch

Fair veteran chaser; goes well at Kempton; likes to front-run, but prone to the odd jumping error; stays three miles and best with a little cut in the ground; has worn a visor.

Tremezzo

75

6-y-o b g Mind Games-Rosa Van Fleet (Sallust)
B R Millman G Battocchi

Placings:0413432/FP (4735)
2003/04: 16⁶G, 17⁰G,

	Starts	1st	2nd	3rd	Win & Pl
Hurdles	2	0	0	0	
Career Total	9	1	1	2	3015
75	11/01 Tntn 2m1f	G Hdl	G-S	£1669

Total win prize-money £1670

Going:	Sf: 0-0 GS: 0-0 Gd: 0-2 GF: - Fm: 0-0
Distance:	2m/2m3: 0-2 2m4-2m7: 0-0 3m+: 0-0
Track:	LH: 0-1 RH: 0-1 Tight: 0-1 Gall: 0-0
Aids:	Bl: 0-0 Vi: 0-0 Tstrap: 0-2 Ckp: 0-0
Best Rating:	75 4/02 Winc 2m good Hdl

Trenance

91 **83**

6-y-o b g Alflora (IRE)-Carmel's Joy (IRE) (Carlingford Castle)
T R George Mr & Mrs D A Gamble

Placings:0-PP60 (4946)
2003/04: 20⁰GS, 24²S, 16⁶GS, 16⁹GS,

	Starts	1st	2nd	3rd	Win & Pl
Hurdles	4	0	0	0	0
Career Total	5	0	0	0	0

Going:	Sf: 0-1 GS: 0-2 Gd: 0-1 GF: - Fm: 0-0
Distance:	2m/2m3: 0-2 2m4-2m7: 0-1 3m+: 0-0
Track:	LH: 0-1 RH: 0-3 Tight: 0-1 Gall: 0-0
Aids:	Bl: 0-0 Vi: 0-0 Tstrap: 0-0 Ckp: 0-0
Best Rating:	83 3/04 Sand 2m110y good Hdl

Tresor De Mai (FR)

104 **149**

10-y-o ch g Grand Tresor (FR)-Lady Night (FR) (Pompon Rouge)
M C Pipe Joe Moran

Placings:1112/151225/4F1334/P224UFP/1P1/4305-304505 (4450)
2003/04: 16⁵GY, 21³F, 20⁰GS, 24⁴S, 19⁵GS, 24⁰S, 24⁵GS,

	Starts	1st	2nd	3rd	Win & Pl
Chases	7	0	0	1	7919
Career Total	36	8	5	4	167799
160	2/02 Asct	2m3f110yA Ch	G-S	£37700
153	1/02 Asct	2m3f110yB HCh	GD	£10250
151	12/99 Asct	3m110y B HCh	G-S	£29050
142	1/99 Ling	2m E Ch	HVY	£2684
	10/98 Segr	2m3f Ch	SFT	£2727
	3/98 Vire	2m1f Hdl	HLD	£2525
	11/97 Vire	2m1f Hdl	GD	£3143

Total win prize-money £88080

Going:	Sf: 0-2 GS: 0-3 Gd: 0-0 GF: - Fm: 0-1
Distance:	2m/2m3: 0-1 2m4-2m7: 0-3 3m+: 0-3
Track:	LH: 0-1 RH: 0-6 Tight: 0-0 Gall: 0-1
Aids:	Bl: 0-0 Vi: 0-0 Tstrap: 0-0 Ckp: 0-0
Best Rating:	160 2/02 Asct 2m3f110y gd-sft Ch

Very useful chaser; has won over three miles, but effective at shorter; not the best of jumpers, but has run well in decent contests and appears to like Ascot; best suited by an easy surface; falling in the weights.

Tresor Preziniere (FR)

98(105h) (111h)**115**

6-y-o b/br g Grand Tresor (FR)-Rose De Martine (FR) (The Quiet Man (FR))
P J Hobbs Bob Jevon

Placings:050/P05FO1331034F-1363F036F6 (4734)
2003/04: 20¹GF, 20³GF, 22⁶G, 19³GS, 20⁵G, 21⁰G, 20³HY, 21⁶G, 24⁶G, 26⁶G,

	Starts	1st	2nd	3rd	Win & Pl
Hurdles	4	1	0	2	6654
Chases	6	0	0	1	1620
Career Total	26	3	0	6	18146
102	10/03 Chep 2m4f	E Hdl	G-F	£2590
	10/02 Ange 2m3f	Ch	SFT	£3979
	8/02 Joss 2m2f	Ch	SFT	£2061

Total win prize-money £8630

Going:	Sf: 0-1 GS: 0-1 Gd: 0-6 GF: - Fm: 1-2
Distance:	2m/2m3: 0-0 2m4-2m7: 1-8 3m+: 0-1
Track:	LH: 1-8 RH: 0-2 Tight: 0-3 Gall: 0-1
Aids:	Bl: 0-6 Vi: 0-0 Tstrap: 0-0 Ckp: 0-0
Best Rating:	115 12/03 Chep 2m3f110y gd-sft Ch

Modest hurdler/chaser; twice a winner over fences on soft ground in the French provinces; bits and pieces of form over

both hurdles and fences since arriving in Britain; acts on most types of ground; suited by around 2m 4f; often blinkered.

Tribal Dancer (IRE)

108(109h)   (118h) 118

10-y-o ch g Commanche Run-Cute Play (Salluceva)
Miss Venetia Williams You Can Be Sure

Placings:1/P5/0423115210/24152-FP4PPP0P2341 **(4784)**
2003/04: 25²G, 24⁵G, 26⁴G, 24⁵GS, 29²G, 24⁵GS, 22⁰S, 20⁷HY, 26²G, 24³G, 26⁴GS, 24¹G,

	Starts	1st	2nd	3rd	Win & Pl
Hurdles	4	0	1	0	1534
Chases	8	1	0	1	8447
Career Total	**30**	**6**	**5**	**2**	**35286**
116 4/04 Hntg	3m	D(0-120)HCh		GD	£5694
109 2/03 Tntn	3m	E Ch		G-S	£4403
118 2/02 Sand	2m4fl110yD(0-120)HHdl			SFT	£4465
104 12/01 Ludl	2m5f	E(0-105)HHdl		GD	£2733
105 11/01 Ludl	3m	F(0-105)HHdl		G-F	£3513
118 4/00 Hntg	2m110y	H NHF		GD	£1715
			Total win prize-money £22526		

Going:	Sf: 0-2 GS: 0-3 Gd: 1-7 GF: - Fm: 0-0
Distance:	2m/2m3: 0-0 2m4-2m7: 0-2 **3m+: 1-10**
Track:	LH: 0-3 **RH: 1-9** Tight: 0-2 Gall: 1-1
Aids:	Bl: 0-1 Vi: 0-0 Tstrap: 0-0 Ckp: 0-0
Best Rating:	**118** 4/03 Bang 3m110y gd-fm Ch

Fair chaser/modest hurdler; recorded second success over fences at Huntingdon in April; stays three miles; acts on a sound surface, but has been successful on soft ground.

Tribal Dispute

94   114

7-y-o b g Primitive Rising (USA)-Coral Princess (Imperial Fling (USA))
T D Easterby Mrs Jennifer E Pallister

Placings:4/040212210-0   **(4513)**
2003/04: 16⁹GS,

	Starts	1st	2nd	3rd	Win & Pl
Hurdles	1	0	0	0	
Career Total	**11**	**2**	**3**	**0**	**10804**
113 4/03 Kels	2m110y	E Hdl	GD	£3575
107 1/03 Newc	2m	E(0-100)HHdl	HVY	£3380
			Total win prize-money £6955

Going:	Sf: 0-0 GS: 0-1 Gd: 0-0 GF: - Fm: 0-0
Distance:	2m/2m3: 0-1 2m4-2m7: 0-0 3m+: 0-0
Track:	LH: 0-1 RH: 0-0 Tight: 0-0 Gall: 0-0
Aids:	Bl: 0-0 Vi: 0-0 Tstrap: 0-0 Ckp: 0-0
Best Rating:	**114** 3/03 Newc 2m gd-sft Hdl

Fair novice hurdler; suited by cut in the ground effective on faster; effective over two miles, but does stay further; scored at Wetherby in January 2003 and Kelso in April; progressive.

Tribal Run (IRE)

95   108

9-y-o ch g Be My Native (USA)-Queen's Run (IRE) (Deep Run)
C Grant Trevor Hemmings

Placings:6/0P0/PFP/1222-632   **(4457)**
2003/04: 25⁵S, 24³HY, 24²HY,

	Starts	1st	2nd	3rd	Win & Pl
Chases	3	0	1	0	2330
Career Total	**14**	**1**	**4**	**1**	**11021**
102 11/02 Hexm	3m1f	F Ch	HVY	£2746
			Total win prize-money £2746

Going:	Sf: 0-3 GS: 0-0 Gd: 0-0 GF: - Fm: 0-0
Distance:	2m/2m3: 0-0 2m4-2m7: 0-0 3m+: 0-3
Track:	LH: 0-3 RH: 0-0 Tight: 0-1 Gall: 0-2
Aids:	Bl: 0-0 Vi: 0-0 Tstrap: 0-3 Ckp: 0-0
Best Rating:	**108** 2/03 Catt 3m6f good Ch

Modest staying chaser, won a maiden chase at Hexham in November and has run well since. Acts in testing ground, wears a tongue tie.

Tribal Tract (IRE)

10-y-o b g Alphabatim (USA)-Wiji Damar (Laurence O)
P H Morris G E Evans

Placings:432/3P52P/P-0   **(0073)**
2003/04: 24⁰S,

	Starts	1st	2nd	3rd	Win & Pl
Chases	1	0	0	0	
Career Total	**10**	**0**	**2**	**2**	**3224**

Going:	Sf: 0-1 GS: 0-0 Gd: 0-0 GF: - Fm: 0-0
Distance:	2m/2m3: 0-0 2m4-2m7: 0-0 3m+: 0-1
Track:	LH: 0-1 RH: 0-0 Tight: 0-1 Gall: 0-0
Aids:	Bl: 0-0 Vi: 0-0 Tstrap: 0-0 Ckp: 0-0
Best Rating:	**100** 10/01 Bang 3m110y soft Ch

Trickey Nick

5-y-o b g Nomadic Way (USA)-Nicky's Choice (Baron Blakeney)
B N Doran Dave Nicholls

Placings:P   **(4374)**
2003/04: 16⁶GF,

	Starts	1st	2nd	3rd	Win & Pl
NH Flat	1	0	0	0	
Career Total	**1**	**0**	**0**	**0**	

Going:	Sf: 0-0 GS: 0-0 Gd: 0-0 GF: - Fm: 0-1
Distance:	2m/2m3: 0-1 2m4-2m7: 0-0 3m+: 0-0
Track:	LH: 0-0 RH: 0-0 Tight: 0-0 Gall: 0-0
Aids:	Bl: 0-0 Vi: 0-0 Tstrap: 0-0 Ckp: 0-0

Tricky Thyne (IRE)

68   47

5-y-o b g Good Thyne (USA)-Cuban Vacation (Ovac (ITY))
R Dickin T M T Racing

Placings:000P   **(4915)**
2003/04: 17⁰GS, 16⁰G, 19⁰G, 16⁶GS,

	Starts	1st	2nd	3rd	Win & Pl
NH Flat	1	0	0	0	
Hurdles	3	0	0	0	0
Career Total	**4**	**0**	**0**	**0**	

Going:	Sf: 0-0 GS: 0-2 Gd: 0-2 GF: - Fm: 0-0
Distance:	2m/2m3: 0-3 2m4-2m7: 0-1 3m+: 0-0
Track:	LH: 0-1 RH: 0-3 Tight: 0-0 Gall: 0-0
Aids:	Bl: 0-0 Vi: 0-0 Tstrap: 0-1 Ckp: 0-0
Best Rating:	**47** 3/04 Sand 2m110y good Hdl

Tricky Trevor (IRE)

11-y-o b/br g Arctic Lord-Chancer's Last (Foggy Bell)

Mrs H J Cobb Mrs H J Cobb

Placings:3/022P0/5F5F/P-2F   **(4122)**
2003/04: 21²GF, 21⁶G,

	Starts	1st	2nd	3rd	Win & Pl
Chases	2	0	1	0	436
Career Total	**13**	**0**	**3**	**1**	**1800**

Going:	Sf: 0-0 GS: 0-0 Gd: 0-1 GF: - Fm: 0-1
Distance:	2m/2m3: 0-0 2m4-2m7: 0-2 3m+: 0-0
Track:	LH: 0-0 RH: 0-2 Tight: 0-2 Gall: 0-0
Aids:	Bl: 0-0 Vi: 0-0 Tstrap: 0-0 Ckp: 0-0
Best Rating:	**98** 4/98 MRas 1m5f110y soft NHF

Trigger Castle

9-y-o b m Henbit (USA)-Jane's Daughter (Pitpan)
P T Midgley (J S Wainwright 3/8) S Birkinshaw

Placings:PPP   **(1375)**
2003/04: 21⁶GF, 20⁸GF, 23⁸GF,

	Starts	1st	2nd	3rd	Win & Pl
Hurdles	1	0	0	0	0
Chases	2	0	0	0	0
Career Total	**3**	**0**	**0**	**0**	

Going:	Sf: 0-0 GS: 0-0 Gd: 0-0 GF: - Fm: 0-3
Distance:	2m/2m3: 0-0 2m4-2m7: 0-2 3m+: 0-1
Track:	LH: 0-2 RH: 0-1 Tight: 0-1 Gall: 0-0
Aids:	Bl: 0-0 Vi: 0-0 Tstrap: 0-0 Ckp: 0-0

Triggerlino

91f   74f

4-y-o b f Double Trigger (IRE)-Voolino (Relkino)
Miss Venetia Williams Mrs Valerie Nock-Sampson

Placings:00   **(3968)**
2003/04: 17⁰GS, 16⁹GS,

	Starts	1st	2nd	3rd	Win & Pl
NH Flat	2	0	0	0	
Career Total	**2**	**0**	**0**	**0**	

Going:	Sf: 0-0 GS: 0-2 Gd: 0-0 GF: - Fm: 0-0
Distance:	2m/2m3: 0-2 2m4-2m7: 0-0 3m+: 0-0
Track:	LH: 0-0 RH: 0-1 Tight: 0-0 Gall: 0-0
Aids:	Bl: 0-0 Vi: 0-0 Tstrap: 0-0 Ckp: 0-0
Best Rating:	**74** 1/04 Tntn 2m1f gd-sft NHF

Trillionaire

107   81

6-y-o ch g Dilum (USA)-Madam Trilby (Grundy)
Miss C J E Caroe Miss N F Thesiger

Placings:05/F4635000P3051-43065U00   **(3759)**
2003/04: 23⁴GF, 20³GF, 24⁰GF, 22⁶G, 24⁵GF, 21⁰GS, 21⁰GS, 22⁰G,

	Starts	1st	2nd	3rd	Win & Pl
Hurdles	8	0	0	1	724
Career Total	**23**	**1**	**0**	**3**	**5149**
81 4/03 MRas	2m6f	F(0-100)HHdl	GD	£3144
			Total win prize-money £3144

Going:	Sf: 0-0 GS: 0-2 Gd: 0-2 GF: - Fm: 0-4
Distance:	2m/2m3: 0-0 2m4-2m7: 0-5 3m+: 0-3
Track:	LH: 0-5 RH: 0-2 Tight: 0-2 Gall: 0-2
Aids:	Bl: 0-0 Vi: 0-0 Tstrap: 0-0 Ckp: 0-0
Best Rating:	**81** 6/03 Strf 2m6f110y good Hdl

Plating-class hurdler; finally broke his duck at the 15th attempt at Market Rasen in April 2003; acts on good ground.

Trinket (IRE)

99   101

6-y-o b g Definite Article-Alamiya (IRE) (Doyoun)
H D Daly Mrs Strachan, Mrs Gabb & Jim Morris

Placings:5/123-1   (4650)
2003/04: 19¹G,

	Starts	1st	2nd	3rd	Win & Pl
Hurdles	1	1	0	0	4300
Career Total	5	2	1	1	7546
101 4/04 Hrfd	2m3f110yE Hdl			GD	£4299
101 5/02 Worc	2m	H NHF		G-F	£1678
			Total win prize-money £5979		

Going:	Sf: 0-0 GS: 0-0 Gd: 1-1 GF: 0-0
Distance:	2m/2m3: 0-0 2m4-2m7: 1-1 3m+: 0-0
Track:	LH: 0-0 RH: 1-1 Tight: 0-0 Gall: 0-0
Aids:	Bl: 0-0 Vi: 0-0 Tstrap: 0-0 Ckp: 0-0
Best Rating:	101 4/04 Hrfd 2m3f110y good Hdl

Moderate novice hurdler; stays 2m4f; acts on a sound surface.

Triple Glory (IRE)

85(94h)   (68 h)51

5-y-o b m Goldmark (USA)-Trebles (IRE) (Kenmare (FR))
Mrs P N Dutfield Mrs Pat Scott

Placings:24UP-00P   (4672)
2003/04: 16⁹G, 19⁹G, 25²⁵G,

	Starts	1st	2nd	3rd	Win & Pl
Hurdles	1	0	0	0	0
Chases	2	0	0	0	0
Career Total	7	0	1	0	1268

Going:	Sf: 0-0 GS: 0-0 Gd: 0-3 GF: - Fm: 0-0
Distance:	2m/2m3: 0-1 2m4-2m7: 0-1 3m+: 0-1
Track:	LH: 0-0 RH: 0-3 Tight: 0-0 Gall: 0-0
Aids:	Bl: 0-0 Vi: 0-0 Tstrap: 0-0 Ckp: 0-0
Best Rating:	68 9/02 Font 2m2f110y gd-fm Hdl

Triple Play (IRE)

5-y-o br g Tagula (IRE)-Shiyra (Darshaan)
Lady Susan Watson (Don Enrico Incisa 26/8) Lady Susan Watson

Placings:P0   (4959)
2003/04: 17⁵G, 19⁴G,

	Starts	1st	2nd	3rd	Win & Pl
Hurdles	2	0	0	0	
Career Total	2	0	0	0	

Going:	Sf: 0-0 GS: 0-0 Gd: 0-2 GF: - Fm: 0-0
Distance:	2m/2m3: 0-1 2m4-2m7: 0-1 3m+: 0-0
Track:	LH: 0-0 RH: 0-2 Tight: 0-2 Gall: 0-0
Aids:	Bl: 0-0 Vi: 0-0 Tstrap: 0-0 Ckp: 0-0

Trisons Star (IRE)

99f   111f

6-y-o b g Roselier (FR)-Delkusha (Castle Keep)
Mrs L B Normile Taylor Martin Scoular and White

Placings:2   (4866)
2003/04: 16²S,

	Starts	1st	2nd	3rd	Win & Pl
NH Flat	1	0	1	0	1092
Career Total	1	0	1	0	1092

Going:	Sf: 0-1 GS: 0-0 Gd: 0-0 GF: - Fm: 0-0
Distance:	2m/2m3: 0-1 2m4-2m7: 0-0 3m+: 0-0
Track:	LH: 0-1 RH: 0-0 Tight: 0-0 Gall: 0-0
Aids:	Bl: 0-0 Vi: 0-0 Tstrap: 0-0 Ckp: 0-0
Best Rating:	111 4/04 Ayr 2m soft NHF

Did not complete in Irish points in 2003 but shaped well on debut at Ayr in April 2004 when runner-up to promising sort in bumper; sure to win a small race; acts on soft ground.

Tristana

39f

5-y-o b m Efisio-Michelle's Ella (IRE) (Ela-Mana-Mou)
J M Bradley Paul M Hicks

Placings:0   (3968)
2003/04: 16⁹GS,

	Starts	1st	2nd	3rd	Win & Pl
NH Flat	1	0	0	0	
Career Total	1	0	0	0	

Going:	Sf: 0-0 GS: 0-1 Gd: 0-0 GF: - Fm: 0-0
Distance:	2m/2m3: 0-1 2m4-2m7: 0-0 3m+: 0-0
Track:	LH: 0-0 RH: 0-1 Tight: 0-0 Gall: 0-0
Aids:	Bl: 0-0 Vi: 0-0 Tstrap: 0-0 Ckp: 0-0

Triumph Of Dubai (IRE)

98   84

4-y-o b g Eagle Eyed (USA)-Jack-N-Jilly (IRE) (Anita's Prince)
J S Moore Bob Reynolds

Placings:6100   (2819)
2003/04: 16⁸S, 17¹GF, 16⁹Gd, 16⁹GF,

	Starts	1st	2nd	3rd	Win & Pl
Hurdles	4	1	0	0	1862
Career Total	4	1	0	0	1862
79 11/03 Tntn	2m1f	G Hdl		G-F	£1862
			Total win prize-money £1862		

Going:	Sf: 0-1 GS: 0-0 Gd: 0-0 GF: - Fm: 1-3
Distance:	2m/2m3: 1-4 2m4-2m7: 0-0 3m+: 0-0
Track:	LH: 0-1 RH: 1-3 Tight: 1-1 Gall: 0-1
Aids:	Bl: 0-0 Vi: 0-0 Tstrap: 0-0 Ckp: 0-0
Best Rating:	84 12/03 Ludl 2m gd-fm Hdl

Plating-class hurdler; effective at around two miles.

Trivial (IRE)

(84c)   (64c)88

12-y-o b m Rakaposhi King-Miss Rubbish (Rubor)
J E Brockbank T Brockbank

Placings:54UP623/130R535-P   (0476)
2003/04: 20³G, 22²⁵GS,

	Starts	1st	2nd	3rd	Win & Pl
Hurdles	1	0	0	0	0
Chases	1	0	0	0	0
Career Total	15	1	1	3	5419
88 5/02 Prth	2m4f110yE Hdl			G-F	£3220
			Total win prize-money £3220		

Going:	Sf: 0-0 GS: 0-1 Gd: 0-1 GF: - Fm: 0-0
Distance:	2m/2m3: 0-0 2m4-2m7: 0-2 3m+: 0-0
Track:	LH: 0-2 RH: 0-0 Tight: 0-1 Gall: 0-0
Aids:	Bl: 0-0 Vi: 0-0 Tstrap: 0-0 Ckp: 0-0
Best Rating:	88 4/03 Hexm 2m4f110y good Hdl

Troedrhiwdalar

84   54

7-y-o b m Gunner B-Delladear (Sonnen Gold)
Mrs D A Hamer Mrs L G Foster

Placings:0/003P-364   (0611)
2003/04: 19³GS, 20⁶S, 26⁴GF,

	Starts	1st	2nd	3rd	Win & Pl
Hurdles	3	0	0	1	601
Career Total	8	0	0	2	977

Going:	Sf: 0-1 GS: 0-1 Gd: 0-0 GF: - Fm: 0-1
Distance:	2m/2m3: 0-0 2m4-2m7: 0-2 3m+: 0-1
Track:	LH: 0-1 RH: 0-2 Tight: 0-1 Gall: 0-1
Aids:	Bl: 0-0 Vi: 0-1 Tstrap: 0-0 Ckp: 0-0
Best Rating:	66 5/02 Extr 2m1f good NHF

Trojan Wolf

78   41

9-y-o ch g Wolfhound (USA)-Trojan Lady (USA) (Irish River (FR))
P Howling Max Pocock

Placings:0   (0156)
2003/04: 16⁹GF,

	Starts	1st	2nd	3rd	Win & Pl
Hurdles	1	0	0	0	
Career Total	1	0	0	0	

Going:	Sf: 0-0 GS: 0-0 Gd: 0-0 GF: - Fm: 0-1
Distance:	2m/2m3: 0-1 2m4-2m7: 0-0 3m+: 0-0
Track:	LH: 0-1 RH: 0-0 Tight: 0-1 Gall: 0-0
Aids:	Bl: 0-0 Vi: 0-0 Tstrap: 0-0 Ckp: 0-0
Best Rating:	41 5/03 Fknm 2m gd-fm Hdl

Troodos Valley (IRE)

97f   90f

5-y-o b g Executive Perk-Valleymay (IRE) (King's Ride)
H D Daly D Sandells

Placings:520   (4920)
2003/04: 16⁵HY, 16²GF, 16⁹GS,

	Starts	1st	2nd	3rd	Win & Pl
NH Flat	3	0	1	0	1174
Career Total	3	0	1	0	1174

Going:	Sf: 0-1 GS: 0-1 Gd: 0-0 GF: - Fm: 0-1
Distance:	2m/2m3: 0-3 2m4-2m7: 0-0 3m+: 0-0
Track:	LH: 0-2 RH: 0-0 Tight: 0-0 Gall: 0-0
Aids:	Bl: 0-0 Vi: 0-0 Tstrap: 0-0 Ckp: 0-0
Best Rating:	90 3/04 Strf 2m110y gd-fm NHF

Has shown ability in bumpers.

Trooper

103(98h)   93

10-y-o b g Rock Hopper-Silica (USA) (Mr Prospector (USA))
A Crook R M Bakes

Placings:14/2P015/2662212/5435303/562P2125P3P31-
10F424404B4P   (4432)
2003/04: 27¹S, 27⁰S, 25⁶G, 27⁴G, 27²GF, 27⁴GF, 25⁴GS, 27⁰G,
25⁴GS, 30⁸G, 27⁴GS, 32²G,

	Starts	1st	2nd	3rd	Win & Pl
Hurdles	1	0	0	0	0
Chases	11	1	1	0	6448
Career Total	48	6	9	6	32075

93	5/03	Sedg	3m3f	E(0-110)HCh	SFT	£4767
92	4/03	Sedg	3m3f	E Ch	G-F	£4342
93	10/02	Sedg	3m3f	F(0-90)HCh	GD	£3513
103	12/00	Leic	2m	G Hdl	HVY	£1876
98	3/00	Catt	2m	G Hdl	G-F	£1578
107	1/98	Muss	2m	E Hdl	GD	£2402

Total win prize-money £18479

Going:	Sf: 1-2 GS: 0-3 Gd: 0-5 GF: - Fm: 0-2
Distance:	2m2m3: 0-0 2m4-2m7: 0-0 3m+: 1-12
Track:	LH: 1-12 RH: 0-0 Tight: 1-10 Gall: 0-0
Aids:	Bl: 0-7 Vi: 1-5 Tstrap: 0-0 Ckp: 0-0
Best Rating:	107 2/98 Weth 2m good Hdl

Plating-class chaser; stays beyond three miles and goes
well on fast ground; likes Sedgefield; can run in snatches
and tends to sulk; usually blinkered or visored.

Trooper Kit

5-y-o b g Petoski-Rolling Dice (Balinger)
Mrs L Richards Leonard Howard

Placings:F0   (2489)
2003/04: 18⁷GS, 16⁰GS,

	Starts	1st	2nd	3rd	Win & Pl
NH Flat	2	0	0	0	
Career Total	2	0	0	0	

Going:	Sf: 0-0 GS: 0-1 Gd: 0-1 GF: - Fm: 0-0
Distance:	2m2m3: 0-2 2m4-2m7: 0-0 3m+: 0-0
Track:	LH: 0-2 RH: 0-0 Tight: 0-0 Gall: 0-1
Aids:	Bl: 0-0 Vi: 0-0 Tstrap: 0-0 Ckp: 0-0

Trouble Ahead (IRE)
109   131

13-y-o b g Cataldi-Why 'O' Why (Giolla Mear)
Miss Venetia Williams Mrs Sharon C Nelson

Placings:5/3/22111/UP2F11R/330/P1RP/5353-
135P53014P   (4912)
2003/04: 16¹G, 16³GS, 17⁵GS, 20⁶G, 16⁵G, 19³GS, 19⁰S, 19¹G,
21⁴GF, 20⁸PS,

	Starts	1st	2nd	3rd	Win & Pl
Chases	10	2	0	2	23617
Career Total	35	8	3	7	77351

129	2/04	Asct	2m3f110yB(0-140)HCh	GD	£10251
131	5/03	Prth	2m	C(0-130)HCh	GD	£8092
134	3/02	Winc	2m5f	C(0-130)HCh	GD	£6857
151	3/00	Sand	3m110y	C(0-135)HCh	GD	£7085
137	3/00	Sand	3m110y	B(0-145)HCh	GD	£19140
131	5/99	Hrfd	2m3f	D Ch	GD	£3850
136	3/99	Hntg	2m4f110yE Ch	G-S	£2815
133	3/99	Tntn	3m	E Ch	SFT	£3192

Total win prize-money £61285

Going:	Sf: 0-2 GS: 0-3 Gd: 2-4 GF: - Fm: 0-1
Distance:	2m2m3: 1-5 2m4-2m7: 1-5 3m+: 0-0
Track:	LH: 0-4 RH: 2-8 Tight: 0-1 Gall: 0-1
Aids:	Bl: 0-0 Vi: 0-0 Tstrap: 0-0 Ckp: 0-0
Best Rating:	151 3/00 Sand 3m110y good Ch

Fair chaser; stays three miles but effective over shorter; best
going right-handed; prone to mistakes; suited by good
ground or softer.

Trouble At Bay (IRE)
111   136+

4-y-o b g Slip Anchor-Fight Right (FR) (Crystal Glitters
(USA))
A King Nigel Bunter

Placings:4111110   (4422)
2003/04: 16⁴GF, 17¹GF, 16¹G, 16¹GS, 17¹G, 16¹G, 17⁰G,

	Starts	1st	2nd	3rd	Win & Pl
Hurdles	7	5	0	0	43271
Career Total	7	5	0	0	43271

136	2/04	Kemp	2m	A Hdl	GD	£17400
124	1/04	Chel	2m1f	B Hdl	GD	£9613
132	12/03	Chel	2m110y	B Hdl	G-S	£11086
111	12/03	Winc	2m	E Hdl	GD	£1946
120	11/03	Hrfd	2m1f	E Hdl	G-F	£2443

Total win prize-money £42489

Going:	Sf: 0-0 GS: 1-1 Gd: 3-4 GF: - Fm: 1-2
Distance:	2m2m3: 5-7 2m4-2m7: 0-0 3m+: 0-0
Track:	LH: 2-3 RH: 3-4 Tight: 0-0 Gall: 1-2
Aids:	Bl: 0-0 Vi: 0-0 Tstrap: 0-0 Ckp: 0-0
Best Rating:	136 2/04 Kemp 2m good Hdl

Very useful novice hurdler; good Flat handicapper; a little
disappointing on hurdles debut having been the subject of
good reports, but went on to win his next starts including
good races at Cheltenham (twice) and Kempton; effective
on fast ground and with cut; tough.

Troubleinallenwood (IRE)
74f   51f

5-y-o b g Big Sink Hope (USA)-Gometra (Lomond (USA))
B D Leavy M A Hill

Placings:0   (4816)
2003/04: 16⁶G,

	Starts	1st	2nd	3rd	Win & Pl
NH Flat	1	0	0	0	
Career Total	1	0	0	0	

Going:	Sf: 0-0 GS: 0-0 Gd: 0-1 GF: - Fm: 0-0
Distance:	2m2m3: 0-1 2m4-2m7: 0-0 3m+: 0-0
Track:	LH: 0-1 RH: 0-0 Tight: 0-0 Gall: 0-0
Aids:	Bl: 0-0 Vi: 0-0 Tstrap: 0-0 Ckp: 0-0
Best Rating:	51 4/04 Chep 2m110y good NHF

Troysgreen (IRE)
78   (0c)23

6-y-o b g Warcraft (USA)-Moylena (Bustomi)
P D Niven Ian G M Dalgleish

Placings:0FPPPP-U540   (0644)
2003/04: 20⁰GF, 25⁴G, 24⁵GS, 24⁴GF, 20⁰GF,

	Starts	1st	2nd	3rd	Win & Pl
Hurdles	4	0	0	0	0
Chases	1	0	0	0	0
Career Total	10	0	0	0	0

Going:	Sf: 0-0 GS: 0-1 Gd: 0-1 GF: - Fm: 0-3
Distance:	2m2m3: 0-0 2m4-2m7: 0-2 3m+: 0-3
Track:	LH: 0-4 RH: 0-1 Tight: 0-0 Gall: 0-1
Aids:	Bl: 0-0 Vi: 0-0 Tstrap: 0-0 Ckp: 0-0
Best Rating:	80 11/02 Winc 2m good NHF

Truckers Tavern (IRE)
99(105h)   (121h)167

9-y-o ch g Phardante (FR)-Sweet Tulip (Beau Chapeau)
Ferdy Murphy Mrs M B Scholey

Placings:1/111246/3F132-42FUP   (4424)
2003/04: 22⁴S, 24²S, 25⁴GS, 25⁴GS, 26⁸G,

	Starts	1st	2nd	3rd	Win & Pl
Hurdles	1	0	0	0	441
Chases	4	0	1	0	13200
Career Total	17	5	3	2	179919

156	1/03	Hayd	3m	A HCh	G-S	£34800
148	1/02	Towc	2m110y	B Ch	HVY	£13552
119	1/02	Newc	2m110y	E Ch	SFT	£3110
115	12/01	Ayr	2m	D Ch	SFT	£3887
120	10/00	Weth	2m	C Hdl	HVY	£5105

Total win prize-money £60456

Going:	Sf: 0-2 GS: 0-2 Gd: 0-1 GF: - Fm: 0-0
Distance:	2m2m3: 0-0 2m4-2m7: 0-1 3m+: 0-4
Track:	LH: 0-5 RH: 0-0 Tight: 0-0 Gall: 0-2
Aids:	Bl: 0-0 Vi: 0-0 Tstrap: 0-5 Ckp: 0-0
Best Rating:	167 3/03 Chel 3m2f110y good Ch

Smart chaser; surprise second to Best Mate in Cheltenham
Gold Cup in 2003 on good ground; a decent second to Keen
Leader in the Tommy Whittle later that year on his return to
chasing; let down by jumping since; stays 3m 2f; suited by
soft ground; wears a tongue tie.

Trudi Bay

7-y-o b m Terimon-Letterewe (Alias Smith (USA))
N B King Mrs E H Vestey

Placings:P   (3427)
2003/04: 23⁰GS,

	Starts	1st	2nd	3rd	Win & Pl
Hurdles	1	0	0	0	
Career Total	1	0	0	0	

Going:	Sf: 0-0 GS: 0-1 Gd: 0-0 GF: - Fm: 0-0
Distance:	2m2m3: 0-0 2m4-2m7: 0-0 3m+: 0-1
Track:	LH: 0-1 RH: 0-0 Tight: 0-1 Gall: 0-0
Aids:	Bl: 0-0 Vi: 0-0 Tstrap: 0-0 Ckp: 0-0

True Beauty (FR)
95f   73f

4-y-o ch f Shemazar-Re-Release (Baptism)
N G Richards Jim Ennis

Placings:54   (4144)
2003/04: 16⁵HY, 16⁴G,

	Starts	1st	2nd	3rd	Win & Pl
NH Flat	2	0	0	0	0
Career Total	2	0	0	0	0

Going:	Sf: 0-1 GS: 0-0 Gd: 0-1 GF: - Fm: 0-0
Distance:	2m2m3: 0-2 2m4-2m7: 0-0 3m+: 0-0
Track:	LH: 0-1 RH: 0-1 Tight: 0-0 Gall: 0-0
Aids:	Bl: 0-0 Vi: 0-0 Tstrap: 0-0 Ckp: 0-0
Best Rating:	73 3/04 Ludl 2m good NHF

True Chimes

13-y-o ch g True Song-Ballytina (Rugantino)

Mrs J Owen Mrs E V Cardew

Placings:000/4/35/4/P   (0028)
2003/04: 21PG,

	Starts	1st	2nd	3rd	Win & Pl
Chases	1	0	0	0	
Career Total	8	0	0	1	539

Going:	Sf: 0-0 GS: 0-0 Gd: 0-1 GF: - Fm: 0-0
Distance:	2m/2m3: 0-0 2m4-2m7: 0-1 3m+: 0-0
Track:	LH: 0-1 RH: 0-0 Tight: 0-0 Gall: 0-1
Aids:	Bl: 0-0 Vi: 0-0 Tstrap: 0-0 Ckp: 0-0
Best Rating:	84 2/99 Folk 2m5f gd-sft Ch

True Lover (GER)
103   126+

7-y-o b g Winged Love (IRE)-Truneba (GER) (Nebos (GER))
J W Mullins   First Impressions Racing Group

Placings:62-50211   (4931)
2003/04: 19JS, 16OGS, 24²GF, 21¹GS, 22¹G,

	Starts	1st	2nd	3rd	Win & Pl
Hurdles	5	2	1	0	11692
Career Total	7	2	2	0	11692
126 4/04 Font 2m6f110yE Hdl				GD	£3549
112 3/04 Newb 2m5f D Hdl				G-S	£7047
Total win prize-money £10596					

Going:	Sf: 0-1 GS: 1-2 Gd: 1-1 GF: - Fm: 0-1
Distance:	2m/2m3: 0-2 2m4-2m7: 2-2 3m+: 0-1
Track:	LH: 2-4 RH: 0-1 Tight: 1-1 Gall: 1-2
Aids:	Bl: 0-0 Vi: 0-0 Tstrap: 0-0 Ckp: 0-0
Best Rating:	126 4/04 Font 2m6f110y good Hdl

Fair hurdler; stays three miles; appreciates soft ground.

True North (IRE)
99   118

9-y-o b g Black Monday-Slip A Loop (The Parson)
D R MacLeod   Maurice W Chapman

Placings:4/33/P031112-00   (3694)
2003/04: 20JS, 25OG,

	Starts	1st	2nd	3rd	Win & Pl
Hurdles	2	0	0	0	
Career Total	12	3	1	3	13459
113 1/03 Newc 3m F(0-100)HHdl			HVY	£2646
118 1/03 Ayr 3m110y D(0-110)HHdl			HVY	£4881
112 12/02 Kels 2m6f110yE(0-105)HHdl			HVY	£3536
Total win prize-money £11064					

Going:	Sf: 0-1 GS: 0-0 Gd: 0-1 GF: - Fm: 0-0
Distance:	2m/2m3: 0-0 2m4-2m7: 0-1 3m+: 0-1
Track:	LH: 0-2 RH: 0-0 Tight: 0-0 Gall: 0-0
Aids:	Bl: 0-0 Vi: 0-0 Tstrap: 0-0 Ckp: 0-0
Best Rating:	118 1/03 Ayr 3m110y heavy Hdl

Modest hurdler; completed a hat-trick at Newcastle in January with all three wins coming in heavy ground; stays 3m; looks sure to make a chaser.

True Rose (IRE)
108(100h)   (84h)99

8-y-o ch m Roselier (FR)-Naar Chamali (Salmon Leap (USA))
J R Turner   Robin Ellerbeck

Placings:501533-3423   (3984)
2003/04: 21³GF, 20⁴G, 16²HY, 21³GS,

	Starts	1st	2nd	3rd	Win & Pl
Hurdles	1	0	0	1	332

	Starts	1st	2nd	3rd	Win & Pl
Chases	3	0	1	1	2137
Career Total	10	1	1	4	7261
83 2/03 Catt 2m E Hdl			GD	£3710
Total win prize-money £3710					

Going:	Sf: 0-0 GS: 0-1 Gd: 0-1 GF: - Fm: 0-1
Distance:	2m/2m3: 0-1 2m4-2m7: 0-3 3m+: 0-0
Track:	LH: 0-4 RH: 0-0 Tight: 0-2 Gall: 0-1
Aids:	Bl: 0-0 Vi: 0-0 Tstrap: 0-2 Ckp: 0-0
Best Rating:	99 2/04 Newc 2m110y heavy Ch

Irish point winner, moderate hurdler; has run with credit in novice chases; stays two and a half miles; acts on any ground.

True Tanner
65f   52f

6-y-o b g Lyphento (USA)-True Nell (Neltino)
Miss C Dyson   Miss C Dyson

Placings:00   (4594)
2003/04: 16OG, 16OG,

	Starts	1st	2nd	3rd	Win & Pl
NH Flat	2	0	0	0	
Career Total	2	0	0	0	

Going:	Sf: 0-0 GS: 0-0 Gd: 0-2 GF: - Fm: 0-0
Distance:	2m/2m3: 0-2 2m4-2m7: 0-0 3m+: 0-0
Track:	LH: 0-0 RH: 0-2 Tight: 0-0 Gall: 0-2
Aids:	Bl: 0-0 Vi: 0-0 Tstrap: 0-0 Ckp: 0-2
Best Rating:	52 3/04 Hntg 2m110y good NHF

Truicear

7-y-o b g Petoski-Fit For A King (Royalty)
L Corcoran   The A T P Racing Partnership

Placings:00/P   (4635)
2003/04: 24PG,

	Starts	1st	2nd	3rd	Win & Pl
Chases	1	0	0	0	
Career Total	3	0	0	0	

Going:	Sf: 0-0 GS: 0-0 Gd: 0-1 GF: - Fm: 0-0
Distance:	2m/2m3: 0-0 2m4-2m7: 0-0 3m+: 0-1
Track:	LH: 0-0 RH: 0-1 Tight: 0-1 Gall: 0-0
Aids:	Bl: 0-0 Vi: 0-0 Tstrap: 0-0 Ckp: 0-0
Best Rating:	37 4/02 Hntg 2m5f110y gd-fm Hdl

Trump Card
87   92+

7-y-o b g Distant Relative-Tell No Lies (High Line)
C J Mann   The Whitcombe Partnership

Placings:00/02l004F30 1-4P   (1454)
2003/04: 24⁴GF, 16PGF,

	Starts	1st	2nd	3rd	Win & Pl
Hurdles	2	0	0	0	
Career Total	13	1	1	1	5958
101 4/03 Cork 2m3f NHF			G-F	£4480
Total win prize-money £4481					

Going:	Sf: 0-0 GS: 0-0 Gd: 0-0 GF: - Fm: 0-2
Distance:	2m/2m3: 0-1 2m4-2m7: 0-0 3m+: 0-1
Track:	LH: 0-2 RH: 0-0 Tight: 0-1 Gall: 0-0
Aids:	Bl: 0-0 Vi: 0-0 Tstrap: 0-0 Ckp: 0-0
Best Rating:	101 4/03 Cork 2m3f gd-fm NHF

Plating-class ex-Irish-trained hurdler; usually wore blinkers.(DEAD)

Trumpington
75   92

6-y-o ch m First Trump-Brockton Flame (Emarati (USA))
D G Bridgwater   R Paul Russell

Placings:6532/63224-5P0   (4914)
2003/04: 24⁵GF, 23PGS, 24⁰GS,

	Starts	1st	2nd	3rd	Win & Pl
Hurdles	3	0	0	0	0
Career Total	12	0	3	2	3838

Going:	Sf: 0-0 GS: 0-2 Gd: 0-0 GF: - Fm: 0-1
Distance:	2m/2m3: 0-0 2m4-2m7: 0-1 3m+: 0-2
Track:	LH: 0-3 RH: 0-0 Tight: 0-0 Gall: 0-0
Aids:	Bl: 0-0 Vi: 0-0 Tstrap: 0-0 Ckp: 0-0
Best Rating:	92 7/02 Worc 3m gd-fm Hdl

Plating-class hurdler; stays well; acts on any ground.

Trusted Instinct (IRE)
78   47

4-y-o b c Polish Precedent (USA)-Trust In Luck (IRE) (Nashwan (USA))
C A Dwyer (D K Weld 12/10)   Cedar Lodge 2000 Syndicate

Placings:0P   (2008)
2003/04: 16⁰GF, 16PG,

	Starts	1st	2nd	3rd	Win & Pl
Hurdles	2	0	0	0	
Career Total	2	0	0	0	

Going:	Sf: 0-0 GS: 0-0 Gd: 0-1 GF: - Fm: 0-1
Distance:	2m/2m3: 0-2 2m4-2m7: 0-0 3m+: 0-0
Track:	LH: 0-0 RH: 0-2 Tight: 0-0 Gall: 0-1
Aids:	Bl: 0-0 Vi: 0-0 Tstrap: 0-0 Ckp: 0-0
Best Rating:	47 11/03 Hntg 2m110y gd-fm Hdl

Trusting Paddy (IRE)
100   (87c)84

7-y-o b g Synefos (USA)-Homefield Girl (IRE) (Rahotep (FR))
L A Dace   D Newman

Placings:5/06443-5PFF56   (4917)
2003/04: 17⁵GS, 21PGF, 16FGF, 20FG, 23⁵GS, 20⁶GS,

	Starts	1st	2nd	3rd	Win & Pl
Hurdles	4	0	0	0	0
Chases	2	0	0	0	0
Career Total	12	0	0	1	1185

Going:	Sf: 0-0 GS: 0-3 Gd: 0-1 GF: - Fm: 0-0
Distance:	2m/2m3: 0-2 2m4-2m7: 0-4 3m+: 0-0
Track:	LH: 0-2 RH: 0-4 Tight: 0-2 Gall: 0-0
Aids:	Bl: 0-0 Vi: 0-0 Tstrap: 0-0 Ckp: 0-0
Best Rating:	87 11/03 Folk 2m gd-fm Ch

Trusting Tom
111   118+

9-y-o b g Teamster-Florista (Oats)
C C Bealby   T P Radford

Placings:3F2P/124U2523-1252PP   (4778)
2003/04: 25³GY, 26¹G, 28²G, 25⁵GS, 24²GS, 24PGS, 21PG,

	Starts	1st	2nd	3rd	Win & Pl
Chases	7	1	2	1	11078
Career Total	18	2	6	2	23050

118 11/03 Sthl 3m2f D(0-115)HCh GD £4108
108 10/02 MRas 2m6f110y E(0-105)HCh
G-S £4533

Total win prize-money £8642

Going: Sf: 0-0 GS: 0-3 Gd: 1-3 GF: - Fm: 0-0
Distance: 2m/2m3: 0-0 2m4-2m7: 0-1 3m+: 1-6
Track: LH: 1-3 RH: 0-4 Tight: 0-2 Gall: 0-0
Aids: Bl: 0-0 Vi: 0-0 Tstrap: 0-0 Ckp: 0-3
Best Rating: 118 2/04 Kemp 3m gd-sft Ch

Modest handicap chaser, hobdayed before making a successful return at Southwell in November 2003; unable to win again since; stays well; suited by give underfoot; has been tried in cheekpieces.

Try Me And See
96(84h)   (53h)84+
10-y-o ch g Rock City-Al Raja (King's Lake (USA))
A M Crow A M Crow

Placings:250/0/050-UU6 (4794)
2003/04: 25UG, 25UG, 21PG,

	Starts	1st	2nd	3rd	Win & Pl
Chases	3	0	0	0	
Career Total	10	0	1	0	354

Going: Sf: 0-0 GS: 0-0 Gd: 0-3 GF: - Fm: 0-0
Distance: 2m/2m3: 0-0 2m4-2m7: 0-1 3m+: 0-2
Track: LH: 0-3 RH: 0-0 Tight: 0-3 Gall: 0-0
Aids: Bl: 0-0 Vi: 0-0 Tstrap: 0-0 Ckp: 0-0
Best Rating: 113 3/98 Chel 2m110y good NHF

Tsar Party (IRE)
88   78
7-y-o b g Moscow Society (USA)-Full Choke (Shirley Heights)
Mrs Susan Nock Gerard Nock

Placings:5F (4782)
2003/04: 19GS, 24FG,

	Starts	1st	2nd	3rd	Win & Pl
Chases	2	0	0	0	0
Career Total	2	0	0	0	0

Going: Sf: 0-0 GS: 0-1 Gd: 0-1 GF: 0-0 Fm: 0-0
Distance: 2m/2m3: 0-0 2m4-2m7: 0-1 3m+: 0-1
Track: LH: 0-0 RH: 0-2 Tight: 0-0 Gall: 0-1
Aids: Bl: 0-0 Vi: 0-0 Tstrap: 0-0 Ckp: 0-0
Best Rating: 78 3/04 Extr 2m3f110y gd-sft Ch

Tsar's Twist
78   47
5-y-o b g Presidium-Kabs Twist (Kabour)
Mrs S Gardner D V Gardner

Placings:0004500P (4519)
2003/04: 16PGS, 170GF, 170GF, 174GF, 205GF, 170G, 160G, 22PGS,

	Starts	1st	2nd	3rd	Win & Pl
NH Flat	4	0	0	0	0
Hurdles	4	0	0	0	0
Career Total	8	0	0	0	0

Going: Sf: 0-0 GS: 0-2 Gd: 0-2 GF: - Fm: 0-4

Distance: 2m/2m3: 0-6 2m4-2m7: 0-2 3m+: 0-0
Track: LH: 0-2 RH: 0-6 Tight: 0-0 Gall: 0-0
Aids: Bl: 0-0 Vi: 0-0 Tstrap: 0-0 Ckp: 0-0
Best Rating: 76 10/03 Extr 2m1f gd-fm NHF

Tschiertschen
79f   64f
4-y-o ch g Master Willie-Smocking (Night Shift (USA))
M W Easterby Lord Daresbury

Placings:5 (4284)
2003/04: 16SGS,

	Starts	1st	2nd	3rd	Win & Pl
NH Flat	1	0	0	0	0
Career Total	1	0	0	0	0

Going: Sf: 0-0 GS: 0-1 Gd: 0-0 GF: - Fm: 0-0
Distance: 2m/2m3: 0-1 2m4-2m7: 0-0 3m+: 0-0
Track: LH: 0-0 RH: 0-1 Tight: 0-0 Gall: 0-0
Aids: Bl: 0-0 Vi: 0-0 Tstrap: 0-0 Ckp: 0-0
Best Rating: 64 3/04 Towc 2m gd-sft NHF

Tsuki (FR)
64   46
6-y-o b m Perrault-Tsunami (FR) (Shafaraz (FR))
S J Gilmore S N Wilshire

Placings:0P6P0P (3081)
2003/04: 16PHY, 16PG, 166GF, 16PS, 19PGS, 16PGS,

	Starts	1st	2nd	3rd	Win & Pl
Hurdles	6	0	0	0	0
Career Total	6	0	0	0	0

Going: Sf: 0-2 GS: 0-2 Gd: 0-1 GF: - Fm: 0-1
Distance: 2m/2m3: 0-6 2m4-2m7: 0-0 3m+: 0-0
Track: LH: 0-5 RH: 0-1 Tight: 0-2 Gall: 0-0
Aids: Bl: 0-1 Vi: 0-0 Tstrap: 0-0 Ckp: 0-0
Best Rating: 46 5/03 Uttx 2m heavy Hdl

Tsunami
(103h)   (87h)38
8-y-o b m Beveled (USA)-Alvecote Lady (Touching Wood (USA))
B D Leavy S H Riley

Placings:042322320/33154345614/00666U-P0P2000P (4782)
2003/04: 22PGS, 16PS, 20PGS, 20PHY, 20PGS, 21PG, 17PG, 24PG,

	Starts	1st	2nd	3rd	Win & Pl
Hurdles	6	0	1	0	714
Chases	2	0	0	0	0
Career Total	34	2	5	5	12624

87 11/01 Aint 2m4f F(0-100)HHdl G-S £4602
85 6/01 Worc 2m F Hdl G-F £2030
Total win prize-money £6632

Going: Sf: 0-2 GS: 0-3 Gd: 0-3 GF: - Fm: 0-0
Distance: 2m/2m3: 0-2 2m4-2m7: 0-5 3m+: 0-1
Track: LH: 0-4 RH: 0-4 Tight: 0-1 Gall: 0-3
Aids: Bl: 0-1 Vi: 0-0 Tstrap: 0-0 Ckp: 0-1
Best Rating: 87 1/04 Uttx 2m4f110y heavy Hdl

Plating-class hurdler; stays two and a half miles; has won on good to firm and soft.

Tubber Roads (IRE)
11-y-o b g Un Desperado (FR)-Node (Deep Run)
M G Hazell W F Caudwell

Placings:30/431/30U0/5631110/P-P (0031)
2003/04: 21PG,

	Starts	1st	2nd	3rd	Win & Pl
Chases	1	0	0	0	
Career Total	18	4	0	4	9637

117 3/02 Newb 2m6f110yH Ch G-S £2077
111 3/02 Newb 3m H Ch SFT £1918
111 2/02 Fknm 2m5f110yH Ch G-S £2167
111 4/00 Fknm 2m5f110yH Ch GD £2008
Total win prize-money £8172

Going: Sf: 0-0 GS: 0-0 Gd: 0-1 GF: - Fm: 0-0
Distance: 2m/2m3: 0-0 2m4-2m7: 0-1 3m+: 0-0
Track: LH: 0-1 RH: 0-0 Tight: 0-0 Gall: 0-1
Aids: Bl: 0-0 Vi: 0-0 Tstrap: 0-0 Ckp: 0-0
Best Rating: 117 3/02 Newb 2m6f110y gd-sft Ch

Tubber Streams (IRE)
72   26
7-y-o b g Great Marquess-Much Obliged (Crash Course)
R T Phillips The Donnington Drinkers

Placings:6-0 (4918)
2003/04: 20PGS,

	Starts	1st	2nd	3rd	Win & Pl
Hurdles	1	0	0	0	
Career Total	2	0	0	0	

Going: Sf: 0-0 GS: 0-1 Gd: 0-0 GF: - Fm: 0-0
Distance: 2m/2m3: 0-0 2m4-2m7: 0-1 3m+: 0-0
Track: LH: 0-1 RH: 0-0 Tight: 0-0 Gall: 0-0
Aids: Bl: 0-0 Vi: 0-0 Tstrap: 0-0 Ckp: 0-0
Best Rating: 79 4/03 Gowr 2m gd-fm NHF

Tucacas (FR)
98(109h)   (131h)131
7-y-o gr m Highest Honor (FR)-Three Well (FR) (Sicyos (USA))
M C Pipe Mrs Belinda Harvey

Placings:611311012/61P0P-4511510 (4842)
2003/04: 224GF, 195GS, 191G, 211S, 215GS, 171G, 21PG,

	Starts	1st	2nd	3rd	Win & Pl
Hurdles	2	0	0	0	1556
Chases	5	3	0	0	13241
Career Total	21	9	1	1	82828

115 4/04 Plum 2m1f E Ch GD £3926
131 1/04 Winc 2m5f D Ch SFT £5395
113 12/03 Extr 2m3f110yE Ch GD £3380
141 11/02 Chel 2m4f C(0-135)HHdl G-S £16965
142 4/02 Asct 2m4f C(0-130)HHdl G-F £6418
125 2/02 Sand 2m110y D Hdl SFT £4543
130 1/02 Leic 2m E Hdl SFT £3178
11/02 Engh 2m2f Hdl HVY £13579
10/01 Engh 2m1f110y Hdl HLD £12124
Total win prize-money £69510

Going: Sf: 1-1 GS: 0-2 Gd: 2-3 GF: - Fm: 0-1
Distance: 2m/2m3: 1-1 2m4-2m7: 2-6 3m+: 0-0
Track: LH: 1-4 RH: 2-3 Tight: 1-1 Gall: 0-2
Aids: Bl: 0-0 Vi: 0-0 Tstrap: 0-0 Ckp: 0-0
Best Rating: 142 4/02 Chel 2m5f110y good Hdl

Useful performer over hurdles at her best; useful novice chaser; stays 2m 5f; acts on most ground; once tried in a visor.

Tudor Blonde

13-y-o ch m Pablond-Cottage Melody (Super Song)
P D Purdy P D Purdy

Placings:600/0/000/P/P (0487)
2003/04: 22PGF,

	Starts	1st	2nd	3rd	Win & Pl
Hurdles	1	0	0	0	
Career Total	9	0	0	0	0

Going: Sf: 0-0 GS: 0-0 Gd: 0-0 GF: 0-0 Fm: 0-1
Distance: 2m/2m3: 0-0 2m4-2m7: 0-1 3m+: 0-0
Track: LH: 0-1 RH: 0-0 Tight: 0-1 Gall: 0-0
Aids: Bl: 0-0 Vi: 0-0 Tstrap: 0-0 Ckp: 0-0
Best Rating: 34   5/99   Strf   2m110y   gd-sft   Hdl

Tudor Cottage

14-y-o ch g Town And Country-Cottage Melody (Super Song)
P D Purdy P D Purdy

Placings:6P6/P/0P/P (0140)
2003/04: 21PG,

	Starts	1st	2nd	3rd	Win & Pl
Hurdles	1	0	0	0	
Career Total	7	0	0	0	0

Going: Sf: 0-0 GS: 0-0 Gd: 0-1 GF: - Fm: 0-0
Distance: 2m/2m3: 0-0 2m4-2m7: 0-1 3m+: 0-0
Track: LH: 0-0 RH: 0-1 Tight: 0-0 Gall: 0-0
Aids: Bl: 0-0 Vi: 0-0 Tstrap: 0-0 Ckp: 0-0
Best Rating: 68   2/98   Tntn   2m1f   gd-fm   Hdl

Tudor King (IRE)

104(101h) (71h)90
10-y-o br g Orchestra-Jane Bond (Good Bond)
J S King J R Kinloch

Placings:0/00000/4430/06U421FU/4401P260/601UU03P01
-6PU1PP231U0 (3052)
2003/04: 25PGF, 22PGF, 21UGF, 211G, 21PGF, 26PGF, 202GF,
213GF, 251GF, 20UF, 249G,

	Starts	1st	2nd	3rd	Win & Pl
Chases	11	2	1	1	9088
Career Total	47	6	3	3	24942
85	11/03	Folk	3m1f	F(0-100)HCh	G-F	£2999
90	7/03	Sthl	2m5f110yE(0-105)HCh	GD	£4431
90	4/03	Plum	2m4f	F(0-100)HCh	G-F	£3360
90	8/02	Sthl	2m5f110yF(0-90)HCh	G-F	£3052
89	8/01	Uttx	3m	F(0-100)HCh	G-F	£3045
90	10/00	Font	2m2f	E(0-105)HCh	G-S	£3395
				Total win prize-money £20283		

Going: Sf: 0-0 GS: 0-0 Gd: 1-2 GF: - Fm: 1-9
Distance: 2m/2m3: 0-0 2m4-2m7: 1-7 3m+: 1-4
Track: LH: 1-5 RH: 1-4 Tight: 1-6 Gall: 0-0
Aids: Bl: 0-0 Vi: 0-0 Tstrap: 0-0 Ckp: 0-0
Best Rating: 90   7/03   Sthl   2m5f110y   good   Ch

Moderate chaser; likes fast ground and just about stays three miles; suited by forcing tactics.

Tudor Native

8-y-o b m Distinct Native-Tudorfield Girl (Tudorville)
A Parker Mrs Cathrine Matthews

Placings:P-PP (3322)
2003/04: 17PHY, 21PGS,

	Starts	1st	2nd	3rd	Win & Pl
Hurdles	2	0	0	0	
Career Total	3	0	0	0	

Going: Sf: 0-1 GS: 0-1 Gd: 0-0 GF: - Fm: 0-0
Distance: 2m/2m3: 0-1 2m4-2m7: 0-1 3m+: 0-0
Track: LH: 0-1 RH: 0-1 Tight: 0-1 Gall: 0-0
Aids: Bl: 0-0 Vi: 0-0 Tstrap: 0-0 Ckp: 0-0

Tudor Nickola

12-y-o ch m Nicholas Bill-Cottage Melody (Super Song)
P D Purdy P D Purdy

Placings:00/00U/PPP/060/P/UP-PP (0547)
2003/04: 19PGF, 22PGF,

	Starts	1st	2nd	3rd	Win & Pl
Hurdles	2	0	0	0	
Career Total	16	0	0	0	0

Going: Sf: 0-0 GS: 0-0 Gd: 0-0 GF: - Fm: 0-2
Distance: 2m/2m3: 0-0 2m4-2m7: 0-2 3m+: 0-0
Track: LH: 0-1 RH: 0-1 Tight: 0-1 Gall: 0-0
Aids: Bl: 0-0 Vi: 0-0 Tstrap: 0-0 Ckp: 0-0
Best Rating: 43   1/98   Ling   2m110y   gd-sft   NHF

Tuftex King

79 75
7-y-o b g Syrtos-More Laughter (Oats)
Mrs S Gardner D V Gardner

Placings:0000000O0-4 (0854)
2003/04: 224GF,

	Starts	1st	2nd	3rd	Win & Pl
Hurdles	1	0	0	0	422
Career Total	10	0	0	0	422

Going: Sf: 0-0 GS: 0-0 Gd: 0-0 GF: - Fm: 0-1
Distance: 2m/2m3: 0-0 2m4-2m7: 0-1 3m+: 0-0
Track: LH: 0-1 RH: 0-0 Tight: 0-1 Gall: 0-0
Aids: Bl: 0-0 Vi: 0-0 Tstrap: 0-0 Ckp: 0-0
Best Rating: 87   11/02   Wwck   2m   gd-sft   Hdl

Modest hurdles form to date.

Tullimoss (IRE)

93 77
9-y-o b m Husyan (USA)-Ballynattin Moss (Le Moss)
J N R Billinge Mrs S E Billinge & Mrs C G Braithwaite

Placings:4060/3462F60P0-2620 (2864)
2003/04: 162G, 18PG, 202G, 16PGS,

	Starts	1st	2nd	3rd	Win & Pl
Hurdles	4	0	2	0	2748
Career Total	17	0	3	1	4777

Going: Sf: 0-0 GS: 0-1 Gd: 0-3 GF: - Fm: 0-0
Distance: 2m/2m3: 0-3 2m4-2m7: 0-1 3m+: 0-0
Track: LH: 0-3 RH: 0-1 Tight: 0-1 Gall: 0-1

Aids: Bl: 0-0 Vi: 0-0 Tstrap: 0-0 Ckp: 0-0
Best Rating: 77   11/03   Ayr   2m4f   good   Hdl

Modest form in bumpers and novice hurdles; acts on good ground or softer.

Tullons Lane

94 (73h)97
9-y-o b g Riverwise (USA)-Pallanda (Pablond)
N R Mitchell Mrs E Mitchell

Placings:0/05P550/0F45P/P166422P0PP-0PU412 (3421)
2003/04: 20PG, 20PG, 19UG, 224G, 211GS, 212S,

	Starts	1st	2nd	3rd	Win & Pl
Chases	6	1	1	0	4488
Career Total	29	2	3	0	11069
87	1/04	Folk	2m5f	F(0-90)HCh	G-S	£3412
97	11/02	Font	2m2f	E(0-110)HCh	G-S	£3766
				Total win prize-money £7179		

Going: Sf: 0-1 GS: 1-1 Gd: 0-4 GF: - Fm: 0-0
Distance: 2m/2m3: 0-0 2m4-2m7: 1-6 3m+: 0-0
Track: LH: 0-1 RH: 1-3 Tight: 1-4 Gall: 0-0
Aids: Bl: 0-0 Vi: 0-0 Tstrap: 0-0 Ckp: 0-0
Best Rating: 97   2/03   Font   2m4f   gd-sft   Ch

Moderate chaser, stays two miles five; acts on good to soft or heavier ground.

Tullynagardy

4-y-o ch g Sabrehill (USA)-Moorefield Girl (IRE) (Gorytus (USA))
J M Jefferson David Bamber

Placings:00 (4866)
2003/04: 13OS, 16PS,

	Starts	1st	2nd	3rd	Win & Pl
NH Flat	2	0	0	0	
Career Total	2	0	0	0	

Going: Sf: 0-2 GS: 0-0 Gd: 0-0 GF: - Fm: 0-0
Distance: 2m/2m3: 0-1 2m4-2m7: 0-0 3m+: 0-0
Track: LH: 0-1 RH: 0-0 Tight: 0-0 Gall: 0-0
Aids: Bl: 0-0 Vi: 0-0 Tstrap: 0-0 Ckp: 0-0

Tumbleweed Glen (IRE)

91 (85h)85
8-y-o ch g Mukaddamah (USA)-Mistic Glen (IRE) (Mister Majestic)
P Kelsall Peter Kelsall

Placings:524335U23/34U0000/P50230/642-P04 (0482)
2003/04: 16PG, 19UGF, 204GF,

	Starts	1st	2nd	3rd	Win & Pl
Chases	3	0	0	0	314
Career Total	28	0	4	5	9203

Going: Sf: 0-0 GS: 0-0 Gd: 0-1 GF: - Fm: 0-2
Distance: 2m/2m3: 0-2 2m4-2m7: 0-1 3m+: 0-0
Track: LH: 0-1 RH: 0-2 Tight: 0-0 Gall: 0-1
Aids: Bl: 0-0 Vi: 0-0 Tstrap: 0-0 Ckp: 0-0
Best Rating: 106   4/00   Chel   2m1f   soft   Hdl

Moderate hurdler/chaser; missed 2002; fair efforts since returning; stays 2m 4f, effective over shorter, acts on fast ground.

Turaath (IRE)

105   106

8-y-o b g Sadler's Wells (USA)-Diamond Field (USA) (Mr Prospector (USA))
A J Deakin (D J Wintle 6/3) A J Deakin

Placings:05P11/2PP10F0-U25PF200 (4870)
2003/04: 22^0S, 24^UGF, 22^0GS, 21^5G, 24^PS, 20^0G, 20^2HY, 22^0G, 24^0GS,

	Starts	1st	2nd	3rd	Win & Pl
Hurdles	9	0	2	0	2871
Career Total	20	3	3	0	12559

103	1/03	Tntn	2m3f110yE(0-105)HHdl	SFT	£3808
94	4/02	MRas	2m5f110yF(0-100)HHdl	GD	£2579
85	4/02	MRas	2m5f110yF(0-95)HHdl	GD	£2401

Total win prize-money £8789

Going: Sf: 0-3 GS: 0-2 Gd: 0-3 GF: - Fm: 0-1
Distance: 2m/2m3: 0-2 2m4-2m7: 0-6 3m+: 0-3
Track: LH: 0-3 RH: 0-5 Tight: 0-2 Gall: 0-2
Aids: Bl: 0-5 Vi: 0-1 Tstrap: 0-0 Ckp: 0-2
Best Rating: 106 3/04 Carl 2m4f heavy Hdl

Modest hurdler; stays two miles five; effective on good and fast ground.

Turbo (IRE)

103   110

5-y-o b g Piccolo-By Arrangement (IRE) (Bold Arrangement)
G B Balding Peter Richardson

Placings:630P-0 (2486)
2003/04: 16^0GS,

	Starts	1st	2nd	3rd	Win & Pl
Hurdles	1	0	0	0	
Career Total	5	0	0	1	1087

Going: Sf: 0-0 GS: 0-1 Gd: 0-0 GF: - Fm: 0-0
Distance: 2m/2m3: 0-1 2m4-2m7: 0-0 3m+: 0-0
Track: LH: 0-1 RH: 0-0 Tight: 0-0 Gall: 0-1
Aids: Bl: 0-1 Vi: 0-0 Tstrap: 0-0 Ckp: 0-1
Best Rating: 110 11/03 Newb 2m110y gd-sft Hdl

Useful middle-distance performer on the Flat, won November Handicap in 2003; fair maiden over hurdles; often wears cheekpieces; best at 2m.

Turgeonev (FR)

113   152

9-y-o gr g Turgeon (USA)-County Kerry (FR) (Comrade In Arms)
T D Easterby D F Sills

Placings:05/56121/31P25/41111P0U2/302U6200-1612542 (4850)
2003/04: 20^1G, 16^6G, 20^1S, 20^2G, 20^5G, 25^4G, 20^2GS,

	Starts	1st	2nd	3rd	Win & Pl
Chases	7	2	2	0	53979
Career Total	36	9	7	2	142142

152	2/04	Weth	2m4f110yB HCh	SFT	£12374
149	11/03	Weth	2m4f110yB(0-150)HCh	GD	£10289
150	1/02	Asct	2m A HCh	GD	£34800
138	12/01	Weth	2m A HCh	G-S	£13500
133	11/01	Weth	2m B(0-150)HCh	GD	£8895
129	11/01	Newc	2m110y E(0-115)HCh	GD	£3360
131	11/00	MRas	2m1f110yE Ch	SFT	£3096
122	4/00	MRas	2m1f110yD Hdl	G-F	£3212
126	2/00	Kels	2m110y D Hdl	G-S	£3721

Total win prize-money £93252

Going: Sf: 1-1 GS: 0-1 Gd: 1-5 GF: - Fm: 0-0
Distance: 2m/2m3: 0-1 2m4-2m7: 2-5 3m+: 0-1
Track: LH: 2-6 RH: 0-1 Tight: 0-1 Gall: 0-2
Aids: Bl: 0-0 Vi: 0-0 Tstrap: 0-0 Ckp: 0-0
Best Rating: 155 3/02 Chel 2m gd-sft Ch

Smart chaser; had a fine season in 2001/2, winning a Grade 2 chase at Ascot; back to winning form at Wetherby in November 2003 and recorded fourth win at that track in February 2004; stays two and a half miles and acts on most types of ground.

Turkestan (FR)

97   98

7-y-o b/br g Petit Loup (USA)-Turkeina (FR) (Kautokeino (FR))
M C Pipe Gerald Myers

Placings:5424/511121500/00 (4559)
2003/04: 16^2HY, 16^0GS,

	Starts	1st	2nd	3rd	Win & Pl
Hurdles	2	0	0	0	
Career Total	15	4	2	0	31412

124	11/01	Asct	2m110y C Hdl	GD	£4953
120	9/01	Plum	2m E Hdl	G-F	£2646
102	8/01	Worc	2m E Hdl	G-F	£3178
120	8/01	Strf	2m110y E Hdl	G-F	£3062

Total win prize-money £13840

Going: Sf: 0-1 GS: 0-1 Gd: 0-0 GF: - Fm: 0-0
Distance: 2m/2m3: 0-2 2m4-2m7: 0-0 3m+: 0-0
Track: LH: 0-1 RH: 0-1 Tight: 0-1 Gall: 0-1
Aids: Bl: 0-0 Vi: 0-0 Tstrap: 0-0 Ckp: 0-0
Best Rating: 130 3/02 Chel 2m110y gd-sft Hdl

Fair hurdler; lightly raced of late; best at around two miles; best on a sound surface.

Turn Of Phrase (IRE)

103   114+

5-y-o b g Cadeaux Genereux-Token Gesture (IRE) (Alzao (USA))
R A Fahey Jacksons Transport (West Riding) Ltd

Placings:50125-115U04P (4662)
2003/04: 16^1GF, 16^1G, 16^5G, 19^UGF, 17^0GS, 19^4S, 20^PS,

	Starts	1st	2nd	3rd	Win & Pl
Hurdles	7	2	0	0	7788
Career Total	12	3	1	0	13291

114	5/03	Weth	2m	E(0-110)HHdl	GD	£3626
109	5/03	Weth	2m	E(0-110)HHdl	GD	£3626
97	5/03	Weth	2m	E Hdl	G-F	£3464

Total win prize-money £10717

Going: Sf: 0-2 GS: 0-1 Gd: 1-2 GF: - Fm: 1-2
Distance: 2m/2m3: 2-4 2m4-2m7: 0-3 3m+: 0-0
Track: LH: 2-7 RH: 0-0 Tight: 0-0 Gall: 0-1
Aids: Bl: 2-5 Vi: 0-0 Tstrap: 0-0 Ckp: 0-0
Best Rating: 114 5/03 Weth 2m good Hdl

Fair hurdler; suited by fast ground; usually wears blinkers.

Turned Out Nice

97   94

6-y-o b m Ezzoud (IRE)-Green Seed (IRE) (Lead On Time (USA))
P Beaumont Robert Gibbons

Placings:403-5P (0718)
2003/04: 16^5G, 20^PG,

	Starts	1st	2nd	3rd	Win & Pl
Hurdles	2	0	0	0	0
Career Total	5	0	0	1	1168

Going: Sf: 0-0 GS: 0-0 Gd: 0-2 GF: - Fm: 0-0
Distance: 2m/2m3: 0-1 2m4-2m7: 0-1 3m+: 0-0
Track: LH: 0-0 RH: 0-2 Tight: 0-0 Gall: 0-0
Aids: Bl: 0-0 Vi: 0-0 Tstrap: 0-0 Ckp: 0-0
Best Rating: 94 4/03 Prth 2m110y good Hdl

Plating-class hurdler; acts on good ground or softer.

Turtle Love (IRE)

87   70

5-y-o b m Turtle Island (IRE)-A Little Loving (He Loves Me)
B D Leavy (Miss V Haigh 26/7) Mrs Renee Farrington-Kirkham

Placings:P60602-60 (0680)
2003/04: 20^6GF, 16^0GF,

	Starts	1st	2nd	3rd	Win & Pl
Hurdles	2	0	0	0	0
Career Total	8	0	1	0	686

Going: Sf: 0-0 GS: 0-0 Gd: 0-0 GF: - Fm: 0-2
Distance: 2m/2m3: 0-1 2m4-2m7: 0-1 3m+: 0-0
Track: LH: 0-2 RH: 0-0 Tight: 0-1 Gall: 0-0
Aids: Bl: 0-0 Vi: 0-0 Tstrap: 0-0 Ckp: 0-0
Best Rating: 70 4/03 MRas 2m1f110y good Hdl

Plating-class both on the flat and over hurdles; runner-up in seller at Market Rasen in April.

Turtle Quest (IRE)

5-y-o b g Turtle Island (IRE)-Brook's Quest (IRE) (Ahonoora)
J M Jefferson Mrs T H Barclay/Mrs F D McInnes Skinner

Placings:00 (3474)
2003/04: 16^5HY, 16^0G,

	Starts	1st	2nd	3rd	Win & Pl
NH Flat	2	0	0	0	
Career Total	2	0	0	0	

Going: Sf: 0-1 GS: 0-0 Gd: 0-0 GF: - Fm: 0-1
Distance: 2m/2m3: 0-2 2m4-2m7: 0-0 3m+: 0-0
Track: LH: 0-1 RH: 0-1 Tight: 0-1 Gall: 0-1
Aids: Bl: 0-0 Vi: 0-0 Tstrap: 0-0 Ckp: 0-0

Turtle Recall (IRE)

5-y-o b g Turtle Island (IRE)-Nora Yo Ya (Ahonoora)
F Jordan The Coventry Academy

Placings:PPPP (4589)
2003/04: 16^PS, 17^PS, 25^PS, 16^PG,

	Starts	1st	2nd	3rd	Win & Pl
Hurdles	4	0	0	0	
Career Total	4	0	0	0	

Going: Sf: 0-3 GS: 0-0 Gd: 0-1 GF: - Fm: 0-0
Distance: 2m/2m3: 0-3 2m4-2m7: 0-0 3m+: 0-1
Track: LH: 0-1 RH: 0-3 Tight: 0-1 Gall: 0-1
Aids: Bl: 0-0 Vi: 0-0 Tstrap: 0-0 Ckp: 0-0

Turtle Soup (IRE)

111   140

8-y-o b g Turtle Island (IRE)-Lisa's Favourite (Gorytus (USA))

T R George M K George

Placings:43/41234/4315345   **(3714)**
2003/04: 22⁴G, 20³GS, 21¹S, 21⁵G, 23³G, 20⁴HY, 22⁵S,

	Starts	1st	2nd	3rd	Win & Pl
Hurdles	7	1	0	2	21677
Career Total	14	2	1	4	30968

140	12/03	Wwck	2m3f	B(0-150)HHdl	SFT	£10257
119	1/02	Newb	2m3f	D Hdl	G-S	£4433
				Total win prize-money £14690		

Going:	Sf: 1-3 GS: 0-1 Gd: 0-3 GF: - Fm: 0-0
Distance:	2m/2m3: 0-0 2m4-2m7: 1-6 3m+: 0-1
Track:	LH: 1-5 RH: 0-2 Tight: 0-1 Gall: 0-1
Aids:	Bl: 0-0 Vi: 0-0 Tstrap: 0-0 Ckp: 0-1
Best Rating:	140 12/03 Wwck 2m5f soft Hdl

Very useful hurdler; just about stays three miles but better around two and a half; acts well with cut in the ground.

Tuscan Tempo
86

5-y-o ch g Perugino (USA)-Fact Of Time (Known Fact (USA))
G F Edwards G F Edwards

Placings:606FPP-P   **(1122)**
2003/04: 22⁵GF,

	Starts	1st	2nd	3rd	Win & Pl
Hurdles	1	0	0	0	
Career Total	7	0	0	0	0

Going:	Sf: 0-0 GS: 0-0 Gd: 0-0 GF: - Fm: 0-1
Distance:	2m/2m3: 0-0 2m4-2m7: 0-1 3m+: 0-0
Track:	LH: 0-1 RH: 0-0 Tight: 0-1 Gall: 0-0
Aids:	Bl: 0-0 Vi: 0-0 Tstrap: 0-0 Ckp: 0-0
Best Rating:	86 1/03 Extr 2m1f gd-sft Hdl

Tusk
105   120

4-y-o ch g Fleetwood (IRE)-Farmer's Pet (Sharrood (USA))
Miss H C Knight (M R Channon 4/10) Hogarth Racing

Placings:41100   **(4625)**
2003/04: 16⁴GS, 16¹G, 16¹S, 17⁰G, 16⁰G,

	Starts	1st	2nd	3rd	Win & Pl
Hurdles	5	2	0	0	11580
Career Total	5	2	0	0	11580

120	2/04	Sand	2m110y	C Hdl	SFT	£6206
106	1/04	Kemp	2m	D Hdl	G-S	£4940
				Total win prize-money £11146		

Going:	Sf: 1-1 GS: 0-1 Gd: 1-3 GF: - Fm: 0-0
Distance:	2m/2m3: 2-5 2m4-2m7: 0-0 3m+: 0-0
Track:	LH: 0-2 RH: 2-3 Tight: 0-1 Gall: 0-1
Aids:	Bl: 0-0 Vi: 0-0 Tstrap: 0-0 Ckp: 0-0
Best Rating:	120 4/04 Aint 2m110y good Hdl

Juvenile hurdler; useful front-runner on the Flat; good run came to an end in the Triumph; effective over two miles; acts on any ground; progressive type who will jump a fence in time; tough sort.

Tuttons
82f   65f

6-y-o ch m Whittingham (IRE)-Avonmouthsecretary (Town And Country)
N J Hawke Mrs Jackie Tutton

Placings:00   **(4509)**
2003/04: 17⁰GF, 14⁰GS,

	Starts	1st	2nd	3rd	Win & Pl
NH Flat	2	0	0	0	
Career Total	2	0	0	0	

Going:	Sf: 0-0 GS: 0-1 Gd: 0-0 GF: - Fm: 0-1
Distance:	2m/2m3: 0-1 2m4-2m7: 0-0 3m+: 0-1
Track:	LH: 0-0 RH: 0-1 Tight: 0-0 Gall: 0-0
Aids:	Bl: 0-0 Vi: 0-0 Tstrap: 0-0 Ckp: 0-0
Best Rating:	65 11/03 Hrfd 2m1f gd-fm NHF

Tuxedo Junction (NZ)
83(106h)   (91h)96

9-y-o br g Little Brown Jug (NZ)-Just Kay (NZ) (St Puckle)
P J Hobbs D A Gascoigne

Placings:2404/43P0/341-365P   **(4814)**
2003/04: 21³G, 19⁶G, 21⁵G, 19⁰G,

	Starts	1st	2nd	3rd	Win & Pl
Chases	4	0	0	1	427
Career Total	15	1	1	3	5959

111	6/02	Worc	2m4f110yD(0-110)HCh	GD	£4075
			Total win prize-money £4076		

Going:	Sf: 0-0 GS: 0-0 Gd: 0-4 GF: - Fm: 0-0
Distance:	2m/2m3: 0-0 2m4-2m7: 0-4 3m+: 0-0
Track:	LH: 0-2 RH: 0-2 Tight: 0-2 Gall: 0-0
Aids:	Bl: 0-0 Vi: 0-0 Tstrap: 0-0 Ckp: 0-0
Best Rating:	111 6/02 Worc 2m4f110y good Ch

Moderate chaser; lightly raced; made a successful chasing debut at Worcester June 2002; off for 16 months afterwards; acts on a sound surface.

Tweli
94   80

7-y-o b g Deploy-Flying Fantasy (Habitat)
I A Wood Mrs A M Riney

Placings:32004-UP60PF03   **(4700)**
2003/04: 21⁰G, 20⁰G, 16⁶S, 21⁰S, 20⁰G, 17⁰GS, 24⁰G, 20³G,

	Starts	1st	2nd	3rd	Win & Pl
Hurdles	8	0	0	1	336
Career Total	13	0	1	2	1426

Going:	Sf: 0-2 GS: 0-1 Gd: 0-5 GF: - Fm: 0-0
Distance:	2m/2m3: 0-2 2m4-2m7: 0-5 3m+: 0-1
Track:	LH: 0-1 RH: 0-6 Tight: 0-3 Gall: 0-1
Aids:	Bl: 0-1 Vi: 0-0 Tstrap: 0-0 Ckp: 0-2
Best Rating:	84 3/03 Hntg 2m110y gd-fm Hdl

Placed form in bumpers; yet to show much over hurdles.

Twenty Bucks
98   122

10-y-o b g Buckley-Sweet N' Twenty (High Top)
M Madgwick W E Baird

Placings:0/60/2454351/2F/3U/3P5F   **(4754)**
2003/04: 17³GS, 24⁵GS, 18⁵G, 20⁰FG,

	Starts	1st	2nd	3rd	Win & Pl
Chases	4	0	0	1	1038
Career Total	18	1	2	3	6904

105	4/00	Winc	2m6f	E Hdl	G-S	£2968
				Total win prize-money £2968		

Going:	Sf: 0-0 GS: 0-2 Gd: 0-2 GF: - Fm: 0-0
Distance:	2m/2m3: 0-2 2m4-2m7: 0-1 3m+: 0-1
Track:	LH: 0-3 RH: 0-1 Tight: 0-2 Gall: 0-1

	Starts	1st	2nd	3rd	Win & Pl
NH Flat	2	0	0	0	
Career Total	2	0	0	0	

Going:	Sf: 0-0 GS: 0-1 Gd: 0-0 GF: - Fm: 0-1
Distance:	2m/2m3: 0-1 2m4-2m7: 0-0 3m+: 0-1
Track:	LH: 0-0 RH: 0-1 Tight: 0-0 Gall: 0-0
Aids:	Bl: 0-0 Vi: 0-0 Tstrap: 0-0 Ckp: 0-0
Best Rating:	65 11/03 Hrfd 2m1f gd-fm NHF

Aids:	Bl: 0-0 Vi: 0-0 Tstrap: 0-0 Ckp: 0-0
Best Rating:	112 10/01 Font 2m4f gd-sft Ch

Fair novice chaser; ran encouragingly on return from a over two years off; stays two and threequarter miles and is suited by cut, although handles faster.

Twenty Degrees
100   103

6-y-o ch g Beveled (USA)-Sweet N' Twenty (High Top)
G L Moore W E Baird

Placings:14420   **(4560)**
2003/04: 18¹S, 16⁴S, 18⁴GS, 16²GS, 21⁰GS,

	Starts	1st	2nd	3rd	Win & Pl
NH Flat	2	1	0	0	2898
Hurdles	3	0	1	0	2748
Career Total	5	1	1	0	5646

105	12/03	Plum	2m2f	H NHF	SFT	£2341
				Total win prize-money £2342		

Going:	Sf: 1-2 GS: 0-3 Gd: 0-0 GF: - Fm: 0-0
Distance:	2m/2m3: 1-4 2m4-2m7: 0-1 3m+: 0-0
Track:	LH: 1-3 RH: 0-2 Tight: 0-1 Gall: 0-1
Aids:	Bl: 0-0 Vi: 0-0 Tstrap: 0-0 Ckp: 0-0
Best Rating:	105 12/03 Asct 2m110y soft NHF

Winner of a Plumpton bumper on his debut; pleasing hurdles bow at Fontwell in February when fourth and again ran well next time; should stay 2m 4f; acts best on soft ground.

Twentytwosilver (IRE)
100   77+

4-y-o gr/ro g Emarati (USA)-St Louis Lady (Absalom)
N J Hawke (J G M O'Shea 3/4) C E Handford

Placings:FP6F33   **(4854)**
2003/04: 16⁶GF, 16⁶PS, 16⁴G, 17⁶GS, 17³G, 17³GF,

	Starts	1st	2nd	3rd	Win & Pl
Hurdles	6	0	0	2	1065
Career Total	6	0	0	2	1065

Going:	Sf: 0-1 GS: 0-1 Gd: 0-2 GF: - Fm: 0-2
Distance:	2m/2m3: 0-6 2m4-2m7: 0-0 3m+: 0-0
Track:	LH: 0-2 RH: 0-4 Tight: 0-2 Gall: 0-1
Aids:	Bl: 0-0 Vi: 0-0 Tstrap: 0-0 Ckp: 0-0
Best Rating:	77 4/04 Tntn 2m1f gd-fm Hdl

Plating-class hurdler; seven furlong winner on the Flat; has fallen twice over hurdles; well beaten third in selling company; will need to settle to get the trip.

Twice As Good (IRE)
82   94+

10-y-o b g Good Thyne (USA)-Twice As Fluffy (Pollerton)
K C Bailey Graham And Alison Jelley

Placings:1/0/3324/64PP-FP03   **(2820)**
2003/04: 24⁶GF, 24⁵GS, 16⁰GS, 20³GF,

	Starts	1st	2nd	3rd	Win & Pl
Chases	4	0	0	1	648
Career Total	14	1	1	3	4247

115	4/00	Hntg	2m110y	H NHF	GD	£1715
				Total win prize-money £1715		

Going:	Sf: 0-0 GS: 0-2 Gd: 0-0 GF: - Fm: 0-2
Distance:	2m/2m3: 0-2 2m4-2m7: 0-1 3m+: 0-1
Track:	LH: 0-1 RH: 0-3 Tight: 0-1 Gall: 0-1
Aids:	Bl: 0-0 Vi: 0-0 Tstrap: 0-0 Ckp: 0-1

Best Rating: 115 4/00 Hntg 2m110y good NHF

Plating-class chaser; stays 3m; has worn cheekpieces.

Twiscombe

9-y-o br m Arctic Lord-Flying Cherub (Osiris)
Mrs J G Retter Mrs J G Retter

| Placings:60/P-P | | | | (0058) |
| 2003/04: 19⁰GS, | | | | |

	Starts	1st	2nd	3rd	Win & Pl
Hurdles	1	0	0	0	
Career Total	4	0	0	0	0

Going:	Sf: 0-0 GS: 0-1 Gd: 0-0 GF: - Fm: 0-0
Distance:	2m/2m3: 0-0 2m4-2m7: 0-1 3m+: 0-0
Track:	LH: 0-0 RH: 0-1 Tight: 0-0 Gall: 0-0
Aids:	Bl: 0-0 Vi: 0-0 Tstrap: 0-0 Ckp: 0-0
Best Rating:	29 4/02 Chel 2m1f good NHF

Never at the races on bumper debut.

Twist Of Faith (IRE)
81   **54**

5-y-o b g Fresh Breeze (USA)-Merry And Bright (Beau Chapeau)
N J Henderson Studwell Three Partnership

| Placings:00 | | | | (4560) |
| 2003/04: 16⁰GS, 21⁰GS, | | | | |

	Starts	1st	2nd	3rd	Win & Pl
NH Flat	1	0	0	0	0
Hurdles	1	0	0	0	0
Career Total	2	0	0	0	0

Going:	Sf: 0-0 GS: 0-2 Gd: 0-0 GF: - Fm: 0-0
Distance:	2m/2m3: 0-1 2m4-2m7: 0-1 3m+: 0-0
Track:	LH: 0-0 RH: 0-1 Tight: 0-0 Gall: 0-1
Aids:	Bl: 0-0 Vi: 0-0 Tstrap: 0-0 Ckp: 0-0
Best Rating:	83 2/04 Sand 2m110y gd-sft NHF

Finished midfield on debut in bumper at Sandown; will be capable of better once sent hurdling.

Twisted Logic (IRE)
105(89h)   (81+h)**125**

11-y-o b g Tremblant-Logical View (Mandalus)
R H Alner P M De Wilde

Placings:533P3/1P2110151/F63U5/451410U/2533013P21	
5-533363311	(4694)
2003/04: 24⁵GF, 24³GF, 24³GF, 26³GF, 32⁶G, 24³S, 30¹G, 23⁴G,	

	Starts	1st	2nd	3rd	Win & Pl
Hurdles	1	0	0	0	
Chases	8	2	0	5	26016
Career Total	46	11	3	12	91303
126	4/04	Extr	2m7f110yD(-125)HCh	GD	£7065
125	3/04	Extr	3m6f110yD(-125)HCh	GD	£12922
126	3/03	Extr	2m7f110yD(-125)HCh	FRM	£7686
126	12/02	Extr	3m1f110yC(-135)HCh	G-S	£8320
131	12/01	Extr	3m1f110yD(-135)HCh	GD	£6994
126	10/01	Chel	3m110y E(0-125)HCh	GD	£7247
136	4/00	Bang	3m110y C(0-135)HCh	G-S	£7410
127	3/00	Font	3m2f110yD(-125)HCh	G-S	£4616
118	1/00	Wwck	3m1f110yE(0-115)HCh	SFT	£3000
119	12/99	Tntn	3m	F(0-105)HCh	SFT	£3395
106	5/99	Towc	2m6f	E Ch	G-F	£3042
			Total win prize-money £71700		

Going:	Sf: 0-1 GS: 0-0 Gd: 2-4 GF: - Fm: 0-4
Distance:	2m/2m3: 0-0 2m4-2m7: 0-0 **3m+: 2-9**
Track:	LH: 0-4 **RH: 2-3** Tight: 0-1 Gall: 0-1
Aids:	Bl: 0-0 Vi: 0-0 Tstrap: 0-0 Ckp: 0-0
Best Rating:	**136** 4/00 Bang 3m110y gd-sft Ch

Fair staying chaser; suited by stiff tracks and small fields; acts on most types of ground; goes well at Exeter; consistent.

Two A Penny
89f   **52f**

4-y-o b f Classic Cliche (IRE)-Pennypot Bay (Suave Dancer (USA))
R H York R H York

| Placings:00 | | | | (4345) |
| 2003/04: 16⁰G, 16⁰GS, | | | | |

	Starts	1st	2nd	3rd	Win & Pl
NH Flat	2	0	0	0	
Career Total	2	0	0	0	0

Going:	Sf: 0-0 GS: 0-1 Gd: 0-1 GF: - Fm: 0-0
Distance:	2m/2m3: 0-2 2m4-2m7: 0-0 3m+: 0-0
Track:	LH: 0-1 RH: 0-1 Tight: 0-0 Gall: 0-0
Aids:	Bl: 0-0 Vi: 0-0 Tstrap: 0-0 Ckp: 0-0
Best Rating:	52 3/04 Kemp 2m good NHF

Two Ewe

5-y-o b g Endoli (USA)-Kelsey Lady (Pongee)
W Storey F W W Chapman

| Placings:0 | | | | (3231) |
| 2003/04: 16⁰GF, | | | | |

	Starts	1st	2nd	3rd	Win & Pl
Hurdles	1	0	0	0	
Career Total	1	0	0	0	0

Going:	Sf: 0-0 GS: 0-0 Gd: 0-0 GF: - Fm: 0-1
Distance:	2m/2m3: 0-1 2m4-2m7: 0-0 3m+: 0-0
Track:	LH: 0-0 RH: 0-1 Tight: 0-1 Gall: 0-0
Aids:	Bl: 0-0 Vi: 0-0 Tstrap: 0-0 Ckp: 0-0

Two Huge
62   **41**

6-y-o gr g Norton Challenger-Rainy Miss (IRE) (Cheval)
N A Twiston-Davies The Really Huge Partnership

| Placings:0-0 | | | | (0149) |
| 2003/04: 20⁰GF, | | | | |

	Starts	1st	2nd	3rd	Win & Pl
Hurdles	1	0	0	0	
Career Total	2	0	0	0	0

Going:	Sf: 0-0 GS: 0-0 Gd: 0-0 GF: - Fm: 0-1
Distance:	2m/2m3: 0-0 2m4-2m7: 0-1 3m+: 0-0
Track:	LH: 0-1 RH: 0-0 Tight: 0-0 Gall: 0-0
Aids:	Bl: 0-0 Vi: 0-0 Tstrap: 0-0 Ckp: 0-0
Best Rating:	82 4/03 Asct 2m110y good NHF

Two Jacks (IRE)

7-y-o b g Fayruz-Kaya (GER) (Young Generation)
W S Cunningham Ann And David Bell

| Placings:O | | | | (0040) |
| 2003/04: 16⁰G, | | | | |

	Starts	1st	2nd	3rd	Win & Pl
Hurdles	1	0	0	0	
Career Total	1	0	0	0	

Going:	Sf: 0-0 GS: 0-0 Gd: 0-1 GF: - Fm: 0-0
Distance:	2m/2m3: 0-1 2m4-2m7: 0-0 3m+: 0-0
Track:	LH: 0-1 RH: 0-0 Tight: 0-1 Gall: 0-0
Aids:	Bl: 0-0 Vi: 0-0 Tstrap: 0-0 Ckp: 0-0

Two Of Diamonds

10-y-o b g Mr Fluorocarbon-Shelleys Rocky Gem (Kemal (FR))
Miss R Williams Miss R Williams

| Placings:P | | | | (0353) |
| 2003/04: 21PGF, | | | | |

	Starts	1st	2nd	3rd	Win & Pl
Chases	1	0	0	0	
Career Total	1	0	0	0	

Going:	Sf: 0-0 GS: 0-0 Gd: 0-0 GF: - Fm: 0-1
Distance:	2m/2m3: 0-0 2m4-2m7: 0-1 3m+: 0-0
Track:	LH: 0-0 RH: 0-1 Tight: 0-1 Gall: 0-0
Aids:	Bl: 0-0 Vi: 0-0 Tstrap: 0-0 Ckp: 0-0

Two Rivers (IRE)
95f   **64f**

5-y-o b g Over The River (FR)-Clarin River (IRE) (Mandalus)
Mrs J Candlish Martin Jump

| Placings:P50 | | | | (3285) |
| 2003/04: 17PG, 17⁵GS, 16⁰HY, | | | | |

	Starts	1st	2nd	3rd	Win & Pl
NH Flat	3	0	0	0	0
Career Total	3	0	0	0	0

Going:	Sf: 0-1 GS: 0-1 Gd: 0-1 GF: - Fm: 0-0
Distance:	2m/2m3: 0-3 2m4-2m7: 0-0 3m+: 0-0
Track:	LH: 0-1 RH: 0-2 Tight: 0-0 Gall: 0-0
Aids:	Bl: 0-0 Vi: 0-0 Tstrap: 0-0 Ckp: 0-0
Best Rating:	64 12/03 Hrfd 2m1f gd-sft NHF

Hung badly left when pulled up on his debut at Carlisle in October 2003; well-beaten fifth in soft ground Hereford bumper in December.

Twotensforafive
100(101h)   (80h)**85**

11-y-o b g Arctic Lord-Sister Of Gold (The Parson)
S C Burrough Mrs Christine Priest

Placings:0000/000300/602P0/F443/P4F31655-2P36FP	
	(1305)
2003/04: 21²GF, 23⁸GF, 21³G, 20⁶GF, 20FGF, 23PGF,	

	Starts	1st	2nd	3rd	Win & Pl
Hurdles	1	0	0	0	0
Chases	5	0	1	1	2142
Career Total	33	1	2	4	8123
84	10/02	Chep	2m3f110yG(0-90)HCh	GD	£2597
			Total win prize-money £2597		

Going:	Sf: 0-0 GS: 0-0 Gd: 0-1 GF: - Fm: 0-5
Distance:	2m/2m3: 0-0 2m4-2m7: 0-4 3m+: 0-2
Track:	LH: 0-5 RH: 0-0 Tight: 0-3 Gall: 0-0

Aids: Bl: 0-0 Vi: 0-0 Tstrap: 0-0 Ckp: 0-0
Best Rating: 89   7/99   Gway 2m   good   NHF

Poor chaser, inconsistent; stays 2m 5f; acts on good and good to firm.

Tyndarius (IRE)
113   **122**

13-y-o b g Mandalus-Lady Rerico (Pamroy)
J Hetherton   Alex Shaw

Placings:0/0101P/03U0/2211F/01450P/150/3PPP6-60630214113PP5235   (4726)
2003/04: 24⁶GF, 22⁶G, 24⁰G, 30⁶G, 21³G, 16⁰GF, 25²G, 20¹GF, 22⁴GS, 24¹GS, 26¹G, 28³G, 25⁵GS, 24ᴾS, 25⁵GS, 25²GF, 32³G, 24⁵G,

	Starts	1st	2nd	3rd	Win & Pl
Chases	18	3	2	3	23310
Career Total	46	9	4	5	58677
122	12/03	Donc	3m2f	B(0-140)HCh	GD	£8762
111	11/03	Uttx	3m	F(0-100)HCh	G-S	£3143
100	11/03	Hexm	2m4f110yE(0-105)HCh	G-F	£2247
122	2/02	MRas	2m1f110yD(0-115)HCh	SFT	£4143
122	12/00	Fair	3m1f	HCh	Y-S	£10400
104	3/00	Leop	2m2f	HCh	GD	£5520
104	3/00	Navn	2m1f	Ch	Y-S	£3864
116	4/98	List	2m4f	(0-109)HHdl	Y-S	£2978
103	2/98	Clon	2m4f	Hdl	Y-S	£1935

Total win prize-money £42995

Going: Sf: 0-1 GS: 1-4 Gd: 1-9 GF: - Fm: 1-4
Distance: 2m/2m3: 0-1 2m4-2m7: 1-4 **3m+: 2-13**
Track: **LH: 3-14** RH: 0-3 Tight: 0-5 **Gall: 1-3**
Aids: Bl: 0-0 Vi: 0-0 Tstrap: 0-0 Ckp: 0-0
Best Rating: 122   12/03   Donc 3m2f   good   Ch

Modest veteran chaser; ex-Irish; effective over two miles but stays really well; acts on ground good or softer.

Tyneandthyneagain
109   **153+**

9-y-o b g Good Thyne (USA)-Radical Lady (Radical)
R C Guest   N B Mason

Placings:222333122121/PP10/22P2101PP   (4861)
2003/04: 21²G, 23⁶G, 26ᴾG, 24²GS, 24¹S, 24⁰S, 33¹G, 24ᴾG, 33ᴾGS,

	Starts	1st	2nd	3rd	Win & Pl
Chases	9	2	3	0	76148
Career Total	25	6	9	3	120131
153	2/04	Newc	4m1f	B(0-150)HCh	HVY	£40600
150	1/04	Donc	3m	A(0-145)HCh	SFT	£29000
135	3/02	Donc	3m110y	B(0-140)HHdl	G-S	£13546
140	4/01	Prth	3m110y	B Hdl	HVY	£8814
128	3/01	Hayd	2m4f	C Hdl	HVY	£6136
107	1/01	Sthl	2m4f110yE(0-105)HHdl	HVY	£2597

Total win prize-money £100693

Going: Sf: 1-2 GS: 0-2 Gd: 1-5 GF: - Fm: 0-0
Distance: 2m/2m3: 0-0 2m4-2m7: 0-1 **3m+: 2-8**
Track: **LH: 2-8** RH: 0-0 Tight: 0-0 **Gall: 2-4**
Aids: Bl: 0-0 Vi: 0-0 Tstrap: 0-0 **Ckp: 1-3**
Best Rating: 153   2/04   Newc 4m1f   good   Ch

Smart chaser; won the Skybet Chase (Great Yorkshire) at Doncaster in January 2004 and Tote Eider at Newcastle the following month; pulled up at Cheltenham and Aintree; still inclined to make mistakes; stays four miles one furlong; best on soft ground; successful in cheekpieces.

Tynedale (IRE)
102f   **89f**

5-y-o b g Good Thyne (USA)-Book Of Rules (IRE)

(Phardante (FR))
Mrs A Hamilton   Ian Hamilton

Placings:253   (3766)
2003/04: 16²GF, 16⁵GF, 17³GS,

	Starts	1st	2nd	3rd	Win & Pl
NH Flat	3	0	1	1	925
Career Total	3	0	1	1	925

Going: Sf: 0-0 GS: 0-1 Gd: 0-0 GF: - Fm: 0-2
Distance: 2m/2m3: 0-3 2m4-2m7: 0-0 3m+: 0-0
Track: LH: 0-1 RH: 0-2 Tight: 0-3 Gall: 0-0
Aids: Bl: 0-0 Vi: 0-0 Tstrap: 0-0 Ckp: 0-0
Best Rating: 87   2/04   Sedg 2m1f   gd-sft   NHF

Moderate form in bumpers on varying ground.

Tyro's Bid
95f   **86f**

6-y-o b g Greensmith-Two Hearts (Nearly A Hand)
Jane Southcombe   Major R P Thorman

Placings:46   (1226)
2003/04: 17⁴GF, 17⁶GF,

	Starts	1st	2nd	3rd	Win & Pl
NH Flat	2	0	0	0	0
Career Total	2	0	0	0	0

Going: Sf: 0-0 GS: 0-0 Gd: 0-0 GF: - Fm: 0-2
Distance: 2m/2m3: 0-2 2m4-2m7: 0-0 3m+: 0-0
Track: LH: 0-2 RH: 0-0 Tight: 0-2 Gall: 0-0
Aids: Bl: 0-0 Vi: 0-0 Tstrap: 0-0 Ckp: 0-0
Best Rating: 86   7/03   NAbb 2m1f   gd-fm   NHF

Tyrrellspass (IRE)
101   **76**

7-y-o b g Alzao (USA)-Alpine Chime (IRE) (Tirol)
J D Frost   R G Frost

Placings:000P/00-503U2   (4266)
2003/04: 17⁵GF, 17⁰GF, 17³GS, 16ᵁG, 16²GF,

	Starts	1st	2nd	3rd	Win & Pl
Hurdles	5	0	1	1	997
Career Total	11	0	1	1	997

Going: Sf: 0-0 GS: 0-1 Gd: 0-2 GF: - Fm: 0-2
Distance: 2m/2m3: 0-5 2m4-2m7: 0-0 3m+: 0-0
Track: LH: 0-2 RH: 0-3 Tight: 0-0 Gall: 0-0
Aids: Bl: 0-0 Vi: 0-0 Tstrap: 0-3 Ckp: 0-0
Best Rating: 76   3/04   Chep 2m110y   gd-fm   Hdl

Ex-Irish; poor form; lucky to finish a distant third in 2m 1f amateur riders' handicap hurdle at Hereford December 2003.

Tysou (FR)
108   (146h)**142**

7-y-o b/br g Ajdayt (USA)-Pretty Point (Crystal Glitters (USA))
N J Henderson   W J Brown

Placings:2155612110/421300/1331F1-F2305P   (4627)
2003/04: 16ᶠGF, 16²GS, 16⁰G, 16⁶S, 16⁵G, 16ᴾG,

	Starts	1st	2nd	3rd	Win & Pl
Chases	6	0	1	1	7059
Career Total	28	8	4	4	74710
137	4/03	Ayr	2m	C Ch	GD	£13385
137	3/03	Winc	2m	D Ch	G-F	£5382
135	11/02	Sand	2m	D Ch	G-S	£4777

141	12/01	Donc	2m110y	B(0-140)HHdl	GD	£8112
133	2/01	Muss	2m	D Hdl	GD	£3444
128	2/01	Catt	2m	E Hdl	SFT	£2775
107	11/00	Catt	2m	D Hdl	G-S	£3900
	7/00	Claf	2m	Hdl	SFT	£5764

Total win prize-money £47541

Going: Sf: 0-1 GS: 0-1 Gd: 0-3 GF: - Fm: 0-1
Distance: 2m/2m3: 0-6 2m4-2m7: 0-0 3m+: 0-0
Track: LH: 0-5 RH: 0-1 Tight: 0-1 Gall: 0-3
Aids: Bl: 0-0 Vi: 0-0 Tstrap: 0-0 Ckp: 0-0
Best Rating: 146   1/02   Kemp 2m   gd-sft   Hdl

Very useful chaser; best over two miles; suited by good ground.

Ulshaw
87   **72**

7-y-o ch g Salse (USA)-Kintail (Kris)
B J Llewellyn   Mrs Vicki Guy

Placings:P600   (4117)
2003/04: 19ᴾS, 17⁶GS, 21⁰G, 22⁰G,

	Starts	1st	2nd	3rd	Win & Pl
Hurdles	4	0	0	0	0
Career Total	4	0	0	0	0

Going: Sf: 0-1 GS: 0-1 Gd: 0-2 GF: - Fm: 0-0
Distance: 2m/2m3: 0-2 2m4-2m7: 0-2 3m+: 0-0
Track: LH: 0-1 RH: 0-3 Tight: 0-1 Gall: 0-1
Aids: Bl: 0-1 Vi: 0-0 Tstrap: 0-0 Ckp: 0-0
Best Rating: 72   1/04   Tntn 2m1f   gd-sft   Hdl

Ultra Marine (IRE)
79   **72**

4-y-o b c Blues Traveller (IRE)-The Aspecto Girl (IRE) (Alzao (USA))
J S Wainwright   Walker & Briggsy Rules

Placings:00   (2528)
2003/04: 16⁰GS, 16⁰GS,

	Starts	1st	2nd	3rd	Win & Pl
Hurdles	2	0	0	0	
Career Total	2	0	0	0	

Going: Sf: 0-0 GS: 0-2 Gd: 0-0 GF: - Fm: 0-0
Distance: 2m/2m3: 0-2 2m4-2m7: 0-0 3m+: 0-0
Track: LH: 0-2 RH: 0-0 Tight: 0-1 Gall: 0-0
Aids: Bl: 0-1 Vi: 0-0 Tstrap: 0-0 Ckp: 0-0
Best Rating: 72   12/03   Catt 2m   gd-sft   Hdl

Ultra Pontem
105   (36h)**98**

12-y-o b m Governor General-Rocquelle (Coquelin (USA))
S C Burrough   L Kirkwood

Placings:500603/0/000P/111   (0974)
2003/04: 23ᴾGS, 20¹GF, 21¹GF, 21¹GS,

	Starts	1st	2nd	3rd	Win & Pl
Chases	4	3	0	0	14127
Career Total	14	3	0	1	14778
98	7/03	NAbb	2m5f110yD(0-125)HCh	G-S	£6044
98	6/03	NAbb	2m5f110yE(0-100)HCh	G-F	£4075
89	6/03	Worc	2m4f110yE(0-100)HCh	G-F	£4007

Total win prize-money £14127

Going: Sf: 0-0 GS: 1-1 Gd: 0-1 GF: - Fm: 2-2
Distance: 2m/2m3: 0-0 **2m4-2m7: 3-3** 3m+: 0-1
Track: **LH: 3-4** RH: 0-0 **Tight: 2-2** Gall: 0-0
Aids: Bl: 0-0 Vi: 0-0 Tstrap: 0-0 Ckp: 0-0

Best Rating: 98 7/03 NAbb 2m5f110y gd-sft   Ch

Moderate chaser; sprang 50/1 shock when landing 2m 4f novice handicap chase at Worcester June 2003 when 4lb 'wrong'; followed up from 12lb higher mark in Newton Abbot 2m 5f handicap next time; completed the hat-trick back at Newton Abbot; acts on good ground; seems to be improving despite her advancing years.

Ulundi

145

9-y-o b g Rainbow Quest (USA)-Flit (USA) (Lyphard (USA))
P R Webber D Heath

Placings:3111510/51/063/6   (2916)
2003/04: 16⁶G,

	Starts	1st	2nd	3rd	Win & Pl
Hurdles	1	0	0	0	1200
Career Total	13	5	0	2	33166
145	4/01	Ayr	2m	A HHdl	G-F	£15600
122	10/99	Chel	2m110y	B HHdl	GD	£6872
111	9/99	Font	2m2f110y	E Hdl	GD	£2285
124	8/99	NAbb	2m1f	H NHF	GD	£2263
101	7/99	NAbb	2m1f	H NHF	G-S	£1871
			Total win prize-money £28894

Going: Sf: 0-0 GS: 0-0 Gd: 0-1 GF: - Fm: 0-0
Distance: 2m/2m3: 0-1 2m4-2m7: 0-0 3m+: 0-0
Track: LH: 0-0 RH: 0-1 Tight: 0-0 Gall: 0-0
Aids: Bl: 0-0 Vi: 0-0 Tstrap: 0-0 Ckp: 0-0
Best Rating: 145 11/01 Winc 2m   good   Hdl

High-class hurdler; lightly raced these days; Group-class on the Flat; must have fast ground.

Ulusaba

109(100h)   (106h)**106+**

8-y-o b g Alflora (IRE)-Mighty Fly (Comedy Star (USA))
Ferdy Murphy (R C Guest 21/5) Dorothy Clinton, Chris McHugh, Jon King

Placings:06P/22124/0023133/4456124001461-5321236   (3473)
2003/04: 16⁵GF, 20³G, 20²GF, 19¹GF, 19²GS, 20³GS, 20⁶GF,

	Starts	1st	2nd	3rd	Win & Pl
Chases	7	1	2	4	8962
Career Total	35	6	7	5	32184
106	11/03	Hrfd	2m3f	E(0-110)HCh	G-F	£4224
96	2/03	Donc	2m3f	E(0-110)HCh	GD	£3861
104	10/02	MRas	2m1f110y	D(0-120)HHdl	G-F	£4810
97	8/02	Sthl	2m1f	E(0-100)HCh	G-F	£3526
106	3/02	Catt	2m	G Hdl	G-S	£1708
88	3/01	MRas	2m1f110y	G(0-95)HHdl	GD	£1561
			Total win prize-money £19690

Going: Sf: 0-0 GS: 0-2 Gd: 0-1 GF: - Fm: 1-4
Distance: 2m/2m3: 1-3 2m4-2m7: 0-0 3m+: 0-0
Track: LH: 0-2 RH: 1-5 Tight: 0-1 Gall: 0-3
Aids: Bl: 0-4 Vi: 0-0 Tstrap: 0-3 Ckp: 0-0
Best Rating: 106 12/03 Newc 2m4f   gd-sft   Ch

Moderate handicap chaser; stays 2m 4f; acts on fast ground; wears blinkers and a tongue tie.

Umista (IRE)

68   **28**

5-y-o b m Tagula (IRE)-Nishiki (USA) (Brogan (USA))
A S T Holdsworth (M Quinn 4/6) N J Holdsworth

Placings:0PP   (3841)
2003/04: 19⁰G, 16⁶GS, 19⁷GS,

	Starts	1st	2nd	3rd	Win & Pl
Hurdles	3	0	0	0	

Career Total   3   0   0   0

Going: Sf: 0-0 GS: 0-2 Gd: 0-1 GF: - Fm: 0-0
Distance: 2m/2m3: 0-2 2m4-2m7: 0-1 3m+: 0-0
Track: LH: 0-0 RH: 0-1 Tight: 0-0 Gall: 0-0
Aids: Bl: 0-0 Vi: 0-0 Tstrap: 0-0 Ckp: 0-0
Best Rating: 28 12/03 Extr 2m3f   good   Hdl

Un Autre Espere

80   **69**

5-y-o b g Golden Heights-Drummer's Dream (IRE) (Drumalis)
T Wall Snax Catering Services Limited

Placings:54000   (1945)
2003/04: 17⁵GF, 16⁴F, 16⁰F, 16⁵GF, 16⁰G,

	Starts	1st	2nd	3rd	Win & Pl
Hurdles	5	0	0	0	319
Career Total	5	0	0	0	319

Going: Sf: 0-0 GS: 0-0 Gd: 0-1 GF: - Fm: 0-4
Distance: 2m/2m3: 0-5 2m4-2m7: 0-0 3m+: 0-0
Track: LH: 0-1 RH: 0-4 Tight: 0-0 Gall: 0-0
Aids: Bl: 0-0 Vi: 0-0 Tstrap: 0-0 Ckp: 0-0
Best Rating: 69 10/03 Towc 2m   firm   Hdl

Un Jour A Vassy (FR)

109   (115h)**136**

9-y-o b g Video Rock (FR)-Bayalika (FR) (Kashtan (FR))
P F Nicholls Mrs Bunty Millard

Placings:64/532F/33U11/1P15330P/2F622-122P15433   (4637)
2003/04: 25¹GF, 25²GF, 24²G, 26⁶GF, 24¹GF, 25⁵GF, 22⁴GS, 25³G, 25³G,

	Starts	1st	2nd	3rd	Win & Pl
Chases	9	2	2	2	26050
Career Total	33	6	6	7	60539
136	10/03	Chel	3m110y	E(0-125)HCh	G-F	£6955
127	5/03	Winc	3m1f110y	D(0-120)HCh	G-F	£5486
115	11/01	Tntn	3m110y	D Hdl	GD	£5889
126	5/01	Sthl	2m4f110y	B(0-145)HCh	G-F	£10790
115	4/01	Tntn	3m	D(0-110)HCh	G-F	£4046
114	4/01	Fknm	2m5f110y	H Ch	G-S	£2298
			Total win prize-money £35464

Going: Sf: 0-0 GS: 0-1 Gd: 0-3 GF: - Fm: 2-5
Distance: 2m/2m3: 0-0 2m4-2m7: 0-1 3m+: 2-8
Track: LH: 1-5 RH: 1-3 Tight: 0-3 Gall: 1-2
Aids: Bl: 0-0 Vi: 0-0 Tstrap: 0-0 Ckp: 0-0
Best Rating: 136 10/03 Chel 3m110y   gd-fm   Ch

Fair chaser; effective at two and a half miles, but stays three on an easy track; most effective on good or fast ground.

Uncle Batty

98f   **75f**

4-y-o b g Bob Back (USA)-Aunt Sadie (Pursuit Of Love)
G A Harker Park View Partnership

Placings:60   (4663)
2003/04: 16⁶GF, 16⁰S,

	Starts	1st	2nd	3rd	Win & Pl
NH Flat	2	0	0	0	0
Career Total	2	0	0	0	0

Going: Sf: 0-1 GS: 0-0 Gd: 0-0 GF: - Fm: 0-1
Distance: 2m/2m3: 0-2 2m4-2m7: 0-0 3m+: 0-0
Track: LH: 0-2 RH: 0-0 Tight: 0-1 Gall: 0-0
Aids: Bl: 0-0 Vi: 0-0 Tstrap: 0-0 Ckp: 0-0
Best Rating: 75 3/04 Catt 2m   gd-fm   NHF

Uncle Bert (IRE)

91

14-y-o b g Ovac (ITY)-Sweet Gum (USA) (Gummo)
Miss Lucinda V Russell Mrs C G Greig

Placings:5/400361115/345126/F4/31225133314P24/241/P
3325522-P   (0314)
2003/04: 21⁶PS,

	Starts	1st	2nd	3rd	Win & Pl
Chases	1	0	0	0	
Career Total	44	8	8	8	49073
101	10/00	Aint	2m4f	D(0-125)HCh	GD	£12499
103	10/98	Sedg	2m110y	E(0-115)HCh	GD	£3185
101	9/98	Sedg	2m5f	E(0-115)HCh	GD	£3470
103	6/98	Prth	2m	E(0-115)HCh	G-F	£3436
106	11/96	Plum	2m	E(0-115)HCh	SFT	£2906
96	3/96	Tntn	2m2f	E(0-100)HCh	G-F	£3234
94	3/96	Tntn	2m110y	F(0-105)HCh	GD	£2697
93	2/96	Tntn	2m110y	E(0-100)HCh	G-S	£2927
			Total win prize-money £34355

Going: Sf: 0-1 GS: 0-0 Gd: 0-0 GF: - Fm: 0-0
Distance: 2m/2m3: 0-0 2m4-2m7: 0-0 3m+: 0-0
Track: LH: 0-1 RH: 0-0 Tight: 0-1 Gall: 0-0
Aids: Bl: 0-0 Vi: 0-0 Tstrap: 0-0 Ckp: 0-0
Best Rating: 106 11/96 Plum 2m   soft   Ch

Plating-class handicap chaser; one-time useful performer, but in the veteran stage now and without a win for more than two years; stays two and a half miles; acts on a sound surface; suited by a sharp track.

Uncle Max (IRE)

96   **94**

4-y-o b g Victory Note (USA)-Sunset Park (IRE) (Red Sunset)
N A Twiston-Davies (J A Osborne 20/9) The Yes - No - Wait Sorries

Placings:3142P000   (4573)
2003/04: 16³GF, 16¹GF, 16⁴GF, 16²GS, 16⁶S, 17⁰GS, 24⁰G, 19⁰G,

	Starts	1st	2nd	3rd	Win & Pl
Hurdles	8	1	1	1	7548
Career Total	8	1	1	1	7548
94	11/03	Asct	2m110y	D Hdl	G-F	£4407
			Total win prize-money £4407

Going: Sf: 0-1 GS: 0-2 Gd: 0-2 GF: - Fm: 1-3
Distance: 2m/2m3: 1-7 2m4-2m7: 0-0 3m+: 0-0
Track: LH: 0-5 RH: 1-3 Tight: 0-1 Gall: 0-3
Aids: Bl: 0-1 Vi: 0-0 Tstrap: 0-0 Ckp: 0-0
Best Rating: 94 12/03 Sand 2m110y   gd-sft   Hdl

Fair novice hurdler; effective over two miles; effective with cut in the ground, but only win to date has come on fast ground.

Uncle Mick (IRE)

111(106h)   (117h)**120+**

9-y-o b g Ikdam-Kandy Kate (Pry)
C L Tizzard D J Hinks

Placings:5/015/FUF2033/F42046021-4221342435   (3102)
2003/04: 26⁴G, 25²GF, 23²GF, 26¹GF, 23³GF, 24⁴GF, 24²GF, 32⁴GF, 24³S, 28⁶G,

	Starts	1st	2nd	3rd	Win & Pl
Chases	10	1	3	2	12225
Career Total	30	3	6	4	25331
120 9/03 Uttx	3m2f	E Ch		G-F	£3646
101 4/03 NAbb	3m2f110yE Ch			GD	£4124
100 1/01 Plum	3m1f110yE Hdl			HVY	£2387
				Total win prize-money £10158	

Going: Sf: 0-1 GS: 0-0 Gd: 0-2 GF: - Fm: 1-7
Distance: 2m/2m3: 0-0 2m4-2m7: 0-1 3m+: 1-9
Track: LH: 1-7 RH: 0-1 Tight: 0-2 Gall: 0-2
Aids: Bl: 0-0 Vi: 0-0 Tstrap: 0-0 Ckp: 0-0
Best Rating: 120 12/03 Ling 3m soft Ch

Fair chaser/hurdler; has proved most consistent since switching to fences with wins at Newton Abbot and Uttoxeter in 2003; stays well and suited by 3m2f; acts on most types of ground.

Uncle Sam

5-y-o ch g Superpower-Treasure Time (IRE) (Treasure Kay)
M Scudamore J Huckle

Placings: P   (2795)
2003/04: 17PGS,

	Starts	1st	2nd	3rd	Win & Pl
Hurdles	1	0	0	0	
Career Total	1	0	0	0	

Going: Sf: 0-0 GS: 0-1 Gd: 0-0 GF: - Fm: 0-0
Distance: 2m/2m3: 0-1 2m4-2m7: 0-1 3m+: 0-0
Track: LH: 0-1 RH: 0-0 Tight: 0-1 Gall: 0-0
Aids: Bl: 0-0 Vi: 0-0 Tstrap: 0-0 Ckp: 0-0

Uncle Teddy (IRE)

100   (82h)**87**

11-y-o b g Arctic Cider (USA)-Ishtar (Dike (USA))
Miss E C Lavelle Miss N Henton

Placings: 551/P/50CP41/35125-2PP   (1174)
2003/04: 21²G, 24PG, 22PGF,

	Starts	1st	2nd	3rd	Win & Pl
Chases	3	0	1	0	1254
Career Total	18	3	2	1	11695
91 6/02 Hrfd	3m1f110yG(0-90)HCh			G-F	£3178
97 4/02 Extr	2m3f110yE Ch			FRM	£3962
85 10/99 Towc	2m5f	G Hdl		GD	£1562
				Total win prize-money £8702	

Going: Sf: 0-0 GS: 0-0 Gd: 0-2 GF: - Fm: 0-1
Distance: 2m/2m3: 0-0 2m4-2m7: 0-2 3m+: 0-1
Track: LH: 0-2 RH: 0-0 Tight: 0-3 Gall: 0-0
Aids: Bl: 0-0 Vi: 0-0 Tstrap: 0-0 Ckp: 0-0
Best Rating: 97 7/02 Worc 2m7f110y good Ch

Moderate lightly-raced hurdler/chaser; took advantage of the odds-on favourite's mistake when winning three runner novice chase at Exeter April 2002; not disgraced on ground softer than he prefers when returning after nearly a year off at Newton Abbot July 2003; stays an extended three miles one; suited by a sound surface.

Undeniable

116   **123+**

6-y-o b g Unfuwain (USA)-Shefoog (Kefaah (USA))
Mrs S J Smith Keith Nicholson

Placings: 160P/F020021   (4219)
2003/04: 20FG, 20UGS, 20²GF, 19UG, 20US, 20²GS, 24¹G,

	Starts	1st	2nd	3rd	Win & Pl
Hurdles	7	1	2	0	9091
Career Total	11	2	2	0	12080
123 3/04 MRas	3m	D(0-115)HHdl		GD	£5027
102 1/02 Newc	2m	E Hdl		SFT	£2989
				Total win prize-money £8017	

Going: Sf: 0-1 GS: 0-2 Gd: 1-3 GF: - Fm: 0-1
Distance: 2m/2m3: 0-0 2m4-2m7: 0-0 3m+: 1-1
Track: LH: 0-6 RH: 1-1 Tight: 1-4 Gall: 0-1
Aids: Bl: 0-0 Vi: 0-0 Tstrap: 0-0 Ckp: 0-0
Best Rating: 123 3/04 MRas 3m good Hdl

Modest hurdler; convincing winner at Market Rasen in March; stays three miles; acts on soft ground; has worn tongue tie.

Under The Sand (IRE)

112(108h)   (127dh)**120+**

7-y-o b g Turtle Island (IRE)-Occupation (Homing)
P J Hobbs R Triple H

Placings: 140/2/6203F00-40F32F12   (4930)
2003/04: 16⁴S, 16⁶GS, 19FGS, 22³G, 23²S, 22FGS, 25¹G, 22²G,

	Starts	1st	2nd	3rd	Win & Pl
Chases	8	1	2	1	9039
Career Total	19	2	4	2	23829
114 4/04 Winc	3m1f110yD Ch			GD	£5395
122 3/01 Hntg	2m110y E Hdl			SFT	£2933
				Total win prize-money £8328	

Going: Sf: 0-2 GS: 0-3 Gd: 1-3 GF: - Fm: 0-0
Distance: 2m/2m3: 0-3 2m4-2m7: 0-3 3m+: 1-2
Track: LH: 0-1 RH: 1-5 Tight: 0-2 Gall: 0-0
Aids: Bl: 0-0 Vi: 0-0 Tstrap: 0-0 Ckp: 0-0
Best Rating: 129 1/03 Chel 2m1f gd-sft Hdl

Modest handicap hurdler/novice chaser; has not won since his debut in 2001; acts on soft ground; effective over two miles.

Under Wraps (IRE)

79(90h)   (81h)**38**

10-y-o b g In The Wings-Wrapping (Kris)
A C Whillans G Brown

Placings: 400/542120146/11122/0P0/PPPP0-PP0   (3437)
2003/04: 25PG, 30PGS, 24UHY,

	Starts	1st	2nd	3rd	Win & Pl
Chases	3	0	0	0	
Career Total	28	5	5	4	25062
120 10/00 Carl	2m4f110yD Ch			GD	£4557
121 5/00 Prth	3m110y D(0-120)HHdl			GD	£3464
121 5/00 Towc	2m5f	D(0-125)HHdl		SFT	£3334
101 2/00 Ayr	2m6f	E Hdl		HVY	£2905
121 12/99 Uttx	3m110y F(0-100)HHdl			SFT	£2379
				Total win prize-money £16641	

Going: Sf: 0-1 GS: 0-1 Gd: 0-1 GF: - Fm: 0-0
Distance: 2m/2m3: 0-0 2m4-2m7: 0-0 3m+: 0-3
Track: LH: 0-3 RH: 0-0 Tight: 0-1 Gall: 0-1
Aids: Bl: 0-0 Vi: 0-0 Tstrap: 0-0 Ckp: 0-1
Best Rating: 129 11/00 Hayd 2m4f heavy Ch

Underley Park (IRE)

106(101h)   (81h)**101**

10-y-o ch g Aristocracy-Even Bunny Vii (Damsire Unregistered)
R Ford David & Zoe Greenwood

Placings: 650/56/U/PPP/F-1F20PP4P   (4882)
2003/04: 26¹G, 26FGS, 26²GF, 24US, 27PGS, 24PG, 24⁴HY, 26PGS,

	Starts	1st	2nd	3rd	Win & Pl
Hurdles	3	0	1	0	1014
Chases	5	1	0	0	2737
Career Total	18	1	1	0	3751
101 5/03 Ctml	3m2f	H Ch		GD	£2184
				Total win prize-money £2184	

Going: Sf: 0-2 GS: 0-3 Gd: 1-2 GF: - Fm: 0-1
Distance: 2m/2m3: 0-0 2m4-2m7: 0-0 3m+: 1-8
Track: LH: 1-6 RH: 0-2 Tight: 1-3 Gall: 0-0
Aids: Bl: 0-0 Vi: 0-0 Tstrap: 0-0 Ckp: 0-0
Best Rating: 101 5/03 Ctml 3m2f good Ch

Dual point winner; jumped much better than in the past when easily winning maiden hunter chase at Cartmel in May 2003; acts on a sound surface.

Uneven Line

100   (56h)**86**

8-y-o b m Jurado (USA)-Altovise (Black Minstrel)
Miss S E Forster D J Simpson

Placings: 00/43   (4794)
2003/04: 21⁴GS, 21³G,

	Starts	1st	2nd	3rd	Win & Pl
Chases	2	0	0	1	1131
Career Total	4	0	0	1	1131

Going: Sf: 0-0 GS: 0-1 Gd: 0-1 GF: - Fm: 0-0
Distance: 2m/2m3: 0-0 2m4-2m7: 0-2 3m+: 0-0
Track: LH: 0-2 RH: 0-0 Tight: 0-2 Gall: 0-0
Aids: Bl: 0-0 Vi: 0-0 Tstrap: 0-0 Ckp: 0-0
Best Rating: 86 4/04 Sedg 2m5f good Ch

Point winner in 2002; well beaten fourth on return in mares' only novices' chase at Sedgefield in February.

Ungaretti (GER)

101(103h)   (105h)**91+**

7-y-o b g Law Society (USA)-Urena (GER) (Dschingis Khan)
Ian Williams Brian Hiskey

Placings: 30/3032120/404F100-455PP4241P   (4916)
2003/04: 26⁴GS, 24⁵S, 26⁵G, 22PS, 24PG, 26⁴G, 29²GS, 24⁴G, 26¹G, 23PGS,

	Starts	1st	2nd	3rd	Win & Pl
Hurdles	3	0	0	0	711
Chases	7	1	1	0	5073
Career Total	26	3	3	3	16839
91 4/04 Plum	3m2f	F(0-95)HCh		GD	£3444
105 2/03 Ludl	3m	E(0-130)HHdl		GD	£5655
105 2/02 Hntg	2m4f110yF(0-100)HHdl			SFT	£2018
				Total win prize-money £11118	

Going: Sf: 0-2 GS: 0-2 Gd: 1-5 GF: - Fm: 0-1
Distance: 2m/2m3: 0-0 2m4-2m7: 0-1 3m+: 1-9
Track: LH: 1-5 RH: 0-5 Tight: 1-2 Gall: 0-1
Aids: Bl: 0-2 Vi: 0-0 Tstrap: 0-0 Ckp: 0-0
Best Rating: 105 2/03 Ludl 3m good Hdl

Modest hurdler/chaser; stays well; suited by good ground; has worn blinkers.

Ungaro (FR)

110f   **117+f**

5-y-o b g Epervier Bleu-Harpyes (FR) (Quart De Vin (FR))
Mrs M Reveley Sir Robert Ogden

Placings: 102   (4578)

2003/04: 16¹G, 16⁰GS, 16²G,

	Starts	1st	2nd	3rd	Win & Pl
NH Flat	3	1	1	0	2936
Career Total	3	1	1	0	2936
99 11/03 Ayr	2m		H NHF	GD	£1988
			Total win prize-money £1988

Going: Sf: 0-0 GS: 0-1 Gd: 1-2 GF: - Fm: 0-0
Distance: 2m2/m3: 1-3 2m4-2m7: 0-0 3m+: 0-0
Track: LH: 1-3 RH: 0-0 Tight: 0-0 Gall: 0-2
Aids: Bl: 0-0 Vi: 0-0 Tstrap: 0-0 Ckp: 0-0
Best Rating: 117 3/04 Newb 2m110y good NHF

Fair bumper performer; suited by good ground.

Unicorn Reward (IRE)

101   102

4-y-o b c Turtle Island (IRE)-Kingdom Pearl (Statoblest)
M D Hammond (R Hannon 28/9) Mrs A Kane & Mrs M Crane

Placings:5422   (4310)
2003/04: 16⁵GF, 16⁴GF, 16²GS, 16²G,

	Starts	1st	2nd	3rd	Win & Pl
Hurdles	4	0	2	0	2652
Career Total	4	0	2	0	2652

Going: Sf: 0-0 GS: 0-1 Gd: 0-0 GF: - Fm: 0-3
Distance: 2m2/m3: 0-4 2m4-2m7: 0-0 3m+: 0-0
Track: LH: 0-2 RH: 0-2 Tight: 0-3 Gall: 0-0
Aids: Bl: 0-0 Vi: 0-0 Tstrap: 0-0 Ckp: 0-0
Best Rating: 102 3/04 Ayr 2m gd-fm Hdl

Moderate miler on the Flat; satisfactory efforts over hurdles to date; capable of winning a modest event.

Union Deux (FR)

96   79

5-y-o ch g Nikos-Sanhia (FR) (Sanhedrin (USA))
Ferdy Murphy Mrs M B Scholey

Placings:00433   (4658)
2003/04: 16⁰G, 20⁰G, 24⁴G, 20³HY, 20³S,

	Starts	1st	2nd	3rd	Win & Pl
Hurdles	5	0	0	2	1465
Career Total	5	0	0	2	1465

Going: Sf: 0-2 GS: 0-0 Gd: 0-3 GF: - Fm: 0-0
Distance: 2m2/m3: 0-1 2m4-2m7: 0-3 3m+: 0-1
Track: LH: 0-4 RH: 0-1 Tight: 0-0 Gall: 0-1
Aids: Bl: 0-0 Vi: 0-0 Tstrap: 0-0 Ckp: 0-0
Best Rating: 82 4/04 Hexm 2m4f110y soft Hdl

Brother to fair hurdler/chaser Nonantais; only modest form to date but turned in improved effort on handicap debut at Newcastle in March; open to further improvement; acts on soft.

Unknown Warrior

5-y-o b g Mtoto-Ayodhya (IRE) (Astronef)
Mrs A L M King Aiden Murphy

Placings:P   (0837)
2003/04: 16ᴾGF,

	Starts	1st	2nd	3rd	Win & Pl
NH Flat	1	0	0	0	
Career Total	1	0	0	0	

Unleash (USA)

111   146+

5-y-o ch g Benny The Dip (USA)-Lemhi Go (USA) (Lemhi Gold (USA))
P J Hobbs Mrs David Thompson

Placings:3311-122   (4628)
2003/04: 16¹G, 16²GF, 20²G,

	Starts	1st	2nd	3rd	Win & Pl
Hurdles	3	1	2	0	26595
Career Total	7	3	2	2	44155
130 5/03 Worc	2m	B(0-140)HHdl	GD	£13711
126 4/03 Strf	2m110y	B HHdl	G-F	£12122
96 3/03 Ludl	2m	E Hdl	GD	£3669
		Total win prize-money £29503

Going: Sf: 0-0 GS: 0-0 Gd: 1-2 GF: - Fm: 0-1
Distance: 2m2/m3: 1-2 2m4-2m7: 0-0 3m+: 0-0
Track: LH: 1-3 RH: 0-0 Tight: 0-1 Gall: 0-0
Aids: Bl: 0-0 Vi: 0-0 Tstrap: 0-0 Ckp: 0-0
Best Rating: 146 4/04 Aint 2m4f good Hdl

Smart hurdler; completing a hat-trick in spring 2003; won the Northumberland Plate on the Flat in June; good effort when runner-up in Free Handicap Hurdle at Chepstow in October, and filled the same position in a big handicap at Aintree in the spring; stays 2m 4f; acts well on a sound surface.

Unlimited Free (IRE)

10-y-o ch g Ile De Chypre-Merry Madness (Raise You Ten)
Mrs S Alner The Hon Miss D Harding

Placings:0365/502125P23/465-130   (4626)
2003/04: 25¹GS, 26²GS, 21⁰G,

	Starts	1st	2nd	3rd	Win & Pl
Chases	3	1	0	1	1790
Career Total	19	2	3	3	12903
109 2/04 Folk	3m1f	H Ch	G-S	£1561
109 1/02 Leic	2m7f110yD(0-110)HCh	GD	£5882
		Total win prize-money £7444

Going: Sf: 0-0 GS: 1-2 Gd: 0-1 GF: - Fm: 0-0
Distance: 2m2/m3: 0-0 2m4-2m7: 0-0 3m+: 1-2
Track: LH: 0-2 RH: 1-1 Tight: 1-2 Gall: 0-0
Aids: Bl: 0-0 Vi: 0-0 Tstrap: 0-0 Ckp: 0-0
Best Rating: 109 3/04 Wwck 3m2f gd-sft Ch

Lightly raced gelding, built for chasing; won two this season, one point and one hunter chase; stays three miles plus; acts on good ground.

Unlocked (IRE)

(106h)   (103+h)

6-y-o b g Supreme Leader-Shunnagh Lass (IRE) (Buckskin (FR))
P J Hobbs Capt E J Edwards-Heathcote

Placings:22656F   (4521)
2003/04: 19²G, 20²G, 19⁶G, 22⁵S, 24⁶G, 19ᶠGS,

	Starts	1st	2nd	3rd	Win & Pl
Hurdles	5	0	2	0	2088
Chases	1	0	0	0	0
Career Total	6	0	2	0	2088

Moderate novice hurdler; stays two and a half miles; acts on good ground.

Unmistakably (IRE)

100(80h)   (91h)102+

7-y-o br g Roselier (FR)-Decent Debbie (Decent Fellow)
Ms Bridget Nicholls (T M Walsh 16/5) Sir Robert Ogden

Placings:00-1U44PU4   (4672)
2003/04: 17¹G, 17ᵁG, 20⁴G, 24⁴G, 23ᴾG, 24ᵁG, 25⁴G,

	Starts	1st	2nd	3rd	Win & Pl
Hurdles	1	1	0	0	4481
Chases	6	0	0	0	831
Career Total	7	1	0	0	5312
91 5/03 Dpat	2m1f172y Hdl	GD	£4480
		Total win prize-money £4481

Going: Sf: 0-0 GS: 0-0 Gd: 1-7 GF: - Fm: 0-0
Distance: 2m2/m3: 1-2 2m4-2m7: 0-1 3m+: 0-4
Track: LH: 0-0 RH: 1-7 Tight: 0-2 Gall: 0-0
Aids: Bl: 0-0 Vi: 0-0 Tstrap: 0-0 Ckp: 0-0
Best Rating: 102 12/03 Tntn 3m good Ch

Moderate ex-Irish hurdler/chaser; won a maiden hurdle on his final start in his native country; held over fences in Britain; acts on good ground.

Unshaken

10-y-o b h Environment Friend-Reel Foyle (USA) (Irish River (FR))
W G Young (E J Alston 14/10) W G Young

Placings:00   (3335)
2003/04: 16⁰GF, 16⁰GS,

	Starts	1st	2nd	3rd	Win & Pl
Hurdles	2	0	0	0	
Career Total	2	0	0	0	

Going: Sf: 0-0 GS: 0-1 Gd: 0-0 GF: - Fm: 0-0
Distance: 2m2/m3: 0-2 2m4-2m7: 0-0 3m+: 0-0
Track: LH: 0-1 RH: 0-1 Tight: 0-2 Gall: 0-0
Aids: Bl: 0-0 Vi: 0-0 Tstrap: 0-0 Ckp: 0-0

Moderate Flat performer at around a mile; well beaten over hurdles.

Unsigned (USA)

104   88

6-y-o b/br g Cozzene (USA)-Striata (USA) (Gone West (USA))
R H Buckler F F Racing Services Partnership II

Placings:0-21F5   (1250)
2003/04: 17²GF, 20¹GF, 21ᶠGF, 19⁵GF,

	Starts	1st	2nd	3rd	Win & Pl
Hurdles	4	1	1	0	4724
Career Total	5	1	1	0	4724
88 6/03 Worc	2m4f	E Hdl	G-F	£3500
		Total win prize-money £3500

Going: Sf: 0-0 GS: 0-0 Gd: 0-0 GF: - Fm: 1-4
Distance: 2m2/m3: 0-1 2m4-2m7: 1-3 3m+: 0-0
Track: LH: 1-2 RH: 0-2 Tight: 0-1 Gall: 0-0
Aids: Bl: 0-0 Vi: 0-0 Tstrap: 0-0 Ckp: 0-0
Best Rating: 92 8/03 MRas 2m3f110y gd-fm Hdl

Plating-class hurdler; appreciated the longer trip when winning 2m 4f novice hurdle at Worcester in June; likes fast ground.

Untidy Daughter

110   101

5-y-o b m Sabrehill (USA)-Branitska (Mummy's Pet)
B Ellison Alderclad Roofing,S Rutter,G Hamilton

Placings:0025051-10262262   (4799)
2003/04: 17¹S, 16⁰G, 21²GF, 16⁶S, 17²G, 17²GS, 16⁶GS, 17²G,

	Starts	1st	2nd	3rd	Win & Pl
Hurdles	8	1	4	0	8333
Career Total	15	2	5	0	12887
88	5/03	Sedg	2m1f	E(0-105)HHdl	SFT £3867
82	4/03	Sedg	2m1f	E(0-105)HHdl	G-F £3373

Total win prize-money £7242

Going:	Sf: 1-2 GS: 0-2 Gd: 0-3 GF: - Fm: 0-1
Distance:	2m/2m3: 1-7 2m4-2m7: 0-1 3m+: 0-0
Track:	LH: 1-7 RH: 0-1 Tight: 1-6 Gall: 0-0
Aids:	Bl: 0-0 Vi: 0-0 Tstrap: 0-0 Ckp: 1-8
Best Rating:	101 4/04 Sedg 2m1f good Hdl

Plating-class hurdler; goes well at Sedgefield; stays 2m 5f; acts on any ground; has worn cheekpieces.

Untwist (IRE)

5-y-o b g Un Desperado (FR)-Pearltwist (Roi Guillaume (FR))
D R Gandolfo G C Hartigan

Placings:0   (4936)
2003/04: 18⁰G,

	Starts	1st	2nd	3rd	Win & Pl
NH Flat	1	0	0	0	
Career Total	1	0	0	0	

Going:	Sf: 0-0 GS: 0-0 Gd: 0-1 GF: - Fm: 0-0
Distance:	2m/2m3: 0-1 2m4-2m7: 0-0 3m+: 0-0
Track:	LH: 0-1 RH: 0-0 Tight: 0-1 Gall: 0-0
Aids:	Bl: 0-0 Vi: 0-0 Tstrap: 0-0 Ckp: 0-0

Unusual Suspect

91f   89f

5-y-o b g Syrtos-Sally Maxwell (Roscoe Blake)
M Pitman The Tsar Partnership

Placings:0   (3927)
2003/04: 16⁰GS,

	Starts	1st	2nd	3rd	Win & Pl
NH Flat	1	0	0	0	
Career Total	1	0	0	0	

Going:	Sf: 0-0 GS: 0-1 Gd: 0-0 GF: - Fm: 0-0
Distance:	2m/2m3: 0-1 2m4-2m7: 0-0 3m+: 0-0
Track:	LH: 0-0 RH: 0-1 Tight: 0-0 Gall: 0-0
Aids:	Bl: 0-0 Vi: 0-0 Tstrap: 0-0 Ckp: 0-0
Best Rating:	89 2/04 Sand 2m110y gd-sft NHF

Up At Midnight

93   77

4-y-o b f Midnight Legend-Uplift (Bustino)
R Rowe D R L Evans

Placings:056066   (4591)
2003/04: 12⁰S, 12⁵GF, 17⁹HY, 16⁰S, 16⁶G, 16⁶G,

	Starts	1st	2nd	3rd	Win & Pl
NH Flat	2	0	0	0	0
Hurdles	4	0	0	0	0
Career Total	6	0	0	0	0

Going:	Sf: 0-3 GS: 0-0 Gd: 0-2 GF: - Fm: 0-1
Distance:	2m/2m3: 0-4 2m4-2m7: 0-0 3m+: 0-0
Track:	LH: 0-2 RH: 0-3 Tight: 0-1 Gall: 0-2
Aids:	Bl: 0-0 Vi: 0-0 Tstrap: 0-0 Ckp: 0-0
Best Rating:	82 3/04 Newb 2m110y good Hdl

Up The Glen (IRE)

88(99h)   (105 h)105+

10-y-o b g Tale Quale-Etrenne (Happy New Year)
A W Carroll (R T Phillips 7/5) Pursuit Media

Placings:16664P/5P/1235-1453   (4811)
2003/04: 20¹S, 20⁴HY, 22⁵GS, 24³G,

	Starts	1st	2nd	3rd	Win & Pl
Hurdles	2	1	0	0	2541
Chases	2	0	0	1	1044
Career Total	16	3	1	2	8511
105	5/03	Uttx	2m4f110yG(0-100)HHdl	SFT £2541
105	11/02	Hexm	2m4f110yG(0-90)HHdl	HVY £1890
104	11/00	Wwck	2m	H NHF	HVY £1659

Total win prize-money £6090

Going:	Sf: 1-2 GS: 0-1 Gd: 0-1 GF: - Fm: 0-0
Distance:	2m/2m3: 0-0 2m4-2m7: 1-3 3m+: 0-1
Track:	LH: 1-4 RH: 0-0 Tight: 0-0 Gall: 0-0
Aids:	Bl: 0-0 Vi: 0-0 Tstrap: 0-0 Ckp: 0-0
Best Rating:	105 4/04 Chep 3m good Ch

Plating-class hurdler, won a Hexham seller in November 2002 and followed up in similar event at Uttoxeter in May 2003; good effort over fences when third in 3m novice chase at Chepstow April 2004; likely to prove best at distances short of 3m; best going left-handed; appreciates heavy ground.

Up The Souths (IRE)

66   27

6-y-o ch g Aahsaylad-Siberian Princess (Northfields (USA))
Jonjo O'Neill (C Roche 3/5) John P McManus

Placings:F0/00P-P0PP   (0884)
2003/04: 24⁵PY, 16⁰G, 26⁸GF, 20⁴G,

	Starts	1st	2nd	3rd	Win & Pl
Hurdles	4	0	0	0	
Career Total	9	0	0	0	

Going:	Sf: 0-0 GS: 0-0 Gd: 0-2 GF: - Fm: 0-1
Distance:	2m/2m3: 0-1 2m4-2m7: 0-1 3m+: 0-2
Track:	LH: 0-3 RH: 0-1 Tight: 0-1 Gall: 0-0
Aids:	Bl: 0-0 Vi: 0-0 Tstrap: 0-0 Ckp: 0-0
Best Rating:	63 5/02 Clon 2m yld-sft Hdl

Up Your Street

9-y-o b m Petoski-Air Streak (Air Trooper)
C Roberts F J Ayres

Placings:5S0/2006PUP22/3-00   (2854)
2003/04: 22⁰G, 26⁰GS,

	Starts	1st	2nd	3rd	Win & Pl
Hurdles	2	0	0	0	
Career Total	15	0	3	1	2778

Going:	Sf: 0-0 GS: 0-1 Gd: 0-1 GF: - Fm: 0-0
Distance:	2m/2m3: 0-2 2m4-2m7: 0-1 3m+: 0-1
Track:	LH: 0-0 RH: 0-2 Tight: 0-0 Gall: 0-0
Aids:	Bl: 0-0 Vi: 0-0 Tstrap: 0-0 Ckp: 0-0
Best Rating:	93 6/01 Worc 2m4f good Hdl

Upgrade

118   158

10-y-o b g Be My Guest (USA)-Cantanta (Top Ville)
M C Pipe Matt Archer & Miss Jean Broadhurst

Placings:P15111P/3F0F30/26F126F1/210/6531251/2F5P3-220156   (4964)
2003/04: 16²GF, 16²S, 16⁹GS, 16¹G, 21⁵GF, 16⁶GF,

	Starts	1st	2nd	3rd	Win & Pl
Chases	6	1	2	0	41584
Career Total	42	10	7	4	255159
158	2/04	Hayd	2m	B HCh	GD £20133
158	4/02	Asct	2m3f110yB HCh	G-F £24900
158	2/02	Winc	2m5f	B Ch	SFT £10188
158	11/00	Asct	2m3f110yA HCh	SFT £30000
154	4/00	Chel	2m	A Ch	SFT £21000
158	2/00	Sand	2m4f110yA Ch	GD £24000
147	3/98	Chel	2m1f	A Hdl	GD £43460
127	2/98	Sand	2m110y	D Hdl	GD £2853
140	2/98	Wwck	2m	E Hdl	GD £2827
133	12/97	Kemp	2m	B Hdl	SFT £5288

Total win prize-money £184653

Going:	Sf: 0-1 GS: 0-1 Gd: 1-1 GF: - Fm: 0-3
Distance:	2m/2m3: 1-5 2m4-2m7: 0-1 3m+: 0-0
Track:	LH: 1-2 RH: 0-4 Tight: 0-0 Gall: 0-1
Aids:	Bl: 0-0 Vi: 0-0 Tstrap: 0-0 Ckp: 0-0
Best Rating:	158 2/04 Hayd 2m good Ch

Very useful chaser on his day, but a lazy type; has refused to start in the past and has pulled himself up, but better in that respect in 2003/4; suited by forcing tactics; best between two miles and two and a half miles; acts on firm and soft ground; has been tried in blinkers.

Upham Lord (IRE)

11-y-o b g Lord Americo-Top O The Mall (Don)
P Beaumont Mrs E W Wilson

Placings:3/3242/51F40104F1/4/3/13F5   (4872)
2003/04: 21¹G, 24³G, 26⁶G, 24⁵S,

	Starts	1st	2nd	3rd	Win & Pl
Chases	4	1	0	1	2919
Career Total	21	4	2	4	20487
112	2/04	Fknm	2m5f110yH Ch	GD £2590
120	4/00	Chep	E Hdl	HVY £2716
120	2/00	Sand	2m4f110yD(0-120)HHdl	SFT £5369
117	11/99	Newb	3m	D(0-120)HCh	G-F £5670

Total win prize-money £16345

Going:	Sf: 0-1 GS: 0-0 Gd: 1-3 GF: - Fm: 0-0
Distance:	2m/2m3: 0-0 2m4-2m7: 1-1 3m+: 0-3
Track:	LH: 1-4 RH: 0-0 Tight: 1-3 Gall: 0-1
Aids:	Bl: 0-0 Vi: 0-0 Tstrap: 0-0 Ckp: 0-0
Best Rating:	120 4/00 Chep 2m4f heavy Hdl

Useful Hunter Chaser/Point-To-Pointer; won a total of 20 races in a row, 19 in points and a hunter chase; effective at up to three miles acts well in a sound surface.

Upright Ima

97   77

5-y-o b m Perpendicular-Ima Delight (Idiots Delight)
Mrs P Sly Mrs P M Sly

Placings:3-46400 (4404)
2003/04: 16^{4}G, 20^{6}GS, 16^{4}S, 16^{0}GS, 16^{0}G,

	Starts	1st	2nd	3rd	Win & Pl
NH Flat	1	0	0	0	0
Hurdles	4	0	0	0	0
Career Total	**6**	**0**	**0**	**1**	**280**

Going: Sf: 0-1 GS: 0-2 Gd: 0-2 GF: - Fm: 0-0
Distance: 2m/2m3: 0-4 2m4-2m7: 0-1 3m+: 0-0
Track: LH: 0-2 RH: 0-3 Tight: 0-1 Gall: 0-2
Aids: Bl: 0-0 Vi: 0-0 Tstrap: 0-0 Ckp: 0-0
Best Rating: 77 12/03 Hntg 2m4f110y gd-sft Hdl

Upswing

98(94c) (74c)81
7-y-o b g Perpendicular-Moorfield Lady (Vicomte)
S B Bell (R Johnson 24/1) C H P Bell

Placings:00P-040632 (4393)
2003/04: 16^{0}G, 16^{4}G, 16^{0}GS, 18^{6}S, 16^{3}G, 17^{2}G,

	Starts	1st	2nd	3rd	Win & Pl
Hurdles	5	0	1	0	1034
Chases	1	0	0	1	632
Career Total	**9**	**0**	**1**	**1**	**1666**

Going: Sf: 0-1 GS: 0-1 Gd: 0-4 GF: - Fm: 0-0
Distance: 2m/2m3: 0-6 2m4-2m7: 0-0 3m+: 0-0
Track: LH: 0-6 RH: 0-0 Tight: 0-3 Gall: 0-0
Aids: Bl: 0-0 Vi: 0-0 Tstrap: 0-0 Ckp: 0-0
Best Rating: 81 3/04 Sedg 2m1f good Hdl

Plating-class novice hurdler/chaser; controversial third on chasing debut at Catterick in January; headstrong and best suited by two miles; will need to brush up his jumping..

Uptown Lad (IRE)

110 109+
5-y-o b g Definite Article-Shoka (FR) (Kaldoun (FR))
R Johnson C Grindell

Placings:0602-533110010040 (4729)
2003/04: 16^{5}GF, 20^{3}GF, 20^{3}GS, 17^{1}HY, 17^{1}GS, 16^{0}S, 16^{0}S, 18^{1}HY, 16^{0}GS, 22^{0}GS, 18^{4}G, 20^{0}G,

	Starts	1st	2nd	3rd	Win & Pl
Hurdles	12	3	0	2	14852
Career Total	**16**	**3**	**1**	**2**	**16312**

112	2/04	Kels	2m2f	D(0-115)HHdl	HVY	£5746
98	12/03	MRas	2m1f110y	D(0-115)HHdl	G-S	£3427
106	11/03	Carl	2m1f	D(0-120)HHdl	HVY	£4192

Total win prize-money £13366

Going: Sf: 2-4 GS: 1-4 Gd: 0-2 GF: - Fm: 0-2
Distance: **2m/2m3: 3-8** 2m4-2m7: 0-4 3m+: 0-0
Track: LH: 1-7 **RH: 2-5 Tight: 2-5** Gall: 0-1
Aids: Bl: 0-0 Vi: 0-0 **Tstrap: 3-9** Ckp: 0-0
Best Rating: 112 2/04 Kels 2m2f heavy Hdl

Moderate hurdler; best over two miles; suited by give; usually wears a tougue tie.

Urban Hymn (IRE)

89(96h) (111h)111
8-y-o ch g College Chapel-Soltura (IRE) (Sadler's Wells (USA))
Ferdy Murphy D A Johnson

Placings:140/5P/3053/63464-12 (2377)
2003/04: 21^{1}G, 21^{2}GF,

	Starts	1st	2nd	3rd	Win & Pl
Chases	2	1	1	0	4029
Career Total	**16**	**2**	**1**	**3**	**10903**

117	10/03	Sedg	2m5f	E Ch	GD	£2996
103	2/00	Sand	2m110y	D Hdl	G-S	£4329

Total win prize-money £7326

Going: Sf: 0-0 GS: 0-0 Gd: 1-1 GF: - Fm: 0-1
Distance: 2m/2m3: 0-0 **2m4-2m7: 1-2** 3m+: 0-0
Track: **LH: 1-2** RH: 0-0 **Tight: 1-2** Gall: 0-0
Aids: Bl: 0-0 Vi: 0-0 Tstrap: 0-0 **Ckp: 1-2**
Best Rating: 117 11/03 Sedg 2m5f gd-fm Ch

Modest novice chaser; stays 2m5f; acts on good ground, but possibly will be better on soft.

Usk Valley (IRE)

95(101h) (88+h)82
9-y-o b g Tenby-Penultimate (USA) (Roberto (USA))
P R Chamings Inhurst Farm Stables Partnership

Placings:2/20/3/3P05/4F-42P012 (4919)
2003/04: 20^{4}G, 25^{2}S, 21^{P}S, 24^{0}S, 22^{1}GF, 20^{2}GS,

	Starts	1st	2nd	3rd	Win & Pl
Hurdles	5	1	1	0	3183
Chases	1	0	1	0	1129
Career Total	**16**	**1**	**4**	**2**	**6409**

88	3/04	Font	2m6f110yG(0-95)HHdl	G-F	£2450

Total win prize-money £2450

Going: Sf: 0-3 GS: 0-1 Gd: 0-1 GF: - Fm: 1-1
Distance: 2m/2m3: 0-0 **2m4-2m7: 1-4** 3m+: 0-2
Track: **LH: 1-4** RH: 0-1 **Tight: 1-1** Gall: 0-1
Aids: Bl: 0-0 Vi: 0-0 Tstrap: 0-0 Ckp: 0-0
Best Rating: 109 2/00 Sand 2m110y soft NHF

Plating-class hurdler/chaser; has shown ability in bumpers and over hurdles; stays an extended three miles one; acts on a soft surface.

Vague Idea

110(94h) (69h)101
11-y-o gr g Tout Ensemble-Roodle Doodle (Rugantino)
O J Carter O J Carter

Placings:P6RP/P30/135U665-12100PPPU (3263)
2003/04: 26^{1}G, 26^{2}GF, 26^{1}GS, 27^{0}G, 24^{0}G, 26^{P}G, 32^{P}G, 29^{P}S, 25^{U}HY,

	Starts	1st	2nd	3rd	Win & Pl
Hurdles	1	0	0	0	0
Chases	8	2	1	0	11372
Career Total	**23**	**3**	**1**	**2**	**14483**

101	7/03	NAbb	3m2f110yE(0-110)HCh	G-S	£4980
97	6/03	NAbb	3m2f110yD(0-120)HCh	GD	£5356
92	5/02	Hrfd	3m1f110yH Ch	G-F	£2450

Total win prize-money £12786

Going: Sf: 0-2 GS: 1-1 Gd: 1-5 GF: - Fm: 0-1
Distance: 2m/2m3: 0-0 2m4-2m7: 0-0 **3m+: 2-9**
Track: **LH: 2-7** RH: 0-2 **Tight: 2-7** Gall: 0-0
Aids: Bl: 0-0 Vi: 0-0 Tstrap: 0-0 Ckp: 0-0
Best Rating: 101 7/03 NAbb 3m2f110y gd-sft Ch

Moderate chaser; a bit of a character; landed a big gamble when winning at Newton Abbot in June 2003; won three-runner race at same course after remounting; stays 3m 2f well; acts on a sound surface; inclined to go left-handed under pressure.

Vaigly North

72 36
6-y-o b m Minshaanshu Amad (USA)-Straight Gold (Vaigly Great)
J A Moore Mrs J M Moore

Placings:5/036P-0 (0417)
2003/04: 17^{0}G,

	Starts	1st	2nd	3rd	Win & Pl
Hurdles	1	0	0	0	
Career Total	**6**	**0**	**0**	**1**	**225**

Going: Sf: 0-0 GS: 0-0 Gd: 0-1 GF: - Fm: 0-0
Distance: 2m/2m3: 0-1 2m4-2m7: 0-0 3m+: 0-0
Track: LH: 0-0 RH: 0-1 Tight: 0-1 Gall: 0-0
Aids: Bl: 0-0 Vi: 0-0 Tstrap: 0-0 Ckp: 0-0
Best Rating: 78 7/02 NAbb 2m1f gd-fm NHF

Vain Minstrel (IRE)

12-y-o b/br g Royal Fountain-Minstrel Top (Black Minstrel)
P Jones M J Parr

Placings:6/00P2102FF/2000411FP0/0/F (0457)
2003/04: 23^{F}HY,

	Starts	1st	2nd	3rd	Win & Pl
Chases	1	0	0	0	
Career Total	**22**	**3**	**3**	**0**	**15050**

102	1/00	Cork	2m	(0-123)HCh	SH	£6900
98	12/99	Thur	2m	(0-95)HCh	SFT	£2926
102	1/99	Tram	2m4f	Ch	HVY	£2915

Total win prize-money £12742

Going: Sf: 0-1 GS: 0-0 Gd: 0-0 GF: - Fm: 0-0
Distance: 2m/2m3: 0-0 2m4-2m7: 0-1 3m+: 0-0
Track: LH: 0-1 RH: 0-0 Tight: 0-0 Gall: 0-0
Aids: Bl: 0-0 Vi: 0-0 Tstrap: 0-0 Ckp: 0-0
Best Rating: 102 1/00 Cork 2m sft-hvy Ch

Val De Fleurie (GER)

104 121
9-y-o b m Mondrian (GER)-Valbonne (Master Willie)
J G M O'Shea Mrs Mary Konig

Placings:34501/11030P/11P31F1120P60 (4397)
2003/04: 17^{1}GS, 19^{1}G, 16^{P}GF, 18^{3}GF, 17^{1}GF, 16^{F}GF, 21^{1}G, 22^{1}GF, 16^{2}GF, 16^{0}GS, 20^{P}HY, 16^{6}G, 21^{0}G,

	Starts	1st	2nd	3rd	Win & Pl
Hurdles	13	5	1	1	22261
Career Total	**24**	**8**	**1**	**3**	**31269**

121	10/03	MRas	2m6f	D(0-125)HHdl	G-F	£4932
118	9/03	Sedg	2m5f110y	D(0-125)HHdl	GD	£3867
101	9/03	NAbb	2m1f	F(0-100)HHdl	G-F	£2982
101	7/03	NAbb	2m3f	F(0-100)HHdl	GD	£3435
97	7/03	NAbb	2m1f	F(0-90)Hdl	G-S	£2968
99	5/00	NAbb	2m1f	F(0-90)Hdl	G-F	£1932
119	5/00	Strf	2m110y	G Hdl	G-F	£2075
81	4/00	Tntn	2m1f	E Hdl	G-S	£2492

Total win prize-money £24686

Going: Sf: 0-1 GS: 1-2 Gd: 2-4 GF: - Fm: 2-6
Distance: **2m/2m3: 3-9** 2m4-2m7: 2-4 3m+: 0-0
Track: **LH: 3-10** RH: 0-1 **Tight: 3-5** Gall: 0-1
Aids: Bl: 0-0 Vi: 0-0 Tstrap: 0-0 Ckp: 0-0
Best Rating: 121 10/03 Chel 2m110y gd-fm Hdl

Fair hurdler; in good form in summer 2003 winning four times; has won four out of four at Newton Abbot; effective at up to 2m6f; acts well on a sound surface.

Val Du Don (FR)

102 131
4-y-o b c Garde Royale-Vallee Normande (FR) (Bellypha)

G Macaire J Detre

Placings:33132 (3485)
2003/04: 15^{3}HO, 16^{3}GS, 18^{1}HO, 17^{3}G, 17^{2}GS,

	Starts	1st	2nd	3rd	Win & Pl
Hurdles	5	1	1	3	23017
Career Total	**5**	**1**	**1**	**3**	**23017**

12/03 Bord 2m2f Hdl HLD £7792
Total win prize-money £7792

Going: Sf: 0-0 GS: 0-2 Gd: 0-1 GF: - Fm: 0-0
Distance: **2m/2m3: 1-4** 2m4-2m7: 0-0 3m+: 0-0
Track: LH: 0-2 RH: 0-1 Tight: 0-0 Gall: 0-3
Aids: Bl: 0-0 Vi: 0-0 Tstrap: 0-0 Ckp: 0-0
Best Rating: **131** 1/04 Chel 2m1f gd-sft Hdl

Useful French juvenile hurdler; twice placed at Cheltenham; stays two miles two; acts on soft ground.

Valance (IRE)

107 **104**

4-y-o br g Bahhare (USA)-Glowlamp (IRE) (Glow (USA))
C R Egerton M Haynes, A & J Allison, J Weatherby

Placings:1F (2096)
2003/04: 16^{1}GF, 16^{F}GF,

	Starts	1st	2nd	3rd	Win & Pl
Hurdles	2	1	0	0	2751
Career Total	**2**	**1**	**0**	**0**	**2751**

104 11/03 Hntg 2m110y E Hdl G-F £2751
Total win prize-money £2751

Going: Sf: 0-0 GS: 0-0 Gd: 0-0 GF: - Fm: 1-2
Distance: **2m/2m3: 1-2** 2m4-2m7: 0-0 3m+: 0-0
Track: LH: 0-1 **RH: 1-1** Tight: 0-0 **Gall: 1-2**
Aids: Bl: 0-0 Vi: 0-0 Tstrap: 0-0 Ckp: 0-0
Best Rating: **104** 11/03 Hntg 2m110y gd-fm Hdl

Modest hurdler; won juvenile hurdle on debut; beaten when fell last next time; acts on fast ground.

Valderrama

62f **25f**

4-y-o ch g Lahib (USA)-Silky Heights (IRE) (Head For Heights)
C J Down G Waterman

Placings:00 (4739)
2003/04: 16^{0}G, 17^{0}G,

	Starts	1st	2nd	3rd	Win & Pl
NH Flat	2	0	0	0	
Career Total	2	0	0	0	

Going: Sf: 0-0 GS: 0-0 Gd: 0-2 GF: - Fm: 0-0
Distance: 2m/2m3: 0-2 2m4-2m7: 0-0 3m+: 0-0
Track: LH: 0-1 RH: 0-1 Tight: 0-1 Gall: 0-0
Aids: Bl: 0-0 Vi: 0-0 Tstrap: 0-0 Ckp: 0-0
Best Rating: **25** 3/04 Winc 2m good NHF

Valerun (IRE)

91 **102**

8-y-o b g Commanche Run-Glenreigh Moss (Le Moss)
Miss E C Lavelle (Timothy Doyle 30/8) Investment Ab Rustningen

Placings:003100/3035446F060-0561020 (4307)
2003/04: 20^{0}S, 22^{5}Y, 22^{6}F, 24^{1}F, 22^{0}F, 22^{2}G, 22^{0}G,

	Starts	1st	2nd	3rd	Win & Pl
Hurdles	7	1	1	0	6209
Career Total	**24**	**2**	**1**	**3**	**12236**

96 8/03 Kbgn 3m Hdl FRM £4480
105 11/01 Naas 2m NHF YLD £3895
Total win prize-money £8376

Going: Sf: 0-1 GS: 0-0 Gd: 0-2 GF: - Fm: 1-3
Distance: 2m/2m3: 0-0 2m4-2m7: 0-6 **3m+: 1-1**
Track: LH: 0-1 RH: 0-1 Tight: 0-1 Gall: 0-0
Aids: Bl: 0-0 Vi: 0-0 Tstrap: 0-0 Ckp: 0-0
Best Rating: **106** 8/02 Tral 2m1f good NHF

Moderate hurdler; ex-Irish; acts on good; stays 3m.

Valeureux

107 **114**

6-y-o ch g Cadeaux Genereux-La Strada (Niniski (USA))
J Hetherton Eureka Racing

Placings:620/F333-1F2P312 (4618)
2003/04: 16^{1}GF, 17^{F}G, 16^{2}GS, 17^{P}GS, 16^{3}S, 17^{1}G, 21^{2}G,

	Starts	1st	2nd	3rd	Win & Pl
Hurdles	7	2	2	1	9010
Career Total	**14**	**2**	**3**	**4**	**11511**

114 3/04 MRas 2m1f110yE Hdl GD £3609
106 10/03 Hexm 2m110y E Hdl G-F £2555
Total win prize-money £6164

Going: Sf: 0-1 GS: 0-2 Gd: 1-3 GF: - Fm: 1-1
Distance: **2m/2m3: 2-6** 2m4-2m7: 0-1 3m+: 0-0
Track: LH: 1-4 RH: 1-3 **Tight: 1-3** Gall: 0-0
Aids: Bl: 0-0 Vi: 0-0 Tstrap: 0-0 Ckp: 0-0
Best Rating: **114** 3/04 Sedg 2m5f110y good Hdl

Modest novice hurdler; finally off the mark in very modest event at Hexham in October; scored again at Market Rasen in March; suited by two miles; acts on fast ground and with cut.

Valfonic

6-y-o b g Zafonic (USA)-Valbra (Dancing Brave (USA))
F Jordan (M C Pipe 31/5) Done It Again

Placings:60U1/11543650P-0P0 (4634)
2003/04: 16^{0}GF, 19^{P}G, 19^{0}G,

	Starts	1st	2nd	3rd	Win & Pl
Hurdles	3	0	0	0	
Career Total	**16**	**3**	**0**	**1**	**9444**

111 5/02 Worc 2m E(0-110)HHdl GD £3003
96 5/02 Sthl 2m F(0-95)HHdl GD £2443
89 4/02 Wwck 2m F(0-95)HHdl G-F £2985
Total win prize-money £8432

Going: Sf: 0-0 GS: 0-0 Gd: 0-2 GF: - Fm: 0-1
Distance: 2m/2m3: 0-2 2m4-2m7: 0-1 3m+: 0-0
Track: LH: 0-1 RH: 0-2 Tight: 0-2 Gall: 0-0
Aids: Bl: 0-0 Vi: 0-0 Tstrap: 0-1 Ckp: 0-0
Best Rating: **111** 6/02 Hrfd 2m1f gd-fm Hdl

Modest hurdler, acts on a sound surface.

Valigan (IRE)

11-y-o gr g Roselier (FR)-Wonderful Lilly (Prince Hansel)
N B King Martin Bailey

Placings:6/310231/641150/42F1/241004/4-4PP (2469)
2003/04: 26^{4}GF, 28^{P}G, 24^{P}S,

	Starts	1st	2nd	3rd	Win & Pl
Hurdles	1	0	0	0	0
Chases	2	0	0	0	364
Career Total	**27**	**6**	**3**	**2**	**28528**

130 12/01 Muss 3m D(0-120)HCh G-F £4134
108 2/01 Sedg 3m3f D Ch SFT £4010
127 12/99 Muss 3m D(0-125)HHdl G-S £5498
135 12/99 Hexm 3m F(0-105)HHdl HVY £2343
120 3/99 Ayr 3m110y D(0-115)HHdl SFT £3574
106 11/98 Sedg 3m3f110yE Hdl G-S £2302
Total win prize-money £21864

Going: Sf: 0-1 GS: 0-0 Gd: 0-1 GF: - Fm: 0-1
Distance: 2m/2m3: 0-0 2m4-2m7: 0-0 3m+: 0-3
Track: LH: 0-1 RH: 0-2 Tight: 0-2 Gall: 0-0
Aids: Bl: 0-1 Vi: 0-0 Tstrap: 0-0 Ckp: 0-0
Best Rating: **135** 12/99 Hexm 3m heavy Hdl

Valjean (IRE)

8-y-o b g Alzao (USA)-Escape Path (Wolver Hollow)
Mrs Myfanwy Miles P B Miles

Placings:0/0U/P4-0P (3778)
2003/04: 19^{0}GF, 24^{P}G,

	Starts	1st	2nd	3rd	Win & Pl
Chases	2	0	0	0	
Career Total	**7**	**0**	**0**	**0**	**0**

Going: Sf: 0-0 GS: 0-0 Gd: 0-1 GF: - Fm: 0-1
Distance: 2m/2m3: 0-0 2m4-2m7: 0-1 3m+: 0-1
Track: LH: 0-0 RH: 0-2 Tight: 0-1 Gall: 0-0
Aids: Bl: 0-0 Vi: 0-0 Tstrap: 0-1 Ckp: 0-0
Best Rating: **60** 4/03 Hrfd 2m gd-fm Ch

Valley Erne (IRE)

13-y-o b g King's Ride-Erne Gold Vii (Damsire Unregistered)
Norman Sanderson (Michael Cunningham 1/5) Norman Sanderson

Placings:225050141140l/3/F333F413F51/3005/004200F3/66502P506-35P (4798)
2003/04: 25^{3}GY, 21^{5}GF, 27^{P}G,

	Starts	1st	2nd	3rd	Win & Pl
Chases	3	0	0	1	2922
Career Total	**49**	**6**	**4**	**8**	**57295**

116 4/00 List 2m4f HCh SFT £10400
112 2/00 Punc 2m4f Ch SFT £4692
132 4/97 Punc 2m4f (0-123)HHdl GD £4069
119 2/97 Punc 2m (0-109)HHdl SFT £3730
108 1/97 Punc 2m (0-116)HHdl YLD £3051
113 12/96 Navn 2m NHF Y-S £2824
Total win prize-money £28768

Going: Sf: 0-0 GS: 0-0 Gd: 0-1 GF: - Fm: 0-1
Distance: 2m/2m3: 0-0 2m4-2m7: 0-1 3m+: 0-2
Track: LH: 0-2 RH: 0-1 Tight: 0-1 Gall: 0-0
Aids: Bl: 0-0 Vi: 0-0 Tstrap: 0-0 Ckp: 0-0
Best Rating: **136** 7/97 Gway 2m yield Hdl

Valley Henry (IRE)

106 (88h)**166**

9-y-o b g Step Together (USA)-Pineway Vii (Damsire Unregistered)
J Howard Johnson (P F Nicholls 22/11) Andrea & Graham Wylie

Placings:15/1134/11FU2F11/114144-F3FP6 (4624)
2003/04: 25^{F}G, 20^{3}GS, 24^{F}G, 25^{P}GS, 25^{6}G,

	Starts	1st	2nd	3rd	Win & Pl
Chases	5	0	0	1	7750
Career Total	**25**	**10**	**1**	**2**	**187582**

166 2/03 Newb 3m A Ch GD £41650
162 12/02 Sand 3m110y B Ch G-S £10972
161 10/02 Winc 2m5f A HCh GD £23800

158	4/02	Ayr	2m4f	A Ch	GD	£15600
99	3/02	Extr	3m1f110yD Ch		GD	£5304
153	11/01	Newb	3m	A Ch	GD	£17850
124	10/01	Chep	2m3f110yC Ch		GD	£6776
140	11/00	Winc	2m6f	C Hdl	SFT	£6286
134	11/00	Chep	2m4f	A Hdl	SFT	£12000
122	3/00	Leop	2m	NHF	Y-S	£3588
				Total win prize-money		£143826

Going:	Sf: 0-0 GS: 0-2 Gd: 0-3 GF: - Fm: 0-0
Distance:	2m/2m3: 0-0 2m4-2m7: 0-1 3m+: 0-4
Track:	LH: 0-3 RH: 0-2 Tight: 0-0 Gall: 0-2
Aids:	Bl: 0-0 Vi: 0-0 Tstrap: 0-0 Ckp: 0-0
Best Rating: 166 2/03 Newb 3m good Ch	

Smart chaser; winner of the 2003 Aon Chase at Newbury and good fourth in Cheltenham Gold Cup after not appearing to quite see out the 3m 2f trip; has had jumping problems; stays three miles and best on good ground; bought out of Paul Nicholls' yard for a large sum in late 2003 and has not had much luck for new connections.

Valley Warrior
81 — 86

7-y-o b g Michelozzo (USA)-Mascara Vii (Damsire Unregistered)
J S Smith Mrs J A Benson

Placings:L55P (4588)
2003/04: 16⁵GS, 17⁵HY, 20⁵G, 21ᴾG,

	Starts	1st	2nd	3rd	Win & Pl
NH Flat	1	0	0	0	0
Hurdles	3	0	0	0	0
Career Total	4	0	0	0	0

Going:	Sf: 0-1 GS: 0-1 Gd: 0-2 GF: - Fm: 0-0
Distance:	2m/2m3: 0-2 2m4-2m7: 0-2 3m+: 0-0
Track:	LH: 0-1 RH: 0-3 Tight: 0-0 Gall: 0-1
Aids:	Bl: 0-0 Vi: 0-0 Tstrap: 0-0 Ckp: 0-0
Best Rating: 86 3/04 Carl 2m4f good Hdl	

Small amount of ability over hurdles.

Valleymore (IRE)
101(114h) — (129+h)117

8-y-o br g Jolly Jake (NZ)-Glamorous Brush (IRE) (Brush Aside (USA))
S A Brookshaw T G K Construction Ltd

Placings:042311P-F332PP (4570)
2003/04: 20ᶠGS, 16³GS, 20³G, 22²S, 22ᴾG, 24ᴾGS,

	Starts	1st	2nd	3rd	Win & Pl
Chases	6	0	1	2	5608
Career Total	13	2	2	3	29130
127	3/03	Uttx	2m6f110yB(0-140)HHdl	SFT	£9222
121	2/03	Hayd	2m4f	B HHdl	G-S	£12412
			Total win prize-money £21634		

Going:	Sf: 0-1 GS: 0-3 Gd: 0-2 GF: - Fm: 0-0
Distance:	2m/2m3: 0-1 2m4-2m7: 0-4 3m+: 0-1
Track:	LH: 0-5 RH: 0-1 Tight: 0-2 Gall: 0-0
Aids:	Bl: 0-0 Vi: 0-0 Tstrap: 0-0 Ckp: 0-0
Best Rating: 127 3/03 Uttx 2m6f110y soft Hdl	

Fair hurdler/chaser; easy winner over brush obstacles at Haydock in February 2003, and followed up at Uttoxeter; pulled up when hating fast ground subsequently; best effort over fences when strong-finishing runner-up at Haydock in February; will be suited by three miles.

Vallica
101 — 90

5-y-o b m Bishop Of Cashel-Vallauris (Faustus (USA))

Mrs A M Thorpe A T Bailey

Placings:5000P0002 (4569)
2003/04: 19⁵GF, 20ᵁG, 16⁵GS, 19⁰GS, 16ᴾS, 19⁰S, 24⁰GS, 21⁰S, 17²GS,

	Starts	1st	2nd	3rd	Win & Pl
Hurdles	9	0	1	0	757
Career Total	9	0	1	0	757

Going:	Sf: 0-3 GS: 0-4 Gd: 0-1 GF: - Fm: 0-1
Distance:	2m/2m3: 0-4 2m4-2m7: 0-4 3m+: 0-1
Track:	LH: 0-5 RH: 0-4 Tight: 0-3 Gall: 0-0
Aids:	Bl: 0-0 Vi: 0-0 Tstrap: 0-0 Ckp: 0-0
Best Rating: 90 3/04 Bang 2m1f gd-sft Hdl	

Valman (IRE)
72

8-y-o b/br g Valville (FR)-Omania (Runnett)
C J Down Mrs L M Edwards

Placings:0P/P-PPU3 (0888)
2003/04: 26ᴾS, 19ᴾGF, 24ᴾG, 23ᵁGF, 24³G,

	Starts	1st	2nd	3rd	Win & Pl
Hurdles	1	0	0	1	491
Chases	4	0	0	0	0
Career Total	7	0	0	1	491

Going:	Sf: 0-1 GS: 0-0 Gd: 0-2 GF: - Fm: 0-2
Distance:	2m/2m3: 0-1 2m4-2m7: 0-0 3m+: 0-4
Track:	LH: 0-4 RH: 0-1 Tight: 0-2 Gall: 0-0
Aids:	Bl: 0-3 Vi: 0-1 Tstrap: 0-0 Ckp: 0-0
Best Rating: 72 4/03 NAbb 3m2f110y soft Ch	

Vals Well (IRE)
73 — (13h)

9-y-o b g Be My Native (USA)-Castle-Lady (Little Buskins)
G Prodromou George Prodromou

Placings:0/P5P0P (3427)
2003/04: 21ᴾG, 21⁵G, 22ᴾS, 26ᴾG, 23ᴾGS,

	Starts	1st	2nd	3rd	Win & Pl
Hurdles	1	0	0	0	0
Chases	4	0	0	0	0
Career Total	6	0	0	0	0

Going:	Sf: 0-2 GS: 0-1 Gd: 0-2 GF: - Fm: 0-0
Distance:	2m/2m3: 0-0 2m4-2m7: 0-3 3m+: 0-2
Track:	LH: 0-4 RH: 0-1 Tight: 0-3 Gall: 0-0
Aids:	Bl: 0-2 Vi: 0-0 Tstrap: 0-0 Ckp: 0-0
Best Rating: 13 6/01 Worc 2m gd-fm Hdl	

Valtar (FR)
102 — 101+

4-y-o b f Tot Ou Tard (IRE)-Valiance (FR) (Akarad (FR))
Y-M Porzier E Letendre

Placings:30 (4625)
2003/04: 16³GS, 16⁰G,

	Starts	1st	2nd	3rd	Win & Pl
Hurdles	2	0	0	1	760
Career Total	2	0	0	1	760

Going:	Sf: 0-0 GS: 0-1 Gd: 0-1 GF: - Fm: 0-0
Distance:	2m/2m3: 0-2 2m4-2m7: 0-0 3m+: 0-0
Track:	LH: 0-1 RH: 0-1 Tight: 0-1 Gall: 0-0
Aids:	Bl: 0-0 Vi: 0-0 Tstrap: 0-2 Ckp: 0-0

Best Rating: 101 3/04 Asct 2m110y gd-sft Hdl	

French-trained filly; jumped well and only run out of it late on on hurdling debut at Ascot; held in good race at Aintree subsequently; effective at two miles; acts on soft ground.

Valuable (IRE)
76 — 36

7-y-o b m Jurado (USA)-Can't Afford It (IRE) (Glow (USA))
R Johnson The Jolly Boys Partnership

Placings:00-0PP0P (4937)
2003/04: 16⁰G, 20⁰G, 16ᴾGS, 16ᴾHY, 16ᴾGS,

	Starts	1st	2nd	3rd	Win & Pl
Hurdles	5	0	0	0	
Career Total	7	0	0	0	

Going:	Sf: 0-1 GS: 0-2 Gd: 0-2 GF: - Fm: 0-0
Distance:	2m/2m3: 0-4 2m4-2m7: 0-1 3m+: 0-0
Track:	LH: 0-4 RH: 0-1 Tight: 0-1 Gall: 0-3
Aids:	Bl: 0-0 Vi: 0-0 Tstrap: 0-3 Ckp: 0-0
Best Rating: 64 12/02 Muss 2m gd-fm NHF	

No worthwhile form so far in bumpers and hurdles.

Van De Velde
87 — 84+

5-y-o ch g Alhijaz-Lucky Flinders (Free State)
P A Blockley Ms Ellen Arbuthnott-Rook

Placings:000-6P (4762)
2003/04: 21⁶G, 19ᴾS,

	Starts	1st	2nd	3rd	Win & Pl
Hurdles	2	0	0	0	0
Career Total	5	0	0	0	0

Going:	Sf: 0-1 GS: 0-0 Gd: 0-1 GF: - Fm: 0-0
Distance:	2m/2m3: 0-0 2m4-2m7: 0-2 3m+: 0-0
Track:	LH: 0-1 RH: 0-0 Tight: 0-1 Gall: 0-0
Aids:	Bl: 0-0 Vi: 0-0 Tstrap: 0-0 Ckp: 0-0
Best Rating: 84 3/04 Sedg 2m5f110y good Hdl	

Vandal
94 — 73

4-y-o b g Entrepreneur-Vax Star (Petong)
Mrs L Wadham (J A R Toller 17/9) R B Holt

Placings:60 (4915)
2003/04: 17⁶GS, 16⁰GS,

	Starts	1st	2nd	3rd	Win & Pl
Hurdles	2	0	0	0	0
Career Total	2	0	0	0	0

Going:	Sf: 0-0 GS: 0-1 Gd: 0-1 GF: - Fm: 0-0
Distance:	2m/2m3: 0-2 2m4-2m7: 0-0 3m+: 0-0
Track:	LH: 0-1 RH: 0-1 Tight: 0-1 Gall: 0-0
Aids:	Bl: 0-0 Vi: 0-0 Tstrap: 0-0 Ckp: 0-0
Best Rating: 73 3/04 MRas 2m1f110y good Hdl	

Vandas Choice (IRE)
110 — 121

6-y-o b g Sadler's Wells (USA)-Morning Devotion (USA) (Affirmed (USA))
Mrs L B Normile J Petterson

Placings:43551-511PP554 (4942)
2003/04: 20⁵G, 16¹G, 16¹GF, 16⁸S, 20⁹S, 16⁵F, 20⁵G, 20⁴GS,

	Starts	1st	2nd	3rd	Win & Pl
Hurdles	8	2	0	0	33208
Career Total	13	3	0	1	38082
121 11/03 DRoy 2m	(0-140)HHdl		G-F		£27435
121 9/03 Prth 2m110y	D(0-115)HHdl		GD		£4108
101 4/03 Prth 2m110y	D Hdl		GD		£5603
	Total win prize-money				£37146

Going:	Sf: 0-2 GS: 0-1 Gd: 1-3 GF: - Fm: 1-2
Distance:	**2m/2m3: 2-4** 2m4-2m7: 0-4 3m+: 0-0
Track:	LH: 0-1 **RH: 1-6** Tight: 0-1 Gall: 0-0
Aids:	Bl: 0-0 Vi: 0-0 Tstrap: 0-0 Ckp: 0-0
Best Rating:	121 11/03 DRoy 2m gd-fm Hdl

Fair hurdler; best at around two miles; acts on good ground but handles softer.

Vanormix (FR)
109   122+
5-y-o gr g Linamix (FR)-Vadsa Honor (FR) (Highest Honor (FR))
M C Pipe Jim Weeden

Placings:2U0114-606143 (4528)
2003/04: 16⁵G, 17⁰G, 17⁶G, 17¹GS, 21⁴G, 20³GS,

	Starts	1st	2nd	3rd	Win & Pl
Hurdles	6	1	0	1	6524
Career Total	12	3	1	1	15722
125 1/04 Tntn 2m1f	D(0-120)HHdl		G-S		£4907
112 2/03 Extr 2m3f	E Hdl		G-S		£3737
100 1/03 Extr 2m3f	E Hdl		G-S		£3794
	Total win prize-money				£12440

Going:	Sf: 0-0 GS: 1-2 Gd: 0-4 GF: - Fm: 0-0
Distance:	**2m/2m3: 1-4** 2m4-2m7: 0-2 3m+: 0-0
Track:	LH: 0-3 **RH: 1-3 Tight: 1-1** Gall: 0-2
Aids:	Bl: 0-0 **Vi: 1-5** Tstrap: 0-0 Ckp: 0-0
Best Rating:	125 1/04 Tntn 2m1f gd-sft Hdl

Fair hurdler; resumed winning ways when winning 2m 1f handicap at Taunton January 2004; stays 2m 3f; acts on good to soft ground; wears a visor.

Veiled Dancer (IRE)
100(79h)   (71 h)75
11-y-o b m Shareef Dancer (USA)-Fatal Distraction (Formidable (USA))
A S T Holdsworth N J Holdsworth

Placings:620P/56FPPP/0666P4-5P5P (0836)
2003/04: 24⁵GF, 24⁴S, 26⁵GF, 23⁹GF,

	Starts	1st	2nd	3rd	Win & Pl
Hurdles	2	0	0	0	0
Chases	2	0	0	0	0
Career Total	20	0	1	0	942

Going:	Sf: 0-1 GS: 0-0 Gd: 0-0 GF: - Fm: 0-3
Distance:	2m/2m3: 0-0 2m4-2m7: 0-0 3m+: 0-4
Track:	LH: 0-3 RH: 0-1 Tight: 0-1 Gall: 0-0
Aids:	Bl: 0-0 Vi: 0-0 Tstrap: 0-0 Ckp: 0-0
Best Rating:	75 3/03 Font 3m4f good Ch

Point winner; maiden over both hurdles and fences; stays well.

Veinte Siete (USA)
4-y-o ch g Trempolino (USA)-Satz (USA) (The Minstrel (CAN))
P R Webber (J A R Toller 1/9) P J Smith

Placings:P (1872)
2003/04: 16⁵GF,

	Starts	1st	2nd	3rd	Win & Pl
Hurdles	1	0	0	0	
Career Total	1	0	0	0	

Going:	Sf: 0-0 GS: 0-0 Gd: 0-0 GF: - Fm: 0-1
Distance:	2m/2m3: 0-1 2m4-2m7: 0-0 3m+: 0-0
Track:	LH: 0-0 RH: 0-1 Tight: 0-0 Gall: 0-0
Aids:	Bl: 0-0 Vi: 0-0 Tstrap: 0-0 Ckp: 0-0

Veleta
95f   89f
5-y-o b m Shaamit (IRE)-Keel Row (Relkino)
N J Henderson The Queen

Placings:43 (0675)
2003/04: 17⁴GF, 17³GF,

	Starts	1st	2nd	3rd	Win & Pl
NH Flat	2	0	0	1	275
Career Total	2	0	0	1	275

Going:	Sf: 0-0 GS: 0-0 Gd: 0-0 GF: - Fm: 0-2
Distance:	2m/2m3: 0-2 2m4-2m7: 0-0 3m+: 0-0
Track:	LH: 0-1 RH: 0-1 Tight: 0-0 Gall: 0-0
Aids:	Bl: 0-0 Vi: 0-0 Tstrap: 0-0 Ckp: 0-0
Best Rating:	89 5/03 MRas 2m1f110y gd-fm NHF

Velvet Rose
10-y-o ch m Cheyenne Dance (FR)-Privy Rose (Privy Seal)
Mrs S M Johnson I D S Jones

Placings:PPP (0563)
2003/04: 26⁸GS, 22²G, 24²GF,

	Starts	1st	2nd	3rd	Win & Pl
Hurdles	3	0	0	0	
Career Total	3	0	0	0	

Going:	Sf: 0-0 GS: 0-1 Gd: 0-1 GF: - Fm: 0-1
Distance:	2m/2m3: 0-0 2m4-2m7: 0-1 3m+: 0-2
Track:	LH: 0-2 RH: 0-1 Tight: 0-1 Gall: 0-0
Aids:	Bl: 0-0 Vi: 0-0 Tstrap: 0-0 Ckp: 0-0

Veneguera (IRE)
101(108h)   (97h)95+
11-y-o b g Satco (FR)-Orlita (Master Buck)
K C Bailey The Sporting Has Beens

Placings:4006P60/5441440412140/4/0253623411130464/P 4610P6-1336322305 (4590)
2003/04: 21¹GF, 21³GF, 24³G, 24⁶GF, 19³G, 25²G, 20²GF, 24³GS, 24⁹G, 24⁵G,

	Starts	1st	2nd	3rd	Win & Pl
Hurdles	6	1	1	3	6340
Chases	4	0	1	1	1930
Career Total	53	7	5	7	32854
97 5/03 Hntg 2m5f110y	E(0-110)HHdl		G-F		£3500
97 10/02 Ludl 3m	F(0-95)HHdl		FRM		£3423
106 10/01 Kemp 2m5f	D(0-125)HHdl		G-S		£5073
106 10/01 Hntg 3m2f	F(0-110)HHdl		GD		£1862
103 3/00 Dpat 2m4f110y	(0-95)HHdl		G-F		£2345
93 11/99 Dpat 2m6f	(0-95)HHdl		YLD		£2002
81 8/99 Naas 2m4f	Hdl		G-F		£3696
	Total win prize-money				£21902

Going:	Sf: 0-0 GS: 0-1 Gd: 0-5 GF: - Fm: 1-4
Distance:	2m/2m3: 0-0 **2m4-2m7: 1-4** 3m+: 0-6
Track:	LH: 0-0 **RH: 1-9** Tight: 0-3 **Gall: 1-4**
Aids:	Bl: 0-0 Vi: 0-0 Tstrap: 0-0 **Ckp: 1-10**
Best Rating:	113 6/01 MRas 2m6f110y gd-fm Ch

Moderate chaser/hurdler; out-and-out stayer, but a little quirky, he goes particularly well for amateur riders; suited by decent ground; has worn cheekpieces.

Venn Ottery
152(71h)   152
9-y-o b g Access Ski-Tom's Comedy (Comedy Star (USA))
P F Nicholls (O J Carter 19/12) O J Carter

Placings:P/P/PF/P4P04F0F-P34F2P46P401112150FP (4860)
2003/04: 20⁵GS, 16³GF, 16⁴GS, 16⁶G, 16²GF, 17⁸G, 16⁴G, 20⁶GS, 17⁸G, 16⁴GS, 16¹G, 16¹G, 17¹G, 17²GS, 16¹GF, 16⁵G, 16⁶GS, 20⁸GS,

	Starts	1st	2nd	3rd	Win & Pl
Chases	20	4	2	1	36445
Career Total	32	4	2	1	36910
152 3/04 Hrfd 2m	E(0-110)HCh		G-F		£4332
140 3/04 Newb 2m1f	C(0-130)HCh		GD		£8820
125 2/04 Ludl 2m	E(0-110)HCh		GD		£6708
119 2/04 Leic 2m	E Ch		GD		£4143
	Total win prize-money				£24004

Going:	Sf: 0-0 GS: 0-7 Gd: 3-10 GF: - Fm: 1-3
Distance:	**2m/2m3: 4-17** 2m4-2m7: 0-3 3m+: 0-0
Track:	**LH: 1-13 RH: 3-7** Tight: 1-11 Gall: 1-3
Aids:	Bl: 0-0 Vi: 0-0 **Tstrap: 4-8** Ckp: 0-0
Best Rating:	152 3/04 Chel 2m good Ch

Smart chaser; poor form for his owner, but showed dramatic improvement after joining Paul Nicholls, winning four times in around three weeks; was travelling best of all until coming under pressure in the straight and retreating, mistakably ran without usual tongue-tie in the Queen Mother; disappointed at Aintree and at Ayr; best at two miles; headstrong; acts on good and fast ground; usually; wears a tongue tie.

Venture To Fly (IRE)
104(97c)   (112c)112
10-y-o ch g Roselier (FR)-Fly Run (Deep Run)
N G Richards Ashleybank Investments Limited

Placings:2325/1134/F4P-00240 (4948)
2003/04: 24⁰G, 23⁹GS, 27²GS, 24⁴HY, 27⁹GS,

	Starts	1st	2nd	3rd	Win & Pl
Hurdles	5	0	1	0	2150
Career Total	16	2	3	2	10968
108 1/01 Ayr 2m6f	E Hdl		SFT		£2954
117 11/00 Newc 3m	E Hdl		SFT		£2583
	Total win prize-money				£5537

Going:	Sf: 0-1 GS: 0-3 Gd: 0-1 GF: - Fm: 0-0
Distance:	2m/2m3: 0-0 2m4-2m7: 0-0 3m+: 0-5
Track:	LH: 0-3 RH: 0-1 Tight: 0-1 Gall: 0-1
Aids:	Bl: 0-0 Vi: 0-0 Tstrap: 0-0 Ckp: 0-0
Best Rating:	117 1/01 Ayr 3m110y gd-sft Hdl

Modest hurdler; has been a little disappointing over fences; acts on soft ground; stays three miles.

Verde Luna
(101h)   (54h)49
12-y-o b g Green Desert (USA)-Mamaluna (USA) (Roberto (USA))
A G Hobbs Jason Parfitt

Placings:0600106/2133F445/2332435053400/4312012/0/P 060U4/00015066-P5P (1040)

2003/04: 24PG, 23SG, 26PGF,

	Starts	1st	2nd	3rd	Win & Pl
Hurdles	1	0	0	0	0
Chases	2	0	0	0	0
Career Total	53	5	5	7	20548
79	8/02	Font	3m2f110yF(0-90)HCh	G-F	£2940
94	3/99	Font	2m3f	H Ch	G-F	£2390
96	8/98	Sthl	2m4f110yE(0-105)HCh	G-F	£2650
87	8/96	NAbb	2m1f	F(0-100)HHdl	G-F	£1948
87	4/96	Plum	2m4f	E(0-100)HHdl	FRM	£2364

Total win prize-money £12293

Going:	Sf: 0-0 GS: 0-0 Gd: 0-2 GF: - Fm: 0-1
Distance:	2m/2m3: 0-0 2m4-2m7: 0-0 3m+: 0-3
Track:	LH: 0-2 RH: 0-1 Tight: 0-2 Gall: 0-0
Aids:	Bl: 0-0 Vi: 0-3 Tstrap: 0-0 Ckp: 0-0
Best Rating:	100 7/97 Worc 2m good Ch

Modest hurdler/chaser, acts on fast; stays well.

Veridian

(104h)   (92h)82

11-y-o b g Green Desert (USA)-Alik (FR) (Targowice (USA))
G F Bridgwater Mrs Gail Bridgwater

Placings:F42126/5/14025/15/045006/434PP55-0P (4531)
2003/04: 16OG, 16PGS,

	Starts	1st	2nd	3rd	Win & Pl
Hurdles	1	0	0	0	0
Chases	1	0	0	0	0
Career Total	29	3	3	1	27635
136	9/00	Bang	2m1f	C(0-135)HHdl	G-F	£6825
137	12/99	Kemp	2m	B(0-145)HHdl	SFT	£10259
116	3/98	Folk	2m1f110yE Hdl	GD	£2630

Total win prize-money £19714

Going:	Sf: 0-0 GS: 0-1 Gd: 0-1 GF: - Fm: 0-0
Distance:	2m/2m3: 0-2 2m4-2m7: 0-0 3m+: 0-0
Track:	LH: 0-1 RH: 0-1 Tight: 0-0 Gall: 0-0
Aids:	Bl: 0-0 Vi: 0-0 Tstrap: 0-0 Ckp: 0-0
Best Rating:	137 12/99 Kemp 2m soft Hdl

Vero Beach

79   88

8-y-o ch g Nicholas Bill-My Moody Girl (IRE) (Alzao (USA))
Mrs S D Williams Bideford Tool Ltd

Placings:0/5P-0 (0758)
2003/04: 27PS, 24OG,

	Starts	1st	2nd	3rd	Win & Pl
Hurdles	2	0	0	0	0
Career Total	4	0	0	0	0

Going:	Sf: 0-1 GS: 0-0 Gd: 0-1 GF: - Fm: 0-0
Distance:	2m/2m3: 0-0 2m4-2m7: 0-0 3m+: 0-2
Track:	LH: 0-2 RH: 0-0 Tight: 0-1 Gall: 0-0
Aids:	Bl: 0-0 Vi: 0-0 Tstrap: 0-0 Ckp: 0-0
Best Rating:	85 4/03 NAbb 3m3f gd-fm Hdl

Versus (GER)

102   101+

4-y-o gr c Highest Honor (FR)-Very Mighty (FR) (Niniski (USA))
C J Mann The Safest Syndicate

Placings:236 (4452)
2003/04: 17PHY, 16PS, 16PGS,

	Starts	1st	2nd	3rd	Win & Pl
Hurdles	3	0	1	1	2185
Career Total	3	0	1	1	2185

Going:	Sf: 0-2 GS: 0-1 Gd: 0-0 GF: - Fm: 0-0
Distance:	2m/2m3: 0-3 2m4-2m7: 0-0 3m+: 0-0
Track:	LH: 0-0 RH: 0-3 Tight: 0-0 Gall: 0-0
Aids:	Bl: 0-0 Vi: 0-0 Tstrap: 0-0 Ckp: 0-0
Best Rating:	101 2/04 Sand 2m110y soft Hdl

Moderate novice hurdler; acts on soft ground; effective over two miles.

Vert Espere

100   (0c)96

11-y-o ch g Green Adventure (USA)-Celtic Dream (Celtic Cone)
Mrs J Candlish P S Daly

Placings:P/0P000F0/40P5406/2310/25122P-U45 (0363)
2003/04: 17UG, 214GF, 20PS,

	Starts	1st	2nd	3rd	Win & Pl
Hurdles	2	0	0	0	0
Chases	1	0	0	0	0
Career Total	28	2	4	1	12830
96	8/02	MRas	2m3f110yD(0-115)HHdl	G-S	£4537
90	6/01	Worc	3m	F(0-100)HHdl	GD	£2037

Total win prize-money £6574

Going:	Sf: 0-1 GS: 0-0 Gd: 0-1 GF: - Fm: 0-0
Distance:	2m/2m3: 0-1 2m4-2m7: 0-2 3m+: 0-0
Track:	LH: 0-2 RH: 0-1 Tight: 0-0 Gall: 0-0
Aids:	Bl: 0-0 Vi: 0-0 Tstrap: 0-0 Ckp: 0-0
Best Rating:	96 9/02 Worc 2m4f good Hdl

Modest handicap hurdler; stays three miles; acts on a sound surface.

Vertedanz (IRE)

4-y-o b f Sesaro (USA)-Blade Of Grass (Kris)
Miss I E Craig Mrs D C Samworth

Placings:P (3245)
2003/04: 16PGS,

	Starts	1st	2nd	3rd	Win & Pl
Hurdles	1	0	0	0	0
Career Total	1	0	0	0	0

Going:	Sf: 0-0 GS: 0-1 Gd: 0-0 GF: - Fm: 0-0
Distance:	2m/2m3: 0-1 2m4-2m7: 0-0 3m+: 0-0
Track:	LH: 0-1 RH: 0-0 Tight: 0-0 Gall: 0-0
Aids:	Bl: 0-0 Vi: 0-0 Tstrap: 0-0 Ckp: 0-0

Very Exclusive (USA)

5-y-o b g Royal Academy (USA)-Exclusive Davis (USA) (Our Native (USA))
G L Moore (R M H Cowell 26/7) Danny Bloor

Placings:P (0852)
2003/04: 16PGF,

	Starts	1st	2nd	3rd	Win & Pl
Hurdles	1	0	0	0	0
Career Total	1	0	0	0	0

Going:	Sf: 0-0 GS: 0-0 Gd: 0-0 GF: - Fm: 0-1
Distance:	2m/2m3: 0-1 2m4-2m7: 0-0 3m+: 0-0
Track:	LH: 0-1 RH: 0-0 Tight: 0-1 Gall: 0-0
Aids:	Bl: 0-0 Vi: 0-0 Tstrap: 0-0 Ckp: 0-1

Very Optimistic (IRE)

107   135

6-y-o b g Un Desperado (FR)-Bright Future (IRE) (Satco (FR))
Jonjo O'Neill Mrs G Smith

Placings:f-110 (4394)
2003/04: 201S, 161GS, 21OG,

	Starts	1st	2nd	3rd	Win & Pl
Hurdles	3	2	0	0	7813
Career Total	4	3	0	0	10386
130	12/03	Hayd	2m	D Hdl	G-S	£3861
130	12/03	Hayd	2m4f	D Hdl	SFT	£3952
110	4/03	Asct	2m110y	H NHF	GD	£2572

Total win prize-money £10386

Going:	Sf: 1-1 GS: 1-1 Gd: 0-1 GF: - Fm: 0-0
Distance:	2m/2m3: 1-1 2m4-2m7: 1-2 3m+: 0-0
Track:	LH: 2-3 RH: 0-0 Tight: 0-0 Gall: 0-1
Aids:	Bl: 0-0 Vi: 0-0 Tstrap: 0-0 Ckp: 0-0
Best Rating:	135 3/04 Chel 2m5f good Hdl

Useful hurdler; made a good winning debut in a decent Ascot bumper in early April 2003; easy winner of two Haydock novice hurdles in December; found step up in grade too much at Cheltenham; stays two and a half miles; effective on good and soft ground.

Very Tasty (IRE)

7-y-o ch g Be My Native (USA)-Jasmine Melody (Jasmine Star)
Mrs Dianne Sayer Mrs Dianne Sayer

Placings:0UP-P-P (4319)
2003/04: 20PS,

	Starts	1st	2nd	3rd	Win & Pl
Hurdles	1	0	0	0	0
Career Total	4	0	0	0	0

Going:	Sf: 0-1 GS: 0-0 Gd: 0-0 GF: - Fm: 0-0
Distance:	2m/2m3: 0-0 2m4-2m7: 0-1 3m+: 0-0
Track:	LH: 0-1 RH: 0-0 Tight: 0-0 Gall: 0-1
Aids:	Bl: 0-0 Vi: 0-0 Tstrap: 0-0 Ckp: 0-0
Best Rating:	57 4/02 Carl 2m1f good NHF

Very Very Noble (IRE)

100   120+

10-y-o ch g Aristocracy-Hills Angel (IRE) (Salluceva)
A M Hales Coach House Racing

Placings:12F/0/13113/1F5P (4371)
2003/04: 21IG, 24PFG, 21SG, 24PG,

	Starts	1st	2nd	3rd	Win & Pl
Chases	4	1	0	0	4023
Career Total	13	5	1	2	18730
120	12/03	Folk	2m5f	D(0-120)HCh	GD	£3497
117	12/01	Folk	3m1f	F(0-110)HCh	GD	£2947
111	11/01	Wwck	3m110y	F(0-95)HCh	GD	£2656
115	10/01	Sthl	2m4f110yF(0-110)HCh	GD	£3391
89	3/00	Dpat	3m	Ch	SFT	£2345

Total win prize-money £14839

Going:	Sf: 0-0 GS: 0-0 Gd: 1-4 GF: - Fm: 0-0
Distance:	2m/2m3: 0-0 2m4-2m7: 1-2 3m+: 0-2
Track:	LH: 0-2 RH: 1-2 Tight: 1-2 Gall: 0-1
Aids:	Bl: 0-0 Vi: 0-0 Tstrap: 0-4 Ckp: 0-0
Best Rating:	121 12/01 Newb 3m good Ch

Fair lightly-raced handicap chaser; stays three miles plus, but effective at shorter; acts on good ground but handles softer; wears a tongue tie.

Vi Et Virtite

5-y-o b m Dancing Spree (USA)-Princess Scully (Weld)
R C Guest (Mrs A Dobloug Talbot 26/9) Ms A D Talbot

Placings:PP　　　　　　　　　　　　　　　　　　(2089)
2003/04: 20PG, 16PG,

	Starts	1st	2nd	3rd	Win & Pl
Hurdles	2	0	0	0	
Career Total	2	0	0	0	

Going:	Sf: 0-0 GS: 0-0 Gd: 0-0 GF: - Fm: 0-0
Distance:	2m/2m3: 0-1 2m4-2m7: 0-1 3m+: 0-0
Track:	LH: 0-2 RH: 0-0 Tight: 0-2 Gall: 0-0
Aids:	Bl: 0-0 Vi: 0-0 Tstrap: 0-1 Ckp: 0-0

Vic Plum (IRE)

6-y-o b/br m Lord Americo-Naujella (Malinowski (USA))
W G Young W G Young

Placings:000-P　　　　　　　　　　　　　　　　(0472)
2003/04: 17PGS,

	Starts	1st	2nd	3rd	Win & Pl
Hurdles	1	0	0	0	
Career Total	4	0	0	0	

Going:	Sf: 0-0 GS: 0-1 Gd: 0-0 GF: - Fm: 0-0
Distance:	2m/2m3: 0-1 2m4-2m7: 0-0 3m+: 0-0
Track:	LH: 0-1 RH: 0-0 Tight: 0-1 Gall: 0-0
Aids:	Bl: 0-0 Vi: 0-0 Tstrap: 0-0 Ckp: 0-0
Best Rating:	26　2/03　Muss　2m　　　good　NHF

Vic Toto (FR)

112　　　　　　　　　　　　　　　　　　**148+**
7-y-o b h Kaid Pous (FR)-Koberta (FR) (Don Roberto (USA))
F Doumen M Benavides

Placings:211331/3112/2211444-40432　　　(3958)
2003/04: 19AVS, 20DVS, 24AVS, 20DVS, 20PG,

	Starts	1st	2nd	3rd	Win & Pl
Hurdles	5	0	1	1	46520
Career Total	22	7	5	4	367913
	10/02	Autl	2m4f110y Hdl		VS	£30368
	9/02	Autl	2m3f110y Hdl		SFT	£30368
	3/02	Autl	2m2f		HVY	£30368
	6/01	Autl	2m3f110y Hdl		VS	£48497
	4/01	Autl	2m3f110y Hdl		VS	£38797
	11/00	Autl	1m7f	Hdl	HVY	£10567

Total win prize-money £194728

Going:	Sf: 0-0 GS: 0-0 Gd: 0-1 GF: - Fm: 0-0
Distance:	2m/2m3: 0-0 2m4-2m7: 0-4 3m+: 0-1
Track:	LH: 0-3 RH: 0-0 Tight: 0-1 Gall: 0-0
Aids:	Bl: 0-0 Vi: 0-0 Tstrap: 0-0 Ckp: 0-0
Best Rating:	158　2/04　Font　2m4f　good　Hdl

Smart French-trained hurdler; multiple winner in his native France; runner-up to Starzaan in the National Spirit Hurdle at Fontwell on his British debut; stays three miles; likes soft ground.

Vic's Brush (IRE)

12-y-o b g Brush Aside (USA)-Fair Vic (Fair Turn)

G Chambers　R A B Brassey

Placings:00/056/P　　　　　　　　　　　　　　(0490)
2003/04: 26PGF,

	Starts	1st	2nd	3rd	Win & Pl
Chases	1	0	0	0	
Career Total	6	0	0	0	

Going:	Sf: 0-0 GS: 0-0 Gd: 0-0 GF: - Fm: 0-1
Distance:	2m/2m3: 0-0 2m4-2m7: 0-0 3m+: 0-1
Track:	LH: 0-1 RH: 0-0 Tight: 0-1 Gall: 0-0
Aids:	Bl: 0-0 Vi: 0-0 Tstrap: 0-0 Ckp: 0-0
Best Rating:	57　6/00　Wxfd　2m4f　　gd-yld　Hdl

Vicar's Lad

105　　　　　　　　　　　　　　　　　　**109+**
8-y-o b g Terimon-Proverbial Rose (Proverb)
N A Twiston-Davies Mrs P Duncan

Placings:405-2556　　　　　　　　　　　　　　(4519)
2003/04: 22DG, 20SG, 25SS, 22GGS,

	Starts	1st	2nd	3rd	Win & Pl
Hurdles	4	0	1	0	1311
Career Total	7	0	1	0	1311

Going:	Sf: 0-1 GS: 0-1 Gd: 0-2 GF: - Fm: 0-0
Distance:	2m/2m3: 0-0 2m4-2m7: 0-3 3m+: 0-1
Track:	LH: 0-3 RH: 0-1 Tight: 0-2 Gall: 0-0
Aids:	Bl: 0-0 Vi: 0-0 Tstrap: 0-0 Ckp: 0-0
Best Rating:	109　11/03　Aint　2m4f　　good　Hdl

Shown a little ability in bumpers and novice hurdles; keen sort.

Vicars Destiny

107　　　　　　　　　　　　　　　　　　**118**
6-y-o b m Sir Harry Lewis (USA)-Church Leap (Pollerton)
Mrs S Lamyman Terence Deal

Placings:4/022314P-420U41515020　　　　(4842)
2003/04: 19AG, 21ZG, 23GGF, 16UGS, 19AG, 19IG, 20SS, 20IS, 20SS, 20AGS, 24ZG, 21GG,

	Starts	1st	2nd	3rd	Win & Pl
Hurdles	12	2	2	0	15380
Career Total	20	3	4	1	20864
116	1/04	Weth	2m4f110yD(0-115)HHdl	SFT	£4956
107	12/03	MRas	2m3f110yD(0-125)HHdl	GD	£3818
97	3/03	Weth	2m4f110yE Hdl	GD	£3474

Total win prize-money £12249

Going:	Sf: 1-3 GS: 0-2 Gd: 1-6 GF: - Fm: 0-1
Distance:	2m/2m3: 0-1 **2m4-2m7: 2-9** 3m+: 0-2
Track:	LH: 1-10 RH: 1-2 **Tight: 1-2** Gall: 0-0
Aids:	Bl: 0-0 Vi: 0-0 Tstrap: 0-0 **Ckp: 2-8**
Best Rating:	118　3/04　Donc　3m110y　good　Hdl

Fair hurdler; bounced back to form at Market Rasen in December 2003; successful again at Wetherby the following month; stays 2m5f; suited by testing ground; has worn cheekpieces.

Vicentio

99　　　　　　　　　　　　　　　　　　**77**
5-y-o br g Vettori (IRE)-Smah (Mtoto)
T J Fitzgerald Shaw Thing Partnership

Placings:0060-024F5U06P　　　　　　　　　(4796)
2003/04: 17UGS, 16ZGF, 17AG, 16FGS, 16SGS, 20UGS, 19DGF, 20RS, 21PG,

	Starts	1st	2nd	3rd	Win & Pl
Hurdles	9	0	1	0	770

Career Total　　13　0　1　0　　770

Going:	Sf: 0-1 GS: 0-4 Gd: 0-2 GF: - Fm: 0-2
Distance:	2m/2m3: 0-6 2m4-2m7: 0-3 3m+: 0-0
Track:	LH: 0-8 RH: 0-1 Tight: 0-5 Gall: 0-1
Aids:	Bl: 0-0 Vi: 0-0 Tstrap: 0-0 Ckp: 0-0
Best Rating:	77　11/03　MRas　2m1f110y　good　Hdl

Plating-class novice hurdler; stays 2m4f; seems best on fast ground.

Viciana

98　　　　　　　　　　　　　　　　　　**107**
5-y-o b m Sir Harry Lewis (USA)-Ludoviciana (Oats)
J W Payne G W Paul

Placings:20F2　　　　　　　　　　　　　　　　(4664)
2003/04: 16ZG, 16DGF, 19FG, 19ZGS,

	Starts	1st	2nd	3rd	Win & Pl
NH Flat	2	0	1	0	588
Hurdles	2	0	1	0	1159
Career Total	4	0	2	0	1747

Going:	Sf: 0-0 GS: 0-1 Gd: 0-2 GF: - Fm: 0-1
Distance:	2m/2m3: 0-2 2m4-2m7: 0-2 3m+: 0-0
Track:	LH: 0-2 RH: 0-2 Tight: 0-2 Gall: 0-0
Aids:	Bl: 0-0 Vi: 0-0 Tstrap: 0-0 Ckp: 0-0
Best Rating:	107　4/04　Ling　2m3f110y　gd-sft　Hdl

Moderate hurdler; placed twice in bumpers; in process of running a sound first race over hurdles when crashing out at Market Rasen in February; suited by two and a half miles; acts on good and easy ground.

Vicomte Thomas (FR)

73　　　　　　　　　　　　　　　　　　**20**
4-y-o b g Highest Honor (FR)-Vigorine (FR) (Shakapour)
R Dickin T M T Racing

Placings:0050　　　　　　　　　　　　　　　　(3841)
2003/04: 14DG, 17DGS, 17SGS, 19DGS,

	Starts	1st	2nd	3rd	Win & Pl
NH Flat	1	0	0	0	0
Hurdles	3	0	0	0	0
Career Total	4	0	0	0	0

Going:	Sf: 0-0 GS: 0-3 Gd: 0-1 GF: - Fm: 0-0
Distance:	2m/2m3: 0-2 2m4-2m7: 0-1 3m+: 0-0
Track:	LH: 0-1 RH: 0-0 Tight: 0-0 Gall: 0-0
Aids:	Bl: 0-1 Vi: 0-0 Tstrap: 0-0 Ckp: 0-1
Best Rating:	25　1/04　Hrfd　2m1f　gd-sft　Hdl

Victoria Ryan (IRE)

6-y-o b m Good Thyne (USA)-No Not (Ovac (ITY))
J R Norton G A Hancock & A Parsonage

Placings:00-PP　　　　　　　　　　　　　　　(4216)
2003/04: 21PGS, 22PG,

	Starts	1st	2nd	3rd	Win & Pl
Hurdles	2	0	0	0	
Career Total	4	0	0	0	

Going:	Sf: 0-0 GS: 0-1 Gd: 0-1 GF: - Fm: 0-0
Distance:	2m/2m3: 0-0 2m4-2m7: 0-2 3m+: 0-0
Track:	LH: 0-1 RH: 0-0 Tight: 0-1 Gall: 0-0

Aids: Bl: 0-0 Vi: 0-0 Tstrap: 0-0 Ckp: 0-0
Best Rating: 58 4/03 Hexm 2m110y   good   NHF

Victoria's Boy (IRE)

11-y-o b g Denel (FR)-Cloghroe Lady (Hard Boy)
J J Coates J J Coates

Placings:/00/00/1526/P506543204/0P-1   (0475)
2003/04: 26¹GS,

	Starts	1st	2nd	3rd	Win & Pl
Chases	1	1	0	0	2363
Career Total	21	2	2	1	7578
92	5/03	Ctml	3m2f	H Ch	G-S £2362
102	5/00	Hexm	3m1f	H Ch	G-F £2366

Total win prize-money £4729

Going: Sf: 0-0 GS: 1-1 Gd: 0-0 GF: - Fm: 0-0
Distance: 2m/2m3: 0-0 2m4-2m7: 0-0 3m+: 1-1
Track: LH: 1-1 RH: 0-0 Tight: 1-1 Gall: 0-0
Aids: Bl: 0-0 Vi: 0-0 Tstrap: 0-0 Ckp: 0-0
Best Rating: 102 5/00 Hexm 3m1f   gd-fm   Ch

Winning pointer and hunter chaser; jumps well; best at three miles; effective on fast ground.

Victory Bell

75   61

6-y-o b g Komaite (USA)-Shikabell (Kala Shikari)
A P Jones P Newell

Placings:060U0   (4783)
2003/04: 18⁰G, 17⁵GS, 16⁶S, 20ᵁGS, 21⁰G,

	Starts	1st	2nd	3rd	Win & Pl
NH Flat	3	0	0	0	0
Hurdles	2	0	0	0	0
Career Total	5	0	0	0	0

Going: Sf: 0-1 GS: 0-2 Gd: 0-2 GF: - Fm: 0-0
Distance: 2m/2m3: 0-3 2m4-2m7: 0-2 3m+: 0-0
Track: LH: 0-1 RH: 0-4 Tight: 0-1 Gall: 0-2
Aids: Bl: 0-0 Vi: 0-0 Tstrap: 0-0 Ckp: 0-0
Best Rating: 73 1/04 Hntg 2m110y   soft   NHF

Victory Gunner (IRE)

102   105

6-y-o ch g Old Vic-Gunner B Sharp (Gunner B)
C Roberts Ron Bartlett

Placings:0520-5P10120   (4838)
2003/04: 22⁵G, 20⁶G, 19¹G, 22⁰GS, 19¹GS, 24²GS, 20⁴GF,

	Starts	1st	2nd	3rd	Win & Pl
Hurdles	7	2	1	0	8097
Career Total	11	2	2	0	8657
107	2/04	Tntn	2m3f110yE(0-110)HHdl	G-S £3786
96	12/03	Tntn	2m3f110yE Hdl	GD £2754

Total win prize-money £6541

Going: Sf: 0-0 GS: 1-3 Gd: 1-3 GF: - Fm: 0-1
Distance: 2m/2m3: 0-0 2m4-2m7: 2-5 3m+: 0-2
Track: LH: 0-3 RH: 2-4 Tight: 2-3 Gall: 0-1
Aids: Bl: 0-0 Vi: 0-0 Tstrap: 0-0 Ckp: 0-0
Best Rating: 107 2/04 Tntn 2m3f110y   gd-sft   Hdl

Moderate hurdler; suited by trips of around two and a half miles although stays three; appreciates a decent surface.

Victory Roll

93(97h)   (104h)92

8-y-o b g In The Wings-Persian Victory (IRE) (Persian Bold)
Miss E C Lavelle Sir Gordon Brunton

Placings:004143/01131320/00-50F   (3807)
2003/04: 17⁵S, 20⁴G, 20⁶G,

	Starts	1st	2nd	3rd	Win & Pl
Chases	3	0	0	0	0
Career Total	19	4	1	3	20469
107	12/01	Hntg	2m110y D(0-125)HHdl	G-S £8287
110	11/01	Folk	2m1f110yF(0-105)HHdl	SFT £2681
104	10/01	Folk	2m1f110yF(0-110)HHdl	HVY £2919
82	1/01	Folk	2m1f110yF(0-115)HHdl	HVY £2387

Total win prize-money £16275

Going: Sf: 0-1 GS: 0-0 Gd: 0-2 GF: - Fm: 0-0
Distance: 2m/2m3: 0-1 2m4-2m7: 0-2 3m+: 0-0
Track: LH: 0-1 RH: 0-2 Tight: 0-1 Gall: 0-0
Aids: Bl: 0-0 Vi: 0-0 Tstrap: 0-0 Ckp: 0-0
Best Rating: 110 2/02 Winc 2m   soft   Hdl

Moderate hurdler/chaser; goes particularly well over the extended two miles one furlong on heavy ground at Folkestone, but has shown decent form on other right-handed tracks and acts on a faster surface.

Victory Sign (IRE)

98   87

4-y-o b g Forzando-Mo Ceri (Kampala)
Miss M P Bryant (K R Burke 28/8) Miss M Bryant

Placings:3446   (4788)
2003/04: 18³G, 16⁴S, 16⁴GS, 16⁶G,

	Starts	1st	2nd	3rd	Win & Pl
Hurdles	4	0	0	1	654
Career Total	4	0	0	1	654

Going: Sf: 0-1 GS: 0-1 Gd: 0-2 GF: - Fm: 0-0
Distance: 2m/2m3: 0-4 2m4-2m7: 0-0 3m+: 0-0
Track: LH: 0-4 RH: 0-0 Tight: 0-4 Gall: 0-0
Aids: Bl: 0-0 Vi: 0-0 Tstrap: 0-0 Ckp: 0-3
Best Rating: 87 1/04 Plum 2m   soft   Hdl

Vidi Caesar (NZ)

106(98h)   (84h)98+

9-y-o b g Racing Is Fun (USA)-Vidi Vici (NZ) (Roman Empire)
R C Guest Mark Barrett

Placings:03-3P60252354U540   (4315)
2003/04: 17⁴GS, 20⁴GF, 17⁶G, 20⁷G, 17²GS, 21⁵GF, 17²GS, 20³GS, 20⁵GS, 16⁴G, 20ᵁS, 24⁵G, 20⁴GF, 16⁹GF,

	Starts	1st	2nd	3rd	Win & Pl
Hurdles	2	0	0	1	566
Chases	12	0	2	3	3081
Career Total	16	0	2	3	4205

Going: Sf: 0-1 GS: 0-3 Gd: 0-6 GF: - Fm: 0-4
Distance: 2m/2m3: 0-6 2m4-2m7: 0-7 3m+: 0-1
Track: LH: 0-11 RH: 0-7 Tight: 0-7 Gall: 0-1
Aids: Bl: 0-4 Vi: 0-0 Tstrap: 0-0 Ckp: 0-4
Best Rating: 95 11/03 Sthl 2m1f   good   Ch

Moderate chaser; placed in testing ground on the Flat in New Zealand; showed some ability when moderate third in novices' hurdle at Catterick in March; third again at Cartmel in May; narrowly denied over fences at Southwell in November; best suited by two miles.

Vigoureux (FR)

96   98+

5-y-o b g Villez (USA)-Rouge Folie (FR) (Agent Bleu (FR))
S Gollings Ian Hesketh & John Webb

Placings:2153-446000   (4718)
2003/04: 16⁴G, 16⁶S, 21⁹GS, 16⁹GS, 16⁹G,

	Starts	1st	2nd	3rd	Win & Pl
Hurdles	6	0	0	0	727
Career Total	10	1	1	1	17768
	11/02	Engh	2m1f110y Hdl	HVY £10601

Total win prize-money £10601

Going: Sf: 0-1 GS: 0-2 Gd: 0-3 GF: - Fm: 0-0
Distance: 2m/2m3: 0-5 2m4-2m7: 0-1 3m+: 0-0
Track: LH: 0-4 RH: 0-2 Tight: 0-1 Gall: 0-0
Aids: Bl: 0-0 Vi: 0-0 Tstrap: 0-0 Ckp: 0-0
Best Rating: 98 12/03 Wwck 2m   good   Hdl

Moderate hurdler; ex-French; has shown promise over here, including on the Flat; effective at around two miles; acts on soft ground.

Vigzol

89   45

6-y-o br g Relief Pitcher-Hammerhill (Grisaille)
R J King Mrs S King

Placings:000   (3750)
2003/04: 17⁰GS, 24⁰S, 18⁰GS,

	Starts	1st	2nd	3rd	Win & Pl
NH Flat	1	0	0	0	0
Hurdles	2	0	0	0	0
Career Total	3	0	0	0	0

Going: Sf: 0-1 GS: 0-1 Gd: 0-0 GF: - Fm: 0-0
Distance: 2m/2m3: 0-2 2m4-2m7: 0-0 3m+: 0-0
Track: LH: 0-2 RH: 0-1 Tight: 0-0 Gall: 0-0
Aids: Bl: 0-0 Vi: 0-0 Tstrap: 0-0 Ckp: 0-0
Best Rating: 56 1/04 Chep 3m   soft   Hdl

Viking Buoy (IRE)

76(91c)   (70c)70

12-y-o ch g Pimpernel's Tune-Clare's Crystal (Tekoah)
Mrs P Townsley Paul Townsley

Placings:S353/2.22UP4132FP/11104023/2263U0/00/03005 3-0   (0152)
2003/04: 20⁰GF,

	Starts	1st	2nd	3rd	Win & Pl
Hurdles	1	0	0	0	0
Career Total	38	4	7	7	22822
90	7/98	Wxfd	2m4f	(0-116)HCh	G-F £3586
111	5/98	Gowr	3m1f	(0-116)HHdl	GD £4765
98	5/98	Klny	2m4f	(0-109)HCh	Y-S £2978
107	2/98	Clon	3m	Hdl	Y-S £1935

Total win prize-money £13266

Going: Sf: 0-0 GS: 0-0 Gd: 0-0 GF: - Fm: 0-1
Distance: 2m/2m3: 0-0 2m4-2m7: 0-1 3m+: 0-0
Track: LH: 0-1 RH: 0-0 Tight: 0-0 Gall: 0-0
Aids: Bl: 0-0 Vi: 0-0 Tstrap: 0-0 Ckp: 0-0
Best Rating: 111 5/98 Gowr 3m1f   good   Hdl

Plating-class hurdler/chaser; stays two miles five; seems to act on any ground.

Villa

101   93

8-y-o b g Jupiter Island-Spoonhill Wood (Celtic Cone)

M C Pipe Matt Archer & Miss Jean Broadhurst

Placings:*61/1-550*   (4560)
2003/04: 24⁵GS, 21⁵G, 21⁹GS,

	Starts	1st	2nd	3rd	Win & Pl
Hurdles	3	0	0	0	
Career Total	6	2	0	0	4718
120 11/02 Chep	2m110y H NHF			HVY	£2401
108 1/02 Towc	2m H NHF			HVY	£2317

Total win prize-money £4718

Going:	Sf: 0-0 GS: 0-2 Gd: 0-1 GF: - Fm: 0-0
Distance:	2m/2m3: 0-0 2m4-2m7: 0-2 3m+: 0-1
Track:	LH: 0-2 RH: 0-1 Tight: 0-0 Gall: 0-2
Aids:	Bl: 0-0 Vi: 0-1 Tstrap: 0-0 Ckp: 0-0
Best Rating:	120 11/02 Chep 2m110y heavy NHF

Moderate hurdler; dual bumper winner on heavy ground back in 2002; will stay three miles; acts on very soft ground; has worn a visor.

Village King (IRE)
93   143

11-y-o b g Roi Danzig (USA)-Honorine (USA) (Blushing Groom (FR))
P J Hobbs Capt E J Edwards-Heathcote

Placings:45210320/111123122/1336F0/0223F0/001P1/24-2   (1501)
2003/04: 24²GF,

	Starts	1st	2nd	3rd	Win & Pl
Chases	1	0	1	0	3975
Career Total	37	9	9	5	95698
135 4/02 Chel	3m2f110yC(0-135)HCh		G-F	£13071
128 2/02 Font	3m2f110yD(0-125)HCh		SFT	£4153
147 12/99 Chel	2m5f C(0-130)HCh		SFT	£10796
139 3/99 Extr	2m3f E(0-115)HCh		GD	£4040
134 10/98 Chel	2m4f110yD(0-110)HCh		GD	£4856
107 10/98 NAbb	2m5f110yE(0-120)Ch		GD	£3126
107 9/98 Worc	2m7f110yD Ch		G-F	£3556
99 8/98 NAbb	2m110y D Ch		G-F	£3501
112 1/98 Ludl	2m5f110yF Hdl		SFT	£2095

Total win prize-money £49198

Going:	Sf: 0-0 GS: 0-0 Gd: 0-0 GF: - Fm: 0-1
Distance:	2m/2m3: 0-0 2m4-2m7: 0-0 3m+: 0-1
Track:	LH: 0-1 RH: 0-0 Tight: 0-0 Gall: 0-0
Aids:	Bl: 0-0 Vi: 0-0 Tstrap: 0-0 Ckp: 0-0
Best Rating:	147 12/99 Chel 2m5f soft Ch

Very useful handicap chaser who stays well and acts on varying ground; off the track since November 2002 until a unlucky second after nearly unseating his rider at the penultimate fence in Class B handicap at Chepstow October 2003; not the most consistent; best efforts when ridden positively.

Villair (IRE)
107(99h)   (84h)114+

9-y-o b g Valville (FR)-Brackenair (Fairbairn)
C J Mann The Safest Syndicate

Placings:3004/00526F/1245F21-43234113   (4941)
2003/04: 20⁴S, 19³S, 22²HY, 26³S, 24⁴S, 29¹GS, 26¹G, 31³GS,

	Starts	1st	2nd	3rd	Win & Pl
Chases	8	2	1	3	14922
Career Total	25	4	4	4	24904
114 4/04 NAbb	3m2f110yD(0-115)HCh		GD	£5590
111 3/04 Wwck	3m5f E(0-110)HCh		G-S	£4241
101 3/03 Plum	2m4f E(0-110)HCh		SFT	£4065
83 5/02 Towc	2m G Hdl		G-S	£2016

Total win prize-money £15913

Going:	Sf: 0-5 GS: 1-2 Gd: 1-1 GF: - Fm: 0-0

Distance: 2m/2m3: 0-0 2m4-2m7: 0-3 3m+: 2-5
Track: LH: 2-4 RH: 0-1 Tight: 1-4 Gall: 0-0
Aids: Bl: 0-0 Vi: 0-0 Tstrap: 0-0 Ckp: 0-0
Best Rating: 114 4/04 NAbb 3m2f110y good Ch

Modest chaser; stays well and appreciated a step up to 3m 5f when winning Class E handicap at Warwick March 2004; best on soft ground; has not always looked keen under pressure.

Villon (IRE)
104f   129+f

5-y-o b g Topanoora-Deep Adventure (Deep Run)
L Lungo R A Bartlett

Placings:*1*   (4886)
2003/04: 17¹GS,

	Starts	1st	2nd	3rd	Win & Pl
NH Flat	1	1	0	0	2078
Career Total	1	1	0	0	2078
129 4/04 Carl	2m1f H NHF		G-S	£2077

Total win prize-money £2078

Going:	Sf: 0-0 GS: 1-1 Gd: 0-0 GF: - Fm: 0-0
Distance:	2m/2m3: 1-1 2m4-2m7: 0-0 3m+: 0-0
Track:	LH: 0-0 RH: 1-1 Tight: 0-0 Gall: 0-0
Aids:	Bl: 0-0 Vi: 0-0 Tstrap: 0-0 Ckp: 0-0
Best Rating:	129 4/04 Carl 2m1f gd-sft NHF

Half-brother to several winners and created very favourable impression when wide-margin bumper winner on debut in April 2004; looks one to keep on the right side.

Vilprano
111   95

13-y-o b g Ra Nova-Village Princess (Rolfe (USA))
James Moffatt The Vilprano Partnership

Placings:0603/313/P012/223625342201/321366/54323216
56/0450141/4535045633300-6105   (0980)
2003/04: 24⁶G, 26¹G, 24⁰GF, 27⁵GF,

	Starts	1st	2nd	3rd	Win & Pl
Hurdles	4	1	0	0	5054
Career Total	63	8	9	13	46437
97 5/03 Ctml	3m2f E(0-110)HHdl	GD	£5053
114 1/02 Catt	3m1f110yD(0-115)HHdl	SFT	£5122
107 11/01 Ayr	3m110y D(0-125)HHdl	G-S	£3477
120 12/00 Newc	3m C(0-135)HHdl	SFT	£5086
113 11/99 Ayr	3m110y D(0-125)HHdl	GD	£3554
103 4/99 Bang	3m D(0-125)HHdl	GD	£4474
87 2/98 Newc	3m F(0-105)HHdl	GD	£2102
88 5/96 Ctml	2m6f F(0-95)HHdl	G-F	£2528

Total win prize-money £31420

Going:	Sf: 0-0 GS: 0-0 Gd: 1-2 GF: - Fm: 0-2
Distance:	2m/2m3: 0-0 2m4-2m7: 0-0 3m+: 1-4
Track:	LH: 1-4 RH: 0-0 Tight: 1-2 Gall: 0-0
Aids:	Bl: 0-0 Vi: 0-0 Tstrap: 0-0 Ckp: 0-0
Best Rating:	120 12/00 Newc 3m soft Hdl

Modest hurdler; stays well; acts on a soft surface; has worn cheekpieces.

Vin Du Pays
69   39

4-y-o b g Alzao (USA)-Royale Rose (FR) (Bering)
M Blanshard J Oliver, W Garrett & Lady Page

Placings:0   (3449)
2003/04: 17⁰GS,

	Starts	1st	2nd	3rd	Win & Pl
Hurdles	1	0	0	0	
Career Total	1	0	0	0	

Going:	Sf: 0-0 GS: 0-1 Gd: 0-0 GF: - Fm: 0-0
Distance:	2m/2m3: 0-1 2m4-2m7: 0-0 3m+: 0-0
Track:	LH: 0-0 RH: 0-1 Tight: 0-1 Gall: 0-0
Aids:	Bl: 0-0 Vi: 0-0 Tstrap: 0-0 Ckp: 0-0
Best Rating:	39 1/04 Tntn 2m1f gd-sft Hdl

Fair stayer on Fibresand on the Flat; will appreciate more than two miles in time.

Vincent Van Gogh (IRE)
98   103

9-y-o b g Executive Perk-Rare Picture (Pollerton)
R J Hodges The Trojan Partnership

Placings:00/P0U2246F1/006521P143P6/126025-346   (3450)
2003/04: 21³G, 25⁴S, 27⁶GS,

	Starts	1st	2nd	3rd	Win & Pl
Chases	3	0	0	1	1088
Career Total	32	4	5	2	29281
103 10/02 Tntn	3m D(0-120)HCh	FRM	£5492
100 2/02 Tntn	3m D(0-115)HCh	SFT	£4771
98 12/01 Ludl	3m F(0-100)HCh	GD	£4550
90 4/01 Tntn	2m110y F(0-105)HCh	GD	£3029

Total win prize-money £17843

Going:	Sf: 0-1 GS: 0-1 Gd: 0-1 GF: - Fm: 0-0
Distance:	2m/2m3: 0-0 2m4-2m7: 0-1 3m+: 0-2
Track:	LH: 0-0 RH: 0-3 Tight: 0-1 Gall: 0-0
Aids:	Bl: 0-0 Vi: 0-0 Tstrap: 0-0 Ckp: 0-0
Best Rating:	103 2/03 Winc 2m5f gd-sft Ch

Moderate chaser; effective between two and a half and three miles; goes well on fast ground; acts on soft and must go right-handed; has broken blood vessels in the past.

Vingis Park (IRE)
105   105

6-y-o b g Old Vic-Lady Glenbank (Tarboosh (USA))
V R A Dartnall Nick Viney

Placings:2-02432   (4483)
2003/04: 17²S, 17⁰GS, 16²S, 24⁴S, 22³G, 18²G,

	Starts	1st	2nd	3rd	Win & Pl
NH Flat	3	0	2	0	1437
Hurdles	3	0	1	1	2079
Career Total	6	0	3	1	3516

Going:	Sf: 0-3 GS: 0-1 Gd: 0-2 GF: - Fm: 0-0
Distance:	2m/2m3: 0-2 2m4-2m7: 0-1 3m+: 0-1
Track:	LH: 0-4 RH: 0-2 Tight: 0-5 Gall: 0-1
Aids:	Bl: 0-0 Vi: 0-0 Tstrap: 0-2 Ckp: 0-0
Best Rating:	116 4/03 NAbb 2m1f soft NHF

Vino Tinto (IRE)

10-y-o b g Glacial Storm (USA)-Pure Spec (Fine Blade (USA))
Mrs C M Mulhall Mrs C M Mulhall

Placings:00/000000/6640004/0/2/3-1   (0079)
2003/04: 21¹S,

	Starts	1st	2nd	3rd	Win & Pl
Chases	1	1	0	0	1505
Career Total	19	1	1	1	2736
96 5/03 Sedg	2m5f H Ch	SFT	£1505

Total win prize-money £1505

Going:	Sf: 1-1 GS: 0-0 Gd: 0-0 GF: - Fm: 0-0
Distance:	2m/2m3: 0-0 **2m4-2m7: 1-1** 3m+: 0-0
Track:	LH: **1-1** RH: 0-0 **Tight: 1-1** Gall: 0-0
Aids:	Bl: 0-0 Vi: 0-0 Tstrap: 0-0
Best Rating:	96 5/03 Sedg 2m5f soft Ch

Former maiden Irish hurdler; winning pointer and narrowly denied in hunter chases.

Vintage Premium

93   107+

7-y-o b g Forzando-Julia Domna (Dominion)
R A Fahey J C Parsons

Placings:235   (3831)
2003/04: 16²G, 16³G, 16⁶G,

	Starts	1st	2nd	3rd	Win & Pl
Hurdles	3	0	1	1	4818
Career Total	3	0	1	1	4818

Going:	Sf: 0-0 GS: 0-1 Gd: 0-2 GF: - Fm: 0-0
Distance:	2m/2m3: 0-3 2m4-2m7: 0-0 3m+: 0-0
Track:	LH: 0-3 RH: 0-0 Tight: 0-0 Gall: 0-1
Aids:	Bl: 0-0 Vi: 0-0 Tstrap: 0-0 Ckp: 0-0
Best Rating:	114 2/04 Newb 2m110y good Hdl

Modest novice hurdler; Listed-class on the Flat; shaped well in a slowly-run race on hurdles debut over two miles at Ayr in November, but failed to stay in a soundly run race next time; should do better, but not a natural over timber.

Violent

78   65

6-y-o b m Deploy-Gentle Irony (Mazilier (USA))
Miss A M Newton-Smith (Jamie Poulton 14/5) James Etheridge

Placings:5/0-P56   (2531)
2003/04: 16⁶G, 23⁵G, 21⁶S,

	Starts	1st	2nd	3rd	Win & Pl
Hurdles	3	0	0	0	0
Career Total	5	0	0	0	0

Going:	Sf: 0-1 GS: 0-0 Gd: 0-2 GF: - Fm: 0-0
Distance:	2m/2m3: 0-1 2m4-2m7: 0-2 3m+: 0-0
Track:	LH: 0-3 RH: 0-0 Tight: 0-0 Gall: 0-0
Aids:	Bl: 0-0 Vi: 0-0 Tstrap: 0-0 Ckp: 0-0
Best Rating:	65 11/03 Ling 2m7f good Hdl

Virac Lad (IRE)

10-y-o b g Brush Aside (USA)-Garryduff Lass (Green Shoon)
Mrs G Harvey Virac Marketing Ltd

Placings:0/00P/00P/P   (0446)
2003/04: 24⁶G,

	Starts	1st	2nd	3rd	Win & Pl
Chases	1	0	0	0	
Career Total	8	0	0	0	

Going:	Sf: 0-0 GS: 0-0 Gd: 0-1 GF: - Fm: 0-0
Distance:	2m/2m3: 0-0 2m4-2m7: 0-0 3m+: 0-1
Track:	LH: 0-0 RH: 0-1 Tight: 0-0 Gall: 0-1
Aids:	Bl: 0-0 Vi: 0-0 Tstrap: 0-0 Ckp: 0-1
Best Rating:	75 11/99 Leic 2m gd-sft Hdl

Virgin Soldier (IRE)

111(108h)   (128 h)124

8-y-o ch g Waajib-Never Been Chaste (Posse (USA))
G A Swinbank J David Abell

Placings:414/1132-FU1115146   (4599)
2003/04: 16⁶GF, 16⁰GF, 21¹GF, 16¹GF, 21¹GF, 16⁵F, 25¹GF, 24⁴G, 18⁶G,

	Starts	1st	2nd	3rd	Win & Pl
Hurdles	2	0	0	0	0
Chases	7	4	0	0	21185
Career Total	16	7	1	1	40118

124	10/03	MRas	3m1f	C(0-130)HCh	G-F	£9060
116	9/03	Sedg	2m5f	E Ch	G-F	£3269
113	8/03	Sedg	2m110y	E Ch	G-F	£3896
110	7/03	Sedg	2m5f	E Ch	G-F	£3896
125	9/02	Bang	2m1f	C(0-135)HHdl	GD	£6695
118	9/02	Strf	2m110y	D(0-125)HHdl	G-F	£4810
116	12/01	Donc	2m4f	E Hdl	GD	£3402
				Total win prize-money		£35030

Going:	Sf: 0-0 GS: 0-0 Gd: 0-2 GF: - Fm: 4-7
Distance:	2m/2m3: 1-5 **2m4-2m7: 2-2** 3m+: 1-2
Track:	**LH: 3-7** RH: 1-2 **Tight: 4-5** Gall: 0-0
Aids:	Bl: 0-0 Vi: 0-0 Tstrap: 0-0 Ckp: 0-0
Best Rating:	128 10/02 Weth 2m gd-fm Hdl

Fair novice chaser/useful hurdler; useful stayer on the Flat; stays three miles one but is effective at shorter; looks most effective on a sound surface.

Viscount Bankes

6-y-o ch g Clantime-Bee Dee Dancer (Ballacashtal (CAN))
Mrs Rosemary Gasson Mrs Rosemary Gasson

Placings:60/P-22   (4655)
2003/04: 19²GS, 16²G,

	Starts	1st	2nd	3rd	Win & Pl
Chases	2	0	2	0	1204
Career Total	5	0	2	0	1204

Going:	Sf: 0-0 GS: 0-1 Gd: 0-1 GF: - Fm: 0-0
Distance:	2m/2m3: 0-2 2m4-2m7: 0-0 3m+: 0-0
Track:	LH: 0-0 RH: 0-2 Tight: 0-0 Gall: 0-0
Aids:	Bl: 0-0 Vi: 0-0 Tstrap: 0-0 Ckp: 0-0
Best Rating:	88 4/04 Hrfd 2m good Ch

Visibility (FR)

116   138

5-y-o gr g Linamix (FR)-Visor (USA) (Mr Prospector (USA))
M C Pipe Jim Weeden

Placings:32145-1P500   (4559)
2003/04: 16¹GF, 16⁶G, 16⁵S, 16⁹G, 16⁰GS,

	Starts	1st	2nd	3rd	Win & Pl
Hurdles	5	1	0	0	25700
Career Total	10	2	1	1	34508

138	11/03	Asct	2m110y	C(0-135)HHdl	G-F	£23200
126	2/03	Leic	2m	D Hdl	HVY	£5135
				Total win prize-money		£28335

Going:	Sf: 0-1 GS: 0-1 Gd: 0-2 GF: - Fm: 1-1
Distance:	**2m/2m3: 1-5** 2m4-2m7: 0-0 3m+: 0-0
Track:	LH: 0-3 **RH: 1-2** Tight: 0-0 Gall: 0-2
Aids:	Bl: 0-0 Vi: 0-3 Tstrap: 0-0 Ckp: 0-0
Best Rating:	138 11/03 Asct 2m110y gd-fm Hdl

Useful ex-French hurdler; decent juvenile hurdler in 2002/3; won valuable handicap at Ascot in November 2003; unable to defy rise in the weights since, and tried in a visor last

twice; should stay two and a half miles; acts on most ground; not a fluent jumper.

Visitation

6-y-o b m Bishop Of Cashel-Golden Envoy (USA) (Dayjur (USA))
Mrs J C McGregor Discounted Cashflow

Placings:PPP   (0976)
2003/04: 20⁶G, 16⁶GF, 17⁶GF,

	Starts	1st	2nd	3rd	Win & Pl
Hurdles	3	0	0	0	
Career Total	3	0	0	0	

Going:	Sf: 0-0 GS: 0-0 Gd: 0-1 GF: - Fm: 0-2
Distance:	2m/2m3: 0-2 2m4-2m7: 0-1 3m+: 0-0
Track:	LH: 0-1 RH: 0-2 Tight: 0-0 Gall: 0-0
Aids:	Bl: 0-1 Vi: 0-0 Tstrap: 0-0 Ckp: 0-0

Vista Verde

102   103

6-y-o b g Alflora (IRE)-Legata (IRE) (Orchestra)
A King Mrs L Field

Placings:06535   (4561)
2003/04: 16⁰G, 16⁵S, 22⁵GS, 24³G, 24⁵GS,

	Starts	1st	2nd	3rd	Win & Pl
NH Flat	2	0	0	0	0
Hurdles	3	0	0	1	762
Career Total	5	0	0	1	762

Going:	Sf: 0-1 GS: 0-2 Gd: 0-2 GF: - Fm: 0-0
Distance:	2m/2m3: 0-2 2m4-2m7: 0-1 3m+: 0-2
Track:	LH: 0-2 RH: 0-3 Tight: 0-0 Gall: 0-1
Aids:	Bl: 0-0 Vi: 0-0 Tstrap: 0-0 Ckp: 0-0
Best Rating:	108 2/04 Asct 3m good Hdl

Showed ability in two bumpers; sound effort when modest third at Ascot in February; suited by three miles; acts on good or softer.

Vital Hesitation

12-y-o br m Vital Season-Jim's Darleen (Jimsun)
M H Wood M H Wood

Placings:P   (0350)
2003/04: 21⁶GF,

	Starts	1st	2nd	3rd	Win & Pl
Chases	1	0	0	0	
Career Total	1	0	0	0	

Going:	Sf: 0-0 GS: 0-0 Gd: 0-0 GF: - Fm: 0-1
Distance:	2m/2m3: 0-0 2m4-2m7: 0-1 3m+: 0-0
Track:	LH: 0-0 RH: 0-1 Tight: 0-1 Gall: 0-0
Aids:	Bl: 0-0 Vi: 0-0 Tstrap: 0-0 Ckp: 0-0

Vitelli

97f   87f

4-y-o b g Vettori (IRE)-Mourne Trix (Golden Love)
G A Swinbank Scotnorth Racing Ltd

Placings:2023   (4594)
2003/04: 13²GF, 13⁰S, 16²G, 16³G,

	Starts	1st	2nd	3rd	Win & Pl
NH Flat	4	0	2	1	1732

| Career Total | 4 | 0 | 2 | 1 | 1732 |

Going:	Sf: 0-1 GS: 0-0 Gd: 0-2 GF: - Fm: 0-1
Distance:	2m/2m3: 0-2 2m4-2m7: 0-0 3m+: 0-0
Track:	LH: 0-1 RH: 0-1 Tight: 0-1 Gall: 0-1
Aids:	Bl: 0-0 Vi: 0-0 Tstrap: 0-0 Ckp: 0-0
Best Rating:	87 3/04 Hntg 2m110y good NHF

Modest form in bumpers on a sound surface.

Vitelucy

104   82

5-y-o b m Vettori (IRE)-Classic Line (Last Tycoon)
Miss S J Wilton John Pointon And Sons

Placings:42-1U430   (1815)
2003/04: 20¹GF, 20ᵁG, 19⁴GF, 22³GF, 20⁰G,

	Starts	1st	2nd	3rd	Win & Pl
Hurdles	5	1	0	1	4031
Career Total	7	1	1	1	5295
77 8/03 Worc 2m4f		E Hdl		G-F	£3493
			Total win prize-money £3493		

Going:	Sf: 0-0 GS: 0-0 Gd: 0-2 GF: - Fm: 1-3
Distance:	2m/2m3: 0-0 2m4-2m7: 1-5 3m+: 0-0
Track:	LH: 1-4 RH: 0-1 Tight: 0-3 Gall: 0-0
Aids:	Bl: 0-0 Vi: 0-0 Tstrap: 0-0 Ckp: 0-0
Best Rating:	82 10/03 Strf 2m6f110y gd-fm Hdl

Plating-class hurdler; probably only just got the trip having been in front plenty soon enough when winning slowly-run two and a half mile novices' hurdle at Worcester August 2003; acts on good to firm.

Vito Andolini

78   40

6-y-o br g Faustus (USA)-Sunshine Gal (Alto Volante)
Mrs Jane Galpin Mrs Jane Galpin

Placings:00PP   (3309)
2003/04: 17⁰G, 19⁰S, 19⁰G, 22PHY,

	Starts	1st	2nd	3rd	Win & Pl
NH Flat	1	0	0	0	0
Hurdles	3	0	0	0	0
Career Total	4	0	0	0	

Going:	Sf: 0-2 GS: 0-0 Gd: 0-2 GF: - Fm: 0-0
Distance:	2m/2m3: 0-1 2m4-2m7: 0-3 3m+: 0-0
Track:	LH: 0-3 RH: 0-1 Tight: 0-4 Gall: 0-0
Aids:	Bl: 0-1 Vi: 0-0 Tstrap: 0-0 Ckp: 0-0
Best Rating:	58 11/03 NAbb 2m1f good NHF

Viva Bingo (IRE)

(0c)46

8-y-o ch g Phardante (FR)-Kitty Frisk (Prince Tenderfoot (USA))
C L Popham (M J Gingell 26/5) Peter Williams

Placings:0/23500PP00-R0P   (4700)
2003/04: 16⁶GF, 16⁰G, 20PG,

	Starts	1st	2nd	3rd	Win & Pl
Hurdles	2	0	0	0	0
Chases	1	0	0	0	0
Career Total	13	0	1	1	1270

Going:	Sf: 0-0 GS: 0-0 Gd: 0-0 GF: - Fm: 0-1
Distance:	2m/2m3: 0-2 2m4-2m7: 0-1 3m+: 0-0
Track:	LH: 0-1 RH: 0-1 Tight: 0-2 Gall: 0-1
Aids:	Bl: 0-1 Vi: 0-0 Tstrap: 0-0 Ckp: 0-0
Best Rating:	96 9/02 DRoy 2m good NHF

Viva Forever (FR)

86   59

5-y-o br m Lando (GER)-Very Mighty (FR) (Niniski (USA))
A M Hales P A Deal

Placings:50   (2100)
2003/04: 17⁵G, 19⁴GF,

	Starts	1st	2nd	3rd	Win & Pl
Hurdles	2	0	0	0	0
Career Total	2	0	0	0	0

Going:	Sf: 0-0 GS: 0-0 Gd: 0-1 GF: - Fm: 0-1
Distance:	2m/2m3: 0-2 2m4-2m7: 0-0 3m+: 0-0
Track:	LH: 0-1 RH: 0-1 Tight: 0-1 Gall: 0-1
Aids:	Bl: 0-0 Vi: 0-0 Tstrap: 0-0 Ckp: 0-0
Best Rating:	59 11/03 Folk 2m1f110y good Hdl

Vivaldi Rose (IRE)

78(89c)   (47c)63

9-y-o b m Cataldi-Peaceful Rose (Roselier (FR))
L Lungo Mrs S J Matthews

Placings:0600/P03P4-00   (0466)
2003/04: 16⁰G, 16⁰G,

	Starts	1st	2nd	3rd	Win & Pl
Hurdles	2	0	0	0	
Career Total	11	0	0	1	818

Going:	Sf: 0-0 GS: 0-0 Gd: 0-2 GF: - Fm: 0-0
Distance:	2m/2m3: 0-2 2m4-2m7: 0-0 3m+: 0-0
Track:	LH: 0-1 RH: 0-1 Tight: 0-0 Gall: 0-0
Aids:	Bl: 0-0 Vi: 0-0 Tstrap: 0-0 Ckp: 0-1
Best Rating:	87 5/01 Ayr 2m gd-fm NHF

Plating-class hurdler/chaser, held in weak company; best effort on soft ground.

Vivante (IRE)

86f   65f

6-y-o b m Toulon-Splendidly Gay (Lord Gayle (USA))
A J Wilson P A Deal

Placings:00   (4186)
2003/04: 16⁰G, 16⁰G,

	Starts	1st	2nd	3rd	Win & Pl
NH Flat	2	0	0	0	
Career Total	2	0	0	0	

Going:	Sf: 0-0 GS: 0-0 Gd: 0-2 GF: - Fm: 0-0
Distance:	2m/2m3: 0-2 2m4-2m7: 0-0 3m+: 0-0
Track:	LH: 0-1 RH: 0-1 Tight: 0-0 Gall: 0-2
Aids:	Bl: 0-0 Vi: 0-0 Tstrap: 0-0 Ckp: 0-0
Best Rating:	65 3/04 Hntg 2m110y good NHF

Vivid Imagination (IRE)

100   56

5-y-o b g Moonax (IRE)-Sezu (IRE) (Mister Lord (USA))
M C Pipe D A Johnson

Placings:4   (1043)
2003/04: 22⁴GF,

	Starts	1st	2nd	3rd	Win & Pl
Hurdles	1	0	0	0	418
Career Total	1	0	0	0	418

Going:	Sf: 0-0 GS: 0-0 Gd: 0-0 GF: - Fm: 0-1
Distance:	2m/2m3: 0-0 2m4-2m7: 0-1 3m+: 0-0
Track:	LH: 0-1 RH: 0-0 Tight: 0-1 Gall: 0-0
Aids:	Bl: 0-0 Vi: 0-0 Tstrap: 0-0 Ckp: 0-0
Best Rating:	56 8/03 NAbb 2m6f gd-fm Hdl

Vizulize

5-y-o b m Robellino (USA)-Euridice (IRE) (Woodman (USA))
A W Carroll (B R Millman 11/9) Last Day Racing Partnership

Placings:PP   (2795)
2003/04: 16PS, 17PGS,

	Starts	1st	2nd	3rd	Win & Pl
Hurdles	2	0	0	0	
Career Total	2	0	0	0	

Going:	Sf: 0-1 GS: 0-1 Gd: 0-0 GF: - Fm: 0-0
Distance:	2m/2m3: 0-2 2m4-2m7: 0-0 3m+: 0-0
Track:	LH: 0-1 RH: 0-1 Tight: 0-1 Gall: 0-0
Aids:	Bl: 0-0 Vi: 0-0 Tstrap: 0-0 Ckp: 0-0

Vodka Bleu (FR)

112   121+

5-y-o b g Pistolet Bleu (IRE)-Viva Vodka (FR) (Crystal Glitters (USA))
M C Pipe D A Johnson

Placings:11U-325053   (4838)
2003/04: 19³G, 16²S, 16⁵GS, 22⁰G, 20⁵HY, 24³GF,

	Starts	1st	2nd	3rd	Win & Pl
Hurdles	6	0	1	2	8065
Career Total	9	2	1	2	15731
117 3/03 Hayd 2m		H NHF		GD	£2065
112 1/03 Leop 2m		NHF		SFT	£5600
			Total win prize-money £7666		

Going:	Sf: 0-2 GS: 0-1 Gd: 0-2 GF: - Fm: 0-1
Distance:	2m/2m3: 0-3 2m4-2m7: 0-2 3m+: 0-1
Track:	LH: 0-2 RH: 0-4 Tight: 0-0 Gall: 0-2
Aids:	Bl: 0-0 Vi: 0-1 Tstrap: 0-0 Ckp: 0-0
Best Rating:	121 4/04 Chel 3m gd-fm Hdl

Fair novice hurdler; dual bumper winner; stays two and a half miles; acts on ground good or softer.

Vodka Inferno (IRE)

101   81

7-y-o ch g Moscow Society (USA)-Corrie Lough (IRE) (The Parson)
C R Egerton Madgenta

Placings:03/30P-224   (1012)
2003/04: 24²G, 24²G, 24⁴G,

	Starts	1st	2nd	3rd	Win & Pl
Hurdles	3	0	2	0	2101
Career Total	8	0	2	2	2700

Going:	Sf: 0-0 GS: 0-0 Gd: 0-3 GF: - Fm: 0-0
Distance:	2m/2m3: 0-0 2m4-2m7: 0-0 3m+: 0-3
Track:	LH: 0-2 RH: 0-1 Tight: 0-2 Gall: 0-0
Aids:	Bl: 0-1 Vi: 0-0 Tstrap: 0-0 Ckp: 0-0
Best Rating:	97 11/02 Chel 2m110y gd-sft NHF

Plating-class hurdler; showed ability in bumpers; runner-up in weak novice hurdles at Hexham and Market Rasen in the summer; stays three miles; poor jumper.

Volano (FR)

111   **131+**

6-y-o b g Pistolet Bleu (IRE)-Vouivre (FR) (Matahawk)
N J Henderson Thurloe Finsbury

Placings:12P/504F-05P1P   (1699)
2003/04: 20⁰GS, 16⁵GS, 16P G, 16¹GF, 19⁹GF,

	Starts	1st	2nd	3rd	Win & Pl
Hurdles	5	1	0	0	5848
Career Total	12	2	1	0	13307
131	10/03	Hntg	2m110y	C(0-130)HHdl	G-F	£5434
126	2/02	Sand	2m110y	D Hdl	SFT	£4348
				Total win prize-money £9783

Going:	Sf: 0-1 GS: 0-1 Gd: 0-1 GF: - Fm: 1-2
Distance:	2m/2m3: 1-4 2m4-2m7: 0-1 3m+: 0-0
Track:	LH: 0-4 RH: 1-1 Tight: 0-3 Gall: 1-1
Aids:	Bl: 0-0 Vi: 0-0 Tstrap: 0-0 Ckp: 0-0
Best Rating:	131 10/03 Hntg 2m110y gd-fm Hdl

Useful hurdler; best a t2m; acts on any ground.

Volcano Snow

92   **72**

4-y-o ch f Zilzal (USA)-Ash Glade (Nashwan (USA))
M F Harris (C Von Der Recke 6/3) M Harris

Placings:4524   (4736)
2003/04: 16⁴GS, 16⁵G, 16²S, 17⁴G,

	Starts	1st	2nd	3rd	Win & Pl
NH Flat	2	0	0	0	
Hurdles	2	0	1	0	1286
Career Total	4	0	1	0	1286

Going:	Sf: 0-1 GS: 0-1 Gd: 0-2 GF: - Fm: 0-0
Distance:	2m/2m3: 0-4 2m4-2m7: 0-0 3m+: 0-0
Track:	LH: 0-3 RH: 0-1 Tight: 0-1 Gall: 0-2
Aids:	Bl: 0-0 Vi: 0-0 Tstrap: 0-0 Ckp: 0-0
Best Rating:	91 3/04 Newb 2m110y good NHF

Showed ability in two starts in bumpers; runner-up in weak juvenile hurdle at Newcastle in March; acts on soft.

Vulcan Lane (NZ)

85(99h)   (81+h)**79+**

7-y-o ch g Star Way-Smudged (NZ) (Nassipour (USA))
R C Guest Blaydon Racers Partnership

Placings:004-02P03U514000   (3847)
2003/04: 16⁶G, 16²F, 17P G, 21⁹G, 17³GF, 16U G, 16⁵GS, 17¹G,
16⁴GF, 16⁰G, 17⁰GS, 16⁰GS,

	Starts	1st	2nd	3rd	Win & Pl
Hurdles	8	1	1	1	3381
Chases	4	0	0	0	312
Career Total	15	1	1	1	4042
88	12/03	MRas	2m1f110yG(0-95)HHdl	GD	£1863
				Total win prize-money £1863

Going:	Sf: 0-0 GS: 0-3 Gd: 1-6 GF: - Fm: 0-3
Distance:	2m/2m3: 1-11 2m4-2m7: 0-1 3m+: 0-0
Track:	LH: 0-8 RH: 1-4 Tight: 1-6 Gall: 0-0
Aids:	Bl: 1-4 Vi: 0-0 Tstrap: 0-0 Ckp: 0-4
Best Rating:	88 12/03 MRas 2m1f110y good Hdl

Plating-class hurdler; Flat winner in native New Zealand; won a weak seller in first-time blinkers; has also worn cheekpieces.

Vulcan's Ash

61f   **12f**

5-y-o ch g Royal Vulcan-Ashraf (Gold Song)

S J Gilmore Mrs A Crook

Placings:0   (2159)
2003/04: 16⁰GS,

	Starts	1st	2nd	3rd	Win & Pl
NH Flat	1	0	0	0	
Career Total	1	0	0	0	

Going:	Sf: 0-0 GS: 0-1 Gd: 0-0 GF: - Fm: 0-0
Distance:	2m/2m3: 0-1 2m4-2m7: 0-0 3m+: 0-0
Track:	LH: 0-1 RH: 0-0 Tight: 0-0 Gall: 0-0
Aids:	Bl: 0-0 Vi: 0-0 Tstrap: 0-0 Ckp: 0-0
Best Rating:	12 11/03 Uttx 2m gd-sft NHF

Wages

99   **86**

4-y-o b g Lake Coniston (IRE)-Green Divot (Green Desert (USA))
P M Phelan (A M Hales 17/5) Andrew L Cohen

Placings:36000   (4892)
2003/04: 16³G, 16⁵GS, 16⁹G, 17⁹G, 16⁹GF,

	Starts	1st	2nd	3rd	Win & Pl
Hurdles	5	0	0	1	1698
Career Total	5	0	0	1	1698

Going:	Sf: 0-0 GS: 0-1 Gd: 0-3 GF: - Fm: 0-1
Distance:	2m/2m3: 0-5 2m4-2m7: 0-0 3m+: 0-0
Track:	LH: 0-1 RH: 0-4 Tight: 0-1 Gall: 0-1
Aids:	Bl: 0-0 Vi: 0-0 Tstrap: 0-0 Ckp: 0-0
Best Rating:	86 11/03 Hntg 2m10y gd-sft Hdl

Modest handicapper on the level; third on hurdles debut but held subsequently.

Waggy (IRE)

8-y-o b g Cataldi-Energance (IRE) (Salmon Leap (USA))
S E H Sherwood Mrs A Gordon

Placings:05P-PF   (3403)
2003/04: 26²S, 19²G,

	Starts	1st	2nd	3rd	Win & Pl
Hurdles	2	0	0	0	
Career Total	5	0	0	0	0

Going:	Sf: 0-1 GS: 0-0 Gd: 0-1 GF: - Fm: 0-0
Distance:	2m/2m3: 0-0 2m4-2m7: 0-1 3m+: 0-1
Track:	LH: 0-2 RH: 0-0 Tight: 0-0 Gall: 0-0
Aids:	Bl: 0-0 Vi: 0-0 Tstrap: 0-0 Ckp: 0-0
Best Rating:	81 6/02 Hntg 2m110y gd-fm NHF

Wagner (IRE)

108(112h)   (118h)**132**

7-y-o b/br g Lure (USA)-Tapaculo (Tap On Wood)
Jonjo O'Neill Ossian Construction Ltd

Placings:21/00120143-31211F026   (4385)
2003/04: 27³G, 22¹GF, 20²G, 20¹GF, 23¹GF, 21²GF, 24⁰GF,
20²GF, 24⁶G,

	Starts	1st	2nd	3rd	Win & Pl
Hurdles	3	1	1	1	8312
Chases	6	2	1	0	14322
Career Total	19	6	4	2	37312
126	8/03	Uttx	2m7f	E Ch	G-F	£4647
110	7/03	MRas	2m4f	D Ch	G-F	£6734
122	6/03	NAbb	2m6f	D(0-120)HHdl	G-F	£5447
118	3/03	MRas	3m	D(0-115)HHdl	G-S	£4667

109	10/02	Bang	2m4f	E(0-110)HHdl	SFT	£4134
88	10/00	Hexm	2m	E Hdl	HVY	£2327
				Total win prize-money £27958

Going:	Sf: 0-0 GS: 0-0 Gd: 0-3 GF: - Fm: 3-6
Distance:	2m/2m3: 0-0 2m4-2m7: 3-6 3m+: 0-3
Track:	LH: 2-8 RH: 1-1 Tight: 2-4 Gall: 0-2
Aids:	Bl: 0-0 Vi: 0-0 Tstrap: 0-0 Ckp: 0-0
Best Rating:	135 11/03 Newb 2m4f gd-fm Ch

Fair hurdler, useful novice chaser; ready winner of first two starts over fences; stays 3m plus; likes soft ground but handles good to firm.

Wahiba Sands

114   **151**

11-y-o b g Pharly (FR)-Lovely Noor (USA) (Fappiano (USA))
M C Pipe D A Johnson

Placings:11230/12/112U6/P2125/110022/36643553-
F244320300P60   (4964)
2003/04: 21²FF, 17²G, 16⁴GF, 16⁴G, 16³GS, 16²G, 16⁹GS, 17³G,
20⁴G, 16⁰G, 21²GF, 16⁵G, 16⁹GF,

	Starts	1st	2nd	3rd	Win & Pl
Chases	13	0	2	2	25968
Career Total	44	8	9	6	251621
161	12/01	Asct	B HCh	GD	£16825
154	11/01	Asct	2m3f110yA HCh	GD	£30000
141	1/01	Donc	2m110y D Ch	GD	£4088
159	11/99	Asct	2m4f	A Hdl	GD	£15475
161	11/99	Winc	2m	A HHdl	GD	£14875
155	11/98	Newb	2m110y	A(0-145)HHdl	SFT	£19290
131	12/97	Asct	2m110y	A Hdl	G-S	£8918
123	12/97	Leic	2m	E Hdl	SFT	£2784
				Total win prize-money £112256

Going:	Sf: 0-0 GS: 0-2 Gd: 0-8 GF: - Fm: 0-3
Distance:	2m/2m3: 0-10 2m4-2m7: 0-3 3m+: 0-0
Track:	LH: 0-7 RH: 0-6 Tight: 0-1 Gall: 0-6
Aids:	Bl: 0-0 Vi: 0-0 Tstrap: 0-0 Ckp: 0-0
Best Rating:	161 4/02 Aint 2m4f good Ch

Smart chaser; best form includes defeat of Best Mate in the First National Gold Cup in November 2001; can go well fresh; effective from two miles to two miles five, does not stay three miles; acts on any ground; has not won since 2001; has worn cheekpieces and more recently a visor. Reportedly retired.

Waimea Bay

95   **96+**

5-y-o b m Karinga Bay-Smart In Sable (Roscoe Blake)
P R Hedger M McD Hooker

Placings:2-044553   (4929)
2003/04: 16⁰G, 16⁴G, 17⁴GS, 17⁵GS, 16⁵GS, 18³G,

	Starts	1st	2nd	3rd	Win & Pl
NH Flat	1	0	0	0	0
Hurdles	5	0	0	1	855
Career Total	7	0	1	1	1711

Going:	Sf: 0-0 GS: 0-3 Gd: 0-3 GF: - Fm: 0-0
Distance:	2m/2m3: 0-6 2m4-2m7: 0-0 3m+: 0-0
Track:	LH: 0-2 RH: 0-4 Tight: 0-3 Gall: 0-0
Aids:	Bl: 0-0 Vi: 0-0 Tstrap: 0-0 Ckp: 0-0
Best Rating:	96 4/04 Font 2m2f110y good Hdl

Moderate second in a bumper on her debut.

Wain Mountain

107   (114h)**138**

8-y-o b g Unfuwain (USA)-Mountain Memory (High Top)

J A B Old W J Smith And M D Dudley

Placings:1/5321P/**1122/24-322P**   **(4046)**
2003/04: 19³S, 25²S, 24²HY, 28⁵G,

	Starts	1st	2nd	3rd	Win & Pl
Chases	4	0	2	1	7695
Career Total	16	4	6	2	40121
131	1/02	Uttx	3m2f	E Ch		HVY £3207
128	12/01	Uttx	2m5f	D Ch		SFT £4104
136	2/01	Hayd	2m7f110yB HHdl			HVY £8767
120	2/00	Leic	2m	E Hdl		HVY £2800
				Total win prize-money £18880

Going:	Sf: 0-3 GS: 0-0 Gd: 0-1 GF: - Fm: 0-0
Distance:	2m/2m3: 0-0 2m4-2m7: 0-1 3m+: 0-3
Track:	LH: 0-4 RH: 0-0 Tight: 0-0 Gall: 0-0
Aids:	Bl: 0-0 Vi: 0-0 Tstrap: 0-0 Ckp: 0-0
Best Rating:	138 1/04 Hayd 3m heavy Ch

Plating-class; stays 2m6f; acts on any ground.

Wainak (USA)
89   87
6-y-o b g Silver Hawk (USA)-Cask (Be My Chief (USA))
Miss Lucinda V Russell William A Powrie

Placings:50/22342433-3   **(0162)**
2003/04: 22³G,

	Starts	1st	2nd	3rd	Win & Pl
Hurdles	1	0	0	1	536
Career Total	11	0	3	4	7379

Going:	Sf: 0-0 GS: 0-0 Gd: 0-1 GF: - Fm: 0-0
Distance:	2m/2m3: 0-0 2m4-2m7: 0-1 3m+: 0-0
Track:	LH: 0-1 RH: 0-0 Tight: 0-0 Gall: 0-0
Aids:	Bl: 0-0 Vi: 0-0 Tstrap: 0-0 Ckp: 0-1
Best Rating:	91 12/02 Ayr 2m4f gd-sft Hdl

A big disappointment on the Flat, he finished runner-up in a poor event at Perth on his hurdling debut and was second again next time. Effective on good ground.

Waindale Flyer
91f   79f
5-y-o ch g Abzu-Mellouise (Handsome Sailor)
J R Norton P J Bamforth

Placings:0   **(4962)**
2003/04: 17⁰G,

	Starts	1st	2nd	3rd	Win & Pl
NH Flat	1	0	0	0	
Career Total	1	0	0	0	

Going:	Sf: 0-0 GS: 0-0 Gd: 0-1 GF: - Fm: 0-0
Distance:	2m/2m3: 0-1 2m4-2m7: 0-0 3m+: 0-0
Track:	LH: 0-0 RH: 0-1 Tight: 0-1 Gall: 0-0
Aids:	Bl: 0-0 Vi: 0-0 Tstrap: 0-0 Ckp: 0-0
Best Rating:	79 4/04 MRas 2m1f110y good NHF

Wait For The Will (USA)
112   115
8-y-o ch g Seeking The Gold (USA)-You'd Be Surprised (USA) (Blushing Groom (FR))
G L Moore Rdm Racing

Placings:3/3/2-124   **(1503)**
2003/04: 17¹GF, 17²G, 16⁴GF,

	Starts	1st	2nd	3rd	Win & Pl
Hurdles	3	1	1	0	8224

			Starts	1st	2nd	3rd		
Career Total	6		1	2	2			9860
115	5/03	NAbb	2m1f	D Hdl			G-F	£5616
				Total win prize-money £5616

Going:	Sf: 0-0 GS: 0-0 Gd: 0-1 GF: - Fm: 1-2
Distance:	2m/2m3: 1-3 2m4-2m7: 0-0 3m+: 0-0
Track:	LH: 1-3 RH: 0-0 Tight: 1-2 Gall: 0-0
Aids:	Bl: 1-3 Vi: 0-0 Tstrap: 0-0 Ckp: 0-0
Best Rating:	115 10/03 Chep 2m1y10y gd-fm Hdl

Fair hurdler; best at around two miles; acts on fast ground; does not always find much for pressure.

Wait For This (IRE)
(71c)
9-y-o b g Torus-Bar You Try (Bargello)
C J Down J B Radford

Placings:0442/41PP**21/4PP**00-PPP   **(1971)**
2003/04: 22⁰GF, 22⁵GF, 24⁸G,

			Starts	1st	2nd	3rd		
Hurdles			3	0	0	0		
Career Total	18		2	2	0			7465
105	4/02	Asct	3m110y	H Ch			G-F	£2749
105	5/01	Tntn	3m110y	E Hdl			FRM	£3087
				Total win prize-money £5837

Going:	Sf: 0-0 GS: 0-0 Gd: 0-1 GF: - Fm: 0-2
Distance:	2m/2m3: 0-0 2m4-2m7: 0-2 3m+: 0-1
Track:	LH: 0-2 RH: 0-1 Tight: 0-0 Gall: 0-0
Aids:	Bl: 0-0 Vi: 0-0 Tstrap: 0-1 Ckp: 0-0
Best Rating:	105 4/02 Asct 3m110y gd-fm Ch

Wakeup Smiling (IRE)
107   126+
6-y-o b g Norwich-Blackmiller Lady (Bonne Noel)
Miss E C Lavelle The Wakeup Partnership

Placings:033-0P40112   **(4813)**
2003/04: 16⁹GF, 21⁵S, 19⁴GF, 20⁰G, 16¹G, 19¹GS, 16²G,

			Starts	1st	2nd	3rd		
Hurdles			7	2	1	0		12715
Career Total	10		2	1	0			13560
117	3/04	Newb	2m3f	E(0-110)HHdl		G-S	£3549
110	3/04	Newb	2m110y	D(0-110)HHdl		GD	£7000
				Total win prize-money £10550

Going:	Sf: 0-1 GS: 1-1 Gd: 1-3 GF: - Fm: 0-2
Distance:	2m/2m3: 2-5 2m4-2m7: 0-2 3m+: 0-0
Track:	LH: 2-4 RH: 0-3 Tight: 0-0 Gall: 2-4
Aids:	Bl: 0-0 Vi: 0-0 Tstrap: 0-0 Ckp: 0-0
Best Rating:	126 4/04 Chep 2m110y good Hdl

Useful hurdler; broke his duck when causing a surprise in two mile novice event at Newbury March 2004; followed up over an extra three furlongs at the same venue in a handicap next time; good effort off much higher mark when second in hat-trick bid at Chepstow; acts on a sound surface; has been tried in a visor.

Walcot Lad (IRE)
106(99h)   (83h)83+
8-y-o b g Jurado (USA)-Butty Miss (Menelek)
A Ennis Boddington, Burke, Camis

Placings:300/0U0000040/30553-P643441404333   **(4933)**
2003/04: 21⁸G, 16⁸G, 20⁴G, 20³G, 22⁴HY, 21⁴GS, 18¹G, 18⁴GS, 25¹⁰G, 21⁴GS, 20³S, 20⁵G, 26⁵G,

	Starts	1st	2nd	3rd	Win & Pl
Hurdles	3	0	0	0	0

			Starts	1st	2nd	3rd		
Chases	10		1	0	4			7591
Career Total	30		1	0	7			9188
83	1/04	Font	2m2f	E(0-100)HCh		GD	£4312
				Total win prize-money £4313

Going:	Sf: 0-2 GS: 0-3 Gd: 1-8 GF: - Fm: 0-0
Distance:	2m/2m3: 1-3 2m4-2m7: 0-4 3m+: 0-2
Track:	LH: 0-6 RH: 0-2 Tight: 1-12 Gall: 0-0
Aids:	Bl: 0-3 Vi: 0-1 Tstrap: 0-0 Ckp: 1-9
Best Rating:	102 1/01 Chep 2m110y gd-sft NHF

Poor handicap chaser; effective at around two miles two; acts on good ground.

Wally Wonder (IRE)
94   (61c)91
6-y-o ch g Magical Wonder (USA)-Sally Gap (Sallust)
R Bastiman (R C Guest 6/1) Richard Long

Placings:3145-0P000000PP   **(4658)**
2003/04: 20⁰S, 20⁶YS, 20³GY, 17⁰Y, 20⁹F, 17⁰GF, 16⁰S, 16⁹GS, 16⁶GS, 20⁸S,

			Starts	1st	2nd	3rd	Win & Pl
Hurdles			7	0	0	0	0
Chases			3	0	0	0	0
Career Total	14		1	0	1	4011
90	9/02	Dpat	2m1f172y	NHF		GD	£3386
				Total win prize-money £3387

Going:	Sf: 0-3 GS: 0-2 Gd: 0-0 GF: - Fm: 0-2
Distance:	2m/2m3: 0-5 2m4-2m7: 0-0 3m+: 0-0
Track:	LH: 0-5 RH: 0-0 Tight: 0-1 Gall: 0-0
Aids:	Bl: 0-1 Vi: 0-0 Tstrap: 0-0 Ckp: 0-0
Best Rating:	90 9/02 Dpat 2m1f172y good NHF

Plating-class hurdler/chaser; ex-Irish; best on good ground or softer.

Walsingham (IRE)
93   75
6-y-o b g Presenting-Lets Compromise (No Argument)
P J Hobbs Sir Robert Ogden

Placings:P000   **(3897)**
2003/04: 20⁵S, 21³GS, 21⁰GS, 16⁸GS,

	Starts	1st	2nd	3rd	Win & Pl
Hurdles	4	0	0	0	
Career Total	4	0	0	0	

Going:	Sf: 0-1 GS: 0-3 Gd: 0-0 GF: - Fm: 0-0
Distance:	2m/2m3: 0-2 2m4-2m7: 0-3 3m+: 0-0
Track:	LH: 0-1 RH: 0-3 Tight: 0-0 Gall: 0-0
Aids:	Bl: 0-0 Vi: 0-0 Tstrap: 0-0 Ckp: 0-0
Best Rating:	75 1/04 Ludl 2m5f gd-sft Hdl

Walter Plinge
77(108c)   (76c)75
8-y-o b g Theatrical Charmer-Carousel Zingira (Reesh)
A G Juckes Tony Cocum

Placings:36/5/F0615300/35PPP01-0P00   **(4441)**
2003/04: 20⁰HY, 22⁷GF, 19⁰GS, 21⁰S,

			Starts	1st	2nd	3rd	Win & Pl
Hurdles			4	0	0	0	
Career Total	22		2	0	3		5223
75	4/03	Uttx	2m4f110yG(0-90)HHdl		GD	£2513
72	7/01	Wolv	2m4f110yG Hdl		G-F	£1570
				Total win prize-money £4084

Going:	Sf: 0-2 GS: 0-0 Gd: 0-1 GF: - Fm: 0-1
Distance:	2m/2m3: 0-0 2m4-2m7: 0-4 3m+: 0-0

Track: LH: 0-3 RH: 0-1 Tight: 0-1 Gall: 0-0
Aids: Bl: 0-0 Vi: 0-0 Tstrap: 0-4 Ckp: 0-0
Best Rating: 76 5/02 Sedg 2m5f   gd-fm Ch

Plating-class hurdler; has only ever won in selling company; effective at around two and a half miles; acts on good ground.

Walter's Destiny
105 **108**
12-y-o ch g White Prince (USA)-Tearful Sarah (Rugantino)
C W Mitchell C W Mitchell

Placings:60/0505/22P1144/3263401/F3/3U1UP4P/341/P44 3P3P-0365330066   (4820)
2003/04: 23⁰G, 25³GF, 25⁶G, 25⁵G, 25³G, 25³S, 24⁰G, 30⁰G, 25⁶GS, 25⁶GF,

	Starts	1st	2nd	3rd	Win & Pl
Chases	10	0	0	3	2771
Career Total	49	5	3	10	34802
115 11/01 Extr	2m7f110yD(0-125)HCh		G-F		£5050
114 12/00 Winc	3m1f110yD(0-125)HCh		G-S		£9441
101 4/99 Extr	2m7f D(0-125)HHdl		G-S		£3078
95 2/98 Ling	2m3f110yF(0-100)HHdl		GD		£2126
86 1/98 Winc	2m6f F(0-105)HHdl		GD		£2122
				Total win prize-money	£21819

Going: Sf: 0-1 GS: 0-1 Gd: 0-6 GF: - Fm: 0-2
Distance: 2m/2m3: 0-0 2m4-2m7: 0-0 3m+: 0-10
Track: LH: 0-0 RH: 0-10 Tight: 0-0 Gall: 0-0
Aids: Bl: 0-0 Vi: 0-0 Tstrap: 0-0 Ckp: 0-0
Best Rating: 115 11/01 Extr 2m7f110y gd-fm Ch

Modest handicap chaser; stays three miles; does not want the ground too soft.

Waltzing Along (IRE)
88 **71**
6-y-o b g Presenting-Clyduffe Fairy (Belfalas)
L Lungo Andrew Duncan,Vicky Royds & James Barber

Placings:34-000   (4732)
2003/04: 16⁰GS, 20⁵GS, 17⁰G,

	Starts	1st	2nd	3rd	Win & Pl
Hurdles	3	0	0	0	
Career Total	5	0	0	1	277

Going: Sf: 0-0 GS: 0-1 Gd: 0-1 GF: - Fm: 0-1
Distance: 2m/2m3: 0-2 2m4-2m7: 0-1 3m+: 0-0
Track: LH: 0-2 RH: 0-1 Tight: 0-1 Gall: 0-0
Aids: Bl: 0-0 Vi: 0-0 Tstrap: 0-0 Ckp: 0-0
Best Rating: 96 4/03 Hexm 2m110y good NHF

Wam
9f
4-y-o b g Distinctly North (USA)-Valise (Salse (USA))
Mrs M Reveley T S Child

Placings:0   (2101)
2003/04: 12⁰GF,

	Starts	1st	2nd	3rd	Win & Pl
NH Flat	1	0	0	0	
Career Total	1	0	0	0	

Going: Sf: 0-0 GS: 0-0 Gd: 0-0 GF: - Fm: 0-0
Distance: 2m/2m3: 0-0 2m4-2m7: 0-0 3m+: 0-0
Track: LH: 0-1 RH: 0-0 Tight: 0-0 Gall: 0-0
Aids: Bl: 0-0 Vi: 0-0 Tstrap: 0-0 Ckp: 0-0

Best Rating: 9 11/03 Newb 1m4f110y gd-fm NHF

Wandering Light (IRE)
15-y-o b g Royal Fountain-Pleaseme (Javelot)
R B Francis R B Francis

Placings:5/00/111/30/12/45P/PP   (0361)
2003/04: 24⁰G, 34⁰HY,

	Starts	1st	2nd	3rd	Win & Pl
Chases	2	0	0	0	
Career Total	15	4	1	1	37699
126 3/01 Hayd	3m	D(0-125)HCh	HVY		£7735
130 3/98 Chel	4m	B Ch	GD		£21135
108 11/97 Ludl	3m	E(0-100)HCh	GD		£3178
109 11/97 Worc	2m7f110yD Ch		GD		£3550
				Total win prize-money	£35598

Going: Sf: 0-1 GS: 0-0 Gd: 0-1 GF: - Fm: 0-0
Distance: 2m/2m3: 0-0 2m4-2m7: 0-0 3m+: 0-2
Track: LH: 0-2 RH: 0-0 Tight: 0-1 Gall: 0-0
Aids: Bl: 0-0 Vi: 0-0 Tstrap: 0-0 Ckp: 0-0
Best Rating: 130 3/98 Chel 4m   good Ch

Wanna Shout
59 **51**
6-y-o b m Missed Flight-Lulu (Polar Falcon (USA))
R Dickin E R C Beech & B Wilkinson

Placings:6/P060-6P   (3229)
2003/04: 16⁶F, 19⁷GS,

	Starts	1st	2nd	3rd	Win & Pl
Hurdles	2	0	0	0	0
Career Total	7	0	0	0	0

Going: Sf: 0-0 GS: 0-1 Gd: 0-0 GF: - Fm: 0-1
Distance: 2m/2m3: 0-1 2m4-2m7: 0-1 3m+: 0-0
Track: LH: 0-0 RH: 0-2 Tight: 0-0 Gall: 0-0
Aids: Bl: 0-0 Vi: 0-0 Tstrap: 0-0 Ckp: 0-1
Best Rating: 51 11/01 Wwck 2m   good Hdl

Wansbeck
11-y-o b g Dancing High-Mother Machree (Bing li)
S B Bell J A Riddell

Placings:P   (4660)
2003/04: 24²S,

	Starts	1st	2nd	3rd	Win & Pl
Hurdles	1	0	0	0	
Career Total	1	0	0	0	

Going: Sf: 0-0 GS: 0-0 Gd: 0-0 GF: - Fm: 0-0
Distance: 2m/2m3: 0-0 2m4-2m7: 0-0 3m+: 0-0
Track: LH: 0-1 RH: 0-0 Tight: 0-0 Gall: 0-0
Aids: Bl: 0-0 Vi: 0-0 Tstrap: 0-0 Ckp: 0-0

Wansford Lady
71 **56**
8-y-o b m Michelozzo (USA)-Marnie's Girl (Crooner)
A P Jones Mrs T Lewis

Placings:0/00   (4268)
2003/04: 17⁰G, 24⁰GF,

	Starts	1st	2nd	3rd	Win & Pl
Hurdles	2	0	0	0	
Career Total	3	0	0	0	

Going: Sf: 0-0 GS: 0-0 Gd: 0-1 GF: - Fm: 0-1
Distance: 2m/2m3: 0-1 2m4-2m7: 0-0 3m+: 0-1
Track: LH: 0-1 RH: 0-1 Tight: 0-0 Gall: 0-0
Aids: Bl: 0-0 Vi: 0-0 Tstrap: 0-1 Ckp: 0-0
Best Rating: 56 5/01 Extr 2m1f   gd-sft Hdl

War Of Attrition (IRE)
114 **152**
5-y-o br g Presenting-Una Juna (IRE) (Good Thyne (USA))
M F Morris Gigginstown House Stud

Placings:201102   (4381)
2003/04: 16²GY, 16⁰G, 16¹Y, 16¹S, 20⁰S, 16²G,

	Starts	1st	2nd	3rd	Win & Pl
Hurdles	6	2	2	0	34792
Career Total	6	2	2	0	34792
114 12/03 Navn	2m	Hdl	SFT		£6272
103 12/03 Punc	2m	Hdl	YLD		£5376
				Total win prize-money	£11650

Going: Sf: 1-2 GS: 0-0 Gd: 0-2 GF: - Fm: 0-0
Distance: 2m/2m3: 2-5 2m4-2m7: 0-1 3m+: 0-0
Track: LH: 1-3 RH: 1-2 Tight: 0-0 Gall: 0-0
Aids: Bl: 0-0 Vi: 0-0 Tstrap: 0-0 Ckp: 0-0
Best Rating: 152 3/04 Chel 2m110y good Hdl

Smart Irish novice hurdler; won two on the bounce in December 2003; found to have mucus in lungs next time; proved that form wrong when runner-up in the Supreme Novices' at Cheltenham; appreciates soft ground.

War Tune
73(107h)   (99h)**101**
8-y-o b g Warrshan (USA)-Keen Melody (USA) (Sharpen Up)
Ian Williams The Five Nations Partnership

Placings:04/63/056F32FP20/521-31   (4221)
2003/04: 20⁰GS, 22¹GS,

	Starts	1st	2nd	3rd	Win & Pl
Hurdles	1	0	0	1	400
Chases	1	1	0	0	4076
Career Total	19	2	3	3	12811
101 3/04 MRas	2m6f110yE(0-105)HCh		G-S		£4075
95 6/02 Worc	2m4f E Hdl		GF		£2681
				Total win prize-money	£6757

Going: Sf: 0-0 GS: 1-2 Gd: 0-0 GF: - Fm: 0-0
Distance: 2m/2m3: 0-0 2m4-2m7: 1-2 3m+: 0-0
Track: LH: 0-0 RH: 1-2 Tight: 1-1 Gall: 0-1
Aids: Bl: 0-0 Vi: 0-0 Tstrap: 0-0 Ckp: 0-0
Best Rating: 101 3/04 MRas 2m6f110y gd-sft Ch

Plating class hurdler/modest chaser; looked reluctant when narrow winner at Market Rasen in March; stays two miles six; seems effective on most ground.

Wareyth (USA)
28
5-y-o b/br g Shuailaan (USA)-Bahr Alsalaam (USA) (Riverman (USA))
R H Buckler Chris Pugsley

Placings:P0P0U-0   (0123)
2003/04: 18⁰G,

	Starts	1st	2nd	3rd	Win & Pl
Hurdles	1	0	0	0	
Career Total	6	0	0	0	

Going: Sf: 0-0 GS: 0-0 Gd: 0-1 GF: - Fm: 0-0
Distance: 2m/2m3: 0-1 2m4-2m7: 0-0 3m+: 0-0
Track: LH: 0-1 RH: 0-0 Tight: 0-0 Gall: 0-0
Aids: Bl: 0-0 Vi: 0-0 Tstrap: 0-0 Ckp: 0-0
Best Rating: 31 2/03 Extr 2m1f gd-sft Hdl

Warminghamsharpish
91   90+
7-y-o b m Nalchik (USA)-Tilstock Maid (Rolfe (USA))
W M Brisbourne The Bentley Boys

Placings:0521-11   (0976)
2003/04: 16^{1}GF, 17^{1}GF,

	Starts	1st	2nd	3rd	Win & Pl
Hurdles	2	2	0	0	7495
Career Total	6	3	1	0	10603
87	7/03	Sedg	2m1f	E Hdl	G-F	£3458
90	5/03	Ludl	2m	E Hdl	G-F	£4036
86	10/02	Ludl	2m	H NHF	FRM	£2586

Total win prize-money £10082

Going: Sf: 0-0 GS: 0-0 Gd: 0-0 GF: - Fm: 2-2
Distance: 2m/2m3: 2-2 2m4-2m7: 0-0 3m+: 0-0
Track: LH: 1-1 RH: 1-1 Tight: 1-1 Gall: 0-0
Aids: Bl: 0-0 Vi: 0-0 Tstrap: 0-0 Ckp: 0-0
Best Rating: 92 10/02 Hexm 2m110y gd-fm NHF

Moderate hurdler; won minor bumper at Ludlow October 2002; first run since; won novice hurdle at same track May 2003; narrow winner under a penalty on her return at Sedgefield in July; handles fast ground.

Warrlin
97(106c)   (106c)90
10-y-o b g Warrshan (USA)-Lahin (Rainbow Quest (USA))
C W Fairhurst Glasgow House Racing Syndicate

Placings:202562360/1523123F/044031134/03200030U0/0 2P3343/2F1-006P0   (4956)
2003/04: 19^{9}G, 20^{5}S, 19^{6}GF, 24^{8}G, 22^{9}G,

	Starts	1st	2nd	3rd	Win & Pl
Hurdles	5	0	0	0	
Career Total	51	5	8	10	34001
87	9/02	MRas	2m6f110yC Ch		G-F	£7540
107	2/00	MRas	2m1f110yF(0-110)HHdl		G-S	£1858
100	2/00	Kels	2m2f	E(0-115)HHdl	G-S	£5850
103	12/98	Sedg	2m1f	E(0-110)HHdl	SFT	£2757
93	8/98	Ctml	2m1f110yE Hdl		G-S	£2477

Total win prize-money £20485

Going: Sf: 0-1 GS: 0-0 Gd: 0-3 GF: - Fm: 0-1
Distance: 2m/2m3: 0-2 2m4-2m7: 0-3 3m+: 0-1
Track: LH: 0-4 RH: 0-0 Tight: 0-0 Gall: 0-0
Aids: Bl: 0-0 Vi: 0-0 Tstrap: 0-0 Ckp: 0-0
Best Rating: 109 11/00 Newc 2m gd-sft Hdl

Plating-class chaser; winner over hurdles, he has shown fair form over fences. Acts on most types of ground and is effective at around two miles.

Warton Crag
8-y-o b g Tina's Pet-Majestic Form (IRE) (Double Schwartz)
James Moffatt Greengate Lease Syndicate

Placings:0/P-P0   (4612)
2003/04: 20^{0}G, 21^{0}G,

	Starts	1st	2nd	3rd	Win & Pl
Hurdles	2	0	0	0	
Career Total	4	0	0	0	

Going: Sf: 0-0 GS: 0-0 Gd: 0-2 GF: - Fm: 0-0
Distance: 2m/2m3: 0-2 2m4-2m7: 0-2 3m+: 0-0
Track: LH: 0-1 RH: 0-1 Tight: 0-1 Gall: 0-0
Aids: Bl: 0-0 Vi: 0-0 Tstrap: 0-0 Ckp: 0-0

Wartorn (IRE)
(108h)   (99h)
9-y-o b g Warcraft (USA)-Alice Minkthorn (Party Mink)
J S King Miss S Douglas-Pennant

Placings:450/50022031-226P3   (4693)
2003/04: 22^{2}G, 24^{2}GF, 21^{6}G, 24^{4}GS, 22^{3}G,

	Starts	1st	2nd	3rd	Win & Pl
Hurdles	5	0	2	1	3333
Career Total	16	1	4	2	9531
101	3/03	Winc	2m6f	F(0-100)HHdl	SFT	£3346

Total win prize-money £3346

Going: Sf: 0-0 GS: 0-0 Gd: 0-3 GF: - Fm: 0-1
Distance: 2m/2m3: 0-0 2m4-2m7: 0-3 3m+: 0-2
Track: LH: 0-1 RH: 0-4 Tight: 0-0 Gall: 0-1
Aids: Bl: 0-0 Vi: 0-0 Tstrap: 0-0 Ckp: 0-0
Best Rating: 101 5/03 Extr 3m110y gd-fm Hdl

Moderate hurdler; stays 3m; seems to act on all types of ground; consistent in his grade.

Was A Drive (IRE)
96(74h)   (18h)81
10-y-o b g Yashgan-Alan's Rosalinda (Prefairy)
Miss Kate Milligan E C Gordon

Placings:PP/30P14P/P3F0-6400663   (4661)
2003/04: 20^{6}G, 20^{4}GF, 22^{0}S, 21^{9}GS, 20^{0}HY, 20^{6}G, 25^{3}S,

	Starts	1st	2nd	3rd	Win & Pl
Hurdles	1	0	0	0	0
Chases	6	0	0	1	682
Career Total	19	1	0	3	5018
89	3/02	Hexm	2m4f110yF(0-100)HCh		HVY	£3066

Total win prize-money £3066

Going: Sf: 0-3 GS: 0-1 Gd: 0-2 GF: - Fm: 0-1
Distance: 2m/2m3: 0-0 2m4-2m7: 0-6 3m+: 0-1
Track: LH: 0-7 RH: 0-0 Tight: 0-2 Gall: 0-1
Aids: Bl: 0-1 Vi: 0-0 Tstrap: 0-0 Ckp: 0-1
Best Rating: 89 3/02 Carl 2m4f gd-sft Ch

Moderate chaser, suited by two and a half miles; handles good ground and has won on heavy.

Wassl Street (IRE)
89(85h)   (15h)55
12-y-o b g Dancing Brave (USA)-One Way Street (Habitat)
R Lee Rex Norton

Placings:1/41P412/P4/4201/113/P-PP0PP0   (4183)
2003/04: 24^{0}S, 25^{0}S, 23^{0}G, 24^{0}HY, 16^{0}GS, 26^{0}G,

	Starts	1st	2nd	3rd	Win & Pl
Hurdles	3	0	0	0	0
Chases	3	0	0	0	0
Career Total	23	6	2	1	18252
108	6/00	MRas	2m4f	E Ch	G-S	£3715
110	5/00	Worc	2m7f110yE Ch		GD	£2983
104	4/00	MRas	2m5f110yF(0-100)HHdl		SFT	£1551
109	3/97	Towc	2m	D(0-120)HHdl	SFT	£2714
107	12/96	Leic	2m4f110yD(0-120)HHdl		G-S	£3028
111	4/96	Prth	2m4f110yE Hdl		SFT	£2108

Total win prize-money £16100

Going: Sf: 0-3 GS: 0-1 Gd: 0-2 GF: - Fm: 0-0
Distance: 2m/2m3: 0-1 2m4-2m7: 0-0 3m+: 0-5
Track: LH: 0-1 RH: 0-5 Tight: 0-0 Gall: 0-1
Aids: Bl: 0-2 Vi: 0-1 Tstrap: 0-6 Ckp: 0-0
Best Rating: 111 4/96 Prth 2m4f110y soft Hdl

Wasted Talent (IRE)
104   112+
4-y-o b f Sesaro (USA)-Miss Garuda (Persian Bold)
J G Portman Wasted Talent Partnership

Placings:2221   (4929)
2003/04: 16^{2}G, 17^{2}G, 17^{2}G, 18^{1}G,

	Starts	1st	2nd	3rd	Win & Pl
Hurdles	4	1	3	0	6775
Career Total	4	1	3	0	6775
112	4/04	Font	2m2f110yE Hdl		GD	£3438

Total win prize-money £3439

Going: Sf: 0-0 GS: 0-0 Gd: 1-4 GF: - Fm: 0-0
Distance: 2m/2m3: 1-4 2m4-2m7: 0-0 3m+: 0-0
Track: LH: 1-3 RH: 0-1 Tight: 1-2 Gall: 0-1
Aids: Bl: 0-1 Vi: 0-0 Tstrap: 0-0 Ckp: 1-2
Best Rating: 112 4/04 Font 2m2f110y good Hdl

Modest hurdler; stays two miles two; acts on good ground; wears cheekpieces.

Watch It
60
6-y-o b g Sea Raven (IRE)-Magic Penny (Sharrood (USA))
M Todhunter Mrs Allison Stamper

Placings:6/04-0   (2403)
2003/04: 17^{0}HY,

	Starts	1st	2nd	3rd	Win & Pl
Hurdles	1	0	0	0	
Career Total	4	0	0	0	0

Going: Sf: 0-1 GS: 0-0 Gd: 0-0 GF: - Fm: 0-0
Distance: 2m/2m3: 0-1 2m4-2m7: 0-0 3m+: 0-0
Track: LH: 0-0 RH: 0-1 Tight: 0-0 Gall: 0-0
Aids: Bl: 0-0 Vi: 0-0 Tstrap: 0-0 Ckp: 0-0
Best Rating: 83 4/03 Newc 2m good NHF

Watch The Dove
102(105h)   (108+h)106+
7-y-o b g Afzal-Spot The Dove (Riberetto)
C L Tizzard Mrs M J Tizzard

Placings:024/3622465-2202PF3F4   (4701)
2003/04: 27^{5}S, 25^{2}GF, 24^{2}G, 19^{0}G, 20^{2}HY, 23^{8}S, 24^{4}GS, 24^{3}G, 21^{8}GF, 22^{4}G,

	Starts	1st	2nd	3rd	Win & Pl
Hurdles	4	0	2	0	3730
Chases	6	0	1	1	2331
Career Total	19	0	6	2	10974

Going: Sf: 0-3 GS: 0-1 Gd: 0-4 GF: - Fm: 0-2
Distance: 2m/2m3: 0-0 2m4-2m7: 0-4 3m+: 0-6
Track: LH: 0-2 RH: 0-6 Tight: 0-6 Gall: 0-1
Aids: Bl: 0-0 Vi: 0-1 Tstrap: 0-0 Ckp: 0-1
Best Rating: 108 11/03 Asct 3m good Hdl

Modest novice chaser; has shown ability in bumpers and over hurdles and fences without winning; stays three miles; acts on good or heavy.

Watchful Witness

101   **94+**

4-y-o ch c In The Wings-Eternal (Kris)
G L Moore   J F Reeves

Placings:4146   (4444)
2003/04: 16⁴S, 16¹S, 16⁴S, 16⁶S,

	Starts	1st	2nd	3rd	Win & Pl
Hurdles	4	1	0	0	4319
Career Total	4	1	0	0	4319
94	1/04 Plum 2m		E Hdl	SFT	£3630

Total win prize-money £3630

Going:	Sf: 1-4 GS: 0-0 Gd: 0-0 GF: - Fm: 0-0
Distance:	2m/2m3: 1-4 2m4-2m7: 0-0 3m+: 0-0
Track:	LH: 1-3 RH: 0-1 Tight: 1-2 Gall: 0-0
Aids:	Bl: 0-1 Vi: 0-0 Tstrap: 0-0 Ckp: 0-0
Best Rating:	94 1/04 Plum 2m soft Hdl

Watchyourback (NZ)

10-y-o ch g Watchman (NZ)-English Lass (NZ) (English Harbour)
M Trott   M Trott

Placings:23150P/2F-3   (4218)
2003/04: 25³GS,

	Starts	1st	2nd	3rd	Win & Pl
Chases	1	0	0	1	192
Career Total	9	1	2	2	3293
91	7/00 Wolv	2m4f110yG Hdl		GD	£1463

Total win prize-money £1463

Going:	Sf: 0-0 GS: 0-1 Gd: 0-0 GF: - Fm: 0-0
Distance:	2m/2m3: 0-0 2m4-2m7: 0-0 3m+: 0-1
Track:	LH: 0-1 RH: 0-1 Tight: 0-1 Gall: 0-1
Aids:	Bl: 0-0 Vi: 0-0 Tstrap: 0-0 Ckp: 0-0
Best Rating:	91 7/00 Wolv 2m4f110y good Hdl

Moderate pointer/hunter chaser; stays three miles; acts on a sound surface; not the best of jumpers.

Water King (USA)

99   **89**

5-y-o b g Irish River (FR)-Brookshield Baby (IRE) (Sadler's Wells (USA))
G Brown   M D Killick

Placings:00435-6051204   (4171)
2003/04: 17⁶GF, 16⁹G, 16⁵G, 16¹G, 16²GS, 20⁰GS, 19⁴G,

	Starts	1st	2nd	3rd	Win & Pl
Hurdles	7	1	1	0	3019
Career Total	12	1	1	1	4032
89	11/03 Fknm 2m	G(0-90)HHdl		GD	£1841

Total win prize-money £1841

Going:	Sf: 0-0 GS: 0-2 Gd: 1-4 GF: - Fm: 0-1
Distance:	2m/2m3: 1-6 2m4-2m7: 0-0 3m+: 0-0
Track:	LH: 1-3 RH: 0-4 Tight: 1-3 Gall: 0-2
Aids:	Bl: 0-0 Vi: 0-0 Tstrap: 0-0 Ckp: 0-0
Best Rating:	89 3/04 Newb 2m3f good Hdl

Water Nymph (IRE)

4-y-o ch f Be My Guest (USA)-Justitia (Dunbeath (USA))
N J Henderson (B A McMahon 24/5) Paul Murphy

Placings:PP   (4783)

2003/04: 17⁶G, 21⁶G,

	Starts	1st	2nd	3rd	Win & Pl
Hurdles	2	0	0	0	
Career Total	2	0	0	0	

Going:	Sf: 0-0 GS: 0-0 Gd: 0-2 GF: - Fm: 0-0
Distance:	2m/2m3: 0-1 2m4-2m7: 0-1 3m+: 0-0
Track:	LH: 0-0 RH: 0-2 Tight: 0-0 Gall: 0-1
Aids:	Bl: 0-0 Vi: 0-0 Tstrap: 0-0 Ckp: 0-0

Water Quirl (GER)

107   **134+**

5-y-o ch h Dr Devious (IRE)-Water Quest (IRE) (Rainbow Quest (USA))
C Von Der Recke (A Schutz 18/10) Stall Weissenhof

Placings:1FP41   (2385)
2003/04: 16¹G, 17⁵S, 16⁶S, 17⁴S, 16¹GF,

	Starts	1st	2nd	3rd	Win & Pl
Hurdles	3	1	0	0	1688
Chases	2	1	0	0	8830
Career Total	5	2	0	0	10518
137	11/03 Wwck	2m110y C Ch		G-F	£7336
	7/03 Brem	2m Hdl		GD	£1688

Total win prize-money £9024

Going:	Sf: 0-3 GS: 0-0 Gd: 1-1 GF: - Fm: 1-1
Distance:	2m/2m3: 2-5 2m4-2m7: 0-0 3m+: 0-0
Track:	LH: 1-1 RH: 0-0 Tight: 0-0 Gall: 0-0
Aids:	Bl: 0-0 Vi: 0-0 Tstrap: 0-0 Ckp: 0-0
Best Rating:	137 11/03 Wwck 2m110y gd-fm Ch

Useful novice chaser; effective over two miles; acts well on decent ground.

Water Sports (IRE)

111   **101+**

6-y-o b m Marju (IRE)-Water Splash (USA) (Little Current (USA))
N A Twiston-Davies   John Duggan

Placings:00P3-11100P10PP   (4508)
2003/04: 24¹GF, 20¹G, 20¹G, 22⁰S, 20⁹G, 24⁶GS, 24¹GS, 24⁰G, 22⁸G, 26⁰GS,

	Starts	1st	2nd	3rd	Win & Pl
Hurdles	10	4	0	0	10602
Career Total	14	4	0	1	10987
101	2/04 Tntn	3m110y F(0-100)HHdl		G-S	£2978
101	11/03 Newc	2m4f F(0-90)HHdl		GD	£2149
101	11/03 Fknm	2m4f G(0-110)HHdl		GD	£2114
101	11/03 Uttx	3m110y D(0-115)HHdl		G-F	£3360

Total win prize-money £10602

Going:	Sf: 0-1 GS: 1-3 Gd: 2-5 GF: - Fm: 1-1
Distance:	2m/2m3: 0-0 2m4-2m7: 2-5 3m+: 2-5
Track:	LH: 3-5 RH: 1-5 Tight: 2-3 Gall: 1-1
Aids:	Bl: 1-2 Vi: 0-0 Tstrap: 0-0 Ckp: 0-0
Best Rating:	101 2/04 Tntn 3m110y gd-sft Hdl

Moderate hurdler; completed a hat-trick in November 2003; stays three miles and looks best on a sound surface.

Waterberg (IRE)

113(96h)   (92h)**124**

9-y-o b g Sadler's Wells (USA)-Pretoria (Habitat)
H D Daly   R M Kirkland

Placings:1/142/122/161311/2P4044-2U112P   (1617)
2003/04: 20²G, 24⁴GF, 24¹G, 24¹GS, 24²G, 24⁶G,

	Starts	1st	2nd	3rd	Win & Pl
Chases	6	2	2	0	21530

				Career Total	25	9	6	1	57761
121	7/03	Strf	3m	D(0-120)HCh	G-S	£8053
123	6/03	Strf	3m	D(0-125)HCh	GD	£10101
121	4/02	Prth	3m	C Ch	GD	£7241
107	4/02	Carl	2m4f	C Ch	G-F	£6987
118	2/02	Ludl	3m	D Ch	G-S	£4134
116	5/01	Hntg	2m4f110yD Hdl		GD	£3892
119	1/01	Leic	2m4f110yD Hdl		HVY	£3510
119	12/99	Uttx	2m	H NHF	SFT	£1742
112	4/99	MRas	1m5f110yH NHF		SFT	£1517

Total win prize-money £47179

Going:	Sf: 0-0 GS: 1-1 Gd: 1-4 GF: - Fm: 0-1
Distance:	2m/2m3: 0-0 2m4-2m7: 0-1 3m+: 2-5
Track:	LH: 2-6 RH: 0-0 Tight: 2-4 Gall: 0-0
Aids:	Bl: 0-0 Vi: 0-0 Tstrap: 0-0 Ckp: 0-0
Best Rating:	124 8/03 Bang 3m110y good Ch

Fair chaser; recorded back-to-back wins at Stratford in the summer of 2003; stays three miles well; likes fast ground; has worn blinkers; has broken blood vessels.

Waterhall

88   **81**

11-y-o b g River God (USA)-Tuneful Queen (Queens Hussar)
J M P Eustace   Mrs T S Matthews

Placings:FP/0030255/F/05P26-4P   (0449)
2003/04: 21⁴GF, 20²GF,

	Starts	1st	2nd	3rd	Win & Pl
Hurdles	2	0	0	0	0
Career Total	17	0	2	1	1683

Going:	Sf: 0-0 GS: 0-0 Gd: 0-0 GF: - Fm: 0-2
Distance:	2m/2m3: 0-0 2m4-2m7: 0-2 3m+: 0-0
Track:	LH: 0-0 RH: 0-2 Tight: 0-0 Gall: 0-2
Aids:	Bl: 0-0 Vi: 0-0 Tstrap: 0-0 Ckp: 0-0
Best Rating:	84 11/99 MRas 2m1f110y gd-sft Hdl

Waterlaw (IRE)

106   **120+**

10-y-o b g Kahyasi-Shuss (USA) (Princely Native (USA))
M C Pipe   Waterlaw Limited

Placings:1023110/00/22/1445/P11P   (3378)
2003/04: 19⁰GS, 21¹G, 21¹G, 21⁴PS,

	Starts	1st	2nd	3rd	Win & Pl
Chases	4	2	0	0	17083
Career Total	19	6	3	1	30438
118	1/04	Chel	2m5f	C(0-130)HCh	GD	£12792
118	12/03	Winc	2m5f	D(0-115)HCh	GD	£4290
94	8/01	Bang	2m4f110yD Ch		GD	£4173
97	6/99	Plum	2m4f	E Hdl	GD	£2337
91	8/98	Bang	2m4f	E Hdl	GD	£2410
93	5/98	Uttx	2m	H NHF	G-F	£1222

Total win prize-money £27227

Going:	Sf: 0-1 GS: 0-1 Gd: 2-2 GF: - Fm: 0-0
Distance:	2m/2m3: 0-0 2m4-2m7: 2-4 3m+: 0-0
Track:	LH: 1-2 RH: 1-2 Tight: 0-0 Gall: 1-1
Aids:	Bl: 0-0 Vi: 0-0 Tstrap: 2-4 Ckp: 0-0
Best Rating:	118 1/04 Chel 2m5f good Ch

Modest chaser; returned from two years off in late 2003, winning at Wincanton and Cheltenham; stays two miles-five; best on good ground.

Waterliner

82   **65**

5-y-o b m Merdon Melody-Double Touch (FR) (Nonoalco (USA))

P S McEntee Fernhurst Racing

Placings:0630 (1543)
2003/04: 16[0]GF, 16[6]GF, 18[3]GF, 16[0]GF,

	Starts	1st	2nd	3rd	Win & Pl
Hurdles	4	0	0	1	374
Career Total	4	0	0	1	374

Going: Sf: 0-0 GS: 0-0 Gd: 0-0 GF: - Fm: 0-4
Distance: 2m/2m3: 0-4 2m4-2m7: 0-0 3m+: 0-0
Track: LH: 0-3 RH: 0-1 Tight: 0-2 Gall: 0-1
Aids: Bl: 0-0 Vi: 0-0 Tstrap: 0-0 Ckp: 0-0
Best Rating: 75 9/03 Worc 2m gd-fm Hdl

Poor form over hurdles.

Watermouse
89 / **66**

4-y-o b g Alhaarth (IRE)-Heavenly Waters (Celestial Storm (USA))
R Dickin Mrs C M Dickin

Placings:61 (2226)
2003/04: 16[6]G, 16[1]GS,

	Starts	1st	2nd	3rd	Win & Pl
Hurdles	2	1	0	0	1890
Career Total	2	1	0	0	1890
71 11/03 Towc 2m	G Hdl			G-S	£1890

Total win prize-money £1890

Going: Sf: 0-0 GS: 1-1 Gd: 0-1 GF: - Fm: 0-0
Distance: 2m/2m3: 1-2 2m4-2m7: 0-0 3m+: 0-0
Track: LH: 0-1 RH: 1-1 Tight: 0-0 Gall: 0-0
Aids: Bl: 0-0 Vi: 0-0 Tstrap: 0-0 Ckp: 0-0
Best Rating: 71 11/03 Towc 2m gd-sft Hdl

Moderate hurdler; acts on easy ground.

Waterspray (AUS)
107 / **100+**

6-y-o ch g Lake Coniston (IRE)-Forain (NZ) (Nassipour (USA))
J L Spearing Bache Silk

Placings:0351-06431224 (2215)
2003/04: 16[0]G, 17[6]GS, 17[4]GF, 16[3]GF, 17[1]F, 16[2]GF, 16[2]GF, 16[4]GF,

	Starts	1st	2nd	3rd	Win & Pl
Hurdles	8	1	2	1	7446
Career Total	12	2	2	2	11528
99 9/03 Extr 2m1f	D(0-120)HHdl			FRM	£3919
101 4/03 Tntn 2m1f	E(0-110)HHdl			FRM	£3640

Total win prize-money £7560

Going: Sf: 0-0 GS: 0-1 Gd: 0-1 GF: - Fm: 1-6
Distance: 2m/2m3: 1-8 2m4-2m7: 0-0 3m+: 0-0
Track: LH: 0-5 RH: 1-3 Tight: 0-1 Gall: 0-0
Aids: Bl: 0-0 Vi: 0-0 Tstrap: 0-0 Ckp: 0-0
Best Rating: 101 11/03 Hayd 2m gd-fm Hdl

Moderate hurdler; showed ability on the Flat in native Australia; tends to pull hard over hurdles; best at around two miles; acts on a sound surface.

Wave Rock
107(107h) / (124 h)**136d**

9-y-o br g Tragic Role (USA)-Moonscape (Ribero)
P J Hobbs Sterling Racing Syndicate

Placings:23223413/23U1312F3211F3/141332P1/6523552/ 12530P4FPU-254063400 (4572)
2003/04: 20[2]G, 20[5]G, 20[4]GF, 20[0]GS, 19[6]G, 21[3]G, 18[4]S, 19[0]G, 24[0]G,

	Starts	1st	2nd	3rd	Win & Pl
Chases	9	0	1	1	6442
Career Total	56	9	11	12	120085
124 5/02 Hrfd	2m3f110yD(0-120)HHdl			GD	£3406
134 4/01 Ayr	B HCh			G-F	£13474
134 11/00 Chel 2m	B(0-145)HCh			G-S	£14088
124 5/00 Punc 2m2f	Ch			GD	£6072
129 3/00 Hntg 2m110y	E Ch			SFT	£2983
122 2/00 Chep 2m110y	D Ch			SFT	£4134
114 11/99 Wwck 2m	D Ch			GD	£4290
110 8/99 Worc 2m	D(0-125)HHdl			G-S	£3029
109 2/99 Sand 2m110y	D Hdl			G-S	£2853

Total win prize-money £54334

Going: Sf: 0-1 GS: 0-1 Gd: 0-6 GF: - Fm: 0-1
Distance: 2m/2m3: 0-1 2m4-2m7: 0-7 3m+: 0-1
Track: LH: 0-7 RH: 0-2 Tight: 0-2 Gall: 0-5
Aids: Bl: 0-5 Vi: 0-0 Tstrap: 0-0 Ckp: 0-0
Best Rating: 144 1/02 Asct 2m good Ch

Modest handicap chaser these days; usually blinkered; tends to carry his head awkwardly; stays two and a half miles; appears to act on any ground; has won over hurdles, but has not won over fences since April 2001.

Waverley Road
100 / **91**

7-y-o ch g Pelder (IRE)-Lillicara (FR) (Caracolero (USA))
M Madgwick (A P Jarvis 25/9) All Four Corners

Placings:5554 (4698)
2003/04: 19[5]S, 19[0]HY, 16[5]G, 18[4]G,

	Starts	1st	2nd	3rd	Win & Pl
Hurdles	4	0	0	0	0
Career Total	4	0	0	0	0

Going: Sf: 0-2 GS: 0-0 Gd: 0-2 GF: - Fm: 0-0
Distance: 2m/2m3: 0-4 2m4-2m7: 0-0 3m+: 0-0
Track: LH: 0-4 RH: 0-0 Tight: 0-1 Gall: 0-2
Aids: Bl: 0-0 Vi: 0-0 Tstrap: 0-0 Ckp: 0-0
Best Rating: 91 4/04 Font 2m2f110y good Hdl

Winning stayer on the Flat; twice beaten in the soft over hurdles; will do better at around 2m4f on decent ground.

Waydale Hill
68

5-y-o ch m Minster Son-Buckby Folly (Netherkelly)
T D Walford Mrs E C York

Placings:06 (4663)
2003/04: 16[6]GS, 16[6]S,

	Starts	1st	2nd	3rd	Win & Pl
NH Flat	2	0	0	0	0
Career Total	2	0	0	0	0

Going: Sf: 0-1 GS: 0-1 Gd: 0-0 GF: - Fm: 0-0
Distance: 2m/2m3: 0-2 2m4-2m7: 0-0 3m+: 0-0
Track: LH: 0-2 RH: 0-0 Tight: 0-0 Gall: 0-0
Aids: Bl: 0-0 Vi: 0-0 Tstrap: 0-0 Ckp: 0-0
Best Rating: 75 4/04 Hexm 2m110y soft NHF

Waynesworld (IRE)
97(95h) / (90+h)

6-y-o b g Petoski-Mariners Mirror (Julio Mariner)
M Scudamore F J Mills & W Mills

Placings:00P-3PP0F2P (4665)
2003/04: 20[3]GS, 21[P]S, 20[P]G, 22[0]S, 19[2]GS, 24[P]S,

	Starts	1st	2nd	3rd	Win & Pl
Hurdles	4	0	0	1	393
Chases	3	0	1	0	1764
Career Total	10	0	1	1	2157

Going: Sf: 0-4 GS: 0-2 Gd: 0-1 GF: - Fm: 0-0
Distance: 2m/2m3: 0-0 2m4-2m7: 0-6 3m+: 0-1
Track: LH: 0-4 RH: 0-3 Tight: 0-2 Gall: 0-1
Aids: Bl: 0-0 Vi: 0-0 Tstrap: 0-0 Ckp: 0-0
Best Rating: 91 12/02 Donc 2m110y gd-sft NHF

Modest chaser/hurdler; acts on easy ground.

Wayward Buttons
98 / (76h)**96**

10-y-o b g Nomadic Way (USA)-Lady Buttons (New Brig)
M Todhunter Mrs A W Scott-Harden And Mrs A Nicholson

Placings:06145PP/45-0 (0195)
2003/04: 16[0]G,

	Starts	1st	2nd	3rd	Win & Pl
Chases	1	0	0	0	
Career Total	10	1	0	0	3409
95 11/01 Sedg 2m5f	E Ch			SFT	£3090

Total win prize-money £3091

Going: Sf: 0-0 GS: 0-0 Gd: 0-1 GF: - Fm: 0-0
Distance: 2m/2m3: 0-1 2m4-2m7: 0-0 3m+: 0-0
Track: LH: 0-1 RH: 0-0 Tight: 0-0 Gall: 0-0
Aids: Bl: 0-0 Vi: 0-0 Tstrap: 0-0 Ckp: 0-0
Best Rating: 108 12/01 Muss 3m gd-fm Ch

Modest winning chaser/pointer; rarely finds as much as he promises and is finding it hard to add to his record; has worn a tongue strap.

Wayward Melody
98 / **83+**

4-y-o b f Merdon Melody-Dubitable (Formidable (USA))
G L Moore (S Dow 5/12) BHW Partnership

Placings:431650401 (4700)
2003/04: 18[4]G, 16[3]GF, 18[1]GF, 16[6]GF, 16[5]F, 20[0]GF, 20[4]GF, 19[0]GS, 20[1]G,

	Starts	1st	2nd	3rd	Win & Pl
Hurdles	9	2	0	1	6050
Career Total	9	2	0	1	6050
83 4/04 Font 2m4f	G(0-90)HHdl			GD	£2352
78 9/03 Font	2m2f110yE Hdl			G-F	£2541

Total win prize-money £4893

Going: Sf: 0-0 GS: 0-1 Gd: 1-1 GF: - Fm: 1-7
Distance: 2m/2m3: 1-6 2m4-2m7: 1-3 3m+: 0-0
Track: LH: 1-4 RH: 0-4 Tight: 2-4 Gall: 0-0
Aids: Bl: 0-0 Vi: 0-0 Tstrap: 0-0 Ckp: 0-0
Best Rating: 83 4/04 Font 2m4f good Hdl

Modest hurdler; stays two and a half miles and acts on fast ground; goes well at Fontwell.

We'll Make It (IRE)
103 / **116+**

6-y-o b g Spectrum (IRE)-Walliser (Niniski (USA))
G L Moore Wayne Barr,John Ripley,D Goff,S Moss

Placings:4342430/0200123-21 (2006)
2003/04: 21[2]GS, 20[1]G,

	Starts	1st	2nd	3rd	Win & Pl
Hurdles	2	1	1	0	4094
Career Total	16	4	3	4	14975
116 11/03 Sand	2m4f110yE(0-105)HHdl			GD	£2954
109 3/03 Folk	2m1f110yE(0-105)HHdl			GD	£3474

Total win prize-money £6428

Going: Sf: 0-0 GS: 0-0 Gd: 1-1 GF: - Fm: 0-1
Distance: 2m2/m3: 0-0 **2m4-2m7: 1-2** 3m+: 0-0
Track: LH: 0-1 **RH: 1-1** Tight: 0-0 Gall: 0-0
Aids: Bl: **1-2** Vi: 0-0 Tstrap: 0-0 Ckp: 0-0
Best Rating: 116 11/03 Sand 2m4f110y good Hdl

Moderate hurdler; stays 2m4f; acts on good ground; usually wears blinkers.

Wearerich

7-y-o ch m Alflora (IRE)-Weareagrandmother (Prince Tenderfoot (USA))
P M Rich P M Rich

Placings:0P-UPP   (3445)
2003/04: 19UGS, 20PS, 21PG,

	Starts	1st	2nd	3rd	Win & Pl
Hurdles	3	0	0	0	
Career Total	5	0	0	0	

Going: Sf: 0-1 GS: 0-1 Gd: 0-1 GF: - Fm: 0-0
Distance: 2m2/m3: 0-0 2m4-2m7: 0-0 3m+: 0-0
Track: LH: 0-1 RH: 0-2 Tight: 0-0 Gall: 0-0
Aids: Bl: 0-0 Vi: 0-0 Tstrap: 0-0 Ckp: 0-0
Best Rating: 55 12/02 Hrfd 2m1f soft NHF

Weaver George (IRE)

112(99h)   (94h)118
14-y-o b g Flash Of Steel-Nephrite (Godswalk (USA))
W Storey Regent Decorators Ltd

Placings: 342U/3403F015/15241211123/11223/33F612241/
52P26324/64621245/604211111F50/3P426531P05P5P-
5U22524B6P035P4   (4882)
2003/04: 22SG, 24UG, 20GF, 25PG, 24PS, 25PGS, 20PGS, 25PS,
30SG, 24PHY, 27PGS, 24PS, 24PHY, 21PG, 26PGS,

	Starts	1st	2nd	3rd	Win & Pl
Chases	15	0	3	1	7779
Career Total	106	20	20	13	123038
118	10/02	Kels	3m1f	D(0-125)HCh	GD	£6773
125	12/01	Kels	3m1f	B(0-145)HCh	G-S	£10707
125	10/01	Kels	3m1f	D(0-125)HCh	G-S	£4173
121	10/01	Carl	3m2f	E(0-115)HCh	GD	£3477
110	10/01	Kels	3m1f	D(0-125)HCh	GD	£4290
105	10/01	Sedg	2m5f	E(0-115)HCh	GD	£3987
119	11/00	Newc	2m5f	D(0-125)HCh	SFT	£5404
4/99	Sedg	2m5f	D(0-125)HCh	G-S	£4432
129	3/99	Newc	2m4f	D(0-125)HCh	SFT	£3694
118	5/97	Prth	2m4f110yD(0-125)HCh	SFT	£3436
118	5/97	Sedg	2m5f	D(0-125)HCh	G-F	£3821
118	2/97	Catt	2m	E(0-115)HCh	G-S	£2842
116	2/97	Catt	2m3f	E(0-110)HCh	GD	£2706
115	1/97	Catt	2m3f	D(0-120)HCh	GD	£3470
108	12/96	Sedg	2m1f110y	E(0-115)HCh	GD	£2877
105	5/96	Sedg	2m1f10y	E Ch	FRM	£2945
105	3/96	Sedg	2m1f	E Ch	GD	£3185
107	12/94	Weth	2m	(0-135)HHdl	GD	£2565
102	5/94	Weth	2m	Hdl	G-F	£2075
91	4/94	Weth	2m	Hdl	GD	£2337
				Total win prize-money £79203		

Going: Sf: 0-5 GS: 0-4 Gd: 0-5 GF: - Fm: 0-1
Distance: 2m2/m3: 0-0 2m4-2m7: 0-4 3m+: 0-11
Track: LH: 0-11 RH: 0-4 Tight: 0-7 Gall: 0-4
Aids: Bl: 0-0 Vi: 0-0 Tstrap: 0-0 Ckp: 0-14
Best Rating: 129 3/99 Newc 2m4f soft Ch

Modest performer; veteran staying chaser, stays well; best on good or easy ground; wears cheekpieces.

Weaver Of Dreams (IRE)

80   52
4-y-o b g Victory Note (USA)-Daziyra (IRE) (Doyoun)
G A Swinbank McRonif Partnership

Placings:0   (4795)
2003/04: 17PG,

	Starts	1st	2nd	3rd	Win & Pl
Hurdles	1	0	0	0	
Career Total	1	0	0	0	

Going: Sf: 0-0 GS: 0-0 Gd: 0-1 GF: - Fm: 0-0
Distance: 2m2/m3: 0-1 2m4-2m7: 0-0 3m+: 0-0
Track: LH: 0-1 RH: 0-0 Tight: 0-1 Gall: 0-0
Aids: Bl: 0-0 Vi: 0-0 Tstrap: 0-0 Ckp: 0-0
Best Rating: 52 4/04 Sedg 2m1f good Hdl

Weavers Choice

11-y-o ch g Sunley Builds-Wedding Song (True Song)
Mrs Joan Tice Mrs Joan Tice

Placings:4/P6-P   (3785)
2003/04: 24PS,

	Starts	1st	2nd	3rd	Win & Pl
Chases	1	0	0	0	
Career Total	4	0	0	0	165

Going: Sf: 0-1 GS: 0-0 Gd: 0-0 GF: - Fm: 0-0
Distance: 2m2/m3: 0-0 2m4-2m7: 0-0 3m+: 0-1
Track: LH: 0-0 RH: 0-1 Tight: 0-0 Gall: 0-1
Aids: Bl: 0-0 Vi: 0-0 Tstrap: 0-0 Ckp: 0-0
Best Rating: 75 3/02 Leic 2m7f110y soft Ch

Web Master (FR)

103   96
6-y-o b g Arctic Tern (USA)-Inesperada (Cariellor (FR))
C Grant Miss S J Turner

Placings:30-05003135   (4948)
2003/04: 16PS, 24SGS, 24PS, 25PGS, 24SHY, 27TGS, 24SHY,
27SGS,

	Starts	1st	2nd	3rd	Win & Pl
NH Flat	1	0	0	0	0
Hurdles	7	1	0	2	7168
Career Total	10	1	0	3	7456
96	2/04	Sedg	3m3f110yE(0-110)HHdl	G-S	£5512
				Total win prize-money £5512		

Going: Sf: 0-4 GS: 1-4 Gd: 0-0 GF: - Fm: 0-0
Distance: 2m2/m3: 0-1 2m4-2m7: 0-0 **3m+: 1-7**
Track: **LH: 1-7** RH: 0-0 Tight: **1-1** Gall: 0-1
Aids: Bl: 0-0 Vi: 0-0 Tstrap: 0-0 Ckp: 0-0
Best Rating: 103 2/03 Ayr 2m gd-sft NHF

Moderate French-bred gelding; stays three miles and acts on heavy ground.

Web Perceptions (USA)

101   123
4-y-o ch c Distant View (USA)-Squaw Time (USA) (Lord At War (ARG))
M F Harris (P F I Cole 16/9) Let's Live Racing

Placings:1112300   (4422)
2003/04: 16TGF, 16TGF, 16TGF, 16PG, 16PS, 16PG, 17PG,

	Starts	1st	2nd	3rd	Win & Pl
Hurdles	7	3	1	1	18197
Career Total	7	3	1	1	18197
123	10/03	Chel	2m110y	C Hdl	G-F	£6409
100	10/03	Chep	2m110y	D Hdl	G-F	£3555
100	9/03	Hntg	2m110y	E Hdl	G-F	£2744
				Total win prize-money £12709		

Going: Sf: 0-1 GS: 0-0 Gd: 0-3 GF: - Fm: 3-3
Distance: 2m2/m3: **3-7** 2m4-2m7: 0-0 3m+: 0-0
Track: **LH: 2-4** RH: 1-3 Tight: 0-0 Gall: **1-2**
Aids: Bl: **3-7** Vi: 0-0 Tstrap: 3-7 Ckp: 0-0
Best Rating: 123 10/03 Chel 2m110y gd-fm Hdl

Fair juvenile hurdler; decent handicapper on the Flat; won first three juvenile hurdles before finding life tough against progressive types under his penalties; best on fast ground, but can handle cut; wears blinkers and a tongue tie.

Wedger's Way (IRE)

95(83c)   (76c)82+
7-y-o ch g Glacial Storm (USA)-Officer's Lady (General Ironside)
Mrs H Dalton C B Brookes

Placings:23   (1373)
2003/04: 22PGF, 24SGF,

	Starts	1st	2nd	3rd	Win & Pl
Hurdles	1	0	0	1	288
Chases	1	0	1	0	1233
Career Total	2	0	1	1	1521

Going: Sf: 0-0 GS: 0-0 Gd: 0-0 GF: - Fm: 0-2
Distance: 2m2/m3: 0-0 2m4-2m7: 0-1 3m+: 0-1
Track: LH: 0-1 RH: 0-0 Tight: 0-1 Gall: 0-0
Aids: Bl: 0-0 Vi: 0-0 Tstrap: 0-0 Ckp: 0-0
Best Rating: 82 9/03 Worc 3m gd-fm Hdl

Overcame mistakes when runner-up on debut in 2m 6f Fontwell maiden chase August 2003; did not seem to get 3m when third over the brush hurdles at Worcester next time.

Wee Danny (IRE)

105   105+
7-y-o b g Mandalus-Bonne Bouche (Bonne Noel)
L A Dace The De Vitos

Placings:00600/0645-6321111005   (4932)
2003/04: 21SGF, 24SGF, 24PGF, 27TG, 24TGF, 26TGF, 24TGF,
24PG, 21PG, 27SG,

	Starts	1st	2nd	3rd	Win & Pl
Hurdles	10	4	1	1	14440
Career Total	19	4	1	1	14440
105	10/03	Extr	3m110y	D(0-115)HHdl	G-F	£3380
101	9/03	Hrfd	3m2f	E(0-110)HHdl	G-F	£2625
93	8/03	Worc	3m	F(0-95)HHdl	G-F	£2933
84	7/03	NAbb	3m3f	E(0-105)HHdl	GD	£4065
				Total win prize-money £13004		

Going: Sf: 0-0 GS: 0-0 Gd: 1-4 GF: - Fm: 3-6
Distance: 2m2/m3: 0-0 2m4-2m7: 0-0 **3m+: 4-8**
Track: LH: 2-5 RH: 2-4 **Tight: 1-3** Gall: 0-2
Aids: Bl: 0-0 Vi: 0-0 Tstrap: 0-0 Ckp: 0-0
Best Rating: 105 10/03 Extr 3m110y gd-fm Hdl

Moderate hurdler; improved form since stepped up to three miles; completed a four-timer in the summer of 2003; acts on fast ground; genuine; should continue to improve.

Wee River (IRE)

88   **67**

15-y-o b g Over The River (FR)-Mahe Reef (Be Friendly)
J Barclay   Miss L Wood

Placings:*0006/60500/PF11211113/13412/541243/4P6/P56*
00/33564/0/PP/53P540F040   (4315)
2003/04: 17⁵G, 20³GF, 20⁵G, 16⁵S, 20⁴GF, 20⁰GF, 17⁵S, 24⁵G,
20⁴F, 16⁰GF,

	Starts	1st	2nd	3rd	Win & Pl
Hurdles	1	0	0	0	0
Chases	9	0	0	1	835
Career Total	56	9	3	6	48975
132	1/97	Kels	2m1f	C(0-135)HCh	GD	£4421
132	3/96	Newb	2m1f	C(0-135)HCh	G-S	£4349
129	10/95	Worc	2m	D(0-125)HCh	GD	£3465
110	4/95	Sedg	C Ch		FRM	£5507
100	3/95	Kels	2m1f	D Ch	G-F	£3501
114	1/95	Muss	2m	E Ch	G-S	£3061
89	1/95	Muss	2m	E Ch	GD	£2801
102	12/94	Sedg	2m1f110y	(0-100)HHdl		
G-S	£1992					
97	11/94	Muss	2m110y	(0-100)HHdl	G-F	£2775

Total win prize-money £31874

Going:	Sf: 0-2 GS: 0-0 Gd: 0-3 GF: - Fm: 0-5
Distance:	2m/2m3: 0-4 2m4-2m7: 0-5 3m+: 0-1
Track:	LH: 0-6 RH: 0-4 **Tight:** 0-6 Gall: 0-1
Aids:	Bl: 0-0 Vi: 0-0 Tstrap: 0-0 Ckp: 0-0
Best Rating:	132 4/97 Aint 2m good Ch

Plating-class chaser; a light of other days.

Wee Willow

102   **81+**

10-y-o b m Minster Son-Peak Princess (Charlottown)
D W Whillans   Chas N Whillans

Placings:*050/3443-210F242P*   (4913)
2003/04: 27²S, 21¹GF, 20⁰HY, 24⁴GF, 24²HY, 24⁴GF, 27⁴G, 24P S,

	Starts	1st	2nd	3rd	Win & Pl
Hurdles	8	1	3	0	6257
Career Total	15	1	3	2	7541
81	11/03	Sedg	2m5f110yF(0-100)HHdl	G-F	£2324

Total win prize-money £2324

Going:	Sf: 0-4 GS: 0-0 Gd: 0-1 GF: - Fm: 1-3
Distance:	2m/2m3: 0-0 **2m4-2m7:** 1-2 3m+: 0-6
Track:	**LH:** 1-5 RH: 0-0 **Tight:** 1-3 Gall: 0-0
Aids:	Bl: 0-0 Vi: 0-0 Tstrap: 0-0 Ckp: 0-0
Best Rating:	82 3/04 Ayr 3m110y gd-fm Hdl

Moderate mare; suited to forcing tactics; modest form over hurdles; stays three miles; acts on heavy and fast ground.

Welburn Lady

64f   **30f**

5-y-o b m Primitive Rising (USA)-Tommys Dream (Le Bavard (FR))
G P Kelly   C I Ratcliffe

Placings:*00*   (1622)
2003/04: 17⁰GF, 17⁰G,

	Starts	1st	2nd	3rd	Win & Pl
NH Flat	2	0	0	0	
Career Total	2	0	0	0	

Going:	Sf: 0-0 GS: 0-0 Gd: 0-1 GF: - Fm: 0-1
Distance:	2m/2m3: 0-2 2m4-2m7: 0-0 3m+: 0-1
Track:	LH: 0-1 RH: 0-1 **Tight:** 0-2 Gall: 0-0
Aids:	Bl: 0-0 Vi: 0-0 Tstrap: 0-1 Ckp: 0-0
Best Rating:	30 9/03 MRas 2m1f110y gd-fm NHF

Welcome Archie

14f

4-y-o ch g Most Welcome-Indefinite Article (IRE) (Indian Ridge)
J S Haldane   D Young

Placings:*0*   (2482)
2003/04: 13⁰GF,

	Starts	1st	2nd	3rd	Win & Pl
NH Flat	1	0	0	0	
Career Total	1	0	0	0	

Going:	Sf: 0-0 GS: 0-0 Gd: 0-0 GF: - Fm: 0-1
Distance:	2m/2m3: 0-0 2m4-2m7: 0-0 3m+: 0-0
Track:	LH: 0-0 RH: 0-0 Tight: 0-0 Gall: 0-0
Aids:	Bl: 0-0 Vi: 0-0 Tstrap: 0-0 Ckp: 0-0
Best Rating:	17 11/03 Donc 1m5f gd-fm NHF

Welcome News

82f   **51f**

6-y-o ch m Bob Back (USA)-Rosie O'Keeffe (IRE) (Royal Fountain)
Mrs H Dalton   Mrs Caroline Shaw

Placings:*0-0*   (0705)
2003/04: 17⁰GF,

	Starts	1st	2nd	3rd	Win & Pl
NH Flat	1	0	0	0	
Career Total	2	0	0	0	

Going:	Sf: 0-0 GS: 0-0 Gd: 0-0 GF: - Fm: 0-1
Distance:	2m/2m3: 0-1 2m4-2m7: 0-0 3m+: 0-0
Track:	LH: 0-0 RH: 0-1 Tight: 0-1 Gall: 0-0
Aids:	Bl: 0-0 Vi: 0-0 Tstrap: 0-1 Ckp: 0-0
Best Rating:	59 3/03 Wwck 2m soft NHF

Welcome To Unos

103   **116+**

7-y-o ch g Exit To Nowhere (USA)-Royal Loft (Homing)
M C Pipe (Mrs M Reveley 24/5) J & M Leisure / Unos Restaurant

Placings:*343/342332-041301P*   (4870)
2003/04: 16⁰G, 17⁴G, 16¹G, 16³G, 17⁰G, 20¹G, 24PGS,

	Starts	1st	2nd	3rd	Win & Pl
Hurdles	7	2	0	1	8410
Career Total	16	2	2	6	16331
116	12/03	Leic	2m4f110yD(0-120)HHdl	GD	£4153
116	10/03	Strf	2m110y	E(0-100)HHdl	GD	£3445

Total win prize-money £7599

Going:	Sf: 0-0 GS: 0-1 Gd: 2-6 GF: - Fm: 0-0
Distance:	2m/2m3: 1-5 2m4-2m7: 1-1 3m+: 0-1
Track:	LH: 1-5 RH: 1-2 **Tight:** 1-5 Gall: 0-0
Aids:	Bl: 0-0 **Vi:** 1-3 Tstrap: 0-0 Ckp: 0-0
Best Rating:	116 12/03 Leic 2m4f110y good Hdl

Fair hurdler; stays two and a half miles; acts on any ground; has worn a visor.

Weldman

5-y-o b g Weld-Manettia (IRE) (Mandalus)
Mrs M Reveley   Guy Stevenson

Placings:*46000*   (4461)
2003/04: 16⁴G, 16⁶GS, 18⁰S, 19⁰G, 16⁰HY,

	Starts	1st	2nd	3rd	Win & Pl
NH Flat	2	0	0	0	0

Hurdles	3	0	0	0	0
Career Total	5	0	0	0	0

Going:	Sf: 0-2 GS: 0-1 Gd: 0-2 GF: - Fm: 0-0
Distance:	2m/2m3: 0-4 2m4-2m7: 0-1 3m+: 0-0
Track:	LH: 0-5 RH: 0-0 **Tight:** 0-1 Gall: 0-1
Aids:	Bl: 0-0 Vi: 0-0 Tstrap: 0-0 Ckp: 0-0
Best Rating:	100 11/03 Weth 2m good NHF

Well Chief (GER)

117(115h)   (146+h) **156+**

5-y-o ch g Night Shift (USA)-Wellesiena (GER) (Scenic)
M C Pipe   D A Johnson

Placings:*1123-15111*   (4645)
2003/04: 16¹GF, 16⁶GS, 16¹S, 16¹G, 16¹G,

	Starts	1st	2nd	3rd	Win & Pl
Hurdles	2	1	0	0	19225
Chases	3	3	0	0	143321
Career Total	9	6	1	1	219279
156	4/04	Aint	2m	A Ch	GD	£58000
153	3/04	Chel	2m	A Ch	GD	£81200
133	2/04	Tntn	2m110y	E Ch	SFT	£4121
146	11/03	Winc	2m	A HHdl	G-F	£18600
121	2/03	Kemp	2m	A Hdl	GD	£17400
107	2/03	Tntn	2m1f	D Hdl	SFT	£5232

Total win prize-money £184554

Going:	Sf: 1-1 GS: 0-1 Gd: 2-2 GF: - Fm: 1-1
Distance:	**2m/2m3:** 4-5 2m4-2m7: 0-0 3m+: 0-0
Track:	LH: 2-3 RH: 2-2 **Tight:** 2-2 Gall: 1-2
Aids:	Bl: 0-0 Vi: 0-0 Tstrap: 0-0 Ckp: 0-0
Best Rating:	156 4/04 Aint 2m good Ch

High-class novice chaser; consistent efforts in the top juvenile hurdles of the 2002/3 season and was placed in both the Triumph Hurdle at Cheltenham and the Grade Two Anniversary Hurdle at Aintree; won on his seasonal reappearance at Wincanton in November 2003 but found out in the Gerry Feilden; made a winning chase debut at Taunton and followed up in determined fashion in the Arkle at the Festival, a great effort considering his inexperience over fences; good winner of Grade 1 at Aintree; has only run at around 2m; effective on fast and soft ground, better on the former.

Well Gone

96   **81**

7-y-o b g Sanglamore (USA)-Well Away (IRE) (Sadler's Wells (USA))
Ian Williams   A L R Morton

Placings:*0/013P3*   (1297)
2003/04: 16⁰G, 17¹GF, 20³GF, 19PGF, 16³GF,

	Starts	1st	2nd	3rd	Win & Pl
NH Flat	2	1	0	0	2947
Hurdles	3	0	0	2	1188
Career Total	6	1	0	2	4135
89	7/03	NAbb	2m1f	H NHF	G-F	£2947

Total win prize-money £2947

Going:	Sf: 0-0 GS: 0-0 Gd: 0-1 GF: - Fm: 1-4
Distance:	**2m/2m3:** 1-3 2m4-2m7: 0-2 3m+: 0-0
Track:	**LH:** 1-4 RH: 0-1 **Tight:** 1-3 Gall: 0-0
Aids:	Bl: 0-0 Vi: 0-0 Tstrap: 0-0 Ckp: 0-0
Best Rating:	89 7/03 NAbb 2m1f gd-fm NHF

Backed down from 25/1 to 10/1 when getting up close home to win Newton Abbot bumper July 2003; disappointing over hurdles; acts on fast ground.

Well Said Sam

8-y-o b g Weld-Auto Sam (Even Say)
P C Handley Mrs S E Handley

Placings:P   (4607)
2003/04: 25PGS,

	Starts	1st	2nd	3rd	Win & Pl
Chases	1	0	0	0	
Career Total	1	0	0	0	

Going:	Sf: 0-0 GS: 0-1 Gd: 0-0 GF: - Fm: 0-0
Distance:	2m/2m3: 0-0 2m4-2m7: 0-0 3m+: 0-1
Track:	LH: 0-0 RH: 0-1 Tight: 0-0 Gall: 0-0
Aids:	Bl: 0-0 Vi: 0-0 Tstrap: 0-0 Ckp: 0-0

Wellfranko (IRE)

62   40

9-y-o b g Camden Town-Electana (Electrify)
Miss Z C Davison The Secret Circle

Placings:U0001P/00-F50   (4752)
2003/04: 16FG, 16S GF, 16PG,

	Starts	1st	2nd	3rd	Win & Pl
Hurdles	3	0	0	0	0
Career Total	11	1	0	0	2667
97	4/02	Uttx	2m	E(0-100)HHdl	G-F	£2667
				Total win prize-money £2667		

Going:	Sf: 0-0 GS: 0-0 Gd: 0-2 GF: - Fm: 0-1
Distance:	2m/2m3: 0-3 2m4-2m7: 0-0 3m+: 0-0
Track:	LH: 0-1 RH: 0-2 Tight: 0-1 Gall: 0-0
Aids:	Bl: 0-0 Vi: 0-0 Tstrap: 0-0 Ckp: 0-0
Best Rating:	97 4/02 Uttx 2m gd-fm Hdl

Wellie (IRE)

100   93

11-y-o b/br g Aristocracy-Sweet View (King's Ride)
S J Gilmore S J Gilmore

Placings:06000UP523/54/54U30F4/PP521-22F   (1169)
2003/04: 202GA, 202GF, 18FGF,

	Starts	1st	2nd	3rd	Win & Pl
Chases	3	0	2	0	2950
Career Total	27	1	4	2	10303
93	4/03	Chep	2m3f110yG(0-90)HCh	G-F	£2646
				Total win prize-money £2646		

Going:	Sf: 0-0 GS: 0-0 Gd: 0-0 GF: - Fm: 0-3
Distance:	2m/2m3: 0-1 2m4-2m7: 0-2 3m+: 0-0
Track:	LH: 0-0 RH: 0-2 Tight: 0-1 Gall: 0-2
Aids:	Bl: 0-0 Vi: 0-0 Tstrap: 0-0 Ckp: 0-0
Best Rating:	103 1/01 Donc 2m110y good Ch

Plating-class front-running chaser; took advantage of a drop in grade when winning selling chase at Chepstow April 2003; prone to the odd mistake; stays 2m 4f; seems to act on any ground.

Welsh And Wylde (IRE)

91   82

4-y-o b g Anita's Prince-Waikiki (GER) (Zampano (GER))
B Palling Mrs M M Palling

Placings:62   (4714)
2003/04: 16SGS, 162G,

	Starts	1st	2nd	3rd	Win & Pl
Hurdles	2	0	1	0	1063
Career Total	2	0	1	0	1063

Going:	Sf: 0-0 GS: 0-1 Gd: 0-1 GF: - Fm: 0-0
Distance:	2m/2m3: 0-2 2m4-2m7: 0-0 3m+: 0-0
Track:	LH: 0-1 RH: 0-1 Tight: 0-0 Gall: 0-0
Aids:	Bl: 0-0 Vi: 0-0 Tstrap: 0-0 Ckp: 0-0
Best Rating:	82 4/04 Ludl 2m good Hdl

Runner-up in weak hurdler at Ludloww in April on good ground.

Welsh Crystal

97f   66f

5-y-o gr m Muqadar (USA)-Rupert's Daughter (Rupert Bear)
Mrs L Williamson Mrs Lisa Williamson

Placings:6300   (2945)
2003/04: 186GJ, 163GF, 17QGS, 16QGS,

	Starts	1st	2nd	3rd	Win & Pl
NH Flat	4	0	0	1	258
Career Total	4	0	0	1	258

Going:	Sf: 0-0 GS: 0-2 Gd: 0-0 GF: - Fm: 0-2
Distance:	2m/2m3: 0-4 2m4-2m7: 0-0 3m+: 0-0
Track:	LH: 0-2 RH: 0-2 Tight: 0-1 Gall: 0-0
Aids:	Bl: 0-0 Vi: 0-0 Tstrap: 0-0 Ckp: 0-0
Best Rating:	66 8/03 Font 2m2f110y gd-fm NHF

Welsh Dream

103   101

7-y-o b g Mtoto-Morgannwg (IRE) (Simply Great (FR))
Miss S E Forster Should Be Fun Racing

Placings:3/2-1   (0473)
2003/04: 171GS,

	Starts	1st	2nd	3rd	Win & Pl
Hurdles	1	1	0	0	3874
Career Total	3	1	1	1	5224
101	5/03	Ctml	2m1f110yE Hdl	G-S	£3874
				Total win prize-money £3874		

Going:	Sf: 0-0 GS: 1-1 Gd: 0-0 GF: - Fm: 0-0
Distance:	2m/2m3: 1-1 2m4-2m7: 0-0 3m+: 0-0
Track:	LH: 1-1 RH: 0-0 Tight: 1-1 Gall: 0-0
Aids:	Bl: 0-0 Vi: 0-0 Tstrap: 0-0 Ckp: 0-0
Best Rating:	101 5/03 Ctml 2m1f110y gd-sft Hdl

Moderate novice hurdler; lightly raced; broke his duck in a fair race at Cartmel; should stay further than two miles; effective with cut in the ground.

Welsh Gold

74   31

5-y-o ch g Zafonic (USA)-Trying For Gold (USA) (Northern Baby (CAN))
S T Lewis D Thompson

Placings:00P6   (2032)
2003/04: 16QGF, 17QGF, 16PG, 20PGF,

	Starts	1st	2nd	3rd	Win & Pl
NH Flat	2	0	0	0	0
Hurdles	2	0	0	0	0
Career Total	4	0	0	0	0

Going:	Sf: 0-0 GS: 0-0 Gd: 0-1 GF: - Fm: 0-3
Distance:	2m/2m3: 0-3 2m4-2m7: 0-1 3m+: 0-0
Track:	LH: 0-2 RH: 0-2 Tight: 0-1 Gall: 0-0

Aids:	Bl: 0-0 Vi: 0-0 Tstrap: 0-0 Ckp: 0-0
Best Rating:	55 6/03 MRas 2m1f110y gd-fm NHF

Welsh Main

102   118+

7-y-o br g Zafonic (USA)-Welsh Daylight (Welsh Pageant)
F Jordan Marcus Reeder

Placings:1U/33F21-000260   (4911)
2003/04: 16QG, 20QS, 16QG, 162G, 16SGS, 16QS,

	Starts	1st	2nd	3rd	Win & Pl
Hurdles	6	0	1	0	1752
Career Total	13	2	2	2	16788
118	10/02	Weth	2m	B(0-140)HHdl	G-F	£8014
102	3/02	Catt	2m	E Hdl	G-S	£3332
				Total win prize-money £11347		

Going:	Sf: 0-2 GS: 0-1 Gd: 0-3 GF: - Fm: 0-0
Distance:	2m/2m3: 0-5 2m4-2m7: 0-1 3m+: 0-0
Track:	LH: 0-2 RH: 0-4 Tight: 0-1 Gall: 0-0
Aids:	Bl: 0-0 Vi: 0-0 Tstrap: 0-0 Ckp: 0-0
Best Rating:	118 10/02 Weth 2m gd-fm Hdl

Fair hurdler; effective over two miles; acts on fast ground but handles cut.

Welsh Whisper

5-y-o b m Overbury (IRE)-Grugiar (Red Sunset)
S A Brookshaw S A Brookshaw

Placings:F   (1334)
2003/04: 17FGF,

	Starts	1st	2nd	3rd	Win & Pl
NH Flat	1	0	0	0	
Career Total	1	0	0	0	

Going:	Sf: 0-0 GS: 0-0 Gd: 0-0 GF: - Fm: 0-1
Distance:	2m/2m3: 0-1 2m4-2m7: 0-0 3m+: 0-0
Track:	LH: 0-0 RH: 0-1 Tight: 0-0 Gall: 0-0
Aids:	Bl: 0-0 Vi: 0-0 Tstrap: 0-0 Ckp: 0-0

Wemyss Quest

110   (129h)116

9-y-o b g Rainbow Quest (USA)-Wemyss Bight (Dancing Brave (USA))
Miss Venetia Williams Four Blokes

Placings:2515223/21110P0/1-15P4P   (1766)
2003/04: 231G, 205GF, 24PG, 264GF, 24PG,

	Starts	1st	2nd	3rd	Win & Pl
Chases	5	1	0	0	4330
Career Total	20	6	4	1	27980
116	6/03	Worc	2m7f110yE(0-110)HCh	GD	£3939
96	6/02	MRas	2m4f	E Ch	G-F	£3802
129	10/01	Chel	3m1f110yB Hdl	GD	£7117
109	10/01	Weth	2m4f110yD Hdl	GD	£3801
116	6/01	MRas	3m	E Hdl	G-F	£2614
86	8/00	Rosc	2m	NHF	FRM	£3036
				Total win prize-money £24312		

Going:	Sf: 0-0 GS: 0-0 Gd: 1-3 GF: - Fm: 0-2
Distance:	2m/2m3: 0-2 2m4-2m7: 0-1 3m+: 1-4
Track:	LH: 1-4 RH: 0-1 Tight: 0-2 Gall: 0-0
Aids:	Bl: 0-0 Vi: 0-0 Tstrap: 0-1 Ckp: 0-0
Best Rating:	129 10/01 Chel 3m1f110y good Hdl

Modest chaser; returned after a year off with tendon trouble when making all in 3m Worcester handicap chase on first start for new stable despite jumping right in June 2003; acts on fast ground; goes well when fresh.

Wensley Blue (IRE)
88   **82**

5-y-o b g Blues Traveller (IRE)-Almasa (Faustus (USA))
P C Haslam Mrs B M Hawkins & R Young

Placings:561-   (0002)
2003/04: 20¹G,

	Starts	1st	2nd	3rd	Win & Pl
Hurdles	1	1	0	0	2562
Career Total	3	1	0	0	2562
77 4/03 Hexm	2m4f110yG Hdl			GD	£2562

Total win prize-money £2562

Going:	Sf: 0-0 GS: 0-0 Gd: 1-1 GF: - Fm: 0-0
Distance:	2m/2m3: 0-0 2m4-2m7: 1-1 3m+: 0-0
Track:	LH: 1-1 RH: 0-0 Tight: 0-0 Gall: 0-0
Aids:	Bl: 0-0 Vi: 0-0 Tstrap: 0-0 Ckp: 0-0
Best Rating:	82 10/02 Hrfd 2m1f good Hdl

Dropped in class won a selling hurdle all out at Hexham in April on good.

Were Not Stoppin
95   **87**

9-y-o b g Mystiko (USA)-Power Take Off (Aragon)
R Bastiman I B Barker

Placings:5/46/5313526PP-430   (4603)
2003/04: 16⁴G, 16³GS, 17⁹G,

	Starts	1st	2nd	3rd	Win & Pl
Hurdles	3	0	0	1	351
Career Total	15	1	1	3	5920
87 6/02 Uttx	2m	E(0-105)HHdl	G-F	£3630

Total win prize-money £3630

Going:	Sf: 0-0 GS: 0-0 Gd: 0-2 GF: - Fm: 0-1
Distance:	2m/2m3: 0-3 2m4-2m7: 0-0 3m+: 0-0
Track:	LH: 0-2 RH: 0-1 Tight: 0-2 Gall: 0-0
Aids:	Bl: 0-0 Vi: 0-0 Tstrap: 0-0 Ckp: 0-0
Best Rating:	87 3/04 Catt 2m gd-fm Hdl

Modest hurdler, suited to hold up tactics; best at two miles; acts on fast.

Wesley's Lad (IRE)
96   **101**

10-y-o b/br g Classic Secret (USA)-Galouga (FR) (Lou Piguet (FR))
D Burchell Brian Williams

Placings:043151/262425321/2P/30/606-040PPFP   (4760)
2003/04: 16⁹S, 16⁴S, 17⁰GS, 24⁹GS, 20⁹GS, 16⁶G, 16⁶S,

	Starts	1st	2nd	3rd	Win & Pl
Hurdles	7	0	0	0	320
Career Total	29	3	5	3	18253
127 3/99 Strf	2m110y C(0-135)HHdl	HVY	£4930
115 3/98 Plum	2m1f	E Hdl	SFT	£2490
114 1/98 Folk	2m1f110yE Hdl	G-S	£1976

Total win prize-money £9397

Going:	Sf: 0-3 GS: 0-3 Gd: 0-1 GF: - Fm: 0-0
Distance:	2m/2m3: 0-5 2m4-2m7: 0-1 3m+: 0-1
Track:	LH: 0-3 RH: 0-4 Tight: 0-1 Gall: 0-0
Aids:	Bl: 0-0 Vi: 0-0 Tstrap: 0-0 Ckp: 0-0
Best Rating:	130 11/99 Leic 2m gd-sft Hdl

Moderate hurdler nowadays; suited by soft ground.

Wessex (USA)

4-y-o ch c Gone West (USA)-Satin Velvet (USA) (El Gran Senor (USA))

James Moffatt (M Johnston 25/6) The Vilprano Partnership

Placings:P   (3732)
2003/04: 16⁶G,

	Starts	1st	2nd	3rd	Win & Pl
Hurdles	1	0	0	0	
Career Total	1	0	0	0	

Going:	Sf: 0-0 GS: 0-0 Gd: 0-1 GF: - Fm: 0-0
Distance:	2m/2m3: 0-0 2m4-2m7: 0-0 3m+: 0-0
Track:	LH: 0-0 RH: 0-1 Tight: 0-1 Gall: 0-0
Aids:	Bl: 0-0 Vi: 0-0 Tstrap: 0-1 Ckp: 0-0

West Aside (IRE)
80   (0c)**66**

10-y-o b g Brush Aside (USA)-Chancy Belle (Le Bavard (FR))
T P McGovern B C J Enterprise

Placings:06/00/U-6PPPP0P4   (4750)
2003/04: 25⁶GS, 25⁷S, 26⁶G, 26⁶G, 25⁷GS, 22⁹GF, 25⁹GS, 21⁴G,

	Starts	1st	2nd	3rd	Win & Pl
Hurdles	3	0	0	0	0
Chases	5	0	0	0	0
Career Total	13	0	0	0	0

Going:	Sf: 0-1 GS: 0-4 Gd: 0-2 GF: - Fm: 0-1
Distance:	2m/2m3: 0-0 2m4-2m7: 0-2 3m+: 0-6
Track:	LH: 0-3 RH: 0-3 Tight: 0-5 Gall: 0-0
Aids:	Bl: 0-5 Vi: 0-0 Tstrap: 0-1 Ckp: 0-0
Best Rating:	66 5/01 Hntg 2m4f110y good Hdl

West Coaster (IRE)
87   **88**

6-y-o gr g Be My Native (USA)-Donegal Grey (IRE) (Roselier (FR))
Miss H C Knight White Rabbit Partnership

Placings:00/F0360-400   (4716)
2003/04: 20⁴GF, 21⁹GS, 21⁹G,

	Starts	1st	2nd	3rd	Win & Pl
Hurdles	3	0	0	0	0
Career Total	10	0	0	1	551

Going:	Sf: 0-0 GS: 0-1 Gd: 0-1 GF: - Fm: 0-0
Distance:	2m/2m3: 0-0 2m4-2m7: 0-3 3m+: 0-0
Track:	LH: 0-2 RH: 0-1 Tight: 0-1 Gall: 0-0
Aids:	Bl: 0-0 Vi: 0-0 Tstrap: 0-0 Ckp: 0-0
Best Rating:	91 1/03 Donc 2m110y gd-sft Hdl

West Paces (IRE)
98   **102**

10-y-o br g Lord Americo-Spanish Royale (Royal Buck)
G B Balding Baldings (training) Ltd

Placings:0PF32-43   (0443)
2003/04: 25⁴GF, 25³GF,

	Starts	1st	2nd	3rd	Win & Pl
Chases	2	0	0	1	969
Career Total	7	0	1	2	1569

Going:	Sf: 0-0 GS: 0-0 Gd: 0-0 GF: - Fm: 0-2
Distance:	2m/2m3: 0-0 2m4-2m7: 0-0 3m+: 0-2
Track:	LH: 0-0 RH: 0-2 Tight: 0-0 Gall: 0-0

Aids:	Bl: 0-0 Vi: 0-0 Tstrap: 0-0 Ckp: 0-0
Best Rating:	102 4/03 Ludl 3m good Ch

Moderate, lightly-raced novice chaser; stays 3m 2f; acts on fast ground.

West Pal (IRE)

10-y-o ch g Lancastrian-Buck And Roll (Buckskin (FR))
Mrs S J Humphrey (R H York 25/8) Mrs S J Humphrey

Placings:P0/00FF/122P64F   (4891)
2003/04: 26¹GF, 24²G, 26²G, 26⁹GF, 25⁸G, 25⁴GS, 24⁴GF,

	Starts	1st	2nd	3rd	Win & Pl
Chases	7	1	2	0	6503
Career Total	13	1	2	0	6503
84 7/03 Sthl	3m2f	E Ch	G-F	£3802

Total win prize-money £3803

Going:	Sf: 0-0 GS: 0-1 Gd: 0-3 GF: - Fm: 1-3
Distance:	2m/2m3: 0-0 2m4-2m7: 0-0 3m+: 1-7
Track:	LH: 1-4 RH: 0-2 Tight: 0-4 Gall: 0-0
Aids:	Bl: 0-0 Vi: 0-0 Tstrap: 0-0 Ckp: 0-0
Best Rating:	91 8/03 Sthl 3m2f good Ch

Plating-class novice chaser; impressive winner of maiden open point May 2003; won weak 3m2f novice chase at Southwell in July; jumps best when held up; acts on a sound surface.

West Point

7-y-o ch g Unfuwain (USA)-Western Reel (USA) (Gone West (USA))
Mrs L Williamson Turner Technology Ltd

Placings:10/000   (2795)
2003/04: 16⁶GS, 17⁰GS, 17⁰GS,

	Starts	1st	2nd	3rd	Win & Pl
NH Flat	2	0	0	0	0
Hurdles	1	0	0	0	0
Career Total	5	1	0	0	1631
93 2/01 Catt	2m	H NHF	SFT	£1631

Total win prize-money £1631

Going:	Sf: 0-0 GS: 0-3 Gd: 0-0 GF: - Fm: 0-0
Distance:	2m/2m3: 0-3 2m4-2m7: 0-0 3m+: 0-0
Track:	LH: 0-2 RH: 0-1 Tight: 0-1 Gall: 0-0
Aids:	Bl: 0-0 Vi: 0-0 Tstrap: 0-0 Ckp: 0-0
Best Rating:	93 2/01 Catt 2m soft NHF

Westbourne (IRE)
74f   **68f**

6-y-o b m King's Ride-Give Me Hope (IRE) (Be My Native (USA))
A King Aiden Murphy

Placings:06   (4636)
2003/04: 16⁹GF, 17⁶G,

	Starts	1st	2nd	3rd	Win & Pl
NH Flat	2	0	0	0	0
Career Total	2	0	0	0	0

Going:	Sf: 0-0 GS: 0-0 Gd: 0-1 GF: - Fm: 0-1
Distance:	2m/2m3: 0-2 2m4-2m7: 0-0 3m+: 0-0
Track:	LH: 0-0 RH: 0-0 Tight: 0-0 Gall: 0-0
Aids:	Bl: 0-0 Vi: 0-0 Tstrap: 0-0 Ckp: 0-0
Best Rating:	68 4/04 Tntn 2m1f good NHF

Westcoast

13-y-o b g Handsome Sailor-Pichon (Formidable (USA))
Miss Joanne Priest O I F Davies

Placings:4/3/0/00600452/5006F45100/B2215015/6PP/0033
6/0   (0483)
2003/04: 24⁰GF,

	Starts	1st	2nd	3rd	Win & Pl
Chases	1	0	0	0	
Career Total	38	3	3	3	14370
107 3/00 Bang	3m	D(0-120)HHdl	GD	£4719
96 1/00 Ludl	3m	E(0-115)HHdl	GD	£3591
96 3/99 Ludl	2m5f110yE Hdl		SFT	£2542

Total win prize-money £10852

Going:	Sf: 0-0 GS: 0-0 Gd: 0-0 GF: - Fm: 0-1
Distance:	2m/2m3: 0-0 2m4-2m7: 0-0 3m+: 0-1
Track:	LH: 0-0 RH: 0-1 Tight: 0-0 Gall: 0-1
Aids:	Bl: 0-0 Vi: 0-0 Tstrap: 0-0 Ckp: 0-0
Best Rating:	**107** 3/00 Bang 3m good Hdl

Westender (FR)
121   164

8-y-o b g In The Wings-Trude (GER) (Windwurf (GER))
M C Pipe Matt Archer & Miss Jean Broadhurst

Placings:P11111022/323-P6533   (4954)
2003/04: 16⁶G, 16⁶G, 16⁵G, 20³G, 16³G,

	Starts	1st	2nd	3rd	Win & Pl
Hurdles	5	0	0	2	33575
Career Total	17	5	3	4	191601
151 11/01 Chel	2m110y A HHdl	GD	£32500
144 10/01 Chel	2m110y B HHdl	GD	£10432
128 10/01 Chep	2m110y D Hdl	GD	£3552
119 9/01 Uttx	2m D Hdl	GD	£3591
125 6/01 Strf	2m110y D Hdl	G-F	£3848

Total win prize-money £53924

Going:	Sf: 0-0 GS: 0-0 Gd: 0-5 GF: - Fm: 0-0
Distance:	2m/2m3: 0-4 2m4-2m7: 0-1 3m+: 0-0
Track:	LH: 0-4 RH: 0-1 Tight: 0-1 Gall: 0-2
Aids:	Bl: 0-0 Vi: 0-0 Tstrap: 0-0 Ckp: 0-0
Best Rating:	**159** 3/03 Chel 2m110y good Hdl

High-class hurdler, though without a win since November
2001; runner-up in the 2003 Champion Hurdle and would
have finished closer but for losing ground at the start; fifth in
the 2004 Champion Hurdle and an excellent third in the
Aintree Hurdle; suited by two miles a sound surface; regularly blinkered; should make a smart chaser.

Western (IRE)

4-y-o ch g Gone West (USA)-Madame Est Sortie (FR)
(Longleat (USA))
J Akehurst (Mrs A J Perrett 14/6) H R Hunt

Placings:P   (4452)
2003/04: 16⁰GS,

	Starts	1st	2nd	3rd	Win & Pl
Hurdles	1	0	0	0	
Career Total	1	0	0	0	

Going:	Sf: 0-0 GS: 0-1 Gd: 0-0 GF: - Fm: 0-0
Distance:	2m/2m3: 0-1 2m4-2m7: 0-0 3m+: 0-0
Track:	LH: 0-0 RH: 0-1 Tight: 0-0 Gall: 0-0
Aids:	Bl: 0-0 Vi: 0-0 Tstrap: 0-0 Ckp: 0-0

Western Bluebird (IRE)
98   69

6-y-o b g Bluebird (USA)-Arrastra (Bustino)
Miss Kate Milligan The W Bees

Placings:0/00PP-015P6   (2511)
2003/04: 19⁰G, 20¹GF, 22⁵GF, 21⁸G, 18⁶S,

	Starts	1st	2nd	3rd	Win & Pl
Hurdles	5	1	0	0	2338
Career Total	10	1	0	0	2338
69 6/03 Hexm	2m4f110yG(0-95)HHdl	G-F	£2338

Total win prize-money £2338

Going:	Sf: 0-1 GS: 0-0 Gd: 0-2 GF: - Fm: 1-2
Distance:	2m/2m3: 0-1 **2m4-2m7: 1-4** 3m+: 0-0
Track:	LH: **1-4** RH: 0-1 Tight: 0-4 Gall: 0-0
Aids:	Bl: 0-0 Vi: 0-0 Tstrap: 0-0 **Ckp: 1-3**
Best Rating:	**70** 1/02 Newb 2m110y gd-sft Hdl

Plating-class hurdler; first worthwhile form when narrow
winner at Hexham in June; stays two and a half miles; acts
on fast ground.

Western Fort (IRE)

14-y-o ch g Saher-Moon Away (Mount Hagen (FR))
P R Rodford Mrs M Elston

Placings:0/U060/334P   (2569)
2003/04: 23³F, 23³GF, 25⁴GF, 29²G,

	Starts	1st	2nd	3rd	Win & Pl
Chases	4	0	0	2	1502
Career Total	9	0	0	2	1502

Going:	Sf: 0-0 GS: 0-0 Gd: 0-1 GF: - Fm: 0-3
Distance:	2m/2m3: 0-0 2m4-2m7: 0-0 3m+: 0-4
Track:	LH: 0-1 RH: 0-3 Tight: 0-0 Gall: 0-0
Aids:	Bl: 0-0 Vi: 0-0 Tstrap: 0-0 Ckp: 0-0
Best Rating:	**75** 5/01 NAbb 2m5f110y gd-fm Ch

Western Ridge (FR)
107   109+

7-y-o b g Darshaan-Helvellyn (USA) (Gone West (USA))
B J Llewellyn D H Driscoll

Placings:0/002-251611243   (1832)
2003/04: 16²GF, 20⁵G, 17¹GF, 17⁶G, 17¹GF, 16¹G, 17²GF, 16⁴GF,
16⁸GF,

	Starts	1st	2nd	3rd	Win & Pl
Hurdles	9	3	2	1	21533
Career Total	13	3	3	1	22549
109 7/03 Strf	2m110y D(0-120)HHdl	GD	£5382
97 7/03 NAbb	2m1f	D(0-115)HHdl	G-F	£4737
88 5/03 NAbb	2m1f	E(0-105)HHdl	G-F	£3503

Total win prize-money £13623

Going:	Sf: 0-0 GS: 0-0 Gd: 1-3 GF: - Fm: 2-6
Distance:	**2m/2m3: 3-8** 2m4-2m7: 0-1 3m+: 0-0
Track:	LH: **3-8** RH: 0-1 Tight: **3-7** Gall: 0-0
Aids:	Bl: 0-0 Vi: 0-0 Tstrap: 0-0 Ckp: 0-0
Best Rating:	**109** 10/03 Chel 2m110y gd-fm Hdl

Modest handicap hurdler; well suited by hold-up tactics;
improved form in the summer of 2003 with back-to-back
wins at Newton Abbot and Stratford; not disgraced subsequently; best at around two miles; acts on fast ground; suited by a flat left-handed track.

Westernmost
102   107

6-y-o b g Most Welcome-Dakota Girl (Northern State (USA))
M Todhunter Steve Baron

Placings:S3F52/21222-005001   (4911)
2003/04: 16⁶G, 17⁰HY, 16⁵S, 23⁹GS, 21⁹GS, 16¹S,

	Starts	1st	2nd	3rd	Win & Pl
Hurdles	6	1	0	0	7066
Career Total	16	2	5	1	16782
99 4/04 Prth	2m110y D(0-120)HHdl	SFT	£7065
97 6/02 Ctml	2m1f110yD Hdl	GD	£3653

Total win prize-money £10719

Going:	Sf: 1-3 GS: 0-2 Gd: 0-1 GF: - Fm: 0-0
Distance:	**2m/2m3: 1-4** 2m4-2m7: 0-1 3m+: 0-1
Track:	LH: 0-4 RH: **1-2** Tight: 0-2 Gall: 0-0
Aids:	Bl: 0-0 Vi: 0-0 Tstrap: 0-0 Ckp: 0-1
Best Rating:	**107** 10/02 Sedg 2m5f110y gd-fm Hdl

Moderate handicap hurdler, effective at up to two miles five;
acts best on a sound surface.

Westerton (IRE)

11-y-o b g Glacial Storm (USA)-Killiney Rose (Buckskin
(FR))
F A Hutsby F A Hutsby

Placings:52I3410P/25/PF/31-P1P   (3898)
2003/04: 25²G, 25¹G, 20⁶G,

	Starts	1st	2nd	3rd	Win & Pl
Chases	3	1	0	0	3122
Career Total	17	4	2	2	10580
93 5/03 Kels	3m1f	H Ch	GD	£3122
90 3/03 MRas	3m1f	H Ch	G-S	£1477
112 3/99 Uttx	2m4f110yD Hdl	HVY	£2957
96 10/98 Sedg	2m1f	H NHF	G-S	£1255

Total win prize-money £8812

Going:	Sf: 0-0 GS: 0-0 Gd: 1-3 GF: - Fm: 0-0
Distance:	2m/2m3: 0-0 2m4-2m7: 0-1 **3m+: 1-2**
Track:	LH: **1-2** RH: 0-1 Tight: **1-1** Gall: 0-1
Aids:	Bl: 0-0 Vi: 0-0 Tstrap: 0-0 Ckp: 0-0
Best Rating:	**112** 3/99 Uttx 2m4f110y heavy Hdl

Modest hunter chaser; stays three miles; acts well on good
ground.

Westfield John

9-y-o ch g Little Wolf-Moonbreaker (Twilight Alley)
J M Turner J M Turner

Placings:00/0004/3-2P   (4775)
2003/04: 26²G, 21⁸G,

	Starts	1st	2nd	3rd	Win & Pl
Chases	2	0	1	0	434
Career Total	9	0	1	1	770

Going:	Sf: 0-0 GS: 0-0 Gd: 0-1 GF: - Fm: 0-1
Distance:	2m/2m3: 0-0 2m4-2m7: 0-1 3m+: 0-1
Track:	LH: 0-1 RH: 0-1 Tight: 0-2 Gall: 0-0
Aids:	Bl: 0-1 Vi: 0-0 Tstrap: 0-0 Ckp: 0-0
Best Rating:	**96** 10/00 Chel 2m110y good NHF

Westgate Run
103   95

7-y-o b m Emperor Jones (USA)-Glowing Reference
(Reference Point)

R A Fahey Mark A Leatham

Placings:433102-33220 (0794)
2003/04: 16³G, 16³G, 16²GF, 16²G, 16⁶G,

	Starts	1st	2nd	3rd	Win & Pl
Hurdles	5	0	2	2	4425
Career Total	11	1	3	4	9104
90	10/02 Hexm 2m110y E Hdl			GD	£2936

Total win prize-money £2937

Going:	Sf: 0-0 GS: 0-0 Gd: 0-4 GF: - Fm: 0-1
Distance:	2m/2m3: 0-5 2m4-2m7: 0-0 3m+: 0-1
Track:	LH: 0-2 RH: 0-3 Tight: 0-0 Gall: 0-0
Aids:	Bl: 0-0 Vi: 0-0 Tstrap: 0-0 Ckp: 0-0
Best Rating:	95 6/03 Prth 2m110y good Hdl

Plating-class hurdler; effective at around two miles and acts on a sound surface; consistent.

Westmeath Flyer
99   111
9-y-o b g Deploy-Re-Release (Baptism)
N G Richards Jim Ennis

Placings:2/22221/2F312/5F (3360)
2003/04: 16⁵S, 16⁶S,

	Starts	1st	2nd	3rd	Win & Pl
Hurdles	2	0	0	0	0
Career Total	13	2	7	1	17688
124	12/01 Hayd 2m4f			C(0-135)HHdl	HVY £5343
110	2/01 Catt 2m3f			E Hdl	SFT £3262

Total win prize-money £8605

Going:	Sf: 0-2 GS: 0-0 Gd: 0-0 GF: - Fm: 0-0
Distance:	2m/2m3: 0-2 2m4-2m7: 0-0 3m+: 0-0
Track:	LH: 0-2 RH: 0-0 Tight: 0-1 Gall: 0-0
Aids:	Bl: 0-0 Vi: 0-0 Tstrap: 0-0 Ckp: 0-0
Best Rating:	129 1/02 Hayd 2m4f soft Hdl

Fair hurdler; made jumping errors when tried over fences; acts well on a soft surface; effective at around two and a half miles.

Westmorland (IRE)

(105h)   (108+h)
8-y-o b g Phardante (FR)-Ticking Over (IRE) (Decent Fellow)
D R MacLeod Maurice W Chapman

Placings:000P/001F1/1-F (4274)
2003/04: 20ᶠG,

	Starts	1st	2nd	3rd	Win & Pl
Chases	1	0	0	0	
Career Total	11	3	0	0	7816
108	5/02 Hexm 3m			F(0-100)HHdl	GD £2943
97	4/02 Carl 3m110y			E(0-105)HHdl	GD £3108
85	3/02 Sedg 2m5f110yG(0-90)HHdl				SFT £1764

Total win prize-money £7816

Going:	Sf: 0-0 GS: 0-0 Gd: 0-1 GF: - Fm: 0-0
Distance:	2m/2m3: 0-0 2m4-2m7: 0-1 3m+: 0-0
Track:	LH: 0-0 RH: 0-1 Tight: 0-0 Gall: 0-0
Aids:	Bl: 0-0 Vi: 0-0 Tstrap: 0-0 Ckp: 0-0
Best Rating:	108 5/02 Hexm 3m good Hdl

Modest hurdler/chaser; acts on any ground; stays three miles.

Weston Rock
106   99
5-y-o b g Double Eclipse (IRE)-Mossberry Fair (Mossberry)
T D Walford Mrs H Spath

Placings:6-2534530 (4255)
2003/04: 17²GF, 16⁵G, 16³S, 20⁴S, 16⁵G, 19³G, 24⁹G,

	Starts	1st	2nd	3rd	Win & Pl
NH Flat	3	0	1	1	892
Hurdles	4	0	0	1	885
Career Total	8	0	1	2	1777

Going:	Sf: 0-2 GS: 0-0 Gd: 0-4 GF: - Fm: 0-1
Distance:	2m/2m3: 0-5 2m4-2m7: 0-1 3m+: 0-1
Track:	LH: 0-6 RH: 0-1 Tight: 0-2 Gall: 0-1
Aids:	Bl: 0-0 Vi: 0-0 Tstrap: 0-0 Ckp: 0-0
Best Rating:	99 3/04 Bang 3m good Hdl

Moderate bumper performer who showed ability on hurdles debut in December 2003; effective over two miles but looks to need further; acts on fast and soft ground.

Wet Lips (AUS)
112   108+
6-y-o ch g Grand Lodge (USA)-Kissing (AUS) (Somalia (AUS))
R C Guest Concertina Racing Three

Placings:3F2213 (4210)
2003/04: 17³GF, 16ᶠS, 16²GS, 20²GF, 16¹F, 16³G,

	Starts	1st	2nd	3rd	Win & Pl
Hurdles	6	1	2	2	13195
Career Total	6	1	2	2	13195
108	2/04 Muss 2m			C(0-130)HHdl	FRM £10023

Total win prize-money £10023

Going:	Sf: 0-1 GS: 0-1 Gd: 0-1 GF: - Fm: 1-3
Distance:	2m/2m3: 1-5 2m4-2m7: 0-1 3m+: 0-0
Track:	LH: 0-3 RH: 1-3 Tight: 1-4 Gall: 0-1
Aids:	Bl: 0-0 Vi: 0-0 Tstrap: 0-0 Ckp: 1-2
Best Rating:	108 3/04 Kemp 2m good Hdl

Modest novice hurdler; ex-Australian; effective at around two and two and a half miles; acts on most types of ground; has worn cheekpieces.

Wethaab (USA)

7-y-o b g Pleasant Colony (USA)-Binntastic (USA) (Lyphard's Wish (FR))
Miss A Stokell Ms Caron Stokell

Placings:P/P0/P (0466)
2003/04: 16ᴾG,

	Starts	1st	2nd	3rd	Win & Pl
Hurdles	1	0	0	0	0
Career Total	4	0	0	0	0

Going:	Sf: 0-0 GS: 0-0 Gd: 0-1 GF: - Fm: 0-0
Distance:	2m/2m3: 0-1 2m4-2m7: 0-0 3m+: 0-0
Track:	LH: 0-1 RH: 0-0 Tight: 0-0 Gall: 0-0
Aids:	Bl: 0-0 Vi: 0-0 Tstrap: 0-0 Ckp: 0-1

Wexford (IRE)

10-y-o ch g Be My Native (USA)-Mizuna (Ballymore)
Miss S K Lamb Miss S K Lamb

Placings:0/500/0322P/00F603000P/P (0044)
2003/04: 25ᴾG,

	Starts	1st	2nd	3rd	Win & Pl
Chases	1	0	0	0	
Career Total	20	0	2	2	3745

Whaleef

(102h)   (110 h)
6-y-o br g Darshaan-Wilayif (USA) (Danzig (USA))
P R Webber Mrs P Sherwood

Placings:60-115103 (2074)
2003/04: 17¹G, 16¹GF, 17⁵GF, 17¹G, 16⁹GF, 16³GF,

	Starts	1st	2nd	3rd	Win & Pl
Hurdles	6	3	0	1	15368
Career Total	8	3	0	1	15368
110	10/03 Bang 2m1f			D(0-115)HHdl	GD £5694
110	8/03 Prth 2m110y E Hdl				G-F £4095
85	8/03 Bang 2m1f			D Hdl	GD £4907

Total win prize-money £14697

Going:	Sf: 0-0 GS: 0-0 Gd: 2-2 GF: - Fm: 1-4
Distance:	2m/2m3: 3-6 2m4-2m7: 0-0 3m+: 0-0
Track:	LH: 2-4 RH: 1-2 Tight: 2-2 Gall: 0-1
Aids:	Bl: 0-0 Vi: 0-0 Tstrap: 0-0 Ckp: 0-0
Best Rating:	110 10/03 Bang 2m1f good Hdl

Modest hurdler; ready winner of a couple of novice hurdles in August 2003; disappointing on handicap debut but bounced back to land a handicap at Bangor in October; best at around 2m; needs the top of the ground.

What A Fiddler (IRE)

11-y-o ch g Orchestra-Crowenstown Miss (Over The River (FR))
J S Haldane J S Haldane

Placings:2/24/5P23/15/16-P3 (0360)
2003/04: 25ᴾG, 25³G,

	Starts	1st	2nd	3rd	Win & Pl
Chases	2	0	0	1	446
Career Total	13	2	3	2	8106
89	6/02 Ctml 3m2f			H Ch	G-S £2730
105	5/01 Hexm 3m1f			H Ch	SFT £2483

Total win prize-money £5213

Going:	Sf: 0-0 GS: 0-0 Gd: 0-2 GF: - Fm: 0-0
Distance:	2m/2m3: 0-0 2m4-2m7: 0-0 3m+: 0-2
Track:	LH: 0-2 RH: 0-0 Tight: 0-1 Gall: 0-0
Aids:	Bl: 0-0 Vi: 0-0 Tstrap: 0-0 Ckp: 0-0
Best Rating:	105 5/01 Hexm 3m1f soft Ch

Moderate hunter chaser; stays three miles; acts on good ground.

What A Monday
94   96
6-y-o b g Beveled (USA)-Raise Memories (Skyliner)
K Bell North Farm Partnership

Placings:103-40 (3042)
2003/04: 17⁴G, 16⁹GS,

	Starts	1st	2nd	3rd	Win & Pl
NH Flat	1	0	0	0	0
Hurdles	1	0	0	0	0
Career Total	5	1	0	1	1810
104	6/02 Worc 2m			H NHF	SFT £1523

Total win prize-money £1523

Going:	Sf: 0-0 GS: 0-1 Gd: 0-1 GF: - Fm: 0-0
Distance:	2m/2m3: 0-2 2m4-2m7: 0-0 3m+: 0-0

Track:	LH: 0-2 RH: 0-0 Tight: 0-1 Gall: 0-1
Aids:	Bl: 0-0 Vi: 0-0 Tstrap: 0-0 Gall: 0-1
Best Rating:	105 12/03 Newb 2m110y gd-sft Hdl

Has done well in bumpers under his penalty since winning on his debut; effective at two miles; acts on good ground.

What A Racket

59   28

5-y-o b/br m Beveled (USA)-Bunny Gee (Last Tycoon)
Mrs D A Hamer M Duthie

Placings:0P   (2116)
2003/04: 16⁰G, 16⁰GF,

	Starts	1st	2nd	3rd	Win & Pl
Hurdles	2	0	0	0	
Career Total	2	0	0	0	

Going:	Sf: 0-0 GS: 0-0 Gd: 0-1 GF: - Fm: 0-1
Distance:	2m/2m3: 0-2 2m4-2m7: 0-0 3m+: 0-0
Track:	LH: 0-0 RH: 0-2 Tight: 0-0 Gall: 0-0
Aids:	Bl: 0-0 Vi: 0-1 Tstrap: 0-0 Ckp: 0-1
Best Rating:	28 11/03 Towc 2m good Hdl

What A Wonder (IRE)

95(95h)   (114h)82

9-y-o gr g Roselier (FR)-Lady Abednego Vii (Damsire Unregistered)
Ferdy Murphy The Sheepscar Syndicate

Placings:0/222121/24U4P01/554540-4FP   (2932)
2003/04: 28⁴GS, 25⁴S, 27⁰G,

	Starts	1st	2nd	3rd	Win & Pl
Chases	3	0	0	0	0
Career Total	23	3	5	0	17648
116	4/02	Prth	3m110y	E(0-105)HHdl	GD	£4654
120	4/01	Prth	3m110y	F(0-105)HHdl	HVY	£3514
106	2/01	Muss	3m	D(0-110)HHdl	GD	£3458
				Total win prize-money £11626	

Going:	Sf: 0-1 GS: 0-1 Gd: 0-1 GF: - Fm: 0-0
Distance:	2m/2m3: 0-0 2m4-2m7: 0-0 3m+: 0-3
Track:	LH: 0-1 RH: 0-2 Tight: 0-2 Gall: 0-0
Aids:	Bl: 0-3 Vi: 0-0 Tstrap: 0-0 Ckp: 0-0
Best Rating:	120 4/01 Prth 3m110y heavy Hdl

Plating-class chaser/modest hurdler; suited by a sharp right-handed track; acts on any ground; stays really well.

What Do'In (IRE)

108f   110f

6-y-o b/br g Good Thyne (USA)-Della Wee (IRE) (Fidel)
N A Twiston-Davies C Cornes

Placings:14   (2187)
2003/04: 16¹G, 16⁴G,

	Starts	1st	2nd	3rd	Win & Pl
NH Flat	2	1	0	0	2762
Career Total	2	1	0	0	2762
107	9/03	Prth	2m110y	H NHF	GD	£1918
				Total win prize-money £1918	

Going:	Sf: 0-0 GS: 0-0 Gd: 1-2 GF: - Fm: 0-0
Distance:	2m/2m3: 1-2 2m4-2m7: 0-0 3m+: 0-0
Track:	LH: 0-1 RH: 1-1 Tight: 0-0 Gall: 0-0
Aids:	Bl: 0-0 Vi: 0-0 Tstrap: 0-0 Ckp: 0-0
Best Rating:	107 11/03 Chel 2m110y good NHF

What If (IRE)

105   101

7-y-o b g Lord Americo-Romany River (Over The River (FR))
I Buchanan I Buchanan

Placings:33-5240   (2107a)
2003/04: 16⁵G, 16²GF, 16⁴GF, 20⁰GY,

	Starts	1st	2nd	3rd	Win & Pl
Hurdles	4	0	1	0	1766
Career Total	6	0	1	2	2473

Going:	Sf: 0-0 GS: 0-0 Gd: 0-1 GF: - Fm: 0-2
Distance:	2m/2m3: 0-3 2m4-2m7: 0-1 3m+: 0-0
Track:	LH: 0-2 RH: 0-1 Tight: 0-0 Gall: 0-0
Aids:	Bl: 0-0 Vi: 0-0 Tstrap: 0-0 Ckp: 0-0
Best Rating:	107 1/03 DRoy 2m soft NHF

What Odds (IRE)

99   131

8-y-o b g Torus-Merrywell (Mugatpura)
T K Geraghty Dee Racing Syndicate

Placings:P1-113PPP0   (4805a)
2003/04: 25¹G, 29¹S, 29³GS, 28⁰HY, 33⁰PG, 28⁰GY, 29⁰Y,

	Starts	1st	2nd	3rd	Win & Pl
Chases	7	2	0	1	38691
Career Total	9	3	0	1	43171
131	11/03	Fair	3m5f	(0-140)HCh	SFT	£16038
112	4/03	Punc	3m1f	Ch	GD	£10551
110	2/03	Fair	3m1f	Ch	Y-S	£4480
				Total win prize-money £31072	

Going:	Sf: 1-2 GS: 0-1 Gd: 1-2 GF: - Fm: 0-0
Distance:	2m/2m3: 0-0 2m4-2m7: 0-0 3m+: 2-7
Track:	LH: 0-2 RH: 2-3 Tight: 0-0 Gall: 0-0
Aids:	Bl: 0-0 Vi: 0-0 Tstrap: 0-0 Ckp: 0-0
Best Rating:	131 11/03 Fair 3m5f soft Ch

Useful Irish staying chaser; likes to front run; former decent point-to-point winner; stays three miles five; acts on most ground, but prefers cut; progressing.

What You Know (IRE)

105   86+

10-y-o b g Be My Guest (USA)-Flamme D'Amour (Gift Card (FR))
Mrs D A Hamer Mrs Ashley Davies

Placings:305/04PP/011000-22P146   (2364)
2003/04: 17²GF, 22²GF, 20⁶G, 21¹GF, 24⁴G, 24⁶GF,

	Starts	1st	2nd	3rd	Win & Pl
Hurdles	6	1	2	0	5063
Career Total	19	3	2	1	9815
86	10/03	Ludl	2m5f	F(0-90)Hdl	G-F	£2905
81	10/02	Extr	2m3f	G(0-95)HHdl	FRM	£2282
79	9/02	Worc	2m	G(0-90)HHdl	GD	£2301
				Total win prize-money £7489	

Going:	Sf: 0-0 GS: 0-0 Gd: 0-2 GF: - Fm: 1-4
Distance:	2m/2m3: 0-1 2m4-2m7: 1-3 3m+: 0-2
Track:	LH: 0-3 RH: 1-3 Tight: 0-3 Gall: 0-0
Aids:	Bl: 0-0 Vi: 0-0 Tstrap: 0-0 Ckp: 0-0
Best Rating:	89 9/98 Hntg 2m110y gd-fm NHF

Plating-class hurdler; stays 2m 6f; acts on fast ground.

What's A Filly

80f   55f

4-y-o b f Bob's Return (IRE)-Pearly-B (IRE) (Gunner B)
R C Guest The Don't Tell Pat Partnership

Placings:00   (3887)
2003/04: 16⁰HY, 16⁰G,

	Starts	1st	2nd	3rd	Win & Pl
NH Flat	2	0	0	0	
Career Total	2	0	0	0	

Going:	Sf: 0-1 GS: 0-0 Gd: 0-1 GF: - Fm: 0-0
Distance:	2m/2m3: 0-2 2m4-2m7: 0-0 3m+: 0-0
Track:	LH: 0-1 RH: 0-1 Tight: 0-1 Gall: 0-0
Aids:	Bl: 0-0 Vi: 0-0 Tstrap: 0-0 Ckp: 0-0
Best Rating:	59 2/04 Muss 2m good NHF

What's The Count

97(104h)   (107h)107+

8-y-o gr g Theatrical Charmer-Yankee Silver (Yankee Gold)
B R Johnson The Twenty Five Club

Placings:0/500/P/5342200-033   (4791)
2003/04: 20⁶GD, 20⁰S, 20⁰G,

	Starts	1st	2nd	3rd	Win & Pl
Hurdles	1	0	0	0	0
Chases	2	0	0	2	1041
Career Total	15	0	2	3	4659

Going:	Sf: 0-1 GS: 0-0 Gd: 0-1 GF: - Fm: 0-1
Distance:	2m/2m3: 0-0 2m4-2m7: 0-3 3m+: 0-0
Track:	LH: 0-2 RH: 0-1 Tight: 0-1 Gall: 0-0
Aids:	Bl: 0-0 Vi: 0-0 Tstrap: 0-2 Ckp: 0-0
Best Rating:	107 2/03 Plum 2m5f heavy Hdl

Modest maiden hurdler; stays two miles five furlongs; acts on a soft surface; often tongue tied.

What's Up Boys (IRE)

98   123

10-y-o gr g Supreme Leader-Maryville Bick (Malacate (USA))
P J Hobbs Mrs J F Deithrick

Placings:62126/11P313/12F1112/14P52/F-4BP   (4965)
2003/04: 25⁴G, 36⁶G, 29⁰GF,

	Starts	1st	2nd	3rd	Win & Pl
Chases	3	0	0	0	2500
Career Total	27	9	5	2	354890
157	12/01	Newb	3m2f110yA HCh	SFT	£58000
155	4/01	Aint	3m1f	A Ch	SFT	£50250
141	2/01	Ludl	3m	E Ch	G-S	£3750
123	12/00	Muss	2m4f	D Ch	GD	£4641
149	5/00	Punc	2m4f	Hdl	GD	£24800
149	3/00	Chel	2m5f	A HHdl	GD	£39000
146	2/99	Sand	2m6f	A Hdl	G-S	£9525
119	11/99	Folk	2m4f110yF Hdl	G-S	£1499
104	12/98	Punc	2m	NHF	SH	£2989
			Total win prize-money £194455	

Going:	Sf: 0-0 GS: 0-0 Gd: 0-2 GF: - Fm: 0-1
Distance:	2m/2m3: 0-0 2m4-2m7: 0-0 3m+: 0-3
Track:	LH: 0-1 RH: 0-2 Tight: 0-1 Gall: 0-0
Aids:	Bl: 0-3 Vi: 0-0 Tstrap: 0-0 Ckp: 0-0
Best Rating:	160 4/02 Aint 4m4f good Ch

High-class chaser; formerly very smart hurdler; game winner of the 2001 Hennessy and a fine second in the 2002 Grand

National; took a heavy fall in the Charlie Hall Chase on his reappearance in November 2002 and absent until satisfactory return in February; early casualty in the Grand National; stays well and is usually a very sound jumper; effective on good ground or softer; tough; blinkered nowadays.

Whatacharlie

(79h)   (51h)**52**
10-y-o b g Nicholas Bill-Zulu Dancer (Sula Bula)
D P Keane D P Keane

Placings:PF/03-5   (0273)
2003/04: 22⁵GF,

	Starts	1st	2nd	3rd	Win & Pl
Hurdles	1	0	0	0	0
Career Total	5	0	0	1	480

Going: Sf: 0-0 GS: 0-0 Gd: 0-0 GF: - Fm: 0-1
Distance: 2m/2m3: 0-0 2m4-2m7: 0-0 3m+: 0-0
Track: LH: 0-0 RH: 0-1 Tight: 0-0 Gall: 0-0
Aids: Bl: 0-0 Vi: 0-0 Tstrap: 0-0 Ckp: 0-0
Best Rating: 52 4/03 Asct 2m3f110y good Ch

Poor chaser; winning pointer; yet to show any worthwhile form under Rules.

Whatashock

97   93+
9-y-o b g Never So Bold-Lady Electric (Electric)
A King J L Frampton & A J Coombes

Placings:00/P-443   (4821)
2003/04: 19⁴S, 21⁴GF, 19³GF,

	Starts	1st	2nd	3rd	Win & Pl
Chases	3	0	0	1	1419
Career Total	6	0	0	1	1419

Going: Sf: 0-1 GS: 0-1 Gd: 0-0 GF: - Fm: 0-1
Distance: 2m/2m3: 0-0 2m4-2m7: 0-3 3m+: 0-0
Track: LH: 0-1 RH: 0-2 Tight: 0-0 Gall: 0-0
Aids: Bl: 0-0 Vi: 0-0 Tstrap: 0-0 Ckp: 0-0
Best Rating: 98 12/03 Chep 2m3f110y soft Ch

A multiple point-to-point winner; he stays three miles; acts on a sound surface.

Whatasucker (IRE)

(90h)   (40h)
10-y-o ch g Meneval (USA)-Tuney Blade (Fine Blade (USA))
B D Leavy M Braycotton

Placings:0/PUF/P/F0   (4000)
2003/04: 24⁴S, 26⁰G,

	Starts	1st	2nd	3rd	Win & Pl
Hurdles	1	0	0	0	0
Chases	1	0	0	0	0
Career Total	7	0	0	0	

Going: Sf: 0-1 GS: 0-0 Gd: 0-1 GF: - Fm: 0-0
Distance: 2m/2m3: 0-0 2m4-2m7: 0-0 3m+: 0-2
Track: LH: 0-1 RH: 0-1 Tight: 0-0 Gall: 0-0
Aids: Bl: 0-0 Vi: 0-0 Tstrap: 0-0 Ckp: 0-1
Best Rating: 40 2/04 Ludl 3m2f110y good Hdl

Whatchowillie (IRE)

10-y-o br g Un Desperado (FR)-Hooch (Warpath)

M A Kemp I A Low

Placings:14335000/041010/FPFP00/5   (0160)
2003/04: 24⁵GF,

	Starts	1st	2nd	3rd	Win & Pl
Chases	1	0	0	0	0
Career Total	21	3	0	2	14115
102 8/00 Gway 2m4f	(0-116)HHdl		G-Y		£6072
95 7/00 Bell 3m	Hdl			G-F	£3174
90 7/99 Gway 2m2f	NHF			G-F	£3836
			Total win prize-money £13083		

Going: Sf: 0-0 GS: 0-0 Gd: 0-0 GF: - Fm: 0-0
Distance: 2m/2m3: 0-0 2m4-2m7: 0-0 3m+: 0-1
Track: LH: 0-1 RH: 0-0 Tight: 0-1 Gall: 0-0
Aids: Bl: 0-0 Vi: 0-0 Tstrap: 0-0 Ckp: 0-0
Best Rating: 102 8/00 Gway 2m4f gd-yld Hdl

Whatdo You Want (IRE)

79f   39f
4-y-o b f Spectrum (IRE)-Soviet Pretender (USA) (Alleged (USA))
M W Easterby Guy Reed

Placings:00   (4885)
2003/04: 16⁰S, 17⁹GS,

	Starts	1st	2nd	3rd	Win & Pl
NH Flat	2	0	0	0	
Career Total	2	0	0	0	

Going: Sf: 0-1 GS: 0-1 Gd: 0-0 GF: - Fm: 0-0
Distance: 2m/2m3: 0-2 2m4-2m7: 0-0 3m+: 0-0
Track: LH: 0-1 RH: 0-1 Tight: 0-0 Gall: 0-0
Aids: Bl: 0-0 Vi: 0-0 Tstrap: 0-0 Ckp: 0-0
Best Rating: 39 2/04 Weth 2m soft NHF

Whats Good (IRE)

61f   39f
6-y-o b/br g Religiously (USA)-Islet Time (Burslem)
K C Bailey Mrs Bettine Evans

Placings:00   (4594)
2003/04: 17⁰GS, 16⁰G,

	Starts	1st	2nd	3rd	Win & Pl
NH Flat	2	0	0	0	
Career Total	2	0	0	0	

Going: Sf: 0-0 GS: 0-1 Gd: 0-1 GF: - Fm: 0-0
Distance: 2m/2m3: 0-2 2m4-2m7: 0-0 3m+: 0-0
Track: LH: 0-0 RH: 0-2 Tight: 0-0 Gall: 0-1
Aids: Bl: 0-0 Vi: 0-0 Tstrap: 0-0 Ckp: 0-0
Best Rating: 39 12/03 Hrfd 2m1f gd-sft NHF

Where's Trigger

85f   69f
4-y-o ch g Aristocracy-Queens Connection (Bay Express)
N A Twiston-Davies C Cornes

Placings:0   (4816)
2003/04: 16⁰G,

	Starts	1st	2nd	3rd	Win & Pl
NH Flat	1	0	0	0	
Career Total	1	0	0	0	

Going: Sf: 0-0 GS: 0-0 Gd: 0-1 GF: - Fm: 0-0

Distance: 2m/2m3: 0-1 2m4-2m7: 0-0 3m+: 0-0
Track: LH: 0-1 RH: 0-0 Tight: 0-0 Gall: 0-0
Aids: Bl: 0-0 Vi: 0-0 Tstrap: 0-0 Ckp: 0-0
Best Rating: 69 4/04 Chep 2m10y good NHF

Whereareyounow (IRE)

120(97h)   (115h)**147**
7-y-o ch g Mister Lord (USA)-Angies Delight (London Gazette)
N A Twiston-Davies H R Mould

Placings:4553420-1134100F2   (4910)
2003/04: 20¹G, 24¹GF, 21³GS, 25⁴G, 21¹G, 21⁹GS, 20⁹G, 21⁶G, 24⁴S,

	Starts	1st	2nd	3rd	Win & Pl
Chases	9	3	1	1	51606
Career Total	16	3	2	2	63799
144 1/04 Chel 2m5f	B HCh		GD		£23200
133 11/03 Chel 3m110y	B Ch		G-F		£14137
140 10/03 Strf 2m4f	D Ch		GD		£5088
			Total win prize-money £42425		

Going: Sf: 0-1 GS: 0-2 Gd: 2-5 GF: - Fm: 1-1
Distance: 2m/2m3: 0-0 **2m4-2m7: 2-6** 3m+: 1-3
Track: **LH: 3-8** RH: 0-1 Tight: 1-3 **Gall: 2-5**
Aids: Bl: 0-0 Vi: 0-0 Tstrap: 0-0 Ckp: 0-0
Best Rating: 144 1/04 Chel 2m5f good Ch

Useful novice chaser; highly tried in 2002/3; stays three miles but possibly better at shorter, winning a valuable handicap at Cheltenham on New Year's Day 2004; held since in better company; acts on any ground.

Whether The Storm (IRE)

8-y-o b g Glacial Storm (USA)-Minimum Choice (IRE) (Miners Lamp)
Miss I E Craig Miss I E L Craig

Placings:3/441/0/44P-13   (4675)
2003/04: 24¹G, 25³G,

	Starts	1st	2nd	3rd	Win & Pl
Chases	2	1	0	1	2616
Career Total	10	2	0	2	7211
112 3/04 Bang 3m110y	H Ch		GD		£2299
109 12/00 Newb 2m3f	D Hdl		SFT		£3623
			Total win prize-money £5924		

Going: Sf: 0-0 GS: 0-0 Gd: 1-2 GF: - Fm: 0-0
Distance: 2m/2m3: 0-0 2m4-2m7: 0-0 **3m+: 1-2**
Track: **LH: 1-1** RH: 0-1 **Tight: 1-1** Gall: 0-0
Aids: Bl: 0-0 Vi: 0-0 Tstrap: 0-0 Ckp: 0-0
Best Rating: 112 3/04 Bang 3m110y good Ch

Hunter chaser; stays three miles; acts on good ground.

Whispered Secret (GER)

102   116+
5-y-o b g Selkirk (USA)-Wells Whisper (FR) (Sadler's Wells (USA))
M C Pipe (R C Guest 28/3) D Levine

Placings:43P2   (4892)
2003/04: 16⁴G, 17³G, 16⁶G, 16²GF,

	Starts	1st	2nd	3rd	Win & Pl
Hurdles	4	0	1	1	2701
Career Total	4	0	1	1	2701

Going:	Sf: 0-0 GS: 0-0 Gd: 0-3 GF: - Fm: 0-1
Distance:	2m/2m3: 0-4 2m4-2m7: 0-0 3m+: 0-0
Track:	LH: 0-2 RH: 0-2 Tight: 0-2 Gall: 0-1
Aids:	Bl: 0-0 Vi: 0-0 Tstrap: 0-0 Ckp: 0-0
Best Rating:	116 4/04 Strf 2m110y gd-fm Hdl

Fair hurdler; suited by a spund surface.

Whispering Holly
87   43

5-y-o b g Holly Buoy-Stuart's Gem (Meldrum)
R S Wood   R S Wood

Placings:0-00006   (4660)
2003/04: 17⁰GF, 17⁰GF, 16⁶GS, 16⁰HY, 24⁶S,

	Starts	1st	2nd	3rd	Win & Pl
NH Flat	3	0	0	0	0
Hurdles	2	0	0	0	0
Career Total	**6**	**0**	**0**	**0**	

Going:	Sf: 0-2 GS: 0-1 Gd: 0-0 GF: - Fm: 0-2
Distance:	2m/2m3: 0-4 2m4-2m7: 0-0 3m+: 0-1
Track:	LH: 0-4 RH: 0-1 Tight: 0-1 Gall: 0-1
Aids:	Bl: 0-0 Vi: 0-0 Tstrap: 0-0 Ckp: 0-0
Best Rating:	50 4/04 Hexm 3m soft Hdl

Whispering John
(IRE)
96(104h)   (111h)107+

8-y-o b g Grand Plaisir (IRE)-London Anne (London Bells (CAN))
Ms Bridget Nicholls   Premiership Racing

Placings:200F-4   (2569)
2003/04: 23⁴G,

	Starts	1st	2nd	3rd	Win & Pl
Chases	1	0	0	0	301
Career Total	**5**	**0**	**1**	**0**	**1980**

Going:	Sf: 0-0 GS: 0-0 Gd: 0-1 GF: - Fm: 0-0
Distance:	2m/2m3: 0-0 2m4-2m7: 0-0 3m+: 0-1
Track:	LH: 0-0 RH: 0-1 Tight: 0-0 Gall: 0-0
Aids:	Bl: 0-0 Vi: 0-0 Tstrap: 0-0 Ckp: 0-0
Best Rating:	111 11/02 Extr 2m3f gd-sft Hdl

Modest chaser/hurdler; acts on good or easier.

Whispering Moor
95f   78f

5-y-o br g Terimon-Larksmore (Royal Fountain)
N W Alexander   Mrs Nicholas Alexander

Placings:604   (4952)
2003/04: 16⁶HY, 16⁰GS, 16⁴GS,

	Starts	1st	2nd	3rd	Win & Pl
NH Flat	3	0	0	0	0
Career Total	**3**	**0**	**0**	**0**	

Going:	Sf: 0-1 GS: 0-2 Gd: 0-0 GF: - Fm: 0-0
Distance:	2m/2m3: 0-3 2m4-2m7: 0-0 3m+: 0-0
Track:	LH: 0-2 RH: 0-1 Tight: 0-0 Gall: 0-0
Aids:	Bl: 0-0 Vi: 0-0 Tstrap: 0-0 Ckp: 0-0
Best Rating:	78 4/04 Prth 2m110y gd-sft NHF

Full-brother to bumper winner Roman Ark; hinted at ability on debut in heavy ground Ayr bumper in January 2004; may be capable of better.

Whispering Storm
(IRE)
90f   88f

6-y-o br g Good Thyne (USA)-Ballybride Gale (IRE) (Strong Gale)
A King   Mrs A Shutes,A Sheppard,A Humbert

Placings:0-5   (4550)
2003/04: 17⁰S, 16⁵GS,

	Starts	1st	2nd	3rd	Win & Pl
NH Flat	2	0	0	0	0
Career Total	**2**	**0**	**0**	**0**	

Going:	Sf: 0-1 GS: 0-1 Gd: 0-0 GF: - Fm: 0-0
Distance:	2m/2m3: 0-2 2m4-2m7: 0-0 3m+: 0-0
Track:	LH: 0-1 RH: 0-1 Tight: 0-1 Gall: 0-0
Aids:	Bl: 0-0 Vi: 0-0 Tstrap: 0-0 Ckp: 0-0
Best Rating:	88 3/04 Winc 2m gd-sft NHF

Whist Drive
101   99

4-y-o ch g First Trump-Fine Quill (Unfuwain (USA))
Mrs N Smith (J L Dunlop 13/6)   Tony Hayward And Barry Fulton

Placings:63434   (4452)
2003/04: 17⁶S, 16³G, 16⁴GS, 18³G, 16⁴GS,

	Starts	1st	2nd	3rd	Win & Pl
Hurdles	5	0	0	2	1174
Career Total	**5**	**0**	**0**	**2**	**1174**

Going:	Sf: 0-0 GS: 0-2 Gd: 0-3 GF: - Fm: 0-0
Distance:	2m/2m3: 0-5 2m4-2m7: 0-0 3m+: 0-0
Track:	LH: 0-1 RH: 0-4 Tight: 0-0 Gall: 0-0
Aids:	Bl: 0-0 Vi: 0-0 Tstrap: 0-0 Ckp: 0-0
Best Rating:	99 3/04 Asct 2m110y gd-sft Hdl

Moderate juvenile hurdler; acts on a sound surface.

Whistling Song
88   42

9-y-o ch m True Song-Sancal (Whistlefield)
R Dickin   Haydn Gott And Claire Dickin

Placings:04P/F-43   (0441)
2003/04: 20⁴HY, 19³GF,

	Starts	1st	2nd	3rd	Win & Pl
Chases	2	0	0	1	972
Career Total	**6**	**0**	**0**	**1**	**1231**

Going:	Sf: 0-1 GS: 0-0 Gd: 0-0 GF: - Fm: 0-1
Distance:	2m/2m3: 0-1 2m4-2m7: 0-1 3m+: 0-0
Track:	LH: 0-1 RH: 0-1 Tight: 0-0 Gall: 0-0
Aids:	Bl: 0-0 Vi: 0-0 Tstrap: 0-0 Ckp: 0-0
Best Rating:	75 3/02 Hrfd 3m1f110y good Ch

Poor form over fences; headstrong.

Whitaside (IRE)
104

10-y-o b/br g Brush Aside (USA)-Flying Silver (Master Buck)
Mrs S J Smith   Ashleybank Investments Limited

Placings:212-P   (0412)
2003/04: 20²PG,

	Starts	1st	2nd	3rd	Win & Pl
Hurdles	1	0	0	0	

Career Total	4	1	2	0	4805
104	10/02 Hexm	2m4f110y		E Hdl	GD
£2936					

Total win prize-money £2937

Going:	Sf: 0-0 GS: 0-0 Gd: 0-1 GF: - Fm: 0-0
Distance:	2m/2m3: 0-0 2m4-2m7: 0-1 3m+: 0-0
Track:	LH: 0-1 RH: 0-0 Tight: 0-0 Gall: 0-0
Aids:	Bl: 0-0 Vi: 0-0 Tstrap: 0-0 Ckp: 0-0
Best Rating:	104 11/02 MRas 2m3f110y soft Hdl

Moderate hurdler, stays 2m4f; acts on good or softer.

White Dove (FR)
97(97h)   (84h)87

6-y-o b m Beaudelaire (USA)-Hermine And Pearls (FR) (Shirley Heights)
Ian Williams   Creme de la Creme

Placings:U634-2166   (4961)
2003/04: 16²GS, 16¹GS, 16⁶G, 20⁶GS,

	Starts	1st	2nd	3rd	Win & Pl
Hurdles	1	0	1	0	650
Chases	3	1	0	0	3848
Career Total	**8**	**1**	**1**	**1**	**5438**
87	2/04 Hrfd	2m	F(0-100)HCh	G-S	£3848

Total win prize-money £3848

Going:	Sf: 0-0 GS: 1-3 Gd: 0-1 GF: - Fm: 0-0
Distance:	2m/2m3: 1-3 2m4-2m7: 0-1 3m+: 0-0
Track:	LH: 0-2 RH: 1-2 Tight: 0-1 Gall: 0-2
Aids:	Bl: 0-0 Vi: 0-0 Tstrap: 0-0 Ckp: 0-0
Best Rating:	87 2/04 Hrfd 2m gd-sft Ch

Moderate novice hurdler; narrowly denied after a lengthy break at Doncaster in December; made a winning chase debut at Hereford in February.

White Park Bay
(IRE)

4-y-o b f Blues Traveller (IRE)-Valiant Friend (USA) (Shahrastani (USA))
J Gallagher (J J Quinn 20/9)   Tony Absolom

Placings:0   (4569)
2003/04: 17⁰GS,

	Starts	1st	2nd	3rd	Win & Pl
Hurdles	1	0	0	0	
Career Total	**1**	**0**	**0**	**0**	

Going:	Sf: 0-0 GS: 0-1 Gd: 0-0 GF: - Fm: 0-0
Distance:	2m/2m3: 0-1 2m4-2m7: 0-0 3m+: 0-0
Track:	LH: 0-1 RH: 0-0 Tight: 0-1 Gall: 0-0
Aids:	Bl: 0-0 Vi: 0-0 Tstrap: 0-0 Ckp: 0-0

Whitestone

8-y-o b m Sula Bula-Flying Cherub (Osiris)
Mrs J G Retter   Mrs J G Retter

Placings:0/0P0P   (4812)
2003/04: 21⁵GS, 21⁰GS, 16⁶PG,

	Starts	1st	2nd	3rd	Win & Pl
Hurdles	3	0	0	0	
Career Total	**4**	**0**	**0**	**0**	

Going:	Sf: 0-0 GS: 0-2 Gd: 0-1 GF: - Fm: 0-0
Distance:	2m/2m3: 0-1 2m4-2m7: 0-2 3m+: 0-0

Track:	LH: 0-2 RH: 0-1 Tight: 0-0 Gall: 0-1
Aids:	Bl: 0-0 Vi: 0-0 Tstrap: 0-0 Ckp: 0-0

Whitfield Warrior

70   **58**

6-y-o ch g Husyan (USA)-Valentines Day (Doctor Pangloss)
J R Turner Yarm Racing Partnership

Placings:4-PP0   (4732)
2003/04: 21PS, 20PGS, 17PG,

	Starts	1st	2nd	3rd	Win & Pl
Hurdles	3	0	0	0	
Career Total	4	0	0	0	0

Going:	Sf: 0-1 GS: 0-1 Gd: 0-1 GF: - Fm: 0-0
Distance:	2m/2m3: 0-1 2m4-2m7: 0-2 3m+: 0-0
Track:	LH: 0-1 RH: 0-2 Tight: 0-0 Gall: 0-1
Aids:	Bl: 0-0 Vi: 0-0 Tstrap: 0-0 Ckp: 0-0
Best Rating:	94 2/03 Weth 2m gd-sft NHF

Whitford Don (IRE)

106   **111**

6-y-o b g Accordion-Whitford Breeze (Le Bavard (FR))
P F Nicholls J Hales

Placings:U231   (4197)
2003/04: 19UGS, 22²GS, 24³HY, 241G,

	Starts	1st	2nd	3rd	Win & Pl
Hurdles	4	1	1	1	8319
Career Total	4	1	1	1	8319
110 3/04 Newb 3m110y D Hdl			GD		£6786

Total win prize-money £6786

Going:	Sf: 0-1 GS: 0-2 Gd: 1-1 GF: 0-0
Distance:	2m/2m3: 0-0 2m4-2m7: 0-2 3m+: 1-2
Track:	LH: 1-2 RH: 0-2 Tight: 0-1 Gall: 1-1
Aids:	Bl: 0-0 Vi: 0-0 Tstrap: 0-0 Ckp: 0-0
Best Rating:	110 3/04 Newb 3m110y good Hdl

Modest novice hurdler; broke his duck at Newbury over three miles in March; stays really well; acts on good or softer.

Whitley Grange Boy

87   (55h)**77**

11-y-o b g Hubbly Bubbly (USA)-Choir (High Top)
A J Lockwood Mrs Carole Sykes

Placings:103/P0/6FU63-0   (0414)
2003/04: 25⁰G,

	Starts	1st	2nd	3rd	Win & Pl
Chases	1	0	0	0	
Career Total	11	1	0	2	4193
107 10/99 Weth 2m4f110yD Hdl			G-F		£3187

Total win prize-money £3188

Going:	Sf: 0-0 GS: 0-0 Gd: 0-1 GF: - Fm: 0-0
Distance:	2m/2m3: 0-0 2m4-2m7: 0-0 3m+: 0-1
Track:	LH: 0-1 RH: 0-0 Tight: 0-0 Gall: 0-0
Aids:	Bl: 0-0 Vi: 0-0 Tstrap: 0-0 Ckp: 0-0
Best Rating:	107 10/99 Weth 2m4f110y gd-fm Hdl

Plating-class novice chaser; lightly raced of late; best on fast ground; stays well.

Whitton Park

95   **87**

4-y-o b g Sillery (USA)-Lady Golconda (FR) (Kendor (FR))

P F Nicholls (F Rohaut 24/8) The Eight Amigos Racing Syndicate

Placings:0B4   (3422)
2003/04: 16⁰S, 16⁸GS, 174HY,

	Starts	1st	2nd	3rd	Win & Pl
Hurdles	3	0	0	0	0
Career Total	3	0	0	0	0

Going:	Sf: 0-2 GS: 0-1 Gd: 0-0 GF: - Fm: 0-0
Distance:	2m/2m3: 0-3 2m4-2m7: 0-0 3m+: 0-0
Track:	LH: 0-1 RH: 0-2 Tight: 0-1 Gall: 0-0
Aids:	Bl: 0-0 Vi: 0-0 Tstrap: 0-0 Ckp: 0-0
Best Rating:	87 1/04 Folk 2m1f110y heavy Hdl

Moderate hurdler; winner in France at up to nine furlongs; looks to be struggling to get the trip over hurdles; acts on soft ground.

Who Cares Wins

105   **104**

8-y-o ch g Kris-Anne Bonny (Ajdal (USA))
J R Jenkins The B C W Partnership

Placings:44/1/P20-P512P43P32   (4873)
2003/04: 21PGF, 225G, 191G, 20²G, 22PGS, 20⁴G, 20³S, 23PG, 16³GS, 20²GS,

	Starts	1st	2nd	3rd	Win & Pl
Hurdles	10	1	2	2	5862
Career Total	16	2	3	2	10916
92 10/03 Towc 2m3f110yF(0-100)HHdl			GD		£1904
100 7/01 Strf 2m6f110yD Hdl			GD		£3374

Total win prize-money £5278

Going:	Sf: 0-1 GS: 0-3 Gd: 1-5 GF: - Fm: 0-1
Distance:	2m/2m3: 0-1 2m4-2m7: 1-8 3m+: 0-1
Track:	LH: 0-5 RH: 0-4 Tight: 0-5 Gall: 0-0
Aids:	Bl: 0-0 Vi: 0-0 Tstrap: 0-0 Ckp: 0-2
Best Rating:	105 3/01 Hntg 2m110y soft Hdl

Moderate hurdler; suited by trips of at least two and a half miles; acts on most types of ground.

Who Dares Wins

11-y-o b g Kala Shikari-Sarah's Venture (Averof)
Ms S Duell J A V Duell

Placings:322/32202/331363/31/23UP3023/330465-433   (4798)
2003/04: 254S, 27³G, 27³G,

	Starts	1st	2nd	3rd	Win & Pl
Chases	3	0	0	2	425
Career Total	33	2	7	14	26035
112 11/00 Uttx 3m2f F(0-100)HCh			HVY		£2961
106 2/00 Carl 3m2f D Ch			HVY		£4368

Total win prize-money £7329

Going:	Sf: 0-1 GS: 0-0 Gd: 0-2 GF: - Fm: 0-0
Distance:	2m/2m3: 0-0 2m4-2m7: 0-0 3m+: 0-3
Track:	LH: 0-3 RH: 0-0 Tight: 0-2 Gall: 0-0
Aids:	Bl: 0-0 Vi: 0-0 Tstrap: 0-0 Ckp: 0-0
Best Rating:	116 3/99 Carl 3m110y soft Hdl

Very modest staying chaser/hunter chaser; suited by marathon trips and very soft ground.

Whose Line Is It

80   **39**

6-y-o gr g Sharp Deal-Madame Ruby (FR) (Homing)
N J Hawke Mrs D A Wetherall

Placings:623-000   (3654)
2003/04: 16⁰G, 17⁰GF, 24⁰S,

	Starts	1st	2nd	3rd	Win & Pl
NH Flat	1	0	0	0	0
Hurdles	2	0	0	0	0
Career Total	6	0	1	1	1090

Going:	Sf: 0-1 GS: 0-1 Gd: 0-1 GF: 0-1 Fm: 0-1
Distance:	2m/2m3: 0-2 2m4-2m7: 0-0 3m+: 0-1
Track:	LH: 0-2 RH: 0-1 Tight: 0-2 Gall: 0-0
Aids:	Bl: 0-0 Vi: 0-0 Tstrap: 0-0 Ckp: 0-0
Best Rating:	94 4/03 NAbb 2m1f gd-fm NHF

Why The Big Paws

6-y-o ch m Minster Son-Springdale Hall (USA) (Bates Motel (USA))
R C Guest Blaydon Racers Partnership

Placings:F   (4881)
2003/04: 17FGS,

	Starts	1st	2nd	3rd	Win & Pl
Hurdles	1	0	0	0	
Career Total	1	0	0	0	

Going:	Sf: 0-0 GS: 0-1 Gd: 0-0 GF: - Fm: 0-0
Distance:	2m/2m3: 0-1 2m4-2m7: 0-0 3m+: 0-0
Track:	LH: 0-0 RH: 0-1 Tight: 0-0 Gall: 0-0
Aids:	Bl: 0-0 Vi: 0-0 Tstrap: 0-0 Ckp: 0-0

Why The Long Face (NZ)

105   **116+**

7-y-o ch g Grosvenor (NZ)-My Charm (NZ) (My Friend Paul (USA))
R C Guest Oliver & Rogers

Placings:051055   (4799)
2003/04: 21⁰GS, 16⁵S, 21¹GS, 20⁰GS, 20⁵GF, 17⁵G,

	Starts	1st	2nd	3rd	Win & Pl
Hurdles	6	1	0	0	3624
Career Total	6	1	0	0	3624
116 2/04 Sedg 2m5f110yE Hdl			G-S		£3623

Total win prize-money £3624

Going:	Sf: 0-1 GS: 1-3 Gd: 0-1 GF: - Fm: 0-1
Distance:	2m/2m3: 0-2 2m4-2m7: 1-4 3m+: 0-0
Track:	LH: 1-5 RH: 0-1 Tight: 1-2 Gall: 0-1
Aids:	Bl: 0-0 Vi: 0-0 Tstrap: 0-0 Ckp: 0-0
Best Rating:	116 2/04 Sedg 2m5f110y gd-sft Hdl

Fair hurdler; winner in native New Zealand; has shown ability over hurdles, winning at Sedgefield in February; stays two miles five.

Wibbley Wobbley

12-y-o b g Arctic Lord-Burrow Star (Four Burrow)
T Ellis Mrs Susan E Busby

Placings:5/5   (0151)
2003/04: 24⁵GF,

	Starts	1st	2nd	3rd	Win & Pl
Chases	1	0	0	0	0
Career Total	2	0	0	0	0

Going:	Sf: 0-0 GS: 0-0 Gd: 0-0 GF: - Fm: 0-1

Distance: 2m/2m3: 0-0 2m4-2m7: 0-0 3m+: 0-1
Track: LH: 0-1 RH: 0-0 Tight: 0-0 Gall: 0-0
Aids: Bl: 0-0 Vi: 0-0 Tstrap: 0-0 Ckp: 0-0
Best Rating: 65 5/03 Chep 3m   gd-fm Ch

Wichway Now (IRE)
96f   92f
5-y-o b g Norwich-Proverb's Way (Proverb)
Miss E C Lavelle Telluride Racing

Placings:43   (4936)
2003/04: 16⁴G, 18³G,

	Starts	1st	2nd	3rd	Win & Pl
NH Flat	2	0	0	1	556
Career Total	2	0	0	1	556

Going: Sf: 0-0 GS: 0-0 Gd: 0-2 GF: - Fm: 0-0
Distance: 2m/2m3: 0-2 2m4-2m7: 0-0 3m+: 0-0
Track: LH: 0-1 RH: 0-1 Tight: 0-1 Gall: 0-0
Aids: Bl: 0-0 Vi: 0-0 Tstrap: 0-0 Ckp: 0-0
Best Rating: 92 4/04 Font 2m2f110y good NHF

Moderate form in bumpers on good ground.

Wicked Weasel (IRE)
104f   109+f
6-y-o b g Religiously (USA)-Just A Maid (Rarity)
K C Bailey D A Halsall

Placings:1   (2797)
2003/04: 17¹GS,

	Starts	1st	2nd	3rd	Win & Pl
NH Flat	1	1	0	0	2086
Career Total	1	1	0	0	2086
109 12/03 Bang	2m1f		H NHF	G-S	£2086

Total win prize-money £2086

Going: Sf: 0-0 GS: 1-1 Gd: 0-0 GF: - Fm: 0-0
Distance: 2m/2m3: 1-1 2m4-2m7: 0-0 3m+: 0-0
Track: LH: 1-1 RH: 0-0 Tight: 1-1 Gall: 0-0
Aids: Bl: 0-0 Vi: 0-0 Tstrap: 0-0 Ckp: 0-0
Best Rating: 109 12/03 Bang 2m1f   gd-sft NHF

Winning debut in a bumper on easy ground.

Widemouth Bay (IRE)
110   120+
6-y-o br g Be My Native (USA)-Lisaleen River (Over The River (FR))
P J Hobbs Mrs J F Deithrick

Placings:113-1046   (4895)
2003/04: 17¹G, 16⁰G, 21⁴G, 22⁶G,

	Starts	1st	2nd	3rd	Win & Pl
Hurdles	4	1	0	0	4891
Career Total	7	3	0	1	11685
120 11/03 Extr	2m1f		D Hdl	GD	£4355
113 11/02 Winc	2m		H NHF	GD	£2394

Total win prize-money £6749

Going: Sf: 0-0 GS: 0-0 Gd: 1-4 GF: - Fm: 0-0
Distance: 2m/2m3: 1-2 2m4-2m7: 0-2 3m+: 0-0
Track: LH: 0-0 RH: 1-4 Tight: 0-0 Gall: 0-0
Aids: Bl: 0-0 Vi: 0-0 Tstrap: 0-0 Ckp: 0-0
Best Rating: 141 3/03 Chel 2m110y good NHF

Fair novice hurdler; third in bumper at Cheltenham Festival in 2003; got off the mark in easy fashion on hurdling debut; failed to go on from that; acts on good and soft ground.

Wigmo Princess
100   72
5-y-o ch m Factual (USA)-Queen Of Shannon (IRE) (Nordico (USA))
S C Burrough (A W Carroll 8/9) Mrs Christine Priest

Placings:0004F   (4493)
2003/04: 17⁹G, 17⁰GS, 16⁹HY, 17⁴G, 16⁶G,

	Starts	1st	2nd	3rd	Win & Pl
Hurdles	5	0	0	0	0
Career Total	5	0	0	0	0

Going: Sf: 0-1 GS: 0-1 Gd: 0-3 GF: - Fm: 0-0
Distance: 2m/2m3: 0-5 2m4-2m7: 0-0 3m+: 0-0
Track: LH: 0-2 RH: 0-3 Tight: 0-3 Gall: 0-0
Aids: Bl: 0-0 Vi: 0-0 Tstrap: 0-0 Ckp: 0-0
Best Rating: 72 3/04 Extr 2m1f   good Hdl

Wilberforce
88   71
7-y-o ch g Elegant Monarch-Eskimo Slave (New Member)
N J Henderson S An S Racing

Placings:5P4P   (4279)
2003/04: 19⁵S, 23⁶GS, 25⁴G, 25⁵G,

	Starts	1st	2nd	3rd	Win & Pl
Chases	4	0	0	0	425
Career Total	4	0	0	0	425

Going: Sf: 0-1 GS: 0-1 Gd: 0-2 GF: - Fm: 0-0
Distance: 2m/2m3: 0-0 2m4-2m7: 0-1 3m+: 0-3
Track: LH: 0-0 RH: 0-4 Tight: 0-0 Gall: 0-0
Aids: Bl: 0-0 Vi: 0-0 Tstrap: 0-0 Ckp: 0-0
Best Rating: 75 1/04 Extr 2m3f110y soft Ch

Wild About Harry
90   72
7-y-o ch g Romany Rye-Shylyn (Hay Chas)
A R Dicken Ron Affleck

Placings:400-0000P0   (4690)
2003/04: 16⁶G, 16⁹S, 20⁰HY, 20⁰S, 22⁰GS, 22⁰G,

	Starts	1st	2nd	3rd	Win & Pl
NH Flat	1	0	0	0	0
Hurdles	5	0	0	0	0
Career Total	9	0	0	0	0

Going: Sf: 0-3 GS: 0-1 Gd: 0-2 GF: - Fm: 0-0
Distance: 2m/2m3: 0-2 2m4-2m7: 0-4 3m+: 0-0
Track: LH: 0-5 RH: 0-0 Tight: 0-3 Gall: 0-2
Aids: Bl: 0-0 Vi: 0-0 Tstrap: 0-0 Ckp: 0-0
Best Rating: 103 12/02 Wwck 2m   soft NHF

Wild Cane Ridge (IRE)
100f   119f
5-y-o gr g Roselier (FR)-Shuil Na Lee (IRE) (Phardante (FR))
L Lungo Ashleybank Investments Limited

Placings:11   (4866)
2003/04: 17¹HY, 16¹S,

	Starts	1st	2nd	3rd	Win & Pl
NH Flat	2	2	0	0	5474
Career Total	2	2	0	0	5474

| 119 4/04 Ayr | 2m | | H NHF | SFT | £3549 |
| 115 3/04 Carl | 2m1f | | H NHF | HVY | £1925 |

Total win prize-money £5474

Going: Sf: 2-2 GS: 0-0 Gd: 0-0 GF: - Fm: 0-0
Distance: 2m/2m3: 2-2 2m4-2m7: 0-0 3m+: 0-0
Track: LH: 1-1 RH: 1-1 Tight: 0-0 Gall: 0-0
Aids: Bl: 0-0 Vi: 0-0 Tstrap: 0-0 Ckp: 0-0
Best Rating: 119 4/04 Ayr 2m   soft NHF

Fair bumper performer; half-brother to fair bumper and hurdles winner River City; has created favourable impression when winning bumpers at Carlisle and Ayr; type to do better over obstacles and will stay further; fair prospect.

Wild Edgar (IRE)
7-y-o ch g Invited (USA)-Ou La La (IRE) (Be My Native (USA))
Miss Lucinda V Russell A R Trotter

Placings:S   (0270)
2003/04: 16⁵G,

	Starts	1st	2nd	3rd	Win & Pl
NH Flat	1	0	0	0	0
Career Total	1	0	0	0	0

Going: Sf: 0-0 GS: 0-0 Gd: 0-1 GF: - Fm: 0-0
Distance: 2m/2m3: 0-1 2m4-2m7: 0-0 3m+: 0-0
Track: LH: 0-0 RH: 0-1 Tight: 0-0 Gall: 0-0
Aids: Bl: 0-0 Vi: 0-0 Tstrap: 0-0 Ckp: 0-0

Wild Knight (IRE)
99(103h)   (111h)120+
7-y-o b g Jurado (USA)-Knight's Maid (Giolla Mear)
P F Nicholls Hunt & Co (bournemouth) Ltd

Placings:21F4P23-31PUUP3   (4286)
2003/04: 19³G, 21¹G, 20⁴G, 21ᵁS, 21ᵁG, 22⁶G, 21³GF,

	Starts	1st	2nd	3rd	Win & Pl
Chases	7	1	0	2	6093
Career Total	14	2	3	3	10366
120 12/03 Winc	2m5f		D Ch	GD	£4212
86 10/02 Chep	2m110y		H NHF	G-F	£1883

Total win prize-money £6095

Going: Sf: 0-1 GS: 0-0 Gd: 1-5 GF: - Fm: 0-1
Distance: 2m/2m3: 0-0 2m4-2m7: 1-7 3m+: 0-0
Track: LH: 0-0 RH: 1-6 Tight: 0-0 Gall: 0-1
Aids: Bl: 0-0 Vi: 0-0 Tstrap: 0-0 Ckp: 0-0
Best Rating: 120 3/04 Winc 2m5f   gd-fm Ch

Fair novice chaser; stays 2m 5f; best on a sound surface.

Wild Oats
99   105+
6-y-o b g Primitive Rising (USA)-Miss Nosey Oats (Oats)
P J Hobbs J & B Gibbs & Sons Ltd

Placings:0-61P0P0   (4897)
2003/04: 17⁰S, 17⁶GF, 19¹G, 24⁵S, 21⁰G, 22⁶G, 22⁴G,

	Starts	1st	2nd	3rd	Win & Pl
NH Flat	2	0	0	0	0
Hurdles	5	1	0	0	4225
Career Total	7	1	0	0	4225
105 11/03 Extr	2m3f		D Hdl	GD	£4225

Total win prize-money £4225

Going: Sf: 0-2 GS: 0-0 Gd: 1-4 GF: - Fm: 0-1
Distance: 2m/2m3: 1-3 2m4-2m7: 0-3 3m+: 0-1
Track: LH: 0-2 RH: 1-5 Tight: 0-1 Gall: 0-1

Aids: Bl: 0-0 Vi: 0-0 Tstrap: 0-0 Ckp: 0-0
Best Rating: 105 11/03 Extr 2m3f good Hdl

Modest hurdler; stays two miles three; acts on good ground.

Wild Passion (GER)
121

4-y-o b g Acatenango (GER)-White On Red (GER) (Konigsstuhl (GER))
Noel Meade (R Suerland 5/10) D P Sharkey

Placings:2F (4422)
2003/04: 16²Y, 17²G,

	Starts	1st	2nd	3rd	Win & Pl
Hurdles	2	0	1	0	4708
Career Total	2	0	1	0	4708

Going: Sf: 0-0 GS: 0-0 Gd: 0-1 GF: 0-0 Fm: 0-0
Distance: 2m/2m3: 0-2 2m4-2m7: 0-0 3m+: 0-0
Track: LH: 0-1 RH: 0-1 Tight: 0-0 Gall: 0-1
Aids: Bl: 0-0 Vi: 0-0 Tstrap: 0-0 Ckp: 0-0
Best Rating: 126 2/04 Fair 2m yield Hdl

Useful on the Flat when trained in Germany; very promising runner-up to stablemate Power Elite on hurdles debut at Fairyhouse.

Wild Power (GER)
104 98+

6-y-o br g Turtle Island (IRE)-White On Red (GER) (Konigsstuhl (GER))
Ian Williams Direct Sales UK Ltd

Placings:24/40422-45631625 (4548)
2003/04: 16⁴GF, 16⁵GF, 20⁶GF, 16³GF, 16¹GF, 16⁶G, 17²G, 16⁵GS,

	Starts	1st	2nd	3rd	Win & Pl
Hurdles	8	1	1	1	5034
Career Total	15	1	4	1	9391
95 10/03 Strf	2m1110y F(0-100)HHdl	G-F			£3010
	Total win prize-money £3010				

Going: Sf: 0-0 GS: 0-0 Gd: 0-2 GF: 1-5
Distance: 2m/2m3: 1-7 2m4-2m7: 0-1 3m+: 0-0
Track: LH: 1-5 RH: 0-3 Tight: 1-3 Gall: 0-1
Aids: Bl: 0-0 Vi: 0-0 Tstrap: 0-0 Ckp: 0-0
Best Rating: 100 3/04 Winc 2m gd-sft Hdl

Moderate hurdler; suited by two miles and acts on a sound surface; goes well for an inexperienced rider.

Wild Romance (IRE)
101 105+

9-y-o b g Accordion-Mandy's Last (Krayyan)
D J Wintle B E T Partnership

Placings:60/40110021/3310/F255-04420P (3706)
2003/04: 16⁹G, 16⁴G, 20⁴G, 23⁹GS, 22⁹S, 20⁶HY,

	Starts	1st	2nd	3rd	Win & Pl
Hurdles	6	0	1	0	1780
Career Total	24	4	3	2	28100
125 12/01 Limk	2m	Hdl	SFT	£7862
124 2/01 Gowr	2m	Hdl	HVY	£5564
90 7/00 Tipp	2m	NHF	G-F	£3032
6/00 Tipp	2m1f	NHF	G-Y	£3588
	Total win prize-money £20048			

Going: Sf: 0-2 GS: 0-1 Gd: 0-3 GF: - Fm: 0-0
Distance: 2m/2m3: 0-2 2m4-2m7: 0-3 3m+: 0-1
Track: LH: 0-2 RH: 0-4 Tight: 0-0 Gall: 0-0
Aids: Bl: 0-0 Vi: 0-0 Tstrap: 0-0 Ckp: 0-4
Best Rating: 125 12/01 Limk 2m soft Hdl

Moderate hurdler; acts on soft ground; stays two miles-seven; has worn cheekpieces.

Wild Spice (IRE)
109(99h) (121h)114

9-y-o b g Mandalus-Curry Lunch (Pry)
Miss Venetia Williams M Crabb, B Ead, P May, M Moore

Placings:5330/1/0/1U16052F25-32FO511 (1106)
2003/04: 26³G, 23²G, 26²G, 32⁰GF, 26⁵GF, 23¹G, 26¹G,

	Starts	1st	2nd	3rd	Win & Pl
Chases	7	2	1	1	9719
Career Total	23	5	3	3	24089
103 8/03 Sthl	3m2f	E Ch	GD	£4030
107 8/03 Worc	2m7f110yE Ch	GD	£3851
121 5/02 Strf	3m3f	D(0-125)HHdl	G-F	£4127
121 5/02 Extr	2m6f110yD(0-115)HHdl	GD	£3689
114 5/00 Hrfd	3m2f	E Hdl	GD	£2600
	Total win prize-money £18298			

Going: Sf: 0-0 GS: 0-0 Gd: 2-5 GF: - Fm: 0-2
Distance: 2m/2m3: 0-0 2m4-2m7: 0-0 3m+: 2-7
Track: LH: 2-4 RH: 0-0 Tight: 0-3 Gall: 0-0
Aids: Bl: 0-0 Vi: 0-0 Tstrap: 0-0 Ckp: 0-0
Best Rating: 121 5/02 Strf 3m3f gd-fm Hdl

Modest hurdler/chaser; has not always impressed with his jumping; benefitted from the fall of Three Eagles when left clear in 3m beginners' chase at Worcester August 2003; acts well on a decent surface; stays very well.

Wild Tide
67f 27f

5-y-o b m Runnett-Polly Two (Reesh)
D W Thompson Michael Howitt and R C Davison

Placings:00 (4780)
2003/04: 16⁹G, 16⁰S,

	Starts	1st	2nd	3rd	Win & Pl
NH Flat	2	0	0	0	
Career Total	2	0	0	0	

Going: Sf: 0-1 GS: 0-0 Gd: 0-1 GF: - Fm: 0-0
Distance: 2m/2m3: 0-2 2m4-2m7: 0-0 3m+: 0-0
Track: LH: 0-1 RH: 0-1 Tight: 0-0 Gall: 0-0
Aids: Bl: 0-0 Vi: 0-0 Tstrap: 0-0 Ckp: 0-0
Best Rating: 27 2/04 Muss 2m good NHF

Wild Walter (GER)
88 70+

5-y-o b h Leone (GER)-Welena (GER) (Nebos (GER))
Frau A Bertram W Renggli

Placings:344 (2783)
2003/04: 16³G, 16⁴GS, 22⁴GS,

	Starts	1st	2nd	3rd	Win & Pl
Hurdles	3	0	0	1	1474
Career Total	3	0	0	1	1474

Going: Sf: 0-1 GS: 0-1 Gd: 0-1 GF: - Fm: 0-0
Distance: 2m/2m3: 0-2 2m4-2m7: 0-1 3m+: 0-0
Track: LH: 0-0 RH: 0-1 Tight: 0-1 Gall: 0-0
Aids: Bl: 0-0 Vi: 0-0 Tstrap: 0-0 Ckp: 0-0
Best Rating: 79 12/03 Folk 2m6f110y gd-sft Hdl

Wildfield Rufo (IRE)
104(108h) (114h)102

9-y-o b g Celio Rufo-Jersey Girl (Hard Boy)
Mrs K Walton Mrs Carol Holroyd

Placings:14/FF2210-1P12P (4941)
2003/04: 25¹G, 21²GF, 24¹GS, 24²HY, 31²GS,

	Starts	1st	2nd	3rd	Win & Pl
Hurdles	3	2	0	0	10316
Chases	2	0	1	0	2210
Career Total	13	4	3	0	20861
114 12/03 Newc	3m	C(0-135)HHdl	G-S	£5512
114 5/03 Weth	3m1f	D Hdl	GD	£4803
99 2/03 Ayr	3m110y	E Hdl	SFT	£3549
114 3/02 Catt	3m1f110yH Ch	G-S	£1475
	Total win prize-money £15341			

Going: Sf: 0-1 GS: 1-2 Gd: 1-1 GF: - Fm: 0-1
Distance: 2m/2m3: 0-0 2m4-2m7: 0-1 3m+: 2-4
Track: LH: 2-3 RH: 0-1 Tight: 0-0 Gall: 1-1
Aids: Bl: 0-0 Vi: 0-0 Tstrap: 0-0 Ckp: 0-0
Best Rating: 114 12/03 Newc 3m gd-sft Hdl

Modest hurdler; winning hunter chaser; had jumping problems in the autumn of 2002 and was switched to hurdles in 2003, winning three times over three miles; best on soft ground but handles quicker.

Wilfie Wild

8-y-o b g Nomadic Way (USA)-Wild Child (Grey Ghost)
Mrs Lynne Ward A Jackson

Placings:P-0 (0430)
2003/04: 26⁹G,

	Starts	1st	2nd	3rd	Win & Pl
Chases	1	0	0	0	
Career Total	2	0	0	0	

Going: Sf: 0-0 GS: 0-0 Gd: 0-1 GF: - Fm: 0-0
Distance: 2m/2m3: 0-0 2m4-2m7: 0-0 3m+: 0-1
Track: LH: 0-1 RH: 0-0 Tight: 0-1 Gall: 0-0
Aids: Bl: 0-0 Vi: 0-0 Tstrap: 0-0 Ckp: 0-0
Best Rating: 66 5/03 Ctml 3m2f good Ch

Wilfram
102 80

7-y-o b g Fraam-Ming Blue (Primo Dominie)
J M Bradley Robert Bailey

Placings:002640-60 (1013)
2003/04: 20⁶GF, 20⁹GF,

	Starts	1st	2nd	3rd	Win & Pl
Hurdles	2	0	0	0	0
Career Total	8	0	1	0	1666

Going: Sf: 0-0 GS: 0-0 Gd: 0-0 GF: - Fm: 0-2
Distance: 2m/2m3: 0-0 2m4-2m7: 0-2 3m+: 0-0
Track: LH: 0-2 RH: 0-0 Tight: 0-0 Gall: 0-0
Aids: Bl: 0-2 Vi: 0-0 Tstrap: 0-0 Ckp: 0-0
Best Rating: 80 4/03 Strf 2m6f110y gd-fm Hdl

Moderate novice hurdler; suited by two and a half miles; has worn cheekpieces and blinkers.

Will He Wish
91 65

8-y-o b g Winning Gallery-More To Life (Northern Tempest (USA))

S Gollings Mrs D Dukes

Placings:*00/6* (0130)
2003/04: 16⁶GF,

	Starts	1st	2nd	3rd	Win & Pl
Hurdles	1	0	0	0	0
Career Total	3	0	0	0	0

Going:	Sf: 0-0 GS: 0-0 Gd: 0-0 GF: - Fm: 0-1
Distance:	2m/2m3: 0-1 2m4-2m7: 0-0 3m+: 0-0
Track:	LH: 0-0 RH: 0-1 Tight: 0-0 Gall: 0-1
Aids:	Bl: 0-0 Vi: 0-0 Tstrap: 0-0 Ckp: 0-0
Best Rating:	65 5/03 Hntg 2m110y gd-fm Hdl

Will Of The People (IRE)

101 **117**

9-y-o b g Supreme Leader-Another Partner (Le Bavard (FR))
M C Pipe Drss D Silk,M Gillard,P Walker,R Purkis

Placings:*2/4135/2023* (4567)
2003/04: 20²S, 21⁰S, 24²GS, 24³GS,

	Starts	1st	2nd	3rd	Win & Pl
Hurdles	4	0	2	1	3822
Career Total	9	1	3	2	7414
95 12/01 Hrfd	2m3f110yE Hdl			GD	£2523
				Total win prize-money	£2524

Going:	Sf: 0-2 GS: 0-1 Gd: 0-1 GF: - Fm: 0-0
Distance:	2m/2m3: 0-2 2m4-2m7: 0-2 3m+: 0-2
Track:	LH: 0-3 RH: 0-1 Tight: 0-3 Gall: 0-0
Aids:	Bl: 0-0 Vi: 0-0 Tstrap: 0-0 Ckp: 0-0
Best Rating:	117 3/04 Bang 3m gd-sft Hdl

Modest hurdler, suited by good ground; effective at up to three miles.

Will Tell

50+

6-y-o b g Rainbow Quest (USA)-Guillem (USA) (Nijinsky (CAN))
Mrs S J Smith Apb Racing

Placings:*04-03* (1109)
2003/04: 16⁶G, 17³GS,

	Starts	1st	2nd	3rd	Win & Pl
NH Flat	1	0	0	0	0
Hurdles	1	0	0	1	488
Career Total	4	0	0	1	488

Going:	Sf: 0-0 GS: 0-1 Gd: 0-0 GF: - Fm: 0-0
Distance:	2m/2m3: 0-2 2m4-2m7: 0-0 3m+: 0-0
Track:	LH: 0-2 RH: 0-0 Tight: 0-0 Gall: 0-0
Aids:	Bl: 0-0 Vi: 0-0 Tstrap: 0-0 Ckp: 0-0
Best Rating:	93 4/03 Prth 2m110y good NHF

Modest form in bumpers and hurdles on good and easy ground.

Will'Sillyshankers

98(77h) (47h)**72**

9-y-o b g Silly Prices-Hannah's Song (Saintly Song)
Mrs E B Scott Mrs E B Scott

Placings:*06/00P00P/0P-P4* (3466)
2003/04: 23²F, 26⁴S,

	Starts	1st	2nd	3rd	Win & Pl
Chases	2	0	0	0	301

Career Total   12   0   0   0   301

Going:	Sf: 0-1 GS: 0-0 Gd: 0-0 GF: - Fm: 0-1
Distance:	2m/2m3: 0-0 2m4-2m7: 0-0 3m+: 0-2
Track:	LH: 0-1 RH: 0-1 Tight: 0-0 Gall: 0-0
Aids:	Bl: 0-0 Vi: 0-0 Tstrap: 0-0 Ckp: 0-0
Best Rating:	85 4/01 Winc 2m soft NHF

William Lionheart

90 **74**

10-y-o b g Henbit (USA)-Come To Tea (IRE) (Be My Guest (USA))
Mrs Jane Galpin G P Galpin & Mrs J Dowson

Placings:*00004/0/0U54-6P0* (0435)
2003/04: 23⁶GS, 25²GF, 18⁶GF,

	Starts	1st	2nd	3rd	Win & Pl
Chases	3	0	0	0	0
Career Total	13	0	0	0	373

Going:	Sf: 0-0 GS: 0-1 Gd: 0-0 GF: 0-0 Fm: 0-2
Distance:	2m/2m3: 0-0 2m4-2m7: 0-0 3m+: 0-2
Track:	LH: 0-1 RH: 0-1 Tight: 0-0 Gall: 0-0
Aids:	Bl: 0-0 Vi: 0-0 Tstrap: 0-0 Ckp: 0-0
Best Rating:	74 1/03 Font 2m6f heavy Ch

Willie John Daly (IRE)

112 **129+**

7-y-o b g Mister Lord (USA)-Murphys Lady (IRE) (Over The River (FR))
P J Hobbs (Donal Coffey 5/6) D R Peppiatt

Placings:*5/4216-2421231FP* (4948)
2003/04: 20²S, 20⁴GY, 22²GS, 22¹HY, 24²GS, 24³G, 24¹G, 24²FG, 27⁶GS,

	Starts	1st	2nd	3rd	Win & Pl
Hurdles	9	2	3	1	14093
Career Total	14	3	4	1	19414
127 3/04 Tntn	3m110y E Hdl			GD	£4842
113 1/04 Font	2m6f110yE Hdl			HVY	£3432
120 1/03 Naas	2m3f			NHF	SFT	£4032
				Total win prize-money	£12307

Going:	Sf: 1-2 GS: 0-3 Gd: 1-3 GF: - Fm: 0-0
Distance:	2m/2m3: 0-0 2m4-2m7: 1-4 3m+: 1-5
Track:	LH: 1-4 RH: 1-2 Tight: 2-4 Gall: 0-1
Aids:	Bl: 0-0 Vi: 0-0 Tstrap: 0-0 Ckp: 0-0
Best Rating:	131 2/04 Kemp 3m110y gd-sft Hdl

Useful novice hurdler; stays three miles well and acts on good ground; progressive.

Willie Makeit (IRE)

14-y-o b g Coquelin (USA)-Turbina (Tudor Melody)
Mrs A L Tory Mrs A L Tory

Placings:*000F0/P26P/P21116332U/45P5/F/1P555/4/40P-4* (0354)
2003/04: 21⁴GF,

	Starts	1st	2nd	3rd	Win & Pl
Chases	1	0	0	0	0
Career Total	34	4	3	2	18087
84 5/99 MRas	2m6f110yH Ch			G-F	£2442
90 8/96 Sthl	2m4f110yD(0-105)HCh			GD	£4150
90 8/96 Worc	2m	E(0-100)HCh			GD	£2877
88 7/96 Worc	2m	E(0-100)HCh			G-F	£3556
				Total win prize-money	£13025

Willie The Fish (IRE)

7-y-o b g King's Ride-Bricon Lady (Proverb)
J M Jefferson Ashleybank Investments Limited

Placings:*FF* (4273)
2003/04: 25⁵GS, 24⁵FG,

	Starts	1st	2nd	3rd	Win & Pl
Hurdles	2	0	0	0	0
Career Total	2	0	0	0	0

Going:	Sf: 0-0 GS: 0-1 Gd: 0-1 GF: - Fm: 0-0
Distance:	2m/2m3: 0-0 2m4-2m7: 0-0 3m+: 0-2
Track:	LH: 0-1 RH: 0-1 Tight: 0-0 Gall: 0-0
Aids:	Bl: 0-0 Vi: 0-0 Tstrap: 0-0 Ckp: 0-0

Williemind

4-y-o b g Mind Games-No Exchange (Master Willie)
Mrs Lucinda Featherstone Heart Of England Racing

Placings:*PP* (2071)
2003/04: 16⁵GF, 16⁵GF,

	Starts	1st	2nd	3rd	Win & Pl
Hurdles	2	0	0	0	0
Career Total	2	0	0	0	0

Going:	Sf: 0-0 GS: 0-0 Gd: 0-0 GF: - Fm: 0-2
Distance:	2m/2m3: 0-2 2m4-2m7: 0-0 3m+: 0-0
Track:	LH: 0-0 RH: 0-2 Tight: 0-0 Gall: 0-0
Aids:	Bl: 0-0 Vi: 0-0 Tstrap: 0-0 Ckp: 0-0

Willow Run (NZ)

94 **80**

10-y-o b g Conquistarose (USA)-Crazy Lady (NZ) (One Pound Sterling)
B Ellison Brian Ellison

Placings:*6560/1252503/000006-0FP* (0618)
2003/04: 16⁶GF, 16⁰G, 16⁶G, 19⁰G,

	Starts	1st	2nd	3rd	Win & Pl
Hurdles	4	0	0	0	0
Career Total	20	1	2	1	3671
89 10/01 Sedg	2m1f	F(0-95)HHdl		G-S	£2299
				Total win prize-money	£2300

Going:	Sf: 0-0 GS: 0-0 Gd: 0-3 GF: - Fm: 0-1
Distance:	2m/2m3: 0-3 2m4-2m7: 0-1 3m+: 0-0
Track:	LH: 0-2 RH: 0-2 Tight: 0-1 Gall: 0-1
Aids:	Bl: 0-0 Vi: 0-0 Tstrap: 0-0 Ckp: 0-2
Best Rating:	89 10/01 Sedg 2m1f gd-sft Hdl

Willows Gate

95f **90f**

6-y-o b h Petoski-Croix Val Mer (Deep Run)
P R Webber Swigalot

Placings:*5* (2602)

2003/04: 16⁵G,

	Starts	1st	2nd	3rd	Win & Pl
NH Flat	1	0	0	0	0
Career Total	1	0	0	0	0

Going:	Sf: 0-0 GS: 0-0 Gd: 0-1 GF: - Fm: 0-0
Distance:	2m/2m3: 0-1 2m4-2m7: 0-0 3m+: 0-0
Track:	LH: 0-1 RH: 0-0 Tight: 0-0 Gall: 0-0
Aids:	Bl: 0-0 Vi: 0-0 Tstrap: 0-0 Ckp: 0-0
Best Rating:	90 12/03 Wwck 2m good NHF

Willows Roulette

12-y-o b g High Season-Willows Casino (Olympic Casino)
A G Hobbs Miss Jayne Brace & Gwyn Brace

Placings:40044/2U304/41005/P/635321124/P352F04/PPF
U   **(1107)**
2003/04: 21ᴾGF, 23ᴾGF, 23ᶠG, 21ᵁG,

	Starts	1st	2nd	3rd	Win & Pl
Chases	4	0	0	0	
Career Total	36	3	4	4	16409
98	8/00	Worc	2m4f110yF(0-100)HCh	G-F	£3513
92	8/00	Worc	2m4f110yE(0-105)HCh	G-F	£3523
82	5/98	Extr	2m7f	E(0-100)HHdl	FRM	£2640
			Total win prize-money £9676

Going:	Sf: 0-0 GS: 0-0 Gd: 0-2 GF: - Fm: 0-2
Distance:	2m/2m3: 0-0 2m4-2m7: 0-2 3m+: 0-2
Track:	LH: 0-4 RH: 0-0 Tight: 0-1 Gall: 0-0
Aids:	Bl: 0-0 Vi: 0-0 Tstrap: 0-0 Ckp: 0-0
Best Rating:	98 9/00 MRas 2m4f gd-fm Ch

Willy Willy

90(100h)   **72**
11-y-o ch g Master Willie-Monsoon (Royal Palace)
G Brown Mrs Amanda Killick

Placings:00411663420/113F00/PP551/255P-00PP **(1455)**
2003/04: 18⁰GF, 20⁰GF, 23ᴾGF, 21ᴾGF,

	Starts	1st	2nd	3rd	Win & Pl
Hurdles	2	0	0	0	0
Chases	2	0	0	0	0
Career Total	30	5	2	2	20041
93	10/01	Ludl	2m5f	F(0-90)Hdl	G-F	£2670
104	8/00	MRas	2m4f	D Ch	G-F	£5331
109	7/00	MRas	2m1f110yF(0-105)HCh	G-F	£4056
109	10/99	Winc	2m	F(0-100)HHdl	GD	£2374
109	9/99	MRas	2m1f110yF(0-100)HHdl	G-F	£2318
			Total win prize-money £16751

Going:	Sf: 0-0 GS: 0-0 Gd: 0-0 GF: - Fm: 0-4
Distance:	2m/2m3: 0-1 2m4-2m7: 0-2 3m+: 0-1
Track:	LH: 0-3 RH: 0-0 Tight: 0-2 Gall: 0-0
Aids:	Bl: 0-1 Vi: 0-0 Tstrap: 0-0 Ckp: 0-0
Best Rating:	109 7/00 MRas 2m1f110y gd-fm Ch

Plating-class front-running hurdler/chaser, stays two miles-five, suited by fast ground.

Willywont He

60
5-y-o b g Bollin William-Scalby Clipper (Sir Mago)
P T Midgley A Dimmock

Placings:0346   **(4886)**
2003/04: 16⁰GF, 17³GF, 17⁴GF, 17⁶GS,

	Starts	1st	2nd	3rd	Win & Pl
NH Flat	4	0	0	1	274
Career Total	4	0	0	1	274

Going:	Sf: 0-0 GS: 0-1 Gd: 0-0 GF: - Fm: 0-3
Distance:	2m/2m3: 0-1 2m4-2m7: 0-0 3m+: 0-0
Track:	LH: 0-1 RH: 0-3 Tight: 0-0 Gall: 0-0
Aids:	Bl: 0-0 Vi: 0-0 Tstrap: 0-0 Ckp: 0-0
Best Rating:	77 10/03 MRas 2m1f110y gd-fm NHF

Wimbledonian

98   **93**
5-y-o b m Sir Harry Lewis (USA)-Ardent Love (IRE)
(Ardross)
R T Phillips OWRC Partnership No 1

Placings:041   **(4118)**
2003/04: 17⁰GF, 20⁴G, 22¹G,

	Starts	1st	2nd	3rd	Win & Pl
NH Flat	1	0	0	0	0
Hurdles	2	1	0	0	3762
Career Total	3	1	0	0	3762
93	3/04	Folk	2m6f110yE Hdl	GD	£3500
			Total win prize-money £3500

Going:	Sf: 0-0 GS: 0-0 Gd: 1-2 GF: - Fm: 0-1
Distance:	2m/2m3: 0-1 **2m4-2m7: 1-2** 3m+: 0-0
Track:	LH: 0-0 **RH: 1-2 Tight: 1-2** Gall: 0-0
Aids:	Bl: 0-0 Vi: 0-0 Tstrap: 0-0 Ckp: 0-0
Best Rating:	93 3/04 Folk 2m6f110y good Hdl

Disappointing favourite on debut in Hereford bumper in September 2003, when found to have muscle problems; showed true form two outings later when winning mares' only novice hurdle at Folkestone in March; acts on good ground; stays 2m 6f.

Win Alot

100   **89**
6-y-o b g Aragon-Having Fun (Hard Fought)
M C Chapman Coverscope Ductwork & Reedkleen
Supplies

Placings:P0R531/2P65-245060B   **(3405)**
2003/04: 19²GF, 17⁴GF, 17⁵GS, 16⁹GS, 19⁶G, 16⁹GS, 19⁸G,

	Starts	1st	2nd	3rd	Win & Pl
Hurdles	7	0	1	0	1628
Career Total	17	1	2	1	4236
83	4/02	MRas	2m1f110yG(0-95)HHdl	GD	£1750
			Total win prize-money £1750

Going:	Sf: 0-0 GS: 0-3 Gd: 0-2 GF: - Fm: 0-2
Distance:	2m/2m3: 0-4 2m4-2m7: 0-3 3m+: 0-0
Track:	LH: 0-2 RH: 0-5 Tight: 0-4 Gall: 0-1
Aids:	Bl: 0-0 Vi: 0-0 Tstrap: 0-0 Ckp: 0-0
Best Rating:	89 8/03 MRas 2m3f110y gd-fm Hdl

Moderate hurdler; seemed to excel himself when runner-up in non-seller at Market Rasen in August; suited by two and a half miles; best on a sound surface.

Win The Toss

12-y-o b g Idiots Delight-Mayfield (USA) (Alleged (USA))
P York (R H York 13/6) Mrs Lola Lim

Placings:0/0/220554P201/442UP/6004/0/06UP-560P   **(3898)**

2003/04: 16⁵G, 20⁶GF, 17⁰GF, 20ᴾG,

	Starts	1st	2nd	3rd	Win & Pl
Hurdles	1	0	0	0	0
Chases	3	0	0	0	0
Career Total	30	1	4	0	4609
94	5/99	Uttx	2m4f110yG(0-100)HHdl	GD	£1784
			Total win prize-money £1784

Going:	Sf: 0-0 GS: 0-0 Gd: 0-2 GF: - Fm: 0-2
Distance:	2m/2m3: 0-0 2m4-2m7: 0-0 3m+: 0-0
Track:	LH: 0-2 RH: 0-2 Tight: 0-1 Gall: 0-0
Aids:	Bl: 0-0 Vi: 0-0 Tstrap: 0-0 Ckp: 0-0
Best Rating:	111 5/98 Uttx 2m gd-sft NHF

Windfola

92   **88+**
5-y-o b m Sovereign Water (FR)-Sainte Martine (Martinmas)
R D E Woodhouse Miss J M Slater

Placings:5-054P056P   **(4515)**
2003/04: 17⁰G, 19⁵GF, 20⁴GS, 16ᴾS, 16⁰GS, 21⁵GS, 19⁶G, 25ᴾGS,

	Starts	1st	2nd	3rd	Win & Pl
NH Flat	1	0	0	0	0
Hurdles	7	0	0	0	376
Career Total	9	0	0	0	376

Going:	Sf: 0-1 GS: 0-4 Gd: 0-2 GF: - Fm: 0-1
Distance:	2m/2m3: 0-4 2m4-2m7: 0-3 3m+: 0-1
Track:	LH: 0-6 RH: 0-2 Tight: 0-3 Gall: 0-1
Aids:	Bl: 0-2 Vi: 0-0 Tstrap: 0-0 Ckp: 0-0
Best Rating:	88 12/03 Hntg 2m4f110y gd-sft Hdl

Moderate form in bumpers and hurdles; handles cut in the ground.

Windhund (GER)

4-y-o ch g Surako (GER)-Windblume (GER) (Nebos (GER))
C Von Der Recke Gestut Rangau Stall Fairy Tale

Placings:P   **(3329)**
2003/04: 16ᴾS,

	Starts	1st	2nd	3rd	Win & Pl
Hurdles	1	0	0	0	
Career Total	1	0	0	0	

Going:	Sf: 0-1 GS: 0-0 Gd: 0-0 GF: - Fm: 0-0
Distance:	2m/2m3: 0-1 2m4-2m7: 0-0 3m+: 0-0
Track:	LH: 0-1 RH: 0-0 Tight: 0-0 Gall: 0-1
Aids:	Bl: 0-0 Vi: 0-0 Tstrap: 0-0 Ckp: 0-0

Winding River (IRE)

91(86h)   (99+h)**98**
7-y-o b g Montelimar (USA)-Bellora (IRE) (Over The River
(FR))
C R Egerton Elite Racing Club

Placings:34   **(3431)**
2003/04: 25³GS, 24⁴GS,

	Starts	1st	2nd	3rd	Win & Pl
Hurdles	1	0	0	1	391
Chases	1	0	0	0	417
Career Total	2	0	0	1	808

Going:	Sf: 0-0 GS: 0-2 Gd: 0-0 GF: - Fm: 0-0
Distance:	2m/2m3: 0-0 2m4-2m7: 0-0 3m+: 0-2
Track:	LH: 0-2 RH: 0-0 Tight: 0-1 Gall: 0-0
Aids:	Bl: 0-0 Vi: 0-0 Tstrap: 0-0 Ckp: 0-0
Best Rating:	99 1/04 Weth 3m1f gd-sft Hdl

Irish point winner; satisfactory third on first outing here in novices' hurdle at Wetherby in January; fourth on chase debut; should do better; suited by three miles.

Windross

107   **133**

12-y-o b g Ardross-Dans Le Vent (Pollerton)
A King Mrs Peter Prowting

Placings: 221140/221F12/3P60/1/PF-P105P0   (4640)
2003/04: 24PHY, 241GS, 25RG, 26SG, 24PGS, 21QG,

	Starts	1st	2nd	3rd	Win & Pl
Chases	6	1	0	0	8881
Career Total	25	6	5	1	46795
128	5/03	Strf	3m	C(0-135)HCh	G-S	£8209
140	12/01	Newb	3m	D(0-125)HCh	GD	£11193
145	2/00	Kemp	3m	C Ch	G-S	£7595
130	12/99	Uttx	2m5f	D Ch	SFT	£4102
124	1/99	Hayd	2m4f	E Hdl	SFT	£2340
123	12/98	Wwck	2m3f	E Hdl	G-S	£2897

Total win prize-money £36340

Going: Sf: 0-1 GS: 1-2 Gd: 0-3 GF: - Fm: 0-0
Distance: 2m/2m3: 0-0 2m4-2m7: 1-3 3m+: 1-5
Track: LH: 1-5 RH: 0-1 Tight: 1-2 Gall: 0-1
Aids: Bl: 0-0 Vi: 0-1 Tstrap: 0-0 Ckp: 0-0
Best Rating: 145   2/00   Kemp   3m   gd-sft   Ch

Fair veteran chaser; injured after winning the Mandarin at Newbury in December 2001; absent until returning in February 2003; bounced back to form when winning handicap at Stratford May 2003; held in three starts since; stays three miles; acts on good and soft ground.

Windsor Beauty (IRE)

83   **69**

6-y-o b/br g Woods Of Windsor (USA)-Tumble Dale (Tumble Wind (USA))
R Rowe Capt A Pratt

Placings: 505/0P   (3145)
2003/04: 16QG, 22PS,

	Starts	1st	2nd	3rd	Win & Pl
Hurdles	2	0	0	0	
Career Total	5	0	0	0	0

Going: Sf: 0-1 GS: 0-0 Gd: 0-1 GF: - Fm: 0-0
Distance: 2m/2m3: 0-1 2m4-2m7: 0-1 3m+: 0-0
Track: LH: 0-0 RH: 0-2 Tight: 0-0 Gall: 0-0
Aids: Bl: 0-0 Vi: 0-0 Tstrap: 0-0 Ckp: 0-0
Best Rating: 69   1/02   Font   2m2f110y   soft   Hdl

Winged Angel

76   **104+**

7-y-o ch g Prince Sabo-Silky Heights (IRE) (Head For Heights)
L Lungo Four Up One Down Partnership

Placings: 0P/5211-P0P   (3763)
2003/04: 17PG, 16QHY, 17PGS,

	Starts	1st	2nd	3rd	Win & Pl
Hurdles	3	0	0	0	
Career Total	9	2	1	0	6064
93	6/02	Hexm	2m4f110yE(0-105)HHdl		GD	£2530
104	6/02	Hexm	2m4f110yE(0-105)HHdl		GD	£2467

Total win prize-money £4999

Going: Sf: 0-1 GS: 0-1 Gd: 0-1 GF: - Fm: 0-0
Distance: 2m/2m3: 0-3 2m4-2m7: 0-0 3m+: 0-0
Track: LH: 0-3 RH: 0-0 Tight: 0-2 Gall: 0-1
Aids: Bl: 0-0 Vi: 0-0 Tstrap: 0-0 Ckp: 0-0
Best Rating: 104   6/02   Hexm   2m4f110y   good   Hdl

Moderate hurdler; stays two and a half miles; acts on good ground.

Winged Hussar

103 (99h)   (106h) **107**

11-y-o b g In The Wings-Akila (FR) (Top Ville)
D R Gandolfo A E Frost

Placings: 2PF2P4/420522-13   (2157)
2003/04: 212S, 201S, 213QG,

	Starts	1st	2nd	3rd	Win & Pl
Chases	3	1	1	1	6715
Career Total	14	1	5	1	12349
106	5/03	Bang	2m4f110yE(0-100)HCh	SFT	£4199

Total win prize-money £4199

Going: Sf: 1-2 GS: 0-1 Gd: 0-0 GF: - Fm: 0-0
Distance: 2m/2m3: 0-0 2m4-2m7: 1-3 3m+: 0-0
Track: LH: 1-3 RH: 0-0 Tight: 1-2 Gall: 0-0
Aids: Bl: 0-0 Vi: 0-0 Tstrap: 0-0 Ckp: 0-0
Best Rating: 107   11/03   Uttx   2m5f   gd-sft   Ch

Modest hurdler; stays two and a half miles; acts on soft ground.

Winged Lady (GER)

96   **69**

5-y-o b m Winged Love (IRE)-Wonderful Lady (GER) (Surumu (GER))
A G Juckes Whistlejacket Partnership

Placings: 0-F0404   (3997)
2003/04: 16FGF, 16QGF, 16KG, 16QGF, 21KG,

	Starts	1st	2nd	3rd	Win & Pl
Hurdles	5	0	0	0	262
Career Total	6	0	0	0	262

Going: Sf: 0-0 GS: 0-0 Gd: 0-2 GF: - Fm: 0-3
Distance: 2m/2m3: 0-4 2m4-2m7: 0-1 3m+: 0-0
Track: LH: 0-4 RH: 0-1 Tight: 0-1 Gall: 0-0
Aids: Bl: 0-0 Vi: 0-0 Tstrap: 0-0 Ckp: 0-0
Best Rating: 69   2/04   Ludl   2m5f   good   Hdl

Plating-class hurdler; Flat winner in Germany; disappointing so far over hurdles, but may be capable of better.

Wings Of Hope (IRE)

88   **93**

8-y-o b g Treasure Hunter-She's Got Wings (Bulldozer)
C J Hemsley Mrs M L Sell

Placings: 22535P/FU62535110P-0BP   (1193)
2003/04: 20QGF, 22BGF, 20PGF,

	Starts	1st	2nd	3rd	Win & Pl
Hurdles	3	0	0	0	
Career Total	20	2	3	2	10011
93	10/02	Ludl	2m5f	E(0-105)HHdl	FRM	£3402
86	10/02	Ludl	2m5f	F(0-90)Hdl	FRM	£3347

Total win prize-money £6750

Going: Sf: 0-0 GS: 0-0 Gd: 0-0 GF: - Fm: 0-3
Distance: 2m/2m3: 0-0 2m4-2m7: 0-3 3m+: 0-0
Track: LH: 0-3 RH: 0-0 Tight: 0-1 Gall: 0-0
Aids: Bl: 0-0 Vi: 0-0 Tstrap: 0-0 Ckp: 0-0
Best Rating: 102   12/01   Strf   2m6f110y   soft   Hdl

Modest hurdler; stays 2m 5f; acts on fast ground; reportedly difficult to train at home because he is quite a character.

Winnie The Pooh

10-y-o br g Landyap (USA)-Moorland Nell (Neltino)
J D Frost J E Blake

Placings: 024P/F600/062PP-P4   (1221)
2003/04: 16PGS, 19KGF,

	Starts	1st	2nd	3rd	Win & Pl
Hurdles	1	0	0	0	262
Chases	0	0	0	0	0
Career Total	15	0	2	0	1752

Going: Sf: 0-0 GS: 0-1 Gd: 0-0 GF: - Fm: 0-1
Distance: 2m/2m3: 0-2 2m4-2m7: 0-0 3m+: 0-0
Track: LH: 0-1 RH: 0-0 Tight: 0-1 Gall: 0-0
Aids: Bl: 0-0 Vi: 0-0 Tstrap: 0-0 Ckp: 0-1
Best Rating: 92   8/00   NAbb   2m1f   good   NHF

Winnie Wild

7-y-o b m Primitive Rising (USA)-Wild Child (Grey Ghost)
Miss T Jackson H L Thompson

Placings: P6P   (3481)
2003/04: 25PGS, 216GS, 25PG,

	Starts	1st	2nd	3rd	Win & Pl
Hurdles	3	0	0	0	0
Career Total	3	0	0	0	0

Going: Sf: 0-0 GS: 0-2 Gd: 0-1 GF: - Fm: 0-0
Distance: 2m/2m3: 0-0 2m4-2m7: 0-1 3m+: 0-2
Track: LH: 0-3 RH: 0-0 Tight: 0-2 Gall: 0-0
Aids: Bl: 0-0 Vi: 0-0 Tstrap: 0-0 Ckp: 0-0

Winning Leader (IRE)

8-y-o b g Supreme Leader-Cromogue Lady (Golden Love)
Miss L Blackford R C Skinner

Placings: P   (4306)
2003/04: 24PG,

	Starts	1st	2nd	3rd	Win & Pl
Chases	1	0	0	0	
Career Total	1	0	0	0	

Going: Sf: 0-0 GS: 0-0 Gd: 0-1 GF: - Fm: 0-0
Distance: 2m/2m3: 0-0 2m4-2m7: 0-0 3m+: 0-1
Track: LH: 0-0 RH: 0-1 Tight: 0-0 Gall: 0-0
Aids: Bl: 0-0 Vi: 0-0 Tstrap: 0-0 Ckp: 0-0

Winsley

103   **101**

6-y-o gr g Sula Bula-Dissolve (Sharrood (USA))
O Sherwood Absolute Solvents Ltd

Placings: 1013044   (4959)
2003/04: 171G, 17QG, 211GS, 213G, 22QG, 244G, 19KG,

	Starts	1st	2nd	3rd	Win & Pl
NH Flat	2	1	0	0	1512
Hurdles	5	1	0	1	5064
Career Total	7	2	0	1	6576
100	1/04	Ludl	2m5f	E Hdl	G-S	£3669
105	11/03	Folk	2m1f110yH NHF	GD	£1512

Total win prize-money £5181

Going:	Sf: 0-0 GS: 1-1 Gd: 1-6 GF: - Fm: 0-0
Distance:	2m/2m3: 1-2 2m4-2m7: 1-4 3m+: 0-1
Track:	LH: 0-0 RH: 2-6 Tight: 1-3 Gall: 0-1
Aids:	Bl: 0-0 Vi: 0-0 Tstrap: 0-0 Ckp: 0-1
Best Rating:	105 11/03 Folk 2m1f110y good NHF

Moderate novice hurdler; bumper winner; won on hurdles debut; looks a thorough stayer.

Winsome Winnie
82

9-y-o b m Teamster-G W Supermare (Rymer)
M J Weeden M J Weeden

Placings:0/0065/P (3415)
2003/04: 24PGS,

	Starts	1st	2nd	3rd	Win & Pl
Hurdles	1	0	0	0	
Career Total	6	0	0	0	0

Going:	Sf: 0-0 GS: 0-1 Gd: 0-0 GF: - Fm: 0-0
Distance:	2m/2m3: 0-0 2m4-2m7: 0-0 3m+: 0-1
Track:	LH: 0-0 RH: 0-1 Tight: 0-0 Gall: 0-0
Aids:	Bl: 0-0 Vi: 0-0 Tstrap: 0-0 Ckp: 0-0
Best Rating:	82 3/02 Winc 2m6f soft Hdl

Winter Gale (IRE)

12-y-o b/br g Strong Gale-Winter Fox (Martinmas)
Mrs G B Walford Mrs J E Eddery

Placings:00/4330/P30/11123/02F66/0P6-2P (0389)
2003/04: 24²GF, 25²G,

	Starts	1st	2nd	3rd	Win & Pl
Chases	2	0	1	0	826
Career Total	24	3	3	4	16151
106 7/00 Wolv	3m1f	E(0-115)HCh	GD	£3978
100 7/00 MRas	2m6f110yF(0-105)HCh	GD	£3770
93 7/00 Worc	2m	F(0-95)HCh	GD	£2463
		Total win prize-money £10212

Going:	Sf: 0-0 GS: 0-0 Gd: 0-1 GF: - Fm: 0-1
Distance:	2m/2m3: 0-0 2m4-2m7: 0-0 3m+: 0-2
Track:	LH: 0-1 RH: 0-1 Tight: 0-0 Gall: 0-1
Aids:	Bl: 0-0 Vi: 0-0 Tstrap: 0-0 Ckp: 0-0
Best Rating:	108 8/00 MRas 3m1f gd-fm Ch

Hunter chaser; stays three miles; effective from good to firm to good to soft.

Winter Garden
108(94h) (100h)101

10-y-o ch g Old Vic-Winter Queen (Welsh Pageant)
Miss Lucinda V Russell A A Bissett

Placings:013015/6052/2204/R055/6503-23222FP00225 (4880)
2003/04: 16³G, 17²G, 16³G, 16²G, 20²GF, 16²GF, 17²S, 20²S, 24⁴GF, 16⁶G, 16²GF, 25²G, 20⁵GS,

	Starts	1st	2nd	3rd	Win & Pl
Hurdles	1	0	0	0	0
Chases	12	0	6	2	9315
Career Total	34	2	9	3	34995
129 4/99 Fair	2m4f	Hdl	YLD	£11049
113 1/99 DRoy	2m	Hdl	HVY	£2455
		Total win prize-money £13504

Going:	Sf: 0-2 GS: 0-1 Gd: 0-6 GF: - Fm: 0-4
Distance:	2m/2m3: 0-8 2m4-2m7: 0-3 3m+: 0-2
Track:	LH: 0-8 RH: 0-4 Tight: 0-4 Gall: 0-0

| Aids: | Bl: 0-0 Vi: 0-0 Tstrap: 0-0 Ckp: 0-11 |
| Best Rating: | 141 5/00 Punc 2m good Hdl |

Moderate hurdler/chaser these days; best effort for some time when second over two miles at Ayr in March 2004; just stays three miles; best on quick ground.

Winter Man (IRE)
(94h) (85h)46

10-y-o b g Aristocracy-Jane Eyre (Master Buck)
J Howard Johnson (Cathal McCarthy 5/5) J Howard Johnson

Placings:005P3/1353/12500006/40U0P0-P00 (2802)
2003/04: 20PG, 19⁴GS, 16⁶S,

	Starts	1st	2nd	3rd	Win & Pl
Hurdles	1	0	0	0	
Chases	2	0	0	0	
Career Total	26	2	1	3	9877
114 10/01 Dpat	2m1f172y Hdl	G-Y	£3477
113 10/00 Fair	2m	NHF	SFT	£3312
		Total win prize-money £6790

Going:	Sf: 0-1 GS: 0-1 Gd: 0-1 GF: - Fm: 0-0
Distance:	2m/2m3: 0-2 2m4-2m7: 0-1 3m+: 0-0
Track:	LH: 0-2 RH: 0-0 Tight: 0-1 Gall: 0-0
Aids:	Bl: 0-0 Vi: 0-0 Tstrap: 0-1 Ckp: 0-0
Best Rating:	127 11/01 Punc 2m soft Hdl

Winter Star
75f 52f

4-y-o b g Overbury (IRE)-Pepper Star (IRE) (Salt Dome (USA))
Miss Venetia Williams M Crabb, B Ead, P May, M Moore

Placings:00 (4787)
2003/04: 16⁶GS, 16⁶G,

	Starts	1st	2nd	3rd	Win & Pl
NH Flat	2	0	0	0	
Career Total	2	0	0	0	

Going:	Sf: 0-0 GS: 0-1 Gd: 0-1 GF: - Fm: 0-0
Distance:	2m/2m3: 0-2 2m4-2m7: 0-0 3m+: 0-0
Track:	LH: 0-0 RH: 0-2 Tight: 0-0 Gall: 0-1
Aids:	Bl: 0-0 Vi: 0-0 Tstrap: 0-0 Ckp: 0-0
Best Rating:	52 4/04 Hntg 2m110y good NHF

Winter Whisper (IRE)

9-y-o b g Jurado (USA)-Princess Annabelle (English Prince)
Mrs S E Busby Mrs Susan E Busby

Placings:001P0/U242P12PP05/P4U0-3 (0204)
2003/04: 20³GF,

	Starts	1st	2nd	3rd	Win & Pl
Chases	1	0	0	1	223
Career Total	21	2	3	1	14615
98 9/01 Dund	2m3f	Ch	G-F	£5008
102 12/00 Thur	2m	Hdl	SH	£4140
		Total win prize-money £9148

Going:	Sf: 0-0 GS: 0-0 Gd: 0-0 GF: - Fm: 0-1
Distance:	2m/2m3: 0-0 2m4-2m7: 0-1 3m+: 0-0
Track:	LH: 0-1 RH: 0-0 Tight: 0-0 Gall: 0-0
Aids:	Bl: 0-0 Vi: 0-0 Tstrap: 0-1 Ckp: 0-0
Best Rating:	102 12/00 Thur 2m sft-hvy Hdl

Wintertide
110 130+

8-y-o b g Mtoto-Winter Queen (Welsh Pageant)
C J Mann J E Brown

Placings:11/02/42-14F1421 (4840)
2003/04: 20¹GF, 20⁴GF, 21FGF, 22¹GF, 25⁴GS, 24²G, 24¹G,

	Starts	1st	2nd	3rd	Win & Pl
Hurdles	7	3	1	0	23874
Career Total	13	5	3	0	30107
130 4/04 Chel	3m	B(0-145)HHdl	GD	£12017
115 11/03 Winc	2m6f	C Hdl	G-F	£5352
99 8/03 Worc	2m4f	F Hdl	G-F	£3052
109 2/00 Muss	2m	H NHF	G-S	£1683
104 1/00 Catt	2m	H NHF	GD	£1725
		Total win prize-money £23832

Going:	Sf: 0-0 GS: 0-1 Gd: 1-2 GF: - Fm: 2-4
Distance:	2m/2m3: 0-0 2m4-2m7: 2-4 3m+: 1-3
Track:	LH: 2-5 RH: 1-2 Tight: 0-0 Gall: 1-3
Aids:	Bl: 0-0 Vi: 0-0 Tstrap: 0-0 Ckp: 0-0
Best Rating:	130 4/04 Chel 3m good Hdl

Fair hurdler; acts on most types of ground; stays two miles six furlongs; regularly held up.

Wise King
104 121

14-y-o b g Rakaposhi King-Sunwise (Roi Soleil)
J A B Old Wise King Partnership

Placings:412/3F2/2311/311/542/520/5325/F4153-442F (2996)
2003/04: 24⁴GS, 26⁴G, 20²GF, 20FGF,

	Starts	1st	2nd	3rd	Win & Pl
Chases	4	0	1	0	2492
Career Total	32	6	7	5	54973
121 2/03 Winc	2m5f	D(0-120)HCh	G-S	£11115
144 4/99 Asct	2m3f110yB HCh	G-F	£9885
149 2/99 Kemp	2m4f110yD(0-125)HCh	GF	£5038
131 12/97 Sand	2m4f110y D Ch	GD	£4065
124 11/97 Newb	2m110y D(0-110)HHdl	GD	£4810
111 3/96 Uttx	2m	H NHF	GD	£1551
		Total win prize-money £36465

Going:	Sf: 0-0 GS: 0-1 Gd: 0-1 GF: - Fm: 0-2
Distance:	2m/2m3: 0-0 2m4-2m7: 0-2 3m+: 0-2
Track:	LH: 0-2 RH: 0-2 Tight: 0-2 Gall: 0-0
Aids:	Bl: 0-0 Vi: 0-0 Tstrap: 0-0 Ckp: 0-0
Best Rating:	149 4/00 Asct 2m3f110y good Ch

Modest handicap chaser; now at the veteran stage; does not win very often; at his best at around two and a half miles on good ground.

Wise Man (IRE)
104(103h) (105h)135+

9-y-o ch g Mister Lord (USA)-Ballinlonig Star (Black Minstrel)
N W Alexander Nicholas Alexander

Placings:03/65253/0032-111P1P (4865)
2003/04: 21¹S, 25¹HY, 25¹GS, 22PGS, 20¹HY, 25PS,

	Starts	1st	2nd	3rd	Win & Pl
Chases	6	4	0	0	21884
Career Total	17	4	2	3	26516
131 3/04 Carl	2m4f	D Ch	HVY	£5746
135 2/04 Ayr	3m1f	D(0-120)HCh	G-S	£5564
130 2/04 Kels	3m1f	D Ch	HVY	£5453
107 12/03 Ayr	2m5f110yE Ch	SFT	£5120
		Total win prize-money £21884

| Going: | Sf: 3-4 GS: 1-2 Gd: 0-0 GF: - Fm: 0-0 |

Distance: 2m/2m3: 0-0 2m4-2m7: 2-3 3m+: 2-3
Track: LH: 3-5 RH: 1-1 Tight: 1-2 Gall: 0-0
Aids: Bl: 0-0 Vi: 0-0 Tstrap: 0-0 Ckp: 0-0
Best Rating: 135 2/04 Ayr 3m1f gd-sft Ch

Useful chaser; progressive; stays 3m 1f; type to improve further and should continue to go well when conditions place the emphasis on stamina.

Wise Reflection (IRE)

10-y-o b g Detroit Sam (FR)-Hester Ann (Proverb)
N J Gifford Mrs M C Sweeney

Placings:2P1545/3352P/2/P   (1906)
2003/04: 24PGF,

	Starts	1st	2nd	3rd	Win & Pl
Chases	1	0	0	0	
Career Total	13	1	3	2	11598

107 11/99 Asct 2m4f E Hdl GD £5015
Total win prize-money £5016

Going: Sf: 0-0 GS: 0-0 Gd: 0-0 GF: - Fm: 0-1
Distance: 2m/2m3: 0-0 2m4-2m7: 0-0 3m+: 0-1
Track: LH: 0-0 RH: 0-1 Tight: 0-0 Gall: 0-1
Aids: Bl: 0-0 Vi: 0-0 Tstrap: 0-0 Ckp: 0-0
Best Rating: 116 5/01 Sthl 3m110y gd-fm Ch

Wise Tale
98   86

5-y-o b g Nashwan (USA)-Wilayif (USA) (Danzig (USA))
P D Niven B Ll Parry

Placings:0F0-404020   (1743)
2003/04: 174G, 22⁰GF, 16⁴F, 17⁰GF, 17²GF, 16⁰GF,

	Starts	1st	2nd	3rd	Win & Pl
Hurdles	6	0	1	0	1151
Career Total	9	0	1	0	1151

Going: Sf: 0-0 GS: 0-0 Gd: 0-0 GF: 0-1 Fm: 0-5
Distance: 2m/2m3: 0-5 2m4-2m7: 0-1 3m+: 0-0
Track: LH: 0-3 RH: 0-2 Tight: 0-2 Gall: 0-0
Aids: Bl: 0-0 Vi: 0-3 Tstrap: 0-0 Ckp: 0-0
Best Rating: 86 9/03 Hexm 2m110y firm Hdl

Plating-class; effective over two miles; acts on fast ground.

Wiseguy (IRE)
95   95

5-y-o b g Darshaan-Bibliotheque (USA) (Woodman (USA))
J Howard Johnson (M P Tregoning 25/10) Andrea & Graham Wylie

Placings:0FP   (4908)
2003/04: 16⁰GF, 17²G, 20⁰S,

	Starts	1st	2nd	3rd	Win & Pl
Hurdles	3	0	0	0	
Career Total	3	0	0	0	

Going: Sf: 0-1 GS: 0-0 Gd: 0-1 GF: - Fm: 0-1
Distance: 2m/2m3: 0-2 2m4-2m7: 0-0 3m+: 0-0
Track: LH: 0-0 RH: 0-3 Tight: 0-1 Gall: 0-0
Aids: Bl: 0-0 Vi: 0-0 Tstrap: 0-0 Ckp: 0-0
Best Rating: 95 4/04 Carl 2m1f good Hdl

Wishful Valentine
86   78

8-y-o ch g Riverwise (USA)-Wishful Dream (Crawter)
C W Mitchell C W Mitchell

Placings:0/000/PP0-6   (0182)
2003/04: 16⁶GF,

	Starts	1st	2nd	3rd	Win & Pl
Hurdles	1	0	0	0	0
Career Total	8	0	0	0	0

Going: Sf: 0-0 GS: 0-0 Gd: 0-0 GF: - Fm: 0-1
Distance: 2m/2m3: 0-1 2m4-2m7: 0-0 3m+: 0-0
Track: LH: 0-0 RH: 0-1 Tight: 0-0 Gall: 0-0
Aids: Bl: 0-0 Vi: 0-0 Tstrap: 0-0 Ckp: 0-0
Best Rating: 82 1/01 Kemp 2m soft NHF

Plating-class hurdler; shown little so far.

Witch's Brew
101   104

7-y-o b m Simply Great (FR)-New Broom (IRE) (Brush Aside (USA))
T D Easterby Mrs Bridget Tranmer

Placings:63221423-03P0   (3885)
2003/04: 19⁰GS, 16³G, 16⁶S, 16⁰G,

	Starts	1st	2nd	3rd	Win & Pl
Hurdles	4	0	0	1	1057
Career Total	12	1	3	3	8575

104 2/03 Catt 2m F(0-95)HHdl GD £2646
Total win prize-money £2646

Going: Sf: 0-1 GS: 0-1 Gd: 0-2 GF: - Fm: 0-0
Distance: 2m/2m3: 0-4 2m4-2m7: 0-0 3m+: 0-0
Track: LH: 0-3 RH: 0-0 Tight: 0-3 Gall: 0-0
Aids: Bl: 0-0 Vi: 0-0 Tstrap: 0-0 Ckp: 0-0
Best Rating: 104 2/03 Catt 2m good Hdl

Modest hurdler; stays 2m 4f; acts on good and soft ground.

With A Dash

6-y-o ch g Afzal-Oh So Ripe (Deep Run)
N A Twiston-Davies Miss S Wood

Placings:0-0P   (4340)
2003/04: 21⁰G, 25⁷G,

	Starts	1st	2nd	3rd	Win & Pl
Hurdles	2	0	0	0	
Career Total	3	0	0	0	

Going: Sf: 0-0 GS: 0-0 Gd: 0-0 GF: - Fm: 0-0
Distance: 2m/2m3: 0-0 2m4-2m7: 0-0 3m+: 0-1
Track: LH: 0-1 RH: 0-1 Tight: 0-0 Gall: 0-0
Aids: Bl: 0-0 Vi: 0-0 Tstrap: 0-0 Ckp: 0-0
Best Rating: 72 2/03 Kemp 2m good NHF

Without A Doubt
91f   104f

5-y-o b g Singspiel (IRE)-El Rabab (USA) (Roberto (USA))
M Pitman Malcolm C Denmark

Placings:30-260   (4649)
2003/04: 16²GY, 16⁶GS, 17⁰G,

	Starts	1st	2nd	3rd	Win & Pl
NH Flat	3	0	1	0	533
Career Total	5	0	1	1	997

Going: Sf: 0-0 GS: 0-1 Gd: 0-1 GF: - Fm: 0-1
Distance: 2m/2m3: 0-3 2m4-2m7: 0-0 3m+: 0-0
Track: LH: 0-0 RH: 0-2 Tight: 0-0 Gall: 0-1
Aids: Bl: 0-0 Vi: 0-0 Tstrap: 0-0 Ckp: 0-0
Best Rating: 104 4/04 Aint 2m1f good NHF

Without Pretense (USA)
91   73

6-y-o b g St Jovite (USA)-Spark Of Success (USA) (Topsider (USA))
N G Ayliffe Derek Jones

Placings:0/00P04-0PP   (4897)
2003/04: 17⁰G, 17⁶G, 22⁸G,

	Starts	1st	2nd	3rd	Win & Pl
Hurdles	3	0	0	0	
Career Total	9	0	0	0	309

Going: Sf: 0-0 GS: 0-0 Gd: 0-3 GF: - Fm: 0-0
Distance: 2m/2m3: 0-2 2m4-2m7: 0-1 3m+: 0-0
Track: LH: 0-0 RH: 0-3 Tight: 0-1 Gall: 0-0
Aids: Bl: 0-0 Vi: 0-0 Tstrap: 0-0 Ckp: 0-0
Best Rating: 78 8/02 Kbgn 2m gd-fm Hdl

Without Words
68   54

6-y-o ch m Lion Cavern (USA)-Sans Escale (USA) (Diesis)
W M Brisbourne F F Racing Services I

Placings:6P   (0528)
2003/04: 16⁶HY, 16⁰GF,

	Starts	1st	2nd	3rd	Win & Pl
Hurdles	2	0	0	0	0
Career Total	2	0	0	0	0

Going: Sf: 0-1 GS: 0-0 Gd: 0-0 GF: - Fm: 0-0
Distance: 2m/2m3: 0-2 2m4-2m7: 0-0 3m+: 0-0
Track: LH: 0-2 RH: 0-0 Tight: 0-0 Gall: 0-0
Aids: Bl: 0-0 Vi: 0-0 Tstrap: 0-0 Ckp: 0-0
Best Rating: 54 5/03 Uttx 2m heavy Hdl

Withthelads (IRE)
99   99+

6-y-o b g Tidaro (USA)-Quayside Charm (Quayside)
L Wells Birch & Pines Syndicate

Placings:42P06451   (4790)
2003/04: 16⁴G, 16²GS, 24PGS, 20⁰S, 18⁶GS, 21⁴G, 22⁵G, 21¹G,

	Starts	1st	2nd	3rd	Win & Pl
NH Flat	2	0	1	0	480
Hurdles	6	1	0	0	4100
Career Total	8	1	1	0	4580

99 4/04 Plum 2m5f E(0-105)HHdl GD £3640
Total win prize-money £3640

Going: Sf: 0-1 GS: 0-3 Gd: 1-4 GF: - Fm: 0-0
Distance: 2m/2m3: 0-3 2m4-2m7: 1-4 3m+: 0-0
Track: LH: 1-5 RH: 0-3 Tight: 1-4 Gall: 0-0
Aids: Bl: 1-1 Vi: 0-0 Tstrap: 0-0 Ckp: 0-0
Best Rating: 101 11/03 Sand 2m110y good NHF

Moderate hurdler; stays two miles five; effective on good ground and with cut; has worn blinkers.

Witness Time (IRE)

(100h)   (97+h)
8-y-o b g Witness Box (USA)-Lisnacoilla (Beau Chapeau)
B J Eckley Brian Eckley

Placings:304/0551-PPP   (3466)
2003/04: 24PS, 19PGS, 26PS,

	Starts	1st	2nd	3rd	Win & Pl
Hurdles	1	0	0	0	0
Chases	2	0	0	0	0
Career Total	10	1	0	1	3712

101 2/03 Hrfd 3m2f E Hdl   GD £3474
Total win prize-money £3474

Going: Sf: 0-2 GS: 0-1 Gd: 0-0 GF: - Fm: 0-0
Distance: 2m/2m3: 0-2 2m4-2m7: 0-0 3m+: 0-2
Track: LH: 0-1 RH: 0-2 Tight: 0-0 Gall: 0-0
Aids: Bl: 0-0 Vi: 0-0 Tstrap: 0-0 Ckp: 0-0
Best Rating: 101 2/03 Hrfd 3m2f good Hdl

Witney O'Grady (IRE)

11-y-o ch g Ring Of Ford-C B M Girl (Diamonds Are Trump (USA))
Miss L V Davis Miss Louise Davis

Placings:0/0/0P5/PP-P   (0626)
2003/04: 21PGF,

	Starts	1st	2nd	3rd	Win & Pl
Chases	1	0	0	0	0
Career Total	8	0	0	0	0

Going: Sf: 0-0 GS: 0-0 Gd: 0-0 GF: - Fm: 0-1
Distance: 2m/2m3: 0-0 2m4-2m7: 0-1 3m+: 0-0
Track: LH: 0-1 RH: 0-0 Tight: 0-0 Gall: 0-0
Aids: Bl: 0-0 Vi: 0-0 Tstrap: 0-0 Ckp: 0-0
Best Rating: 68 4/02 MRas 2m3f110y gd-fm Hdl

Wittering

5-y-o b m Keen-Club Elite (Salse (USA))
J G M O'Shea W J Dobson

Placings:0P   (4636)
2003/04: 16PGS, 17PG,

	Starts	1st	2nd	3rd	Win & Pl
NH Flat	2	0	0	0	0
Career Total	2	0	0	0	0

Going: Sf: 0-0 GS: 0-1 Gd: 0-1 GF: - Fm: 0-0
Distance: 2m/2m3: 0-2 2m4-2m7: 0-0 3m+: 0-0
Track: LH: 0-0 RH: 0-1 Tight: 0-0 Gall: 0-0
Aids: Bl: 0-0 Vi: 0-0 Tstrap: 0-0 Ckp: 0-0

Wizard O' Wass

6-y-o ch g Imp Society (USA)-Sabeel (Local Suitor (USA))
J R Turner R C Shedden

Placings:550-P00   (3356)
2003/04: 16PS, 16PGS, 18PS,

	Starts	1st	2nd	3rd	Win & Pl
Hurdles	3	0	0	0	0
Career Total	6	0	0	0	0

Wizard Of Edge

92   77
4-y-o b g Wizard King-Forever Shineing (Glint Of Gold)
G B Balding Peter Richardson

Placings:004   (4489)
2003/04: 16PS, 16PG, 16PG,

	Starts	1st	2nd	3rd	Win & Pl
Hurdles	3	0	0	0	265
Career Total	3	0	0	0	265

Going: Sf: 0-1 GS: 0-0 Gd: 0-2 GF: - Fm: 0-0
Distance: 2m/2m3: 0-3 2m4-2m7: 0-0 3m+: 0-0
Track: LH: 0-2 RH: 0-1 Tight: 0-0 Gall: 0-1
Aids: Bl: 0-0 Vi: 0-0 Tstrap: 0-0 Ckp: 0-0
Best Rating: 82 3/04 Newb 2m110y good Hdl

Wizard Of The West

55   90
4-y-o b g Wizard King-Rose Burton (Lucky Wednesday)
Miss Sheena West Mrs Sue Flight

Placings:F0P   (3512)
2003/04: 16FG, 16OG, 18PG,

	Starts	1st	2nd	3rd	Win & Pl
Hurdles	3	0	0	0	0
Career Total	3	0	0	0	0

Going: Sf: 0-0 GS: 0-0 Gd: 0-3 GF: - Fm: 0-0
Distance: 2m/2m3: 0-3 2m4-2m7: 0-0 3m+: 0-0
Track: LH: 0-1 RH: 0-2 Tight: 0-0 Gall: 0-0
Aids: Bl: 0-0 Vi: 0-0 Tstrap: 0-0 Ckp: 0-0
Best Rating: 86 12/03 Kemp 2m good Hdl

Wizardtree

49f
5-y-o ch g Presidium-Snow Tree (Welsh Pageant)
R S Brookhouse R S Brookhouse

Placings:0-P   (0087)
2003/04: 16PGS,

	Starts	1st	2nd	3rd	Win & Pl
NH Flat	1	0	0	0	0
Career Total	2	0	0	0	0

Going: Sf: 0-0 GS: 0-1 Gd: 0-0 GF: - Fm: 0-0
Distance: 2m/2m3: 0-1 2m4-2m7: 0-0 3m+: 0-0
Track: LH: 0-1 RH: 0-0 Tight: 0-0 Gall: 0-0
Aids: Bl: 0-0 Vi: 0-0 Tstrap: 0-0 Ckp: 0-0
Best Rating: 49 2/03 Winc 2m gd-sft NHF

Woman

33
6-y-o b m Homo Sapien-La Princesse (Le Bavard (FR))
H J Manners H J Manners

Placings:00U-6PFU6P   (4929)
2003/04: 17PGF, 17PGF, 16FGF, 19UG, 19PS, 18PG,

	Starts	1st	2nd	3rd	Win & Pl
NH Flat	1	0	0	0	0
Hurdles	5	0	0	0	0
Career Total	9	0	0	0	0

Going: Sf: 0-1 GS: 0-0 Gd: 0-2 GF: - Fm: 0-3
Distance: 2m/2m3: 0-5 2m4-2m7: 0-1 3m+: 0-0
Track: LH: 0-4 RH: 0-1 Tight: 0-4 Gall: 0-0
Aids: Bl: 0-0 Vi: 0-0 Tstrap: 0-0 Ckp: 0-0
Best Rating: 79 6/03 Hrfd 2m1f gd-fm NHF

Won Too Phar (IRE)

77   (54h)48
8-y-o b g Phardante (FR)-Townandcountrygirl (Buckskin (FR))
G L Moore Pietro Addis & Sons Ltd

Placings:4F6   (2532)
2003/04: 21LG, 24FGF, 20PS,

	Starts	1st	2nd	3rd	Win & Pl
Hurdles	1	0	0	0	272
Chases	2	0	0	0	0
Career Total	3	0	0	0	272

Going: Sf: 0-1 GS: 0-0 Gd: 0-0 GF: - Fm: 0-1
Distance: 2m/2m3: 0-0 2m4-2m7: 0-2 3m+: 0-1
Track: LH: 0-1 RH: 0-2 Tight: 0-1 Gall: 0-0
Aids: Bl: 0-0 Vi: 0-0 Tstrap: 0-0 Ckp: 0-0
Best Rating: 54 11/03 Kemp 2m5f good Hdl

Wonder Brook

64f   52f
4-y-o b f Alderbrook-Wordy's Wonder (Welsh Captain)
Mrs C A Dunnett Wordingham Plant Hire

Placings:60   (4780)
2003/04: 16FG, 16OS,

	Starts	1st	2nd	3rd	Win & Pl
NH Flat	2	0	0	0	0
Career Total	2	0	0	0	0

Going: Sf: 0-1 GS: 0-0 Gd: 0-1 GF: - Fm: 0-0
Distance: 2m/2m3: 0-2 2m4-2m7: 0-0 3m+: 0-0
Track: LH: 0-2 RH: 0-0 Tight: 0-2 Gall: 0-0
Aids: Bl: 0-0 Vi: 0-0 Tstrap: 0-0 Ckp: 0-0
Best Rating: 55 2/04 Fknm 2m good NHF

Wonder Weasel (IRE)

105   (101h)142
11-y-o b g Lancastrian-The She Weasel (Gulf Pearl)
K C Bailey D A Halsall

Placings:513/1/511PP5U/4134F-5FPP030P   (4647)
2003/04: 21LG, 27FG, 29PS, 25PS, 24OS, 29OGS, 32OG, 36PG,

	Starts	1st	2nd	3rd	Win & Pl
Hurdles	1	0	0	0	0
Chases	7	0	0	1	909
Career Total	24	5	0	3	45518

139	12/02	Weth	3m1f	C(0-130)HCh	G-S	£7475
142	12/01	Hayd	3m	D(0-125)HCh	HVY	£6464
142	12/01	Hayd	3m	E(0-115)HCh	SFT	£3558
123	1/01	Donc	2m3f110y	C(0-130)HCh	GD	£7182
120	4/00	Hayd	2m6f	D Ch	GD	£5655

Total win prize-money £30336

Going: Sf: 0-3 GS: 0-1 Gd: 0-4 GF: - Fm: 0-0
Distance: 2m2/m3: 0-0 2m4-2m7: 0-1 3m+: 0-7
Track: LH: 0-7 RH: 0-1 Tight: 0-3 Gall: 0-0
Aids: Bl: 0-0 Vi: 0-2 Tstrap: 0-0 Ckp: 0-5
Best Rating: 142 12/01 Hayd 3m   heavy   Ch

Fair staying handicap chaser; gets three miles plus; suited by good and soft ground; has worn cheekpieces with success.

Wonder Wings
71   **34**

7-y-o ch g Lir-Ginger Wings (Ginger Boy)
G L Moore D J Forehead

Placings:4-00   (0587)
2003/04: 16^3G, 20^0GF,

	Starts	1st	2nd	3rd	Win & Pl
NH Flat	1	0	0	0	0
Hurdles	1	0	0	0	0
Career Total	3	0	0	0	0

Going: Sf: 0-0 GS: 0-0 Gd: 0-1 GF: - Fm: 0-1
Distance: 2m2/m3: 0-1 2m4-2m7: 0-1 3m+: 0-0
Track: LH: 0-2 RH: 0-0 Tight: 0-0 Gall: 0-0
Aids: Bl: 0-0 Vi: 0-0 Tstrap: 0-0 Ckp: 0-0
Best Rating: 74 4/03 Font 2m2f110y   gd-fm   NHF

Wonderful Man
89   (0c)**89d**

8-y-o ch g Magical Wonder (USA)-Gleeful (Sayf El Arab (USA))
R D E Woodhouse M K Oldham

Placings:P640/00/F22350-U506   (1095)
2003/04: 16^6G, 17^0U, 16^5G, 17^0GF, 16^6GF,

	Starts	1st	2nd	3rd	Win & Pl
Hurdles	4	0	0	0	0
Chases	1	0	0	0	0
Career Total	16	0	2	1	2142

Going: Sf: 0-0 GS: 0-0 Gd: 0-3 GF: - Fm: 0-2
Distance: 2m2/m3: 0-5 2m4-2m7: 0-0 3m+: 0-0
Track: LH: 0-4 RH: 0-1 Tight: 0-3 Gall: 0-0
Aids: Bl: 0-0 Vi: 0-0 Tstrap: 0-0 Ckp: 0-1
Best Rating: 89 2/03 Weth 2m   good   Hdl

Modest, lightly-raced hurdler, suited by fast ground; best when held up.

Wonderful Remark
(90h)   (63h)

8-y-o b m Golden Heights-Queen Of Dreams (Ti King (FR))
P T Dalton Mrs Joanne Woods

Placings:00/0P60/0P-PP0P   (1105)
2003/04: 20^0G, 19^0G, 17^0GF, 17^0GS,

	Starts	1st	2nd	3rd	Win & Pl
Hurdles	3	0	0	0	0
Chases	1	0	0	0	0
Career Total	12	0	0	0	0

Going: Sf: 0-0 GS: 0-1 Gd: 0-2 GF: - Fm: 0-1
Distance: 2m2/m3: 0-3 2m4-2m7: 0-1 3m+: 0-0
Track: LH: 0-3 RH: 0-1 Tight: 0-2 Gall: 0-0
Aids: Bl: 0-0 Vi: 0-0 Tstrap: 0-0 Ckp: 0-1
Best Rating: 59 6/02 MRas 2m1f110y   gd-fm   Hdl

Wontcostalotbut
(104h)   (114h)**105**

10-y-o b m Nicholas Bill-Brave Maiden (Three Legs)
B De Haan Wontcostalot Partnership

Placings:U36230210/432041532444/22112640/0PP0/3060
33/32100341-253P0P   (2855)
2003/04: 26^2GF, 27^5G, 25^3G, 30^4GS, 24^0GS, 25^0GS,

	Starts	1st	2nd	3rd	Win & Pl
Hurdles	4	0	1	1	2099
Chases	2	0	0	0	0
Career Total	53	6	9	10	48022

105 4/03 Hrfd	3m1f110yE Ch		G-F	£4932
104 12/02 Font	3m2f110yE Ch		GD	£4336
135 12/99 Kemp	3m110y B(0-140)HHdl		SFT	£7061
118 11/99 Newb	3m110y C(0-135)HHdl		G-F	£4695
108 12/98 NAbb	2m6f (0-125)HHdl		SFT	£2684
106 4/98 Uttx	2m4f110yE Hdl		SFT	£2211

Total win prize-money £25920

Going: Sf: 0-0 GS: 0-3 Gd: 0-2 GF: - Fm: 0-1
Distance: 2m2/m3: 0-0 2m4-2m7: 0-0 3m+: 0-6
Track: LH: 0-3 RH: 0-3 Tight: 0-1 Gall: 0-1
Aids: Bl: 0-0 Vi: 0-0 Tstrap: 0-0 Ckp: 0-1
Best Rating: 135 1/00 Uttx 3m110y   soft   Hdl

Modest chaser/fair hurdler; loves the mud, but acts on decent ground; stays three miles plus; has worn cheekpieces; a little quirky.

Wood Be King

5-y-o b h Prince Sabo-Sylvan Dancer (IRE) (Dancing Dissident (USA))
A P James Anne & Mahendra Ramkaran

Placings:P   (0210)
2003/04: 16^0G,

	Starts	1st	2nd	3rd	Win & Pl
Hurdles	1	0	0	0	
Career Total	1	0	0	0	

Going: Sf: 0-0 GS: 0-0 Gd: 0-1 GF: - Fm: 0-0
Distance: 2m2/m3: 0-1 2m4-2m7: 0-0 3m+: 0-0
Track: LH: 0-1 RH: 0-0 Tight: 0-0 Gall: 0-0
Aids: Bl: 0-0 Vi: 0-0 Tstrap: 0-0 Ckp: 0-0

Wood Colony (USA)

6-y-o b g Woodman (USA)-Promenade Colony (USA) (Pleasant Colony (USA))
M F Harris Let's Live Racing

Placings:P   (2415)
2003/04: 16^0GS,

	Starts	1st	2nd	3rd	Win & Pl
Hurdles	1	0	0	0	
Career Total	1	0	0	0	

Going: Sf: 0-0 GS: 0-0 Gd: 0-0 GF: - Fm: 0-0
Distance: 2m2/m3: 0-1 2m4-2m7: 0-0 3m+: 0-0
Track: LH: 0-1 RH: 0-0 Tight: 0-0 Gall: 0-0
Aids: Bl: 0-0 Vi: 0-0 Tstrap: 0-0 Ckp: 0-0

Wood Street (IRE)
105   **87**

5-y-o b g Eagle Eyed (USA)-San-Catrinia (IRE) (Knesset (USA))

R J Baker (Mrs A J Bowlby 14/6) Churchill Property Services Ltd

Placings:002P0P   (4735)
2003/04: 16^6G, 16^9GF, 16^2GF, 16^0GS, 17^0GS, 17^0G,

	Starts	1st	2nd	3rd	Win & Pl
Hurdles	6	0	1	0	740
Career Total	6	0	1	0	740

Going: Sf: 0-0 GS: 0-2 Gd: 0-2 GF: - Fm: 0-2
Distance: 2m2/m3: 0-6 2m4-2m7: 0-0 3m+: 0-0
Track: LH: 0-4 RH: 0-1 Tight: 0-1 Gall: 0-1
Aids: Bl: 0-0 Vi: 0-0 Tstrap: 0-0 Ckp: 0-0
Best Rating: 89 10/03 Chep 2m110y   gd-fm   Hdl

Plating-class novice hurdler; has ability but a hard puller.

Woodland Warrior
83   **77**

7-y-o b g Lyphento (USA)-Dutch Majesty (Homing)
C Roberts William John Day

Placings:5600PS0/0   (4632)
2003/04: 24^0G,

	Starts	1st	2nd	3rd	Win & Pl
Hurdles	1	0	0	0	
Career Total	8	0	0	0	0

Going: Sf: 0-0 GS: 0-0 Gd: 0-1 GF: - Fm: 0-0
Distance: 2m2/m3: 0-0 2m4-2m7: 0-0 3m+: 0-1
Track: LH: 0-0 RH: 0-1 Tight: 0-1 Gall: 0-0
Aids: Bl: 0-0 Vi: 0-0 Tstrap: 0-0 Ckp: 0-0
Best Rating: 77 11/01 Font 2m4f   gd-sft   Hdl

Woodlands Beau (IRE)

12-y-o b g Beau Sher-Never Intended (Sayyaf)
Mrs S Alner Club Ten

Placings:2U130U22U/234P25PP23U6/2241521U0/03U555
552/42-232F   (4425)
2003/04: 33^2G, 25^3GF, 31^2GF, 26^6G,

	Starts	1st	2nd	3rd	Win & Pl
Chases	4	0	2	1	3578
Career Total	45	3	13	5	34764

113 1/01 Folk	3m1f F(0-110)HCh		HVY	£6838
110 10/00 Winc	3m1f110yF(0-110)HCh		G-S	£5362
117 11/98 Towc	3m1f D Ch		G-S	£3692

Total win prize-money £15894

Going: Sf: 0-0 GS: 0-0 Gd: 0-2 GF: - Fm: 0-2
Distance: 2m2/m3: 0-0 2m4-2m7: 0-0 3m+: 0-4
Track: LH: 0-2 RH: 0-2 Tight: 0-1 Gall: 0-2
Aids: Bl: 0-4 Vi: 0-0 Tstrap: 0-0 Ckp: 0-0
Best Rating: 117 3/99 Plum 3m1f110y   heavy   Ch

Hunter Chaser; suited by three miles plus, soft ground and a right-handed track; usually wears blinkers.

Woodlands Genpower (IRE)
114f   **122+f**

6-y-o gr g Roselier (FR)-Cherished Princess (IRE) (Kemal (FR))
P A Pritchard Woodland Generators

Placings:11330   (4400)
2003/04: 17^1G, 16^1GS, 16^2S, 16^3GS, 16^0G,

	Starts	1st	2nd	3rd	Win & Pl
NH Flat	5	2	0	2	6648
Career Total	5	2	0	2	6648
122 11/03 Chep	2m110y	H NHF		G-S	£1680
100 6/03 NAbb	2m1f	H NHF		GD	£2954

Total win prize-money £4634

Going:	Sf: 0-1 GS: 1-2 Gd: 1-2 GF: - Fm: 0-0
Distance:	2m/2m3: 2-5 2m4-2m7: 0-0 3m+: 0-0
Track:	LH: 2-4 RH: 0-1 Tight: 1-1 Gall: 0-0
Aids:	Bl: 0-0 Vi: 0-0 Tstrap: 0-0 Ckp: 0-0
Best Rating:	122 2/04 Sand 2m110y gd-sft NHF

Useful bumper performer; winner of first two bumpers, posting a particularly decent time on the last of them; not disgraced in two hot bumpers since; effective over two miles; acts on good and soft ground.

Woodlands Lass

8-y-o ch m Nearly A Hand-Maranzi (Jimmy Reppin)
P A Pritchard Woodland Generators

Placings:	0000P/4FPP				(4632)
2003/04:	21⁴GS, 25⁵FS, 20⁵PS, 24⁵PG,				

	Starts	1st	2nd	3rd	Win & Pl
Hurdles	4	0	0	0	0
Career Total	9	0	0	0	0

Going:	Sf: 0-2 GS: 0-1 Gd: 0-1 GF: - Fm: 0-0
Distance:	2m/2m3: 0-0 2m4-2m7: 0-2 3m+: 0-2
Track:	LH: 0-1 RH: 0-3 Tight: 0-1 Gall: 0-0
Aids:	Bl: 0-0 Vi: 0-0 Tstrap: 0-3 Ckp: 0-0
Best Rating:	59 4/02 Wwck 2m gd-fm NHF

Woodybetheone

101   91

4-y-o b g Wolfhound (USA)-Princesse Zelda (FR) (Defensive Play (USA))
O Sherwood (R Hannon 13/6) Miss J A Challen

Placings:	32P				(1414)
2003/04:	17³G, 18²GF, 18ᴾGF,				

	Starts	1st	2nd	3rd	Win & Pl
Hurdles	3	0	1	1	1578
Career Total	3	0	1	1	1578

Going:	Sf: 0-0 GS: 0-0 Gd: 0-1 GF: - Fm: 0-2
Distance:	2m/2m3: 0-3 2m4-2m7: 0-0 3m+: 0-0
Track:	LH: 0-3 RH: 0-0 Tight: 0-3 Gall: 0-0
Aids:	Bl: 0-0 Vi: 0-0 Tstrap: 0-0 Ckp: 0-1
Best Rating:	91 9/03 Font 2m2f110y gd-fm Hdl

Modest juvenile hurdler; had the race won when going lame on the run-in at Fontwell on his third start over hurdles.

Word Gets Around (IRE)

93f   97+f

6-y-o b g King's Ride-Kate Fisher (IRE) (Over The River (FR))
L Lungo Mr & Mrs Raymond Anderson Green

Placings:	3411				(3737)
2003/04:	16³G, 16⁴S, 16¹G, 16¹G,				

	Starts	1st	2nd	3rd	Win & Pl
NH Flat	4	2	0	1	2321
Career Total	4	2	0	1	2321
97 1/04 Catt	2m	H NHF		GD	£2037

Total win prize-money £2037

Going:	Sf: 0-1 GS: 0-0 Gd: 2-3 GF: - Fm: 0-0
Distance:	2m/2m3: 2-4 2m4-2m7: 0-0 3m+: 0-0
Track:	LH: 1-3 RH: 1-1 Tight: 2-2 Gall: 0-0
Aids:	Bl: 0-0 Vi: 0-0 Tstrap: 0-0 Ckp: 0-0
Best Rating:	97 2/04 Muss 2m good NHF

Modest bumper performer; off the mark in bumper on third try at Catterick in January; has plenty of speed and likely to be always best at two miles; acts on good; looks a long-term chasing prospect.

Words And Deeds (USA)

93   95

5-y-o ch g Shadeed (USA)-Millfit (USA) (Blushing Groom (FR))
R A Fahey Northumbria Leisure Ltd

Placings:	25				(0796)
2003/04:	16⁴G, 16⁵G,				

	Starts	1st	2nd	3rd	Win & Pl
Hurdles	2	0	1	0	1704
Career Total	2	0	1	0	1704

Going:	Sf: 0-0 GS: 0-0 Gd: 0-2 GF: - Fm: 0-0
Distance:	2m/2m3: 0-2 2m4-2m7: 0-0 3m+: 0-0
Track:	LH: 0-0 RH: 0-2 Tight: 0-0 Gall: 0-0
Aids:	Bl: 0-0 Vi: 0-0 Tstrap: 0-0 Ckp: 0-0
Best Rating:	89 6/03 Prth 2m110y good Hdl

Workaway

100(102h)   (94h)105+

8-y-o b g Alflora (IRE)-Annicombe Run (Deep Run)
A Parker Mr & Mrs Raymond Anderson Green

Placings:	14/540/315265-F1P4P3P				(4686)
2003/04:	16ᶠGF, 17¹S, 16³GF, 20⁴G, 16ᴾG, 20³F, 17ᴾG,				

	Starts	1st	2nd	3rd	Win & Pl
Hurdles	1	0	0	0	0
Chases	6	1	0	1	4122
Career Total	18	3	1	2	11735
105 12/03 Kels	2m1f	E(0-100)HCh	SFT	£3094
94 10/02 Kels	2m110y	D(0-115)HHdl	GD	£4069
104 11/00 Carl	2m1f	H NHF	HVY	£1977

Total win prize-money £9141

Going:	Sf: 1-1 GS: 0-0 Gd: 0-3 GF: - Fm: 0-3
Distance:	2m/2m3: 1-5 2m4-2m7: 0-2 3m+: 0-0
Track:	LH: 1-2 RH: 0-5 Tight: 1-6 Gall: 0-0
Aids:	Bl: 0-0 Vi: 0-0 Tstrap: 0-0 Ckp: 0-0
Best Rating:	105 12/03 Kels 2m1f soft Ch

Plating-class hurdler/headstrong moderate chaser; acts on good and heavy ground; stays two and a half miles; possibly best with a positive ride over fences.

Working Girl

93   70

7-y-o b m Morpeth-Workamiracle (Teamwork)
J D Frost R G Frost

Placings:	0003-P03				(4518)
2003/04:	22ᴾG, 19ᴾS, 17³GS,				

	Starts	1st	2nd	3rd	Win & Pl
Hurdles	3	0	0	1	436
Career Total	7	0	0	2	857

Going:	Sf: 0-1 GS: 0-1 Gd: 0-1 GF: - Fm: 0-0
Distance:	2m/2m3: 0-2 2m4-2m7: 0-1 3m+: 0-0
Track:	LH: 0-0 RH: 0-3 Tight: 0-0 Gall: 0-0
Aids:	Bl: 0-0 Vi: 0-0 Tstrap: 0-0 Ckp: 0-0
Best Rating:	73 3/04 Extr 2m1f gd-sft Hdl

Worlaby Dale

92   93

8-y-o b g Terimon-Restandbethankful (Random Shot)
Mrs S Lamyman P Lamyman

Placings:	00030/P/44F				(4511)
2003/04:	16⁴GS, 17⁴G, 20ᶠGS,				

	Starts	1st	2nd	3rd	Win & Pl
Hurdles	3	0	0	0	564
Career Total	9	0	0	1	812

Going:	Sf: 0-0 GS: 0-2 Gd: 0-1 GF: - Fm: 0-0
Distance:	2m/2m3: 0-2 2m4-2m7: 0-1 3m+: 0-0
Track:	LH: 0-1 RH: 0-2 Tight: 0-1 Gall: 0-0
Aids:	Bl: 0-0 Vi: 0-0 Tstrap: 0-0 Ckp: 0-0
Best Rating:	98 3/04 Weth 2m4f110y gd-sft Hdl

Plating-class chaser; would have finished third but for falling two out at Wetherby in March; suited by two and a half miles.

World Vision (IRE)

103   96+

7-y-o ch g Denel (FR)-Dusty Lane (IRE) (Electric)
Ferdy Murphy R & M J Partnership

Placings:	430000-413034				(4617)
2003/04:	24⁴GF, 24¹G, 24³GF, 22⁹G, 27³GS, 27⁴G,				

	Starts	1st	2nd	3rd	Win & Pl
Hurdles	6	1	0	2	4025
Career Total	12	1	0	3	4607
92 11/03 Newc	3m	E Hdl	GD	£2520

Total win prize-money £2520

Going:	Sf: 0-0 GS: 0-1 Gd: 1-3 GF: - Fm: 0-2
Distance:	2m/2m3: 0-0 2m4-2m7: 0-1 3m+: 1-5
Track:	LH: 1-5 RH: 0-1 Tight: 0-3 Gall: 1-1
Aids:	Bl: 0-0 Vi: 0-0 Tstrap: 0-0 Ckp: 0-0
Best Rating:	97 2/04 Sedg 3m3f110y gd-sft Hdl

Moderate hurdler; stays 3m; best on good ground.

World Wide Web (IRE)

112(108h)   (125+h)128+

8-y-o b g Be My Native (USA)-Meldrum Lass (Buckskin (FR))
Jonjo O'Neill John P McManus

Placings:	414/56214F5/4005110-121P				(4046)
2003/04:	20¹GS, 19²GS, 24¹S, 28ᴾG,				

	Starts	1st	2nd	3rd	Win & Pl
Chases	4	2	1	0	70205
Career Total	21	6	2	0	92512
128 12/03 Leop	3m	(0-140)HCh	SFT	£63116
117 11/03 Hntg	2m4f110yD(0-115)HCh	G-S	£4478
127 2/03 Chep	2m110y D(0-125)HHdl	G-S	£5050
120 2/03 Sand	2m110y E(0-115)HHdl	HVY	£4446
117 2/02 DRoy	2m4f	Hdl	SFT	£3809
117 12/00 Leop	2m	NHF	SH	£5520

Total win prize-money £86423

Going:	Sf: 1-1 GS: 1-2 Gd: 0-1 GF: - Fm: 0-0
Distance:	2m/2m3: 0-0 2m4-2m7: 1-2 3m+: 1-2

Track: LH: 1-3 RH: 1-1 Tight: 0-0 **Gall: 1-1**
Aids: Bl: 0-0 Vi: 0-0 Tstrap: 0-0 Ckp: 0-0
Best Rating: 128 12/03 Leop 3m   soft   Ch

Fair hurdler, useful and improving chaser; won valuable Paddy Power Handicap Chase at Leopardstown; stays three miles; acts well on a soft surface.

Worthy Man

64   50

7-y-o b g Homo Sapien-Marnworth (Funny Man)
T R George Mrs W H Walter

Placings:0/P-05   (0631)
2003/04: 16⁰GF, 17⁵GF,

	Starts	1st	2nd	3rd	Win & Pl
Hurdles	2	0	0	0	0
Career Total	4	0	0	0	0

Going: Sf: 0-0 GS: 0-0 Gd: 0-0 GF: - Fm: 0-2
Distance: 2m/2m3: 0-2 2m4-2m7: 0-0 3m+: 0-0
Track: LH: 0-2 RH: 0-0 Tight: 0-1 Gall: 0-0
Aids: Bl: 0-0 Vi: 0-0 Tstrap: 0-0 Ckp: 0-0
Best Rating: 55 2/02 Asct 2m110y   soft   NHF

Wot No Cash

110   82

12-y-o gr g Ballacashtal (CAN)-Madame Non (My Swanee)
R C Harper R C Harper

Placings:P5P/F5/P012005PP/35P5-44213FF63P   (4789)
2003/04: 20⁴F, 19⁴GF, 17²GF, 19¹GF, 16³GF, 18⁵GF, 20⁵G, 19⁹G, 16³GS, 17⁹G,

	Starts	1st	2nd	3rd	Win & Pl
Chases	10	1	1	2	4049
Career Total	28	2	2	3	7716
81 10/03 Chep	2m3f110yG(0-90)HCh		G-F	£2002	
77 5/01 Font	2m2f	G(0-90)HCh	G-F	£2383	

Total win prize-money £4386

Going: Sf: 0-0 GS: 0-1 Gd: 0-3 GF: - Fm: 1-6
Distance: 2m/2m3: 0-7 **2m4-2m7: 1-3** 3m+: 0-0
Track: **LH: 1-8** RH: 0-1 Tight: 0-3 Gall: 0-0
Aids: Bl: 0-0 Vi: 0-0 Tstrap: 1-3 Ckp: 0-0
Best Rating: 84 6/01 NAbb 2m110y   gd-sft   Ch

Plating-class chaser; stays 2m 4f; loves a fast surface.

Wotan (FR)

5-y-o ch g Beaudelaire (USA)-Woglinde (USA) (Sunny's Halo (CAN))
Miss I E Craig Mrs M L Luck

Placings:P   (2336)
2003/04: 16⁵S,

	Starts	1st	2nd	3rd	Win & Pl
Hurdles	1	0	0	0	0
Career Total	1	0	0	0	0

Going: Sf: 0-1 GS: 0-0 Gd: 0-0 GF: - Fm: 0-0
Distance: 2m/2m3: 0-1 2m4-2m7: 0-0 3m+: 0-0
Track: LH: 0-1 RH: 0-0 Tight: 0-1 Gall: 0-0
Aids: Bl: 0-0 Vi: 0-0 Tstrap: 0-0 Ckp: 0-0

Would You Believe

102   115

8-y-o gr g Derrylin-Ramelton (Precipice Wood)

K C Bailey D Allen

Placings:0/F3-2UF3   (4534)
2003/04: 22²S, 26ᵁHY, 25⁵GS, 22³GS,

	Starts	1st	2nd	3rd	Win & Pl
Chases	4	0	1	1	1666
Career Total	7	0	1	2	2856

Going: Sf: 0-2 GS: 0-2 Gd: 0-0 GF: - Fm: 0-0
Distance: 2m/2m3: 0-0 2m4-2m7: 0-2 3m+: 0-2
Track: LH: 0-1 RH: 0-3 Tight: 0-0 Gall: 0-0
Aids: Bl: 0-0 Vi: 0-0 Tstrap: 0-0 Ckp: 0-0
Best Rating: 115 12/03 Towc 2m6f   soft   Ch

Lightly raced ex-Irish chaser; prefers soft ground; stays three miles.

Wouldn't You Agree (IRE)

97(107h)   (131h)124

8-y-o ch g Toulon-Mention Of Money (Le Bavard (FR))
Jonjo O'Neill (C Roche 29/7) John P McManus

Placings:2/11112-012616F0   (3924)
2003/04: 20⁰YS, 22¹GY, 20²F, 22⁶S, 16¹S, 16⁶G, 16⁵S, 16⁹G,

	Starts	1st	2nd	3rd	Win & Pl
Hurdles	1	0	0	0	0
Chases	7	2	1	0	12627
Career Total	14	6	3	0	49312
123 11/03 Towc	2m110y	D Ch	SFT	£4071	
124 6/03 Tral	2m6f	Ch	G-Y	£5824	
126 10/02 Tipp	2m	Hdl	G-F	£15153	
110 8/02 Tipp	2m4f	Hdl	G-F	£4656	
114 8/02 Gway	2m	Hdl	G-Y	£6773	
110 7/02 Gway	2m	(—)NHF	SFT	£5503	

Total win prize-money £41982

Going: Sf: 1-3 GS: 0-0 Gd: 0-2 GF: - Fm: 0-1
Distance: 2m/2m3: 1-4 2m4-2m7: 1-4 3m+: 0-0
Track: LH: 0-1 **RH: 1-6** Tight: 0-0 Gall: 0-0
Aids: Bl: 0-0 Vi: 0-0 **Tstrap: 1-3** Ckp: 0-0
Best Rating: 131 11/02 Chel 2m5f   gd-sft   Hdl

Useful ex-Irish trained novice chaser; winner of a bumper and three hurdle races; winner of his first chase in Ireland; won at Towcester over two miles in very bad ground on British debut; stays two miles six; acts on any ground; has worn a tongue tie.

Wozzeck

72   83

4-y-o b g Groom Dancer (USA)-Opera Lover (IRE) (Sadler's Wells (USA))
R H Buckler (J R Fanshawe 3/9) Mrs P J Buckler

Placings:F00   (3856)
2003/04: 16⁶GS, 17⁰S, 16⁹S,

	Starts	1st	2nd	3rd	Win & Pl
Hurdles	3	0	0	0	0
Career Total	3	0	0	0	0

Going: Sf: 0-2 GS: 0-1 Gd: 0-0 GF: - Fm: 0-0
Distance: 2m/2m3: 0-3 2m4-2m7: 0-0 3m+: 0-0
Track: LH: 0-1 RH: 0-2 Tight: 0-2 Gall: 0-0
Aids: Bl: 0-0 Vi: 0-0 Tstrap: 0-0 Ckp: 0-1
Best Rating: 83 1/04 Winc 2m   gd-sft   Hdl

Wrags To Riches (IRE)

105   102

7-y-o b g Tremblant-Clonea Lady (IRE) (Lord Ha Ha)
J D Frost No Illusions Partnership

Placings:052-3532P00   (4691)
2003/04: 17³G, 17⁵GS, 16³S, 18²FH, 20²S, 22⁹G, 17⁰G,

	Starts	1st	2nd	3rd	Win & Pl
NH Flat	1	0	0	1	427
Hurdles	6	0	1	1	1427
Career Total	10	0	2	2	2442

Going: Sf: 0-3 GS: 0-1 Gd: 0-3 GF: - Fm: 0-0
Distance: 2m/2m3: 0-5 2m4-2m7: 0-2 3m+: 0-0
Track: LH: 0-4 RH: 0-3 Tight: 0-3 Gall: 0-0
Aids: Bl: 0-0 Vi: 0-0 Tstrap: 0-0 Ckp: 0-0
Best Rating: 108 1/04 Font 2m2f110y   heavy   Hdl

Moderate maiden; showed some ability in bumpers, but best form has come at around two miles on soft over hurdles; stays 2m2f; acts on soft.

Wrangel (FR)

101(88c)   (66c)90+

10-y-o ch g Tropular-Swedish Princess (Manado)
B J Llewellyn Miss Emily Jane Jones

Placings:0/P62/4061320UF0/064210/34/50P06336-41P0   (3050)
2003/04: 17⁴G, 17¹GF, 18⁰GF, 17⁰G,

	Starts	1st	2nd	3rd	Win & Pl
Hurdles	3	1	0	0	2213
Chases	1	0	0	0	321
Career Total	34	3	3	4	12262
91 10/03 Sthl	2m1f	G(0-95)HHdl	G-F	£2213	
100 10/00 Fknm	2m	F(0-105)HHdl	GD	£3331	
100 10/99 Strf	2m110y	F(0-100)HHdl	G-S	£2495	

Total win prize-money £8039

Going: Sf: 0-0 GS: 0-0 Gd: 0-2 GF: - Fm: 1-2
Distance: **2m/2m3: 1-4** 2m4-2m7: 0-0 3m+: 0-0
Track: **LH: 1-3** RH: 0-1 Tight: 0-3 Gall: 0-0
Aids: Bl: 0-0 Vi: 0-0 Tstrap: 0-0 Ckp: 0-1
Best Rating: 101 12/99 Donc 2m110y   gd-fm   Hdl

Plating-class hurdler; best at around two miles; suited by a sound surface.

Wreford Lake

82f   63f

4-y-o ch g Karinga Bay-Sporting Annie (Teamster)
J D Frost N W Lake

Placings:0   (4739)
2003/04: 17⁰G,

	Starts	1st	2nd	3rd	Win & Pl
NH Flat	1	0	0	0	
Career Total	1	0	0	0	

Going: Sf: 0-0 GS: 0-0 Gd: 0-1 GF: - Fm: 0-0
Distance: 2m/2m3: 0-1 2m4-2m7: 0-0 3m+: 0-0
Track: LH: 0-1 RH: 0-0 Tight: 0-1 Gall: 0-0
Aids: Bl: 0-0 Vi: 0-0 Tstrap: 0-0 Ckp: 0-0
Best Rating: 63 4/04 NAbb 2m1f   good   NHF

Wrens Island (IRE)

107   105

10-y-o br g Yashgan-Tipiton (Balboa)

R Dickin Wholebuild Ltd

Placings:P/P1162P5450/P11P055-020 (0747)
2003/04: 24^0GF, 23^2GF, 24^0G,

	Starts	1st	2nd	3rd	Win & Pl
Chases	3	0	1	0	2170
Career Total	21	4	2	0	15234

105	8/02	Uttx	3m	F(0-100)HCh	G-F	£3412
97	7/02	Worc	2m7f110yE(0-110)HCh		G-F	£3565
102	5/01	Chel	2m110y	H Ch	GD	£3178
100	5/01	Strf	2m4f	H Ch	G-F	£1657
					Total win prize-money £11814

Going: Sf: 0-0 GS: 0-0 Gd: 0-1 GF: - Fm: 0-2
Distance: 2m/2m3: 0-0 2m4-2m7: 0-0 3m+: 0-3
Track: LH: 0-3 RH: 0-0 Tight: 0-1 Gall: 0-0
Aids: Bl: 0-0 Vi: 0-0 Tstrap: 0-0 Ckp: 0-0
Best Rating: 105 6/03 Worc 2m7f110y gd-fm Ch

Moderate hurdler; improved form when winning back-to-back three miles handicaps in July and August 2002; signs of a return to form when runner-up at Worcester June 2003; acts on ground good or faster.

Wrong Impression (IRE)
53   38
6-y-o b m Executive Perk-Adare Boreen (Boreen (FR))
Miss Lucinda V Russell White Horse Racing Club

Placings:0F0 (2145)
2003/04: 16^0G, 16^2GF, 16^0G,

	Starts	1st	2nd	3rd	Win & Pl
NH Flat	1	0	0	0	0
Hurdles	2	0	0	0	0
Career Total	3	0	0	0	

Going: Sf: 0-0 GS: 0-0 Gd: 0-2 GF: - Fm: 0-1
Distance: 2m/2m3: 0-3 2m4-2m7: 0-0 3m+: 0-0
Track: LH: 0-1 RH: 0-1 Tight: 0-0 Gall: 0-0
Aids: Bl: 0-0 Vi: 0-0 Tstrap: 0-0 Ckp: 0-0
Best Rating: 57 9/03 Prth 2m110y good NHF

Wuchowsen (IRE)
88f   54f
6-y-o b m King's Ride-Our Sioux (IRE) (Jolly Jake (NZ))
J M Jefferson Yorkshire Racing Club Owners Group

Placings:000 (3438)
2003/04: 17^0G, 16^0GS, 16^0HY,

	Starts	1st	2nd	3rd	Win & Pl
NH Flat	3	0	0	0	
Career Total	3	0	0	0	

Going: Sf: 0-1 GS: 0-1 Gd: 0-1 GF: - Fm: 0-0
Distance: 2m/2m3: 0-3 2m4-2m7: 0-0 3m+: 0-0
Track: LH: 0-3 RH: 0-0 Tight: 0-1 Gall: 0-0
Aids: Bl: 0-0 Vi: 0-0 Tstrap: 0-0 Ckp: 0-0
Best Rating: 54 11/03 Weth 2m gd-sft NHF

Wun Chai (IRE)
103   95+
5-y-o b g King's Theatre (IRE)-Flower From Heaven (Baptism)
R J Baker (F Jordan 29/5) Graham Brown

Placings:P510-40200401 (4859)
2003/04: 17^4S, 16^0G, 19^2GS, 19^0S, 19^0GS, 19^4GF, 17^0GS, 19^1GF,

	Starts	1st	2nd	3rd	Win & Pl
Hurdles	8	1	1	0	7274
Career Total	12	2	1	0	10648

95	4/04	Tntn	2m3f110yD(0-115)HHdl	G-F	£5716
87	3/03	Hrfd	2m1f	E Hdl	G-F	£3373
				Total win prize-money £9091	

Going: Sf: 0-2 GS: 0-3 Gd: 0-1 GF: - Fm: 1-2
Distance: 2m/2m3: 0-4 2m4-2m7: 1-4 3m+: 0-0
Track: LH: 0-1 RH: 1-7 Tight: 1-3 Gall: 0-0
Aids: Bl: 1-3 Vi: 0-0 Tstrap: 0-0 Ckp: 0-0
Best Rating: 95 4/04 Tntn 2m3f110y gd-fm Hdl

Modest hurdler;scored on third start in blinkers when allowed a soft lead in 2m 3f handicap at Taunton April 2004; acts on a sound surface.

Wuxi Venture
103(106h)   (115h)114+
9-y-o b g Wolfhound (USA)-Push A Button (Bold Lad (IRE))
R A Fahey R G Leatham

Placings:43242/365162-0P12546U (4516)
2003/04: 17^0G, 16^2G, 19^1GS, 16^2S, 16^4G, 16^6GS, 16^0GS,

	Starts	1st	2nd	3rd	Win & Pl
Hurdles	1	0	0	0	0
Chases	7	1	1	0	6449
Career Total	19	2	4	2	17864

114	1/04	Catt	2m3f	E Ch	G-S	£3981
115	2/03	Bang	2m1f	E(0-110)HHdl	G-S	£4387
					Total win prize-money £8369

Going: Sf: 0-1 GS: 1-3 Gd: 0-3 GF: - Fm: 0-1
Distance: 2m/2m3: 1-7 2m4-2m7: 0-3 3m+: 0-1
Track: LH: 1-3 RH: 0-5 Tight: 1-3 Gall: 0-1
Aids: Bl: 0-0 Vi: 0-0 Tstrap: 0-0 Ckp: 0-0
Best Rating: 115 3/03 Font 2m2f110y good Hdl

Modest hurdler/novice chaser; pulled up on debut over fences but made amends at Catterick in January; suited by ground good or softer; best at two miles and two miles four.

Wylde Winter (IRE)
19
6-y-o b g Fourstars Allstar (USA)-Wintry Shower (Strong Gale)
P Spottiswood P Spottiswood

Placings:P0-PPP0 (4258)
2003/04: 16^5S, 16^5S, 20^2F, 16^0GF,

	Starts	1st	2nd	3rd	Win & Pl
Hurdles	4	0	0	0	
Career Total	6	0	0	0	

Going: Sf: 0-2 GS: 0-0 Gd: 0-0 GF: - Fm: 0-2
Distance: 2m/2m3: 0-3 2m4-2m7: 0-1 3m+: 0-0
Track: LH: 0-3 RH: 0-1 Tight: 0-3 Gall: 0-0
Aids: Bl: 0-0 Vi: 0-0 Tstrap: 0-3 Ckp: 0-0
Best Rating: 19 4/03 Slig 2m good Hdl

Wyn Dixie (IRE)
99   95+
5-y-o b g Great Commotion (USA)-Duchess Affair (IRE) (Digamist (USA))
M C Pipe D A Johnson

Placings:23600 (3097)
2003/04: 16^2GF, 17^3G, 16^6GS, 16^0GS, 17^0G,

	Starts	1st	2nd	3rd	Win & Pl
Hurdles	5	0	1	1	1439
Career Total	5	0	1	1	1439

Going: Sf: 0-0 GS: 0-2 Gd: 0-2 GF: - Fm: 0-1
Distance: 2m/2m3: 0-5 2m4-2m7: 0-0 3m+: 0-0
Track: LH: 0-5 RH: 0-0 Tight: 0-0 Gall: 0-1
Aids: Bl: 0-0 Vi: 0-0 Tstrap: 0-0 Ckp: 0-0
Best Rating: 95 11/03 Aint 2m110y gd-sft Hdl

Moderate novice hurdler; looks a tricky ride.

Wynbury Flyer
105   85+
9-y-o ch g Risk Me (FR)-Woolcana (Some Hand)
Ferdy Murphy Mrs G P Seymour

Placings:45031443/43614FU1342/0543/F4F/06P-32265P (4458)
2003/04: 16^3GF, 16^2GS, 16^2GS, 16^6G, 16^6HY,

	Starts	1st	2nd	3rd	Win & Pl
Chases	6	0	2	1	2286
Career Total	35	3	3	6	17336

109	2/00	Carl	2m	D Ch	HVY	£4173
109	12/99	Donc	2m3f110yD Ch		G-S	£4261
93	1/99	Catt	2m	G Hdl	GD	£1646
					Total win prize-money £10080

Going: Sf: 0-1 GS: 0-2 Gd: 0-2 GF: - Fm: 0-1
Distance: 2m/2m3: 0-6 2m4-2m7: 0-0 3m+: 0-0
Track: LH: 0-4 RH: 0-2 Tight: 0-4 Gall: 0-2
Aids: Bl: 0-0 Vi: 0-0 Tstrap: 0-0 Ckp: 0-0
Best Rating: 109 3/00 Kels 2m1f gd-sft Ch

Plating-class chaser these days; has not won since 2000; effective at two miles; acts on fast and easy ground.

Wynyard Dancer
10-y-o b m Minster Son-The White Lion (Flying Tyke)
Miss T Jackson A Jackson

Placings:3305/260P/1-F (0079)
2003/04: 21^0FS,

	Starts	1st	2nd	3rd	Win & Pl
Chases	1	0	0	0	
Career Total	10	1	1	2	2908

74	6/02	Hexm	2m4f110yH Ch	G-F	£1575
				Total win prize-money £1575	

Going: Sf: 0-1 GS: 0-0 Gd: 0-0 GF: - Fm: 0-0
Distance: 2m/2m3: 0-0 2m4-2m7: 0-1 3m+: 0-0
Track: LH: 0-1 RH: 0-0 Tight: 0-0 Gall: 0-0
Aids: Bl: 0-0 Vi: 0-0 Tstrap: 0-0 Ckp: 0-1
Best Rating: 85 3/99 Hexm 2m gd-sft NHF

Xaipete (IRE)
111(108h)   (104h)122
12-y-o b g Jolly Jake (NZ)-Rolfete (USA) (Tom Rolfe)
R C Guest N B Mason

Placings:43622114211352U/1122320152244U5301/16411 334340453003F/3262F/306403332326416331F-335310334F12342U32332 (4912)
2003/04: 18^3G, 20^3G, 17^5G, 17^3G, 20^1G, 20^4GF, 16^3G, 20^3G, 20^4GF, 17^2G, 16^1G, 17^3G, 16^3F, 21^4GF, 20^2G, 22^4G, 19^3G, 21^2G, 21^3GS, 21^3G, 20^2S,

	Starts	1st	2nd	3rd	Win & Pl
Hurdles	9	2	1	5	11636
Chases	12	0	3	4	13510
Career Total	111	17	19	29	126082

94	9/03	Prth	2m110y	F Hdl	GD	£3471
104	7/03	Worc	2m4f	E(0-110)HHdl	GD	£3474
122	3/03	Carl	2m4f	E(0-110)HCh	GD	£4621
113	1/03	Ayr	2m	D(0-115)HCh	HVY	£5414

Xtra (continued)

120	8/00	Cntml	2m1f110yD(0-125)HHdl	GD	£3581	
134	8/00	Bang	2m4f110yD(0-125)HCh	GD	£5642	
123	5/00	Kels	2m110y D(0-125)HHdl	GD	£4706	
112	4/00	Kels	2m110y D(0-125)HHdl	SFT	£2941	
127	8/99	Bang	2m4f110yD(0-125)HCh	GD	£4810	
134	5/99	Aint	2m D(0-125)HCh	G-F	£4485	
127	5/99	Weth	2m (0-135)HCh	G-F	£5572	
113	1/99	Muss	2m D(0-125)HCh	G-S	£3597	
109	12/98	Sedg	2m110y E(0-110)HCh	G-S	£3488	
110	11/98	Sedg	2m (0-110)HCh	G-S	£3397	
105	10/98	Fknm	2m F(0-105)HHdl	G-S	£3326	
93	11/97	Sedg	2m110y F(0-100)HCh	GD	£2784	
77	3/96	Sedg	2m1f E Hdl	G-F	£2372	
				Total win prize-money	£67689	

Going: Sf: 0-1 GS: 0-1 Gd: 2-15 GF: - Fm: 0-0
Distance: 2m/2m3: 1-8 2m4-2m7: 1-13 3m+: 0-0
Track: LH: 1-17 RH: 1-3 Tight: 0-14 Gall: 0-0
Aids: Bl: 0-0 Vi: 0-0 Tstrap: 0-0 Ckp: 0-0
Best Rating: 134 9/00 Worc 2m gd-fm Ch

Modest hurdler/fair chaser; has continued to run well since winning two and a half mile handicap hurdle at Worcester July 2003 despite hanging left; effective from two miles to two miles four; acts on most ground; needs thing to go his way.

Xellance (IRE)
111 ... 128

7-y-o b g Be My Guest (USA)-Excellent Alibi (USA) (Exceller (USA))
P J Hobbs The Five Nations Partnership

Placings:5000331-40232211122212 (4963)
2003/04: 21^{4}G, 20^{9}G, 20^{2}GF, 22^{3}G, 22^{2}GF, 20^{2}G, 22^{1}GF, 22^{1}GF, 19^{1}GF, 20^{2}GF, 24^{2}GF, 24^{2}GF, 21^{1}GF, 20^{2}G,

	Starts	1st	2nd	3rd	Win & Pl		
Hurdles	14	4	7	1	42305		
Career Total	21	5	7	3	47241		
124	4/04	Chel	2m5f110yB HHdl	G-F	£11780		
107	8/03	MRas	2m3f110yD(0-115)HHdl	G-F	£5291		
105	8/03	NAbb	2m6f D Hdl	G-F	£4725		
95	8/03	NAbb	2m6f D Hdl	G-F	£5434		
89	4/03	Hrfd	2m3f110yE(0-105)HHdl	G-F	£3614		
			Total win prize-money	£30846			

Going: Sf: 0-0 GS: 0-0 Gd: 0-5 GF: - Fm: 4-9
Distance: 2m/2m3: 0-0 2m4-2m7: 4-12 3m+: 0-2
Track: LH: 3-9 RH: 1-5 Tight: 3-6 Gall: 1-1
Aids: Bl: 0-0 Vi: 0-0 Tstrap: 0-0 Ckp: 0-0
Best Rating: 128 4/04 Sand 2m4f110y good Hdl

Fair hurdler; multiple winner on the Flat; in good form in the summer of 2003 completing a hat-trick; returned from a break with victory in a handicap at Cheltenham; loves fast ground; stays two miles six; tough and consistent.

Xixita
95 ... 79

4-y-o ch f Fleetwood (IRE)-Conquista (Aragon)
Dr J D Scargill J P T Partnership

Placings:00P (4756)
2003/04: 16^{9}G, 16^{9}G, 19^{P}S,

	Starts	1st	2nd	3rd	Win & Pl
Hurdles	3	0	0	0	
Career Total	3	0	0	0	

Going: Sf: 0-1 GS: 0-0 Gd: 0-2 GF: - Fm: 0-0
Distance: 2m/2m3: 0-2 2m4-2m7: 0-1 3m+: 0-0
Track: LH: 0-0 RH: 0-2 Tight: 0-0 Gall: 0-2
Aids: Bl: 0-0 Vi: 0-0 Tstrap: 0-0 Ckp: 0-0
Best Rating: 79 3/04 Hntg 2m110y good Hdl

Xtra
97+

6-y-o b g Sadler's Wells (USA)-Oriental Mystique (Kris)
J A B Old W E Sturt

Placings:3-P (2837)
2003/04: 16^{P}G,

	Starts	1st	2nd	3rd	Win & Pl
Hurdles	1	0	0	0	
Career Total	2	0	0	1	697

Going: Sf: 0-0 GS: 0-0 Gd: 0-1 GF: - Fm: 0-0
Distance: 2m/2m3: 0-1 2m4-2m7: 0-0 3m+: 0-0
Track: LH: 0-0 RH: 0-1 Tight: 0-0 Gall: 0-0
Aids: Bl: 0-0 Vi: 0-0 Tstrap: 0-0 Ckp: 0-0
Best Rating: 98 1/03 Tntn 2m1f soft Hdl

Modest novice hurdler; formerly smart performer on the Flat; acts on fast ground, but especially suited by soft

Xyphor Seeker (IRE)
69f

4-y-o b g Moonax (IRE)-Vera Dodd (IRE) (Riot Helmet)
R H Alner Miss H J Flower

Placings:0 (4374)
2003/04: 16^{9}GF,

	Starts	1st	2nd	3rd	Win & Pl
NH Flat	1	0	0	0	
Career Total	1	0	0	0	

Going: Sf: 0-0 GS: 0-0 Gd: 0-0 GF: - Fm: 0-1
Distance: 2m/2m3: 0-1 2m4-2m7: 0-0 3m+: 0-0
Track: LH: 0-0 RH: 0-1 Tight: 0-0 Gall: 0-0
Aids: Bl: 0-0 Vi: 0-0 Tstrap: 0-0 Ckp: 0-0
Best Rating: 69 3/04 Strf 2m110y gd-fm NHF

Yaiyna Tango (FR)
81 ... 72

9-y-o br g Fijar Tango (FR)-Yaiyna (FR) (Lashkari)
R Ford D W Watson

Placings:1422/2/65P (4455)
2003/04: 23^{6}G, 19^{5}G, 24^{7}HY,

	Starts	1st	2nd	3rd	Win & Pl		
Hurdles	3	0	0	0			
Career Total	8	1	3	0	5153		
118	11/99	Worc	2m H NHF	G-S	£1786		
			Total win prize-money	£1786			

Going: Sf: 0-1 GS: 0-1 Gd: 0-1 GF: - Fm: 0-0
Distance: 2m/2m3: 0-0 2m4-2m7: 0-2 3m+: 0-1
Track: LH: 0-3 RH: 0-1 Tight: 0-0 Gall: 0-1
Aids: Bl: 0-0 Vi: 0-0 Tstrap: 0-0 Ckp: 0-1
Best Rating: 118 11/99 Worc 2m gd-sft NHF

Moderate hurdler, stays 2m4f, but likely to stay further; acts on most ground; showed promise on his comeback after three years off the track.

Yankee Crossing (IRE)
67 ... 14

6-y-o b g Lord Americo-Ath Leathan (Royal Vulcan)
Jonjo O'Neill Trevor Hemmings

Placings:00-0 (2289)
2003/04: 20^{0}G,

	Starts	1st	2nd	3rd	Win & Pl
Hurdles	1	0	0	0	
Career Total	3	0	0	0	

Going: Sf: 0-0 GS: 0-0 Gd: 0-1 GF: - Fm: 0-0
Distance: 2m/2m3: 0-0 2m4-2m7: 0-1 3m+: 0-0
Track: LH: 0-1 RH: 0-0 Tight: 0-0 Gall: 0-0
Aids: Bl: 0-0 Vi: 0-0 Tstrap: 0-0 Ckp: 0-0
Best Rating: 76 3/03 Hayd 2m good NHF

Yankee Jamie (IRE)
107(105c) ... (124c)**112**

10-y-o b g Strong Gale-Sparkling Opera (Orchestra)
L Lungo R J Gilbert

Placings:6660/P11/PP2111-50P6P (4948)
2003/04: 24^{5}G, 21^{9}GS, 24^{P}GS, 22^{6}G, 27^{P}GS,

	Starts	1st	2nd	3rd	Win & Pl		
Hurdles	5	0	0	0			
Career Total	18	5	1	0	19551		
114	1/03	Muss	3m E(0-110)HHdl	GD	£4075		
124	12/02	Ayr	3m1f E(0-110)HCh	SFT	£3601		
119	12/02	Ayr	2m5f110yD(0-110)HCh	G-S	£4654		
103	12/01	Kels	2m6f110yE(0-105)HHdl	G-S	£3080		
84	11/01	Kels	2m6f110yF(0-100)HHdl	G-S	£3010		
			Total win prize-money	£18421			

Going: Sf: 0-0 GS: 0-3 Gd: 0-2 GF: - Fm: 0-0
Distance: 2m/2m3: 0-0 2m4-2m7: 0-2 3m+: 0-3
Track: LH: 0-3 RH: 0-1 Tight: 0-3 Gall: 0-0
Aids: Bl: 0-0 Vi: 0-0 Tstrap: 0-0 Ckp: 0-0
Best Rating: 124 12/02 Ayr 3m1f soft Ch

Fair hurdler/chaser; in fine form in 2002/3; acts on good and soft ground; stays three miles.

Yankie Lord (IRE)
106 ... 95

12-y-o b g Lord Americo-Coolstuff (Over The River (FR))
Mrs J C McGregor The Good To Soft Firm

Placings:12/P1212/2301/55FFP/0PFPU5431/F2P55P535 6-433U4F (3882)
2003/04: 20^{4}G, 20^{3}GF, 16^{9}G, 17^{U}G, 20^{4}G, 24^{F}G,

	Starts	1st	2nd	3rd	Win & Pl		
Chases	6	0	0	2	2719		
Career Total	42	5	5	5	37770		
100	2/02	Muss	2m4f D(0-115)HCh	G-S	£5694		
131	4/00	Hayd	3m D(0-125)HCh	GD	£7572		
118	3/99	Fknm	2m5f110yD(0-120)HCh	GD	£4281		
130	1/99	Hntg	2m4f110yF(0-105)HCh	SFT	£2600		
98	2/97	Naas	2m Ch	SFT	£3051		
			Total win prize-money	£23201			

Going: Sf: 0-0 GS: 0-1 Gd: 0-4 GF: - Fm: 0-0
Distance: 2m/2m3: 0-2 2m4-2m7: 0-3 3m+: 0-0
Track: LH: 0-2 RH: 0-4 Tight: 0-2 Gall: 0-0
Aids: Bl: 0-0 Vi: 0-0 Tstrap: 0-0 Ckp: 0-0
Best Rating: 131 4/00 Hayd 3m good Ch

Plating-class chaser; formerly a fair sort but on the downgrade now; probably best when able to dictate over two and a half miles; looks best suited by a sound surface.

Yann's (FR)
102(99h) ... (125h)**125**

8-y-o b g Helios (USA)-Listen Gyp (USA) (Advocator)
R T Phillips Darren Bloom & Matthew Miller

Placings:0/1103/206S/42212-366 (4871)
2003/04: 23^{3}G, 20^{6}GS, 24^{6}S,

	Starts	1st	2nd	3rd	Win & Pl
Chases	3	0	0	1	1350
Career Total	**17**	**3**	**4**	**2**	**19249**

120	2/03	Tntn	3m	D Ch		SFT	£5726
125	1/01	Ludl	2m	E(0-105)HHdl		SFT	£3041
109	11/00	Wwck	2m	E Hdl		SFT	£2119

Total win prize-money £10889

Going:	Sf: 0-1 GS: 0-1 Gd: 0-1 GF: - Fm: 0-0
Distance:	2m/2m3: 0-0 2m4-2m7: 0-1 3m+: 0-2
Track:	LH: 0-2 RH: 0-1 Tight: 0-2 Gall: 0-0
Aids:	Bl: 0-0 Vi: 0-0 Tstrap: 0-0 Ckp: 0-0
Best Rating:	125 4/03 Extr 2m7f110y good Ch

Fair novice chaser in 2002/3; stays three miles and acts on soft ground; effective under forcing tactics.

Yardbird (IRE)
105   114+

5-y-o b g Moonax (IRE)-Princess Lizzie (IRE) (Homo Sapien)
Miss H C Knight Gilco

Placings: 10-4425101   (4819)
2003/04: 17⁴G, 16⁴GS, 20²G, 21⁵G, 24¹G, 21⁰G, 22¹GF,

	Starts	1st	2nd	3rd	Win & Pl
Hurdles	7	2	1	0	12376
Career Total	**9**	**3**	**1**	**0**	**15792**

114	4/04	Extr	2m6f110y	E Hdl	G-F	£4160
118	2/04	Asct	3m	D Hdl	GD	£4953
93	3/03	Newb	2m110y	H NHF	GD	£3416

Total win prize-money £12529

Going:	Sf: 0-0 GS: 0-1 Gd: 1-5 GF: - Fm: 1-1
Distance:	2m/2m3: 0-2 2m4-2m7: 1-4 3m+: 1-1
Track:	LH: 0-2 RH: 2-5 Tight: 0-0 Gall: 0-2
Aids:	Bl: 0-0 Vi: 0-0 Tstrap: 0-0 Ckp: 0-0
Best Rating:	118 2/04 Asct 3m good Hdl

Modest novice hurdler; made a winning bumper debut at Newbury in March 2003; has shown ability over hurdles and broke his duck with hard-fought success at Ascot in February; suited by three miles; acts on decent ground.

Yassar (IRE)
81   92

9-y-o b g Yashgan-Go Hunting (IRE) (Abednego)
D J Wintle (Patrick Heffernan 6/6) Lavender Hill Stud L L C

Placings: 4-20P2   (4442)
2003/04: 24²Y, 20⁰YS, 24⁴HY, 20²GS,

	Starts	1st	2nd	3rd	Win & Pl
Hurdles	1	0	0	0	
Chases	3	0	2	0	2334
Career Total	**5**	**0**	**2**	**0**	**2821**

Going:	Sf: 0-1 GS: 0-1 Gd: 0-0 GF: - Fm: 0-0
Distance:	2m/2m3: 0-0 2m4-2m7: 0-2 3m+: 0-2
Track:	LH: 0-2 RH: 0-1 Tight: 0-0 Gall: 0-0
Aids:	Bl: 0-0 Vi: 0-0 Tstrap: 0-0 Ckp: 0-0
Best Rating:	92 5/03 Navn 3m yield Ch

Ex-Irish; dual point winner in 2002; finished tired in soft ground when eventually well beaten second in weak 2m 4f beginners' chase at Warwick March 2004.

Yellow River (IRE)

4-y-o b g Sesaro (USA)-Amtico (Bairn (USA))
R Curtis Yellow River Partnership

Placings: PP   (4899)
2003/04: 16ᵖGS, 16ᵖG,

	Starts	1st	2nd	3rd	Win & Pl
Hurdles	2	0	0	0	
Career Total	**2**	**0**	**0**	**0**	

Going:	Sf: 0-0 GS: 0-1 Gd: 0-1 GF: - Fm: 0-0
Distance:	2m/2m3: 0-2 2m4-2m7: 0-0 3m+: 0-0
Track:	LH: 0-1 RH: 0-1 Tight: 0-0 Gall: 0-0
Aids:	Bl: 0-0 Vi: 0-0 Tstrap: 0-0 Ckp: 0-1

Yellow Sky
66   26

6-y-o b m Gildoran-Summer Sky (Skyliner)
K G Wingrove L T Woodhouse

Placings: 000-P0PR   (4370)
2003/04: 16ᵖGS, 16⁰GS, 19ᴿGF,

	Starts	1st	2nd	3rd	Win & Pl
Hurdles	4	0	0	0	
Career Total	**7**	**0**	**0**	**0**	

Going:	Sf: 0-0 GS: 0-3 Gd: 0-0 GF: - Fm: 0-1
Distance:	2m/2m3: 0-4 2m4-2m7: 0-0 3m+: 0-0
Track:	LH: 0-2 RH: 0-2 Tight: 0-1 Gall: 0-0
Aids:	Bl: 0-0 Vi: 0-0 Tstrap: 0-3 Ckp: 0-0
Best Rating:	38 8/02 NAbb 2m1f gd-fm NHF

Yellow Soil Star (IRE)
89   91

5-y-o b m Perugino (USA)-Standing Ovation (Godswalk (USA))
J J Lambe (V Bowens 19/6) Edward O'Connor

Placings: F00050403-0600   (1188)
2003/04: 16⁰F, 17⁰GF, 16⁰GF, 17⁰G,

	Starts	1st	2nd	3rd	Win & Pl
Hurdles	4	0	0	0	0
Career Total	**13**	**0**	**0**	**1**	**740**

Going:	Sf: 0-0 GS: 0-0 Gd: 0-0 GF: - Fm: 0-3
Distance:	2m/2m3: 0-4 2m4-2m7: 0-0 3m+: 0-0
Track:	LH: 0-2 RH: 0-1 Tight: 0-0 Gall: 0-0
Aids:	Bl: 0-1 Vi: 0-0 Tstrap: 0-0 Ckp: 0-0
Best Rating:	91 4/03 Thur 2m gd-fm Hdl

Yer 'Umble (IRE)
15

13-y-o b g Lafontaine (USA)-Miners Girl (Miners Lamp)
J K Cresswell J K S Cresswell

Placings: 60P/5423F00/0046/00164P/000P/6341444/PP03-P   (0329)
2003/04: 26ᵖGF,

	Starts	1st	2nd	3rd	Win & Pl
Chases	1	0	0	0	
Career Total	**36**	**2**	**1**	**3**	**11549**

94	7/00	Strf	3m	D Ch	G-F	£4368
89	3/99	Strf	2m6f110y	D Hdl	HVY	£3961

Total win prize-money £8329

Going:	Sf: 0-0 GS: 0-0 Gd: 0-0 GF: - Fm: 0-0
Distance:	2m/2m3: 0-0 2m4-2m7: 0-0 3m+: 0-1
Track:	LH: 0-1 RH: 0-0 Tight: 0-0 Gall: 0-0
Aids:	Bl: 0-0 Vi: 0-0 Tstrap: 0-0 Ckp: 0-0

Best Rating:	94 7/00 Strf 3m gd-fm Ch

Yesyes (IRE)
87   110+

9-y-o b g Supreme Leader-Barton Bay (IRE) (Kambalda)
Miss E C Lavelle The Yomali Partnership

Placings: P01P-0   (4704)
2003/04: 18⁰G,

	Starts	1st	2nd	3rd	Win & Pl
Hurdles	1	0	0	0	
Career Total	**5**	**1**	**0**	**0**	**4251**

108	11/02	Plum	2m	D Hdl	SFT	£4251

Total win prize-money £4251

Going:	Sf: 0-0 GS: 0-0 Gd: 0-1 GF: - Fm: 0-0
Distance:	2m/2m3: 0-1 2m4-2m7: 0-0 3m+: 0-0
Track:	LH: 0-1 RH: 0-0 Tight: 0-1 Gall: 0-0
Aids:	Bl: 0-0 Vi: 0-0 Tstrap: 0-0 Ckp: 0-0
Best Rating:	108 11/02 Plum 2m soft Hdl

Yogi (IRE)
113   141

8-y-o ch g Glacial Storm (USA)-Good Performance Vii (Damsire Unregistered)
Thomas Foley Patrick Delaney Jnr

Placings: 2U5203/4340205/154610/0004P0002415111050-16226   (4423)
2003/04: 20⁰GY, 20¹YS, 16⁰GS, 24²S, 22²S, 24⁶G,

	Starts	1st	2nd	3rd	Win & Pl
Hurdles	6	1	2	0	29243
Career Total	**42**	**7**	**6**	**2**	**66217**

128	11/03	Clon	2m4f	(0-135)HHdl	Y-S	£7840
120	3/03	Naas	2m	(81-116)HHdl	HVY	£5600
108	3/03	Thur	2m4f	(67-102)HHdl	SFT	£4480
106	2/03	Clon	2m	(67-95)HHdl	SFT	£4480
95	1/03	Thur	2m	(74-109)HHdl	SFT	£5600
107	1/02	Gowr	2m	NHF	HVY	£6349
107	11/01	Thur	2m2f	NHF	Y-S	£3338

Total win prize-money £37694

Going:	Sf: 0-2 GS: 0-1 Gd: 0-1 GF: - Fm: 0-0
Distance:	2m/2m3: 0-1 2m4-2m7: 1-3 3m+: 0-2
Track:	LH: 0-1 RH: 0-3 Tight: 0-0 Gall: 0-1
Aids:	Bl: 0-0 Vi: 0-0 Tstrap: 0-0 Ckp: 0-0
Best Rating:	141 3/04 Chel 3m good Hdl

Very useful Irish-trained hurdler; stays three miles, but also effective at shorter; acts well on soft ground.

York Rite (AUS)
94(98c)   (74c) 77+

8-y-o ch g Grand Lodge (USA)-Amazaan (NZ) (Zamazaan (FR))
R C Guest Miss C Metcalfe

Placings: P00-51-P1423056   (1530)
2003/04: 16ᵖG, 24¹G, 21⁴GF, 23²GF, 20³F, 20⁰G, 19⁵GF, 22⁶F,

	Starts	1st	2nd	3rd	Win & Pl
Hurdles	6	1	0	1	3078
Chases	2	0	1	0	850
Career Total	**13**	**2**	**1**	**1**	**6140**

77	8/03	Bang	3m	F(0-95)HHdl	GD	£2744
75	11/02	Fknm	2m4f	G(0-95)HHdl	G-S	£2212

Total win prize-money £4956

Going:	Sf: 0-0 GS: 0-0 Gd: 1-3 GF: - Fm: 0-5
Distance:	2m/2m3: 0-1 2m4-2m7: 0-5 3m+: 1-2
Track:	LH: 1-6 RH: 0-2 Tight: 1-3 Gall: 0-1
Aids:	Bl: 0-1 Vi: 0-0 Tstrap: 0-1 Ckp: 1-6

Best Rating: 77 8/03 Bang 3m good Hdl

Plating-class hurdler; took time to get the hang of things over jumps; has shown ability over fences; stays three miles; wears cheekpieces and a tongue tie these days.

Yorkie

5-y-o b g Aragon-Light The Way (Nicholas Bill)
P A Blockley (D Carroll 8/3) Mrs Joanna Hughes

Placings:P   (1480)
2003/04: 17PG,

	Starts	1st	2nd	3rd	Win & PI
Hurdles	1	0	0	0	
Career Total	1	0	0	0	

Going:	Sf: 0-0 GS: 0-0 Gd: 0-1 GF: - Fm: 0-0
Distance:	2m/2m3: 0-1 2m4-2m7: 0-0 3m+: 0-0
Track:	LH: 0-1 RH: 0-0 Tight: 0-1 Gall: 0-0
Aids:	Bl: 0-0 Vi: 0-0 Tstrap: 0-1 Ckp: 0-0

Yorkie Morgans

8-y-o b g Manhal-Placid Fury (Sovereign King)
Mrs D A Hamer Ms Diane Morgans

Placings:0PF0-PP   (3081)
2003/04: 20PGF, 16PGS,

	Starts	1st	2nd	3rd	Win & PI
Hurdles	2	0	0	0	
Career Total	6	0	0	0	

Going:	Sf: 0-0 GS: 0-1 Gd: 0-0 GF: - Fm: 0-1
Distance:	2m/2m3: 0-1 2m4-2m7: 0-1 3m+: 0-0
Track:	LH: 0-2 RH: 0-0 Tight: 0-1 Gall: 0-0
Aids:	Bl: 0-0 Vi: 0-0 Tstrap: 0-0 Ckp: 0-0
Best Rating:	61 11/02 Tntn 2m1f gd-sft NHF

Yorkshire (IRE)

90 (0c)**128**
10-y-o ch g Generous (IRE)-Ausherra (USA) (Diesis)
D L Williams Girls On Top Racing 2000

Placings:1111132466P6-UFP00F   (4270)
2003/04: 20UGF, 24FG, 20PHY, 24UG, 20PG, 16FGF,

	Starts	1st	2nd	3rd	Win & PI
Hurdles	4	0	0	0	0
Chases	2	0	0	0	0
Career Total	18	5	1	1	20746
137	7/02	MRas	2m3f110yD Hdl	G-F	£4143
137	7/02	Strf	2m3f E Hdl	G-F	£3052
125	5/02	Hntg	2m110y E Hdl	GD	£2478
125	5/02	Bang	2m1f E Hdl	SFT	£2849
107	5/02	Chep	2m4f D Hdl	G-F	£3659

Total win prize-money £16183

Going:	Sf: 0-1 GS: 0-0 Gd: 0-3 GF: - Fm: 0-2
Distance:	2m/2m3: 0-1 2m4-2m7: 0-3 3m+: 0-2
Track:	LH: 0-2 RH: 0-0 Tight: 0-1 Gall: 0-2
Aids:	Bl: 0-0 Vi: 0-2 Tstrap: 0-0 Ckp: 0-0
Best Rating:	137 7/02 MRas 2m3f110y good Hdl

Fair hurdler/chaser; a good stayer on the Flat, he took advantage of some uncompetitive novice hurdles in the summer of 2002, winning five in a row; did not seemed to take to fences; stays two and a half miles; acts on any ground; has been tried in blinkers and a visor.

You Got Me

48 **16**
5-y-o gr g First Trump-Simply Sooty (Absalom)
Evan Williams If You're Lucky

Placings:0   (4812)
2003/04: 16RG,

	Starts	1st	2nd	3rd	Win & PI
Hurdles	1	0	0	0	
Career Total	1	0	0	0	

Going:	Sf: 0-0 GS: 0-0 Gd: 0-1 GF: - Fm: 0-0
Distance:	2m/2m3: 0-1 2m4-2m7: 0-0 3m+: 0-0
Track:	LH: 0-1 RH: 0-0 Tight: 0-0 Gall: 0-0
Aids:	Bl: 0-0 Vi: 0-0 Tstrap: 0-0 Ckp: 0-0
Best Rating:	16 4/04 Chep 2m10y good Hdl

You Never No (IRE)

96 **79**
4-y-o b g Eagle Eyed (USA)-Nordic Doll (IRE) (Royal Academy (USA))
Paul A Roche (E J O'Neill 9/10) Liam Mulryan

Placings:005400   (4679a)
2003/04: 17QG, 16PGF, 16SGF, 16AGF, 16QGF, 16PYS,

	Starts	1st	2nd	3rd	Win & PI
Hurdles	6	0	0	0	0
Career Total	6	0	0	0	0

Going:	Sf: 0-0 GS: 0-0 Gd: 0-1 GF: - Fm: 0-4
Distance:	2m/2m3: 0-6 2m4-2m7: 0-0 3m+: 0-0
Track:	LH: 0-3 RH: 0-2 Tight: 0-2 Gall: 0-1
Aids:	Bl: 0-3 Vi: 0-0 Tstrap: 0-3 Ckp: 0-0
Best Rating:	79 9/03 Hntg 2m110y gd-fm Hdl

Plating-class hurdler; acts on fast; has worn tongue tie and blinkers; not straightforward.

You Owe Me (IRE)

107 **110+**
7-y-o b g Jurado (USA)-Bodyline (Crash Course)
N A Twiston-Davies C Cornes

Placings:311   (2939)
2003/04: 20QGS, 21LG, 20LGS,

	Starts	1st	2nd	3rd	Win & PI
Hurdles	3	2	0	1	7546
Career Total	3	2	0	1	7546
120	12/03	Uttx	2m4f110yE Hdl	G-S	£3472
110	12/03	Wwck	2m5f E Hdl	GD	£3514

Total win prize-money £6986

Going:	Sf: 0-0 GS: 1-2 Gd: 1-1 GF: - Fm: 0-0
Distance:	2m/2m3: 0-0 **2m4-2m7: 2-3** 3m+: 0-0
Track:	**LH: 2-3** RH: 0-0 Tight: 0-0 Gall: 0-0
Aids:	Bl: 0-0 Vi: 0-0 Tstrap: 0-0 Ckp: 0-0
Best Rating:	120 12/03 Uttx 2m4f110y gd-sft Hdl

Progressive novice hurdler; back-to-back wins at around 2m 5f at Warwick and Uttoxeter December 2003; will now be stepped up in class; considered a chaser in the making; acts on good and soft ground.

You're A Diamond

6-y-o ch m Superlative-Diamond Tip (Homing)
T P Walshe Mrs Penny Walshe

Placings:PP-PP   (0804)

2003/04: 17FGF, 17PG,

	Starts	1st	2nd	3rd	Win & PI
Hurdles	2	0	0	0	
Career Total	4	0	0	0	

Going:	Sf: 0-0 GS: 0-0 Gd: 0-1 GF: - Fm: 0-1
Distance:	2m/2m3: 0-2 2m4-2m7: 0-0 3m+: 0-0
Track:	LH: 0-2 RH: 0-0 Tight: 0-1 Gall: 0-0
Aids:	Bl: 0-0 Vi: 0-0 Tstrap: 0-0 Ckp: 0-0

You're Agoodun

107 **148**
12-y-o ch g Derrylin-Jennie Pat (Rymer)
M C Pipe J S Lammiman

Placings:00000/2R53211/104F2003/114UU2B0/143540P/1P20U-356   (4384)
2003/04: 24JG, 28SG, 24RG,

	Starts	1st	2nd	3rd	Win & PI
Chases	3	0	0	1	10800
Career Total	146	7	5	4	98008
148	11/02	Asct	3m110y B(0-140)HCh	G-S	£10757
148	11/01	Asct	3m110y B(0-150)HCh	GD	£9854
132	10/00	Hrfd	3m1f110yE Ch	GD	£3493
132	9/00	Hrfd	3m1f110yD Ch	G-S	£3701
142	10/99	Towc	3m C(0-135)HHdl	GD	£4840
138	4/99	Chel	3m D(0-120)HHdl	GD	£5425
130	12/98	Hayd	2m7f110yD(0-110)HHdl	SFT	£2997

Total win prize-money £41069

Going:	Sf: 0-0 GS: 0-0 Gd: 0-3 GF: - Fm: 0-0
Distance:	2m/2m3: 0-0 2m4-2m7: 0-0 3m+: 0-3
Track:	LH: 0-3 RH: 0-0 Tight: 0-0 Gall: 0-1
Aids:	Bl: 0-0 Vi: 0-3 Tstrap: 0-0 Ckp: 0-0
Best Rating:	148 3/03 Hayd 3m4f110y good Ch

Very useful chaser; stays extreme distances and suited by good ground or softer; sometimes let down by his jumping; goes well at Ascot; usually wears a visor.

You're Special (USA)

109 (122h)**130+**
7-y-o b g Northern Flagship (USA)-Pillow Mint (USA) (Stagedoor Johnny)
P C Haslam Les Buckley

Placings:123P14/2-11125222   (3038)
2003/04: 20LGS, 26LG, 20LGF, 25PGF, 25SG, 16PGF, 20PGS,

	Starts	1st	2nd	3rd	Win & PI
Chases	8	3	4	0	24433
Career Total	15	5	5	4	33859
119	6/03	Hexm	2m4f110yE Ch	G-F	£3861
117	5/03	Cttml	2m3f E Ch	GD	£4485
114	5/03	Aint	2m4f D Ch	G-S	£5827
121	4/02	Weth	2m4f110yE Hdl	GD	£3143
122	11/01	Newc	2m4f E Hdl	GD	£2625

Total win prize-money £19942

Going:	Sf: 0-0 GS: 1-2 Gd: 1-3 GF: - Fm: 1-3
Distance:	2m/2m3: 0-1 **2m4-2m7: 2-4** 3m+: 1-3
Track:	**LH: 3-8** RH: 0-0 Tight: 2-3 Gall: 0-2
Aids:	Bl: 0-0 Vi: 0-0 Tstrap: 0-1 Ckp: 0-0
Best Rating:	130 12/03 Chel 2m4f110y good Ch

Fair chaser; completed a hat-trick in the spring of 2003; limitations exposed since; stays beyond three miles, but effective at shorter; acts on most types of ground; has been tried in a tongue tie.

You're The Man (IRE)

105   **76**

7-y-o b g Lapierre-Another Advantage (IRE) (Roselier (FR))
Mrs Dianne Sayer (Mrs E Slack 14/11) A Slack

Placings:0/6050P20P10P   (4913)
2003/04: 16⁶G, 20⁰G, 20⁵GF, 19⁹G, 24⁸GF, 24²GS, 20⁰G, 20⁵HY, 24¹G, 24⁰HY, 24⁴S,

	Starts	1st	2nd	3rd	Win & Pl
NH Flat	1	0	0	0	0
Hurdles	9	1	1	0	3464
Chases	1	0	0	0	0
Career Total	12	1	1	0	3464
76	3/04	Hexm	3m		F(0-100)HHdl	GD	£2730

Total win prize-money £2730

Going:	Sf: 0-3 GS: 0-1 Gd: 1-5 GF: - Fm: 0-2
Distance:	2m/2m3: 0-1 2m4-2m7: 0-5 3m+: 1-5
Track:	LH: 1-3 RH: 0-7 Tight: 0-1 Gall: 0-1
Aids:	Bl: 0-1 Vi: 0-0 Tstrap: 0-0 Ckp: 1-2
Best Rating:	86 5/03 Kels 2m110y good NHF

Modest hurdler who got off the mark over three miles at Hexham in March; may be capable of better over hurdles granted a suitable test of stamina.

Youlbesolucky (IRE)

99f   **90f**

5-y-o b g Accordion-Gaye Humour (IRE) (Montelimar (USA))
Jonjo O'Neill Mrs G Smith

Placings:0   (4447)
2003/04: 16⁵S,

	Starts	1st	2nd	3rd	Win & Pl
NH Flat	1	0	0	0	
Career Total	1	0	0	0	

Going:	Sf: 0-1 GS: 0-0 Gd: 0-0 GF: - Fm: 0-0
Distance:	2m/2m3: 0-1 2m4-2m7: 0-0 3m+: 0-0
Track:	LH: 0-1 RH: 0-0 Tight: 0-0 Gall: 0-0
Aids:	Bl: 0-0 Vi: 0-0 Tstrap: 0-0 Ckp: 0-0
Best Rating:	90 3/04 Wwck 2m soft NHF

Out of an unraced half-sister to Kingsmark from the family of Gaye Brief and Gaye Chance; failed to live up to strong market support on debut in soft ground bumper.

Young American (IRE)

92   **128d**

8-y-o br g Hamas (IRE)-Banana Peel (Green Dancer (USA))
Jonjo O'Neill John P McManus

Placings:51402/0402/06P03031/261PP6P-0   (4255)
2003/04: 24⁰G,

	Starts	1st	2nd	3rd	Win & Pl
Hurdles	1	0	0	0	0
Career Total	25	3	3	2	28876
128	11/02	Hayd	2m6f	B(0-140)HHdl	SFT	£10093
123	4/02	Bang	3m	D(0-120)HHdl	GD	£5687
116	12/99	Leop	2m	Hdl	SH	£4620

Total win prize-money £20402

Going:	Sf: 0-0 GS: 0-0 Gd: 0-1 GF: - Fm: 0-0
Distance:	2m/2m3: 0-0 2m4-2m7: 0-0 3m+: 0-1
Track:	LH: 0-1 RH: 0-0 Tight: 0-1 Gall: 0-0
Aids:	Bl: 0-0 Vi: 0-0 Tstrap: 0-0 Ckp: 0-0
Best Rating:	129 11/00 Naas 2m sft-hvy Hdl

Fair handicap hurdler; stays three miles; acts on good and soft ground; out of form of late.

Young Bounder (FR)

71   **56**

5-y-o b/br g Septieme Ciel (USA)-Far But Near (USA) (Far North (CAN))
N A Twiston-Davies Mrs M Slade and G MacEchern

Placings:0-00   (3831)
2003/04: 17⁰G, 16⁰G,

	Starts	1st	2nd	3rd	Win & Pl
NH Flat	1	0	0	0	0
Hurdles	1	0	0	0	0
Career Total	3	0	0	0	

Going:	Sf: 0-0 GS: 0-0 Gd: 0-2 GF: - Fm: 0-0
Distance:	2m/2m3: 0-2 2m4-2m7: 0-0 3m+: 0-0
Track:	LH: 0-1 RH: 0-0 Tight: 0-0 Gall: 0-1
Aids:	Bl: 0-0 Vi: 0-0 Tstrap: 0-0 Ckp: 0-0
Best Rating:	61 2/04 Newb 2m110y good Hdl

Young Buck (IRE)

(97c)   **(48c)110**

10-y-o ch g Glacial Storm (USA)-Lady Buck (Pollerton)
A G Juckes Barry Benton and Partners

Placings:12/21360/1PP0/06006/4523246-PPP   (1015)
2003/04: 21⁹GF, 20⁶GF, 20⁰GF,

	Starts	1st	2nd	3rd	Win & Pl
Hurdles	3	0	0	0	
Career Total	26	3	4	2	20283
119	11/00	DRoy	2m	Hdl	Y-S	£7800
120	11/99	Navn	2m	Hdl	Y-S	£4004
100	10/98	Fair	2m	NHF	YLD	£2690

Total win prize-money £14494

Going:	Sf: 0-0 GS: 0-0 Gd: 0-0 GF: - Fm: 0-3
Distance:	2m/2m3: 0-0 2m4-2m7: 0-3 3m+: 0-0
Track:	LH: 0-2 RH: 0-1 Tight: 0-0 Gall: 0-1
Aids:	Bl: 0-0 Vi: 0-3 Tstrap: 0-3 Ckp: 0-0
Best Rating:	126 12/99 Punc 2m soft Hdl

Modest ex-Irish hurdler/chaser. Suited by cut in the ground.

Young Butt

101   **78**

11-y-o ch g Bold Owl-Cymbal (Ribero)
L A Dace D Newman

Placings:03/0/P605-6   (0057)
2003/04: 17⁶GS,

	Starts	1st	2nd	3rd	Win & Pl
Hurdles	1	0	0	0	0
Career Total	8	0	0	1	364

Going:	Sf: 0-0 GS: 0-1 Gd: 0-0 GF: - Fm: 0-0
Distance:	2m/2m3: 0-0 2m4-2m7: 0-0 3m+: 0-0
Track:	LH: 0-0 RH: 0-1 Tight: 0-0 Gall: 0-0
Aids:	Bl: 0-1 Vi: 0-0 Tstrap: 0-0 Ckp: 0-0
Best Rating:	88 4/00 Plum 2m gd-sft Hdl

Young Chevalier

103(93h)   **(78h)107+**

7-y-o b g Alflora (IRE)-Mrs Teasdale (Idiots Delight)
M Todhunter James R Adam

Placings:00/0506/F000-26116   (4686)
2003/04: 22²S, 16⁶HY, 16¹G, 16¹G, 17⁶G,

	Starts	1st	2nd	3rd	Win & Pl
Chases	5	2	1	0	9408

Career Total		15	2	1	0		9408
103	3/04	Carl	2m	E(0-105)HCh	GD	£4329
107	3/04	Donc	2m110y	E(0-105)HCh	GD	£3991

Total win prize-money £8320

Going:	Sf: 0-2 GS: 0-0 Gd: 2-3 GF: - Fm: 0-0
Distance:	2m/2m3: 2-4 2m4-2m7: 0-1 3m+: 0-0
Track:	LH: 1-4 RH: 1-1 Tight: 0-2 Gall: 1-2
Aids:	Bl: 0-0 Vi: 0-0 Tstrap: 0-0 Ckp: 0-0
Best Rating:	107 3/04 Donc 2m110y good Ch

Moderate but progressive novice chaser; easy first success over fences at Doncaster in March; might be best suited going right-handed; best suited by two miles.

Young Claude

(95h)   **(89+h)59**

7-y-o b g Le Moss-Deirdres Dream (The Parson)
P Beaumont Read O'Gorman Racing

Placings:033P-PPP204PP   (4514)
2003/04: 24⁵S, 24⁰GS, 24⁴GS, 25²GS, 25⁰G, 24⁴HY, 32⁸G, 25⁹GS,

	Starts	1st	2nd	3rd	Win & Pl
Hurdles	3	0	1	0	811
Chases	5	0	0	0	434
Career Total	12	0	1	2	2370

Going:	Sf: 0-2 GS: 0-4 Gd: 0-2 GF: - Fm: 0-0
Distance:	2m/2m3: 0-0 2m4-2m7: 0-0 3m+: 0-8
Track:	LH: 0-7 RH: 0-1 Tight: 0-3 Gall: 0-0
Aids:	Bl: 0-5 Vi: 0-0 Tstrap: 0-0 Ckp: 0-0
Best Rating:	89 12/03 Weth 3m1f gd-sft Hdl

Plating-class chaser/hurdler; acts on soft ground.

Young Collier

104   **110**

5-y-o b g Vettori (IRE)-Cockatoo Island (High Top)
J A B Old W E Sturt

Placings:140   (4561)
2003/04: 19¹S, 23⁴G, 24⁰GS,

	Starts	1st	2nd	3rd	Win & Pl
Hurdles	3	1	0	0	5140
Career Total	3	1	0	0	5140
110	1/04	Newb	2m3f	E Hdl	SFT	£3640

Total win prize-money £3640

Going:	Sf: 1-1 GS: 0-1 Gd: 0-1 GF: - Fm: 0-0
Distance:	2m/2m3: 1-1 2m4-2m7: 0-1 3m+: 0-2
Track:	LH: 1-3 RH: 0-0 Tight: 0-0 Gall: 1-2
Aids:	Bl: 0-0 Vi: 0-0 Tstrap: 0-0 Ckp: 0-0
Best Rating:	110 1/04 Newb 2m3f soft Hdl

Modest hurdler; half-brother to the Champion Hurdle winner Collier Bay; modest handicapper on the level; made a winning debut over hurdles; stays two miles three, but will get a lot further; acts well on easy ground.

Young Dancer (IRE)

104   **108**

6-y-o b g Eurobus-Misquested (Lord Ha Ha)
V R A Dartnall D G Staddon

Placings:0-0FP2   (4735)
2003/04: 16⁰GS, 16⁶S, 19⁰S, 17²G,

	Starts	1st	2nd	3rd	Win & Pl
Hurdles	4	0	1	0	1508
Career Total	5	0	1	0	1508

Going:	Sf: 0-2 GS: 0-1 Gd: 0-1 GF: - Fm: 0-0
Distance:	2m/2m3: 0-4 2m4-2m7: 0-0 3m+: 0-0
Track:	LH: 0-2 RH: 0-2 Tight: 0-1 Gall: 0-1
Aids:	Bl: 0-0 Vi: 0-0 Tstrap: 0-0 Ckp: 0-0
Best Rating:	108 4/04 NAbb 2m1f good Hdl

Modest hurdler; acts on good.

Young Devereaux (IRE)

105(94h)   (91h)151

11-y-o b/br g Lord Americo-Miss Iverk (Torus)
P F Nicholls Paul K Barber,Mick Coburn,Colin Lewis 2

Placings:45/31/F11/2/11P-003   (4537)
2003/04: 16⁸GS, 21⁰GS, 16³GS,

	Starts	1st	2nd	3rd	Win & Pl
Hurdles	1	0	0		424
Chases	2	0	0	0	
Career Total	14	5	1	2	97971

151	1/03	Kemp	2m	A HCh	GD	£46400
141	12/02	Asct	2m	B HCh	SFT	£31000
135	1/00	Folk	2m	E Ch	G-S	£3217
144	1/00	Uttx	2m	D Ch	SFT	£5330
115	12/98	Chep	2m110y	D Hdl	GD	£3116
				Total win prize-money £89064		

Going:	Sf: 0-0 GS: 0-3 Gd: 0-0 GF: - Fm: 0-0
Distance:	2m/2m3: 0-0 2m4-2m7: 0-1 3m+: 0-0
Track:	LH: 0-1 RH: 0-2 Tight: 0-0 Gall: 0-1
Aids:	Bl: 0-0 Vi: 0-0 Tstrap: 0-0 Ckp: 0-1
Best Rating:	151 2/03 Asct 2m3f110y gd-sft Ch

Very useful but fragile two-mile chaser; seems on the downgrade; all of his wins have come over two miles, although he does stay further; winner of the re-scheduled Victor Chandler Chase in 2003; acts on good and soft ground, but reportedly prefers a sound surface; well beaten in a claiming hurdle at Ludlow in March 2004.

Young Garrick (IRE)

6-y-o b g Old Vic-Youngandfair (IRE) (Phardante (FR))
P R Webber Mrs Richard Lay

Placings:0P   (4664)
2003/04: 16⁰G, 19ᴾGS,

	Starts	1st	2nd	3rd	Win & Pl
NH Flat	1	0	0	0	0
Hurdles	1	0	0	0	0
Career Total	2	0	0	0	0

Going:	Sf: 0-0 GS: 0-0 Gd: 0-1 GF: - Fm: 0-0
Distance:	2m/2m3: 0-1 2m4-2m7: 0-1 3m+: 0-0
Track:	LH: 0-2 RH: 0-0 Tight: 0-1 Gall: 0-1
Aids:	Bl: 0-0 Vi: 0-0 Tstrap: 0-0 Ckp: 0-0
Best Rating:	37 3/04 Newb 2m110y good NHF

Young Harry

64f   84f

6-y-o b g Karinga Bay-Heathfield Gale (Strong Gale)
M C Pipe A E Ford

Placings:0   (4824)
2003/04: 17⁰GF,

	Starts	1st	2nd	3rd	Win & Pl
NH Flat	1	0	0	0	
Career Total	1	0	0	0	

Young Lirrup

78f   80f

6-y-o ch g Lir-Blue-Bird Express (Pony Express)
W S Kittow W G Kittow

Placings:0/60-0   (0251)
2003/04: 17⁰GF,

	Starts	1st	2nd	3rd	Win & Pl
NH Flat	1	0	0	0	
Career Total	4	0	0	0	0

Going:	Sf: 0-0 GS: 0-0 Gd: 0-0 GF: - Fm: 0-1
Distance:	2m/2m3: 0-1 2m4-2m7: 0-0 3m+: 0-0
Track:	LH: 0-0 RH: 0-1 Tight: 0-0 Gall: 0-0
Aids:	Bl: 0-0 Vi: 0-0 Tstrap: 0-0 Ckp: 0-0
Best Rating:	74 5/03 Extr 2m1f gd-fm NHF

Young Monash (IRE)

6-y-o b g General Monash (USA)-Sound Pet (Runnett)
A C Wilson Cooper Wilson

Placings:P/P   (3762)
2003/04: 21ᴾGS,

	Starts	1st	2nd	3rd	Win & Pl
Hurdles	1	0	0	0	
Career Total	2	0	0	0	

Going:	Sf: 0-0 GS: 0-1 Gd: 0-0 GF: - Fm: 0-0
Distance:	2m/2m3: 0-2 2m4-2m7: 0-1 3m+: 0-0
Track:	LH: 0-1 RH: 0-0 Tight: 0-1 Gall: 0-0
Aids:	Bl: 0-0 Vi: 0-0 Tstrap: 0-0 Ckp: 0-0

Young Owen

101   80

6-y-o b g Balinbarbi-Polly Potter (Pollerton)
Mrs L B Normile (R A Fahey 2/6) Alf Chadwick

Placings:60/5PP-0330F   (2842)
2003/04: 16⁰F, 16³GF, 16³GF, 18⁰S, 16⁶GS,

	Starts	1st	2nd	3rd	Win & Pl
Hurdles	5	0	0	2	673
Career Total	10	0	0	2	673

Going:	Sf: 0-0 GS: 0-1 Gd: 0-0 GF: - Fm: 0-3
Distance:	2m/2m3: 0-5 2m4-2m7: 0-0 3m+: 0-0
Track:	LH: 0-5 RH: 0-0 Tight: 0-1 Gall: 0-0
Aids:	Bl: 0-0 Vi: 0-0 Tstrap: 0-0 Ckp: 0-0
Best Rating:	76 10/03 Hayd 2m gd-fm Hdl

Plating-class hurdler; suited by two miles; acts on soft and fast ground.

Young Rab

9-y-o b g Nomadic Way (USA)-Penny Pink (Spartan General)
M J Brown M J Brown

Placings:00P/5						(0269)
2003/04: 20⁵G,						
		Starts	1st	2nd	3rd	Win & Pl
Chases		1	0	0	0	0
Career Total		4	0	0	0	0

Going:	Sf: 0-0 GS: 0-0 Gd: 0-0 GF: - Fm: 0-0
Distance:	2m/2m3: 0-0 2m4-2m7: 0-1 3m+: 0-0
Track:	LH: 0-0 RH: 0-1 Tight: 0-0 Gall: 0-0
Aids:	Bl: 0-0 Vi: 0-0 Tstrap: 0-0 Ckp: 0-0
Best Rating:	52 5/03 Prth 2m4f110y good Ch

Young Scotton

100f   107+f

4-y-o b g Cadeaux Genereux-Broken Wave (Bustino)
K A Ryan The I B & B D F Partnership

Placings:112   (4649)
2003/04: 16¹S, 16¹G, 17²G,

	Starts	1st	2nd	3rd	Win & Pl
NH Flat	3	2	1	0	11605
Career Total	3	2	1	0	11605

87	2/04	Muss	2m	H NHF	GD	£2947
90	1/04	Weth	2m	H NHF	SFT	£2058
				Total win prize-money £5005		

Going:	Sf: 1-1 GS: 0-0 Gd: 1-2 GF: - Fm: 0-0
Distance:	2m/2m3: 2-3 2m4-2m7: 0-0 3m+: 0-0
Track:	LH: 1-1 RH: 1-1 Tight: 1-1 Gall: 0-0
Aids:	Bl: 0-0 Vi: 0-0 Tstrap: 0-0 Ckp: 0-0
Best Rating:	107 4/04 Aint 2m1f good NHF

Flat-bred; took an ordinary bumper in bad ground on debut at Wetherby in January, but achieved a lot more when winning under a penalty on next outing at Musselburgh; runner-up in the Aintree Champion Bumper; acts on good and soft ground.

Young Spartacus

113   157

11-y-o b g Teenoso (USA)-Celtic Slave (Celtic Cone)
H D Daly B G Hellyer

Placings:6161/15102/11222F/13211U/306/1-440   (2720)
2003/04: 25⁴G, 20⁴G, 20⁰GS,

	Starts	1st	2nd	3rd	Win & Pl
Chases	3	0	0	0	8617
Career Total	28	10	5	2	192245

157	3/03	Chel	2m4f110y	A HCh	GD	£43500
157	2/01	Kemp	3m	A HCh	GD	£46400
152	1/01	Chel	2m5f	B HCh	SFT	£20800
148	11/00	Chep	2m4f	B HHdl	SFT	£22750
147	12/99	Chep	2m3f110y	D Ch	GD	£3891
136	11/99	Towc	2m110y	E Ch	GD	£3265
133	2/99	Wwck	2m	C(0-135)HHdl	G-S	£4828
128	12/98	Wwck	2m	C(0-130)HHdl	SFT	£5487
119	4/98	Ludl	2m	E HHdl	GD	£2836
120	12/97	Strf	2m110y	E Hdl	SFT	£2710
				Total win prize-money £156469		

Going:	Sf: 0-0 GS: 0-1 Gd: 0-2 GF: - Fm: 0-0
Distance:	2m/2m3: 0-2 2m4-2m7: 0-2 3m+: 0-1
Track:	LH: 0-2 RH: 0-1 Tight: 0-0 Gall: 0-2
Aids:	Bl: 0-0 Vi: 0-0 Tstrap: 0-0 Ckp: 0-0
Best Rating:	157 3/03 Chel 2m4f110y good Ch

Smart chaser; wins include the Ladbroke Trophy Chase at Cheltenham and the 2001 Racing Post Chase; first run for over a year; won the Mildmay of Flete at the 2003 Cheltenham Festival; fourth in Paddy Power Gold Cup on reappearance; stays three miles, effective over shorter; suited by good ground or softer.

Young Tomo (IRE)

12-y-o b g Lafontaine (USA)-Siege Queen (Tarqogan)
Miss C J Goodall Mrs J E Goodall

Placings:20151/241FP2/4F1/20P/5331FP2/P34-P   **(4283)**
2003/04: 25PG,

	Starts	1st	2nd	3rd	Win & Pl
Chases	1	0	0	0	
Career Total	28	5	5	3	21732
102	11/01	Sedg	3m3f	F(0-90)HCh	GD £2947
90	10/99	Sedg	3m3f	F(0-110)HCh	GD £2882
98	12/98	Muss	3m	E Ch	G-F £2901
99	2/98	Muss	2m4f	D Hdl	GD £2895
71	12/97	Sedg	2m5f110yE Hdl	GD £2022

Total win prize-money £13649

Going: Sf: 0-0 GS: 0-0 Gd: 0-1 GF: - Fm: 0-0
Distance: 2m/2m3: 0-0 2m4-2m7: 0-0 3m+: 0-1
Track: LH: 0-0 RH: 0-1 Tight: 0-1 Gall: 0-0
Aids: Bl: 0-1 Vi: 0-0 Tstrap: 0-0 Ckp: 0-0
Best Rating: 105 5/97 Prth 2m110y gd-sft NHF

Young Tot (IRE)
97   84

6-y-o b g Torus-Lady-K (IRE) (Rock Chanteur)
Mrs A Duffield North Briton Racing

Placings:00003P   **(4690)**
2003/04: 16DG, 16PS, 19PG, 16PGF, 20PGS, 22PG,

	Starts	1st	2nd	3rd	Win & Pl
NH Flat	2	0	0	0	
Hurdles	4	0	0	1	392
Career Total	6	0	0	1	392

Going: Sf: 0-1 GS: 0-1 Gd: 0-3 GF: - Fm: 0-1
Distance: 2m/2m3: 0-3 2m4-2m7: 0-3 3m+: 0-0
Track: LH: 0-5 RH: 0-1 Tight: 0-3 Gall: 0-0
Aids: Bl: 0-0 Vi: 0-0 Tstrap: 0-0 Ckp: 0-0
Best Rating: 90 3/04 Weth 2m4f110y gd-sft Hdl

Modest novice hurdler; best effort so far when third at Wetherby in March; stays two and a half miles.

Young Whack (IRE)
109   (94h) 127+

10-y-o br g Phardante (FR)-Flash Parade (Boreen (FR))
J Howard Johnson Gordon Brown/bert Watson

Placings:4/623/521224/016322262P/130P1-3165F   **(4850)**
2003/04: 16³GD, 20¹G, 20⁶G, 21⁵G, 20FGS,

	Starts	1st	2nd	3rd	Win & Pl
Chases	5	1	0	1	8733
Career Total	30	5	8	4	51376
127	11/03	Ayr	2m4f	D(0-120)HCh	GD £5427
127	4/03	List	2m4f	HCh	G-F £11607
81	5/02	Dpat	2m6f	Ch	G-F £4656
104	5/01	Tipp	2m4f	Ch	G-F £6677
103	8/00	Kbgn	2m3f	Hdl	G-F £2980

Total win prize-money £31349

Going: Sf: 0-0 GS: 0-1 Gd: 1-3 GF: - Fm: 0-1
Distance: 2m/2m3: 0-1 2m4-2m7: 1-4 3m+: 0-0
Track: LH: 1-5 RH: 0-0 Tight: 0-2 Gall: 0-0
Aids: Bl: 0-0 Vi: 0-0 Tstrap: 0-0 Ckp: 0-0
Best Rating: 127 4/04 Aint 2m5f110y good Ch

Fair chaser; ex-Irish; best over two and a half miles, but stays further; won for Howard Johnson at Ayr in November; acts on soft but suited by fast ground.

Youpeeveecee (IRE)
(91 h)

(86h)
8-y-o b g Little Bighorn-Godlike (Godswalk (USA))
Mrs J Candlish Greencard Golfers

Placings:042/P436U-PP   **(2841)**
2003/04: 25PGS, 20PGS,

	Starts	1st	2nd	3rd	Win & Pl
Chases	2	0	0	0	
Career Total	10	0	1	1	1347

Going: Sf: 0-0 GS: 0-2 Gd: 0-0 GF: - Fm: 0-0
Distance: 2m/2m3: 0-0 2m4-2m7: 0-1 3m+: 0-1
Track: LH: 0-1 RH: 0-1 Tight: 0-0 Gall: 0-0
Aids: Bl: 0-0 Vi: 0-2 Tstrap: 0-0 Ckp: 0-0
Best Rating: 97 4/02 MRas 2m1f110y good NHF

Modest novice hurdler; has shown signs of temperament; stays two and a half miles.

Your A Gassman (IRE)
106   104

6-y-o b g King's Ride-Nish Bar (Callernish)
Ferdy Murphy W J Gott

Placings:3-10222   **(4908)**
2003/04: 17¹GF, 18⁶S, 19²G, 21²G, 20²S,

	Starts	1st	2nd	3rd	Win & Pl
NH Flat	1	1	0	0	2079
Hurdles	4	0	3	0	3862
Career Total	6	1	3	1	6447
106	5/03	Sthl	2m1f	H NHF	G-F £2079

Total win prize-money £2079

Going: Sf: 0-2 GS: 0-0 Gd: 0-2 GF: - Fm: 1-1
Distance: 2m/2m3: 1-2 2m4-2m7: 0-3 3m+: 0-0
Track: LH: 1-4 RH: 0-1 Tight: 0-2 Gall: 0-0
Aids: Bl: 0-0 Vi: 0-0 Tstrap: 0-0 Ckp: 0-0
Best Rating: 106 5/03 Sthl 2m1f gd-fm NHF

Modest hurdler; Southwell bumper winner; game runner-up in novices' hurdles at Doncaster and Sedgefield in March; suited by two and a half miles; suited by a sound surface; capable of better.

Your Advantage (IRE)
101   100+

4-y-o b g Septieme Ciel (USA)-Freedom Flame (Darshaan)
Jonjo O'Neill (R Gibson 9/7) Mrs G Smith

Placings:P0001OP   **(4638)**
2003/04: 16PGF, 16PGS, 16PGS, 16PG, 16¹S, 10PGS, 16PG,

	Starts	1st	2nd	3rd	Win & Pl
Hurdles	7	1	0	0	3705
Career Total	7	1	0	0	3705
104	3/04	Wwck	2m	E(0-105)HHdl	SFT £3705

Total win prize-money £3705

Going: Sf: 1-1 GS: 0-3 Gd: 0-2 GF: - Fm: 0-1
Distance: 2m/2m3: 1-7 2m4-2m7: 0-0 3m+: 0-0
Track: LH: 1-4 RH: 0-3 Tight: 0-1 Gall: 0-0
Aids: Bl: 1-3 Vi: 0-0 Tstrap: 0-0 Ckp: 0-0
Best Rating: 104 3/04 Ludl 2m gd-sft Hdl

Moderate novice hurdler; won modest novices' handicap at Warwick in first-time blinkers in March 2004 and may have followed up at Ludlow had he not taken the wrong course; acts on soft ground; seemed to improve in blinkers.

Your My Angel (IRE)
90   72

8-y-o b m Commanche Run-Marshtown Fair (IRE) (Camden Town)
Ferdy Murphy S Hubbard Rodwell

Placings:4-64U4   **(0910)**
2003/04: 20⁶G, 20⁴G, 26UG, 26⁴GF,

	Starts	1st	2nd	3rd	Win & Pl
Hurdles	4	0	0	0	0
Career Total	5	0	0	0	266

Going: Sf: 0-0 GS: 0-0 Gd: 0-3 GF: - Fm: 0-1
Distance: 2m/2m3: 0-0 2m4-2m7: 0-2 3m+: 0-2
Track: LH: 0-4 RH: 0-0 Tight: 0-0 Gall: 0-0
Aids: Bl: 0-0 Vi: 0-0 Tstrap: 0-0 Ckp: 0-0
Best Rating: 74 7/03 Sthl 3m2f gd-fm Hdl

Ex-Irish pointer; has shown just moderate performer over hurdles.

Your So Cool
105   117+

7-y-o ch g Karinga Bay-Laurel Diver (Celtic Cone)
M C Pipe Matt Archer & Miss Jean Broadhurst

Placings:0/3-21   **(3654)**
2003/04: 21²S, 24¹S,

	Starts	1st	2nd	3rd	Win & Pl
Hurdles	2	1	1	0	5446
Career Total	4	1	1	1	5973
117	2/04	Tntn	3m110y	E Hdl	SFT £4368

Total win prize-money £4368

Going: Sf: 1-2 GS: 0-0 Gd: 0-0 GF: - Fm: 0-0
Distance: 2m/2m3: 0-0 2m4-2m7: 0-1 **3m+: 1-1**
Track: LH: 0-1 **RH: 1-1 Tight: 1-2** Gall: 0-0
Aids: Bl: 0-1 **Vi: 1-1** Tstrap: 0-0 Ckp: 0-0
Best Rating: 117 2/04 Tntn 3m110y soft Hdl

Showed ability when blinkered on his hurdling debut on testing ground.

Yourman (IRE)
89   76

4-y-o b g Shernazar-Lantern Lover (Be My Native (USA))
M C Pipe D A Johnson

Placings:050P   **(3856)**
2003/04: 16⁰G, 16⁵GF, 17⁰GS, 16PS,

	Starts	1st	2nd	3rd	Win & Pl
Hurdles	4	0	0	0	0
Career Total	4	0	0	0	0

Going: Sf: 0-1 GS: 0-1 Gd: 0-1 GF: - Fm: 0-1
Distance: 2m/2m3: 0-4 2m4-2m7: 0-0 3m+: 0-0
Track: LH: 0-2 RH: 0-2 Tight: 0-1 Gall: 0-1
Aids: Bl: 0-0 Vi: 0-0 Tstrap: 0-0 Ckp: 0-0
Best Rating: 76 12/03 Newb 2m110y gd-fm Hdl

Yvanovitch (FR)
102(94h)   (98h) 109+

6-y-o b g Kaldounevees (FR)-County Kerry (FR) (Comrade In Arms)
Mrs L C Taylor Robert Frostel

Placings:0550-53F26   **(4049)**
2003/04: 18⁵GS, 16³GF, 21⁶GS, 18²G, 20⁶G,

	Starts	1st	2nd	3rd	Win & Pl
Hurdles	1	0	0	0	0

	Starts	1st	2nd	3rd	Win & Pl
Chases	4	0	1	1	2436
Career Total	9	0	1	1	2436

Going: Sf: 0-0 GS: 0-2 Gd: 0-2 GF: - Fm: 0-1
Distance: 2m/2m3: 0-3 2m4-2m7: 0-2 3m+: 0-0
Track: LH: 0-2 RH: 0-2 Tight: 0-1 Gall: 0-1
Aids: Bl: 0-0 Vi: 0-0 Tstrap: 0-0 Ckp: 0-0
Best Rating: 109 1/04 Font 2m2f good Ch

Moderate hurdler; shown promise over fences.

Zaajer (USA)
88   76

8-y-o ch g Silver Hawk (USA)-Crown Quest (USA) (Chief's Crown (USA))
Mrs G Harvey Mrs J Draper, C Jefferies, R Smith

Placings:244P/5-0   (0527)
2003/04: 20QGF,

	Starts	1st	2nd	3rd	Win & Pl
Hurdles	1	0	0	0	
Career Total	6	0	1	0	846

Going: Sf: 0-0 GS: 0-0 Gd: 0-0 GF: - Fm: 0-1
Distance: 2m/2m3: 0-2 2m4-2m7: 0-1 3m+: 0-0
Track: LH: 0-1 RH: 0-0 Tight: 0-0 Gall: 0-0
Aids: Bl: 0-0 Vi: 0-0 Tstrap: 0-0 Ckp: 0-0
Best Rating: 90 1/02 Hntg 2m110y gd-sft Hdl

Zabadi (IRE)
104

12-y-o b g Shahrastani (USA)-Zerzaya (Beldale Flutter (USA))
Miss Venetia Williams Miss V M Williams

Placings:051101/1005052/32F3332F3/52/221222223P206 3/2212111P3/656465-PPPP   (1335)
2003/04: 21PGF, 17PG, 21PG, 19PGF,

	Starts	1st	2nd	3rd	Win & Pl
Chases	4	0	0	0	
Career Total	57	9	15	8	100568
119 12/01 Towc	2m110y	D(0-120)HCh		HVY	£5486
113 12/01 Plum	2m4f	D(0-125)HCh		SFT	£3802
119 11/01 Towc	2m110y	F(0-105)HCh		SFT	£3900
117 10/01 Fknm	2m5f110y	F(0-100)HCh		SFT	£3435
91 6/00 Uttx	D Ch			G-F	£4225
149 11/96 Newb	2m110y	A Hdl		GD	£12120
138 3/96 Aint	2m110y	A Hdl		GD	£28424
139 2/96 Kemp	2m	A Hdl		SFT	£9002
135 1/96 Kemp	2m	D Hdl		GD	£3061
				Total win prize-money	£73457

Going: Sf: 0-0 GS: 0-0 Gd: 0-2 GF: - Fm: 0-2
Distance: 2m/2m3: 0-2 2m4-2m7: 0-2 3m+: 0-0
Track: LH: 0-2 RH: 0-2 Tight: 0-3 Gall: 0-0
Aids: Bl: 0-1 Vi: 0-0 Tstrap: 0-0 Ckp: 0-0
Best Rating: 150 4/97 Ayr 2m good Hdl

One-time smart hurdler; low-grade chaser these days; does not always put it all in; suited by two to two and a half miles and soft ground.

Zabriskie Point
84   42

5-y-o b m Overbury (IRE)-Brownhill Lass (Sunyboy)
Mrs J C McGregor (R Allan 17/12) Drew McClelland

Placings:00-0P00PP   (4909)
2003/04: 16QG, 24PS, 20PHY, 24QGS, 24PGF, 24PS,

	Starts	1st	2nd	3rd	Win & Pl
NH Flat	1	0	0	0	0
Hurdles	5	0	0	0	0
Career Total	8	0	0	0	

Going: Sf: 0-3 GS: 0-1 Gd: 0-1 GF: - Fm: 0-1
Distance: 2m/2m3: 0-1 2m4-2m7: 0-1 3m+: 0-4
Track: LH: 0-5 RH: 0-1 Tight: 0-0 Gall: 0-0
Aids: Bl: 0-0 Vi: 0-0 Tstrap: 0-0 Ckp: 0-0
Best Rating: 61 11/03 Hexm 2m110y good NHF

Zacopani (IRE)
41

12-y-o b g Lafontaine (USA)-Take A Dare (Pragmatic)
R Ford Mr & Mrs T D Williams

Placings:0P0P/041616132/5PF04000P5P/P3300/1F1/P4P 24/0PU-P   (0471)
2003/04: 24PG,

	Starts	1st	2nd	3rd	Win & Pl
Hurdles	1	0	0	0	
Career Total	41	5	2	3	20034
98 7/00 Sedg	3m3f110y	F(0-110)HHdl		FRM	£2618
95 5/00 Hexm	3m1f	E Ch		G-F	£3159
101 8/97 Cork	3m	(0-116)HHdl		Y-S	£4069
96 7/97 Klny	2m6f	(0-109)HHdl		G-Y	£3051
101 6/97 Tral	2m	NHF		FRM	£3391
				Total win prize-money	£16289

Going: Sf: 0-0 GS: 0-0 Gd: 0-1 GF: - Fm: 0-0
Distance: 2m/2m3: 0-0 2m4-2m7: 0-0 3m+: 0-1
Track: LH: 0-1 RH: 0-0 Tight: 0-0 Gall: 0-0
Aids: Bl: 0-0 Vi: 0-0 Tstrap: 0-0 Ckp: 0-0
Best Rating: 106 8/97 Tral 2m4f heavy Hdl

Zafarabad (IRE)
107   (130h) 130

10-y-o gr g Shernazar-Zarafa (Blushing Groom (FR))
P J Hobbs Mrs Elaine Baines

Placings:11141/1323F4/12221U/P03133/1304-0532S0   (3878)
2003/04: 22PY, 24SGF, 20QGF, 25QGF, 23SF, 23QG,

	Starts	1st	2nd	3rd	Win & Pl
Chases	6	0	1	1	3741
Career Total	33	9	5	7	135045
146 10/02 Kemp	3m	B(0-145)HCh		G-F	£17400
140 2/02 Kemp	2m4f110y	C(0-130)HCh		G-S	£11212
135 1/00 Hntg	3m	D Ch		GD	£4381
132 11/99 Extr	2m3f	C Ch		G-S	£6385
150 11/98 Newb	2m110y	B Hdl		G-S	£5095
143 4/98 Punc	2m			HVY	£26956
142 2/98 Newb	2m110y	C HHdl		GD	£4272
137 1/98 Chel	2m1f	A Hdl		G-S	£9645
134 1/98 Kemp	2m	D Hdl		SFT	£2996
				Total win prize-money	£88345

Going: Sf: 0-0 GS: 0-0 Gd: 0-1 GF: - Fm: 0-4
Distance: 2m/2m3: 0-0 2m4-2m7: 0-2 3m+: 0-4
Track: LH: 0-0 RH: 0-6 Tight: 0-0 Gall: 0-0
Aids: Bl: 0-6 Vi: 0-0 Tstrap: 0-0 Ckp: 0-0
Best Rating: 156 1/99 Leop 2m heavy Hdl

Fair handicap chaser; stays three miles, effective at shorter; acts on a fast surface, but also effective on soft ground; best going right-handed; regularly blinkered.

Zaffamore (IRE)
116   (97h) 130

8-y-o ch g Zaffaran (USA)-Furmore (Furry Glen)

Zaffaran Express (IRE)
89f   76f

5-y-o b m Zaffaran (USA)-Majestic Run (Deep Run)
N G Richards A Clark/W B Morris/J Dudgeon

Placings:5   (4867)
2003/04: 16SS,

	Starts	1st	2nd	3rd	Win & Pl
NH Flat	1	0	0	0	0
Career Total	1	0	0	0	0

Going: Sf: 0-1 GS: 0-0 Gd: 0-0 GF: - Fm: 0-0
Distance: 2m/2m3: 0-1 2m4-2m7: 0-0 3m+: 0-0
Track: LH: 0-1 RH: 0-0 Tight: 0-0 Gall: 0-0
Aids: Bl: 0-0 Vi: 0-0 Tstrap: 0-0 Ckp: 0-0
Best Rating: 76 4/04 Ayr 2m soft NHF

Out of a winning hurdler and is a full-sister to useful hurdler Glenmoss Tara; only hinted at ability in Ayr bumper on debut in April 2004 but in good hands and may well be capable of better.

Zaffre (IRE)
102f   96f

5-y-o gr m Mtoto-Zeferina (IRE) (Sadler's Wells (USA))
Miss Z C Davison Rags to Riches

Placings:100   (4846)
2003/04: 16TGF, 17QG, 17PG,

	Starts	1st	2nd	3rd	Win & Pl
NH Flat	3	1	0	0	2331
Career Total	3	1	0	0	2331
93 11/03 Wwck	2m	H NHF		G-F	£2331
				Total win prize-money	£2331

Going: Sf: 0-0 GS: 0-1 Gd: 0-1 GF: - Fm: 1-1
Distance: 2m/2m3: 1-3 2m4-2m7: 0-0 3m+: 0-0
Track: LH: 1-2 RH: 0-1 Tight: 0-1 Gall: 0-1
Aids: Bl: 0-0 Vi: 0-0 Tstrap: 0-0 Ckp: 0-0
Best Rating: 96 4/04 Chel 2m1f good NHF

Won Warwick bumper on debut, but unable to defy a penalty on a couple of occasions since; should get further over hurdles; acts well on fast going.

Zaffre Noir (IRE)
101 (94h)   (101h) 106

8-y-o b g Zaffaran (USA)-Massinetta (Bold Lad (IRE))

Miss H C Knight Martin Broughton

Placings:0/4/52/1510P2-441214   (4953)
2003/04: 22QGS, 24QGF, 20TG, 20PG, 21TGF, 20QG,

	Starts	1st	2nd	3rd	Win & Pl
Chases	6	2	1	0	26050
Career Total	16	4	3	0	38076
132 3/04 Winc	2m5f	C(0-130)HCh		G-F	£8095
132 1/04 Kemp	2m4f110y	B(0-140)HCh		G-D	£12035
126 1/03 Ludl	2m4f	E Ch		SFT	£4953
121 11/02 Ludl	2m4f	E Ch		GD	£4472
				Total win prize-money	£29556

Going: Sf: 0-0 GS: 0-1 Gd: 1-3 GF: - Fm: 1-2
Distance: 2m/2m3: 0-0 2m4-2m7: 2-5 3m+: 0-1
Track: LH: 0-0 RH: 2-6 Tight: 0-2 Gall: 0-0
Aids: Bl: 0-0 Vi: 0-0 Tstrap: 0-0 Ckp: 0-0
Best Rating: 132 3/04 Winc 2m5f gd-fm Ch

Useful chaser; effective at up to 2m 5f; does not stay three miles; acts on good and soft ground; goes well on a flat, right-handed track.

T D McCarthy Mrs D Salmon

Placings:*260/261F31/3054/P-650U0P36* **(4888)**
2003/04: 16⁶S, 20⁵G, 21⁰G, 24⁰UGS, 24⁰G, 22⁹GS, 24³G, 24⁶GF,

	Starts	1st	2nd	3rd	Win & Pl
Hurdles	5	0	0	0	
Chases	3	0	0	1	606
Career Total	22	2	2	3	11249
120 4/01 Winc	2m6f		E Hdl	SFT	£2408
120 12/00 Newb	2m3f		D Hdl	SFT	£3607
				Total win prize-money	£6016

Going:	Sf: 0-1 GS: 0-2 Gd: 0-4 GF: - Fm: 0-1
Distance:	2m/2m3: 0-1 2m4-2m7: 0-3 3m+: 0-4
Track:	LH: 0-3 RH: 0-4 Tight: 0-3 Gall: 0-2
Aids:	Bl: 0-0 Vi: 0-0 Tstrap: 0-0 Ckp: 0-0
Best Rating: 120 12/01 Kemp 2m5f	good Hdl

Modest hurdler/novice chaser; stays three miles; appreciates cut in the ground.

Zaggy Lane

102   119

12-y-o b g Prince Of Peace-Meldon Lady (Ballymoss)
P R Rodford (S C Burrough 3/5) E T Wey

Placings:*6¹006/5F422/3F111F2/P56/FP306153/3462423P/
224425443-60005* **(3639)**
2003/04: 24⁶HY, 25⁰G, 24⁰S, 27⁰GS, 25⁵S,

	Starts	1st	2nd	3rd	Win & Pl
Chases	5	0	0	0	311
Career Total	49	4	8	6	45066
119 2/01 Wwck	3m5f	F(0-110)HCh	SFT	£3558
123 1/99 Tntn	3m3f	C(0-130)HCh	SFT	£7197
117 12/98 Uttx	3m	D(0-120)HCh	SFT	£3598
112 12/98 NAbb	2m5f110y (0-100)HCh	SFT	£3080
			Total win prize-money	£17436

Going:	Sf: 0-3 GS: 0-1 Gd: 0-1 GF: - Fm: 0-0
Distance:	2m/2m3: 0-0 2m4-2m7: 0-0 3m+: 0-5
Track:	LH: 0-2 RH: 0-3 Tight: 0-1 Gall: 0-0
Aids:	Bl: 0-0 Vi: 0-0 Tstrap: 0-0 Ckp: 0-0
Best Rating: 123 2/99 Newb 3m2f110y	gd-sft Hdl

Fair staying chaser; suited by marathon trips and soft ground; consistent; does not win very often these days.

Zahaalie (USA)

108   83

12-y-o ch g Zilzal (USA)-Bambee Tt (USA) (Better Bee)
J A Pickering Christian Wroe

Placings:*3612363P/50022225/00P5P/321F040/4-3406*
(3317)
2003/04: 20³S, 21⁴GF, 20⁰G, 16⁶S,

	Starts	1st	2nd	3rd	Win & Pl
Hurdles	4	0	0	1	413
Career Total	33	2	6	5	10233
94 11/00 Leic	2m4f110yG(0-90)HHdl	HVY	£1932
84 12/97 Bang	2m1f	G Hdl	GD	£2305
			Total win prize-money	£4238

Going:	Sf: 0-2 GS: 0-0 Gd: 0-1 GF: - Fm: 0-1
Distance:	2m/2m3: 0-1 2m4-2m7: 0-3 3m+: 0-0
Track:	LH: 0-1 RH: 0-3 Tight: 0-1 Gall: 0-1
Aids:	Bl: 0-0 Vi: 0-0 Tstrap: 0-0 Ckp: 0-0
Best Rating: 97 3/99 Bang 3m	gd-sft Hdl

Plating-class hurdler; stays two and a half miles; acts on fast ground.

Zaleem (IRE)

7-y-o b g Kahyasi-Zallaka (IRE) (Shardari)
Mrs J Candlish N Heath

Placings:*034/P-P* **(0308)**
2003/04: 17⁰G,

	Starts	1st	2nd	3rd	Win & Pl
Hurdles	1	0	0	0	
Career Total	5	0	0	1	283

Going:	Sf: 0-0 GS: 0-0 Gd: 0-1 GF: - Fm: 0-0
Distance:	2m/2m3: 0-1 2m4-2m7: 0-0 3m+: 0-0
Track:	LH: 0-1 RH: 0-0 Tight: 0-1 Gall: 0-0
Aids:	Bl: 0-0 Vi: 0-0 Tstrap: 0-0 Ckp: 0-0
Best Rating: 94 12/01 Ludl 2m	good NHF

Zambezi River

5-y-o ch g Zamindar (USA)-Double River (USA) (Irish River (FR))
J M Bradley J M Bradley

Placings:*0P* **(1361)**
2003/04: 16⁰GF, 16⁶GF,

	Starts	1st	2nd	3rd	Win & Pl
NH Flat	1	0	0	0	0
Hurdles	1	0	0	0	0
Career Total	2	0	0	0	

Going:	Sf: 0-0 GS: 0-0 Gd: 0-0 GF: - Fm: 0-0
Distance:	2m/2m3: 0-2 2m4-2m7: 0-0 3m+: 0-0
Track:	LH: 0-2 RH: 0-0 Tight: 0-0 Gall: 0-0
Aids:	Bl: 0-0 Vi: 0-0 Tstrap: 0-0 Ckp: 0-0

Zan Lo (IRE)

52

4-y-o ch f Grand Lodge (USA)-Zanella (IRE) (Nordico (USA))
B S Rothwell D J Coles

Placings:*0* **(3529)**
2003/04: 16⁰S,

	Starts	1st	2nd	3rd	Win & Pl
Hurdles	1	0	0	0	
Career Total	1	0	0	0	

Going:	Sf: 0-1 GS: 0-0 Gd: 0-0 GF: - Fm: 0-0
Distance:	2m/2m3: 0-1 2m4-2m7: 0-0 3m+: 0-0
Track:	LH: 0-0 RH: 0-1 Tight: 0-0 Gall: 0-0
Aids:	Bl: 0-0 Vi: 0-0 Tstrap: 0-0 Ckp: 0-0

Zanoora (IRE)

66f   27f

6-y-o br m Topanoora-Zagliarelle (FR) (Rose Laurel)
R J Price R J Price

Placings:*000* **(4345)**
2003/04: 16⁰GS, 16⁰GS, 16⁰GS,

	Starts	1st	2nd	3rd	Win & Pl
NH Flat	3	0	0	0	
Career Total	3	0	0	0	

Going:	Sf: 0-0 GS: 0-2 Gd: 0-1 GF: - Fm: 0-0
Distance:	2m/2m3: 0-3 2m4-2m7: 0-0 3m+: 0-0

Track:

Track:	LH: 0-2 RH: 0-1 Tight: 0-0 Gall: 0-0
Aids:	Bl: 0-0 Vi: 0-0 Tstrap: 0-0 Ckp: 0-0
Best Rating: 27 12/03 Wwck 2m	good NHF

Zantana Boy (IRE)

99(89h)   (53h)86

6-y-o ch g Zaffaran (USA)-Ardtana (IRE) (Cidrax (FR))
M Scudamore (D J Caro 7/6) The Carried Away Syndicate

Placings:*0-05PF54UP4635* **(4446)**
2003/04: 16⁶GS, 20⁵GF, 16⁸GF, 17⁶G, 24⁵GS, 16⁴GS, 25⁵UGS,
19⁰HY, 18⁴G, 19⁶HY, 16³GF, 16⁵GS,

	Starts	1st	2nd	3rd	Win & Pl
NH Flat	1	0	0	0	0
Hurdles	5	0	0	0	0
Chases	6	0	0	1	1153
Career Total	13	0	0	1	1153

Going:	Sf: 0-2 GS: 0-5 Gd: 0-2 GF: - Fm: 0-0
Distance:	2m/2m3: 0-8 2m4-2m7: 0-2 3m+: 0-2
Track:	LH: 0-5 RH: 0-5 Tight: 0-3 Gall: 0-0
Aids:	Bl: 0-3 Vi: 0-0 Tstrap: 0-0 Ckp: 0-0
Best Rating: 86 3/04 Leic 2m	gd-fm Ch

Poor form over fences including in blinkers.

Zapata Highway

68

7-y-o ch g Bold Arrangement-Trailing Rose (Undulate (USA))
Mrs M Reveley R & H Burridge and M Matheson

Placings:*0/0P0-PPO0* **(3760)**
2003/04: 16⁶G, 20⁰PHY, 16⁰HY, 17⁰GS,

	Starts	1st	2nd	3rd	Win & Pl
Hurdles	4	0	0	0	
Career Total	8	0	0	0	

Going:	Sf: 0-2 GS: 0-1 Gd: 0-1 GF: - Fm: 0-0
Distance:	2m/2m3: 0-3 2m4-2m7: 0-1 3m+: 0-0
Track:	LH: 0-3 RH: 0-1 Tight: 0-1 Gall: 0-1
Aids:	Bl: 0-0 Vi: 0-0 Tstrap: 0-0 Ckp: 0-0
Best Rating: 68 10/02 Winc 2m	good Hdl

Zarakash (IRE)

81   75

4-y-o b g Darshaan-Zarannda (IRE) (Last Tycoon)
Jonjo O'Neill (John M Oxx 12/8) John P McManus

Placings:*00* **(4732)**
2003/04: 16⁰G, 17⁰G,

	Starts	1st	2nd	3rd	Win & Pl
Hurdles	2	0	0	0	
Career Total	2	0	0	0	

Going:	Sf: 0-0 GS: 0-0 Gd: 0-2 GF: - Fm: 0-0
Distance:	2m/2m3: 0-2 2m4-2m7: 0-0 3m+: 0-0
Track:	LH: 0-1 RH: 0-1 Tight: 0-0 Gall: 0-1
Aids:	Bl: 0-0 Vi: 0-0 Tstrap: 0-0 Ckp: 0-0
Best Rating: 73 4/04 Carl 2m1f	good Hdl

Zarbari (IRE)

5-y-o b g Kahyasi-Zarlana (IRE) (Darshaan)
D McCain The Acrobats

Placings:0-P   (0192)
2003/04: 16^PG,

	Starts	1st	2nd	3rd	Win & Pl
Hurdles	1	0	0	0	
Career Total	2	0	0	0	

Going: Sf: 0-0 GS: 0-0 Gd: 0-1 GF: - Fm: 0-0
Distance: 2m/2m3: 0-1 2m4-2m7: 0-0 3m+: 0-0
Track: LH: 0-1 RH: 0-0 Tight: 0-0 Gall: 0-0
Aids: Bl: 0-0 Vi: 0-0 Tstrap: 0-1 Ckp: 0-0
Best Rating: 44 4/03 Carl 2m1f   gd-fm NHF

Zarza Bay (IRE)
76

5-y-o b g Hamas (IRE)-Frill (Henbit (USA))
R M Stronge (K R Burke 28/4) A P Holland

Placings:0-0   (0449)
2003/04: 20⁰GF,

	Starts	1st	2nd	3rd	Win & Pl
Hurdles	1	0	0	0	
Career Total	2	0	0	0	

Going: Sf: 0-0 GS: 0-0 Gd: 0-0 GF: - Fm: 0-1
Distance: 2m/2m3: 0-0 2m4-2m7: 0-1 3m+: 0-0
Track: LH: 0-0 RH: 0-1 Tight: 0-0 Gall: 0-1
Aids: Bl: 0-0 Vi: 0-0 Tstrap: 0-0 Ckp: 0-0
Best Rating: 74 12/02 Fknm 2m   gd-sft Hdl

Zawoyski (IRE)

7-y-o b g Posen (USA)-Cri Basque (Gay Fandango (USA))
Jonjo O'Neill Mrs J Mason

Placings:30U/13/PP   (3930)
2003/04: 17^PG, 16^PG,

	Starts	1st	2nd	3rd	Win & Pl
Hurdles	2	0	0	0	
Career Total	7	1	0	2	4747
109	5/01	Thur	2m	Hdl	G-F £3895
			Total win prize-money £3895		

Going: Sf: 0-0 GS: 0-0 Gd: 0-2 GF: 0-0 Fm: 0-0
Distance: 2m/2m3: 0-2 2m4-2m7: 0-0 3m+: 0-0
Track: LH: 0-1 RH: 0-1 Tight: 0-1 Gall: 0-0
Aids: Bl: 0-0 Vi: 0-0 Tstrap: 0-0 Ckp: 0-0
Best Rating: 110 6/01 Clon 2m   firm Hdl

Moderate hurdler; ex-Irish; acts on fast ground; only raced at two miles.

Zawrak (IRE)

5-y-o ch g Zafonic (USA)-Gharam (USA) (Green Dancer (USA))
I W McInnes New Century Windows Ltd

Placings:P   (4214)
2003/04: 17^PG,

	Starts	1st	2nd	3rd	Win & Pl
Hurdles	1	0	0	0	
Career Total	1	0	0	0	

Going: Sf: 0-0 GS: 0-0 Gd: 0-1 GF: - Fm: 0-0
Distance: 2m/2m3: 0-1 2m4-2m7: 0-0 3m+: 0-0
Track: LH: 0-0 RH: 0-1 Tight: 0-1 Gall: 0-0
Aids: Bl: 0-0 Vi: 0-0 Tstrap: 0-0 Ckp: 0-0

Zelensky (IRE)
87   67

5-y-o b g Danehill Dancer (IRE)-Malt Leaf (IRE) (Nearly A Nose (USA))
G Brown C F Stratford

Placings:P-0050B   (4435)
2003/04: 16^PS, 16^PS, 16^PG, 19^PG, 16^PGS,

	Starts	1st	2nd	3rd	Win & Pl
Hurdles	5	0	0	0	0
Career Total	6	0	0	0	0

Going: Sf: 0-2 GS: 0-1 Gd: 0-2 GF: - Fm: 0-0
Distance: 2m/2m3: 0-4 2m4-2m7: 0-1 3m+: 0-0
Track: LH: 0-3 RH: 0-2 Tight: 0-4 Gall: 0-0
Aids: Bl: 0-0 Vi: 0-0 Tstrap: 0-0 Ckp: 0-0
Best Rating: 66 1/04 Leic 2m   soft Hdl

Zen (IRE)
78(92h)   (99h)87

9-y-o b g Shernazar-Mary Mary (Moulton)
T P McGovern Ahmed Abdel-Khaleq

Placings:2155/544/6PPPP0   (4917)
2003/04: 25^PG, 25^PGS, 22^PS, 24^PG, 20^PGS,

	Starts	1st	2nd	3rd	Win & Pl
Hurdles	1	0	0	0	0
Chases	5	0	0	0	0
Career Total	13	1	1	0	2579
111	12/00	Folk	2m1f110yH NHF	HVY	£1725
			Total win prize-money £1726		

Going: Sf: 0-1 GS: 0-2 Gd: 0-3 GF: - Fm: 0-0
Distance: 2m/2m3: 0-0 2m4-2m7: 0-2 3m+: 0-4
Track: LH: 0-3 RH: 0-3 Tight: 0-3 Gall: 0-1
Aids: Bl: 0-0 Vi: 0-0 Tstrap: 0-0 Ckp: 0-0
Best Rating: 111 12/00 Folk 2m1f110y   heavy NHF

Heavy-ground bumper winner; maiden over hurdles; no show over fences to date.

Zero Risk (IRE)
102   117+

8-y-o ch g Insan (USA)-Serenade Run (Deep Run)
L Wells Paul Zetter

Placings:16U3/0133/412UF0   (4307)
2003/04: 16^FGS, 20¹G, 21²G, 23^UHY, 24^FG, 22⁰G,

	Starts	1st	2nd	3rd	Win & Pl
Hurdles	6	1	1	0	8134
Career Total	14	3	1	3	17624
108	12/03	Font	2m4f	C(0-130)HHdl	GD £5785
101	9/01	Bang	2m1f	D Hdl	GD £3542
112	12/00	Folk	2m1f110yH NHF	HVY	£1662
			Total win prize-money £10990		

Going: Sf: 0-1 GS: 0-1 Gd: 1-4 GF: - Fm: 0-0
Distance: 2m/2m3: 0-1 2m4-2m7: 1-3 3m+: 0-2
Track: LH: 0-3 RH: 0-2 Tight: 1-2 Gall: 0-1
Aids: Bl: 0-0 Vi: 0-0 Tstrap: 0-0 Ckp: 0-0
Best Rating: 117 1/04 Kemp 2m5f   good Hdl

Fair hurdler; effective at around two and a half miles; acts on most ground; sometimes wears a tongue strap.

Zeta's River (IRE)
115

6-y-o g Over The River (FR)-Laurebon (Laurence O)
M C Pipe D A Johnson

Placings:U2   (1935)
2003/04: 17^UG, 19²G,

	Starts	1st	2nd	3rd	Win & Pl
Chases	2	0	1	0	2096
Career Total	2	0	1	0	2096

Going: Sf: 0-0 GS: 0-0 Gd: 0-2 GF: - Fm: 0-0
Distance: 2m/2m3: 0-1 2m4-2m7: 0-1 3m+: 0-0
Track: LH: 0-1 RH: 0-1 Tight: 0-1 Gall: 0-0
Aids: Bl: 0-0 Vi: 0-0 Tstrap: 0-0 Ckp: 0-0
Best Rating: 120 11/03 Extr 2m3f110y good Ch

Modest novice chaser; unseated on debut in October 2003 at Bangor; better effort when touched off on second start at Exeter in November by useful rival; should stay 2m4f; acts on good ground.

Zibeline (IRE)
107   141+

7-y-o b g Cadeaux Genereux-Zia (USA) (Shareef Dancer (USA))
B Ellison (B R Millman 12/7) Ashley Carr

Placings:1345401   (4628)
2003/04: 21¹G, 17³G, 16⁴G, 16⁵G, 16⁴G, 16⁰G, 20¹G,

	Starts	1st	2nd	3rd	Win & Pl
Hurdles	7	2	0	1	30881
Career Total	7	2	0	1	30881
141	4/04	Aint	2m4f	A HHdl	GD £23200
88	9/03	Sedg	2m5f110yE Hdl	GD	£2450
			Total win prize-money £25650		

Going: Sf: 0-0 GS: 0-0 Gd: 2-7 GF: - Fm: 0-0
Distance: 2m/2m3: 0-5 2m4-2m7: 2-2 3m+: 0-0
Track: LH: 2-6 RH: 0-1 Tight: 2-3 Gall: 0-0
Aids: Bl: 1-5 Vi: 0-0 Tstrap: 0-0 Ckp: 0-0
Best Rating: 141 4/04 Aint 2m4f   good Hdl

Very useful hurdler; useful on the Flat; stays two and a half miles; suited by fast ground; keen sort; has been tried in blinkers and cheekpieces in the past.

Ziet D'Alsace (FR)
82   64

4-y-o b f Zieten (USA)-Providenc Mill (FR) (French Stress (USA))
A W Carroll (G C Bravery 16/9) Dennis Deacon

Placings:56   (2331)
2003/04: 16⁵GF, 16⁶G,

	Starts	1st	2nd	3rd	Win & Pl
Hurdles	2	0	0	0	0
Career Total	2	0	0	0	0

Going: Sf: 0-0 GS: 0-0 Gd: 0-1 GF: - Fm: 0-1
Distance: 2m/2m3: 0-2 2m4-2m7: 0-0 3m+: 0-0
Track: LH: 0-2 RH: 0-0 Tight: 0-1 Gall: 0-0
Aids: Bl: 0-0 Vi: 0-0 Tstrap: 0-0 Ckp: 0-0
Best Rating: 63 11/03 Wwck 2m   gd-fm Hdl

Zigali

5-y-o b g Zilzal (USA)-Aililisa (USA) (Alydar (USA))
John A Harris Ms Annie Glanfield

Placings:PUP   (3315)
2003/04: 16^PGS, 16^UG, 16^PS,

	Starts	1st	2nd	3rd	Win & Pl
Hurdles	3	0	0	0	
Career Total	3	0	0	0	

Going:	Sf: 0-1 GS: 0-1 Gd: 0-1 GF: - Fm: 0-0
Distance:	2m/2m3: 0-3 2m4-2m7: 0-0 3m+: 0-0
Track:	LH: 0-2 RH: 0-1 Tight: 0-0 Gall: 0-1
Aids:	Bl: 0-0 Vi: 0-0 Tstrap: 0-0 Ckp: 0-0

Ziggy Zen

105   131+

5-y-o b g Muhtarram (USA)-Springs Welcome (Blakeney)
C J Mann (C A Cyzer 17/5) All For One & One For All
Partnership 2

Placings:1U   (3779)
2003/04: 21¹G, 21ᴜG,

	Starts	1st	2nd	3rd	Win & Pl
Hurdles	2	1	0	0	5057
Career Total	2	1	0	0	5057

128 1/04   Kemp   2m5f   D Hdl   GD   £5057
                      Total win prize-money £5057

Going:	Sf: 0-0 GS: 0-0 Gd: 1-2 GF: - Fm: 0-0
Distance:	2m/2m3: 0-0 2m4-2m7: 1-2 3m+: 0-0
Track:	LH: 0-0 RH: 1-2 Tight: 0-0 Gall: 0-0
Aids:	Bl: 0-0 Vi: 0-0 Tstrap: 0-0 Ckp: 0-0
Best Rating:	128 1/04 Kemp 2m5f good Hdl

Fair novice hurdler; winning stayer on the Flat; surprise winner on hurdles debut; stays 2m 5f; keen sort.

Ziggy's Way

103   (85h)99+

9-y-o b g Teenoso (USA)-Onaway (Commanche Run)
Mrs A Barclay Mrs Althea Barclay

Placings:54P/40/P-153   (4916)
2003/04: 20¹GS, 22⁵G, 23³GS,

	Starts	1st	2nd	3rd	Win & Pl
Chases	3	1	0	1	5235
Career Total	9	1	0	1	5557

90   3/04   Wwck   2m4f110yE Ch   G-S   £4533
                      Total win prize-money £4533

Going:	Sf: 0-0 GS: 1-2 Gd: 0-1 GF: - Fm: 0-0
Distance:	2m/2m3: 0-0 2m4-2m7: 1-2 3m+: 0-1
Track:	LH: 1-3 RH: 0-0 Tight: 0-0 Gall: 0-1
Aids:	Bl: 0-0 Vi: 0-0 Tstrap: 0-0 Ckp: 0-0
Best Rating:	99 4/04 Worc 2m7f110y gd-sft Ch

Moderate novice chaser; achieved little when causing 33/1 shock in 2m 4f beginners' chase in soft ground at Warwick March 2004.

Zilarator (USA)

105

8-y-o b g Zilzal (USA)-Allegedly (USA) (Sir Ivor)
P J Hobbs Jay Dee Bloodstock Limited

Placings:5/2425R-P   (0248)
2003/04: 19⁰GF,

	Starts	1st	2nd	3rd	Win & Pl
Hurdles	1	0	0	0	
Career Total	7	0	2	0	3602

Going:	Sf: 0-0 GS: 0-0 Gd: 0-0 GF: - Fm: 0-0
Distance:	2m/2m3: 0-1 2m4-2m7: 0-0 3m+: 0-0
Track:	LH: 0-0 RH: 0-1 Tight: 0-0 Gall: 0-0
Aids:	Bl: 0-1 Vi: 0-0 Tstrap: 0-0 Ckp: 0-0
Best Rating:	123 2/02 Kemp 2m gd-sft Hdl

Modest novice hurdler; useful middle-distance handicapper on the Flat; stays two and a half miles and acts on ground

good or softer; yet to win over timber; sometimes not the easiest of rides.

Zimbabwe

108   118

4-y-o b g Kahyasi-Zeferina (IRE) (Sadler's Wells (USA))
G L Moore (John M Oxx 12/10) Sargent Gillespie

Placings:24102   (4839)
2003/04: 16⁶S, 17⁴G, 18¹G, 17⁹G, 17²GF,

	Starts	1st	2nd	3rd	Win & Pl
Hurdles	5	1	2	0	13296
Career Total	5	1	2	0	13296

118 1/04   Font   2m2f110yE Hdl   GD   £3354
                      Total win prize-money £3354

Going:	Sf: 0-1 GS: 0-0 Gd: 1-3 GF: - Fm: 0-1
Distance:	2m/2m3: 1-5 2m4-2m7: 0-0 3m+: 0-0
Track:	LH: 1-5 RH: 0-0 Tight: 1-2 Gall: 0-3
Aids:	Bl: 0-0 Vi: 0-0 Tstrap: 0-0 Ckp: 0-0
Best Rating:	118 1/04 Font 2m2f110y good Hdl

Very useful juvenile hurdler; stays two miles two; acts on easy ground, but thought capable of better on faster ground.

Zoffany (IRE)

106(101h)   (108+h)120+

7-y-o b g Synefos (USA)-Shining Green (Green Shoon)
M Todhunter Sir Robert Ogden

Placings:10-23   (2232)
2003/04: 17²G, 16³G,

	Starts	1st	2nd	3rd	Win & Pl
Chases	2	0	1	1	1620
Career Total	4	1	1	1	5683

108 12/02 Hayd   2m   D Hdl   GD   £4062
                      Total win prize-money £4063

Going:	Sf: 0-0 GS: 0-0 Gd: 0-2 GF: - Fm: 0-0
Distance:	2m/2m3: 0-2 2m4-2m7: 0-0 3m+: 0-0
Track:	LH: 0-2 RH: 0-0 Tight: 0-1 Gall: 0-0
Aids:	Bl: 0-0 Vi: 0-0 Tstrap: 0-0 Ckp: 0-0
Best Rating:	120 10/03 Bang 2m1f110y good Ch

Fair chaser/hurdler; lightly-raced performer; fortunate winner on hurdling debut over two miles at Haydock in December 2002 and well beaten next time; but fair effort behind Thisthatandtother on chasing bow at Bangor in October 2003; best at around two miles; acts on good/good to soft.

Zoltano (GER)

98   104

6-y-o b g In The Wings-Zarella (GER) (Anatas)
M Todhunter Leeds Plywood And Doors Ltd

Placings:42F2-565   (4459)
2003/04: 17⁵GS, 22⁶G, 20⁵HY,

	Starts	1st	2nd	3rd	Win & Pl
Hurdles	3	0	0	0	0
Career Total	7	0	2	0	4417

Going:	Sf: 0-1 GS: 0-1 Gd: 0-1 GF: - Fm: 0-0
Distance:	2m/2m3: 0-1 2m4-2m7: 0-2 3m+: 0-0
Track:	LH: 0-2 RH: 0-1 Tight: 0-0 Gall: 0-1
Aids:	Bl: 0-0 Vi: 0-0 Tstrap: 0-0 Ckp: 0-0
Best Rating:	112 12/02 Weth 2m soft Hdl

Winner on the Flat in his native Germany; has shown promise over hurdles but tends to run too free; acts on soft ground..

Zonergem

111   102

6-y-o ch g Zafonic (USA)-Anasazi (IRE) (Sadler's Wells (USA))
Lady Herries Tony Perkins

Placings:2   (2069)
2003/04: 16²GF,

	Starts	1st	2nd	3rd	Win & Pl
Hurdles	1	0	1	0	820
Career Total	1	0	1	0	820

Going:	Sf: 0-0 GS: 0-0 Gd: 0-0 GF: - Fm: 0-1
Distance:	2m/2m3: 0-1 2m4-2m7: 0-0 3m+: 0-0
Track:	LH: 0-0 RH: 0-0 Tight: 0-0 Gall: 0-1
Aids:	Bl: 0-0 Vi: 0-0 Tstrap: 0-0 Ckp: 0-0
Best Rating:	105 11/03 Hntg 2m110y gd-fm Hdl

Very useful, but quirky on the level; second on hurdles debut at Huntingdon in November 2003; best at two miles; acts on good/good to firm.

Zoralo (IRE)

111

8-y-o gr g Toulon-Another Yankee (Le Moss)
D C Turner Mrs M E Turner

Placings:0/P/P   (1121)
2003/04: 21⁰GF,

	Starts	1st	2nd	3rd	Win & Pl
Chases	1	0	0	0	
Career Total	3	0	0	0	

Going:	Sf: 0-0 GS: 0-0 Gd: 0-0 GF: - Fm: 0-1
Distance:	2m/2m3: 0-0 2m4-2m7: 0-1 3m+: 0-0
Track:	LH: 0-1 RH: 0-0 Tight: 0-1 Gall: 0-0
Aids:	Bl: 0-0 Vi: 0-0 Tstrap: 0-0 Ckp: 0-0

Zorro Real

111

7-y-o b g Rakaposhi King-Sharp Vixen (Laurence O)
R Rowe John Sturgess, Noel Bonner

Placings:0/P   (4931)
2003/04: 22⁰G,

	Starts	1st	2nd	3rd	Win & Pl
Hurdles	1	0	0	0	
Career Total	2	0	0	0	

Going:	Sf: 0-0 GS: 0-0 Gd: 0-0 GF: - Fm: 0-0
Distance:	2m/2m3: 0-0 2m4-2m7: 0-1 3m+: 0-0
Track:	LH: 0-1 RH: 0-0 Tight: 0-1 Gall: 0-0
Aids:	Bl: 0-0 Vi: 0-0 Tstrap: 0-0 Ckp: 0-0
Best Rating:	39 1/02 Hntg 2m110y gd-sft NHF

Zsarabak

99(105h)   (111h)92

7-y-o br g Soviet Lad (USA)-Moorefield Girl (IRE) (Gorytus (USA))
P D Niven C D Carr

Placings:331P0/3223P/1403-343F043   (1132)
2003/04: 20³G, 20⁴G, 16³G, 17FGF, 17⁰G, 16⁴GF, 20³G,

	Starts	1st	2nd	3rd	Win & Pl
Chases	7	0	0	3	3150
Career Total	21	2	2	8	15985

112 5/02 Bang   2m1f   D(0-115)HHdl   GD   £4329

97 9/00 Bang 2m1f   D Hdl   G-F £3172
                        Total win prize-money £7501

Going: Sf: 0-0 GS: 0-0 Gd: 0-5 GF: - Fm: 0-2
Distance: 2m/2m3: 0-4 2m4-2m7: 0-3 3m+: 0-0
Track: LH: 0-5 RH: 0-2 Tight: 0-5 Gall: 0-0
Aids: Bl: 0-0 Vi: 0-0 Tstrap: 0-0 Ckp: 0-0
Best Rating: 112 5/02 Bang 2m1f   good   Hdl

Moderate chaser; fair handicap hurdler at his best; moderate
over fences so far; has broken blood vessels; one to avoid.

Zum See (IRE)
113   122+
5-y-o ch g Perugino (USA)-Drew (IRE) (Double Schwartz)
Noel Meade Alex Syndicate

Placings:61-010210   (4381)
2003/04: 16⁵G, 16¹GY, 16⁶GF, 16²S, 16¹Y, 16⁶G,

	Starts	1st	2nd	3rd	Win & Pl
NH Flat	1	0	0	0	0
Hurdles	5	2	1	0	14302
Career Total	8	3	1	0	20126

122 3/04 Naas 2m   Hdl   YLD £7785
111 11/03 Naas 2m   Hdl   G-Y £4928
111 2/03 Punc 2m   NHF   SH   £5824
                        Total win prize-money £18540

Going: Sf: 0-1 GS: 0-0 Gd: 0-2 GF: - Fm: 0-1
Distance: 2m/2m3: 2-6 2m4-2m7: 0-0 3m+: 0-0
Track: LH: 2-5 RH: 0-1 Tight: 0-0 Gall: 0-0
Aids: Bl: 0-0 Vi: 0-0 Tstrap: 0-0 Ckp: 0-0
Best Rating: 122 3/04 Naas 2m   yield   Hdl

Irish novice hurdler; won one of three bumpers; scored in
maiden hurdle on debut, but well held in next two outings
when found to have scoped badly; successful on most
recent start at Naas in March; raced only at two miles; likes
soft ground.

Zurs (IRE)
101   104
11-y-o b g Tirol-Needy (High Top)
H J Collingridge Mrs M Liston

Placings:0/50/213/4/00031134430/3F26244P-5PP0 (0761)
2003/04: 16⁵GS, 21ᴾGF, 16ᴾGF, 16⁹G,

	Starts	1st	2nd	3rd	Win & Pl
Hurdles	4	0	0	0	0
Career Total	30	3	3	5	28822

118 10/01 Chel 2m110y E(0-135)HHdl GD   £7182
112 10/01 Bang 2m1f   F(0-110)HHdl GD   £5824
112 11/99 Plum 2m   F(0-110)HHdl G-F £2818
                        Total win prize-money £15826

Going: Sf: 0-0 GS: 0-1 Gd: 0-1 GF: - Fm: 0-2
Distance: 2m/2m3: 0-3 2m4-2m7: 0-1 3m+: 0-0
Track: LH: 0-4 RH: 0-0 Tight: 0-0 Gall: 0-0
Aids: Bl: 0-0 Vi: 0-1 Tstrap: 0-0 Ckp: 0-0
Best Rating: 121 2/02 Kemp 2m   gd-sft Hdl

One-time decent handicap hurdler; disappointing of late and
is slipping down the handicap.

Zygomatic
106   85
6-y-o ch g Risk Me (FR)-Give Me A Day (Lucky Wednesday)
R F Fisher S P Marsh

Placings:330P0000-631   (1136)
2003/04: 21⁶S, 17⁹GF, 20¹G,

	Starts	1st	2nd	3rd	Win & Pl
Hurdles	3	1	0	1	4013

Career Total   11   1   0   3   4475
85 8/03 Bang 2m4f   E Hdl   GD   £3558
                        Total win prize-money £3559

Going: Sf: 0-1 GS: 0-0 Gd: 0-0 GF: 1-1 Fm: 0-1
Distance: 2m/2m3: 0-1 **2m4-2m7: 1-2** 3m+: 0-0
Track: **LH: 1-3** RH: 0-0 **Tight: 1-3** Gall: 0-0
Aids: Bl: 0-0 Vi: 0-0 Tstrap: 0-0 Ckp: 0-0
Best Rating: 92 6/02 Hexm 2m110y   good   NHF

Moderate novice hurdler; best effort when winning maiden
race at Bangor in August 2003; stays two and a half miles.

TOP JUMPS OWNERS IN BRITAIN 2003/4

OWNER	HORSE WITH MOST WIN & PLACE PRIZE-MONEY	WINS-RUNS	WNRS-HORSES	2ND	3RD	4TH	£WIN	£PLACE	£ TOTAL
D A Johnson	Well Chief	49-288	25-63	37	33	20	590,480	334,299	924,779
John P McManus	Clan Royal	36-264	26-81	30	17	19	369,302	465,127	834,430
Jim Lewis	Best Mate	8-29	4-9	11	3	0	377,018	89,739	466,757
Trevor Hemmings	Southern Star	31-165	17-42	18	19	13	338,365	111,995	450,361
Sir Robert Ogden	Iris Royal	35-152	17-41	16	14	12	363,765	85,666	449,432
Halewood International Ltd	Amberleigh House	4-16	4-16	3	7	6	358,206	29,393	387,599
J Hales	Azertyuiop	5-28	4-8	5	3	0	192,734	54,765	247,499
Mrs J Stewart	Cenkos	9-52	5-11	7	6	11	121,960	93,970	215,931
C G Roach	Thisthatandtother	13-31	5-6	5	3	0	149,225	50,053	199,278
B C Marshall	Strong Flow	8-22	4-4	2	1	3	161,931	32,811	194,743
Laurence Byrne	Hardy Eustace	1-2	1-1	1	0	0	174,000	11,000	185,000
Andrea & Graham Wylie	Inglis Drever	16-45	8-14	7	2	2	125,785	55,300	181,086
Terry Warner	Rooster Booster	2-26	2-8	6	0	2	26,826	152,086	178,912
Sir Peter And Lady Gibbings	Isio	3-8	2-2	1	0	0	134,200	34,250	168,450
H R Mould	Bindaree	12-42	8-12	6	3	3	131,589	34,436	166,025
Mr & Mrs Mark Woodhouse	Rigmarole	6-11	1-1	2	0	1	142,605	21,107	163,713
Terry Neill	Puntal	7-28	3-8	2	1	2	145,837	13,279	159,116
N B Mason	Tyneandthyneagain	11-97	8-16	15	15	8	102,968	49,279	152,247
Mrs John Magnier	Rhinestone Cowboy	3-8	1-4	0	3	0	122,653	29,150	151,803
The Liars Poker Partnership	Tiutchev	1-5	1-1	1	1	1	87,000	64,200	151,200
Brian Kearney	Moscow Flyer	2-3	1-1	0	0	0	147,250	0	147,250
Mr & Mrs Raymond Anderson Green	Paddy The Piper	18-118	10-30	7	24	8	98,502	41,967	140,469
A Hordle	Sir Rembrandt	2-7	2-2	2	0	0	32,914	95,650	128,564
Ashleybank Investments Limited	Skippers Cleuch	15-133	12-41	18	10	7	74,086	51,344	125,430
B A Kilpatrick	Tango Royal	9-51	4-13	7	8	4	78,362	38,208	116,570
Keith Nicholson	Gottabe	12-78	11-19	13	17	6	69,926	45,694	115,620
Robert Lester	Iris's Gift	2-3	1-1	1	0	0	110,200	3,960	114,160
M G St Quinton	Monkerhostin	5-12	3-4	2	2	1	80,713	33,382	114,095
R Owen	Ballycassidy	7-10	1-3	0	1	0	106,780	1,280	108,060
Interskyracing.Com & Mrs Jonjo O'Neill	Intersky Falcon	1-6	1-1	1	2	1	46,400	60,400	106,800
Terry Evans	Made In Japan	3-9	2-2	1	4	0	69,998	34,875	104,873
Matt Archer & Miss Jean Broadhurst	Upgrade	5-43	5-12	5	4	2	38,839	65,739	104,578
The 1961 Partnership	Thesis	6-12	2-2	3	2	0	91,080	11,379	102,460
Leslie John Garrett	Our Armageddon	7-17	2-2	2	1	1	94,692	7,360	102,052
W J Brown	Fondmort	1-16	1-3	2	3	2	63,800	34,860	98,660
Ken Roper,Elinor M Roper,Norman Furness	Grey Abbey	3-4	1-1	0	0	0	94,241	750	94,991
Keith Middleton	Cill Churnain	12-38	4-5	7	6	2	75,108	19,322	94,431
M A Ryan	Al Eile	2-4	1-2	1	0	0	76,652	15,400	92,052
Million In Mind Partnership	Garde Champetre	7-22	4-5	3	5	2	63,527	28,040	91,567
Mrs F Montauban	Jair Du Cochet	2-3	1-1	0	0	0	91,400	0	91,400
Let's Live Racing	Mondul	7-43	3-11	4	1	3	68,431	20,014	88,445
Thurloe Finsbury	Geos	2-9	2-2	1	0	0	77,934	10,313	88,247
Patrick Burling Developments Ltd	Hand Inn Hand	1-9	1-2	2	2	1	59,500	28,014	87,514
John P Lynch	Rule Supreme	1-3	1-1	0	1	0	81,200	6,050	87,250
Miss B Swire	Accipiter	5-11	1-3	1	1	0	82,866	3,128	85,994
Mike Charlton And Rodger Sargent	Tikram	3-9	1-2	3	1	1	57,817	27,544	85,361
J E Brown	Bear On Board	8-22	3-5	3	1	2	51,576	31,215	82,791
The Earl Cadogan	Jakari	7-25	3-6	1	6	1	63,246	18,765	82,012
F F Racing Services Partnership III	Hasty Prince	2-8	1-1	1	2	0	58,000	23,800	81,800
Mrs S M Richards	Ei Ei	3-25	1-2	4	5	6	25,567	55,086	80,654
Peter Bowling	Swansea Bay	4-5	1-1	0	0	0	79,743	0	79,743
J B Webb	Royal Shakespeare	7-40	5-10	8	6	3	52,863	24,967	77,831
Hogarth Racing	Keiran	8-42	3-10	7	8	1	63,426	14,270	77,697
The Macca & Growler Partnership	Seebald	6-24	3-4	1	2	3	50,930	24,224	75,154
J R Cornwall	Strong Magic	10-80	6-10	8	14	9	40,514	33,658	74,172
Sandicroft Stud I	Exit Swinger	5-21	4-4	10	1	0	45,252	28,861	74,113
Nigel Bunter	Trouble At Bay	9-20	3-4	0	2	1	70,601	3,270	73,872
Howard Parker	Shardam	2-8	1-1	1	0	1	48,083	22,600	70,683
Mrs D A La Trobe	Grey Report	4-13	1-3	4	2	0	27,907	42,431	70,338
Mrs Jill Eynon & Robin Eynon	Hot Shots	3-9	1-1	2	0	0	59,536	10,764	70,300
B T Stewart-Brown	Lord Of The River	4-15	2-3	3	1	0	46,775	23,051	69,826
Gripen	Fundamentalist	2-3	1-1	1	0	0	62,953	6,600	69,553
Tony Fisher & Mrs Jeni Fisher	Crystal d'Ainay	2-8	1-3	3	1	1	41,122	28,112	69,234
Jim Ennis	The French Furze	4-21	2-5	1	3	2	57,967	10,956	68,924
Clive D Smith	Royal Auclair	0-13	0-2	3	1	3	0	67,908	67,908
R V Shaw	Kings Mistral	2-6	1-1	1	1	1	55,100	11,651	66,751
Widdop Wanderers	Royal Emperor	2-19	1-5	3	0	0	24,361	37,998	62,359
Mrs M Liston	Feel The Pride	6-15	1-2	1	1	0	57,625	3,560	61,185
Mrs Belinda Harvey	Chicuelo	6-39	3-9	1	4	3	35,772	25,225	60,997
Mr & Mrs F C Welch	Fork Lightning	3-9	1-4	1	3	0	54,824	4,912	59,736
Mr & Mrs Peter Orton	Lord Maizey	10-39	7-9	4	6	2	43,447	16,145	59,593
B Ridge & D Hewitt	Cassia Heights	2-8	1-1	3	1	1	44,142	15,385	59,527
Novices Syndicate	Brave Inca	1-1	1-1	0	0	0	58,000	0	58,000
Favourites Racing	Limerick Boy	3-49	3-12	9	4	5	38,665	18,985	57,651
Elite Racing Club	Dancing Bay	9-38	5-11	1	7	4	50,431	6,494	56,925
C H Stevens	Silver Knight	6-43	4-8	10	6	3	24,893	31,685	56,578
Mrs L C Taylor	Monte Cristo	7-41	5-8	5	7	2	40,870	15,622	56,492
W E Sturt	Sir Talbot	8-61	8-21	7	7	5	30,246	25,332	55,578
Islands Racing Connection	Magical Bailiwick	4-8	1-1	1	1	0	36,642	18,700	55,342
J C, J R And S R Hitchins	Native Emperor	2-11	1-3	3	0	0	34,264	20,900	55,164
Mrs Stewart Catherwood	Keen Leader	3-11	3-5	2	1	0	38,636	16,515	55,151
J A G Meaden	Dear Deal	2-25	1-5	3	4	0	19,114	35,945	55,059
O J Carter	Venn Ottery	7-50	3-4	3	2	4	40,008	14,448	54,456
John Galvanoni	His Nibs	3-10	1-1	2	0	3	39,404	15,030	54,435
D F Sills	Turgeonev	2-10	1-3	2	0	1	22,664	31,315	53,979
Mrs M Fisher	Tidour	3-6	1-1	2	0	0	47,869	5,183	53,052

TOP JUMPS TRAINERS IN BRITAIN 2003/4

WINS-RUNS	TRAINER	WIN & PLACE £PRIZE-MONEY	WIN £PRIZE-MONEY	2ND	3RD	£1STAKE	INDIVIDUAL WNRS-HORSES	FIRST-TIME WINS	HURDLES & NH Flat WINS-RUNS	WNRS	CHASES WNS-RUNS	WNRS
175-1069 16%	M C Pipe	2,407,356	1,561,899	121	106	−242.22	96-236	44 19%	104-684 15%	66	71-385 18%	38
127-650 20%	P F Nicholls	2,191,809	1,371,712	129	78	−95.59	73-153	32 21%	61-332 18%	37	66-318 21%	39
102-632 16%	Jonjo O'Neill	1,543,697	1,034,435	72	50	−106.21	63-172	31 18%	74-428 17%	50	28-204 14%	20
121-706 17%	P J Hobbs	1,507,914	810,153	120	81	−140.44	68-160	26 16%	65-437 15%	41	56-269 21%	30
79-370 21%	N J Henderson	1,197,814	870,073	35	50	+14.72	56-115	32 28%	45-238 19%	36	34-132 26%	22
89-562 16%	Miss Venetia Williams	935,615	599,244	86	72	−38.29	51-119	21 18%	55-325 17%	31	34-237 14%	21
42-257 16%	Miss H C Knight	842,796	646,481	39	29	−28.22	30-76	13 17%	20-148 14%	16	22-109 20%	14
79-386 20%	N A Twiston-Davies	759,880	560,101	48	41	+43.00	44-87	14 16%	54-267 20%	30	25-119 21%	15
69-428 16%	Mrs S J Smith	741,110	477,296	54	76	+9.58	41-96	13 14%	23-237 10%	18	46-191 24%	25
47-260 18%	A King	521,335	345,981	32	31	−4.45	26-73	9 12%	31-183 17%	18	16-77 21%	8
41-197 21%	J Howard Johnson	474,401	353,112	29	16	+5.92	24-64	11 17%	25-134 19%	15	16-63 25%	12
46-401 11%	R C Guest	426,817	306,909	48	48	−26.49	29-72	6 8%	20-235 9%	15	26-166 16%	15
28-281 10%	R H Alner	424,288	193,809	34	42	−118.67	18-65	5 8%	9-137 7%	8	19-144 13%	11
8-133 6%	D McCain	421,107	380,194	7	7	−73.17	8-31	2 6%	3-75 4%	3	5-58 9%	5
41-354 12%	Mrs M Reveley	418,179	242,737	57	47	−105.18	28-83	10 12%	33-252 13%	21	8-102 8%	7
50-302 17%	T R George	409,557	244,140	49	38	−63.85	32-65	13 20%	22-132 17%	15	28-170 16%	17
38-126 30%	P Bowen	395,670	344,878	16	10	+55.07	14-32	7 22%	20-76 26%	8	18-50 36%	6
43-209 21%	H D Daly	391,517	269,556	30	28	+10.11	24-60	10 17%	20-106 19%	12	23-103 22%	13
37-231 16%	C J Mann	365,425	239,304	34	28	+20.90	22-66	11 17%	25-129 19%	15	12-102 12%	8
35-226 15%	P R Webber	348,884	238,908	28	26	+1.94	21-70	10 14%	19-121 16%	13	16-105 15%	8
50-358 14%	Ian Williams	338,217	231,257	41	35	−45.63	31-99	9 9%	31-238 13%	20	19-120 16%	14
36-234 15%	G L Moore	330,948	197,498	48	23	−38.27	30-64	12 19%	30-198 15%	26	6-36 17%	4
38-170 22%	N G Richards	309,572	210,347	27	13	+6.33	21-55	9 16%	32-144 22%	17	6-26 23%	4
47-303 16%	L Lungo	295,215	218,867	32	23	−111.35	32-84	15 15%	37-242 15%	25	10-61 16%	8
7-23 30%	F Doumen	249,314	137,595	4	1	+2.11	5-12	5 42%	6-15 40%	4	1-8 13%	1
31-318 10%	Ferdy Murphy	231,833	132,735	37	36	−90.33	24-82	10 12%	14-151 9%	12	17-167 10%	13
22-190 12%	C L Tizzard	213,712	117,629	30	21	+18.53	13-34	7 21%	6-77 8%	5	16-113 14%	9
18-117 15%	G B Balding	205,291	158,573	11	10	−4.79	10-32	4 13%	10-82 12%	6	8-35 23%	5
24-235 10%	K C Bailey	196,441	108,406	24	38	−33.42	16-57	5 8%	13-125 10%	10	11-110 10%	8
22-155 14%	O Sherwood	195,524	107,118	27	16	−83.44	14-44	8 18%	16-108 15%	11	6-47 13%	3
2-7 29%	D T Hughes	193,681	179,681	1	0	+30.00	2-6	1 17%	2-5 40%	2	0-2 0%	0
22-120 18%	M Pitman	192,382	145,215	14	9	+14.57	14-38	6 16%	10-81 12%	6	12-39 31%	9
23-219 11%	J W Mullins	184,547	119,761	26	23	+4.66	12-53	6 11%	7-123 6%	4	16-96 17%	8
18-123 15%	T D Easterby	178,214	91,301	20	17	−23.56	12-32	3 9%	10-68 15%	8	8-55 15%	5
14-201 7%	Miss Lucinda V Russell	164,595	60,982	29	27	−35.89	8-43	2 5%	3-90 3%	3	11-111 10%	5
2-10 20%	Mrs John Harrington	154,500	147,250	0	0	−5.50	1-8	1 13%	0-5 0%	0	2-5 40%	1
24-181 13%	M W Easterby	154,073	107,029	27	17	+15.21	12-54	5 9%	18-137 13%	9	6-44 14%	4
15-104 14%	B Ellison	148,133	92,657	17	15	−25.14	8-25	6 24%	11-88 13%	6	4-16 25%	3
17-128 13%	R J Hodges	139,306	99,279	11	13	−0.92	11-29	2 7%	9-69 13%	6	8-59 14%	5
16-189 8%	G M Moore	136,088	78,154	25	21	−72.83	10-37	6 16%	11-85 13%	8	4-17 24%	3
15-102 15%	R A Fahey	134,674	92,815	16	10	−7.70	11-30	5 17%	11-85 13%	8	6-37 16%	4
13-113 12%	Miss E C Lavelle	133,498	83,667	17	7	−31.92	7-36	5 14%	7-76 9%	5	6-37 16%	4
20-163 12%	R Lee	133,483	97,407	15	15	−4.25	14-31	2 6%	9-70 13%	8	11-93 12%	7
17-142 12%	P Monteith	132,033	84,847	12	19	−7.17	10-28	3 11%	10-97 10%	7	7-45 16%	3
22-131 17%	M Todhunter	131,615	96,188	12	9	+37.11	15-43	6 14%	10-70 14%	8	12-61 20%	7
18-186 10%	R Dickin	130,561	79,005	19	19	−79.63	11-47	3 6%	4-92 4%	3	14-94 15%	8
1-29 3%	W P Mullins	129,650	81,200	1	2	−3.00	1-19	0 0%	0-15 0%	0	1-14 7%	1
3-16 19%	G Macaire	129,368	84,540	5	5	−6.01	2-7	2 29%	0-7 0%	0	3-9 33%	2
20-219 9%	B G Powell	126,923	85,139	17	20	−73.93	14-72	3 4%	8-127 6%	6	12-92 13%	8
9-79 11%	S A Brookshaw	122,041	83,267	11	12	+49.94	5-14	1 7%	5-40 13%	3	4-26 15%	2
13-102 13%	R J Price	116,095	62,567	15	10	+36.25	9-26	2 8%	9-76 12%	8	4-12 33%	2
18-50 36%	P C Haslam	113,736	88,288	10	4	+12.29	10-16	6 38%	14-38 37%	8	4-12 33%	2
10-56 18%	H Morrison	113,452	80,658	8	2	−0.37	8-15	4 27%	9-46 20%	7	1-10 10%	1
9-151 6%	M F Harris	108,721	73,002	11	11	−112.06	5-40	4 10%	9-129 7%	6	0-22 0%	0
14-162 9%	R H Buckler	105,766	60,714	19	19	−45.32	11-33	2 6%	7-95 7%	6	7-67 10%	5
9-115 8%	S Gollings	104,431	65,379	8	21	−39.80	4-28	2 7%	9-110 8%	4	0-5 0%	0
18-124 15%	J Mackie	103,819	70,033	16	6	−6.80	12-28	4 14%	15-114 13%	11	3-10 30%	2
7-100 7%	M C Chapman	101,528	35,598	10	10	−28.50	5-22	0 0%	4-76 5%	4	3-24 13%	2
17-93 18%	Noel T Chance	99,692	67,781	13	14	−14.79	12-32	9 28%	13-84 15%	10	4-9 44%	2
10-100 10%	Mrs S C Bradburne	99,395	47,043	17	22	−31.50	8-13	0 0%	5-62 8%	5	5-16 31%	3
8-29 28%	A M Balding	97,487	79,000	5	1	+19.33	6-8	1 13%	3-13 23%	3	5-38 13%	2
17-152 11%	Mrs H Dalton	97,261	66,697	11	23	−32.77	10-53	0 0%	8-99 8%	6	9-53 17%	4
7-150 5%	P Beaumont	94,656	45,286	13	17	−103.84	5-32	2 6%	0-69 0%	0	7-81 9%	5
2-4 50%	John Queally	92,052	76,652	1	0	+31.00	1-2	1 50%	2-4 50%	1	0-0 0%	0
11-171 6%	J D Frost	90,535	42,215	18	22	−102.96	9-50	1 2%	8-137 6%	7	3-34 9%	3
10-88 11%	A Parker	89,768	63,386	5	15	−9.60	7-22	0 0%	1-34 3%	1	9-54 17%	6
12-180 7%	J M Jefferson	89,459	57,673	16	14	−73.58	10-47	3 6%	9-137 7%	7	3-43 7%	3
9-88 10%	Mrs L Wadham	87,894	42,164	10	17	−41.50	8-20	3 15%	9-79 11%	8	0-9 0%	0
17-95 18%	C R Egerton	87,735	49,971	10	13	−16.61	11-31	5 16%	14-78 18%	9	3-17 18%	2
10-141 7%	R Rowe	86,892	43,159	15	13	−64.50	5-32	2 6%	6-86 7%	2	4-55 7%	3
4-36 11%	P R Chamings	84,277	60,871	7	4	−8.50	3-8	1 25%	1-17 6%	1	3-19 16%	2
7-39 18%	V R A Dartnall	81,267	48,213	9	5	−4.77	4-15	3 20%	4-33 12%	3	3-6 50%	1
14-139 10%	R Johnson	81,260	59,659	7	14	+67.00	6-27	0 0%	10-111 9%	10	3-36 8%	2
13-147 9%	R T Phillips	80,813	49,206	12	10	−89.82	11-55	3 5%	2-23 9%	2	7-44 16%	5
9-67 13%	Mrs L C Taylor	75,646	50,227	7	10	+7.50	6-14	0 0%	6-87 7%	6	3-38 8%	3
9-125 7%	J A B Old	74,595	32,507	12	13	−37.80	9-43	4 9%	6-87 7%	6	3-38 8%	3
13-102 13%	D P Keane	74,320	55,707	7	7	+42.78	8-26	2 8%	7-76 9%	5	6-26 23%	4
10-80 13%	J R Cornwall	74,172	40,514	8	14	+14.00	6-10	1 10%	0-5 0%	0	10-75 13%	9
13-73 18%	G A Swinbank	72,528	55,710	7	8	+19.14	9-31	5 16%	9-61 15%	8	4-12 33%	1
11-71 15%	L A Dace	72,419	66,149	4	3	+19.46	3-20	1 9%	11-58 19%	3	0-13 0%	0
9-82 11%	N J Gifford	71,327	41,740	9	8	−2.50	8-26	4 15%	6-43 14%	5	3-39 8%	3
4-195 2%	Dr P Pritchard	69,951	18,334	16	29	−173.80	3-29	0 0%	1-109 1%	1	3-86 3%	2
6-101 6%	A C Whillans	68,767	33,664	13	14	−52.25	5-27	1 4%	4-63 6%	3	2-38 5%	2
11-127 9%	J R Jenkins	67,865	37,758	15	14	−58.33	7-28	1 4%	11-120 9%	4	0-7 0%	0
10-145 7%	C J Down	67,749	39,955	15	14	−26.75	8-41	1 2%	4-108 4%	4	6-37 16%	5

TOP JUMPS JOCKEYS IN BRITAIN 2003/4

WINS-RIDES	JOCKEY AND LOWEST RIDING WEIGHT IN LAST 12 MONTHS	●CONDITIONAL JOCKEY / TRAINER GIVING MOST WINNERS WINS-RIDES	2ND	3RD	£1 STAKE	WIN& PLACE £PRIZE-MONEY	NH FLAT & HURDLES WINS-RIDES	CHASES WINS-RIDES	FAVOURITES WINS-RIDES	LAST 14 DAYS WINS-RIDES	RIDES SINCE WIN
209-800	26% A P McCoy 10-3	M C Pipe 116-443 26%	144	111	−131.24	2,032,216	133-522	76-278	139-329	10-39	2
186-891	21% R Johnson 10-0	P J Hobbs 85-418 20%	158	107	+41.67	1,974,603	100-549	86-342	97-260	7-43	9
94-625	15% G Lee 9-7	J Howard Johnson 35-135 26%	87	68	+77.20	1,356,423	56-402	38-223	33-92	6-46	9
89-499	18% A Dobbin 10-0	L Lungo 33-114 29%	61	45	−172.43	660,681	65-339	24-160	47-131	6-30	4
86-528	16% A Thornton 10-0	R H Alner 19-115 17%	68	64	+19.99	832,736	37-290	49-238	36-87	2-25	11
73-521	14% R Thornton 10-0	A King 30-171 18%	59	70	−60.46	699,160	44-351	29-170	31-81	3-32	18
65-420	15% C Llewellyn 10-0	N A Twiston-Davies 50-247 20%	48	37	+52.57	715,967	43-301	22-119	26-75	4-25	6
62-294	21% R Walsh 10-1	P F Nicholls 58-245 24%	66	41	−29.05	1,463,043	30-165	32-129	40-113	0-0	6
61-470	13% J Tizzard 10-0	P F Nicholls 30-168 18%	69	54	−184.13	625,678	26-249	35-221	27-74	1-37	8
58-367	16% J Culloty 9-7	Miss H C Knight 34-180 19%	48	49	+21.59	1,055,994	30-243	28-124	21-51	2-17	8
57-411	14% T J Murphy 9-7	M Pitman 16-51 31%	53	41	+70.70	737,791	33-244	24-167	18-54	3-20	7
52-377	14% N Fehily 10-0	C J Mann 29-171 17%	54	41	+140.88	452,138	26-223	26-154	22-57	3-23	10
51-338	15% M A FitzGerald 10-4	N J Henderson 42-204 21%	29	47	−126.01	754,644	28-222	23-116	32-85	2-28	20
49-230	21% D Elsworth 9-13	Mrs S J Smith 43-177 24%	26	29	+97.29	475,555	18-125	31-105	18-48	2-8	0
49-396	12% J A McCarthy 10-0	O Sherwood 9-75 12%	36	49	+16.59	394,286	31-269	18-127	14-44	0-26	33
48-372	13% T Doyle 10-0	P R Webber 27-153 18%	38	41	−88.47	399,251	27-232	21-140	20-39	2-23	14
48-411	12% ●J E Moore 9-9	M C Pipe 22-166 13%	53	42	−180.43	478,586	35-314	13-97	24-78	7-39	3
47-298	16% J M Maguire 10-3	T R George 31-191 16%	33	36	+2.41	345,210	20-158	27-140	21-51	2-14	0
47-337	14% ●S Thomas 9-8	Miss Venetia Williams 36-228 16%	48	37	−34.43	445,658	31-211	16-126	24-77	3-21	3
47-541	9% L Aspell 10-0	Mrs L Wadham 8-59 14%	67	65	−224.95	396,739	32-381	15-160	14-37	3-31	14
45-285	16% L Cooper 10-0	Jonjo O'Neill 45-281 16%	30	22	−100.02	733,740	33-197	12-88	24-74	3-16	6
43-263	16% ●A Tinkler 9-9	N J Henderson 11-55 20%	17	18	+87.38	252,018	38-206	5-57	14-33	1-18	6
40-360	11% R McGrath 10-0	A Parker 6-31 19%	30	42	−76.21	359,214	16-205	24-155	15-40	2-28	7
39-328	12% J P McNamara 10-0	K C Bailey 17-149 11%	40	44	−72.95	310,644	18-191	21-137	18-40	2-18	4
39-394	10% S Durack 10-0	Noel T Chance 7-37 19%	34	28	−143.70	318,911	19-264	20-130	13-36	1-16	3
39-402	10% M Bradburne 10-0	H D Daly 11-75 15%	37	55	−106.21	481,435	19-225	20-177	6-23	5-29	2
38-488	8% ●James Davies 9-7	B G Powell 5-56 9%	38	50	−115.37	238,275	18-321	20-167	5-21	1-22	4
36-380	9% P Flynn 10-0	P J Hobbs 18-138 13%	31	30	−59.72	249,025	18-235	18-145	6-43	2-17	3
34-322	11% D R Dennis 10-0	Ian Williams 18-167 11%	31	39	−70.15	267,390	15-214	19-108	8-38	1-15	1
33-441	7% W Marston 10-0	Mrs S J Smith 9-97 9%	50	61	−167.64	293,775	20-304	13-137	12-56	2-19	7
30-261	11% B Fenton 10-0	Miss E C Lavelle 8-60 13%	28	20	−4.35	263,378	13-160	17-101	8-28	0-0	3
30-492	6% R Greene 10-0	M C Pipe 11-121 9%	34	45	−171.51	334,984	17-312	13-180	8-23	1-32	19
29-206	14% ●L McGrath 9-9	R C Guest 23-131 18%	26	22	−10.07	242,801	12-115	17-91	12-36	0-11	32
28-207	14% D N Russell 10-0	Ferdy Murphy 23-128 18%	28	24	−42.03	193,653	16-118	12-89	11-32	0-2	23
28-268	10% J Crowley 10-0	G A Swinbank 5-25 20%	19	18	−38.07	183,679	17-181	11-87	6-20	2-14	10
27-249	11% P Moloney 9-12	Ian Williams 9-62 15%	17	12	+43.91	184,153	7-147	20-102	5-17	2-16	9
27-361	7% T Scudamore 10-0	M C Pipe 15-124 12%	37	31	−116.28	250,028	17-242	10-119	7-36	0-7	46
25-199	13% T Siddall 10-0	Jonjo O'Neill 22-108 20%	18	17	−48.54	178,133	13-130	12-69	10-19	0-1	11
25-266	9% ●A O'Keeffe 9-9	Miss Venetia Williams 18-112 15%	35	34	−146.62	191,737	15-171	10-95	13-36	1-16	13
24-216	11% ●Christian Williams 9-11	P F Nicholls 8-64 13%	31	26	−10.14	233,318	18-148	6-68	5-32	3-15	4
23-173	13% ●Antony Evans 9-11	N A Twiston-Davies 9-44 20%	12	15	+12.70	129,221	19-134	4-39	10-17	2-11	0
23-264	9% R Garritty 10-7	T D Easterby 10-72 14%	36	41	−138.44	224,962	12-149	11-115	10-28	0-9	40
23-323	7% B Hitchcott 10-0	R Dickin 11-133 8%	27	26	−135.37	176,691	9-200	14-123	8-19	1-22	4
23-337	7% B Harding 9-9	N G Richards 9-53 17%	26	28	−140.08	235,882	13-226	10-111	3-17	0-8	23
21-176	12% B J Crowley 10-0	Miss Venetia Williams 17-106 16%	19	25	−30.82	265,076	14-119	7-57	5-23	0-0	28
21-188	11% M Foley 10-0	N J Henderson 9-49 18%	20	19	−50.93	279,292	19-140	2-48	6-22	0-0	11
21-232	9% ●R Walford 9-11	R H Alner 8-111 7%	24	37	−55.64	157,941	13-152	8-80	4-11	1-14	1
20-217	9% ●W Hutchinson 9-11	R J Price 7-37 19%	22	17	+12.75	179,478	12-158	8-59	5-15	3-21	2
20-261	8% A Dempsey 10-0	Mrs M Reveley 8-92 9%	33	39	−104.38	199,752	12-181	8-80	10-34	3-18	0
20-272	7% H Oliver 10-0	R C Guest 16-185 9%	30	25	−54.12	217,210	10-170	10-102	1-16	0-8	11
19-187	10% ●P Whelan 10-0	R A Fahey 14-73 19%	21	16	+0.30	146,315	16-139	3-48	5-19	0-4	11
19-200	10% D O'Meara 9-11	T D Easterby 6-37 16%	23	21	−50.54	189,863	8-121	11-79	4-10	1-18	6
19-274	7% ●P J Brennan 9-9	P J Hobbs 7-56 13%	26	22	−133.44	173,572	9-185	10-89	5-15	1-20	14
18-256	7% ●P Aspell 9-11	Mrs M Reveley 8-55 15%	27	29	−103.32	150,803	15-183	3-73	5-19	0-0	70
17-253	7% ●D Crosse 9-9	C J Mann 4-34 12%	19	26	−31.70	108,558	13-195	4-58	2-9	2-12	3
16-176	9% ●P Robson 9-11	N G Richards 5-21 24%	21	20	−99.13	103,141	7-120	9-56	3-24	1-12	11
16-196	8% A Ross 10-0	G M Moore 7-46 15%	18	10	+19.00	116,495	10-128	6-68	3-9	2-13	5
16-214	9% R Hobson 9-9	J R Cornwall 9-44 20%	12	29	−29.00	111,451	4-131	12-83	0-5	2-6	4
16-217	7% K Renwick 10-0	P Monteith 10-82 12%	20	22	−28.32	173,090	7-129	9-88	3-14	0-10	27
16-244	7% ●V T Keane 10-2	B Ellison 10-62 16%	30	24	−137.14	130,918	13-189	3-55	7-19	0-16	24
15-112	13% ●T Greenway 9-7	N A Twiston-Davies 6-12 50%	6	11	+87.31	64,345	11-76	4-36	6-12	0-0	8
15-184	8% K Johnson 10-0	R Johnson 12-126 10%	10	18	−57.50	55,534	4-115	11-69	5-12	0-10	13
15-202	7% ●F King 9-13	Mrs M Reveley 7-66 11%	18	24	−69.26	162,802	10-133	5-69	3-13	2-27	13
14-130	11% Mr O Nelmes 9-7	Mrs M Reveley 6-36 17%	12	16	−19.38	85,945	12-93	2-37	4-13	1-15	1
13-76	17% B J Geraghty 10-3	Jonjo O'Neill 6-30 20%	14	3	−16.83	687,746	6-47	7-29	7-21	2-7	1
13-135	10% ●N P Mulholland 9-7	Ferdy Murphy 6-65 9%	13	14	+10.70	76,112	7-89	6-46	3-7	0-0	12
13-212	6% ●A Honeyball 9-11	P F Nicholls 4-25 16%	19	13	−7.62	85,199	9-131	4-81	1-9	0-6	25
12-110	11% Mr T Greenall 9-11	M W Easterby 8-66 12%	15	9	+22.63	86,722	8-80	4-30	6-21	1-8	3
12-147	8% ●R Young 9-9	J W Mullins 9-80 11%	15	14	+10.00	72,925	6-85	6-62	1-9	2-11	1
12-224	5% ●C Bolger 9-9	Miss Suzy Smith 4-21 19%	13	19	−93.62	92,314	6-165	6-59	2-7	0-20	45
11-87	13% ●T Best 9-9	G B Balding 9-55 16%	7	5	−7.25	121,670	11-87	0-0	0-3	0-3	7
11-111	10% ●G Richards 9-9	J G M O'Shea 9-66 14%	12	12	−61.67	62,534	11-93	0-18	7-13	0-0	18
11-114	10% ●N Hannity 10-4	G A Harker 8-60 13%	8	3	−46.00	50,992	11-103	0-11	4-11	1-5	2
11-137	8% ●G Carenza 10-0	M W Easterby 8-41 20%	14	20	−79.58	66,551	10-84	1-53	3-19	1-6	1
11-153	7% ●B Gibson 10-0	L Lungo 5-87 6%	19	7	−80.00	64,469	7-116	4-37	3-16	2-9	5
11-170	6% F Keniry 10-0	N M L Ewart 3-14 21%	9	7	+23.17	81,225	7-116	4-54	2-5	1-10	6
10-72	14% Mr N Williams 9-7	P F Nicholls 2-18 11%	11	4	−21.62	48,354	4-32	6-40	4-12	0-5	6
10-80	13% ●J R Ryan 9-0	Mrs S J Smith 10-71 14%	12	12	−15.12	96,225	3-47	7-33	3-9	0-3	3
10-84	12% ●W A Worthington 10-0	Ian Williams 8-41 20%	11	5	−12.26	56,807	10-82	0-2	4-12	0-6	7
10-88	11% ●J P Byrne 9-11	H D Daly 6-32 19%	12	10	−4.25	53,068	10-74	0-14	2-5	1-11	10
10-137	7% ●C Honour 9-11	J D Frost 5-81 6%	11	20	−65.75	67,452	10-121	0-16	3-8	0-9	33
10-137	7% ●D McGann 9-6	D W Thompson 4-35 11%	8	13	−66.52	48,988	9-114	1-23	5-8	1-6	0
10-144	7% ●R P McNally 9-11	P F Nicholls 7-48 15%	17	13	−96.08	160,235	5-76	5-68	5-11	0-15	56

RACEFORM TOP RATED CHASERS

Moscow Flyer (IRE) 176
Azertyuiop (FR)...176
Best Mate (IRE) 174
Edredon Bleu (FR) 172
Sir Rembrandt (IRE) 172
Tiutchev..171
First Gold (FR) 171
Harbour Pilot (IRE)..170
Jair Du Cochet (FR) 170
Keen Leader (IRE) 170
Beef Or Salmon (IRE) 170
Strong Flow (IRE) 169
Behrajan (IRE) 168
Kingscliff (IRE) 168
Cenkos (FR)..167
Isio (FR) 167
Florida Pearl (IRE) 166
Flagship Uberalles (IRE)......................................166
Marlborough (IRE) 166
Kadarann (IRE)...166
Grey Abbey (IRE)..165

RACEFORM TOP RATED HURDLERS

Baracouda (FR) 176
Iris's Gift...176
Rooster Booster...173
Rhinestone Cowboy (IRE) 170
Hardy Eustace (IRE) 170

WINNERS OF PRINCIPAL RACES (LAST TEN YEARS)

PADDY POWER GOLD CUP (HANDICAP CHASE)
formerly Thomas Pink, Murphy's & Mackeson Gold Cup
Cheltenham 2m 4f 110y

1994	Bradbury Star	9-11-11	14
1995	Dublin Flyer	9-11-08	12
1996	Challenger du Luc	6-10-02	12
1997	Senor El Betrutti	8-10-00	9
1998	Cyfor Malta	5-11-03	12
1999	The Outback Way	9-10-00	14
2000	Lady Cricket	6-10-13	15
2001	Shooting Light	8-11-3	14
2002	Cyfor Malta	9-11-9	15
2003	Fondmort	7-10-13	9

FIRST NATIONAL BANK GOLD CUP (HANDICAP CHASE)
Ascot 2m 4f

1994	Raymylette	7-11-10	11
1995	Sound Man	7-12-00	5
1996	Strong Promise	5-10-05	8
1997	Simply Dashing	9-10-05	15
1998	Red Marauder	8-10-11	11
1999	Nordance Prince	8-10-09	11
2000	Upgrade	6-11-08	4
2001	Wahiba Sands	8-10-4	4
2002	Abandoned due to waterlogging		
2003	Iris Royal	7-10-4	5

HENNESSY COGNAC GOLD CUP (HANDICAP CHASE)
Newbury 3m 2f 110y

1994	One Man	6-10-00	16
1995	Couldnt Be Better	8-10-08	11
1996	Coome Hill	7-10-00	11
1997	Suny Bay	8-11-08	14
1998	Teeton Mill	9-10-05	16
1999	Ever Blessed	7-10-00	13
2000	King's Road	7-10-07	17
2001	What's Up Boys	7-10-12	14
2002	Gingembre	8-10-13	25
2003	Strong Flow	6-11-0	21

TRIPLEPRINT GOLD CUP (HANDICAP CHASE)
Cheltenham 2m 4f

1994	Dublin Flyer	8-10-02	11
1995	Abandoned due to frost		
1996	Addington Boy	8-11-10	10
1997	Senor El Betrutti	8-11-03	9
1998	Northern Starlight	7-10-01	13
1999	Legal Right	6-10-13	9
2000	Go Roger Go	8-11-00	12
2001	Abandoned due to frost		
2002	Fondmort	6-10-5	9
2003	Iris Royal	7-10-13	17

BONUSPRINT CHRISTMAS HURDLE
Kempton 2m

1994	Absaloms's Lady	6-11-02	6
1995	Abandoned due to frost		
1996	Abandoned due to frost		
1997	Kerawi	4-11-07	5
1998	French Holly	7-11-07	5
1999	Dato Star	8-11-07	4
2000	Geos	5-11-07	7

2001	Landing Light	6-11-7	5
2002	Intersky Falcon	5-11-7	6
2003	Intersky Falcon	6-11-7	6

PERTEMPS KING GEORGE VI CHASE
Kempton 3m

1994	Algan	6-11-10	9
1995	*One Man	8-11-10	11
1996	One Man	8-11-10	5
1997	See More Business	7-11-10	8
1998	Teeton Mill	9-11-10	9
1999	See More Business	9-11-10	9
2000	First Gold	7-11-10	9
2001	Florida Pearl	9-11-10	8
2002	Best Mate	7-11-10	10
2003	Edredon Bleu	11-11-10	12

(*Run at Sandown Jan 6th 1996)

CORAL WELSH NATIONAL (HANDICAP CHASE)
Chepstow 3m 6f

1994	*Master Oats	8-11-06	8
1995	Abandoned due to frost		
1996	Abandoned due to frost		
1997	Earth Summit	9-10-13	14
1998	Kendal Cavalier	8-10-08	14
1999	Edmond	7-10-00	16
2000	Jocks Cross	9-10-04	19
2001	Supreme Glory	8-10-00	13
2002	Mini Sensation	9-10-4	16
2003	Bindaree	9-10-9	14

(*Run at Newbury)

PIERSE HANDICAP HURDLE
(formerly Ladbroke Handicap Hurdle)
Leopardstown 2m

1995	Anusha	5-10-02	17
1996	Dance Beat	5-09-12	22
1997	Master Tribe	7-10-04	23
1998	Graphic Equaliser	6-10-00	20
1999	Archive Footage	7-11-08	25
2000	Mantles Prince	6-9-12	14
2001	Grinkov	6-10-07	24
2002	Adamant Approach	8-11-1	26
2003	Xenophon	7-10-11	28
2004	Dromlease Express	6-10-4	19

VICTOR CHANDLER HANDICAP CHASE
Ascot 2m

1995	Martha's Son	8-10-09	8
1996	Big Matt	9-10-04	11
1997	*Ask Tom	8-10-10	8
1998	Jeffell	8-10-11	9
1999	*Call Equiname	9-11-03	7
2000	Nordance Prince	9-10-00	10
2001	Function Dream	9-10-11	10
2002	Turgeonev	7-10-4	8
2003	**Young Devereaux	10-10-4	9
2004	Isio	8-10-5	13

(*Run at Kempton)
(**Run at Kempton as Tote Exacta Chase)

TOTE GOLD TROPHY (HANDICAP HURDLE)
Newbury 2m 110y

1995	Mysilv	5-10-08	8
1996	Squire Silk	7-10-12	18
1997	Make a Stand	6-11-07	18
1998	Sharpical	6-11-01	14
1999	Decoupage	7-11-10	18
2000	Geos	5-11-03	17
2001	Landing Light	6-10-02	20
2002	Copeland	7-11-07	16
2003	Spirit Leader	7-10-00	27
2004	Geos	9-10-9	25

HENNESSY COGNAC GOLD CUP CHASE
Leopardstown 3m

1995	Jodami	10-12-00	6
1996	Imperial Call	7-12-00	8
1997	Danoli	9-12-00	8
1998	Dorans Pride	9-12-00	8
1999	Florida Pearl	7-12-00	7
2000	Florida Pearl	8-12-00	7
2001	Florida Pearl	9-12-00	7
2002	Alexander Banquet	9-12-00	5
2003	Beef Or Salmon	7-12-00	5
2004	Florida Pearl	12-11-12	7

RACING POST HANDICAP CHASE
Kempton 3m

1995	Val D'Alene	8-11-02	9
1996	Rough Quest	10-10-08	9
1997	Mudahim	11-10-02	9
1998	Super Tactics	10-10-10	7
1999	Dr Leunt	8-11-05	8
2000	Gloria Victis	6-11-10	13
2001	Young Spartacus	8-11-03	15
2002	Gunther McBride	7-10-03	14
2003	La Landiere	8-11-07	14
2004	Marlborough	12-11-12	11

SUNDERLANDS IMPERIAL CUP
(HANDICAP) HURDLE
Sandown 2m 110y

1995	Collier Bay	5-10-02	10
1996	Amancio	5-10-08	11
1997	Carlito Brigante	5-10-00	18
1998	Blowing Wind	5-11-10	15
1999	Regency Rake	7-10-07	9
2000	Magic Combination	7-10-00	18
2001	Ibal	5-9-09	23
2002	Polar Red	5-11-01	16
2003	Korelo	5-11-06	17
2004	Scorned	9-10-3	23

IRISH INDEPENDENT ARKLE CHALLENGE
TROPHY NOVICES' CHASE
(formerly Guinness Arkle Challenge Trophy)
Cheltenham 2m

1995	Klairon Davis	6-11-08	11
1996	Ventana Canyon	7-11-08	16
1997	Or Royal	6-11-08	9
1998	Champleve	5-11-00	16
1999	Flagship Uberalles	5-11-00	14
2000	Tiutchev	7-11-08	12
2001	Abandoned- Foot & Mouth		
2002	Moscow Flyer	8-11-08	12
2003	Azertyuiop	6-11-08	9
2004	Well Chief	5-11-03	16

SMURFIT CHAMPION HURDLE
Cheltenham 2m 110y

1995	Alderbrook	6-12-00	14
1996	Collier Bay	6-12-00	16
1997	Make a Stand	6-12-00	17
1998	Istabraq	6-12-00	18
1999	Istabraq	7-12-00	14
2000	Istabraq	8-12-00	12
2001	Abandoned - Foot & Mouth		
2002	Hors La Loi III	7-12-00	15
2003	Rooster Booster	9-12-00	17
2004	Hardy Eustace	7-11-10	14

QUEEN MOTHER CHAMPION CHASE
Cheltenham 2m

1995	Viking Flagship	8-12-00	10
1996	Klairon Davis	7-12-00	7
1997	Martha's Son	10-12-00	6
1998	One Man	10-12-00	8
1999	Call Equiname	9-12-00	13
2000	Edredon Bleu	8-12-00	13
2001	Abandoned - Foot & Mouth		
2002	Flagship Uberalles	8-12-00	12
2003	Moscow Flyer	9-12-00	11
2004	Azertyuiop	7-11-10	8

ROYAL & SUNALLIANCE (NOVICES') CHASE
Cheltenham 3m

1995	Brief Gale	8-10-13	13
1996	Nahthen Lad	7-11-04	12
1997	Hanakham	8-11-04	14
1998	Florida Pearl	6-11-04	10
1999	Looks Like Touble	7-11-04	14
2000	Lord Noelie	7-11-04	9
2001	Abandoned - Foot & Mouth		
2002	Hussard Collonges	7-11-04	19
2003	One Knight	7-11-04	9
2004	Rule Supreme	8-11-04	10

JCB TRIUMPH HURDLE
(formerly Daily Express & Elite Racing Club
Triumph Hurdle) Cheltenham 2m 1f (4-y-o)

1995	Kissair	11-00	26
1996	Paddy's Return	11-00	29
1997	Commanche Court	11-00	28
1998	Upgrade	11-00	25
1999	Katarino	11-00	23
2000	Snow Drop	10-09	28
2001	Abandoned - Foot & Mouth		
2002	Scolardy	11-00	28
2003	Spectroscope	11-00	27
2004	Made In Japan	11-00	23

TOTE CHELTENHAM GOLD CUP (CHASE)
Cheltenham 3m 2f

1995	Master Oats	9-12-00	15
1996	Imperial Call	7-12-00	10
1997	Mr Mulligan	9-12-00	14
1998	Cool Dawn	10-12-00	17
1999	See More Business	9-12-00	12
2000	Looks Like Trouble	8-12-00	12
2001	Abandoned - Foot & Mouth		
2002	Best Mate	7-12-00	18
2003	Best Mate	8-12-00	15
2004	Best Mate	9-11-10	10

MARTELL COGNAC CUP CHASE
Aintree 3m 1f

1995	Merry Gale	7-11-09	6
1996	Scotton Banks	7-11-05	6
1997	Barton Bank	11-11-05	5
1998	Escartefigue	6-11-13	8
1999	Macgeorge	9-11-05	5
2000	See More Business	10-12-00	4
2001	First Gold	8-12-00	7
2002	Florida Pearl	10-11-12	6
2003	First Gold	10-11-2	7
2004	Tiutchev	11-11-12	8

UNWINS WINE GROUP ANNIVERSARY HURDLE
(formerly GLENLIVET ANNIVERSARY HURDLE)
(4-y-o) Aintree 2m 110y

1995	Stompin	11-00	18
1996	Zabadi	11-00	11
1997	Quakers Field	11-00	12
1998	Deep Water	11-00	14
1999	Hors La Loi III	11-04	6
2000	Lord Brex	11-00	12
2001	Bilboa	10-13	14
2002	Quazar	11-04	17
2003	Le Duc	11-00	19
2004	Al Eile	11-00	18

MARTELL COGNAC MELLING CHASE
Aintree 2m 4f

1995	Viking Flagship	8-11-10	6
1996	Viking Flagship	9-11-10	4
1997	Martha's Son	10-11-10	4
1998	Opera Hat	10-11-05	5
1999	Direct Route	8-11-10	6
2000	Direct Route	9-11-10	5
2001	Fadalko	8-11-10	7
2002	Native Upmanship	9-11-10	8
2003	Native Upmanship	10-11-10	6
2004	Moscow Flyer	10-11-10	7

MARTELL COGNAC RED RUM CHASE
(LIMITED HANDICAP)
Aintree 2m

1995	Coulton	8-11-08	12
1996	Arctic Kinsman	8-11-00	10
1997	Down the Fell	8-10-07	10
1998	Jeffell	8-12-00	5
1999	Flying Instructor	9-11-05	7
2000	Jungli	7-10-07	7
2001	Aghawadda Gold	9-11-02	12
2002	Dark'n Sharp	7-10-08	15
2003	Golden Alpha	9-10-13	16
2004	Tidour	8-10-11	14

MARTELL AINTREE HURDLE
Aintree 2m 4f

1995	Danoli	7-11-07	6
1996	Urubande	6-11-07	8
1997	Bimsey	7-11-07	7
1998	Pridwell	8-11-07	6
1999	Istabraq	7-11-7	7
2000	Mister Morose	10-11-07	10
2001	Barton	8-11-07	8
2002	Ilnamar	6-11-07	14
2003	Sacundai	6-11-07	5
2004	Rhinestone Cowboy	8-11-07	11

MARTELL GRAND NATIONAL
(HANDICAP CHASE) 4m 4f

1971	Specify	9-10-13	42
1972	Well To Do	9-10-01	42
1973	Red Rum	8-10-05	38
1974	Red Rum	9-12-00	42
1975	L'Escargot	12-11-03	31
1976	Rag Trade	10-10-12	32
1977	Red Rum	12-11-08	42
1978	Lucius	9-10-09	37
1979	Rubstic	10-10-00	34
1980	Ben Nevis	12-10-12	30
1981	Aldaniti	11-10-13	39
1982	Grittar	9-11-05	39
1983	Corbiere	8-11-04	41
1984	Hallo Dandy	10-10-02	40
1985	Last Suspect	11-10-05	40
1986	West Tip	9-10-11	40
1987	Maori Venture	11-10-13	40
1988	Rhyme 'N' Reason	9-11-00	40
1989	Little Polveir	12-10-03	40
1990	Mr Frisk	11-10-06	38
1991	Seagram	11-10-06	40
1992	Party Politics	8-10-07	40
1993	Void Race		
1994	Miinnehoma	11-10-08	36
1995	Royal Athlete	12-10-06	35
1996	Rough Quest	10-10-07	27
1997	Lord Gyllene	9-10-00	36
1998	Earth Summit	10-10-05	37
1999	Bobbyjo	9-10-00	32
2000	Papillon	9-10-12	40
2001	Red Marauder	11-10-11	40
2002	Bindaree	8-10-04	40
2003	Monty's Pass	10-10-07	40
2004	Amberleigh House	12-10-10	39

GALA CASINOS DAILY RECORD SCOTTISH
GRAND NATIONAL (HANDICAP CHASE)
Ayr 4m 1f

1995	Willsford	12-10-12	22
1996	Moorcroft Boy	11-10-02	20
1997	Belmont King	9-11-10	17
1998	Baronet	8-10-00	18
1999	Young Kenny	8-11-10	15
2000	Paris Pike	8-11-0	18
2001	Gingembre	7-11-02	30
2002	Take Control	8-10-06	18
2003	Ryalux	10-10-05	19
2004	Grey Abbey	10-11-12	28

BETFRED GOLD CUP (HANDICAP CHASE)
(formerly ATTHERACES & WHITBREAD GOLD CUP)
Sandown 3m 5f 110y

1995	Cache Fleur	9-10-01	14
1996	Life of a Lord	10-11-10	17
1997	Harwell Lad	8-10-0	9
1998	Call It A Day	8-10-10	19
1999	Eulogy	9-10-00	19
2000	Beau	7-10-9	20
2001	Ad Hoc	7-10-04	25
2002	Bounce Back	6-10-09	20
2003	Ad Hoc	9-10-10	16
2004	Puntal	8-11-04	18

RACEFORM JUMP MEDIAN TIMES 2003-2004

Some distances have been omitted where insufficient data exists to establish a reliable median time.

AINTREE
Chase (Mildmay)
2m	3m 58.7
2m4f	5m 7.3
3m1f	6m 29.2

Chase (National)
2m 6f	5m 40.1
3m3f	7m 15.7
4m4f	9m 8.6

Hurdles
2m110y	4m 7.2
2m4f	4m 59.2
3m110y	6m 11.7

ASCOT
Chase
2m	4m
2m3f110y	4m 58.1
3m110y	6m 23.2

Hurdles
2m110y	4m 2.3
2m4f	4m 59.7
3m	5m 55.9
3m1f 110y	6m 25.4

AYR
Chase
2m	4m 4.2
2m4f	5m 18.6
2m5f110y	5m 58.7
3m1f	6m 38.1
3m3f110y	7m 7.4
4m1f	8m 20.8

Hurdles
2m	3m 54.7
2m4f	5m 7.3
2m6f	5m 43.8
3m110y	6m 22
3m2f110y	6m 37.7

BANGOR
Chase
2m1f110y	4m 26.2
2m4f110y	5m 15.6
3m110y	6m 23.7
3m6f	8m 22.7
4m1f	9m 16.7

Hurdles
2m1f	4m 9
2m4f	4m 53.8
3m	5m 54.3

CARLISLE
Chase
2m	4m 13.4
2m4f	5m 15.2
3m	6m 23.9
3m2f	7m 8.5

Hurdles
2m1f	4m 22.5
2m4f110y	5m 16.6
3m110y	6m 19.6

CARTMEL
Chase
2m1f110y	4m 21.6
2m5f110y	5m 22.3
3m2f	6m 37.9

Hurdles
2m1f110y	4m 11
2m6f	5m 29.2
3m2f	6m 21.7

CATTERICK
Chase
2m	4m 2.9
2m3f	4m 56.4
3m1f110y	6m 46
3m4f110y	7m 46.8

Hurdles
2m	3m 55.8
2m3f	4m 49.5
3m1f110y	6m 34

CHELTENHAM (NEW)
Chase
2m110y	4m 10.6
2m5f	5m 28.9
3m1f110y	6m 47.8
3m2f110y	6m 50.8
4m1f	8m 57.2

Hurdles
2m1f	4m 14.6
2m5f110y	5m 28.6
3m	6m 1.2

CHELTENHAM (OLD)
Chase
2m	3m 59.3
2m4f110y	5m 12.4
3m110y	6m 26.1
3m3f110y	7m 17.3
4m	8m 23.6

Hurdles
2m110y	4m 1.7
2m5f	5m 14.3
3m1f110y	6m 36.5

Cross Country Chases
3m	6m 19
3m7f	8m 37.4

CHEPSTOW
Chase
2m110y	4m 19.2
2m3f110y	5m 13.5
3m	6m 16.6
3m2f110y	7m 22.8
3m5f110y	8m 11.0

Hurdles
2m110y	4m 12.8
2m4f	5m 5.1
3m	6m 17.7

DONCASTER
Chase
2m110y	4m 6.8
2m3f110y	4m 59.4
3m	6m 12.7
3m2f	6m 37.8

Hurdles
2m110y	4m 4.1
2m4f	4m 55.5
3m110y	6m 2.5

EXETER
Chase
2m1f110y	4m 20.0
2m3f110y	4m 52.3
2m7f110y	5m 59.3
3m1f110y	6m 26.4

Hurdles
2m1f	4m 7
2m3f	4m 33.3
2m6f110y	5m 34.2
3m110y	6m 8.4

FAKENHAM
Chase
2m110y	4m 14.4
2m5f110y	5m 34
3m110y	6m 28

Hurdles
2m	4m 3
2m4f	5m 0.7
2m7f110y	5m 47.8

FOLKESTONE
Chase
2m	4m 8.9
2m5f	5m 30.6
3m1f	6m 32.8
3m2f	6m 44.8
3m7f	8m 0.4

Hurdles
2m1f110y 4m 28.9
2m4f110y 5m 23.8
2m6f110y 6m

FONTWELL
Chase
2m2f 4m 38.6
2m4f 5m 2.3
2m6f 5m 37.4
3m2f110y 7m 4.5
Hurdles
2m2f110y 4m 33.3
2m4f 4m 59.8
2m6f110y 5m 38.8
3m3f 6m 37.5

HAYDOCK
Chase
2m 4m 14.8
2m4f 5m 28.3
2m6f 5m 48.8
3m 6m 34.6
3m4f110y 7m 40.2
4m110y 9m 11.2
Hurdles
2m 3m 59.8
2m4f 5m 8.2
2m6f 5m 48.1
2m7f110y 6m 9.9

HEREFORD
Chase
2m 4m 3.7
2m3f 4m 48.7
3m1f110y 6m 33.8
Hurdles
2m1f 4m 4.0
2m3f110y 4m 48.5
3m2f 6m 29.1

HEXHAM
Chase
2m110y 4m 10.1
2m4f110y 5m 13.2
3m1f 6m 32.8
4m 9m 12.4
Hurdles
2m110y 4m 14.0
2m4f110y 5m 6.9
3m 6m 11.2

HUNTINGDON
Chase
2m110y 4m 9.1
2m4f110y 5m 4.9
3m 6m 12
3m6f110y 8m 10.1

Hurdles
2m110y 3m 55.7
2m4f110y 4m 49.9

2m5f110y 5m 10
3m2f 6m 20.6

KELSO
Chase
2m1f 4m 20.5
2m6f110y 5m 55
3m1f 6m 28.4
3m4f 7m 24.1
4m 8m 39
Hurdles
2m110y 4m
2m2f 4m 31.5
2m6f110y 5m 37.8
3m3f 6m 34.7

KEMPTON
Chase
2m 3m 56.6
2m4f110y 5m 15.5
3m 6m 13.2
Hurdles
2m 3m 57.5
2m5f 5m 16.1
3m110y 6m 13.1

LEICESTER
Chase
2m 4m 17.9
2m4f110y 5m 25.5
2m7f110y 6m 12.3
Hurdles
2m 4m 6.4
2m4f110y 5m 22.7
3m 6m 17.1

LINGFIELD
Chase
2m 4m 20.5
2m4f110y 5m 34.8
3m 6m 36.1
Hurdles
2m110y 4m 14.3
2m3f110y 5m10.7
2m7f 6m 13.4

LUDLOW
Chase
2m 4m 4.2
2m4f 5m 5.8
3m 6m 9.1
Hurdles
2m 3m 47.6
2m5f 5m 13.5
3m 5m 54.6

MARKET RASEN
Chase
2m1f110y 4m 28.7
2m4f 5m 6.5
2m6f110y 5m 44.7

3m 6m 28
3m1f 6m 34
3m4f110y 7m 54.3
4m1f 9m 12.1
Hurdles
2m1f110y 4m 16.1
2m3f110y 4m 49
2m5f110y 5m 25.3
3m 6m 6.8

MUSSELBURGH
Chase
2m 3m 58.3
2m4f 5m 4.4
3m 6m 9.6
Hurdles
2m 3m 49.8
2m4f 4m 53.8
3m 5m 55.2

NEWBURY
Chase
2m1f 4m 15.9
2m2f110y 5m 41.4
2m4f 5m 12
2m6f110y 5m 47.7
3m 6m 10.2
3m2f110y 6m 51.9
Hurdles
2m110y 4m 4.3
2m3f 4m 48
2m5f 5m 15.3
3m110y 6m 9.6

NEWCASTLE
Chase
2m110y 4m 16
2m4f 5m 16
3m 6m 10.2
3m6f 8m 6.2
4m1f 8m 48.1
Hurdles
2m 4m 2.6
2m4f 5m 8.1
3m 6m 6.0

NEWTON ABBOT
Chase
2m110y 4m 7.2
2m5f110y 5m 25
3m2f110y 6m 49
Hurdles
2m1f 4m 7.1

2m6f......................... 5m 21.7
3m3f......................... 6m 46

PERTH
Chase

2m............................. 3m 59.9
2m4f110y 5m 9.8
3m............................. 6m 12.4

Hurdles

2m110y 3m 56.7
2m4f110y 5m 2.4
3m110y 6m 5.8

PLUMPTON
Chase

2m1f........................ 4m 23.6
2m4f........................ 5m 23.2
3m2f........................ 7m 5.4
Hurdles
2m............................. 3m 50.3
2m5f........................ 5m 30.3
3m1f110y 6m 57.1

SANDOWN
Chase

2m............................. 4m 3.2
2m4f110y 5m 21.5
3m110y 6m 31.5
3m5f110y 7m 41
Hurdles
2m110y 4m 7.1
2m4f110y 5m 23.9
2m6f......................... 5m 33.5

SEDGEFIELD
Chase

2m110y 4m 11.6
2m5f........................ 5m 19.6
3m3f......................... 7m 2.4
3m4f......................... 7m 11.3
Hurdles
2m1f........................ 4m 3
2m5f110y 5m 10.7
3m3f110y 6m 56.5

SOUTHWELL
Chase

2m1f........................4m 11.7
2m5f110y 5m 25.1
3m2f........................6m 37.9
Hurdles
2m1f........................ 4m 2.9
2m5f110y 5m 15.8
3m2f......................... 6m 27

STRATFORD
Chase

2m1f110y 4m 14.7
2m4f......................... 5m 1.2
2m5f110y 5m 22.6
3m............................. 6m 4.2
3m4f......................... 7m 11.7
Hurdles
2m110y 3m 59.9
2m3f......................... 4m 34.9
2m6f110y 5m 33.7
3m3f......................... 6m 33.8

TAUNTON
Chase

2m110y 4m 9.4
2m3f......................... 4m 55
3m............................. 6m 16.3
3m3f......................... 7m 18.6
4m2f110y 9m 38.9
Hurdles
2m1f........................ 4m 3.5
2m3f110y 4m 43.3
3m110y 6m 9.8

TOWCESTER
Chase

2m110y 4m 16.3
2m6f......................... 5m 52.2
3m1f........................ 6m 42.3
Hurdles
2m............................. 4m 2.8
2m5f........................ 5m 32.3
3m............................. 6m 16.6

UTTOXETER
Chase

2m............................. 4m 2.2
2m4f......................... 5m 14.7
2m5f........................ 5m 19.3
2m7f......................... 5m 54.1
3m............................. 6m 30.4
3m2f......................... 6m 55
4m2f......................... 8m 54.3
Hurdles
2m............................. 3m 52.4
2m4f110y 5m 2.6
2m6f110y 5m 36.5
3m110y 5m 58.7

WARWICK
Chase

2m110y 4m 0.3
2m4f110y 5m 16.5
3m110y 6m 13.8
3m2f......................... 6m 48.4
3m5f......................... 7m 48.9

Hurdles

2m............................. 3m 54.3
2m3f......................... 4m 38.7
2m5f........................ 5m 13.5
3m1f........................ 6m 28.4

WETHERBY
Chase

2m............................. 4m 3.5
2m4f110y 5m 19.4
3m1f........................ 6m 36.1
3m5f......................... 7m 23.1
Hurdles
2m............................. 3m 57.2
2m4f110y 5m 7.5
2m7f......................... 5m 59.6
3m1f........................ 6m 14

WINCANTON
Chase

2m............................. 4m 4.4
2m5f........................ 5m 22.6
3m1f110y 6m 44.4
Hurdles
2m............................. 3m 48
2m6f......................... 5m 23.4

WORCESTER
Chase

2m............................. 3m 58.6
2m4f110y 5m 15.5
2m7f110y 6m 1.1
Hurdles
2m............................. 3m 50.2
2m4f......................... 4m 53

3m............................. 5m 51.9

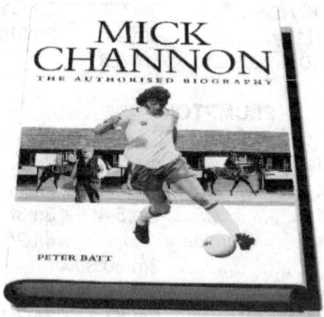

SPLIT SECOND SPEED RATINGS

The following list shows the fastest performances of chasers and hurdlers which have recorded a speed figure of 100 or over during the 2003-2004 season. Additional information in parentheses following the speed figure shows the distance of the race in furlongs, course, state of going and the date on which the figure was achieved.

CHASING

Abalvino 107 (16f,Utt,HY,Jan 10)
Abbeytown 101 (32f,Chl,G,Mar 17)
Able Native 100 (16½f,Hex,G,May 10)
Acoustic 102 (24½f,Fak,GF,May 7)
Act In Time 110 (22½f,Kel,G,May 7)
Ad Hoc 106 (27½f,Chl,G,Nov 15)
Adalie 101 (19f,Tau,G,Dec 29)
Aegean 104 (25f,Ain,GS,May 16)
Aelred 109 (20f,Ncs,GS,Dec 20)
Again An Again 113 (17f,Fai,Y,Apr 13)
Agincourt 102 (25f,Tow,GS,Nov 18)
Ah Yeah 106 (25f,Tow,G,Mar 11)
Aimees Mark 108 (19f,Leo,YS,Jan 25)
Ain Tecbalet 102 (26f,Plu,G,Mar 1)
Aircon 100 (20½f,Wor,G,May 21)
Alakdar 105 (23½f,Wor,G,Jly 16)
Alcapone 112 (25f,Wet,G,Nov 1)
Alcatras 103 (24f,Tau,G,Mar 4)
Alexander Banquet 113 (24f,Leo,YS,Feb 8)
All Sonsilver 103 (20f,Ncs,HY,Jan 21)
Alleged Slave 101 (20½f,Ban,G,Mar 10)
Allimac 103 (20½f,Hun,GF,Sep 28)
Almire Du Lia 101 (25f,Kel,G,Mar 28)
Alpha Blues 105 (25f,Fai,S,Dec 13)
Alphazar 112 (17f,Leo,S,Dec 26)
Alpine Slave 105 (24f,Str,GF,Apr 18)
Alvino 109 (17½f,Mar,GS,Dec 4)
Amberleigh House 113 (36f,Ain,G,Apr 3)
Ambience Lady 101 (17f,Plu,GF,Oct 6)
Ambushed 101 (16½f,Hex,G,Mar 18)
American Duchess 107 (20f,Thu,S,Feb 1)
Ammieanne 102 (21f,Leo,YS,Dec 29)
Amplifi 101 (16f,Lei,G,Feb 18)
Amptina 109 (17½f,Ban,G,Aug 1)
An Modh Direach 107 (18f,Pun,GY,Nov 15)
Andiamo 109 (24f,Naa,GY,Nov 22)
Ankles Back 100 (23½f,Lei,GF,Dec 27)
Annie Byers 105 (20½f,San,G,Dec 5)
Annshoon 110 (17f,Fai,Y,Apr 13)
Another Chance 102 (24f,Mus,G,Feb 8)
Another Joker 104 (19f,Her,GF,May 13)
Antartic Prince 100 (24f,Hun,S,Jan 9)
Anxious Moments 113 (16f,Pun,GY,Nov 16)
Apple Joe 102 (24½f,Ban,G,Oct 27)
Ar Muin Na Muice 109 (24f,Utt,S,Dec 26)
Arctic Challenge 111 (21½f,Str,G,May 31)
Arctic Copper 111 (16f,Pun,GY,Apr 29)
Arctic Fancy 108 (20½f,Ban,S,May 2)
Arctic Lagoon 107 (16½f,Hex,S,Dec 17)
Ardent Scout 112 (24f,Hay,S,Feb 14)
Argento 107 (17½f,Mar,GS,Dec 4)
Arlas 100 (24f,Don,G,Mar 6)
Armaturk 116 (16f,Ain,G,Apr 1)
Around Before 107 (24f,Hun,GF,Sep 28)
Artemesia 103 (20½f,Hex,GF,Jun 20)
Artic Jack 112 (24f,Hay,G,Jan 10)
Ashley Muck 103 (20½f,Wor,GF,Jun 18)
Ashstorm 107 (25f,Pun,Y,Dec 6)
Asparagus 108 (16f,Utt,HY,Jan 10)

Astral Prince 101 (17f,Sth,GF,Oct 11)
Athnowen 110 (20f,Utt,GS,Dec 19)
Atlantic Rhapsody 100 (16f,Pun,Y,Dec 6)
Atlastaboy 107 (27f,Tau,GS,Jan 22)
Atomic Breeze 102 (28½f,Mar,GF,Oct 5)
Atum Re 113 (16f,San,G,Dec 6)
Auburn Spirit 109 (25f,Tow,S,Dec 26)
Auditty 103 (17½f,Ban,G,Oct 11)
Aura About Him 108 (17f,Fai,HY,Jan 31)
Avalanche 115 (20½f,Kem,G,Feb 13)
Avalon Buck 106 (26½f,Nab,G,Jun 9)
Azertyuiop 121 (16f,Asc,GS,Jan 10)

Bacardi Boy 103 (24f,Hun,S,Feb 12)
Back On Top 116 (25f,Pun,GY,May 1)
Backdoor Champion 100 (17f,Fai,HY,Jan 31)
Bak To Bill 105 (24f,Kem,G,Mar 7)
Bal De Nuit 112 (16f,Asc,GS,Jan 10)
Ballinclay King 102 (20½f,Chl,GS,Dec 13)
Ballyamber 110 (21f,Leo,S,Jan 11)
Ballybough Rasher 125 (25f,Wet,G,Nov 1)
Ballybrophy 105 (25f,Ain,GS,May 16)
Ballycassidy 117 (20f,Mar,GF,Jly 19)
Ballyconnell 107 (25½f,Chl,G,Dec 31)
Ballylusky 111 (25f,Ain,G,Nov 23)
Ballynattin Buck 102 (20f,Nav,YS,Mar 6)
Ballyrobert 101 (18½f,Nby,GS,Nov 30)
Ballystone 103 (24f,Crl,G,Apr 10)
Ballyvaddy 110 (24f,Lud,G,May 5)
Bandit Brown 103 (22f,Tow,GS,Mar 24)
Banjo Hill 111 (20f,Mar,GF,Jly 19)
Banker Count 108 (24½f,San,S,Feb 7)
Barito 103 (20½f,Chl,GF,Oct 29)
Barnards Green 102 (16f,Fol,G,Mar 3)
Baron Allfours 106 (26½f,Nab,GF,Aug 4)
Barrow Drive 117 (25f,Wet,G,Nov 1)
Barton 109 (20½f,Wet,G,Nov 1)
Barton Nic 101 (16½f,Chp,GS,Mar 24)
Bathwick Annie 103 (24f,Hun,GS,Dec 11)
Batman Senora 112 (29f,Aut,VS,May 25)
Batswing 107 (21½f,Str,G,May 31)
Be My Belle 108 (24f,Leo,S,Jan 11)
Be My Destiny 109 (16f,Lei,G,Jan 13)
Be My Manager 109 (20½f,Wet,G,Dec 26)
Be Upstanding 103 (24f,Don,G,Jan 19)
Beachcomber Bay 111 (17f,Fai,S,Jan 18)
Bear On Board 109 (33f,Chl,G,Jan 1)
Beausheram 109 (24f,Nav,YS,Mar 6)
Beaver Lodge 100 (23½f,Wor,G,Jly 23)
Bee An Bee 111 (24f,Nby,G,Mar 27)
Beef Or Salmon 115 (26½f,Chl,G,Mar 18)
Beefy Nova 104 (24f,Utt,GS,Nov 15)
Behrajan 113 (24½f,Asc,S,Dec 20)
Belisario 105 (24f,Ncs,S,Mar 13)
Belski 105 (23½f,Exe,GS,Mar 23)
Belvento 100 (26½f,Fon,G,May 5)
Benbecula 103 (24f,Lud,G,Feb 11)
Bengal Boy 100 (21f,Sed,GF,Jly 28)
Bennie's Pride 110 (19f,Leo,YS,Jan 25)
Benrajah 108 (22½f,Kel,GS,Mar 6)
Berkley 104 (24f,Thu,GY,Dec 21)

Berlin Blue 104 (24f,Chp,GF,May 7)
Best Mate 117 (26½f,Chl,G,Mar 18)
Best Wait 109 (20f,Thu,S,Feb 1)
Better Days 104 (20f,Ayr,GS,Apr 16)
Bigjames 100 (21f,Leo,YS,Dec 29)
Biliverdin 105 (19½f,Exe,GS,Mar 23)
Bill Owen 103 (18f,Fon,GF,Aug 22)
Billie John 107 (16½f,Sed,GF,Jly 22)
Billywill 100 (20½f,Hun,S,Jan 16)
Bindaree 116 (26½f,Chp,GS,Dec 6)
Bit O Magic 110 (22½f,Kel,G,May 7)
Bit Of A Snob 106 (19½f,Chp,GF,Oct 22)
Bizet 101 (16f,Naa,GY,Nov 22)
Blackchurch Mist 105 (21½f,Str,GF,Sep 6)
Blakeney Coast 108 (17f,Plu,GF,Sep 27)
Blame The Ref 103 (25f,Fai,S,Dec 13)
Blazing Batman 105 (24f,Str,GS,Mar 21)
Bleu Superbe 115 (16f,Asc,S,Dec 20)
Blowing Wind 102 (20½f,San,G,Apr 23)
Blunham Hill 105 (22f,Tow,S,Mar 24)
Bob's Buster 109 (16f,Wet,GS,Mar 22)
Bob's The Business 103 (25f,Tow,GS,Feb 22)
Bobayaro 103 (24f,Per,GF,Jun 5)
Bold King 100 (24½f,Ban,S,May 22)
Bold Navigator 102 (27f,Sed,G,Dec 26)
Boneyarrow 114 (21f,Leo,YS,Feb 8)
Bonus Bridge 111 (16f,Lud,G,Jan 9)
Boom Economy 101 (25f,Fai,S,Dec 13)
Borehill Joker 104 (16f,Lei,G,Jan 27)
Boring Goring 103 (25f,Fol,GF,Nov 4)
Borzov 103 (25f,Mar,GF,Aug 3)
Boss Royal 103 (19f,Tau,GS,Jan 22)
Boston Lass 107 (26f,Crt,G,May 24)
Brady Boys 105 (16½f,Tau,G,Mar 4)
Bramblehill Duke 105 (27f,Tau,GS,Jan 22)
Brandsby Stripe 100 (17½f,Ban,S,May 2)
Brave Effect 101 (16½f,Hex,F,Sep 14)
Brave Spirit 101 (24f,Hun,G,Mar 17)
Brave Thought 105 (20½f,Per,GS,Apr 23)
Brereton 102 (21½f,Str,GS,May 30)
Briar Rose 108 (30f,Ncs,G,Nov 29)
Broadgate Flyer 110 (24f,Per,G,Jun 6)
Broken Dream 104 (26½f,Nab,G,Apr 10)
Bronhallow 108 (21½f,Str,GS,May 30)
Bronzesmith 100 (20½f,Wor,G,May 21)
Brooklyn Breeze 105 (20f,Crl,S,Nov 27)
Brooklyn's Gold 101 (16f,Lei,G,Jan 13)
Brother Joe 109 (21½f,Fak,G,Oct 24)
Brownie Returns 101 (25f,Pun,GY,Apr 29)
Builtes And Fadas 107 (33f,Pun,G,May 1)
Buckby Lane 109 (20½f,Chl,GS,Dec 13)
Bungee Jumper 111 (16f,Utt,GF,Jun 5)
Bunkum 105 (21f,Sed,G,Mar 16)
Burning Truth 108 (20f,Lud,GF,Oct 9)
Burundi 104 (20½f,San,G,Mar 12)
Burwood Breeze 104 (24f,Per,G,May 15)
Bush Park 109 (24f,Nby,GS,Dec 29)
Business Class 101 (20f,Mar,GS,Apr 24)
Buzybakson 108 (24f,Hun,S,Feb 12)
Byron Lamb 106 (16f,Wet,G,Nov 26)

Cad A Ra Leat 101 (20f,Pun,GY,Nov 15)

Cadou Royal 112 (20f,Nav,S,Dec 20)

Caishill 111 (16f,Pun,GY,Nov 16)

Caitriona's Choice 107 (16f,Per,GS,May 23)

Calling Brave 116 (20¹/₂f,Kem,G,Feb 28)

Calvados 100 (16f,Lei,GF,Mar 2)

Camden Tanner 107 (21f,Leo,YS,Feb 8)

Camden West 109 (24f,Naa,GY,Nov 22)

Cameron Bridge 105 (20¹/₂f,Kem,GF,Nov 19)

Camp Hill 112 (20f,Crl,HY,Mar 21)

Canadiane 107 (20f,Mar,GF,Jun 21)

Canary Tan 108 (17f,Fai,GY,Feb 28)

Capricorn Princess 105 (17f,Sth,GF,Oct 11)

Caracciola 103 (16f,Hay,S,Dec 13)

Carbury Cross 102 (21¹/₂f,Str,GF,Oct 18)

Cardinal Mark 104 (21f,Sed,G,Mar 30)

Carnacrack 108 (26f,Crt,GF,Jly 17)

Carneys Cross 103 (21f,Leo,YS,Feb 8)

Carrick Troop 115 (17f,Nby,GS,Nov 29)

Cassia Heights 106 (24¹/₂f,Ban,G,Oct 11)

Castle Doret 108 (17f,Fai,HY,Jan 31)

Castle Oliver 101 (20f,Pun,GY,Nov 15)

Castle Prince 113 (16f,Asc,GF,Nov 1)

Castleford 103 (24¹/₂f,San,G,Feb 20)

Catalpa Cargo 108 (20f,Fai,S,Nov 30)

Ceanannas Mor 103 (23¹/₂f,Exe,G,Nov 4)

Ceannaireceach 104 (17f,Leo,S,Dec 26)

Cedar Green 105 (25f,Wet,S,Jan 26)

Celestial Gold 105 (32f,Chl,G,Mar 17)

Celioso 113 (20¹/₂f,Wet,G,Nov 1)

Celtic Ross 102 (20f,Nav,YS,Mar 6)

Cenkos 118 (16f,San,GF,Apr 24)

Central House 118 (17f,Leo,S,Dec 26)

Ceresfield 105 (16f,Mus,G,Feb 18)

Cerilly 105 (29f,Aut,VS,May 25)

Channahrlie 110 (24f,Nby,GS,Dec 29)

Chapeltown 107 (19¹/₂f,Exe,GF,Apr 13)

Charlies Future 110 (19¹/₂f,Exe,S,Feb 2)

Charliesmedarlin 103 (24f,Utt,GF,Jun 12)

Charming Admiral 103 (25¹/₂f,Cat,GS,Dec 3)

Chateau Rose 100 (24f,Nby,GS,Dec 29)

Chauvinist 110 (16f,San,G,Dec 6)

Chergan 111 (19f,Don,G,Mar 6)

Cherry Gold 100 (26¹/₂f,Fon,GF,Aug 18)

Cherry Hunter 100 (24f,Nav,GY,Nov 23)

Chevalier Errant 109 (22¹/₂f,Kel,G,Nov 1)

Chicago Bulls 111 (25¹/₂f,Chl,G,Dec 12)

Chicuelo 114 (24f,Kem,G,Feb 28)

Christopher 106 (19¹/₂f,Exe,S,Jan 1)

Cill Churnain 107 (20f,Ain,G,Oct 26)

Circus Maximus 101 (24f,Hun,GF,Oct 10)

City Hall 102 (16f,Pun,Y,Dec 6)

Clan Royal 112 (36f,Ain,G,Apr 3)

Classic Lash 110 (20¹/₂f,Per,GF,Jun 5)

Claymore 110 (20f,Nby,GS,Nov 29)

Clear Dawn 106 (22¹/₂f,Mar,GS,Dec 4)

Clonmel's Minella 111 (25f,Pun,G,Apr 30)

Cloudy Bays 114 (24f,Nav,GY,Nov 23)

Club Royal 100 (20f,Mar,G,Jun 11)

Cobbet 112 (20f,Mar,GF,Jly 19)

Cobreces 106 (20f,Lud,GS,Mar 25)

Colca Canyon 117 (17f,Leo,YS,Jan 25)

Cold Encounter 106 (24¹/₂f,Ban,G,Oct 27)

Collinstown 101 (20f,Pun,GY,Nov 15)

Colnel Rayburn 117 (24f,Nav,YS,Mar 6)

Colonel Braxton 107 (24f,Leo,YS,Dec 28)

Colonel Frank 116 (24f,Nby,GF,Dec 10)

Colquhoun 105 (21¹/₂f,Nab,GF,Jun 28)

Comanche War Paint 111 (25¹/₂f,Wcn,GF,Nov 20)

Come In Moscow 103 (20f,Pun,GY,Apr 29)

Commanche Hero 108 (24f,Hun,GF,Sep 28)

Commanche Jim 107 (29f,War,G,Dec 6)

Commanche Quest 107 (25f,Hex,G,May 3)

Commonchero 106 (17f,Leo,YS,Jan 25)

Compostello 113 (18f,Fai,GF,Oct 22)

Compton Chick 103 (20¹/₂f,Wor,G,Aug 15)

Con Tricks 101 (20f,Plu,GS,Dec 15)

Conquer 102 (24f,Hun,G,Apr 12)

Contract Scotland 103 (23¹/₂f,Wet,G,Apr 25)

Cool Monty 105 (20¹/₂f,Kem,G,Feb 28)

Cool Song 103 (25f,Mar,G,Nov 20)

Coolnahilla 106 (24f,Naa,S,Jan 24)

Coppeen Cross 103 (20f,Mar,G,Jun 11)

Copper Shell 101 (25f,Fol,GS,Feb 17)

Coq Hardi Diamond 100 (24f,Nav,GY,Nov 23)

Corston Jigthyme 101 (20f,Pun,GY,Nov 15)

Count Campioni 105 (26¹/₂f,Chp,HY,Feb 7)

Count Oski 103 (24f,Hun,G,Apr 12)

Count Rossini 103 (24f,Thu,GY,Dec 21)

County Flyer 106 (25¹/₂f,Her,GS,May 1)

Courage Under Fire 103 (23¹/₂f,Lei,G,Feb 18)

Coursing Run 105 (24f,Nby,S,Jan 14)

Creative Time 105 (24f,Str,G,Mar 15)

Cregg House 100 (24f,Nav,GY,Nov 23)

Creon 102 (22f,Tow,S,Nov 29)

Cresswell Quay 105 (26f,Plu,GS,Dec 15)

Croc An Oir 112 (26¹/₂f,Nab,GF,Aug 4)

Cromwell 103 (28¹/₂f,Mar,GF,Oct 5)

Cruise Leader 101 (20¹/₂f,Wet,GS,Dec 27)

Curly Spencer 111 (20f,Crl,HY,Mar 21)

Curtins Hill 109 (24f,Lud,G,May 5)

Cyanara 107 (26¹/₂f,Fon,GF,Sep 23)

Cyborsun 107 (19f,Naa,S,Jan 4)

Cyfor Malta 102 (20¹/₂f,Chl,G,Nov 15)

D'Argent 103 (26f,War,G,Dec 6)

Dads Lad 103 (26f,Utt,HY,May 26)

Dalcassian King 104 (16f,Lei,F,Nov 17)

Dale Creek 100 (26¹/₂f,Nab,GF,Aug 12)

Dalus Park 106 (24f,Hun,S,Feb 12)

Dam The Breeze 101 (25¹/₂f,Her,GF,May 26)

Dan De Man 101 (21f,Sed,G,Mar 30)

Danaeve 101 (24f,Naa,GY,Nov 22)

Dante Citizen 103 (24f,Lud,GS,Mar 25)

Dante's Brook 106 (17¹/₂f,Ban,G,Aug 1)

Danteco 106 (27f,Sed,G,Oct 14)

Dantie Boy 102 (20f,Str,G,Jun 27)

Dark Room 105 (20¹/₂f,Hun,GF,Nov 2)

Darnley 110 (16¹/₂f,Ncs,GS,Dec 20)

Davids Lad 108 (17f,Fai,S,Jan 18)

Davoski 103 (16¹/₂f,Chl,G,Apr 15)

Day Du Roy 107 (20f,Str,GF,Apr 18)

Dead-Eyed Dick 101 (19¹/₂f,Exe,G,Nov 21)

Dealer Del 111 (26¹/₂f,Nab,GF,Jun 21)

Dealer's Choice 105 (20f,Lud,G,Feb 11)

Dear Deal 107 (24¹/₂f,Chl,GF,Nov 14)

Deckie 103 (24f,Naa,GY,Nov 22)

Deep Water 105 (19f,Cat,G,Feb 6)

Delaware Bay 100 (19¹/₂f,Exe,S,Feb 2)

Deliceo 108 (20f,Lud,G,Jan 22)

Demasta 105 (16¹/₂f,Fak,GS,Jan 21)

Deneises Blossom 100 (27f,Sed,GF,Nov 11)

Desailly 113 (24f,Nby,GS,Dec 29)

Devon View 108 (20f,Nby,GS,Nov 29)

Diceman 105 (20f,Ncs,G,Nov 29)

Dick The Taxi 102 (16¹/₂f,Sed,S,May 17)

Didifon 107 (16¹/₂f,Sed,GF,Nov 25)

Die Fledermaus 108 (20¹/₂f,Wor,GF,Aug 23)

Direct Bearing 116 (19f,Leo,YS,Dec 29)

Dirk Cove 106 (24f,Chp,GF,May 7)

Divet Hill 108 (25f,Mar,GF,Oct 18)

Doberman 102 (20f,Lud,GF,Oct 9)

Doc Davis 107 (24f,Thu,GY,Dec 21)

Doe Nal Rua 100 (25¹/₂f,Cat,GF,Mar 10)

Dominikus 109 (24f,Per,G,Jun 22)

Don Fernando 104 (20f,Plu,G,Mar 1)

Doora Volunteer 107 (18f,Pun,GY,Nov 15)

Double Honour 109 (24¹/₂f,Asc,G,Feb 21)

Double You Cubed 108 (20f,Ayr,GF,Mar 12)

Dragon King 111 (24¹/₂f,Fak,GF,May 18)

Dream On Willie 114 (20¹/₂f,Wet,G,Nov 1)

Dream With Me 101 (20f,Mar,GF,May 24)

Drom Wood 105 (25f,Ain,G,Oct 26)

Drombeag 104 (32f,Chl,G,Mar 17)

Dual Star 105 (16¹/₂f,Hun,GF,Aug 25)

Duchamp 103 (21¹/₂f,Str,GF,Oct 18)

Duke Of Buckingham 113 (16f,Ain,G,Apr 1)

Dunlea 106 (17f,Fai,S,Jan 18)

Dunmanus Bay 111 (26¹/₂f,Nab,GF,Sep 3)

Dunowen 101 (16¹/₂f,Fak,GS,Jan 21)

Dunraven 103 (16f,Lei,F,Nov 17)

Dunster Castle 110 (26¹/₂f,Fon,G,May 5)

Dunston Bill 107 (24¹/₂f,San,GS,Mar 13)

Durham Dandy 100 (22¹/₂f,Mar,GF,Oct 5)

Early Edition 104 (25¹/₂f,Wcn,GS,Mar 25)

Eastern Tribute 110 (16¹/₂f,Ncs,HY,Jan 21)

Eau De Cologne 105 (24f,Kem,GF,Oct 25)

Ebony Light 108 (26f,Crl,G,Nov 10)

Echo Du Lac 104 (24¹/₂f,Ban,G,Mar 10)

Ede'Iff 105 (16f,Lei,G,Jan 13)

Edmo Heights 109 (16¹/₂f,Ncs,S,Mar 13)

Edredon Bleu 117 (24f,Kem,G,Dec 26)

Ei Ei 116 (16f,Ain,G,Apr 1)

El Bandito 102 (20¹/₂f,San,G,Apr 23)

El Cordobes 106 (24¹/₂f,Fak,G,Nov 13)

El Hombre Del Rio 107 (24f,Hun,S,Feb 12)

Elenas River 111 (25¹/₂f,Wcn,G,Apr 18)

Emotional Moment 112 (21f,Leo,S,Jan 11)

Emperor Ross 101 (24f,Per,G,Jun 22)

Emperor's Magic 104 (25f,Ain,GS,May 16)

Emperors Guest 110 (16f,Naa,Y,Mar 7)

Ennel Boy 109 (21¹/₂f,Str,GS,May 30)

Enrique 108 (24f,Crl,G,Oct 25)

Enzo De Baune 113 (20¹/₂f,San,G,Apr 23)

Eoins Pride 104 (24f,Pun,GY,Apr 29)

Erin Alley 106 (16f,Crl,HY,Feb 11)

Esendi 104 (24¹/₂f,Ban,G,Oct 27)

Even More 106 (25¹/₂f,Wcn,S,Jan 17)

Executive Decision 102 (16f,San,G,Feb 20)

Executive Director 101 (16f,Pun,YS,Mar 2)

Executive Games 101 (22¹/₂f,Kel,G,Nov 1)

Existential 101 (24f,Tau,GS,Feb 19)
Exit Swinger 106 (16½f,Don,S,Jan 31)
Exit To Wave 114 (24½f,Asc,S,Nov 22)
Exstoto 100 (24f,Don,G,Mar 5)
Extra Jack 109 (20½f,Ban,S,May 2)
Extra Proud 104 (22½f,Kel,G,Nov 1)
Eye Of The Tiger 109 (17f,Fai,S,Jan 18)
Eyze 101 (25f,Kel,G,Nov 12)

Fable 110 (17f,Fai,Y,Apr 13)
Fadoudal Du Cochet 113 (17f,Fai,Y,Apr 11)
Falcon Du Coteau 102 (24f,Str,GF,Sep 6)
Family Venture 105 (21½f,Ayr,G,Nov 16)
Fanion De Neulliac 100 (21f,Leo,YS,Dec 29)
Far Horizon 103 (16f,Lei,G,Jan 13)
Farinel 112 (24f,Nav,YS,Mar 6)
Farlington 102 (19f,Cat,GS,Jan 15)
Farmer Jack 106 (16f,Asc,GS,Jan 10)
Fasgo 108 (33f,Chl,G,Jan 1)
Fashion House 100 (24f,Lud,GF,Oct 9)
Fashions Monty 103 (27f,Sed,GS,Feb 24)
Father Paddy 102 (21f,Sed,G,Apr 12)
Favoured Option 105 (25½f,Wcn,GF,May 9)
Fayrway Rhythm 103 (16½f,Hex,S,Apr 4)
Fear Siuil 108 (24f,Str,GF,Sep 6)
Fielding's Hay 104 (24f,Hun,GF,May 5)
Fields Of Home 105 (21f,Sed,GS,Feb 24)
Fiery Peace 110 (16f,Lud,GF,Dec 18)
Fiery Ring 109 (19f,Leo,YS,Jan 25)
Figawin 101 (24½f,Fak,G,Feb 20)
Fin Bec 108 (22f,Tow,G,Nov 6)
Final Finish 106 (24f,Thu,GY,Dec 21)
Finbar's Revenge 106 (24f,Str,GS,Mar 21)
Finians Ivy 107 (18f,Pun,YS,May 3)
Fiori 113 (20f,Mar,GF,Jun 21)
First Flight 103 (22½f,Nby,S,Jan 14)
First Gold 120 (25f,Pun,G,Apr 30)
First Love 107 (24f,Per,G,May 14)
Flagship Uberalles 115 (16f,San,G,Dec 6)
Flahive's First 112 (20f,Str,GF,Jly 13)
Flame Creek 105 (17½f,Ban,S,May 22)
Flash Gordon 111 (20f,Mar,GF,Jun 21)
Flecthefawna 102 (24½f,San,G,Feb 20)
Flinders 109 (24½f,Fak,G,Nov 23)
Flinders Chase 105 (20½f,San,G,Feb 20)
Flora Muck 102 (24f,Hun,GF,Nov 11)
Florida Pearl 119 (17f,Fai,S,Jan 18)
Florries Son 105 (20½f,Hex,G,Apr 28)
Fluff 'N' Puff 105 (20f,Lud,G,Jan 22)
Flying Instructor 113 (23½f,Wor,GF,Aug 8)
Flying Trix 107 (24f,Kem,G,Mar 7)
Follow The Flow 102 (26f,Utt,HY,May 26)
Follow The Trend 100 (24f,Tau,G,Mar 15)
Foly Pleasant 116 (21f,Chl,G,Jan 1)
Fondmort 115 (20½f,Chl,G,Nov 15)
Force Twelve 105 (20f,Fon,G,Dec 9)
Forest Dante 103 (24½f,Sth,GF,Dec 5)
Fork Lightning 116 (25½f,Wcn,G,Feb 12)
Forrestfield 110 (17f,Fai,Y,Apr 13)
Fox In The Box 100 (24f,Utt,GF,Nov 7)
Foxchapel King 106 (25f,Pun,G,Apr 30)
Foxies Lad 101 (19½f,Exe,G,Apr 30)
Francines-Boy 111 (20f,Nav,S,Dec 20)
Fred's In The Know 103 (19f,Cat,G,Feb

6)
Free To Run 107 (23½f,Wor,G,Jun 28)
French Executive 104 (28f,Str,G,Oct 30)
Frentzen 102 (23½f,Wor,GF,Jly 9)
Freteval 100 (19f,Her,GS,Feb 15)
Frontis 101 (24f,Mus,G,Feb 18)
Full Irish 116 (16f,Ayr,GS,Apr 16)
Full Minty 108 (20½f,Ban,G,Sep 13)
Full On 104 (20½f,San,G,Mar 12)

Galen 101 (25f,Tow,G,Mar 11)
Game On 107 (20f,Plu,GF,Oct 6)
Gangsters R Us 106 (20f,Mus,GF,Jan 23)
Garden Party Ii 103 (16f,Ayr,GF,Mar 13)
Garolsa 105 (26f,Plu,S,Nov 23)
Garvivonnian 112 (29f,Fai,Y,Apr 12)
Gatorade 102 (21f,Sed,GF,Jly 28)
Gaucho 107 (16½f,Sed,G,Mar 30)
General 100 (17f,Plu,S,Jan 4)
General Claremont 108 (24f,Chp,GF,May 7)
Generous Ways 102 (16f,Lei,G,Jan 27)
Get The Point 103 (16½f,Tow,GS,Nov 18)
Ghadames 102 (21f,Sed,G,Sep 30)
Ghutah 104 (16½f,Hun,GF,May 5)
Gigs Gambit 110 (26½f,Fon,GF,Sep 23)
Giocomo 109 (19f,Cat,G,Jan 24)
Givenchy De Solzen 101 (16f,Pun,YS,May 2)
Glanmerin 100 (20½f,Hun,S,Feb 12)
Glenelly Gale 115 (16f,Nav,GF,Nov 9)
Glenfarclas Boy 101 (20f,Ayr,S,Dec 26)
Glinger 110 (20½f,Per,GF,Aug 16)
Glynn Dingle 109 (20½f,Per,GF,Aug 16)
Go White Lightning 103 (26f,Plu,GS,Feb 16)
Gofagold 107 (16f,Crl,HY,Feb 11)
Golden Alpha 112 (16f,Asc,GF,Nov 1)
Golden Rod 101 (24½f,Ban,G,Sep 13)
Golden Row 110 (16f,Pun,GY,Nov 16)
Golden Storm 116 (29f,Fai,Y,Apr 12)
Goldnecu 106 (17f,Fai,S,Jan 18)
Goldstreet 112 (20f,Mar,GF,Jly 19)
Golly 109 (22½f,Mar,GF,Oct 5)
Good Bone 100 (25f,Fol,GS,Feb 17)
Good Outlook 106 (24f,Kem,G,Mar 7)
Good Vintage 107 (25f,Pun,G,Apr 30)
Goodtime George 100 (22½f,Nby,GF,Nov 12)
Got One Too 117 (16f,Asc,GS,Jan 10)
Gottabe 111 (24f,Don,G,Jan 19)
Graineuaile 106 (24f,Naa,S,Jan 24)
Granit D'Estruval 117 (29f,Fai,Y,Apr 12)
Grate Deel 103 (27f,Sed,GF,Sep 5)
Grattan Lodge 101 (21f,Sed,GS,Jan 13)
Grayslake 106 (20f,Utt,GS,Dec 19)
Great Travel 107 (16f,San,G,Feb 20)
Greco 103 (18f,Pun,GY,Nov 15)
Green Go 101 (21½f,Crt,G,Aug 23)
Green Ideal 104 (17½f,Mar,GS,Dec 4)
Gregorio 102 (20f,Nav,S,Feb 15)
Grey Abbey 113 (33f,Ayr,GS,Apr 17)
Grey Ciseaux 100 (21f,Wcn,GF,May 9)
Ground Ball 114 (16½f,Chl,G,Mar 18)
Guard Duty 105 (20f,Plu,S,Dec 3)
Guilsborough Gorse 105 (25f,Wet,G,May 29)
Gunner Welburn 118 (25f,Wet,GS,Dec 27)
Gunther McBride 120 (24f,Kem,G,Feb 28)
Gus Des Bois 105 (24f,Tau,G,Apr 1)

Hades De Sienne 106 (28f,Kel,G,Nov 12)
Haditovski 104 (20½f,Ban,GS,Mar 27)

Hakim 100 (20½f,Wor,G,Aug 2)
Halexy 105 (20½f,Wet,G,Nov 1)
Hallrule 101 (26f,Crl,GS,Apr 18)
Hallyards Gael 105 (24f,Per,G,May 15)
Hand Inn Hand 112 (25f,Ain,G,Apr 1)
Handyman 102 (23½f,Exe,G,Nov 4)
Happy Change 104 (19½f,Exe,G,Apr 30)
Harbour Pilot 116 (26½f,Chl,G,Mar 18)
Hardiman 102 (24½f,Ban,G,Oct 27)
Harik 102 (16f,Lin,G,Nov 11)
Harlov 104 (30f,Ban,GS,Dec 17)
Harvis 103 (16f,San,G,Feb 20)
Haut Cercy 110 (25½f,Chl,G,Dec 12)
Hawk's Landing 112 (21f,Fol,GS,Feb 17)
Hazeljack 105 (21f,Chl,G,Mar 18)
Heads Onthe Ground 109 (17f,Fai,S,Jan 18)
Heart Midoltian 117 (20f,Pun,GY,Apr 29)
Heartache 104 (17½f,Ban,GS,Mar 27)
Hedgehunter 115 (26½f,Nby,GS,Nov 29)
Heezapistol 101 (16f,Pun,YS,May 2)
Hehasalife 100 (20f,Mar,GS,Apr 24)
Heidi Iii 106 (20½f,Ban,GS,Mar 27)
Helixir Du Theil 103 (26½f,Nab,G,Nov 18)
Helvetius 102 (23½f,Lei,GF,Mar 2)
Henrianjames 106 (16f,Wet,GF,May 7)
Heracles 102 (26½f,Chl,GF,Apr 14)
Heraclitean Fire 105 (17f,Leo,S,Dec 26)
Here Comes Henry 103 (26f,Plu,GS,Dec 15)
Hermes Iii 109 (24f,Utt,HY,May 3)
Heroic 109 (25f,Fai,S,Dec 13)
Hersov 107 (33f,Chl,G,Jan 1)
Hey Ref 101 (16f,Utt,GS,Dec 19)
Hi Cloy 117 (20f,Fai,Y,Apr 13)
Hidden Valley 102 (21½f,Nab,GS,Jly 27)
Hiers De Brouage 107 (19½f,Chp,GS,Nov 26)
Hisar 100 (18f,Fon,GF,Aug 22)
Historic 106 (24½f,Chl,G,Mar 17)
Hit Royal 105 (20½f,Hun,GF,Sep 28)
Hombre 106 (20f,Utt,GS,Dec 19)
Hopeful Chance 102 (16½f,Sed,G,Mar 30)
Hors La Loi 105 (17½f,Str,GF,Oct 7)
Horus 114 (24½f,Asc,S,Nov 22)
Hot Shots 119 (16f,Asc,S,Dec 20)
How Ran On 102 (16½f,Nab,GF,Jun 28)
Howaya Pet 106 (20f,Thu,S,Feb 1)
Howdydoody 106 (25½f,Wcn,S,Jan 8)
Howrwenow 105 (24f,Str,GS,Dec 30)
Hugo De Grez 101 (25f,Kel,S,Dec 1)
Hume Castle 109 (24f,Thu,GY,Dec 21)
Hunters Tweed 113 (21f,Chl,GS,Jan 24)
Hurlers Cross 103 (26f,Plu,G,Mar 15)
Hurricane Bay 109 (25f,Wet,G,May 29)
Hussard Collonges 103 (24f,Hay,GS,Nov 16)

I Got It 103 (17f,Fai,S,Nov 29)
I'Vehadit 113 (20f,Pun,GY,Apr 29)
Iacacia 102 (17½f,Str,GF,Oct 7)
Ibin St James 102 (28½f,Mar,GS,Dec 4)
Ibis Rochelais 105 (24½f,San,G,Feb 19)
Ice Cool Lad 103 (26½f,Fon,GF,Nov 10)
Ichi Beau 104 (20f,Pun,YS,May 2)
Idaho D'Ox 104 (17½f,Exe,G,Apr 30)
Ideal Du Bois Beury 102 (20½f,Per,G,Sep 25)
Idealko 105 (20½f,Lei,GF,Mar 2)
Idiome 108 (16f,Her,HY,Feb 6)
Ifni Du Luc 101 (20½f,Kem,G,Mar 7)
Il Capitano 113 (20f,Mar,GF,Jly 19)
Ilare 109 (29f,Aut,VS,May 25)
Ile De Librate 100 (28f,Str,GS,May 30)

Imaginaire 104 (16½f,Chp,S,Jan 23)
Impek 119 (16f,Pun,GY,May 1)
Imperial De Thaix 104 (24f,Nby,G,Mar 27)
Impertio 101 (22½f,Kel,HY,Feb 5)
In The Rough 104 (24f,Utt,HY,May 3)
Inaki 100 (17f,Plu,S,Jan 4)
Inca Trail 102 (16½f,Hun,GF,Nov 2)
Incas 115 (17f,Fai,Y,Apr 13)
Indeed To Goodness 104 (22f,Tow,S,Nov 29)
Indian Chance 107 (25½f,Wcn,G,Dec 4)
Indian Scout 108 (25f,Wet,G,Nov 15)
Indian Venture 102 (16f,Per,G,May 14)
Indiscret 109 (26f,War,GF,Nov 5)
Infrasonique 108 (24½f,San,S,Feb 7)
Inigo Jones 107 (16f,Her,GS,Mar 22)
Initiative 101 (16½f,Sed,GF,Aug 8)
Inn Antique 112 (20½f,Chl,G,Mar 17)
Innox 109 (24½f,San,G,Feb 19)
Interdit 108 (22½f,Kel,HY,Feb 5)
Intrepid Mogal 103 (25f,Wet,S,Jan 26)
Iris Royal 118 (20½f,Chl,GS,Dec 13)
Irish Hussar 107 (24f,Nby,G,Feb 14)
Irishman 105 (24f,Utt,GS,Nov 15)
Iron Express 108 (25f,Hex,G,Apr 28)
Isam Top 105 (16f,Fol,G,Mar 3)
Isard III 104 (20½f,Chl,GS,Dec 13)
Isio 122 (16f,Asc,GS,Jan 10)
Island Faith 103 (16f,Ain,G,Nov 22)
Isotop 103 (24f,Lud,G,Feb 11)
It Takes Time 107 (20½f,Chl,GS,Dec 13)
Its Over 110 (17f,Fai,Y,Apr 13)
Itsonlyme 110 (24½f,Chl,GF,Nov 14)
Ivanoph 109 (24½f,Ban,S,Apr 17)
Iverain 105 (20f,Ain,G,Oct 26)
Iznogoud 120 (24f,Kem,G,Feb 28)

Jaboune 108 (16f,San,G,Dec 6)
Jacdor 108 (24f,Tau,GS,Feb 19)
Jack Fuller 106 (16½f,Tau,G,Mar 4)
Jack High 108 (20f,Nav,YS,Mar 6)
Jack Ross 102 (16f,Naa,Y,Mar 7)
Jacksonville 107 (20½f,Per,GS,Apr 23)
Jahash 110 (16½f,Fak,GS,Jan 21)
Jair Du Cochet 123 (25½f,Chl,GS,Jan 24)
Jakari 116 (21f,Chl,GF,Apr 14)
Jaloux D'Estruval 105 (23½f,Exe,S,Jan 1)
Jamerosier 103 (22½f,Nby,S,Jan 14)
Jamica Plane 110 (17f,Fai,Y,Apr 13)
Jamorin Dancer 104 (17½f,Mar,GF,May 24)
Janiture 103 (20½f,Kem,GF,Nov 19)
Janus Du Cochet 111 (23½f,Exe,GS,Jan 20)
Jardin De Beaulieu 109 (20½f,War,GS,Jan 10)
Jasmin D'Oudairies 102 (20f,Nav,S,Feb 15)
Jasmin Guichois 101 (20½f,Chl,G,Dec 12)
Jazz Du Forez 102 (26f,Crt,G,May 24)
Jefertiti 106 (20½f,Hun,GF,Oct 10)
Jenniferjo 102 (24f,Leo,S,Dec 27)
Jeremy Spider 104 (25f,Pun,GY,Apr 29)
Jericho Iii 105 (20f,Lud,G,Apr 8)
Jetowa Du Bois Hue 108 (16½f,Hun,GF,May 5)
Jeu De Brook 100 (19f,Naa,S,Jan 4)
Jim 116 (24f,Naa,S,Jan 24)
Jimmy Tennis 112 (24f,Kem,G,Feb 28)
Jivaros 102 (25½f,Wcn,GS,Mar 25)
Jodante 106 (16½f,Hex,S,Apr 4)
Joe Blake 106 (20f,Ayr,GS,Feb 14)
Joe Cullen 100 (16½f,Tow,GF,Oct 26)
Joe Deane 103 (20f,Plu,S,Jan 19)
Joe Di Capo 105 (30f,Ncs,G,Nov 29)

John James 108 (20f,Fai,Y,Apr 13)
John Rich 101 (25f,Mar,G,Nov 20)
Joint Authority 106 (16½f,Sed,GF,Nov 25)
Jolly Giant 101 (30f,Ban,GS,Dec 17)
Joly Bey 115 (20f,Pun,GY,Apr 29)
Jordan's Ridge 113 (25f,Kel,G,Nov 12)
Jorodama King 101 (25f,Tow,F,Oct 8)
Joss Naylor 115 (26½f,Nby,GS,Nov 29)
Julie's Leader 103 (26½f,Nab,GF,Jun 28)
Julies Boy 103 (24f,Tau,G,Mar 15)
Jumbo's Dream 105 (25f,Hex,G,Nov 19)
June's River 104 (16f,Lei,G,Jan 27)
Jungle Jinks 116 (25f,Wet,G,Nov 1)
Jupon Vert 105 (20f,Lud,GS,Mar 25)
Jurado Express 105 (16f,Pun,GY,May 1)
Juralan 109 (20f,Ayr,GS,Apr 16)
Jurancon II 110 (29f,War,GS,Jan 10)
Just In Debt 107 (25f,Pun,G,Apr 30)
Just Muckin Around 103 (17f,Plu,S,Nov 23)
Just Murphy 105 (17f,Kel,G,May 21)
Just Reuben 107 (20f,Fon,G,Dec 9)
Just Sooty 107 (21f,Sed,G,Apr 12)

Kadarann 114 (17½f,Exe,G,Nov 4)
Kadoun 110 (29f,Fai,Y,Apr 12)
Kaki Crazy 109 (21½f,Nab,GF,May 29)
Kalca Mome 109 (16f,Hay,HY,Jan 24)
Kalisko 106 (24f,Utt,GS,Nov 15)
Karajan 101 (20½f,Per,G,Sep 25)
Karo De Vindecy 100 (17½f,Crt,G,May 24)
Keen Leader 107 (24f,Nby,G,Feb 14)
Keen To The Last 107 (22½f,Mar,GS,Dec 4)
Keiran 109 (25f,Wet,G,Nov 15)
Kelami 110 (24½f,Chl,G,Mar 16)
Kelantan 104 (24f,Hun,GS,Dec 26)
Kelrev 114 (16f,Utt,HY,Jan 10)
Keltic Bard 114 (20f,Ain,G,Apr 3)
Keltic Heritage 102 (28f,Str,G,Oct 30)
Kerrigand 105 (23½f,Wor,G,May 10)
Kerry Lads 105 (24f,Crl,S,Nov 27)
Kety Star 108 (16½f,Don,GF,Nov 30)
Kew Gardens 101 (16f,Naa,Y,Mar 7)
Khan Kicker 101 (21f,Sed,G,Oct 29)
Khayal 102 (26½f,Nab,GF,Jun 21)
Kick For Touch 104 (26½f,Nab,G,Nov 5)
Kicking King 120 (17f,Leo,YS,Jan 25)
Kilbyrne King 110 (17f,Fai,Y,Apr 13)
Killultagh Storm 108 (16f,Pun,GY,Apr 29)
Killultagh Thunder 107 (25f,Pun,G,Apr 30)
Kilmore Quay 100 (25f,Tow,G,Oct 30)
Kimdaloo 103 (16½f,Hex,G,May 3)
Kind Sir 108 (16f,Her,GF,Mar 9)
King Bee 106 (24f,Hun,G,Mar 28)
King Plato 100 (20f,Mar,GS,Apr 24)
King's Bounty 109 (22½f,Kel,GS,Mar 6)
Kings Castle 100 (21½f,Nab,G,Nov 18)
Kings Mistral 114 (24½f,San,S,Feb 7)
Kings Orchard 107 (20f,Nav,S,Dec 14)
Kingscliff 120 (24½f,Asc,S,Nov 22)
Kingsmoor 106 (20½f,Lei,GF,Mar 2)
Kitimat 100 (18f,Fon,G,Jan 26)
Kittenkat 102 (30f,Ban,GS,Dec 17)
Klondike Charger 106 (26½f,Fon,GF,Aug 18)
Knife Edge 113 (17f,Fai,S,Jan 18)
Kock De La Vesvre 106 (20f,Ain,G,Oct 26)
Konker 101 (19f,Cat,G,Feb 6)
Koquelicot 107 (24f,Tau,G,Apr 1)
Korakor 104 (20½f,Wet,G,May 22)
Korelo 110 (17½f,Exe,G,Dec 5)
Kroisos 107 (26½f,Fon,G,Apr 22)

Kung Hei Fat Choi 106 (24f,Per,G,Jun 6)
Kymandjen 109 (24f,Leo,S,Dec 27)

L'Ange Au Ciel 112 (17½f,Exe,G,Dec 5)
L'Aventure 108 (20½f,San,S,Feb 7)
L'Etang Bleu 100 (17f,Plu,S,Nov 23)
L'Orphelin 104 (19f,Tau,GS,Jan 22)
La Landiere 109 (21f,Chl,GS,Jan 24)
Labula Bay 103 (26½f,Fon,GF,Mar 8)
Ladalko 112 (16f,Fol,GS,Jan 2)
Lady Brookvale 108 (20f,Nav,S,Feb 16)
Lakeside Lad 104 (26½f,Nab,GF,Aug 4)
Lancero 105 (24f,Naa,GY,Nov 22)
Lanmire Tower 100 (24f,Str,GS,May 16)
Lannkaran 103 (24f,Kem,GS,Feb 2)
Latalomne 107 (16f,Pun,GY,Apr 29)
Latensaani 101 (16½f,Hex,G,May 27)
Latitude 107 (22f,Fon,G,Mar 21)
Lauderdale 109 (22½f,Kel,G,Nov 1)
Le Coudray 116 (24f,Leo,YS,Feb 8)
Le Duc 113 (16f,Chl,G,Mar 16)
Le Roi Miguel 122 (16f,Pun,GY,May 1)
Leaburn 107 (16f,Wcn,G,Dec 26)
Left Bank 104 (20f,Ayr,GF,Mar 12)
Liberthine 101 (20f,Str,G,Mar 15)
Lights And Music 100 (20f,Pun,Y,Dec 7)
Lilium De Cotte 104 (16f,Utt,GS,Nov 27)
Lime Supreme 105 (18f,Thu,GY,Dec 21)
Lincoln Place 104 (20½f,Chl,G,Nov 16)
Linden's Lotto 104 (24f,Pun,GY,Apr 29)
Line Marine 115 (29f,Aut,VS,May 25)
Lirfox 106 (19f,Her,GF,May 26)
Lisaan 108 (18f,Pun,GY,Nov 15)
Liscannor Lad 110 (17f,Fai,Y,Apr 13)
Lisdante 109 (24f,Str,GS,Jly 26)
Lislaughtin Abbey 108 (23½f,Wor,GF,Jun 1)
Little Big Horse 107 (25f,Mar,GS,Mar 7)
Little Brown Bear 112 (24½f,Fak,GF,May 18)
Little Docker 106 (16½f,Ncs,GS,Dec 20)
Little Herman 103 (26f,War,GF,Nov 25)
Little Task 103 (16f,Per,G,Jun 22)
Lochiedubs 100 (20f,Crl,HY,Feb 11)
Lodestar 108 (20½f,Wet,G,Nov 1)
Log On Intersky 106 (20f,Ain,G,Oct 26)
Long Walk 104 (24f,Lud,G,Feb 11)
Longshanks 105 (20f,Ayr,GS,Nov 28)
Longstone Boy 108 (24f,Lud,G,May 5)
Look Collonges 104 (24f,Kem,GS,Feb 2)
Looking Forward 109 (21f,Sed,G,Mar 16)
Lord 'N' Master 111 (24½f,San,GS,Mar 13)
Lord Atterbury 111 (36f,Ain,G,Apr 3)
Lord Broadway 109 (25½f,Wcn,G,Feb 12)
Lord Capitaine 102 (26f,Crl,G,Mar 11)
Lord Halfnothin 108 (21f,Fol,GF,Nov 17)
Lord Jack 107 (20f,Ayr,HY,Jan 31)
Lord Maizey 105 (19½f,Chp,GS,Dec 6)
Lord Noelie 108 (27½f,Chl,G,Nov 15)
Lord Of The Hill 107 (20½f,Hun,GF,Oct 10)
Lord Of The Land 104 (25½f,Cat,GS,Dec 3)
Lord Of The River 113 (25f,Ain,G,Apr 2)
Lord Sam 119 (20½f,Hun,GS,Nov 22)
Lord Seamus 103 (24f,Kem,GF,Nov 5)
Lord Transcend 110 (25f,Ayr,GS,Nov 28)
Lord Warford 102 (21½f,Str,GS,May 30)
Lord Who 117 (24f,Naa,S,Jan 24)
Lord Youky 106 (20f,Utt,GF,Nov 7)
Lorenzino 106 (20½f,Ban,G,Sep 13)
Lost In Normandy 107 (24½f,Ban,G,Sep 13)

Lou Du Moulin Mas 106 (20f,Fon,G,Feb 22)
Lucky Bay 108 (25f,Wet,G,Nov 15)
Lucky Clover 105 (26¹/₂f,Nab,GF,Aug 12)
Lucky Leader 104 (23¹/₂f,Exe,GS,Mar 23)
Lucky Sinna 102 (24¹/₂f,Fak,GS,Mar 19)
Luneray 105 (22f,Fon,G,Mar 21)
Luzcadou 108 (20f,Ayr,HY,Jan 31)
Lynrick Lady 103 (26f,Plu,GS,Feb 16)

Mac Hine 110 (20¹/₂f,Wet,G,Nov 1)
Maceo 103 (16¹/₂f,Hun,GF,May 29)
Madam Flora 105 (19¹/₂f,Exe,S,Jan 1)
Madam's Man 107 (25¹/₂f,Chl,G,Dec 31)
Magic Of Sydney 100 (24f,Nby,GS,Dec 29)
Magical Bailiwick 114 (25¹/₂f,Chl,G,Dec 31)
Maidstone Monument 106 (26¹/₂f,Nab,GF,Sep 3)
Majed 104 (23¹/₂f,Exe,GS,Mar 23)
Major Benefit 103 (22f,Tow,S,Dec 15)
Majority Verdict 110 (20f,Hay,S,Nov 29)
Malek 104 (24f,Crl,S,Nov 27)
Mallory 103 (19f,Tau,GS,Jan 22)
Mamideos 105 (24¹/₂f,Fak,GS,Mar 19)
Man On The Hill 103 (20f,Ncs,G,Feb 21)
Manawanui 109 (16f,Fol,G,Dec 16)
Mandy's Rose 105 (25f,Wet,G,May 29)
Manolito 101 (24f,Hun,GF,May 5)
Maragun 103 (17¹/₂f,Ban,S,May 22)
Marcus Du Berlais 116 (29f,Fai,Y,Apr 12)
Marigliano 102 (16¹/₂f,Hun,S,Jan 16)
Mark Equal 106 (16f,Fol,G,Dec 16)
Marked Man 114 (16f,Lud,GF,Apr 25)
Marlborough 123 (25f,Wet,G,Nov 1)
Master Henry 102 (17¹/₂f,Crt,G,Aug 23)
Master Rex 106 (16f,Lei,GF,Mar 2)
Master Tern 106 (24¹/₂f,Chl,G,Mar 16)
Masters Of War 101 (17¹/₂f,Ban,G,Oct 11)
Maximize 109 (25¹/₂f,Wcn,GF,Nov 8)
Mensch 102 (24f,Tau,GF,Apr 16)
Mercato 106 (24¹/₂f,San,G,Mar 12)
Merchants Friend 112 (26¹/₂f,Nby,GS,Nov 29)
Message Recu 105 (16f,Lei,F,Nov 17)
Mestre Sala 103 (20f,Str,G,Jun 27)
Mexican 100 (16f,Cat,GS,Jan 15)
Michael Mor 109 (20f,Pun,YS,May 2)
Midland Flame 110 (25f,Ain,G,Apr 2)
Midlem Melody 106 (17f,Kel,G,Apr 5)
Midnight Gunner 106 (26¹/₂f,Chl,GF,Apr 14)
Mighty Fine 101 (16f,Wet,GF,May 7)
Mighty Montefalco 105 (23¹/₂f,Wor,GF,Sep 13)
Mighty Strong 110 (20f,Nby,GF,Nov 12)
Millcroft Seaspray 101 (23¹/₂f,Exe,G,Nov 4)
Millennium Gold 101 (26¹/₂f,Nab,GF,Aug 12)
Miners Dance 103 (24¹/₂f,Chl,GF,Nov 14)
Mini Dare 103 (24¹/₂f,Fak,G,Nov 23)
Minster Glory 105 (17¹/₂f,Ban,G,Oct 11)
Minster York 106 (16¹/₂f,Tow,GF,Oct 26)
Mister Banjo 105 (20¹/₂f,Ban,GS,Dec 17)
Mister Bigtime 100 (24f,Mus,G,Feb 8)
Mister Dave'S 105 (25f,Hex,G,Apr 28)
Mister Friday 103 (20f,Mar,GS,Apr 24)
Mister Magpie 100 (21¹/₂f,Str,GS,Mar 21)
Mister McGoldrick 117 (16f,Ayr,GS,Apr 16)
Mister Moss 103 (17¹/₂f,Ban,G,Aug 1)
Mister One 106 (25¹/₂f,Wcn,G,Dec 4)

Mistletoeandwine 109 (20f,Thu,S,Feb 1)
Misty Future 108 (25f,Ain,G,Nov 23)
Misty Ramble 102 (25f,Hex,G,May 10)
Mixsterthetrixster 100 (17¹/₂f,Ban,S,Apr 17)
Mollycarrsbrekfast 100 (24f,Str,G,Aug 9)
Monbonami 110 (24f,Utt,GS,Nov 15)
Mondial Jack 114 (20¹/₂f,San,G,Apr 23)
Monger Lane 100 (22f,Tow,HY,Jan 9)
Montayral 113 (29f,Fai,Y,Apr 12)
Monte Cristo 111 (17¹/₂f,Str,G,Oct 30)
Montemoss 101 (25f,Tow,GS,Feb 22)
Montpelier 104 (24f,Don,G,Jan 19)
Montreal 103 (24f,Hun,G,Apr 12)
Monty's Double 102 (25f,Mar,GS,Mar 7)
Monty's Pass 105 (36f,Ain,G,Apr 3)
Monty's Quest 106 (25f,Hex,G,May 3)
Moon Glow 102 (16¹/₂f,Nab,G,Jly 30)
Moonlake 103 (16¹/₂f,Hex,F,Sep 14)
Moor Lane 102 (24¹/₂f,Asc,GF,Nov 1)
Moral Justice 105 (20¹/₂f,Wor,GF,Jun 18)
Moral Support 101 (26f,Plu,GS,Dec 15)
Moreluck 103 (24f,Mus,G,Feb 8)
Moscow Flyer 121 (16f,San,G,Dec 6)
Moscow Leader 105 (24f,Crl,HY,Mar 21)
Mose Harper 110 (17f,Fai,Y,Apr 13)
Moss Harvey 106 (20¹/₂f,Per,S,Apr 21)
Mossy Green 117 (17f,Leo,YS,Jan 25)
Motcomb Jam 106 (20f,Plu,GF,Oct 6)
Mounsey Castle 114 (23¹/₂f,Wor,GF,Sep 14)
Mount Prague 101 (20¹/₂f,Hun,GS,Nov 22)
Moving Earth 109 (20¹/₂f,Wet,G,May 22)
Mr Baxter Basics 108 (20¹/₂f,Wor,G,May 10)
Mr Bossman 111 (22¹/₂f,Kel,G,May 7)
Mr Cospector 114 (24f,Hay,S,Feb 14)
Mr Dow Jones 105 (29f,War,GS,Mar 14)
Mr Flowers 101 (16f,Pun,YS,May 2)
Mr Laggan 101 (22¹/₂f,Mar,G,Jun 11)
Mr Ventura 108 (24f,Naa,S,Feb 7)
Mr Woodentop 107 (24f,Crl,S,Nov 27)
Ms Trude 105 (24f,Str,G,Jly 31)
Muck Savage 109 (23¹/₂f,Exe,G,Nov 21)
Muharib Lady 102 (26¹/₂f,Fon,GF,Aug 18)
Mulkev Prince 104 (20f,Lud,G,Jan 22)
Mullacash 107 (25f,Fai,S,Dec 13)
Mulligatawny 109 (24f,Hun,S,Feb 12)
Multeen River 109 (17f,Sth,GF,Oct 11)
Multi Talented 108 (24¹/₂f,San,GF,Nov 8)
Mumaris 104 (20f,Crl,G,Feb 23)
Munster 113 (19f,Leo,YS,Dec 29)
Murphy's Cardinal 107 (20f,Plu,S,Dec 3)
Musally 102 (20¹/₂f,Wor,G,Aug 2)
Mutakarrim 105 (16f,Naa,GY,Nov 22)
Myson 103 (16f,Fol,GS,Jan 2)
Mystic Lord 110 (25f,Pun,G,Apr 30)

Nas Na Riogh 111 (17¹/₂f,Exe,G,Dec 5)
Native Beat 109 (24f,Pun,GY,Apr 29)
Native Commander 111 (17f,Fai,Y,Apr 13)
Native Eire 102 (21f,Sed,GS,Jan 13)
Native Emperor 116 (24f,Nby,GS,Nov 30)
Native Jack 115 (29f,Fai,Y,Apr 12)
Native Performance 105 (25f,Pun,GY,Apr 29)
Native Scout 119 (16f,Pun,HY,Feb 1)
Native Sessions 110 (24f,Nav,S,Feb 15)
Native Upmanship 115 (25f,Pun,G,Apr 30)
Natural 108 (16f,Crl,HY,Feb 11)
Navarone 104 (24f,Str,G,Mar 15)
Nearly A Moose 114 (20f,Pun,GY,Apr 29)

Nephite 103 (16¹/₂f,Nab,GF,Aug 4)
New Bird 108 (16¹/₂f,Nab,GF,Aug 25)
Newick Park 108 (16f,Lei,G,Jan 27)
Newratking 115 (24f,Naa,GY,Nov 22)
Newsplayer 104 (16¹/₂f,Nab,GS,Jly 27)
Niagara 100 (16¹/₂f,Tow,F,Oct 8)
Nick The Jewel 106 (17¹/₂f,Str,GF,Oct 7)
Night Fighter 105 (17¹/₂f,Mar,G,Jly 6)
Nijway 101 (27f,Sed,GF,Sep 5)
Nil Desperandum 114 (20f,Fai,S,Nov 30)
No Forecast 101 (24¹/₂f,Asc,G,Nov 21)
No Messin' 102 (24f,Naa,S,Feb 7)
No Retreat 100 (24¹/₂f,Ban,G,Mar 10)
No Sam No 103 (24f,Per,G,Jly 3)
No Visibility 112 (20¹/₂f,Kem,G,Feb 13)
Noble Comic 103 (16¹/₂f,Nab,GF,Aug 25)
Noisetine 109 (19f,Cat,G,Feb 6)
Nomadic 100 (24f,Nav,GY,Nov 23)
Non So 109 (17f,Plu,S,Jan 4)
Nonantais 109 (21f,Fol,GS,Feb 17)
Nonchalant 105 (24f,Nav,S,Feb 15)
Norbrook 103 (24f,Mus,G,Feb 8)
North Of Kala 100 (18f,Fon,GF,May 26)
Northern Edition 105 (26f,Plu,GS,Feb 16)
Northern Flash 101 (16¹/₂f,Sed,G,Mar 30)
Nosam 105 (25f,Kel,F,Oct 5)
Noshinannikin 107 (19¹/₂f,Asc,G,Feb 21)

October Mist 100 (19f,Cat,G,Feb 6)
Old Marsh 107 (16f,Her,HY,Feb 6)
Old Opry 107 (17f,Fai,S,Nov 29)
One Nation 107 (17¹/₂f,Exe,G,Dec 5)
One Night Out 106 (17f,Fai,S,Nov 30)
Orswell Crest 111 (24¹/₂f,San,GF,Nov 8)
Our Armageddon 119 (21f,Chl,G,Mar 18)
Our Jolly Swagman 110 (24f,Chp,GF,May 7)
Our Kev 100 (24f,Mus,G,Feb 8)
Our Vic 116 (24¹/₂f,Chl,G,Mar 17)
Outlaw Express 100 (24f,Hun,G,Mar 6)
Over The First 111 (20f,Nav,S,Feb 15)
Over The Storm 112 (24¹/₂f,San,G,Jan 3)
Over Zealous 108 (29f,War,G,Dec 6)

Paco Venture 100 (24f,Hun,GF,Oct 10)
Paddy The Duke 101 (16f,Pun,YS,May 2)
Paddy The Optimist 104 (20¹/₂f,Per,GS,Apr 23)
Palarshan 106 (16f,Asc,GS,Jan 10)
Palua 107 (20¹/₂f,Hun,GF,Nov 11)
Pamela Anshan 102 (19f,Tau,GS,Jan 22)
Panchovillas Gleam 111 (24f,Naa,GY,Nov 22)
Pangeran 105 (26f,War,GF,Nov 3)
Panmure 108 (16f,Crl,G,Oct 25)
Papua 110 (16f,Utt,GF,Jly 16)
Parlour Game 111 (25f,Tow,G,Oct 30)
Party Animal 104 (25¹/₂f,Her,GS,May 1)
Passing Wind 105 (24¹/₂f,Ban,G,Sep 13)
Patriarch 101 (21f,Fol,GS,Feb 17)
Patricksnineteenth 112 (24¹/₂f,Chl,G,Mar 17)
Pay It Forward 104 (21f,Leo,YS,Feb 8)
Peacemaker 102 (25f,Tow,F,Oct 8)
Peccadillo 110 (24f,Kem,GF,Oct 25)
Penthouse Minstrel 106 (20¹/₂f,Chl,GF,Oct 29)
Per Amore 106 (21¹/₂f,Nab,GF,Jun 13)
Perange 108 (19f,Tau,S,Feb 3)
Perchancer 102 (16¹/₂f,Sed,GF,Aug 8)
Percy Parkeeper 105 (24f,Str,GS,May

29)

16)
Perfect Fellow 112 (24½f,San,GS,Mar 13)
Perk Alert 103 (24f,Hun,GF,May 5)
Persian King 104 (16f,Wor,GF,Sep 7)
Pertino 104 (17f,Kel,G,Apr 5)
Pessimistic Dick 105 (24f,Chp,GF,May 7)
Petolinski 102 (23½f,Exe,GS,Mar 23)
Pettree 109 (24f,Chp,GF,May 7)
Phar City 100 (23½f,Exe,GF,May 14)
Phar From A Fiddle 104 (22f,Fon,G,Oct 5)
Pharaway Citizen 106 (24f,Tau,G,Apr 1)
Pharbeitfrome 106 (16½f,Sed,GF,Jly 22)
Pharpost 107 (20f,Utt,GF,Jun 29)
Phildari 109 (24f,Lud,G,May 5)
Pietro Bembo 106 (24f,Str,GS,Jly 26)
Pizarro 117 (21f,Leo,YS,Feb 8)
Plumier 103 (24f,Lin,S,Apr 4)
Point Of Origin 101 (20½f,Hun,S,Jan 16)
Poitiers 109 (16f,Lud,GF,Apr 25)
Polar Red 113 (20½f,Chl,G,Mar 17)
Poliantas 111 (20½f,Chl,G,Nov 15)
Polish Pilot 106 (17½f,Mar,GF,May 24)
Polished 109 (16½f,Ncs,HY,Feb 4)
Polligana 110 (26½f,Nab,GF,Sep 3)
Poly Amanshaa 109 (20½f,Hun,GF,Nov 2)
Polyphon 107 (16f,Ayr,GF,Mar 13)
Pontius 106 (22½f,Kel,G,May 22)
Pornic 103 (21f,Sed,G,Mar 30)
Potoffairies 105 (20f,Nav,YS,Mar 6)
Pounsley Mill 100 (20f,Fon,G,May 5)
Prairie Minstrel 101 (20½f,Wor,GF,Nov 9)
Prancing Blade 110 (26f,War,GF,Nov 25)
Primitive Way 106 (25f,Hex,GF,Oct 3)
Prince Sorinieres 102 (23½f,Exe,G,Apr 30)
Princelou 104 (29f,Aut,VS,May 25)
Princely Sword 102 (18f,Pun,YS,May 3)
Princess Symphony 107 (25f,Pun,G,Apr 30)
Prokofiev 102 (20½f,Ban,G,Oct 11)
Prominent Profile 110 (17½f,Str,G,Oct 30)
Proper Squire 105 (24½f,Fak,GF,May 7)
Punchy 112 (23½f,Exe,F,Oct 21)
Puntal 109 (16f,San,G,Dec 6)

Quainton Hills 106 (22f,Tow,S,Nov 29)
Quality First 103 (20f,Str,GF,Apr 18)
Quarterstaff 107 (25f,Kel,G,Apr 30)

Radcliffe 107 (26f,Plu,G,Nov 3)
Ragdale Hall 107 (20½f,Per,G,Sep 25)
Rainbow Dance 107 (20½f,Per,G,Jun 22)
Rainbows Aglitter 102 (16½f,Tow,GF,Oct 26)
Raise A McGregor 100 (20½f,Wor,GF,Sep 7)
Random Harvest 102 (24f,Don,G,Jan 19)
Rathgar Beau 118 (16f,Pun,GY,May 1)
Ray Source 105 (24½f,Ban,G,Sep 13)
Reach The Clouds 102 (16½f,Hex,G,May 3)
Red Gold 109 (24f,Utt,GS,Nov 15)
Red Guard 103 (20½f,Wor,GF,Jun 18)
Red Mail 104 (17f,Kel,G,Apr 30)
Red Perk 100 (32f,Hex,G,Mar 18)
Red Rampage 104 (24f,Crl,G,Apr 10)
Red Red Red 101 (20f,Pun,GY,Nov 15)

Red Society 106 (21f,Sed,G,Mar 16)
Redde 103 (23f,Utt,HY,May 26)
Redemption 114 (20f,Nby,GS,Nov 29)
Redskin Raider 106 (25½f,Wcn,G,Apr 4)
Reel Dancer 100 (19½f,Chp,GS,Dec 6)
Reflective Way 100 (20f,Crl,HY,Feb 11)
Regal Exit 103 (20½f,Kem,G,Jan 17)
Reggae Rhythm 102 (16f,Crl,G,Mar 11)
Reiziger 111 (16½f,Chl,G,Mar 18)
Renvyle 103 (20½f,Ban,G,Mar 10)
Repunzel 101 (16½f,Tow,GS,Nov 18)
Restless Wind 106 (24f,Tau,G,Apr 1)
Rheindross 101 (20f,Pun,Y,Dec 7)
Ricardo 107 (16f,Naa,GY,Nov 22)
Rift Valley 109 (23½f,Exe,GF,May 14)
Rigmarole 100 (18f,Fon,G,May 5)
Rince Ri 119 (25½f,Chl,GS,Jan 24)
Rio Diamond 111 (24f,Naa,GY,Nov 22)
Risk Accessor 117 (20½f,Chl,GS,Dec 13)
River Amora 105 (20½f,Lin,S,Apr 4)
River Cora 101 (16f,Pun,YS,May 2)
River Quoile 103 (24f,Kem,G,Mar 7)
River Rising 100 (16½f,Hex,G,May 3)
River Styx 106 (13½f,Chp,GF,Oct 22)
River Trix 109 (26½f,Nab,GF,Jun 21)
Robbo 108 (33f,Ncs,G,Feb 21)
Roberty Bob 109 (24f,Utt,HY,May 3)
Rockspring Hero 105 (24f,Thu,GY,Dec 21)
Rodalko 109 (24f,Lud,G,Mar 4)
Rodber 108 (16½f,Ncs,S,Mar 13)
Roddy The Vet 103 (23½f,Lei,G,Jan 27)
Rosalyons 107 (30f,Ncs,G,Nov 29)
Rose Perk 116 (24f,Nav,YS,Mar 6)
Rose Tina 101 (22f,Fon,G,Oct 5)
Rosie Redman 105 (25f,Mar,G,Dec 26)
Ross Minster 103 (25½f,Wcn,S,Jan 8)
Ross Moff 106 (17f,Fai,S,Nov 30)
Rosslea 111 (25½f,Chl,G,Dec 12)
Rougenoir 112 (29f,Aut,VS,May 25)
Royal Auclair 112 (20½f,Chl,GS,Dec 13)
Royal Beluga 104 (20f,Ncs,GS,Dec 20)
Royal Castle 105 (21½f,Crt,G,May 26)
Royal County Buck 101 (32f,Chl,GF,Nov 14)
Royal Emperor 120 (22½f,Kel,S,Dec 1)
Ruby Gale 106 (21f,Wcn,GS,Jan 8)
Rudetski 103 (16½f,Don,G,Jan 19)
Rudi Knight 111 (21½f,Nab,S,Apr 29)
Rufius 104 (20½f,Hun,GF,Oct 9)
Rule Supreme 118 (24½f,Chl,G,Mar 17)
Rum Pointer 110 (24f,Utt,S,Dec 26)
Runaway Bishop 103 (25f,Tow,S,Apr 11)
Runner Bean 108 (16f,Lud,GF,Dec 18)
Running Machine 106 (24½f,San,G,Feb 20)
Running Mute 108 (20½f,Per,G,Jun 22)
Running On 101 (20f,Pun,GY,Nov 15)
Russian Gigolo 108 (25½f,Chl,G,Dec 31)
Ryders Storm 108 (17f,Sth,GF,Oct 11)

Saby 100 (16f,Wcn,G,Apr 4)
Sad Mad Bad 101 (25f,Hex,G,Apr 28)
Saffron Sun 104 (24f,Kem,GF,Oct 25)
Salford 102 (25½f,Wcn,F,Oct 26)
Salvage 105 (17f,Kel,G,Apr 5)
Sam Adamson 108 (16f,Wcn,GF,May 15)
Same Old Story 109 (20f,Nav,S,Feb 16)
Samon 100 (20f,Fon,GF,May 26)
Samuel Wilderspin 107 (33f,Chl,G,Jan 1)
San Peire 103 (27f,Sed,GS,Feb 10)
Santa Lucia 102 (20½f,Per,G,Sep 25)
Santenay 111 (20½f,Kem,G,Feb 28)

Saragann 111 (16½f,Hun,S,Jan 16)
Satco Express 108 (24f,Leo,YS,Dec 28)
Satcoslam 108 (24f,Leo,S,Dec 27)
Saxo Du Rocher 101 (20f,Pun,GY,Nov 15)
Say Again 111 (17f,Fai,Y,Apr 11)
Scotmail Boy 105 (20f,Crl,G,Feb 23)
Scotmail Lad 107 (16½f,Sed,GF,Nov 11)
Scots Grey 104 (20½f,Kem,G,Dec 27)
Search And Destroy 111 (20½f,Per,GF,Jun 5)
Seasquill 102 (16f,Hay,GF,Oct 23)
Secret Drinker 104 (26f,Plu,GS,Dec 15)
Secret Native 107 (24f,Leo,S,Dec 27)
See You Around 102 (26½f,Nab,G,Nov 18)
See You Sometime 104 (20f,Nby,G,Mar 6)
Seebald 118 (21f,Chl,GF,Apr 14)
Selberry 106 (16f,Lin,G,Nov 11)
Shampooed 113 (20f,Str,GF,Jly 13)
Shardam 119 (24f,Kem,G,Feb 28)
Shardante 109 (26f,Don,G,Dec 13)
Sharmy 106 (16f,Lud,G,Dec 11)
Sharp Single 102 (16½f,Hex,G,Mar 18)
Sharp Steel 107 (17½f,Ban,G,Aug 1)
Sharpastrizam 104 (17f,Kel,G,Apr 5)
Shays Lane 101 (25f,Hex,G,May 24)
Sheer Frustration 112 (20f,Thu,S,Feb 1)
Shelu 100 (25f,Hex,GF,Nov 7)
Shepherds Rest 105 (24½f,Ban,G,Aug 16)
Shooting Light 108 (24f,Nby,G,Feb 14)
Shoulton 105 (26½f,Chp,S,Jan 23)
Sidewinder 108 (23½f,Exe,F,Oct 21)
Silent Snipe 107 (27f,Sed,G,Oct 14)
Silk Trader 105 (19f,Cat,G,Jan 24)
Silver Birch 115 (25½f,Wcn,G,Feb 12)
Silver Knight 106 (25f,Mar,GS,Mar 7)
Silver Streak 104 (24½f,Asc,S,Nov 22)
Simber Hill 111 (24f,Str,GS,Jly 26)
Simlet 104 (21f,Sed,G,Mar 16)
Simply Gifted 116 (16f,Ain,G,Apr 1)
Simply Supreme 112 (25f,Ain,G,Apr 2)
Single Sourcing 107 (25f,Hex,G,Apr 28)
Sir Frosty 105 (25f,Ain,G,Apr 2)
Sir Norman 109 (25f,Hay,May 21)
Sir Rembrandt 119 (26½f,Chp,GS,Dec 6)
Sir Storm 114 (16f,Per,GS,Apr 22)
Sir Talbot 110 (16f,Lei,G,Jan 13)
Sir Toby 109 (21½f,Fak,G,Apr 12)
Sireric 106 (25f,Hex,G,Apr 28)
Six Pack 101 (16f,Lei,F,Dec 10)
Skippers Cleuch 116 (25f,Wet,GS,Dec 27)
Sky Warrior 105 (24½f,San,S,Feb 7)
Skycab 103 (25f,Kel,G,May 22)
Smarty 104 (24f,Nby,G,Mar 27)
Snowy Ford 112 (24f,Nav,YS,Mar 6)
Solar System 108 (24f,Nav,YS,Mar 6)
Solway Rose 101 (26f,Crl,G,Mar 11)
Some Ticket 109 (24f,Naa,GY,Nov 22)
Something Dandy 107 (19½f,Chp,GS,Nov 26)
Son Of A Gun 105 (17f,Sth,GF,Oct 11)
Sossus Vlei 106 (17f,Plu,S,Jan 4)
Soul 103 (16½f,Hun,S,Jan 16)
Sound Of Cheers 112 (16½f,Ncs,HY,Mar 20)
Sounds Cool 102 (16½f,Sed,S,May 17)
Soundtrack 100 (24f,Per,G,Jun 6)
Southbay 104 (24f,Str,G,Mar 15)
Southern Star 111 (29f,War,GS,Jan 10)
Southerndown 106 (26f,Sth,GF,Oct 11)
Spanish Point 101 (24½f,San,G,Feb 20)
Sparkling Cascade 101 (19½f,Exe,G,Apr 30)
Special Agenda 100 (16f,Utt,HY,Jan 10)

Spendid 111 (26f,Don,G,Dec 13)
Spokesman 102 (16f,Ain,G,Nov 22)
Spot Thedifference 105 (36f,Ain,G,Apr 3)
Spread The Word 110 (25f,Tow,G,Oct 30)
Spring Grove 117 (21f,Chl,G,Jan 1)
Springwood White 100 (25f,Hex,GF,Jun 20)
St Pirran 116 (16½f,Chl,G,Mar 18)
Stamparland Hill 112 (16f,Wet,GS,Mar 22)
Stand Easy 103 (26f,Utt,HY,May 21)
Standing Bloom 101 (24f,Hun,S,Jan 16)
Stanmore 103 (24f,Str,GF,Sep 6)
Star Clipper 108 (16f,Pun,GY,May 1)
Star Performance 107 (25f,Pun,G,Apr 30)
Star Storm 111 (17f,Leo,S,Dec 26)
Star Trooper 104 (16½f,Sed,G,Mar 30)
Stars Out Tonight 100 (22½f,Nby,GS,Nov 30)
Starting Again 101 (20f,Lud,G,Feb 11)
Stashedaway 118 (20f,Thu,S,Feb 1)
Stavordale Lad 100 (23½f,Exe,G,Nov 21)
Steel Mill 102 (25f,Tow,GS,Mar 24)
Step Quick 100 (22f,Fon,G,Oct 5)
Stocks 'n Shares 105 (19f,Tau,GS,Jan 22)
Stone Cold 103 (25f,Kel,G,Apr 30)
Stonebridge Chance 105 (24f,Nav,YS,Mar 6)
Stormez 109 (27½f,Chl,G,Nov 15)
Stormhill Stag 101 (23½f,Exe,G,Apr 30)
Stormy Beech 109 (16f,Crl,HY,Feb 11)
Strawman 108 (21½f,Fak,G,Apr 12)
Stromness 108 (23½f,Wor,GS,May 2)
Strong Flow 120 (26½f,Nby,GS,Nov 29)
Strong Magic 108 (20f,Utt,GS,Dec 19)
Strong Resolve 104 (25f,Ayr,GS,Nov 28)
Strong Run 104 (16½f,Lud,G,Mar 18)
Strong Tartan 109 (24f,Str,GS,Jly 26)
Strongtrooper 109 (24½f,Fak,GF,May 18)
Sum Leader 106 (20f,Nav,S,Dec 14)
Sunday Habits 102 (24f,Utt,GF,Jun 12)
Sunday Rain 106 (20½f,Per,G,Sep 25)
Sunnycliff 101 (25½f,Cat,GS,Dec 3)
Sunshan 103 (24f,Tau,GF,Apr 16)
Super Fellow 105 (26½f,Chl,GF,Apr 14)
Super Nomad 110 (19f,Don,G,Mar 6)
Super Sammy 108 (17½f,Mar,GS,Dec 4)
Superb Leader 100 (20½f,Lei,GF,Mar 2)
Superior Weapon 111 (16½f,Ncs,HY,Mar 20)
Supreme Arrow 107 (24f,Hun,GF,Nov 11)
Supreme Breeze 106 (26f,Crt,G,May 24)
Supreme Catch 109 (24½f,San,S,Feb 7)
Supreme Prince 108 (23½f,Exe,G,Nov 21)
Supreme Touch 111 (20f,Thu,S,Feb 1)
Surefast 108 (20½f,Lin,S,Apr 4)
Surprising 104 (28½f,Mar,G,Nov 20)
Suspendid 108 (20½f,Wor,GF,Jun 18)
Swan Knight 104 (17½f,Mar,GS,Dec 4)
Swansea Bay 111 (24f,Kem,GF,Oct 25)
Swincombe 104 (24f,Nby,S,Jan 14)
Sylphide 101 (22f,Fon,G,Apr 7)
Sylviesbuck 103 (27f,Sed,GS,Jan 13)

Ta Ta For Now 100 (24f,Per,G,Jun 6)
Tacolino 114 (20f,Mar,GF,Jun 21)
Tagar 106 (16f,Per,G,Sep 24)
Takagi 105 (25f,Pun,GY,May 1)
Take Control 115 (26½f,Nby,GS,Nov 29)

Take The Stand 112 (25½f,Exe,G,Dec 18)
Talbot Lad 109 (20f,Lud,G,Apr 8)
Tamango 112 (16f,Asc,GF,Nov 1)
Tambo 106 (21½f,Fak,GS,Mar 19)
Tango Royal 114 (17f,Nby,GS,Nov 29)
Tanikos 107 (20f,Plu,S,Jan 19)
Tara-Brogan 102 (26f,Plu,GF,Sep 27)
Tarbolton Moss 104 (25f,Kel,S,Jan 16)
Tarongo 104 (16f,Wcn,GF,May 15)
Tarxien 110 (19½f,Asc,S,Nov 22)
Teaatral 105 (20½f,Hun,GF,May 5)
Team Captain 104 (25½f,Her,G,Apr 3)
Telemoss 112 (20½f,Chl,GS,Dec 13)
Tell Me See 106 (25f,Fai,S,Dec 13)
Teme Valley 108 (16½f,Sed,G,Mar 30)
Terek 101 (16½f,Tau,G,Mar 15)
Thalys 103 (19f,Her,GS,Feb 15)
Thari 107 (25f,Pun,G,Apr 30)
The Alleycat 109 (19½f,Chp,GF,Oct 22)
The Bandit 112 (20f,Ain,G,Apr 3)
The Dark Flasher 100 (16f,Naa,GY,Nov 22)
The Extra Man 106 (20½f,Hun,GS,Nov 22)
The Galway Man 113 (20f,Nav,S,Dec 14)
The Hearty Joker 103 (22½f,Mar,G,Jly 6)
The Kew Tour 102 (25f,Wet,GF,Oct 31)
The Merry Mason 100 (25f,Hex,GF,Jun 20)
The Moyne Machine 109 (17f,Fai,HY,Jan 31)
The Newsman 104 (20f,Plu,G,Nov 3)
The Nomad 108 (16½f,Hex,S,Apr 4)
The Pennys Dropped 106 (25½f,Chl,G,Dec 31)
The River Joker 110 (25f,Tow,S,Dec 26)
The Sawdust Kid 100 (26½f,Nab,GF,Jun 28)
The Staggery Boy 104 (16½f,Nab,GF,Jun 13)
The Tall Guy 104 (20½f,Chl,GF,Oct 29)
The Tinker 108 (16f,Per,GS,Apr 22)
The Villager 107 (21f,Chl,GS,Jan 24)
Themanfromcarlisle 108 (20f,Plu,GF,Oct 6)
Therealbandit 114 (25½f,Chl,G,Dec 12)
Thisthatandtother 117 (16f,Wcn,G,Feb 21)
Three Days Reign 113 (20½f,Wor,G,May 21)
Three Eagles 115 (24½f,Nab,G,Aug 16)
Thunderpoint 109 (24f,Str,G,Aug 9)
Tidour 121 (16f,Ain,G,Apr 1)
Tierkely 102 (24f,Per,G,Jly 3)
Tikram 117 (21f,Chl,GF,Apr 14)
Timbera 114 (29f,Fai,Y,Apr 12)
Tino 105 (21f,Fol,GF,Nov 4)
Tipp Top Lord 107 (25f,Tow,G,Mar 11)
Tipsy Mouse 105 (24f,Hay,HY,Jan 24)
Tirley Storm 100 (22f,Fon,G,Oct 5)
Tiutchev 116 (24f,Kem,G,Dec 26)
Tobesure 106 (25f,Hex,G,Nov 19)
Toi Express 103 (16f,Lin,G,Nov 11)
Tollbrae 104 (16f,Lei,G,Feb 18)
Tom Costalot 105 (21f,Chl,G,Jan 1)
Tom's Prize 108 (24½f,Ban,S,Apr 17)
Tom's River 104 (19½f,Exe,G,Apr 30)
Tommy Carson 103 (20f,Plu,G,Mar 15)
Tonoco 113 (24f,Hay,S,Feb 14)
Top Buck 101 (20½f,Hun,GF,Nov 11)
Topol 102 (16f,Her,GS,Dec 2)
Tor Head 103 (16½f,Hex,G,Mar 18)
Torduff Boy 110 (20f,Pun,YS,May 2)
Torrid Kentavr 110 (16½f,Sed,S,May 17)
Toto Caelo 103 (18f,Pun,YS,May 3)
Towns Ender 107 (16f,Lei,G,Jan 27)
Transit 102 (16f,Mus,G,Feb 18)

Translucid 104 (16f,San,G,Dec 6)
Tremallt 113 (25½f,Ncs,S,Jan 17)
Tresor De Mai 104 (24½f,Asc,S,Dec 20)
Tribal Dancer 108 (24f,Hun,G,Apr 12)
Tristernagh 106 (20f,Pun,HY,Feb 1)
Trooper 103 (27f,Sed,S,May 2)
Trouble Ahead 109 (19½f,Asc,G,Feb 21)
True Blue Victory 108 (19f,Leo,YS,Jan 25)
True Rose 108 (16½f,Ncs,HY,Feb 4)
Trusting Tom 111 (25f,Pun,GY,Apr 29)
Tudor King 104 (25f,Fol,GF,Nov 4)
Turgeonev 113 (20½f,Chl,G,Mar 17)
Turn Two 112 (25f,Pun,G,Apr 30)
Twisted Logic 105 (23½f,Exe,G,Apr 6)
Twotensforafive 100 (21½f,Nab,GF,Jun 3)
Tyndarius 113 (26f,Don,G,Dec 13)
Tyneandthyneagain 109 (33f,Ncs,G,Feb 21)
Tysou 108 (16f,San,G,Jan 3)

Ultra Pontem 105 (21½f,Nab,GS,Jly 27)
Ulusaba 109 (20½f,Wor,G,May 21)
Un Jour A Vassy 109 (25½f,Exe,G,Dec 18)
Uncle Mick 111 (23½f,Wor,GF,Sep 14)
Uncle Teddy 100 (21½f,Nab,G,Jly 30)
Under The Sand 112 (25½f,Wcn,G,Apr 4)
Underley Park 102 (24f,Crl,HY,Mar 21)
Uneven Line 100 (21f,Sed,G,Apr 12)
Ungaretti 101 (26f,Plu,G,Apr 11)
Unmistakably 100 (20½f,San,G,Dec 5)
Upgrade 118 (16f,Asc,S,Dec 20)
Urga 112 (29f,Aut,VS,May 25)

Vague Idea 110 (26½f,Nab,GF,Jun 21)
Valley Erne 109 (25f,Pun,GY,May 1)
Valley Henry 106 (25f,Ain,G,Apr 1)
Valleymore 101 (22f,Hay,S,Feb 14)
Veiled Dancer 100 (26½f,Nab,GF,Jun 21)
Veneguera 101 (20f,Lud,GF,Nov 24)
Venn Ottery 116 (16f,Her,GF,Mar 9)
Verchoyles Lad 103 (17f,Nav,S,Feb 16)
Very Very Noble 100 (21f,Fol,G,Dec 16)
Victor Boy 110 (17f,Leo,S,Dec 26)
Vidi Caesar 106 (20f,Utt,GS,Dec 19)
Villair 107 (26½f,Nab,G,Apr 10)
Virgin Soldier 111 (25f,Mar,GF,Oct 18)

Wagner 108 (20f,Nby,GF,Nov 12)
Wahiba Sands 114 (17½f,Exe,G,Nov 4)
Wain Mountain 107 (25f,Wet,S,Jan 17)
Walcot Lad 106 (26½f,Fon,G,Apr 22)
Walter's Destiny 105 (25½f,Wcn,G,Dec 26)
Watch The Dove 102 (24f,Tau,G,Mar 4)
Water Quirl 107 (16½f,War,GF,Nov 25)
Waterberg 113 (24f,Str,GS,Jly 26)
Waterlaw 106 (21f,Chl,G,Jan 1)
Wave Rock 107 (20½f,Wor,G,May 10)
Weaver George 112 (25f,Kel,G,Nov 12)
Well Chief 117 (16f,Chl,G,Mar 16)
Wellie 100 (20½f,Hun,GF,May 5)
Wemyss Quest 110 (23½f,Wor,G,Jun 28)
West Pal 102 (24f,Str,G,Jly 31)
Western View 100 (24f,Nav,GY,Nov 23)
What's The Score 113 (25f,Pun,GY,Apr 29)
Whatatouch 112 (25f,Pun,GY,Apr 29)
Whereareyounow 120 (21f,Chl,G,Jan 1)
Wild Spice 109 (26½f,Fon,G,May 5)
Wildfield Rufo 104 (24f,Crl,HY,Mar 21)

Windross 107 (24f,Str,GS,May 16)
Winged Hussar 103 (21½f,Nab,S,Apr 29)
Winter Garden 108 (16f,Ayr,GF,Mar 13)
Wise King 104 (24f,Str,GS,May 16)
Wise Man 104 (20f,Crl,HY,Mar 21)
Wonder Weasel 105 (29f,War,GS,Mar 14)
Workaway 100 (17f,Kel,S,Dec 1)
World Wide Web 112 (24f,Leo,S,Dec 27)
Wot No Cash 110 (19½f,Chp,GF,Oct 22)
Wotsitooya 109 (25f,Pun,GY,May 1)
Would You Believe 102 (22f,Tow,S,Dec 15)
Wrens Island 107 (23½f,Wor,GF,Jun 1)
Wuxi Venture 103 (19f,Cat,GS,Jan 15)
Wynbury Flyer 105 (16½f,Sed,GF,Nov 25)

Xaipete 111 (20f,Mar,GF,Jly 19)
Xenophon 111 (20f,Nav,S,Dec 14)

Yankie Lord 106 (20½f,Per,GF,Jun 5)
Yann's 102 (23½f,Exe,G,Apr 30)
Yeoman's Point 108 (19f,Naa,S,Jan 4)
You're Special 109 (26f,Crt,G,May 24)
You're Agoodun 107 (24½f,Chl,G,Mar 16)
Younevertoldme 107 (20f,Nav,S,Feb 16)
Young Chevalier 103 (16f,Crl,G,Mar 11)
Young Devereaux 105 (21f,Chl,GS,Jan 24)
Young Spartacus 113 (25f,Pun,G,Apr 30)
Young Whack 109 (20f,Ayr,G,Nov 15)
Yvanovitch 102 (18f,Fon,G,Jan 26)

Zafarabad 107 (25½f,Wcn,GF,Nov 20)
Zaffamore 116 (20½f,Kem,G,Feb 13)
Zaffre Noir 101 (24f,Hun,G,Apr 12)
Zaggy Lane 102 (24f,Utt,HY,May 3)
Ziggy's Way 103 (23½f,Wor,GS,Apr 21)
Zoffany 106 (17½f,Ban,G,Oct 27)

HURDLES

A Few Bob Back 106 (22f,Hay,S,Nov 29)
Able Native 104 (16½f,Hex,G,May 24)
Above The Cut 105 (22½f,Exe,G,Apr 30)
Abzuson 111 (20f,Ncs,S,Mar 13)
Accepting 105 (24½f,Per,G,Jun 6)
Accipiter 109 (20f,Asc,GS,Mar 20)
Accordion Etoile 115 (16f,Nav,GF,Nov 9)
Adalpour 101 (16½f,Kel,G,Apr 5)
Adamant Approach 111 (17f,Chl,G,Mar 18)
Adarma 109 (20f,Naa,S,Jan 4)
Adelphi Boy 103 (16½f,Per,GF,Jun 5)
Adiysha 106 (16f,Fak,G,Oct 24)
Admiral Brown 109 (16f,Fai,S,Nov 29)
Admiral Peary 100 (26f,Hun,GF,May 5)
Adolphus 101 (20f,Fai,GF,Oct 22)
Adopted Hero 108 (17f,Chl,G,Mar 18)
Adradee 101 (16f,Wcn,GF,May 15)
Aerleon Pete 100 (16½f,Str,G,Jly 26)
Afro Man 103 (21f,Kem,G,Nov 5)
After Eight 106 (16f,Kem,G,Dec 27)
After Me Boys 100 (24½f,Don,G,Mar 6)
After Puck 101 (24f,Hun,G,Apr 12)
Agitando 111 (16½f,Ain,GS,May 16)
Aine Dubh 117 (21f,Chl,G,Mar 17)
Air Of Confusion 100 (17f,Sed,GF,Aug 8)

Airolo 104 (16f,Nav,GF,Nov 9)
Akrabad 106 (20f,Pun,GY,Nov 16)
Al Eile 114 (16½f,Ain,G,Apr 1)
Al Mabrook 107 (17f,Sed,GS,Jan 13)
Al Towd 115 (22f,Fai,Y,Apr 12)
Alam 108 (16½f,Hex,S,Dec 17)
Albany 100 (16f,Hay,S,Feb 14)
Albatros 116 (16f,Leo,S,Jan 11)
Albuhera 110 (16½f,Asc,GF,Nov 1)
Albuquerque 112 (24f,Pun,YS,May 2)
Alchemystic 102 (19f,Nby,G,Mar 27)
Alexanderthegreat 113 (22f,San,S,Feb 7)
Alexandra Parade 103 (20f,Ayr,S,Dec 26)
Alfa Sunrise 105 (19f,Nby,GF,Dec 10)
Alfy Rich 104 (17f,Exe,GS,Mar 23)
Algarve 107 (22f,Hay,G,Jan 10)
Aliabad 106 (22½f,Exe,GF,Oct 8)
Aliby 100 (16f,Pun,GY,Nov 16)
Alice Cooney 101 (16f,Pun,Y,Dec 6)
Alicudi 102 (16f,Fai,HY,Jan 31)
All Bleevable 102 (16f,Fak,G,Feb 20)
All Fours 105 (16f,Fai,GF,Oct 22)
All In The Stars 100 (20f,Chp,GS,Dec 6)
All Rock Hard 104 (16f,Mus,F,Feb 29)
Allineedisamiracle 100 (20f,Fai,GF,Oct 22)
Allofasudden 118 (24f,Pun,YS,May 2)
Allude 107 (16½f,Str,GF,Jly 13)
Almaravide 107 (20f,Asc,S,Jan 10)
Almaydan 107 (17f,Tau,GS,Feb 19)
Almnadia 104 (21½f,Chl,G,Apr 15)
Alpha Rose 107 (16½f,Hun,GF,Oct 9)
Alphabetic 107 (19f,Nby,GF,Dec 10)
Alphazar 108 (20f,Pun,GY,Apr 29)
Alpine Fox 101 (16½f,Nby,GS,Nov 30)
Alpine Hideaway 105 (17f,Sed,GF,Aug 8)
Alsyati 103 (16½f,Chp,GF,Mar 10)
Altareek 105 (16f,Fak,G,Oct 24)
Altay 112 (16f,Hay,GS,May 3)
Altitude Dancer 104 (16f,Lei,G,Dec 4)
Alvaro 100 (22f,Nab,GF,Aug 4)
Always 106 (16f,Fai,S,Nov 30)
Always Rainbows 101 (16f,Wet,GS,Mar 22)
Amalita 101 (16f,Nav,GF,Jun 22)
Amber Go Go 101 (27½f,Sed,G,Mar 16)
Amberleigh House 103 (23½f,Hay,GF,Oct 23)
Ambry 110 (20f,Ban,G,Aug 1)
Ambushed 105 (16½f,Per,G,Jun 22)
Ameras 104 (24f,Hex,S,Dec 17)
Americanconnection 107 (22½f,Exe,GF,Oct 21)
Amicelli 106 (20f,Fon,GF,Mar 8)
Ammonias 101 (16½f,Nby,GS,Dec 29)
Among Equals 110 (16½f,Nby,GS,Mar 26)
Ampertaine 109 (20f,Fai,Y,Apr 13)
Amplified 106 (20f,Pun,GY,Nov 16)
An Culainn Beag 105 (20f,Fai,Y,Apr 11)
Analogy 108 (24f,Lud,G,Apr 8)
Analyze 101 (17f,Exe,GF,Oct 21)
Anatar 102 (21f,Chl,G,Mar 17)
Andromache 101 (17½f,Fol,HY,Jan 2)
Angels Venture 111 (16f,Wcn,GF,Nov 20)
Anglosprinter 103 (16f,Fai,GY,Feb 28)
Anna Walhaan 101 (16½f,Hun,GF,Nov 11)
Anns Gamble 108 (16f,Pun,GY,Nov 15)
Another Aspect 106 (16f,Fai,GY,Nov 12)
Another Chance 107 (20½f,Hex,S,Apr 4)
Another Copper 102 (22f,Nab,GF,Jun 21)
Another Dollar 103 (20f,Leo,Y,Jan 25)
Another Dude 108 (16f,Mus,G,Feb 18)

Another Moose 105 (23½f,Hay,S,Feb 14)
Another Rum 104 (22f,Ayr,G,Nov 16)
Antony Ebeneezer 103 (16½f,Str,G,Jly 26)
Anzal 101 (20f,Wor,G,Jun 28)
Apadi 101 (17½f,Crt,G,Aug 23)
Apollo Theatre 101 (21f,Nby,GS,Mar 26)
April Allegro 112 (24f,Pun,YS,May 2)
Ar Muin Na Muice 110 (25½f,Chl,G,Mar 16)
Araf 101 (17½f,Crt,GF,Jly 17)
Araglin 105 (16½f,Chp,GF,Oct 22)
Arch Stanton 118 (16f,Leo,S,Jan 11)
Archie Babe 107 (16f,Wet,GS,Nov 26)
Arctic Lagoon 100 (16½f,Per,G,May 15)
Arctic Rainbow 101 (21f,Plu,GS,Dec 15)
Arctic Spirit 102 (16f,Tow,S,Apr 11)
Ardashir 110 (24f,Ban,GS,Apr 17)
Arden Hills 104 (17f,Nab,GF,Jun 13)
Arellano 106 (20f,Pun,GY,Nov 16)
Arijaz 102 (24½f,Ayr,GF,Mar 13)
Arimero 101 (16½f,Ain,G,Apr 1)
Ark Admiral 101 (16f,Wcn,G,Apr 18)
Arkadian 106 (16f,Fai,GY,Nov 12)
Armen 104 (17f,Chl,G,Dec 31)
Around Before 101 (24f,Tow,F,Oct 16)
Artemesia 101 (20f,Fak,GF,May 7)
Artic Plain 100 (16f,Pun,GY,Nov 16)
Artic Reason 105 (16f,Naa,S,Jan 4)
Ashcroft 105 (16f,Fai,GF,Oct 22)
Ashgar 111 (21f,Tow,F,Oct 8)
Ashlawn 101 (16f,Nav,GY,Nov 23)
Ashley Brook 106 (17f,Exe,G,Nov 21)
Ashleybank House 105 (16f,Ayr,S,Dec 26)
Ashnaya 108 (20f,Ncs,G,Nov 14)
Ashtaroute 101 (16f,Cat,GF,Mar 10)
Ashwell 101 (19½f,Mar,G,Feb 10)
Ask Me What 101 (16f,Lud,G,Dec 11)
Ask The Builder 108 (16f,Pun,GY,Nov 15)
Assoon 103 (18½f,Fon,G,Oct 5)
Astafort 100 (16½f,Kel,G,May 21)
Aston 101 (16f,Mus,GF,Jan 23)
Aston Mara 102 (21½f,Hun,GF,May 29)
Astronaut 103 (16f,Utt,GF,Jly 16)
Athenian Law 104 (16f,Wor,GF,Jly 9)
Atlantic Rhapsody 101 (18f,Fai,S,Nov 29)
Atticus Finch 100 (21½f,Sth,GF,Oct 11)
Attorney General 113 (17f,Chl,GS,Jan 24)
Audiostreetdotcom 104 (20f,Chp,HY,Feb 7)
Avalanche 105 (21f,War,GS,Mar 14)
Avas Delight 101 (17f,Tau,G,Mar 15)
Avitta 101 (18½f,Fon,G,May 5)
Away Home 112 (20f,Naa,S,Jan 4)
Aye Aye Popeye 107 (16½f,San,GS,Dec 6)

Baby Gee 105 (20½f,Per,GF,Jun 5)
Back In Front 115 (16f,Pun,YS,May 2)
Back Nine 109 (16f,Pun,GY,Nov 15)
Back On Top 107 (25½f,Chl,G,Mar 16)
Backcraft 104 (20½f,Per,GF,Jun 5)
Bacyan 103 (25½f,Cat,G,Jan 24)
Bahlino 102 (16f,Cat,GF,Mar 10)
Baily Mist 101 (20f,Fai,Y,Apr 11)
Bak To Bill 101 (22f,Nab,S,Apr 29)
Bakiri 101 (19f,Str,GF,Mar 15)
Balakar 102 (17½f,Mar,GF,May 24)
Balapour 117 (17f,Chl,G,Mar 18)
Ball Games 101 (16½f,Hex,GF,Oct 3)
Ball O Malt 105 (24f,Pun,Y,May 3)
Balladeer 103 (21f,Lud,GF,Nov 24)
Ballina Belle 106 (16f,Fai,GY,Nov 12)

Ballybough Rasher 112 (24½f,Ain,G,Oct 26)

Ballygill Heights 101 (20f,Pun,Y,May 3)

Ballylusky 104 (23½f,Hay,HY,Jan 24)

Ballystone 108 (25½f,Cat,G,Feb 6)

Ballyvaddy 110 (24f,Chp,GF,Nov 8)

Baloo 105 (27f,Nab,GF,Jun 28)

Banningham Blaze 101 (16½f,Hun,G,Mar 17)

Baracouda 120 (25½f,Asc,G,Dec 19)

Barcelona 109 (20f,Wor,GF,Jun 7)

Barcham Again 100 (22½f,Utt,S,May 3)

Barneys Lyric 101 (16½f,Per,G,Sep 24)

Baron De Feypo 100 (24f,Nav,GF,Jun 22)

Barrack Buster 101 (16f,Pun,G,Apr 30)

Barresbo 104 (22f,Crt,GS,May 28)

Barton Gate 103 (16f,War,GS,Jan 10)

Barton Hill 100 (19½f,Mar,G,Dec 26)

Barton Nic 111 (20f,Ban,S,May 2)

Basinet 101 (17f,Sed,GF,Aug 8)

Battle Warning 117 (25½f,Chl,G,Dec 12)

Bay Kenny 106 (24f,Lud,G,Apr 8)

Bay Magic 100 (22f,Ayr,G,Nov 16)

Be Fair 107 (21½f,Hun,GF,Nov 2)

Be My Belle 115 (24f,Leo,YS,Dec 28)

Be On Time 101 (16f,Nav,GF,Jun 22)

Be The Tops 105 (20½f,Per,G,Jun 22)

Beamish Prince 105 (16f,Ncs,GS,Dec 20)

Bearaway 102 (16f,Tow,F,Oct 8)

Beat The Heat 104 (16½f,Kel,G,Nov 12)

Beau Artiste 101 (16f,Mus,GF,Jan 7)

Beau Supreme 105 (21f,Nby,G,Mar 5)

Beau Torero 101 (16f,Lud,GF,Nov 13)

Beauly 100 (16f,War,G,Dec 6)

Beausejour 103 (19f,Exe,G,Mar 9)

Bed Bug 102 (21f,Kem,G,Dec 26)

Bedford Leader 101 (24f,Chp,S,Jan 23)

Beechcourt 109 (18f,Leo,S,Dec 26)

Begsy's Bullet 101 (20f,Hay,S,Nov 29)

Behzad 104 (20½f,Per,G,Jun 22)

Bell Lane Lad 109 (20f,Asc,G,Dec 19)

Bella Bambina 100 (16f,Plu,S,Jan 4)

Bellaficient 103 (16f,Nav,S,Dec 20)

Ben Ewar 102 (16f,Wor,G,May 21)

Benbyas 114 (17f,Chl,G,Mar 18)

Benefit 104 (24f,Mar,G,Mar 7)

Benjis Treasure 107 (16f,Fai,GY,Nov 12)

Bergamo 107 (17½f,Mar,GS,Dec 4)

Berkeley Hall 104 (16½f,Str,G,May 16)

Berkeley Note 106 (16f,Fai,S,Nov 29)

Bermaho 100 (16f,Pun,GY,Nov 16)

Bernardon 109 (18f,Kel,G,Mar 28)

Bertiebanoo 103 (21f,Plu,S,Nov 23)

Beseiged 105 (16½f,Per,G,May 15)

Best Wait 109 (16f,Thu,GY,Dec 21)

Better Think Again 116 (24f,Pun,YS,May 2)

Beyond Borders 103 (16½f,Hun,S,Jan 16)

Beyond Control 104 (25½f,Asc,G,Dec 19)

Bid Me Again 107 (16f,Naa,G,Aug 4)

Bid Spotter 104 (16½f,Hun,S,Jan 16)

Biennale 102 (16f,Nav,GF,Nov 9)

Big King 100 (16f,Fai,S,Nov 29)

Big Maggie 104 (22f,Fai,GY,Feb 28)

Big Max 105 (19f,Exe,S,Feb 2)

Big Moment 121 (21f,Nby,GS,Dec 29)

Billy Bonnie 112 (22f,Fai,Y,Apr 12)

Billy Two Rivers 100 (16½f,Kel,G,Apr 5)

Bison King 101 (24f,Ban,G,Mar 10)

Bisquet-De-Bouche 101 (24f,Hex,G,May 10)

Bitter Sweet 102 (17½f,Mar,GF,Oct 5)

Black Church Lad 111 (20f,Pun,Y,Dec 7)

Blackchurch Mist 109 (20f,Wor,GF,Aug 23)

Blame The Ref 112 (24f,Pun,YS,May 2)

Blanc C'Est Blanc 103 (20f,Fai,GF,Oct 22)

Blasket Sound 101 (26f,Her,GS,Mar 22)

Blitzy Boy 101 (20f,Fai,GF,Oct 22)

Blue Americo 103 (17f,Tau,S,Feb 3)

Blue Away 111 (20f,Pun,GY,Apr 29)

Blue Business 107 (24½f,Tau,G,Mar 4)

Blue Corrig 109 (16f,Fai,GF,Oct 22)

Blue Derby 103 (17f,Exe,GS,Dec 5)

Blue Endeavour 102 (17f,Exe,G,Apr 6)

Blue Hawk 105 (16f,Utt,GF,Sep 7)

Blue Leader 103 (16½f,Hun,G,Mar 17)

Blue Ride 105 (25½f,Chl,G,Nov 15)

Blue Streak 104 (16f,Plu,GF,Oct 6)

Blunham Hill 104 (21f,Tow,S,Nov 29)

Bob Ar Aghaidh 102 (20½f,Utt,GS,Nov 27)

Bob Justice 115 (24f,Leo,YS,Dec 28)

Bob The Piler 107 (16f,Ncs,HY,Jan 21)

Bob's Gone 105 (22½f,Str,G,Jly 26)

Bobalong 108 (24f,Chp,S,Jan 23)

Bobanvi 103 (22f,Crt,G,Aug 23)

Bobbi Rose Red 102 (20f,Ban,G,May 17)

Bobby Dazzler 107 (20½f,Per,S,Apr 21)

Bobsbest 108 (21f,Lud,GF,May 15)

Bobsleigh 105 (16f,Plu,S,Jan 19)

Bodakker 107 (20f,Fai,S,Jan 18)

Bodfari Creek 108 (22½f,Fon,GF,Aug 18)

Bodfari Rose 102 (16f,Utt,GF,Jun 29)

Bodfari Signet 109 (22½f,Kel,G,Nov 1)

Bohemian Boy 104 (21f,Plu,S,Jan 19)

Bohill Lad 100 (17f,Nab,GF,Aug 25)

Boing Boing 101 (17f,Ban,G,Nov 28)

Bold Bishop 115 (16½f,San,S,Mar 13)

Boleyknowsbest 105 (18f,Fai,S,Nov 30)

Bolshoi Ballet 107 (16f,Wet,G,Nov 15)

Bolton Barrie 111 (20f,Crl,GF,Oct 10)

Bonnie Parker 100 (21½f,Sed,GS,Jan 13)

Book's Way 108 (26f,Hun,GF,Sep 28)

Boom Or Bust 100 (17f,Tau,G,Mar 15)

Border Tale 102 (17f,Chl,G,Mar 18)

Borora 106 (17f,Her,GF,Oct 2)

Bosham Mill 108 (24½f,Crl,GF,Oct 25)

Boss White 104 (19f,Naa,S,Jan 4)

Bound 114 (16½f,Hun,GS,Dec 11)

Bourbon Manhattan 112 (20f,Ayr,GS,Apr 16)

Bourgeois 109 (16f,Cat,GF,Mar 10)

Bow Strada 110 (21f,Chl,G,Mar 17)

Bracey Run 100 (20f,Wor,GF,Jun 1)

Brackney Boy 103 (24f,Hex,G,May 27)

Bramlynn Brook 108 (21f,Tow,S,Nov 29)

Brave Inca 118 (16f,Nav,S,Dec 14)

Breathtaking View 107 (19½f,Mar,G,Jun 11)

Breeze Home 100 (17½f,Mar,GF,Oct 5)

Breknen Le Noir 111 (16½f,Asc,HY,Jan 31)

Bressbee 102 (16½f,Str,GF,Oct 18)

Brewster 114 (23½f,Hay,S,Feb 14)

Bridge Hotel 106 (20f,Pun,GY,Nov 16)

Brief Promise 101 (16f,Nav,GY,Nov 23)

Bright Green 100 (16½f,Chp,HY,Feb 7)

Brooklyn's Gold 106 (16f,Hay,GS,May 3)

Brush A King 109 (25½f,Cat,G,Feb 6)

Bubble Up 100 (16½f,Str,G,May 16)

Bude 103 (16f,Utt,GF,Jun 5)

Bulougun 124 (19½f,Aut,VS,May 25)

Bunkum 100 (20½f,Utt,S,May 3)

Buoni Island 104 (19f,Naa,F,Jun 18)

Burdens Girl 109 (17f,Her,G,Apr 3)

Burning Shore 105 (16f,Fak,G,Nov 23)

Burnt Out 107 (20f,Fai,Y,Apr 11)

Burntoakboy 106 (20f,Fai,Y,Apr 12)

Bush Park 103 (25½f,Plu,GF,Oct 20)

Bushido 107 (19f,Cat,GS,Jan 15)

Business Traveller 107 (19f,Nby,G,Mar 27)

C'Est Fantastique 101 (16f,Leo,S,Dec 27)

Ca Na Trona 102 (21f,Nby,G,Mar 5)

Cadou Royal 104 (19f,Naa,Y,Mar 7)

Caesar's Palace 107 (24½f,Per,G,May 14)

Calamintha 108 (17f,Ban,G,Nov 28)

Calatagan 106 (17½f,Mar,GS,Dec 4)

Calcot Flyer 102 (22½f,Utt,S,May 3)

Calling Brave 104 (24½f,Ain,G,Nov 22)

Calling Classy 106 (20f,Pun,GY,Nov 16)

Calvic 103 (21f,Tow,S,Nov 29)

Cameron Bridge 103 (20f,Asc,GS,Mar 20)

Cameron Jack 100 (27½f,Sed,GF,Jly 28)

Campaign Trail 109 (25f,Wet,G,Dec 26)

Campanello Blu 105 (16f,Fai,GF,Oct 22)

Camptect 108 (16f,Pun,GY,Nov 15)

Candarli 100 (16½f,Hun,GS,Jan 16)

Cane Brake 109 (18f,Leo,S,Dec 26)

Cape Teal 106 (16f,Fai,GY,Nov 12)

Capriccio 100 (24½f,Per,G,Sep 24)

Capricorn Princess 104 (16½f,Ain,GS,May 16)

Capriolo 102 (22f,Nab,GF,Jun 13)

Captain Flinders 100 (17f,Exe,G,Nov 21)

Captain Hardy 103 (17½f,Fol,G,Mar 3)

Captain Zinzan 113 (20f,Wor,GF,Jun 7)

Caracciola 113 (16½f,Chl,G,Nov 16)

Carapuce 100 (17f,Crl,HY,Feb 11)

Cardenas 110 (16½f,Chl,G,Mar 16)

Cardinal Mark 102 (25½f,Cat,GF,Nov 22)

Caribbean Cove 100 (21f,War,GF,May 10)

Carlovent 104 (20½f,San,G,Apr 24)

Carly Bay 103 (16f,Plu,S,Jan 4)

Carlys Quest 104 (20f,Crl,GS,Apr 18)

Carranduff 100 (16f,Pun,GY,Nov 16)

Carrigeensnowflake 109 (20f,Fai,Y,Apr 13)

Casadei 106 (16f,Fai,GY,Nov 12)

Case Of Poteen 103 (20f,Mus,GF,Jan 23)

Cashel Dancer 105 (17f,Her,GF,Oct 2)

Castanet 105 (21f,Kem,G,Feb 13)

Castle Kevin 112 (24f,Pun,YS,May 2)

Castle Richard 102 (20f,Crl,G,Feb 23)

Castle River 102 (16½f,Chp,GF,Oct 22)

Castlemore 102 (21f,Kem,G,Nov 5)

Castleshane 107 (16f,Wcn,GF,Nov 8)

Catalpa Cargo 109 (20f,Pun,Y,May 3)

Celebration Town 105 (16f,Hay,GF,Oct 23)

Celestial Light 109 (20f,Fai,S,Jan 18)

Celtic Blaze 101 (16½f,San,GS,Jan 3)

Celtic Fame 100 (20f,Fai,GF,Oct 22)

Celtic Grian Ard 105 (20f,Fai,GY,Nov 12)

Celtic Star 103 (20f,Chp,GF,Oct 22)

Cetti's Warbler 108 (16f,Tow,S,Dec 15)

Chabrimal Minster 108 (24½f,Crl,G,Mar 11)

Chamoss Royale 106 (22f,Wcn,GS,Mar 25)

Champagne Harry 111 (25½f,Chl,GS,Dec 13)

Champagne Lil 112 (20f,Wor,GF,Jun 7)

Champagnesupernova 104 (20f,Fai,GF,Oct 22)

Chan Move 101 (19½f,Mar,G,Jun 11)

Chancers Dante 108 (24f,Hex,G,May 10)
Chanticlier 107 (21f,Tow,G,Nov 6)
Charlies Future 103 (22f,Nab,S,Apr 29)
Charlies Memory 106 (16f,Cat,GF,Mar 10)
Chase The Sunset 108 (17f,Chl,GS,Jan 24)
Chateau Rose 105 (24¹⁄2f,Tau,G,Mar 4)
Cheeky Lady 101 (24f,Nav,GF,Nov 9)
Cheler 112 (19¹⁄2f,Aut,VS,May 25)
Chem's Truce 106 (16¹⁄2f,Hun,GS,Dec 11)
Cherokee Bay 102 (19¹⁄2f,Tau,G,Mar 15)
Cherub 113 (17f,Chl,G,Mar 18)
Chevet Girl 106 (16f,Ayr,S,Nov 28)
Chicago Bulls 108 (21f,Tow,G,Nov 6)
Chicuelo 108 (24f,Wor,GF,Aug 2)
Chief Odin 106 (16f,Fai,GY,Nov 12)
Chief Yeoman 114 (17f,Chl,G,Mar 18)
Chirouble 106 (16f,Fai,GY,Nov 12)
Chivalry 105 (16¹⁄2f,Kel,S,Jan 16)
Chivite 110 (17f,Exe,G,Dec 18)
Chockdee 105 (16f,Kem,G,Feb 28)
Ciara's Delight 110 (16f,Nav,S,Dec 20)
Cigarillo 101 (16¹⁄2f,Nby,GF,Dec 10)
Cill Churnain 107 (24f,Wor,GF,Aug 2)
Circle Of Wolves 105 (21f,Plu,G,Nov 3)
Cita Verda 110 (16f,Hay,GS,May 3)
Clarendon 107 (17f,Nab,GF,Jun 3)
Classic Native 107 (20f,Ain,G,Nov 22)
Classic Note 107 (16f,Nav,GF,Jun 22)
Classical Ben 104 (19f,Cat,G,Feb 6)
Classify 105 (18¹⁄2f,Fon,G,Mar 21)
Claude Greengrass 100 (17f,Crl,GS,Nov 2)
Claymore 112 (21f,Chl,G,Mar 17)
Clifton Mist 105 (19¹⁄2f,Tau,GF,Nov 27)
Cliquey 103 (19f,Str,GF,Mar 15)
Cloudy Grey 114 (16¹⁄2f,Asc,S,Jan 10)
Clounties Hill 111 (20f,Leo,Y,Jan 25)
Coccinelle 105 (22f,Nav,S,Dec 20)
Coctail Lady 101 (16¹⁄2f,Str,G,Jly 26)
Code Sign 102 (16f,Wor,G,May 10)
Cody 101 (24¹⁄2f,Tau,G,Apr 1)
Collectedcoppers 102 (16f,Pun,Y,Dec 6)
Collier County 111 (19f,Naa,S,Jan 24)
Collier Hill 111 (16¹⁄2f,Kel,S,Dec 1)
Colonel Frank 101 (19f,Nby,GF,Nov 12)
Colonel Monroe 113 (24f,Pun,GY,May 1)
Colorado Falls 103 (16¹⁄2f,Kel,S,Jan 16)
Colourful Life 113 (20f,Ncs,GS,Feb 21)
Columba 107 (16f,Leo,S,Jan 11)
Columbus 117 (24f,Pun,YS,May 2)
Comfortable Call 104 (19¹⁄2f,Mar,G,Jun 11)
Commanche Court 116 (24f,Pun,GY,May 1)
Commanche Hero 102 (24f,Wor,GF,Sep 14)
Commercial Flyer 102 (19f,Exe,S,Feb 2)
Commonchero 113 (16f,Pun,GY,Nov 15)
Commonwealth 105 (17¹⁄2f,Crt,G,May 24)
Comply Or Die 115 (25¹⁄2f,Chl,GS,Dec 13)
Compton Commander 101 (21f,Lud,G,Apr 8)
Confey Lass 104 (20f,Fai,GY,Feb 28)
Conroy 102 (16¹⁄2f,Hun,GF,May 29)
Constantine 103 (17¹⁄2f,Fol,HY,Jan 20)
Contraband 113 (17f,Tau,GF,Nov 27)
Control Man 115 (20¹⁄2f,San,S,Mar 13)
Coogans Bluff 100 (16f,Pun,GY,Nov 16)
Cool Roxy 108 (16f,Fak,G,Oct 24)
Cool Spice 111 (17f,Chl,GS,Jan 24)
Cooling Off 100 (20f,Fak,GF,May 7)
Copeland 118 (17f,Chl,G,Mar 18)
Copplestone 103 (17¹⁄2f,Crt,G,Aug 23)

Copsale Lad 106 (21¹⁄2f,Chl,GF,Apr 14)
Corbie Lynn 103 (22f,Ayr,G,Nov 16)
Cordilla 101 (20¹⁄2f,Per,GS,Apr 23)
Cornish Rebel 122 (21f,Nby,GS,Dec 29)
Corrage 106 (22f,Nab,G,Jly 30)
Corrib Boy 112 (16f,Naa,Y,Mar 7)
Corroboree 104 (16f,Kem,G,Nov 5)
Corrycroar 109 (20f,Fai,Y,Apr 13)
Corskeagh Thunder 106 (20f,Pun,GY,Nov 16)
Cosmic Case 112 (17¹⁄2f,Mar,GF,Jly 19)
Cosmic Ranger 100 (17¹⁄2f,Crt,G,May 26)
Cosmocrat 106 (16f,Utt,HY,Jan 10)
Cotopaxi 103 (21f,Kem,G,Jan 17)
Count Campioni 108 (24¹⁄2f,Nby,GS,Nov 29)
Count Fosco 102 (16¹⁄2f,Kel,G,Apr 5)
Count Tony 105 (22¹⁄2f,Fon,G,Dec 9)
Countess Camilla 109 (22f,Hay,HY,Jan 24)
Court Champagne 105 (20¹⁄2f,Utt,S,May 21)
Court Of Justice 107 (16f,Lei,S,Jan 13)
Court Shareef 119 (21f,Chl,G,Mar 17)
Covent Garden 102 (22f,San,GS,Dec 6)
Cowboyboots 103 (24f,Chl,G,Apr 15)
Craobh Rua 108 (16f,Pun,GY,Nov 15)
Crazy Horse 107 (23¹⁄2f,Hay,GS,May 3)
Creon 111 (25¹⁄2f,Chl,G,Mar 16)
Criaire Princess 102 (24f,Fai,S,Jan 18)
Crimson Dancer 107 (16f,Fak,GS,Jan 21)
Crimson Flower 105 (16f,Fai,Y,Apr 13)
Cristoforo 105 (16f,Kem,G,Nov 19)
Cristophe 101 (24f,Wor,GS,Apr 21)
Crocadee 101 (21f,Kem,G,Feb 28)
Croix De Guerre 107 (20f,Fon,GF,Mar 8)
Cromer Pier 100 (19¹⁄2f,Her,GF,May 26)
Cronin's Boy 114 (16f,Leo,S,Jan 11)
Crooked Mile 110 (16f,Fai,S,Nov 29)
Crystal D'Ainay 128 (20¹⁄2f,Chl,GS,Jan 24)
Crystal Gift 111 (20¹⁄2f,Hex,S,Apr 4)
Culcabock 107 (16f,Ayr,G,Nov 16)
Cullian 102 (16f,Wcn,G,Apr 4)
Cumbrian Knight 110 (16f,Wet,GS,Dec 27)
Cupla Cairde 107 (16f,Naa,S,Jan 24)
Curtistown 106 (16f,Fai,GY,Nov 12)
Curzon Ridge 106 (16f,Fai,GY,Nov 12)
Cush Jewel 105 (26f,Hun,GF,Sep 28)
Cyanara 103 (24¹⁄2f,Tau,GS,Feb 19)
Cyborg De Sou 108 (16¹⁄2f,Per,GS,Apr 23)
Cyindien 100 (22f,Wcn,G,Apr 18)
Czar Of Peace 106 (20f,Pun,GY,Nov 16)

Dabus 108 (17f,Sed,GF,Sep 5)
Dalaram 104 (16f,Mus,G,Feb 8)
Dalblair 100 (16f,Mus,GF,Jan 7)
Dam The Breeze 109 (24¹⁄2f,Utt,GF,Jly 16)
Dan De Man 101 (16f,Wet,GS,Jan 6)
Danakil 106 (16¹⁄2f,Hun,GF,Nov 11)
Dancer Life 113 (16¹⁄2f,Hun,GF,Nov 11)
Dancing Bay 111 (16¹⁄2f,Hex,S,Dec 17)
Dancing Impact 102 (16f,Naa,S,Jan 4)
Dancing Pearl 107 (16¹⁄2f,Don,G,Mar 5)
Dancing Phantom 101 (16¹⁄2f,Hex,S,Dec 17)
Danehill Miss 101 (16f,Nav,G,Nov 23)
Dangerously Good 109 (21¹⁄2f,Chl,GF,Apr 14)
Daniels Hymn 112 (24f,Pun,YS,May 2)
Danish Decorum 100 (16¹⁄2f,Str,GF,Oct 18)
Dannytom 109 (20f,Fai,Y,Apr 13)
Dante's Banker 106 (22¹⁄2f,Utt,GF,Oct 4)

Dante's Battle 101 (17f,Sed,GF,Sep 5)
Dantes Reef 114 (20f,Fai,GY,Feb 28)
Dantie Boy 109 (20f,Wor,GF,Jun 7)
Dare To Dance 103 (16f,Fai,GY,Feb 28)
Dark Vocation 101 (16f,Nav,GY,Nov 23)
Darnley 103 (16¹⁄2f,Per,GS,May 23)
Dashing Home 113 (16f,Pun,GY,May 1)
Davenport Milenium 109 (20f,Fai,S,Nov 30)
Dawn Invasion 102 (16f,Fai,Y,Apr 12)
Day Du Roy 107 (20f,Hay,GF,Nov 6)
Dbest 101 (16f,Nav,YS,Mar 6)
Dd's Glenalla 105 (21f,Nby,G,Mar 27)
De Blanc 103 (16¹⁄2f,Str,G,Mar 21)
Dealer's Choice 103 (27f,Nab,S,Apr 29)
Deanery Nellie 103 (20f,Fai,Y,Apr 11)
Deano's Beeno 112 (24¹⁄2f,Nby,GS,Nov 29)
Deep Return 105 (22f,Thu,S,Feb 1)
Definate Spectacle 107 (16f,Nav,YS,Mar 6)
Deja Vu 103 (20f,Mus,GF,Jan 7)
Del Trotter 107 (16¹⁄2f,Hex,GF,Nov 7)
Delgany Rose 112 (22f,Fai,Y,Apr 12)
Delphina 103 (16f,Fai,GY,Feb 28)
Demi Beau 116 (17f,Chl,G,Dec 31)
Demophilos 109 (16f,Leo,YS,Dec 28)
Dempsey 107 (16f,Wcn,G,Apr 4)
Denadoon 101 (16f,Nav,G,Nov 23)
Deponey 104 (24f,Nav,GF,Jun 22)
Derawar 112 (22f,Fai,Y,Apr 12)
Derivative 113 (24¹⁄2f,Nby,G,Feb 14)
Derring Bridge 104 (27f,Nab,GF,Jun 28)
Desert Air 105 (16¹⁄2f,San,S,Mar 13)
Designer Label 108 (22f,Nab,GF,Aug 4)
Desperado Queen 113 (20f,Fai,Y,Apr 13)
Detonateur 101 (16f,Plu,GF,Sep 27)
Di's Dilemma 102 (16¹⁄2f,Hun,S,Jan 16)
Diamant Noir 109 (16f,Tow,G,Nov 6)
Diamond Maxine 110 (16f,Fak,G,Nov 23)
Diamond Monroe 102 (24f,Lud,GF,Nov 24)
Diamond Orchid 104 (16¹⁄2f,Str,GF,Mar 15)
Diamonds Will Do 106 (20f,Wor,GF,Aug 23)
Dick Turpin 109 (16f,Utt,G,May 12)
Dickens 103 (16¹⁄2f,San,GS,Jan 3)
Dickensbury Lad 103 (17¹⁄2f,Mar,G,Feb 10)
Dictum 107 (16¹⁄2f,Asc,HY,Jan 31)
Diego Garcia 103 (16f,Fai,Y,Apr 12)
Dilly Stars 106 (16f,Fai,GY,Nov 12)
Dinofelis 105 (16f,Fak,GF,May 18)
Direct Descendant 104 (16¹⁄2f,Hex,GF,Oct 3)
Discovery Walk 106 (16f,Fai,GF,Oct 22)
Distant Prospect 103 (16¹⁄2f,Nby,GF,Dec 10)
Distant Thunder 102 (20¹⁄2f,San,S,Mar 13)
Diversity 101 (26f,Hun,G,Mar 17)
Divet Hill 102 (20f,Mus,GF,Dec 16)
Divinshki 101 (16f,Nav,GY,Nov 23)
Divulge 103 (17¹⁄2f,Mar,GF,Aug 3)
Dix Bay 103 (16¹⁄2f,Hun,GS,Feb 12)
Dixie Melody 105 (20f,Fai,GY,Nov 12)
Dizzy Tart 104 (17f,Nab,GF,May 29)
Dizzy's Dream 110 (16f,Fai,HY,Jan 31)
Do It On Dani 110 (24f,Chp,GF,Nov 8)
Do L'Enfant D'Eau 105 (21f,Chl,GS,Dec 13)
Doberman 103 (17f,Her,GS,May 1)
Doce Vida 100 (17f,Ban,G,Mar 10)
Doe Nal Rua 105 (23f,Wet,G,Dec 6)
Doire-Chrinn 115 (16f,Leo,S,Jan 11)
Dolmur 101 (16f,Nav,GY,Nov 23)
Domenico 105 (16f,Plu,GF,Sep 27)

Don Fernando 103 (17f,Nab,GF,Aug 25)
Don't Sioux Me 111 (17½f,Mar,GF,Jly 19)
Doonaree 109 (20f,Pun,GY,Nov 16)
Double Account 109 (25½f,Chl,G,Dec 12)
Double Blade 105 (17f,Sed,G,Sep 30)
Double Honour 110 (20f,Hay,S,Dec 13)
Double You Cubed 101 (20f,Ayr,GS,Feb 14)
Douceur Des Songes 109 (20f,Wor,GF,Aug 8)
Downpour 111 (16½f,Asc,G,Nov 21)
Downtherefordancin 102 (16½f,San,GS,Dec 6)
Dr Charlie 103 (22f,Wcn,G,Apr 18)
Dr Sharp 101 (18f,Kel,HY,Feb 5)
Dragon's Dream 101 (24½f,Tau,G,Mar 4)
Drakestone 108 (20f,Ban,S,May 2)
Dream Falcon 106 (16f,Lud,GS,Jan 9)
Dromhale Lady 109 (20f,Pun,Y,Dec 7)
Dromlease Express 126 (16f,Leo,S,Jan 11)
Drum Bar 110 (20f,Fai,Y,Apr 13)
Dueling B'Anjiz 100 (20f,Fai,GF,Oct 22)
Dun An Doras 102 (22f,Nab,GF,Jun 13)
Dunbrody Millar 108 (22f,Fai,Y,Apr 12)
Dunlea 102 (24f,Hex,GF,Oct 11)
Dunraven 108 (16f,Fak,GF,May 18)
Dusty Bandit 101 (19½f,Tau,G,Mar 4)
Dusty Too 108 (18½f,Fon,GF,Sep 23)
Dynamic Lifter 104 (27f,Nab,GF,Jun 28)

Eagle Thyme 109 (16f,Fai,GY,Nov 12)
Eagles High 106 (16f,Nav,S,Dec 20)
Earl Sigurd 109 (17f,Ban,G,May 17)
Early Start 107 (16f,Tow,G,Nov 6)
Easibrook Jane 103 (21f,Plu,S,Nov 23)
East Hill 105 (22f,Wcn,GF,Nov 20)
East Tycoon 106 (24f,Ain,GS,Nov 23)
Easter Present 100 (16½f,Hun,S,Jan 16)
Eau Pure 102 (20f,Wor,GS,Apr 21)
Ebinzayd 111 (18f,Kel,G,Apr 30)
Ede'Iff 101 (16f,Wcn,G,Dec 4)
Edge Dancer 101 (16f,Nav,GF,Nov 23)
Edmo Heights 114 (16½f,Ain,GS,May 16)
Edmo Yewkay 103 (16f,Ncs,G,Nov 29)
Ehab 100 (17½f,Fol,GS,Dec 16)
Ei Ei 106 (17½f,Crt,G,Aug 23)
El Vaquero 105 (22f,Wcn,G,Apr 18)
Ela Agori Mou 103 (20f,Mus,G,Feb 8)
Ela D'Argent 102 (17f,Nab,GF,Jun 3)
Ela Jay 101 (17½f,Fol,G,Nov 4)
Ela La Senza 112 (20f,Wor,GF,Jun 18)
Ela Re 114 (17f,Chl,GS,Jan 24)
Elegant Clutter 106 (17f,Ban,G,Oct 27)
Elgar 103 (22½f,Utt,S,May 3)
Elheba 106 (17f,Her,G,Apr 3)
Ella Falls 101 (24f,Wor,GF,Sep 14)
Emanic 102 (16f,War,S,Dec 20)
Emerging Star 100 (16f,Wet,GS,Nov 26)
Emotional Moment 117 (21f,Chl,G,Mar 17)
Emperor Ross 101 (20½f,Hex,G,May 27)
Emphatic 106 (24f,Lud,G,Jan 22)
Encore Cadoudal 104 (16f,Ayr,S,Dec 26)
End Of An Error 109 (24½f,Per,G,Sep 24)
Endless Magic 112 (24f,Pun,YS,May 2)
Ennel Boy 100 (25½f,Chl,G,Nov 15)
Ennistown Lady 106 (16f,Fai,Y,Apr 11)
Enrique 106 (24f,Mar,GF,Aug 30)
Entertainer 109 (20f,Crl,G,Feb 23)
Envious 109 (17½f,Crt,GF,Jly 17)

Epicure 101 (16½f,Per,G,Jun 22)
Eric's Charm 114 (21f,Kem,G,Feb 28)
Erinella 109 (16f,Nav,GF,Jun 22)
Erins Lass 102 (16½f,Chp,GF,May 7)
Eskaddle 109 (20f,Fai,Y,Apr 13)
Essex 109 (16f,Fai,Y,Apr 12)
Euro Bleu 105 (20½f,Utt,S,May 3)
Euro Falcon 100 (20f,Wor,GF,Aug 23)
Euro Leader 107 (16f,Pun,HY,Feb 1)
Euro Warrior 106 (20f,Fai,GY,Nov 12)
Eurolink Rooster 100 (16f,Thu,GY,Dec 21)
Eva So Charming 103 (24f,Lud,G,Apr 8)
Ever Present 106 (20½f,Wet,G,Nov 1)
Excellent Vibes 107 (22½f,Exe,F,Sep 30)
Existential 100 (22½f,Exe,GS,Dec 5)
Exodous 102 (16½f,Asc,G,Feb 21)
Expedient 108 (16f,Pun,GY,Nov 15)
Experimental 101 (16f,Pun,GY,May 1)
Exstoto 104 (24½f,Ayr,G,Nov 15)
Eyze 110 (22½f,Kel,G,Nov 1)

Fabrezan 108 (22½f,Exe,GF,Oct 8)
Factor Fifteen 109 (16f,Mus,GF,Dec 16)
Fadie's Island 100 (16f,Nav,YS,Mar 6)
Fadoudal Du Cochet 101 (16f,Nav,S,Dec 14)
Fair Prospect 102 (23f,Wet,G,May 22)
Fair Question 106 (21½f,Hun,G,Mar 28)
Fairtoto 109 (21f,Tow,F,Oct 8)
Fairwood Present 109 (20f,Fai,Y,Apr 11)
Fairy Skin Maker 103 (16½f,Kel,G,Apr 5)
Falchion 109 (20f,Crl,G,Feb 23)
Famous Grouse 101 (16½f,Str,G,Mar 21)
Fantastic Champion 108 (20f,Fon,GF,Mar 8)
Fantastico 101 (16f,Ncs,G,Nov 14)
Far Pavilions 107 (16½f,Kel,G,May 7)
Far To Fall 105 (24½f,Nby,G,Mar 6)
Fard Du Moulin Mas 107 (22f,San,G,Mar 12)
Farington Lodge 101 (23f,Wet,G,Dec 6)
Farnaheezview 105 (24½f,Nby,G,Mar 6)
Fast Mix 101 (19½f,Tau,GS,Feb 19)
Feanor 107 (16½f,Hex,S,Dec 17)
Feel The Pride 110 (16f,Ayr,S,Nov 28)
Feichead Ghra 105 (16f,Leo,YS,Dec 28)
Felix The Great 105 (16f,Fai,Y,Apr 13)
Fencote 103 (16½f,Kel,G,Apr 5)
Fenix 113 (16½f,San,S,Mar 13)
Field Marshal 109 (18f,Leo,S,Dec 26)
Fiery Peace 101 (19½f,Her,GF,Jun 11)
Fifteen Reds 100 (24f,Hex,G,May 10)
Fifty Franks 100 (20f,Crl,G,Apr 10)
Figaro Du Rocher 106 (17f,Exe,GS,Mar 23)
Finians Ivy 112 (20f,Fai,GY,Feb 28)
Fiolino 102 (24f,Hex,G,May 10)
Firey Steel 106 (24f,Nav,GY,Nov 23)
First Ballot 110 (16f,Wet,F,Oct 15)
First Diploma 109 (16f,Fai,S,Dec 13)
Fishki's Lad 107 (22½f,Kel,G,Nov 1)
Fit The Cove 100 (16f,Pun,GY,Nov 16)
Fiza 106 (16f,Fai,GY,Nov 12)
Flake 103 (17f,Ban,G,Nov 28)
Flame Creek 114 (16f,Leo,Y,Dec 29)
Flaming Cheek 105 (16½f,Hun,GF,Nov 11)
Fleet Street 111 (16½f,Chl,G,Mar 16)
Flight Command 100 (20f,Ban,GS,Apr 17)
Florida Coast 111 (20f,Fai,S,Nov 30)
Flower Hunter 103 (24f,Nav,GF,Jun 22)
Flower Of Pitcur 104 (17f,Her,GS,Feb 15)
Fly Kicker 103 (16f,Wet,G,Nov 15)

Flying Spirit 105 (18½f,Fon,GF,Aug 22)
Flyoff 103 (16½f,Hun,GF,Oct 9)
Fnan 116 (24f,Pun,GY,May 1)
Foly Pleasant 111 (21f,Chl,G,Mar 17)
Fontanesi 106 (18½f,Fon,G,Apr 7)
Fool On The Hill 111 (16½f,Ain,G,Apr 2)
Fools Rush In 101 (16f,Fai,GY,Feb 28)
Football Crazy 104 (19½f,Her,GF,Mar 9)
For Your Ears Only 102 (16½f,Kel,G,Apr 5)
Forbearing 102 (16f,War,GS,Jan 10)
Foreman 113 (16½f,Chl,G,Mar 16)
Forest Ivory 103 (24½f,Nby,G,Feb 14)
Forest Tune 103 (17f,Her,GS,Feb 15)
Forever Dream 108 (19f,Nby,GF,Dec 10)
Forever Eyesofblue 101 (24½f,Crl,HY,Mar 21)
Forget The Past 111 (20f,Fai,Y,Apr 13)
Formal Bid 110 (20f,Pun,GY,Apr 29)
Fortunate Dave 108 (20½f,Hun,G,Mar 6)
Forzacurity 106 (17f,Her,GS,Feb 15)
Fota Island 111 (16½f,Chl,G,Mar 16)
Fountain Bank 100 (22½f,Str,GF,Jly 13)
Fountain Hill 110 (21f,Nby,G,Mar 5)
Francys Fancy 105 (16f,Fai,Y,Apr 13)
Fred's In The Know 100 (20f,Hay,S,Dec 13)
Frederic Forever 100 (16½f,Asc,G,Nov 21)
Free Quotation 101 (24f,Pun,Y,May 3)
Free Return 102 (19f,Nby,GF,Nov 12)
Freiwind 108 (16f,Pun,GY,Nov 15)
French Mannequin 107 (17f,Exe,GS,Jan 20)
French Tune 101 (17f,Sed,GF,Aug 8)
Friedhelmo 105 (16f,Mus,G,Feb 8)
Fromragstoriches 106 (24½f,Crl,G,Mar 11)
Frontier 100 (17f,Tau,S,Feb 3)
Full House 110 (16½f,Asc,G,Feb 21)
Fullards 113 (22f,Hay,G,Jan 10)
Fundamental 108 (16½f,Ain,G,Apr 3)
Fundamentalist 115 (21f,Chl,G,Mar 17)

G V A Ireland 111 (20f,Pun,Y,Dec 7)
Gabla 101 (16½f,Per,G,Sep 25)
Gabor 102 (16½f,Hun,GF,Nov 11)
Galaxy Sam 101 (24½f,Nby,GS,Mar 26)
Galey River 102 (16½f,Hun,GF,Mar 17)
Galileo 111 (21f,Chl,G,Mar 17)
Gallant Hero 100 (16½f,Ain,G,Oct 26)
Galwaybay Stan 101 (22½f,Fol,HY,Jan 2)
Gan Eagla 107 (16½f,Hun,GF,Nov 11)
Gandon 103 (17f,Nab,GF,Jun 13)
Gaora Bridge 105 (16f,Wcn,G,Apr 4)
Garde Champetre 113 (16½f,San,GS,Jan 3)
Gardor 101 (16½f,Kel,G,May 21)
Gargoyle Girl 105 (16½f,Per,G,Sep 25)
Garw Valley 102 (16f,Utt,GF,Sep 7)
Gary's Pimpernel 103 (16½f,Per,GS,Apr 23)
Gazump 101 (21f,Lud,G,Apr 8)
Gebora 106 (19½f,Tau,GF,Nov 27)
Gemster 106 (24½f,Tau,GS,Feb 19)
General Cloney 105 (16f,Fai,Y,Apr 13)
General Duroc 105 (24f,Ncs,HY,Mar 20)
General Gossip 100 (22½f,Utt,GS,Nov 27)
Generous Ways 101 (17f,Exe,G,Mar 9)
Gentle Beau 101 (19f,Exe,G,Mar 9)
Georges Girl 124 (16f,Leo,S,Jan 11)
Geos 123 (16½f,Nby,G,Feb 14)
Geri Roulette 103 (16f,Ncs,HY,Jan 21)
Gielgud 104 (21½f,Sth,GF,Oct 11)
Gigs Bounty 100 (16f,Utt,GF,Oct 15)
Gilou 103 (16½f,Hex,GF,Oct 11)
Gimme Shelter 101 (20f,Ncs,G,Nov 14)

Gimmick 112 (16f,Wet,F,Oct 15)
Gin Palace 110 (16½f,San,S,Mar 13)
Gingerbread House 107 (20f,Ayr,GS,Apr 16)
Giuliani 101 (23f,Wet,G,Apr 25)
Glacial Evening 109 (23f,Wet,S,Feb 7)
Glacial Sunset 104 (20½f,San,G,Apr 24)
Glen Warrior 111 (24½f,Per,G,May 14)
Glenbar 105 (24f,Nav,GY,Nov 23)
Glencoyle 105 (19f,Nby,G,Mar 27)
Glendamah 101 (17f,Sed,S,May 17)
Glenelly Gale 101 (16f,Leo,YS,Dec 28)
Glenmore Boy 103 (16f,Nav,YS,Mar 6)
Glenmoss Tara 108 (16f,Ayr,S,Nov 28)
Glenogue 108 (21f,Nby,G,Mar 27)
Glynn Dingle 101 (20f,Fai,Y,Apr 12)
Go Lassie Go 100 (16f,Pun,GY,Nov 16)
Goblet Of Fire 111 (16½f,Asc,S,Nov 22)
Gods Token 111 (16½f,San,GS,Dec 5)
Going Global 109 (16½f,Asc,G,Nov 21)
Gola Supreme 100 (24½f,Tau,S,Feb 3)
Goldbrook 113 (17f,Exe,G,Dec 18)
Golden Cross 117 (16f,Pun,GY,May 1)
Golden Crusader 106 (16f,Lud,G,May 5)
Golden Thunderbolt 101 (17f,Sed,G,Mar 30)
Golden Triangle 105 (16f,Fai,S,Nov 29)
Golfagent 100 (19½f,Tau,G,Mar 15)
Gone Dancing 101 (16f,Nav,GY,Nov 23)
Gone Far 102 (17f,Chl,G,Dec 31)
Gone No More 103 (16f,Naa,G,Aug 4)
Gone Too Far 101 (16½f,Chl,G,Nov 15)
Good Fortune 109 (20f,Fai,Y,Apr 13)
Good Lord Murphy 102 (26f,Her,GS,Mar 22)
Good Thyne Guy 101 (22½f,Exe,G,Dec 18)
Goodtimelady 110 (24½f,Tau,GS,Feb 19)
Gormans Best 102 (16f,Nav,S,Dec 20)
Gortinard 109 (24f,Nav,GF,Jun 22)
Gospel Song 104 (16f,Ncs,HY,Jan 21)
Governor Daniel 108 (17f,Nab,GF,Jun 3)
Graceful Dancer 104 (24½f,Tau,GS,Feb 19)
Gracilis 101 (17f,Ban,GS,Mar 27)
Gralmano 111 (16f,Hay,GS,May 3)
Grand Finale 104 (16f,Wor,GS,May 2)
Grand Prairie 106 (17½f,Fol,G,Mar 3)
Grand Prompt 102 (19f,Str,G,Jly 26)
Grande Jete 104 (17f,Ban,GS,Dec 17)
Granite Steps 106 (20f,Crl,HY,Mar 21)
Graphic Approach 111 (20½f,Wet,GS,Jan 6)
Grave Doubts 110 (17f,Chl,G,Mar 18)
Gravy Train 109 (16f,Naa,S,Jan 4)
Gray's Eulogy 103 (26f,Hun,G,Mar 6)
Great As Gold 111 (23f,Wet,G,Dec 6)
Great Chaos 101 (16f,Naa,GY,Nov 22)
Great Crusader 108 (27f,Str,G,May 16)
Great Jubilee 100 (20f,Chp,GF,Oct 22)
Great Love 102 (21½f,Aut,VS,May 25)
Green Belt Flyer 113 (16f,Nav,GF,Nov 9)
Green Go 102 (20f,Ban,G,Aug 1)
Green Tango 102 (16½f,Hun,S,Jan 16)
Greenfield 100 (16f,Wcn,G,Feb 12)
Greenfort Brave 109 (20f,Fai,Y,Apr 13)
Greenhall Rambler 108 (20f,Fai,Y,Apr 11)
Greenhope 111 (17f,Chl,G,Mar 18)
Greensmith Lane 107 (20f,Fon,G,Oct 5)
Gregorian 104 (17f,Nab,GF,Jun 3)
Grey Abbey 114 (25½f,Cat,G,Feb 6)
Grey Brother 103 (19f,Exe,G,Mar 9)
Grey Report 115 (21f,Nby,GS,Dec 29)
Grimshaw 100 (19½f,Her,GF,Sep 10)
Ground Ball 114 (16f,Pun,GY,Nov 15)
Gumley Gale 102 (22f,Wcn,S,Jan 17)

Guru 108 (16½f,Nby,GS,Nov 30)

Haikal 101 (24f,Wor,GF,Sep 14)
Hallyards Gael 111 (22½f,Kel,G,Nov 1)
Hamadeenah 105 (17f,Her,GF,Jun 11)
Hand Inn Hand 110 (20f,Ain,GS,Nov 23)
Handy Money 101 (19½f,Mar,G,May 24)
Hanover Square 102 (24½f,Nby,S,Jan 14)
Happy Hussar 112 (19f,Exe,GF,Oct 8)
Harapour 102 (19f,Exe,S,Feb 2)
Harbour Bay 101 (16f,Nav,GY,Nov 23)
Harbour Pilot 105 (24f,Nav,GY,Nov 23)
Harbour View 110 (20f,Fai,HY,Jan 31)
Harchibald 117 (17f,Chl,G,Mar 18)
Hard Shoulder 103 (16f,Fai,GY,Feb 28)
Hard Winter 107 (20f,Leo,Y,Dec 29)
Hardrada 106 (20f,Pun,GY,Nov 16)
Hardy Duckett 111 (16f,Naa,Y,Mar 7)
Hardy Eustace 126 (20½f,Chl,GS,Jan 24)
Harmony Hall 102 (16f,Wor,G,Jly 23)
Harpoon Harry 111 (20f,Ncs,S,Mar 13)
Harry Collins 101 (22½f,Fol,GS,Feb 17)
Harry Husyan 107 (19f,Naa,F,Jun 18)
Harry The Ear 112 (16f,Naa,G,Aug 4)
Hasty Prince 116 (16f,Hay,G,Jan 10)
Hatsnall 100 (22½f,Utt,S,May 3)
Hawadeth 118 (17f,Chl,G,Mar 18)
Hawaiian Son 105 (24f,Nav,GY,Nov 23)
Hawk's Landing 106 (22½f,Str,G,Oct 30)
Hawkes Run 104 (24f,Wor,G,May 10)
Hawthorn Prince 101 (20½f,Sth,GF,Dec 5)
Hayaain 100 (24½f,Ayr,GS,Nov 28)
Haydens Field 106 (20½f,Utt,S,May 3)
Haystacks 105 (22f,Crt,GS,May 28)
He's The Biz 101 (24½f,Tau,G,Dec 11)
He's The Boss 100 (20f,Asc,G,Nov 21)
Hell-Of-A-Shindy 102 (20f,Fon,G,Oct 5)
Henbridge 108 (17f,Nab,GF,Jun 13)
Henrietta 105 (21f,Tow,GS,Nov 18)
Henry Hammond 102 (19f,Naa,Y,Mar 7)
Henry Pearson 100 (17f,Sed,GS,Jan 13)
Heron's Ghyll 105 (17f,Chl,G,Dec 31)
Hersov 103 (22f,San,GS,Dec 6)
Hever Golf Glory 101 (19½f,Mar,G,Jun 11)
Hey Ref 100 (20f,Hay,G,Feb 28)
Hi Cloy 109 (20f,Pun,YS,May 2)
Hi Fi 108 (17f,Exe,GS,Mar 23)
Hickleton Dream 100 (16½f,Hex,GF,Oct 3)
Hidden Bounty 117 (20f,Ncs,GS,Feb 21)
Hidden Smile 105 (16f,Utt,GF,Jly 16)
High Drama 110 (22½f,Exe,G,Apr 30)
High Paddy 102 (16f,Plu,GS,Mar 15)
High Prospect 105 (16f,Fai,Y,Apr 13)
High Rank 106 (21f,War,GS,Mar 14)
Highland Tracker 101 (21½f,Sed,G,Oct 29)
Hill Port 105 (16f,Leo,S,Feb 8)
Hill Track 102 (17f,Sed,G,Mar 30)
Hilltime 100 (17f,Sed,GF,Aug 8)
Hirvine 106 (24½f,Kem,GS,Feb 2)
His Nibs 111 (25½f,Chl,G,Dec 12)
His Song 101 (24f,Chp,S,Dec 27)
Ho Pang Yau 103 (16f,Wet,G,Apr 25)
Hoh Viss 106 (16½f,San,GS,Feb 19)
Holland Park 108 (20½f,San,S,Mar 13)
Hollows Mill 108 (20f,Mus,GF,Dec 16)
Hollows Mist 100 (16½f,Kel,G,Apr 5)
Holy Orders 122 (24f,Pun,GY,May 1)
Home Office 111 (16f,Naa,G,Aug 4)
Homeleigh Mooncoin 100 (22f,Wcn,G,Dec 26)
Honest Yer Honour 108 (18f,Leo,S,Dec 26)

Honey's Gift 101 (16f,War,G,Mar 14)
Honeybunch 106 (19f,Naa,S,Jan 4)
Hopbine 105 (22f,Wcn,S,Jan 17)
Hope Diamond 101 (20f,Crl,GF,Oct 10)
Hope Sound 102 (16f,Ncs,G,Nov 29)
Horner Rocks 110 (20f,Pun,GY,Apr 29)
Hors La Loi 115 (16½f,Str,GF,Jly 13)
Hot Produxion 110 (20f,Wor,GF,Jun 7)
Hot Shots 103 (16f,Wcn,G,Mar 11)
Houghton Bay 106 (22f,San,G,Mar 12)
Hour Of Need 105 (16f,Fai,S,Dec 13)
Howle Hill 111 (17f,Chl,G,Mar 18)
Howrwenow 105 (24½f,Kem,G,Feb 13)
Hugo De Perro 109 (22½f,Kel,G,May 22)
Hulysse Royal 101 (20½f,San,G,Apr 24)
Hunters Bar 110 (16f,Pun,GY,Nov 16)
Hunters Creek 108 (20f,Ncs,G,Nov 14)
Hunting Yuppie 101 (21f,Lud,GS,Mar 25)
Hurry Bob 112 (24f,Pun,YS,May 2)
Hutch 104 (17f,Ban,GS,Mar 27)
Hyderabad 105 (24f,Nav,GY,Nov 23)

I D Technology 101 (16f,Plu,G,Apr 12)
I Got Rhythm 110 (16f,Wet,GS,Dec 27)
I'Ll Fly 101 (16½f,Hun,G,Mar 17)
I'Lleveit Tou 101 (22½f,Fol,HY,Jan 2)
Icare D'Oudairies 104 (21f,Chl,G,Nov 14)
Ichi Beau 105 (20½f,Hex,GF,Jun 20)
Icy River 110 (20f,Crl,GF,Oct 10)
Idaho D'Ox 106 (20½f,San,G,Apr 24)
Ideal Du Bois Beury 101 (16f,Mus,F,Feb 29)
Idole First 100 (19f,Str,G,Jly 31)
Igloo D'Estruval 103 (23f,Lin,G,Nov 11)
Ikdam Melody 106 (24f,Nav,GF,Jun 22)
Il Cavaliere 104 (21f,Kem,G,Dec 26)
Ilabon 103 (20½f,Lei,S,Jan 27)
Ile Michel 107 (16½f,Str,GF,Oct 18)
Iloveturtle 100 (17½f,Mar,G,Mar 28)
Imazulutoo 111 (16f,Fai,S,Nov 29)
Imperative 100 (16½f,Hun,GF,Nov 2)
Imperial De Thaix 116 (25½f,Chl,G,Dec 12)
Imperial Rocket 102 (16½f,Str,G,Jly 31)
Impish Jude 104 (16f,Lei,G,Dec 4)
Impressive Way 108 (16f,Pun,GY,Nov 15)
Imtihan 105 (22½f,Str,G,Mar 21)
In Contrast 111 (16f,Hay,GS,May 3)
In Good Faith 103 (19f,Cat,GS,Jan 15)
In The Forge 111 (16f,Pun,YS,May 2)
In The Frame 112 (16f,Wcn,G,Apr 18)
Inca Trail 107 (21f,Chl,G,Mar 17)
Inching Closer 103 (25½f,Chl,G,Mar 16)
Inchinnan 100 (16f,Wcn,S,Jan 8)
Indalo Grey 102 (16f,Pun,GY,May 1)
Indeed 105 (20½f,San,G,Apr 24)
Indeed To Goodness 106 (24f,Chp,S,Dec 27)
Indian Beat 105 (17f,Nab,GF,Jun 13)
Indian Solitaire 101 (17f,Sed,GS,Feb 10)
Indian Star 103 (17f,Nab,GF,Aug 12)
Indian Sun 105 (17f,Nab,G,Apr 10)
Inexorable 106 (24f,Fai,S,Jan 18)
Inglis Drever 115 (20½f,San,GS,Dec 5)
Ingres 100 (16f,Fai,Y,Apr 12)
Inigo Jones 105 (16f,Lei,S,Feb 18)
Inn Antique 102 (16½f,Hex,S,Dec 17)
Innisfree 109 (20f,Fai,Y,Apr 13)
Intersky Falcon 116 (16f,Ncs,G,Nov 29)
Intersky Native 105 (20f,Crl,GS,Apr 18)
Intox Iii 100 (17f,Nab,GF,Jun 21)
Intymcginty 100 (24½f,Nby,GS,Mar 26)
Investor Relations 102 (16f,Plu,GF,Sep 27)
Invitado 101 (17f,Sed,GF,Sep 5)
Iorana 105 (16f,Wor,GS,May 2)

Ireland's Eye 109 (20½f,Hex,S,Apr 4)
Iris's Gift 116 (23½f,Hay,S,Feb 14)
Irish Distinction 108 (16f,Wet,G,May 29)
Irish Flight 104 (16f,Plu,S,Jan 19)
Irish Sea 105 (20f,Wor,GF,Aug 8)
Irishkawa Bellevue 104 (22f,Wcn,G,Apr 18)
Isard III 106 (24f,Chl,G,Apr 15)
Isio 111 (16½f,San,GS,Dec 6)
Island Sound 107 (16½f,Str,GF,Sep 6)
Island Stream 110 (17f,Chl,GS,Jan 24)
Istaralla 100 (16f,Pun,GY,Nov 16)
It Was'Nt Me 105 (24f,Nav,GY,Nov 23)
It's Harry 105 (20½f,Wet,G,Dec 26)
It's Wallace 109 (20½f,Hun,G,Mar 6)
Italian Counsel 116 (17½f,Mar,GF,Jly 19)
Itcanbedone Again 103 (16f,Utt,GF,Jun 29)
Itch 102 (16f,Fak,GF,May 18)
Its Wallace Jnr 103 (18½f,Fon,G,Oct 5)
Itsallgreektome 109 (20f,Fai,Y,Apr 13)
Izmir 106 (16f,Naa,G,Aug 4)

Jaboune 113 (16½f,Asc,GF,Nov 1)
Jaccout 104 (22½f,Kel,G,Nov 1)
Jacdor 100 (20½f,Utt,S,May 3)
Jack Cousteau 108 (16f,Pun,GY,Nov 15)
Jack Dawson 106 (16½f,Ain,G,Apr 3)
Jack High 113 (20f,Pun,YS,May 2)
Jack Martin 109 (20f,Ayr,GS,Apr 16)
Jack Pot II 104 (20f,Crl,HY,Nov 27)
Jackie Cullen 111 (16f,Fai,S,Nov 29)
Jacks Craic 101 (16½f,Don,G,Jan 19)
Jahash 112 (24f,Pun,YS,May 2)
Jake Black 102 (16f,Ncs,G,Nov 14)
Jake The Jumper 101 (26f,Hun,G,Mar 17)
Jallastep 110 (20f,Ayr,GF,Mar 13)
Jaloux D'Estruval 102 (23f,Lin,GS,Apr 4)
Jamaican Flight 103 (19½f,Mar,GF,Aug 3)
Jaseur 106 (26f,Crt,G,May 26)
Javelin 111 (20½f,Wet,G,Nov 1)
Jawwala 102 (19½f,Don,GF,Nov 30)
Jazz D'Estruval 112 (24½f,Per,G,May 14)
Jeff De Chalamont 112 (24f,Pun,YS,May 2)
Jewel Of India 100 (16f,Plu,GF,Oct 20)
Jim 108 (16f,Pun,GY,Nov 15)
Jim Jam Joey 106 (24½f,Nby,S,Jan 14)
Jiran 108 (16f,Pun,GY,Nov 15)
Jivaty 100 (22½f,Fon,G,Feb 22)
Joe Hill 109 (16f,Nav,S,Dec 14)
Joes Edge 105 (20½f,Utt,GS,Dec 26)
John Magical 101 (16f,Naa,GY,Nov 22)
Johnjoe's Express 105 (16f,Fai,Y,Apr 13)
Johnny Oscar 101 (17½f,Crt,GS,May 28)
Johnston's Art 107 (24½f,Utt,GF,Jly 16)
Joint Authority 100 (18f,Kel,G,Nov 1)
Jolika 102 (20f,Ayr,GS,Feb 14)
Jolly Moonbeam 104 (16f,Pun,GY,May 1)
Jolly Sharp 111 (20f,Fai,GY,Feb 28)
Jollyolly 111 (20½f,Utt,GF,Oct 4)
Joly Bey 114 (24½f,Nby,G,Feb 14)
Jomasoma 111 (20f,Fai,Y,Apr 13)
Jonalton 105 (22½f,Str,G,Jly 31)
Jonanaud 108 (20f,Chp,HY,Feb 7)
Jordan's Ridge 101 (21½f,Sed,GS,Jan 13)
Joseph Vernet 113 (20f,Pun,Y,Dec 7)
Joshua's Bay 106 (23f,Lin,G,Nov 11)
Joueur D'Estruval 107 (20f,Pun,YS,May

2)
Joyeux Royal 108 (24f,Chp,S,Dec 27)
Jug Of Punch 101 (21f,Lud,G,Apr 8)
Juralan 102 (16½f,Don,G,Jan 19)
Just In Time 111 (19f,Exe,GF,Oct 8)
Just Kate 103 (21f,Lud,G,Apr 8)
Just Maybe 113 (25½f,Cat,G,Feb 6)
Just Midas 106 (16f,Utt,GF,Jly 16)
Just Sal 108 (16½f,Hex,G,Mar 18)
Just Superb 107 (16f,War,GS,Jan 10)
Justupyourstreet 105 (16½f,Per,G,Jun 6)

Kadara 108 (24½f,Kem,G,Feb 28)
Kadiskar 105 (20f,Nav,S,Dec 14)
Kadlass 105 (17f,Her,GS,May 1)
Kadoun 102 (20f,Ban,GS,Apr 17)
Kadount 105 (16f,Hay,GS,Nov 16)
Kahuna 111 (16f,Pun,HY,Feb 1)
Kaikovra 107 (16½f,Str,GF,Sep 6)
Kaki Crazy 109 (20½f,Wet,G,May 22)
Kald River 103 (16f,Fai,GY,Feb 28)
Kali Des Obeaux 102 (22½f,Str,G,Mar 21)
Kalinnjar 102 (16f,Naa,G,Aug 4)
Kaoutchou 104 (20f,Leo,Y,Dec 29)
Kaparolo 105 (18½f,Fon,G,Mar 21)
Kapok 104 (16f,Pun,GY,May 1)
Karatchi 101 (24½f,Ayr,GS,Nov 28)
Karinga City 100 (17f,Exe,G,Apr 6)
Karju 100 (16½f,Per,G,Jly 3)
Karly Flight 106 (21½f,Aut,VS,May 25)
Kasthari 104 (20f,Ncs,S,Mar 13)
Kathakali 104 (16f,Wor,G,Jly 16)
Kathella 101 (22f,Nab,GF,Aug 4)
Katiki 100 (21½f,Aut,VS,May 25)
Katmandu 101 (20f,Ncs,HY,Feb 4)
Katoune 120 (19½f,Aut,VS,May 25)
Kavi 100 (16½f,Str,G,Jly 26)
Kedge Anchor Man 100 (22½f,Exe,G,Apr 30)
Keepatem 109 (25½f,Chl,G,Mar 16)
Keepers Mead 104 (25½f,Chl,GS,Dec 13)
Keepthedreamalive 104 (21f,Plu,G,Mar 1)
Kelly's Craft 108 (16f,Pun,GY,Nov 15)
Kelnik Glory 102 (24f,Wor,GF,Jly 9)
Kelrev 101 (21f,Plu,S,Feb 16)
Ken Scott 101 (18½f,Fon,G,Mar 21)
Ken'tucky 109 (24f,Lud,G,Jan 22)
Kentford Grebe 109 (21f,Nby,G,Mar 27)
Kentucky Blue 101 (16f,Wet,GS,Nov 26)
Kercabellec 105 (16f,War,G,Nov 25)
Kerry Lads 110 (24½f,Crl,HY,Mar 21)
Kety Star 102 (16½f,Chp,GF,May 7)
Kevins View 100 (20f,Fai,GF,Oct 22)
Khaladjistan 105 (17f,Her,GF,Mar 9)
Kharak 112 (20f,Crl,G,Feb 23)
Khaysar 104 (17f,Her,G,Apr 3)
Kidithou 104 (27½f,Sed,G,Dec 26)
Kilbeggan Lad 110 (16f,Naa,S,Jan 4)
Kilcullen Girl 108 (16f,Fai,GY,Nov 12)
Kildare 111 (20f,Leo,Y,Jan 25)
Kildee Lass 100 (17f,Exe,GS,Jan 20)
Killalongford 100 (24f,Lud,GF,Nov 24)
Killers Fury 100 (24½f,Kem,G,Mar 7)
Kiltulaa Lad 102 (17½f,Mar,G,Mar 28)
Kim Fontaine 115 (18f,Leo,S,Feb 8)
Kim Fontenail 106 (17f,Her,GS,Jan 7)
Kimbambo 101 (16f,Ncs,GS,Feb 21)
Kimberley 107 (24f,Chp,S,Dec 27)
Kimoe Warrior 106 (17½f,Mar,GF,May 24)
Kind Word 106 (21f,Lud,GF,May 15)
King Carew 105 (16f,Fai,Y,Apr 13)
King Of Arms 105 (24f,Hex,S,Dec 17)
King Of The Arctic 106 (16½f,Kel,G,Apr 5)

King Revo 108 (16½f,Ain,G,Apr 1)
King Solomon 108 (17f,Ban,GS,Mar 27)
King's Equerry 107 (24f,Nav,GY,Nov 23)
Kingkohler 103 (16f,Mus,GF,Jan 7)
Kings Orchard 107 (20f,Pun,YS,May 2)
Kippanour 109 (26f,Hun,GF,Sep 28)
Kirisnippa 101 (22½f,Exe,GF,Oct 8)
Kitty Star 104 (20f,Pun,Y,Dec 7)
Kivotos 114 (20f,Ncs,GS,Feb 21)
Klakos 119 (19½f,Aut,VS,May 25)
Kniaz 105 (16f,Fai,Y,Apr 13)
Knightsbridge King 105 (17f,Her,GS,May 1)
Knockdoo 107 (24½f,Per,G,May 14)
Knockrigg 100 (16f,Tow,GS,Feb 22)
Kombinacja 108 (16½f,Str,G,May 30)
Konker 105 (16f,Wet,G,Nov 15)
Korelo 116 (21f,Chl,G,Mar 17)
Kristoffersen 105 (16f,Kem,G,Dec 27)
Kylie Time 104 (16½f,Per,GS,Apr 23)
Kymberlya 108 (20f,Wor,GF,Jun 7)

L'Interprete 118 (19½f,Aut,VS,May 25)
L'Orage Lady 101 (16f,Lud,G,Dec 11)
La Luna 107 (22½f,Kel,GF,Oct 18)
La Marette 101 (16f,Tow,GS,Feb 22)
Labelthou 101 (16½f,Asc,S,Jan 10)
Lacdoudal 104 (17f,Exe,G,Apr 6)
Lady Danehill 100 (16f,Pun,GY,Nov 16)
Lady Harriet 101 (16f,Plu,S,Feb 16)
Lady Ward 109 (17f,Nab,GF,Jun 13)
Lafayette 106 (16f,Pun,GY,May 1)
Lago 102 (24½f,Crl,HY,Mar 21)
Lalagune 102 (22f,Wcn,GS,Mar 25)
Lambhill Stakes 103 (24½f,Crl,HY,Mar 21)
Lancashire Lass 101 (24½f,Tau,GF,Nov 27)
Lanmire Gale 105 (20f,Fai,GY,Nov 12)
Lantern Leader 103 (24½f,Ayr,GS,Nov 28)
Lanzlo 107 (17½f,Crt,G,May 24)
Laoch Na Mara 101 (16f,Pun,GY,May 1)
Laouen 109 (18f,Kel,G,May 22)
Larkhill Jo 106 (16f,Pun,Y,Dec 6)
Lasquini Du Moulin 104 (20f,Fai,S,Jan 18)
Latalomne 111 (17½f,Mar,GF,Jly 19)
Late Claim 100 (16f,Kem,G,Feb 13)
Laughing Lesa 102 (16f,Naa,G,Aug 4)
Lazerito 104 (20½f,Fol,GS,Feb 17)
Lazy But Lively 100 (22f,Hay,S,Nov 29)
Lazzaz 105 (17f,Her,GS,May 1)
Le Duc 118 (16½f,Nby,G,Feb 14)
Le Passing 111 (16½f,Asc,S,Jan 10)
Le Royal 105 (20f,Ain,G,Nov 22)
Le-Monde 112 (24f,Pun,YS,May 2)
Leaders Way 105 (24f,Nav,GY,Nov 23)
Learn To Dance 101 (16f,Nav,YS,Mar 6)
Lease 106 (16½f,Per,GF,Aug 16)
Legal Lunch 105 (24f,Lud,G,Jan 22)
Leinster 108 (16f,Pun,GY,Nov 15)
Leith Hill Star 105 (21f,Kem,G,Feb 13)
Leophin Dancer 100 (16f,Fak,G,Oct 24)
Lesdream 102 (19f,Exe,S,Jan 1)
Letitia's Loss 106 (27½f,Sed,G,Dec 26)
Lets Go Dutch 100 (22½f,Exe,G,Apr 30)
Lets Try Again 103 (19f,Naa,F,Jun 18)
Lewis Island 105 (19½f,Her,GF,Mar 9)
Liberty Seeker 107 (17f,Sed,GF,Nov 11)
Lightning Star 101 (17½f,Fol,G,Mar 3)
Lik Wood Power 100 (16½f,Ain,G,Oct 26)
Like A Bee 101 (20f,Fai,Y,Apr 12)
Lilac 100 (16f,Wcn,G,Apr 4)
Limerick Boy 108 (16f,Pun,GY,Apr 29)
Limerick Leader 105 (24½f,Kem,G,Mar 7)

Lincoln Place 104 (19½f,Tau,GF,Nov 27)
Lingo 114 (16½f,San,GS,Jan 3)
Linus 104 (22f,Nab,GF,Sep 3)
Lisa Du Chenet 107 (20f,Fon,G,Jan 26)
Lisa's Dream 104 (20f,Fai,GY,Feb 28)
Listenlads 105 (20f,Fai,GY,Nov 12)
Little Big Horse 100 (23f,Wet,G,May 22)
Little Bud 101 (21f,Plu,G,Mar 1)
Little Docker 105 (16f,Wet,G,Nov 15)
Little Rort 103 (18f,Fai,S,Nov 29)
Little Ross 101 (17½f,Fol,G,Mar 3)
Litzinsky 101 (20f,Ncs,S,Mar 13)
Live Our Dreams 113 (24f,Pun,YS,May 2)
Locksmith 110 (16f,Kem,G,Feb 28)
Lodestar 107 (24f,Wor,G,May 10)
Long Shot 105 (19f,Nby,GF,Nov 12)
Longshanks 107 (22½f,Utt,S,May 3)
Look To The Future 108 (22f,Hay,G,Jan 10)
Loop The Loup 109 (16f,Hay,GS,May 3)
Lord Buckingham 101 (16½f,Nby,GF,Dec 10)
Lord Dal 103 (17f,Exe,GS,Mar 23)
Lord Dundaniel 101 (20f,Hay,G,Feb 28)
Lord Lington 110 (17½f,Fol,GS,Dec 16)
Lord Of Beauty 105 (16f,Kem,G,Dec 27)
Lord Of The Land 108 (17½f,Crt,G,May 24)
Lord Of The Loch 104 (21½f,Sed,G,Apr 12)
Lord Pat 100 (21½f,Sed,G,Apr 12)
Lord Strickland 105 (22½f,Exe,G,Apr 30)
Lord Ville 105 (17f,Exe,F,Sep 30)
Lord York 106 (20½f,Wet,G,May 29)
Lordofourown 109 (20f,Leo,Y,Jan 25)
Lorenzino 106 (24f,Mar,GF,Aug 30)
Lorgnette 107 (26f,Hun,G,Mar 6)
Lorient Express 100 (16f,Plu,S,Jan 19)
Lorraine's Pride 105 (20f,Pun,Y,May 3)
Lotier 101 (19½f,Her,GS,Dec 20)
Lotomore Lad 113 (20f,Fai,HY,Jan 31)
Lotus Des Pictons 107 (24f,Chp,S,Jan 23)
Lough Derg 100 (16f,War,GS,Jan 10)
Loughanelteen 105 (16f,Fai,Y,Apr 13)
Loughinlae 100 (20f,Fai,GF,Oct 22)
Louisville 106 (16f,Fai,GY,Nov 12)
Loulou Nivernais 106 (16f,Fai,GY,Nov 12)
Loup 104 (16f,Hay,GS,Nov 16)
Love Connection 101 (16f,Nav,GY,Nov 23)
Love On Request 105 (16f,Fai,S,Dec 13)
Lowe Go 102 (16f,War,GS,Jan 10)
Lubinas 109 (20f,Wor,GS,Apr 21)
Lucifer Bleu 104 (19½f,Tau,G,Mar 4)
Lucky Duck 107 (16½f,Kel,G,Apr 5)
Lucky Slipper 101 (16f,Fai,GY,Feb 28)
Lustral Du Seuil 106 (16f,Plu,G,Mar 1)
Lynrick Lady 105 (24f,Chp,S,Dec 27)

Maceo 112 (20f,Ayr,GF,Mar 13)
Macnance 107 (17f,Exe,GS,Jan 20)
Macs Joy 124 (16f,Leo,S,Jan 11)
Macs-Bet 108 (16f,Naa,S,Jan 4)
Made In Japan 115 (17f,Chl,G,Mar 18)
Madge Carroll 109 (24½f,Tau,GS,Feb 19)
Magalina 103 (19½f,Tau,G,Mar 15)
Magenko 105 (20f,Crl,HY,Nov 27)
Magenta Rising 103 (17f,Her,GF,Mar 9)
Magic Mistress 104 (17f,Nab,G,Apr 10)
Magical Field 102 (19½f,Don,GF,Nov 30)
Maharbal 105 (16½f,Nby,GF,Dec 10)
Maiden Voyage 108 (20f,Ban,S,May 22)

Maidstone Monument 108 (25½f,Plu,GF,Oct 20)
Maith An Fear 105 (20f,Pun,Y,Dec 7)
Major Burns 105 (16f,Fai,Y,Apr 11)
Major Drive 105 (21½f,Sed,GS,Jan 13)
Major Euro 105 (20½f,San,GS,Feb 19)
Major Shark 103 (19½f,Her,GF,Mar 9)
Majority Verdict 106 (22½f,Utt,S,May 3)
Maldoun 104 (17f,Her,GF,May 13)
Mallory 101 (20f,Ncs,GF,Apr 28)
Mama Jaffa 100 (16f,Nav,YS,Mar 6)
Mambo 105 (16f,Wet,G,Dec 26)
Mamboesque 106 (20f,Hay,GF,Nov 6)
Man From Highworth 104 (16½f,Str,G,Mar 21)
Man O'Mystery 119 (16½f,Nby,G,Feb 14)
Man On The Nile 107 (16f,Fai,S,Dec 13)
Mana-Mou Bay 102 (16½f,Hun,GF,May 29)
Manawanui 102 (17f,Exe,GF,Apr 13)
Mandingo Chief 109 (24½f,Crl,HY,Mar 21)
Mango Catcher 104 (16f,Fai,S,Dec 13)
Manhunter 108 (22½f,Utt,GF,Oct 4)
Maniatis 102 (17f,Ban,GS,Mar 27)
Manly Money 105 (19½f,Her,GS,Dec 20)
Manoram 102 (20f,Wor,G,May 21)
Mansony 101 (16f,Thu,S,Feb 1)
Mantilla 105 (19f,Exe,GF,Oct 8)
Maragun 104 (17½f,Fol,G,Mar 3)
Maraud 109 (26f,Crt,G,May 26)
Mariah Rollins 115 (18f,Leo,S,Feb 8)
Marico 103 (20f,Fon,G,Oct 5)
Marjina 103 (22f,Wcn,GS,Mar 25)
Mark The Begining 106 (16f,Fai,GY,Nov 12)
Mark The Man 103 (16f,Leo,S,Dec 27)
Mark The Shark 105 (16f,Fai,GF,Oct 22)
Marked Man 113 (17f,Ban,G,May 17)
Markino 106 (16f,Fai,GY,Nov 12)
Marrakech 113 (16½f,Asc,S,Nov 22)
Marrel 106 (16½f,Str,GF,Jly 13)
Massenet 106 (22f,Nav,S,Dec 20)
Master Billyboy 104 (20f,Asc,GS,Mar 20)
Master Florian 102 (22f,San,GS,Dec 6)
Master Gatemaker 104 (17½f,Mar,GF,Aug 3)
Master Glow 105 (16f,Fai,GY,Feb 28)
Master Papa 108 (18f,Kel,G,May 22)
Master Ride 100 (19½f,Her,GS,Dec 20)
Master T 103 (16½f,Chl,GF,Oct 29)
Master Trix 112 (20f,Asc,G,Dec 19)
Masters Of War 100 (20½f,Per,GS,Apr 23)
Material World 108 (21f,Nby,G,Mar 27)
Max Time 107 (16f,Nav,S,Feb 15)
Mccracken 104 (16½f,Hun,GS,Feb 12)
Mcgruders Cross 113 (20f,Naa,S,Jan 4)
Meggie's Lad 107 (16f,Tow,G,Oct 30)
Meggies Gamble 111 (19f,Cat,G,Feb 6)
Meldrum Star 108 (20f,Wor,GF,Aug 23)
Meltonian 101 (16f,Tow,GF,Oct 26)
Melusina 100 (18½f,Fon,GF,Aug 25)
Members Only 100 (17f,Tau,S,Feb 3)
Mendosino 102 (18½f,Fon,GS,Feb 9)
Merryvale Man 105 (16f,Ncs,HY,Mar 20)
Metal Detector 105 (20½f,Utt,S,May 3)
Michael Mor 100 (19f,Naa,Y,Mar 7)
Michaels Dream 106 (17f,Sed,GF,Nov 11)
Mickey Campbell 101 (16f,Fai,GY,Feb 28)
Mickey Croke 102 (21f,Plu,GS,Dec 15)
Middlethorpe 112 (16f,Wet,GS,Dec 27)
Midnight Creek 111 (20f,Crl,G,Feb 23)
Mighty Fine 109 (17f,Sed,S,May 17)
Milan King 102 (19½f,Mar,G,Jun 11)
Mildon 107 (17f,Sed,GF,Sep 5)

Mill Emerald 101 (20½f,Utt,HY,May 26)
Millkom Elegance 101 (17f,Sed,G,Oct 29)
Millys Filly 101 (20f,Wor,GF,Aug 2)
Milord Lescribaa 105 (16f,Lei,S,Feb 18)
Mindanao 105 (22½f,Kel,G,Apr 30)
Minivet 106 (19½f,Don,G,Mar 5)
Minster Glory 112 (16f,Lei,GF,Nov 17)
Minstrel Hall 100 (16f,Cat,GF,Mar 10)
Mio Caro 102 (16½f,San,GS,Jan 3)
Mioche D'Estruval 101 (16f,Plu,GS,Dec 15)
Mirant 109 (17f,Nab,GF,May 29)
Mirjan 103 (20½f,Wet,G,Apr 25)
Mirpour 108 (16f,Pun,GY,May 1)
Misbehaviour 100 (17f,Nab,S,Apr 29)
Mishead 103 (17½f,Mar,GF,Aug 3)
Miss Chinchilla 104 (21f,Nby,G,Mar 27)
Miss Cool 103 (25½f,Chl,G,Dec 12)
Miss Lacroix 105 (21f,Lud,GF,May 15)
Mistanoora 110 (22f,San,S,Feb 7)
Mister Arjay 103 (16f,Fak,GS,Mar 19)
Mister Chisum 109 (18f,Kel,G,Apr 30)
Mister Dave'S 103 (23f,Wet,S,Feb 7)
Mister Felix 103 (19½f,Don,G,Jan 19)
Mister Flint 107 (16½f,Per,GF,Apr 23)
Mister McGoldrick 106 (16f,Wet,GF,Oct 31)
Mister Mustard 104 (20f,Hay,GS,Nov 16)
Mister Webb 104 (22f,Nab,GF,Jun 21)
Mistrio 102 (16½f,Hun,G,Mar 28)
Misty Future 104 (17f,Her,GS,May 1)
Mobasher 105 (19½f,Don,G,Mar 6)
Mocharamor 102 (22f,Thu,S,Feb 1)
Model Son 101 (20f,Fai,S,Dec 13)
Modem 100 (16f,Utt,GF,Sep 7)
Momentous Jones 100 (22½f,Fon,G,Dec 9)
Mon Villez 110 (20½f,Utt,GS,Dec 19)
Mondeed 102 (23½f,Fak,G,Apr 12)
Mondul 114 (16½f,Lin,S,Dec 13)
Monet's Garden 107 (24½f,Per,GS,Apr 22)
Monjoyau 104 (16f,Fai,S,Nov 29)
Monkerhostin 122 (16½f,Nby,G,Feb 14)
Monksford 103 (17f,Exe,GS,Mar 23)
Monolith 110 (20f,Crl,G,Apr 10)
Monsieur Tagel 105 (19½f,Don,G,Mar 5)
Montagnette 102 (24½f,Tau,GS,Feb 19)
Montel Girl 102 (27f,Nab,G,Jly 30)
Montemoss 109 (23f,Wet,G,Dec 6)
Montesino 102 (16f,Utt,GF,Nov 7)
Montevideo 101 (16½f,Str,G,Mar 21)
Montoya 105 (16f,Wor,G,May 21)
Monty's Pass 101 (16f,Naa,Y,Mar 7)
Moon Colony 103 (16f,Utt,HY,May 26)
Moon Emperor 102 (16½f,Asc,G,Feb 21)
Moon Spinner 106 (16½f,Str,G,May 16)
Moonlass 101 (16f,Nav,GY,Nov 23)
Moratorium 103 (16f,Hay,GS,May 3)
Moscow Dancer 108 (18f,Kel,S,Dec 1)
Moscow Fields 101 (19f,Nby,GF,Dec 10)
Moscow Leader 104 (24½f,Crl,GS,Nov 2)
Moscow Whisper 103 (20f,Wor,GF,Jun 1)
Moss Run 101 (22½f,Fon,G,Dec 9)
Moulin Riche 107 (17f,Chl,G,Mar 18)
Mounsey Castle 108 (22½f,Exe,G,Apr 30)
Mount Karinga 110 (20f,Ayr,GS,Apr 16)
Moving Earth 106 (20f,Chp,GF,Oct 22)
Moving Onwards 104 (20f,Leo,Y,Dec 29)
Mr Cool 116 (20f,Asc,G,Nov 21)
Mr Copperfield 105 (16f,Fai,GF,Oct 22)
Mr Ed 100 (19f,Exe,F,Sep 30)
Mr Fluffy 102 (21½f,Hun,GF,May 26)

Mr Houdini 105 (16f,Fai,Y,Apr 11)
Mr Lear 103 (16f,Wet,GS,Mar 22)
Mr Whizz 101 (16½f,Hun,G,Apr 12)
Mrs Ritchie 100 (19½f,Tau,G,Mar 15)
Mughas 122 (16½f,Nby,G,Feb 14)
Mujarad 101 (16f,Nav,GY,Nov 23)
Mullacash 107 (20f,Pun,Y,May 3)
Mumbling 101 (16f,Lei,GF,Nov 17)
Muntasir 102 (19f,Nby,G,Mar 27)
Murat 107 (17f,Her,GS,Jan 7)
Murphy's Retreat 104 (24f,Pun,Y,May 3)
Murray River 106 (20f,Wor,GF,Jun 7)
Musally 109 (21f,Lud,GF,May 15)
Musical Stage 104 (16½f,Hun,G,Mar 28)
Mutadarra 102 (20f,Wor,GF,Jun 1)
Mutineer 115 (16f,Pun,GY,May 1)
My Ace 104 (16f,Lud,GF,Nov 13)
My Bold Boyo 100 (22½f,Exe,G,Apr 30)
My Galliano 104 (16½f,San,G,Nov 8)
My Good Son 100 (22½f,Str,GF,Jly 13)
My Last Bean 107 (16f,Mus,GF,Jan 23)
My Legal Eagle 109 (16½f,Str,GF,Sep 6)
My Line 109 (22f,Hay,G,Jan 10)
My Retreat 100 (16f,Plu,S,Jan 19)
My Sharp Grey 106 (16f,Lud,G,Dec 11)
My Will 110 (16½f,Ain,G,Apr 1)
Mylo 103 (19½f,Mar,G,Jly 6)
Mysteri Dancer 108 (16½f,Str,GF,Aug 9)
Mystic Forest 107 (22f,Nab,G,Jly 30)
Mythical King 103 (20f,Hay,G,Feb 28)

Naked Oat 101 (17½f,Mar,G,Mar 28)
Nameless Wonder 100 (21½f,Sed,GS,Jan 13)
Narwhal 105 (20½f,San,S,Feb 7)
Nathos 106 (16f,Utt,GS,Nov 27)
Native Cunning 104 (25½f,Plu,GS,Mar 15)
Native Dara 105 (20f,Fai,GY,Feb 28)
Native Ivy 103 (25f,War,S,Mar 19)
Native Stag 108 (16f,Nav,S,Dec 14)
Natural 101 (20f,Ncs,G,Nov 14)
Naunton Brook 102 (25f,War,G,Mar 14)
Navado 107 (17½f,Mar,G,Mar 7)
Nawamees 109 (16f,Kem,G,Dec 26)
Needwood Spirit 105 (16½f,Hex,S,Dec 17)
Nemisto 100 (21f,War,GF,May 10)
Never 109 (16½f,Nby,G,Feb 14)
Never Can Tell 100 (16f,Lud,G,May 5)
New Mischief 102 (16f,Wcn,G,Apr 18)
Newhall 109 (20f,Hay,S,Dec 13)
Newlands Gold 106 (22f,Fai,Y,Apr 12)
Newmill 117 (18f,Leo,S,Feb 8)
Next To Nothing 100 (24½f,Ayr,GS,Nov 28)
Niagara 101 (20½f,Utt,GF,Jun 29)
Nicely Presented 103 (16½f,Per,GS,Apr 23)
Niciara 102 (19½f,Don,G,Mar 5)
Nick's Choice 103 (16f,Plu,S,Nov 23)
Nickel Sun 105 (20½f,Utt,S,May 3)
Nickname 119 (19½f,Aut,VS,May 25)
Niembro 106 (16f,Lei,G,Dec 4)
No Picnic 107 (24f,Hex,S,Apr 4)
No Sam No 104 (24½f,Tau,GS,Feb 19)
No Small Plans 110 (20f,Naa,S,Jan 4)
Noble Baron 103 (22½f,Exe,GS,Mar 23)
Noble Calling 100 (17f,Tau,G,Dec 11)
Noble House 102 (20f,Ncs,G,Nov 14)
Nobody Told Me 115 (20f,Pun,YS,May 2)
Nolans Pride 104 (20f,Pun,Y,Dec 7)
Nonchalant 105 (20f,Fai,GY,Feb 28)
Nopekan 109 (16½f,Ain,G,Apr 1)
Normandy Sands 101 (24f,Ncs,HY,Feb 4)
Northern Echo 100 (17f,Sed,GF,Sep 5)

Northern Minster 100 (20f,Crl,GS,Nov 10)
Northern Rambler 100 (23f,Wet,GF,Oct 31)
Noshinannikin 106 (16½f,Don,G,Dec 13)
Novatara 105 (26f,Hun,G,Mar 6)
Now Then Sid 101 (20½f,Hex,GF,Nov 7)
Nowator 109 (17f,Her,GS,May 1)
Nowell House 111 (16f,Wet,GS,Mar 22)
Numbersixvalverde 110 (22f,Fai,Y,Apr 12)
Numitas 105 (16½f,Nby,G,Mar 5)
Nurzyk 103 (27½f,Sed,S,May 2)

Ocean Dancer 101 (16½f,Ain,G,Oct 26)
October Mist 108 (23½f,Hay,GS,May 3)
Odagh Odyssey 100 (20f,Asc,G,Dec 19)
Oh Be The Hokey 115 (16f,Leo,S,Jan 11)
Oh So Wisley 103 (24½f,Exe,G,Nov 4)
Old Bean 102 (21f,Plu,S,Jan 4)
Old Nosey 104 (20f,Crl,GS,Apr 18)
Old Rolla 101 (27½f,Sed,G,Dec 26)
Oliverjohn 105 (19f,Naa,S,Jan 24)
Ollie Magern 112 (21f,Chl,G,Mar 17)
Olney Lad 103 (20½f,Utt,GS,Nov 15)
On The Jetty 110 (20f,Pun,Y,Dec 7)
Once Seen 103 (16f,Plu,S,Feb 16)
One Day 100 (20f,Crl,GS,Nov 2)
One For Me 102 (19f,Exe,GF,Oct 21)
One More Stride 101 (21f,Lud,GF,Oct 9)
One Night Out 113 (22f,Fai,Y,Apr 12)
One Shot Sheehan 110 (20f,Fai,GY,Nov 12)
One Won One 100 (16f,Fai,GY,Feb 28)
Onefortheroadpaddy 101 (16f,Nav,GY,Nov 23)
Onefourseven 102 (21½f,Sed,GF,Aug 8)
Oneofthesimpsons 112 (24f,Pun,YS,May 2)
Only One Matty 104 (20f,Mus,G,Feb 8)
Only Words 105 (16f,Wet,GS,Jan 6)
Ontos 102 (16f,Ncs,G,Nov 29)
Onwardsandupwards 108 (17f,Exe,G,Nov 4)
Optimaite 103 (16½f,Asc,GF,Nov 1)
Oracle Des Mottes 112 (17f,Exe,G,Dec 18)
Orange Order 101 (22f,Crt,GS,May 28)
Orbicularis 102 (22½f,Exe,G,Dec 18)
Orient Bay 102 (21f,Lud,G,Apr 8)
Osiris 111 (20f,Fai,HY,Jan 31)
Ososhot 102 (22f,Wcn,S,Jan 17)
Ottoman 101 (19½f,Mar,G,Dec 26)
Oulton Broad 107 (16f,Lud,GS,Mar 25)
Our Dream 105 (22f,Hay,HY,Jan 24)
Our Prima Donna 102 (21f,Lud,GS,Jan 9)
Our Vic 116 (16½f,San,GS,Dec 6)
Outside Investor 100 (16f,Mus,GF,Jan 7)
Over Bridge 101 (19f,Nby,GS,Mar 26)
Overstrand 119 (16½f,San,GS,Dec 6)

Paddy The Piper 112 (18f,Kel,GS,Mar 6)
Pailitas 107 (16½f,Hun,GF,Aug 25)
Pantarez 105 (16f,Fai,S,Dec 13)
Paperprophet 107 (20f,Hay,G,Feb 28)
Papillon De Iena 108 (18½f,Fon,G,Mar 21)
Pardishar 113 (17f,Chl,GS,Jan 24)
Pardon What 101 (25½f,Plu,GS,Mar 15)
Park City 104 (16f,Wor,GS,May 2)
Parknasilla 102 (16f,Lei,S,Feb 18)
Parshawar 100 (16f,Pun,GY,Nov 16)
Parsifal 109 (17f,Sed,S,May 17)

Parsons Legacy 111 (19f,Nby,GF,Nov 12)
Parsons Pride 103 (22½f,Exe,F,Sep 30)
Party Airs 109 (16f,Pun,GY,May 1)
Party Games 102 (16f,Plu,S,Jan 19)
Pass Me By 106 (20f,Hay,GS,Nov 16)
Pasteur's Legacy 104 (16f,Fai,GY,Feb 28)
Patriarch Express 107 (18f,Kel,GS,Mar 6)
Patsy Veale 111 (16f,Hay,GS,May 3)
Patton 100 (20f,Fai,GF,Oct 22)
Paumafi 108 (20f,Fai,GY,Nov 12)
Pawn Broker 109 (16½f,Asc,S,Nov 22)
Pay It Forward 111 (20f,Pun,YS,May 2)
Peace In Ireland 108 (16f,Pun,GY,May 1)
Pease Blossom 101 (16f,Pun,Y,Dec 6)
Pedina 104 (16f,Pun,HY,Feb 1)
Peeyoutwo 100 (16½f,Str,GF,Sep 6)
Penny Pictures 100 (16½f,Asc,G,Feb 21)
Penric 100 (19f,Nby,G,Mar 27)
Pepe Galvez 106 (19f,Nby,GF,Nov 12)
Per Amore 106 (17f,Exe,F,Sep 30)
Percipient 102 (16f,Fak,GS,Jan 21)
Perfect Liaison 103 (19f,Exe,S,Feb 2)
Periwinkle Lad 112 (24f,Pun,YS,May 2)
Perle De Puce 111 (16½f,Asc,G,Dec 19)
Perouse 115 (17f,Chl,G,Dec 31)
Persian King 108 (16½f,Str,G,May 31)
Persian Tiger 112 (24f,Pun,YS,May 2)
Persian Waters 110 (23½f,Hay,GS,May 3)
Personal Assurance 108 (21½f,Sth,GF,Oct 11)
Perugino's Shadow 106 (16f,Fai,GF,Oct 22)
Petanque 110 (17f,Chl,G,Dec 31)
Peter's Imp 100 (22f,Crt,G,Aug 23)
Petite Margot 111 (24½f,Per,S,Apr 21)
Petrea 102 (24f,Ncs,HY,Feb 4)
Petrozzino 106 (16f,Fai,GY,Nov 12)
Petrula 110 (16f,Wet,GS,Mar 22)
Peveril Pride 107 (24½f,Tau,GF,Mar 4)
Phar From A Fiddle 106 (22½f,Exe,GF,Oct 21)
Phar From Frosty 114 (25½f,Chl,GS,Dec 13)
Piercing Sun 110 (18f,Leo,S,Dec 26)
Pillar Of Fire 100 (24f,Mar,GF,Sep 27)
Pipssalio 100 (20½f,San,S,Mar 13)
Pirandello 113 (16½f,Hun,GS,Dec 11)
Pizarro 110 (20f,Pun,YS,May 2)
Plenty Courage 105 (24½f,Per,G,Jun 6)
Plenty Of Ice 101 (16f,Pun,G,Apr 30)
Poachin Again 107 (18f,Leo,S,Dec 26)
Point Barrow 111 (20f,Fai,Y,Apr 11)
Poitiers 103 (16f,Lud,GS,Mar 25)
Polish Cloud 104 (22f,Wcn,S,Jan 17)
Polished 106 (17f,Sed,GS,Jan 13)
Political Sox 110 (24½f,Per,G,May 14)
Polly's Joy 106 (16f,Fai,GY,Nov 12)
Pompeii 104 (16f,Wet,GS,Jan 6)
Popular Deb 101 (16f,Nav,GY,Nov 23)
Port Moreno 102 (17f,Her,G,Apr 3)
Portant Fella 105 (16f,Fai,Y,Apr 13)
Posh Pearl 107 (20f,Ban,S,May 22)
Positive Profile 114 (25½f,Chl,G,Dec 12)
Pougatcheva 105 (21f,Kem,G,Feb 13)
Powder Creek 104 (16f,Ncs,GS,Feb 21)
Power Elite 108 (16f,Fai,Y,Apr 13)
Precious Mystery 108 (16f,Fak,GS,Jan 21)
Predestine 108 (17f,Her,GS,Jan 7)
Premier Drive 103 (16f,Wet,GS,Dec 27)
Premier Estate 105 (22½f,Exe,GS,Dec 5)
Preston Brook 100 (16f,Tow,S,Apr 11)

Sharp Jack 103 (20f,Ncs,S,Mar 13)
Sharp Rigging 105 (16f,Plu,G,Apr 12)
Sharpaten 106 (16f,Lei,S,Feb 18)
Shaunas Vision 111 (16f,Nav,S,Dec 14)
Shayadi 112 (16f,Ncs,GS,Dec 20)
Shazal 101 (16½f,Per,G,Jun 6)
She'll Be Lucky 100 (16f,Leo,S,Feb 8)
She's Our Native 103 (16f,Lud,GF,Nov 13)
Shean Town 108 (20f,Pun,GY,Apr 29)
Shelovesmenot 109 (16f,Fai,S,Nov 29)
Sherbet Lad 112 (24f,Pun,YS,May 2)
Shifting Moon 103 (22½f,Str,GF,Jly 13)
Shivermetimber 106 (22f,Nav,S,Dec 20)
Short Change 103 (16f,War,GF,Nov 3)
Showpiece 112 (17½f,Mar,GF,Jly 19)
Shuhood 106 (16f,Kem,G,Feb 28)
Sidekick 101 (16f,Nav,GY,Nov 23)
Silent Sound 104 (20f,Wor,GF,Aug 2)
Silent Thoughts 100 (16f,Pun,GY,Nov 16)
Silk Screen 102 (16f,Pun,GY,Nov 16)
Silk Trader 110 (18f,Kel,G,Mar 28)
Silogue 101 (17½f,Mar,GF,Aug 3)
Silver Buzzard 112 (16½f,Ain,GS,May 16)
Silver Charmer 108 (21½f,Chl,G,Apr 15)
Silver Coin 105 (16f,Mus,F,Feb 29)
Silver Gift 101 (27f,Nab,GF,Jun 28)
Silver Prophet 104 (16½f,Hun,G,Mar 17)
Simlet 109 (20f,Ncs,G,Nov 14)
Simoski 101 (16f,Wor,GF,Aug 8)
Simoun 102 (17f,Tau,S,Feb 3)
Simply Supreme 104 (23½f,Hay,G,Jan 10)
Sindapour 109 (16f,Plu,G,Mar 1)
Sir Brastias 103 (16½f,Hun,G,Mar 17)
Sir Edward Burrow 101 (20½f,Per,G,May 15)
Sir Homo 100 (17f,Sth,GF,Oct 11)
Sir Oj 103 (22f,Fai,GY,Feb 28)
Sir Rowland Hill 100 (20f,Ncs,G,Nov 14)
Sir Walter 106 (17f,Ban,G,May 17)
Six Love 106 (16f,Fai,GY,Nov 12)
Six Of One 112 (17f,Exe,G,Dec 18)
Sixo 112 (16½f,San,GS,Dec 5)
Skenfrith 102 (20f,Ncs,HY,Feb 4)
Skiddaw Rose 100 (17½f,Crt,GF,Jly 17)
Slaney Native 112 (24f,Pun,YS,May 2)
Sleep Bal 101 (20f,Fon,G,Feb 22)
Sleeping Night 108 (24½f,Nby,GS,Nov 29)
Sloane Street 105 (16½f,Hun,GF,Oct 9)
Slyboots 100 (20f,Wor,GF,Jly 9)
Smart Savannah 104 (17f,Tau,GS,Jan 22)
Smithlyn 100 (21½f,Hun,G,Mar 28)
Smiths Landing 113 (20½f,Hex,S,Apr 4)
Snapper Creek 108 (16f,Fai,Y,Apr 13)
Snob Wells 114 (16f,Nav,S,Dec 14)
Snowy 105 (20f,Crl,GS,Apr 18)
Snowy Ford 102 (20f,Pun,GY,Apr 29)
So Sure 104 (16f,Lei,G,Dec 4)
Society Affair 108 (26f,Hun,G,Mar 6)
Society Buck 104 (22½f,Str,G,Mar 21)
Soho Fields 100 (16f,Lud,G,May 5)
Solerina 115 (20f,Fai,S,Nov 30)
Solo Dancer 102 (21f,Plu,G,Mar 1)
Solway Minstrel 104 (24½f,Crl,GF,Oct 10)
Some Buzz 101 (16f,Leo,YS,Dec 28)
Son Of Ross 102 (27½f,Sed,G,Mar 16)
Son Of Snurge 109 (20f,Crl,GF,Oct 10)
Sonevafushi 112 (16½f,Ain,GS,May 16)
Sonny Jim 109 (20f,Wor,GF,Jun 1)
Sono 103 (16f,Wet,G,Dec 26)
Southerncrosspatch 100 (24½f,Tau,G,Apr 1)
Sovereign 108 (24f,Mar,GF,Aug 30)
Sovereign State 109 (16f,Fak,GF,May 18)

Space Cowboy 100 (16f,Plu,G,Mar 1)
Space Star 102 (17f,Tau,GF,Apr 16)
Spanchil Hill 100 (16f,Pun,GY,Nov 16)
Spandau 107 (17f,Nab,GF,Aug 12)
Sparkling Water 106 (22½f,Fon,GF,Aug 18)
Special Conquest 104 (24½f,Nby,GS,Mar 26)
Special Rate 109 (20½f,Wet,GS,Jan 6)
Spectroscope 119 (16f,Pun,GY,May 1)
Specular 111 (16f,Hay,G,Jan 10)
Speed Kris 101 (16½f,Per,S,Apr 21)
Speed Venture 105 (17f,Ban,S,May 2)
Spinaround 102 (17f,Her,GS,Feb 15)
Spirit Leader 115 (16f,Leo,Y,Dec 29)
Sporazene 120 (16f,Pun,GY,May 1)
Sports Express 104 (20f,Crl,GS,Apr 18)
Spree Vision 103 (18f,Kel,G,Apr 30)
Spring Gamble 107 (19f,Cat,G,Feb 6)
Spring Grove 105 (22½f,Exe,G,Apr 30)
Spring Pursuit 112 (17f,Chl,GS,Jan 24)
Springfield Scally 109 (24½f,Nby,GS,Nov 29)
Stacumny Bridge 110 (16f,Thu,GY,Dec 21)
Stance 106 (18½f,Fon,G,Apr 7)
Star Councel 110 (26f,Crt,G,May 26)
Star Of Bethlehem 110 (18f,Fai,S,Nov 30)
Star Trooper 109 (20f,Crl,HY,Nov 27)
Stars Delight 101 (21½f,Hun,GF,May 10)
Start From Scratch 106 (16f,Fai,GY,Nov 12)
Starzaan 116 (16f,Pun,GY,May 1)
Stashedaway 108 (20f,Pun,GY,Apr 29)
State Power 104 (20½f,Per,GF,Jun 5)
Station Island 106 (26f,Her,GS,Mar 22)
Steach Maoilin 106 (16f,Fai,GY,Nov 12)
Steel Band 118 (16f,Leo,S,Jan 11)
Steppes Of Gold 111 (18f,Kel,GS,Mar 6)
Stero Heights 105 (24f,Nav,GY,Nov 23)
Steve The Fish 105 (24f,Tow,S,Nov 29)
Sting Like A Bee 100 (20½f,Hex,GF,Nov 7)
Stitches 106 (16f,Fai,GY,Nov 12)
Stolen Song 103 (16½f,Hun,G,Mar 28)
Storm Clear 100 (16f,Plu,S,Jan 19)
Storm Prince 107 (21f,War,GS,Mar 14)
Stormez 115 (23½f,Hay,S,Feb 14)
Stormy Beech 104 (17f,Sed,S,May 2)
Strawberry Bob 112 (24f,Pun,YS,May 2)
Streets Of Steel 104 (16f,Fai,S,Nov 29)
Strictly Speaking 102 (20f,Ban,G,Aug 16)
Strife Leader 104 (18f,Leo,S,Dec 26)
Strike Alliance 101 (16f,Naa,G,Aug 4)
Strike Back 106 (16f,Fai,S,Nov 30)
Stromness 105 (25½f,Chl,G,Nov 15)
Strong Project 110 (20f,Nav,GF,Nov 9)
Sud Bleu 119 (16½f,Asc,S,Dec 20)
Suggest 110 (25½f,Cat,G,Feb 6)
Sully Shuffles 114 (20f,Ncs,GS,Feb 21)
Sum Leader 106 (20f,Pun,GY,Apr 29)
Sun Bird 108 (18f,Kel,G,May 22)
Sun Cat 101 (20f,Ayr,GF,Mar 13)
Sun King 110 (16½f,Hun,GS,Dec 11)
Sunday Rain 103 (18f,Kel,G,Apr 30)
Sungates 103 (22½f,Fol,HY,Jan 2)
Sunny Native 101 (20f,Crl,GF,Oct 25)
Sunnyside Royale 105 (17f,Sed,GS,Feb 10)
Sunray 100 (16½f,Chp,S,Dec 27)
Sunshine Boy 107 (21f,Lud,GF,May 15)
Super Lucky 100 (25½f,Per,G,Jly 2)
Super Sammy 106 (20½f,Hex,S,Apr 4)
Supergood 107 (22f,Fai,Y,Apr 12)
Supreme Arrow 108 (22½f,Str,GF,Oct 7)

Supreme Being 106 (20f,Fai,GY,Feb 28)
Supreme Dawn 104 (16f,War,G,Nov 25)
Supreme Piper 102 (20f,Fon,G,Apr 7)
Supreme Priority 112 (21f,Tow,F,Oct 8)
Supreme Serenade 108 (21f,Nby,G,Mar 27)
Supreme Touch 112 (24f,Pun,YS,May 2)
Sure Future 106 (25½f,Chl,G,Dec 12)
Swan Knight 102 (16f,Utt,HY,Jan 10)
Sweet Diversion 109 (16½f,San,GS,Dec 5)
Swift Spirit 105 (16f,Fai,GF,Oct 22)
Sword Lady 106 (21f,Tow,GS,Mar 11)
Swordplay 105 (16f,Fai,Y,Apr 13)

Tacin 111 (24f,Pun,Y,May 3)
Tactful Remark 103 (16½f,Str,G,May 31)
Taffy Dancer 103 (20½f,Fol,GS,Feb 17)
Tai Lass 102 (16½f,Hun,G,Mar 28)
Take Five 103 (16f,Nav,S,Feb 16)
Take The Oath 108 (16f,Pun,GY,Nov 15)
Talama Lady 104 (17f,Ban,GS,Mar 27)
Talarive 107 (16f,Utt,HY,Jan 10)
Tales Of Bounty 106 (24f,Wor,G,May 10)
Tam O'Shanter 100 (24½f,Tau,G,Apr 1)
Tamarinbleu 105 (17f,Chl,G,Mar 18)
Tango Royal 110 (16½f,Str,G,May 31)
Tanners Court 103 (22½f,Str,G,Mar 21)
Tanterari 105 (24½f,Tau,G,Mar 4)
Tarboush 100 (16f,Wcn,G,Apr 4)
Tardar 117 (23½f,Hay,S,Feb 14)
Tarn Ridge 100 (16f,Pun,GY,Nov 16)
Tarque 112 (16f,Kem,G,Dec 27)
Tarski 106 (22½f,Exe,F,Sep 30)
Tarxien 116 (20½f,Chl,GS,Jan 24)
Tasman 106 (16f,Nav,YS,Mar 6)
Teaatral 103 (16½f,San,S,Feb 7)
Tealby 103 (16f,Fak,GS,Jan 21)
Team Tassel 107 (19½f,Mar,G,Feb 10)
Technohead 105 (20f,Fai,GY,Nov 12)
Tee-Jay 110 (24f,Hex,G,May 10)
Tees Components 104 (22½f,Kel,G,May 7)
Teknash 108 (20f,Pun,GY,Apr 29)
Tell Me See 101 (20f,Pun,Y,May 3)
Teme Valley 106 (20f,Mus,GF,Dec 16)
Temple Dog 108 (20f,Crl,G,Feb 23)
Tensile 103 (23½f,Hay,GS,May 3)
Teorban 103 (26f,Hun,G,Mar 6)
Terdad 110 (26f,Crt,G,May 26)
Terek 109 (17f,Sed,S,May 17)
Terre De Java 100 (20½f,Wet,GS,Mar 22)
Thames 106 (20f,Ain,G,Nov 22)
The Bajan Bandit 110 (20f,Ayr,HY,Jan 31)
The Bandit 102 (20f,Asc,GF,Nov 1)
The Bar Maid 105 (21f,Tow,GS,Mar 11)
The Card Shark 100 (16f,Pun,GY,Nov 16)
The Dark Lord 105 (19½f,Mar,G,Feb 10)
The Flyer 101 (20f,Ain,GS,Nov 23)
The French Furze 121 (20½f,Chl,GS,Jan 24)
The Gene Genie 103 (16f,Wcn,S,Jan 8)
The Grey Butler 105 (22½f,Str,GS,Dec 30)
The Indispensable 104 (21½f,Hun,GF,Nov 2)
The Joker 103 (16f,Ncs,G,Nov 29)
The Kelt 100 (21½f,Hun,G,Apr 12)
The Kop End 106 (16f,Pun,Y,Dec 6)
The Last Cast 102 (20f,Asc,GS,Mar 20)
The Local 104 (16f,Plu,S,Feb 16)
The Masareti Kid 101 (27½f,Sed,G,Dec 26)
The Mighty Sparrow 104

(20½f,Utt,GF,Jun 29)
The Miner 104 (18f,Kel,HY,Feb 5)
The Newsman 102 (18½f,Fon,G,Oct 5)
The Parishioner 113 (22f,Thu,S,Feb 1)
The Phair Crier 103 (22f,Hay,S,Nov 29)
The Posh Paddy 104 (16f,Fai,S,Dec 13)
The Proof 101 (17½f,Fol,G,Mar 3)
The Rile 103 (16f,Ayr,S,Dec 26)
The River Joker 104 (24f,Tow,S,Nov 29)
The Sister 102 (24f,Ban,GS,Apr 17)
The Stillard 109 (20f,Fai,Y,Apr 13)
Therealbandit 109 (25½f,Chl,G,Nov 15)
Thesis 120 (16½f,Asc,S,Dec 20)
Thieves'Glen 110 (25½f,Chl,GS,Dec 13)
This Is Serious 107 (20f,Pun,GY,Nov 16)
Thrashing 104 (24½f,Tau,G,Apr 1)
Three Eagles 107 (21½f,Sth,GF,Oct 11)
Through The Rye 108 (17f,Chl,G,Mar 18)
Thumper 102 (16½f,Per,G,Sep 25)
Thunder Alley 106 (16f,Fai,S,Nov 29)
Tianyi 107 (16½f,Hun,GF,Oct 9)
Tiawana 102 (20f,Pun,Y,May 3)
Tickton Flyer 107 (24f,Hex,G,May 3)
Tidjani 107 (20f,Chp,HY,Feb 7)
Tiger Cry 108 (16f,Fai,HY,Jan 31)
Tiger Frog 102 (16f,Tow,S,Apr 11)
Tiger Talk 103 (19½f,Mar,G,Jun 11)
Tiger Tips Lad 103 (16f,Plu,GS,Mar 15)
Tighten Your Belt 110 (21f,Chl,G,Mar 17)
Tik-A-Tai 108 (20f,Chp,GF,Nov 8)
Tikram 114 (16½f,Asc,GF,Nov 1)
Time To Reflect 107 (17f,Exe,G,Nov 4)
Time To Shine 110 (16½f,Asc,G,Feb 21)
Timeless Chick 102 (20f,Wor,GF,Aug 2)
Timidjar 108 (17f,Nab,GF,Jun 13)
Timpeall An Ti 103 (19f,Naa,F,Jun 18)
Tinoveritas 112 (19f,Nby,GF,Dec 10)
Tirikumba 106 (21f,Nby,G,Mar 27)
Tisho 104 (21½f,Chl,G,Apr 15)
Tiutchev 107 (20f,Chp,GF,Nov 8)
Toejam 100 (17f,Sed,S,May 17)
Toi Express 103 (17f,Exe,GF,Oct 21)
Tom Paddington 115
(16½f,Nby,GS,Nov 30)
Tom Sayers 109 (20f,Fai,Y,Apr 13)
Tom's Prize 111 (24½f,Nby,GS,Mar 26)
Tomenoso 106 (20f,Ncs,G,Nov 14)
Toms Gone Grey 102 (17½f,Fol,G,Mar 3)
Tomwontpayalot 101 (16f,Utt,GF,Jun 12)
Too Technical 104 (19f,Str,G,Jly 26)
Toon Trooper 104 (25f,War,S,Dec 20)
Top Of The Left 107 (20½f,Wet,G,Dec 26)
Top Strategy 113 (17f,Chl,G,Mar 18)
Top Trees 105 (17f,Exe,F,Sep 30)
Torche 100 (25f,War,S,Dec 20)
Torrid Kentavr 110 (17f,Ban,G,Sep 13)
Tosawi 106 (17f,Exe,G,Mar 9)
Totally Scottish 108 (18f,Kel,G,Mar 28)
Totland Bay 101 (22f,Nab,GF,Aug 4)
Touch Closer 104 (20f,Asc,G,Dec 19)
Town Crier 105 (16f,Utt,GF,Aug 7)
Towns Ender 102 (19f,Nby,GF,Dec 10)
Toy Boy 105 (19f,Nby,GF,Dec 10)
Trabolgan 108 (20f,Asc,G,Dec 19)
Tragic Ohio 104 (17f,Her,HY,Feb 6)
Tramantano 110 (16f,Hay,GS,May 3)
Transatlantic 103 (16f,Lei,G,Dec 4)
Translucid 103 (16½f,Chl,GF,Oct 29)
Travellers Rest 117 (16f,Chl,G,Dec 31)
Travello 101 (16f,Lei,G,Dec 4)
Tresor Preziniere 105 (20f,Chp,HY,Feb 7)
Tribal Dancer 103 (26½f,Lud,G,Feb 25)
Tribal Princess 105 (16f,Nav,G,Jun 22)

Trillionaire 107 (20f,Wor,GF,Jun 1)
Trouble At Bay 111 (16f,Kem,G,Feb 28)
Truckers Tavern 105 (22f,Hay,S,Nov 29)
True Lover 103 (21f,Nby,GS,Mar 26)
Truly Gold 105 (16f,Nav,S,Dec 20)
Trusting Paddy 100 (17f,Her,GS,May 1)
Tucacas 100 (21½f,Chl,G,Apr 15)
Tumbling Dice 103 (16f,Pun,Y,Dec 6)
Tuppenny Cody 111 (16f,Nav,GF,Nov 9)
Turaath 105 (20f,Crl,HY,Mar 21)
Turbo 103 (16½f,Nby,GS,Nov 30)
Turn Of Phrase 103 (16f,Wet,G,Nov 15)
Turtle Soup 111 (21f,War,S,Dec 20)
Turtleback 115 (16f,Leo,S,Jan 11)
Tusk 105 (16½f,Ain,G,Apr 1)
Twenty Degrees 100 (18½f,Fon,GS,Feb 9)
Twentytwosilver 100 (17f,Tau,GF,Apr 16)
Twist 'n Shout 107 (16f,Fai,S,Nov 29)
Twotensforafive 101 (20f,Wor,GF,Aug 2)
Tyrrellspass 101 (16½f,Chp,GF,Mar 10)

Ultimate Accolade 106 (16f,Pun,S,Feb 12)
Ummoon 109 (20f,Fai,Y,Apr 13)
Undeniable 116 (20f,Ncs,GS,Feb 21)
Underley Park 101 (24f,Hex,S,Dec 17)
Unicorn Reward 101 (16f,Mus,GF,Jan 23)
Unleash 111 (16f,Wor,G,May 21)
Unlocked 106 (20f,Chp,G,Nov 26)
Unsigned 104 (20f,Wor,GF,Jun 1)
Untidy Daughter 110 (17f,Sed,S,May 17)
Uptown Lad 110 (18f,Kel,HY,Feb 5)
Ursumman 106 (16f,Fai,GY,Nov 12)
Usk Valley 101 (25½f,Plu,S,Dec 3)

Val De Fleurie 104 (16½f,Chl,GF,Oct 29)
Val Du Don 102 (16½f,Hun,GS,Nov 22)
Valance 107 (16½f,Hun,GF,Nov 2)
Valeureux 107 (16½f,Hex,GF,Oct 3)
Vallica 101 (24½f,Tau,GS,Feb 19)
Valtar 102 (16½f,Asc,GS,Mar 20)
Vandas Choice 110 (16½f,Per,G,Sep 25)
Vanormix 109 (17f,Chl,G,Dec 31)
Veneguera 108 (24½f,Per,G,Jun 6)
Venture To Fly 104 (24½f,Per,G,May 14)
Verrocchio 101 (16f,Pun,GY,Nov 16)
Versus 102 (17½f,Fol,HY,Jan 20)
Vert Espere 100 (20½f,Utt,S,May 21)
Very Optimistic 107 (21f,Chl,G,Mar 17)
Vic Toto 112 (20f,Fon,G,Feb 22)
Vic Ville 108 (16f,Naa,S,Jan 24)
Vicar's Lad 105 (22½f,Str,G,Oct 30)
Vicars Destiny 107 (19½f,Mar,G,Dec 26)
Victory Gunner 102 (19½f,Tau,GS,Feb 19)
Villa 101 (21f,Nby,G,Mar 5)
Vilprano 111 (26f,Crt,G,May 26)
Vingis Park 105 (18½f,Fon,G,Mar 21)
Virgin Soldier 104 (16f,Wet,F,Oct 15)
Visibility 116 (16½f,Asc,GF,Nov 1)
Vista Verde 102 (24½f,Nby,GS,Mar 26)
Vitelucy 104 (22½f,Str,GF,Oct 7)
Vivid Imagination 100 (22f,Nab,GF,Aug 4)
Vodka Bleu 112 (16½f,Asc,S,Nov 22)
Vodka Inferno 101 (24f,Hex,G,May 3)
Volano 111 (16½f,Ain,GS,May 16)

Waffles Of Amin 101 (20f,Fai,S,Dec 13)
Wagner 106 (22f,Nab,GF,Jun 13)
Wait For The Will 112 (17f,Nab,GF,May 29)
Wakeup Smiling 107 (19f,Nby,GF,Dec 10)
Walk Over 100 (22f,Fai,GY,Feb 28)
War Of Attrition 114 (16½f,Chl,G,Mar 16)
Warrens Castle 102 (20f,Pun,Y,May 3)
Wartorn 108 (22½f,Exe,G,Apr 30)
Wasted Talent 104 (16½f,Nby,G,Mar 5)
Watch The Dove 105 (25½f,Chl,GF,Oct 28)
Watchful Witness 101 (16f,Plu,S,Jan 4)
Water Sports 111 (24½f,Tau,GS,Feb 19)
Waterspray 107 (17f,Exe,F,Sep 30)
Watson Lake 114 (20f,Leo,Y,Jan 25)
Waverley Road 100 (18½f,Fon,G,Apr 7)
We'Ll Make It 103 (20½f,San,G,Nov 8)
Web Master 103 (27½f,Sed,GS,Feb 24)
Web Perceptions 101 (16½f,Hun,GF,Sep 28)
Wee Danny 105 (24f,Wor,GF,Jly 9)
Wee Willow 102 (27½f,Sed,S,May 2)
Wekiwa Springs 100 (16f,Fai,S,Dec 13)
Welcome To Unos 103 (16½f,Str,G,Oct 30)
Well Chief 111 (16f,Wcn,GF,Nov 8)
Well Presented 114 (22f,Fai,Y,Apr 12)
Welsh Dream 103 (17½f,Crt,GS,May 28)
Welsh Main 102 (16f,Wet,GS,Mar 22)
Westender 121 (16½f,Nby,G,Feb 14)
Western Ridge 107 (16½f,Str,G,Jly 31)
Westernmost 102 (17½f,Per,S,Apr 21)
Westgate Run 103 (16½f,Per,G,Jun 22)
Weston Rock 106 (19f,Cat,G,Feb 6)
Wet Lips 112 (16f,Mus,F,Feb 29)
Whaleef 102 (17f,Ban,G,Oct 11)
What If 105 (20f,Fai,GY,Nov 12)
What You Know 105 (17f,Nab,GF,Aug 12)
Whatareyouhaving 113 (22f,Fai,Y,Apr 12)
Whispered Secret 102 (16f,Wet,G,Dec 26)
Whist Drive 101 (18½f,Fon,G,Jan 26)
Whistling Dixie 109 (20f,Pun,GY,Apr 29)
Whitford Don 106 (24½f,Nby,G,Mar 6)
Who Cares Wins 105 (20f,Asc,G,Dec 19)
Who Dares 100 (16f,Pun,S,Feb 12)
Why The Long Face 105 (20f,Ayr,GF,Mar 13)
Widemouth Bay 110 (17f,Exe,G,Nov 4)
Wigmo Princess 100 (17f,Exe,G,Mar 9)
Wild Power 104 (16½f,Hun,GF,Oct 9)
Wild Romance 101 (16½f,Asc,G,Nov 21)
Wildfield Rufo 101 (24f,Ncs,GS,Dec 20)
Wilfram 102 (20f,Wor,GF,Jun 1)
Will Of The People 101 (20½f,Lei,S,Jan 27)
Willie John Daly 112 (24½f,Nby,G,Feb 14)
Willoughby Joe 103 (24f,Nav,GF,Jun 22)
Win Alot 100 (19½f,Mar,GF,Aug 30)
Windsor Boy 101 (16f,Pun,GY,May 1)
Winning Dream 106 (16f,Naa,Y,Mar 7)
Winsley 103 (21f,Lud,GS,Jan 9)
Wintertide 110 (25½f,Chl,GS,Dec 13)
Witch's Brew 101 (16f,Cat,G,Jan 24)
Wood Street 105 (16½f,Chp,GF,Oct 22)
Woodstamp 101 (16f,Nav,GY,Nov 23)
Woodybetheone 101 (18½f,Fon,GF,Aug 25)
Workaway 102 (20f,Mus,G,Feb 8)
World Vision 103 (24½f,Crl,GF,Oct 25)
Wotsitooya 100 (22f,Fai,GY,Nov 12)
Wouldn't You Agree 107 (20f,Pun,YS,May 2)
Wrags To Riches 105 (16f,Tow,S,Dec

15)
Wrangel 101 (17f,Sth,GF,Oct 11)
Wrapitup 105 (20f,Fai,GF,Oct 22)
Wun Chai 103 (19½f,Her,GF,Mar 9)

Xaipete 108 (20f,Ban,G,Aug 1)
Xellance 111 (22f,Nab,GF,Aug 4)

Yankee Jamie 107 (24½f,Per,G,May 14)
Yardbird 105 (20f,Asc,G,Dec 19)
Yogi 113 (22f,San,S,Feb 7)
Yorkshire Grey 109 (20f,Fai,Y,Apr 13)
You Need Luck 108 (16f,Fai,S,Nov 29)
You Owe Me 107 (20½f,Utt,GS,Dec 26)
You'Re The Man 105 (24½f,Crl,GS,Nov 2)
Young Butt 101 (17f,Her,GS,May 1)
Young Collier 104 (19f,Nby,S,Jan 14)
Young Dancer 104 (17f,Nab,G,Apr 10)
Young Owen 101 (16f,Hay,GF,Oct 23)
Young Vintage 107 (16f,Fai,GF,Oct 22)
Youngblood 103 (16f,Naa,S,Jan 4)
Your A Gassman 106 (20½f,Per,S,Apr 21)
Your Advantage 101 (16f,War,S,Mar 19)
Your Almost There 111 (16f,Pun,S,Feb 12)
Your Father 100 (16f,Pun,GY,Nov 16)
Your So Cool 105 (24½f,Tau,S,Feb 3)

Zahaalie 108 (20f,Ban,S,May 2)
Zarenas Treasure 103 (20f,Fai,Y,Apr 11)
Zero Risk 102 (21f,Kem,G,Jan 17)
Zero To Hero 102 (19f,Naa,S,Jan 4)
Zibeline 107 (16½f,Chl,G,Mar 16)
Ziggy Zen 105 (21f,Kem,G,Jan 17)
Zimbabwe 108 (16½f,Lin,S,Dec 13)
Zonergem 111 (16½f,Hun,GF,Nov 11)
Zum See 113 (16f,Naa,Y,Mar 7)
Zurs 101 (16f,Wor,GS,May 2)

Zygomatic 106 (17½f,Crt,GF,Jly 17)

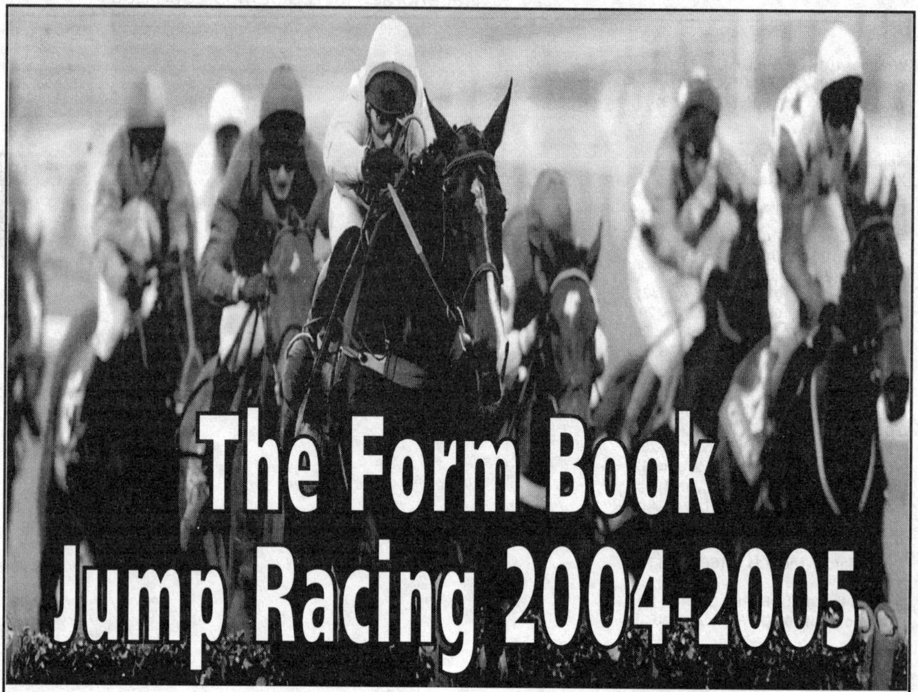

Notes